ULRICH'S INTERNATIONAL PERIODICALS DIRECTORY

31st Edition

1992-93

Ulrich's International Periodicals Directory
is compiled by
R.R. Bowker
Serials Department

Judith Salk, Executive Editor
Edvika Popilskis, Senior Editor

Frank McDermott, Senior Associate Editor
Egill Halldorsson, Ewa Kowalska, Associate Editors

Lisa Finan, Laura Forbes, Christopher King, Dawn Lombardy, Henry Wessells, Pu Xiang,
Assistant Editors

Mary Crouthers, Editorial Assistant
Ila Joseph, Mail Processing Clerk
Brenda Worthy, Secretary

Barry Barish, Terence Carlson, Karl Dusza, Dorothy Hodges,
Margareta Leon, Inna Levine, Lucy Setteducato, and
Eline van de Poel, Contributing Editors

Max Kobrinsky, Systems Communications Manager
Jack Murphy, Supervisor, Computer Operations
Karen Strong, Senior Account Manager, International Computaprint Corporation

James P. Murray, Senior Vice President and General Manager
Peter Simon, Vice President, Database Publishing Group

31st Edition

ULRICH'S™
INTERNATIONAL PERIODICALS DIRECTORY
1992-93

including
Irregular Serials & Annuals

Volume 2
Subjects I-Z

THE BOWKER INTERNATIONAL SERIALS DATABASE

R.R. BOWKER
A Reed Reference Publishing Company
New Providence, New Jersey

Published by R.R. Bowker
A Reed Reference Publishing Company
121 Chanlon Rd., New Providence, NJ 07974

Ulrich's Hotline (U.S. only): 1-800-346-6049
Editorial (Canada only, call collect): 1-908-665-2870, 2875
Serials Fax (overseas users): 908-771-7725

Copyright © 1992 by Reed Publishing (USA) Inc.
All rights reserved.

Ulrich's is a trademark of Reed Properties Inc., used under license.

No part of this publication may be reproduced or transmitted in any form or by any means, stored in any information storage and retrieval system, without prior written permission of R.R. Bowker, 121 Chanlon Rd., New Providence, NJ 07974

International Standard Book Number 0-8352-3264-6
(3 Volume set)
International Standard Book Number 0-8352-3265-4
(Volume 1)
International Standard Book Number 0-8352-3266-2
(Volume 2)
International Standard Book Number 0-8352-3267-0
(Volume 3)
International Standard Serial Number 0000-0175
Library of Congress Catalog Card Number 32-16320

Printed and bound in the United States of America.

No payment is either solicited or accepted for the inclusion of entries in this publication. R.R. Bowker has used its best efforts in collecting and preparing material for inclusion in this publication, but does not warrant that the information herein is complete or accurate, and does not assume, and hereby disclaims, any liability to any person for any loss or damage caused by errors or omissions in this publication, whether such errors or omissions result from negligence, accident or any other cause.

3 Volume Set

ISBN 0-8352-3264-6

9 780835 232647

Contents

PREFACE vii

USER'S GUIDE ix

INTERNATIONAL STANDARD SERIAL NUMBER xvii

ABBREVIATIONS
    General Abbreviations and Special Symbols xix
    Money Symbols xx
    Micropublishers and Distributors xxi
    Reprint Services xxv
    Country of Publication Codes xxvi
    Abstracting and Indexing Services xxviii

SUBJECT GUIDE TO ABSTRACTING AND INDEXING xl

SUBJECTS xlii

CROSS-INDEX TO SUBJECTS xlviii

VOLUME 1

CLASSIFIED LIST OF SERIALS/SUBJECTS A to H 1

VOLUME 2

CLASSIFIED LIST OF SERIALS/SUBJECTS I to Z 2521

VOLUME 3

REFEREED SERIALS 4863

CONTROLLED CIRCULATION SERIALS 4961

SERIALS AVAILABLE ON CD-ROM 5031

PRODUCER LISTING/SERIALS ON CD-ROM 5043

SERIALS AVAILABLE ONLINE 5045

VENDOR LISTING/SERIALS ONLINE 5109

CESSATIONS 5127

INDEX TO PUBLICATIONS OF INTERNATIONAL ORGANIZATIONS ... 5311
    International Organizations 5311
    International Congress Proceedings 5321
    European Communities 5324
    United Nations 5325

ISSN INDEX 5331

TITLE INDEX 5855

Preface

Ulrich's International Periodicals Directory has been the premier serials reference source since 1932. The 31st edition, which is the 60th anniversary edition of **Ulrich's**, continues to uphold its reputation for excellence in the provision of serials bibliographic information. With the publication of this edition, we not only unveil a new look for this venerable serials authority, but we also include a multitude of new features which will enhance your access to and use of the serials information we provide.

Foremost among the physical changes introduced in this edition of **Ulrich's** is the new typeface which is intended to improve the readability of the text. Boldfaced data elements, particularly in the title field, now appear in each listing to help users locate vital bibliographic information at a glance. Not so obvious to the user are other internal changes, such as improved punctuation between data elements.

Noteworthy new features such as full-page advertising rates and an advertising contact name appear when provided by the publisher; and, when known, years of coverage of serials by specific A&I services are included. We also now note the shelfmark numbers of serials held by the British Library indicating their availability for document delivery through the British Library Document Supply Centre (BLDSC). For a full explanation of the BLDSC and the shelfmark number, please refer to page xiii in the User's Guide in this volume. In addition, we have expanded our coverage of serials reprint services. Such services are an important resource, providing access to back issues and otherwise hard-to-find serials. While many microform publishers also function as reprint services, we have highlighted the reprint services in a separate list on page xxv.

In a year full of enormous political changes, **Ulrich's** has kept pace with the emergence of new nations from the former Soviet Union and Yugoslavia. Entries for publications from these 19 new countries reflect both actual correspondence with publishers in the new nations and revisions according to the latest USMARC Code List for Countries.

Numerous additions and refinements were made to our subject heading file this year, reflecting our acknowledgement of the increasingly specialized nature of serials publishing. New subject classifications in this edition fall into two groups: those with separate headings for publications in such diverse areas as Women's Studies, Men's Studies, Singles' Interests and Lifestyles, Leisure and Recreation, Matrimony, and How-to and Do-It-Yourself; and, as a result of extensive research and discussion, many specialized subheadings such as ten new headings within the Law classification; Pollution, Toxicology and Environmental Safety, and Waste Management within the Environmental Studies category; Bioengineering and Biotechnology within the Biology category; Science Fiction, Fantasy, Horror and Mystery and Detective within the Literature category; and Solar Energy, Wind Energy, Geothermal Energy within the Energy category, to name only a few.

Serials continue to be important as primary sources of current and topical news in all fields of endeavor, as evidenced by the vast number of serials published and their rapid development into electronic formats. The availability of serials in electronic formats, either online or on CD-ROM, continues to grow. This edition of **Ulrich's** includes 2,941 serials available exclusively online or in addition to hardcopy, and 558 serials available on CD-ROM. These serials are indicated by a notation and a bullet (●) in the main entry.

The 31st edition of **Ulrich's** contains information on nearly 126,000 serials published throughout the world, arranged under 788 subject headings. More than 66,000 entries from the 30th edition have been updated to reflect the most current information available and nearly 10,000 serials have been added. Also included in this edition is information on 8,304 titles that are known to have ceased or suspended publication in the last three years. The ceased or suspended titles are preceded by a dagger (†) in the "Title Index" for instant identification. Users can identify newer serials, over 3,800 of which are known to have begun publication since January 1, 1990, by looking for an upside-down solid triangle (▼) preceding entries in both the "Classified List of Serials" and the "Title Index." In addition, over 5,000 refereed serials notations, 42,000 brief descriptions, 30,300 LC Classification Numbers, 14,100 CODEN, and 2,142 vendor file names or numbers for 2,941 titles available in an online format appear in this edition.

International data inquiries are mailed annually to some 67,000 publishers to secure accurate and up-to-date information directly from the publishers on current titles, as well as new titles, titles changes, and cessations. In addition, updating of the database occurs daily from information received from publishers throughout the year. All post office returns are researched, and entries from publishers whose addresses cannot be located are suspended from the file. Information about title changes, cessations, and new titles not received by the deadline for this edition will appear in **Ulrich's Update**; in the online database available through DIALOG Information Services, Inc., BRS Information Technologies, Inc., and the European Space Agency (ESA-ISA); on **Ulrich's *Plus*™** CD-ROM; and on **Ulrich's Microfiche**. In addition, users are encouraged to call our editorial office for help in solving serials questions.

Included in **Ulrich's** are serials which are currently available, issued more frequently than once a year and usually published at regular intervals, as well as publications issued annually or less frequently than once a year, or irregularly. Due to the vast number of serials, we have established certain criteria for inclusion, while maintaining our aim of maximum title coverage that will satisfy the widest range of use. We include all publications that meet the definition of a serial except general daily newspapers, newspapers of local scope or local interest, administrative publications of major government agencies below state level that can be easily found elsewhere, membership directories, comic books, and puzzle and game books. This edition of **Ulrich's** is arranged in eleven sections within three volumes: the first two volumes comprise the "Classified List of Serials;" the third volume contains the "Refereed Serials," "Controlled Circulation Serials," "Serials Available on CD-ROM," "Producer Listing/Serials on CD-ROM," "Serials Available Online," "Vendor Listing/Serials Online," "Cessations," "Index to International Organizations," "ISSN," and "Title" indexes.

Your purchase and use of **Ulrich's** is complemented with some additional services. **Ulrich's Update**, provided free of charge, three times per year—in November, February, and May—is a supplemental service to the annual directory. The **Ulrich's Hotline** is a toll-free number that customers can call to get help in solving their periodicals and serials research problems and questions. Canadian users are asked to call a special number collect, and our overseas users are asked to use a designated fax number. (Please see page iv for our address and telephone and fax numbers.) **Ulrich's News**, previously a free quarterly publication sent to subscribers of **Ulrich's**, was recently merged with a new quarterly newsletter from R.R. Bowker, **The Cornerstone**. (The last issue of of **Ulrich's News** was published in 1992, and the first issue of **The Cornerstone** will debut in September, 1992.) **The Cornerstone** will include not only valuable information about serials and **Ulrich's**, as had **Ulrich's News**, but will also contain news about other Bowker titles and pertinent topics.

As always, we continue to research, plan, and implement enhancements to the **Ulrich's** database and our database maintenance system. The 32nd edition is sure to include some new developments that will enhance your usage of **Ulrich's**. We consider feedback from our users to be essential, so please contact us and let us know your thoughts. We want **Ulrich's** and its family of products to provide all necessary reference information quickly and effectively. Comments and suggestions are encouraged in order to help keep our database and its bibliographic publications of the highest quality.

My sincere appreciation is extended to the senior staff of **Ulrich's**, Edvika Popilskis, Frank McDermott, and Ewa Kowalska, and to our fine staff of serials editors for their unflagging dedication and hard work in updating and maintaining the serials database in preparation of the 31st edition of **Ulrich's**. Thanks also to Peter Simon, Vice President of the Database Publishing Group, and to all others at R.R. Bowker for their contributions toward the completion of this 60th anniversary edition. Profound gratitude goes to Karen Strong, Senior Account Manager at International Computaprint Corporation, for her competence, diligence, and patience in working closely with us this past year to program all the special features contained herein. Finally, I would like to thank the various information specialists throughout the world who have taken it upon themselves to provide us with hard-to-find serials data. We consider their participation and interest in the dissemination of accurate and comprehensive serials information to be of great value to **Ulrich's** and its users.

Judith Salk
Executive Editor

User's Guide

This directory offers two primary access methods for locating periodicals: by subject in the CLASSIFIED LIST OF SERIALS, and alphabetically in the TITLE INDEX. Ceased serials are listed in a separate CESSATIONS section and are also accessible by means of the TITLE INDEX. Other indexes provide listings of selected periodicals in specific categories. These indexes are REFEREED SERIALS, CONTROLLED CIRCULATION SERIALS, SERIALS AVAILABLE ON CD-ROM, PRODUCER LISTING/SERIALS ON CD-ROM, SERIALS AVAILABLE ONLINE, VENDOR LISTING/SERIALS ONLINE, PUBLICATIONS OF INTERNATIONAL ORGANIZATIONS, and ISSN INDEX.

In addition, separate subheadings for "Abstracting, Bibliographies and Statistics" under major subject headings provide convenient access to these types of publications. Page references for these subheadings are given in the "Subject Guide to Abstracting and Indexing" on p. xl. This Subject Guide provides an overview of subjects for which abstracting and indexing publications have been identified.

This "User's Guide" is separated into three divisions for ease of use: (I) Section Descriptions, (II) Full Entry Content Description, and (III) Cataloging Rules for Main Entry Title.

Section Descriptions

CLASSIFIED LIST OF SERIALS

This is the main section of the book, containing bibliographic information for currently published serials classified by subject. Entries are arranged alphabetically by title within each subject heading. Subject cross-references in the text direct the user to the location of subheadings.

Volume 1 contains subjects A-H, from "Abstracting and Indexing" through "Humanities." Volume 2 contains subjects I-Z, "Instruments" through "Zoology."

A complete listing of the "Subjects" used in the CLASSIFIED LIST OF SERIALS appears on p. xlii. To aid international users, this list is translated into four languages. For additional guidance on the subject classification scheme, the user should also consult the "Cross-Index to Subjects" on p. xlviii, which contains additional key word references.

Each serial is listed with full bibliographic information only once. If a serial covers several subjects, title cross-references appear under the related headings, directing the user to the heading where the full entry is listed.

New serials (beginning publication within the last three years) are highlighted by a ▼ in front of the title.

The "Cataloging Rules for Main Entry Title" section of this "User's Guide" explains the title cataloging rules followed in compiling the **Ulrich's International Periodicals Directory.**

REFEREED SERIALS

This section is an alphabetical listing by title of all serials known to be refereed, or peer reviewed. It includes the publisher name, address, and telephone number, if known. The italicized number at the end of each entry is the page number where the full entry appears in the CLASSIFIED LIST OF SERIALS.

CONTROLLED CIRCULATION SERIALS

This section is an alphabetical listing of all serials known to have controlled circulations. It includes the publisher name and address, telephone and fax numbers, and circulation figure, if known. The italicized number at the end of each entry is a reference to the page on which the full entry appears in the CLASSIFIED LIST OF SERIALS.

SERIALS AVAILABLE ON CD-ROM

This section is an alphabetical listing of all serials known to be available on CD-ROM, either in addition to hardcopy, or on CD-ROM only. It includes the publisher name, address, telephone and fax numbers, if known. It also includes the name of CD-ROM producers, when known. The italicized number at the end of each entry is the page number where the full entry appears in the CLASSIFIED LIST OF SERIALS.

PRODUCER LISTING/SERIALS ON CD-ROM

This section is an alphabetical listing of identified producers of serials on CD-ROM. Entries include the producer address, telephone and fax numbers, and an alphabetical listing of all serials titles known to be available. If known, the serial on CD-ROM product name is listed in parentheses after the serial title. All serials listed in this index also have full bibliographic entries in the CLASSIFIED LIST OF SERIALS. Consult the TITLE INDEX or the SERIALS AVAILABLE ON CD-ROM listing for page numbers.

SERIALS AVAILABLE ONLINE

This section is an alphabetical listing of all serials known to be available online, either in addition to hardcopy, or online only. Entries include publisher name, address, telephone and fax numbers, plus names of online vendors and file names or numbers, if known. The number in parentheses at the end of each entry is the page number where the full entry appears in the CLASSIFIED LIST OF SERIALS.

VENDOR LISTING/SERIALS ONLINE

This section is an alphabetical listing of identified vendors of online periodicals. Entries include addresses, telephone and fax numbers for the vendor, and an alphabetical listing of all titles known to be available, with file names or numbers, if known. All serials listed in this index also have full bibliographic entries in the CLASSIFIED LIST OF SERIALS. Consult the TITLE INDEX or the SERIALS AVAILABLE ONLINE listing for page numbers.

CESSATIONS

In this section, entries for serials which have ceased in the past three years are listed alphabetically by title. The cessation entry includes: title, Dewey Decimal Classification number, former frequency of publication, publisher name and address, country-of-publication code, and, if available, other information such as ISSN, CODEN, LC number, subtitle, corporate author, year of first issue and year ceased. Titles which were originally planned as continuing series but which have closed are included in the CESSATIONS section although back issues may still be available.

If a title has "ceased" because a new title is being used, there will not be an entry in the CESSATIONS section. Instead, the entry is maintained in the CLASSIFIED LIST OF SERIALS under the new title, with a "Formerly" or "Former title" indication.

INDEX TO PUBLICATIONS OF INTERNATIONAL ORGANIZATIONS

Complexity of corporate author structure, as well as title page variations in multilingual texts, compound the problems in cataloging international publications. This special index is provided so that the user may have one reference point for these titles. This index consists of four sections:

International Organizations
International Congress Proceedings
European Communities
United Nations

The index contains all current titles listed in the Bowker International Serials Database. The user must consult the CLASSIFIED LIST OF SERIALS for the full bibliographic information pertaining to these titles. Page references are provided.

ISSN INDEX

The ISSN INDEX lists serials in order by ISSN number. It includes all serials contained in the Bowker International Serials Database, whether current, ceased, or inactive, to which an ISSN has been assigned in our file. A dagger symbol (†) indicates that the title is ceased. If an ISSN appears twice, it usually indicates that the serial has split into two or more parts. Titles which have changed, and for which new ISSNs have been assigned, will show cross-references from one ISSN to the new ISSN. If no new ISSN has been assigned, the cross-reference is from ISSN to new title. Entries for inactive titles do not appear in the book.

A full description of the ISSN and its use is provided on p. xvii.

TITLE INDEX

The TITLE INDEX, which is at the end of Volume 3, is the second major access point for serials. To locate a serial by its title, the user should be familiar with title cataloging rules as described in the "Cataloging Rules for Main Entry Title" paragraphs of this "User's Guide."

The TITLE INDEX lists all current and ceased serials included in this directory. **Boldface** type indicates the page number where the complete entry will be found; page numbers in roman type refer to related subject categories.

USER'S GUIDE   xi

For serials with identical titles published within a country, the city of publication is added in parentheses, and sometimes the year of first publication is given to further distinguish the titles.

If a serial title consists of or contains an acronym, a cross-reference is provided from the full name to the acronym form of the title.

Cross-references are provided from former titles and variant titles, and from the alternate language titles of multiple-language publications. Recent title changes are noted, with a reference to the current title. The TITLE INDEX also lists the country code for all serials, along with the ISSN, if known.

The ▼ used in the Classified List to indicate new serials also appears in this index, preceding the title. A † appears preceding the title if the publication has ceased.

Full Entry Content Description

Basic Information

The following items are mandatory for listing and appear in all entries: main entry title, frequency of publication, publisher address, country code, and Dewey Decimal Classification number.

Dewey Decimal Classification Number

The Dewey Decimal number is printed at the top left of each entry. More than one Dewey number may have been assigned if a serial covers several subjects.

LC Classification Number

The Library of Congress classification number, if known, appears directly below the Dewey Decimal number. Shelf numbers are not included.

SAMPLE ENTRY

(1) 930.198 490.996   **(2)** US   **(3)** ISSN 1055-7644
(4) DZ991   **(5)** CODEN: JAAPL9
(6) JOURNAL OF ANTARCTIC ARCHAEOLOGY AND PROTOLINGUISTICS; **(7)** international communications and research. **(8)** (Supplement avail.) **(9)** (Text in English, French, Polynesian languages) **(10)** 1986. **(11)** 2/yr. **(12)** $39 to individuals; institutions $99 (includes Supplement) (effective 1993). **(13)** (Societe d'Archaeologie et de Linguistique Pacifiques—Society of Pacific Archaeology and Linguistics) **(14)** W.A. Translations (Subsidiary of: Temporary Culture), **(15)** Box 43072, Upper Montclair, NJ 07043-7072. **(16)** TEL 908-665-2869. **(17)** FAX 508-555-0010. **(18)** TELEX 123458. **(19)** (Subscr. to: Department of Archaeology and Proto-Linguistics, 7 Old College Walk, Arkham, MA 01901-1011. TEL 508-555-0110. **(20)** Dist. in Europe by: Editions d'Erlette, Ch. de Kerangat, Plumelec 56120, France. TEL 33-76-63-94). (Co-sponsor: Miskatonic University, Department of Archaeology and Proto-Linguistics) **(21)** Eds. A.H. Whateley, J.M. Snyrnat. **(22)** adv. contact: Arthur Dunwich; **(23)** B&W page $400; trim 8⅛ x 10; **(24)** bk.rev.; abstr.; bibl.; illus.; index; **(25)** circ. 500 (paid); 500 (controlled). **(26)** (also avail. in microform from SWZ, UMI; also avail. on diskette; back issues avail.; reprint service avail. from SWZ, UMI). **(27)** Indexed: Abstr. Anthropol., Br.Archaeol.Abstr. **(28)** (1991—), Onoma (1986—), Ref.Zh.
(29) • Also avail. online. **(30)** Vendor(s): UTOPIA (Miskatonic).
(31) Also avail. on CD-ROM. **(32)** Producers: TEMPCULT (Miskatonic).
(33) —BLDSC shelfmark: 4939.001100.
(34) Supersedes (1927-1986): Miskatonic Annals of Antarctic Archaeology and Extraterrestrial Linguistics **(35)** (ISSN 0055-1298).
(36) Description: Publishes archaeological field research on prehistoric civilizations in the Pacific Islands and Antarctica, with relevant contributions discussing worldwide linguistic evidence of contacts among civilizations.
(37) *Refereed Serial*

KEY

1. Dewey Decimal Classification
2. Country Code
3. ISSN
4. LC Classification
5. CODEN
6. Main Entry Title
7. Subtitle
8. Bibliographic Note
9. Language
10. First Published
11. Frequency
12. Price
13. Sponsoring Body
14. Publisher
15. Address
16. Telephone
17. Fax
18. Telex
19. Subscription Address & Tel
20. Distributor Address & Tel
21. Editor
22. Advertising Contact
23. Advertising Rate
24. Special Features
25. Circulation
26. Format
27. Indexed In
28. Years of Coverage
29. Online Availability
30. Online Vendor/File Name
31. CD-ROM Availability
32. CD-ROM Producer
33. British Library Document Supply Centre Shelfmark Number
34. Title Changes
35. Former ISSN
36. Brief Description
37. Refereed

Country Code
The Country Code is printed at the top right of each entry following the Dewey Decimal number. A complete list of country codes used will be found on p. xxvi.

ISSN
The ISSN for the main entry title is printed immediately following the country code. Not all publications have been assigned an ISSN, and lack of a number does not render a publication ineligible for listing.

CODEN
The CODEN designation, if known, is printed directly below the country code and ISSN. The CODEN is an alphanumeric code, applied uniquely to a specific publication. Devised by the American Society for Testing and Materials, it is used primarily for scientific and technical titles. New CODEN are assigned by Chemical Abstracts Service.

Title Information
The main title is printed in upper case as the first item in the entry. Titles are cataloged according to rules described below in the "Cataloging Rules for Main Entry Title" section. For multiple-language publications, the parallel language title is also printed in uppercase, immediately following the main entry title, and is separated from it by a slash.

A ▼ printed before the title indicates that the title began publishing within the last three years.

An asterisk printed after the title indicates that the information in the entry was not verified by the publisher for this edition.

The subtitle is printed in lower case after the title.

Variant titles or translated edition titles are given within the entry and are labeled as such.

Former titles are given at the end of the entry, along with publication dates if known. If a former title also had an ISSN, the ISSN is listed in parentheses after the former title. Many entries contain extensive former title information, providing a history of changes which may be useful for bibliographic record-keeping.

The Key Title, which is assigned at the time of ISSN assignment by the responsible center of the International Serials Data System, is given only if it is different from the main entry title.

Year First Published
The year first published is given if provided by the publisher. If information is lacking, a volume number and specific year may be provided to indicate the approximate age of the publication.

Frequency
The frequency of publication is given in abbreviated form, such as "a." for annual, "irreg." for irregular, "m." for monthly, "3/yr." for three times per year. All abbreviations used are listed in the "General Abbreviations" on p. xix.

Price
Unless otherwise indicated, the price given is the annual price for an individual subscription in the currency of the country of origin. The price in U.S. dollars may also be given in parentheses if it is provided by the publisher. No attempt is made to convert foreign currency to U.S. dollars. Separate postage information is not given, since postal rates vary widely.

Publisher Information
Many serials are editorially controlled by a sponsoring organization or corporate author and published by a commercial publisher. In these instances, the commercial publisher's name and address are given, and the name of the corporate author is given in parentheses immediately preceding. In other instances, either a sponsoring organization or a commercial publisher has sole responsibility, and only one name is given. We avoid listing printers as publishers, preferring the name and address of someone with editorial responsibility. For the same reason, we avoid listing distributors as publishers.

If no publisher name is given, it is assumed that the publisher name is the same as the title.

If the publisher is also the editor, the person's name is given with the notation "Ed. & Pub."

Subscription or Distribution Address
A second address is given only if the address for ordering subscriptions is different from the publisher's address. Distributors are listed only if we have been informed that a particular organization is the exclusive distributor. Additional subscription and/or distribution offices of international publishers are listed, if known.

Telephone, Fax and Telex Numbers
Telephone, Fax and Telex numbers are given when provided by the publisher. U.S. and Canadian numbers are given in standard North American format. Numbers

in other countries are provided in the same format as supplied by the publisher, resulting in some inconsistencies. Users are advised to consult an international operator before placing calls. Telephone numbers for subscription and/or distribution offices appear if provided by the publisher.

Editor
Usually only one name is given, preceded by the notation "Ed." Advanced degrees and titles are omitted, except for medical, military and religious titles; absence of a title does not mean that the editor has none. The abbreviation "Ed.Bd." indicates editorship by three or more persons.

Advertising Rates and Contact Name
When provided by the publisher, full-page advertising rates and trim size information are indicated, as is the name of the advertising contact.

Special Features
A listing of special features may include such items as book or other types of reviews, advertising (usually meaning commercial, not classified advertising), charts, illustrations, bibliography section, article abstracts, and an annual index to the periodical's contents.

Reprint Services
If a serial is known to be available from a reprint service, a code referring to the service appears in the entry. More than one code may be listed. For a list of reprint services and a translation of the codes, please refer to p. xxv.

Circulation
All circulation figures used are approximate. Circulation is given only if provided by the publisher. The notation "controlled" indicates that the publication is available only to qualified persons, usually members of a particular trade or profession.

Format
Formats other than standard magazine format are noted in parentheses. Other formats may be looseleaf, duplicated (mimeographed), tabloid, newspaper. If a publication is available in microform, a notation is made which includes a three-letter code for the vendor, if known. A list of names, addresses, telephone and fax numbers of micropublishers is provided on p. xxi.

Abstracting and Indexing
The notation "Indexed:" precedes a list of abbreviations for all abstracting and indexing services known to cover the serial on a regular basis. Years of coverage immediately follow each abstracting and indexing service code, if known. The complete names of the abstracting and indexing services are listed with their abbreviations on p. xxviii. All currently published abstracting and indexing services are also listed as entries in the CLASSIFIED LIST OF SERIALS.

Online Availability and CD-ROM Availability
If a serial is known to be available in a full-text online format and/or on CD-ROM, a bullet symbol (●) precedes the information. Online and CD-ROM availability are noted whether they exist in addition to hardcopy or in one or both formats exclusively. Online vendors and CD-ROM producers are also listed, if known.

For a listing of serials available online, consult the SERIALS AVAILABLE ONLINE index on p. 5045. Complete names and addresses of vendors, with a listing of serials known to be available through them, are in a separate index, VENDOR LISTING/SERIALS ONLINE on p. 5109.

For a listing of serials available on CD-ROM, consult the SERIALS AVAILABLE ON CD-ROM index on p. 5031. Complete names and addresses of producers, with a list of CD-ROMs known to be available through them, are in a separate index, PRODUCER LISTING/ SERIALS ON CD-ROM on p. 5043.

British Library Document Supply Centre (BLDSC)
Serials holdings of the British Library, available for document delivery through the British Library Document Supply Centre (BLDSC), are noted. The British Library shelfmark number, the unique identifier of each serial, is preceded by an em-dash (—) which is followed by the notation "BLDSC shelfmark: 0000.000000." The format of the shelfmark is four digits, a decimal, then 6 digits.

While the **Ulrich's** and BLDSC's titles were matched on the presence of ISSNs, not all titles have ISSNs, and the absence of a shelfmark number in an **Ulrich's** record does not necessarily mean that title is unavailable from the BLDSC. For further information about BLDSC's services, contact: Customer Services, British Library Document Supply Centre, Boston Spa, Wetherby, LS23 7BQ, UK; Tel: +44 (937) 546060, Fax: +44 (937) 546333.

Brief Description
A brief description of the contents and editorial focus of the publication may be provided, preceded by the word "Description:" at the end of the entry. These descriptions were submitted by the publisher or were written by editorial staff after examination of sample copies or publisher catalogs.

Refereed Serial
The manuscript peer review and evaluation system is utilized to protect, maintain and raise the quality of scholarly material published in serials. If a serial is known to be refereed or juried, the notation "Refereed Serial" appears in italics at the end of the entry. This information is generally provided by the serial publisher.

Cataloging Rules for Main Entry Title

The majority of titles in the Bowker International Serials Database were cataloged according to *Anglo-American Cataloging Rules* prior to 1978, the date of the new edition of *Anglo-American Cataloging Rules*. The new *AACR II* reflects a trend toward the Key Title concept of cataloging as used by the International Serials Data System (ISDS) and published in its *International Standard Bibliographic Description for Serials* (1974).

Because recataloging a database the size of Bowker's was not feasible, our cataloging rules were modified but not radically changed. Cross-references are provided in the TITLE INDEX from variant forms of title, such as Key Title, to aid users searching by other methods.

Whenever possible, main entry title cataloging is done from a sample of the title page of the most recent issue, according to the following rules:

Articles at the beginning of titles are omitted, or are bypassed in filing.

Serials with distinctive titles are usually entered under title. For example:

Annual Bulletin of Historical Literature
Business Week
Milton Studies

If a title consists only of a generic term followed by the name of the issuing body, or if the name of the issuing body clarifies the content of the publication, entry is under the name of the issuing body. For example:

Newsletter of the American Theological Library Association
is entered as
American Theological Library Association. Newsletter

Economic Performance and Prospects, issued by the Private Development Corporation of the Philippines
is entered as
Private Development Corporation of the Philippines. Economic Performance and Prospects

A title which consists of a subject modified generic term followed by the name of the issuing body is considered nondistinctive and is entered under the name of the issuing body. For example:

Annual Meeting Scientific Proceedings of the American Animal Hospital Association
is entered as
American Animal Hospital Association. Annual Meeting Scientific Proceedings

Government publications with nondistinctive titles are entered under the name of the government jurisdiction of the issuing body, although distinctive titles of government organizations may be entered directly under title. For example:

Great Britain. Economic and Social Research Council. Annual Report
but
Statistical Abstract of Iceland

Titles which begin with the initials of the issuing body are entered under the initials. Cross-references from the full name are provided in the TITLE INDEX.

If a geographic name is part of the name of the issuing body, entry will be under the common form of the name of the body. For example:

University of the West Indies. Vice-Chancellor's Report
not
West Indies. University. Vice-Chancellor's Report

Note, however, that government publications retain similar cataloging as government jurisdiction.

Canada. Statistics Canada. Field Crop Reporting Series

Multilingual titles are entered under the first title given on the title page, or the first title reported by the publisher if the title page is not available. Titles in other languages are entered directly after the main entry title. Cross-references are provided in the TITLE INDEX for each language title.

FILING RULES
Due to the restrictions imposed by computer filing of titles, the following special filing rules should be noted.

Articles and prepositions within titles are alphabetized as words:

Journal of the West
precedes
Journal of Theological Studies

Hyphenated words are treated as separate words:

Pre-Text

precedes

Preaching

However, words indicating compass points (northeast, southwest, etc.) are filed as one word regardless of how printed:

Northeast Agriculture
North East Coast Institution of Engineers and Shipbuilders Transactions
Northeast Folklore Society Newsletter
North-East India Council for Social Science Research Journal

Titles entered under corporate author or government jurisdiction are sequenced before distinctive titles that begin with the same words:

British Columbia. Ministry of Energy, Mines and Petroleum Resources. Mineral Market Update

precedes

British Columbia Catholic

Acronyms and initials are treated as such and are listed at the beginning of each letter of the alphabet. Exceptions are the abbreviations U.N. (United Nations), U.S. (United States), Gt. Britain (Great Britain), and St. (Saint), which are filed as words:

U W I P A Newsletter
United Mutual Fund Selector
U.S. Environmental Protection Agency. Clean Water: Report to Congress

Titles in excess of 36 characters which are identical may not sort sequentially. The editors suggest that users scan the entire sequence of identical titles to locate specific entries.

Diacritical marks have been omitted. The German and Scandinavian umlaut has been replaced by the letter "e" following the vowels a, e, o, and u. In Danish, Norwegian and Swedish, the letter å is sequenced as "aa" and the letter ø as "oe."

International Standard Serial Number (ISSN)

1. *What is the ISSN?*

An internationally accepted, concise, unique and unambiguous code for the identification of serial publications. One ISSN represents one serial.

The ISSN consists of seven numbers with an eighth check digit calculated according to Modulus 11 and used to verify the number in computer processing. A hyphen is printed after the fourth digit, as a visual aid, and the abbreviation ISSN precedes the number.

A code indicating country of publication may be printed preceding the ISSN as an additional identifier; for example, UK ISSN 1234-5679.

2. *How did the ISSN evolve as an international system?*

The International Organization for Standardization Technical Committee 46 (ISO/TC 46) is the agency responsible for the development of the ISSN as an international standard. The organization responsible for the administration and assignment of ISSN is the International Center (IC) of the International Serials Data System (ISDS). The IC/ISDS, supported by the French government and Unesco, is located in Paris.

The implementation of the ISSN system started with the numbering of the 70,000 titles in the serials database of the R.R. Bowker Company (*Ulrich's International Periodicals Directory* and *Irregular Serials and Annuals*). The next serials database numbered was the *New Serial Titles 1950-70* cumulation listing 220,000 titles, cumulated, converted to magnetic tape and published by the R.R. Bowker Company in collaboration with the Serials Record Division of the Library of Congress. These two databases were used as the starting base for the implementation of the ISSN.

3. *What types of publications are assigned ISSN?*

For assignment of an ISSN, a serial is defined by the International Serials Data System as: "a publication in print or in non-print form, issued in successive parts, usually having numerical or chronological designations, and intended to be continued indefinitely."

4. *How is ISSN used?*

ISSN, the tool for communication of basic information about a serial title with a minimum of error, is used for such processes as ordering, billing, inventory control, abstracting, and indexing. Authors use ISSN for copyright. In library processes, ISSN is used in operations such as acquisitions, claiming, binding, accessioning, shelving, cooperative cataloging, circulation, interlibrary loans, and retrieval of requests.

5. *May a publication have an International Standard Book Number (ISBN) and an ISSN?*

Yes! Monographic series (separate works issued indefinitely under a common title, generally in a uniform format with numeric designations) and annuals or titles planned to be issued indefinitely under the same title may be defined as serials. The ISSN is assigned to the serial title, while an ISBN is assigned to each individual title or monograph in the series.

A new ISBN is assigned to each volume or edition by the publisher, while the ISSN, which is assigned by the International Center, national or regional center, remains the same for each issue. Both numbers should be printed on the copyright page of each volume, with initials or words preceding each number for immediate identification. With the availability of both ISSN and ISBN, the problem of defining the overlap of serials and monographs has been resolved.

SAMPLE TITLE

ADVANCES IN THE BIOSCIENCES
ISSN 0065-3446
Vol. 1 Proceedings: Berlin. Schering Symposium of Endocrinology, Berlin. Ed. by Gerhard Raspe. 1969. 40.00 (ISBN 0-08-013395-9). Pergamon.
Vol. 2 Proceedings. Schering Symposium on Biodynamics & Mechanims of Action of Steroid Hormones, Berlin. Ed. by Gerhard Raspe. 1969. 41.25 (ISBN 0-08-006942-8). Pergamon.
Vol. 3 Proceedings. Schering Workshop on Steroid Metabolism "in Vitro Versus in Vivo," Berlin. Ed. by Gerhard Raspe. 1969. 41.25 (ISBN 0-08-017544-9). Pergamon.
Vol. 4 Proceedings. Schering Symposium on Mechanisms Involved in Conception. Berlin. Ed. by Gerhard Raspe. 1970. text ed. 41.25 (ISBN 0-08-017546-5) Pergamon.
Vol. 25 Development of Responsiveness to Steroid Hormones. Alvin M. Kaye & Myra Kaye et al. LC 79-42938. 1980. 66.00 (ISBN 0-08-024940-X). Pergamon Press.

6. *Where should the ISSN appear on the serial?*

In a prominent position on or in each issue of the serial, such as front cover, back cover, title or copyright pages. ISDS recommends that the ISSN of a periodical be printed, whenever possible, in the upper right corner of the front cover.

Promotional and description materials about the serial should include the ISSN.

7. *When a title changes is a new ISSN assigned?*

In most instances, a new ISSN is assigned when a title changes. However, the determination is made by the International Center or the National or regional center of ISDS. Publishers should report all title changes to their respective centers.

8. *How does a publisher apply for an ISSN?*

The publisher should maintain contact with the national, regional or International Center of ISDS. They require bibliographic evidence of the serial, including a copy of the title page and cover. There is no charge to the publisher for the assignment of ISSN.

For full information, publishers should contact the national library or bibliographic center in the country where they are publishing. The address for the International Center is:

> International Serials Data System (ISDS)
> International Center (for the Registration of Serial Publications)
> 20 rue Bachaumont
> 75002 Paris, France

The address for the National Center in the United States is:

> National Serials Data Program
> Library of Congress
> Washington, DC 20540
> (202) 707-6452

9. *What is SISAC?*

SISAC stands for the Serials Industry Systems Advisory Committee. SISAC is an industry group formed to develop voluntary standardized formats for electronically transmitting serial business transaction information. SISAC provides a forum where serial (particularly journal) publishers, library system vendors, and librarians can discuss mutual concerns regarding the electronic transmission of serial information and develop cooperative solutions, in the form of standardized formats, to efficiently address these concerns. *(Reprinted with permission from SISAC.)*

10. *SISAC Codes*

The serial identification code, also called the SIID, is a string of letters and/or numbers which follows the International Standard Serials Number (ISSN) and identifies a particular issue. The identification code and the machine-scannable bar code presentation was tested in libraries in 1986.

The SIID is a new presentation of existing codes. The code begins with the International Standard Serials Number (ISSN) and then adds issue information comprised of the date (chronology) and the volume/issue numbers (enumeration). *(Reprinted with permission from SISAC.)*

Abbreviations
General Abbreviations and Special Symbols

a.	annual	music rev.	music reviews
abstr.	abstracts	N.S.	New Series
adv.	advertising	pat.	patents
approx.	approximately	play rev.	play reviews (theatre reviews)
BLDSC	British Library Document Supply Centre	Prof.	Professor
bi-m.	every two months	q.	quarterly
bi-w.	biweekly	record rev.	record reviews
bibl.	bibliographies	s-a.	twice annually
bk.rev.	book reviews	s-m.	twice monthly
c/o	care of	s-w.	twice weekly
charts	charts (diagrams, graphs, tables)	stat.	statistics
circ.	circulation	subscr.	subscription
contr.	controlled	tele. rev.	television reviews
cum.index	cumulative index	3/m.	3 times a month
Cy.	county	3/yr.	3 times a year
d.	daily	tr. lit.	trade literature (manufacturers' catalogues, reader response cards)
dance rev.	dance reviews		
Dir.	Director	tr. mk.	trade marks
Ed., Eds.	Editor, Editors	video rev.	video reviews
Ed.Bd.	Editorial Board	w.	weekly
film rev.	film reviews	‡	not available from a subscription agency
fortn.	fortnightly		
ISSN	International Standard Serial Number	*	not updated/unverified
illus.	illustrations	●	online and/or CD-ROM availability
irreg.	irregular	▼	new serial
m.	monthly	†	ceased
mkt.	market prices		

Money Symbols

SYMBOL	UNIT	COUNTRY
A.	austral	Argentina
Arg.$	peso	Argentina
Aus.$	dollar	Australia
B.	baht	Thailand
B.$	dollar	Brunei Darussalam, Belize
BEF	franc	Belgium
Bl.	balboa	Panama
Bol.$	peso	Bolivia
Br.	birr	Ethiopia
Bs.	bolivar	Venezuela
BTN	bonus do tesouro nacional	Brazil
BTNF	bonus do tesouro nacional fiscal	Brazil
C.$	cordoba; dollar	Nicaragua, Cayman Islands
Can.$	dollar	Canada
CFPF	franc	New Caledonia
Col.	colon	Costa Rica, El Salvador
Col.$	peso	Colombia
Cr.$	cruzeiro	Brazil
Cz.$	cruzado	Brazil
D.	dalasi	Gambia
DH., Dh.	dirham	Morocco, United Arab Emirates
DKK	krone	Denmark
DM.	mark	Germany
din.	dinar	Algeria, Jordan, Kuwait, Libya, Tunisia, Yugoslavia
$	dollar; peso	various
Dr.	drachma	Greece
E.	emalangeni	Swaziland
EAs.	shilling	East Africa, Somalia, Tanzania, Uganda
EC$.	dollar	Dominica, St. Lucia
ECU	European currency unit	European Communities
Esc.	escudo	Angola, Portugal, Mozambique
F.	franc	Djibouti, France, Guadeloupe, Mali, Martinique, Monaco, Rwanda
F$	dollar	Fiji
FIM	markka	Finland
fl.	guilder; florin	Netherlands, Netherlands Antilles, Surinam
FMG.	franc	Malagasy Republic
Fmk.	mark; markka	Finland
Fr.	franc	Belgium, Liechtenstein, Luxembourg, Switzerland
Fr. CFA	franc	African Financial Community, Benin, Burkina Faso, Burundi, Cameroon, Central African Republic, Chad, Congo, Gabon, Ivory Coast, Niger, Reunion, Senegal, Togo
Ft.	forint	Hungary
g.	guarani	Paraguay
Gde.	gourde	Haiti
G.$	dollar	Guyana
HK$	dollar	Hong Kong
I£	pound	Ireland
I.D.	dinar	Iran, Iraq
IRI.	riyal	Iran
IS	shekel	Israel
ISK	krona	Iceland
J.$	dollar	Jamaica
Jam.$	dollar	Jamaica
K.	kina; kwacha	Malawi, Papua New Guinea, Zambia
Kcs.	koruny	Czechoslovakia
kip	kip	Laos
Kr.	krona; krone	Scandinavian countries
KShs.	shilling	Kenya
L.	lempira; lira	Honduras, Italy
Le.	leone	Sierra Leone
lei	lei	Rumania
Lit.	lira italiana	Italy
lv.	lev	Bulgaria
M.$	dollar; ringgit	Malaysia
Mex.$	peso	Mexico
$m.n.	moneda nacional	various
mt.	metical	Mozambique
N$	new Uruguay peso	Uruguay
NC.	cedi	Ghana
NOK	krone	Norway
NT.$	dollar	Republic of China (Taiwan)
N.Z.$	dollar	New Zealand
ORI.	riyal	Oman
P.	pula; peso	Botswana, Philippines, various
QRI.	riyal	Qatar
£	pound	Ireland, Gt. Britain, Malta
£C	pound	Cyprus
£E	pound	Egypt
£L	pound; dinar	Lebanon
£N	pound; naira	Nigeria
£S	pound	Syria
ptas.	peseta	Spain
Q.	quetzal	Guatemala
R.	rand	South Africa, Lesotho, Namibia
RD.$	peso	Dominican Republic
Rps.	rupiah	Indonesia
Rs.	riel; rial; rupee	Cambodia, India, Iran, Mauritius, Nepal, Pakistan, Seychelles, Sri Lanka
Rub.	ruble	former U.S.S.R.
S/	sucre; sole	Ecuador, Peru
S.	schilling	Austria
S.$	dollar	Singapore
SEK	krona	Sweden
SFr.	franc	Liechtenstein, Switzerland
SI$	dollar	Solomon Islands
SL.	pound	Sudan
SLT	talar	Slovenia
SRl.	riyal	Saudia Arabia
$T.	dollar	Tonga
TK.	taka	Bangladesh
TL.	pound; lira	Turkey
T.T.$	dollar	Trinidad and Tobago
tugrik	tugrik	Mongolia
UM	ouguiya	Mauritania
Urg.$	peso	Uruguay
vatu	vatu	Vanuatu
VN.$	dollar	Vietnam
Won	won (hwan)	Korea
Y	yuan	People's Republic of China
Yen	yen	Japan
YRl.	rial	Yemen
Z	zaire	Zaire
Z.$	dollar	Zimbabwe
Zl.	zloty	Poland

Micropublishers and Distributors

ACR **A.C.R.P.P.**
(Association pour la Conservation et la Reproduction photographique de la Presse)
B.P. 221, 77313 Marne-La-Vallee
Cedex 2, France
Tel: 331-60177213 Fax: 331-60176805

ADL **Advanced Library Systems, Inc.**
100 Brickstone Sq.
Andover, MA 01810-3894
Tel: 508-470-0610 Fax: 508-475-1072

AFS **Fertility and Sterility**
2140 11 Avenue South
Suite 200
Birmingham, AL 35205-2800
Tel: 205-933-8494; Fax: 205-930-9904

AGU **American Geophysical Union**
2000 Florida Ave., NW
Washington, DC 20009
Tel: 202-462-6903 Fax: 202-328-0566

AIP **American Institute of Physics**
335 East 45th St.
New York, NY 10017
Tel: 212-661-9409; Fax: 212-949-0473

AIR **Aircraft Technical Publishers**
101 South Hill Dr.
Brisbane, CA 94005
Tel: 415-468-1705; Fax: 415-468-1596

AJP **American Jewish Periodical Center**
Hebrew Union College-Jewish Institute of Religion
3101 Clifton Ave.
Cincinnati, OH 45220
Tel: 513-221-1875; Fax: 513-221-0321

ALP **Alpha Com**
Ueberseering 9, 2000
Hamburg 60, Germany
Tel: 49-40-513020; Fax: 49-40-51302000

AMP **Adam Matthew Publications**
44 Royal Ave., Calcot
Reading, Berkshire RG3 5UP England
Tel: 44-734-422765; Fax: 44-0380830300

AMS **AMS Press, Inc.**
56 E. 13th St.
New York, NY 10003
Tel: 212-777-4700; Fax: 212-995-5413

ATL **American Theological Library Association, Preservation Board**
820 Church St., Suite 300
Evanston, IL 60201
Tel: 708-869-7788; Fax: 708-869-8513

ATP **Appropriate Technology Project**
P.O. Box 4543
Stanford, CA 94309
Tel: 415-326-8581; Fax: 415-326-3475

BAR **Barbour Index Plc**
New Lodge, Drift Rd., Windsor
Berkshire SL4 4RQ England
Tel: 44-344884121; Fax: 44-344884845

BHP **Brookhaven Press**
P.O. Box 2287
La Crosse, WI 54602-2287
Tel: 608-781-0850; Fax: 608-781-3883

BIO **BIOSIS**
2100 Arch St.
Philadelphia, PA 19103-1399
Tel: 215-587-4800, 800-523-4806; Fax: 215-587-2041

BKR **Bowker A&I Publishing**
A Reed Reference Publishing Company
121 Chanlon Rd.
New Providence, NJ 07974
Tel: 908-665-2847, 800-227-2477; Fax: 908-771-7725

BLC **Bloch & Company**
P.O. Box 18058
Cleveland, OH 44118
Tel: 216-371-0979

BLH **Bell & Howell**
(Micropublishing now operated by UMI)

BLI **Balch Institute**
Research Library
18 S. 7th St.
Philadelphia, PA 19106
Tel: 215-925-8090; Fax: 215-922-3201

BNB **British Library National Bibliographic Service**
Boston Spa, Wetherby
West Yorkshire LS23 7BQ England
Tel: 44-71-937546585; Fax: 44-71-937546586

BNQ **Bibliotheque national de Quebec**
Service de Microphotographie
1700 St. Denis
Montreal, PQ H2X 3K6 Canada
Tel: 514-873-1100; Fax: 514-873-9932

BWC **Butterworth & Co., Ltd.**
88 Kingsway
London WC2B 6AB England
Tel: 44-71-4056900; Fax: 44-71-4051332

CCM **Core Collection Micropublishers**
Div. of Roth Publishing, Inc.
185 Great Neck Rd.
Great Neck, NY 11021
Tel: 516-466-3636, 800-327-0295; Fax: 516-829-7746

CDS **Current Digest of the Soviet Press**
3857 N. High St.
Columbus, OH 43214
Tel: 614-292-4234; Fax: 614-267-6310

CHL	**Chadwyck-Healey Ltd.** Cambridge Place Cambridge CB2 1NR England **Tel:** 223-311479; **Fax:** 223-66440	**HAW**	**The Haworth Press** 10 Alice St. Binghamton, NY 13904 **Tel:** 607-722-7259; **Fax:** 607-722-1424
	Chadwyck-Healey, Inc. N.A. Distributors 1101 King St. Alexandria, VA 22314 **Tel:** 703-683-4890; **Fax:** 703-683-7589	**HPL**	**Harvester Press Microfilm Publications Ltd.** (Now wholly owned and operated by Research Publications, Inc.)
		IAM	**SIAM Publications** 3600 University City Science Center Philadelphia, PA 19104-2688 **Tel:** 215-382-9800; **Fax:** 215-386-7999
CIH	**Canadian Institute for Historical Microreproductions** P.O. Box 2428, Station D Ottawa, ON K1P 5W5 Canada **Tel:** 613-235-2628; **Fax:** 613-235-9752	**ICS**	**Editions I.C.S.** 23 Ave. Villemain 75014 Paris, France **Tel:** 33-1-45392244; **Fax:** 33-1-45434680
CIS	**Congressional Information Services** 4520 East-West Hwy., Ste. 800 Bethesda, MD 20814-3389 **Tel:** 301-654-1550, 800-638-8380; **Fax:** 301-654-4033	**IDC**	**Inter Documentation Co., AG.** Hoge Woerd 151 Leiden, 2301 EE The Netherlands **Tel:** 31-71142700; **Fax:** 31-71131721
CLA	**Canadian Library Association** (no longer producer) Microfile Program 200 Elgin St., Ste. 602 Ottawa, ON K2P 1L5 Canada **Tel:** 613-232-9625; **Fax:** 613-563-9895	**IFA**	**International Federation of Film Archives (FIAF)** 113 Canalot Studios 222 Kensal Rd., London W10 5BN England **Tel:** 44-81-9601001; **Fax:** 44-81-960-8907
CLS	**CLASS** (Cooperative Library Agency for Systems & Services) 1415 Koll Circle, Ste. 101 San Jose, CA 95112-4698 **Tel:** 408-453-0444; **Fax:** 408-453-5379	**ILO**	**ILO Publications** 1828 L St., N.W., Ste 801 Washington, DC 20036 **Tel:** 202-653-7652 **Fax:** 202-653-7687
		IMI	**Irish Microforms, Ltd.** Unit 56 Sandyford Industrial Estate Dublin 18 Ireland **Tel:** 353-1-2893626; **Fax:** 353-1-2954270
CMC	**Computer Microfilm Corp.** 3900 Wheeler Ave. Alexandria, VA 22304 **Tel:** 703-823-0500; **Fax:** 703-823-0505		
CML	**Commonwealth Microfilm Products** 3395 American Dr., Unit 11 Mississauga, ON L4V 1T5 Canada **Tel:** 416-671-4173; **Fax:** 416-671-8361	**IPC**	**Institute of Paper Science & Technology, Inc.** 575 14th St., N.W. Atlanta, GA 30318 **Tel:** 404-853-9500; **Fax:** 404-853-9510
EDR	**Eric Document Reproduction Service** (See: CMC)	**IRE**	**International Research and Evaluation** 21098 IRE—Control Center Eagan, MN 55121 **Tel:** 612-888-9635; **Fax:** 612-888-9124
EEE	**Institute of Electrical and Electronics Engineers** 345 East 47th St. New York, NY 10017 **Tel:** 212-705-7900; **Fax:** 212-705-7682	**ISI**	**Institute for Scientific Information** 3501 Market St. Philadelphia, PA 19104 **Tel:** 215-386-0100; **Fax:** 215-386-6362; 215-386-2911
EMP	**Emmett Publishing, Ltd.** West House 21, West St. Haslemere, Surrey GU27 2AB England **Tel:** 44-428-654443; **Fax:** 44-428-661582	**JAI**	**JAI Press Inc.** 55 Old Post Rd., No. 2 P.O. Box 1678 Greenwich, CT 06836-1678 **Tel:** 203-661-7602; **Fax:** 203-661-0792
FCM	**Fairchild Microfilms** Fairchild Book Division 7 West 34th St. New York, NY 10001 **Tel:** 212-630-3880; **Fax:** 212-630-3868	**JOH**	**Johnson Reprint Microeditions** (Microeditions phased out) 111 Fifth Ave. New York, NY 10003 **Tel:** 212-614-3200; **Fax:** 212-614-3221
GCS	**Preston Publications** P.O. Box 48312 7800 Merrimac Ave. Niles, IL 60714 **Tel:** 708-965-0566; **Fax:** 708-965-7639	**JSC**	**J. S. Canner & Co.** 10 Charles St. Needham Heights, MA 02194 **Tel:** 617-449-9103; **Fax:** 617-449-1767
GMC	**General Microfilm Co.** (acquired by OMNISYS Corp.)		

KGS	**K.G. Saur** A Reed Reference Publishing Company 121 Chanlon Rd. New Providence, NJ 07974 **Tel:** 908-464-6800; **Fax:** 908-771-7725
KHS	**Kansas State Historical Society** **Microfilm Publications** 120 West Tenth Ave. Topeka, KS 66612-1291 **Tel:** 913-296-3251; **Fax:** 913-296-1005
KTO	**Kraus Microform** 358 Saw Mill River Rd. Millwood, NY 10546-1035 **Tel:** 914-762-2200; **Fax:** 914-762-1195
LCP	**The Library of Congress** **Photoduplication Service** 10 First St., S.E. Washington, DC 20540 **Tel:** 202-707-5650; **Fax:** 202-707-1771
LIB	**Library Microfilms** 1115 E. Arques Ave. Sunnyvale, CA 94086 **Tel:** 408-736-7444; **Fax:** 408-736-4397
LOP	**Lomond Publications** P.O. Box 88 Mt. Airy, MD 21771 **Tel:** 301-829-1496, 800-443-6299
MCA	**Microfilming Corporation of America** (Acquired by UMI; operation phased out)
MCE	**Microcard Editions** (See: CIS)
MDX	**Micromedex Inc.** 600 Grant St. Denver, CO 80203 **Tel:** 303-831-1400; **Fax:** 303-837-1717
MEL	**Metropolitan Library Service Agency** (MELSA) S-322 Griggs Midway Bldg., 1821 University Ave. St. Paul, MN 55104-3083 **Tel:** 612-645-5731; **Fax:** 612-649-3169
MIM	**Pergamon Press** 660 White Plains Rd. Tarrytown, NY 10591-5153 **Tel:** 914-524-9200; **Fax:** 914-333-2444
MIS	**Moody's Investors Service** Sales Department 99 Church St. New York, NY 10007 **Tel:** 212-553-0300; **Fax:** 212-553-4700
MML	**Micromedia Limited** 20 Victor St. Toronto, ON M5H 2N8 Canada **Tel:** 416-362-5211, 800-387-2689; **Fax:** 416-362-6161
MMP	**McLaren Micropublishing Ltd.** P.O. Box 972, Station F Toronto, ON M4Y 2N9 Canada **Tel:** 416-960-4801; **Fax:** 416-964-3745
MUE	**University Music Editions, Inc.** P.O. Box 192, Fort George Station New York, NY 10040 **Tel:** 718-569-5340, 5393; **Fax:** 718-601-7226
NBI	**Newsbank, Inc.** 58 Pine St. New Canaan, CT 06840 **Tel:** 203-966-1100, 800-243-7694; **Fax:** 203-966-6254
NRP	**Norman Ross Publishing, Inc.** 330 West 58th St. New York, NY 10019 **Tel:** 212-765-8200, 800-648-8850; **Fax:** 212-765-2393
NTI	**National Technical Information Service** 5285 Port Royal Rd. Springfield, VA 22161 **Tel:** 703-487-4600; **Fax:** 703-321-8547
NYL	**New York Law Publishing Co.** 111 Eighth Ave. New York, NY 10011 **Tel:** 212-741-8300; **Fax:** 212-741-3985
NYT	**New York Times Information Bank** (Operation phased out) 229 W. 43rd St. New York, NY 10036 **Tel:** 212-556-1234
OEC	**Organization for Economic Cooperation &** **Development, Publications & Information Center** 2001 L St., N.W., Ste. 700 Washington, DC 20036 **Tel:** 202-785-6323; **Fax:** 202-785-0350
OMN	**OMNISYS Corp.** 211 Second Ave. Waltham, MA 02154 **Tel:** 617-684-1234; **Fax:** 617-684-1245
OMP	**Oxford Microform Publication Ltd.** (Acquired by UMI)
PMC	**Princeton Microfilm Corp.** P.O. Box 2073 Princeton, NJ 08543 **Tel:** 609-452-2066, 800-257-9502; **Fax:** 609-275-6201
PSL	**The Pretoria State Library** P.O. Box 397 Pretoria 0001, Republic of South Africa **Tel:** 27-12-218931; **Fax:** 27-12-3255984
RPI	**Research Publications** 12 Lunar Dr. Drawer AB Woodbridge, CT 06525 **Tel:** 203-397-2600; **Fax:** 203-397-3893
RRI	**Fred B. Rothman & Co.** 10368 W. Centennial Rd. Littleton, CO 80127 **Tel:** 303-979-5657, 800-457-1986; **Fax:** 303-978-1457

SAS	**Society for Applied Spectroscopy** P.O. Box 1438 Frederick, MD 21701 **Tel:** 301-694-8122; **Fax:** 301-694-6860	**VCI**	**VCH Publishers, Inc.** 303 N.W. 12th Ave. Deerfield Beach, FL 33442-1788 **Tel:** 305-428-5566; **Fax:** 305-428-8201
SOC	**Societe Canadienne du Microfilm Inc–Canadian Microfilming Co. Ltd.** 464 rue Saint-Jean, Ste. 110 Montreal, PQ H2Y 2S1 Canada **Tel:** 514-288-5404; **Fax:** 514-843-4690	**VFN**	**The Voltaire Foundation** at the Taylor Institution St. Giles' Oxford OX1 3NA England **Tel:** 44-865270250; **Fax:** 44-865270740
TMI	**Tennessee Microfilms** P.O. Box 23075 Nashville, TN 37202 **Tel:** 615-242-3632	**WDS**	**Dawson Microfiche** (Distributor only) Cannon House Parkfarm Rd. Folkestone, Kent CT19 5EE England **Tel:** 303-850-101; **Fax:** 303-850-440
UMI	**University Microfilms International** (A Bell & Howell Company) 300 N. Zeeb Rd. Ann Arbor, MI 48106 **Tel:** 313-761-4700, 800-521-0600; **Fax:** 313-761-1203	**WMP**	**World Microfilm Publications Ltd.** Microworld House 2-6 Foscote Mews London, W92 HH England **Tel:** 44-71-2662200; **Fax:** 44-71-2662314
UNM	**University of Michigan Library** Microform Reading Room 2 South Hatcher c/o Graduate Library Ann Arbor, MI 48109 **Tel:** 313-764-0503; **Fax:** 313-764-0259	**WPI**	**Waverly Press, Inc.** 428 East Preston St. Baltimore, MD 21202 **Tel:** 410-528-4288 **Fax:** 410-528-4312
UNW	**University of Wisconsin Library** Interlibrary Loan Department 728 State St., Rm. 231 Madison, WI 53706 **Tel:** 608-262-3193; **Fax:** 608-262-4649	**WSH**	**William S. Hein & Co., Inc.** Hein Building 1285 Main St. Buffalo, NY 14209 **Tel:** 716-882-2600, 800-828-7571; **Fax:** 716-883-8100
UPD	**Updata Publications Inc.** 1736 Westwood Blvd. Los Angeles, CA 90024 **Tel:** 310-474-5900; **Fax:** 310-474-4095	**WWS**	**Williams & Wilkins** 428 East Preston St. Baltimore, MD 21202 **Tel:** 410-528-4309; **Fax:** 410-528-4312

Reprint Services

ISI   **Institute for Scientific Information**
3501 Market St.
Philadelphia, PA 19104
Tel: 215-386-0100; **Fax:** 215-386-6362; 215-386-2911

JOH   **Johnson Reprint Microeditions**
111 Fifth Ave.
New York, NY 10003
Tel: 212-614-3200; **Fax:** 212-614-3221

KTO   **Kraus Microform**
358 Saw Mill River Rd.
Millwood, NY 10546-1035
Tel: 914-762-2200; **Fax:** 914-762-1195

RRI   **Fred B. Rothman & Co.**
10368 W. Centennial Rd.
Littleton, CO 80127
Tel: 303-979-5657, 800-457-1986; **Fax:** 303-978-1457

SCH   **Schmidt Periodicals GmbH**
Dettendorf
D-8201 Bad Feilnbach 2
Germany
Tel: 49-8064221; **Fax:** 49-8064557

SWZ   **Swets & Zeitlinger B.V.**
P.O. Box 810
Heereweg 347 B
2160 SZ Lisse
The Netherlands
Tel: 31-2521-35111; **Fax:** 31-2521-15888

UMI   **University Microfilms International**
(A Bell & Howell Company)
300 N. Zeeb Rd.
Ann Arbor, MI 48106
Tel: 313-761-4700, 800-521-0600; **Fax:** 313-761-1203

WDS   **Dawson Microfiche**
Cannon House
Parkfarm Rd.
Folkestone, Kent CT19 5EE England
Tel: 303-850-101; **Fax:** 303-850-440

WSH   **William S. Hein & Co., Inc.**
428 East Preston St.
Baltimore, MD 21202
Tel: 410-528-4309; **Fax:** 410-528-4312

Country of Publication Codes

This list of countries and their codes has been taken from the list used by the Library of Congress in the MARC II format, 1972. The list used here is not the complete list of the MARC II format and is limited to presently existing national entities. The states of the United States, provinces and territories of Canada, and divisions of the United Kingdom are not listed separately.

The codes are mnemonic in most cases. Special codes not in the MARC format are used for publications of two international organizations: EI for European Communities and UN for United Nations and related organizations, and KR for Ukraine, respectively.

Country Code Sequence

AA -ALBANIA
AE -ALGERIA
AF -AFGHANISTAN
AG -ARGENTINA
AI -ARMENIA
AJ -AZERBAIJAN
AN -ANDORRA
AO -ANGOLA
AQ -ANTIGUA
AS -AMERICAN SAMOA
AT -AUSTRALIA
AU -AUSTRIA
AY -ANTARCTICA
BA -BAHRAIN
BB -BARBADOS
BD -BURUNDI
BE -BELGIUM
BF -BAHAMAS
BG -BANGLADESH
BH -BELIZE
BL -BRAZIL
BM -BERMUDA
BN -BOSNIA HERCEGOVINA
BO -BOLIVIA
BP -SOLOMON ISLANDS
BR -UNION OF MYANMAR (FORMERLY BURMA)
BS -BOTSWANA
BT -BHUTAN
BU -BULGARIA
BW -BELARUS
BX -BRUNEI DARUSSALAM
CB -CAMBODIA
CC -CHINA, PEOPLE'S REPUBLIC OF
CD -CHAD
CE -SRI LANKA
CF -CONGO (BRAZZAVILLE)
CH -CHINA, REPUBLIC OF
CI -CROATIA
CJ -CAYMAN ISLANDS
CK -COLOMBIA
CL -CHILE
CM -CAMEROON
CN -CANADA
CR -COSTA RICA
CS -CZECHOSLOVAKIA
CU -CUBA
CV -CAPE VERDE
CX -CENTRAL AFRICAN REPUBLIC
CY -CYPRUS
CZ -CANAL ZONE
DK -DENMARK
DM -BENIN
DQ -DOMINICA
DR -DOMINICAN REPUBLIC
EC -ECUADOR
EG -EQUATORIAL GUINEA
EI -EUROPEAN COMMUNITIES
ER -ESTONIA
ES -EL SALVADOR
ET -ETHIOPIA
FA -FAEROE ISLANDS
FG -FRENCH GUIANA
FI -FINLAND
FJ -FIJI
FK -FALKLAND ISLANDS
FM -FEDERATED STATES OF MICRONESIA
FP -FRENCH POLYNESIA
FR -FRANCE
FT -DJIBOUTI
GD -GRENADA
GH -GHANA

GI -GIBRALTAR
GL -GREENLAND
GM -GAMBIA
GO -GABON
GP -GUADELOUPE
GR -GREECE
GS -GEORGIA
GT -GUATEMALA
GU -GUAM
GV -GUINEA
GW -GERMANY
GY -GUYANA
HK -HONG KONG
HO -HONDURAS
HT -HAITI
HU -HUNGARY
IC -ICELAND
IE -IRELAND
II -INDIA
IO -INDONESIA
IQ -IRAQ
IR -IRAN
IS -ISRAEL
IT -ITALY
IV -IVORY COAST
JA -JAPAN
JM -JAMAICA
JO -JORDAN
KE -KENYA
KG -KYRGYZSTAN
KN -KOREA, NORTH
KO -KOREA, SOUTH
KR -UKRAINE
KU -KUWAIT
KZ -KAZAKHSTAN
LB -LIBERIA
LE -LEBANON
LH -LIECHTENSTEIN
LI -LITHUANIA
LO -LESOTHO
LS -LAOS
LU -LUXEMBOURG
LV -LATVIA
LY -LIBYA
MC -MONACO
ME -MAURITIUS
MG -MALAGASY REPUBLIC (MADAGASCAR)
MH -MACAO
MJ -MONTSERRAT
MK -SULTANATE OF OMAN
ML -MALI
MM -MALTA
MP -MONGOLIA
MQ -MARTINIQUE
MR -MOROCCO
MU -MAURITANIA
MV -MOLDOVA
MW -MALAWI
MX -MEXICO
MY -MALAYSIA
MZ -MOZAMBIQUE
NA -NETHERLANDS ANTILLES
NE -NETHERLANDS
NG -NIGER
NL -NEW CALEDONIA
NN -VANUATU (NEW HEBRIDES)
NO -NORWAY
NP -NEPAL
NQ -NICARAGUA
NR -NIGERIA
NU -NAURU

NZ -NEW ZEALAND
PE -PERU
PG -GUINEA-BISSAU
PH -PHILIPPINES
PK -PAKISTAN
PL -POLAND
PN -PANAMA
PO -PORTUGAL
PP -PAPUA NEW GUINEA
PR -PUERTO RICO
PY -PARAGUAY
QA -QATAR
RE -REUNION
RH -ZIMBABWE
RM -RUMANIA
RU -RUSSIA
RW -RWANDA
SA -SOUTH AFRICA
SE -SEYCHELLES
SF -SAO TOME PRINCIPE
SG -SENEGAL
SI -SINGAPORE
SJ -SUDAN
SL -SIERRA LEONE
SM -SAN MARINO
SO -SOMALIA
SP -SPAIN
SQ -SWAZILAND
SR -SURINAM
SU -SAUDI ARABIA
SW -SWEDEN
SX -NAMIBIA (FORMERLY SOUTH-WEST AFRICA)
SY -SYRIA
SZ -SWITZERLAND
TA -TAJIKISTAN
TC -TURKS AND CAICOS ISLANDS
TG -TOGO
TH -THAILAND
TI -TUNISIA
TK -TURKMENISTAN
TO -TONGA
TR -TRINIDAD & TOBAGO
TS -UNITED ARAB EMIRATES
TU -TURKEY
TZ -TANZANIA
UA -EGYPT (ARAB REPUBLIC OF EGYPT)
UG -UGANDA
UI -UNITED KINGDOM MISC. ISLANDS
UK -UNITED KINGDOM
UN -UNITED NATIONS
US -UNITED STATES
UV -BURKINA FASO
UY -URUGUAY
UZ -UZBEKISTAN
VB -BRITISH VIRGIN ISLANDS
VC -VATICAN CITY
VE -VENEZUELA
VI -U.S. VIRGIN ISLANDS
VN -VIETNAM
WS -WESTERN SAMOA
XC -MALDIVE ISLANDS
XE -MARSHALL ISLANDS
XI -ST. KITTS-NEVIS
XK -SAINT LUCIA
XM -SAINT VINCENT
XN -MACEDONIA
XV -SLOVENIA
YE -YEMEN, REPUBLIC OF
YU -YUGOSLAVIA
ZA -ZAMBIA
ZR -ZAIRE

COUNTRY OF PUBLICATION CODES xxvii

Country Sequence

AFGHANISTAN - AF
ALBANIA - AA
ALGERIA - AE
AMERICAN SAMOA - AS
ANDORRA - AN
ANGOLA - AO
ANTARTICA - AY
ANTIGUA - AQ
ARGENTINA - AG
ARMENIA - AI
AUSTRALIA - AT
AUSTRIA - AU
AZERBAIJAN - AJ
BAHAMAS - BF
BAHRAIN - BA
BANGLADESH - BG
BARBADOS - BB
BELARUS - BW
BELGIUM - BE
BELIZE - BH
BENIN - DM
BERMUDA - BM
BHUTAN - BT
BOLIVIA - BO
BOSNIA HERCEGOVINA - BN
BOTSWANA - BS
BRAZIL - BL
BRITISH VIRGIN ISLANDS - VB
BRUNEI DARUSSALAM - BX
BULGARIA - BU
BURKINA FASO - UV
BURUNDI - BD
CAMBODIA - CB
CAMEROON - CM
CANADA - CN
CANAL ZONE - CZ
CAPE VERDE - CV
CAYMAN ISLANDS - CJ
CENTRAL AFRICAN REPUBLIC - CX
CHAD - CD
CHILE - CL
CHINA, PEOPLE'S REPUBLIC OF - CC
CHINA, REPUBLIC OF - CH
COLOMBIA - CK
CONGO (BRAZZAVILLE) - CF
COSTA RICA - CR
CROATIA - CI
CUBA - CU
CYPRUS - CY
CZECHOSLOVAKIA - CS
DENMARK - DK
DJIBOUTI - FT
DOMINICA - DQ
DOMINICAN REPUBLIC - DR
ECUADOR - EC
EGYPT (ARAB REPUBLIC OF EGYPT) - UA
EL SALVADOR - ES
EQUATORIAL GUINEA - EG
ESTONIA - ER
ETHIOPIA - ET
EUROPEAN COMMUNITIES - EI
FAEROE ISLANDS - FA
FALKLAND ISLANDS - FK
FEDERATED STATES OF MICRONESIA - FM
FIJI - FJ
FINLAND - FI
FRANCE - FR
FRENCH GUIANA - FG
FRENCH POLYNESIA - FP
GABON - GO
GAMBIA - GM
GEORGIA - GS

GERMANY - GW
GHANA - GH
GIBRALTAR - GI
GREECE - GR
GREENLAND - GL
GRENADA - GD
GUADELOUPE - GP
GUAM - GU
GUATEMALA - GT
GUINEA - GV
GUINEA - BISSAU - PG
GUYANA - GY
HAITI - HT
HONDURAS - HO
HONG KONG - HK
HUNGARY - HU
ICELAND - IC
INDIA - II
INDONESIA - IO
IRAN - IR
IRAQ - IQ
IRELAND - IE
ISRAEL - IS
ITALY - IT
IVORY COAST - IV
JAMAICA - JM
JAPAN - JA
JORDAN - JO
KAZAKHSTAN - KZ
KENYA - KE
KOREA, NORTH - KN
KOREA, SOUTH - KO
KUWAIT - KU
KYRGYZSTAN - KG
LAOS - LS
LATVIA - LV
LEBANON - LE
LESOTHO - LO
LIBERIA - LB
LIBYA - LY
LIECHTENSTEIN - LH
LITHUANIA - LI
LUXEMBOURG - LU
MACAO - MH
MACEDONIA - XN
MALAGASY REPUBLIC
    (MADAGASCAR) - MG
MALAWI - MW
MALAYSIA - MY
MALDIVE ISLANDS - XC
MALI - ML
MALTA - MM
MARSHALL ISLANDS - XE
MARTINIQUE - MQ
MAURITANIA - MU
MAURITIUS - MF
MEXICO - MX
MOLDOVA - MV
MONACO - MC
MONGOLIA - MP
MONTSERRAT - MJ
MOROCCO - MR
MOZAMBIQUE - MZ
NAMIBIA (FORMERLY SOUTH-WEST
    AFRICA) - SX
NAURU - NU
NEPAL - NP
NETHERLANDS - NE
NETHERLANDS ANTILLES - NA
NEW CALEDONIA - NL
NEW ZEALAND - NZ
NICARAGUA - NQ

NIGER - NG
NIGERIA - NR
NORWAY - NO
PAKISTAN - PK
PANAMA - PN
PAPUA NEW GUINEA - PP
PARAGUAY - PY
PERU - PE
PHILIPPINES - PH
POLAND - PL
PORTUGAL - PO
PUERTO RICO - PR
QATAR - QA
REUNION - RE
RUMANIA - RM
RUSSIA - RU
RWANDA - RW
SAINT KITTS-NEVIS-XI
SAINT LUCIA - XK
SAINT VINCENT - XM
SAN MARINO - SM
SAO TOME E PRINCIPE - SF
SAUDI ARABIA - SU
SENEGAL - SG
SEYCHELLES - SE
SIERRA LEONE - SL
SINGAPORE - SI
SLOVENIA - XV
SOLOMON ISLANDS - BP
SOMALIA - SO
SOUTH AFRICA - SA
SPAIN - SP
SRI LANKA - CE
SUDAN - SJ
SULTANATE OF OMAN - MK
SURINAM - SR
SWAZILAND - SQ
SWEDEN - SW
SWITZERLAND - SZ
SYRIA - SY
TAJIKISTAN - TA
TANZANIA - TZ
THAILAND - TH
TOGO - TH
TONGA - TO
TRINIDAD & TOBAGO - TR
TUNISIA - TI
TURKEY - TU
TURKMENISTAN - TK
TURKS AND CAICOS ISLANDS - TC
UGANDA - UG
UKRAINE - KR
UNION OF MYANMAR (FORMERLY BURMA) - BR
UNITED ARAB EMIRATES - TS
UNITED KINGDOM - UK
UNITED KINGDOM MISC. ISLANDS - UI
UNITED NATIONS - UN
UNITED STATES - US
URUGUAY - UY
U.S VIRGIN ISLANDS - VI
UZBEKISTAN - UZ
VANUATU (NEW HEBRIDES) - NN
VATICAN CITY - VC
VENEZUELA - VE
VIETNAM - VN
WESTERN SAMOA - WS
YEMEN, REPUBLIC OF - YE
YUGOSLAVIA - YU
ZAIRE - ZR
ZAMBIA - ZA
ZIMBABWE - RH

Abstracting and Indexing Services

This list contains the full names of all abstracting and indexing services whose abbreviations are used in entries in the Classified List of Serials. For all currently published abstracting and indexing services, entries containing full bibliographic information will be found in the Classified List of Serials. Consult the Title Index for page numbers. (Bibliographic information for ceased titles can be found in the Bowker International Serials Database online.)

A

A.A.P.P.Abstr.	Amino Acids, Peptides & Proteins Abstracts (Now: Cambridge Scientific Biochemistry Abstracts, Part 3: Amino Acids, Peptides & Proteins)
AAR	Accounting Articles
ABC	Abstracts in BioCommerce
A.B.C.Pol.Sci.	ABC Pol Sci; A Bibliography of Contents: Political Science and Government
ABI Inform.	A B I-INFORM
ABTICS	Abstracts and Book Title Index Card Services (Ceased)
A.D.& D.	Alcohol, Drugs and Driving: Abstracts and Reviews (Now: Alcohol, Drugs and Driving)
AESIS	A E S I S Quarterly (Australian Earth Sciences Information System)
A.I.Abstr.	Artificial Intelligence Abstracts (United States)
A.I.C.P.	Anthropological Index to Current Periodicals in the Library of the Museum of Mankind Library
A.I.D.Res.Dev. Abstr.	A.I.D. Research & Development Abstracts (Agency for International Development)
A.I.P.P.	Annual Index to Poetry in Periodicals (Now: Roth's American Poetry Annual)
AIT Reports	A I T Reports and Publications on Renewable Energy Resources. Abstracts (Asian Institute of Technology) (Now: A I T Reports and Publications on Energy. Abstracts)
API Abstr.	A P I Abstracts: Literature (American Petroleum Institute) (Now: Literature Abstracts)
ALISA	A L I S A (Australian Library and Information Science Abstracts)
API Catal.	A P I Abstracts: Catalysts & Catalysis (Now: Literature Abstracts: Catalysts & Catalysis)
API Hlth.& Environ.	A P I Abstracts: Health & Environment (Now: Literature Abstracts: Health & Environment)
API Oil.	A P I Abstracts: Oilfield Chemicals (Now: Literature and Patent Abstracts: Oilfield Chemicals)
API Pet.Ref.	A P I Abstracts: Petroleum Refining and Petrochemicals (Now: Literature Abstracts: Petroleum Refining and Petrochemicals)
API Pet.Subst.	A P I Abstracts: Petroleum Substitutes (Now: Literature Abstracts: Petroleum Substitutes)
API Transport.	A P I Abstracts: Transportation and Storage (Now: Literature Abstracts: Transportation and Storage)
A.S.& T.Ind.	Applied Science & Technology Index
ASCA	Automatic Subject Citation Alert (Now: Research Alert (Philadelphia))
ASEAN Manage. Abstr.	A S E A N Management Abstracts (Association of South East Asian Nations)
ASSIA	A S S I A (Applied Social Sciences Index & Abstracts)
ASTIS	A S T I S Bibliography (Arctic Science & Technology Information System)
Abr.R.G.	Abridged Readers' Guide to Periodical Literature
Abstr.Anthropol.	Abstracts in Anthropology
Abstr.Bk.Rev. Curr.Leg.Per.	Abstracts of Book Reviews in Current Legal Periodicals (Ceased)
Abstr.Bulg.Sci. Med.Lit.	Abstracts of Bulgarian Scientific Medical Literature
Abstr.Bull.Inst. Pap.Chem.	Institute of Paper Chemistry. Abstract Bulletin
Abstr.Crim.& Pen.	Abstracts on Criminology and Penology (Now: Criminology, Penology & Police Science Abstracts)
Abstr.Engl.Stud.	Abstracts of English Studies
Abstr.Folk.Stud.	Abstracts of Folklore Studies (Ceased)
Abstr.Health Care Manage. Stud.	Abstracts of Health Care Management Studies (Ceased)
Abstr.Health Eff. Environ. Pollut.	Abstracts on Health Effects of Environmental Pollutants (Ceased)

Abstr.Hosp. Manage.Stud.	Abstracts of Hospital Management Studies (Now: Abstracts of Health Care Management Studies)	Anbar	Anbar Publications Ltd. Accounting & Data Processing Abstracts Marketing & Distribution Abstracts Personnel & Training Abstracts Top Management Abstracts Work Study & O and M Abstracts (Now: Management Services & Production Abstracts)
Abstr.Hum.Comp. Inter.	Abstracts in Human-Computer Interaction		
Abstr.Hyg.	Abstracts on Hygiene and Communicable Diseases		
Abstr.Inter.Med.	Abstracts in Internal Medicine (Now: Abstracts in Medicine and Key Word Index)		
		Anim.Behav. Abstr.	Animal Behavior Abstracts
Abstr.J.Earthq. Eng.	Abstract Journal in Earthquake Engineering	Anim.Breed. Abstr.	Animal Breeding Abstracts
Abstr.Mil.Bibl.	Abstracts of Military Bibliography	Ap.Ind.	Apple Index
Abstr.Musl.Rel.	European Muslims and Christian-Muslim Relations. Abstracts. (Ceased)	Apic.Abstr.	Apicultural Abstracts
		Appl.Ecol.Abstr.	Applied Ecology Abstracts (Now: Ecology Abstracts)
Abstr.N.Amer. Geol.	Abstracts of North American Geology (Ceased)	Appl.Mech.Rev.	Applied Mechanics Reviews
		Aqua.Sci.& Fish.Abstr.	Aquatic Sciences & Fisheries Abstracts (Parts 1, 2)
Abstr.Pop.Cult.	Abstracts of Popular Culture (Ceased)		
Abstr.Rural Dev.Trop.	Abstracts on Rural Development in the Tropics	Aquacult.Abstr.	A S F A Aquaculture Abstracts
		Archit.Per.Ind.	Architectural Periodicals Index
Abstr.Soc.Geront.	Abstracts in Social Gerontology: Current Literature on Aging	Arct.Bibl.	Arctic Bibliography (Ceased)
		Art & Archaeol. Tech.Abstr.	Art and Archaeology Technical Abstracts
Abstr.Soc.Work.	Abstracts for Social Workers (Now: Social Work Research & Abstracts)		
		Art Ind.	Art Index
		Art.Int.Abstr.	Artificial Intelligence Abstracts (England) (Ceased)
Abstr.Trop.Agri.	Abstracts on Tropical Agriculture		
Acad.Ind.	Academic Index	Artbibl.	Artbibliographies Current Titles
Access	Access: the Supplementary Index to Periodicals	Artbibl.Mod.	Artbibliographies Modern
		Arts & Hum. Cit.Ind.	Arts & Humanities Citation Index
Account.& Data Proc.Abstr.	Accounting & Data Processing Abstracts (Now: Accounting & Finance Abstracts) (see: Anbar)	Ash.G.Bot.Per.	Asher's Guide to Botanical Periodicals (Now: Guide to Botanical Periodicals) (Ceased)
Account.Ind.	Accountant's Index		
Acid Pre.Dig.	Acid Precipitation Digest	Asian-Pac.Econ.Lit.	Asian-Pacific Economic Literature
Acid Rain Abstr.	Acid Rain Abstracts (Now: Environment Abstracts)	Astron.& Astrophys. Abstr.	Astronomy and Astrophysics Abstracts
Acid Rain Ind.	Acid Rain Annual Index (Now: Environment Abstracts Annual)		
		Astron. Jahresber.	Astronomischer Jahresbericht (Now: Astronomy and Astrophysics Abstracts)
Acoust.Abstr.	Acoustics Abstracts		
Adol.Ment. Hlth.Abstr.	Adolescent Mental Health Abstracts (Ceased)		
		Aus.Educ.Ind.	Australian Education Index
Agri.Eng.Abstr.	Agricultural Engineering Abstracts	Aus.Leg.Mon. Dig.	Australian Legal Monthly Digest
Agri.Ind.	Agriculture Index (Now: Biological & Agricultural Index)	Aus.P.A.I.S.	Australian Public Affairs Information Service (Now: A P A I S: Australian Public Affairs Information Service)
Agrindex	Agrindex		
Agroforest.Abstr.	Agroforestry Abstracts		
Air Un.Lib.Ind.	Air University Library Index to Military Periodicals		
		Aus.Rd.Ind.	Australian Road Index (Ceased)
Alloys Ind.	Alloys Index	Aus.Sci.Ind.	Australian Science Index (Ceased)
Alt.Press Ind.	Alternative Press Index	Aus.Speleo Abstr.	Australian Speleo Abstracts
Amer.Bibl.Slavic & E.Eur.Stud.	American Bibliography of Slavic and East European Studies	Avery Ind. Archit.Per.	Avery Index to Architectural Periodicals
Amer.Hist.& Life	America: History & Life (Parts A, B, C, D)	**B**	
Amer.Hum.Ind.	American Humanities Index	B.C.I.R.A.	B.C.I.R.A. Abstracts of International Foundry Literature (British Cast Iron Research Association) (Now: B C I R A Abstracts on International Literature on Metal Casting Production)
Amer.Stat.Ind.	American Statistics Index		
Anal.Abstr.	Analytical Abstracts		

BIM	Bibliography and Index of Micropaleontology	Biul.Inst.Hod. Aklim.Rosl.	Instytut Hodowli i Aklimatyzacji Roslin. Biuletyn
BMT	B M T Abstracts (British Maritime Technology)	Biwk.Pap.Rad. Chem.& Photochem.	Biweekly List of Papers on Radiation Chemistry and Photochemistry
B.P.I.	Business Periodicals Index	Bk.Rev.Dig.	Book Review Digest
BPIA	Business Publications Index and Abstracts (Ceased)	Bk.Rev.Ind.	Book Review Index
B.R.I.	BioResearch Index (Now: Biological Abstracts/R R M (Reports, Reviews, Meetings)	Bk.Rev.Mo.	Book Reviews of the Month (Ceased)
		Br.Archaeol. Abstr.	British Archaeological Abstracts (Now: British Archaeological Bibliography)
BSL Biol.	Abstracts of Bulgarian Scientific Literature. Biology	Br.Ceram.Abstr.	British Ceramic Abstracts (Now: World Ceramic Abstracts)
BSL Econ.	Abstracts of Bulgarian Scientific Literature. Economics and Law	Br.Educ.Ind.	British Education Index
BSL Geo.	Abstracts of Bulgarian Scientific Literature. Geosciences	Br.Geol.Lit.	British Geological Literature
		Br.Hum.Ind.	British Humanities Index
BSL Indus.	Abstracts of Bulgarian Scientific Literature. Industry, Building and Transport	Br.Rail.Bd.	British Railways Board. Monthly Review of Technical Literature (Ceased)
BSL Math.	Abstracts of Bulgarian Scientific Literature. Mathematical and Physical Sciences	Br.Tech.Ind.	British Technology Index (Now: Current Technology Index)
Bangladesh Agr. Sci.Abstr.	Bangladesh Agricultural Sciences Abstracts	Build.Manage. Abstr.	Building Management Abstracts (Now: Technical Information Service–TIS)
Bank.Lit.Ind.	Banking Literature Index	Bull.Anal.Ent. Med.Vet.	Bulletin Analytique d'Entomologie Medicale et Veterinaire (Ceased)
Behav.Abstr.	Behavioural Abstracts (Ceased)	Bull.Signal.	Bulletin Signaletique (Now: P A S C A L Explore, P A S C A L Folio, P A S C A L Thema) (Programme Applique a la Selection et la Compilation Automatique de la Literature)
Behav.Med.Abstr.	Behavioral Medicine Abstracts (Now: Annals of Behavioral Medicine)		
Ber.Biochem. Biol.	Berichte Biochemie und Biologie (Ceased)		
Bibl.Agri.	Bibliography of Agriculture		
Bibl.& Ind.Geol.	Bibliography & Index of Geology (see: GeoRef)	Bull.Thermodyn.& Thermochem.	Bulletin of Thermodynamics & Thermochemistry (Now: Bulletin of Chemical Thermodynamics) (Ceased)
Bibl.Cart.	Bibliographia Cartographica	Bus.Comput.Ind.	Business Computer Index
Bibl.Dev.Med.& Child Neur.	Bibliography of Developmental Medicine & Child Neurology. Books and Articles Received	Bus.Educ.Ind.	Business Education Index
		Bus.Ind.	Business Index
Bibl.Engl.Lang. & Lit.	Bibliography of English Language and Literature (Now: Annual Bibliography of English Language and Literature)	**C**	
		CAD CAM Abstr.	C A D/C A M Abstracts
		CALL	C A L L (Current Awareness—Library Literature)
Bibl.Ind.	Bibliographic Index	C.C.L.P.	Contents of Current Legal Periodicals (Now: Legal Contents) (Ceased)
Bibl.IULA	Bibliographia I U L A (International Union of Local Authorities) (Ceased)	C.C.M.J.	Contents of Contemporary Mathematical Journals (Now: Current Mathematical Publications)
Bibl.Repro.	Bibliography of Reproduction		
Bibliogr.Bras. Odontol.	Bibliografia Brasileira de Odontologia		
Bio-Contr.News & Info.	Bio-Control News and Information	CCR	Current Christian Abstracts (Now: Current Thoughts & Trends)
Biodet.Abstr.	Biodeterioration Abstracts	CERDIC	Universite de Strasbourg. Centre de Recherche et de Documentation des Institutions Chretiennes. Bulletin du CERDIC (Ceased)
Bioeng.Abstr.	Bioengineering Abstracts		
Biog.& Gen.Master Ind.	Biography and Genealogy Master Index		
Biog.Ind.	Biography Index		
Biol.Abstr.	Biological Abstracts	CHNI	Consumer Health & Nutrition Index
Biol.& Agr.Ind.	Biological & Agricultural Index	C.I.J.E.	Current Index to Journals in Education
Biol.Dig.	Biology Digest		
Biostat.	Biostatistica	CINAHL (also C.I.N.L.)	Cumulative Index to Nursing and Allied Health Literature
Biotech.Abstr.	Biotechnology Research Abstracts		

CIRF Abstr.	C I R F Abstracts (Now: IRD Abstracts) (Ceased)		College Student Personnel Abstracts (Now: Higher Education Abstracts)
C.I.S. Abstr.	C I S Abstracts (Centre International d'Information de Securité et Hygiène du Travail) (Now: Safety and Health at Work)		Communication Abstracts
			Community Mental Health Review (Now: Prevention in Human Services)
C.I.S. Ind.	C I S Index (Congressional Information Service)		Compumath Citation Index
CJPI	Criminal Justice Periodical Index		Computer and Information Systems Abstracts Journal
C.L.I.	Current Law Index		Computer Abstracts
CLOA	Current Literature on Aging (Now: Abstracts in Social Gerontology: Current Literature on Aging)		Computer & Control Abstracts (Also see: INSPEC; also see: Sci. Abstr.)
CMI	Canadian Magazine Index		Computer Business
C.P.I.	Current Physics Index		Computer Contents (Ceased)
C.R.E.J.	Contents of Recent Economics Journals		Computer Database
			Computer Industry Update
C.R.I. Abstr.	C R I Abstracts (Central Research Institute of India)		Computer Literature Index
CS Ind.	Canadian Statistics Index		Computing Reviews
CSI Fed.Ind.	C S I Federal Index (Capitol Services, Inc.)		Concrete Abstracts
			Consumers Index
CWHM	Current Work in the History of Medicine		Contents Pages in Education
Cab.Vid.Ind.	Cable-Video Index		Contents Pages in Management
Cadscan	Cadscan		Copper Abstracts (Now: International Copper Information Bulletin)
Cal.Per.Ind.	California Periodicals Index		
Cal.Tiss.Abstr.	Calcified Tissue Abstracts		Corrosion Abstracts
Can.B.P.I.	Canadian Business Periodicals Index (Now: Canadian Business Index)		Cotton and Tropical Fibres Abstracts (Now: Cotton and Tropical Fibres)
Can.Educ.Ind.	Canadian Education Index		Criminal Justice Abstracts
Can.Lit.Ind.	Canadian Literature Index		Crime and Delinquency Abstracts (Ceased)
Can.Per.Ind.	Canadian Periodical Index		
Can.Rev.Comp. Lit.	Canadian Review of Comparative Literature		Crime & Delinquency Literature (Now: Criminal Justice Abstracts)
Can.Wom.Per.Ind.	Canadian Women's Periodicals Index		Crop Physiology Abstracts
Canadiana	Canadiana		Current Advances in Biochemistry (Now: Current Advances in Protein Biochemistry)
Canon Law Abstr.	Canon Law Abstracts		
Carcinog.Abstr.	Carcinogenesis Abstracts (Now: Cancergram)		
			Current Advances in Cancer Research
Cath.Ind.	Catholic Periodical and Literature Index		
Ceram.Abstr.	Ceramic Abstracts		Current Advances in Cell and Developmental Biology
Chem.Abstr.	Chemical Abstracts		
Chem.Eng.Abstr.	Chemical Engineering Abstracts		Current Advances in Clinical Chemistry
Chem.Indus.Notes	Chemical Industry Notes		
Chem.Infd.	Chemischer Informationsdienst (Now: ChemInform)		Current Advances in Ecological Sciences (Now: Current Advances in Ecological and Environmental Sciences)
Chem.Titles	Chemical Titles		
Chemorec.Abstr.	Chemoreception Abstracts		
Chicago Psychoanal. Lit.Ind.	Chicago Psychoanalytic Literature Index (Ceased)		Current Advances in Genetics and Molecular Biology
Chic.Per.Ind.	Chicano Periodical Index (Now: Chicano Index)		Current Advances in Immunology (Now: Current Advances in Immunology & Infectious Diseases)
Child.Auth.& Illus.	Children's Authors and Illustrators		Current Advances in Microbiology (Now: Current Advances in Applied Microbiology & Biotechnology)
Child.Bk.Rev.Ind.	Children's Book Review Index		
Child Devel.Abstr.	Child Development Abstracts and Bibliography		
Child.Lit.Abstr.	Children's Literature Abstracts		Current Advances in Neuroscience
Chr.Per.Ind.	Christian Periodical Index		Current Advances in Pharmacology & Toxicology (Now: Current Advances in Toxicology)
Clin-Alert	Clin-Alert		

Curr.Adv.Physiol.	Current Advances in Physiology (Now: Current Advances in Endocrinology & Metabolism)	Dok.Arbeitsmed.	Dokumentation Arbeitsmedizin (Now: Arbeitsmedizin)
Curr.Adv.Plant Sci.	Current Advances in Plant Science	Dok.Raum.	Dokumentation zur Raumentwicklung (Ceased)
Curr.Aus.N.Z.Leg. Lit.Ind.	Current Australian and New Zealand Legal Literature Index	Dok.Str.	Dokumentation Strasse

E

Curr.Bibl.Aquatic Sci.& Fish	Current Bibliography for Aquatic Sciences & Fisheries (Now: Aquatic Sciences and Fisheries Abstracts. Parts 1,2,3)
Curr.Biotech.Abstr.	Current Biotechnology Abstracts
Curr.Bk.Rev.Cit.	Current Book Review Citations (Ceased)
Curr.Chem.React.	Current Chemical Reactions
Curr.Cont.	Current Contents
Curr.Cont.Africa	Current Contents Africa
Curr.Cont.M.E.	Current Contents of Periodicals on the Middle East
Curr.Dig.Sov. Press	Current Digest of Soviet Press (Now: Current Digest of the Post-Soviet Press)
Curr.Ind. Commonw. Leg.Per.	Current Index to Commonwealth Legal Periodicals (Now: Index to Commonwealth Legal Periodicals) (Ceased)
Curr.Ind.Stat.	Current Index to Statistics
Curr.Leather Lit.	Current Leather Literature (Now: Leather Science Abstracts)
Curr.Lit.Blood	Current Literature of Blood (Ceased)
Curr.Lit.Fam.Plan.	Current Literature in Family Planning
Curr.Pack.Abstr.	Current Packaging Abstracts
Curr.Pap.Phys.	Current Papers in Physics (Also see: INSPEC)
Curr.Tit.Dent.	Current Titles in Dentistry
Curr.Tit. Electrochem.	Current Titles in Electrochemistry
Curr.Tit.Ocean	Current Titles in Ocean, Coastal, Lake & Waterway Sciences (Ceased)
Cyb.Abstr.	Cybernetics Abstracts

EC Ind.	E C Index (European Communities)
E.I.	E I (Excerpta Indonesica)
ERIC	Eric Clearinghouse (See: C.I.J.E.)
Ecol.Abstr.	Ecological Abstracts
Econ.Abstr.	Economic Abstracts (Now: Key to Economic Science)
Educ.Admin.Abstr.	Educational Administration Abstracts
Educ.Ind.	Education Index
Educ.Tech.Abstr.	Educational Technology Abstracts
Ekist.Ind.	Ekistic Index
Elec.& Electron. Abstr.	Electrical & Electronics Abstracts (Also see: INSPEC; also see: Sci.Abstr.)
Electroanal.Abstr.	Electroanalytical Abstracts (Ceased)
Electron.& Communic.Abstr.J.	Electronics and Communications Abstracts Journal
Endocrin.Abstr.	Endocrinology Abstracts (Now: C S A Neurosciences Abstracts)
Endocrin.Ind.	Endocrinology Index (Ceased)
Energy Abstr.	Energy Abstracts
Energy Ind.	Energy Index (Now: Energy Information Abstracts Annual)
Energy Info.Abstr.	Energy Information Abstracts
Energy Res.Abstr.	Energy Research Abstracts
Energy Rev.	Energy Review (Santa Barbara)
Eng.Ind.	Engineering Index (Now: Engineering Index Monthly)
Eng.Mat.Abstr.	Engineered Materials Abstracts
Entomol.Abstr.	Entomology Abstracts
Environ.Abstr.	Environment Abstracts
Environ.Ind.	Environment Index (Now: Environment Abstracts Annual)
Environ.Per.Bibl.	Environmental Periodicals Bibliography
Ergon.Abstr.	Ergonomics Abstracts
Except.Child Educ. Abstr.	Exceptional Child Education Abstracts (Now: Exceptional Child Education Resources)
Excerp.Bot.	Excerpta Botanica (Sections A, B)
Excerp.Criminol.	Excerpta Criminologica (Now: Criminology and Penology Abstracts)
Excerp.Med.	Excerpta Medica

D

DAAI	Design and Applied Arts Index
DM& T	Defense Markets and Technology (Now: Aerospace Defense Markets and Technology) (Ceased)
DNP	Digest of Neurology & Psychiatry
DSH Abstr.	D S H Abstracts (Deafness, Speech and Hearing) (Ceased)
Dairy Sci.Abstr.	Dairy Science Abstracts
Data Process.Dig.	Data Processing Digest
Deep Sea Res.& Oceanogr.Abstr.	Deep Sea Research & Oceanographic Abstracts (Now: Deep-Sea Research. Parts A, B)
Dent.Abstr.	Dental Abstracts
Dent.Ind.	Index to Dental Literature
Devindex	Devindex (Ceased)
Diab.Lit.Ind.	Diabetes Literature Index (Ceased)
Doc.Geogr.	Documentatio Geographica (Now: Dokumentation zur Raumentwicklung) (Ceased)

F

F.A.C.T.	Fuel Abstracts and Current Titles (Now: Fuel and Energy Abstracts)
FAMLI	F A M L I (Family Medicine Literature Index)
F.R.	Fanatic Reader
Fababean Abstr.	Fababean Abstracts
Farm & Garden Ind.	Farm & Garden Index (Ceased)
Fed Print	Fed in Print
Fert.Abstr.	Fertilizer Abstracts (Ceased)

Field Crop Abstr.	Field Crop Abstracts	Graph.Arts Abstr.	Graphic Arts Abstracts (Now: G A T F World)
Film Lit.Ind.	Film Literature Index	Graph.Arts Lit. Abstr.	Graphic Arts Literature Abstracts (Now: Institute of Paper Science and Technology. Graphic Arts Bulletin)
Fluidex	Fluidex Consists of: Civil Engineering Hydraulics Abstracts Current Fluid Engineering Titles (Ceased) Fluid Flow Measurement Abstracts Fluid Power Abstracts Fluid Sealing Abstracts Industrial Aerodynamics Abstracts Industrial Jetting Report Pipelines Abstracts Pumps and Other Fluids Machinery Abstracts Pumps and Turbines (Ceased) River and Flood Control Abstracts (Ceased) Solid-Liquid Flow Abstracts Tribos-Tribology Abstracts World Ports and Harbours Abstracts World Ports and Harbours News (Ceased)		

H

HMA	Healthcare Marketing Abstracts
HR Rep.	Human Rights Internet Reporter
HRIS	H R I S Abstracts (Now: Highway Research Abstracts)
Helminthol.Abstr.	Helminthological Abstracts. Series A (Now: Helminthological Abstracts) Helminthological Abstracts. Series B (Now: Nematological Abstracts)
Herb.Abstr.	Herbage Abstracts
High.Educ.Abstr.	Higher Education Abstracts
High.Educ.Curr. Aware.Bull.	Higher Education Current Awareness Bulletin (Ceased)
Hisp.Amer.Per.Ind.	Hispanic American Periodicals Index
Hist.Abstr.	Historical Abstracts (Parts A, B)
Hlth.Dev.Alerts	Health Devices Alerts
Hlth.Ind.	Health Index
Hlth.Phys.Educ.& Rec.	Health, Physical Education and Recreation Microform Publication Bulletin
Hort.Abstr.	Horticultural Abstracts
Hosp.Abstr.	Hospital Abstracts (Now: Health Service Abstracts)
Hosp.Abstr.Serv.	Hospital Abstracts Service (Ceased)
Hosp.Lit.Ind.	Hospital Literature Index
Hospit.Ind.	Hospitality Index
Hum.Ind.	Humanities Index
Human Resour. Abstr.	Human Resources Abstracts
Hung.Build.Bull.	Hungarian Building Bulletin (Ceased)
Hung.Lib.& Info. Sci.Abstr.	Hungarian Library and Information Science Abstracts
Hwy.Res.Abstr.	Highway Research Abstracts (Now: Transportation Research Abstracts) (Ceased)

Food Sci.&Tech. Abstr.	Food Science and Technology Abstracts
Foreign Leg.Per.	Index to Foreign Legal Periodicals
Forest.Abstr.	Forestry Abstracts
Forest Prod.Abstr.	Forest Products Abstracts
Foul.Prev.Res.Dig.	Fouling Prevention Research Digest (Now: Heat Transfer & Fluid Flow Service Digest)
Fuel & Energy Abstr.	Fuel & Energy Abstracts
Fut.Abstr.	Future - Abstracts
Fut.Surv.	Future Survey

G

G.Indian Per.Lit.	Guide to Indian Periodical Literature
G.Perf.Arts	Guide to the Performing Arts (Ceased)
G.Soc.Sci.& Rel. Per.Lit.	Guide to Social Science and Religion in Periodical Literature
Gard.Lit.	Garden Literature
Gas Abstr.	Gas Abstracts
Gastroenterol: Abstr.& Cit.	Gastroenterology: Abstracts & Citations (Ceased)
Gdlns.	Guidelines
Gen.Phys.Adv. Abstr.	General Physics Advance Abstracts
Gen.Sci.Ind.	General Science Index
Geneal.Per.Ind.	Genealogical Periodical Annual Index
Genet.Abstr.	Genetics Abstracts
Geo.Abstr.	Geographical Abstracts
Geophys.Abstr.	Geophysical Abstracts (Ceased)
GeoRef	Bibliography and Index of Geology (Also known as GeoRef)
Geosci.Doc.	Geoscience Documentation
Geotech.Abstr.	Geotechnical Abstracts
Ger.J.Psych.	German Journal of Psychology
Gleanings	Gleanings

I

IBM PC Ind.	I B M PC Index (Personal Computer)
IBR	I B R (International Bibliography of Book Reviews of Scholarly Literature)
IBZ	Internationale Bibliographie der Zeitschriftenliteratur aus allen Gebieten des Wissens/International Bibliography of Periodicals from all Fields of Knowledge
I.C.U.I.S.Abstr.	I C U I S Abstracts Service (Institute on the Church in Urban Industrial Society) (Now: I C U I S Justice Ministries) (Ceased)
I D A	International Development Abstracts
IIS	Index to International Statistics

I.M.M.Abstr.	I M M Abstracts (Institute of Mining & Metallurgy) (Now: I M M Abstracts and Index)	I.P.A.	International Pharmaceutical Abstracts
		I.R.A.	Information Resources Annual (Ceased)
I.N.E.P.	Index to New England Periodicals	ISMEC	I S M E C Bulletin (Information Service in Mechanical Engineering (Now: I S M E C: Mechanical Engineering Abstracts)
INIS Atomind.	I N I S Atomindex (International Nuclear Information System)		
INSPEC	INSPEC (The Institution of Electrical Engineers):		
	Computers & Control Abstracts (Alternative title: INSPEC, Section C. Represents: Science Abstracts. Section C) (Also see: Comput. & Contr.Abstr.; also see: Sci.Abstr.)	Immun.Abstr.	Immunology Abstracts
		Ind.Agri.Am.Lat. Caribe	Indice Agricole de America Latina y el Caribe (Ceased)
		Ind.Amer.Per. Verse	Index of American Periodical Verse
		Ind.Artic.Jew.Stud.	Index of Articles on Jewish Studies
	Current Papers in Computers & Control	Ind.Bk.Rev.Hum.	Index to Book Reviews in the Humanities (Ceased)
		Ind.Bus.Rep.	Index to Business Reports
	Current Papers in Electrical & Electronics Engineering	Ind.Can.L.P.L.	Index to Canadian Legal Periodical Literature
	Current Papers in Physics (Also see: Curr.Pap.Phys.)	Ind.Chem.	Index Chemicus
		Ind.Child.Mag.	Subject Index to Children's Magazines (Now: Children's Magazine Guide)
	Electrical & Electronics Abstracts (Alternative title: INSPEC, Section B. Represents: Science Abstracts. Section B.) (Also see: Elec.&Electron.Abstr.; also see: Sci.Abstr.)	Ind.Curr.Urb.Doc.	Index to Current Urban Documents
		Ind.Develop.Abstr.	Industrial Development Abstracts
		Ind.Free Per.	Index to Free Periodicals
		Ind.Heb.Per.	Index to Hebrew Periodicals
		Ind.How To Do It	Index to How to Do It Information
	Key Abstracts Advanced Materials	Ind.Hyg.Dig.	Industrial Hygiene Digest
	Key Abstracts Antennas & Propagation	Ind.India	Index India
		Ind.Islam.	Index Islamicus
	Key Abstracts Artificial Intelligence	Ind.Jew.Per.	Index to Jewish Periodicals
	Key Abstracts Business Automation	Ind.Lit.Amer. Indian	Index to Literature on the American Indian (Ceased)
	Key Abstracts Computer Communication and Storage	Ind.Lit.Dent.	Indice de la Literatura Dental Periodica en Castellano
	Key Abstracts Computing in Electronics & Power		
	Key Abstracts Electronic Circuits	Ind.Little Mag.	Index to Little Magazines (Ceased)
	Key Abstracts Electronic Instrumentation	Ind.Med.	Index Medicus
		Ind.Med.Esp.	Indice Medico Espanol
	Key Abstracts Factory Automation	Ind.N.Z.Per.	Index to New Zealand Periodicals (Now: Index New Zealand)
	Key Abstracts High-Temperature Superconductors		
	Key Abstracts Human-Computer Interaction	Ind.Per.Art.Relat. Law	Index to Periodical Articles Related to Law
	Key Abstracts Machine Vision	Ind.Per.Blacks	Index to Periodical Articles by and about Blacks (Now: Index to Black Periodicals)
	Key Abstracts Measurements in Physics		
	Key Abstracts Microelectronics & Printed Circuits	Ind.Per.Lit.	Index to Indian Periodical Literature (Ceased)
	Key Abstracts Microwave Technology	Ind.Per.Negroes	Index to Periodical Articles by & about Negroes (Now: Index to Black Periodicals)
	Key Abstracts Neural Networks		
	Key Abstracts Optoelectronics	Ind.Phil.Per.	Index to Philippine Periodicals
	Key Abstracts Power Systems & Applications	Ind.Rheum.	Annual Index of Rheumatology (Ceased)
	Key Abstracts Robotics & Control		
	Key Abstracts Semiconductor Devices	Ind.S.A.Per.	Index to South African Periodicals
		Ind.Sci.Rev.	Index to Scientific Reviews
	Key Abstracts Software Engineering	Ind.Sel.Per.	Index to Selected Periodicals (Now: Index to Black Periodicals)
	Key Abstracts Telecommunications		
	Physics Abstracts (Alternative title: INSPEC, Section A. Represents: Science Abstracts. Section A) (Also see: Phys.Abstr.; also see: Sci.Abstr.)	Ind.SST.	Index to Spanish Science and Technolog
		Ind.U.S.Gov.Per.	Index to U.S. Government Periodical:
		Ind.Vet.	Index Veterinarius
		Indian Educ.Abstr.	Indian Education Abstracts

Indian Lib.Sci. Abstr.	Indian Library Science Abstracts	JCT	Japan Computer Technology and Applications Abstracts (Ceased)
Indian Psychol. Abstr.	Indian Psychological Abstracts	JTA	Japanese Technical Abstracts (Now: Japan Technology Series) (Ceased)
Indian Sci.Abstr.	Indian Science Abstracts	J.Cont. Quant.Meth.	Journal Contents in Quantitative Methods
Indian Sci.Ind.	Indian Science Index (Ceased)		
Info.Media & Tech.	Information Media and Technology	J.Curr.Laser Abstr.	Journal of Current Laser Abstracts
Inform.Sci.Abstr.	Information Science Abstracts	J.of Abstr.Int. Educ.	Journal of Abstracts in International Education
Inpharma	InPharma		
Instrum.Abstr.	Instrument Abstracts (Now: Metron) (Ceased)	J.of Econ.Abstr.	Journal of Economic Abstracts (Now: Journal of Economic Literature)
Int.Abstr.Biol.Sci.	International Abstracts of Biological Sciences (Now: Current Awareness in Biological Sciences)	J.of Ferroc.	Journal of Ferrocement
		Jap.Per.Ind.	Japanese Periodicals Index (Humanities and Social Science Section; Medical Sciences and Pharmacology (Ceased); Science and Technology)
Int.Abstr.Oper.Res.	International Abstracts in Operations Research		
Int.Aerosp.Abstr.	International Aerospace Abstracts	Jazz Ind.	Jazz Index (Ceased)
Int.Bibl.Soc.Sci.	International Bibliography of the Social Sciences: Anthropology, Political Science, Economics, Sociology (Ceased)	Jun.High Mag. Abstr.	Junior High Magazine Abstracts
		K	
Int.Build.Serv. Abstr.	International Building Services Abstracts	Key to Econ.Sci.	Key to Economic Science
		Key Word Ind.Ser. Titl.	Keyword Index to Serial Titles
Int.Dredg.Abstr.	International Dredging Abstracts (Now: World Ports and Harbours Abstracts; see: Fluidex)	Key Word Ind. Wildl.Res.	Key Word Index of Wildlife Research
Int.G.Class.Stud.	International Guide to Classical Studies (Ceased)	**L**	
Int.Ind.Film Per.	International Index to Film Periodicals		
Int.Lab.Doc.	International Labor Documentation	LAMP	L A M P (Literature Analysis of Microcomputer Publications)
Int.Nurs.Ind.	International Nursing Index		
Int.Packag.Abstr.	International Packaging Abstracts	LCR	Literary Criticism Register
Int.Polit.Sci.Abstr.	International Political Science Abstracts	LHTN	Library Hi Tech News
Int.Sci.Rev.	International Science Review Series (Ceased)	L.I.I.	Life Insurance Index (Ceased)
		LISA	Library & Information Science Abstracts
Int.Z.Bibelwiss.	Internationale Zietschriften fuer Bibel- wissenschaft und Grenzgebiete (Ceased)	L.R.I.	Legal Resource Index
		Lab.Haz.Bull	Laboratory Hazards Bulletin
Intl.Bibl.Burns	International Bibliography on Burns	Landwirt. Zentralbl.	Landwirtschaftliches Zentralblatt (Now: Agroselekt)
Intl.Bibl.S.S.Econ.	International Bibliography of the Social Sciences: Economics		
Intl.Bibl.S.S.Pol. Sci.	International Bibliography of the Social Sciences: Political Science	Lang.& Lang. Behav.Abstr.	Language and Language Behaviour Abstracts (Now: Linguistics and Language Behavior Abstracts)
Intl.Bibl.S.S. Soc.Cult.Anthro.	International Bibliography of the Social Sciences. Anthropology	Lang.Teach.& Ling.Abstr.	Language Teaching and Linguistics Abstracts (Now: Language Teaching)
Intl.Civil Eng. Abstr.	International Civil Engineering Abstracts	Lat.Lit.Fam.Plan.	Latest Literature in Family Planning (Ceased)
Intl.Ind.TV.	International Index to Television Periodicals	Law Ofc.Info.Svc.	Law Office Information Service
		Lead Abstr.	Lead Abstracts (Now: Leadscan)
Intl.Mgmt.Info.	International Management Information Business Digest (Ceased)	Left Ind.	Left Index
		Leg.Cont.	Legal Contents (Ceased)
Intl.Polym.Sci.& Tech.	International Polymer Science and Technology	Leg.Info.Manage. Ind.	Legal Information Management Index
Iron & Steel Indus. Pr.	Iron and Steel Industry Profiles (Ceased)	Leg.Per.	Index to Legal Periodicals
		Lib.Lit.	Library Literature
Irr.& Drain.Abstr.	Irrigation & Drainage Abstracts	Lib.Sci.Abstr.	Library Science Abstracts (Now: Library & Information Science Abstracts)
J			
JAMA	JAMA: The Journal of the American Medical Association	Lit.Automat.	Literature on Automation (Now: New Literature on Automation)

M

MEDOC	MEDOC: Index to U.S. Government Publications in the Medical and Health Sciences
MEDSOC	Medical Socioeconomic Research Sources (Ceased)
MELSA	MELSA Messenger (Metropolitan Library Service) (Ceased)
M.L.A.	M L A Abstracts of Articles in Scholarly Journals (Ceased)
M.M.R.I.	Multi-Media Reviews Index (Now: Media Review Digest)
Mag.Ind.	Magazine Index
Maize Abstr.	Maize Abstracts
Manage.Abstr.	Management Abstracts (India) (Now: Indian Management)
Manage.Cont.	Management Contents (Ceased)
Mar.Aff.Bibl.	Marine Affairs Bibliography
Mar.Sci.Cont.Tab.	Marine Science Contents Tables
Mark.Res.Abstr.	Market Research Abstracts
Mass Spectr.Bull.	Mass Spectrometry Bulletin
Math.R.	Mathematical Reviews
Med.Abstr.	Medical Abstract Service (Ceased)
Med.Care Rev.	Medical Care Review
Med.Res.Ind.	Medical Research Index (Now: Medical Research Centres)
Media Rev.Dig.	Media Review Digest
Ment.Retard.Abstr.	Mental Retardation Abstracts (Now: Developmental Disabilities Abstracts) (Ceased)
Met.Abstr.	Metallurgical Abstracts (Now: Metals Abstracts) see also: Cleaning/Finishing/Coating Digest Corrosion Prevention/Inhibition Digest Heat Processing Digest
Met.Finish.Abstr.	Metal Finishing Abstracts (Now: Surface Treatment Technology Abstracts)
Meteor.& Geo-astrophys. Abstr.	Meteorological & Geoastrophysical Abstracts
Meth.Per.Ind.	Methodist Periodical Index (Now: United Methodist Periodical Index) (Ceased)
Mgmt.Abstr.	Management Abstracts (Trinidad)
Mgmt.& Market. Abstr.	Management & Marketing Abstracts
Mich.Mag.Ind.	Michigan Magazine Index (Ceased)
Microbiol.Abstr.	Microbiological Abstracts (Sections A, B, C)
Microcomp.Ind.	Microcomputer Index
Microcomp.Indus.Up.	Microcomputer Industry Update
Mid.East: Abstr. & Ind.	Middle East: Abstracts and Index (Ceased)
Mineral.Abstr.	Mineralogical Abstracts
Mkt.Inform.Guide	Marketing Information Guide (Ceased)
Multi.Scler.Abstr.	Multiple Sclerosis Indicative Abstracts (Ceased)
Music Artic.Guide	Music Article Guide
Music Ind.	Music Index
Mycol.Abstr.	Abstracts of Mycology

N

NAA	N A A (Nordic Archaeological Abstracts)
NASA	N A S A Patent Abstracts Bibliography: A Continuing Bibliography. Section 2. Indexes (National Aeronautics and Space Administration)
NRN	Nutrition Research Newsletter
Nav.Abstr.	Naval Abstracts (Ceased)
Neurosci.Abstr.	Neurosciences Abstracts (Now: C S A Neurosciences Abstracts)
New Per.Ind.	New Periodicals Index (Ceased)
New Sil.Tech	New Silver Technology (Ceased)
New Test.Abstr.	New Testament Abstracts
Noise Pollut. Publ.Abstr.	Noise Pollution Publications Abstracts (Ceased)
Nucl.Sci.Abstr.	Nuclear Science Abstracts (Superseded by: I N I S Atomindex)
Numis.Lit.	Numismatic Literature
Nurs.Abstr.	Nursing Abstracts
Nurs.Res.Abstr.	Nursing Research Abstracts
Nutr.Abstr.	Nutrition Abstracts & Reviews (Now: Nutrition Abstracts and Reviews Series A: Human and Experimental; Nutrition Abstracts and Reviews Series B: Livestock Feeds and Feeding)
Nutr.Plan.	Nutrition Planning (Ceased)

O

Occup.Saf.& Health Abstr.	Occupational Safety & Health Abstracts (Now: Safety at Health at Work)
Ocean.Abstr.	Oceanic Abstracts
Ocean.Abstr.Bibl.	Oceanic Abstracts and Bibliography (Now: Deep Sea Research. Parts A, B)
Ocean.Ind.	Oceanic Index (Now: Oceanic Abstracts)
Old Test.Abstr.	Old Testament Abstracts
Oncol.Abstr.	Oncology Abstracts (Ceased)
Oper.Res.Manage. Sci.	Operations Research/Management Science
Ophthal.Lit.	Ophthalmic Literature
Oral Res.Abstr.	Oral Research Abstracts (Ceased)
Ornam.Hort.	Ornamental Horticulture

P

P.A.I.S.	P A I S Bulletin (Public Affairs Information Service) (Now: P A I S International in Print)
P.A.I.S.For. Lang.Ind.	Public Affairs Information Service Foreign Language Index (Now: P A I S International in Print)
PC Abstr.	P C Abstracts (Personal Computing) (Ceased)
PCR2	P C R2 (Personal Computer Review—Squared)
PHRA	Poverty & Human Resources Abstracts (Now: Human Resources Abstracts)
P.I.R.A.	P.I.R.A. Marketing Abstracts (Packaging Industry Research Association) (Now: Management and Marketing Abstracts)
P.L.I.I.	Property & Liability Insurance Index (Ceased)
P.M.I.	Photography Magazine Index (Ceased)
PMR	Popular Magazine Review (Now: Magazine Article Summaries)
P.N.I.	Pharmaceutical News Index
PROMT	Predicasts Overview of Markets and Technologies
PSI	Philanthropic Studies Index
Packag.Abstr.	Packaging Abstracts (Now: International Packaging Abstracts)
Packag.Sci.Tech.	Packaging Science and Technology Abstracts
Paper.& Bd.Abstr.	Paper and Board Abstracts
Past.Care & Couns. Abstr.	Pastoral Care & Counseling Abstracts (Now: Abstracts of Research in Pastoral Care and Counseling)
Peace Res.Abstr.	Peace Research Abstracts Journal
Peat Abstr.	Peat Abstracts
Perf.Arts Biog. Master Ind.	Performing Arts Biography Master Index
Periodex	Periodex (Now: Point de Repere)
Pers.Lit.	Personnel Literature
Pers.Manage. Abstr.	Personnel Management Abstracts
Petrol.Abstr.	Petroleum Abstracts
Petrol.Energy B.N.I.	Petroleum/Energy Business News Index
Pharmacog.Tit.	Pharmacognosy Titles (Ceased)
Phil.Ind.	Philosopher's Index
Philip.Abstr.	Philippine Abstracts (Now: Philippine Science & Technology Abstracts)
Photo.Abstr.	Photographic Abstracts (Now: Imaging Abstracts)
Photo.Ind.	Photography Index
Phys.Abstr.	Physics Abstracts (Also see: INSPEC; also see: Sci.Abstr.)
Phys.Ber.	Physikalische Berichte (Now: Physics Briefs)
Phys.Ed.Ind.	Physical Education Index
Pig News & Info.	Pig News and Information
Pinpointer	Pinpointer
Plant Breed.Abstr.	Plant Breeding Abstracts
Plant Grow.Reg. Abstr.	Plant Growth Regulator Abstracts
Plast.Abstr.	Plastics Abstracts (Ceased)
Pol.Tech.Abstr.	Polish Technical Abstracts (Now: Polish Technical and Economic Abstracts)
Polit.Sci.Abstr.	Political Science Abstracts
Pollut.Abstr.	Pollution Abstracts
Pop.Mus.Per.Ind.	Popular Music Periodicals Index (Ceased)
Pop.Per.Ind.	Popular Periodical Index
Popul.Ind.	Population Index
Potato Abstr.	Potato Abstracts
Poult.Abstr.	Poultry Abstracts
Pr.Briefs	Predi-Briefs
Predi.F & S Ind.Eur.	Predicasts F & S Index Europe
Predi.F & S Ind.Intl.	Predicasts F & S Index International
Predi.F & S Ind. U.S.	Predicasts F & S Index United States
Print.Abstr.	Printing Abstracts
Protozool.Abstr.	Protozoological Abstracts
Psychoanal.Abstr.	Psychoanalytic Abstracts (Now: PsychScan: Psychoanalysis)
Psychol.Abstr.	Psychological Abstracts
Psychol.R.G.	Psychological Reader's Guide (Ceased)
Psychopharmacol. Abstr.	Psychopharmacology Abstracts (Ceased)
Psycscan	Psycscan: Applied Psychology
Psycscan C.P.	Psycscan: Clinical Psychology
Psycscan D.P.	Psycscan: Development Psychology
Pt.de Rep.	Point de Repere (Formed by the merger of: Periodex and RADAR)
Pub.Admin.Abstr.	Public Administration Abstracts and Index of Articles (Now: Documentation in Public Administration & Sage Public Administration Abstracts)

Q

Qual.Contr. Appl.Stat.	Quality Control and Applied Statistics

R

RADAR	Repertoire Analytique d'Articles des Revues du Quebec (Now: Point de Repere)
RAPRA	R A P R A Abstracts (Rubber and Plastics Research Association of Great Britain)
R.G.	Readers' Guide to Periodical Literature
R.G.Abstr.	Readers' Guide Abstracts
RICS	R I C S Abstracts and Reviews (Now: R I C S Library Information Service Abstracts and Reviews) (Royal Institute of Chartered Surveyors)
RILA	R I L A (International Repertory of the Literature of Art) (Now: B H A (Bibliography of the History of Art))

RILM	R I L M Abstracts of Music Literature (International Repertory of Music Literature)	Sage Urb.Stud. Abstr.	Sage Urban Studies Abstracts
Reac.	Reactions	Sci.Abstr.	Science Abstracts
Ref.Pt.Food Indus.Abstr.	Reference Point: Food Industry Abstracts		A. Physics Abstracts (Also see INSPEC; also see: Phys.Abstr.)
Ref.Sour.	Reference Sources (Ceased)		B. Electrical & Electronics Abstracts (Also see: Elec.&Electron.Abstr.; also see: INSPEC)
Ref.Zh.	Referativnyi Zhurnal		
Refug.Abstr.	Refugee Abstracts		
Rehabil.Lit.	Rehabilitation Literature (Ceased)		
Rel.& Theol.Abstr.	Religious & Theological Abstracts		C. Computer & Control Abstracts (Also see: Comput.&Cont.Abstr.; also see: INSPEC)
Rel.Ind.One	Religion Index One: Periodicals		
Rel.Ind.Two	Religion Index Two: Multi-Author Works	Sci.Cit.Ind.	Science Citation Index
		Sci.Res.Abstr.	Science Research Abstracts (Now: Solid State and Superconductivity Abstracts)
Rel.Per.	Index to Religious Periodical Literature (Now: Religion Index One: Periodicals)		
		Search	Search
Res.Educ.	Research in Education (Now: Resources in Education)	Seed Abstr.	Seed Abstracts
		Sel.Bibl.Homosex.	Selected Bibliography of Homosexuality
Res.High.Educ. Abstr.	Research into Higher Educaton Abstracts		
		Sel.J.Water	Selected Journals on Water (Ceased)
Resour.Ctr.Ind.	Resource Center Index	Sel.Water Res. Abstr.	Selected Water Resources Abstracts
Rev.Appl.Entomol.	Review of Applied Entomology (Series A, B) (Now: Review of Agricultural Entomology & Review of Medical and Veterinary Entomology)	Ship Abstr.	Ship Abstracts
		Sh.& Vib.Dig.	Shock and Vibration Digest
		Sinop.Odontol.	Sinopse de Odontologia (Ceased)
		Small Anim.Abstr.	Small Animal Abstracts (Now: Small Animals)
Rev.Appl.Mycol.	Review of Applied Mycology (Now: Review of Plant Pathology)		
		So.Pac.Per.Ind.	South Pacific Periodicals Index
Rev.Med.& Vet.Mycol.	Review of Medical and Veterinary Mycology	Soc.Sci.Ind.	Social Sciences Index
		Soc.Work Res.& Abstr.	Social Work Research & Abstracts
Rev.Plant Path.	Review of Plant Pathology		
Rheol.Abstr.	Rheology Abstracts	Sociol.Abstr.	Sociological Abstracts
Rice Abstr.	Rice Abstracts	Sociol.Educ.Abstr.	Sociology of Education Abstracts
Risk Abstr.	Risk Abstracts	Soft.Abstr.Eng.	Software Abstracts for Engineers
Robomat.	Robomatix Reporter (Now: Robotics Abstracts)	Soils & Fert.	Soils & Fertilizers
		Solid St.Abstr.	Solid State Abstracts (Now: Solid State and Superconductivity Abstracts)
Rom.Sci.Abstr.	Romanian Scientific Abstracts		
Rural Devel.Abstr.	Rural Development Abstracts		
Rural Ext.Educ.& Tr.Abstr.	Rural Extension, Education and Training Abstracts (Ceased)	Sorghum & Millets Abstr.	Sorghum and Millets Abstracts
		South.Bap.Per.Ind.	Southern Baptist Periodical Index (Ceased)
Rural Recreat. Tour.Abstr.	Rural Recreation and Tourism Abstracts (Now: Leisure, Recreation and Tourism Abstracts)		
		Soyabean Abstr.	Soyabean Abstracts
		Sp.Ed.Needs Abstr.	Special Educational Needs Abstracts
		Speleol.Abstr.	Speleological Abstracts
S		Sport Fish.Abstr.	Sport Fishery Abstracts (Now: Fisheries Review) (Ceased)
S.A.Waterabstr.	S.A. Waterabstracts (South Africa) (Ceased)		
		Sports Per.Ind.	Sports Periodicals Index
SCIMP	S C I M P (Selective Cooperative Index of Management Periodicals)	Sportsearch	Sportsearch
		Sri Lanka Sci.Ind.	Sri Lanka Science Index
SOPODA	Social Planning, Policy and Development Abstracts	St.Educ.J.Ind.	State Education Journal Index
		Stamp J.Ind.	Stamp Journals Index
SRI	Statistical Reference Index	Stat.Theor. Meth.Abstr.	Statistical Theory and Method Abstracts
SSCI	Social Science Citation Index		
Saf.Sci.Abstr.	Safety Science Abstracts Journal (Now: Health and Safety Science Abstracts)	Steel Cas.Abstr.	Steel Castings Abstracts (Ceased)
		Stud.Wom.Abstr.	Studies on Women Abstracts
		Sugar Ind.Abstr.	Sugar Industry Abstracts
Sage Fam.Stud. Abstr.	Sage Family Studies Abstracts		
		T	
Sage Pub.Admin. Abstr.	Sage Public Administration Abstracts	TBRI	Technical Book Review Index (Ceased

T.C.E.A.	Theoretical Chemical Engineering Abstracts	Vis.Ind.	Vision Index (Ceased)
TOM	T O M (Text on Microfilm)	VITIS	Vitis – Viticulture and Enology Abstracts
Tech.Educ.Abstr.	Technical Education Abstracts		
Tel.Abstr.	Telecommunications Abstracts (Ceased)		

W

Tel.Alert	Telecommunications Alert	W.R.C.Inf.	W.R.C. Information (Water Research Centre) (Now: Aqualine Abstracts)
Telegen	Telegen Reporter (Now: Telegen Abstracts) (Ceased)	Water Pollut.Abstr.	Water Pollution Abstracts (Now: Aqualine Abstracts)
Text.Dig.	Textile Digest (Ceased)	Water Resour.Abstr.	Water Resources Abstracts (Now: Hydro-Abstracts)
Text.Tech.Dig.	Textile Technology Digest		
Therm.Abstr.	Thermal Abstracts (Now: International Building Services Abstracts)	Weed Abstr.	Weed Abstracts
Tob.Abstr.	Tobacco Abstracts	Wild Life Rev.	Wildlife Review (Ceased)
Tob.Bibl.	Tobacco Bibliography (Ceased)	Wom.Stud.Abstr.	Women Studies Abstracts
Top Manage.Abstr.	Top Management Abstracts (See: Anbar)	Work Rel.Abstr.	Work Related Abstracts
Tox.Abstr.	Toxicology Abstracts	World Agri.Econ.& Rural Sociol. Abstr.	World Agricultural Economics & Rural Sociology Abstracts
Tr.& Indus.Ind.	Trade & Industry Index		
Trans.Res.Abstr.	Transportation Research Abstracts (Ceased)	World Alum.Abstr.	World Aluminum Abstracts
		World Bank.Abstr.	World Banking Abstracts
Triticale Abstr.	Wheat, Barley and Triticale Abstracts	World Bibl.Soc.Sec.	World Bibliography of Social Security
Trop.Abstr.	Tropical Abstracts (Now: Abstracts on Tropical Agriculture)	World Fish.Abstr.	World Fisheries Abstracts (Ceased)
		World Surf.Coat.	World Surface Coatings Abstracts
Trop.Dis.Bull.	Tropical Diseases Bulletin	World Text.Abstr.	World Textile Abstracts
Trop.Oil Seeds Abstr.	Tropical Oil Seeds Abstracts (Now: Tropical Oil Seeds)		

Y

		Yrbk.Assoc.Educ.& Rehab.Blind	Association for Education and Rehabilitation of the Blind and Visually Impaired. Yearbook (Ceased)

U

Urb.Aff.Abstr.	Urban Affairs Abstracts

V

Z

Va.Hist.Abstr.	Virginia Historical Abstracts (Ceased)	Zent.Math.	Zentralblatt fuer Mathematik und ihre Grenzgebiete
Vert.File Ind.	Vertical File Index		
Vet.Bull.	Veterinary Bulletin	Zinscan	Zinscan
Virol.Abstr.	Virology Abstracts (Now: Virology and A I D S Abstracts)	Zion.Lit.	Zionist Literature
		Zoo.Rec.	Zoological Record

Subject Guide to Abstracting and Indexing

The 124 subject headings listed below are major subjects which contain a sub-category headed "Abstracting, Bibliographies, Statistics." This sub-category, which follows the major subject headings in the Classified List of Serials, identifies publications which abstract and/or index publications in the relevant subject. Bibliographies and statistical publications pertaining to the subject are also included in this sub-category. This guide will enable users to quickly locate subject areas of interest for which abstracting and indexing publications have been identified and to build profiles by combination of relevant subject areas. Page numbers refer to the first page on which the sub-category appears.

SUBJECT CATEGORY	PAGE
A	
Advertising and Public Relations	40
Aeronautics and Space Flight	66
Agriculture	131
Anthropology	253
Archaeology	290
Architecture	309
Art	351
Arts and Handicrafts	357
Astronomy	371
B	
Beauty Culture	375
Beverages	388
Biography	424
Biology	461
Birth Control	598
Building and Construction	636
Business and Economics	701
C	
Ceramics, Glass and Pottery	1167
Chemistry	1191
Children and Youth	1247
Civil Defense	1274
Classical Studies	1281
Cleaning and Dyeing	1282
Clothing Trade	1288
Communications	1346
Computers	1402
Conservation	1501
Consumer Education and Protection	1509
Criminology and Law Enforcement	1524

SUBJECT CATEGORY	PAGE
D	
Dance	1532
Drug Abuse and Alcoholism	1540
E	
Earth Sciences	1549
Education	1673
Encyclopedias and General Almanacs	1782
Energy	1797
Engineering	1841
Environmental Studies	1972
Ethnic Interests	2030
F	
Fire Prevention	2035
Fish and Fisheries	2050
Folklore	2060
Food and Food Industries	2084
Forests and Forestry	2111
G	
Gardening and Horticulture	2141
Genealogy and Heraldry	2168
Geography	2267
Gerontology and Geriatrics	2280
H	
Handicapped	2285
Heating, Plumbing and Refrigeration	2304
History	2327
Hobbies	2444

SUBJECT CATEGORY	PAGE
Home Economics	2450
Homosexuality	2458
Hospitals	2470
Hotels and Restaurants	2482
Housing and Urban Planning	2499
Humanities: Comprehensive Works	2519

I

Instruments	2525
Insurance	2545
Interior Design and Decoration	2556

J

Jewelry, Clocks and Watches	2566
Journalism	2577

L

Labor Unions	2592
Law	2697
Leather and Fur Industries	2738
Library and Information Sciences	2792
Linguistics	2854
Literary and Political Reviews	2890
Literature	2980

M

Machinery	3025
Mathematics	3062
Medical Sciences	3165
Meetings and Congresses	3395
Metallurgy	3424
Meteorology	3444
Metrology and Standardization	3449
Military	3476
Mines and Mining Industry	3498
Motion Pictures	3519
Museums and Art Galleries	3536
Music	3588

N

Nutrition and Dietetics	3613

O

Occupational Health and Safety	3623
Occupations and Careers	3631
Oriental Studies	3646

P

Packaging	3652
Paints and Protective Coatings	3656

SUBJECT GUIDE TO ABSTRACTING AND INDEXING, CONTINUED

SUBJECT CATEGORY	PAGE
Paleontology	3661
Paper and Pulp	3667
Parapsychology and Occultism	3672
Patents, Trademarks and Copyrights	3679
Petroleum and Gas	3704
Pharmacy and Pharmacology	3747
Philosophy	3738
Photography	3798
Physical Fitness and Hygiene	3811
Physics	3836
Plastics	3868
Political Science	3936
Population Studies	3989
Printing	4006
Psychology	4051
Public Administration	4078
Public Health and Safety	4116
Publishing and Book Trade	4139

R

Real Estate	4159
Religions and Theology	4211
Rubber	4294

S

Sciences: Comprehensive Works	4354
Shoes and Boots	4362
Social Sciences: Comprehensive Works	4394
Social Services and Welfare	4425
Sociology	4457
Sound Recording and Reproduction	4462
Sports and Games	4498

T

Technology: Comprehensive Works	4613
Textile Industries and Fabrics	4628
Theater	4643
Tobacco	4646
Transportation	4661
Travel and Tourism	4798

V

Veterinary Science	4820

W

Water Resources	4834
Women's Interests	4858
Women's Studies	4861

Subjects

ENGLISH	SPANISH
Abstracting and Indexing Services	Servicios de Extractos e Indices
Advertising and Public Relations	Publicidad y Relaciones Públicas
Aeronautics and Space Flight	Aeronáutica y Vuelo Espacial
Computer Applications	Aplicaciones de los Ordenadores
Agriculture	Agricultura
Agricultural Economics	Economía Agrícola
Agricultural Equipment	Aparatos Agrícolas
Computer Applications	Aplicaciones de los Ordenadores
Crop Production and Soil	Producción de Cosecha, Tierra
Dairying and Dairy Products	Lechería y Productos Lácteos
Feed, Flour and Grain	Forraje, Granos y Harina
Poultry and Livestock	Ganadería
Animal Welfare	Bienestar Animal
Anthropology	Antropología
Antiques	Antigüedades
Archaeology	Arqueología
Computer Applications	Aplicaciones de los Ordenadores
Architecture	Arquitectura
Computer Applications	Aplicaciones de los Ordenadores
Art	Arte
Computer Applications	Aplicaciones de los Ordenadores
Arts and Handicrafts	Artes y Obras de Mano
Astrology	Astrología
Astronomy	Astronomía
Computer Applications	Aplicaciones de los Ordenadores
Beauty Culture	Belleza Personal
Perfumes and Cosmetics	Perfumes y Cosméticos
Beverages	Bebidas
Bibliographies	Bibliografías
Biography	Biografía
Biology	Biología
Bioengineering	Bio-ingeniería
Biological Chemistry	Química Biológica
Biophysics	Biofísica
Biotechnology	Biotecnología
Botany	Botánica
Cytology and Histology	Citología e Histología
Entomology	Entomología
Genetics	Genética
Microbiology	Microbiología
Microscopy	Microscopia
Ornithology	Ornitología
Physiology	Fisiología
Zoology	Zoología
Birth Control	Reglamentación del Nacimiento
Building and Construction	Edificios y Construcción
Carpentry and Woodwork	Carpintería y Ebanistería
Hardware	Quincalla

SUBJECTS xliii

Business and Economics	Affaires et Economie	Wirtschaft und Handel	Negocios y Economía
Accounting	Comptabilité	Rechnungswesen	Contabilidad
Banking and Finance	Banque et Finance	Bank- und Finanzwesen	Bancos y Finanzas
Banking and Finance-Computer Applications	Banque et Finance-Applications des Ordinateurs	Bank- und Finanzwesen-Computer Anwendung	Bancos y Finanzas-Aplicaciones de los Ordenadores
Chamber of Commerce Publications	Publications des Chambres de Commerce	Veröffentlichungen von Handelskammern	Publicaciones de las Cámaras de Comercio
Computer Applications	Applications des Ordinateurs	Computer Anwendung	Aplicaciones de los Ordenadores
Cooperatives	Coopératives	Genossenschaften	Cooperativos
Domestic Commerce	Commerce Interieur	Binnenhandel	Comercio Interior
Economic Situation and Conditions	Situations et Conditions Economiques	Wirtschaftliche Situation und Verhältnisse	Situaciones y Condiciones Económicas
Economic Systems and Theories, Economic History	Systèmes et Theories Economiques, Histoire Economique	Ökonomische Systeme und Theorien, Wirtschaftsgeschichte	Sistemas y Teorías Económicos, Historia Económica
International Commerce	Commerce International	Aussenhandel	Comercio Internacional
International Development and Assistance	Développement et Assistance Internationaux	Internationale Entwicklungshilfe	Desarrollo y Asistencia Internacionales
Investments	Investissements	Investitionen	Inversiones
Labor and Industrial Relations	Travail et Relations Industrielles	Arbeits- und Industrielle Beziehungen	Trabajo y Relaciones Industriales
Macroeconomics	Macroeconomique	Makroökonomie	Macroeconomía
Management	Gestion	Betriebsführung	Gerencia
Marketing and Purchasing	Cours et Achats	Marketing und Kauf	Compra y Venta
Office Equipment and Services	Matériel et Entretien de Bureaux	Büroeinrichtung und Service	Equipo y Servicios de Oficinas
Personnel Management	Direction de Personnel	Personal Führung	Dirección de Empleados
Production of Goods and Services	Production	Produktion	Producción
Public Finance, Taxation	Finance Publique, Impots	Staatsfinanzen, Steuerwesen	Finanza Publica, Impuestos
Small Business	Petites et Moyennes Affaires	Kleinbetrieb	Negocios Pequeños
Trade and Industrial Directories	Directoires de Commerce et Industrie	Firmenverzeichnisse	Directorios de Comercio e Industria
Ceramics, Glass and Pottery	Céramique, Verrerie et Poterie	Keramik, Glas und Töpferei	Cerámica, Vidrio y Porcelana
Chemistry	Chimie	Chemie	Química
Analytical Chemistry	Chimie Analytique	Analytische Chemie	Química Analítica
Computer Applications	Applications des Ordinateurs	Computer Anwendung	Aplicaciones de los Ordenadores
Crystallography	Cristallographie	Kristallographie	Cristalografía
Electrochemistry	Electrochimie	Elektrochemie	Electroquímica
Inorganic Chemistry	Chimie Inorganique	Anorganische Chemie	Química Inorgánica
Organic Chemistry	Chimie Organique	Organische Chemie	Química Orgánica
Physical Chemistry	Chimie Physique	Physikalische Chemie	Fisicoquímica
Children and Youth	Enfance et Adolescence	Kinder und Jugend	Niños y Jóvenes
About	Au Sujet de	Über	Acerca
For	Pour	Für	Para
Civil Defense	Defense Civile	Ziviler Bevölkerungsschutz	Defensa Civil
Classical Studies	Etudes Classiques	Klassische Studien	Estudios Clásicos
Cleaning and Dyeing	Nettoyage et Teinturerie	Reinigen und Farben	Limpieza y Tintura
Clothing Trade	Vêtement	Bekleidungsgewerbe	Industria de Vestidos
Fashions	Mode	Moden	Modas
Clubs	Clubs	Klubs	Clubes
College and Alumni	Université et Diplomés	Universitäten und Hochschul-Absolventen	Universidades y Exalumnos
Communications	Communications	Nachrichtentechnik	Comunicaciones
Computer Applications	Applications des Ordinateurs	Computer Anwendung	Aplicaciones de los Ordenadores
Postal Affairs	Postes	Postwesen	Correo
Radio	Radio	Rundfunk	Radio
Telephone and Telegraph	Téléphone et Télégraphe	Telephon und Telegraph	Teléfono y Telégrafo
Television and Cable	Télévision	Fernsehen und Bildfrequenzkanal	Televisión y Cable
Video	Vidéo	Video	Video
Computers	Ordinateurs	Computer	Ordenadores
Artificial Intelligence	Intelligence Artificielle	Künstliche-Intelligenz	Inteligencia Artificial
Automation	Automation	Automatisierung	Automación
Calculating Machines	Calculateurs	Rechenmaschine	Calculadoras
Circuits	Circuits	Kreisbewegung	Circuitos
Computer Architecture	Architecture de la Machine	Computer Architektur	Arquitectura de los Ordenadores
Computer-Assisted Instruction	Enseignement Assisté par Ordinateur	Computer Beistande Anweisung	Instrucción con la Ayuda de Ordenador
Computer Engineering	Technique d'Ordinateur	Computer Bewerkstellingen	Ingeniería de Ordenador
Computer Games	Jeux des Ordinateurs	Computer Spiele	Juegos de Ordenadores
Computer Graphics	Conception Assistée par Ordinateur	Computergraphik	Diseño con la Ayuda de Ordenador
Computer Industry	Industrie d'Ordinateur	Computer Fleiss	Industrias de los Ordenadores
Computer Industry Directories	Annuaire de la Industrie Ordinateur	Computer Fleiss Fernsprechbuch	Directorios de los Ordenadores
Computer Industry, Vocational Guidance	Industrie d'Ordinateur, Orientation Professionnelle	Computer Fleiss Berufsberatung Ratschlag	Industria de los Ordenadores Gobierno Práctico
Computer Music	Musique d'Ordinateur	Computer Musik	Música de Ordenadores
Computer Networks	Reseaux des Ordinateurs	Computer Netzwerk	Red para Transmición de Datos
Computer Programming	Programme Machine	Computer Programm	Programa de Ordenador
Computer Sales	Ventes des Ordinateurs	Computer Verkaufen	Ventas de Ordenadores
Computer Security	Protection des Ordinateurs	Computer Sicherheit	Protección de los Ordenadores
Computer Simulation	Simulation des Ordinateurs	Computer Verstellung	Simulación de los Ordenadores
Computer Systems	Systemes des Ordinateurs	Computer Systemen	Sistemas de los Ordenadores
Cybernetics	Cybernetiques	Kybernetik	Cibernéticas
Data Communications, Data Transmission Systems	Données de Communication	Daten Bekanntmachung, Daten Verschickung Systems	Datos de Comunicación

SUBJECTS

Data Base Management	Gestion de Base de Données	Datenbank Verwaltung	Gestión de Banco de Datos
Electronic Data Processing	Traitement de l'Information Electronique	Elektrisiert-Daten Aufbereitung	Proceso de Datos Electronico
Hardware	Materiel	Eisenwaren	Equipo Físico
Information Science, Information Theory	Théorie de l'Information	Nachrichtenswissenschaft, Nachrichtenstheorie	Ciencia, Teoría de la Información
Machine Theory	Theorie de Machine	Maschinetheorie	Teoría de la Maquina
Microcomputers	Micro-Ordinateurs	Mikrocomputer	Microordenadores
Minicomputers	Mini-Ordinateurs	Minicomputer	Miniordenadores
Personal Computers	Ordinateurs Privé	Persoenlichecomputer	Ordenador Personal
Software	Logiciel	Weichwaren	Soporte Lógico
Theory of Computing	Théorie de Traitement	Computertheorie	Theoria de Cálculo
Word Processing	Traitement de Textes	Wortbehandlung	Proceso de la Palabras
Conservation	Conservation	Landschaftsschutz	Conservación
Consumer Education and Protection	Protection de Consommateur	Verbraucherswirtschaftsschutz	Protección del Consumidor
Criminology and Law Enforcement	Criminologie et Police	Kriminologie und Strafvollzug	Criminologia y Accion Policial
Computer Applications	Applications des Ordinateurs	Computer Anwendung	Aplicaciones de los Ordenadores
Security	Securité	Sicherheit	Seguridad
Dance	Danse	Tanz	Baile
Drug Abuse and Alcoholism	Toxicomanie et Alcoolisme	Rauschgiftsucht und Alkoholismus	Drogadismo y Alcoholismo
Earth Sciences	Sciences Géologiques	Wissenschaften der Erde	Ciencias Geológicas
Computer Applications	Applications des Ordinateurs	Computer Anwendung	Aplicaciones de los Ordenadores
Geology	Géologie	Geologie	Geología
Geophysics	Géophysique	Geophysik	Geofísica
Hydrology	Hydrologie	Hydrologie	Hidrología
Oceanography	Océanographie	Ozeanographie	Oceanografía
Education	Education	Bildungswesen	Educación
Adult Education	Enseignement des Adultes	Erwachsenenbildung	Enseñanza de Adultos
Computer Applications	Applications des Ordinateurs	Computer Anwendung	Aplicaciones de los Ordenadores
Guides to Schools and Colleges	Guides d'Ecoles et Colleges	Führer zur Schulen und Universitaten	Guías de Escuelas y Colegios
Higher Education	Enseignement Supérieur	Hochschulwesen	Enseñanza Superior
International Education Programs	Programmes de'Education Internationale	Internazionale Erziehungs-Programme	Programas de Enseñanza Internacional
School Organization and Administration	Organisation et Administration de l'Ecole	Organisation und Verwaltung von dem Schule	Administración y Dirección de la Escuela
Special Education and Rehabilitation	Enseignement Special et Réhabilitation	Fachunterricht und Rehabilitierung	Enseñanza Especial y Rehabilitación
Teaching Methods and Curriculum	Méthodes Pédagogiques et Programmes Scolaires	Lehrmethoden und Lehrplan	Métodos de Enseñanza y Planes de Estudios
Electronics	Electronique	Elektronik	Electrónicos
Computer Applications	Applications des Ordinateurs	Computer Anwendung	Aplicaciones de los Ordenadores
Encyclopedias and General Almanacs	Encyclopédies et Almanachs Générales	Enzyklopädien und Allgemeine Nachschlagewerke	Enciclopedias y Almanaques Generales
Energy	Energie	Energie	Energía
Computer Applications	Applications des Ordinateurs	Computer Anwendung	Aplicaciones de los Ordenadores
Electrical Energy	Energie Eléctrique	Elektrizitätsenergie	Energía Eléctrica
Geothermal Energy	Energie Géothermique	Thermalenergie	Energía Geotérmica
Hydroelectrical Energy	Energie Hydraulique	Hydroelektroenergie	Energía Hidroeléctrica
Nuclear Energy	Energie Nucléaire	Kernenergie	Energía Nuclear
Solar Energy	Energie Solaire	Sonnenenergie	Energía Solar
Wind Energy	Energie à Vent	Windenergie	Energía del Viento
Engineering	Génie	Ingenieurwesen	Ingeniería
Chemical Engineering	Génie Chimique	Chemieingenieurwesen	Ingeniería Química
Civil Engineering	Génie Civil	Bauingenierurwesen	Ingeniería Civil
Computer Applications	Applications des Ordinateurs	Computer Anwendung	Aplicaciones de los Ordenadores
Electrical Engineering	Génie Eléctrique	Elektrotechnik	Ingeniería Eléctrica
Engineering Mechanics and Materials	Mechánique de Génie et Materiels	Ingenieurwesen Mechanik und Materialien	Mecanica de Ingeniería y Materiales
Hydraulic Engineering	Génie Hydraulique	Wasserbau	Ingeniería Hidráulica
Industrial Engineering	Génie Industriel	Industrieingenieurwesen	Ingeniería Industrial
Mechanical Engineering	Génie Mécanique	Maschinenbau	Ingeniería Mecánica
Environmental Studies	Science de l'Environnement	Umweltschutz	Ciencias Ecológicas
Computer Applications	Applications des Ordinateurs	Computer Anwendung	Aplicaciones de los Ordenadores
Pollution	Pollution	Umweltverschmutzung	Contaminación
Toxicology and Environmental Safety	Toxicologie et Sécurité de l'Environnement	Toxokologie und Umweltsicherheit	Toxicología y Seguridad Ambiental
Waste Management	Gestion des Déchets	Abfallwirtschaft	Manejo de la Basura
Ethnic Interests	Publications de l'Orientation Ethnique	Veröffentlichungen von Minoritäten	Publicaciones de Temas Etnicos
Fire Prevention	Précaution contre l'Incendie	Brandbekaempfung	Prevención del Fuego
Fish and Fisheries	Poisson et Peche	Fische und Fischerei	Pesca y Pesquerías
Folklore	Folklore	Volkskunde	Folklore
Food and Food Industries	Alimentation et Industries Alimentaires	Nahrungsmittel und Lebensmittelindustrie	Alimentos e Industrias Alimenticias
Bakers and Confectioners	Boulangerie et Confiserie	Bäcker- und Konditorgewerbe	Panaderías y Dulcerías
Grocery Trade	Epicerie	Kolonialwarenhandel	Abacerías
Forest and Forestry	Forêts et Exploitation Forestiére	Forstwesen und Waldwirtschaft	Bosques y Selvicultura
Lumber and Wood	Bois	Holz	Maderas
Funerals	Funérailles	Beerdigungen	Funerales
Gardening and Horticulture	Jardinage et Horticulture	Gartenpflege und Gartenbau	Jardinería y Horticultura
Florist Trade	Commerce des Fleurs	Blumenhandel	Floristas
Genealogy and Heraldry	Généalogie et Science Héraldique	Genealogie und Wappenkunde	Genealogía y Heráldica
Computer Applications	Applications des Ordinateurs	Computer Anwendung	Aplicaciones de los Ordenadores

SUBJECTS

General Interest Periodicals (Subdivided by country)	Publications d'Intérêt Général (Selon pays)	Allgemeine Zeitschriften (nach Land)	Periódicos de Interés General (por país)
Geography	Géographie	Geographie	Geografía
Computer Applications	Applications des Ordinateurs	Computer Anwendung	Aplicaciones de los Ordenadores
Gerontology and Geriatrics	Gérontologie	Gerontologie	Gerontología y Geriátrica
Giftware and Toys	Cadeaux et Jouets	Geschenkartikel und Spielwaren	Regalos y Juguetes
Handicapped	Handicapés	Behinderung	Desventajados
Computer Applications	Applications des Ordinateurs	Computer Anwendung	Aplicaciones de los Ordenadores
Hearing Impaired	Sourds	Schwerhörigkeit	Debilitado del Oído
Physically Impaired	Handicapés Physique	Körperbehinderung	Debilitado Físicamente
Visually Impaired	Aveugles	Blindheit	Debilitado Visualmente
Heating, Plumbing, and Refrigeration	Chauffage, Plomberie et Réfrigeration	Heizung, Kühlung und Installation	Calefaccion, Plomería y Refrigeración
History	Histoire	Geschichte	Historia
Computer Applications	Applications des Ordinateurs	Computer Anwendung	Aplicaciones de los Ordenadores
History of Africa	Histoire de l'Afrique	Geschichte-Afrika	Historia de Africa
History of Asia	Histoire de l'Asie	Geschichte-Asien	Historia de Asia
History of Australasia	Histoire de l'Australasie	Geschichte-Australasien	Historia de Australasia
History of Europe	Histoire de l'Europe	Geschichte-Europa	Historia de la Europa
History of North and South America	Histoire de l'Amérique du Nord et du Sud	Geschichte-Nord- und Südamerika	Historia de la América del Norte y de la del Sur
History of Near East	Histoire du Proche-Orient	Geschichte-Nahe Osten	Historia del Cercano Oriente
Hobbies	Passe-Temps	Hobbies	Pasatiempos
Home Economics	Enseignement Ménager	Hauswirtschaft	Economía Doméstica
Homosexuality	Homosexualisme	Homosexualität	Homosexualismo
Hospitals	Hôpitaux	Krankenhäuser	Hospitales
Computer Applications	Applications des Ordinateurs	Computer Anwendung	Aplicaciones de los Ordenadores
Hotels and Restaurants	Hôtels et Restaurants	Hotels und Restaurants	Hoteles y Restaurantes
Computer Applications	Applications des Ordinateurs	Computer Anwendung	Aplicaciones de los Ordenadores
Housing and Urban Planning	Lógement et Urbanisme	Wohnungswesen und Stadtplanung	Viviendas y Urbanismo
Computer Applications	Applications des Ordinateurs	Computer Anwendung	Aplicaciones de los Ordenadores
How-To and Do-It-Yourself	Bricolage	Selbstanfertigung	Cómo Hacerlo y Hágalo Si Mismo
Humanities: Comprehensive Works	Humanités: Oeuvres Comprehensives	Geisteswissenschaften	Humanidades: Obras Comprensivas
Computer Applications	Applications des Ordinateurs	Computer Anwendung	Aplicaciones de los Ordenadores
Instruments	Instruments	Instrumente	Instrumentos
Insurance	Assurances	Versicherungswesen	Seguros
Computer Applications	Applications des Ordinateurs	Computer Anwendung	Aplicaciones de los Ordenadores
Interior Design and Decoration	Agencements Intérieurs et Décoration	Innenarchitektur und Innenausstattung	Diseño del Interior y Ornamentación
Furniture and House Furnishing	Meubles et Articles pour la Maison	Möbel and Wohnungseinrichtung	Muebles y Articulos para el Hogar
Jewelry, Clocks und Watches	Bijouterie et Horlogerie	Schmuck und Uhren	Joyería y Relojería
Journalism	Journalisme	Journalismus	Periodismo
Labor Unions	Syndicalisme	Gewerkschaften	Sindicatos
Law	Droit	Recht	Derecho
Civil Law	Droit Civil	Zivilrecht	Derecho Civil
Computer Applications	Applications des Ordinateurs	Computer Anwendung	Aplicaciónes de los Ordenadores
Constitutional Law	Droit Constitutionel	Verfassungsrecht	Derecho Constitucional
Corporate Law	Droit Commercial	Handelsrecht	Derecho Corporativo
Criminal Law	Droit Penal	Strafrecht	Derecho Criminal
Estate Planning	Succession	Mobiliarvermögensrecht	Planificación de los Bienes
Family And Matrimonial Law	Droit Familial et Matrimonial	Ehegesetz und Familienrecht	Derecho Familial y Matrimonial
International Law	Droit International	Völkerrecht	Derecho Internacional
Judicial Systems	Système Judiciaire	Gerichtswesen	Sistemas Judiciales
Legal Aid	Assistance Judiciaire	Rechtshilfe	Ayuda Legal
Maritime Law	Droit Maritime	Seerecht	Derecho Marítimo
Military Law	Droit Militaire	Kriegsrecht	Derecho Militar
Leather and Fur Industries	Maroquinerie et Pelleterie	Leder und Pelz	Pieles y Cuero
Leisure and Recreation	Loisirs et Récréation	Freizeit und Unterhaltung	Ocio y Recreo
Library and Information Science	Bibliothéconomie et Informatique	Bibliothek- und Informationswissenschaft	Bibliotecología y Ciencia de la Información
Computer Applications	Applications des Ordinateurs	Computer Anwendung	Aplicaciones de los Ordenadores
Linguistics	Linguistique	Sprachwissenschaft	Lingüística
Computer Applications	Applications des Ordinateurs	Computer Anwendung	Aplicaciones de los Ordenadores
Literary and Political Reviews	Revues Littéraires et Politiques	Literarische und Politische Zeitschriften	Revistas Literarias y Politicas
Literature	Litterature	Literatur	Literatura
Adventure and Romance	Aventure et Romance	Abenteuer und Romantik	Aventura y Romance
Mystery and Detective	Mystere et Policier	Geheimnis und Detektivroman	Misterio y Detective
Poetry	Poésie	Poesie	Poesía
Science Fiction, Fantasy, Horror	Science-Fiction, Oeuvres Fantastiques, Oeuvre d'Epouvante	Zukunftsroman, Phantasiegebilde, Grausen	Ciencia Ficción, Fantasía, Horror
Machinery	Machines	Maschinenwesen	Maquinaria
Computer Applications	Applications des Ordinateurs	Computer Anwendung	Aplicaciones de los Ordenadores
Mathematics	Mathématiques	Mathematik	Matemática
Computer Applications	Applications des Ordinateurs	Computer Anwendung	Aplicaciones de los Ordenadores
Matrimony	Mariage	Ehestand	Matrimonio
Computer Applications	Applications des Ordinateurs	Computer Anwendung	Aplicaciones de los Ordenadores
Medical Sciences	Sciences Médicales	Medizinische Wissenschaften	Ciencias Médicas
Allergology and Immunology	Allergologie et Immunologie	Allergie und Immunologie	Alergología e Imunología
Anaesthesiology	Anesthésiologie	Anaesthesiologie	Anestesiología
Cancer	Cancer	Krebs	Cancer
Cardiovascular Diseases	Maladies Cardiovasculaires	Kreislauferkrankungen	Enfermedades Cardiovasculares

Chiropractic, Homeopathy, Osteopathy	Chiropraxie, Homépathie, Ostéopathie	Chiropraktik, Homöopathie, Osteopathie	Quiropractica, Homeopatia Osteopatía
Communicable Diseases	Maladies Contagieuses	Infektiöse Krankheiten	Enfermedades Contagiosas
Computer Applications	Applications des Ordinateurs	Computer Anwendung	Aplicaciónes de los Ordenadores
Dentistry	Dentisterie	Zahnmedizin	Dentistería
Dermatology and Venereology	Dermatologie et Maladies Vénériennes	Dermatologie und Geschlechtskrankheiten	Dermatología y Venereología
Endocrinology	Endocrinologie	Endokrinologie	Endocrinología
Experimental Medicine Laboratory Technique	Médicine Expérimentale, Techniques de Laboratoire	Versuchsmedizin, Laboratoriumstechnik	Medicina Experimental, Tecnicas del Laboratorio
Forensic Sciences	Médecine Légale	Gerichtliche Medizin	Ciencias Forenses
Gastroenterology	Gastroentérologie	Gastroenterologie	Gastroenterología
Hematology	Hématologie	Hämatologie	Hematología
Hypnosis	Hypnose	Hypnose	Hipnotismo
Nurses and Nursing	Personnel et Soins Infirmiers	Krankenpflege	Enfermeros y Enfermería
Obstetrics and Gynecology	Obstétrique et Gynécologie	Gynäkologie und Geburtshilfe	Obstetricia y Ginecología
Ophthalmology and Optometry	Ophtalmologie et Optométrie	Opthalmologie und Optometrie	Oftalmología y Optometría
Orthopedics and Traumatology	Orthopédie et Traumatologie	Orthopädie und Traumatologie	Ortopedia y Traumatologia
Otorhinolaryngology	Otorhinolaryngologie	Otorhinolaryngologie	Otorinolaringología
Pediatrics	Pédiatrie	Pädiatrie	Pediatría
Psychiatry and Neurology	Psychiatrie et Neurologie	Psychiatrie und Neurologie	Psiquiatría y Neurología
Radiology and Nuclear Medicine	Radiologie et Médecine Nucléaire	Radiologie und Nuklearmedizin	Radiología y Medicina Nuclear
Respiratory Diseases	Maladies Respiratoires	Atmungskrankheiten	Enfermedades Respiratorios
Rheumatology	Rhumatologie	Rheumatologie	Reumatología
Sports Medicine	Médecine du Sport	Sportmedizin	Medicina de Deportes
Surgery	Chirurgie	Chirurgie	Cirugía
Urology and Nephrology	Urologie et Néphrologie	Urologie und Nephrologie	Urología y Nefrología
Men's Health	Santé de l'Homme	Gesundheit von Mannern	Salud Masculina
Men's Interests	Publications d'Interêt Masculin	Männer Interessen	Intereses Masculinos
Men's Studies	Etudes de l'Homme	Männerstudien	Estudios de los Hombres
Meetings and Congresses	Réunions et Congrès	Tagungen und Kongresse	Conferencias y Congresos
Metallurgy	Métallurgie	Metallurgie	Metalurgia
Computer Applications	Applications des Ordinateurs	Computer Anwendung	Aplicaciones de los Ordenadores
Welding	Soudure	Schweissen	Soldadura
Meteorology	Météorologie	Meteorologie	Meteorología
Computer Applications	Applications des Ordinateurs	Computer Anwendung	Aplicaciones de los Ordenadores
Metrology and Standardization	Métrologie et Standardisation	Mass- und Gewichtskunde, Normung	Metrología y Normalización
Computer Applications	Applications des Ordinateurs	Computer Anwendung	Aplicaciones de los Ordenadores
Military	Militaires	Militärwesen	Militares
Mines and Mining Industry	Mines et Resources Minières	Bergwesen und Bergbauindustrie	Mines y Minerales
Computer Applications	Applications des Ordinateurs	Computer Anwendung	Aplicaciones de los Ordenadores
Motion Pictures	Cinéma	Film und Kino	Películas
Museums and Art Galleries	Musées et Galleries	Museen und Kunstgalerien	Museos y Galerías del Arte
Music	Musique	Musik	Música
Computer Applications	Applications des Ordinateurs	Computer Anwendung	Aplicaciones de los Ordenadores
Needlework	Travaux à l'Aiguille	Nedelarbeiten	Bordados
New Age	Nouvelle Ere	New Age	Nueva Epoca
Numismatics	Numismatique	Numismatik	Numismática
Nutrition and Dietetics	Nutrition et Diététique	Ernährung und Diätetik	Nutrición y Dietética
Occupational Health and Safety	Medicine du Travail et Prevention	Berufsgesundheitspflege und -Sicherheit	Sanidad y Seguridad de Oficio
Occupations and Careers	Occupations et Carrières	Berufe	Empleos y Ocupaciones
Oriental Studies	Etudes Orientales	Orientalistik	Estudios Orientales
Packaging	Emballage	Verpackung	Empaque
Computer Applications	Applications des Ordinateurs	Computer Anwendung	Aplicaciones de los Ordenadores
Paints and Protective Coatings	Couleurs et Peintures	Farben	Pinturas y Revestimientos Protectores
Paleontology	Paléontologie	Paleontologie	Paleontología
Computer Applications	Applications des Ordinateurs	Computer Anwendung	Aplicaciones de los Ordenadores
Paper and Pulp	Papier et Pulpe	Papier und Papierstoff	Papel y Pasta
Parapsychology and Occultism	Parapsychologie et Occultisme	Parapsychologie und Okkultismus	Parapsicología y Ocultismo
Patents, Trademarks and Copyrights	Brevets, Marques de Fabrique et Droits d'Auteur	Patente, Schutzmarken und Urheberrechte	Patentes, Marcas de Fabrica y Derechos de Autor
Petroleum and Gas	Pétrole et Gas Naturel	Petroleum und Gas	Petróleo y Gas Natural
Computer Applications	Applications des Ordinateurs	Computer Anwendung	Aplicaciones de los Ordenadores
Pets	Animaux Familiers	Haustiere	Animales Domésticos
Pharmacy and Pharmacology	Pharmacie et Pharmacologie	Pharmazie und Pharmakologie	Farmacia y Farmacología
Computer Applications	Applications des Ordinateurs	Computer Anwendung	Aplicaciones de los Ordenadores
Philately	Philatelie	Philatélie	Filatelia
Philosophy	Philosophie	Philosophie	Filosofía
Photography	Photographie	Photographie	Fotografía
Computer Applications	Applications des Ordinateurs	Computer Anwendung	Aplicaciones de los Ordenadores
Physical Fitness and Hygiene	Santé Physique et Hygiène	Gesundheitszustand und Hygiene	Salud Física e Higiene
Physics	Physique	Physik	Física
Computer Applications	Applications des Ordinateurs	Computer Anwendung	Aplicaciones de los Ordenadores
Electricity	Electricité	Elektrizität	Electricidad
Heat	Chaleur	Wärme	Calor
Mechanics	Mécanique	Mechanik	Mecánica
Nuclear Physics	Physique Nucléaire	Kernphysik	Física Nuclear
Optics	Optique	Optik	Optica
Sound	Son	Schall	Sonido
Plastics	Plastiques	Kunststoffe	Plásticos
Computer Applications	Applications des Ordinateurs	Computer Anwendung	Aplicaciones de los Ordenadores
Political Science	Sciences Politiques	Politische Wissenschafte	Ciencias Políticas
Civil Rights	Droits Civiques	Bürgerrechte	Derechos Civiles
International Relations	Relations Internationales	Internationale Beziehungen	Relaciones Internacionales
Population Studies	Démographie	Bevölkerungswissenschaft	Demografía

SUBJECTS xlvii

Printing	Imprimerie	Druck	Imprenta
Computer Applications	Applications des Ordinateurs	Computer Anwendung	Aplicaciónes de los Ordenadores
Psychology	Psychologie	Psychologie	Psicología
Public Administration	Administration Publique	Öffentliche Verwaltung	Administración Pública
Computer Applications	Applications des Ordinateurs	Computer Anwendung	Aplicaciónes de los Ordenadores
Municipal Government	Gouvernement Municipal	Kommunalverwaltung	Gobierno Municipal
Public Health and Safety	Santé Publique et Prevention	Öffentliche Gesundheitspflege	Salud Pública y Seguridad
Publishing and Book Trade	Edition et Commerce du Livre	Verlagswesen und Buchhandel	Editoriales y Libreria
Computer Applications	Applications des Ordinateurs	Computer Anwendung	Aplicaciónes de los Ordenadores
Real Estate	Immobilières	Grundbesitz und Immobilien	Bienes Raíces
Computer Applications	Applications des Ordinateurs	Computer Anwendung	Aplicaciónes de los Ordenadores
Religions and Theology	Religions et Théologie	Religion und Theologie	Religión y Teología
Buddhist	Bouddhisme	Buddhist	Budista
Eastern Orthodox	Eglises Orthodoxes	Griechischkatolische Kirche	Ortodoxo Oriental
Hindu	Hindou	Hindu	Hindú
Islamic	Islamique	Islamische	Islámico
Judaic	Judaique	Jüdäistische	Judaico
Protestant	Protestant	Evangelische	Protestante
Roman Catholic	Catholique romain	Römisch-katholische	Católico Romano
Other Sects	Autres sectes	Andere Sekte	Otras Sectas
Rubber	Caoutchouc	Gummi	Caucho
Computer Applications	Applications des Ordinateurs	Computer Anwendung	Aplicaciones de los Ordenadores
Sciences: Comprehensive Works	Sciences: Oeuvres Comprehensives	Wissenschaften: Umfassende Werke	Ciencias: Obras Comprensivas
Computer Applications	Applications des Ordinateurs	Computer Anwendung	Aplicaciónes de los Ordenadores
Shoes and Boots	Chaussures et Bottes	Schuhe und Stiefel	Zapatos y Botas
Singles' Interests and Lifestyles	Intérêts et Style de Vie Célibataire	Ledigenstandinteressen	Intereses y Estilos de Vivir de los Solteros
Social Sciences: Comprehensive Works	Sciences Sociales: Oeuvres Comprehensives	Sozialwissenschaften: Umfassende Werke	Ciencias Sociales: Obras Comprensivas
Social Service and Welfare	Service Social et Protection Sociale	Sozialpflege und Fürsorge	Asistencia Social y Bienestar
Sociology	Sociologie	Soziologie	Sociología
Computer Applications	Applications des Ordinateurs	Computer Anwendung	Aplicaciónes de los Ordenadores
Sound Recording and Reproduction	Enregistrement et Reproduction du Son	Tonaufnahme und Tonwiedergabe	Grabaciones y Reproducciones Sonoras
Computer Applications	Applications des Ordinateurs	Computer Anwendung	Aplicaciones de los Ordenadores
Sports and Games	Sports et Jeux	Sport und Spiele	Deportes y Juegos
Ball Games	Jeux de Balle	Ballspiele	Juegos de Pelota
Bicycles and Motorcycles	Bicyclettes et Motorcyclettes	Fahrräder und Motorräder	Bicicletas y Motocicletas
Boats and Boating	Bateaux et Canotage	Boote und Bootssport	Botes y Bartelaje
Horses and Horsemanship	Equitation	Pferde und Reitsport	Caballos y Equitación
Outdoor Life	Vie en Plein Air	Im Freien	Vida de Campo
Statistics	Statistique	Statistik	Estadísticas
Technology: Comprehensive Works	Technologie: Oeuvres Comprehensives	Technologie: Umfassende Werke	Tecnologia: Obras Comprensivas
Textile Industries and Fabrics	Textiles	Textil	Textiles y Telas
Computer Applications	Applications des Ordinateurs	Computer Anwendung	Aplicaciones de los Ordenadores
Theater	Théâtre	Theater	Teatro
Tobacco	Tabac	Tabak	Tabaco
Transportation	Transports	Transport	Transportación
Air Transport	Transport Aérien	Luftverkehr	Transporte Aéreo
Automobiles	Automobiles	Kraftfahrzeugen	Automóviles
Computer Applications	Applications des Ordinateurs	Computer Anwendung	Aplicaciónes de los Ordenadores
Railroads	Chemins de Fer	Eisenbahnen	Ferrocarriles
Roads and Traffic	Routes et Circulation	Strassen und Strassenverkehr	Caminos y Tráfico
Ships and Shipping	Navires et Transport Maritimes	Schiffe und Schiffahrt	Barcos y Embarques
Trucks and Trucking	Transports Routiers	Lastkraftwagen	Camiones
Travel and Tourism	Voyages et Tourisme	Reisen und Tourismus	Viaje y Turismo
Airline Inflight and Hotel Inroom	Revues en Vol des Lignes Aérienne et en Chambre des Hôtels	Fluggesellschaft und Hotel Veröffentlichungen	Aerolínea En-Vuelo y Hotel En-Cuarto
Veterinary Sciences	Science Vétérinaire	Tierheilkunde	Veterinaria
Computer Applications	Applications des Ordinateurs	Computer Anwendung	Aplicaciónes de los Ordenadores
Water Resources	Ressources de l'Eau	Wasserwirtschaft	Recursos de Aqua
Computer Applications	Applications des Ordinateurs	Computer Anwendung	Aplicaciónes de los Ordenadores
Women's Health	Santé de la Femme	Gesundheit von Frauen	Salud Feminina
Women's Interests	Publications d'Intérêt Feminin	Veröffentlichungen für Frauen	Intereses Femininas
Women's Studies	Etudes de la Femme	Frauenstudien	Estudios de las Mujeres

Cross-Index to Subjects

A I D S see MEDICAL SCIENCES - Communicable Diseases 3216
Abortions see BIRTH CONTROL 595, see also MEDICAL SCIENCES - Obstetrics And Gynecology 3288
Abrasives see MACHINERY 3015, see also METALLURGY 3401
ABSTRACTING AND INDEXING SERVICES 1
Accident Prevention see OCCUPATIONAL HEALTH AND SAFETY 3614, see also TRANSPORTATION - Roads and Traffic 4717
ACCOUNTING 25
Acoustics see PHYSICS - Sound 3858, see also SOUND RECORDING AND REPRODUCTION 4459
Acquired Immunodeficiency Syndrome see MEDICAL SCIENCES - Communicable Diseases 3216
Activation Analysis see PHYSICS - Nuclear Physics 3846
Actuarial Science see INSURANCE 2525, see also MATHEMATICS 3025
Acupuncture see MEDICAL SCIENCES 3068
Addictions see DRUG ABUSE AND ALCOHOLISM 1532
Adhesives see ENGINEERING - Chemical Engineering 1847
ADULT EDUCATION 25
ADVENTURE AND ROMANCE 25
ADVERTISING AND PUBLIC RELATIONS 25
ADVERTISING AND PUBLIC RELATIONS — Abstracting, Bibliographies, Statistics 40
Advertising Art see ADVERTISING AND PUBLIC RELATIONS 25
Aerobics see PHYSICAL FITNESS AND HYGIENE 3798, see also SPORTS AND GAMES 4463
Aerodynamics see PHYSICS - Mechanics 3842
AERONAUTICS AND SPACE FLIGHT 42, see also ENGINEERING - Mechanical Engineering 1926, TRANSPORTATION - Air Transport 4669
AERONAUTICS AND SPACE FLIGHT — Abstracting, Bibliographies, Statistics 66
AERONAUTICS AND SPACE FLIGHT — Computer Applications 66
Aerophysics see PHYSICS - Mechanics 3842
Aerospace Medicine see MEDICAL SCIENCES 3068
Aesthetics see ART 309, see also PHILOSOPHY 3759
African History see HISTORY - History of Africa 2330
African Studies see HISTORY - History of Africa 2330
Agricultural Aviation see AERONAUTICS AND SPACE FLIGHT 42
Agricultural Chemistry see AGRICULTURE 67, see also CHEMISTRY 1168
AGRICULTURAL ECONOMICS 67
Agricultural Engineering see AGRICULTURE 67, see also ENGINEERING 1813
AGRICULTURAL EQUIPMENT 67
Agricultural Marketing see AGRICULTURE - Agricultural Economics 145, see also FOOD AND FOOD INDUSTRIES - Grocery Trade 2090
AGRICULTURE 67, see also FOOD AND FOOD INDUSTRIES 2060, FORESTS AND FORESTRY 2094, GARDENING AND HORTICULTURE 2120
AGRICULTURE — Abstracting, Bibliographies, Statistics 131
AGRICULTURE — Agricultural Economics 145
AGRICULTURE — Agricultural Equipment 161
AGRICULTURE — Computer Applications 165
AGRICULTURE — Crop Production And Soil 165
AGRICULTURE — Dairying And Dairy Products 197
AGRICULTURE — Feed, Flour And Grain 204
AGRICULTURE — Poultry And Livestock 209
Agronomy see AGRICULTURE 67
Air Conditioning see HEATING, PLUMBING AND REFRIGERATION 2297
Air Defense see MILITARY 3449
Air Force see MILITARY 3449
Air Law see AERONAUTICS AND SPACE FLIGHT 42, see also LAW 2592, TRANSPORTATION - Air Transport 4669
Air Navigation see AERONAUTICS AND SPACE FLIGHT 42
Air Pollution see ENVIRONMENTAL STUDIES - Pollution 1975

AIR TRANSPORT 229
AIRLINE INFLIGHT AND HOTEL INROOM 229
Airplanes see AERONAUTICS AND SPACE FLIGHT 42, see also TRANSPORTATION - Air Transport 4669
Airports see AERONAUTICS AND SPACE FLIGHT 42, see also TRANSPORTATION - Air Transport 4669
Alcoholic Beverages see BEVERAGES 377
Alcoholism see DRUG ABUSE AND ALCOHOLISM 1532
Algae see BIOLOGY - Botany 491
ALLERGOLOGY AND IMMUNOLOGY 229
Almanacs, General see ENCYCLOPEDIAS AND GENERAL ALMANACS 388
Alumni see COLLEGE AND ALUMNI 1302
Amateur Radio see COMMUNICATIONS - Radio 1354
Amusement Guides see COMMUNICATIONS - Television And Cable 1368, see also MUSIC 3536, THEATER 4629, TRAVEL AND TOURISM 4750
ANAESTHESIOLOGY 229
Analogue Computation see COMPUTERS - Hardware 1453, see also COMPUTERS - Theory of Computing 1481
ANALYTICAL CHEMISTRY 229
Anatomy see BIOLOGY 424, see also MEDICAL SCIENCES 3068
Ancient History see ARCHAEOLOGY 260, see also HISTORY 2305
Angiology see MEDICAL SCIENCES - Cardiovascular Diseases 3203
ANIMAL WELFARE 229
Animals see AGRICULTURE - Poultry and Livestock 209, see also ANIMAL WELFARE 229, BIOLOGY - Zoology 575, LEATHER AND FUR INDUSTRIES 2735, PETS 3707, SPORTS AND GAMES - Horses and Horsemanship 4531, VETERINARY SCIENCE 4804
ANTHROPOLOGY 232, see also ARCHAEOLOGY 260
ANTHROPOLOGY — Abstracting, Bibliographies, Statistics 253
Anti-Vivisection see ANIMAL WELFARE 229
Antibiotics see PHARMACY AND PHARMACOLOGY 3714
ANTIQUES 254
Antiquities see CLASSICAL STUDIES 1274
Apparel see CLOTHING TRADE 1282
Appliances see HEATING, PLUMBING AND REFRIGERATION 2297, see also INTERIOR DESIGN AND DECORATION - Furniture and House Furnishings 2556, PHYSICS - Electricity 3840
Applied Mechanics see ENGINEERING - Engineering Mechanics and Materials 1911
Apprenticeship see OCCUPATIONS AND CAREERS 3624
Aquariums see BIOLOGY - Zoology 575, see also FISH AND FISHERIES 2035, PETS 3707
ARCHAEOLOGY 260, see also ANTHROPOLOGY 232, ART 309, HISTORY 2305
ARCHAEOLOGY — Abstracting, Bibliographies, Statistics 290
ARCHAEOLOGY — Computer Applications 290
Archery see SPORTS AND GAMES 4463
ARCHITECTURE 291, see also BUILDING AND CONSTRUCTION 598, ENGINEERING - Civil Engineering 1861, HOUSING AND URBAN PLANNING 2482
ARCHITECTURE — Abstracting, Bibliographies, Statistics 309
ARCHITECTURE — Computer Applications 309
Archives see HISTORY 2305, see also LIBRARY AND INFORMATION SCIENCES 2739
Area Planning see HOUSING AND URBAN PLANNING 2482
Armed Forces see MILITARY 3449
ART 309
ART — Abstracting, Bibliographies, Statistics 351
ART — Computer Applications 352
Art Exhibitions see MUSEUMS AND ART GALLERIES 3520
Art History see ART 309
Arteriosclerosis see MEDICAL SCIENCES - Cardiovascular Diseases 3203
Arthritis see MEDICAL SCIENCES - Rheumatology 3368

ARTIFICIAL INTELLIGENCE 352
Arts see ART 309, see also DANCE 1528, LITERATURE 2890, MOTION PICTURES 3502, MUSIC 3536, THEATER 4629
ARTS AND HANDICRAFTS 352
ARTS AND HANDICRAFTS — Abstracting, Bibliographies, Statistics 357
Asbestos see BUILDING AND CONSTRUCTION 598
Asian History see HISTORY - History of Asia 2336
Asphalt see BUILDING AND CONSTRUCTION 598, see also ENGINEERING - Civil Engineering 1861, TRANSPORTATION - Roads and Traffic 4717
Asthma see MEDICAL SCIENCES - Respiratory Diseases 3364
ASTROLOGY 357
Astronautics see AERONAUTICS AND SPACE FLIGHT 42
ASTRONOMY 359
ASTRONOMY — Abstracting, Bibliographies, Statistics 371
Astrophysics see ASTRONOMY 359
Athletics see MEDICAL SCIENCES - Sports Medicine 3370, see also SPORTS AND GAMES 4463
Atmospheric Sciences see METEOROLOGY 3431
Atomic Energy see ENERGY - Nuclear Energy 1803
Audio Equipment see ELECTRONICS 1764, see also SOUND RECORDING AND REPRODUCTION 4459
Audio-Visual Education see EDUCATION - Teaching Methods and Curriculum 1742, see also MOTION PICTURES 3502
Audiology see MEDICAL SCIENCES - Otorhinolaryngology 3312
Auditing see BUSINESS AND ECONOMICS - Accounting 744
AUTOMATION 371
Automobile Racing see SPORTS AND GAMES 4463
AUTOMOBILES 371
Aviation see AERONAUTICS AND SPACE FLIGHT 42, see also TRANSPORTATION - Air Transport 4669
Aviculture see BIOLOGY - Ornithology 561
Bacteriology see BIOLOGY - Microbiology 548, see also MEDICAL SCIENCES - Communicable Diseases 3216
Badminton see SPORTS AND GAMES 4463
BAKERS AND CONFECTIONERS 371
BALL GAMES 371
Ballet see DANCE 1528
BANKING AND FINANCE 371
BANKING AND FINANCE - Computer Applications see also COMPUTERS - Electronic Data Processing 1448
Banking Law see BUSINESS AND ECONOMICS - Banking and Finance 757, see also LAW 2592
Barbering see BEAUTY CULTURE 371
Baseball see SPORTS AND GAMES - Ball Games 4499
Batteries see PHYSICS - Electricity 3840, see also TRANSPORTATION - Automobiles 4678
BEAUTY CULTURE 371
BEAUTY CULTURE — Abstracting, Bibliographies, Statistics 375
BEAUTY CULTURE — Perfumes And Cosmetics 375
Beekeeping see AGRICULTURE 67
Beer see BEVERAGES 377
Behavioral Sciences see PSYCHOLOGY 4007, see also SOCIOLOGY 4427
BEVERAGES 377, see also FOOD AND FOOD INDUSTRIES 2060
BEVERAGES — Abstracting, Bibliographies, Statistics 388
Biblical Studies see RELIGIONS AND THEOLOGY 4161
BIBLIOGRAPHIES 388, see also ABSTRACTING AND INDEXING SERVICES 1, LIBRARY AND INFORMATION SCIENCES 2739, PUBLISHING AND BOOK TRADE 4119
BICYCLES AND MOTORCYCLES 417
Billiards see SPORTS AND GAMES - Ball Games 4499
Biochemistry see BIOLOGY - Biological Chemistry 470
Biocybernetics see MEDICAL SCIENCES 3068
Bioenergetics see BIOLOGY 424, see also PHYSICAL FITNESS AND HYGIENE 3798
BIOENGINEERING 417
Biofeedback see MEDICAL SCIENCES 3068, see also PHYSICAL FITNESS AND HYGIENE 3798
BIOGRAPHY 417
BIOGRAPHY — Abstracting, Bibliographies, Statistics 424
BIOLOGICAL CHEMISTRY 424
BIOLOGY 424, see also MEDICAL SCIENCES 3068
BIOLOGY — Abstracting, Bibliographies, Statistics 461
BIOLOGY — Bioengineering 468
BIOLOGY — Biological Chemistry 470
BIOLOGY — Biophysics 484
BIOLOGY — Biotechnology 487
BIOLOGY — Botany 491
BIOLOGY — Cytology And Histology 522
BIOLOGY — Entomology 527
BIOLOGY — Genetics 539
BIOLOGY — Microbiology 548
BIOLOGY — Microscopy 559
BIOLOGY — Ornithology 561
BIOLOGY — Physiology 568
BIOLOGY — Zoology 575
Biometeorology see METEOROLOGY 3431
Biometry see BIOLOGY 424, see also STATISTICS 4560
Bionics see COMPUTERS - Cybernetics 1440
BIOPHYSICS 595
BIOTECHNOLOGY 595
Birds see BIOLOGY - Ornithology 561, see also CONSERVATION 1482, PETS 3707
BIRTH CONTROL 595
BIRTH CONTROL — Abstracting, Bibliographies, Statistics 598
Black Studies see ETHNIC INTERESTS 1988
Blind see EDUCATION - Special Education and Rehabilitation 1732, see also HANDICAPPED - Visually Impaired 2290, MEDICAL SCIENCES - Ophthalmology And Optometry 3297, SOCIAL SERVICES AND WELFARE 4396
Blood Transfusion see MEDICAL SCIENCES - Cardiovascular Diseases 3203, see also MEDICAL SCIENCES - Hematology 3270

BOATS AND BOATING 598
Bobsleighing see SPORTS AND GAMES - Outdoor Life 4539
Bodybuilding see PHYSICAL FITNESS AND HYGIENE 3798, see also SPORTS AND GAMES 4463
Bond Market see BUSINESS AND ECONOMICS - Investments 937
Book Collecting see PUBLISHING AND BOOK TRADE 4119
Book Illustrating see PUBLISHING AND BOOK TRADE 4119
Book Reviews see LITERATURE 2890, see also PUBLISHING AND BOOK TRADE 4119
Book Trade see BIBLIOGRAPHIES 388, see also PRINTING 3997, PUBLISHING AND BOOK TRADE 4119
Bookbinding see PUBLISHING AND BOOK TRADE 4119
Bookkeeping see BUSINESS AND ECONOMICS - Accounting 744
Booksellers see PUBLISHING AND BOOK TRADE 4119
Boots see SHOES AND BOOTS 4360
BOTANY 598
Bottling see BEVERAGES 377, see also PACKAGING 3647
Bowling see SPORTS AND GAMES - Ball Games 4499
Boxes see PACKAGING 3647
Boxing see SPORTS AND GAMES 4463
Braille see HANDICAPPED - Visually Impaired 2290
Brass Instruments see MUSIC 3536
Brewing see BEVERAGES 377
Bricks see BUILDING AND CONSTRUCTION 598, see also CERAMICS, GLASS AND POTTERY 1160
Brides And Bridal Apparel see CLOTHING TRADE - Fashions 1289, see also MATRIMONY 3066
Bridge see SPORTS AND GAMES 4463
Bridge Construction see ENGINEERING - Civil Engineering 1861
Broadcasting see COMMUNICATIONS - Radio 1354, see also COMMUNICATIONS - Television And Cable 1368
Bryology see BIOLOGY - Botany 491
BUDDHISM 598
BUILDING AND CONSTRUCTION 598, see also ARCHITECTURE 291, ENGINEERING - Civil Engineering 1861, HOUSING AND URBAN PLANNING 2482
BUILDING AND CONSTRUCTION — Abstracting, Bibliographies, Statistics 636
BUILDING AND CONSTRUCTION — Carpentry And Woodwork 639
BUILDING AND CONSTRUCTION — Hardware 641
Bullfighting see SPORTS AND GAMES 4463
Burns see MEDICAL SCIENCES - Orthopedics and Traumatology 3306
Buses see TRANSPORTATION - Automobiles 4678
Business Administration see BUSINESS AND ECONOMICS - Management 1000
BUSINESS AND ECONOMICS 643
BUSINESS AND ECONOMICS — Abstracting, Bibliographies, Statistics 701
BUSINESS AND ECONOMICS — Accounting 744
BUSINESS AND ECONOMICS — Banking And Finance 757
BUSINESS AND ECONOMICS — Banking And Finance - Computer Applications 804
BUSINESS AND ECONOMICS — Chamber Of Commerce Publications 806
BUSINESS AND ECONOMICS — Computer Applications 825
BUSINESS AND ECONOMICS — Cooperatives 828
BUSINESS AND ECONOMICS — Domestic Commerce 833
BUSINESS AND ECONOMICS — Economic Situation And Conditions 841
BUSINESS AND ECONOMICS — Economic Systems And Theories, Economic History 888
BUSINESS AND ECONOMICS — International Commerce 899
BUSINESS AND ECONOMICS — International Development And Assistance 925
BUSINESS AND ECONOMICS — Investments 937
BUSINESS AND ECONOMICS — Labor And Industrial Relations 970
BUSINESS AND ECONOMICS — Macroeconomics 998
BUSINESS AND ECONOMICS — Management 1000
BUSINESS AND ECONOMICS — Marketing And Purchasing 1032
BUSINESS AND ECONOMICS — Office Equipment And Services 1057
BUSINESS AND ECONOMICS — Personnel Management 1062
BUSINESS AND ECONOMICS — Production Of Goods And Services 1071
BUSINESS AND ECONOMICS — Public Finance, Taxation 1087
BUSINESS AND ECONOMICS — Small Business 1112
BUSINESS AND ECONOMICS — Trade And Industrial Directories 1119
Business Law see LAW - Corporate Law 2706
Butane see PETROLEUM AND GAS 3680
Cable Television see COMMUNICATIONS - Television And Cable 1368
Cables see COMMUNICATIONS - Telephone and Telegraph 1361, see also ENGINEERING - Electrical Engineering 1880
Cafeterias see HOTELS AND RESTAURANTS 2471
Calendars of Events see MEETINGS AND CONGRESSES 3390, see also TRAVEL AND TOURISM 4750
Calligraphy see ART 309
Camping see LEISURE AND RECREATION 2738, see also SPORTS AND GAMES - Outdoor Life 4539, TRAVEL AND TOURISM 4750
Canals see TRANSPORTATION - Ships and Shipping 4723
CANCER 1160
Candy see FOOD AND FOOD INDUSTRIES - Bakers and Confectioners 2086
Canning and Preserving see FOOD AND FOOD INDUSTRIES 2060, see also HOME ECONOMICS 2444
Canoeing see SPORTS AND GAMES - Boats and Boating 4521
Canon Law see RELIGIONS AND THEOLOGY 4161
Canvas see TEXTILE INDUSTRIES AND FABRICS 4615
Carboniferous Geology see EARTH SCIENCES - Geophysics 1586
Cardiology see MEDICAL SCIENCES - Cardiovascular Diseases 3203
CARDIOVASCULAR DISEASES 1160
Cardiovascular Surgery see MEDICAL SCIENCES - Surgery 3373
Careers see OCCUPATIONS AND CAREERS 3624
Cargo Handling see TRANSPORTATION - Ships and Shipping 4723
Caribbean History see HISTORY - History of North and South America 2397
CARPENTRY AND WOODWORK 1160
Carpets and Rugs see INTERIOR DESIGN AND DECORATION - Furniture and House Furnishings 2556
Cartography see GEOGRAPHY 2240
Cartoons see ART 309

Catering see HOTELS AND RESTAURANTS 2471
Cattle see AGRICULTURE - Poultry and Livestock 209
Caves see EARTH SCIENCES - Geology 1552
Cement see BUILDING AND CONSTRUCTION 598
Cemeteries see FUNERALS 2119
CERAMICS, GLASS AND POTTERY 1160, see also ART 309, ARTS AND HANDICRAFTS 352
CERAMICS, GLASS AND POTTERY — Abstracting, Bibliographies, Statistics 1167
Cereals see AGRICULTURE - Feed, Flour and Grain 204, see also FOOD AND FOOD INDUSTRIES 2060
Cerebral Palsy see MEDICAL SCIENCES - Psychiatry and Neurology 3327
CHAMBER OF COMMERCE PUBLICATIONS 1168
Chaplains see MILITARY 3449, see also RELIGIONS AND THEOLOGY 4161
Charities see SOCIAL SERVICES AND WELFARE 4396
CHEMICAL ENGINEERING 1168
Chemical Wastes see ENVIRONMENTAL STUDIES - Pollution 1975, see also ENVIRONMENTAL STUDIES - Waste Management 1984
CHEMISTRY 1168
CHEMISTRY — Abstracting, Bibliographies, Statistics 1191
CHEMISTRY — Analytical Chemistry 1203
CHEMISTRY — Crystallography 1210
CHEMISTRY — Electrochemistry 1211
CHEMISTRY — Inorganic Chemistry 1213
CHEMISTRY — Organic Chemistry 1215
CHEMISTRY — Physical Chemistry 1224
Chemotherapy see BIOLOGY - Biological Chemistry 470, see also MEDICAL SCIENCES 3068, PHARMACY AND PHARMACOLOGY 3714
Chess see SPORTS AND GAMES 4463
Chest Diseases see MEDICAL SCIENCES - Respiratory Diseases 3364
Child Psychology see PSYCHOLOGY 4007
Child Welfare see CHILDREN AND YOUTH - About 1231, see also SOCIAL SERVICES AND WELFARE 4396
CHILDREN AND YOUTH — About 1231
CHILDREN AND YOUTH — Abstracting, Bibliographies, Statistics 1247
CHILDREN AND YOUTH — For 1248
Chromatography see CHEMISTRY - Analytical Chemistry 1203
Church History see RELIGIONS AND THEOLOGY 4161
Cigarettes and Cigars see TOBACCO 4643
Cinematography see MOTION PICTURES 3502, see also PHOTOGRAPHY 3788
CIRCUITS 1273
Circulatory System see MEDICAL SCIENCES - Cardiovascular Diseases 3203
Circus see THEATER 4629
Cities and Towns see HOUSING AND URBAN PLANNING 2482, see also PUBLIC ADMINISTRATION - Municipal Government 4083
Citizenship see POLITICAL SCIENCE 3869
Citrus Fruits see AGRICULTURE - Crop Production and Soil 165, see also FOOD AND FOOD INDUSTRIES 2060, GARDENING AND HORTICULTURE 2120
City Planning see HOUSING AND URBAN PLANNING 2482
Civil Aeronautics see TRANSPORTATION - Air Transport 4669
CIVIL DEFENSE 1273, see also MILITARY 3449
CIVIL DEFENSE — Abstracting, Bibliographies, Statistics 1274
CIVIL ENGINEERING 1274
CIVIL LAW 1274
Civil Liberties see LAW - Constitutional Law 2705, see also POLITICAL SCIENCE - Civil Rights 3939
CIVIL RIGHTS 1274
Civil Service see OCCUPATIONS AND CAREERS 3624, see also PUBLIC ADMINISTRATION 4052
Clairvoyance see NEW AGE PUBLICATIONS 3593, see also PARAPSYCHOLOGY AND OCCULTISM 3668
CLASSICAL STUDIES 1274, see also ARCHAEOLOGY 260, HISTORY 2305, LINGUISTICS 2799, LITERATURE 2890
CLASSICAL STUDIES — Abstracting, Bibliographies, Statistics 1281
CLEANING AND DYEING 1281
CLEANING AND DYEING — Abstracting, Bibliographies, Statistics 1282
Climatology see METEOROLOGY 3431
Clinical Medicine see MEDICAL SCIENCES 3068
CLOTHING TRADE 1282
CLOTHING TRADE — Abstracting, Bibliographies, Statistics 1288
CLOTHING TRADE — Fashions 1289
CLUBS 1295
CLUBS — Abstracting, Bibliographies, Statistics 1302
Coaching see SPORTS AND GAMES 4463
Coastal Engineering see ENGINEERING - Hydraulic Engineering 1923
Coffee see BEVERAGES 377
Cognitive Studies see PSYCHOLOGY 4007
Coins see NUMISMATICS 3597
Collectibles see ANTIQUES 254
Collectors and Collecting see ANTIQUES 254, see also HOBBIES 2432
COLLEGE AND ALUMNI 1302, see also CLUBS 1295, EDUCATION - Higher Education 1698
College Management see EDUCATION - Higher Education 1698, see also EDUCATION - School Organization and Administration 1724
Colloids see CHEMISTRY - Physical Chemistry 1224, see also PHYSICS 3812
Combustion see CHEMISTRY - Physical Chemistry 1224, see also PHYSICS - Heat 3840
Commerce see BUSINESS AND ECONOMICS - Domestic Commerce 833, see also BUSINESS AND ECONOMICS - International Commerce 899
Commercial Art see ADVERTISING AND PUBLIC RELATIONS 25, see also ART 309
Commercial Education see EDUCATION - Teaching Methods and Curriculum 1742
Commercial Law see BUSINESS AND ECONOMICS 643, see also LAW 2592
COMMUNICABLE DISEASES 1331
COMMUNICATIONS 1331, see also JOURNALISM 2566
COMMUNICATIONS — Abstracting, Bibliographies, Statistics 1346
COMMUNICATIONS — Computer Applications 1349
COMMUNICATIONS — Postal Affairs 1352
COMMUNICATIONS — Radio 1354
COMMUNICATIONS — Telephone And Telegraph 1361

COMMUNICATIONS — Television And Cable 1368
COMMUNICATIONS — Video 1384
Communism see BUSINESS AND ECONOMICS - Economic Systems and Theories, Economic History 888, see also POLITICAL SCIENCE 3869
Community Affairs see PUBLIC ADMINISTRATION - Municipal Government 4083
Comparative Psychology see PSYCHOLOGY 4007
Compressed Air see ENGINEERING - Mechanical Engineering 1926
COMPUTERS 1388, see also COMPUTERS - Information Science and Information Theory 1455
COMPUTERS — Abstracting, Bibliographies, Statistics 1402
COMPUTERS — Artificial Intelligence 1406, see also COMPUTERS - Cybernetics 1440
COMPUTERS — Automation 1411
COMPUTERS — Circuits 1416, see also COMPUTERS - Computer Engineering 1417
COMPUTERS — Computer Architecture 1416, see also COMPUTERS - Computer Engineering 1417
COMPUTERS — Computer Assisted Instruction 1416, see also EDUCATION - Computer Applications 1688
COMPUTERS — Computer Engineering 1417, see also COMPUTERS - Computer Architecture 1416
COMPUTERS — Computer Games 1418
COMPUTERS — Computer Graphics 1420, see also PRINTING - Computer Applications 4007
COMPUTERS — Computer Industry 1423
COMPUTERS — Computer Industry Directories 1424
COMPUTERS — Computer Industry, Vocational Guidance 1425, see also EDUCATION 1612, OCCUPATIONS AND CAREERS 3624
COMPUTERS — Computer Music 1426, see also MUSIC - Computer Applications 3589
COMPUTERS — Computer Networks 1426
COMPUTERS — Computer Programming 1429, see also COMPUTERS - Software 1475
COMPUTERS — Computer Sales 1432, see also BUSINESS AND ECONOMICS - Marketing and Purchasing 1032
COMPUTERS — Computer Security 1433
COMPUTERS — Computer Simulation 1435
COMPUTERS — Computer Systems 1436, see also COMPUTERS - Computer Architecture 1416
COMPUTERS — Cybernetics 1440, see also COMPUTERS - Artificial Intelligence 1406
COMPUTERS — Data Base Management 1443
COMPUTERS — Data Communications And Data Transmission Systems 1445
COMPUTERS — Electronic Data Processing 1448, see also BUSINESS AND ECONOMICS - Banking and Finance - Computer Applications 804
COMPUTERS — Hardware 1453
COMPUTERS — Information Science And Information Theory 1455, see also COMPUTERS 1388
COMPUTERS — Machine Theory 1457
COMPUTERS — Microcomputers 1457, see also COMPUTERS - Personal Computers 1466
COMPUTERS — Minicomputers 1466
COMPUTERS — Personal Computers 1466, see also COMPUTERS - Microcomputers 1457
COMPUTERS — Software 1475, see also COMPUTERS - Computer Programming 1429
COMPUTERS — Theory Of Computing 1481
COMPUTERS — Word Processing 1482
Conchology see BIOLOGY - Zoology 575
Confectioners see FOOD AND FOOD INDUSTRIES - Bakers and Confectioners 2086
Congenital Abnormalities see BIOLOGY - Genetics 539, see also MEDICAL SCIENCES 3068
Congresses see MEETINGS AND CONGRESSES 3390
CONSERVATION 1482, see also ENVIRONMENTAL STUDIES 1941, FISH AND FISHERIES 2035, FORESTS AND FORESTRY 2094, WATER RESOURCES 4821
CONSERVATION — Abstracting, Bibliographies, Statistics 1501
CONSTITUTIONAL LAW 1502
Construction see BUILDING AND CONSTRUCTION 598, see also ENGINEERING - Civil Engineering 1861
Consumer Credit see BUSINESS AND ECONOMICS - Banking and Finance 757
CONSUMER EDUCATION AND PROTECTION 1502
CONSUMER EDUCATION AND PROTECTION — Abstracting, Bibliographies, Statistics 1509
Consumer Electronics see ELECTRONICS 1764
Contact Lenses see MEDICAL SCIENCES - Ophthalmology and Optometry 3297
Containers see PACKAGING 3647
Contraception see BIRTH CONTROL 595
Contractors see BUILDING AND CONSTRUCTION 598
Convention Dates see MEETINGS AND CONGRESSES 3390
Cookery see HOME ECONOMICS 2444, see also HOTELS AND RESTAURANTS 2471
COOPERATIVES 1509
Copying and Duplicating see PHOTOGRAPHY 3788, see also PRINTING 3997
Copyrights see PATENTS, TRADEMARKS AND COPYRIGHTS 3672
CORPORATE LAW 1509
Correspondence Education see EDUCATION - Adult Education 1681
Corrosion see METALLURGY 3401, see also PAINTS AND PROTECTIVE COATINGS 3652
Cosmetics see BEAUTY CULTURE - Perfumes and Cosmetics 375
Counseling see EDUCATION 1612, see also PSYCHOLOGY 4007, SOCIAL SERVICES AND WELFARE 4396
Crafts see ARTS AND HANDICRAFTS 352
Credit and Collections see BUSINESS AND ECONOMICS - Banking and Finance 757
Credit Unions see BUSINESS AND ECONOMICS - Banking and Finance 757
Cricket see SPORTS AND GAMES 4463
CRIMINAL LAW 1509
CRIMINOLOGY AND LAW ENFORCEMENT 1509
CRIMINOLOGY AND LAW ENFORCEMENT — Abstracting, Bibliographies, Statistics 1524

CRIMINOLOGY AND LAW ENFORCEMENT — Security 1525
CROP PRODUCTION AND SOIL 1528
Croquet see SPORTS AND GAMES - Ball Games 4499
Cryogenic Engineering see ENGINEERING - Mechanical Engineering 1926
Cryogenics see PHYSICS - Heat 3840
CRYSTALLOGRAPHY 1528
Currency see BUSINESS AND ECONOMICS - Banking and Finance 757
Curriculum and Teaching Methods see EDUCATION - Teaching Methods and Curriculum 1742
Customs and Excise see BUSINESS AND ECONOMICS - Public Finance, Taxation 1087
Cybernetic Medicine see MEDICAL SCIENCES 3068
CYBERNETICS 1528
Cystic Fibrosis see MEDICAL SCIENCES 3068
CYTOLOGY AND HISTOLOGY 1528
DAIRYING AND DAIRY PRODUCTS 1528
DANCE 1528, see also MUSIC 3536, THEATER 4629
DANCE — Abstracting, Bibliographies, Statistics 1532
DATA BASE MANAGEMENT 1532
DATA COMMUNICATIONS AND DATA TRANSMISSION SYSTEMS 1532
Data Processing see COMPUTERS - Electronic Data Processing 1448
Deaf see EDUCATION - Special Education and Rehabilitation 1732, see also HANDICAPPED - Hearing Impaired 2285, MEDICAL SCIENCES - Otorhinolaryngology 3312, SOCIAL SERVICES AND WELFARE 4396
Decoration see INTERIOR DESIGN AND DECORATION 2547
Defense see CIVIL DEFENSE 1273, see also MILITARY 3449
Delinquency see CHILDREN AND YOUTH - About 1231, see also CRIMINOLOGY AND LAW ENFORCEMENT 1509, SOCIAL SERVICES AND WELFARE 4396
Demography see POPULATION STUDIES 3979
DENTISTRY 1532
Department Stores see BUSINESS AND ECONOMICS - Marketing and Purchasing 1032
DERMATOLOGY AND VENEREOLOGY 1532
Desalination see ENVIRONMENTAL STUDIES 1941, see also WATER RESOURCES 4821
Design see ART 309
Detective Magazines see LITERATURE - Mystery And Detective 2985
Detectives see CRIMINOLOGY AND LAW ENFORCEMENT 1509
Diabetes see MEDICAL SCIENCES - Endocrinology 3250
Dialysis see MEDICAL SCIENCES - Urology and Nephrology 3386
Diecasting see ENGINEERING 1813
Diesel Engines see ENGINEERING - Mechanical Engineering 1926
Dietetics see NUTRITION AND DIETETICS 3602
Digestive System see MEDICAL SCIENCES - Gastroenterology 3266
Digital Computers see COMPUTERS - Hardware 1453
Diplomatic Service see POLITICAL SCIENCE - International Relations 3948
Disability, Disabled see HANDICAPPED 2283, see also INSURANCE 2525, OCCUPATIONAL HEALTH AND SAFETY 3614, SOCIAL SERVICES AND WELFARE 4396
Disarmament see MILITARY 3449, see also POLITICAL SCIENCE 3869
Disk Drives see COMPUTERS - Hardware 1453
Distilling see BEVERAGES 377
Divorce see MATRIMONY 3066
Documentation see COMPUTERS - Computer Programming 1429, see also COMPUTERS - Software 1475
Domestic Animals and Birds see ANIMAL WELFARE 229, see also PETS 3707, VETERINARY SCIENCE 4804
DOMESTIC COMMERCE 1532
Drafting see ENGINEERING 1813, see also TECHNOLOGY: COMPREHENSIVE WORKS 4592
Drama see LITERATURE 2890, see also THEATER 4629
Drawing and Sketching see ART 309
DRUG ABUSE AND ALCOHOLISM 1532
DRUG ABUSE AND ALCOHOLISM — Abstracting, Bibliographies, Statistics 1540
Drugs see PHARMACY AND PHARMACOLOGY 3714
Dry Goods see CLOTHING TRADE 1282, see also TEXTILE INDUSTRIES AND FABRICS 4615
Dyes and Dyeing see CLEANING AND DYEING 1281, see also TEXTILE INDUSTRIES AND FABRICS 4615
E C G see MEDICAL SCIENCES - Cardiovascular Diseases 3203
E E G see MEDICAL SCIENCES - Psychiatry and Neurology 3327
EARTH SCIENCES 1540
EARTH SCIENCES — Abstracting, Bibliographies, Statistics 1549
EARTH SCIENCES — Geology 1552
EARTH SCIENCES — Geophysics 1586
EARTH SCIENCES — Hydrology 1596
EARTH SCIENCES — Oceanography 1601
EASTERN ORTHODOX 1612
Ecclesiastical Art see ART 309, see also RELIGIONS AND THEOLOGY 4161
Ecclesiastical Law see RELIGIONS AND THEOLOGY 4161
Ecology see BIOLOGY 424, see also CONSERVATION 1482, ENVIRONMENTAL STUDIES 1941
Economic Geology see EARTH SCIENCES - Geology 1552
ECONOMIC SITUATION AND CONDITIONS 1612
ECONOMIC SYSTEMS AND THEORIES, ECONOMIC HISTORY 1612
ECONOMICS 1612
Editing see JOURNALISM 2566, see also PUBLISHING AND BOOK TRADE 4119
EDUCATION 1612, see also CHILDREN AND YOUTH - About 1231
EDUCATION — Abstracting, Bibliographies, Statistics 1673
EDUCATION — Adult Education 1681
EDUCATION — Computer Applications 1688, see also COMPUTERS - Computer Assisted Instruction 1416
EDUCATION — Guides To Schools And Colleges 1691
EDUCATION — Higher Education 1698
EDUCATION — International Education Programs 1721
EDUCATION — School Organization And Administration 1724
EDUCATION — Special Education And Rehabilitation 1732
EDUCATION — Teaching Methods And Curriculum 1742

Educational Films see EDUCATION - Teaching Methods and Curriculum 1742, see also MOTION PICTURES 3502
Educational Psychology see PSYCHOLOGY 4007
Egyptology see ARCHAEOLOGY 260, see also ART 309, HISTORY - History of Africa 2330
ELECTRICAL ENERGY 1764
ELECTRICAL ENGINEERING 1764
ELECTRICITY 1764
ELECTROCHEMISTRY 1764
ELECTRONIC DATA PROCESSING 1764
ELECTRONICS 1764
ELECTRONICS — Computer Applications 1779
Electroplating see ENGINEERING - Electrical Engineering 1880, see also METALLURGY 3401
Electrotherapy see MEDICAL SCIENCES - Psychiatry and Neurology 3327, see also MEDICAL SCIENCES - Radiology and Nuclear Medicine 3356
Embroidery and Needlework see NEEDLEWORK 3590
Embryology see BIOLOGY 424, see also MEDICAL SCIENCES 3068
Emigration see POPULATION STUDIES 3979
Emotionally Disturbed Children see CHILDREN AND YOUTH - About 1231, see also EDUCATION - Special Education and Rehabilitation 1732
Employment see BUSINESS AND ECONOMICS - Labor and Industrial Relations 970, see also OCCUPATIONS AND CAREERS 3624
Encephalitis see MEDICAL SCIENCES - Psychiatry and Neurology 3327
ENCYCLOPEDIAS AND GENERAL ALMANACS 1779
ENCYCLOPEDIAS AND GENERAL ALMANACS — Abstracting, Bibliographies, Statistics 1782
ENDOCRINOLOGY 1783
ENERGY 1783
ENERGY — Abstracting, Bibliographies, Statistics 1797
ENERGY — Electrical Energy 1801
ENERGY — Geothermal Energy 1802
ENERGY — Hydroelectrical Energy 1802
ENERGY — Nuclear Energy 1803
ENERGY — Solar Energy 1810
ENERGY — Wind Energy 1812
ENGINEERING 1813
ENGINEERING — Abstracting, Bibliographies, Statistics 1841
ENGINEERING — Chemical Engineering 1847
ENGINEERING — Civil Engineering 1861
ENGINEERING — Computer Applications 1877
ENGINEERING — Electrical Engineering 1880
ENGINEERING — Engineering Mechanics And Materials 1911
ENGINEERING — Hydraulic Engineering 1923
ENGINEERING — Industrial Engineering 1925
ENGINEERING — Mechanical Engineering 1926
Engines see ENGINEERING - Mechanical Engineering 1926, see also TRANSPORTATION 4646
English Language - Study and Teaching see LINGUISTICS 2799
Engraving see ART 309, see also PRINTING 3997
Entertainment see COMMUNICATIONS - Radio 1354, see also COMMUNICATIONS - Television And Cable 1368, COMMUNICATIONS - Video 1384, DANCE 1528, MOTION PICTURES 3502, MUSIC 3536, SPORTS AND GAMES 4463, THEATER 4629, TRAVEL AND TOURISM 4750
ENTOMOLOGY 1941
Environmental Health see ENVIRONMENTAL STUDIES 1941, see also PUBLIC HEALTH AND SAFETY 4096
ENVIRONMENTAL STUDIES 1941, see also CONSERVATION 1482
ENVIRONMENTAL STUDIES — Abstracting, Bibliographies, Statistics 1972
ENVIRONMENTAL STUDIES — Computer Applications 1975
ENVIRONMENTAL STUDIES — Pollution 1975
ENVIRONMENTAL STUDIES — Toxicology And Environmental Safety 1980
ENVIRONMENTAL STUDIES — Waste Management 1984
Enzymes see BIOLOGY - Biological Chemistry 470, see also MEDICAL SCIENCES 3068
Ephemerides see ASTRONOMY 359
Epidemiology see PUBLIC HEALTH AND SAFETY 4096
Epilepsy see MEDICAL SCIENCES - Psychiatry and Neurology 3327
Ergonomics see BUSINESS AND ECONOMICS - Labor and Industrial Relations 970, see also PSYCHOLOGY 4007
Erosion see AGRICULTURE - Crop Production and Soil 165, see also CONSERVATION 1482
Esperanto see LINGUISTICS 2799
ESTATE PLANNING LAW 1988
ETHNIC INTERESTS 1988
ETHNIC INTERESTS — Abstracting, Bibliographies, Statistics 2030
Ethnography see ANTHROPOLOGY 232, see also SOCIOLOGY 4427
Eugenics see BIOLOGY - Genetics 539
European History see HISTORY - History of Europe 2346
Exceptional Children, Education see EDUCATION - Special Education and Rehabilitation 1732
EXPERIMENTAL MEDICINE, LABORATORY TECHNIQUE 2030
Exports and Imports see BUSINESS AND ECONOMICS - International Commerce 899
Extrasensory Perception see PARAPSYCHOLOGY AND OCCULTISM 3668
Eye Care see MEDICAL SCIENCES - Ophthalmology and Optometry 3297
Fabrics see TEXTILE INDUSTRIES AND FABRICS 4615
FAMILY AND MATRIMONIAL LAW 2030
Family Planning see BIRTH CONTROL 595
Family Therapy see MATRIMONY 3066
Farm Equipment see AGRICULTURE - Agricultural Equipment 161, see also MACHINERY 3015
Farm Management see AGRICULTURE 67
FASHIONS 2030
FEED, FLOUR AND GRAIN 2030
Fellowships see EDUCATION - Higher Education 1698
Feminist Movement see POLITICAL SCIENCE - Civil Rights 3939, see also WOMEN'S INTERESTS 4836, WOMEN'S STUDIES 4858
Fencing see SPORTS AND GAMES 4463

Fertilizers see AGRICULTURE - Crop Production and Soil 165
Fiction see LITERATURE 2890
Filmmaking see MOTION PICTURES 3502
Finance see BUSINESS AND ECONOMICS - Banking and Finance 757, see also BUSINESS AND ECONOMICS - Investments 937
Finishing see PAINTS AND PROTECTIVE COATINGS 3652
FIRE PREVENTION 2030
FIRE PREVENTION — Abstracting, Bibliographies, Statistics 2035
Firearms see HOBBIES 2432, see also SPORTS AND GAMES 4463
First Aid see MEDICAL SCIENCES 3068, see also PUBLIC HEALTH AND SAFETY 4096
FISH AND FISHERIES 2035, see also BIOLOGY - Zoology 575
FISH AND FISHERIES — Abstracting, Bibliographies, Statistics 2050
Fishing, Sport see SPORTS AND GAMES - Outdoor Life 4539
Flax see AGRICULTURE - Crop Production and Soil 165, see also TEXTILE INDUSTRIES AND FABRICS 4615
Floor Coverings see INTERIOR DESIGN AND DECORATION - Furniture and House Furnishings 2556
Floral Decorations see ART 309, see also GARDENING AND HORTICULTURE 2120
FLORIST TRADE 2052
Flowers see BIOLOGY - Botany 491, see also GARDENING AND HORTICULTURE 2120
Fluid Power see ENGINEERING - Mechanical Engineering 1926
Flying see AERONAUTICS AND SPACE FLIGHT 42, see also TRANSPORTATION - Air Transport 4669
Flying Saucers see AERONAUTICS AND SPACE FLIGHT 42, see also LITERATURE - Science Fiction, Fantasy, Horror 3010
FOLKLORE 2052
FOLKLORE — Abstracting, Bibliographies, Statistics 2060
FOOD AND FOOD INDUSTRIES 2060
FOOD AND FOOD INDUSTRIES — Abstracting, Bibliographies, Statistics 2084
FOOD AND FOOD INDUSTRIES — Bakers And Confectioners 2086
FOOD AND FOOD INDUSTRIES — Grocery Trade 2090
Football see SPORTS AND GAMES - Ball Games 4499
Footwear see LEATHER AND FUR INDUSTRIES 2735, see also SHOES AND BOOTS 4360
Foreign Affairs see POLITICAL SCIENCE - International Relations 3948
Foreign Aid see BUSINESS AND ECONOMICS - International Development and Assistance 925
Foreign Commerce see BUSINESS AND ECONOMICS - International Commerce 899
Foreign Legion see MILITARY 3449
FORENSIC SCIENCES 2094
Forest Fires see FIRE PREVENTION 2030, see also FORESTS AND FORESTRY 2094
FORESTS AND FORESTRY 2094
FORESTS AND FORESTRY — Abstracting, Bibliographies, Statistics 2111
FORESTS AND FORESTRY — Lumber And Wood 2113
Foundry Practices see METALLURGY 3401
Fraternal Organizations see CLUBS 1295, see also COLLEGE AND ALUMNI 1302
Freight see TRANSPORTATION 4646
French Language - Study and Teaching see LINGUISTICS 2799
Frequency Modulation see COMMUNICATIONS - Radio 1354, see also COMMUNICATIONS - Television And Cable 1368, SOUND RECORDING AND REPRODUCTION 4459
Fretted Instruments see MUSIC 3536
Frozen Food see FOOD AND FOOD INDUSTRIES 2060
Fruit see AGRICULTURE - Crop Production and Soil 165, see also FOOD AND FOOD INDUSTRIES 2060, GARDENING AND HORTICULTURE 2120
Fuel see ENERGY 1783, see also HEATING, PLUMBING AND REFRIGERATION 2297, MINES AND MINING INDUSTRY 3477, PETROLEUM AND GAS 3680
Fundraising see SOCIAL SERVICES AND WELFARE 4396
FUNERALS 2119
Fur see LEATHER AND FUR INDUSTRIES 2735
Furnaces see HEATING, PLUMBING AND REFRIGERATION 2297, see also METALLURGY 3401
FURNITURE AND HOUSE FURNISHINGS 2120
Galleries see MUSEUMS AND ART GALLERIES 3520
Gambling see SPORTS AND GAMES 4463
Game Breeding see AGRICULTURE - Poultry and Livestock 209
Games see SPORTS AND GAMES 4463
Garages see TRANSPORTATION - Automobiles 4678
GARDENING AND HORTICULTURE 2120, see also AGRICULTURE 67, BIOLOGY - Botany 491
GARDENING AND HORTICULTURE — Abstracting, Bibliographies, Statistics 2141
GARDENING AND HORTICULTURE — Florist Trade 2141
Gas Chromatography see CHEMISTRY - Analytical Chemistry 1203
Gas Dynamics see PHYSICS - Mechanics 3842
Gas Turbines see ENGINEERING - Mechanical Engineering 1926
GASTROENTEROLOGY 2143
Gastronomy see HOME ECONOMICS 2444
Gemstones see JEWELRY, CLOCKS AND WATCHES 2562
Gender Studies see MEN'S STUDIES 3400, see also WOMEN'S STUDIES 4858
GENEALOGY AND HERALDRY 2143
GENEALOGY AND HERALDRY — Abstracting, Bibliographies, Statistics 2168
GENEALOGY AND HERALDRY — Computer Applications 2168
GENERAL INTEREST PERIODICALS — Africa 2168
GENERAL INTEREST PERIODICALS — Argentina 2170
GENERAL INTEREST PERIODICALS — Australasia 2171
GENERAL INTEREST PERIODICALS — Australia 2171
GENERAL INTEREST PERIODICALS — Austria 2173
GENERAL INTEREST PERIODICALS — Bahrain 2173
GENERAL INTEREST PERIODICALS — Bangladesh 2173
GENERAL INTEREST PERIODICALS — Belarus 2174
GENERAL INTEREST PERIODICALS — Belgium 2174
GENERAL INTEREST PERIODICALS — Bermuda 2175
GENERAL INTEREST PERIODICALS — Bolivia 2175
GENERAL INTEREST PERIODICALS — Brazil 2175
GENERAL INTEREST PERIODICALS — Bulgaria 2175
GENERAL INTEREST PERIODICALS — Canada 2175

GENERAL INTEREST PERIODICALS — Central America 2180
GENERAL INTEREST PERIODICALS — Chile 2180
GENERAL INTEREST PERIODICALS — China 2180
GENERAL INTEREST PERIODICALS — Colombia 2183
GENERAL INTEREST PERIODICALS — Cuba 2184
GENERAL INTEREST PERIODICALS — Cyprus 2184
GENERAL INTEREST PERIODICALS — Czechoslovakia 2184
GENERAL INTEREST PERIODICALS — Denmark 2185
GENERAL INTEREST PERIODICALS — Dominican Republic 2185
GENERAL INTEREST PERIODICALS — Ecuador 2185
GENERAL INTEREST PERIODICALS — Egypt 2185
GENERAL INTEREST PERIODICALS — Estonia 2186
GENERAL INTEREST PERIODICALS — Ethiopia 2186
GENERAL INTEREST PERIODICALS — Finland 2186
GENERAL INTEREST PERIODICALS — France 2186
GENERAL INTEREST PERIODICALS — Germany 2188
GENERAL INTEREST PERIODICALS — Ghana 2192
GENERAL INTEREST PERIODICALS — Great Britain 2193
GENERAL INTEREST PERIODICALS — Greece 2196
GENERAL INTEREST PERIODICALS — Greenland 2196
GENERAL INTEREST PERIODICALS — Guatemala 2196
GENERAL INTEREST PERIODICALS — Guyana 2196
GENERAL INTEREST PERIODICALS — Haiti 2197
GENERAL INTEREST PERIODICALS — Hong Kong 2197
GENERAL INTEREST PERIODICALS — Hungary 2197
GENERAL INTEREST PERIODICALS — Iceland 2198
GENERAL INTEREST PERIODICALS — India 2198
GENERAL INTEREST PERIODICALS — Indonesia 2202
GENERAL INTEREST PERIODICALS — Iran 2202
GENERAL INTEREST PERIODICALS — Iraq 2202
GENERAL INTEREST PERIODICALS — Ireland 2202
GENERAL INTEREST PERIODICALS — Israel 2203
GENERAL INTEREST PERIODICALS — Italy 2204
GENERAL INTEREST PERIODICALS — Japan 2207
GENERAL INTEREST PERIODICALS — Jordan 2208
GENERAL INTEREST PERIODICALS — Kenya 2208
GENERAL INTEREST PERIODICALS — Korea 2209
GENERAL INTEREST PERIODICALS — Kuwait 2209
GENERAL INTEREST PERIODICALS — Latvia 2209
GENERAL INTEREST PERIODICALS — Lebanon 2209
GENERAL INTEREST PERIODICALS — Libya 2209
GENERAL INTEREST PERIODICALS — Lithuania 2209
GENERAL INTEREST PERIODICALS — Malagasy Republic 2209
GENERAL INTEREST PERIODICALS — Malawi 2209
GENERAL INTEREST PERIODICALS — Malaysia 2209
GENERAL INTEREST PERIODICALS — Mexico 2210
GENERAL INTEREST PERIODICALS — Middle East 2210
GENERAL INTEREST PERIODICALS — Mozambique 2211
GENERAL INTEREST PERIODICALS — Nepal 2211
GENERAL INTEREST PERIODICALS — Netherlands 2211
GENERAL INTEREST PERIODICALS — New Zealand 2212
GENERAL INTEREST PERIODICALS — Nigeria 2212
GENERAL INTEREST PERIODICALS — Norway 2212
GENERAL INTEREST PERIODICALS — Oceania 2213
GENERAL INTEREST PERIODICALS — Pakistan 2213
GENERAL INTEREST PERIODICALS — Panama 2213
GENERAL INTEREST PERIODICALS — Paraguay 2213
GENERAL INTEREST PERIODICALS — Peru 2213
GENERAL INTEREST PERIODICALS — Philippines 2213
GENERAL INTEREST PERIODICALS — Poland 2214
GENERAL INTEREST PERIODICALS — Portugal 2214
GENERAL INTEREST PERIODICALS — Puerto Rico 2215
GENERAL INTEREST PERIODICALS — Rumania 2215
GENERAL INTEREST PERIODICALS — Russia 2215
GENERAL INTEREST PERIODICALS — Saudi Arabia 2216
GENERAL INTEREST PERIODICALS — Scandinavia 2216
GENERAL INTEREST PERIODICALS — Singapore 2216
GENERAL INTEREST PERIODICALS — South Africa 2216
GENERAL INTEREST PERIODICALS — South America 2217
GENERAL INTEREST PERIODICALS — Spain 2217
GENERAL INTEREST PERIODICALS — Sri Lanka 2218
GENERAL INTEREST PERIODICALS — Sudan 2218
GENERAL INTEREST PERIODICALS — Sweden 2218
GENERAL INTEREST PERIODICALS — Switzerland 2218
GENERAL INTEREST PERIODICALS — Syria 2219
GENERAL INTEREST PERIODICALS — Taiwan 2219
GENERAL INTEREST PERIODICALS — Tanzania 2219
GENERAL INTEREST PERIODICALS — Thailand 2219
GENERAL INTEREST PERIODICALS — Turkey 2220
GENERAL INTEREST PERIODICALS — Uganda 2220
GENERAL INTEREST PERIODICALS — Ukraine 2220
GENERAL INTEREST PERIODICALS — Union Of Myanmar 2220
GENERAL INTEREST PERIODICALS — United Arab Emirates 2220
GENERAL INTEREST PERIODICALS — United States 2220
GENERAL INTEREST PERIODICALS — Uruguay 2238
GENERAL INTEREST PERIODICALS — Venezuela 2238
GENERAL INTEREST PERIODICALS — Vietnam 2238
GENERAL INTEREST PERIODICALS — West Indies 2239
GENERAL INTEREST PERIODICALS — Yugoslavia 2239
GENERAL INTEREST PERIODICALS — Zambia 2240
GENERAL INTEREST PERIODICALS — Zimbabwe 2240
Generators see ENGINEERING - Electrical Engineering 1880, see also PHYSICS - Electricity 3840
GENETICS 2240
Geochemistry see EARTH SCIENCES - Geology 1552
Geodesy see EARTH SCIENCES - Geophysics 1586, see also GEOGRAPHY 2240
GEOGRAPHY 2240, see also TRAVEL AND TOURISM 4750
GEOGRAPHY — Abstracting, Bibliographies, Statistics 2267

GEOGRAPHY — Computer Applications 2268
GEOLOGY 2269
Geomagnetism see EARTH SCIENCES - Geophysics 1586
GEOPHYSICS 2269
GEOTHERMAL ENERGY 2269
German Language - Study and Teaching see LINGUISTICS 2799
GERONTOLOGY AND GERIATRICS 2269
GERONTOLOGY AND GERIATRICS — Abstracting, Bibliographies, Statistics 2280
GIFTWARE AND TOYS 2280
Glaciology see EARTH SCIENCES - Geology 1552
Glass see CERAMICS, GLASS AND POTTERY 1160
Glasses, Eye see MEDICAL SCIENCES - Ophthalmology and Optometry 3297
Glaucoma see MEDICAL SCIENCES - Ophthalmology and Optometry 3297
Gliders see AERONAUTICS AND SPACE FLIGHT 42
Golf see SPORTS AND GAMES - Ball Games 4463
Government see POLITICAL SCIENCE 3869, see also PUBLIC ADMINISTRATION 4052
Graphic Arts see ART 309, see also PRINTING 3997
Graphology see PSYCHOLOGY 4007
Greenhouses see GARDENING AND HORTICULTURE 2120
Greeting Cards see GIFTWARE AND TOYS 2280
GROCERY TRADE 2283
GUIDES TO SCHOOLS AND COLLEGES 2283
Guns see SPORTS AND GAMES 4463
Gymnastics see SPORTS AND GAMES 4463
Gynecology see MEDICAL SCIENCES - Obstetrics and Gynecology 3288
Hair Removal see BEAUTY CULTURE 371
Hairdressing see BEAUTY CULTURE 371
Handbags see CLOTHING TRADE 1282, see also LEATHER AND FUR INDUSTRIES 2735
HANDICAPPED 2283
HANDICAPPED — Abstracting, Bibliographies, Statistics 2285
HANDICAPPED — Computer Applications 2285
HANDICAPPED — Hearing Impaired 2285
HANDICAPPED — Physically Impaired 2290
HANDICAPPED — Visually Impaired 2290
Handicrafts see ARTS AND HANDICRAFTS 352
Harbors see TRANSPORTATION - Ships and Shipping 4723
HARDWARE 2297
HARDWARE (COMPUTER) 2297
Harnesses see LEATHER AND FUR INDUSTRIES 2735
Hazardous Substances see ENVIRONMENTAL STUDIES - Waste Management 1984
Health Foods see FOOD AND FOOD INDUSTRIES 2060, see also NUTRITION AND DIETETICS 3602, PHYSICAL FITNESS AND HYGIENE 3798
Health Insurance see INSURANCE 2525
Hearing see MEDICAL SCIENCES - Otorhinolaryngology 3312
HEARING IMPAIRED 2297
Heart Diseases see MEDICAL SCIENCES - Cardiovascular Diseases 3203
HEAT 2297
HEATING, PLUMBING AND REFRIGERATION 2297, see also BUILDING AND CONSTRUCTION 598, ENGINEERING - Mechanical Engineering 1926
HEATING, PLUMBING AND REFRIGERATION — Abstracting, Bibliographies, Statistics 2304
Helicopters see AERONAUTICS AND SPACE FLIGHT 42
HEMATOLOGY 2305
Heraldry see GENEALOGY AND HERALDRY 2143
Herbs see AGRICULTURE 67, see also GARDENING AND HORTICULTURE 2120
Heredity see BIOLOGY - Genetics 539
Hides see LEATHER AND FUR INDUSTRIES 2735
HIGHER EDUCATION 2305
Highways see ENGINEERING - Civil Engineering 1861, see also TRANSPORTATION - Roads and Traffic 4717
HINDUISM 2305
Histochemistry see BIOLOGY - Cytology and Histology 522
Histology see BIOLOGY - Cytology and Histology 522
Historic Sites see HISTORY 2305, see also TRAVEL AND TOURISM 4750
HISTORY 2305, see also ARCHAEOLOGY 260, BIOGRAPHY 417, CLASSICAL STUDIES 1274
HISTORY — Abstracting, Bibliographies, Statistics 2327
HISTORY — Computer Applications 2330
HISTORY — History Of Africa 2330
HISTORY — History Of Asia 2336
HISTORY — History Of Australasia And Other Areas 2343
HISTORY — History Of Europe 2346
HISTORY — History Of North And South America 2397
HISTORY — History Of The Near East 2427
HOBBIES 2432, see also SPORTS AND GAMES 4463
HOBBIES — Abstracting, Bibliographies, Statistics 2444
Hockey see SPORTS AND GAMES 4463
HOME ECONOMICS 2444
HOME ECONOMICS — Abstracting, Bibliographies, Statistics 2450
Home Improvement see HOW-TO AND DO-IT-YOURSELF 2500
Home Remodeling And Repairs see HOW-TO AND DO-IT-YOURSELF 2500
Homeopathy see MEDICAL SCIENCES - Chiropractic, Homeopathy, Osteopathy 3213
HOMOSEXUALITY 2450
HOMOSEXUALITY — Abstracting, Bibliographies, Statistics 2458
Hormones see MEDICAL SCIENCES - Endocrinology 3250
Horology see JEWELRY, CLOCKS AND WATCHES 2562
HORSES AND HORSEMANSHIP 2458
Horticulture see GARDENING AND HORTICULTURE 2120
Hosiery see CLOTHING TRADE 1282
Hospices see HOSPITALS 2458
Hospital Supplies see HOSPITALS 2458, see also PHARMACY AND PHARMACOLOGY 3714
HOSPITALS 2458, see also MEDICAL SCIENCES 3068
HOSPITALS — Abstracting, Bibliographies, Statistics 2470
HOTELS AND RESTAURANTS 2471
HOTELS AND RESTAURANTS — Abstracting, Bibliographies, Statistics 2482

House Furnishings see INTERIOR DESIGN AND DECORATION - Furniture and House Furnishings 2556
Household Management see HOME ECONOMICS 2444
HOUSING AND URBAN PLANNING 2482, see also BUILDING AND CONSTRUCTION 598, PUBLIC ADMINISTRATION 4052, REAL ESTATE 4144
HOUSING AND URBAN PLANNING — Abstracting, Bibliographies, Statistics 2499
HOW-TO AND DO-IT-YOURSELF 2500
Human Ecology see SOCIOLOGY 4427
Human Geography see GEOGRAPHY 2240, see also POPULATION STUDIES 3979
Human Rights see POLITICAL SCIENCE - Civil Rights 3939
Humanism see PHILOSOPHY 3759
HUMANITIES: COMPREHENSIVE WORKS 2501
HUMANITIES: COMPREHENSIVE WORKS — Abstracting, Bibliographies, Statistics 2519
HUMANITIES: COMPREHENSIVE WORKS — Computer Applications 2520
Hunting see SPORTS AND GAMES - Outdoor Life 4539
HYDRAULIC ENGINEERING 2520
Hydroelectric Engineering see ENGINEERING - Electrical Engineering 1880
HYDROELECTRICAL ENERGY 2520
Hydrography see WATER RESOURCES 4821
HYDROLOGY 2520
Hygiene see OCCUPATIONAL HEALTH AND SAFETY 3614, see also PHYSICAL FITNESS AND HYGIENE 3798, PUBLIC HEALTH AND SAFETY 4096
Hypertension see MEDICAL SCIENCES - Cardiovascular Diseases 3203
Illumination see ENGINEERING - Electrical Engineering 1880, see also PHYSICS - Electricity 3840
Immigration see POPULATION STUDIES 3979
Immunology see MEDICAL SCIENCES - Allergology and Immunology 3182
Imports see BUSINESS AND ECONOMICS - International Commerce 899
Indexing Services see ABSTRACTING AND INDEXING SERVICES 1
Indoor Games and Amusements see HOBBIES 2432, see also SPORTS AND GAMES 4463
Industrial Arts see TECHNOLOGY 4592
Industrial Chemistry see ENGINEERING - Chemical Engineering 1847
Industrial Design see ENGINEERING 1813, see also TECHNOLOGY: COMPREHENSIVE WORKS 4592
INDUSTRIAL ENGINEERING 2521
Industrial Relations see BUSINESS AND ECONOMICS - Labor and Industrial Relations 970, see also BUSINESS AND ECONOMICS - Personnel Management 1062
Industry see BUSINESS AND ECONOMICS - Production of Goods and Services 1071
Infectious Diseases see MEDICAL SCIENCES - Communicable Diseases 3216, see also PUBLIC HEALTH AND SAFETY 4096
INFORMATION SCIENCE AND INFORMATION THEORY 2521
INORGANIC CHEMISTRY 2521
Input-Output Systems see COMPUTERS - Hardware 1453
Insects see BIOLOGY - Entomology 527
INSTRUMENTS 2521
INSTRUMENTS — Abstracting, Bibliographies, Statistics 2525
Insulation see BUILDING AND CONSTRUCTION 598, see also HEATING, PLUMBING AND REFRIGERATION 2297
INSURANCE 2525
INSURANCE — Abstracting, Bibliographies, Statistics 2545
INSURANCE — Computer Applications 2547
Intensive Care Medicine see MEDICAL SCIENCES 3068
INTERIOR DESIGN AND DECORATION 2547, see also HOME ECONOMICS 2444
INTERIOR DESIGN AND DECORATION — Abstracting, Bibliographies, Statistics 2556
INTERIOR DESIGN AND DECORATION — Furniture And House Furnishings 2556
Internal Medicine see MEDICAL SCIENCES 3068
International Affairs see BUSINESS AND ECONOMICS - International Development and Assistance 925, see also LITERARY AND POLITICAL REVIEWS 2857, POLITICAL SCIENCE - International Relations 3948
INTERNATIONAL COMMERCE 2562
INTERNATIONAL DEVELOPMENT AND ASSISTANCE 2562
INTERNATIONAL EDUCATION PROGRAMS 2562
INTERNATIONAL LAW 2562
INTERNATIONAL RELATIONS 2562
Interplanetary Flight see AERONAUTICS AND SPACE FLIGHT 42
INVESTMENTS 2562
Ionization see CHEMISTRY - Electrochemistry 1211
Irrigation see AGRICULTURE 67, see also CONSERVATION 1482, ENGINEERING - Hydraulic Engineering 1923, WATER RESOURCES 4821
ISLAM 2562
Italian Language - Study and Teaching see LINGUISTICS 2799
JEWELRY, CLOCKS AND WATCHES 2562
JEWELRY, CLOCKS AND WATCHES — Abstracting, Bibliographies, Statistics 2566
Job Opportunities see BUSINESS AND ECONOMICS - Labor and Industrial Relations 970, see also OCCUPATIONS AND CAREERS 3624
Jogging see PHYSICAL FITNESS AND HYGIENE 3798
JOURNALISM 2566
JOURNALISM — Abstracting, Bibliographies, Statistics 2577
JUDAISM 2579
JUDICIAL SYSTEMS 2579
Judo see SPORTS AND GAMES 4463
Jury see LAW - Criminal Law 2712
Jute see TEXTILE INDUSTRIES AND FABRICS 4615
Juvenile Delinquency see CHILDREN AND YOUTH - About 1231, see also CRIMINOLOGY AND LAW ENFORCEMENT 1509
Juvenile Literature see CHILDREN AND YOUTH - For 1248, see also PUBLISHING AND BOOK TRADE 4119
Karate see SPORTS AND GAMES 4463
Kinetics see CHEMISTRY - Organic Chemistry 1215, see also CHEMISTRY - Physical Chemistry 1224, PHYSICS 3812
Knit Goods see CLOTHING TRADE 1282, see also TEXTILE INDUSTRIES AND FABRICS 4615
Knitting see NEEDLEWORK 3590
LABOR AND INDUSTRIAL RELATIONS 2579
Labor Law see BUSINESS AND ECONOMICS - Labor and Industrial Relations 970, see also LAW 2592

LABOR UNIONS 2579
LABOR UNIONS — Abstracting, Bibliographies, Statistics 2592
Laboratory Animals see MEDICAL SCIENCES - Experimental Medicine, Laboratory Technique 3256
LABORATORY TECHNIQUE 2592
Laboratory Techniques see INSTRUMENTS 2521, see also MEDICAL SCIENCES - Experimental Medicine, Laboratory Technique 3256
Land Management see CONSERVATION 1482
Land Reclamation see AGRICULTURE - Crop Production and Soil 165
Landscaping see ARCHITECTURE 291, see also GARDENING AND HORTICULTURE 2120
Language, Study and Teaching see LINGUISTICS 2799
Laryngology see MEDICAL SCIENCES - Otorhinolaryngology 3312
Lasers see PHYSICS - Optics 3851
Lathes see MACHINERY 3015
Latin American History see HISTORY - History of North and South America 2397
Latin Language and Literature see CLASSICAL STUDIES 1274, see also LINGUISTICS 2799
Laundries see CLEANING AND DYEING 1281
LAW 2592
LAW — Abstracting, Bibliographies, Statistics 2697
LAW — Civil Law 2701
LAW — Computer Applications 2705
LAW — Constitutional Law 2705
LAW — Corporate Law 2706
LAW — Criminal Law 2712
Law Enforcement see CRIMINOLOGY AND LAW ENFORCEMENT 1509
LAW — Estate Planning 2714
LAW — Family And Matrimonial Law 2716
LAW — International Law 2719
LAW — Judicial Systems 2731
LAW — Legal Aid 2734
LAW — Maritime Law 2734
LAW — Military Law 2735
Lawns see GARDENING AND HORTICULTURE 2120
LEATHER AND FUR INDUSTRIES 2735, see also SHOES AND BOOTS 4360
LEATHER AND FUR INDUSTRIES — Abstracting, Bibliographies, Statistics 2738
LEGAL AID 2738
Legislation see LAW 2592, see also POLITICAL SCIENCE 3869, PUBLIC ADMINISTRATION 4052
LEISURE AND RECREATION 2738
Leprosy see MEDICAL SCIENCES - Communicable Diseases 3216
Leukemia see MEDICAL SCIENCES - Hematology 3270
Lexicography see LINGUISTICS 2799
LIBRARY AND INFORMATION SCIENCES 2739, see also BIBLIOGRAPHIES 388, COMPUTERS - Information Science and Information Theory 1455, PUBLISHING AND BOOK TRADE 4119
LIBRARY AND INFORMATION SCIENCES — Abstracting, Bibliographies, Statistics 2792
LIBRARY AND INFORMATION SCIENCES — Computer Applications 2796
Library Bookbinding see LIBRARY AND INFORMATION SCIENCES 2739, see also PUBLISHING AND BOOK TRADE 4119
Lighting see INTERIOR DESIGN AND DECORATION - Furniture and House Furnishings 2556, see also PHYSICS - Electricity 3840
Limnology see EARTH SCIENCES - Hydrology 1596
LINGUISTICS 2799
LINGUISTICS — Abstracting, Bibliographies, Statistics 2854
LINGUISTICS — Computer Applications 2856
Liquor see BEVERAGES 377
LITERARY AND POLITICAL REVIEWS 2857, see also LITERATURE 2890
LITERARY AND POLITICAL REVIEWS — Abstracting, Bibliographies, Statistics 2890
Literary Criticism see LITERARY AND POLITICAL REVIEWS 2857, see also LITERATURE 2890
LITERATURE 2890, see also LINGUISTICS 2799, LITERARY AND POLITICAL REVIEWS 2857
LITERATURE — Abstracting, Bibliographies, Statistics 2980
LITERATURE — Adventure And Romance 2983
LITERATURE — Mystery And Detective 2985
LITERATURE — Poetry 2986, see also LITERARY AND POLITICAL REVIEWS 2857
LITERATURE — Science Fiction, Fantasy, Horror 3010
Lithography see PRINTING 3997
Little Magazines see LITERARY AND POLITICAL REVIEWS 2857
Livestock see AGRICULTURE - Poultry and Livestock 209, see also VETERINARY SCIENCE 4804
Locks see BUILDING AND CONSTRUCTION -Hardware 641
Lubrication and Lubricants see ENGINEERING - Mechanical Engineering 1926, see also PETROLEUM AND GAS 3680
Luggage see LEATHER AND FUR INDUSTRIES 2735
LUMBER AND WOOD 3015
MACHINE THEORY 3015
Machine Translating see COMPUTERS - Computer Programming 1429, see also LINGUISTICS 2799
MACHINERY 3015, see also AGRICULTURE - Agricultural Equipment 161, ENGINEERING - Mechanical Engineering 1926, TECHNOLOGY: COMPREHENSIVE WORKS 4592
MACHINERY — Abstracting, Bibliographies, Statistics 3025
MACHINERY — Computer Applications 3025
MACROECONOMICS 3025
Macromolecules see CHEMISTRY - Organic Chemistry 1215
Magazine Business see PUBLISHING AND BOOK TRADE 4119
Magic see HOBBIES 2432
Magnetism see PHYSICS 3812
Mail Order Business see BUSINESS AND ECONOMICS - Marketing and Purchasing 1032
Malacology see BIOLOGY - Zoology 575
Malpractice see LAW - Civil Law 2701, see also MEDICAL SCIENCES 3068
MANAGEMENT 3025

Manufacturing see BUSINESS AND ECONOMICS - Production of Goods and Services 1071
Marijuana see DRUG ABUSE AND ALCOHOLISM 1532
Marine Biology see BIOLOGY 424, see also EARTH SCIENCES - Oceanography 1601
Marine Engineering see ENGINEERING 1813, see also TRANSPORTATION - Ships and Shipping 4723
Marine Policy see LAW - Maritime Law 2734
MARITIME LAW 3025
MARKETING AND PURCHASING 3025
Marxism see BUSINESS AND ECONOMICS - Economic Systems and Theories, Economic History 888, see also POLITICAL SCIENCE 3869
Masonry see BUILDING AND CONSTRUCTION 598
Mass Transit see TRANSPORTATION 4646
Mathematical Geography see GEOGRAPHY 2240
Mathematical Physics see PHYSICS 3812
MATHEMATICS 3025
MATHEMATICS — Abstracting, Bibliographies, Statistics 3062
MATHEMATICS — Computer Applications 3063
MATRIMONY 3066
Mechanical Drawing see ENGINEERING 1813, see also TECHNOLOGY: COMPREHENSIVE WORKS 4592
MECHANICAL ENGINEERING 3068
Mechanical Handling see MACHINERY 3015, see also TECHNOLOGY: COMPREHENSIVE WORKS 4592, TRANSPORTATION 4646
Mechanical Translating see COMPUTERS - Computer Programming 1429, see also LINGUISTICS 2799
MECHANICS 3068
Medical Bacteriology see MEDICAL SCIENCES - Communicable Diseases 3216
Medical Engineering see MEDICAL SCIENCES 3068
Medical Jurisprudence see MEDICAL SCIENCES - Forensic Sciences 3263
Medical Parasitology see MEDICAL SCIENCES - Communicable Diseases 3216
MEDICAL SCIENCES 3068, see also BIOLOGY 424, DRUG ABUSE AND ALCOHOLISM 1532, GERONTOLOGY AND GERIATRICS 2269, HOSPITALS 2458, NUTRITION AND DIETETICS 3602, OCCUPATIONAL HEALTH AND SAFETY 3614, PHARMACY AND PHARMACOLOGY 3714, PHYSICAL FITNESS AND HYGIENE 3798, PUBLIC HEALTH AND SAFETY 4096
MEDICAL SCIENCES — Abstracting, Bibliographies, Statistics 3165
MEDICAL SCIENCES — Allergology And Immunology 3182
MEDICAL SCIENCES — Anaesthesiology 3189
MEDICAL SCIENCES — Cancer 3192
MEDICAL SCIENCES — Cardiovascular Diseases 3203
MEDICAL SCIENCES — Chiropractic, Homeopathy, Osteopathy 3213
MEDICAL SCIENCES — Communicable Diseases 3216
MEDICAL SCIENCES — Computer Applications 3224
MEDICAL SCIENCES — Dentistry 3226
MEDICAL SCIENCES — Dermatology And Venereology 3245
MEDICAL SCIENCES — Endocrinology 3250
MEDICAL SCIENCES — Experimental Medicine, Laboratory Technique 3256
MEDICAL SCIENCES — Forensic Sciences 3263
MEDICAL SCIENCES — Gastroenterology 3266
MEDICAL SCIENCES — Hematology 3270
MEDICAL SCIENCES — Hypnosis 3274
MEDICAL SCIENCES — Nurses And Nursing 3274
MEDICAL SCIENCES — Obstetrics And Gynecology 3288
MEDICAL SCIENCES — Ophthalmology And Optometry 3297
MEDICAL SCIENCES — Orthopedics And Traumatology 3306
MEDICAL SCIENCES — Otorhinolaryngology 3312
MEDICAL SCIENCES — Pediatrics 3317
MEDICAL SCIENCES — Psychiatry And Neurology 3327
MEDICAL SCIENCES — Radiology And Nuclear Medicine 3356
MEDICAL SCIENCES — Respiratory Diseases 3364
MEDICAL SCIENCES — Rheumatology 3368
MEDICAL SCIENCES — Sports Medicine 3370
MEDICAL SCIENCES — Surgery 3373
MEDICAL SCIENCES — Urology And Nephrology 3386
Medieval Studies see HISTORY - History of Europe 2346, see also LITERATURE 2890, PHILOSOPHY 3759
MEETINGS AND CONGRESSES 3390
MEETINGS AND CONGRESSES — Abstracting, Bibliographies, Statistics 3395
Memory Structures see COMPUTERS - Hardware 1453
MEN'S HEALTH 3395
MEN'S INTERESTS 3395
MEN'S STUDIES 3400
Menswear see CLOTHING TRADE 1282
Mental Health see PSYCHOLOGY 4007
Mental Hygiene see PUBLIC HEALTH AND SAFETY 4096
Mental Retardation see EDUCATION - Special Education and Rehabilitation 1732, see also MEDICAL SCIENCES - Psychiatry and Neurology 3327, PSYCHOLOGY 4007
Merchandising see BUSINESS AND ECONOMICS - Marketing and Purchasing 1032
Metabolism see BIOLOGY - Physiology 568, see also MEDICAL SCIENCES 3068
Metal Industries see METALLURGY 3401
METALLURGY 3401, see also MINES AND MINING INDUSTRY 3477
METALLURGY — Abstracting, Bibliographies, Statistics 3424
METALLURGY — Welding 3429
Metaphysics see PHILOSOPHY 3759
METEOROLOGY 3431
METEOROLOGY — Abstracting, Bibliographies, Statistics 3444
METROLOGY AND STANDARDIZATION 3444
METROLOGY AND STANDARDIZATION — Abstracting, Bibliographies, Statistics 3449
MICROBIOLOGY 3449
MICROCOMPUTERS 3449
Microfilming see PHOTOGRAPHY 3788
Microphotography see PHOTOGRAPHY 3788
MICROSCOPY 3449
Microwaves see ELECTRONICS 1764
Midwifery see MEDICAL SCIENCES - Obstetrics and Gynecology 3288
Migration see POPULATION STUDIES 3979
MILITARY 3449

MILITARY — Abstracting, Bibliographies, Statistics 3476
Military Engineering see ENGINEERING 1813
MILITARY LAW 3477
Military Medicine see MEDICAL SCIENCES 3068
Millinery see CLOTHING TRADE 1282
Milling see AGRICULTURE - Feed, Flour and Grain 204
Mineral Resources see EARTH SCIENCES - Geology 1552, see also MINES AND MINING INDUSTRY 3477
Mineralogy see MINES AND MINING INDUSTRY 1552
MINES AND MINING INDUSTRY 3477
MINES AND MINING INDUSTRY — Abstracting, Bibliographies, Statistics 3498
MINICOMPUTERS 3502
Missiles see AERONAUTICS AND SPACE FLIGHT 42
Mobile Homes see HOUSING AND URBAN PLANNING 2482, see also TRANSPORTATION 4646
Models and Model Building see HOBBIES 2432
Modems see COMPUTERS - Hardware 1453
Mollusca see BIOLOGY - Zoology 575
Monitors see COMPUTERS - Hardware 1453
Morphology see BIOLOGY 424, see also MEDICAL SCIENCES 3068
Mosses see BIOLOGY - Botany 491
Motels see HOTELS AND RESTAURANTS 2471
MOTION PICTURES 3502
MOTION PICTURES — Abstracting, Bibliographies, Statistics 3519
Motor Scooters see SPORTS AND GAMES - Bicycles and Motorcycles 4515
Motorcycles see SPORTS AND GAMES - Bicycles and Motorcycles 4515
Mountaineering see SPORTS AND GAMES - Outdoor Life 4539
Movies see MOTION PICTURES 3502
Multiple Sclerosis see MEDICAL SCIENCES - Psychiatry and Neurology 3327
MUNICIPAL GOVERNMENT 3520
Municipal Law see LAW 2592, see also PUBLIC ADMINISTRATION - Municipal Government 4083
Municipal Transportation see TRANSPORTATION 4646
MUSEUMS AND ART GALLERIES 3520
MUSEUMS AND ART GALLERIES — Abstracting, Bibliographies, Statistics 3536
MUSIC 3536
MUSIC — Abstracting, Bibliographies, Statistics 3588
MUSIC — Computer Applications 3589, see also COMPUTERS - Computer Music 1426
Music Therapy see EDUCATION - Special Education and Rehabilitation 1732, see also MUSIC 3536
Mutual Funds see BUSINESS AND ECONOMICS - Investments 937
Mycology see BIOLOGY - Botany 491
MYSTERY AND DETECTIVE 3590
Mysticism see NEW AGE PUBLICATIONS 3593, see also PARAPSYCHOLOGY AND OCCULTISM 3668
Mythology see FOLKLORE 2052
Narcotics see DRUG ABUSE AND ALCOHOLISM 1532, see also PHARMACY AND PHARMACOLOGY 3714
Natural Food see NUTRITION AND DIETETICS 3602
Natural Resources see CONSERVATION 1482, see also ENVIRONMENTAL STUDIES 1941
Naturalization see POLITICAL SCIENCE 3869
Nautical Arts and Sciences see TRANSPORTATION - Ships and Shipping 4723
Naval Architecture see TRANSPORTATION - Ships and Shipping 4723
Naval Engineering see TRANSPORTATION - Ships and Shipping 4723
Naval Medicine see MEDICAL SCIENCES 3068
NEEDLEWORK 3590
Nephrology see MEDICAL SCIENCES - Urology and Nephrology 3386
Neurology see MEDICAL SCIENCES - Psychiatry and Neurology 3327
Neurophysiology see MEDICAL SCIENCES - Psychiatry and Neurology 3327
Neuroradiology see MEDICAL SCIENCES - Radiology and Nuclear Medicine 3356
Neurosurgery see MEDICAL SCIENCES - Psychiatry and Neurology 3327, see also MEDICAL SCIENCES - Surgery 3373
NEW AGE PUBLICATIONS 3593, see also PARAPSYCHOLOGY AND OCCULTISM 3668
Newspaper Business see JOURNALISM 2566
Noise Control see ENGINEERING - Mechanical Engineering 1926
Noise Pollution see ENVIRONMENTAL STUDIES - Pollution 1975
North American History see HISTORY - History of North and South America 2397
NUCLEAR ENERGY 3597
Nuclear Medicine see MEDICAL SCIENCES - Radiology and Nuclear Medicine 3356
NUCLEAR PHYSICS 3597
Nudism see PHYSICAL FITNESS AND HYGIENE 3798
NUMISMATICS 3597
NUMISMATICS — Abstracting, Bibliographies, Statistics 3602
Nurseries see GARDENING AND HORTICULTURE - Florist Trade 2141
NURSES AND NURSING 3602
Nursing Homes see HOSPITALS 2458, see also SOCIAL SERVICES AND WELFARE 4396
NUTRITION AND DIETETICS 3602, see also FOOD AND FOOD INDUSTRIES 2060, HOSPITALS 2458, PHARMACY AND PHARMACOLOGY 3714, PHYSICAL FITNESS AND HYGIENE 3798
NUTRITION AND DIETETICS — Abstracting, Bibliographies, Statistics 3613
OBSTETRICS AND GYNECOLOGY 3614
Occultism see PARAPSYCHOLOGY AND OCCULTISM 3668
OCCUPATIONAL HEALTH AND SAFETY 3614
OCCUPATIONAL HEALTH AND SAFETY — Abstracting, Bibliographies, Statistics 3623
Occupational Therapy see EDUCATION - Special Education and Rehabilitation 1732, see also MEDICAL SCIENCES 3068
OCCUPATIONS AND CAREERS 3624, see also BUSINESS AND ECONOMICS - Labor and Industrial Relations 970
OCCUPATIONS AND CAREERS — Abstracting, Bibliographies, Statistics 3631
OCEANOGRAPHY 3632
OFFICE EQUIPMENT AND SERVICES 3632
Oils and Fats see CHEMISTRY - Organic Chemistry 1215
Old Age see GERONTOLOGY AND GERIATRICS 2269
OPHTHALMOLOGY AND OPTOMETRY 3632

OPTICS 3632
Optometry see MEDICAL SCIENCES - Ophthalmology and Optometry 3297
ORGANIC CHEMISTRY 3632
ORIENTAL STUDIES 3632, see also HISTORY - History of Asia 2336, LINGUISTICS 2799, LITERATURE 2890, PHILOSOPHY 3759
ORIENTAL STUDIES — Abstracting, Bibliographies, Statistics 3646
ORNITHOLOGY 3647
Orthodontics see MEDICAL SCIENCES - Dentistry 3226
ORTHOPEDICS AND TRAUMATOLOGY 3647
Osteopathy see MEDICAL SCIENCES - Chiropractic, Homeopathy, Osteopathy 3213
Otology see MEDICAL SCIENCES - Otorhinolaryngology 3312
OTORHINOLARYNGOLOGY 3647
OUTDOOR LIFE 3647
PACKAGING 3647
PACKAGING — Abstracting, Bibliographies, Statistics 3652
PAINTS AND PROTECTIVE COATINGS 3652
PAINTS AND PROTECTIVE COATINGS — Abstracting, Bibliographies, Statistics 3656
Paleobotany see BIOLOGY - Botany 491
PALEONTOLOGY 3656
PALEONTOLOGY — Abstracting, Bibliographies, Statistics 3661
PAPER AND PULP 3661, see also FORESTS AND FORESTRY - Lumber and Wood 2113
PAPER AND PULP — Abstracting, Bibliographies, Statistics 3667
Papyrus see PAPER AND PULP 3661
Parachuting see SPORTS AND GAMES 4463
Paraplegia see MEDICAL SCIENCES - Psychiatry and Neurology 3327
PARAPSYCHOLOGY AND OCCULTISM 3668, see also NEW AGE PUBLICATIONS 3593
PARAPSYCHOLOGY AND OCCULTISM — Abstracting, Bibliographies, Statistics 3672
Parasitology see BIOLOGY 424
Parent Teacher Associations see EDUCATION - School Organization and Administration 1724
Parenting see CHILDREN AND YOUTH - About 1231
Parks and Recreation Areas see CONSERVATION 1482, see also SPORTS AND GAMES - Outdoor Life 4539, TRAVEL AND TOURISM 4750
PATENTS, TRADEMARKS AND COPYRIGHTS 3672
PATENTS, TRADEMARKS AND COPYRIGHTS — Abstracting, Bibliographies, Statistics 3679
Paving see BUILDING AND CONSTRUCTION 598, see also TRANSPORTATION - Roads and Traffic 4717
Peat see HEATING, PLUMBING AND REFRIGERATION 2297
PEDIATRICS 3680
Penology see CRIMINOLOGY AND LAW ENFORCEMENT 1509
Pensions see BUSINESS AND ECONOMICS - Labor and Industrial Relations 970, see also INSURANCE 2525, SOCIAL SERVICES AND WELFARE 4396
Performing Arts see DANCE 1528, see also MOTION PICTURES 3502, MUSIC 3536, THEATER 4629
PERFUMES AND COSMETICS 3680
Peripherals see COMPUTERS - Hardware 1453
PERSONAL COMPUTERS 3680
PERSONNEL MANAGEMENT 3680
Pest Control see AGRICULTURE 67, see also BIOLOGY - Entomology 527, PUBLIC HEALTH AND SAFETY 4096
PETROLEUM AND GAS 3680
PETROLEUM AND GAS — Abstracting, Bibliographies, Statistics 3704
Petrology see EARTH SCIENCES - Geology 1552
PETS 3707
PHARMACY AND PHARMACOLOGY 3714, see also MEDICAL SCIENCES 3068
PHARMACY AND PHARMACOLOGY — Abstracting, Bibliographies, Statistics 3747
Philanthropy see SOCIAL SERVICES AND WELFARE 4396
PHILATELY 3748
PHILATELY — Abstracting, Bibliographies, Statistics 3759
Philology see LINGUISTICS 2799
PHILOSOPHY 3759
PHILOSOPHY — Abstracting, Bibliographies, Statistics 3787
Phonetics see LINGUISTICS 2799
Phonographs see MUSIC 3536, see also SOUND RECORDING AND REPRODUCTION 4459
Photogrammetry see GEOGRAPHY 2240, see also PHOTOGRAPHY 3788
Photographic Surveying see ENGINEERING - Civil Engineering 1861
PHOTOGRAPHY 3788, see also MOTION PICTURES 3502
PHOTOGRAPHY — Abstracting, Bibliographies, Statistics 3798
Photomechanical Processing see PRINTING 3997
PHYSICAL CHEMISTRY 3798
Physical Education see EDUCATION - Teaching Methods and Curriculum 1742, see also PHYSICAL FITNESS AND HYGIENE 3798, SPORTS AND GAMES 4463
PHYSICAL FITNESS AND HYGIENE 3798
PHYSICAL FITNESS AND HYGIENE — Abstracting, Bibliographies, Statistics 3811
Physical Therapy see MEDICAL SCIENCES 3068
PHYSICALLY IMPAIRED 3812
PHYSICS 3812
PHYSICS — Abstracting, Bibliographies, Statistics 3836
PHYSICS — Computer Applications 3840
PHYSICS — Electricity 3840
PHYSICS — Heat 3840
PHYSICS — Mechanics 3842
PHYSICS — Nuclear Physics 3846
PHYSICS — Optics 3851
PHYSICS — Sound 3858
PHYSIOLOGY 3860
Planned Parenthood see BIRTH CONTROL 595
Plant Breeding see AGRICULTURE - Crop Production and Soil 165, see also BIOLOGY - Botany 491, GARDENING AND HORTICULTURE 2120
Plasma Physics see PHYSICS 3812
Plastic Surgery see MEDICAL SCIENCES - Surgery 3373
PLASTICS 3860, see also CHEMISTRY - Physical Chemistry 1224, ENGINEERING - Chemical Engineering 1847
PLASTICS — Abstracting, Bibliographies, Statistics 3868

Plays see LITERATURE 2890, see also THEATER 4629
Plumbing see HEATING, PLUMBING AND REFRIGERATION 2297
POETRY 3869
Police see CRIMINOLOGY AND LAW ENFORCEMENT 1509
Poliomyelitis see MEDICAL SCIENCES - Psychiatry and Neurology 3327
Political Reviews see LITERARY AND POLITICAL REVIEWS 2857
POLITICAL SCIENCE 3869, see also LITERARY AND POLITICAL REVIEWS 2857, PUBLIC ADMINISTRATION 4052
POLITICAL SCIENCE — Abstracting, Bibliographies, Statistics 3936
POLITICAL SCIENCE — Civil Rights 3939
POLITICAL SCIENCE — International Relations 3948
POLLUTION 3979
Polymers see CHEMISTRY 1168, see also ENGINEERING - Chemical Engineering 1847
POPULATION STUDIES 3979
POPULATION STUDIES — Abstracting, Bibliographies, Statistics 3989
Ports see TRANSPORTATION - Ships and Shipping 4723
Portuguese LANGUAGE - Study and Teaching see LINGUISTICS 2799
POSTAL AFFAIRS 3997
Pottery see CERAMICS, GLASS AND POTTERY 1160
POULTRY AND LIVESTOCK 3997
Power Plants see ENERGY 1783
Pre-school Education see EDUCATION 1612
Precision Mechanics see INSTRUMENTS 2521
Prefabricated Houses see BUILDING AND CONSTRUCTION 598
Preventive Medicine see PUBLIC HEALTH AND SAFETY 4096
PRINTING 3997
PRINTING — Abstracting, Bibliographies, Statistics 4006
PRINTING — Computer Applications 4007, see also COMPUTERS - Computer Graphics 1420
Prisons see CRIMINOLOGY AND LAW ENFORCEMENT 1509
Private Schools see EDUCATION - Guides to Schools and Colleges 1691, see also EDUCATION - School Organization and Administration 1724
Produce see FOOD AND FOOD INDUSTRIES 2060
PRODUCTION OF GOODS AND SERVICES 4007
Programmed Instruction see EDUCATION - Teaching Methods and Curriculum 1742
Programming, Automatic see COMPUTERS - Computer Programming 1429
Proofreading see JOURNALISM 2566, see also PRINTING 3997
Prosthetics see MEDICAL SCIENCES - Orthopedics and Traumatology 3306
Protective Coatings see PAINTS AND PROTECTIVE COATINGS 3652
PROTESTANTISM 4007
Protozoology see BIOLOGY - Zoology 575
PSYCHIATRY AND NEUROLOGY 4007
Psychic Phenomena see PARAPSYCHOLOGY AND OCCULTISM 3668
Psychical Research see PARAPSYCHOLOGY AND OCCULTISM 3668
Psychoanalysis see PSYCHOLOGY 4007
Psychological Testing see PSYCHOLOGY 4007
PSYCHOLOGY 4007
PSYCHOLOGY — Abstracting, Bibliographies, Statistics 4051
Psychosomatic Medicine see MEDICAL SCIENCES 3068
Psychotherapy see MEDICAL SCIENCES - Psychiatry and Neurology 3327
PUBLIC ADMINISTRATION 4052, see also POLITICAL SCIENCE 3869
PUBLIC ADMINISTRATION — Abstracting, Bibliographies, Statistics 4078
PUBLIC ADMINISTRATION — Computer Applications 4083
PUBLIC ADMINISTRATION — Municipal Government 4083
Public Affairs see POLITICAL SCIENCE 3869, see also PUBLIC ADMINISTRATION 4052, SOCIAL SCIENCES 4364
PUBLIC FINANCE, TAXATION 4096
PUBLIC HEALTH AND SAFETY 4096, see also DRUG ABUSE AND ALCOHOLISM 1532, ENVIRONMENTAL STUDIES 1941, FIRE PREVENTION 2030, HOSPITALS 2458, MEDICAL SCIENCES 3068, OCCUPATIONAL HEALTH AND SAFETY 3614
PUBLIC HEALTH AND SAFETY — Abstracting, Bibliographies, Statistics 4116
Public Relations see ADVERTISING AND PUBLIC RELATIONS 25
Public Transportation see TRANSPORTATION 4646
Public Utilities see PETROLEUM AND GAS 3680, see also PUBLIC ADMINISTRATION 4052
Public Welfare see SOCIAL SERVICES AND WELFARE 4396
Public Works see BUILDING AND CONSTRUCTION 598, see also ENGINEERING - Civil Engineering 1861, HOUSING AND URBAN PLANNING 2482, PUBLIC ADMINISTRATION 4052
Publicity see ADVERTISING AND PUBLIC RELATIONS 25
PUBLISHING AND BOOK TRADE 4119, see also BIBLIOGRAPHIES 388, LIBRARY AND INFORMATION SCIENCES 2739, PATENTS, TRADEMARKS AND COPYRIGHTS 3672, PRINTING 3997
PUBLISHING AND BOOK TRADE — Abstracting, Bibliographies, Statistics 4139
PUBLISHING AND BOOK TRADE — Computer Applications 4143
Pulp see PAPER AND PULP 3661
Puppets see HOBBIES 2432, see also THEATER 4629
Puzzles see SPORTS AND GAMES 4463
Quality Control see BUSINESS AND ECONOMICS - Management 1000, see also METROLOGY AND STANDARDIZATION 3444
Quantum Chemistry see CHEMISTRY - Physical Chemistry 1224
Quarries see MINES AND MINING INDUSTRY 3477
Race Relations see POLITICAL SCIENCE - Civil Rights 3939, see also SOCIOLOGY 4427
Racing see SPORTS AND GAMES - Horses and Horsemanship 4531, see also TRANSPORTATION - Automobiles 4678
Radar see COMMUNICATIONS 1331
Radiation see ASTRONOMY 359, see also BIOLOGY - Biophysics 484, CHEMISTRY - Physical Chemistry 1224, MEDICAL SCIENCES - Radiology and Nuclear Medicine 3356, PHYSICS - Nuclear Physics 3846
RADIO 4144
Radio Advertising see ADVERTISING AND PUBLIC RELATIONS 25, see also COMMUNICATIONS - Radio 1354
Radiobiology see BIOLOGY 424
Radiocarbon see PHYSICS - Nuclear Physics 3846
RADIOLOGY AND NUCLEAR MEDICINE 4144
Railroad Engineering see TRANSPORTATION - Railroads 4707

RAILROADS 4144
Railway Ties see FORESTS AND FORESTRY - Lumber and Wood 2113, see also TRANSPORTATION - Railroads 4707
Rare Earths see CHEMISTRY - Inorganic Chemistry 1213
Reading Guides and Aids see ABSTRACTING AND INDEXING SERVICES 1, see also BIBLIOGRAPHIES 388, EDUCATION - Teaching Methods and Curriculum 1742, LIBRARY AND INFORMATION SCIENCES 2739
REAL ESTATE 4144, see also BUILDING AND CONSTRUCTION 598, BUSINESS AND ECONOMICS 643, HOUSING AND URBAN PLANNING 2482, LAW 2714
REAL ESTATE — Abstracting, Bibliographies, Statistics 4159
Recorded Music see MUSIC 3536, see also SOUND RECORDING AND REPRODUCTION 4459
Recreation see DANCE 1528, see also HOBBIES 2432, LEISURE AND RECREATION 2738, SPORTS AND GAMES 4463
Recreation Areas see CONSERVATION 1482, see also TRAVEL AND TOURISM 4750
Recreational Vehicles see TRANSPORTATION - Automobiles 4678
Red Cross see SOCIAL SERVICES AND WELFARE 4396
Refrigeration see HEATING, PLUMBING AND REFRIGERATION 2297, see also PHYSICS - Heat 3840
Regional Planning see HOUSING AND URBAN PLANNING 2482
Rehabilitation see EDUCATION - Special Education and Rehabilitation 1732, see also MEDICAL SCIENCES 3068, SOCIAL SERVICES AND WELFARE 4396
Reincarnation see NEW AGE PUBLICATIONS 3593, see also PARAPSYCHOLOGY AND OCCULTISM 3668, RELIGIONS AND THEOLOGY 4161
RELIGIONS AND THEOLOGY 4161
RELIGIONS AND THEOLOGY — Abstracting, Bibliographies, Statistics 4211
RELIGIONS AND THEOLOGY — Buddhist 4213
RELIGIONS AND THEOLOGY — Eastern Orthodox 4217
RELIGIONS AND THEOLOGY — Hindu 4217
RELIGIONS AND THEOLOGY — Islamic 4217
RELIGIONS AND THEOLOGY — Judaic 4221
RELIGIONS AND THEOLOGY — Other Denominations And Sects 4279
RELIGIONS AND THEOLOGY — Protestant 4227
RELIGIONS AND THEOLOGY — Roman Catholic 4254
Religious History see RELIGIONS AND THEOLOGY 4161
Repairs see HOW-TO AND DO-IT-YOURSELF 2500
Reproduction and Fertility see BIOLOGY 424, see also MEDICAL SCIENCES 3068
Research and Development see TECHNOLOGY: COMPREHENSIVE WORKS 4592
Resins see PLASTICS 3860
Resorts see HOTELS AND RESTAURANTS 2471, see also TRAVEL AND TOURISM 4750
RESPIRATORY DISEASES 4290
Restaurants see HOTELS AND RESTAURANTS 2471
Retailing see BUSINESS AND ECONOMICS - Marketing and Purchasing 1032
Rheology see PHYSICS - Mechanics 3842
RHEUMATOLOGY 4290
Rhinology see MEDICAL SCIENCES - Otorhinolaryngology 3312
ROADS AND TRAFFIC 4290
Robotics see COMPUTERS - Artificial Intelligence 1406
Rockets see AERONAUTICS AND SPACE FLIGHT 42
Rodeo see SPORTS AND GAMES - Horses and Horsemanship 4531
Roller Skating see SPORTS AND GAMES 4463
ROMAN CATHOLICISM 4290
RUBBER 4290, see also ENGINEERING - Chemical Engineering 1847, PLASTICS 3860
RUBBER — Abstracting, Bibliographies, Statistics 4294
Rugby see SPORTS AND GAMES - Ball Games 4499
Safety Education see BUSINESS AND ECONOMICS - Labor and Industrial Relations 970, see also INDUSTRIAL HEALTH AND SAFETY 3614, PUBLIC HEALTH AND SAFETY 4096, TRANSPORTATION - Roads and Traffic 4717
Sailing see SPORTS AND GAMES - Boats and Boating 4521
Salesmanship see BUSINESS AND ECONOMICS - Marketing and Purchasing 1032
Sanitary Engineering see PUBLIC HEALTH AND SAFETY 4096
Sanitation see ENGINEERING - Civil Engineering 1861, see also PHYSICAL FITNESS AND HYGIENE 3798, PUBLIC HEALTH AND SAFETY 4096
Savings and Loan see BUSINESS AND ECONOMICS - Banking and Finance 757
Scholarships see EDUCATION - Higher Education 1698
SCHOOL ORGANIZATION AND ADMINISTRATION 4295
SCIENCE FICTION, FANTASY, HORROR 4295
SCIENCES: COMPREHENSIVE WORKS 4295
SCIENCES: COMPREHENSIVE WORKS — Abstracting, Bibliographies, Statistics 4354
SCIENCES: COMPREHENSIVE WORKS — Computer Applications 4358
Scooters see SPORTS AND GAMES - Bicycles and Motorcycles 4515
Sculpture see ART 309
Seaweed see BIOLOGY - Botany 491, see also EARTH SCIENCES - Oceanography 1601
Securities see BUSINESS AND ECONOMICS - Investments 937
SECURITY 4360
Sediment Data see ENGINEERING - Hydraulic Engineering 1923
Sedimentology see EARTH SCIENCES - Geophysics 1586
Seeds see AGRICULTURE - Crop Production and Soil 165
Seismology see EARTH SCIENCES - Geophysics 1586
Selling see ADVERTISING AND PUBLIC RELATIONS 25, see also BUSINESS AND ECONOMICS - Marketing and Purchasing 1032
Semantics see LINGUISTICS 2799
Semiconductors see PHYSICS - ELECTRICITY 3840
Senior Citizens see GERONTOLOGY AND GERIATRICS 2269
Service Stations see PETROLEUM AND GAS 3680, see also TRANSPORTATION - Automobiles 4678
Sewage and Waste Treatment see PUBLIC ADMINISTRATION 4052, see also PUBLIC HEALTH AND SAFETY 4096
Sewing see CLOTHING TRADE - Fashions 1289, see also NEEDLEWORK 3590
Sex Education see PHYSICAL FITNESS AND HYGIENE 3798
Sheet Metal see METALLURGY 3401
Shipbuilding see TRANSPORTATION - Ships and Shipping 4723
SHIPS AND SHIPPING 4360
SHOES AND BOOTS 4360, see also LEATHER AND FUR INDUSTRIES 2735
SHOES AND BOOTS — Abstracting, Bibliographies, Statistics 4362

Shooting see SPORTS AND GAMES - Outdoor Life 4539
Short Wave see COMMUNICATIONS - Radio 1354
Shorthand see BUSINESS AND ECONOMICS - Office Equipment and Services 1057
Sign Manufacturing see ADVERTISING AND PUBLIC RELATIONS 25
Silicosis see MEDICAL SCIENCES 3068
SINGLES' INTERESTS AND LIFESTYLES 4362
Site Selection see HOUSING AND URBAN PLANNING 2482, see also REAL ESTATE 4144
Skating see SPORTS AND GAMES 4463
Skeet Shooting see SPORTS AND GAMES - Outdoor Life 4539
Skiing see SPORTS AND GAMES - Outdoor Life 4539
Slavonic Languages - Study and Teaching see LINGUISTICS 2799
SMALL BUSINESS 4364
Smoking see DRUG ABUSE AND ALCOHOLISM 1532, see also PHYSICAL FITNESS AND HYGIENE 3798, PUBLIC HEALTH AND SAFETY 4096, TOBACCO 4643
Snack Foods see FOOD AND FOOD INDUSTRIES - Bakers and Confectioners 2086
Soap see BEAUTY CULTURE - Perfumes and Cosmetics 375
Soccer see SPORTS AND GAMES - Ball Games 4499
Social Insurance see INSURANCE 2525, see also SOCIAL SERVICES AND WELFARE 4396
Social Psychology see PSYCHOLOGY 4007, see also SOCIOLOGY 4427
SOCIAL SCIENCES: COMPREHENSIVE WORKS 4364
SOCIAL SCIENCES: COMPREHENSIVE WORKS — Abstracting, Bibliographies, Statistics 4394
Social Security see INSURANCE 2525, see also SOCIAL SERVICES AND WELFARE 4396
SOCIAL SERVICES AND WELFARE 4396
SOCIAL SERVICES AND WELFARE — Abstracting, Bibliographies, Statistics 4425
Socialism see BUSINESS AND ECONOMICS - Economic Systems and Theories, Economic History 888, see also POLITICAL SCIENCE 3869
SOCIOLOGY 4427, see also POPULATION STUDIES 3979
SOCIOLOGY — Abstracting, Bibliographies, Statistics 4457
SOCIOLOGY — Computer Applications 4458
Soft Drinks see BEVERAGES 377
SOFTWARE 4459
Soil see AGRICULTURE - Crop Production and Soil 165, see also CONSERVATION 1482, ENGINEERING - Civil Engineering 1861
Soil Pollution see ENVIRONMENTAL STUDIES - Pollution 1975
SOLAR ENERGY 4459
Solid Waste see ENVIRONMENTAL STUDIES - Waste Management 1984
SOUND 4459
SOUND RECORDING AND REPRODUCTION 4459
SOUND RECORDING AND REPRODUCTION — Abstracting, Bibliographies, Statistics 4462
South American History see HISTORY - History of North and South America 2397
Space Flight see AERONAUTICS AND SPACE FLIGHT 42
Spanish Language - Study and Teaching see LINGUISTICS 2799
Spearfishing see SPORTS AND GAMES - Outdoor Life 4539
SPECIAL EDUCATION AND REHABILITATION 4463
Spectroscopy see PHYSICS - Optics 3851
Speech and Hearing Disorders see EDUCATION - Special Education and Rehabilitation 1732, see also HANDICAPPED - Hearing Impaired 2285, MEDICAL SCIENCES - Psychiatry and Neurology 3327
Speech - Study and Teaching see EDUCATION - Special Education and Rehabilitation 1732, see also LINGUISTICS 2799
Speleology see EARTH SCIENCES - Geophysics 1586
Spices see FOOD AND FOOD INDUSTRIES 2060
Spinning see NEEDLEWORK 3590
Spiritualism see NEW AGE PUBLICATIONS 3593, see also PARAPSYCHOLOGY AND OCCULTISM 3668
Sporting Goods see SPORTS AND GAMES 4463
SPORTS AND GAMES 4463
SPORTS AND GAMES — Abstracting, Bibliographies, Statistics 4498
SPORTS AND GAMES — Ball Games 4499
SPORTS AND GAMES — Bicycles And Motorcycles 4515
SPORTS AND GAMES — Boats And Boating 4521
SPORTS AND GAMES — Horses And Horsemanship 4531
SPORTS AND GAMES — Outdoor Life 4539
Sports Cars see TRANSPORTATION - Automobiles 4678
Sportswear see CLOTHING TRADE 1282
Stained Glass see ART 309, see also ARTS AND HANDICRAFTS 352, CERAMICS, GLASS AND POTTERY 1160
Standards see METROLOGY AND STANDARDIZATION 3444
Stationery and Office Equipment see BUSINESS AND ECONOMICS - Office Equipment and Services 1057
STATISTICS 4560, see also POPULATION STUDIES 3979
Stenography see BUSINESS AND ECONOMICS - Office Equipment and Services 1057
Sterilization see BIRTH CONTROL 595
Stock and Stock-Breeding see AGRICULTURE - Poultry and Livestock 209
Stocks and Bonds see BUSINESS AND ECONOMICS - Investments 937
Store Display and Promotion see ADVERTISING AND PUBLIC RELATIONS 25
Stress see PSYCHOLOGY 4007
Student Aid see EDUCATION 1612
Supermarkets see FOOD AND FOOD INDUSTRIES - Grocery Trade 2090
Surfing see SPORTS AND GAMES - Outdoor Life 4539
SURGERY 4592
Surgical Instruments see MEDICAL SCIENCES - Surgery 3373
Surveying see ENGINEERING - Civil Engineering 1861, see also GEOGRAPHY 2240
Swimming see SPORTS AND GAMES 4463
Synthetic Fabrics see TEXTILE INDUSTRIES AND FABRICS 4615
Table Tennis see SPORTS AND GAMES - Ball Games 4499
Tailoring see CLOTHING TRADE 1282
Talking Books see HANDICAPPED - Visually Impaired 2290
Tape Drives see COMPUTERS - Hardware 1453
Tape Recording see SOUND RECORDING AND REPRODUCTION 4459
Tariffs see BUSINESS AND ECONOMICS - International Commerce 899, see also BUSINESS AND ECONOMICS - Public Finance, Taxation 1087

TAXATION 4592, see also BUSINESS AND ECONOMICS - Public Finance, Taxation 1087
Taxicabs see TRANSPORTATION - Automobiles 4678
Tea see BEVERAGES 377
TEACHING METHODS AND CURRICULUM 4592
TECHNOLOGY: COMPREHENSIVE WORKS 4592
TECHNOLOGY: COMPREHENSIVE WORKS — Abstracting, Bibliographies, Statistics 4613
Telecommunications see COMMUNICATIONS 1331, see also ENGINEERING - Electrical Engineering 1880
Telepathy see NEW AGE PUBLICATIONS 3593, see also PARAPSYCHOLOGY AND OCCULTISM 3668
TELEPHONE AND TELEGRAPH 4615
TELEVISION AND CABLE 4615
Tennis see SPORTS AND GAMES - Ball Games 4499
Terminals see COMPUTERS - Hardware 1453
Textbooks see EDUCATION - Teaching Methods and Curriculum 1742, see also PUBLISHING AND BOOK TRADE 4119
TEXTILE INDUSTRIES AND FABRICS 4615
TEXTILE INDUSTRIES AND FABRICS — Abstracting, Bibliographies, Statistics 4628
Thanatology see MEDICAL SCIENCES 3068
THEATER 4629
THEATER — Abstracting, Bibliographies, Statistics 4643
Theology see RELIGIONS AND THEOLOGY 4161
THEORY OF COMPUTING 4643
Theosophy see PHILOSOPHY 3759, see also RELIGIONS AND THEOLOGY 4161
Thermodynamics see CHEMISTRY - Physical Chemistry 1224, see also PHYSICS - Heat 3840
Thoracic Surgery see MEDICAL SCIENCES - Surgery 3373
Thrombosis see MEDICAL SCIENCES - Cardiovascular Diseases 3203
Timber see FORESTS AND FORESTRY - Lumber and Wood 2113
Timetables see TRANSPORTATION 4646
Tires see RUBBER 4290, see also TRANSPORTATION - Automobiles 4678
TOBACCO 4643
TOBACCO — Abstracting, Bibliographies, Statistics 4646
Toiletries see BEAUTY CULTURE 371
Tools see MACHINERY 3015
Touring see TRAVEL AND TOURISM 4750
Tourist Camps see HOTELS AND RESTAURANTS 2471, see also TRAVEL AND TOURISM 4750
Town Planning see HOUSING AND URBAN PLANNING 2482
Toxicology see MEDICAL SCIENCES 3068, see also PHARMACY AND PHARMACOLOGY 3714
TOXICOLOGY AND ENVIRONMENTAL SAFETY 4646
Toys see GIFTWARE AND TOYS 2280
Track and Field see SPORTS AND GAMES 4463
Tractors see AGRICULTURE - Agricultural Equipment 161
Trade see BUSINESS AND ECONOMICS - Domestic Commerce 833, see also BUSINESS AND ECONOMICS - International Commerce 899
TRADE AND INDUSTRIAL DIRECTORIES 4646
Trade Shows see MEETINGS AND CONGRESSES 3390
Trade Unions see LABOR UNIONS 2579
Trademarks see PATENTS, TRADEMARKS AND COPYRIGHTS 3672
Traffic see TRANSPORTATION - Roads and Traffic 4717
Trailers see TRANSPORTATION 4646
Transistors see ELECTRONICS 1764
Translation Services see LINGUISTICS 2799
TRANSPORTATION 4646
TRANSPORTATION — Abstracting, Bibliographies, Statistics 4661
TRANSPORTATION — Air Transport 4669
TRANSPORTATION — Automobiles 4678
TRANSPORTATION — Computer Applications 4706
Transportation Law see LAW 2592
TRANSPORTATION — Railroads 4707
TRANSPORTATION — Roads And Traffic 4717
TRANSPORTATION — Ships And Shipping 4723
TRANSPORTATION — Trucks And Trucking 4742
Trapping see LEATHER AND FUR INDUSTRIES 2735
Trapshooting see SPORTS AND GAMES - Outdoor Life 4539
Traumatology see MEDICAL SCIENCES - Orthopedics and Traumatology 3306
TRAVEL AND TOURISM 4750, see also GEOGRAPHY 2240, HOTELS AND RESTAURANTS 2471
TRAVEL AND TOURISM — Abstracting, Bibliographies, Statistics 4798
TRAVEL AND TOURISM — Airline Inflight And Hotel Inroom 4801
Treaties see LAW - International Law 2719
Trees see FORESTS AND FORESTRY 2094, see also GARDENING AND HORTICULTURE 2120
Trial Law see LAW - Criminal Law 2712
Tropical Diseases see MEDICAL SCIENCES - Communicable Diseases 3216
Tuberculosis see MEDICAL SCIENCES - Respiratory Diseases 3364
Typewriters see BUSINESS AND ECONOMICS - Office Equipment and Services 1057
Typography see PRINTING 3997
Ultrasonics see PHYSICS - Sound 3858
Underground Periodicals see LITERARY AND POLITICAL REVIEWS 2857, see also POLITICAL SCIENCE 3869
Underwear see CLOTHING TRADE 1282
Unemployment see BUSINESS AND ECONOMICS - Labor and Industrial Relations 970
Unidentified Flying Objects see AERONAUTICS AND SPACE FLIGHT 42
Unions see LABOR UNIONS 2579
U. S. Armed Forces see MILITARY 3449
Universities and Colleges see EDUCATION - Higher Education 1698
Upholstery see INTERIOR DESIGN AND DECORATION - Furniture and House Furnishings 2556
Urban Renewal see HOUSING AND URBAN PLANNING 2482
UROLOGY AND NEPHROLOGY 4804
Utilities see ENGINEERING - Electrical Engineering 1880, see also PUBLIC ADMINISTRATION 4052
Vaccines see PHARMACY AND PHARMACOLOGY 3714

Vacuum Sciences see ENGINEERING - Mechanical Engineering 1926, see also PHYSICS - Mechanics 3842
Vegetarianism see NUTRITION AND DIETETICS 3602
Vending Machines see BUSINESS AND ECONOMICS - Marketing and Purchasing 1032
Venereology see MEDICAL SCIENCES - Dermatology and Venereology 3245
Ventilation see HEATING, PLUMBING AND REFRIGERATION 2297
Veterans see MILITARY 3449
VETERINARY SCIENCE 4804
VETERINARY SCIENCE — Abstracting, Bibliographies, Statistics 4820
VETERINARY SCIENCE — Computer Applications 4821
VIDEO 4821
Virology see BIOLOGY - Microbiology 548
VISUALLY IMPAIRED 4821
Vital Statistics see POPULATION STUDIES 3979
Vitamins see PHARMACY AND PHARMACOLOGY 3714
Viticulture see AGRICULTURE - Crop Production and Soil 165
Vocational Education see EDUCATION - Teaching Methods and Curriculum 1612, see also OCCUPATIONS AND CAREERS 3624
Volume Feeding see HOTELS AND RESTAURANTS 2471
Wages see BUSINESS AND ECONOMICS - Labor and Industrial Relations 970
WASTE MANAGEMENT 4821
Waste Reclamation see ENVIRONMENTAL STUDIES 1941
Watchmaking see JEWELRY, CLOCKS AND WATCHES 2562
Water Pollution see ENVIRONMENTAL STUDIES - Pollution 1975
WATER RESOURCES 4821, see also AGRICULTURE 67, CONSERVATION 1482, ENVIRONMENTAL STUDIES 1941, PUBLIC HEALTH AND SAFETY 4096
WATER RESOURCES — Abstracting, Bibliographies, Statistics 4834
Water Sports see SPORTS AND GAMES 4463
Weather see METEOROLOGY 3431
Weaving see NEEDLEWORK 3590, see also TEXTILE INDUSTRIES AND FABRICS 4615
Weddings see MATRIMONY 3066
Weightlifting see PHYSICAL FITNESS AND HYGIENE 3798, see also SPORTS AND GAMES 4463

WELDING 4835
Welfare see SOCIAL SERVICES AND WELFARE 4396
Wildlife see BIOLOGY 424, see also CONSERVATION 1482
WIND ENERGY 4835
Window Covering see INTERIOR DESIGN AND DECORATION - Furniture and House Furnishings 2556
Windows see BUILDING AND CONSTRUCTION 598, see also CERAMICS, GLASS AND POTTERY 1160
Wine see BEVERAGES 377
Wire see MACHINERY 3015, see also METALLURGY 3015
Wit and Humor see LITERARY AND POLITICAL REVIEWS 2857
WOMEN'S HEALTH 4835, see also MEDICAL SCIENCES - Obstetrics and Gynecology 4835
WOMEN'S INTERESTS 4836
WOMEN'S INTERESTS — Abstracting, Bibliographies, Statistics 4858
Women's Liberation Movement see POLITICAL SCIENCE - Civil Rights 3939, see also WOMEN'S INTERESTS 4836
WOMEN'S STUDIES 4858
WOMEN'S STUDIES — Abstracting, Bibliographies, Statistics 4861
Women's Wear see CLOTHING TRADE 1282
Wood see BUILDING AND CONSTRUCTION - Carpentry and Woodwork 639, see also FORESTS AND FORESTRY - Lumber and Wood 2113
Wood Pulp see PAPER AND PULP 3661
Woodwork see BUILDING AND CONSTRUCTION - Carpentry and Woodwork 639
WORD PROCESSING 4861
Wrestling see SPORTS AND GAMES 4463
Writers and Writing see JOURNALISM 2566, see also LITERATURE 2890, PUBLISHING AND BOOK TRADE 4119
Yachting see SPORTS AND GAMES - Boats and Boating 4521
Yoga see PHILOSOPHY 3759, see also PHYSICAL FITNESS AND HYGIENE 3798
Youth see CHILDREN AND YOUTH - About 1231
Zoning see HOUSING AND URBAN PLANNING 2482
ZOOLOGY 4861
Zootechniques see AGRICULTURE - Poultry and Livestock 209, see also VETERINARY SCIENCE 4804

Classified List of Serials
Subjects I-Z

INDUSTRIAL ENGINEERING

see Engineering–Industrial Engineering

INFORMATION SCIENCE AND INFORMATION THEORY

see Computers–Information Science and Information Theory

INORGANIC CHEMISTRY

see Chemistry–Inorganic Chemistry

INSTRUMENTS

see also Jewelry, Clocks and Watches; Metrology and Standardization

681   US   ISSN 0739-0270
A A M I NEWS. bi-m. $75. Association for the Advancement of Medical Instrumentation, 3330 Washington Blvd., Ste. 400, Arlington, VA 22201-4598. TEL 703-525-4890. circ. 5,500. (back issues avail.)
Description: Keeps readers informed of government standards, and AAMI activities regarding medical instrumentation.

681.2   US   ISSN 0065-2814
TA165   CODEN: AVINBP
ADVANCES IN INSTRUMENTATION. (Consists of: Instrument Society of America. International Conference Proceedings) a. price varies. Instrument Society of America, 67 Alexander Dr., Box 12277, Research Triangle Park, NC 27709. TEL 919-549-8411. FAX 919-549-8288. TELEX 802540 ISA DURM. (reprint service avail. from ISI,UMI) **Indexed:** Chem.Abstr., Excerp.Med. —BLDSC shelfmark: 0709.241000.
Refereed Serial

681   GW   ISSN 0932-2655
ALTE UHREN UND MODERNE ZEITMESSUNG. 1978. bi-m. DM.123 (students DM.91.20). Verlag D.W. Callwey, Streitfeldstr. 35, Postfach 800409, 8000 Munich 80, Germany. Ed. Ch. Pfeiffer-Belli. adv.; bk.rev.; circ. 6,000.
Formerly: Alte Uhren (ISSN 0343-7140)

681   US   ISSN 0882-5785
                                 CODEN: AINSB8
ANALYSIS INSTRUMENTATION. (Includes: Analysis Instrumentation Symposium Proceedings) 1963. a. price varies. Instrument Society of America, 67 Alexander Dr., Box 12277, Research Triangle Park, NC 27709. TEL 919-549-8411. FAX 919-549-8288. TELEX 802540 ISA DURM. (reprint service avail. from ISI,UMI) **Indexed:** INIS Atomind.
Refereed Serial

681.2 643   UK   ISSN 0265-3435
ANALYTICAL INSTRUMENT INDUSTRY REPORT. 1984. s-m. £275($495) A I I Report, P.O. Box 78, E. Grinstead, W. Sussex RH19 2YW, England. TEL 0342-323382. FAX 0342-315939. Ed. Gordon Wilkinson. bk.rev. (back issues avail.)
Description: Provides market information on laboratory equipment and analytical instrument business.

ATOMIZATION AND SPRAYS. see *ENGINEERING — Chemical Engineering*

681   AT   ISSN 0045-0626
QC53   CODEN: AJICA9
AUSTRALIAN JOURNAL OF INSTRUMENTATION AND CONTROL. 1944-1985; N.S. 1986. q. Aus.$25($7.50) South Australian Institute of Technology, Measurement and Instrumentation Systems Centre, P.O. Box 1, Ingle Farm, South Australia, Australia. TEL (08)343 3342. (Co-sponsor: Institute of Instumentation and Control, Australia (I.I.C.A.)) Ed. David Aspinall. adv.; bk.rev.; circ. 850. **Indexed:** Aus.Rd.Ind., Aus.Sci.Ind., Chem.Abstr., Curr.Cont., Sci.Abstr.
Description: Covers control instrumentation and data systems for manufacturing and non-manufacturing industries.

681   GW   ISSN 0178-2320
AUTOMATISIERUNGSTECHNISCHE PRAXIS; Zeitschrift fuer Mess- und Automatisierungstechnik. 1959. m. DM.124.60. R. Oldenbourg Verlag GmbH, Rosenheimerstr. 145, 8000 Munich 80, Germany. TEL 089-4112-232. Ed. K.F. Frueh. adv.; bk.rev.; charts; illus.; tr.lit.; index; circ. 8,000. **Indexed:** Appl.Mech.Rev., Chem.Abstr., Cyb.Abstr., Eng.Ind., Excerp.Med., Fluidex, INIS Atomind., Sci.Abstr.
Formerly: Regelungstechnik Praxis (ISSN 0340-4730)
Description: Articles on the use of automatic controls and automation in industrial processes. Includes software applications, detailed descriptions of actual automated systems, industry news, new products.

AUTOMATIZALAS/AUTOMATION. see *ENGINEERING — Mechanical Engineering*

681   IT   ISSN 0393-3911
AUTOMAZIONE INTEGRATA. 1968. 11/yr. L.70000 (foreign L.180000)(effective 1992). Tecniche Nuove s.p.a., Via Menotti 14, 20129 Milan, Italy. TEL 02-75701. FAX 02-7570205. Ed. G. Nardella. adv.; bk.rev.; abstr.; charts; illus.; pat.; tr.lit.; circ. 7,000. **Indexed:** Cyb.Abstr.
Former titles: Controlli Numerici Macchine a C N Robot Industriali (ISSN 0392-6036); Controlli Numerici e Macchine (ISSN 0010-8081)
Description: Articles on advanced automation factories with employees, flexible working systems and robotics.

681   GW   ISSN 0005-755X
                                 CODEN: BECRBZ
BECKMAN REPORT. 1959. q. free. Beckman Instruments GmbH, Frankfurter Ring 115, 8000 Munich 40, Germany. TEL 089-3887-1. FAX 089-3887-490. TELEX 5215761. Ed. B. Maneck. adv.; bk.rev.; charts; stat.; circ. 12,000. **Indexed:** Chem.Abstr.
Description: Reports on research and development of new products in analytical measurement systems for biochemistry and biotechnology, lab automation systems and systems for laboratory data management.

BIOMEDICAL SCIENCES INSTRUMENTATION. see *MEDICAL SCIENCES*

681   BL   ISSN 0101-0794
C & I. (Controle & Instrumentacao - Automatizacao) 1972. m. $85. Editora Gruenwald Ltda., Caixa Postal 3798, Sao Paulo, Brazil. FAX 011-829-0042. TELEX 1130410. adv.; bk.rev.; tr.lit.; circ. 26,000.

C L R. (Clinical Laboratory Reference) see *MEDICAL SCIENCES — Experimental Medicine, Laboratory Technique*

681   II   ISSN 0304-9841
                                 CODEN: CSIOBT
C S I O COMMUNICATIONS. (Text in English) 1974. q. Rs.30($10) Central Scientific Instruments Organization, Sector 30, Chandigarh 160 020, India. FAX 0172-43633. TELEX 0395-300 CSIO IN. (Affiliate: Council of Scientific and Industrial Research) Ed. M.G.Joshi. adv.; bk.rev.; illus.; index; circ. 250. (back issues avail.) **Indexed:** Eng.Ind, Excerp.Med., Indian Sci.Abstr., Indian Sci.Ind., Phys.Ber., Sci.Abstr.

INSTRUMENTS

681   CN
CANADIAN INFORMATION & IMAGE MANAGEMENT SOCIETY. NEWSLETTERS. 1973. q. Can.$45. Canadian Information and Image Management Society, 86 Wilson St., Oakville, Ont. L6K 3G5, Canada. TEL 416-842-6067. Ed. D.F. Donoahue. adv.; bk.rev.; circ. 500.
Former titles: Canadian Information and Image Management Society. Micro Notes; Canadian Micrographic Society. Micro Notes (ISSN 0315-9337)

CHEMICAL MONITOR. see CHEMISTRY — Analytical Chemistry

681   US
CLINICAL ENGINEERING SECTION NEWSLETTER. 1987. bi-m. membership. (American Hospital Association) American Society for Hospital Engineering, 840 N. Lake Shore Dr., Chicago, IL 60611. TEL 312-280-5223. Ed. Kerry Hutchinson. charts; illus.; circ. 5,400. (back issues avail.)
Description: Information on the maintenance and upkeep of diagnostic equipment in hospitals. Geared toward clinical engineers and biomedical equipment technicians.

CONFERENCE ON PRECISION ELECTROMAGNETIC MEASUREMENTS. DIGEST. see ENGINEERING — Electrical Engineering

681   US
CONTROL (CHICAGO). 1988. 12/yr. Putman Publishing Co., 301 E. Erie St., Chicago, IL 60611. TEL 312-644-2020. Ed. Peggy Smedley. circ. 75,000.
Description: Covers all aspects of instrumentation and process control through features and news.

681   US
CONTROL AD - LITS. 1988. q. Putman Publishing Co., 301 E. Erie St., Chicago, IL 60611. TEL 312-644-2020. FAX 312-644-1131. Ed. Nick Cappelletti. adv.; circ. 75,026.
Description: Contains literature and reviews of process control industries products and services.

681 617.6   SP
DENTAL EQUIP; guia de equipamiento dental. q. free. Ediciones Doyma S.A., Travesera de Gracis, 17-21, 08021 Barcelona, Spain. TEL 200-07-11. FAX 209-11-36. TELEX 51964 INK E. Ed. Celia Ribera Banus. adv.: page 265000 ptas.; trim 305 x 420; adv. contact: Jose Luis Campos. circ. 6,300.
Description: List equipment available to dental professionals.

681.2   CC   ISSN 1001-1390
DIANCE YU YIBIAO/ELECTRONIC MEASURING AND METERS. (Text in Chinese) m. Harbin Diangong Yibiao Yanjiusuo - Harbin Institute of Electrical Engineering and Instruments, 1 Gongli Chu, Haping Lu, Harbin, Heilongjiang 150040, People's Republic of China. TEL 63097. Ed. Wang Yi.

DRUG AND DEVICE PRODUCT APPROVAL LIST. see MEDICAL SCIENCES — Experimental Medicine, Laboratory Technique

EXPERIMENTAL ASTRONOMY; an international journal on astronomical instrumentation and data analysis. see ASTRONOMY

681   HU   ISSN 0231-2662
TS176   CODEN: FNMKAY
FINOMMECHANIKA, MIKROTECHNIKA. 1961. m. $26. (Optikai, Akusztikai es Filmtechnikai Egyesulet) Lapkiado Vallalat, Lenin korut 9-11, 1073 Budapest 7, Hungary. TEL 222-408. (Subscr. to: Kultura, Box 149, H-1389 Budapest, Hungary) illus. **Indexed:** Excerp.Med., INIS Atomind., Sci.Abstr.
Formerly: Finommechanika.

681.2   UK   ISSN 0955-5986
TA357.5.M43   CODEN: FMEIEJ
FLOW MEASUREMENT AND INSTRUMENTATION. 1989. q. £125 (Europe £140; elsewhere £120). Butterworth - Heinemann Ltd. (Subsidiary of: Reed International PLC), Linacre House, Jordan Hill, Oxford OX2 8DP, England. TEL 0865-310366. FAX 0865-310898. TELEX 83111 BHPOXF G. (Subscr. to: Turpin Transactions Ltd., Distribution Centre, Blackhorse Rd., Letchworth, Herts SG6 1HN, England. TEL 0462-672555) Ed. Michael Sanderson. (also avail. in microform from UMI; back issues avail.)
—BLDSC shelfmark: 3958.300000.
Description: International journal containing refereed technical papers, review articles and case studies on the latest advances in flowmeters and the theory of their operation.
Refereed Serial

681   US   ISSN 0196-626X
KF3827.M4
G M P LETTER. (Good Manufacturing Practice) 1980. m. $297. Washington Business Information, Inc., c/o Karen Harrington, 1117 N. 19th St., Ste. 200, Arlington, VA 22209. TEL 703-247-3434. FAX 703-247-3421. Ed. Samuel Gilston. bk.rev. (looseleaf format)
●Also available online. Vendor(s): BRS (DIOG), Data-Star, DIALOG.
Description: Covers Good Manufacturing Practice according to FDA rules dictating controls on production and quality control.

681.2 621.329   CC
GUANGXUE YIQI/OPTICAL INSTRUMENTS. (Text in Chinese) bi-m. Shanghai Guangxue Yiqi Yanjiusuo, 115 Changling Lu, Shanghai 200093, People's Republic of China. TEL 5433311. Ed. Peng Dingsang.

681   MX
GUIA DE LA INDUSTRIA: LABORATORIOS DE ESPECIALADES Y CONTROL. 1963. a. Mex.$100000($50) Informatica Cosmos, S.A. de C.V., Fernandez Arrieta 5-101, Col. Los Cipreses, 04830 Mexico D.F., Mexico. TEL 677-48-68. FAX 679-35-75. Dir. Cesar Macazaga Orodono. circ. 5,000.

681 619   SP
GUIA DE MATERIAL DE LABORATORIO. Short title: M L. 1986. q. free. Ediciones Doyma S.A., Travesera de Gracia, 17-21, 08021 Barcelona, Spain. TEL 200-07-11. FAX 209-11-36. TELEX 51964 INK E. Ed. Celia Ribera Banus. adv.: page 265000 ptas.; trim 305 x 420; adv. contact: Jose Luis Campos. circ. 6,900.
Description: Lists laboratory equipment, components and materials, from the simplest to the most sophisticated.

681 610   SP
GUIA DEL EQUIPAMIENTO HOSPITALARIO. Short title: Equip H. 1986. q. free. Ediciones Doyma S.A., Travesera de Gracia, 17-21, 08021 Barcelona, Spain. TEL 200-07-11. FAX 209-11-36. TELEX 51964 INK E. Ed. Celia Ribera Banus. adv.: page 265000 ptas.; trim 305 x 420; adv. contact: Jose Luis Campos. circ. 6,346.
Description: Lists technical, material resources available for the health profession. Contains their properties, characteristics, techniques and applications.

GUIDE TO BIOTECHNOLOGY PRODUCTS AND INSTRUMENTS. see BIOLOGY — Biotechnology

HEALTH TECHNOLOGY TRENDS; for health care executives. see HOSPITALS

681   NE   ISSN 0020-4358
HONEYWELL INSTRUMENTATIE NIEUWS. 1965. q. free. Honeywell B.V., Marketing Division, Postbus 12683, 1100 AR Amsterdam; Netherlands. illus.; circ. 5,000.

681   GW
I C F A INSTRUMENTATION BULLETIN. (Text in English) 1986. 2/yr. free. International Committee for Future Accelerators, c/o University of Siegen, Physics Department, Adolf-Reichwein-Str., 5900 Siegen, Germany. TEL 0271-740-4140. FAX 0271-74515. TELEX 872337. Ed. A.H. Walenta. adv.; bk.rev.; circ. 2,000.
Formerly: Instrumentation Bulletin.
Description: Reports on research and progress in the field of instrumentation, with emphasis on application.

681   US
I E C O N: INTERNATIONAL CONFERENCE ON INDUSTRIAL ELECTRONICS, CONTROL AND INSTRUMENTATION. PROCEEDINGS. Variant title: I E E E Industrial Electronics Society Conference. (Former name of issuing body: Industrial Electronics and Control Instrumentation Society) a. (I E E E, Industrial Electronics Society) Institute of Electrical and Electronics Engineers, Inc., 345 E. 47th St., New York, NY 10017. TEL 212-705-7900. FAX 212-705-7682. (Subscr. to: 445 Hoes Lane, Box 1331, Piscataway, NJ 08855-1331)
Former titles (until 1983): I E E E - I E C O N. Proceedings; (until 1981): I E C I Industrial and Control Applications of Microprocessors. Proceedings; Industrial Applications of Microprocessors.
Description: Covers the enhancement of industrial and manufacturing processes through the application of electronics and electrical sciences.

681.2   US
I E E E INSTRUMENTATION AND MEASUREMENT TECHNOLOGY CONFERENCE. PROCEEDINGS.. Short title: I M T C. 1984. a. price varies. (I E E E, Instrumentation and Measurement Society) Institute of Electrical and Electronics Engineers, Inc., 345 E. 47th St., New York, NY 10017-2394. TEL 212-705-7366. FAX 212-705-7682. (Subscr. to: Box 1331, 445 Hoes Lane, Piscataway, NJ 08855-1331. TEL 908-562-3948)

681   US   ISSN 0272-8141
HD9706.6.U6
I S A DIRECTORY OF INSTRUMENTATION. (Instrument Society of America) 1979. a. $100. I S A Services, Inc., 67 Alexander Dr., Box 12277, Research Triangle Park, NC 27709. TEL 919-549-8411. FAX 919-549-8288. TELEX 802540 ISA DURM. Ed. T.L. Laughter. adv.; circ. 43,000.
Incorporates: I S A Transducer Compendium.

681 610   JA   ISSN 0019-1736
IKAKIKAI GAKU ZASSHI/JOURNAL OF MEDICAL INSTRUMENTS. (Text in Japanese) 1923. m. 6000 Yen. Medical Instrument Society of Japan - Nihon Ikakikai Gakkai, 3-39-15 Hongo, Bunkyo-ku, Tokyo 113, Japan. Ed. Muramatsu Atsuyoshi.

681   UK
INDUSTRIAL AND SCIENTIFIC INSTRUMENTS. 1960. m. Maxwell Business Publications, Audit House, Field End Road, Eastcote, Ruslip, Middlesex HA4 9LT, England. FAX 081-429-3117. adv.; circ. 22,000.
Indexed: BMT, Br.Ceram.Abstr., Fluidex, Met.Abstr., World Alum.Abstr.

681.2   UK   ISSN 0142-3312
TJ212   CODEN: TICODG
INSTITUTE OF MEASUREMENT AND CONTROL. TRANSACTIONS. 1979. 5/yr. £130 (foreign £153). Institute of Measurement and Control, 87 Gower St., London WC1E 6AA, England. Ed. T. Flanagan.
Indexed: Br.Tech.Ind., Chem.Eng.Abstr., Cyb.Abstr., Fluidex, ISMEC, Sci.Abstr., Sh.& Vib.Dig., T.C.E.A.
—BLDSC shelfmark: 8940.500000.

681   US
INSTRUMENTATION & AUTOMATION NEWS; instruments, scientific equipment, electronic and mechanical components. 1953. m. $35. Chilton Co., Chilton Way, Radnor, PA 19089. TEL 215-964-4419. FAX 215-964-4947. (Subscr. to: Box 2005, Radnor, PA 19089) Ed. Patricia Pool. adv.; illus.; tr.lit.; circ. 117,227. (tabloid format; also avail. in microfilm from UMI; microfiche from UMI; reprint service avail. from UMI) **Indexed:** Bus.Ind., Tr.& Indus.Ind.
Former titles: Chilton's I A N; Chilton's Instrument and Apparatus News (ISSN 0193-6174); Instrument and Apparatus News (ISSN 0020-4293)
Description: Presents news, state-of-the-art products, plus applications for existing products for the instrumentation and control engineer.

681 TA165 US CODEN: CHISDY
INSTRUMENTATION AND CONTROL SYSTEMS; the publication of control technology for engineers and engineering management. 1928. m. $60. Chilton Co., Chilton Way, Radnor, PA 19089. TEL 215-964-4417. FAX 215-964-4947. (Subscr. to: Box 2026, Radnor, PA 19080-9526) Ed. John E. Hickey Jr. adv.; bk.rev.; charts; illus.; tr.lit.; index; circ. 88,641. (also avail. in microfilm from UMI; microfiche from UMI; reprint service avail. from UMI) **Indexed:** A.S.& T.Ind., API Abstr., API Catal., API Hlth.& Environ., API Oil., API Pet.Ref., API Pet.Subst., API Transport., Appl.Mech.Rev., Biol.Abstr., Ceram.Abstr., Chem.Abstr., Chem.Eng.Abstr., Comput.Cont., Comput.Dtbs., Curr.Cont., Cyb.Abstr., Deep Sea Res.& Oceanogr.Abstr., Eng.Ind., Excerp.Med., Fluidex, Fuel & Energy Abstr., Met.Abstr., PROMT, Robomat, Sci.Abstr.
●Also available online. Vendor(s): DIALOG.
Former titles: Chilton's I and C S (ISSN 0746-2395); (until 1983): Chilton's Instruments and Control Systems (ISSN 0164-0089); Instruments and Control Systems (ISSN 0020-4404)
Description: Technical features on engineering applications related to control technology.

681.2 TP157 US
INSTRUMENTATION FOR THE PROCESS INDUSTRIES. 35th, 1980. a. price varies. Instrument Society of America, 67 Alexander Dr., Box 12277, Research Triangle Park, NC 27709. TEL 919-549-8411. FAX 919-549-8288. TELEX 802540-ISA DURM. (reprint service avail. from ISI,UMI) **Indexed:** Chem.Abstr.
Formerly: Instrumentation Symposium for the Process Industries (ISSN 0738-3231)
Refereed Serial

681 660 TP157 US ISSN 0074-0551 CODEN: INCPAW
INSTRUMENTATION IN THE CHEMICAL AND PETROLEUM INDUSTRIES. (Includes: International Instrument Society of America Chemical and Petroleum Instrumentation Symposium Proceedings) 1965. a. price varies. Instrument Society of America, 67 Alexander Dr., Box 12277, Research Triangle Park, NC 27709. TEL 919-549-8411. FAX 919-549-8288. TELEX 802-540 ISA DURM. (reprint service avail. from ISI,UMI) **Indexed:** API Catal., API Hlth.& Environ., API Oil., API Pet.Ref., API Pet.Subst., API Transport.
Refereed Serial

681 664 TP373 US CODEN: IFDBB8
INSTRUMENTATION IN THE FOOD AND PHARMACEUTICAL INDUSTRIES. irreg., vol.3, 1980. price varies. Instrument Society of America, 67 Alexander Dr., Box 12277, Research Triangle Park, NC 27709. TEL 919-549-8411. FAX 919-832-0237. TELEX 802540 ISA DURM. (reprint service avail. from ISI,UMI)
Formerly: Instrumentation in the Food Industry (ISSN 0095-0777)
Refereed Serial

681.7 TJ5 US ISSN 0074-056X CODEN: IPWIAN
INSTRUMENTATION IN THE POWER INDUSTRY. (Includes: International Instrument Society of America Power Symposium Proceedings) 1967. a. price varies. Instrument Society of America, 67 Alexander Dr., Box 12277, Research Triangle Park, NC 27709. TEL 919-549-8411. FAX 919-549-8288. TELEX 802540 ISA DURM. (reprint service avail. from UMI,ISI) **Indexed:** INIS Atomind.
Refereed Serial

681 US
INSTRUMENTATION NEWSLETTER. q. National Instruments Corporation, 6504 Bridge Point Parkway, Austin, TX 78730. TEL 512-794-0100. FAX 512-338-9119. Ed. Traci Hensley. circ. 130,000.

681 FR
INSTRUMENTATION SYSTEMS. m. 350 F. (foreign 480 F.). Promotion Presse International, 7 ter, Tour des Petites-Ecuries, 75010 Paris, France. Ed. H. Thiron. adv.; circ. 20,000.

681 US
INSTRUMENTOS Y CONTROLES INTERNACIONALES. q. Keller International Publishing Corp., 150 Great Neck Rd., Great Neck, NY 11021-3309. TEL 516-829-9210. FAX 516-829-5414. Ed. Felicia Morales. circ. 62,000.

681 QC53 US ISSN 0020-4412 CODEN: INETAK
INSTRUMENTS AND EXPERIMENTAL TECHNIQUES. English translation of: Pribory i Tekhnika Eksperimenta. 1958. m. $1175 (foreign $1375)(effective 1992). (Russian Academy of Sciences, RU) Plenum Publishing Corp., Consultants Bureau, 233 Spring St., New York, NY 10013-1578. TEL 212-620-8468. FAX 212-463-0742. TELEX 23-421139. Ed. M.S. Khaikin. (also avail. in microfilm from JSC; back issues avail.) **Indexed:** Appl.Mech.Rev., Cadscan, Chem.Titles, Comput.Abstr., Comput.& Info.Sys., Curr.Cont., Electron.& Communic.Abstr.J., Energy Res.Abstr., Eng.Ind., INIS Atomind., Lead Abstr., Mass Spectr.Bull., Solid St.Abstr., Zincscan.
—BLDSC shelfmark: 0412.700000.
Refereed Serial

681 II ISSN 0047-0376 CODEN: ISIDBS
INSTRUMENTS INDIA. Variant title: I M D A Journal. (Text in English) 1957. bi-m. Rs.30. All India Instrument Manufacturers and Dealers Association, A-32 Navyug Niwas, 167, Dr. D. Bhadkamkar Rd., Bombay 400007, India. Ed. V.K. Vasudevan. adv.; bk.rev.; circ. 2,000. **Indexed:** Sci.Abstr.

681 TA165 US ISSN 0192-303X CODEN: INTCDD
INTECH; the international journal of instrumentation and control. 1954. m. $60 (foreign $90). (Instrument Society of America) I S A Services, Inc., 67 Alexander Dr., Box 12277, Research Triangle Park, NC 27709. TEL 919-549-8411. FAX 919-549-8288. TELEX 802540 ISA DURM. Ed. Walter J. Maczka. adv.; bk.rev.; charts; illus.; tr.lit.; index; circ. 53,000. (also avail. in microfilm from UMI; reprint service avail. from ISI,UMI) **Indexed:** A.S.& T.Ind., Abstr.Bull.Inst.Pap.Chem., API Catal., API Hlth.& Environ., API Oil., API Pet.Ref., API Pet.Subst., API Transport., Appl.Mech.Rev., Biol.Abstr., Chem.Abstr., Chem.Eng.Abstr., Comput.Cont., Comput.Cont., Comput.Dtbs., Comput.Rev., Curr.Cont., Deep Sea Res.& Oceanogr.Abstr., Eng.Ind., Excerp.Med., Fluidex, Fuel & Energy Abstr., Gas Abstr., Ind.Sci.Rev., Met.Abstr., Ocean.Abstr., Petrol.Abstr., Pollut.Abstr., PROMT, Risk Abstr., Sci.Abstr., Sci.Cit.Ind., Sh.& Vib.Dig., World Alum.Abstr.
—BLDSC shelfmark: 4531.804000.
Former titles: Instrumentation Technology (ISSN 0020-4382); I S A Journal (ISSN 0096-0810)

681.2 540 UK
INTERNATIONAL GUIDE TO SCIENTIFIC INSTRUMENTS & CHEMICALS. 1976. a. £70. Labmate Ltd., 12 Alban Park, Hatfield Rd., St. Albans AL4 0JJ, England. Ed. M.H. Pattison. circ. 45,000. (back issues avail.)

681 US
INTERNATIONAL INSTRUMENTATION & CONTROLS. 1975. 6/yr. Keller International Publishing Corporation, 150 Great Neck Rd., Great Neck, NY 11021. TEL 516-829-9210. FAX 516-829-5414. TELEX 221 574 KELLE. Ed. Felicia M. Morales. adv.; abstr.; illus.; circ. 31,184. (tabloid format) **Indexed:** Mass Spectr.Bull.
Formerly: International Instrumentation - Instrumentacion Internacional.

INTERNATIONAL JOURNAL OF REMOTE SENSING. see EARTH SCIENCES

INTERNATIONAL LABMATE. see MEDICAL SCIENCES — Experimental Medicine, Laboratory Technique

681 US
▼**INTERNATIONAL MEDICAL DEVICE AND DIAGNOSTIC INDUSTRY**. 1990. bi-m. free. Canon Communications, Inc., 3340 Ocean Park Blvd., Ste. 1000, Santa Monica, CA 90405-3207. TEL 310-392-5509. FAX 310-392-4920.

681 542 II ISSN 0047-1070
INTERNATIONAL PRESS CUTTING SERVICE: SCIENTIFIC INSTRUMENTS, LABORATORY EQUIPMENT & CHEMICALS. 1970. w. $65. International Press Cutting Service, Box 63, Allahabad 211001, India. Ed. N. Khanna. bk.rev.; index; circ. 1,200. (processed)

681 RU ISSN 0021-3349
IZMERITEL'NAYA TEKHNIKA. 1939. m. 31.80 Rub. Gosudarstvennyi Komitet Standartov Mer i Izmeritel'nykh Priborov, Shchuseva 4, Moscow K-1, Russia. Ed. G.D. Burdun. bk.rev.; charts; index. **Indexed:** Chem.Abstr., INIS Atomind., ISMEC, Sci.Abstr.

681 RU ISSN 0021-3454 CODEN: IVUBAY
IZVESTIYA VYSSHIKH UCHEBNYKH ZAVEDENII. SERIYA PRIBOROSTROENIE. 1958. m. 10.80 Rub. Leningradskii Institut Tochnoi Mekhaniki i Optiki, Leningrad, Russia. Ed. L.F. Porfiriev. charts; illus.; index; circ. 2,500. (tabloid format) **Indexed:** Chem.Abstr., INIS Atomind., Sci.Abstr.
—BLDSC shelfmark: 0077.700000.

681 JA ISSN 0385-4418
J E O L NEWS: ANALYTICAL INSTRUMENTATION. (Text in English) 1963. 2/yr. exchange basis. J E O L Ltd. - Nihon Denshi K.K., 1-2 Musashino 3-chome, Akishima, Tokyo 196, Japan. TEL 0425-42-2161. FAX 0425-46-3353. TELEX 0-2842-135. Ed. Shunich Enomoto. circ. 12,000. **Indexed:** Chem.Abstr., Mass Spectr.Bull., Sci.Abstr.
—BLDSC shelfmark: 4665.280000.
Formerly: J E O L News - Analytical Instruments: Application.

629 JA ISSN 0385-4426 CODEN: JNEIDZ
J E O L NEWS: ELECTRON OPTICS INSTRUMENTATION. (Text in English) 1963. 2/yr. exchange basis. J E O L Ltd. - Nihon Denshi K.K., 1-2 Musasiino 3-chome, Akishima, Tokyo 196, Japan. TEL 0425-42-2161. FAX 0425-46-3353. TELEX 02842135. Ed. Shunich Enomoto. circ. 18,000. **Indexed:** Mass Spectr.Bull.
—BLDSC shelfmark: 4665.300000.
Formerly: J E O L News - Electron Optics Instruments - Application.

681 JA ISSN 0916-782X
JAPAN SOCIETY FOR PRECISION ENGINEERING. INTERNATIONAL JOURNAL. (Text in European languages) 1963. q. $48. Japan Society for Precision Engineering - Seimitsu Kogakkai, Ceramics Bldg., 22-17 Hyakunincho 2-chome, Shinjuku-ku, Tokyo 169, Japan. FAX 81-3-3367-0994. **Indexed:** Chem.Abstr., Curr.Cont., Fluidex, ISMEC, JCT, JTA, Met.Abstr., Sci.Abstr., Sci.Cit.Ind.
—BLDSC shelfmark: 4541.467000.
Formerly: Japan Society of Precision Engineering. Bulletin (ISSN 0582-4206)

JOURNAL OF ELECTROPHYSIOLOGICAL TECHNOLOGY. see BIOLOGY — Biophysics

KYOWA ENGINEERING NEWS. see ENGINEERING

681.2 CC
L S I ZHIZHAO YU CESHI. (Text in Chinese) bi-m. Shanghai Yibiao Dianxun Ju, Guangxue Hangye Chu, Room 201, 450 Jiangxi Zhonglu, Shanghai 200020, People's Republic of China. TEL 3230383. Ed. Zhuang Songlin.

LABORATORIUM PRAKTIJK/LABORATORY MAGAZINE. see MEDICAL SCIENCES — Experimental Medicine, Laboratory Technique

338.4 UK ISSN 0141-8963
LABORATORY EQUIPMENT DIRECTORY. 1972. a. £65. Benn Business Information Services Ltd., PO Box 20, Sovereign Way, Tonbridge, Kent TN9 1RQ, England. TEL 0732-362666. FAX 0732-770483. TELEX 95454-BBIS-G. Ed. Peter Bealin. circ. 1,500.
Formerly: Laboratory Equipment Directory and Buyers Guide.

681.2 607 US
LASER QUEST. 1971. a. free. Metrologic Instruments Inc., Coles Rd. at Rte. 42, Blackwood, NJ 08012. TEL 609-228-8100. FAX 609-228-6673. Ed. Herbert H. Gottlieb. adv.; bk.rev.; charts; illus.; circ. 5,000.
Formerly: Education News from Metrologic (ISSN 0046-144X)

INSTRUMENTS

621 US
M & C DATA ACQUISITION AND RECORDER HANDBOOK & BUYERS GUIDE. 1982. a. $15. Measurements & Data Corp., 2994 W. Liberty Ave., Pittsburgh, PA 15216. TEL 412-343-9666. Eds. Harish Saluja, Elisa Behnk. adv.; circ. 10,000.
Former titles: M and C Temperature Handbook and Buyers Guide; M and C Pressure and Force Handbook Buyers Guide.

681 UK
MARCONI INSTRUMENTS CONTACT; international newsletter. 1967. q. free. Marconi Instruments Ltd., Longacres, St. Albans, Herts. AL4 OJN, England. TEL 0727-59292. FAX 0727-57481. (U.S. subscr. addr.: 3 Pearl Court, Allendale, NJ 07401) Ed. Nitin Dahad. circ. 50,000.
Formerly: M I Contact (ISSN 0024-8207)

681.2 UK ISSN 0020-2940
TJ212 CODEN: MEACBX
MEASUREMENT AND CONTROL. 1968. m. (10/yr.). £78 uK (foreign £103). Institute of Measurement and Control, 87 Gower St., London WC1E 6AA, England. Ed. J. Barrell. adv.; bk.rev.; charts; illus.; index; circ. 6,560. Indexed: Br.Tech.Ind., Chem.Eng.Abstr., Cyb.Abstr., Eng.Ind., Fluidex, Fuel & Energy Abstr., ISMEC, Met.Abstr., Sci.Abstr., T.C.E.A., World Text.Abstr.
—BLDSC shelfmark: 5413.560000.
Supersedes: Society of Instrument Technology. Transactions.

681 530 UK ISSN 0957-0233
QC39 CODEN: MSTCEP
MEASUREMENT SCIENCE AND TECHNOLOGY. 1968. m. £245($409) (effective 1991). (Institute of Physics) I O P Publishing, Techno House, Redcliffe Way, Bristol BS1 6NX, England. TEL 0272 297481. FAX 0272-294318. TELEX 449149-INSTP-G. (U.S. addr.: American Institute of Physics, Subscr. Services, 500 Sunnyside Blvd., Woodbury, NY 11797-2999) Ed. P.A. Payne. adv.; bk.rev.; bibl.; charts; illus.; index. (also avail. in microfiche; microfilm; back issues avail.) Indexed: A.S.& T.Ind., Abstr.Bull.Inst.Pap.Chem., AESIS, Agri.Eng.Abstr., Anal.Abstr., Appl.Mech.Rev., Biol.Abstr., BMT, Br.Ceram.Abstr., Br.Tech.Ind., C.I.S. Abstr., Chem.Abstr., Chem.Eng.Abstr., Curr.Cont., Deep Sea Res.& Oceanogr.Abstr., Eng.Ind., Excerp.Med., Fluidex, Fuel & Energy Abstr., GeoRef, Hort.Abstr., Ind.Sci.Rev., Ind.Vet., INIS Atomind., Int.Aerosp.Abstr., Int.Build.Serv.Abstr., Mass.Spectr.Bull., Met.Abstr., Nutr.Abstr., Phys.Ber., Sci.Abstr., Sh.& Vib.Dig., Soils & Fert., T.C.E.A., W.R.C.Inf., World Alum.Abstr., World Text.Abstr.
—BLDSC shelfmark: 5413.568000.
Former titles (until 1990): Journal of Physics E: Scientific Instruments (ISSN 0022-3735); Journal of Scientific Instruments (ISSN 0368-4253)
Description: Discusses the construction of new instruments for industry and research laboratories.

681 US ISSN 0148-0057
T50
MEASUREMENTS AND CONTROL. (Supplement avail.: M & C: Measurement & Control News.) 1967. bi-m. $22. Measurements & Data Corp., 2994 W. Liberty Ave., Pittsburgh, PA 15216. TEL 412-343-9666. Ed. Harish Saluja. adv.; bk.rev.; illus.; cum.index; circ. 100,000. (reprint service avail. from UMI) Indexed: Excerp.Med., Petrol.Abstr.
Formerly: Measurements and Data (ISSN 0025-6323)
Refereed Serial

681 US ISSN 0194-1461
MEASUREMENTS & CONTROL NEWS. (Supplement to: Measurements & Control) 6/yr. Measurements & Data Corp., 2994 W. Liberty Ave., Pittsburgh, PA 15216. TEL 412-343-9666. Ed. Harish C. Saluja. (reprint service avail. from UMI)

681 US ISSN 0194-844X
CODEN: MDIIDI
MEDICAL DEVICE & DIAGNOSTIC INDUSTRY. 1979. m. free to qualified personnel. Canon Communications, Inc., 3340 Ocean Park Blvd., Ste. 1000, Santa Monica, CA 90405-3207. TEL 310-392-5509. FAX 310-392-4920. Ed. John Bethune. adv.; charts; illus.; pat.; tr.lit.; index; circ. 35,000. (back issues avail.) Indexed: Chem.Abstr., Curr.Adv.Ecol.Sci., Curr.Pack.Abstr., Telegen.
—BLDSC shelfmark: 5527.055000.
Description: Emphasizes applied technology in product design, manufacturing and marketing. Covers market trends, business news, regulatory and legal issues and management for manufacturers of medical devices and medical electronics.

MEDICAL DEVICE APPROVAL LETTER. see MEDICAL SCIENCES — Experimental Medicine, Laboratory Technique

MEDICAL DEVICES, DIAGNOSTICS & INSTRUMENTATION REPORTS: THE GRAY SHEET. see MEDICAL SCIENCES

681 610 US
MEDICAL EQUIPMENT DESIGNER. bi-m. Huebcore Communications, Inc., 29100 Aurora Rd., Ste. 200, Cleveland, OH 44139. TEL 216-248-1125. FAX 216-248-0187. Ed. Michael F. Malley. circ. 12,000.

MEDICAL INDUSTRY EXECUTIVE. see MEDICAL SCIENCES

MEDICAL LABORATORY PRODUCTS. see MEDICAL SCIENCES — Experimental Medicine, Laboratory Technique

681 338 US ISSN 0893-6250
R856.A1
MEDICAL PRODUCT MANUFACTURING NEWS. 1985. 10/yr. free to qualified personnel. Canon Communications, Inc., 3340 Ocean Park Blvd., Ste. 1000, Santa Monica, CA 90405-3207. TEL 310-392-5509. FAX 310-392-4920. Ed. John Bethune. adv.; circ. 30,000. (tabloid format; back issues avail.) Indexed: Telegen.
Description: Covers product news of equipment, materials, components, and services for original equipment manufacturers of medical devices and medical electronics.

MEDICAL PRODUCTS SALES. see MEDICAL SCIENCES

681.2 UK
MEDINDEX. a. £18. Reed Business Publishing Group, Reed Healthcare Communications (Subsidiary of: Reed International PLC), Quadrant House, The Quadrant, Sutton, Surrey SM2 5AS, England. TEL 081-661-3500. FAX 081-661-8946. circ. 6,000.

681 SZ ISSN 0026-2854
QC81 CODEN: MITCAJ
MICROTECNIC. (Includes Micro-News) (Text in English, French and German) 1947. q. 178 Fr. AGIFA Verlag AG, Bruggacherstr. 26, Postfach, CH-8117 Faellanden, Switzerland. TEL 01-8256464. Ed. Rudolf Weber. adv.; bk.rev.; abstr.; bibl.; illus.; stat.; index,cum.index; circ. 7,000. (also avail. in microfilm from UMI; reprint service avail. from UMI) Indexed: C.I.S. Abstr., Chem.Abstr., Curr.Cont., Eng.Ind., Fluidex, ISMEC, Sci.Abstr., Sh.& Vib.Dig.
—BLDSC shelfmark: 5761.000000.

681 RU ISSN 0236-3933
▼**MOSKOVSKII GOSUDARSTVENNYI TEKHNICHESKII UNIVERSITET. VESTNIK. PRIBOROSTROENIE.** 1990. 4/yr. 1.40 Rub. Moskovskii Gosudarstvennyi Tekhnicheskii Universitet, 2-ya Baumanskaya, 5 MGTU, 107005 Moscow, Russia. TEL 263-60-45. Ed. A.S. Eliseev.

681.2 PL ISSN 0257-3881
Q184 CODEN: NAAPEO
NAUCHNAYA APPARATURA/SCIENTIFIC INSTRUMENTATION. (Text in English, Russian) 1986. q. $48. (Polish Academy of Sciences, Institute of Physical Chemistry) Ossolineum, Publishing House of the Polish Academy of Sciences, Rynek 9, 50-106 Wroclaw, Poland. TEL 386-25. (Dist. by: Ars Polona, Krakowskie Przedmiescie 7, 00-068 Warsaw, Poland) Ed. Wojciech Zielenkiewicz.
—BLDSC shelfmark: 8181.035000.
Description: Forum for the exchange of experiences between the academies of sciences of the socialist countries in the field of production of research instrumentation and laboratory equipment.

NEWSMETER. see ADVERTISING AND PUBLIC RELATIONS

681 621.9 US
NOTICIARIO DE TESTES E LABORATORIOS. (Text in Portuguese) 3/yr. Thomas Publishing Company, Five Penn Plaza, 8th Fl., New York, NY 10001. TEL 212-629-1549. FAX 212-629-1542. adv.; circ. 12,000.
Description: Covers the Brazilian market of analytical instruments, information systems, statistical quality control products, and measurement and inspection equipment.

OPTOELECTRONICS, INSTRUMENTATION AND DATA PROCESSING. see ELECTRONICS

681 SZ ISSN 0255-6944
PRECISION; Zeitschrift fuer Mikromechanik, Elektronik, Automaton und Zulieferindustrie. (Text in French and German) 1927. m. 90 Fr. Vogt-Schild Ag, Zuchwilerstr. 21, CH-4501 Solothurn 1, Switzerland. TEL 065-247247. FAX 065-247335. TELEX 934646. Ed. Robert Meier. adv.; bk.rev.; bibl.; charts; illus.; stat.; index; circ. 9,200.
Former titles: Uhren Rundschau; Schweizer Uhr (ISSN 0036-7478)

681 RU ISSN 0032-8162
QC53 CODEN: PRTEAJ
PRIBORY I TEKHNIKA EKSPERIMENTA. 1963. m. 54.90 Rub. (Akademiya Nauk S.S.S.R.) Izdatel'stvo Nauka, 90 Profsoyuznaya ul., 117864 Moscow, Russia. Ed. A.I. Shal'nikov. index. (tabloid format)
Indexed: Chem.Abstr., Sci.Abstr.
—BLDSC shelfmark: 0131.700000.

REMOTE SENSING OF ENVIRONMENT. see GEOGRAPHY

681 US ISSN 0034-6748
Q184 CODEN: RSINAK
REVIEW OF SCIENTIFIC INSTRUMENTS. 1930. m. $650. American Institute of Physics, 335 E. 45th St., New York, NY 10017. TEL 212-661-9404. (Subscr. to: Member and Subscriber Service, 500 Sunnyside Blvd., Woodbury, NY 11797-2999) Ed. Thomas H. Braid. adv.; bk.rev.; bibl.; illus.; index. cum.index. (also avail. in microfiche; back issues avail.) Indexed: A.S.& T.Ind., Abstr.Bull.Inst.Pap.Chem., Agri.Eng.Abstr., Anal.Abstr., Appl.Mech.Rev., Biol.Abstr., Br.Ceram.Abstr., C.P.I., Chem.Abstr., Curr.Cont., Deep Sea Res.& Oceanogr.Abstr., Eng.Ind., Excerp.Med., Fluidex, Fuel & Energy Abstr., Gas Abstr., Gen.Phys.Adv.Abstr., GeoRef, Int.Aerosp.Abstr., Mass Spectr.Bull., Met.Abstr., Meteor.& Geoastrophys.Abstr., Phys.Ber., Psychol.Abstr., RAPRA, Sci.Abstr., Sh.& Vib.Dig., World Alum.Abstr.
—BLDSC shelfmark: 7795.000000.
Refereed Serial

S M T TRENDS. (Surface Mount Technology) see PACKAGING

681.2 918 US
SCIENTIFIC INSTRUMENTS: LATIN AMERICAN INDUSTRIAL REPORT. 1985. a. $235 per country report. Aquino Productions, Box 15760, Stamford, CT 06901. TEL 203-325-3138. Ed. Andres C. Aquino.

681 US
SECOND SOURCE BIOMEDICAL. bi-m. Satellite Publishing Company, Inc., 2900 E. Carolina Center, Charlotte, NC 28208. TEL 704-391-9306. FAX 704-394-8060. Ed. John McGillicuddy. circ. 10,500.

681　　　　　　GW　ISSN 0179-9592
SENSOR REPORT; Anwenderorientierte Fachzeitschrift fuer Sensorik und Messtechnik. 1985. bi-m. DM.99.30 (foreign DM.141). P. Keppler GmbH und Co. KG, Industrie. 2, Postfach, 6056 Heusenstamm, Germany. TEL 06104-6060. FAX 06104-606333. TELEX 410131. Ed. Dr. G.A. Weissler. adv.; bk.rev.; illus.; circ. 10,000 (controlled).

681 001.53　　　US　ISSN 0746-9462
TA165
SENSORS; the journal of machine perception. 1984. m. $55 (free to qualified personnel). Helmers Publishing, Inc., 174 Concord St., Box 874, Peterborough, NH 03458-0874. TEL 603-924-9631. FAX 603-924-7408. Ed. Dorothy Rosa. adv.; tr.lit.; circ. 52,580. **Indexed:** A.I.Abstr., CAD CAM Abstr., Robomat., Telegen.
—BLDSC shelfmark: 8241.784500.
Description: For users of sensing devices and related products for use in product design and manufacture.
Refereed Serial

681 001.53　　　US
SENSOR'S BUYERS GUIDE. 1984. a. Helmers Publishing, Inc., 174 Concord St., Peterborough, NH 03458. TEL 603-924-9631. FAX 603-924-7408. adv.: B&W page $3435; trim 8 1/8 x 10 7/8. circ. 50,419.
Description: Contains information on over 1200 companies in the sensor industry.

SEPARATION. see *MEDICAL SCIENCES — Experimental Medicine, Laboratory Technique*

681　　　　　　UK
SIRA REVIEW ANNUAL BROCHURE. 1980. a. Sira Ltd., South Hill, Chislehurst, Kent BR7 5EH, England. TEL 081-467-2636. FAX 081-467-6515. TELEX 896649-SIRA-G. circ. 3,000.
Formerly: Sira Review.

681 629.8 681　　UK
SIRA SPOTLIGHT. 1971. 2/yr. free to qualified personnel. Sira Ltd., South Hill, Chislehurst, Kent BR7 5EH, England. TEL 081-467-2636. FAX 081-467-6515. TELEX 896649-SIRA-G. Ed. F.E. Jones. charts; circ. 10,000. **Indexed:** Br.Ceram.Abstr., Fluidex, World Surf.Coat., World Text.Abstr.
Incorporates: Measurement and Automation News; Which superseded: Sira Limited. Annual Report; Which was formerly: British Scientific Instrument Research Association. Annual Report.
Description: Provides information on automation application in scientific and industrial measurement. Areas covered include process instrumentation, software programs, industrial instrumentation and sensors.

SOLID STATE NUCLEAR MAGNETIC RESONANCE. see *CHEMISTRY — Analytical Chemistry*

SOVIET JOURNAL OF OPTICAL TECHNOLOGY. see *PHYSICS — Optics*

SPECTRUM. see *PHYSICS — Optics*

681.2　　　　US　ISSN 0074-0527
TA165
STANDARDS AND PRACTICES FOR INSTRUMENTATION. 1963. biennial. price varies. Instrument Society of America, 67 Alexander Dr., Box 12277, Research Triangle Park, NC 27709. TEL 919-549-8411. FAX 919-549-8288. TELEX 802540-ISA-DURM. (Dist. in Japan by: Intercontinental Marketing Corp., I.P.O. Box 5056, Tokyo 100-31, Japan) index. (reprint service avail. from ISI,UMI)

681　　　　　　RU　ISSN 0038-9811
CODEN: STINA4
STANKI I INSTRUMENTY. English translation: Soviet Engineering Research (US ISSN 0144-6622) 1930. m. $21. Izdatel'stvo Mashinostroenie, 4, Stromynsky Lane, Moscow, 107076, Russia. Ed. A.A. Pavlov. adv.; bk.rev.; bibl.; charts; illus.; index. **Indexed:** Chem.Abstr., Eng.Ind., ISMEC, Met.Abstr., Sci.Abstr., World Alum.Abstr.
—BLDSC shelfmark: 0168.000000.

681　　　　　　GW　ISSN 0171-8096
TA165　　　　　　CODEN: TMTMDL
TECHNISCHES MESSEN - T M. 1931. m. DM.184.60. (Archiv fuer Technisches Messen) R. Oldenbourg Verlag München, Rosenheimerstr. 145, 8000 Munich 80, Germany. Ed. Prof. Hesse. adv.; bk.rev.; charts; illus.; tr.lit.; index; circ. 4,000. **Indexed:** Appl.Mech.Rev., ASCA, C.I.S. Abstr., Chem.Abstr., Curr.Cont., Eng.Ind., Excerp.Med., Met.Abstr., Sci.Abstr., Sh.& Vib.Dig.
—BLDSC shelfmark: 8753.780000.
Former titles: Technisches Messen - A T M (ISSN 0340-837X); A T M und Messtechnische Praxis; Archiv fuer Messen - A T M (ISSN 0003-9411)
Description: Devoted to new developments in measurement techniques. News on surface analysis, signal processing, temperature and pressure measurement technology and new products.

001.64 681.2　　UK
TEST; state of the art review. 1975. m (9/yr.). £46($174) (elsewhere £58). Angel Publishing Ltd., Kingsland House, 361 City Rd., London EC1V 1LR, England. TEL 071-417-7400. FAX 071-417-7500. Ed. David Evans. adv.; bk.rev.; illus.; tr.lit.; circ. 14,500. (tabloid format)
Former titles: Test-Cadmat; Test; (until Feb. 1979): Journal of A T E (ISSN 0307-2649)

TEST & MEASUREMENT WORLD BUYER'S GUIDE. see *ENGINEERING — Electrical Engineering*

681　　　　　　US
ULTRA PRODUCT FOCUS. 4/yr. Cahners Publishing Company (Des Plaines) (Subsidiary of: Reed International PLC), Division of Reed Publishing (USA) Inc., 1350 E. Touhy Ave., Box 5080, Des Plaines, IL 60017-5080. TEL 708-635-8800. Ed. Bob Compton. circ. 65,000. (tabloid format)
Description: Showcases the leading-edge equipment and materials required to develop and manufacture high-tech products.

V W D - MASCHINEN. (Vereinigte Wirtschaftsdienste GmbH) see *BUSINESS AND ECONOMICS — Investments*

681　　　　　　US
V X I JOURNAL. bi-m. 25875 Jefferson, St. Clair Shores, MI 48081. TEL 313-774-8180. FAX 313-774-8182. Ed. Wayne Kristoff. circ. 5,000.

WEIGHING & MEASURING DIRECTORY; buyers guide. see *ENGINEERING*

WHAT'S NEW IN PROCESSING. see *ENGINEERING — Chemical Engineering*

681　　　　　　CC
YIBIAO JISHU/TECHNOLOGY OF METERS AND INSTRUMENTS. (Text in Chinese) bi-m. Shanghai Yiqi Yibiao Yanjiusuo - Shanghai Instrument and Meter Research Institute, 225 Longjiang Lu, Shanghai 200082, People's Republic of China. TEL 5417350. Ed. Ding Yinyun.

681.2 001.6　　CC　ISSN 1000-0380
ZIDONGHUA YIBIAO. (Text in Chinese) m. Shanghai Gongye Zidonghua Yibiao Yanjiusuo - Shanghai Institute of Industrial Automation Instruments, 103 Caobao Lu, Shanghai 200233, People's Republic of China. TEL 4360791. (Co-sponsor: Zhongguo Yiqi Yibiao Xuehui) Ed. Fan Jianruan.
—BLDSC shelfmark: 6849.983470.

INSTRUMENTS — Abstracting, Bibliographies, Statistics

AUTOMATIZALASI, SZAMITASTECHNIKAI ES MERESTECHNIKAI SZAKIRODALMI TAJEKOZTATO/AUTOMATION, COMPUTING, COMPUTERS & MEASUREMENT ABSTRACTS. see *PHYSICS — Abstracting, Bibliographies, Statistics*

681.2　　　　US　ISSN 0195-4938
CODEN: CCHIDW
C A SELECTS. CHEMICAL INSTRUMENTATION. s-w. $195. Chemical Abstracts Service (Subsidiary of: American Chemical Society), 2540 Olentangy River Rd., Box 3012, Columbus, OH 43210. TEL 614-447-3600. FAX 614-447-3713. TELEX 6842086.
Description: Covers the use of analyzers, detectors, and meters in chemistry related areas; and the construction and modification of such instrumentation.

681 016　　　　RU　ISSN 0131-7997
EKSPRESS-INFORMATSIYA. ISPYTATEL'NYE PRIBORY I STENDY. 1961. 48/yr. 52.80 Rub. Vsesoyuznyi Institut Nauchno-Tekhnicheskoi Informatsii (VINITI), Baltiiskaya ul., 14, Moscow A-219, Russia. (Subscr. to: Mezhdunarodnaya Kniga, Dimitrova ul. 39, 113095 Moscow, Russia)

681 016　　　　RU　ISSN 0131-0224
EKSPRESS-INFORMATSIYA. KONTROL'NO-IZMERITEL'NAYA TEKHNIKA. 1957. 48/yr. 52.80 Rub. Vsesoyuznyi Institut Nauchno-Tekhnicheskoi Informatsii (VINITI), Baltiiskaya ul., 14, Moscow A-219, Russia. (Subscr. to: Mezhdunarodnaya Kniga, Dimitrova ul. 39, 113095 Moscow, Russia)

KEY ABSTRACTS - MEASUREMENTS IN PHYSICS. see *METROLOGY AND STANDARDIZATION — Abstracting, Bibliographies, Statistics*

SACHGUETERERZEUGUNG SCHNELLBERICHT. see *CERAMICS, GLASS AND POTTERY — Abstracting, Bibliographies, Statistics*

INSURANCE

368　　　　　　US
A A I S VIEWPOINT. 1976. q. American Association of Insurance Services, 1035 S. York Rd., Bensenville, IL 60106. TEL 708-595-3225. FAX 708-595-4647. Ed. Carol Poynter. circ. 1,500. (back issues avail.)
Description: Discusses property and casualty insurance issues.

368　　　　　　AT　ISSN 0314-8580
A I I JOURNAL. 1919. 5/yr. Aus.$30. Australian Insurance Institute, 31 Queen St., Melbourne, Vic. 3000, Australia. TEL 03-629-4021. FAX 03-629-4204. Ed. G.E. Taylor. adv.; bk.rev.; circ. 16,500.
Formerly: Australian Insurance Institute Journal (ISSN 0084-7453)

368　　　　　　US
A L F I NEWS. (Auto, Life, Fire, Insurance) 1936. bi-w. State Farm Insurance Cos., One State Farm Plaza, Bloomington, IL 61710. TEL 309-766-2628. circ. 8,000.
Description: Information for employees at State Farm's home office.

368　　　　　　US
A L I C O NEWS; Caribbean, Americas, Europe & New Zealand. 1964. 3/yr. American Life Insurance Co., One ALICO Plaza, Box 2226, Wilmington, DE 19899. TEL 301-594-2900. Ed. Ellen J. Roberts. circ. 5,000.
Description: Conveys company and industry news to worldwide field force.

A M C R A'S MANAGED CARE MONITOR. (American Managed Care & Review Association) see *HOSPITALS*

A P P A DIGEST. (American Professional Practice Association) see *BUSINESS AND ECONOMICS — Investments*

368　　　　　　US　ISSN 0001-3730
ACACIA CLARION. 1940. bi-m. Acacia Mutual Life Insurance Co., 51 Louisiana Ave. N.W., Washington, DC 20001. TEL 202-628-4506. adv.; bk.rev.; charts; illus.; stat.; circ. 2,000.

ACCIDENTS CLAIMS JOURNAL. see *LAW*

ACCOUNTANCY, BUSINESS & INSURANCE REVIEW. see *BUSINESS AND ECONOMICS — Accounting*

INSURANCE

368   FR   ISSN 0761-7593
ACTU'A G F. 1970. bi-m. free. Assurances Generales de France, 87 rue de Richelieu, 75002 Paris, France. TEL 42-44-19-50. FAX 42-44-19-56. Eds. Alain de la Baume, Dimitri Thanassekos. bk.rev.; circ. 18,000.
    Formerly: Assurances Generales de France. Informations (ISSN 0066-989X)

368   SP
ACTUALIDAD ASEGURADORA; el eco del seguro. 1891. fortn. 10000 ptas.($80) Sede Editorial, Santa Engracia, 151, 28003 Madrid, Spain. Ed. Manuel Maestro Lopez. adv.; bk.rev.; circ. 12,000.

368   US
ACTUARIAL DIGEST. 1982. bi-m. $22. Actuarial Digest Publishing Company, 5600 Roswell Rd., N.E., Ste. 276N, Atlanta, GA 30342-1103. TEL 404-256-5871. FAX 404-843-1964. Ed. Gene Hubbard. circ. 18,000.
    Description: Articles of interest to the working professional actuary.

368 657   US
ACTUARIAL UPDATE. 1972. m. membership. American Academy of Actuaries, 1720 I St., N.W., 7th Fl., Washington, DC 20006. TEL 202-223-8196. FAX 202-872-1948. (Subscr. to: 475 N. Martingale Rd., Ste. 800, Schaumburg, IL 60173) Ed. Jeanne Casey. circ. 10,000. (back issues avail.)
    Description: Covers insurance, pensions and employee benefits.

368.01   NE
ACTUARIEEL GENOOTSCHAP. MEDEDELINGENBLAD. 1963. 6/yr. membership. Actuarieel Genootschap - Actuarial Society of the Netherlands, Postbus 259, 1000 AG Amsterdam, Netherlands. Ed. H.F. Haan. adv.; bibl.; circ. 1,300. (looseleaf format)

368.01   US   ISSN 0001-7825
ACTUARY. 1967. m. (Sep.-Jun.). $15 (foreign $22.50)(effective 1991). Society of Actuaries, 475 N. Martingale, No. 800, Schaumburg, IL 60173-2226. TEL 708-706-3500. FAX 708-706-3599. Ed. Linda Emory. adv.; circ. 14,000.
    Description: Publishes articles on professional issues and SOA activities.

368   US
ADJUSTERS' REFERENCE GUIDE. 1960. q. $425 ($190 for 4 supplements). Insurance Field Company, 1812 Production Ct., Louisville, KY 40299. TEL 502-491-5857. FAX 502-491-5905. (Subscr. to: Box 24244, Louisville, KY 40224) Eds. Ralph Wm. Bourne, Ron Anderson. (looseleaf format)

368.012   US
ADVANCED UNDERWRITING SERVICE. 1935. m. $395 for 8 vol. set. Dearborn - R & R Newkirk, 520 N. Dearborn, Chicago, IL 60610-4901. TEL 312-836-4400. circ. 3,400.

368.3   US   ISSN 0001-9585
AETNAIZER. vol.52,1970. bi-m. free. Aetna Life and Casualty, 151 Farmington Ave., TS4N, Hartford, CT 06156. TEL 203-273-6245. adv.; charts; illus.; circ. 15,000 (controlled).

368   SA
AFRICAN INSURANCE & FINANCE RECORD. 1924. m. R.24. P.O. Box 2651, Cape Town 8001, South Africa. TEL 021 46-6932. Ed. Fred Roffey. adv.; bk.rev.; charts; illus.; circ. 3,000. **Indexed:** Ind.S.A.Per.
    Incorporates: African Insurance Record (ISSN 0002-001X)

368.4   SZ   ISSN 0379-7074
HD7237
AFRICAN NEWS SHEET. French edition: Nouvelles Africaines de Securite Sociale. 1967. irreg. International Social Security Association, Box 1, 1211 Geneva 22, Switzerland. (Dist. by: I S S A Regional Office for Africa, Boite Postale 10113, Lome, Togo)
    Formerly: African Social Security Series (ISSN 0065-4043)
    Description: News and information on ISSA's activities in the region, and on developments in African social security schemes.

368   US
AGENCY NEWS. 1905. bi-w. free to qualified personnel. Equitable Life Assurance Society of the U.S., 787 Seventh Ave., Area 39N, New York, NY 10019. TEL 212-554-2100. Ed. Tom Donlon. adv.; charts; illus.; circ. 15,000.
    Former titles: Agency News Items; Agency Items (ISSN 0002-0788)

AGENT NEWSLETTER. see *AGRICULTURE — Agricultural Economics*

368   US
AGENTS INFORMATION SERVICE. 1984. m. $27. Insurance Field Company, 1812 Production Ct., Louisville, KY 40299. TEL 502-491-5857. FAX 502-491-5905. (Subscr. to: Box 24244, Louisville, KY 40224) Ed. Tad De Santo. charts; illus.; stat.; tr.lit.; circ. 5,500. (looseleaf format; back issues avail.)
    Description: Marketing tool for insurance companies, excess and surplus lines brokers, and MGAs.

368   US
AIM (BOSTON). 1977. bi-m. membership only. Commercial Union Insurance Companies, One Beacon St., Boston, MA 02108. TEL 617-725-6000. Ed. Susan Kaplovitz. charts; illus.; stat.; circ. 10,000.
    Description: Contains information of the Company's insurance products for the salesforce.

ALBERTA HAIL AND CROP INSURANCE CORPORATION. ANNUAL REPORT. see *AGRICULTURE — Crop Production And Soil*

368   CN   ISSN 0712-9343
ALBERTA INSURANCE DIRECTORY; insurance companies, agents and adjusters. 1982. a. Can.$20. Arbutus Publications Ltd., P.O. Box 35070, Sta. E., Vancouver, B.C. V6M 4G1, Canada. TEL 604-687-8003. Ed. W.D.S. Earle. adv.; circ. 1,000.

368.4   NE   ISSN 0401-331X
ALGEMEEN WERKLOOSHEIDSFONDS. JAARVERSLAG. 1949. a. fl.15. Bureau Centrale Fondsen - Social Security Council, Postbus 100, 2700 AC Zoetermeer, Netherlands. circ. 1,000.

368   US
ALL ABOUT MEDICARE. 1987. a. $7.95. National Underwriter Co., 505 Gest St., Cincinnati, OH 45203. TEL 513-721-2140. FAX 513-721-0126.
    Description: Provides comprehensive information on Medicare benefits and costs in a question and answer format.

368   BE
ALLE RISICO'S. (Text in Flemish) s-m. 1990 Fr. C E D Samson (Subsidiary of: Wolters Samson Belgie n.v.), Louizalaan 485, B-1050 Brussels, Belgium. TEL 02-7231111. FAX 02-6498480. TELEX CEDSAM 64130.
    Description: Reports on various aspects of the insurance industry.

ALLENSBACHER MARKT-ANALYSE - WERBETRAEGER-ANALYSE. see *BUSINESS AND ECONOMICS — Marketing And Purchasing*

368   GW
ALLIANZ ZEITUNG; Zeitschrift fuer den Aussen- und Innendienst der Allianz-Gesellschaften. 1919. m. free. Allianz Versicherungs-AG, Koeniginstr. 28, Postfach 440124, 8000 Munich 44, Germany. Ed.Bd.

368.01   US   ISSN 0569-2032
HG8754
AMERICAN ACADEMY OF ACTUARIES. YEARBOOK. a. $25. American Academy of Actuaries, 1720 I St., N.W., 7th Fl., Washington, DC 20006. TEL 202-223-8196. FAX 202-872-1948. (Subscr. to: 475 N. Martingale Rd., Ste. 800, Schaumburg, IL 60173) index; circ. 10,000.
    Description: Directory of the Academy's board of directors and committees. Includes bylaws, qualification standards, and guides to professional conduct.

368   US   ISSN 0002-7200
HG9651
AMERICAN AGENT AND BROKER. 1929. m. $12 (free to qualified personnel). Commerce Publishing Co., 408 Olive St., St. Louis, MO 63102. TEL 314-421-5445. Ed. D.A. Baetz. adv.; bk.rev.; illus.; circ. 39,125. (also avail. in microfilm from UMI) **Indexed:** ABI Inform.
    Formerly: Local Agent.
    Description: Provides sales management information to help multi-line independent insurance agents serve their clients better.

AMERICAN ASSOCIATION OF CROP INSURERS WASHINGTON UPDATE. see *AGRICULTURE — Agricultural Economics*

368.32   US
AMERICAN COUNCIL OF LIFE INSURANCE. COUNCIL REVIEW. 1976. 6/yr. membership only. American Council of Life Insurance, 1001 Pennsylvania Ave., N.W., Washington, DC 20004-2599. TEL 202-624-2000. Ed. Martin W.G. King.

368   US
AMERICAN INSURANCE NEWSLETTER. 1979. fortn. $75. John David Thomas Inc., 876 Duncan St., San Francisco, CA 94131. TEL 415-647-0830. Ed. John D. Thomas. bk.rev.; circ. 200.

AMERICAN MARITIME CASES. see *LAW*

AMERICAN SOCIETY OF APPRAISERS. NEWSLINE. see *REAL ESTATE*

AMERISURE SAFETY NEWS. see *PUBLIC HEALTH AND SAFETY*

ANALYSIS OF WORKERS' COMPENSATION LAWS. see *BUSINESS AND ECONOMICS — Labor And Industrial Relations*

DIE ANGESTELLTENVERSICHERUNG. see *PUBLIC ADMINISTRATION*

368   FR
ANNUAIRE DES ASSURANCES. 1909. a. 930 F. (effective July 1992). 2 rue de Chateaudun, 75009 Paris, France. FAX 48-78-36-59. TELEX 643 040 F.
    Formerly: Annuaire des Assurances et l'Assureur-Conseil.

368   IT   ISSN 0084-6635
ANNUARIO ITALIANO DELLE IMPRESE ASSICURATRICI. 1925. a. L.100000. Associazione Nazionale fra le Imprese Assicuratrici, Via della Frezza, 70, 00186 Rome, Italy. TEL 06-3227141. FAX 06-3227135. Ed. Fabrizio Moretti. circ. 5,000.

368   SP
ANUARIO ESPANOL DE SEGUROS. 1910. a. 14000 ptas. Sede Editorial, Santa Engracia, 151, 28003 Madrid, Spain. circ. 7,500.

APPRAISERS' INFORMATION EXCHANGE. see *BUSINESS AND ECONOMICS — Investments*

368.4   NE
ARBEIDSONGESCHIKTHEIDSFONDS EN ALGEMEEN ARBEIDSONGESCHIKTHEIDSFONDS. JAARVERSLAG. 1977. a. fl.15. Bureau Centrale Fondsen - Social Security Council, Postbus 100, 2700 AC Zoetermeer, Netherlands. circ. 1,000.
    Former titles: Algemeen Arbeidsongeschiktheidsfonds. Jaarverslag; Arbeidsongeschiktheidsfonds. Jaarverslag.

368.4   AG   ISSN 0004-1025
ARGENTINA. DIRECCION NACIONAL DE ASISTENCIA NACIONAL. DAS.* 1961. q. Direccion Nacional de Asistencia Nacional, Cangallo 524, Buenos Aires, Argentina. Ed.Bd. bibl.; illus.

368   FR   ISSN 0004-1173
ARGUS; journal international des assurances. 1877. w. 780 F. Securitas, 2 rue de Chateaudun, 75009 Paris, France. TEL 1-48-78-36-59. FAX 1-48-78-36-59. Ed. Brigitte Raymond. adv.; bk.rev.; bibl.; charts; stat.; index; circ. 21,436.

368   SP   ISSN 0004-430X
ASEGURADORES. 1968. 10/yr. 3500 ptas. Colegios de Agentes y Corredores de Seguros, Consejo General, Nunez de Balboa 116, 28006 Madrid, Spain. FAX 2622702. TELEX 43779 CACS E. Dir. Jose Espinosa Gasco. adv.; bk.rev.; illus.; stat.; circ. 29,000 (controlled).

368   SZ   ISSN 0518-8881
HD7090
ASIAN NEWS SHEET. (Text in English) 1972. s-a. free. International Social Security Association, Box 1, 1211 Geneva 22, Switzerland. (Dist. by: I S S A Regional Office for Asia and Oceania, B-66 Defence Colony, New Delhi 110 024, India) **Indexed:** World Bibl.Soc.Sec.
  Formerly: Social Security Series for Asia and Oceania.
  Description: Information on social security in Asia and the Pacific, also giving information about ISSA activities in the region.

368.32   US
ASSETS (BRYN MAWR). (Former name of issuing body: American Society of Chartered Life Underwriters) 1980. bi-m. membership. American Society of C L U & Ch F C, 270 Bryn Mawr Ave., Bryn Mawr, PA 19010. TEL 215-526-2500. Ed. Michael Rogers. circ. 1,200.

368   IT   ISSN 0004-511X
ASSICURAZIONI; rivista di diritto, economia e finanza delle assicurazioni private. 1934. bi-m. L.92000. Istituto Nazionale delle Assicurazioni, Via Sallustiana 51, 00187 Rome, Italy. TEL 06-4882497. FAX 06-47224559. TELEX 610336 INA RM1. (Subscr. to: Casa Editrice Felice Le Monnier, Via Antonio Meucci, 2, 50010 (Grassina) Florence, Italy) Ed. Dott. Brando Battistig. adv.; bk.rev.; abstr.; tr.lit.; index; circ. 2,600.
  —BLDSC shelfmark: 1746.650000.

368.3   US   ISSN 0066-9598
ASSOCIATION OF LIFE INSURANCE MEDICAL DIRECTORS OF AMERICA. TRANSACTIONS. 1889. a. $15. Association of Life Insurance Medical Directors of America, Southeastern Head Office, Metropolitan Plaza, Tampa, FL 33607. Ed. Dr. Walter S. Clough. cum.index every 5 yrs.; circ. 1,000 (controlled). (also avail. in microform from UMI) **Indexed:** Ind.Med.

368   FR   ISSN 0004-6019
ASSURANCE FRANCAISE. 1947. bi-m. 940 F. Societe d'Editions et de Publications l'Assurance Francaise, 55 rue de Chateaudun, 75009 Paris, France. FAX 42-80-45-93. TELEX 283-392F. Ed.Bd. adv.; bk.rev.; circ. 9,500.

368   FR
ASSURANCE MUTUELLE. (Text in French) 1925. q. free. Reunion des Organismes d'Assurance Mutuelle, 114 rue la Boetie, 75008 Paris, France. TEL 1-42-25-59-37. FAX 1-42-56-04-49. Ed. R. Choplin. bk.rev.; circ. 4,500.

368   CN   ISSN 0004-6027
HG8015
ASSURANCES; revue trimestrielle consacree a l'etude theorique et pratique de l'assurance au Canada. (Text mainly in French; occasionally in English) 1933. q. Can.$32($39) Sodarcan, Inc., 1140 Ouest, Blvd. de Maisonneuve, 7e etage, Montreal, Que. H3A 3H1, Canada. TEL 514-282-1112. FAX 514-282-1364. TELEX 055-60657. Dir. Remi Moreau. adv.; bk.rev.; bibl.; charts; circ. 1,300. **Indexed:** Can.Per.Ind., Ind.Can.L.P.L., P.A.I.S.For.Lang.Ind., P.A.I.S., Pt.de Rep. (1983-).
  —BLDSC shelfmark: 1746.790000.

368   DK   ISSN 0109-1875
ASSURANDOEREN. vol.37, 1946. m. DKK 200 to non-members. Centralforeningen for Danske Assurandoerer, Vester Voldgade 100, 1552 Copenhagen V, Denmark. FAX 33-12-09-29. Ed. Peter Hemicke. adv.; illus.; circ. 2,500.
  Former titles: Danske Assurandoerer (ISSN 0109-145X); Tidsskrift for Danske Assurandoerer (ISSN 0109-1468)

368   NE   ISSN 0167-3882
ASSURANTIE MAGAZINE. (Text in Dutch) 1979. bi-w. fl.89. Samsom BedrijfsInformatie, Postbus 4, Prinses Margrietlaan 3, 2404 MA Alphen aan den Rijn, Netherlands. TEL 01720-66571. FAX 01720-22892. TELEX 39682. Ed. Richard Vroom. adv.; bk.rev.; circ. 30,000 (controlled).

368   UK   ISSN 0515-0361
ASTIN BULLETIN. (Text in English or French) 1958. s-a. £25($49) (International Actuarial Association, Astin Section) Tieto Ltd., Bank House, 8A Hill Rd., Clevedon, Bristol BS21 7HH, England. Eds. H. Buhlmann, D.H. Reid. adv.; bk.rev.; index; circ. 2,000. (back issues avail.) **Indexed:** World Bank.Abstr.
  —BLDSC shelfmark: 1747.065000.

368.01   US
ATLANTIC STATES INSURANCE.* 1986. bi-m. $20. Independent Insurance Agents Association of Maryland, Pennsylvania, Delaware & Washington, D.C., 8501 La Salle Rd., Ste. 206, Baltimore, MD 21204. (Subscr. to: Chase Communications Group, 495 New Rochelle Rd., Bronxville, NY 10708) Ed. George Boue. adv.; circ. 4,000. (back issues avail.)
  Formerly (until vol.2, 1987): I Magazine.

ATTORNEY'S GUIDE TO SOCIAL SECURITY DISABILITY CLAIMS. see LAW — Legal Aid

368   GW   ISSN 0933-8357
AUSSENDIENST INFORMATIONEN; Trainingskurs fuer systematische Akquisition. 1970. m. DM.117. Verlag Norbert Mueller AG und Co. KG, Englschalkingerstr. 152, Postfach 810605, 8000 Munich 81, Germany. TEL 089-9989000. Ed. Adolf Bauer. cum.index: 1985-1991; circ. 10,000. (back issues avail.)

368.4   AT
AUSTRALIA. DEPARTMENT OF SOCIAL SECURITY. ANNUAL REPORT OF THE DIRECTOR-GENERAL. 1972. a. price varies. Australian Government Publishing Service, Publishing Branch, G.P.O. Box 84, Canberra 2601, A.C.T., Australia. illus.; stat.

328.94 368.9   AT
AUSTRALIA. INSURANCE COMMISSIONER. ANNUAL REPORT. 1974. a. price varies. Australian Government Publishing Service, G.P.O. Box 84, Canberra, A.C.T. 2601, Australia. illus.; stat.

368   AT   ISSN 0728-6864
AUSTRALIA. OFFICE OF THE LIFE INSURANCE COMMISSIONER. HALF YEARLY FINANCIAL & STATISTICAL BULLETIN. (Text and summaries in English) s-a. Aus.$2.25 per no. (Office of the Life Insurance Commissioner) Australian Government Publishing Service, G.P.O. Box 84, Canberra 2601, Australia. Ed.Bd. circ. 1,020.

368   AT
AUSTRALIAN AND NEW ZEALAND INSURANCE REPORTER. (In 3 vols.) 1979. 12/yr. C C H Australia Ltd., P.O. Box 230, North Ryde, N.S.W. 2113, Australia. TEL 888-2555. FAX 02-888-7324.

AUSTRALIAN SUPERANNUATION LAW AND PRACTICE. see SOCIAL SERVICES AND WELFARE

368.3   US   ISSN 0093-0466
HG9970.A5
AUTOMOBILE INSURANCE LOSSES, COLLISION COVERAGES, VARIATIONS BY MAKE AND SERIES. (Subseries of its Research Report) 1972. s-a. free. Highway Loss Data Institute, c/o Stephen L. Oesch, General Counsel, Sec.-Treas., 1005 N. Glebe Rd., Ste. 800, Arlington, VA 22201. TEL 703-247-1600. FAX 703-247-1678. illus.; stat.; circ. 2,500. **Indexed:** SRI.

368   US
AUTOMOBILE LAW REPORTS - INSURANCE CASES. 1966. fortn. $980. Commerce Clearing House, Inc., 4025 W. Peterson Ave., Chicago, IL 60646. TEL 312-583-8500. Ed. D. Newquist. charts; stat.; circ. 703. (looseleaf format)
  Former titles: Automobile Law Reports Insurance Decisions (ISSN 0005-1411); Automobile Law Reports.

368   CN   ISSN 0707-7114
B.C. AGENT. 1949. bi-m. Can.$15 to non-members. (Insurance Agents' Association of British Columbia) Arbutus Publications Ltd., P.O. Box 35070, Sta. E, Vancouver, B.C. V6M 4G1, Canada. TEL 604-687-8003. Ed. William D. S. Earle. adv.; illus.; circ. 1,100.

INSURANCE 2527

368   CN
B.C. BROKER. (British Columbia) 1949. 6/yr. Insurance Publications Ltd., Box 35070, Sta. E, Vancouver, B.C. V6M 4G1, Canada. TEL 604-687-8003. FAX 604-687-2733. Ed. Patrick Durrant. adv.

368   GW   ISSN 0723-7561
DIE B G; Fachzeitschrift fuer Arbeitssicherheit und Unfallversicherung. 1876. m. DM.112.80. (Hauptverband der Gewerblichen Berufsgenossenschaften e.V.) Erich Schmidt Verlag GmbH & Co. (Bielefeld), Viktoriastr. 44A, Postfach 7330, 4800 Bielefeld 1, Germany. TEL 0521-583080. Ed. Dr. Sokoll. adv.; bk.rev. **Indexed:** INIS Atomind., World Bibl.Soc.Sec.
  —BLDSC shelfmark: 1947.487000.
  Formerly: Berufsgenossenschaft (ISSN 0005-9544)

368   GW   ISSN 0937-0811
B G W MITTEILUNGEN. 1970. s-a. Berufsgenossenschaft fuer Gesundheitsdienst und Wohlfahrtspflege, Technischer Aufsichtsdienst, Pappelallee 35-37, 2000 Hamburg 76, Germany. TEL 040-202070. FAX 040-20207-525. TELEX 2174949.
  Formerly (until 1988): B G W Mitteilungsblatt (ISSN 0178-8574)

B I F U REPORT. (Banking Insurance & Finance Union) see BUSINESS AND ECONOMICS — Banking And Finance

B N A PENSION REPORTER. see BUSINESS AND ECONOMICS — Labor And Industrial Relations

BANKINSURANCE NEWS. see BUSINESS AND ECONOMICS — Banking And Finance

BANKS IN INSURANCE REPORT. see BUSINESS AND ECONOMICS — Banking And Finance

368   GW
DIE BARMER. 1928. 4/yr. free. Barmer Ersatzkasse, Untere Lichtenplatzer Str. 100, Postfach 200108, 5600 Wuppertal 2, Germany. bk.rev.; charts; illus.; index; circ. 4,400,000.
  Formerly: Barmer Ersatzkasse (ISSN 0005-5980)

368   GW
BARMER BRUECKE; Zeitschrift fuer die Vertrauensleute der Barmer Ersatzkasse. 1951. 4/yr. free. Barmer Ersatzkasse, Untere Lichtenplatzer Str. 100, Postfach 200108, 5600 Wuppertal 2, Germany. bk.rev.; charts; illus.; index; circ. 140,000.
  Formerly: B E K - Bruecke (ISSN 0005-8238)

368   BE   ISSN 0046-9726
BELGIUM. INSTITUT NATIONAL D'ASSURANCE MALADIE INVALIDITE. I.N.A.M.I. BULLETIN D'INFORMATION/BELGIUM. RIJKSINSTITUUT VOOR ZIEKTE- EN INVALIDITEITSVERZEKERING. R.I.Z.I.V. INFORMATIEBLAD. (Editions in Dutch, French) 1964. 6/yr. 800 Fr. Institut National d'Assurance Maladie-Invalidite - Rijksinstituut voor Ziekte- en Invaliditeitsverzekering, Av. de Tervuren 211, B-1150 Brussels, Belgium. TEL 02-739-71-11. FAX 02-739-72-19. Ed. Raphael Schutyser. bk.rev.; charts; stat.; index, cum.index; circ. 4,500 (2,100 Dutch ed.; 2,400 French ed.).
  —BLDSC shelfmark: 2862.800000.

368.4   BE
BELGIUM. INSTITUT NATIONAL D'ASSURANCES SOCIALES POUR TRAVAILLEURS INDEPENDANTS. RAPPORT ANNUEL. Flemish edition: Belgium. Rijksinstituut voor de Sociale Verzekeringen der Zelfstandigen. Jaarverslag. 1970. a. free. Institut National d'Assurances Sociales pour Travailleurs Independants, Bibliotheque - Bureau 4-7 (Wat.), Place Jean Jacobs 6, B-1000 Brussels, Belgium. TEL 02-507-6211. FAX 02-511-2153.
  Description: Details activities for each branch of the institute.

I J K

INSURANCE

331.252 368 UK ISSN 0268-764X
BENEFITS & COMPENSATION INTERNATIONAL. 1971. 10/yr. $380 (foreign £210)(effective 1992). Pension Publications Ltd., East Wing, Fourth Floor, Hope House, 45 Great Peter St., London SW1P 3LT, England. TEL 071-222-0288. FAX 071-799-2163. TELEX 261401-BENINT-G. Ed. Irena St. John-Brooks. adv.; bk.rev.; charts; index; circ. 1,190. (also avail. in microform from UMI; back issues avail.) **Indexed:** ABI Inform., BPIA, Bus.Ind., Manage.Cont., World Bibl.Soc.Sec.
  Formerly (until 1985): Benefits International (ISSN 0045-172X)
  Description: Covers international employee benefits and compensation trends. Emphasis on design of private pension plans and pension fund investment.

BENEFITS LAW JOURNAL. see *LAW — Legal Aid*

BERGBAU-BERUFSGENOSSENSCHAFT. JAHRESBERICHT. see *LABOR UNIONS*

368 US ISSN 0094-9973
HG8943
BEST'S AGENTS GUIDE TO LIFE INSURANCE COMPANIES. 1974. a. $65. A.M. Best Co., Ambest Rd., Oldwick, NJ 08858. TEL 908-439-2200. FAX 908-439-3363. TELEX 837744. Ed. Robert J. King. stat.

368 US
BEST'S DIRECTORY OF RECOMMENDED INSURANCE ADJUSTERS. 1930. a. $55. A.M. Best Co., Ambest Rd., Oldwick, NJ 08858. TEL 908-439-2200. FAX 908-439-3363. TELEX 837744. Ed. E.C. Krisak.
  Former titles: Best's Directory of Recommended Independent Insurance Adjusters (ISSN 0271-0927); Best's Recommended Independent Insurance Adjusters (ISSN 0091-830X); Best's Recommended Insurance Adjusters.

368 US ISSN 0277-1551
KF195.I5
BEST'S DIRECTORY OF RECOMMENDED INSURANCE ATTORNEYS. 1928. a. $65. A.M. Best Co., Ambest Rd., Oldwick, NJ 08858. TEL 908-439-2200. FAX 908-439-3363. TELEX 837744. Ed. E.C. Krisak.
  Formerly: Best's Recommended Insurance Attorneys.

368 US
BEST'S INSURANCE MANAGEMENT REPORTS: LIFE - HEALTH EDITION. 1957. w. $275. A.M. Best Co., Ambest Rd., Oldwick, NJ 08858. TEL 908-439-2200. FAX 908-439-3363. TELEX 837744. Ed. D. Hall. charts; stat.
  Former titles (until 1979): Best's Insurance News Digest: Life - Health Edition; Best's Weekly Digest (ISSN 0005-9722)

368 US
BEST'S INSURANCE MANAGEMENT REPORTS: PROPERTY - CASUALTY EDITION. 1957. w. $275. A.M. Best Co., Ambest Rd., Oldwick, NJ 08858. TEL 908-439-2200. FAX 908-439-3363. TELEX 837744. Ed. D. Hall. charts; stat.
  Formerly (until 1979): Best's Insurance News Digest: Property - Casualty Edition.

368 US
BEST'S INSURANCE REPORT: LIFE - HEALTH. 1906. a. $530. A.M. Best Co., Ambest Rd., Oldwick, NJ 08858. TEL 908-439-2200. FAX 908-439-3363. TELEX 837744. Ed. Robert J. King. stat.

368 US ISSN 0148-3218
HG9655
BEST'S INSURANCE REPORT: PROPERTY - CASUALTY. 1900. a. $530. A.M. Best Co., Ambest Rd., Oldwick, NJ 08858. TEL 908-439-2200. FAX 908-439-3363. TELEX 837744. Ed. C. Burton Kellogg II. stat.
  Formerly: Best's Insurance Report: Property - Liability.

368 US
BEST'S RETIREMENT INCOME GUIDE. 1979. s-a. $55. A.M. Best Co., Ambest Rd., Oldwick, NJ 08858. TEL 908-439-2200. FAX 908-439-3363. TELEX 837744. Ed. A.D. Gold.

368 US ISSN 0005-9706
HG8751 CODEN: BRLHB5
BEST'S REVIEW. LIFE - HEALTH INSURANCE EDITION. 1899. m. $16. A.M. Best Co., Ambest Rd., Oldwick, NJ 08858. TEL 908-439-2200. FAX 908-439-3363. TELEX 837744. Ed. Doris Fenske. adv.; bk.rev.; charts; illus.; stat.; s-a. index, cum.index; circ. 40,300. (also avail. in microform from UMI; reprint service avail. from UMI) **Indexed:** ABI Inform., Account.Ind. (1974-), B.P.I., BPIA, Bus.Ind., Comput.Lit.Ind., Data Process.Dig., Hlth.Ind., L.I.I., Pers.Lit., PROMT, PSI, Sci.Abstr., SRI, Tr.& Indus.Ind., Work Rel.Abstr.
  ●Also available online. Vendor(s): DIALOG.
  Formerly: Best's Insurance News. Life Edition.

368 US ISSN 0161-7745
HG8011 CODEN: BRPIDU
BEST'S REVIEW. PROPERTY - CASUALTY INSURANCE EDITION. 1899. m. $16. A.M. Best Co., Ambest Rd., Oldwick, NJ 08858. TEL 908-439-2200. FAX 908-439-3363. TELEX 837744. Ed. Doris Fenske. adv.; bk.rev.; charts; illus.; stat.; tr.lit.; index, cum.index; circ. 36,800. (also avail. in microform from UMI; reprint service avail. from UMI) **Indexed:** ABI Inform., Account.Ind. (1974-), B.P.I., BPIA, Bus.Ind., Comput.Lit.Ind., Data Process.Dig., PSI, Sci.Abstr., SRI, Tr.& Indus.Ind.
  ●Also available online. Vendor(s): DIALOG.
  —BLDSC shelfmark: 1942.389000.
  Former titles: Best's Review. Property - Liability Insurance Edition (ISSN 0005-9714); Best's Insurance News. Fire and Casualty Edition.
  Description: Highlights fire and casualty coverage.

368.4 GW ISSN 0005-9951
BETRIEBLICHE ALTERSVERSORGUNG. 1946. 8/yr. membership. Arbeitsgemeinschaft fuer Betriebliche Altersversorgung e.V., Postfach 101208, 6900 Heidelberg 1, Germany. TEL 06221-21422. FAX 06221-24210. Ed. Michael Lubnow. bk.rev.; circ. 1,700. **Indexed:** World Bibl.Soc.Sec.

368.4 GW ISSN 0342-0817
DIE BETRIEBSKRANKENKASSE. 1908. m. DM.62.40. Bundesverband der Betriebskrankenkassen, Kronprinzenstr. 6, Postfach 100531, 4300 Essen 1, Germany. TEL 0201-1791140. FAX 0201-1791003. adv.; bk.rev.; circ. 7,500. (also avail. in microfiche) **Indexed:** World Bibl.Soc.Sec.

368 NE ISSN 0006-0313
BEURSBENGEL. 1938. m. (bi-m. July). fl.30. Stichting Vakontwikkeling Verzekeringsbedrijf, Postbus 9791, 3506 GT Utrecht, Netherlands. (Co-sponsor: Federatie van Verenigingen tot Bevordering van de Assurantie-Wetenschap) Ed. W.M.Th. Adriaansens. adv.; bk.rev.; bibl.; index; circ. 24,000.

368.382 GW
BLEIB GESUND. 1960. bi-m. DM.5. (AOK-Bundesverband) Wirtschaftsdienst Gesellschaft fuer Medien & Kommunikation mbH & Co. OHG, Lange Str. 13, 6000 Frankfurt 1, Germany. Ed. Werner Stuetzel. circ. 12,861,600.

368 CN ISSN 0831-6503
BLUE CHART REPORT. 1984. a. Can.$22.50 (foreign Can.$25.50). Stone and Cox Ltd., 111 Peter St., Ste. 202, Toronto, Ont. M5V 2H1, Canada. TEL 416-599-0772. FAX 416-599-0867. Ed. John D. Wyndham.
  Suepersedes: Underwriting Results: The Blue Chart.
  Description: Performance and solvency ratios for Canadian property and casualty insurance companies.

368 CK
BOLIVAR. 1941. q. Compania de Seguros Bolivar, Medellin, Colombia. **Indexed:** Amer.Hist.& Life, Hist.Abstr.

368 BO
BOLIVIA. SUPERINTENDENCIA NACIONAL DE SEGUROS Y REASEGUROS. COLECCION ESTUDIOS. 1976. irreg. Superintendencia Nacional de Seguros y Reaseguras, La Paz, Bolivia.

BOND. see *RELIGIONS AND THEOLOGY — Protestant*

368 US ISSN 0006-9256
BRATRSKY VESTNIK/FRATERNAL HERALD. 1897. m. $10. Western Fraternal Life Association, 1900 First Ave., N.E., Cedar Rapids, IA 52402. TEL 319-363-2653. Ed. Cathy M. Langer. bk.rev.; stat.; circ. 50,000.

368 US ISSN 0006-9779
BRICKBATS & BOUQUETS. Short title: B & B. 1934. bi-m. free to qualified personnel. Employers Insurance of Texas, Box 2759, Dallas, TX 75221. TEL 214-760-6282. FAX 214-760-3751. Ed. Denise Brooke. illus.; circ. 2,100 (controlled).

BRIEF (CHICAGO). see *LAW*

368.4 CN
BRITISH COLUMBIA. WORKERS' COMPENSATION BOARD. WORKERS' COMPENSATION REPORTER. 1973. irreg. Can.$50 per vol. Workers' Compensation Board, Community Relations Department, 6951 Westminster Highway, Richmond, B.C. V7C 1C6, Canada. TEL 604-276-3068. FAX 604-276-7406. circ. 1,522.
  Description: Covers matters of policy and interpretation of the British Columbia Workers Compensation Act.

BRITISH COLUMBIA DECISIONS - INSURANCE LAW CASES. see *LAW*

368 CN ISSN 0068-1598
BRITISH COLUMBIA INSURANCE DIRECTORY. INSURANCE COMPANIES, AGENTS AND ADJUSTERS. 1964. a. Can.$23. Arbutus Publications Ltd., P.O. Box 35070, Sta. E, Vancouver, B.C. V6M 4G1, Canada. TEL 604-687-8003. Ed. W.D.S. Earle. adv.; bk.rev.; circ. 1,400.

368 UK
BROKER. 1977. q. £12. Lloyd's List International, 1 Singer Street, London EC2A 4LQ, England. TEL 071-250-1500. FAX 071-250-0998. TELEX 987321 LLOYDS G. Ed. Edward Ion. adv.; bk.rev.; bibl.; tr.lit.; circ. 20,000.
  Formerly (until 1988): British Insurance Broker (ISSN 0141-6197)

368 US
THE BROKER. bi-m. Western Association of Insurance Brokers, 235 Montgomery St., Rm. 962, San Francisco, CA 94104-3002. TEL 415-392-5383. FAX 415-392-5644. Ed. Michael S. Cabot.

368 US ISSN 0273-6551
BROKER WORLD. 1980. m. $9. Insurance Publications, Inc., 10709 Barkley, Ste. 3, Overland Park, KS 66211. TEL 800-762-3387. FAX 913-383-1247. Ed. Sharon Chace. adv.; circ. 26,474. (back issues avail.)
  Description: Contains information pertinent to independent life and health insurance agents and brokers.

368 UK ISSN 0260-2385
BROKERS' MONTHLY & INSURANCE ADVISER. 1950. m. £27.50. Insurance Publishing & Printing Co., 7 Stourbridge Rd., Lye, Stourbridge, West Midlands DY9 7DG, England. Ed. Brian Susman. adv.; bk.rev.; charts; illus.; mkt.; tr.lit.; index, cum.index; circ. 9,500.
  —BLDSC shelfmark: 2349.490000.
  Formerly: Insurance Brokers' Monthly (ISSN 0020-4633)

368 CN ISSN 0585-3680
HG8550.A4
THE BROWN CHART. PROVINCIAL RESULTS. Short title: Brown Chart. (Text in English, French) 1935. a. Can.$68. Stone & Cox Ltd., 111 Peter St., Ste. 202, Toronto, Ont. M5V 2H1, Canada. TEL 416-599-0772. FAX 416-599-0867. Ed. John D. Wyndham. circ. 500. (also avail. on diskette)
  Incorporates: Provincial Results in Canada of Fire and Casualty Companies & Provincial Results in Canada of General Insurance Companies; **Formerly:** Brown Chart for All Lines of General Insurance. Provincial Results. Reports (ISSN 0227-437X)
  Description: Breakdown of business in each province by class of insurance for Canadian property-casualty companies.

368 AG
BRUJULA. Variant title: Compania Argentina de Seguros. Memoria y Balance General. no.14, 1975. irreg. Compania Argentina de Seguros, San Martin 439, Buenos Aires, Argentina.

368 US ISSN 0007-3261
BUILDER (COLUMBUS). 1909. 6/yr. free. Midland Mutual Life Insurance Company, 250 E. Broad St., Columbus, OH 43215. TEL 614-228-2001. Ed. M. Pollman. illus.; tr.lit.; circ. 1,300 (controlled).

INSURANCE 2529

368.32 US ISSN 0739-9413
HD7653
BUSINESS AND HEALTH. 1983. m. $99 (foreign $136). Medical Economics Company Inc., Five Paragon Dr., Montvale, NJ 07645. TEL 201-358-7200. FAX 201-573-1045. Ed. Karen Hunt. adv.; bk.rev.; circ. 35,000. **Indexed:** ABI Inform., Abstr.Health Care Manage.Stud., Abstr.Soc.Geront., B.P.I.
—BLDSC shelfmark: 2933.205000.
Description: Examine the full range of healthcare concerns affecting corporations, including cost management, quality assurance, health promotion and wellness, disability and rehabilitation.

368 US ISSN 0007-6864
HG8011 CODEN: BUINEW
BUSINESS INSURANCE; news magazine for corporate risk, employee benefit and financial executives. 1967. w. $80. Crain Communications, Inc. (Chicago), 740 Rush St., Chicago, IL 60611. TEL 312-649-5286. FAX 312-280-3174. (Subscr. to: 965 E. Jefferson Ave., Detroit, MI 48207-9966. TEL 800-992-9970) Ed. Jim Burcke. bk.rev.; circ. 50,176. (tabloid format; also avail. in microform from UMI,MIM; reprint service avail. from UMI) **Indexed:** ABI Inform, B.P.I, BPIA, Bus.Ind., CINAHL, Hlth.Ind., L.I.I., PROMT, PSI, Tr.& Indus.Ind.
●Also available online. Vendor(s): Mead Data Central.
—BLDSC shelfmark: 2933.830000.

368 US ISSN 0199-2414
C A L UNDERWRITER. 1970. m. $5. California Association of Life Underwriters, 333 Hegenberger Rd., Ste. 211, Box 6459, Oakland, CA 94603. TEL 415-638-2450. FAX 415-638-2474. Ed. Dan Crouch. adv.; bk.rev.; circ. 11,000. (reprint service avail.)
Description: News and articles on legislative, regulatory, tax, and political issues of interest to the California Association of Life Underwriters. Includes regular columns on membership benefits, public relations, education, trends and sales techniques.

368.01 UK ISSN 0957-4883
C I I JOURNAL. 1976. 6/yr. £12. Chartered Insurance Institute, 20 Aldermanbury, London EC2V 7HY, England. TEL 071-606-3835. FAX 071-726-0131. Ed. S. Bolam. adv.; bk.rev.; circ. 70,000. **Indexed:** RICS.
—BLDSC shelfmark: 4725.200000.
Formerly: Chartered Insurance Institute, London. Journal (ISSN 0309-4928); Incorporating: Chartered Insurance Institute, London. Yearbook (ISSN 0069-2808); Contact (London, 1955) (ISSN 0010-7247)
Description: Provides information on CII activities and articles on matters of interest to insurance people.

368 CN ISSN 0382-7038
C L U COMMENT (ENGLISH EDITION). (French edition: Commentaires (ISSN 0382-7046) ceased) 1967. 6/yr. (Canadian Institute Chartered Life Underwriters) Life Underwriters Association of Canada, 41 Lesmill Rd., Don Mills, Ont. M3B 2T3, Canada. TEL 416-444-5251. (Co-sponsor: Chartered Financial Consultants) cum.index every 5 yrs.; circ. 29,000.

368 US ISSN 0007-8883
C P C U NEWS. 1952. m. (except May-June & Sep.-Oct. combined). $3. Society of Chartered Property & Casualty Underwriters, Box 3009, 720 Providence Rd., Malvern, PA 19355. TEL 215-251-2728. Ed. Lisa A. Fittipaldi. circ. 21,000. (tabloid format; avail. on records) **Indexed:** P.L.I.I.

368 US
C P C U PUBLIC AFFAIRS FORUM; a digest of current events about insurance & related issues. irreg. Society of Chartered Property & Casualty Underwriters, Box 3009, 720 Providence Rd., Malvern, PA 19355. TEL 215-251-2728.

368 US
C P C U UPDATE; a summary of current financial trends affecting the property and casualty industy. q. Society of Chartered Property & Casualty Underwriters, Box 3009, 720 Providence Rd., Malvern, PA 19355. TEL 215-251-2728. Ed. Lisa A. Fittipaldi.

368 US
C S R CONNECTION. (Customer Service Representative) q. National Association of Professional Agents, 400 N. Washington St., Alexandria, VA 22314-2312. TEL 703-836-9340. Ed. Karen L. Stallings.

368.4 355.115 US
CAL - VET INSURANCE PLANS. ANNUAL REPORT. 1980. a. Department of Veterans Affairs, 1227 O St., Sacramento, CA 95814. TEL 916-322-1796.

CALIFORNIA COMPENSATION CASES. see *LAW*

CALIFORNIA INSURANCE LAW AND PRACTICE. see *LAW*

368 US
CALIFORNIA INSURANCE LAW AND REGULATION REPORTER. 1989. m. $355. Shepard's - McGraw-Hill, Inc., Box 35300, Colorado Springs, CO 80935-3530. TEL 719-475-7230.

CALIFORNIA LAW OF EMPLOYEE INJURIES AND WORKMEN'S COMPENSATION. see *LAW*

368 US
CALUNDERWRITER. m. California Association of Life Underwriters, 333 Hegenberger Rd., Ste. 211, Oakland, CA 94621-1453. TEL 510-638-2450. FAX 415-638-2474. Ed. Dan Crouch. circ. 12,376.

332 368 CN ISSN 0068-7383
CANADA. DEPARTMENT OF INSURANCE. REPORT. CO-OPERATIVE CREDIT ASSOCIATIONS. 1956. a. price varies. (Department of Insurance) Supply and Services Canada, Publishing Centre, Ottawa, Ont. K1A OS9, Canada. TEL 819-997-2560.

368 CN ISSN 0068-7405
HG8550
CANADA. DEPARTMENT OF INSURANCE. REPORT OF THE SUPERINTENDENT OF INSURANCE. (In 3 vols.) a. price varies. (Department of Insurance) Supply and Services Canada, Publishing Centre, Ottawa, Ont. K7A OS9, Canada. TEL 819-997-2560.

332 CN ISSN 0068-7413
CANADA. DEPARTMENT OF INSURANCE. REPORT. SMALL LOANS COMPANIES AND MONEY-LENDERS. a. price varies. (Department of Insurance) Supply and Services Canada, Publishing Centre, Ottawa, Ont. K1A OS9, Canada. TEL 819-997-2560.

332.1 368 CN ISSN 0068-7391
CANADA. DEPARTMENT OF INSURANCE. REPORT. TRUST AND LOAN COMPANIES. a. price varies. (Department of Insurance) Supply and Services Canada, Publishing Centre, Ottawa, Ont. K1A OS9, Canada. TEL 819-997-2560.

CANADIAN CASES ON THE LAW OF INSURANCE (2ND SERIES). see *LAW*

368 331.8 CN
CANADIAN EMPLOYMENT BENEFITS & PENSION GUIDE. m. Can.$600. C C H Canadian Ltd., 6 Garamond Ct., Don Mills, Ont. M3C 1Z5, Canada. TEL 416-441-2992. FAX 416-444-9011.
Formerly: Canadian Employment Benefits and Pension Guide Reports.
Description: Canada and Quebec pension plans and provincial legislation regulating private pension plans.

368 CN
CANADIAN FORESTER. (Text in English, French) 1895. a. Can.$10. Canadian Foresters Life Insurance Society, Box 850, Brantford, Ont. N3T 5S3, Canada. TEL 519-753-3461. circ. 16,000.

368.382 CN
CANADIAN HEALTH CARE MANAGEMENT. 1986. 12/yr. Can.$349. M P L Communications Inc., 700-133 Richmond St. W., Toronto, Ont. M5H 3M8, Canada. TEL 416-869-1177. FAX 416-869-0456. Eds. Sheila Brawn, Chris Garbutt. circ. 500. (looseleaf format)
Description: Provides current, need-to-know information for health care administrators, senior personnel.

368 CN ISSN 0008-3828
CANADIAN INDEPENDENT ADJUSTER. (Text in English and French) 1958. q. Can.$5. (Canadian Independent Adjusters' Conference) Journal Management, 216 Market Square, Newmarket, Ont. L3Y 4A8, Canada. Ed. Vernn Newton. adv.; bk.rev.; circ. 3,400 (controlled). (processed)

368 CN ISSN 0008-3879
HG8015
CANADIAN INSURANCE. 1905. m. (13/yr.). Can.$28 (foreign $42). Stone and Cox Ltd., 111 Peter St., Ste. 202, Toronto, Ont. M5V 2H1, Canada. TEL 416-599-0772. FAX 416-599-0867. Ed. M.F. Steeler. adv.; illus.; stat.; circ. 11,041. **Indexed:** ABI Inform., BPIA, Can.B.P.I.
Incorporates: Corporate Insurance in Canada (ISSN 0315-8098); Insurance Agent and Broker in Canada (ISSN 0020-4595)
Description: Industry magazine for the insurance industry, covers statistics, computerization, marine, reinsurance and office management.

368.014 CN
CANADIAN INSURANCE CLAIMS DIRECTORY. 1932. a. $35. University of Toronto Press, Directories Department, 10 Mary St., Ste. 700, Toronto, Ont. M4Y 2W8, Canada. TEL 416-978-8651. Ed. Kieran Simpson. adv.

368.91 CN ISSN 0068-9033
CANADIAN INSURANCE LAW BULLETIN SERVICE. 1929. m. Can.$175. Stone & Cox Ltd., 11 Peter St., Ste. 202, Toronto, Ont. M5V 2H1, Canada. TEL 416-599-0772. FAX 416-599-0867. Ed. Blair C.F. Fraser. circ. 800.
Description: Statute law and bulletin service covering the laws and regulations governing insurance enterprises in Canada and the provinces.

CANADIAN INSURANCE LAW REPORTER. see *LAW*

CANADIAN INSURANCE LAW REVIEW. see *LAW*

368 CN ISSN 0822-109X
KE1142
CANADIAN JOURNAL OF INSURANCE LAW. 1983. 6/yr. Can.$145. Butterworths Canada Ltd., 75 Clegg Rd., Markham, Ont. L6G 1A1, Canada. TEL 800-668-6481. FAX 416-479-2826. Ed. Lazer Sarna. (back issues avail.)
Description: Covers insurance, pensions and benefits; reviews recent laws and cases. For insurance professionals and legal practitioners.

368.3 CN ISSN 0706-5582
CANADIAN JOURNAL OF LIFE INSURANCE. 1978. 3/m. Can.$63. P.M.L.R. Publications, Box 365, Elmira, Ont. N3B 2Z7, Canada. TEL 519-669-2693. Ed. R Alastair Rickard. bk.rev. (also avail. in microfilm) **Indexed:** Can.B.P.I.

368 CN ISSN 0068-9157
CANADIAN LIFE AND HEALTH INSURANCE FACTS; an authoritative source of factual information about life and health insurance in Canada. (Editions in English, French) 1955. a. free. Canadian Life and Health Insurance Association Inc., Communications Department, 1 Queen St., E., Ste. 1700, Toronto, Ont. M5C 2X9, Canada. TEL 416-777-2221. FAX 416-777-1895. Ed. Alice Freeburn, Giuliano Tolusso. circ. 8,000. **Indexed:** CS Ind.
Formed by the 1985 merger of: Canadian Health Insurance Facts & Canadian Life Insurance Facts.

368 CN ISSN 0008-5251
CANADIAN UNDERWRITER. 1934. 13/yr. Can.$26.70($40) Southam Business Communications Inc., 1450 Don Mills Rd., Don Mills, Ont. M3B 2X7, Canada. TEL 416-445-6641. Ed. Lawrence Welsh. adv.; bk.rev.; charts; illus.; stat.; tr.lit.; index; circ. 7,500. **Indexed:** Can.B.P.I.
—BLDSC shelfmark: 3046.050000.
Description: Committed to the Canadian insurance industry.

368 UK ISSN 0262-7701
CAPTIVE INSURANCE COMPANY REVIEW. 1981. m. £195($350) R I R G Ltd., 4 Henrietta St., Covent Garden, London WC2E 8PS, England. TEL 071-836-0614. FAX 071-379-6335. Ed. C.F. Best. bk.rev.

CASE MANAGER. see *MEDICAL SCIENCES*

368 282 US
CATHOLIC AID NEWS. 1895. m. membership. Catholic Aid Association, 3499 N. Lexington Ave., St. Paul, MN 55126-8098. TEL 612-490-0170. FAX 612-490-0746. Ed. David E. Brown. circ. 35,000.
Description: News articles and announcements pertaining to the members and activities of this association.

2530 INSURANCE

CATHOLIC FORESTER. see *GENERAL INTEREST PERIODICALS — United States*

368   US
CATHOLIC KNIGHT MAGAZINE. 1909. q. membership. Catholic Knights Insurance Society, 1100 W. Wells St., Milwaukee, WI 53233. TEL 414-273-6266. FAX 414-223-3201. Ed. Dorothy Deer. circ. 57,000.
   Description: News, announcements, and features pertaining to the members and activities of this society.

368   US
CLAIMS. 1953. m. $36. 1001 4th Ave. Plaza, Ste. 3029, Seattle, WA 98154. TEL 206-624-6965. FAX 206-624-5021. Ed. Bill Thorness. adv.; bk.rev.; illus.; circ. 8,012.
   Formerly: Insurance Adjuster (ISSN 0020-4579)

THE CLAIMS FORUM. see *BUSINESS AND ECONOMICS — Labor And Industrial Relations*

368   SA
COLIMPEX INSURANCE BROKERS EXECUPAD. (Text in Afrikaans and English) a. Colimpex Africa (Pty.) Ltd., P.O. Box 5838, Johannesburg 2000, South Africa. adv.

368.01   US
COLLEGE OF INSURANCE. ACADEMIC BULLETIN. 1962. biennial. free. College of Insurance, 101 Murray St., New York, NY 10007. TEL 212-962-4111. FAX 212-964-3381. circ. 20,000.
   Formerly: College of Insurance. General Bulletin (ISSN 0069-5718)

COLOMBIA. MINISTERIO DE TRABAJO Y SEGURIDAD SOCIAL. MEMORIA AL CONGRESO NACIONAL. see *BUSINESS AND ECONOMICS — Labor And Industrial Relations*

COLOMBIA. SUPERINTENDENCIA BANCARIA. SEGUROS Y CAPITALIZACION. see *BUSINESS AND ECONOMICS*

368   US
▼**COLUMNS (MINNEAPOLIS).** 1990. fortn. free. Northwestern National Life Insurance Companies, Inc., 20 Washington Ave., S., Minneapolis, MN 55401. TEL 612-372-5628. FAX 612-342-3002. Ed. Ruth Weber. circ. 3,500. (back issues avail.)
   Description: Provides news of the companies' activities, and financial information.

368   CN   ISSN 0382-7046
COMMENTAIRE (DON MILLS)/COMMENT. 1967. bi-m. membership. Institut Canadien des Assureurs-Vie Agrees et des Conseillers Financiers Agrees - Canadian Institute of Chartered Life Underwriters and Chartered Financial Consultants, 41 Lesmill, Don Mills, Ont. M3B 2T3, Canada. TEL 416-444-5251. FAX 416-444-8031. Ed.Bd. circ. 5,000.
   Description: Examines financial planning.

COMPANY LAW INSTITUTE OF INDIA. REPORTS OF COMPANY CASES INCLUDING BANKING & INSURANCE. see *LAW — Corporate Law*

368   US
COMPARISON OF STATE UNEMPLOYMENT INSURANCE LAWS. 1938. s-a. $45. U.S. Department of Labor, Unemployment Insurance Service, Washington, DC 20210. TEL 202-535-0200. (Dist. by: U.S. Govt. Printing Office, Supt. of Documents, Washington, DC 20402) Ed. Diana Runner. circ. 3,000.

COMPENSATION & BENEFITS MANAGEMENT. see *BUSINESS AND ECONOMICS — Personnel Management*

368.32   US   ISSN 0010-5287
CONCORDIA TORCH. 1909. q. membership. Concordia Mutual Life Association, 3041 Woodcreek Dr., Downers Grove, IL 60515. TEL 312-971-8000. Ed. Lee Strouse. circ. 17,000.

368 340   US
CONNECTICUT INSURANCE LAW REVIEW. 1981. a. $15. Yules & Yules, Box 3597, Hartford, CT 06103. Ed. Robert B. Yules. index; circ. 2,000. (back issues avail.)

368   FR
CONSEILLER DES ASSURANCES ET DE LA FINANCE. 1879. m. 60 F. 129 bd. St. Michel, 75005 Paris, France. Ed. Rene Colin.

CONSTRUCTION RISK MANAGEMENT. see *BUILDING AND CONSTRUCTION*

CONSUMERS FOR HEALTH CARE REFORM NEWSLETTER. see *CONSUMER EDUCATION AND PROTECTION*

368   US   ISSN 0010-7697
CONTINENTAL BULLETIN. 1903. 4/yr. free. Continental Corp., Corporate Communications, 180 Maiden Lane, New York, NY 10038. TEL 212-440-7735. FAX 212-440-3263. Ed. Abbe Bates. illus.; circ. 23,000.

368   US
CONTINGENCIES. 1989. bi-m. $24. American Academy of Actuaries, 1720 I St., N.W., Washington, DC 20006. TEL 202-223-8196. FAX 202-872-1948. Ed. Janice Radak. circ. 22,000 (controlled).
   Description: Reports on and analyzes actuarial trends and the insurance business.

368 366   US   ISSN 0364-1066
RA626
CORRESPONDENT (APPLETON). 1904. q. membership. Aid Association for Lutherans, 4321 N. Ballard Rd., Appleton, WI 54919. TEL 414-734-5721. FAX 414-730-3757. Ed. Cindy S. Zirbel. circ. 920,000.

368   UK   ISSN 0084-9405
COVER; a magazine for insurance brokers & agents. 1948. s-a. free. Provincial Insurance plc, Stramongate, Kendal, Cumbria LA9 4BE, England. Ed. John Shiels. bk.rev.; illus.; circ. 20,000.

368   AT
COVER NOTE. 1975. w. Aus.$350 (effective Jan. 1991). Newsletter Information Services, P.O.Box 693, Manly, Sydney, N.S.W. 2095, Australia. FAX 02-977-3310. Ed. Anna Lockwood. adv.; bk.rev.; circ. 550. (back issues avail.)

368   US
CRITTENDEN EXCESS & SURPLUS INSIDER. w. Crittenden Publishing, Inc., Box 1150, Novato, CA 94948-1150. TEL 415-382-2458. FAX 415-382-2476. Ed. James Church. circ. 10,000.

368   US
CRITTENDEN INSURANCE MARKETS NEWSLETTER. w. Crittenden Publishing, Inc., Box 1150, Novato, CA 94948-1150. TEL 415-382-2440. FAX 415-382-2416. Ed. Colleen Pestana.

368   SZ   ISSN 0379-0290
CURRENT RESEARCH IN SOCIAL SECURITY/RECHERCHES EN SECURITE SOCIALE/FORSCHUNG IN DER SOZIALEN SICHERHEIT/INVESTIGACIONES EN LA SEGURIDAD SOCIAL. (Text in English, French, German and Spanish) 1978. s-a. free. International Social Security Association, Box 1, 1211 Geneva 22, Switzerland. circ. 1,500. **Indexed:** Abstr.Hyg., HR Rep.
   —BLDSC shelfmark: 3501.994000.
   Description: Summaries of projects undertaken by social security institutions, government departments, research institutes and universities, includes results of research and addresses of those in charge of research projects.

CYPRUS. MINISTRY OF LABOUR AND SOCIAL INSURANCE. ANNUAL REPORT. see *BUSINESS AND ECONOMICS — Labor And Industrial Relations*

D O K: POLITIK - PRAXIS RECHT. see *LAW*

368   DK   ISSN 0106-2735
DANSK FORSIKRINGS AARBOG. 1900. a. DKK 240. Forlaget Forsikring, Amaliegade 10, DK-1256 Copenhagen K, Denmark. Ed. Joergen Nielsensen. circ. 1,400.

368   US
DATA BASE REPORTS. m. $75. Insurance Information Institute, 110 William St., New York, NY 10038. TEL 212-699-9200. FAX 212-732-1916.
   ●Also available online. Vendor(s): Mead Data Central.
   Formerly: Data Base Plus.

368   DK
HG8655
DENMARK. FINANSTILSYNET. BERETNING. BILAG 1: PENGEINSTITUTTERM.V.. (Supplement to: Denmark. Finanstilsynet. Beretning (ISSN 0905-0965)) (Text in Danish, English and French) 1989. a. DKK 210 for main vol. with 5 suppls. Finanstilsynet, Gl. Kongevej 74A, DK-1850 Frederiksberg C, Denmark. (Dist. by: Danske Boghendleres Kommissionsanstalt, Siljangade 6, 2300 Copenhagen S, Denmark) circ. 1,500.

368.8   II   ISSN 0304-6966
HG1662.I4
DEPOSIT INSURANCE CORPORATION. ANNUAL REPORT: DIRECTORS' REPORT, BALANCE SHEET AND ACCOUNTS. (Text in English) 1962. a. Deposit Insurance & Credit Guarantee Corp., New India Centre, 17 Cooperage Rd., Bombay 400039, India. TEL 202-02-99. circ. 4,000.

368   GW   ISSN 0012-0200
DEUTSCHE GESELLSCHAFT FUER VERSICHERUNGSMATHEMATIK. BLAETTER. 1950. s-a. DM.45($5) Deutsche Gesellschaft fuer Versicherungsmathematik, Gothaer Platz 8, 3400 Goettingen, Germany. TEL 0551-7012021. Ed. E. Neuburger. bk.rev.; abstr.; charts; circ. 1,000.
   —BLDSC shelfmark: 2109.100000.

368   GW   ISSN 0070-4237
DIE DEUTSCHE LEBENSVERSICHERUNG. JAHRBUCH. a. free. Verband der Lebensversicherungs Unternehmen e.V., Eduard-Pflueger-Str. 55, 5300 Bonn 1, Germany. TEL 0228-5300841. FAX 0228-53-00-820. (Subscr. to: Verlag Versicherungswirtschaft e.V., Klosestr. 22, 7500 Karlsruhe 1, Germany) Ed. Michael Glueck. circ. 22,000. (back issues avail.)

368.4   GW   ISSN 0012-0618
DEUTSCHE RENTENVERSICHERUNG. 1929. m. DM.192. (Verband Deutscher Rentenversicherungstraeger) Wirtschaftsdienst Gesellschaft fuer Medien & Kommunikation MbH & Co. OHG, Lange Str. 13, 6000 Frankfurt 1, Germany. Ed. R. Kolb. adv.; bk.rev.; charts; illus.; index; circ. 3,350. **Indexed:** World Bibl.Soc.Sec.
   —BLDSC shelfmark: 3573.400000.

368   US   ISSN 0070-5691
DIRECTORY OF INSURANCE COMPANIES LICENSED IN NEW YORK STATE. a. $1 per no. (single copies free to NY residents). Insurance Department, Publications Unit, Empire State Plaza, Agency Bldg. No. 1, Albany, NY 12257. circ. 5,000.

DIRITTO E PRATICA NELL'ASSICURAZIONE. see *LAW*

368.012   US   ISSN 0742-5619
HG9336
DISABILITY INCOME AND HEALTH INSURANCE; time saver. a. $25.95. National Underwriter Co., 505 Gest St., Cincinnati, OH 45203. TEL 513-721-2140. FAX 513-721-0126. Ed. Price Gaines. stat.

368.4   SZ   ISSN 0250-6041
DOCUMENTACION DE LA SEGURIDAD SOCIAL AMERICANA. (Text in Spanish) 1980. a. 15 Fr. per no. International Social Security Association, Publications, Case Postale 1, CH-1211 Geneva 22, Switzerland. Ed.Bd.
   Description: Includes regional reports, round tables and other meetings' proceedings on Social Security.

346.71   CN   ISSN 0706-8964
DUNHILL LIABILITY LOSS REPORT. 1977. m. Can.$115. Dunhill Publishing Company, 6389 Coburg Rd., Halifax, N.S. B3H 2A5, Canada.

346.71   CN
DUNHILL PERSONAL INJURY & DEATH REPORTS. 1976. m. Can.$115. Dunhill Publishing Company, 6389 Coburg Rd., Halifax, N.S. B3H 2A5, Canada.
   Former titles: Dunhill Personal Injury Awards Annotator; Dunhill Insurance Law Report (ISSN 0706-8956)

E B R I ISSUE BRIEF. (Employee Benefit Research Institute) see *BUSINESS AND ECONOMICS — Personnel Management*

INSURANCE 2531

368 UK
EAST EUROPEAN INSURANCE REPORT. m. £342($572) Financial Times Business Information Ltd., Tower House, Southampton St., London WC2E 7HA, England. TEL 071-240-9391.
   Description: International service for East Europe's insurance and reinsurance management.

368 US ISSN 0740-9087
EMPLOYERS' HEALTH COSTS SAVINGS LETTER. 1983. m. $157. American Business Publishing, 3100 Hwy. 138, Box 1442, Wall Township, NJ 07719-1442. TEL 908-681-1133. FAX 908-681-0490. Ed. Robert K. Jenkins. index. (back issues avail.)
   Description: For business and industry vice presidents, personnel, fringe benefit managers and other executives. Provides current information on how to save money in health care costs.

368 CN
HD7096.C2
EMPLOYMENT AND IMMIGRATION CANADA. ANNUAL REPORT/EMPLOI ET IMMIGRATION CANADA. RAPPORT ANNUEL. (Text in English and French) 1978. a. free. Public Enquiries Centre, Public Affairs Division, Employment and Immigration, Ottawa, Ont. K1A 0J9, Canada. charts; stat.; circ. 10,000.
   Incorporates: Employment and Immigration Commission. Annual Report; Unemployment Insurance Canada. Annual Report (ISSN 0576-4157)

EMPLOYMENT SERVICE AND UNEMPLOYMENT INSURANCE OPERATIONS; a monthly summary. see *OCCUPATIONS AND CAREERS*

EN MARCHE; journal bimensuel d'information pour les beneficiaires des soins de sante. see *PHYSICAL FITNESS AND HYGIENE*

368 657 US
ENROLLED ACTUARIES REPORT. 1976. q. membership. American Academy of Actuaries, 1720 I St., N.W., 7th Fl., Washington, DC 20006. TEL 202-223-8196. FAX 202-872-1948. Ed. Jeanne Casey. circ. 5,000. (back issues avail.)
   Description: Newsletter for pension actuaries on pension and employee benefit topics.

368 US
ENTERPRISE (NEW YORK). 1956. fortn. free to qualified personnel. Equitable Life Assurance Society of the U.S., Corporate Communications Department, Internal Communications Division, 787 Seventh Ave., Area 37K, New York, NY 10019. TEL 212-554-4738. Ed. James Lacey. charts; illus.; circ. 22,000.
   Formerly: Equinews (ISSN 0013-984X)

340 US
▼**ENVIRONMENTAL INSURANCE COVERAGE;** state law and regulation. 1991. base vol. (plus a. suppl.). $125. Butterworth Legal Publishers (Salem) (Subsidiary of: Reed International PLC), 90 Stiles Rd., Salem, NH 03079. TEL 800-548-4001. FAX 603-898-9858. Ed. Mitchell L. Lathrop. (looseleaf format)
   Description: Overview of judicial decisions involving insurance coverage arising from environmental and toxic tort claims.

368.4 SZ ISSN 0379-0266
ESTUDIOS DE LA SEGURIDAD SOCIAL. (Text in Spanish) irreg. price varies. International Social Security Association, Publications, Case Postale 1, CH-1211 Geneva 22, Switzerland. (Orders to: Oficina para las Americas de la A I S S, Zuviria 20, Temperley 1834, Buenos Aires, Argentina) (Co-sponsors: Secretariat of State for Social Security of Argentina; Family Allowances Fund for Industrial Personnel, Dockers and Commercial Employees) Ed.Bd.

368.012 US ISSN 0740-1388
EXCESS EXPRESS. 1979. m. $487. Merritt Company, 1661 Ninth St., Box 955, Santa Monica, CA 90406. TEL 213-450-7234. FAX 213-396-4563. Ed. W. Feldhaus. circ. 1,155. (looseleaf format)
   Description: Information on excess and surplus insurance, specialty insurance and unique insurance coverages.

368 UK
EXECUTIVES' AND DIRECTORS' PENSIONS (YEAR). 1976. irreg. Financial Times Business Information, 102 Clerkenwell Rd., London EC1M 5SA, England. circ. 4,500. (tabloid format)
   Formerly: Executive Pensions.

EXPATRIATE. see *BUSINESS AND ECONOMICS — Labor And Industrial Relations*

EXPATXTRA!. see *BUSINESS AND ECONOMICS — Banking And Finance*

368 SZ ISSN 0014-4932
EXPERIODICA. Includes: Sigma (ISSN 0037-4857) (Editions in English, French, German, Spanish) 1960. 8-10/yr. free. Schweizerische Rueckversicherungs-Gesellschaft - Swiss Reinsurance Company, Economic Department, Mythenquai 50-60, Zurich, Switzerland. TEL 01-208-2121. FAX 1-208-2999. TELEX 815722 SRE CH. abstr.
   Description: Topical news items pertaining to the international insurance press.

368 CN ISSN 0839-1041
EXPERTS. (Text in English, French) 1987. 6/yr. $24. Publications Mar-Lu, 10790 Hamel, Montreal, Que. H2C 2X8, Canada. TEL 514-385-9000. FAX 514-385-9002. Ed. Marcellin Lupien. adv.; circ. 5,000.

368 NO
F F-AVISEN. bi-m. Forsikringsfunksjonaerenes Landsforbund, Bygdoe Alle 19, Oslo 2, Norway. adv.; circ. 4,800.

368.08 UK ISSN 0071-3686
FACULTY OF ACTUARIES IN SCOTLAND. TRANSACTIONS. 1901. irreg. (approx. 2/yr.) £9 per issue to non-members. Faculty of Actuaries, 23 St. Andrew Sq., Edinburgh EH2 1AQ, Scotland. TEL 031-655-6000. FAX 031-662-4053. Ed. Leslie J.G. Purdie. bk.rev.; index; circ. 1,100.
   Description: Publishes actuarial papers and discussions from the Faculty's sessional meetings.

368 US
FEDERAL & STATE INSURANCE WEEK. w. $327. J R Publishing, Box 6654, McLean, VA 22106. TEL 703-532-2235.

FEDERAL BENEFITS FOR VETERANS AND DEPENDENTS, IS-1 FACT SHEET. see *MILITARY*

368.8 332.2 US
FEDERAL HOME LOAN BANK SYSTEM. LIST OF MEMBER INSTITUTIONS.* 1962. a. U.S. Federal Home Loan Bank Board, Box 37248, Washington, DC 20013. TEL 202-377-6000. Ed. John Ghizzoni. circ. 500. Key Title: List of Member Institutions - Federal Saving and Loan Insurance Corporation.
   Formerly: Federal Savings and Loan Insurance Corporation. List of Member Institutions (ISSN 0428-1365)

FEDERAL RESERVE BANK OF CLEVELAND. WORKING PAPER. see *BUSINESS AND ECONOMICS — Banking And Finance*

FEDERAL TAXATION OF INSURANCE COMPANIES. see *BUSINESS AND ECONOMICS — Public Finance, Taxation*

368.4 NE ISSN 0071-4151
HC321
FEDERATIE VAN BEDRIJFSVERENIGINGEN. JAARVERSLAG. 1930. a. free. Federatie van Bedrijfsverenigingen, Postbus 8300, 1005 C A Amsterdam, Netherlands. TEL 020-879111. circ. 400.
   Description: Covers unemployment law, insurance, union dues, salaries, work environment, legal protection, scientific research, international affairs, financial situation and more.

FEDERATION OF INSURANCE AND CORPORATE COUNSEL QUARTERLY. see *LAW*

368 MG
FEON'NY MAMA. m. B.P. 185, 101 Antananarivo, Malagasy Republic. TEL 25433. Ed. Richard Ramanandraibe. circ. 2,000.

368 FR
FEUX ET FLAMMES. 1927. q. 20 rue de Madrid, 75008 Paris, France. Ed. L.M. Balcet.

FIDELITY AND SURETY NEWS. see *LAW*

368 US
FIELD GUIDE TO ESTATE PLANNING, BUSINESS PLANNING & EMPLOYEE BENEFITS. 1989. a. $23.95. National Underwriter Co., 505 Gest St., Cincinnati, OH 45203. TEL 513-721-2140. FAX 513-721-0126.
   Description: Practical guide to the uses of life insurance in estate planning, business planning, and employee benefits.

368 US ISSN 0423-4596
FINANCIAL ESTATE PLANNERS QUARTERLY. 1956. q. $175 for 2 vol. set. Dearborn - R & R Newkirk, 520 N. Dearborn, Chicago, IL 60610-4901. TEL 312-836-4400. Ed. Georgia Mann. index; circ. 1,000. (looseleaf format; back issues avail.)
   Formerly: Estate Planners Quarterly.

368 US
FINANCIAL REVIEW OF ALIEN INSURERS. a. $275. National Association of Insurance Commissioners, 120 W. 12th St., Kansas City, MO 64105. TEL 816-842-3600. (Subscr. to: N A I C Publications, Box 263 Department 42, Kansas City, MO 64193-0042)
   Description: Provides current financial and corporate data for alien insurance companies.

368 UK ISSN 0309-751X
FINANCIAL TIMES INTERNATIONAL YEAR BOOKS: WORLD INSURANCE. a. £105. Longman Group UK Ltd., Westgate House, The High, Harlow, Essex CM20 1YR, England. TEL 0279-442601.

368 CN
FINANCIAL TIMES OF CANADA. R R S PS (YEAR). 1983. a. Can.$14.95. Financial Times of Canada, 440 Front St. W., Toronto, Ont. M5V 3E6, Canada. TEL 416-585-5000. FAX 416-585-5547.
   Formerly: Financial Times of Canada. Guide to R R S Ps.

368 CN
FINK AND BORSTEIN WORKERS' COMPENSATION NEWSLETTER. 4/yr. Can.$75. Fink and Bornstein, Barristers & Solicitors, 720 Spadina Ave., Ste. 507, Toronto, Ont. M5S 2T9, Canada. TEL 416-926-0400. FAX 416-926-0072.

368.38 610 FI ISSN 0355-4813
FINLAND. KANSANELAKELAITOS. JULKAISUJA. SARJA AL. (Text in English and Finnish; summaries in English) 1975. irreg., no. AL32, 1990. Kansanelakelaitos - Social Insurance Institution of Finland, Research Institute for Social Security, P.O. Box 78, SF-00381 Helsinki 38, Finland.

368.38 610 FI ISSN 0355-4856
FINLAND. KANSANELAKELAITOS. JULKAISUJA. SARJA EL. (Text in English and Finnish; summaries in English) 1973. irreg., no. EL84, 1992. Kansanelakelaitos - Social Insurance Institution of Finland, Research Institute for Social Security, P.O. Box 78, SF-00381 Helsinki 38, Finland.

368.38 610 FI ISSN 0355-483X
FINLAND. KANSANELAKELAITOS. JULKAISUJA. SARJA ML. (Text in Finnish and English; summaries in English) 1973. irreg., no.ML111, 1991. Kansanelakelaitos - Social Insurance Institution of Finland, Research Institute for Social Security, P.O. Box 78, SF-00381 Helsinki 38, Finland.

368.1 FI ISSN 0355-5003
FINLAND KANSANELAKELAITOS. TOIMINTAKERTOMUS. English edition: Finland. Social Insurance Institution. Annual Report. Swedish edition: Finland. Folkpensionsanstalten. Beraettelse. 1938. a. Social Insurance Institution, Information Division, P.O. Box 450, SF-00101 Helsinki 10, Finland. FAX 90-412-358. circ. 18,000.

368 US
FIRE, CASUALTY & SURETY BULLETIN. 5 base vols. (plus m. updates). $267.50. National Underwriter Co., 505 Gest St., Cincinnati, OH 45203. TEL 513-721-2140. FAX 513-721-0126.
   Description: Provides current information on all aspects of property and casualty insurance.

368.11
FIRE MARK CIRCLE OF THE AMERICAS JOURNAL. 1985. a. $30 membership. Fire Mark Circle of the Americas, 2859 Marlin Dr., Chamblee, GA 30341-5119. TEL 404-451-2651. Ed. Edward R. Tufts. circ. 350. (tabloid format; back issues avail.)

INSURANCE

368.11 US
FIRE MARK CIRCLE OF THE AMERICAS NEWSLETTER. q. Fire Mark Circle of the Americas, 2859 Marlin Dr., Chamblee, GA 30341. TEL 404-451-2651.

FLOOD REPORT. see *EARTH SCIENCES — Hydrology*

368 US
FLORIDA UNDERWRITER. 1984. m. $16.50. National Underwriter Co., 505 Gest St., Cincinnati, OH 45203. TEL 513-721-2140. FAX 513-721-0126. Ed. James Seymour. adv.; circ. 10,000. (reprint service avail.)
Description: Covers the insurance industry in Florida, including regulatory and legislative decisions and trends.

368 US
FOCUS (AUSTIN). 1956. q. membership only. Professional Insurance Agents of Texas, Box 3175, Austin, TX 78764. TEL 512-462-9222. FAX 512-462-1314. Ed. Becky Sloan. adv.; circ. 3,000.
Description: Covers news and issues of interest to independent insurance agents in Texas.

368 SW ISSN 0015-7880
HG8015
FOERSAAKRINGSTIDNINGEN. 1946. 11/yr. SEK 385. Foersaakringsbranschens Serviceaktiebolag, 11587 Stockholm, Sweden. FAX 08-7836739. Ed. Rune Lundberg. adv.; bk.rev.; illus.; circ. 5,400.

368 SW ISSN 0345-3901
FOERSAEKRINGS VAERLDEN. 1945. m. (10/yr). SEK 150. Foersaekringsjaenstemannafoerbundet, Box 45166, 104 30 Stockholm, Sweden. TEL 08-247455. FAX 08-102271. Ed. Peter Hennix. adv.; circ. 20,294. (also avail. in microfiche)

368 SW
FOERSAEKRINGSANSTAELLD. m. (11/yr.). Foersaekringsanstaelldas Foerbund, Vasagatan 44, Box 1119, 111 81 Stockholm, Sweden. adv.; circ. 23,150.

368 FI ISSN 0355-7308
FOERSAEKRINGSTIDNING. (Text in Swedish) 1935. 4/yr. FIM 277 in the Nordic countries; elsewhere FIM 346. Vakuutussanomia Oy, Bulevardi 28, 00120 Helsinki 12, Finland. TEL 358-0-680-401. FAX 358-0-640-469. Ed. Reijo Ollikainen. adv.; circ. 1,300.

368 CN
FOREFRONT. 1976. m. free. Sun Life Assurance Company of Canada, Marketing Services, 200 University Ave., Toronto, Ont. M5H 3C7, Canada. TEL 416-595-8422. FAX 416-595-8001. Ed. Elizabeth Chong. circ. 5,000.
Former titles (until 1984): Sunbeat; Sun Life Assurance Company of Canada. Field News.

368 CN ISSN 0384-5958
FORESIGHT. French edition: Regards (ISSN 0384-594X) 1923. bi-m. Can.$25. Insurance Brokers Association of the Province of Quebec, 300 Leo-Pariseau St., Montreal, Que. H2W 2N1, Canada. TEL 514-842-2591. FAX 514-842-3138. Ed. Sophie B. Brzozowska. adv.; bk.rev.; illus.; circ. 6,500. Indexed: Can.Per.Ind.
Formerly: Insurance Broker (ISSN 0020-4617)

368 DK ISSN 0105-4260
FORSIKRING. 1969. fortn. (except July). DKK 430. Forlaget Forsikring, Amaliegade 10, DK-1256 Copenhagen K, Denmark. TEL 45-33-13 75 55. FAX 45-33-33-02-71. Ed. Joergen Nielsen. adv.; bk.rev.; bibl.; charts; illus.; stat.; index; circ. 3,300 (controlled).
Formerly: Dansk Forsikrings Tidende - Assurandoeren (ISSN 0300-4732)

368 NO ISSN 0015-7929
FORSIKRINGSTIDENDE. 1897. 10/yr. NOK 340. Forsikringslitteratur, Box 2473, Solli, 0202 Oslo 2, Norway. Ed. Egil Tannaes. adv.; bk.rev.; charts; illus.; circ. 3,785.

368 US ISSN 0013-6743
FORUM (SYRACUSE). 1927. m. $24. Independent Insurance Agents Association of New York State, Inc., Box 9001, Mt. Vernon, NY 10552. TEL 914-699-2020. FAX 914-664-1503. Stephen H. Acunto. adv.; bk.rev.; illus.; circ. 3,000 (controlled). (back issues avail.)
Formerly: Empire State Agency Forum.

346 368 FR
FRANCE. MINISTERE DE L'ECONOMIE ET DES FINANCES. BULLETIN ADMINISTRATIF DES ASSURANCES. q. 15 F. Ministere de l'Economie et des Finances, Imprimerie Nationale, 2 Rue Paul Hervieu, Paris 15, France.

FRAT. see *HANDICAPPED — Hearing Impaired*

368 US ISSN 0016-0105
FRATERNAL MONITOR. 1890. m. $23. Dearborn - R & R Newkirk, 520 N. Dearborn, Chicago, IL 60610-4901. TEL 312-836-4400. Ed. James A. Ballew. adv.; illus.; circ. 5,000.

368 US ISSN 0016-1233
FRIDAY FLASH. 1940. fortn. $125 to non-members. National Association of Insurance Brokers, Inc., 1401 New York Ave., N.W., No. 720, Washington, DC 20005. TEL 202-628-6700. Ed. Ann O. Riser. stat.; circ. controlled.

FRIENDLY EXCHANGE. see *GENERAL INTEREST PERIODICALS — United States*

368 US ISSN 0016-1748
FROM THE STATE CAPITALS. INSURANCE REGULATION. 1946. w. $215 (foreign $235)(effective Dec. 1990). Wakeman-Walworth, Inc., 300 N. Washington St., Alexandria, VA 22314. TEL 703-549-8606. FAX 703-549-1372. (processed)
●Also available online. Vendor(s): WESTLAW.
Description: Regulation of policy, rates and benefits for all types of insurance - life, health, automobile, homeowner, malpractice. Covers self-insurance and innovations such as life style considerations.

368 AU ISSN 0016-2728
FUNDAMENT; das erste allgemeine Generali-Magazin. 1951. 6/yr. membership. Erste Allgemeine Versicherungs-AG, Generali Allgemeine Lebensversicherung AG, Landskrongasse 1-3, A-1011 Vienna, Austria. FAX 53401-593. (Co-sponsor: Generali Rueckversicherung AG) Ed. Beate Manndorff. bk.rev.; circ. 8,000.

368 US
G A M A NEWS JOURNAL. 1983. bi-m. $20. General Agents and Managers Association, 1922 F St., N.W., Washington, DC 20006-4389. TEL 202-331-6088. FAX 202-785-5712. adv.; circ. 9,157.
Description: Provides information on the art and science of agency management.

368 914.306 US
G B U REPORTER. 1893. bi-m. free. Greater Beneficial Union of Pittsburgh, 4254 Clairton Blvd., Pittsburgh, PA 15227-3394. TEL 412-884-5100. FAX 412-884-9815. Ed. Frederick W. Schwesinger. circ. 10,300. (also avail. in microfiche)
Formerly (until 1958): Union Reporter.
Description: Contains news of members of the society and of insurance products available to them.

G D S - ZEITUNG. (Gewerkschaft Der Sozialversicherung) see *LABOR UNIONS*

368 US
G E I C O DIRECT. 1986. q. (Government Employees Insurance Company) Maxwell Custom Publishing, 1999 Shepard Rd., St. Paul, MN 55666. TEL 612-690-7200. FAX 612-690-7357. Ed. Sharon Ross. circ. controlled.

368 SP
G E S. BOLETIN DE INFORMACION. Running title: General Espanola de Seguros. Boletin de Informacion. 1940. q. free. General Espanola de Seguros, S.A., Plaza de las Cortes, 2, Madrid 28014, Spain. charts; illus.; stat.; circ. 1,500 (controlled).

368 AG
GALICIA Y RIO DE LA PLATA. COMPANIA DE SEGUROS. MEMORIA Y BALANCE GENERAL. 1974. a. Compania de Seguros, Rivadavia 717, Buenos Aires, Argentina. stat.

368 US ISSN 0016-6545
GENERAL INSURANCE GUIDE. (In 3 vols.) 1936. q. $110 1st yr.; thereafter $52; foreign $65. Werbel Publishing Co., Inc., 20 Oser Ave., Hauppauge, NY 11788-3813. Ed. Harold Luckstone, Jr. circ. 3,500. (looseleaf format)

368 NE ISSN 0926-4957
GENEVA PAPERS ON RISK AND INSURANCE THEORY. 1975. 6/yr. fl.147($75) (effective 1992). (Geneva Association) Kluwer Academic Publishers, P.O. Box 17, 3300 AA Dordrecht, Netherlands. TEL 078-334911. FAX 078-334254. (Dist. by: Kluwer Academic Publishers Group, P.O. Box 322, 3300 AH Dordrecht, Netherlands. TEL 078-524400; Dist. in U.S. and Canada by: Kluwer Academic Publishers Boston, Box 358, Accord Sta., Hingham, MA 02018-0358. TEL 617-871-6600) Eds. Henri Louberg, Harris Schlesinger.
Formerly (until 1992): Geneva Papers on Risk and Insurance (ISSN 0252-1148)
Description: Publishes theoretical, empirical and experimental articles on the economics of risk and insurance.
Refereed Serial

368 GW ISSN 0302-5608
GERMANY (FEDERAL REPUBLIC, 1949-). BUNDESAUFSICHTSAMT FUER DAS VERSICHERUNGSWESEN. GESCHAEFTSBERICHT. 1953. a. DM.80. Bundesaufsichtsamt fuer das Versicherungswesen, Ludwigkirchplatz 3-4, Postfach 180, 1000 Berlin 15, Germany. TEL 030-88930. FAX 030-8893494. bk.rev.; stat.; index; circ. 1,700.

368 GW ISSN 0170-236X
GERMANY (FEDERAL REPUBLIC, 1949-) BUNDESAUFSICHTSAMT FUER DAS VERSICHERUNGSWESEN. VEROEFFENTLICHUNGEN. m. DM.72. Bundesaufsichtsamt fuer das Versicherungswesen, Ludwigkirchplatz 3-4, Postfach 180, D-1000 Berlin 15, Germany. TEL 030-88930. FAX 030-8893494. circ. 2,400.

368 IT
GIORNALE DELLE ASSICURAZIONI - ESPANSION; mensile di finanza e assicurazioni. 1981. m. L.81000 (foreign L.82200). Arnoldo Mondadori Editore S.p.A., Casella Postale 1833, 20101 Milan, Italy. Ed. Redento Mori. circ. 8,144.

368.32 355.15 US
GOVERNMENT LIFE INSURANCE PROGRAMS FOR VETERANS AND MEMBERS OF THE SERVICES. ANNUAL REPORT. a. U.S. Veterans Administration, Department of Veterans Benefits, Washington, DC 20420.

368 355 US
GOVERNMENTAL RISK MANAGEMENT MANUAL. 1976. bi-m. $125 (renewal $90). Risk Management Publishing Co., 2030 E. Broadway, Ste. 106, Tucson, AZ 85719. TEL 602-622-5174. FAX 602-792-2814. Ed. Sabina Dunton. cum.index: 1976-1989; circ. 1,000. (looseleaf format; back issues avail.)

368 US
GOVERNORS' JOURNAL. 1971. s-a. free. International Insurance Society, Inc., Tuscaloosa, AL 35487. TEL 205-348-8974. FAX 205-348-8973. Ed. Mary B. Silberberg. circ. 2,000.

368 UK ISSN 0308-499X
GREAT BRITAIN. DEPARTMENT OF TRADE. INSURANCE BUSINESS: ANNUAL REPORT. a. H.M.S.O., P.O.Box 276, London SW8 5DT, England. (Co-sponsor: Department of Trade) stat. (reprint service avail. from UMI)
—BLDSC shelfmark: 4531.691600.
Supersedes: Great Britain. Board of Trade. Insurance Business: Annual Report (ISSN 0072-5684)

368.382 US ISSN 1050-9038
H M O MAGAZINE. (Health Maintenance Organization) 1959. 6/yr. $75 (effective Jan. 1989). Group Health Association of America, Inc., 1129 Twentieth St., N.W., Ste. 600, Washington, DC 20036. TEL 202-778-3247. FAX 202-331-7487. Ed. Lisa Lopez. bk.rev.; circ. 5,000. Indexed: Med.Care Rev.
Former titles (until vol.31, no.2, 1990): G H A A News (ISSN 0887-9087); (until Dec. 1986): Group Health News (ISSN 0164-0542); (until Dec. 1975): Group Health and Welfare News (ISSN 0017-470X)
Description: Provides analysis and news on HMO market trends and legislative and regulatory issues. Includes ideas on management information systems, pharmacy benefits, and health care finances.

INSURANCE

368.382   IS
HADASHOT KUPOT HOLIM. m. (General Labor Federation of Israel) Kupot Holim, 101 Arlozorof St., Tel Aviv 62 098, Israel. TEL 03-433340. Ed. David Tagar.

368   US   ISSN 0017-7482
HANOVER NEWS. vol.9, 1970. q. free to qualified personnel. Hanover Insurance Co., 100 N. Parkway, Worcester, MA 01605. TEL 617-852-1000. Ed. Robert K. Newman. adv.; illus.; stat.; circ. 2,500.

368   US   ISSN 0017-7962
THE HARTFORD AGENT. 1909. 4/yr. (plus bulletins as needed). free to qualified personnel. I T T Hartford Insurance Group, Hartford Plaza, Hartford, CT 06115. TEL 203-547-4976. FAX 203-547-3799. Ed. Susan R.A. Honeyman. charts; illus.; circ. 30,000 (controlled).
    Description: Provides current information about Hartford and its products, and insurance issues in general for agents and Hartford employees.

368   US   ISSN 0073-1110
HAWAII. INSURANCE DIVISION. REPORT OF THE INSURANCE COMMISSIONER OF HAWAII. 1903. a. free. Department of Commerce and Consumer Affairs, Insurance Division, Box 3614, Honolulu, HI 96811. TEL 808-586-2790. circ. 1,000.

HAZARDOUS WASTE AND TOXIC TORTS LAW AND STRATEGY. see *LAW*

HEALTH AFFAIRS; the journal of the health policy sphere. see *PUBLIC HEALTH AND SAFETY*

HEALTH CARE FINANCING ADMINISTRATION MANUALS. see *HOSPITALS*

368.382   US
HEALTH CARE FINANCING NOTES. irreg. free. Health Care Financing Administration, Office of Research and Demonstrations, Oak Meadows Bldg., Rm. 2230, 6325 Security Blvd., Baltimore, MD 21207. TEL 301-966-6584. (Subscr. to: Supt. of Documents, Washington, DC 20402. TEL 202-783-3238)
    Description: Presents data highlights or selected summary information on various aspects of the Medicare and Medicaid programs.

368.3   US   ISSN 0017-9019
HG9371
HEALTH INSURANCE UNDERWRITER. 1951. m. (except July-Aug. combined). $40 to non-members; members $18. National Association of Health Underwriters, 1000 Connecticut Ave., N.W., Ste. 1111, Washington, DC 20036. TEL 202-223-5533. FAX 202-785-2274. Ed. Paul E. Van Heuklom. adv.; illus.; circ. 10,300.
    Description: Provides information, instruction, facts and opinions of interest to individuals and corporations selling health and disability insurance products.

HIGHLIGHTS OF STATE UNEMPLOYMENT COMPENSATIONS LAWS. see *LAW — Legal Aid*

368   US
HINE'S DIRECTORY OF INSURANCE ADJUSTERS. 1936. a. $25. Hine's Legal Directory, Inc., Box 280, Glen Ellyn, IL 60138. TEL 708-462-9670. Ed. James R. Collins. circ. 7,000 (controlled).

HINE'S INSURANCE COUNSEL. see *LAW*

368 340 330   GW
HINWEIS. 1959. q. Muenchener Lebensversicherung Aktiengesellschaft, Leopold Str. 6, D-8000 Munich 40, Germany. Ed. Ekkehard Renz. charts; illus.; stat.; circ. 2,000. (back issues avail.)

368   GW   ISSN 0073-3350
HOPPENSTEDT VERSICHERUNGS-JAHRBUCH. 1958. a. DM.536. Verlag Hoppenstedt und Co., Havelstr. 9, Postfach 4006, 6100 Darmstadt, Germany. TEL 06151-380-0. FAX 06151-380-360. adv.

368   US
HUEBNER FOUNDATION MONOGRAPH. 1972. irreg. price varies. University of Pennsylvania, Wharton School, S.S. Huebner Foundation for Insurance, 430 Vance Hall, Philadelphia, PA 19104-6301. TEL 215-898-9631. FAX 215-898-0310. (Dist. by: Boyertown Publishing, Boyertown, PA 195512) Ed. J. David Cummins. circ. 1,000. Indexed: J.of Econ.Lit.
    Description: Presents scholarly research studies in risk and insurance.

368   US
I A D A BULLETIN. q. Independent Automotive Damage Appraisers Association, 710 E. Ogden Ave., Ste. 113, Naperville, IL 60563-8603. TEL 414-541-7556.

368 360   US
I B I S REVIEW. 1986. m. $90 (foreign $110). (International Benefits Information Service) Charles D. Spencer & Associates, Inc., 250 S. Wacker Dr., Ste. 600, Chicago, IL 60606. TEL 312-993-7900. Eds. Bruce F. Spencer, Laurie W. Letts. charts; stat.; index; circ. 2,500. (back issues avail.)
    Description: Provides descriptions and commentary on topics of importance to international benefits specialists, such as pensions, death benefits and health care.

368   AT
I C A BULLETIN. 1975. q. Insurance Council of Australia Inc., 31 Queen St., 5th Fl., Melbourne, Vic. 3000, Australia. Ed. Judy Robertson. circ. 4,800. (back issues avail.)

368.382   GW
I K K STUTTGART AKTUELL. 1985. q. DM.2. Volker Rothfuss Verlag, Wollgrasweg 31, 7000 Stuttgart 70, Germany. TEL 0711-4567179. FAX 0711-4567180. Ed. Volker Rothfuss. circ. 45,000.

368   BL   ISSN 0019-0446
I R B REVISTA. 1940. 4/yr. free. Instituto de Resseguros do Brasil, Secretaria Geral da Presidencia (SECR-GP), Av. Marechal Camara 171-8, Rio de Janeiro, Brazil. TEL 021-2971212. FAX 021-2408820. TELEX IRBR 021-21019, 21237,30105. Ed. Lilia Maria G. Ferreira Leite. adv.; bk.rev.; charts; illus.; index; circ. 6,000.

368.4   SZ   ISSN 0255-7592
I S S A. COMMITTEE ON PROVIDENT FUNDS. REPORTS. (Text in English) 1977. irreg., no.9, 1990. 10 Fr. International Social Security Association, Publications, Case Postale 1, CH-1211 Geneva 22, Switzerland. FAX 22-7986385. Ed.Bd.
    Description: Details aspects of converting provident to pension funds, training and capital investment.

368.4   SZ   ISSN 0254-0576
I S S A. SOCIAL SECURITY DOCUMENTATION. CARIBBEAN SERIES. (Text in English) 1984. irreg., no.5, 1990. 15 Fr. per no. International Social Security Association, Publications, Case Postale 1, CH-1211 Geneva 22, Switzerland. Ed.Bd.

368   US   ISSN 0094-7660
HG8538.I3
ILLINOIS INSURANCE. 1969. bi-m. free. Department of Insurance, 320 W. Washington St., Springfield, IL 62767. TEL 217-782-4515. Ed. Nan Nases. circ. 5,000. (also avail. in microform from UMI; reprint service avail. from UMI)
    Description: Regulatory newsletter of the Illinois Department of Insurance.

IMPULS; Zeitung fuer Sicherheit im Betrieb. see *BUSINESS AND ECONOMICS — Management*

368   CN   ISSN 0225-1701
IN ONTARIO. 1976. q. membership. Insurance Institute of Ontario, 18 King St., E., 6th Fl., Toronto, Ont. M5C 1C4, Canada. TEL 416-362-8586. FAX 416-362-1126. Ed. Ingrid Taheri. bk.rev.; circ. 12,500. (reprint service avail. from UMI)
    Formerly: Insurance Institute of Ontario. Newsletter.

368   US   ISSN 0019-3658
INDEPENDENT ADJUSTER.* vol.35, 1970. q. free. National Association of Independent Insurance Adjusters, 300 W. Washington St., No. 805, Chicago, IL 60606-2001. TEL 312-427-7965. Ed. Richard Christopher. adv.; charts; illus.

368   US   ISSN 0002-7197
HG9651
INDEPENDENT AGENT. 1903. m. $24. Independent Insurance Agents of America - M S I, 127 S. Peyton St., Alexandria, VA 22314. TEL 703-706-5411. FAX 703-683-7556. Ed. H.P. Hoskins. adv.; bk.rev.; charts; illus.; circ. 45,000. (also avail. in microform from UMI; reprint service avail. from UMI)
    Formerly: American Agency Bulletin.

368   US
INDEX OF INSURANCE AND EMPLOYEE BENEFITS PROCEEDINGS. 1982. a. $50. Badger Infosearch, Box 11943, Milwaukee, WI 53211. TEL 414-964-2377. Ed. Darlene E. Waterstreet. (looseleaf format; back issues avail.)

368.012   US
INDIANA UNDERWRITER. m. $16.50. National Underwriter Co., 505 Gest St., Cincinnati, OH 45203. TEL 513-721-2140. FAX 513-721-0126. Ed. Marianne Coil. circ. 10,000.
    Description: Covers the insurance industry in Indiana, including regulatory and legislative decisions and trends.

INDIVIDUAL INVESTOR'S GUIDE TO LOW-LOAD INSURANCE PRODUCTS. see *BUSINESS AND ECONOMICS — Investments*

368 340   CK   ISSN 0120-1875
INFORMATIVO JURIDICO. 1977. bi-m. $30. Union de Aseguradores Colombianos, Carrera 7a. No. 26-20, Piso 11, Apdo. Aereo 5233, Bogota, Colombia. circ. 800.
    Description: Contains main pieces of Colombian legislation relevant to the insurance sector.

368   CK
INFORMATIVO TECNICO. 1977. q. $15. Union de Aseguradores Colombianos, Carrera 7a. No. 26-20, Piso 11, Apdo. Aereo 5233, Bogota, Colombia. circ. 250.
    Formerly (until 1990): Informativo Fasecolda (ISSN 0120-1921)
    Description: Contains technical articles on insurance lines in Colombia.

INJURY VALUATION REPORTS AND SPECIAL RESEARCH REPORTS. see *LAW*

INSIGHT (CHATSWORTH). see *LAW*

368   FR   ISSN 0007-4438
INSTITUT DE SCIENCE FINANCIERE ET D'ASSURANCES. BULLETIN DES ACTUAIRES DIPLOMES.* 1958. s-a. 500 F. (foreign 480 F.). F I C O M, 5 av. de l'Opera, 75001 Paris, France. Ed. J. Dulac. index.

368   UK   ISSN 0020-2681
INSTITUTE OF ACTUARIES. JOURNAL. 1851. 3/yr. price varies. Alden Press Ltd., Osney Mead, Oxford OX2 0EF, England. Ed. W.H.P. Davies. adv.; bk.rev.; charts; stat.; index, cum.index; circ. 6,500. **Indexed:** Abstr.Hyg., Popul.Ind., Trop.Dis.Bull., World Bank.Abstr.

368.4   EC
INSTITUTO ECUATORIANO DE SEGURIDAD SOCIAL. BOLETIN. NORMAS RESOLUCIONES Y JURISPRUDENCIAS. 1938. s-a. exchange basis. Instituto Ecuatoriano de Seguridad Social, Apdo. Postal 2640, Quito, Ecuador. circ. 10,000.
    Supersedes (since 1970): Boletin de Informaciones y de Estudios Sociales y Economicos.

368.4   HO   ISSN 0074-0233
INSTITUTO HONDURENO DE SEGURIDAD SOCIAL. DEPARTAMENTO DE ESTADISTICA Y PROCESAMIENTO DE DATOS. ANUARIO ESTADISTICO. a. (with supplements). exchange basis. Instituto Hondureno de Seguridad Social, Departamento de Estadistica y Actuarial, Apartado 555, Tegucigalpa, D.C., Honduras.

368.4   CR
INSTITUTO NACIONAL DE SEGUROS MEMORIA ANUAL. 1934. a. free. Instituto Nacional de Seguros, Apdo. 10061, San Jose, Costa Rica. charts; illus.; stat.; circ. 2,000.
    Former titles: Instituto Nacional de Seguros. Memoria Anual I.N.S; Instituto Nacional de Seguros. Informe Anual (ISSN 0074-0268).

I J K

INSURANCE

368.382   GW
▼**INSTRUKTIV.** 1990. q. DM.8. Volker Rothfuss Verlag, Wollgrasweg 31, 7000 Stuttgart 70, Germany. TEL 0711-4567179. FAX 0711-4567180. Ed. Volker Rothfuss. circ. 4,000.

368   US   ISSN 0020-4587
INSURANCE ADVOCATE. 1889. w. $40. Roberts Publishing Corp., Box 9001, Mt. Vernon, NY 10552-9001. TEL 914-699-2020. FAX 914-664-1503. Ed. Emanuel Levy. adv.; bk.rev.; illus.; stat.; tr.lit.; circ. 8,500. (also avail. in microform from UMI; back issues avail.; reprint service avail. from UMI) **Indexed:** P.L.I.I.
    Description: Covers all aspects of the insurance business, including feature articles for insurance specialists and professionals. Provides stock listings of 60 insurers, reinsurers and publicly held brokers.

368   UK   ISSN 0142-6265
INSURANCE AGE. 1979. m. £28($109) United Trade Press Ltd., U.T.P. House, 33-35 Bowling Green Ln., London EC1R 0DA, England. TEL 01-837 1212. Ed. David Worsfold. circ. 14,604. (tabloid format)

368   US   ISSN 0074-0675
INSURANCE ALMANAC; WHO, WHAT, WHEN AND WHERE IN INSURANCE. 1912. a. $105. Underwriter Printing and Publishing Co., 50 E. Palisade Ave., Englewood, NJ 07631. TEL 201-569-8808. Ed. Donald E. Wolff. adv.; circ. 10,000.
    Description: Lists 2,000 agencies and brokerages; over 3,000 U.S. and Canadian insurance companies; adjusters, auditors, investigators, insurance officials, and organizations.

368   US   ISSN 0736-0126
HG8011
INSURANCE AND FINANCIAL REVIEW. 1978. m. $365. Philo Smith & Co., Inc., 2950 Summer St., Stamford, CT 06905-4303. TEL 203-348-7365. FAX 203-348-4307. TELEX 317785. Ed. James A. Amen. circ. 1,000.
    Former titles: Insurance Review (Stamford); Insurance Stock Review (ISSN 0579-529X)
    Description: Short analytical progress reports discussing current results and point of view on insurance and other financial service companies.

INSURANCE AND FINANCIAL SERVICES CAREERS. see *OCCUPATIONS AND CAREERS*

368   US
INSURANCE & LIABILITY REPORTER. s-m. N I L S Publishing Company, 21625 Prairie St., Chatsworth, CA 91311. TEL 800-423-5910. FAX 818-718-8482. Ed. Mark S. Rhodes.

368 332.6   US   ISSN 0892-5887
INSURANCE AND RISK MANAGEMENT. 1987. bi-w. $348 (foreign $370). Buraff Publications (Subsidiary of: Millin Publications, Inc.), 1350 Connecticut Ave. N.W., Ste. 1000, Washington, DC 20036. TEL 202-862-0990. FAX 202-862-0999. Ed. Louis LaBrecque. (also avail. in looseleaf format; back issues avail.)
    Description: Covers risk management and loss prevention and control, including news briefs, tax tips, state developments, and coverage of specific insurance and risk management topics.

368   AT
INSURANCE BROKER. 1977. bi-m. Aus.$35. National Insurance Brokers Association, 2 Jocelyn Ct., Doncaster East, Vic. 3109, Australia. TEL 61-3-848-9540. FAX 61-3-848-6908. Ed. John Heath. adv.; bk.rev.; circ. 3,400. (back issues avail.)
    Description: Covers current topics in insurance, insurance broking and related fields in Australia, New Zealand and Asia.

INSURANCE CASE LAW DIGEST. see *LAW*

368   PH
INSURANCE COMPANY PROFILE. 1982. biennial. price varies. Philippine Insurance Commission, Statistics and Research Division - Ministry ng Pananalapi, Komisyon ng Seguro, Insurance Commission Bldg., 1071 United Nations Ave., P.O. Box 3589, Manila, Philippines. TEL 02-599221. FAX 02-522-1434. circ. 300.
    Description: Provides a brief history of each company authorized to transact insurance business in the Philippines, including comparative highlights on the financial situation, operating results, and business done.

INSURANCE CONFERENCE PLANNER. see *MEETINGS AND CONGRESSES*

368   UK   ISSN 0074-0691
INSURANCE DIRECTORY AND YEAR BOOK. (In 3 vols.) 1841. a. £175. Buckley Press Ltd., 131-135 Temple Chambers, Temple Ave., London EC4Y 0BP, England. TEL 071-583-3030. FAX 071-583-4068. adv.; charts.
    —BLDSC shelfmark: 4531.699000.
    Formerly: Post Magazine Almanack. Insurance Directory.

368   NZ
INSURANCE DIRECTORY OF NEW ZEALAND. a. NZ.$12. Mercantile Gazette Marketing Ltd., P.O. Box 20-034, Christchurch 5, New Zealand. Ed. B.M. Stoop.

368   US   ISSN 0020-4684
INSURANCE FIELD. 1888. a. free. Insurance Field Company, 1812 Production Ct., Louisville, KY 40299. TEL 502-491-5857. FAX 502-491-5905. (Subscr. to: Box 24244, Louisville, KY 40224) Ed. Charles Kaltenthaler. adv.; bk.rev.; illus.; stat.; circ. 3,000 (controlled).
    Description: Covers the American Association of Managing General Agents and the National Association of Professional Surplus Lines Offices' annual conventions.

368   US   ISSN 0095-2923
HG8501
INSURANCE FORUM. 1974. m. $50. Insurance Forum, Inc., Box 245, Ellettsville, IN 47429. Ed. Joseph M. Belth. bk.rev.; index. (also avail. in microform from UMI; reprint service avail. from UMI) **Indexed:** L.I.I.

368   AT
INSURANCE IN AUSTRALIA. 1966. a. Aus.$45. Craftsman Publishing Pty. Ltd., 125 Highbury Rd., Burwood, Vic. 3000, Australia. TEL 03-808-9622. FAX 03-808-0317. Ed. Edward Morgan. adv.; bk.rev.; circ. 1,000.
    Formerly: Insurance in Australia and New Zealand (ISSN 0811-0905)

368   FI   ISSN 0356-9993
INSURANCE IN FINLAND. (Text in English) s-a. FIM 66. Vakuutussanomia Oy - Insurance News Ltd., Bulvardi 28, 00120 Helsinki 12, Finland. TEL 358-0-19251. FAX 90-64-04-69. TELEX 123511 VAKES SF. Ed. Eeva Koskinen. circ. 5,000.
    Description: Covers a broad range of insurance related topics for a non-specialist audience.

368   US
INSURANCE INDUSTRY NEWSLETTER. 1969. w. $117. Insurance Field Company, 1812 Production Ct., Louisville, KY 40299. TEL 502-491-5857. FAX 502-491-5905. (Subscr. to: Box 24244, Louisville, KY 40224) Ed. George V.R. Smith. bk.rev.; circ. 450. (looseleaf format)
    Description: Condensation of a wide range of reading matter on the insurance industry.

368   CN
INSURANCE INSTITUTE OF CANADA. PERSPECTIVES. 1972. q. membership. Insurance Institute of Canada, 18 King St. E., 6th fl., Toronto, Ont. M5C 1C4, Canada. TEL 416-362-8586. FAX 416-362-1126. Ed. Ingrid Taheri. bk.rev.; circ. 29,000.
    Former titles: Insurance Institute of Canada. Newsletter (ISSN 0225-168X); Insurance Institute of Canada. Report (ISSN 0074-0721)

368   II
INSURANCE INSTITUTE OF INDIA. JOURNAL. 1975. s-a. Rs.15 per issue. Insurance Institute of India, 6th Fl., Universal Insurance Bldg., Sir Pherozshah Mehta Rd., Bombay 400 001, India. TEL 22-2872923. TELEX 11-85705-INST-IN. Ed. V.H.P. Pinto. bk.rev.; circ. 9,000.
    Formerly (until 1987): Federation of Insurance Institutes Journal.
    Description: Explores insurance education, training and research in India and neighboring countries.

368.9   BG
INSURANCE JOURNAL. (Text in English) 1975. m. Tk.150($8) Bangladesh Insurance Academy, 53 Mohakhali Commercial Area, Dhaka 1212, Bangladesh. Ed. C.M. Rahman. adv.
    Formerly: Bangladesh Insurance Academy. Journal.

INSURANCE LAW & PRACTICE. see *LAW*

368   US   ISSN 0892-4422
K9
INSURANCE LAW ANTHOLOGY. 1986. a. $149.95. International Library Law Book Publishers, Inc., 101 Lakeforest Blvd., Ste. 270, Gaithersburg, MD 20877. TEL 301-990-7755. FAX 301-990-7642. Ed. Allison P. Zabriskie. bibl.; index.
    Description: Selected best U.S. law review articles, printed in their entirety, in the field of insurance culled from over 900 U.S. law review journals.

INSURANCE LAW CITATIONS. see *LAW*

INSURANCE LAW JOURNAL. see *LAW*

368   UK
INSURANCE LAW MONTHLY. m. £114 (foreign £129). Monitor Press, Rectory Road, Great Waldingfield, Sudbury, Suffolk CO10 0TL, England. TEL 0787-78607. FAX 0787-880201. (back issues avail.)
    Description: Covers pending and new legislation and developments on insurance law.

368 340   US   ISSN 0020-4730
INSURANCE LAW REPORTS: FIRE & CASUALTY. 1929. fortn. $775. Commerce Clearing House, Inc., 4025 W. Peterson Ave., Chicago, IL 60646. TEL 312-583-8500. charts; stat. (looseleaf format)

368 340   US
INSURANCE LAW REPORTS: LIFE, HEALTH & ACCIDENT. 1975. m. $750. Commerce Clearing House, Inc., 4025 W. Peterson Ave., Chicago, IL 60646. TEL 312-583-8500. charts; stat. (looseleaf format)

INSURANCE LITIGATION REPORTER; recent decisions of national significance. see *LAW*

368   UK   ISSN 0020-4773
INSURANCE MAIL. 1904. m. £12. Stone & Cox (Publications) Ltd., 44 Fleet St., London EC4Y 1BS, England. Ed. Richard Blausten. adv.; bk.rev.
    Description: Sales and marketing magazine for the insurance industry.

368   US   ISSN 0892-1458
INSURANCE MARKETING INSIDER. 1987. m. $118. Shelby Publishing Corp., 155 Federal St., Boston, MA 02110. TEL 617-423-0978. Ed. Robert Montgomery. circ. 1,760. (back issues avail.)
    Description: Insurance marketing information for insurance professionals.

368   US   ISSN 0538-2629
HG8523
INSURANCE MARKETPLACE; the agents and brokers guide to non-standard & specialty lines, aviation, marine & international insurance. 1962. a. $6.50. Rough Notes Co., Inc., 1200 N. Meridian, Box 564, Indianapolis, IN 46206. TEL 800-428-4384. FAX 317-634-1041. Ed. Wallace L. Clapp, Jr. circ. 100,000.

368 510   NE   ISSN 0167-6687
                       CODEN: IMECDX
INSURANCE: MATHEMATICS & ECONOMICS. (Text in English) 1982. q. fl.387 (effective 1992). North-Holland (Subsidiary of: Elsevier Science Publishers B.V.), P.O. Box 211, 1000 AE Amsterdam, Netherlands. TEL 020-5803911. FAX 020-5803598. TELEX 18582 ESPA NL. (Subscr. in U.S. and Canada to: Elsevier Science Publishing Co., Inc., Box 882, Madison Sq. Sta., New York, NY 10159. TEL 212-989-5800) Ed. F. De Vylder. adv.; bk.rev.; index; circ. 1,000. (also avail. in microform; back issues avail.) **Indexed:** ABI Inform., BPIA, Bus.Ind., Compumath, Int.Abstr.Oper.Res., Manage.Cont., Math.R., Phys.Abstr., Risk Abstr., SSCI.
    Description: Includes the theory, models and computational methods of life insurance, non-life insurance, and of reinsurance and other risk-sharing arrangements.
    Refereed Serial

368.32   US
INSURANCE PRODUCT NEWS. q. $12.95. Investment Dealers' Digest, Two World Trade Center, 18th Fl., New York, NY 10048. TEL 212-227-1200. FAX 212-321-2336. Ed. Gail Brown. adv.; circ. 22,692.
    Description: Contains new product information for life insurance salespeople.

INSURANCE

368 US
INSURANCE PULSE. 2/yr. $60. Insurance Information Institute, 110 William St., New York, NY 10038. TEL 212-699-9200. FAX 212-732-1916.

368 US ISSN 0020-4803
INSURANCE RECORD. 1934. fortn. $15. Record Publishing Co. (Dallas), Box 225770, Dallas, TX 75222. TEL 214-630-0687. FAX 214-631-2476. Ed. Glen E. Hargis. adv.; illus.; circ. 2,100.

368 368 AT ISSN 0725-4644
INSURANCE RECORD OF AUSTRALIA & NEW ZEALAND; journal of insurance, banking and finance. 1877. m. (except Jan.). Aus.$55. Craftsman Publishing Pty. Ltd., 125 Highbury Rd., Burwood, Vic. 3165, Australia. TEL 03-808-9622. FAX 03-808-0317. Ed. Edward Morgan. adv.; bk.rev.; mkt.; stat.; index; circ. 1,200.
—BLDSC shelfmark: 4531.761000.
Former titles: Insurance and Banking Record (ISSN 0311-0192); Australasian Insurance and Banking Record (ISSN 0004-8372).

368 PK ISSN 0020-4811
INSURANCE REVIEW. (Text in English) 1964. q. Rs.10($2) Pakistan Insurance Corporation, Pakistan Insurance Bldg., Bunder Rd., Karachi 2, Pakistan. Ed. Jauher Hussain. adv.; charts; illus. **Indexed:** Tr.& Indus.Ind.

368 RH
INSURANCE REVIEW. 1955. m. Z.$20 (foreign Z.$28). (Insurance Institute, Zimbabwe) Thomson Publications Zimbabwe (Pvt) Ltd., Thomson House, P.O. Box 1683, Harare, Zimbabwe. TEL 736835. TELEX 24705 ZW. Ed. A. Francis. adv.
Formerly: Rhodesian Insurance Review (ISSN 0035-4805)

368 US ISSN 0749-8667
HG9956 CODEN: INRVER
INSURANCE REVIEW (NEW YORK). 1940. m. $36. Journal of Commerce - Knight-Ridder Inc., 2 World Trade Center, 27th Fl., New York, NY 10048. TEL 212-837-7000. FAX 212-837-7035. Ed. Olga B. Sciortino. adv.: B&W page $3180; trim 7 x 10; adv. contact: Robert R. Frump. charts; illus.; index; circ. 71,905. (also avail. in microfilm from UMI; reprint service avail. from UMI) **Indexed:** ABI Inform., BPIA, Bus.Ind., HRIS, P.A.I.S., Tr.& Indus.Ind.
Former titles (until 1983): Journal of Insurance (ISSN 0022-1929); Journal of Insurance Information.
Description: Covers important news, issues and developments affecting the property and casualty insurance industry. Assists agents, brokers and corporate policy makers in responding to legal, financial, regulatory and consumer concerns.

INSURANCE SETTLEMENTS JOURNAL. see LAW

368 US
INSURANCE SOUTH MAGAZINE. bi-m. Ronald W. Vinson, Ed. & Pub., 8517 Cherry Valley, Alexandria, VA 22309. TEL 703-799-1430.

368 US ISSN 0888-4935
INSURANCE TIMES.* 1982. w. $34.95. 437 Newtoville Ave., Newton, MA 02160-1934. TEL 617-244-1240. FAX 617-244-7147. Ed. David Isgur. adv.; circ. 14,000. (reprint service avail.)
Formerly: New England Insurance Times.
Description: Insurance newspaper covering Northeast region.

368 US ISSN 0020-4846
INSURANCEWEEK. 1933. w. $30. I W Publications, Inc., 1001 Fourth Ave. Plaza, Ste. 3029, Seattle, WA 98154. TEL 206-624-6965. FAX 206-624-5021. Ed. Richard Rambeck. adv.; illus.; circ. 9,000.
Description: Western States property and casualty news weekly.

368 US
INTERBEN. 1983. m. $250. Interben Publications, Box 896, Southport, CT 06490. (And: P.O. Box 4, Kirriemuir, Agnus DD8 4YG, Scotland) Ed. Peter A. Boylan. bk.rev.; circ. 110.

368 GW ISSN 0177-8722
INTERN; Nachrichten fuer die Mitarbeiter. 1935. bi-m. D B V Versicherungen, Frankfurterstr. 50, 6200 Wiesbaden, Germany. TEL 0611-3632593. FAX 0611-3634161. circ. 20,000.

368 US
INTERNATIONAL CLAIM ASSOCIATION PROCEEDINGS. 1910. a. $12. International Claim Association, c/o Ernest Beane, Modern Woodmen of America, Mississippi River at 17th St., Rock Island, IL 61201. (Dist. by: Professional Book Distributors, Inc., Box 100120, Roswell, GA 30077) Ed. James F. Adams. circ. 3,000.

368 US
INTERNATIONAL CONFERENCE OF INSURANCE REGULATORY OFFICIALS. PROCEEDINGS. a. $50. National Association of Insurance Commissioners, 120 W. 12th St., Kansas City, MO 64105. TEL 816-842-3600. (Subscr. to: N A I C Publications, Box 263 Department 42, Kansas City, MO 64193-0042)
Description: Publishes papers on international insurance topics submitted during the annual conference.

368.4 SZ ISSN 0444-1583
INTERNATIONAL CONFERENCE OF SOCIAL SECURITY ACTUARIES AND STATISTICIANS. REPORTS. (Text and summaries in English, French, German, Spanish) fifth, 1971. irreg., no.9, 1990. 40 Fr. per no. International Social Security Association, Publications, Case Postale 1, Ch-1211 Geneva 22, Switzerland. Ed.Bd.

368.4 SZ ISSN 0251-7469
INTERNATIONAL CONFERENCE ON DATA PROCESSING IN THE FIELD OF SOCIAL SECURITY. REPORTS. (Text and summaries in English, French, German, Spanish) second, 1978. quadrennial. 25 Fr. per no. International Social Security Association, Publications, Case Postale 1, CH-1211 Geneva 22, Switzerland. Ed.Bd.

INTERNATIONAL FOUNDATION OF EMPLOYEE BENEFIT PLANS. DIGEST. see BUSINESS AND ECONOMICS — Labor And Industrial Relations

368 US ISSN 0020-6997
HG8011
INTERNATIONAL INSURANCE MONITOR. 1947. m. $25 (foreign $35). International Insurance Monitor, Box 9001, Mt. Vernon, NY 10552. TEL 914-699-2020. Ed. M. Martin. adv.; bk.rev.; circ. 3,200. (also avail. in microform from UMI; reprint service avail. from UMI) **Indexed:** ABI Inform., BPIA.
—BLDSC shelfmark: 4541.430000.

368.4 SZ ISSN 0251-1339
INTERNATIONAL SOCIAL SECURITY ASSOCIATION. REPORTS OF THE GENERAL ASSEMBLIES OF THE ISSA. triennial, 23rd, 1989, Vienna. price varies. International Social Security Association, Box 1, CH-1211 Geneva 22, Switzerland.
Formerly: International Social Security Association. Technical Reports of Assemblies (ISSN 0074-8439)
Description: International comparative studies dealing with different branches or aspects of social security.

368.4 SZ
INTERNATIONAL SOCIAL SECURITY ASSOCIATION. STUDIES AND RESEARCH. (Editions in English and French) 1970. irreg. (1-2/yr.). 25 Fr. per no. International Social Security Association, Box 1, CH-1211 Geneva 22, Switzerland.
Description: Specialized conferences and meetings organized by the ISSA.

368.4 SZ ISSN 0020-871X
HD7090
INTERNATIONAL SOCIAL SECURITY REVIEW. French edition: Revue Internationale de Securite Sociale (ISSN 0379-0312); German edition: Internationale Revue fuer Sociale Sicherheit (ISSN 0379-0282); Spanish edition: Revista Internacional de Seguridad Social (ISSN 0250-605X) (Text in English) 1947. q. 50 Fr. International Social Security Association, Secretariat General, Case Postale 1, CH-1211 Geneva 22, Switzerland. TEL 799-6295. Ed. Michael Gautrey. bk.rev.; bibl.; charts; illus.; stat.; index; circ. 5,000. (back issues avail.; reprint service avail. from SCH) **Indexed:** Abstr.Hyg., ASSIA, C.I.S. Abstr., CERDIC, CLOA, Excerp.Med., Int.Lab.Doc., Med.Care Rev., Mid.East: Abstr.& Ind., P.A.I.S., Soc.Work Res.& Abstr., Stud.Wom.Abstr., Trop.Dis.Bull.
—BLDSC shelfmark: 4549.470000.
Formerly: International Social Security Association Bulletin.
Description: Articles and studies of social security around the world. Includes analyses of technical and administrative aspects of social insurance and commments on new social security legislation.

368 IT ISSN 0021-2482
ISTITUTO ITALIANO DEGLI ATTUARI. GIORNALE. (Text mainly in Italian; occasionally in other languages) 1930. s-a. L.18000. Istituto Italiano degli Attuari, Via del Corea 3, 00186 Rome, Italy. Ed. Giuseppe Ottaviani. bk.rev.; circ. 700.

368 IT ISSN 0021-2520
HD7182
ISTITUTO NAZIONALE DELLA PREVIDENZA SOCIALE. ATTI UFFICIALI. 1925. m. L.45000. Istituto Nazionale della Previdenza Sociale, Via Ciro II Grande 21, 00144 Rome, Italy. index; circ. 8,500.

368 GW
J O. (Junge Ortskrankenkasse) 1974. bi-m. DM.6. (AOK-Bundesverband) Wirtschaftsdienst Gesellschaft fuer Medien & Kommunikation mbH & Co. OHG, Lange Str. 13, 6000 Frankfurt 1, Germany. Ed. Wolfgang Frenken. adv.; circ. 936,400.

368 JM
JAMAICA. MINISTRY OF SOCIAL SECURITY. REPORT. irreg. free. Ministry of Social Security, 14 National Heroes Circle, Box 10, Kingston 5, Jamaica.
Formerly: Jamaica. Ministry of Pensions and Social Security. Report; Incorporates: Jamaica. National Insurance Scheme. Annual Reports (ISSN 0077-5053)

368 JA ISSN 0910-4534
JAPAN INSURANCE NEWS. (Text in English) 1974. bi-m. 950 Yen($64) Hoken Kenkyujo Ltd. - Insurance Research Institute Ltd., 17-3 Hon-machi 1-chome, Shibuya-ku, Tokyo, Japan. TEL 03-376-3331. FAX 03-376-7125. Ed. Toshiaki Shirai. adv.; bk.rev.; circ. 5,000.

THE JEWELRY APPRAISER. see JEWELRY, CLOCKS AND WATCHES

368 CC
JIANGSU BAOXIAN/JIANGSU INSURANCE. (Text in Chinese) bi-m. Jiangsu Baoxian Xuehui - Jiangsu Insurance Association, 57 Beijing Donglu, Nanjing, Jiangsu 210018, People's Republic of China. TEL 714055. (Co-sponsor: Zhongguo Renmin Baoxian Gongsi Jiangsu Fengongsi) Ed. Li Jiming.

368 US ISSN 0021-7204
JOHN LINER LETTER. 1963. m. $138. Shelby Publishing Corp., 155 Federal St., Boston, MA 02110. TEL 617-423-0978. Ed. Robert Montgomery. index; circ. 6,000.

368 332.6 US
JOHN LINER REVIEW. 1987. q. $78. Shelby Publishing Corp., 155 Federal St., Boston, MA 02110. TEL 617-423-0978. Ed. Roger Pierce. circ. 2,000.

JOURNAL OF FINANCIAL SERVICES RESEARCH. see BUSINESS AND ECONOMICS — Banking And Finance

INSURANCE

368 610   US   ISSN 0743-6661
CODEN: JINNER
JOURNAL OF INSURANCE MEDICINE. 1969. q. $45 (foreign $55). American Academy of Insurance Medicine, Box 82446, Kenmore, WA 98028-0446. Ed. Dr. Roger H. Butz. circ. 1,200.
Description: Original articles concerning insurance medicine, including actuariomedical analysis for development of life table, mortality, morbidity, and survival data, underwriting, claims, disability and health insurance issues.

368   US
JOURNAL OF INSURANCE REGULATION. 1983. q. $40 (foreign $55). National Association of Insurance Commissioners, 120 W. 12th St., Kansas City, MO 64105. TEL 816-842-3600. (Subscr. to: N A I C Publications, Box 263 Department 42, Kansas City, MO 64193-0042) Ed. Barbara Haney. cum.index: 1983-1986; circ. 1,600. (back issues avail.)
Description: Covers current insurance topics. Includes case studies and legal reviews.

368   JA
JOURNAL OF INSURANCE SCIENCE. q. 5000 Yen. Japanese Society of Insurance Science, Life Insurance Association of Japan, 3-4-1 Marunouchi, Chiyoda-ku, Tokyo 100, Japan. TEL 03-286-2734. Ed. Kuroda.

368   US   ISSN 0022-4367
HG8011
JOURNAL OF RISK AND INSURANCE. 1933. q. $75 in US and Canada; elsewhere $80 (effective Jan. 1992). American Risk and Insurance Association, c/o Dr. Patricia Cheshier, Executive Director, Clifornia State University, Sacramento, School of Business, BUS-3059, 6000 J Street, Sacramento, CA 95819-6088. Ed. Jerry Jorgensen. adv.; bk.rev.; abstr.; bibl.; charts; index, cum.index: 1932-1967, 1968-1975; circ. 2,200. (also avail. in microform from UMI; reprint service avail. from ISI,UMI)
Indexed: ABI Inform., B.P.I., BPIA, Bus.Ind., Cont.Pg.Manage., Curr.Cont., J.of Econ.Lit., L.I.I., Manage.Cont., Med.Care Rev., P.A.I.S., Risk Abstr., SSCI, Tr.& Indus.Ind.
●Also available online. Vendor(s): DIALOG.
—BLDSC shelfmark: 5052.100000.
Formerly: Journal of Insurance.
Description: Presents scholarly articles on theory and practice relevant to insurance and related areas.

368.4 331   US
▼**JOURNAL OF WORKERS COMPENSATION.** 1991. q. (John Liner Organization) Shelby Publishing Corp., 155 Federal St., Boston, MA 02110. TEL 617-457-0600. FAX 617-482-7820. adv.; circ. 2,000.
Description: Gives information and advice on workers compensation management.

368   FR   ISSN 0022-6823
JURISPRUDENCE AUTOMOBILE. 1929. m. 435 F. L' Argus, 2 rue de Chateaudun, 75441 Paris Cedex 09, France. TEL 45-96-13-00. FAX 48-78-36-59. Ed. Gerard DeFrance. adv.; bk.rev.; charts; tr.lit.; index; circ. 2,550.

368.382   GW
K K H NACHRICHTEN; Beratungsdienst der Kaufmaennischen Krankenkasse fuer Firmen. 1967. q. Kaufmaennische Krankenkasse Hauptverwaltung, Hindenburgstr. 43-45, 3000 Hannover 1, Germany. TEL 0511-28020.

368   US   ISSN 0194-634X
KANSAS INSURANCE. 1979. bi-m. $30. Independent Insurance Agents of Kansas, 817 S.W. Topeka Ave., Topeka, KS 66612. TEL 913-232-0561. FAX 913-232-6817. Ed. Deborah L. Harvey. adv.; stat.; circ. 1,200. (back issues avail.)

368   GW
KARLSRUHER GREIF. 1955. m. Karlsruher Lebensversicherung AG, Friedrich-Scholl-Platz, Postfach 3649, 7500 Karlsruhe, Germany. TEL 0721-1392232. FAX 0721-1392699. Ed. Werner Hampel. adv.; bk.rev. (back issues avail.)

368.3   JA   ISSN 0022-989X
KENPO NYUSU. (Text in Japanese) 1957. 3/m. 10080 Yen. National Federation of Health Insurance Societies, 1-24-4 Minami-Aoyama, Minato-ku, Tokyo, Japan. FAX 03-5410-2091. adv.; bk.rev.; stat.; index.

368 622   GW   ISSN 0342-0809
KOMPASS; Zeitschrift fuer Sozialversicherung im Bergbau. 1886. m. DM.85.70. (Bergbau-Berufsgenossenschaft) Verlag Glueckauf GmbH, Postfach 103945, 4300 Essen 1, Germany. FAX 0201-293630. *Indexed:* World Bibl.Soc.Sec.
—BLDSC shelfmark: 5105.600000.
Description: Covers insurance for the mining industry (accident, medical, retirement and social security). Includes information on the prevention of accidents and illness, association news, and a list of events.

368   KO
KOREA NON-LIFE INSURANCE. (Text in English) 1979. a. free. Korea Non-Life Insurance Association, 80 Soosong-dong, 6th Fl., Chongno-ku, Seoul, S. Korea. Ed. Su-Ung Cho. circ. 1,500.
Formerly: Korea Non-Life Insurance Industry.

368   GW   ISSN 0301-4835
HD7102.G3
DIE KRANKENVERSICHERUNG. 1949. m. DM.143.40. (Bundesverband der Innungskrankenkassen) Erich Schmidt Verlag GmbH & Co. (Bielefeld), Viktoriastr. 44A, Postfach 7330, 4800 Bielefeld 1, Germany. TEL 0521-58308-0. illus. *Indexed:* World Bibl.Soc.Sec.

368   US   ISSN 0889-0986
L I M R A'S MARKETFACTS. 1982. m. $90 to non-members; members $45. Life Insurance Marketing and Research Association (LIMRA), Box 208, Hartford, CT 06141. TEL 203-674-4267. Ed. Heather Waldron. bk.rev.; circ. 2,500. *Indexed:* ABI Inform.
—BLDSC shelfmark: 5220.080000.
Formerly: Marketfacts.

368   US
L.O.M.A. RESOURCE. 1974. m. $36. Life Office Management Association, Inc., 5770 Powers Ferry Rd., Atlanta, GA 30327. TEL 404-951-1770. FAX 404-984-0441. Ed. Ron Clark. adv.; bk.rev.; charts; illus.; circ. 26,000.
Incorporates: Life Office Management Association. Annual Conference. Proceedings of Concurrent Sessions; Which was formerly: Life Office Management Association. Annual Conference. Highlights; Supersedes: Systems and Procedures Review (ISSN 0024-3191); Personnel Quarterly (ISSN 0031-5834); Life Office Management Association. Bulletin (ISSN 0024-3183) Former titles: Keynotes (ISSN 0023-0979); Group Administration Topics.
Description: Articles of interest to life insurance management personnel.

368.32   CN   ISSN 0380-3147
L U A C FORUM. 1914. 10/yr. Can.$30. Life Underwriters Association of Canada, 41 Lesmill Rd., Don Mills, Ont. M3B 2T3, Canada. TEL 416-444-5251. FAX 416-444-8031. Ed. Valerie Osborne. adv.; bk.rev.; illus.; circ. 18,000. *Indexed:* L.I.I.
Incorporates: Revue des Assureurs-Vie.

LABOUR AND NATIONAL INSURANCE/AVODA UBITUACH LEUMI. see *BUSINESS AND ECONOMICS — Labor And Industrial Relations*

368   GW   ISSN 0023-7922
LANDESVERSICHERUNGSANSTALT HESSEN. NACHRICHTEN. 1951. 6/yr. free. Landesversicherungsanstalt Hessen, Staedelstr. 28, 6000 Frankfurt a.M. 70, Germany. Ed. Manfred Brenda. bk.rev.; illus.; stat.; index; circ. 22,000.

368   US   ISSN 0094-0623
KF1164.A1
LEGAL NOTES FOR INSURANCE. 1982. m. $87. Data Research, Inc., 4635 Nicols Rd., Ste. 100, Eagan, MN 55122. TEL 612-452-8267. FAX 612-452-8694. (Subscr. to: Box 490, Rosemount, MN 55068. TEL 800-365-4900) Ed. David Greven. index; circ. 1,000.
Description: Reports recent state and federal court decisions and legislation affecting insurance.

369   US
LEGISLATIVE REPORTER. 1945. fortn. membership only. National Association of Independent Insurers, 2600 River Rd., Des Plaines, IL 60018. TEL 708-297-7800. Ed. Therese Sheehy. circ. 750. (looseleaf format)
Description: Provides comprehensive coverage of state legislative actions affecting the property-casualty insurance industry.

LESLIE AND BRITTS: MOTOR VEHICLE LAW IN N.S.W.. see *LAW*

368   US   ISSN 0742-5120
KF1165
LICENSING, COUNTERSIGNING AND SURPLUS LINE LAWS. a. $17. National Underwriter Co., 505 Gest St., Cincinnati, OH 45203. TEL 513-721-2140. FAX 513-721-0126. Ed. Michael McCracken.
Description: Compilation of the laws and regulations governing licensing and countersigning requirements of insurance agents for all 50 states, Puerto Rico and Virgin Islands.

368.3   US   ISSN 1053-2838
HG8751
LIFE & HEALTH INSURANCE SALES. 1878. m. $22.50 (foreign $35). Rough Notes Co., Inc., 1200 N. Meridian, Box 564, Indianapolis, IN 46206. TEL 800-428-4384. FAX 317-634-1041. Ed. Ray Werner. adv.; bk.rev.; illus.; s-a. index; circ. 30,000. *Indexed:* ABI Inform., L.I.I., PSI.
Former titles (until 1990): Insurance Sales (ISSN 0199-4581); Insurance Salesman (ISSN 0020-482X)

368.32   US   ISSN 0024-3078
HG8751
LIFE ASSOCIATION NEWS. 1906. m. $6 to non-members (foreign $22). National Association of Life Underwriters, 1922 F St., N.W., Washington, DC 20006. TEL 202-331-6070. FAX 202-331-2179. Ed. Ian MacKenzie. adv.; bk.rev.; illus.; index; circ. 144,000. (also avail. in microform from UMI) *Indexed:* ABI Inform., BPIA, L.I.I., PSI.
—BLDSC shelfmark: 5208.916500.
Incorporates (1956-1986): Probe (Rockville Centre) (ISSN 0032-9193)

LIFE COMMUNICATIONS. see *ADVERTISING AND PUBLIC RELATIONS*

368   CH
LIFE INSURANCE BUSINESS IN TAIWAN (YEAR). (Text in Chinese, English) 1972. a. free. Taipei Life Insurance Association, Ste. 152, 5th Fl., Sung Chiang Rd., Taipei, Taiwan, Republic of China. Ed.Bd.
Formerly: Annual Report of Life Insurance, Republic of China.

368.3   US   ISSN 0075-9406
HG8943
LIFE INSURANCE FACT BOOK. 1946. biennial. single copy free; additional copies $2 per no. American Council of Life Insurance, 1001 Pennsylvania Ave., N.W., Washington, DC 20004-2599. TEL 202-624-2000. Ed. Suzanne K. Stemnock. circ. 80,000. *Indexed:* L.I.I., SRI.

368.32   IE
LIFE INSURANCE INTERNATIONAL. m. I£495. Lafferty Publications Ltd., The Tower, IDA Enterprise Centre, Pearse St., Dublin 2, Ireland. TEL 01-718022. FAX 01-718240. (US subscr. to: 1422 W. Peachtree St., Ste. 800, Atlanta, GA 30309. TEL 404-874-5120) Ed. Nessa O'Mahony.
Description: Market intelligence for the life insurance industry worldwide.

368.32   US   ISSN 0024-3132
LIFE INSURANCE PLANNING. 1966. base vol. (plus m. updates; s-m. Life Insurance Planning Ideas). $261. Maxwell Macmillan, Professional and Business Reference Publishing, 910 Sylvan Ave., Englewood Cliffs, NJ 07632. TEL 800-562-0245. FAX 201-816-3569. (looseleaf format)

368.32   US   ISSN 0024-3140
HG8751
LIFE INSURANCE SELLING. 1926. m. $10. Commerce Publishing Co., 408 Olive St., St. Louis, MO 63102. TEL 314-421-5445. Ed. Larry Albright. adv.; illus.; circ. 43,528. (also avail. in microform from UMI) *Indexed:* L.I.I.
Description: Information for life insurance salespeople to serve clients better, increase sales and profits.

368.32 US
LIFE LINES. free. Monumental Life Insurance Company, 2 E. Chase St., Baltimore, MD 21202. TEL 301-685-2900. FAX 301-347-8666. Ed. Alice Simon-Curry. circ. 850 (controlled).
Formerly: Monumental News.
Description: Company news for employees and retirees.

368 CN
LIFELINE (KINGSTON). 1936. m. Empire Life Insurance Co., Head Office, 259 King St.E., Kingston, Ont. K7L 3A8, Canada. TEL 613-548-1881. FAX 613-541-4104. Ed. Nancy McIver. circ. 1,800 (controlled).
Formerly: Builder (ISSN 0045-3382)

368 US
LIFETIME. m. Kansas City Life Insurance Company, Box 419139, Kansas City, MO 64141. TEL 816-753-7000. Ed. Eileen Jenkins. index; circ. 2,500. (back issues avail.)
Description: Articles on issues affecting the insurance industry for members of the agency force of the Kansas City Life Insurance Company.

368.32 US ISSN 0194-4312
LIFETIMES. 1962. bi-m. $3 to non-members. Tennessee Association of Life Underwriters, 500 Interstate Blvd. S., Ste. 310, Box 100745, Nashville, TN 37224. TEL 615-256-8258. Ed. Terry Scalos. adv.; illus.; circ. 4,200.
Formerly: Tennessee Life Insurance News (ISSN 0040-330X)

LITIGATION AND PREVENTION OF INSURER BAD FAITH. see *LAW*

368 GW
LLOYD REPORT. 1959. bi-m. Deutscher Lloyd Versicherungen, Karlstr. 10, 8000 Munich 2, Germany. FAX 089-5908203. Ed. Peter Frank. bk.rev.; circ. 6,800.

368 US
LLOYD'S INSURANCE INTERNATIONAL. 1987. m. $225 (foreign $245). Lloyd's of London Press, Inc., 611 Broadway, Ste. 308, New York, NY 10012-2608. TEL 212-529-9500. FAX 212-529-9826. Ed. Jeff Myhre.

LLOYD'S LIST INTERNATIONAL. see *TRANSPORTATION — Ships And Shipping*

368 UK ISSN 0024-550X
LLOYD'S LOG. 1930. bi-m. £32. Lloyd's of London, 1 Lime St., London E.C.3, England. Ed. M. Wynn Jones. adv.; bk.rev.; illus.; circ. 37,000. Indexed: BMT.

368.2 387 UK ISSN 0047-4908
LLOYD'S WEEKLY CASUALTY REPORTS. vol.207, 1972. w. (4 vols./yr.). $610. Lloyd's of London Press Ltd., Sheepen Place, Colchester, Essex CO3 3LP, England. TEL 0206-772277. FAX 0206-46273. TELEX 987321 LLOYDS G. (US subscr. to: 611 Broadway, Ste. 308, New York, NY 10012. TEL 212-529-9500) q. index.
Description: Provides information on marine, non-marine aviation and miscellaneous casualties, port conditions and weather information.

368 US
LONG ISLAND TELEPHONE TICKLER FOR INSURANCE MEN & WOMEN. a. $6. Underwriter Printing and Publishing Co., 50 E. Palisade Ave., Englewood, NJ 07631. TEL 201-569-8808. Ed. Donald E. Wolff. adv.; circ. 17,000.
Description: Directory of names, addresses and telephone numbers of insurance companies, agents, brokers and related suppliers in the Long Island, NY area.

368 US
LOUISIANA SURPLUS LINE REPORTER. m. Reporter Publishing Company, Box 52193, New Orleans, LA 70152-2193. TEL 504-366-8797. Ed. Carol J. DeGraw.

368.4 LU
▼**LUXEMBOURG. INSPECTION GENERALE DE LA SECURITE SOCIALE. APERCU SUR LA LEGISLATION DE LA SECURITE SOCIALE AU GRAND-DUCHE DE LUXEMBOURG.** 1991. a. 160 Fr. Inspection Generale de la Securite Sociale, Ministere de la Securite Sociale, Luxembourg, Luxembourg. FAX 49921-2325. TELEX 2985 MINTSS LU. circ. 1,600.

368 US
M D R T ANNUAL MEETING. PROCEEDINGS. 1927. a. $20. Million Dollar Round Table, 325 Touhy, Park Ridge, IL 60068. TEL 708-692-6378. FAX 708-518-8921. Ed. H. William Woulfe. circ. 20,000. (audio cassette; video cassette) Indexed: L.I.I.
Description: Presents motivational and technical life insurance sessions from annual meetings.

368 US ISSN 0024-8282
M O N Y NEWS; for its employees and field force. 1959. fortn. Mutual of New York Life Insurance Co., Public Relations Department, 1740 Broadway, New York, NY 10019. TEL 212-708-2000. Ed. Georgianna Hinsch. charts; illus.; stat.; circ. 13,000. (newspaper)

368 MW ISSN 0076-3349
MALAWI. REGISTRAR OF INSURANCE. REPORT. a., latest 1972. K.0.50. Government Printer, P.O. Box 37, Zomba, Malawi.

368 650 US ISSN 0025-1968
HG8751
MANAGER'S MAGAZINE. 1926. m. $65 to non-members; members $45. Life Insurance Marketing and Research Association (LIMRA), Box 208, Hartford, CT 06141. TEL 203-677-0033. Ed. Daniel J. Nahorney. bk.rev.; illus.; index; circ. 10,000. Indexed: ABI Inform., BPIA, Bus.Ind., Manage.Cont.
—BLDSC shelfmark: 5359.280000.

368 631 CN ISSN 0542-5395
HG9968.C75
MANITOBA CROP INSURANCE CORPORATION. ANNUAL REPORT. 1962. a. free. Manitoba Crop Insurance Corporation, 25 Tupper St., N., Portage la Prairie, Man. R1N 3K1, Canada. FAX 204-239-3401. charts; circ. 325.

368 UK ISSN 0265-8410
MARINE AND AVIATION INSURANCE REPORT. 1984. m. £230($460) D Y P Insurance and Reinsurance Research Group, Bridge House, 181 Queen Victoria St., London EC4V 4DD, England. TEL 071-236 2175. FAX 071-489-1487. Ed. J.S. Bannister. bk.rev.; charts; stat. (back issues avail.)

368 JA
MARINE & FIRE INSURANCE ASSOCIATION OF JAPAN. FACT BOOK; non-life insurance in Japan. (Text in English) 1975. a. 750 Yen($5) (effective 1991; typically set in Dec.). Marine & Fire Insurance Association of Japan Inc., Non-Life Insurance Building, 9 Kanda Awajicho 2-Chome, Chiyoda-Ku, Tokyo, Japan. FAX 03-3255-1234. TELEX 222-4829 SONPO J. circ. 4,500.

MATECON; materiali di finanza, credito e assicurazioni. see *BUSINESS AND ECONOMICS — Banking And Finance*

368 MF
MAURITIUS. MINISTRY OF FINANCE. INSURANCE UNIT. CONTROLLER OF INSURANCE. REPORT. 1972. a. Rs.50. Ministry of Finance, Insurance Unit, Controller of Insurance, 7 Leoville l'Homme St., Port Louis, Mauritius. FAX 088622. TELEX 4249 EXTERN 1W. (Dist. by: Government Printing Office, Elizabeth II Ave., Port Louis, Mauritius) stat.
Formerly: Mauritius. Registrar of Insurance. Annual Report.

MEALEY'S LITIGATION REPORT: ASBESTOS. see *LAW — Civil Law*

MEALEY'S LITIGATION REPORT: BAD FAITH. see *LAW — Civil Law*

MEALEY'S LITIGATION REPORT: INSURANCE. see *LAW — Civil Law*

MEALEY'S LITIGATION REPORT: INSURANCE INSOLVENCY. see *LAW — Civil Law*

MEALEY'S LITIGATION REPORT: PUNITIVE DAMAGES AND TORT REFORM. see *LAW — Civil Law*

MEALEY'S LITIGATION REPORT: REINSURANCE. see *LAW — Civil Law*

MEDICAL LIABILITY ADVISORY SERVICE. see *LAW — Civil Law*

346.73 US ISSN 0732-9636
MEDICAL LIABILITY MONITOR; newsletter on professional liability and risk management. 1975. m. $150. Malpractice Lifeline, Inc., Box 9011, Winnetka, IL 60093-9011. FAX 708-998-1930. Ed. Carol Brierly Golin. bk.rev.; index; circ. 1,750.
Formerly (until 1981): Malpractice Lifeline (ISSN 0361-8412)
Description: News updates on legal and policy issues that affect premiums for malpractice insurance.

MEDICAL LIABILITY REPORTER; recent decisions of national significance. see *LAW — Civil Law*

MEDICAL OFFICE REPORT. see *MEDICAL SCIENCES*

368.382 340 US ISSN 1061-4192
▼**MEDICAL RECORD RISKS: CLAIMS & LITIGATION.** 1992. m. $250. Cox Publications, Box 20316, Billings, MT 59104-0316. TEL 406-256-8822. Ed. Meridith B. Cox.
Description: For those who review medical records for claims and litigation.

368 610 US
MEDICARE ADVISOR. m. Shannon Publications, Inc., 11651 Plano Rd., Ste. 160, Dallas, TX 75243-5256. TEL 214-343-8897. Ed. Brian Buchan.

368.382 US
MEDICARE AND MEDICAID DATA BOOK. a. Health Care Financing Administration, Office of Research and Demonstrations, Oak Meadows Bldg., Rm. 2230, 6325 Security Blvd., Baltimore, MD 21207. TEL 301-966-6584. (Subscr. to: Supt. of Documents, Washington, DC 20402. TEL 202-783-3238) stat.
Formerly: Data on the Medicaid Program: Eligibility - Service - Expenditures.
Description: Provides an overview, descriptive and comparative data and analyses of the Medicare and Medicaid programs. Includes trends and statistics on enrolees, recipients, utilization and expenditures.

368.382 610 US
MEDICARE COMPLIANCE ALERT. (Supplement avail.: Civil Money Penalties Reporter) 1989. bi-w. $370. United Communications Group, 11300 Rockville Pike, Ste. 1100, Rockville, MD 20852-3030. TEL 301-816-8950. FAX 301-816-8945. Ed. Carol Sardinha.
Formerly: Medicare Compliance Report.
Description: Examines enforcement trends in Medicare and Medicaid fraud, abuse law and billing practices. Also gives health care providers and attorneys analysis of administrative law rulings in Civil Money Penalties Reporter.

368.382 US
MEDICARE - MEDICAID GUIDE. 1969. fortn. $995. Commerce Clearing House, Inc., 4025 W. Peterson Ave., Chicago, IL 60646. TEL 312-583-8500. Ed. D. Newquist. (looseleaf format)

368 610 US
MEDICARE REVIEW. m. Shannon Pubications, Inc., 11651 Plano Rd., Ste. 160, Dallas, TX 75243-5256. TEL 214-343-8897. Ed. Brian Buchan. circ. 3,226.

368 CN ISSN 0714-6914
MERCER BULLETIN. 1951. m. free. William M. Mercer Ltd., BCE Place, 161 Bay St., P.O. Box 501, Toronto, Ont. M5J 2S5. TEL 416-868-2522. FAX 416-868-7555. Ed. Robert C. Dowsett. circ. 8,500. Indexed: World Bibl.Soc.Sec.
Formerly (until Jan. 1982): Mercer Actuarial Bulletin (ISSN 0025-9845)

368 US ISSN 0742-3446
MERRITT RISK MANAGEMENT REVIEW. 1983. m. $327. Merritt Company, 1661 Ninth St., Box 955, Santa Monica, CA 90406. TEL 213-450-7234. FAX 213-396-4563. Eds. Mary Ann Giorgio, Allon J. Greene. circ. 3,000. (looseleaf format)
Description: Information of risk management and insurance.

INSURANCE

368 US
MESSENGER REPORTER. vol.13, 1977. 10/yr. free. (Council of Insurance Brokers of Greater New York) Chase Communications Group, Inc., c/o Linda S. Warren, Asst. VP, 25-35 Beechwood Ave., Mount Vernon, NY 10550. TEL 914-699-2020. FAX 914-664-1503. adv.; illus.; circ. 800.
  Incorporating: Brooklyn Insurance Brokers Association. Bulletin (ISSN 0007-2354)

368 331 US ISSN 0746-1461
KFM4542.A59
MICHIGAN WORKERS' COMP DIGEST. 1982. m. $70. Pathfinder Associates Inc., 1906 Mills Ave., Box 5240, North Muskegon, MI 49445. TEL 616-744-8462. FAX 616-744-0509. Ed. Ronald E. Hauxwell. adv.; circ. 400. (back issues avail.)
  Description: Offers a summary of Michigan workers' compensation cases and laws.

368 US ISSN 0026-2935
MID-AMERICA INSURANCE. 1891. m. $10. Insurance Publications, Inc., Box 11310, Overland Park, KS 66207. FAX 913-383-1247. Ed. James M. Willman. adv.; charts; illus.; stat.; circ. 13,196. **Indexed:** ABI Inform.

368 US
MINNESOTA INSURANCE. 1982. m. $14. Meusey Communications, 5871 Cedar Lake Rd., S., Minneapolis, MN 55416-1481. TEL 612-544-8666. Ed. Jack Meusey. adv.; circ. 4,500.
  Description: Covers people, events, and issues affecting insurance in Minnesota.

368.2 340 US
MINNESOTA NO-FAULT AUTOMOBILE INSURANCE. 2nd ed., 1989. 2 base vols. (plus suppl.). $140. Butterworth Legal Publishers (Salem) (Subsidiary of: Reed International PLC), 90 Stiles Rd., Salem, NH 03079. TEL 800-548-4001. FAX 603-898-9858. Ed. Michael K. Steenson. (looseleaf format)
  Description: Reviews the history, amendment and development of the no-fault statute since 1974 and discusses the case law that has arisen under the act.

368 US
MISSOURI. DEPARTMENT OF INSURANCE. ANNUAL REPORT AND STATISTICAL DATA. 1870. a. $10. Department of Insurance, Administrative Section, Box 690, Jefferson City, MO 65102. TEL 314-751-4439. FAX 314-751-1165. stat.; circ. 750.
  Formerly: Missouri. Division of Insurance. Annual Report and Statistical Data.
  Description: Contains division operations summaries and listing of insurance companies licensed in Missouri.

368 BE
LE MONITEUR DES ASSURANCES; journal independant de l'assurance privee. 2250. w. 1995 Fr. (Office des Assureurs de Belgique) Wolters-Kluwer Belgium, 485 Av. Louise, B-1050 Brussels, Belgium. Ed. F. Claes. adv.; bk.rev.; bibl.; circ. 5,200.
  Formerly: Petit Moniteur des Assurances (ISSN 0031-627X)

368 US
MUTUAL PIPER. irreg. Professional Insurance Communicators of America, Box 68700, Indianapolis, IN 46268. TEL 317-875-5250. FAX 317-879-8408.
  Formerly: Communique.

368 FR ISSN 0027-5239
HG8057
MUTUALITE/GEGENSEITIGKEIT/ MUTUALISMO/MUTUALITY. (Text in English, French, German, Spanish) 1965. s-a. free. Association Internationale des Societes d'Assurance Mutuelle - International Association of Mutual Insurance Companies, 114 rue la Boetie, 75008 Paris, France. FAX 1-42-56-04-49. Ed. R. Choplin. bk.rev.; bibl.; illus.; circ. 2,500 (controlled).

N A D E ADVOCATE. (National Association of Disability Examiners) see SOCIAL SERVICES AND WELFARE

368 US
N A I C NEWSLETTER. (Includes: N A I C Bulletin) m. $150. National Association of Insurance Commissioners, 120 W. 12th St., Kansas City, MO 64105. TEL 816-842-3600. (Subscr. to: N A I C Publications, Box 263 Department 42, Kansas City, MO 64193-0042)
  Description: Provides summaries of insurance regulatory activities.

N A I F A CONVENTION. PROCEEDINGS. (National Association of Independent Fee Appraisers) see REAL ESTATE

N A I F A TECHNICAL MANUAL. (National Association of Independent Fee Appraisers) see REAL ESTATE

368 US
N A M I C MAGAZINE. 1895. m. $12. National Association of Mutual Insurance Companies, 3707 Woodview Terr., Box 68700, Indianapolis, IN 46268. TEL 317-875-5250. FAX 317-879-8408. Ed. Tonya H. McGue. adv.; bk.rev.; illus.; circ. 3,200.
  Formerly: Mutual Insurance Bulletin.

368 340 UK
N A P F PENSIONS LEGISLATION SERVICE. irreg. (approx. 5/yr.). $450. Butterworth & Co. (Publishers) Ltd. (Subsidiary of: Reed International PLC), 88 Kingsway, London WC2B 6AB, England. TEL 71-405-6900. FAX 71-405-1332. TELEX 95678. (US addr.: Butterworth Legal Publishers, 90 Stiles Rd., Salem, NH 03079. TEL 800-548-4001)

368 US ISSN 0027-5964
N A P I A BULLETIN. vol.13, 1970. q. membership. National Association of Public Insurance Adjusters, 1101 14th St., N.W., Ste. 1100, Washington, DC 20005. TEL 202-371-1258. FAX 202-371-1090. adv.; circ. 900.

N A R I STETHOSCOPE. (National Association of Residents and Interns) see BUSINESS AND ECONOMICS — Investments

N F R A NEWSLETTER. (National Forest Recreation Association) see CONSERVATION

368 US
N R R A NEWS. m. National Risk Retention Association, 3421 M St., N.W., Box 1740, Washington, DC 20007. TEL 800-999-4505. Ed. Leslea Dummer.

368.32 US ISSN 0027-7142
N Y L I C REVIEW. 1933. m. free. New York Life Insurance Co., Agency Dept. for the Field Representatives, 51 Madison Ave., New York, NY 10010. TEL 212-567-7000. Ed. Douglas S. Davin. bk.rev.; charts; illus.; index; circ. 16,500.

368.5 BE
NAAMLOZE VENNOOTSCHAPPEN. Short title: N V. (Supplement avail.) (Text in Flemish) s-m. 4558 Fr. C E D Samson (Subsidiary of: Wolters Samson Belgie n.v.), Louizalaan 485, B-1050 Brussels, Belgium. TEL 02-7231111. FAX 02-6498480. TELEX CEDSAM 64130.
  Description: Examines limited liability.

368 US
NATIONAL ASSOCIATION OF INSURANCE COMMISSIONERS. COMPILATION OF REPORTS. s-a. $200. National Association of Insurance Commissioners, 120 W. 12th St., Kansas City, MO 64105. TEL 816-842-3600. (Subscr. to: N A I C Publications, Box 263 Department 42, Kansas City, MO 64193-0042) (looseleaf format)
  Description: Provides immediate access to meeting records.

368 US
NATIONAL ASSOCIATION OF INSURANCE COMMISSIONERS. LIFE AND HEALTH ACTUARIAL REPORT. irreg. (6-8/yr.). $150. National Association of Insurance Commissioners, 120 W. 12th St., Kansas City, MO 64105. TEL 816-842-3600. (Subscr. to: N A I C Publications, Box 263 Department 42, Kansas City, MO 64193-0042)
  Description: Provides reports of task force research studies and meetings.

368 US
NATIONAL ASSOCIATION OF INSURANCE COMMISSIONERS. LISTING OF COMPANIES. s-a. $125. National Association of Insurance Commissioners, 120 W. 12th St., Kansas City, MO 64105. TEL 816-842-3600. (Subscr. to: N A I C Publications, Box 263 Department 42, Kansas City, MO 64193-0042) (also avail. in magnetic tape)
  Description: Provides information on more than 5,000 insurance companies.

368 US ISSN 0363-0358
HG8016
NATIONAL ASSOCIATION OF INSURANCE COMMISSIONERS. PROCEEDINGS. 1871. s-a. $200. National Association of Insurance Commissioners, 120 W. 12th St., Kansas City, MO 64105. TEL 816-842-3600. (Subscr. to: N A I C Publications, Box 263 Department 42, Kansas City, MO 64193-0042) Ed. Karen Miller. charts; stat.; cum.index: 1950-1970, 1970-1979; circ. 800. (back issues avail.)
  ●Also available online. Vendor(s): Mead Data Central.
  Description: Official record of transactions from all of the association's meetings.

368 TZ
NATIONAL INSURANCE CORPORATION OF TANZANIA. ANNUAL REPORT AND ACCOUNTS. (Text in English) a. National Insurance Corporation of Tanzania Ltd., Box 9264, Dar es Salaam, Tanzania.

368.01 IS ISSN 0075-1324
NATIONAL INSURANCE INSTITUTE, JERUSALEM. FULL ACTUARIAL REPORT. (Text in English and Hebrew) triennial. price varies. National Insurance Institute, 13 Sderot Weizman, Jerusalem, Israel.

NATIONAL INSURANCE LAW REVIEW. see LAW

368 US ISSN 0028-033X
HG8751
NATIONAL UNDERWRITER. LIFE & HEALTH INSURANCE EDITION. w. $74 (foreign $159). National Underwriter Co., 505 Gest St., Cincinnati, OH 45203. TEL 513-721-2140. FAX 513-721-0126. adv.; charts; illus.; stat.; circ. 29,260. (also avail. in microfilm from UMI; reprint service avail. from UMI) **Indexed:** ABI Inform., B.P.I., BPIA, Bus.Ind., Hlth.Ind., L.I.I., PSI, Tr.& Indus.Ind.
  Description: News on legislation, products and general facts on the life, health and financial services industries.

368.012 US ISSN 0163-8912
HG8011
NATIONAL UNDERWRITER. PROPERTY & CASUALTY INSURANCE EDITION. 1896. w. $74 (foreign $159). National Underwriter Co., 505 Gest St., Cincinnati, OH 45203. TEL 513-721-2410. FAX 513-721-0126. (also avail. in microform from UMI; reprint service avail. from UMI) **Indexed:** ABI Inform., B.P.I, BPIA, Bus.Ind., Hlth.Ind., P.L.I.I., PSI, Tr.& Indus.Ind.
  —BLDSC shelfmark: 6033.235000.
  Description: Discusses products, market, legislation, risk management and employee benefits.

368.1 US
HG9765
NATIONAL UNDERWRITER PROFILES. (In 3 editions: Life Insurors, Health Insurors, and Property-Casualty Insurors) a. $36.50. National Underwriter Co., 505 Gest St., Cinncinnati, OH 45203. TEL 513-721-2140. FAX 513-721-0126.
  Former titles (until 1990): Argus F C and S Chart (ISSN 0360-8921); Argus Insurance Chart.
  Description: Provides financial information on insurance companies' performances.

368 UK
NATIONAL UNION OF INSURANCE WORKERS. PRUDENTIAL SECTION. GAZETTE. 4/w. National Union of Insurance Workers, Prudential Section, 27 Old Gloucester St., London WC1N 3AF, England. TEL 071-405-6798. FAX 071-404-8150. circ. 13,000.
  Supersedes: Prudential Staff Gazette.

368 NE ISSN 0077-5975
NATIONALE-NEDERLANDEN. ANNUAL REPORT. (Text in Dutch and English) 1963. a. free. Nationale-Nederlanden N.V., Johan de Wittlaan 3, Box 29701, 2502 LS The Hague, Netherlands. TEL 70-581210. circ. 37,000.

INSURANCE

368   GW
NESSELBLATT. 1971. bi-m. Provinzial Versicherungen, Sophienblatt 33, 2300 Kiel 1, Germany. FAX 0431-6032804. TELEX 292977. Ed. Guenther Jesumann. bk.rev.; circ. 3,500.
Description: Insurance company publication including annual report, reports of meetings and events, company news, and list of exhibitions.

NEW HAMPSHIRE PRACTICE SERIES. VOLS. 8 AND 9: PERSONAL INJURY - TORT AND INSURANCE PRACTICE. see *LAW*

368   US
NEW YORK (STATE). INSURANCE DEPARTMENT. ANNUAL REPORT OF THE SUPERINTENDENT OF INSURANCE TO THE NEW YORK LEGISLATURE. a. free. Insurance Department, Publications Unit, Empire State Plaza, Agency Bldg. No. 1, Albany, NY 12257. circ. 2,000. **Indexed:** SRI.

368   US
NEW YORK (STATE). INSURANCE DEPARTMENT. BULLETIN. 1961. m. free. Insurance Department, Research Bureau, 160 W. Broadway, 21st Fl., New York, NY 10013. TEL 212-602-0473. FAX 212-602-0437. Ed. Wayne Cotter. circ. 4,100 (controlled). (back issues avail.)

368   US
NEW YORK (STATE). INSURANCE DEPARTMENT. FEES AND TAXES CHARGED INSURANCE COMPANIES UNDER THE LAWS OF NEW YORK TOGETHER WITH ABSTRACTS OF FEES, TAXES AND OTHER REQUIREMENTS OF OTHER STATES. 1906. a. $2.50. Insurance Department, Publications Unit, Empire State Plaza, Agency Bldg. No. 1, Albany, NY 12257. circ. 1,000.

368.4   US
NEW YORK (STATE). WORKMEN'S COMPENSATION BOARD. SUMMARY OF ACTIVITIES. 1956. a. free. Worker's Compensation Board, 180 Livingston St., Brooklyn, NY 11201. TEL 718-488-4141. circ. 700.

368.32   US
NEW YORK CITY ASSOCIATION OF LIFE UNDERWRITERS. 1922. m. $5. New York City Association of Life Underwriters, Inc., 500 Fifth Ave., New York, NY 10110. FAX 212-764-8693. Ed. C. Jennings. adv.; bk.rev.; charts; illus.; stat; circ. 3,400.
Formerly: Life Underwriters Association of the City of New York. Bulletin (ISSN 0024-3221)

NEW YORK NO-FAULT ARBITRATION REPORTS. see *LAW*

368   US
NEW YORK TELEPHONE TICKLER FOR INSURANCE MEN AND WOMEN. a. $12.95. Underwriter Printing and Publishing Co., 50 E. Palisade Ave., Englewood, NJ 07631. TEL 201-569-8808. Ed. Donald E. Wolff. adv.; circ. 27,500.
Formerly: Telephone Tickler for Insurance Men and Women (ISSN 0082-2663)
Description: Directory of names, addresses and telephone numbers of insurance companies, agents, brokers and related suppliers in the New York City area.

368   ZR
NGABU; revue Zairoise des assurances. 1973. q. £120. Societe Nationale d'Assurance, Sonas Sankuru Bldg., Blvd. du 30 Juin, P.O. Box 3443, Kinshasa-Gombe, Zaire. TEL 23051. TELEX 21653. Ed. Utshudiema Luhaka. adv.; illus.

368.9   TZ   ISSN 0856-1222
NGAO. (Text in English) 1972. q. National Insurance Corporation of Tanzania Ltd., Insurance House, Box 9264, Dar es Salaam, Tanzania. Ed. Theresia Mshuza. illus.; circ. 3,000.

368   NR   ISSN 0048-0398
NIGERIAN INSURANCE MONITOR.* 1971. m. EAs.34. Nara Advertising Ltd., 30 Idoluwo St., Box 4236, Lagos, Nigeria. Ed. Obiora Okeke. adv.; illus.

368   KO
NON-LIFE INSURANCE. (Text in English) 1961. m. free. Korea Non-Life Insurance Association, 80 Soosong-dong, 6th floor, Chongno-ku, Seoul, S. Korea. Ed. Su-Ung Cho. circ. 9,000.

368   SW   ISSN 0348-6516
NORDISK FOERSAEKRINGSTIDSKRIFT/SCANDINAVIAN INSURANCE QUARTERLY. Short title: N F T. (Jointly edited by the Insurance Societies of Denmark, Finland, Norway and Sweden) (Text in Danish, English, French, German, Norwegian or Swedish) 1921. q. SEK 75($12) Svenska Foersaekringsfoereningen - Swedish Insurance Society, Tegeluddsvaegen 100, S-11587 Stockholm, Sweden. FAX 009-46-8-6632235. Ed. Anders Kleverman. adv.; bk.rev.; illus.; cum.index every 5 yrs.; circ. 9,000. (processed)

368   US
NORTH JERSEY TELEPHONE TICKLER FOR INSURANCE MEN & WOMEN. a. $6. Underwriter Printing and Publishing Co., 50 E. Palisade Ave., Englewood, NJ 07631. TEL 201-569-8808. Ed. Donald E. Wolff. adv.; circ. 17,000.
Description: Directory of names, addresses and telephone numbers of insurance companies, agents, brokers and related suppliers in the northern New Jersey area.

368   CK
NOTICIAS DEL SEGURO. 1989. m. $10. Union de Aseguradores Colombianos, Carrera 7a No. 26-20, Piso 11, Apdo. Aereo 5233, Bogota, Colombia. circ. 500.

368   IT
NOTIZIARIO ASSICURATIVO. 1919. m. L.60000. Publiass s.r.l., Via Dei Gracchi, 30, 20146 Milan, Italy. TEL 39-2-58313538. FAX 39-2-58313730. Ed. Sergio Scotti. adv.; bk.rev.; circ. 16,800.

368   NE   ISSN 0165-8220
NU. 1971. m. free. Nationale-Nederlanden N.V., Johan de Wittlaan 3, Box 29701, 2502 LS The Hague, Netherlands. TEL 70-581726. Ed. Anneke Rijk. circ. 19,000.

368   US
O S H A NEWS. m. $387. Merritt Company, 1661 Ninth St., Box 955, Santa Monica, CA 90406. TEL 213-450-7234. FAX 213-396-4563.

368.4 331   UK   ISSN 0952-231X
OCCUPATIONAL PENSIONS. 1987. 12/yr. £99 (foreign £110). Eclipse Publications Ltd., 18-20 Highbury Place, London N5 1QP, England. TEL 071-354-5858. FAX 071-359-4000. Ed. Colin Sherwood. circ. 1,000. (back issues avail.)
—BLDSC shelfmark: 6229.760000.
Description: Provides guidelines on new legislation and changes to regulations. Includes comprehensive surveys on named organizations.

368   US   ISSN 0198-683X
OHIO UNDERWRITER; insurance news of Ohio. 1967. m. $16.50. National Underwriter Co., 505 Gest St., Cincinnati, OH 45203. TEL 513-721-2410. FAX 513-721-0126. Ed. Gilbert McLean. adv.; bk.rev.; stat.; tr.lit.; circ. 10,000. (tabloid format; also avail. in microform from UMI; back issues avail.; reprint service avail. from UMI)
Formerly (until 1980): State Underwriter (ISSN 0039-0178)
Description: Covers the insurance industry in Ohio, including regulatory and legislative decisions and trends.

368 331   RU   ISSN 0030-1590
OKHRANA TRUDA I SOTSIAL'NOE STRAKHOVANIE. 1913. m. 10.80 Rub. (Vsesoyuznyi Tsentral'nyi Sovet Professional'nykh Soyuzov) Profizdat, Ul. Myasnitskaya 13, 101000 Moscow, Russia. Ed. K.S. Khromov. adv.; bk.rev.; charts; illus.; stat.; circ. 560,000. **Indexed:** World Bibl.Soc.Sec.

368   CN
ONTARIO INSURANCE DIRECTORY; a comprehensive listing of Ontario brokers, general and reinsurance company personnel, adjusters, appraisers, associations, and buyers guide. 1985. a. Can.$29.96. (Toronto Insurance Conference) Southam Business Communications Inc., 1450 Don Mills Rd., Don Mills, Ont. M3B 2X7, Canada. TEL 416-445-6641. FAX 416-442-2261. circ. 3,000.

368.4   US
OPINION MANUAL LETTERS (CHRONOLOGICAL). q. $48 in US, Canada, Mexico; elsewhere $96. (Pension Benefit Guaranty Corporation) U.S. National Technical Information Service, 5825 Port Royal Rd., Springfield, VA 22161. TEL 703-487-4630. (back issues avail.)
Description: Consists of issuances that are responses to issues raised under Employee Retirement Income Security Act (ERISA.)

368.4   US
OPINION MANUAL UPDATES (SECTIONAL). q. $48 in US, Canada, Mexico; elsewhere $96. (Pension Benefit Guaranty Corporation) U.S. National Technical Information Service, 5825 Port Royal Rd., Springfield, VA 22161. TEL 703-487-4630.

368   CI   ISSN 0030-6193
OSIGURANJE I PRIVREDA; casopis za teoriju i praksu osiguranja. (Text in Croatian; summaries in English, French or German) 1960. m. 600 din.($30) Croatia Osiguranje, d.d., Savska 41, 4100 Zagreb, Croatia. TEL 041-630-622. FAX 041-535-616. TELEX 21216. Ed. Vladimir Miletic. adv.; bk.rev.; index; circ. 3,000.

368   US   ISSN 0030-6932
OUR PAPER. 1913. m. free. Grain Dealers Mutual Insurance Co., 1752 N. Meridian St., Box 1747, Indianapolis, IN 46206. TEL 317-923-2453. Ed. John C. Knox. illus.; circ. 2,500.

368   US
OUR VOICE.* (Text in English and Slovenian) 1910. s-m. membership. American Mutual Life Association, 19424 S. Waterloo Rd., Cleveland, OH 44119-3250. Ed. Margot Ann Klima. adv.; circ. 8,500 (controlled). (tabloid format; back issues avail.)

368 387   UK   ISSN 0950-4044
P & I INTERNATIONAL. (Protection & Indemnity); monthly review of mutual insurance. 1987. m. $305. Lloyd's of London Press Ltd., Sheepen Place, Colchester, Essex CO3 3LP, England. TEL 0206-772277. FAX 0206-46273. TELEX 987321 LLOYDS G. (US subscr. to: 611 Broadway, Ste. 308, New York, NY 10012. TEL 212-529-9500) Ed. W. Robertson. bk.rev. (back issues avail.)
Description: Covers developments affecting insurance companies, brokers, and adjusters, including legislation, case law, personal injury, cargo, pollution, and more.

P I P E R. (Pensions & Investments Performance Evaluation Reports) see *BUSINESS AND ECONOMICS — Investments*

368.3   GW   ISSN 0343-9321
P K V INFORMATIONDIENST. (Private Krankenversicherung) 1946. w. DM.536. Egon Siller Verlag, Tussmannstr. 17, Postfach 7024, 4000 Dusseldorf, Germany. Ed. H.U. Hill. circ. 200. (looseleaf format)
Formerly: Informationsdienst fuer die Private Krankenversicherung (ISSN 0020-031X)

368   GW   ISSN 0176-3261
P K V PUBLIK. 1964. 9/yr. DM.6.30. (Verband der Privaten Krankenversicherung e.V.) Verlag Versicherungswirtschaft e.V., Klosestr. 20-24, 7500 Karlsruhe 1, Germany. Ed. Christoph Uleer. charts.
Formerly: Private Krankenversicherung.

P P O LETTER. (Preferred Provider Organization) see *BUSINESS AND ECONOMICS*

368.382 610   US
PART B NEWS. 1987. bi-w. $396. United Communications Group, 11300 Rockville Pike, Ste. 1100, Rockville, MD 20852-3030. TEL 301-816-8950. FAX 301-816-8945. Eds. Roxanne Bollinger, Carol Monaco.
Description: Reports on the changes in Medicare reimbursement rules for physicians, plus ways they can get their share of "Part B" dollars.

INSURANCE

362.6   UK   ISSN 0140-6647
PENSION FUNDS & THEIR ADVISERS. 1978. a. £62.50. A.P. Information Services Ltd., 33 Ashbourne Ave., London NW11 0DU, England. TEL 081-458-1607. FAX 081-455-6381. (Dist. in U.S. by: Money Market Directories Inc., 300 Eastmarket St., Charlottesville, VA 22901) Ed. Alan Philipp. adv.; circ. 3,500. (avail. on diskette)
—BLDSC shelfmark: 6422.710000.

368 331   US
PENSION PLAN GUIDE. w. $870. Commerce Clearing House, Inc., 4025 W. Peterson Ave., Chicago, IL 60646. TEL 312-583-8500.
   Supersedes: Pension Plan Guide Summary.

PENSION WORLD. see *BUSINESS AND ECONOMICS — Banking And Finance*

368   UK
PENSIONS TODAY. 1979. m. £145 (foreign £160). Monitor Press, Rectory Rd., Great Waldingfield, Sudbury, Suffolk CO10 0TL, England. TEL 0787-78607. FAX 0787-880201. (back issues avail.)
   Description: For pension-fund managers, trustees, company secretaries, pensions specialists in broking and insurance companies.

368   UK   ISSN 0307-191X
PENSIONS WORLD. 1972. m. £22. (National Association of Pension Funds) Tolley Publishing Co. Ltd., Tolley House, 2 Addiscombe Rd., Croydon, Surrey CR9 5AF, England. TEL 01-686 9141. Ed. K.D. Ladbrook. adv.; bk.rev.; stat.; index; circ. 4,850.
Indexed: Account.& Data Proc.Abstr., Account.Ind. (1974-), Anbar, Work Rel.Abstr.
—BLDSC shelfmark: 6422.720500.

PERSONAL INJURY NEWSLETTER. see *LAW*

PERSONAL INJURY VALUATION HANDBOOKS; injury valuation & special research reports. see *LAW*

368.5   US
PERSONAL INJURY VERDICT REVIEWS. 1982. w. $375. Jury Verdict Research Inc., 30700 Bainbridge Rd., Ste. H, Solon, OH 44139. TEL 800-321-6910. TELEX 216-349-JURY. (back issues avail.)
   Description: Up-to-date case examples and research provided on various liability areas in personal damage litigation.

368.5   US
PERSONAL INJURY VERDICT SURVEY. (Edition for the 50 US States) a. $29.50. Jury Verdict Research, Inc., 30700 Bainbridge Rd., Ste. H, Solon, OH 44139. TEL 216-248-7960. TELEX 216-349-JURY. (back issues avail.)
   Description: Analysis of personal damage verdict trends by state.

368   UK
PERSONAL PENSIONS (YEAR). 1975. irreg. Financial Times Business Information, 102 Clerkenwell Rd., London EC1M 5SA, England. TEL 01-799-2002. circ. 3,500. (tabloid format)
   Former titles: Self-Employed Pensions; Handbook of Self-Employed Pensions.

368   US   ISSN 0737-6839
PERSONAL PROPERTY SECTION NEWS. 1980. q. $40 membership. International Association of Assessing Officers, 1313 E. 60th St., Chicago, IL 60637-9990. TEL 312-947-2042. Ed. Pam Madgett. circ. 655. (back issues avail.)

PERSPECTIVES IN HEALTHCARE RISK MANAGEMENT. see *HOSPITALS*

368   PH
PHILIPPINE INSURANCE COMMISSION ANNUAL REPORT. 1949. a. price varies. Insurance Commission, Insurance Commission Bldg., 1071 United Nations Ave., P.O. Box 3589, Manila, Philippines. TEL 599-221. FAX 632-522-1434. circ. 1,000.
   Description: Provides the insurance industry and the public with information on the results of business operations and other insurance information.

368   CS   ISSN 0032-2393
POJISTNY OBZOR. 1923. m. 18 Kcs.($15.40) (Ceska Statni Pojistovna, Prague) Nakladatelstvi Technicke Literatury, Spalena 51, 113 02 Prague 1, Czechoslovakia. (Dist. by: Artia, Ve Smeckach 30, 111 27 Prague 1, Czechoslovakia) (Co-sponsor: Slovenska Statni Pojistovna, Bratislava) Ed. Eva Trojanova. bk.rev.; circ. 4,800.

368   US
POL-AM JOURNAL. (Text in English and Polish) 1911. m. $5. Polish National Alliance of Brooklyn, 155 Noble St., Brooklyn, NY 11222. TEL 718-389-4704. (Subscr. to: 413 Cedar Ave., Scranton, PA 18505) Ed. Henry J. Dende. adv.; bk.rev.; illus.; circ. 9,118. (tabloid format)

365   US
POLICIES REVIEW. 1988? m. $192. Shelby Publishing Corp., 155 Federal St., Boston, MA 02110. TEL 617-423-0978. Ed. Roger Peirce.

368   UK   ISSN 0263-6700
POLICY MARKET. 1902. m. £24. Stone and Cox (Publications) Ltd., 44 Fleet St., London EC4Y 1BS, England. Ed. David Vaughan-Williams. adv.; illus.; stat.; index.
   Formerly: Policy (ISSN 0032-2652)
   Description: Covers life and non-life insurance industries, of special interest to the broker.

368   UK   ISSN 0032-5252
HG8013
POST MAGAZINE AND INSURANCE MONITOR. 1840. w. £75. Buckley Press Ltd., 131-135 Temple Chambers, Temple Ave., London EC4Y 0BP, England. TEL 071-583-3030. FAX 071-583-4068. Ed. V.J.F. Betson. adv.; charts; illus.; stat.
—BLDSC shelfmark: 6558.879000.

368 610   YU   ISSN 0032-5880
POVRATAK U ZIVOT. 1952. bi-m. $4.80. Institut za Rehabilitaciju, Belgrade, Sokobanjska, Belgrade, Yugoslavia. Ed. Zivojin Zec.

368.4   IT   ISSN 0032-8065
HD7090
PREVIDENZA SOCIALE. (Text in Italian; summaries in English) 1945. bi-m. L.30000. Istituto Nazionale della Previdenza Sociale, Via Ciro Il Grande 21, Rome, Italy. Ed. Aldo Stranges. adv.; bk.rev.; bibl.; stat.; index; circ. 6,000. **Indexed:** P.A.I.S.For.Lang.Ind., World Bibl.Soc.Sec.

368   IT   ISSN 0032-809X
PREVIDENZA SOCIALE NELL'ARTIGIANATO. vol.11, 1970. bi-m. L.3000. Confederazione delle Libere Associazioni Artigiane Italiane, Piazzetta Pattari 4, Milan, Italy. Ed. Gabriele Maria Lanfredini. bk.rev.; abstr.

PREVISIONS GLISSANTES DETAILLEES EN PERSPECTIVES SECTORIELLES (VOL.31): ASSURANCES. see *BUSINESS AND ECONOMICS — Economic Situation And Conditions*

PRINCIPAL'S REPORT. see *BUSINESS AND ECONOMICS — Management*

368   US
PRODUCER NEWS. 1976. m. $27. Insurance Field Company, 1812 Production Ct., Louisville, KY 40299. TEL 502-491-5857. FAX 502-491-5905. (Subscr. to: Box 24244, Louisville, KY 40224) Ed. George V.R. Smith. circ. 16,350. (looseleaf format; back issues avail.)
   Description: Newsletter for independent insurance agents.

368   GW   ISSN 0723-3604
PRODUKTHAFTPFLICHT INTERNATIONAL. 1982. bi-m. DM.170. Verlag Versicherungswirtschaft e.V., Klosestr. 22, Postfach 6469, 7500 Karlsruhe 1, Germany. TEL 0221-7759516. FAX 0221-7759571. (Subscr. to: Cologne RE, Theodor-Heuss-Ring 11, P.O. Box 108016, 5000 Cologne 1, Germany) Ed. Wilhelm Zeller. bk.rev.; index; circ. 1,000. (back issues avail.)
   Description: Covers product liability and related matters.

368   US   ISSN 0148-8899
HG8011
PROFESSIONAL AGENT. 1937. m. $24 to non-members; members $12. National Association of Professional Insurance Agents, 400 N. Washington St., Alexandria, VA 22314. TEL 703-836-9340. FAX 703-836-1279. Ed. Alan Prochoroff. adv.; bk.rev.; charts; illus.; stat.; circ. 30,414.
   Formerly (until 1976): Mutual Review (ISSN 0027-5204)

368.01   US
PROFESSIONAL INSURANCE AGENTS OF NEW YORK - NEW JERSEY - CONNECTICUT. 1948. m. (except July). $25. P I A Management Services, Inc., Box 997, Glenmont, NY 12077-0997. TEL 518-434-3111. FAX 518-434-2342. Ed. Mary Vanniere. adv.; index; circ. 5,000.
   Description: Covers technical subjects, general business management information, and Association activities.

368.5   UK   ISSN 0268-9669
PROFESSIONAL LIABILITY TODAY. 1986. m. £380. Lloyds' of London Press Ltd., Sheepen Place, Colchester, Essex CO3 3LP, England. TEL 0206-772277. FAX 0206-46273. TELEX 987321 LLOYDS G. (US subscr. to: 611 Broadway, New York, NY 10012. TEL 212-529-9500) Ed. J.S. Ashworth. (back issues avail.)
—BLDSC shelfmark: 6859.528000.
   Description: Advises on law, insurance, and practical means to avoid and minimize liability.

368   UK
PROSPECT (LONDON).* 1972. m. £3.50 per no. (Life Insurance Association) Citadel HSC, Sta. Approach, Chorleywood, Rickmansworth, Herts WD3 5PF, England. FAX 01-636-8120. Ed. Stewart Farr. adv.; bk.rev.; circ. 11,500.

PUBLIC RISK. see *PUBLIC ADMINISTRATION — Municipal Government*

Q R C ADVISOR. (Quality, Risk and Cost) see *HOSPITALS*

QUALITY ASSURANCE AND UTILIZATION REVIEW. see *BUSINESS AND ECONOMICS — Management*

368   US
QUARTERLY LISTING OF ALIEN INSURERS. q. $150 (with supplement $250). National Association of Insurance Commissioners, 120 W. 12th St., Kansas City, MO 64105. TEL 816-842-3600. (Subscr. to: N A I C Publications, Box 263, Department 42, Kansas City, MO 64193-0042) stat.
   Description: Provides information on alien insurance companies.

368   CN   ISSN 0701-5666
HG1662.C3
QUEBEC (PROVINCE) REGIE DE L'ASSURANCE-DEPOTS DU QUEBEC. RAPPORT ANNUEL. a. Can.$2. Ministere des Communications, Direction Generale des Publications Gouvernementales, 2e etage, 1279 boul. Charest Ouest, Quebec, Que. G1N 4K7, Canada. TEL 413-643-3895.

368   US   ISSN 0033-6270
QUERY. (Former name of issuing body: American Society of Chartered Life Underwriters) 1946. m. membership. American Society of C L U & Ch F C, 270 Bryn Mawr Ave., Bryn Mawr, PA 19010. TEL 215-526-2500. Ed. Fred J. Dopheide.

368   US
R E I D QUARTERLY. (Real Estate Investment Quarterly) 1973. q. free. Prudential Insurance Co. of America, Public Relations & Advertising Dept., 5 Plaza, Newark, NJ 07101. TEL 201-877-6000. Ed. Carol Abaya. circ. 3,000 (controlled).
   Supersedes: Mirror.

368   GW
R UND V GRUPPENBILD. 1985. m. R und V Versicherung, Taunusstr. 1, 6200 Wiesbaden, Germany. TEL 0611-5330. FAX 0611-533375. Ed. Renate Killmer. bk.rev.; circ. 14,000. (back issues avail.)

INSURANCE

368 GW
R UND V REPORT. 1986. q. free. R und V Versicherung, Taunusstr. 1, Postfach 4840, 6200 Wiesbaden, Germany. TEL 0611-533-4672.
FAX 0611-533-375. Ed. Renate Killmer. index; circ. 33,000.

368.382 US
R V S FEE SCHEDULE. (Relative Value Scale) base vol. (plus updates 9/yr.). $370. United Communications Group, 11300 Rockville Pike, Ste. 1100, Rockville, MD 20852-3030. TEL 301-816-8950.
FAX 301-816-8945. Ed. Carol Monaco.
 Description: Examines the Medicare payment system for physicians; includes data and worksheet to calculate reimbursement.

368 US
RALPH H. BLANCHARD MEMORIAL ENDOWMENT SERIES.* 1977. irreg. $10. University of Pennsylvania, Wharton School of Finance and Commerce, Pension Research Council, 3373 Vance Hall, Philadelphia, PA 19104-6358.

368.3 GW ISSN 0033-9989
DER RATGEBER; Monatshefte fuer die Aus- und Fortbildung der Krankenkassenangestellten. m. DM.29.40. Verlag der Ratgeber, Postfach 3004, 6200 Wiesbaden, Germany. Ed. H.A. Aye. bk.rev.; index. (also avail. in record)

368 UK ISSN 0953-5640
REACTIONS. m. £110. ReActions Ltd., 39-41 North Rd., London N7 9DP, England. TEL 071-609-8661.
FAX 071-609-0139. TELEX 27142-REACT-G. Ed. Valerie Denney. adv. contact: Simon Hitches.
—BLDSC shelfmark: 7300.280200.

366 UK ISSN 0034-1215
RECHABITE. 1840. q. 25p. Independent Order of Rechabites, Rechabite Bldgs., One N. Parade, Deansgate, Manchester 3, England. Ed. F.S. Tucker.

RECUEIL JURIDIQUE DE L'EST SECURITE SOCIALE; doctrine jurisprudence, documents administratifs.
see *LAW*

368 US
RED SHIELD NEWS. 1940. m. free to employees. Royal Insurance, Corporate Communications Dept., 9300 Arrowpoint Blvd., Charlotte, NC 28217.
TEL 704-522-2000. FAX 704-522-2055. Ed. Dene Hellman. charts; illus.; stat.; circ. 10,000.
 Formerly: Red Shield (ISSN 0034-2041)

368 NE ISSN 0034-2947
REFLECTOR. 1949. m. fl.60. Nederlandse Vereniging van Makelaars in Assurantien en Assurantieadviseurs, Postbus 235, 3800 AE Amersfoort, Netherlands. TEL 033-631414. Ed.Bd. adv.; bk.rev.; illus.; circ. 4,000.

368 CN
REGARDS LA REVUE DE L'ASSURANCE. (Text in French, summaries in English) 1923. bi-m. $30. Association des Courtiers d'Assurances de la Province de Quebec - Insurance Broker's Association of the Province of Quebec, 300 rue Leo-Pariseau, Montreal, Que. H2W 2N1, Canada. TEL 514-842-2591.
FAX 514-842-3138. Ed. Sophie B. Brzozowska. adv.; circ. 5,799.

REIMBURSEMENT ADVISOR. see *HOSPITALS*

368 UK ISSN 0048-7171
HG8059.R4
REINSURANCE; the monthly international reinsurance magazine. 1969. m. £50. Buckley Press Ltd., 131-135 Temple Chambers, Temple Ave., London EC4Y 0BP, England. TEL 071-583-3030.
FAX 071-583-4068. Ed. V.J.F. Betson. adv.; charts; illus.; stat. Indexed: P.A.I.S.
—BLDSC shelfmark: 7351.800000.

368 US ISSN 0747-5276
HG8083
REINSURANCE DIRECTORY; Bermuda, Canada, & the U.S.A. 1984. a. $75. Robert W. Strain Publishing & Seminars, Box 1520, Athens, TX 75751.
TEL 914-677-5974. Ed. Robert W. Strain. adv.; index; circ. 1,000 (controlled).
●Also available online.

368 UK ISSN 0266-8653
REINSURANCE MARKET REPORT. 1983. fortn. £255($510) D Y P Insurance and Reinsurance Research Group, Bridge House, 181 Queen Victoria St., London EC4V 4DD, England.
TEL 071-236-2175. Ed. J.S. Bannister. bk.rev.; charts; stat. (back issues avail.)

368 US ISSN 0034-3641
REINSURANCE REPORTER. 1958. q. free. Lincoln National Life Insurance Co., Reinsurance Division, 1300 S. Clinton St., Fort Wayne, IN 46801.
FAX 219-455-2738. Ed. Barbara W. Warden. adv.; charts; illus.; stat.; circ. 3,500.

368 GW ISSN 0340-5753
DIE RENTENVERSICHERUNG. 1959. m. DM.80. Asgard-Verlag Dr. Werner Hippe KG, Einsteinstr. 10, Postfach 1465, 5205 St. Augustin, Germany.
TEL 02241-3164-0. Ed. W. Hippe. adv.; bk.rev.; bibl.; circ. 1,000.

368 340 US
RESPONSIBILITIES OF INSURANCE AGENTS AND BROKERS. 1974. s-a. $375. Matthew Bender & Co., Inc., 11 Penn Plaza, New York, NY 10001.
TEL 212-967-7707. (Subscr. to: 1275 Broadway, Box 989, Albany, NY 12201) Ed. Bertram Harnett. index, cum.index: 1974-1988; circ. 1,683.
 Description: Updates to comprehensive treatises on insurance agency law.

368 UK ISSN 0034-6349
HG8013
REVIEW: WORLDWIDE REINSURANCE. 1869. m. £50($174) United Trade Press Ltd., U.T.P. House, 33-35 Bowling Green Ln., London EC1R 0DA, England. TEL 01-837 1212. Ed. Ann Myers. adv.; charts; stat.; index; circ. 4,995.

368 CK ISSN 0120-1972
REVISTA FASECOLDA. 1977. q. $30. Union de Aseguradores Colombianos, Carrera 7a. No. 26-20, Piso. 11, Apdo. Aereo 5233, Bogota, Colombia. circ. 1,000.
 Formerly: Fasecolda.

REVISTA PARA JUBILADOS Y PENSIONADOS. see *GERONTOLOGY AND GERIATRICS*

368 FR
REVUE DU COURTAGE. 1923. m. 260 F. Syndicat National des Courtiers d'Assurances et des Reassurances, 31 rue d'Amsterdam, 75008 Paris, France. TEL 33-1-48-74-19-12. FAX 42-82-91-10. Ed. Alain Farshian. adv.; bk.rev.; bibl.; illus.; index; circ. 2,000.
 Former titles: Revue l'Assureur Conseil; Assureur Counseil (ISSN 0004-6043)
 Description: Deals with insurance, security and prevention, risk management, pensions, law and cases, international relations, insurance companies and products, broking.

368 FR ISSN 0035-3167
REVUE GENERALE DES ASSURANCES TERRESTRES. 1930. q. 500 F. (foreign 520 F.) (Librairie Generale de Droit et de Jurisprudence) Editions Juridiques Associees, 26 rue Vercingetorix, 75014 Paris, France. TEL 1-43-35-01-67.
FAX 43-20-07-42. TELEX EJA 203 918 F. Ed. Jean Bigot. bk.rev.; circ. 1,350.
—BLDSC shelfmark: 7905.600000.
 Description: Presents articles, chronicles, miscellanea and jurisprudence of insurance.

368 US
▼**RISK AND BENEFITS JOURNAL.** 1991. bi-m. Curant Communications, Inc., 1849 Sawtelle Blvd., Ste. 770, Los Angeles, CA 90025. TEL 213-479-1769. FAX 213-479-6275. adv.; circ. 14,000.
 Description: Includes case histories, features, industry news, legislative information and pragmatic information for risk and benefits managers.

368 658 US ISSN 0893-2654
RISK & BENEFITS MANAGEMENT. 1986. m. $48. Stevens Publishing Corp., 225 N. New Rd., Waco, TX 76710. TEL 817-776-9000. (Subscr. to: Box 2178, Santa Monica, CA 90406-2178) adv.; bk.rev.; charts; illus.; index; circ. 16,000. (back issues avail.)

368 US
▼**RISK & INSURANCE.** 1990. bi-m. Axon Group, 747 Dresher Rd., Ste. 500, Box 980, Horsham, PA 19044. TEL 215-784-0860. FAX 215-784-0870. Ed. Karen McCone-Berney. circ. 40,000. (tabloid format)
 Description: For insurance industry executives and risk and insurance managers at corporations, nonprofit institutions and government agencies. Covers professional liability, environmental liability, captive administration, health benefits and workers' compensation.

368 US ISSN 0035-5593
HG8059.C7 CODEN: RMGTDN
RISK MANAGEMENT. 1954. 12/yr. $48. (Risk and Insurance Management Society) Risk Management Society Publishing, Inc., 205 E. 42nd St., New York, NY 10017. TEL 212-286-9364.
FAX 212-986-9716. TELEX 968289. Ed. Alice Oshins. adv.; bk.rev.; charts; mkt.; index; circ. 10,700. (also avail. in microfilm from UMI; reprint service avail. from UMI; back issues avail.) Indexed: ABI Inform., Account.Ind. (1974-), BPIA, Bus.Ind., Hlth.Ind., Manage.Cont., PROMT, Sci.Abstr., Tr.& Indus.Ind.
●Also available on CD-ROM.
 Formerly: National Insurance Buyer.
 Description: Official publication of the Risk and Insurance Management Society with how-to and interpretive articles relating to risk analysis and funding techniques, safety and loss prevention, employee benefits planning, and federal/state legislative and regulatory developments.

368 US ISSN 0732-2666
RISK MANAGEMENT FOR EXECUTIVE WOMEN. 1982-1985; resumed 1990. bi-m. $85 to individuals; institutions $125. Cox Publications, Box 20316, Billings, MT 59104-0316.
TEL 406-256-8822. Ed. Meridith B. Cox. circ. 350.
 Formerly (until 1983): California Risk Management Report: For the Female Executive.
 Description: Reports on court decisions affecting insurance, personnel, health records and safety issues which expand liability or set up new areas of risk.

368 US
RISK MANAGEMENT NEWSLETTER. m. $283. Merritt Company, 1661 Ninth St., Box 955, Santa Monica, CA 90406. TEL 213-450-7234.
FAX 213-396-4563.

368 US
RISK REPORT. m. International Risk Management Institute, Inc., 12222 Merit Dr., Ste. 1660, Dallas, TX 75251-2276. TEL 214-960-7693. Ed. Jack P. Gibson.

368 450 US
RISKWATCH. 1985. bi-w. $100. Public Risk Management Association, 1117 N. 19th St., Ste. 900, Arlington, VA 22209. FAX 703-528-7966. Eds. Kathy Walsh. circ. 2,500.
 Description: A current events watchdog for public sector risk managers.

368 US ISSN 0035-8525
HG8011
ROUGH NOTES; property, casualty, surety. 1878. m. $25 (foreign $35). Rough Notes Co., Inc., 1200 N. Meridian, Box 564, Indianapolis, IN 46206.
TEL 800-428-4384. FAX 317-634-1041. Ed. Thomas McCoy. adv.; bk.rev.; illus.; tr.lit.; index; circ. 40,000. Indexed: ABI Inform.
—BLDSC shelfmark: 8025.750000.

368 US
ROUND THE TABLE. 1973. bi-m. $10. Million Dollar Round Table, 325 Touhy, Park Ridge, IL 60068.
TEL 708-692-6378. FAX 708-518-8921. Ed. Mary Kay Ams. bk.rev.; charts; illus.; tr.lit.; circ. 21,000. (back issues avail.) Indexed: L.l.l.
 Description: Contains sales ideas and organizational information for life underwriters.

368 UK
ROYAL INSURANCE NEWSLETTER. m. Royal Insurance, P.O. Box 144, New Hall Place, Liverpool L69 3EN, England. Ed. Bill Curran.

368 GW
RUNDE TISCH. 1956. bi-m. Vereinte Versicherung, Postfach 202522, 8000 Munich 2, Germany.
TEL 089-6785-0. FAX 089-67856523. illus.

IJK

INSURANCE

368 US ISSN 0036-2409
SAFECO AGENT. 1923. bi-m. free. (Safeco Insurance Companies) Safeco Corporation, Safeco Plaza, Seattle, WA 98185. TEL 206-545-5000. Ed. Dan Pedersen. adv.; charts; illus.; stat.; circ. 14,000 (controlled).

368 US ISSN 0036-3669
SALVAGE BIDS. 1963. fortn. $410. John B. Tamke, Ed. & Pub., Box 5, Laconia, NH 03246. TEL 603-528-3039. FAX 603-366-5734. charts; tr.lit.; circ. 1,322. (looseleaf format)
Description: Compilation of major industrial actions worldwide.

SASKATCHEWAN. PRESCRIPTION DRUG PLAN. ANNUAL REPORT. see *PHARMACY AND PHARMACOLOGY*

368.3 CN
HD7102.C22
SASKATCHEWAN HEALTH. ANNUAL REPORT. (Supplements avail.: Saskatchewan Health. Mental Health Service Branch; Saskatchewan Health. Medical Care Insurance Branch; Saskatchewan Health. Labor and Distribution Control Branch; Saskatchewan Health. Community Health - Preventitive Service Branch; Saskatchewan Health. Hospital Service Branch; Saskatchewan Health. Continuing Care Branch; Saskatchewan Health. Prescription Drug Service Branch; Saskatchewan Health. Vital Statistics Branch.) 1962. a. free. Medical Care Insurance Branch, T.C. Douglas Bldg., 3475 Albert St., Regina, Sask. S4S 6X6, Canada. TEL 306-787-3475. FAX 306-787-9000. circ. 2,500.
Incorporates: Saskatchewan Health. Medical Care Insurance Branch. Annual Report; Which was formerly: Saskatchewan. Medical Care Insurance Commission. Annual Report (ISSN 0080-6544)

368.4 US
SAVING SOCIAL SECURITY. 1983. 8/yr. $1.25 per no. National Committee to Preserve Social Security and Medicare, 2000 K St., N.W., Ste. 800, Washington, DC 20006. TEL 202-822-9459. FAX 202-822-9459. Ed. Denise S. Fremeau. adv.; circ. 2,028,551.
Description: Covers federal agencies, congressional committees and political leaders with jurisdiction over social security, medicare, nursing home reform and more.

368 UK ISSN 0308-1729
SAVINGS MARKET. 1976. q. £2. United Trade Press Ltd., U.T.P. House, 33-35 Bowling Green Lane, London EC1R 0DA, England. TEL 01-837 1212. Ed. Mike Hockings.

368.01 SW ISSN 0346-1238
HG8751 CODEN: SAJODI
SCANDINAVIAN ACTUARIAL JOURNAL. (Supplements avail.) (Text in English) 1918. q. SEK 460 incl. supplements. (Swedish Society of Actuaries) Almqvist & Wiksell Periodical Company, Box 638, S-101 28 Stockholm, Sweden. Co-sponsors: Danish Society of Actuaries; Actuarial Society of Finland; Norwegian Society of Actuaries) Ed. Bjoern Pelmgren. adv.; bk.rev.; circ. 1,500. (tabloid format) Indexed: J.Cont.Quant.Meth., Math.R.
—BLDSC shelfmark: 8087.468000.
Formerly: Skandinavisk Aktuarientidskrift (ISSN 0037-606X)

368 SZ
SCHWEIZER VERSICHERUNG; Magazin fuer Fuehrungskraefte aus der Versicherungswirtschaft. 1988. q. 30 Fr. (foreign 35 Fr.) S H Z Fachverlag AG, Alte Landstr. 43, 8700 Kuesnacht, Switzerland. TEL 01-910-80-22. FAX 01-910-51-55. circ. 10,000.

368 SZ ISSN 0042-3815
SCHWEIZERISCHE VEREINIGUNG DER VERSICHERUNGSMATHEMATIKER. MITTEILUNGEN. (Text and summaries in English, French and German) 1901. s-a. 160 Fr.($105) Staempfli und Cie AG, Postfach, CH-3001 Berne, Switzerland. FAX 031-276699. TELEX 911987. Ed. Hans Buehlman. bk.rev.

368 SZ
SCHWEIZERISCHE VERSICHERUNGSZEITSCHRIFT/REVUE SUISSE D'ASSURANCES. (Text in French and German) 1933. bi-m. $69. Verlag Peter Lang AG, Jupiterstr. 15, CH-3015 Bern, Switzerland. TEL 031-321122. FAX 031-321131. TELEX 912651-PELA-CH. Ed.Bd. adv.; bk.rev.; bibl.; index; circ. 2,000. Indexed: World Bibl.Soc.Sec.

368.4 CK
SEGURIDAD SOCIAL. 1948. q. Instituto Colombiana de Seguros Sociales, Transversal 17, no. 25-39, Bogota, Colombia.

368.4 BO
SEGURIDAD SOCIAL. 1938. m. Caja Nacional de Seguridad Social, Casilla 697, Plaza Murillo, Esquina Ingavi, La Paz, Bolivia. bibl.
Formerly (1938-1954): Proteccion Social.

368 UY
SEGUROS. 1975. irreg. Banco de Seguros, Av. Libertador Brigadier General Juan A. Lavalleja No. 1465, Montevideo, Uruguay. illus.
Formerly: Bancoseguros.

368.382 GW ISSN 0342-2186
SELBSTVERWALTUNG UND SELBSTVERANTWORTUNG. 1951. m. DM.13.20. Bundesverband der Betriebskrankenkassen, Kronprinzen Str. 6, 4300 Essen 1, Germany. TEL 0201-1791140. FAX 0201-1791003. circ. 12,500. (back issues avail.)

368 CC
SHANDONG BAOXIAN/SHANDONG INSURANCE. (Text in Chinese) m. Shandong Sheng Baoxian Gongsi - Shandong Insurance Company, No. 4, Gongqingtuan Lu, Jinan, Shandong 250012, People's Republic of China. TEL 25103. Ed. Huang Shanhua.

368 CC
SHANGHAI BAOXIAN/SHANGHAI INSURANCE. (Text in Chinese) m. Zhongguo Renmin Baoxian Gongsi, Shanghai Fengongsi, Baoxian Yanjiusuo - China People's Insurance Company, Shanghai Branch, Insurance Research Institute, No.1, Alley 590, Room 101, Yuanping Nanlu, Shanghai 200030, People's Republic of China. TEL 4386301. Ed. Wu Yue.

SHEPARD'S INSURANCE LAW CITATIONS. see *LAW*

368.012 US
SHORTCUT. 1948. q. $720. National Underwriter Co., 505 Gest St., Cincinnati, OH 45203. TEL 513-721-2140. FAX 513-721-0126. adv. (avail. on diskette)
Formerly (until 1986): Agent's and Buyer's Guide (ISSN 0065-4272)
Description: Provides data on available markets for standard, excess and surplus insurance coverages on a state by state basis, as well as those markets with binding authority.

368 CC
SICHUAN BAOXIAN/SICHUAN INSURANCE. (Text in Chinese) bi-m. Zhongguo Renmin Baoxian Gongsi, Sichuan Fengongsi - China People's Insurance Company, Sichuan Branch, Baoxian Dalou, Donggan Dao, Chengdu, Sichuan 610016, People's Republic of China. TEL 25738. Ed. Zheng Zhenhua.

368 IT
SICURTA. 1945. m. L.12000. Nuova Mercurio S.p.A., Via S. Paolo 15, 20121 Milan, Italy. Ed. Luigi Giudice. adv.; circ. 12,000.

368 SZ ISSN 0037-4857
SIGMA. Issued with: Experiodica (ISSN 0014-4932) (Editions in English, French, German) 1958. irreg. (8-10/yr.) free. Schweizerische Rueckversicherungs-Gesellschaft - Swiss Reinsurance Company, Economic Department, Mythenquai 50-60, Zurich, Switzerland. TEL 01-2082121. FAX 01-2082999. TELEX 815722-SRE-CH. charts; stat.
Description: Studies of problems concerning the economics and insurance fields.

368 US ISSN 0736-8348
SMARTS INSURANCE BULLETIN. 1956. 48/yr. $195. James Whitaker & Associates, 870 Market St., Ste. 459 459, San Francisco, CA 94102. TEL 415-982-1480. FAX 415-982-3504. Ed. James Whitaker. bk.rev.; charts; stat.; tr.lit.; q. index; circ. 1,000. (looseleaf format)
Description: California legislative, regulatory, judicial news and opinion relating to insurance.

368.4 IS
SOCIAL SECURITY; journal of welfare and social security studies. (Text in Hebrew; summaries in English) 1971. s-a. IS.24. National Insurance Institute, 13 Sderot Weizman, Jerusalem, Israel. Ed.Bd. bibl.; cum.index; circ. 500. (tabloid format; back issues avail.) Indexed: Ind.Heb.Per., World Bibl.Soc.Sec.
Description: Discusses contemporary social security problems from sociological, economic and legal perspectives.

368.4 US ISSN 0037-7910
HD7123 CODEN: SSYBA
SOCIAL SECURITY BULLETIN. 1938. q. plus a. supplement. $19 (foreign $23.75). U.S. Social Security Administration, Office of Research and Statistics, Van Ness Centre Bldg., Rm. 209, 4301 Connecticut Ave., N.W., Washington, DC 20008. TEL 202-282-7138. FAX 202-282-7219. (Subscr. to: Supt. of Documents, Washington, DC 20402) Ed. Marylin R. Thomas. adv.; bk.rev.; bibl.; charts; stat.; index, cum.index: 1938-1979, 1980-1988. (also avail. in microform from MIM,UMI; reprint service avail. from UMI) Indexed: ABI Inform., Abstr.Soc.Geront., Amer.Stat.Ind., ASCA, B.P.I., Bus.Ind., C.L.I., CLOA, Excerp.Med., Ind.Med., Ind.U.S.Gov.Per., J.of Econ.Lit., L.I.I., L.R.I., Leg.Per., Med.Care Rev., MEDOC, P.A.I.S., Pers.Lit., PROMT, Rehabil.Lit., Soc.Work Res.& Abstr., SSCI, Tr.& Indus.Ind., Work Rel.Abstr., World Bibl.Soc.Sec.
●Also available online. Vendor(s): DIALOG.
—BLDSC shelfmark: 8318.195100.

368 SZ ISSN 0379-704X
SOCIAL SECURITY DOCUMENTATION: AFRICAN SERIES. 1977. irreg. 15 Fr. per no. International Social Security Association, Box 1, CH-1211 Geneva 22, Switzerland. Indexed: Int.Lab.Doc.
—BLDSC shelfmark: 8318.195500.
Description: Includes reports of regional conferences, round tables and study groups, as well as articles and studies on regional problems.

368 SZ ISSN 0250-4057
SOCIAL SECURITY DOCUMENTATION: ASIAN SERIES. 1979. irreg. 15 Fr. per no. International Social Security Association, Box 1, CH-1211 Geneva 22, Switzerland.
Description: Includes reports of regional conferences, round tables and other meetings, as well as studies on problems specific to the region.

368 SZ
SOCIAL SECURITY DOCUMENTATION: EUROPEAN SERIES. (Editions in English, French, German and Spanish) 1979. irreg. 20 Fr. per no. International Social Security Association, Box 1, CH-1211 Geneva 22, Switzerland. Indexed: World Agri.Econ.& Rural Sociol.Abstr.
Description: Studies and reports of meetings concerning aspects of social security which are of special interest to industrialized countries.

360 UK
SOCIAL SECURITY LIBRARY BULLETIN. (Text in English, French) 1971. m. £7.50. Departments of Health and Social Security, Adelphi, 1-11, John Adam St., London WC2N 6HT, England. (Subscr. to: DHSS (Leaflets), P.O. Box 21, Stanmore, Middlesex HA7 1AY, England) Ed. Martin Gilbert. circ. 750. Indexed: L.R.I.
Formerly: Current Literature on Social Security.

368 US
SOCIAL SECURITY MANUAL. a. $11.95. National Underwriter Co., 505 Gest St., Cincinnati, OH 45203. TEL 513-721-2140. FAX 513-721-0126.
Description: Guide providing explanations of rules and rights under Social Security in a question and answer format.

INSURANCE

368.4 US
SOCIAL SECURITY PRACTICE GUIDE. (Issued in 4 base vols. with supplements) 1984. irreg. Matthew Bender & Co., Inc., 11 Penn Plaza, New York, NY 10001. TEL 212-967-7707. (looseleaf format)
Description: Comprehensive information on understanding Social Security regulations pertaining to the standards used in evaluating medical and vocational aspects of disability claims.

368.4 AT ISSN 0817-3524
SOCIAL SECURITY REPORTER. 1981. bi-m. Aus.$35 (foreign Aus.$47). Legal Service Bulletin Co., Ltd., c/o Monash University, Faculty of Law, Wellington Rd., Clayton, Vic. 3168, Australia.
TEL 64-3-544-0974. FAX 643-565-5305.

368.4 US
SOCIAL SECURITY RULINGS, ACQUIESCENCE RULINGS ON FEDERAL OLD-AGE, SURVIVORS, DISABILITY, SUPPLEMENTAL SECURITY INCOME AND BLACK LUNG BENEFITS. q. (plus annual cum.). $9.50. U.S. Social Security Administration, 6401 Security Blvd., Baltimore, MD 21235. TEL 202-953-3600. (Orders to: Supt. of Documents, Washington, DC 20402)
Former titles (until 1987): Social Security Rulings on Federal Old-Age, Survivors, Disability, Supplemental Security Income and Black Lung Benefits; Social Security Rulings on Federal Old-Age, Survivors, Disability and Health Insurance, Supplemental Security Income and Miners Benefits (ISSN 0037-7929)

368 DK ISSN 0107-5047
SOCIALE YDELSER, HVEM, HVAD, OG HVORNAAR; en Kort oversigt over Danmarks Sociale lovgivning med Regler og Ydelser. 1968. a. DKK 23.50. Forsikringsoplysningen, Amaliegade 10, 1256 Copenhagen K, Denmark. illus.

SOCIALNA POLITIKA. see SOCIAL SCIENCES: COMPREHENSIVE WORKS

SOCIETA LOMBARDA DI MEDICINA LEGALE E DELLE ASSICURAZIONI. ARCHIVIO. see MEDICAL SCIENCES — Forensic Sciences

368 US
SOCIETY OF ACTUARIES. RECORD. 1975. q. $60 (foreign $90)(effective 1991). Society of Actuaries, 475 N. Martingale, No. 800, Schaumburg, IL 60173-2226. TEL 708-706-3500. FAX 708-706-3599. Ed. James G. Cochran. circ. 14,000.
Description: Proceedings of three spring meetings and the annual meetin of the SOA, and discussions of all sessions.

368 US ISSN 0037-9794
HG8754
SOCIETY OF ACTUARIES. TRANSACTIONS (GENERAL). 1949. a. $55 (foreign $82.50). Society of Actuaries, 475 N. Martingale, Ste. 800, Schaumburg, IL 60173-2226. TEL 708-706-3500. FAX 708-706-3599. Ed. Jerry Enoch. bk.rev.; abstr.; bibl.; charts; index, cum.index every 5 yrs.; circ. 14,000. (also avail. in microform from UMI) **Indexed:** L.I.I.
Description: Prosents formal and scholarly papers contributed by SOA members.
Refereed Serial

368 US
SOCIETY OF ACTUARIES. TRANSACTIONS: REPORTS OF MORTALITY AND MORBIDITY EXPERIENCE. 1951. a. $14.50 (foreign $21.75)(effective 1991). Society of Actuaries, 475 N. Martingale, Ste. 800, Schaumburg, IL 60173-2226. TEL 708-706-3599. FAX 708-706-3599. charts; index; circ. 14,000.
Description: Presents results of experience studies.

368 US
SOCIETY OF ACTUARIES. YEARBOOK. 1950. a. $75 (foreign $112.50)(effective 1991). Society of Actuaries, 475 N. Martingale, Ste. 800, Schaumburg, IL 60173-2226. TEL 708-706-3500. FAX 708-706-3599. Ed. Barbara A. Simmons. index; circ. 14,000.
Description: Lists officers, committees, members, constitution and by-laws, and other items of insterest to SOA members.

368 US ISSN 0162-2706
HG8011
SOCIETY OF CHARTERED PROPERTY AND CASUALTY UNDERWRITERS. JOURNAL. Short title: C P C U Journal. 1949. q. $16. Society of Chartered Property & Casualty Underwriters, Box 3009, 720 Providence Rd., Malvern, PA 19355.
TEL 215-251-2728. adv.; bk.rev.; charts; stat.; index; circ. 22,000. **Indexed:** ABI Inform., BPIA, P.L.I.I.
Formerly: Society of Chartered Property and Casualty Underwriters. Annals (ISSN 0037-9824)

368 US ISSN 0038-0075
SOCIETY PAGE. (Former name of issuing body: American Society of Chartered Life Underwriters) 1961. bi-m. membership. American Society of C L U & Ch F C, 270 Bryn Mawr Ave., Bryn Mawr, PA 19010. TEL 215-526-2500. Ed. Deanne L. Sherman. charts; illus.; stat.; circ. 21,000.

368 US ISSN 0038-1152
SOLIDARITY (HICKSVILLE). 1906. bi-m. $1. Workmen's Benefit Fund of the United States of America, 99 N. Broadway, Hicksville, NY 11801-2936.
TEL 516-938-6060. Ed. C. Robert Muck. bk.rev.; charts; illus.; tr.lit.; circ. 16,000. **Indexed:** Abstr.Engl.Stud.

SOSIAL TRYGD. see SOCIAL SERVICES AND WELFARE

368.4 RU ISSN 0038-1713
SOTSIAL'NOE OBESPECHENIE. 1926. m. 7.20 Rub. Izdatel'stvo Sovetskaya Rossiya, Proezd Sapunova, 13, Moscow K-12, Russia. (Co-sponsor: Ministerstvo Sotsial'nogo Obespecheniya) Ed. L.S. Malanchev. bk.rev.; illus.; index; circ. 100,000. **Indexed:** World Bibl.Soc.Sec.

368.38 US ISSN 0073-148X
HG9396
SOURCE BOOK OF HEALTH INSURANCE DATA. 1959. a. single copy free. Health Insurance Association of America, 1025 Connecticut Ave., N.W., Washington, DC 20036-3998. index; circ. 45,000. **Indexed:** SRI.

368.4 331.2 SA
SOUTH AFRICA. UNEMPLOYMENT INSURANCE FUND. REPORT/SOUTH AFRICA. WERKLOOSHEIDVERSEKERINGSFONDS. VERSLAG. (Text in Afrikaans, English) a. R.1. Unemployment Insurance Fund, Box 1851, Pretoria 0001, South Africa.
Description: Report of the Unemployment Insurance Fund consisting of the balance sheet and income and expenditure accounts for the year.

368 US
SOUTHERN INSURANCE. m. Chase Communications, Box 9001, Mt. Vernon, NY 10552-9001.
TEL 212-320-2727. FAX 914-699-2025. Ed. Stephen Acunto. circ. 3,400.

368 GW ISSN 0038-6057
SOZIALE SELBSTVERWALTUNG; Informationsdienst fuer die Mitgieder der Selbstverwaltung in der Sozialversicherung. 1953. m. DM.28.80. (Bundesvereinigung der Deutschen Arbeitgeberverbaende E.V) Heider Verlag, Paffrather Str. 102, Postfach 200540, 5060 Bergisch Gladbach, Germany. TEL 02202-53047.
FAX 02202-21531. Eds. J. Husmann, E. Mueller. adv.; bk.rev.; upd 00819 88110; circ. 6,700.

368.43 AU ISSN 0038-6065
HD7090
SOZIALE SICHERHEIT; Fachzeitschrift fuer die Oesterreichische Sozialversicherung. 1948. m. S.298.50. Hauptverband der Oesterreichischen Sozialversicherungstraeger, Kundmanng. 21, A-1030 Vienna 3, Austria. TEL 0222-71132. FAX 0222-71132-3777. Ed. Ralph Mace. adv.; bk.rev.; charts; illus.; stat.; index, cum.index; circ. 7,500. **Indexed:** World Bibl.Soc.Sec.
Description: Covers social insurance in Austria.

368 UK ISSN 0038-8637
SPRINKLER BULLETIN. 1892. every 6-9 mos. Mather and Platt Ltd., Park Works, Manchester M10 6BA, England. Ed. M.L.A. Jones. charts; illus.; stat.; circ. 10,000 (controlled).

368 US ISSN 0038-9390
HG9651
STANDARD (QUINCY); New England's insurance weekly. 1865. w. $25. Standard Publishing (Quincy), 21 McGrath Hwy., Quincy, MA 02169.
TEL 617-773-7702. Ed. Frank R. Pote. adv.; bk.rev.; illus.; stat.; index; circ. 5,675. (also avail. in microform from UMI; back issues avail.; reprint service avail. from UMI) **Indexed:** P.L.I.I.

368 US
STANDARD'S SUMMARY LIFE REPORT AND RATIO ANALYSIS.* 1988. a. $5. Standard Analytical Services, Inc., 5960 Howdershell Rd., Ste. 101, Hazelwood, MO 63042-1115. TEL 314-727-5151. FAX 314-727-4167. Ed. John B. LaMacchia, Jr.
Description: Reports on individual insurance companies featuring financial information compared with that of the 25 largest companies.

368 US
STANDARD'S SUMMARY REPRODUCTIONS.* 1988. a. $5. Standard Analytical Services, Inc., 5960 Howdershell Rd., Ste. 101, Hazelwood, MO 63042-1115. TEL 314-727-5151. Ed. John B. LaMacchia, Jr.
Description: Financial summary sheets from annual statements of insurance companies, showing the financial conditions of individual companies.

368 CN ISSN 0380-223X
HG9783
STONE AND COX GENERAL INSURANCE REGISTER. 1920. a. Can.$34. Stone and Cox Ltd., 111 Peter St., Suite 202, Toronto, Ont. M5V 2H1, Canada. TEL 416-599-0772. FAX 416-599-0867. Ed. John D. Wyndham. adv.; circ. 4,230.
Formerly: Stone and Cox General Insurance Year Book (ISSN 0081-5772)
Description: Directory of property-casualty services in Canada: companies and management groups, adjusters, appraisers, legal counsel, brokers and agents, includes financial supplement.

368.3 CN ISSN 0835-2933
STONE AND COX LIFE INSURANCE TABLES. (Text in English, French) 1912. a. Can.$27.50. Stone and Cox Ltd., 111 Peter St., Suite 202, Toronto, Ont. M5V 2H1, Canada. TEL 416-599-0772. FAX 416-599-0867. Ed. John D. Wyndham. adv.; circ. 3,700.
Description: Life insurance rates, values, dividends and special features of plans for the top 60 writers of individual life insurance in Canada.

368 UK
STONE AND COX ORDINARY BRANCH LIFE ASSURANCE HANDBOOK (AND UP-DATES). 1953. m. £60 including monthly up-date sheets. Stone and Cox (Publications) Ltd., 44 Fleet St., London EC4Y 1BS, England. TEL 01-353 1622. (Subscr. to: 73-75 Gammons Lane, Watford, Herts WD2 5HU, England) Ed. Ernest Holland. adv. (looseleaf format; back issues avail.)
Formerly: Stone and Cox Ordinary Branch Life Assurance Tables.
Description: Covers nearly all UK and Irish life insurance offices.

368 UK
STONE AND COX UNIT LINKED LIFE ASSURANCE HANDBOOK (AND UP-DATES). 1970. m. £56 including monthly up-date sheets. Stone & Cox (Publications) Ltd., 44 Fleet St., London EC4Y 1BS, England. (Subscr. to: 73-75 Gammons Ln., Watford, Herts WD2 5HU, England) (looseleaf format)
Formerly: Stone and Cox Unit Linked Assurance and Annuity Tables.
Description: Covers UK and Irish life insurance offices.

368 PL ISSN 0137-9704
STUDIA UBEZPIECZENIOWE. (Text in Polish; summaries in English, Russian) 1973. irregr., vol.10, 1989. price varies. (Polskie Towarzystwo Ekonomiczne, Oddzial w Poznaniu) Panstwowe Wydawnictwo Naukowe, Miodowa 10, 00-251 Warsaw, Poland. Ed. Tadeusz Sangowski. bibl.; illus.

SUEDDEUTSCHE EISEN- UND STAHL-BERUFSGENOSSENSCHAFT. MITTEILUNGEN. see OCCUPATIONAL HEALTH AND SAFETY

INSURANCE

368.3   JA
SUKOYAKA KENPO. (Text in Japanese) 1959. m. 720 Yen. National Federation of Health Insurance Societies, 1-24-4 Minami-Aoyama, Minato-ku, Tokyo, Japan. FAX 03-5410-2091. Ed. Jiro Hirose. adv.; bk.rev.; film rev.; abstr.; bibl.; stat.; circ. 7,200.
Formerly: Kenko Hoken Shinbun (ISSN 0022-992X)

368   FI   ISSN 0356-7826
SUOMEN VAKUUTUSVUOSIKIRJA/FINNISH INSURANCE YEARBOOK. Swedish edition: Foersaekringsaarsbok foer Finland (ISSN 0356-7834) (Text in Finnish, Swedish) 1912. a. Fmk.150. Suomen Vakuutusyhdistys - Finnish Insurance Society, Bulevardi 28, 00120 Helsinki 12, Finland. FAX 358-0-192526. adv.; stat.; circ. 1,000 (Finnish ed.); 400 (Swedish ed.).

368   AT   ISSN 0729-3828
SUPERFUNDS. 1962. q. Aus.$66. (Association of Superannuation Funds of Australia) Rala Publications, 203-205 Darling St., Balmain, N.S.W. 2041, Australia. (Subscr. to: Federal Secretary, ASFA, 8th Floor, 37 York St., Sydney, N.S.W. 2000, Aus) Ed.Bd. adv.; bk.rev.; index; circ. 2,400. **Indexed:** Aus.P.A.I.S.

368 333.33   CN
HG8550
SUPERINTENDENT OF INSURANCE ANNUAL REPORT. 1976. a. free. Alberta Consumer and Corporate Affairs, 10025 Jasper Ave., Edmonton, Alta. T5J 3Z5, Canada. TEL 403-422-1592. FAX 403-422-0775. stat.; circ. 600.
Former titles: Alberta Insurance Report (ISSN 0229-7108); (until 1984): Alberta. Office of the Superintendent of Insurance and Real Estate. Annual Report (ISSN 0705-596X)

368   US
SURPLUS LINE REPORTER. 1978. m. $20. Reporter Publishing Co., Box 52193, New Orleans, LA 70152. TEL 504-366-8797. Ed. Carol DeGraw. circ. 3,100. (tabloid format; back issues avail.)

368.4   SW   ISSN 0082-0075
HA1521
SWEDEN. RIKSFOERSAEKRINGSVERKET. ALLMAEN FOERSAEKRING. (Text in Swedish; summaries in English) 1963. a. SEK 142. Riksfoersaekringsverket - National Social Insurance Board, S-103 51 Stockholm, Sweden. (Dist. by: Liber Foerlag, S-162 89 Stockholm, Sweden) circ. 1,200.

368   US
TARGET ARSON: UPDATE. m. q. Insurance Committee for Arson Control, 110 William St., 4th Fl., New York, NY 10038-3901. TEL 212-669-9245. Ed. Loretta Worters. circ. 1,500.

368   US
TAX FACTS 1; taxation on life insurance. a. $15.95. National Underwriter Co., 505 Gest St., Cincinnati, OH 45203. TEL 513-721-2140. FAX 513-721-0126. (also avail. in microform from UMI) **Indexed:** L.I.I.
Formerly: Tax Facts on Life Insurance (ISSN 0145-1847)
Description: Provides answers to federal, income, estate and gift tax questions.

368   US
TENNESSEE AGENT. 1951. bi-m. $15. Professional Insurance Agents of Tennessee, 500 Wilson Pike Cir., No. 212, Brentwood, TN 37027-5252. Ed. Lochiel Gaines. adv.; bk.rev.; circ. 800.

TEXAS INSURANCE LAW JOURNAL. see *LAW*

368   US
TEXAS INSUROR. 1923. bi-m. $20. Box 1663, Austin, TX 78767. Ed. Amy B. Wick. adv.; circ. 4,000.

368   US
TEXAS SURPLUS LINE REPORTER. 1984. m. $20. Reporter Publishing Co., Box 52193, New Orleans, LA 70152. TEL 504-366-8797. Ed. Carol DeGraw. circ. 5,100. (tabloid format; back issues avail.)
Description: Local coverage of political and financial organizations.

368   US   ISSN 0892-4414
TODAY'S INSURANCE WOMAN. 1946. bi-m. $15. National Association of Insurance Women (International), 1847 E. 15th St., Box 4410, Tulsa, OK 74159. TEL 918-744-5195. (Subscr. to: Box 4410, Tulsa OK 74159) Ed. Stephanie Darling. adv.: B&W page $1200; trim 8 5/8 x 10 7/8. circ. 20,000.
Description: Covers industry related news on a local, state, regional and national level.

TOXIC TORTS; litigation of hazardous substance cases. see *PUBLIC HEALTH AND SAFETY*

TRAFFIC SAFETY SERIES. see *TRANSPORTATION — Roads And Traffic*

TREASURY. see *BUSINESS AND ECONOMICS — Banking And Finance*

368   US   ISSN 0041-2384
TRENDS IN ADJUSTING. 1962. 3/yr. free to qualified personnel. Daynard & Van Thunen Co., Inc., Two World Trade Center, Ste. 3324, New York, NY 10048. TEL 212-432-1100. Ed. William C. Van Thunen. bk.rev.; tr.lit.; circ. 500. (processed)

368   FR   ISSN 0395-9406
TRIBUNE DE L'ASSURANCE. 1946. 14/yr. 790 F. La Tribune de L'Assurance, 39 rue de Trevise, 75009 Paris, France. TEL 1-48-01-01-10. FAX 1-48-01-04-35. adv.; bk.rev.; circ. 12,000.

368   XN   ISSN 0041-3445
TRUDOV INVALID. (Text in Macedonian) vol.8, 1966. m. $2 din. per no. Sojuzot na Trudovite Invalidi na Makedonija, Marsala Tita, Box 437, Skopje, Macedonia. Ed. Blagoja Trajkovski.

368   AG
TUTORA. MEMORIA Y BALANCE GENERAL. no.13, 1975. a. Compania Sudamericana de Seguros, Rivadavia 717, Buenos Aires, Argentina.

368   NE   ISSN 0041-4581
TWEE N. 1937. m. free. Nationale-Nederlanden N.V., Johan de Wittlaan 3, Box 29701, 2502 LS The Hague, Netherlands. TEL 70-581726. Ed. Anneke Rijk. circ. 9,700.

U C A N S S. BULLETIN JURIDIQUE. (Union des Caisses Nationales de Securite Sociale) see *LAW*

368 331.8   US   ISSN 0041-5189
U L L I C O BULLETIN. 1938. bi-m. membership. Union Labor Life Insurance Co., 111 Massachusetts Ave., N.W., Washington, DC 20001. TEL 202-682-4907. Ed. Doyle Niemann. illus.; circ. 25,000.

368   US
UNDERWRITERS' HANDBOOK. a. $39.50. National Underwriter Co., 505 Gest St., Cincinnati, OH 45203. TEL 513-721-2140. FAX 513-721-0126.
Description: Provides comprehensive information about the US domestic insurance market.

368.012   US   ISSN 0041-6622
UNDERWRITERS' REPORT; the west's weekly insurance newsmagazine. 1905. w. $35. Underwriters' Report, Inc., 667 Mission St., San Francisco, CA 94105. TEL 415-981-3221. FAX 415-974-5041. Ed. Roy Pasini. adv.; charts; illus.; circ. 5,918.

368 331   US
UNEMPLOYMENT INSURANCE REPORTS WITH SOCIAL SECURITY. 1934. w. $1750. Commerce Clearing House, Inc., 4025 W. Peterson Ave., Chicago, IL 60646. TEL 312-583-8500. Ed. D. Newquist. (looseleaf format)

UNITED CHURCH OF CHRIST. PENSION BOARDS (ANNUAL REPORT). see *RELIGIONS AND THEOLOGY — Other Denominations And Sects*

UNITED RETIREMENT BULLETIN. see *GERONTOLOGY AND GERIATRICS*

U.S. DEPARTMENT OF LABOR. EMPLOYEE RETIREMENT INCOME SECURITY ACT. REPORT TO CONGRESS. see *BUSINESS AND ECONOMICS — Labor And Industrial Relations*

332.17 368.85   US   ISSN 0083-0658
U.S. FEDERAL DEPOSIT INSURANCE CORPORATION. ANNUAL REPORT. 1934. a. U.S. Federal Deposit Insurance Corporation, 550 17th St., N.W., Washington, DC 20429. TEL 202-393-8400.

U.S. VETERANS ADMINISTRATION. ANNUAL REPORT. see *MILITARY*

368   US
UPPER CASE. q. National Life Insurance Company of Vermont, Montpelier, VT 05604. TEL 802-229-3333. Ed. Jack Fehr. bk.rev.; charts; illus.; stat.; index; circ. 3,000 (controlled).
Supersedes (until 1983): National Messenger (ISSN 0027-9714)
Description: Geared toward Vermont's insurance agents. Includes articles and information on industry developments and issues.

368 332.6   US
V A R D S REPORT. 1988. m. $698. Financial Planning Resources, Inc., 15120 S.W. 145th St., Box 161998, Miami, FL 33116. TEL 305-252-4600. Ed. R.H. Rick Carey. circ. 500.
Description: Reports on two essential elements of variable annuity analysis - investment performance and contract features.

368   GW   ISSN 0170-9690
V G A NACHRICHTEN. 1952. bi-m. DM.48. Bundesverband der Geschaeftsstellenleiter der Assekuranz, Kaiser Wilhelm-Ring 15, 5000 Cologne 1, Germany. TEL 0221-527321. FAX 0221-523615. adv.; bk.rev.; circ. 1,500. (back issues avail.)

368   NE
VADEMECUM VOOR HET VERZEKERINGSWEZEN. (Issued in 2 Parts) a. fl.241. Nijgh Periodieken B.V., Postbus 122, 3100 AC Schiedam, Netherlands. TEL 010-4274100. FAX 010-4739911. TELEX 22680. adv.; circ. 1,850.
Formed by merger of: Vademecum voor Het Nederlandsche Verzekeringswezen; Jaarboek voor Het Assurantie- en Hypotheekwezen.

368   FI   ISSN 0355-7294
VAKUUTUSSANOMAT. 1903. 8/yr. FIM 277 in the Nordic countries; elsewhere FIM 222. Vakuutussanomia Oy, Bulevardi 28, 00120 Helsinki 12, Finland. TEL 358-0-640-469. FAX 358-0-640-469. Ed. Reijo Ollikainen. adv.; circ. 9,000.

VALUATION MAGAZINE. see *REAL ESTATE*

368   GW
VERSICHERUNGS BETRIEBSWIRT. 1966. bi-m. Vereinigung der Versicherungs Betriebswirte e.V., Landgrafenstr. 1, 5000 Cologne 41, Germany. TEL 0221-404398. Ed. Rudolf Slate. adv.; bk.rev.; circ. 1,600.

368   GW
VERSICHERUNGS JAHRBUCH. 1957. a. DM.506. Verlag Hoppenstedt und Co., Havelstr. 9, 6100 Darmstadt 1, Germany. TEL 6151-380-1. FAX 6151-380-360. circ. 700.

368   GW   ISSN 0344-6379
VERSICHERUNGSBETRIEBE; journal fuer Automation Betriebsorganisation und Einrichtung. 1970. 6/yr. DM.111. Hans Holzmann Verlag KG, Gewerbestr. 2, Postfach 1342, 8939 Bad Woerishofen, Germany. Ed. Erwin Stroebele. adv.; circ. 4,000.

368.01   GW   ISSN 0049-6006
VERSICHERUNGSKAUFMANN; Fachmagazin fuer die Versicherungsbranche. 1954. m. DM.115 (foreign DM.129). Betriebswirtschaftlicher Verlag Dr. Th. Gabler GmbH, Taunusstr. 54, Postfach 1546, 6200 Wiesbaden 1, Germany. TEL 0611-534-0. FAX 0611-534-89. TELEX 04186567. bk.rev.; abstr.; bibl.; illus.; stat.; tr.lit.; index.

368   GW
VERSICHERUNGSRECHT; Juristische Rundschau fuer die Individualversicherung. 1950. 36/yr. DM.292. Verlag Versicherungswirtschaft e.V., Klosestr. 20-24, 7500 Karlsruhe 1, Germany. TEL 0721-3509126. FAX 0721-31833. Eds. Egon Lorenz, Karl-Heinz Rehnert. adv.; bk.rev.; bibl.; index; circ. 8,000. (back issues avail.; reprint service avail. from SCH)
●Also available online.

INSURANCE — ABSTRACTING, BIBLIOGRAPHIES, STATISTICS

368   GW   ISSN 0049-6014
VERSICHERUNGSVERMITTLUNG; Zeitschrift selbstaendiger Versicherungskaufleute und Bausparkaufleute. 1901. m. DM.78. Bundesverband Deutscher Versicherungskaufleute (BVK), Kekulestr. 12, 5300 Bonn 1, Germany. TEL 0228-224315. FAX 0228-261157. Ed. Hans-Dieter Schaefer. adv.; bk.rev.; circ. 18,000.

368   GW   ISSN 0042-4358
VERSICHERUNGSWIRTSCHAFT. 1946. fortn. DM.144. Verlag Versicherungswirtschaft e.V., Klosestr. 20-24, 7500 Karlsruhe 1, Germany. Ed. Karl-Heinz Rehnert. adv.; bk.rev.; charts; illus.; circ. 11,600. (back issues avail.)
—BLDSC shelfmark: 9195.700000.

368   NE   ISSN 0042-4528
VERZEKERINGS-ARCHIEF. (Text in Dutch, English and French) 1920. q. fl.26. (Nederlandse Vereniging ter Bevordering van het Levensverzekeringwezen) Kluwer Academic Publishers, Box 17, 3300 AA Dordrecht, Netherlands. TEL 078-334911. FAX 078-334254. TELEX 29245. (Dist. by: Kluwer Academic Publishers Group, P.O. Box 322, 3300 AH Dordrecht, Netherlands) Ed.Bd. bk.rev.; bibl.; index. **Indexed:** Excerp.Med., Math.R.
—BLDSC shelfmark: 9218.350000.

368   NE
VERZEKERINGS MAGAZINE V V P. w. fl.132.50. Nijgh Periodieken B.V., Postbus 122, 3100 AC Schiedam, Netherlands. TEL 010-4274100. FAX 010-4739911. TELEX 22680. circ. 4,100.
Formerly: V V P Magazine.

368   BE
VERZEKERINGSNIEUWS. (Supplement avail.) (Text in Flemish) s-m. 4558 Fr. C E D Samson (Subsidiary of: Wolters Samson Belgie n.v.), Louizalaan 485, B-1050 Brussels, Belgium. TEL 02-7231111. FAX 02-6498480. TELEX CEDSAM 64130.
Description: Insurance industry news from national and European Community perspectives.

VIERTELJAHRESSCHRIFT FUER SOZIALRECHT. see *LAW*

368   SA   ISSN 0259-0026
VITAE; the South African insurance magazine. (Text in English) 1980. m. R.85 (typically set in Jan.). Vitae Insurance Publications (Pty) Ltd., P.O. Box 849, Highlands North, 2037, South Africa. TEL 011-882-6105. FAX 011-882-6104. Ed. S.W. Bishop. adv.; bk.rev.; index; circ. 2,100.
Incorporates (March 1982): S.A. Insurance Magazine.

368   US
WAVELENGTH (NEWPORT BEACH). 1966? 6/yr. free. Pacific Mutual Life Insurance, 700 Newport Center Dr., Newport Beach, CA 92663. TEL 714-640-3768. Ed. Barbara Assadi. illus.
Formerly (until 1989): Soundings; **Supersedes:** P M L - Life (ISSN 0030-8765)

368   US
WHO WRITES WHAT IN LIFE AND HEALTH INSURANCE. a. $22.95. National Underwriter Co., 505 Gest St., Cincinnati, OH 45203. TEL 513-721-2140. FAX 513-721-0126. adv.
Description: Provides information for coverages and services for unusual and hard to place risks.

368   US   ISSN 0083-9574
HG8523
WHO'S WHO IN INSURANCE. a. $105. Underwriter Printing and Publishing Co., 50 E. Palisade Ave., Englewood, NJ 07631. TEL 201-569-8808. Ed. Donald E. Wolff. circ. 6,000.
Description: Contains over 5,000 biographies of insurance officials, leading agents and brokers, high-ranking company officers. Each biography includes position-title, educational background, club and professional associations and career synopsis.

368   US
WHO'S WHO IN RISK MANAGEMENT. 1971. a. $60. Underwriter Printing and Publishing Co., 50 E. Palisade Ave., Englewood, NJ 07631. TEL 201-569-8808. Ed. Donald E. Wolff. circ. 10,000.
Description: Contains specialized biographies of insurance buyers for large business and industrial firms throughout the U.S. Includes indexes by company and location.

368.32   AT
WICKEN'S THE LAW OF LIFE INSURANCE IN AUSTRALIA. 4/yr. Aus.$240. Law Book Co. Ltd., 44-50 Waterloo Rd., North Ryde, N.S.W. 2113, Australia. TEL 02-887-0177. FAX 02-888-9706. TELEX ASBOOK 27995. Eds. Brian Sharpe, Cathy Manolios.
Description: Examines the law of life insurance including taxation, mortgages on policies, trusts and trustees, agency and brokers and reinsurance.

368   GW
WIR (COLOGNE). 1932. bi-m. Berlin-Koelnische Versicherungen, Clever Str. 36, Postfach 140134, 5000 Cologne 1, Germany. TEL 0221-7724-0. FAX 0221-7724-200. Ed. Rudolf A.P. Slate. bk.rev.; circ. 2,800.
Formerly: Bruecke (Cologne).

368   US
WISCONSIN INSUROR.* vol.40, 1977. m. $10. Independent Insurance Agents of Wisconsin, 725 John Nolen Dr., Madison, WI 53713-1421. Ed. Robert C. Jartz. adv.; charts; illus.; stat.; circ. 1,200.
Former titles: Wisconsin Insurance; Wisconsinsuror (ISSN 0043-6704)

368   CN   ISSN 0833-1278
WITHOUT PREJUDICE. 1936. 10/yr.(Sept.-June). Can.$60 to non-members; (foreign Can.$75). Ontario Insurance Adjusters Association, c/o C. W. Gibula, Ed., 55 Devins Dr., Aurora, Ont. L4G 2Z3, Canada. TEL 416-542-0576. FAX 416-542-1301. (Subscr. to: Business Manager, OIAA, 132 Bonham Blvd., Mississauga, Ont. L5M 1C7, Canada) adv.; charts; circ. 1,300.

368   US   ISSN 0043-7751
HS1510.W78
WOODMEN OF THE WORLD MAGAZINE. 1890. m. $2.40. Woodmen of the World Life Insurance Society, 1700 Farnam St., Omaha, NE 68102. TEL 402-342-1890. FAX 402-271-7269. Ed. Geroge M. Herriott. bk.rev.; illus.; circ. 480,000 (controlled).
Description: Contains articles on insurance, Woodmen of the World operations, health, lodges and fraternal activities.

368   US
WORKERS' COMPENSATION LAW REPORTER. a. (plus fortn. updates). $825. Commerce Clearing House, Inc., 4025 W. Peterson Ave., Chicago, IL 60646. TEL 312-583-8500. Ed. D. Newquist. (also avail. in looseleaf format)

368.014   US
WORKER'S COMPENSATION LAW REVIEW. Variant title: Workmens' Compensation Law Review. 1974. a. $63. William S. Hein & Co., Inc., 1285 Main St., Buffalo, NY 14209. TEL 800-828-7571. FAX 716-883-8100. TELEX 91-209 WU 7 HEIN BUF. Ed. William Moran. circ. 300.
Description: Legal articles on workers' compensation.

WORKERS' COMPENSATION LAWS OF CALIFORNIA. see *LAW*

368   UK
WORLD INSURANCE REPORT. s-m. £565($915) (foreign £513). Financial Times Business Information Ltd., Tower House, Southampton St., London WC2E 7HA, England. TEL 071-240 9391. FAX 071-240-7946. TELEX 296926-BUSINF-G. (Subscr. to: Maggie Lutteridge, Tower House, Southampton St., London WC2E 7HA, England)
Description: International service for the world's insurance and reinsurance management.

368   UK
WORLD POLICY GUIDE; a monthly analysis of insurance policies available in the U.K. 1983. m. £695($713) Financial Times Business Information Ltd., Tower House, Southampton St., London WC2E 7HA, England. TEL 071-240-9391. FAX 071-240-7946. TELEX 296926-BUSINF-G. Ed. Sue Copeman.
●Also available online.
Former titles: F T London Policy Guide (ISSN 0263-5569); World Policy Checklist.
Description: Provides analysis of commercial, corporate, and group insurances offered by UK-based insurers.

368   NE
WORLDWIDE NEWS. (Text in English) 1962. 5/yr. free. Nationale-Nederlanden N.V., Johan de Wittlaan 3, Box 29701, 2502 LS The Hague, Netherlands. TEL 70-3581315. Ed. Sharon Lewis. bk.rev.; circ. 13,000.

368   CS   ISSN 0044-1708
ZABRANA SKOD; damage prevention: fire prevention, road safety, work safety, agriculture and industry protection. 1953. m. 12 Kcs.($11.45) (Ceska Statni Pojistovna, Prague) Nakladatelstvi Technicke Literatury, Spalena 51, 113 02 Prague 1, Czechoslovakia. (Dist. by: Artia, Ve Smecckach 30, 111 27 Prague 1, Czechoslovakia) (Slovenska Statni Pojistovna, Bratislava) Ed. Eva Trojanova. circ. 10,000.

368   ZA
ZAMBIA STATE INSURANCE CORPORATION. REPORT AND ACCOUNTS. 1971. a. free. Zambia State Insurance Corporation, Box 894, Lusaka, Zambia. circ. 3,000.

368   GW   ISSN 0044-2585
HG8015
ZEITSCHRIFT FUER DIE GESAMTE VERSICHERUNGSWISSENSCHAFT. 1901. 4/yr. DM.127. (Deutscher Verein fuer Versicherungswissenschaft e.V.) Duncker und Humblot GmbH, Postfach 410329, 1000 Berlin 41, Germany. TEL 030-7900060. FAX 030-79000631. (And: Verlag Versicherungswirtschaft, Klosestr. 22, 7500 Karlsruhe, Germany) Ed. Reimer Schmidt. bk.rev.; bibl.; index. (tabloid format)

368   GW
ZEITSCHRIFT FUER VERSICHERUNGSWESEN. (Text in English and German) 1950. s-m. DM.188.75. Allgemeiner Fachverlag Rolf Mathern GmbH, Agnesstr. 1, 2000 Hamburg 60, Germany. TEL 040-473500. Ed. Eva Mathern. circ. 6,000.

368   CC   ISSN 1001-4489
ZHONGGUO BAOXIAN/INSURANCE IN CHINA. (Text in Chinese) m. Zhongguo Renmin Baoxian Gongsi - China People's Insurance Company, 22 Xijiaominxiang, Beijing 100031, People's Republic of China. TEL 654231. Ed. Pan Lufu.

368   UK
7-DAY RATE UPDATE. w. £180. Financial Times Business Information Ltd., Tower House, Southampton St., London WC2E 7HA, England. TEL 071-240-9391. FAX 071-240-7946. TELEX 296926-BUSINF-G. (Subscr. to: John McLachlan, Financial Times Business Information, Bracken House, 10 Cannon St., London EC4P 4BY, England)
Description: Guide to life assurance rates and contract details, including annuities, bonds, pensions, term assurance and endowments.

INSURANCE — Abstracting, Bibliographies, Statistics

368   US   ISSN 1046-5081
ACTUARIAL REVIEW. 1973. q. $5 to non-members. Casualty Actuarial Society, 1100 N. Glebe Rd., Ste. 600, Arlington, VA 22201. TEL 703-276-3100. bk.rev.; charts.

AUSTRALIA. OFFICE OF THE LIFE INSURANCE COMMISSIONER. HALF YEARLY FINANCIAL & STATISTICAL BULLETIN. see *INSURANCE*

368 319 332   HO
BANCO CENTRAL DE HONDURAS. DIVISION DE SEGUROS. BOLETIN DE ESTADISTICAS DE SEGUROS. 1974. a. free. Banco Central de Honduras, Division de Seguros, Tegucigalpa, M.D.C., Honduras. FAX 504-37-1791. TELEX 1121 BANTRAL HO. charts; illus.; stat.; circ. 250.
Description: Covers insurance market statistics.

INSURANCE — ABSTRACTING, BIBLIOGRAPHIES, STATISTICS

368   BE
BELGIUM. INSTITUT NATIONAL D'ASSURANCES SOCIALES POUR TRAVAILLEURS INDEPENDANTS. STATISTIQUES DES BENEFICIAIRES DE PRESTATIONS DE RETRAITE ET DE SURVIE/BELGIUM. RIJKSINSTITUUT VOOR DE SOCIALE VERZEKERINGEN DER ZELFSTANDIGEN. STATISTIEK VAN DE PERSONEN DIE EEN RUST- EN OVERLEVINGSPRESTATIE GENIETEN. (Text in Flemish and French) 1970. a. free. Institut National d'Assurances Sociales pour Travailleurs Independants, Bibliotheque - Bureau 4-7 (Wat.), Place Jean Jacobs, 6, B-1000 Brussels, Belgium. TEL 02-507-6211. FAX 02-511-2153.

314 368.4   BE
BELGIUM. INSTITUT NATIONAL D'ASSURANCES SOCIALES POUR TRAVAILLEURS INDEPENDANTS. STATISTIQUE DES ENFANTS BENEFICIAIRES D'ALLOCATIONS FAMILIALES/BELGIUM. RIJKSINSTITUUT VOOR DE SOCIALE VERZEKERINGEN DER ZELFSTANDIGEN. STATISTIEK VAN DE KINDEREN DIE RECHT GEVEN OP KINDERBIJSLAG. (Text in Dutch and French) 1970. a. Institut National d'Assurances Sociales pour Travailleurs Independants, 6 place Jean Jacobs, B-1000 Brussels, Belgium. TEL 02-507-6211. FAX 02-511-2153.

368.4   BE
BELGIUM. INSTITUT NATIONAL D'ASSURANCES SOCIALES POUR TRAVAILLEURS INDEPENDANTS. STATISTIQUES DES PERSONNES ASSUJETTIES AU STATUT SOCIAL DES TRAVAILLEURS INDEPENDANTS/BELGIUM. RIJKSINSTITUUT VOOR DE SOCIALE VERZEKERINGEN DER ZELFSTANDIGEN. STATISTIEK VAN DE PERSONEN DIE ONDER DE TOEPASSING VALLEN VAN HET SOCIAAL STATUUT VAN DE ZELFSTANDIGEN. (Text in Flemish and French) 1970. a. free. Institut National d'Assurances Sociales pour Travailleurs Independants, Bibliotheque - Bureau 4-7 (Wat.), Place Jean Jacobs, 6, B-1000 Brussels, Belgium. TEL 02-507-6211. FAX 02-511-2153.
    Description: Employment statistics covering a wide variety of professions.

368   CN   ISSN 0701-5488
HD7106.C2
CANADA. STATISTICS CANADA. PENSION PLANS IN CANADA. (Catalogue 74-401) (Text in English and French) 1970. biennial. Can.$35($42) (foreign $42) per issue. Statistics Canada, Publications Sales and Services, Ottawa, Ont. K1A 0T6, Canada. TEL 613-951-7277. FAX 613-951-1584. (also avail. in microform from MML)
    Description: Includes all occupational pension plans sponsored by employers in both the public and private sectors. Includes sections on recipients of pension benefits and contributors to RRSPs.

368   CN   ISSN 0068-9025
CANADIAN INSURANCE. ANNUAL STATISTICAL ISSUE. 1905. a. Can.$32. Stone and Cox Ltd., 111 Peter St., Ste. 202, Toronto, Ont. M5V 2H1, Canada. TEL 416-599-0772. FAX 416-599-0867. Ed. M. Steeler. adv.; circ. 11,338. (back issues avail.)
    Description: Round-up of the underwriting statistics for the Canadian property-casualty and life insurance industry, with informed comment.

368   US
CASUALTY ACTUARIAL SOCIETY. DISCUSSION PAPER PROGRAM. 1982. a. price varies. Casualty Actuarial Society, 1100 N. Glebe Rd., Ste. 600, Arlington, VA 22201. TEL 703-276-3100.

368   US
CASUALTY ACTUARIAL SOCIETY. FORUM. 1987. s-a. $30. Casualty Actuarial Society, 1100 N. Glebe Rd., Ste. 600, Arlington, VA 22201. TEL 703-276-3100.

368.01   US   ISSN 0893-2980
CASUALTY ACTUARIAL SOCIETY. PROCEEDINGS. 1914. a. $50. Casualty Actuarial Society, 11009 N. Glebe Rd., Ste. 600, Arlington, VA 22201. TEL 703-276-3100. (also avail. in microform from UMI; reprint service avail. from UMI)

368   US   ISSN 0895-6022
CASUALTY ACTUARIAL SOCIETY. YEARBOOK. a. $20 (effective 1991). Casualty Actuarial Society, 1100 N. Glebe Rd., Ste. 600, Arlington, VA 22201. TEL 703-276-3100.

368.4   CL
CHILE. SUPERINTENDENCIA DE SEGURIDAD SOCIAL. SEGURIDAD SOCIAL: ESTADISTICAS. 1969. irreg. exchange basis. Superintendenica de Seguridad Social, Santiago, Chile.
    Formerly: Chile. Superintendencia de Seguridad Social. Boletin de Estadisticas de Seguridad.

368   CK
DATASEGUROS. 1987. a. $60. Union de Aseguradores Colombianos, Carrera 7a No. 26-20, Piso 11, Apdo. Aereo 5233, Bogota, Colombia. circ. 150.
    Description: Contains statistics organized by insurance company, balance sheets and insurance lines.

368   ES
HG8555.A4
EL SALVADOR. SUPERINTENDENCIA DEL SISTEMA FINANCIERO. JUNTA MONETARIA. ANUARIO ESTADISTICO: SEGUROS, FIANZAS, BANCOS. Variant title: Estadisticas, Seguros, Fianzas, Bancos. 1963. a. free. Superintendencia del Sistema Financiero, Asesoria Actuarial y Estadistica, Junta Monetaria, Apdo. Postal 2942, San Salvador, El Salvador. Dir. Jorge Barraza Ibarra. stat.; circ. 750.
    Former titles: El Salvador. Superintendencia de Bancos y Otras Instituticiones Financieras. Estadisticas: Seguros, Finanzas, Bancos; (until no.14, 1976): El Salvador. Superintendencia de Bancos y Otras Instituciones Financieras. Estadisticas: Seguros, Finanzas, Capitalization (ISSN 0067-3234)

368.4 314   FI   ISSN 0071-5247
FINLAND. KANSANELAKELAITOS. TILASTOLLINEN VUOSIKIRJA/FINLAND. FOLKPENSIONSANSTALT. STATISTISK AARSBOK/FINLAND. SOCIAL INSURANCE INSTITUTION. STATISTICAL YEARBOOK. (Subseries of its Julkaisuja. Series T: 1) (Text in Finnish, Swedish; summaries in English) 1965. a. Kansanelakelaitos - Social Insurance Institution of Finland, Estimating and Statistics Department, Nordenskioldinkatu 12, SF-00250 Helsinki 25, Finland. Ed. F. Gustafsson. charts; stat.; circ. 4,000.

368 314   GW   ISSN 0435-7442
GESAMTSTATISTIK DER KRAFTFAHRTVERSICHERUNG. 1958. a. free. Verband der Haftpflicht- , Unfall- und Kraftverkehrsversicherer e.V., Glockengiesserwall 1, 2000 Hamburg 1, Germany. stat.; circ. controlled.

368   GY
GUYANA. NATIONAL INSURANCE BOARD. ANNUAL REPORT: GUYANA NATIONAL INSURANCE SCHEME. 1970. a. free. National Insurance Board, Brickdam and Winter Place, Georgetown, Guyana. TEL 02-66797. stat.; circ. 300.
    Description: Yearly information and tabular statistics on the activities and members of the board, focusing on employers, benefits branches, claims adjudication issues, training and staffing, and income expenditures, with an appendix of industrial statistics.

368 314   AU
HANDBUCH DER OESTERREICHISCHEN SOZIALVERSICHERUNG. 1971. a. (2 vols.). S.135 for vol.1; S.175 for vol.2. Hauptverband der Oesterreichischen Sozialversicherungstraeger, Kundmanng. 21, A-1030 Vienna, Austria.
    Formerly: Statistisches Handbuch der Oesterreichischen Sozialversicherung; Which superseded in part: Jahrbuch der Oesterreichischen Sozialversicherung.

368 314   IT   ISSN 0021-2539
I N A I L NOTIZIARIO STATISTICO. 1951. q. L.16320. Istituto Nazionale per l'Assicurazione Contro gli Infortuni sul Lavoro, Via 4 Novembre 144, 00187 Rome, Italy. Ed. Carla Maciocci. charts; index; circ. 2,500.
    Description: Statistics on work accidents.

368.4 331   US
INDIANA. DEPARTMENT OF EMPLOYMENT AND TRAINING SERVICES. UNEMPLOYMENT INSURANCE CLAIMS BY AREA. w. free. Department of Employment and Training Services, Statistical Services, 10 Senate Ave., Rm. 313, Indianapolis, IN 46204. TEL 317-232-7704. FAX 317-232-6950.
    Description: Tabulates initial and continued claims under the State and Federal Unemployment Insurance programs for all local offices.

368.4 331   US
INDIANA. DEPARTMENT OF EMPLOYMENT AND TRAINING SERVICES. UNEMPLOYMENT INSURANCE PAYMENTS BY INDUSTRY. m. free. Department of Employment and Training Services, Statistical Services, 10 Senate Ave., Rm. 313, Indianapolis, IN 46204. TEL 317-232-7704. FAX 317-232-6950.
    Description: Reports number and amount of State Unemployment Insurance payments by selected industries.

368   CK
INDUSTRIA ASEGURADORA COLOMBIANA. ESTADISTICAS ANUALES. 1976. a. $30. Union de Aseguradores Colombianos, Carrera 7a. No. 26-20, Piso 11, Apdo. Aereo 5233, Bogota, Colombia. TEL 571-287-6611. FAX 571-287-5764.
    Description: Principal data from balance sheets and statistics on Colombian businesses.

368 016   US
INSURANCE AND EMPLOYEE BENEFITS LITERATURE. 1950. bi-m. Can.$15($15) (foreign $20). Special Libraries Association, Insurance and Employee Benefits Division, c/o Beth Dominianni, Aetna, Ste. 5112, 151 Farmington Ave., Hartford, CT 06156. FAX 203-636-2044. Ed. Sara Jane McDavid. bk.rev.; bibl.; circ. 375.
    Formerly: Insurance Literature (ISSN 0020-4765)
    Description: Features an annoted current bibliography and buying guide regarding books, pamphlets and government documents concerning insurance and employee benefits.

368.01   US   ISSN 0074-0713
HG8523
INSURANCE FACTS. 1961. a. $22.50. Insurance Information Institute, 110 William St., New York, NY 10038. TEL 212-669-9200. circ. 7,500. **Indexed:** SRI.
    Description: Comprehensive statistical yearbook about property-liability insurance business.

368 016   US   ISSN 0074-073X
HG8011
INSURANCE PERIODICALS INDEX. 1962. a. $100. (Special Libraries Association, Insurance and Employee Benefits Division) N I L S Publishing Company, 21625 Prairie St., Box 2507, Chatsworth, CA 91311. TEL 818-998-8830. FAX 818-718-8482. (Addr. of Association: 1700 19th St., N.W., Washington, DC 20009) Ed. Oriole Anderson. circ. 450. (back issues avail.)
    ●Also available online. Vendor(s): DIALOG (File no.169), Mead Data Central (NEXIS/LEXIS), WESTLAW.
    —BLDSC shelfmark: 4531.750000.
    Description: Indexes the 35 most significant journals in insurance. Online databases include abstracts.

368   US
INSURANCE REGULATORY INFORMATION SYSTEM RATIO RESULTS. a. $50. National Association of Insurance Commissioners, 120 W. 12th St., Kansas City, MO 64105. TEL 816-842-3600. (Subscr. to: N A I C Publications, Box 263 Department 42, Kansas City, MO 64193-0042) stat. (also avail. in magnetic tape)
    Description: Provides statistical evaluations for the financial condition of 5,000 insurance companies.

368 319   FJ
INSURANCE REPORT AND STATISTICS OF FIJI. 1969. a. free. Commissioner of Insurance, Government Printer, Box 1220, Suva, Fiji. TEL 679 301688. stat.; circ. 200.
    Formerly: Insurance Statistics of Fiji.

368   UK   ISSN 0950-3668
INSURANCE STATISTICS (YEARS). 1952. a. free. Association of British Insurers, 51 Gresham St., London EC2V 7HQ, England. TEL 071-248-4477. FAX 071-489-1120. TELEX 937035-ABINS-G. circ. 10,000.
    —BLDSC shelfmark: 4531.770800.
    Supersedes (in 1985): Insurance Facts and Figures & Life Insurance in the United Kingdom.

368 315   IS   ISSN 0074-0705
ISRAEL. CENTRAL BUREAU OF STATISTICS. INSURANCE IN ISRAEL/ISKE HA-BITUAH BE-YISRAEL. (Subseries of the Bureau's Special Series) (Text in English, Hebrew) 1950. a. price varies. Central Bureau of Statistics, P.O. Box 13015, Jerusalem 91 130, Israel. TEL 02-21 12 11.

368.382 315   JA   ISSN 0911-8454
JAPAN. MINISTRY OF HEALTH AND WELFARE. STATISTICS AND INFORMATION DEPARTMENT. REPORT ON SURVEY OF NATIONAL MEDICAL CARE INSURANCE SERVICES. (Text in Japanese) 1976. a. 5300 Yen. Ministry of Health and Welfare, Statistics and Information Department - Kosei-sho Daijin Kanbo Tokei Joho-bu, 7-3 Ichigaya-Honmura-cho, Shinjuku-ku, Tokyo 162, Japan. TEL 03-3586-3361. (Orders to: Health & Welfare Statistics Association, 5-13-14 Roppongi, Minato-ku, Tokyo, Japan) Key Title: Shakai Iryo Shinryo Koibetsu Chosa Hokoku.

368   LU
LUXEMBOURG. INSPECTION GENERALE DE LA SECURITE SOCIALE. RAPPORT GENERAL SUR LA SECURITE SOCIALE AU GRAND-DUCHE DE LUXEMBOURG. 1974. a. 1100 Fr. Inspection Generale de la Securite Sociale, Ministere de la Securite Sociale, Luxembourg, Luxembourg. FAX 49921-2325. TELEX 2985 MINTSS LU. circ. 850.
 Description: Covers statistics on demography, economics, and finances.

368 016   US   ISSN 0743-8079
MEDICAL BENEFITS. 1984. s-m. $144. Panel Publishers, Inc., Box 1007, Charlottesville, VA 22902. TEL 804-979-4947. FAX 804-979-5164. Ed. Bruce G. Carveth. charts.

368.4 613.62   MX
MEXICO. CENTRO DE INFORMACION TECNICA Y DOCUMENTACION. INDICE DE ARTICULOS SOBRE SEGURIDAD E HIGIENE INDUSTRIAL. 1979. 3/yr. Mex.$140($13) (Centro de Informacion Tecnica y Documentacion) Mexico. Servicio Nacional de Adiestramiento Rapido de la Mano de Obra en la Industria, Calzada Atzcapotzalco-la Villa 209, Apdo. 16-099, Mexico 16, D.F., Mexico. Ed. Javier Pedraza Garcia. circ. 2,000.

368   MX
MEXICO. COMISION NACIONAL BANCARIA Y DE SEGUROS. ANUARIO ESTADISTICO DE SEGUROS. 1945. a. free. Comision Nacional Bancaria y de Seguros, Codigo Postal 06080, Republica de el Salvador No. 47, 1 Mexico, D.F., Mexico. stat.; index.

310   IS
NATIONAL INSURANCE INSTITUTE, JERUSALEM. ANNUAL SURVEY. 1981. a. free. National Insurance Institute, 13 Sderot Weizman, Jerusalem, Israel. Ed. Lea Achduz. circ. 1,000.
 Formerly: National Insurance Institute, Jerusalem. Statistical Abstracts.

368.4 314   NE   ISSN 0168-4108
NETHERLANDS. CENTRAAL BUREAU VOOR DE STATISTIEK. DIAGNOSESTATISTIEK BEDRIJFSVERENIGINGEN (OMSLAGLEDEN). (Text in Dutch and English) 1958. a. Centraal Bureau voor de Statistiek, Prinses Beatrixlaan 428, Voorburg, Netherlands. (Dist. by: SDU - Publishers, Christoffel Plantijnstraat, The Hague, Netherlands)

368 317   US
NEW YORK (STATE) INSURANCE DEPARTMENT. STATISTICAL TABLES FROM ANNUAL STATEMENTS. 1944. a. $11.50 (single copy free to NY residents). Insurance Department, Publications Unit, Empire State Plaza, Agency Bldg. No. 1, Albany, NY 12257. circ. 1,000. (back issues avail.)

368   NZ   ISSN 0111-0225
HG8784.N45
NEW ZEALAND. DEPARTMENT OF STATISTICS. NEW ZEALAND LIFE TABLES. quinquennial. NZ.$30.65. Department of Statistics, P.O. Box 2922, Wellington, New Zealand.
 Formerly: New Zealand. Department of Statistics. Life Annuity Tables.

368.4   PP
PAPUA NEW GUINEA. DEPARTMENT OF LABOUR AND EMPLOYMENT. WORKER'S COMPENSATION CLAIMS. (Text in English) 1966. a. K.1.50. Department of Labour and Employment, Publication Section, P.O. Box 417, Papua New Guinea. circ. 110.
 Former titles: Papua New Guinea. National Statistical Office. Worker's Compensation Claims & Papua New Guinea. Bureau of Statistics. Industrial Accidents; Papua New Guinea. Bureau of Statistics. Workers' Compensation Statistics (ISSN 0078-9267)
 Description: Contains tables on the value of workers' compensation premiums collected and claims paid; number of claims lodged, by age, sex and occupation of claimant, location and nature of injury, cause of accident, duration of absence from work, industry of employer, and province.

368 314   PL   ISSN 0079-2853
POLAND. GLOWNY URZAD STATYSTYCZNY. UBEZPIECZENIA MAJATKOWE I OSOBOWE/POLAND. CENTRAL STATISTICS OFFICE. PROPERTY AND PERSONAL INSURANCE. 1969. a. Glowny Urzad Statystyczny, Al. Niepodleglosci 208, 00-925 Warsaw, Poland. TEL 48 22 25-03-45.

368   US
PROFITABILITY BY LINE BY STATE. a. $100. National Association of Insurance Commissioners, 120 W. 12th St., Kansas City, MO 64105. TEL 816-842-3600. (Subscr. to: N A I C Publications, Box 263 Department 42, Kansas City, MO 64193-0042) stat.
 Description: Provides comparative statistics for evaluating insurance company performance.

368.4 317   CN   ISSN 0226-5346
QUEBEC (PROVINCE) REGIE DE L'ASSURANCE-MALADIE. STATISTIQUES ANNUELLES. (Text in French) 1971. a. free. Regie de l'Assurance-Maladie, Case Postale 6600, Quebec, Que. G1K 7T3, Canada. TEL 418-682-5168. FAX 418-643-7312. Ed.Bd. circ. 1,000.

368   IT
STATISTICHE PER LA PREVENZIONE. 1974. s-a. L.16320. Istituto Nazionale per l'Assicurazione Contro gli Infortuni sul Lavoro, Via 4 Novembre 144, 00187 Rome, Italy. Ed. Carla Maciocci. charts; stat.; index; circ. 2,000.

368 310   JA   ISSN 0910-5727
STATISTICS OF JAPANESE NON-LIFE INSURANCE BUSINESS. (Text in English and Japanese) 1948. a. $35. Hoken Kenkyujo Ltd. - Insurance Research Institute Ltd., 17-3, Hon-machi 1-chome, Shibuya-ku, Tokyo, Japan. TEL 03-3376-3331. FAX 03-3376-7125. Ed. Kazuaki Shimada. circ. 10,000. Key Title: Insurance. Songai Hoken Tokubetsu Tokei-go.
 Formerly: Japanese Insurance Business Statistics: Non-Life; Which supersedes in part: Insurance - Non-Life Annual Statistics (ISSN 0085-1930)
 Description: Annual business figures for the non-life industry and all domestic individual companies.

368   JA   ISSN 0910-5719
STATISTICS OF LIFE INSURANCE BUSINESS IN JAPAN. (Text in English and Japanese) 1948. a. $28. Hoken Kenkyujo Ltd. - Insurance Research Institute Ltd., 17-3, Hon-machi 1-chome, Shibuya-ku, Tokyo, Japan. TEL 03-3376-3331. FAX 03-3376-7125. Ed. Kazuaki Shimada. circ. 10,000. Key Title: Insurance. Seimei Hoken Tokei-go.
 Formerly: Japanese Insurance Business Statistics: Life; Which supersedes in part: Insurance - Non-Life Annual Statistics (ISSN 0085-1930)
 Description: Annual business figures for the life industry and all domestic individual companies.

368   FR
STATISTICS ON INSURANCE. (Text and summaries in English, French) 1983. a. free. Organization for Economic Cooperation and Development, 2 rue Andre Pascal, 75775 Paris Cedex 16, France. TEL 33-1-45-24-82-00. FAX 33-1-45-24-85-00. (U.S. orders to: O.E.C.D. Publications and Infromation Center, 2001 L St., N.W., Ste. 700, Washington, DC 20036-4910. TEL 202-785-6323) stat. (back issues avail.)
 Description: Comparitive tables of insurance statistics covering 24 OECD member countries.

368.382   DK   ISSN 0107-8437
SYGESIKRINGSSTATISTIK. 1981. a. free. Sygesikrings Forhandlingsudvalg, c/o Amtsraadsforeningen i Danmark, Landmaerket 10, 1119 Copenhagen K, Denmark. TEL 33-912161. FAX 33-15-12-44. Ed. Frank I. Jensen. circ. 500.
 Formerly: Statistik over Afregning af Ydelser Inden for den Offentlige Sygesikring.
 Description: Statistical information about public expenditure in health insurance.

368.32   US   ISSN 0739-4691
HG8961.T4
TEXAS BLUE BOOK OF LIFE INSURANCE STATISTICS. 1944. a. $30. Record Publishing Co. (Dallas), Box 225770, Dallas, TX 75222. TEL 214-630-0687. FAX 214-631-2476. Ed. John H. Leslie. circ. 1,300.

333.33 016 368   US   ISSN 0040-8190
TITLE NEWS. 1925. bi-m. $30. American Land Title Association, 1828 L St. N.W., Washington, DC 20036. TEL 202-296-3671. FAX 202-223-5843. Ed. Adina Conn. adv.; bk.rev.; charts; illus.; pat.; tr.mk.; index; circ. 4,600. Indexed: C.L.I., L.R.I., Leg.Per., P.A.I.S., Tr.& Indus.Ind.

368   RH   ISSN 0556-8692
ZIMBABWE. REGISTRAR OF INSURANCE. REPORT. (Text in English) 1974. a. Z.$4.50. Registrar of Insurance, Private Bag 7705, Causeway, Harare, Zimbabwe. stat.; circ. 500.
 Rhodesia. Central Statistical Office. Insurance Statistics.

INSURANCE — Computer Applications

368   US   ISSN 1054-0733
HG8075   CODEN: INSREK
INSURANCE AND TECHNOLOGY. 1976. bi-m. free to qualified personnel. Miller Freeman Inc. (New York) (Subsidiary of: United Newspapers Group), 1515 Broadway, New York, NY 10036. TEL 212-869-1300. FAX 212-302-6273. Ed. Kathleen Burger. adv.; charts; illus.; stat.; tr.lit.; circ. 18,000. (back issues avail.) **Indexed:** ABI Inform., Comput.Cont., Comput.Lit.Ind.
 Former titles: Insurance Software Review (ISSN 0892-8533); Interface. Insurance Industry (ISSN 0745-0419); Insurance Industry (ISSN 0362-8817)
 Description: Articles on information strategies for insurance management.

368   UK   ISSN 0268-1935
INSURANCE SYSTEMS BULLETIN; the essential monthly management review of information technology in the insurance industry. 1985. m. £195. Eurostudy, 36-38 Willesden Ln., London NW6 7SW, England. TEL 071-625-8656. FAX 071-625-6223. (Subscr. addr.: Stonehart Subscription Services, Unit, Hainault Rd., Little Heath, Romford, Essex RN6 5NP, England) Ed. Kathryn Custance. bk.rev. (tabloid format; back issues avail.)

INTERIOR DESIGN AND DECORATION

see also Interior Design and Decoration–Furniture and House Furnishings

A D ARCHITECTURAL DIGEST, EDIZIONE ITALIANA. see *ARCHITECTURE*

A D ARCHITECTURE. (Architectural Digest) see *ARCHITECTURE*

A I T. (Architektur, Innenarchitektur, Technischer Ausbau) see *ARCHITECTURE*

A PROPOS DE BAIN ET CUISINE. see *BUILDING AND CONSTRUCTION*

747   US
A S I D REPORT. 1975. bi-m. membership only. American Society of Interior Designers, 608 Massachusetts Ave., N.E., Washington, DC 20002-6006. TEL 202-546-3480. FAX 202-546-3240. Ed. Joseph Pryweller. bk.rev.; circ. 35,000 (controlled).

ABITARE. see *ARCHITECTURE*

INTERIOR DESIGN AND DECORATION

688 US
ACCESSORIES - TODAY; the business and fashion newspaper of the decorative accessories industry. (Avail. only as suppl. to: Furniture - Today) 1986. 6/yr. $69.95. Cahners Business Newspapers (Subsidiary of: Reed International PLC), Division of Reed Publishing (USA) Inc., 200 Main St., Box 2754, High Point, NC 27261. TEL 919-889-0113. FAX 919-841-8256. Ed. Judith Z. Cushman. adv.; circ. 25,000. (newspaper)
  Description: Aimed at decorative accessory buyers shopping the major furniture markets in High Point, Dallas, Atlanta and San Francisco.

747 US
ACCESSORY MERCHANDISING. 1980. q. $10. Market Place Publications, 170 World Trade Center, Box 58421, Dallas, TX 75258. TEL 214-747-4274. Ed. Nancy Miller. adv.; circ. 17,000.

ADRICHALUT YISRAELIT/ARCHITECTURE OF ISRAEL. see *ARCHITECTURE*

ALLT I HEMMET. see *INTERIOR DESIGN AND DECORATION — Furniture And House Furnishings*

747 GW
AMBIENTE. 1980. 10/yr. $120. Burda Verlag GmbH, Postfach 1230, 7600 Offenburg, Germany. FAX 089-9250-3519. (U.S. dist.: GLP International, 153 S. Dean St., Englewood, NJ 07631) **Indexed:** Excerp.Med.

747 IT ISSN 0392-5730
L'AMBIENTE CUCINA/KITCHEN. (Text in English and Italian) 1977. bi-m. $77. Editoriale P E G SpA, Via Fratelli Bressan 2, 20126 Milan, Italy. TEL 02-25-79-841. FAX 02-25-52-779. TELEX 323088 PEGMOS I. Ed. Fabrizio Gomarasca. adv.; circ. 27,000.
  Description: Covers kitchen interior design, surveys on updated production, reports from main sectorial exhibitions in Italy and abroad.

747 US
AMERICAN BUNGALOW. bi-m. Brinkmann Design Offices, Inc., 123 S. Baldwin Ave., Sierra Madre, CA 91024. TEL 818-355-3363. Ed. George B. Murray.

747 155.67 IT
▼**ANCHE NOI.** 1991. 6/yr. $25. Alberto Greco Editore, Via del Fusaro, 8, 20146 Milan, Italy. TEL 02-4189086. FAX 02-4189091. Ed. Pieralberto Greco. circ. 80,000.
  Description: Contains information and research about the world of the handicapped and senior citizens.

747 US
APPLIANCES: LATIN AMERICAN INDUSTRIAL REPORT. (Avail. for each of 22 Latin American countries) 1985. a. $435 per country report. Aquino Productions, Box 15760, Stamford, CT 06901. TEL 203-325-3138.

747 FR ISSN 0294-8567
ARCHI-CREE. bi-m. 710.09 F. (foreign 725 F.). Societe d'Edition et de Presse, 106 bd. Malesherbes, 75017 Paris, France. adv.; circ. 20,000. **Indexed:** Avery Ind.Archit.Per.
  Formerly: Architecture Interieure.
  Description: International architecture magazine that covers the development of architecture, draftmanship, building details and interior arrangements.

ARCHIMAGE. see *ARCHITECTURE*

ARCHITECT. see *ARCHITECTURE*

ARCHITECTURAL DESIGNS. see *ARCHITECTURE*

ARCHITECTURAL DIGEST; the international magazine of fine interior design. see *ARCHITECTURE*

ARCHITECTURAL LIGHTING. see *ARCHITECTURE*

ARCHITEKTUR UND LADENBAU; europaeische Fachzeitschrift fuer modernen Ladenbau, Schaufenster und Auslage. see *ARCHITECTURE*

747 FR ISSN 0004-3168
N2
ART ET DECORATION; la revue de la maison. 1897. 8/yr. 205 F. Editions Charles Massin, 16-18 rue de l'Amiral Mouchez, 75686 Paris Cedex 14, France. TEL 1-45-65-48-48. FAX 1-45-65-47-00. TELEX 240 918 TRACE. adv.; bk.rev.; illus.; index; circ. 451,443. **Indexed:** Art Ind.

051 US
▼**AT HOME.** 1990. bi-m. K Q E D, Inc., 680 Eighth St., San Francisco, CA 94103. TEL 415-553-2800. circ. 85,000.
  Description: Covers service information and articles about home decoration.

338 FR ISSN 0980-9465
L'ATELIER;* le magazine de la creation contemporaine. 1975. 6/yr. 340 F. S N E C, 18 rue Wurtz, 75013 Paris, France. TEL 45-67-67-21. FAX 43-06-42-69. Dir. Colette Save. adv.
  Formerly: Atelier des Metiers d'Art.

747 US
ATLANTA HOMES AND LIFESTYLES. 1966. bi-m. $15.95. Wiesner Publishing, 5775-B Glenridge Dr., Ste. 120, Atlanta, GA 30328. TEL 404-252-6670. FAX 404-252-6673. Ed. Barbara Tapp. adv.; bk.rev.; circ. 50,000.
  Formerly (until 1991): Southern Homes.
  Description: Southern home magazine filled with ideas about interior design, architecture, remodeling, the kitchens and bath, gardening, food and entertaining, plus stories about people who live in Atlanta.

AUSTRALIAN ANTIQUE TRADER. see *ANTIQUES*

747 AT
AUSTRALIAN DESIGN SERIES. 1981. m. 54 Park St., Sydney, N.S.W. 2000, Australia. TEL 02-282-8450. FAX 02-267-2150. TELEX 120514. Ed. Stephanie King. circ. 24,000.
  Description: Covers domestic and commercial design and interiors.

747 AT ISSN 0004-928X
AUSTRALIAN HOME BEAUTIFUL. 1926. m. Aus.$42 (foreign Aus.$60). Southdown Press, 32 Walsh St., Melbourne, Vic. 3000, Australia. Ed. Tony Fawcett. adv.; bk.rev.; charts; illus.; circ. 151,000. **Indexed:** Pinpointer.

747 AT ISSN 0004-931X
AUSTRALIAN HOUSE AND GARDEN. 1948. m. Aus.$59.50. Australian Consolidated Press, 54-58 Park St., Sydney, N.S.W. 2000, Australia. TEL 02-282-8413. FAX 02-282-8116. TELEX 20514. Ed. Rosemarie Hillier. adv.; bk.rev.; illus.; tr.lit.; index; circ. 120,500. **Indexed:** Pinpointer.
  Description: Covers building, furnishing, decorating, handicrats, gardening, entertaining.

645 AT ISSN 0814-107X
AUSTRALIANA. 1978. q. Aus.$35. Australiana Society Inc., P.O. Box 288, Lindfield N.S.W. 2070, Sydney, Australia. FAX 02-569-7246. Ed. Kevin Fahy. adv.; bk.rev.; index; circ. 747. (back issues avail.)

747 FI ISSN 0355-2950
AVOTAKKA. 1948. m. FIM 420. A-Lehdet Oy, Hitsaajankatu 7, 00810 Helsinki 81, Finland. FAX 0-783-582. Ed. Leena Nokela. adv.; illus.; circ. 51,985.
  Formerly: Kaunis Koti (ISSN 0022-9482)
  Description: Devoted to housing and interior decoration.

747 CN ISSN 0829-982X
AZURE MAGAZINE. 1985. 8/yr. Can.$18 (foreign Can.$32). Azure Publishing Inc., 2 Silver Ave., Toronto, Ont. M6R 3A2, Canada. TEL 416-588-2588. FAX 416-588-2357. Ed. Nelda Rodger. adv.; bk.rev.; abstr.; illus.; circ. 10,000. (back issues avail.)
  Description: Covers interior design, graphic design and industrial design, architecture and art.

744 728 IT ISSN 1120-5407
BAGNO E CUCINA ARCHITETTURA E INTERIOR DESIGN. q. L.22000 (foreign L.65000)(effective 1992). Tecniche Nuove s.p.a., Via C. Mennotti, 14, 20129 Milan, Italy. TEL 02-75701. FAX 02-7570205.

747 IT ISSN 0392-2715
IL BAGNO OGGI E DOMANI/BAIN AUJOURD'HUI ET DEMAIN/BATHROOM TODAY AND TOMORROW/BAD HEUTE UND MORGEN. (Text in English, French, German and Italian) 1974. m. $134. Editoriale P E G SpA, Via Fratelli Bressan 2, 20126 Milan, Italy. TEL 02-25-79-841. FAX 25-52-779. TELEX 323088 PEGMOS I. Ed. Oscar G. Colli. adv.; illus.; circ. 31,700.
  Description: Covers bathroom interior design, surveys on updated production, reports from main sectorial exhibitions in Italy and abroad.

747 IT
BAGNOGUIDA. 1978. a. L.20000 (foreign L.25000). Gruppo Editoriale Faenza Editrice s.p.a., Via Pier de Crescenzi no.44, 48018 Faenza (RA), Italy. TEL 0546 663488. adv.

747 690 UK ISSN 0260-9169
BARBOUR COMPENDIUM BUILDING PRODUCTS. 1977. a. £56.50. Barbour Index Plc., New Lodge, Drift Rd., Windsor, Berks SL4 4RQ, England. FAX 0344-884845. Ed. Carol Barnes. adv.; circ. 22,000. (also avail. in microfiche from BAR)

658.8 690 CN
BATH & KITCHEN MARKETER. 6/yr. Can.$16.85($19.50) (foreign $32). Southam Business Communications Inc. (Subsidiary of: Southam), 1450 Don Mills Rd., Don Mills, Ont. M3B 2X7, Canada. TEL 416-445-6641. FAX 416-442-2214. TELEX 06 966612 - SOUTHMAG TOR. Ed. Sophie Kneisel. (back issues avail.)
  Description: For retailers, contractors and designers involved in the residential bathroom and kitchen markets.

749 UK ISSN 0950-0197
BATHROOMS. 1986. m. £42. Maclean Hunter Ltd., Maclean Hunter House, Chalk Lane, Cockfosters Rd., Barnet, Herts EN4 OBU, England. TEL 081-975-9759. FAX 081-440-1796. TELEX 299072 MACHUN G. Ed. Barbara Field. circ. 6,975.

747 US
BAY AREA HOMESTYLE RESOURCE MAGAZINE. m. Bay Area Publishing Group Inc., 455 Los Gatos Blvd., Ste. 103, Los Gatos, CA 95032-5523. TEL 408-358-0081. FAX 408-356-4903. circ. 30,000.

BEAUTIFUL HOMES. see *ARCHITECTURE*

747 US
BEDROOMS & BATHS. 3/yr. Harris Publications, Inc., 1115 Broadway, New York, NY 10010-2803. TEL 212-807-7100. FAX 212-627-4678. Ed. Barbara Jacksier.

BELLE. see *HOME ECONOMICS*

747 US
BEST SELLING HOME PLANS. bi-m. $3.50 per no. Hachette Magazines, Inc., 1633 Broadway, 45th Fl., New York, NY 10019. TEL 212-767-6000.

747 641 US ISSN 0006-0151
NA7100
BETTER HOMES AND GARDENS. (Regional editions: New England, Middle Atlantic (including Metro New York), East North Central, West North Central, Central, Southwest and Pacific) 1922. m. $17. Meredith Corporation, 1716 Locust St., Des Moines, IA 50336. TEL 515-284-3000. Ed. David Jordan. adv.; circ. 8,002,000. (also avail. in microform from UMI; reprint service avail. from UMI) **Indexed:** Hlth.Ind., Ind.How To Do It (1971-), Jun.High.Mag.Abstr., Mag.Ind., MELSA, PMR, R.G., TOM.
  Description: Provides ideas and how-to-information on interior decorating, landscape design, home entertainment, parenting, food, money, automotives.

747 US
BETTER HOMES AND GARDENS BEDROOM AND BATH IDEAS. 1988. a. $3.50. Meredith Corporation, Special Interest Publications, 1716 Locust St., Des Moines, IA 50336. TEL 515-284-3000. adv.; illus.; circ. 500,000.
  Supersedes (1977-1983): Better Homes and Gardens Bedroom and Bath Decorating Ideas (ISSN 0164-0186)

INTERIOR DESIGN AND DECORATION 2549

747 US
BETTER HOMES AND GARDENS DECORATING. 1941. q. $3.50. Meredith Corporation, Special Interest Publications, 1716 Locust St., Des Moines, IA 50336. TEL 515-284-3000. adv.; illus.; circ. 500,000.
Former titles: Better Homes and Gardens Decorating Ideas (ISSN 0731-7441); Better Homes and Gardens Furnishings and Decorating Ideas (ISSN 0092-7961)

643.3 US ISSN 0731-5600
TH4816
BETTER HOMES AND GARDENS KITCHEN & BATH IDEAS. 1973. q. $3.50 per no. Meredith Corporation, Special Interest Publications, 1716 Locust St., Des Moines, IA 50336. TEL 515-284-3000. illus.; circ. 450,000.

747 US
▼**BETTER HOMES AND GARDENS PRIZEWINNING REMODELING.** 1992. a. Meredith Corporation, 1716 Locust St., Des Moines, IA 50309. TEL 515-284-3000. FAX 515-284-2700. adv.: B&W page $17200, color page $24725; trim 8 x 10 1/2. circ. 450,000.
Description: Focuses on top winners of the magazine's home improvement contests. Contains before and after photos and product information.

747 US ISSN 0277-836X
NK2121
BETTER HOMES AND GARDENS WINDOW & WALL IDEAS. 1975. s-a. $3.50 per no. Meredith Corporation, Special Interest Publications, 1716 Locust St., Des Moines, IA 50336. TEL 515-284-3000. illus.; circ. 500,000.
Formerly: Window and Wall Decorating Ideas (ISSN 0363-5406)

747 IS
BINIAN DEIR; quarterly of building and interior decorating. 1984. q. $98 for 6 nos. 4 Namal St., Tel Aviv 63-506, Israel. TEL 03-448897. FAX 03-5465027. adv.; circ. 50,000.

747 DK
BO BEDRE. 1961. m. DKK 34.50. Bonniers Specialmagasiner A-S, Strandboulevarden 130, 2100 Copenhagen OE, Denmark. TEL 45-31-29-55-00. FAX 45-31-29-01-99. Ed. Karen Lyager Horve.
Description: Home decorating, design gardening and cooking for the Danish family.

747 GW ISSN 0006-5463
BODEN, WAND, DECKE. 1954. m. DM.144. Lobrecht Verlag Max Rauscher KG, Postfach 1454, 8939 Bad Woerishofen, Germany. FAX 08247-5894. Ed. Max Rauscher. adv.; bk.rev.; charts; illus.; mkt.; pat.; tr.lit.; index; circ. 6,800.
Description: Information on coverings for ceilings, floors and walls.

747 NO ISSN 0800-1936
BONYTT/DESIGN FOR LIVING; Norsksspesialblad for Arkitektur boliginnredning. 1941. 10/yr. NOK 350. Forlaget Bonytt AS, Bygdoey Alle 9, 0257 Oslo 2, Norway. Ed. Tore Giljane. adv.; circ. 70,000.
Former titles: Nye Bonytt (ISSN 0029-6783); Bonytt (ISSN 0006-7199)

747 UK
BRITISH DECORATOR. 1930. bi-m. £12. British Decorators Association, 6 Haywra St., Harrogate, North Yorkshire HG1 5BL, England. TEL 0423-567292. Ed. S.M. Broughton. adv.; charts; illus.; stat.; tr.lit.; circ. 2,500. **Indexed:** World Surf.Coat.
Formerly: Masterpainter (ISSN 0025-5092)

747 UK ISSN 0263-2047
BRITISH INSTITUTE OF INTERIOR DESIGN MEMBERS' REFERENCE BOOK. 1983. a. £20. Sterling Publications Ltd., 86-88 Edgware Road, London, W2 2YW, England. TEL 01-258 0066. adv.

BROOKLYN HOME JOURNAL. see *HOME ECONOMICS*

747 US
BUDGET WISE HOME PLANS. a. Archway Press, Inc., 19 W. 44th St., New York, NY 10036. TEL 212-757-5580.

BUILDER'S BEST HOME DESIGNS. see *BUILDING AND CONSTRUCTION*

CAMINO. see *ARCHITECTURE*

747 CN
CANADIAN HOME STYLE MAGAZINE. 1989. 6/yr. Can.$24 (foreign $39). Lorell Communications Inc., 10 Byam Place, Uxbridge, Ont. L9P 1A6, Canada. TEL 416-852-9019. FAX 416-852-9019. Ed. Laurie Merckel. adv.; circ. 7,600.

747 CN ISSN 0008-3887
CANADIAN INTERIORS. 1964. 8/yr. Can.$33. Maclean-Hunter Ltd., Business Publication Division, Maclean-Hunter Bldg., 777 Bay St., Toronto, Ont. M5W 1A7, Canada. TEL 416-596-5881. FAX 416-596-5526. Ed. Dean Shalden. adv.; bk.rev.; charts; illus.; index; circ. 8,700. (also avail. in microform from UMI; reprint service avail. from UMI) **Indexed:** CMI.

CARTER'S PRICE GUIDE TO ANTIQUES IN AUSTRALIA. see *ANTIQUES*

747 720 BL
CASA CLAUDIA; a revista para morar melhor. 1975. m. $100. Editora Abril, S.A., R. Geraldo Flausino Gomes, 61, 04575 Sao Paolo, Brazil. TEL 011-8239222. FAX 011-8643796. TELEX 011-80360 EDAB BR. (Subscr. to: Rua do Curtume, 769 CEP 05065 Lapa, Sao Paulo, Brazil.) Ed. Victor Civita. adv.; charts; illus.; circ. 113,860.
Description: Contains decorating ideas to personalize one's home, new furniture styles, appliance reviews, architecture styles and gardening tips.

747 BL
CASA & DECORACAO. m. Cr.$40. Editora Vecchi, Rua do Resende 144, Rio de Janeiro, Brazil. illus.

747 BL
CASA E JARDIM. 1953. m. Rua Felizbelo Freire 671, 20071 Rio de Janeiro, RJ, Brazil. TEL 21-270-6262. Ed. Milton Madeira. illus.; circ. 80,000.

699 IT
CASA STILE. 1962. bi-m. L.50000. Agenzia Gestione Periodici, Via D. Trentacoste 9, 20134 Milan, Italy. TEL 02-2640009. Ed. G. Artuffo. bk.rev.; charts; illus.; stat.; circ. 19,000 (controlled).
Former titles: Stile Casa (ISSN 0039-1441) & Casalinghi Stile.

747 IT ISSN 0008-7173
CASA VOGUE. 1969. m. L.62000 (foreign L.124000). Edizioni Conde Nast S.p.A., Piazza Castello 27, 20121 Milan, Italy. TEL 02-85611. FAX 02-870686. Ed. Isa Vercelloni. adv.; charts; illus.; circ. 51,322. **Indexed:** Artbibl.Mod.

747 IT
CASARREDO & CONTRACT. (Text in English, French, German, Spanish) 1977. q. L.30000. Editore RIMA s.r.l., Via Vincenzo Da Filicaia 7, 20162 Milan, Italy. TEL 02-66103539. FAX 02-66103558. adv.; circ. 17,500.
Formerly: Casarredo International.
Description: Covers Italian design, office and contract furniture.

CASE AL MARE. see *ARCHITECTURE*

CASE DI CAMPAGNA. see *ARCHITECTURE*

CASE DI MONTAGNA. see *ARCHITECTURE*

747 CN ISSN 0838-9330
CENTURY HOME. (Text in English) 1983. 7/yr. Can.$19.95. Bluestone House Inc., 12 Mill St. S., Port Hope, Ont. L1A 2S5, Canada. TEL 416-885-2449. FAX 416-885-5355. Ed. Joan Rumgay. adv.; bk.rev.; circ. 35. (back issues avail.)
Formerly: Canada Century Home (ISSN 0821-5774)

747 CN ISSN 0715-5689
CITY & COUNTRY HOME. 1982. 10/yr. Can.$24($50) Canadian Home Decor Magazines, 227 Front St., E., Ste. 100, Toronto, Ont. M5A 1E8, Canada. TEL 416-368-7889. FAX 416-941-9113. Ed. Anita Draycott. adv.; illus.; circ. 78,378. **Indexed:** CMI.
Former titles: Home Decor Canada; Canadian Home Decor.

747 FR
CLUB MAISON. 1978. 4/yr. 48 F. (foreign 60 F.). Publications Conde Nast S.A., 10 Bd. du Montparnasse, 75724 Paris Cedex 15, France. Ed. Patrick Delcroix.

COLONIAL HOMES. see *BUILDING AND CONSTRUCTION*

747 SP
COLOR Y DECORACION EN EL HOGAR. irreg. price varies. Editorial Gustavo Gili S.A., Rosellon 87-89, Barcelona 15, Spain.

747 635 301 US ISSN 0272-6904
TX301
COLORADO HOMES & LIFESTYLES. 1980. bi-m. $15. Wiesner Publishing, Inc., 7009 S. Potomac St., Englewood, CO 80112. TEL 303-397-7600. FAX 303-397-7619. Ed. Ann McGregor Parsons. adv.; bk.rev.; circ. 18,000.

747 UK
COMMERCIAL INTERIORS INTERNATIONAL. 1985. a. $29.95. Grosvenor Press International, Holford Mews, Cruickshack St., London WC1X 9HD, England. TEL 01-2783000. FAX 01-2781674. TELEX 23931 GPI G. Ed. Richard Parkes. circ. 30,000.

747 FR ISSN 0395-2673
CONSEILS SOLS ET MURS. 1976. m. 230 F. Editions A4, 32, av. Charles-de-Gaulle, 92200 Neuilly-sur-Seine, France. FAX 47-22-70-04. Ed. Messaline Guedj. adv.; bk.rev.; circ. 6,000.

747 US ISSN 0010-7832
TS840
CONTRACT; the business magazine of commerical and institutional interior design and architecture, planning and construction. 1960. m. $65 ($35 to qualified personnel). Miller Freeman Inc. (New York) (Subsidiary of: United Newspapers Group), 1515 Broadway, New York, NY 10036. TEL 212-869-1300. FAX 212-302-6273. Ed. Roger Yee. adv.; illus.; tr.lit.; index; circ. 29,500. (also avail. in microform from UMI) **Indexed:** Search (1990-).

747 CN ISSN 0833-9406
CONTRACT MAGAZINE. (Text in English, French) 1981. bi-m. Can.$29($40) Victor Publishing Co. Ltd., 312 Dolomite Dr., Ste. 217, Downsview, Ont. M3J 2N2, Canada. TEL 416-667-9609. FAX 416-667-9715. Ed. David Lasker. adv.; circ. 13,500. (back issues avail.)
Formerly: Canada's Contract Magazine.

747 GW
COUNTRY. (Text in German; summaries in English) 1988. q. DM.56. Jahreszeiten Verlag GmbH, Possmoorweg 5, Postfach 132150, 2000 Hamburg 60, Germany. TEL 040-27170. FAX 040-27172056. Ed. Christa von Hantelmann. (back issues avail.)

COUNTRY ALMANAC. see *HOME ECONOMICS*

747 US
COUNTRY DECORATING IDEAS. 1980. q. $8. Harris Publications, Inc., 1115 Broadway, 8th fl., New York, NY 10010. TEL 212-807-7100. adv.

747 US
THE COUNTRY DECORATOR. q. G C R Publishing Group, 1700 Broadway, New York, NY 10019-5905. TEL 212-541-7100. FAX 212-245-1241. Ed. Marilyn Hansen.

747 US ISSN 0737-3740
TH4850
COUNTRY HOME. 1979. 6/yr. $17.97. Meredith Corporation, 1716 Locust St., Des Moines, IA 50336. TEL 515-284-3000. Ed. Jean Lemmon. circ. 1,000,000. **Indexed:** Access (1984-), Gard.Lit. (1992-).

747 745.1 UK ISSN 0951-3019
COUNTRY HOMES & INTERIORS. 1986. m. £23.40 (foreign £33). Southbank Publishing Group, King's Reach Tower, London SE1 9LS, England. TEL 071-261-5000. FAX 071-261-6895. (Subscr. to: Quadrant Subscr. Service Ltd., Oakfield House, Perrymount Rd., Haywards Heath, W. Sussex RH16 3DH, England) Ed. Julia Watson. circ. 90,252. (back issues avail.)

IJK

INTERIOR DESIGN AND DECORATION

747 US
COUNTRY KITCHENS. 3/yr. Harris Publications, Inc., 1115 Broadway, New York, NY 10010-2803. TEL 212-807-7100. FAX 212-627-4678. Ed. Kathleen Fredrick.

747 US ISSN 0732-2569
TX1
COUNTRY LIVING (NEW YORK). 1978. m. $17.97 (foreign $33.97). Hearst Magazines, Country Living, 224 W. 57th St., New York, NY 10019. TEL 800-888-0128. Ed. Rachel Newman. adv.; circ. 1,700,000. **Indexed:** Gard.Lit. (1992-), PMR.
Formerly: Good Housekeeping's Country Living (ISSN 0274-4791)

747 US
COUNTRY LIVING REMODELING. a. $2.95 per no. Hearst Magazines, 250 W. 55th St., New York, NY 10019. TEL 212-649-4203.

747 US
COUNTRY VICTORIAN ACCENTS. bi-m. $3.50 per no. G C R Publishing Group, Inc., 1700 Broadway, 34th Fl., New York, NY 10019. TEL 212-541-7100. FAX 212-245-1241.

747 US
COUNTRY VICTORIAN DECORATING. q. G C R Publishing Group, 1700 Broadway, New York, NY 10019-5905. TEL 212-541-7100. FAX 212-245-1241. Ed. Marilyn Hansen.

747 CN
CUISINES ET SALLES DE BAINS. a. Publicor Inc., 7 Chemin Bates, Outremont, Que. H2V 1A6, Canada. TEL 514-270-1100. FAX 514-270-6900.
Description: Features new designs in kitchen and bathroom furnishing and accessories.

747 GW ISSN 0172-2867
D L W NACHRICHTEN; Zeitschrift fuer Architektur und Innenausbau. (Text in English, French and German) 1927. a. free. D L W Aktiengesellschaft, Postfach 140, 7120 Bietigheim-Bissingen, Germany. Ed. Frank Werner. bk.rev.; bibl.; illus.; circ. 35,000.
Formerly: D L W Informationen zur Bau- und Einrichtungspraxis (ISSN 0011-5002)

747 GW
DECO; Wohnen mit Textilien. 1979. a. DM.10. Peter Winkler Verlag, Maximiliansplatz 9, 8000 Munich 2, Germany. TEL 089-555701. FAX 089-553752. circ. 40,000.

747 720 US
DECOR ELEGANTE.* 1989. q. $20. C.Q. Publications, Inc., 505 N. Tustin Ave., Ste. 148, Santa Ana, CA 92705. TEL 714-938-3220. adv.; circ. 10,000.
Description: For affluent new home owners in Southern California. Focuses on interior and exterior design ideas and previews trends in materials and accessories, along with product information and industry services.

747 CN
DECORATING & DESIGN SOURCEBOOK. q. Selective Media Ventures, Inc., 1300 Yonge St., Ste. 500, Toronto, Ont. M4T 1X3, Canada. TEL 416-961-5002. FAX 416-961-5584. Ed. Kathleen Sloan. circ. 200,000.

747 UK ISSN 0070-3192
DECORATING CONTRACTOR ANNUAL DIRECTORY. 1903. a. £13.50. Kingslea Press Ltd., 137 Newhall Street, Birmingham B3 1SF, England. TEL 021-236-8112. FAX 021-200-1480. Ed. Sam Ichbia. adv.; bk.rev.; circ. 1,000.

747 US ISSN 0889-2210
DECORATING DIGEST; craft & home projects. 1987. bi-m. $21. Women's Publishing Company, 950 Third Ave., 16th Fl., New York, NY 10022. TEL 212-888-1855. FAX 212-838-8420. (Subscr. to: Box 11276, Des Moines, IA 50340-1276) Ed. Christine Burns Roth. circ. 250,000. (back issues avail.)

676.284 US
DECORATING PRODUCTS RETAIL SALES REPORT; an analysis of sales through decorating products dealers. a. $950. National Decorating Products Association, 1050 N. Lindbergh Blvd., St. Louis, MO 63132. TEL 314-991-3470. FAX 314-991-5039. Ed. David Weiss. circ. 400.
Former titles: Decorating Products Sales Report.

667.6 767.284 US
DECORATING PRODUCTS TRENDS ADVISORY; marketing newsletter for the decorating products industry. q. membership. National Decorating Products Association, 1050 N. Lindbergh Blvd., St. Louis, MO 63132. TEL 314-991-3470. FAX 314-991-5039. Ed. Ernest W. Stewart. circ. 500.
Formerly: Italics.

747 US
DECORATING REMODELING. 1986. bi-m. $16. Family Circle, Inc. (Subsidiary of: New York Times Company, Inc.), 110 Fifth Ave., New York, NY 10011. TEL 212-463-1636. Eds. Catherine George, Karen Saks. adv.; circ. 684,447.
Formed by the merger of: Remodeling Made Easy & Decorating Made Easy; Which was formerly titled: Family Circle's Home Decorating Guide (ISSN 0090-8630)

747 US
▼**DECORATING REMODELING BEST KITCHEN PLAN DESIGNS.** 1990. 3/yr. New York Times Company, Magazine Group, 110 Fifth Ave., New York, NY 10011. TEL 212-463-1574. adv.; circ. 450,000.
Description: Features popular configurations, island plans, L-shapes, U-shapes, and galleys.

676.284 US ISSN 0011-7404
DECORATING RETAILER. 1964. m. $20. National Decorating Products Association, 1050 N. Lindbergh Blvd., St. Louis, MO 63132. TEL 314-991-3470. FAX 314-991-5039. Ed. Diane Capuano. adv.; charts; illus.; index; circ. 32,786.

747 US
▼**DECORATING RETAILER'S DECORATING REGISTRY.** 1992. a. National Decorating Products Association, 1050 N. Lindbergh Blvd., St. Louis, MO 63132. TEL 314-991-3470. FAX 314-991-5039. Ed. Kristin Pratt. adv.; circ. 32,786.
Description: Provides information on manufacturers, distributors and suppliers serving the decorating products industry.

676.284 US
DECORATING RETAILER'S DIRECTORY OF THE WALLCOVERING INDUSTRY; the gold book. 1972. a. $25. National Decorating Products Association, 1050 N. Lindbergh Blvd., St. Louis, MO 63132. TEL 314-991-3470. FAX 314-991-5039. Ed. Kristin Pratt. adv.; index; circ. 8,000. (back issues avail.)
Description: Source of wallcoverings from manufacturer to distributor. Current collections and their distributors listed for dealers.

745 FR
DECORATION. 9/yr. 360 F. (foreign 432 F.). Editions Rusconi, 90 rue de Flandre, 75019 Paris, France.

747 CN ISSN 0705-1093
DECORATION CHEZ-SOI.* 1977. m. Can.$24. Les Editions Le Nordais Ltee, 7 Chemin Bates, Outremont, Que. H2V 1A6, Canada. TEL 514-735-6361. Ed. Claude Durocher. adv.; illus.; circ. 91,000.

747 CN ISSN 0315-047X
DECORMAG. (Text in French) 1972. 10/yr. Can.$23.50. Editions du Feu Vert, Inc., 5148 St. Laurent Blvd., Montreal, Que. H2T 1R8, Canada. TEL 514-273-9773. FAX 514-273-9034. Ed. Dominique Lamarche. adv.; bk.rev.; illus.; circ. 63,492. **Indexed:** Pt.de Rep. (1981-).

747 CN
DEL CONDOMINIUM LIFE. 1986. 4/yr. Can.$10. Del Property Management Inc., 4800 Dufferin St., Downsview, Ont. M3H 5S9, Canada. TEL 416-661-3640. FAX 416-661-8923. Ed. Patricia Mackellar. adv.; circ. 25,000 (controlled).

DESIGN. see ART

DESIGN BOOK REVIEW. see ARCHITECTURE

DESIGN FIRM DIRECTORY; a listing of firms and consultants in industrial and graphic design in the U.S. and Canada. see BUSINESS AND ECONOMICS — Trade And Industrial Directories

747 DK ISSN 0108-0695
NK1457.A1
DESIGN FROM SCANDINAVIA; a Scandinavian production in furniture, textiles, illumination, arts and crafts and industrial design. (Text in English, French, German and Scandinavian languages) 1966. a. $19. World Pictures, Martinsvej 8, DK-1926 Frederiksberg C, Denmark. FAX 31-270481. (U.S. dist. by: Rockport Publishers, Inc., P.O. Box 396, Five Smith St., Rockport, MA 01966) Ed. Kirsten Bjerregaard. illus.; circ. 50,000.
—BLDSC shelfmark: 3560.185000.
Formerly: Design from Denmark.

747 FI ISSN 0782-4327
DESIGN IN FINLAND. 1960. a. FIM 58. Finnish Foreign Trade Association, P.O. Box 908, 00101 Helsinki, Finland. illus.; circ. 55,000.
Formerly: Designed in Finland (ISSN 0418-7717)

DESIGN LINE. see ARCHITECTURE

DESIGN QUARTERLY. see ARCHITECTURE

747 720 US ISSN 0277-3538
NA2750
DESIGN SOLUTIONS. 1981. q. $18. Architectural Woodwork Institute, Box 1550, Centreville, VA 22020-8550. TEL 703-222-1100. FAX 703-222-2499. Ed. Elaine Ferri. adv.; circ. 25,000. **Indexed:** Avery Ind.Archit.Per.
Description: Devoted to interior design solutions and custom use of wood, metals, plastics, and fabrics. Combines interior design and structural architecture with detailed draqings.

747 720 US ISSN 1041-0422
DESIGN TIMES; style of New England. 1988. bi-m. $30 (effective Jan. 1992). Regis Publishing, Inc., 715 Boylston St., Boston, MA 02116. TEL 617-859-9690. FAX 617-859-0002. Ed. Nancy Zerbey. adv.; bk.rev.; circ. 20,000.

747 720 AT ISSN 0810-6029
NK1490.A1
DESIGN WORLD. 1983. q. $37.50. Design Editorial Pty. Ltd., 11 School Rd., Ferny Creek, Vic. 3786, Australia. FAX 03-755-1155. (Dist. in U.S. by: Expediters of the Printed Word, 2323 Randolph Ave., Avenel, NJ 07001) Ed. Colin Wood. adv.; bk.rev.; circ. 18,000.
—BLDSC shelfmark: 3560.216000.
Description: For those who are interested in all the related aspects of design.

747 728 US
DESIGNER HOME PLANS. 1986. 2/yr. $15.95 (includes Architectural Designs). Davis Publications, Inc., 380 Lexington Ave., New York, NY 10168-0035. TEL 212-557-9100. Ed. Stephen Wagner. circ. 75,000.

DESIGNERS' COLLECTION HOME PLANS. see BUILDING AND CONSTRUCTION

747 301 US
DESIGNERS ILLUSTRATED. bi-m. $15.95. Select Communications, Inc., 4410 El Camino Real, Ste. 111, Los Altos, CA 94022. TEL 415-941-6200. FAX 415-941-6263. Ed. Paul D. Nyberg. adv.; illus.
Description: Resource guide for interior design and home furnishings for consumers.

747 728 UK ISSN 0264-8148
NK2043
DESIGNERS' JOURNAL. 1983. 10/yr. £30. Architectural Press Ltd., 9 Queen Anne's Gate, London SW1H 9BY, England. TEL 01-222-4333. FAX 01-222-5196. TELEX 8953505-MBC-QAG-G. Ed. Alastair Best. adv.; bk.rev.; illus.; circ. 13,000. **Indexed:** Artbibl.Mod., Avery Ind.Archit.Per., Ergon.Abstr.
—BLDSC shelfmark: 3560.305500.

745 724 US ISSN 0192-1487
NK2004
DESIGNERS WEST. 1953. m. $30 (includes annual Resource Directory). Designers World Corp., 8914 Santa Monica Blvd., The Penthouse, Box 69660, Los Angeles, CA 90069. TEL 310-657-8231. Ed. Carol King. adv.; bk.rev.; tr.lit.; circ. 36,789.
Description: For interior designers, architects and industrial designers professionally interested in the United States Sunbelt states.

INTERIOR DESIGN AND DECORATION

645 720   US   ISSN 0192-1487
DESIGNERS WEST RESOURCE DIRECTORY. (Supplement to: Designers West) 1973. a. $10 (for single copy). Designers World Corp., 8914 Santa Monica Blvd., The Penthouse, Box 69660, Los Angeles, CA 90069. TEL 310-657-8231. Ed. Carol S. King. adv.; index; circ. 38,564.

747   US   ISSN 1057-8277
NK1700
▼**DESIGNERS WORLD.** 1991. m. $30. Designers World Corp., 8914 Santa Monica Blvd., The Penthouse, Box 69660, Los Angeles, CA 90069. TEL 310-657-8231. Ed. Carol King.
 Description: Provides the southern and southwestern design professional with an expanded and comprehensive pictorial portfolio of outstanding hospitality, residential, and corporate design projects.

747 728   US
DESIGNMENT. 1986. a. $8. (Simpson Door Company) Northwest Home Designing, Inc., N H D Marketing Division, 10901 Bridgeport Way, S.W., Tacoma, WA 98499. TEL 206-584-6309. FAX 206-588-0607. Ed. Todd Lord. adv.; bk.rev.; illus.; circ. 120,000. (back issues avail.)
 Description: Discusses home plans.

747   CN   ISSN 0835-2526
DESIGNS. (Text English, French) 1986. 4/yr. Can.$8 (foreign Can.$16). Association Communication Innovation Designs 4, C.P. 692, succ. Place D'Armes, Montreal, Que. H2Y 3H8, Canada. TEL 514-842-4436. FAX 514-848-9730. Ed. Bill Taillefer. adv.; circ. 13,900 (controlled).
 Description: Addressed to architects, interior and industrial designers, graphists, manufacturers, retailers, government agencies.

DIRECTORY OF CONTRACT WALLCOVERINGS AND SPECIFICATIONS. see *BUSINESS AND ECONOMICS — Trade And Industrial Directories*

747   II   ISSN 0256-4025
DIRECTORY OF INTERIOR DESIGNERS. (Text in English) 1984. biennial. $15. Architects Publishing Corp. of India, 51 Sujata, Ground Floor, Rani Sati Marg, Malad East, Bombay 400 097, India. TEL 6804442. Ed. A.K. Gupta. adv.; charts; illus.; circ. 5,000.
 Description: Listing of professional interior designers, manufacturers, dealers and contractors.

747   US   ISSN 1049-9172
DISPLAY & DESIGN IDEAS. 1988. 10/yr. $49. Shore Communications, Inc., 180 Allen Rd., N.E., Ste. 300 N., Atlanta, GA 30328. TEL 404-252-8831. FAX 404-252-4436. Ed. Karen Benning. adv.; bk.rev.; circ. 18,039 (controlled).
 Description: Discusses new products and display ideas in the visual merchandising and store design field.

747   CS   ISSN 0012-5369
DOMOV. (Text in Czech; summaries in English, French, German, Russian) 1960. m. 300 Kcs. Premiera, a.s., Radlicka 103, 150 02 Prague 5, Czechoslovakia. Ed. Lenka Zizkova - Eibel. circ. 50,000.

DOMUS; architettura arredamento arte. see *ARCHITECTURE*

DOSSIER COMPONENTI; international lighting technology and lighting accessories magazine. see *ENGINEERING — Electrical Engineering*

747   US   ISSN 0279-4918
DRAPERIES & WINDOW COVERINGS. 1981. 13/yr. $30. L.C. Clark Publishing Co., Inc., 450 Skokie Blvd., Ste. 507, Northbrook, IL 60062. FAX 407-627-3447. (Or: 800 US Hwy. 1, Ste. 330, North Palm Beach, FL 33408-3833) Ed. Katie Sosnowchik. adv.; tr.lit.; circ. 25,115. (reprint service avail.)

EARLY AMERICAN LIFE; decorating, crafts and history. see *INTERIOR DESIGN AND DECORATION — Furniture And House Furnishings*

747   NE
EIGEN HUIS EN INTERIEUR. 1967. m. fl.42. Eska Tijdschriften, PB 2252, 3500 MD Utrecht, Netherlands. TEL 030-822511. FAX 030-898388. TELEX 40349-ESKA. Ed. l. Kluvers. adv.; bk.rev.; charts; illus.; circ. 91,400. **Indexed:** Key to Econ.Sci.
 Formerly: Eigen Huis (ISSN 0013-2519)

747   GW
ESQUIRE; Das Deutsche Lifestyle Magazin. 1987. m. $80. Heinrich Bauer Verlag (Munich), Charles-de-Gaulle-Str. 8, 8000 Munich 83, Germany. TEL 089-6786-406. FAX 089-676433. (Dist. by: German Language Publications Inc., 560 Sylvan Ave., Englewood Cliffs, NJ 07632. TEL 201-871-1010) Ed. Rolf Diekhof. circ. 56,607.

747 658   UK
FACILITY DESIGN AND MANAGEMENT. 1986. m. £30. Maple Publishing Ltd., 21A Brighton Rd., South Croydon, Surrey CR2 6EA, England. TEL 081 686 0141. FAX 081-680-1825. Ed. Malcolm Bowen. adv.; bk.rev.; circ. 9,500.
 Formerly: Facility Management.
 Description: Discusses all the individual elements that create the modern office environment.

747   CN   ISSN 0319-616X
FLOOR COVERING NEWS. 1955. 10/yr. Can.$30. Style Communications Inc., 1448 Lawrence Ave. E., Ste. 302, Toronto, Ont. M4A 4V6, Canada. TEL 416-755-5199. FAX 416-755-9123. Ed. Michael J. Knell. adv.; circ. 7,224.

747   US
FLOOR COVERING NEWS. 1986. w. $20. Altron Communications, Inc., 29-10 Thomson Ave., Long Island City, NY 11101. TEL 718-706-7830. Ed. Albert Wahnon. adv.; circ. 912.

747 330   US
FLOORING MARKET SHOPPER. s-a. free to convention attendees. Avanstar Communications, Inc., 7500 Old Oak Blvd., Cleveland, OH 44130. TEL 216-826-2839. FAX 216-891-2726. (Subscr. to: 1 E. First St., Duluth, MN 55802) Ed. Dan Alaimo. circ. 4,570.

747   UK   ISSN 0263-7693
FLOORS. 1982. m. £20. Maple Publishing Limited, 21A Brighton Rd., South Croydon, Surrey, England. TEL 01 686 0141. FAX 01-680-1825. Ed. Penelope Brook. adv.; bk.rev.; circ. 14,000. (tabloid format)
 Formerly (until 1987): Floor and Flooring.
 Description: Information on new products and developments within the flooring industry for the retail and commercial purchasing sectors, retail outlets and buyers for distributors in the U.K.

051 635   US   ISSN 0898-9494
FLORIDA HOME & GARDEN. 1984. m. $24 (foreign $39). Florida Media Affiliates, Inc. (Subsidiary of: Micromedia Affiliates), 600 Brickell Ave., Ste. 207, Miami, FL 33131. TEL 305-445-4500. FAX 305-374-7691. (Subscr. to: Box 2052, Marion, OH 44306) Ed. Kathryn Howard. adv.; bk.rev.; circ. 80,000.
 Formerly: South Florida Home and Garden (ISSN 0743-863X)
 Description: Features home interior design, gardening, homecare and travel.

747   GW   ISSN 0015-7678
FORM; Zeitschrift fuer Gestaltung. 1957. q. DM.61. Verlag Form GmbH, Ernsthoefer Str. 12, 6104 Seeheim-Jugenheim, Germany. TEL 06257-81395. Ed.Bd. adv.; bk.rev.; illus.; mkt.; index; circ. 9,500.
 Indexed: Graph.Arts Lit.Abstr.
 —BLDSC shelfmark: 4008.290000.

747   SW   ISSN 0015-766X
FORM. (Text in Swedish; summaries in English; editions in English) 1905. 8/yr. SEK 650 in Nordic countries; elsewhere SEK 690. Foereningen Svensk Form - Swedish Society of Crafts and Design, Renstiernas Gata 12, S-116 28 Stockholm, Sweden. TEL 8-6443303. FAX 8-6442285. Ed. Ulf Beckman. adv.; bk.rev.; illus.; index, cum.index; circ. 11,000.
 —BLDSC shelfmark: 4008.300000.

FORM & ZWECK; Fachzeitschrift fuer industrielle Formgestaltung. see *BUILDING AND CONSTRUCTION*

FRAMING AND ART. see *ART*

FRANK LLOYD WRIGHT NEWSLETTER. see *ARCHITECTURE*

747   US
FURNITURE: LATIN AMERICAN INDUSTRIAL REPORT. (Avail. for each of 22 Latin American countries) 1985. a. $435 per country report. Aquino Productions, Box 15760, Stamford, CT 06901. TEL 203-325-3138. Ed. Andres C. Aquino.

747   IT   ISSN 0393-4500
GIORNALE DELL'ARREDAMENTO. 1982. m. L.50000. Editore Rima s.r.l., Via Vincenzo Da Filicaia 7, 20162 Milan, Italy. TEL 02-66103539. FAX 02-66103558. Ed. Flavio Maestrini. circ. 16,000.
 Description: Magazine about Italian interior design.

747   US   ISSN 0362-5419
TT1
GLORIA VANDERBILT DESIGNS FOR YOUR HOME.*
1975. q. $1.25. McCall Pattern Co., 11 Penn Plaza, Ste. 18, New York, NY 10001-2065. TEL 212-580-2600. TELEX 649212. Ed. Phyllis Hingston Roderick. illus.

747 641   US
NA7100
H G. 1901. m. $24. Conde Nast Publications Inc., House & Garden Magazine, 350 Madison Ave., New York, NY 10017. TEL 212-880-8800. Ed. Nancy Novogrod. adv.; bk.rev.; illus.; tr.lit.; index; circ. 650,000. (also avail. in microform from UMI; reprint service avail. from UMI) **Indexed:** Artbibl.Mod., Avery Ind.Archit.Per., Biog.Ind., Gard.Lit. (1992-), Mag.Ind., PMR, R.G.
 Formerly: House and Garden (ISSN 0018-6406); Incorporating: Living for Young Homemakers.
 Description: Interior and landscape architecture and design. Articles profile architects, designers, historical places and current design ideas.

747 651.2   IT   ISSN 1120-236X
HABITAT UFFICIO. (Text in English and Italian) 1981. 6/yr. $80. Alberto Greco Editore, Via del Fusaro 8, 20146 Milan, Italy. TEL 02-4819086. FAX 02-4819091. Ed. Paola Pianzola. circ. 21,500.

HARDWOOD FLOORS. see *BUILDING AND CONSTRUCTION — Carpentry And Woodwork*

747   GW
DAS HAUS. 10/yr. $36. Burda Verlag GmbH, Postfach 1230, 7600 Offenburg, Germany. (U.S. dist.: GLP International, 153 S. Dean St., Englewood, NJ 07631)

747   US
▼**HAUT DECOR.** 1990. 10/yr. $19. Haut Decor, Inc., 3290 N.E. 12th Ave., Oakland Park, FL 33334. TEL 305-568-9444. FAX 305-568-9445. Ed. Janet Verdeguer. adv.; circ. 16,000.
 Description: Reports on the upper-end furnishings community, both residential and commercial, for professional interior designers.

747   US
HAWAIIAN ISLAND HOME. bi-m. Pacific Publishing, 677 Ala Moana Blvd., Penthouse Ste., Honolulu, HI 96813. TEL 808-522-7400. FAX 808-522-7408. Ed. Rob Sandler.

HEIM UND HOBBY; Kundenfachzeitschrift fuer Heimwerker in Haus, Hof und Garten. see *HOME ECONOMICS*

747   GW   ISSN 0017-9876
HEIMTEX; trade journal for interior decoration. 1949. m. DM.132. (Fachverband des Deutschen Teppich- und Gardinenhandels e.V.) Westdeutsche Verlagsanstalt GmbH, Ahmser Str. 190, Postfach 3054, 4900 Herford, Germany. TEL 05221-775-0. FAX 05221-775215. TELEX 17-5221-855. Ed. H. Russ. adv.; illus.
 Description: Focuses on interior decoration and trading with carpets.

HOME; creative ideas for home design. see *ARCHITECTURE*

747   IT
HOME; tessile d'arredamento nell'architettura d'interni. (Text in English and Italian) m. (11/yr.). L.60000 (foreign L.150000). Editoriale Galfa s.r.l., Viale Monza 57, 20125 Milan, Italy. TEL 02-2840574. FAX 2610923. TELEX 315614 SISTAR. adv.
 Formerly: Ambientare Home.
 Description: Trade magazine covering the furnishing textiles and interior design industry.

2552 INTERIOR DESIGN AND DECORATION

747   US
HOME & HOLIDAY INTERNATIONAL. bi-m. $3.95 per no. Hyde Park Group, 2001 W. Main St., Stamford, CT 06902. TEL 203-969-2533. FAX 203-348-3555.

HOME FURNISHINGS REVIEW. see *INTERIOR DESIGN AND DECORATION — Furniture And House Furnishings*

747   HK
HOME JOURNAL. 1980. m. HK.$250. Communication Management Ltd., 1811, Hong Kong Plaza, 188 Connaught Rd. W., Hong Kong. TEL 547-7117. FAX 858-2671. Ed. Lina Ross. adv.; circ. 302,800.

747   US
HOME PLANS. 3/yr. $3.95 per no. New York Times Company, Magazine Group, 110 Fifth Ave., New York, NY 10011. TEL 212-463-1124.

747   CN
HOMES AND COTTAGES. 8/yr. In-Home Show Ltd., 6557 Mississauga Rd., No. D, Mississauga, Ont. L5N 1A6, Canada. TEL 416-567-1440. FAX 416-567-1442. Ed. Janice B. Naisby. circ. 28,000.

747 635   UK   ISSN 0018-4233
HOMES AND GARDENS. 1919. m. £25($49.50) (foreign £34). I P C Magazines Ltd., Southbank Publishing (Subsidiary of: Reed International PLC), King's Reach Tower, Stamford St., London SE1 9LS, England. TEL 071-261-5000. FAX 071-261-6247. (Subscr. to: Oakfield House, 35 Perrymount Rd., Haywards Heath, Sussex RH1 3DH, England; U.S. subscr. to: ISI, Box 186, North Bergen, NJ 07047) Ed. Amanda Evans. adv.; bk.rev.; illus.; index; circ. 192,000. (back issues avail.)
    Incorporates: A la Carte.

747   CN
HOMES AND IDEAS MAGAZINE. 6/yr. N H R Publishing Ltd., 17th Ave., S.W., Ste. 330-1302, Calgary, Alta. T2T 0A5, Canada. TEL 403-244-4239. FAX 403-228-0529. Ed. John Hromyk. circ. 220,000.

HOTEL SPECIFICATION INTERNATIONAL. see *HOTELS AND RESTAURANTS*

HOUSE & BUNGALOW; quarterly journal of the Architectural Service Planning Partnership. see *ARCHITECTURE*

747 641   UK   ISSN 0043-5759
HOUSE & GARDEN (LONDON). 1934. 12/yr. £32.20 (foreign £42.20). Conde Nast Publications Ltd., Vogue House, Hanover Sq., London W1R OAD, England. TEL 071-499-9080. FAX 071-493-1345. (Subscr. to: Quadrant Subscription Services, Oakfield House, Perrymount Rd., Haywards Heath, W. Sussex RH16 3DH, England) Ed. Robert Harling. adv.; bk.rev.; illus.; circ. 147,857. Indexed: Artbibl.Mod., Br.Tech.Ind., Search.
    Incorporating: Wine and Food.

747   JA
HOUSE & HOME. (Text in Japanese) 1981. bi-m. 5280 Yen. Gakken Co. Ltd., 40-5, 4-chome, Kamiikedai, Ohta-ku, Tokyo 145, Japan. Ed. Takanari Taguchi.

747   US   ISSN 0018-6422
NA7100
HOUSE BEAUTIFUL. 1896. m. $17.95. Hearst Magazines, House Beautiful, 1700 Broadway, New York, NY 10019-5970. TEL 212-903-5101. FAX 212-765-8292. Ed. Louis O. Gropp. adv.; bk.rev.; illus.; tr.lit.; circ. 1,000,000. (also avail. in microform from UMI; reprint service avail. from UMI) **Indexed:** Access, Avery Ind.Archit.Per., Consum.Ind., Gard.Lit. (1992-), Mag.Ind., PMR, R.G.

HOUSE BEAUTIFUL'S HOME BUILDING. see *BUILDING AND CONSTRUCTION*

747   US
HOUSE BEAUTIFUL'S HOME REMODELING & DECORATING. 1964. q. $2.95 per no. Hearst Corporation, 1700 Broadway, Ste. 2801, New York, NY 10019. TEL 212-903-5050. FAX 212-262-9401. Ed. John Driemen. adv.; illus.; circ. 250,000.
    Formed by the **1987 merger of:** House Beautiful's Home Decorating (ISSN 0018-6457) & House Beautiful's Home Remodeling (ISSN 0018-6465)

747   US
HOUSE BEAUTIFUL'S KITCHENS - BATHS. 1980. 3/yr. $2.95 per no. Hearst Corporation, 1700 Broadway, Ste. 2801, New York, NY 10019. TEL 212-903-5050. FAX 212-262-9401. Ed. Timothy Drew. adv.; circ. 250,000.

747   US
HOUSE PLAN FAVORITES. s-a. $2.95 per no. Archway Press, Inc., 19 W. 44th St., New York, NY 10036. TEL 212-757-5580.

747 645   IC
HUS & HIBYLI/HOME AND FAMILY. 1973. bi-m. ISK 3150($70) Sam-utgafan sf, Haaleitisbraut 1, 105 Reykjavik, Iceland. FAX 354-1-680101. Ed. Thorarinn J. Magnusson. circ. 14,000. (back issues avail.)

747   US   ISSN 0161-1895
I.D.E.A.S.. (Interiors, Design, Environment, Arts, Structures) 1976. q. $14. DoDi Publishing Corporation Inc., Box 343392, Coral Gables, FL 33114. TEL 305-662-8924. Ed. Sam Hirsch. adv.; illus.; circ. 16,000.

747 658.788   US   ISSN 0192-3021
TS1
I D: INTERNATIONAL DESIGN MAGAZINE; planning-design-marketing. Alternative title: I D Magazine of International Design. (Includes: Annual Design Review) 1954. bi-m. $40. Design Publications, Inc., 250 W. 57th St., New York, NY 10107. TEL 212-956-0535. FAX 212-246-3891. Ed. Annetta Hanna. adv.; bk.rev.; illus.; tr.lit.; index; circ. 19,500. (also avail. in microfilm from UMI; back issues avail.; reprint service avail. from UMI) **Indexed:** A.S.& T.Ind., Art Ind., Artbibl.Mod., Avery Ind.Archit.Per., Ind.Sci.Rev.
    —BLDSC shelfmark: 4362.217000.
    Formerly (until vol. 26, 1979): Industrial Design (ISSN 0019-8110)

747   DK   ISSN 0109-4505
IDE-NYT: TIL LEJLIGHEDER I ETAGEBEBYGGELSE. Variant title: Ide-nyt Til Lejligheder. q. free. Forlaget Ide-nyt A-S, Klausdalsbrovej 495, DK-2730 Herlev, Denmark. TEL 45-44-53-40-00. FAX 44-92-11-21. TELEX 35 148 KDB DK. Ed. Suzanne LeMaire. adv.: B&W page DKK 76100, color page DKK 77800. charts; illus.; stat.; tr.lit.; circ. 830,000.
    Formerly: Ide-nyt Hus og Have til Villa - Raekkehuse.
    Description: Provides tips on improving the lifestyle of Danish apartment dwellers. Includes recipes and occasionally patterns.

747 635   DK   ISSN 0906-0952
IDE-NYT: TIL VILLA, RAEKKEHUSE OG JORDBRUGERE. 1959. q. free. Forlaget Ide-Nyt AS, Gl. Klausdalsbrovej 495, DK-7230 Herlev, Denmark. TEL 45-44-53-40-00. FAX 45-44-92-11-21. Ed. Suzanne LeMaire. adv.; charts; illus.; stat.; tr.lit.; circ. 1,600,000.
    Formed by the **1984 merger of:** Ide-Nyt: Til Jordbrugere (ISSN 0109-4513); (1973-1984): Ide-Nyt: Til Villa og Raekkehuse (ISSN 0107-007X); Which incorporates (1959-1982): Vi Med Hus og Have (ISSN 0109-3983)
    Description: Provides ideas and information to people living in single-family houses or row houses, either with or without gardens.

747   UK   ISSN 0019-1361
IDEAL HOME. 1920. m. £19.95 (foreign £21.15). World Press Network, 551 Hatton Gardens, London EC1N 8HT, England. TEL 0444-440421. TELEX 915748 MAGDIV G. (Subscr. to: Quadrant Subscription Services Ltd., Haywards Heath, W. Sussex, England) Ed. T. Whelan. adv.; bk.rev.; illus.; circ. 282,429.
    —BLDSC shelfmark: 4362.373500.

747   US
IDEAL HOME PLANS. s-a. $1.95 per no. Archway Press, Inc., 19 W. 44th St., New York, NY 10036. TEL 212-757-5580.

747 332.6   US
IDEAS FOR BETTER LIVING. 1945. m. free to qualified personnel. Boulevard Publications, 1755 Northwest Blvd., Columbus, OH 43212. TEL 614-488-8252. FAX 614-488-9124. Ed. Steve Bulkley. adv.; bk.rev.; illus.; circ. 350,000 (controlled).
    Description: Includes home decorating articles, as well as articles on health, pets, good money sense, travel, interesting hobbies (available commercially), and gardening.

747   CN   ISSN 0840-8130
IDEES DE MA MAISON. 1983. 10/yr. Can.$44 for 24 issues. Publicor Inc., 7 Chemin Bates, Outremont, Que. H2V 1A6, Canada. TEL 514-270-1100. FAX 514-270-6900. adv.; circ. 86,118.

ILLUMINOTECNICA; international lighting magazine. see *ENGINEERING — Electrical Engineering*

747   CN
IMAGE.* (Text in French) 1986. q. Societe des Decorateurs Ensembliers du Quebec, 20 Elmira, C.P. 1122, Place Bonaventure, Montreal, Que. H5A 1G4, Canada. TEL 514-288-9046. FAX 514-288-7090. adv.: B&W page Can.$1000; trim 8 1/2 x 11; adv. contact: Edgar Donelle. circ. 1,500.

INDIVIDUAL HOMES; designing, building & renovating your own home. see *BUILDING AND CONSTRUCTION*

747   II   ISSN 0970-1761
NK2076.A1
INSIDE - OUTSIDE; the Indian design magazine. (Text in English) 1977. bi-m. Rs.90. Business India Group of Publications, Wadia Bldg., 17-19 Dalal St., Bombay 400 023, India. TEL 22-274161. FAX 22-2871901. TELEX 011-3557-BZIN-IN. Ed. Sheila Shahani. adv.; illus.; circ. 39,000. **Indexed:** Br.Tech.Ind.

INTER ARCHITECTURE. see *ARCHITECTURE*

747 643.6   DK
INTERIEUR. 1925. m. (8/yr.). DKK 250 (typically set in Oct.); free to qualified personnel. Forlaget Cahier, Box 244, Langebjergvej 139, DK-3050 Humlebaek, Denmark. TEL 45-42-19-08-55. FAX 45-42-19-01-25. Ed. Laila Ramnaes. adv.; circ. 6,781 (controlled).
    Formerly: Huset Ude og Inde (ISSN 0108-9072)

747   US
INTERIOR DECORATORS' HANDBOOK. 1922. s-a. $30. Columbia Communications, Inc., 370 Lexington Ave., New York, NY 10017. TEL 212-532-9290. FAX 212-779-8345. Ed. Diane Gumple. adv.; illus.; circ. 20,000 (controlled).

747   UK   ISSN 0020-5494
INTERIOR DESIGN. 1957. m. £25. A G B Publications Ltd., Audit House, Field End Rd., Ruislip, Middx HA4 9LT, England. TEL 01-868-4499. FAX 01-429-3117. TELEX 926726. Ed. Katherine Tickle. adv.; bk.rev.; charts; illus.; tr.lit.; index; circ. 9,736. **Indexed:** Artbibl.Mod., Br.Tech.Ind., Bus.Ind., Tr.& Indus.Ind.
    ●Also available online. Vendor(s): DIALOG.
    Incorporating: Decor and Contract Furnishing (ISSN 0010-2946)
    Description: Professional facts for the designer working in the commercial interior field.

747   US   ISSN 0020-5508
NK1700
INTERIOR DESIGN. 1932. 17/yr. $47.95 (Canada $74.95; elsewhere $97.95). Cahners Publishing Company (New York), Interior Design Group (Subsidiary of: Reed International PLC), Division of Reed Publishing (USA) Inc., 249 W. 17th St., New York, NY 10011. TEL 212-645-0067. FAX 212-645-6987. (Subscr. to: Box 1970, Marion, OH 43305) Ed. Stanley Abercrombie. adv.; bk.rev.; illus.; circ. 57,000. (also avail. in microform from UMI; reprint service avail. from UMI) **Indexed:** Art Ind., Artbibl.Mod., Avery Ind.Archit.Per., Bus.Ind., Tr.& Indus.Ind.
    Description: For the professional designer, provides information on trends and new products.

INTERIOR DESIGN BUYERS GUIDE. see *BUSINESS AND ECONOMICS — Trade And Industrial Directories*

747   CN   ISSN 0836-3803
INTERIOR DESIGN ONTARIO. 1985. 9/yr. membership. Association of Registered Interior Designers of Ontario (ARIDO), 168 Bedford Road, Toronto, Ont. M5R 2K9, Canada. TEL 416-921-2127. FAX 416-921-3660. Ed. Phillip Moody. adv.; bk.rev.; circ. 6,400.
    Description: Devoted to the encouragement of the design industry and the enhancement of the profession.

INTERIOR DESIGN AND DECORATION

747 UK
INTERIOR DESIGNER'S HANDBOOK. 1981. a. £19.95. Grosvenor Press International, Holford Mews, Cruikshack St., London WC1X 9HD, England. TEL 01-2783000. FAX 01-2786174. TELEX 23931 GPI G. Ed. Richard Parkes. adv.; circ. 10,000.

INTERIOR LANDSCAPE INDUSTRY. see *GARDENING AND HORTICULTURE*

747 US ISSN 0164-8470
TS1300
INTERIORS: FOR THE CONTRACT DESIGN PROFESSIONAL. 1888. m. $35. B P I Communicatins, Inc. (New York) (Subsidiary of: Affiliated Publications, Inc.), 1515 Broadway, 39th Fl., New York, NY 10036. TEL 212-764-7300. FAX 212-944-1719. (Subscr. to: Box 2073, Mahopac, NY 10541. TEL 914-628-7771) Ed. Paula Rice Jackson. adv.; bk.rev.; illus.; tr.lit.; index; circ. 29,200. (also avail. in microform from UMI,MIM) Indexed: Art Ind., Artbibl.Mod., Avery Ind.Archit.Per., Br.Tech.Ind. Key Title: Interiors (New York, 1978).
—BLDSC shelfmark: 4534.350000.
Former titles: Contract Interiors (ISSN 0148-012X); Interiors (ISSN 0020-5516)

747 AT
INTERIORS MAGAZINE. 1984. bi-m. Aus.$3.95. Magazine Group Pty. Ltd., 3 Montague St., Balmain, N.S.W. 2041, Australia. TEL 02-555-1455. FAX 02-555-7822. Eds. Patsy Hollis, Mandy Nolan. circ. 70,000.
Former titles: Gabriel's Interiors Magazine & Gabriel's Interiors Annual.
Description: Details domestic decorating, building and furnishings. Reviews global trends and their application to Australia.

747 UK
INTERIORS QUARTERLY. 1987. q. £14. Grosvenor Press International, Ltd., Holford Mews, Cruikshank St., London WC1X 9HD, England. TEL 01-278-3000. FAX 01-278-1674. Ed. Richard Parkes. adv.; circ. 15,000.
Description: Covers topical preoccupations of the international interior-design world.

747 US ISSN 0744-8635
INTERIORSCAPE.* 1977. 6/yr. $12. Brantwood Publications, Inc., 3023 Eastland Blvd., Ste. 103, Clearwater, FL 34621-4106. TEL 813-796-3877. Ed. Jeffrey A. Morey. adv.; bk.rev.; circ. 7,500 (controlled).

747 UK ISSN 0268-2966
INTERNATIONAL CARPET BULLETIN. 1970. 6/yr. £58. W.R. Publications Ltd., 76 Kirkgate, Bradford BD1 1T8, England. FAX 0274-735045. TELEX 517617-WOOLMN-G. Ed. Jennifer Bradley. bk.rev.; stat.; tr.lit. (back issues avail.)
—BLDSC shelfmark: 4538.396700.
Description: Covers technical information for the carpet trade.

747 UK
INTERNATIONAL COLLECTION OF CONTRACT DESIGN. 1985. a. Grosvenor Press International, Holford Mews, Cruikshack St., London WC1X 9HD, England. TEL 01-2783000. FAX 01-2781674. TELEX 23931 GPI G. adv.

747 UK
INTERNATIONAL COLLECTION OF INTERIOR DESIGN. 1984. a. $29.95. Grosvenor Press International, Holford Mews, Cruickshack St., London WC1X 9HD, England. TEL 01-2783000. FAX 01-2781674. TELEX 23931 GPI G. Ed. Richard Parkes. adv.; circ. 30,000.

INTERNATIONAL LIGHTING REVIEW. see *BUILDING AND CONSTRUCTION*

747 FR
JOURNAL DE LA MAISON.* 1968. m. 138 F. 20 rue Billancourt, 92103 Boulogne-Billancourt Cedex, France. Ed. Jean Yves Bonhommet. adv.; circ. 20,300.

JOURNAL OF DESIGN HISTORY. see *ART*

747 US ISSN 0147-0418
NK1700
JOURNAL OF INTERIOR DESIGN EDUCATION AND RESEARCH.* 1976. s-a. $20 for individuals; libraries and institutions $25. Interior Design Educators Council, Inc., c/o Paul Eshelman, Design & Env. Analysis, MVR Hall, Cornell University, Ithaca, NY 14853. TEL 515-294-8898. (Subscr. to: Jeanne S. Rymer, Circulation Manager, College of Human Resources, Univ. of Delaware, Newark, DE 19716) bk.rev.; cum.index: 1976-1988; circ. 650. (back issues avail.)
Description: Focuses on research in interior design profession and education, including related fields.

643.3 US
KITCHEN & BATH DESIGN NEWS. 1983. 12/yr. free. K B C Publications, Inc., Two University Plaza, Hackensack, NJ 07601. TEL 201-487-7800. Ed. Tom Garry. adv.; tr.lit.; circ. 41,700. (reprint service avail.)

747 US
KITCHEN PLANS. s-a. $3.95 per no. New York Times Company, Magazine Group, 110 Fifth Ave., New York, NY 10011. TEL 212-463-1018.

749 UK
KITCHENS & BATHROOMS. 1975. m. £20. A G B Publications Ltd., Audit House, Field End Rd., Ruislip, Middx. HA4 9LT, England. TEL 01-868-4499. Ed. Grahame Morrison. adv.; bk.rev.; circ. 11,902.

747 GW ISSN 0722-9917
KUECHENPLANER; Partner des Kuechen-Fachhandels. 1966. bi-m. DM.52. Verlag A. Strobel KG, Postfach 5654, 5760 Arnsberg 2, Germany. TEL 02931-8900-0. FAX 02931-890038. TELEX 17293136. Ed. Claus Birkner. circ. 2,900. (back issues avail.)
Description: Trade journal for planning, furnishing and mounting of kitchens and household appliances and techniques.

L D & A. (Lighting Design & Application) see *ENGINEERING — Electrical Engineering*

747 HU ISSN 0047-391X
LAKASKULTURA. 1966. 6/yr. $24.50. (Belkereskedelmi Miniszterium) Lapkiado Vallalat, Lenin korut 9-11, 1073 Budapest 7, Hungary. TEL 222-408. (Subscr. to: Kultura, Box 149, H-1389 Budapest, Hungary) Ed. Maria Pataki. adv.; circ. 130,000.

747 IT
LIBRO DI CASA. 1935. a. Editoriale Domus, Via Grandi 5-7, 20089 Rozzano (MI), Italy. TEL 02 82472266. FAX 02-8255033. adv.

LICHT JOURNAAL; vakblad over verlichting en projektinrichting. see *ENGINEERING — Electrical Engineering*

LIGHTING DIMENSIONS. see *ARCHITECTURE*

747 US
LUXURY HOME IDEAS. 2/yr. Cahners Publishing Company (Des Plaines) (Subsidiary of: Reed Publishing PLC), Division of Reed Publishing (USA) Inc., 1350 E. Touhy Ave., Box 5080, Des Plaines, IL 60017-5080. TEL 708-635-8800. Ed. Roy L. Diez. circ. 120,000.
Description: Aimed at custom home buying consumers.

747 US
LUXURY HOMES. q. $4.95 per no. Cahners Publishing Company (New York) (Subsidiary of: Reed International PLC), Division of Reed Publishing (USA) Inc., 475 Park Ave. S., New York, NY 10016. TEL 212-545-5315. FAX 212-545-5356.

747 GW ISSN 0343-0642
M D. (Moebel Interior Design) (Text in English, French and German) 1955. m. DM.214.20. Konradin Verlag Robert Kohlhammer GmbH, Ernst-Mey-Str. 8, 7022 Leinfelden-Echterdingen, Germany. TEL 0711-7594-0. FAX 0711-7594-390. Ed. Gisela Schultz. adv.; illus.; circ. 14,125. (back issues avail.) Indexed: Artbibl.Mod., Br.Tech.Ind., CERDIC.
—BLDSC shelfmark: 5413.509200.
Formerly: M D Moebel Interior Design (ISSN 0024-8029); Formed by the merger of: Innenarchitektur und Moebel; Decoration.
Description: Offers a unique editorial and advertising platform for trendsetting problems and solutions in the fields of furniture, interior furnishings and design.

M I N FAX. (Marketing Information Network) see *HOUSING AND URBAN PLANNING*

747 UK
MAGAZINE FOR LONDON LIVING. 1982. m. £15. Magazine Publishing Co. Ltd., Fredrica House, 12 Oval Rd., London NW1 7DH, England. TEL 01-485-0975. Ed. Lucy Tuck. adv.; bk.rev.; film rev.; play rev.; circ. 65,000.

747 FR ISSN 0025-0945
MAISON ET JARDIN. (Supplement avail.: Maison et Jardin Hors Serie) 1950. 10/yr. 250 F.($59) (foreign 400 F.)(effective Aug. 1990). Publications Conde Nast S.A., 4 place du Palais-Bourbon, 75341 Paris Cedex 07, France. TEL 1-45-67-35-05. FAX 1-45-67-99-60. TELEX 204 191. (Subscr. to: 60732 Sainte-Genevieve Cedex, France. TEL 16-44-03-44-00; In U.S. subscr. to: International Subscriptions Inc., 1305 Paterson Plank Rd., North Bergen, NJ 07047-1890. TEL 201-867-9381) Ed. Patrick Delcroix. index; circ. 95,581.

747 FR
MAISON ET JARDIN HORS SERIE. (Supplement to: Maison et Jardin (ISSN 0025-0945)) 1978. 2/yr. 310 F.($59) Publications Conde Nast S.A., 4 place du Palais-Bourbon, 75341 Paris Cedex 07, France. (Subscr. to: 60732 Sainte-Genevieve Cedex, France. TEL 16-44-03-44-00; In U.S. subscr. to: International Subscriptions Inc., 1305 Paterson Plank Rd., North Bergen, NJ 07047-1890. TEL 201-867-9381) Ed. Patrick Delcroix. adv.; illus.
Formerly: Maison Magazine.

747 FR ISSN 0025-0953
TX1
MAISON FRANCAISE. 1946. 12/yr. 250 F. P.D.L., 17 rue d'Uzes, 75002 Paris, France. FAX 40-26-10-97. TELEX 680876. Ed. R. Glauveau. adv.; bk.rev.; charts; illus.; circ. 97,000. Indexed: Avery Ind.Archit.Per.

747 FR
MAISON INDIVIDUELLE. 1970. 9/yr. Publications du Moniteur, 17 rue d'Uzes, 75002 Paris, France. TEL 40-13-30-30. FAX 40-41-93-63. TELEX UPRESSE 680876F. circ. 160,000.

747 FR ISSN 0180-4561
MAISONS & DECORS MEDITERRANEE. 1974. bi-m. 151 Fr. Compagnie Mediterraneene d'Edition, Collines de Cuque, Av. de l'Armee d'Afrique, 13100 Aix en Provence, France. TEL 42-27-29-53. adv.

747 CN
MANDARIN HOME. bi-m. Home - Sweet - Home Publishing Inc., 226 Esna Park Dr., Ste. 202, Markham, Ont. L3R 1H3, Canada. TEL 416-479-5666. FAX 416-479-5667. Ed. Roks Lam. circ. 12,000.

MANHATTAN COOPERATOR; the co-op and condo monthly. see *REAL ESTATE*

747 CN
MANITOBA LIVING GUIDE. q. 826 Erin St., Winnipeg, Man. R3G 2W4, Canada. TEL 204-775-8918. Ed. Frank Chalmers. adv.; circ. 36,666.

MEANS INTERIOR COST DATA (YEAR). see *BUILDING AND CONSTRUCTION*

747 US
METRO - ORLANDO HOME. m. NewTech Solutions Inc., 1330 Palmetto Ave., Winter Park, FL 32789-4916. TEL 407-629-2393. FAX 407-629-5448. Ed. William P. Marino. adv.; circ. 20,000.

INTERIOR DESIGN AND DECORATION

METROPOLIS; the architecture and design magazine of New York. see *ARCHITECTURE*

747 US ISSN 0273-2858
NK1700
METROPOLITAN HOME; style for our generation. 1969. m. $19.95. Meredith Corporation, Special Interest Publications, 750 Third Ave., 11th fl., New York, NY 10017. TEL 212-557-6600. Ed. Dorothy Kalins. adv.; bk.rev.; bibl.; charts; illus.; tr.lit.; circ. 729,000. (also avail. in microform from UMI) **Indexed**: Access (1984-), Ind.How To Do It (1978-1980), Mag.Ind., PMR, Search.
  Former titles (until 1981): Apartment Life (ISSN 0092-0444); (until 1970): Apartment Ideas (ISSN 0003-6366)
  Description: Articles on home design and entertainment. Includes product profiles and menu ideas.

747 IT
LA MIA CASA - MENSILE DI ARREDAMENTO. 1968. m. (10/yr.). L.50000. Alberto Peruzzo Editore, Viale Marelli 165, 20099 Sesto S. Giovanni, Milan, Italy. TEL 02 24202284. FAX 2402723. TELEX 314386 APER I. Ed. Alessandra Burgiana. adv.; circ. 55,000.

MOBILA. see *INTERIOR DESIGN AND DECORATION — Furniture And House Furnishings*

747 NE ISSN 0165-5302
MOBILIA; vakblad voor interieurspecialisten. 1959. m. (foreign fl.107). Uitgeverij Mobilia BV, Prof. Tulpstr. 17, 1018 GZ Amsterdam, Netherlands. TEL 020-6206934. FAX 020-6207624. Ed. Olga Smalhout-Holst. adv.; bk.rev.; circ. 6,500.

MODERN LIVING. see *HOME ECONOMICS*

747 SZ ISSN 0026-8712
MODERNES WOHNEN/HABITATION MODERNE.* 1958. q. 20 Fr. Verlag H. G. Franke, 8126 Zumikon, Switzerland. adv.; charts.

747 GW ISSN 0026-8844
MOEBEL UND WOHNRAUM; Fachzeitschrift fuer Moebelindustrie und Raumgestaltung. (Text in German; index in English and Russian) 1947. 8/yr. DM.18 (foreign DM.27.60). Fachbuchverlag, Karl-Heine-Str. 16, 7031 Leipzig, Germany. adv.; bk.rev.; bibl.; charts; illus.; index.
  Description: Trade publication for the furniture industry, featuring new furniture designs, woodworking technology, surface technology, product development, and reports of events.

647 641 SP ISSN 0027-2930
EL MUEBLE ACTUAL; la gran revista del hogar. 1961. m. Editorial Quiris S.A., Rocafort 142, 8o, 08015 Barcelona, Spain. TEL 93-2246503. Ed. Isabel Castellet. adv.; charts; illus.; circ. 38,823. (tabloid format)

N Y HABITAT; for co-op, condominium and loft living. see *REAL ESTATE*

747 UK
NATIONAL FEDERATION OF PAINTING AND DECORATING CONTRACTORS YEAR BOOK. 1982. a. Comprint Ltd., 177 Hagden Lane, Watford WD1 8LW, England. adv.

747 IT
NEGOZIO MODERNO.* 1981. bi-m. L.20000. EDIBA Editrice Varese, Via Ponte Rotto, 21056 Induno Olona, Italy. Ed. Bagnasco Antonio. adv.; circ. 40,000.

747 640 GW ISSN 0863-4076
NEUES WOHNEN. 1956. m. DM.38.40. Verlagsgesellschaft Neues Wohnen mbH, Karl-Liebknecht-Str. 29, 1026 Berlin, Germany. TEL 030-23275270. FAX 030-23276325. (Subscr. to: Postfach 102525, 2000 Hamburg 1, Germany) Ed. Monika Grams. adv. contact: Bernd-Rainer Buettner. bk.rev.
  —BLDSC shelfmark: 6080.619200.
  Formerly (until 1990): Kultur im Heim (ISSN 0323-4967)
  Description: Devoted to new design in interior furnishings, interior decorating, architecture and interior architecture, renovations, and artwork; includes tips.

NEW ZEALAND HOME AND BUILDING. see *BUILDING AND CONSTRUCTION*

747 DK
NORDIC CONTRACT; commercial furnishings and interior design. (Text in English, French and German) 1983. a. DKK 75. N O V A Kommunikation A-S, Solvang 23, P.O. Box 146, DK-3450 Alleroed, Denmark. TEL 42-27-00-78. FAX 42-27-13-05. Ed. Poul Jacobson. adv.; illus.; circ. 22,000 (controlled).
  Formerly: Danish Contract (ISSN 0108-982X)

747 635 US ISSN 0898-1191
NORTHERN CALIFORNIA HOME & GARDEN. 1987. m. $16. Westar Media, Inc., 656 Bair Island Rd., 2nd Fl., Redwood City, CA 94063. TEL 415-368-8800. FAX 415-368-6251. Ed. Ann Bertelsen. adv.; circ. 40,000.
  Description: Covers the architecture, interior design, cooking, gardening, antiques, collectibles, home furnishings and art of this region.

NUESTRA ARQUITECTURA. see *ARCHITECTURE*

747 IT ISSN 1120-2386
OFFICE FURNITURE; annual of Italian design for the office. (Supplement to: Habitat Ufficio) 1986. a. $30. Alberto Greco Editore, Via del Fusaro 8, 20146 Milan, Italy. TEL 02-4819086. FAX 02-4819091. Ed. Paola Pianzola. adv.; circ. 21,500.

747 IT ISSN 0391-7487
OTTAGONO; design, art, architecture. 1966. q. L.50000 (foreign L.70000). CO.P.IN.A, Via Melzi d'Eril 26, 20154 Milan, Italy. Ed. Marco De Michelis. adv.; bk.rev.; circ. 24,000. (back issues avail.) **Indexed**: Artbibl.Mod., Avery Ind.Archit.Per., Br.Tech.Ind.

PAINTER & ALLIED TRADES JOURNAL. see *LABOR UNIONS*

747 UK
PAINTING & DECORATING. 1880. 6/yr. £12.30. (National Federation of Painting & Decorating Contractors) Turret-Wheatland Ltd., 12 Greycaine Rd., Watford, Herts. WD2 4JP, England. Ed. Alison Davis. adv.; bk.rev.; circ. 3,850. **Indexed**: World Surf.Coat.

PAINTING AND WALLCOVERING CONTRACTOR. see *PAINTS AND PROTECTIVE COATINGS*

747 330 US
PATHWAYS TO PROFITABILITY; a financial analysis of the decorating products centers in the U.S. a. $695. National Decorating Products Association, 1050 N. Lindbergh Blvd., St. Louis, MO 63132. TEL 314-991-3470. FAX 314-991-5039. circ. 400.
  Former titles: Sales and Operations Comparison; Pathways to Retail Profits; Cost of Doing Business Study.

747 635 US ISSN 0270-9341
TX311
PHOENIX HOME & GARDEN. 1980. m. $18. P H G, Inc., Box 34308, Phoenix, AZ 85067. TEL 602-234-0840. Ed. Manya Winsted. adv.; bk.rev.; circ. 37,362.

747 720 UK ISSN 0263-7553
PICTURE HOUSE. 1982. s-a. £7.50($12) Cinema Theatre Association, 44 Warlingham Rd., Thorton Heath, Surrey CR4 7DE, England. (Subscr. addr.: 53 Wenham Dr., Westcliff-on-Sea, Essex SS0 9BJ, England) Ed. Allen Eyles. illus.; circ. 1,350. (back issues avail.) **Indexed**: Film Lit.Ind. (1989-).
  —BLDSC shelfmark: 6498.627000.

747 CN
PISCINES, TERRASSES ET PATIOS. a. Publicor Inc., 7 Chemin Bates, Outremont, Que. H2V 1A6, Canada. TEL 514-270-1100. FAX 514-270-6900.
  Description: Focuses on exterior design, landscaping and outdoor furniture.

PLANAHOME HOME IMPROVEMENT GUIDE. see *BUILDING AND CONSTRUCTION*

747 333.33 CN ISSN 0826-4392
PLANS DE MAISONS DU QUEBEC. 4/yr. Can.$2 per no. Quebecor Inc., 7 Chemin Bates, Outremont, Que. H2V 1A6, Canada. TEL 514-270-1100. adv.; illus. **Indexed**: Pt.de Rep. (1981-).
  Formerly (until 1983): Maisons du Quebec.

PRACTICAL HOUSEHOLDER. see *BUILDING AND CONSTRUCTION*

PROFESSIONAL BUILDER & REMODELER CUSTOM - LUXURY TRENDS. see *BUILDING AND CONSTRUCTION*

747 UK
PROFESSIONAL HOTEL AND RESTAURANT INTERIORS. 1988. bi-m. £24. Scroll Communications Ltd., P.O. Box 45, Dorking, Surrey RH5 5YZ, England. Ed. Tony Ellis. adv.; circ. 5,500. (back issues avail.)
  Formerly: Professional Interiors.

QUEST: MANHATTAN PROPERTIES & COUNTRY ESTATES. see *REAL ESTATE*

747 721 UK
R I B A INTERIOR DESIGN SELECTOR. 1985. a. £35. (Royal Institute of British Architects) R I B A Services Ltd., Finsbury Mission, 39 Moreland St., London EC1V 8BB, England. TEL 071-251-5885. FAX 071-253-1085. Ed. Sue Quirk. adv.; circ. 10,000.
  Formerly: R I B A Interior Design Product Selector (ISSN 0267-0801)
  Description: Contains directory of products and suppliers within the UK interiors market.

RAKAM; mensile di moda e lavori femminili. see *WOMEN'S INTERESTS*

747 IT
RASSEGNA BAGNO CUCINA. 1979. 4/yr. $55. Alberto Greco Editore, Via del Fusaro 8, 20146 Milan, Italy. TEL 02-4819086. FAX 02-4819091. Ed. Ezio Corti. adv.; circ. 45,000.
  Formerly: Rassegna del Bagno.
  Description: Discusses furniture and accessories for bath and kitchen.

747 US
REMODELED HOMES. 2/yr. Cahners Publishing Company (Des Plaines) (Subsidiary of: Reed International PLC), Division of Reed Publishing (USA) Inc., 1350 E. Touhy Ave., P.O. Box 5080, Des Plaines, IL 60017-5080. TEL 708-635-8800. Ed. Roy L. Diez. circ. 120,000.
  Description: Offers residential remodeling ideas for the consumer.

747 694 US
RENOVATOR'S SUPPLY. 1978. 6/yr. $3 per no. Renovator's Supply, Inc., Renovator's Old Mill, Millers Falls, MA 01349. TEL 413-659-2241. FAX 413-659-3796. adv.
  Description: Concentrates on products for decorating, remodeling, restoring and building.

547 720 CN
▼**RESIDENCES**. (Text in English, French) 1990. 5/yr. Can.$3.50 per no. Marketing R.N.H. Inc., 223 rue du Limousin, Saint-Lambert, Que. J4S 1X5, Canada. TEL 514-393-7285. FAX 514-672-9962. Ed. Regine Thomasset. adv.; circ. 82,738.

747 US ISSN 0745-4929
NA7800
RESTAURANT - HOTEL DESIGN INTERNATIONAL. 1979. 12/yr. $40 (foreign $90). Bill Communications, Inc., 633 Third Ave., New York, NY 10017. TEL 212-986-4800. Ed. M.J. Madigan. adv.; charts; illus.; circ. 36,000. (also avail. in microform from UMI; reprint service avail. from UMI) **Indexed**: Bus.Ind., Tr.& Indus.Ind.
  Former titles (until 1987): Restaurant and Hotel Design; (until 1982): Restaurant Design (ISSN 0191-345X)
  Description: Edited for interior designers and architects of hotels, restaurants, clubs, and senior living facilities and for the developers, owners, and operators of such projects.

747 US ISSN 1047-8841
▼**RETAIL STORE IMAGE**. 1990. bi-m. $32 (foreign $102). Communication Channels, Inc., 6255 Barfield Rd., Atlanta, GA 30328-4369. TEL 404-256-9800. FAX 404-256-3116. TELEX 4611074 COMCHANI. Ed. Katherine Field. adv.; circ. 25,000.
  Description: For store planners, visual merchandisers, interior designers, architects, retail headquarter executives, and store owners who create and implement an image for national and local retail stores. Focuses on the in-line and freestanding store.

INTERIOR DESIGN AND DECORATION

747 BE
REVUE DES PEINTURES BELGES. (Editions in Flemish and French) bi-m. (Federation Nationale Belge des Entrepeneurs de Peinture, de Decoration et de Recouvrement des Murs et du Sol.) Editions Coppieters, S.P.R.L., Bd. de Smet de Nayer 393, Boite 5, B-1090 Brussels, Belgium. TEL 02-478-40-98. FAX 02-478-35-02. adv.; circ. 2,000.

747 CN
RICKY MCMOUNTAIN BUYER'S GUIDE. 1988. 5/yr. free. Ricky McMountain Enterprises, Ltd., 2256A Sheppard Ave. W., Toronto, Ont. M9M 1L7, Canada. TEL 416-740-0731. FAX 416-740-0980. Ed. Ylva Van Buuren. adv.; circ. 700,000.

747 FR
RUSTICA. 1928. w. 330 F. Dargaud Editeur, 12 rue Blaise-Pascal, 92200 Neuilly-sur-Seine, France. adv.; circ. 174,862.

SADELMAGER-OG TAPETSERER TIDENDE. see *INTERIOR DESIGN AND DECORATION — Furniture And House Furnishings*

747 635 US
SAN DIEGO HOME-GARDEN. 1979. m. $16. San Diego Home-Garden Ltd., 655 Fourth Ave., San Diego, CA 92101. TEL 619-233-4567. Ed. Peter Jensen. adv.; circ. 36,000. (also avail. in microfiche)

640 747 GW
SCHOENER WOHNEN. 1960. m. DM.54. Gruner und Jahr AG und Co., Am Baumwall 11, 2000 Hamburg 11, Germany. TEL 040-3703-0. FAX 040-37035631. Ed. Angelika Jahr. adv.; illus.; circ. 488,000. (also avail. in microfilm from UMI; reprint service avail. from UMI)

747 CN
SELECT HOMES & FOOD. 8/yr. Telemedia Publishing Inc., 50 Holly St., Toronto, Ont. M4S 3B3, Canada. TEL 416-482-8260. FAX 416-482-1239. Ed. David Titcombe. adv.; circ. 138,000.

747 CC
SHINEI SHEJI/INTERIOR DESIGN. (Text in Chinese) q. (Chongqing Jianzhu Gongcheng Xueyuan - Chongqing Architectural and Civil Engineering Institute) Zhongguo Jianzhu Gongye Chubanshe - China Architectural Industry Press, Shapingba, Chongqing, Sichuan 630045, People's Republic of China. TEL 661989. (Co-sponsor: Chongqing Jianzhu Kance Sheji Yanjiuyuan)

747 US
SINGLE FAMILY HOME PLANS. s-a. $2 per no. Archway Press, Inc., 19 W. 44th St., New York, NY 10036. TEL 212-757-5580.

747 700 SW
SKOENA HEM. (Text in Swedish; summaries in English) 1979. q. SEK 175($30) Bonniers Maanadstidningar, Sveavaagen 53, S-105 44 Stockholm, Sweden. TEL 08-7365300. FAX 08-346908. TELEX 10043-BONMAG-S. Ed. Boerge Bengtsson. adv.; circ. 73,000.

SLOVENIJALES; glasilo mednarodnega podjetja za trgovino, inzeniring, proizvodnjo, zastopanje in konsignacijo. see *BUSINESS AND ECONOMICS*

SOL ET MURS MAGAZINE. see *TECHNOLOGY: COMPREHENSIVE WORKS*

SOUNDINGS (DEERFIELD); briefings on timely topics. see *BUILDING AND CONSTRUCTION*

SOUTH AFRICAN GARDEN & HOME. see *GARDENING AND HORTICULTURE*

747 635 US ISSN 0149-516X
NK2002
SOUTHERN ACCENTS. 1977. bi-m. $24.95 (foreign $30)(effective Jan. 1992). Southern Progress Corp. (Subsidiary of: Time, Inc. Magazine Co.), c/o H. Jahnson, V.P. Circulation, 2100 Lakeshore Dr., Birmingham, AL 35209. TEL 205-877-6263. (Subscr. to: Box 10411, Birmingham, AL 35202) Ed. Karen Phillips Irons. adv.; bk.rev.; illus.; tr.lit.; circ. 265,000. **Indexed:** Avery Ind.Archit.Per., Gard.Lit., Search (until 1989).

SPACIOLOGY. see *ARCHITECTURE*

747 US ISSN 0039-1859
STORE PLANNING SERVICE. 1941. m. $34.50 per no. Retail Reporting Bureau, 101 Fifth Ave., New York, NY 10003. TEL 212-255-9595. Ed.Bd. illus.

747.85 US ISSN 0192-8732
NK2195.S89
STORES OF THE YEAR; a pictorial report on store interiors. biennial. Retail Reporting Bureau, 101 Fifth Ave., New York, NY 10003. TEL 212-255-9595. illus.

747 US
SWEET'S CONTRACT INTERIORS FILE. a. $39.80 to qualified personnel. Sweet's Catalog Files (Subsidiary of: McGraw-Hill, Inc.), 1221 Ave. of the Americas, New York, NY 10020. TEL 212-512-4750. FAX 212-512-2348. circ. 10,000.

SYNTHESIS/COMPOSITION. see *CLOTHING TRADE*

747 IT
TEX HOME; mensile della biancheria per la casa. (Text in English and Italian) 1971. m. (10/yr.) L.60000 (foreign L.90000). Editoriale Galfa s.r.l., Viale Monza 57, 20125 Milan, Italy. TEL 02-2840574. FAX 2610923. TELEX 315614 SISTAR I. Ed. Franco Battaglini. adv.
Former titles: Tessilcasa Tex Home; Tex Home.
Description: Trade magazine covering the household linen industry.

TILE NEWS. see *CERAMICS, GLASS AND POTTERY*

720 651 747 US
TODAY'S FACILITY MANAGER; the magazine of facilities - interior planning team. 1982. bi-m. $35. BusFac Publishing Co., Inc., 121 Monmouth St., Box 2060, Red Bank, NJ 07701. TEL 908-842-7433. Ed. Heidi Schwartz. adv.; bk.rev.; illus.; circ. 31,000. (tabloid format; back issues avail.)
Formerly (until Sep. 1991): Business Interiors (ISSN 1044-3584); Incorporates (1987-1987): Corporate Design (ISSN 0894-3575); Which was formerly (until 1987): Corporate Design and Realty (ISSN 8750-8206); (until 1984): Corporate Design (ISSN 0744-2750)

TODAY'S FAMILY HOME PLANS. see *ARCHITECTURE*

747 HK
TODAY'S LIVING. (Text in Chinese, English) 1987. m. HK.$306 (foreign $534)(effective 1992). Kenneth Li, Ed. & Pub., 1905 Westlands Centre, 20 Westlands Rd., Quarry Bay, Hong Kong. TEL 5659900. FAX 5658846. TELEX 49505. circ. 30,000.

TOKYO NO IKEBANA. see *ARTS AND HANDICRAFTS*

747 CN
TORONTO LIFE HOMES. 1978. 4/yr. Toronto Life Publishing Co. Ltd., 59 Front St. E., Toronto, Ont. M5E 1B3, Canada. TEL 416-364-3333. Ed. Marq de Villiers. adv.; illus.; circ. 103,000.
Formerly: Toronto Life Design and Decor Guide.

TOY AND DECORATION FAIR DIRECTORY. see *BUSINESS AND ECONOMICS — Trade And Industrial Directories*

747 US
TRADITIONAL HOME. 1978. 6/yr. $14.97. Meredith Corporation, Special Interest Publications, 1716 Locust St., Des Moines, IA 50336. TEL 515-284-3000. Ed. Karol DeWulf Nickell. adv.; circ. 600,000.
Former titles: Better Homes and Gardens Traditional Home; Traditional Home Ideas (ISSN 0162-1386).

TRE OG MOEBLER. see *INTERIOR DESIGN AND DECORATION — Furniture And House Furnishings*

TUTTOVILLE. see *INTERIOR DESIGN AND DECORATION — Furniture And House Furnishings*

UNIVERSITA DEGLI STUDI DI PARMA. ISTITUTO DI STORIA DELL'ARTE. CATALOGHI. see *ART*

747 US ISSN 1040-8150
VERANDA; a gallery of Southern style. 1987. q. $12. 3116 Maple Dr., N.E., Atlanta, GA 30305. Ed. Lisa Newsom. adv.; bk.rev.
Description: Covers Southern interior decorating, antiques and gracious living.

747 US ISSN 0744-415X
NK2115.5.V53
VICTORIAN HOMES. 1982. 6/yr. $18. Vintage Publications, Inc., Box 61, Millers Falls, MA 01349. TEL 413-659-3785. FAX 413-659-3113. Ed. Carolyn Flaherty. adv.; bk.rev.; illus.; circ. 120,000. (back issues avail.) **Indexed:** Avery Ind.Archit.Per., Gard.Lit. (1992-).
Description: For owners and lovers of homes built in the late 19th and early 20th centuries. Provides how-to information on decorating.

747 BL
VIDA DOMESTICA. m. Carlos Goncalves Fidalgo, Ed. & Pub., Rua Riachuelo 414, Rio de Janeiro GB, Brazil.

747 FR
VOGUE DECORATION. 6/yr. 180 F. (foreign 270 F.) (effective 1991). Publications Conde Nast S.A., 4 place du Palais Bourbon, 75341 Paris Cedex 07, France. (Subscr. to: 60732 Sainte-Genevieve Cedex, France. TEL 16-44-03-44-00; In U.S. subscr. to: International Subscriptions Inc., 1305 Paterson Plank Rd., North Bergen, NJ 07470-1890. TEL 201-867-9381)

747 FR ISSN 0042-8973
VOTRE MAISON; l'officiel de la maison individuelle et de la decoration. (Text in French, German, Italian, Japanese, Portuguese and Spanish) 1947. bi-m. $20. Editions du Croissant, 6 av. Delcasse, 75008 Paris, France. (Dist. by: European Publishers, 11-03 46th Avenue, Long Island City, N.Y. 11101) Dir. Felix M. Portal. adv.; bk.rev.; charts; illus.; circ. 315,000.

747 US ISSN 0273-6837
THE WALL PAPER; the only monthly journal serving the wallcovering trade exclusively. 1980. m. $21 (Canada $35; elsewhere $65). Tapis Publishing Co., Inc., 570 7th Ave., Ste. 500, New York, NY 10018. TEL 212-869-4960. FAX 212-869-1141. Ed. Marita Thomas. adv.; bk.rev.; illus.; circ. 17,500. (tabloid format; back issues avail.)
Description: Edited for wallcovering dealers and others in the industry. Reports on product selling, merchandising, sales training, advertising, promotions, new products and procedures.

747 US
WALLCOVERINGS LETTER. m. Publishing Dynamics, Inc., 15 Bank St., Ste.101, Stamford, CT 06901-3017. TEL 203-357-0028. FAX 203-357-0075. Ed. Martin Johnson. circ. 500.

WALLCOVERINGS, WINDOWS & INTERIOR FASHION. see *PAPER AND PULP*

747 US
WALLPAPER REPRODUCTION NEWS. 4/yr. Box 187, Lee, MA 01238-0187. TEL 413-243-3489. Ed. Robert Kelly.

747 635 US
▼**WASHINGTON HOME & GARDEN.** 1990. q. $12. Regardie's, Inc., 1010 Wisconsin Ave. N.W., Ste. 600, Washington, DC 20007. TEL 202-342-0410. FAX 202-342-0515. Ed. William A. Regardie. adv.; circ. 105,000.
Description: For affluent Washington area homeowners and luxury home buyers with coverage of available upper-bracket homes, as well as trends in architecture, interior design, landscape design and home furnishings. Includes profiles of prominent area residents.

747 JA
WATASHI NO HEYA/MY ROOM. (Text in Japanese) 1972. bi-m. 5460 Yen. Fujin Seikatsu Sha, 19-5, 2-chome, Yushima, Bunkyo-ku, Tokyo, Japan. Ed. Hanaho Yagi.

WEST COAST PEDDLER; oldest journal of antiques, art & collectibles in the Pacific states. see *ANTIQUES*

747 380.1 UK ISSN 0262-2742
WHAT'S NEW IN INTERIORS. m. £25($50) Morgan-Grampian (Construction Press) Ltd., 30 Calderwood St., Woolwich, London SE18 6QH, England. TEL 01-855-7777. FAX 01-854-7476. Ed. Anthea Bain. circ. 10,685.

747 US
WINDOW & WALL IDEAS. q. Harris Publications, Inc., 1115 Broadway, New York, NY 10010-2803. TEL 212-807-7100. FAX 212-627-4678. Ed. Kathleen Fredrick.

INTERIOR DESIGN AND DECORATION — Abstracting, Bibliographies, Statistics

747 GW
WOHNIDEE; wohnen und leben. 1984. m. DM.54. Heinrich Bauer Verlag, Burchardstr. 11, 2000 Hamburg 1, Germany. TEL 040-30195273. FAX 040-326589. Ed. Ute Stahmann. adv.; circ. 261,196.

747.05 US ISSN 0361-638X
TX311
WOMAN'S DAY HOME DECORATING IDEAS. Short title: Home Decorating Ideas. 3/yr. $2.25. Hachette Magazines, Inc., Woman's Day Special Publications, 1633 Broadway, 45th Fl., New York, NY 10019. TEL 212-767-6000. adv.; illus.

747
WOMAN'S DAY HOME IMPROVEMENTS. 1984. 3/yr. $2.75 per no. Hachette Magazines, Inc., Woman's Day Special Publications, 1633 Broadway, 45th Fl., New York, NY 10019. TEL 212-767-6000. adv.; circ. 450,000.
Description: Covers various aspects of maintaining and upgrading the home.

WOMAN'S DAY KITCHEN & BATH NEW PRODUCT IDEAS. see *INTERIOR DESIGN AND DECORATION — Furniture And House Furnishings*

747 US
WOMAN'S DAY KITCHENS AND BATHS. 1971. q. $2.75 per no. Hachette Magazines, Inc., Woman's Day Special Publications, 1633 Broadway, 45th Fl., New York, NY 10019. TEL 212-719-6000. adv.
Description: Concentrates on the remodeling and decorating of the kitchen and bath.

747 UK ISSN 0264-083X
NK1700
THE WORLD OF INTERIORS. 1981. 11/yr. £33 (foreign £40). Conde Nast Publications Ltd., 234 King's Rd., London SW3 5UA, England. FAX 351-3709. TELEX 914549-INTMAG-G. (Subsr. to: Quadrant Subscriptions Services, Oakfield House, Perrymount Rd., Haywards Heath, W. Sussex RH16 3DH, England) Ed. Min Hogg. adv.; bk.rev.; circ. 73,210. (back issues avail.) Indexed: Artbibl.Mod., Avery Ind.Archit.Per.
—BLDSC shelfmark: 9356.071480.

747 CC
XIANDAI ZHUANGSHI/MODERN DECORATION. (Text in Chinese) 1985. q. Y9.60 (HK$20) per no. Shenzhen Zhuangshi Gongcheng Gongye Zonggongsi - Shenzhen Corporation of Interior Design Engineering Industy, Zhuangshi Gongye Dasha, 2nd Floor, Baguailing 10 Dong, Shenzhen, Guangdong 518029, People's Republic of China. TEL 0755-263855. Ed. Gao Shouquan.

YISHU - SHENGHUO/ART - LIFE. see *ARTS AND HANDICRAFTS*

747 NZ ISSN 1170-3229
▼**YOUR HOME.** 1990. 6/yr. NZ.$19.70. Associated Group Media Ltd., Private Bag 99-915, Newmarket, Auckland, New Zealand. TEL 09-795-393. Ed. Sharon Newey. adv.; charts; illus.; tr.lit.; circ. 20,000.
Description: Seasonal coverage of topics pertinent to people in their first year living in a different home, including redecorating, finances, new products, home improvements, working with contractors and professionals.

747 GW
ZUHAUSE; Wohnung, Haus und Garten. 1967. m. DM.76. Jahreszeiten Verlag GmbH, Possmoorweg 5, 2000 Hamburg 60, Germany. TEL 040-27170. FAX 040-27172056. TELEX 213214. Ed. E.-H. Schlichting. circ. 346,000.

INTERIOR DESIGN AND DECORATION — Abstracting, Bibliographies, Statistics

643.3 US
ASSOCIATION OF HOME APPLIANCE MANUFACTURERS. M A C A P STATISTICAL REPORT. a. free. Association of Home Appliance Manufacturers, Major Appliance Consumer Action Panel, 20 N. Wacker Dr., Chicago, IL 60606. TEL 312-984-5800. FAX 312-984-5823. circ. 700.

338.4 US
CARPET AND RUG INDUSTRY REVIEW. a. $15. Carpet and Rug Institute, 310 Holiday Ave., S., Box 2048, Dalton, GA 30720-2048. TEL 404-278-3176. FAX 404-278-8835. **Indexed:** SRI.
Formerly: Carpet and Rug Institute. Review-State of the Industry (ISSN 0092-0495)

680 FR
FRANCE. SERVICE D'ETUDE DES STRATEGIES ET DES STATISTIQUES INDUSTRIELLES. RESULTATS MENSUELS DES ENQUETES DE BRANCHE. AMEUBLEMENT. m. 260 F. (foreign 310 F.)(effective 1991). Service d'Etude des Strategies et des Statistiques Industrielles (SESSI), 85 Bd. du Montparnasse, 75270 Paris Cedex 06, France. TEL 45-56-42-34. FAX 45-56-40-71. stat.
Description: Follows developments in the furnishings industry through the performance of selected indicators.

680 FR
FRANCE. SERVICE D'ETUDE DES STRATEGIES ET DES STATISTIQUES INDUSTRIELLES. RESULTATS TRIMESTRIELS DES ENQUETES DE BRANCHE. INDUSTRIE DE L'AMEUBLEMENT. q. 180 F. (foreign 210 F.)(effective 1991). Service d'Etude des Strategies et des Statistiques Industrielles (SESSI), 85 Bd. du Montparnasse, 75270 Paris Cedex 06, France. TEL 45-56-42-34. FAX 45-56-40-71. stat.
Description: Provides detailed industry-wide performance statistics for comparative evaluations.

684 016 RU ISSN 0484-2286
REFERATIVNYI ZHURNAL. KOMMUNAL'NOE, BYTOVOE I TORGOVOE OBORUDOVANIE. 1959. m. 50.40 Rub. (52.50 Rub. including index). Vsesoyuznyi Institut Nauchno-Tekhnicheskoi Informatsii (VINITI), Baltiiskaya ul., 14, Moscow A-219, Russia. (Subscr. to: Mezhdunarodnaya Kniga, Dimitrova ul. 39, 113095 Moscow, Russia)

INTERIOR DESIGN AND DECORATION — Furniture And House Furnishings

749 US
A & D BUSINESS.* (Architects & Designers) bi-m. Aztex Inc., Box 5059, Hoboken, NJ 07030-1501. TEL 212-545-0055. FAX 212-545-0119. Ed. Laura A. Fentress.

690 664 US
A H A M MAJOR APPLIANCE FACTORY SHIPMENT REPORT. m. $35 to non-members by mail; by fax $70. Association of Home Appliance Manufacturers, 20 N. Wacker Dr., Chicago, IL 60606. TEL 312-984-5800. FAX 312-984-5823. Eds. Mary Gillespie, Craig Schulz. circ. 1,000. (looseleaf format)
Description: Factory unit shipments on major appliances, by month, year-to-date, and quarterly (in "units" for current periods and "percent change" from year-ago periods) for 12 product categories.

690 664 US
A H A M MAJOR APPLIANCE INDUSTRY FACTS BOOK (YEAR). a. $20 to members. Association of Home Appliance Manufacturers, 20 N. Wacker Dr., Chicago, IL 60606. TEL 312-984-5800. FAX 312-984-5823. charts; illus.
Description: Comprehensive reference book on the United States' major home appliance industry. Discusses industry market and products.

645 635 FR
L'ACTUALITE; de l'amenagement et decoration de l'habitat. 1986. 10/yr. 300 F. (foreign 410 F.). Editions G. M. Perrin, 88, Blvd. de Charonne, 75020 Paris, France. TEL 43-48-99-51. FAX 43-48-56-60. TELEX GMPPAR 216219F. adv.; circ. 7,000.

645 IT
AD. 1981. 12/yr. L.53000. Giorgio Mondadori e Associati S.p.A., Centro Direzionale, Palazzo Canova, 20090 Milan 2 - Segrate, Italy. Ed. Ettore Mocchetti. adv.; bk.rev.; charts; illus.; circ. 75,000. **Indexed:** CERDIC.

749 SW ISSN 0002-6182
ALLT I HEMMET. 1956. m. SEK 85. Specialtidningsforelaget AB, Sveavaegen 53, S-105 44 Stockholm, Sweden. Ed. Signe Rolf. adv.; charts; illus.; mkt.; circ. 126,800.

747 US
THE AMERICAN DREAM. 1984. a. $3.95 free. Yorktown Publishing, 2454 Ridge St., Yorktown Heights, NY 10598. TEL 914-962-2565. adv.: B&W page $2150 (Fairfield Ed.), $2480 (Westchester Ed.), $1890 (Rockland Ed., Dutchess & Putnam Ed.); trim 8 x 10 3/4. circ. 11,350 (controlled).
Description: For new homeowners in Westchester, Fairfield, Rockland, Dutches and Putnam counties.

AMI DES JARDINS ET DE LA MAISON. see *GARDENING AND HORTICULTURE*

684 FR
ANNUAIRE DE L'AMEUBLEMENT. 1908. a. 545 F. Editions Louis Johanet, 68 rue Boursault, 75017 Paris, France.
Former titles: Annuaire de l'Ameublement et des Industries s'y Rattachant (ISSN 0066-2615); Annuaire de l'Ameublement.

645 666 IT
ANNUARIO ARTICOLI CASALINGHI E ARTICOLI REGALO. (Editions in English, French and Italian) 1980. a. L.16000($30) Edispe s.n.c., Via Melchiorre Gioia 71, 20144 Milan, Italy. Ed. Vincenzo Vaccaro. adv.; circ. 9,500.

684.1 GW
ANZEIGEN BEOBACHTER MOEBEL. 1978. m. DM.1176. Team Work Werbung & Verlag GmbH, Heinrich-Heine-Str. 1, Postfach 1411, 6368 Bad Vilbel, Germany. TEL 06101-64007. FAX 06101-7918. stat.; circ. 190. (back issues avail.)

645.1 US ISSN 0044-8974
ARMSTRONG LOGIC. 1915. 4/yr. free to qualified personnel. Armstrong World Industries, Inc., Floor Division, Box 3001, Lancaster, PA 17604. TEL 717-397-0611. Ed. Shannon M. Oates. charts; illus.; circ. 80,000 (controlled). (tabloid format)
Description: Provides selling tips and installation information to flooring retailers, contractors and installers.

749 IT ISSN 0004-2854
ARREDORAMA. 1969. m. L.140000. Industria del Mobile s.r.l., Via Giambologna 21, Milan, Italy. TEL 02 8394780. FAX 02-8372547. adv.; illus.; circ. 18,000.

684.1 740 FR
ART ET VALEURS. 11/yr. 300 F. (foreign 420 F.). Editions G.M. Perrin, 88 Blvd. de Charonne, 75980 Paris Cedex 20, France. TEL 43-48-99-51. FAX 43-48-56-60. TELEX GMPPAR 216219F.

749 IT
ARTICOLI CASALINGHI ED ELETTROCASALINGHI. 1958. m. L.140000. Pubbliemme s.r.l., Via Caracciolo 77, 20155 Milan, Italy. TEL 02-33100954. FAX 02-313864. Ed. Massimo Martini. adv.; bk.rev.; illus.; index; circ. 17,600.
Formerly: Articoli Casalinghi (ISSN 0004-3672)

ASIAN SOURCES GIFTS & HOME PRODUCTS. see *GIFTWARE AND TOYS*

ASSOCIATION OF HOME APPLIANCE MANUFACTURERS. GREEN REPORT. see *ENVIRONMENTAL STUDIES*

AUDIO - VIDEO INTERIORS. see *ELECTRONICS*

645 AT
AUSTRALIAN CONTRACT FURNISHING CYCLOPAEDIA. 1972. a. Aus.$50. Furnishing Publications Pty. Ltd., 251 Hawthorn Rd., Caulfield, Vic. 3162, Australia. TEL 03-523-8444. FAX 03-523-0291. Ed. Keith Dunn. adv.; illus.; pat.; tr.lit.; circ. 5,951.
Formerly: Australian Contract Yearbook.
Description: For manufacturers, suppliers and retailers of commercial furniture, flooring and furnishings as well as architects, specifiers and government departments federal, state and local.

645 AT ISSN 0045-0456
AUSTRALIAN FURNISHING TRADE JOURNAL. 1949. bi-m. Aus.$46. Furnishing Publications Pty. Ltd., 251 Hawthorn Rd., Caulfield, Vic. 3162, Australia. TEL 03-523-8444. FAX 03-523-0291. Ed. Keith Dunn. adv.; illus.; circ. 4,125.
Description: For retailers, manufacturers, distributors, suppliers and affiliated industres.

AVOTAKKA. see *INTERIOR DESIGN AND DECORATION*

INTERIOR DESIGN AND DECORATION — FURNITURE AND HOUSE FURNISHINGS

670 676 GW
B T H - TAPETENZEITUNG. (Boden - Tapeten - Heimtextilien) 1888. 11/yr. DM.120. S N Verlag Michael Steinert, An der Alster 21, 2000 Hamburg 1, Germany. TEL 040-240852. TELEX 2165704-AGZG-D. adv.; bk.rev.; charts; illus.; mkt.; pat.; stat.; tr.lit.; circ. 6,000.
  Formerly: B T H Fussboden-Forum - Tapetenzeitung; Incorporates: Tapetenzeitung (ISSN 0720-6593); Fussboden-Zeitung; Tapetenzeitung Tapete und Bodenbelag (ISSN 0039-9566)

747 TS
BAIT AL-IMARAT/EMIRATES HOME. (Text in Arabic) 1987. q. International Publications, P.O. Box 6872, Sharjah, United Arab Emirates. TEL 595777. TELEX 68715. Ed. Abdullah Ahmed Ibrahim. circ. 1,000.

684.16 GW ISSN 0341-3659
BAU- UND MOEBELSCHREINER. (Abbreviated Title: B M) 1946. m. DM.176.40. (Verband des holz- und kunststoffverarbeitenden Handwerks) Konradin Verlag Robert Kohlhammer GmbH, Ernst-Mey-Str. 8, 7022 Leinfelden-Echterdingen, Germany. TEL 0711-7594-0. FAX 0711-7594-390. Eds. Peter Nagel, Manfred Maier. adv.; bk.rev.; charts; illus.; circ. 30,196. (back issues avail.) **Indexed:** Excerp.Med.
  Description: Trade publication for the furniture and building industry. Covers building materials, construction, manufacturing, interior design, architecture, and marketing. Includes events and exhibitions, and positions available.

BAUSPAR-JOURNAL. see *BUILDING AND CONSTRUCTION*

747.77 US ISSN 0273-7469
BEDROOM. 1976. m. $32 (Canada $38; elsewhere $48). Bobit Publishing Company, 2512 Artesia Blvd., Redondo Beach, CA 90278. TEL 310-376-8788. FAX 310-376-9043. Ed. Kathy Knoles. bk.rev.; circ. 21,000. (controlled).
  Formerly: Waterbed.
  Description: Retail focus on bedding, linens, furniture and accessories.

684.15 US ISSN 0893-5556
TX315 CODEN: BEDTEF
BEDTIMES. 1917. m. $30 (foreign $35). International Sleep Products Association, 333 Commerce St., Alexandria, VA 22314-2801. TEL 703-683-8371. FAX 703-683-4503. Ed. Tracy F. Savidge. adv.; bk.rev.; charts; illus.; mkt.; pat.; tr.lit.; tr.mk.; circ. 2,450. (back issues avail.) **Indexed:** Text.Tech.Dig.
  Formerly: Bedding (ISSN 0005-7568)
  Description: Geared towards mattress manufacturing industry and its suppliers, and other related sleep products trades.

645 US
▼**BETTER HOMES AND GARDENS HOME FURNISHINGS PRODUCTS GUIDE.** 1992. a. Meredith Corporation, 1716 Locust St., Des Moines, IA 50309. TEL 515-284-3000. FAX 515-284-2700. adv.: B&W page $19100, color page $27300; trim 8 x 10 1/2. circ. 450,000.
  Description: Surveys what is available in home furnishings for consumers and professionals.

645 US
▼**BETTER HOMES AND GARDENS KITCHEN AND BATH PRODUCTS GUIDE.** 1990. a. $3.50. Meredith Corporation, 1716 Locust St., Des Moines, IA 50309. TEL 515-284-3000. FAX 515-284-2700. adv.: B&W page $17200, color page $24725; trim 8 x 10 1/2. circ. 450,000.
  Description: Lists products in categories, including: cabinetry, appliances, sinks and faucets, bath fixtures, tile, flooring, lighting, laundry equipment and accessories.

747.3 UK ISSN 0305-733X
BLINDS AND SHUTTERS. 1952. q. $52. (British Blind & Shutter Association) Turret Group Plc., Turret House, 171 High St., Rickmasworth, Herts. WD3 1SN, England. TEL 0923-777000. FAX 0923-771297. TELEX 888095 DX. Ed. Colin Bryer. adv.; bk.rev.; circ. 3,200.
  Formerly: Blindmaker (ISSN 0006-4874)

679.6 US
BROOM, BRUSH & MOP. 1912. m. $20. 118 E. Main, Arcola, IL 61910. TEL 217-268-4950. FAX 217-268-4815. (Subscr. to: Box 130, Arcola, IL 61910) Ed. Don Rankin. adv.; tr.lit.; stat.; circ. 1,200. (tabloid format; also avail. in microfilm)
  Formerly: Broom and Broom Corn News (ISSN 0007-2400)
  Description: Covers industry news, sales analysis, market conditions, supplier's surveys, new product news and monthly import and export figures on both raw materials and finished products.

BRUSHWARE. see *BUILDING AND CONSTRUCTION — Hardware*

684.16 UK
CABINET MAKER. 1880. w. £73 (foreign £98). Benn Publications Ltd., Sovereign Way, Tonbridge, Kent TN9 1RW, England. TEL 0732-364422. Ed. Sandra Danby. adv.; bk.rev.; charts; illus.; mkt.; tr.lit.; circ. 8,289. **Indexed:** Key to Econ.Sci.
  Former titles: Cabinet Maker and Retail Furnisher (ISSN 0007-9278); Carpet World & Furniture Record; Incorporates: Furnishing World (ISSN 0016-3015)

684.1 US
CABINETMAKER. 1987. bi-m. $25 (free to qualified personnel). Delta Communications, Inc. (Chicago) (Subsidiary of: Elsevier Business Press, Inc. (New York)), 400 N. Michigan Ave., Ste. 1200, Chicago, IL 60611. TEL 312-222-2000. FAX 312-222-2026. Ed. Bruce Plantz. adv.; circ. 25,000.

381 AG
CAMARA DE COMERCIANTES EN ARTEFACTOS PARA EL HOGAR. REVISTA. irreg. Camara de Comerciantes en Artefactos para el Hogar, Bartolome Mitre 2162, Buenos Aires, Argentina. illus.

684.1 CN ISSN 0711-0030
CANADA'S FURNITURE MAGAZINE. (Text in English, French) 1981. 4/yr. Can.$16 for 2 yrs. Manor Publishing Co. Ltd., 312 Dolomite Dr., Ste. 217, Downsview, Ont. M3J 2N2, Canada. TEL 416-667-9609. FAX 416-667-9715. Ed. Don Douloff. adv.: B&W page Can.$2241, color page Can.$3213; trim 9 1/2 x 12 1/2; adv. contact: Victor Sibilia. circ. 11,000. (back issues avail.)

CANADIAN FURNITURE & FURNISHINGS DIRECTORY. see *BUSINESS AND ECONOMICS — Trade And Industrial Directories*

CANADIAN FURNITURE, CABINETRY & WOODWORKING SUPPLY DIRECTORY. see *BUSINESS AND ECONOMICS — Trade And Industrial Directories*

749 CN
CANADIAN WOOD PROCESSING. 1900. 6/yr. Can.$30. Sentinel Business Publications, P.O. Box 14, Lachine, Que. H8S 4A5, Canada. TEL 514-333-1116. FAX 514-631-8858. Ed. Keith Fredericks. adv.; illus.
  Former titles: Furniture Production and Design; Furniture Production and Design Meubles (ISSN 0703-9514); Canadian Wood Products.

CARE AND REPAIR. see *BUILDING AND CONSTRUCTION*

670 747.4 UK ISSN 0263-4236
CARPET & FLOORCOVERINGS REVIEW. 1946. 22/yr. £55 (foreign £73). Benn Publications Ltd., Sovereign Way, Tonbridge, Kent TN9 1RW, England. TEL 0732-364422. Ed. Mrs. Joy Lawrence. adv.; bk.rev.; illus.; stat.; tr.lit.; tr.mk.; index; circ. 5,720. **Indexed:** World Text.Abstr.
  Former titles: Carpet Review Weekly (ISSN 0308-4507); Carpet Review (ISSN 0008-6851)

CARPET & RUG INDUSTRY. see *TEXTILE INDUSTRIES AND FABRICS*

747 PO
CASA E DECORACAO. 1967. 10/yr. Esc.7800. Meriberica - Liber Editores, Lda., Rua D. Filipa de Vilhena, 8, 3o Dto., 1000 Lisbon, Portugal. TEL 01-3530485. FAX 01-576344. circ. 10,000.
  Description: Covers art, architecture, design, decoration, rebuilding and garden.

747 635 PO
CASA E JARDIM. 1978. m. Esc.8250 (in Europe Esc.14500; elsewhere Esc.16000). Rua da Misericordia 137, s-l esq., 1200 Lisbon, Portugal. TEL 01-347-21-27. FAX 01-342-14-90. Dir. Eduardo Fortunato de Almeida. circ. 20,000.

747 AG ISSN 0008-7203
CASAS Y JARDINES. 1932. 6/yr. $30. Editorial Contempora s.r.l., Sarmiento 643, Piso 5, 1382 Buenos Aires, Argentina. TEL 1-45-1793. Ed. Norberto M. Muzio. adv.; circ. 35,000.

645 IT
CASAVIVA. 1973. m. L.60000 (foreign L.84600). Arnoldo Mondadori Editore S.p.A., Casella Postale 1833, 20101 Milan, Italy. TEL 3199345. Ed. Maria Pia Rosignoli. circ. 190,135.

749 US
CASUAL LIVING. 1960. m. $15. Columbia Communications, Inc., 370 Lexington Ave., New York, NY 10017. TEL 212-532-9290. FAX 212-779-8345. Ed. Eileen Smith. adv.; charts; illus.; stat.; tr.lit.; circ. 11,500.
  Formerly: Casual Living and Summer and Casual Furniture (ISSN 0008-7564)

CATALOG CONNECTION. see *GIFTWARE AND TOYS*

645 CN
CHAMBRES A COUCHER. a. Publicor Inc., 7 Chemin Bates, Outremont, Que. H2V 1A6, Canada. TEL 514-270-1100. FAX 514-270-6900.
  Description: Features new designs in bedroom furnishing and accessories.

643.3 621.56 US
CONSUMER SELECTION GUIDE FOR REFRIGERATORS AND FREEZERS (YEAR). 1983. a. $2. Association of Home Appliance Manufacturers, 20 N. Wacker Dr., Chicago, IL 60606. TEL 312-984-5800. FAX 312-984-5823. Ed. Marian Stamos. circ. 9,000.
  Description: Discusses key facts to consider before purchase of refrigerators and freezers and lists annual operating costs for specific models for consumers.

643.3 330.9 US
CONSUMER SELECTION GUIDE FOR ROOM AIR CONDITIONERS (YEAR). 1983. a. $2. Association of Home Appliance Manufacturers, 20 N. Wacker Dr., Chicago, IL 60606. TEL 312-984-5800. FAX 312-984-5823. Ed. Marian Stamos. circ. 9,000.
  Description: Discusses key facts to consider before purchase of room air conditioners and lists EER for specific models, aimed at consumers.

645 US
CONTACT (HIGH POINT). vol.26, 1989. m. $3.50. International Home Furnishings Representatives Association, 209 S. Main St., Space M1215, Box 670, High Point, NC 27261. TEL 919-889-3920. Ed. Danielle M. Conte.
  Description: For home furnishings representatives. Gives facts on taxes, markets, legislation and membership benefits and ideas on how to enhance sales.

645 US
COUNTRY ACCENTS. 1986. q. G C R Publishing Group, Inc., 1700 Broadway, 34th Fl., New York, NY 10019. TEL 212-541-7100. adv.; circ. 300,000.

COUNTRY ALMANAC. see *HOME ECONOMICS*

COUNTRY DECORATING IDEAS. see *INTERIOR DESIGN AND DECORATION*

COUNTRY HOME. see *INTERIOR DESIGN AND DECORATION*

747.3 FR ISSN 0751-6320
COURRIER DU MEUBLE. 1957. w. 540 F. (foreign 940 F.). Editions du Tigre, 23 rue Joubert, 75009 Paris, France. TEL 48-74-52-50. FAX 1-40-16-43-65. TELEX COUMEUB 283769F. adv.; circ. 9,600.

643.3 IT
CUCINA BELLA. 1978. 3/yr. L.6500. Di Baio Editore s.r.l., Via Settembrini 11, 20124 Milan, Italy. Ed. Giuseppe Maria Jonghi-Lavarini. adv.; circ. 60,000.

INTERIOR DESIGN AND DECORATION — FURNITURE AND HOUSE FURNISHINGS

684.1   GW   ISSN 0341-8839
D D S - DER DEUTSCHER SCHREINER UND TISCHLER; Fachzeitschrift fuer die Holz- und Kunststoffverarbeitung. 1901. m. DM.148.20 (foreign DM.154.20). Deutsche Verlags-Anstalt GmbH, Neckarstr. 121, Postfach 106012, 7000 Stuttgart 10, Germany. TEL 0711-26310. FAX 0711-2631-292. TELEX 7111193. Ed. Ulrich Mueller. adv.; bk.rev.; charts; illus.; tr.lit.; index; circ. 20,000.
   Former titles: Deutscher Schreiner (ISSN 0012-0685); Deutsche Moebel- und Bauschreiner.
   Description: Trade publication for the wood and plastics industry. Features design and construction, technology, materials, business, economics, and education. Includes positions available.

747.5   US
DALTON CARPET JOURNAL. 1981. m. $12. Daily Citizen-News, 308 S. Thornton Ave., Dalton, GA 30720. TEL 404-278-1011. Ed. Louise Hackney. adv.; bk.rev.; circ. 20,000.

684.1   IT   ISSN 0393-330X
DATALIGNUM. (Text in English, German and Italian) 1982. m. L.80000($100) Milla Editrice srl, Via Mugello 6, 20137 Milan, Italy. TEL 02-7610878. FAX 02-7490037. TELEX 322210 MILLA I. Ed. Pietro Stroppa. adv.; bk.rev.; circ. 9,000.

DEALERSCOPE MERCHANDISING; the marketing magazine for consumer electronics and major appliance retailing. see ELECTRONICS

749   US   ISSN 0011-7358
N8610
DECOR; the magazine of fine interior accessories. 1880. m. $20. Commerce Publishing Co., 408 Olive St., St. Louis, MO 63102. TEL 314-421-5445. Ed. M. Humberg. adv.; illus.; mkt.; circ. 22,122.
   Formerly: Picture and Gift Journal.
   Description: Provides merchandizing and operating ideas to help retailers of art, frames and related materials increase sales.

347.5   US   ISSN 1045-8816
DECORATIVE RUG. 1987. m. $48. Oriental Rug Auction Review, Inc., Box 709, Meredith, NH 03253. TEL 603-744-9191. FAX 603-744-6933. Ed. Ron O'Callaghan. adv.; bk.rev.; illus.; circ. 10,000.
   Formerly: Decorative Rug Review.
   Description: Covers new oriental rugs at the wholesale and retail levels.

747   BE   ISSN 0773-4034
DECORS NEW EDITIONS. (Editions in French and Dutch) 1965. q. 2000 Fr. Decors New Editions S.A., Av. des Mimosas 33, B-1150 Brussels, Belgium. Ed. Euroset. circ. 40,000.
   Former titles: Decors; S.A. Decors New Editions; Meubles et Decors (ISSN 0026-1653)

645.4   US
DIGEST FOR HOME FURNISHERS.* 1919. q. $3.50. Minnesota 300, 300 Prairie Center Dr., Ste. 210, Eden Prairie, MN 55344. Ed. Richard L. English. adv.; circ. 3,000.
   Formerly: Furniture Digest.

DIRECTORY OF HOME CENTER OPERATORS & HARDWARE CHAINS (YEAR). see BUSINESS AND ECONOMICS — Trade And Industrial Directories

DIRECTORY OF HOME FURNISHINGS RETAILERS (YEAR). see BUSINESS AND ECONOMICS — Trade And Industrial Directories

DIRECTORY OF MATERIALS SUPPLIERS. see FIRE PREVENTION

684.1   UK   ISSN 0070-6604
DIRECTORY TO THE FURNISHING TRADE; cabinet maker directory. 1957. a. £72 (foreign £85). Benn Business Information Services Ltd., P.O. Box 20, Sovereign Way, Tonbridge, Kent TN9 1RQ, England. TEL 0732-362666. FAX 0732-770483. TELEX 95162-BENTON-G. Ed. Andrea Vizard. adv.; index; circ. 2,500.
   —BLDSC shelfmark: 3593.730000.
   Description: Features manufacturers and wholesalers, classified buyers guides, retailers, agents, business information and trade associations.

DOMOV. see INTERIOR DESIGN AND DECORATION

DREAM HOME MAGAZINE. see BUILDING AND CONSTRUCTION

749.63   GW
E R C O LICHTBERICHT. 1977. 3/yr. E R C O Leuchten GmbH, Brockhauser Weg 80-82, 5880 Ludenscheid, Germany. TEL 02351-551-0. illus.; circ. 45,000.

749   US   ISSN 0012-8155
E162
EARLY AMERICAN LIFE; decorating, crafts and history. 1970. bi-m. $16.95 (foreign $21). (Early American Society) Cowles Magazines, Inc. (Subsidiary of: Cowles Media Company), 6405 Flank Dr., Box 8200, Harrisburg, PA 17105-8200. TEL 717-657-9555. FAX 717-657-9526. (Subscr. to: Box 1620, Mt. Morris, IL 61054. TEL 800-435-9601) Ed. Frances Carnahan. adv.; bk.rev.; illus.; tr.lit.; circ. 207,990. (also avail. in microform from UMI; reprint service avail. from UMI)
   Indexed: Access (1976-), Amer.Hist.& Life, Hist.Abstr., Ind.How To Do It (1977-), Mag.Ind.

747.4   US
▼**EASTERN FLOORS.** 1990. q. $20. Specialist Publications, Inc., 17835 Ventura Blvd., Ste. 312, Encino, CA 91316. TEL 818-345-3550. FAX 818-344-9647. Ed. Howard Olansky. circ. 17,500.
   Description: For floor covering and tile retailers, distributors, agents and manufacturers in the eastern half of the United States, with an emphasis on markets, shows, conventions and industry meetings.

645   BE   ISSN 0772-6287
ECHO DU MEUBLE. Flemish edition: Meubel Echo (ISSN 0772-6279) (Editions in Flemish, French) bi-m. 1300 Fr. Hayez S.A., Rue Fin 4, 1080 Brussels, Belgium. TEL 02-424-0064. FAX 021-424-03-78. TELEX 63467 HAYEZ B. adv.; circ. 4,500.

EIGEN HUIS EN INTERIEUR. see INTERIOR DESIGN AND DECORATION

643.3   SW
ELECTROLUX. ANNUAL REPORT. (Text in English) a. free to qualified personnel. Electrolux, Lilla Essingen, S-10545 Stockholm, Sweden.
   Description: Reports on electrical appliances.

645   US   ISSN 1046-1957
NK1700
ELLE DECOR. (American edition) 1989. 6/yr. $27. Elle Publishing (Subsidiary of: Hachette Publications), 1633 Broadway, New York, NY 10019. TEL 800-876-8775. FAX 212-489-4216. Ed. Barbara L. Dixon. adv.; bk.rev.; circ. 20,000.
   Indexed: Access (1991-).
   Description: Provides an international design showcase of home products. Encourages readers to use their own creativity.

643.3   SP
EQUIPO DOMESTICO - ELECTRODOMESTICOS; revista especializada del mundo de los aparatos que dan confort al hogar. 7/yr. 5300 ptas. (foreign 8000 ptas.). Antonio Duarte Cifuentes, Ed.& Pub.; Fermin Caballero 64 (Larra 1), 6 D, 28034 Madrid, Spain. TEL 201-8240. adv.; charts; illus.; stat.; circ. 5,600.

645   FR
EURODECO. q. 300 F. (foreign 300 F.). Editions G.M. Perrin, 88 Blvd. de Charonne, 75980 Paris Cedex 20, France. TEL 43-48-99-51. FAX 43-48-56-60. TELEX GMPPAR 216219 F.

684.1   SP   ISSN 0210-5489
EUROMUEBLE. 1965. m. $45. Editorial Oifce, German Perez Carrasco, 63, 28027 Madrid, Spain. Ed. Ch.G. Robba. circ. 10,000. (back issues avail.)

645   GW
EUROPAEISCHER WIRTSCHAFTSDIENST. EINKAUFSBERATER FUER DIE MOEBELINDUSTRIE. m. DM.360. Casimir Katz Verlag, Bleichstr. 20-22, 7562 Gernsbach, Germany. TEL 07224-3091. FAX 07224-3094. TELEX 78915-DBV-D.

684.1   GW
EUROPAEISCHER WIRTSCHAFTSDIENST. MOEBEL-DIENST. 1926. w. DM.410. Casimir Katz Verlag, Bleichstr. 20-22, 7562 Gernsbach, Germany. TEL 07224-3091. FAX 07224-3094. TELEX 78915-DBV-D. Eds. Richard Barth, Stefan Lang. circ. 980.

380.1   GW
EUROPEAN FURNITURE REVIEW. (Text in English, French, German) a. $53. A B C Publishing Group, P.O. Box 4034, D-6100 Darmstadt 1, Germany. TEL 6151-33411. FAX 6151-33164. TELEX 4 19 257. (Dist. in US by: Western Hemisphere Publishing Corporation, Box 710, Newcastle, CA 95654) adv.
   Description: Reviews European furniture export industries.

684.1   GW
EUROPEAN OFFICE FURNITURE. 1987. a. DM.10. Verlagsanstalt Alexander Koch GmbH, Fasanenweg 18, 7022 Leinfelden - Echterdingen, Germany. TEL 0711-7591-1. Eds. L. Drabarczyk, K-H. Weinbrenner.

684.1   GW
EUROPEAN WOODWORKING MACHINERY AND ACCESSORIES. (Text in English) 1986. a. free. D R W-Verlag Weinbrenner GmbH & Co., Fasanenweg 18, 7022 Leinfelden-Echterdingen, Germany. TEL 0711-7591-1. Ed. Karl-Heinz Weinbrenner. circ. 25,000.

684.1   US   ISSN 0192-8058
TS880
F D M - FURNITURE DESIGN & MANUFACTURING. 1959. m. $40. Delta Communications, Inc. (Chicago) (Subsidiary of: Elsevier Business Press, Inc. (New York), 400 N. Michigan Ave., Ste. 1200, Chicago, IL 60611. TEL 312-222-2000. FAX 312-222-2026. Ed. Michael Chazin. adv.; illus.; tr.lit.; circ. 50,000. (also avail. in microform from UMI,MIM) **Indexed:** Key to Econ.Sci.
   Formerly: Furniture Design and Manufacturing (ISSN 0016-304X)
   Description: Articles on the furniture, bedding and upholstering industries.

684.1   UK   ISSN 0014-5904
TS840
F I R A BULLETIN; the quarterly for the furniture industry. 1962. q. £60 (effective 1991). Furniture Industry Research Association (F I R A), Maxwell Rd., Stevenage, Herts. SG1 2EW, England. TEL 0438-313433. FAX 0438-727607. TELEX 827653 FIRA G. Ed. P.R. Hinton. adv.; abstr.; illus.; circ. 1,000. **Indexed:** Br.Ceram.Abstr., C.I.S. Abstr., Fluidex, Forest.Abstr., World Surf.Coat., World Text.Abstr.
   Formerly: F I R A Technical Bulletin.
   Description: Contains articles on developments in the industry.

747.4   US   ISSN 0015-3761
FLOOR COVERING WEEKLY.* 1952. w. $25. Hearst Business Communications, Inc., F C W Division, 60 E. 42nd St., Ste. 234, New York, NY 10165-0006. Ed. John P. McGrath. adv.; bk.rev.; illus.; circ. 21,000. (tabloid format) **Indexed:** Text.Tech.Dig.

747.4   US
FLOOR COVERING WEEKLY MARKET GUIDE SERIES.* 1979. s-a. Hearst Business Communications, Inc., F C W Division, 60 E. 42nd St., Ste. 234, New York, NY 10165-0006. circ. 21,000. (tabloid format)

747.4   US
FLOOR COVERINGS INTERNATIONAL.* 1980. s-a. Hearst Business Communications, Inc., F C W Division, 60 E. 42nd St., No. 234, New York, NY 10165-0006. (Subscr. to: Foor Covering Weekly, 645 Stewart Ave., Garden City, NY 11530) Ed. Albert Wahnon.

747.4   US   ISSN 0162-881X
TH2521
FLOORING; the magazine of interior surfaces. 1931. m. $20. Avanstar Communications, Inc., 7500 Old Oak Blvd., Cleveland, OH 44130. TEL 216-826-2839. FAX 216-891-2726. (Subscr. to: 1 E. First St., Duluth, MN 55802) Ed. Mark S. Kuhar. adv.; circ. 24,546. **Indexed:** Text.Tech.Dig.

FORESTA; Rumanian wood and furniture review. see FORESTS AND FORESTRY — Lumber And Wood

FRAMES ARCHITETTURA DEI SERRAMENTI; rivista internazionale degli infissi e dei sistemi di chiusura nell'edilizia. see BUILDING AND CONSTRUCTION

FRAMES BOOK (YEAR). see BUSINESS AND ECONOMICS — Trade And Industrial Directories

684.1 643.3   NZ
FURNISHING & APPLIANCE WORLD. m. Tricom, P.O. Box 9072, Auckland, New Zealand. adv.; circ. 3,206.

INTERIOR DESIGN AND DECORATION — FURNITURE AND HOUSE FURNISHINGS

747.4   AT
FURNISHING FLOORS; national magazine for the flooring trade. 6/yr. Aus.$44. Furnishing Publications Pty. Ltd., 251 Hawthorn Rd., Caulfield, Vic. 3162, Australia. TEL 03-523-8444. FAX 03-523-0291. Ed. Keith Dunn. adv.; illus.; pat.; tr.lit.; circ. 4,800.
   Description: For floor covering industry both domestic and commercial, suppliers, manufacturers, retailers, architects, specifiers, and government departments, federal, state and local.

684.3   IE
FURNISHING RETAILER & CONTRACTOR. 1975. m. Acorn Publishing Co. Ltd., 105 Aradara Ave., Raheny, Dublin 13, Ireland. Ed. David Collins. adv.

747 677   UK
FURNISHINGS RECORD. 1981. s-a. free with Drapers Record. International Thomson Business Publishing, 100 Avenue Road, London NW3 3TP, England. TEL 01-935-6611. Ed. Cliff Waller. adv.; illus.; stat.
   Former titles (until 1986): Furnishings International; Home Furnishings International.

645   PH
FURNITURE. 6/yr. $12. Leverage International (Consultants) Inc., PS Bank Bldg. 5F, C.P.O. Box 2296, Ayala Ave., Makati MM, Philippines. FAX 632-8101594. Ed. Cecilia Sanchez.

684.1   UK   ISSN 0964-0940
▼**FURNITURE COMPONENTS & PRODUCTION INTERNATIONAL.** 1991. m. £20 (foreign £32). Nigel Gearing Ltd., No.4 Red Barn Mews, High St., Battle, E. Sussex TN33 0AG, England. TEL 04246-4982. FAX 04246-4321. Ed. David Young. adv.; circ. 11,000.

684.1   US
THE FURNITURE EXECUTIVE. 1983. m. American Furniture Manufacturers Association, Box HP-7, High Point, NC 27261. TEL 919-884-5000. Ed. Nancy High. circ. 2,500.

749   UK   ISSN 0016-3058
NK2528
FURNITURE HISTORY. 1965. a. £20($36) (subscr. includes q. newsletter). Furniture History Society, c/o B. Austen, One Mercedes Cottages, St. John's Rd., Haywards Heath, West Sussex RH16 4EH, England. TEL 0444-413845. Ed. Simon Jervis. adv.; bk.rev.; abstr.; bibl.; illus.; cum.index every 10 yrs.; circ. 1,500. (tabloid format; back issues avail.) **Indexed:** Artbibl.Mod., Avery Ind.Archit.Per., Br.Archaeol.Abstr., RILA.
   Description: Includes information about antiques, art, interior design, and decoration, furniture and house furnishing.

684.1   UK   ISSN 0306-0519
FURNITURE MANUFACTURER; the international journal for the furniture manufacturer. 1935. m. £62. Publex International Ltd., 110-112 Station Rd. E., Oxted, Surrey RH8 0QA, England. TEL 0883-717755. FAX 0883-714554. Ed. Ann Von Klosst-Dohna. adv.; bk.rev.; illus.; circ. 7,723. **Indexed:** Key to Econ.Sci., PROMT.
   —BLDSC shelfmark: 4059.239500.
   Formerly: Furniture and Bedding Production.

684.1   US   ISSN 0192-799X
FURNITURE MANUFACTURING MANAGEMENT.* 1954. m. $20 (free to qualified personnel). Associations Publications, Inc., Box 640, Collierville, TN 38027-9986. TEL 901-853-7470. adv.; bk.rev.; circ. 27,560.
   Formerly (until 1978): Furniture Methods and Materials.

749 658   US
FURNITURE RETAILER (GREENSBORO). 1927. m. $48. Pace Communications, 1301 Carolina St., Greensboro, NC 27401. TEL 919-378-6065. FAX 919-275-2864. Ed. Patricia N. Bowling. adv.; charts; illus.; stat.; tr.lit.; circ. 16,780.
   Former titles (until 1989): Competitivedge (ISSN 0149-2276); N H F A Reports (ISSN 0027-6944); N R F A Reports.

749   US   ISSN 0194-360X
FURNITURE - TODAY; the weekly business newspaper of the furniture industry. 1976. w. $69.95 includes Accessories - Today. Cahners Business Newspapers (Subsidiary of: Reed International PLC), Division of Reed Publishing (USA) Inc., 200 S. Main St., Box 2754, High Point, NC 27261. TEL 919-889-0113. FAX 919-841-8256. (Subscr. to: Box 1424, Riverton, NJ 08077) Ed. Lester Craft. adv.; bk.rev.; charts; illus.; stat.; circ. 27,500. (tabloid format; also avail. in microform from UMI; back issues avail.)
   Supersedes: Furniture News (ISSN 0016-3066)
   Description: Articles are geared toward the furniture retailer and manufacturer.

FURNITURE WORKERS PRESS. see *LABOR UNIONS*

749   US
FURNITURE WORLD. 1870. 13/yr. $16. Towse Publishing Co., 530 Fifth Ave., Pelham, NY 10803. TEL 914-738-6744. FAX 914-738-6820. Ed. B.I. Bienenstock. adv.; illus.; circ. 20,100.
   Formerly: Furniture South (ISSN 0016-3074)
   Description: Information on finance, operations, marketing and sales management for homefurnishings retailers.

749   US   ISSN 0016-3104
FURNITURE WORLD AND FURNITURE BUYER AND DECORATOR. 1870. m. $16. Towse Publishing Co., 530 Fifth Ave., Pelham, NY 10803. TEL 914-738-6744. FAX 914-738-6820. Ed. R.A. Bienenstock. adv.; bk.rev.; illus.; mkt.; stat.; circ. 18,814.
   Description: For homefurnishings retailers. Covers finance, operations, marketing and sales.

FUTURE HOME TECHNOLOGY NEWS. see *ENGINEERING — Computer Applications*

677   NE   ISSN 0923-3660
GAAF GOED;* vakblad voor de interieur-textiel-branche. Short title: G G. (Text in Dutch) 1986. bi-m. Buro Jet b.v., Trenkstraat 1N, 2288 EG Rijswijk, Netherlands. Ed. M.J. van der Drift. adv.; circ. 11,000. (tabloid format; back issues avail.)
   Description: Business magazine for home decorating and the home textile market.

645   IT
GAP CASA. m. (10/yr.). L.115000 in Europe; America L.160000. Publimedia Societa Editrice, Corso Venezia 18, 20121 Milan, Italy. TEL 02-77521. FAX 02-781068. Ed. Francesco Buffa di Perrero. adv.; circ. 20,000.

643.3   US
▼**GLOBAL APPLIANCE REPORT.** 1990. m. $350 to non-members; members $250. Association of Home Appliance Manufacturers, 20 N. Wacker Dr., Chicago, IL 60606. TEL 312-984-5800. FAX 312-984-5823. Ed. Craig Schulz. (looseleaf format)
   Description: Digest of international news affecting the home appliance industry.

747.5   SW   ISSN 0345-3979
GOLV TILL TAK; Skandinavisk tidskrift am golv, vaeggar och tak/Scandinavian magazine for floor coverings, wallcoverings and ceilings. (Text in Swedish; summaries in English) 1972. 8/yr. SEK 280. (Golventreprenoerernas Branschorganisation) Foerlags AB Golv till Tak, P.O. Box 4604, 116 91 Stockholm, Sweden. TEL 08-644 09 05. FAX 08-643-98-11. (Co-sponsor: Sveriges Golvhandlares Riksfoerbund) Ed. Inger Rosengren. adv.; circ. 3,708.

749   US   ISSN 0162-9158
HF5001
H F D - RETAILING HOME FURNISHINGS. 1929. w. $38. Fairchild Publications, Inc., H F D-Retailing Home Furnishings, 7 W. 34th St., New York, NY 10001. TEL 212-630-4000. (Subscr. to: 55 Fifth Ave., New York, NY 10003) Ed. Geri Brin. adv.; illus.; mkt.; circ. 31,769. (also avail. in microform from MIM) **Indexed:** Bus.Ind., PROMT, Text.Tech.Dig., Tr.& Indus.Ind.
   ●Also available online. Vendor(s): DIALOG.
   Formerly (until 1976): Home Furnishings Daily (ISSN 0018-4047)
   Description: Ideas for retailers, wholesalers, manufacturers and supliers, covers furniture, bedding, floor coverings, giftware and housewares.

H G. see *INTERIOR DESIGN AND DECORATION*

645   IT
HARPER'S GRAN BAZAAR. 1978. 6/yr. L.40000. Edizioni S Y D S Italia s.r.l., Viale Stelvio 57, 20159 Milan, Italy. Ed. Giuseppe Della Schiava. adv.; circ. 44,000.

684.1   GW
HAUSTEX. 1950. m. DM.104.40. Westdeutsche Verlagsanstalt GmbH, Ahmser Str. 190, Postfach 3054, 4900 Herford, Germany. TEL 05221-775-0. FAX 05221-775215. TELEX 17-5221855. Ed. H. Russ. adv.; illus.
   Formerly: Aussteuer Bett und Couch (ISSN 0004-8259)
   Description: Information, insider news on interior design and decoration.

HEARTH & HOME; the magazine of specialty retailing. see *ENERGY*

684.1   AU   ISSN 0018-3776
HOLZ IM HANDWERK; oesterreichische Moebelzeitschrift. 1959. m. S.460. Zeitschriftenverlag Dr. Hildegard Braig, Anton Frankgasse 17, A-1181 Vienna, Austria. TEL 0222-343439. FAX 0222-342309.

684.1   GW
TS840
HOLZ- UND MOEBELINDUSTRIE. (Text in English, French, German) 1965. 11/yr. DM.165. D R W-Verlag Weinbrenner GmbH & Co., Fasanenweg 18, 7022 Leinfelden-Echterdingen, Germany. Ed. Karl-Heinz Weinbrenner. adv.; bk.rev.; bibl.; illus.; stat.; circ. 8,500. **Indexed:** Packag.Sci.Tech.
   Former titles: Holz- und Kunststoffverarbeitung (ISSN 0721-2585); Moderne Holzverarbeitung.

747   SI
HOME & DECOR. 1981. bi-m. S.41. Times Periodicals Private Ltd., 422 Thomson Rd., Time Industrial Bldg., Singapore 1129, Singapore. TEL 2550011. FAX 2568016. Ed. Sophie Kho. adv.; illus.; circ. 12,000.
   Formerly: Decor Guide (ISSN 0129-8194)
   Description: A guide to home designing and decor, features on decor trends and ideas.

684.3   US   ISSN 0896-7962
TS1760
HOME FASHIONS MAGAZINE. 1979. m. $30 (foreign $60). Fairchild Publications, Inc., Home Fashions Magazine, 7 W. 34th St., New York, NY 10001. TEL 212-630-3700. Ed. Lauren Payne. adv.; circ. 11,000.
   Formerly: Home Fashion Textiles (ISSN 0195-654X)

658.8 684.1   US
HOME FURNISHINGS REVIEW. 1927. q. $10. Southwest Homefurnishings Association, 110 World Trade Center, Box 581207, Dallas, TX 75258. TEL 214-741-7632. Ed. Darrell Hofheinz. adv.; bk.rev.; charts; illus.; mkt.; tr.lit.; index; circ. 18,419.
   Former titles: Home Furnishings; Southwest Homefurnishings News (ISSN 0199-8854); Southwest Furniture News (ISSN 0038-4666)
   Description: Presents business information drawn from a variety of publications and other sources, digested into brief articles aimed at helping the home furnishings retailer operate a more profitable business.

644.3   US   ISSN 0162-9077
HOME LIGHTING & ACCESSORIES. 1923. m. $30 (effective Jan. 1991). Doctorow Communications, Inc., 1115 Clifton Ave., Clifton, NJ 07013. TEL 201-779-1600. FAX 201-779-3242. Ed. Peter Wulff. adv.; bk.rev.; charts; illus.; mkt.; pat.; tr.lit.; circ. 10,300.
   —BLDSC shelfmark: 4326.070000.
   Formerly: Lamp Journal (ISSN 0023-7426)
   Description: Describes lamps and fixtures.

747   US
HOMEMARKET TRENDS. 6/yr. Lebhar-Friedman, Inc., 425 Park Ave., New York, NY 10022. TEL 212-756-5000. Ed. Tony Lisanti. adv.; circ. 14,329.
   Description: Covers the home fashions industry. Includes furniture, bed and bath, table top and window treatments.

I J K

INTERIOR DESIGN AND DECORATION — FURNITURE AND HOUSE FURNISHINGS

645 US
HOMEWORLD BUSINESS; the newspaper for the housewares decision maker. 1989. m. $25 (Canada $35; elsewhere $200). I C D Publications, Box 14307, Hauppauge, NY 11788-0477. TEL 516-979-7878. FAX 516-979-8182. Ed. Ian Gittlitz. adv.; circ. 12,800 (controlled). (tabloid format)
Description: Provides statistical analysis and coverage of the houseware industry.

747 SA
HOUSE AND HOME/HUIS EN TUIS. (Text in English) m. R.7. Furniture Traders Association of South Africa, Albert & Eloff Sts., Box 5492, Johannesburg 2001, South Africa. Ed. Wally Kriek. adv.

HOUSE BEAUTIFUL. see *INTERIOR DESIGN AND DECORATION*

645 UK
HOUSE BEAUTIFUL. 1989. m. £13.20. National Magazine Co. Ltd., 72 Broadwick St., London W1V 2BP, England. TEL 071-439-5000. FAX 071-437-6886. Ed. Pat Roberts. circ. 283,193.

643.6 UK ISSN 0264-8563
HOUSEWARES. 1983. 11/yr. £36 (foreign £52). Benn Publications Ltd., Sovereign Way, Tonbridge, Kent TN9 1RW, England. TEL 0732-364422. Ed. Sarah Burling. adv.; circ. 9,250.

645 CN ISSN 0829-9889
HOUSEWARES CANADA.* 1985. bi-m. Can.$21.40($38.50) (foreign $38.50). Centre Publications Ltd. (Subsidiary of: Southam Communications), 1450 Don Mills Rd., Don Mills, Ont. M3B 2X7, Canada. TEL 416-438-1153. Ed. Laurie Merckel. adv.; circ. 18,000.

HOUSEWARES SHOW STOPPERS (A.M. AND P.M. EDITIONS). see *HOME ECONOMICS*

747 635 US
HOUSTON METROPOLITAN. 1974. m. $18. A R C Communications, Inc., 5615 Kirby Dr., Box 25386, Houston, TX 77265. TEL 713-524-3000. FAX 713-524-8213. Ed. Chris Kelly. illus.; circ. 96,950. **Indexed:** Access (1980-).
Formerly (until 1988): Houston Home and Garden (ISSN 0360-2087)

HUS & HIBYLI/HOME AND FAMILY. see *INTERIOR DESIGN AND DECORATION*

640.73 NO ISSN 0018-7976
HUSET VAART. 1958. 3/yr. free. A-S Informa Reklame, Akersgt. 64, Oslo 1, Norway. Ed. Jan R. Landmark. adv.; illus.; circ. 610,000.

747 US
IDEAS (CORAL GABLES). q. Dodi Publishing, Box 343392, Coral Gables, FL 33134. TEL 305-238-0557. Ed. Sam Hirsch. circ. 17,000.

684.1 IT ISSN 0019-753X
INDUSTRIA DEL MOBILE. 1959. m. L.160000. Industria del Mobile s.r.l., 21 via Giambologna, Milan, Italy. TEL 02 8394780. FAX 02-8372547. adv.; illus.; circ. 6,000.
—BLDSC shelfmark: 4441.550000.

INDUSTRIEL SUR BOIS. see *BUILDING AND CONSTRUCTION — Carpentry And Woodwork*

684.1 GW
INSIDE. 1974. s-m. DM.332.98. Inside-Verlag, Kaiserstr. 12, Postfach 440328, 8000 Munchen 40, Germany. Ed. Peter Wulff.

747.4 US ISSN 0192-1657
TS1779.5
INSTALLATION & CLEANING SPECIALIST. 1963. m. $22. Specialist Publications, Inc., 17835 Ventura Blvd., Ste. 312, Encino, CA 91316. TEL 213-873-1411. FAX 818-344-9647. Ed. Howard Olansky. adv.; circ. 16,639.
Formerly: Installation Specialist (ISSN 0446-3161)

INTERIEUR. see *INTERIOR DESIGN AND DECORATION*

747 US
INTERIOR DESIGN MARKET. 3/yr. Cahners Publishing Company (New York), Interior Design Group (Subsidiary of: Reed International PLC), Division of Reed Publishing (USA) Inc., 249 W. 17th St., New York, NY 10011. TEL 212-645-0067. FAX 212-645-5409. (Subscr. to: Box 1970, Marion, OH 43305) Ed. Stanley Abercrombie. circ. 47,122.

747 US
INTERIORS & SOURCES. bi-m. $18. L C Clark Publishing, 840 US Highway One, 330, N. Palm Beach, FL 33408. TEL 407-627-3393. FAX 407-627-3447. Ed. Katie Sosnowchick. circ. 18,780.

INTERIORS MAGAZINE. see *INTERIOR DESIGN AND DECORATION*

684.1 IT
INTERNI. m. L.100000($65) Electa Periodici SRL, Via Trentacoste 7, 20134 Milan, Italy. TEL 02-215631. FAX 26410847. Ed. Dorothea Balluff. circ. 60,000.
Formerly: Arredamento Interni.

684 US ISSN 0022-7161
HD9999.I473
JUVENILE MERCHANDISING. 1946. m. $12. Columbia Communications, Inc., 370 Lexington Ave., New York, NY 10017. TEL 212-532-9290. FAX 212-779-8345. Ed. Claudia Desimone. adv.; charts; illus.; mkt.; tr.lit.; circ. 12,000.

643.3 NE
KEUKEN & INTERIEUR MAGAZINE. 1983. bi-m. Bruil Tijdschriften, Keppelsweg 44, Postbus 100, 7000 AC Doetinchem, Netherlands. TEL 08340-24033. FAX 08340-33433. Ed. Bert Bruil. adv.; circ. 5,200.
Description: For kitchen and interior design specialists.

643.3 NE
KEUKEN MAGAZINE. bi-m. Bruil Tijdschriften, Keppelswag 44, Postbus 100, 7000 AC Doetinchem, Netherlands. TEL 08340-24033. FAX 08340-33433. Ed. Bert Bruil. adv.
Description: For the customer who wants to buy a kitchen.

KITCHEN & BATH DESIGN NEWS. see *INTERIOR DESIGN AND DECORATION*

KITCHENS & BATHROOMS. see *INTERIOR DESIGN AND DECORATION*

643.3 GW
KUECHENPROFI; Moebel, Geraete, Zubehoer. 1988. s-a. free. Ferdinand Holzmann Verlag GmbH und Co., Mexikoring 37, 2000 Hamburg 60, Germany. TEL 040-632018-0. Ed. Dieter Reinbender. circ. 10,500.
Description: News for the kitchen furniture and appliance trade.

677 US ISSN 0892-743X
HD9850.1
L D B INTERIOR TEXTILES. 1928. m. $25. Columbia Communications Inc., 370 Lexington Ave., New York, NY 10017. TEL 212-532-9290. FAX 212-779-8345. Ed. Renee Bennett. adv.; illus.; stat.; index; circ. 32,000. (back issues avail.) **Indexed:** Text.Tech.Dig.
Formed by the 1988 merger of: Interior Textiles; Which was formerly: Curtain, Drapery and Bedspread Magazine (ISSN 0011-4065) & Linens, Domestics and Bath Products (ISSN 0024-3833); Which was formerly: Linens and Domestics.
Description: Retailing magazine for home furnishing, textiles and bath products, including linens.

674 IT
L M L'INDUSTRIA DEL LEGNO E DEL MOBILE. 1949. bi-m. L.100000. Centro Studi Industria Leggera, Via Gesu 17, 20121 Milan, Italy. TEL 02-79-66-30. adv.; bk.rev.; illus.; stat.; tr.lit.; cum.index; circ. 5,500. **Indexed:** Chem.Abstr.
Formerly: Industria del Legno e del Mobile (ISSN 0019-7521)

684.1 IT
IL LEGNO (MILAN). 1986. m (10/yr.). L.110000. Industria del Mobile s.r.l., Via Giambologna 21, Milan, Italy. FAX 02-8372547.

749.63 621.32 UK ISSN 0024-3418
LIGHTING EQUIPMENT NEWS. 1967. m. £50. Maclean Hunter Ltd., Maclean Hunter House, Chalk Lane, Cockfosters Rd., Barnet, Herts EN4 0BU, England. TEL 081-975-9759. FAX 081-440-1796. TELEX 299072 MACHUN G. Ed. Judy Sewell. adv.; bk.rev.; illus.; circ. 14,160. **Indexed:** C.I.S. Abstr., Int.Build.Serv.Abstr., Sci.Abstr.
—BLDSC shelfmark: 5214.400000.

677 US
LINENS, DOMESTICS & BATH - INTERIOR TEXTILE ANNUAL DIRECTORY. 1927. a. $10. Columbia Communications, Inc., 370 Lexington Ave., New York, NY 10017. TEL 212-532-9290. FAX 212-779-8345. adv.; circ. 18,000.
Former titles: Curtain, Drapery and Bedspread National Buyers Guide (ISSN 0084-9502); (until 1987): Linens, Domestics and Bath Products Annual Directory; Incorporates (1987): Interior Textiles National Buyers Guide.

644.3 749.63 FR
LUMINAIRES ET ECLAIRAGE. q. 45 F. Publicite Larrey, 73 bis Avenue de Wagram, 75017 Paris, France. Ed. Francoise Launois. adv.

LYS; miljoe-design-teknik. see *ENGINEERING — Electrical Engineering*

643.3 US
M A C A P CONSUMER BULLETINS. irreg., latest no.13. $0.25. Association of Home Appliance Manufacturers, Major Appliance Consumer Action Panel, 20 N. Wacker Dr., Chicago, IL 60606. TEL 312-984-5800. FAX 312-984-5823.

684.1 IT
MACCHINE ACCESSORI COMPONENTI. Short title: M A C. 1977. m. L.40000. Editore RIMA s.r.l., Via Vincenzo Da Filicaia 7, 20162 Milan, Italy. TEL 02-66103539. FAX 02-66103558. adv.; circ. 16,000.
Formerly: Informobili (ISSN 0393-4403)
Description: For the furniture and accessories industry.

684.1 FR ISSN 0025-3537
MARKET; commerce de l'equipement du cadre de vie. 1969. m. 200 F. Editions Presse Professionnelle, 96 rue de la Victoire, 75009 Paris, France. Ed. Jacqueline Peron. adv.; circ. 62,000.
Formerly: Equipment des Jardins; Incorporates: Quincaillier Equipement Menager.

747.4 AT
▼**MASTER PAINTER AND DECORATIONS TRADE JOURNAL.** 1990. bi-m. Aus.$33. (Master Painter and Decorations Association of Victoria) Furnishing Publications Pty. Ltd., 251 Hawthorn Rd., Caulfield, Vic. 3162, Australia. TEL 03-523-8444. FAX 03-523-0291. circ. 2,100.

684.1 GW
MATERIAL UND TECHNIK. 1985. 3/yr. DM.21.30. Verlag Matthias Ritthammer GmbH, Burgschmietstr. 25, Postfach 3850, 8500 Nuernberg 90, Germany. TEL 0911-37374. Ed. Franz Schaefer. circ. 17,000.

METROPOLITAN HOME; style for our generation. see *INTERIOR DESIGN AND DECORATION*

684.1 NE ISSN 0165-4543
MEUBEL; the weekly business newspaper for the furnishing market. (Text in Dutch) 1919. w. fl.151 (foreign fl.375). Drukkerij-Uitgeverij Lakerveld B.V., P.O. Box 43250, Mangaanstraat 86, 2504 AG The Hague, Netherlands. TEL 070-3218218. FAX 070-3298744. Ed. Martijn van der Drift. adv.; bk.rev.; illus.; circ. 7,000. (back issues avail.) **Indexed:** Key to Econ.Sci.
Formerly: Vakblad voor de Meubelindustrie (ISSN 0042-2231)

MIDWEST RETAILER. see *BUSINESS AND ECONOMICS — Marketing And Purchasing*

747.8 US
MIRROR NEWS MAGAZINE. q. Market Power, Inc., Box 471, Hopkins, MN 55343-0471. TEL 612-935-3666. W.L. Tiller. bk.rev.; circ. 93,321.

INTERIOR DESIGN AND DECORATION — FURNITURE AND HOUSE FURNISHINGS

747 RM ISSN 0026-7104
MOBILA. (Text in Rumanian; occasionally in English; abstracts and summaries in English, French, Rumanian, Russian) 1964. q. $180. Ministerul Industrializarii Lemnului si Materialelor de Constructii, Oficiul de Informare Documentara, Bd. Magheru Nr. 31, sector 1, Bucharest, Rumania. TEL 59-68-65. Ed. Claudiu Lazarescu. adv.; bk.rev.; abstr.; illus.; circ. 6,000. **Indexed:** Forest Prod.Abstr.

684.1 IT ISSN 0026-7112
IL MOBILE; quindicinale indipendente di economia e informazione. 1957. s-m. L.120000($81) Mobile s.r.l., Viale Renato Serra 14, 20148 Milan, Italy. TEL 3270337. FAX 02-39210192. Ed. Roberto Salardi. adv.; bk.rev.; circ. 12,000. (tabloid format)

645
MOBILE - ARREDAMENTO DESIGN. (Supplement avail.) (Text in Italian; summaries in English) Editrice Il Mobile S.r.l., Viale Renato Serra, 14, 20148 Milan, Italy. TEL 3270337. FAX 02-39210192. Ed. Roberto Salardi. circ. 25,000.

643.3 GW ISSN 0026-864X
DIE MODERNE KUECHE. 1958. bi-m. DM.50. (Arbeitsgemeinschaft die Moderne Kueche) Die Planung Verlagsgesellschaft mbH, Holzhofallee 25-31, 6100 Darmstadt, Germany. TEL 06151-314104. FAX 06151-387307. Ed. Horst Bach. adv.; charts; illus.; tr.lit.; circ. 7,000.
Description: Covers remodeling and appliances.

684 GW ISSN 0077-0205
MOEBEL-INDUSTRIE UND IHRE HELFER. 1957. a. DM.38. Industrieschau-Verlagsgesellschaft, Berliner Allee 8, 6100 Darmstadt, Germany.

684.1 GW ISSN 0047-7796
MOEBEL-KULTUR; Fachzeitschrift fuer die Moebelwirtschaft. 1949. m. DM.118.80. Ferdinand Holzmann Verlag, P.O.B. 60 10 49, 2000 Hamburg 60, Germany. TEL 040-632018-0. adv.; bk.rev.; index; circ. controlled.

MOEBEL UND WOHNRAUM; Fachzeitschrift fuer Moebelindustrie und Raumgestaltung. see INTERIOR DESIGN AND DECORATION

684.1 GW
MOEBELFERTIGUNG. (Text in English and German) 1985. s-a. free. Ferdinand Holzmann Verlag GmbH und Co., Mexicoring 37, 2000 Hamburg 60, Germany. TEL 040-632018-0. Eds. Joern Holzmann, Jochen Holzmann.
Description: Covers furniture production, from concept to market place.

684.1 NO ISSN 0333-354X
MOEBELHANDLEREN. 1929. m. (10/yr. NOK 350. Moebelhandlernes Landsforbund, Drammensvn. 30, 0255 Oslo 2, Norway. Ed. Jan Erik Bjeorn. adv.; circ. 4,500.

684.1 GW
MOEBELMARKT. 1960. m. DM.138. Verlag Matthias Ritthammer GmbH, Burgschmietstr. 25, Postfach 3850, 8500 Nuernberg 90, Germany. FAX 0911-334400. TELEX 622839. Eds. Franz Schaefer, Klaus Ritthammer. adv.; bk.rev.; abstr.; illus.; stat.; index; circ. 13,500 (controlled).

684.1 SW ISSN 0345-7737
MOEBLER OCH MILJOE. 1921. 9/yr. SEK 395. Sveriges Moebelhandlares Centralfoerbund - Swedish Furniture Retailers' Association, Kungsgatan 21, S-105 61 Stockholm, Sweden. Ed. Birgit Johansson. adv.; bk.rev.; circ. 4,616.
Formerly: Moebelvaerlden (ISSN 0026-7090)

684.1 US
MONDAY MORNING MESSAGE. 1966. w. $88. John H. Tobin, Ed. & Pub., Box 6415, High Point, NC 27262-6415. TEL 919-884-5732. FAX 919-884-4038. bk.rev.; circ. 5,000.

MONDOCUCINA. see BUILDING AND CONSTRUCTION

EL MUEBLE ACTUAL; la gran revista del hogar. see INTERIOR DESIGN AND DECORATION

643.3 US
N A P S A. RESULTS. bi-m. $50. National Appliance Parts Suppliers Association, 600 S. Federal St., Ste. 400, Chicago, IL 60605. TEL 312-922-6222.

NATIONWIDE DIRECTORY OF GIFT, HOUSEWARES & HOME TEXTILE BUYERS. see GIFTWARE AND TOYS

684.1 FR
NOUVEL OFFICIEL DE L'AMEUBLEMENT. 1950. m. 430 F. Editions G. M. Perrin, 88 bd. de Charonne, 75020 Paris, France. adv.; bk.rev.; illus.; circ. 8,000. **Indexed:** Key to Econ.Sci.
Formerly: Officiel de l'Ameublement: Ameublement Informations (ISSN 0030-0446)

684 UK
NURSERY TRADER. 1874. m. £20 (foreign £27.50). Turret Group Plc., Turret House, 177 Hagden Lane, Watford, Herts. WD1 8LN, England. TEL 0923-777000. FAX 0923-771297. TELEX 9419706. Ed. Alison Davis. adv.; bk.rev.; illus.; circ. 3,726.
Former titles (until 1983): Pram and Nursery Trader (ISSN 0032-6844); Pram World; Nursery Times International.

749 AU ISSN 0029-9081
OESTERREICHISCHE FUSSBODENZEITUNG.* 1965. bi-m. S.48. Verlag Piletzky, Nikolsdorfer Gasse 7, A-1050 Vienna, Austria. Ed. Heinrich Piletzky. adv.; charts; illus.; stat.; circ. 4,300.
Description: Concerns floor coverings.

749 684.1 AU ISSN 0029-9405
OESTERREICHISCHE RAUMAUSSTATTERZEITUNG.* 1966. bi-m. S.48. Verlag Piletzky, Nikolsdorfer Gasse 7, 1050 Vienna, Austria. Ed. Heinrich Piletzky. adv.; charts; illus.; stat.; circ. 4,100.

OFFICIEL DU BOIS (EDITION ROUGE). see BUILDING AND CONSTRUCTION — Carpentry And Woodwork

677.643 US ISSN 0030-5332
ORIENTAL RUG.* 1928. q. $15 (Canada & Mexico $20; elsewhere $40). Oriental Rug Importers Association of America, 15 E. 30th St., No.4-W, New York, NY 10016. Ed. Archie Cherkezian. adv.; bk.rev.; illus.; stat.; tr.lit.; circ. controlled.
Description: For retailers and others in the home furnishings industry. Contains educational articles about all types of oriental rugs, with wholesale and retail market analysis, and more.

747.5 US ISSN 1044-4807
NK2808
ORIENTAL RUG REVIEW. 1981. bi-m. $48. Oriental Rug Auction Review, Inc., Box 709, Meredith, NH 03253. TEL 603-744-9191. FAX 603-744-6933. Ed. Ron O'Callaghan. adv.; bk.rev.; illus.; circ. 4,500.
Description: Covers oriental rugs and other textiles for collectors and dealers.

684.1 US ISSN 0048-2633
PACIFIC MARKETER;* the Northwest's only home furnishings magazine. 1926. bi-m. $4. Northwest Furniture Retailers' Association, 12233 Ashwoth N., No. 15, Seattle, WA 98133. TEL 206-623-1510. Ed. Lucy Hazelton. adv.; illus.; circ. 4,000.

747.4 GW ISSN 0934-9014
PARKETT MAGAZIN. 1988. 6/yr. DM.70 (foreign DM.75). S N Verlag Michael Steinert, An der Alster 21, 2000 Hamburg 1, Germany. TEL 040-240852. FAX 040-2803788.

684.1 UK ISSN 0964-0959
PINE NEWS INTERNATIONAL. 1986. m. £15 (foreign £25). Nigel Gearing Ltd., No.4 Red Barn Mews, High St., Battle, E. Sussex TN33 0AG, England. TEL 04246-4982. FAX 04246-4321. Ed. David Young. adv.; circ. 4,000.
Description: News and information on all aspects of the pine furniture industry and related softwood markets.

645 FR
PRATIQUE. 1966. m. 95 F. S.E.B.A.M., 42 rue de Louvre, Paris, France. Ed. J.P. Renau. adv.; bk.rev.; circ. 90,000.
Former titles: Bricolage; Bricolage Maison Pratique.

PREVISIONS GLISSANTES DETAILLEES EN PERSPECTIVES SECTORIELLES (VOL.4): INDUSTRIES DU BOIS ET DE L'AMEUBLEMENT. see BUSINESS AND ECONOMICS — Economic Situation And Conditions

REMODELING. see BUILDING AND CONSTRUCTION

643.3 US
▼**RETAIL OBSERVER.** 1990. m. $5. 1442 Sierra Creek Way, San Jose, CA 95132. TEL 408-272-8974. FAX 408-251-6511. adv.; circ. 3,888 (controlled).
Description: Covers the retailing of appliances, electronics, and kitchen and bath items.

684.1 FR ISSN 0242-8903
REVUE DE L'AMEUBLEMENT. (Includes Centre de Liaison et d'Ameublement des Fournisseurs de l'Ameublement et de la Literie. Cahier Mensuel) vol.65, 1977. 10/yr. 400 F. (foreign 830 F.). Editions du Tigre, 23 rue Joubert, 75009 Paris, France. TEL 48-74-52-50. FAX 1-40-16-43-65. TELEX COUMEUB 283769F. Ed. Francois Prevot. adv.; illus.

747 IT
RIVISTA ARREDOS; rivista mensile specializzata nel settore dell'arredamento. (Text in English, Italian) m. Stampacolor, Via Grazia Deledda 13, 07100 Sassari, Italy. TEL 079-241215. TELEX 315528 SIAP MI I. Ed. Dott. Sebastiano Ibba. adv.

747.5 DK ISSN 0036-228X
SADELMAGER-OG TAPETSERER TIDENDE.* 1899. m. DKK 42. Saddlers and Upholsterer's Guild, Fortunstraede 5, 1065 Copenhagen K, Denmark. Ed. Frithiof Larsen. adv.; index; circ. 3,200 (controlled).

747 SP
SALA BANO; revista trimestral de decoracion. 1981. q. 800 ptas. (foreign 950 ptas.). Faenza Editrice Iberica, S.A., Calle Navarra 85, 7o, 12002 Castellon, Spain. TEL 964-21-65-70. FAX 964-24-10-10. Ed. Benjamin Cervera. adv.; bk.rev.; circ. 300. (back issues avail.)

SCHORNSTEINFEGERHANDWERK. see BUILDING AND CONSTRUCTION

SCHWEIZERISCHE SCHREINERZEITUNG. see BUILDING AND CONSTRUCTION — Carpentry And Woodwork

684.1 FR
SEMAINE AMEUBLEMENT INFORMATIONS. 48/yr. 500 F. (foreign 1100 F.). Editions G.M. Perrin, 88 Blvd. de Charonne, 75980 Paris Cedex 20, France. TEL 43-48-99-51. FAX 43-48-56-60. TELEX GMPPAR 216219 F.

749.63 IT
SHOWCASE. (Text in English, Italian) 1989. 3/yr. L.70000 (typically set in Sep.). Editrice Habitat s.r.l., Via Luchino del Maino 12, 20147 Milan, Itlay. TEL 48-14-800. FAX 48-19-3013. adv.; circ. 50,000.
Description: For entepreneurs in the design sector, including import-exporters, dealers, architects, and designers.

SLOVENIJALES; glasilo mednarondega podjetja za trgovino, inzeniring, proizvodnjo, zastopanje in konsignacijo. see BUSINESS AND ECONOMICS

684 US ISSN 0037-7260
SMALL WORLD; the magazine of nursery furniture, wheel goods, toys and accessories. 1949. m. $18. Earnshaw Publications, Inc., 225 W. 34th St., Ste. 1212, New York, NY 10001. TEL 212-563-2742. Ed. Thomas W. Hudson. adv.; bk.rev.; charts; illus.; mkt.; tr.lit.; index; circ. 10,200.

747 635.9 IT
SPAZIO CASA. no.28, 1989. m. L.52800. Rusconi Editore Associati S.p.A., Viale Sarca 235, 20126 Milan, Italy. TEL 02-66191. FAX 02-66192686. adv.; bk.rev.
Description: Covers furniture for the home and gardening.

747.4 US
SPECIFIER'S GUIDE TO CONTRACT FLOOR COVERINGS.* 1977. a. $15. Hearst Business Communications, Inc., F C W Division, 60 E. 42nd St., No,234, New York, NY 10165-0006. (Subscr. to: Floor Covering Weekly, 645 Stewart Ave., Garden City, NY 11530) Ed. Albert Wahnon.
Formerly: Handbook of Contract Floor Covering.

645 677 UK ISSN 0950-5032
STOCKLISTS COLOUR MAGAZINE. a. Mayville Publishing Co., Ltd., Mayville House, 142 Park Rd., Timperley, Altrincham WA15 6QT, England. TEL 061-973-8858. Ed. Roy P. Spragg. circ. 13,000.

684.1   GW
SUMMERTIME; Garten und Freizeitmoebel. (Text in English, German) 1987. a. free. Ferdinand Holzmann Verlag GmbH und Co., Mexikoring 37, 2000 Hamburg 60, Germany. TEL 040-632018-0. Eds. Jorn Holzmann, Joern Holzmann. circ. 8,398.
  Description: News for the outdoor and garden furniture trade.

SUPPLIERS SANITARY - TABLEWARE BOOK. see *HEATING, PLUMBING AND REFRIGERATION*

747.4   CN
SURFACE. (Text in French) 1985. 8/yr. free. Institut Quebecois de Revetements de Sol Inc. - Quebec Institute of Floor Covering, 9420 rue Pascal Gagnon, St-Leonard, Montreal, Que. H1P 1Z7. TEL 514-323-8480. FAX 514-323-1511. adv.; circ. 4,000.
  Description: Discusses such floor covering topics as ceramic, fiber, wood, natural stone, installation and resiliency, as well as wall and window decoration.

642.7 666   FR   ISSN 0039-8780
TABLE ET CADEAU. (Editions in English, French, German, Italian, Spanish) 1961. 10/yr. 350 F. (foreign 485 F.). Editions Ampere, Groupe C.E.P.P., 25, rue Dagorno, 75012 Paris, France. TEL 43-47-30-20. FAX 43-48-56-60. TELEX GMPPAR 216219F. circ. 6,000 (controlled).
  Formerly: Arts et Decor de la Table et du Foyer.

749   CH
TAIWAN FURNITURE. (Text in English) irreg. (approx. 3/yr.). NT.$1400($60) for Middle East, Asia, Oceania; elsewhere $70. China Economic News Service, 561 Chung Hsiao E. Rd. Sec. 4, Taipei, Taiwan 10516, Republic of China. TEL 2-642-2629. FAX 2-642-7422. TELEX 27710-CENSPC. (Subscr. to: P.O. Box 43-60, Taipei, Taiwan, R.O.C.)

749.63   CH
TAIWAN LIGHTING. (Text in English) q. NT.$1600($70) in Asia, Middle East, Oceania; elsewhere $80. China Economic News Service, 561 Chunghsiao E. Rd. Sec. 4, Taipei, Taiwan 10516, Republic of China. TEL 02-642-2629. FAX 02-642-7422. TELEX 27710-CENSPC.

747.5   IT
TAPPEZZIERE IN STOFFA.* 1952. q. (Associazione Tappezzori in Stoffa e Affini) A.T.I.S.E.A., Corso Porta Vigentina 15-a, 20122 Milan, Italy. adv.; circ. 2,500.

TORONTO LIFE HOMES. see *INTERIOR DESIGN AND DECORATION*

684.1   NO
TRE OG MOEBLER. 1969. m. (10/yr.). NOK 250 in Nordic countries; elsewhere NOK 350. (Norske Trevarefabrikkers Landsforbund) John A. Antonsen A-S, Postboks 78 Sentrum, 0101 Oslo 1, Norway. TEL 02-33-67-76. FAX 02-33-23-61. (Co-sponsor: Moebelprodusentenes Landsforbund) Ed. John A. Antonsen. adv.; circ. 2,528.
  Description: Directed to the woodworking and furniture industry, building and furniture architects, and furniture trade and agents.

749   IT   ISSN 0041-445X
TUTTOVILLE. 1967. q. L.16000. Gruppo Editoriale Electa S.p.A., Via Goldoni 1, 20129 Milano, Italy. adv.; illus.; circ. 9,000.
  Supersedes: Furniture Arredamento - Furniture Italy.

U F A C (YEAR). (Upholstered Furniture Action Council) see *FIRE PREVENTION*

U F A C VOLUNTEER. (Upholstered Furniture Action Council) see *FIRE PREVENTION*

674 749   US   ISSN 0199-8714
HD9774.U54
UNFINISHED FURNITURE INDUSTRY; the voice of the unfinished furniture industry. 1979. bi-m. $15. (Unfinished Furniture Industry Institute) U S Expositions, Inc., 1850 Oak St., Northfield, IL 60093. TEL 708-446-8434. FAX 708-446-3523. Ed. Lynda Utterback.
  Description: Provides trade news and information on new product items.

UNIVERSIDADE DE SAO PAULO. MUSEU PAULISTA. COLECAO. SERIE DE MOBILIARIO. see *MUSEUMS AND ART GALLERIES*

747.5   US
UPHOLSTERY DESIGN & MANUFACTURING. Short title: U D M. 1988. m. Delta Communications, Inc. (Chicago) (Subsidiary of: Elsevier Business Press, Inc. (New York), 400 N. Michigan Ave., 13th Fl., Chicago, IL 60611. TEL 312-222-2000. Ed. Michael Chazin. adv.; circ. 18,000.
  Incorporates (in 1990): Upholstery Manufacturing.

V D T A NEWS. (Vacuum Dealers Trade Association) see *BUSINESS AND ECONOMICS — Marketing And Purchasing*

V D T A PHONE DIRECTORY AND PRODUCT GUIDE. (Vacuum Dealers Trade Association) see *BUSINESS AND ECONOMICS — Marketing And Purchasing*

VOGUE DECORATION. see *INTERIOR DESIGN AND DECORATION*

747   AT   ISSN 0042-8035
VOGUE LIVING. 1967. 6/yr. Aus.$30 (foreign Aus.$45)(effective June 1992). Conde Nast Publications Pty. Ltd., 170 Pacific Highway, Greenwich, N.S.W. 2065, Australia. TEL 02-964-3888. FAX 02-964-3882. Ed. Virginia Rayner. adv.; bk.rev.; circ. 40,840. Indexed: Gdlns.
  Formerly: Vogue's Guide to Living.

WATASHI NO HEYA/MY ROOM. see *INTERIOR DESIGN AND DECORATION*

747.3   US   ISSN 0886-9669
WINDOW FASHIONS. 1981. m. $30. G & W McNamara Publishing, Inc., 6 Fifth St. W., Ste. 300, St. Paul, MN 55102-1420. TEL 612-293-1544. FAX 612-293-9497. Ed. Susan Schultz. adv.; charts; illus.; stat.; circ. 23,000. (back issues avail.)
  Former titles: W E S: Voice of the Window Treatment Industry (ISSN 0746-7400); (until 1983): Window Energy Systems (ISSN 0277-0709)
  Description: Articles and information on design, decoration, and treatment (motorized and mechanical shading), with installation and sales advice, business prospects, and an advertisement index.

645   GW   ISSN 0178-2509
WOHNBADEN. s-a. DM.25.20. Krammer Verlag, Hermannstr. 3, 4000 Duesseldorf 1, Germany. TEL 0211-67972-0. FAX 0211-6797231. TELEX 8586639-KRVG-D. Ed.Bd. adv. contact: adv. contact: Heinz Martin.
  Description: Bathroom, kitchen and heating industry news and features. Includes latest designs, practical information, new ideas.

645   GW
WOHNMAGAZIN. 1959. 10/yr. DM.85 (foreign DM.128). Wohnteam-Verlag, Deutz-Muelheimer-Str. 30, 5000 Cologne 21, Germany. TEL 0221-813353. FAX 0221-814732. Ed. Josef Nuxoll. adv.; circ. 4,000.

WOMAN'S DAY HOME DECORATING IDEAS. see *INTERIOR DESIGN AND DECORATION*

643
▼**WOMAN'S DAY KITCHEN & BATH NEW PRODUCT IDEAS.** 1990. a. $3.50. Hachette Magazines, Inc., Woman's Day Special Publications, 1633 Broadway, New York, NY 10019. TEL 212-767-6000. adv.; circ. 450,000.
  Description: Provides information about products that are available to help in remodeling kitchens or baths.

684.1   US   ISSN 0746-1089
TS840
WOOD DIGEST. 1984. m. $65 (Canada and Mexico $80; elsewhere $120). Johnson Hill Press, Inc., 1233 Janesville Ave., Ft. Atkinson, WI 53538. TEL 414-563-6388. FAX 414-563-1701. Ed. Steve Ehle. adv.; illus.; circ. 52,000 (controlled). (tabloid format) Indexed: Tr.& Indus.Ind.
  Formerly: Furniture Wood Digest.
  Description: Provides productivity solutions for manufacturers of furniture, cabinets, millwork and specialty wood products.

XIANDAI SHENGHUO YONGPIN/MODERN DAILY NECESSITIES. see *CONSUMER EDUCATION AND PROTECTION*

ZUHAUSE; Wohnung, Haus und Garten. see *INTERIOR DESIGN AND DECORATION*

INTERNATIONAL COMMERCE

see *Business and Economics–International Commerce*

INTERNATIONAL DEVELOPMENT AND ASSISTANCE

see *Business and Economics–International Development and Assistance*

INTERNATIONAL EDUCATION PROGRAMS

see *Education–International Education Programs*

INTERNATIONAL LAW

see *Law–International Law*

INTERNATIONAL RELATIONS

see *Political Science–International Relations*

INVESTMENTS

see *Business and Economics–Investments*

ISLAM

see *Religions and Theology–Islamic*

JEWELRY, CLOCKS AND WATCHES

739   US   ISSN 0192-7507
ACCENT (NEW YORK). 1976. m. $28. Larkin Group, 485 Seventh Ave., Ste. 1400, New York, NY 10018. TEL 212-594-0880. FAX 212-594-8556. (And: 100 Wells Ave., Newton, MA 02159) Ed. Deanna Vincent. adv.; circ. 15,000. (also avail. in microfilm from UMI; microfiche from UMI; reprint service avail. from UMI)
  Description: Primarily targeted to users of fashion jewelry and fashion watches - fashion forward editorials.

553.8   US
AMERICAN DIAMOND INDUSTRY ASSOCIATION NEWSLETTER. 1982. irreg. American Diamond Industry Association Inc., 71 W. 47th St., New York, NY 10023. TEL 212-575-0525. Ed. Lloyd Jaffe.

739.27   US   ISSN 0002-9041
AMERICAN JEWELRY MANUFACTURER. 1956. m. $16. (Manufacturing Jewelers and Silversmiths of America, Inc) Chilton Co., Chilton Way, Radnor, PA 19089. TEL 215-964-4483. Ed. Mitch Plotnick. adv.; charts; illus.; stat.; circ. 5,200. (reprint service avail. from UMI)
  —BLDSC shelfmark: 0820.910000.
  Description: Includes manufacturing technology, management and marketing topics, industry trends and news.

681.11   UK   ISSN 0003-5785
ANTIQUARIAN HOROLOGY AND THE PROCEEDINGS OF THE ANTIQUARIAN HOROLOGICAL SOCIETY. 1953. q. membership. Antiquarian Horological Society, New House, High St., Ticehurst, Wadhurst, Sussex TN5 7AL, England. TEL 0580 200155. Ed. David Penney. adv.; bk.rev.; illus.; index; circ. 3,000.
  —BLDSC shelfmark: 1549.900000.

JEWELRY, CLOCKS AND WATCHES

745.5 629.288 UK
ANTIQUE CLOCKS; magazine for horological collectors and restorers. 1978. m. £28.60($49) Argus Specialist Publications Ltd., Argus House, Boundary Way, Hemels, Hampstead, Herts HP2 7ST, England. TEL 0442-876661. Ed. John Hunter. adv.; circ. 4,815.
Formerly: Clocks (ISSN 0141-5107)

ANTIQUE COMB COLLECTOR. see *ANTIQUES*

681.11 SP ISSN 0066-510X
ANUARIO DE RELOJERIA Y ARTE EN METAL PARA ESPANA E HISPANOAMERICA. 1959. a. 5000 ptas. Ediciones CEDEL, Calle Mallorca 257, Barcelona 8, Spain. TEL 343-215-6039. FAX 343-215-6088.
Formerly: Anuario de la Relojeria en Espana.

ART AUREA; Schmuck Mesch Objekte. see *ART*

739.27 681.11 IT
ARTEREGALO ORO ARGENTO; trimestrale inviato in abbonamento agli operatori commerciali dei settori oreficeria, gioielleria, argenteria. 1984. q. L.110000. Pubbliemme s.r.l., Via Caracciolo 77, 20155 Milan, Italy. TEL 02-33100954. FAX 02-313864. Dir. Massimo Martini. adv.; circ. 12,700.
Formerly: Arteregalo - Oreficeria, Argenteria, Vetri d'Arte.
Description: Covers production of jewelry, silverware, and watches.

681.11 US ISSN 0254-1173
ASIAN SOURCES TIMEPIECES. 1980. m. $60. Asian Sources Trade Journals, c/o Wordright Enterprises Inc., 1020 Church St., Evanston, IL 60201. TEL 708-475-1900. FAX 708-475-2794. (Subscr. in Asia to: ASIMAG Ltd., P.O. Box 12367, Hong Kong) adv.; circ. 19,700.

739.27 BE
AURIFEX. 1978. irreg., vol.7, 1988. price varies. Association des Diplomes Histoire Art et Archeologie, Centre d'Archeologie Grecque, College Erasme, Place Blaise Pascal 1, B-1348 Louvain-la-Neuve, Belgium. FAX 10-472579. Ed. T. Hackens.

739.27 553.8 AT ISSN 0004-9174
CODEN: AGMLB2
AUSTRALIAN GEMMOLOGIST. 1958. q. Aus.$20. Gemmological Association of Australia, P.O. Box 35, South Yarra, Vic. 3141, Australia. TEL 03-826-9003. Ed. W.H. Hicks. adv.; bk.rev.; index, cum.index; circ. 2,356. (tabloid format; back issues avail.) **Indexed**: AESIS, Chem.Abstr., GeoRef., Mineral.Abstr.

739.27 301 CN ISSN 0829-8726
BEAD FORUM. 1981. s-a. Can.$18($15) Society of Bead Researchers, 1600 Liverpool Ct., Ottawa, Ont. K1A OH3, Canada. TEL 613-990-4814. FAX 613-952-1756. Ed. Karlis Karklins. bibl.; illus.; circ. 300. (back issues avail.)

739.27 301 CN ISSN 0843-5499
BEADS. 1989. a. Can.$18($15) (effective 1992). Society of Bead Researchers, 1600 Liverpool Ct., Ottawa, Ont. K1A OH3, Canada. TEL 613-990-4814. FAX 613-952-1756. Ed. Karlis Karklins. adv.; bk.rev.; illus.; circ. 1,000. (back issues avail.)
Description: Fosters serious research on beads of all materials and periods.
Refereed Serial

739.27 681.11 FR
BIJOUTIER. 1940. m. 460 F. Pierre Johanet et ses Fils, 7 av. Franklin D. Roosevelt, 75008 Paris, France. TEL 33-1-43-59-08-91. FAX 33-1-42-25-59-47. TELEX 649712. adv.; illus.
Formerly: Revue Francaise des Bijoutiers Horlogers (ISSN 0035-2993)

745 SP
BISUTERIA Y BISUTEROS. w. 5000 ptas. (foreign 9000 ptas.). Tecnipublicaciones, S.A., Fernando VI, 27, 28004 Madrid, Spain. TEL 91-419 90 66. TELEX 43905 YEBE E.
Formerly: Catalogo Bisuteria y Bisuteros.

739.27 681.11 UK
BRITISH JEWELLER & WATCH BUYER. 1933. m. £36. E M A P Response Publishing Ltd., Wentworth House, Wentworth St., Peterborough PE1 1DS, England. TEL 0733-63100. FAX 0733-62656. Ed. Alison Marshall. adv.; bk.rev.; illus.; mkt.; stat.; circ. 7,000.
Formerly: British Jeweller (ISSN 0007-0866)

681.11 UK
BRITISH JEWELLER & WATCH BUYER. YEARBOOK. a. £20. E M A P Response Publishing Ltd., Wentworth House, Wentworth St., Peterborough PE1 1DS, England. TEL 0733-63100. FAX 0733-62656. Ed. Alison Marshall. circ. 7,000.
Former titles: British Jeweller. Yearbook; British Jeweller. Buyer's Guide.

551 739.27 CN ISSN 0226-7446
CANADIAN GEMMOLOGIST. 1976. q. Can.$25($25) (typically set in Jan.). Canadian Gemmological Association, 21 Dundas Square, Ste. 1209, Toronto, Ont. M5B 1B7, Canada. TEL 416-603-0451. Ed. Willow Wight. adv.; bk.rev.; index; circ. 600. (back issues avail.)
Description: Covers all aspects of gemmology, new gemstones and localities.
Refereed Serial

739.27 CN ISSN 0008-3917
CANADIAN JEWELLER. 1879. m. Can.$29. Maclean-Hunter Ltd., Business Publication Division, Maclean-Hunter Bldg., 777 Bay St., Toronto, Ont. M5W 1A7, Canada. TEL 416-596-5733. FAX 416-596-5526. Ed. Simon Hally. adv.; charts; illus.; tr.lit.; circ. 6,883. **Indexed**: Can.B.P.I.

CANADIAN JEWELLERY & GIFTWARE DIRECTORY. see *BUSINESS AND ECONOMICS — Trade And Industrial Directories*

CATALOG CONNECTION. see *GIFTWARE AND TOYS*

681.11 SP
CATALOGO RELOJES Y RELOJEROS. a. 2000 ptas. Tecnipublicaciones, S.A., Fernando VI, 27, 28004 Madrid, Spain. TEL 91-319-7889. FAX 91-319-7089. TELEX 43905 YEBE E.

681.11 US
CATALYST (LONG BEACH); happenings of the Self Winding Clock Association. 1979. q. $25. (Self Winding Clock Association) S W C Publications (Long Beach), Box 7704, Long Beach, CA 90807-7704. TEL 310-427-8001. Ed. Bengt E. Honning. bk.rev.; cum.index; circ. 250. (looseleaf format) **Indexed**: Amer.Hist.& Life.

739.27 US ISSN 0194-2905
TS720
CHILTON'S JEWELERS' CIRCULAR-KEYSTONE. 1869. 14/yr. $29. Chilton Co., Chilton Way, Radnor, PA 19089. TEL 215-964-4474. Ed. George Holmes. adv.; bk.rev.; charts; illus.; mkt.; pat.; tr.lit.; index; circ. 37,000. (also avail. in microfilm from UMI; microfiche from UMI; reprint service avail. from UMI) **Indexed**: Bus.Ind., SRI, Tr.& Indus.Ind.
●Also available online. Vendor(s): DIALOG.
Formerly: Jewelers' Circular-Keystone (ISSN 0021-6267)

739.27 IT ISSN 0009-8752
CLESSIDRA. 1945. m. L.100000. Sothis Editrice srl, Via di Monteverde, 74, 00152 Rome, Italy. FAX 06-5374140. Ed. Gianfranco di Mario. adv.; bk.rev.; circ. 16,000.
Description: Focuses on the jewelry and watch industry. Advertises the latest trends in the jewelry market. Covers trade shows and various related events.

739.27 622 US ISSN 1046-462X
COLORED STONE; the international reporter of the gemstone trade. 1988. bi-m. $15. Lapidary Journal, Inc., 60 Chestnut Ave., Ste. 201, Devon, PA 19333. TEL 215-293-1112. FAX 215-293-1717. Ed. Deborah Catalano. adv.; circ. 10,000. (back issues avail.)

688.2 US
COSTUME JEWELRY REVIEW. 1936. s-m. $108. Retail Reporting Bureau, 101 Fifth Ave., New York, NY 10003. TEL 212-255-9595. Ed.Bd. illus.
Formerly: Jewelry Clip Review (ISSN 0021-6283)

553.8 GW ISSN 0343-7892
DEUTSCHE GEMMOLOGISCHE GESELLSCHAFT. ZEITSCHRIFT. 1951. a. DM.84. E. Schweizerbart'sche Verlagsbuchhandlung, Johannesstr. 3A, 7000 Stuttgart 1, Germany. TEL 0711-625001. FAX 0711-625005. TELEX 723363-SCHB-D. Eds. H. Bank, G. Lenzen. adv.; charts; illus.; index. **Indexed**: GeoRef.

681.1 GW ISSN 0070-4040
DEUTSCHE GESELLSCHAFT FUER CHRONOMETRIE. JAHRBUCH. 1950. a. DM.35. Deutsche Gesellschaft fuer Chronometrie e.V., Christopherstr. 5, Postfach 590, 7000 Stuttgart 1, Germany.

739.27 382 US ISSN 0954-5581
DIAMOND INSIGHT; penetrating the multi-faceted world of diamonds. 1988. m. $295. Tryon Mercantile Inc., 790 Madison Ave., Ste. 602, New York, NY 10021. TEL 212-570-4180. FAX 212-772-1286. Ed. Guido Giovannini-Torelli. adv.; bk.rev.; abstr.; bibl.; charts; illus.; index, cum.index; circ. 200. (looseleaf format; back issues avail.)
Description: Intelligence on the world's most important diamonds, future price indicators and key individuals in the industry.

739.27 US ISSN 0199-9753
DIAMOND REGISTRY. BULLETIN. 1969. m. $97 (foreign $125). Diamond Registry, 580 Fifth Ave., New York, NY 10036. TEL 212-575-0444. FAX 212-575-0722. Ed. Joseph Schlussel. bk.rev. (back issues avail.)
Description: Provides information, forecasts trends, wholesale diamond prices, and diamond jewelry news.

739 II ISSN 0970-7727
DIAMOND WORLD. (Text in English) 1973. bi-m. Rs.125($40) Diamond World, International House, A-95 Journal House, Janta Colony, Jaipur 302 004, India. TEL 44398. FAX 91-141-67760. TELEX 365 2410 KALA IN. Ed. Vidya Vinod Kala. adv.; illus.; stat.; tr.lit.

739.27 IS ISSN 0333-5380
DIAMOND WORLD REVIEW. (Text in English) 1974. 6/yr. $78. (World Federation of Diamond Bourses) International Diamond Publications Ltd., P.O. Box 3237, Ramat Gan 52131, Israel. TEL 03-7512165. FAX 03-5752201. TELEX 341730 SPEED IL. Ed. Joseph Sela. adv.; bk.rev.; circ. 6,400.

739.27 669 NE
EDELMETAAL. m. Centraal Orgaan voor de Detailhandel in Juwelen, Goud, Zilver, Uurwerken en Aanver Wante Artikelen en het Uuwerkmakersambacht, Treubstraat 25, 2288 Rijswijk, Netherlands.

681.11 NE
EDELMETAAL UURWERKEN EDELSTENEN. 1946. m. avail. on request. Federatie Goud en Zilver, Van der Spiegelstraat 3, 2518 ES The Hague, Netherlands. TEL 070-469607. FAX 070-643431. TELEX 31468-EDMET. Ed. P.L. Renes. adv.; bk.rev.; bibl.; illus.; stat.; circ. 4,500. **Indexed**: Key to Econ.Sci.

739.27 SZ ISSN 0014-2603
EUROPA STAR - INTERNATIONAL JEWELLERY MAGAZINE. (6 eds. avail.) bi-m. $50. Hugo Buchser S.A., Route des Acacias 25, P.O. Box 30, CH-1211 Geneva 24, Switzerland. TEL 022-3003737. FAX 022-3003748. adv.; bk.rev.; illus.; circ. 38,000.

739.27 GW
EUROPEAN JEWELER SPECIAL. (Text in English, German) 1988. s-a. free. Ruehle - Diebener Verlag GmbH und Co. KG, Postfach 700450, 7000 Stuttgart 70, Germany. TEL 0711-765075. FAX 0711-766551. adv.; charts; illus.; stat.; circ. 12,490. (back issues avail.)
Description: Information and statistics on imports and exports of jewelry, gems, pearls, stones, watches and clocks from all over the world.

553.8 US
FACETS (PEARLAND). q. membership. Association of Women Gemmologists, Box 1844, Pearland, TX 77588. TEL 713-485-1606.
Description: Provides a forum for the exchange of technical and business information.

I J K

JEWELRY, CLOCKS AND WATCHES

688.2 — US — ISSN 0014-8644
FASHION ACCESSORIES. 1951. m. $22. S.C.M. Publications, Inc., 65 W. Main St., Bergenfield, NJ 07621-1696. TEL 201-384-3336. FAX 201-384-6776. Ed. Samuel Mendelson. adv.; bk.rev.; illus.; stat.; circ. 8,000. (tabloid format; back issues avail.)
Description: Directed to manufacturing and wholesaling jewlery exectives.

739.27 — CH
FASHION JEWELRY & ACCESSORIES. m. $60. Taiwan Trade Pages Corp., P.O. Box 72-50, Taipei, Taiwan, Republic of China. TEL 02-3050759. FAX 866-2-3071000. TELEX 24838 TRADEPAG. Eds. Michelle Cheng, Jennifer Yeh.
Formerly: Gifts and Sundries.

739.27 — US
FASHION JEWELRY PLUS. bi-m. Larkin - Pluznick - Larkin, Inc., Box 9103, Newton, MA 02159. TEL 617-964-5100. Ed. Sari Botton Lido.

739.27 669 — NE
FEDERATIE GOUD EN ZILVER. VADEMECUM. a. Federatie Goud en Zilver, Van de Spiegelstraat 3, 2518 The Hague, Netherlands. TEL 070-469607.

681.11 — SZ
FEDERATION DE L'INDUSTRIE HORLOGERE SUISSE. ANNUAL REPORT. (Text in French and German) 1925. a. free. Federation de l'Industrie Horlogere Suisse - Federation of the Swiss Watch Manufacturers Industry, 6 rue d'Argent, 2501 Bienne, Switzerland. TEL 032-225911. FAX 032-233191. TELEX 934239-FHBI. (Dist. in U.S. by: Watchmakers of Switzerland Information Center, Inc., 608 Fifth Ave., 8th Fl., NY 10020) circ. 3,300.
Formerly: Federation Horlogere Suisse. Annual Report (ISSN 0071-4259)

681.11 — SZ
FEDERATION DE L'INDUSTRIE HORLOGERE SUISSE. REVUE. Short title: Revue F H. (Text in French and German) fortn. (22/yr.). 360 Fr. Federation de l'Industrie Horlogere Suisse - Federation of the Swiss Watch Manufacturers, 6 rue d'Argent, 2501 Bienne, Switzerland. TEL 032-225911. FAX 032-233191. TELEX 934239-FHBI.
Formerly: Federation Horlogere Suisse. Bulletin.

681.11 739.27 — FR — ISSN 0015-9573
FRANCE HORLOGERE; revue de l'horlogerie, bijouterie, orfevrerie cadeaux. 1901. m. 500 F. Societe d'Editions Millot et Cie, 20 rue Gambetta, B.P. 169, 25014 Besancon Cedex, France. TEL 81-82-14-90. FAX 87-83-36-82. TELEX 362 976 F. adv.; bk.rev.; illus.; stat.; tr.lit.; circ. 8,450.

736 553.8 — II
GEM & JEWELLERY YEARBOOK. 1974. a. Rs.250($45) International Journal House, A-95 Janta Colony, Jaipur 302 004, India. TEL 44398. FAX 91-141-67760. TELEX 365 2410 KALA IN. Eds. Vidya Vinod Kala, Alok Kala. adv.; bk.rev.; charts; illus.; stat.; tr.lit.; circ. 4,500.

553.8 — US — ISSN 0016-626X
TS720 — CODEN: GEGEA2
GEMS & GEMOLOGY. 1934. q. $49.95. Gemological Institute of America, 1660 Stewart St., Santa Monica, CA 90404. TEL 213-829-2991. Ed. Alice S. Keller. bk.rev.; charts; illus.; index; circ. 10,000. *Indexed:* AESIS, Chem.Abstr, GeoRef.
Description: Industry news and technological and historical information on gems.

739.27 — IT
GIOIELLI & FASCINO. 1978. 4/yr. L.29000. Giorgio Mondadori e Associati S.p.A., Centro Direzionale, Palazzo Canova, 20090 Milan 2 - Segrate, Italy. Ed. Renato Olivieri. adv.; bk.rev.; charts, illus.; circ. 15,000.
Former titles: Gioielli (Milan, 1978); BolaffiArte Gioielli.

739.2 — GW — ISSN 0017-1573
GOLD UND SILBER - UHREN UND SCHMUCK. 1948. m. DM.201.60. Konradin Verlag Robert Kohlhammer GmbH, Ernst-Mey-Str. 8, Postfach 100252, 7022 Leinfelden-Echterdingen, Germany. TEL 0711-7594-0. FAX 0711-7594-390. TELEX 7 255 421. Ed. Klaus Hallwass. adv.; bk.rev.; charts; illus.; pat.; tr.lit.; circ. 10,322. (back issues avail.)
Formed by merger of: Gold und Silber & Uhren und Schmuck (ISSN 0041-5847)
Description: Trade publication for the watch and jewelry industry. Covers the latest trends in designs and styles. Includes reports and announcements of exhibitions and events, list of courses, and positions available.

739 681 — GW
GOLDSCHMIEDE- UND UHRMACHER-JAHRBUCH. 1903. a. DM.20. Ruehle-Diebener Verlag GmbH und Co. KG, Wolfschlugener Str. 5a, Postfach 700450, 7000 Stuttgart 70, Germany. TEL 0711-765075. FAX 0711-766551. adv.; circ. 2,500.
Formerly: Diebeners Goldschmiede- und Uhrmacher-Jahrbuch (ISSN 0070-4814)

739.27 — GW — ISSN 0932-464X
GOLDSCHMIEDE UND UHRMACHER ZEITUNG - EUROPEAN JEWELER. (Supplements avail.) 1892. m. DM.173.40. (Zentralverband fuer das Juwelier-, Gold- und Silberschmiedhandwerk) Ruehle-Diebener Verlag GmbH und Co. KG, Wolfschlugener Str. 5a, Postfach 700450, 7000 Stuttgart 70, Germany. TEL 0711-765075. FAX 0711-766551. adv.; bk.rev.; illus.; tr.lit.; circ. 15,100. *Indexed:* Chem.Abstr.
Formerly: Goldschmiede Zeitung - European Jeweler und Uhrmacherzeitschrift (ISSN 0017-1689); *Incorporates:* Deutsche Urmacher-Zeitschrift (ISSN 0012-0863)

739.27 — DK — ISSN 0017-5544
GULDSMEDEBLADET. 1917. m. (11/yr.). DKK 590. Guldsmedefagets Faellesrad, DK-4894 Oester Ulslev, Denmark. TEL 53-86-55-66. FAX 53-86-55-66. Ed. Bendix Bech-Thostrup. adv.; bk.rev.; bibl.; illus.; stat.; index, cum.index; circ. 1,625.

739.2 — SW — ISSN 0282-4175
GULDSMEDSTIDNINGEN. 1915. m. (8/yr.). SEK 425 (foreign SEK 600). Sveriges Juvelerare- och Guldsmedsfoerbund - Swedish Jewellers and Goldsmiths Association, Gamla Brogatan 19, S-111 20 Stockholm, Sweden. FAX 08-248025. adv.; bk.rev.; illus.; index; circ. 1,550.
Formerly: Svensk Guldsmeds Tidning (ISSN 0039-6559)

739.27 — NO — ISSN 0046-6603
GULLSMEDKUNST. 1910. 11/yr. NOK 275. Norges Gullsmedforbund - Norwegian Goldsmiths' Association, Storgaten 14, 0184 Oslo 1, Norway. Ed. Berit Roehne. adv.; bk.rev.; index; circ. 1,825. (back issues avail.)

HENRY'S AUKTIONEN. see *ANTIQUES*

739.27 681.11 — HK
HONG KONG JEWELLERY BI-ANNUAL. (Text in English) 1985. s-a. $48 (free to qualified personnel). Hong Kong Trade Development Council, 36-39th Fl., Office Tower, Convention Plaza, 1 Harbour Rd., Wanchai, Hong Kong. TEL 584-4333. FAX 824-0249. Ed. Saul Lockhart. circ. 20,000.
Formerly: Hong Kong Jewellery Annual; Which supersededs in part: Hong Kong Jewellery and Watches.

739.27 — HK
HONG KONG JEWELLERY MAGAZINE. (Text in Chinese, English) 1978. q. HK.$120($16) Ridgeville Ltd., Unit 7, 3 Fl., Block A, Focal Industrial Centre, 21 Man Lok St., Hunghom, Kowloon, Hong Kong. TEL 3344311. FAX 852-7641956. Eds. Robin Savidge, Catherine Chan. circ. 15,000.
Description: Carries advertisements of jeweleries. Aimed at jewellers and jewelry traders throughout the world.

681.11 — HK
HONG KONG WATCHES & CLOCKS. (Text in English) 1988. s-a. $48 (free to qualified personnel). Hong Kong Trade Development Council, 36-39th Fl., Office Tower, Convention Plaza, 1 Harbour Rd., Wanchai, Hong Kong. TEL 584-4333. FAX 824-0249. Ed. Saul Lockhart. circ. 20,000.
Supersedes in part: Hong Kong Jewellery and Watches.

681.11 — US — ISSN 0145-9546
TS540
HOROLOGICAL TIMES. 1977. m. $40. American Watchmakers Institute, 3700 Harrison Ave., Box 11011, Cincinnati, OH 45211. TEL 513-661-3838. FAX 513-661-3131. Ed. Milton C. Stevens. adv.; bk.rev.; circ. 9,000.

739.27 — IT
INDUSTRIA ORAFA ITALIANA; mensile di arte orafa, orologi, argento. 1917. m. L.60000. Globo Editoriale s.r.l., Via S. Calimero, 1, 20122 Milan, Italy. TEL 02-58309823. FAX 02-58309739. adv.; circ. 8,000.

681.11 — US
INTERNATIONAL WRIST WATCH. bi-m. $5.95 per no. Hyde Park Group, 2001 W. Main St., Stamford, CT 06902. TEL 203-969-2533. FAX 203-348-3555.

739.27 — IS — ISSN 0021-2016
ISRAEL DIAMONDS. (Text in English) 1966. bi-m. $78. International Diamond Publications Ltd., P.O. Box 3237, Ramat Gan 52131, Israel. TEL 03-7512165. FAX 03-5752201. TELEX 341730 SPEED IL. Ed. Joseph Sela. adv.; bk.rev.; illus.; circ. 4,500.

739.27 — CN
J W PLUS. 1982. 6/yr. $65 (foreign $100). Jewellery World Ltd., 20 Eglinton Ave. W., Ste. 1203, Toronto, Ont. M4R 1K8, Canada. TEL 416-480-1450. FAX 416-480-2342. Ed. Joanne McGarry. adv.; circ. 9,015. (tabloid format)

745.594 — US
JEWELERS' BOOK CLUB NEWS. 1979. q. (Jewelers' Book Club) Chilton Co. (Subsidiary of: A B C, Inc.), Chilton Way, Radnor, PA 19089-0140. TEL 215-964-4490. Ed. Donald S. McNeil. bk.rev.; circ. 13,000.
Description: Geared to retail and manufacturing jewelers. Offers educational and coffee table publications pertinent to the industry.

739.27 — US
JEWELERS, INC.. 1910. m. $24. Trades Publishing Co., 142 W. Main St., Albert Lea, MN 56007. TEL 507-373-2316. FAX 507-373-0605. Ed. Patti Reick. adv.; circ. 4,8,000.
Formerly: Northwestern Jeweler (ISSN 0029-3490)
Description: For retail jewelers. Features news on conventions, seminars, selling techniques, new products in the industry, regional items on jewelers, and state association news.

739.27 — AT
JEWELLERS ASSOCIATION OF AUSTRALIA. NATIONAL NEWSLETTER. 1968. q. free to members (foreign Aus.$25). Jewellers Association of Australia Limited, P.O. Box E 446, Queen Victoria Terrace, Canberra, A.C.T. 2600, Australia. TEL 06-282-3211. FAX 06-282-2725. Ed. Kim Hilliard. adv.; bk.rev.; circ. 1,500.
Former titles: Jewellers Association of Australia. Federal Newsletter (ISSN 0816-6706); Australian Jewellers Association. Federal Newsletter; Australian Jewellers Association. Jewellers News.

681.1 739.27 — UK
JEWELLERS' REFERENCE BOOK. 1931. a. £19.50. Whitehall Press Ltd., Earl House, Maidstone ME14 1PE, England. TEL 0622-759841. FAX 0622-675734. adv.
Formerly (until 1986): Watchmaker, Jeweller and Silversmith Directory of Trade Names and Punch Marks (ISSN 0083-7628)

JEWELRY, CLOCKS AND WATCHES

745.594   UK
JEWELLERY. 6th ed., 1987. every 18 mos. £155 per no. Key Note Publications Ltd., Field House, Old Field Rd., Hampton TW12 2HQ, England. TEL 01-783-0755.
Description: Review of the jewelry industry in the U.K., including industry structure, market size and trends, recent developments, prospects and company profiles.

739.27   HK
JEWELLERY NEWS ASIA. (Text in English) 1983. m. HK.$240($89) Jewellery News Asia Ltd., 1st Fl., Washington Plaza, 230 Wanchai Rd., Wanchai, Hong Kong. TEL 8322011. FAX 8329208. Ed. Peter Brindisi. adv.; charts; illus.; stat.; tr.lit.; circ. 8,000. (back issues avail.)
Description: News for executives in jewelry, gemstone and watch and clock trades. Covers new products, manufacturing and marketing techniques.

681.11   NZ
JEWELLERY TIME. 1925. m. (11/yr.). NZ.$96. Jewellers and Matchmakers of NZ Inc., Box 386, Auckland, New Zealand. FAX 099-3097-798. Ed. Carol Bucknell. adv.; bk.rev.; circ. 709.
Former titles: New Zealand Jeweller and Watchmaker; New Zealand Horological Journal (ISSN 0028-8195)

745.594   CN   ISSN 0823-1346
JEWELLERY WORLD. 1976. 6/yr. Can.$65 (foreign Can.$100). Jewellery World Ltd., 20 Eglington Ave. W., Ste. 1203, Toronto, Ont. M4R 1K8, Canada. TEL 416-480-1450. FAX 416-480-2342. Ed. Joanne McGarry. adv.; circ. 9,015.

681.11   AT   ISSN 0811-2274
JEWELLERY WORLD. 1981. bi-m. Aus.$24($40) Jewellery World Pty. Ltd., P.O. Box 63, Eastwood, N.S.W. 2122, Australia. TEL 2-804-6517. FAX 2-804-6517. Ed. D.D. Michel. adv.; circ. 3,050.

553   US
THE JEWELRY APPRAISER. 1980. q. $39 (foreign $59)(effective 1992). National Association of Jewelry Appraisers, Box 6558, Annapolis, MD 21401-0558. TEL 301-261-8270. Ed. James V. Jollitt. adv.; bk.rev.; circ. 1,200. (back issues avail.)
Description: Discusses the value and evaluation techniques of jewels and gems.

658   US
▼**JEWELRY BUYERS.** 1990. a. $197. Salesman's Guide, Inc., A Reed Reference Publishing Company, Division of Reed Publishing (USA) Inc., 121 Chanlon Rd., New Providence, NJ 07974. TEL 800-521-8110. FAX 609-665-6688. (Subscr. to: Order Dept., Box 31, New Providence, NJ 07974)
Description: Lists jewelry buyers nationwide.

739.27   US
JEWELRY FASHION GUIDE. 1976. a. Miller Freeman Inc. (New York) (Subsidiary of: United Newspapers Group), 1515 Broadway, New York, NY 10036. TEL 212-869-1300. FAX 212-302-6273. Ed. Lynn Diamond. adv.; illus.; circ. 37,000 (controlled).

681   US   ISSN 0738-7261
JEWELRY NEWSLETTER INTERNATIONAL. 1973. m. $250. Newsletters International, Inc., 2600 South Gessner Rd., Houston, TX 77063. TEL 713-783-0100. Ed. Len Fox.

736.2   II   ISSN 0022-1244
TS720
JOURNAL OF GEM INDUSTRY. (Text in English) 1963. bi-m. Rs.200($45) Journal of Gem Industry, A-95 Journal House, Janta Colony, Jaipur 302 004, India. TEL 44398. FAX 91-141-42973. TELEX 365-2410-KALA-IN. Ed. Alok Kala. adv.; bk.rev.; charts; illus.; stat.

553.8   UK
JOURNAL OF GEMMOLOGY. 1947. q. £80. Gemmological Association and Gem Testing Laboratory of Great Britain, 27 Greville St., London EC1N 8SU, England. TEL 071-404-3334. FAX 071-404-8843. Ed. E.A. Jobbins. adv.; bk.rev.; abstr.; bibl.; cum.index every 2 yrs.; circ. 4,000. (also avail. in microform from UMI; reprint service avail. from UMI) *Indexed:* AESIS, Chem.Abstr., GeoRef.
Formerly: Journal of Gemmology and Proceedings of the Gemmological Association of Great Britain (ISSN 0022-1252)

739.27   SP   ISSN 0213-120X
JOYAS & JOYEROS; revista independiente para el profesional de la joyeria relojeria y orfebreria. 1985. bi-m. 6500 ptas. (foreign 10000 ptas.). Tecnipublicaciones, S.A., Fernando VI, 27, 28004 Madrid, Spain. TEL 91-319-7889. FAX 91-319-7089. TELEX 43905 YEBE E. Ed. Jose Arquero Hidalgo. adv.; circ. 10,000.
Incorporates: Diamantes Oro.

681   FI   ISSN 0085-2600
KULTASEPPIEN LEHTI. 1926. 8/yr. FIM 135. Suomen Kultaseppien Liitto r. y. - Finnnish Goldsmith Association, Vuorikatu 3 A 10, 00100 Helsinki 10, Finland. Ed. Pekka Kautto. adv.; bk.rev.; index; circ. 1,500.

LAPIDARY JOURNAL. see *HOBBIES*

LAPIS; die aktuelle Monatsschrift fuer Liebhaber und Sammler von Mineralien und Edelsteinen. see *MINES AND MINING INDUSTRY*

745.594 659.152   IT
MODA E BIJOUX. (Text in English and Italian) 1987. s-a. $55. Edizioni Gold S.r.l., Viale Zara 7-9, 20159 Milan, Italy. TEL 02-680189. FAX 02-685888. TELEX 311271 MIPP. Ed. Florinda Gaudio.
Description: Covers costume jewelry and fashion accessories.

739.27 681.11   US   ISSN 0193-208X
MODERN JEWELER. NATIONAL EXECUTIVE. 1901. m. $25 (foreign $100). Vance Publishing Corporation, 7950 College Blvd., Shawnee Mission, KS 66210. TEL 913-451-2200. FAX 913-451-5821. Ed. Joseph Thompson. adv.; bk.rev.; illus.; mkt.; index; circ. 38,000. (also avail. in microform from UMI)
Supersedes in part: Modern Jeweler (ISSN 0026-7864)

739.27   US   ISSN 0744-2513
MODERN JEWELER NATIONAL. 1901. m. $35 (foreign $100). Vance Publishing Corporation, 7950 College Blvd., Shawnee Mission, KS 66210. TEL 913-451-2200. (Subscr. to: Box 1416, Lincolnshire, IL 60069) Ed. Joseph Thompson. circ. 38,000 (controlled). (also avail. in microfilm; back issues avail.)

739.27   IT   ISSN 0392-6079
MONDO DEI GIOIELLI. (Text in English and Italian) 1977. 3/yr. L.40000 (foreign L.110000)(effective 1992). Tecniche Nuove s.p.a., Via Menotti 14, 20129 Milan, Italy. TEL 02-75701. FAX 02-7570205. adv.; illus.; circ. 14,000.
Formerly: Alam al Mugiauharat.
Description: Information on the exhibitions and collections of Italian goldsmiths and jewelers.

332.743   UK   ISSN 0047-9020
N.P.A. JOURNAL. 1959. bi-m. £2. National Pawnbrokers Association (Inc.), Park 1 Bell Yard, London WC2, England.

681.11   US   ISSN 0027-8688
NK11
NATIONAL ASSOCIATION OF WATCH AND CLOCK COLLECTORS. BULLETIN. 1946. 6/yr. $25. National Association of Watch and Clock Collectors, Inc., 514 Poplar St., Columbia, PA 17512. TEL 717-684-8261. FAX 717-684-0878. Ed. Kathy I. Everett. bk.rev.; abstr.; charts; illus.; index, cum.index every 9 to 10 yrs.; circ. 35,000. (back issues avail.)

739.27 681.11   US   ISSN 0027-9544
NATIONAL JEWELER. 1906. bi-m. $480. Miller Freeman Inc. (New York) (Subsidiary of: United Newspapers Group), 1515 Broadway, New York, NY 10036. TEL 212-869-1300. FAX 212-302-6273. Ed. Lynn Diamond. adv.; bk.rev.; charts; illus.; mkt.; tr.lit.; index; circ. 34,700.
●Also available online.
Formerly: National Jeweler and National Watchmaker.

646
NATIONAL JEWELER'S IN STYLE. 1976. a. Miller Freeman Inc. (New York) (Subsidiary of: United Newspapers Group), 1515 Broadway, New York, NY 10036. TEL 212-869-1300. FAX 212-302-6273. adv.; circ. 34,700.
Formerly: National Jeweler Annual Fashion Guide.

681.11   JA   ISSN 0029-0416
NIHON TOKEI GAKKAISHI/HOROLOGICAL INSTITUTE OF JAPAN. JOURNAL.* (Text in Japanese; summaries in English) 1957. q. 2000 Yen. Nihon Gakkai Jimu Senta, 4-16, Yayoi 2-chome, Bunkyo-ku, Tokyo 113, Japan. Ed. G. Nishimura. adv. *Indexed:* JTA, Sci.Abstr.

739.27   JA
▼**NIKKEI JEWELLERY.** (Text in Japanese) 1991. m. 20000 Yen. Nikkei Business Publications, Inc., 3-3-23, Misakicho, Chiyoda-ku, Tokyo 101, Japan. TEL 03-5210-8502. FAX 03-5210-8119. Ed. Osamu Hasuike.
Description: Covers information for retailers, wholesalers, and other specialists in all areas of Japan's jewelry market. Includes management methods, new trends, consumer survey results and more.

739.27 681.11   JA   ISSN 0029-0653
NIPPON KIKINZOKU TOKEI SHINBUN/JAPAN PRECIOUS METALS AND WATCH NEWS. (Text in Japanese) every 10 days. 5000 Yen. Nippon Kikinzoku Tokei Shinbunsha, Tokyo Kikokaikan Bldg., 2-19-16 Negishi, Taito-ku, Tokyo 110, Japan. Ed. Chosaburo Someya. adv.

739.27   IT   ISSN 0471-7376
ORAFO ITALIANO. 1947. m. L.190. L'Orafo Italiano S.r.l., Via Nervesa 2, 20139 Milan, Italy. TEL 92-5392288. FAX 92-5695814. Ed. Gianni Roggini. adv.; illus.; circ. 10,000.
Description: Includes color editorials on jewelry, precious stones, watches and trade fairs.

739   IT   ISSN 0473-1174
ORAFO ITALIANO NEL MONDO/ITALIAN GOLDSMITH IN THE WORLD. (Text in English and Italian) 1956. 3/yr. free. L'Orafo Italiano S.r.l., Via Nervesa 2, 20139 Milan, Italy. TEL 92-5392288. FAX 92-5695814. adv.; charts; illus.; circ. 20,000.
Description: Includes color editorials on jewelry, precious stones, watches and production methods.

681.11   IT   ISSN 0030-4182
ORAFO OROLOGIAIO. 1945. bi-m. L.10000. Associazione Piemontese Orafi Orologiai, Via Bogino N. 1, 10123 Turin, Italy. Ed. Italo Ambrosio. adv.; charts; illus.; circ. 2,500.

745.5   US   ISSN 0148-3897
NK7300
ORNAMENT; a quarterly of jewelry and personal adornment. 1974. q. $25. Ornament Inc., Box 2349, San Marcos, CA 92079-2349. TEL 619-599-0222. FAX 619-599-0228. Eds. Robert K. Liu, Carolyn L.E. Benesh. adv.; bk.rev.; circ. 35,000. (back issues avail.) *Indexed:* A.I.C.P., Art Ind., Artbibl.Mod.; Br.Archaeol.Abstr.
Formerly (until 1979): Bead Journal (ISSN 0094-2448)
Description: Covers ancient, ethnic, and contemporary jewelry, costumes and artist-made clothing.

681.11   IT
OROLOGI; le misure del tempo. 1987. m. L.77000 (foreign L.215000). Technimedia s.r.l., Via Carlo Perrier, 9, 00157 Rome, Italy. TEL 06-4180300. FAX 06-4512524. Ed. Marco Marinacci.

745.594   IT
OROLOGI DA POLSO. 1987. bi-m. L.40000 (foreign L.80000). Studio Zeta S.r.l., Via S. Fruttuoso, 10, 20052 Monza, Italy. TEL 039-731952. FAX 736500. Ed. Elena Introna.

PLATINUM (YEAR). see *MINES AND MINING INDUSTRY*

736.2   AT
POINTER.* q. Combined Victorian Gem Clubs Association, P.O. 121, Doncaster, Vic. 3108, Australia. adv. *Indexed:* Educ.Ind.

739.27 681.11   UK   ISSN 0034-6063
RETAIL JEWELLER; for retailers, wholesalers and manufacturers of jewelry, clocks, watches, silverware, etc., dealers and designers. 1963. fortn. £58.40($95.19) International Thomson Business Publishing, 100 Avenue Road, London NW3 3TP, England. TEL 01-935-6611. Ed. Jill Bousoulengas. adv.; bk.rev.; illus.; circ. 10,031. (newspaper; also avail. in microfilm from UMI)
Incorporates: Gemmologist; Goldsmiths Journal & Horological Review.

2566 JEWELRY, CLOCKS AND WATCHES — ABSTRACTING, BIBLIOGRAPHIES, STATISTICS

SAN FRANCISCO GIFTCENTER AND JEWELRYMART BUYER'S GUIDE. see *GIFTWARE AND TOYS*

739.27 GW ISSN 0341-9002
SCHMUCK UND UHREN. 1947. 8/yr. DM.90 (including special insert DM.144). Ebner Verlag GmbH, Postfach 3060, D-7900 Ulm, Germany. Ed. R.J. Ludwig. adv.; bk.rev.; bibl.; charts; illus.; mkt.; pat.; tr.lit.; index; circ. 15,000.
  Formerly: Neue uhrmacher-Zeitung (ISSN 0028-341X)

681.11 SZ
SCHWEIZERISCHE UHRMACHER- UND GOLDSCHMIEDE-ZEITUNG/JOURNAL SUISSE DES HORLOGERS ET DES BIJOUTIERS-ORFEVRES. (Text in French, German) 1878. m. 140 Fr. (Zentralverband Schweizerischer Uhrmacher) Editions Scriptar S.A., Ch. Creux de Corey 25, CH-1093 La Conversion-Lausanne, Switzerland. (Co-sponsor: Vereinigung Schweizerischer Juwelen- und Edelmetallbranchen) adv.; bk.rev.; charts; illus.; index; circ. 2,500.
  Formerly: Schweizerische Uhrmacher Zeitung (ISSN 0036-7761)

681.11 SW
SVENSK URMAKARTIDNING.* 1887. m. SEK 250. (Sveriges Urmakarefoerbund) Ohlsson Reklam Information AB, Everoed 13, S-27300 Tomlille, Sweden. Ed. Elbe Oldenburg. adv.; bk.rev.; charts; illus.; tr.lit.; index; circ. 1,800.
  Former titles: Ur Optik; Svensk Ur- Optik Tidning (ISSN 0039-680X)

681.11 739.27 SZ ISSN 0039-7520
SWISS WATCH AND JEWELRY JOURNAL. 1876. m. 75 Fr.($54) (European Watch, Clocks and Jewellery Fair) Editions Scriptar S.A., Ch. Creux de Corsy 25, 1093 La Conversion-Lausanne, Switzerland. adv.; bk.rev.; illus.; circ. 20,000.

TAIWAN GIFTS & HOUSEWARES. see *BUSINESS AND ECONOMICS — Trade And Industrial Directories*

745.594 BE
TECHNICA. 1948. m. 3000 Fr. Comite National de la Bijouterie, Horlogerie, Joaillerie, Orfevrerie, Blvd. de Smet de Naeyer 290a, 1090 Brussels, Belgium. TEL 2-4282245. FAX 2-4283078. adv.; bk.rev.; circ. 2,400.

681.11 617.752 DK
TID OG SYN. m. (except Aug.). DKK 303.25. Urmagernes- og Optikernes Landssammenslutning, Upsalagade 20, 4, DK-Copenhagen Oe, Denmark. TEL 31-265419. FAX 35-43-21-04. adv.; circ. 1,850.
  Description: Directed to members of the trade union for watchmakers and opticians.

681.11 SZ
U B A H REVUE. q. Union des Associations de Fabricants de Parties Detachees Horlogeres, Rue Daniel Jeanrichard 44, CH-2301 Chaux-de-Fonds, Switzerland. TEL 231672.

681.11 SZ
U S F B INFORMATIONS. 1968. m. (10/yr.). $25. Union Suisse des Fabricants de Boites de Montres, Case Postale 75, 2500 Bienne 4, Switzerland. stat.; circ. controlled.

739.27 AU ISSN 0041-5839
UHREN JUWELEN. 1960. m. S.780. Oesterreichischer Wirtschaftsverlag, Nikolsdorfer Gasse 7-11, A-1050 Vienna, Austria. TEL 0222-555585. TELEX 1-11669. tr.mk.; index; circ. 3,400.
  Formerly: Ein- und Verkaufsfuehrer der Oesterreichischen Uhren- und Schmuckwirtschaft (ISSN 0013-2632)

739.2 GW
UHREN - JUWELEN - SCHMUCK. 1946. s-m. DM.145.20. Bielefelder Verlagsanstalt GmbH & Co. KG, Niederwall 53, Postfach 1140, 4800 Bielefeld, Germany. TEL 0521-595-520. adv.; bk.rev.; charts; illus.; mkt.; pat.; tr.lit.; index; circ. 9,000.
  Formerly: Uhr (ISSN 0041-5820)

681.11 GW
UHREN UND SCHMUCK JOURNEL. 1950. m. DM.27.50. (Bundesgrosshandelsverband fuer Uhren- und Uhrentechnischen Bedarf e.V.) MC Wolf GmbH und Co., Fabrikstr. 17, 4630 Herne, Germany. Ed. J.P. Polzin. adv.; bk.rev.; circ. 5,200.
  Formerly: Uhrenjournel (ISSN 0041-5855)

681.11 SZ ISSN 0049-5042
UHRENFACHGESCHAEFT/MAGASIN D'HORLOGERIE SPECIALISE. vol.22, 1971. bi-m. 16 Fr. to non-members. (Verband Schweizerischer Uhrenfachgeschaefte - Swiss Watch Shops Association) Buchdruckerei K. Furter, Scheidgasse 48, CH-3800 Unterseen-Interlaken, Switzerland. adv.; charts; illus.; circ. 1,250.

739.27 DK
URE & OPTIK. 1893. m. (10/yr.). DKK 250. A-Reklame, Autoriseret Reklamebureau A-S - A-Reklame, Authorized Advertising Co., Ltd., Lillehoejvej 10, Postbox 306, DK-8600 Silkeborg, Denmark. Ed. Harry Krojgaard. adv.; bk.rev.; bibl.; charts; illus.; stat.; tr.lit.; index; circ. 1,300.
  Former titles (until Jan. 1979): Urmager-Tidende (ISSN 0042-1081); Dansk Tidsskrift for Urmagere.

739.2 IT
VALENZA GIOIELLI. 1958. q. L.75000. (Associazione Orafa Valenzana) A O V Service s.r.l., Piazza Don Minzoni 1, 15048 Valenza, Italy. TEL 31-941851. FAX 31-946609. (Subscr. to: A I E, Via Gadames, 89, I-20152 Milan, Italy) Dir. Rosanna Comi. adv.; circ. 16,000.
  Formerly (until Jan. 1987): Orafo Valenzano (ISSN 0030-4190)

745.594 IT
VICENZAORO MAGAZINE. (Text in English and Italian) 1984. 3/yr. $60. (Vicenza Trade Fair Board) Pentastudio, Corso Palladio 114, 36100 Vicenza, Italy. TEL 0444 238687. (Subscr. to: Ente Fiera di Vicenza, Via dell'Oreficeria, 36100 Vicenza, Italy)

VINTAGE FASHIONS; clearing house for information on vintage clothing, jewelry, fashion accessories. see *CLOTHING TRADE — Fashions*

739.27 IT ISSN 1120-7817
VOGUE GIOIELLO. s-a. L.19000 (foreign L.38000). Edizioni Conde Nast S.p.A., Piazza Castello 27, 20121 Milan, Italy. TEL 02-85611. FAX 02-870686. Ed. A. Milella. adv.; circ. 45,000.

681.11 739.27 US ISSN 0279-6198 TS540
WATCH AND CLOCK REVIEW. 1936. m. $15. Bell Publications, 2403 Champa St., Denver, CO 80205. TEL 303-296-1600. Ed. Jayne Barrick. adv.; illus.; circ. 14,000. (also avail. in microform from UMI)
  Formerly (until 1981): American Horologist and Jeweler (ISSN 0002-8797)

681.11 739.27 UK ISSN 0043-1079
WATCHMAKER, JEWELLER & SILVERSMITH. 1875. m. £40. Whitehall Press Ltd., Earl House, Maidstone, Kent ME14 1PE, England. TEL 0622-759841. FAX 0622-675734. Ed. Maggie Gebbett. adv.; bk.rev.; illus.; circ. 5,500.

739.27 380.1 HK
WORLD JEWELOGUE (YEAR). (Text and summaries in English) 1986. a. HK.$190($35) Headway International Publications Co., 907 Great Eagle Centre, 23 Harbour Road, Hong Kong. TEL 852-827-5121. FAX 852-827-7064. TELEX 72554 HEWAY HX. (Dist. in U.S. by: Leonard Estrin Publications, 20832 Roscoe Blvd., Canoga Park, CA 91304) Eds. Rebecca Yung, Doreen Wong. pat.; tr.lit.; cum.index: 1986-1992; circ. 100,00. (back issues avail.)
  Description: Color catalogue with references and order guides for the international jewelry industry.

681.11 380.1 HK
WORLD TIME CATALOGUE (YEAR). (Text and summaries in English) 1987. a. HK.$190($35) Headway International Publications Co., 907 Great Eagle Centre, 23 Harbour Road, Hong Kong. TEL 852-827-5121. FAX 853-827-7064. TELEX 72554 HEWAY HX. (Dist. in U.S. by: Leonard Estrin Publications, 20832 Roscoe Blvd., Canoga Park, CA 91204) Eds. Rebecca Yung, Doreen Wong. illus.; pat.; tr.lit.; cum.index: 1987-1992; circ. 50,000. (back issues avail.)
  Description: Color catalogue with references and order guides for the international horological industry.

739.27 IT
18 KARATI GOLD & FASHION. 1971. bi-m. $85. Edizioni Gold s.r.l., Viale Zara, 7-9, 20159 Milan, Italy. TEL 02-680189. FAX 02-685888. TELEX 311271 MIPP. Ed. Florinda Gaudio. adv.

JEWELRY, CLOCKS AND WATCHES — Abstracting, Bibliographies, Statistics

739.27 US
JEWELERS' BOOK CLUB CATALOG. 1979. a. $3. (Jewelers' Book Club) Chilton Co. (Subsidiary of: A B C, Inc.), Chilton Way, Radnor, PA 19089. TEL 215-964-4478. Ed. Donald S. McNeil. bk.rev.; circ. 13,000.
  Description: Geared to the retail and manufacturing jeweler, offering educational and coffee table publications pertinent to the industry.

JEWELERS' BOOK CLUB NEWS. see *JEWELRY, CLOCKS AND WATCHES*

JOURNALISM

A A F COMMUNICATOR. (American Advertising Federation) see *ADVERTISING AND PUBLIC RELATIONS*

070 UK
A B C CIRCULATION REVIEW. 1931. s-a. membership. Audit Bureau of Circulations, 207-209 High St., Berkhamsted, Hertfordshire HP4 1AD, England. TEL 44-442-870800. FAX 44-442-877407.

070.172 347.9 US
A C C N BULLETIN.* q. (Associated Court and Commercial Newspapers) Daily Journal of Commerce, Box 10127, Portland, OR 97210. TEL 503-226-1311. Ed. Stutz Maul. circ. 100. (looseleaf format; back issues avail.)
  Description: Information regarding newspaper issues and Associated Court and Commercial Newspapers' activities.

070 US
A I M REPORT. 1972. s-m. $22.95. Accuracy in Media, Inc., 1275 K St., N.W., Ste. 1150, Washington, DC 20005. TEL 202-371-6710. FAX 202-371-9054. Ed. Reed J. Irvine. index; circ. 27,000. (back issues avail.; reprint service avail.)
  ●Also available online.

070 US
A P F REPORTER. 1977. q. free. Alicia Patterson Foundation, 1001 Pennsylvania Ave., N.W., Ste. 1250, Washington, DC 20004. TEL 202-393-5995. FAX 301-951-8512. Ed. Margaret Engel. circ. 3,200 (paid); 3,200 (controlled). (back issues avail.)
  ●Also available online. Vendor(s): DIALOG.
  Description: Investigative reporting and photojournalism based on the year-long research projects of the foundation's fellows.

070 US
A S N E. PROCEEDINGS (YEAR). (Proceedings of the Society's annual convention) a. $25. American Society of Newspaper Editors, Box 17004, Washington, DC 20041. TEL 703-648-1144.
  Formerly: Problems of Journalism.

808.02 371.3 US
A W P CHRONICLE. 1970. 6/yr. $18. Associated Writing Programs, Norfolk, VA 23529-0079. TEL 804-683-3839. Ed. D.W. Fenza. adv.; bk.rev.; circ. 12,000. (tabloid format)
  Formerly: A W P Newsletter (ISSN 0194-6498)

AARETS PRESSEFOTO. see *PHOTOGRAPHY*

070 GW ISSN 0065-0323
ABHANDLUNGEN UND MATERIALEN ZUR PUBLIZISTIK. 1962. irreg. price varies. (Freie Universitaet Berlin, Institut fuer Publizistik) Colloquium Verlag, Luetzowstr. 105, 1000 Berlin 30, Germany. Ed. Bernd Soesemann. circ. 1,000.

070 301.16 KE
AFRICA MEDIA MONOGRAPH SERIES. 1986. irreg. $13 (outside Africa $16). African Council for Communication Education, P.O. Box 47495, Nairobi, Kenya. TEL 227043. TELEX 25148 ACCE KE.
  Description: Presents various issues related to journalism and communication by African and other communication scholars, researchers and practitioners.

070   SZ
AFRIKA BULLETIN. (Text in German) 1976. q. 15 Fr.($8) Afrika Komitee, Postfach 1072, CH-4001 Basel, Switzerland. FAX 061-25-61-16. Ed.Bd. adv.; bk.rev.; circ. 1,200. (back issues avail.)

AGENDA IN BRIEF. see *ETHNIC INTERESTS*

AIR ACCIDENTS & THE NEWS MEDIA. see *AERONAUTICS AND SPACE FLIGHT*

070   200   US   ISSN 0002-5542
ALL-CHURCH PRESS NEWSPAPERS.* 1912. w. subscriptions through local congregations only. c/o Lambuth Tomlinson, Box 1159, Fort Worth, TX 76101. TEL 817-926-9580. Ed. Walter Winsett. adv.; bk.rev.; illus.; circ. 207,088. (newspaper)

070   US   ISSN 1046-0470
AMERICAN AMATEUR JOURNALIST. 1936. bi-m. membership only. American Amateur Press Association, 1923 20th St., Portsmouth, OH 45662. TEL 614-353-6358. Ed. Linda Donaldson. circ. 325. (back issues avail.)
    Description: Covers writing and printing for fun; any age, any level of experience, any subject, any technology.

070   US   ISSN 0882-1127
PN4700
AMERICAN JOURNALISM. 1982. q. $25 (typically set in Oct.). American Journalism Historians Association, Communication Dept., University of Tulsa, 600 S. College Ave., Tulsa, OK 74104-3189. TEL 918-631-2830. Ed. John Pauly. adv.; bk.rev.; circ. 350.
    —BLDSC shelfmark: 0840.135000.
    Description: Publishes articles, and research notes on the history of journalism and mass communication.

070   369   US   ISSN 0002-9742
AMERICAN LEGION PRESS ASSOCIATION NEWS-LETTER. 1946. bi-m. membership. National American Legion Press Association, Box 1184, Decatur, GA 30031-1184. TEL 404-377-5602. Ed. George W. Hooten. bk.rev.; circ. 2,600.

070   US
AMERICAN NEWSPAPER MARKETS CIRCULATION. Cover title: Circulation. 1961. a. $90. Standard Rate & Data Services, 3004 Glenview Rd., Wilmette, IL 60091. Ed. Peter S. Sinding. adv.; circ. 5,000.

808.02   617.585   US
AMERICAN PODIATRIC MEDICAL WRITERS ASSOCIATION. NEWSLETTER. 1985. bi-m. $12 to non-members; free to members. American Podiatric Medical Writers Association, Box 50, Island Sta., New York, NY 10044. TEL 212-355-5216. FAX 212-486-7706. Ed. Barry Block. adv.; bk.rev.; circ. 200. (back issues avail.)
    Description: For professional writers of podiatric literature.

070   US   ISSN 0003-1178
PN4700
AMERICAN SOCIETY OF NEWSPAPER EDITORS. BULLETIN. 1926. 9/yr. $20. American Society of Newspaper Editors, Box 17004, Washington, DC 20041. TEL 703-648-1144. Ed. Craig Klugman. index; circ. 2,500. (back issues avail.)
    Description: Forum for the editors of daily newspapers to discuss their work.

070   US   ISSN 1061-4230
▼**AMERICA'S CENSORED NEWSLETTER.** 1992. m. $30 (foreign $40). (Project Censored) Censored Publications, Box 310, Cotati, CA 94931. TEL 707-664-2500. FAX 707-664-0597. Ed. Carl Jensen. bk.rev.; film rev.; index.
    Description: Analysis and discussion of news media censorship; includes stories that were overlooked or undercovered by the national press.

070   FR   ISSN 0066-2585
ANNUAIRE DE LA PRESSE ET DE LA PUBLICITE. 1879. a. 24 Place du General Catroux, 75017 Paris, France. adv.
    Formerly (until 1969): Annuaire de la Presse Francaise et Etrangere.

ARCHIV FUER PRESSERECHT; Zeitschrift fuer das gesamte Medienrecht. see *LAW*

079   KO
ASIAN PRESS.* a. $3. Institute for Communication Research, Readership Research Center, Seoul National University, Dong Song-dong, Seoul, S. Korea. illus.

ASSOCIATION DES JOURNALISTES AGRICOLES. ANNUAIRE. see *AGRICULTURE*

AUSTRALIAN JOURNAL OF COMMUNICATION. see *COMMUNICATIONS — Television And Cable*

070   AT   ISSN 0810-2686
PN4701
AUSTRALIAN JOURNALISM REVIEW. 1979. a. Aus.$6 to individuals; institutions Aus.$25. Journalism Education Association, c/o School of Media and Journalism, Queensland University of Technology, G.P.O. Box 2434, Birsbane, Qld. 4001, Australia. TEL 07-864-2656. FAX 07-869-1513. Ed. Len Granato. adv.; bk.rev.; circ. 500.

AUTHORS & ARTISTS FOR YOUNG ADULTS. see *CHILDREN AND YOUTH — For*

AUTOMATIC I D NEWS. see *COMPUTERS — Automation*

070   UK   ISSN 0306-1000
B A I E NEWS. 1972. m. £15. British Association of Industrial Editors, 3 Locks Yard, High St., Sevenoaks, Kent TN13 1LT, England. FAX 0732-4617574. adv.; bk.rev.; circ. 1,250.

070   895.1   CC   ISSN 0257-0149
BAOGAO WENXUE/REPORTAGE LITERATURE. (Text in Chinese) 1984. m. $56.70. Renmin Ribao Chubanshe, 2, Jintai Xilu, Chaoyangmenwai, Beijing 100733, People's Republic of China. (Dist. in US by: China Books & Periodicals, Inc., 2929 24th St., San Francisco, CA 94110. TEL 415-282-2994)

BEITRAEGE ZUR KOMMUNIKATIONSWISSENSCHAFT UND MEDIENFORSCHUNG. see *COMMUNICATIONS*

070   UK
BENN'S MEDIA DIRECTORY. INTERNATIONAL EDITION. a. £90 (foreign £105). Benn Business Information Services Ltd., P.O. Box 20, Sovereign Way, Tonbridge, Kent TN9 1RQ, England. Ed. Christine Johnson. adv.; index; circ. 5,700.
    Formerly: Benn's Media Directory. Overseas Press (ISSN 0269-8366)

070   659.1   UK
BENN'S MEDIA DIRECTORY. U.K. EDITION. 1846. a. £90 (foreign £105). Benn Business Information Services Ltd., P.O. Box 20, Sovereign Way, Tonbridge, Kent TN9 1RQ, England. TEL 0732-362666. FAX 0732-770483. TELEX 95162-BENTON-G. Ed. Ann Guest. adv.; index; circ. 5,700.
    Former titles: Benn's Media Directory. U.K. Media (ISSN 0269-8358); Benn's Press Directory (ISSN 0141-1772); Newspaper Press Directory (ISSN 0078-043X)
    Description: Details of newspapers, periodicals, directories and broadcasting services.

081   US   ISSN 0195-895X
PN4726
BEST NEWSPAPER WRITING; winners, The American Society of Newspaper Editors' competition. 1979. a. $10.95 (typically set. in Apr.). Poynter Institute for Media Studies, 801 Third St. S., St. Petersburg, FL 33701. TEL 813-821-9494. FAX 813-821-0583. Ed. Karen Brown. circ. 6,000.

081   US   ISSN 0737-2612
Z253.5
BEST OF NEWSPAPER DESIGN. 1979. a. Society of Newspaper Design, c/o Newspaper Center, Dulles International Airport, Box 17290, Washington, DC 20041. TEL 703-620-1083. FAX 703-620-4557. circ. 7,000.
    Description: Features winners of the society's newspaper design and graphics competition.

BETWEEN THE LINES (WASHINGTON). see *POLITICAL SCIENCE*

JOURNALISM   2567

070   CC
BIANJI XUEBAO/ACTA EDITOLOGICA. (Text in Chinese, table of contents and a few abstracts in English) 1989. q. Y10. (Zhongguo Kexue Jishu Qikan Bianji Xuehui - China Editology Society of Science Periodicals) Science Press, Marketing and Sales Department, 16 Donghuangchenggen Beijie, Beijing 100707, People's Republic of China. TEL 4010642. FAX 4012180. TELEX 210247 SPBJ CN. Ed. Wang Yong-qing.
    Description: Covers the science of editing sci-tech journals.

BIANJI ZHI YOU/COMPILERS' FRIEND. see *PUBLISHING AND BOOK TRADE*

BORDER WATCH. see *PRINTING*

808.02   GW   ISSN 0939-3498
▼**BRIEF BERATER.** 1991. q. DM.150. Verlag Norman Rentrop, Theodor-Heuss-Str. 4, 5300 Bonn 2, Germany. TEL 0228-8205-0. FAX 0228-364411. (looseleaf format)

070   US   ISSN 0885-4890
BRILLIANT IDEAS FOR PUBLISHERS. 1983. bi-m. $49 (free to qualified personnel). Creative Brilliance Associates, Box 44237, Madison, WI 53744-4237. TEL 608-233-2669. Ed. Naomi K. Shapiro. adv.; bk.rev.; tr.lit.; circ. 15,000 (controlled). (back issues avail.; reprint service avail.)
    Description: Idea magazine for the newspaper and publishing industries of the United States, Canada, and worldwide. Covers sales tips, management advice, advertising promotion ideas and production hints.

070   UK   ISSN 0007-0238
BRITISH AMATEUR JOURNALIST. 1890. 3/yr. £5 membership. British Amateur Press Association, Cimarron Close, South Woodham Ferrers, Essex CM3 5PB, England. Ed. Allan Bula. bk.rev.; circ. 200.
    Description: Includes articles, stories, poems and line drawings by Association members.

BRITISH NEWSPAPER AND MAGAZINES INDUSTRY. see *BUSINESS AND ECONOMICS — Trade And Industrial Directories*

070   940   070   BU   ISSN 0323-956X
BULGARSKI ZHURNALIST/BULGARIAN JOURNALIST. 1959. m. 30 lv.($47) (Suiz na Bulgarskite Zhurnalisti - Union of Bulgarian Journalists) Bulgarian Journalist, Editor's Office, Bogdanovets 2, Sofia 1606, Bulgaria. TEL 52-53-48. TELEX 022635. Ed. Yordanka Blagoeva. adv.; bk.rev.; circ. 3,000.

BULLDOG WEEKLY. see *COLLEGE AND ALUMNI*

070.172   GW
BUNDESVERBAND DEUTSCHER ZEITUNGSVERLEGER. ZEITUNG. 1973. m. Bundesverband Deutscher Zeitungsverleger, Riemenschneiderstr. 10, Postfach 205002, 5300 Bonn 2, Germany. TEL 0228-810040. FAX 0228-8100415. TELEX 885461. bk.rev.; circ. 12,000.

070   US   ISSN 1055-3568
▼**BUSINESS SPEAKER'S DIGEST.** 1990. bi-m. $195. Lime Rock Press, Inc., Box 363, Salisbury, CT 06068. TEL 800-228-5297. FAX 203-435-8937.
    Description: Contains digests of speeches and articles.

808.02   US   ISSN 0744-4249
BYLINE. 1981. m. (Jul.-Aug. combined). $18. Marcia Preston, Ed. & Pub., Box 130596, Edmond, OK 73013. TEL 405-348-5591. adv.; circ. 2,500.
    Description: Offers information and encouragement for writers.

070   CN   ISSN 1184-0641
C A J BULLETIN. (Text in English, French) 1978. q. Can.$55 membership; libraries Can.$25. Canadian Association of Journalists, Carleton University, St. Patrick's Bldg., Ottawa, Ont. K1S 5B6, Canada. FAX 613-788-5604. adv.; bk.rev.; circ. 2,000. (also avail. in microform from MML)
    Formerly: C I J Bulletin (ISSN 0822-207X)
    Description: Reports on news from behind the scenes, written for journalists by journalists.

070　　　　　　　　　UK
C P U NEWS. 1968. 6/yr. £12 (foreign £20). Commonwealth Press Union, Studio House, 184 Fleet St., London EC4A 2DU, England. FAX 01-831-4923. Ed. Eric Blott. adv.; bk.rev.; circ. 1,800.
 Formerly (until 1989): C P U Quarterly.

070　　　CS　　ISSN 0590-501X
C T K DOKUMENTACNI PREHLED. 1967. w. (plus 2-3 supplements per yr.). $156. Ceskoslovenska Tiskova Kancelar, Dokumentacni Redakce - Czechoslovak News Agency, Opletalova 5, 111 44 Prague 1, Czechoslovakia. Ed. Pavel Hanus. circ. 1,400. (processed)

070　　　　　　　　US
CALIFORNIA NEWSPAPER PUBLISHERS ASSOCIATION. DIRECTORY AND RATE BOOK. 1923. a. $50. California Newspaper Publishers Association, Inc., 1311 I St., Ste. 200, Sacramento, CA 95814-2913. TEL 916-443-5991. FAX 916-443-6447. Ed. Jackie Nava. adv.; circ. 2,800.
 Formerly: California Newspaper Publishers' Association. Newspaper Directory; Which supersedes: California Newspaper Directory (ISSN 0068-5763)

070　　　　US　　ISSN 0008-1434
PN4700
CALIFORNIA PUBLISHER. 1918. m. $15. California Newspaper Publishers Association, Inc., 1311 I St., Ste. 200, Sacramento, CA 95814-2912. TEL 916-443-5991. FAX 916-443-6447. Ed. Jackie Nava. adv.; bk.rev.; illus.; tr.lit.; circ. 1,700. (tabloid format)

070.4 283　　　　US
CATHEDRAL. 1986. q. Cathedral Church of St. John the Divine, 1047 Amsterdam Ave. at 112th St., New York, NY 10025. TEL 212-316-7441. FAX 212-316-7404. circ. 8,000.
 Formerly: Heights.

070 282　　US　　ISSN 0008-8129
CATHOLIC JOURNALIST. 1945. m. $12. Catholic Press Association (Rockville Centre), 119 North Park Ave., Rockville Centre, NY 11570. TEL 516-766-3400. Ed. Owen P. Govern. adv.; bk.rev.; illus.; stat.; tr.lit.; circ. 2,700. (tabloid format) **Indexed:** Cath.Ind.

342　　　　US　　ISSN 0749-6001
CENSORSHIP NEWS. 1975. q. $25. National Coalition Against Censorship, 2 W. 64th St., New York, NY 10023. TEL 212-724-1500. FAX 212-724-5875. Ed. Leanne Katz. bk.rev.; circ. 5,000. (back issues avail.)
 Description: Covers current school book censorship controversies, threats to the free flow of information, obscenity laws, and creationism and school textbooks.

070　　　US　　ISSN 0887-0594
CENTRAL AMERICA NEWSPAK; a bi-weekly news & resource update. 1986. fortn. $38. Central America Resource Center, Box 2327, Austin, TX 78768. TEL 512-476-9841. Eds. Eva Llorens, Billy Pope. circ. 325. (back issues avail.)

794.1　　　　　US
CHESS JOURNALIST.* 1972. 4/yr. $5. Chess Journalists of America, c/o Bill Merrell, 13 Gloria Lane, St. Peters, MO 63376. TEL 215-449-4294. (Subscr. to: Bill Wall, 626-B Perimeter Rd., Mountain View, CA 94043) Ed. John Hillery.

070　　　　　　　　IT
CHI E' CHI DEL GIORNALISMO DELL'AUTO. (Text in English, Italian) 1986. a. L.40000. Crisalide Editrice, Via Brusuglio 66, 20161 Milan, Italy. TEL 6464663. Ed. Bianca Carretto. circ. 50,000.

070　　　　　　　　US
CHICAGO MEDIA DIRECTORY. 1989. a. $5 to non-members. Chicago Convention and Tourism Bureau, Inc., McCormick Place on the Lake, Chicago, IL 60616. TEL 312-567-8500. FAX 312-567-8533. Ed. Kate Haymaker. circ. 1,000.

CHINA NEWS ANALYSIS. see *GENERAL INTEREST PERIODICALS — China*

070　　　US　　ISSN 1045-2958
CHIPS OFF THE WRITER'S BLOCK. 1986. bi-m. $12. Chips Off the Writer's Block, Box 83371, Los Angeles, CA 90083. Ed. Wanda Windham. adv.; bk.rev.; circ. 500. (back issues avail.)
 Description: How-to articles and inspiration for writers, with market and contest information.

070　　　　　　　　BL
COLECAO JORNALISMO CATARINENSE. 1978. irreg. (Sindicato dos Jornalistos) Editora Lunardelli, Rua Victor Meirelles 28, 880000 Florianopolis SC, Brazil.

070 378　　US　　ISSN 0739-1056
COLLEGE MEDIA REVIEW. 1956. q. $15 to non-members. College Media Advisers, c/o Department of Journalism, Memphis State University, Memphis, TN 38152. TEL 901-678-2403. Ed. David Nelson. adv.; bk.rev.; illus.; stat.; cum.index: 1959-1972; circ. 1,000. (also avail. in microfilm) **Indexed:** Coll.Stud.Pers.Abstr.
 Formerly: College Press Review (ISSN 0010-1117)

COLLEGE PRESS SERVICE. see *EDUCATION — Higher Education*

070　　　　US　　ISSN 0010-1567
COLORADO EDITOR. 1926. m. $5. Colorado Press Association, 1336 Glenarm Place, Denver, CO 80204. TEL 303-571-5117. FAX 303-571-1803. Ed. Marge Easton. adv.; bk.rev.; illus.; circ. 948.

070 378　　US　　ISSN 0010-194X
PN4700
COLUMBIA JOURNALISM REVIEW. 1961. bi-m. $19.95. Columbia University, Graduate School of Journalism, 700 Journalism Bldg., New York, NY 10027. TEL 212-854-1881. FAX 212-854-8580. (Subscr. to: Box 1943, Marion OH 43302) Ed. Suzanne Braun Levine. adv.; bk.rev.; illus.; circ. 31,000. (also avail. in microform from UMI,MIM; reprint service avail. from UMI,WSH) **Indexed:** Acad.Ind., Amer.Bibl.Slavic & E.Eur.Stud.; Bk.Rev.Ind. (1980-), C.L.I., Child.Bk.Rev.Ind. (1980-), Curr.Cont., Film Lit.Ind. (1976-), HR Rep., Hum.Ind., Leg.Per., Mid.East: Abstr.& Ind., P.A.I.S., PMR, SSCI. —BLDSC shelfmark: 3323.220000.
 Incorporates: More Magazine & Public Interest Alert & Media and Consumer (ISSN 0047-6439)
 Description: Reports and comments critically on developments and trends in the world of journalism.

COMMUNICARE; journal of communication sciences. see *COMMUNICATIONS*

COMMUNICATION. see *COMMUNICATIONS*

COMMUNICATION: JOURNALISM EDUCATION TODAY. see *EDUCATION*

COMMUNICATIONS CONCEPTS; the best ideas in print for professional communicators. see *ADVERTISING AND PUBLIC RELATIONS*

070　　　　　　　　US
COMMUNITY COLLEGE JOURNALIST. 1972. q. $35 to individuals; libraries $40. Community College Journalism Association, c/o Tom Pasqua, Ed., Southwestern College, 900 Otay Lakes Rd., Chula Vista, CA 91910. TEL 619-421-6700. FAX 619-482-6412. (Subscr. to: c/o W.B. Daugherty, San Antonio College, 1300 San Pedro Ave., San Antonio, TX 78284) adv.; bk.rev.; circ. 250. (also avail. in microform from EDR) **Indexed:** ERIC.
 Formerly: Junior College Journalist.

COMPUTERITER; microcomputer news and views for the writer-editor. see *COMPUTERS — Personal Computers*

CONGRES INTERNATIONAL D'HISTOIRE DES SCIENCES. ACTES. see *SCIENCES: COMPREHENSIVE WORKS*

CONNECTICUT NEWS HANDBOOK. see *JOURNALISM — Abstracting, Bibliographies, Statistics*

070 051　　　　US
CONVERSATIONS WITH WRITERS. 1977. irreg. $50 per vol. Gale Research Inc., 835 Penobscot Bldg., Detroit, MI 48226. TEL 313-961-2242. FAX 313-961-6083. TELEX 810-221-7086. Ed.Bd. illus.

070　　　　　　　　II
COOPERATIVE PRESS IN SOUTH-EAST ASIA. 1965. irreg. Rs.7.50($1) International Co-Operative Alliance, Regional Office and Education Centre for South-East Asia, Box 3312, 43 Friends Colony, New Delhi 110014, India.

070　　　　　　　　US
COPY EDITOR. bi-m. Box 604, Ansonia Sta., New York, NY 10023-0604. Ed. Mary Beth Protomastro.

COPYRIGHT SOCIETY OF THE U.S.A. JOURNAL. see *LAW*

CORPORATE ANNUAL REPORT NEWSLETTER. see *COMMUNICATIONS*

070.43　　　　　　FR
CORRESPONDANCE DE LA PRESSE. 1951. d. 19210 F. (effective Jan. 1992). Societe Generale de Presse et d'Editions, 13 av. de l'Opera, 75001 Paris, France. TEL 40-15-17-89. FAX 40-15-17-15. TELEX SOGPRESS 230023. Dir. G. Berard Quelin. adv.
 Description: Provides professional news and data on the media industry.

CRITERION. see *COLLEGE AND ALUMNI*

CRITIC. see *MOTION PICTURES*

CROSS AND QUILL. see *RELIGIONS AND THEOLOGY — Protestant*

070.172　　　　　　NE
D I DAGBLADPERS. m. Vereniging de Nederlandse Dagbladpers, Johannes Vemeerstraat 14, Postbus 50570, 1007 DB Amsterdam, Netherlands. TEL 020-763366.

070　　　　NO　　ISSN 0011-5304
DAGSPRESSEN. 1924. 18/yr. NOK 350 (foreign NOK 500)(typically set in Aug.-Sep.). Norwegian Newspapers Association, Storgaten 32, Oslo 1, Norway. FAX 02-171127. (Co-sponsor: Association of Norwegian Newspaper Editors) Ed. Helge Iversen. adv.; bk.rev.; illus.; circ. 4,100.

DANMARKS JOURNALISTHOEJSKOLES AARSKRIFT. see *EDUCATION — Higher Education*

070　　　　　　　　MG
DANS LES MEDIA, DEMAIN. m. Immeuble Jeune Afrique, 58 rue Tsiombikibo, B.P. 1734, Ambatovinaky, 101 Antananarivo, Malagasy Republic. TEL 27788. Ed. Honore Razafintsalama.

070　　　　DK　　ISSN 0106-0120
DANSK FAGPRESSE. 1932. 6/yr. DKK 175. Dansk Fagpresse Service ApS, Sommerstedgade 7, 1718 Copenhagen V, Denmark. Ed. Kurt Boelsgaard. adv.; bk.rev.; illus.; index; circ. 3,832.
 Formerly: Nordisk Fagpresse (ISSN 0029-1331)

070 658.8　　DK　　ISSN 0106-5343
DANSK PRESSE. 1918. 10/yr. DKK 310. Danske Dagblades Forening - Danish Newspapers Association, Pressens Hus, Skindergade 7, 1159 Copenhagen K, Denmark. TEL 45-33-122115. FAX 45-33-142325. Ed. Hans Joergen Vonsild. adv.; bk.rev.; index; circ. 8,000.

070 327　　　　US
DEADLINE. 1986. q. $25 includes membership. Center for War, Peace, and the News Media, 10 Washington Place, New York, NY 10003. TEL 212-998-7960. FAX 212-995-4143. circ. 6,000. (back issues avail.)
 Description: Press criticism of US media coverage of US-Soviet relations, the Soviet Union, arms control, and international security.

070　　　　CS　　ISSN 0011-8214
DEMOCRATIC JOURNALIST. French edition: Journaliste Democratique. Russian edition: Demokraticheskii Zhurnalist. Spanish edition: El Periodista Democrata. (Editions in English, French, Spanish and Russian) 1953. m. $10. International Organization of Journalists, Parizska 9, 110 01 Prague 1, Czechoslovakia. TEL 0422-341533. FAX 2320426. (Subscr. to: Rooseveltova 18, 160 00 Prague 6, Czechoslovakia) adv.; bk.rev.; illus.; index; circ. 15,000.
 Description: Analyses the development of communication media in different countries and regions of the world, the status of journalist, activities of their organizations.

070 GR
DEMOSIOGRAFIKI/JOURNALISM. (Text in Greek) 1987. m. Prokopion 7-9, 171 24 Athens, Greece. TEL 973-1388. Ed. John Menounos. circ. 2,000.

070 PH
DEPTHNEWS. 1969. w. $2500. Press Foundation of Asia, Box 1843, Manila, Philippines. Ed. M. Jara. bibl.; illus.
  Formerly: Press Forum (ISSN 0048-5209)

073 GW
DEUTSCHE PRESSEFORSCHUNG. 1958. irreg., vol.27, 1990. price varies. (Deutsche Presseforschung e.V.) K.G. Saur Verlag KG, Ortlerstr. 8, Postfach 701620, 8000 Munich 70, Germany. TEL 089-76902-0. FAX 089-76902150. Ed. Elger Bluehm.
  Formerly (until 1985): Studien zur Publizistik. Bremer Reihe (ISSN 0585-6175)

DHARMA COMBAT; a magazine about spirituality, metaphysics, reality and other conspiracies. see *RELIGIONS AND THEOLOGY*

070.43 BE ISSN 0417-5271
DIRECT LINE. French edition (ISSN 0773-7386); German edition (ISSN 0258-4344); Spanish Edition (ISSN 0258-4352) (Text in English) 1963. m. free. International Federation of Journalists, International Press Centre, 1 Bd. Charlemagne, Bte. 5, B-1041 Brussels, Belgium. TEL 02-2380951. FAX 02-2303633. TELEX 61275 IPC. Ed. Aidan White. bk.rev.; circ. 2,500. (back issues avail.)
  Description: Consists of short news and information of federation activities.

DIRECTORY OF EDITORS & PUBLISHERS. see *PUBLISHING AND BOOK TRADE*

073 GW ISSN 0417-9994
DORTMUNDER BEITRAEGE ZUR ZEITUNGSFORSCHUNG. 1958. irreg., vol.4, 1991. price varies. (Institut fuer Zeitschriftforschung der Stadt Dortmund) K.G. Saur Verlag KG, Ortlerstr. 8, Postfach 701620, 8000 Munich 70, Germany. TEL 089-76902-0. FAX 089-76902150. Ed. Kurt Koszyk.

070 US
DOW JONES NEWSPAPER FUND. ADVISOR UPDATE. 1970. s-a. free. Dow Jones Newspaper Fund, Box 300, Princeton, NJ 08543-0300. TEL 609-452-2820. FAX 609-520-5804. Ed. Elaine Reed. circ. 1,500.
  Description: Covers scholastic journalism.

070 FR ISSN 0012-9232
ECHO DE LA PRESSE ET DE LA PUBLICITE. 1945. w. 1370 F. Editions Jacquemart, Maison du Livre en Bourgogne, 14 rue Chaptal, B.P. 82, 92303 Levallois-Perret Cedex, France. Ed. Noel Jacquemart. adv.; illus.; index; circ. 8,100.
  Incorporates: Echo de l'Imprimerie et des Arts Graphiques (ISSN 0012-9259)

070.172 SP
ECO DE SITGES. 1886. w. 40 ptas. Bonaire 6, D.L.B. 2908-1960, Sitges, Spain. Dir. J.M. Soler.

070 FR ISSN 0070-8321
ECOLE FRANCAISE DES ATTACHES DE PRESSE. ASSOCIATION DES ANCIENS ELEVES. ANNUAIRE. 2nd ed., 1962. a. price varies. Association des Anciens Eleves de l'Ecole Francaise des Attaches de Presse, 61 rue Pierre-Charron, 75008 Paris, France. adv.; circ. 5,000.

070 SA ISSN 0256-0054
ECQUID NOVI; journal for journalism in Southern Africa/tydskrif vir joernalistiek in Suider-Afrika. (Text in Afrikaans, English) 1980. s-a. $20 to individuals; institutions $30. Institute for Communication Research, Potchefstroom University, Potchefstroom 2520, South Africa. TEL 0148-99-1641. FAX 0148-992799. TELEX 267666 SA. (Subscr. to: Argo Publications, P.O. Box 1475, Johannesburg 2000, South Africa) Ed. Arnold S. de Beer. adv.; bibl.; illus.; circ. 800. (also avail. in microfiche; back issues avail.) **Indexed:** Ind.S.A.Per.
  ●Also available online.
  Refereed Serial

EDITOR & PUBLISHER INTERNATIONAL YEAR BOOK; encyclopedia of the newspaper industry. see *COMMUNICATIONS*

070 US
EDITOR & PUBLISHER SYNDICATE DIRECTORY; annual directory of syndicate services. 1925. a. $6. Editor & Publisher Co., Inc., 11 W. 19th St., New York, NY 10011. TEL 212-675-4380. FAX 212-929-1259. Ed. Robert U. Brown. circ. 28,000.
  Description: Lists syndicates, syndicated features, syndicated cartoonists, columnists by subject. Used by newspaper industry and others.

070 659.1 US ISSN 0013-094X
PN4700
EDITOR & PUBLISHER - THE FOURTH ESTATE; spot news and features about newspapers, advertisers & agencies. (Annual Numbers: International Year Book; Market Guide; Syndicate Directory) 1884. w. $50. Editor & Publisher Co., Inc., 11 W. 19th St., New York, NY 10011. TEL 212-675-4380. FAX 212-929-1259. Ed. Robert U. Brown. adv.; bk.rev.; illus.; circ. 27,641. (also avail. in microform from UMI,MIM; reprint service avail. from UMI) **Indexed:** B.P.I, Chic.Per.Ind., Graph.Arts Lit.Abstr.
  —BLDSC shelfmark: 3661.077000.

EDITORIAL EYE; focusing on publications standards and practices. see *PUBLISHING AND BOOK TRADE*

070 US
EDITORIAL PACE. (Text in English, Spanish) 1955. s-a. free. Derus Media Service, Inc., 500 N. Dearborn, Chicago, IL 60610. TEL 312-644-4360. Ed. Pat Derus. adv.; bk.rev.; charts; illus.; tr.lit.; circ. 10,000(controlled). (tabloid format)

070 US ISSN 0746-3014
EDITORS' FORUM. 1980. m. $75. Editors' Forum Publishing Co., Box 411806, Kansas City, MO 64141. TEL 913-236-9235. Ed. William R. Brinton. adv.; bk.rev.; illus.; circ. 1,000.
  Formerly (until 1985): Newsletter Forum.
  Description: Educational journal which deals with writing, editing, proofreading, layout and design.

EDITORS' NOTES. see *PUBLISHING AND BOOK TRADE*

070 US ISSN 0735-8490
EDITORS ONLY. 1982. m. $89 in U.S.; Canada $95; elsewhere $105. Editors Only Publications, P.O. Box 17108, Fountain Hills, AZ 85269. TEL 602-837-6492. FAX 602-837-6872. Ed. William Dunkerley. bk.rev.; circ. 450. (back issues avail.)
  ●Also available online. Vendor(s): NewsNet (PB13).

070 370 US
EDITOR'S REVENGE. 1979. m. $10 in US, Canada and Mexico; elsewhere $12. Box 805, Morristown, NJ 07960. Ed. John T. Harding. circ. 500.
  Description: Memorandum on the use, misuse and abuse of the English language in America.

070 US
EDITOR'S WORKSHOP NEWSLETTER. 1984. w. $119. Lawrence Ragan Communications, Inc., 407 S. Dearborn, Chicago, IL 60605. TEL 312-922-8245. Ed. Charles Shields. bk.rev.; circ. 6,000.

070 US
EIGHT BALL. 1947. m. (plus a. edition). membership. Greater Los Angeles Press Club, 2005 N. Highland Ave., Los Angeles, CA 90068-3272. TEL 213-874-3003. FAX 213-874-3005. adv.; bk.rev.; circ. 2,500. (tabloid format)

070.4 330 FR
ENTREPRESSE. 1976. q. 200 F. Union des Journaux et Journalistes d'Entreprise de France (UJJEF), 63 Ave. de la Bourdonnais, 75007 Paris, France. FAX 47-05-22-54. Ed. Jacques Dehedin. adv.; circ. 1,500.

EUROP. see *LITERARY AND POLITICAL REVIEWS*

070 FR ISSN 0071-2299
EUROPA. REVUE DE PRESSE EUROPEENNE. 1969. irreg. 0.50 f. each. Cercle Europe de la Faculte de Droit et des Sciences Economiques de Paris, 92 rue d'Assas, 75006 Paris, France. **Indexed:** Hist.Abstr.

EUROPEAN ECONOMICS EDITOR; news for managers and economic journalists. see *BUSINESS AND ECONOMICS — Management*

070.43 US
F O I A UPDATE. (Freedom of Information Act) 1979. q. $5 (foreign $6.25; government agencies free). U.S. Department of Justice, Office of Information and Privacy, Constitution Ave. & 10th Sts., N.W., Washington, DC 20530. TEL 202-514-3642. (Subscr. to: Supt. of Documents, Washington, DC 20402) Ed. Pamela Maida. circ. 5,000. (also avail. in microfiche) **Indexed:** Ind.U.S.Gov.Per.
  ●Also available online.
  Description: Provides information and guidance to federal agencies.

070 DK ISSN 0108-2027
FAGPRESSENOEGLEN. 1976. a. membership (Kr.50 to non-members). Dansk Fagpresse Service ApS, Sommerstedgade 7, 1718 Copenhagen V, Denmark. illus.
  Formerly: Dansk Fagpresseforenings Medlemsliste.
  Description: Gives facts about members, addresses, phone numbers and publisher names.

FAULKNER NEWSLETTER & YOKNAPATAWPHA REVIEW. see *BIOGRAPHY*

070.5 FJ
FIJI. PRINTING DEPARTMENT REPORT. (Text in English) a. price varies. Government Printing Department, Box 98, Suva, Fiji.

070 US ISSN 0739-0033
FILLERS FOR PUBLICATIONS; the editorial tool that eliminates deadline pressures. 1956. m. $68. Publications Co., 7015 Prospect Pl., N.E., Albuquerque, NM 87110. TEL 505-884-7636. FAX 505-888-0477. Ed. Pat Johnston. (back issues avail.)
  Description: Publishes short articles, cartoons, artwork and puzzles.

070 FI ISSN 0071-5301
FINLAND. POSTI-JA LENNATINLAITOS. ULKOMAISTEN SANOMALEHTIEN HINNASTO. UTLANDSK TIDNINGSTAXA. (Text in Finnish and Swedish) 1853. a. FIM 7. Posti- ja Lennatinlaitos - General Direction of Posts and Telegraphs, Mannerheimintie 11, SF-00100 Helsinki 10, Finland. index.

070 US
FLORIDA FLAMBEAU. 1913. d. Florida Flambeau Foundation, Inc., Box 20287, Tallahassee, FL 32316. TEL 904-681-6695. FAX 904-681-3577. Ed. Jim Richardson. circ. 21,000. (tabloid format; back issues avail.)

070 SW ISSN 0025-8547
FOERFATTAREN. 1970. 8/yr. SEK 195 (typically set in Jan.) Sveriges Foerfattarfoerbund, Drottninggatan 88 B, 111 36 Stockholm, Sweden. TEL 08-791-22-80. FAX 08-791-22-85. Ed. Inger Aerlemalm.
  Supersedes: Sveriges Foerfattareforening. Medlemsblad.

070 US ISSN 0888-3955
FOLLOW UP FILE. 1975. w. $144. Editorial Services, Inc., 24 Vinka Ln., Irvington, NY 10333-2333. FAX 914-591-6526. Ed. Steve Hess. index. (tabloid format; back issues avail.)
  Description: News idea service for radio and TV stations, newspaper, and magazines.

070 JA ISSN 0387-5040
FOREIGN PRESS CENTER JAPAN. PRESS GUIDE. 12/yr. Foreign Press Center - Forin Puresu Senta, Nippon Press Center Bldg., 2-1 Uchisaiwai-cho 2-chome, Chiyoda-ku, Tokyo 100, Japan. TEL 03-501-3401. FAX 03-501-3622.

070 CN ISSN 0015-9190
FOURTH ESTATE; Canada's national press journal. 1967. m. Fourth Estate Partnership, P.O. Box 971, Cornwall, P.E.I. COA 1HO, Canada. Ed. A.L. O'Neill. bk.rev.; circ. 1,500 (controlled).
  ●Also available online.

070 700 UK ISSN 0016-0385
FREE-LANCE WRITING & PHOTOGRAPHY. 1965. q. £11.50. Weavers Press Publishing, Tregeraint House, Zennor, St. Ives, Cornwall TR26 3DB, England. TEL 0736-797061. Ed. John T. Wilson. adv.; bk.rev. (back issues avail.)
  Formerly: Free-Lance Writing.
  Description: Practical articles and features to help freelance writers and photographers into print.

2570 JOURNALISM

070 384.54 323.4 US
FREE PRESS NETWORK. 1982. bi-m. $25. Free Press Association, Box 15548, Columbus, OH 43215. TEL 614-236-1908. Ed. Michael Grossberg. adv.; bk.rev.; circ. 450. (looseleaf format; back issues avail.)
Description: Debates First Amendment issues and reports on controversies in the area of communication.

070 US
FREEDOM MAGAZINE. 1968. m. $18. Church of Scientology International, 6331 Hollywood Blvd., Ste. 1200, Los Angeles, CA 90028. TEL 213-960-3500. FAX 213-960-3508. Ed. Thomas G. Whittle. bk.rev.; illus.; circ. 100,000.

808.02 070.5 659.1 US ISSN 0731-549X
FREELANCE WRITER'S REPORT. 1982. m. $39. Cassell Communications, Inc., Box 9844, Ft. Lauderdale, FL 33310-9844. TEL 305-485-0795. FAX 305-485-0806. Ed. Dana K. Cassell. bk.rev.; circ. 2,000. (looseleaf format; back issues avail.)
Description: Contains market information, news of interest and how-to features for the professional.

808.02 US
FREELANCER'S NEWS. 8/yr. Creative Independent Communications, Inc., Box 437, Murray Hill Sta., New York, NY 10156-0437. TEL 212-686-3514. Ed. Barbara Gordon.

FRONTPAGE. see LABOR UNIONS

070 US
G C GOVERNMENT COMMUNICATIONS. 1976. 10/yr. $50. National Association of Government Communicators, 609 S. Washington St., Alexandria, VA 22304. TEL 703-519-3902. FAX 703-519-7732. Ed. Michael Stirens. adv.; circ. 1,000.
Former titles: Journal of Public Communication and Membership Directory; Journal of Public Communication.

GADNEY'S GUIDES TO INTERNATIONAL CONTESTS, FESTIVALS & GRANTS IN FILM & VIDEO, PHOTOGRAPHY, TV-RADIO BROADCASTING, WRITING & JOURNALISM. see COMMUNICATIONS

070 301.16 NE ISSN 0016-5492
CODEN: GIJMAZ
GAZETTE; international journal for mass communication studies. (Text in English) 1955. bi-m. $189. (Institute of the Science of the Press) Kluwer Academic Publishers, Postbus 17, 3300 AA Dordrecht, Netherlands. TEL 078-334911. FAX 078-334254. TELEX 29245. (Dist. by: Kluwer Academic Publishers Group, P.O. Box 322, 3300 AH Dordrecht, Netherlands; N. America dist. addr.: Box 358, Accord Station, Hingham, MA 02018-0358. TEL 617-871-6600) Ed. Wim Noomen. adv.; bk.rev.; bibl.; charts; illus.; index; circ. 800. (also avail. in microform from SWZ; reprint service avail. from SWZ) **Indexed:** Amer.Hist.& Life, Commun.Abstr., E.I., Hist.Abstr., P.A.I.S.
—BLDSC shelfmark: 4092.700000.

070 FR
GAZETTE DE LA PRESSE DE LANGUE FRANCAISE. 1974. bi-m. 200 F. Union Internationale des Journalistes et de la Presse de Langue Francaise, 3 Cite Bergere, 75009 Paris, France. Ed. Georges Gros. adv.; bk.rev.; circ. 15,000.

GAZETTE OF LAW JOURNALISM. see LAW

GENERAL DIRECTORY OF THE PRESS AND PERIODICALS IN JORDAN AND KUWAIT. see PUBLISHING AND BOOK TRADE

GENERAL DIRECTORY OF THE PRESS AND PERIODICALS IN SYRIA. see PUBLISHING AND BOOK TRADE

070 IT
GIORNALISMO. m. L.5000. Viale Montesanto, 7, 20124 Milan, Italy. TEL 02-6552874. Ed. Giorgio Santerini. circ. 15,000.

070 IT ISSN 0017-0518
GIORNALISMO EUROPEO. (Text in French, German and Italian) 1966. bi-m. Comunita Europea dei Giornalisti, Via Venti Settembre 26, 00187 Rome, Italy. Ed. Karol Kleszczynski. circ. 10,000.

070 US ISSN 0017-3541
GRASSROOTS EDITOR. 1960. q. $14. International Society of Weekly Newspaper Editors, c/o Donald F. Brod, Ed., Northern Illinois University, Dept. of Journalism, DeKalb, IL 60115. TEL 815-753-1925. FAX 815-753-1824. circ. 1,000. (also avail. in microform from UMI; reprint service avail. from UMI)
—BLDSC shelfmark: 4213.600000.
Formerly: Grassroots (Carbondale) (ISSN 0046-6328)
Description: Geared to those interested in community journalism.

GUIDE TO FLORIDA WRITERS. see BUSINESS AND ECONOMICS — Trade And Industrial Directories

GUILD OF AGRICULTURAL JOURNALISTS YEAR BOOK. see AGRICULTURE

070 UK
GUILD OF BRITISH NEWSPAPER EDITORS GUILD JOURNAL. 1947. 4/yr. membership. Guild of British Newspaper Editors, Bloomsbury House, Bloomsbury Square, 74-77 Great Russell St., London WC1B 3DA, England. TEL 071-636-7014. Ed. E. Price. adv.; bk.rev.; circ. 450.

GUILD REPORTER. see LABOR UNIONS

070 UK ISSN 0954-9021
HEADLINES (LONDON). 1981. 6/yr. Newspaper Society, Bloomsbury House, Bloomsbury Sq., 74-77 Gt. Russell St., London WC1B 3DA, England. TEL 071-636-7014. FAX 071-631-5119. Ed. Gary Cullum. adv.; illus.; charts; circ. 9,000 (controlled). (tabloid format) **Indexed:** Print.Abstr.
Formerly (until 1988): Newstime (London) (ISSN 0262-6373); Formed by the merger of: Newspaper Society News & Newspaper Sales & Talking Points.
Description: Articles about the local and regional press.

070 614.7 US ISSN 0191-5657
HIGH COUNTRY NEWS. 1970. bi-w. $24 to individuals (foreign $30); institutions $34 (foreign $40). High Country Foundation, Box 1090, Paonia, CO 81428. TEL 303-527-4898. FAX 303-527-3313. Ed. Betsy Marston. adv.; bk.rev.; index; circ. 10,500. (tabloid format; also avail. in microfiche; back issues avail.) **Indexed:** Acid Rain Abstr., Acid Rain Ind., Energy Info.Abstr., Energy Rev., Environ.Abstr., Environ.Per.Bibl.
Description: Environmental newspaper that covers conservation and natural resource issues in the Western United States.

070 US ISSN 0742-5538
HISTORICAL GUIDES TO THE WORLD'S PERIODICALS AND NEWSPAPERS. 1982. irreg. price varies. Greenwood Press, Inc. (Subsidiary of: Greenwood Publishing Group Inc.), 88 Post Rd. W., Box 5007, Westport, CT 06881-5007. TEL 203-226-3511. FAX 203-222-1502.

370 US
HOME SCHOOL GAZETTE.* bi-m. $20. Brackin and Sons Publishing, 3512 Fontaine St., Pland, TX 75075-6213. TEL 301-421-1473.
Description: Christian-oriented student newspaper written by home-schooled students under the guidance of professional journalists.

HOSPITAL EDITORS' IDEA EXCHANGE. see HOSPITALS

070 AA
HOSTENI/AIGUILLON. reviste politike, satiro-humoristike. 1945. fortn. $14. Bashkimi i Gazetareve te Shqiperise - Union of Journalists of Albania, Punetoret e Rilindjes St., Tirana, Albania. TEL 75-10. Ed. Niko Nikolla. circ. 30,000. **Indexed:** Apic.Abstr.

HOTLINE (STONY BROOK); news service on the missing children field. see CHILDREN AND YOUTH — About

070 CC
HUBEI FANGZHI. (Text in Chinese) bi-m. Hubei Sheng Difangzhi Bianzuan Weiyuanhui Bangongshi, Wuchang, Hubei 430071, People's Republic of China. Eds. Ren Ping, Zhao Hui.
Description: Covers the editing and compilation of local records.

070 US ISSN 1046-8110
PN4784.N5
HUDSON'S SUBSCRIPTION NEWSLETTER DIRECTORY. 1977. a. $118. Hudson Associates, 44 W. Market St., Box 311, Rhinebeck, NY 12572. TEL 914-876-2081. FAX 914-876-2561. adv.; circ. 1,500.
Former titles: Hudson's Newsletter Directory; Hudson's Directory; Newsletter Yearbook Directory.
Description: Lists 4,139 business, professional and consumer newsletters worldwide in 52 major subject headings, broken down into 169 categories.

070 US ISSN 0441-389X
Z6953.W2
HUDSON'S WASHINGTON NEWS MEDIA CONTACTS DIRECTORY. 1968. a. $129. Hudson Associates, 44 W. Market St., Box 311, Rhinebeck, NY 12572. TEL 914-876-2081. FAX 914-876-2561. Ed. Howard Penn Hudson. adv.
Description: Comprehensive listing of Washington Press Corps (1989) 4,145 newspapers, magazines, radio-TV, 4,529 correspondents and editors, with names, assignments, addresses and phone numbers.

070 US ISSN 0018-8409
PN4712
I A P A NEWS. no.216, April-May, 1973. m. $60 to non-members. Inter American Press Association, 2911 N.W. 39th St., Miami, FL 33142. TEL 305-634-2465. TELEX 522873. Ed.Bd. bibl.; illus. **Indexed:** HR Rep.
Formerly: Bulletin Press of the Americas.

070 US ISSN 0018-8824
P87
I C B.* (International Communication Bulletin) 1966. q. $4. Association for Education in Journalism, International Division, Box 820172, Tuscaloosa, Box 1482, AL 35487-0172. TEL 301-454-2228. adv.; bk.rev.; abstr.; bibl.; circ. 1,600. (looseleaf format)

I E E E TRANSACTIONS ON PROFESSIONAL COMMUNICATION. see ENGINEERING — Electrical Engineering

070.43 BE
I F J INFORMATION. (Text in English, French, Spanish) 1953. a. free. International Federation of Journalists, International Press Centre, 1 Bd. Charlemagne, Bte. 5, B-1041 Brussels, Belgium. TEL 02-2380951. FAX 02-2303633. TELEX 61275 IPC. Ed. Aidan White. bk.rev. (tabloid format; back issues avail.)
Description: Contains studies of relevance to professionals, including freelancers' working conditions, freedom of the press and licensing.

070 331 US
I L C A REPORTER. (Former name of issuing body: International Labor Press Association) 1956. m. membership only. International Labor Communications Association, 815 16th St., N.W., Washington, DC 20006. TEL 202-637-5068. circ. 750.
Formerly: I L P A Reporter (ISSN 0018-9995)

070 CS
I O J NEWSLETTER. French edition: Nouvelles de l'O I J. German edition: I O J Nachrichten. Spanish edition: Correo de la O I P. (Editions also in Arabic, Portuguese and Russian) 1974. fortn. $12.50 to non-members. International Organization of Journalists, Parizska 9, 110 01 Prague 1, Czechoslovakia. TELEX 122631.
Formerly (until 1980): Journalists' Affairs.
Description: Provides up-to-date information about the activities of IOJ, its member organizations and clubs.

070 UK ISSN 0019-0314
I P I REPORT. 1952. m. 180 Fr. International Press Institute, London Secretariat, Dilke House, Malet St., London WC1E 7JA, England. (Subscr. to: International Press Institute, Mangoldweg 2, 8142 Uitikon-Waldegg, Switzerland) Ed. Adam Feinstein. adv.; bk.rev.; illus.; index, cum.index; circ. 2,000. **Indexed:** HR Rep.
Description: Coverage of journalists and journalism, both print and broadcast.

JOURNALISM

070 US
I S W N E NEWSLETTER. 1976. m. (10/yr.). $30 membership. International Society of Weekly Newspaper Editors, Northern Illinois University, Department of Journalism, Dekalb, IL 60115. TEL 815-753-1925. FAX 815-753-1824. Ed. Donald Brod. circ. 350.
Description: Covers developments in community journalism.

808.82 808 US
I W I NEWSLETTER. 1976? bi-m. $20 to institutions; membership $20. Illinois Writers, Inc., Dept. of English, Illinois State University, Normal, IL 61701-6901. TEL 309-438-7705. Ed. Lynn DeVore. bk.rev.; circ. 500.
Formerly: I W I Monthly (ISSN 0733-8929); Supersedes (in 1981): Illinois Writers' Newsletter.

070 US
IDEAS UNLIMITED; for company editors. m. $137. Newsletter Services, Inc., 1545 New York Ave., N.E., Washington, DC 20002. TEL 202-529-5700. FAX 202-636-3992. (back issues avail.)
Description: Contains camera-ready art and helpful editorial features and information on safety, health, good work and business practices for incorporation in to company newsletters and publications.

070 US
ILLINOIS PUBLISHER. 1939. q. $4. Illinois Press Association, Inc., 701 S. Grand Ave., W., Springfield, IL 62704. TEL 217-523-5092. FAX 217-523-5103. Ed. David Porter. adv.; bk.rev.; circ. 3,000. (back issues avail.)

IMPRESOR; al servicio de las artes graficas. see *PRINTING*

070.43 US
IN HOUSE. 1980. 2/yr. Center for Investigative Reporting, 530 Howard St., 2nd Fl., San Francisco, CA 94105. TEL 415-543-1200. FAX 415-543-8311. circ. 2,500.

070 US
IN PRINT. 1934. 10/yr. $12 (students $8). New Jersey Press Association, 206 W. State St., Trenton, NJ 08608. TEL 609-695-3366. FAX 609-695-8729. Ed. Elisabeth Hagen. adv.; bk.rev.; illus.; circ. 1,000.
Formerly (until Dec. 1989, vol.57, no.9): Jersey Publisher (ISSN 0021-5961)
Description: Covers events, issues and personalities in the New Jersey newspaper industry.

INDEPENDENT NATIONAL EDITION; a monthly journal for thoughtful Canadians. see *ENVIRONMENTAL STUDIES*

808.02 070.5 US
INDEPENDENT PUBLISHING REPORT. 1980. 12/yr. $36. Publishers Media, 116 E. Main St., Box 546, El Cajon, CA 92022. Ed. Russ A. Von Hoelscher. adv.; bk.rev.; circ. 1,500.
Formerly (until 1984): Free Lance Writing and Publishing.

079 II
INDIAN & EASTERN NEWSPAPER SOCIETY PRESS HANDBOOK. Spine title: I.E.N.S. Press Handbook. (Text in English) irreg. Rs.25. Indian and Eastern Newspaper Society, I.E.N.S. Bldgs., Rafi Marg, New Delhi 110001, India.

070 II ISSN 0445-801X
INDIAN PRESS. 1962-1964; N.S. March 1974. m. Rs.25($20) Indian and Eastern Newspaper Society, I.E.N.S. Bldgs., Rafi Marg, New Delhi 110001, India. Ed.Bd. adv.; illus. (also avail. in microform from UMI; reprint service avail. from UMI)

070 US ISSN 0019-6711
INDIANA PUBLISHER. 1936. m. $5. Hoosier State Press Association, Inc., 300 Consolidated Building, 115 N. Pennsylvania St., Indianapolis, IN 46204. TEL 317-637-3966. FAX 317-631-1199. Ed. Grace A. Falvey. adv.; bk.rev.; circ. controlled.

070 AU
INFORMATION UND MEINUNG. 1970. q. S.35. Niederoesterreichisches Pressehaus, Gutenbergstr. 12, A-3100 St. Poelten, Austria. Ed. Hans Stroebitzer. circ. 2,000.

INKWORLD. see *LABOR UNIONS*

INTER AMERICAN PRESS ASSOCIATION. COMMITTEE ON FREEDOM ON THE PRESS. REPORT. see *POLITICAL SCIENCE*

070 US
INTER AMERICAN PRESS ASSOCIATION. MINUTES OF THE ANNUAL MEETING. a. $100. Inter American Press Association, 2911 N.W. 39th St., Miami, FL 33142. TEL 305-634-2465. TELEX 522873.

INTERNATIONAL FEDERATION OF JOURNALISTS AND TRAVEL WRITERS. OFFICIAL LIST/REPERTOIRE OFFICIEL. see *TRAVEL AND TOURISM*

070 US ISSN 0020-837X
INTERNATIONAL PRESS JOURNAL; international press news and views. 1957. q. $20. Drawer G, Kenmore, NY 14217. Ed. Edward Howard Barr. adv.; bk.rev.; illus.; circ. 7,000. (tabloid format)

070.43 US ISSN 0164-7016
INVESTIGATIVE REPORTERS & EDITORS JOURNAL. 1978. bi-m. $25. Investigative Reporters & Editors, Inc., 100 Neff Hall, School of Journalism, University of Missouri, Columbia, MO 65211. TEL 314-882-2042. Ed. Steve Weinberg. bk.rev.; circ. 3,000. (also avail. in microfiche from UMI)

070.43 US
INVESTIGATIVE REPORTS. 1978. a. $5. Center for Investigative Reporting, 530 Howard St., 2nd Fl., San Francisco, CA 94105. TEL 415-543-1200. FAX 415-543-8311. (Alt. addr.: 309 Pennsylvania Ave., S.E., 3rd Fl., Washington, DC 20003) Ed.Bd. circ. 500.

070 378 US ISSN 0897-0696
CODEN: ISWRE7
ISSUES IN WRITING; education, government, arts and humanities, business and industry, science and technology. 1988. s-a. $12 (foreign $15) (typically set in Sep.). University of Wisconsin at Stevens Point, Department of English, Stevens Point, WI 54481. TEL 715-346-3568. Ed. Robert Stokes, David Holborn. adv.; bk.rev.; index. (also avail. in video cassette) **Indexed:** Lang.&Lang.Behav.Abstr.
Refereed Serial

070 301.16 US ISSN 0196-3031
PN4700
J Q: JOURNALISM QUARTERLY; devoted to research in journalism and mass communication. 1924. q. $30 to individuals (foreign $40); institutions $40 (foreign $50). Association for Education in Journalism and Mass Communication, 1621 College St., University of South Carolina, Columbia, SC 29208-0251. TEL 803-777-2005. Ed. Donald Shaw. adv.; bk.rev.; bibl.; charts; index, cum.index; circ. 4,100. (also avail. in microform from UMI; reprint service avail. from UMI) **Indexed:** Acad.Ind., Amer.Bibl.Slavic & E.Eur.Stud, Amer.Hist.& Life, Bk.Rev.Ind. (1976-), C.I.J.E., Chic.Per.Ind., Child.Bk.Rev.Ind. (1976-), Commun.Abstr., Cont.Pg.Educ., Curr.Cont., E.I., Hist.Abstr., Hum.Ind., Lang.& Lang.Behav.Abstr., M.L.A., Mid.East: Abstr.& Ind., P.A.I.S., Psychol.Abstr., Ref.Sour., Sage Pub.Admin.Abstr., Sage Urb.Stud.Abstr., SSCI.
Formerly: Journalism Quarterly (ISSN 0022-5533)

070 GW
JAHRBUCH DER KOELNER JUGENDPRESSE. 1974. biennial. DM.5.20. Junge Presse Koeln Arbeitsgemeinschaft, Hansaring 64, Postfach 420390, 5000 Cologne 1, Germany. TEL 0221-137677. adv.; bk.rev.; circ. 1,000.

070 JA
THE JAPANESE PRESS. (Text in English) 1949. a. 3500 Yen. Japan Newspaper Publishers & Editors Association, Nippon Press Center Bldg., 2-2-1 Uchisaiwaicho, Chiyoda-ku, Tokyo 100, Japan. TEL 03-3591-4401. FAX 03-3591-6149. Ed. Izumi Tadokoro.

JEWISH WORLD. see *ETHNIC INTERESTS*

070 II ISSN 0021-6976
JIWAN DHARA. (Text in Hindi; summaries in English and Hindi) 1966. 8/yr. Rs.5. Ram Ballabh Tapuriah, Pub., Naya Shaher, Sikar, Rajasthan, India. adv.; illus.

070 CC
JIZHE YAOLAN/JOURNALISTS CRADLE. (Text in Chinese) m. Liaoning Ribao, Xinwen Yanjiusuo - Liaoning Daily, Journalism Institute, 339 Zhongshan Lu, Shenhe Qu, Shenyang, Liaoning 110014, People's Republic of China. TEL 472417. Ed. Li Qingmin.

070 GW
JOJO. (Journal der Fachjournalisten); Geschichte und Geschichten. 1985. s-a. free. c/o Siegfried Quandt, Pub., Justus-Liebig-Universitaet Giessen, Fachbereich 08, 6300 Giessen, Germany. TEL 0641-7025505. FAX 0641-48199. Ed. Gunter Stemmler. circ. 1,500.

071 CN ISSN 0380-2051
JOURNAL DU NORD-OUEST. 1974. d. Can.$1.50. Publications du Nord-Ouest, 167 Dallaire, c.p. 490, Rouyn, Que. J9X 4T3, Canada. illus.

JOURNAL OF COMMUNICATION. see *COMMUNICATIONS*

070 371.0025 US ISSN 0895-6545
PN4788
JOURNALISM AND MASS COMMUNICATION DIRECTORY. 1983. a. $20 (foreign $30). Association for Education in Journalism and Mass Communication, University of South Carolina, 1621 College St., Columbia, SC 29208-0251. TEL 803-777-2005. Ed. James A. Crook. adv.; circ. 2,500. (also avail. in microfilm)
Formerly: J D: Journalism Directory (ISSN 0735-3103)

070 US
JOURNALISM CAREER AND SCHOLARSHIP GUIDE; information on journalism career scholarships available for the study of journalism and directory of college journalism programs. 1962. a. free. Dow Jones Newspaper Fund, Inc., Box 300, Princeton, NJ 08543-0300. TEL 609-452-2820. bibl.; stat.; index.
Formerly: Journalism Scholarship Guide (ISSN 0449-3362)
Description: Provides information on career preparation, salary data, list of more than 330 schools offering degrees and financial aid for this study.

JOURNALISM CAREER GUIDE FOR MINORITIES. see *OCCUPATIONS AND CAREERS*

070.07 370 US ISSN 0022-5517
PN4788
JOURNALISM EDUCATOR. 1945. q. $20 to individuals; institutions $25; foreign institutions $30. Association for Education in Journalism and Mass Communication, 1621 College St., University of South Carolina, Columbia, SC 29208-0251. TEL 803-777-2005. Ed. Thomas A. Bowers. bk.rev.; stat.; circ. 2,500. (also avail. in microform from UMI; reprint service avail. from UMI) **Indexed:** C.I.J.E., Commun.Abstr., Cont.Pg.Educ., Educ.Ind., SRI.
—BLDSC shelfmark: 5072.827000.

070 US ISSN 0094-7679
PN4700
JOURNALISM HISTORY. 1974. q. $9 to individuals; institutions $15. (C S U N Foundation) California State University, Northridge, Department of Journalism, Northridge, CA 91330. TEL 818-885-3135. Ed. Susan Henry. adv.; bk.rev.; bibl.; circ. 800. (also avail. in microform from UMI; reprint service avail. from UMI) **Indexed:** Amer.Hist.& Life, Hist.Abstr., Hum.Ind., Mid.East: Abstr.& Ind.
—BLDSC shelfmark: 5072.830000.

070 US ISSN 0022-5525
PN4722
JOURNALISM MONOGRAPHS. 1966. 4/yr. $25 to individuals (foreign $30); institutions $30 (foreign $35). Association for Education in Journalism and Mass Communication, 1621 College St., University of South Carolina, Columbia, SC 29208-0251. TEL 803-777-2005. Ed. James Tankard. circ. 2,300. (also avail. in microform from UMI; reprint service avail. from UMI,ERIC) **Indexed:** Amer.Hist.& Life, Commun.Abstr., ERIC, Hist.Abstr.
—BLDSC shelfmark: 5072.840000.

070 IS ISSN 0334-2948
JOURNALISM YEARBOOK. a. Association of Journalists, 4 Kaplan St., Tel Aviv, Israel. TEL 03-256141. Ed. Dov Atzman.

JOURNALISM

070   GW   ISSN 0022-5576
PN4703
DER JOURNALIST. 1950. m. DM.132. (Deutscher Journalisten-Verband e.V) Verlag Rommerskirchen und Co. KG, Rolandshof, 5480 Remagen-Rolandseck, Germany. TEL 0228-222974. FAX 0228-214917. TELEX 886567-JOUR-D. Ed. Thomas Rommerskirchen. adv.; bk.rev.; illus.; cum.index; circ. 21,700.

070   NE   ISSN 0022-555X
PN4705
JOURNALIST. 1946. a. fl.152. Nederlandse Vereniging van Journalisten - Netherlands Association of Journalists, Johannes Vermeerstraat 55, Amsterdam, Netherlands. TEL 20-6766771. FAX 20-6624901. Ed. W. Verbei. adv.; bk.rev.; circ. 8,500. Indexed: Key to Econ.Sci.
Description: Articles cover freedom of the press, newspaper managing, publishing, and schooling. Includes Association news, and positions available.

070   UK   ISSN 0022-5541
JOURNALIST. 1908. m. £9.50 (foreign £13). National Union of Journalists, 314-320 Grays Inn Rd., London WC1X 8DP, England. TEL 071-278-7916. FAX 071-837-8143. TELEX 892384. adv.; bk.rev.; illus.; circ. 34,000. (tabloid format)

070   SW   ISSN 0022-5592
JOURNALISTEN. 1904. 39/yr. SEK 400. Svenska Journalistfoerbundet - Swedish Association of Journalists, Vasagatan 50, 111 20 Stockholm, Sweden. Ed. Lars-G. Holmstroem. adv.; bk.rev.; illus.; stat.; circ. 16,141.

070   NO
JOURNALISTEN. 1917. 20/yr. NOK 350. Norwegian Union of Journalists, Box 8793, Youngstorget, 0028 Oslo 1, Norway. TEL 02-173825. FAX 02-171783. Ed. Jan Otto Hauge. adv.; bk.rev.; circ. 7,500.

070 301.16   GW   ISSN 0176-9707
JOURNALISTEN JAHRBUCH. 1983. a. DM.39.80. Verlag Oelschlaeger GmbH, Kegelhofstr. 54, 2000 Hamburg 20, Germany. TEL 040-470081. FAX 040-474676. Ed. Bernd-Juergen Martini. adv.; circ. 3,000. (back issues avail.)

070 621.384   UK   ISSN 0269-1736
JOURNALIST'S HANDBOOK. 1985. q. £16. Carrick Publishing, 28 Miller Rd., Ayr KA7 2AY, Scotland. FAX 0292-266679. Ed. Kenneth Roy. adv.; bk.rev.; circ. 2,600 (paid); 2,600 (controlled).
Description: Presents review of the media, mainly of interest to working journalists in the U.K.

JUGENDPRESSEREPORT; Magazin fuer engagierte Schueler und Nachwuchsjournalisten. see *CHILDREN AND YOUTH — For*

808.02 740   US
JUNIOR AUTHORS AND ILLUSTRATORS SERIES. 1951. irreg., 6th ed., 1989. price varies. H.W. Wilson Co., 950 University Ave., Bronx, NY 10452. TEL 800-367-6770. FAX 212-538-2716. TELEX 4990003HWILSON. Ed. Sally Holmes Holtze. index.
Description: Biographical sketches of outstanding creators of children's literature.

070   US   ISSN 0022-8737
KANSAS PUBLISHER. 1923. m. $7. Kansas Press Association, Box 1773, Topeka, KS 66601. TEL 913-233-7421. Ed. Donald Fitzgerald. adv.; bk.rev.; illus.; circ. 700.
Description: Newspaper layout and typography.

070.48
KAPPA TAU ALPHA. NEWSLETTER; National Society Honoring Scholarship in Journalism and Communication. 1983. irreg. (3-4/yr.). membership. Kappa Tau Alpha, U M School of Journalism, Box 838, Columbia, MO 65205. TEL 314-882-7685. FAX 314-882-4823. Ed. Keith Sanders. circ. 1,700 (controlled).
Description: Covers news in journalism and mass communications.

070   US   ISSN 0023-0324
KENTUCKY PRESS. 1929. m. $4. Kentucky Press Association, 101 Consumer Lane, Frankfort, KY 40601. TEL 502-223-8821. FAX 502-875-2624. Ed. Pam Shingler. adv.; bk.rev.; circ. 638.

073   GW
KOMMUNIKATION UND POLITIK. irreg., no.16, 1983. price varies. K.G. Saur Verlag KG, Ortlerstr. 8, Postfach 701620, 8000 Munich 70, Germany. TEL 089-76902-0. FAX 089-76902150. Ed.Bd.

070   KO
KOREAN PRESS. Korean edition: Korean Press Annual. (Text in English) 1984. a. Korean Press Institute, Korea Press Center Bldg., 12th Fl., 1-25 Taepyung-ro, Chung-ku, Seoul, S. Korea. FAX 02-737-7170.
Description: Introduces Korean press to both domestic and foreign countries.

070.43   KO
KOREAN PRESS ANNUAL/HANGUK SINMUN PANGSONG YONGAM. English edition: Korean Press. (Text in Korean) 1977. a. 38000 Won (effective 1991). Korean Press Institute, Korea Press Center Bldg., 12th fl., 1-25 Taepyung-ro, Chung-ku, Seoul, S. Korea. FAX 02-737-7170. Ed. Han Dorng-Won. adv.; circ. 45,000.
Description: Includes up-to-date statistics of journalism-related information and Who's Who of the Korean press. Also covers activities of domestic media for the past one year.

070   UZ
KORRESPONDENT. (Editions in Russian and Uzbek) 1918. m. (Soyuz Zhurnalistov Uzbekistana) Izdatel'stvo Kommunisticheskaya Partiya Uzbekistana, Ul. Pravdy Vostoka, 26, Tashkent 700000, Uzbekistan. Ed. N. Uvarov. illus.; circ. 1,123.

070   PL   ISSN 0137-2998
PN5355.P6
KWARTALNIK HISTORII PRASY POLSKIEJ. (Text in Polish; summaries in English) 1962. q. $30. (Polska Akademia Nauk, Instytut Badan Literackich) Ossolineum, Publishing House of the Polish Academy of Sciences, Rynek 9, Wroclaw, Poland. TELEX 0712771 OSS PL. (Dist. by: Ars Polona-Ruch, Krakowskie Przedmiescie 7, Warsaw, Poland) Ed. J. Myslinski. bk.rev.; abstr.; bibl.; charts; illus.; cum.index: 1962-1974; circ. 640.
Formerly: Rocznik Historii Czasopismiennictwa Polskiego (ISSN 0035-7669)
Description: History of Polish dailies and periodicals.

070   GW
LANDBOTE. 1952. 5/yr. DM.20. Junge Presse Baden-Wuerttemberg e.V., Postfach 1127, 7140 Ludwigsburg, Germany. TEL 6221-384765.

918   AU
LATEINAMERIKA PRESSESPIEGEL. 1981. 5/yr. S.50. Oesterreichisches Lateinamerika Institut, Schmerlingplatz 8, A-1010 Vienna, Austria. TEL 0222-5233315.

070.49 770   CC
LIANHUAN HUABAO/PICTURE STORIES. (Text in Chinese) m. $90. Renmin Meishu Chubanshe - People's Fine Arts Publishers, 32 Beizongbu Hutong, Beijing 100735, People's Republic of China. TEL 5122587. (Dist. in US by: China Books & Periodicals, Inc. 2929 24th St., San Francisco, CA 94110. TEL 415-282-2994) Ed. Meng Qingjiang. illus.

070.172 301   US
▼**LIES OF OUR TIMES;** a magazine to correct the record. 1990. m. $24 (foreign $32). (Institute for Media Analysis) Sheridan Square Press, 145 W. 4th St., New York, NY 10012.

LITERARY AGENTS OF NORTH AMERICA. see *LITERATURE*

LITERARY MAGAZINE REVIEW. see *LITERATURE*

070   US
M P A BULLETIN. m. free to qualified personnel. Maine Press Association, 107 Lord Hall, University of Maine, Orono, ME 04469-0141. TEL 207-581-1283. Ed. Albert F. Barnes. stat.; tr.lit.; circ. 300. (looseleaf format; back issues avail.)

070 659.1   UK
MACCLESFIELD EXPRESS ADVERTISER. 1811. w. Lancashire and Cheshire County Newspapers Ltd., 37 Chestergate, Macclesfield, Cheshire, England. TEL 0625-24445. Ed. D.J. Pickford. circ. 18,000.

070   DK
MAGASINET NU. 1983. bi-m. DKK 35 per no. Danmarks Journalisthoejskole, Olof Palmes alle 11, 8200 Aarhus N, Denmark. TEL 86-161122. FAX 86-168910. Ed. Hans-Henrik Holm. illus.; circ. 1,000.
Formerly: Nu (ISSN 0109-5072)

070   US   ISSN 0025-5122
PN4700
MASTHEAD. 1948. q. $25 to non-members. National Conference of Editorial Writers, 6223 Executive Blvd., Rockville, MD 20852. TEL 301-984-3015. FAX 301-231-0026. Ed. Sue Ryon. bk.rev.; circ. 1,000. (back issues avail.) Indexed: Amer.Hist.& Life, Hist.Abstr.
Description: Devoted to all aspects of producing editorials, from determining editorial policy to writing and design.

MASTHEAD; the magazine about magazines. see *PUBLISHING AND BOOK TRADE*

MATERIALY SAMIZDATA. see *POLITICAL SCIENCE*

MEDIA; Asia's media & marketing newspaper. see *ADVERTISING AND PUBLIC RELATIONS*

MEDIA ASIA. see *COMMUNICATIONS*

MEDIA OWNERSHIP IN AUSTRALIA. see *BUSINESS AND ECONOMICS — Trade And Industrial Directories*

070   UK   ISSN 0309-0256
PN4701
MEDIA REPORTER. 1976. q. Brennan Publications, 148 Birchover Way, Allestree, Derby, England. Ed. James Brennan. adv.; bk.rev.; circ. 15,000. Indexed: Intl.Ind.TV.
Description: Covers the mass media: professional standards and education and training in all media.

MEDIA REPORTER. see *HOMOSEXUALITY*

MEDIAFILE. see *COMMUNICATIONS*

070   FR
MEDIAS POUVOIRS. 1955. 9/yr. 315 F. Bayard Presse, 5 rue Bayard, 75380 Paris Cedex 08, France. Ed. Jean Gelamur. bk.rev.; abstr.; charts; illus.; circ. 9,000.
Formerly: Presse Actualite (ISSN 0032-7832)

070.43 320   US   ISSN 1053-8321
MEDIAWATCH. 1987. m. $36. Media Research Center, 113 S. West St., 2nd fl., Alexandria, VA 22314. TEL 703-683-9733. FAX 703-683-9736. Ed. Brent H. Baker. circ. 15,000.
Description: Analyzes the liberal political bias in reporting from major media outlets, especially the television networks.

MEDIEN-KRITIK. see *COMMUNICATIONS — Television And Cable*

070   GW   ISSN 0932-7886
MEDIEN UND PUBLICUM; Medien fuer den Dialog mit den Medien. 1987. m. DM.34.80. (Studienzentrum fuer Publizistische Bildung) Publicum Verlagsgesellschaft mbH, Otto-Hahn-Str. 10, 7141 Benningen, Germany. TEL 07144-18002. (back issues avail.)

070   US   ISSN 0026-6671
MISSOURI PRESS NEWS. 1938. m. $7.50. Missouri Press Association, Eighth and Locust, Columbia, MO 65201. TEL 314-449-4167. FAX 314-874-5894. Ed. Kent M. Ford. adv.; bk.rev.; illus.; index; circ. 1,215. (also avail. in microfilm)

070   RU
MOSKOVSKII UNIVERSITET. VESTNIK. SERIYA 11: ZHURNALISTIKA. (Text in Russian; table of contents in English) bi-m. 13.50 Rub. Moskovskii Universitet, Ul. Gertsena 5-7, 103009 Moscow, Russia. bk.rev.; bibl.; index.

MUNDO ISRAELITA; actualidad de la semana en Israel y en el mundo judio. see *GENERAL INTEREST PERIODICALS — Israel*

N A B J JOURNAL. (National Association of Black Journalists) see *ETHNIC INTERESTS*

JOURNALISM

070.172 US
N N A NATIONAL DIRECTORY OF WEEKLY NEWSPAPERS. 1921. a. $50. National Newspaper Association, 1627 K St., N.W., Ste. 400, Washington, DC 20006. TEL 202-466-7200. adv.; charts; stat.; circ. 3,000.
Description: Lists more than 7,000 weekly newspapers by city, state and county groupings.

070.172 JA ISSN 0916-295X
N.S.K. NEWS BULLETIN. (Text in English) q. Japan Newspaper Publishers and Editors Association, Nippon Press Center Bldg., 2-2-1, Uchisaiwai-cho 2-chome, Chiyoda-ku, Tokyo 100, Japan. TEL 03-3591-4401. FAX 03-3591-6149.

070 UK
N U J FREELANCE DIRECTORY. biennial. £8. National Union of Journalists, Acorn House, 314-320 Grays Inn Rd., London WC1X 8DP, England. TEL 071-278-7916. FAX 071-837-8143. TELEX 892384.

808.02 US
N W C MARKET UPDATE. 1978. 6/yr. $18. National Writers Club, 1450 S. Havana, Ste. 620, Aurora, CO 80012. TEL 303-751-7844. Ed. Sandy Whelchel. circ. 6,000. (back issues avail.)
Formerly (until 1984): Freelancers Market.

070 800 US
N W C NEWSLETTER. 10/yr. membership only. National Writers Club, 1450 S. Havana, Ste. 620, Aurora, CO 80012. TEL 303-751-7844. Ed. Sandy Whelchel. circ. 5,000. (looseleaf format; back issues avail.)
Description: For freelance writers of all categories, genres, and types.

070 US ISSN 0342-9148
NACHRICHTENTECHNIK. (Text in German) 1977. irreg. price varies. Springer-Verlag, 175 Fifth Ave., New York, NY 10010. TEL 212-460-1500. (Also Berlin, Heidelberg, Tokyo and Vienna) Ed. H. Marko. (reprint service avail. from ISI)

070 YU ISSN 0027-8149
NASA STAMPA. (Text in Serbo-Croation) 1951. m. 400 din. Savez Novinara Jugoslavije, Trg Republike 5, Belgrade, Yugoslavia. Ed. Miodrag Avramovic.

070 790.13 US ISSN 0027-8521
NATIONAL AMATEUR. 1878. q. $8. National Amateur Press Association, 972 Wakefield Ct., El Cajon, CA 92020. TEL 619-464-1971. bk.rev.; charts; circ. 400.

808.02 694 US
NATIONAL ASSOCIATION OF HOME AND WORKSHOP WRITERS NEWSLETTER. 1973. bi-m. membership only. National Association of Home and Workshop Writers, c/o Richard Day, Man. Ed., Box 10, Palomar Mountain, CA 92060-0010. bk.rev.; circ. 65.
Description: Presents marketing and other information for the home-and-workshop freelance writer.

070 US ISSN 0027-9927
NATIONAL PRESS CLUB RECORD. 1949. 48/yr. membership only. National Press Club, National Press Bldg., Washington, DC 20045. TEL 202-662-7500. FAX 202-879-6725. circ. 5,500.
Description: Covers activities and events of the Club. Includes a listing of employment opportunities.

070 US ISSN 0028-1913
PN4700
NEBRASKA NEWSPAPER. 1949. bi-m. $10.50. Nebraska Press Association, 1120 K St., Lincoln, NE 68508. TEL 402-476-2851. FAX 402-476-2942. Ed. MaryJo Chatelain. adv.; bk.rev.; illus.; circ. 568.

808.02 301.412 US ISSN 1044-1476
NETWORK (NEW YORK); an alliance and network for those connected to the written word. 1980. bi-m. $35 (foreign $45). International Women's Writing Guild, Box 810, Gracie Sta., New York, NY 10028. Ed. Tatiana Stoumen. adv.; circ. 3,000. **Indexed:** Abstr.Hyg.
Description: News of and by women writers.

070 GW ISSN 0323-4339
NEUE DEUTSCHE PRESSE. 1947. m. Verband der Journalisten der DDR, Friedrichstr. 101, 1086 Berlin, Germany. Ed. Erika Gelhauer. adv.; bk.rev.; illus. (microfiche)

NEWES. see *HOBBIES*

070 XK ISSN 1010-5735
NEWS ADVERTISER. 1985. q. $10. A L K I M Communication Production Company, Box MA 020, Marchand Post Office, Castries, St. Lucia, W.I. Ed. Albert De Terville. adv.; circ. 5,000.

070 US
NEWS BUREAU CONTACTS (YEAR). a. (plus m. updates). $120. B P I Communications, Inc. (Schenectady) (Subsidiary of: B P I Media Services), 210 Canal Sq., Schenectady, NY 10036. TEL 212-536-5263. FAX 212-536-5351. (And: 1515 Broadway, 37th Fl., New York, NY 10036. TEL 800-753-6675) Ed. Mitch Tebo. circ. 350. (back issues avail.)
Description: Lists publications, newspapers, trade magazines with news bureau.

NEWS COMPUTING JOURNAL; a quarterly journal on microcomputer use in journalism and mass communication. see *PUBLISHING AND BOOK TRADE — Computer Applications*

070 340 US ISSN 0149-0737
KF2750.A15
NEWS MEDIA AND THE LAW. 1973. 4/yr. $20 (foreign $35). Reporters Committee for Freedom of the Press, 1735 Eye St. N.W., Rm. 504, Washington, DC 20006. TEL 202-466-6312. Ed. Jane E. Kirtley. adv.; circ. 3,500. (also avail. in microform from UMI; back issues avail.; reprint service avail. from UMI,WSH) **Indexed:** C.L.I.; HR Rep., L.R.I., Leg.Per.
Supersedes (as of 1977): Press Censorship Newsletter.

070 US
NEWSLETTER DESIGN. 1987. 12/yr. $95. Newsletter Clearinghouse (Rhinebeck), 44 W. Market St., Box 311, Rhinebeck, NY 12572. TEL 914-876-2081. FAX 914-876-2561. illus.
Description: News and reviews for the desktop generation. Features illustrated critiques of 20 newsletters chosen from those entered in the Newsletter Clearinghouse's annual award competition.

070 US ISSN 0028-9507
NEWSLETTER ON NEWSLETTERS; reporting on the newsletter world: editing, graphics, management, promotion, newsletter reviews, and surveys. 1964. s-m. $120 (foreign $140). Newsletter Clearinghouse (Rhinebeck), 44 W. Market St., Box 311, Rhinebeck, NY 12572. TEL 914-876-2081. FAX 914-876-2561. Ed. Howard Penn Hudson. bk.rev. (looseleaf format)

070 II ISSN 0028-9531
NEWSMAN.* (Text in English) vol.9, 1968. m. Madras Reporters Guild, Government Estate, Madras 2, India. Ed. V. Ramakrishna Aiyar. adv.

070 KO
NEWSPAPER AND BROADCASTING. (Text in Korean) 1964. m. 10000 Won. Korean Press Institute, Korea Press Center Bldg., 12 Fl., 1-25 Taepyung-ro, Chung-ku, Seoul, S. Korea. circ. 2,500.
Description: Comprises specific issues and feature stories along with activities of Korean media and data related to journalism and mass communication.

NEWSPAPER FINANCIAL EXECUTIVES JOURNAL. see *BUSINESS AND ECONOMICS — Management*

070 US
NEWSPAPER FUND ADVISER UPDATE. vol.15, 1974. 4/yr. (during school year). free. Dow Jones Newspaper Fund, Inc., Box 300, Princeton, NJ 08543-0300. TEL 609-452-2820. Ed. Elaine Wells Reed. bk.rev.; circ. 1,500.
Formerly: Newspaper Fund Newsletter.
Description: Aimed at high school journalism teachers, publication advisers and others interested in scholastic journalism.

070.4 US ISSN 0090-2209
HD6515.N4
NEWSPAPER GUILD. ANNUAL T.N.G. CONVENTION OFFICERS' REPORT. a. Newspaper Guild, AFL-CIO, CLC., 8611 Second Ave., Silver Spring, MD 20910. TEL 301-585-2990. FAX 301-585-0668. Key Title: Annual T N G Convention Officers' Report.

070.4 US ISSN 0741-7950
HD6515.N4
NEWSPAPER GUILD. PROCEEDINGS OF THE ANNUAL CONVENTION. 1940. a. Newspaper Guild, AFL-CIO, 8611 Second Ave., Silver Spring, MD 20910. TEL 301-585-2990. FAX 301-585-0668. (also avail. in microform from UMI; reprint service avail. from UMI)

070 UK
NEWSPAPER PUBLISHERS HANDBOOK. a. £15. E C N Special Publications, 69 Thorpe Rd., Norwich, Norfolk NR1 1TB, England. FAX 0603-615973. circ. 4,000.

070.172 US
NEWSPAPER RESEARCH JOURNAL. 1979. q. $20 to individuals; institutions $30; libraries $40. Association for Education in Journalism and Mass Communication, 1621 College St., Newspaper Division, University of South Carolina, Columbia, SC 29208-0251. TEL 803-777-2005. (Subscr. to: School of Journalism, Ohio University, Athens, OH 45701) Ed. Ralph Izardo. bk.rev.; circ. 900. (also avail. in microform from UMI; reprint service avail. from UMI) **Indexed:** Commun.Abstr., Sage Urb.Stud.Abstr.

070.172 US
NEWSPAPERS & TECHNOLOGY. m. Transmedia Partners, 50 S. Steele St., Ste. 500, Denver, CO 80209. TEL 303-355-2101. FAX 303-355-2144. Ed. Chuck Moozahis. adv.; circ. 18,900.

070
▼**NEWSPAPERS AND VOICE.** 1991. m. Virgo Publishing, Inc., 4141 N. Scottsdale Rd., No. 316, Scottsdale, AZ 85251. TEL 602-990-1101. FAX 602-990-0819. adv.: B&W page $2270; trim 8 1/8 x 10 7/8. circ. 10,000.
Description: Covers voice services offered by the international newspaper community.

070 378
NEWSWIRE (MANHATTAN). 1972. 4/yr. $35 to individuals; institutions $40. Journalism Education Association, Kedzie Hall 103, Kansas State University, Manhattan, KS 66506. TEL 913-532-5532. FAX 913-532-7309. Ed. Nancy Hall. adv.; circ. 2,000. (reprint service avail. from ERIC)

070 US ISSN 0028-9817
PN4700
NIEMAN REPORTS. 1947. q. $15 (foreign $25). Nieman Foundation, Harvard University, One Francis Ave., Cambridge, MA 02138. (Subscr. to: Box 4951, Manchester, NH 03108) Ed. Robert H. Phelps. bk.rev.; circ. 1,363. (also avail. in microform from UMI; reprint service avail. from UMI) **Indexed:** Mid.East: Abstr.& Ind.
—BLDSC shelfmark: 6110.800000.
Description: Provides a forum for discussion of media-related issues by journalists, educators, and public figures.

070.172 JA
NIHON KAIJI SHINBUN/JAPAN MARITIME DAILY. d. 66000 Yen. Nihon Kaiji Shinbun Sha, 13-4, 5-chome, Shinbashi, Minato-ku, Tokyo 105, Japan. TEL 03-436-3221. Ed. Shoji Miyazawa.

NORTHERN ADVOCATE. see *ADVERTISING AND PUBLIC RELATIONS*

070 301.16 YU ISSN 0029-5175
NOVINARSTVO. (Text in Serbo-Croatian; abstract in English) 1965. q. 10000 din. Jugoslovenski Institut za Novinarstvo Beograd, Njegoseva 72, Box 541, 11000 Belgrade, Yugoslavia. TEL 11-444-22-51. FAX 11-444-842. Ed. Zdravko Lekovic. adv.; bk.rev.; bibl.; stat.; index. cum.index; circ. 3,000.
—BLDSC shelfmark: 6180.405000.

NUMERO ZERO. see *LABOR UNIONS*

NURSE AUTHOR AND EDITOR. see *MEDICAL SCIENCES — Nurses And Nursing*

070 DK
OGSA EN AVIS. 1973. 10/yr. DKK 50. Danmarks Journalisthojskole, Olof Palmes Alle 11, 8200 Aarhus N., Denmark. FAX 45-86-16-89-10. adv.; circ. 3,500.

OHIO STATE LANTERN. see *COLLEGE AND ALUMNI*

JOURNALISM

070   IT
ORDINE DEI GIORNALISTI DELLA LOMBARDIA. m. Ordine Lombardo dei Giornalisti, Corso Venezia, 16, 20121 Milan, Italy. TEL 76009007. FAX 02-784058. TELEX 324683. Ed. Franco Abruzzo. circ. 12,000.

070.48   CS
OTAZKY ZURNALISTIKY. q. $29. (Journalist Study Institute) Obzor, Ceskoslovenskej Armady 35, 815 85 Bratislava, Czechoslovakia.

070.4   US   ISSN 0195-6124
PN4871
OUTDOOR WRITERS ASSOCIATION OF AMERICA. DIRECTORY. a. Outdoor Writers Association of America, Inc., 2017 Cato Ave., Ste. 101, State College, PA 16801. TEL 814-234-1011.
   Formerly: O W A A Outdoor Writers Directory.

OUTDOORS UNLIMITED. see *CONSERVATION*

070   US
OVERSEAS PRESS CLUB BULLETIN.* vol.28, 1973. s-m. membership. Overseas Press Club of America, Inc., 310 Madison Ave., New York, NY 10017. TEL 212-679-9650. adv.; bk.rev.; illus.; tr.lit.; circ. 1,700.
   Formerly: Overseas Press Bulletin (ISSN 0048-2544)

059.95   JA   ISSN 0910-4607
BJ1545
P H P INTERSECT.* (Peace, Happiness and Prosperity) (Text in English) 1970. m. 3600 Yen($18) P H P Institute International, Inc., International Division, 3-10 Sanban-cho, Chiyoda-ku, Tokyo 102, Japan. TEL 03-239-6238. Ed. Robert J. Wargo. adv.; bk.rev.; circ. 70,000.
   Formerly (until 1985): P H P (ISSN 0030-798X)
   Description: Intended to promote mutual understanding and trust between the U.S. and Japan. Offers valuable insight into Japan and the Japanese people. Touches on problems - and their possible solutions - that affect the two countries.

070   US   ISSN 0030-8196
P N P A PRESS. 1929. 10/yr. $17.75. Pennsylvania Newspaper Publishers Association, 2717 N. Front St., Harrisburg, PA 17110. TEL 717-234-4067. FAX 717-234-0746. Ed. Jodie Morris. adv.; illus.; circ. 985.

070.1   CN   ISSN 0845-8499
P.W.A.CONTACT. 1976. bi-m. Can.$125 to non-members. Periodical Writers Association of Canada, 24 Ryerson Ave., Toronto, Ont. M5T 2P3, Canada. TEL 416-868-6913. Ed. Kathe Lieber. adv.; circ. 450.
   Former titles (until 1988): P.W.A.C. National Newsletter (ISSN 0822-4706) & P.W.A.C. Newsletter (ISSN 0711-5946); (until 1979): Periodical Writers Association Newsletter (ISSN 0701-0826)

070   US   ISSN 0883-6752
PAGES; editorial and filler service. 1969. 12/yr. $185 (diskette service $235). Berry Publishing Company, 300 N. State St., Chicago, IL 60610. TEL 312-222-9245. FAX 312-222-9637. bk.rev.; illus.
   Description: Contains editing resources for the newsletter publishing world.

070   FI   ISSN 0030-9443
PAIKALLISLEHDISTO. 1958. 6/yr. Fmk.150. Paikallislehtien Liitto - Association of Local Newspapers, Arkadiankatu 18 A, 00100 Helsinki 11, Finland. TEL 90-441366. FAX 90-443836. Ed. Pentti Kurunmaeki. adv.; bk.rev.; illus.; circ. 2,500.

070 808.8   US   ISSN 0895-0180
PEN IN HAND. 1987. m. $25. Brooklyn Writers' Network, 2509 Avenue K, Brooklyn, NY 11210. TEL 718-377-4945. Ed. Vicki Karen Hershowitz. adv.; bk.rev.; circ. 500. (back issues avail.)

070.1   CN   ISSN 0829-0857
PERIODICAL WRITERS ASSOCIATION OF CANADA. DIRECTORY OF MEMBERS. 1982. a. Can.$15. Periodical Writers Association of Canada, 24 Ryerson Ave., Toronto, Ont. M5T 2P3, Canada. TEL 416-868-6913. circ. 2,000.
   Formerly: Periodical Writers Association of Canada. Directory.
   Description: Listing of 350 of Canada's freelance magazine writers listed geographically, by area of specialty and related skills, and in alphabetical index.

070.1   CN   ISSN 0829-0865
PERIODICAL WRITERS ASSOCIATION OF CANADA. MAGAZINE MARKETS AND FEES. 1979. s-a. Can.$16. Periodical Writers Association of Canada, 24 Ryerson Ave., Toronto, Ont. M5T 2P3, Canada. TEL 416-868-6913. circ. 2,000.
   Formerly: Periodical Writers Association of Canada. Fees Survey.
   Description: Guide to over 300 Canadian magazines with rates and requirements.

070   VE   ISSN 0048-3370
PERIODISTA. 1967. bi-m. Bs.2. Colegio Nacional de Periodistas, Casa Nacional del Periodista, Avda. Andres Bello, Caracas, Venezuela. Ed.Bd. adv.; bk.rev.; charts; illus.; circ. 500. (also avail. in microform)

PHOTOJOURNALIST (NEWARK). see *PHOTOGRAPHY*

PIMS EUROPEAN CONSUMER DIRECTORY. see *BIBLIOGRAPHIES*

PIMS EUROPEAN NEWSPAPERS DIRECTORY. see *BIBLIOGRAPHIES*

PIMS MEDIA TOWNSLIST. see *PUBLISHING AND BOOK TRADE*

PIMS U K MEDIA DIRECTORY. see *PUBLISHING AND BOOK TRADE*

PIMS U S A CONSUMER DIRECTORY. see *BIBLIOGRAPHIES*

PIMS U S A NEWSPAPER DIRECTORY. see *BIBLIOGRAPHIES*

PIMS U S A TRADE & TECHNICAL DIRECTORY. see *BIBLIOGRAPHIES*

070 236   US
PITTSBURGH JEWISH CHRONICLE. w. American Jewish Press Association, 5600 Baum Blvd., Pittsburgh, PA 15206. TEL 412-687-1000. FAX 412-687-5119. circ. 13,500.
   Formerly: American Jewish Press Association. Bulletin.

070.172   FR   ISSN 0220-5157
PLUME LIMOUSINE. 1977. 3/yr. Association de la Presse Limousine, 52 Av. Garibaldi, 8700 Limoges, France.

070.48   US
POLISH DAILY NEWS/NOWY DZIENNIK. d. Bicentennial Publishing Corp., 21 W. 38th St., New York, NY 10018. TEL 212-354-0490. Ed. Boleslaw Wierzbianski.

070 323.44   II
PRESS COUNCIL OF INDIA REVIEW. (Text in English) 1980. q. free. Press Council of India, Faridkot House, Copernicus Marg, New Delhi 110 001, India. TEL 388885. Ed. G.L. Ahuja. illus.; circ. 2,000.
   Description: Covers the press world, articles and adjudications of the Council.

070   CH
PRESS COUNCIL OF THE REPUBLIC OF CHINA. 1967. m. National Press Council of the Republic of China, Nanchang Rd. Sec. 1, Lane 9, No. 4, 3rd Fl., Taipei, Taiwan 107, Republic of China. Ed.Bd. circ. 4,000(controlled).
   Formerly: P C O T Bulletin.

070   CN
PRESS REVIEW. 1976. 4/yr. Can.$20. Press Review Ltd., Box 368, Sta. A, Toronto, Ont. M5W 1C2, Canada. TEL 416-368-0512. FAX 416-366-0104. Ed. Michael Cassidy. adv.; bk.rev.; circ. 16,000.

070   US   ISSN 0032-7824
PRESS WOMAN. 1937. bi-m. $20. National Federation of Press Women, Inc., c/o. Lois Lauer Wolfe, Ed., 1105 Main St., Box 99, Blue Springs, MO 64013. TEL 816-229-1666. adv.; bk.rev.; illus.; circ. 5,000.

070.1   BE   ISSN 0478-1546
PRESSE/PERS. (Text in Dutch, French) 1954. q. 700 Fr. Association Belge des Editeurs de Journaux, Rue Belliard 20, B-1040 Brussels, Belgium. TEL 02-512-17-32. FAX 02-511-9969. Ed. J. Hoet. adv.; bk.rev.; bibl.; circ. 1,500.

PRESSE REPORT; Magazin fuer den Presseeinzelhandel. see *PUBLISHING AND BOOK TRADE*

070.172   GW
PRESSE UND SPRACHE. (Text in English, French and German) 1959. m. DM.18. Eilers und Schuenemann Verlag GmbH und Co., Postfach 10 60 67, 2800 Bremen 1, Germany.
   Formerly: Unsere Zeitung.
   Description: Press review with articles from German newspapers with explanations or translations of difficult words in English and French.

PRESSEHANDBUCH (YEAR). see *PUBLISHING AND BOOK TRADE*

070   SW   ISSN 0032-7883
PRESSENS TIDNING. 1920. 20/yr. SEK 325. (Svenska Tidningsutgivarefoereningen - Swedish Newspaper Publishers Association) TU: S Foerlags AB, Box 22500, 104 22 Stockholm, Sweden. Ed. Jan Lindeberg. adv.; bk.rev.; circ. 18,632.

070   US
PRESSNEWS. 1947. m. $5. Maryland-Delaware-D.C. Press Association, University of Maryland, College of Journalism, College Park, MD 20742. TEL 301-454-0245. FAX 301-314-9166. Ed. Patricia Marshall. adv.; charts; illus.; circ. 300. (tabloid format; also avail. in microfilm)
   Former titles: Md De D C Press News (ISSN 0025-4215); Maryland-Delaware Press News.
   Description: Articles and announcements on the newspaper industry, largely in the Maryland-Delaware-D.C. area.

070.172 686.2   US   ISSN 0194-3243
PN4700
PRESSTIME. 1979. m. $100. American Newspaper Publishers Association, Box 17407, Dulles Airport, Washington, DC 20041. TEL 703-648-1000. Ed. Maurice Fliess. adv.; bk.rev.; charts; illus.; stat.; index; circ. 12,600. *Indexed:* Abstr.Bull.Inst.Pap.Chem., Graph.Arts Lit.Abstr., SRI. —BLDSC shelfmark: 6612.555000.
   Supersedes (1979): American Newspaper Publishers Association, Research Institute. R I Bulletins (ISSN 0001-205X)
   Description: Deals with newspaper business.

PRIMA COMUNICAZIONE. see *COMMUNICATIONS*

PRODUCTION JOURNAL. see *PRINTING*

070 800   US
PROFESSIONAL FREELANCE WRITERS DIRECTORY. 1970. a. $15. National Writers Club, 1450 S. Havana, Ste. 620, Aurora, CO 80012. TEL 303-751-7844. Ed. Sandy Whelchel. circ. 1,500. (processed; back issues avail.) *Indexed:* Text.Tech.Dig.
   Supersedes: National Writers Club. Bulletin for Professional Members (ISSN 0028-0429)

PRZEKAZY I OPINIE. see *COMMUNICATIONS — Television And Cable*

PUBLIC OPINION REPORT. see *POLITICAL SCIENCE*

070   US   ISSN 0048-5942
PN4700
PUBLISHERS' AUXILIARY. 1865. fortn. $50. National Newspaper Association, 1627 K St., N.W., Ste. 400, Washington, DC 20006. TEL 202-466-7200. Ed. Edward Holahan. adv.; bk.rev.; charts; illus.; tr.lit.; circ. 9,000. (tabloid format) *Indexed:* Graph.Arts Lit.Abstr.

PUBLIZISTIK. see *COMMUNICATIONS*

070   GW
PUBLIZISTIK UND KUNST. 1951. m. DM.48. Industriegewerkschaft Medien, Postfach 102451, 7000 Stuttgart 10, Germany. TEL 0711-2018-0. Ed.Bd. adv.; bk.rev.; illus.; index; circ. 11,000.
   Formerly (until 1990): Feder (ISSN 0014-8970)

070   US   ISSN 0105-8126
▼**PULSO**; del periodismo. (Text in Spanish; table of contents in English) 1990. 4/yr. $15. Universidad de la Florida en Miami, Programa Centroamericano de Periodismo - University of Florida at Miami, Central American Journalism Program, Biscayne Blvd. and N.E. 151st St., North Miami, FL 33181. TEL 305-940-5672. FAX 305-956-5498. (And: Apdo. 1253-1002, San Jose, Costa Rica. TEL 506-533-280) Ed. Gerardo Bolanos. adv.; circ. 4,500. (back issues avail.)
   Description: Covers problems in journalism with a heavy emphasis on Latin American media.

070　　　　　　　　　　IS
QESHER/CONNECTION. (Text in Hebrew; summaries in English) 1987. s-a. $22 per no. (effective 1992). Tel Aviv University, Institute for Research of the Jewish Press, Journalism Studies Program, P.O. Box 39040, Tel Aviv 69978, Israel. TEL 03-6413404. FAX 03-6422318. Ed. Mordecai Naor.
　　Description: Covers the history of Jewish journalism and journalists throughout the world.

QINGNIAN ZUOJIA/YOUNG WRITERS; wenxue shuang yuekan. see LITERATURE

070　　　　　　　　　　IT　　ISSN 0302-5063
QUARTO POTERE; rassegna di storia, tecnica ed esperienze del giornalismo. 1973. q. Via Bartolomeo Gosio 59, 00191 Rome, Italy. Ed. Gino Pallotta.

070　　　　　　　　　　US　　ISSN 0480-7898
QUILL (GREENCASTLE); a magazine for journalists. 1912. m. $25 (foreign $30). Society of Professional Journalists, Box 77, Greencastle, IN 46135-0077. FAX 317-653-4631. Ed. Brian Steffens. adv.; bk.rev.; illus.; circ. 22,000. (also avail. in microform from UMI) **Indexed:** Hum.Ind.

070 373　　　　　　　　US　　ISSN 0033-6505
QUILL AND SCROLL. 1926. 4/yr. $11. (International Honorary Society for High School Journalists) Quill & Scroll Society, School of Journalism and Mass Communication, Univ. of Iowa, Iowa City, IA 52242. TEL 319-335-5795. Ed. Richard P. Johns. adv.; bk.rev.; illus.; circ. 13,500. (also avail. in microform from UMI; reprint service avail. from UMI) **Indexed:** C.I.J.E.

070 200　　　　　　　　US　　ISSN 0034-4109
R N A NEWSLETTER.* 1953. bi-m. $5. Religion Newswriters Association, c/o Ben Kaufman, Cincinnati Enquirer, 617 Vine St., Cincinnati, OH 45202. circ. 125. (processed)

R T N D A COMMUNICATOR. (Radio-Television News Directors Association) see COMMUNICATIONS — Radio

070　　　　　　　　　　RU　　ISSN 0033-9318
RASPROSTRANENIE PECHATI. 1929. m. 15.60 Rub. (Komitet po Pechati Soveta Ministrov) Izdatel'stvo Kniga, 50, Gorky St., 125047 Moscow, Russia. Ed. K.F. Takoyev.

070　　　　　　　　　　BE
REDACTUEL. 1979. bi-m. membership. Association Belge de la Presse d'Enterprise, Hammeveld 2, B-1785 Hamme, Belgium. FAX 02-210-07-02. Ed. Christiane Asselberghs. bk.rev.; circ. 200.
　　Formerly: Informations pour Jounalistes d'Entreprise - Informatie voor Bedrijfsjournalisten.

808.02　　　　　　　　US
REGISTERED WRITER'S COMMUNIQUE - CONTACTS AND ASSIGNMENTS; magazine for professional freelance writers. 1986. m. $18. (Registered Writer's Guild) Gibbs Publishing Company, Box 600927, N. Miami Beach, FL 33160. Ed. James Calvin Gibbs. adv.; bk.rev.
　　Formerly: Registered Writer's Forum - Assignments.

070　　　　　　　　　　RU
▼REPORTER. 1990. w. Soyuz Zhurnalistov S.S.S.R., Kemerovskaya Oblastnaya Organizatsiya, Pr. Lenina 124, 650056 Kemerovo, Russia. TEL 55-81-21. Ed. Aleksandr Kosvintsev. circ. 50,000. (newspaper)

RESOURCE-MAG; a marketing report for publishing professionals. see PUBLISHING AND BOOK TRADE

070　　　　　　　　　　MG
REVUE DE LA PRESSE DE L'OCEAN INDIEN. (Text in French) 1981. bi-m. $23. Communication et Media Ocean Indien, B.P. 46, Antananarivo, Malagasy Republic. Ed. Georges Ranaivosoa. adv.; bk.rev.; circ. 3,000.

REVUE TUNISIENNE DE COMMUNICATION. see COMMUNICATIONS

RIGHTING WORDS; the journal of language and editing. see LINGUISTICS

808.06 978　　　　　　　US　　ISSN 0035-855X
PS374.W4
ROUNDUP (EL PASO). 1953. q. $30. Texas Christian University Press for Western Writers of America, Inc., Box 823, Sheridan, WY 82801-0823. TEL 307-672-0889. Ed. Judy Alter. bk.rev.; circ. 600.
　　Description: Covers the study of literature and history of the American West.

070　　　　　　　　　　AT
ROY MORGAN MAGAZINE & NEWSPAPER SURVEY. 1971. s-a. Roy Morgan Research Centre Pty. Ltd., Box 2282U, Melbourne, Vic. 3001, Australia. FAX 03-629-1250.

070 320　　　　　　　　US　　ISSN 0036-2948
ST. LOUIS COUNTIAN. 1902. d. $95. Legal Communications Corp., 111 S. Bemiston Ave., Ste. 504, St. Louis, MO 63105-1912. TEL 314-727-6111. Ed. Will Connagham. adv.; circ. 1,956. (tabloid format; also avail. in microform)

070　　　　　　　　　　US　　ISSN 0036-2972
PN4899.S25
ST. LOUIS JOURNALISM REVIEW. 1970. m. (except Dec.-Jan. and Jul.-Aug. combined). $25. Charles L. Klotzer, Ed. & Pub., 8380 Olive Blvd., St. Louis, MO 63132. TEL 314-991-1699. FAX 314-997-1898. adv.; bk.rev.; illus.; circ. 7,500. (tabloid format; back issues avail.) **Indexed:** Alt.Press Ind., Amer.Hist.& Life, Hist.Abstr., Mid.East: Abstr.& Ind., P.A.I.S.
　　Incorporates (after no.95, 1984): Focus - Midwest (ISSN 0015-508X)
　　Description: Evaluates media print, broadcast, communications, advertising, and public relations, and issues ignored by media.

070　　　　　　　　　　FI　　ISSN 0036-4479
SANOMALEHTIMIES/JOURNALISTEN. (Text in Finnish, Swedish) 1924. 22/yr. Fmk.200. Suomen Sanomalehtimiesten Liitto, Hietalahdenkatu 2B22, 00180 Helsinki, Finland. FAX 640-361. Ed. Timo Vuortama. adv.; bk.rev.; illus.; circ. 10,300.

070　　　　　　　　　　BU　　ISSN 0205-1656
P87
SAVREMENNA ZHURNALISTIKA/MODERN JOURNALISM. 1982. q. 10 lv. Research and Information Centre of Journalism, Editor's Office, Bratya Miladinovi 12, Sofia 1000, Bulgaria. TEL 88 42 33. TELEX 022635. (Co-sponsor: Union of Bulgarian Journalists) Ed. Todor Abazov. bk.rev.; circ. 1,000.
　　—BLDSC shelfmark: 0161.560000.

070 808　　　　　　　　US　　ISSN 0894-2617
SCAVENGER'S NEWSLETTER. 1984. m. $11.50. 519 Ellinwood, Osage City, KS 66523-1329. TEL 913-528-3538. Ed. Janet Fox. bk.rev.; circ. 1,000.
　　Description: Information on small press markets for science fiction and fantasy-horror writers and artists with an interest in the small press.

070 370　　　　　　　　US　　ISSN 0036-6730
LB3621.A2
SCHOOL PRESS REVIEW; high school and college level. 1925. q. $12. (Columbia Scholastic Press Association) Columbia University, Box 11, Central Mail Room, New York, NY 10027-6969. TEL 212-854-3311. Ed. Edmund J. Sullivan. adv.; bk.rev.; charts; illus.; circ. 3,000. (also avail. in microform from UMI; reprint service avail. from UMI) **Indexed:** ERIC.

070　　　　　　　　　　SZ
SCHWEIZER FACHPRESSE/PRESSE SPECIALISEE SUISSE/STAMPA SPECIALIZATA SVIZZERA. (Text in French, German and Italian) 1925. bi-m. 18 F. Schweizerischer Fachpresse-Verband - Union Suisse de la Presse Specialisee, Secretariat, Hintere Hauptgasse 9, Postfach 2, CH-4800 Zofingen, Switzerland. Ed. Jaroslaw Trachsel. adv.; bk.rev.; circ. 1,000.
　　Formerly: Fachpresse (ISSN 0014-6382)

SE LA VIE WRITER'S JOURNAL. see LITERATURE — Poetry

070　　　　　　　　　　MP
SETGUULCH/JOURNALIST. (Text in Mongolian) 1982. bi-m. Union of Journalists, Ulan Bator, Mongolia. TEL 25388. Ed. T. Baasansuren. circ. 4,000.
　　Description: Covers journalism, politics, literature, art and economy.

070　　　　　　　　　　KO
SHIN DONG-A/NEW EAST ASIA. 1931. m. Dong-A Ilbo, 17 Yeoido-dong, Yongdeungpo-ku, Seoul 150 010, S. Korea. TEL 02-781-0611. FAX 02-785-4547. Ed. Kwon O-Kie. circ. 335,000.

070　　　　　　　　　　CC
SICHUAN XINWEN TUPIAN/SICHUAN NEWS PHOTO PRESS. (Text in Chinese) 1980. q. $0.60. Sichuan Xiwen Tupianshe - Sichuan News Photo Agency, Chongqing, Sichuan 630010, People's Republic of China. TEL 45856. circ. 50,000.
　　Formerly (until 1992): Sichuan News Photo.

070.48 500　　　　　　　US　　ISSN 0737-0350
SIPISCOPE. 1970. q. $25 (free to qualified personnel). Scientists' Institute for Public Information, 355 Lexington Ave., New York, NY 10017. TEL 212-661-9110. FAX 212-599-6432. Ed. fred Jerome. circ. 10,000.
　　Description: Discusses media coverage of science and technology.

070.48 796.93　　　　　US
SKI WRITERS BULLETIN. 1964. q. membership. United States Ski Writers Association, 7 Kensington Rd., Glens Falls, NY 12801. circ. 350.

SMALL PRESS REVIEW. see PUBLISHING AND BOOK TRADE

SOCIAL RESPONSIBILITY: BUSINESS, JOURNALISM, LAW, MEDICINE. see PHILOSOPHY

070　　　　　　　　　　FR
SOCIETE GENERALE DE PRESSE ET D'EDITIONS. INDEX. d. 18160 F. (effective Jan. 1992). Societe Generale de Presse et d'Editions, Siege 13, Avenue de l'Opera, 75001 Paris, France. TEL 40-15-17-89. FAX 40-15-17-15. TELEX SOGPRES 230023.

EL SOL. see ETHNIC INTERESTS

070 378　　　　　　　　US　　ISSN 0038-3716
SOUTHEASTERNER. 1965. m. (Sep.-May). free. University of Kentucky, Southeast Community College, Cumberland, KY 40823. TEL 606-589-2145. Ed. Ed Boggs. adv.; illus.; circ. 2,500 (paid); 3,500 (controlled). (newspaper)

SPECTRUM (OLATHE); a guide to the independent press and informative organizations. see LIBRARY AND INFORMATION SCIENCES

808.02 330　　　　　　　US　　ISSN 0272-8079
SPEECHWRITER'S NEWSLETTER. 1980. w. $287. Lawrence Ragan Communications, Inc., 407 S. Dearborn, Chicago, IL 60605. TEL 312-922-8245. Ed. John Cowan. bk.rev.; circ. 1,500.

070　　　　　　　　　　FI　　ISSN 0039-5587
SUOMEN LEHDISTO/FINLANDS PRESS. (Text in Finnish; summaries in Swedish) 1930. m. $70. Sanomalehtien Liitto - Tidningarnas Foerbund (Finnish Newspaper Publishers Association), Kalevankatu 4, 00100 Helsinki 10, Finland. TEL 358-0-607786. FAX 358-0-607989. Ed. Olavi Rantalainen. adv.; bk.rev.; circ. 4,047 (controlled).

070 327 980　　　　　　US　　ISSN 0743-4324
PN4748.L29
SURVEY OF PRESS FREEDOM IN LATIN AMERICA. 1983. a. $8.95. Council on Hemispheric Affairs, 724 9th St., N.W., Ste. 401, Washington, DC 20001. TEL 202-393-3322. FAX 202-393-3423. (Co-sponsor: Newspaper Guild) Ed.Bd. circ. 4,000.

070　　　　　　　　　　US
SYNDICATED COLUMNISTS CONTACTS (YEAR). 1975. a. (plus m. updates). $30. B P I Communications, Inc. (Schenectady) (Subsidiary of: B P I Media Services), 210 Canal Sq., Schenectady, NY 12305. TEL 518-374-7640. FAX 518-374-7889. (And: 1515 Broadway, 37th Fl., New York, NY 10036. TEL 212-536-5263) Ed. Richard Weiner. bibl.; circ. 1,000.

070　　　　　　　　　　US
T P A MESSENGER. 1926. m. $6. Texas Press Association, 718 W. 5th St., Austin, TX 78701. TEL 512-477-6755. Ed. Lyndell Williams. adv.; bk.rev.; charts; illus.; circ. 1,015. (tabloid format)
　　Formerly (until vol.54, no.77, Jul. 1979): Texas Press Messenger (ISSN 0040-4624)

TASCHENBUCH FUER AGRARJOURNALISTEN. see AGRICULTURE

2576 JOURNALISM

810 760   US   ISSN 0492-3901
TAYLOR TALK; the yearbook magazine. 1960. q. $10. Taylor Publishing Co., 1550 W. Mockingbird Lane, Dallas, TX 75235. TEL 800-677-2800. FAX 214-951-0135. Ed. Leigh-Ellen Clark. illus.; circ. 25,000.

TECHNICAL COMMUNICATION. see *COMMUNICATIONS*

070   UK   ISSN 0959-7808
▼**TEES VALLEY WRITER**. 1990. s-a. £1.90. 57 the Avenue, Linthorpe, Middlesbrough, Cleveland TS5 6QU, England. TEL 0642-819102. Ed. Derek Gregory. adv.; bk.rev.; circ. 1,000.
Description: Provides an outlet for creative writers from the Northeast.

070   US
TENNESSEE PRESS. 1938? m. $1.50. Tennessee Press Service, Inc., Box 8123, Knoxville, TN 37996. FAX 615-974-4493. Ed. Don Campbell. adv.; circ. 775.

070   US
TEXT TECHNOLOGY. bi-m. Wright State University, Lake Campus, Celina, OH 45822-2921. TEL 419-586-2365. FAX 419-586-9048. Ed. Jim Schwartz. circ. 800.

THEATRE RECORD. see *THEATER*

TIDNINGSTEKNIK. see *PRINTING*

070   TZ
TORCH. (Text in English) 1975. m. Sh.101. Tanzania School of Journalism, Box 4067, Dar es Salaam, Tanzania. TELEX 41344 MASCOM. adv.; bk.rev.; circ. 5,000.
Formerly (until 1978): Tanzanian Journalist.

TRAVEL JOURNALIST/JOURNALISTE DE TOURISME. see *TRAVEL AND TOURISM*

070.48 910   US
TRAVEL WRITER. 1959. 10/yr. membership. Society of American Travel Writers, 1155 Connecticut Ave., Ste. 500, Washington, DC 20036. TEL 202-429-6639. Eds. Victor Block, Peter Vandevanter. circ. 1,000. (looseleaf format)

808.02 910   US   ISSN 0738-9094
TRAVELWRITER MARKETLETTER. 1979. m. $60 (foreign $70). At the Waldorf-Astoria, Ste. 1850, New York, NY 10022. TEL 212-759-6744. Ed. Robert Scott Milne. bk.rev.; circ. 1,000.
Description: Marketing information for travel writers and photographers. Includes information on free trips for professionals.

070 028.5   GW
TREFFPUNKT JUGENDPRESSE. 1960. s-a. Junge Presse Koeln Arbeitsgemeinschaft, Hansaring 64, Postfach 420390, 5000 Cologne 1, Germany. TEL 0221-137677. Ed. Angela Meuter. adv.; bk.rev.; bibl.; chart.; film rev.; illus.; play rev.; stat.; circ. 500.

070 370   US
LB3620
TRENDS IN COLLEGE MEDIA. 1921. bi-m. (Sep.-May). $18. National Scholastic Press Association, 620 Rarig Center, 330 21st Ave., S., University of Minnesota, Minneapolis, MN 55455. TEL 612-625-8335. (Co-sponsor: Associated College Press) Ed. Tom E. Rolnicki. adv.; bk.rev.; charts; illus.; index; circ. 2,300. (processed; also avail. in microform from UMI; reprint service avail. from UMI)
Supersedes in part: Scholastic Editor's Trends in Publications (ISSN 0745-2357); Former titles (until 1982): Scholastic Editor; (until Sep. 1975): Scholastic Editor Graphics - Communications (ISSN 0036-6390)

070 370   US
TRENDS IN HIGH SCHOOL MEDIA. 4/yr. National Scholastic Press Association, 620 Rarig Center, 330 21st Ave. S., University of Minnesota, Minneapolis, MN 55455. TEL 612-625-8335.
Supersedes in part: Scholastic Editor's Trends in Publications (ISSN 0745-2357)

070   AA
TRIBUNA E GAZETARIT. 1964. bi-m. $14. Bashkimi i Gazetareve te Shqiperise - Union of Journalists of Albania, Punetoret e Rilindjes St., Tirana, Albania. TEL 27977.

THE TYNDALL REPORT. see *COMMUNICATIONS — Television And Cable*

070   UK   ISSN 0041-5170
U K PRESS GAZETTE; journalism's newspaper. 1965. w. £49.50. Maclean Hunter Ltd., Maclean Hunter House, Chalk Lane, Cockfosters Rd., Barnet, Herts EN4 0BU, England. TEL 081-975-9759. FAX 081-440-1796. Ed. John Gerard. adv.; bk.rev.; charts; illus.; circ. 8,000.
Incorporates (1990): Magazine Week.

U S B W A TIP-OFF. (United States Basketball Writers Association) see *SPORTS AND GAMES — Ball Games*

070.48 796.93   US
U S SKI WRITERS ASSOCIATION NEWSLETTER. 1963. bi-m. membership. United States Ski Writers Association, 7 Kensington Rd., Glens Falls, NY 12801. TEL 518-793-1202. circ. 300.
Description: News of interest to ski journalist members.

070   US
U.S. LIBRARY OF CONGRESS. NEWSPAPERS RECEIVED CURRENTLY. 1968. biennial. price varies. U.S. Library of Congress, Washington, DC 20540. TEL 202-707-6100. (Subscr. to: Supt. of Documents, Washington, DC 20402)
Formerly: Newspapers Currently Received and Permanently Retained in the Library of Congress (ISSN 0083-1646)

070   SP
UNIVERSIDAD DE NAVARRA. FACULTAD DE CIENCIAS DE LA INFORMACION. COLECCION DE TRABAJO. 1964. irreg., no.56, 1990. price varies. Ediciones Universidad de Navarra, S.A., Apdo. 396, 31080 Pamplona, Spain. TEL 94 825 6850.

070   SP   ISSN 0078-8783
UNIVERSIDAD DE NAVARRA. FACULTAD DE CIENCIAS DE LA INFORMACION. MANUALES: PERIODISMO. 1967. irreg., no.13, 1988. price varies. Ediciones Universidad de Navarra, S.A., Apdo. 396, 31080 Pamplona, Spain. TEL 94 825 6850.

070   US   ISSN 0077-6378
UNIVERSITY OF NEBRASKA. SCHOOL OF JOURNALISM. DEPTH REPORT. 1961. a. free. University of Nebraska, Lincoln, College of Journalism, Lincoln, NE 68508. TEL 402-472-3047. Ed. Daryl Frazell. circ. 2,500.

070   CS   ISSN 0083-422X
UNIVERZITA KOMENSKEHO. FILOZOFICKA FAKULTA. ZBORNIK: ZURNALISTIKA. (Text in Slovak; summaries in German and Russian) 1968. irreg. exchange basis. Univerzita Komenskeho, Filozoficka Fakulta, c/o Ustredna Kniznica Filozofickej Fakulty, Gondova 2, 818 01 Bratislava, Czechoslovakia. Ed. Lubos Sefcak. circ. 600.

070 800   US   ISSN 0709-4698
PN5124.P4
VICTORIAN PERIODICALS REVIEW. 1968. q. $13 to individuals (foreign $17); institutions $18 (foreign $22). Research Society for Victorian Periodicals, English Department, Ed. Barbara Quinn Schmidt, Southern Illinois University, Edwardsville, IL 62026-1436. TEL 618-692-2326. FAX 618-692-3509. adv.; bk.rev.; stat.; circ. 650. (processed; also avail. in microfilm from UMI; reprint service avail. from UMI) **Indexed:** Amer.Hum.Ind., Hist.Abstr., M.L.A.
Formerly: Victorian Periodicals Newsletter (ISSN 0049-6189)

070   US   ISSN 0887-5227
VIRGINIA'S PRESS. 1918. w. $15 to non-members. Virginia Press Association, Inc., Box C-32015, Richmond, VA 23261-2015. TEL 804-550-2361. FAX 804-550-2407. Ed. Ray Hall. adv.; bk.rev.; illus.; circ. 731.
Formerly: Virginia Publisher and Printer (ISSN 0042-6741)

320.9 051   US   ISSN 0042-742X
PN6121
VITAL SPEECHES OF THE DAY. 1934. s-m. $35. City News Publishing Co. Inc., Box 1247, Mt. Pleasant, SC 29465-1247. TEL 803-881-8733. Ed. Thomas F. Daly III. index. cum.index: 1934-1959; circ. 18,000. (also avail. in microfilm; microfiche)
Indexed: ABI Inform, Acad.Ind., BPIA, Bus.Ind., Fut.Surv., Hlth.Ind., Mag.Ind., Manage.Cont., Mid.East: Abstr.& Ind., Pers.Lit., PMR, PSI, R.G., TOM.
—BLDSC shelfmark: 9241.855000.

070   II
VRITTA VIDYA; experimental journal. (Text in English and Marathi) 1965. bi-m. free. University of Poona, Department of Communication and Journalism, Ranade Institute, Poona 411 004, India. Ed. P.N. Paranjpe. adv.; bk.rev.; film rev.; play rev.; circ. 600. (tabloid format)

070   CS
VYBER. w. $78. (Union of Slovak Journalists) Obzor, Ceskoslovenskej Armady 35, 815 85 Bratislava, Czechoslovakia. **Indexed:** Sci.Abstr.

070   US   ISSN 0741-8876
AP2
WASHINGTON JOURNALISM REVIEW. Short title: W J R. 1977. m. $24. Washington Journalism Review Associates, Inc., 4716 Pontiac St., Ste. 310, College Park, MD 20740. TEL 301-513-0001. FAX 301-441-9495. Ed. Rem Rieder. adv.; bk.rev.; circ. 27,000. (also avail. in microform from UMI; back issues avail.) **Indexed:** Access (1980-), Bk.Rev.Ind. (1981-), Child.Bk.Rev.Ind. (1981-), Dent.Abstr.

070   US   ISSN 0043-0684
WASHINGTON NEWSPAPER. 1914. m. $8 to non-member Wash. residents; others $10. Washington Newspaper Publishers' Association, Inc., 3838 Stone Way North, Seattle, WA 98103. TEL 206-634-3838. FAX 206-634-3842. Ed. Miles Turnbull. adv.; tr.lit.; circ. 700.

301.16 070   US
WASHINGTON STATE UNIVERSITY. DAILY EVERGREEN. 1894. 5/wk. (Mon.-Fri.). $28. W.S.U. Student Publications, 113 Murrow Communications Center, Pullman, WA 99164. circ. 14,000. (tabloid format)

070   US
WEST VIRGINIA FOURTH ESTATESMAN. 1941. q. West Virginia University, School of Journalism, 112 Martin Hall, Box 6010, Morgantown, WV 26506-6010. TEL 304-293-3505. FAX 304-293-3505. Ed. Emery L. Sasser. circ. 2,900.

WHO'S WHO OF AUSTRALIAN WRITERS. see *BIOGRAPHY*

WILLIAM WINTER COMMENTS; a twice monthly personal newsletter on current world affairs. see *POLITICAL SCIENCE — International Relations*

070 500   GW   ISSN 0938-6300
▼**WISSENSCHAFT IN DEN MEDIEN**. 1990. 3/yr. DM.45. Georg Thieme Verlag, Ruedigerstr. 14, Postfach 104853, 7000 Stuttgart 10, Germany. TEL 0711-89310. FAX 0711-8931298. TELEX 07252275-GTV-D.

070.43   II
WORKING JOURNALIST. (Text in English) 1955. m. Rs.12. Indian Federation of Working Journalists, Fl. 101, M.S. Apt., Kasturba Gandhi Marg, New Delhi 110001, India. TEL 384956. Ed. K. Vikram Rao. adv.; bk.rev.; circ. 25,000.

070   US   ISSN 0084-1323
WORKING PRESS OF THE NATION. (Issued in 5 vols.: Vol.1 The Newspaper Directory, Vol.2 The Magazine Directory, Vol.3 The Radio and Television Directory, Vol.4 The Feature Writers and Photographer Directory, Vol.5 Internal Publications Directory) 1949. a. $150 per vol., $310 per set. National Research Bureau, Inc. (Burlington), 424 N. Third St., Box 1, Burlington, IA 52601-0001. TEL 319-752-5415. FAX 319-752-3421. Ed. Nancy Veatch.

JOURNALISM — ABSTRACTING, BIBLIOGRAPHIES, STATISTICS

070   UK
WORLD PRESS FREEDOM REVIEW. 1952. a. International Press Institute, London Secretariat, Dilke House, Malet St., London WC1E 7JA, England. FAX 071-580-8349. TELEX 25950 IPILON G. (Subscr. to: International Press Institute, Mangoldweg 2, 8142 Uitikon-Waldegg, Switzerland)
  Former titles: Annual Review of World Press Freedom & International Press Institute. Survey (ISSN 0085-2198)

070 800   US   ISSN 0043-9517
PN101
WRITER (BOSTON). 1887. m. $27. Writer, Inc., 120 Boylston St., Boston, MA 02116. TEL 617-423-3157. Ed. Sylvia K. Burack. adv.; bk.rev.; index; circ. 58,174. (microform; also avail. in microform from UMI) **Indexed:** Child.Lit.Abstr., Mag.Ind., PMR, R.G.
  Description: Articles of instruction on all writing fields.

WRITERS CONNECTION. see *PUBLISHING AND BOOK TRADE*

070 800   US   ISSN 0043-9525
PN101
WRITER'S DIGEST. 1920. m. $24. F & W Publications, Inc., 1507 Dana Ave., Cincinnati, OH 45207. TEL 513-531-2222. (Subscr. to: Box 2123, Harlan, IA 51593) Ed. Bruce Woods. adv.; bk.rev.; illus.; mkt.; index; circ. 229,320. (also avail. in microform from UMI,MIM; reprint service avail. from UMI) **Indexed:** Access (1979-), Ind.How To Do It (1990-), Mag.Ind., Pop.Per.Ind., R.G.
  —BLDSC shelfmark: 9364.681000.
  Description: Provides "how-to" instruction, information and inspiration for people who love to write. Includes advice from bestselling authors, tips and techniques for creating better manuscripts, and information on how and where to sell fiction, nonfiction, poetry and scripts.

808.02   US   ISSN 1053-1793
WRITERS' GUIDELINES MAGAZINE; a roundtable for writers and editors. 1988. bi-m. $18. Writers' Guidelines, Inc., Box 608, Pittsburg, MO 65724. TEL 417-993-5544. Ed. Susan Salaki. adv.; bk.rev.; circ. 750. (back issues avail.)
  Former titles: Guidelines Magazine (ISSN 1046-9184); Guidelines Newsletter.
  Description: Inspiration and support for writers, and a guideline service in which 300 editors supply current guidelines.

WRITERS GUILD OF AMERICA, WEST. JOURNAL. see *LITERATURE*

WRITERS' JOURNAL (N. ST. PAUL). see *LITERATURE*

WRITERS NEWS. see *LITERATURE*

070   US   ISSN 0890-9504
WRITER'S NOOK NEWS. 1985. q. $18. Writer's Nook Press, 38114 Second St., Ste. 181, Willoughby, OH 44094. TEL 216-975-8965. FAX 216-354-6403. Ed. Eugene Ortiz. adv.; bk.rev.; index; circ. 1,000.
  Description: News and tips for working and aspiring writers.

070 800   AT   ISSN 0043-9576
WRITERS' WORLD. 1952. bi-m. Aus.$10 (typically set in Jan.). Australian Writers' Professional Service, Stott House, 140 Flinders St., Melbourne, Vic. 3000, Australia. TEL 03-654-6211. FAX 03-650-9648. Ed. J. Thornton. bk.rev.; circ. 5,000. (processed)
  Description: Newsletter for freelance writers and journalists. Competitions and articles of interest to writers.

WRITING (NORTHBROOK); the continuing guide to written communication. see *LITERATURE*

070   US   ISSN 1050-4788
▼**WRITING CONCEPTS;** the newsletter on writing & editing. 1990. m. $59. Communication Concepts Inc., 2100 National Press Bldg., Washington, DC 20045. TEL 703-425-7751. FAX 703-425-8930. (Subscr. to: Box 1608, Springfield, VA 22151-0608)
  Description: Provides practical advice from peers for nonfiction writers and editors and addresses new problems they are facing.

808.02   US
XIE ZUO/WRITING. (Text in Chinese) m. $36.80. China Books & Periodicals, Inc., 2929 24th St., San Francisco, CA 94110. TEL 415-282-2994. FAX 415-282-0994.

070   CC
XINWEN JIZHE/JOURNALISTS. (Text in Chinese) m. Shanghai Shehui Kexueyuan, Xinwen Yanjiusuo - Shanghai Academy of Social Sciences, Institute of Journalism, No.20, Alley 18, Gao'an Road, Shanghai 200030, People's Republic of China. TEL 4337049. Ed. Wei Yongzheng.

070.808.02   CC
XINWEN XUEKAN. (Text in Chinese) bi-m. Y1.20 per no. (Zhongguo Xinwen Xuehui, Lianhehui) Xinwen Xuekan Bianjibu, 2, Jintai Xilu, Beijing, People's Republic of China. (Subscr. to: P.O. Box 8811, Beijing 100733, P.R.C.) (Co-sponsor: Zhongguo Shehui Kexueyuan, Xinwen Yanjiusuo) Ed. Qian Xinbo.
  Description: Examines issues related to journalism and the news media.

070   CC
XINWEN YANJIU ZILIAO/JOURNALISM RESEARCH MATERIALS. (Text in Chinese) q. Zhongguo Shehui Kexueyuan, Xinwen Yanjiusuo - Chinese Academy of Social Sciences, Institute of Journalism, 2, Jintan Xilu, Beixiang, Building No. 9, Beijing 100026, People's Republic of China. TEL 5022868. Ed. Yan Huanshu.

070   CC
XINWEN YU CHENGCAI. (Text in Chinese) m. Jiefangjun Baoshe, 34, Fuchengmenwai Dajie, Beijing 100832, People's Republic of China. TEL 6846991. Ed. Yuan Liang.

070   CC
XINWEN YU XIEZUO/JOURNALISM AND WRITING. (Text in Chinese) m. Beijing Ribao, 34, Biaobei Hutong, Dongdan, Beijing 100734, People's Republic of China. TEL 546218. Ed. Qi Shoucheng.

070 796   CC   ISSN 0257-5930
XINWEN ZHANXIAN. (Text in Chinese) m. Y12($36.80) People's Daily Publishing House - Renmin Ribao Chubanshe, 2, Jintai Xilu, Chaoyang Menwai, Beijing 100733, People's Republic of China. (Dist. outside China by: China International Book Trading Corp., P.O. Box 2820, Beijing, P.R.C.; Dist. in US by: China Books & Periodicals, Inc., 2929 24th St., San Francisco, CA 94110. TEL 415-272-2994) Ed. Cao Xianwen. adv.

070   CC
XINWENJIE/PRESS CIRCLES. (Text in Chinese) bi-m. Sichuan Daily, Sichuan Ribaoshe, Hongxing Zhonglu Erduan (Sec. 2), Chengdu, Sichuan 610012, People's Republic of China. TEL 667450. (Co-sponsor: Sichuan Journalists Association)

070   GR
YEARBOOK OF GREEK PRESS. 1965. a. free. Secretariat General of Press and Information, Zalokosta 10, Athens, Greece. Ed.Bd. index; circ. 2,000. (tabloid format)

070   CC
ZHONGGUO JIZHE/CHINESE JOURNALIST. (Text in Chinese) m. $42.20. Xinhua Tongxunshe - Xinhua News Agency, 57 Xuanwumen Xidajie, Beijing 100803, People's Republic of China. TEL 3073780. (Dist. in US by: China Books & Periodicals, Inc., 2929 24th St., San Francisco, CA 94110. TEL 415-282-2994) Ed. Yu Zhenpeng.

070   RU   ISSN 0022-5568
ZHURNALIST. 1967. m. 16.20 Rub. (Soyuz Zhurnalistov S.S.S.R.) Izdatel'stvo Pravda, Ul. Pravdy, 24, Moscow 125047, Russia. Ed. V. Zhidkov. bk.rev.; abstr.; bibl.; illus.; stat.; circ. 120,000.
  Indexed: Curr.Dig.Sov.Press.
  Supersedes: Sovetskaya Pechat'

070 296 956.940   IS
ZSHURNALIST. (Text in Yiddish) 1974. irreg. World Federation of Jewish Journalists, P.O. Box 7009, Tel Aviv 64734, Israel. (Co-sponsor: World Zionist Organization. Information Department)

070   US
10 BEST CENSORED STORIES. a. free. Project Censored, Sonoma State University, Rohnert Park, CA 94928. TEL 707-664-2149.
  Description: Top 10 censored stories of the previous year are capsulized. A combination of journalism review and bibliographic listing, and an innovative approach to constructive media criticism.

JOURNALISM — Abstracting, Bibliographies, Statistics

A B C NEWS INDEX. see *COMMUNICATIONS — Abstracting, Bibliographies, Statistics*

011   UA   ISSN 0303-2728
AHRAM INDEX. 1974. m. $60. Mu'assasat al-Ahram, Sharia al-Galaa, Cairo, Egypt. TEL 02-758333. FAX 02-745888. TELEX 20185 AHRAM UN. Ed. Muhammed M. Daoud. adv.; circ. 300. (also avail. in microfilm)
  Description: Index analysis of every item (articles, news) of Al-Ahram daily newspaper.

070   AU
AUSTRIAN JOURNALISTS INDEX; lists 6800 journalists. (Text in German) 1983. s-a. S.880($88) Presseverlag Wien, Frimmelgasse 41, Vienna 1190, Austria. TEL 371577. FAX 37-46-93. TELEX 115126. Ed. Peter Hoffer. adv.; index; circ. 1,200. (back issues avail.)

BENN'S MEDIA DIRECTORY. INTERNATIONAL EDITION. see *JOURNALISM*

BENN'S MEDIA DIRECTORY. U.K. EDITION. see *JOURNALISM*

CALIFORNIA NEWSPAPER PUBLISHERS ASSOCIATION. DIRECTORY AND RATE BOOK. see *JOURNALISM*

070 016   CN   ISSN 0225-7459
AI3
CANADIAN NEWS INDEX. 1977. m. (with a. cumulation). price varies. Micromedia Ltd., 20 Victoria St., Toronto, Ont. M5C 2N8, Canada. TEL 416-362-5211. FAX 416-362-6161. Ed. Tom McGreevy. index.
  ●Also available online. Vendor(s): CISTI, DIALOG (File no.262), IST-INFORMATHEQUE, QL Systems Ltd.. Also available on CD-ROM. Producer(s): Dialog Information Services.
  Formerly: Canadian Newspaper Index (ISSN 0384-983X)
  Description: Indexes nearly 100,000 articles per year from seven major Canadian daily newspapers.

070 011   US   ISSN 0893-245X
AI21.C462
CHRISTIAN SCIENCE MONITOR INDEX. 1945. m. (plus q. & a. cum.). $375. University Microfilms International, Data Courier, c/o Bonnie Maxwell, VP, 620 S. Third St., Louisville, KY 40202. TEL 800-626-2823. FAX 502-589-5572. **Indexed:** Bk.Rev.Ind., Bus.Ind., Child.Bk.Rev.Ind., Tr.& Indus.Ind.
  ●Also available online. Vendor(s): DIALOG.
  Former titles: Index to the Christian Science Monitor (ISSN 0098-1184); Christian Science Monitor. Cumulated Index (ISSN 0578-0152)

070.172   UK
CLOVER NEWSPAPER INDEX. 1986. 46/yr. £148 (foreign £252). Clover Publications, 32 Ickwell Rd., Northill, Biggleswade, Beds. SG18 9AB, England. TEL 076-727-363.
  Description: Indexes articles from daily and Sunday newspapers.

070 011   MX
COLEGIO DE MEXICO. BIBLIOTECA. LISTA DE OBRAS EN CANJE. PUBLICACIONES PERIODICAS. 1973. q. free. Colegio de Mexico, Biblioteca, Camino al Ajusco 20, Mexico 20, D.F., Mexico. FAX 652-06-19. bibl.; circ. 300.

808.02   US   ISSN 0277-5956
AI21.H37
CONNECTICUT NEWS HANDBOOK. 1977. a. $99.95. Connecticut Information Co., Box 460, Clinton, CT 06413. TEL 203-669-4917. Ed. Thomas C. Clarie. circ. 50.
  Description: Index and abstract service to 2,000 Hartford Courant stories about Connecticut.

JOURNALISM — ABSTRACTING, BIBLIOGRAPHIES, STATISTICS

CURRENT DIGEST OF THE POST-SOVIET PRESS. see POLITICAL SCIENCE — Abstracting, Bibliographies, Statistics

070 915.2   JA
DAILY SUMMARY OF THE JAPANESE PRESS. d. Embassy of the United States in Japan, 1-10-5 Akasaka, Minato-ku, Tokyo, Japan. (also avail. in microfilm)

011   DK   ISSN 0106-147X
DANSK ARTIKELINDEKS: AVISER OG TIDSSKRIFTER/DANISH INDEX OF ARTICLES: NEWSPAPERS AND PERIODICALS. 1940. m. (plus a. cum.) DKK 7243.75. Bibliotekscentralen, Tempovej 7-11, DK-2750 Ballerup, Denmark. TEL 2-974000. FAX 2-655310. bibl.; index; circ. 300. (back issues avail.)
●Also available online.
Formed by the merger of: Avis-Kronik-Index (ISSN 0005-2280); Dansk Tidsskrift Index.

070   DK   ISSN 0109-0968
DANSK FAGPRESSEKATALOG. 1984. a. DKK 175. Dansk Fagpresse Service ApS, Sommerstedgade 7, 1718 Copenhagen V, Denmark. circ. 3,832.
Description: Gives facts on media data, prices, sizes, circulation and members per year.

070   US   ISSN 0893-2441
AI21.D44
DENVER POST INDEX. 1979. m. (plus q. & a. cum.). $680. University Microfilms International, Data Courier, c/o Bonnie Maxwell, VP, 620 S. Third St., Louisville, KY 40202. TEL 800-626-2823. FAX 502-589-5572.
●Also available online. Vendor(s): DIALOG.
Formerly: Index to the Denver Post (ISSN 0195-6434)

070 011   US   ISSN 0893-2433
AI21.D46
DETROIT NEWS INDEX. 1976. m. (plus q. & a. cum.index). $680. University Microfilms International, Data Courier, c/o Bonnie Maxwell, VP, 620 S. Third St., Louisville, KY 40202. TEL 800-626-2823. FAX 502-589-5572.
●Also available online. Vendor(s): DIALOG.
Former titles: Index to the Detroit News; Detroit News. Newspaper Index (ISSN 0361-6983)

070 016   FR
FICHIERS-PRESSE. (Available in the following catagories: Mode et Beaute, Maison et Decoration, Economie et Finances, Arts et Spectacles, Tourisme et Loisirs, Alimentation et Distribution, Industries et Techniques, Medecine et Pharmacie, Fichier General, Presse Regionale, Agriculture, Fichier des Radios et Televisions) 1971. 5/yr. price varies for each category. Argus des Fichiers Presse, 19 bd. Montmartre, 75002 Paris, France. TEL 40-20-02-59. FAX 42-86-04-61. Ed. Stephanie Duriez. (looseleaf format)

070   JM   ISSN 0259-0336
GLEANER INDEX. 1975. q. $101. National Library of Jamaica, 12 East St., P.O. Box 823, Kingston, Jamaica, W.I. TEL 809-92-20620. FAX 809-92-25567. TELEX 596. Ed. Valerie G. Francis. circ. 35.
Formerly: Airs - Index to the Daily Gleaner.
Description: Personal name and subject index of articles of political, social, economic or cultural significance to Jamaica and the West Indies, appearing in the Gleaner.

070   CC
GUANGMING RIBAO SUOYIN/INDEX TO THE GUANGMING RIBAO. (Text in Chinese) m. $21.50. Guangming Ribao Chubanshe, 106, Yong'an Lu, Beijing 100050, People's Republic of China. (Dist. outside China by: China International Book Trading Corp., P.O. Box 2820, Beijing, P.R.C.; Dist. in US by: China Books & Periodicals, Inc., 2929 24th St., San Francisco, CA 94110. TEL 415-282-2994)

070 011   US   ISSN 0893-2476
AI21.H68
HOUSTON POST INDEX. 1976. m. (plus q. & a. cum.). $680. University Microfilms International, Data Courier, c/o Bonnie Maxwell, VP, 620 S. Third St., Louisville, KY 40202. TEL 800-626-2823. FAX 502-589-5672.
●Also available online. Vendor(s): DIALOG.
Former titles: Index to the Houston Post; Houston Post. Newspaper Index (ISSN 0363-7824)

011   MY   ISSN 0126-9062
AI3
INDEKS SURATKHABAR MALAYSIA. English Edition: Malaysian Newspaper Index (ISSN 0127-7448) (Editions in Bahasa Malaysia and English) 1979. q. M.$40 per no. National Library of Malaysia, Bibliography and Indexing Division, 3rd Fl., Wisma, Sachdev, Jalan Raja Laut, 50572 Kuala Lumpur, Malaysia. TEL 2923144. TELEX MA 30092. (Order to: University of Malaya Co-operative Bookshop Ltd, Library Building, University of Malaya, 59100 Kuala Lumpur, Malaysia) Ed. Zahariah Sharoon. circ. 320.

011   US
INDEX OF THE MINNEAPOLIS STAR AND TRIBUNE. m. University Microfilms International, Serials Data Management, 300 N. Zeeb Rd., Ann Arbor, MI 48106. TEL 313-761-4700. (back issues avail.)

070   US   ISSN 0741-5281
AI21.B63
INDEX TO THE BOSTON GLOBE. 1983. m. (plus a. cumulation). $680. University Microfilms International, Serials Data Management, 300 N. Zeeb Rd., Ann Arbor, MI 48106. TEL 313-761-4700.

011   US
INDEX TO THE NATIONAL OBSERVER. irreg. University Microfilms International, Data Courier, c/o Bonnie Maxwell, 620 S. Third St., Louisville, KY 40202. TEL 800-626-2823. FAX 502-589-5572. (Or: 300 N. Zeeb Rd., Ann Arbor, MI 48106) (back issues avail.)
Formerly: National Observer Newspaper Index (ISSN 0363-7832)

011   US
INDEX TO THE ST. PAUL PIONEER PRESS. 1967. m. (plus a. cumulation). $212 to non tax-exempt organizations. St. Paul Public Library, 90 W. Fourth St., St. Paul, MN 55102. TEL 612-292-6306. FAX 612-292-6141. Ed. Norman Lathrop. bk.rev.; circ. 36. (looseleaf format; back issues avail.)
Former titles: Index to the St. Paul Pioneer Press and Dispatch; St. Paul Dispatch and Pioneer Press Newspaper Index (ISSN 0048-900X)

954 015   II   ISSN 0019-6177
AI3
INDIAN PRESS INDEX. (Text in English) 1968. m. Rs.300($70) Delhi Library Association, Box 1270, c/o Hardinge Public Library, Queen's Gardens, Delhi 6, India. Ed. Shri C.P. Vashisth. index.

070 016   US   ISSN 0742-3985
INTERNATIONAL PERIODICALS AND REFERENCE WORKS. 1974. irreg. free to libraries. Maxwell Scientific International (Subsidiary of: Pergamon Press, Inc.), Fairview Park, Elmsford, NY 10523. TEL 914-592-7700. Ed. Edward Gray. adv.; bibl.; circ. 15,000.
Former titles: Guide to International Periodicals & Librarians' Guide to Back Issues of International Periodicals; Reference Guide and Comprehensive Catalog of International Serials (ISSN 0094-0151)

070   US
JIEFANG RIBAO SUOYIN/LIBERATION DAILY. INDEX. (Text in Chinese) m. $329.80. China Books & Periodicals, Inc., 2929 24th St., San Francisco, CA 94110. TEL 415-282-2994. FAX 415-282-0994.

070 016   US   ISSN 0075-4412
PN4725
JOURNALISM ABSTRACTS; M.A., M.S., and Ph.D. theses in journalism and mass communication. 1963. a. $15 to individuals (foreign $25); institutions $20 (foreign $30). Association for Education in Journalism and Mass Communication, 1621 College St., University of South Carolina, Columbia, SC 29208-0251. TEL 803-777-2005. Ed. Gilbert Fowler. circ. 700. (also avail. in microform from UMI; reprint service avail. from UMI)
—BLDSC shelfmark: 5072.825000.

016   US
LATHROP REPORT ON NEWSPAPER INDEXES. 1979. irreg. $60. Norman Lathrop Enterprises, 2342 Star Dr., Box 198, Wooster, OH 44691. TEL 216-262-5587. illus.
Description: Detailed descriptions of all known published and unpublished newspaper indexes in the United States and Canada.

070 011   US   ISSN 0742-4817
AI21.L65
LOS ANGELES TIMES INDEX. 1972. m. (plus q. & a. cum.) $680. University Microfilms International, Data Courier, c/o Bonnie Maxwell, VP, 620 S. Third St., Louisville, KY 40202. TEL 800-626-2823. FAX 502-589-5572. *Indexed:* Art & Archaeol.Tech.Abstr., Bus.Ind., Med.Care Rev.
●Also available online. Vendor(s): DIALOG.
Former titles: Index to the Los Angeles Times (ISSN 0195-6418); Los Angeles Times. Newspaper Index (ISSN 0098-1192)

070   GW   ISSN 0170-4192
Z6956.G3
MEDIA DATEN: FACHZEITSCHRIFTEN. 7/yr. DM.804. Media Daten Verlag GmbH, Heidesheimer Str. 49, D-6500 Mainz, Germany. TEL 06131-40024.

070   GW   ISSN 0170-4176
Z6956.G3
MEDIA DATEN: ZEITSCHRIFTEN. 7/yr. DM.804. Media Daten Verlag GmbH, Heidesheimer Str. 49, D-6500 Mainz, Germany. TEL 06131-40024.

070   GW   ISSN 0931-3265
MEDIA DATEN: ZEITUNGEN. (Text in German) 1961. 7/yr. DM.804. Media Daten Verlag Gmbh, Heidesheimer Str. 49, D-6500 Mainz, Germany. TEL 06131-40024. adv.; circ. 2,580.
Formerly: Media Daten (ISSN 0038-951X)

070 011   US   ISSN 0893-2484
AI21.T66
NEW ORLEANS TIMES-PICAYUNE INDEX. 1972. m. (plus q. & a. cum.). $680. University Microfilms International, Data Courier, c/o Bonnie Maxwell, VP, 620 S. Third St., Louisville, KY 40202. TEL 800-626-2823. FAX 502-589-5572.
Former titles: Index to the New Orleans Times-Picayune (ISSN 0195-640X); New Orleans Times-Picayune. Newspaper Index (ISSN 0098-1206)

070   US   ISSN 0147-538X
AI21
NEW YORK TIMES INDEX. 1913. s-m. (plus 3 quarterly & a. cumulations). $495 for s-m.; a. only $525; s-m., q., & a. $760. (New York Times Company) University Microfilms International, Serials Data Management, 300 N. Zeeb Rd., Ann Arbor, MI 48106. TEL 313-761-4700.
●Also available online.
Also available on CD-ROM.

070 016   US
NEW YORK TIMES INDEX HIGHLIGHTS. 1977. q. free to New York Times Index subscribers. (New York Times Company) University Microfilms International, Serials data Management, 300 N. Zeeb Rd., Ann Arbor, MI 48106.

070   PP
P N G POST-COURIER INDEX. 1972. a. price varies. National Research Institute, P.O. Box 5854, Boroko, NCD, Papua New Guinea. TEL 675-26-0300. FAX 675-26-0312.

070   PP
P N G TIMES INDEX. 1980. irreg. price varies. National Research Institute, P.O. Box 5854, Boroko, NCD, Papua New Guinea. TEL 675-26-0300. FAX 675-26-0312.

P O M P I. (Popular Music Periodicals Index) see MUSIC — Abstracting, Bibliographies, Statistics

PROGRESSIVE PERIODICALS DIRECTORY. see PUBLISHING AND BOOK TRADE — Abstracting, Bibliographies, Statistics

070   CC
RENMIN RIBAO SUOYIN/PEOPLE'S DAILY. INDEX. (Text in Chinese) m. $32.30. People's Daily Publishing House - Renmin Ribao Chubanshe, 2 Jintai Xilu, Chaoyangmenwai, Beijing 100733, People's Republic of China. (Dist. in US by: China Books & Periodicals, Inc., 2929 24th St., San Francisco, CA 94019. TEL 415-282-0994)

070 US ISSN 0893-2417
AI21.S79
ST. LOUIS POST-DISPATCH INDEX. Variant title: Index to the St. Louis Post-Dispatch. 1980. m. (plus q. & a. cum.). $580. University Microfilms International, Data Courier, c/o Bonnie Maxwell, VP, 620 S. Third St., Louisville, KY 40202. TEL 800-626-2823. FAX 502-589-5572.
  Formerly: Bell & Howell Newspaper Index to the St. Louis Post-Dispatch (ISSN 0275-858X)

070 011 US ISSN 0893-2425
AI21.S25
SAN FRANCISCO CHRONICLE INDEX. 1976. m. (plus q. & a. cum.). $680. University Microfilms International, Data Courier, c/o Bonnie Maxwell, VP, 620 S. Third St., Louisville, KY 40202. TEL 800-626-2823. FAX 502-589-5572.
  Former titles: Index to the San Francisco Chronicle (ISSN 0195-6396); San Francisco Chronicle. Newspaper Index (ISSN 0363-7816)

011 MF
SUBJECT INDEX TO ARTICLES IN NEWSPAPERS IN MAURITIUS. Cover title: Newspapers Index: Mauritius. (Text in English) publication begun and suspended 1978; resumed 1983. s-a. City Library, City Hall, Port Louis, Mauritius.

948 011 FI ISSN 0355-4074
SUOMEN SANOMALEHTIEN MIKROFILMIT/MICROFILMED NEWSPAPERS OF FINLAND. (Text in English, Finnish, Swedish) 1971. quinquennial. free. Helsingin Yliopiston Kirjasto - Helsinki University Library, Box 312, 00171 Helsinki, Finland. circ. 300.
  Description: Contains bibliographic data on Finnish newspapers microfilmed by Helsinki University Library.

011 UK
TIMES INDEX. 1906. m. $760. Research Publications Ltd., P.O. Box 45, Reading RG1 8HF, England. FAX 0734-5912325. (Dist. in U.S. by: Research Publications Inc., 12 Lunar Dr., Drawer AB, Woodbridge, CT 06525) index; circ. 1,000. (also avail. in microfilm) **Indexed:** Ind.Bus.Rep.
  Formerly: Index to the Times (ISSN 0046-8924)

070 011 US ISSN 0041-1116
Z7403
TRANSDEX INDEX. Variant title: Bell and Howell Transdex. 1974. m. (plus microform a. cum.). $885. University Microfilms International, Research Information Services, c/o Amy Seeto, Mgr., 300 N. Zeeb Rd., Ann Arbor, MI 48106. TEL 313-761-4700. Key Title: Transdex.
  —BLDSC shelfmark: 9020.581300.

070 US ISSN 0893-2409
AI21.U8
U S A TODAY INDEX. 1982. m. (plus q. & a. cum.). $265. University Microfilms International, Data Courier, c/o Bonnie Maxwell, VP, 620 S. Third St., Louisville, KY 40202. TEL 800-626-2823. FAX 502-589-5572.
  Formerly: Index to USA Today (ISSN 0736-9999)

WHO'S WHO IN WRITERS, EDITORS & POETS IN THE UNITED STATES & CANADA; a biographical directory. see LITERATURE — Abstracting, Bibliographies, Statistics

053 073 015 GW ISSN 0340-0107
ZEITUNGS - INDEX; Verzeichnis wichtiger Aufsaetze aus deutschsprachigen Zeitungen. (Supplement: Buchrezensionen) 1974. q. DM.448. K.G. Saur Verlag KG, Ortlerstr. 8, Postfach 701620, 8000 Munich 70, Germany. TEL 089-76902-0. FAX 089-76902150. Ed. Willi Gorzny. index; circ. 1,000.
  ●Also available on CD-ROM.
  Description: Indexes 19 German-language daily and weekly newspapers.

JUDAISM

see Religions and Theology–Judaic

JUDICIAL SYSTEMS

see Law–Judicial Systems

LABOR AND INDUSTRIAL RELATIONS

see Business and Economics–Labor and Industrial Relations

LABOR UNIONS

see also Business and Economics–Labor and Industrial Relations

331.8 US ISSN 0001-009X
HD6856
A A L C REPORTER. (Editions in Arabic, English, French) 1965(English, French); 1977(Arabic). bi-m. free. African-American Labor Center, A F L - C I O, 1400 K St., Ste. 700, Washington, DC 20005. TEL 202-789-1020. FAX 202-842-0730. TELEX 710-822-1115. Ed. John T. Sarr. illus.; cum.index: 1970-1974; 1975-1977; 1978-1980; 1981-84; 1985-89; circ. 3,850(combined circ. for all 3 editions). **Indexed:** HR Rep.
  Description: Reports on the activities and policies of the center in its cooperative program with African labor movements to promote free and democratic labor.

331.8 US
A A U C G INSIDER. m. free. Public Service Research Council, Americans Against Union Control of Government, 1761 Business Center Dr., Ste. 230, Reston, VA 22090-5333. TEL 703-438-3966. FAX 703-438-3935.

331 GW ISSN 0001-1126
A F A INFORMATIONEN. 1951. 6/yr. DM.14. (Deutscher Gewerkschaftsbund, Arbeitskreis fuer Arbeitsstudien) Bund-Verlag GmbH, Hansestr. 63a, Postfach 900840, 5000 Cologne 90, Germany. bibl.; charts; circ. 4,200. **Indexed:** Dok.Arbeitsmed.

331.8 327 US ISSN 0890-6165
A F L - C I O. DEPARTMENT OF INTERNATIONAL AFFAIRS. BULLETIN. m. American Federation of Labor - Congress of Industrial Organizations, Department of International Affairs, 815 16th St., N.W., Washington, DC 20006. Dir. Tom Kahn.

331.8 US
A F L - C I O CONVENTION PROCEEDINGS. 1955. biennial. $15. A F L - C I O, 815 16th St., N.W., Washington, DC 20006. TEL 202-637-5041. index; circ. 5,000. (back issues avail.)

331.88 US ISSN 0001-1185
A F L - C I O NEWS. 1956. bi-w. $10. American Federation of Labor - Congress of Industrial Organizations, 815 16th St., N.W., Washington, DC 20006. TEL 202-637-5032. FAX 202-637-5058. Ed. Michael Byrne. bk.rev.; illus.; circ. 75,000. (tabloid format; also avail. in microform from UMI) **Indexed:** Med.Care Rev., Pers.Lit.
  ●Also available online. Vendor(s): DIALOG.

331.88 370 US
A F T ISSUES BULLETIN. irreg. American Federation of Teachers, 555 New Jersey Ave., N.W., Washington, DC 20001. TEL 202-879-4400. (reprint service avail. from UMI)

331.88 384.5 US
A F T R A. 1968. q. free. American Federation of Television and Radio Artists, 260 Madison Ave., 7th Fl., New York, NY 10016-2401. Ed. Dick Moore. adv.; bk.rev.; charts; illus.; circ. 80,000.
  Formerly: American Federation of Television and Radio Artists. A F T R A (ISSN 0044-7676)

LABOR UNIONS 2579

791 US
A G V A NEWSLETTER.* 1958. irreg. membership. American Guild of Variety Artists, 184 Fifth Ave., New York, NY 10010. TEL 212-675-1003. adv.; bk.rev.; illus.; circ. 16,500.
  Formerly: A G V A News (ISSN 0001-1371)

331.3 SP
A HOMBROS DE TRABAJADORES. m. Juan de Austria 9, 28010 Madrid, Spain. TEL 91-4464290. Dir. Juan Gonzalez Castejon.

331.88 650 UK
A P E X. 1908. 6/yr. £5 (foreign £7). Association of Professional, Executive, Clerical and Computer Staff, 22 Worple Rd., Wimbledon, London SW19 4DF, England. Ed. Neil Hamilton. adv.; bk.rev.; abstr.; illus.; circ. 60,000.
  Formerly: Clerk (ISSN 0009-8744)

331.88 384.5 US ISSN 0001-2289
A R A LOG.* 1949. 2/yr. membership only. American Radio Association, 26 Journal Sq., Ste. 1501, Jersey City, NJ 07306. Ed. W.R. Steinberg. adv.; bk.rev.; charts; illus.; stat.; circ. 3,000.

331.8 AT
A S U NATIONAL. 1986. q. free. Australian Services Union, National Executive, 116-124 Queensberry St., Carlton South, Vic. 3053, Australia. TEL 03-348-1788. FAX 03-374-5050. Ed. S.P. Gibbs. bk.rev.; circ. 72,000. (back issues avail.)
  Formerly: Foreword (ISSN 0819-2006)

A T F ANNUAL REPORT. (Australian Teachers Union) see EDUCATION

331.3 AO
A VOZ DO TRABALHADOR. m. Uniao Nacional de Trabalhadores Angolanos, CP 28, Luanda, Angola.

331.8 AT
ABOUT U. a. Australian Council of Trade Unions, 393-397 Swanston St., Melbourne, Vic. 3000, Australia. TEL 03-663-5266. (Co-sponsors: BTR Nylex; Ericsson)

331.3 SP
ACCION SINDICALISTA. m. Via Layetana 16 y 18, 08003 Barcelona, Spain. TEL 93-3105192. Dir. Joaquin Jose Saurina.

331.88 FR ISSN 0181-2874
ACTION JURIDIQUE (PARIS, 1978). 1978. bi-m. 250 F. (foreign 307 F.)(effective Jan. 1992). Confederation Francaise Democratique du Travail, 4 Blvd. de la Villette, 75955 Paris Cedex 19, France. TEL 42-03-81-40. Ed. Loic Richard.

AEROVOZ. see AERONAUTICS AND SPACE FLIGHT

331.88 LB ISSN 0002-0044
AFRICAN LABOUR NEWS.* vol.3, 1967. w. International Confederation of Free Trade Unions, African Regional Organisation, P.O.B. 415, Monrovia, Liberia. Ed. Gab Atitsogbui. illus. (tabloid format)

331.88 BE ISSN 0065-4027
AFRICAN REGIONAL TRADE UNION CONFERENCE. REPORT. 1957. irreg., 4th, 1964, Addis Ababa. (African Regional Organization of ICFTU) International Confederation of Free Trade Unions, 37-47, rue Montagne aux Herbes Potageres, B-1000 Brussels, Belgium. TEL 02-217-80-85. FAX 02-217-80-85. TELEX 26785 ICFTU BRU.

331.88 TG
AFRICAN TRADE UNION NEWS. bi-m. Regional Economic Research and Documentation Center, Box 7138, Lome, Togo. **Indexed:** HR Rep.

331.88 387 US ISSN 0002-2411
AIR LINE EMPLOYEE. 1952. bi-m. $5 or membership. Air Line Employees Association, 5600 S. Central, Chicago, IL 60638. TEL 312-767-3333. Ed. Quentin David, Jr. illus.; circ. 12,000.

AIR LINE PILOT; the magazine of professional flight deck crews. see AERONAUTICS AND SPACE FLIGHT

L

LABOR UNIONS

331.88 780   US   ISSN 0002-5704
ML1
ALLEGRO. 1921. 11/yr. $20 to non-members. Associated Musicians of Greater New York, Local 802, A F M, 330 W. 42nd St., New York, NY 10036. TEL 212-239-4802. FAX 212-268-8696. Ed. Tim Ledwith. adv.; bk.rev.; illus.; circ. 20,000 (controlled). (newspaper)

L'ALLIANCE (MONTREAL). see *EDUCATION*

ALLIANCE (OTTAWA). see *PUBLIC ADMINISTRATION*

331.88   US   ISSN 0002-6107
ALLIED INDUSTRIAL WORKER. 1956. m. $6. Allied Industrial Workers of America, A F L - C I O, 3520 W. Oklahoma Ave., Milwaukee, WI 53215. TEL 414-645-9500. FAX 414-645-5530. Ed. Dominick D'Ambrosio. bk.rev.; illus.; circ. 76,000. (tabloid format)

AMERICAN EDUCATOR. see *EDUCATION*

AMERICAN FEDERATION OF MUSICIANS LOCAL 325. see *MUSIC*

331.88 371.1   US   ISSN 0894-8208
AMERICAN FEDERATION OF TEACHERS. ACTION. w. American Federation of Teachers, 555 New Jersey Ave., N.W., Washington, DC 20001. TEL 202-879-4400. Ed. Trish Gorman. (reprint service avail. from UMI)
   Former titles: A F T - Action; A F T in Action.

331.88   US   ISSN 0002-8525
HD6350.G5
AMERICAN FLINT. 1909. m. membership. American Flint Glass Workers' Union, 1440 S. Byrne Rd., Toledo, OH 43614. FAX 419-385-8839. Ed. Richard Morgan. circ. 12,000.

331.88 387.5   US   ISSN 0002-9882
AMERICAN MARITIME OFFICER. 1971. m. free. Marine Engineers Beneficial Association - Associated Maritime Officers, A F L - C I O, District 2, 650 Fourth Ave., Brooklyn, NY 11232. TEL 718-965-6750. Ed. Paul Doell. adv.; charts; illus.; circ. 21,000. (tabloid format)

AMERICAN POSTAL WORKER. see *COMMUNICATIONS — Postal Affairs*

331.88 370   US   ISSN 0003-1380
AMERICAN TEACHER. 1916. m. $10 or membership. American Federation of Teachers, 555 New Jersey Ave., N.W., Washington, DC 20001. TEL 202-879-4430. Ed. Trish Gorman. adv.; bk.rev.; illus.; circ. 700,000. (also avail. in microform from UMI,MIM; reprint service avail. from UMI) **Indexed:** Biog.Ind., Educ.Ind.

331.8   GW   ISSN 0341-017X
ANGESTELLTEN MAGAZIN; Wirtschaft und Wissen. 1950. m. DM.18. (Deutscher Gewerkschaftsbund) Bund-Verlag GmbH, Hansestr. 63a, Postfach 900840, 5000 Cologne 90, Germany. Ed. Hermann A. Grontzki. adv.; bk.rev.; abstr.; charts; illus.; stat.; circ. 430,000.
   Formerly: Wirtschaft und Wissen (ISSN 0043-616X)

331.8   AU   ISSN 0003-7656
HD4809
ARBEIT UND WIRTSCHAFT. 1923. m. S.142($7) Oesterreichischer Gewerkschaftsbund, Hohenstaufengasse 10-12, A-1010 Vienna, Austria. Ed. Gottfried Duvaz. bk.rev.; charts; illus.; index; circ. 30,000. **Indexed:** C.I.S. Abstr., Int.Lab.Doc.

331.8   GW
ARBEITNEHMER. 1953. m. DM.10.50. Arbeitskammer des Saarlandes, Fritz-Dobisch-Str. 6-8, 6600 Saarbruecken, Germany. TEL 0681-4005-0. FAX 0681-4005-401. Ed. Hans-Arthur Klein. adv.; bk.rev.; charts; illus.; stat.; tr.lit.; circ. 23,000. **Indexed:** Dok.Arbeitsmed.
   Former titles: Saarlaendischer Arbeitnehmer (ISSN 0003-7737); Arbeitskammer.

331.8   SW   ISSN 0003-7842
ARBETSLEDAREN. 1908. m. SEK 160 (typically set in Jan.). Sveriges Arbetsledarefoerbund, P.O. Box 12069, 102 22 Stockholm 12, Sweden. FAX 08-539968. Ed. Anders Arhammar. adv.; bk.rev.; illus.; stat.; circ. 93,000.

ARC-BOUTANT; organe d'information des questions scolaires et familiales. see *SOCIAL SERVICES AND WELFARE*

331 630   LY
AL-ARDH. w. Agricultural Trade Union, P.O. Box 7528, Tripoli, Libya.

331.88 690   US   ISSN 0004-4245
HD6515.A55
ASBESTOS WORKER. 1916. q. free. International Association of Asbestos Workers, Machinists Bldg., 1300 Connecticut Ave., N.W., Washington, DC 20036. TEL 202-785-2388. Ed. Andrew T. Haaf. illus.; circ. controlled.

331.8   II
ASIAN AND PACIFIC LABOUR. (Text in English) 1963. bi-m. Rs.48($25) International Confederation of Free Trade Unions (ICFTU), Asian and Pacific Regional Organization, P-20, Green Park Extension, Delhi 110016, India. Ed. V.S. Mathur. adv.; bk.rev.; illus.; stat.; circ. 25,000.
   Formerly: Asian Labour (ISSN 0004-4601)

792.028 331.88   AG
ASOCIACION ARGENTINA DE ACTORES. MEMORIA Y BALANCE.* no.58, 1977. a. free. Asociacion Argentina de Actores, Alsina 1766, Buenos Aires, Argentina. circ. 3,000.

331.88   II   ISSN 0970-8626
ASSOCIATION OF SCIENTIFIC WORKERS OF INDIA. BULLETIN. (Text in English) 1947. 9/yr. Rs.10. Association of Scientific Workers of India, 10 Rajendra Park, New Delhi 110 060, India. TEL 11-587625. Ed. Ram Prasad. adv.; bk.rev.; circ. 2,000.
   Formerly (until 1968): Vijnan Karmee.

331.8   GW   ISSN 0004-8119
AUSBLICK (DUSSELDORF). 1948. m. DM.10. Gewerkschaft Handel, Banken und Versicherungen, Tersteegenstr. 30, 4000 Dusseldorf 30, Germany. TEL 0211-4582-0. FAX 0211-4582239. TELEX 08584653. Ed. Detlef Feldhoff. bk.rev.; film rev.; play rev.; abstr.; charts; illus.; mkt.; stat.; circ. 400,000. **Indexed:** M.L.A.

331   AT
AUSTRALIAN CONGRESS OF TRADE UNIONS. DECISIONS. biennial. Aus.$3. Australian Council of Trade Unions, 393-397 Swanston St., Melbourne, Vic. 3000, Australia.

331 385   AT
AUSTRALIAN RAILWAYS UNION. FEDERAL OFFICE NEWS. 1960. q. free. Percival Publishing Co. Pty. Ltd., 862-870 Elizabeth St., Waterloo, N.S.W. 2017, Australia.

AUSTRALIAN TEACHER. see *EDUCATION*

331.88   AT   ISSN 0045-0979
AUSTRALIAN WORKER. 1891. bi-m. Aus.$6($6.50) to non-members. (Australian Workers Union) D.F. Austin Publishing, Post Office Building, 148 Harris St., Pyrmont, N.S.W. 2009, Australia. FAX 02-6901020. TELEX AA73231. Ed.Bd. adv.; circ. 105,000. (tabloid format)
   Incorporates: Queensland Worker (ISSN 0043-8065)

AUTOTECNICA. see *TRANSPORTATION — Automobiles*

331.88 664   US   ISSN 0163-447X
B C & T NEWS. 1969. 10/yr. free to qualified personnel. Bakery, Confectionery and Tobacco Workers International Union, 10401 Connecticut Ave., Kensington, MD 20895. TEL 301-933-8600. bk.rev.; illus.; circ. 175,000. (tabloid format)
   Supersedes: B and C News (ISSN 0001-043X); Which was formed by the merger of: A B C News; Bakers and Confectioners Journal.

331.88   US   ISSN 1049-3921
HD6350.R43
B M W E RAILWAY JOURNAL. 1892. m. (10/yr.). $16. Brotherhood of Maintenance of Way Employes, 12050 Woodward Ave., Detroit, MI 48203-3596. TEL 313-868-0490. Ed. Charles F. Fountain. illus.; circ. 65,000.
   Former titles: B M W E Railway Journal (ISSN 0146-0625); Brotherhood of Maintenance of Way Employes. Journal (ISSN 0007-2443)

331.8   IS
BAMAARACHOT. m. Technical Engineers Union, 93 Arlozorov St., Tel Aviv 62 098, Israel.

331.88 332.1   II   ISSN 0005-5077
BANK KARAMCHARI. (Text in English) 1963. m. Rs.5($3.) All India Bank Employees Federation, c/o V.N. Sekhri, 26-104 Birhana Rd., Kanpur 208001, India. Ed. Shri V.K. Agarwal. adv.; bk.rev.; circ. 2,000.

BANKVAERLDEN. see *BUSINESS AND ECONOMICS — Banking And Finance*

331.8   ML
BARAKELA. m. Union Nationale des Travailleurs du Mali, Bamako, Mali.

331.8   GW   ISSN 0933-0615
BEAMTE HEUTE. 1949. m. DM.14. (Deutscher Gewerkschaftsbund) Bund-Verlag GmbH, Hansestr. 63a, Postfach 900840, 5000 Cologne 90, Germany. Ed. Dieter Benthien. adv.; bk.rev.; abstr.; index; circ. 94,000.
   Formerly: Deutsche Beamte (ISSN 0011-9938)

331.8   GW
DER BEAMTE IN DER BUNDESANSTALT FUER ARBEIT. 1954. bi-m. membership. Verband der Beamten der Bundesanstalt fuer Arbeit, Dientzenhofer Str. 9a, D-8500 Nuremberg, Germany. adv.; bk.rev.; circ. 5,000.

331.3   CC
BEIJING GONGREN/BEIJING WORKERS. (Text in Chinese) m. Beijing Shi Zonggonghui, 2, Taijichang Santiao, Beijing 100005, People's Republic of China. TEL 544207. Ed. Zheng Shouting.

331.8   SW   ISSN 0005-8262
BEKLAEDNADSFOLKET. 1944. m. SEK 100. Beklaednadsarbetarnes Foerbund, P.O. Box 1120, 111 81 Stockholm, Sweden. FAX 08-242354. Ed. Ingemar Dahlkvist. adv.; charts; illus.; circ. 31,000 (controlled).

331.8   IS
BEMOATZA. bi-m. Jerusalem Labour Federation, 17 Strauss St., Jerusalem 91 000, Israel. TEL 02-233863.

331.88 622   GW   ISSN 0933-0127
BERGBAU-BERUFSGENOSSENSCHAFT. JAHRESBERICHT. 1887. a. free. Bergbau-Berufsgenossenschaft, Hunscheidtstr. 18, 4630 Bochum, Germany. TEL 0234-316352. FAX 0234-316300. adv.; bk.rev.; stat.; circ. 1,600. **Indexed:** GeoRef.
   Formerly: Bergbau-Berufsgenossenschaft. Geschaeftsbericht (ISSN 0343-0510)
   Description: Annual and statistical report of insurance companies for the mining industry. Covers mine accidents, work related illnesses, injuries, and workers' compensation.

331.8   CS   ISSN 0006-0453
BEZPECNOST A HYGIENA PRACE/SAFETY AND HYGIENE OF WORK.* 1951. m. $39.20. Prace, Publishing House of the Trade Union Movement, c/o Artia, Ve Smeckach 30, 111 37 Prague 1, Czechoslovakia. Ed. Jiri Pehe. adv.; bk.rev.; circ. 48,000. **Indexed:** C.I.S. Abstr.

331   US
BOILERMAKERS - BLACKSMITHS REPORTER. 1961? 6/yr. $1.50. International Brotherhood of Boilermakers, Iron Ship Builders, Blacksmiths, Forgers and Helpers, 753 State Ave., Ste. 565, Kansas City, KS 66101. TEL 913-371-2640. Ed. Charles W. Jones. index; circ. 95,000. (tabloid format; back issues avail.)
   Description: AFL-CIO, CFL union membership newspaper.

BRIEFING SESSIONS ON COLLECTIVE BARGAINING AND EMPLOYEE RELATIONS. see *BUSINESS AND ECONOMICS — Labor And Industrial Relations*

331.88   SZ
BUILDING AND WOOD.* q. International Federation of Building and Woodworkers, c/o Ulf Asp, ICC Building A, 20 route de Pre-Bois, Postfach 733, 1215 Geneve 15 Aeorport, Switzerland.

LABOR UNIONS 2581

690 331.88   US   ISSN 0007-3717
BUILDING TRADESMAN.* 1952. w. $8. Greater Detroit Building Trade Council, 1640 Porter St., Detroit, MI 48216. Ed. Donald Constantineau. adv.; illus.; circ. 67,000. (newspaper)

331.8 664   BU
BULGARIAN FEDERATION OF AGRICULTURAL WORKERS' INDEPENDENT UNIONS. BULLETIN. bi-m. Bulgarian Federation of Agricultural Workers' Independent Unions, Dimo Hajidimov 29, 1606 Sofia, Bulgaria. TEL 5-16-51.
Formerly: U A F I W Bulletin.

331.88   BU   ISSN 0007-3954
BULGARIAN TRADE UNIONS. 1948. bi-m. $5. (Bulgarski Profesionalni Suiuzi) Izdatelstvo Profizdat, 82, Dondukov Blvd., Sofia, Bulgaria. (Dist. by: Hemus, 6, Rouski Blvd., 1000 Sofia Bulgaria) Ed. Kiril Panauotov. illus.; circ. 3,850. **Indexed:** BSL Econ.

331.88   II   ISSN 0045-348X
BULLET. (Text in English or Hindi) no.19, 1971. m. Rs.1.20. All India Administrative Offices Employees Union, C-1-2 Baird Rd., New Delhi 110001, India. Ed. L.A. Prasad. adv.; stat.; circ. 7,500.

331.8   FR   ISSN 0294-8397
C F D T AUJOURD'HUI. 1973. bi-m. 309 F. (foreign 349 F.)(effective Jan. 1992). Confederation Francaise Democratique du Travail, 4 Blvd. de la Villette, 75955 Paris Cedex 19, France. TEL 42-03-81-40. Ed. A. Mercier.

C H C G PULSE. (Canadian Health Care Guild) see MEDICAL SCIENCES — Nurses And Nursing

331   SR
C L O BULLETIN. 1973. irreg. Centrale Landsdienaren Organisatie, Gemenelandsweg 95, Paramaribo, Surinam.

C N V - OPINIE. (Christelijk Nationaal Vakverbond in Nederland) see RELIGIONS AND THEOLOGY

331.88 384   US   ISSN 0007-9227
C W A NEWS. 1948. m. $2. Communications Workers of America, 501 Third St., N.W., Washington, DC 20001. TEL 202-434-1100. FAX 202-434-1482. Ed. Jeffery M. Miller. bk.rev.; charts; illus.; circ. 525,000. (also avail. in microfrom from UMI; microfilm from KTO; reprint service avail. from UMI)

331.88   FR   ISSN 0398-3145
CADRES C F D T. 1948. bi-m. 230 F. Union Confederale des Ingenieurs et Cadres, 47 av. Simon Bolivar, 75948 Paris Cedex 19, France. FAX 42-47-72-04. Ed. Marie-Noelle Auberger. adv.; bk.rev.; circ. 30,000.
Formerly: Cadres and Profession (ISSN 0007-9472)

CAHIERS D'ETUDE ET DE RECHERCHE. see BUSINESS AND ECONOMICS — Economic Systems And Theories, Economic History

331.88   BG
CALAMANA.* (Text in Bengali) q. Tk.1. Chalaman Sanskritik Sibir, Kendriya Samsada, S-1 Nurjahan Rd., Mohammadpur, Dhaka 7, Bangladesh.

331.116   CN   ISSN 0381-4130
CALENDAR OF EXPIRING COLLECTIVE AGREEMENTS (YEAR). a. Can.$11.20. Ministry of Labour and Consumer Services, Parliament Bldgs., Victoria, B.C. V8V 1X4, Canada. (Subscr. to: Crown Publications, 546 Yates St., Victoria, B.C. V8W 1K8, Canada. TEL 604-386-4636)
Description: Compiles major collective agreements in BC which are scheduled to expire in the coming year.

331.88   US   ISSN 0008-0802
CALIFORNIA A F L - C I O NEWS. 1959. w. $10 to individuals; corporations $20. California Labor Federation, A F L - C I O, 417 Montgomery St., San Francisco, CA 94104. TEL 415-986-3535. FAX 415-956-7838. Ed. Floyd Tucker. bk.rev.; stat.; circ. 5,200.

353.93   US
CALIFORNIA PRIDE. 1931. 10/yr. $10. California State Employees Association, 1108 O St., Sacramento, CA 95814. TEL 916-444-8134. FAX 916-326-4214. Ed. Robert Striegel. adv.; bk.rev.; illus.; circ. 60,000. **Indexed:** Cal.Per.Ind. (1990-).
Formerly: California State Employee (ISSN 0008-1566)

CALIFORNIA TEACHER. see EDUCATION

331.8   CN
CANADA WORKS!. (Text in English, French) 1971. bi-m. Service Employees International, One Credit Union Dr., Toronto, Ont. M4A 2S6, Canada. TEL 416-752-4770. FAX 416-752-1966. Ed. Lou Volpentesta. circ. 45,000. (back issues avail.)
Formerly: Canadian Service Employee.

CANADIAN EMPLOYMENT BENEFITS & PENSION GUIDE. see INSURANCE

383   CN   ISSN 0008-4794
CANADIAN POSTMASTER/MAITRE DE POSTE CANADIEN. (Text in English, French) 1926. 4/yr. membership. Canadian Postmasters and Assistants Association, 281 Queen Mary, Ottawa, Ont. K1K 1X1, Canada. TEL 613-745-2095. FAX 613-745-5559. Ed. Gaston Gelinas. circ. 11,000.

CANADIAN TRANSPORT. see TRANSPORTATION

350   CN
CANADIAN UNION OF PUBLIC EMPLOYEES. THE PUBLIC EMPLOYEE. 1964. m. membership. Canadian Union of Public Employees, 21 Florence St., Ottawa, Ont. K2P 0W6, Canada. TEL 613-237-1590. Ed. Fred Tabachnick. bk.rev.; circ. 11,000.
Formerly: Canadian Union of Public Employees. Journal (ISSN 0045-5512)

331.8   BB
CARIBBEAN CONGRESS OF LABOUR. LABOUR VIEWPOINT. q. Caribbean Congress of Labour, Norman Centre, Rm. 405, Broad St., Bridgetown, Barbados, W.I.
Formerly: Caribbean Congress of Labour. Perspectives on Caribbean Labour.
Description: Reports on trade union developments and economic factors affecting the Caribbean.

331.8   BB   ISSN 0576-7547
CARIBBEAN CONGRESS OF LABOUR. REPORT. 1962. triennial. Caribbean Congress of Labour, Norman Centre, Rm. 405, Broad St., Bridgetown, Barbados, W.I.
Description: Reports on the activities of the congress.

CARPENTER. see BUILDING AND CONSTRUCTION — Carpentry And Woodwork

331.88 642.5   US   ISSN 0008-7815
CATERING INDUSTRY EMPLOYEE. 1890. m. $5. Hotel Employees & Restaurant Employees International Union, A F L - C I O, 1219 28th St., N.W., Washington, DC 20007-3316. TEL 202-393-4373. FAX 202-333-0468. Ed. Herman Leavitt. illus.; index; circ. 250,000.
Description: Provides news and features of the Union, other unions and overall labor issues, both domestic and international.

331.88   US   ISSN 0069-1615
CENTRAL CONFERENCE OF TEAMSTERS. OFFICERS' REPORT. 1954. irreg., latest 1979. membership. Central Conference of Teamsters, 8550 W. Bryn Mawr Ave., Ste. 707, Chicago, IL 60631. TEL 312-693-6200. circ. 200,000.
Formerly: Central Conference of Teamsters. Chairman's Report.

CESKOSLOVENSKY HORNIK A ENERGETIK. see MINES AND MINING INDUSTRY

696 331.88   FR
CHAUDRONNERIE TOLERIE. m. 250 F. Syndicat National de la Chaudronnerie, de la Tolerie et de la Tuyauterie Industrielle, 10 Av. Hoche, 75352 Paris Cedex 8, France. Ed. P.M. Gougaud. adv.

331.88 660   US   ISSN 0162-637X
CHEMICAL WORKER. 1944. m. $12 for non-members; $2 for libraries and schools. International Chemical Workers Union, International Chemical Workers Bldg., 1655 W. Market St., Akron, OH 44313. TEL 216-867-2444. FAX 216-867-0544. Ed. Frank D. Martino. bk.rev.; illus.; circ. 85,000. (tabloid format)
Formerly: International Chemical Worker (ISSN 0020-6334)

331.88 385   SZ   ISSN 0009-2916
CHEMINOT. (Text in French) 1919. w. 30 Fr. (foreign 34 Fr.). Schweizerischer Eisenbahnerverband - Federation Suisse des Cheminots, Steinerstr. 35, Case Postale 186, 3000 Berne 16, Switzerland. Ed. Michel Beguelin. adv.; charts; illus.

385 331.88   FR   ISSN 0245-7318
CHEMINOT DE FRANCE. 1917. bi-m. 50 F. Federation des Cheminots, 22 rue Pajol, 75018 Paris, France. TEL 46-07-15-19. FAX 40-38-49-11. Dir. Y. Tasserie. adv.
Description: Publication of the railway transportation organization.

385 331.88   FR
CHEMINOT RETRAITE. 1945. m. Federation Generale des Retraites des Chemins de Fer de France et d'Outre-Mer, 1 place Franz Liszt, 75010 Paris, France. adv.

CIVIL AVIATION NEWS; the paper that unites all aviation workers. see TRANSPORTATION — Air Transport

331.795   MF
CIVIL SERVICE NEWS. (Text in English or French) m. Federation of Civil Service Unions, 10, La Chausee, Port Louis, Mauritius.

647.94 331.88   FR
CLEFS D'OR. 5/yr. Union Professionnelle des Portiers des Grands Hotels, 12 rue Cambon, 75001 Paris, France. adv.

687 331.8   SA
CLOTHES LINE. (Text in English) 1979. w. membership. Garment Workers Union of the Western Province, 350 Victoria Rd., Box 194, Salt River 7925, Cape Town, South Africa. Ed. C.E. Petersen. adv.; circ. 53,000.

COLLECTIVE BARGAINING IN HIGHER EDUCATION AND THE PROFESSIONS. ANNUAL BIBLIOGRAPHY. see EDUCATION — Higher Education

331.116   CN   ISSN 0826-8800
COLLECTIVE BARGAINING INFORMATION MONTHLY. m. Can.$50. Industrial Relations Council, 1125 Howe St., Vancouver B.C. V6Z 2K8, Canada. (Subscr. to: Crown Publications, 546 Yates St., Victoria, B.C. V8W 1K8, Canada. TEL 604-386-4636)
Description: Contains information of wage settlement, work stoppages and collective agreement settlements.

331.8   MQ
COMBAT OUVRIER. w. B.P. 386, 97258 Fort-de-France, Martinique. Ed. M.G. Beaujour.

331.8   EI
COMMISSION OF THE EUROPEAN COMMUNITIES. TRADE UNION INFORMATION BULLETIN. (Text in various languages) bi-m. Commission of the European Communities, 200 rue de la Loi, 1049 Brussels, Belgium. circ. 20,000. (tabloid format; back issues avail.)

331.88 350   IE
COMMUNICATIONS WORKER. 1923. m. Communications Workers Union, 575 N. Circular Rd., Dublin 1, Ireland. Ed. D. Begg. adv.; bk.rev.; stat.; circ. 18,000. (tabloid format)
Former titles (until 1991): Postal and Telecommunications Journal (ISSN 0790-6277); (until 1983): Postal Worker (ISSN 0032-5392)

331.8   CN
COMPASS.* 1983. bi-m. Canadian Union of Public Employees, Peel District Council, 21 Florence St., Ottawa, Ont. K2P 0W6, Canada. TEL 416-826-5041. Ed. Edna Toth. circ. 4,000.

LABOR UNIONS

331.88   CE   ISSN 0045-6217
CONGRESS NEWS. (Text in English) vol.4, 1971. s-m. free. Ceylon Workers' Congress, P.O. Box 1294, 72 Ananda Coomaraswamy Mawatha, Colombo 7, Sri Lanka. Ed. Ponniah Krishnaswamy. circ. 5,000. (processed)

331.88   IT   ISSN 0010-6348
CONQUISTE DEL LAVORO. 1948. w. L.16000. (Confederazione Italiana Sindacati Lavoratori) Editrice Finlavoro, 23 via Po 23, 00198 Rome, Italy. Dir. Bruno Storti. bk.rev.; film rev.; illus.; index; circ. 150,000. (tabloid format)

331.88   AG   ISSN 0589-5081
CONTACTO. 1968. m. (Federacion Argentina de Trabajadores de Luz y Fuerza) Editorial Sleil S.A., Calao 1764, Buenos Aires, Argentina. (Dist. by: Macht y Cla S.R.L. Carlos Calvo, 2426 Argentina) Ed. Carlos Garcia Martinez. illus. **Indexed:** Excerp.Med.

331.8   NE   ISSN 0921-500X
CONTRIBUTIONS TO THE HISTORY OF LABOR AND SOCIETY. (Text in English) 1988. irreg., vol.3, 1991. price varies. E.J. Brill, P.O. Box 9000, 2300 PA Leiden, Netherlands. TEL 071-312624. FAX 071-317532. TELEX 39296 BRILL NL. (In N. America: E.J. Brill, 24 Hudson St., Kinderhook, NY 12106. TEL 800-962-4406)
—BLDSC shelfmark: 3458.623000.

331   AT
COUNSELLOR. 1965. q. Aus.$0.05 per no. Federated Municipal and Shire Council Employees' Union of Australia, Victorian Division, 1-3 O'Connell St., N. Melbourne, Vic. 3051, Australia. TEL 03-3266001. Ed. Paul Slape. adv.; bk.rev.; circ. 15,000.

331.8   US   ISSN 1062-7863
CRITIQUE OF TRADE UNION RIGHTS IN COUNTRIES AFFILIATED WITH THE LEAGUE OF ARAB STATES. (Documentation Supplement avail.) 1989. a. free. Jewish Labor Committee, 25 E. 21st St., New York, NY 10010. TEL 212-477-0707. FAX 212-477-1918. Ed. Michael S. Perry. bibl.; circ. 5,000. (back issues avail.)
Description: Comprehensive country by country review of labor policies, practices and conditions in the Arab countries of the Middle East and North Africa, compiled from ILO and U.S. State Department reports as well as newspaper, radio and broadcast news sources.

CRITIQUE OF TRADE UNION RIGHTS IN COUNTRIES AFFILIATED WITH THE LEAGUE OF ARAB STATES. DOCUMENTATION SUPPLEMENT. see *LABOR UNIONS — Abstracting, Bibliographies, Statistics*

331.8   GW   ISSN 0935-6592
D A G - JOURNAL. 1948. 10/yr. DM.55. (Deutsche Angestellten-Gewerkschaft) Waren Einkaufs- und Vertriebs-Gesellschaft mbH, Karl-Muck-Platz 1, 2000 Hamburg 36, Germany. TEL 040-34915-1. FAX 040-34915-400. TELEX 211642-AGHV-D. adv.; index; circ. 500,000.
Former titles: Angestellten (ISSN 0028-307X); Neue Angestellte.

331.8   GW
D B B MAGAZIN. 1949. m. DM.12.80. Deutscher Beamtenbund, Dreizehnmorgenweg 36, 5300 Bonn 2, Germany. Eds. W. Schmitz, F.J. Schmitz. adv.; bk.rev.; illus.; circ. 600,000.
Formerly (until 1991): Der Beamten-Bund (ISSN 0405-1033)

331.8   US
DALLAS CRAFTSMAN. w. Reilly Echols Printing, Inc., 1710 S. Harwood, Box 15866, Dallas, TX 75215. TEL 214-428-8385.

331.88 355.133   FR
DEFENSE DES GRADES DE LA POLICE NATIONALE. m. 20 F. Syndicat des Grades de la Police Nationale, 11 rue des Ursins, 75004 Paris, France.

331.8   XV   ISSN 0011-7722
DELAVSKA ENOTNOST. (Text in Slovenian) 1942. w. 10400 din.($23) T.O.Z.D. Delavska Enotnost, CGP Delo, n.sol.o., Celovska 43, 61001 Ljubljana, Slovenia. Eds. Dusan Gacnik, Francek Kavcic. adv.; bk.rev.

331.88 658.87   US   ISSN 0011-8915
DEPARTMENT STORE WORKERS' UNION. LOCAL 1-S NEWS. 1949. m. $6 to members. Department Store Workers' Union, Local 1- S, Retail, Wholesale and Dept. Store Union, A F L - C I O, 140 W. 31st St., New York, NY 10001. Eds. Joseph Pascarella, Harold H. Hollabaugh. circ. 10,000(controlled). (tabloid format; also avail. in microfilm from UMI)

331.8   US
DETROIT LABOR NEWS. 1914. bi-w. $11. Metropolitan Detroit A F L - C I O, 2550 W. Grand Blvd., Detroit, MI 48208. FAX 313-896-1078. Ed. Aldo Vagnozzi. adv.; bk.rev.; circ. 4,500. (also avail. in microform from UMI; back issues avail.; reprint service avail. from UMI)

DETROIT TEACHER. see *EDUCATION*

331.88 383   GW   ISSN 0012-0596
DEUTSCHE POST (FRANKFURT). 1949. m. DM.36 to non-members. Deutsche Postgewerkschaft, Rhonestr. 2, 6000 Frankfurt a.M. 71, Germany. Ed. Joachim Scherzer. circ. 620,000.

331.88   IT
DIMENSIONE LAVORO. 1980. m. L.15000. Editrice Dimensione Lavoro, Via Cavour 108, 00184 Rome, Italy. TEL 4755774. adv.; bk.rev.; circ. 120,000.

331.8   US   ISSN 0419-2052
PN1998.A1
DIRECTORS GUILD OF AMERICA. DIRECTORY OF MEMBERS. 1967. a. $22. Directors Guild of America, 7920 Sunset Blvd., Hollywood, CA 90046. TEL 213-289-2000. FAX 213-289-2029. adv.; circ. 15,000.

DIRECTORY OF FACULTY CONTRACTS AND BARGAINING AGENTS IN INSTITUTIONS OF HIGHER EDUCATION. see *EDUCATION — Higher Education*

331.8   US
DIRECTORY OF LABOR ORGANIZATIONS. a. Labor Cabinet, Office of the Secretary, 1049 US 127 S., Frankfort, KY 40601.

331.8   US
DIRECTORY OF LABOR UNIONS AND EMPLOYEE ORGANIZATIONS IN NEW YORK STATE. 1948. biennial. $15. Department of Labor, Division of Research and Statistics, One Main St., Brooklyn, NY 11201. Ed. Eileen DeVeau. circ. 5,000.
Formerly: Directory of Labor Organizations in New York State.

331.88   CN   ISSN 0075-7578
DIRECTORY OF LABOUR ORGANIZATIONS IN CANADA/REPERTOIRE DES ORGANISATIONS DE TRAVAILLEURS ET TRAVAILLEUSES AU CANADA. (Catalog no. L2-2-1990) (Text in English and French) 1911. a. Can.$21 (foreign $25.20). Canada Communiation Group, Publishing Division, Ottawa, Ont. K1A 0S9, Canada. TEL 819-956-2560. circ. 6,000.
Description: Names of officials, telephone numbers, and addresses of all labor organizations in Canada with data on union membership and international affiliations.

331.8   US
DIRECTORY OF MAINE LABOR ORGANIZATIONS. (Subseries of: Maine. Bureau of Labor Standards. B L S Bulletin) 1969. a. Department of Labor, Bureau of Labor Standards, Division of Research & Statistics, State House Station 45, Augusta, ME 04333-0045. TEL 207-289-6440. Ed. Terry M. Hathaway. circ. 1,000.

331.8   US   ISSN 0734-6786
HD6504
DIRECTORY OF U.S. LABOR ORGANIZATIONS (YEAR). 1982. irreg. $30. B N A Books (Subsidiary of: The Bureau of National Affairs, Inc.), 1520 23rd St., N.W., Washington, DC 20037. TEL 201-225-1900. FAX 201-417-0482. (Subscr. to: BNA Books Distribution Center, 30 Raritan Center Pkwy., Box 7816, Edison, NJ 08818-7816) Ed. Courtney D. Gifford.

DIREKTE AKTION; Anarchosyndikalistische Zeitung. see *BUSINESS AND ECONOMICS — Economic Situation And Conditions*

331.88   US   ISSN 0012-3765
DISPATCHER (SAN FRANCISCO, 1942). 1942. m. $2.50 membership or exchange basis. International Longshoremen's & Warehousemen's Union, 1188 Franklin St., San Francisco, CA 94109. TEL 415-775-0533. FAX 415-775-1302. Ed. Danny Beagle. bk.rev.; charts; illus.; circ. 42,000. (tabloid format; also avail. in microform from UMI)

ECHO. see *EDUCATION*

370.7 331.88   FR   ISSN 0982-5339
ECOLE DU GRAND PARIS. 1922. m. (during academic year). 3 F. Syndicat National des Instituteurs et Professeurs du College, 69 rue du Faubourg St. Martin, 75010 Paris, France. adv.

331.88 621   US   ISSN 0041-686X
ELECTRICAL UNION WORLD. vol.30, 1940. every 4 wks. International Brotherhood of Electrical Workers, A F L - C I O, Local Union No. 3, 158-11 Harry Van Arsdale Jr. Ave., Flushing, NY 11365. TEL 718-591-4000. Ed. Thomas Van Arsdale. adv.; bk.rev.; illus.; circ. 44,500. (also avail. in microform from UMI)

331.88   SA
EMPLO REVIEW/TYDSKRIF. (Text in Afrikaans and English) 1935. m. membership. South African Railways and Harbours Employees' Union, Boston House, Rm. 335, Waterkant St., Cape Town 8001, South Africa. Ed. G. Janse van Rensburg. adv.; illus.; circ. 10,000 (controlled).
Formerly: S.A.R. and H. Employees' Review (ISSN 0036-0929)

EMPLOYERS NEGOTIATING SERVICE. see *EDUCATION — School Organization And Administration*

023   UK   ISSN 0963-5548
EMPLOYMENT NEWS. 1978. 3/yr. free. Library Association, Professional Practice Division, 7 Ridgmount St., London WC1E 7AE, England. TEL 071-636-7543. FAX 071-436-7218. Ed. V.E. Fraser. circ. 4,500.
Formerly (until 1991): L A Trade Union News (ISSN 0144-6827)
Description: Contains news and informational articles on a range of topics which have implications for library and information staff who have an interest in trade union matters across all library sectors including job-sharing arrangements and equal employment opportunities.

331.88   AT   ISSN 0818-9846
ENTERTAINMENT WORKER. q. Australian Theatrical and Amusement Employees Association, P.O. Box 2, Trades Hall, Carlton South, Vic. 3053, Australia. Ed. C. Livingston. bk.rev.; circ. 13,000.
Formerly: In Focus.

ERZIEHUNG UND WISSENSCHAFT NIEDERSACHSEN. see *EDUCATION*

ESSOR DE L'ELECTRICITE ET DE L'ELECTRONIQUE. see *ENGINEERING — Electrical Engineering*

ESTANDARTE OBRERO. see *BUSINESS AND ECONOMICS — Labor And Industrial Relations*

EUROPEAN INFORMATION BULLETIN; a quarterly publication for European Trade Unionists. see *BUSINESS AND ECONOMICS — Labor And Industrial Relations*

331.88   CS
EUROPEAN TRADE UNION. CONTACTS. (Editions in English, French) 1988. bi-m. free. World Federation of Trade Unions, Commission for Europe, Branicka 112, 140 00 Prague 4, Czechoslovakia. TEL 46-21-40. FAX 46-13-783.

F A P U Q NOUVELLES UNIVERSITAIRES. (Federation des Associations de Professeurs des Universites du Quebec) see *EDUCATION — Higher Education*

331   NE
F N V - MAGAZINE (WOERDEN). 1881. fortn. fl.2.25 (free to members). Dienstenbond F N U, P.O. Box 550, 3440 AN Woerden, Netherlands. TEL 03480-75922. FAX 03480-23610. Ed.Bd. adv.; illus.; circ. 80,000.
Formerly (until 1978): Mercurius (ISSN 0025-9950)

LABOR UNIONS

331.88   NE
F N V NEWS. (Text in English) 1977. 3/yr. free. Federatie Nederlandse Vakbeweging - Confederation Netherlands Trade Union Movement, Maritaweg 10, Amsterdam, Netherlands. FAX 20-6844541. TELEX 16660 FNV NL. bk.rev.; circ. 550.
Supersedes: Netherlands Federation of Trade Unions. Information Bulletin (ISSN 0466-7530)

791.4 331.8   UK   ISSN 0015-1106
F T T AND BETA NEWS. 1935. m. £20.00 per no. (typically set in Jan.). Broadcasting Entertainment and Cinematograph Technicians Union, 111 Wardour St., London W1V 4AY, England. FAX 437-8268. Ed. Janice Turner. adv.; bk.rev.; illus.; index; circ. 58,000.
Formerly: Film and Television Technician.

331.88   CN   ISSN 0705-856X
FACTS. 1978. 10/yr. free. Canadian Union of Public Employees, 21 Florence St., Ottawa, Ont. K2P 0W6, Canada. TEL 613-237-1590.

331.88   BL
FEDERACAO DOS TRABALHADORES NA AGRICULTURA DO ESTADO DO PARANA. RELATORIO. irreg. Federacao dos Trabalhadores na Agricultura do Estado do Parana, Curitiba, Brazil.

331.88   UK   ISSN 0014-9411
FEDERATION NEWS. 1950. irreg. (3-4/yr.). free. General Federation of Trade Unions, Central House, Upper Woburn Pl., London WC1H 0HY, England. TEL 071-387-2578. FAX 071-383-0820. bk.rev.; charts; illus.; stat.; circ. 1,000.

331.88   US   ISSN 0014-942X
FEDERATION NEWS. vol.85, 1973. m. $3. Chicago Federation of Labor and Industrial Union Council, 130 E. Randolph, Ste. 1710, Chicago, IL 60601-6221. FAX 312-565-6769. Ed. Robert L. Kite. adv.; bk.rev.; illus.; circ. 3,800.

FEDERATION NEWS (SYDNEY). see *BUSINESS AND ECONOMICS — Labor And Industrial Relations*

331.88   AT   ISSN 0014-9276
FEDERATION OF INDUSTRIAL, MANUFACTURING AND ENGINEERING EMPLOYEES. LABOR NEWS. 1945. bi-m. membership. Magazine Printers, 51-65 Bathurst St., Sydney, N.S.W. 2000, Australia. TEL 264-2877. FAX 261-1701. Ed. Steve Harrison. adv.; bk.rev.; circ. 75,000.
Formerly (until July 1991): Federated Ironworkers' Association of Australia. Labor News.

331.8 350   US
FEDNEWS. 1962. q. $2.40. National Association of Government Employees, 285 Dorchester Ave., Boston, MA 02127. TEL 617-268-5002. FAX 617-268-2142. Ed. Ed Gillooly. adv.; circ. 35,000. (tabloid format) **Indexed:** Pers.Lit.

331.8   MG
FEON'NY MPIASA. (Text in Malagasy) m. Lot M8, Isotry, 101 Antananarivo, Malagasy Republic. Ed. M. Razakanaivo. circ. 2,000.

331.88 385   SZ   ISSN 0015-0215
FERROVIERE. w. 30 Fr. (foreign 34 Fr.). Schweizerischer Eisenbahnerverband - Federation Suisse des Cheminots, Steinerstr. 35, Case Postale 186, 3000 Berne 16, Switzerland. Ed. Franco Robbiani. adv.; charts; illus.; stat.

331.88   US
FIRE LINES. vol.12, 1973. m. membership. Uniformed Firefighters Association of Greater New York, Local 94, 225 Broadway, New York, NY 10007. TEL 212-233-4234. Ed. Robert di Virgilio. adv.; charts; illus.

331.8   BE
FLASH. (Text in Dutch, English, French, German, Spanish) fortn. 250 Fr.($6) (effective 1992). World Confederation of Labour, 33 rue de Treves, B-1040 Brussels, Belgium. TEL 02-230-62-95. FAX 02-230-87-22. TELEX 26966.

331.88   CS
FLASHES FROM THE TRADE UNIONS. (Editions in English, French, Spanish) 1972. bi-m. $24. World Federation of Trade Unions, Branicka 112, 140 00 Prague 4, Czechoslovakia. TEL 46-21-40. FAX 46-13-78. illus.; circ. 4,000.
Formerly: Trade Union Press (ISSN 0041-0527)
Description: Monitors the activities of trade unions world-wide. Covers congresses, sessions, meetings, seminars, strikes and demonstrations.

331.8 350   SZ
FONCTION PUBLIQUE. (Text in French, Italian) 1927. m. 7.50 Fr. (Union Romande et Tessinoise des Societes de Fonctionaires Cantonaux) Presses Centrales Laussanne, Case Postale, CH-1002 Laussanne, Switzerland. TEL 021-289977. Ed. Gerard Laurent. adv.; charts; illus.; stat.; circ. 11,500.

331.88 350   SA   ISSN 0015-6809
FOOTPLATE/VOETPLAAT. (Text in Afrikaans, English) 1925. m. membership. South African Footplate Staff Association - Suid Afrikanse Voetplaatpersoneelvereniging, P.O. Box 31100, Braamfontein, Johannesburg 2001, South Africa. FAX 339-2888. Ed. H.C. Kidson. adv.; circ. 9,000.
Description: Covers news of the different divisions within the trade union.

FRANKFURTER LEHRERZEITUNG. see *EDUCATION — School Organization And Administration*

331.88   BE   ISSN 0016-0350
FREE LABOUR WORLD. Spanish edition: Mundo del Trabajo Libre (ISSN 0027-3260) (Editions in English, French, German, Spanish) 1950. fortn. 1000 Fr. International Confederation of Free Trade Unions (ICFTU), 37-41 rue Montagne aux Herbes Potageres, B-1000 Brussels, Belgium. TEL 02-2178085. FAX 02-2188415. TELEX 26785 ICFTU B. Ed. B. Russell. bk.rev.; illus.; index; circ. 16,000. **Indexed:** HR Rep., Mid.East: Abstr.& Ind., P.A.I.S.

331.88 070   US   ISSN 0016-2183
FRONTPAGE. 1942. irreg $5. Newspaper Guild of New York, A F L - C I O, C L C, 133 W. 44th St., New York, NY 10036. TEL 212-575-1580. Ed. Dona Fowler. charts; illus.; stat.; circ. 6,500. (tabloid format)

331.88 684.1   US   ISSN 0016-3090
FURNITURE WORKERS PRESS.* vol.31, 1970. m. $1. United Furniture Workers of America, A F L - C I O, 1910 Air Ln. Dr., Nashville, TN 37210. Ed. Carl Scarbrough. adv.; charts; illus.; stat. (tabloid format)

331.8 368.4   GW   ISSN 0173-2323
G D S - ZEITUNG. 1971. m. DM.71. (Gewerkschaft Der Sozialversicherung) G. Grote'sche Verlagsbuchhandlung GmbH und Co.KG, Postfach 400263, Max-Planck-Strasse 12, 5000 Cologne 40, Germany. Ed. G. Paetz. adv. (reprint service avail.)
Formerly: Sozialversicherungs-Beamte und -Angestellte BSBA (ISSN 0340-367X)

G E O: GRASSROOTS ECONOMIC ORGANIZING NEWSLETTER. see *OCCUPATIONS AND CAREERS*

331.88 350   UK
G M B WORKING TOGETHER. 1924. m. free. G M B, Thorne House, Ruxley Ridge, Esher, Surrey KT10 0TL, England. FAX 0372-67164. Ed.Bd. adv.; bk.rev.; charts; illus.; circ. 80,000.
Former titles: General, Municipal, Boilermakers and Allied Trades Union Journal; General and Municipal Workers' Union (ISSN 0016-6499)

331.88 687   US   ISSN 0016-4712
GARMENT WORKER.* 1902. m. membership. United Garment Workers of America, 4207 Lebanon Rd., Hermitage, TN 37076. Ed. Catherine C. Peters. illus. (tabloid format; also avail. in microform from UMI)

LA GAUCHE. see *POLITICAL SCIENCE*

331.15 331.8   GW   ISSN 0016-9447
HD4809
GEWERKSCHAFTLICHE MONATSHEFTE. 1950. m. DM.108. (Deutscher Gewerkschaftsbund) Bund-Verlag GmbH, Hansestr. 63a, Postfach 900840, 5000 Cologne 90, Germany. Ed. Hans Otto Hemmer. adv.; bk.rev.; abstr.; bibl.; index; circ. 6,100. **Indexed:** INIS Atomind., Key to Econ.Sci., P.A.I.S.For.Lang.Ind.
—BLDSC shelfmark: 4165.595000.

331.88 383   GW
GEWERKSCHAFTLICHE PRAXIS. 1955. m. DM.13 to non-members. Deutsche Postgewerkschaft, Rhonestr. 2, 6000 Frankfurt a.M. 71, Germany. Ed. Reinhold Kohlmeier. circ. 45,000.

331.88   SZ   ISSN 0016-9455
GEWERKSCHAFTLICHE RUNDSCHAU. 1909. 4/yr. 36 SFr. Schweizerischer Gewerkschaftsbund - Swiss Federation of Trade Unions, Monbijoustr. 61, CH-3000 Berne 23, Switzerland. Ed. Ewald Ackermann. bk.rev.; bibl.; charts; stat.; index; circ. 5,000. **Indexed:** Chem.Abstr., World Bibl.Soc.Sec.

331.88 282   BE
GIDS OP MAATSCHAPPELIJK GEBIED; tijdschrift voor syndicale, culturele en sociale problemen. 1902. m. (10/yr.). 1200 Fr. (Algemeen Christelijk Werknemersverbond - Catholic Workers Movement) V.Z.W. Vormingscentrum Ter Munk, Wetstraat 121, 1040 Brussels, Belgium. FAX 2373300. TELEX 61770 CSC ACV. Ed. A. Vanempten. bk.rev. **Indexed:** Key to Econ.Sci.

GLOS NAUCZYCIELSKI. see *EDUCATION*

331 622   PL   ISSN 0017-226X
GORNIK. 1945. w. 26000 Zl. Zwiazkowe Przedsiebiorstwo Wydawniczo-Handlowe "Gornik", Ul. Dabrowskiego 23, 40-033 Katowice, Poland. TEL 48 32 517-892. Ed. Wlodzimierz Kotowicz. adv.; bk.rev.; circ. 55,000.

331.88 350   US   ISSN 1041-5335
GOVERNMENT STANDARD. 1933. 4/yr. membership. American Federation of Government Employees, A F L - C I O, 80 F St., N.W., Washington, DC 20001. TEL 202-639-6423. FAX 202-639-6441. Ed. Janice Lachance. illus.; circ. 222,000. (tabloid format) **Indexed:** Pers.Lit.
Description: Covers working conditions, legislation; and organizing regarding federal and DC employees.

331.88 655   US   ISSN 0746-3626
GRAPHICOMMUNICATOR. 1978. 8/yr. $12 in US and Canada; elsewhere $15. Graphic Communications International Union, 1900 L St., N.W., Washington, DC 20036. TEL 202-462-1400. Ed. James J. Norton. adv.; charts; illus.; circ. 180,000. (tabloid format; also avail. in microform from UMI; reprint service avail. from UMI) **Indexed:** Chem.Abstr., Graph.Arts Lit.Abstr.
Formerly (until Jun. 1983): Union Tabloid; **Supersedes:** Graphic Arts Unionist (ISSN 0017-3363); Which was formed by the 1964 merger of: International Bookbinder; American Photo-Engraver (ISSN 0097-3297); Lithographer Journal. Also supersedes (as of 1983): International Printing and Graphic Communications Union. News and Views; Which was formerly: International Printing Pressmen and Assistants Union of North America. News and Views (ISSN 0020-8388).

331.8   CN
GUARDIAN. 1952. m. Can.$10. Guardian of Windsor Inc., 1855 Turner Rd., Windsor, Ont. N8W 3K2, Canada. TEL 519-258-6400. Ed. Tom Burton. circ. 35,000.

331.88 070   US   ISSN 0017-5404
HD6350.N4
GUILD REPORTER. 1933. tri-w. $20. Newspaper Guild, AFL-CIO, CLC, 8611 Second Ave., Silver Spring, MD 20910. TEL 301-585-2990. FAX 301-585-0668. Ed. James M. Cesnik. bk.rev.; charts; illus.; stat.; circ. 32,000. (tabloid format; also avail. in microform from UMI; reprint service avail. from UMI) **Indexed:** HR Rep.

GURU MALAYSIA. see *EDUCATION*

331.88 655   SZ   ISSN 0017-5811
LE GUTENBERG; relieur et cartonnier. 1871. w. 30 Fr. Syndicat du Livre et du Papier, Monbijoustrasse 33, 3011 Berne, Switzerland. Ed. Florence Rouiller. adv.; bk.rev.; charts; illus.; stat.; circ. 7,000.

331.8 381   SW   ISSN 0017-7326
HANDELSNYTT. 1908. m. SEK 65. Handelsanstaelldas Foerbund, Fack 5074, 200 71 Malmoe, Sweden. Ed. Lars Jonson. circ. 161,000. (tabloid format)

LABOR UNIONS

331.8   LU
HANDWIERK. (Text in French and German) 1945. m. 450 Fr. Federation des Artisans, 2, circuit de la Foire Internationale, L-1347 Luxembourg, Luxembourg. TEL 40-00-22-1. FAX 48-97-02. TELEX 2215. (Co-sponsor: Chambre des Metiers) Ed.Bd. adv.; bk.rev.; circ. 7,500. **Indexed:** Key to Econ.Sci.

331.88   US
HAWAII A F L - C I O NUPEPA. 1966. m. membership. Hawaii State A F L - C I O, 320 Ward Ave., Ste. 205, Honolulu, HI 96814. TEL 808-536-4945. Ed. Ethel A. Miyachi. adv.; bk.rev.; illus.; circ. 300.
   Former titles: Hawaii A F L - C I O News (ISSN 0017-8535); Hawaii State Fed. News.

778.5 331.88   AG
HECHOS DE MASCARA. m. free. Asociacion Argentina de Actores, Alsina 1766, Buenos Aires, Argentina. Ed. Victor Bruno. adv.; illus.; circ. 6,500.

HESSISCHE BEITRAEGE ZUR GESCHICHTE DER ARBEITERBEWEGUNG. see *HISTORY — History Of Europe*

331.88   UK   ISSN 0018-1676
HIGHWAY. 1939. bi-m. free. Transport & General Workers Union, Transport House, Smith Sq., London S.W.1., England. Ed. B. Henderson. illus. **Indexed:** CINAHL.

331.88   II   ISSN 0073-2273
HIND MAZDOOR SABHA. REPORT OF THE ANNUAL CONVENTION. 1952. a. price varies. Hind Mazdoor Sabha, Nagindas Chambers, 167 P. d'Mello Rd., Bombay 400001, India.

331.88   GW   ISSN 0018-3806
HOLZARBEITER-ZEITUNG. Abbreviated title: H Z. 1893. m. DM.16 to non-members. Gewerkschaft Holz und Kunststoff, Sonnenstr. 14, D-4000 Dusseldorf, Germany. Ed. Peter Riemer. adv.; bk.rev.; illus.; stat.; circ. 125,000.

331.8 385   SA
HOOFLIG/HEADLIGHT. (Text in Afrikaans and English) 1930. m. Transport Worker's Union of S.A., P.O.B. 31415, Braamfontein 2017, South Africa. Ed. Mari Gerber. adv.; circ. 7,000. (back issues avail.)

HOSPITAL WORKER. see *HOSPITALS*

331.88 642.55   US
HOTEL VOICE. (Text in English and Spanish) 1940. w. $10. Hotel, Motel & Club Employees Union Local 6, AFL- CIO, 707 Eighth Ave., New York, NY 10036. TEL 212-245-8100. (Co-sponsor: New York Hotel and Motel Trades Council) Ed.Bd. illus.; circ. 28,000.
   Former titles: Motel, Restaurant Voice; Hotel Voice; Hotel and Club Voice (ISSN 0018-6074); Hotel (ISSN 0018-6066)

331.88   HU   ISSN 0018-778X
HUNGARIAN TRADE UNION NEWS. (Text in English. Editions in six languages.) 1957. m. free. Szakszervezetek Orszagos Tanacsa, Dozsa Gyorgy ut 84B, Budapest 6, Hungary. TEL 2122-4810. Ed. Emoke Nandori. charts; illus.; stat.

331.88 621   US   ISSN 0018-859X
I B E W - A F L - C I O. LOCAL 1470 JOURNAL. 1952. m. $1. International Brotherhood of Electrical Workers, A F L - C I O, Local 1470, 2 Central Ave., Kearny, NJ 07032. TEL 201-589-3605. Ed. Adam F. Papasavas. bk.rev.; bibl.; charts; illus.; stat.; circ. 15,000. (tabloid format)

331.88 621   US   ISSN 0897-2826
HD6350.E3
I B E W JOURNAL. 1893. m. $4. International Brotherhood of Electrical Workers, A F L - C I O, 1125 15th St., N.W., Washington, DC 20005. TEL 202-863-7000. FAX 202-728-7664. Ed. J.J. Barry. illus.; circ. 900,000.
   Formerly: Electrical Workers' Journal (ISSN 0013-4449)

331.88   SY   ISSN 0018-8816
I C A T U REVIEW. (Text in English) 1968. m. International Confederation of Arab Trade Unions, P.O. Box 3225, Sahat al-Tahrir, Damascus, Syria. Ed. El-Sayed. charts; illus.

331.88   MX
I C F T U - O R I T INTER-AMERICAN LABOR NEWS. (Text in English and Spanish) bi-m. free to qualified personnel. Organizacion Regional Interamericana de Trabajadores, Vallarta 8, 3 Piso, Mexico, D.F. 06030, Mexico. FAX 592-73-29. TELEX 1771699 ORITME. Ed. Luis A. Anderson. illus.; circ. 3,000.
   Supersedes (as of 1984): Revista Sindical Interamericana.

I E A - N E A ADVOCATE. (Illinois Education Association, National Education Association) see *EDUCATION*

331.88   UK
I T F NEWS. (Editions in English, French, German, Spanish and Swedish) 1905. m. International Transport Workers' Federation, 133-135 Great Suffolk St., London SE1 1PD, England. TEL 01-403 2733. index; circ. 1,500 (English edt.); 205 (French edt.); 1,000 (German edt.); 510 (Spanish edt.); 400 (Swedish edt.).
   Formerly: I T F Newsletter (ISSN 0019-0799)
   Description: Industrial and labor issues of interest to transport workers.

331.88 655   US   ISSN 0019-0853
I T U REVIEW. 1958. w. free. International Typographical Union, 316 Wilcox St., Castle Rock, CO 80104-2441. Ed. Robert S. McMichen. bk.rev.; illus.; circ. 35,000.

331.8   US   ISSN 0199-3704
I U D DIGEST. 10/yr. A F L - C I O, Industrial Union Department, 815 16th St., N.W., Washington, DC 20006. TEL 202-842-7800.

331.88 621   US   ISSN 0019-0861
HD6350.E3
I U E NEWS. 1949. m. $2. International Union of Electronic, Electrical, Salaried, Machine and Furniture Workers, A F L - C I O, 1126 16th St., N.W., Washington, DC 20036. TEL 202-296-1200. Ed. William H. Bywater. bk.rev.; charts; illus.; stat.; circ. 200,000. (tabloid format; also avail. in microform from UMI; reprint service avail. from UMI)

331.88 940   GW   ISSN 0046-8428
HD8448
I W K. (Internationale Wissenschaftliche Korrespondenz zur Geschichte der Deutschen Arbeiterbewegung.) (Text in English, French and German) 1965. 4/yr. DM.72 to individuals; students DM.45. Historische Kommission zu Berlin, Kirchweg 33, 1000 Berlin 38, Germany. TEL 030-81600141.
FAX 030-81600134. Ed. Henryk Skrzypczak. adv.; bk.rev.; abstr.; circ. 1,400. **Indexed:** A.B.C.Pol.Sci., Amer.Hist.& Life, Hist.Abstr.
—BLDSC shelfmark: 4554.960000.

I Z A. (Illustrierte Zeitschrift fuer Arbeitssicherheit) see *OCCUPATIONAL HEALTH AND SAFETY*

IDEAS & ACTION. see *BUSINESS AND ECONOMICS — Labor And Industrial Relations*

331.3   RM
IFJUMUNKAS. (Text in Hungarian) 1957. w. Piata Presei Libere 1, 71341 Bucharest, Rumania. Ed. Jozsef Varga. circ. 22,000.

ILLINOIS LABOR HISTORY SOCIETY REPORTER. see *BUSINESS AND ECONOMICS — Labor And Industrial Relations*

331.88 686   FR
IMPRIMERIE SYNDICALISTE. 1949. bi-m. Federation Force Ouvriere du Livre, 198 Av. du Maine, 75014 Paris, France.

331.88   NZ   ISSN 0019-3054
IMPRINT. vol.22, 1970. m. free. New Zealand Printing & Related Trades Industrial Union of Workers, 195 Victori St., P.O. Box 6413, Wellington, New Zealand. FAX 40-844-841. Ed. W.D.J. Down. adv.; bk.rev.; charts; illus.; tr.lit.; circ. 13,300.

331.88   US   ISSN 0019-3291
IN TRANSIT. 1892. m. $5. Amalgamated Transit Union, 5025 Wisconsin Ave., N.W., Washington, DC 20016. TEL 202-537-1645. FAX 202-244-7824. Ed. Betty Curran. illus.; circ. 160,000. (tabloid format)
   Incorporates: Union Leader (ISSN 0161-9292)

331.88   II
INDIAN WORKER; English weekly journal of labour movement in India led by INTUC. (Text in English) vol.20, 1972. w. Rs.100($9) Indian National Trade Union Congress, 1-B Maulana Azad Rd., New Delhi 110011, India. Ed. S.N. Rao. adv.; charts; illus.

331.88   EI   ISSN 0073-7909
INFORMATION SERVICE OF THE EUROPEAN COMMUNITIES. TRADE UNION NEWS. 1965. irreg. (approx. 4/yr.). limited distribution. Commission of the European Communities, Direction Generale de la Presse et Information, 200 rue de la Loi, B-1049 Brussels, Belgium.

311.3   PN
INFORMATIVO INDUSTRIAL. m. Sindicato de Industriales de Panama, Apdo. 6-4798, El Dorado, Panama City 1, Panama. TEL 60-0077. FAX 36-0166. Ed. Jose Chirino R.

331.88 070   II   ISSN 0377-0087
PN4701
INKWORLD. (Text in English) 1972. q. Rs.24. National Union of Journalists (India), 7 Jantar Mantar Rd., New Delhi 110 001, India. Ed. K.N. Gupta. adv.; bk.rev.; illus.; circ. 2,000.

331.8 370   US
INSIDER'S REPORT; a special bulletin for leaders. 1983. q. free. Concerned Educators Against Forced Unionism, 8001 Braddock Rd., Ste. 500, Springfield, VA 22160. TEL 703-321-8519. Ed. Jo Seker. circ. 7,500.
   Description: Discusses coercive unionism in education, in relation to legislation, litigation and other areas.

331.8   GW   ISSN 0084-9782
INSTITUT DER DEUTSCHEN WIRTSCHAFT. GEWERKSCHAFTSREPORT. 8/yr. DM.46.71. Deutscher Instituts Verlag GmbH, Gustav-Heinemann-Ufer 84-88, Postfach 510670, 5000 Cologne 51, Germany. TELEX 8882768-IWKD.
   Formerly: Deutsches Industrieinstitut. Berichte zu Gewerkschaftsfragen.

943 331 327   GW   ISSN 0173-2471
INSTITUT ZUR ERFORSCHUNG DER EUROPAEISCHEN ARBEITERBEWEGUNG. MITTEILUNGSBLATT. 2/yr. DM.14.80 per no. Ruhr-Universitaet, Institut zur Erforschung der Europaeischen Arbeiterbewegung, Postfach 10 21 48, 4630 Bochum 1, Germany. TEL 0234-7006332. FAX 0234-2001. circ. 500.

331.88   FR
INTENDANCE ET SYNDICALISME. 1953. bi-m. 60 F. S.N.I.E.N., 22 bis rue de Paradis, 75010 Paris, France. TEL 48-24-70-90. FAX 45-23-33-11. adv.; bk.rev.; circ. 91,000.

331.88 385   US
INTERCHANGE (ROCKVILLE). 1901. 9/yr. $5. Transportation Communications International Union, 3 Research Pl., Rockville, MD 20850.
TEL 301-948-4910. Ed. R.I. Kilroy. charts; illus.; mkt.; circ. 150,000.
   Former titles (until 1985): Railway Clerk - Interchange (ISSN 0033-8869); Railway Clerk.

331.88 790   US   ISSN 0020-5885
INTERNATIONAL ALLIANCE OF THEATRICAL STAGE EMPLOYES AND MOVING PICTURE MACHINE OPERATORS OF THE UNITED STATES AND CANADA. OFFICIAL BULLETIN. 1910. q. $3. International Alliance of Theatrical Stage Employes and Moving Picture Machine Operators of the United States and Canada, 1515 Broadway, Ste. 601, New York, NY 10036. TEL 212-730-1770. FAX 212-921-7699. Ed. James J. Riley. bk.rev.; illus.; circ. 61,000.

331.8   BE   ISSN 0074-2872
INTERNATIONAL CONFEDERATION OF FREE TRADE UNIONS. WORLD CONGRESS REPORTS. 1949. quadrennial, 14th, 1988, Melbourne. 600 Fr. International Confederation of Free Trade Unions (ICFTU), 37-41 rue Montagne aux Herbes Potageres, B-1000 Brussels, Belgium.
TEL 02-2178085. FAX 02-2188415. TELEX 26785 ICFTU B. Ed. John Vanderveken. circ. 1,500.

LABOR UNIONS

331.88   SZ
INTERNATIONAL FEDERATION OF COMMERCIAL CLERICAL, PROFESSIONAL AND TECHNICAL EMPLOYEES. NEWSLETTER. (Editions in English, French, German and Spanish) 1974. 11/yr. International Federation of Commercial Clerical, Professional and Technical Employees, 15, Avenue de Balexert, 1219 Chatelaine-Geneva, Switzerland. FAX 022-79653211. TELEX 418736-FIET-CH. Ed. Philip Jennings. charts; illus.; circ. 3,000.
    Formerly: International Federation of Commercial Clerical and Technical Employees. Newsletter; **Supersedes:** Non-Manual Worker in the Free Labour World (ISSN 0029-1056); International Non-Manual Workers Bulletin.

INTERNATIONAL FEDERATION OF PLANTATION, AGRICULTURAL AND ALLIED WORKERS. REPORT OF THE SECRETARIAT TO THE I F P A A W WORLD CONGRESS. see AGRICULTURE — Agricultural Economics

331.88   BE   ISSN 0074-6177
INTERNATIONAL GRAPHICAL FEDERATION. REPORT OF ACTIVITIES. (Text in English, French, German, Spanish and Swedish) 1950. triennial. International Graphical Federation, Rue des Fripiers 17, Bloc 2, Galerie du Centre, 1000 Brussels, Belgium. TEL 02-223-18-14. FAX 02-223-02-20. circ. 1,800.

INTERNATIONAL MUSICIAN. see MUSIC

331.8   US   ISSN 0020-8159
INTERNATIONAL OPERATING ENGINEER. 1896. m. $5. International Union of Operating Engineers, 1125 17th St. N.W., Washington, DC 20036. TEL 202-429-9100. Ed. Frank Hanley. illus.; circ. 360,000.

331.8   US   ISSN 0161-9314
INTERNATIONAL PRESIDENT'S BULLETIN. 1937. q. Transportation Communications International Union, 3 Research Pl., Rockville, MD 20850. TEL 301-948-4910. Ed. R.I. Kilroy. circ. 3,500. (back issues avail.)

331.88   US   ISSN 0020-8892
HD6350.A76
INTERNATIONAL TEAMSTER. 1903. m. $12. International Brotherhood of Teamsters, A F L - C I O, 25 Louisiana Ave., N.W., Washington, DC 20001. TEL 202-624-6800. Ed. Linda Fisher. charts; illus.; circ. 1,800,000. (also avail. in microform from UMI; reprint service avail. from UMI)

INTERNATIONAL TRADE CONFERENCE OF WORKERS OF THE BUILDING, WOOD AND BUILDING MATERIALS INDUSTRIES. (BROCHURE). see BUILDING AND CONSTRUCTION

331.88   UK   ISSN 0539-0915
INTERNATIONAL TRANSPORT WORKERS' FEDERATION REPORT ON ACTIVITIES. (Editions in English, French, German, Spanish and Swedish) 1897. 4/yr. International Transport Workers' Federation, 133-135 Great Suffolk St., London SE1 1PD, England. circ. 500 (controlled).

331.88 691   US   ISSN 0362-3696
HD6350.B9
INTERNATIONAL UNION OF BRICKLAYERS AND ALLIED CRAFTSMEN. JOURNAL. 1898. m. $1.50. International Union of Bricklayers and Allied Craftsmen, 815 15th St., N.W., Washington, DC 20005. TEL 202-783-3788. Ed. Mary T. Dresser. adv.; charts; illus.; circ. 105,000.
    Former titles (until 1975): Bricklayers', Masons' and Plasterers' International Union of America. Journal (ISSN 0360-6058); Bricklayer, Mason and Plasterer.

331.88 664   SZ   ISSN 0579-8299
INTERNATIONAL UNION OF FOOD AND ALLIED WORKERS' ASSOCIATIONS. MEETING OF THE EXECUTIVE COMMITTEE. I. DOCUMENTS OF THE SECRETARIAT. II. SUMMARY REPORT. a. 100 Fr. International Union of Food and Allied Workers' Associations - Union Internationale des Travailleurs de l'Alimentation et des Branches Connexes, Secretariat, Rampe du Pont-Rouge 8, CH-1213 Petit-Lancy - Geneva, Switzerland.

331.88 664   SZ   ISSN 0020-9074
INTERNATIONAL UNION OF FOOD AND ALLIED WORKERS' ASSOCIATIONS. NEWS BULLETIN. (Editions in a Scandinavian language, English, French, German, Spanish) 1920. bi-m. 180 Fr. International Union of Food and Allied Workers' Associations, Secretariat, Rampe du Pont-Rouge 8, CH-1213 Petit-Lancy - Geneva, Switzerland. Ed. Dan Gallin. index.

331.88   US   ISSN 0021-163X
HD6350.I5
IRONWORKER. 1901. m. $2.50 or membership. International Association of Bridge, Structural and Ornamental Iron Workers, 1750 New York Ave., N.W., Washington, DC 20006. TEL 202-383-4810. Ed. W.M. Lawbaugh. bk.rev.; charts; illus.; circ. 135,000.

331.88   MM   ISSN 0021-2725
IT-TORCA. (Text in Maltese) 1944. w. £6.24. (General Workers Union) Union Print Co., Ltd., South St., Valletta, Malta. FAX 243454. TELEX 1724 UNWOR RAW. Ed. Joe A. Vella. adv.; bk.rev.; film rev.; play rev.; circ. 24,000. (tabloid format)

331.88 688.2   US   ISSN 0021-6291
JEWELRY WORKERS' BULLETIN. vol.34, 1970. s-m. membership only. Amalgamated Jewelry, Diamond and Watchcase Worker's Union, Local No. 1-J, A F L - C I O 133 W. 44th St., New York, NY 10036. TEL 212-246-2335. Ed. Joseph Tarantola. adv.; illus.; circ. 3,250. (tabloid format; also avail. in microfilm from AJP)

331.8 622   FR   ISSN 0397-1511
JOURNAL DU MINEUR. no.96, 1975. m. 12 F. Federation Nationale des Mineurs CFDT, 35 rue des Ferronniers, 59500 Douai, France. Ed. M. Provost Jean-Gerant. charts; stat. (tabloid format)

JOURNAL OF COMMUNICATION BETWEEN RURAL COMMUNITIES AND TOWNS/NOSON TO TOSHI O MUSUBU. see AGRICULTURE — Agricultural Economics

JOURNAL OF LABOR RESEARCH. see BUSINESS AND ECONOMICS — Labor And Industrial Relations

331.88 687   US   ISSN 0022-7013
HD6350.C6
JUSTICE. Spanish edition: Justicia (ISSN 0195-3737) 1919. m. $2. International Ladies' Garment Workers' Union, 1710 Broadway, New York, NY 10019. TEL 212-265-7000. Ed. Dwight Burton. illus.; circ. 280,000. (tabloid format; also avail. in microform from MIM; microfilm from BHP,KTO)
Indexed: HR Rep.

331.88 687   US   ISSN 0195-3737
JUSTICIA. English edition: Justice (ISSN 0022-7013) m. $2. International Ladies' Garment Workers' Union, 1710 Broadway, New York, NY 10019. TEL 212-265-7000. Ed. Felicita Vargas. illus.; circ. 35,000. (tabloid format)

331.88   CS
KALENDAR ODBORARA. a. 8 Kcs. (Slovenska Odborova Rada) Praca, Publishing House of the Slovak Trade Unions Council, Stefanikava 19, 812 71 Bratislava, Czechoslovakia. TEL 7-222779. FAX 7-330046. Ed. Michal Zaleta.

331   US   ISSN 0023-0251
KENTUCKY LABOR NEWS.* 1942. bi-m. $10.50. Kentucky State A F L - C I O, Box 5445, Louisville, KY 40205-0445. Ed. Tom Brimm. adv.; bk.rev.; charts; illus.; stat.; circ. 10,000.

331.8   RU
KLUB I KHUDOZHESTVENNAYA SAMODEYATEL'NOST'. 1951. s-m. 26.40 Rub. (Vsesoyuznyi Tsentral'nyi Sovet Professional'nykh Soyuzov) Profizdat, Ul. Kirova 13, Moscow, Russia. adv.; bk.rev.; bibl.; illus.; index; circ. 92,000.
    Formerly: Klub (ISSN 0023-219X)

331.88   KN   ISSN 0454-4196
HD6835.6
KOREAN TRADE UNIONS.* (Text in English) no.142, 1974. m. General Federation of Trade Unions of Korea, Central Committee, Pyongyang, N. Korea. illus.

331.88   DK   ISSN 0109-2057
KRISTELIG FAGFORENING. MEDLEMSBLAD. vol.41, 1984. m. free. Kristelig Fagforening, Postbox 239, 8900 Randers, Denmark. FAX 86-417301. Ed. Per Boysen. bk.rev.; circ. 36,000.
    Supersedes in part: Kristelig Fagforening, Kristelig Funktionaer-Organisation. Medlemsblad (ISSN 0109-2936); Which was formerly: Kristelig Fagforening og K F O (ISSN 0107-8860)

331.88   DK   ISSN 0109-1131
KRISTELIG FUNKTIONAER-ORGANISATION. MEDLEMSBLAD. vol.14, 1984. m. free. Kristelig Funktionaer-Organisation, Postbox 239, 8900 Randers, Denmark. FAX 86-417301. Ed. Per Boysen. illus.; circ. 27,000.
    Supersedes in part: Kristelig Fagforening, Kristelig Funktionaer-Organisation. Medlemsblad (ISSN 0109-2936); Which was formerly: Kristelig Fagforening og K F O (ISSN 0107-8860)

DIE KUENSTLERGILDE; ein Mitteilungsblatt fuer unsere Mitglieder. see ART

331.3   KN
KULLOJA/WORKERS. (Text in Korean) 1946. m. Central Committee of the Korean Workers' Party, 1 Munshin Dong, Tongdaewon, Pyongyang, N. Korea. Ed. Li Jong-Nam. circ. 300,000.

331.88   DK   ISSN 0105-032X
HD8542
L O BLADET. 1904. 24/yr. DKK 100 (typically set in Jan.). Landsorganisationen i Danmark - Danish Federation of Trade Unions, Danasvej 7, 1910 Frederiksberg C, Denmark. FAX 45-31-31-79-89. Ed. Finn Thorgrimson. bk.rev.; charts; illus.; stat.; index; circ. 36,000. (tabloid format) **Indexed:** C.I.S. Abstr.
    Formerly: Lon og Virke (ISSN 0024-5976)

331.88   SW   ISSN 0346-895X
L O TIDNINGEN. 1921. 40/yr. SEK 150. Landsorganisationen i Sverige, Barnhusgatan 18, 105 53 Stockholm, Sweden. Ed. Elon Johanson. adv.; bk.rev.; illus.; circ. 70,000.
    Formerly (until 1976): Fackfoereningsroerelsen (ISSN 0014-6455)

LABOR AND EMPLOYMENT LAW ANTHOLOGY. see LAW

331.8 332.6   US
LABOR AND INVESTMENTS. 1981. 4/yr. $40. A F L - C I O, Industrial Union Department, 815 16th St., N.W., Washington, DC 20006. TEL 202-842-7860.

LABOR LAW REPORTS. see LAW

331.8   US   ISSN 0023-6594
LABOR LEADER.* 1906. m. $10. San Diego-Imperial Counties Labor Council, 4265 Fairmount Ave., San Diego, CA 92105-1265. Ed. Gabe DeNunzio. adv.; bk.rev.; film rev.; circ. 33,000 (controlled). (tabloid format)

331.8   US
THE LABOR PAGE; news for Boston area workers. 1982. bi-m. $8. Workplace Committee for City Life - Vida Urbana, 335 Lamerine St., Jamaica Plains, MA 02130. TEL 617-524-3541. circ. 3,500.

LABOR PAPER. see BUSINESS AND ECONOMICS — Labor And Industrial Relations

331.88   BE
LABOR PRESS AND INFORMATION; revue on trade union information and training. (Editions in Dutch, English, French, German, Spanish) 1971. 8/yr. 600 Fr.($15) World Confederation of Labour, 33 rue Treves, 1040 Brussels, Belgium. TEL 02-230-62-95. FAX 02-230-87-22. TELEX 26966. Ed.Bd. charts; circ. 2,700.
    Formed by the merger of: Labor (ISSN 0047-3871) & World Confederation of Labour. Information Bulletin.

L

2586 LABOR UNIONS

331.8   US   ISSN 0023-6640
LABOR TODAY;* a monthly journal and independent forum for organized labor. 1962. 4/yr. $7. Labor Today Associates, Box 25704, Chicago, IL 60625-0704. Eds. John Kailin, Jim Williams. bk.rev.; charts; illus.; stat.; circ. 12,000. (tabloid format; also avail. in microform from UMI) **Indexed:** Alt.Press Ind., Bus.Ind., C.I.S. Abstr., Mag.Ind., Tr.& Indus.Ind., Work Rel.Abstr.
    Description: Recommended for rank-and-file labor activitists. Union democracy, organizing drives and articles on past and present workers' struggles are among the many topics covered.

331.88 687   US   ISSN 0271-5848
LABOR UNITY. (Text in English, French, Spanish) 1976. 11/yr. $1.50 domestic; Canada $1.75. Amalgamated Clothing and Textile Workers Union, A F L - C I O, 15 Union Sq., New York, NY 10003. TEL 212-242-0700. FAX 212-255-7230. Ed. Anne Rivera. bk.rev.; illus.; circ. 383,000. **Indexed:** Text.Tech.Dig.
    Incorporating: Textile Labour - Canadian Edition (ISSN 0049-3562); Formed by the merger of: Advance (New York) (ISSN 0001-8597); Textile Labor (ISSN 0040-5027)

331.88   US   ISSN 0023-6667
LABOR WORLD. 1896. bi-w. $10. (Duluth A F L - C I O Central Labor Body) Labor World, Inc., 2002 London Rd., Rm. 108, Duluth, MN 55812. TEL 218-728-4469. Ed. Larry Sillanpa. adv.; bk.rev.; circ. 14,000. (tabloid format)

331.88   US   ISSN 0023-6888
HD6350.B89
LABORER. 1947. bi-m. $2. Laborers' International Union of North America, 905 16th St., N.W., Washington, DC 20006. TEL 202-737-8320. FAX 202-737-2754. Ed. Angelo Fosco. bk.rev.; circ. 500,000.

LABOUR/TRAVAIL; journal of Canadian labour studies - revue d'etudes ouvrieres Canadiennes. see *BUSINESS AND ECONOMICS — Labor And Industrial Relations*

320.531   UK   ISSN 0953-3494
LABOUR & TRADE UNION REVIEW. 1968. bi-m. £11 in U.K.; Europe £13; elsewhere £15. Bevin Society, 114 Lordship Rd., London N16 0QP, England. Ed. Dick Barry. adv.; bk.rev.; circ. 1,000.
    Formerly: Socialist; **Supersedes:** Communist.

LABOUR ARBITRATION. see *LAW*

331.8   IS   ISSN 0023-6969
LABOUR IN ISRAEL. French edition: Israel au Travail (ISSN 0021-1966); German edition: Histadrut Nachrichten (ISSN 0333-7782); Spanish edition: Trabajo en Israel (ISSN 0041-0225) 1947. irreg. (3-4/yr.). free. Histadrut, 93 Arlosoroff St., 62 098 Tel Aviv, Israel. TEL 03-431111. TELEX 342-488-HISTD-IL. Ed. Raffel Benkler-Barkan. illus.; circ. 24,000 (9,000 English ed.; 3,500 French ed.; 3,500 German ed.; 8,000 Spanish ed.).
    Description: News about trade unions in Israel and socio-economic issues.

331.88   CN   ISSN 0383-3437
HD6529.N63
LABOUR ORGANIZATIONS IN NOVA SCOTIA. 1970. a. free. Department of Labour, Research Division, P.O. Box 697, Halifax, N.S. B3J 2T8, Canada. TEL 902-424-4313. FAX 902-424-3239. (processed)
    Formerly: Directory of Labour Unions in Nova Scotia.
    Description: Directory of union locals in the province of Nova Scotia.

LABOUR RESOURCER. see *BUSINESS AND ECONOMICS — Labor And Industrial Relations*

331.8   SW
LANDSORGANISATIONEN I SVERIGE. YTTRANDEN TILL OFFENTLIG MYNDIGHET. irreg. Landsorganisationen i Sverige, Barnhusgatan 18, 105 53 Stockholm, Sweden.

LANDWORKER. see *AGRICULTURE*

331.88   US   ISSN 0023-8384
LANSING LABOR NEWS. 1945. fortn. $13 to non-members. U.A.W., 342 Clare St., Lansing, MI 48917. TEL 517-484-7408. Ed. Harold Foster. adv.; bk.rev.; illus.; circ. 29,000. (tabloid format)

331.3   LS
LAO DONG/LABOR. (Text in Lao) 1986. fortn. Lao Federation of Trade Unions, 87 ave Lane Xang, BP 780, Vientiane, Laos. circ. 46,000.

331.8   IT
IL LAVORO. 1946. a. free. Camera Confederale del Lavoro UIL, V. Polonio, 5, 34100 Trieste, Italy. TEL 040-302633. Dir. Fabricci Carlo.
    Description: Focuses on labor union activities in the Trieste economic area.

331.8 340   IT   ISSN 1120-947X
LAVORO E DIRITTO. 1987. q. L.110000. Societa Editrice Il Mulino, Strada Maggiore, 37, 40125 Bologna, Italy. TEL 051-256011. FAX 051-256034. Ed. Umberto Romagnoli. adv.; index; circ. 900. (back issues avail.)

331.8   IT   ISSN 0023-9089
LAVORO ITALIANO.* vol.18, 1966. fortn. L.5000. Unione Italiana del Lavoro, Via Cavour 108, 00184 Rome, Italy. Ed. Camillo Benevento. charts; illus.; stat.

LITERARY AGENT. see *PUBLISHING AND BOOK TRADE*

LOCOMOTIVE ENGINEER NEWSLETTER. see *TRANSPORTATION — Railroads*

LOCOMOTIVE ENGINEERS JOURNAL. see *TRANSPORTATION — Railroads*

LOCOMOTIVE JOURNAL. see *TRANSPORTATION — Railroads*

331.88   US   ISSN 0024-6549
LOS ANGELES CITIZEN. 1896? s-m. $5. Los Angeles County Federation of Labor, A F L - C I O, 2130 W. 9th St., Los Angeles, CA 90006. TEL 213-381-5611. Ed. Sal Perrotta. adv.; illus. (tabloid format)

385 331.3   RM
LUPTA C F R. 1932. w. Rumanian Railway Workers (C F R), Bd. Dinicu Golescu 38, Bucharest, Rumania. Ed. Ionel Chiru. circ. 150,000.

331.8   FR   ISSN 0024-7650
LUTTE OUVRIERE. 1968. w. 250 F. (foreign 320 F.). B.P. 233, 75865 Paris Cedex 18, France. Ed. Michel Rodinson.

620   UK
M S F JOURNAL. 1914. m. £7 to non-members. M S F, 79 Camden Rd., London NW1 9ES, England. adv.; bk.rev.; charts; illus.; circ. 400,000.
    Former titles: Tass News and Journal; Tass Journal (ISSN 0307-3424); Data Journal (ISSN 0011-6823)

331.8 630   FI
MAASEUTUTYOVAEN VIESTI. m. Suomen Maaseututyovaen Liitto - Finnish Forest and Agricultural Workers Union, Haapaniemenk 7-9, SF-00530 Helsinki 53, Finland.

331.88 621.9   US   ISSN 0047-5378
MACHINIST. 1946. m. $4. International Association of Machinists and Aerospace Workers, 1300 Connecticut Ave., N.W., Washington, DC 20036. TEL 202-857-5200. Ed. Robert J. Kalaski. bk.rev.; charts; illus.; tr.lit.; circ. 780,000. (tabloid format)

331 614.7   US   ISSN 0731-0323
MALCRIADO. (Text in English, Spanish) 1964-1990; N.S. 1992. m. $5. United Farm Workers of America, Box 62, La Paz, Keene, CA 93531. TEL 805-822-5571. FAX 805-822-6537. adv.; circ. 25,000.

MARITIME NEWSLETTER. see *TRANSPORTATION — Ships And Shipping*

MARITIME WORKER. see *TRANSPORTATION — Ships And Shipping*

MASARYKOVA UNIVERZITA. FILOZOFICKA FAKULTA. SBORNIK PRACI. G: RADA SOCIALNEVEDNA. see *BUSINESS AND ECONOMICS — Economic Systems And Theories, Economic History*

331.88   US   ISSN 0025-4894
MASSACHUSETTS STATE LABOR COUNCIL A F L - C I O NEWSLETTER. 1960. m. free. Massachusetts State Labor Council, A F L - C I O, 8 Beacon St., Boston, MA 02108. TEL 617-227-8260. FAX 617-227-2010. Ed. John S. Laughlin. circ. 8,000 (controlled).

MEATWORKER. see *FOOD AND FOOD INDUSTRIES*

MECHANIST. see *AERONAUTICS AND SPACE FLIGHT*

MEDECINE HOSPITALIERE/HOSPITAL MEDICINE. see *HOSPITALS*

331.88   US   ISSN 0047-679X
MESSAGE (BRONX).* 1972. m. Union of Telephone Workers, 702 Rhinelander Ave., Bronx, NY 10462. Ed. H. Curran. charts; illus.

670   DK   ISSN 0026-0517
METAL. 1912. 3/w. DKK 100. Dansk Metalarbejderforbund, Nyropsgade 38, 1602 Copenhagen V, Denmark. TEL 33 12 82 12. FAX 33-12-82-28. Ed. Kjeld Hammer. adv.; bk.rev.; index; circ. 150,000.

338.11   AT   ISSN 0727-1115
METAL WORKER. 1939. m. membership. Metals and Engineering Workers' Union, National Council, 136 Chalmers St., Surry Hills, N.S.W. 2010, Australia. FAX 02-6987516. Ed. Chris Lindsay. bk.rev.; circ. 191,000.
    Former titles: A M W S U Journal; A M W U Journal; A E U Monthly Journal.

331.88 670   US   ISSN 0047-6870
METALETTER. vol.3, 1972. m. free. A F L - C I O, Metal Trades Department, 815 16th St., N.W., Washington, DC 20006. TEL 202-637-5000. Ed.Bd. charts.

METALLARBETAREN. see *METALLURGY*

331.88   US   ISSN 0026-1998
MICHIGAN A F L - C I O NEWS. 1939. m. $2.50. Michigan A F L - C I O News, Inc., 419 Washington Square South, Ste. 200, Lansing, MI 48933. TEL 517-487-5966. Ed. Jon Ogar. adv.; bk.rev.; illus.; stat.; circ. 30,000. (tabloid format; also avail. in microfilm from UMI; reprint service avail. from UMI)
    Description: Articles and news on issues affecting the Michigan labor movement.

331.8   US
MILWAUKEE LABOR PRESS, A F L - C I O. 1942. m. $8.50. Milwaukee County Labor Council, A F L - C I O, 633 S. Hawley Rd., Milwaukee, WI 53214. TEL 414-771-7070. Ed. Carole Casamento. adv.; circ. 76,800. (tabloid format)

331.88   US   ISSN 0026-6728
MISSOURI TEAMSTER. 1963. q. $3. Teamsters Joint Council 13, 5730 Elizabeth, St. Louis, MO 63110. TEL 314-647-2002. Ed. Gus Lumpe. bk.rev.; charts; illus.; stat.; circ. 42,000. (tabloid format; back issues avail.)

331.88   AT   ISSN 0047-7753
MODERN UNIONIST. 1970. q. Aus.$5 to individuals; institutions Aus.$10. Trade Union Information and Research Centre, P.O. Box K535, Haymarket, N.S.W. 2000, Australia. Ed. W.J. Brown. adv.; bk.rev.; circ. 10,000.

331.3   RM
MUNKASELET. (Text in Hungarian) 1957. w. General Trade Union Confederation, Piata Presei Libere 1, 41917 Bucharest, Rumania. TEL 185795. Ed. Aurel Moja. circ. 12,000.

331.88 380.5   FR
MUTUALISTE DU METRO. 1947. q. Societe Mutualiste du Personnel de la Regie Autonome des Transports Parisiens, 18 rue de Naples, 75381 Paris Cedex 8, France. adv.; illus.

331.88 384   US   ISSN 0027-5697
HD6350.B86
N A B E T NEWS. vol.24, 1975. bi-m. $2. National Association of Broadcast Employees and Technicians, A F L - C I O, 7101 Wisconsin Ave., Ste. 800, Bethesda, MD 20814. TEL 301-659-8420. FAX 301-657-9478. Ed. John J. Krieger. illus.; circ. 14,000.

LABOR UNIONS

N A S U W T CAREER TEACHER JOURNAL. see *EDUCATION*

N E A ADVOCATE; a publication for NEA members in higher education. (National Education Association of the United States) see *EDUCATION — Higher Education*

N E A ALMANAC OF HIGHER EDUCATION. (National Education Association of the United States) see *EDUCATION — Higher Education*

331.88 US ISSN 0279-540X
HD8009.03
N T E U BULLETIN. 1973. m. membership. National Treasury Employees Union, 901 E St., N.W., Ste. 600, Washington, DC 20004. TEL 202-783-4444. FAX 202-783-4085. Ed. Eve Berton. illus.; stat.; circ. 81,000. (tabloid format)
 Formerly: National Treasury Employees Union. Bulletin (ISSN 0095-4748) Continues the bulletin issued by the union under its earlier name: National Association of Internal Revenue Employees.

331 US
N T L NEWS. 1986. q. membership. International Brotherhood of Boilermakers, Iron Ship Builders, Blacksmiths, Forgers and Helpers, National Transient Lodge, 753 State Ave., Ste. 765, Kansas City, KS 66101. TEL 913-371-2640. Ed. George Santos. circ. 4,000.

331.88 350 US ISSN 0027-8513
HE6499
NATIONAL ALLIANCE (WASHINGTON). 1917. m. $9. National Alliance of Postal and Federal Employees, National Executive Board, 1628 Eleventh St., N.W., Washington, DC 20001. TEL 202-939-6325. FAX 800-939-6389. Ed. Jacquelyn C. Moore. adv.; illus.; circ. 18,500.
 Formerly: Postal Alliance.

NATIONAL CENTER FOR THE STUDY OF COLLECTIVE BARGAINING IN HIGHER EDUCATION AND THE PROFESSIONS. ANNUAL CONFERENCE PROCEEDINGS. see *EDUCATION — Higher Education*

331.8 622 JA
NATIONAL UNION OF COAL MINE WORKERS. JOURNAL. q. National Union of Coal Mine Workers, 20-12 Shiba, 2-chome, Minato-ku, Tokyo 105, Japan.

NEW JERSEY EDUCATION LAW REPORT; the authority on labor relations in New Jersey schools. see *EDUCATION*

621.38 US ISSN 0028-7245
NEW YORK GENERATOR. 1960. m. $2. Communications Workers of America, Local 1101, C W A, A F L - C I O, 275 7th Ave., 17th Fl., New York, NY 10001. TEL 212-683-2666. Eds. Angel Feliciano, Cecilia E. Mallia. adv.; bk.rev.; illus.; circ. 14,000.

331.88 350 US ISSN 0028-7342
NEW YORK LETTER CARRIERS' OUTLOOK. 1939. m. $6. National Association of Letter Carriers, N Y L C Branch 36, 249 W. 49th St., New York, NY 10019. TEL 212-956-3110. Eds. Lenny Goldman, Sid Klein. adv.; illus.; circ. 9,200. (tabloid format)

331.88 370 US
NEW YORK TEACHER. 1917. bi-w. $4. New York State United Teachers, 159 Wolf Rd., Box 15-008, Albany, NY 11212-5008. TEL 212-254-7660. (Or: 260 Park Ave. S., New York, NY 10010) Ed. Ted Bleecker. adv.; bk.rev.; charts; illus.; stat.; circ. 311,000.
 Formerly: United Teacher (ISSN 0041-8161)

331.88 686.2 US ISSN 0049-4968
NEW YORK TYPOGRAPHICAL UNION NUMBER SIX. BULLETIN. 1898. irreg. membership. New York Typographical Union Number Six, 817 Broadway, New York, NY 10003. TEL 212-533-2000. FAX 212-475-0536. Ed. Gunnar Janger. bk.rev.; charts; illus.; circ. 7,000.

331.88 NZ ISSN 1170-7887
NEW ZEALAND COUNCIL OF TRADE UNIONS. OFFICIAL TRADE UNION DIRECTORY. 1971. a. free. New Zealand Council of Trade Unions, P.O. Box 6645, Wellington, New Zealand. FAX 3856-051. Ed.Bd. adv.
 Formerly: New Zealand Federation of Labour. Official Trade Union Directory.

331 AT
NEWSMONTH. 1981. 8/yr. Aus.$38. New South Wales Independent Teachers Association, G.P.O. Box 116, Sydney, N.S.W. 2001, Australia. Eds. Dick Shearman, Leith Hamilton. adv.; bk.rev.; circ. 16,000. (tabloid format; back issues avail.)

383 331.88
NEWSPAPER AND MAIL DELIVERERS' UNION BULLETIN. vol.73, 1976. m. membership. Newspaper and Mail Deliverers' Union, 41-18 27th St., Long Island City, NY 11101. TEL 718-392-8367. charts; circ. 4,000.

NIKKYOSO KYOIKU SHINBUN. see *EDUCATION*

331.88 SW
NORDISKA SAMARBETSORGAN. 1975. irreg. Nordisk Raad, Tyrgatan 7, Boks 19506, S-104 32 Stockholm, Sweden.

NORSK SJOEMANNSFORBUND. MEDLEMSBLAD. see *TRANSPORTATION — Ships And Shipping*

331 US
NORTHERN CALIFORNIA LABOR. 1951. m. $6. (San Francisco Labor Council, A F L - C I O) San Francisco Labor Council Newspaper Association, 510 Harrison St., San Francisco, CA 94105. Ed. Gerald Holl. adv.; bk.rev.; illus.; circ. 38,000. (tabloid format)
 Formerly: San Francisco Labor (ISSN 0036-4134)

331.8 331 US ISSN 0894-444X
NORTHWEST LABOR PRESS. 1900. s-m. $10. Oregon Labor Press Publishing Co., 4313 N.E. Tillamook, Ste. 206, Box 13150, Portland, OR 97213. TEL 503-288-3311. FAX 503-288-3320. Ed. Michael Gutwig. adv.; circ. 52,000. (tabloid format; also avail. in microfilm)
 Description: Covers issues of interest to labor.

NOUVEAU CENTRE DE SANTE. see *MEDICAL SCIENCES*

331.88 070 IT
NUMERO ZERO. 1945. m. L.1800 per no. Federazione Nazionale Stampa Italiana, Corso Vittorio Emanuele 349, Rome 00186, Italy. TEL 65681. TELEX 221121. Ed. Sergio Borsi. bk.rev.; charts; illus.; circ. 25,000.
 Supersedes: Stampa Italiana.

331.88 US ISSN 8756-1727
HD6350.P415
O C A W REPORTER. 1944. bi-m. $6. Oil, Chemical and Atomic Workers International Union, A F L - C I O, Box 2812, Denver, CO 80201. TEL 303-987-2229. Ed. Rodney Rogers. bk.rev.; illus.; circ. 120,000. (also avail. in microfilm from UMI; reprint service avail. from UMI)
 Formerly (until 1988): Oil, Chemical and Atomic Workers International Union. Union News (ISSN 0030-1426)

331.8 LU
O G B - L AKTUELL. 1919. m. Confederation of Independent Trade Unions of Luxembourg, 1002 Esch-sur-Alzette, Luxembourg. TEL 54-05-45. FAX 54-16-20. TELEX 1368. circ. 28,000.

OBRERO FERROVIARIO. see *TRANSPORTATION — Railroads*

331.88 US ISSN 0030-0772
OHIO A F L - C I O NEWS AND VIEWS. vol.19, 1970. w. free. Ohio A F L - C I O, 271 E. State St., Columbus, OH 43215. TEL 614-224-8271. FAX 614-224-2671. Ed. Kent Darr. stat.; circ. 14,000. (processed)

331.88 II ISSN 0030-1329
OIL & CHEMICAL WORKER. (Text in English) 1965. m. National Federation of Petroleum Workers, Tel-Rasayan Bhavan, Tilak Rd., Dadar, Bombay 400 014, India. (Co-sponsor: Indian National Chemical Workers' Federation) Ed. Raja Kulkarni. adv.; stat.; circ. 500. (avail. in talking book)

662 665.5 TU
OIL CHEMICAL RUBBER WORKERS TRADE UNION OF TURKEY. YEARBOOK. a. Turkiye Petrol, Kimya, Lastik Iscileeri Sendikasi - Oil Chemical Rubber Workers Trade Union of Turkey, Yildiz, Posta Cad P.O. Box 284, Evren Sitesi Gayrettepe, Istanbul 80280, Turkey. TEL 1748896. FAX 1747446.

331.88 US ISSN 0030-4840
OREGON TEAMSTER.* 1946. m. membership. Joint Council of Teamsters No. 37, 1866 N.E. 162nd Ave., Portland, OR 97230-5642. TEL 503-231-2618. Ed. Frank Flori. bk.rev.; circ. 37,000.

OSIM INYAN. see *SOCIAL SERVICES AND WELFARE*

331.88 687 US ISSN 0048-2390
OUR LOCAL SIXTY SIX.* vol.24, 1971. q. membership. International Ladies Garment Workers Union, Local 66, 1710 Broadway, NY 10019. Ed. Rafael Martinez. charts; illus.

331.8 CN ISSN 0822-6377
OUR TIMES MAGAZINE; independent Canadian labour magazine. 1981. 8/yr. Can.$20 to individuals; institutions Can.$32. Our Times Publishing Ltd., 390 Dufferin St., Toronto, Ont. M6K 2A3, Canada. TEL 416-531-5762. FAX 416-533-2397. Ed. Lorraine Endicott. adv.; bk.rev.; circ. 5,000. (also avail. in microfilm; back issues avail.; reprint service avail. from MML) Indexed: Can.Per.Ind., CMI.
 Description: Reports and opinions, profiles and interviews, creative writing and photography, reflecting the current state of the union movement in Canada.

331.9 AT
OVER 2 U. a. Australian Council of Trade Unions, 393-397 Swanston St., Melbourne, Vic. 3000, Australia. TEL 03-663-5266. (Co-sponsors: BTR Nylex Ltd.; OTC Ltd.; Lane Lease)

331.8 US
P E D FORUM. 1975. q. free. A F L - C I O, Public Employee Department, 816 16th St., N.W., Ste. 308, Washington, DC 20006. TEL 202-393-2820. FAX 202-347-1825. Ed. Laura Ginsburg. bk.rev.; circ. 3,500.
 Formerly: In Public Service (ISSN 0161-9330)

331.8 CN
P S A C UNION UPDATE. (Text in English and French) 1976. fortn. free. Public Service Alliance of Canada, 233 Gilmour Street, Ottawa, Ont. K2P 0P1, Canada. TEL 613-560-4200. FAX 613-236-1654. Ed. Francine Filion. stat.; illus.; circ. 30,000. (back issues avail.)
 Former titles: Your Union; (until 1989): Public Service Alliance of Canada. Weekly Newsletter.

331.8 AT
P S A INDUSTRIAL BULLETIN. 1988. s-m. Public Service Association of New South Wales, G.P.O. Box 3365, Sydney, N.S.W. 2001, Australia. TEL 02-290-1555. FAX 02-262-1623. Ed. Allan Gibson. circ. 9,000.
 Description: Reports on current industrial issues.

331.8 AT ISSN 0812-7573
P S A REPORTER. 1983. s-m. Public Service Association of New South Wales, G.P.O. Box 3365, Sydney, N.S.W. 2001, Australia. TEL 02-290-1555. FAX 02-262-1623. Ed. Allan Gibson. circ. 9,000.
 Description: Reports of decisions and industrial disputes.

P S C CLARION. (Professional Staff Congress) see *EDUCATION — Higher Education*

331.8 FR
PAGES JURIDIQUES DE LA VIE OUVRIERE. a. Vie Ouvriere, 33 rue Bouret, 75940 Paris cedex, France.

331.88 698 US ISSN 0030-9532
HD6350.P2
PAINTER & ALLIED TRADES JOURNAL. 1887. m. $2. International Brotherhood of Painters & Allied Trades, 1750 New York Ave., N.W., Washington, DC 20006. TEL 202-637-0700. Ed. K.A. Berlin. illus.; circ. 210,000.
 Formerly: Painter and Decorator.

331.3 NZ
PAPER CLIP. 5/yr. New Zealand Clerical Workers' Association, P.O. Box 9781, Wellington, New Zealand. TEL 04-843-749. circ. 40,000.

LABOR UNIONS

331.88 676 US ISSN 0363-6437
HD6350.P27
PAPERWORKER. 1972. m. membership. United Paperworkers International Union, 3340 Perimeter Hill Dr., Box 1475, Nashville, TN 37202. TEL 615-834-8590. FAX 615-834-7741. Ed. Dick Blin. bk.rev.; illus.; stat.; circ. 265,000. (tabloid format; back issues avail.)
Supersedes: Pulp and Paper Worker; United Paper (ISSN 0041-7459)

331.88 US
PATTERN MAKERS & ALLIED CRAFTS JOURNAL. 1890. a. membership. Pattern Makers' League of North America, 501 15th St., No. 204, Moline, IL 61265-2180. Ed. Jack L. Gabelhausen, Sr. adv.; illus.; circ. 17,500.
Former titles: Pattern Makers' Journal (ISSN 0031-319X); Pattern Makers and Allied Crafts Journal.

331.8 HU
PEDAGOGUSOK LAPJA. fortn. $21. Hungarian Union of Teachers, Gorkij fasor 10, 1068 Budapest, Hungary. circ. 20,000.

PENNSYLVANIA EDUCATION LAW REPORT. see *EDUCATION*

331.88 FR ISSN 0031-661X
PEUPLE. 1921. bi-m. 520 F. (Confederation Generale du Travail) Edition de Publications et Journaux Syndicaux, 263 rue de Paris, Case 432, 93516 Montreuil Cedex, France. TEL 48-51-83-06. FAX 48-59-28-31. TELEX 235091F. Ed. Lucien Postel. stat.; index; circ. 23,500.

331.8 384.54 UK
PHI PI EPSILON B E T A NEWS. 1946. m. £20. Broadcasting, Entertainment, Cinematograph, and Theatre Union, 111 Wardour St., London W1V 4AY, England. TEL 071-437-8506. FAX 071-437-8268. Ed. Janice Turner. adv.; bk.rev.; circ. 60,000.
Formerly: B E T A News; Which incorporates (in 1985): A B Stract & Nattke News.
Description: Includes association news, radio, television and cinema industry and theatre news.

331.88 PE
PONTIFICIA UNIVERSIDAD CATOLICA. TALLER DE ESTUDIOS URBANO INDUSTRIALES. SERIE: ESTUDIOS SINDICALES. no.3, 1976. irreg. Pontificia Universidad Catolica, Taller de Estudios Urbanos Industriales, Fundo Pando s-n, Lima, Peru.

331.8 620.85 US
PORTLAND ALLIANCE. (Text in English, Spanish) 1981. m. $15. Northwest Alliance for Alternative Media & Education, 2807 S.E. Stark, Portland, OR 97214. TEL 503-239-4991. Ed. Tarso Luis Ramos. adv.; bk.rev.; film rev.; play rev.; illus.; circ. 7,000. (back issues avail.)
Description: Covers local and regional political, cultural and environmental issues from a radical perspective.

331.88 350 UK ISSN 0032-5236
POST. 1920. m. £1. Union of Communication Workers, U.C.W. House, Crescent Ln., Clapham, London SW4 9RN, England. FAX 01-720-6853. Ed. Jean Jacques. adv.; bk.rev.; circ. 80,000.

331.88 350 US ISSN 0032-5376
HD6350.P75
POSTAL RECORD. 1888. m. $8. National Association of Letter Carriers, A F L - C I O, 100 Indiana Ave., N.W., Washington, DC 20001. TEL 202-393-4695. Ed. Vincent R. Sombrotto. illus.; circ. 315,000.

POTRAVINAR. see *NUTRITION AND DIETETICS*

POWER. see *BUSINESS AND ECONOMICS — Labor And Industrial Relations*

331.8 NO
PRAUSIS. 1905. 10/yr. NOK 50. Arbeidernes Ungdomsfylking, Arbeidersamfunnets Plass 1, Oslo 1, Norway. Ed. Jens Ove Kristiansen. adv.; bk.rev.; circ. 31,811.
Formerly: Arbeidrungdommen.

PROCESSED WORLD. see *COMPUTERS*

331.88 AT ISSN 0048-5454
PROFESSIONAL OFFICER. 1914. bi-m. Aus.$2 to members only. Queensland Professional Officers Association, 32 Peel St., South Brussane, Qld. 4101, Australia. FAX 07-846-3359. Ed. Donald Martindale. adv.; circ. 11,000.

331.8 IT ISSN 0391-7797
HD6706
PROSPETTIVA SINDACALE. 1970. q. L.57000 (Europe L.79000; elsewhere L.88000). Rosenberg & Sellier, Via Andrea Doria 14, 10123 Turin, Italy. TEL 011-561-39-07. FAX 011-532188. Ed. Guido Baglioni. adv.; bk.rev.; film rev.; index; circ. 3,500. (back issues avail.)
Description: Covers various topics in Italian work unions. Includes representation, organization, and procedures.

331.88 US ISSN 0161-7494
HD8008.A1
PUBLIC EMPLOYEE (WASHINGTON). 1935. 8/yr. membership. American Federation of State, County & Municipal Employees, A F L - C I O, 1625 L St., N.W., Washington, DC 20036. TEL 202-429-1144. FAX 202-429-1293. Ed. Marshall O. Donley. bk.rev.; circ. 1,400,000. (also avail. in microform from UMI)
Indexed: Pers.Lit.
Description: Official publication with matters of interest to the American Federation of State, County and Municipal Employees.

331.88 350 US ISSN 0033-345X
PUBLIC EMPLOYEE PRESS. 1959. fortn. (m. in Jan., July, Aug.). $15 to non-members. American Federation of State, County & Municipal Employees, A F L - C I O, District Council 37, 125 Barclay St., New York, NY 10007. TEL 212-815-1000. Ed. Walter Balcerak. bk.rev.; illus.; circ. 165,000. (tabloid format)

PUBLIC SERVICE ASSOCIATION JOURNAL. see *PUBLIC ADMINISTRATION*

331.88 PR
PUERTO RICO. DEPARTMENT OF LABOR. DIRECTORIO DE ORGANIZACIONES DEL TRABAJO. 1965. a. free. Department of Labor, Bureau of Labor Statistics, 505 Munoz Rivera Ave., Hato Rey, PR 00918. Ed. Federico Irizarry. circ. 900. (also avail. in microform)

331.8 AA
PUNA/TRAVAIL. (Editions in Albanian and French) q. $1.54. Unions Professionnelles d'Albanie, Tirana, Albania.

QUARTERNOTE. see *MUSIC*

331.8 GW ISSN 0033-6246
HD4809
DIE QUELLE; Funktionaerzeitschrift des Deutschen Gewerkschaftsbundes. 1951. m. DM.12($6) (Deutscher Gewerkschaftsbund) Bund-Verlag GmbH, Hansestr. 63a, Postfach 900840, 5000 Cologne 90, Germany. adv.; bk.rev.; illus.; circ. 269,000.
Indexed: Dok.Arbeitsmed.
—BLDSC shelfmark: 7216.100000.

331.88 US ISSN 0033-7196
R W D S U RECORD. 1954. bi-m. $3. Retail Wholesale and Department Store Union, AFL-CIO, CLC, 30 E. 29th St., New York, NY 10016. TEL 212-684-5300. Ed. Pat Evans. bk.rev.; charts; illus.; circ. 260,000. (tabloid format; also avail. in microform from UMI; reprint service avail. from UMI)

331.8 US
RACINE LABOR; Racine's voice of working people. 1941. bi-w. $17. Union Labor Publishing Co., Inc., 1840 Sycamore Ave., Racine, WI 53406. TEL 414-634-7186. Ed. Roger Bybee, Jr. adv.; circ. 12,225. (tabloid format; back issues avail.)
Description: Covers local and national labor issues.

331.8 YU ISSN 0033-7463
RAD. 1945. a. 320 din. Savez Sindikata Jugoslavije, Trg Marksa i Engelsa 5, 11000 Belgrade, Yugoslavia. Ed. Stanislav Marinkovic. (also avail. in microfilm from NRP) **Indexed:** Math.R.

385 FR
RAIL SYNDICALISTE. 1947. m. Federation Syndicaliste Force Ouvriere des Cheminots, 60 rue Vergniand, 75640 Paris Cedex 13, France. adv.

RASANT; Zeitschrift der D A G-Jugend. see *CHILDREN AND YOUTH — For*

331.8 IT ISSN 0033-9849
RASSEGNA SINDACALE. 1956. w. L.20000. (C G I L) Editrice Sindacale Italia s.r.l., Corso d'Italia 25, Rome, Italy. Ed. Francesco Cuozzo. adv.; bk.rev.; charts; illus.; stat.; index; circ. 30,000.

331.8 385 BE ISSN 0048-6949
RECHTE LIJN. vol.52, 1971. s-m. membership. Christelijke Vakbond van Communicatiemiddelen en Cultuur, Oudergemselaan 26-32, 1040 Brussels, Belgium. Ed. Michel Bovy. film rev.; stat.; circ. 40,000.

331.88 US ISSN 0034-1541
RECORD (NEW YORK, 1940). 1940. 4/yr. membership. Utility Workers Union of America A F L - C I O Local 1-2, 386 Park Ave. S., New York, NY 10016. TEL 212-532-7110. Ed. James Beamish. illus.
Indexed: Rehabil.Lit.

331.8 AT ISSN 1030-0740
RED TAPE. bi-m. Aus.$20. Public Service Association of New South Wales, G.P.O. Box 3365, Sydney, N.S.W. 2001, Australia. TEL 02-290-1555. FAX 02-262-1623. Ed. Allan Gibson. circ. 55,000. (tabloid format)
Description: Covers wages, conditions of public sector employees and broader industrial and political issues for union members.

REEL. see *MOTION PICTURES*

331.88 665.538 SP
REVISTA PROFESIONAL DEL GREMIO DE ESTACIONES DE SERVICIO. Short title: A E S D I. vol.8, 1978. m. 800 ptas.($10) Estaciones de Servicio, Torre de Madrid Plt. 8, Madrid, Spain. Ed. Julio Carpallo Abadia. adv.; bibl.; illus.

331.8 SZ ISSN 0035-421X
REVUE SYNDICALE SUISSE. 1909. 6/yr. 35 Fr. Union Syndicale Suisse - Swiss Federation of Trade Unions, Monbijoustr. 61, CH-3000 Berne 23, Switzerland. FAX 031-450837. Ed. Fernand Quartenoud. bk.rev.; index. **Indexed:** C.I.S. Abstr., World Bibl.Soc.Sec.

331.8 340 IT ISSN 0392-7229
RIVISTA GIURIDICA DEL LAVORO E DELLA PREVIDENZA SOCIALE. DOTTRINA. 1949. irreg., no.38, 1987. L.180000. Societa Edizioni Giuridiche del Lavoro, Via dei Giordani, 22, 00198 Rome, Italy. TEL 06-421941. index; circ. 2,000. (back issues avail.)
—BLDSC shelfmark: 7986.620000.

331.88 CS ISSN 0557-1693
ROCENKA ODBORARA. a. 15 Kcs. (Slovenska Odborova Rada) Praca, Publishing House of the Slovak Trade Unions Council, Stefanikova 19, 812 71 Bratislava, Czechoslovakia. TEL 7-333779. FAX 7-330046. Ed. Michal Zaleta.

331.8 SW ISSN 0347-0342
S A C O - S R-TIDNINGEN.* 1954. 8/yr. SEK 110. Centralorganisationen S A C O-S R - Swedish Confederation of Professional Associations, P.O. Box 2206, 114 89 Stockholm, Sweden. FAX 08-20-40-49. TELEX 810-52-25. Ed. Lars-Goeran Heldt. adv.; charts; illus.; stat.; circ. 35,000.
Formerly: S A C O Tidningen (ISSN 0036-0597)

331.88 SA ISSN 0036-1011
S.A. WORKER/S.A. WERKER. (Text in Afrikaans and English) 1948. m. R.4.80. South African Iron, Steel and Allied Industries Union, 430 Church St. West, P.O.Box 19299, Pretoria, South Africa. Ed. J.A. van Niekerk-Venter. adv.; bk.rev.; circ. 28,000.

331.88 US
S E I U UPDATE. (Building Service, Office Worker Healthcare, Public and Industrial & Allied Division Editions) 1977. q. free. Service Employees International Union, AFL-CIO, CLC, 1313 L St., N.W., Washington, DC 20005. TEL 202-898-3200. FAX 202-898-3438. Ed. Joyce Moscato. circ. 50,000 (controlled).
Formerly (until 1986): S E I U Leadership News Update.
Description: Consists of five quarterly news magazines for union leaders in the building service, clerical, health care, public sector and other industries.

S P E E A SPOTLITE. (Seattle Professional Engineering Employees Association) see *ENGINEERING*

331.88   US   ISSN 0036-2247
SACRAMENTO VALLEY UNION LABOR BULLETIN. 1928. m. $10. Sacramento Area Central Labor Council, Building Trades Council, 2840 El Centro Rd., No. 109, Sacramento, CA 95833-9700. TEL 916-898-3200. Ed. Rita A. Carroll. adv.; bk.rev.; charts; illus.; stat.; circ. 14,000. (tabloid format)

331.88   US
ST. LOUIS - SOUTHERN ILLINOIS LABOR TRIBUNE; the official weekly A F L - C I O newspaper. 1937. w. $25. Labor Tribune Publishing Co., 505 S. Ewing Ave., St. Louis, MO 63103. TEL 314-535-9660. FAX 314-535-9013. Ed. Sherwood Kerker. adv.; circ. 95,000. (tabloid format; also avail. in microfilm)
  Formerly: St. Louis Labor Tribune (ISSN 0190-0870); Incorporates: Southern Illinois Labor Tribune (ISSN 0490-0200)

331.8 780.65   YU
SAVEZ ORGANIZACIJA KOMPOZITORA JUGOSLAVIJE. BILTEN. English edition: Union of Yugoslav Composers' Organizations. Bulletin. (Text in Serbo-Croatian) 1971. m. free. Savez Organizacija Kompozitora Jugoslavije (SOKOJ), Misarska 12-14, 11000 Belgrade, Yugoslavia. TEL 38-11-334771. FAX 33-11-336-168. Ed. Ivan Kovac. circ. 1,500.
  Description: Publishes news on union's activities in the country and abroad.

331.8   YU
SAVEZ SINDIKATA JUGOSLAVIJE. VECA S S J. BILTEN. 1953. m. Savez Sindikata Jugoslavije, Veca S S J, Trg Marksa i Engelsa 5, Belgrade, Yugoslavia. Ed. Radovan Vukovic. circ. 5,000.
  Formerly: Savez Sindikata Jugoslavije. Centralni Vec. Bilten (ISSN 0006-2561)

331.8   SJ
SAWT AL UMMAL/WORKER'S VOICE. m. £S025 per no. Sudan Federation of Trade Unions, P.O. Box 2285, Khartoum, Sudan.

331.8 791   US   ISSN 0036-956X
PN1993
SCREEN ACTOR. 1934. q. $7. Screen Actors Guild, 7065 Hollywood Blvd., Hollywood, CA 90028. TEL 213-856-6650. FAX 213-856-6603. Ed. Mark Locher. adv.; bk.rev.; illus.; circ. 75,000. (back issues avail.) Indexed: Film Lit.Ind. (1982-).
  Formerly (until 1959): Screen Actor News (ISSN 0745-7243)
  Description: Official publication with news and events of the Screen Actors Guild. Includes articles of general interest about motion pictures.

331.88 387   US
HD6350.S4
SEAFARERS LOG. 1939. m. free. Seafarers' International Union, A F L - C I O, 5201 Auth Way, Camp Springs, MD 20746. TEL 301-899-0675. FAX 301-899-7355. Ed. Jessica Smith. bk.rev.; charts; illus.; circ. 50,000. (tabloid format; also avail. in microfilm from BHP) Indexed: Rehabil.Lit.
  Former titles (until Dec. 1988): Log (ISSN 0160-2047); (until 1976): Seafarer's Log (ISSN 0037-0096); Incorporates: Inland Boatman.

331.88 387   UK   ISSN 0037-0142
SEAMAN. 1911. m. membership. National Union of Rail, Maritime and Transport Workers, Maritime House, Old Town, Clapham, London SW4 0JP, England. TEL 071-622-5581. FAX 071-738-8636. Ed. Jim Jump. adv.; bk.rev.; illus.; index; circ. 13,000.

331.88 669.142   CN   ISSN 0037-041X
SEARCHER. vol.7, 1970. m. membership. United Steelworkers of America, Local 6500, 92 Frood Rd., Sudbury, Ont., Canada. TEL 705-675-1383. Ed. Ron MacDonald. illus.

331.88   US
SERVICE EMPLOYEES INTERNATIONAL UNION. INTERNATIONAL CONVENTION OFFICIAL PROCEEDINGS. 17th ed., 1980. quadrennial. Service Employees International Union, 1313 L St., N.W., Washington, DC 20005. TEL 202-898-3200.

331.88   US
SERVICE EMPLOYEES UNION. 1921. q. $12 to non-members. Service Employees International Union, AFL-CIO, CLC, 1313 L St., N.W., Washington, DC 20005. TEL 202-898-3200. FAX 202-898-3438. Ed. Susan Calhoun. bk.rev.; film rev.; illus.; circ. 950,000. (controlled)
  Formerly (until 1986): Service Employees (ISSN 0037-2609)
  Description: Features opinions, advice and news of interest to union and non-union workers.

331.88   IS   ISSN 0037-413X
SHUROTE. 1938. m. $4.50. General Federation of Labour, P.O. Box 303, Tel Aviv, Israel. Ed. Hayim Yaari. adv.; circ. 20,000.

331.88 385   US   ISSN 0037-5020
HD6350.R39
SIGNALMAN'S JOURNAL. 1920. m. $5. Brotherhood of Railroad Signalmen, 601 W. Golf Rd., Mt. Prospect, IL 60056. Ed. Robert W. McKnight. adv.; bk.rev.; charts; illus.; tr.lit.; index; circ. 18,000.

331.8   IT   ISSN 0037-5543
SINDACATO MODERNO.* vol.6, 1969. m. L.2000. Federazione Impiegati Operai Metallurgici, Via Maroncelli 34, 47100 Forlì, Italy. Ed. Alberto Bellocchio. bk.rev.; charts; illus.

331.8   SP
SINDICALISMO EN ESPANA/TRADE UNIONISM IN SPAIN.* (Text in English, French, Spanish) bi-m. Servicio de Relaciones Exteriores Sindicales, Paseo del Prado, 18-20, Madrid-14, Spain. illus.

331.8   ISSN 0280-9060
SINDIKALNE NOVOSTI. (Text in Serbo-Croation) 1982. 8/yr. free. Landsorganisationen i Sverige, Barnhusgaran 18, 105 53 Stockholm, Sweden. Ed. Penti Lehto. adv.; circ. 16,000.

331.88
SKILL; the UAW's international magazine for skilled trades members. 1981. q. $5 to non-members. United Automobile, Aerospace, and Agricultural Implement Workers of America, 8000 E. Jefferson, Detroit, MI 48214. TEL 313-926-5277. Ed. Peter Laarman. circ. 180,000.

SLUZBA LIDU. see BUSINESS AND ECONOMICS — Management

SOCIALIST CHALLENGE. see POLITICAL SCIENCE

SOCIALISTICKY ZEMEDELEC. see AGRICULTURE

331.8   US   ISSN 0164-856X
SOLIDARITY (DETROIT). 1958. 10/yr. $5. International, United Automobile, Aerospace and Agricultural Implement Workers of America, 8000 E. Jefferson, Detroit, MI 48114. TEL 313-926-5291. FAX 313-331-1520. Ed. David Elsila. bk.rev.; charts; illus.; circ. 1,417,000.
  Description: News of the labor movement; economic and political reports.

SOLIDARITY (HICKSVILLE). see INSURANCE

331.8   MG
SOSIALISMA MPIASA. 1979. m. B.P. 1128, 101 Antananarivo, Malagasy Republic. TEL 21989. Ed. Paul Rabemananjara. circ. 5,000.

SOUTH AFRICAN JOURNAL OF LABOUR RELATIONS. see BUSINESS AND ECONOMICS — Labor And Industrial Relations

331.8 655   SA   ISSN 0038-2787
Z119
SOUTH AFRICAN TYPOGRAPHICAL JOURNAL/SUID-AFRIKAANSE TIPOGRAFIESE JOERNAAL. (Text in Afrikaans and English) 1898. m. R.1.80. South African Typographical Union, P.O. Box 1993, 166 Visagie St., Pretoria, South Africa. Ed. E. Van Tonder. adv.; bk.rev.; illus.; circ. 18,000.

SOUTH INDIAN TEACHER. see EDUCATION

331.88   US   ISSN 0038-3953
SOUTHERN CALIFORNIA TEAMSTER. 1941. 12/yr. $5. Joint Council of Teamsters No. 42, 1616 W. Ninth St., Los Angeles, CA 90015. TEL 213-383-4242. Ed. Paul J. Mihalow. bk.rev.; charts; illus.; circ. 160,000. (tabloid format)

LABOR UNIONS   2589

331.8   RU   ISSN 0038-5174
SOVETSKIE PROFSOYUZY. 1917. s-m. 15.60 Rub. (Vsesoyuznyi Tsentral'nyi Sovet Professional'nykh Soyuzov) Profizdat, Ul. Kirova, 13, Moscow, Russia. (Dist. by: Mezhdunarodnaya Kniga, Moscow, G-200, Russia) Ed. M.P. Mudrov. bk.rev.; illus.; circ. 269,970.

331.8   LU
SOZIALE FORTSCHRETT. (Text in French, German) 1920. fortn. 500 Fr. Letzeburger Chreschtleche Gewerkschaftsbond - Confederation of Christian Trade Unions of Luxembourg, 11 rue du Commerce, B.P. 1208, L-1012 Luxembourg, Luxembourg. TEL 49-94-24-1. FAX 49-94-24-49. TELEX 2116 LCGB. Ed. Weber Robert. circ. 21,000. (back issues avail.)

SPLINTER. see CHILDREN AND YOUTH — For

331.8   GW   ISSN 0172-9527
DER STANDPUNKT (HAMBURG). (Supplement to D A G Journal) 1962. 5/yr. DM.55. (Deutsche Angestellten-Gewerkschaft) Waren Einkaufs- und Vertriebs-Gesellschaft mbH, Karl-Muck-Platz 1, 2000 Hamburg 36, Germany. Ed. Peter Stueber. bk.rev.; bibl.; charts; illus.; index; circ. 55,000.
  Indexed: CERDIC.

331.8   AT
STATE SERVICE; the official journal of the Queensland State Service Union. 1904. m. membership. Queensland State Service Service Union (Q.S.S.U.), 96 Albert St., Brisbane, Qld. 4000, Australia. TEL 07-221-1633. FAX 07-221-5250. Ed. L.M.J. Gillespie. adv.; circ. 17,000. (back issues avail.)
  Description: Industrial issues of interest to union members.

STAVEBNIK. see BUILDING AND CONSTRUCTION

331.88 669.142   US
STEELABOR. (Text in English, French, Spanish) 1936. bi-m. $5. United Steelworkers of America, Five Gateway Center, Pittsburgh, PA 15222. TEL 412-562-2442. FAX 412-562-2445. Ed. Gary Hubbard. bk.rev.; illus.; circ. 900,000.
  Formerly: Steel Labor (ISSN 0039-0941)

331.88   SW
STUDIER I ARBETARROERELSENS HISTORIA. irreg. Saellskapet foer Studier i Arbetarroerelsens Historia, P.O. Box 16 393, Stockholm, Sweden.

STUDIES FOR TRADE UNIONISTS. see BUSINESS AND ECONOMICS — Labor And Industrial Relations

331.88   MY   ISSN 0126-7191
SUARA BURUH. (Text in English) 1956. m. $7.20. Malaysian Trades Union Congress, 19 Jalan Barat, 3rd Fl., P.O. Box 38, Petaling Jaya, Selangor, Malaysia. TEL 03-7560224. Ed. V. David. adv.; charts; illus.; circ. 50,000. (tabloid format)
  Description: Labor, trade unions and related news.

332.1 331.88   MY
SUARA N U B E. (Text in English) 1968. bi-m. free. National Union of Bank Employees, 114 Jalan Tuanku Abdul Rahman, Nube Bldg., 5th Fl., P.O. Box 12488, 50780 Kuala Lumpur, Malaysia. Ed. K. Sanmugam. charts; illus.; circ. 12,000. (tabloid format)

SUGAR WORLD; a newsletter on issues of concern to sugar workers. see FOOD AND FOOD INDUSTRIES

331.88   FR   ISSN 0039-775X
SYNDICALISME C F T C. 1965. m. 22 F. Confederation Francaise des Travailleurs Chretiens, 13 rue des Ecluses Saint-Martin, 75483 Paris, France. FAX 42-00-44-04. Ed. G. Drilleaud. adv.; bk.rev.; charts; illus.; circ. 160,000.

331.88   FR
SYNDICALISME HEBDO. w. 307 F. (foreign 446 F.)(effective Jan. 1992). Confederation Francaise Democratique du Travail, 4 Blvd. de la Villette, 75955 Paris Cedex 19, France. TEL 42-03-81-40. Ed. Loic Richard. charts; illus.; stat.
  Former titles: Syndicalisme C F D T; Syndicalisme Hebdo (ISSN 0039-7741)

331.8   VN   ISSN 0049-2744
SYNDICATS VIETNAMIENS.* (Editions in English and French) vol.13, 1971. q. Federation des Syndicats du Vietnam, 82 Tran Hung Dao, Hanoi, Socialist Republic of Vietnam. charts; illus.

LABOR UNIONS

331.3 700   HU
SZOVETKEZETI HIRLAP. fortn. National Union of Artisans, Pesti Barnabas u. 6, 1052 Budapest, Hungary. TEL 117-0181. Ed. Maria Dolezsal. circ. 12,000.

331.88   UK
T & G RECORD. 1922. m. free. Transport and General Workers Union, Transport House, Smith Sq., London S.W.1, England. Ed. Chris Kaufman. circ. 350,000. (tabloid format)
   Formerly: T G W U Record.

331.88   GH
T U C NEWS. vol.4, 1970. m. $0.15 per copy. Trades Union Congress of Ghana, Hall of Trade Unions, P.O. Box 701, Accra, Ghana. Ed. C.A. Quansah. adv.; illus.; circ. 10,000 (controlled).
   Former titles: T U C Newsletter; Ghana Workers' Bulletin (ISSN 0016-9617)

331.88 630 634   RU
T U I A F P W INFORMATION. (Text in Arabic, English, French, Russian, Spanish) 1974. bi-m. exchange basis. Trade Union International of Agricultural, Forestry and Plantation Workers, Bol'shaya Serpokhovskaya, 44, 113093 Moscow, Russia. TEL 230-2070. TELEX 411040 UISAG SU. illus.

331.88   US   ISSN 0039-8659
T W U EXPRESS. 1949. m. $2. Transport Workers Union of America, 1980 Broadway, New York, NY 10023. TEL 212-873-6000. Ed. Jim Cannon. bk.rev.; illus.; circ. 124,000. (tabloid format; also avail. in microform from UNW)

331.8   IS   ISSN 0002-4074
TA'AWUN; cooperation, economics and social welfare. (Text in Arabic) 1960. irreg. (2-3/yr.). Histadrut, Arab Workers' Department, P.O. Box 303, Tel Aviv, Israel. TEL 03-431111. TELEX 342-488-HISTD-IL. Ed. Mahmoied Youners.

371.3 331.8   AT
TEACHER. 1918. 8/yr. Aus.$15. Tasmanian Teachers' Federation, 32 Patrick St., Hobart, Australia. TEL 002-349500. FAX 002-343052. Ed. C. Duhig. adv.; bk.rev.; illus.; circ. 5,200.
   Formerly: Tasmanian Teacher (ISSN 0813-6580)

TEACHERS OF THE WORLD; international pedagogical and trade union review. see EDUCATION

TECHNICKY TYDENIK; casopis pro novou techniku a otazky zlepsovatelskeho a vynalezcovskeho hnuti. see TECHNOLOGY: COMPREHENSIVE WORKS

621.38 331.8   NO
TELE TJENESTEN. 10/yr. Norsk Tele Tjeneste Forbund, Moellergt. 10, 0179 Oslo 1, Norway. TEL 02-202-843. Ed. Asbjoern Gardsjord. adv.; circ. 14,000.

331.88 642.5   US   ISSN 0040-6546
THREE HUNDRED THIRTY-EIGHT NEWS; labor monthly of the food service industry. 1940. bi-m. $3. Retail, Wholesale and Department Store Union, 30 E. 29th St., New York, NY 10016. adv.; bk.rev.; rec.rev.; illus.; circ. 12,000. (tabloid format)

331.88   US   ISSN 0041-0497
TRADE UNION COURIER.* 1936. m. $18.50. (New York Teamsters Joint Council, Carpenters District Council) Socio-Economic Publications, Inc., 386 Park Ave. S., Ste. 1108, New York, NY 10016. Ed. Maxwell C. Raddock. adv.; bk.rev.; charts; illus.; stat. (tabloid format)

331.8   US   ISSN 1053-7007
TRADE UNION HANDBOOK. 1950. a. $25 (effective 1992). New York City Central Labor Council, A F L - C I O, 386 Park Ave. S., New York, NY 10016. TEL 212-685-9552. FAX 212-685-9557. Ed. Ted. H. Jacobsen.
   Formerly: New York City Trade Union Handbook (ISSN 0545-6061)
   Description: Contains current information on American labor history, scholarships, publications and services of the AFL-CIO affiliated unions in New York City and State, as well as names and addresses of officers of AFL-CIO unions at city, state, national and international levels.

331.8   SW
TRADE UNION NEWS. (Editions in Arabic, English, Finnish, Greek, Serbo-Croatian, Spanish and Turkish) 1983. 8/yr. SEK 50. Labor Unions, LO - Landsorganisationen i Sverige, Barnhusgatan 18, 105 53 Stockholm, Sweden. FAX 08-200358. TELEX 19145-LO-PRESS. Ed. Pentti Lehto. adv.; bk.rev.; circ. 15,000. (back issues avail.; reprint service avail.)
   Formerly: Sindikalistika Nea (ISSN 0281-0557)

331.88   II   ISSN 0041-0535
TRADE UNION RECORD. (Text in English) 1930. s-m. Rs.20($7) All India Trade Union Congress, Rani Jhansi Rd., New Delhi 55, India. Ed. P. Krishnan. adv.

331.88   UK   ISSN 0144-7106
TRADE UNION STUDIES JOURNAL. 1980. s-a. £5.50. (Trade Union Studies Advisory Committee) Workers' Educational Association, 9 Upper Berkeley St., London W1H 8BY, England. Eds. Mel Doyle, Peter Caldwell. bk.rev.; circ. 1,000.
   —BLDSC shelfmark: 8881.027940.
   Description: Theory and practice for tutors and students involved with union studies and workers' education.

331.88   II   ISSN 0445-6289
TRADE UNIONS IN INDIA. (Text in English) biennial. Rs.34($12.24) Labour Bureau, Simla 171004, India. (Order from: Controller of Publications, Government of India, Civil Lines, Delhi 110054, India)
   Supersedes: Review on the Working of the Trade Unions Act, 1926.

943.9   HU
TRADE UNIONS INTERNATIONAL OF CHEMICAL, OIL AND ALLIED WORKERS. INFORMATION BULLETIN. q. Trade Unions International of Chemical, Oil and Allied Workers, Benczur ut 45, 1415 Budapest VI, Hungary.

331.88   HU   ISSN 0084-1544
TRADE UNIONS INTERNATIONAL OF CHEMICAL, OIL AND ALLIED WORKERS. INTERNATIONAL TRADE CONFERENCE. DOCUMENTS. irreg., 7th, Tarnow, Poland. free. Trade Unions International of Chemical, Oil and Allied Workers, Benczur u. 45, Budapest 6, Hungary.

331.88 380   CS   ISSN 0049-433X
TRADE UNIONS INTERNATIONAL OF WORKERS IN COMMERCE. BULLETIN. (Text in English, French, German, Russian and Spanish) 1959. q. free. Trade Unions International of Workers in Commerce, Opletalova 57, 110 00 Prague 1, Czechoslovakia. TEL 22-05-01. TELEX 121525 WFTU. Ed.Bd.
   Description: Focuses on living and working conditions and new technologies in the field.

331.88 380   CS
TRADE UNIONS INTERNATIONAL OF WORKERS IN COMMERCE. NEWS. (Editions in English, French, German, Russian, Spanish) 1958. m. free. Trade Unions International of Workers in Commerce, Opletalova 57, 110 00 Prague 1, Czechoslovakia. TEL 22-05-01. TELEX 121525 WFTU C. Ed.Bd (processed)
   Description: Covers trade treaties and unions, labor laws and solidarity.

331.88   UK
TRADES UNION CONGRESS. REPORT. Cover title: T U C Report. 1868. a. £30. Trades Union Congress, Congress House, Great Russell St., London WC1B 3LS, England. FAX 071-636-0632. TELEX 268-328-TUC-G. Ed. M.J. Smith. circ. 1,000. (also avail. in microform)

331.88 385   US   ISSN 0041-0837
HD6350.R318
TRAIN DISPATCHER. 1919. 4/yr. $12 to non-members; members $5. American Train Dispatchers Association, 1401 S. Harlem Ave., Berwyn, IL 60402. TEL 708-795-5656. Ed. R.L. Rafferty. adv.; bk.rev.; illus.; circ. 3,550.
   Formerly: Transit.

331.88 380.5   HU
TRANSPORT WORKERS OF THE WORLD. (Editions in English, French, Spanish) 1973. q. $15. Trade Unions International of Transport Workers, Vaci ut 73, H-1139 Budapest, Hungary. TEL 209-601. Ed. K.C. Mathew. charts; illus.; circ. 2,000.

331.8   CM
TRAVAILLEUR/WORKER. (Text in English and French) 1972. m. Organisation des Syndicats des Travailleurs Camerounais, B.P.K 1610, Yaounde, Cameroon. circ. 15,000.

331.8   GV
TRAVAILLEUR DE GUINEE. m. Conakry, Guinea.

331.8   UK   ISSN 0041-2821
TRIBUNE. 1937. w. £0.80 per no. Tribune Publications Ltd., 308 Grays Inn Rd., London WC1X 8DY, England. adv.; bk.rev.; illus.; circ. 40,000. (also avail. in microform)

331.8   XN   ISSN 0041-3437
TRUDBENIK; vesnik na sindikalnite organizacii vo Makedonija. (Text in Macedonian) 1945. w. 50 din. Sojuzot na Sindikatite na Makedonija, 12 Udarne brigade 3 a, Skopje, Macedonia. Ed. Simo Ivanovski.

TYGODNIK SOLIDARNOSC/SOLIDARITY WEEKLY. see BUSINESS AND ECONOMICS — Economic Situation And Conditions

331.88 655   US   ISSN 0041-4832
TYPOGRAPHICAL JOURNAL.* 1889. m. $6 to non-members. International Typographical Union, 316 Wilcox St., Castle Rock, CO 80104-2441. Ed. Thomas W. Kopeck. adv.; bk.rev.; illus.; circ. 75,000.
   Indexed: Graph.Arts Lit.Abstr.
   Incorporating (1912-1979): International Typographical Union. Bulletin.

331.88   US
U A W AMMO. 1960. m. $1.50. United Automobile, Aerospace, and Agricultural Implement Workers of America, 8000 E. Jefferson Ave., Detroit, MI 48214. TEL 313-926-5291. Ed. Frank Joyce. circ. 180,000.
   Formerly: U A W Ammunition (ISSN 0502-9392)

331.88   US   ISSN 0041-4980
U A W WASHINGTON REPORT. vol.9, 1969. w. free. United Automobile, Aerospace, and Agricultural Implement Workers of America (Washington), 1757 N St., N.W., Washington, DC 20036. Ed. Frank Wallick. bk.rev.; charts; illus.; index; circ. 60,000.

331.88   US   ISSN 0041-5065
U E NEWS. 1937. every 3 weeks. $5 to individuals; institutions $10. United Electrical, Radio & Machine Workers of America, 2400 Oliver Bldg., 535 Smithfield St., Pittsburgh, PA 15222-2304. TEL 412-471-8919. Ed. Peter Gilmore. bk.rev.; charts; illus. (also avail. in microfilm)

331.88   CN
U E NEWS MAGAZINE. vol.33, 1970. bi-m. free. United Electrical Radio and Machine Workers of Canada, 10 Codeco Court, Don Mills, Ont. M3A 1A2, Canada. TEL 416-447-5196. FAX 416-447-5709. Ed. Elias Stavrides. adv.; bk.rev.; charts; illus.; circ. 10,000. (also avail. in microform)
   Former titles (until 1990): U E News (ISSN 0041-5049); U E Canadian News.

331.8   US   ISSN 0195-0363
HD6350.F7
U F C W ACTION. 1979. bi-m. United Food and Commercial Workers International Union, 1175 K St., N.W., Washington, DC 20006-1598. Ed. William H. Wynn.

331.88 690   FI
U I T B B BULLETIN. (Text in English) 1955. q. Trade Unions International of Workers of the Building, Wood and Building Materials Industries, P.O. Box 281, 00101 Helsinki 10, Finland. charts; illus.
   Formerly: U I T B B Information (ISSN 0356-8105)

U L L I C O BULLETIN. (Union Labor Life Insurance Co.) see INSURANCE

331.88 350   US   ISSN 0041-5464
U S A RECORD. vol.10, 1973. m. membership. Uniformed Sanitationmen's Association, 23-25 Cliff St., New York, NY 10038. TEL 212-964-8900. Ed. Edward T. Ostrowski. charts; illus.

331.88 UK
U S D A W TODAY. 1973. m. £15. Union of Shop Distributive and Allied Workers, Oakley, 188 Wilmslow Rd. Fallowfield, Manchester, England. FAX 061-257-2566. Ed. P.H. Jones. adv.; bk.rev.; charts; illus.; stat.; index; circ. 100,000.
  Formerly: Dawn; Supersedes: New Dawn (ISSN 0028-4521)

331.88 UA
AL-UMMAL. w. Egyptian Trade Union Federation, 90 Sharia Galal, Cairo, Egypt. TEL 02-740362. TELEX 93255. Ed. Ahmed Hara.

UNIFICACION. see TRANSPORTATION — Railroads

331.1 US
UNION DEMOCRACY REVIEW. 1972. bi-m. $10 to individuals; institutions $15. Association for Union Democracy, Inc., 500 State St., Brooklyn, NY 11217. TEL 718-855-6650. Ed. Herman Benson. bk.rev.; circ. 3,000.
  Supersedes: Union Democracy in Action (ISSN 0041-6835)
  Description: Reports movements for reform and development in law affecting union democracy and movements against corruption in labor unions.

331.88 630 MY ISSN 0049-528X
HD6820.6.Z6
UNION HERALD. (Text in English) vol.65, 1985. m. M.$0.50 per no. National Union of Plantation Workers, Plantation House, P.O. Box 73, 46000 Petaling Jaya, Selangor, Malaysia. TEL 7927861. Ed.Bd. bk.rev.; abstr.; stat.; circ. 1,000. (processed)
  Description: News about workers and agriculture in Southeast Asia.

331.8 US
UNION LABOR JOURNAL. 1903. q. $3. Kern-Inyo-Mono County Central Labor Council, 200 W. Jeffrey, Bakersfield, CA 93305. TEL 805-324-6451. circ. 6,300.

331.88 US ISSN 0041-6924
UNION LABOR NEWS. 1937. m. $6. Union Labor News Publishers, Ltd., 1602 S. Park, Rm. 228, Madison, WI 53715. TEL 608-256-5111. Ed. James A. Cavanaugh. adv.; bk.rev.; illus.; circ. 17,000. (tabloid format; also avail. in microform)

UNION LABOR REPORT. see BUSINESS AND ECONOMICS — Labor And Industrial Relations

UNION LABOR REPORT WEEKLY NEWSLETTER. see BUSINESS AND ECONOMICS — Labor And Industrial Relations

UNION LABOR REPORT'S - ON THE LINE; a guide for union stewards. see BUSINESS AND ECONOMICS — Labor And Industrial Relations

331.88 CN
UNION MATTERS. 1927. 6/yr. free. Saskatchewan Government Employees' Union, 1440 Broadway Ave., Regina, Sask. S4P 1E2, Canada. TEL 306-522-8571. FAX 306-352-1969. Ed. Beth Smillie. charts; illus.; stat.; circ. 17,500 (controlled).
  Former titles: Common Ground; (until 1986): Dome (ISSN 0319-8588)

331.8 SZ ISSN 0503-2334
UNION MONDIALE DES ORGANISATIONS SYNDICALES SUR BASES ECONOMIQUE ET SOCIALE LIBERALES. CONFERENCES: RAPPORT. 1960. a. World Union of Liberal Trade Union Organisations, 41 Badenerstr., CH-8004 Zurich, Switzerland.

331.8 IT
L'UNIONE DEI SEGRETARI. 1952; N.S. 1987. bi-m. L.68000. (Unione dei Segretari) Maggioli Editore, Via Crimea, 1, Casella Postale 290, 47037 Rimini, Italy. TEL 0541-626777. FAX 0541-622020. Ed. Antonino Saija.

331.88 360 US ISSN 0041-7092
UNIONIST. 1965. m. membership. Social Service Employees Union, Local 371, District Council 37, A F S C M E, A F L - C I O, 817 Broadway, New York, NY 10003. TEL 212-677-3900. Ed. Martin Fishgold. bk.rev.; illus.; circ. 17,000.
  Formerly: S S E U News.

331.88 696.1 US ISSN 0041-7181
UNITED ASSOCIATION JOURNAL. 1889. m. free. United Association of Journeymen and Apprentices of the Plumbing and Pipe Fitting Industry of the United States and Canada, 901 Massachusetts Ave., N.W., Washington, DC 20001. TEL 202-628-5823. Ed. Charles J. Habig. charts; illus.; circ. 250,000.

331.88 622 US ISSN 0041-7327
HD6350.M6
UNITED MINE WORKERS JOURNAL. 1891. m. $10 to individuals; institutions $25; corporations $100. United Mine Workers, 900 Fifteenth St., N.W., Washington, DC 20005. TEL 202-842-7200. Ed. Greg Hawthorne. bk.rev.; film rev.; circ. 200,000. (also avail. in microform; back issues avail.)

331.88 678 US ISSN 0162-3869
HD6350.R9
UNITED RUBBER WORKER. 1935. bi-m. $10 for 12 nos. to non-members. United Rubber, Cork, Linoleum, & Plastic Workers of America, AFL-CIO, CLC, Public Relations Office, 87 S. High St., Akron, OH 44308. TEL 216-376-6181. FAX 216-434-5230. Ed. Curt Brown. bk.rev.; circ. 160,000.

331.88 669.142 CN ISSN 0566-0963
UNITED STEELWORKERS OF AMERICA. INFORMATION. (Text in English and French) bi-m. United Steelworkers of America, 92 Frood Rd., Sudbury, Ont., Canada. TEL 705-675-1383. illus.

331.88 312 UK
UNITY. 1968. q. membership. Society of Registration Officers, Register Office, St. Peter's Square, Wolverhampton WV1 1RU, England. Ed. Philp Yeardley. adv.; circ. 1,000. (processed)

UNIVERSITETSLAERAREN. see EDUCATION

331.8 SZ
V O REALITES. (Text in French) 1944. w. 100 Fr. Parti Suisse du Travail, 4-6, rue du Pre-Jerome, 1205 Geneva, Switzerland. TEL 022-206335.
  Formerly (until 1986): Voix Ouvriere.

331.88 621.3 FI ISSN 0049-5883
VASAMA. 1957. s-m. Fmk.105. Suomen Sahkoalantyontekijain Liitto - Finnish Electric Workers' Union, P.O. Box 747, 33101 Tampere, Finland. FAX 931-520210. Ed. Seppo Salisma. adv.; charts; illus. (tabloid format)

VIE DE LA RECHERCHE SCIENTIFIQUE. see SCIENCES: COMPREHENSIVE WORKS

331.8 FR ISSN 0399-1164
VIE OUVRIERE. 1909. w. 500 F. (Confederation Generale du Travail) Vie Ouvriere, 33 rue Bouret, 75940 Paris Cedex 19, France. TEL 40-40-36-51. FAX 42-09-99-65. Ed. Roger Guilbert. adv.; bk.rev.; circ. 264,555. Indexed: RADAR.

331.8 IT ISSN 0042-7357
VITA SINDACALE BERGAMASCA. 1960. fortn. Unione Sindacale Provinciale, G. Paglia 16, 24100 Bergamo, Italy. Ed. Dir. Dino T. Donadoni. illus. (tabloid format)

331.8 IT
LA VOCE DELLA U I L. 1961. m. free. Unione Italiana del Lavoro, Piazzetta Padenna, 26, 48100 Ravenna, Italy. TEL 0544-36059. FAX 0544-36899. stat.; tr.lit.; index.
  Formerly: Nessuno.
  Description: Covers various topics on the Italian labor union.

331.8 GH
VOICE OF AFRICAN WORKERS. (Text in English, French) 1977. q. Organization of African Trade Union Unity - Organisation de l'Unite Syndical Africaine, Box M 386, Accra, Ghana. TELEX 2673 OATUU GH. circ. 4,000.

331.88 JO
VOICE OF JORDANIAN LABOURERS/SAWT UMMAL AL-URDON.* (Text in Arabic) 1973. m. General Federation of Jordania Trade Unions, Wadi as-Sir Rd., P.O. Box 1065, Amman, Jordan. Ed. Salim Jedoun.

331.8 US
VOICE OF LOCAL 399. 1976. m. membership. Hospital & Service Employees Union, Local 399, 1247 W. Seventh St., Los Angeles, CA 90017. TEL 213-680-9567. Ed. Tom Ramsay. bk.rev.; circ. 22,000. (tabloid format; back issues avail.)

VOICE OF THE UNIONS. see BUSINESS AND ECONOMICS — Labor And Industrial Relations

VOICES; the magazine of Ontario public sector workers. see BUSINESS AND ECONOMICS — Labor And Industrial Relations

331.8 BE
VOIX DE L'UNION. (Text in French) 1948. w. 2400 Fr. Ediclam, 32 av. des Gaulois, B-1040 Brussels, Belgium. TEL 02-736-1198. FAX 02-736-2555. Ed. Vincent Gernay. adv.; circ. 25,000.

331.8 CF
VOIX DE LA CLASSE OUVRIERE. Short title: Voco. 6/yr. B.P. 2311, Brazzaville, Congo. TEL 83-36-66. Ed. Marie-Joseph Tsengou. circ. 4,500.

331.8 BE ISSN 0042-854X
VOLKSMACHT; weekblad van de christelijke arbeidersbeweging. 1945. w. 950 Fr. (foreign 1000 Fr.)(effective 1992). Algemeen Christelijk Werknemersverbond - Catholic Workers Movement, Wetstraat 121, B-1040 Brussels, Belgium. FAX 02-2373300. TELEX 61770 CSCACV. Ed. Leo Pauwels. bk.rev.; circ. 1,118,800.

331.88 655.55 AU ISSN 0042-8930
VORWAERTS. 1867. m. membership. Gewerkschaft Druck und Papier, Seidengasse 15, A-1070 Vienna, Austria. Ed. Josef Keller. bk.rev.; illus.; circ. 26,000.

331.8 RU
▼**VREMYA**. 1990. w. 10.44 Rub. Nezavisimye Profsoyuzy Kuzbassa, Pr. Sovetskii 56, Kemerovo, Russia. circ. 24,799. (newspaper)
  Formerly (until Oct. 1990): Profsoyuzy i Vremya.

331.8 RU ISSN 0042-9236
VSEMIRNOE PROFSOYUZNOE DVIZHENIE. (Editions in several languages) 1949. m. 7.20 Rub. (World Federation of Trade Unions) Profizdat, Ul. Kirova 13, Moscow, Russia. (Dist. by: Mezhdunarodnaya Kniga, Moscow, G-200, Russia) Ed. A.V. Byhovskii. illus.; stat.

331.116 664.9 AT
W.A. MEAT WORKER. s-a. free. Australasian Meat Industry Employees' Union, W.A. Branch, 1 St. Floor, 102 Beaufort St., Perth, W.A. 6000, Australia. Ed. D.J. Beaton.

W S I MITTEILUNGEN. (Wirtschafts- und Sozialwissenschaftliches Institut) see SOCIAL SCIENCES: COMPREHENSIVE WORKS

331.8 674 CN ISSN 0049-7371
WESTERN CANADIAN LUMBER WORKER. 1939. m. Can.$2. International Woodworkers of America, Regional Council No. 1, 1285 W. Pender St., 500, Vancouver, B.C. V6E 4B2, Canada. TEL 604-683-1117. Ed. Clay Perry. adv.; bk.rev.; circ. 34,000. (tabloid format; also avail. in microfilm)

WESTERN TEACHER. see EDUCATION

331.88 US ISSN 0043-4876
WHITE COLLAR. no.322, May 1973. q. $1 per no. Office and Professional Employees International Union, AFL-CIO, CLC, Rm. 610, 265 W. 14th St., New York, NY 10011. Ed. John Kelly. charts; illus.; stat.; circ. 120,000.

331.88 694 US
WOODWORKER. 1987. m. $5. International Woodworkers of America, U.S. - A F L - C I O, 25 Cornell Ave., Gladstone, OR 97027-2547. Ed. Glenn Blaylock. bk.rev.; illus.; circ. 26,000. (tabloid format)
  Formerly: International Woodworker (ISSN 0020-9139)

WORK IN PROGRESS. see POLITICAL SCIENCE — Civil Rights

WORKER'S DEMOCRACY. see POLITICAL SCIENCE

LABOR UNIONS — ABSTRACTING, BIBLIOGRAPHIES, STATISTICS

331.88 ZA
WORKERS VOICE. 1972. fortn. 2000 n. per no. Zambia Congress of Trade Unions, P.O. Box 20652, Kitwe, Zambia. TEL 211446. Ed. Reuben S. Muchimba. adv.; bk.rev.; illus.; circ. 15,000.

331.88 II ISSN 0377-6611
WORKING CLASS. 1971. m. Rs.20. Centre of Indian Trade Unions, 6 Talkatora Rd., New Delhi 110001, India. TEL 384071. Ed. P.K. Ganguly. adv.; bk.rev.; charts; illus.; index; circ. 5,000.

331.8 AT ISSN 1036-5117
WORKPLACE. q. Aus.$4.50. Australian Council of Trade Unions, 393-397 Swanston St., Melbourne, Vic. 300, Australia. TEL 03-663-5266. Ed. Andrew Casey.
  Description: Presents union movement perspectives on industrial, economic, social and other issues.

WORLD FEDERATION OF TEACHERS' UNIONS. INFORMATION LETTER. see *EDUCATION*

YA'AD. see *POLITICAL SCIENCE*

YORKSHIRE MINER. see *MINES AND MINING INDUSTRY*

331.8 CN
YOUR UNION LOCAL 480 U S W A. 1974. m. Local 480 U S W A, 910 Portland St., Trail, B.C. V1R 3X7, Canada. TEL 604-368-9131. FAX 604-368-5568. Ed. Jim Hill. adv.; circ. 2,000. (back issues avail.)
  Description: Discusses membership information, safety, health and grievance issues and affairs of provincial and national interest.

331.88 YU ISSN 0044-135X
YUGOSLAV TRADE UNIONS. (Editions in English, French, Russian, Spanish) 1960. bi-m. Savez Sindikata Jugoslavije, Trg Marksa i Engelsa 5, 11000 Belgrade, Yugoslavia. Ed. Milos Marinovic. illus.; circ. 10,000. Indexed: P.A.I.S.

331.88 YU ISSN 0022-6041
YUGOSLAVSKIE PROFSOYUZY; gazeta Soyuza profsoyuzov Yugoslavii. (Text in Russian) 1960. bi-m. 9 Kop.per no. Savez Sindikata Jugoslavije, Trg Marksa i Engelsa 5, 11000 Belgrade, Yugoslavia. Ed. Milos Marinovic.

331.8 664 BU
ZEMIA. d. 11 Avgust St., 1000 Sofia, Bulgaria. TEL 835033.
  Formerly (until 1990): Cooperative Village.

331.3 CC
ZHONGGUO GONGYUN XUEYUAN XUEBAO/CHINESE INSTITUTE OF LABOR MOVEMENT. JOURNAL. (Text in Chinese) bi-m. Zhongguo Gongyun Xueyuan, 2, Huayuancun, Fucheng Lu, Beijing 100037, People's Republic of China. TEL 8314477. Ed. Yu Shixiong.

331.3 US
32E EVENTS. q. membership. Service Employees International Union, Local 32E, 4234 Bronx Blvd., Bronx, NY 10466-2611. TEL 212-324-6556. FAX 212-994-4910. Ed. Diana D. Degroat. circ. 10,000.
  Description: Information for members; covers benefits, union events; and lists contacts.

331.88 US
1814 UNION NEWS. 1960. q. free. International Longshoremen's Association, A F L - C I O, Local 1814, 343 Court St., Brooklyn, NY 11231. TEL 718-834-7800. Ed. Jon Visel. bk.rev.; illus.; circ. 15,750.
  Formerly (until 1978): Brooklyn Longshoreman (ISSN 0007-2370)

LABOR UNIONS — Abstracting, Bibliographies, Statistics

331.8 011 US ISSN 0001-1150
A F L - C I O LIBRARY ACQUISITION LIST. 1967. bi-m. free. A F L - C I O, Library, 815 16th St., N.W., Washington, DC 20006. TEL 202-637-5000. bibl. (processed)

331.8 AT ISSN 0312-1437
AUSTRALIA. BUREAU OF STATISTICS. TRADE UNION STATISTICS, AUSTRALIA. 1969. a. Aus.$10 (foreign Aus.$11.30)(effective 1991). Australian Bureau of Statistics, P.O. Box 10, Belconnen, A.C.T. 2616, Australia. TEL 062-527911. FAX 062-516009. illus.; circ. 413.
  Description: Number of separate trade unions; financial and total members classified by state, territory and sex; proportion of employed wage and salary earners who were members of unions.

331.8 011 US
CRITIQUE OF TRADE UNION RIGHTS IN COUNTRIES AFFILIATED WITH THE LEAGUE OF ARAB STATES. DOCUMENTATION SUPPLEMENT. 1989. a. free. Jewish Labor Committee, 25 E. 21st St., New York, NY 10010. TEL 212-477-0707. FAX 212-477-1918. Ed. Michael S. Perry. circ. 5,000. (back issues avail.)
  Description: Bibliography of sources for the review of labor policies in the Middle East and North Africa.

FUNDHEFT FUER ARBEITS- UND SOZIALRECHT; systematischer Nachweis der deutschen Rechtsprechung, Zeitschriftenaufsaetze und selbstaendigen Schriften. see *LAW — Abstracting, Bibliographies, Statistics*

NATIONAL TRADE AND PROFESSIONAL ASSOCIATIONS OF THE UNITED STATES AND LABOR UNIONS. see *BUSINESS AND ECONOMICS — Trade And Industrial Directories*

331.881 314 NE ISSN 0168-4035
STATISTIEK DER VAKBEWEGING IN NEDERLAND/STATISTICS OF THE TRADE UNIONS IN THE NETHERLANDS. (Text in Dutch and English) 1946. a. Centraal Bureau voor de Statistiek, Prinses Beatrixlaan 428, Voorburg, Netherlands. (Orders to: SDU - Publishers, Christoffel Plantijnstraat, The Hague)
  Formerly: Omvang der Vakbeweging in Nederland (ISSN 0077-6904)

331.11 US
UNION LABOR IN CALIFORNIA. 1939. biennial. free. Department of Industrial Relations, Division of Labor Statistics and Research, Box 420603, San Francisco, CA 94142-0603. TEL 415-703-3451.

LABORATORY TECHNIQUE

see *Medical Sciences–Experimental Medicine, Laboratory Technique*

LAW

see also Law–Civil Law; Law–Computer Applications; Law–Constitutional Law; Law–Corporate Law; Law–Criminal Law; Law–Estate Planning; Law–Family and Matrimonial Law; Law–International Law; Law–Judicial Systems; Law–Legal Aid; Law–Maritime Law; Law–Military Law; Criminology and Law Enforcement; Patents, Trademarks and Copyrights

345.01 US
A A A ANNUAL REPORT. a. American Arbitration Association, 140 W. 51st St., New York, NY 10020-1203. TEL 212-484-4011. FAX 212-765-4874.

020 US ISSN 0065-7255
A A L L PUBLICATIONS SERIES. 1960. irreg., no.39, 1990. price varies. (American Association of Law Libraries) Fred B. Rothman & Co., 10368 W. Centennial Rd., Littleton, CO 80127. TEL 303-979-5657. FAX 303-978-1457. (back issues avail.)

A A M P LIFIER. (American Association of Meat Processors) see *AGRICULTURE — Poultry And Livestock*

340 US ISSN 0740-4050
A B A - B N A LAWYERS' MANUAL ON PROFESSIONAL CONDUCT. (Subseries of: Trial Practice Series) 1984. bi-w. $570. (American Bar Association) The Bureau of National Affairs, Inc., 1231 25th St., N.W., Washington, DC 20037. TEL 202-452-4200. FAX 202-822-8092. TELEX 285656 BNAI WSH. (Subscr. to: 9435 Key West Ave., Rockville, MD 20850. TEL 800-372-1033) Ed. Robert A. Robbins. bk.rev.; index, cum.index. (looseleaf format; back issues avail.)
  Description: Notification and reference service covering a broad range of issues dealing with ethics and professional responsibiliity.

A B A BANK COMPLIANCE. (American Bankers Association) see *BUSINESS AND ECONOMICS — Banking And Finance*

340 US ISSN 0747-0088
K1
A B A JOURNAL; the lawyer's magazine. 1915. 12/yr. $66 to non-members (effective June 1991). American Bar Association, 750 N. Lake Shore Dr., Chicago, IL 60611. TEL 312-988-5000. FAX 312-988-6014. Ed. Gary A. Hengstler. adv.; bk.rev.; illus.; index; 50 yr. cum.index; circ. 431,000. (also avail. in microfilm from UMI; microfiche from UMI) Indexed: Amer.Bibl.Slavic & E.Eur.Stud., Amer.Hist.& Life, Bk.Rev.Ind. (1990-), C.L.I., Child.Bk.Rev.Ind. (1990-), CJPI, Crim.Just.Abstr., Curr.Cont., Hist.Abstr., Hlth.Ind., L.R.I., Law Ofc.Info.Svc., Leg.Cont., Leg.Per., P.A.I.S., Pers.Lit., Risk Abstr., SSCI.
  ●Also available online. Vendor(s): Mead Data Central, WESTLAW.
  —BLDSC shelfmark: 0537.721400.
  Formerly (until 1983): American Bar Association Journal (ISSN 0002-7596)
  Description: Trade journal of the ABA.

A B A JUVENILE AND CHILD WELFARE LAW REPORTER. (American Bar Association) see *CHILDREN AND YOUTH — Law*

340 US ISSN 0516-9968
KF200
A B A WASHINGTON LETTER. m. $25 to non-members; members $20. American Bar Association, Governmental Affairs Office, 1800 M St., N.W., Washington, DC 20036. TEL 202-331-2609. Ed. Rhonda J. McMillion.
  ●Also available online.
  Description: Reports congressional actions on legislative issues of interest to the legal profession.

A C A UPDATE; news for arts leaders. (American Council for the Arts) see *ART*

A C C A DOCKET. (American Corporate Counsel Association) see *BUSINESS AND ECONOMICS*

A C C N BULLETIN. (Associated Court and Commercial Newspapers) see *JOURNALISM*

340 GW
A D A C HANDBUCH: REISERECHT ENTSCHEIDUNGEN. irreg. DM.48. (Allgemeiner Deutscher Automobil-Club e.V.) A D A C GmbH, Am Westpark 8, Postfach 70 01 26, D-8000 Munich, Germany. TEL 089-7676-0.

340 GW
A D A C HANDBUCH: SCHADENERSATZ BEI VERLETZUNG. irreg. DM.48. (Allgemeiner Deutscher Automobil-Club e.V.) A D A C GmbH, Am Westpark 8, Postfach 70 01 26, D-8000 Munich, Germany. TEL 089-7676-0.

340 GW
A D A C HANDBUCH: UNFALL IM AUSLAND - SCHADENSREGULIERUNG. irreg. DM.38. (Allgemeiner Deutscher Automobil-Club e.V.) A D A C GmbH, Am Westpark 8, Postfach 70 01 26, D-8000 Munich, Germany. TEL 089-7676-0.

340 GW
A D A C HANDBUCH: UNFALL RATGEBER. irreg. DM.34. (Allgemeiner Deutscher Automobil-Club e.V.) A D A C GmbH, Am Westpark 8, Postfach 70 01 26, D-8000 Munich, Germany. TEL 089-7676-0.

LAW

340 296 US
A D L LAW REPORT. 1965. irreg. (1-2/yr.). Anti-Defamation League of B'nai B'rith, 823 United Nations Plaza, New York, NY 10017. TEL 212-490-2525. Ed.Bd. circ. 5,000 (controlled). (reprint service avail. from UMI)
Formerly: Law (ISSN 0023-916X)

346 US ISSN 0090-2411
K1
A E LEGAL NEWSLETTER. (Architects and Engineers) 1973. m. $200. Victor O. Schinnerer & Co., Two Wisconsin Circle, Chevy Chase, MD 20815. TEL 301-961-9800. Ed. Milton F. Lunch. bk.rev.; circ. 500. (looseleaf format)

340 US
A F I REPORT.* 1957. m. Association of Federal Investigators, 3299 K St., N.W., Ste. 7, Washington, DC 20007-4415. TEL 202-466-7288. Ed. Clark Blight. circ. 2,000.
Description: Law enforcement initiatives and techniques.

A F R A ADVICE SHEET. (Association for Rural Advancement) see POLITICAL SCIENCE — Civil Rights

340 US
A G REPORT. 10/yr. $55. National Association of Attorneys General, 444 N. Capitol St., N.W., Ste. 403, Washington, DC 20001. TEL 202-628-0435. circ. 200.

340 616.9 US
A I D S & FLORIDA LAW. 1989. 2 base vols. (plus suppl.). $120. Butterworth Legal Publishers (Salem) (Subsidiary of Reed International PLC), 90 Stiles Rd., Salem, NH 03079. TEL 800-548-4001. FAX 603-898-9858. (looseleaf format)

A I D S & PUBLIC POLICY JOURNAL. see MEDICAL SCIENCES — Communicable Diseases

A I D S LAW & LITIGATION REPORTER. see MEDICAL SCIENCES — Communicable Diseases

340 610 US ISSN 0899-1464
KF3803.A54
A I D S LITIGATION REPORTER. (Acquired Immune Deficiency Syndrome); the national journal of record of AIDS-related litigation. 1987. s-m. $700. Andrews Publications, 1646 West Chester Pike, Box 1000, Westtown, PA 19395. TEL 215-399-6600. FAX 215-399-6610. Ed. Ronald V. Baker. s-a. index. (looseleaf format; back issues avail.)

A I D S POLICY AND LAW; the bi-weekly newsletter on legislation, regulation, and litigation concerning AIDS. see MEDICAL SCIENCES — Communicable Diseases

A I D S UPDATE (NEW YORK). see MEDICAL SCIENCES — Communicable Diseases

340 US ISSN 0898-1663
KF4802
A I L A MONTHLY MAILING. 1982. m. $295. American Immigration Lawyers Association, 1400 I St., N.W., Ste. 1200, Washington, DC 20005-2208. TEL 202-371-9377. circ. 3,000. (back issues avail.)
Description: Covers recent developments in immigration law.

340 608.7 US
A I P L A BULLETIN. 5/yr. $40 to non-members. American Intellectual Property Law Association, 2001 Jefferson Davis Hwy., Ste. 203, Arlington, VA 22202. FAX 703-415-0786.

346 US ISSN 0883-6078
K1
A I P L A QUARTERLY JOURNAL. 1972. q. $45. American Intellectual Property Law Association, 2001 Jefferson Hwy., Ste. 203, Arlington, VA 22202. FAX 703-415-0786. Ed. Donald Chisum. illus.; circ. 4,700. (also avail. in microform from WSH; reprint service avail. from WSH) Indexed: C.L.I., L.R.I., Leg.Per.
Formerly: A P L A Quarterly Journal (American Patent Law Association) (ISSN 0091-0538)

347 US
A J A BENCHMARK. q. $25 (includes subscr. to: Court Review). (American Judges Association) National Center for State Courts, 300 Newport Ave., Williamsburg, VA 23187-8798. TEL 804-253-2000. FAX 804-220-0449. Ed. Joseph Burtell. circ. 2,000.
Description: Notifies members of the association's activities.

375 340 US
A L A NEWS. 1960. 4/yr. membership. American Lawyers Auxiliary, 750 N. Lake Shore Dr., Chicago, IL 60611. TEL 312-988-6387. Ed. Susan Hendricks. circ. 2,000.

340 US ISSN 0044-7560
A L I - A B A - C L E REVIEW. 1970. fortn. (except June). free. American Law Institute, Committee on Continuing Professional Education, 4025 Chestnut St., Philadelphia, PA 19104. TEL 215-243-1604. FAX 215-243-1664. (Co-sponsor: American Bar Association) Ed. Mark T. Carroll. adv.; bk.rev.; circ. 60,000. (also avail. in microform from UMI)
Description: Looks at courses, books, humor, reviews, lawyer news and other educational materials for lawyers.

340 US ISSN 0145-6342
K1
A L I - A B A COURSE MATERIALS JOURNAL. 1976. bi-m. $40. American Law Institute, Committee on Continuing Professional Education, 4025 Chestnut St., Philadelphia, PA 19104. TEL 215-243-1604. FAX 215-243-1664. (Co-sponsor: American Bar Association) Ed. Mark T. Carroll. adv.; bibl.; cum.index; circ. 4,500. (back issues avail.; reprint service avail. from UMI) Indexed: C.L.I., L.R.I., Law Ofc.Info.Svc., Leg.Per.
Description: Collections of outlines presented at various ALI-ABA courses.

340 US ISSN 0164-5757
KF200
A L I REPORTER. 1978. q. free to qualified personnel. American Law Institute, 4025 Chestnut St., Philadelphia, PA 19104. TEL 215-243-1600. FAX 215-243-1664. (Co-sponsor: American Bar Association) Ed. Michael Greenwald. circ. 3,300.
Description: Information on the institute, its projects and members.

340 AT
A L R C REPORT SERIES. (Australia Law Reform Commission) 1975. irreg. price varies. Australian Government Publishing Service, G.P.O. Box 84, Canberra, A.C.T. 2601, Australia. Indexed: Aus.Leg.Mon.Dig.

A M P L A BULLETIN. (Australian Mining and Petroleum Law Association Ltd.) see MINES AND MINING INDUSTRY

A M P L A YEARBOOK. (Australian Mining and Petroleum Law Association Ltd.) see MINES AND MINING INDUSTRY

A M S STUDIES IN CRIMINAL JUSTICE. see CRIMINOLOGY AND LAW ENFORCEMENT

340 IT
▼**A N D I G.** 1990. irreg., no.3, 1991. price varies. (Associazione Nazionale Docenti Informatica Giuridica) Ligouri Editrice s.r.l., Via Mezzocannone 19, 80134 Naples, Italy. TEL 081-5527139. Ed. Vittorio Frosini.

340 UK
A P A S NEWS. 1924. 4/yr. free. Association of Personal Assistants and Secretaries Ltd., 14 Victoria Terrace, Leamington Spa, Warwickshire, England. FAX 0926-451988. Ed. Jacqueline Cameron. bk.rev.; circ. 1,000.

A S A E ASSOCIATION LAW AND POLICY. (American Society of Association Executives) see BUSINESS AND ECONOMICS — Management

A S C P WASHINGTON REPORT ON NATIONAL AND STATE ISSUES. (American Society of Clinical Pathologists) see MEDICAL SCIENCES

340 613 US ISSN 1048-907X
A S H SMOKING AND HEALTH REVIEW. vol.8, 1968. 6/yr. $15 (foreign $25). Action on Smoking & Health, 2013 H St., N.W., Washington, DC 20006. TEL 202-659-4310. FAX 202-659-4322. Ed. John F. Banzhaf, III. illus.; circ. 32,000.
Formerly: A S H Newsletter.

976 340 US
A S L H NEWSLETTER. 1970. s-a. $35 to individuals (foreign $38); institutions $50 (foreign $53). American Society for Legal History, Department of History, University of Mississippi, University, MS 38677. TEL 601-232-7148. FAX 601-232-5918. Ed. Robert J. Haws. circ. 1,500.
Description: Provides members with news about the society and other items of interest to legal historians.

340 US ISSN 0746-4177
A T L A ADVOCATE. 11/yr. membership. Association of Trial Lawyers of America, 1050 31st St., N.W., Washington, DC 20007. TEL 202-965-3500. Ed. Donald C. Dilworth.

347.91 US ISSN 0364-8125
KF294.A8
A T L A LAW REPORTER. 1957. 10/yr. $135. Association of Trial Lawyers of America, 1050 31st St., N.W., Washington, DC 20007. TEL 202-965-3500. Ed. Jean Hellwege. abstr.; index; circ. 75,000. (also avail. in microfilm from UMI) Indexed: C.L.I.
Former titles (until vol.19, no.10, 1976): Association of Trial Lawyers of America. Newsletter (ISSN 0093-1160); American Trial Lawyers Association Newsletter (ISSN 0003-1437)

340 US
A U L INSIGHTS. 4/yr. price varies. Americans United for Life, 343 S. Dearborn St., Ste. 1804, Chicago, IL 60604. TEL 312-786-9494. Ed. Melodie Schlenker Gage. (back issues avail.)
Description: Factual review of pro-life topics.

340 US
A U L STUDIES IN LAW, MEDICINE & SOCIETY. irreg. $3. Americans United for Life, 343 S. Dearborn St., Ste. 1804, Chicago, IL 60604. TEL 312-786-9494. Ed. Melodie Schlenker Gage. (back issues avail.)
Description: Monograph series on issues involving the human right to life.

A V A ADVISOR. (Asbestos Victims of America) see MEDICAL SCIENCES — Cancer

349 HU ISSN 0001-592X
ACADEMIA SCIENTIARUM HUNGARICA. ACTA JURIDICA. (Text in English, French, German, Russian) 1959. q. $62. (Magyar Tudomanyos Akademia) Akademiai Kiado, Publishing House of the Hungarian Academy of Sciences, Alkotmany u. 21, 0154 Budapest, Hungary. TEL 111-010. Ed. Gy. Eorsi. adv.; bk.rev.; index. Indexed: Abstr.Crim.& Pen., P.A.I.S.For.Lang.Ind. Key Title: Acta Juridica.

ACADEMIE DE STIINTE A R.S.S. MOLDOVA. FILOSOFIE SI DREPT/AKADEMIYA NAUK S.S.R. MOLDOVA. FILOSOFIYA I PRAVO. see PHILOSOPHY

347 II
ACADEMY LAW REVIEW. (Text in English) 1977. s-a. Rs.50($10) Kerala Law Academy, Punnen Rd, Trivandrum 695 039, India. Ed. K. Parameswaran. bk.rev.; circ. 5,000.

340 AT
ACCIDENT COMPENSATION VICTORIA. 6/yr. $445. Butterworths Pty Ltd., 271-273 Lane Cove Rd., P.O. Box 345, North Ryde, N.S.W. 2113, Australia. TEL 02-335-4444. FAX 02-335-4655. (looseleaf format)

340 614.19 US ISSN 1057-8153
ACCIDENT RECONSTRUCTION JOURNAL. 1989. bi-m. $39. 3004 Charleton Ct., Waldorf, MD 20602-2527. TEL 201-843-1371. (Subscr. to: Box 234, Waldorf, MD 20604-0234) Ed. Victor T. Craig. adv.; index; circ. 2,100. (back issues avail.)
Description: Covers traffic accident investigation and reconstruction, traffic safety news, and related legal developments.

340 368 — II — ISSN 0001-4583
ACCIDENTS CLAIMS JOURNAL. (Text in English) 1966. m. Rs.330 (typically set in Jan.). 12 Malka Ganj, Delhi 110007, India. TEL 2917483. Ed. R.L. Kumar. adv.; circ. 6,000.

340 — CK
ACCION Y CRITICA. 1975. fortn. Apdo. Aereo 52150, Bogota, Colombia. Ed. Juan F. Londono.

ACCOUNTANCY LAW REPORTS. see *BUSINESS AND ECONOMICS — Accounting*

ACCOUNTING FOR BANKS. see *BUSINESS AND ECONOMICS — Accounting*

ACCOUNTING FOR LAW FIRMS. see *BUSINESS AND ECONOMICS — Accounting*

ACCOUNTING SYSTEMS FOR LAW OFFICES. see *BUSINESS AND ECONOMICS — Accounting*

ACID RAIN UPDATE. see *ENVIRONMENTAL STUDIES*

340 320 — HU — ISSN 0524-904X
ACTA FACULTATIS POLITICO-JURIDICAE UNIVERSITATIS SCIENTIARUM BUDAPESTIENSIS DE ROLANDO EOTVOS NOMINATAE. (Text in Hungarian; summaries in German and Russian) 1959. irreg. Eotvos Lorand Tudomanyegyetem, Allam- es Jogtudomanyi Kar, Pf. 109, 1364 Budapest, Hungary. TEL 1-174-930. FAX 1-1174-114. TELEX 225467. **Indexed:** Amer.Hist.& Life, Hist.Abstr.

340 — SA — ISSN 0065-1346
LAW
ACTA JURIDICA. 1947. a. R.75. Juta & Co. Ltd., P.O. Box 14373, Kenwyn 7790, South Africa. TEL 021-797-5101. FAX 021-761-5010. Ed.Bd. circ. 500. **Indexed:** Ind.S.A.Per., Leg.Per., P.A.I.S.For.Lang.Ind.
—BLDSC shelfmark: 0628.400000.
Formerly (until 1959): Butterworths South African Law Review.
Description: Articles and discussions on recent legal problems in South Africa.

ACTA TECNOLOGIAE ET LEGIS MEDICAMENTI. see *MEDICAL SCIENCES*

340 320 — HU — ISSN 0563-0606
ACTA UNIVERSITATIS DE ATTILA JOZSEF NOMINATAE. ACTA IURIDICA ET POLITICA. (Text in English, French, German, Hungarian or Russian) 1955. a. exchange basis. Attila Jozsef University, c/o E. Szabo, Exchange Librarian, Dugonics ter 13, P.O.B. 393, Szeged H-6701, Hungary. (Subscr. to: Kultura, Box 149, H-1389 Budapest, Hungary) Ed.Bd. circ. 500.
Description: Law and political science with special reference to Hungary and the socialist countries.

340 370 — PL — ISSN 0208-6069
K1
ACTA UNIVERSITATIS LODZIENSIS: FOLIA IURIDICA. (Text in Polish; summaries in various languages) 1955-1974; N.S. 1980. irreg. Wydawnictwo Uniwersytetu Lodzkiego, Ul. Jaracza 34, Lodz, Poland. (Dist. by: Ars Polona-Ruch, Krakowskie Przedmiescie 7, Warsaw, Poland)
—BLDSC shelfmark: 0585.207200.
Supersedes in part: Uniwersytet Lodzki. Zeszyty Naukowe. Seria 1: Nauki Humanistyczno-Spoleczne (ISSN 0076-0358).
Description: Separate issues include sets of articles, monographs or conference papers of particular branches of law.

340 — PL — ISSN 0208-5283
ACTA UNIVERSITATIS NICOLAI COPERNICI. PRAWO. 1961. irreg. price varies. Uniwersytet Mikolaja Kopernika, Fosa Staromiejska 3, Torun, Poland. (Dist. by: Osrodek Rozpowszechniania Wydawnictw Naukowych PAN, Palac Kultury i Nauki, 00-901 Warsaw, Poland)
Formerly: Uniwersytet Mikolaja Kopernika, Torun. Nauki Humanistyczno-Spoleczne. Prawo (ISSN 0083-4513).

340 — FR — ISSN 0339-6851
ACTES "CAHIERS D'ACTION JURIDIQUE". 1973. q. 237.03 F. to individuals; institutions 242 F. (foreign 260 F.). 39 rue Bobillot, 75013 Paris, France. Ed.Bd. bk.rev.; circ. 5,000.

340 310.412 — US
ACTION ALERT (WASHINGTON, 1980). 1980. m. $25 to non-members; members $20. American Association of University Women, 1111 16th St., N.W., Washington, DC 20036. TEL 202-785-7700. FAX 202-785-7797. Ed. Carolin Head. index. (back issues avail.)
Description: Covers pending legislation, regulations and court decisions affecting women's issues, with emphasis on education, work and family issues.

658 340 — US
ACTION KIT FOR HOSPITAL LAW. 1972. m. $495. Action Kit Publications, 4614 Fifth Ave., Pittsburgh, PA 15213. TEL 800-245-1205. Ed. John Horty. circ. 2,000. (looseleaf format)

ACTION KIT FOR HOSPITAL TRUSTEES. see *HOSPITALS*

345 — US
ACTS AND CASES BY POPULAR NAMES, FEDERAL AND STATE. 1968. base vol. (plus supplements 6/yr.). $316. Shepard's - McGraw-Hill, Inc., Box 35300, Colorado Springs, CO 80935-3530. TEL 800-525-2474.
Formerly (until 1979): Shepard's Acts and Cases by Popular Names, Federal and State (ISSN 0080-9233).

340 — CK
ACTUALIDAD JURIDICA. 1975. m. Avda. Jimenez 12-42, Apdo. Aereo 27248, Bogota, Colombia. Ed. Carlos A. Useque.

340 — SP
▼**ACTUALIDAD JURIDICA ARANZADI**; pliego semanal de actualidad juridica. 1991. w. free to qualified personnel. Editorial Aranzadi, S.A., Avda. Carlos III, 34, Apdo. 111, 31080 Pamplona, Spain. TEL 948-331212. FAX 948-330919. Ed. Juan Miguel Perez. illus.

340 — FR — ISSN 0044-6157
ACTUALITE FIDUCIAIRE. 1927. 11/yr. 260 F. (foreign 310 F.)(effective Jan. 1992). Nouvelles Editions Fiduciaires, 2 bis rue de Villiers, 92300 Levallois-Perret, France. Ed. Sodie Robert. adv.; bk.rev.; circ. 35,000.

349 333 — FR
L'ACTUALITE JURIDIQUE: DROIT ADMINISTRATIF. 1945. m. 620 F. (foreign 690 F.). 17 rue d'Uzes, 75002 Paris, France. TEL 40-13-30-30. FAX 40-26-55-87. TELEX 680-876F. Ed. Pierre le Mire. adv.; bk.rev.; abstr.; bibl.; index; circ. 6,385. (reprint services avail. from SCH)
Formerly: Actualite Juridique: Edition Droit Administratif (ISSN 0001-7728); **Incorporates:** Actualite Juridique: Edition Propriete Immobiliere (ISSN 0001-7736)
Description: Property and real estate from a juridical and economical point of view.

340 — FR
ACTUALITE JURIDIQUE PROPRIETE IMMOBILIERE. 1950. m. 695 F. (foreign 755 F.). Publications du Moniteur, 17 rue d'Uzes, 75002 Paris, France. TEL 1-40-13-30-30. FAX 1-40-26-04-01. TELEX UPRESSE 680876F. Ed. Jean-Marc Pilpoul. circ. 6,000.

340 — FR
ACTUALITE LEGISLATIVE DALLOZ. bi-m. 450 F. (foreign 570 F.). Editions Dalloz, 11 rue Soufflot, 75240 Paris Cedex 05, France. (Subscr. to: 35, rue Tournefort, 75240 Paris Cedex 05, France. TEL 40-51-54-54) bk.rev.; index.
Formerly: Bulletin Legislatif Dalloz.

340 — FR
ACTUALITES COMMUNAUTAIRES; bulletin mensuel du dictionnaire du Marche Commun. vol.11, 1979. m. 680 F. G L N - Joly Editions, 1 av. Franklin D. Roosevelt, 75008 Paris, France. TEL 1-42-25-47-40. FAX 1-45-63-89-39. Eds. Xavier de Roux, Dominique Voillemot. circ. 700.
Formerly: Notes d'Informations Communautaires (ISSN 0339-6460)

330 297 — TS
AL-ADALAH/JUSTICE. (Text in Arabic) 1975. q. Ministry of Justice, P.O. Box 260, Abu Dhabi, United Arab Emirates. TEL 652224. FAX 664944. Ed. Khalifa Sultan al-Aqroubi. circ. 3,000.
Description: Covers the revival of the Islamic legal heritage, contemporary legal scholarship, foreign legal research, and important legal cases in the UAE.

340 — AT — ISSN 0065-1915
LAW
ADELAIDE LAW REVIEW. 1960. 2/yr. $20. Adelaide Law Review Association, c/o Department of Law, University of Adelaide, North Terrace, Adelaide, S.A. 5000, Australia. TEL 08-228-5063. FAX 08-232-4679. (Dist. in U.S. by: William S. Hein & Co., 1285 Main St., Buffalo, NY 14209) Ed.Bd. adv.; bk.rev.; index; circ. 500. (also avail. in microform from UMI) **Indexed:** Aus.P.A.I.S., C.L.I., L.R.I., Leg.Per.
—BLDSC shelfmark: 0680.300000.

340 — US
ADELPHIA LAW JOURNAL.* 1972-19??; resumed 1982. a. $10. Sigma Nu Phi Legal Fraternity, 9700 Fernwood Rd., W. Bethesda, Washington, DC 20817. bk.rev.; cum.index: 1982-1984; circ. 2,000. (back issues avail.) **Indexed:** Leg.Per.
Formerly: Adelphia.

340 — US
ADMINISTRATION OF JUSTICE MEMORANDA. 1975. irreg. price varies. University of North Carolina at Chapel Hill, Institute of Government, Knapp Bldg., CB 3330, Chapel Hill, NC 27599-3330. FAX 919-962-0654. Ed. Robert L. Farb. circ. 400.
Description: Discusses current issues of concern to North Carolina law enforcement and judicial officials.

340 364 — US
ADMINISTRATION OF JUVENILE JUSTICE IN CALIFORNIA. Department of Justice, Division of Law Enforcement, 4949 Broadway, Box 13427, Sacramento, CA 95813.

342 — BE — ISSN 0771-4084
ADMINISTRATION PUBLIQUE. 1976. q. 3800 Fr. (foreign 4000 Fr.). Institut Belge des Sciences Administratives - Belgian Institute of Administrative Sciences, Rue Saint-Bernard, 98, B-1060 Brussels, Belgium. TEL 02-536-59-38. FAX 02-536-59-11.
Formerly: Recueil de Jurisprudence de Droit Administrative et du Conseil d'Etat.

340 — AT — ISSN 0813-779X
ADMINISTRATIVE APPEAL REPORTS. 1984. m. price varies. Law Book Co. Ltd., 44-50 Waterloo Rd., North Ryde, N.S.W. 2113, Australia. TEL 02-887-0177. FAX 02-888-9706. TELEX ASBOOK 27995. Ed. Matthew Smith. cum.index. (back issues avail.)
Description: Provides reports of decisions of the Administrative Appeals Tribunal.

346.066 — US
ADMINISTRATIVE INTERPRETATIONS OF THE UNIFORM CONSUMER CREDIT CODE. 1989. base vol. (plus suppl.). $110. Butterworth Legal Publishers (Salem) (Subsidiary of: Reed International PLC), 90 Stiles Rd., Salem, NH 03079. TEL 800-548-4001. FAX 603-898-9858. Ed. Fred H. Miller. (looseleaf format)

340 — US
ADMINISTRATIVE JUDICIARY NEWS AND JOURNAL. 1978. q. membership only. American Bar Association, National Conference of Administrative Law Judges, 750 N. Lake Shore Dr., Chicago, IL 60611. TEL 312-988-5000. Ed. John M. Vittone. circ. 450.
Formerly: American Bar Association. Conference of Administrative Law Judges. Newsletter.

340 — US
ADMINISTRATIVE LAW. 1977. 6 base vols. (plus irreg. supplements). Matthew Bender & Co., Inc., 11 Penn Plaza, New York, NY 10001. TEL 212-967-7707. Ed. Glenn A. Mitchell. (looseleaf format)
Description: Analyzes all aspects of administrative law and the administrative process.

340 — AT — ISSN 0726-5816
ADMINISTRATIVE LAW DECISIONS. 1976. irreg. Aus.$95 per vol. Butterworths Pty. Ltd., 271-273 Lane Cove Rd., North Ryde, N.S.W. 2113, Australia. TEL 02-335-4444. FAX 02-335-4655. (Subscr. to: P.O. Box 345, North Ryde, N.S.W. 2113, Australia) Ed. D.C. Pearce.

340 US ISSN 0567-9494
LAW
ADMINISTRATIVE LAW NEWS. 1974. q. membership only. American Bar Association, Administrative Law and Regulatory Practice Section, 750 N. Lake Shore Dr., Chicago, IL 60611. TEL 312-988-6068. Ed. William Funk. circ. 8,000. **Indexed:** C.L.I., L.R.I.
Description: Provides information about meetings, committees, and council activities; chairman's report; and decisions of interest on the practice of administrative law.

340 CN ISSN 0824-2615
KE5015.A49
ADMINISTRATIVE LAW REPORTS. 1983. 12/yr. (in 6 vols.). Can.$115. Carswell Publications, Corporate Plaza, 2075 Kennedy Rd., Scarborough, Ont. M1T 3V4, Canada. TEL 416-609-8000. FAX 416-298-5094. Ed. David J. Mullan. **Indexed:** Ind.Can.L.P.L.

340 UK ISSN 0957-9710
ADMINISTRATIVE LAW REPORTS. 1989. 26/yr. £96.50. Barry Rose Law Periodicals, Little London, Chichester, West Sussex PO19 1PG, England. TEL 0243-787841. FAX 0243-779278. Ed. Ian McLeod.
Description: Reports on recent developments in administrative law in England.

340 US ISSN 0001-8368
ADMINISTRATIVE LAW REVIEW. 1973. q. $35 to non-members (foreign $40). American Bar Association, Administrative Law and Regulatory Practice Section, 750 N. Lake Shore Dr., Chicago, IL 60611. TEL 312-988-6068. Ed. Charles H. Koch, Jr. adv.; abstr.; cum.index; circ. 8,000. (reprint service avail. from RRI) **Indexed:** Abstr.Bk.Rev.Curr.Leg.Per., BPIA, Bus.Ind., C.L.I., Curr.Cont., Energy Ind., Energy Info.Abstr., L.R.I., Leg.Cont., Leg.Per., Pers.Lit., SSCI.
—BLDSC shelfmark: 0696.450000.
Description: Scholarly approach to the study of developments in the field of adminstrative law.

340 US
ADMINISTRATIVE RULEMAKING. 1983. base vol. (plus a. suppl.). $95. Shepard's - McGraw-Hill, Inc., Box 35300, Colorado Springs, CO 80935-3530. TEL 800-525-2474.
Description: Addresses the development of rulemaking. Covers the petition process, OMB input and includes regulatory analysis and judicial reviews.

340 II ISSN 0970-1060
LAW
ADMINISTRATIVE TRIBUNALS CASES. (Text in English) 1986. fortn. $95. Eastern Book Company, 34 Lalbagh, Lucknow 226 001, India. FAX 0091-522-242061. TELEX 535 436 FAST IN. Ed. Surendra Malik. adv.; bk.rev.; circ. 1,000. (back issues avail.)
Description: Contains the decisions of the Central Administrative Tribunals, and of the Supreme Court of India.

344 US
ADMIRALTY LAW NEWSLETTER. s-a. $15. American Bar Association, Young Lawyers Division, 750 N. Lake Shore Dr., Chicago, IL 60611. TEL 312-988-5000.
Description: Focuses on summaries of recent case law developments, CLE programs in maritime law area, and information and articles on programs and projects.

ADOPTION. see *SOCIAL SERVICES AND WELFARE*

ADOPTION AND FOSTERING. see *SOCIAL SERVICES AND WELFARE*

ADOPTION FACTBOOK; United States data, issues, regulations and resources. see *SOCIAL SERVICES AND WELFARE*

ADVANCES IN LAW AND CHILD DEVELOPMENT. see *CHILDREN AND YOUTH — About*

340 US
ADVANCES SESSION LAWS. 1932. irreg. price varies. Commerce Clearing House, Inc., 4025 W. Peterson Ave., Chicago, IL 60646. TEL 312-583-8500. Ed. D. Newquist.

ADVERTISING COMPLIANCE SERVICE NEWSLETTER. see *ADVERTISING AND PUBLIC RELATIONS*

346.066 US
ADVERTISING LAW ANTHOLOGY. 1973. a. $149.95. International Library Law Book Publishers, Inc., 101 Lakeforest Blvd., Ste. 270, Gaithersburg, MD 20877. TEL 301-990-7755. FAX 301-990-7642. Ed. Donald J. Hoyes. bibl.; index, cum.index.
Description: Selected best U.S. law review articles, printed in their entirety, in the field of advertising, culled from over 900 American law review journals.

340 US ISSN 0462-3134
ADVOCACY INSTITUTE. PROCEEDINGS (YEAR). 23rd, 1972. a. Institute of Continuing Legal Education, 1020 Greene St., Ann Arbor, MI 48109-1444. TEL 313-764-0533.
Description: Transcripts of the proceedings of the Annual Advocacy Institutes.

340 US
ADVOCACY: THE ART OF PLEADING A CAUSE, 2-E. 1980. base vol. (plus a. suppl.). $95. Shepard's - McGraw-Hill, Inc., Box 35300, Colorado Springs, CO 80935-3530. TEL 800-525-2474.
Description: Provides "how-to" information on eliciting truthful answers from various types of witnesses.

340 975 US ISSN 0515-4987
KF200
THE ADVOCATE (BOISE). 1957. m. $28. Idaho State Bar, 204 W. State St., Box 895, Boise, ID 83701. TEL 208-342-8958. Ed. Linda C. Watkins. adv.; bk.rev.; circ. 3,200. (also avail. in microfiche; back issues avail.) **Indexed:** C.L.I.

THE ADVOCATE (INDIANAPOLIS). see *POLITICAL SCIENCE — Civil Rights*

347.91 US ISSN 0199-1876
KFC1025.A15
ADVOCATE (LOS ANGELES, 1973). 1973. m. $50. Los Angeles Trial Lawyers Association, 3435 Wilshire Blvd., Ste. 2870, Los Angeles, CA 90010-1912. TEL 213-487-1212. FAX 213-487-1224. Ed. Christine Spagnoli. adv.; circ. 2,700.
Description: Covers both substantive law and practice tips.

340 CN ISSN 0382-456X
ADVOCATE (TORONTO). 1964. irreg. University of Toronto, Faculty of Law, Toronto, Ont. M5S 2C5, Canada. TEL 416-978-3725.

340 CN ISSN 0044-6416
ADVOCATE (WEST VANCOUVER). 1943. bi-m. Can.$21.40. Vancouver Bar Association, 4765 Pilot House Rd., W. Vancouver, B.C. V7W 1J2, Canada. TEL 604-925-2122. FAX 604-925-2065. Ed. David Roberts. adv.; cum.index; circ. 1943-1986; circ. 7,750. (back issues avail.) **Indexed:** Ind.Can.L.P.L.

340 CN ISSN 0704-0288
K1
ADVOCATES QUARTERLY; a Canadian journal for practitioners of civil litigation. 1977. q. Can.$107. Canada Law Book Inc., 240 Edward St., Aurora, Ont. L4G 3S9, Canada. TEL 416-841-6472. Ed. P. Theodore Matlow. adv.; bk.rev. **Indexed:** C.L.I., Ind.Can.L.P.L., L.R.I., Leg.Per.
—BLDSC shelfmark: 0719.560000.

340 NO
ADVOKATBLADET. 1931. m. (10/yr.). NOK 250. Norske Advokatforening - Norwegian Bar Association, Juristenes Hus, Kristian Augusts gate 9, N-0167 Oslo 1, Norway. TEL 47 2 11 68 68. FAX 47-2-11-53-25. Ed. Per Wang. adv.; circ. 4,700.
Formerly: Norsk Advokatblad (ISSN 0332-5466)

349 SW ISSN 0281-3505
LAW
ADVOKATEN. m. (8/yr.). SEK 250. Sveriges Advokatsamfund - Swedish Bar Association, P.O. Box 27321, S-102 54 Stockholm, Sweden. Ed. Lars Bentelius. adv.; charts.
Formerly: Sveriges Advokatsamfund. Tidskrift (ISSN 0040-6902)

340 DK
ADVOKATEN. 1921. 11/yr. free to members. Danske Advokatsamfund - Danish Law Society, Kronprinsessegade 28, 1306 Copenhagen K, Denmark. FAX 33-321831. Ed. Ole Stig Anderson. adv.; bk.rev.; index; circ. 5,500 (controlled).
Formerly: Advokatbladet.

349 YU ISSN 0017-0933
ADVOKATSKA KOMORA VOJVODINE. GLASNIK; Chasopis za pravnu teoriju i praksu. (Text in Serbo-Croatian) 1928. m. 246000 din. Advokatska Komora Vojvodine, Zmaj Jovina 20, 21000 Novi Sad, Yugoslavia. TEL 021 29-459. (Co-sponsor: Samoupravna Interesna Zajednica za Naucni Rad Vojvodine) Ed. Miroslav Zdjelar. adv.; bk.rev.; circ. 1,000.
Description: Provides articles on law theory and practice.

340 YU
ADVOKATURA. 1975. q. 60 din. Advokatska Komora Srbije, Mose Pijade 13, Belgrade, Yugoslavia. Ed. Aleksander Mikulic.

347 BN
ADVOKATURA BOSNE I HERCEGOVINE. 1975. q. 150 din. Advokatska Komora Bosne i Hercegovine, Saloma Albaharija 2, Sarajevo, Bosnia Hercegovina. Ed. Seid Hadziselimovic.

AE K - K V W L AKTUELL; berufspolitische Informationen fuer die Aerzte in Westfalen-Lippe. (Aerztkammer Westfalen-Lippe, Kassenaerztliche Vereinigung Westfalen-Lippe) see *MEDICAL SCIENCES*

AEROSPACE MANAGEMENT AND LAW. see *AERONAUTICS AND SPACE FLIGHT*

340 US ISSN 0360-5485
KF325.26
AFFILIATE (CHICAGO). 6/yr. $15 (free to qualified personnel). American Bar Association, Young Lawyers Division, Affiliate Outreach Committees, 750 N. Lake Shore Dr., Chicago, IL 60611. TEL 312-988-5555.

347 AF
AFGHANISTAN. MINISTRY OF JUSTICE. LAW JOURNAL. (Text in Persian or Pushto) 1976. m. $3. Ministry of Justice, Darrul Aman, Kabul, Afghanistan.

342 AF
AFGHANISTAN. MINISTRY OF JUSTICE. OFFICIAL GAZETTE/RASMI JARIDAH. (Text in Persian) irreg. AF.21. Ministry of Justice, Judicial Relations and Planning Department, Darrul Aman, Kabul, Afghanistan. circ. 10,500.

349 ET ISSN 0002-0052
LAW
AFRICAN LAW DIGEST. (Name of issuing body varies: Haile Sellassie I University, University of Addis Ababa, National University) 1966. 3/yr. Eth.$15($40) Addis Ababa University, Faculty of Law, P.O. Box 1176, Addis Ababa, Ethiopia. Ed. Yeshak Teshome. bibl.; index; circ. 250. (processed; also avail. in microfiche from SWZ; reprint service avail. from SWZ)
Description: Summaries of important African legislation and inter-African treaties.

340 GW ISSN 0722-2181
AFRIKANISCHES RECHT. JAHRBUCH. (Text in English, French and German; summaries in English and French) 1980. a. price varies. C.F. Mueller Juristischer Verlag GmbH, Postfach 102640, 6900 Heidelberg 1, Germany. TEL 06221-489281. FAX 06221-489279. bk.rev.

610 355.115 US
AGENT ORANGE REVIEW; for veterans who served in Vietnam. 1982. irreg., 2-3/yr. free. U.S. Department of Veterans Affairs, Environmental Agents Service (116A), 810 Vermont Ave., N.W., Washington, DC 20420. TEL 202-535-7183. Ed. Donald J. Rosenblum. circ. controlled. (looseleaf format)
Description: Provides information on Agent Orange exposure, examination, compensation, and other related matters, including legislation, for Vietnam veterans, families, and others concerned about the effects of herbicides used in Vietnam.

AGRARRECHT. see *AGRICULTURE*

340 630 US
AGRICULTURAL LAW. 1980. 15 base vols. (plus irreg. supplements). Matthew Bender & Co. Inc., 11 Penn Plaza, New York, NY 10001. TEL 212-967-7760. (looseleaf format)
Description: Covers the pertinence of all case and statutory law to farms, ranches, and other agricultural interests.

340 630　　　　US
AGRICULTURAL LAW MANUAL. 1985. base vol. (plus irreg. supplements). Matthew Bender & Co., Inc., 11 Penn Plaza, New York, NY 10001.
TEL 212-967-7707. (looseleaf format)
　Description: Covers taxation of farm income, government regulation of agriculture, agricultural estate and business planning, agricultural cooperatives, farm bankruptcy and foreclosure and organizing the farm or ranch.

AGRICULTURAL LAW UPDATE. see *AGRICULTURE — Agricultural Economics*

340 630　　　　US　　ISSN 0002-1741
LAW
AGRICULTURE DECISIONS. 1942. m. U.S. Department of Agriculture, Office of Administrative Law Judges, 14th St. & Independence Ave., S.W., Washington, DC 20250. TEL 202-655-4000. (also avail. in microform from UMI)

347　　　　　　US　　ISSN 0098-9738
KFH510.A73
AHA'ILONO; to report the news. vol.6, 1978. bi-m. free. Hawaii State Judiciary, Public Information Office, Box 2560, Honolulu, HI 96804. TEL 808-548-4634. FAX 808-548-6002. Ed. Chapman Lam. illus.; circ. 4,500.
　Description: Reports current events and departmental updates for the Hawaii State Judiciary.

340 629.1　　　US　　ISSN 0747-7449
KF2400.A15
AIR AND SPACE LAWYER. vol.3, 1986. q. $20 membership. American Bar Association, Forum on Air and Space Law, 750 N. Lake Shore Dr., Chicago, IL 60611. TEL 312-988-5579. Ed. Robert J. O'Connell.
　Description: News on significant developments in air and space law, as well as reports of committee activities.

340　　　　　　US　　ISSN 0094-8381
K25
AIR FORCE LAW REVIEW. 1959. s-a. $5 (foreign $6.25). U.S. Air Force, Judge Advocate General School, CPD-JAL, Maxwell AFB, AL 36112-5712. TEL 205-953-2802. (Subscr. to: Supt. of Documents, Washington, D.C. 20402) Ed. Eric D. Placke. bk.rev.; charts; index; circ. 1,800. (also avail. in microform from MIM,UMI) **Indexed:** Abstr.Bk.Rev.Curr.Leg.Per., Air Un.Lib.Ind., C.C.L.P., C.L.I., Ind.U.S.Gov.Per., L.R.I., Leg.Cont., Leg.Per., PROMT.
　Former titles: J A G Law Review & J A G Bulletin (ISSN 0021-3527)
　Description: Articles of interest to Air Force judge advocates, civilian attorneys and other military lawyers.

AIR SAFETY WEEK; the newsletter of air safety regulation. see *AERONAUTICS AND SPACE FLIGHT*

AIR TRAFFIC CONTROL ASSOCIATION. BULLETIN. see *TRANSPORTATION — Air Transport*

340　　　　　　BL
AJURIS. 1974. irreg. (Associacao dos Juizes do Rio Grande do Sul) Livraria Sulina, Av. Borges de Medeiros 1030-1036, Porto Alegre, Brazil.

AKADEMIYA NAUK AZERBAIDZHANSKOI S.S.R. IZVESTIYA. SERIYA ISTORIYA, FILOSOFIYA I PRAVO. see *HISTORY*

340　　　　　　US　　ISSN 0002-371X
K1
AKRON LAW REVIEW. 1967. 4/yr. $20. University of Akron, School of Law, Akron, OH 44325. TEL 216-972-7335. adv.; bk.rev.; circ. 1,500. (also avail. in microfilm from PMC,WSH; microfiche from WSH; back issues avail.; reprint service avail. from WSH) **Indexed:** C.C.L.P., C.L.I., L.R.I., Leg.Cont., Leg.Per., R.G.
　—BLDSC shelfmark: 0785.641000.

340　　　　　　US　　ISSN 1049-9369
▼**ALABAMA EMPLOYMENT LAW LETTER.** 1990. 12/yr. $127. M. Lee Smith Publishers & Printers, 162 Fourth Ave. N., Box 2678, Nashville, TN 37219. TEL 615-242-7395. FAX 615-256-6601.
(Co-sponsor: Sirote & Permutt) Ed.Bd.
　Description: Reports the latest Alabama employment law developments that affect Alabama employers.

340　　　　　　US　　ISSN 0002-4279
K1
ALABAMA LAW REVIEW. 1948. 3/yr. $24. University of Alabama, School of Law, Box 870382, University, AL 35487-0382. TEL 205-348-7191. bk.rev.; index, cum.index every 5 yrs.; circ. 1,500. (also avail. in microform from WSH; reprint service avail. from WSH) **Indexed:** C.L.I., Crim.Just.Abstr., L.R.I., Leg.Cont., Leg.Per., P.A.I.S.
　●Also available online. Vendor(s): WESTLAW.
　—BLDSC shelfmark: 0786.521500.

340　　　　　　US　　ISSN 0002-4287
KF200
ALABAMA LAWYER. 1940. q. $15. State Bar of Alabama, Lock Box 4156, Montgomery, AL 36101. TEL 205-269-1515. Ed. Margaret Lacey. adv.; bk.rev.; index, cum.index: vols.1-25; circ. 9,000. **Indexed:** C.L.I., L.R.I., Leg.Per.
　●Also available online. Vendor(s): WESTLAW.
　—BLDSC shelfmark: 0786.522000.

ALABAMA TODAY. see *BUSINESS AND ECONOMICS — Chamber Of Commerce Publications*

ALAN GUTTMACHER INSTITUTE. WASHINGTON MEMO. see *MEDICAL SCIENCES — Obstetrics And Gynecology*

340　　　　　　US
ALASKA BAR RAG. 1963. bi-m. $25. Alaska Bar Association, Box 100279, Anchorage, AK 99510. TEL 907-272-7469. Ed.Bd. adv.; bk.rev.; index; circ. 3,000. (looseleaf format)
　Former titles: Alaska Bar Brief (ISSN 0093-1039); Alaska Law Journal (ISSN 0002-452X)

340　　　　　　US　　ISSN 0883-0568
K1
ALASKA LAW REVIEW. vol.8, 1991. s-a. $20 (foreign $23). Duke University, School of Law, Rm. 006, Durham, NC 27706-2580. TEL 919-684-5966. FAX 919-684-3417. (reprint service avail. from RRI)

340　　　　　　US　　ISSN 0002-4678
LAW
ALBANY LAW REVIEW. 1936. 4/yr. $25. Albany Law School, 80 New Scotland Ave., Albany, NY 12208. TEL 518-445-2375. FAX 518-445-2315. Ed. Robert Laing. adv.; bk.rev.; index; circ. 1,000. (also avail. in microfilm from PMC,WSH; back issues avail.) **Indexed:** Abstr.Bk.Rev.Curr.Leg.Per., C.L.I., Crim.Just.Abstr., Geo.Abstr., L.R.I., Leg.Cont., Leg.Per.
　—BLDSC shelfmark: 0786.568000.

340　　　　　　CN
ALBERTA CORPORATIONS LAW GUIDE. m. Can.$475. C C H Canadian Ltd., 6 Garamond Court, Don Mills, Ont. M3C 1Z5, Canada. TEL 416-441-2992. FAX 416-444-9011.
　Description: Covers Alberta business corporations act and regulations.

342　　　　　　CN　　ISSN 0824-7277
ALBERTA DECISIONS. RULES AND STATUTE CITATOR. 1981. m. Can.$105. Western Legal Publications, 301-1 Alexander St., Vancouver, B.C. V6A 1B2, Canada. TEL 604-687-5671. FAX 604-687-2796. (looseleaf format)
　Description: Provides notes on all current judgements of the Supreme Court of Canada and the Alberta Courts, and case citations for all decisions of the Alberta Courts in which an Alberta Rule of Court or statute was cited.

340　　　　　　CN　　ISSN 0319-7980
ALBERTA DECISIONS, CIVIL AND CRIMINAL CASES. 1974. m. Can.$310. Western Legal Publications, 301-1 Alexander St., Vancouver, B.C. V6A 1B2, Canada. TEL 604-687-5671. FAX 604-687-2796.
　●Also available online.
　Description: Provides detailed summaries of judgements from the Alberta Court of Appeals, Court of Queen's Bench and selected decisions of the Provincial Courts of Alberta.

340　　　　　　CN
ALBERTA FAMILY LAW. 4/yr. Can.$175. Butterworths Canada Ltd., 75 Clegg Rd., Markham, Ont. L6G 1A1, Canada. TEL 416-479-2665. FAX 416-479-2826. (looseleaf format)
　Description: All federal and provincial statutes, rules and regulations pertaining to family law practice in Alberta.

340　　　　　　CN　　ISSN 0703-3117
ALBERTA LAW REPORTS (2ND SERIES). 1976. 26/yr. (in 6 vols.). Can.$110. Carswell Publications, 800 Rocky Mountain Plaza, 615 MacLeod Trail S.E., Calgary, Alta. T2G 4T8, Canada.
TEL 416-609-8000. FAX 416-298-5094. (Subscr. to: Carswell Publications, Corporate Plaza, 2075 Kennedy Rd., Scarborough, Ont. M1T 3V4, Canada) Ed. Margaret James. cum.index.

340　　　　　　CN　　ISSN 0002-4821
ALBERTA LAW REVIEW. 1955. 4/yr. Can.$30. University of Alberta, Faculty of Law, Edmonton, Alta. T6G 2H5, Canada. TEL 403-492-5559. FAX 403-492-4924. adv.; bk.rev.; illus.; index; circ. 5,500. (also avail. in microform from UMI; reprint service avail. from UMI) **Indexed:** Abstr.Bk.Rev.Curr.Leg.Per., C.L.I., Can.Per.Ind., Ind.Can.L.P.L., L.R.I., Leg.Cont., Leg.Per., Mar.Aff.Bibl.
　—BLDSC shelfmark: 0786.587000.

340　　　　　　CN
ALBERTA LIMITATIONS MANUAL. 2/yr. Can.$180. Butterworths Canada Ltd., 75 Clegg Rd., Markham, Ont. L6G 1A1, Canada. TEL 416-479-2665. FAX 416-479-2826. (looseleaf format)
　Description: A reference of time limits specified in Alberta's legal statutes.

340　　　　　　CN
ALBERTA REPORTS. 1976. irreg. Can.$83 per vol. Maritime Law Book Ltd., Box 302, Fredericton, N.B. E3B 4Y9, Canada. TEL 506-454-9921. (back issues avail.)
　●Also available online. Vendor(s): QL Systems Ltd..

343　　　　　　CN　　ISSN 0715-3155
ALBERTA, SASKATCHEWAN, MANITOBA - CRIMINAL CONVICTION CASES. 1976. m. Can.$150. Western Legal Publications, 301-1 Alexander St., Vancouver, B.C. V6A 1B2, Canada. TEL 604-687-5671. FAX 604-687-2796. q. index. (looseleaf format)
　Description: Summaries of criminal conviction decisions made available by the Appellate and Trial Divisions of the Superior Courts of Alberta, Saskatchewan and Manitoba.

340　　　　　　CN　　ISSN 0713-892X
ALBERTA WEEKLY LAW DIGEST. 1982. w. (50/yr.). Can.$375. Carswell Publications, 800 Rocky Mountain Plaza, 615 MacLeod Trail S.E., Calgary, Alta. T2G 4T8, Canada. TEL 416-291-8421. FAX 416-291-3426. (Subscr. to: Carswell Publications, 2330 Midland Ave., Agincourt, Ont. M1S 1P7, Canada) Ed. Margaret James. cum.index; circ. 380.

ALCOHOL ISSUES INSIGHTS. see *BEVERAGES*

344.73　　　　　US　　ISSN 0098-0757
KF3919
ALCOHOL, TOBACCO AND FIREARMS BULLETIN. q. $5.80. U.S. Department of the Treasury, Bureau of Alcohol, Tobacco and Firearms, 15th & Pennsylvania Ave., N.W., Washington, DC 20224.
TEL 202-566-7777. (Dist. by: Supt. of Documents, Washington, DC 20402)

ALERT (LOS ANGELES). see *SOCIAL SERVICES AND WELFARE*

340　　　　　　BE
ALGEMENE PRACTISCHE RECHTVERZAMELING. Short title: A P R. 1972. irreg. price varies. E. Story-Scientia, De Jamblinne de Meuplien 34-35, B-1040 Brussels, Belgium. TEL 32-2-36-89-80.

343 365　　　　FI　　ISSN 0357-542X
ALIBI. m. FIM 291. Yhtyneet Kuvalehdet Oy, Maistraatinportti 1, 00240 Helsinki, Finland. TEL 0-15661. FAX 0-1566505. TELEX 121364. Ed. Antero Maunula. adv.; circ. 70,405.
　Description: Focuses on criminal cases and legal issues.

340　　　　　　CN　　ISSN 0705-1360
ALL CANADA WEEKLY SUMMARIES - NATIONAL. 1977. w. Can.$145. Canada Law Book Inc., 240 Edward St., Aurora, Ont. L4G 3S9, Canada.
TEL 416-841-6472.
　●Also available online.

340　　　　　　UK　　ISSN 0002-5569
ALL ENGLAND LAW REPORTS. 1936. w. Butterworth & Co. (Publishers) Ltd. (Subsidiary of: Reed International PLC), 88 Kingsway, London WC2B 6AB, England. TEL 71-405-6900. FAX 71-405-1332. (US addr.: Butterworth Legal Publishers, 90 Stiles Rd., Salem, NH 03079. TEL 800-548-4001) Ed. Peter Hutchesson. adv.; cum.index: 1936-1981; circ. 15,000. Indexed: RICS.
●Also available online. Vendor(s): Mead Data Central.

340　　　　　　UK　　ISSN 0265-766X
ALL ENGLAND LAW REPORTS. ANNUAL REVIEW. 1983. a. £25($85) Butterworth & Co. (Publishers) Ltd. (Subsidiary of: Reed International PLC), 88 Kingsway, London WC2B 6AB, England. TEL 71-405-6900. FAX 71-405-1332. TELEX 95678. (US addr.: Butterworth Legal Publishers, 90 Stiles Rd., Salem, NH 03079. TEL 800-548-4001) —BLDSC shelfmark: 0788.642000.
Description: Survey of developments in English law during the year, including analyses of decisions handed down by the higher courts.

349　　　　　　II　　ISSN 0002-5593
ALL INDIA REPORTER; full reports of all reportable (civil, criminal and revenue) cases of the High Courts and Supreme Court in India. 1922. m. Rs.540($168) All India Reporter Ltd., P.O. Box 209, Nagpur 440012, India. Ed. V.R. Manohar. adv.; bk.rev.; index; circ. 34,000.

340　　　　　　II
ALL INDIA SERVICES LAW JOURNAL. (Text in English) 1973. m. Rs.160. Bahri Brothers, Box 2032, 742 Lajpat Rai Market, Delhi 6, India. adv.; bk.rev.; circ. 2,000.

340　　　　　　PK　　ISSN 0030-9958
ALL PAKISTAN LEGAL DECISIONS. 1949. m. Rs.500. P.L.D. Publishers, Nabha Rd., Lahore 1, Pakistan. Ed. Malik Muhammad Saeed. (reprint service avail. from UMI)

340　　　　　　II
ALLAHABAD LAW JOURNAL. (Text in English) vol.75, 1977. w. Rs.65. Allahabad Law Journal Co., Ltd., 5 Prayag St., Allahabad, India. Ed. B.C. Dey. bibl.

340　 350　　HU　　ISSN 0324-7171
JA26
ALLAM ES IGAZGATAS. 1951. m. $22.50. (Minisztertanacs) Lapkiado Vallalat, Lenin korut 9-11, 1073 Budapest 7, Hungary. TEL 222-408. (Subscr. to: Kultura, Box 149, H-1389 Budapest, Hungary) Ed. Tibor Kovacs. adv.; bk.rev.; bibl. Indexed: Rural Recreat.Tour.Abstr., World Agri.Econ.& Rural Sociol.Abstr.

349　320　　HU　　ISSN 0002-564X
ALLAM- ES JOGTUDOMANY/POLITICAL SCIENCE AND JURISPRUDENCE. (Text in Hungarian; summaries in French and Russian) 1957. q. $29. (Magyar Tudomanyos Akademia, Allam-es Jogtudomanyi Intezet) Akademiai Kiado, Publishing House of the Hungarian Academy of Sciences, PO Box 24, H-1363 Budapest, Hungary. Eds. I. Szabo, F. Madl. adv.; bk.rev.; index. Indexed: Rural Recreat.Tour.Abstr., World Agri.Econ.& Rural Sociol.Abstr.

340　　　　　　US
ALLEGHENY LAWYER. 1959. m. free to members. Allegheny County Bar Association, 436 7th Ave., Ste. 400, Pittsburgh, PA 15219-1818. TEL 412-261-6161. FAX 412-261-3622. Ed. James I. Smith. circ. 6,300. (back issues avail.)
Description: Membership news of the Allegheny County Bar Association.

340　　　　　　US
ALTERNATIVES NEWSLETTER. 3/yr. $12. American Bar Association, Young Lawyers Division, 750 N. Lake Shore Dr., Chicago, IL 60611. TEL 312-988-5000.
Description: Features editorials on the subject of Alternative Dispute Resolution, articles on young lawyers and ADR programs in operation, as well as federal and state case law updates.

AMERICAN ACADEMY OF PSYCHIATRY AND THE LAW. BULLETIN. see MEDICAL SCIENCES — Psychiatry And Neurology

340　616.8　　US　　ISSN 0896-5633
KF8922
AMERICAN ACADEMY OF PSYCHIATRY AND THE LAW. NEWSLETTER. 1975. 3/yr. $25. American Academy of Psychiatry and the Law, 819 Park Ave., Baltimore, MD 21201. TEL 301-539-0379. FAX 301-385-0154. Ed. Dr. Alan R. Felthous. circ. 1,750. (back issues avail.)
Description: Law and practice in psychiatry and forensic psychiatry.

AMERICAN AUTOMOBILE ASSOCIATION. DIGEST OF MOTOR LAWS. see TRANSPORTATION — Automobiles

340　　　　　　US　　ISSN 0027-9048
K1
AMERICAN BANKRUPTCY LAW JOURNAL. 1927. q. $50. National Conference of Bankruptcy Judges, Box 11516, Fort Wayne, IN 46858-1516. TEL 219-486-6574. FAX 219-486-6474. Ed. Sam Bufford. bk.rev.; illus.; index, cum.index: vols.24-27 (1950-1973); circ. 3,408. (also avail. in microfilm from UMI; reprint service avail. from WSH) Indexed: Bank.Lit.Ind., C.L.I., Curr.Cont., L.R.I., Leg.Cont., Leg.Per., SSCI.
—BLDSC shelfmark: 0810.723000.
Formerly: National Conference of Referees in Bankruptcy. Journal (ISSN 0197-2669)

340　　　　　　US
AMERICAN BAR ASSOCIATION. I.R.R. SECTION NEWSLETTER. 1969. 3/yr. $30 to non-members; members $18. American Bar Association, Section of Individual Rights and Responsibilities, 750 N. Lake Shore Dr., Chicago, IL 60611. TEL 312-988-5000. Ed. Vicki Quade.
Formerly: American Bar Association. Section of Individual Rights and Responsibilities. Newsletter (ISSN 0572-3590)

340　　　　　　US
AMERICAN BAR ASSOCIATION. LAW PRACTICE MANAGEMENT SECTION. NETWORK. q. membership only. American Bar Association, Law Practice Management Section, 750 N. Lake Shore Dr., Chicago, IL 60611. TEL 312-988-5555.
Formerly: American Bar Association. Economics of Law Practice Section. Network.

340　　　　　　US
AMERICAN BAR ASSOCIATION. OFFICE OF POLICY ADMINISTRATION. SUMMARY AND REPORTS. s-a. $10. American Bar Association, Office of Policy Administration, 750 N. Lake Shore Dr., Chicago, IL 60611. TEL 312-988-6101. FAX 312-988-6281.
Description: Contains recommendations and informational reports to and summary of actions of the ABA House of Delegates.

340　336　　US　　ISSN 0277-2361
KF6272
AMERICAN BAR ASSOCIATION. SECTION OF TAXATION. NEWSLETTER. q. $15 to non-members. American Bar Association, Taxation Section, 1800 M St., N.W., 2nd Fl., S. Lobby, Washington, DC 20036-5886. TEL 202-331-2231. FAX 202-331-2220. Ed. Phyllis Horn Epstein. (looseleaf format; back issues avail.) Indexed: C.L.I., Leg.Per.
Description: Update on current tax developments, committee projects, meeting information.

340　352　　US　　ISSN 0569-3349
KF2077
AMERICAN BAR ASSOCIATION. UTILITY SECTION. NEWSLETTER. 1960. q. membership only. American Bar Association, Public Utility Law Section, 750 N. Lake Shore Dr., Chicago, IL 60611. TEL 312-988-5602. Indexed: C.L.I.
Description: Articles pertaining to the field of public utility law.

340　　　　　　US　　ISSN 0094-3584
LAW
AMERICAN BAR - THE CANADIAN BAR - THE INTERNATIONAL BAR. 1919. a. $255. Forster-Long, Inc., 3280 Ramos Circle, Sacramento, CA 95827. TEL 916-362-3276. Ed. Marie Finn. circ. 34,000.
Description: Biographical directory of preeminent lawyers of the world with abridged handbook.

347.9　　　　US
AMERICAN BENCH; judges of the nation. 1977. biennial. $250. Forster-Long, Inc., 3280 Ramos Circle, Sacramento, CA 95827. TEL 916-362-3276. Ed. Marie Hough.
Description: Biographical reference guide listing approximately 18,000 judges serving all levels of federal, state and local courts.

346.066　　US　　ISSN 0002-7766
K1　　　　　　　　　CODEN: ABLJAN
AMERICAN BUSINESS LAW JOURNAL. 1963. 4/yr. $24 (foreign $27). Academy of Legal Studies in Business, c/o Daniel J. Herron, School of Business, Western Carolina University, Cullowhee, NC 28723. TEL 704-586-1423. FAX 704-227-7414. Ed. Michael J. Phillips. adv.; bk.rev.; charts; illus.; index, cum.index; circ. 2,000. (also avail. in microform from UMI) Indexed: ABI Inform., Abstr.Bk.Rev.Curr.Leg.Per., Account.Ind. (1974-), B.P.I., BPIA, Bus.Ind., C.C.L.P., C.L.I., Curr.Cont., L.R.I., Leg.Cont., Leg.Per., SSCI, Tr.& Indus.Ind.
—BLDSC shelfmark: 0811.500000.
Refereed Serial

AMERICAN CRIMINAL LAW REVIEW. see CRIMINOLOGY AND LAW ENFORCEMENT

340　　　　　　US
AMERICAN FOREIGN LAW ASSOCIATION NEWSLETTER. no.24, 1974. 3/yr. $20. American Foreign Law Association, c/o Richard Lutringer, 200 Park Ave., 28th Fl., New York, NY 10017. TEL 212-836-8000. FAX 212-351-3131. Ed. James R. Maxeiner. circ. controlled. (processed)
Description: Reports on programs sponsored by the Association and on other activities related to foreign, international and comparative law and international affairs of interest to Association members and practitioners.

AMERICAN GROUP PRACTICE ASSOCIATION. EXECUTIVE NEWS SERVICE. see MEDICAL SCIENCES

AMERICAN INDIAN JOURNAL. see HISTORY — History Of North And South America

AMERICAN INDIAN LAW NEWSLETTER. see ETHNIC INTERESTS

340　970.1　　US　　ISSN 0094-002X
K1
AMERICAN INDIAN LAW REVIEW. 1973. s-a. $15. University of Oklahoma, College of Law, 300 Timberdell Rd., Norman, OK 73019. TEL 405-325-2840. Ed. Dena Silliman. adv.; bk.rev.; circ. 650. (also avail. in microfilm from WSH,PMC; reprint service avail. from WSH) Indexed: C.L.I., L.R.I., Leg.Cont., Leg.Per., Sel.Water Res.Abstr.
●Also available online. Vendor(s): WESTLAW.
Description: Articles, student notes and federal developments on American Indian law and education.

AMERICAN JOURNAL OF CRIMINAL LAW. see CRIMINOLOGY AND LAW ENFORCEMENT

340　　　　　　US　　ISSN 0891-6330
K1
AMERICAN JOURNAL OF FAMILY LAW. 1987. q. $120 (foreign $136). John Wiley & Sons, Inc., Journals, 605 Third Ave., New York, NY 10158-0012. TEL 212-850-6000. FAX 212-850-6088. cum.index; circ. 800. (back issues avail.) Indexed: C.L.I.
Description: Provides in-depth, relevant commentary on current issues in practice; includes sample forms, checklists, and useful guidelines for day-to-day use for family law practitioners, paralegals, or judges.

AMERICAN JOURNAL OF FORENSIC PSYCHIATRY. see MEDICAL SCIENCES — Forensic Sciences

AMERICAN JOURNAL OF FORENSIC PSYCHOLOGY; interfacing issues of psychology and law. see PSYCHOLOGY

340 US ISSN 0065-8995
K14
AMERICAN JOURNAL OF JURISPRUDENCE. 1956. a.
$11. (University of Notre Dame, Law School)
Western Publishing, 537 E. Ohio St., Indianapolis, IN
46204-2173. TEL 219-255-2938. Eds. Charles E.
Rice, Robert E. Rodes. adv.; bk.rev.; circ. 1,000.
(also avail. in microform from UMI,WSH,PMC; back
issues avail.; reprint service avail. from UMI,WSH)
Indexed: A.B.C.Pol.Sci., C.L.I., Cath.Ind., L.R.I.,
Leg.Cont., Leg.Per.
—BLDSC shelfmark: 0826.850000.
 Formerly: Natural Law Forum.

340 610 US ISSN 0098-8588
K1 CODEN: AJLMDN
AMERICAN JOURNAL OF LAW & MEDICINE. 1975. q.
$70 (foreign $100). American Society of Law &
Medicine, Inc., 765 Commonwealth Ave., Ste. 1634,
Boston, MA 02215. TEL 617-262-4990.
FAX 617-437-7596. (Co-sponsor: Boston University,
School of Law) Ed. Frances H. Miller. bk.rev.; bibl.;
circ. 6,500 (controlled). (also avail. in microfilm
from WSH,PMC; reprint service avail. from WSH)
Indexed: Abstr.Bk.Rev.Curr.Leg.Per., Abstr.Health
Care Manage.Stud., Biol.Abstr., C.L.I., Curr.Cont.,
Dok.Arbeitsmed., Excerp.Med., Hlth.Ind.,
Hosp.Lit.Ind., Ind.Med., INIS Atomind., L.R.I.,
Leg.Cont., Leg.Per., Med.Care Rev., SSCI, Telegen.
—BLDSC shelfmark: 0826.880000.
 Description: Interdisciplinary law review providing
in-depth legal analysis of current medicolegal issues.
Refereed Serial

340 US ISSN 0002-9319
AMERICAN JOURNAL OF LEGAL HISTORY. 1957. q.
$20. Temple University School of Law, Philadelphia,
PA 19122. TEL 215-787-1256.
FAX 215-787-1785. Ed. Diane C. Maleson. adv.;
bk.rev.; bibl.; charts; index, cum.index every 5 yrs.;
circ. 1,200. (also avail. in microfilm from RRI; reprint
service avail. from RRI) Indexed: A.B.C.Pol.Sci.,
Abstr.Bk.Rev.Curr.Leg.Per., Amer.Hist.& Life, C.L.I.,
Chic.Per.Ind., Hist.Abstr., L.R.I., Leg.Cont., Leg.Per.,
SSCI.
●Also available online. Vendor(s): WESTLAW.
—BLDSC shelfmark: 0826.900000.

347.91 US ISSN 0160-0281
K1
AMERICAN JOURNAL OF TRIAL ADVOCACY. 1977. 3/yr.
$24. Samford University, Cumberland School of
Law, 800 Lakeshore Dr., Box 2263, Birmingham, AL
35229. TEL 205-870-2959. Ed.Bd. bk.rev.; index;
circ. 2,000. (also avail. in microform from UMI;
reprint service avail. from RRI) Indexed: C.C.L.P.,
C.L.I., CJPI, Hlth.Ind., L.R.I., Leg.Cont., Leg.Per.
—BLDSC shelfmark: 0838.900000.

340 US ISSN 0732-1031
KF294.A4
AMERICAN JUDICATURE SOCIETY. ANNUAL REPORT.
1917. a. free. American Judicature Society, 25 E.
Washington, Ste. 1600, Chicago, IL 60602-1805.
Ed. David Richert. circ. 20,000. (reprint service avail.
from ISI,UMI)

340 US ISSN 0065-9045
**AMERICAN LAW INSTITUTE. ANNUAL MEETING.
PROCEEDINGS.** 1923. a. $60. American Law
Institute, 4025 Chestnut St., Philadelphia, PA
19104. TEL 215-243-1600. FAX 215-243-1664.
(Co-sponsor: American Bar Association) index from
1967. (also avail. in microfiche from BHP)
 Description: Edited transcipt of the American Law
Institute's annual meeting, the American Law
Institute Annual Report and items of interest on ALI
and ALI-ABA projects.

340 US ISSN 0162-3397
K1
AMERICAN LAWYER. 1979. m. American Lawyer Media,
L.P. (New York), 600 Third Ave., New York, NY
10016. TEL 212-973-2800. FAX 212-972-6258.
Ed. Michael Orey. adv.; bk.rev.; circ. 18,000. (tabloid
format) Indexed: Access (1982-), C.L.I., L.R.I.,
Leg.Info.Manage.Ind., Leg.Per.
 Description: News and features about the legal
profession including the people and management
issues shaping the legal field.

340 US
AMERICAN LAWYER MANAGEMENT SERVICE. 1984. 3
base vols. (plus q. updates). $295 for set; q. update
$135. American Lawyer Media, L.P. (San Francisco),
625 Polk, Ste. 500, San Francisco, CA 94102.
TEL 415-749-5407. Ed. Sara Seigel.
 Description: Practical management advice for law
firm partners and adminstration.

374.75 US ISSN 0002-9874
AMERICAN MARITIME CASES. 1923. m. (except Aug.).
$685. American Maritime Cases, Inc., 28 E. 21st
St., Baltimore, MD 21218. TEL 410-752-2939.
FAX 410-625-1174. Ed. Elliot B. Nixon. index; circ.
1,064. (back issues avail.)
●Also available online. Vendor(s): Mead Data Central.

347 US ISSN 0044-7773
AMERICAN NOTARY. 1965. bi-m. $9. American Society
of Notaries, 918 16th St., N.W., Washington, DC
20006. TEL 202-955-6162. Ed. Eugene E. Hines.
adv.; bk.rev.; circ. 27,000. (also avail. in microform
from UMI)

**AMERICAN SOCIETY OF CORPORATE SECRETARIES. LOS
ANGELES CHAPTER. NEWSLETTER.** see *BUSINESS
AND ECONOMICS — Management*

340 US ISSN 0003-1453
LAW
AMERICAN UNIVERSITY LAW REVIEW. 1952. 4/yr. $30.
American University, Washington College of Law,
4400 Massachusetts Ave., N.W., Washington, DC
20016. TEL 202-885-2652. Ed. Kelly Grems. adv.;
bk.rev.; index; circ. 1,600. (also avail. in microform
from UMI) Indexed: C.L.I., CJPI, Crim.Just.Abstr.,
L.R.I., Leg.Cont., Leg.Per.
●Also available online. Vendor(s): WESTLAW.
—BLDSC shelfmark: 0858.070000.

342 940 US ISSN 0740-0470
**AMERICAN UNIVERSITY STUDIES. SERIES 10. POLITICAL
SCIENCE.** 1983. irreg. Peter Lang Publishing, Inc.,
62 W. 45th St., 4th Fl., New York, NY 10036.
TEL 212-302-6740. Ed. Kathryn Earle.
—BLDSC shelfmark: 0858.078400.

AMISTAD. see *HISTORY — History Of North And South
America*

340 GW
**AMTLICHE BEKANNTMACHUNGEN DER UNIVERSITAET
GESAMTHOCHSCHULE ESSEN.** 1972. m. Universitaet
Gesamthochschule Essen, Universitaetsstr. 2, 4300
Essen 1, Germany. TEL 0201-183-2075. circ. 500.

**AMTLICHES SCHULBLATT FUER DEN
REGIERUNGSBEZIRK DUESSELDORF.** see *EDUCATION*

340 AU ISSN 0003-2220
**AMTSBLATT DER OESTERREICHISCHEN
JUSTIZVERWALTUNG.** 1923. S.460.
(Bundesministerium fuer Justiz) Oesterreichische
Staatsdruckerei, Rennweg 12a, 1037 Vienna,
Austria. TEL 0222-787631. index; circ. 1,400.

349 GW ISSN 0003-2336
DER AMTSVORMUND. 1927. m. DM.60($33)
Deutsches Institut fuer Vormundschaftswesen,
Zaehringerstr. 10, Postfach 102020, 6900
Heidelberg, Germany. Ed. Walter Zarbock. adv.;
bk.rev.; circ. 1,500.
 Description: Discusses legal problems involving
minor children.

349 AG ISSN 0034-6985
LAW
ANALES DE LEGISLACION ARGENTINA. 1940. every 10
days (plus q. cum.). Arg.$150($600) Ediciones la
Ley S.A., 1471 Tucuman, Buenos Aires, Argentina.
adv.; abstr.; index, cum.index; circ. 11,000
(controlled).

ANALYSIS OF WORKERS' COMPENSATION LAWS. see
*BUSINESS AND ECONOMICS — Labor And Industrial
Relations*

340 US
ANDREWS ADVISOR; quarterly newsletter for law
librarians. 1989. q. Andrews Publications, 1646
West Chester Pike, Box 1000, Westtown, PA
19395. TEL 215-399-6600. FAX 215-399-6610.

ANESTHESIA MALPRACTICE PROTECTOR. see *MEDICAL
SCIENCES — Anaesthesiology*

ANESTHESIOLOGY MALPRACTICE REPORTER. see
MEDICAL SCIENCES

340 UK ISSN 0308-6569
K1
ANGLO-AMERICAN LAW REVIEW. 1972. q. £75
(typically set in Sep.). Barry Rose Law Periodicals,
East Row, Little London, Chichester, Sussex PO19
1PG, England. TEL 0243-787841.
FAX 0243-779278. Ed. Martin Partington. adv.;
bk.rev. Indexed: C.L.I., L.R.I., Leg.Cont., Leg.Per.
—BLDSC shelfmark: 0902.803000.
 Description: Covers major legal issues in the
United Kingdom and the United States and
throughout the common law world.

340 US
ANIMAL LAW REPORT. s-a. $10. American Bar
Association, Young Lawyers Division, 750 N. Lake
Shore Dr., Chicago, IL 60611. TEL 312-988-5555.
 Description: Summarizes recent legislation, case
decisions, and literature.

343 DK ISSN 0108-7169
ANKLAGEMYNDIGHEDENS AARSBERETNING. 1973. a.
free. Rigsadvokaturen, Rigspolitchefen, Porthusgade
3, 1213 Copenhagen K, Denmark. FAX 33-147008.
circ. 3,000.

340 BE ISSN 0770-6472
K1
ANNALES DE DROIT; revue trimestrielle de droit belge.
1965. q. 3300 Fr. Universite Catholique de Louvain,
Association des Anciens Etudiants de la Faculte de
Droit, 1348 Louvain-la-Neuve, Belgium.
FAX 217-41-75. adv.; bk.rev.; bibl.

340 PL ISSN 0458-4317
**ANNALES UNIVERSITATIS MARIAE CURIE-SKLODOWSKA.
SECTIO G. IUS.** (Text in English, French, German,
Polish; summaries in French, German, Polish) 1954.
a. price varies. Uniwersytet Marii Curie-Sklodowskiej,
Wydawnictwo, Pl. M. Curie-Sklodowskiej 5, 20-031
Lublin, Poland. TEL 48-81-375304.
FAX 48-81-336699. TELEX 0643223. Ed. W.
Skrzydlo. circ. 500. Indexed: Amer.Hist.& Life,
Hist.Abstr., World Agri.Econ.& Rural Sociol.Abstr.
—BLDSC shelfmark: 0962.200000.

**ANNALS OF AIR AND SPACE LAW/ANNALES DE DROIT
AERIEN ET SPATIAL.** see *AERONAUTICS AND SPACE
FLIGHT*

340 FR ISSN 0066-2658
ANNUAIRE DE LEGISLATION FRANCAISE ET ETRANGERE.
a. price varies. (Centre National de la Recherche
Scientifique, Service de Recherches Juridiques
Comparatives) Editions du C N R S, 1 Place Aristide
Briand, 92195 Meudon Cedex, France.
TEL 1-45-34-75-50. FAX 1-46-36-38-49. TELEX
LABOBEL 204 135 F. (Subscr. to: Presses du C N R
S, 20-22, rue Saint Amand, 75015 Paris, France.
TEL 1-45-33-16-00) adv.; bk.rev.; index; circ. 1,250
(controlled).
 Description: Studies on the evolution and
development of law in different countries.

340 630 US
ANNUAL AGRICULTURAL INSTITUTE. a. $47.50.
Hamline University School of Law, Advanced Legal
Education, 1536 Hewitt Ave., St. Paul, MN 55104.
TEL 612-641-2336. Ed.Bd.

ANNUAL INSTITUTE ON SECURITIES REGULATION. see
*BUSINESS AND ECONOMICS — Banking And
Finance*

ANNUAL REVIEW OF BANKING LAW. see *BUSINESS AND
ECONOMICS — Banking And Finance*

340 CN
ANNUAL REVIEW OF CRIMINAL LAW. 1982. a. Can.$72.
Carswell Publications, Corporate Plaza, 2075
Kennedy Rd., Scarborough, Ont. M1T 3V4, Canada.
TEL 416-609-8000. FAX 416-298-5094. Ed. Alan
D. Gold.
 Description: Covers important developments in
Canadian criminal law, practice and evidence.

340 US
ANNUAL REVIEW OF POVERTY LAW. a. $6. National
Clearinghouse for Legal Services, Inc., 407 S.
Dearborn, Ste. 400, Chicago, IL 60605.
TEL 312-939-3830.

340   UK   ISSN 0066-4405
ANNUAL SURVEY OF AFRICAN LAW. 1970. a. price varies. Rex Collings Ltd., 6 Paddington St., London W.1., England. Eds. N.N. Rubin, E. Cotran. index.

345   US   ISSN 0066-4413
KF178
ANNUAL SURVEY OF AMERICAN LAW. 1945. a. price varies. (New York University, Law Publications) Oceana Publications, Inc., 75 Main St., Dobbs Ferry, New York, NY 10522. TEL 914-693-1320. FAX 914-693-0402. circ. 800. (back issues avail.) **Indexed:** C.L.I., L.R.I., Leg.Per.
—BLDSC shelfmark: 1534.905000.
  Description: Focuses on developments and issues which affect the legal system in America.

340   AT   ISSN 0727-4076
K1
ANNUAL SURVEY OF AUSTRALIAN LAW. 1976. a. price varies. Law Book Co. Ltd., 44-50 Waterloo Rd., North Ryde, N.S.W. 2113, Australia. TEL 02-887-0177. FAX 02-888-9706. TELEX ASBOOK 27995. Eds. R. Baxt, G. Kewley. **Indexed:** Leg.Per.
  Description: Presents developments in major areas of Australian law.

340   US
ANNUAL SURVEY OF BANKRUPTCY LAW. 1979. a. $98.50. Callaghan & Co., 155 Pfingsten Rd., Deerfield, IL 60015. TEL 800-323-1336. Ed. William L. Norton. index. (back issues avail.)

340   II   ISSN 0570-2666
LAW
ANNUAL SURVEY OF INDIAN LAW. (Text in English) 1965. a. $16. Indian Law Institute, Bhagwandas Rd., New Delhi 110001, India. bibl.
—BLDSC shelfmark: 1534.913000.

ANNUARIO EUROPEO DELL'AMBIENTE. see *ENVIRONMENTAL STUDIES*

340   UK   ISSN 0262-3234
ANTHONY AND BERRYMAN'S MAGISTRATES' COURT GUIDE. a. $51. Butterworth & Co. (Publishers) Ltd. (Subsidiary of: Reed International PLC), 88 Kingsway, London WC2B 6AB, England. TEL 71-405-6900. FAX 71-405-1332. TELEX 95678. (US addr.: Butterworth Legal Publishers, 90 Stiles Rd., Salem, NH 03079. TEL 800-548-4001) Ed. A.P. Carr.
—BLDSC shelfmark: 1542.399500.

353.73   US   ISSN 0162-7996
KF1632
ANTITRUST. 1978. 3/yr. $22 (foreign $27). American Bar Association, Antitrust Law Section, 750 N. Lake Shore Dr., Chicago, IL 60611. TEL 312-988-5555. **Indexed:** C.L.I.
●Also available online. Vendor(s): WESTLAW (ANTITR).
  Description: Informs members of Section calendar, upcoming publications, and developments in antitrust law.

347.7   US
ANTITRUST ADVISER, 3-E. irreg. $95. Shepard's - McGraw-Hill, Inc., Box 35300, Colorado Springs, CO 80935-3530. TEL 800-525-2474.
  Description: Pragmatic discussions of the Sherman Act, the Clayton Act, the Robinson-Patman Act and the Federal Trade Commission Act.

347.7   US
ANTITRUST AND AMERICAN BUSINESS ABROAD, 2-E. 1981. 2 base vols. (plus a. suppl.) $210. Shepard's - McGraw-Hill, Inc., Box 35300, Colorado Springs, CO 80935-3530. TEL 800-525-2474.
  Description: For litigants, counselors and scholars. Reflects the sweeping changes taking place in American law related to the worldwide issues of antitrust.

347.7   US
ANTITRUST & COMMERCE REPORT. 1974. 10/yr. $145. National Association of Attorneys General, 444 N. Capitol St., N.W., Ste. 403, Washington, DC 20001. TEL 202-628-0435. Ed. Elena Boisuert. index; circ. 250. (back issues avail.)

ANTITRUST & TRADE REGULATION REPORT. see *BUSINESS AND ECONOMICS — Production Of Goods And Services*

347.7   US   ISSN 0003-603X
K1   CODEN: ATBUAU
ANTITRUST BULLETIN. 1955. q. $85 to individuals; academic & government personnel $52. Federal Legal Publications, Inc., 157 Chambers St., New York, NY 10007. TEL 212-619-4949. Ed. William J. Curran, III. adv.; bk.rev.; bibl.; charts; cum.index: 1955-1977; circ. 2,000. (also avail. in microfilm from UMI; back issues avail.; reprint service avail. from UMI) **Indexed:** ABI Inform., Abstr.Bk.Rev.Curr.Leg.Per., BPIA, Bus.Ind., C.L.I., C.R.E.J., J.of Econ.Lit., L.R.I., Leg.Per., P.A.I.S., SCIMP, Tr.& Indus.Ind.
—BLDSC shelfmark: 1552.400000.

347.7   US
ANTITRUST COUNSELING AND LITIGATION TECHNIQUES. 1984. 4 base vols., with a. supplements. Matthew Bender & Co., Inc., 11 Penn Plaza, New York, NY 10001. TEL 212-967-7707. (looseleaf format)
  Description: Practical guide to corporate antitrust counseling and successful antitrust litigation, complementing von Kalinowski's treatise on antitrust.

ANTITRUST FREEDOM OF INFORMATION LOG. see *BUSINESS AND ECONOMICS — International Commerce*

347.7 338.8   US   ISSN 0003-6048
ANTITRUST LAW AND ECONOMICS REVIEW. 1967. q. $87.50. Antitrust Law and Economics Review, Inc., Beach P.O. Box 3532, Vero Beach, FL 32964-9990. Ed. Charles E. Mueller. bk.rev. **Indexed:** ABI Inform., B.P.I., BPIA, Bus.Ind., C.L.I., C.R.E.J., L.R.I., Leg.Per., P.A.I.S.

340   US   ISSN 0738-5919
KF1632.5
ANTITRUST LAW HANDBOOK. 1984. a. $79.50. Clark - Boardman - Callaghan Company, Ltd., 375 Hudson St., New York, NY 10014. TEL 212-929-7500. FAX 212-924-0460. Ed. Robert Bouchard.

347.7   US   ISSN 0003-6056
LAW
ANTITRUST LAW JOURNAL. 1968. 3/yr. $30 (foreign $35). American Bar Association, Antitrust Law Section, 750 N. Lake Shore Dr., Chicago, IL 60611. TEL 312-988-5605. Ed. Tina Miller. cum.index: 1960-1967, 1968-1980; circ. 15,000. (also avail. in microfilm from RRI; reprint service avail. from RRI) **Indexed:** C.L.I., L.R.I., Leg.Cont., Leg.Per., Tr.& Indus.Ind.
●Also available online. Vendor(s): Mead Data Central, WESTLAW (ANTITRLJ).
—BLDSC shelfmark: 1552.800000.
  Description: Covers meeting proceedings, section reports and positions on legislation, especially those of the national institutes on anti-trust law.

347.7   US
ANTITRUST LAWS AND TRADE REGULATION. (Issued with Antitrust Laws and Trade Regulation Newsletter) 1969. 4/yr. Matthew Bender & Co., Inc., 11 Penn Plaza, New York, NY 10001. TEL 212-967-7707. (looseleaf format)
  Description: Detailed treatise on antitrust.

340   US
ANTITRUST LAWS AND TRADE REGULATION: DESK EDITION. 1981. 2 base vols. (plus irreg. supplements). Matthew Bender & Co., Inc., 11 Penn Plaza, New York, NY 10001. TEL 212-967-7707. (looseleaf format)
  Description: Examines the essence of von Kalinowski's master treatise.

340   UY
ANUARIO DE DERECHO CIVIL URUGUAYO. 1970. a. $40. Fundacion de Cultura Universitaria, 25 de Mayo, No. 568, Casilla de Correo No. 1155, Montevideo, Uruguay. TEL 961152. FAX 962540.

340 320   SP
ANUARIO DE DERECHO PUBLICO Y ESTUDIOS POLITICOS. 1988. a. 2500 ptas. Universidad de Granada, Servicio de Publicaciones, Antiguo Colegio Maximo, Campus de Cartuja, 18071 Granada, Spain. TEL 281356.

340   MX   ISSN 0185-3295
ANUARIO JURIDICO. 1974. a. $30. Universidad Nacional Autonoma de Mexico, Instituto de Investigaciones Juridicas, Ciudad Universitaria, Delegacion Coyoacan, 04510 Mexico, DF, Mexico. Ed. Eugenio Hurtado Marquez. adv.; bk.rev.; abstr.; bibl.; index.

340   MX
ANUARIO MEXICANO DE HISTORIA DEL DERECHO. 1989. a. $20. Universidad Nacional Autonoma de Mexico, Instituto de Investigaciones Juridicas, Ciudad Universitaria, Coyoacan, 04510 Mexico D.F., Mexico.

340   GW   ISSN 0171-7227
ANWALTSBLATT. 1950. m. DM.165. (Deutscher Anwaltverein e.V.) Deutscher Anwaltverlag GmbH, Bocholder 259, 4300 Essen, Germany. TEL 0201-611114. Ed. P. Hamacher. adv.; bk.rev.; stat.; index; circ. 26,000.

AOYAMA JOURNAL OF SOCIAL SCIENCES/AOYAMA SHAKAI KAGAKU KIYO. see *SOCIAL SCIENCES: COMPREHENSIVE WORKS*

APARTMENT AGE; the voice of the industry. see *HOUSING AND URBAN PLANNING*

346.066   US
APPEALS TO THE ELEVENTH CIRCUIT. 1984. 3 base vols. (plus suppl. 2-3/yr.). $120. Butterworth Legal Publishers (Salem) (Subsidiary of: Reed International PLC), 90 Stiles Rd., Salem, NH 03079. TEL 800-548-4001. FAX 603-898-9858. (looseleaf format)

346.066   US
APPEALS TO THE FIFTH CIRCUIT. 1977. 2 base vols. (plus suppl. 1-2/yr.). $150. Butterworth Legal Publishers (Salem) (Subsidiary of: Reed International PLC), 90 Stiles Rd., Salem, NH 03079. TEL 800-548-4001. FAX 603-898-9858. (looseleaf format)

346.066   US
APPEALS TO THE THIRD CIRCUIT. 1986. 2 base vols. (plus suppl.). $130. Butterworth Legal Publishers (Salem) (Subsidiary of: Reed International PLC), 90 Stiles Rd., Salem, MA 03079. TEL 800-548-4001. FAX 603-898-9858. (looseleaf format)

APPLIED COMPUTER AND COMMUNICATIONS LAW. see *COMPUTERS*

340   CN
APPORTIONMENT OF LIABILITY IN BRITISH COLUMBIA. 4/yr. Can.$160. Butterworths Canada Ltd., 75 Clegg Rd., Markham, Ont. L6G 1A1, Canada. TEL 416-479-2665. FAX 416-479-2826. (looseleaf format)
  Description: Practical digest of all the British Columbia cases that address liability in motor vehicle accidents.

340   CE
AQUINAS LAW JOURNAL. (Text in English) 1972. irreg. Rs.15. Aquinas College of Higher Studies, Colombo 8, Sri Lanka.

340 300   SP
▼**ARANZADI SOCIAL.** (Includes bound vols. with indexes.) 1991. w. 56000 ptas. (effective 1991). Editorial Aranzadi, S.A., Avda. Carlos III, 34, Apdo. 111, 31080 Pamplona, Spain. TEL 948-331212. FAX 948-330919. index.

ARBEIT UND ARBEITSRECHT; Zeitschrift fuer betriebliche Praxis. see *BUSINESS AND ECONOMICS — Labor And Industrial Relations*

347.9 331   GW   ISSN 0003-7648
ARBEIT UND RECHT; Zeitschrift fuer Arbeitsrechtspraxis. 1953. m. DM.132. (Deutscher Gewerkschaftsbund) Bund-Verlag GmbH, Hansestr. 63a, Postfach 900840, 5000 Cologne 90, Germany. Ed. Albert Gnade. adv.; bk.rev.; index; circ. 3,600. **Indexed:** P.A.I.S.For.Lang.Ind.

340   GW   ISSN 0934-7100
ARBEITSRECHT-BLATTEI (A R); Handbuch fuer die Praxis. 1949. m. DM.487.80. Forkel Verlag GmbH, Felsenstr. 23, 6200 Wiesbaden 1, Germany. TEL 0611-42785. FAX 0611-419575. Eds. Werner Oehmann, Thomas Dieterich. (looseleaf format; back issues avail.)
  Description: Compilation of verdicts and texts, with a list of reference texts.

ARBEITSRECHT DER GEGENWART. see *BUSINESS AND ECONOMICS — Labor And Industrial Relations*

ARBEITSRECHT IN STICHWORTEN; Arbeitsrechtliche Entscheidungssammlung. see *BUSINESS AND ECONOMICS — Labor And Industrial Relations*

ARBEJDSRETLIGT TIDSSKRIFT; arbejdsrettens domme, arbejdsretlige kendelser. see *BUSINESS AND ECONOMICS — Labor And Industrial Relations*

ARBITRATION INTERNATIONAL. see *BUSINESS AND ECONOMICS — Labor And Industrial Relations*

ARBITRATION JOURNAL. see *BUSINESS AND ECONOMICS — Labor And Industrial Relations*

349　　　　　　　GW　　ISSN 0003-8911
JA14
ARCHIV DES OEFFENTLICHEN RECHTS. 1886. q. DM.182. Verlag J.C.B. Mohr (Paul Siebeck), Wilhelmstr. 18, Postfach 2040, 7400 Tuebingen, Germany. TEL 07071-26064. FAX 07071-51104. TELEX 7262872-MOHR-D. Ed.Bd. adv.; bk.rev.; index. **Indexed:** A.B.C.Pol.Sci., INIS Atomind.
Description: All aspects of German public law.

341　　　　　　　GW　　ISSN 0003-892X
JX5
ARCHIV DES VOELKERRECHTS. 1948. q. DM.240. Verlag J.C.B. Mohr (Paul Siebeck), Wilhelmstr. 18, Postfach 2040, 7400 Tuebingen, Germany. TEL 07071-26064. FAX 07071-51104. TELEX 7262872-MOHR-D. Ed.Bd. adv.; bk.rev.; bibl.; index. **Indexed:** A.B.C.Pol.Sci., Amer.Hist.& Life, Hist.Abstr., INIS Atomind., Mar.Aff.Bibl., P.A.I.S.For.Lang.Ind.
Description: Analysis and reports on international public law court decisions.

349　　　　　　　GW　　ISSN 0003-8997
ARCHIV FUER DIE CIVILISTISCHE PRAXIS. 1828. bi-m. DM.204. Verlag J.C.B. Mohr (Paul Siebeck), Wilhelmstr. 18, Postfach 2040, 7400 Tuebingen, Germany. TEL 07071-26064. FAX 07071-51104. TELEX 7262872-MOHR-D. Ed.Bd.; bk.rev.; index, cum.index.
Description: Covers all aspects of German civil law.

340 070.43　　　　　GW　　ISSN 0341-5198
ARCHIV FUER PRESSERECHT; Zeitschrift fuer das gesamte Medienrecht. 1970. q. Handelsblatt GmbH, Kasernenstr. 67, 4000 Duesseldorf 1, Germany. TEL 0211-8870. Ed. Georg Wallraf. (reprint services avail. from SCH)

ARCHIV FUER RECHTS- UND SOZIALPHILOSOPHIE/ARCHIVES DE PHILOSOPHIE DU DROIT ET DE PHILOSOPHIE SOCIALE/ARCHIVES FOR PHILOSOPHY OF LAW AND SOCIAL PHILOSOPHY. see *PHILOSOPHY*

ARCHIV FUER RECHTS- UND SOZIALPHILOSOPHIE. BEIHEFTE. see *PHILOSOPHY*

340　　　　　　　FR　　ISSN 0066-6564
ARCHIVES DE PHILOSOPHIE DU DROIT. 1952. a. price varies. Editions Sirey-Diffusion Dalloz, 11 rue Soufflot, 75240 Paris Cedex 05, France. TEL 1-40-51-54-54. FAX 1-45-87-37-48. TELEX 206 446 F.

340 011　　　　　　IT　　ISSN 0391-5646
ARCHIVIO GIURIDICO. 1868. s-a. L.70000 (foreign L.90000). Mucchi Editore s.r.l., Via Emilia Est. 1527, 41100 Modena, Italy. Ed. Lorenzo Spinelli. adv. (back issues avail.)

340　　　　　　　PL　　ISSN 0066-6882
ARCHIVUM IURIDICUM CRACOVIENSE. (Text in English, French and German) 1968. a. price varies. (Polska Akademia Nauk, Oddzial w Krakowie, Komisja Nauk Prawnych) Ossolineum, Publishing House of the Polish Academy of Sciences, Rynek 9, Wroclaw, Poland. TELEX 0712771 OSS PL. (Dist. by: Ars Polona-Ruch, Krakowskie Przedmiescie 7, Warsaw, Poland) Ed. Franciszek Studnicki. circ. 600.
—BLDSC shelfmark: 1659.525000.
Description: Legal theory and jurisprudence, constitutional, administrative, civil, penal laws, law of labor, international laws, comparativistic studies.

L'ARGUS DE LA LEGISLATION LIBANAISE. see *PUBLIC ADMINISTRATION*

349　　　　　　　YU　　ISSN 0004-1270
ARHIV ZA PRAVNE I DRUSTVENE NAUKE. (Text in Serbo-Croatian; summaries in English) 1906. q. $20. Savez Udruzenja Pravnika Jugoslavije, Proleterskih Brigada 74, P.O. Box 179, Belgrade, Yugoslavia. TEL 11-452-848. Ed. Jovan Dordevic. adv.; bk.rev.; circ. 4,000. **Indexed:** Amer.Hist.& Life, Foreign Leg.Per., Hist.Abstr.

340　　　　　　　US　　ISSN 0004-1386
ARIZONA ADVOCATE. 1966. 6/yr. free to qualified personnel. University of Arizona, College of Law, Tucson, AZ 85721. TEL 602-626-1373. Ed. Sara L. Pratt. adv.; bk.rev.; illus.; circ. 6,200. (tabloid format; also avail. in microfilm; reprint service avail. from UMI)

348　　　　　　　US
ARIZONA APPEAL REPORTS. 1913. irreg. (Supreme Court) West Publishing Co., Box 64526, St. Paul, MN 55164-0526. TEL 800-328-9352.
Formerly: Report of Cases Argued and Determined in the Supreme Court of the State of Arizona.

340　　　　　　　US　　ISSN 1040-4090
K1
ARIZONA ATTORNEY. 1965. 11/yr. $30. State Bar of Arizona, 363 N. First Ave., Phoenix, AZ 85003. TEL 602-252-4804. FAX 602-271-4930. Ed. Patricia Gannon. adv.; bk.rev.; stat.; circ. 12,000. **Indexed:** C.L.I., L.R.I., Law Ofc.Info.Svc., Leg.Per.
Formerly: Arizona Bar Journal (ISSN 0004-1424)
Description: General interest publication for the Arizona legal profession.

614.7 340　　　　　US　　ISSN 1049-9342
▼**ARIZONA ENVIRONMENTAL LAW LETTER.** 1990. 12/yr. $147. M. Lee Smith Publishers & Printers, 162 Fourth Ave. N., Box 2678, Nashville, TN 37219. TEL 615-242-7395. FAX 615-256-6601. (Co-sponsor: Brown & Bain) Ed.Bd.
Description: Reports the latest Arizona environmental law developments that affect Arizona companies.

ARIZONA FARM BUREAU NEWS. see *AGRICULTURE*

340　　　　　　　US　　ISSN 0004-153X
K1
ARIZONA LAW REVIEW. 1959. 4/yr. $20. University of Arizona, College of Law, Tucson, AZ 85721. TEL 602-621-1764. FAX 602-621-9140. Ed. David Earl. adv.; bk.rev.; index; circ. 2,000. (also avail. in microform from UMI; reprint service avail. from RRI,UMI) **Indexed:** C.L.I., Crim.Just.Abstr., INIS Atomind., L.R.I., Leg.Cont., Leg.Per.
—BLDSC shelfmark: 1668.439000.

348　　　　　　　US　　ISSN 0094-4246
KFA2431
ARIZONA LEGISLATIVE SERVICE. Cover title: A R S Legislative Service. irreg. West Publishing Co., Box 64526, St. Paul, MN 55164-0526. TEL 800-328-9352.

340　　　　　　　US　　ISSN 0164-4297
K1
ARIZONA STATE LAW JOURNAL. 1969. q. $20. Arizona State University, College of Law, Tempe, AZ 85287. TEL 602-965-6287. Ed.Bd. adv.; bk.rev.; bibl.; circ. 1,500. (also avail. in microfilm from WSH,PMC) **Indexed:** C.L.I., L.R.I., Leg.Cont., Leg.Per., P.A.I.S. ●Also available online. Vendor(s): WESTLAW.
Supersedes: Law and the Social Order (ISSN 0023-9224)

340　　　　　　　US
ARKANSAS BAR ASSOCIATION. NEWS BULLETIN. 1975. bi-m. Arkansas Bar Association, 400 W. Markham, Little Rock, AR 72201. TEL 501-375-4605. Ed. Paige Beavers. circ. 4,000. (back issues avail.)

340　　　　　　　US　　ISSN 0004-1831
K1
ARKANSAS LAW REVIEW. 1946. q. $15 (foreign $17.50). University of Arkansas, School of Law, Waterman Hall, Fayetteville, AR 72701. TEL 501-575-5609. Ed. Charles E. Harris. adv.; bk.rev.; index; circ. 4,000. (also avail. in microfilm from WSH,PMC; back issues avail.; reprint service avail. from WSH) **Indexed:** C.L.I., L.R.I., Leg.Cont., Leg.Per.

340　　　　　　　US
ARKANSAS LAWYER. 1967. q. $15. Arkansas Bar Association, 400 W. Markham, Little Rock, AR 72201. TEL 501-375-4605. Ed. Paige Beavers. adv.; bk.rev.; charts; illus.; index; circ. 4,100. (back issues avail.) **Indexed:** C.L.I.

340　　　　　　　US
ARKANSAS REGISTER. 1977. m. $40. Office of the Secretary of State, State Capitol, Little Rock, AR 72201-1094. TEL 501-682-3578. FAX 501-682-1284. Ed. Ricky B. Hearne. cum.index: 1977-1985; circ. 300. (back issues avail.)

ARKANSAS REPORT. see *PUBLIC ADMINISTRATION*

ARKANSAS REPORT - WEEKLY LEGISLATIVE EDITION. see *PUBLIC ADMINISTRATION*

ARMCHAIR ARCHAEOLOGIST. see *ARCHAEOLOGY*

340　　　　　　　US　　ISSN 0364-1287
KF7209.A1
ARMY LAWYER. 1971. m. $24. U.S. Army, Judge Advocate General's School, Charlottesville, VA 22903-1781. TEL 804-972-6395. (Orders to: Supt. of Documents, Washington, DC 20402) Ed. Benjamin T. Kash. index; circ. 7,600. (also avail. in microform from MIM,UMI) **Indexed:** C.L.I., Ind.U.S.Gov.Per., L.R.I., Leg.Cont., Leg.Per.
Description: Articles of interest to attorneys practicing military law.

343　　　　　　　US　　ISSN 8755-8300
KF9625.A59
ARREST LAW BULLETIN.* m. $39.95. Quinlan Publishing Co., Inc., 23 Drydock Ave, 2nd Fl., Boston, MA 02210-2307. Ed. E. Michael Quinlan. (also avail. in microform from UMI) **Indexed:** CJPI.

349　　　　　　　NE　　ISSN 0004-2870
ARS AEQUI; juridisch studentenblad. 1950. 11/yr. fl.47.85 (students fl.34.65). Stichting Ars Aequi, Postbus 1043, 6501 BA Nijmegen, Netherlands. TEL 080-223506. FAX 080-241108. Ed. E. Thissen. adv.; bk.rev.; index; circ. 28,000. **Indexed:** Excerp.Med.

340　　　　　　　US
ARSON REPORTER; arson cases and legislation. m. $15. American Bar Association, Young Lawyers Division, 750 N. Lake Shore Dr., Chicago, IL 60611. TEL 312-988-5555.
Description: Reports on court decisions pertaining to arson and legislation at both the state and national level.

340 001.535　　　　NE　　ISSN 0924-8463
▼**ARTIFICIAL INTELLIGENCE AND THE LAW**; an international journal. 1992. 4/yr. Kluwer Academic Publishers, Postbus 17, 3300 AA Dordrecht, Netherlands. TEL 078-334911. FAX 078-334254. TELEX 29245. (Dist. by: Kluwer Academic Publishers Group, P.O. Box 322, 3300 AH Dordrecht, Netherlands; N. America dist. addr.: Box 358, Accord Sta., Hingham, MA 02018-0358. TEL 617-871-6600) Eds. Donald H. Berman, Carole D. Hafner.

ARZTRECHT; Kompendium des Gesamten Rechtes der Medizin. see *MEDICAL SCIENCES*

340 613.62　　　　　US
ASBESTOS CASE LAW QUARTERLY. q. $85. Butterworth Legal Publishers (Salem), 90 Stiles Rd., Salem, NH 03079. TEL 800-548-4001. FAX 603-898-9858. Ed. Jerry Nates.

340　　　　　　　US　　ISSN 0273-3048
KF1297.A73
ASBESTOS LITIGATION REPORTER; the national journal of record of asbestos litigation. 1979. s-m. $900. Andrews Publications, 1646 West Chester Pike, Box 1000, Westtown, PA 19395. TEL 215-399-6600. FAX 215-399-6610. Ed. Thomas M. Hennessey. abstr.; bibl.; stat.; s-a. index. (looseleaf format; back issues avail.)
Description: Focuses on the most recent developments in suits alleging personal injuries from exposure to asbestos. Reports selected developments in suits brought to recover the cost of removing or encapsulating asbestos building materials.

340　　　　　　　　US
▼ASBESTOS M D L 875 UPDATE. 1991. s-m. $650. Andrews Publications, 1646 West Chester Pike, Box 1000, Westtown, PA 19395. FAX 215-399-6610. Ed. Thomas Hennessey. bibl.; stat.; s-a. index. (looseleaf format; back issues avail.)
  Description: Covers developments in the consolidated pretrial proceedings pending in Philadelphia before US District Court Judge Charles R. Weiner.

340　　　　　　　　US　　ISSN 1041-5130
KF1950.A59
ASBESTOS PROPERTY LITIGATION REPORTER; the national journal of asbestos property litigation. 1988. s-m. $650. Andrews Publications, 1646 West Chester Pike, Box 1000, Westtown, PA 19395. TEL 215-399-6600. FAX 215-399-6610. Ed. Jay Steinberg. abstr.; bibl.; stat.; s-a. index. (looseleaf format; back issues avail.)
  Description: Covers current developments in suits brought to recover the cost of removing or encapsulating asbestos-containing building materials.

340 614.7　　　　US　　ISSN 1055-9493
KF3964.A73
▼ASBESTOS REGULATORY REPORTER - NEW YORK EDITION; reports decision by NYC Environmental Control Board in actions by NYC to enforce Asbestos Control Code. 1990. m. $425. Andrews Publications, 1646 West Chester Pike, Box 1000, Westtown, PA 19395. TEL 215-399-6600. FAX 215-399-6610. Ed. Michael Rinker. bibl.; stat.; s-a. index. (looseleaf format; back issues avail.)

340　　　　　　　　HK　　ISSN 1015-5562
▼ASIA LAW & PRACTICE. (Text in English) 1992. 10/yr. HK.$2450($315) Asia Law & Practice Ltd., 2-F, 29 Hollywood Rd., Central, Hong Kong. TEL 852-544-9918. FAX 852-543-7617.
  —BLDSC shelfmark: 1742.249100.

340　　　　　　　　UY　　ISSN 0376-5024
ASOCIACION DE ESCRIBANOS DEL URUGUAY. REVISTA. 1904. s-a. price varies. Asociacion de Escribanos del Uruguay, Av. 18 de Julio 1730, Piso 11, Montevideo, Uruguay. TEL 40-64-00. FAX 41-06-37. Ed. Gerardo Rocca Couture. bk.rev.; bibl.; index; circ. 5,000.
  Description: Covers all matters of Uruguyan law.

ASSET BASED FINANCING: A TRANSACTIONAL GUIDE. see BUSINESS AND ECONOMICS — Banking And Finance

ASSIA. see MEDICAL SCIENCES

340　　　　　　　　US
ASSOCIATION OF AMERICAN LAW SCHOOLS. NEWSLETTER. 1964. 5/yr. $30. Association of American Law Schools, 1201 Connecticut Ave., N.W., Ste. 800, Washington, DC 20036. TEL 202-296-8851. Ed. Carl Monk. circ. controlled. (processed)

346　　　　　　　　US　　ISSN 0066-9407
ASSOCIATION OF AMERICAN LAW SCHOOLS. PROCEEDINGS. 1901. a. $10 per no. Association of American Law Schools, 1201 Connecticut Ave., N.W., Ste. 800, Washington, DC 20036. TEL 202-296-8851. Ed. Jan Kulick. cum.index: 50 yr. (processed; also avail. in microfiche from BHP)

ASSOCIATION OF FOOD AND DRUG OFFICIALS. JOURNAL. see FOOD AND FOOD INDUSTRIES

340　　　　　　　　US　　ISSN 0004-5837
ASSOCIATION OF THE BAR OF THE CITY OF NEW YORK. RECORD. 1946. 8/yr. $55. Association of the Bar of the City of New York, 42 W. 44th St., New York, NY 10036. TEL 212-382-6650. FAX 212-398-6634. Ed.Bd. adv.; bibl.; index, cum.index every 3 yrs.; circ. 19,400. (also avail. in microform from UMI; microfiche from WSH; reprint service avail. from UMI) Indexed: C.L.I., L.R.I., Law Ofc.Info.Svc., Leg.Info.Manage.Ind., Leg.Per., P.A.I.S.
  —BLDSC shelfmark: 7313.500000.

340　　　　　　　　CN
ATLANTIC PROVINCES REPORTERS. 1974. irreg. Can.$67 per vol. Maritime Law Book Ltd., Box 302, Fredericton, N.B. E3B 4Y9, Canada. TEL 506-454-9921. (back issues avail.)

ATOMIC ENERGY LAW JOURNAL. see ENERGY — Nuclear Energy

340　　　　　　　　US
ATTORNEY FEE AWARDS. base vol. (plus s-a. suppl.). $95 price varies. Shepard's - McGraw-Hill, Inc., Box 35300, Colorado Springs, CO 80935-3530. TEL 800-525-2474.
  Description: Analysis of federal fee opinion and fee award precedents.

340　　　　　　　　US
▼ATTORNEY FEES IN WASHINGTON; annotated statutes, cases and commentary. 1991. base vol. (plus irreg. suppl.). $85. Butterworth Legal Publishers (Salem) (Subsidiary of: Reed International PLC), 90 Stiles Rd., Salem, NH 03079. TEL 800-548-4001. FAX 603-898-9858. Ed. Philip A. Talmadge. (looseleaf format)
  Description: Complete guide to the granting or allowing of attorney fees in Washington. Contains statutes from the Washington State code concerning attorneys fees along with annotations, case summaries, and helpful commentary.

340　　　　　　　　US
ATTORNEY'S FEES IN FLORIDA. 1989. 3 base vols. (plus suppl.). $120. Butterworth Legal Publishers (Salem) (Subsidiary of: Reed International PLC), 90 Stiles Rd., Salem, MA 03079. TEL 800-548-4001. FAX 603-898-9858. (looseleaf format)

ATTORNEYS MARKETING REPORT. see BUSINESS AND ECONOMICS — Marketing And Purchasing

ATTORNEYS PERSONNEL REPORT. see BUSINESS AND ECONOMICS — Personnel Management

346　　　　　　　　NZ　　ISSN 0067-0510
K1
AUCKLAND UNIVERSITY LAW REVIEW. 1967. a. NZ.$15. Auckland University Law Students Society, Inc., Private Bag, Auckland, New Zealand. FAX 64-9-33429. Eds. Andrew Simester, Bruce McLintoch. adv.; bk.rev.; circ. 1,500. Indexed: C.L.I., L.R.I., Leg.Per.

340　　　　　　　　US
AUDIO LAWYER. 8/yr. $99. American Law Institute, Committee on Continuing Professional Education, 4025 Chestnut St., Philadelphia, PA 19104. TEL 215-243-1697. FAX 215-243-1664. (Co-sponsor: American Bar Association) Ed. William S. Stevens. circ. 125. (audio cassette)
  Description: Articles of practical interest to the general practitioner.

340　　　　　　　　US
▼AUDIO LITIGATOR. 1990. q. $75. American Law Institute, Committee on Continuing Professional Education, 4025 Chestnut St., Philadelphia, PA 19104. TEL 215-243-1697. FAX 215-243-1664. (Co-sponsor: American Bar Association) Ed. William S. Stevens. circ. 60. (audio cassette)
  Description: Articles of practical interest to litigation attorneys.

340 333.33　　　　US
AUDIO REAL ESTATE LAWYER. 4/yr. $75. American Law Institute, Committee on Continuing Professional Education, 4025 Chesnut St., Philadelphia, PA 19104. TEL 215-243-1697. FAX 215-243-1664. (Co-sponsor: American Bar Association) Ed. William S. Stevens. circ. 200. (audio cassette)
  Description: Collection of articles of practical interest to attorneys specializing in real estate.

AUSSENWIRTSCHAFTSRECHT (YEAR); Einfuehrung - Fundstellen - Vorschriftentexte. see BUSINESS AND ECONOMICS — International Commerce

328.94 328.9　　　　AT
AUSTRALASIAN AND PACIFIC REGIONAL PARLIAMENTARY SEMINAR. SUMMARY REPORT OF PROCEEDINGS. 1972. biennial. free. Commonwealth Parliamentary Association, Regional Secretariat, Canberra, A.C.T. 2600, Australia. TEL 61-62-774340. FAX 61-62-772000. TELEX 61884 PRO. circ. 250.
  Former titles: Australasian and Pacific Parliamentary Seminar. Summary Report of Proceedings; (until 1980): Australia Parliamentary Seminar. Summary Report of Proceedings.

340　　　　　　　　AT　　ISSN 0312-6994
AUSTRALIA. LAW REFORM COMMISSION. ANNUAL REPORT. 1975. a. price varies. Australian Government Publishing Service, G.P.O. Box 84, Canberra, A.C.T. 2601, Australia. FAX 061-957295. TELEX AA62013. (back issues avail.) Indexed: Aus.Leg.Mon.Dig.

340　　　　　　　　AT　　ISSN 0814-5733
AUSTRALIAN AND NEW ZEALAND CITATOR TO UK REPORTS. CUMULATIVE SUPPLEMENT. 1973. a. Aus.$93. Butterworths Pty. Ltd., 271-273 Lane Cove Rd., North Ryde, N.S.W. 2113, Australia. TEL 02-335-4444. FAX 02-335-4655. Eds. Kingsley Siebel, Helen Findlay. (back issues avail.)
  Description: Covers law reports of the United Kingdom.

340　　　　　　　　AT
AUSTRALIAN AND NEW ZEALAND EQUAL OPPORTUNITY LAW AND PRACTICE. (In 2 vols.) 1984. bi-m. C C H Australia Ltd., P.O. Box 230, North Ryde, N.S.W. 2113, Australia. TEL 02-888-2555. FAX 02-888-7324.
  Description: Includes guidelines issued by various boards and authorities.

AUSTRALIAN AND NEW ZEALAND INSURANCE REPORTER. see INSURANCE

230　　　　　　　　AT
AUSTRALIAN BANKRUPTCY LEGISLATION. 1989. irreg., as required for all legislative changes. C C H Australia Ltd., P.O. Box 230, North Ryde, N.S.W. 2113, Australia. TEL 02-888-2555. FAX 02-888-7324.

340　　　　　　　　AT　　ISSN 0814-8589
K1
AUSTRALIAN BAR REVIEW. 1986. 3/yr. Aus.$135. Butterworths Pty. Ltd., P.O. Box 345, North Ryde, N.S.W. 2113, Australia. TEL 02-335-4444. FAX 02-335-4655.

AUSTRALIAN BUSINESS LAW REVIEW. see LAW — Corporate Law

340　　　　　　　　AT
AUSTRALIAN CASE CITATOR. 1983. 5/yr. Aus.$120. Law Book Co. Ltd., 44-50 Waterloo Rd., North Ryde, N.S.W. 2113, Australia. TEL 02-887-0177. FAX 02-888-9796. TELEX ASBOOK 27995. Ed.Bd.
  Description: Contains the most recent case citations, covering almost the entire length of Australian reporting.

340　　　　　　　　AT
AUSTRALIAN COMPANY PRACTICE. q. (plus bi-w. bulletin). $315. Butterworths Pty. Ltd., 271-273 Lane Cove Rd., P.O. Box 345, North Ryde, N.S.W. 2113, Australia. TEL 02-335-4444. FAX 02-335-4655.

347 330　　　　AT
AUSTRALIAN CONSUMER SALES AND CREDIT LAW REPORTER. (In 4 vols.) 1978. 12/yr. C C H Australia Ltd., P.O. Box 230, North Ryde, N.S.W. 2113, Australia. TEL 888-2555. FAX 02-888-7324. charts.

346.066　　　　　　AT
▼AUSTRALIAN CONTRACT LAW REPORTER. (In 2 vols.) 1991. q. C C H Australia Ltd., P.O. Box 230, North Ryde, N.S.W. 2113, Australia. TEL 02-888-2555. FAX 02-888-7324.
  Description: Includes case reporting.

340　　　　　　　　AT
AUSTRALIAN CORPORATION LAW. 6 base vols. (plus updates every 3 weeks). $745. Butterworths Pty. Ltd., 271-273 Lane Cove Rd., P.O. Box 345, North Ryde, N.S.W. 2113, Australia. TEL 02-335-4444. FAX 02-335-4655. (looseleaf format)
  Formerly: Australian Company Law.

AUSTRALIAN CRIMINAL REPORTS. see CRIMINOLOGY AND LAW ENFORCEMENT

340　　　　　　　　AT
AUSTRALIAN CURRENT LAW LEGISLATION. (Annual cumulation avail.) 1963. m. price on application. Butterworths Pty. Ltd., 271-273 Lane Cove Rd., North Ryde, N.S.W. 2113, Australia. TEL 02-335-4444. FAX 02-335-4655. Ed. F. Smith. bk.rev.
  Supersedes in part: Australian Current Law (ISSN 0045-0405)

LAW

340 AT
AUSTRALIAN CURRENT LAW REPORTER. 1963. fortn. Butterworths Pty. Ltd., 271-273 Lane Cove Rd., North Ryde, N.S.W. 2113, Australia. TEL 02-335-4444. FAX 02-335-4655.
Supersedes in part: Australian Current Law (ISSN 0045-0405)

340 382 AT
▼**AUSTRALIAN CUSTOMS LAW AND PRACTICE.** 1990. 10/yr. C C H Australia Ltd., P.O. Box 230, North Ryde, N.S.W. 2113, Australia. TEL 02-888-2555. FAX 02-888-7324.

340 AT
AUSTRALIAN DE FACTO RELATIONSHIPS LAW. 1985. bi-m. C C H Australia Ltd., P.O. Box 230, North Ryde, N.S.W. 2113, Australia. TEL 02-888-2555. FAX 02-888-7324.
Description: Includes case reporting.

346 AT ISSN 0067-1843
AUSTRALIAN DIGEST. 1988. irreg. price varies. Law Book Co. Ltd., 44-50 Waterloo Rd., North Ryde, N.S.W. 2113, Australia. TEL 02-887-0177. FAX 02-888-9706. TELEX ASBOOK 27995. Ed. J. Benett.
Incorporates: Australian Digest Annual Supplement (ISSN 0813-5959)

340 AT ISSN 1034-3059
AUSTRALIAN DISPUTE RESOLUTION JOURNAL. q. Aus.$132. Law Book Co. Ltd., 44-50 Waterloo Rd., North Ryde, N.S.W 2113, Australia. TEL 02-887-0177. FAX 02-888-9706. TELEX ASBOOK 27995. Eds. Micheline Dewdney, Ruth Charlton.
Description: Discusses and promotes the use of alternative dispute resolution processes in Australia and New Zealand.

340 AT
AUSTRALIAN HEALTH AND MEDICAL LAW REPORTER. 1988. bi-m. C C H Australia Ltd., P.O. Box 230, North Ryde, N.S.W. 2113, Australia. TEL 02-888-2555. FAX 02-888-7324.

342 AT
AUSTRALIAN HIGH COURT AND FEDERAL COURT PRACTICE. (In 2 vols.) 1980. every 6 weeks. C C H Australia Ltd., P.O. Box 230, North Ryde, N.S.W. 2113, Australia. TEL 888-2555. FAX 02-888-7324. charts.

340 336 AT
AUSTRALIAN INCOME TAX RULINGS. (In 3 vols.) 1983. fortn. C C H Australia Ltd., P.O. Box 230, North Ryde, N.S.W. 2113, Australia. TEL 02-888-2555. FAX 02-888-7324.

340 338 AT
AUSTRALIAN INDUSTRIAL AND INTELLECTUAL PROPERTY. (In 2 vols.) 1983. every 3 weeks. C C H Australia Ltd., P.O. Box 230, North Ryde, N.S.W. 2113, Australia. TEL 02-888-2555. FAX 02-888-7324.
Description: Includes full text case reporting of all court and patent office decisions.

AUSTRALIAN INDUSTRIAL SAFETY, HEALTH & WELFARE. see *OCCUPATIONAL HEALTH AND SAFETY*

340 336 AT
AUSTRALIAN INTERNATIONAL TAX AGREEMENTS. (In 2 vols.) 1982. irreg. C C H Australia Ltd., P.O. Box 230, North Ryde, N.S.W. 2113, Australia. TEL 02-888-2555. FAX 02-888-7324.

340 AT ISSN 0729-3356
K1
AUSTRALIAN JOURNAL OF LAW AND SOCIETY. 1982. a. Aus.$12 to individuals; institutions Aus.$16. School of Law, Macquarie University, Sydney, N.S.W. 2109, Australia. FAX 612-805-7686. TELEX MACUNI AA122377. adv.; bk.rev.; circ. 500. (back issues avail.) **Indexed:** C.L.I., Leg.Per.
—BLDSC shelfmark: 1809.140000.

340 AT ISSN 0004-9611
LAW
AUSTRALIAN LAW JOURNAL. 1927. m. Aus.$265. Law Book Co. Ltd., 44-50 Waterloo Rd., North Ryde, N.S.W. 2113, Australia. TEL 02-887-01776. FAX 02-888-9706. TELEX ASBOOK 27995. bk.rev.; index, cum.index; circ. 7,400. **Indexed:** Aus.P.A.I.S., C.L.I., Curr.Aus.N.Z.Leg.Lit.Ind., L.R.I., Leg.Cont., Leg.Per., Refug.Abstr.
—BLDSC shelfmark: 1813.300000.
Description: Contains advance reports of High Court cases, including headnotes and the full text of reasons for decisions.

340 AT ISSN 0159-7531
AUSTRALIAN LAW NEWS. 1964. m. Aus.$49. Law Council of Australia, G.P.O. Box 1989, Canberra, A.C.T. 2601, Australia. TEL 062 47-3788. FAX 062-480-639. Ed. Barrie Virtue. adv.; bk.rev.; circ. 26,784. (back issues avail.)
Formerly: Law Council of Australia. Law Council Newsletter (ISSN 0047-4177)
Description: Covers activities of the Law Council of Australia, national issues of interest to lawyers, case reports and more.

348 AT ISSN 0310-0014
LAW
AUSTRALIAN LAW REPORTS. fortn. Aus.$110. Butterworths Pty. Ltd., 271-273 Lane Cove Rd., North Ryde, N.S.W. 2113, Australia. TEL 02-335-4444. FAX 02-335-4655.

340 658.3 AT
AUSTRALIAN LEAVE AND HOLIDAYS PRACTICE MANUAL. 1981. q. C C H Australia Ltd., P.O. Box 230, North Ryde, N.S.W. 2113, Australia. TEL 02-888-2555. FAX 02-888-7324.

AUSTRALIAN LEGAL DIRECTORY. see *BUSINESS AND ECONOMICS — Trade And Industrial Directories*

340 AT ISSN 0004-9646
AUSTRALIAN LEGAL MONTHLY DIGEST. 1967. m. Aus.$420. Law Book Co. Ltd., 44-50 Waterloo Rd., North Ryde, N.S.W. 2113, Australia. TEL 02-887-0177. FAX 02-888-9706. TELEX ASBOOK 27995. Ed.Bd. adv.; bk.rev.; illus.; index; circ. 3,500.
Description: Covers Australian case law and legislation.

340 AT ISSN 0728-6309
LAW
AUSTRALIAN PLANNING APPEAL DECISIONS. 1980. irreg. (approx. 16/yr.). price varies. Law Book Co. Ltd., 44-50 Waterloo Rd., North Ryde, N.S.W. 2113, Australia. TEL 02-887-0177. FAX 02-888-9706. TELEX ASBOOK 27995. Ed. Carolyn May. (back issues avail.)
Description: Covers all planning and environmental appeal decisions.

340 614.7 AT
▼**AUSTRALIAN POLLUTION LAW (CONTROL).** 1991. q. C C H Australia Ltd., P.O. Box 230, North Ryde, N.S.W. 2113, Australia. TEL 02-888-2555. FAX 02-888-7324.
Description: To be used together with Australian Pollution Law New South Wales and Australian Pollution Law Victoria.

340 614.7 AT
▼**AUSTRALIAN POLLUTION LAW NEW SOUTH WALES.** 1991. q. C C H Australia Ltd., P.O. Box 230, North Ryde, N.S.W. 2113, Australia. TEL 02-888-7324. FAX 02-888-7324.
Description: To be used together with Australian Pollution Law (Control).

340 614.7 AT
▼**AUSTRALIAN POLLUTION LAW VICTORIA.** 1991. q. C C P Australia Ltd., P.O. Box 230, North Ryde, N.S.W 2113, Australia. TEL 02-888-2555. FAX 02-888-7324.
Description: To be used together with Australian Pollution Law (Control).

AUSTRALIAN TAX CASES. see *BUSINESS AND ECONOMICS — Public Finance, Taxation*

AUSTRALIAN TAX FORUM; a journal of taxation policy, law and reform. see *BUSINESS AND ECONOMICS — Public Finance, Taxation*

AUSTRALIAN TAX REVIEW. see *BUSINESS AND ECONOMICS — Public Finance, Taxation*

340 AT
AUSTRALIAN TENANCY PRACTICE & PRECEDENTS. 2 base vols. (plus s-a. updates). $235. Butterworths Pty. Ltd., 271-273 Lane Cove Rd., P.O. Box 345, North Ryde, N.S.W. 2113, Australia. TEL 02-335-4444. FAX 02-335-4655. (looseleaf format)

340 AT
AUSTRALIAN TORTS REPORTER. (In 3 vols.) 1984. 10/yr. C C H Australia Ltd., P.O. Box 230, North Ryde, N.S.W. 2113, Australia. TEL 888-2555. FAX 02-888-7324.
Description: Details relevant cases on the practice and procedure of the High Court, Federal Court and Administrative Appeals Tribunal.

AUSTRALIAN TRADE PRACTICES REPORTER. see *BUSINESS AND ECONOMICS*

AUTHORS GUILD BULLETIN. see *LITERATURE*

340 388 US
AUTOMOBILE DESIGN LIABILITY. 1970. a. Clark - Boardman - Callaghan Company Ltd., 375 Hudson St., New York, NY 10014. TEL 212-929-7500. FAX 212-924-0460. Ed. Richard M. Goodman.

340 US
AUTOMOTIVE LITIGATION REPORTER; the twice monthly national reporting service of litigation concerning common automotive defects. 1981. s-m. $825. Andrews Publications, 1646 West Chester Pike, Box 1000, Westtown, PA 19395. TEL 215-399-6600. FAX 215-399-6610. Ed. Nicholas W. Sullivan. bibl.; stat.; cum.index every 6 mos. (looseleaf format; back issues avail.)

AVIATION LAW REPORTS. see *TRANSPORTATION — Air Transport*

340 629.13 US
AVIATION LITIGATION. 1986. base vol. (plus a. suppl.) $95. Shepard's - McGraw-Hill, Inc., Box 35300, Colorado Springs, CO 80935-3530. TEL 800-525-2474.
Description: Covers major commercial crashes as well as small aircraft and military accidents. Describes the substantive law of liability, the damages recoverable, the technical steps involved in aviation litigation, alternative theories and defenses of liability.

340 US ISSN 0737-7746
KF2454.A59
AVIATION LITIGATION REPORTER; the national journal of record of aviation litigation. 1983. s-m. $825. Andrews Publications, 1646 West Chester Pike, Box 1000, Westtown, PA 19395. TEL 215-399-6600. FAX 215-399-6610. Ed. Nicholas W. Sullivan. bibl.; stat.; cum.index every 6 mos. (looseleaf format; back issues avail.)
Description: Covers developments in lawsuits arising from commercial carrier, military, private plane and helicopter crashes.

AZIONE NONVIOLENTA. see *CIVIL DEFENSE*

340 US
B A R - B R I BAR REVIEW. (Consists of 13 parts: Civil Procedure, Community Property, Constitutional Law, Contracts, Corporations, Criminal Law, Evidence, Professional Responsibility, Real Property, Remedies, Torts, Trusts, Wills) a. $1,295. B A R - B R I Bar Review, 3280 Motor Ave., Los Angeles, CA 90034-3710. TEL 213-477-2542.

346 US
B A R - B R I BAR REVIEW. COMMUNITY PROPERTY. a. $395. B A R - B R I Bar Review, 3280 Motor Ave., Los Angeles, CA 90034-3710. TEL 213-477-2542.

346.73 US ISSN 0098-762X
KF801.Z9
B A R - B R I BAR REVIEW. CONTRACTS. a. $395. B A R - B R I Bar Review, 3280 Motor Ave., Los Angeles, CA 90034-3710. TEL 213-477-2542.

347.73 US
B A R - B R I BAR REVIEW. EVIDENCE. a. $395. B A R - B R I Bar Review, 3280 Motor Ave., Los Angeles, CA 90034-3710. TEL 213-477-2542.

LAW

174 US
B A R - B R I BAR REVIEW. PROFESSIONAL RESPONSIBILITY. a. $395. B A R - B R I Bar Review, 3280 Motor Ave., Los Angeles, CA 90034-3710. TEL 213-477-2542.
  Formerly: Bay Area Review Course. Legal Ethics (ISSN 0098-7980)

346.73 US
B A R - B R I BAR REVIEW. REAL PROPERTY. a. $395. B A R - B R I Bar Review, 3280 Motor Ave., Los Angeles, CA 90034-3710. TEL 213-477-2542.

347 US ISSN 0098-7999
KF9010.Z9
B A R - B R I BAR REVIEW. REMEDIES. a. $395. B A R - B R I Bar Review, 3280 Motor Ave., Los Angeles, CA 90034-3710. TEL 213-477-2542.

346.066 GW
B B K BUCHFUEHRUNG, BILANZ, KOSTENRECHNUNG. 1954. fortn. DM.150. Verlag Neue Wirtschafts-Briefe GmbH, Eschstr. 22, Postfach 1620, D-4690 Herne 1, Germany. circ. 16,000.

340 CN
B C GAZETTE. PART 1. vol.26, 1986. w. Can.$114. Queen's Printer, Victoria, 563 Superior St., Victoria, B.C. V8V 1X4, Canada. (Dist. by: Crown Publications, 546 Yates St., Victoria, B.C. V8W 1K8, Canada. TEL 604-386-4636) index. (back issues avail.)
  Description: Contains legal notices including forestry tenders, notices to creditors, changes of name and company incorporations.

340 CN
B C GAZETTE. PART 2. vol.29, 1986. fortn. Can.$72. Queen's Printer, Victoria, 563 Superior St., Victoria, B.C. V8V 1X4, Canada. (Dist. by: Crown Publications, 546 Yates St., Victoria, B.C. V8W 1K8, Canada. TEL 604-386-4636) (back issues avail.)
  Description: Contains new B C regulations.

340 301.435 US
B I F O C A L. (Bar Associations in Focus on Aging and the Law) 1979. q. free. American Bar Association, Young Lawyers Division, Commission on Legal Problems of the Elderly, 750 N. Lake Shore Dr., Chicago, IL 60611. TEL 312-988-5555. Ed. Norma B. Gregerman. circ. 3,000.

340 US
B N A ADMINISTRATIVE PRACTICE MANUAL. 1986. base vol. (plus a. suppl.). $245 includes Supplement. The Bureau of National Affairs, Inc., 1231 25th St., N.W., Washington, DC 20037. TEL 202-452-4200. FAX 202-822-8092. (Subscr. to: 9435 Key West Ave., Rockville, MD 20850. TEL 800-372-1033) Ed. Bertram R. Cottine. index. (looseleaf format)

340 US
B N A ADMINISTRATIVE PRACTICE MANUAL. SUPPLEMENT. 1989. a. $98. The Bureau of National Affairs, Inc., 1231 25th St., N.W., Washington, DC 20037. TEL 202-452-4200. FAX 202-822-8092. (Subscr. to: 9435 Key West Ave., Rockville, MD 20850-3397. TEL 800-372-1033) Ed. Bertram Robert Cottine. (looseleaf format)
  Description: Reflects changes in every area of administrative law.

B N A CALIFORNIA - ENVIRONMENT REPORTER. see ENVIRONMENTAL STUDIES

B N A LABOR RELATIONS REPORTER. STATE LABOR LAWS. see BUSINESS AND ECONOMICS — Labor And Industrial Relations

346.066 336 US ISSN 0891-0634
KF967
B N A'S BANKING REPORT. 1965. w. $860. The Bureau of National Affairs, Inc., 1231 25th St., N.W., Washington, DC 20037. TEL 202-452-4200. FAX 202-822-8092. TELEX 285656 BNAI WSH. (Subscr. to: 9435 Key West Ave., Rockville, MD 20850. TEL 800-372-1033) Ed. Susan Webster. index. (looseleaf format; back issues avail.) **Indexed:** Bank.Lit.Ind.
  ●Also available online. Vendor(s): Bureau of National Affairs, Human Resources Information Network (CDD,HDD), Mead Data Central (BNABNK), WESTLAW (BNA-BNK).
  Formerly (until 1987): Washington Financial Reports (ISSN 0511-3172)
  Description: Covers major developments and competitors.

340 US ISSN 1044-7474
KF1507
B N A'S BANKRUPTCY LAW REPORTER. 1989. w. $716. The Bureau of National Affairs, Inc., 1231 25th St., N.W., Washington, DC 20037. TEL 202-452-4200. FAX 202-822-8092. TELEX 285656 BNAI WSH. (Subscr. to: 9435 Key West Ave., Rockville, MD 20850. TEL 800-372-1033) Ed. Wendell Yee. index. (back issues avail.)
  Description: Notification service covering various areas of bankruptcy law.

B N A'S CORPORATE COUNSEL WEEKLY. see BUSINESS AND ECONOMICS — Management

B N A'S DIRECTORY OF STATE COURTS, JUDGES, AND CLERKS. see BUSINESS AND ECONOMICS — Trade And Industrial Directories

340 614.7 US
▼**B N A'S ENVIRONMENTAL DUE DILIGENCE GUIDE.** 1992. m. $595. The Bureau of National Affairs, Inc., 1231 25th St., N.W., Washington, DC 20037. TEL 202-452-4200. FAX 202-822-8092. TELEX 285656 BNAI WSH. (Subscr. to: 9435 Key West Ave., Rockville, MD 20850. TEL 800-372-1033) Ed. Wallis McClain. (looseleaf format; back issues avail.)
  Description: Reference manual which describes how environmental law affects real estate transactions and how "due diligence" can provide protection against Superfund (CERCLA) and RCRA cleanup liabilities.

B N A'S MEDICARE REPORT. see MEDICAL SCIENCES

B N A'S WORKERS' COMPENSATION REPORT. see BUSINESS AND ECONOMICS — Labor And Industrial Relations

B O C A NATIONAL BUILDING CODE. (Building Officials and Code Administrators International) see BUILDING AND CONSTRUCTION

B O C A NATIONAL MECHANICAL CODE. (Building Officials and Code Administrators International) see BUILDING AND CONSTRUCTION

B O C A NATIONAL PLUMBING CODE. (Building Officials and Code Administrators International) see HEATING, PLUMBING AND REFRIGERATION

B O C A NATIONAL PROPERTY MAINTENANCE CODE. (Building Officials and Code Administrators International) see BUILDING AND CONSTRUCTION

340 GW ISSN 0722-6934
B R A K - MITTEILUNGEN. 1969. q. DM.30. Verlag Dr. Otto Schmidt KG, Unter den Ulmen 96-98, 5000 Cologne 51, Germany. TEL 0221-3498-0. FAX 0221-3498-181. TELEX 8883381. index; circ. 62,700. (back issues avail.)

340 333.33 AT ISSN 0727-8047
BAALMAN & WELL'S LAND TITLES OFFICE PRACTICE. 1980. 3/yr. Aus.$205. Law Book Co. Ltd., 44-50 Waterloo Rd., N. Ryde, N.S.W. 2113, Australia. TEL 02-887-0177. FAX 02-888-9706. TELEX ASBOOK 27995. Ed. Kevin Nettle. (looseleaf format; back issues avail.)
  ●Also available online.

BALDWIN'S OHIO LEGISLATIVE SERVICE. see PUBLIC ADMINISTRATION

BALDWIN'S OHIO SCHOOL LAW JOURNAL. see EDUCATION

342 BG
BANGLADESH JATIYA AINJIBI SAMITY SOUVENIR. Variant title: Bangladesh Jatiya Ainjibi Samity. Annual Law Journal. (Text in English or Bengali) 1977. a. Tk.25. Bangladesh Jatiya Ainjibi Samity - National Bar Associaton of Bangladesh, Dhanmandi R.A. 87, Road 7A, Dhaka, Bangladesh. Ed. Mr.Sobhan. adv.; bk.rev.; circ. 10,000.

342 BG
BANGLADESH SUPREME COURT REPORTS. (Text in English) 1975. q. $20. Bangladesh Institute of Law and International Affairs, 501 Dhanmondi Residential Area, Rd. No. 7, Dhaka 5, Bangladesh. (Dist. by: Karim International, Padmalochon Roy Lane, Mahuttuly, Dacca 1, Bangladesh) Ed.Bd. circ. 2,500.

BANK ASSET - LIABILITY MANAGEMENT. see BUSINESS AND ECONOMICS — Banking And Finance

BANK BAILOUT LITIGATION NEWS. see BUSINESS AND ECONOMICS — Banking And Finance

340 332.1 US
BANK HOLDING COMPANY COMPLIANCE MANUAL. 1986. base vol. (plus irreg. suppl.). Matthew Bender & Co., Inc., 11 Penn Plaza, New York, NY 10001. TEL 212-967-7707. Ed. Joseph G. Beckford. (looseleaf format)
  Description: Guide to the day-to-day compliance responsibilities faced by bank holding company line officers.

BANK INCOME TAX RETURN MANUAL. see BUSINESS AND ECONOMICS — Banking And Finance

BANK OFFICERS HANDBOOK OF COMMERCIAL BANKING LAW (SUPPLEMENT). see BUSINESS AND ECONOMICS — Banking And Finance

340 TU
BANKA VE TICARET HUKUKU DERGISI. 1961. s-a. TL.122400($25) Ankara Universitesi, Hukuk Fakultesi - University of Ankara, Faculty of Law, 06590 Cebeci - Ankara, Turkey. circ. 1,000. (back issues avail.)

BANKER'S LETTER OF THE LAW. see BUSINESS AND ECONOMICS — Banking And Finance

BANKING AND FINANCE LAW REVIEW. see BUSINESS AND ECONOMICS — Banking And Finance

346.066 US
BANKING ATTORNEY. w. $645. American Banker Newsletters, Box 30240, Bethesda, MD 20824. TEL 301-654-5580. Ed. Dave Postal. adv. (back issues avail.)
  Formerly: Thrift Attorney.

340 332.1 US
BANKING LAW. 1981. 12 base vols. (plus irreg. suppl.). Matthew Bender & Co., Inc., 11 Penn Plaza, New York, NY 10001. TEL 212-967-7707. (looseleaf format)
  Description: Operational guidance for bank officers, with analysis of statutory law and agency regulations.

340 332.1 US ISSN 0737-2159
K2
BANKING LAW ANTHOLOGY. 1983. a. $149.95. International Library Law Book Publishers, Inc., 101 Lakeforest Blvd., Ste. 270, Gaithersburg, MD 20877. TEL 301-990-7755. FAX 301-990-7642. Ed. Allison P. Zabriskie. bibl.; index; cum.index. **Indexed:** Leg.Per.
  Description: Selected best U.S. law review articles, printed in their entirety, in the field of banking, selected from over 900 American law review journals.

BANKING LAW BRIEFS. see BUSINESS AND ECONOMICS — Banking And Finance

346.066 US
BANKING LAW IN THE UNITED STATES. 1988. base vol. (plus a. suppl.). $95. Butterworth Legal Publishers (Salem) (Subsidiary of: Reed International PLC), 90 Stiles Rd., Salem, NH 03079. TEL 800-548-4001. FAX 603-898-9858. Ed.Bd.
  Description: Reviews and analyses of the laws and regulations governing banking practice in the US.

BANKING LAW JOURNAL. see BUSINESS AND ECONOMICS — Banking And Finance

LAW

BANKING LAW JOURNAL DIGEST (SUPPLEMENT). see *BUSINESS AND ECONOMICS — Banking And Finance*

340 332 US
BANKING LAW MANUAL: LEGAL GUIDE TO COMMERCIAL BANKS, THRIFT INSTITUTIONS AND CREDIT UNIONS. 1983. base vol. (plus irreg. suppl.). Matthew Bender & Co., Inc., 11 Penn Plaza, New York, NY 10001. TEL 212-967-7707. (looseleaf format)
Description: Examines the basic legal issues related to financial institutions and the regulatory framework within which they operate. Includes a comparative analysis of the powers of various types of financial institutions.

BANKING LAW REVIEW; practical legal guidance for bankers and their attorneys. see *BUSINESS AND ECONOMICS — Banking And Finance*

BANKRUPTCY LAW LETTER. see *BUSINESS AND ECONOMICS — Banking And Finance*

340 CE
BAR ASSOCIATION OF SRI LANKA. NEWSLETTER. (Text in English) 1975. m. Bar Association of Sri Lanka, Law Library, Colombo 12, Sri Lanka.

340 US
BAR DIRECTORY OF MAINE. 1970. a. $29.50. Tower Publishing Co., 34 Diamond St., Box 7220, Portland, ME 04112. TEL 207-775-1740. FAX 207-775-1740. adv. (avail. on diskette)
Description: Directory of lawyers, law firms and legal services for Maine.

340 US ISSN 0005-5824
LAW
BAR EXAMINER. 1931. 4/yr. free to judges and lawyers engaged in the field of admissions to the bar. National Conference of Bar Examiners, 333 N. Michigan Ave., Ste. 1025, Chicago, IL 60601. TEL 312-641-0963. FAX 312-641-2052. Ed. Stuart Duhl. circ. 2,500. (also avail. in microform from UMI; reprint service avail. from UMI) **Indexed:** C.L.I., L.R.I., Leg.Per.

340 IS ISSN 0334-0716
K13
BAR-ILAN LAW STUDIES. (Text in Hebrew) a. $38. Bar-Ilan University Press, Ramat Gat 52900, Israel. TEL 03-5318401. (back issues avail.)
Description: Direct and theoretical studies of general and Jewish law.

340.06 US ISSN 0099-1031
KF200
BAR LEADER. 1975. bi-m. $21 (free to qualified personnel). American Bar Association, Bar Services Division, 750 N. Lake Shore Dr., Chicago, IL 60611. TEL 312-988-5000. Ed. George Gold. illus.; circ. 8,000. **Indexed:** C.L.I., L.R.I., Leg.Cont.
—BLDSC shelfmark: 1863.188000.
Formed by the merger of: American Bar Association. Section of Bar Activities. Bar Activities; American Bar Association. Section of Bar Activities. Bar Keys; American Bar Association. Section of Bar Activities. Communications Coordinator.

340 US
BAR NEWS (WASHINGTON). 1946. m. $24. Washington State Bar Association, 500 Westin Bldg., 2001 Sixth Ave., Seattle, WA 98121-2599. TEL 206-448-0441. adv.; bk.rev.; circ. 1,800. (also avail. in microform from WSH; reprint service avail.) **Indexed:** C.L.I.

340 US ISSN 0164-3835
K2
BARCLAYS LAW MONTHLY. 1979. m. Matthew Bender & Co., Inc., 11 Penn Plaza, New York, NY 10001. TEL 212-967-7707.

342 US
BARCLAYS UNITED STATES EIGHTH CIRCUIT SERVICE. s-m. Barclays Law Publishers, 400 Oyster Point Blvd., Ste. 500, S. San Francisco, CA 94080. TEL 415-588-1155.

342 US
BARCLAYS UNITED STATES TENTH CIRCUIT SERVICE. s-m. Barclays Law Publishers, 400 Oyster Point Blvd., Ste. 500, S. San Francisco, CA 94080. TEL 415-588-1155.

340.1 NR ISSN 0331-0086
K2
BARRISTER. 1967; N.S. 1970. irreg. 6 n. University of Nigeria, Law Student's Association, Nsukka, Nigeria. Ed. Mr. Anyadike. adv.; bk.rev.; circ. 2,000. **Indexed:** Leg.Per.
Description: Articles by law students at the University of Nigeria, Enuqu Campus.

340 US ISSN 0094-5277
K2
BARRISTER (CHICAGO). 1973. q. $20. American Bar Association, Young Lawyers Division, 750 N. Lake Shore Dr., Chicago, IL 60611. TEL 312-988-6047. Ed. Anthony Monahan. adv.; bk.rev.; circ. 151,421. (reprint service avail.) **Indexed:** Anbar, C.L.I., L.R.I., Law Ofc.Info.Svc., Leg.Cont., Leg.Per.
—BLDSC shelfmark: 1863.824000.
Incorporates: Law Notes (ISSN 0023-9305)
Description: General articles about the legal profession, the law, and society.

340 US ISSN 0739-2494
KF200
BARRISTER (PHILADELPHIA). 1970. q. $32. Pennsylvania Trial Lawyers Association, 121 S. Broad St., Ste. 800, Philadelphia, PA 19107-4594. TEL 215-546-6451. FAX 215-546-5430. Ed. Lee C. Swartz. adv.; bk.rev.; cum.index; circ. 4,000. (back issues avail.)
Description: Advice and information for advocates practicing trial law in Pennsylvania.

340 SZ
BASLER STUDIEN ZUR RECHTSWISSENSCHAFT. 1932. irreg. price varies. Helbing und Lichtenhahn Verlag AG, Freie Str. 82, CH-4051 Basel, Switzerland. (Subscr. to: Sauerlaender AG, Postfach, CH-5001 Aarau, Switzerland)

BAURECHT; Zeitschrift fuer das gesamte oeffentliche und zivile Baurecht. see *BUILDING AND CONSTRUCTION*

340 SZ
BAURECHT/DROIT DE LA CONSTRUCTION. (Text in French and German) 1979. q. 49 SFr. (Seminar fuer Schweizerisches Baurecht) Union Walter AG, Postfach, Kapuzinerstr. 6, CH-4502 Solothurn, Switzerland. TEL 065-238161. FAX 065-222931. Ed.Bd. adv.; bk.rev.; circ. 3,900. (tabloid format; back issues avail.)

340 350 GW ISSN 0522-5337
BAYERISCHE VERWALTUNGSBLAETTER; Zeitschrift fuer oeffentliches Recht und oeffentliche Verwaltung. 1955. s-m. DM.261.60. Richard Boorberg Verlag (Munich), Levelingstr. 6a, Postfach 800340, D-8000 Munich 80, Germany. Ed. Herbert von Golitschek. **Indexed:** Dok.Str., INIS Atomind.

340 GW
BAYERISCHEN OBERLANDESGERICHTE. ENTSCHEIDUNGEN IN STRAFSACHEN. 1951. irreg. (12-25/yr.). DM.58. C.H. Beck'sche Verlagsbuchhandlung, Wilhelmstr. 9, 8000 Munich 40, Germany. TEL 089-381890.

349 GW ISSN 0005-7142
BAYERISCHES JUSTIZMINISTERIALBLATT. 1863. m. DM.46. Staatsministerium der Justiz, Justizpalast, 8000 Munich 35, Germany. FAX 089-55973566. (Subscr. to: J. Schweizer Sortiment, Lenbachplatz 1, 8000 Munich 2, Germany) index; circ. 2,300.

340 US ISSN 0005-7274
K2
BAYLOR LAW REVIEW. 1948. q. $28. Baylor University, Law School, 1400 S. 5th St., Waco, TX 76706. TEL 817-755-3487. (Subscr. to: Box 97156, Waco, TX 76798) Ed. Charles Wesky Rhodes IV. adv.; index, cum.index every 5 yrs.: vols.1-43 (1984-1991); circ. 1,200. (also avail. in microfilm from WSH,PMC) **Indexed:** C.L.I., Curr.Cont., L.R.I., Leg.Cont., Leg.Per., P.A.I.S., SSCI.
—BLDSC shelfmark: 1871.241500.

BEER MARKETER'S INSIGHTS. see *BEVERAGES*

BEHAVIORAL SCIENCES AND THE LAW. see *PSYCHOLOGY*

340 AU
BEITRAEGE ZUM UNIVERSITAETSRECHT. 1982. irreg. vol.13, 1991. price varies. Manzsche Verlags- und Universitaetsbuchhandlung, Kohlmarkt 16, A-1014 Vienna, Austria. TEL 0222-531610. FAX 0222-5316181. Ed. Rudolf Strasser. circ. 1,500.
Description: Collects articles on university law.

343 BE
BELGIUM. COUR DE CASSATION. BULLETIN DES ARRETS. Cover title: Arrets de la Cour de Cassation de Belgique. m. 8250 Fr. Etablissements Emile Bruylant, 67 rue de la Regence, B-1000 Brussels, Belgium. TEL 02-512-9845.
Formerly: Belgium. Cour de Cassation. Bulletin.

340 US ISSN 0276-1505
KF200
BENCH & BAR OF MINNESOTA. 1931. 11/yr. $20 to non-members. Minnesota State Bar Association, 514 Nicollet Ave., Ste. 300, Minneapolis, MN 55402. TEL 612-333-1183. FAX 612-333-4927. Ed. Judson Haverkamp. adv.; bk.rev.; index; circ. 13,000. (also avail. in microform; back issues avail.) **Indexed:** C.L.I., L.R.I., Law Ofc.Info.Svc.
Description: Law related topics of interest to Minnesota lawyers.

343.73 US ISSN 0270-5206
KF6385
BENDER'S DICTIONARY OF 1040 DEDUCTIONS. 1980. a. Matthew Bender & Co., Inc., 11 Penn Plaza, New York, NY 10001. TEL 212-967-7707. Ed. Kevin Egan.

349 YU ISSN 0003-2565
BEOGRADSKI UNIVERZITET. PRAVNI FAKULTET. ANALI. (Text in Serbo-Croatian) 1953. bi-m. 72500 din.($15) Univerzitet u Beogradu, Pravni Fakultet, Bulevar Revolucije 67, Belgrade, Yugoslavia. Ed. Obren Stankovic. bk.rev.; circ. 1,500.

340 US ISSN 0882-4312
K2
BERKELEY WOMEN'S LAW JOURNAL. 1986. a. $17 to individuals (foreign $21); institutions $38 (foreign $42); students $9 (foreign $13). University of California Press, Journals Division, 2120 Berkeley Way, Berkeley, CA 94720. TEL 510-642-4191. FAX 510-643-7127. Ed.Bd. adv.; bk.rev.; circ. 550. (back issues avail.)
—BLDSC shelfmark: 1940.630000.
Description: Explores racial, cultural and socio-economic issues concerning women and the law.
Refereed Serial

340 GW
BERLINER ANWALTSBLATT. 1951. m. DM.90. C B Verlag Carl Boldt, Baseler Str. 80, 1000 Berlin 45, Germany. TEL 030-8337087. FAX 030-8339125. circ. 4,800.

658 340 GW ISSN 0340-7918
BETRIEBS-BERATER; Zeitschrift fuer Recht und Wirtschaft. 1946. 3/m. DM.417.60. Verlag Recht und Wirtschaft GmbH, Haeusserstr. 14, Postfach 105960, 6900 Heidelberg 1, Germany. TEL 06221-906-1. adv.; bk.rev.; circ. 20,000. **Indexed:** INIS Atomind., Key to Econ.Sci.
—BLDSC shelfmark: 1946.830000.

340 GW ISSN 0179-2776
K2
BETRIFFT JUSTIZ. 1985. q. DM.40($20) Neuthor-Verlag, P.O. Box 3402, D-6120 Michelstadt, Germany. Ed.Bd. index; circ. 1,500. (back issues avail.)

340 US ISSN 1051-628X
K2
BEVERLY HILLS BAR ASSOCIATION JOURNAL. vol.4, 1970. q. $40 (foreign $45). Beverly Hills Bar Association, 300 S. Beverly Dr., Ste. 201, Beverly Hills, CA 90212. TEL 213-553-6644. FAX 213-284-8290. adv.; bk.rev.; illus.; circ. 3,000. (also avail. in microfiche) **Indexed:** C.L.I., L.R.I., Leg.Per.
Description: Scholarly journal dealing with substantive and procedural issues in the law.

BIANJI ZHI YOU/COMPILERS' FRIEND. see *PUBLISHING AND BOOK TRADE*

340　　　　　　　　　II
BIHAR LAW JOURNAL REPORTS. (Text in English)
vol.21, 1973. w. Rs.50. Allahabad Law Journal Co.,
Ltd., 5 Prayag St., Allahabad, India. Ed. Harihar Nath
Sinha. bibl.

BIJBLAD BIJ DE INDUSTRIELE EIGENDOM. see *PATENTS,
TRADEMARKS AND COPYRIGHTS*

349　　　　　　YU　　ISSN 0006-2731
BILTEN PRAVNE SLUZBE J N A. (Text in Serbo-Croatian)
1961. q. Savezni Sekretarijat za Narodnu Odbranu,
Kneza Milosa 37, Belgrade, Yugoslavia. Ed. Vuko
Gozze-Gucetic.

340 020　　　　　　US
▼**BIMONTHLY REVIEW OF LAW BOOKS.** 1990. bi-m.
$75. Fred B. Rothman & Co., 10368 W. Centennial
Rd., Littleton, CO 80127. TEL 303-979-5657.
FAX 303-978-1457. Eds. Edward Bander, Michael
Rustad. (back issues avail.)
  Description: Provides law librarians, legal
academics and lawyers with reviews of
contemporary legal topics.

**BIOLAW: A LEGAL AND ETHICAL REPORTER ON
MEDICINE, HEALTH CARE, AND BIOENGINEERING.** see
BIOLOGY — Bioengineering

BIOTECHNOLOGY LAW REPORT. see *BIOLOGY —
Biotechnology*

340　　　　　　US　　ISSN 0006-3711
BIRMINGHAM BAR ASSOCIATION. BULLETIN.* 1964. q.
$10. Birmingham Bar Association, 109 N. 20th St.,
Birmingham, AL 35203. TEL 205-251-8006. Ed.
Warren B. Lightfoot. adv.; bk.rev.; circ. 1,600.
(controlled). (tabloid format)

349　　　　　　SZ　　ISSN 0006-4491
BLAETTER FUER ZUERCHERISCHE RECHTSPRECHUNG.
10/yr. 98 SFr. (foreign 114 SFr.). Orell Fuessli
Graphische Betriebe AG, Dietzingerstr. 3, CH-8036
Zurich, Switzerland. Ed.Bd. adv.; circ. 1,700.

346.066 340　　　　CN
BLAKES REPORT - INTELLECTUAL PROPERTY. 1986. q.
Blake, Cassels & Graydon, Box 25, Commerce Court
West, Toronto, Ont. M5L 1A9, Canada.
TEL 416-863-2400. FAX 416-863-2653. TELEX
06-219687. Ed. Victor V. Butsky. index; circ. 7,000.
(back issues avail.)

340　　　　　　US
BLUE SKY COMPLIANCE MANUAL; a state-by-state
guide. 1987. base vol. (plus suppl.). $75.
Butterworth Legal Publishers (Salem) (Subsidiary of:
Reed International PLC), 90 Stiles Rd., Salem, NH
03079. TEL 800-548-4001. FAX 603-898-9858.
Ed. Bobby G. Palmer. (looseleaf format)
  Description: For attorneys, legal assistants,
paralegal and legal secretaries; includes a directory
of all state securities administrators' addresses and
telephone numbers, necessary forms for compliance
in every state and sample filings and cover letters.

340　　　　　　US
BLUE SKY LAW REPORTS. 1928. s-m. $775.
Commerce Clearing House, Inc., 4025 W. Peterson
Ave., Chicago, IL 60646. TEL 312-583-8500. Ed.
D. Newquist.

346.006　　　　　US
**BOARD OF CONTRACT APPEALS BID PROTEST
DECISIONS.** m. $412. Federal Publications, Inc.,
1120 20th St., N.W., Ste. 500 S., Washington, DC
20036. TEL 202-337-7000. FAX 202-223-0755.
  Description: Reports on government contracts.

340　　　　　　US
▼**BOHANNON'S NEW MEXICO ENVIRONMENTAL LAW
HANDBOOK;** a practical guide to New Mexico laws
and regulations. 1990. base vol. (plus irreg. suppl.).
$95. Butterworth Legal Publishers (Salem)
(Subsidiary of: Reed International PLC), 90 Stiles
Rd., Salem, NH 03079. TEL 800-548-4001.
FAX 603-898-9858. Ed. Paul M. Bohannon.
(looseleaf format)
  Description: Provides a current review of all
environmental programs operating in New Mexico.

340　　　　　　CL
BOLETIN DE DERECHO PUBLICO. 1979. m. Universidad
de Chile, Facultad de Derecho, Santiago, Chile.
bk.rev.; circ. 500.

340　　　　　　EC
BOLETIN DE LEGISLACION E INFORMACION JURIDICA.
no.20, 1979. m. Camara de Comercio de Quito,
Avenidas Amazonas y de la Republica, Apdo. 202,
Quito, Ecuador.

BOLETIN JURIDICO MILITAR. see *MILITARY*

340.5　　　　　MX　　ISSN 0041-8633
LAW
BOLETIN MEXICANO DE DERECHO COMPARADO. 1948.
3/yr. Mex.$50($42) Universidad Nacional
Autonoma de Mexico, Instituto de Investigaciones
Juridicas, Delegacion Coyoacan, Ciudad
Universitaria, 04510 Mexico, DF, Mexico. Ed.
Eugenio Hurtado Marquez. adv.; bk.rev.; abstr.; bibl.;
index. **Indexed:** A.B.C.Pol.Sci.; HR Rep., Mar.Aff.Bibl.
  Formerly: Universidad Nacional Autonoma de
Mexico. Instituto de Investigaciones Juridicas.
Boletin.

347　　　　　　SP
BOLETIN OFICIAL DE LAS CORTES ESPANOLES. s-w.
34100 ptas. Congreso de los Diputados, C.
Floridablanca s-n., 28014 Madrid, Spain.

340　　　　　　IT　　ISSN 0394-6592
BOLLETTINO DEL LAVORO E DEI TRIBUTI; settimanale di
dottrina legislazione circolari giurisprudenza. 1971.
w. L.410000. Casa Editrice Edis s.r.l., Via S. Franca
60, 29100 Piacenza, Italy. TEL 0523-25684.
FAX 0523-36782. Ed. Giuseppe Sgroi. (back issues
avail.)
  Formerly (until 1987): Bollettino del Lavoro (ISSN
0391-822X)

340　　　　　　II
BOMBAY LAW REPORTER. (Text in English) 1899. m.
Rs.200 (foreign Rs.400). Bombay Law Reporter Pvt.
Ltd., Krishna Mahal 63, Marine Dr., Bombay 20,
India. Eds. A.P. Yajnik, A.G. Joshi. adv.; bk.rev.; bibl.;
index; circ. 2,500.

340　　　　　　US
BOSTON BAR JOURNAL. 1959. 6/yr. $40. Boston Bar
Association, 16 Beacon St., Boston, MA 02108.
TEL 617-742-0615. FAX 617-523-0127. adv.;
bk.rev.; circ. 8,500. **Indexed:** C.L.I.

**BOSTON COLLEGE ENVIRONMENTAL AFFAIRS LAW
REVIEW.** see *ENVIRONMENTAL STUDIES*

341.57　　　　　US　　ISSN 0161-6587
K2
BOSTON COLLEGE LAW REVIEW. 1959. 5/yr. $20.
Boston College, School of Law, 885 Centre St.,
Newton, MA 02159. TEL 617-969-0100. index,
cum.index; circ. 1,200. (also avail. in microfiche
from RRI; reprint service from RRI) **Indexed:**
Bank.Lit.Ind., BPIA, Bus.Ind., C.L.I., L.R.I., Leg.Per.,
Ocean.Abstr., P.A.I.S., Pollut.Abstr.
  ●Also available online. Vendor(s): WESTLAW.
  —BLDSC shelfmark: 2251.812300.
  Formerly (until vol.19, 1977): Boston College
Industrial and Commercial Law Review (ISSN
0006-7954)

BOSTON UNIVERSITY JOURNAL OF TAX LAW. see
*BUSINESS AND ECONOMICS — Public Finance,
Taxation*

340　　　　　　US　　ISSN 0006-8047
LAW
BOSTON UNIVERSITY LAW REVIEW. 1897. 5/yr. $18.
Boston University, School of Law, 765
Commonwealth Ave., Boston, MA 02215.
TEL 617-353-3118. Ed. Robert G. Holdway. adv.;
bk.rev.; index. cum.index: vols.1-26; circ. 5,200.
(also avail. in microfiche from RRI) **Indexed:** BPIA,
Bus.Ind., C.L.I., Crim.Just.Abstr., Curr.Cont., L.R.I.,
Leg.Cont., Leg.Per., P.A.I.S., Risk Abstr., SSCI.
  ●Also available online. Vendor(s): WESTLAW.
  —BLDSC shelfmark: 2251.840000.

BOTTLE - CAN RECYCLING UPDATE. see
ENVIRONMENTAL STUDIES — Waste Management

340　　　　　　US　　ISSN 0162-1726
BOYCOTT LAW BULLETIN. 1977. m. $495. Nu-Tec
Publishing, 4715 Strack Rd., Ste. 211, Houston, TX
77069-1617. TEL 713-444-6522.
FAX 713-444-6564.

**BRANDEIS UNIVERSITY. BIGEL INSTITUTE FOR HEALTH
POLICY. RESEARCH NEWS.** see *MEDICAL SCIENCES*

340　　　　　　BL
**BRAZIL. SUPREMO TRIBUNAL FEDERAL. INDICES DE
LEGISLACAO FEDERAL.** (Subseries of:
D.I.N.-Divulgacao) a. price varies. Supremo Tribunal
Federal, Departamento de Imprensa Nacional, SIG
-Quadra 6- Lote 800, CEP 70604 Brasilia-DF, Brazil.

340　　　　　　BL
**BRAZIL. SUPREMO TRIBUNAL FEDERAL. RELATORIO DOS
TRABALHOS REALIZADOS.** Title varies slightly. 1916.
a. Supremo Tribunal Federal, Departamento de
Imprensa Nacional, SIG - Quadra 6- Lote 800, CEP
70604 Brasilia-DF, Brazil.

340　　　　　　BL　　ISSN 0076-8855
**BRAZIL. TRIBUNAL REGIONAL DO TRABALHO. TERCERA
REGIAO. REVISTA.** 1965. s-a. Cr.$15000. Tribunal
Regional do Trabalho, Tercera Regiao, Rua Curitiba
835, 30000 Belo Horizonte, MG, Brazil. TELEX 31
11 76. Ed.Bd. bibl.; circ. 1,000.

340 613.9　　　UK　　ISSN 0309-7978
BREAKING CHAINS. 1977. q. £8.50 to members.
Abortion Law Reform Association, 88 Islington High
St., London N.1., England. Ed.Bd. adv.; bk.rev.; circ.
2,000.
  Formerly: A L R A Newsletter.
  Description: Pro-choice publication of the
Association.

368 340　　　　US　　ISSN 0273-0995
KF1164.A1
BRIEF (CHICAGO). q. $18 to non-members; members
$4 per no. American Bar Association, Tort and
Insurance Practice Section, 750 N. Lake Shore Dr.,
Chicago, IL 60611. TEL 312-988-5555. Ed. Lucia
Ann Lockwood. (also avail. in microform)
  ●Also available online. Vendor(s): WESTLAW (BRIEF).
  Formerly: American Bar Association. Section of
Insurance, Negligence and Compensation Law. I N C
L Brief.
  Description: News and features on current events
in the fields of tort and insurance law.

BRIEFING PAPERS. see *BUSINESS AND ECONOMICS —
Economic Situation And Conditions*

658.8 001.642　　US　　ISSN 1051-0036
▼**BRIEFLY....** 1990. m. $50. Allison & Associates, 303
Staley Dr., LeRoy, IL 61752. TEL 309-962-9410.
Ed. Kathleen E. Allison. circ. 300.
  Description: Assists small law firms in areas of
marketing, management, hardware and software
selection.

340 367　　　　CN　　ISSN 0715-3759
BRIEFLY SPEAKING. 1979. m. membership. Canadian
Bar Association - Ontario, 20 Toronto St., Ste. 200,
Toronto, Ont. M5C 2B8, Canada.
FAX 416-869-1390. Ed. Lucinda Falconer. circ.
16,000.

340.05　　　　US　　ISSN 0360-151X
K2
BRIGHAM YOUNG UNIVERSITY LAW REVIEW. 1975. q.
$20. Brigham Young University, J. Reuben Clark
Law School, 453 JRCB, Provo, UT 84602.
TEL 801-378-5678. FAX 801-378-3595. adv.;
bk.rev.; circ. 850. (also avail. in microform from
UMI; reprint service avail. from RRI,UMI) **Indexed:**
C.L.I., L.R.I., Leg.Cont., Leg.Per.
  ●Also available online. Vendor(s): WESTLAW.

340　　　　　　CN　　ISSN 0381-2510
LAW
**BRITISH COLUMBIA. LAW REFORM COMMISSION.
ANNUAL REPORT.** 1970. a. Law Reform
Commission, 601-865 Hornby St., Vancouver, B.C.
V6Z 2G3, Canada. TEL 604-660-2366.
FAX 604-660-2378. Ed. Arthur L. Close. circ. 2,000
(controlled).

340　　　　　　CN
**BRITISH COLUMBIA. LAW REFORM COMMISSION.
REPORTS.** irreg. price varies. Law Reform
Commission, 601-865 Hornby St., Vancouver, B.C.
V6Z 2G3, Canada. TEL 604-660-2366.
FAX 604-660-2378. (Subscr. to: Crown
Publications, 546 Yates St., Victoria, B.C. V8W 1K8,
Canada. TEL 604-386-4636) (back issues avail.)

340   CN
BRITISH COLUMBIA ANNOTATED INDUSTRIAL RELATIONS ACT. 4/yr. Can.$295. Butterworths Canada Ltd., 75 Clegg Rd., Markham, Ont. L6G 1A1, Canada. TEL 416-479-2665. FAX 416-479-2826. (looseleaf format)
 Formerly: British Columbia Labour Code.
 Description: British Columbia Labour Court and Labour Board decisions.

340   CN
BRITISH COLUMBIA ANNUAL PRACTICE. a. Can.$75. Western Legal Publications, 301 One Alexander St., Vancouver, B.C. V6A 1B2, Canada. TEL 604-687-5671. FAX 604-687-2796.
 Description: Provides access to the current text of the B.C. Rules of Court, fully annotated with more than 850 decisions, a History of the Rules and all available Practice Directions for the Rules of Court and the Court of Appeals Rules.

346   CN
BRITISH COLUMBIA CORPORATIONS LAW GUIDE. m. Can.$435. C C H Canadian Ltd., 6 Garamond Ct., Don Mills, Ont. M3C 1Z5, Canada. TEL 416-441-2992. FAX 416-444-9011. index.
 Description: Covers British Columbia company act and regulations.

340   CN
BRITISH COLUMBIA COURT FORMS. 2/yr. Can.$550. Butterworths Canada Ltd., 75 Clegg Rd., Markham, Ont. L6G 1A1, Canada. TEL 416-479-2665. FAX 416-479-2826. Eds. Beverly M. McLachlin, James P. Taylor. (looseleaf format)
 Description: Precedents and court forms for important court procedures encountered by British Columbia lawyers.

340 368   CN   ISSN 0824-720X
BRITISH COLUMBIA DECISIONS - INSURANCE LAW CASES. 1981. m. Can.$265. Western Legal Publications, 301-1 Alexander St., Vancouver, B.C. V6A 1B2, Canada. TEL 604-687-5671. FAX 604-687-2796. m.index. (looseleaf format)
 ●Also available online.
 Description: Digests of cases concerning insurance, motor vehicle liability, personal injury damages, negligence and relevant practice issues are included.

BRITISH COLUMBIA DECISIONS, LABOUR ARBITRATION. see BUSINESS AND ECONOMICS — Labor And Industrial Relations

340 352   CN   ISSN 0824-7188
BRITISH COLUMBIA DECISIONS - MUNICIPAL LAW CASES. 1980. m. Can.$75. Western Legal Publications, 301-1 Alexander St., Vancouver, B.C. V6A 1B2, Canada. TEL 604-687-5671. FAX 604-687-2796. m.index. (looseleaf format)
 ●Also available online.

342   CN   ISSN 0715-4798
BRITISH COLUMBIA DECISIONS - STATUTE CITATOR. 1978. m. Can.$105. Western Legal Publications, 301-1 Alexander St., Vancouver, B.C. V6A 1B2, Canada. TEL 604-687-5671. FAX 604-687-2796. (looseleaf format)
 Description: Provides all current judicial decisions pertaining to the interpretation and application of British Columbia statutes decided by the Supreme Court of Canada and the British Columbia Courts.

340   CN   ISSN 0703-3060
KEB104
BRITISH COLUMBIA LAW REPORTS (3RD SERIES). 1976. 30/yr. (10 vols./yr.). Can.$110. Carswell Publications, 800 Rocky Mountain Plaza, 615 MacLeod Trail S.E., Calgary, Alta. T2G 4T8, Canada. TEL 416-609-8000. FAX 416-298-5094. (Subscr. to: Carswell Publications, Corporate Plaza, 2075 Kennedy Rd., Scarsborough, Ont. M1T 3V4, Canada) Ed. Darrell Burns. cum.index.

340   CN
BRITISH COLUMBIA PRACTICE. a. Can.$425. Butterworths Canada Ltd., 75 Clegg Rd., Markham, Ont. L6G 1A1, Canada. TEL 416-479-2665. FAX 416-479-2826. Eds. Beverly M. McLachlin, James P. Taylor. (looseleaf format)
 Description: Text of each rule and subrule of the Canadian Supreme Court and Court of Appeals.

BRITISH COLUMBIA REAL ESTATE LAW GUIDE. see REAL ESTATE

340   CN
BRITISH COLUMBIA RULES CITATOR. 1977. m. Can.$99.50. Western Legal Publications, 301 One Alexander St., Vancouver, B.C. V6A 1B2, Canada. TEL 604-687-5671. FAX 604-687-2796. (looseleaf format)
 Description: Covers case citations for all decisions of the B.C. Courts since February 1977.

340   CN   ISSN 0713-8865
BRITISH COLUMBIA WEEKLY LAW DIGEST. 1982. w (50/yr.). Can.$495. Carswell Publications, 800 Rocky Mountain Plaza, 615 MacLeod Trail S.E., Calgary, Alta. T2G 4T8, Canada. TEL 416-609-8000. FAX 416-298-5094. (Subscr. to: Carswell Publications, Corporate Plaza, 2075 Kennedy Rd., Scarsborough, Ont. M1T 3V4, Canada) Ed. Leanne Berry. cum.index.

340   AT
BRITTS: COMPARABLE VERDICTS IN PERSONAL INJURY CLAIMS. 1973. 6/yr. Law Book Co. Ltd., 44-50 Waterloo Rd., N. Ryde, N.S.W. 2113, Australia. TEL 02-887-0177. FAX 02-888-9706. TELEX ASBOOK 27995. Ed. M.G. Britts. (looseleaf format)
 Description: Covers damages, personal injury claims and jurisdiction in Australia.

BROADCASTING AND THE LAW. see COMMUNICATIONS — Television And Cable

BROADCASTING LAW AND PRACTICE. see COMMUNICATIONS — Television And Cable

340 333.33   US
BROKER-DEALERS AND SECURITIES MARKETS. 1977. base vol. (plus a. suppl.). $95. Shepard's - McGraw-Hill, Inc., Box 35300, Colorado Springs, CO 80935-3530. TEL 800-525-2474.
 Description: Focuses on Securities and Exchange Commission rules, their various interpretations and their many relationships to the brokerage industry and regulatory process.

340   US   ISSN 0007-232X
BROOKLYN BARRISTER. 1950. q. membership. Brooklyn Bar Association, 123 Remsen St., Brooklyn, NY 11201. TEL 718-624-0675. Ed. John L. Leventhal. adv.; bk.rev.; index; circ. 2,600. (also avail. in microform from UMI; reprint service avail. from UMI) **Indexed:** C.L.I., Leg.Per.

340   US   ISSN 0007-2362
K2
BROOKLYN LAW REVIEW. 1935. 4/yr. $18. Brooklyn Law School, 250 Joralemon St., Brooklyn, NY 11201. TEL 718-780-7968. bk.rev.; bibl.; index; circ. 3,000. (also avail. in microfilm from MIM,RRI; back issues avail.; reprint service avail. from RRI) **Indexed:** Abstr.Bk.Rev.Curr.Leg.Per., C.L.I., Crim.Just.Abstr., L.R.I., Leg.Cont., Leg.Per.
 ●Also available online. Vendor(s): Mead Data Central.
 —BLDSC shelfmark: 2350.150000.
 Description: Analyzes a wide variety of legal topics.

BROWARD REVIEW. see BUSINESS AND ECONOMICS

340   UK
BUCKLEY ON THE COMPANIES ACTS. (15th ed.) s-a. $450. Butterworth & Co. (Publishers) Ltd. (Subsidiary of: Reed International PLC), 88 Kingsway, London WC2B 6AB, England. TEL 71-405-6900. FAX 71-405-1332. (US addr.: Butterworth Legal Publishers, 90 Stiles Rd., Salem, NH 03079. TEL 800-548-4001) (looseleaf format)

340   US   ISSN 0407-5501
BUCKS COUNTY LAW REPORTER. 1951. w. $42. Bucks County Bar Association, 135 E. State St., Box 300, Doylestown, PA 18901. TEL 215-348-9413. Ed. Dianne C. Magee. adv.; cum.index; circ. 700. (also avail. in microfiche; back issues avail.)

340   US   ISSN 0023-9356
K2
BUFFALO LAW REVIEW. 1951. 3/yr. $21. State University of New York at Buffalo, Buffalo Law Review, 605 John Lord O'Brian Hall, Amherst Campus, Amherst, NY 14260. TEL 716-626-2059. FAX 716-636-2064. Ed. Nancy L. Shulman. bk.rev.; circ. 600. (also avail. in microfilm from WSH,PMC; reprint service avail.; reprint service avail. from WSH) **Indexed:** Abstr.Bk.Rev.Curr.Leg.Per., C.L.I., Crim.Just.Abstr., Curr.Cont., Environ.Abstr., L.R.I., Lang.& Lang.Behav.Abstr., Leg.Cont., Leg.Per., Mar.Aff.Bibl., SSCI.
 ●Also available online. Vendor(s): WESTLAW.
 —BLDSC shelfmark: 2357.600000.
 Description: Publishes scholarly writings addressing contemporary issues in all areas of law.

BUILDING AND CONSTRUCTION CONTRACTS IN AUSTRALIA. see BUILDING AND CONSTRUCTION

BUILDING AND CONSTRUCTION LAW. see BUILDING AND CONSTRUCTION

340   UK
BUILDING CONTRACTS & PRACTICE. (8th ed.) irreg. (2-3/yr.). $616. Butterworth & Co. (Publishers) Ltd. (Subsidiary of: Reed International PLC), 88 Kingsway, London WC2B 6AB, England. TEL 71-405-6900. FAX 71-405-1332. (US addr.: Butterworth Legal Publishers, 90 Stiles Rd., Salem, NH 03079. TEL 800-548-4001) (looseleaf format)

340 690   UK
BUILDING LAW MONTHLY. m. £115 (foreign £130). Monitor Press, Rectory Rd., Great Waldingfield, Sudbury, Suffolk CO10 0TL, England. FAX 0787-880201. (back issues avail.)
 Description: Advisory service for specialists in the building and construction industries.

340 690   UK   ISSN 0141-5875
BUILDING LAW REPORTS. 1976. 5/yr. £139($262). Longman Group UK Ltd., Longman House, Burnt Mill, Harlow, Essex CM20 2JE, England. TEL 0279-426721. FAX 0279-431059. Ed.Bd. (back issues avail.)
 Description: Comprehensive and up-to-date collection of legal construction cases for all those with a professional interest in construction law.

BUILDING SERVICE. see BUILDING AND CONSTRUCTION

340   FR   ISSN 0007-411X
BULLETIN ANNOTE DES LOIS ET DECRETS. 1825. m. 320 F. Publications Paul Dupont, 38 rue Croix des Petits Champs, 75001 Paris, France.

340   FR   ISSN 0007-4519
BULLETIN DES TRANSPORTS. 1895. w. 830 F. (effective 1991). Lamy S.A., 155, rue Legendre, 75850 Paris Cedex 17, France. TEL 1-46-27-28-90. FAX 42-29-86-81. TELEX 214 398. adv.; charts; illus.; index; circ. 7,000.
 Description: Covers the law, regulation, jurisprudence, and professional news of all forms of transport.

BULLETIN FIDUCIAIRE. see BUSINESS AND ECONOMICS — Banking And Finance

342   BE
BULLETIN LEGISLATIF BELGE. (Supplement avail: Tables Chronologiques et Alphabetiques du Moniteur Belge) w. 9450 Fr. Maison Ferdinand Larcier S.A., Rue des Minimes 39, 1000 Brussels, Belgium.

340   CS   ISSN 0323-2719
BULLETIN OF CZECHOSLOVAK LAW. (Text in English) 1960. q. $40. Asociace Pravniku C S F R - Association of Lawyers of the Czech and Slovak Federal Republic, Nam. Curieovych 7, 116 40 Prague 1, Czechoslovakia. (Dist. by: Pegas Press Distributor, Artia, Ve Smeckach 30, 111 27 Prague 1, Czechoslovakia) **Indexed:** Geo.Abstr.

340 US ISSN 0362-3769
KF325.188
BULLETIN OF LAW, SCIENCE & TECHNOLOGY. 1976. bi-m. membership only. American Bar Association, Science and Technology Section, 750 N. Lake Shore Dr., Chicago, IL 60611. TEL 312-988-6067. Ed. Bertram R. Cottine. bk.rev.; circ. 5,400. **Indexed:** C.L.I., L.R.I.
    Description: Developments in areas of science and technology, and related legal issues and court decisions; news of section activities.

340 UK ISSN 0007-4969
BULLETIN OF LEGAL DEVELOPMENTS; a fortnightly survey of U.K., European, foreign, commonwealth and international legal events. 1966. fortn. £85($170) British Institute of International and Comparative Law, 17 Russell Square, London WC1B 5DR, England. TEL 071-636-5802. FAX 071-323-2016. s-a.index; circ. 350. **Indexed:** Ocean.Abstr., Pollut.Abstr.
    —BLDSC shelfmark: 2865.600000.

348 US ISSN 0146-2989
BULLETIN OF MEDIEVAL CANON LAW. NEW SERIES. (Text in English, French, German, Italian, Latin and Spanish) 1971. a. $20. Institute of Medieval Canon Law, University of California, Berkeley, Boalt Hall, Berkeley, CA 94720. TEL 415-642-5094. Ed. Kenneth Pennington. bibl.; circ. 500. **Indexed:** Canon Law Abstr., CERDIC.

320 UK ISSN 0260-6550
K2
BULLETIN OF NORTHERN IRELAND LAW. 1981. 10/yr. £92. S L S Legal Publications, School of Law, Queens University of Belfast, Belfast BT7 1NN, N. Ireland. TEL 0232-245133. FAX 0232-247895. TELEX 74487. Ed. Deborah J. McBride. adv.; circ. 650.

340 CN
BULLETIN ON CURRENT RESEARCH IN SOVIET AND EAST EUROPEAN LAW. 1970. 3/yr. $9 (effective Feb. 1991). University of Toronto, Centre for Russian and East European Studies, 100 St. George St., Toronto, Ont. M5S 1A1, Canada. TEL 416-978-3330. Ed. Peter Solomon, Jr. adv.; bk.rev.; bibl.; circ. 200. (processed; back issues avail.)

BULLETIN RAPIDE DE DROIT DES AFFAIRES. see BUSINESS AND ECONOMICS — Management

340 BE
BULLETIN USUEL DES LOIS ET ARRETES. 1850. fortn. 20000 Fr. Etablissements Emile Bruylant, 67 rue de la Regence, B-1000 Brussels, Belgium. TEL 02-512-9845.

340 351.06 GW
BUNDESWEHRVERWALTUNG; Fachzeitschrift fuer Administration. m. DM.138. Carl Heymanns Verlag KG, Luxemburgerstr. 449, 5000 Cologne 41, Germany. TEL 0221-46010-0. FAX 0221-4601069.

340 BD
BURUNDI. MINISTERE DE LA JUSTICE. BULLETIN OFFICIEL. (Text in French) vol.10, 1971. m. Ministere de la Justice, Bujumbura, Burundi. (Subscr. to: Impr. du Gouvernement, B.P. 991, Bujumbura, Burundi)

BUSINESS ACCOUNTING FOR LAWYERS NEWSLETTER; summary, analysis, and application of current accounting concepts in the practice of law. see BUSINESS AND ECONOMICS — Accounting

BUSINESS FRANCHISE GUIDE. see BUSINESS AND ECONOMICS — Small Business

340 UK ISSN 0263-4430
BUSY SOLICITORS' DIGEST. 1982. m. £55($90) Longman Group UK Ltd., Law, Tax and Finance Division, 21-27 Lamb's Conduit St., London WC1N 3NJ, England. TEL 071-242-2548. FAX 071-831-8119. TELEX 295445. Eds. S. Vaulkhard, C. Spencer.
    Description: Changes and developments in the law for solicitors.

340 NZ
BUTTERWORTHS ANNOTATIONS TO THE NEW ZEALAND STATUTES. 4 base vols. (plus m. update). Butterworths of New Zealand Ltd., 203-207 Victoria St., P.O. Box 472, Wellington, New Zealand. TEL 04-385-1479. FAX 04-385-1598. Ed. Stuart Coghill. (looseleaf format)
    Description: Full text of all amendments to New Zealand public Acts, regularly updated, plus case notes and annotations.

340 NZ ISSN 0111-9656
BUTTERWORTHS CONVEYANCING BULLETIN. 1982. 8/yr. Butterworths of New Zealand Ltd., P.O. Box 472, 203-207 Victoria St., Wellington, New Zealand. TEL 04-385-1479. FAX 04-385-1598. Ed. Peter Haig.
    Formerly: New Zealand Conveyancing Bulletin (ISSN 0113-115X)
    Description: Articles and case notes dealing with significant developments in conveyancing and property transactions.

340 UK
BUTTERWORTHS COSTS SERVICE. 3/yr. $525. Butterworth & Co. (Publishers) Ltd. (Subsidiary of: Reed International PLC), 88 Kingsway, London WC2B 6AB, England. TEL 71-405-6900. FAX 71-405-1332. (US addr.: Butterworth Legal Publishers, 90 Stiles Rd., Salem, NH 03079. TEL 800-548-4001) Ed. F. Berkeley. (looseleaf format)

340 UK
BUTTERWORTHS COUNTY COURT PRECEDENTS & PLEADINGS. 3/yr. $406. Butterworth & Co. (Publishers) Ltd. (Subsidiary of: Reed International PLC), 88 Kingsway, London WC2B 6AB, England. TEL 71-405-6900. FAX 71-405-1332. (US addr.: Butterworth Legal Publishers, 90 Stiles Rd., Salem, NH 03079. TEL 800-548-4001) (looseleaf format)

340.093 NZ ISSN 0110-070X
LAW
BUTTERWORTHS CURRENT LAW. 24/yr. Butterworths of New Zealand Ltd., P.O. Box 472, 203-207 Victorian St., Wellington, New Zealand. TEL 04-385-1479. FAX 04-385-1598. Ed. Christine O'Brien.
    Description: Notes on cases of significance in New Zealand.

340 NZ
BUTTERWORTHS DISTRICT COURT REPORTS. 1981. m. NZ.$464. Butterworths of New Zealand Ltd., P.O. Box 472, 203-207 Victoria St., Wellington, New Zealand. TEL 04-385-1479. FAX 04-385-1598. Ed. Judge Robert Kerr.
    Formerly: New Zealand District Court Reports (ISSN 0111-4239)
    Description: Reports on a large selection of District Court cases from throughout New Zealand.

340 332 UK ISSN 0269-2694
K2
BUTTERWORTHS JOURNAL OF INTERNATIONAL BANKING AND FINANCIAL LAW. 1986. m. $975. Butterworth & Co. (Publishers) Ltd. (Subsidiary of: Reed International PLC), 88 Kingsway, London WC2B 6AB, England. TEL 71-405-6900. FAX 71-405-1332. (US addr.: Butterworth Legal Publishers, 90 Stiles Rd., Salem, NH 03079. TEL 800-548-4001) Ed. Josephine McAfee. bk.rev. **Indexed:** World Bank.Abstr.
    —BLDSC shelfmark: 2935.632050.
    Description: Presents news and comment from international financial centers.

340 UK
BUTTERWORTHS LAW DIRECTORY AND DIARY. 1985. a. £49. Reed Information Services Ltd., Specialist Publications, Windsor Court, East Grinstead House, East Grinstead, W. Sussex RH19 1XA, England. TEL 0342-326972. FAX 0342-317422. Ed. C. Stratton. circ. 14,000.
    Description: Directory of law firms and lawyers in the United Kingdom.

340 UK
BUTTERWORTHS LAW OF FOOD & DRUGS. (In 6 vols.) 3/yr. $1650. Butterworth & Co. (Publishers) Ltd. (Subsidiary of: Reed International PLC), 88 Kingsway, London WC2B 6AB, England. TEL 71-405-6900. FAX 71-405-1332. (US addr.: Butterworth Legal Publishers, 90 Stiles Rd., Salem, NH 03079. TEL 800-548-4001) Ed. Anthony A. Painter. (looseleaf format)

340 UK
BUTTERWORTHS LEGAL SERVICES DIRECTORY. 1987. a. £25. Reed Information Services Ltd., Specialist Publications, Windsor Court, East Grinstead House, East Grinstead, W. Sussex RH19 1XA, England. TEL 0342-326972. FAX 0342-317422. Ed. C. Stratton.

340 UK
BUTTERWORTHS LEGISLATION SERVICE. irreg. (7-10/yr.) $844. Butterworth & Co. (Publishers) Ltd. (Subsidiary of: Reed International PLC), 88 Kingsway, London WC2B 6AB, England. TEL 71-405-6900. FAX 71-405-1332. TELEX 95678. (US addr.: Butterworths Legal Publishers, 90 Stiles Rd., Salem, NH 03079. TEL 800-548-4001)

340 SA
BUTTERWORTHS LEGISLATION SERVICE. MONTHLY BULLETIN. (Text in English) 1958. m. (plus q. update). price varies. Butterworth Publishers (Pty.) Ltd., 8 Walter Pl., Waterval Park, Durban 4000, South Africa. FAX 2731-286350. Ed. T. Juul. circ. 2,500.
    Formerly: Butterworths Consolidated Legislation Service of South Africa. Monthly Bulletin (ISSN 0007-7321)

340 333.33 UK
BUTTERWORTHS PROPERTY LAW HANDBOOK. 3/yr. (plus bi-m. Bulletins). $66. Butterworth & Co. (Publishers) Ltd. (Subsidiary of: Reed International PLC), 88 Kingsway, London WC2B 6AB, England. TEL 71-405-6900. FAX 71-405-1332. TELEX 95678. (US addr.: Butterworth Legal Publishers, 90 Stiles Rd., Salem, NH 03079. TEL 800-548-4001) (looseleaf format)

340 388.31 UK
BUTTERWORTHS ROAD TRAFFIC SERVICE. irreg. (approx 3/yr.). $450. Butterworths & Co. (Publishers) Ltd., 88 Kingsway, London WC2B 6AB, England. TEL 071-405-6900. FAX 071-405-1332. (US addr.: Butterworth Legal Publishers, 90 Stiles Rd., Salem, NH 03079. TEL 603-898-9664) (looseleaf format)
    Formerly: Mahaffy & Dodson on Road Traffic.

340 UK
BUTTERWORTHS U K TAX GUIDE. a. $48. Butterworth & Co. (Publishers) Ltd. (Subsidiary of: Reed International PLC), 88 Kingsway, London WC2B 6AB, England. TEL 71-405-6900. FAX 71-405-1332. (US addr.: Butterworth Legal Publishers, 90 Stiles Rd., Salem, NH 03079. TEL 800-548-4001)

340 331 CN
BUTTERWORTH'S WRONGFUL DISMISSAL PRACTICE MANUAL. q. Can.$240. Butterworths Canada Ltd., 75 Clegg Rd., Markham, Ont. L6G 1A1, Canada. TEL 416-479-2665. FAX 416-479-2826. Ed. Ellen E. Mole. (looseleaf format)
    Description: Examines all aspects of wrongful dismissal in Canada.

BUY OR SELL YOUR BUSINESS. see BUSINESS AND ECONOMICS — Small Business

340 320 US
BYERS ELECTION LAW. a. $80. New York Legal Publishing Corp., 6 Charles Park, Guilderland, NY 12084. TEL 800-541-2681. FAX 518-456-0828.

340 323.4 UK
C A B NEWS. 1972. 4/yr. free. National Association of Citizens Advice Bureaux, 115 Pentonville Rd., London N1 9LZ, England. Eds. Jo Gibbons, Jacqui Roach. circ. 6,000. **Indexed:** Ind.Child.Mag.
    Formerly: Owl.

C A C S W NEWS. (Canadian Advisory Council on the Status of Women) see WOMEN'S INTERESTS

340 US ISSN 0892-1822
KF200
C B A RECORD.* 1987. bi-m. $12. Chicago Bar Association, 321 S. Plymouth Ct., Chicago, IL 60604-3907. Ed. Paul C. Kimball. adv.; bk.rev.; circ. 19,000. (also avail. in microfilm; back issues avail.; reprint service avail. from RRI) **Indexed:** C.L.I., L.R.I., Law Ofc.Info.Svc., Leg.Per.
●Also available online. Vendor(s): WESTLAW.
    —BLDSC shelfmark: 3095.110000.
    Formerly (until 1987): Chicago Bar Record (ISSN 0009-3505)

LAW 2607

C C A NEWS. (Consumer Credit Association) see *BUSINESS AND ECONOMICS — Banking And Finance*

C C H JOURNAL OF ASIAN PACIFIC TAXATION. see *BUSINESS AND ECONOMICS — International Commerce*

340 300　　　　UA　ISSN 0752-4412
DT43
▼**C E D E J EGYPTE - MONDE ARABE.** 1990. 4/yr. $80. Centre d'Etudes et de Documentation Economique, Juridique et Sociale, 14 Sharia Gameyet al-Nisr, Mohandessin-Dokki, Cairo, Egypt. TEL 3611932. TELEX 93088 CEFEC UN. Ed. J.C. Vatin. adv.; bk.rev.; circ. 600.
　Formed by the 1989 merger of: Revue de la Presse Egyptienne & C E D E J Departement des Sciences Sociales. Bulletin (ISSN 0255-755X); Formerly: Centre de Documentation d'Etudes Juridiques, Economiques et Sociales. Bulletin.

346.013　　　　PY　ISSN 1017-2785
C E D H U. 1988. bi-m. $12. Centro de Estudios Humanitarios, Azara 3267, Asuncion, Paraguay. (Dist. by: D.I.P.P., Box 2507, Asuncion, Paraguay) Ed. Esther Prieto. circ. 500.

C E I UPDATE. (Competitive Enterprise Institute) see *BUSINESS AND ECONOMICS*

C H I L D NEWSLETTER. (Children's Healthcare is a Legal Duty) see *CHILDREN AND YOUTH — About*

C L E A R EXAM REVIEW. (Council on Licensure, Enforcement & Regulation) see *PUBLIC HEALTH AND SAFETY*

340 378　　　　US
KF275
C L E JOURNAL AND REGISTER. 1965. 6/yr. $75. American Law Institute, Committee on Continuing Professional Education, 4025 Chestnut St., Philadelphia, PA 19104. TEL 215-243-1604. FAX 215-243-1664. (Co-sponsor: American Bar Association) Ed. Mark T. Carroll. circ. 525.
●Also available online.
　Former titles (until 1987): C L E Register (ISSN 0193-693X); (until 1979): C L E Catalog of Continuing Legal Education Programs in the United States.
　Description: Catalogue of continuing legal education courses for lawyers and articles on continuing legal education.

340　　　　US
C L E T V. (Continuing Legal Education) 1988. 24/yr. $700. American Law Institute, Committee on Continuing Professional Education, 4025 Chestnut St., Philadelphia, PA 19104. TEL 215-243-1617. FAX 215-243-1664. Ed. Eileen Kenney. (video cassette)
　Description: Video programs of practical interest to the general practitioner.

340 200　　　　US　ISSN 0736-0142
KF200
C L S QUARTERLY. 1980. 4/yr. $20. Christian Legal Society, 4208 Evergreen Lane, Ste. 222, Annandale, VA 22003. TEL 703-642-1070. FAX 703-642-1075. Ed. Karen Heal. adv.; bk.rev.; circ. 6,000. (also avail. in microform from UMI; back issues avail.; reprint service avail. from WSH) **Indexed:** C.L.I., L.R.I., Leg.Per.
　Formerly (until 1981): Christian Legal Society Quarterly (ISSN 0275-6765); Which was formed by the merger of: Christian Legal Society Newsletter; Christian Lawyer.
　Description: Platform for views held by Christian attorneys, judges, law students and law professors.

340 320 350　　　　US
C O G E L GUARDIAN. 1980. bi-m. $54 to non-members; members $25. Council on Governmental Ethics Laws, Iron Works Pike, Box 11910, Lexington, KY 40578. TEL 606-231-1909. FAX 606-231-1858. Ed. Joyce Bullock. bk.rev.; abstr.; bibl.; stat.; circ. 400.
　Formerly: C O G E L Newsletter.
　Description: Reports on campaign finance, conflict of interest and lobbying issues, legislation and litigation.

340 350　　　　US
C S I CONGRESSIONAL RECORD REPORT.* d. (following session of Congress). price varies. (Capitol Services, Inc.) National Standards, 1200 Quince Orchard Blvd., Gaithersburg, MD 20878. Ed. Lisa Joy.

340 350　　　　US
C S I FEDERAL REGISTER.* d. price varies. (Capitol Services, Inc.) National Standards, 1200 Quince Orchard Blvd., Gaithersburg, MD 20878. Ed. Gregory Friedman.

347.91　　　　US　ISSN 0889-7751
C T L A FORUM.* 1979. 10/yr. $40 (avail. to law libraries only). California Trial Lawyers Association, 980 Ninth St., Ste. 200, Sacramento, CA 95814-2721. Ed. Sharon E. Scott. adv.; circ. 8,000.
　Formerly: California Trial Lawyers Forum; Supersedes: California Trial Lawyers Association. Journal (ISSN 0730-4919); California Trial Lawyers Journal (ISSN 0575-6316).

340 384.55　　　　US
KF2844.A15
CABLE T V AND NEW MEDIA LAW & FINANCE. 1983. m. $195 (effective Sep. 1991). Leader Publications, Inc. (Subsidiary of: New York Law Publishing Co.), 111 Eighth Ave., Ste. 900, New York, NY 10011. TEL 800-888-8300. FAX 212-463-5523. Eds. Michael Botein, David M. Rice. bk.rev.
　Formerly: Cable T V Law and Finance (ISSN 0736-489X)
　Description: Interprets and analyzes the latest developments in cable and video.

CABLE T V LAW REPORTER. see *COMMUNICATIONS — Television And Cable*

CABLE T V PROGRAMMING; newsletter on programs for pay cable T V and analysis of basic cable networks. see *COMMUNICATIONS — Television And Cable*

340　　　　BL
CADERNO DE DIREITO ECONOMICO. 1983. irreg. $15. Centro de Estudos de Extensao Universitaria, Av. Alfonso Bovero, 175, 01254 Sao Paulo SP, Brazil. TEL 011-872-1877. circ. 1,000.
　Description: Debates objective questions on an economic law doctrine theme.

340　　　　BL
CADERNO DE DIREITO NATURAL. 1985. irreg. $10. Centro de Estudos de Extensao Universitaria, Av. Prof. Alfonso Bovero, 175, 01254 Sao Paulo, SP, Brazil. TEL 011-872-1877. circ. 1,000.
　Description: Discusses several views of a specific theme in natural law.

340　　　　BL
CADERNO DE PESQUISAS TRIBUTARIAS. 1976. a. $75. Centro de Estudos de Extensao Universitaria, Av. Alfonso Bovero, 175, 01254 Sao Paulo SP, Brazil. TEL 011-872-1877. circ. 5,000.
　Description: Debates objective questions on a theme of tributary law doctrine.

340　　　　MG
CAHIERS D'HISTOIRE JURIDIQUE ET POLITIQUE. 1966. s-a. Universite de Madagascar, Etablissement d'Enseignement Superieur de Droit, d'Economie, de Gestion et de Sociologie, B.P. 905, Antananarivo, Malagasy Republic.
　Formerly (until no.10, 1974): Universite de Madagascar. Centre d'Etudes des Coutumes. Cahiers (ISSN 0496-8018)

340　　　　CN　ISSN 0007-974X
LAW
CAHIERS DE DROIT. (Text in English and French) vol.1, 1954. q. Can.$42.80 to individuals; institutions Can.$53.50. (Universite Laval) Wilson et Lafleur Ltee., C.P. 24, Place d'Armes, Montreal, Que. H2Y 3L2, Canada. Ed. Pierre Verge. adv.; bk.rev.; bibl.; index, cum.index; circ. 1,200. (also avail. in microform from UMI,MML; reprint service avail. from UMI,WSH) **Indexed:** C.L.I., Ind.Can.L.P.L., L.R.I., Leg.Per., Mar.Aff.Bibl., Pt.de Rep. (1982-).
　—BLDSC shelfmark: 2948.853000.

349　　　　BE　ISSN 0007-9758
CAHIERS DE DROIT EUROPEEN. 1965. bi-m. 4900 Fr. Maison Ferdinand Larcier S.A., Rue des Minimes 39, 1000 Brussels, Belgium. TEL 02-5124712. FAX 02-5139009. Ed. Leon Goffin. adv.; bk.rev.; index. cum.index; circ. 1,000.
　—BLDSC shelfmark: 2948.855000.
　Description: Publishes legal and jurisprudential commentary on the application of European law, reports of significant cases before the Court of Justice of the European Communities, the Human Rights Court, the Courts of Belgium, Luxembourg and the Netherlands, and in addition provides coverage of legislative developments.
　Refereed Serial

CAHIERS DE L'UNIVERSITE DE PERPIGNAN. see *LITERATURE*

CAHIERS DU TOURISME. SERIE E: LEGISLATION. see *TRAVEL AND TOURISM*

340　　　　FR　ISSN 0981-1761
CAHIERS TERRITOIRES. 1983. 2/yr. 350 F. Association Territoires, 31, rue de la Cerisaie, 75004 Paris, France. TEL 4274-7461.
　Formerly: Territoires (ISSN 0761-7143)

CAISSES CENTRALES DE MUTUALITE SOCIALE AGRICOLE. STATISTIQUES.. see *BUSINESS AND ECONOMICS — Abstracting, Bibliographies, Statistics*

340　　　　II　ISSN 0045-3854
CALCUTTA WEEKLY NOTES; a journal of law notes of the Calcutta high court. (Text in English) 1896. w. Rs.55($16) Weekly Notes Printing Works, Pvt. Ltd., 34 Ballygunge Circular Rd., Calcutta 700019, India. Ed. Ranadeb Chaudhuri. adv.; bibl.
　Description: Law notes and reports of Calcutta High Court.

CALENDARS OF THE UNITED STATES HOUSE OF REPRESENTATIVES AND HISTORY OF LEGISLATION. see *MEETINGS AND CONGRESSES*

340　　　　US
CALIFORNIA. LAW REVISION COMMISSION. REPORTS, RECOMMENDATIONS AND STUDIES. 1955. irreg., vol.20, 1990. pamphlets $35; bound vols. $50. Law Revision Commission, 4000 Middlefield Rd., Ste. D-2, Palo Alto, CA 94303-4739. index; circ. 1,500.
　Description: Includes its Annual Reports, Recommendations and Studies issues as pamphlets, bound every two years.

CALIFORNIA. STATE BOARD OF COSMETOLOGY. RULES AND REGULATIONS.. see *BEAUTY CULTURE*

346.066　　　　US
▼**CALIFORNIA ADMINISTRATIVE AND ANTITRUST LAW**; regulation of business, trades and professions. 1991. 2 base vols. (plus suppl.). $160. Butterworth Legal Publishers (Salem) (Subsidiary of: Reed International PLC), 90 Stiles Rd., Salem, NH 03079. TEL 800-548-4001. FAX 603-898-9858. Eds. Robert C. Fellmeth, Ralph H. Folsom. (looseleaf format)

340　　　　US
CALIFORNIA AND NEVADA LEGAL SERVICES PROGRAMS DIRECTORY. 1974. a. $6. Western Center on Law and Poverty, Inc., 3535 W. Sixth St., Los Angeles, CA 90020-2898. TEL 213-487-7211. circ. 120.

340　　　　US
CALIFORNIA ATTORNEY PRACTICE: REQUIREMENTS, ETHICS, AND RESPONSIBILITIES. 1986. 3 base vols. (plus irreg. supplements). Matthew Bender & Co., Inc., 11 Penn Plaza, New York, NY 10001. TEL 212-967-7707. Eds. Mary Yen, Tom Low. (looseleaf format)
　Description: Discusses such topics as admission to the bar, establishment of a law practice, advertising and solicitation, fee agreements, recovery of attorney's fees, ethical duties to clients and discipline for professional misconduct.

CALIFORNIA CABLE LETTER; current community perspectives and directions. see *COMMUNICATIONS*

CALIFORNIA CLOSELY HELD CORPORATIONS: TAX PLANNING AND PRACTICE GUIDE. see *BUSINESS AND ECONOMICS — Public Finance, Taxation*

340 331 US
CALIFORNIA COMPENSATION CASES. a. (plus m. supplements). Matthew Bender & Co., Inc., 11 Penn Plaza, New York, NY 10001. TEL 212-967-7707. Ed. W.H. Ryan.
Description: Covers all en banc and selected panel decisions of Workers' Compensation Appeals Board. Includes digests of significant Appeals Board decisions denied judicial review and digests of related state and federal court opinions.

340 690 US
▼**CALIFORNIA CONSTRUCTION LAW MANUAL, 3-E.** 1990. base vol. (plus a. suppl.). $95. Shepard's - McGraw-Hill, Inc., Box 35300, Colorado Springs, CO 80935-3530. TEL 800-525-2474.
Description: For construction executives, architects, engineers and lawyers who work in California.

340 352 US ISSN 0068-5879
CALIFORNIA COUNTY LAW LIBRARY BASIC LIST. 1961. irreg. free. State Library, Law Library, Box 942837, Sacramento, CA 94237-0001. TEL 916-324-4868. circ. 600.

340 US ISSN 1049-9334
▼**CALIFORNIA EMPLOYMENT LAW LETTER.** 1990. 12/yr. $127. M. Lee Smith Publishers & Printers, 162 Fourth Ave. N., Box 2678, Nashville, TN 37219. TEL 615-242-7395. FAX 615-256-6601. (Co-sponsor: O'Melveny & Myers) Ed.Bd.
Description: Reports the latest California employment law developments that affect California employers.

347.91 US
CALIFORNIA FORMS OF JURY INSTRUCTION. 1985. 3 base vols. (plus irreg. supplements). Matthew Bender & Co., Inc., 11 Penn Plaza, New York, NY 10001. TEL 212-967-7707. (looseleaf format)
Description: Comprehensive source for jury instructions in contract, business tort and real property cases. Enables litigators to draft instructions that accurately reflect the law and are comprehensible to the average juror.

340 368 US
CALIFORNIA INSURANCE LAW AND PRACTICE. 1986. 4 base vols. (plus irreg. supplements). Matthew Bender & Co., Inc., 11 Penn Plaza, New York, NY 10001. TEL 212-967-7707. Ed.Bd. (looseleaf format)
Description: Provides detailed coverage of life, health and disability insurance, property and liability insurance, agents and brokers, and carriers. Examines common insurance law problems and considerations, with an analysis of California statutes, case law, regulations, and other administrative material.

340 331 US
CALIFORNIA LAW OF EMPLOYEE INJURIES AND WORKMEN'S COMPENSATION. 1953. 4 base vols. (plus irreg. supplements). Matthew Bender & Co., Inc., 11 Penn Plaza, New York, NY 10001. Ed.Bd. (looseleaf format)
Description: Covers every stage of workers' compensation cases in California and all related proceedings. Includes principles of substantive law (California workers' compensation liability and federal and state law of employee injuries).

340 US ISSN 0008-1221
K3 CODEN: CLARDJ
CALIFORNIA LAW REVIEW. 1912. 6/yr. $38 (foreign $47). University of California Press, Journals Division, 2120 Berkeley Way, Berkeley, CA 94720. TEL 510-642-4191. FAX 510-643-7127. adv.; bk.rev.; bibl.; index; circ. 1,900. (also avail. in microfiche from RRI; back issues avail.; reprint service avail. from RRI) **Indexed:** A.B.C.Pol.Sci., ABI Inform, C.L.I., Commun.Abstr., Crim.Just.Abstr., Curr.Cont., L.R.I., Leg.Cont., Leg.Per., P.A.I.S., SSCI.
—BLDSC shelfmark: 3015.020000.
Description: Articles on problems and developments in all areas of California law.
Refereed Serial

340 US ISSN 0279-4063
KF200
CALIFORNIA LAWYER. 1928. m. $24. Daily Journal Corporation (San Francisco), 1390 Market St., Ste. 1016, San Francisco, CA 94102. TEL 415-558-9888. FAX 415-558-8469. Ed. Ray Reynolds. adv.; bk.rev.; bibl.; illus.; circ. 120,00. (also avail. in microform from UMI,WSH,PMC; reprint service avail. from UMI,WSH) **Indexed:** C.L.I., Cal.Per.Ind. (1984-), L.R.I., Law Ofc.Info.Svc., Leg.Per., So.Pac.Per.Ind.
—BLDSC shelfmark: 3015.022000.
Former titles (until 1981): California State Bar Journal (ISSN 0161-9241); State Bar of California. Journal (ISSN 0039-002X)
Description: Discusses legal affairs, with news, analysis and practical advice on products and services.

CALIFORNIA LEAGUE OF SAVINGS INSTITUTIONS. LEGISLATION AND REGULATION UPDATE. see *BUSINESS AND ECONOMICS — Banking And Finance*

340 US
CALIFORNIA NOTARY LAW PRIMER. a. $9.95. National Notary Association, 8236 Remmet Ave., Box 7184, Canoga Park, CA 91304-7184. TEL 818-713-4000. FAX 818-713-9061. Ed. Charles N. Faerber. (reprint service avail. from UMI)

340 US
CALIFORNIA OFFICIAL REPORTS; official advance sheets of the Supreme Court, Courts of Appeal, and Appellate Departments of the Superior Court. 1850. 35/yr. $416.44. Bancroft-Whitney Company, Box 7005, San Francisco, CA 94120-7005. TEL 415-986-4410. Ed. Jay Nicolaisen. circ. 7,560.

340 US ISSN 1040-2640
CALIFORNIA PARALEGAL MAGAZINE. 1989. q. $22. California Parlegal Magazine, Box 6960, Los Osos, CA 93412. TEL 805-526-8705. Ed. Valerie Goodman-Plater. adv.; bk.rev.; circ. 2,000.
Description: Forum for paralegal networking. Contains updates on continuing education seminars and reports on paralegal literature.

340 US
CALIFORNIA POINTS AND AUTHORITIES. 1965. 24 base vols. (plus irreg. supplements). Matthew Bender & Co., Inc., 11 Penn Plaza, New York, NY 10001. TEL 212-967-7707. Ed.Bd. (looseleaf format)
Description: Provides the necessary statutory and case law required in law and motion picture proceedings.

340 640.73 US
CALIFORNIA PRODUCTS LIABILITY ACTIONS. 1970. base vol. with supplements. Matthew Bender & Co., Inc., 11 Penn Plaza, New York, NY 10001. TEL 212-967-7707. Ed.Bd. (looseleaf format)
Description: Covers every aspect of California products liability law for both plaintiff and defendant: investigation, role of experts, pleadings, discovery, proof, defenses, damages and trials.

340 350 US
CALIFORNIA PUBLIC AGENCY PRACTICE. 1988. 3 base vols. (plus irreg. supplements). Matthew Bender & Co., Inc., 11 Penn Plaza, New York, NY 10001. TEL 212-967-7707. Ed. Gregory L. Ogden. (looseleaf format)
Description: Covers both the theoretical and practical aspects of administrative law practice in California.

340 US ISSN 0739-7860
KFC430.A15
CALIFORNIA REGULATORY LAW REPORTER. 1981. q. $45. University of San Diego, School of Law, Center for Public Interest Law, Alcala Park, San Diego, CA 92110. TEL 619-260-4806. FAX 619-260-4753. Ed. Robert C. Fellmeth. circ. 1,200. (back issues avail.)
Description: Provides information on 60 California administrative agencies which regulate business, trades and professions. Includes pending litigation and legislation, feature articles and commentaries.

CALIFORNIA SCHOOL LAW DIGEST. see *EDUCATION — School Organization And Administration*

340 US
CALIFORNIA TORT REPORTER. 1980. 10/yr. $290. Shepard's - McGraw-Hill, Inc., Box 35300, Colorado Spring, CO 80935-3530. TEL 719-475-7230. Ed.Bd.

340 US ISSN 0008-1639
LAW
CALIFORNIA WESTERN LAW REVIEW. 1965. 2/yr. $15 (foreign $17). California Western School of Law, 350 Cedar St., San Diego, CA 92101. TEL 619-239-0391. FAX 619-696-9999. adv.; bk.rev.; circ. 1,300. (also avail. in microfilm from RRI; reprint service avail. from RRI) **Indexed:** C.L.I., L.R.I., Leg.Cont., Leg.Per., P.A.I.S.
—BLDSC shelfmark: 3015.360000.

340 331 US ISSN 0363-129X
KFC592.A15
CALIFORNIA WORKERS' COMPENSATION REPORTER. 1973. m. $240 (effective June 1991). California Workers' Compensation Reporter, Box 975, Berkeley, CA 94701. TEL 415-841-5575. Ed. Melvin S. Witt. bk.rev.; cum.index; circ. 1,350. (back issues avail.)
Description: News articles and briefs on legislative, policy, and judicial developments pertaining to the state law.

340 UK ISSN 0084-8328
K3
CAMBRIAN LAW REVIEW. 1970. a. $20. University College of Wales, Aberystwyth, Department of Law, Aberystwyth, Wales. TEL 0970-622271. FAX 0970-622729. adv.; bk.rev.; illus.; circ. 700. (also avail. in microfilm from WSH,PMC) **Indexed:** Abstr.Bk.Rev.Curr.Leg.Per., C.L.I., L.R.I., Leg.Per.

340 UK ISSN 0008-1973
LAW
CAMBRIDGE LAW JOURNAL. 1921. 3/yr. $64. (Cambridge University, Law Faculty) Cambridge University Press, Edinburgh Bldg., Shaftesbury Rd., Cambridge CB2 2RU, England. TEL 0223-312393. FAX 0223-315052. TELEX 851817256. (North American addr.: Cambridge University Press, 40 W. 20th St., New York, NY 10011) Ed. C.C. Turpin. adv.; bk.rev.; index; circ. 1,600. (also avail. in microform from UMI) **Indexed:** Abstr.Bk.Rev.Curr.Leg.Per., BPIA, Br.Hum.Ind., Bus.Ind., C.L.I., L.R.I., Leg.Per., Soc.Work Res.& Abstr.
—BLDSC shelfmark: 3015.960000.
Description: Articles on issues such as tort, constitutional law, legal history, and criminal law, with emphasis on current developments.

340 341 UK
CAMBRIDGE STUDIES IN INTERNATIONAL AND COMPARATIVE LAW: NEW SERIES. 1967. irreg. price varies. Cambridge University Press, Edinburgh Bldg., Shaftesbury Rd., Cambridge CB2 2RU, England. TEL 0223-312393. FAX 0223-315052. TELEX 851817256.
Formerly (until 1982): Cambridge Studies in International and Comparative Law (ISSN 0068-6751)

340 AT ISSN 0729-2570
CAMERON: SUPREME AND DISTRICT COURTS PRACTICE N.S.W. 1982. 6/yr. Aus.$320. Law Book Co. Ltd., 44-50 Waterloo Rd., N. Ryde, N.S.W. 2113, Australia. TEL 02-887-0177. FAX 02-888-9706. TELEX ASBOOK 27995. Ed. J. Lemaine. (looseleaf format; back issues avail.)
Description: Covers courts, jurisdiction, offices, judgement and enforcement, admiralty rules.

340 US ISSN 0198-8174
K3
CAMPBELL LAW REVIEW. 1979. 3/yr. $15. Campbell University, Box 1165, Buies Creek, NC 27506. TEL 919-893-4111. Ed. Elizabeth H. McCullough. adv.; bk.rev.; cum.index; circ. 1,000. (back issues avail.) **Indexed:** C.L.I., Leg.Per.

340 US ISSN 0742-8987
CAMPBELL'S LIST; a directory of selected lawyers. 1879. a. (plus suppl.). $10. Campbell's List, Inc., Campbell Bldg., 100 E. Ventris Ave., Maitland, FL 32751. TEL 407-644-8298. FAX 407-740-6494. Ed. John A. Campbell, Jr. circ. 6,000.

2610 LAW

340 CN
CANADA. LAW REFORM COMMISSION. ADMINISTRATIVE LAW SERIES. STUDY PAPERS. (Text in English, French) 1976. irreg. free. Law Reform Commission, 130 Albert St., Ottawa, Ont. K1A 0L6, Canada. TEL 613-996-7844. FAX 613-996-8599. (back issues avail.; reprint service avail. from MML)
Description: Monographs on Administrative Law.

340 CN ISSN 0382-1463
CANADA. LAW REFORM COMMISSION. ANNUAL REPORT. (Text in English, French) 1971. a. free. Law Reform Commission, 130 Albert St., Ottawa, Ont. K1A 0L6, Canada. TEL 613-996-7844. FAX 613-996-8599. (reprint service avail. from MML)

340 CN
CANADA. LAW REFORM COMMISSION. MODERNIZATION OF STATUTES. STUDY PAPERS. (Text in English and French) 1981. irreg. free. Law Reform Commission, 130 Albert St., Ottawa, Ont. K1A 0L6, Canada. TEL 613-996-7844. FAX 613-996-8599. (reprint service avail. from MML)

340 CN
CANADA. LAW REFORM COMMISSION. PROTECTION OF LIFE SERIES. STUDY PAPERS. (Text in English and French) 1979. irreg. free. Law Reform Commission, 130 Albert St., Ottawa, Ont. K1A 0L6, Canada. TEL 613-996-7844. FAX 613-996-8599. (back issues avail., reprint service avail. from MML)
Description: Monographs on medico-legal and environmental issues.

340 CN
CANADA. LAW REFORM COMMISSION. REPORT TO PARLIAMENT. (Text in English and French) 1975. irreg. free. Law Reform Commission, 130 Albert St., Ottawa, Ont. K1A 0L6, Canada. TEL 613-996-7844. FAX 613-996-8599. (back issues avail.; reprint service avail. from MML)
Description: Monographs on various issues in Canadian law.

340 CN
CANADA. LAW REFORM COMMISSION. WORKING PAPER. (Text in English, French) irreg. free. Law Reform Commission, 130 Albert St., Ottawa, Ont. K1A 0L6, Canada. TEL 613-996-7844. FAX 613-996-8599. circ. 10,000 (controlled). (back issues avail.; reprint service avail. from MML)
Description: Monographs on various issues in Canadian law.

CANADA. WOMEN'S BUREAU. WOMEN IN THE LABOUR FORCE. see *BUSINESS AND ECONOMICS — Labor And Industrial Relations*

340 CN ISSN 0045-4192
CANADA GAZETTE: PART 1: GOVERNMENT, DIVORCE, BANKRUPTCY NOTICES, ETC. (Catalog no. SP2-1) (Text in English, French) w. Can.$135($162) Canada Communication Group, Publishing Division, Ottawa, Ont. K1A 0S9, Canada. TEL 819-997-2560. (also avail. in microfilm from MIM,UMI,BHP,KTO)

340 CN
CANADA GAZETTE: PART 2: STATUTORY INSTRUMENTS. (Catalog SP2-2) (Text in English, French) s-m. Can.$67.50($79.80) Canada Communication Group, Publishing Division, Ottawa, Ont. K1A 0S9, Canada. TEL 819-997-2560. (also avail. in microform from MIM,UMI)
Formerly: Canada Gazette: Part 2: Statutory Orders and Regulations (ISSN 0045-4206)

340 CN
CANADA LEGAL DIRECTORY. 1911. a. Can.$105. Carswell Publications, Corporate Plaza, 2075 Kennedy Rd., Scarborough, Ont. M1T 3V4, Canada. TEL 416-609-8000. FAX 416-298-5094. circ. 3,000. (back issues avail.)

340 CN
CANADA PENSION PLAN, OLD AGE SECURITY ACT AND PENSION BENIFITS STANDARDS ACT. irreg., 8th ed., 1992. Can.$18.95. C C H Canadian Ltd., 6 Garamond St., Don Mills, Ont. M3C 1Z5, Canada. TEL 416-441-2992. FAX 416-444-9011.
Formerly: Canada Pension and Old Age Security Legislation.

340 CN
CANADA STATUTE CITATOR. irreg. (4-5/yr.). Can.$178.50. Canada Law Book Inc., 240 Edward St., Aurora, Ont. L4G 3S9, Canada. TEL 416-841-6472. (also avail. in looseleaf format)

340 336 CN
CANADA'S TAX TREATIES. q. Can.$285. Butterworths Canada Ltd., 75 Clegg Rd., Markham, Ont. L6G 1A1, Canada. TEL 416-479-2665. FAX 416-479-2826. (looseleaf format)
Description: Reference guide for tax practitioners and companies involved in cross-border transactions.

340 CN ISSN 0318-4935
CANADIAN BAR ASSOCIATION. ANNUAL REPORT OF PROCEEDINGS. a. Can.$45. Canadian Bar Foundation, 50 O'Connor, Suite 902, Ottawa, Ont. K1P 6L2, Canada. TEL 613-237-2925. FAX 613-237-0185.
Description: Transcript of proceedings of Canadian Bar Association's annual meeting.

340 CN ISSN 0384-5753
CANADIAN BAR ASSOCIATION. BRITISH COLUMBIA BRANCH. PROGRAM REPORT.* 1971. irreg. Canadian Bar Association, British Columbia Branch, 50 O'Connor St., Ottawa, Ont. K1P 6L2, Canada.
Indexed: Ind.Can.L.P.L.

340 CN ISSN 0315-2286
LAW
CANADIAN BAR NATIONAL. (Text in English, French) 1974. 10/yr. Can.$40. Canadian Bar Foundation, 50 O'Connor, Ste. 902, Ottawa, Ont. K1P 6L2, Canada. TEL 613-237-2925. FAX 613-237-0185. Ed. Hannah Bernstein. bk.rev.; bibl.; illus.; circ. 37,315. (tabloid format; also avail. in microfilm)

340 CN ISSN 0008-3003
CANADIAN BAR REVIEW. 1923. q. Can.$100. Canadian Bar Foundation, 50 O'Connor, Ste. 902, Ottawa, Ont. K1P 6L2, Canada. TEL 613-237-2925. FAX 613-237-0185. Ed. A.J. MacClean. adv.; bk.rev.; index. cum.index; circ. 35,000. (also avail. in microfilm from WSH,PMC) **Indexed:** Amer.Bibl.Slavic & E.Eur.Stud, C.L.I., Crim.Just.Abstr., Ind.Can.L.P.L., L.R.I., Leg.Per., Refug.Abstr., Risk Abstr., SSCI, Tr.& Indus.Ind.

340 658.3 CN
CANADIAN CASES ON EMPLOYMENT LAW. 1983. 12/yr. (4 vols./yr.). Can.$115. Carswell Publications, Corporate Plaza, 2075 Kennedy Rd., Scarborough, Ont. M1T 3V4, Canada. TEL 416-609-8000. FAX 416-298-5094. Ed. David Harris. **Indexed:** Ind.Can.L.P.L.
Former titles: Canadian Cases on Employment Law Reports (ISSN 0824-2607); Employment Law Reports.

340 368 CN ISSN 0824-2585
CANADIAN CASES ON THE LAW OF INSURANCE (2ND SERIES). 1983. 12/yr. (4 vols./yr.). Can.$115. Carswell Publications, Corporate Plaza, 2075 Kennedy Rd., Scarborough, Ont. M1T 3V4, Canada. TEL 416-609-8000. FAX 416-298-5094. Eds. Marvin F. Baer, James A. Rendall. **Indexed:** Ind.Can.L.P.L.

340 CN ISSN 0701-1733
KE1232.A45
CANADIAN CASES ON THE LAW OF TORTS (2ND SERIES). 1976. 12/yr. (4 vols./yr.). Can.$115. Carswell Publications, Corporate Plaza, 2075 Kennedy Rd., Scarborough, Ont. M1T 3V4, Canada. TEL 416-609-8000. FAX 416-298-5094. Ed. John Irvine. **Indexed:** C.L.I., Ind.Can.L.P.L., L.R.I.

340 CN
CANADIAN CHARTER OF RIGHTS ANNOTATED. 9/yr. Can.$194.25. Canada Law Book Inc., 240 Edward St., Aurora, Ont. L4G 3S9, Canada. TEL 416-841-6472. (looseleaf format)

342 CN ISSN 0821-719X
CANADIAN CHARTER OF RIGHTS DECISIONS. 1982. fortn. (3 vols./yr.). Can.$156.50 per vol. Western Legal Publications, 301-1 Alexander St., Vancouver, B.C. V6A 1B2, Canada. TEL 604-687-5671. FAX 604-687-2796. index. (back issues avail.)
Description: Information on all available decisions pertaining to the Canadian Charter of Rights and Freedoms and the Canadian Bill of Rights.

340 CN ISSN 0835-9776
KE173
CANADIAN CITATIONS. 20/yr. Can.$555 includes Canadian Current Law. Carswell Publications, Corporate Plaza, 2075 Kennedy Rd., Scarborough, Ont. M1T 3V4, Canada. TEL 416-609-8000. FAX 416-298-5094.
Supersedes in part: Canadian Current Law and Canadian Citations.

340 CN ISSN 0228-1961
CANADIAN COMPETITION POLICY RECORD. 1980. q. Can.$250 to individuals; institutions Can.$125. Fraser Beatty Legal Publications, 180 Elgin Street, Ste.1201, Ottawa, Ont. K2P 2K7, Canada. TEL 613-235-0690. FAX 613-563-7800. Ed. Lawson Hunter. bk.rev.; circ. 280. (back issues avail.) **Indexed:** Can.Per.Ind.

CANADIAN COMPUTER LAW REPORTER. see *COMPUTERS*

CANADIAN CORPORATE SECRETARY'S GUIDE. see *BUSINESS AND ECONOMICS — Management*

340 CN ISSN 0835-9768
KE173
CANADIAN CURRENT LAW. 1948. 40/yr. Can.$555 includes Canadian Citations. Carswell Publications, Corporate Plaza, 2075 Kennedy Rd., Scarborough, Ont. M1T 3V4, Canada. TEL 416-609-8000. FAX 416-298-5094.
Supersedes in part: Canadian Current Law and Canada Citations.

347.9 CN
CANADIAN EMPLOYMENT LAW GUIDE. bi-m. Can.$230. C C H Canadian Ltd., 6 Garamond Ct., Don Mills, Ont. M3C 1Z5, Canada.
Description: Covers collective bargaining, minimum wage, personnel reporrts, work hours, overtime, payment of wages, vacations, holidays, leaves of absence, termination, human rights, equal pay and unemployment insurance.

346.066 CN
CANADIAN EMPLOYMENT LAW TODAY. fortn. Can.$278. M P L Communications Inc., 700-133 Richmond St. W., Toronto, Ont. M5H 3M8, Canada. TEL 416-869-1177. FAX 416-869-0456.
Description: Focuses on the field of Canadian employment law and how it affects management-employee relations.

CANADIAN EMPLOYMENT SAFETY AND HEALTH GUIDE. see *OCCUPATIONAL HEALTH AND SAFETY*

340 614.7 CN
CANADIAN ENVIRONMENTAL LAW. q. Can.$725. Butterworths Canada Ltd., 75 Clegg Rd., Markham, Ont. L6G 1A1, Canada. TEL 416-479-2665. FAX 416-479-2826. Eds. Robert T. Franson, Alastair R. Lucas. (looseleaf format)
Description: Reference on waste management and other aspects of pollution control.

CANADIAN ENVIRONMENTAL LAW REPORT. NEW SERIES. see *ENVIRONMENTAL STUDIES*

CANADIAN ENVIRONMENTAL PROTECTION. see *ENVIRONMENTAL STUDIES*

340 332.1 CN
CANADIAN FINANCIAL SERVICES ALERT. 1988. 8/yr. Can.$225. Carswell Publications, 2330 Midland Ave., Agincourt, Ont. M1S 1P7, Canada. TEL 416-291-8421. FAX 416-291-3426. Eds. Ron Marshall, William Chambers. circ. 175.
Formerly (until Jun.1991): Canadian Banking Law Newsletter.
Description: Legal information for chartered banks, trust companies, investment and insurance communities, and their legal counsel.

CANADIAN HEALTH CASE LAW DIGEST. see *MEDICAL SCIENCES*

340 614 CN
CANADIAN HEALTH FACILITIES LAW GUIDE. m. Can.$490. C C H Canadian Ltd., 6 Garamond Court, Don Mills, Ont. M3C 1Z5, Canada. TEL 416-441-2992. FAX 416-444-9011. index.
Description: Statutes and commentary related to health care facilities (i.e. hospitals, nursing homes, clinics, chronic care homes, etc.). Text of approximately 70 statutes and selected regulations are reproduced.

340 336   CN
CANADIAN INDUSTRIAL INCENTIVES LEGISLATION. 6/yr.
Can.$155. Butterworths Canada Ltd., 75 Clegg Rd.,
Markham, Ont. L6G 1A1, Canada.
TEL 416-479-2665. FAX 416-479-2826. Eds. Les
Soloman, Jeff Carbell. (looseleaf format)
    Description: Both Federal and Provincial assistance
and tax incentive programs. A reference for business
and industry managers.

346.086   CN   ISSN 0045-4990
CANADIAN INSURANCE LAW REPORTER. m. Can.$430.
C C H Canadian Ltd., 6 Garamond Ct., Don Mills,
Ont. M3C 1Z5, Canada. TEL 416-441-2992.
FAX 416-444-9011. index.
    Description: Contains text decisions from provincial
and federal courts on insurance contracts: life,
health, accident, fire, casualty and automobiles.
Comprehensive digests of tort decisions, quantum of
damages chart.

346.066   CN
CANADIAN INSURANCE LAW REVIEW. 1988. 3/yr.
Can.$128($102) Carswell Publications, 800 Rocky
Mountain Plaza, 615 MacLeod Trail S.E., Calgary,
Alta. T2G 4T8, Canada. TEL 416-609-8000.
FAX 416-298-5094. (Subscr. to: Carswell
Publications, Corporate Plaza, 2075 Kennedy Rd.,
Scarsborough, Ont. M1T 3V, Canada) Ed. J.F.
Graham. cum.index.
    Description: Confronts the most topical issues
being faced by the insurance industry today.

CANADIAN INTELLECTUAL PROPERTY REVIEW. see
PATENTS, TRADEMARKS AND COPYRIGHTS

340   CN   ISSN 0835-6742
K3
**CANADIAN JOURNAL OF ADMINISTRATIVE LAW &
PRACTICE.** 1987. 3/yr. (plus bound vol.).
Can.$128($102) (Council of Canadian
Administrative Tribunals) Carswell Publications,
Corporate Plaza, 2075 Kennedy Rd., Scarborough,
Ont. M1T 3V4, Canada. TEL 416-609-8000.
FAX 413-298-5094. Ed. Michael I. Jeffery. adv.;
bk.rev.; cum.index.
    Description: Case comments and articles focusing
on administrative law issues, particularly the role
played by tribunals, boards and commissions.

CANADIAN JOURNAL OF INSURANCE LAW. see
INSURANCE

345   CN   ISSN 0703-900X
K27
CANADIAN JOURNAL OF LAW & JURISPRUDENCE. 1961.
s-a. Can.$24($20) to individuals; institutions
Can.$48($40). University of Western Ontario,
Faculty of Law, London, Ont. N6A 3K7, Canada.
TEL 519-679-2111. FAX 519-661-3790. Eds.
Richard Bronaugh, Peter Barton. adv.; bk.rev.; circ.
600. (also avail. in microfilm from WSH) **Indexed:**
C.L.I., Ind.Can.L.P.L., L.R.I., Leg.Cont., Leg.Per.
—BLDSC shelfmark: 3031.792000.
    Former titles (until 1988): Western Ontario Law
Review (ISSN 0083-8950); University of Western
Ontario Law Review.
    Description: Serves as a forum for the publication
of scholarly writing in the area of general
jurisprudence and legal philosophy.

340 301   CN   ISSN 0829-3201
K3
**CANADIAN JOURNAL OF LAW AND SOCIETY/REVUE
CANADIENNE DE DROIT ET SOCIETE.** (Text in English,
French) biennial. Can.$32 to individuals (foreign
$30); institutions Can.$55 (foreign $50). University
of Calgary Press, 2500 University Dr., N.W.,
Calgary, Alta. T2N 1N4, Canada.
TEL 403-220-7578. FAX 403-282-0085. TELEX
03-821545. Ed. C. Thomassett. circ. 300. (back
issues avail.)
—BLDSC shelfmark: 3031.795000.
    Description: Articles broadly relating to law and
society.
    Refereed Serial

340 305.4   CN   ISSN 0832-8781
**CANADIAN JOURNAL OF WOMEN AND THE LAW/REVUE
FEMMES ET DROIT.** (Text in English, French) 1986.
s-a. Can.$42.80 to individuals; institutions
Can.$69.55; students Can.$21.40. National
Association of Women and the Law, 575 King
Edward Ave., Ottawa, Ont. K1N 6N5, Canada.
TEL 613-238-1545. FAX 613-236-3339. Eds.
Marlene Cano, T. Brettel Dawson. bk.rev.; circ.
1,250. (also avail. in microfilm from MML; back
issues avail.) **Indexed:** C.L.I., Can.Per.Ind.,
Can.Wom.Per.Ind., Ind.Can.L.P.L., Leg.Per.,
Stud.Wom.Abstr., Wom.Stud.Abstr. (1986-).
—BLDSC shelfmark: 3036.750000.
    Description: Concentrates on criminal activity and
how it relates to women.

CANADIAN LABOUR LAW REPORTER. see *BUSINESS
AND ECONOMICS — Labor And Industrial Relations*

CANADIAN LABOUR RELATIONS BOARD REPORTS. see
*BUSINESS AND ECONOMICS — Labor And Industrial
Relations*

**CANADIAN LAW LIBRARIES/BIBLIOTHEQUES DE DROIT
CANADIENNES.** see *LIBRARY AND INFORMATION
SCIENCES*

340   CN   ISSN 0084-8573
CANADIAN LAW LIST. a. Can.$95. Canada Law Book
Inc., 240 Edward St., Aurora, Ont. L4G 3S9,
Canada. TEL 416-841-6472. Ed. Mrs. P. Egan.

340   CN   ISSN 0703-2129
K3
CANADIAN LAWYER.* 1977. 6/yr. Can.$10. H P
Publications, 240 Edward St., Aurora, Ontario L4G
3S9, Canada. Ed. Kim Kockhart. adv.; bk.rev.; circ.
30,000. (also avail. in microfilm from UMI; reprint
service avail. from UMI) **Indexed:** C.L.I., Can.Per.Ind.,
CMI, Ind.Can.L.P.L., L.R.I., Law Ofc.Info.Svc.

450 917.106   CN   ISSN 0225-2279
KE7705.8
CANADIAN NATIVE LAW REPORTER. Short title: C N L R.
1977. q. Can.$50 (typically set in Nov.). University
of Saskatchewan, Native Law Centre, Diefenbaker
Centre, Saskatoon, Sask. S7N 0W0, Canada.
TEL 306-966-6189. FAX 306-966-8517. Ed.
Zandra MacEachern. bk.rev.; cum.index; circ. 300.
(back issues avail.) **Indexed:** C.L.I., Ind.Can.L.P.L.
    Description: Comprehensive coverage and full text
reporting of Canadian native law judgments.

CANADIAN OCCUPATIONAL SAFETY & HEALTH LAW. see
OCCUPATIONAL HEALTH AND SAFETY

CANADIAN OIL & GAS. see *PETROLEUM AND GAS*

340 608.7   CN   ISSN 0008-4689
CANADIAN PATENT REPORTER. 1942. fortn. Can.$244.
Canada Law Book Inc., 240 Edward St., Aurora, Ont.
L4G 3S9, Canada. TEL 416-841-6472. Ed. G.F.
Henderson. index. **Indexed:** Ind.Can.L.P.L.
●Also available online.

342 917.1   CN   ISSN 0715-4860
KE4381.5.A45
CANADIAN RIGHTS REPORTER. a.(12 parts and 6 vols.).
Can.$105. Butterworths Canada Ltd., 75 Clegg Rd.,
Markham, Ont. L6G 1A1, Canada.
TEL 416-479-2665. FAX 416-479-2826. (looseleaf
format)
    Description: Reports of cases decided under the
Canadian Charter of Rights and Freedoms.

346.092   CN   ISSN 0045-5342
CANADIAN SECURITIES LAW REPORTER. m. Can.$700.
C C H Canadian Ltd., 6 Garamond Ct., Don Mills,
Ont. M3C 1Z5, Canada. TEL 416-441-2992.
FAX 416-444-9011. index.
    Description: Full texts of provincial securities acts,
regulations, related federal and provincial statutes.
Policy statements by securities commissions.
By-laws of self-regulatory bodies.

340.6   CN   ISSN 0008-5030
    CODEN: JCFSBP
**CANADIAN SOCIETY OF FORENSIC SCIENCE
JOURNAL/SOCIETE CANADIENNE DES SCIENCES
JUDICIAIRES JOURNAL.** 1967. q. Can.$50 (foreign
Can.$60). Canadian Society of Forensic Science,
2660 Southvale Crescent, Ste. 215, Ottawa, Ont.
K1B 4W5, Canada. TEL 613-731-2096. Ed. Brian T.
Hodgson. adv.; bk.rev.; charts; illus.; circ. 900.
Indexed: Biol.Abstr., Chem.Abstr, Excerp.Med.
—BLDSC shelfmark: 4723.120000.
    Supersedes: Canadian Society of Forensic Science
Newsletter.
    Description: Includes forensic chemistry, blood
alcohol analysis, forensic toxicology, questioned
documents, forensic odontology, firearms
examination, forensic pathology and forensic biology.

**CANADIAN TAX OBJECTIONS AND APPEAL
PROCEDURES.** see *BUSINESS AND ECONOMICS —
Public Finance, Taxation*

340 380.5   CN
▼**CANADIAN TRANSPORTATION LAW REPORTER.** 1990.
m. Can.$385. C C H Canadian Ltd., 6 Garamond
Ct., Don Mills, Ont. M3C 1Z5, Canada.
TEL 416-441-2992. FAX 416-444-9011.
    Description: Covers the Canadian Transportation
Regulations environment including transportation by
rail, road, water, air and pipeline.

340   CN   ISSN 0008-5308
CANADIAN WEEKLY LAW SHEET. 1959. w. Can.$265.
Butterworths Canada Ltd., 75 Clegg Rd., Markham,
Ont. L6G 1A1, Canada. TEL 416-292-1421.
FAX 416-292-6970. Ed.Bd. q. index; circ. 650.
(looseleaf format)
    Description: Digests reports on all fields of
Canadian law.

340   CN
CANNONS OF CONSTRUCTION. 1970. q. free to
qualified personnel. W. 234 Law Centre, University
of Alberta, Edmonton, Alta. T6G 2H5, Canada.
TEL 403-492-5121. FAX 403-492-4929. Ed. Paul
T. Babie. adv.; bk.rev.; circ. 1,600.

CAPITOL LINE-UP. see *AGRICULTURE — Poultry And
Livestock*

CAPITULO CRIMINOLOGICO. see *CRIMINOLOGY AND
LAW ENFORCEMENT*

340 301.16   US   ISSN 0736-7694
K3
CARDOZO ARTS & ENTERTAINMENT LAW JOURNAL.
1981. s-a. $15. Cardozo School of Law, 55 Fifth
Ave., New York, NY 10003. TEL 212-790-0292.
Ed. Gary T. Holtzer. cum.index; circ. 1,300. (also
avail. in microform from WSH; back issues avail.;
reprint service avail. from WSH) **Indexed:** C.L.I., Film
Lit.Ind. (1985-), Leg.Per.
—BLDSC shelfmark: 3051.530000.
    Description: Covers current legal issues in the arts,
entertainment, communications, intellectual property
and sports.

340   US
CARDOZO LAW REVIEW. 1979. bi-m. $20. Cardozo
School of Law, 55 Fifth Ave., New York, NY 10003.
TEL 212-790-0292. (back issues avail.; reprint
service avail. from RRI) **Indexed:** C.L.I., Leg.Per.

340 800   US
CARDOZO STUDIES IN LAW AND LITERATURE. 1989.
s-a. $20 to individuals; institutions $50; students
$18. Jacob Burns Institute for Advanced Legal
Studies, Cardozo School of Law, Yeshiva University,
55 Fifth Ave., New York, NY 10003.
TEL 212-790-0292. FAX 212-790-0345. Ed.
Richard H. Weisberg. adv.; circ. 500.

340   CN   ISSN 0706-5388
KE01115.8
CARSWELL'S PRACTICE CASES. (3RD SERIES). 1976.
24/yr. (in 6 vols.). Can.$115. Carswell Publications,
Corporate Plaza, 2075 Kennedy Rd., Scarborough,
Ont. M1T 3V4, Canada. TEL 416-609-8000.
FAX 416-298-5094. Ed. Michael McGowan. (also
avail. in looseleaf format) **Indexed:** C.L.I.,
Ind.Can.L.P.L., L.R.I.

CARTA DE GERENCIA. see *BUSINESS AND
ECONOMICS — Management*

LAW

340 US ISSN 0008-7238
K3
CASE AND COMMENT MAGAZINE (ROCHESTER). 1894. bi-m. $18 (free to attorneys). Robert E. Weber, 50 Broad St. E., Rochester, NY 14694. TEL 716-546-5530. FAX 716-262-4075. Ed. Joseph J. Marticelli. adv.; bk.rev.; index; circ. 110,000 (controlled). (also avail. in microform from UMI) **Indexed:** C.L.I., Crim.Just.Abstr., L.R.I.

340 US ISSN 0008-7262
K3
CASE WESTERN RESERVE LAW REVIEW. 1948. 4/yr. $20. Case Western Reserve University, School of Law, Cleveland, OH 44106. TEL 216-368-3313. Ed. Dean David Gamin. adv.; bk.rev.; charts; index; circ. 1,100. (also avail. in microform from RRI,WSH; back issues avail.; reprint service avail. from WSH) **Indexed:** C.L.I., L.R.I., Leg.Per.
●Also available online. Vendor(s): WESTLAW.
—BLDSC shelfmark: 3058.244000.
Formerly: Western Reserve Law Review (ISSN 0270-2150)

340 US
CASES AND MATERIALS ON TRADE REGULATION. irreg. price varies. Foundation Press, Inc., 615 Merrick Ave., Westbury, NY 11590-6607.

343 IT ISSN 0008-7424
CASSAZIONE PENALE; rivista mensile di giurisprudenza. 1961. m. L.220000 (foreign L.330000). Casa Editrice Dott. A. Giuffre, Via Busto Arsizio 40, 20151 Milan, Italy. TEL 02-38000905. FAX 02-38009582. Ed. Giorgio Lattanzi. adv.; bk.rev.; index; circ. 5,500. (looseleaf format)

CATALOG OF CURRENT LAW TITLES; recent acquisitions of major legal libraries. see *LIBRARY AND INFORMATION SCIENCES — Abstracting, Bibliographies, Statistics*

340 330 IT
CATALOGO LEGALE. 1886. q. Libreria Gozzini, Via Ricasoli 49-103r, 50122 Florence, Italy. TEL 55-212433. FAX 55-211105. circ. 3,500.

340 US ISSN 0008-8137
K3
CATHOLIC LAWYER. 1955. q. $5. St. John's University, School of Law, Grand Central and Utopia Parkways, Jamaica, NY 11439. TEL 718-990-6654. FAX 718-990-6649. Ed. Edward Fagan. bk.rev.; illus.; index. cum.index; circ. 2,500. (also avail. in microfilm from RRI; reprint service avail. from RRI) **Indexed:** C.L.I., Canon Law Abstr., Cath.Ind., CERDIC, L.R.I., Leg.Cont., Leg.Per.
—BLDSC shelfmark: 3093.075000.

340 US ISSN 0008-8390
K3
CATHOLIC UNIVERSITY LAW REVIEW. 1950. q. $25 (foreign $30). Catholic University of America, Law School, Washington, DC 20064. TEL 202-319-5159. Ed. Martin V. Kirkwood. adv.; bk.rev.; index; circ. 1,200. (also avail. in microfilm from WSH,PMC; reprint service avail. from UMI,WSH) **Indexed:** Abstr.Bk.Rev.Curr.Leg.Per., C.L.I., Cath.Ind., Curr.Cont., L.R.I., Leg.Cont., Leg.Per., SSCI.
●Also available online. Vendor(s): Mead Data Central.
—BLDSC shelfmark: 3093.249000.

340 US
CAUSES OF ACTION. a. $18.90. Shepard's - McGraw-Hill, Inc., Box 35300, Colorado Springs, CO 80935-3530. TEL 800-525-2474.
Description: Analysis of issues involved in establishing or defending a "prima facie" case.

340 352 CJ
CAYMAN GAZETTE. (Issues usually accompanied by numbered supplements) 1975. fortn. C.$221($269.52) Government Information Service, Tower Bldg., Grand Cayman, Cayman Islands, British W.I. FAX 809-94-98487. TELEX 4260 CIGOVT CP. Ed. Pat Ebanks. circ. 500.
Description: Official publication for government and other legal notices including liquidations, trade marks and probate.

CENTER FOR LAW AND EDUCATION. NEWSNOTES. see *EDUCATION*

CENTRO DE ESTUDIOS PUBLICOS. DOCUMENTO DE TRABAJO. see *BUSINESS AND ECONOMICS — Economic Situation And Conditions*

340 US ISSN 0886-2435
KF8727.A15
CHANGE EXCHANGE; the newsletter for reduction of litigation cost and delay. q. $10 (free to qualified personnel). American Bar Association, Judicial Administration Division Lawyers Conference, 750 N. Lake Shore Dr., Chicago, IL 60611. TEL 312-988-5555.
Description: News on programs from state courts.

340 630 US
CHAPTER 12: FARM REORGANIZATIONS. 1987. base vol. (plus a. suppl.). $110. Shepard's - McGraw-Hill, Inc., Box 35300, Colorado Springs, CO 80935-3500. TEL 800-525-2474. (looseleaf format)
Description: Comprehensive review of theory and practice under Chapter 12, including examination of history, filing procedures, cram-down procedures against creditors and improved debtor protection.

340 US
CHAPTER 13: PRACTICE AND PROCEDURE. 1983. base vol. (plus a. suppl.). $95. Shepard's - McGraw-Hill, Inc., Box 35300, Colorado Springs, CO 80935-3530. TEL 800-525-2474. (looseleaf format)
Description: Covers legal history, current practices and provides procedural advice.

CHEMICAL SUBSTANCES CONTROL. see *CHEMISTRY*

CHEMICAL WASTE LITIGATION REPORTER. see *ENVIRONMENTAL STUDIES*

340 US ISSN 0362-6148
CHICAGO DAILY LAW BULLETIN. 1854. d. $125. Law Bulletin Publishing Co., 415 N. State St., Chicago, IL 60610-4674. TEL 312-644-7800. Ed. Bernard Judge. adv.; bk.rev.; index; circ. 7,000. (also avail. in microfilm; back issues avail.) **Indexed:** C.L.I., Hlth.Ind., L.R.I.

340 US
CHICAGO - KENT LAW REVIEW. 1923. 3/yr. $23. Chicago - Kent College of Law, 77 S. Wacker Dr., Chicago, IL 60606. TEL 312-567-5013. FAX 312-567-5880. Ed. Mary N. Cameli. adv.; bk.rev.; cum.index; circ. 1,800. (also avail. in microform from WSH,PMC; reprint service avail. from WSH) **Indexed:** C.L.I., L.R.I., Leg.Cont., Leg.Per.
●Also available online. Vendor(s): WESTLAW. Also available on CD-ROM.
Former titles: I I T Chicago - Kent Law Review; Chicago - Kent Law Review (ISSN 0009-3599)
Description: Each issue is in symposium format, with one issue each year focusing on the US Court of Appeals for the 7th Circuit located in Chicago.

340 US ISSN 0199-8374
K3
CHICAGO LAWYER.* 1978. m. $38. Chicago Lawyer Publishing, Inc., 703 W. Roscoe St., Ste. 2, Chicago, IL 60657-2416. Ed. Rob Warden. circ. 5,820. (back issues avail.)

340 US
CHICANO - LATINO LAW REVIEW. 1972. a. $10. (U C L A Chicano Studies Center) University of California, Los Angeles, School of Law, 405 Hilgard Ave., Los Angeles, CA 90024. TEL 213-825-2894. adv.; circ. 600. (back issues avail.; reprint service avail. from RRI) **Indexed:** C.L.I., L.R.I., Leg.Per.
●Also available online. Vendor(s): WESTLAW.
Formerly: Chicano Law Review.

CHILDREN AND THE LAW. see *CHILDREN AND YOUTH — About*

340 US
CHILDREN BEFORE THE COURT; reflections on legal issues affecting minors. irreg., 2nd ed., 1991. $45. Butterworth Legal Publishers (Salem) (Subsidiary of: Reed International PLC), 90 Stiles Rd., Salem, NH 03079. TEL 800-548-4001. FAX 603-898-9664. Ed. Paul R. Kfoury.
Description: Examines the role of the court in protecting and advocating children's rights; challenges the juvenile justice system to expand its approaches to guarantee the rights of privacy, confidentiality and permanency.

340 US ISSN 0278-7210
CHILDREN'S LEGAL RIGHTS JOURNAL. 1979. q. $52.50. William S. Hein & Co., Inc., 1285 Main St., Buffalo, NY 14209. TEL 800-828-7571. FAX 716-883-8100. TELEX 91-209 WU 7 HEIN BUF. Ed. Robert Horowitz. (also avail. in microform from WSH; back issues avail.; reprint service avail. from WSH) **Indexed:** C.I.J.E., C.L.I., Child Devel.Abstr., Except.Child Educ.Abstr., Leg.Cont.
—BLDSC shelfmark: 3172.990340.
Description: Focuses on the relationship between the legal professional and children.
Refereed Serial

340 HK ISSN 1011-2359
LAW
CHINA CURRENT LAWS. (Text in English) 1987. 11/yr. HK.$1940($275) Longman Group (Far East) Ltd., 18th Fl. House, Tong Chong St., Quarry Bay, Hong Kong. TEL 8118168. FAX 5657440. TELEX 73051 LGHK HX. Ed.Bd. (back issues avail.)
Description: News for lawyers and businesses involved in China trade and investment.

340 US ISSN 0009-4609
K3
CHINESE LAW AND GOVERNMENT; a journal of translations. 1968. q. $285 to institutions. M.E. Sharpe, Inc., 80 Business Park Dr., Armonk, NY 10504. TEL 914-273-1800. FAX 914-273-2106. Eds. Michael Y.M. Kau, James Tong. adv.; index. (also avail. in microfilm from WSH; back issues avail.; reprint service avail. from WSH) **Indexed:** C.L.I., Curr.Cont., Leg.Per., P.A.I.S., SSCI.
Refereed Serial

CHRONICLE OF PARLIAMENTARY ELECTIONS AND DEVELOPMENTS. see *POLITICAL SCIENCE*

340 320 HT
CHRONIQUE JUDICIAIRE D'HAITI; revue juridique et culturelle Haitienne. (Text in English and French) 1980. m. $24. Imprimerie des Antilles, P.O. Box 1453, Port-au-Prince, Haiti, W.I. Ed. Lucien Lacarriere. adv.; bk.rev.; circ. 10,000. (back issues avail.)

349 JA ISSN 0009-6296
CHUO LAW REVIEW/HOGAKU SHINPO. (Text in Japanese; title and contents page in English) 1891. m. exchange basis. Chuo Daigaku, Hogakubu - Chuo University, Faculty of Law, 3-9 Kanda-Surugadai, Chiyoda-ku, Tokyo, Japan. Ed. Toichiro Kigawa. index; circ. 650.
—BLDSC shelfmark: 3189.722000.

340 200 US
CHURCH LAW & TAX REPORT. q. Christian Ministry Resources, c/o Bernice Bush Company, 15052 Springdale St., Huntington Beach, CA 92649-1178. TEL 714-891-3344.

340 ES
CIENCIAS JURIDICAS Y SOCIALES.* 1947. s-a. Universidad de El Salvador, Associacion de Estudiantes de Derecho, Final 25 Avda Norte, Ciudad Universitaria, San Salvador, El Salvador.

340 US ISSN 0009-6881
K25
CINCINNATI LAW REVIEW. Variant title: University of Cincinnati Law Review. 1932. q. $20 (foreign $22). University of Cincinnati, College of Law, Rm. 300, Cincinnati, OH 45221-0040. TEL 513-556-5101. Ed. James Englert. adv.; bk.rev.; cum.index: vols.1-43; circ. 1,200. (also avail. in microfilm from RRI,WSH; reprint service avail. from RRI) **Indexed:** Abstr.Bk.Rev.Curr.Leg.Per., C.L.I., Curr.Cont., Energy Ind., Energy Info.Abstr., L.R.I., Leg.Cont., Leg.Per.
●Also available online. Vendor(s): WESTLAW.
—BLDSC shelfmark: 9106.600000.

CIRCLE (JAMAICA PLAIN); a paper for Native American People. see *ETHNIC INTERESTS*

CITIZEN ACTION. see *SOCIOLOGY*

340 UK
CITIZENS ADVICE NOTES SERVICE. 1940. 3/yr. £75. C A N S Trust, 1 Stockwell Green, London SW9 9HP, England. TEL 071-326-0356. FAX 071-737-3237. Ed. Flavia Wade. circ. 5,200. (looseleaf format)
Description: Digest of British social legislation.

CITY OF CHICAGO BUILDING CODE. see *BUILDING AND CONSTRUCTION*

340 US
▼**CITY OF NEW YORK COUNCIL DIGEST**; a cumulative record of the councilmanic session. 1990. 24/yr. $600. New York Legal Publishing Corp., 6 Charles Park, Guilderland, NY 12084. TEL 800-541-2681. FAX 518-456-0828.
Description: Covers budget modifications, public hearing schedules, bills and local laws, zoning, landmarking, and land use issues.

340 US
CIVIL ACTIONS AGAINST THE UNITED STATES: ITS AGENCIES, OFFICES, AND EMPLOYEES. 1982. base vol. (plus a. suppl.). $95. Shepard's - McGraw-Hill, Inc., Box 35300, Colorado Springs, CO 80935-3530. TEL 800-525-2474.
Description: Covers the problems that arise when the United States is named a party defendant to a suit.

340 320 355 301 US
CIVILIAN CONGRESS; includes a directory of persons holding executive branch-military office in Congress contrary to constitutional prohibition (Art.1, Sec.6, Cl.2) of concurrent office-holding. 1964. biennial. $10. 2361 Mission St., Rm. 238, San Francisco, CA 94110-1868. TEL 415-695-1597. Ed. Jack Fitch. bk.rev.; circ. 500. (looseleaf format; back issues avail.)

THE CLAIMS FORUM. see *BUSINESS AND ECONOMICS — Labor And Industrial Relations*

CLARKE HALL & MORRISON ON CHILDREN. see *CHILDREN AND YOUTH — About*

340 US ISSN 0009-868X
KF336
CLEARINGHOUSE REVIEW. 1969. m. $75 (foreign $95). (Legal Services Corporation) National Clearinghouse for Legal Services, Inc., 407 S. Dearborn, Ste. 400, Chicago, IL 60605. TEL 312-939-3838. Ed. Stephen Spitz. bk.rev.; bibl.; tr.lit.; index; cum.index: 1967-1984; circ. 9,000. (looseleaf format; also avail. in microform from UMI) **Indexed:** Abstr.Health Care Manage.Stud., Bus.Ind., C.L.I., Hlth.Ind., L.R.I., Law Ofc.Info.Svc., Leg.Cont., Leg.Per., Med.Care Rev.
—BLDSC shelfmark: 3278.539000.

340 US ISSN 0009-8876
K3
CLEVELAND STATE LAW REVIEW. 1951. 4/yr. $20. Cleveland State University, Cleveland-Marshall College of Law, 1983 E. 24th St., Cleveland, OH 44115. TEL 216-687-2236. adv.; bk.rev.; circ. 3,000. (also avail. in microform from WSH; microfiche from WSH) **Indexed:** C.L.I., L.R.I., Leg.Cont., Leg.Per.
●Also available online. Vendor(s): WESTLAW.
—BLDSC shelfmark: 3278.655000.
Formerly: Cleveland-Marshall Law Review.

340 US
CLIENT UPDATE. q. $39.90. (American Bar Association) A B A Press, 750 N. Lake Shore Dr., Chicago, IL 60611. TEL 312-988-6122.
Description: Short items on the latest legal trends intended for laymen. Distributed by individual law offices to their clients.

340 US
CLOSING OFFICER'S GUIDE. 1983. base vol. (plus a. suppl.). $70. Butterworth Legal Publishers (Salem) (Subsidiary of: Reed International PLC), 90 Stiles Rd., Salem, NH 03079. TEL 800-548-4001. FAX 609-898-9858. Ed. Fred B. Phillips, Jr. (looseleaf format)

346.066 US
CODE AND REGULATIONS. 1946. m. $445. Commerce Clearing House, Inc., 4025 W. Peterson Ave., Chicago, IL 60646. TEL 312-583-8500. Ed. D. Newquist.

CODE NEWS (CLEVELAND). see *BUILDING AND CONSTRUCTION*

353 US
CODE OF FEDERAL REGULATIONS. a. $620. U.S. Office of the Federal Register, National Archives and Records Administration, Washington, DC 20408. TEL 202-523-5240. (Orders to: Supt. of Documents, Box 371954, Pittsburgh, PA 15250-7954) (also avail. in microfiche; magnetic tape)

CODE OF MARYLAND REGULATIONS. see *PUBLIC ADMINISTRATION*

349 BE ISSN 0010-0188
CODES LARCIER. (Includes Mise a Jour; supplements avail.) a. 24490 Fr. Maison Ferdinand Larcier S.A., Rue des Minimes 39, 1000 Brussels, Belgium. TEL 02-5124712. charts; index.
Description: Compendium of Belgian legal codes.

349 SA ISSN 0010-020X
CODICILLUS. (Text in Afrikaans, English) 1960. s-a. R.7.70($6) University of South Africa, Faculty of Law, P.O. Box 392, Pretoria 0001, South Africa. TEL 012-322-8944. FAX 012-429-3221. TELEX 350068. Ed. G.J. van Nickerk. adv.; bk.rev.; charts; illus.; circ. 6,400. (also avail. in microform from UMI; reprints service avail. from UMI) **Indexed:** Ind.S.A.Per.
Description: Covers legal history and recent legislation.

340 320 US ISSN 0741-9333
K3 CODEN: SWTEEN
COGITATIONS ON LAW AND GOVERNMENT. 1983. q. $16. (Cogitations on Law and Government, Inc.) Bill Keyes, Ed. & Pub., Drawer 6865, McLean, VA 22106-6865. Ed. Jonathan W. Emord. adv.; bk.rev.; circ. 2,000. **Indexed:** Sage Pub.Adm.Abstr.

342 VE
COLECCION TEXTOS LEGISLATIVOS. a. Editorial Juridica Venezolana, Apdo. 17598 Parque Central, Caracas, Venezuela.

349 CR ISSN 0010-0587
COLEGIO DE ABOGADOS. REVISTA.* vol.24, 1969. 3/yr. Colegio de Abogados, Apdo. 3161, San Jose, Costa Rica. Ed. Luis Antonio Murillo. charts; index.

349 AG ISSN 0325-8955
COLEGIO DE ABOGADOS DE BUENOS AIRES. REVISTA. 1921. 3/yr. free. Colegio de Abogados de Buenos Aires, Montevideo 640, 1019 Buenos Aires, Argentina. Ed. Julian del Campo. adv.; bk.rev.; circ. 1,200.
Former titles: Colegio de Abogados de la Ciudad de Buenos Aires. Revista & Colegio de Abogados de la Ciudad de Buenos Aires. Boletin Informativo (ISSN 0010-0560)

349 PR ISSN 0010-0579
LAW
COLEGIO DE ABOGADOS DE PUERTO RICO. REVISTA. (Text in English, Spanish) 1914. q. $20. Colegio de Abogados de Puerto Rico, Box 1900, San Juan, PR 00903. Ed. Carmelo Delgado Cintron. adv.; bk.rev.; circ. 7,000. **Indexed:** C.L.I., L.R.I., Leg.Per.

340 378 US ISSN 0192-1371
KF4225.A59
COLLEGE ADMINISTRATOR AND THE COURTS; briefs of selected court cases affecting the administration of institutions of higher education. 1977. q. $110.50. College Administration Publications, Inc., School Administration Publications, 21 Mt. Vernon Pl., Box 8492, Asheville, NC 28814. TEL 704-252-0883. Ed. Robert D. Bickel. index; circ. 1,200.
Description: Peer editorial research briefs on court cases that affect the administrative staff and activities of institutions of higher education, with a yearly cumulative index cross-referenced by case name, topic, and subject.

340 US ISSN 0045-737X
KF4225.A59
COLLEGE LAW DIGEST. 1970. m. $30. (National Association of College and University Attorneys) Fred B. Rothman & Co., 10368 West Centennial Rd., Littleton, CO 80127. TEL 800-457-1986. FAX 303-978-1457. index; circ. 2,200. (reprint service avail. from RRI) **Indexed:** C.L.I., Leg.Per.

340 378 US ISSN 0145-1472
KF4243.A59
COLLEGE STUDENT AND THE COURTS; briefs of selected court cases involving student-institutional relationships in higher education. 1973. q. $110.50. College Administration Publications, Inc., School Administration Publications, 21 Mt. Vernon Pl., Box 8492, Asheville, NC 28814. TEL 704-252-0883. Eds. D. Parker Young, Donald D. Gehring. index; circ. 2,200. (back issues avail.)
Description: Peer editorial research briefs on court cases that affect the relationship between students and institutions in higher education, with a yearly cumulative index cross-referenced by case name, topic, and subject.

COLLIER BANKRUPTCY COMPENSATION GUIDE. see *BUSINESS AND ECONOMICS — Banking And Finance*

COLLIER BANKRUPTCY MANUAL. see *BUSINESS AND ECONOMICS — Banking And Finance*

COLLIER HANDBOOK FOR CREDITORS' COMMITTEES. see *BUSINESS AND ECONOMICS — Banking And Finance*

COLLIER LENDING INSTITUTIONS AND THE BANKRUPTCY CODE. see *BUSINESS AND ECONOMICS — Banking And Finance*

COLLIER ON BANKRUPTCY. see *BUSINESS AND ECONOMICS — Banking And Finance*

340 CE ISSN 0069-5939
COLOMBO LAW REVIEW.* 1969. a. Rs.15($3) (Sri Lanka University Law Review) Hansa Publishers Ltd., Hansa House, Clifford Ave., Colombo 3, Sri Lanka.

COLORADO LAWS ENACTED AFFECTING MUNICIPAL GOVERNMENTS. see *PUBLIC ADMINISTRATION — Municipal Government*

340 US ISSN 0363-7867
K3
COLORADO LAWYER. 1971. m. $75. Colorado Bar Association, 1900 Grant St., Ste. 940, Denver, CO 80203-4309. TEL 303-860-1118. FAX 303-894-0821. Ed. Arlene Abady. adv.; bk.rev.; index; circ. 12,000. (also avail. in microfiche from WSH) **Indexed:** C.L.I.
—BLDSC shelfmark: 3321.525000.
Description: Provides practical information to the Colorado legal profession. Includes articles on substantive law, full appellate opinions, law-related features and certain federal court opinion summaries.

COLTIVATORE DIRETTO. see *AGRICULTURE*

382 US ISSN 0898-0721
K3
COLUMBIA BUSINESS LAW REVIEW. 1986. 3/yr. $30. Columbia University, School of Law, 435 W. 116th St., New York, NY 10027. (also avail. in microform from WSH; back issues avail.; reprint service avail. from WSH) **Indexed:** C.L.I., Leg.Per.

340 US ISSN 0090-7944
K3
COLUMBIA HUMAN RIGHTS LAW REVIEW. 1967. 2/yr. $26. Columbia University, School of Law, 435 W. 116th St., New York, NY 10027. TEL 212-854-2171. FAX 212-854-7946. Ed. Ivan Sacks. bk.rev.; circ. 600. (also avail. in microfiche from WSH; microfiche from WSH; back issues avail.) **Indexed:** C.L.I., Leg.Per.
—BLDSC shelfmark: 3323.030000.
Description: Domestic and international issues in human and civil rights.

340 US ISSN 0098-4582
K3 CODEN: CJELE8
COLUMBIA JOURNAL OF ENVIRONMENTAL LAW. 1973. s-a. $25. Columbia University, School of Law, Box B-28, 435 W. 116th St., New York, NY 10027. TEL 212-280-2539. adv.; bk.rev.; index; circ. 900. (also avail. in microfilm from WSH; back issues avail.; reprint service avail. from WSH) **Indexed:** Abstr.Bk.Rev.Curr.Leg.Per., C.L.I., Energy Ind., Energy Info.Abstr., Environ.Abstr., L.R.I., Leg.Cont., Leg.Per, Pollut.Abstr., Sel.Water Res.Abstr.
—BLDSC shelfmark: 3323.040000.
Description: Local, national and international issues in environmental and public health law.

340 US ISSN 0010-1923
LAW
COLUMBIA JOURNAL OF LAW AND SOCIAL PROBLEMS. 1965. q. $30. (Columbia University, School of Law) Darby Publishing, 435 W. 116th St., New York, NY 10027. TEL 212-854-2640. adv.; index; circ. 800. (also avail. in microfilm from WSH; microfiche from WSH) **Indexed:** A.B.C.Pol.Sci., Adol.Ment.Hlth.Abstr., C.L.I., Curr.Cont., L.R.I., Leg.Cont., Leg.Per., P.A.I.S., SSCI.
—BLDSC shelfmark: 3323.050000.
  Description: General interest, student-written law journal.

340 US ISSN 0093-304X
KF292.C6
COLUMBIA LAW ALUMNI OBSERVER. 1971. 5/yr. free. Columbia University, School of Law, 435 W. 116th St., New York, NY 10027. TEL 212-280-2156. Ed. C. Davidson. circ. 15,500. (tabloid format)
  Formerly: Columbia Law Observer.

340 US ISSN 0010-1958
K3
COLUMBIA LAW REVIEW. 1901. m. (Oct.-Jan., Mar.-Jun.). $36 (foreign $42). Columbia Law Review Association, 435 W. 116th St., New York, NY 10027. TEL 212-854-4398. Ed. Daniel Penn. adv.; bk.rev.; index; circ. 3,000. (also avail. in microfiche from RRI,WSH; microfilm from WSH; reprint service avail. from RRI) **Indexed:** A.B.C.Pol.Sci., Abstr.Bk.Rev.Curr.Leg.Per., Account.Ind. (1974-), BPIA, Bus.Ind., C.L.I., Chic.Per.Ind., Crim.Just.Abstr., Curr.Cont., L.R.I., Leg.Per., Mar.Aff.Bibl., P.A.I.S., Pers.Lit., SSCI.
●Also available online. Vendor(s): Mead Data Central.
—BLDSC shelfmark: 3323.250000.

COLUMBIA LAW SCHOOL NEWS. see *COLLEGE AND ALUMNI*

COLUMBIA - V L A JOURNAL OF LAW & THE ARTS. see *ART*

340 CN ISSN 0832-7688
KE1492
COMMERCIAL INSOLVENCY REPORTER. 1987. 6/yr. Can.$195. Butterworths Canada Ltd., 75 Clegg Rd., Markham, Ont. L6G 1A1, Canada. TEL 800-668-6481. FAX 416-479-2826. Ed. E. Bruce Leonard. (back issues avail.)
  Description: For accounting professionals. Contains case digests and comments, legislation, analyses of secured transactions and creditors' rights.

346.066 US
COMMERCIAL LAW BULLETIN. bi-m. Commercial Law League of America, 175 W. Jackson, Ste. 1541, Chicago, IL 60604. TEL 312-431-1305. FAX 312-431-1669. Ed. Linda Saghir.

340 US ISSN 0010-3055
COMMERCIAL LAW JOURNAL.* 1912. m. (10/yr.). $25. Commercial Law League of America, 175 W. Jackson Blvd., Ste. 1541, Chicago, IL 60604-2703. TEL 312-236-4942. Ed. Leo E. Smith. adv.; bk.rev.; bibl.; index; circ. 7,000. (also avail. in microform from UMI; microfilm from WSH) **Indexed:** ABI Inform, BPIA, Bus.Ind., C.L.I., L.R.I., Leg.Cont., Leg.Per.
—BLDSC shelfmark: 3336.965000.
  Description: Discusses legal aspects of business.

346.066 347.7 US
COMMERCIAL LAW REPORT. 1987. m. $205. Matthew Bender & Co., Inc., 11 Penn Plaza, New York, NY 10001. TEL 212-967-7707. Ed.Bd.

340 UK ISSN 0141-7258
LAW
COMMERCIAL LAWS OF EUROPE. (Text in English and original language) 1978. m. £290. (European Law Centre Ltd.) Sweet & Maxwell, South Quay Plaza, 8th Fl., 183 Marsh Wall, London E14 9FT, England. TEL 071-538-8686. FAX 071-538-9508. Ed. Neville March Hunnings. index. (back issues avail.)
  Description: Reports national and international legislation.

COMMERCIAL LEASE LAW INSIDER; the practical, plain-English, monthly newsletter for owners, managers, attorneys and other real estate professionals. see *REAL ESTATE*

COMMERCIAL LOAN DOCUMENTATION GUIDE. see *BUSINESS AND ECONOMICS — Banking And Finance*

340 US
▼**COMMERCIAL PAPER AND PAYMENT SYSTEMS.** 1990. 2 base vols. (plus a. suppl.). $150. Butterworth Legal Publishers (Salem) (Subsidiary of: Reed International PLC), 90 Stiles Rd., Salem, NH 03079. TEL 800-548-4001. FAX 603-898-9858. Ed. William H. Lawrence. (looseleaf format)
  Description: Discusses traditional payment systems while analyzing the role of new, alternative payment methods as they complement or compete with historical modes of payment.

COMMISSION ROYALE DES ANCIENNES LOIS ET ORDONNANCES DE BELGIQUE. BULLETIN/KONINKLIJKE COMMISSIE VOOR DE UITGAVE DER OUDE WETTEN EN VERORDENINGEN VAN BELGIE. HANDELINGEN. see *HISTORY*

COMMISSIONE TRIBUTARIA CENTRALE. see *BUSINESS AND ECONOMICS — Public Finance, Taxation*

340 US ISSN 0277-2930
KF1085.A15
COMMODITIES LAW LETTER. 1981. m. $285. Commodities Law Press Associates, 900 Third Ave., New York, NY 10022. TEL 212-935-0638. FAX 212-371-1084. Ed. Richard A. Miller. bk.rev. (looseleaf format; back issues avail.) **Indexed:** C.L.I.
  Description: Covers legal developments affecting commodity futures in U.S. and world-wide.

340 US ISSN 0887-784X
KF1085.A59
COMMODITIES LITIGATION REPORTER; the national journal of record of commodities litigation. 1985. s-m. $750. Andrews Publications, 1646 West Chester Pike, Box 1000, Westtown, PA 19395. TEL 215-399-6600. FAX 215-399-6610. Ed. Barbara Pizzirani. abstr.; bibl.; stat.; cum.index every 6 mos. (looseleaf format; back issues avail.)
  Description: Covers reparations and enforcements actions involving the scope of the Commodity Exchange Act.

346.066 332.6 US
COMMODITY FUTURES LAW REPORTS. 1974. s-m. $640. Commerce Clearing House, Inc., 4025 W. Peterson Ave., Chicago, IL 60646. TEL 312-940-4600. Ed. D. Newquist.

341 UK ISSN 0588-7445
COMMON MARKET LAW REPORTS. (Supplement avail.) 1962. w. £445 with supplement. (European Law Centre Ltd.) Sweet & Maxwell, South Quay Plaza, 8th Fl., 183 Marsh Wall, London E14 9FT, England. TEL 071-538-8686. FAX 071-538-9508. Ed. Neville March Hunnings. cum.index: vol. 1-50 (1962-1987). (back issues avail.)
  Description: Up-to-date reports of community case law.

340 UK ISSN 0305-0718
LAW
COMMONWEALTH LAW BULLETIN. q. £20. Commonwealth Secretariat, Publications Division, Marlborough House, Pall Mall, London S1Y 5HX, England. **Indexed:** RICS.
—BLDSC shelfmark: 3340.880000.

COMMUNICATIONS AND THE LAW. see *COMMUNICATIONS*

340 AT
COMMUNICATIONS LAW & POLICY IN AUSTRALIA. base vol. (plus q. update). $395. Butterworths Pty. Ltd., 271-273 Lane Cove Rd., P.O. Box 345, North Ryde, N.S.W. 2113, Australia. TEL 02-335-4444. FAX 02-335-4655. (looseleaf format)

340 301.16 US ISSN 0737-7622
KF2750.A15
COMMUNICATIONS LAWYER. 1983. 4/yr. $15 to non-members. (American Bar Association, Forum Committee on Communications Law) A B A Press, 750 N. Lake Shore Dr., Chicago, IL 60611. TEL 312-988-6067. Ed. Marla Hillery. bk.rev.; bibl.; circ. 2,020.
  Description: Newsletter reviews significant activities and developments in communications law and reports on Forum Committee events.

COMMUNICATIONS UPDATE; a monthly round-up of media and communications. see *COMMUNICATIONS*

COMMUNITY ASSOCIATION LAW REPORTER. see *HOUSING AND URBAN PLANNING*

340 US
COMMUNITY LAW WEEK NEWSLETTER. irreg. $6. American Bar Association, Young Lawyers Division, 750 N. Lake Shore Dr., Chicago, IL 60611. TEL 312-988-5555.

360 FR
COMPAGNIE NATIONALE DES COMMISSAIRES AUX COMPTES. CONSEIL NATIONAL. BULLETIN. 1970. q. 360 F. Compagnie Nationale des Commissaires aux Comptes, 6 rue de l'Amiral de Coligny, 75001 Paris, France. FAX 42-61-37-73. TELEX CINACO 240564F. bk.rev.; index; circ. 20,000.
  Formerly: Federation des Associations de Commissaires de Societes. Bulletin de Liason.

COMPANY DIRECTOR. see *BUSINESS AND ECONOMICS — Management*

342.085 SZ
COMPARATIVA. (Text in French) 1972. irreg., no.44, 1991. price varies. (Universite de Lausanne, Centre de Droit Compare) Librairie Droz S.A., 11 rue Massot, CH-1211 Geneva 12, Switzerland. TEL 022-466666. (Subscr. to: Base Postale 389, 1211 Geneva 12, Switzerland) Ed.Bd.

340 US ISSN 0069-7893
COMPARATIVE JURIDICAL REVIEW. (Text in English and Spanish) 1964. a. free. (Rainforth Foundation) Pan American Institute of Comparative Law, 3001 Ponce de Leon Blvd., Coral Gables, FL 33134. TEL 305-446-7856. Ed. Mario Diaz Cruz. bk.rev.; cum.index in vol.11, 1973; circ. 1,000. **Indexed:** C.L.I., L.R.I.

347.9 US ISSN 0147-9202
K3
COMPARATIVE LABOR LAW JOURNAL. 1976. q. $25 (foreign $30). (International Society for Law and Social Security, United States National Branch) University of Pennsylvania, Wharton School, 2203 Steinberg-Dietrich Hall, Philadelphia, PA 19104-6369. TEL 215-898-6851. FAX 215-898-2400. Ed. Benjamin Aaron. bk.rev.; abstr.; circ. 700. (also avail. in microform from WSH) **Indexed:** Abstr.Bk.Rev.Curr.Leg.Per., BPIA, C.L.I., Int.Lab.Doc., L.R.I., Leg.Per., World Bibl.Soc.Sec.
—BLDSC shelfmark: 3363.784200.
  Formerly (until vol.8, 1986): International Society for Labor Law and Social Legislation. United States National Committee. Bulletin (ISSN 0146-0234)
  Description: Offers articles and comments dealing comparatively with various aspects of labor and employment, and labor relations matters.

340.5 JA ISSN 0010-4116
COMPARATIVE LAW REVIEW/HIKAKUHO ZASSHI. (Text in Japanese; summaries in English) 1951. q. 900 Yen per no. Institute of Comparative Law in Japan - Nihon Hikakuho Kenkyujo, c/o Chuo University, Higashinakano, Hachioji-shi, Tokyo 192-03, Japan. FAX 0426-74-3301. Ed. Yoshiaki Sanada. bk.rev.; bibl.; pat.; index, cum.index; circ. 1,000.

COMPARATIVE STATE POLITICS. see *POLITICAL SCIENCE*

COMPENSATION OF ATTORNEYS (NON-LAW FIRMS). see *BUSINESS AND ECONOMICS — Labor And Industrial Relations*

COMPENSATION STRATEGY AND MANAGEMENT. see *BUSINESS AND ECONOMICS — Personnel Management*

340 US
KF311.A15
COMPETITIONS (CHICAGO); developments in client counseling, negotiation, and appellate advocacy. 1980. irreg. $6. American Bar Association, Competitions Committee, 750 N. Lake Shore Dr., Chicago, IL 60611. TEL 312-988-5621. FAX 312-988-6281. Ed. Joanne Davis.
  Formerly (until 1989): Client Counseling Update (ISSN 0276-752X)
  Description: Newsletter containing summaries of publications and news articles concerning client counseling, negotiation and appellate advocacy.

340　　　　US　ISSN 0882-9136
KF1262.A29
COMPILATION OF STATE AND FEDERAL PRIVACY LAWS.
(Annual supplement avail.) 1975. irreg., latest
1989. $29. (Privacy Journal) Robert Ellis Smith, Ed.
& Pub., Box 28577, Providence, RI 02908.
TEL 401-274-7861. circ. 2,000. **Indexed:**
Comput.Lit.Ind.
Description: Cites and describes state and federal
laws protecting confidentiality of personal
information.

340　　　　US　ISSN 0741-9066
K3
COMPLEAT LAWYER. 1984. q. $39.90. (American Bar
Association) A B A Press, 750 N. Lake Shore Dr.,
Chicago, IL 60611. TEL 312-988-6122. Ed. Ray
DeLong. adv.; circ. 44,000. (back issues avail.)
Indexed: C.L.I., L.R.I.
—BLDSC shelfmark: 3364.203350.
Formerly (until vol.19, no.3, 1983): Docket Call
(Chicago) (ISSN 0569-3160)
Description: Practical articles directed to the lay
clients of general practitioners on substantive areas
of law.

340　　　　US
**COMPLETE GUIDE TO MECHANIC'S AND
MATERIALMAN'S LIEN LAWS OF TEXAS.** base vol.
(plus suppl. 1-2/yr.), 3rd ed., 1990. $115.
Butterworth Legal Publishers (Salem) (Subsidiary of:
Reed International PLC), 90 Stiles Rd., Salem, NH
03079. TEL 800-548-4001. FAX 603-898-9858.
Eds. Brenda T. Cubbage, Sterling W. Steves.
(looseleaf format)

340 332.1　　　US
COMPLIANCE EXAMINATION UPDATE. 1985. bi-m.
$248. (Consumer Bankers Association) Warren,
Gorham and Lamont, One Penn Plaza, New York, NY
10119. TEL 800-950-1201. FAX 212-971-5240.
(looseleaf format)
Description: Update service written by two lawyers
covers the latest compliance violations in the
industry. Offers helpful curing techniques to protect
your compliance program.

COMPLIANCE PROGRAM GUIDANCE MANUALS. see
PUBLIC HEALTH AND SAFETY

COMPTROLLER GENERAL'S PROCUREMENT DECISIONS.
see *BUSINESS AND ECONOMICS — Economic
Situation And Conditions*

COMPUTER COUNSEL. see *COMPUTERS*

340　　　　US　ISSN 0740-1469
KF390.5.C6
COMPUTER INDUSTRY LITIGATION REPORTER; the
national journal of record of computer industry
litigation. 1983. s-m. $825. Andrews Publications,
1646 West Chester Pike, Box 1000, Westtown, PA
19395. TEL 215-399-6600. FAX 215-399-6610.
Ed. Harry G. Armstrong. bibl.; stat.; cum.index every
6 mos. (looseleaf format; back issues avail.)
Description: Reports on copyright, patent and
trademark claims, theft of secret cases, significant
user - vendor contract-misrepresentation claims,
consultant liability questions, and other evolving
issues as they relate to the computer industry.

COMPUTER LAW & PRACTICE. see *COMPUTERS*

COMPUTER LAW & TAX REPORT; monthly newsletter
covering computer-related law and tax issues. see
COMPUTERS

COMPUTER-LAW JOURNAL; international journal of
computer, communication and information law. see
COMPUTERS

COMPUTER LAW MONITOR. see *COMPUTERS*

COMPUTER LAW REPORTER; a bi-monthly journal of
computer law and practice. see *COMPUTERS*

COMPUTER LAW SERIES. see *COMPUTERS*

COMPUTER LAW STRATEGIST. see *COMPUTERS*

COMPUTER LAWYER. see *COMPUTERS*

COMPUTER SOFTWARE PROTECTION LAW. see
COMPUTERS — Software

COMPUTER SOFTWARE PROTECTION LAW. SUPPLEMENT.
see *COMPUTERS — Software*

340 001.6 621.381　US
COMPUTER TECHNOLOGY AND THE LAW. 1983. base
vol. (plus a. suppl.). $95. Shepard's - McGraw-Hill,
Inc., Box 35300, Colorado Springs, CO
80935-3530.
Description: Explores all facets of proprietary rights
and contract issues. Discusses how computers affect
principles of law and legal procedure, and how law
and regulation affect the development, marketing
and implementation of new data processing
technologies.

COMPUTER UND RECHT; Forum fuer die Praxis des
Rechts der Datenverarbeitung, Kommunikation und
Automation. see *COMPUTERS*

**COMPUTERREPORT DER NEUE JURISTISCHEN
WOCHENSCHRIFT;** Informationsmanagement und
Bueroorganisation in der juristischen Praxis. see
LAW — Computer Applications

340　　　　SP
COMUNIDAD EUROPEA. (Includes q. bound vols.) 1974.
m. (except Aug.). 16000 ptas. Editorial Aranzadi,
S.A., Avda. Carlos III, 34, Apdo. 111, 31080
Pamplona, Spain. TEL 948-331212.
FAX 948-330919. bibl.; index.

COMUNITA MEDITERRANEA; rivista di diritto e relazioni
internazionali, politica economica e finanziari. see
POLITICAL SCIENCE — International Relations

CONCERNS (WASHINGTON). see *EDUCATION*

CONDITIONS OF WORK DIGEST. see *BUSINESS AND
ECONOMICS — Labor And Industrial Relations*

347.91　　　　CN
CONDUCT OF CIVIL LITIGATION IN BRITISH COLUMBIA.
s-a. Can.$425. Butterworths Canada Ltd., 75 Clegg
Rd., Markham, Ont. L6G 1A1, Canada.
TEL 416-479-2665. FAX 416-479-2826. Eds.
Peter Fraser, John Horn. (looseleaf format)
Description: A guide for practitioners and support
staff in British Columbia.

349　　　　PE　ISSN 0573-4347
**CONFERENCIA DE FACULTADES LATINOAMERICANAS DE
DERECHO. (DOCUMENTOS OFICIALES).*** 1959. a.
Universidad Nacional, Apartado 524, Lima, Peru.

340 360　　　US
CONFLICT RESOLUTION NOTES. 1983. q. $20. Conflict
Resolution Center International, Inc., 7101 Hamilton
Ave., Pittsburgh, PA 15208-1828.
TEL 412-371-9884. FAX 412-371-9885. Ed. Paul
Wahrhaftig. adv.; bk.rev.; circ. 600. (back issues
avail.)
●Also available online.
Description: Presents short articles for researchers
or practitioners of conflict resolution. Focuses on
resolution of neighborhood, racial, ethnic and
religious conflicts.

340 350　　　TT
**CONGRESS OF MICRONESIA. HOUSE OF
REPRESENTATIVES. JOURNAL.** q. Congress of
Micronesia, House of Representatives, Capitol Hill,
Saipan 96950, Mariana Islands.

340 350　　　TT
CONGRESS OF MICRONESIA. SENATE. JOURNAL. (Text in
English) irreg. Senate, Capitol Hill, Saipan 96950,
Mariana Islands.

340　　　　US
CONGRESSIONAL ACTION; special reports. 1957. m.
$15 to non-members; members $10. U.S. Chamber
of Commerce, 1615 H St., N.W., Washington, DC
20062. TEL 202-463-5600. Ed. Kevin P. Meath.

340 352　　　US
CONGRESSIONAL LEGISLATIVE REPORTING. 1937.
irreg. price varies. Commerce Clearing House, Inc.,
4025 W. Peterson Ave., Chicago, IL 60646.
TEL 312-583-8500. Ed. D. Newquist.

353.9　　　US　ISSN 0098-8138
KFC4108
CONNECTICUT. JUDICIAL DEPARTMENT. REPORT.
biennial. free. Judicial Department, 231 Capitol Ave.,
Hartford, CT 06106. TEL 203-566-8219.
FAX 203-566-3308. Ed. Faith Mandell. illus. Key
Title: Report of the Judicial Department, State of
Connecticut.

320　　　　US
**CONNECTICUT. LAW REVISION COMMISSION. ANNUAL
REPORT.** 1976. a. Law Revision Commission, State
Capitol, Rm. 509A, Hartford, CT 06106.
TEL 203-240-0220. FAX 203-240-8307.

340　　　　US
CONNECTICUT APPELLATE PRACTICE & PROCEDURE.
1989. base vol. (plus suppl.). $105. Butterworth
Legal Publishers (Salem) (Subsidiary of: Reed
International PLC), 90 Stiles Rd., Salem, NH 03079.
TEL 800-548-4001. FAX 603-898-9858. Ed. Colin
C. Tait. (looseleaf format)
Description: Covers appeals from the Superior
Court to the Appellate Court and the Supreme Court,
and appeals from the Appellate Court to the
Supreme Court. Constitutional and statutory
materials are discussed, as are matters within the
original jurisdiction of the Supreme Court.

340　　　　US　ISSN 0010-6070
LAW
CONNECTICUT BAR JOURNAL. 1927. bi-m. $30.
Connecticut Bar Association, Inc., 101 Corporate Pl.,
Rocky Hill, CT 06067. TEL 203-721-0025. Ed.
William T. Burrank. adv.; bk.rev.; bibl.; index; circ.
10,800. (also avail. in microfilm from WSH) **Indexed:**
C.L.I., L.R.I., Law Ofc.Info.Svc., Leg.Per.
—BLDSC shelfmark: 3417.615000.

**CONNECTICUT EDUCATION ASSOCIATION. LEGISLATIVE
BULLETIN.** see *EDUCATION*

340　　　　US
CONNECTICUT FAMILY LAW JOURNAL. 1982. 6/yr.
$75. Butterworth Legal Publishers (Salem)
(Subsidiary of: Reed International PLC), 90 Stiles
Rd., Salem, NH 03079. TEL 800-548-4001.
FAX 603-898-9858. cum.index. (looseleaf format;
back issues avail.)
Description: Family law articles, case comments,
and Connecticut Superior Court decisions.

CONNECTICUT INSURANCE LAW REVIEW. see
INSURANCE

340　　　　US
CONNECTICUT LAW JOURNAL. 1935. w. $150.
Commission on Official Legal Publications, Office of
Production and Distribution, 111 Phoenix Ave.,
Enfield, CT 06082. TEL 203-741-3027.
FAX 203-745-2178. Dir. Richard J. Hemenway.
Description: Covers Supreme court, Appellate court
and selected Superior court decisions; practice book
rule changes; administrative regulations; and legal
notices.

340　　　　US　ISSN 0010-6151
CONNECTICUT LAW REVIEW. 1968. q. $23.
Connecticut Law Review Association, 65 Elizabeth
St., Hartford, CT 06105-2290. TEL 203-241-4607.
FAX 203-241-7666. Ed. James F. Sullivan. adv.;
bk.rev.; circ. 1,600. (also avail. in microfilm; back
issues avail.; reprint service avail. from RRI,UMI)
Indexed: C.L.I., L.R.I., Leg.Cont., Leg.Per.
●Also available online. Vendor(s): WESTLAW.
—BLDSC shelfmark: 3417.653000.

340　　　　US　ISSN 0198-0289
K3
CONNECTICUT LAW TRIBUNE.* w. $280. 1 Post Rd.,
Fairfield, CT 06430-0215. TEL 203-348-8200.
FAX 203-348-1790. Ed. Laurel Left. adv.; bk.rev.;
index; circ. 3,500. (back issues avail.)
Description: Covers legal issues for the state of
Connecticut.

340　　　　US
CONNECTICUT NOTARY LAW PRIMER. a. $9.95.
National Notary Association, 8236 Remmet Ave.,
Box 7184, Canoga Park, CA 91304-7184.
TEL 818-713-4000. FAX 818-713-9061. Ed.
Charles N. Faerber. (reprint service avail. from UMI)

CONNECTICUT REAL ESTATE LAW JOURNAL. see *REAL
ESTATE*

340 333.33　　　US
CONNECTICUT REAL PROPERTY STATUTES. 1980. base
vol. (plus suppl.). $45. Butterworth Legal Publishers
(Salem) (Subsidiary of: Reed International PLC), 90
Stiles Rd., Salem, NH 03079. TEL 800-548-4001.
FAX 603-898-9858. (looseleaf format)

2616 LAW

340   US
CONNECTICUT TIME LIMITATIONS. 1984. base vol. (plus suppl.). $40. Butterworth Legal Publishers (Salem) (Subsidiary of: Reed International PLC), 90 Stiles Rd., Salem, NH 03079. TEL 800-548-4001. FAX 603-898-9858. (looseleaf format)

CONNECTICUT WORKERS' COMPENSATION REVIEW OPINIONS. see *BUSINESS AND ECONOMICS — Labor And Industrial Relations*

CONSCIOUS CONSUMER; products and services that help the earth and society. see *ENVIRONMENTAL STUDIES*

340   IT   ISSN 0010-6569
CONSIGLIO DI STATO; rassegna di giurisprudenza e dottrina. 1953. m. L.360000. Casa Editrice Italedi, Piazza Cavour 19, Rome 00193, Italy. Ed. Ignazio Scotto. adv.; bk.rev.; bibl.; index, cum.index; circ. 5,000.

342   II   ISSN 1049-4987
K3
CONSTITUTIONAL LAW JOURNAL. (Text in English) 1971. q. Rs.80($20) Law Academy, 1-9-322 Vidyanagar, Hyderabad 500044 (A.P.), India. Ed. G.S. Prasad Rao. adv.; bk.rev
    Description: Covers Indian Supreme Court decisions and includes articles by eminent authorities.

CONSTRUCTION AND DESIGN LAW DIGEST. see *BUILDING AND CONSTRUCTION*

CONSTRUCTION CLAIMS CITATOR. see *BUILDING AND CONSTRUCTION*

CONSTRUCTION CLAIMS MONTHLY; devoted exclusively to the problems of construction contracting. see *BUILDING AND CONSTRUCTION*

CONSTRUCTION CLAIMS TRAINING GUIDE. see *BUILDING AND CONSTRUCTION*

CONSTRUCTION LAW ADVISER; monthly practical advice for lawyers and construction professionals. see *BUILDING AND CONSTRUCTION*

CONSTRUCTION LAW JOURNAL. see *BUILDING AND CONSTRUCTION*

CONSTRUCTION LAW LETTER. see *BUILDING AND CONSTRUCTION*

CONSTRUCTION LAW REPORTS. see *BUILDING AND CONSTRUCTION*

CONSTRUCTION LAWYER. see *BUILDING AND CONSTRUCTION*

CONSTRUCTION LITIGATION REPORTER; recent decisions of national significance. see *BUILDING AND CONSTRUCTION*

340   US   ISSN 0300-6034
KF1039.A15
CONSUMER CREDIT AND TRUTH-IN-LENDING COMPLIANCE REPORT. 1969. m. $158. Warren, Gorham and Lamont, One Penn Plaza, New York, NY 10119. TEL 800-950-1201. FAX 212-971-5240. Ed. Earl Phillips. (also avail. in microform from UMI)
    Description: Focuses on the latest regulatory rulings and findings involving consumer lending and credit activity.

340   UK
CONSUMER CREDIT CONTROL. irreg. £275. Longman Group UK Ltd., Law, Tax and Finance Division, 21-27 Lambs Conduit St., London WC1N 3NJ, England. TEL 071-242-2548. FAX 071-831-8119. TELEX 295445. Ed. Frances Bennion. (looseleaf format)
    Description: Analysis of the Consumer Credit Act.

640.73   US
CONSUMER CREDIT GUIDE REPORTS. 1969. fortn. $810. Commerce Clearing House, Inc., 4025 W. Peterson Ave., Chicago, IL 60646. TEL 312-583-8500. Ed. D. Newquist.

340   UK
CONSUMER CREDIT LEGISLATION. (In 2 vols.) irreg. (approx. 3/yr.). £490. Butterworth & Co. (Publishers) Ltd. (Subsidiary of: Reed International PLC), 88 Kingsway, London WC2B 6AB, England. TEL 71-405-6900. FAX 71-405-1332. TELEX 95678. (US addr.: Butterworth Legal Publishers, 90 Stiles Rd., Salem, NH 03079. TEL 800-548-4001) (looseleaf format)

340 640.73   UK
CONSUMER LAW TODAY. 1977. m. £112 (foreign £127). Monitor Press, Rectory Rd., Great Waldingfield, Sudbury, Suffolk CO10 0TL, England. TEL 0787-78607. FAX 0787-880201. (back issues avail.)
    Description: For senior management who need to know about the latest developments and regulations that concern packaging and advertising, labelling, credit, pricing, contracts, guarantees, insurance and new moves on product liability.

340   US   ISSN 1052-9632
KF1296.A59
▼**CONSUMER PRODUCT LITIGATION REPORTER.** 1990. m. $350. Andrews Publications, 1646 West Chester Pike, Box 1000, Westtown, PA 19395. TEL 215-399-6600. FAX 215-399-6610. Ed. Kathy Knaub. bibl.; stat.; cum.index every 6 mos. (looseleaf format; back issues avail.)
    Description: Covers product liability issues such as strict liability, adequacy of warning and merchantability. Also covers state and federal legislation.

CONTEMPORARY DRUG PROBLEMS. see *DRUG ABUSE AND ALCOHOLISM*

340   CN   ISSN 0381-0925
CONTINUUM. 1973. 2/yr. York University, Osgoode Hall Law School, Rm. 118D, 4700 Keele St., Downsview, Ont. M5J 2R5, Canada. TEL 416-667-3961. illus.; circ. 8,500. **Indexed**: C.I.J.E., Film Lit.Ind. (1989-).

340   US
CONTRACT APPEALS DECISIONS. 1956. fortn. $805. Commerce Clearing House, Inc., 4025 W. Peterson Ave., Chicago, IL 60646. TEL 312-583-8500. Ed. D. Newquist.

340   US   ISSN 0147-1074
CONTRIBUTIONS IN LEGAL STUDIES. 1978. irreg., no.67, 1992. price varies. Greenwood Press, Inc. (Subsidiary of: Greenwood Publishing Group Inc.), 88 Post Rd. W., Box 5007, Westport, CT 06881-5007. TEL 203-226-3571. FAX 203-222-1502. Ed. Paul L. Murphy.
—BLDSC shelfmark: 3458.870000.

CONTROL OF POLLUTION ENCYCLOPEDIA. see *ENVIRONMENTAL STUDIES — Pollution*

CONVEYANCER AND PROPERTY LAWYER. see *REAL ESTATE*

340   SA
CONVEYANCING BULLETIN. base vol. (plus q. suppl.). $59. Butterworth Publishers (Pty.) Ltd., 8 Walter Pl., Waterval Park, Durban 4000, South Africa. TEL 031-294247. FAX 031-283255. (looseleaf format)

340   AT
CONVEYANCING SERVICE NEW SOUTH WALES. 2 base vols. (plus updates 8/yr.). $655. Butterworths Pty. Ltd., 271-273 Lane Cove Rd., P.O. Box 345, North Ryde, N.S.W. 2113, Australia. TEL 02-335-4444. FAX 02-335-4655. (looseleaf format)

340 334   II
COOPERATIVE LAW JOURNAL. (Text in English) 1965. q. Rs.60. National Cooperative Union of India, 3-Siri Institutional Area, Panchshila Marg (Behind Hauz Khas), New Delhi 110016, India. Ed. B.D. Sharma. circ. 1,000.

340   UN   ISSN 0010-8634
COPYRIGHT BULLETIN; quarterly review. (Editions in English, French, Spanish) 1948. q. 60 F.($20) Unesco, 7-9 Place de Fontenoy, 75700 Paris, France. TEL 577-16-10. (Dist. in U.S. by: Unipub, 4611-F Assembly Dr., Lanham, MD 20706-4391. TEL 800-274-4888) Ed. Evgueni Guerassimov. bibl.; charts; circ. 1,590. (also avail. in microform from MIM) **Indexed**: Mid.East: Abstr.& Ind., P.A.I.S.
—BLDSC shelfmark: 3468.790000.

346.066 340   US
COPYRIGHT LAW IN BUSINESS AND PRACTICE. 1989. base vol. (plus s-a. suppl.). Maxwell Macmillan, Rosenfeld Launer, 910 Sylvan Ave., Englewood Cliffs, NJ 07632-3310. TEL 800-562-0245. FAX 201-816-3569. Ed. John W. Hazard, Jr.

340   US   ISSN 0886-3520
KF2987   CODEN: JCUSEZ
COPYRIGHT SOCIETY OF THE U.S.A. JOURNAL. 1953. q. $125 to individuals; institutions $500; non-profit libraries $50. Fred B. Rothman & Co., 10368 W. Centennial Rd., Littleton, CO 80127. TEL 303-979-5657. FAX 303-978-1457. adv.; bk.rev.; bibl.; index; circ. 1,000. (also avail. in microfilm from RRI; back issues avail.; reprint service avail. from RRI,UMI) **Indexed**: C.L.I., Curr.Cont., L.R.I., Leg.Per., SSCI.
    Formerly (until vol.28): Copyright Society of the U.S.A. Bulletin (ISSN 0010-8642)

340   US   ISSN 0010-8839
KF292.C6914
CORNELL LAW FORUM. 1949. 3/yr. free to qualified personnel. Cornell University, Law School, Myron Taylor Hall, Ithaca, NY 14853. TEL 607-255-7477. Eds. John A. Siliciano, Kathleen E. Rourke. illus.; pat.; tr.mk.; circ. 9,000. (reprint service avail. from WSH) **Indexed**: C.L.I., L.R.I., Leg.Per.

340   US   ISSN 0010-8847
K3
CORNELL LAW REVIEW. 1915. 6/yr. $35. Cornell University, Law School, Myron Taylor Hall, Ithaca, NY 14853. TEL 607-255-3387. Ed.Bd. adv.; bk.rev.; charts; illus.; index, cum.index: vol.1-15, 16-38; circ. 3,500. (also avail. in microfiche from RRI,WSH; microfilm from WSH; back issues avail.; reprint service avail. from RRI) **Indexed**: A.B.C.Pol.Sci., Account.Ind. (1974-), Bank.Lit.Ind., BPIA, C.L.I., Crim.Just.Abstr., Curr.Cont., L.R.I., Leg.Cont., Leg.Per., P.A.I.S., SSCI.
●Also available online. Vendor(s): Mead Data Central, WESTLAW.
—BLDSC shelfmark: 3470.955500.
    Former titles: Cornell Law Quarterly; Cornell Law Journal.

340   NE   ISSN 0169-7528
JF1081   CODEN: CORFEM
CORRUPTION AND REFORM; international journal. (Text in English) 1986. 3/yr. $56 to individuals; institutions $121.50. Kluwer Academic Publishers, Postbus 17, 3300 AA Dordrecht, Netherlands. TEL 078-334911. FAX 078-334254. TELEX 29245. (Dist. by: Kluwer Academic Publishers, P.O. Box 322, 3300 AH Dordrecht, Netherlands; N. America dist. addr.: Box 358, Accord Station, Hingham, MA 02018-0358. TEL 617-871-6600) Eds. Michael Johnston, Stephen Riley. (reprint service avail. from SWZ)
—BLDSC shelfmark: 3477.027500.

340   US
COUNCIL FOR COURT EXCELLENCE ANNUAL REPORT. 1982. a. $50. Council for Court Excellence, 1025 Vermont Ave., N.W., Ste. 510, Washington, DC 20005. TEL 202-783-7736. FAX 202-783-7697. Ed. Samuel F. Harahan. circ. 2,000. (back issues avail.)
    Description: Report of public interest group working to improve the administration of justice.

340   FR   ISSN 0252-0877
LAW
COUNCIL OF EUROPE. DIRECTORATE OF LEGAL AFFAIRS. INFORMATION BULLETIN ON LEGISLATIVE ACTIVITIES. 1972. 4/yr. $4. Council of Europe, Directorate of Legal Affairs, Publications Section, 67006 Strasbourg, France. (Dist. in U.S. by: Manhattan Publishing Co., 80 Brook St., P.O. Box 650, Croton, NY 10520)
—BLDSC shelfmark: 4485.480000.
    Formerly (until 1978): Council of Europe. Directorate of Legal Affairs. Newsletter on Legislative Activities.

340   US   ISSN 0279-9626
KF200
COUNTY BAR UPDATE. 1981. m. membership. Los Angeles County Bar Association, Box 55020, Los Angeles, CA 90055. TEL 213-896-6410. FAX 213-896-6500. Ed. Karen King. circ. 24,000. (back issues avail.)

| 340 | UK | ISSN 0269-3291 |

COUNTY COURT PRACTICE. a. $339. Butterworth & Co. (Publishers) Ltd. (Subsidiary of: Reed International PLC), 88 Kingsway, London WC2B 6AB, England. TEL 71-405-6900. FAX 71-405-1332. TELEX 95678. (US addr.: Butterworth Legal Publishers, 90 Stiles Rd., Salem, NH 03079. TEL 800-548-4001) Ed. R.C.L. Gregory.

| 340 | CN | ISSN 0316-1234 |

COURS DE PERFECTIONNEMENT DU NOTARIAT. 1962. s-a. Can.$20 per no. Chambre des Notaires du Quebec, 630 Blvd. Rene Levesque, Ste. 1700, Montreal, Que. H3B 1T6, Canada. TEL 514-879-1793. FAX 514-879-1923. bibl.; cum.index: 1962-1985. (also avail. in record; video cassette)

| 347 | US | ISSN 1043-8483 |
K3

▼**COURTS, HEALTH SCIENCE & THE LAW.** 1990. q. $100. Williams & Wilkins, 428 E. Preston St., Baltimore, MD 21202. TEL 301-528-4000. FAX 301-528-4312. Ed. Franklin M. Zweig.
    Description: Examines the problems and opportunities challenging the nation's health care, legal, and scientific communities.

CREDIT (WASHINGTON). see BUSINESS AND ECONOMICS — Banking And Finance

| 340 332.7 | US | |

CREDIT UNION LAW SERVICE. (Issued in 4 base vols. with supplements and a monthly newsletter) 1985. irreg. (Credit Union National Association) Matthew Bender & Co., Inc., 11 Penn Plaza, New York, NY 10001. TEL 212-967-7707. (looseleaf format)
    Description: Acts as a guide to the laws and regulations governing credit unions, with practical analysis and explanations.

CREDIT UNION WEEK. see BUSINESS AND ECONOMICS — Banking And Finance

| 340 | US | ISSN 0011-1155 |
K3

CREIGHTON LAW REVIEW. 1963. q. $25. Creighton University, Creighton Law School, 2133 California St., Omaha, NE 68178. TEL 402-280-2980. (Dist. by: Fred B. Rothman & Co., 10368 W. Centennial Rd., Littleton, CO 80123) Ed. Sharon L. Rosse. adv.; bk.rev.; index; circ. 3,840. (also avail. in microform from UMI; reprint service avail. from RRI,UMI) Indexed: C.L.I., L.R.I., Leg.Cont., Leg.Per.
●Also available online. Vendor(s): WESTLAW.
—BLDSC shelfmark: 3487.297000.

| 340 | IT | |

CRITICA GIUDIZIARIA. bi-m. Via F. Turati 37, 40134 Bologna, Italy. Ed. Giuseppe Delfini.

| 347 945 | | |

CRITICA PENALE.* q. Via Bassi 14, 40121 Bologna, Italy.

CRITICAL ISSUES. see POLITICAL SCIENCE

| 340 658.7 | UK | |

CRONER'S BUYING AND SELLING LAW. 1982. bi-m. £81 effective 1992. Croner Publications Ltd., Croner House, London Road, Kingston, Surrey KT2 6SR, England. TEL 081-547-3333. FAX 081-547-2637. TELEX 267778. Ed. Robert Piper. (looseleaf format)
    Description: Covers the essentials of all areas of the law relevant to buying and selling goods or services.

| 340 658.3 | UK | |

CRONER'S EMPLOYMENT LAW. 1980. bi-m. £96.40 (effective 1992). Croner Publications Ltd., Croner House, London Road, Kingston, Surrey KT2 6SR, England. TEL 081-547-3333. FAX 081-547-2637. TELEX 267778. Ed. Clio Fisher. (looseleaf format)
    Description: Details legislative requirements at each stage of employment from recruitment to termination.

CRONER'S HEALTH AND SAFETY AT WORK. see OCCUPATIONAL HEALTH AND SAFETY

| 340 | UK | |

CROWN OFFICE DIGEST. bi-m. £145. Sweet & Maxwell, South Quay Plaza, 8th Fl., 183 Marsh Wall, London E14 9FT, England. TEL 071-538-8686. FAX 071-538-9508. Ed. Richard Gordon.

| 342 | AG | |

CUADERNOS DE LOS INSTITUTOS. 1957. irreg. Universidad Nacional de Cordoba, Instituto de Derecho Constitucional, Calle Obispo Trejo y Sanabria 242, Cordoba, Argentina.

| 340 | US | ISSN 0360-8298 |
K3

CUMBERLAND LAW REVIEW. 1970. 3/yr. $24. Samford University, Cumberland School of Law, 800 Lakeshore Dr., Birmingham, AL 35229. TEL 205-870-2757. Ed.Bd. adv.; bk.rev.; circ. 1,700. (also avail. in microfilm from UMI; back issues avail.; reprint service avail. from RRI,UMI) Indexed: C.L.I., L.R.I., Leg.Cont., Leg.Per.
●Also available online. Vendor(s): WESTLAW.
    Formerly: Cumberland-Samford Law Review (ISSN 0045-9275)

| 340 | US | |

CURRENT AWARD TRENDS. 1960. a. $29.50. Jury Verdict Research, Inc., 30700 Bainbridge Rd., Ste. H, Solon, OH 44139. TEL 800-321-6910. FAX 216-349-5879. TELEX 216-349-JURY. Ed. Brian Shenker. circ. 5,000.

| 340 | II | ISSN 0253-6579 |

CURRENT CENTRAL LEGISLATION; central acts, ordinances, regulations, rules & notifications. (Text and summaries in English) 1975. m. $41. Eastern Book Company, 34 Lalbagh, Lucknow 226 001, India. TEL 43171. FAX 0091-522-242061. TELEX 535 436 FAST IN. Eds. P.L. Malik, K.K. Malik. adv.; bk.rev.; circ. 2,500. (back issues avail.)

CURRENT INCOME TAX LAW. see BUSINESS AND ECONOMICS — Public Finance, Taxation

| 340 | II | ISSN 0011-3573 |

CURRENT INDIAN STATUTES. (Text in English) 1923. m. Rs.300. 36, Sector 9-A, Chandigarh 160009, India. Ed. Lalit Mohan Suri. adv.; bk.rev.; index, cum.index; circ. 2,500. (back issues avail.)

| 340 | UK | ISSN 0011-362X |

CURRENT LAW. 1947. m. £235. Sweet & Maxwell, South Quay Plaza, 8th Fl., 183 Marsh Wall, London E14 9FT, England. TEL 071-538-8686. FAX 071-538-9508. (Dist. in U.S. & Canada by: Carswell Co. Ltd., 2330 Midland Ave., Agincourt, Ont. M1S 1P7, Canada) Indexed: Leg.Per.
—BLDSC shelfmark: 3499.100000.

| 340 | SA | |

CURRENT LAW SERVICE. (Supplement to: Laws of South Africa) m. $345. Butterworth Publishers (Pty.) Ltd., 8 Walter Pl., Waterval Park, Durban 4000, South Africa. TEL 031-294247. FAX 031-283255. (looseleaf format)
    Description: Details current developments in South African law.

CURRENT MUNICIPAL PROBLEMS. see PUBLIC ADMINISTRATION — Municipal Government

CUSTOMS BULLETIN; regulations, rulings, decisions, and notices concerning customs and related matters and decisions of Court of Customs and Patent Appeals and Customs Court. see BUSINESS AND ECONOMICS — Public Finance, Taxation

| 349 | GW | ISSN 0012-1231 |

D A R. (Deutsches Autorecht) 1926. m. DM.120. (Allgemeiner Deutscher Automobil-Club e.V.) A D A C Verlag GmbH, Am Westpark 8, Postfach 700126, 8000 Munich 70, Germany. TEL 089-7676-0. Ed. Johann Seehon. adv.; bk.rev.; bibl.; circ. 6,200. Indexed: Dok.Str.
—BLDSC shelfmark: 3576.287000.

| 340 | US | |

D C B A BRIEF. 1987. 10/yr. $40. DuPage County Bar Association, 800 Roosevelt Rd., Bldg. E, Ste. 120, Glen Ellyn, IL 60137. TEL 708-653-7779. FAX 708-653-7870. adv.; circ. 1,532.
    Description: Provides updates on current case law, tips on business management and on trial preparation.

D.C. CODE UPDATER. see PUBLIC ADMINISTRATION — Municipal Government

D.C. REAL ESTATE REPORTER. see REAL ESTATE

LAW 2617

| 340 | US | ISSN 0276-5675 |
KF1297.D7

D E S LITIGATION REPORTER; the national journal of record of diethylstilbestrol litigation. 1981. s-m. $800. Andrews Publications, 1646 West Chester Pike, Box 1000, Westtown, PA 19395. TEL 215-399-6600. FAX 215-399-6610. Ed. Edith McFall. bibl.; stat.; cum.index every 6 mos. (looseleaf format; back issues avail.)

D I N. CATALOGUE OF TECHNICAL RULES. (Deutsches Institut fuer Normung e.V. (D I N)) see TECHNOLOGY: COMPREHENSIVE WORKS

| 349 | DK | ISSN 0108-3627 |
LAW

D J OE F - HAANDBOGEN; opslagsbog for tillidsrepraesentanter i D J OE F. 1981. biennial. DKK 201.30. Danmarks Jurist- og Oekonomforbund, Gothersgade 133, 1123 Copenhagen K, Denmark.

| 340 | US | |

D N A NEWSLETTER. 1968. bi-m. free. D N A - People's Legal Services, Inc., Box 306, Window Rock, AZ 86515. TEL 602-871-4151. Dir. Eddie Tso. adv.; charts; illus.; stat.; circ. 4,500. (also avail. in microfilm from MCA)
    Former titles: D N A in Action; Law in Action.

D.O.; a publication for osteopathic physicians and surgeons. (Doctor of Osteopath) see MEDICAL SCIENCES — Chiropractic, Homeopathy, Osteopathy

| 340 368 | GW | ISSN 0936-6156 |
HD7102.G3

D O K: POLITIK - PRAXIS RECHT. 1914. s-m. DM.120. (A O K - Bundesverband) A O K - Verlag GmbH, Kontrijker Str. 1, Postfach 20 13 54, D-5300 Bonn 2, Germany. FAX 0228-8490930. Ed. M. Petter. adv.; bk.rev.; circ. 7,000. (also avail. in microfilm) Indexed: World Bibl.Soc.Sec.
    Formerly: Ortskrankenkasse (ISSN 0030-5995)

| 342 610 170 301.2 | CN | ISSN 0847-1797 |

D W D NEWSLETTER. 1983. q. membership. Death with Dignity, 600 Eglinton Ave. E., Ste. 401, Toronto, Ont. M4P 1P3, Canada. TEL 416-486-3998. Ed. Sheilagh Hickie. bk.rev.; charts; stat.; circ. 6,500.
    Description: Discusses issues related to end of life decision making. Looks at ethical, legal, moral and social aspects of life-death concerns of Canadians.

D W I JOURNAL: LAW & SCIENCE. see TRANSPORTATION — Automobiles

| 340 330 | US | |

DAILY BULLETIN (BROOKLYN); a daily newspaper serving professionals. 1975. d. $150. Brooklyn Journal Publications, Inc., 129 Montague St., Brooklyn, NY 11201. TEL 718-624-6033. FAX 718-875-5302. Ed. Edward Goldstein. adv.; bk.rev.; circ. 5,200.
    Formerly: Brooklyn Journal.

DAILY ENVIRONMENT REPORT. see ENVIRONMENTAL STUDIES

THE DAILY RECORD. see BUSINESS AND ECONOMICS

| 340 332 | US | ISSN 0360-9510 |
K4

DAILY REPORTER. 1896. w. $139. Daily Reporter of Sioux City Inc., 518 Nebraska St., Sioux City, IA 51101-1306. TEL 712-255-8829. Ed. Jeffrey S. Scotsky. circ. 450.

DAILY TERRITORIAL. see BUSINESS AND ECONOMICS

| 340 | US | |

DAILY WASHINGTON LAW REPORTER. 1874. d. $158.40. Washington Law Reporter Co., 1001 Connecticut Ave., N.W., Ste. 238, Washington, DC 20036-5504. TEL 202-331-1700. FAX 202-785-8476. Ed. James W. Twaddell, Jr.

| 340 | JA | |

DAITO HOGAKU/JOURNAL OF LAW AND POLITICS. (Text in Japanese) 1974. a. free. Daito Bunka University, Law and Politics Society - Daito Bunka Daigaku Hogakkai, 1-9-1 Takashimadaira, Itabashi-ku, Tokyo, Japan. circ. 2,350.

340　　　　　　CN　ISSN 0317-1663
K4
DALHOUSIE LAW JOURNAL. (Text in English and French) 1973. 2/yr. Can.$12.50 per no. Dalhousie University, Faculty of Law, Halifax, N.S. B3H 4H9, Canada. TEL 902-424-2211. (Subscr. to: Carswell Co. Ltd., 2330 Midland Ave., Agincourt, Ont. M1S 1P7) Ed. J. Yogis. bk.rev.; circ. 325. (back issues avail.) **Indexed:** Abstr.Bk.Rev.Curr.Leg.Per., C.L.I., Curr.Cont., Ind.Can.L.P.L., L.R.I., Leg.Per., Mar.Aff.Bibl.
　—BLDSC shelfmark: 3517.730000.

340　　　　　　TZ　ISSN 0418-3770
DAR ES SALAAM UNIVERSITY LAW JOURNAL. Short title: D U L J. (Text in English) 1963-198?; N.S. 1991. q. $100. University of Dar es Salaam, Faculty of Law, P.O. Box 35034, Dar es Salaam, Tanzania. (Co-sponsor: Friedrich Gibert Stiftung) Ed. Kasimbazi, E.B.
　Formerly (until 1971): Denning Law Society. Journal.

340　　　　　　SA
DE JURE. (Text in Afrikaans, English) s-a. $50. (Pretoria University, Faculty of Law) Butterworth Publishers (Pty.) Ltd., 8 Walter Pl., Waterval Park, Durban 4000, South Africa. TEL 031-294247. FAX 031-283255.

340　　　　　　US　ISSN 0011-7188
DE PAUL LAW REVIEW. 1951. q. $21. DePaul University, College of Law, 25 E. Jackson Blvd., Chicago, IL 60604. TEL 312-362-8554. Ed. R. Cabell Morris, Jr. adv.; bk.rev.; index; circ. 2,300. (also avail. in microform from UMI; back issues avail.; reprint service avail. from UMI,ISI) **Indexed:** C.C.L.P., C.L.I., L.R.I., Leg.Per.
　—BLDSC shelfmark: 3535.948000.

340　　　　　　US　ISSN 0011-7250
DECALOGUE JOURNAL. 1950. q. $36. Decalogue Society of Lawyers, 179 W. Washington St., Chicago, IL 60602. TEL 312-263-6493. Ed. Melvin Lewis. adv.; bk.rev.; circ. 1,800. (also avail. in microform from UMI; reprint service avail. from UMI) **Indexed:** C.L.I., L.R.I.

DECENCY REPORTER. see *SOCIOLOGY*

347　　　　　　US
DECISIONS & DEVELOPMENTS. 1979. bi-m. $84. Box 342, Wayland, MA 01778. TEL 617-890-5678. Ed. Joseph S. Iandorio.
　Description: Reports court decisions relating to intellectual property.

340　　　　　　US
DELAWARE LAW MONTHLY. 1978. m. $330. Delaware Law Monthly, Box 262, Wilmington, DE 19899. TEL 302-652-2050. Ed.Bd. circ. 250.
　Description: Covers decisions of Delaware State Courts, with emphasis on corporate and business decisions.

348　　　　　　US　ISSN 0091-5564
KFD47
DELAWARE REPORTER. (Vol. numbering adopted from that of the Atlantic Reporter) irreg. West Publishing Co., Box 64526, St. Paul, MN 55164-0526. TEL 800-328-9352.
　Supersedes: Delaware. Court of Chancery. Delaware Chancery Reports; Delaware. Courts. Delaware Reports.

340　　　　　　II
DELHI LAW REVIEW. 1972. irreg. $2 per no. University of Delhi, Faculty of Law, Delhi 110007, India. adv.; bk.rev.; circ. 275.

349　　　　　　II　ISSN 0011-7846
DELHI LAW TIMES. (Text in English) 1965. fortn. Rs.45. 36 Sector 9-A, Chandigarh 11, India. Eds. Ravinder Mohan Suri, Shashi Mohan Suri. adv.; bk.rev.; cum.index every 5 yrs.

DEMOCRATIC REPUBLIC OF THE SUDAN GAZETTE/JARIDAH AL-RASMIYAH LI-JUMHURIYAT AL-SUDAN AL-DIMUQRATIYAH. see *PUBLIC ADMINISTRATION*

DEMOCRATIC REPUBLIC OF THE SUDAN GAZETTE. LEGISLATIVE SUPPLEMENT. see *PUBLIC ADMINISTRATION*

340　　　　　　IT　ISSN 0416-9565
DEMOCRAZIA E DIRITTO/DEMOCRACY AND LAW. 1960. bi-m. L.61000 (foreign L.81000). Editori Riuniti, Via Serchio 9-11, 00198 Rome, Italy. TEL 06-866383. FAX 06-416096. TELEX EDIRIU I 625292. Ed. Pietro Barcellona. adv.; bk.rev.; circ. 7,000.
　—BLDSC shelfmark: 3550.575000.

DENMARK. LOVINFORMATION FRA MILJOESTYRELSEN. see *ENVIRONMENTAL STUDIES*

340　　　　　　DK　ISSN 0109-1913
KJR3127.A12
DENMARK. MILJOEMINISTERIET. MILJOEMINISTERIETS LOVREGISTER; systematisk register over Miljoeministeriets love, bekendtgoerelser, cirkulaerer og vejledninger. 1984. q. free. (Miljoestyrelsen) Danish Environmental Protection Agency, Environmental Data and Information, Strandgade 29, DK-1401 Copenhagen K, Denmark. TEL 45-31-57-83-10. FAX 45-31-57-24-49. TELEX 31209. Ed. Birgitte Pedersen. circ. 150.
　Description: Provides an introduction to the department's regulations. Includes 2,500 key words to all of the agency's regulations.

340　　　　　　UK　ISSN 0269-1922
K4
DENNING LAW JOURNAL. 1986. a. £12.50 (typically set in Dec). University of Buckingham, Buckingham, Bucks MK18 1EG, England. TEL 0280-814080. FAX 0280-822245. Ed. C.G. Hall. adv. (back issues avail.) **Indexed:** C.L.I., Leg.Per.
　—BLDSC shelfmark: 3553.104500.

340　　　　　　US
DENVER UNIVERSITY LAW REVIEW. 1923. q. $23. University of Denver, College of Law, Porter Adm. Bldg., 7039 E. 18th Ave., Denver, CO 80220-1826. TEL 303-871-6171. Ed. Diana Cachey. adv.; bk.rev.; index, cum.index every 5 and 20 yrs.; circ. 1,500. (also avail. in microfiche from WSH; microfilm from WSH) **Indexed:** C.L.I., Curr.Cont., L.R.I., Law Ofc.Info.Svc., Leg.Cont., Leg.Per., P.A.I.S., Sel.Water Res.Abstr., SSCI.
　●Also available online. Vendor(s): WESTLAW.
　Former titles: Denver Law Journal (ISSN 0011-8834); Dicta.

340　　　　　　PE
DERECHO. 1944. a. $8. Pontificia Universidad Catolica del Peru, Facultad de Derecho, Fondo Editorial, Apdo. 1761, Lima 100, Peru. Ed. Marcial Rubio Correo. adv.; circ. 2,000.

DERECHO DEL TRABAJO; revista critica mensual de jurisprudencia, doctrina y legislacion. see *BUSINESS AND ECONOMICS — Labor And Industrial Relations*

340　　　　　　SP　ISSN 0210-3001
DERECHO PENAL Y CIENCIAS PENALES. ANUARIO. 1948. a. (plus updates 3/yr.). 5000 ptas. (foreign 5400 ptas.). Ministerio de Justicia, Centro de Publicaciones, Secretaria General Tecnica, Gran Via, 76-8, 28013 Madrid, Spain. TEL 247 54 22.

340 300　　　　MX
DERECHO Y CIENCIAS SOCIALES. 1973. q. Universidad Autonoma de Nuevo Leon, Loma Redonda 1515-A, Col. Loma Larga, Monterrey, Mexico. illus.

DETENTION REPORTER; a monthly resource for detention & corrections. see *CRIMINOLOGY AND LAW ENFORCEMENT*

340.05　　　　　US　ISSN 0099-135X
K4
DETROIT COLLEGE OF LAW REVIEW. 1975. q. $14. Detroit College of Law, 130 E. Elizabeth St., Detroit, MI 48201. TEL 313-965-0150. Ed. Juli Hopson Decker. adv.; bk.rev.; circ. 1,500. (also avail. in microfilm from MIM,WSH; reprint service avail. from WSH) **Indexed:** Abstr.Bk.Rev.Curr.Leg.Per., C.L.I., L.R.I., Leg.Per., Mar.Aff.Bibl.

340　　　　　　US　ISSN 0011-9652
KF200
THE DETROIT LAWYER. 1931. q. $10 to non-members. Detroit Bar Association, 2380 Penobscot Bldg., Detroit, MI 48226-4811. FAX 313-965-0842. Ed. Jeffrey J. Alderman. adv.; bk.rev.; charts; illus.; circ. 4,500. **Indexed:** C.L.I., Law Ofc.Info.Svc., Leg.Per.

340　　　　　　GW　ISSN 0138-1644
DEUTSCHE DEMOKRATISCHE REPUBLIK. GESETZBLATT; * Gesetze und andere allgemeinverbindliche Rechtsvorschriften mit Ausnahme von voelkerrechtlichen Vertraegen. 1949. irreg. DM.30. Staatsverlag der DDR, Otto-Grotewohlstr. 17, 1086 Berlin, Germany. Ed.Bd. **Indexed:** Agri.Eng.Abstr.

DEUTSCHE NOTAR-ZEITSCHRIFT. see *PUBLIC ADMINISTRATION*

349　　　　　　GW　ISSN 0012-060X
DEUTSCHE RECHTSPRECHUNG. 1948. 18/yr. DM.387.60. Verlag Neue Wirtschafts-Briefe GmbH, Eschstr. 22, Postfach 1620, D-4690 Herne 1, Germany. adv.; bk.rev.; circ. 5,700.

340　　　　　　GW　ISSN 0340-8612
DEUTSCHE RICHTERZEITUNG. 1950. m. DM.74. (Deutscher Richterbund) Carl Heymanns Verlag KG, Luxemburger Str. 449, 5000 Cologne 41, Germany. TEL 0221-46010-0. index; circ. 1,300. (back issues avail.)

DEUTSCHES STEUERRECHT; Zeitschrift fuer Praxis und Wissenschaft des gesamten Steuerrechts. see *BUSINESS AND ECONOMICS — Public Finance, Taxation*

349　　　　　　GW　ISSN 0012-1363
DEUTSCHES VERWALTUNGSBLATT. (With: Verwaltungsarchiv) 1885. s-m. DM.390. Carl Heymanns Verlag KG, Luxemburgerstr. 449, 5000 Cologne 41, Germany. TEL 0221-46010-0. FAX 0221-4601069. Ed. C.H. Vle. adv.; bk.rev.; abstr.; charts; stat.; index; circ. 3,300. (reprint service avail. from SCH) **Indexed:** Dok.Str., INIS Atomind.
　—BLDSC shelfmark: 3578.300000.

340　　　　　　BG
DHAKA LAW REPORTS: CIVIL DIGEST. (Text in English) 1949-1984; N.S. 1986. irreg. $35. Dhaka Law Reports Office, Malibagh, Dhaka, Bangladesh. TEL 403909. Ed. Obaidul Huq. adv.; bk.rev.; circ. 5,000.
　Formerly: Up-to-Date Civil Reference.
　Description: Contains commentaries and case laws of Bangladesh, India and Pakistan.

340　　　　　　US　ISSN 0012-2459
LAW
DICKINSON LAW REVIEW. 1897. q. $35. Dickinson School of Law, 150 S. College St., Carlisle, PA 17013. TEL 717-243-4611. FAX 717-243-4443. Ed. Jrusteb Beebe. adv.; bk.rev.; charts; index; circ. 1,500. (also avail. in microfilm from WSH) **Indexed:** C.C.L.P., C.L.I., Crim.Just.Abstr., L.R.I., Leg.Per., Mar.Aff.Bibl.
　●Also available online. Vendor(s): WESTLAW.
　—BLDSC shelfmark: 3580.270000.

DICTIONNAIRE DU MARCHE COMMUN. see *BUSINESS AND ECONOMICS — International Commerce*

DICTIONNAIRE JOLY CONCURRENCE. see *BUSINESS AND ECONOMICS*

349　　　　　　FR　ISSN 0012-2475
DICTIONNAIRE PERMANENT DROIT DES AFFAIRES. 1963. fortn. 1412.32 F. Editions Legislatives et Administratives, 80, ave. de la Marne, 92546 Montrouge Cedex, France. TEL 1-40-92-68-68. FAX 1-46-56-00-15. TELEX 632 855 F. bibl.; index; cum.index; circ. 9,000. (looseleaf format)
　Description: Covers commercial, economic and business laws.

340　　　　　　IT　ISSN 0394-9036
LA DIFESA PENALE; rivista trimestrale di eloquenza, diritto e applicazione forense. 1983. q. L.80000($120) Edizioni Bucalo snc., Casella Postale 51, 04100 Latina, Italy. FAX 773-623226. Dir. Enrico Baccino. adv.; bk.rev.; bibl.; cum.index; circ. 5,000.

340　　　　　　FR　ISSN 0292-935X
DIGEST DOCUMENTATION ORGANIQUE. w. Documentation Organique, 11, rue de Teheran, 75008 Paris, France. TEL 45-62-54-35.

340 331　　　　II　ISSN 0419-1293
DIGEST OF CURRENT INDUSTRIAL AND LABOUR LAW. (Text in English) vol.8, 1973. m. Rs.36. Current Law Publishers, PO Box 1268, Delhi 110006, India. Ed. J.D. Jain.

347.9   II   ISSN 0012-2750
DIGEST OF LABOUR CASES. (Text in English) 1960. m. Rs.20. V. Subramanian, Ed. & Pub., 337 Thambu Chetty St., Madras 600001, India. adv.; bk.rev.; index; circ. 280 (controlled).

347   US   ISSN 0070-4857
DIGEST OF LEGAL ACTIVITIES OF INTERNATIONAL ORGANIZATIONS AND OTHER INSTITUTIONS. 1969. irreg. price varies. (Unidroit - International Institute for the Unification of Private Law) Oceana Publications, Inc., Dobbs Ferry, NY 10522. TEL 914-696-1320. FAX 914-693-0402. Ed.Bd. circ. 300. (looseleaf format)
  Description: Provides a comprehensive view of the variety of legal activities conducted in numerous international and inter-federal organizations.

340   US   ISSN 0012-2777
DIGEST OF OPINIONS OF THE ATTORNEY GENERAL. 1965. q. $7.50. Attorney General's Office, Rm. 112, State Capitol, Oklahoma City, OK 73105. TEL 405-521-3921. FAX 405-521-6246. Ed. Cathy Margerum. circ. 780. (processed)

340   CN
DIGEST ON GAY RIGHTS; I: human - civil rights. 1977. a. free. Gays for Equality, P.O. Box 1661, Winnipeg, MB. R3C 2Z6, Canada. TEL 204-284-5208. FAX 204-474-0212. Ed. Chris Vogel. circ. 500.

340   IS   ISSN 0070-4903
DINE ISRAEL; an annual of Jewish law: past and present. (Text in English and Hebrew) 1969. a. $14. Tel Aviv University, Faculty of Law, Ramat Aviv, Tel Aviv, Israel. Ed. Aaron Kirschenbaum. bk.rev.; circ. 500. Indexed: Ind.Heb.Per.
  Incorporates (no.8, 1969): Current Bibliography of Hebrew Law.

340   SP
DIRECCION GENERAL DE LOS REGISTROS Y DEL NOTARIADO. ANUARIO. a. 5000 ptas. Ministerio de Justicia, Centro de Publicaciones, Secretaria General Tecnica, Gran Via, 76-8, 28013 Madrid, Spain. TEL 247 54 22.

342   US
DIRECT CONFRONTATION. 1984. m. $12. Constitutional Revival, 29 Fairfield Rd., Enfield, CT 06082. TEL 203-745-2221. Ed. Andy Mel. circ. 2,000. (back issues avail.)

340   US
DIRECTORY OF BAY AREA PUBLIC INTEREST ORGANIZATIONS. 1980. triennial, 4th ed., 1991. $25 (members $20). Public Interest Clearinghouse, 200 McAllister St., San Francisco, CA 94102. TEL 415-565-4695. FAX 415-621-4859. circ. 1,000.
  Formerly (until 1991): Public Interest Clearinghouse Directory.
  Description: Comprehensive listing describing the services, costs and publications of public interest organizations in the San Francisco Bay Area.

340   EI
DIRECTORY OF COMMUNITY LEGISLATION IN FORCE. (In 2 vols.: Vol.I - Analytical Register; Vol.II - Chronological Index, Alphabetical Index) biennial. $110. (Commission of the European Communities, Legal Service) Office for Official Publications of the European Communities, 2, rue Mercier, L-2985 Luxembourg, Luxembourg. TEL 49-92-81. (Dist. in the U.S. by: Unipub, 4611-F Assembly Dr., Lanham, MD 20706-4391)
  Description: Reference work which enables the user to find the current instruments of Community legislation.

DIRECTORY OF CRIMINAL JUSTICE ISSUES IN THE STATES. see *CRIMINOLOGY AND LAW ENFORCEMENT*

340 333.33   US
DIRECTORY OF INTELLECTUAL PROPERTY ATTORNEYS. 1989. a. Prentice Hall Law & Business (Subsidiary of: Simon & Schuster), 270 Sylvan Ave., Englewood Cliffs, NJ 07632. TEL 201-894-8484.

020
DIRECTORY OF LAW LIBRARIES. 1946. a. $60. American Association of Law Libraries, 53 W. Jackson Blvd., Ste. 940, Chicago, IL 60604. TEL 312-939-4764. FAX 312-431-1097. Ed.Bd. circ. 4,700.

340 378   US   ISSN 0070-573X
DIRECTORY OF LAW TEACHERS. 1922. a. $15. (Association of American Law Schools) West Publishing Co., Box 64526, St. Paul, MN 55164-0526. TEL 800-328-9352. (Order from: Association of American Law Schools, One Dupont Circle, Ste. 370, Washington, DC 20036)

340   CN   ISSN 0383-8358
KE280.D575
DIRECTORY OF LAW TEACHERS/ANNUAIRE DES PROFESSEURS DE DROIT. (Text in English and French) 1972. a. Can.$13.50. Canadian Association of Canadian Law Teachers, c/o Canadian Bar Association, 57 Copernicus, Ottawa, Ont. K1N 6N5, Canada. Ed. Louis Perret. adv.; circ. 500.

340   US
DIRECTORY OF LAWYER REFERRAL SERVICES. 1976. a. $2.50. American Bar Association, Standing Committee on Lawyer Referral and Information Service, 750 N. Lake Shore Dr., Chicago, IL 60611. TEL 312-988-5760. FAX 312-988-5664. circ. 1,000.

345.01   US
KF336
DIRECTORY OF LEGAL AID AND DEFENDER OFFICES IN THE UNITED STATES AND TERRITORIES. biennial. $30. National Legal Aid & Defender Association, 1625 K St., N.W., 8th Fl., Washington, DC 20006. TEL 202-452-0620. FAX 202-872-1031.
  Former titles: Directory of Legal Aid and Defender Offices in the United States (ISSN 0276-5365) & National Legal Aid and Defender Association Directory.
  Description: Lists legal aid and defender offices by state and territory.

340   US   ISSN 0092-9174
KF193.S25
DIRECTORY OF SAN FRANCISCO ATTORNEYS. a. $50 to non-members. Bar Association of San Francisco, 685 Market St., Ste. 700, San Francisco, CA 94105. adv.; circ. 10,000.
  Description: Lists all attorneys in San Francisco and notes which are members of the Bar Association. Also lists San Francisco law firms, federal, state and local courts and governments.

DIRECTORY OF STATE COURT CLERKS & COUNTY COURTHOUSES (YEAR). see *PUBLIC ADMINISTRATION*

340   PO
DIREITO ADMINISTRATIVO. 1980. bi-m. Centelha Promocao do Livro, S.A.R.L., Apartado 241, 3003 Coimbra Codex, Portugal.

340   BL
DIREITO & JUSTICA. 1979. s-a. Pontifica Universidade Catolica do Rio Grande do Sul, Faculdade de Direito, Av. Iparanga 6681, Caixa Postal 1429, Porto Alegre RS, Brazil.

341.57   IT   ISSN 0012-3390
DIRITTO AEREO; rivista di dottrina, giurisprudenza e legislazione aeronautica dei trasporti intermodali e del diritto spaziale. 1962. N.S. 1992. s-a. L.60000($100) International Association of Lawyers and Experts in Air Law, Via Prisciano 8, piano 4, 00136 Rome, Italy. TEL 39-6-3450955. FAX 39-6-343470. TELEX 621600 PPRMMZ I. Ed. Adalberto Tempesta. adv.; bk.rev.; bibl.; index; circ. 500. (back issues avail.)
  Formerly: Diritto Aereo e dei Trasporti Intermodali.
  Description: Forum devoted to air and space law. Includes law cases and articles in international multimodal transport of goods, air traffic control and rights of servitude.

DIRITTO DEL COMMERCIO INTERNAZIONALE. see *BUSINESS AND ECONOMICS — International Commerce*

347.9   IT   ISSN 0012-3404
DIRITTO DEL LAVORO; rivista di dottrina e di giurisprudenza. 1927. bi-m. L.115000 to individuals; libraries L.75000. Fondazione Diritto del Lavoro, Via Gramsci, 14, Rome, Italy. Ed. Raffaele Foglia. bk.rev.; circ. 1,500. Indexed: P.A.I.S.For.Lang.Ind.
  —BLDSC shelfmark: 3595.413500.

DIRITTO DELL'AGRICOLTURA. see *AGRICULTURE*

DIRITTO DELL'INFORMAZIONE E DELL'INFORMATICA. see *LIBRARY AND INFORMATION SCIENCES*

340   IT   ISSN 0012-3412
DIRITTO DELLE RADIODIFFUSIONI E DELLE TELECOMUNICAZIONI. 1969. 3/yr. L.70000 (foreign L.95000). E R I Edizioni R A I, Via Arsenale 41, 10121 Turin, Italy. TEL 011-8800. FAX 011-534732. Ed. Emanuele Santoro. bk.rev.; abstr.

DIRITTO DELLE RELAZIONI INDUSTRIALI. see *BUSINESS AND ECONOMICS — Labor And Industrial Relations*

DIRITTO DI AUTORE. see *PATENTS, TRADEMARKS AND COPYRIGHTS*

340   IT
DIRITTO DI FAMIGLIA E DELLE PERSONE. 1972. q. L.100000 (foreign L.150000). Casa Editrice Dott. A. Giuffre, Via Busto Arsizio 40, 20151 Milan, Italy. TEL 02-38000905. FAX 02-38009582. Ed. V. Lojacono. adv.; bk.rev.; bibl.; circ. 2,600.

349   IT   ISSN 0012-3439
DIRITTO E GIURISPRUDENZA; rassegna trimestrale di dottrina e di giurisprudenza civile. 1945. q. L.75000. Casa Editrice Dott. Eugenio Jovene, Via Mezzocannone 109, Naples 80134, Italy. Ed. Antonio Guarino.
  —BLDSC shelfmark: 3595.408000.

DIRITTO E PRACTICA DELL'AVIAZIONE CIVILE. see *TRANSPORTATION — Air Transport*

347 368   IT   ISSN 0417-6766
DIRITTO E PRATICA NELL'ASSICURAZIONE. 1956. q. L.80000 (foreign L.120000). (Centro Studi Assicurativi di Milano) Casa Editrice Dott. A. Giuffre, Via Busto Arsizio 40, 20151 Milan, Italy. TEL 02-38000905. FAX 02-38009582. Ed. Emilio Pasanisi. adv.; circ. 3,800.

340   IT   ISSN 0012-3447
DIRITTO E PRATICA TRIBUTARIA. 1929. bi-m. L.380000 (foreign L.430000)(effective 1991). Casa Editrice Dott. Antonio Milani, Via Jappelli 5, 35121 Padua, Italy. TEL 049-656677. FAX 049-8752900. Dir. Victor Uckmar. bk.rev.; index; circ. 2,800.

340   IT   ISSN 0390-8542
DIRITTO E SOCIETA (NAPLES). (Numbers not published consecutively) 1976. irreg., no.15, 1984. price varies. Liguori Editore s.r.l., Via Mezzocannone 19, 80134 Naples, Italy. TEL 081-5227139. Ed. Gustavo Minervini.

340   IT
DIRITTO E SOCIETA (PADUA). N.S. 1978. q. L.120000 (foreign L.150000). Casa Editrice Dott. Antonio Milani, Via Jappelli 5, 35121 Padua, Italy. TEL 049-656677. FAX 049-8752900. Ed. Leopoldo Mazzarolli.

340 330   IT
DIRITTO ED ECONOMIA; rivista-dibattito interdisciplinare quadrimestrale. 1988. 3/yr. L.84000 (effective 1992). Maggioli Editore, Via Crimea, 1, Casella Postale 290, 47037 Rimini, Italy. TEL 0541-626777. FAX 0541-622020. Eds. Carlo Ferrari, Gian Maria Gros-Pietro.

340   IT
DIRITTO FALLIMENTARE E DELLE SOCIETA COMMERCIALI. vol.26, 1951. bi-m. L.180000 (foreign L.21000)(effective 1991). Casa Editrice Dott. Antonio Milani, Via Jappelli 5, 35121 Padua, Italy. TEL 049-656677. FAX 049-8752900. Eds. A. Bonsignori, G. Ragusa Maggiori.

347.75   IT   ISSN 0012-348X
DIRITTO MARITTIMO; rivista trimestrale di dottrina giurisprudenza legislazione italiana e straniera. (Text in English, French, Italian) 1899. q. L.210000 (effective Jan. 1992). Dirmar, s.n.c., Via Roma 10-2, Genoa, Italy. FAX 10-594805. TELEX 270687 DIRMAR. bk.rev.; index; circ. 750. Indexed: Mar.Aff.Bibl.

340   IT
DIRITTO PROCESSUALE AMMINISTRATIVO. 1983. q. L.70000 (foreign L.105000). Casa Editrice Dott. A. Giuffre, Via Busto Arsizio 40, 20151 Milan, Italy. TEL 02-38000905. FAX 02-38009582. Ed. Ricardo Villata. adv.; bk.rev.; circ. 1,500.

DISABILITIES REGULATION NEWS. see MEDICAL SCIENCES

DISCIPLINE AND GRIEVANCES FOR SUPERVISORS IN LOCAL, STATE AND FEDERAL GOVERNMENT. see BUSINESS AND ECONOMICS — Labor And Industrial Relations

340 US
DISCOVERY IN ILLINOIS; federal and state practice. 1985. base vol. (plus suppl.). $80. Butterworth Legal Publishers (Salem) (Subsidiary of: Reed International PLC), 90 Stiles Rd., Salem, NH 03079. TEL 800-548-4001. FAX 603-898-9858. Eds. Robert G. Johnston, Kenneth Kandaras.
   Description: Practitioner's guide to the law of discovery in Illinois state and federal courts; provides both the theoretical basis and the practical application of the rules.

340 US
▼DISCOVERY PROCEEDINGS IN FEDERAL PRACTICE, 2-E. 1991. 2 base vol. (plus a. suppl.). $190. Shepard's - McGraw-Hill, Inc., Box 35300, Colorado Springs, CO 80935-3530. TEL 800-525-2474.
   Description: Provides a practical guide to the federal discovery rules and their applications in federal practice.

340 AG
DISCREPANCIAS. 1983. m. Federacion Argentina de Colegios de Abogados, Av. de Mayo 651, Buenos Aires, Argentina. Ed. Gustavo Adolfo Blanco.

340 US ISSN 0271-2709
KF9084.A15
DISPUTE RESOLUTION. 1979. 3/yr. free. American Bar Association, Standing Committee on Dispute Resolution, 1800 M St., N.W., Washington, DC 20036. TEL 202-331-2258. Ed.Bd. bk.rev.; circ. 3,000.

340 US ISSN 0731-4833
KF9084.A15
DISPUTE RESOLUTION PROGRAM DIRECTORY (YEAR). 1982. irreg. American Bar Association (Washington), 1800 M St., N.W., Washington, DC 20036. TEL 202-331-2258. Ed. Prue Kestner.

340 333.33 US ISSN 0892-4198
KF1507
DISTRESSED REAL ESTATE LAW ALERT. 1988. 6/yr. $250. Clark - Boardman - Callaghan Company Ltd., 375 Hudson St., New York, NY 10014. TEL 212-929-7500. FAX 212-924-0460. (looseleaf format)

340 AT
DISTRICT COURT PRACTICE. 1974. 5/yr. Law Book Co. Ltd., 44-50 Waterloo Rd., North Ryde, N.S.W. 2113, Australia. TEL 02-887-0177. FAX 02-888-9706. TELEX ASBOOK 27995. Ed. E.J. O'Grady.
   Description: An annotated reproduction of the District Court Act 1973, the District Court Rules 1973 and other relevant acts, plus the approved forms and fees, costs and practice notes.

340 AT
DISTRICT COURT PROCEDURE (N.S.W.). base vol. (plus updates 8/yr.). $255. Butterworths Pty. Ltd., 271-273 Lane Cove Rd., P.O. Box 345, North Ryde, N.S.W. 2113, Australia. TEL 02-335-4444. FAX 02-335-4655. (looseleaf format)
   Formerly: District Court Act and Rules: New South Wales.

340 US
DISTRICT OF COLUMBIA BAR. BAR REPORT. vol.9, 1981. bi-m. $20. District of Columbia Bar, 1707 L St., N.W., Ste. 600, Washington, DC 20036-4203. TEL 202-331-3883. FAX 202-223-7726. Ed. Cynthia Kuhn. adv.; illus.; circ. 56,000. (tabloid format) Indexed: C.L.I., Leg.Per.

DITCHLEY CONFERENCE REPORTS. see SOCIAL SCIENCES: COMPREHENSIVE WORKS

DITCHLEY NEWSLETTER. see SOCIAL SCIENCES: COMPREHENSIVE WORKS

DIVORCE CHATS. see SOCIOLOGY

340 CU
DIVULGACION JURIDICA.* q. (Ministerio de Justicia, Departamento de Divulgacion) Ediciones Cubanas, Obispo 57, Apdo. 605, Havana, Cuba.

340 CU
DIVULGACION LEGISLATIVA. q. $15 in N. and S. America; Europe $16; elsewhere $18. (Ministerio de Justicia, Departamento de Divulgacion) Ediciones Cubanas, Obispo No. 527, Apdo. 605, Havana, Cuba.

340 NZ
DIXON & MCVEAGH'S ROAD TRAFFIC LAW. base vol. (plus updates 3/yr.). Butterworths of New Zealand Ltd., 203-207 Victoria St., Box 472, Wellington, New Zealand. TEL 04-385-1479. FAX 04-385-1598. Ed. John Cottle. (looseleaf format)
   Description: Statutes and regulations pertaining to road traffic law, with commentary and case notes.

340.05 US
DOCKET CALL (RICHMOND).* 1973. s-a. $1 per no. Virginia State Bar, Young Lawyers Conference, 707 E. Main St., Ste. 1500, Richmond, VA 27219-2803. TEL 804-786-2061. circ. 6,500. Indexed: C.L.I.
   Former titles: Virginia State Bar. Young Lawyers Conference. Newsletter; Virginia State Bar. Younger Members Conference. Newsletter (ISSN 0094-2251)

340 BE
DOCTRINE JURIDIQUE BELGE.* (Text in French) a. price varies. La Charte - Die Keure, Oude Gentweg 108, B-8000 Brugge, Belgium. FAX 050-34-37-68. index.

340 FR
DOCUMENTS D'ETUDES. (Includes 4 Series: Droit Constitutionnel et Institutions Politiques; Droit Administratif; Droit International Publique; Libertes Publiques) 1970. irreg. Documentation Francaise, 29-31 Quai Voltaire, 75340 Paris cedex 07, France. TEL 1-40-15-70-00. Ed. Jean Jenger. bibl. (also avail. in microfiche)

349 AU ISSN 0012-5075
DOKUMENTATION DER GESETZE UND VERORDNUNGEN OSTEUROPAS. 1950. 15/yr. S.4800($312) Oesterreichisches Ost- und Suedosteuropa Institut, Josefsplatz 6, A-1010 Vienna, Austria. Ed. Ilona Slawinski. index; circ. 100.

340 GW ISSN 0175-5293
DOKUMENTATION DEUTSCHE FINANZRECHTSPRECHUNG. 1968. s-a. DM.162. Stollfuess Verlag Bonn GmbH & Co. KG, Dechenstr. 7, 5300 Bonn 1, Germany.

DOLLARS & CENTS. see BUSINESS AND ECONOMICS — Management

340 CN ISSN 0012-5350
KE132
DOMINION LAW REPORTS. 1912. w. Can.$114. Canada Law Book Inc., 240 Edward St., Aurora, Ont. L4G 3S9, Canada. TEL 416-841-6472. Ed. Bruce Dunlop.
●Also available online.

340 AT
▼DOYLES DISPUTE RESOLUTION PRACTICE - ASIA PACIFIC. 1990. q. C C H Australia Ltd., P.O. Box 230, North Ryde, N.S.W. 2113, Australia. TEL 02-888-2555. FAX 02-888-7324.

340 AT
▼DOYLES DISPUTE RESOLUTION PRACTICE - NORTH AMERICA. 1990. q. C C H Australia Ltd., P.O. Box 230, North Ryde, N.S.W. 2113, Australia. TEL 02-888-2555. FAX 02-888-7324.

DR. SAMUEL MUDD NEWSLETTER. see HISTORY — History Of North And South America

340 US ISSN 0012-5938
DRAKE LAW REVIEW. 1951. q. $25 (effective Apr. 1991). Drake University, Law School, Cartwright Hall, Des Moines, IA 50311. TEL 515-271-2930. Ed.Bd. adv.; bk.rev.; circ. 1,300. (also avail. in microform from MIM,RRI; reprint service avail. from RRI) Indexed: C.C.L.P., C.L.I., L.R.I., Lang.& Lang.Behav.Abstr., Leg.Cont., Leg.Per.
●Also available online. Vendor(s): WESTLAW.
—BLDSC shelfmark: 3623.190000.

340 AA ISSN 0304-2731
DREJTESIA POPULLORE/JUSTICE POPULAIRE. 1948. q. $6.16. Cour Supreme et du Parquet General de la Republique Populaire Socialiste d'Albanie, Tirana, Albania. Ed. Eleni Selenica.

340 US
DRINKING DRIVER IN MINNESOTA. 1989. base vol. (plus suppl.). $88. Butterworth Legal Publishers (Salem) (Subsidiary of: Reed International PLC), 90 Stiles Rd., Salem, NH 03079. TEL 800-548-4001. FAX 603-898-9858. Ed. Donald H. Nichols.
   Description: Practical analysis of Minnesota statutes and cases plus expert examination of the psychological, and pharmacological effects of alcohol.

DRINKING DRIVING LAW LETTER. see TRANSPORTATION — Automobiles

340 UA
DROIT/AL-HAQQ. (Text in Arabic and French) 1970. 3/yr. P.T.50 per no. Arab Lawyers Union - Itehad el Mohameen el Arab, 13, rue Itihad el Mohameen el Arab, Garden City, Cairo, Egypt. bk.rev.; circ. 1,000.

340 BE
DROIT DE LA SECURITE SOCIALE. q. 4626 Fr. Maison Ferdinand Larcier S.A., Rue des Minimes 39, 1000 Brussels, Belgium.

340 330 FR ISSN 0012-639X
DROIT ET ECONOMIE. 1958. q. $4. Association Nationale des Docteurs en Droit, 38 bis, rue Fabert, 75007 Paris, France. (Co-sponsor: Club International du Droit et de l'Economie) adv.; bibl.; charts; illus.; stat.; circ. 4,000.
—BLDSC shelfmark: 3627.358000.

340 301 FR
DROIT ET SOCIETE; revue internationale de theorie du droit et de sociologie juridique. 1926. 3/yr. 310 F. (foreign 330 F.). (Librairie Generale de Droit et de Jurisprudence) Editions Juridiques Associees, 26 rue Vercingetorix, 75014 Paris, France. TEL 1-43-35-01-67. FAX 43-20-07-42. TELEX EJA 203 918 F. Ed.Bd.

DROIT NUCLEAIRE. see ENERGY — Nuclear Energy

349 PL ISSN 0070-7325
DROIT POLONAIS CONTEMPORAIN. Russian edition: Sovremennoe Polskoe Pravo (ISSN 0038-5956) (Text in French) 1963. q. $30. (Polska Akademia Nauk, Instytut Panstwa i Prawa) Ossolineum, Publishing House of the Polish Academy of Sciences, Rynek 9, Wroclaw, Poland. TELEX 0712771 OSS PL. (Dist. by: Ars Polona-Ruch, Krakowskie Przedmiescie 7, Warsaw, Poland) Ed. Jerzy Jodlowski. bk.rev.; circ. 700. Indexed: P.A.I.S.For.Lang.Ind.
   Description: Papers on all domains of Polish contemporary law, current legislatives acts.

349 FR ISSN 0012-6438
DROIT SOCIAL. (Includes special numbers) 1938. m. 715.70 F. (foreign 842 F.). Editions Techniques et Economiques, 3 rue Soufflot, 75005 Paris, France. TEL 46-34-10-30. FAX 46-34-55-83. TELEX 260-717 F. Ed. Jean-Jacques Dupeyroux. adv.; bk.rev.; charts; stat.; index; circ. 6,700. (reprint service avail. from SCH) Indexed: Int.Lab.Doc., World Bibl.Soc.Sec.
—BLDSC shelfmark: 3627.375000.
   Description: Studies the problems of labor law, including social security, social policy and jurisprudence.

340 FR
DROITS; revue francaise de theorie juridique. q. 290 F. (foreign 340 F.). Presses Universitaires de France, Departement des Revues, 14 av. du Bois-de-l'Epine, 91003 Evry Cedex, France. TEL 1-60-77-82-05. FAX 1-60-79-20-45. TELEX PUF 600 474 F. Dir. Stephane Rials.

340 US
▼DRUG AND ALCOHOL TESTING; advising the employer. 1990. base vol. (plus a. suppl.). $110. Butterworth Legal Publishers (Salem) (Subsidiary of: Reed International PLC), 90 Stiles Rd., Salem, NH 03079. TEL 800-548-4001. FAX 603-898-9858. Ed. William D. Turkula. (looseleaf format)
   Description: Discusses the law, scientific methodology and practical applications of drug testing programs in the workplace.

DRUG LAW REPORT. see DRUG ABUSE AND ALCOHOLISM

DRUGS AND BIOLOGY GUIDANCE MANUAL. see PUBLIC HEALTH AND SAFETY

340   IE
DUBLIN UNIVERSITY LAW JOURNAL. 1976. a. £15. Dublin University, Law School, Arts Bldg., Trinity College, Dublin 2, Ireland. TEL 01-772941. FAX 01-772694. Eds. Alex Schuster, Tony Kerr. adv.; bk.rev.; circ. 700. **Indexed:** C.L.I., L.R.I., Leg.Per.

340   US   ISSN 0012-7086
K4
DUKE LAW JOURNAL. 1951. 6/yr. $36 (foreign $42). Duke University, School of Law, Rm. 006, Durham, NC 27706-2580. TEL 919-684-5966. FAX 919-684-3417. adv.; bk.rev.; cum. index; circ. 1,400. (processed; also avail. in microfilm from WSH; reprint service avail. from WSH) **Indexed:** Abstr.Health Care Manage.Stud., C.L.I., Commun.Abstr., Crim.Just.Abstr., Curr.Cont., L.R.I., Leg.Cont., Leg.Per., Rel.Per., SSCI.
●Also available online. Vendor(s): Mead Data Central, WESTLAW.
—BLDSC shelfmark: 3630.950000.

DUNHILL PERSONAL INJURY & DEATH REPORTS. see *INSURANCE*

340   US
DUNNELL MINNESOTA DIGEST. 1978. 47 base vols. (plus a. suppl.), 4th ed., 1991. $1350. Butterworth Legal Publishers (Salem) (Subsidiary of: Reed International PLC), 90 Stiles Rd., Salem, NH 03079. TEL 800-548-4001. FAX 603-898-9858. Ed.Bd.
Description: Covers all Minnesota Supreme Court and Court of Appeals cases as well as relevant Minnesota cases decided by the Federal Courts.

340   US   ISSN 0093-3058
K4
DUQUESNE LAW REVIEW. 1963. q. $15. Duquesne University, Duquesne School of Law, 900 Locust St., Pittsburgh, PA 15282. TEL 412-434-5020. Ed. Donn K. Butkovic. adv.; bk.rev.; index; circ. 1,700. (also avail. in microform from WSH; reprint service avail. from WSH) **Indexed:** Abstr.Bk.Rev.Curr.Leg.Per., C.L.I., Crim.Just.Abstr., L.R.I., Leg.Cont., Leg.Per., Mar.Aff.Bibl.
Formerly: Duquesne University Law Review (ISSN 0012-7213)

THE E C GRANTS AND LOANS DATABASES. see *BUSINESS AND ECONOMICS — Banking And Finance*

340   UK   ISSN 0144-3054
LAW
E C L R: EUROPEAN COMPETITION LAW REVIEW; a bi-monthly review. 1980. bi-m. £135. (E S C Publishing Ltd.) Sweet & Maxwell, South Quay Plaza, 8th Fl., 183 Marsh Wall, London E14 9FT, England. TEL 071-538-8686. FAX 071-538-8625. Ed. Julian Maitland-Walker. adv.; bk.rev.; index; circ. 400. (back issues avail.)
—BLDSC shelfmark: 3829.637000.

E D F LETTER. (Environmental Defense Fund) see *ENVIRONMENTAL STUDIES*

E D V & RECHT; Zeitschrift fuer das Recht der Datenverarbeitung. see *COMPUTERS*

E E O COMPLIANCE MANUAL. (Equal Employment Opportunity) see *BUSINESS AND ECONOMICS — Labor And Industrial Relations*

340   UK   ISSN 0142-0461
K5   CODEN: EIPRES
E I P R: EUROPEAN INTELLECTUAL PROPERTY REVIEW. 1978. m. £270. (E S C Publishing Ltd.) Sweet & Maxwell, South Quay Plaza, 8th Fl., 183 Marsh Wall, London E14 9FT, England. TEL 071-538-8686. FAX 071-538-8625. Ed. Hugh Brett. adv.; bk.rev.; index. (back issues avail.)
—BLDSC shelfmark: 3829.720960.
Description: Recent developments and news for intellectual property lawyers, patent agents, trade mark agents, music publishers and academics.

E P A POLICY ALERT. (Environmental Protection Agency) see *ENVIRONMENTAL STUDIES*

E R I S A: THE LAW AND THE CODE. (Employee Retirement Income Security Act) see *BUSINESS AND ECONOMICS — Labor And Industrial Relations*

EARLY IRISH LAW SERIES. see *HISTORY — History Of Europe*

340   KE
EAST AFRICAN LAW JOURNAL. 2/yr. P.O. Box 30197, Nairobi, Kenya. Ed. G.K. Rukwaro. circ. 400.

349   TZ   ISSN 0012-8678
K5
EASTERN AFRICA LAW REVIEW; a journal of law and development. (Text in English) 1968. 2/yr. $25. (University of Dar es Salaam, Faculty of Law) Dar es Salaam University Press, P.O. Box 35093, Dar es Salaam, Tanzania. Ed. N.N.N. Nditi. adv.; bk.rev.; bibl.; circ. 1,000. (back issues avail.)

EASTERN BOWHUNTING. see *SPORTS AND GAMES — Outdoor Life*

340   US   ISSN 0733-6098
KF1819.A2
EASTERN MINERAL LAW FOUNDATION. ANNUAL INSTITUTE. 1980. a. $105. Eastern Mineral Law Foundation, West Virginia University Law Center, Box 6130, Morgantown, WV 26506-6130. TEL 304-293-2470. FAX 304-293-7654. (Dist. by: Matthew Bender & Co., Inc., Box 989, Dept. D.M., Albany, NY 12214-1056) circ. 750. **Indexed:** Leg.Per.

340 622   US   ISSN 0749-7709
EASTERN MINERAL LAW FOUNDATION. CASE UPDATE. 1983. 3/yr. $100. Eastern Mineral Law Foundation, West Virginia University Law Center, Box 6130, Morgantown, WV 26506-6130. TEL 304-293-2470. Ed. Sharon J. Daniels. (back issues avail.) **Indexed:** C.L.I.

340 549   US
EASTERN MINERAL LAW FOUNDATION NEWSLETTER. vol.8, 1988. q. Eastern Mineral Law Foundation, West Virginia University Law Center, Box 6130, Morgantown, WV 26506-6130. TEL 304-293-2470.
Description: Discusses coal legislation and Institute conference topics.

614.7 340   US   ISSN 0046-1121
K5
ECOLOGY LAW QUARTERLY. 1971. q. $29 to individuals (foreign $35); institutions $48 (foreign $54); students $21 (foreign $27). University of California Press, Journals Division, 2120 Berkeley Way, Berkeley, CA 94720. TEL 510-642-4191. FAX 510-643-7127. adv.; bk.rev.; bibl.; index; circ. 1,300. (also avail. in microform from WSH; reprint service avail. from WSH) **Indexed:** Acid Pre.Dig., C.L.I., Curr.Adv.Ecol.Sci., Curr.Cont., Deep Sea Res.& Oceanogr.Abstr., Energy Rev., Environ.Abstr., Environ.Ind., Environ.Per.Bibl., Excerp.Med., Geo.Abstr., GeoRef, Ind.Sci.Rev., INIS Atomind., L.R.I., Leg.Cont., Leg.Per., Mar.Aff.Bibl., P.A.I.S., Pollut.Abstr., Risk Abstr., Sage Pub.Admin.Abstr., Sci.Cit.ind, Sel.Water Res.Abstr., SSCI.
—BLDSC shelfmark: 3650.044000.
Description: Legal issues relating to environmental affairs.
Refereed Serial

ECONOMIA E DIRITTO DEL TERZIARIO. see *BUSINESS AND ECONOMICS*

ECONOMIC DEVELOPMENT AND LAW CENTER REPORT. see *BUSINESS AND ECONOMICS — Economic Situation And Conditions*

ECONOMY AND LAW. see *BUSINESS AND ECONOMICS — Economic Systems And Theories, Economic History*

340 370   CN   ISSN 0838-2875
EDUCATION AND LAW JOURNAL. 1988. 3/yr. (plus bound vol.). Can.$128($102) Carswell Publications, Corporate Plaza, 2075 Kennedy Rd., Scarborough, Ont. M1T 3V4, Canada. TEL 416-609-8000. FAX 413-298-5094. Ed. Greg Dickinson. adv.; bk.rev.; cum.index.
Description: Focuses on issues arising from the interaction of law and education at the elementary, secondary and post-secondary levels.

340   UK   ISSN 0953-9964
EDUCATION AND THE LAW. 1989. q. £30($67) (foreign £35). Longman Group UK Ltd., Longman House, Burnt Mill, Harlow, Essex CM20 2JE, England. TEL 0279-26721. FAX 0279-451946. Ed.Bd. adv.; bk.rev.
—BLDSC shelfmark: 3661.188200.
Description: Covers all aspects of the law relating to primary, secondary, tertiary and higher education.

EDUCATION FOR THE HANDICAPPED LAW REPORT. see *EDUCATION — Special Education And Rehabilitation*

340   AU
EHE- UND FAMILIENRECHTLICHE ENTSCHEIDUNGEN. 1966. a. price varies. Manzsche Verlags- und Universitaetsbuchhandlung, Kohlmarkt 16, A-1014 Vienna, Austria. TEL 0222-531610. FAX 0222-5316181. Eds. Wolfgang Melber, Anton Schwarz. circ. 2,500.
Description: Collects decisions on laws of domestic relations.

DIE EIGENTUMSWOHNUNG; Vorteilhaft erwerben, nutzen und verwalten. see *HOUSING AND URBAN PLANNING*

347.9   GW   ISSN 0341-2261
EILDIENST: BUNDESGERICHTLICHE ENTSCHEIDUNGEN. 1971. w. DM.231.60. Richard Boorberg Verlag GmbH & Co., Levelingstr. 6a, D-8000 Munich, Germany. Ed. Max D. Kleiner. index. (back issues avail.)

342   US
ELECTION LAWS OF HAWAII HANDBOOK. a. free. Office of the Lieutenant Governor, State Capitol, Honolulu, HI 96811. TEL 808-548-2544. FAX 808-548-3844.
Formerly: Election Laws of Hawaii (ISSN 0091-9101)

349   BL   ISSN 0013-6638
EMENTARIO FORENSE; repositorio de jurisprudencia dos triuniais brasileiros e de legislacao federal. 1948. m. Cr.$5600. Editora Ementario Forense Ltda., Rua da Lapa 180, Rio de Janeiro, Brazil. Ed. Aulus Plautius Hiendlmayer De Macedo. circ. 2,000. (processed; also avail. in cards)

340 610   US   ISSN 1042-2978
KF3826.E5
EMERGENCY DEPARTMENT LAW; bi-weekly news and analysis for health professionals, administrators, and counsel. 1989. fortn. $287 (foreign $309). Buraff Publications (Subsidiary of: Millin Publications, Inc.), 1350 Connecticut Ave., N.W., Ste. 1000, Washington, DC 20036. TEL 202-862-0990. FAX 202-862-0999. Ed. William H. Feldman. (back issues avail.)
Description: News and analysis of malpractice and other legal issues as they affect urgent-care facilities. For doctors, health professionals, hospital administrators, and lawyers.

EMERGENCY MEDICAL TECHNICIAN LEGAL BULLETIN. see *MEDICAL SCIENCES*

EMERGENCY MEDICINE REPORTS LEGAL BRIEFINGS. see *MEDICAL SCIENCES*

EMERGENCY NURSE LEGAL BULLETIN. see *MEDICAL SCIENCES — Nurses And Nursing*

EMERGENCY PHYSICIAN LEGAL BULLETIN. see *MEDICAL SCIENCES*

340   US   ISSN 0094-4076
K10
EMORY LAW JOURNAL. 1952. q. $30. Emory University, School of Law, Gambrell Hall, Atlanta, GA 30322. TEL 404-727-6830. FAX 404-727-6820. Ed. Michelle Weisberg. adv.; bk.rev.; charts; index. cum.index every 5 yrs.; circ. 1,100. (also avail. in microfilm from UMI,WSH; reprint service avail. from WSH) **Indexed:** A.B.C.Pol.Sci., C.L.I., Curr.Cont., L.R.I., Leg.Cont., Leg.Per., SSCI.
●Also available online. Vendor(s): WESTLAW.
—BLDSC shelfmark: 3733.560000.
Formerly (until 1974): Journal of Public Law (ISSN 0022-4014)

344.73 US ISSN 0098-8898
K5 CODEN: ERLJDC
EMPLOYEE RELATIONS LAW JOURNAL. 1975. q. $180 in US and Canada; elsewhere $230. Executive Enterprises Publications Co., Inc., 22 W. 21st St., New York, NY 10010-6904. TEL 212-645-7880. FAX 212-645-1160. Ed. Jane G. Bensahel. (also avail. in microfilm from UMI,WSH; reprint service avail. from UMI,WSH) **Indexed:** ABI Inform., B.P.I., Bank.Lit.Ind., BPIA, Bus.Ind., C.L.I., Curr.Cont., L.R.I., Leg.Cont., Leg.Per., Manage.Cont., Pers.Lit., Risk Abstr., Sage Fam.Stud.Abstr., Tr.& Indus.Ind.
●Also available online. Vendor(s): DIALOG.
—BLDSC shelfmark: 3737.053000.
Description: Designed to make employer and personnel manager proficient in handling EEO, occupational health and safety, labor-management relations, employee benefits and compensation problems.

340
EMPLOYERS GUIDE TO LAW SCHOOLS. a. $80 to non-members. National Association for Law Placement, 1666 Connecticut Ave., Ste. 450, Washington, DC 20009. TEL 202-667-1666.
Formerly: Employers Guide to A B A Approved N A L P Member Law Schools (ISSN 0275-2832)
Description: Interprets student resumes, grading systems, standards for honors recognition, and lists law school placement office contacts.

EMPLOYMENT AND LABOUR LAW REPORTER. see BUSINESS AND ECONOMICS — Labor And Industrial Relations

EMPLOYMENT DISCRIMINATION. see BUSINESS AND ECONOMICS — Personnel Management

340 331.1 CN
EMPLOYMENT IN ALBERTA; a guide to conditions of work and employee benefits. s-a. Can.$90. Butterworths Canada Ltd., 75 Clegg Rd., Markham, Ont. L6G 1A1, Canada. TEL 416-479-2665. FAX 416-479-2826. Ed. Philip H. McLarren. (looseleaf format)
Description: Information on laws, regulations, programs, plans and practices affecting conditions of work and employee benefits in the province of Alberta.

340 331.1 CN
EMPLOYMENT IN BRITISH COLUMBIA; a guide to conditions of work and employee benefits. s-a. Can.$90. Butterworths Canada Ltd., 75 Clegg Rd., Markham, Ont. L6G 1A1, Canada. TEL 416-479-2665. FAX 416-479-2826. Ed. Philip H. McLarren. (looseleaf format)
Description: Information on laws, regulations, programs, plans and practices affecting conditions of work and employee benefits in the province of British Columbia.

EMPLOYMENT IN MISSOURI; a guide to employment practice and regulations. see BUSINESS AND ECONOMICS — Labor And Industrial Relations

340 331.1 CN
EMPLOYMENT IN ONTARIO; a guide to conditions of work and employee benefits. s-a. Can.$100. Butterworths Canada Ltd., 75 Clegg Rd., Markham, Ont. L6G 1A1, Canada. TEL 416-479-2665. FAX 416-479-2826. Ed. Phillip H. McLarren. (looseleaf format)
Description: Information on laws, regulations, programs, plans and practices affecting conditions of work and employee benefits in the province of Ontario.

340 331 US
EMPLOYMENT LAW DESK BOOK FOR TENNESSEE EMPLOYERS. 1989. a. $90. M. Lee Smith Publishers & Printers, 162 Fourth Ave. N., Box 2678, Nashville, TN 37219. TEL 615-242-7395. FAX 615-256-6601. Ed. John P. Phillips, Jr.
Description: Reference encyclopedia for all areas of employment law - both state and federal.

346.066
EMPLOYMENT LAW GUIDE (YEAR). a. $70 to non-members; members $35. Pennsylvania Chamber of Business and Industry, 222 N. Third St., Harrisburg, PA 17101. TEL 800-326-3252. FAX 717-255-3298.

340 IE ISSN 0791-2560
▼**EMPLOYMENT LAW REPORTS.** 1990. q. I£90($125) The Round Hall Press, Kill Lane, Blackrock, Co. Dublin, Ireland. TEL 2892922. FAX 2893072. Ed. Noreen Mackey. circ. 400 (controlled).
Description: Reports decisions of the Employment Appeals Tribunal and appeals therefrom to higher courts.

340 US
EMPLOYMENT LITIGATION REPORTER; the national journal of record for termination lawsuits alleging tort and contract claims against employers. 1986. s-m. $750. Andrews Publications, 1646 West Chester Pike, Box 1000, Westtown, PA 19395. TEL 215-399-6600. FAX 215-399-6610. Ed. Linda Coady. cum.index every 6 mos. (looseleaf format; back issues avail.)
Formerly: Wrongful Termination Litigation Reporter (ISSN 0888-1197)

EMPLOYMENT RELATIONS TODAY. see BUSINESS AND ECONOMICS — Labor And Industrial Relations

EMPLOYMENT SAFETY AND HEALTH GUIDE. see OCCUPATIONAL HEALTH AND SAFETY

230 US
EMPLOYMENT TESTING; law and policy reporter. m. $275. University Publications of America (Subsidiary of: Congressional Information Service), 4520 East-West Hwy., Ste. 800, Bethesda, MD 20814-3389. TEL 301-657-3200. FAX 301-657-3203. Ed. Sandra N. Hurd. (looseleaf format)

346.066 UK
ENCYCLOPEDIA OF BANKING LAW. 3 base vols. (plus updates 3/yr.). price varies. Butterworth & Co. (Publishers) Ltd. (Subsidiary of: Reed International PLC), 88 Kingsway, London WC2B 6AB, England. TEL 71-405-6900. FAX 71-405-1332. TELEX 95678. (US addr.: Butterworth Legal Publishers, 90 Stiles Rd., Salem, NH 03079. TEL 800-548-4001) (looseleaf format)

340 531.64 US ISSN 0270-9163
K5
ENERGY LAW JOURNAL. 1980. s-a. $25 (Canada $36; elsewhere $42)(effective 1992). Federal Energy Bar Association, 1900 M St., N.W., Ste. 620, Washington, DC 20036. FAX 202-833-5566. Ed. William A. Mogel. adv.; bk.rev.; index. cum.index; circ. 2,500. (also avail. in microfilm; microfiche; back issues avail.) **Indexed:** C.L.I., INIS Atomind., L.R.I., Leg.Per.
—BLDSC shelfmark: 3747.671700.

ENERGY MANAGEMENT AND FEDERAL ENERGY GUIDELINES. see ENERGY

340 620 US
ENGINEERING EVIDENCE, 2-E. 1987. 2 base vols. (plus a. suppl.). $195. Shepard's - McGraw-Hill, Inc., Box 35300, Colorado Springs, CO 80935-3530. TEL 800-525-2474.
Description: Covers every aspect of locating, obtaining, interpreting, understanding and preparing engineering evidence for use in litigation involving construction, products liability, catastrophic and transportation cases.

340 NE
ENGLISH LEGAL MANUSCRIPTS. (Includes printed guide and bibliography) 1975. irreg. latest section 5. fl.34430. I D C Microform Publishers B.V., P.O. Box 11205, 2301 EE Leiden, Netherlands. FAX 071-131721. (microfiche)
Description: Collections of 16th and 17th century legal manuscripts from Lincoln's Inn, Gray's Inn, the Bodleian, Harvard and Yale libraries.

340 790 US ISSN 0732-1880
KF4290.A15
ENTERTAINMENT AND SPORTS LAWYER. 1982. 4/yr. membership only. (American Bar Association, Forum Committee on the Entertainment and Sports Industries) A B A Press, 750 N. Lake Shore Dr., Chicago, IL 60611. TEL 312-988-6068. Ed. Richard J. Greenston. circ. 2,946. (also avail. in microform) **Indexed:** C.L.I.
Description: Developments in entertainment and sports law.

340 US
▼**ENTERTAINMENT LAW.** 1992. 4 base vols. (plus a. suppl.). $525. Shepard's - McGraw-Hill, Inc., Box 35300, Colorado Springs, CO 80935-3530. TEL 800-525-2474. (looseleaf format)
Description: Focuses on the legal principles and business realities that motivate the entertainment industry, with a systematic discussion and analysis of applicable case law.

346.066 US
ENTERTAINMENT LAW & BUSINESS. 1989. base vol. (plus suppl.). $119. Butterworth Legal Publishers (Salem) (Subsidiary of: Reed International PLC), 90 Stiles Rd., Salem, NH 03079. TEL 800-548-4001. FAX 603-898-9858. Ed. David Sinacore-Guinn. (looseleaf format)

750 US
ENTERTAINMENT LAW & FINANCE. m. $135. New York Law Publishing Co., Marketing Dept., 111 Eighth Ave., New York, NY 10011. TEL 212-741-8300.
Description: Legal and financial developments in music, film, theater, broadcasting, sports, publishing, video and related media arts.

340 US ISSN 0270-3831
KF4290.A59
ENTERTAINMENT LAW REPORTER; motion pictures, television, radio, music, theater, publishing, sports. 1979. m. $175 (effective May 1991). Entertainment Law Reporter Publishing Co., 2210 Wilshire Blvd., No. 311, Santa Monica, CA 90403. TEL 310-892-9335. Ed. Lionel S. Sobel. adv.; bk.rev.; index; circ. 825. **Indexed:** C.L.I., Leg Cont., Leg.Per.

340 UK ISSN 0959-3799
▼**ENTERTAINMENT LAW REVIEW.** 1990. bi-m. £160. E S C Publishing Ltd., Mill St., Oxford OX2 0JU, England. TEL 0865-249248. FAX 0865-792301. Ed. Tony Martino.
—BLDSC shelfmark: 3776.655000.
Description: Provides a regular update on developments in entertainment law.

340 US ISSN 1047-4137
KF4290.A59
ENTERTAINMENT LITIGATION REPORTER; national journal of record covering critical issues in entertainment law field. 1989. s-m. $650. Andrews Publications, 1646 West Chester Pike, Box 1000, Westtown, PA 19395. TEL 215-399-6600. FAX 215-399-6610. Ed. Robert Sullivan. abstr.; bibl.; stat.; cum.index every 6 mos. (looseleaf format; back issues avail.)

340 GW ISSN 0425-1288
ENTSCHEIDUNGEN DER OBERLANDESGERICHTE IN ZIVILSACHEN. 1965. 4/yr. DM.148. C.H. Beck'sche Verlagsbuchhandlung, Wilhelmstr. 9, 8000 Munich 40, Germany. TEL 089-38189-338. FAX 089-38189-398. TELEX 521085-BECK-D. Eds. J. Kuntze, M. Maerz.

340 GW
ENTSCHEIDUNGEN DER OBERVERWALTUNGSGERICHTE FUER DAS LAND NORDRHEIN-WESTFALEN IN MUENSTER SOWIE FUER DIE LAENDER NIEDERSACHSEN UND SCHLESWIG-HOLSTEIN IN LUENEBURG. 1953. irreg. DM.100. Aschendorffsche Verlagsbuchhandlung, Soesterstr. 13, 4400 Muenster, Germany. TEL 0251-690-0. FAX 0251-690405. circ. 1,000.

340 GW ISSN 0435-7124
ENTSCHEIDUNGEN DES BUNDESGERICHTSHOFES IN ZIVILSACHEN. 1951. m. DM.54. Carl Heymanns Verlag KG, Luxemburger Str. 449, 5000 Cologne 41, Germany. TEL 0221-4601000. FAX 0221-4601069. (back issues avail.)

340 GW ISSN 0433-7646
ENTSCHEIDUNGEN DES BUNDESVERFASSUNGSGERICHTS. 1952. irreg. (1-2/yr.). DM.58 per vol. Verlag J.C.B. Mohr (Paul Siebeck), Postfach 2040, 7400 Tuebingen, Germany. TEL 07071-26064. FAX 07071-51104.
Description: Decisions of the German Constitutional Court.

340   GW   ISSN 0013-9106
ENTSCHEIDUNGEN DES BUNDESVERWALTUNGSGERICHTS. 1955. irreg. DM.78. Carl Heymanns Verlag KG, Luxemburger Str. 449, 5000 Cologne 41, Germany. TEL 0221-460100. FAX 0221-4601069. (back issues avail.)

ENTSCHEIDUNGEN ZUM WIRTSCHAFTSRECHT - E W I R. see *BUSINESS AND ECONOMICS — Economic Situation And Conditions*

340 614.7   AT   ISSN 0813-300X
K5   CODEN: EPLJEX
ENVIRONMENTAL AND PLANNING LAW JOURNAL. 1984. q. Aus.$210. Law Book Co. Ltd., 44-50 Waterloo Rd., North Ryde, N.S.W. 2113, Australia. TEL 02-887-0177. FAX 02-888-9706. TELEX ASBOOK 27995. Ed. Gerry Bates. bk.rev. (back issues avail.) **Indexed:** Environ.Per.Bibl.
—BLDSC shelfmark: 3791.383200.
    Description: Discusses environmental policy and administration, national parks and wildlife, cultural and natural heritage and environmental contaminants.

ENVIRONMENTAL APPROVALS IN CANADA; practice and procedure. see *ENVIRONMENTAL STUDIES*

ENVIRONMENTAL AUDITS. see *ENVIRONMENTAL STUDIES*

340   US
▼**ENVIRONMENTAL CITIZEN SUITS.** 1991. base vol. (plus a. suppl.). $95. Butterworth Legal Publishers (Salem) (Subsidiary of: Reed International PLC), 90 Stiles Rd., Salem, NH 03079. TEL 800-548-4001. FAX 603-898-9858. Ed. Michael D. Axline. (looseleaf format)
    Description: Provides both the experienced practitioner and the environmental law novice with information concerning the prosecution and defense of environmental citizen suits.

ENVIRONMENTAL CLAIMS JOURNAL. see *ENVIRONMENTAL STUDIES*

ENVIRONMENTAL COMPLIANCE UPDATE. see *ENVIRONMENTAL STUDIES*

ENVIRONMENTAL INSURANCE COVERAGE; state law and regulation. see *INSURANCE*

ENVIRONMENTAL LAW (PORTLAND). see *ENVIRONMENTAL STUDIES*

344.73   US   ISSN 0748-8769
KF3775.A15
ENVIRONMENTAL LAW (WASHINGTON). 1973. 3/yr. $15 to institutions; free to individuals. American Bar Association, Standing Committee on Environmental Law, 1800 M St., N.W., Washington, DC 20036. TEL 202-331-2276. FAX 202-331-2220. Ed. Elissa C. Lichtenstein. bk.rev.; circ. 5,000. (back issues avail.) **Indexed:** C.L.I., L.R.I.
    Formerly: American Bar Association. Special Committee on Environmental Law. Quarterly Newsletter (ISSN 0093-7797)
    Description: Lists ABA programs and activities in environmental law.

347   US
▼**ENVIRONMENTAL LAW ANTHOLOGY.** 1990. a. $149.95. International Library Law Book Publishers, Inc., 101 Lakeforest Blvd., Ste. 270, Gaithersburg, MD 20877. TEL 301-990-7755. FAX 301-990-7642. Ed. Allison P. Zabriskie. bibl.; index.
    Description: Selected best U.S. law review articles, printed in their entirety, in the field of enviromental law culled from over 900 American law review journals.

ENVIRONMENTAL LAW HANDBOOK. see *ENVIRONMENTAL STUDIES*

ENVIRONMENTAL LAW IN NEW YORK; developments in federal and state law. see *ENVIRONMENTAL STUDIES*

ENVIRONMENTAL LAW JOURNAL OF OHIO. see *ENVIRONMENTAL STUDIES*

340 614.7   US   ISSN 0163-545X
KFT1554.A15
ENVIRONMENTAL LAW NEWSLETTER. q. State Bar of Texas, Box 12487, Capitol Sta., Austin, TX 78711. TEL 512-475-1234. **Indexed:** C.L.I., L.R.I.

ENVIRONMENTAL LAW REPORTER. see *ENVIRONMENTAL STUDIES*

346.066   US
▼**ENVIRONMENTAL LIABILITY;** law and strategy for businesses and corporations. 1990. base vol. (plus a. suppl.). $110. Butterworth Legal Publishers (Salem) (Subsidiary of: Reed International PLC), 90 Stiles Rd., Salem, NH 03079. TEL 800-548-4001. FAX 603-898-9858. Ed. Lawrence P. Schnapf. (looseleaf format)
    Description: Provides guidance on environmental law issues for attorneys handling business venture start-ups and compliance with Superfund cleanup regulations. Includes the text of relevant federal and state environmental statutes.

ENVIRONMENTAL MANAGEMENT REVIEW. see *ENVIRONMENTAL STUDIES*

ENVIRONMENTAL POLICY AND LAW. see *ENVIRONMENTAL STUDIES*

ENVIRONMENTAL STATUTES. see *ENVIRONMENTAL STUDIES*

EPITESUGYI ERTESITO. see *BUILDING AND CONSTRUCTION*

340   US
EQUIPMENT LEASING NEWSLETTER. m. $255. New York Law Publishing Co., Marketing Dept., 111 Eighth Ave., New York, NY 10011. TEL 212-741-8300.
    Description: Legal, business, and tax developments affecting the equipment leasing industry.

347   US   ISSN 0743-247X
KF532.7.A15
EQUITABLE DISTRIBUTION JOURNAL; a monthly review of current developments. m. $105. National Legal Research Group, Inc., 2421 Ivy Rd., Box 7187, Charlottesville, VA 22906-7187. TEL 800-446-1870. FAX 804-295-4667. Ed. Joan L. Cobb.
    Description: Analyses of recent cases in equitable distribution.

340   US
EQUITABLE DISTRIBUTION OF PROPERTY. 1983. base vol. (plus a. suppl.). $70. Shepard's - McGraw-Hill, Inc., Box 35300, Colorado Springs, CO 80935-3530. TEL 800-525-2474.
    Description: Provides classification of marital and separate property and information on how to avoid malpractice. Covers valuation of property, the Uniform Marriage and Divorce Act, discovery techniques, and advocacy and litigation skills.

340   US
ESTATE ADMINISTRATION; a handbook with forms. 1985. base vol. (plus suppl.). $85. Butterworth Legal Publishers (Salem) (Subsidiary of: Reed International PLC), 90 Stiles Rd., Salem, NH 03079. TEL 800-548-4001. FAX 603-898-9858. Ed. Michael H. Riley. (looseleaf format)

340   US   ISSN 0273-7027
KFC195.A15
ESTATE PLANNING AND CALIFORNIA PROBATE REPORTER. 1980. 6/yr. $125. Continuing Education of the Bar - California, University of California Extension, 2300 Shattuck Ave., Berkeley, CA 94704. TEL 510-642-0306. FAX 800-642-3788. (Co-sponsor: State Bar of California) Ed. Jeffrey Strathmeyer. (tabloid format; back issues avail.)

346.73   US   ISSN 0098-2873
KF746.A3
ESTATE PLANNING REVIEW. 1974. m. $130. Commerce Clearing House, Inc., 4025 W. Peterson Ave., Chicago, IL 60646. TEL 312-583-8500. index. (also avail. in microform from UMI) **Indexed:** L.I.I.

340   US
ESTATE PLANNING: WILLS AND TRUSTS. (Number of base vols. varies depending on number of states) base vol. (plus m. Report Bulletins and updates). Maxwell Macmillan, 910 Sylvan Ave., Englewood Cliffs, NJ 07632-3310. FAX 201-816-3569. (looseleaf format)

340   US
ESTATE PLANNING: WILLS, TRUSTS AND FORMS. base vol. (plus bi-m. Report Bulletins and updates). Maxwell Macmillan, 910 Sylvan Ave., Englewood Cliffs, NJ 07632-3310. TEL 800-562-0245. FAX 201-816-3569. (looseleaf format)

349   CK   ISSN 0014-1461
ESTUDIOS DE DERECHO. (Text mainly in Spanish; occasionally in English, French, Italian) 1939. s-a. $15. Universidad de Antioquia, Facultad de Derecho y Ciencias Politicas, Apdo. Aereo 1226, Medellin, Colombia. FAX 638282. Ed. Dr. Benigno Mantilla Pineda. adv.; bk.rev.; abstr.; bibl.; circ. 2,000. (also avail. in microform) **Indexed:** Amer.Hist.& Life, Foreign Leg.Per., Hist.Abstr., P.A.I.S.For.Lang.Ind.

ESTUDIOS PUBLICOS. see *BUSINESS AND ECONOMICS — Economic Situation And Conditions*

340   BL   ISSN 0100-2538
ESTUDOS JURIDICOS. 1971. 3/yr. Cr.$40000($20) or exchange basis. (Universidade do Vale do Rio dos Sinos) Unisinos, Av. Unisinos, 950, 93010 Sao Leopoldo RS, Brazil. TEL 0512-926333. FAX 0512-921035. TELEX 524076. Ed. Bruno Hammes. bibl.; index. cum.index; circ. 250. (back issues avail.)

ETHIK IN DER MEDIZIN. see *PHILOSOPHY*

340   NR
ETHIOPE LAW SERIES. no.4, 1976. irreg. Ethiope Publishing Corporation, 34 Murtala Mohammed St., P.M.B. 1192, Benin City, Nigeria. Ed. T.O. Elias.

340   GW   ISSN 0341-9800
LAW
EUROPAEISCHE GRUNDRECHTE ZEITSCHRIFT. 1974. bi-w. DM.286. N.P. Engel Verlag, Postfach 1670, 7640 Kehl, Germany. TEL 07851-2463. FAX 07851-4234. TELEX 7-53560. Ed. N.P. Engel. adv.; bk.rev.; index; circ. 1,000. **Indexed:** INIS Atomind., Refug.Abstr.
—BLDSC shelfmark: 3829.345000.
    Formerly (until 1977): Grundrechte; die Rechtsprechung in Europa (ISSN 0340-8906)
    Description: Articles, constitutional and Supreme Court decisions and reports, documentation and pending proceedings.

346.066   GW   ISSN 0937-7204
KJE6411.3
▼**EUROPAEISCHE ZEITSCHRIFT FUER WIRTSCHAFTSRECHT.** 1990. s-m. DM.436. C.H. Beck'sche Verlagsbuchhandlung, Wilhelmstr. 9, 8000 Munich 40, Germany. TEL 089-38189-338. FAX 089-38189-398. TELEX 5215085-BECK-D. Ed.Bd.

349 940   FR   ISSN 0531-2671
EUROPEAN ASPECTS, LAW SERIES; a collection of studies relating to European integration. 1962. irreg. Council of Europe, Publishing and Documentation Service, 67000 Strasbourg, France. (Dist. in U.S. by Manhattan Publishing Co., P.O. Box 650, Croton-on-Hudson, N.Y. 10520)

346.066   UK   ISSN 0959-6941
K5
▼**EUROPEAN BUSINESS LAW REVIEW.** 1990. m. £210 fl.670. Graham & Trotman Ltd. (Subsidiary of: Kluwer Academic Publishers Group), Sterling House, 66 Wilton Rd., London SW1V 1DE, England. (Dist. by: Kluwer Academic Publishers Group, P.O. Box 322, 3300 AH Dordrecht, Netherlands; N. America dist. addr.: Box 358, Accord Station, Hingham, MA 02018-0358. TEL 617-871-6600) Ed. Susan Nicholas. adv.
—BLDSC shelfmark: 3829.552700.

340 UK ISSN 0141-7266
LAW
EUROPEAN COMMERCIAL CASES. 1978. q. £255. (European Law Centre) Sweet & Maxwell, South Quay Plaza, 9th Floor, 183 Marsh Wall, London E14 9FT, England. TEL 071-538-8686.
FAX 071-538-8625. Ed. Marina Milmo.
—BLDSC shelfmark: 3829.618500.
Description: Major decisions of European national courts in certain areas of commercial law.

340 UK
EUROPEAN COMMUNITIES LEGISLATION: CURRENT STATUS. a. (plus q. suppl.). price varies. Butterworth & Co. (Publishers) Ltd. (Subsidiary of: Reed International PLC), 88 Kingsway, London WC2B 6AB, England. TEL 71-405-6900.
FAX 71-405-1332. TELEX 95678. (US addr.: Butterworth Legal Publishers, 90 Stiles Rd., Salem, NH 03079. TEL 800-548-4001)

340 323.4 UK ISSN 0260-4868
LAW
EUROPEAN HUMAN RIGHTS REPORTS. 1979. bi-m. £175. (European Law Centre Ltd.) Sweet & Maxwell, South Quay Plaza, 8th Floor, 183 Marsh Wall, London E14 9FT, England. TEL 071-538-8686.
FAX 071-538-9508. Ed. Peter Duffy.
—BLDSC shelfmark: 3829.718500.
Description: Includes articles on criminal procedure, property law and aliens control.

340 UK ISSN 0307-5400
K5
EUROPEAN LAW REVIEW. 1975. 6/yr. £160. Sweet & Maxwell, South Quay Plaza, 8th Floor, 183 Marsh Wall, London E14 9FT, England.
TEL 071-538-8686. FAX 071-538-9505. (Dist. in U.S. & Canada by: Carswell Co Ltd., 233 Midland Ave., Agincourt, Ont., Canada) (reprint service avail. from RRI) **Indexed:** Abstr.Bk.Rev.Curr.Leg.Per., C.L.I., L.R.I., Leg.Per.
—BLDSC shelfmark: 3829.748700.

340 NE
EUROPEAN STUDIES IN LAW. 1977. irreg., vol.9, 1980. price varies. Elsevier Science Publishers B.V., Books Division, P.O. Box 211, 1000 AE Amsterdam, Netherlands. TEL 020-5803911.
FAX 020-5803705. TELEX 18582 ESPA NL. (Subscr. in U.S. and Canada to: Elsevier Science Publishing Co., Inc., Box 882, Madison Sq. Sta., New York, NY 10159. TEL 212-989-5800) Ed. A.G. Chloros.
Refereed Serial

EVANGELISCHE KIRCHE DER KIRCHENPROVINZ SACHSEN. AMTSBLATT. see *RELIGIONS AND THEOLOGY — Protestant*

340 US
EVIDENCE TRIAL MANUAL FOR TEXAS LAWYERS: CIVIL. (Companion to: Evidence Trial Manual for Texas Lawyers - Criminal) 1986. base vol. (plus suppl. 1-2/yr.). $120. Butterworth Legal Publishers (Salem) (Subsidiary of: Reed International PLC), 90 Stiles Rd., Salem, NH 03079. TEL 800-548-4001. FAX 603-898-9858. Ed. Murl A. Larkin. (looseleaf format)
Description: Provides the full text of all state and federal evidence rules and statutes applicable in Texas.

340 US
EVIDENCE TRIAL MANUAL FOR TEXAS LAWYERS: CRIMINAL. (Companion to: Evidence Trial Manual for Texas Lawyers - Civil) 1986. base vol. (plus suppl. 1-2/yr.). $120. Butterworth Legal Publishers (Salem) (Subsidiary of: Reed International PLC), 90 Stiles Rd., Salem, NH 03079. TEL 800-548-4001. FAX 603-898-9858. Ed. Murl A. Larkin. (looseleaf format)

346.066 336 US
EXECUTIVE ACTION REPORT. w. (plus irreg. Special Reports). Warren, Gorham & Lamont, Inc., 210 South Street, Boston, MA 02111.
TEL 617-423-2020. FAX 617-423-2026.

340 US
EXECUTIVE AND PROFESSIONAL EMPLOYMENT CONTRACTS; the major legal issues and forms. 1988. base vol. (plus suppl.). $105. Butterworth Legal Publishers (Salem) (Subsidiary of: Reed International PLC), 90 Stiles Rd., Salem, NH 03079. TEL 800-548-4001. FAX 603-898-9858. Ed. L.J. Kutten. (looseleaf format)

346.066 US
EXECUTIVE COMPENSATION SURVEY REPORT. a. $400. Manufacturers Association of Delaware Valley, Box 770, Valley Forge, PA 19482. TEL 215-666-7330. FAX 215-666-7866.
Description: Provides comparative information about executive compensation practices among businesses in the Mid-Atlantic states.

347 617.1 US ISSN 0891-0278
KF2915.E95
EXERCISE STANDARDS AND MALPRACTICE REPORTER. 1987. 6/yr. $39.95. Professional Reports Corporation, 4571 Stephen Circle, N.W., Canton, OH 44718-3629. TEL 800-336-0083.
FAX 216-499-6609. Eds. David L. Herbert, William G. Herbert. adv.; index; circ. 700. (looseleaf format; back issues avail.)
Description: Current standards of practice for exercise, wellness and health promotion programs. Malpractice and professional concerns and developments are examined.

340 US ISSN 1054-3473
K5
EXPERIENCE. 1986. q. $34.95. (American Bar Association) A B A Press, 750 N. Lake Shore Dr., Chicago, IL 60611. TEL 312-988-6122.
FAX 312-988-6281. Ed. Ray DeLong. adv.; bk.rev.; circ. 7,500.
Supersedes (in 1990): Senior Lawyer.
Description: Articles on practice problems and aspects of retirement for lawyers 60 and older. Includes news of the division.

340 US
EXPERT AND THE LAW. 1979. bi-m. $55. National Forensic Center, Box 3161, Princeton, NJ 08540. TEL 609-883-0550. Ed. Mark Wieckowski.
●Also available online. Vendor(s): Mead Data Central.
Description: Newsletter devoted to the application of scientific, medical, and technical knowledge to litigation.

340 CK
EXTERNADO. 1935. 3/yr. Col.1500. Universidad Externado de Colombia, Publishing Department, Cr. 12, No. 1-17 Este, Bogota, Colombia. Ed. Fernando Hinestrosa. adv.; bk.rev.; circ. 2,500.
Former titles: Universidad Externado de Colombia. Revista (ISSN 0041-8544); (until 1964): Universidad Externado de Colombia. Facultad de Derecho. Revista.

EXTRAORDINARY CONTRACTUAL RELIEF REPORTER. see *BUSINESS AND ECONOMICS — Economic Situation And Conditions*

340 US
EYEWITNESS TESTIMONY: STRATEGIES AND TACTICS. 1984. base vol. (plus a. suppl.). $195. Shepard's - McGraw-Hill, Inc., Box 35300, Colorado Springs, CO 80935-3530. TEL 800-525-2474.
Description: Explains how and where errors in eyewitness perception can occur.

F C C RULEMAKING REPORTS. (Federal Communications Commission) see *COMMUNICATIONS*

F C C WEEK; an exclusive report on domestic and international telecommunications policy and regulation. (Federal Communications Commission) see *COMMUNICATIONS*

F C N L WASHINGTON NEWSLETTER. (Friends Committee on National Legislation) see *POLITICAL SCIENCE*

340 US
F E L A REPORTER & RAILROAD LIABILITY MONITOR. (Federal Employees Liability Act) 1988. m. $350. M. Lee Smith Publishers & Printers, 162 Fourth Ave. N., Box 2678, Nashville, TN 37219.
TEL 615-242-7395. FAX 615-256-6601. Ed. Lewis L. Laska.
Description: Summarizes current information about employment compensation cases involving railroads.

340 US ISSN 0093-7630
HD4903.5.U58
F E P GUIDELINES. (Fair Employment Practices) m. $87. Bureau of Business Practice, 24 Rope Ferry Rd., Waterford, CT 06386. TEL 203-442-4365. FAX 203-434-3341. TELEX 966420. Ed. Rosalie Donlon.

F M A TODAY (JACKSONVILLE). (Florida Medical Association) see *MEDICAL SCIENCES*

F T C FREEDOM OF INFORMATION LOG. (Federal Trade Commission) see *BUSINESS AND ECONOMICS — International Commerce*

340 BE
FACULTE DE DROIT DE NAMUR. TRAVAUX. no.12, 1975. irreg. price varies. (Societe d'Etudes Morales, Sociales et Juridiques) Maison Ferdinand Larcier S.A., Rue des Minimes 39, 1000 Brussels, Belgium.

340 900 FR ISSN 0765-4847
KJV150.A15
FACULTES DE DROIT ET DE LA SCIENCE JURIDIQUE. REVUE D'HISTOIRE. 1984. s-a. 260 F. Societe pour l'Histoire des Facultes de Droit et de la Science Juridique, Universite de Paris V, 10 av. Pierre Larousse, 92241 Malakoff Cedex, France. bk.rev.
Former title (until 1987): Facultes de Droit dt de la Science Juridique. Annales d'Histoire.

340 US
FACULTY BRIEFING; a newsletter for law teachers. bi-m. free. American Bar Association, Membership Department, 750 N. Lake Shore Dr., Chicago, IL 60611. TEL 312-988-5000.
Description: Provides information on ABA programs and resources of interest to law school teachers.

340 FA ISSN 0108-142X
FAEROESK LOVREGISTER. 1966. irreg. DKK 75. Faeroernes Landsstyre, Rigsombudsmanden paa Faeroerne, Postboks 12, FR-110 Toshavn, Faeroe Islands. TELEX 10864. circ. 450.

340 US ISSN 0887-7807
KF971.3
FAILED BANK AND THRIFT LITIGATION REPORTER; the nationwide litigation report of failed national and state banks and savings and loan associations, including F D I C and F S L I C complaints and related actions among shareholders, officers, directors, institutions and insurers. 1986. s-m. $825. Andrews Publications, 1646 West Chester Pike, Box 1000, Westtown, PA 19395.
TEL 215-399-6600. FAX 215-399-6610. Ed. Barbara Murphy. abstr.; bibl.; stat.; cum.index every 6 mos. (looseleaf format; back issues avail.)

340 US
▼**FAILED L B O LITIGATION REPORTER.** (Leveraged Buy-Out); the monthly national journal of litigation concerning leveraged debt liability. 1990. m. $600. Andrews Publications, 1646 West Chester Pike, Box 1000, Westtown, PA 19395. TEL 215-399-6600. FAX 215-399-6610. Ed. Linda H. Coady. bibl.; stat.; cum.index every 6 mos. (looseleaf format; back issues avail.)
Description: Covers leverages, corporate debt liability issues in bankruptcy, federal district and appellate courts.

340 US ISSN 0273-3560
KF506.A3
FAIRSHARE; the matrimonial law monthly. m. $125. Prentice Hall Law & Business, 270 Sylvan Ave., Englewood Cliffs, NJ 07632-2513.
TEL 201-894-8484. FAX 201-894-8666. Ed. Ronald L. Brown.
Description: Information on approaches, techniques, and precedents used by lawyers to solve the financial and economic questions of equitable distribution divorce practice.

340 CC
FALU YU SHENGHUO/LAW & LIFE. (Text in Chinese) m. $41.30. Falu Chubanshe, Law Press, Taiping Lu, Haidian Qu, Beijing 100036, People's Republic of China. TEL 8217301. (Dist. in US by: China Books & Periodicals, Inc., 2929 24th St., San Francisco, CA 94110. TEL 415-282-2994) Ed. Xu Chang.

340 PH ISSN 0046-3272
LAW
FAR EASTERN LAW REVIEW. (Text in English) 2/yr. P.20($5) Far Eastern University, Institute of Law, Quezon Boulevard, Manila, Philippines. Ed. Faustino S. Cruz. (also avail. in microform from UMI; reprint service avail. from UMI) **Indexed:** Mar.Aff.Bibl.
—BLDSC shelfmark: 3865.925000.
Formerly: F E U Quarterly.

340   CC
FAXUE/SCIENCE OF LAW. (Text in Chinese) m. Huadong Zhengfa Xueyuan - East China Institute of Law, 1575 Wanhangdu Lu, Shanghai 200042, People's Republic of China. TEL 2594295. Ed. Zhang Guoquan.

340   CC
FAXUE YANJIU/STUDIES IN LAW. (Text in Chinese) bi-m. $33.80. Zhongguo Shehui Kexueyuan, Faxue Yanjiusuo - Chinese Academy of Social Science, Jurisprudence Institute, 15 Shatan Beijie, Beijing 100720, People's Republic of China. TEL 447471. (Dist. in US by: China Books & Periodicals, Inc., 2929 24th St., San Francisco, CA 94110. TEL 415-282-2994) Ed. Li Buyun.

340   CC
FAXUE YICONG/TRANSLATED LAW LITERATURE. (Text in Chinese) bi-m. Zhongguo Shehui Kexueyuan, Faxueyanjiusuo, 15 Shatan Beijie, Beijing 100720, People's Republic of China. TEL 441580. Ed. Ren Yunzheng.

340   CC
FAXUE YU SHIJIAN/LAW AND PRACTICE. (Text in Chinese) bi-m. Heilongjiang Sheng Faxue Yanjiusuo - Heilongjiang Institute of Law, 43, Hongxia Jie, Daoli-qu, Harbin, Heilongjiang 150010, People's Republic of China. TEL 417707. (Co-sponsor: Heilongjiang Law Society) Ed. Wang Wei.

340   CC   ISSN 1001-618X
FAXUE ZAZHI/JOURNAL OF JURISPRUDENCE. (Text in Chinese) bi-m. $15.80. Beijing Faxuehui - Beijing Jurisprudence Society, 1 Xisanhuan Zhonglu, Beijing 100036, People's Republic of China. TEL 896217-802. (Dist. in US by: China Books & Periodicals, 2929 24th St., San Francisco, CA 94110. TEL 415-282-2994) Ed. Fu Juchuan.
—BLDSC shelfmark: 5161.402500.

340   CC
FAZHI. (Text in Chinese) m. Y12. (Guangdong Sheng Sifa-ting) Guangdong Fazhi Baokan She, No.26, Qiye Lu, Guangzhou, Guangdong 510030, People's Republic of China. TEL 348264. Ed. Zhong Qiliang.

340   CC   ISSN 1000-3568
FAZHI JIANSHE/LAW & ORDER. (Text in Chinese) 1983. m. $41.30. (Zhonghua Renmin Gongheguo Sifabu - Ministry of Justice) Beijing Falu Chubanshe, Baiguang Lu 1, Xuanwu Qu, Beijing, People's Republic of China. (Dist. in US by: China Books & Periodicals, Inc., 2929 24th St., San Francisco, CA 94110. TEL 415-282-2994)

340   US
FAZHI RIBAO/LEGAL DAILY. (Text in Chinese) d. $235.80. China Books & Periodicals, Inc., 2929 24th St., San Francisco, CA 94110. TEL 415-282-2994. FAX 415-282-0994. (newspaper)

340   CC
FAZHI TIANDI. (Text in Chinese) m. Jilin Sheng Sifa Ting, 39, Stalin Street, Changchun, Jilin 130051, People's Republic of China. TEL 36095. Ed. Sun Libo.

340   CC
FAZHI YU WENMING/LEGAL SYSTEM AND CIVILIZATION. (Text in Chinese) m. Liaoning Sheng Sifa Ting, 8, Congshan Donglu 1 Duan, Huanggu-qu, Shenyang, Liaoning 110032, People's Republic of China. TEL 461317. Ed. Ba Wen.

340 350   AT
FEDERAL ADMINISTRATIVE LAW. 1985. 6/yr. Aus.$195. Law Book Co. Ltd., 44-50 Waterloo Rd., North Ryde, N.S.W. 2113, Australia. TEL 02-887-0177. FAX 02-888-9706. TELEX ASBOOK 27995. Ed. Geoffrey Flick.
  Description: Contains all relevant legislation with authoritative and up-to-date legislation and annotations.

340   US
FEDERAL APPEALS: JURISDICTION AND PRACTICE. 1987. base vol. (plus a. suppl.). $95. Shepard's - McGraw-Hill, Inc., Box 35300, Colorado Springs, CO 80935-3530. TEL 800-525-2474.
  Description: Covers all areas of federal jurisdiction and offers practical tips on how to successfully file, brief and argue an appeal.

FEDERAL BANKING LAW REPORTS. see *BUSINESS AND ECONOMICS — Banking And Finance*

FEDERAL BANKING LAWS (SUPPLEMENT). see *BUSINESS AND ECONOMICS — Banking And Finance*

340   US   ISSN 0279-4691
K6
FEDERAL BAR NEWS & JOURNAL. 1981. 10/yr. $25 to non-members. Federal Bar Association, 1815 H St., N.W., Ste. 408, Washington, DC 20006-3697. TEL 202-638-0252. FAX 202-775-0295. Ed. Elaine M. Deering. adv.; bk.rev.; circ. 15,000. (also avail. in microform from WSH; reprint service avail.) **Indexed:** Abstr.Bk.Rev.Curr.Leg.Per., Acid Rain Abstr., Acid Rain Ind., Bank.Lit.Ind., C.L.I., Curr.Cont., HR Rep., L.R.I., Leg.Cont., Leg.Per., Pers.Lit., SSCI.
  ●Also available online. Vendor(s): WESTLAW.
—BLDSC shelfmark: 3901.873200.
  Formed by the 1981 merger of (1953-1981): Federal Bar News (ISSN 0014-9047); (1931-1981): Federal Bar Journal (ISSN 0014-9039)

340   US
FEDERAL CARRIERS CASES. 1937. irreg. $61.50 per no. Commerce Clearing House, Inc., 4025 W. Peterson Ave., Chicago, IL 60646. TEL 312-583-8500. Ed. D. Newquist.

340   US   ISSN 0163-7606
K6
FEDERAL COMMUNICATIONS LAW JOURNAL. vol.30, 1977. 3/yr. $18. University of California, Los Angeles, School of Law, 405 Hilgard Ave., Los Angeles, CA 90024. TEL 213-825-3712. (Co-sponsor: Federal Communications Bar Association) Ed. Keith Nichols. adv.; bk.rev.; circ. 2,000. (also avail. in microform from UMI,WSH; reprint service avail. from UMI,WSH) **Indexed:** ABI Inform., Abstr.Bk.Rev.Curr.Leg.Per., BPIA, Bus.Ind., C.L.I., CAD CAM Abstr., Commun.Abstr., L.R.I., Leg.Cont., Leg.Per., Tel.Abstr.
—BLDSC shelfmark: 3901.873700.
  Formerly: Federal Communications Bar Journal.

330   US   ISSN 0747-9700
KF846.3
FEDERAL CONTRACT DISPUTES. 1983. m. $255.48. Business Publishers, Inc., 951 Pershing Dr., Silver Spring, MD 20910-4464. TEL 301-587-6300. FAX 301-585-9075. Ed. Bruce M. Jervis. index. (looseleaf format; back issues avail.)
  ●Also available online. Vendor(s): NewsNet.
  Description: Studies cases and provides advice for contractors with the federal government who find themselves in disputes over contract terms or payments.

FEDERAL ENVIRONMENTAL REGULATION. see *ENVIRONMENTAL STUDIES*

FEDERAL ESTATE AND GIFT TAXES. see *BUSINESS AND ECONOMICS — Public Finance, Taxation*

340   US
FEDERAL EVIDENCE FOUNDATIONS. 1988. base vol. (plus suppl.). $90. Butterworth Legal Publishers (Salem) (Subsidiary of: Reed International PLC), 90 Stiles Rd., Salem, NH 03079. TEL 800-548-4001. FAX 603-898-9858. Ed. Murl A. Larkin. (looseleaf format)
  Description: Identifies and sets out the requirements for admissibility of all types of evidence in federal courts under the Federal Rules and common law.

FEDERAL HEALTH MONITOR. see *PUBLIC HEALTH AND SAFETY*

340   US
▼**FEDERAL INFORMATION DISCLOSURE, 2-E.** 1990. 2 base vols. (plus s-a. suppl.). $195. Shepard's - McGraw-Hill, Inc., Box 35300, Colorado Springs, CO 80935-3530. TEL 800-525-2474. (looseleaf format)
  Description: Covers the disclosure of information from agency files under the Freedom of Information Act, the mechanics of suing the government for mandatory disclosure of this information, the 1974 Privacy Act and its significant impact on gathering information.

342   AT   ISSN 0085-0462
FEDERAL LAW REPORTS. 1956. irreg. Law Book Co. Ltd., 44-50 Waterloo Rd., North Ryde, N.S.W. 2112, Australia. TEL 02-887-0177. FAX 02-888-9706. TELEX ASBOOK 27995. **Indexed:** C.L.I., Curr.Aus.N.Z.Leg.Lit.Ind.
  Description: Reports all decisions on federal law, includes important rulings in the State and Territory Supreme Courts, Family Court and in the federal tribunals.

FEDERAL LEGISLATION ANNOTATIONS. see *PUBLIC ADMINISTRATION*

340   CN
FEDERAL LIMITATION PERIODS; a handbook of limitation periods and other statutory time limits. s-a. Can.$75. Butterworths Canada Ltd., 75 Clegg Rd., Markham, Ont. L6G 1A1, Canada. TEL 416-479-2665. FAX 416-479-2826. (looseleaf format)
  Description: Tables of time limits.

340   US
FEDERAL LITIGATOR. 1985. 10/yr. $290. Shepard's - McGraw-Hill, Inc., Box 35300, Colorado Springs, CO 80935-3530. TEL 719-488-3000. Eds. Neil Levy, Jeffrey Brand.

353   US   ISSN 0097-6326
KF70   CODEN: FEREAC
FEDERAL REGISTER. d., a. cum. in: Code of Federal Regulations. $340 (microfiche $195). U.S. Office of the Federal Register, National Archives and Records Administration, Washington, DC 20408. TEL 202-523-5240. (Orders to: Supt. of Documents, Box 371954, Pittsburgh, PA 15420-7954) index; circ. 50,000. (also avail. in microfiche from UMI; microfilm from BHP; magnetic tape; reprint service avail. from UMI) **Indexed:** Acid Rain Abstr., Acid Rain Ind., API Abstr., API Catal., API Hlth.& Environ., API Oil., API Pet.Ref., API Pet.Subst., API Transport., Art & Archaeol.Tech.Abstr., C.I.S. Abstr., CAD CAM Abstr., Chem.Abstr., Food Sci.& Tech.Abstr., I.P.A., INIS Atomind., Int.Packag.Abstr., Noise Pollut.Publ.Abstr., Ocean.Abstr., Pollut.Abstr., Rehabil.Lit., Sel.Water Res.Abstr., Telegen, Text.Tech.Dig.
  ●Also available online. Vendor(s): BRS (DIOG), DIALOG (File no.669), Mead Data Central, WESTLAW.
—BLDSC shelfmark: 3901.933000.
  Description: Features federal agency regulations.

340   US
FEDERAL REGISTER HIGHLIGHTS NEWSLETTER. fortn. $35. National Clearinghouse for Legal Services, Inc., 407 S. Dearborn, Ste. 400, Chicago, IL 60605. TEL 312-939-3830.

340   US
FEDERAL REGULATION OF ENERGY. 1983. base vol. (plus a. suppl.). $95. Shepard's - McGraw-Hill, Inc., Box 35300, Colorado Springs, CO 80935-3530. TEL 800-525-2474.
  Description: Provides a historical perspective on energy regulation. Covers current Federal Energy Regulatory Commission regulations on controversial topics such as nuclear waste disposal.

340 540   US
FEDERAL REGULATION OF THE CHEMICAL INDUSTRY. 1980. base vol. (plus suppl. every 2 yrs.). $195. Shepard's - McGraw-Hill, Inc., Box 35300, Colorado Springs, CO 80935-3530. TEL 800-525-2474. (looseleaf format)
  Description: Addresses problems and methods of dealing with plant personnel, regulatory compliance officers, company managers, investment or consultant service executives and recent governmental restraints on the chemical industry.

340   US
▼**FEDERAL RULES CITATIONS.** 1992. 3 base vols. (plus q. suppl.). $450. Shepard's - McGraw-Hill, Inc.., Box 35300, Colorado Springs, CO 80935. TEL 800-525-2474.
  Description: Brings together citations to the Federal Rules and all corresponding state rules from every jurisdiction in the nation.

340   US
FEDERAL RULES OF EVIDENCE NEWS. 1976. m. $130. Callaghan & Co., 155 Pfingsten Rd., Deerfield, IL 60015. TEL 800-323-1336. Ed. John R. Schmertz, Jr. (tabloid format)
  ●Also available online. Vendor(s): WESTLAW.

LAW

FEDERAL RULES SERVICE. see *PUBLIC ADMINISTRATION*

340 332.6 US
FEDERAL SECURITIES LAW REPORT. 1933. w. $1080. Commerce Clearing House, Inc., 4025 W. Peterson Ave., Chicago, IL 60646. TEL 312-583-8500. Ed. D. Newquist.

FEDERAL SENTENCING REPORTER. see *CRIMINOLOGY AND LAW ENFORCEMENT*

FEDERAL TAX COLLECTIONS, LEINS AND LEVIES. see *BUSINESS AND ECONOMICS — Public Finance, Taxation*

FEDERAL TAX REGULATIONS. see *BUSINESS AND ECONOMICS — Public Finance, Taxation*

FEDERAL TAXATION OF OIL AND GAS TRANSACTIONS. see *PETROLEUM AND GAS*

340 US
FEDERAL TRADE COMMISSION. 1979. 2 base vols. (plus a. suppl.). $190. Shepard's - McGraw-Hill, Inc., Box 35300, Colorado Springs, CO 80935-3530. TEL 800-525-2474. (looseleaf format)
   Description: Guide to regulations and procedures of the FTC organized with a topical outline that presents comprehensive information on specific problems.

340 US
FEDERAL TRIAL EVIDENCE. 1984. 2 base vols. (plus suppl. 2-3/yr.). $80. Butterworth Legal Publishers (Salem) (Subsidiary of: Reed International PLC), 90 Stiles Rd., Salem, NH 03079. TEL 800-548-4001. FAX 603-898-9858. Ed. Charles E. Wagner. (looseleaf format)

340 US
FEDERAL TRIAL NEWS. irreg. membership only. American Bar Association, National Conference of Federal Trial Judges, 750 N. Lake Shore Dr., Chicago, IL 60611. TEL 312-988-5688. circ. 750.
   Description: Information to members on conference activities.

FEDERATION NATIONALE DE L'IMMOBILIERS. INFORMATIONS F N A I M: JURIDIQUES ET TECHNIQUES. see *REAL ESTATE*

340 368 US ISSN 0887-0942
K6
FEDERATION OF INSURANCE AND CORPORATE COUNSEL QUARTERLY.* 1950. q. $26 (law college libraries $20). Federation of Insurance and Corporate Counsel, Marquette Univ. Law School, 1103 W. Wisconsin Ave., Milwaukee, WI 53233. TEL 617-639-0698. FAX 617-639-1877. Ed. John J. Kersher. cum.index to 1970; circ. 2,200. (also avail. in microform from UMI; reprint service avail. from RRI,UMI) **Indexed:** ABI Inform, C.L.I., L.R.I., Leg.Per., Mar.Aff.Bibl.
   —BLDSC shelfmark: 7169.616500.
   Formerly (until Oct. 1985): Federation of Insurance Counsel Quarterly (ISSN 0430-2583)

340 FR
FEUILLETS ANALYTIQUES. w. Documentation Organique, 11, rue de Teheran, 75008 Paris, France. TEL 45-62-54-35.

368 340 US ISSN 0747-6582
FIDELITY AND SURETY NEWS. q. $100. American Bar Association, Tort and Insurance Practice Section, Fidelity and Surety Law Committee, 750 N. Lake Shore Dr., Chicago, IL 60611. TEL 312-988-5555. Ed. Donald B. King. (back issues avail.; reprint service avail.)
   Description: Provides a current digest of opinions about construction contract bonds, financial institution and other bonds, court bonds, and surety's rights.

328.96 FJ
FIJI. OFFICE OF THE OMBUDSMAN. ANNUAL REPORT OF THE OMBUDSMAN. (Text in English) 1973. a. price varies. Office of the Ombudsman, Suva, Fiji. circ. 200.

791 FR ISSN 0181-4141
FILMECHANGE; droit, economie, sociologie de l'audiovisuel. 1978. q. 260 F. Editions des Quatre Vents, 6 rue Git le Coeur, 75006 Paris, France. TEL 46-34-28-20. FAX 46-42-53-88. Ed. Jacques Leclere. adv.; bk.rev.; film rev.; abstr.; bibl.; charts; stat.; index; circ. 2,500. **Indexed:** Film Lit.Ind. (1980-), Intl.Ind.TV.
   —BLDSC shelfmark: 3925.725000.

340 SP
FILOSOFIA DEL DERECHO. ANUARIO. 1953-1977; N.S. 1984. a. 3500 ptas. (foreign 3700 ptas.). Ministerio de Justicia, Centro de Publicaciones, Secretaria General Tecnica, Gran Via, 76-8, 28013 Madrid, Spain. TEL 247 54 22. Ed. L. Legaz Lacambra.

FINANCE AND COMMERCE. see *BUSINESS AND ECONOMICS — Banking And Finance*

FINANCIAL REVIEW OF ALIEN INSURERS. see *INSURANCE*

346.066 UK
FINANCIAL SERVICES, LAW & PRACTICE. (In 2 vols.) 3/yr. price varies. Butterworth & Co. (Publishers) Ltd. (Subsidiary of: Reed International PLC), 88 Kingsway, London WC2B 6AB, England. TEL 71-405-6900. FAX 71-405-1332. TELEX 95678. (US addr.: Butterworth Legal Publishers, 90 Stiles Rd., Salem, NH 03079. TEL 800-548-4001) (looseleaf format)

THE FINANCIAL SERVICES LAW LETTER. see *BUSINESS AND ECONOMICS — Banking And Finance*

FINANCIAL SERVICES REPORT; strategic information for the financial executive. see *BUSINESS AND ECONOMICS — Banking And Finance*

346.066 US
▼**FINANCIAL VALUATION: BUSINESSES AND BUSINESS INTERESTS.** 1990. base vol. (plus suppl.). Maxwell Macmillan, Rosenfeld Launer, 910 Sylvan Ave., Englewood Cliffs, NJ 07632-3310. TEL 800-562-0245. FAX 201-816-3569. Ed. James H. Zukin.

FINANZRECHTLICHE ERKENNTNISSE DES VERWALTUNGSGERICHTSHOFES; Beilage zur Oesterreichischen Steuer-Zeitung. see *BUSINESS AND ECONOMICS — Public Finance, Taxation*

340 US
FINE'S WISCONSIN EVIDENCE; a quick guide to courtroom evidence. 1988. base vol. (plus suppl.). $95. Butterworth Legal Publishers (Salem) (Subsidiary of: Reed International PLC), 90 Stiles Rd., Salem, NH 03079. TEL 800-548-4001. FAX 603-898-9858. Ed. Ralph Adam Fine. (looseleaf format)

FIRE AND ARSON INVESTIGATOR. see *CRIMINOLOGY AND LAW ENFORCEMENT*

FISCALITE QUEBECOISE. see *BUSINESS AND ECONOMICS — Public Finance, Taxation*

328 US ISSN 0090-1520
KFF15
FLORIDA. LEGISLATURE. JOINT LEGISLATIVE MANAGEMENT COMMITTEE. SUMMARY OF GENERAL LEGISLATION. 1955. a. free. Legislature, Joint Legislative Management Committee, The Capitol, Tallahassee, FL 32399. TEL 904-488-2812. FAX 904-488-9879. Ed. B. Gene Baker. circ. 500. (processed)

340 US ISSN 0194-4800
KFF440
FLORIDA ADMINISTRATIVE LAW REPORTS. 1979. s-m. $425. Florida Administrative Law Reports, Inc., Box 385, Gainesville, FL 32602. TEL 904-375-8036. Ed. James Konish. cum.index; circ. 230. (back issues avail.)
   Description: Presents lists of public-access publications and indexes on final legal orders after formal proceedings from Florida state agencies and boards, with catalogues of settlements and non-final orders.

340 350 US
FLORIDA ADMINISTRATIVE PRACTICE. 1979. 3 base vols. (plus suppl. 2-3/yr.). $240. Butterworth Legal Publishers (Salem) (Subsidiary of: Reed International PLC), 90 Stiles Rd., Salem, NH 03079. TEL 800-548-4001. FAX 603-898-9858. Eds. Arthur J. England, Jr., L. Harold Levinson. (looseleaf format)

348 US ISSN 0098-874X
KFF36
FLORIDA ADMINISTRATIVE WEEKLY. 1975. w. $165. Department of State, Bureau of Administrative Code, The Capitol, Rm. 2002, Tallahassee, FL 32399-0250. TEL 904-488-8427. Ed. Liz Cloud. adv.; cum.index.
   Description: Informational synopses and data on state administrative procedures as they pertain to regulatory actions, public hearings, petitions, and orders.

340 US
FLORIDA APPELLATE PRACTICE. 1979. 3 base vols. (plus suppl. 2-3/yr.). $240. Butterworth Legal Publishers (Salem) (Subsidiary of: Reed International PLC), 90 Stiles Rd., Salem, NH 03079. TEL 800-548-4001. FAX 603-898-9858. (looseleaf format)

340 US ISSN 0015-3915
KF200
FLORIDA BAR JOURNAL; advancing the competence and public responsiblity of lawyers. 1927. m. $25 (including annual directory number). Florida Bar, 650 Apalachee Pkwy., Tallahassee, FL 32399-2300. TEL 904-561-5600. FAX 904-681-3859. Ed. Judson H. Orrick. adv.; bk.rev.; illus.; index; circ. 47,000. (also avail. in microfiche from WSH; microfilm from UMI,WSH; reprint service avail. from UMI) **Indexed:** C.L.I., HRIS, L.R.I., Law Ofc.Info.Svc., Leg.Per.
   ●Also available online. Vendor(s): WESTLAW.
   —BLDSC shelfmark: 3955.290000.
   Description: Practical legal articles from the Florida Bar.

340.06 US ISSN 0360-0114
KF200
FLORIDA BAR NEWS. s-m. $12. Florida Bar, 650 Apalachee Pkwy., Tallahassee, FL 32399-2300. TEL 904-561-5600. FAX 904-681-3859. Ed. Judson H. Orrick. illus.; circ. 50,000. (reprint service avail. from UMI)
   Description: Articles on activities, programs and concerns of the legal profession in Florida.

340 US
FLORIDA COMMERCIAL LANDLORD - TENANT LAW. 1985. base vol. (plus suppl. 2-3/yr.). $80. Butterworth Legal Publishers (Salem) (Subsidiary of: Reed International PLC), 90 Stiles Rd., Salem, NH 03079. TEL 800-548-4001. FAX 603-898-9858. (looseleaf format)

340 US
FLORIDA CONDOMINIUM LAW MANUAL. 1980. 3 base vols. (plus suppl. 2-3/yr.). $240. Butterworth Legal Publishers (Salem) (Subsidiary of: Reed International PLC), 90 Stiles Rd., Salem, NH 03079. TEL 800-548-4001. FAX 603-898-9858. (looseleaf format)

340 690 US
FLORIDA CONSTRUCTION LAW MANUAL, 2-E. 1988. base vol. (plus a. suppl.). $95. Shepard's - McGraw-Hill, Inc., Box 35300, Colorado Springs, CO 80935-3530. TEL 800-525-2474.
   Description: Explains the principles of the law of contracts, mechanics' liens, bid disputes and surety bonds.

340 640.73 US
FLORIDA CONSUMER LAW MANUAL. 1977. 3 base vols. (plus suppl. 2-3/yr.). $240. Butterworth Legal Publishers (Salem) (Subsidiary of: Reed International PLC), 90 Stiles Rd., Salem, NH 03079. TEL 800-548-4001. FAX 603-898-9858. (looseleaf format)

340   US   ISSN 1041-3537
KFF331.A15
FLORIDA EMPLOYMENT LAW LETTER. 1989. m. $127. M. Lee Smith Publishers & Printers, 162 Fourth Ave. N., Box 2678, Nashville, TN 37219. TEL 615-242-7395. FAX 615-256-6601. (Co-sponsor: Haynsworth, Baldwin, Johnson & Harper) Ed. C. Thomas Harper.
 Description: Review of Florida employment law developments.

614.7 340   US   ISSN 1047-4641
KFF354.A15
▼**FLORIDA ENVIRONMENTAL & LAND USE LETTER.** 1990. 12/yr. $167. M. Lee Smith Publishers & Printers, 162 Fourth Ave. N., Box 2678, Nashville, TN 37219. TEL 615-242-7395. FAX 615-256-6601. (Co-sponsor: Holland & Knight) Ed.Bd.
 Description: Reports the latest Florida environmental law developments that affect Florida companies.

340   US
FLORIDA EVIDENCE MANUAL. 1975. 4 base vols. (plus suppl. 5-6/yr.). $280. Butterworth Legal Publishers (Salem) (Subsidiary of: Reed International PLC), 90 Stiles Rd., Salem, NH 03079. TEL 800-548-4001. FAX 603-898-9858. (looseleaf format)

340   US
FLORIDA LAND USE RESTRICTIONS. 1976. 3 base vols. (plus suppl. 2-3/yr.). $240. Butterworth Legal Publishers (Salem) (Subsidiary of: Reed International PLC), 90 Stiles Rd., Salem, NH 03079. TEL 800-548-4001. FAX 603-898-9858. (looseleaf format)

340   US
FLORIDA LAW OF SECURED TRANSACTIONS IN PERSONAL PROPERTY. 1979. 3 base vols. (plus a. suppl.). $240. Butterworth Legal Publishers (Salem) (Subsidiary of: Reed International PLC), 90 Stiles Rd., Salem, NH 03079. TEL 800-548-4001. FAX 603-898-9858. (looseleaf format)

340   US
FLORIDA LAW REVIEW. 1948. 5/yr. $30. University of Florida, College of Law, Gainesville, FL 32611. TEL 904-392-0421. Ed. Diane Tomlinson. adv.; bk.rev.; index; circ. 1,500. (also avail. in microfiche from WSH; microfilm from WSH) **Indexed:** C.L.I., Crim.Just.Abstr., L.R.I., Leg.Cont., Leg.Per., Sel.Water Res.Abstr.
 ●Also available online. Vendor(s): WESTLAW.
 Formerly: University of Florida Law Review (ISSN 0041-9583)

340   US   ISSN 0274-8533
FLORIDA LAW WEEKLY. 1976. w. $275. Judicial and Administrative Research Association, Inc., 1327 North Adams St., P.O. Box 4284, Tallahassee, FL 32315. TEL 904-222-3171. Ed. E. Neil Young. circ. 4,000. (back issues avail.)
 Description: Includes opinions of Florida Appellate Courts.

340   US
FLORIDA LEGAL RESEARCH & SOURCE BOOK. 1989. base vol. (plus a. suppl.). $35. Butterworth Legal Publishers (Salem) (Subsidiary of: Reed International PLC), 90 Stiles Rd., Salem, NH 03079. TEL 800-548-4001. FAX 603-898-9858. (looseleaf format)

340   US
FLORIDA MECHANICS LEIN MANUAL. 1974. 4 base vols. (plus suppl. 4-5/yr.). $280. Butterworth Legal Publishers (Salem) (Subsidiary of: Reed International PLC), 90 Stiles Rd., Salem, NH 03079. TEL 800-548-4001. FAX 603-898-9858. (looseleaf format)

340   US
FLORIDA MOTOR VEHICLE LIABILITY LAW. 1981. 4 base vols. (plus suppl. 4-5/yr.). Butterworth Legal Publishers (Salem) (Subsidiary of: Reed International PLC), 90 Stiles Rd., Salem, NH 03079. TEL 800-548-4001. FAX 603-898-9858. (looseleaf format)

340   US
FLORIDA NEGLIGENCE LAW MANUAL. 1986. 2 base vols. (plus suppl. 3-4/yr.). $160. Butterworth Legal Publishers (Salem) (Subsidiary of: Reed International PLC), 90 Stiles Rd., Salem, NH 03079. TEL 800-548-4001. FAX 603-898-9858. (looseleaf format)

340   US
FLORIDA NOTARY LAW PRIMER. a. $9.95. National Notary Association, 8236 Remmet Ave., Box 7184, Canoga Park, CA 91304-7184. TEL 818-713-4000. FAX 818-713-9061. Ed. Charles N. Faerber. (reprint service avail. from UMI)

340   US
FLORIDA PARALEGAL SERIES: WILLS, TRUSTS, ESTATES. 1982. base vol. (plus a. suppl.). $60. Butterworth Legal Publishers (Salem) (Subsidiary of: Reed International PLC), 90 Stiles Rd., Salem, NH 03079. TEL 800-548-4001. FAX 603-898-9858. (looseleaf format)

340   US
FLORIDA PRACTICE AND PROCEDURE. a. $59.95. Harrison Company Publishers, 3110 Crossing Park, Norcross, GA 30071. TEL 404-447-9150. circ. 4,450.

340   US
▼**FLORIDA PREMISES LIABILITY.** 1991. base vol. (plus suppl.). $80. Butterworth Legal Publishers (Salem) (Subsidiary of: Reed International PLC), 90 Stiles Rd., Salem, NH 03079. TEL 800-548-4001. FAX 603-898-9858. Ed. Douglas MacGregor.
 Description: Practical examination of factors determining premises liability, including occupation and control of premises, extent of alleged unsafe conditions, status of the injured or deceased person and negligence on the part of the injured or deceased.

340   US
FLORIDA PROBATE CODE MANUAL. 1975. 3 base vols. (plus suppl. 2-3/yr.). $240. Butterworth Legal Publishers (Salem) (Subsidiary of: Reed International PLC), 90 Stiles Rd., Salem, NH 03079. TEL 800-548-4001. FAX 603-898-9858. (looseleaf format)

340   US
▼**FLORIDA REAL ESTATE CLOSINGS.** 1990. base vol. (plus suppl.). $50. Butterworth Legal Publishers (Salem) (Subsidiary of: Reed International PLC), 90 Stiles Rd., Salem, NH 03079. TEL 800-548-4001. FAX 603-898-9858. Ed. Neysa Rich. (looseleaf format)
 Description: Covers basic procedure as well as special situations involving estates, delinquent mortgages, assignments of contracts, mail closings, and escrow closings.

FLORIDA REAL ESTATE CONTRACTS. see *REAL ESTATE*

FLORIDA REAL ESTATE TRANSACTIONS. see *REAL ESTATE*

340 333.33   US
FLORIDA RESIDENTIAL LANDLORD - TENANT LAW MANUAL. 1983. 3 base vols. (plus a. suppl.). $120. Butterworth Legal Publishers (Salem) (Subsidiary of: Reed International PLC), 90 Stiles Rd., Salem, NH 03079. TEL 800-548-4001. FAX 603-898-9858. (looseleaf format)

340   US
FLORIDA RULES OF COURT SERVICE. 1972. 2 base vols. (plus suppl.). $80. Butterworth Legal Publishers (Salem) (Subsidiary of: Reed International PLC), 90 Stiles Rd., Salem, NH 03079. TEL 800-548-4001. FAX 603-898-9858. (looseleaf format)

328.759   US   ISSN 0093-4089
JK4476
FLORIDA SENATE. 1965. biennial. free. Legislature, Senate, The Capitol, Tallahassee, FL 32399. TEL 904-487-5270. Ed. Joe Brown. illus.; stat.; circ. 75,000.

340   US   ISSN 0096-3070
K6
FLORIDA STATE UNIVERSITY LAW REVIEW. 1973. q. $25. Florida State University, College of Law, Tallahassee, FL 32306. TEL 904-644-2045. Ed. Donna E. Blanton. adv.; bk.rev.; circ. 925. (also avail. in microform from WSH; reprint service avail. from WSH) **Indexed:** C.L.I., Crim.Just.Abstr., L.R.I., Leg.Cont., Leg.Per.
 ●Also available online. Vendor(s): WESTLAW.
 —BLDSC shelfmark: 3956.140000.

340   US
FLORIDA SUMMARY CLAIMS HANDBOOK. 1978. 2 base vols. (plus suppl. 2-3/yr.). $160. Butterworth Legal Publishers (Salem) (Subsidiary of: Reed International PLC), 90 Stiles Rd., Salem, NH 03079. TEL 800-548-4001. FAX 603-898-9858. (looseleaf format)

FLORIDA TRAFFIC & D U I PRACTICE. see *TRANSPORTATION — Roads And Traffic*

FLORIDA WORKERS' COMPENSATION MANUAL. see *BUSINESS AND ECONOMICS — Labor And Industrial Relations*

340   US
FLORIDA ZONING LAW MANUAL. 1980. 3 base vols. (plus suppl. 2-3/yr.). $240. Butterworth Legal Publishers (Salem) (Subsidiary of: Reed International PLC), 90 Stiles Rd., Salem, NH 03079. TEL 800-548-4001. FAX 603-898-9858. (looseleaf format)

340   II
FOCUS; fortnightly digest for the law maker. (Text in English) 1970. fortn. free. Kerala Legislature, Secretariat, P.O. Box 62, Trivandrum, India. bk.rev.; bibl.; circ. 350. **Indexed:** Rehabil.Lit.

340 378   US
FOCUS ON LAW STUDIES; teaching about law in the liberal arts. s-a. free. American Bar Association, Commission on College and University Nonprofessional Legal Studies, 750 N. Lakeshore Dr., Chicago, IL 60611. TEL 312-988-5736. (And: 541 N. Fairbanks Ct., Chicago, IL 60611-3314) Ed. John Paul Ryan.
 Description: Offers a forum for ideas, resources, analysis, and opinions on teaching about law in liberal arts and professional programs.

340   SW
FOERTECKNING OEVER ADVOKATER OCH ADVOKATBYRAAER. a. SEK 125. Sveriges Advokatsamfund - Swedish Bar Association, PO Box 27321, 102 54 Stockholm, Sweden.

349   SW   ISSN 0015-8585
FOERVALTNINGSRAETTSLIG TIDSKRIFT. 1938. 6/yr. SEK 75. Norstedts Tryckeri AB, P.O. Box 2080, S-103 12 Stockholm, Sweden. Ed. Ole Westerberg. abstr.; bibl.
 —BLDSC shelfmark: 4024.130000.

FONTES RERUM AUSTRIACARUM. REIHE 3. FONTES JURIS. see *HISTORY — History Of Europe*

658.8 340   UN   ISSN 0015-6221
FOOD AND AGRICULTURAL LEGISLATION. (Editions in English, French, Spanish) 1952. a. $10. Food and Agriculture Organization of the United Nations, Legislation Branch, c/o UNIPUB, 4611-F Assembly Dr., Lanham, MD 20706-4391. FAX 301-459-0056. stat.; index. **Indexed:** Dairy Sci.Abstr., Food Sci.& Tech.Abstr., Forest.Abstr., Forest Prod.Abstr., Nutr.Abstr.

FOOD AND COSMETICS GUIDANCE MANUAL. see *PUBLIC HEALTH AND SAFETY*

340 615   US
FOOD AND DRUG ADMINISTRATION. 1979. 2 base vols. (plus a. suppl.). $180. Shepard's - McGraw-Hill, Inc., Box 35300, Colorado Springs, CO 80935-3530. TEL 800-525-2474. (looseleaf format)
 Description: Provides information for handling FDA cases.

340   US
FOOD DRUG COSMETIC LAW REPORTS. 1938. w. $1780. Commerce Clearing House, Inc., 4025 W. Peterson Ave., Chicago, IL 60646. TEL 312-583-8500. Ed. D. Newquist.

LAW

340 664   UK   ISSN 0262-0030
FOOD LAW MONTHLY; the advisory service for the food, drug and cosmetics industries. 1981. m. £120 (foreign £135). Monitor Press, Rectory Rd., Great Waldingfield, Sudbury, Suffolk CO10 0TL, England. TEL 0787-78607. FAX 0787-880201. (back issues avail.)
    Description: Covers all aspects of the law relating to food manufacture, processing, distribution and importing.

FOOD LEGISLATION SURVEYS. see FOOD AND FOOD INDUSTRIES

FOOD LEGISLATION VICTORIA. see FOOD AND FOOD INDUSTRIES

344   US   ISSN 0015-6884
KF8911.A3
FOR THE DEFENSE.* 1960. m. (Sep.-Jun.). $35. Defense Research Institute, Inc., 750 N. Lake Shore Dr., Ste. 5000, Chicago, IL 60611-3006. Ed. Donald J. Hirsch. bk.rev.; bibl.; charts; illus.; index, cum.index every 10 yrs; circ. 14,500. (looseleaf format) **Indexed:** C.L.I., L.R.I.

340   US
FOR THE RECORD (LAKE OSWEGO). 1987. m. included in Oregon State Bar Bulletin. Oregon State Bar, Box 1689, Lake Oswego, OR 97035-0889. TEL 503-620-0222. FAX 503-684-1366. Ed. Karen McGlone. adv. (tabloid format)

340   US   ISSN 0747-9395
JX1
FORDHAM INTERNATIONAL LAW JOURNAL. 1977. 4/yr. $16. Fordham University, School of Law, 140 W. 62 St., New York, NY 10023. TEL 212-841-5175. adv.; bk.rev.; index; circ. 900. (also avail. in microform from WSH; back issues avail.; reprint service avail. from WSH) **Indexed:** Leg.Cont., Leg.Per.
    ●Also available online. Vendor(s): WESTLAW.
    —BLDSC shelfmark: 3985.850000.
    Formerly: Fordham International Law Forum.

340   US   ISSN 0015-704X
FORDHAM LAW REVIEW. 1914. 6/yr. $18. Fordham University, School of Law, Lincoln Center, 140 W. 62nd St., New York, NY 10023. TEL 212-841-5243. adv.; bk.rev.; charts; index; circ. 2,800. (also avail. in microfilm from UMI,WSH; back issues avail.; reprint service avail. from UMI,WSH) **Indexed:** A.B.C.Pol.Sci., Abstr.Bk.Rev.Curr.Leg.Per., Bank.Lit.Ind., C.L.I., Crim.Just.Abstr., Curr.Cont., L.R.I., Lang.& Lang.Behav.Abstr., Leg.Cont., Leg.Per., SSCI, SSCI.
    ●Also available online. Vendor(s): Mead Data Central, WESTLAW.
    —BLDSC shelfmark: 3985.900000.

340   US
FORDHAM URBAN LAW JOURNAL. 1972. q. $15. Fordham University, School of Law, Lincoln Center, 140 W. 62nd St., New York, NY 10023. TEL 212-841-5243. adv.; bk.rev.; index; circ. 1,700. (back issues avail.; reprint service avail. from RRI) **Indexed:** C.L.I., Crim.Just.Abstr., L.R.I., Leg.Cont., Leg.Per., P.A.I.S.
    ●Also available online. Vendor(s): WESTLAW.

343 336.2   US   ISSN 0095-7291
LAW
FOREIGN TAX LAW BI-WEEKLY BULLETIN. 1947. fortn. $125. Foreign Tax Law Publishers, Box 2189, Ormond Beach, FL 32175. TEL 904-253-5785. FAX 904-257-3003. Ed.Bd. bk.rev.; index; circ. 500.

340   US   ISSN 0192-3145
KF195.E96
FORENSIC SERVICES DIRECTORY; national register of experts, engineers, scientific advisors, medical specialists, technical consultants and sources of specialized knowledge. 1980. a. $89.50. National Forensic Center, Box 3161, Princeton, NJ 08540. TEL 609-883-0550. Ed. Betty S. Lipscher. adv.
    ●Also available online. Vendor(s): Mead Data Central, WESTLAW.

340   IT
FORO AMMINISTRATIVO. 1925. m. L.240000 (foreign L.360000). Casa Editrice Dott. A. Giuffre, Via Busto Arsizio, 40, 20151 Milan, Italy. TEL 02-38000905. FAX 02-38009582. Eds. Eugenio C. Bartoli, Ricardo Chieppa. adv.; bk.rev.; circ. 4,800.

340   IT
FORO COSENTINO. RIVISTA DI PRASSI GUIRIDICA. m. L.40000. Editrice Pellegrini, Via Roma 74, Casella Postale 158, 87100 Cosenza, Italy.

349   IT   ISSN 0015-783X
FORO ITALIANO. 1876. m. L.325000 (foreign L.390000)(effective Feb. 1992). (Societa Editrice del Foro Italiano) Zanichelli Editore S.p.A., Via Irnerio, 34, 40126 Bologna, Italy. TEL 051-293111. FAX 051-249782. index, cum.index.

349   IT   ISSN 0015-7848
FORO NAPOLETANO; rivista di dottrina e di giurisprudenza. 1951. q. L.12000. Societa Editrice Napoletana s.r.l., Corso Umberto I 34, 80138 Naples, Italy. Ed. I. Militerni. bk.rev.; abstr.; index; circ. 1,500.

343   IT   ISSN 0015-7864
FORO PENALE.* 1945. q. L.7000. Libreria Scientifica Editrice, Corso Umberto I 38-40, Naples, Italy. Ed.Bd. index; circ. 800.

340   CK   ISSN 0040-9502
FORO UNIVERSITARIO. 1963. exchange basis. Universidad de Narino, Facultad de Derecho, Apdo. Aereo 505, Pasto, Narino, Colombia.

340   US   ISSN 0071-7657
FORSCHUNGEN AUS STAAT UND RECHT. irreg. price varies. Springer-Verlag, 175 Fifth Ave., New York, NY 10010. TEL 212-460-1500. (Also Berlin, Heidelberg, Tokyo and Vienna) (reprint service avail. from ISI)

340   AU
FORSCHUNGEN ZUR EUROPAEISCHEN UND VERGLEICHENDEN RECHTSGESCHICHTE. 1977. irreg., vol.2, 1979. price varies. Boehlau Verlag GmbH & Co.KG., Sachsenplatz 4-6, Postfach 87, A-1201 Vienna, Austria. TEL 0222-33024270. FAX 0222-3302432. TELEX 114-506-SPRIW-A. Ed. Berthold Sutter. circ. 600. (back issues avail.)

340   SZ
FORSCHUNGEN ZUR RECHTSARCHAEOLOGIE UND RECHTLICHEN VOLKSKUNDE. 1978. irreg., vol.10, 1988. price varies. Schulthess Polygraphischer Verlag AG, Zwingliplatz 2, CH-8022 Zurich, Switzerland. TEL 01-251-9336. Ed. Louis Carlen.

340   PR
FORUM. 1979. q. free. Office of Court Administration, Vela St., Stop 35 1-2, Hato Rey Station, Call Box 917 A, Hato Rey, PR 00919. Ed. Ivette Rossello. bk.rev.; circ. 600 (controlled).

340   US   ISSN 0015-8305
FORUM (WASHINGTON, 1963). 1963. 4/yr. $8. Federal Bar Association, District of Columbia Chapter, 1815 H St., N.W., Washington, DC 20006. TEL 202-638-0252. Ed. Paul A. Pumpian. adv.; illus.; circ. 4,500. **Indexed:** Leg.Per.
    Description: Presents articles on and analysis of current developments and matters of interest pertaining to the Federal Bar Association, its activities and its members, with a calendar of events.

340   PH   ISSN 0015-8968
FOUNDATION LAW REVIEW. vol.6, 1971. q. Foundation University, School of Law, Dumaguete City 6501, Philippines. Ed. Saleto J. Erames. bibl.

FRANCE. DIRECTION GENERALE DES IMPOTS. PRECIS DE FISCALITE. see BUSINESS AND ECONOMICS — Public Finance, Taxation

FRANCE. IFREMER. CENTRE DE BREST. PUBLICATIONS. SERIE: RAPPORTS ECONOMIQUES ET JURIDIQUES. (Institut Francais de Recherche pour l'Exploitation de la Mer (IFREMER)) see EARTH SCIENCES — Oceanography

346.066   US   ISSN 8756-7962
KF2023.A15
FRANCHISE LAW JOURNAL. 1980. 4/yr. $30 to non-members. (American Bar Association, Forum Commission on Franchising) A B A Press, 750 N. Lake Shore Dr., Chicago, IL 60611. TEL 312-988-6068. Ed. W. Michael Garner. circ. 1,500. **Indexed:** C.L.I., L.R.I., Leg.Info.Manage.Ind., Leg.Per.
    Former titles: American Bar Association. Forum Committee on Franchising. Journal (ISSN 0732-1910); Forum Committee on Franchising. Newsletter.
    Description: Legal trends in franchising.

340   US
FRANCHISE LEGAL DIGEST. 1973. q. $195 membership. International Franchise Association, 1350 New York Ave. N.W., Ste. 900, Washington, DC 20005. FAX 202-628-0812. TELEX 323175. Ed. Neil A. Simon. circ. 850. (looseleaf format)
    Formerly: Current Legal Digest.
    Description: Reviews current domestic and international legal and legislative developments concerning franchising.

340 658   US
FRANCHISING ADVISER. 1987. base vol. (plus a. suppl.). $95. Shepard's - McGraw-Hill, Inc., Box 35300, Colorado Springs, CO 80935-3530. TEL 800-525-2474.
    Description: Discusses all the key elements of a successful franchise system: trademark selection and registration, trade secret and copyright licensing, franchise agreements, including state and industry regulations.

340   GW
FRANKFURTER WISSENSCHAFTLICHE BEITRAGE. RECHTS- UND WIRTSCHAFTSWISSENSCHAFTLIHE REIHE. 1939. irreg. Vittorio Klostermann, Frauenlobstr. 22, Postfach 900601, 6000 Frankfurt a.M. 90, Germany. TEL 069-774011. FAX 069-708038.

340   US
▼**FRAUD, WINDOW DRESSING AND NEGLIGENCE IN FINANCIAL STATEMENTS.** 1991. 2 base vols. (plus a. suppl.). $165. Shepard's - McGraw-Hill, Inc., Box 35300, Colorado Springs, CO 80935-3530. TEL 800-525-2474.
    Formerly (until 1990): How to Find Negligence and Misrepresentations in Financial Statements.
    Description: Advice to protect yourself and your clients from being victimized by false or negligently prepared financial statements.

340   AT   ISSN 0817-3532
FREEDOM OF INFORMATION REVIEW. bi-m. Aus.$35 (foreign Aus.$45). Legal Service Bulletin Co., Ltd., c/o Monash University, Faculty of Law, Wellington Rd., Clayton, Vic. 3168, Australia. TEL 64-35-544-0974. FAX 643-565-5305.

340   GW   ISSN 0343-835X
FREIE UNIVERSITAET BERLIN. OSTEUROPA-INSTITUT. RECHTSWISSENSCHAFTLICHE VEROEFFENTLICHUNGEN. 1974. irreg. price varies. Freie Universitaet Berlin, Osteuropa-Institut, Garystr. 55, 1000 Berlin 33 (Dahlem), Germany. Eds. Klaus Westen, Herwig Roggemann. circ. 500.

340   US
FRIENDS OF THE COURT. 1982. q. free. Administrative Office of the Courts, Justice Bldg., 625 Marshall, State Capitol Grounds, Little Rock, AR 72201. TEL 501-376-6655. Ed. Karolyn Bond. bk.rev.; bibl.; circ. 1,400.
    Formerly (until 1982): Amicus Curiae (ISSN 0360-7739)

797.124   FI
FRISK BRIS.* 1904. 5/yr. FIM 130. Frisk Bris Grafisk Industri AB, Mannerheimvagen 18, 00100 Helsingfors, Finland. Ed. Mats Kockberg. adv.; bk.rev.; circ. 6,000.

340　　　　　　　US　　ISSN 0749-2790
FROM THE STATE CAPITALS. JUSTICE POLICIES. 1946. w. $215 (foreign $235)(effective Dec. 1990). Wakeman-Walworth, Inc., 300 N. Washington St., Alexandria, VA 22314. TEL 703-549-8606. FAX 703-549-1372. (processed) Indexed: CJPI.
● Also available online. Vendor(s): WESTLAW.
Incorporates: From the State Capitals. Prison Administration (ISSN 0734-0885)
Description: Covers state and local action affecting judicial administration.

340　346.013　　US　　ISSN 0741-3572
FROM THE STATE CAPITALS. WOMEN AND THE LAW. 1984. m. $215 (foreign $235)(effective Dec. 1990). Wakeman-Walworth, Inc., 300 N. Washington St., Alexandria, VA 22314. TEL 703-549-8606. FAX 703-549-1372.
● Also available online. Vendor(s): WESTLAW.
Description: Compiles information on a wide range of legislative and regulatory subjects concerning women.

340　　　　　　　　US
FULTON COUNTY DAILY REPORT. 1890. d. $425. American Lawyer Media, L.P. (Atlanta), 190 Pryor St., S.W., Atlanta, GA 30303. TEL 404-521-1227. FAX 404-523-5924. Ed. S. Richard Gard, Jr. adv.; bk.rev.; circ. 4,300. (also avail. in microfilm)
Description: Official legal newspaper for Fulton County, Georgia. Covers law and business in Atlanta.

340　　　　　　　US　　ISSN 0741-8736
K12
G M U LAW REVIEW. 1976. s-a. $10 per issue. George Mason University, Law Review, School of Law, 3401 N. Fairfax Dr., Arlington, VA 22201. TEL 403-841-2655. Ed. Laura Jones. adv.; bk.rev.; circ. 300. (back issues avail.; reprint service avail. from RRI) Indexed: C.L.I., L.R.I., Leg.Cont., Leg.Per.
Formerly: International School of Law. Law Review.

340　　　　　　　MX
GACETA INFORMATIVA DE LEGISLACION. 1985. bi-m. $25. Universidad Nacional Autonoma de Mexico, Instituto de Investigaciones Juridicas, Ciudad Universitaria, Delegacion Coyoacan, 04510 Mexico, DF. Ed. Eugenio Hurtado Marquez. bk.rev.; circ. 1,000.
Formerly: Gaceta Informativa de Legislacion, Jurisprudencia y Bibliografia (ISSN 0187-5841)

340　　　　　　　US　　ISSN 0016-4089
GALLAUDET TODAY. ANNUAL LEGAL REVIEW. (Special issue of Gallaudet Today) 1985. a. $7 (foreign $9). Gallaudet University, National Center for Law and the Deaf (NCLD), 800 Florida Ave., N.E., Washington, DC 20002. TEL 202-651-5373. Ed. Jim Stentzel.
Description: Scholarly research articles on the legislative, technological, social, and cultural issues affecting persons with hearing impairments.

349　　　　　　　FR　　ISSN 0016-5514
GAZETTE DE LA REGION DU NORD. 1956. 3/w. 495 F. La Gazette, 7 rue Jacquemars-Gielee, B.P. 1380, 59015 Lille Cedex, France. adv.; abstr.; bibl.; mkt.; stat.; circ. 19,000.
Description: Directory of commercial and legal enterprises in Northern France.

340　　　　　　　FR
GAZETTE DU PALAIS ET DU NOTARIAT. (Includes bimonthly cumulations) 1881. 3/wk. 1190 F. 3 Bd. du Palais, 75180 Paris, France. adv.; index; circ. 21,000.

340　070　　AT　　ISSN 0818-0148
GAZETTE OF LAW JOURNALISM. 1987. 10/yr. Aus.$195. Law Press of Australia, G.P.O. Box 3793, Sydney, N.S.W. 2001, Australia. TEL 02-360-7788. FAX 02-360-7838. Ed. Richard Ackland. (back issuss avail.)

340　　　　　　　CN
GAZETTE OFFICIELLE DU QUEBEC: AVIS JURIDIQUES. w. Can.$53. Ministere des Communications, P.O. Box 1005, Quebec, Que. G1K 7B5, Canada. TEL 514-948-1222. (Subscr. to: Service Abonnements, CP 1190, Outremont, Que. H2V 4S7, Canada)

340　　　　　　　CN
GAZETTE OFFICIELLE DU QUEBEC: LOIS ET REGLEMENTS. w. Can.$77. Ministere des Communications, P.O. Box 1005, Quebec, Que. G1K 7B5, Canada. TEL 514-948-1222. (Subscr. to: Service Abonnements, CP 1190, Outremont, Que. H2V 4S7, Canada) (also avail. in microfilm from BHP)

GENERATOR'S JOURNAL. see ENVIRONMENTAL STUDIES

340　　　　　　　US　　ISSN 0016-8076
K7
GEORGE WASHINGTON LAW REVIEW. 1932. 5/yr. $25. George Washington University, G W Law Review, 716 20th St. N.W., Burns 4th Fl., Washington, DC 20052. TEL 202-994-6835. FAX 202-994-3090. Ed. Cheryl Walker. adv.; bk.rev.; index; circ. 2,000. (also avail. in microfilm from WSH; back issues avail.; reprint service avail. from WSH) Indexed: Abstr.Bk.Rev.Curr.Leg.Per., C.L.I., Curr.Cont., Energy Ind., Energy Info.Abstr., L.R.I., Leg.Cont., Leg.Per., P.A.I.S., Pers.Lit., SSCI.
● Also available online. Vendor(s): Mead Data Central, WESTLAW.
—BLDSC shelfmark: 4158.230000.

340　　　　　　　US　　ISSN 0016-8092
GEORGETOWN LAW JOURNAL. 1912. 6/yr. $35 (foreign $38). (Georgetown Law Journal Association) Georgetown University Law Center, 600 New Jersey Ave., N.W., Washington, DC 20001. TEL 202-662-9468. adv.; bk.rev.; stat.; index; circ. 1,508. (also avail. in microfiche from RRI,WSH; microfilm from WSH) Indexed: Bank.Lit.Ind., C.L.I., Cath.Ind., Crim.Just.Abstr., Curr.Cont., L.R.I., Leg.Cont., Leg.Per., P.A.I.S., Pers.Lit., So.Pac.Per.Ind., SSCI.
● Also available online. Vendor(s): Mead Data Central, WESTLAW.
—BLDSC shelfmark: 4158.270000.

340　　　　　　　US　　ISSN 8750-0515
GEORGIA ADVANCE SHEETS.* 1984. w. $124. Darby Printing Co., 6215 Puroue Dr., S.W., Atlanta, GA 30336-2827. TEL 404-755-4521. Ed. Robert A. Wilkinson. cum.index; circ. 2,000. (back issues avail.)

343　　　　　　　US
GEORGIA ARREST, SEARCH & SEIZURE. 1987. base vol. (plus a. suppl.) $50. Butterworth Legal Publishers (Salem) (Subsidiary of: Reed International PLC), 90 Stiles Rd., Salem, NH 03079. TEL 800-548-4001. FAX 603-898-9858. (looseleaf format)

GEORGIA CONDOMINIUM LAW MANUAL. see REAL ESTATE

246.066　　　　　US
GEORGIA CREDITORS' RIGHTS. 1987. 3 base vols. (plus suppl. 2-3/yr.) $120. Butterworth Legal Publishers (Salem) (Subsidiary of: Reed International PLC), 90 Stiles Rd., Salem, NH 03079. TEL 800-548-4001. FAX 603-898-9858.

340　　　　　　　US　　ISSN 1040-4813
KFG331.A15
GEORGIA EMPLOYMENT LAW LETTER. 1988. m. $127. M. Lee Smith Publishers & Printers, 162 Fourth Ave. N., Box 2678, Nashville, TN 37219. TEL 800-274-6774. FAX 615-256-6601. (Co-sponsor: Clark, Paul, Hoover, & Mallard) Ed. David C. Hagaman.
Description: Survey of Georgia employment law developments.

340　614.7　　US　　ISSN 1044-2324
GEORGIA ENVIRONMENTAL LAW LETTER. 1989. 12/yr. $147. M. Lee Smith Publishers & Printers, 162 Fourth Ave. N., Box 2678, Nashville, TN 37219. TEL 615-242-7395. FAX 615-256-6601. (Co-sponsor: Arnall Golden & Gregory) Ed. A. Jean Tolman.
Description: Reports the latest Georgia environmental law developments that affect Georgia companies.

GEORGIA LANDLORD - TENANT LAW. see REAL ESTATE

340　　　　　　　US　　ISSN 0884-1217
KFG57
GEORGIA LAW LETTER. 1985. 52/yr. $207 to law firms; sole practitioners $177. M. Lee Smith Publishers & Printers, 162 Fourth Ave. N., Box 2678, Nashville, TN 37219. TEL 615-242-7395. FAX 615-256-6601. Ed. Elizabeth Lane. index.
Description: Summarizes opinions of Georgia state Appellate courts and relevant actions of Georgia General Assembly and Georgia Attorney General.

340　　　　　　　US　　ISSN 0016-8300
K7
GEORGIA LAW REVIEW. 1966. q. $22.50. (Georgia Law Review Association Inc.) University of Georgia School of Law, Athens, GA 30602. TEL 404-542-7286. Ed. Laura Woollcott. adv.; bk.rev.; bibl.; charts; stat.; circ. 2,000. (also avail. in microfilm from RRI,WSH) Indexed: C.L.I., L.R.I., Leg.Cont., Leg.Per., P.A.I.S.
● Also available online. Vendor(s): WESTLAW.
—BLDSC shelfmark: 4158.430000.

344　　　　　　　US　　ISSN 0362-5931
KFG15
GEORGIA LEGISLATIVE REVIEW. 1974. irregr. Southern Center for Studies in Public Policy, Clark Atlanta College, Atlanta, GA 30314. TEL 404-880-8085.
Description: Covers law and politics in Georgia and how it affects minorities and the poor.

340　　　　　　　US
GEORGIA PROBATE MANUAL. 1985. 2 base vols. (plus suppl. 2-3/yr.) $80. Butterworth Legal Publishers (Salem) (Subsidiary of: Reed International PLC), 90 Stiles Rd., Salem, NH 03079. TEL 800-548-4001. FAX 603-898-9858. (looseleaf format)

340　333.33　　US
GEORGIA REAL ESTATE LAW LETTER. 1988. 12/yr. $127. M. Lee Smith Publishers & Printers, 162 Fourth Ave. N., Box 2678, Nashville, TN 37219. TEL 615-242-7395. FAX 615-256-6601. Ed. Seth G. Weissman.
Description: Review of Georgia real estate law developments.

340　　　　　　　US　　ISSN 0016-8416
K7
GEORGIA STATE BAR JOURNAL. 1964. q. $10 to non-members. State Bar of Georgia, 800 The Hurt Bldg., Atlanta, GA 30303. TEL 404-527-8700. FAX 404-527-8717. Ed. L. Dale Owens. adv.; bk.rev.; index; circ. 20,000. (also avail. in microfiche from BHP; microfilm from WSH) Indexed: C.L.I., L.R.I., Law Ofc.Info.Svc., Leg.Per.
Supersedes: Georgia Bar Journal.

340　　　　　　　GW
GERICHTSNOTIZEN. 1978. m. free. Amtsgericht Gross-Gerau, Europaring 11-13, 6080 Gross-Gerau 1, Germany. TEL 06152-170458. FAX 06152-53536. Ed. Manfred Franz. adv.; bk.rev.; circ. 170. (looseleaf format; back issues avail.)

340　　　　　　　GW
GESETZ- UND VERORDNUNGSBLATT FUER BERLIN. 1945. irregr. (approx. 60/yr.). DM.104. (Senatsverwaltung fuer Justiz) Kulturbuch Verlag GmbH, Passauerstr. 4, 1000 Berlin 30, Germany. TEL 030-213-6071. FAX 030-213-4449. (back issues avail.) Indexed: Dok.Str.

340　　　　　GW　　ISSN 0174-478X
GESETZBLATT FUER BADEN-WUERTTEMBERG. 1952. s-m. DM.55. Staatsministerium Baden-Wuerttemberg, Richard-Wagner-Str. 15, 7000 Stuttgart 1, Germany. FAX 647-2771. TELEX 722207-STAMID. Ed.Bd. circ. 7,000. (reprint service avail.) Indexed: Dok.Str., INIS Atomind.

349　　　　　GH　　ISSN 0072-436X
LAW
GHANA LAW REPORTS. 1959. a. $79. Council for Law Reporting, P.O. Box M. 165, Accra, Ghana. Ed. S.Y. Bimpong-Buta. adv.; circ. 2,000.

340　　　　　　　US
GILBERT LAW SUMMARIES. ADMINISTRATIVE LAW. irregr., 11th ed., 1988. $14.95. Law Distributors (Subsidiary of: H B J Legal & Professional Publications Inc.), 14415 S. Main St., Gardena, CA 90248. TEL 800-421-1893. FAX 213-324-6381.

LAW

340 US
GILBERT LAW SUMMARIES. CALIFORNIA BAR TEST SKILLS. irreg., 4th ed., 1990. $13.95. Law Distributors (Subsidiary of: H B J Legal & Professional Publications Inc.), 14415 S. Main St., Gardena, CA 90248. TEL 800-421-1893. FAX 213-324-6381.

340 US
GILBERT LAW SUMMARIES. COMMUNITY PROPERTY. irreg., 14th ed., 1986. $12.95. Law Distributors (Subsidiary of: H B J Legal & Professional Publications Inc.), 14415 S. Main St., Gardena, CA 90248. TEL 800-421-1893. FAX 213-324-6381.

340 US
GILBERT LAW SUMMARIES. CONFLICT OF LAWS. irreg., 16th ed., 1990. $15.95. Law Distributors (Subsidiary of: H B J Legal & Professional Publications Inc.), 14415 S. Main St., Gardena, CA 90248. TEL 800-421-1893. FAX 213-324-6381.

340 US
GILBERT LAW SUMMARIES. DICTIONARY OF LEGAL TERMS. 1984. irreg. $10.95. Law Distributors (Subsidiary of: H B J Legal & Professional Publications Inc.), 14415 S. Main St., Gardena, CA 90248. TEL 800-421-1893. FAX 213-324-6381.

340 US
GILBERT LAW SUMMARIES. ESTATE AND GIFT. irreg., 14th ed., 1988. $15.95. Law Distributors (Subsidiary of: H B J Legal & Professional Publications Inc.), 14415 S. Main St., Gardena, CA 90248. TEL 800-421-1893. FAX 213-324-6381.

340 US
GILBERT LAW SUMMARIES. EVIDENCE. irreg., 15th ed., 1989. $15.95. Law Distributors (Subsidiary of: H B J Legal & Professional Publications Inc.), 14415 S. Main St., Gardena, CA 90248. TEL 800-421-1893. FAX 213-324-6381.

340 US
GILBERT LAW SUMMARIES. FUTURE INTERESTS. irreg., 3rd ed., 1982. $10.95. Law Distributors (Subsidiary of: H B J Legal & Professional Publications Inc.), 14415 S. Main St., Gardena, CA 90248. TEL 800-421-1893. FAX 213-324-6381.

340 US
GILBERT LAW SUMMARIES. INCOME TAX 1 (INDIVIDUAL). irreg., 17th ed., 1990. $17.95. Law Distributors (Subsidiary of: H B J Legal & Professional Publications Inc.), 14415 S. Main St., Gardena, CA 90248. TEL 800-421-1893. FAX 213-324-6381.

347.9 US
GILBERT LAW SUMMARIES. LABOR LAW. irreg., 10th ed., 1989. $14.95. Law Distributors (Subsidiary of: H B J Legal & Professional Publications Inc.), 14415 S. Main St., Gardena, CA 90248. TEL 800-421-1893. FAX 213-324-6381.

340 US
GILBERT LAW SUMMARIES. LEGAL ETHICS. irreg., 6th ed., 1987. $12.95. Law Distributors (Subsidiary of: H B J Legal & Professional Publications Inc.), 14415 S. Main St., Gardena, CA 90248. TEL 800-421-1893. FAX 213-324-6381.

340 US
GILBERT LAW SUMMARIES. LEGAL RESEARCH & WRITING. irreg., 5th ed., 1989. $10.95. Law Distributors (Subsidiary of: H B J Legal & Professional Publications Inc.), 14415 S. Main St., Gardena, CA 90248. TEL 800-421-1893. FAX 213-324-6381.

340 US
GILBERT LAW SUMMARIES. MULTISTATE. irreg., 2nd ed., 1984. $12.95. Law Distributors (Subsidiary of: H B J Legal & Professional Publications Inc.), 14415 S. Main St., Gardena, CA 90248. TEL 800-421-1893. FAX 213-324-6381.

340 US
GILBERT LAW SUMMARIES. PERSONAL PROPERTY. irreg., 6th ed., 1980. $8.95. Law Distributors (Subsidiary of: H B J Legal & Professional Publications Inc.), 14415 S. Main St., Gardena, CA 90248. TEL 800-421-1893. FAX 213-324-6381.

340 US
GILBERT LAW SUMMARIES. PROPERTY. irreg., 13th ed., 1991. $18.95. Law Distributors (Subsidiary of: H B J Legal & Professional Publications Inc.), 14415 S. Main St., Gardena, CA 90248. TEL 800-421-1893. FAX 213-324-6381.

340 US
GILBERT LAW SUMMARIES. REMEDIES. irreg., 9th ed., 1991. $17.95. Law Distributors (Subsidiary of: H B J Legal & Professional Publications Inc.), 14415 S. Main St., Gardena, CA 90248. TEL 800-421-1893. FAX 213-324-6381.

340 US
GILBERT LAW SUMMARIES. SALES. irreg., 10th ed., 1986. $13.95. Law Distributors (Subsidiary of: H B J Legal & Professional Publications Inc.), 14415 S. Main St., Gardena, CA 90248. TEL 800-421-1893. FAX 213-324-6381.

346.066 US
GILBERT LAW SUMMARIES. SECURED TRANSACTIONS. irreg., 8th ed., 1987. $13.95. Law Distributors (Subsidiary of: H B J Legal & Professional Publications Inc.), 14415 S. Main St., Gardena, CA 90248. TEL 800-421-1893. FAX 213-324-6381.

340 US
GILBERT LAW SUMMARIES. SECURITIES REGULATION. irreg., 4th ed., 1987. $17.95. Law Distributors (Subsidiary of: H B J Legal & Professional Publications Inc.), 14415 S. Main St., Gardena, CA 90248. TEL 800-421-1893. FAX 213-324-6381.

340 US
GILBERT LAW SUMMARIES. TORTS. irreg., 19th ed., 1988. $17.95. Law Distributors (Subsidiary of: H B J Legal & Professional Publications Inc.), 14415 S. Main St., Gardena, CA 90248. TEL 800-421-1893. FAX 213-324-6381.

340 US
GILBERT LAW SUMMARIES. TRUSTS. irreg., 11th ed., 1990. $14.95. Law Distributors (Subsidiary of: H B J Legal & Professional Publications Inc.), 14415 S. Main St., Gardena, CA 90248. TEL 800-421-1893. FAX 213-324-6381.

GIURISPRUDENZA AGRARIA ITALIANA. see *AGRICULTURE*

346.066 IT
GIURISPRUDENZA DELLE IMPOSTE. 1953. q. L.100000 (foreign L.150000). Casa Editrice Dott. A. Giuffre, Via Busto Arsizio 40, 20151 Milan, Italy. TEL 02-38000905. FAX 02-38009582. Ed. C. Berliri. adv.; circ. 5,800.

340 IT
GIURISPRUDENZA DI MERITO. 1969. bi-m. L.110000 (foreign L.165000). Casa Editrice Dott. A. Giuffre, Via Busto Arsizio 40, 20151 Milan, Italy. TEL 02-38000905. FAX 02-38009582. Ed. A. Jannuzzi. adv.; bk.rev.; circ. 5,000.

349 IT ISSN 0017-0623
GIURISPRUDENZA ITALIANA. 1848. m. L.203000. Unione Tipografico Editrice Torinese, Corso Raffaello 28, 10125 Turin, Italy. index; circ. 13,500.

340 IT
GIUSTIZIA CIVILE. MASSIMARIO ANNOTATO DELLA CASSAZIONE. 1955. m. L.160000 (foreign L.240000). Casa Editrice Dott. A. Giuffre, Via Busto Arsizio 40, 20151 Milan, Italy. TEL 02-38000905. FAX 02-38009582. Eds. Mario Barba, Alfio Finocchiaro. adv.; circ. 5,000.

349 IT ISSN 0017-064X
GIUSTIZIA NUOVA. 1960. m. L.5000($7) Edizioni Giustizia Nuova, Via Bozzi 47-A, Bari, Italy. Ed. Alfredo Zallone. adv.; bk.rev.; abstr.; bibl.; tr.lit.; circ. 15,000. (newspaper)

343 IT ISSN 0017-0658
GIUSTIZIA PENALE. 1895. m. L.70000. Giustizia Penale s.r.l., Via Giovanni Nicotera 10, Rome, Italy. charts; stat.

340 US ISSN 0363-2423
K7
GLENDALE LAW REVIEW. 1976. irreg. $9. Glendale University, College of Law, 220 N. Glendale Ave., Glendale, CA 91206. TEL 818-247-0770. Ed. Robert Cohen. circ. 500. (back issues avail.) Indexed: C.L.I., L.R.I., Leg.Per., P.A.I.S.
—BLDSC shelfmark: 4195.130000.

GLOBAL SHAREHOLDER. see *BUSINESS AND ECONOMICS — Investments*

349 GW ISSN 0016-3570
K22
GMBH-RUNDSCHAU. 1908. m. DM.136.50. (Centrale fuer GmbH Dr. O. Schmidt) Verlag Dr. Otto Schmidt KG, Unter den Ulmen 96-98, 5000 Cologne 51, Germany. TEL 0221-3498-0. FAX 0221-3498-181. TELEX 8883381. Ed. B. Tillmann. bk.rev.; abstr.; bibl.; index; circ. 4,400.

GOETTINGER RECHTSWISSENSCHAFTLICHE STUDIEN. see *LAW — International Law*

340 GW
GOETTINGER STUDIEN ZUR RECHTSGESCHICHTE. 1969. irreg. price varies. Muster-Schmidt Verlag, Gruenbergerweg 6, Postfach 2741, 3400 Goettingen, Germany. FAX 0551-7702774. TELEX 96704-GOFAFI. Ed. Dr. Sellert.

340 US ISSN 0363-0307
K7
GOLDEN GATE UNIVERSITY LAW REVIEW. 1969. 3/yr. $22. Golden Gate University, School of Law, 536 Mission St., San Francisco, CA 94105. TEL 415-442-7250. adv.; bk.rev.; circ. 600. (also avail. in microfiche from WSH; microfilm from WSH; microform from UMI; back issues avail.; reprint service avail. from UMI) Indexed: BPIA, Bus.Ind., C.L.I., Crim.Just.Abstr., L.R.I., Leg.Cont., Leg.Per. •Also available online. Vendor(s): WESTLAW.
Formerly (until 1975): Golden Gate Law Review (ISSN 0098-6631)

340 US ISSN 0046-6115
K7
GONZAGA LAW REVIEW. 1966. 4/yr. $25. Gonzaga University School of Law, Spokane, WA 99258. TEL 509-328-4220. Ed. David Fonda. adv.; bk.rev.; bibl.; index, cum.index every 10 yrs.; circ. 1,000. (also avail. in microfilm from WSH; microfiche from WSH; back issues avail.) Indexed: Abstr.Bk.Rev.Curr.Leg.Per., C.L.I., L.R.I., Leg.Cont., Leg.Per.

GOTHERMAN'S OHIO MUNICIPAL SERVICE. see *PUBLIC ADMINISTRATION*

GOVERNMENT CONTRACT COSTS, PRICING & ACCOUNTING REPORT. see *BUSINESS AND ECONOMICS — Economic Situation And Conditions*

GOVERNMENT CONTRACTOR. see *BUSINESS AND ECONOMICS — Production Of Goods And Services*

GOVERNMENT CONTRACTS CITATOR. see *BUSINESS AND ECONOMICS — Economic Situation And Conditions*

350 US
GOVERNMENT CONTRACTS REPORTS. 9 base vols. (plus w. updates). $1615. Commerce Clearing House, Inc., 4025 W. Peterson Ave., Chicago, IL 60646. TEL 312-583-8500.

GOVERNMENT CONTRACTS SERVICE. see *BUSINESS AND ECONOMICS — Management*

GOVERNMENT REPORT. see *ADVERTISING AND PUBLIC RELATIONS*

GOWER FEDERAL SERVICE - OUTER CONTINENTAL SHELF. see *MINES AND MINING INDUSTRY*

340 UK
GRAYA; magazine for and about Gray's Inn and its members. 1927. a. £5. 8 South Square, Gray's Inn, London WC1R 5EU, England. TEL 01-405-8164. Ed. Francis Cowper. (back issues avail.)

340 UK
GREAT BRITAIN. OFFICE OF FAIR TRADING. REPORT. 1975. a. H.M.S.O., P.O. Box 276, London SW8 5DT, England. (reprint service avail. from UMI)

349 UK ISSN 0080-7915
KDC320
GREAT BRITAIN. SCOTTISH LAW COMMISSION. ANNUAL REPORT. 1965. a. price varies. Scottish Law Commission, 140 Causewayside, Edinburgh EH9 1PR, Scotland. FAX 031-662-4900. (Dist by: H.M.S.O., 71 Lothian Rd., Edinburgh EH3 9AZ, Scotland) circ. 1,000.

347.9 UK
GREENS WEEKLY DIGEST. w. £80. W. Green, 21 Alva St., Edinburgh EH2 4PS, Scotland. Ed. P. Nicholson.

GRIEVANCE BULLETIN. see *BUSINESS AND ECONOMICS — Labor And Industrial Relations*

340 NE ISSN 0167-3831
GROTIANA. (Text in English, French, German, Italian, Latin) 1980. a. fl.70($30) (Grotiana Foundation) Van Gorcum en Co. B.V., P.O. Box 43, 9400 AA Assen, Netherlands. TEL 05920-46864. FAX 05920-72064. Ed. B. Vermeulen. adv.; bk.rev.; circ. 800. (back issues avail.)
   Description: Covers history of law.

340 IT
GUIDA. 1978. m. (11/yr.) L.20000. Libreria Guida, Via Port'Alba 20-23, 80134 Naples, Italy. TEL 081-446377. FAX 081-459822. Ed. Pietro Marino. adv.; circ. 20,000.

GUIDE TO COMPUTER LAW. see *COMPUTERS*

340 US
▼**GUIDE TO TEXAS WORKERS' COMPENSATION REFORM.** 1991. 2 base vols. (plus a. suppl.) $225. Butterworth Legal Publishers (Salem) (Subsidiary of: Reed International PLC), 90 Stiles Rd., Salem, NH 03079. TEL 800-548-4001. FAX 603-898-9858. Ed.Bd. (looseleaf format)
   Description: Analysis of the statutes producing recent changes in the workers' compensation and tort litigation system in Texas.

340 664 UK
GUIDE TO THE FOOD REGULATIONS IN THE U.K.. 1984. a. £350 for base vol; updates £175. Leatherhead Food Research Association, Randalls Rd., Leatherhead, Surrey, KT22 7RY, England. TEL 0372-376761. FAX 0372-386228.

344.73 US ISSN 0196-7975
KF3464.Z9
GUIDEBOOK TO FAIR EMPLOYMENT PRACTICES. (Supplement to: Labor Law Reports: Employment Practices.) a. $15. Commerce Clearing House, Inc., 4025 W. Peterson Ave., Chicago, IL 60646. TEL 312-583-8500.

GUIDEBOOK TO LABOR RELATIONS. see *BUSINESS AND ECONOMICS — Labor And Industrial Relations*

349 II ISSN 0017-551X
GUJARAT LAW REPORTER; reportable judgements of the Supreme Court and the Gujarat High Court. (Text in English) 1960. m. Rs.300. Chandrakant Chimanlal Vora, 57-2 Gandhi Rd., P.O. Box 163, Ahmedabad 380 001, Gujarat, India. adv.; bk.rev.; index; circ. 3,000. (back issues avail.)

349 II ISSN 0017-5528
GUJARAT LAW TIMES; law journal publishing short-notes on the cases decided by the High Court of Gujarat (India) as well as those of Supreme Court of India. (Text in English) 1964. fortn. Rs.175. Chandrakant Chimanlal Vora, 57-2 Gandhi Rd., P.O. Box 163, Ahmedabad 380 001, Gujarat, India. Ed. Babubhai A. Soni. adv.; bk.rev.; index; circ. 2,000. (back issues avail.)

349 II ISSN 0017-5536
GUJARAT REVENUE TRIBUNAL LAW REPORTER; judgements of the Gujarat Revenue Tribunal. (Text in English) 1961. m. Rs.125. Chandrakant Chimanlal Vora, 57-2 Gandhi Rd., P.O. Box 163, Ahmedabad 380 001, Gujarat, India. Ed. N. C. Vakil. adv.; bk.rev.; index; circ. 350. (back issues avail.)

340 US ISSN 0198-7364
K8
HAMLINE LAW REVIEW. 1978. s-a. $15. Hamline University School of Law, Hamline Law Review, 1536 Hewitt Ave., St. Paul, MN 55104-1284. TEL 612-641-2350. FAX 612-641-2435. bk.rev.; illus.; circ. 1,300. (also avail. in microfilm from WSH; reprint service avail. from WSH) Indexed: Abstr.Bk.Rev.Curr.Leg.Per., C.L.I., Crim.Just.Abstr., L.R.I., Leg.Cont., Leg.Per.
   ●Also available online. Vendor(s): WESTLAW.
   Supersedes: Midwestern Advocate (ISSN 0360-5094)

340 GW
HANDBUCH DER JUSTIZ. 1953. biennial. DM.84. (Deutscher Richterbund) R. v. Decker's Verlag, G. Schenck GmbH, Im Weiher 10, 6900 Heidelberg, Germany. TEL 06221-489369. FAX 06221-489-410. TELEX 461727-HUE-HD. Ed. P. Marqua. adv.; circ. 4,000.

340 614.8 US
HANDGUN CONTROL. SEMI-ANNUAL PROGRESS REPORT. 1974. s-a. Handgun Control, Inc., 1225 Eye St., N.W., Washington, DC 20005. TEL 202-898-0792. Ed. Susan Whitmore.
   Formerly (until 1989): Washington Report (Washington, 1974).
   Description: Reports on federal and state legislative efforts toward stronger handgun laws. Cites new studies on handgun issue.

340 AU
HANS KELSEN - INSTITUT. SCHRIFTENREIHE. 1974. irreg., vol.16, 1991. price varies. Manzsche Verlags- und Universitaetsbuchhandlung, Kohlmarkt 16, A-1014 Vienna, Austria. TEL 0222-531610. FAX 0222-5316181.
   Description: Focuses on legal philosophy.

340 323.4 US
HARVARD BLACKLETTER JOURNAL. a. $12 (foreign $14). Harvard University, Law School, Publications Center, Hastings Hall, Cambridge, MA 02138. TEL 617-495-3694. circ. 300. (also avail. in microform from WSH; reprint service avail. from WSH)
   Description: Dedicated to the dissemination of legal literature, thought and ideas which have direct impact on the minority community.

340 US ISSN 0147-8257
K8
HARVARD ENVIRONMENTAL LAW REVIEW. 1976. 2/yr. $24 (foreign $28). Harvard University, Law School, Publications Center, Hastings Hall, Cambridge, MA 02138. TEL 617-495-3694. circ. 1,000. (also avail. in microfilm from WSH; back issues avail.; reprint service avail. from WSH) Indexed: Acid Pre.Dig., Acid Rain Abstr., Acid Rain Ind., C.L.I., Deep Sea Res.& Oceanogr.Abstr., Energy Info.Abstr., Energy Rev., Environ.Abstr., Environ.Per.Bibl., Geo.Abstr., INIS Atomind., L.R.I., Leg.Per., Mar.Aff.Bibl., P.A.I.S., Risk Abstr., Sel.Water Res.Abstr., SSCI, Telegen.
   ●Also available online. Vendor(s): WESTLAW.
   Description: Provides a forum for in-depth technical and legal analysis of complex environmental problems, ranging from energy and urban land use to hazardous wastes and wilderness preservation.

340 US ISSN 0193-4872
K8
HARVARD JOURNAL OF LAW AND PUBLIC POLICY. 1978. 3/yr. $32.50 to individuals and institutions; students $17.50; foreign $35. Harvard Society for Law and Public Policy, Inc., Harvard Law School, Cambridge, MA 02138. TEL 617-495-3105. Ed. Margaret Stock. adv.; bk.rev.; circ. 4,000. (also avail. in microfilm from WSH; back issues avail.; reprint service avail. from WSH) Indexed: C.L.I., L.R.I., Leg.Per., P.A.I.S., Pers.Lit.
   ●Also available online. Vendor(s): WESTLAW.
   Description: Student-run law journal.

340 US ISSN 0017-808X
K8
HARVARD JOURNAL ON LEGISLATION. 1964. 2/yr. $24 (foreign $28). Harvard University, Law School, Publications Center, Hastings Hall, Cambridge, MA 02138. TEL 617-495-3694. adv.; bk.rev.; charts; circ. 800. (also avail. in microform from RRI,UMI; microfilm from WSH; reprint service avail. from RRI,UMI) Indexed: A.B.C.Pol.Sci., Abstr.Bk.Rev.Curr.Leg.Per., BPIA, Bus.Ind., C.L.I., L.R.I., Leg.Cont., Leg.Per., Mar.Aff.Bibl., P.A.I.S., SSCI.
   ●Also available online. Vendor(s): WESTLAW.
   —BLDSC shelfmark: 4267.400000.
   Description: Examines the current state of the law, trends and the theoretical underpinnings of legislation. Presents detailed statements of how the law should be changed, and proposes specific model acts for adoption by legislatures.

HARVARD LAW BULLETIN. see *COLLEGE AND ALUMNI*

340 US ISSN 0017-8101
HARVARD LAW RECORD. 1946. 25/yr. $30. Harvard Law Record Corporation, Harvard Law School, Cambridge, MA 02138. TEL 617-495-4418. Ed. George Borkowski. adv.; B&W page $650. bk.rev.; charts; illus.; stat.; index; circ. 15,000. (tabloid format; also avail. in microform from WSH; reprint service avail. from WSH)
   Description: Serves the students, faculty and alumni of the School.

340 US ISSN 0017-811X
K8 CODEN: HALRAF
HARVARD LAW REVIEW. 1887. m. (8/yr.). $36 (foreign $42). Harvard Law Review Association, Gannett House, Cambridge, MA 02138. TEL 617-495-4650. Ed.Bd. adv.; bk.rev.; bibl.; index, cum.index: 1887-1972, vols.1-86; circ. 8,500. (also avail. in microfiche from WSH; microfilm from WSH; microform from RRI,UMI; reprint service avail. from RRI,UMI) Indexed: A.B.C.Pol.Sci., ABI Inform, Abstr.Bk.Rev.Curr.Leg.Per., Account.Ind. (1974-), Bank.Lit.Ind., Bk.Rev.Ind. (1965-), BPIA, Bus.Ind., C.L.I., Child.Bk.Rev.Ind. (1965-), Crim.Just.Abstr., Curr.Cont., L.R.I., Leg.Per., Mar.Aff.Bibl., Mid.East: Abstr.& Ind., P.A.I.S., Pers.Lit., Risk Abstr., SSCI, SSCI.
   ●Also available online. Vendor(s): Mead Data Central (Lexis), WESTLAW.
   —BLDSC shelfmark: 4267.500000.

349.73 305.4 US ISSN 0270-1456
K8
HARVARD WOMEN'S LAW JOURNAL. 1978. a. $15 (foreign $27). Harvard University, Law School (Women's Law Journal), Publications Center, Hastings Hall, Cambridge, MA 02138. TEL 617-495-3726. FAX 617-495-1110. Ed. Kirstin Dodge. adv.; bk.rev.; circ. 900. (also avail. in microfilm from WSH; back issues avail.; reprint service avail. from WSH) Indexed: Abstr.Bk.Rev.Curr.Leg.Per., Alt.Press Ind., C.L.I., HR Rep., L.R.I., Leg.Per., P.A.I.S., Stud.Wom.Abstr.
   ●Also available online. Vendor(s): WESTLAW.
   Description: Devoted to the development of a feminist jurisprudence, which explores both the impact of the law on women and the impact of women on the law. Legal, political, economical, historical and sociological perspectives are combined in order to clarify legal issues affecting women.

340 001.6 790 US
K3
HASTINGS COMMUNICATIONS AND ENTERTAINMENT LAW JOURNAL (COMM - ENT). 1977. q. $20 (foreign $22). University of California, San Francisco, Hastings College of the Law, 200 McAllister St., San Francisco, CA 94102-4978. TEL 415-565-4731. FAX 415-565-4814. Ed. Janet L. Avery. adv.; bk.rev.; abstr.; circ. 1,300. (tabloid format; also avail. in microfilm from WSH; back issues avail.; reprint service avail. from WSH) Indexed: C.L.I., Commun.Abstr., L.R.I., Leg.Per.
   ●Also available online. Vendor(s): WESTLAW.
   Also available on CD-ROM.
   Formerly: Comm-Ent: Hastings Journal of Communications and Entertainment Law (ISSN 0193-8398)
   Description: Covers telecommunications, broadcasting, cable and other non-broadcast video, the print media, defamation, advertising, the arts, entertainment, sports, computers and high technology information services, copyright, patent, trademark, privacy, film and other first-amendment issues.

340 US ISSN 0017-8322
HASTINGS LAW JOURNAL. 1949. 6/yr. $25 (foreign $27). University of California, San Francisco, Hastings College of the Law, 200 McAllister St., San Francisco, CA 94102-4978. TEL 415-565-4727. FAX 415-565-4814. Ed. Simeon Herskovits. adv.; bk.rev.; bibl.; cum.index: 1947-1969, 1970-1979; circ. 1,800. (tabloid format; also avail. in microfilm from UMI,WSH; reprint service avail.from UMI,WSH; back issues avail.) **Indexed:** Abstr.Bk.Rev.Curr.Leg.Per., C.L.I., L.R.I., Leg.Cont., Leg.Per., SSCI.
● Also available online. Vendor(s): Mead Data Central, WESTLAW.
—BLDSC shelfmark: 4273.050000.
Description: Contributes to the advancement of knowledge in legal thinking through scholarly articles written by experts in the legal community.

340 US
HASTINGS WOMEN'S LAW JOURNAL. 1989. s-a. $25. University of California, San Francisco, Hastings College of the Law, 200 McAllister St., San Francisco, CA 94102. TEL 415-565-4870. FAX 415-464-4814. Ed. Allison Bernstein. adv.; bk.rev.; circ. 800. (tabloid format; back issues avail.)
Description: Promotes feminist legal perspectives and scholarship in issues of concern common to all women.

340 GW ISSN 0930-6692
HAUSBESITZER A B C; Recht - Steuern - Finanzierung - Vorsicherung. 1986. q. DM.48. Wirtschaft Recht und Steuern Verlag, Fraunhoferstr. 5, Postfach 1363, 8033 Planegg-Munich, Germany. TEL 089-8577944. FAX 089-8577990. (looseleaf format)
Description: News about finance and law for the homeowner.

347.9 US
HAWAII. COMMISSION ON JUDICIAL DISCIPLINE. ANNUAL REPORT. 1980. a. Commission on Judicial Discipline, Box 2560, Honolulu, HI 96804. Ed. Sandra L. Gorla. circ. 250.

HAWAII. STATE COMMISSION ON THE STATUS OF WOMEN. ANNUAL REPORT. see WOMEN'S INTERESTS

347.9 US
HAWAII. STATE JUDICIARY. ANNUAL REPORT. 1962. a. Judiciary Department, Box 2560, Honolulu, HI 96804. TEL 808-548-4634. FAX 808-548-6002. (Or: 417 S. King St., Honolulu, HI 96813) illus.; stat.; circ. 4,500.
Formerly: Hawaii. Judiciary Department. Annual Report.

340 US
HAWAII BAR JOURNAL. 1966. a. $8. Hawaii Bar Association, Box 26, Honolulu, HI 96810. TEL 808-537-1868. FAX 808-521-7936. Ed. Edward C. Kemper. adv.; bk.rev.; circ. 4,500. (also avail. in microfilm from WSH; back issues avail.) **Indexed:** C.L.I., L.R.I., Leg.Per.

340 US
HAZARDOUS WASTE AND TOXIC TORTS LAW AND STRATEGY. m. $195. New York Law Publishing Co., Marketing Dept., 111 Eighth Ave., New York, NY 10011. TEL 212-741-8300.
Description: Roundup of significant legislative and regulatory rulings of special interest to manufacturers, insurance companies, trial attorneys, government enforcement agencies, environmental consultants and corporate counsel.

340 US ISSN 0275-0244
KF3946.A59
HAZARDOUS WASTE LITIGATION REPORTER; the national journal of record of hazardous waste-related litigation. 1980. s-m. $850. Andrews Publications, 1646 West Chester Pike, Box 1000, Westtown, PA 19395. TEL 215-399-6600. FAX 215-399-6610. Ed. Harry G. Armstrong. bibl.; stat.; cum.index every 6 mos. (looseleaf format; back issues avail.)

340 UK
HAZELL'S GUIDE TO THE JUDICIARY & THE COURTS WITH THE HOLBORN LAW SOCIETY'S BAR LIST. 1985. a. £24($45) Court & Judicial Publishing Co. Ltd., P.O. Box 39, Henley-on-Thames, Oxfordshire RG9 5UA, England. (Co-publisher: R. Hazell & Co.) Ed. C.G.A. Parker. adv.; index.
Former titles: Hazell's Guide to the Judiciary and the Courts with the Holborn Law Society's Bar List by Chambers; Hazell's Guide to the Judiciary and the Courts with the Holborn Law Society's List of Barristers by Chambers (ISSN 0266-3597)
Description: Directory of all the judiciary, courts and advocates of the United Kingdom.

HEALTH & SAFETY MONITOR. see OCCUPATIONAL HEALTH AND SAFETY

HEALTH CARE LABOR MANUAL. see HOSPITALS

342 613.7 US
HEALTH LAW DIGEST. 1972. m. $195. National Health Lawyers Association, 1620 Eye St., Ste. 900, Washington, DC 20006. TEL 202-833-1100. Ed. David Rapoport. circ. 7,200.

340 613.7 US ISSN 1043-6081
KFO361.A15
HEALTH LAW JOURNAL OF OHIO. 1987. bi-m. $155. Banks - Baldwin Law Publishing Co., University Center, Box 1974, Cleveland, OH 44106. TEL 216-721-7373. FAX 216-721-8055. Ed. Peter A. Pavarini.
Formerly (until 1989): Ohio Health Law Insider (ISSN 0893-8466)
Description: Review of state and national trends; practical guidance; digest of current court decisions, agency opinions, legislation and rules.

340 US ISSN 0736-3443
KF3821.A15
HEALTH LAWYER. irreg. (3-4/yr.). membership only. (American Bar Association, Forum Committee on Health Law) A B A Press, 750 N. Lake Shore Dr., Chicago, IL 60611. TEL 312-988-6067. Ed. Lawrence Manson. circ. 3,220. (also avail. in microform)
Description: Legal trends in health law.

340 614 US
HEALTH LAWYERS NEWS REPORT. 1971. m. $50. National Health Lawyers Association, 1620 Eye St., Ste. 900, Washington, DC 20006. TEL 202-833-1100. Ed. David Rapoport. circ. 7,200. **Indexed:** Med.Care Rev.
Former titles: N H L A News Report; Health Lawyers News Report (ISSN 0145-4129)

HEALTH LEGISLATION AND REGULATION. see MEDICAL SCIENCES

HEALTHSPAN; the report of health business and law. see BUSINESS AND ECONOMICS — Management

340 CN
HEARSAY. 1976. 2/yr. Dalhousie University, Faculty of Law, Halifax, N.S. B3H 4H9, Canada. TEL 902-494-1102. illus.; circ. 4,000.
Formerly: Hearsay, for Dalhousie Law Graduates (ISSN 0704-4860)

340 US
▼**HEARSAY HANDBOOK.** 1991. base vol. (plus a. suppl.). $95. Shepard's - McGraw-Hill, Inc., Box 35300, Colorado Springs, CO 80935-3530. TEL 800-525-2474.
Description: Analyzes the critical contemporary case law generated by the Federal Rules of Evidence. Provides explanations and explanations of the Hearsay Rule and its 40 exceptions as they are currently applied in courts throughout the country.

340 CC
HEBEI FAXUE. (Text in Chinese) bi-m. Hebei Sheng Zhengfa Ganbu Guanli Xueyuan, Wuqi Lu, Shijiazhuang, Hebei 050061, People's Republic of China. TEL 639286. Ed. Xie Shiwen.

347 IS ISSN 0075-9740
HEBREW UNIVERSITY OF JERUSALEM. LIONEL COHEN LECTURES. (Text in English) 1953. irreg. price varies. Magnes Press, Hebrew University of Jerusalem, Jerusalem, Israel.

340 IS
HEDEI DIN. 1977. q. Tel Aviv Bar Association, P.O. Box 16023, Tel Aviv 64 731, Israel. TEL 03-258361.

340 GW
HEIDELBERGER RECHTSVERGLEICHENDE UND WIRTSCHAFTSRECHTLICHE STUDIEN. 1967. a. price varies. Carl Winter Universitaetsverlag GmbH, Lutherstr. 59, 6900 Heidelberg, Germany.

340 GW ISSN 0073-165X
HEIDELBERGER RECHTSWISSENSCHAFTLICHE ABHANDLUNGEN. NEUE FOLGE. 1957. irreg. price varies. (Universitaet Heidelberg, Juristische Fakultaet) Carl Winter Universitaetsverlag GmbH, Lutherstr. 59, 6900 Heidelberg, Germany.

340 US
HEIN CHECKLIST OF STATUTES. s-a. $25. William S. Hein & Co., Inc., 1285 Main St., Buffalo, NY 14209. TEL 800-828-7571. FAX 716-883-8100. TELEX 91-209 WU 7 HEIN BUF. circ. 300.
Formerly: Hein Annual Checklist Statutes (ISSN 0891-6527)

HEMLOCK QUARTERLY. see MEDICAL SCIENCES

340 600 US ISSN 0885-2715
K8
HIGH TECHNOLOGY LAW JOURNAL. 1986. s-a. $48 (foreign $52). University of California Press, Journals Division, 2120 Berkeley Way, Berkeley, CA 94720. TEL 510-642-4191. FAX 510-643-7127. adv.; bk.rev.; circ. 500. (also avail. in microfiche from WSH; microfilm) **Indexed:** ABI Inform, C.L.I., Leg.Per., Tel.Abstr., Telegen.
—BLDSC shelfmark: 4307.363500.
Description: Addresses new legal issues posed by developing technologies.
Refereed Serial

HIGHWAY CODE. see TRANSPORTATION — Roads And Traffic

340 JA ISSN 0439-1365
HIKAKU HO KENKYU/COMPARATIVE LAW JOURNAL. (Text in Japanese) 1949. s-a. (Hikaku Ho Gakkai - Japanese Society of Comparative Law) Yuhikaku Publishing Co. Ltd., 2-17 Kanda Jinbo-cho, Chiyoda-ku, Tokyo 101, Japan.
—BLDSC shelfmark: 3363.785000.

340 US
HILDEBRANDT REPORT; a management and marketing newsletter for law firms. 1985. m. Hildebrandt, Inc. (Somerville), 501 P.O. Plaza, 50 Division St., Somerville, NJ 08876-2900. TEL 201-725-1600. (And: Box 515, Colville, WA 99114) Ed. Edward J. Burke. circ. 3,600.

HILL & REDMAN: LANDLORD & TENANT. see REAL ESTATE

340 US
HINE'S INSURANCE COUNSEL. 1908. a. $25. Hine's Legal Directory, Inc., Box 280, Glen Ellyn, IL 60138. TEL 708-462-9670. Ed. James R. Collins. adv.; circ. 7,000 (controlled).
Description: Lists of law firms handling defense trial cases in the United States and Canada.

HINWEIS. see INSURANCE

340 940 SP ISSN 0304-4319
LAW
HISTORIA DEL DERECHO ESPANOL. ANUARIO. 1924. a. 6420 ptas. (foreign 6500 ptas.). Ministerio de Justicia, Centro de Publicaciones, Secretaria General Tecnica, Gran Via, 76-8, 28013 Madrid, Spain. TEL 247 54 22. bk.rev.; bibl.; index. **Indexed:** Amer.Hist.& Life, Hist.Abstr.

HISTORIJSKI ARHIV RIJEKA. VJESNIK. see HISTORY — History Of Europe

HISTORY AND LAW SERIES. see HISTORY — History Of Europe

320 340 JA ISSN 0073-2796
LAW
HITOTSUBASHI JOURNAL OF LAW AND POLITICS. 1960. a. Hitotsubashi Daigaku, Hitotsubashi Gakkai - Hitotsubashi University, Hitotsubashi Academy, 2-1 Naka, Kunitachi-shi, Tokyo 186, Japan. Ed. O. Ishii. circ. 900. **Indexed:** P.A.I.S.

349   GW   ISSN 0018-3059
HOECHSTRICHTERLICHE FINANZRECHTSPRECHUNG. 1961. m. DM.267. Stollfuss Verlag Bonn, Dechenstr. 7-11, Postfach 2428, 5300 Bonn 1, Germany. TEL 0228-724-0. TELEX 8869477. Ed. Guenther Wauer. adv.; circ. 4,500.

340   US   ISSN 0091-4029
K8
HOFSTRA LAW REVIEW. 1973. q. $26. Hofstra University, School of Law, Hempstead, NY 11550. TEL 516-463-5910. FAX 516-560-7676. adv.; bk.rev.; index; circ. 2,500. (reprint service avail.) **Indexed:** C.L.I., Crim.Just.Abstr., L.R.I., Leg.Per.
●Also available online. Vendor(s): Mead Data Central, WESTLAW.
—BLDSC shelfmark: 4322.010000.

340 320   JA   ISSN 0385-5082
HOGAKU/JOURNAL OF LAW AND POLITICAL SCIENCE. (Text in Japanese) 1932. bi-m. 1000 Yen per no. Tohoku Daigaku, Hogakkai - Tohoku University, Faculty of Law, Association of Law and Political Science, Kawauchi, Aoba-ku, Sendai-shi, Miyagi-ken 980, Japan. TEL 022-222-1800. FAX 022-263-2933. Ed. Hideo Aoi. bk.rev.; circ. 1,500.
—BLDSC shelfmark: 5010.137000.

320 340 301   JA
HOGAKU KENKYU/JOURNAL OF LAW, POLITICS, AND SOCIOLOGY. (Text in Japanese) 1922. m. Keio Gijuku Daigaku, Hogaku Kenkyukai - Keio University, Association for the Study of Law and Politics, 2-2 Mita, Minato-ku, Tokyo 108, Japan. bk.rev.; bibl. **Indexed:** Amer.Hist.& Life (until 1992), Hist.Abstr. (until 1992), Numis.Lit.

340   AF
HOKOUK. (Text in English or Persian) 1972. q. $10. Kabul University, Faculty of Law and Political Science, Djamal-Mina, Kabul, Afghanistan.

340   UK   ISSN 0260-5864
K8
HOLDSWORTH LAW REVIEW. 1974. s-a. £14. University of Birmingham, Faculty of Law, P.O. Box 363, Birmingham B15 2TT, England. TEL 021-472-1301. FAX 021-414-3585. Ed. Jeremy McBride. adv.; bk.rev.; circ. 300. (back issues avail.; reprint service avail.)
—BLDSC shelfmark: 4322.294600.
Description: Covers all fields of law.

HOLZBAU - REPORT. see BUILDING AND CONSTRUCTION — Carpentry And Woodwork

340   HO   ISSN 0016-3791
HONDURAS. CORTE SUPREMA DE JUSTICIA. GACETA JUDICIAL.* 1889. bi-m. L.3($1.50) Corte Suprema de Justicia, Tegucigalpa D.C., Honduras. bk.rev. (tabloid format)

340   HK   ISSN 0378-0600
HONG KONG LAW JOURNAL. (Text in English) 1971. 3/yr. HK.$540 (students HK.$240). Hong Kong Law Journal Ltd., 1424 Prince's Bldg., Hong Kong. TEL 5260318. FAX 5371346. adv.; bk.rev.; cum.index. (back issues avail.)

340 382
HONG KONG REVENUE LEGISLATION. (In 2 vols.) 1989. irreg. (approx. 4-6/yr.) C C H Australia Ltd., P.O. Box 230, North Ryde, N.S.W. 2113, Australia. TEL 02-888-2555. FAX 02-888-7324.
Description: Includes the Inland Revenue Department Interpretation and Practice notes, case reporting.

340   US
HOSPITAL LAW MANUAL. ADMINISTRATORS. q. $599 (including Attorneys section $799). Aspen Publishers, Inc., 200 Orchard Ridge Dr., Gaithersburg, MD 20878. TEL 301-417-7500. FAX 301-417-7550.

340   US
HOSPITAL LAW MANUAL. ATTORNEYS. 1959. q. $725 (including Administrators section $799). Aspen Publishers, Inc., 200 Orchard Ridge Dr., Gaithersburg, MD 20878. TEL 301-417-7500. FAX 301-417-7550. charts; illus.; circ. 450.
Formerly: Hospital Law Manual and Quarterly Service (ISSN 0018-5728)

HOSPITAL LAW NEWSLETTER. see HOSPITALS

HOSPITAL LITIGATION REPORTER. see HOSPITALS

HOSPITAL RISK CONTROL; an information and consultation system. see HOSPITALS

HOSPITALITY LAW; the preventive-law information service for the lodging industry. see HOTELS AND RESTAURANTS

HOTLINE (STONY BROOK); news service on the missing children field. see CHILDREN AND YOUTH — About

340   UK
HOUSING LAW REPORTS. bi-m. £155. Sweet & Maxwell, South Quay Plaza, 8th Fl., 183 Marsh Wall, London E14 9FT, England. TEL 071-538-8686. FAX 071-538-9508. Ed. Andrew Arden.

340 382   US   ISSN 0194-1879
JX1
HOUSTON JOURNAL OF INTERNATIONAL LAW. 1978. 3/yr. $20 (foreign $25). University of Houston, Law Center, 4800 Calhoun Rd., BLB, Ste. 29, Houston, TX 77004-6370. TEL 713-749-3774. Eds. Harold J. Herman, Brent Sadler. adv.; bk.rev.; cum.index; circ. 600. (back issues avail.; reprint service avail. from WSH) **Indexed:** C.L.I., HR Rep., L.R.I., Leg.Per.
●Also available online. Vendor(s): WESTLAW.
—BLDSC shelfmark: 4335.153270.

340   US   ISSN 0018-6694
K8
HOUSTON LAW REVIEW. 1963. 5/yr. $28. (University of Houston, Law Center) Houston Law Review Inc., University of Houston Law Center-University Park, Houston, TX 77004. TEL 713-749-3195. FAX 713-749-4661. Ed. Nicolas Eranoff. adv.; bk.rev.; bibl.; illus.; stat.; index; circ. 1,400. (also avail. in microform from UMI; reprint service avail. from UMI) **Indexed:** C.L.I., Crim.Just.Abstr., Curr.Cont., L.R.I., Leg.Cont., Leg.Per., Ocean.Abstr., Pollut.Abstr., SSCI.
●Also available online. Vendor(s): WESTLAW.

340   US
HOW TO PREPARE WITNESSES FOR TRIAL. 1985. base vol. (plus a. suppl.) $95. Shepard's - McGraw-Hill, Inc., Box 35300, Colorado Springs, CO 80935-3530. TEL 800-525-2474.
Description: Provides practical ideas and insights on evaluating and assessing potential witnesses, educating witnesses and handling expert witnesses.

340   US   ISSN 0018-6813
LAW
HOWARD LAW JOURNAL. 1955. s-a. $22 (foreign $25). Howard University, School of Law, 2900 Van Ness St., N.W., Washington, DC 20008. TEL 202-686-6570. Ed. Alice Thomas. adv.; bk.rev.; index; circ. 1,100. (also avail. in microfilm from WSH; reprint service avail. from WSH) **Indexed:** C.L.I., L.R.I., Lang.& Lang.Behav.Abstr., Leg.Per., P.A.I.S.
●Also available online. Vendor(s): WESTLAW.
—BLDSC shelfmark: 4335.247000.

HSIEN CHENG SSU CH'AO. see POLITICAL SCIENCE

340   IO   ISSN 0125-9687
HUKUM DAN PEMBANGUNAN. 1972. bi-m. Rps.15000. University of Indonesia, Faculty of Law - Universitas Indonesia, Fakultas Hukum, Jl. Cirebon 5, Jakarta 10310, Indonesia. Eds. Koestantinah Soeparno, Mardjono Reksodiputro. adv.; bk.rev.; circ. 3,000. (also avail. in microfiche) **Indexed:** E.I.
Formerly: (until vol.7, no.1, 1977): Universitas Indonesia. Fakultas Hukum. Majalah.

HUMAN RESEARCH REPORT; protecting researchers and research subjects. see MEDICAL SCIENCES — Experimental Medicine, Laboratory Technique

340   MP
▼**HUUL' DZUYN MEDEELE/LEGAL INFORMATION.** (Text in Mongolian) 1990. m. Ulan Bator, Mongolia.

340   MP
HUUL' YOS/LEGALITY. (Text in Mongolian) bi-m. Supreme Court, Procurator's Office, Ulan Bator, Mongolia. (Co-sponsor: Ministry of Law) Ed. R. Hatanbaatar.

HYRESGAESTEN. see HOUSING AND URBAN PLANNING

247 332   US
I B A LAW WATCH. 1986. q. Illinois Bankers Association, 111 N. Canal, Ste. 1111, Chicago, IL 60606. TEL 312-876-9900. FAX 312-876-3826. Ed. James J. Brennan. circ. 350. (looseleaf format; back issues avail.)
Description: Highlights legal developments affecting the Illinois banking industry and preventative banking law.

I C S I D REVIEW: FOREIGN INVESTMENT LAW JOURNAL. (International Center for Settlement of Investment Disputes) see BUSINESS AND ECONOMICS — Investments

340   UN   ISSN 0378-7362
K1704.23
I L O JUDGEMENTS OF THE ADMINISTRATIVE TRIBUNAL. 2/yr. 60 Fr.($48) (International Labour Office) I L O Publications, CH-1211 Geneva 22, Switzerland. TEL 022-7996111. FAX 022-798-6358. TELEX 415-647-ILO-CH. (Dist. in U.S. by: ILO Publications Center, 49 Sheridan Ave., Albany, NY 12210) circ. 1,800.
—BLDSC shelfmark: 5073.828000.

340   US
I L S A JOURNAL OF INTERNATIONAL LAW. 1977. a. $9. International Law Students Association, Tillar House, 2223 Massachusetts Ave., N.W., Washington, DC 20008. FAX 202-797-7133. Ed. Denise M. Hodge. adv.; bk.rev.; circ. 500. **Indexed:** C.L.I., L.R.I., Leg.Per., Peace Res.Abstr.
Formerly: A S I L S International Law Journal (ISSN 0161-1402)

I N T V NEWSLETTER. (Association of Independent Television Stations, Inc.) see COMMUNICATIONS — Television And Cable

340   US
I O L T A UPDATE. q. free. American Bar Association, Commission on Interest on Lawyers' Trust Accounts, 750 N. Lake Shore Dr., Chicago, IL 60611. TEL 312-988-5555.
Description: Discusses trends in lawyers' trust accounts nationwide.

340   US
I P C REPORT. q. $18 to non-members; members $13. (International Procurement Committee) American Bar Association, Public Contract Law Section, 750 N. Lake Shore Dr., Chicago, IL 60611. TEL 312-988-5555.
Description: Newsletter examines the questions involving public contracts in countries other than the U.S.

340   AT
I.R.C. WEEKLY NEWSLETTER. w. Aus.$60. Law Printer, P.O. Box 203, North Melbourne, Vic. 3051, Australia. TEL 03-320-0100. FAX 03-328-1657.

340   US
I S B A NEWS. s-m. Illinois State Bar Association, 424 S. 2nd St., Springfield, IL 62701-1704. TEL 217-525-1760. FAX 217-525-0712. Ed. Stephen Anderson. circ. 31,000.

340   US   ISSN 0019-1205
K9
IDAHO LAW REVIEW. 1964. 4/yr. $26.65. University of Idaho, College of Law, Moscow, ID 83843. TEL 208-885-7241. adv.; cum.index; circ. 750. (also avail. in microfiche from WSH; microfilm from WSH) **Indexed:** C.L.I., L.R.I., Leg.Cont., Leg.Per., Sel.Water Res.Abstr.
●Also available online. Vendor(s): WESTLAW.

347   US   ISSN 0536-3713
KFI1708
ILLINOIS. ADMINISTRATIVE OFFICE OF ILLINOIS COURTS. ANNUAL REPORT TO THE SUPREME COURT OF ILLINOIS. 1959. a. free. Administrative Office of Illinois Courts, Supreme Court Bldg., Springfield, IL 62706. TEL 217-782-7770. FAX 217-785-9114. stat.; circ. 1,500. **Indexed:** SRI. **Key Title:** Annual Report to the Supreme Court of Illinois.
Description: Provides narrative and statistical summaries of what happened in the Illinois judicial system during the calendar year.

LAW

340 US
ILLINOIS. LEGISLATIVE REFERENCE BUREAU. LEGISLATIVE SYNOPSIS AND DIGEST. 1913. w. (during sessions, approx. Feb.-June). $55. Legislative Reference Bureau, Rm. 112, Statehouse, Springfield, IL 62706. TEL 217-782-6625. Ed. Kathleen H. Kenyon. index; circ. 1,800.

340 US
ILLINOIS ATTORNEY GENERAL'S REPORT AND OPINIONS. 1872. irreg., latest 1984. Attorney General, 500 S. Second St., Springfield, IL 62706. TEL 217-782-1090. index; circ. 1,400. (back issues avail.)

340 US ISSN 0019-1876
K9
ILLINOIS BAR JOURNAL. 1931. m. $60 to non-lawyers; $50 to law libraries. Illinois State Bar Association, Illinois Bar Center, Springfield, IL 62701. TEL 217-525-1760. Ed. Mark S. Mathewson. adv.; charts; illus.; index; circ. 30,000. (also avail. in microfiche from WSH; microfilm from WSH,PMC) **Indexed:** C.L.I., HRIS, L.R.I., Law Ofc.Info.Svc., Leg.Per.
—BLDSC shelfmark: 4364.980000.
Description: Articles on new laws, recent court decisions, and developments in the law profession. Includes news of the association's activities.

340 US ISSN 0019-1957
ILLINOIS COURTS BULLETIN. 1955. m. $35 to non-members; members $25. Illinois State Bar Association, Illinois Bar Center, Springfield, IL 62701. TEL 217-525-1760. Ed. Dennis A. Rendleman. bk.rev.; circ. 2,700.
Description: Digest of opinions of the Illinois Supreme Court, Apellate Courts, and Courts of Appeal.

340 US
▼**ILLINOIS ENVIRONMENTAL LAW LETTER.** 1992. 12/yr. $137. M. Lee Smith Publishers & Printers, 162 4th Ave. N., Box 2678, Nashville, TN 37219. TEL 615-242-7385. FAX 615-256-6601. Eds. Sanford Stein, Pat Fleischauer.
Description: Reports the latest developments in Illinois environmental laws.

ILLINOIS FARMWEEK. see AGRICULTURE

340 US
ILLINOIS LEGAL TIMES. 1987. m. $48. Giant Steps Publishing Corporation, 420 W. Grand Ave., Chicago, IL 60610. TEL 312-644-4378. FAX 312-644-0765. Ed. Charles H. Carman. adv.; bk.rev.; circ. 14,307. (tabloid format)
●Also available online. Vendor(s): WESTLAW.
Description: Contains news and analysis of law business for Illinois lawyers and other legal professionals.

340 US
ILLINOIS LIMITATIONS MANUAL. 1989. base vol. (plus suppl.), 2nd ed. $50. Butterworth Legal Publishers (Salem) (Subsidiary of: Reed International PLC), 90 Stiles Rd., Salem, NH 03079. TEL 800-548-4001. FAX 603-898-9858. Ed.Bd. (looseleaf format)

340 US
ILLINOIS STATE BAR ASSOCIATION. LEGISLATIVE BULLETIN. irreg. during Assembly session. $20 to non-members; members $10. Illinois State Bar Association, Illinois Bar Center, Springfield, IL 62701. TEL 217-525-1760.
Description: Digests of recent legislative action on bills of interest to lawyers.

340 US
ILLINOIS TORT LAW. 1986. base vol. (plus suppl.). $120. Butterworth Legal Publishers (Salem) (Subsidiary of: Reed International PLC), 90 Stiles Rd., Salem, NH 03079. TEL 800-548-4001. FAX 603-898-9858. Eds. Bruce L. Ottley, Michael J. Polelle.

340 US
▼**ILLINOIS TRIALS**; law and strategy. 1990. base vol. (plus irreg. suppl.). $88. Butterworth Legal Publishers (Salem) (Subsidiary of: Reed International PLC), 90 Stiles Rd., Salem, NY 03079. TEL 800-548-4001. FAX 603-898-4001. Ed. Jenneth L. Gillis. (looseleaf format)

IMPACT (WASHINGTON). see TRANSPORTATION — Automobiles

347.91 CN
IMPAIRED DRIVING & BREATHALYZER LAW. (Supplement avail.: Monthly Newsletter) s-a. Can.$160. Butterworths Canada Ltd., 75 Clegg Rd., Markham, Ont. L6G 1A1, Canada. TEL 416-479-2665. FAX 416-479-2826. Ed. K.R. Hamilton. (looseleaf format)
Description: Reference to statutes and case law.

IN DEPTH (NEW YORK); report to management. see BUSINESS AND ECONOMICS — Labor And Industrial Relations

IN DEPTH (WASHINGTON). see POLITICAL SCIENCE — International Relations

340 IT
IN IURE PRAESENTIA. 1975. s-a. L.55000 (foreign L.83000). Casa Editrice Dott. A. Giuffre, Via Busto Arsizio 40, 20151 Milan, Italy. TEL 02-38000905. FAX 02-38009582.

INCOME TAXATION OF NATURAL RESOURCES. see BUSINESS AND ECONOMICS — Public Finance, Taxation

340 CE ISSN 0073-5728
INCORPORATED LAW SOCIETY OF SRI LANKA. ANNUAL REPORT.* 1960. a. Incorporated Law Society of Sri Lanka, 129-5 Hultsdorf St., Colombo 12, Sri Lanka.

340 CE ISSN 0073-5736
INCORPORATED LAW SOCIETY OF SRI LANKA. JOURNAL.* irreg. Incorporated Law Society of Sri Lanka, 129-5 Hultsdorf St., Colombo 12, Sri Lanka.

INDEPENDENT POWER REPORT. see ENERGY

340 UK ISSN 0265-2501
INDEPENDENT SOLICITOR.* 1968. s-a. £0.75 per no. to individuals; free to qualified personnel. British Legal Association, 56 Wind St., Swansea SA1 1EG, England. Ed. Stanley Best. adv.; bk.rev.
Formerly: B L A Solicitor.

INDEX - DIGEST BULLETIN. see BUSINESS AND ECONOMICS — Public Finance, Taxation

340 CN ISSN 0701-760X
INDEX OF CURRENT B C REGULATIONS. 1958. 2/yr. Can.$13. Ministry of Attorney General, Parliament Bldgs., Victoria, B.C. V8V 1X4, Canada. (Subscr. to: Crown Publications, 546 Yates St., Victoria, B.C. V8W 1K8, Canada. TEL 604-386-4636)

348.54 II
INDIA. SUPREME COURT. UNREPORTED JUDGMENTS. (Text in English) 1969. s-m. Rs.45. Supreme Court, Jodhpur, High Court Rd., Jodhpur, Rajasthan, India. Ed. Dharm Veer Kalia. adv.; index; circ. 3,000.

349 II ISSN 0019-4301
INDIAN ADVOCATE. (Text in English) 1961. q. Rs.15($5.50) Bar Association of India, Chamber No. 93, Supreme Court Building, Tilak Marg, New Delhi 110001, India. Ed. C. K. Daphtary. adv.; bk.rev.; circ. 2,000. **Indexed:** P.A.I.S.

340 II
INDIAN BAR REVIEW. (Text in English) 1974. q. $25. Bar Council of India, AB-21, Lal Bahadur Shastri Marg, Facing Supreme Court Bldg., New Delhi 110001, India. bk.rev.; circ. 1,500. **Indexed:** C.L.I., Leg.Per.
Formerly (until Jan. 1983): Bar Council of India. Journal.

349 II ISSN 0019-5731
INDIAN LAW INSTITUTE. JOURNAL. (Text in English) 1958. q. Rs.300. Indian Law Institute, Bhagwandas Rd., New Delhi 110001, India. Ed. Dr. Upendra Baxi. bk.rev. (also avail. in microform from UMI; reprint service avail. from UMI) **Indexed:** P.A.I.S.
—BLDSC shelfmark: 4766.300000.

340 917.306 US ISSN 0097-1154
KF8201.A3
INDIAN LAW REPORTER. 1974. m. $396. American Indian Lawyer Training Program, Inc., 319 MacArthur Blvd., Oakland, CA 94610. TEL 510-834-9333. FAX 510-834-3836. Ed. Patricia M. Zell. abstr.; index; circ. 650. (looseleaf format; also avail. in microform from WSH; back issues avail.; reprint service avail. from WSH) **Indexed:** C.L.I., HR Rep.
Description: Comprehensive case reporting service that collects, reports and summarizes all current developments in Indian law from federal, tribal, and state courts as well as administrative agencies.

342 II
INDIAN LAW REPORTS. (Text in English) m. Rs.120($43.20) Ministry of Urban Development, Department of Publication, Controller of Publications, Civil Lines, Delhi 110 054, India. TEL 11-2512527.

340 614.7 US ISSN 1053-6183
▼**INDIANA ENVIRONMENTAL LAW LETTER.** 1991. 12/yr. $147. M. Lee Smith Publishers & Printers, 162 Fourth Ave. N., Box 2678, Nashville, TN 37219. TEL 615-242-7395. FAX 615-256-6601. (Co-sponsor: Barnes & Thornburg) Ed. John M. Kyle, III.
Description: Reports the latest Indiana environmental law developments that affect Indiana companies.

340 US ISSN 0019-6665
K9
INDIANA LAW JOURNAL. 1926. q. $25 (foreign $29). Indiana University, School of Law, Law Building, Bloomington, IN 47405. TEL 812-855-5175. FAX 812-855-7099. adv.; bk.rev.; bibl.; index, cum.index: vols.1-27, 1926-1952; vols.28-36, 1952-1961; circ. 1,165. (also avail. in microfiche from WSH; microfilm from RRI,WSH; reprint service avail. from RRI) **Indexed:** Account.Ind. (1974-), C.L.I., Curr.Cont., L.R.I., Leg.Cont., Leg.Per., SSCI.
●Also available online. Vendor(s): Mead Data Central, WESTLAW.
—BLDSC shelfmark: 4431.750000.

340 ISSN 0046-9106
INDIANA LAW REVIEW. 1967. q. $15. (Indiana University, School of Law-Indianapolis) West Publishing Co., Box 64526, St. Paul, MN 55164-0526. TEL 800-328-9352. Ed. Mark Wenzel. adv.; bk.rev.; index; circ. 2,000. (also avail. in microfiche from WSH; microfilm from RRI,WSH; reprint service avail. from RRI) **Indexed:** C.L.I., L.R.I., Lang.& Lang.Behav.Abstr., Leg.Cont., Leg.Per.
●Also available online. Vendor(s): WESTLAW.
Formerly: Indiana Legal Forum.

340 628.53 US
INDOOR POLLUTION LAW REPORTER. m. $185. New York Law Publishing Co., 111 Eighth Ave., New York, NY 10011. TEL 212-741-8300.
Description: Covers pollution issues such as preventative measures, latest technologies, government regulations and litigation alternatives. For those involved in real estate and environmental areas.

340 628.53 US ISSN 1053-024X
KF3812.A53
▼**INDOOR POLLUTION LITIGATION REPORTER.** 1990. m. $600. Andrews Publications, 1646 West Chester Pike, Box 1000, Westtown, PA 19395. TEL 215-399-6600. FAX 215-399-6610. Ed. Jay Steinberg. bibl.; stat.; s-a. cum.index. (looseleaf format; back issues avail.)
Description: Records verdicts, settlements, appeals and decisions in indoor pollution litigation: radon, asbestos, lead, ETS, and formaldehyde; includes personal injury.

INDOOR POLLUTION NEWS. see CONSERVATION

INDUSTRIAL ACCIDENT LAW BULLETIN. see OCCUPATIONAL HEALTH AND SAFETY

INDUSTRIAL HEALTH & HAZARDS UPDATE. see PUBLIC HEALTH AND SAFETY

INDUSTRIAL HEALTH FOUNDATION. LEGAL SERIES BULLETINS. see OCCUPATIONAL HEALTH AND SAFETY

INDUSTRIAL RELATIONS LAW REPORTS. see BUSINESS AND ECONOMICS — Labor And Industrial Relations

INDUSTRIAL RELATIONS LEGAL INFORMATION BULLETIN. see *BUSINESS AND ECONOMICS — Labor And Industrial Relations*

INFANCIA E JUVENTUDE. see *SOCIAL SERVICES AND WELFARE*

INFANCIA Y SOCIEDAD. see *CHILDREN AND YOUTH — About*

340   CU
INFORMACION JURIDICA. 1975. irreg. Fiscalia General de la Republica, San Rafael 3, Havana, Cuba. illus.

INFORMATICA E DIRITTO. see *LIBRARY AND INFORMATION SCIENCES*

340   NE   ISSN 0920-3745
INFORMATIERECHT. 1977. s-m. fl.85. Uitgeverij Kluwer BV, Postbus 23, 7400 GA Deventer, Netherlands. Ed.Bd. circ. 800.

340   FR
INFORMATIONS SPECIALES. w. Documentation Organique, 11, rue de Teheran, 75008 Paris, France. TEL 45-62-54-35.

INFORMATIVO JURIDICO. see *INSURANCE*

340   323.4   PE
INFORMATIVO LEGAL RODRIGO. 1961. m. $200. Asesores Financieros S.A., Jr. Pachacutec 1133, Jesus Maria, Lima, Peru. FAX 637300. TELEX 25622 PE LUCARO. bk.rev.; circ. 570. (back issues avail.)
    Description: Publishes legal rules with summarized ordered references in chronological and thematical order. Also offers sections of judicial reports and comments on judgements.

INITIAL DECISIONS AND BOARD OPINIONS AND ORDERS IN SAFETY. see *TRANSPORTATION — Air Transport*

340   US   ISSN 0020-1391
INJURY VALUATION REPORTS AND SPECIAL RESEARCH REPORTS. (Supplement to: Personal Injury Valuation Handbooks) 1959. m. $29.50 per no. Jury Verdict Research, Inc., 30700 Bainbridge Rd., Ste. H, Solon, OH 44139. TEL 800-321-6910. TELEX 216-349-JURY. Ed. Virginia M. Hermann. charts; pat.; tr.mk. (looseleaf format)
    Description: Articles on injuries and liability in personal damage litigation. Includes diagrams and graphs.

INQUIRY & ANALYSIS. see *EDUCATION*

340   US   ISSN 0890-7315
KF8911.A3
INSIDE LITIGATION. 1986. m. $325. Prentice Hall Law & Business, 270 Sylvan Ave., Englewood Cliffs, NJ 07632. TEL 201-894-8538. FAX 201-894-8666. Ed. J. Stratton Shartel. index. (back issues avail.)

344.022   US   ISSN 0884-4925
KF1147
INSIGHT (CHATSWORTH). 1985. m. $240. N I L S Publishing Company, 21625 Prairie St., Box 2507, Chatsworth, CA 91311. TEL 818-998-8830. Eds. Deborah von Winckelmann, Chuck Welch.
    Description: Summarizes insurance legislation in all 50 states, with additional analysis of proposed insurance regulations.

340   UK   ISSN 0950-2645
INSOLVENCY INTELLIGENCE. 1988. 10/yr. £95($175) Longman Group UK Ltd., 21-27 Lamb's Conduit St., London WC1 3NJ, England. TEL 01-242-2548. FAX 01-831-8119. Eds. Steven Frieze, David Graham.

340   UK   ISSN 0267-0771
KD2142
INSOLVENCY LAW & PRACTICE. 1985. 6/yr. £110($180) Tolley Publishing Co. Ltd., Tolley House, 2 Addiscombe Rd., Croydon, Surrey CR9 5AF, England. Eds. Steve Hill, Shashi Rajani. adv.; bk.rev.; index. (back issues avail.)
    —BLDSC shelfmark: 4518.365000.
    Description: Covers all areas of insolvency law and practice.

340   FR
INSTITUT DE RECHERCHES JURIDIQUES, POLITIQUES ET SOCIALES DE STRASBOURG. FACULTE DE DROIT ET DE SCIENCE POLITIQUE. ANNALES. a. price varies. Editions Juridiques Associees, 26 rue Vercingetorix, 75014 Paris, France. TEL 1-43-35-01-67. FAX 43-20-07-42. TELEX EJA 203 918 F. (Co-sponsor: Librairie Generale de Droit et de Jurisprudence) (back issues avail.)

340   GW   ISSN 0073-8492
INSTITUT FUER OSTRECHT. STUDIEN. 1958. irreg. price varies. Deutscher Bundes-Verlag, 5300 Bonn, Germany. circ. 1,000.

342   CI   ISSN 0350-0365
INSTITUT ZA JAVNO UPRAVO. VESTNIK. (Text in Slovenian; table of contents in English) 1961. q. 2,500 din.($15) Institut za Javno Upravo - Institute of Public Administration, Trg Osvoboditve 11, P.O. Box 469, 61001 Ljubljana, Slovenia. TEL 061 331-855. (Co-sponsor: Republic Secretatiat for Science, Research and Technology) Ed. Rupko Godec. bk.rev.; abstr.; bibl.; charts; circ. 500. (back issues avail.)

INSTITUTE OF PATENT ATTORNEYS OF AUSTRALIA. ANNUAL PROCEEDINGS. see *PATENTS, TRADEMARKS AND COPYRIGHTS*

INSTITUTE ON ADVANCED TAX PLANNING FOR REAL PROPERTY TRANSACTIONS. see *BUSINESS AND ECONOMICS — Public Finance, Taxation*

INSTITUTE ON OIL AND GAS LAW AND TAXATION. PROCEEDINGS. see *PETROLEUM AND GAS*

340   333.33   US   ISSN 0730-3009
KF5692.A5
INSTITUTE ON PLANNING, ZONING AND EMINENT DOMAIN. PROCEEDINGS. 1971. a. $85. Southwestern Legal Foundation, c/o Carol Holgren, Box 830707, Richardson, TX 75083. TEL 214-690-2370. index. (also avail. in microfilm from RRI; back issues avail.; reprint service avail. from RRI) Indexed: C.L.I., Leg.Per.
    Formed by the merger of: Institute on Planning and Zoning. Proceedings; Institute on Eminent Domain. Proceedings.

340   SP
INSTITUTO DE CIENCIAS PARA LA FAMILIA. 1982. irreg., no.5, 1986. price varies. (Universidad de Navarra, Facultad de Derecho) Ediciones Universidad de Navarra, S.A., Apdo. 396, 31080 Pamplona, Spain. TEL 94 825 6850.
    Formerly: Division Interdisciplinar para la Familia.

349   VE   ISSN 0020-3823
INSTITUTO DE DERECHO PRIVADO. BOLETIN. 1966. s-a. Bs.12 per no. Universidad Central de Venezuela, Instituto de Derecho Privado, Departamento de Distribucion de Publicaciones, Edificio de la Biblioteca Central, Apdo. 47004, Caracas 1041, Venezuela. bk.rev.; abstr.; bibl.; circ. 2,000.

340   SP
INSTITUTO DE ESTUDIOS TARRACONENSES RAMON BERENGUER IV. SECCION DE ESTUDIOS JURIDICOS. PUBLICACION. (Text in Catalan or Spanish) 1972. irreg. Instituto de Estudios Tarraconenses Ramon Berenguer IV, Calle Santa Ana 8, Tarragona, Spain.

340   VE
INSTITUTO DE FILOSOFIA DEL DERECHO. BOLETIN INFORMATIVO. 1973. biennial. free. (Universidad del Zulia, Faculdade de Derecho) Ediluz, Apdo. 526, Maracaibo 72687, Venezuela. TELEX 64287. circ. 1,000.

340   BL
INSTITUTO DOS ADVOGADOS DE S. PAULO. REVISTA. 1985. s-a. (Instituto dos Advogados de Sao Paulo) Editora Resenha Tributaria, Rue Xavier de Toledo 210, Sao Paulo, Brazil.
    Supersedes (1976-19??): Analise Jurisprudencial.

INSTITUTO INTERAMERICANO DEL NINO. JURIDICO SOCIAL. INFORMES TECNICOS. see *SOCIOLOGY*

340   BL
INSTITUTO NACIONAL DE COLONIZACAO E REFORMA AGRARIA. PROCURADORIA GERAL. BOLETIM. PARECERES. 1972. s-a. free. Instituto Nacional de Colonizacao e Reforma Agraria, Procuradoria Geral, Palacio do Desenvolvimento, 21 andar, Setor Bancario Norte, CEP 70437-Brasilia D.F., Brazil. Eds. Agnaldo Jurandyr Silva, Eliene Rodriques da Costa Maia. circ. 800.

INSTITUTO NACIONAL DE MEDICINA LEGAL DE COLOMBIA. REVISTA. see *MEDICAL SCIENCES — Forensic Sciences*

INSTITUTO PERUANO DE DERECHO AGRARIO. CUADERNOS AGRARIOS. see *AGRICULTURE*

340   CN
INSURANCE CASE LAW DIGEST. q. Can.$450. Butterworths Canada Ltd., 75 Clegg Rd., Markham, Ont. L6G 1A1, Canada. TEL 416-479-2665. FAX 416-479-2826. Ed. John Newcombe. (looseleaf format)
    Description: Complete coverage of automobile and property insurance cases in Canada.

340   US   ISSN 0887-7858
KF1159
INSURANCE INDUSTRY LITIGATION REPORTER; the national journal of record for insurance litigation. 1985. s-m. $800. Andrews Publications, 1646 West Chester Pike, Box 1000, Westtown, PA 19395. TEL 215-399-6600. FAX 215-399-6610. Ed. Maureen H. McGuire. abstr.; bibl.; stat.; cum.index every 6 mos. (looseleaf format; back issues avail.)

340   368   UK   ISSN 0962-1385
▼**INSURANCE LAW & PRACTICE.** 1991. 4/yr. £90($145) Tolley Publishing Co. Ltd., Tolley House, 2 Addiscombe Rd., Croydon, Surrey CR9 5AF, England. Eds. Andrew McGee, Ray Hodgin. adv.; bk.rev.
    —BLDSC shelfmark: 4531.719500.
    Description: Covers all aspects of insurance law and practice.

INSURANCE LAW ANTHOLOGY. see *INSURANCE*

340   368   US
INSURANCE LAW CITATIONS. 6 base vols. (plus q. suppl.). $660. Shepard's - McGraw-Hill, Inc., Box 35300, Colorado Springs, CO 80935-3530. TEL 800-525-2474.
    Description: Lists insurance law cases, with citations to cases decided by the U.S. Supreme Court, lower federal courts and state courts.

340   368   AT   ISSN 1030-2379
K9
INSURANCE LAW JOURNAL. 1988. 3/yr. Aus.$115. Butterworths Pty. Ltd., 271-273 Lane Cove Rd., North Ryde, N.S.W. 2113, Australia. TEL 02-335-4444. FAX 02-335-4655. Ed. A.A. Tarr. bk.rev. Indexed: C.L.I.

INSURANCE LAW REPORTS: FIRE & CASUALTY. see *INSURANCE*

INSURANCE LAW REPORTS: LIFE, HEALTH & ACCIDENT. see *INSURANCE*

368   US   ISSN 0195-1858
KF1159
INSURANCE LITIGATION REPORTER; recent decisions of national significance. 1978. m. $320. (Litigation Research Group) Shepard's - McGraw-Hill, Inc., Box 35300, Colorado Springs, CO 80935-3530. Ed. John K. DiMugno. bibl.; index. (looseleaf format; back issues avail.) Indexed: BPIA.
    Description: Analyzes trends and summarizes recent litigation affecting insurance law.

346.086 368.014   US   ISSN 1052-7249
K9
INSURANCE SETTLEMENTS JOURNAL. 1988. q. $95. James Publishing Group, Inc., 3520 Cadillac Ave., Ste. E, Costa Mesa, CA 92626. TEL 714-755-5450. FAX 714-549-8835. Eds. Joan Manno, Stuart Ogilvie. circ. 1,400.

LAW

340   PH   ISSN 0115-138X
K9
INTEGRATED BAR OF THE PHILIPPINES. JOURNAL. (Text in English) 1973. q. $32. Integrated Bar of the Philippines, Dona Julia Vargas Ave., Ortigas Office Bldg. Complex, Pasig, Metro Manila, Philippines. FAX 631-3014. Ed. Beda G. Fajardo. adv.; bk.rev.; circ. 30,000. **Indexed:** Ind.Phil.Per.
—BLDSC shelfmark: 4802.062000.

340 608.7   CN   ISSN 0824-7064
K9
INTELLECTUAL PROPERTY JOURNAL. (Text in English, French) 1984. 3/yr. (plus bound vol.). Can.$128($102) Carswell Publications, Corporate Plaza, 2075 Kennedy Rd., Scarborough, Ont. M1T 3V4, Canada. TEL 416-609-8000. FAX 416-298-5094. Ed. David Vaver. adv.; bk.rev.; circ. 450. **Indexed:** C.L.I., Ind.Can.L.P.L.
—BLDSC shelfmark: 4531.823800.
Description: Covers matters of interest relating to parents, trademarks, copyright, designs, trade secrets, and competitive torts.

340   AT   ISSN 1034-3032
INTELLECTUAL PROPERTY JOURNAL. q. Aus.$210. Law Book Co. Ltd., 44-50 Waterloo Rd., North Ryde, N.S.W. 2113, Australia. TEL 02-887-0177. FAX 02-888-9706. TELEX ASBOOK 27995. Ed. Ann Dufty.
Description: Discusses the developments in intellectual property law in Australia.

340   US   ISSN 0892-2365
K9   CODEN: IPLAEG
INTELLECTUAL PROPERTY LAW. 4/yr. (in 1 vol., 4 nos./vol.). $111. Harwood Academic Publishers, 270 Eighth Ave., New York, NY 10011. TEL 212-206-8900. FAX 212-645-2459. TELEX 236735 GOPUB UR. (Subscr. to: Box 786, Cooper Sta., NY 10276. TEL 800-545-8398; UK subscr. to: P.O. Box 90, Reading, Berkshire RG1 8JI, England. TEL 0734-560-080) Eds. Allam S. Melser, David C. Gryce. (also avail. in microform)
—BLDSC shelfmark: 4531.823900.
Refereed Serial

340   AT   ISSN 0812-2024
INTELLECTUAL PROPERTY REPORTS. 1984. m. Aus.$125. Butterworths Pty. Ltd., P.O. Box 345, North Ryde, N.S.W. 2113, Australia. TEL 02-335-4444. FAX 02-335-4655.

340   US   ISSN 0092-6086
K14
INTER ALIA. 1936. q. $15. State Bar of Nevada, 295 Holcomb Ave., Ste. 2, Reno, NV 89502. TEL 703-329-4100. FAX 702-329-0522. Ed. Christine Cendagorta. adv.; bk.rev.; circ. 3,400. (also avail. in microform from UMI; reprint service avail. from UMI) **Indexed:** C.L.I., L.R.I., Law Ofc.Info.Svc., Leg.Per.
Formerly: Nevada State Bar Journal (ISSN 0028-4092)

340   CN
INTER-AMERICAN ARBITRATION. (Text in English, French, Spanish) 1981. q. Can.$10. Canadian Arbitration, Conciliation and Amicable Composition Centre, Inc., c/o Civil Law Section, University of Ottawa, Ottawa, Ont. K1N 6N5, Canada. TEL 613-232-1476. FAX 613-564-9800. TELEX 0533338. Ed. L. Kos Rabcewicz-Zubkowski. bk.rev.; circ. 400. (back issues avail.)

340   US
INTER-AMERICAN BAR ASSOCIATION. CONFERENCE PROCEEDINGS.* 1941. biennial. $30. Inter-American Bar Association, 815 15th St., N.W., Ste. 921, Washington, DC 20005-2201. TEL 202-789-2747. FAX 202-842-2608.
Description: Papers presented during the biennial conference of the association.

340   US
INTER-AMERICAN BAR ASSOCIATION. LETTER TO MEMBERS.* (Text in English and Spanish) 1961. q. $6. Inter-American Bar Association, 815 15th St., N.W., Ste. 921, Washington, DC 20005-2201. TEL 202-789-2747. FAX 202-842-2608. Ed. Grover Prevatte Hopkins. circ. 3,000. (processed)

340   US
INTERNATIONAL ACADEMY OF TRIAL LAWYERS. JOURNAL. 1959. 3/yr. free. International Academy of Trial Lawyers, 4 N.S. Second St., No. 175, San Jose, CA 95113. TEL 408-275-6767. FAX 408-275-6874. Ed. Barbara V. Laskin. circ. 700.
Formerly: International Academy of Trial Lawyers. Bulletin.

340   BE   ISSN 0074-1604
INTERNATIONAL ASSOCIATION OF DEMOCRATIC LAWYERS. CONGRESS REPORT. quadrennial, 12th, 1984, Athens. International Association of Democratic Lawyers, 263 av. Albert, 1180 Brussels, Belgium.

340   IS
INTERNATIONAL ASSOCIATION OF JEWISH LAWYERS AND JURISTS. BULLETIN. (Text in English) a. International Association of Jewish Lawyers and Jurists, 10 Daniel Frish St., Tel Aviv, Israel.

340 539   UN   ISSN 0074-1868
INTERNATIONAL ATOMIC ENERGY AGENCY. LEGAL SERIES. (Text in English) 1959. irreg. price varies. International Atomic Energy Agency, Wagramer Str. 5, Box 100, A-1400 Vienna, Austria. (Dist. in U.S. by: Unipub, 4611-F Assembly Dr., Lanham, MD 20706-4391)

INTERNATIONAL COMPUTER LAW ADVISER; a monthly research report on the international law of computers, telecommunications & information. see COMPUTERS

INTERNATIONAL CONFERENCE OF INSURANCE REGULATORY OFFICIALS. PROCEEDINGS. see INSURANCE

340   IS
INTERNATIONAL CONGRESS OF COMPARATIVE LAW. ISRAEL REPORTS. (Text in English) quadrennial. IS.50($35) P.O. Box 24100, Mt. Scopus, Jerusalem, Israel.

INTERNATIONAL DIGEST OF HEALTH LEGISLATION. see PUBLIC HEALTH AND SAFETY

340 410   UK   ISSN 0952-8059
INTERNATIONAL JOURNAL FOR THE SEMIOTICS OF LAW; semiotic, linguistic, discursive approach to law. 1988. 3/yr. £51. (International Association for the Semiotics of Law) Deborah Charles Publications, 173 Mather Ave., Liverpool LI8 6JZ, England. TEL 051-724-2500. (Distr. in US by: William Gaunt & Sons, Inc., 3011 Gulf Dr., Holmes Beach, FL 34217-2199) Ed. E. Landowski. adv.; bk.rev.; circ. 400.
—BLDSC shelfmark: 4542.544670.

341   II   ISSN 0020-7098
INTERNATIONAL JOURNAL OF ARBITRATION. 1970. 3/yr. Rs.100($20) K.K. Roy (Private) Ltd., 55 Gariahat Rd., P.O. Box 10210, Calcutta 700 019, India. Ed. K.K. Roy. adv.; bk.rev.; abstr.; bibl.; index; circ. 500. (tabloid format)

340 616.8   US   ISSN 0160-2527
K9
INTERNATIONAL JOURNAL OF LAW AND PSYCHIATRY. 1978. q. £160 (effective 1992). Pergamon Press, Inc., Journals Division, 660 White Plains Rd., Tarrytown, NY 10591-5153. TEL 914-524-9200. FAX 914-333-2444. (And: Headington Hill Hall, Oxford OX3 0BW, England. TEL 0865-794141) Ed. D.N. Weisstub. adv.; circ. 1,100. (also avail. in microform from MIM,UMI; reprint service avail. from UMI) **Indexed:** Adol.Ment.Hlth.Abstr., Amer.Bibl.Slavic & E.Eur.Stud, C.C.L.P., C.L.I., Crim.Just.Abstr., Curr.Cont., Excerp.Med., Ind.Med., L.R.I., Lang.& Lang.Behav.Abstr., Leg.Cont., Leg.Per., Psychol.Abstr., SSCI.
—BLDSC shelfmark: 4542.312500.
Refereed Serial

INTERNATIONAL JOURNAL OF LEGAL INFORMATION. see LIBRARY AND INFORMATION SCIENCES

340   UK   ISSN 0194-6595
K9
INTERNATIONAL JOURNAL OF THE SOCIOLOGY OF LAW. 1972. q. $142 to individuals; institutions £72($134). Academic Press Ltd., 24-28 Oval Rd., London NW1 7DX, England. TEL 071-267-4466. FAX 071-482-2293. TELEX 25775 ACPRES G. (Subscr. to: Academic Press Ltd., Foots Cray, Sidcup, Kent DA14 5HP, England) Eds. S. Picciotto, C. Smart. bk.rev. (back issues avail.) **Indexed:** ASSIA, C.L.I., CJPI, Crim.Just.Abstr., L.R.I., Lang.& Lang.Behav.Abstr., Leg.Per., Psychol.Abstr., Soc.Sci.Ind., Sociol.Abstr. (1979-), SSCI.
—BLDSC shelfmark: 4542.574000.
Formerly (until vol.7, 1979): International Journal of Criminology and Penology (ISSN 0306-3208)
Description: Theoretical and empirical studies of law as a social process with an international perspective.

347.9   NE
INTERNATIONAL LABOUR LAW REPORTS. 1978. a. price varies. Kluwer Academic Publishers, Postbus 17, 3300 AA Dordrecht, Netherlands. TEL 078-334911. FAX 078-334254. TELEX 29245. (Dist. by: Kluwer Academic Publishers Group, P.O. Box 322, 3300 AH Dordrecht, Netherlands; US addr.: P.O. Box 358, Accord Station, Hingham, MA 02018-0358) Ed.Bd.

INTERNATIONAL LABOUR OFFICE. LABOUR LAW DOCUMENTS. see BUSINESS AND ECONOMICS — Labor And Industrial Relations

INTERNATIONAL LAW REPORTS. see LAW — International Law

340   US   ISSN 0738-9728
K120.A2
INTERNATIONAL LAWYERS' NEWSLETTER; a private network of practical international news. 1979. bi-m. $90. Kluwer Law and Taxation Publishers, 6 Bigelow St., Cambridge, MA 02139. TEL 617-354-0140. FAX 617-354-8595. Eds. Carol A. Emory, Arthur G. Kroos. bk.rev.; circ. 1,000.

INTERNATIONAL MONETARY AGREEMENTS ACTS. ANNUAL REPORT. see BUSINESS AND ECONOMICS — Banking And Finance

340   CN   ISSN 0229-2181
INTERNATIONAL OMBUDSMAN INSTITUTE. NEWSLETTER. 1974. 6/yr. $10. International Ombudsman Institute, Faculty of Law, University of Alberta, Edmonton, Alta. T6G 2H5, Canada. TEL 403-492-3196. **Indexed:** HR Rep.

340   CN
INTERNATIONAL OMBUDSMAN INSTITUTE. OCCASIONAL PAPER SERIES. 6/yr. $8 per no. International Ombudsman Institute, Faculty of Law, University of Alberta, Edmonton, Alta. T6G 2H5, Canada. TEL 403-492-3196. **Indexed:** HR Rep.

340   BE   ISSN 0048-7473
INTERNATIONAL REVIEW OF CONTEMPORARY LAW. French edition: Revue Internationale de Droit Contemporain. (None published 1970-1975) (Editions in English, French) 1954. s-a. 600 Fr.($15) International Association of Democratic Lawyers, 263 av. Albert, 1180 Brussels, Belgium. **Indexed:** HR Rep.

340 330   US   ISSN 0144-8188
K9   CODEN: IRLEE8
INTERNATIONAL REVIEW OF LAW AND ECONOMICS. 1981. 4/yr. $150 (foreign $185). Butterworth - Heinemann Ltd. (Subsidiary of: Reed International PLC), 80 Montvale Ave., Stoneham, MA 02180. TEL 617-438-8464. FAX 617-438-1479. TELEX 880052. Ed.Bd. bk.rev.; index. (also avail. in microform from UMI; back issues avail.) **Indexed:** C.L.I., C.R.E.J., J.of Econ.Lit., L.R.I., Leg.Per., P.A.I.S.
—BLDSC shelfmark: 4547.330000.
Description: Research on interface between economics and law including legal institutions, jurisprudence, legal history and political-legal theory.
Refereed Serial

340   US
INTERNATIONAL RIGHT OF WAY. bi-m. International Right of Way Association, 13650 S. Gramercy Place, Gardena, CA 90249-2465. TEL 213-538-0233. FAX 213-538-1471. Ed. David M. Roman. circ. 9,000.

INTERNATIONAL STUDIES. see POLITICAL SCIENCE —
International Relations

342.085   NE   ISSN 0903-9961
INTERNATIONAL STUDIES. NORDIC SEMINAR ON HUMAN RIGHTS. PROCEEDINGS. (Text in English) irreg., no.4, 1989. (Danish Center of Human Rights) Martinus Nijhoff Publishers (Subsidiary of: Kluwer Academic Publishers Group), P.O. Box 163, 3300 AD Dordrecht, Netherlands. TEL 078-1728111. (Dist. by: Kluwer Academic Publishers Group, Box 322, 3300 AH Dordrecht, Netherlands; N. America dist. addr.: Kluwer Academic Publishers, Box 358, Accord Sta., Hingham, MA 02018-0358. TEL 617-871-6600) Eds. Lars Rehof, Claus Gulman.
—BLDSC shelfmark: 4549.787500.

340   AU
INTERNATIONALE GESELLSCHAFT FUER URHEBERRECHT. SCHRIFTENREIHE.* 1955. irreg., vol.61, 1984. price varies. (Internationale Gesellschaft fuer Urheberrecht e.V. - International Copyright Society) Nomos Verlagsgesellschaft mbH und Co. KG, Waldseestr. 3-5, Postfach 610, 7570 Baden-Baden, Germany. TEL 07221-20140. FAX 07221-210427.

INTERPRETER RELEASES; report and analysis of immigration and nationality law. see POPULATION STUDIES

340   US
INTERROGATORIES, DOCUMENTS AND ADMISSIONS. 1989. base vol. (plus a. suppl.). $70. Butterworth Legal Publishers (Salem) (Subsidiary of: Reed International PLC), 90 Stiles Rd., Salem, NH 03079. TEL 800-548-4001. FAX 603-898-9858. Ed. John Hardin Young. (looseleaf format)

INTERVENOR. see ENVIRONMENTAL STUDIES

340   US   ISSN 0578-6533
KF292.I614
IOWA ADVOCATE. s-a. University of Iowa, College of Law, Iowa City, IA 52240. TEL 319-335-9034. (Co-sponsor: Iowa Law School Foundation) illus.

340   US   ISSN 0021-0552
K9
IOWA LAW REVIEW. 1915. 5/yr. $25. University of Iowa, College of Law, Iowa City, IA 52242. TEL 319-335-9061. adv.; bk.rev.; charts; index, cum.index every 10 yrs.; circ. 1,575. (also avail. in microfilm from WSH; reprint service avail. from WSH) Indexed: Account.Ind. (1974-), C.L.I., Curr.Cont., L.R.I., Leg.Per., P.A.I.S., SSCI.
●Also available online. Vendor(s): WESTLAW.
—BLDSC shelfmark: 4566.300000.

340   US
IOWA PLEADING AND CAUSES OF ACTION. 1989. 2 base vols. (plus suppl.). $160. Butterworth Legal Publishers (Salem) (Subsidiary of: Reed International PLC), 90 Stiles Rd., Salem, NH 03079. TEL 800-548-4001. FAX 603-898-9858. Ed. George A. La Marca. (looseleaf format)

340   IE   ISSN 0791-5403
▼IRISH EUROPEAN LAW JOURNAL. 1992. a. I£45($70) The Round Hall Press, Kill Lane, Blackrock, Co. Dublin, Ireland. TEL 2892922. FAX 2893072. Ed. Noreen Mackey. circ. 300 (controlled).
Description: Articles, law reports and case references to the leading decisions of the courts on European Law.

340   IE   ISSN 0021-1273
IRISH JURIST. N.S. 1966. s-a. £25. Jurist Publishing Co., University College, Dublin 4, Ireland. Ed. W.N. Osborough. adv.; bk.rev.; abstr.; circ. 700. (also avail. in microfilm from BHP,RRI) Indexed: C.L.I., Leg.Per.
—BLDSC shelfmark: 4572.500000.

340 340   IE   ISSN 0332-3293
KDK63 1867.A2
▼IRISH LAW REPORTS MONTHLY. 1981. 12/yr. I£190($290) The Round Hall Press, Kill Lane, Blackrock, Dublin, Ireland. TEL 2892922. FAX 2893072. Ed. Bart D. Daly. index; circ. 750. (back issues avail.)
Description: Reports of judgments from the High and Superior Courts in Ireland.

340   IE   ISSN 0021-1281
LAW
IRISH LAW TIMES AND SOLICITORS' JOURNAL. 1867; N.S. 1983. m. I£105($165) The Round Hall Press, Kill Lane, Blackrock, Co. Dublin, Ireland. TEL 2892922. FAX 2893072. Ed. Bart D. Daly. adv.; bk.rev.; cum.index; circ. 1,000. (also avail. in microfiche from BHP)
Description: Reports on a wide range of legal areas. Includes a digest of cases delivered in the Irish Superior Courts.

340   US
▼IRREVOCABLE TRUSTS. 1992. base vol. (plus a. suppl.). $95. Shepard's - McGraw-Hill, Inc., Box 35300, Colorado Springs, CO 80935-3530. TEL 800-525-2474.
Description: Looks at the types of trusts used for estate planning. Examines the income tax implications of an irrevocable trust, involvement with the IRS, and the problems of calculating assets being transferred to the trustee.

340   UK
IS IT IN FORCE?. a. $56. Butterworth & Co. (Publishers) Ltd. (Subsidiary of: Reed International PLC), 88 Kingsway, London WC2B 6AB, England. TEL 71-405-6900. FAX 71-405-1332. TELEX 95678. (US addr.: Butterworth Legal Publishers, 90 Stiles Rd., Salem, NH 03079. TEL 800-548-4001)

340   IS   ISSN 0021-2237
LAW
ISRAEL LAW REVIEW. (Text in English) 1966. q. IS.80($36) Israel Law Review Association, c/o Hebrew University, Faculty of Law, P.O. Box 24100, Mount Scopus, Jerusalem 91240, Israel. TEL 02-882520. FAX 02-823042. Ed.Bd. adv.; bk.rev.; index; circ. 1,500. (also avail. in microfiche from WSH; microfilm from WSH) Indexed: Curr.Cont., Foreign Leg.Per., Lang.& Lang.Behav.Abstr., Leg.Cont., Leg.Per., Sociol.Abstr., SSCI.
—BLDSC shelfmark: 4583.820000.

ISRAEL YEARBOOK ON HUMAN RIGHTS. see POLITICAL SCIENCE — Civil Rights

340 610   US   ISSN 8756-8160
KF480.A15   CODEN: ILAME3
ISSUES IN LAW AND MEDICINE. 1985. q. $36. National Legal Center for the Medically Dependent and Disabled, Inc., Box 1586, Terre Haute, IN 47808-1586. TEL 812-232-0103. (Co-sponsors: Horatio R. Storer Foundation, Inc., American Academy of Medical Ethics, Inc.) Ed. James Bopp, Jr. bk.rev.; circ. 6,000. (back issues avail.) Indexed: C.L.I., Curr.Cont., Hlth.Ind., Hosp.Lit.Ind., Ind.Med., Int.Nurs.Ind., L.R.I., Leg.Per., Psychol.Abstr.
●Also available online. Vendor(s): National Library of Medicine, WESTLAW.
—BLDSC shelfmark: 4584.302000.

340   IT
ISTITUTO DI DIRITTO ROMANO. BOLLETTINO. (Text in various European Languages) 1888. a. price varies. Casa Editrice Dott. A. Giuffre, Via Busto Arsizio 40, Milan 20151, Italy. TEL 02-38000905. FAX 02-3809582. Ed. Marco Talamanca. adv.; bk.rev.; index; circ. 500.

340   IT   ISSN 0021-3241
IURA; rivista internazionale di diritto romano e antico. (Text in various languages) 1950. irreg. price varies. Casa Editrice Dott. Eugenio Jovene, 109 via Mezzocannone, Naples, Italy. Ed. Cesare Sanfilippo. bk.rev.
—BLDSC shelfmark: 4589.058000.

IUS ICCLESIAE; rivista internazionale di diritto canonico. see RELIGIONS AND THEOLOGY — Roman Catholic

340   IT   ISSN 0075-2037
IUS ROMANUM MEDII AEVI. (Text in English, French, German, Italian, Spanish) 1961. irreg. price varies. Casa Editrice Dott. A. Giuffre, Via Busto Arsizio 40, 20151 Milan, Italy. TEL 02-38000905. FAX 02-3809582.

349   IT   ISSN 0021-3268
IUSTITIA. 1948. q. L.40000 (foreign L.60000). (Unione Giuristi Cattolici Italiani) Casa Editrice Dott. A. Giuffre, Via Busto Arsizio 40, 20151 Milan, Italy. TEL 02-38000905. FAX 02-38009582. Ed. Sergio Cotta. adv.; bk.rev.; index; circ. 1,300. Indexed: CERDIC.

340   YU
IZVORI SRPSKOG PRAVA/SOURCES DE DROIT SERBE/SERBISCHE RECHTSQUELLEN. (Subseries of: Srpska Akademija Nauka i Umetnosti. Odeljenje Drustvenih Nauka) (Text in Serbian; summaries in English, French, German, Russian) 1967. irreg. Srpska Akademija Nauka i Umetnosti, Odeljenje Drustvenih Nauka, Knez Mihailova 35, 11001 Belgrade, Serbia, Yugoslavia. FAX 38-11-182-825. TELEX 72593 SANU YU. illus.

340   US
J A D NEWS. s-a. free. American Bar Association, Judicial Administration Division, 750 N. Lake Shore Dr., Chicago, IL 60611. TEL 312-988-5000. (tabloid format)

J.C.H.R. NEWS LETTER. (Jamaica Council of Human Rights) see POLITICAL SCIENCE — Civil Rights

349   IT   ISSN 0022-6955
K10
J U S; rivista di scienze giuridiche. 1940. 3/yr. L.130000($100) (effective 1992). (Universita Cattolica del Sacro Cuore) Vita e Pensiero, Largo Gemelli 1, 20123 Milan, Italy. TEL 02-8856310. FAX 02-8856260. TELEX 321033 UCATMI 1. Ed. Giorgio Berti. adv.; bk.rev.; bibl.; index.
Description: Covers political issues, looks at the contributions of debate within an institution and how this institution is faced by conflict within itself as well as socially.

349   SW   ISSN 1100-620X
J U S E K; tidningen. 1951. m. SEK 150. J U S E K - Foerbundet foer Jurister, Samhaellsvetare och Ekonomer - Swedish Federation of Jurists, Social Scientists and Economists, PO Box 5167, S-102 44 Stockholm, Sweden. FAX 08-6627923. Ed. Ann Marie Bergstroem. adv.; bk.rev.; charts; illus.; index; circ. 32,772.
Formerly (until Sep. 1979): J U S (ISSN 0022-6947)

340   II   ISSN 0448-1054
JABALPUR LAW JOURNAL. (Text in English) 1952. m. Rs.140. Law Journal Publications, Jayendraganj, Gwalior 474009, India. Ed. Harihar Nivas Dvivedi. adv.; bk.rev.; bibl.; circ. 2,683.

JAHRBUCH DES SOZIALRECHTS DER GEGENWART. see SOCIAL SERVICES AND WELFARE

340   GW   ISSN 0075-2746
K10
JAHRBUCH FUER OSTRECHT. (Issued in 2 parts) 1960. a. DM.48. (Institut fuer Ostrecht, Munich) Deutscher Bundes-Verlag, 5300 Bonn, Germany. Ed. Erhardt Gralla. circ. 750.

340   JM
JAMAICAN BAR ASSOCIATION. ANNUAL REPORT. a. Jamaican Bar Association, 11 Duke St., Kingston, Jamaica, W.I. TEL 922-2609.

340   II
JAMMU AND KASHMIR LAW REPORTER. (Text in English) 1970. m. Rs.30. High Court of Jammu and Kashmir, Srinagar, Jammu, India. Ed. Mufti Salah-Ud-Din Arshad. bibl.; circ. 475.

JAPAN BUSINESS LAW GUIDE. see BUSINESS AND ECONOMICS

JERSEY SIERRAN. see CONSERVATION

340 333.33   AT
JESSUP'S LAND TITLES OFFICE PRACTICE S.A.. 1989. 2/yr. Aus.$145. Law Book Co. Ltd., 44-50 Waterloo Rd., North Ryde, N.S.W 2113, Australia. TEL 02-887-0177. FAX 02-888-9706. TELEX ASBOOK-27995. Ed. R.J. White.
Description: Reflects the current practice of the Land Titles Office in S.A. to assist the conveyancer in matters which arise in the course of document preparation.

349   FR   ISSN 0021-6151
JEUNES AVOCATS.* 1963. 6 F. Union des Jeunes Avocats a la Cour de Paris, Palais de Justice, Paris, France. Ed. Jean-Paul Clement.

2638 LAW

340 296   US   ISSN 0276-1432
JEWISH JURISPRUDENCE SERIES. irreg. Harwood Academic Publishers, 270 Eighth Ave., New York, NY 10011. TEL 212-206-8900.
FAX 212-645-2459. TELEX 236735 GOPUB UR. (Subscr. to: Box 786, Cooper Sta., New York, NY 10276. TEL 800-545-8398; U.K. subscr. to: Box 90, Reading, Berkshire RG1 8JL, England. TEL 0734-560-080) Eds. E.B. Quint, N.S. Hecht. (also avail. in microform)
—BLDSC shelfmark: 4668.356000.
Refereed Serial

296   US   ISSN 0169-8354
K10
JEWISH LAW ANNUAL. (Supplement avail.) 1978. a. price varies. Harwood Academic Publishers, 270 Eighth Ave., New York, NY 10011.
TEL 212-206-8900. FAX 212-645-2459. TELEX 236735 GOPUB UR. (Subscr. to: Box 786, Cooper Sta., New York, NY 10276. TEL 800-545-8398; UK subscr. to: Box 90, Reading, Berkshire RG1 8JL, England. TEL 0734-560-080) Ed. Bernard S. Jackson. (also avail. in microform) **Indexed:** Old Test.Abstr.
Description: Presents research on laws in the Old Testament.
Refereed Serial

340   NE   ISSN 0169-8400
JEWISH LAW ANNUAL SUPPLEMENTS. (Supplement to: Jewish Law Annual) 1980. irreg., vol.2, 1980. price varies. E.J. Brill, P.O. Box 9000, 2300 PA Leiden, Netherlands. TEL 071-312624. FAX 071-317532. TELEX 39296 BRILL NL. (In N. America: E.J. Brill, 24 Hudson St., Kinderhook, NY 12106. TEL 800-962-4406) Ed. B.S. Jackson.

340 296   US   ISSN 1045-6015
JEWISH LAW IN CONTEXT. irreg. Harwood Academic Publishers, 270 Eighth Ave., New York, NY 10011. TEL 212-206-8900. FAX 212-645-2459. TELEX 236735 GOPUB UR. (Subscr. to: Box 786, Cooper Sta., New York, NY 10276. TEL 800-545-8398; U.K. subscr. to: Box 90, Reading, Berkshire RG1 8JL, England. TEL 0734-560-080) Ed. N.S. Hecht. (also avail. in microform)
Refereed Serial

340   CC
JIN DUN/GOLDEN SHIELD. (Text in Chinese) m. Jin Dun Zazhishe, No. 25, Dongjiao Minxiang, Beijing 100006, People's Republic of China. TEL 5128871. Ed. Ma Weidong.

340   HU
JOGASZ SZOVETSEGI ERTEKEZESEK. 1977. s-a. Magyar Jogasz Szovetseg, Szemere u.10, 1054 Budapest 5, Hungary. TEL 314-575. Ed. Laszlo Nagy.

349   HU   ISSN 0021-7166
JOGTUDOMANYI KOZLONY/LAW SCIENCES REVIEW. (Summaries in English, German, Russian) 1866. m. $38. Jogtudomanyi Koezloeny, Orszaghaz u. 30, Budapest 1014, Hungary. (Subscr. to: Kultura, Box 149, H-1389 Budapest, Hungary) Ed. Jozsef Halasz. bk.rev.; abstr.; circ. 2,500.
—BLDSC shelfmark: 4670.400000.

JOHN HOWARD SOCIETY OF ALBERTA REPORTER. see *CRIMINOLOGY AND LAW ENFORCEMENT*

340   US   ISSN 0270-854X
K10
JOHN MARSHALL LAW REVIEW. 1967. a. $18. (John Marshall Law School) Christensen Inc. (Chicago), 315 S. Plymouth Ct., Chicago, IL 60604.
TEL 312-987-1415. FAX 312-427-8307. Ed. Lance Peterson. adv.; bk.rev.; bibl.; charts; illus.; index; circ. 2,500. (also avail. in microform from UMI; reprint service avail. from RRI,UMI) **Indexed:** C.L.I., Crim.Just.Abstr., HRIS, L.R.I., Leg.Cont., Leg.Per.
●Also available online. Vendor(s): WESTLAW.
Formerly (until 1979): John Marshall Journal of Practice and Procedure (ISSN 0021-7212)

JORNADAS NACIONALES DE DERECHO AERONAUTICO Y ESPACIAL. TRABAJOS. see *TRANSPORTATION — Air Transport*

340   CN   ISSN 0833-921X
KEQ160
JOURNAL BARREAU; le journal de la communaute juridique. (Text in French) 1969. s-m. Barreau du Quebec, Maison du Barreau, 445 St-Laurent Blvd., Montreal, Que. H2Y 3T8, Canada.
TEL 514-954-3439. FAX 514-954-3451. Ed. Leon Bedard. adv.; bk.rev.; index; circ. 21,500. (tabloid format; back issues avail.)

343   BE
JOURNAL DE DROIT FISCAL. 1927. bi-m. 3200 Fr. Etablissements Emile Bruylant, 67 Rue de Regence, B-1000 Brussels, Belgium. TEL 02-512-9845. index; circ. 1,000.
Formed by the merger of: Journal Pratique de Droit Fiscal et Financier (ISSN 0022-5495); Revue Fiscale (ISSN 0035-2810) & Repertoire Fiscal.

340   BE
JOURNAL DES JUGES DE PAIX. (Text in Dutch, French) 1891. m. (except Jul.-Aug.). 3850 Fr. (4150Fr. outside the EC)(effective 1992). Union Royale des Juges de Paix, c/o M. Benoit, Rue Fransman, 89, 1020 Brussels, Belgium. FAX 050-39-37-68. adv.; bk.rev.

340   FR
JOURNAL DES NOTAIRES ET DES AVOCATS. 1808. bi-m. 800 F. 6, rue de Mezieres, 75006 Paris, France. adv.; circ. 7,900.

349   BE   ISSN 0021-812X
JOURNAL DES TRIBUNAUX; hebdomadaire judiciaire. (Text in French) 1882. w. 9500 Fr. Maison Ferdinand Larcier S.A., Rue des Minimes 39, 1000 Brussels, Belgium. TEL 02-5124712. Ed. Roger O. Dalcq. bk.rev.; charts.
Description: Publishes articles contributing to the understanding of legal theory, reports court decisions and jurisprudential issues, and chronicles the activities of the judiciary.
Refereed Serial

340   BE
JOURNAL DES TRIBUNAUX DU TRAVAIL. 3/mo. 9600 Fr. Maison Ferdinand Larcier S.A., Rue des Minimes 39, 1000 Brussels, Belgium.

340   SA   ISSN 0258-252X
K24
JOURNAL FOR JURIDICAL SCIENCE/TYDSKRIF VIR REGSWETENSKAP. (Text in Afrikaans and English) 1976. s-a. R.20. University of the Orange Free State, P.O. Box 339, Bloemfontein 9300, South Africa. TEL 051-401-2309. Ed. Dirk C. Du Toit. cum.index; circ. 800. (back issues avail.)

341   UK   ISSN 0021-8553
LAW
JOURNAL OF AFRICAN LAW. 1956. 2/yr. £20. University of London, College of Oriental and African Studies, Thornhaugh St., Russell Sq., London WC1H 0XG, England. TEL 071-637-2388.
FAX 071-436-3844. Ed.Bd. adv.; bk.rev.; bibl.; index. (also avail. in microfilm from WSH; reprint service avail. from WSH) **Indexed:** A.I.C.P., C.L.I., Curr.Cont.Africa, L.R.I., Leg.Per., P.A.I.S.
—BLDSC shelfmark: 4919.995000.
Description: Covers all aspects of African customary and modern law.

341.57   US   ISSN 0021-8642
K10
JOURNAL OF AIR LAW AND COMMERCE. 1930. q. $32. Southern Methodist University, School of Law, Dallas, TX 75275. TEL 214-692-2570.
FAX 214-692-4330. adv.; bk.rev.; bibl.; index, cum.index every 10 yrs.; circ. 2,100. (also avail. in microform from UMI; microfilm from WSH; reprint service avail. from UMI,WSH) **Indexed:** C.L.I., Int.Aerosp.Abstr., L.R.I., Leg.Cont., Leg.Per., P.A.I.S.
●Also available online. Vendor(s): WESTLAW.
—BLDSC shelfmark: 4926.420000.

JOURNAL OF APPLIED BIOMATERIALS. see *MEDICAL SCIENCES — Experimental Medicine, Laboratory Technique*

340   US   ISSN 0733-5113
PN2000
JOURNAL OF ARTS MANAGEMENT AND LAW. 1969. q. $38 to individuals; institutions $75. (Helen Dwight Reid Educational Foundation) Heldref Publications, 1319 Eighteenth St., N.W., Washington, DC 20036-1802. TEL 202-296-6267.
FAX 202-296-5149. Ed. Sylvia Nothman. adv.; bk.rev.; charts; illus.; stat.; index; circ. 700. (also avail. in microform from WSH; reprint service avail. from WSH) **Indexed:** Abstr.Bk.Rev.Curr.Leg.Per., Arts & Hum.Cit.Ind., Bk.Rev.Ind. (1985-), C.L.I., CHild.BK.Rev.Ind. (1985-), Commun.Abstr., Curr.Cont., Ind.Bk.Rev.Hum., L.R.I., Leg.Cont., Leg.Per., Music Ind.
Formerly (until 1982): Performing Arts Review (ISSN 0031-5249)
Refereed Serial

340 951   US   ISSN 1041-7567
JOURNAL OF CHINESE LAW. 1987. s-a. (Center for Chinese Legal Studies) Columbia University, School of Law, 435 W. 116th St., Box C-10, New York, NY 10027. TEL 212-854-2628. FAX 212-854-7946. bk.rev.

340 200   US   ISSN 0741-6075
K10
JOURNAL OF CHRISTIAN JURISPRUDENCE. 1980. a. $9.95. Regent University, College of Law and Government, Virginia Beach, VA 23464.
TEL 804-424-7000. Ed. Joseph N. Kickasola. circ. 300. **Indexed:** C.L.I.
—BLDSC shelfmark: 4958.272000.

JOURNAL OF CHURCH AND STATE. see *RELIGIONS AND THEOLOGY*

JOURNAL OF CLINICAL ETHICS. see *MEDICAL SCIENCES*

340   US   ISSN 0093-8688
K10
JOURNAL OF COLLEGE AND UNIVERSITY LAW. 1973. q. $40. (National Association of College and University Attorneys) Fred B. Rothman & Co., 10368 W. Centennial Rd., Littleton, CO 80127.
TEL 303-979-5657. FAX 303-978-1457. Ed. Laura F. Rothstein. (back issues avail.; reprint service avail. from RRI,UMI) **Indexed:** Abstr.Bk.Rev.Curr.Leg.Per., C.I.J.E., C.L.I., Cont.Pg.Educ., L.R.I., Leg.Cont., Leg.Per.
—BLDSC shelfmark: 4958.799700.

JOURNAL OF CONTEMPORARY HEALTH LAW AND POLICY. see *MEDICAL SCIENCES*

340   US   ISSN 0097-9937
K10
JOURNAL OF CONTEMPORARY LAW. 1974. s-a. $10. University of Utah, College of Law, Salt Lake City, UT 84112. TEL 801-581-6833. Ed.Bd. bk.rev.; index; circ. 350. (also avail. in microform from UMI; back issues avail.; reprint service avail. from RRI,UMI) **Indexed:** Abstr.Bk.Rev.Curr.Leg.Per., C.C.L.P., C.L.I., L.R.I., Leg.Cont., Leg.Per.

340   AT   ISSN 1030-7230
K10
JOURNAL OF CONTRACT LAW. 1988. 3/yr. Aus.$115. Butterworths Pty. Ltd., 271-173 Lane Cove Rd., North Ryde, N.S.W. 2113, Australia.
TEL 02-335-4444. FAX 02-335-4655. Ed. J.W. Carter. bk.rev. (back issues avail.)
Description: Forum, discussion and analysis of issues confronting contract lawyers.

653   US
Z54
JOURNAL OF COURT REPORTING. 1905. m. (Nov.-Aug.) $35. National Court Reporters Association, 8224 Old Courthouse Rd., Vienna, VA 22182-3808. Ed. Benjamin M. Rogner. adv.; index; circ. 30,000. **Indexed:** Bus.Educ.Ind.
Formerly: National Shorthand Reporter (ISSN 0028-0178)

JOURNAL OF CRIME & JUSTICE. see *CRIMINOLOGY AND LAW ENFORCEMENT*

345   US   ISSN 0047-2352
HV7231   CODEN: JCJUDJ
JOURNAL OF CRIMINAL JUSTICE; an international journal. 1973. 6/yr. £200 (effective 1992). Pergamon Press, Inc., Journals Division, 660 White Plains Rd., Tarrytown, NY 10591-5153. TEL 914-524-9200. FAX 914-333-2444. (And: Headington Hill Hall, Oxford OX3 0BW, England. TEL 0865-794141) Ed. Kent B. Joscelyn. adv.; bk.rev.; charts; illus.; index; circ. 3,000. (also avail. in microform from MIM,UMI; reprint service avail. from UMI) **Indexed:** Abstr.Bk.Rev.Curr.Leg.Per., ASSIA, C.L.I., CJPI, Crim.Just.Abstr., Curr.Cont., L.R.I., Leg.Per., Mid.East: Abstr.& Ind., P.A.I.S., Psychol.Abstr., SSCI.
—BLDSC shelfmark: 4965.530000.
  Description: Concerned with all aspects of the criminal justice system, and the relationships of individual elements to the entire process. For both legal practitioners and academicians.
  Refereed Serial

340 610   US   ISSN 1044-2073
HV1551
▼**JOURNAL OF DISABILITY POLICY STUDIES.** 1990. s-a. $14 to individuals; institutions $22. University of Arkansas Press, Dept. of Rehabilitation Education and Research, 201 Ozark, Fayetteville, AR 72701. FAX 501-575-6044. Ed. Kay Fletcher Schriner. adv.; bk.rev.; circ. 500. (back issues avail.)
—BLDSC shelfmark: 4969.680000.
  Description: Publishes research, discussion and review articles, and brief reports pertaining to both macro- and micro-policy issues.

346.046   NE   ISSN 0264-6811
JOURNAL OF ENERGY AND NATURAL RESOURCES LAW. (Text in English) vol.9, 1991. 4/yr. $203.50. (International Bar Association, Section on Energy and Natural Resources Law) Kluwer Academic Publishers, Postbus 17, 3300 AA Dordrecht, Netherlands. TEL 078-334911. FAX 078-334254. TELEX 29245. (Dist. by: Kluwer Academic Publishers Group, P.O. Box 322, 3300 AH Dordrecht, Netherlands; N. America dist. addr.: Box 358, Accord Sta., Hingham, MA 02018-0358. TEL 617-871-6600) (Co-sponsor: University of Dundee, Centre for Petroleum and Mineral Law Studies) Ed. T.C. Daintith.
—BLDSC shelfmark: 4978.302000.

JOURNAL OF ENERGY, NATURAL RESOURCES AND ENVIRONMENTAL LAW. see *ENERGY*

JOURNAL OF ENVIRONMENTAL LAW. see *ENVIRONMENTAL STUDIES*

JOURNAL OF ENVIRONMENTAL REGULATION. see *ENVIRONMENTAL STUDIES*

JOURNAL OF HALACHA AND CONTEMPORARY SOCIETY. see *ETHNIC INTERESTS*

JOURNAL OF HEALTH AND HOSPITAL LAW. see *MEDICAL SCIENCES*

JOURNAL OF HEALTH POLITICS, POLICY AND LAW. see *MEDICAL SCIENCES*

JOURNAL OF INDIVIDUAL EMPLOYMENT RIGHTS. see *BUSINESS AND ECONOMICS — Labor And Industrial Relations*

170 340   US
▼**JOURNAL OF INFORMATION ETHICS.** 1992. s-a. $38 (foreign $44)(effective 1992). St. Cloud State University, St. Cloud, MN 56301. TEL 612-255-4822. (Subscr. to: McFarland and Company, Inc., Box 611, Jefferson, NC 28640. TEL 919-246-4460) Ed. Robert Hauptman. bk.rev.; abstr.; bibl. (back issues avail.)
  Description: Deals with ethics in all areas of information or knowledge production and dissemination, with particular emphasis on library and information science, cyberspace, computers, medicine and law, from theoretical, philosophical and applied viewpoints.
  Refereed Serial

JOURNAL OF INSURANCE REGULATION. see *INSURANCE*

340   PL   ISSN 0075-4277
LAW
JOURNAL OF JURISTIC PAPYROLOGY. (Text in English, German, Italian and Russian) 1949. irreg., vol.19, 1983. price varies. (Uniwersytet Warszawski, Instytut Papirologii i Prawa Antycznego - Warsaw University, Institute of Papyrology and Ancient Laws) Panstwowe Wydawnictwo Naukowe, Ul. Miodowa 10, 00-251 Warsaw, Poland. (Dist. by: Ars Polona, Krakowskie Przedmiescie 7, 00-068 Warsaw, Poland) Ed. H. Kupiszewski. bk.rev.; circ. 510.
—BLDSC shelfmark: 5009.700000.

340   US   ISSN 0160-2098
K10
JOURNAL OF JUVENILE LAW. 1977. a. $12. (University of La Verne, College of Law) La Verne Law Review, Inc., 1950 3rd St., La Verne, CA 91750. TEL 714-596-1848. adv.; bk.rev.; circ. 2,000. (also avail. in microform from WSH; back issues avail.; reprint service avail. from WSH) **Indexed:** Adol.Ment.Hlth.Abstr., C.L.I., Crim.Just.Abstr., L.R.I., Leg.Per.

JOURNAL OF LAND USE AND ENVIRONMENTAL LAW. see *ENVIRONMENTAL STUDIES*

340 330   US   ISSN 0022-2186
LAW   CODEN: JLLEA7
JOURNAL OF LAW AND ECONOMICS. 1958. s-a. $26 to individuals; institutions $39; students $15. (University of Chicago Law School) University of Chicago Press, Journals Division, 5720 S. Woodlawn Ave., Chicago, IL 60637. TEL 312-753-3347. FAX 312-702-0694. TELEX 25-4603. (Orders to: Box 37005, Chicago IL 60637) Ed.Bd. adv.; charts; stat.; cum.index: 1958-1972; circ. 3,400. (also avail. in microform from MIM,UMI) **Indexed:** A.B.C.Pol.Sci., ABI Inform, Amer.Hist.& Life, Bank.Lit.Ind., BPIA, Bus.Ind., C.L.I., C.R.E.J., Cont.Pg.Manage., Curr.Cont., Deep Sea Res.& Oceanogr.Abstr., Excerp.Med., Hist.Abstr., Int.Lab.Doc., J.of Econ.Lit., L.R.I., Leg.Per., Oper.Res.Manage.Sci., P.A.I.S., Soc.Sci.Ind., SSCI.
—BLDSC shelfmark: 5010.130000.
  Description: Focuses on the influence of regulation and legal institutions on the operation of economic systems, especially the behavior of markets and the impact of governmental institutions on markets.
  Refereed Serial

340 370   US   ISSN 0275-6072
K10
JOURNAL OF LAW AND EDUCATION. 1972. q. $40 (foreign $48.50). Anderson Publishing Co., 2035 Reading Rd., Cincinnati, OH 45202. TEL 513-421-4142. FAX 513-562-8116. Eds. Laurence W. Knowles, Eldon D. Wedlock, Jr. adv.; bk.rev.; circ. 2,500. (also avail. in microform from UMI; back issues avail.; reprint service avail. from UMI) **Indexed:** Abstr.Bk.Rev.Curr.Leg.Per., C.I.J.E., C.L.I., CJPI, Cont.Pg.Educ., Educ.Admin.Abstr., Educ.Ind., L.R.I., Leg.Cont., Leg.Per., Sp.Ed.Needs Abstr., SSCI.
—BLDSC shelfmark: 5010.132200.

340   US
JOURNAL OF LAW AND HEALTH. 1985. s-a. $15. Cleveland State University, Cleveland-Marshall College of Law, Cleveland, OH 44115. TEL 216-687-2336. **Indexed:** C.L.I., Hlth.Ind., Leg.Per.

320 340   JA   ISSN 0387-2882
JOURNAL OF LAW AND POLITICS/HO-SEI KENKYU. (Text in Japanese; contents page in English) 1931. q. 1,000 Yen. Kyushu University, Institute of Law and Politics - Kyushu Daigaku Hosei Gakkai, c/o Faculty of Law, Kyushu University, Hakozaki, Higashi-ku, Fukuoka 812, Japan. bk.rev. **Indexed:** C.L.I., Jap.Per.Ind., Leg.Per.
—BLDSC shelfmark: 5010.143000.

340 200   US   ISSN 0748-0814
K10
JOURNAL OF LAW AND RELIGION. 1983. s-a. $12. Hamline University School of Law, Journal of Law and Religion, 1536 Hewitt Ave., St. Paul, MN 55104. Eds. Michael Scherschligt, Wilson Yates. (also avail. in microfilm from WSH; reprint service avail. from WSH) **Indexed:** C.L.I., Rel.& Theol.Abstr. (1988-), Rel.Per.

340   UK   ISSN 0263-323X
K2
JOURNAL OF LAW AND SOCIETY. 1974. 4/yr. £26($55) to individuals; institutions £91($193). Basil Blackwell Ltd., 108 Cowley Rd., Oxford OX4 1JF, England. TEL 0865-791100. FAX 0865-791347. TELEX 837022-OXBOOK-G. Ed. P.A. Thomas. adv.; bk.rev.; index; circ. 900. **Indexed:** A.B.C.Pol.Sci., Abstr.Bk.Rev.Curr.Leg.Per., Amer.Hist.& Life, ASSIA, C.L.I., Crim.Just.Abstr., Hist.Abstr., Int.Polit.Sci.Abstr, L.R.I., Lang.& Lang.Behav.Abstr., Leg.Per., Soc.Work Res.& Abstr., Sociol.Abstr., Stud.Wom.Abstr.
—BLDSC shelfmark: 5010.180000.
  Formerly: British Journal of Law and Society (ISSN 0306-3704)

340 330.1   US   ISSN 8756-6222
K10
JOURNAL OF LAW, ECONOMICS, AND ORGANIZATION. 1985. 2/yr. $26 to individuals; institutions $40. Oxford University Press, Journals, 200 Madison Ave., New York, NY 10016. TEL 212-679-7300. FAX 212-725-2972. TELEX 6859654. (Subscr. to: Journals Fulfillment, 2001 Evans Rd., Cary, NC 25713. TEL 919-677-0977) Eds. Roberta Romano, Oliver Williamson. **Indexed:** C.L.I., J.of Econ.Lit.
—BLDSC shelfmark: 5010.190000.
  Description: Interdisciplinary journal integrating legal-economic scholarship with other social science disciplines. Promotes an understanding of complex social phenomena by examining such matters from a legal, economic, and organizational perspective.

340 370   US   ISSN 0022-2208
K10
JOURNAL OF LEGAL EDUCATION. 1937. q. $30 (foreign $34). (Association of American Law Schools) University of Iowa, College of Law, Iowa City, IA 52242. TEL 319-335-9127. Ed. David H. Vernon. bk.rev.; index. (also avail. in microform from UMI; reprint service avail. from RRI,UMI) **Indexed:** Abstr.Bk.Rev.Curr.Leg.Per., C.I.J.E., C.L.I., Cont.Pg.Educ., Curr.Cont., High.Educ.Curr.Aware.Bull., L.R.I., Leg.Per., SSCI.
—BLDSC shelfmark: 5010.250000.
  Formerly (until 1940): National Jounal of Legal Education.
  Description: Focuses on study and teaching.

340   UK   ISSN 0144-0365
K10
JOURNAL OF LEGAL HISTORY. 1980. 3/yr. £30($45) to individuals; institutions £70($105). Frank Cass & Co. Ltd., Gainsborough House, 11 Gainsborough Rd., London E11 1RS, England. TEL 081-530-4226. FAX 081-530-7795. Ed. Andrew Lewis. adv.; bk.rev.; index. (also avail. in microfilm from UMI; back issues avail.) **Indexed:** C.L.I., L.R.I., Lang.& Lang.Behav.Abstr., Leg.Per.
—BLDSC shelfmark: 5010.260000.
  Description: Covers the history of the law of the British Isles as well as all significant developments in the countries of the Commonwealth, the USA and continental Europe.

JOURNAL OF LEGAL MEDICINE. see *MEDICAL SCIENCES*

340   US   ISSN 0732-9113
K1
JOURNAL OF LEGAL PLURALISM AND UNOFFICIAL LAW. 1969. a. $12.50 to individuals; institutions $26. (Foundation for the Journal of Legal Pluralism) Fred B. Rothman & Co., 10368 W. Centennial Rd., Littleton, CO 80127. TEL 303-979-5657. FAX 303-978-1457. (Co-sponsor: University of California, Los Angeles, African Studies Center) Ed. John Griffiths. (back issues avail.) **Indexed:** C.L.I., Curr.Cont.Africa, Foreign Leg.Per., Leg.Per.
—BLDSC shelfmark: 5010.272000.
  Formerly (until 1981): African Law Studies (ISSN 0002-0060)

340 K10 US ISSN 0047-2530
JOURNAL OF LEGAL STUDIES. 1972. s-a. $26 to individuals; institutions $39; students $15. (University of Chicago Law School) University of Chicago Press, Journals Division, 5720 S. Woodlawn Ave., Chicago, IL 60637. TEL 312-753-3347. FAX 312-702-0694. TELEX 25-4603. (Subscr. to: Box 37005, Chicago IL 60637) Ed. Richard Epstein. adv.; bibl.; charts; circ. 1,500. (also avail. in microform from MIM,UMI,WSH; reprint service avail. from UMI,WSH) **Indexed:** A.B.C.Pol.Sci., C.L.I., CJPI, Crim.Just.Abstr., Curr.Cont., J.of Econ.Lit., L.R.I., Lang.& Lang.Behav.Abstr., Leg.Cont., Leg.Per., Risk Abstr., SSCI.
—BLDSC shelfmark: 5010.275000.
Description: Presents theoretical and empirical research on law and legal institutions, emphasizing the use of social science research techniques to obtain new information about the actual functioning of legal systems.
Refereed Serial

340 K14 US ISSN 0146-9584
JOURNAL OF LEGISLATION. 1974. 2/yr. $15. University of Notre Dame, Notre Dame Law School, Notre Dame, IN 46556. TEL 219-239-5918. Ed. Kevin V. Parsons. adv.; bk.rev.; bibl.; circ. 1,500. (also avail. in microform from UMI,WSH; back issues avail.; reprint service avail. from WSH) **Indexed:** A.B.C.Pol.Sci., Abstr.Bk.Rev.Curr.Leg.Per., C.L.I., Energy Abstr., INIS Atomind., L.R.I., Leg.Cont., Leg.Per., P.A.I.S., Sage Fam.Stud.Abstr., Sage Pub.Admin.Abstr., Sage Urb.Stud.Abstr., Sociol.Abstr., Work Rel.Abstr.
—BLDSC shelfmark: 5010.276000.
Formerly: Notre Dame Journal of Legislation (ISSN 0360-4209); Which superseded: New Dimensions in Legislation (ISSN 0300-6018)
Description: Studies current public policy issues facing state, national and international legislative bodies.

340 341 K10 MY ISSN 0126-6322
JOURNAL OF MALAYSIAN AND COMPARATIVE LAW/JERNAL UNDANG-UNDANG. (Text in English and Malay) 1974. s-a. M.$30. (University of Malaya, Faculty of Law) University of Malaya Press, c/o University Library, Pantai Valley, 59100 Kuala Lumpur, Malaysia. FAX 03-7573661. TELEX MA-37453. Eds. P. Balan, Wan Arfah. adv.; bk.rev.; index, cum.index: vols. 1-4; circ. 500.

340 301.16 K10 UK ISSN 0144-0373
JOURNAL OF MEDIA LAW AND PRACTICE. 1980. 4/yr. £90($145) Tolley Publishing Co. Ltd., Tolley House, 2 Addiscombe Rd., Croydon, Surrey CR9 5AF, England. Eds. David Goldberg, Michael Rudin. adv.; bk.rev. **Indexed:** Commun.Abstr., Lang.& Lang.Behav.Abstr.
—BLDSC shelfmark: 5017.045000.
Incorporates: Advertising and Marketing Law and Practice; Which was formerly: Advertising Law and Practice (ISSN 0267-0763)
Description: Covers all aspects of law and practice governing the media in the UK and worldwide.

340 380.5 CN ISSN 0840-7754
JOURNAL OF MOTOR VEHICLE LAW. 1989. 3/yr. Can.$128($102) Carswell Publications, Corporate Plaza, 2075 Kennedy Rd., Scarborough, Ont. M1T 3V4, Canada. TEL 416-609-8000. FAX 416-298-5094. Ed. Murray D. Segal. adv.; bk.rev.; cum.index.
Description: Covers issues relating to driving offences arising from both criminal and highway traffic law.

347.016 US
JOURNAL OF NOTARIAL ACTS AND RECORDKEEPING PRACTICES. 1974. a. $9.95. National Notary Association, 8236 Remmet Ave., Box 7184, Canoga Park, CA 91304-7184. TEL 818-713-4000. FAX 818-713-9061. Ed. Charles N. Faerber. (reprint service avail. from UMI)
Supersedes in part: Customs and Practices of Notaries Public and Digest of Notary Laws in the U.S.

340 K10 UK ISSN 0307-4870
JOURNAL OF PLANNING AND ENVIRONMENT LAW. 1948. m. £90. Sweet & Maxwell, South Quay Plaza, 8th Floor, 183 Marsh Wall, London E14 9FT, England. TEL 071-538-8686. FAX 071-538-9508. (Dist. in U.S. & Canada by: Carswell Co. Ltd., 233 Midland Ave., Agincourt, Ont., Canada) Ed. Victor Moore. adv.; bk.rev.; index. (reprint service avail. from RRI) **Indexed:** ASSIA, Br.Archaeol.Abstr., Br.Tech.Ind., C.L.I., Geo.Abstr., L.R.I., Leg.Cont., Leg.Per., P.A.I.S., RICS, Sage Urb.Stud.Abstr.
●Also available online.
—BLDSC shelfmark: 5040.380000.
Formerly: Journal of Planning and Property Law (ISSN 0022-376X)

340 620 K10 US ISSN 0363-0404 CODEN: JPLIDG
JOURNAL OF PRODUCTS LIABILITY. 1977. q. $255 (effective 1992). Pergamon Press, Inc., Journals Division, 660 White Plains Rd., Tarrytown, NY 10591-5153. TEL 914-524-9200. FAX 914-333-2444. (And: Headington Hill Hall, Oxford, OX3 0BW England. TEL 0865-794141) Eds. Verne L. Roberts, Kenneth Ross. adv.; charts; illus.; circ. 1,000. (also avail. in microform from MIM,UMI; back issues avail.) **Indexed:** ABI Inform, BPIA, Bus.Ind., C.L.I., Consum.Ind., Curr.Cont., L.R.I., Manage.Cont., Risk Abstr., Tr.& Indus.Ind.
—BLDSC shelfmark: 5042.670000.
Description: Publishes original research papers from the legal as well as from technical fields such as engineering and medicine bearing upon issues of product safety and liability.
Refereed Serial

340 616.8 K10 US ISSN 0093-1853 CODEN: JPSLAN
JOURNAL OF PSYCHIATRY AND LAW. 1973. q. $45 to individuals; institutions $36. Federal Legal Publications, Inc., 157 Chambers St., New York, NY 10007. TEL 212-619-4949. Ed. Howard Nashel. adv.; bk.rev.; charts; stat.; circ. 1,500. (also avail. in microfilm from UMI; back issues avail.; reprint service avail. from UMI) **Indexed:** Abstr.Bk.Rev.Curr.Leg.Per., Adol.Ment.Hlth.Abstr., C.L.I., Crim.Just.Abstr., Curr.Cont., Excerp.Med., Hlth.Ind., Ind.Per.Art.Relat.Law., L.R.I., Leg.Cont., Leg.Per., Mid.East: Abstr.& Ind., Psychol.Abstr., SSCI.
—BLDSC shelfmark: 5043.260000.

347.7 K10 US ISSN 0022-4243
JOURNAL OF REPRINTS FOR ANTITRUST LAW & ECONOMICS. 1969. s-a. $55. Federal Legal Publications, Inc., 157 Chambers St., New York, NY 10007. TEL 212-619-4949. Ed. William J. Curran, III. adv.; bk.rev.; mkt.; pat.; tr.mk.; index; circ. 1,500. (back issues avail.; reprint service avail. from UMI) **Indexed:** C.L.I., Leg.Per.
—BLDSC shelfmark: 5049.500000.

JOURNAL OF REPRINTS OF DOCUMENTS AFFECTING WOMEN. see *WOMEN'S INTERESTS*

340 US
JOURNAL OF THE LEGAL PROFESSION. 1976. a. $12. University of Alabama, School of Law, Box 870382, University, AL 35487-0382. TEL 205-348-4996. (also avail. in microform from WSH; reprint service avail. from WSH) **Indexed:** Abstr.Bk.Rev.Curr.Leg.Per., C.L.I., L.R.I., Leg.Per.

342 351.713 K25 US ISSN 8756-0801
JOURNAL OF URBAN & CONTEMPORARY LAW. Variant title: Washington University Journal of Urban & Contemporary Law. 1968. 2/yr. $20. Washington University, One Brookings Dr., Campus Box 1120, St. Louis, MO 63130. TEL 314-889-6436. FAX 314-935-6493. adv.; bk.rev.; cum.index: 1968-1984; circ. 1,000. (also avail. in microfiche from WSH; microfilm from WSH; back issues avail.) **Indexed:** C.L.I., Leg.Cont., Leg.Per.

JOURNAL OF WORLD TRADE. see *LAW — International Law*

346.066 BE
JOURNAL PRATIQUE DE DROIT FISCAL. 6/yr. 3043 Fr. Maison Ferdinand Larcier S.A., Rue des Minimes 39, 1000 Brussels, Belgium.

JOURNAL RECORD. see *BUSINESS AND ECONOMICS*

340 FR ISSN 0756-3825
JOURNEES DE LA SOCIETE DE LEGISLATION COMPAREE. 1979. a. 350 Fr. Societe de Legislation Comparee, 28 rue St. Guillaume, 75007 Paris, France. TEL 45-44-44-67. FAX 19-1-45-49-41-65. (back issues avail.)
Description: Collection of all the papers presented at the society's bilateral international conferences.

347.9 US
JUDICIAL COUNCIL REPORT TO THE GOVERNOR AND LEGISLATURE. 1962. a. free. Judicial Council of California, Administrative Office of the Courts, South Tower, Ste. 400, 303 Second St., San Francisco, CA 94107-1366. Dir. Robert W. Page Jr. circ. 4,000.
Formerly: California. Administrative Office of the Courts. Annual Report (ISSN 0068-5488); **Incorporates:** Judicial Council of California. Annual Report.

340 350 US
JUDICIAL STAFF DIRECTORY. 1986. a. $59. Staff Directories Ltd., Box 62, Mount Vernon, VA 22121. TEL 703-739-0900. FAX 703-739-0234. Eds. Charles B. Brownson, Anna L. Brownson.
●Also available on CD-ROM.
Description: Lists 13,000 federal court personnel, from judges to law clerks. Includes the Supreme Court, circuit courts, district courts and bankruptcy courts.

JUGOSLOVENSKA REVIJA ZA KRIMINOLOGIJU I KRIVICNO PRAVO. see *CRIMINOLOGY AND LAW ENFORCEMENT*

340 K10 GW ISSN 0170-1452
JURA; Juristische Ausbildung. 1979. m. $95 (students $66). Walter de Gruyter und Co., Genthiner Str. 13, 1000 Berlin 30, Germany. TEL 030-26005-0. FAX 030-26005251. TELEX 184027. (US addr.: Walter de Gruyter, 200 Saw Mill Rd., Hawthorne, NY 10532) Ed.Bd. index; circ. 8,000. (back issues avail.)

340 330.9 MG
JURECO. m. Immeuble S O M A G I, 120 rue Rainandriamampandry, 101 Antananarivo, Malagasy Republic. TEL 24145. FAX 20397. TELEX 22365. Ed. Mboara Andrianarimanana.

340 MX
JURIDICA.* (Published under a different title each year.) 1969. a. Mex.$300($12) Universidad Iberoamericana, Departamento de Derecho, Prol. Paseo de la Reforma 880, Col. Lomas de Santa Fe, 01210 Mexico, D.F., Mexico.

349 LAW UK ISSN 0022-6785
JURIDICAL REVIEW; law journal of Scottish universities. 1889. 2/yr. £26. W. Green, 21 Alva St., Edinburgh EH2 4PS, Scotland. Eds. W.A. Wilson, J.P. Grant. adv.; bk.rev.; index. (reprint service avail. from RRI) **Indexed:** Abstr.Bk.Rev.Curr.Leg.Per., Br.Hum.Ind., C.L.I., L.R.I., Leg.Per.
—BLDSC shelfmark: 5075.560000.

349 K24 FI ISSN 0040-6953
JURIDISKA FOERENINGEN I FINLAND. TIDSKRIFT. 1865. 6/yr. FIM 230. Juridiska Foereningen i Finland - Finnish Law Association, c/o Christian Wik, Centralgatan 7A, 00100 Helsinki, Finland. Ed. Edward Andersson. bk.rev.; circ. 1,400. (reprint service avail)

340 001.6 US ISSN 0022-6793 CODEN: JURJAD
JURIMETRICS JOURNAL; journal of law, science and technology. 1959. q. $29 (foreign $33). American Bar Association, Science and Technology Section, 750 N. Lake Shore Dr., Chicago, IL 60611. TEL 312-988-5000. (Co-sponsor: Arizona State University, Center for the Study of Law, Science and Technology) Ed. Mark A. Hall. bk.rev.; abstr.; bibl.; charts; illus.; index, cum.index; circ. 5,000. (also avail. in microform from UMI; reprint service avail. from RRI) **Indexed:** C.L.I., CJPI, Comput.Lit.Ind., Comput.Rev., Data Process.Dig., L.R.I., Law Ofc.Info.Svc., Leg.Per., Sci.Abstr.
—BLDSC shelfmark: 5075.565000.
Formerly: Modern Uses of Logic in Law (MULL).
Description: Legal issues in science and technology.

LAW 2641

340 US ISSN 0022-6807
K10
JURIS. 1967. q. free. Duquesne University, School of Law, 900 Locust St., Pittsburgh, PA 15282. TEL 412-434-6305. Ed. Steven W. Zoffer. adv.; bk.rev.; circ. 5,500.

340 BL
JURISCIVEL DO S T F. Cover title: Revista Juriscivel do S.T.F. 1972. irreg. (Supremo Tribunal Federal) Cultural Distribuidora de Livros, Praca dos Tres Poderes, Brasilia, D.F., Brazil.

346.013 CN ISSN 0835-0892
JURISFEMME. (Editions in English, French) 1975. 3/yr. Can.$30 (effective 1992). National Association of Women & the Law - Association Nationale de la Femme et du Droit, 604 - 1 Nicholas St., Ottawa, Ont. K1N 7B7, Canada. TEL 613-238-1544. FAX 613-238-1545. Eds. Sandra Sellens, Nicole Girard. bk.rev.; index; circ. 1,000. (back issues avail.)

340 JA ISSN 0022-6815
JURISPRUDENCE ASSOCIATION. JOURNAL/HOGAKU KYOKAI ZASSHI. (Text in Japanese; contents page in English) 1853. m. 15000 Yen. Jurisprudence Association - Hogaku Kyokai, c/o Faculty of Law, University of Tokyo, 7-3-1 Hongo, Bunkyo-ku, Tokyo 113, Japan. Ed. Eiichi Hoshino. bk.rev.; index; circ. 1,500.
—BLDSC shelfmark: 4810.050000.

342 BE
JURISPRUDENCE DU DROIT SOCIAL. 1985. q. 3000 Fr. Etablissements Emile Bruylant, 67 Rue de Regence, B-1000 Brussels, Belgium. TEL 02-512-9845.
Formerly: Jurisprudence des Jurisdictions du Travail de Bruxelles.

340 CN
JURISPRUDENCE LOGEMENT. 10/yr. Can.$50. (Regie du Logement et des Tribunaux Civil) Ministere des Communications, P.O. Box 1005, Quebec, Que. G1K 7B5, Canada. TEL 514-948-1222. (Subscr. to: Service Abonnements, CP 1190, Outrement, Que. H2V 4S7, Canada)

348.46 SP
JURISPRUDENCIA ARAGONESA.. 1972. s-a. Colegio de Abogados de Zaragoza, Zaragoza, Spain. Ed. Miguel Monserrat. circ. 1,500.

340 AG ISSN 0326-1190
JURISPRUDENCIA ARGENTINA. (In 5 vols. including an index) 1918. a. $100 per volume. Jurisprudencia Argentina S.A., Talcahuano 650, 1013 Buenos Aires, Argentina. TEL 40-7850. Dir. Ricardo Estevez Boero. circ. 10,000.
Formerly: Anuario de Jurisprudencia Argentina.

349 BL ISSN 0022-684X
JURISPRUDENCIA E DOUTRINA. 1951. q. Cr.$60($12) (Ordem dos Advogados do Brasil, Secao do Ceara) Editora Juridica Ltda., Rua Princesa Isabel 639, Caixa Postal 428, Fortaleza, Ceara, Brazil. (Co-sponsors: Tribunal de Justica do Estado do Ceara; Tribunal de Justica do Estado da Bahia; Tribunal de Justica do Estado de Pernambuca) Ed. Jose Josino Da Costa. bk.rev.; cum.index: nos.1-35, nos.36-75; circ. 7,500.

340 NE ISSN 0924-4824
▼JURISPRUDENTIE VOOR GEMEENTEN. 1990. 10/yr. fl.120. V N G Uitgeverij, P.O. Box 30435, 2500 GK The Hague, Netherlands. TEL 070-3738888. FAX 070-3651826. adv.; circ. 900.

340 US ISSN 0022-6858
JURIST; studies in church order and ministry. 1941. s-a. $35. Catholic University of America, Department of Canon Law, Washington, DC 20064. TEL 202-319-5439. FAX 202-319-4967. Ed. Frederick R. McManus. adv.; bk.rev.; index, cum.index; circ. 2,100. (also avail. in microfilm from UMI; reprint service avail. from UMI) Indexed: Abstr.Bk.Rev.Curr.Leg.Per., C.L.I., Canon Law Abstr., Cath.Ind., CERDIC, L.R.I., Leg.Per.
—BLDSC shelfmark: 5075.577000.

340 378 CN ISSN 0829-5476
JURISTE. (Text in French) 1985. s-a. free. University of Moncton Law School, Moncton, N.B. E1A 3E9, Canada. TEL 506-858-4145. FAX 506-858-4534. bk.rev.; circ. 1,200. (back issues avail.)

349 DK
JURISTEN OG OEKONOMEN; debat og orientering. 1918. s-m. DKK 460. Danmarks Jurist og Oekonomforbund, Gothersgade 133, 1123 Copenhagen K, Denmark.
Formed by the merger of: Juristen (ISSN 0022-6874) & Oekonomen.

349 GW ISSN 0022-6882
LAW
JURISTENZEITUNG. 1951. s-m. DM.246 to individuals; students DM.124. Verlag J.C.B. Mohr (Paul Siebeck), Wilhelmstr. 18, Postfach 2040, 7400 Tuebingen, Germany. TEL 07071-26064. FAX 07071-51104. TELEX 7262872-MOHR-D. Ed.Bd. adv.; bk.rev. Indexed: CERDIC, INIS Atomind.
Description: Current aspects of German law, legislation and jurisdiction.

340 GW ISSN 0449-4342
JURISTISCHE ABHANDLUNGEN. 1964. irreg., vol.20, 1989. price varies. Vittorio Klostermann, Frauenlobstr. 22, Postfach 900601, 6000 Frankfurt 90, Germany. TEL 069-774011. FAX 069-708038.
—BLDSC shelfmark: 5075.592000.

349 US ISSN 0022-6912
LAW CODEN: JUBLA7
JURISTISCHE BLAETTER; mit Beilage WBL Wirtschaftsrechtliche Blaetter. 1872. 24/yr. DM.292($164) Springer-Verlag, Journals, 175 Fifth Ave., New York, NY 10010. TEL 212-460-1500. (Also Berlin, Heidelberg, Tokyo and Vienna) Eds. P. Rummel, H.R. Klecatsky. adv.; bk.rev.; illus.; index. (also avail. in microfiche from UMI; reprint service avail. from ISI)
—BLDSC shelfmark: 5075.595000.
Incorporates: Beilage Wirtschaftsrechtliche Blaetter (ISSN 0930-3855)

349 GW ISSN 0022-6920
JURISTISCHE RUNDSCHAU. 1928. m. $177 (students $72.50). Walter de Gruyter und Co., Genthiner Str. 13, 1000 Berlin 30, Germany. TEL 030-26005-0. FAX 030-26005251. TELEX 184027. (US addr.: Walter de Gruyter, Inc., 200 Saw Mill Rd., Hawthorne, NY 10532) Ed. Olten Troendle. adv.; bk.rev.

349 GW ISSN 0022-6939
LAW
JURISTISCHE SCHULUNG; Zeitschrift fuer Studium und Ausbildung mit JUS-Kartei und JUS-Lernbogen. 1961. m. DM.128. C.H. Beck'sche Verlagsbuchhandlung, Wilhelmstr. 9, 8000 Munich 40, Germany. TEL 089-38189-338. FAX 089-38189-398. TELEX 5215085-BECK-D. Eds. Hermann Weber, K.-P. Schroeder. adv.; bk.rev.; index, cum.index every 5 yrs.; circ. 26,000.

340 NO ISSN 0332-7590
JURISTKONTAKT. 1967. m. (9/yr.). NOK 300. Norges Juristforbund, Juristenes Hus, Kr. Augustgt. 9, 0164 Oslo 1, Norway. TEL 02-11-68-68. FAX 02-11-51-18. Ed. Ulf Ertzaas. adv.; circ. 6,600. (back issues avail.)
Description: News and events affecting the Norwegian legal community.

340 US
▼JURY SELECTION, 2-E. 1990. base vol. (plus a. suppl.). $95. Shepard's - McGraw-Hill, Inc., Box 35300, Colorado Springs, CO 80935-3530. TEL 800-525-2474.
Description: Discusses everyday problems that arise in choosing a jury. Offers practical advice and solutions.

340 PE
JUS; revista peruana de derecho. 1974. m. Editorial Jus, Paseo Colon 270, Of. 202, Lima, Peru.

349 NO ISSN 0022-6971
JUSSENS VENNER; a journal on the study of law. 1952. bi-m. $76. Universitetsforlaget, P.O. Box 2959-Toeyen, N-0608 Oslo 1, Norway. (U.S. addr.: Publications Expediting Inc., 200 Meacham Ave., Elmont, NY 11003) Ed.Bd. adv.; circ. 3,900.

340 ISSN 0738-6494
JUST COMPENSATION. 1957. m. $95. Just Compensation, Inc., Box 5133, Sherman Oaks, CA 91403. TEL 818-848-6765. Ed. Gideon Kanner. bk.rev.; index.

348 CN ISSN 0707-8501
KEQ1170.A72
JUSTICE (SAINTE-FOY). 1979. 10/yr. Can.$21. Magazine Justice Inc., 1200 de l'Eglise Rd., Sainte-Foy, Que. G1V 4M1, Canada. TEL 418-646-3203. FAX 418-646-4449. Ed. Agathe Legare. adv.; bk.rev.; circ. 45,000. Indexed: Pt.de Rep. (1984-).
Description: Covers legal aspects of daily life, with regular columns on court cases.

JUSTICE AND THE J.P.. see CRIMINOLOGY AND LAW ENFORCEMENT

340 US
JUSTICE IN AMERICA SERIES. 1969. irreg. $9.20 for 6 vols. (Law in American Society Foundation) Houghton Mifflin Co., One Beacon St., Boston, MA 02107. TEL 617-725-5000. Ed. Robert H. Ratcliffe. bibl.; illus.
Formerly: Justice in Urban America Series.

JUSTICE INSTITUTE OF BRITISH COLUMBIA. ANNUAL REPORT. see EDUCATION — Higher Education

340 UK ISSN 0264-3731
KD291
JUSTICE OF THE PEACE REPORTS. 1837. 26/yr. £101. Justice of the Peace Ltd., Little London, Chichester, W. Sussex PO19 1PG, England. TEL 0243-787841. FAX 0243-779278. Ed. Nicholas Yell. index. (also avail. in microfiche from BHP; back issues avail.)
Description: Reports on specialist subjects: coroners law, consumer law, domestic proceedings, licensing law, local government law and road traffic law.

JUSTICE QUARTERLY. see CRIMINOLOGY AND LAW ENFORCEMENT

347.9 US ISSN 0098-261X
K10
JUSTICE SYSTEM JOURNAL. 1974. 3/yr. $30. Institute for Court Management, 1331 17th St., no. 402, Denver, CO 80202. FAX 800-296-9007. Ed. Keith Boyum. bk.rev.; circ. 1,000. (also avail. in microform from UMI,WSH; reprint service avail. from UMI,WSH) Indexed: C.L.I., CJPI, Crim.Just.Abstr., Curr.Cont., L.R.I., Leg.Per., SSCI.
—BLDSC shelfmark: 5075.678000.

340 UK
JUSTICES' CLERK. 1943. 3/yr. free. Justices' Clerks' Society, The Law Courts, Castle Hill Ave., Folkestone, Kent CT20 2DH, England. FAX 0303-220512. Ed. P.S. Wallis. adv.; bk.rev.; circ. 800.

349 NA ISSN 0022-7056
JUSTICIA;* rechtsgeleerd periodiek voor de Nederlandse Antillen. (Text in Dutch) 1965. q. fl.6. Stichting tot Bevordering van de Rechtswetenschappen in de Nederlandse Antillen, Emanstraat 68, Oranjestad, Aruba. Eds. P. V. Sjiem Fat, H. Th. Lopez. adv.; bk.rev.; index; circ. 250.

340 UY
JUSTICIA URUGUAYA. 1940. w. 25 de Mayo 555, Montevideo, Uruguay. Ed. Oscar Arias Barbe. circ. 3,000.

340 AT ISSN 0157-5317
JUSTINIAN. 10/yr. Aus.$195. Law Press of Australia, G.P.O. Box 3793, Sydney, N.S.W. 2001, Australia. TEL 02-360-7788. FAX 02-360-7838. Ed. Richard Ackland.

349 GW ISSN 0022-7064
JUSTIZ-MINISTERIAL-BLATT FUER HESSEN. 1949. s-m. DM.34.60. Ministerium der Justiz, Luisenstr. 13, 6200 Wiesbaden, Germany. bk.rev.; index; circ. 2,400. (tabloid format)

340 GW ISSN 0941-6781
JUSTUF; das Juramagazin. 1986. s-a. DM.20($20) Weimann Presse und Verlag, Boellerts Hoefe 3, 4330 Muehlheim, Germany. FAX 0208-428271. Ed. Tom Weimann. bibl.; circ. 52,000. (back issues avail.)
Description: Magazine for young lawyers and law students.

JUVENILE JUSTICE DIGEST. see CRIMINOLOGY AND LAW ENFORCEMENT

L

2642 LAW

340   GW
K11
K T S - ZEITSCHRIFT FUER INSOLVENSRECHT, KONKURS, TREUHAND, SANIERUNG. 1939. q. DM.198. Carl Heymanns Verlag KG, Luxemburgerstr. 449, 5000 Cologne 41, Germany. TEL 0221-46010-0. FAX 0221-4601069. Ed. Juergen Mohrbutter. adv.; bk.rev.; abstr.; index; circ. 1,150.
    Formerly: Konkurs, Treuhand- und Schiedsgerichtswesen (ISSN 0023-3552)

KANAZAWA UNIVERSITY. FACULTY OF LAW AND LITERATURE. STUDIES AND ESSAYS. see *LITERATURE*

KANO STATE OF NIGERIA GAZETTE. see *PUBLIC ADMINISTRATION*

340   AU   ISSN 0259-0727
KANON. 1973. irreg., no.9, 1989. price varies. (Gesellschaft fuer das Recht der Ostkirchen) Verband der Wissenschaftlichen Gesellschaften Oesterreichs, Lindengasse 37, A-1070 Vienna, Austria. TEL 932166. **Indexed:** CERDIC.

340   JA   ISSN 0388-886X
K11
KANSAI UNIVERSITY REVIEW OF LAW AND POLITICS. (Text in English) 1980. a. exchange basis. Kansai University, Faculty of Law - Kansai Daigaku Hogakubu, Exchange Department (LP), Kansai University Library, P.O. Box 50, Suita, Osaka 564, Japan. FAX 06-330-1435. Ed. Katsumi Yamakawa. circ. 750.
    Description: Each number examines a current policy issue of interest to the study of law. A thorough discussion on the structure and content of treaties are presented with conclusions.

340   US   ISSN 0022-8486
K2
KANSAS BAR ASSOCIATION. JOURNAL. 1932. 10/yr. $35 to non-members. Kansas Bar Association, 1200 Harrison, Box 1034, Topeka, KS 66601. TEL 913-234-5696. FAX 913-234-3813. Ed. Patti Slider. adv.; bk.rev.; illus.; index, cum.index every 10 yrs.; circ. 5,500. (also avail. in microform from UMI; reprint service avail. from UMI) **Indexed:** C.L.I., L.R.I., Leg.Per.
    Incorporates (in Feb. 1986): Barletter.
    Description: Covers association news and activities, court digests, practice aid articles.

340   US
▼**KANSAS - IOWA ENVIRONMENTAL LAW LETTER.** 1991. 12/yr. $137. M. Lee Smith Publishers & Printers, 162 4th Ave. N., Box 2678, Nashville, TN 37219. TEL 615-242-7385. FAX 615-256-6601. Ed. George M. von Stamitz.
    Description: Reports the latest developments in Kansas and Iowa environmental laws.

340   IO
KEADILAN. 1973. bi-m. Rps.1000 per no. Islamic University of Indonesia, Faculty of Law - Universitas Islam Indonesia, Fakultas Hukum, Jalan Taman Siswa 158, Yogyakarta 55151, Indonesia. TEL 2978. Ed. Sobirin Malian. adv.; bk.rev.; circ. 2,500 (controlled).

340   US   ISSN 0748-9080
KENTUCKY ATTORNEY GENERAL OPINIONS. 1964. q. $85. Banks - Baldwin Law Publishing Co., University Center, Box 1974, Cleveland, OH 44106. TEL 216-721-7373. FAX 216-721-8055.
    Description: Contains all formal opinions of the Attorney General, in either full text or synopsis treatment, with cumulative research aids.

340   US   ISSN 0164-9345
KENTUCKY BENCH & BAR. 1936. q. $12. Kentucky Bar Association, 514 W. Main St., Frankfort, KY 40601. TEL 502-564-3795. FAX 502-564-3225. Ed. Edwin S. Hopson. adv.; bk.rev.; illus.; index; circ. 16,017. (also avail. in microform from UMI; reprint service avail. from UMI) **Indexed:** C.L.I., L.R.I., Law Ofc.Info.Svc., Leg.Per.
    Formerly: Kentucky State Bar Journal (ISSN 0023-0367)

340   US   ISSN 1052-4371
▼**KENTUCKY EMPLOYMENT LAW LETTER.** 1990. 12/yr. $127. M. Lee Smith Publishers & Printers, 162 Fourth Ave. N., Box 2678, Nashville, TN 37219. TEL 615-242-7395. FAX 615-256-6601. (Co-sponsor: Greenbaum Doll & McDonald) Eds. R. Cleary, P. Nepute.
    Description: Reports the latest Kentucky employment law developments that affect Kentucky employers.

340   US   ISSN 0023-026X
LAW
KENTUCKY LAW JOURNAL. 1912. q. $28. University of Kentucky, College of Law, Lexington, KY 40506. TEL 606-257-4747. FAX 606-258-1061. Ed. Lloyd Chatfield. adv.; bk.rev.; index; circ. 1,000. (also avail. in microfiche from WSH; microfilm from RRI,WSH; back issues avail.) **Indexed:** C.L.I., L.R.I., Lang.& Lang.Behav.Abstr., Leg.Cont., Leg.Per., P.A.I.S., SSCI.
    ●Also available online. Vendor(s): WESTLAW.
    —BLDSC shelfmark: 5089.645000.

340   KE
KENYA. COURT OF APPEAL. DIGEST OF DECISIONS OF THE COURT. (Text in English) 1968. m. Court of Appeal, Box 30187, Nairobi, Kenya.
    Formerly: Court of Appeal for East Africa. Digest of Decisions of the Court.

349   II   ISSN 0023-0510
LAW
KERALA LAW JOURNAL. (Text in English) vol.15, 1971. w. Rs.20. Mathrubhumi Press, c/o Mr. C.P.M. Sundaram, T. D. Road, "Menons", Cochin 682011, Kerala, India.

349   II   ISSN 0023-0529
LAW
KERALA LAW TIMES. (Text in English) 1949. w. Rs.100. High Court Rd., Ernakulam, Cochin 11, Kerala, India. Ed. M.C. Mathew. adv.; bk.rev.; abstr.; index; circ. 5,500.

340   SJ
KHARTOUM LAW REVIEW. 1979. a. (University of Khartoum, Faculty of Law) Khartoum University Press, Box 321, Khartoum, Sudan.

340   UK
KINGS COLLEGE LAW JOURNAL. 1936. a. $20. University of London, Kings College, School of Law, Strand, London WC2R 2LS, England. TEL 071-836-5454. FAX 071-873-2465. (back issues avail.)
    Formerly: Kings Counsel.

340   AU   ISSN 0259-0735
KIRCHE UND RECHT. irreg., no.18, 1989. price varies. Verband der Wissenschaftlichen Gesellschaften Oesterreichs, Lindengasse 37, A-1070 Vienna, Austria. TEL 932166.

340 388.3   UK   ISSN 0308-8987
KITCHIN'S ROAD TRANSPORT LAW. 1959. biennial. Butterworth & Co. (Publishers) Ltd. (Subsidiary of: Reed International PLC), 88 Kingsway, London WC2B 6AB, England. TEL 71-405 6900. FAX 71-405-1332. TELEX 95678. (US addr.: Butterworth Legal Publishers, 90 Stiles Rd., Salem, NH 03079. TEL 800-548-4001) Ed. James Duckworth.
    —BLDSC shelfmark: 5098.334000.

340 350   UK   ISSN 0140-3281
KNIGHT'S LOCAL GOVERNMENT REPORTS. 1902. 12/yr. £220. Charles Knight Publishing, Tolley House, 2 Addiscombe Rd., Croydon CR9 5AF, England. TEL 01-686-9141. FAX 01-686-3155. Ed. E.M. Wellwood. index; circ. 750.
    Formerly (until 1975): Knight's Local Government and Magisterial Reports.

340   JA   ISSN 0075-6423
LAW
KOBE UNIVERSITY LAW REVIEW. INTERNATIONAL EDITION. (Text in English, French, German and other languages) 1961. a. Kobe University Law Review Association, Faculty of Law, Kobe University, Rokkodai, Kobe-shi, Hyogo-ken, Japan. FAX 078-802-3614. Ed. Akira Negishi. circ. 460.
    —BLDSC shelfmark: 5100.612000.

340   GR
KODIX NOMIKOU VEMATOS. s-m. Dr.7500. Athens Bar Association, Academia 60, 106 79 Athens, Greece. TEL 361-4289-290. FAX 36-10-537.

340   DK   ISSN 0108-9811
KOEBENHAVNS UNIVERSITET. RETSVIDENSKABELIGT INSTITUT B. STUDIER. 1983. irreg. free. Koebenhavns Universitet, Retsvidenskabeligt Institut B, Studiegaarden, Studiestraede 6, 1455 Copenhagen K, Denmark. FAX 339-0552. Ed. Peter Blume. circ. 150.

KOKUGAKUIN UNIVERSITY. FACULTY OF LAW AND POLITICS. JOURNAL/KOKUGAKUIN HOGAKU. see *POLITICAL SCIENCE*

340   PL   ISSN 0023-4478
LAW
KRAKOWSKIE STUDIA PRAWNICZE. (Text in Polish; summaries in English, French, German or Russian) 1968. a. price varies. (Polska Akademia Nauk, Oddzial w Krakowie, Komisja Nauk Prawnych) Ossolineum, Publishing House of the Polish Academy of Sciences, Rynek 9, Wroclaw, Poland. TELEX 0712771 OSS PL. (Dist. by: Ars Polona-Ruch, Krakowskie Przedmiescie 7, Warsaw, Poland) Ed. Joseph Filipek.
    Description: Theory of all branches of law. Comparative studies.

KRCKI ZBORNIK. see *HISTORY — History Of Europe*

KRITISCHE JUSTIZ. see *POLITICAL SCIENCE — Civil Rights*

340   GW   ISSN 0179-2830
KRITISCHE VIERTELJAHRESSCHRIFT FUER GESETZGEBUNG UND RECHTSWISSENSCHAFT. 1917. q. DM.138. Duncker und Humblot GmbH, Postfach 410329, 1000 Berlin 41, Germany. TEL 030-7900060. FAX 030-79000631. Ed. P.-A. Albrecht. (reprint service avail. from SCH)

340   DK   ISSN 0108-7878
KROGHS LOVINFORMATION. (Register for: Samling af Bekendtgoerelser, and Cirkulaeresamlingen, Indeholdende Samtlige Gaeldende Lovebestemmelse, Bekendtgoerelser, Anordninger, Cirkulaerer m.m.) 1983. a. DKK 580. Kroghs Forlag A S, Chr. Hansensvej 3, 7100 Vejle, Denmark.
    Formerly: Kroghs Register (ISSN 0106-4878)

340   II
KURUKSHETRA LAW JOURNAL. (Text in English) 1971. a. Rs.7.50($2) Kurukshetra University, Faculty of Law, Kurukshetra 132118, Haryana, Punjab, India. Ed. S.C. Srivastava. bk.rev.; circ. 700.

340 658   US
L A M A MANAGER. 1984. q. $20. Legal Assistant Management Association, Box 40129, Overland Park, KS 66204. TEL 913-381-4458. adv.; bk.rev.; circ. 600.
    Formerly: Legal Assistant Management Newsletter.

346.013   CN
L E A F LINES. (Text in English, French) 1985. q. Can.$40. Women's Legal Education and Action Fund, 489 College St., Ste. 403, Toronto, Ont. M6G 1A5, Canada. TEL 416-963-9654. FAX 416-963-8455. Ed. Jane Craig. circ. 8,500. (also avail. in audio cassette)
    Description: Describes test case litigation undertaken by LEAF based on sexual equality guarantees in Canadian Chartered Rights and Freedoms.

L I R S BULLETIN. (Lutheran Immigration and Refugee Service) see *RELIGIONS AND THEOLOGY — Protestant*

340   US   ISSN 0734-0990
KF4208.5.L3
L R E PROJECT EXCHANGE. (Law-Related Education) 3/yr. free. American Bar Association, Youth Education for Citizenship, 750 N. Lake Shore Dr., Chicago, IL 60611. TEL 312-988-5000. Ed. Charles White.
    Description: For project leaders; emphasizes the practical considerations involved in designing and carrying out LRE programs.

LAW

340   US   ISSN 0731-9711
KF4208.5.L3
L R E REPORT. (Law-Related Education) 3/yr. free. American Bar Association, Youth Education for Citizenship, 750 N. Lake Shore Dr., Chicago, IL 60611. TEL 312-988-5000. Ed. Charles White.
Description: Contains current information on resources, instructional materials, forthcoming conferences, new projects, funding opportunities, and other developments in the field of LRE.

349   IT   ISSN 0023-6462
LABEO; rassegna quadrimestrale di diritto romano. 1955. 3/yr. L.95000. Casa Editrice Dott. Eugenio Jovene, Via Mezzocannone 109, Naples, Italy. Ed. Antonio Guarino.

LABOR AND EMPLOYMENT IN CONNECTICUT. see BUSINESS AND ECONOMICS — Labor And Industrial Relations

LABOR & EMPLOYMENT IN MASSACHUSETTS; a guide to employment laws, regulations and practices. see BUSINESS AND ECONOMICS — Labor And Industrial Relations

LABOR AND EMPLOYMENT IN NEW YORK. see BUSINESS AND ECONOMICS — Labor And Industrial Relations

LABOR & EMPLOYMENT LAW. see BUSINESS AND ECONOMICS — Labor And Industrial Relations

347   US   ISSN 0892-4449
▼**LABOR AND EMPLOYMENT LAW ANTHOLOGY**. 1991. a. $114.95. International Library Law Book Publishers, Inc., 101 Lakeforest Blvd., Ste. 270, Gaithersburg, MD 20877. TEL 301-990-7755. FAX 301-990-7642. Ed. Donald J. Hoyes. bibl.; index.
Description: Selected US review articles on labor and employment, culled from over 900 US law review journals, and printed in their entirety.

340   US
LABOR ARBITRATION AND DISPUTE SETTLEMENTS. (Subseries of: Labor Relations Reporter) 1937. w. $749. The Bureau of National Affairs, Inc., 1231 25th St., N.W., Washington, DC 20037. TEL 201-452-4200. FAX 202-822-8092. TELEX 285656 BANI WSH. (Subscr. to: 9435 Key West Ave., Rockville, MD 20850. TEL 800-372-1033) Ed. Nancy J. Sedmak. (looseleaf format; back issues avail.)
●Also available online. Vendor(s): DIALOG (File no.244).
Description: Contains arbitration cases, and digests of court decisions involving arbitration.

340 331.1   US
LABOR LAW INSTITUTE. 1967. a. $100. Southwestern Legal Foundation, Attn: Carol Holgren, Ed., Box 830707, Richardson, TX 75083. TEL 214-690-2370. (also avail. in microfilm from RRI; reprint service avail. from RRI)
Formerly: Institute on Labor Law. Labor Law Developments. Annual Proceeding.

347.9   US   ISSN 0023-6586
K12
LABOR LAW JOURNAL; to promote sound thinking on labor law problems. 1949. m. $95. Commerce Clearing House, Inc., 4025 W. Peterson Ave., Chicago, IL 60646. TEL 312-583-8500. bk.rev.; abstr.; charts; illus.; stat.; cum.index: 1949-1954, vols.1-5; circ. 3,000. (also avail. in microform from UMI; reprint service avail. from RRI) **Indexed:** B.P.I., BPIA, C.L.I., Curr.Cont., Int.Lab.Doc., L.R.I., Leg.Per., P.A.I.S., Pers.Lit., Risk Abstr., SSCI, Tr.& Indus.Ind., Work Rel.Abstr.
—BLDSC shelfmark: 5137.920000.

340 331.8   US
LABOR LAW REPORTS. 1934. w. $1995. Commerce Clearing House, Inc., 4025 W. Peterson Ave., Chicago, IL 60646. TEL 312-583-8500. Ed. D. Newquist. (looseleaf format)

LABOR LAW REPORTS: SUMMARY. see BUSINESS AND ECONOMICS — Labor And Industrial Relations

347.9   US   ISSN 8756-2995
K12
LABOR LAWYER. 1985. q. $23 (foreign $28). American Bar Association, Labor and Employment Law Section, 750 N. Lake Shore Dr., Chicago, IL 60611. TEL 312-988-6083. Ed. Robert Rabin. circ. 14,240. (back issues avail.) **Indexed:** Leg.Per.
—BLDSC shelfmark: 5137.920100.
Description: Provides discussions of developments in all areas of employment to practitioners, judges, administrators, and public.

LABOR LETTER. see BUSINESS AND ECONOMICS — Labor And Industrial Relations

LABOR RELATIONS IN MAINE. see BUSINESS AND ECONOMICS — Labor And Industrial Relations

LABORATORY REGULATION MANUAL. see MEDICAL SCIENCES — Experimental Medicine, Laboratory Technique

LABORATORY REGULATION NEWS; biweekly news for testing and standards professionals. see MEDICAL SCIENCES — Experimental Medicine, Laboratory Technique

LABOUR AND INDUSTRIAL CASES. see BUSINESS AND ECONOMICS — Labor And Industrial Relations

347.9 331.8   CN   ISSN 0821-2635
KEB404.3
LABOUR ARBITRATION. (Text in English) 1978. a. price varies. Continuing Legal Education Society of British Columbia, 200-1148 Hornby St., Vancouver, B.C. V6Z 2C3, Canada. TEL 604-669-3544. FAX 604-669-9260. Ed. Karen Imeson. circ. 300. (looseleaf format; back issues avail.)

347.9 331   II   ISSN 0023-6977
LABOUR LAW JOURNAL. 1949. m. Rs.300. 18 Daiva Sigamani Rd., Madras 600 014, India. TEL 471621. Ed.Bd. adv.; charts; index every 6 mos, cum.index covering 11 yrs.; circ. 5,000. **Indexed:** Bus.Ind.

LABOUR LEGISLATION IN NOVA SCOTIA. see BUSINESS AND ECONOMICS — Labor And Industrial Relations

340   US   ISSN 0023-7078
LAW
LACKAWANNA JURIST. 1879. w. $35. Lackawanna Bar Association, 205 Davidow Bldg., Corner Spruce and Wyoming Aves., Scranton, PA 18503. TEL 717-969-9161. Ed. Michael B. Keegan. adv.; circ. 600. (also avail. in microform)

LAG OCH AVTAL. see BUSINESS AND ECONOMICS — Labor And Industrial Relations

340   FI   ISSN 0023-7353
LAW
LAKIMIES. 8/yr. FIM 55. Suomen Lakimiesliitto - Society of Finnish Jurists, Vudenmaankatu 4-6 B, 00120 Helsinki, Finland. bk.rev.; index.

340   FI   ISSN 0023-7361
LAKIMIESUUTISET/JURISTNYTT. (Text in Finnish and Swedish) 1945. m. FIM 160. Suomen Lakimiesliitto - Finlands Juristfoerbundet, Uudenmaankatu 4-6 B, 00120 Helsinki, Finland. TEL 90649201. FAX 90-602139. Ed. Liisa Groenroos. adv.; bk.rev.; stat.; circ. 11,600.

LAMBDA UPDATE. see HOMOSEXUALITY

346.066 600   FR
LAMY DROIT DE L'INFORMATIQUE; Informatique, Telematique, Reseaux. (Supplement avail.: Lamy Droit de l'Informatique - Formulaire) a. 1380 F. (with supplement 1640 F.)(effective 1991). Lamy S.A., 155, rue Legendre, 75850 Paris Cedex 17, France. TEL 46-27-28-90. FAX 42-29-86-81. TELEX 214 398.
Description: Treats questions of law raised by new technologies - expert systems, integrated circuits, video games.

346.066 330   FR
LAMY DROIT ECONOMIQUE; concurrence, distribution, consommation. (Supplement avail.: Lamy Droit Economique - Formulaire) a. 1360 F. (with supplement 1620 F.)(effective 1991). Lamy S.A., 155, rue Legendre, 75850 Paris Cedex 17, France. TEL 46-27-28-90. FAX 42-29-86-81. TELEX 214 398.
Description: Provides in-depth analysis of the economics of competition, distribution and consumption.

346.066 332   FR
LAMY FISCAL; l'outil pratique pour connaitre et exploiter la reglementation fiscale. a. 1500 F. Lamy S.A., 155, rue Legendre, 75850 Paris, France. TEL 46-27-28-90. FAX 42-29-86-81. TELEX 214398. charts; index.
Description: Covers corporate, income, state, local and vehicular taxes, Value Added Tax, penal laws and special regulations.

346.066 330   FR
LAMY SOCIAL; droit du travail et de la securite sociale. (Supplement avail.: Lamy Social Formulaire) a. 1340 F. (with supplement 1600 F.)(effective 1991). Lamy S.A., 155, rue Legendre, 75850 Paris Cedex 17, France. TEL 46-27-28-90. FAX 42-29-86-81. TELEX 214398. charts; index.
Description: Aims to evaluate new legislative texts and the fluctuation and evolution of jurisprudence.

340   CC
LAN DUN. (Text in Chinese) m. (Tianji Shi Faxuehui) Tianji Ribao She, 62, Tangshan Dao, Heping-qu, Tianjin 300040, People's Republic of China. TEL 312764. Ed. Mi Qihua.

340   US   ISSN 0023-7612
K12
LAND AND WATER LAW REVIEW. 1966. s-a. $18 to non-members. University of Wyoming, College of Law, Box 3035, University Sta., Laramie, WY 82071. TEL 307-766-3359. FAX 307-766-4044. (Co-sponsors: Wyoming State Bar; Water Resources Research Institute) adv.; bk.rev.; cum.index: vols. 1-20; circ. 2,150. (also avail. in microform from UMI,WSH; reprint service avail. from WSH) **Indexed:** Bibl.& Ind.Geol., C.L.I., Energy Info.Abstr., Environ.Abstr., INIS Atomind., L.R.I., Leg.Per., Ocean.Abstr., Pollut.Abstr., Sel.Water Res.Abstr.
—BLDSC shelfmark: 5146.790000.
Incorporates: Wyoming Law Journal.

340   CN   ISSN 0380-4208
KE5175.A45
LAND COMPENSATION REPORTS. 1971. m. (with quarterly cumulations). Can.$105. Canada Law Book Inc., 240 Edward St., Aurora, Ont. L4G 3S9, Canada. TEL 416-841-6472.

LAND DEVELOPMENT LAW REPORTER. see REAL ESTATE

340 614.7   UK
LAND MANAGEMENT AND ENVIRONMENTAL LAW REPORT. 1989. 6/yr. $295. John Wiley & Sons Ltd., Journals, Baffins Lane, Chichester, Sussex PO19 1UD, England. TEL 0243-779777. FAX 0243-775878. TELEX 86290-WIBOOK-G. Ed. Malcolm Forster. **Indexed:** Environ.Per.Bibl.
Description: Provides information on the entire spectrum of environmental issues in a cross-sectoral manner.

340 333.33   US   ISSN 1058-7012
▼**LAND USE FORUM**; a journal of law, policy, and practice. 1991. 4/yr. $225. Continuing Education of the Bar - California, University of California Extension, 2300 Shattuck Ave., Berkeley, CA 94704. TEL 510-642-8000. FAX 800-642-3788. (Co-sponsor: State Bar of California) Ed. Johanna Sherlin. bk.rev. (tabloid format; back issues avail.)
Description: Addresses land use issues at an advanced level from the standpoints of law, policy, and practice. Explores key issues recently developing as they relate to land use process.

LAND USE LAW AND ZONING DIGEST. see REAL ESTATE

LAND USE LAW REPORT. see HOUSING AND URBAN PLANNING

LAW

340 333.33   US
LANDLORD REMEDIES IN FLORIDA. 1987. base vol. (plus suppl.). $80. Butterworth Legal Publishers (Salem) (Subsidiary of: Reed International PLC), 90 Stiles Rd., Salem, NH 03079. TEL 800-548-4001. FAX 603-898-9858. (looseleaf format)

LANDLORD VS TENANT - N Y C. see *REAL ESTATE*

LANSKY: BIBLIOTHEKSRECHTLICHE VORSCHRIFTEN. see *LIBRARY AND INFORMATION SCIENCES*

LAVORO E DIRITTO. see *LABOR UNIONS*

340   AU   ISSN 0259-0816
K12
LAW & ANTHROPOLOGY; internationales Jahrbuch fuer Rechtsanthropologie. 1986. a. price varies. Verband der Wissenschaftlichen Gesellschaften Oesterreichs, Lindengasse 37, A-1070 Vienna, Austria. TEL 932166. (Co-sponsor: Klaus Renner Verlag)

LAW & BUSINESS DIRECTORY OF BANKRUPTCY ATTORNEYS (YEAR). see *BUSINESS AND ECONOMICS — Trade And Industrial Directories*

340   US   ISSN 0023-9186
K12
LAW AND CONTEMPORARY PROBLEMS. 1933. q. $45 (foreign $51). Duke University, School of Law, Rm. 006, Durham, NC 27706-2580. TEL 919-684-5966. FAX 919-684-3417. Ed. Theresa N. Glover. adv.; index; circ. 2,100. (also avail. in microfilm from RRI; reprint service avail. from KTO,RRI) **Indexed**: A.B.C.Pol.Sci., Account.Ind. (1974-), ASSIA, C.L.I., Commun.Abstr., Crim.Just.Abstr., Curr.Cont., Energy Ind., Energy Info.Abstr., J.of Econ.Lit., L.R.I., Lang.& Lang Behav.Abstr., Leg.Cont., Leg.Per., Mar.Aff.Bibl., Mid.East: Abstr.& Ind., P.A.I.S., Soc.Sci.Ind., SSCI.
—BLDSC shelfmark: 5161.350000.

340   UK   ISSN 0957-8536
CODEN: LACREI
▼**LAW AND CRITIQUE**; journal of critical legal studies. 1990. 2/yr. £37. Deborah Charles Publications, 173 Mather Ave., Liverpool LI8 6JZ, England. TEL 051-724-2500. (Distr. in US by: William Gaunt & Sons, Inc., 3011 Gulf Dr., Holmes Beach, FL 34217-2199) Ed. P. Goodrich. adv.; bk.rev.; circ. 400.
—BLDSC shelfmark: 5161.350700.

340   US
LAW AND ETHICS SERIES. (Former name of issuing body: Academy for Contemporary Problems) 1977. irreg. Academy for State and Local Government, 444 N. Capitol St., N.W., Ste. 349, Washington, DC 20001. TEL 202-638-1445.

340   US   ISSN 0738-2480
K12
LAW AND HISTORY REVIEW. 1983. s-a. $30 to individuals (foreign $33); institutions $50 (foreign $53). (American Society for Legal History) University of Illinois Press, 54 E. Gregory Dr., Champaign, IL 61820. TEL 217-244-0626. FAX 217-244-8082. Ed. Bruce H. Mann. adv.; bk.rev.; circ. 1,350. (also avail. in microfilm from UMI) **Indexed**: C.L.I., Hist.Abstr., Leg.Per.
—BLDSC shelfmark: 5161.351500.
Refereed Serial

340 150   US   ISSN 0147-7307
K12   CODEN: LHBEDM
LAW AND HUMAN BEHAVIOR. 1977. bi-m. $275 (foreign $320)(effective 1992). Plenum Publishing Corp., 233 Spring St., New York, NY 10013-1578. TEL 212-620-8000. FAX 212-463-0742. TELEX 23-421139. Ed. Ronald Roesch. adv. (also avail. in microfilm from JSC; back issues avail.) **Indexed**: Adol.Ment.Hlth.Abstr., Biol.Abstr., C.L.I., Crim.Just.Abstr., Curr.Cont., Excerp.Med., L.R.I., Lang.& Lang.Behav.Abstr., Leg.Per., Psychol.Abstr., Psycscan, Sociol.Abstr., SSCI.
—BLDSC shelfmark: 5161.352500.
Refereed Serial

340   US   ISSN 0737-089X
K12
LAW & INEQUALITY; a journal of theory and practice. 1983. 3/yr. $15. University of Minnesota, Law School, 229 19th Ave. S., Minneapolis, MN 55455. TEL 612-625-8034. Ed. Kendal Tyre. bk.rev.; circ. 5,600. (also avail. in microform from WSH; back issues avail.; reprint service avail. from WSH) **Indexed**: C.L.I., Leg.Per.
—BLDSC shelfmark: 5161.352700.

340   BG
LAW AND INTERNATIONAL AFFAIRS. (Text in English) 1975. s-a. $6. Bangladesh Institute of Law and International Affairs, 501 Dhanmondi Residential Area, Rd. No. 7, Dhaka 5, Bangladesh. (Dist. by: Karim International, 3, Padmalochon Roy Lane, Mahutuly, Dhaka 1, Bangladesh) Ed. Kamruddin Ahmed. bk.rev.; circ. 2,000.

340   UK
LAW & JUSTICE. 1962. s-a. £12.50 (foreign £13.50). Edmund Plowden Trust, 100A Hazellville Rd., London N19 3NA, England. Ed. Mary Welstead. adv.; bk.rev.; abstr.; bibl.; circ. 250. **Indexed**: C.L.I., Canon Law Abstr, CERDIC, L.R.I.
Formerly: Quis Custodiet (ISSN 0033-6610)

340 347   US   ISSN 0740-090X
KF190
LAW AND LEGAL INFORMATION DIRECTORY. 1980. irreg., 6th ed., 1991. $305. Gale Research Inc., 835 Penobscot Bldg., Detroit, MI 48226. TEL 313-961-2242. FAX 313-961-6083. TELEX 810-221-7086. Eds. Jacqueline Wasserman O'Brien, Steven Wasserman.
Description: Guide to law enforcements organizations and legal information in the U.S.

340   GW   ISSN 0458-8460
K12
LAW AND LEGISLATION IN THE GERMAN DEMOCRATIC REPUBLIC. (Text in English) 1959. 2/yr. DM.20. (Vereinigung der Juristen der Deutschen Demokratischen Republik - Lawyers Association of the GDR) Staatsverlag der DDR, Otto-Grotewohl-Str. 17, 1086 Berlin, Germany. Ed.Bd. bibl. **Indexed**: C.L.I., Excerp.Med., Leg.Per.

340 100   NE   ISSN 0167-5249
K12   CODEN: LAWPDG
LAW AND PHILOSOPHY; an international journal for jurisprudence and legal philosophy. 1982. q. $65 to individuals; institutions $153.50. Kluwer Academic Publishers, Postbus 17, 3300 AA Dordrecht, Netherlands. TEL 078-334911. FAX 078-334254. TELEX 29245. (Dist. by: Kluwer Academic Publishers Group, P.O. Box 322, 3300 AH Dordrecht, Netherlands; N. America dist. addr.: Box 358, Accord Station, Hingham, MA 02018-0358. TEL 617-871-6600) Ed. A. Mabe. adv.; bk.rev (reprint service avail. from SWZ) **Indexed**: C.L.I., Curr.Cont., L.R.I., Lang.& Lang.Behav.Abstr., Leg.Cont., Leg.Per., Phil.Ind., Sociol.Abstr., SSCI.
—BLDSC shelfmark: 5161.362600.

340 100   NE
LAW AND PHILOSOPHY LIBRARY. 1985. irreg., vol.2, 1985. price varies. Kluwer Academic Publishers, Spuiboulevard 50, P.O. Box 17, 3300 AA Dordrecht, Netherlands. TEL 078-334911. FAX 078-334254. TELEX 29245. (Dist. by: Kluwer Academic Publishers Group, P.O. Box 322, 3300 AH Dordrecht, Netherlands) Eds. Michael Bayles, Alan Mabe.

340 320   UK   ISSN 0265-8240
K12   CODEN: LAPOE6
LAW & POLICY. 1979. q. £31($45) to individuals; institutions £74($110). Basil Blackwell Ltd., 108 Cowley Rd., Oxford OX4 1JF, England. TEL 0865-791100. FAX 0865-791347. TELEX 837022-OXBOOK-G. Ed.Bd. adv.; bk.rev.; bibl.; charts; stat.; index; circ. 700. (also avail. in microform; reprint service avail. from WSH) **Indexed**: A.B.C.Pol.Sci., Amer.Hist.& Life, C.L.I., Crim.Just.Abstr., Hist.Abstr., L.R.I., Mid.East: Abstr.& Ind., Sage Pub.Admin.Abstr.
—BLDSC shelfmark: 5161.362800.
Formerly: Law and Policy Quarterly (ISSN 0164-0267)

340 320   KO
LAW AND POLITICAL REVIEW. (Text in Korean; table of contents in English) 1958. a. Ewha Women's University, College of Law and Political Science, 11-1 Dai-Hyun-dong, Seodaimoon-ku, Seoul, S. Korea. bibl.

340   II   ISSN 0377-0850
LAW
LAW AND PROGRESS.* (Text in English) 1974. q. Rs.18. Indian Association of Lawyers, 29-B Maharani Bagh, New Delhi, India. Ed. Harish Chandra. bk.rev.; bibl.

340 300 616.8   US   ISSN 0098-5961
K12
LAW AND PSYCHOLOGY REVIEW. 1975. a. $12. University of Alabama, School of Law, Box 870382, Tuscaloosa, AL 35487-0382. TEL 205-348-4527. adv.; bk.rev.; circ. 400. (also avail. in microfilm from WSH; reprint service avail. from WSH) **Indexed**: Adol.Ment.Hlth.Abstr., C.L.I., Crim.Just.Abstr., L.R.I., Leg.Per., Psychol.Abstr., Psycscan.
—BLDSC shelfmark: 5161.363800.

340   US   ISSN 0897-6546
K1
LAW AND SOCIAL INQUIRY. 1976. q. $36 to individuals; institutions $59 (foreign $65); academic $29 (foreign $35). (American Bar Foundation) University of Chicago Press, Journals Division, 5720 S. Woodlawn Ave., Chicago, IL 60637. TEL 312-753-3347. FAX 312-702-0694. TELEX 25-4603. (Subscr. to: Box 37005, Chicago, IL 60637) Ed. T.C. Halliday. bibl.; circ. 6,700. (also avail. in microfilm from UMI; back issues avail.; reprint service avail. from RRI) **Indexed**: Abstr.Bk.Rev.Curr.Leg.Per., C.L.I., CJPI, Crim.Just.Abstr., Curr.Cont., L.R.I., Law Ofc.Info.Svc., Leg.Cont., Leg.Per., SSCI.
—BLDSC shelfmark: 5161.364300.
Formerly: American Bar Foundation Journal (ISSN 0361-9486)
Description: Provides empirical studies on the legal system. Reviews social issues and includes notes annotating recent legal publications in law and social science.
Refereed Serial

340 300   US   ISSN 0023-9216
K12
LAW & SOCIETY REVIEW. 1966. 5/yr. $86 (foreign $91). Law and Society Association, Hampshire House, University of Massachusetts, Amherst, MA 01003. TEL 413-545-4617. FAX 413-545-1640. Ed. Shari S. Diamond. adv.; bk.rev.; bibl.; charts; circ. 2,400. (also avail. in microfilm from RRI,UMI; microfiche from WSH; microfilm from WSH; back issues avail.; reprint service avail. from ISI) **Indexed**: A.B.C.Pol.Sci., Abstr.Crim.& Pen., Acad.Ind., Adol.Ment.Hlth.Abstr., Amer.Hist.& Life, ASSIA, C.L.I., Crim.Just.Abstr., Curr.Cont., E.I., Hist.Abstr, HRIS, Int.Bibl.Soc.Sci., L.R.I., Lang.& Lang.Behav.Abstr., Leg.Cont., Leg.Per., P.A.I.S., Psychol.Abstr., Sage Urb.Stud.Abstr., Soc.Sci.Ind., Soc.Work Res.& Abstr., Sociol.Abstr. (1966-), SSCI.
—BLDSC shelfmark: 5161.365000.
Description: Examines the relationship between society and the legal process. Includes the cultural, economic, political, psychological, and social aspects of law and the legal system.

340   UK   ISSN 0262-7647
LAW & TAX REVIEW. 1982. m. £107($175) Longman Group UK Ltd., Law, Tax and Finance Division, 21-27 Lamb's Conduit St., London WC1N 3NJ, England. TEL 071-242-2548. FAX 071-831-8119. TELEX 295445. Ed. David Martin.
—BLDSC shelfmark: 5161.366100.
Description: Articles on topical issues of law and taxation.

323.42   US
LAW & WOMEN SERIES. 1972. irreg. $2 per no. Today Publications and News Service, Inc., 621 National Press Bldg., Washington, DC 20045. TEL 202-638-0348. Ed. Myra E. Barrer.

LAW AND YOU. see *BUSINESS AND ECONOMICS — Chamber Of Commerce Publications*

LAW BOOKS IN PRINT; books in English published throughout the world. see *BIBLIOGRAPHIES*

340 001.535   UK   ISSN 0962-9580
LAW, COMPUTERS, AND ARTIFICIAL INTELLIGENCE. 3/yr. £54($98) (foreign £60). Triangle Books Ltd., P.O. Box 65, Wallingford, Oxfordshire OX10 0YG, England. TEL 0491-38013. FAX 0491-34968. Ed. Indira Mahalingham Carr.

340   ZA
LAW DEVELOPMENT COMMISSION. ANNUAL REPORT.
(Text in English) 1976. a. K.50. (Law Development Commission) Government Printing Department, P.O. Box 30136, Lusaka, Zambia. TEL 01-215-401. circ. 500.

340   US
LAW ENFORCEMENT LEGAL REPORTER. 1977. m. $24.50. Law Enforcement Legal Reporter, Box 1356, Torrance, CA 90505. TEL 213-379-3214. Ed. Elliot E. Alhadeff. circ. 3,000. (back issues avail.)

340   US
LAW FIRM PROFIT REPORT. 1988. m. $139. Newsletter Services, Inc., 1545 New York Ave., N.E., Washington, DC 20002. TEL 202-529-5700. Ed. Nancy Koran. bk.rev.; index.

LAW FIRMS YELLOW BOOK. see BUSINESS AND ECONOMICS — Trade And Industrial Directories

340.05   US
THE LAW FORUM. 1970. 3/yr. free. University of Baltimore, School of Law, Managing Editor, 1420 N. Charles St., Baltimore, MD 21202. TEL 301-576-2303. Ed. William P. Atkins. circ. 8,000. (also avail. in microform from UMI; reprint service avail. from UMI)
Former titles: Forum Law Journal (ISSN 0360-2044); Forum (Baltimore) (ISSN 0094-1948)

340   AT   ISSN 0811-5796
K12
LAW IN CONTEXT. 1983. s-a. Aus.$36.50 to institutions (foreign Aus.$39.50). La Trobe University Press, Bundoora, Vic. 3083, Australia. TEL 03-479-1234. Ed. Martyn Chanock. adv.; bk.rev.; circ. 500. (back issues avail.)

340   NR   ISSN 0458-8592
LAW IN SOCIETY. 1964. irreg. (1-2/yr.) Ahmadu Bello University, Law Society, Zaria, Nigeria.

340   AT   ISSN 0023-9267
LAW INSTITUTE JOURNAL. 1927. m. (except Jan.). Aus.$74 (foreign Aus.$114). Law Institute of Victoria, 470 Bourke St, Melbourne, Vic. 3000, Australia. TEL 03-607-9342. FAX 03-607-4451. Ed. M. Schiel. adv.; bk.rev.; index; circ. 10,000. (tabloid format; also avail. in microfiche from WSH; microfilm from WSH) **Indexed:** C.L.I., L.R.I., Leg.Per.
—BLDSC shelfmark: 5161.390000.

LAW LIBRARIAN. see LIBRARY AND INFORMATION SCIENCES

026   US
LAW LIBRARIAN'S BULLETIN BOARD. 1989. 8/yr. $36 (foreign $44). Legal Information Services, Box 67, Newton Highlands, MA 02161-0067. TEL 508-443-4087. Ed. Elyse H. Fox.
Description: Provides international coverage of news and developments in law libraries, government information, library organizations, industry news and job listings.

LAW LIBRARY ASSOCIATION OF MARYLAND NEWS. see LIBRARY AND INFORMATION SCIENCES

340   US   ISSN 0268-8336
LAW LIBRARY INFORMATION REPORTS. 1981. irreg. (3-6/yr.). $100 per report. Glanville Publishers, Inc., 75 Main St., Dobbs Ferry, NY 10522. TEL 914-693-5956. FAX 914-693-0402. Ed. Gary R. Hartman. circ. 250.
—BLDSC shelfmark: 5161.399000.
Description: Provides information and recommendations which librarians and administrative personnel can apply in making decisions for the law library.

LAW LIBRARY JOURNAL. see LIBRARY AND INFORMATION SCIENCES

LAW, MEDICINE & HEALTH CARE. see MEDICAL SCIENCES — Forensic Sciences

340   UK   ISSN 0141-5867
LAW NOTES. 1881. m. £1.70 per no. (College of Law) Law Notes Lending Library, 25-26 Chancery Lane, London WC2A 1NB, England. FAX 071-831-5905. Ed. P.J. Hawkins. adv.; bk.rev.; circ. 4,750. (also avail. in microfilm from BHP) **Indexed:** C.L.I., L.R.I.

340 659.1   US
THE LAW OF ADVERTISING. (Issued as 4 base vols. with supplements) 1973. irreg. Matthew Bender & Co., Inc., 11 Penn Plaza, New York, NY 10001. TEL 212-967-7707. Eds. George Eric Rosden, Peter E. Rosden. (looseleaf format)
Description: Covers the rules governing each party to the advertising contract: media, consumers, advertisers, and advertising agencies.

340 361.73   US
LAW OF ASSOCIATIONS: AN OPERATING LEGAL MANUAL FOR EXECUTIVES AND COUNSEL. (Issued as 1 base vol. with supplements) 1971. irreg. Matthew Bender & Co., Inc., 11 Penn Plaza, New York, NY 10001. TEL 212-967-7707. Ed. George D. Webster. (looseleaf format)
Description: Covers all legal and tax aspects of non-profit associations. Provides specialized information regarding tax exemptions and liabilities, executive compensation plans, political action committees, antitrust liability, public relations, and accounting procedures.

LAW OF BANK DEPOSITS, COLLECTIONS AND CREDIT CARDS (SUPPLEMENT). see BUSINESS AND ECONOMICS — Banking And Finance

340   US
LAW OF EVIDENCE IN WASHINGTON. 1986. base vol. (plus a. suppl.). $65. Butterworth Legal Publishers (Salem) (Subsidiary of: Reed International PLC), 90 Stiles Rd., Salem, NH 03079. TEL 800-548-4001. FAX 603-898-9858. Ed. Robert H. Aronson. (looseleaf format)
Description: Contains the full text of the Code plus legislative commentary, applicable Federal Advisory Committee commentary, analysis of the rules and recent court interpretations.

343   US
LAW OF PROBATION AND PAROLE. 1983. base vol. (plus a. suppl.). $95. Shepard's - McGraw-Hill, Inc., Box 35300, Colorado Springs, CO 80935-3530. TEL 800-525-2474.
Description: Covers legal issues such as parole granting, rescission, modification and revocation proceedings.

340   US
▼**LAW OF PRODUCTS LIABILITY.** 1990. 2 base vols. (plus a. suppl.). $185. Butterworth Legal Publishers (Salem) (Subsidiary of: Reed International PLC), 90 Stiles Rd., Salem, NH 03079. TEL 800-548-4001. FAX 603-898-9858. Ed. Marshall S. Shapo.
Description: Study of issues that occur in products liability litigation.

340   AT   ISSN 0725-6892
LAW OF STAMP DUTIES IN QUEENSLAND. 1981. 3/yr. Aus.$175. Law Book Co. Ltd., 44-50 Waterloo Rd., N. Ryde, N.S.W. 2113, Australia. TEL 02-887-0177. FAX 02-888-9706. TELEX ASBOOK 27995. Ed. J.G. Mann. (looseleaf format; back issues avail.)

340   UK
LAW OF WEIGHT & MEASURES. (In 2 vols.) 3/yr. $525 includes Butterworths Consumer Law Bulletin. Butterworth & Co. (Publishers) Ltd. (Subsidiary of: Reed International PLC), 88 Kingsway, London WC2B 6AB, England. TEL 71-405-6900. FAX 71-405-1332. TELEX 95678. (US addr.: Butterworth Legal Publishers, 90 Stiles Rd., Salem, NH 03079. TEL 800-548-4001) (looseleaf format)

LAW OFFICE GUIDE TO SMALL COMPUTERS. see COMPUTERS — Microcomputers

340   US   ISSN 0735-4843
LAW OFFICE MANAGEMENT & ADMINISTRATION REPORT. m. $295. Institute of Management and Administration, 29 W. 35th St., 5th fl., New York, NY 10001-2200. TEL 212-244-0360. FAX 212-564-0465. index. (back issues avail.)

340   CN   ISSN 0843-7076
LAW OFFICE MANAGEMENT JOURNAL. 1989. 3/yr. Can.$128($102) Carswell Publications, Corporate Plaza, 2075 Kennedy Rd., Scarborough, Ont. M1T 3V4, Canada. TEL 416-609-8000. FAX 416-298-5094. Ed. Donna Wannop. adv.; bk.rev.; cum.index.
Description: Provides articles on contemporary issues in law office management.

LAW OFFICE TECHNOLOGY REVIEW. see LAW — Computer Applications

338.4 658   US   ISSN 1045-9081
KF315.A15   CODEN: LEECDA
LAW PRACTICE MANAGEMENT; the magazine of law office management. 1975. 8/yr. $48 (foreign $54). American Bar Association, Law Practice Management Section, 750 N. Lake Shore Dr., Chicago, IL 60611. TEL 312-988-5000. Ed. Delmar L. Roberts. adv.; bk.rev.; illus.; circ. 23,817. (reprint service avail.) **Indexed:** ABI Inform, Account.Ind. (1987-), C.L.I., L.R.I., Law Ofc.Info.Svc., Leg.Cont., Leg.Info.Manage.Ind., P.A.I.S.
●Also available online. Vendor(s): Mead Data Central, WESTLAW.
Formerly: Legal Economics (ISSN 0360-1439)
Description: Includes feature articles, reports on technical innovations and announcements of forthcoming events.

LAW QUADRANGLE NOTES. see COLLEGE AND ALUMNI

340   PK
LAW QUARTERLY. (Text in English) vol. 3, 1970. q. Rs.12($4) Supreme Court, Lahore, Pakistan.

340   UK   ISSN 0023-933X
LAW
LAW QUARTERLY REVIEW. 1885. 4/yr. £62. Sweet & Maxwell, South Quay Plaza, 8th Floor, 183 Marsh Wall, London E14 9FT, England. TEL 071-538-8686. FAX 071-538-9508. (Dist. in U.S. & Canada by: Carswell Co. Ltd., 233 Midland Ave., Agincourt, Ont., Canada) Ed. F.M.B. Reynolds. adv.; bk.rev.; index. (reprint service avail. from RRI) **Indexed:** Abstr.Bk.Rev.Curr.Leg.Per., Br.Hum.Ind., C.L.I., L.R.I., Leg.Cont., Leg.Per., RICS, SSCI.
—BLDSC shelfmark: 5161.410000.

340   II
LAW REFERENCER. (Contains an annotated index to selected Indian legal periodicals) (Text in English) 1958. m. Rs.30($15) 35 Lawyers' Chambers, Supreme Court, New Delhi 110001, India. Ed. S.S. Husain.

340   CN   ISSN 0839-4539
KES168.A72
LAW REFORM COMMISSION OF SASKATCHEWAN. ANNUAL REPORT AND REVIEW. 1980. a. free. Law Reform Commission of Saskatchewan, 122 Third Ave., North Saskatoon, Sask. S7K 2H6, Canada. TEL 306-933-6127. FAX 306-933-6999. index; circ. 400. (back issues avail.)
Supersedes: Law Reform Commission of Saskatchewan. Yearly Review (ISSN 0711-0111)
Description: Contains objectives of the commission, description of the programs and activities carried out, plans for the upcoming year and financial information.

340 332.1   AT
▼**LAW RELATING TO BANKER AND CUSTOMER IN AUSTRALIA.** 1990. 2/yr. Aus.$475. Law Book Co. Ltd., 44-50 Waterloo Rd., North Ryde, N.S.W. 2113, Australia. TEL 02-887-0177. FAX 02-888-9706. TELEX ASBOOK 27995. Eds. G.A. Weaver, C.R. Craigie.
Description: Includes all major developments in case and statute law, including statutes dealing with cheques and corporations.

346.066   UK
LAW RELATING TO TRADE DESCRIPTIONS. (In 2 vols.) 4/yr. $525 includes Butterworths Consumer Law Bulletin. Butterworth & Co. (Publishers) Ltd. (Subsidiary of: Reed International PLC), 88 Kingsway, London WC2B 6AB, England. TEL 71-405-6900. FAX 71-405-1332. TELEX 95678. (US addr.: Butterworth Legal Publishers, 90 Stiles Rd., Salem, NH 03079. TEL 800-548-4001) (looseleaf format)

340   UK   ISSN 0265-122X
LAW REPORTS: APPEAL CASES. m. £51 (typically set in Aug.). Incorporated Council of Law Reporting for England and Wales, 3 Stone Bldgs., Lincoln's Inn, London WC2A 3XN, England. TEL 071-242 6471. FAX 071-831-5247. (also avail. in microfiche from BHP)

340   TZ
LAW REPORTS OF TANZANIA. 1973. s-a. EAs.140. University of Dar es Salaam, Faculty of Law, Box 35093, Dar es Salaam, Tanzania. Ed. B.A. Rwezaura. circ. 500. (back issues avail.)
Formerly: Tanzania High Court Digest.

340　　　　　　　UK　　ISSN 0264-1127
LAW REPORTS: QUEEN'S BENCH DIVISION. 1865. m. £51 (typically set in Aug.). Incorporated Council of Law Reporting for England and Wales, 3 Stone Bldgs., Lincoln's Inn, London WC2A 3XN, England. TEL 071-242 6471. FAX 071-831-5247. Ed. Ms. C.J. Ellis. (also avail. in microfiche from BHP)

340　　　　　　　US　　ISSN 0734-1938
KF250
LAW REVIEW JOURNAL. 1979. 3/yr. $9.75. Legal Institute, 3250 Wilshire Blvd., Ste. 1000, Los Angeles, CA 90010. TEL 213-487-6268. Ed. Herman B. Lancaster. adv.; bk.rev.; bibl.; charts; illus.; stat.; tr.lit.; circ. 200. (back issues avail.)
—BLDSC shelfmark: 5161.441000.

340　　　　　　　US　　ISSN 0741-1170
LAW SCHOOL ADMINISTRATOR'S JOURNAL. 1982. 3/yr. $9.75 per no. Legal Institute, 3250 Wilshire Blvd., Ste. 1000, Los Angeles, CA 90010. TEL 213-487-6268. FAX 213-385-2396. Ed.Bd. circ. 300.

340　　　　　　　US　　ISSN 0737-2590
LAW SCHOOL JOURNAL. 1980. 3/yr. $9.75 per no. Legal Institute, 3250 Wilshire Blvd., Ste. 1000, Los Angeles, CA 90010. TEL 213-487-6268. FAX 213-385-2396. Ed.Bd.

340　378　　　　　　US
LAW SCHOOL RECORD. 1951. s-a. $15 includes Occasional Papers. University of Chicago Law School, 1111 E. 60th St., Chicago, IL 60637. TEL 312-702-9629. FAX 312-702-0730. (Subscr. to: William S. Hein & Co., Inc., 1285 Main St., Buffalo, NY 14209) Ed. Jill Fosse. circ. 8,000. (also avail. in microfilm; microfiche; reprint service avail. from UMI) **Indexed:** C.L.I., L.R.I.

340　　　　　　　US
LAW, SOCIETY, AND POLICY. 1982. irreg., vol.5, 1990. Plenum Publishing Corp., 233 Spring St., New York, NY 10013-1578. TEL 212-620-8000. FAX 212-463-0742. TELEX 23-421139. Ed.Bd.
　　Refereed Serial

340　　　　　　　KE
LAW SOCIETY DIGEST. (Text in English) 1975. q. Law Society of Kenya, Nairobi, Kenya.

340　　　　　　　CN　　ISSN 0023-9364
LAW
LAW SOCIETY GAZETTE. 1967. q. Can.$15 to non-members. Law Society of Upper Canada, Osgoode Hall, Toronto, Ont. M5H 2N6, Canada. TEL 416-366-3726. FAX 416-367-2502. TELEX 065-28013. (Subscr. to: John Honsberger, Rm. 500, 85 Richmond St. W., Toronto, Ont. M5H 2C9, Canada) Ed. John Honsberger. bk.rev.; illus.; circ. 19,000. (tabloid format) **Indexed:** C.L.I., Ind.Can.L.P.L., L.R.I., Leg.Per.

340　　　　　　　AT　　ISSN 0023-9372
LAW
LAW SOCIETY JOURNAL. 1963. 11/yr. Aus.$65 (foreign Aus.$85). Law Society of New South Wales, 170 Phillips St., Sydney, N.S.W. 2000, Australia. FAX 231-5809. TELEX AA73063. Ed. Bob Campbell. adv.; bk.rev.; cum.index; circ. 10,936. **Indexed:** C.L.I., L.R.I.

340　　　　　　　UK　　ISSN 0458-8711
LAW
LAW SOCIETY OF SCOTLAND. JOURNAL (YEAR). 1956. m. £45. Law Society of Scotland, 26 Drumsheugh Gardens, Edinburgh EH3 7YR, Scotland. adv.; bk.rev.; bibl.; charts; illus.; index; circ. 7,600. (tabloid format) **Indexed:** C.L.I., L.R.I.
—BLDSC shelfmark: 4812.965000.

340　　　　　　　AT
LAW SOCIETY OF SOUTH AUSTRALIA. BULLETIN. 1967. m. Aus.$66 to non-members. Law Society of South Australia, 124 Waymouth St., Adelaide, S.A. 5000, Australia. TEL 08-231-9972. FAX 08-231-1929. Ed. B.C. Fitzgerald. adv.; bk.rev.; index; circ. 2,000.

340　　　　　　　CN　　ISSN 0316-5310
KE16
LAW SOCIETY OF UPPER CANADA. SPECIAL LECTURES. 1950. a. price varies. Carswell Publications, Corporate Plaza, 2075 Kennedy Rd., Scarborough, Ont. M1T 3V4, Canada. TEL 416-609-8000. FAX 416-298-5094. **Indexed:** Ind.Can.L.P.L.
—BLDSC shelfmark: 8366.600000.

340　　　　　　　UK　　ISSN 0023-9380
LAW SOCIETY'S GAZETTE. 1903. w. £62. Law Society of England and Wales, 50 Chancery Lane, London WC2A 1SX, England. FAX 01-831-0869. Ed. Sheila Pratt. adv.; bk.rev.; illus.; s-a. index; circ. 64,797.
　Indexed: Leg.Per., RICS.

340　　　　　　　UK
LAW SOCIETY'S GUARDIAN GAZETTE. 1965. m. £62. Law Society of England and Wales, 50 Chancery Lane, London WC2A 1SX, England. Ed. Sheila Pratt. adv.; bk.rev.; charts; illus.; play rev.; circ. 91,562.
　Former titles: Guardian Gazette (ISSN 0306-3348) & Law Guardian (ISSN 0023-9259)

340　　　　　　　UK　　ISSN 0306-9400
K12
LAW TEACHER. 1967. 3/yr. £35. (Association of Law Teachers) Sweet & Maxwell, South Quay Plaza, 8th Floor, 183 Marsh Wall, London E14 9FT, England. TEL 071-538-8686. FAX 071-538-9508. (Dist. in U.S. & Canada by: Carswell Co. Ltd., 233 Midland Ave., Agincourt, Ont., Canada) Ed. Patricia Leighton. adv.; bk.rev.; bibl.; charts. **Indexed:** C.L.I., L.R.I.
—BLDSC shelfmark: 5161.447000.
　Formerly: Association of Law Teachers. Journal (ISSN 0044-9628)

340　　　　　　　US　　ISSN 0741-1197
LAW TEACHER'S JOURNAL. 1984. 3/yr. $9.75 per no. Legal Institute, 3250 Wilshire Blvd., Ste. 1000, Los Angeles, CA 90010. TEL 213-487-6268. FAX 213-385-2396. Ed.Bd.

340　　　　　　　II　　ISSN 0023-9399
K12
LAW THESAURUS. (Text in English) m. Rs.4. University Book House, 15 W.B. Bungalow Rd., Tawehar Nagar, Delhi 7, India. Ed. S.M. Katial. circ. 2,000.

340　　　　　　　CN　　ISSN 0847-5083
▼**LAW TIMES.** 1990. w. $79 (foreign $135). Law Times Inc., 240 Edward St., Aurora, Ont. L4G 3S9, Canada. TEL 416-841-6481. FAX 416-841-5078. Ed. Jim Middlemiss. adv.; circ. 15,000. (tabloid format)

340　　　　　　　US
LAW TOOLS, MATERIALS, CONTACTS. 1985. 3/yr. $9.75 per no. Legal Institute, 3250 Wilshire Blvd., Ste. 1000, Los Angeles, CA 90010. TEL 213-487-6268. FAX 213-385-2396. Ed.Bd.

340　　　　　　　II
LAW WEEKLY. (Text in English) vol.86, 1973. w. Vasantha Vilas, No. 3 South Mada St., Mylapore, Madras 600004, India. Ed. K.S. Desikan. bibl.

LAWDOCS. see *LIBRARY AND INFORMATION SCIENCES*

340　　　　　　　KE
LAWS OF KENYA. SUPPLEMENT. (Text in English) 1963. irreg. Government Printing and Stationery Department, P.O. Box 30128, Nairobi, Kenya.

342　　　　　　　CC
LAWS OF THE PEOPLE'S REPUBLIC OF CHINA. (Editions in Chinese and English) 1987. irreg., vol.3, 1989. $60. (Quanguo Renmin Daibiao Dahui, Changwu Weiyuanhui, Lifa Shiwu Weiyuanhui - National People's Congress, Standing Committee, Legislative Affairs Commission) Kexue Chubanshe, Qikan Bu, 16 Donghuangchenggen Beijie, Beijing 100707, People's Republic of China. TEL 4010642. FAX 4012180. TELEX 210247-SPBJ-CN. (US office: Science Press New York, Ltd., 63-117 Alderton St., Rego Park, NY 11374. TEL 718-459-4638)
　Description: Compiles new laws enacted by the NPC and its standing committee.

340　　　　　　　NR　　ISSN 0023-9437
LAWYER. (Text in English) vol.3, 1968. irreg. (2-3/yr.). University of Lagos, Law Society, P.O. Box 12003, Lagos, Nigeria. Ed. Jonah O. Aghimien. bk.rev.; charts; circ. 500. (tabloid format)
　Description: For the Nigerian lawyer.

340　　　　　　　II
LAWYER. 1969. m. (Indian Law Institute) University of Madras, Chepauk, Triplicane, Madras 600005, Tamil Nadu, India.

658.3　　　　　　　US　　ISSN 0739-1706
KF276.5.A15
LAWYER HIRING & TRAINING REPORT. 1980. m. $249. Prentice Hall Law & Business, 270 Sylvan Ave., Englewood Cliffs, NJ 07632-2513. TEL 201-894-8484. FAX 201-894-8666. Ed. Larry Smith. bk.rev.; charts; stat.; video rev.; index; circ. 1,000. (back issues avail.)
　Incorporates: Henning C L E Reporter.

LAWYER - PILOTS BAR ASSOCIATION JOURNAL. see *AERONAUTICS AND SPACE FLIGHT*

340　　　　　　　US　　ISSN 0887-7777
LAWYER REFERRAL NETWORK. q. free. American Bar Association, Standing Committee on Lawyer Referral and Information Service, 750 N. Lake Shore Dr., Chicago, IL 60611. TEL 312-988-5000. FAX 312-988-6281.
　Description: News briefs on activities of the LRIS Committee and state and local lawyer referral services.

340　　　　　　　US　　ISSN 0278-9817
K12
LAWYERS ALERT. 1981. bi-w. $175. Lawyers Weekly Publications, 30 Court Square, Boston, MA 02108. TEL 617-227-1081. Ed. Joann Flaminio. adv.; bk.rev.; circ. 6,000. (back issues avail.)
　Description: Covers breakthrough court cases and provides how-to feature articles for trial lawyers and others.

346.066　　　　　　　US
LAWYERS' AND ACCOUNTANTS' GUIDE TO PURCHASE - SALE OF SMALL BUSINESS. 1989. base vol. (plus suppl.). Maxwell Macmillan, Rosenfeld Launer, 910 Sylvan Ave., Englewood Cliffs, NJ 07632-3310. TEL 800-562-0245. FAX 201-816-3569. Ed. Willard D. Horwich.

340　　　　　　　US
LAWYERS' ARBITRATION LETTER. 1973. q. $30 to non-members. American Arbitration Association, 140 W. 51st St., New York, NY 10020-1203. TEL 212-484-4014. FAX 212-765-4874. Ed. Vicki Young. index. cum.index.
　Formerly: Lawyers' Arbitration Letter and the Digest of Court Decisions; Formed by the merger of: Lawyers' Arbitration Letter; Arbitration Law.
　Description: Discusses the case history and developments in a specific area of arbitration law. Looks at arbitration and the common law, the enforceability of partial final awards, consolidation, and international arbitration.

341　　　　　　　
LAWYER'S COMMITTEE ON NUCLEAR POLICY NEWSLETTER. 1983. 3/yr. $35. Lawyer's Committee on Nuclear Policy, Inc., 666 Broadway, Ste. 610, New York, NY 10012. TEL 212-674-7790. FAX 212-674-6199. Ed. Brian D'Agostino. adv.; bk.rev.; circ. 2,000.
　Description: Lawyers working for the abolition of nuclear weapons.

340　　　　　　　US
LAWYERS FOR THE ARTS NEWSLETTER. s-a. $10. American Bar Association, Young Lawyers Division, 750 N. Lake Shore Dr., Chicago, IL 60611. TEL 312-988-5000. bk.rev.
　Description: Contains articles by lawyers on issues in art law, summaries of recent cases and legislation in the area.

340　　　　　　　US
LAWYER'S GUIDE TO THE TEXAS DECEPTIVE TRADE PRACTICES ACT. base vol. (plus a. suppl.). $95. Butterworth Legal Publishers (Salem) (Subsidiary of: Reed International PLC), 90 Stiles Rd., Salem, NH 03079. TEL 800-548-4001. FAX 603-898-9858. Ed. Richard M. Alderman. (looseleaf format)

340　　　　　　　US
LAWYERS JOB BULLETIN BOARD. 1975. m. $30. Federal Bar Association, 1815 H St., N.W., Ste. 408, Washington, DC 20006-3697. TEL 202-638-0252. FAX 202-775-0295. Ed. Margaret Simon. circ. 300.

340 US ISSN 0740-0519
KF8700.A15
LAWYERS LETTER. 3/yr. $13. American Bar Association, Judicial Administration Division Lawyers Conference, 750 N. Lake Shore Dr., Chicago, IL 60611. TEL 312-988-5691. Ed. Robert B. Yegge. circ. 2,400.
 Description: Informs lawyers of new developments in court improvement and reports on conference activities.

610 US
LAWYERS' MEDICAL DIGEST. 1984. m. $140. Callaghan & Co., 155 Pfingsten Rd., Deerfield, IL 60015. TEL 800-323-1336. Ed. Steve Babitsky.

340 CN ISSN 0317-8668
LAWYER'S PHONE BOOK (YEAR). a. Can.$36.75. Canada Law Book Inc., 240 Edward St., Aurora, Ont. L4G 3S9, Canada. TEL 416-841-6472. Ed. Patricia Egan. adv.

340 AT
LAWYERS PRACTICE MANUAL N.S.W.. 1983. 4/yr. Aus.$163. (Redfern Legal Centre) Law Book Co. Ltd., 44-50 Waterloo Rd., North Ryde, N.S.W. 2113, Australia. TEL 02-887-0177. FAX 02-888-9706. TELEX ASBOOK 27995.
 Description: Deals with the everyday practice of law and questions which occupy much of the time of practitioners, especially inexperienced lawyers.

340 AT
LAWYERS PRACTICE MANUAL VICTORIA. 1985. 4/yr. Aus.$155. (Springvale Legal Service) Law Book Co. Ltd., 44-50 Waterloo Rd., North Ryde, N.S.W. 2113, Australia. TEL 02-887-0177. FAX 02-888-9706. TELEX ASBOOK 27995.
 Description: Deals with the day-to-day practice of law and the questions which occupy much of the time of practitioners, particularly inexperienced lawyers.

340 US
LAWYERS PROFESSIONAL LIABILITY UPDATE. 1981. a. $100. American Bar Association, Standing Committee on Lawyers Professional Liability, 750 N. Lake Shore Dr., Chicago, IL 60611-3314. TEL 312-988-5763. FAX 312-988-5032. Ed. Alice L. Hughey. bk.rev.; circ. 200.
 Description: Presents articles on loss prevention, and information about recent developments in the law concerning professional liability. Includes state-by-state list of legal malpractice insurance carriers.

340 II ISSN 0023-9488
LAWYERS' RECREATION. (Text in English) 1957. m. Rs.12. The Law Book Co. (P) Ltd., Sardar Patel Marg, P.B. 1-004, Allahabad 211 001, India. TEL 602415. Ed. Rakesh Bagga. bk.rev.; charts; illus.; index, cum.index; circ. 10,000.
 Description: Contains legal articles, comments on important judgements of the superior courts, legal anecdotes, and news about legal publications.

340 US ISSN 0883-2412
LAWYER'S REGISTER BY SPECIALTIES AND FIELDS OF LAW. 1978. a. $119.50. Lawyer's Register Publishing Co., 28790 Chagrin Blvd., Ste. 140, Cleveland, OH 44122. TEL 216-591-1492. FAX 216-591-0265. Ed. Roger Perlmuter. circ. 4,000. (also avail. in microform; back issues avail.)
 Description: A directory listing lawyer specialists, including corporate counsel, for referral or consultation.

340 UK ISSN 0142-7490
LAWYER'S REMEMBRANCER. a. $45. Butterworth & Co. (Publishers) Ltd. (Subsidiary of: Reed International PLC), 88 Kingsway, London WC2B 6AB, England. TEL 71-405-6900. FAX 71-405-1332. TELEX 98678. (US addr.: Butterworth Legal Publishers, 90 Stiles Rd., Salem, NH 03079. TEL 800-548-4001) Ed. L.A. Whitbourn.

346 US ISSN 0361-3763
KF1234.A15
LAWYERS' TITLE GUARANTY FUNDS NEWSLETTER. irreg., 1990. free to qualified personnel. American Bar Association, Standing Committee on Lawyers' Title Guaranty Funds, 750 N. Lake Shore Dr., Chicago, IL 60611. TEL 312-988-5000. circ. 5,000. **Indexed:** C.L.I., L.R.I.
 Description: Information on Bar-related title insurance funds for Bar groups.

347.9 CN ISSN 0830-0151
THE LAWYERS WEEKLY. 1983. w. Can.$149($175) Butterworths Canada Ltd., 75 Clegg Rd., Markham, Ont. L6G 1A1, Canada. TEL 416-479-2665. FAX 416-479-2826. Ed. D. Michael Fitz-James. adv.; bk.rev.; charts; illus.; stat.; index; circ. 9,000 (paid); 29,000 (controlled). (tabloid format; also avail. in microfilm; back issues avail.)
 Formerly: Ontario Lawyers Weekly (ISSN 0822-5745)

340 001.6 US ISSN 0738-0186
KF320.A9
LEADER'S LEGAL TECH NEWSLETTER. 1983. m. $175 (effective Sep. 1991). Leader Publications, Inc. (Subsidiary of: New York Law Publishing Company), 111 Eighth Ave., Ste. 900, New York, NY 10011. TEL 800-888-8300. FAX 212-463-5523. Ed. Rodney Piette. index.
 Description: Newsletter detailing new technologies of interest to lawyers and legal firms. Covers industry news, computer information, product reviews for law office automation.

340 UK
LEASEHOLD LAW. irreg. £215. Longman Group UK Ltd., Law, Tax and Finance Division, 21-27 Lambs Conduit St., London WC1N 3NJ, England. TEL 071-242-2548. FAX 071-831-8119. TELEX 295445. Ed. Trevor Aldridge.
 Description: Analysis of landlord and tenant law.

340 900 AG
LECCIONES DE HISTORIA JURIDICA. irreg. (Universidad de Buenos Aires, Instituto de Historia del Derecho Ricardo Levene) Editorial Perrot, Azcuenaga 1846, Buenos Aires, Argentina.

342 341 AG
LECCIONES Y ENSAYOS. 1956. 3/yr. L.10. (Universidad de Buenos Aires, Facultad de Derecho y Ciencias Sociales) Editorial Astrea, Av. Figueroa Alcorta 2263, Buenos Aires, Argentina. adv.; bk.rev.; bibl.; circ. 1,000.
 Description: Articles and essays on national and international law enforcement, public administration, criminology and philosophy.

345.01 UK
LEGAL ACTION. 1972. m. £42 to individuals & libraries; institutions £69. Legal Action Group, 242-244 Pentonville Rd., London N1 9UN, England. TEL 01-833-2931. FAX 01-837-6094. Ed. Roger Smith. adv.; bk.rev.; cum.index; circ. 5,600. (also avail. in microform from UMI; reprint service avail. from UMI) **Indexed:** C.L.I., L.R.I., RICS.
 Formerly (until 1983): L A G Bulletin (ISSN 0306-7963)

340 UK
LEGAL & GENERAL GAZETTE. 1971. m. free. Legal & General Assurance Society Ltd., Temple Court, 11 Queen Victoria St., London EC4N 4TP, England. Ed. Roy Moore. circ. 7,700.

347.7 658 US
LEGAL ASPECTS OF SELLING AND BUYING. base vol. (plus a. suppl.). $70. Shepard's - McGraw-Hill, Inc., Box 35300, Colorado Springs, CO 80935-3530. TEL 800-525-2474. Ed. Philip F. Zeidman.
 Description: Antitrust and distribution law guide for dealing with the relationships between buyers and sellers.

340 658 US
LEGAL ASSISTANT MANAGEMENT ASSOCIATION. DIRECTORY. 1984. s-a. Legal Assistant Management Association, Box 40129, Overland Park, KS 66204. TEL 913-381-4458. circ. 550.

340 US ISSN 1051-3663
KF320.L4
LEGAL ASSISTANT TODAY. 1983. bi-m. $39.98. James Publishing Group, Inc., 3520 Cadillac Ave., Ste. E, Costa Mesa, CA 92626-1419. TEL 800-882-7855. adv.; circ. 16,500. **Indexed:** ABI Inform.
 Former titles (until 1990): Legal Professional (ISSN 1045-6686); (until Apr. 1989): Legal Assistant Today (ISSN 0741-7772)
 Description: Provides students with information on the day-to-day activities of paralegals, practical advice on working with attorneys, how to handle the case load, and how to get ahead in their careers.

340.023 US ISSN 0272-1961
KF320.L4
LEGAL ASSISTANTS UPDATE. 1980. a. $6. American Bar Association, Standing Committee on Legal Assistants, 750 N. Lake Shore Dr., Chicago, IL 60611. TEL 312-988-5555. FAX 312-988-6281. Ed. Roger Larson. circ. 3,500. **Indexed:** Anbar.

340 US ISSN 0741-1189
LEGAL BIBLIOGRAPHY JOURNAL. 1983. 3/yr. $9.75 per no. Legal Institute, 3250 Wilshire Blvd., Ste. 1000, Los Angeles, CA 90010. TEL 213-487-6268. FAX 213-385-2396. Ed.Bd. circ. 300.

340 658 CK ISSN 0458-9564
LEGAL BULLETIN. 1963. m. $150. Ediciones Juan Caro & Asociados Ltda., Apdo Aereo 241518, Bogota, Colombia. FAX 57-1-3102606. Ed. Juan Caro. index. **Indexed:** C.L.I.

346.066 UK ISSN 0958-4609
▼**LEGAL BUSINESS**. 1990. 10/yr. £245($475) Legalease, 3 Clifton Rd., London W9 1SZ, England. TEL 071-286-1890. FAX 071-289-3289. Ed. John Pritchard. adv.; bk.rev.; circ. 5,500.
 —BLDSC shelfmark: 5181.312300.
 Description: Covers news of commercial law firms and their clients.

340 US ISSN 0270-3424
KF195.C6
LEGAL CONNECTION: CORPORATIONS AND LAW FIRMS; a directory of publicly-held corporations and their law firms. 1979. a. Box 801, Menlo Park, CA 94025. Ed. S.P. Harris.

340 AT
LEGAL COSTS N S W. base vol. (plus m. update). $290. Butterworths Pty. Ltd., 271-273 Lane Cove Rd., P.O. Box 345, North Ryde, N.S.W. 2113, Australia. TEL 02-335-4444. FAX 02-335-4655. (looseleaf format)

340 AT
LEGAL COSTS VICTORIA. base vol. (plus m. update). $295. Butterworths Pty. Ltd., 271-273 Lane Cove Rd., P.O. Box 345, North Ryde, N.S.W. 2113, Australia. TEL 02-335-4444. FAX 02-335-4655.

340 US
THE LEGAL EDGE; the value of strategic market planning. 1987. 6/yr. $145. Coulter King O'Neil, Ltd., Inc., 120 Milk St., Boston, MA 02109. TEL 617-482-1310. FAX 617-482-6528. (And: 370 17th St., Denver, CO 80202. TEL 303-592-5916) adv.; circ. 4,999.

340 UK ISSN 0024-0362
LAW
LEGAL EXECUTIVE. 1963. m. £30 (foreign £46.92). Institute of Legal Executives, Kempston Manor, Kempston, Bedford, England. TEL 0234-840-022. FAX 0234-841-999. Ed. R. Kendrick. adv.; bk.rev.; illus.; index; circ. 19,997 (controlled).

720 US ISSN 0887-1183
KF902
LEGAL HANDBOOK FOR ARCHITECTS, ENGINEERS AND CONTRACTORS. 1986. a. $75. Clark Boardman - Callaghan, 375 Hudson St., New York, NY 10014. TEL 212-929-7500.

340 338 US
LEGAL HANDBOOK FOR SMALL BUSINESS. irreg. $18.95. American Management Association, Amacom Division, 135 W. 50th St., New York, NY 10020. TEL 212-586-8100. FAX 212-903-8168. (Dist. by: Gale Research Inc., Dept. 77748, Detroit, MI 48277-0748; Subscr. to: Box 319, Saranac, NY 12983) Ed. Marc J. Lane.
 Description: Provides practical counsel on the legal obligations of the small business owner, from starting up to successfully running a business. Includes recent changes in FTC regulations, Truth in Lending notices, and tax planning.

342   II   ISSN 0377-0907
K12
LEGAL HISTORY. (Text in English) 1975. q. Rs.390($50) (Indian Institute of Legal History) K.K. Roy (Private) Ltd., 55 Gariahat Rd., P.O. Box 10210, Calcutta 700 019, India. Ed. K.K. Roy. bk.rev.; abstr.; bibl.; circ. 500. (tabloid format) **Indexed:** Amer.Hist.& Life, Hist.Abstr.
—BLDSC shelfmark: 5181.322000.
    Formerly (until 1975): Journal of Constitutional Law (ISSN 0022-0051)

LEGAL INFORMATION ALERT; what's new in legal publications, databases and research techniques. see LAW — Abstracting, Bibliographies, Statistics

026   US
LEGAL INFORMATION MANAGEMENT REPORTS. 1989. q. $50 (foreign $55). Legal Information Services, Box 67, Newton Highlands, MA 02161-0067. TEL 508-443-4087. Ed. Elyse H. Fox.
    Description: Each issue deals with a single topic in the field of law librarianship.

346.066   US
LEGAL INSIGHTS FOR MANAGERS. m. $131.40. Bureau of Business Practice, 24 Rope Ferry Rd., Waterford, CT 06386. TEL 800-243-0876.
FAX 203-437-3555.
    Description: Covers all business management legal issues.

347.91   US
LEGAL INTELLIGENCER. 1843. d. (5/w.). $235. Legal Communications, Ltd., 1617 JFK Blvd., Ste. 1245, Philadelphia, PA 19103. TEL 215-563-2700. Ed. Brian Harris. adv.; circ. 3,000. (back issues avail.)
    Description: Legal news, trial lists, legal notices for the Philadelphia court system.

LEGAL - LEGISLATIVE REPORTER. NEWS BULLETIN. see BUSINESS AND ECONOMICS — Labor And Industrial Relations

340   US   ISSN 0275-4088
KF1
LEGAL LOOSELEAFS IN PRINT. 1981. a. $90. Infosources Publishing, 140 Norma Rd., Teaneck, NJ 07666. TEL 201-836-7072. Ed. Arlene L. Eis. adv.; circ. 1,000.
    Description: Bibliography of 4,000 legal looseleafs with subject and publisher indexes.

658 340   US   ISSN 1043-7355
KF318.A1   CODEN: LEMAEB
LEGAL MANAGEMENT. 1982. bi-m. free. Association of Legal Administrators, 175 E. Hawthorn Pkwy., Ste. 325, Vernon Hills, IL 60061-1428.
TEL 708-816-1212. (Subscr. to: Box 1347, Elmhurst, IL 60126) Ed. Paul Manus. adv.; bk.rev.; index; circ. 17,500.
    Formerly: Legal Administration (ISSN 0745-0532)
    Description: Provides information relating to management of a law practice, for the education and benefit of administrators, managing partners and others.

LEGAL MEDICINE: LEGAL DYNAMICS OF MEDICAL ENCOUNTERS. see MEDICAL SCIENCES

344   US   ISSN 0093-397X
KF4119.A1
LEGAL NOTES FOR EDUCATION. 1973. m. $24.95. Data Research, Inc., 4635 Nicols Rd., Ste. 100, Eagan, MN 55122. TEL 612-452-8267.
FAX 612-452-8694. (Subscr. to: Box 490, Rosemount, MN 55068. TEL 800-365-4900) cum.index.
    Description: Reports court decisions and legislation affecting education.

347   US   ISSN 0886-6678
LEGAL PLAN LETTER. 1982. fortn. $75 to libraries (foreign $95). National Resource Center for Consumers of Legal Services, Box 340, Gloucester, VA 23061. TEL 804-693-9330. Ed. William A. Bolger. bk.rev.; s-a. index; circ. 1,000. (back issues avail.)
    Supersedes: New Directions - Action Line.
    Description: News and resources on legal services plans.

340   US
▼**LEGAL PLANNING FOR THE ELDERLY IN MASSACHUSETTS.** 1991. base vol. (plus a. suppl.). $95. Butterworth Legal Publishers (Salem) (Subsidiary of: Reed International PLC), 90 Stiles Rd., Salem, NH 03079. TEL 800-548-4001.
FAX 603-898-9858. Eds. William J. Brisk, William G. Talis. (looseleaf format)

340 028.1   US   ISSN 0000-1279
KF6
LEGAL PUBLISHING PREVIEW; reviews & listings of new & forthcoming legal products. 1989. 6/yr. $99.95. R.R. Bowker, A Reed Reference Publishing Company, Division of Reed Publishing (USA) Inc., 121 Chanlon Rd., New Providence, NJ 07974.
TEL 800-521-8110. FAX 908-665-6688. TELEX 138 755. (Subscr. to: Order Dept., Box 32, New Providence, NJ 07974) Ed. Lucille Boorstein. adv.; bk.rev.; circ. 5,000 (controlled). **Indexed:** Bk.Rev.Ind. (1990-), Child.Bk.Rev.Ind. (1990-).
    Description: Written for law librarians and legal researchers in both the academic and business communities. Provides authoritative reviews of new and forthcoming legal materials, including books, audio and video-cassettes, and specialized software.

LEGAL QUARTERLY DIGEST OF MINE SAFETY AND HEALTH DECISIONS. see MINES AND MINING INDUSTRY

LEGAL REFERENCE SERVICES QUARTERLY. see LIBRARY AND INFORMATION SCIENCES

345   AT   ISSN 0159-2483
LAW
LEGAL REPORTER. 1980. irreg. (approx. 20/yr.). Aus.$345. Scribe Pty. Ltd., G.P.O. Box 1807, Canberra, A.C.T. 2601, Australia. TEL 062-391282. Ed. David Solomon. bk.rev.; index; circ. 650. (back issues avail.)
    Description: Reports on the Australian High Court.

340   US   ISSN 0146-0382
KF240
LEGAL RESEARCH JOURNAL. 1977. 3/yr. $9.75. Legal Institute, 3250 Wilshire Blvd., No. 1000, Los Angeles, CA 90010. TEL 213-487-6268. Ed. Herman B. Lancaster. bibl.; charts; illus.; stat.; circ. 400. (also avail. in microfilm) **Indexed:** Abstr.Bk.Rev.Curr.Leg.Per., C.L.I.

LEGAL RESOURCES FOR THE MENTALLY DISABLED: A DIRECTORY OF LAWYERS AND OTHER SPECIALISTS. see MEDICAL SCIENCES — Psychiatry And Neurology

340   AT   ISSN 0817-3516
LEGAL SERVICE BULLETIN. 1974. bi-m. Aus.$57 (foreign $75). Legal Service Bulletin Co., Ltd., c/o Monash University, Faculty of Law, Wellington Rd., Clayton, Vic. 3168, Australia. TEL 64-3-544-0974. FAX 64-3-565-5305. bk.rev.; cum.index; circ. 2,000. (back issues avail.) **Indexed:** C.L.I.
●Also available online.
    Incorporates: Aboriginal Law Bulletin (ISSN 0728-5671)

340   UK   ISSN 0261-3875
K12
LEGAL STUDIES. N.S. 1947. 3/yr. £29($126) (Society of Public Teachers of Law) Butterworth & Co. (Publishers) Ltd. (Subsidiary of: Reed International PLC), 88 Kingsway, London WC2B 6AB, England. TEL 71-405-6900. FAX 71-405-1332. TELEX 95678. (US addr.: Butterworth Legal Publishers, 90 Stiles Rd., Salem, NH 03079) Ed. J.A. Andrews. bk.rev. **Indexed:** Abstr.Bk.Rev.Curr.Leg.Per., C.L.I., L.R.I., Leg.Per.
—BLDSC shelfmark: 5181.413000.
    Formerly (until 1981): Society of Public Teachers of Law Journal (ISSN 0038-0016)

340   US   ISSN 0894-5993
K1
LEGAL STUDIES FORUM; an interdisciplinary journal. 1975. q. $50 to institutions (foreign $60). American Legal Studies Association, c/o Law, Policy and Society Program, 305 Cushing Hall, Northeastern University, Boston, MA 02114. TEL 617-437-5211. FAX 617-437-4691. Ed. David R. Papke. adv.; film rev.; bibl.; circ. 500. (also avail. in microfiche from WSH; microfilm from WSH; back issues avail.) **Indexed:** C.L.I., L.R.I., Sociol.Abstr.
    Formerly (until vol.8, 1984): A L S A Forum (ISSN 0162-7937)

340   US
LEGAL TIMES. 1978. w. $175 to individuals; corporations $435. American Lawyer Newspapers Group, Inc. (Washington), 1730 M St., N.W., Ste. 802, Washington, DC 20036. TEL 202-457-0686. FAX 202-457-0718. Ed. Eric Effron. circ. 10,000. (also avail. in microfilm; microfiche) **Indexed:** Bank.Lit.Ind., C.L.I., Hlth.Ind., L.R.I., Leg.Info.Manage.Ind.
●Also available online. Vendor(s): Mead Data Central.
    Former titles: Legal Times of Washington (ISSN 0732-7536); Legal Times (ISSN 0162-7295); Legal Times of Washington.
    Description: Covers law, lobbying, and politics in Washington, D.C.

340 370   US
LEGAL VIDEO REVIEW; a newsletter of the media library at the social law library. 1984. q. $50. Media Library at the Social Law Library, 1200 Courthouse, Boston, MA 02108. TEL 617-495-4840. Ed. Ellen J. Miller. circ. 150. (back issues avail.)
    Description: Focuses on video tapes produced for continuing legal education and law schools. For law practitioners, students and professors.

340   US   ISSN 0732-4529
LEGAL WRITING JOURNAL. 1981. 3/yr. $9.95 per no. Legal Institute, 3250 Wilshire Blvd., Ste. 1000, Los Angeles, CA 90010. TEL 213-487-6268.
FAX 213-385-2396. Ed.Bd.

340   IT
LEGALITA E GIUSTIZIA. 1973. q. L.80000 to individuals; institutions L.100000; foreign L.120000(effective 1992). Edizioni Scientifiche Italiane S.p.A., Via Chiatamone, 7, 80121 Naples, Italy. TEL 081-7645768. FAX 081-7646477. Ed. Giovanni Giacobbe. adv.; circ. 1,000.

349   IT   ISSN 0024-0400
LEGGI. 3/m. L.174000 (foreign L.209000)(effective Feb. 1992). Zanichelli Editore S.p.A., Via Irnerio 34, 40126 Bologna, Italy. TEL 051-293111.
FAX 051-249782. index, cum.index.

LEGI-SOCIAL. see BUSINESS AND ECONOMICS — Investments

340   FR
LEGIPRESSE. m. (10/yr.). 1850 F. Publications Paul Dupont, 38 rue Croix des Petits Champs, 75001 Paris, France.

340   BL   ISSN 0024-158X
LEGISLACAO FEDERAL E MARGINALIA; coletanea de legislacao e jurisprudencia. (Subseries of: Lex-coletanea de Legislacao e Jurisprudencia) 1937. 3/m. Cz$3176($178) Lex Editora S.A., Machado de Assis, Nrs. 47-57-CEP 04106, Caixa Postal 12888, Sao Paulo, Brazil. Ed. Afonso Vitale Sobrinho. bk.rev.; charts; index; circ. 15,000.

340   SP
LEGISLACION COMUNIDADES AUTONOMAS. (In separate vols. for each of the 17 autonomous communities of Spain.) 1982. irreg. (approx. m.). 52000 ptas. for entire series (also avail. separately). Editorial Aranzadi, S.A., Avda. Carlos III, 34, Apdo. 111, 31080 Pamplona, Spain. TEL 948-331212.
FAX 948-330919. index.

340   SP
LEGISLACION COMUNIDADES EUROPEAS. (Includes q. bound vols. with indexes.) 1986. m. 38160 ptas. Editorial Aranzadi, S.A., Avda. Carlos III, 34, Apdo. 111, 31080 Pamplona, Spain. TEL 948-331212. FAX 948-330919. index.

346.066   AG
LEGISLACION ECONOMICA ARGENTINA/ARGENTINE ECONOMIC LEGISLATION. (Text in English, Spanish) 1974. fortn. (with annual cumulation). $350. Consejo Tecnico de Inversiones S.A., Esmeralda 320, Buenos Aires, Argentina. Ed. Jose Luis Blanco. adv.; circ. 180.

340   US
LEGISLATIVE ADVISORY. m. General Merchandise Distributors Council, 1275 Lake Ave., Colorado Springs, CO 80906. TEL 303-576-4260.

340 360 US
LEGISLATIVE ALERT. irreg. free to qualified personnel. Child Welfare League of America, Inc., 440 First St., N.W., Ste. 310, Washington, DC 20001-2085. TEL 202-638-2952. FAX 202-638-4004.
 Description: Presents current information on children's policy decisions at the federal level.

LEGISLATIVE AND REGULATORY UPDATE. see *BUSINESS AND ECONOMICS — Banking And Finance*

LEGISLATIVE NETWORK FOR NURSES. see *MEDICAL SCIENCES — Nurses And Nursing*

LEGISLATIVE SCENE. see *BUSINESS AND ECONOMICS — Personnel Management*

LEGISLATIVE UPDATE (WASHINGTON). see *BUSINESS AND ECONOMICS — Banking And Finance*

LEGISLATVE MEMORANDA. see *HOTELS AND RESTAURANTS*

LEGISLAZIONE E NORMATIVA DELLE COSTRUZIONI. see *BUILDING AND CONSTRUCTION*

340 IT ISSN 0024-0524
LEGISLAZIONE ITALIANA. 1943. fortn. L.173000 (foreign L.260000). Casa Editrice Dott. A. Giuffre, Via Busto Arsizio 40, 20151 Milan, Italy. TEL 02-38000905. FAX 02-3809582. Ed. Renato Borruso. adv.; index; circ. 3,600.

340 NE ISSN 0169-8605
LEIDSE JURIDISCHE REEKS. 1954. irreg., vol.15, 1981. price varies. E.J. Brill, P.O. Box 9000, 2300 PA Leiden, Netherlands. TEL 071-312624. FAX 071-317532. TELEX 39296-BRILL-NL. (N. America dist. addr.: E.J. Brill, 24 Hudson St., Kinderhook, NY 12106. TEL 800-962-4406)

340 332 US
LENDER LIABILITY LAW AND LITIGATION. (Issued in 1 base vol. with supplements) 1989. irreg. Matthew Bender & Co., Inc., 11 Penn Plaza, New York, NY 10001. TEL 212-967-7707. (looseleaf format)
 Description: Complete guide to the theory and practice of lender liability cases. Includes discussions of causes of action and defenses, as well as information on how to litigate these often complex disputes.

340 332.3
LENDER LIABILITY LAW REPORT. 1987. m. $155. Warren, Gorham and Lamont, One Penn Plaza, New York, NY 10019. TEL 800-950-1205. FAX 212-971-5240.
 Description: Articles analyze court decisions and new legislation. Provides suggestions for developing protective mechanisms for lenders and the means of defending borrowers suits.

340 332 US ISSN 1042-5764
KF1301.5.B36
LENDER LIABILITY LITIGATION REPORTER; the national journal of record of lawsuits brought by borrowers against their lending institutions. 1988. s-m. $650. Andrews Publications, 1646 West Chester Pike, Box 1000, Westtown, PA 19395. TEL 215-399-6600. FAX 215-399-6610. Ed. Kathy Knaub. abstr.; bibl.; stat.; s-a. cum.index. (looseleaf format; back issues avail.)

340 332.3 US ISSN 0898-7645
KF1035.A15
LENDER LIABILITY NEWS. 1988. bi-w. $545 (foreign $567). Buraff Publications (Subsidiary of: Millin Publications, Inc.), 1350 Connecticut Ave. N.W., Ste. 1000, Washington, DC 20036. TEL 202-862-0990. FAX 202-822-8092. TELEX 285656 BNAI WSH. Ed. Rose Lally. (back issues avail.)
 Description: Liability issues facing lenders in all areas: fraud, breach of fiduciary duty, environmental cleanup. Covers litigation, legislation and regulation, and new industry practice (how lenders are reducing their exposure in negotiating, administrating and enforcing loan agreements).

LENINGRADSKII UNIVERSITET. VESTNIK. SERIYA EKONOMIKA, FILOSOFIYA I PRAVO. see *BUSINESS AND ECONOMICS*

340 US ISSN 8755-9021
KF4754.5.A15
LESBIAN - GAY LAW NOTES. 1980. m. (except Aug.). $25 (foreign $30). Lesbian & Gay Law Association of Greater New York, Box 1899, Grand Central Sta., New York, NY 10163. TEL 212-302-5100. Ed. Arthur S. Leonard. index; circ. 1,400. (looseleaf format; back issues avail.)
 Description: Summary of legal developments in the areas of lesbian and gay rights and AIDS.

325 AT
LESLIE AND BRITTS: MOTOR VEHICLE LAW IN N.S.W.. 1982. 6/yr. Aus.$290. Law Book Co. Ltd., 44-50 Waterloo Rd., N. Ryde, N.S.W. 2113, Australia. TEL 02-887-0177. FAX 02-888-9706. TELEX ASBOOK 27995. Ed. M.M.G. Britts. (looseleaf format; back issues avail.)

340 LO ISSN 0255-6472
K12 CODEN: JMSCED
LESOTHO LAW JOURNAL; a journal of law and development. 1985. s-a. R.35($35) National University of Lesotho, Faculty of Law, P.O. Roma 180, Lesotho. Ed. N.S. Rembe. adv.; bk.rev.; circ. 500.
—BLDSC shelfmark: 5184.554530.
 Description: Addresses the conflict between the need for governments to govern, and the necessity to protect citizens against the power of the state.

340 336 US ISSN 0883-0487
LETTER OF CREDIT UPDATE. 1985. m. $395 (foreign $425). (International Chamber of Commerce, FR) Government Information Services, 1611 N. Kent St., Ste. 508, Arlington, VA 22209. TEL 703-528-1000. FAX 703-528-6060. Eds. Jim E. Byrne, Clancy Zens. index.
 Description: For businessmen, bankers and lawyers. Covers legislative and judicial developments concerning letter of credit practices.

340 332.7 US
LETTERS OF CREDIT. 1987. base vol. (plus suppl.). Matthew Bender & Co., Inc., 11 Penn Plaza, New York, NY 10001. TEL 212-967-7707. (looseleaf format)
 Description: Illustrates ways to use letters of credit to your client's advantage. Includes case law discussions.

LETTERS OF CREDIT REPORT; bank guaranties and acceptances. see *BUSINESS AND ECONOMICS — Banking And Finance*

340 US
LETTERS OF INTENT AND OTHER PRECONTRACTUAL DOCUMENTS; comparative analysis and forms. base vol. (plus suppl.). $85. Butterworth Legal Publishers (Salem) (Subsidiary of: Reed International PLC), 90 Stiles Rd., Salem, NH 03079. TEL 800-548-4001. FAX 603-898-9858. Ed. Ralph B. Lake.
 Description: Examines the impact of precontractual agreements on subsequently created contracts, comparing civil law and common law countries' practices with regard to the use and enforceability of precontractual documents.

340 IT ISSN 0024-1598
LEX; legislazione Italiana. 1914. q. L.154000. Unione Tipografico Editrice Torinese, Corso Raffaello 28, 10125 Turin, Italy. charts; circ. 33,000.

LEX COLLEGII. see *EDUCATION — Higher Education*

340 US
LEX VITAE; the pro-life legislation and litigation summary. q. $25. Americans United for Life, 343 S. Dearborn St., Ste. 1804, Chicago, IL 60604. TEL 312-786-9494. Ed. Kevin J. Todd. (tabloid format; back issues avail.)
 Description: Summary of cases at all levels of the judiciary and state legislation concerning abortion and euthanasia.

340 330.9 336 GW ISSN 0171-0826
LEXIKON DES STEUER- UND WIRTSCHAFTSRECHTS. 1974. m. DM.98. Wirtschaft Recht und Steuern Verlag, Fraunhofstr. 5, Postfach 1363, 8033 Planegg-Munich, Germany. TEL 089-8577944. FAX 089-857-7990. Ed.Bd. circ. 24,000. (looseleaf format)
 Description: Reference on tax and law.

349 AG ISSN 0024-1636
LEY; revista argentina de jurisprudencia. Alternate title: Revista Juridica Argentina: La Ley. (Text in Spanish) 1935. d. (with q. cum. summaries). Arg.$150($600) Ediciones la Ley S.A., 1471 Tucuman, Buenos Aires (R.34), Argentina. adv.; bk.rev.; bibl.; charts; illus.; stat.; index, cum.index; circ. 12,000 (controlled). (tabloid format)

340 NQ
LEYES DE LA REPUBLICA DE NICARAGUA. 1980. s-a. $10. Ministerio de Justicia, Managua, Nicaragua.

340 332 FR
LIAISONS JURIDIQUES ET FISCALES. d. 1940 F. (typically set in Oct.) Groupe Liaisons, 5 av. de la Republique, 75541 Paris Cedex 11, France. TEL 1-48-05-91-05. FAX 1-48-05-81-20.

LIBERATOR; male call. see *MEN'S INTERESTS*

340 LB
LIBERIA. MINISTRY OF JUSTICE. ANNUAL REPORT TO THE LEGISLATURE.* 1973. a. Ministry of Justice, Monrovia, Liberia.

340 LB ISSN 0024-1970
K12
LIBERIAN LAW JOURNAL.* 1965. s-a. $30. University of Liberia, Louis Arthur Grimes School of Law, Monrovia, Liberia. Eds. Boakai Dukuly, Ruth Jappah. adv.; bk.rev.; charts; circ. 300.

340 UK ISSN 0267-7083
LIBERTARIAN ALLIANCE. LEGAL NOTES. 1985. irreg. £10($20) Libertarian Alliance, 1 Russell Chambers, Covent Garden, London WC2E 8AA, England. TEL 071-821-5502. FAX 071-834-2031. Ed.Bd. adv.; bk.rev.; film rev.; bibl.; circ. 1,000. (back issues avail.)

340 JA
LIBERTY & JUSTICE. m. 4800 Yen. Japan Federation of Bar Associations, 1-1, Kasumigaseki 1-chome, Chiyoda-ku, Tokyo 100, Japan. adv.; bk.rev.

340 301 US ISSN 0075-9120
LIBRARY OF LAW AND CONTEMPORARY PROBLEMS. 1961. irreg., no.19, 1974. price varies. (Duke University, School of Law) Oceana Publications, Inc., Dobbs Ferry, NY 10522. TEL 914-693-1320. FAX 914-693-0402.

340 382 600 US ISSN 0731-5783
KF3145.A152
LICENSING LAW HANDBOOK. 1979. a. $62.50. Clark Boardman - Callaghan, 155 Hudson St., New York, NY 10014. TEL 212-929-7500. index.

340 AT
LICENSING LAWS N S W: LIQUOR ACT & REGULATIONS. base vol. (plus q. update). $265. Butterworths Pty. Ltd., 271-273 Lane Cove Rd., P.O. Box 345, North Ryde, N.S.W. 2113, Australia. TEL 02-335-4444. FAX 02-335-4655. (looseleaf format)

340 US
LIFE DOCKET. m. free. Americans United for Life, 343 S. Dearborn St., Ste. 1804, Chicago, IL 60604. TEL 312-786-9494. Ed. Melodie Schlenker Gage.
 Description: Summary of legal news relating to abortion and euthanasia.

340 AT
LIQUOR LAWS VICTORIA. base vol. (plus updates 3-4/yr.) $155. Butterworths Pty. Ltd., 271-273 Lane Cove Rd., P.O. Box 345, N. Ryde, N.S.W. 2113, Australia. TEL 02-335-4444. FAX 02-335-4655. (looseleaf format)

340 AT
LIQUOR LICENSING LAW AND PRACTICE N.S.W.. 1984. 4/yr. Aus.$175. Law Book Co. Ltd., 44-50 Waterloo Rd., N. Ryde, N.S.W. 2113, Australia. TEL 02-887-0177. FAX 02-888-9706. TELEX ASBOOK 27995. Ed. K.T. Palmer.

340 US
THE LITERATE LAWYER. irreg., 2nd ed., 1991. $25. Butterworth Legal Publishers (Salem) (Subsidiary of: Reed International PLC), 90 Stiles Rd., Salem, NH 03079. TEL 800-548-4001. FAX 603-898-9858. Ed. Robert B. Smith.
 Description: Emphasizes legal writing skills and communication techniques.

2650 LAW

347.7 US
LITIGATING PRIVATE ANTITRUST ACTIONS. 1984. base vol. (plus a. suppl.). Shepard's - McGraw-Hill, Inc., Box 35300, Colorado Springs, CO 80935-3530. TEL 800-525-2474.
 Description: Policy-oriented guidelines to the intricacies of identifying, proving and litigating antitrust violations.

347.73 US ISSN 0097-9813
K12
LITIGATION. 1975. q. $40 to non-members (foreign $45). American Bar Association, Litigation Section, 750 N. Lake Shore Dr., Chicago, IL 60611. TEL 312-988-5555. Ed. Miriam Kass. bk.rev.; illus.; circ. 63,000. (also avail. in microfiche from WSH; microfilm from WSH) **Indexed:** C.L.I., L.R.I., Law Ofc.Info.Svc., Leg.Cont., Leg.Per.
●Also available online. Vendor(s): WESTLAW.
—BLDSC shelfmark: 5277.462000.
 Description: For trial lawyers and judges. Each issue focuses on a particular topic involving trial practice.

340 UK ISSN 0263-2160
LITIGATION. 1981. 8/yr. £46.50. Barry Rose Law Periodicals, East Row, Little London, Chichester, West Sussex PO19 1PG, England. TEL 0243-787841. FAX 0243-779278. Ed. Richard Colbey.
—BLDSC shelfmark: 5277.462030.
 Description: Looks at the litigation business for British lawyers (solicitors and barristers) involving personal injuries, civil practice and procedure, matrimonial law, landlord and tenant, employment law and commercial law.

340 368.5 US
LITIGATION AND PREVENTION OF INSURER BAD FAITH. base vol. (plus a. suppl.). $95. Shepard's - McGraw-Hill, Inc., Box 35300, Colorado Springs, CO 80935-3530. TEL 800-525-2474.
 Description: Traces the development of damages for breach of contract, claims for foreseeable or consequential damages, claims for emotional distress and punitive damages.

340 US
LITIGATION COMMITTEE NEWSLETTER. q. $15. American Bar Association, Young Lawyers Division, 750 N. Lake Shore Dr., Chicago, IL 60611. TEL 312-988-5000. bk.rev.

340 US ISSN 0147-9970
KF200
LITIGATION NEWS. 1975. q. membership only. American Bar Association, Litigation Section, 750 N. Lake Shore Dr., Chicago, IL 60611. TEL 312-988-6063. Ed. Michael Hyman. circ. 63,000. (back issues avail.) **Indexed:** C.L.I., L.R.I.
 Description: Newsletter of council and committee activity, upcoming meetings, legislative activities of interest to trial attorneys.

340 320 US
LITIGATION UNDER THE FEDERAL OPEN GOVERNMENT LAWS. a. $45. American Civil Liberties Union Foundation, 122 Maryland Ave., N.E., Washington, DC 20002. TEL 202-544-1681.
FAX 202-546-0738. Ed. Allan Adler. circ. 2,500.
 Formerly: Litigation Under the Federal Freedom of Information Act and Privacy Act.

347 BL
LITIS; revista trimestral de direito processual. 1974. q. Rua Sao Salvador, 31, ZC-01 Rio de Janeiro, Brazil.

340 UK ISSN 0144-932X
K12
LIVERPOOL LAW REVIEW; a journal of contemporary legal issues. 1979. s-a. £37. (Liverpool Law Review Association) Deborah Charles Publications, 173 Mather Ave., Liverpool LI8 6JZ, England. (Dist. in US by: William Gaunt & Sons, Inc., 3011 Gulf Dr., Holmes Beach, FL 34217-2199. TEL 813-778-5211) Ed. J. Kirkbride. adv.; bk.rev.; circ. 400. **Indexed:** C.L.I., L.R.I., Leg.Per.
—BLDSC shelfmark: 5281.143000.

LLOYD'S AVIATION LAW. see *AERONAUTICS AND SPACE FLIGHT*

340 UK ISSN 0024-5488
KD1815.A2
LLOYD'S LAW REPORTS. 1919. m. $560. Lloyd's of London Press Ltd., Sheepen Place, Colchester, Essex CO3 3LP, England. TEL 0206-772277. FAX 0206-46273. TELEX 987321 LLOYDS G. (Subscr. in US to: Lloyd's of London Press Inc., 611 Broadway, Ste. 308, New York, NY 10012. TEL 212-529-9500) Ed. Mavis d'Souza. s-a. index. (tabloid format; back issues avail.) **Indexed:** RICS.
—BLDSC shelfmark: 5287.250000.
 Formerly: Lloyd's List Law Reports.
 Description: Provides reports of judicial decisions affecting both maritime and commercial spheres. Each report contains a summary of the facts and legal issues raised, followed by the verbatim judgment of the court.

LOAN OFFICERS LEGAL ALERT; the commercial lending law letter. see *BUSINESS AND ECONOMICS — Banking And Finance*

340 350 US ISSN 1057-0594
▼**LOBBYING RESOURCE DIRECTORY;** a practical guide to sources of information and assistance for lobbyists, legislative advocates and citizen activists. 1991. a. $75. Government Research Service, 701 Jackson, Topeka, KS 66603. TEL 913-232-7720. FAX 913-232-1615. Ed. Lynn Hellebust.
 Description: Covers sources of strategic planning assistance, grass roots media, phone and direct mail help, handbooks and manuals, bill status information, policy research organizations and bill drafting manuals.

LOCAL GOVERNMENT AND LAW. see *PUBLIC ADMINISTRATION — Municipal Government*

340 AT ISSN 0727-7830
LOCAL GOVERNMENT LAW & PRACTICE (NEW SOUTH WALES). 1987. 11/yr. Aus.$425. Law Book Co. Ltd., 44-50 Waterloo Rd., N. Ryde, N.S.W. 2113, Australia. TEL 02-887-0177. FAX 02-888-9706. TELEX ASBOOK 27995. Ed. S. White. (looseleaf format)

340 690 AT ISSN 0727-7997
LOCAL GOVERNMENT ORDINANCE 70 "BUILDING" (NEW SOUTH WALES). 1974. 6/yr. Aus.$95. Law Book Co. Ltd., 44-50 Waterloo Rd., N. Ryde, N.S.W. 2113, Australia. TEL 02-887-0177. FAX 02-888-9706. TELEX ASBOOK 27995. (looseleaf format; back issues avail.)
 Description: Covers building regulation and jurisdiction in N.S.W.

340 AT ISSN 0727-8004
LOCAL GOVERNMENT ORDINANCES SERVICES (NEW SOUTH WALES). 1945. q. Aus.$325. Law Book Co. Ltd., 45-50 Waterloo Rd., N. Ryde, N.S.W. 2113, Australia. TEL 02-887-0177. FAX 02-888-9706. TELEX ASBOOK 27995. Ed. K. Kulakowski. (looseleaf format; back issues avail.)

340 UK ISSN 0262-4303
LOCAL GOVERNMENT REVIEW. 1837. w. £146 (typically set in Sep.). Barry Rose Law Periodicals, East Row, Little London, Chichester, Sussex PO19 1PG, England. TEL 0243-787841.
FAX 0243-779278. adv.; bk.rev.; stat.; index, cum.index. **Indexed:** ASSIA, C.L.I.
—BLDSC shelfmark: 5290.027000.
 Description: Covers all aspects of local government law practice and administration in England and Wales; also covers Lands Tribunal and planning appeal decisions.

340 US
LOCAL RULES OF THE DISTRICT COURTS IN TEXAS. 1981. base vol. (plus suppl. 2/yr.). $135. Butterworth Legal Publishers (Salem) (Subsidiary of: Reed International PLC), 90 Stiles Rd., Salem, NH 03079. TEL 800-548-4001. FAX 603-898-9858. Ed. Sterling W. Steves. (looseleaf format)
 Description: Contains the complete local rules of the district courts in Texas' 254 counties, along with a schedule of court costs, names, addresses and phone numbers of the district judges, court reporters, and other personnel.

340 US
LOCAL RULES OF THE SUPERIOR COURT: WASHINGTON STATE. 1981. 2 base vols. (plus suppl. 4-5/yr.). $70. Butterworth Legal Publishers (Salem) (Subsidiary of: Reed International PLC), 90 Stiles Rd., Salem, NH 03079. TEL 800-548-4001. FAX 603-898-9858. Ed.Bd. (looseleaf format)

340 UK
LONDON GAZETTE. 4/w. £290. H.M.S.O., P.O. Box 276, London SW8 5DT, England. (also avail. in microform from UMI; microfilm from KTO; reprint service avail. from UMI)

340 UK
LONGMAN DIRECTORY OF LOCAL AUTHORITIES. a. £16.50. Longman Group UK Ltd., Law, Tax and Finance Division, 21-27 Lambs Conduit St., London WC1N 3NJ, England. TEL 071-242-2548. FAX 071-831-8119. TELEX 295445.
 Description: Reference of names and addresses of all local authorities in Great Britain.

340 US ISSN 0362-5575
LOS ANGELES DAILY JOURNAL. 1888. d. $259. Daily Journal Corporation (Los Angeles), 915 E. First St., Los Angeles, CA 90012. TEL 213-229-5300. FAX 213-680-3682. Ed. T. Sumner Robinson. adv.; bk.rev.; circ. 18,637. (also avail. in microfilm) **Indexed:** C.L.I., Hlth.Ind., L.R.I.

340 US ISSN 0162-2900
KF200
LOS ANGELES LAWYER. 1978. m. $28. Los Angeles County Bar Association, Box 55020, Los Angeles, CA 90055. TEL 213-896-6501.
FAX 213-896-6500. Ed. Susan Pettit. adv.; bk.rev.; illus.; index; circ. 24,000. (also avail. in microfilm from WSH) **Indexed:** C.L.I., Cal.Per.Ind. (1984-), L.R.I., Law Ofc.Info.Svc., Leg.Per.
—BLDSC shelfmark: 5294.722000.
 Formed by the merger of: Barrister Bulletin (ISSN 0094-310X); Los Angeles Bar Journal (ISSN 0362-837X); Which was formerly: Los Angeles Bar Bulletin (ISSN 0024-6530); Bar Bulletin (ISSN 0197-2588)

LOUISIANA ADMINISTRATIVE CODE. see *PUBLIC ADMINISTRATION*

340 US ISSN 0459-8881
KF200
LOUISIANA BAR JOURNAL. 1942. bi-m. $30. Louisiana State Bar Association, 601 St. Charles Ave., New Orleans, LA 70130. TEL 504-566-1600.
FAX 566-0930. Ed. Michael H. Rubin. adv.; circ. 15,100. (also avail. in microfilm from WSH; back issues avail.) **Indexed:** C.L.I.
 Description: Topics of interest to members of the Louisiana Bar.

340 639.2 US
LOUISIANA COASTAL LAW REPORT; coastal zone management, marine resource law, and environmental law related to coastal and marine issues. 1971. irreg. (3-4/yr.). free. Louisiana State University, Sea Grant Legal Program, 170 Law Center, Baton Rouge, LA 70803.
TEL 504-388-1558. Eds. Michael W. Wascom, James G. Wilkins. bibl.; circ. 1,200.

340 333.33 US
LOUISIANA LANDLORD & TENANT LAW. 1987. base vol. (plus a. suppl.). $120. Butterworth Legal Publishers (Salem) (Subsidiary of: Reed International PLC), 90 Stiles Rd., Salem, NH 03079. TEL 800-548-4001. FAX 603-898-9858. (looseleaf format)

340 US ISSN 0024-6859
K12
LOUISIANA LAW REVIEW. 1937. 6/yr. $36. Louisiana State University, Law School, Baton Rouge, LA 70803. TEL 504-388-1681. FAX 504-388-8202. Ed. Neil C. Abramson. adv.; bk.rev.; index, cum.index covering 40 yrs.; circ. 2,200. (also avail. in microfiche from WSH; microfilm from WSH; reprint service avail. from UMI,WSH) **Indexed:** C.L.I., Curr.Cont., INIS Atomind., L.R.I., Leg.Cont., Leg.Per., Mar.Aff.Bibl., SSCI.
●Also available online. Vendor(s): Mead Data Central, WESTLAW.
—BLDSC shelfmark: 5296.100000.

340 US
LOUISIANA LEGAL RESEARCH. irreg., 2nd ed., 1990. $50. Butterworth Legal Publishers (Salem) (Subsidiary of: Reed International PLC), 90 Stiles Rd., Salem, NH 03079. TEL 800-548-4001. FAX 603-898-9858. Ed. Win-Shin S. Chiang.
 Description: Covers governmental bodies and sources of law in the state - the legislative, executive, and judicial branches of state and local government plus the law schools, the practicing bar, and state document depository program.

340 US
LOUISIANA OIL AND GAS LAW. 1988. base vol. (plus a. suppl.). $120. Butterworth Legal Publishers (Salem) (Subsidiary of: Reed International PLC), 90 Stiles Rd., Salem, NH 03079. TEL 800-548-4001. FAX 603-898-9858. Eds. W.R. Irby, Luther L. McDougal, III. (looseleaf format)
Description: Covers mineral servitudes, oil and gas leases, implied obligations in oil and gas leases, oil and gas royalties, and state regulation of development and production.

LOUISIANA REGISTER. see *PUBLIC ADMINISTRATION*

340 US
▼**LOUISIANA SECURITY RIGHTS IN PERSONAL PROPERTY.** 1991. base vol. (plus a. suppl.). $85. Butterworth Legal Publishers (Salem) (Subsidiary of: Reed International PLC), 90 Stiles Rd., Salem, NH 03079. TEL 800-548-4001. FAX 603-898-9858. Ed. Henry D. Gabriel. (looseleaf format)
Description: Provides a complete analysis on all aspects of security rights from creation to default.

345 622 US ISSN 0076-1087
KF1849.A2
LOUISIANA STATE UNIVERSITY. LAW SCHOOL. INSTITUTE ON MINERAL LAW. PROCEEDINGS. 1954. a. $30. Louisiana State University, Center of Continuing Professional Development, Paul M. Hebert Law Center, Baton Rouge, LA 70803-7507. TEL 504-388-5837. FAX 504-388-8202. TELEX 510-993-3414. Ed. Thomas A. Harrell. index; circ. 500. (reprint service avail. from UMI) **Indexed:** Leg.Per.

340 US
LOUISIANA WRONGFUL DEATH & SURVIVAL ACTIONS. 1986. base vol. (plus a. suppl.). $120. Butterworth Legal Publishers (Salem) (Subsidiary of: Reed International PLC), 90 Stiles Rd., Salem, NH 03079. TEL 800-548-4001. FAX 603-898-9858. (looseleaf format)

349 NO ISSN 0024-6980
LOV OG RETT; norsk juridisk tidsskrift. 1962. m. (10/yr.). $93. Universitetsforlaget, P.O. Box 2959-Toeyen, N-0608 Oslo 1, Norway. (US addr.: Publications Expediting Inc., 200 Meacham Ave., Elmont, NY 11003) Ed. Asbjoern Kjoenstad. adv.; bk.rev.; index; circ. 5,000.

340 DK ISSN 0108-9102
LOVE OG BEKENDTGOERELSER M.V.. 1979. s-a. DKK 468. Kroghs Forlag A S, Chr. Hansensvej 3, 7100 Vejle, Denmark.
Formerly: Samling af Bekendtgoerelser (ISSN 0415-3693)

340 DK ISSN 0108-0849
LAW
LOVNOEGLE; register over love og tilhoerende aendringslove, bekendtgoerelser og cirkulaerer m.v. 1982. q. DKK 895. Schultz Information A-S, Ottiliavej 18, DK-2500 Valby, Denmark. circ. 1,100.

340 DK ISSN 0106-8458
LOVTIDENDE A FOR KONGERIGET DANMARK. 1871. s-w. DKK 700. Justisministeriet, Sekretariatet for Retsinformation, Axeltorv 6, 5. sal, D-1609 Copenhagen V, Denmark. TEL 33-32-52-22. FAX 33-91-28-01. index; circ. 3,950.
●Also available online.
Description: Official organ for promulgating statutes, laws and departmental orders in accordance with Danish law.

342 US
LOYOLA LAW REVIEW. 1920. q. $20 (foreign $22). Loyola University, School of Law, 7214 St. Charles, New Orleans, LA 70118. TEL 504-861-5558. bk.rev.; index; circ. 11,000. **Indexed:** Abstr.Bk.Rev.Curr.Leg.Per., C.L.I., Crim.Just.Abstr., L.R.I., Leg.Cont., Leg.Per., Mar.Aff.Bibl.
●Also available online. Vendor(s): WESTLAW.

340 US ISSN 0277-5417
K12
LOYOLA OF LOS ANGELES INTERNATIONAL AND COMPARATIVE LAW JOURNAL. 1978. 4/yr. $35 (foreign $40). Loyola of Los Angeles Law School, 1441 W. Olympic Blvd., Los Angeles, CA 90015-3980. TEL 213-736-1405. FAX 213-380-3769. adv.; bk.rev.; circ. 300. (also avail. in microform from WSH; back issues avail.; reprint service avail. from WSH) **Indexed:** C.L.I., L.R.I., Leg.Per., Mar.Aff.Bibl., P.A.I.S.
●Also available online. Vendor(s): WESTLAW.
—BLDSC shelfmark: 5299.550000.
Formerly (until 1983): Loyola of Los Angeles International and Comparative Law Annual.

340 US ISSN 0024-7081
K12
LOYOLA UNIVERSITY OF CHICAGO LAW JOURNAL. 1970. q. $18. Loyola University of Chicago, Law School, One E. Pearson St., Chicago, IL 60611. TEL 312-915-7182. adv.; bk.rev.; circ. 625. (back issues avail.; reprint service avail. from RRI) **Indexed:** C.L.I., Leg.Cont., Leg.Per.

340 II ISSN 0459-9756
LUCKNOW LAW TIMES; acts, ordinances, rules and notifications of the central and U.P. governments. (Text in English) 1960. m. $41. Eastern Book Company, 34 Lalbagh, Lucknow 226 001, India. TEL 43171. FAX 0091-522-242061. TELEX 535 436 FAST IN. Ed. P.L. Malik. adv.; bk.rev.; index; circ. 3,000. (back issues avail.)

340 CC
LUSHI SHIJIE. (Text in Chinese) m. Hubei Sheng Sifa Ting, No. 16, Hongshan Celu, Wuchang-qu, Wuhan, Hubei 430071, People's Republic of China. TEL 813498. Ed. Chen Hengchu.

340 CC ISSN 1001-6376
LUSHI YU FAZHI/LAWYERS AND LEGAL SYSTEM. (Text in Chinese) bi-m. Zhejiang Sheng Sifa-ting - Zhejiang Provincial Judiciaries, 1 Shengfu Lu, Hangzhou, Zhejiang 310007, People's Republic of China. TEL 754413. Ed. Li Xin.

M & A DEALMAKER. (Mergers and Acquisitions) see *BUSINESS AND ECONOMICS — Investments*

340 350 US ISSN 0884-1667
KF200
M S B A IN BRIEF. 1985. m. $15. Minnesota State Bar Association, 514 Nicollet Ave., Ste. 300, Minneapolis, MN 55402. TEL 612-333-1183. FAX 612-333-4927. Ed. Judson Haverkamp. adv.; circ. 12,700. (back issues avail.)
Description: News of the legal profession in Minnesota.

340 US
M S N NEWSLETTER. 1985. 3/yr. $7.50 (foreign $10). Center for Constitutional Rights, Movement Support Network, 666 Broadway, 7th Fl., New York, NY 10012. TEL 212-614-6422. FAX 212-614-6499. circ. 4,000. (back issues avail.)
Supersedes: Quash.

340 AT
McDONALD, HENRY AND MEEK: AUSTRALIAN BANKRUPTCY LAW AND PRACTICE. 1977. 6/yr. Aus.$325. Law Book Co. Ltd., 44-50 Waterloo Rd., N. Ryde, N.S.W. 2113, Australia. TEL 02-887-0177. FAX 02-888-9706. TELEX ASBOOK 27995. Ed.Bd.
Description: Covers bankruptcy, court practice and jurisdiction in Australia.

340 CN ISSN 0024-9041
LAW
McGILL LAW JOURNAL/REVUE DE DROIT DE McGILL. (Text in English, French) 1952. 4/yr. Can.$37($31.50) McGill University, Faculty of Law, Chancellor Day Hall, 3644 Peel St., Montreal, Que. H3A 1W9, Canada. TEL 514-398-7397. FAX 514-398-4659. Ed.Bd. adv.; bk.rev.; index, cum.index; circ. 1,500. (also avail. in microfilm from RRI; reprint service avail. from RRI) **Indexed:** C.L.I., Can.Per.Ind., Curr.Cont., Ind.Can.L.P.L., L.R.I., Leg.Cont., Leg.Per., Refug.Abstr., SSCI.
—BLDSC shelfmark: 5413.428000.

346.066 US ISSN 0024-9289
MACOMB COUNTY LEGAL NEWS. 1957. w. $25. Adams Publishing Company, 67 Cass Ave., Mt. Clemens, MI 48043. TEL 313-469-4510. (Subscr. to: Box 707, Mt. Clemens, MI 48046) Ed. Diane Kish. adv.; circ. 900. (newspaper; back issues avail.)
Description: Covers general, legal and business news in Macomb County.

340 352 US
McQUILLIN MUNICIPAL LAW REPORT; a monthly review for lawyers, administrators and officials. 1982. m. $110. Callaghan & Co., 155 Pfingsten Rd., Deerfield, IL 60015. TEL 800-323-1336. index; circ. 1,500. (tabloid format)

340 II ISSN 0024-9459
MADHYA PRADESH LAW JOURNAL. (Text in English) 1956. m. Rs.200. Journal Publications, Road No. 12, Dhantoli, Nagpur 440 012, India. Ed. Shri A.G. Dhande. bk.rev.; circ. 4,500.

342 II
MADRAS LAW JOURNAL. (Text in English) 1891. w. Rs.300 (effective 1991). Madras Law Journal Office, Box 604, Mylapore, Madras 4, India. Ed. S. Venkatraman. bk.rev.

343 II
MADRAS LAW JOURNAL (CRIMINAL). (Text in English) 1957. fortn. Rs.200 (effective 1991). Madras Law Journal Office, Box 604, Mylapore, Madras 4, India. Ed. R. Narayanaswamy. bibl.

340 330 UA
AL-MAGALLAH AL-QANUNIYYAH AL-IQTISADIYYAH. 1986. irreg. Zagazig University, Faculty of Law, Zagazig, Egypt.

340 UA
MAGALLAT AL-DIRASAT AL-QANUNIYYAH. vol.10, 1988. m. Assiut University, Faculty of Law, Assiut, Egypt.

340 SA ISSN 0024-9971
MAGISTRATE/LANDDROS. (Text in Afrikaans, English) 1965. q. R.49.50 membership. (Magistrates Association) Digma Publications (Pty) Ltd., 270 Main St., Waterkloof, Pretoria 0181, South Africa. TEL 012-346-3840. FAX 012-346-3845. TELEX 4-25847 SA. (Subscr. to: P.O. Box 95466, Pretoria 0181, South Africa) Ed. P.J. Theron. adv.; bk.rev.; bibl.; circ. 1,900.
Description: Covers a variety of legal topics from a practitioner's point of view, including laws of evidence, jurisdiction, unreported cases, rules of practice, criminal law, civil and criminal procedure, and sentencing.

340 UK ISSN 0024-9920
THE MAGISTRATE. 1921. 10/yr. £27. The Magistrates' Association, 28 Filgron Sq., London W1P 6DD, England. TEL 037-975-519. FAX 037-975-8173. Ed. Caroline Ball. adv.; bk.rev.; circ. 27,000. (also avail. in microform from UMI)
—BLDSC shelfmark: 5334.830000.
Description: For lay magistrates and all professionals working in the magistrates' courts and other parts of the criminal justice and child care systems.

340 HU ISSN 0025-0147
K13
MAGYAR JOG. 1954. m. $38.50. Magyar Jogasz Szovetseg, Szemere u. 10, 1054 Budapest 5, Hungary. TEL 314-574. (Subscr. to: Kultura, Box 149, H-1389 Budapest, Hungary) Ed. Peter Boor. adv.; bk.rev.; index; circ. 29,500.
Former titles: Magyar Jog es Kulfoldi Jogi Szemle (ISSN 0034-6829); Magyar Jog.

340 II ISSN 0025-0465
LAW
MAHARASHTRA LAW JOURNAL. (Text in English) 1963. m. Rs.300. Journal Publications, Road No. 12, Dhantoli, Nagpur 440 012, India. Ed. Shri J.N. Chandurkar. bk.rev.; circ. 5,000.
Supersedes: Nagpur Law Journal.

2652   LAW

340 350   US
MAINE ADMINISTRATIVE PROCEDURE. 1985. base vol. (plus a. suppl.). $65. Butterworth Legal Publishers (Salem) (Subsidiary of: Reed International PLC), 90 Stiles Rd., Salem, NH 03079. TEL 800-548-4001. FAX 603-898-9858. Ed. John N. Ferdico. (looseleaf format)
Description: Covers the Maine Administrative Procedure Act, Maine Freedom of Access Law, selected Maine Rules of Civil Procedure and Maine Administrative Court Rules, plus attorney general opinions.

340   US   ISSN 0885-9973
KF200
MAINE BAR JOURNAL. 1986. bi-m. membership. Maine State Bar Association, 124 State St., Box 788, Augusta, ME 04332-0788. TEL 207-622-7523. Ed. Edward M. Bonney. adv.; bk.rev.; circ. 2,600. (also avail. in microfiche; back issues avail.; reprint service avail.) **Indexed:** C.L.I., Leg.Per.
Description: Presents articles on substantive areas of the law, Maine legal history, Maine bar and court news and other notices of interest to Maine practitioners.

340   US
MAINE EVIDENCE. 1987. base vol. (plus suppl.). $85. Butterworth Legal Publishers (Salem) (Subsidiary of: Reed International PLC), 90 Stiles Rd., Salem, NH 03079. TEL 800-548-4001. FAX 603-898-9858. Ed. Peter L. Murray. (looseleaf format)
Description: Contains the complete text of the Rules of Evidence with advisor's notes and commentary which explains each rule.

340   US
MAINE JURY INSTRUCTION MANUAL. irreg., 2nd ed., 1990. $75. Butterworth Legal Publishers (Salem) (Subsidiary of: Reed International PLC), 90 Stiles Rd., Salem, NH 03079. TEL 800-548-4001. FAX 603-898-9858. Ed. Donald G. Alexander. (looseleaf format)
Description: Covers statutory and judicial developments and offers instructions to assist attorneys and judges in communicating legal issues to jurors.

340   US   ISSN 0025-0651
K13
MAINE LAW REVIEW. 1908. s-a. $20 (Canada $22; Europe $24)(typically set in Jan.). University of Maine, School of Law, 246 Deering Ave., Portland, ME 04102. TEL 207-780-4357. Ed. John P. March. adv.; bk.rev.; bibl.; index; circ. 1,200. (also avail. in microform from UMI; microfiche from WSH; microfilm from WSH; back issues avail.) **Indexed:** C.L.I., L.R.I., Leg.Cont., Leg.Per., Mar.Aff.Bibl.
●Also available online. Vendor(s): WESTLAW.

340   US
MAINE MANUAL ON PROFESSIONAL RESPONSIBILITY. 1986. base vol. (plus a. suppl.). $45. Butterworth Legal Publishers (Salem) (Subsidiary of: Reed International PLC), 90 Stiles Rd., Salem, NH 03079. TEL 800-548-4001. FAX 603-898-9858. (looseleaf format)

MAINE WORKERS' COMPENSATION ACT; practice and procedure. see BUSINESS AND ECONOMICS — Labor And Industrial Relations

MAINE WORKERS COMPENSATION COMMISSION: APPELLATE DIVISION DECISIONS. see BUSINESS AND ECONOMICS — Labor And Industrial Relations

340   CN   ISSN 0842-9960
MAITRES. 1989. bi-m. free. Barreau du Quebec, 445 Bd. St. Laurent, Montreal, Que. H2Y 3T8, Canada. TEL 514-954-3440. FAX 514-954-3477. Ed. Leon Bedard. adv.; index; circ. 25,000. (back issues avail.)

340.59 297   TS
MAJALLAT AL-SHARI'AH WAL-QANUN. (Text in Arabic) 1987. a. exchange basis. United Arab Emirates University, Faculty of Law and Islamic Jurisprudence, P.O. Box 15551, Al-Ain, United Arab Emirates. TEL 643998. TELEX 33521 JAMEAH EM. Ed. Wahbah Mustafa al-Zuhaili. bk.rev.; circ. 1,000.
Description: Publishes research on topics in Islamic jurisprudence and legal issues in the U.A.E. and the Gulf region.

340   US
MAJOR STUDIES AND ISSUE BRIEFS OF THE CONGRESSIONAL RESEARCH SERVICE.. 1975. a. (plus supplements to base vols.). $1135 for latest supp. University Publications of America (Subsidiary of: Congressional Information Service), 4520 East-West Hwy., Ste. 800, Bethesda, MD 20814-3389. TEL 301-657-3200. FAX 301-657-3200. (microfilm)

340   UG
MAKERERE LAW JOURNAL.* 1971. s-a. EAs.250. (Makerere Law Society) Makerere University, Faculty of Law, Box 7062, Kampala, Uganda. Ed.Bd. bk.rev.; circ. 1,000.

340   UG   ISSN 0075-4781
MAKERERE UNIVERSITY. FACULTY OF LAW. HANDBOOK. 1970. a. Makerere University, Faculty of Law, Box 7062, Kampala, Uganda.

347.9   MW   ISSN 0076-3160
LAW
MALAWI. MINISTRY OF JUSTICE. ANNUAL REPORT. a., latest 1969. K.0.50. Government Printer, Box 37, Zomba, Malawi.

340   MW
MALAWI. MINISTRY OF JUSTICE. LAWS AMENDMENTS. (Text in English) 1969. a. Government Printer, Box 37, Zomba, Malawi.

340   MW
MALAWI LAW REPORTS. a. Government Printer, Box 37, Zomba, Malawi. Ed. James B. Kalaile.
Formerly (until 1973): African Law Reports: Malawi Series.

340   SI   ISSN 0025-1283
LAW
MALAYAN LAW JOURNAL. 1932. fortn. S.$370 for Singapore and Brunei; Malaysia M.$595. Butterworths Asia (Subsidiary of: Reed International (Singapore) Pte Ltd.), 3 Shenton Way, No. 14-03, Shenton House, Singapore 0106, Singapore. TEL 220-3684. FAX 225-2939. Ed. Zarinah Marican. adv.; bk.rev.; s-a. index; circ. 1,450. (back issues avail.)
—BLDSC shelfmark: 5356.006000.

340   SI   ISSN 0961-5563
MALLAL'S MONTHLY DIGEST; Malaysia, Singapore, Brunei. (Text in English) 1987. m. S.$299 in Singapore & Brunei; Malaysia M.$418. Butterworths Asia (Subsidiary of: Reed International (Singapore) Pte. Ltd.), 3 Shenton Way, No. 14-03, Shenton House, Singapore 0106, Singapore. TEL 220-3684. FAX 225-2939. Ed.Bd. adv.; circ. 500. (back issues avail.)
Formerly: Butterworths Law Digest (ISSN 0951-5720)
Description: Carries case digests from Malaysia, Singapore and Brunei. Includes summaries of recent Malaysian and Singapore legislation.

MALPRACTICE REPORTER; comprehensive reporting of malpractice issues for the medical, legal, health services, and insurance communities. see MEDICAL SCIENCES

MALPRACTICE REPORTER. HOSPITALS EDITION. see MEDICAL SCIENCES

MALPRACTICE REPORTER. PODIATRY EDITION. see MEDICAL SCIENCES

MANAGED CARE LAW OUTLOOK. see MEDICAL SCIENCES

MANAGEMENT POLICIES & PERSONNEL LAW. see BUSINESS AND ECONOMICS — Management

MANAGERIAL LAW. see BUSINESS AND ECONOMICS — Labor And Industrial Relations

MANAGER'S LEGAL BULLETIN. see BUSINESS AND ECONOMICS — Labor And Industrial Relations

MANAGER'S MANUAL. see BUSINESS AND ECONOMICS — Banking And Finance

340   US
MANAGING THE FLORIDA CONDOMINIUM. 1988. base vol. (plus suppl. 2-3/yr.). $80. Butterworth Legal Publishers (Salem) (Subsidiary of: Reed International PLC), 90 Stiles Rd., Salem, NH 03079. TEL 800-548-4001. FAX 603-898-9858. Ed. William D. Clark. (looseleaf format)
Description: Comprehensive reference for community association managers, developers, owners and attorneys concerned with the legal duties and responsibilities of condominium management.

340 657   US
MANAGING YOUR ACCOUNTING AND CONSULTING PRACTICE. (Issued as 1 base vol. with supplements) 1978. irreg. Matthew Bender & Co., Inc., 11 Penn Plaza, New York, NY 10001. TEL 212-967-7707. Eds. Mary Ann Altman, Robert I. Weil. (looseleaf format)
Description: Comprehensive guidebook for accountants and consultants, including management consultants and engineers, on applying sound management principles to their own practices.

340   CN   ISSN 0380-0008
MANITOBA DECISIONS - CIVIL AND CRIMINAL CASES. 1975. m. Can.$265. Western Legal Publications, 301-1 Alexander St., Vancouver, B.C. V6A 1B2, Canada. TEL 604-687-5671. FAX 604-687-2796. (looseleaf format)
●Also available online.
Description: Provides summaries of both civil and criminal decisions from the Manitoba Court of Appeal, Court of Queen's Bench and selected decisions of the Provicial Court of Manitoba.

340   CN   ISSN 0824-7293
MANITOBA DECISIONS - RULES AND STATUTE CITATOR. 1981. m. Can.$120. Western Legal Publications, 301-1 Alexander St, Vancouver, B.C. V6A 1B2, Canada. TEL 604-687-5671. FAX 604-687-2796.
Description: Provides notes on all current judgments of the Supreme Court of Canada and the Manitoba Courts, case citations for all decisions of the Manitoba Courts in which a Manitoba Rule of Court was cited.

340   CN   ISSN 0076-3861
K13
MANITOBA LAW JOURNAL. (Text in English, French) 1962. 3/yr. $28. University of Manitoba, Faculty of Law, Winnipeg, Man. R3T 2N2, Canada. TEL 204-474-6159. FAX 204-275-5266. Ed. Jonathan Penner. adv.; bk.rev.; cum.index; circ. 800. (also avail. in microfilm from WSH; back issues avail.; reprint service avail. from WSH) **Indexed:** Abstr.Bk.Rev.Curr.Leg.Per., C.C.L.P., C.L.I., Foreign Leg.Per., Ind.Can.L.P.L., L.R.I., Leg.Cont., Leg.Per.
—BLDSC shelfmark: 5360.630000.
Incorporates: Manitoba Bar News.

340   CN
MANITOBA REPORTS. irreg. Can.$84 per vol. Maritime Law Book Ltd., Box 302, Fredericton, N.B. E3B 4Y9, Canada. TEL 506-454-9921. (back issues avail.)
●Also available online. Vendor(s): QL Systems Ltd..

340   US
MANUAL FOR FLORIDA LEGAL SECRETARIES. 1984. 3 base vols. (plus suppl. 3-4/yr.). (Florida Association of Legal Secretaries) Butterworth Legal Publishers (Salem) (Subsidiary of: Reed International PLC), 90 Stiles Rd., Salem, NH 03079. TEL 800-548-4001. FAX 603-898-9858. (looseleaf format)
Description: Practical up-to-date procedural guide providing forms and checklists, plus explanations on everyday use.

330   US
MARKETING FOR LAWYERS NEWSLETTER. 1987. m. $135. New York Law Publishing Co., 111 Eighth Ave., New York, NY 10011. TEL 212-741-8300.
Description: Helps attorneys to expand their practices by covering marketing techniques and strategies such as cross-marketing, using newsletters and seminars, opening branch offices, and servicing existing clients.

340 658 659.1   CN
MARKETING LAW REPORTING SERVICE. 1973. m. Can.$325($295) Businesstek Publishing Inc., P.O. Box 250, Carleton Place, Ont. K7C 3P4, Canada. TEL 613-253-2834. FAX 613-253-2834. Ed. Shaun McLaughlin. circ. 140. (looseleaf format)
  Formerly: Marketing & Advertising Law Reporter (ISSN 0827-2115)
  Description: Covers Canadian federal and provincial laws and regulation regarding marketing, packaging, advertising and labelling of consumer products.

340   US   ISSN 0025-3987
MARQUETTE LAW REVIEW. 1916. q. $20. Marquette University, Law School, 1103 W. Wisconsin Ave., Milwaukee, WI 53233. TEL 414-224-5143. Ed. Laurence M. Brooks. adv.; bk.rev.; index, cum.index; circ. 1,800. (also avail. in microfiche from WSH; microfilm from WSH) **Indexed:** C.L.I., Crim.Just.Abstr., L.R.I., Leg.Cont., Leg.Per., P.A.I.S.
  ●Also available online. Vendor(s): WESTLAW.
  —BLDSC shelfmark: 5382.500000.

MARQUETTE SPORTS LAW JOURNAL. see *SPORTS AND GAMES*

340   AT   ISSN 0728-5981
MARTIN AND MORLEY MOTOR VEHICLE LAW (QUEENSLAND). 1982. 4/yr. Aus.$250. Law Book Co. Ltd., 44-50 Waterloo Rd., N. Ryde, N.S.W. 2113, Australia. TEL 02-887-0177. FAX 02-888-9706. TELEX ASBOOK 27995. Ed. M.G. Martin. (looseleaf format)
  Description: Covers motor vehicles, negligence, traffic regulation, traffic offenses, and motor vehicle insurance in Queensland.

340   US
MARTINDALE-HUBBELL BAR REGISTER OF PREEMINENT LAWYERS. 1917. a. $129.95. R.R. Bowker, A Reed Reference Publishing Company, Division of Reed Publishing (USA) Inc., Box 1001, Summit, NJ 07902-1001. TEL 201-464-6800. FAX 201-464-3553. TELEX 138755. (Subscr. to: Order Dept., Box 31, New Providence, NJ 07974)
  Description: Lists over 7,700 members of the Bar in the United States, Canada, and 90 other countries. Presents complete information on each partnership, including current addresses and telephone numbers, names of members of the firm, and major clients represented.

340   US   ISSN 0191-0221
KF190
MARTINDALE-HUBBELL LAW DIRECTORY. (In 16 vols.) 1868. a. $273. R.R. Bowker, A Reed Reference Publishing Company, Division of Reed Publishing (USA) Inc., Box 1001, Summit, NJ 07902-1001. TEL 800-526-4902. FAX 201-464-3553. TELEX 138755.
  ●Also available online.
  Also available on CD-ROM.
  Description: Lists individuals licensed to practice law in the U.S., Canada and over 50 other countries. Consists of three main parts: practice profiles, professional biographies, and services and suppliers. Includes "Law Digest".

340   US
MARYLAND. GENERAL ASSEMBLY. SUBJECT INDEX TO BILLS INTRODUCED IN THE SESSION. 1976. a. $9. Department of Legislative Reference, 90 State Circle, Annapolis, MD 21401. TEL 410-841-3810.

340   US
MARYLAND. HOUSE OF DELEGATES. JOURNAL OF PROCEEDINGS. REGULAR SESSION. 1826. a. $75. Department of Legislative Reference, 90 State Circle, Annapolis, MD 21401. TEL 410-841-3810.

340   US
MARYLAND. SENATE. JOURNAL OF PROCEEDINGS. REGULAR SESSION. 1826. a. $75. Department of Legislative Reference, 90 State Circle, Annapolis, MD 21401. TEL 410-841-3810.

348.752   US   ISSN 0093-0520
KFM1238
MARYLAND. STATE DEPARTMENT OF LEGISLATIVE REFERENCE. SYNOPSIS OF LAWS ENACTED BY THE STATE OF MARYLAND. 1916. a. $20. Department of Legislative Reference, 90 State Circle, Annapolis, MD 21401. TEL 410-841-3810. Key Title: Synopsis of Laws Enacted by the State of Maryland.

340   US   ISSN 0025-4177
K13
MARYLAND BAR JOURNAL. 1968. bi-m. $25 to non-members. Maryland State Bar Association, 520 W. Fayette St., Baltimore, MD 21201. TEL 301-685-7878. FAX 301-837-0518. Ed. Janet Stidman Eveleth. adv.; bk.rev.; illus.; index; circ. 15,000. **Indexed:** C.L.I., Law Ofc.Info.Svc., Leg.Per.
  —BLDSC shelfmark: 5383.410000.

340   US
MARYLAND JOURNAL OF CONTEMPORARY LEGAL ISSUES. 1989. 2/yr. $15 ($10 per issue). University of Maryland School of Law, Student Bar Association, 500 W. Baltimore St., Baltimore, MD 21201. TEL 301-328-2115. Ed. Rita Edwards. circ. 600.
  Description: Contains current social and political concerns. Explores a separate topic of contemporary significance, and includes pieces from authors prominent in their respective fields.

340   US   ISSN 0025-4282
K13
MARYLAND LAW REVIEW. 1936. q. $20. University of Maryland School of Law, 500 W. Baltimore St., Baltimore, MD 21201. TEL 301-328-7214. Ed. Linda M. Thomas. adv.; bk.rev.; index, cum.index every 10 yrs.; circ. 2,200. (also avail. in microform from RRI,UMI; back issues avail.; reprint service avail. from RRI) **Indexed:** C.L.I., L.R.I., Leg.Cont., Leg.Per., P.A.I.S., Refug.Abstr.
  ●Also available online. Vendor(s): WESTLAW.

340   US   ISSN 0542-836X
MARYLAND LAWYER'S MANUAL. 1968. a. $52.50 to non-members. Maryland State Bar Association, 520 W. Fayette St., Baltimore, MD 21201. TEL 301-685-7878. Ed. Janet Stidman Eveleth. adv.; circ. 18,000.

MARYLAND REGISTER. see *PUBLIC ADMINISTRATION*

MARYLAND REGISTER. STATE CONTRACT SUPPLEMENT. see *PUBLIC ADMINISTRATION*

340   US
MASSACHUSETTS ATTORNEY DISCIPLINE REPORTS. (In 4 vols.) 1980. a. $55 per vol. Butterworth Legal Publishers (Salem) (Subsidiary of: Reed International PLC), 90 Stiles Rd., Salem, NH 03079. TEL 800-548-4001. FAX 603-898-9858.

340   US
MASSACHUSETTS COLLECTIONS MANUAL. irreg., 2nd ed., 1990. $75. Butterworth Legal Publishers (Salem) (Subsidiary of: Reed International PLC), 90 Stiles Rd., Salem, NH 03079. TEL 800-548-4001. FAX 603-898-9858. Ed.Bd. (looseleaf format)
  Description: For practitioners of commercial law who collect business debts for clients and all lawyers who are faced with clients who do not pay them.

340 346   US
MASSACHUSETTS DISCRIMINATION LAW REPORTER. 1978. m. $245 (effective 1992). New England Legal Publishers, Box 425, Weston, MA 02193-0425. TEL 617-891-6200. Ed. J. Ambash. index. (back issues avail.)

340   US   ISSN 0163-1411
K13
MASSACHUSETTS LAW REVIEW. 1915. q. $40 to non-members. Massachusetts Bar Association, 20 West St., Boston, MA 02111-1204. Ed. Majorie Heins. adv.; bk.rev.; index every 2 yrs.; circ. 22,000. (also avail. in microfiche from WSH; microfilm from UMI,WSH; reprint service avail.) **Indexed:** C.L.I., L.R.I., Leg.Cont., Leg.Per.
  Formerly (until vol.60, 1979): Massachusetts Law Quarterly (ISSN 0025-4835)

340   US
MASSACHUSETTS LAWYER WEEKLY. w. Lawyers Weekly Publications, 30 Court Sq., Boston, MA 02108-2553. TEL 617-227-6034. FAX 617-227-8824. Ed. Robert J. Ambrogi. circ. 10,100.

MASSACHUSETTS SALES AND USE TAX MANUAL. see *BUSINESS AND ECONOMICS — Public Finance, Taxation*

340   IT   ISSN 0025-4932
MASSIMARIO DEL FORO ITALIANO. m. L.142000 (foreign L.170000)(effective Feb. 1992). Zanichelli Editore S.p.A., Via Irnerio, 34, 40126 Bologna, Italy. TEL 081-293111. FAX 051-249782. index, cum.index.

340   IT   ISSN 0025-4940
MASSIMARIO DELLA GIURISPRUDENZA ITALIANA. 1931. m. L.109000. Unione Tipografico Editrice Torinese, Corso Raffaello 28, 10425 Turin, Italy. index; circ. 9,000.

340   IT   ISSN 0025-4959
MASSIMARIO DI GIURISPRUDENZA DEL LAVORO. 1929. bi-m. L.120000 (foreign L.150000). Servizio Italiano Pubblicazioni Internazionali s.r.l., Viale L. Pasteur, 6, 00144 Rome, Italy. TEL 06-5918586. FAX 06-5924819. index, cum.index every 10 yrs.; circ. 21,000.

340   GW
MAX-PLANCK-INSTITUT FUER AUSLAENDISCHES OEFFENTLICHES RECHT UND VOELKERRECHT. FONTES IURIS GENTIUM. (Deutsche Rechtsprechung Zum Voelkerrecht 1879-1985) 1931. irreg. price varies. Max-Planck-Institut fuer Auslaendisches Oeffentliches Recht und Voelkerrecht, Berliner Str. 48, 6900 Heidelberg, Germany. FAX 06221-43982. TELEX 461505-MPIMF. (Subscr. to: Springer-Verlag Berlin, Heidelberger Platz 3, 1000 Berlin 33, Germany) Ed.Bd. adv.; circ. 700.
  Formerly: Max-Planck-Institut fuer Auslaendisches Oeffentliches Recht und Voelkerrecht. Fontes (ISSN 0076-5651)

340   GW   ISSN 0579-2428
MAX-PLANCK-INSTITUT FUER EUROPAISCHE RECHTSGESCHICHTE. VEROEFFENTLICHUNGEN. IUS COMMUNE. a. price varies. Vittorio Klostermann, Frauenlobstr. 22, Postfach 900601, 6000 Frankfurt a.M. 90, Germany. TEL 069-774011. FAX 069-708038. Ed. Dieter Simon.

340   GW   ISSN 0175-6532
MAX-PLANCK-INSTITUTE FUER EUROPAISCHE RECHTSGESCHICHTE. VEROEFFENTLICHUNGEN. IUS COMMUNE. SONDERHEFTE. irreg., vol.57, 1991. price varies. Vittorio Klostermann, Frauenlobstr. 22, Postfach 900601, 6000 Frankfurt a.M. 90, Germany. TEL 069-774011. FAX 069-708038.

340 331   NZ   ISSN 0111-6770
MAZENGARB'S INDUSTRIAL LAW BULLETIN. 1981. 8/yr. NZ.$160. Butterworths of New Zealand Ltd., P.O. Box 472, 203-207 Victoria St., Wellington, New Zealand. TEL 04-385-1479. FAX 04-385-1598. Ed. Richard Chan.
  Description: Articles plus notes on all developments of relevance to industrial law in New Zealand.

340   NZ
MAZENGARB'S INDUSTRIAL LAW SERVICE. 2 base vols. (plus updates 3/yr.). NZ.$296. Butterworths of New Zealand Ltd., 203-207 Victoria St., P.O. Box 472, Wellington, New Zealand. TEL 04-385-1479. FAX 04-385-1598. Ed. Richard Chan. (looseleaf format)
  Description: Full text of relevant legislation with case notes and commentary.

346.066   US
MECKLENBURG TIMES. 1924. 2/w. $51. Legal and Business Publishers, Inc., Box 36306, Charlotte, NC 28236. TEL 704-377-6221. Ed. Jill T. Purdy. adv.; bk.rev.; circ. 1,000. (tabloid format; also avail. in microfiche; back issues avail.)

MEDIATION QUARTERLY. see *PSYCHOLOGY*

340 610   US
MEDICAID FRAUD REPORT. 1981. 10/yr. $150. National Association of Medicaid Fraud Control Units, 444 N. Capitol St., Washington, DC 20001. TEL 202-628-0445. FAX 202-347-4882. Ed. Barbara L. Zelner. (back issues avail.)

MEDICAL AND RADIOLOGICAL DEVICES GUIDANCE MANUAL. see *PUBLIC HEALTH AND SAFETY*

MEDICAL DEVICE ESTABLISHMENT REGISTRATION MASTER FILE. see *PUBLIC HEALTH AND SAFETY*

MEDICAL DEVICE PROBLEMS REPORT FROM THE D E N: REPORTS FROM MEDICAL DEVICE USERS. see *PUBLIC HEALTH AND SAFETY*

MEDICAL DEVICE REPORTING FROM THE D E N: REPORTS FROM MEDICAL DEVICE MANUFACTURERS. see *PUBLIC HEALTH AND SAFETY*

MEDICAL DEVICE TECHNOLOGY. see *MEDICAL SCIENCES*

MEDICAL DEVICES, DIAGNOSTICS & INSTRUMENTATION REPORTS: THE GRAY SHEET. see *MEDICAL SCIENCES*

MEDICAL ETHICS ADVISOR. see *MEDICAL SCIENCES*

340   341   AU   ISSN 0257-3822
MEDIEN UND RECHT INTERNATIONAL; Zeitschrift fuer das Recht der Medien und der Werbung. 1983. bi-m. S.980. Verlag Medien und Recht, P.O. Box 83, Danhauserg. 6, 1041 Vienna, Austria. TEL 01-5052766. FAX 01-505276615. Ed. Dr. Heinz Wittmann. adv.; bk.rev.; index; circ. 1,900. (back issues avail.)
   Formerly: Medien und Recht.

340   PP   ISSN 0254-0657
K13
MELANESIAN LAW JOURNAL. 1970. a. K.12. University of Papua New Guinea, Faculty of Law, P.O. Box 317, University P.O., Papua New Guinea. FAX 245187. TELEX NE 22366. (Overseas subscr. to: William Gaunt & Son, Inc., 3011 Gulf Dr., Holmes Beach, FL 34217-2199, USA. TEL 817-778-5211) Ed. Rafiqul Islam. bk.rev.; circ. 1,000. **Indexed:** C.L.I., L.R.I., Leg.Per.

340   AT   ISSN 0025-8938
K13
MELBOURNE UNIVERSITY LAW REVIEW. 1957. s-a. Aus.$15. University of Melbourne, Law School, Parkville 3052, Victoria, Australia. FAX 61-3-347-2392. (Subscr. to: Law Book Co. Ltd., 389 Lonsdale St., Melbourne 3000, Australia) adv.; bk.rev.; index every 2 yrs; circ. 2,000. **Indexed:** Aus.P.A.I.S., C.L.I., L.R.I., Leg.Per.
   —BLDSC shelfmark: 5536.830000.

340   US
MEMBER NET. q. $11. American Bar Association, Young Lawyers Division, 750 N. Lake Shore Dr., Chicago, IL 60611. TEL 312-988-5555.

340   FR
MEMENTO PRATIQUE DES SOCIETES COMMERCIALES. a. 408 F. Editions Francis Lefebvre, 5 rue Jacques Bingen, 75017 Paris, France.

340   US   ISSN 0047-6714
K24
MEMPHIS STATE UNIVERSITY LAW REVIEW. 1970. q. $18. Memphis State University, Cecil C. Humphreys School of Law, Memphis, TN 38152. TEL 901-454-2078. adv.; bk.rev.; index; circ. 800. (also avail. in microfilm from UMI; reprint service avail. from RRI,UMI) **Indexed:** Abstr.Bk.Rev.Curr.Leg.Per., C.L.I., L.R.I., Leg.Cont., Leg.Per.

MENTAL HEALTH WEEKLY; news for policy and program decision-makers. see *PSYCHOLOGY*

340   US   ISSN 0025-987X
LAW
MERCER LAW REVIEW. 1949. 4/yr. $30. Mercer University, Walter F. George School of Law, Macon, GA 31207. TEL 912-752-2622. Ed. Cheryl Long. adv.; index, cum.index; circ. 1,800. (also avail. in microform from UMI; reprint service avail. from UMI) **Indexed:** C.L.I., L.R.I., Leg.Cont., Leg.Per., Mar.Aff.Bibl., SSCI.
   ●Also available online. Vendor(s): WESTLAW.
   —BLDSC shelfmark: 5678.820000.

MERCHANT AND GOULD COMPUTER LAW NEWSLETTER. see *COMPUTERS*

340   296   US   ISSN 0094-9701
BM520
HA-MESIVTA. (Text in Hebrew) 1940. a. $4. Yeshivath Torah Vodaath, Inc., 452 E. Ninth St., Brooklyn, NY 11218. TEL 718-462-6081. Ed. Elie Goldberg. adv.; circ. 1,000.

340   US   ISSN 0164-3576
KF200
MICHIGAN BAR JOURNAL. 1921. m. $35. State Bar of Michigan, 306 Townsend, Lansing, MI 48933. TEL 517-372-9030. Ed. Nancy F. Brown. adv.; bk.rev.; illus.; index; circ. 27,518. (also avail. in microform from UMI; microfilm from WSH) **Indexed:** C.L.I., HRIS, L.R.I., Law Ofc.Info.Svc., Leg.Per.
   ●Also available online. Vendor(s): WESTLAW.
   —BLDSC shelfmark: 5753.625000.
   Formerly (until Jan. 1979): Michigan State Bar Journal (ISSN 0162-5101)

340   US   ISSN 0026-2234
K13
MICHIGAN LAW REVIEW. 1902. 8/yr. $36. Michigan Law Review Association, Ann Arbor, MI 48109-1215. Ed.Bd. adv.; bk.rev.; index, cum.index; circ. 2,420. (also avail. in microform from UMI,WSH; reprint service avail. from WSH) **Indexed:** ABI Inform, Account.Ind. (1974-), Bank.Lit.Ind., BPIA, C.L.I., Crim.Just.Abstr., Curr.Cont., J.of Econ.Lit., L.R.I., Leg.Cont., Leg.Per., P.A.I.S., SSCI.
   ●Also available online. Vendor(s): Mead Data Central, WESTLAW.
   —BLDSC shelfmark: 5755.300000.

340   US
MICHIGAN LAWYERS WEEKLY. 1986. Michigan Lawyers Weekly, 333 S. Washington Sq., No.300, Lansing, MI 48933. TEL 517-374-6200. FAX 517-374-6222. adv.; circ. 3,513.
   Description: Provides summaries of court decisions for all state and federal courts in Michigan. Reports local and state legal news, State Bar news, and includes judicial profiles.

340   614.7   US   ISSN 1049-9350
▼**MIDWEST ENVIRONMENTAL LAW LETTER.** 1990. 12/yr. $147. M. Lee Smith Publishers & Printers, 162 Fourth Ave. N., Box 2678, Nashville, TN 37219. TEL 615-242-7395. FAX 615-256-6601. (Co-sponsor: Armstrong, Teasdale, Schlafly, Davis & Dicus) Ed. George M. von Stamwitz.
   Description: Reports the latest Midwestern environmental law developments that affect Midwestern companies.

340   US
MIDWEST LAW REVIEW. 1981. a. $5. (Midwest Regional Business Law Association) Illinois State University, College of Business, 328 William Hall, Illinois State University, Normal, IL 61761. TEL 309-438-5675. Ed. Dennis Kruse. bk.rev.; circ. 200.
   Description: Covers business law, the legal environment, and government regulation.

MILIEU EN BEDRIJF. see *ENVIRONMENTAL STUDIES*

340   US
MILWAUKEE LAWYER. 1976. q. $12. Milwaukee Bar Association, Inc., 533 E. Wells St., Milwaukee, WI 53202-3806. Ed. James L. Santelle. adv.; circ. 5,200. (back issues avail.) **Indexed:** C.L.I., Law Ofc.Info.Svc., Leg.Per.

MINERAL LAW NEWSLETTER. see *MINES AND MINING INDUSTRY*

340   622   AT
▼**MINING AND PETROLEUM LEGISLATION SERVICE.** 1990. 5/yr. Aus.$275. Law Book Co. Ltd., 44-50 Waterloo Rd., North Ryde, N.S.W. 2113, Australia. TEL 02-887-0177. FAX 02-888-9706. TELEX ASBOOK 27995.
   Description: Contains all legislation from the Australian Commonwealth, states, and territories relating to mining and petroleum; up-to-date and annotated.

MINNESOTA ADMINISTRATIVE PROCEDURE. see *PUBLIC ADMINISTRATION*

340   US
▼**MINNESOTA CONDEMNATION LAW AND PRACTICE.** 1990. base vol. (plus a. suppl.) $95. Butterworth Legal Publishers (Salem) (Subsidiary of: Reed International PLC), 90 Stiles Rd., Salem, NH 03079. TEL 800-548-4001. FAX 603-898-9858. Ed.Bd. (looseleaf format)
   Description: For attorneys representing both the condemning authorities or the property owners.

340   US
MINNESOTA EVIDENCE TRAILBOOK. 1987. base vol. (plus suppl.). $54. Butterworth Legal Publishers (Salem) (Subsidiary of: Reed International PLC), 90 Stiles Rd., Salem, NH 03079. TEL 800-548-4001. FAX 603-898-9858. Ed. Bertrand Poritsky. (looseleaf format)

340   US   ISSN 0026-5535
K13
MINNESOTA LAW REVIEW. 1917. 6/yr. $24. (Minnesota Law Review Foundation) University of Minnesota, Law School, 229 19th Ave. S., Minneapolis, MN 55455. TEL 612-625-8034. adv.; bk.rev.; charts; index, cum.index every 5 yrs.; circ. 1,486. (also avail. in microfilm from WSH; back issues avail.; reprint service avail. from WSH) **Indexed:** A.B.C.Pol.Sci., Abstr.Bk.Rev.Curr.Leg.Per., Bank.Lit.Ind., C.L.I., Crim.Just.Abstr., L.R.I., Leg.Cont., Leg.Per., P.A.I.S., SSCI.
   ●Also available online. Vendor(s): Mead Data Central, WESTLAW.
   —BLDSC shelfmark: 5810.390000.

340   US
MINNESOTA LEGAL REGISTER: MINNESOTA TAX COURT DECISIONS. 1985. a. $48. Philip G. Bradley, Ed. & Pub., Box 372, Long Lake, MN 55356. TEL 612-473-0987. index; circ. 140. (looseleaf format)
   Description: Complete text of all decisions.

340   US   ISSN 0026-5543
MINNESOTA LEGAL REGISTER: OPINIONS OF THE MINNESOTA ATTORNEY GENERAL. 1968. m. $40 for 2 yrs. Philip G. Bradley, Ed. & Pub., Box 372, Long Lake, MN 55356. TEL 612-473-0987. index; circ. 260. (looseleaf format)
   Description: Complete text of all opinions.

340   US
MINNESOTA LEGISLATIVE MANUAL. biennial. free. Secretary of State, 180 State Office Bldg, St. Paul, MN 55155. Ed. Joseph Mansky. circ. 15,000.

340   US
MINNESOTA LIMITATIONS MANUAL. 1989. base vol. (plus a. suppl.), 2nd ed., 1990. $50. Butterworth Legal Publishers (Salem) (Subsidiary of: Reed International PLC), 90 Stiles Rd., Salem, NH 03079. TEL 800-548-4001. FAX 603-898-9858. Ed.Bd. (looseleaf format)

340   US
MINNESOTA MECHANICS' LIENS PRACTICE MANUAL. 1987. base vol. (plus suppl.). $78. Butterworth Legal Publishers (Salem) (Subsidiary of: Reed International PLC), 90 Stiles Rd., Salem, NH 03079. TEL 800-548-4001. FAX 603-898-9858. Ed. James E. Snoxell. (looseleaf format)
   Description: Covers all aspects of a liens claim and includes over 30 forms as well as the complete text of the state statute.

340   US
MINNESOTA MISDEMEANORS AND MOVING TRAFFIC VIOLATIONS. 2nd ed., 1990. 2 base vols. (plus suppl.). $160. Butterworth Legal Publishers (Salem) (Subsidiary of: Reed International PLC), 90 Stiles Rd., Salem, NH 03079. TEL 800-548-4001. FAX 603-898-9858. Ed.Bd. (looseleaf format)
   Description: Guide to the prosecution and defense of misdemeanor, gross, and petty misdemeanor cases in the district courts on Minnesota.

MINNESOTA NO-FAULT AUTOMOBILE INSURANCE. see *INSURANCE*

340   US
MINNESOTA PROBATE LAW DIGEST. 1982. 3 base vols. (plus a. suppl.). $185. Butterworth Legal Publishers (Salem) (Subsidiary of: Reed International PLC), 90 Stiles Rd., Salem, NH 03079. TEL 800-548-4001. FAX 603-898-9858. Ed.Bd. (looseleaf format)

349   US
MINNESOTA RULES. 1983. biennial. $160. Office of Revisor of Statutes, 700 State Office Bldg., St. Paul, MN 55155. TEL 612-296-2868. circ. 1,000.

349   US
MINNESOTA RULES. SUPPLEMENT. 1984. biennial (2/yr. in even-numbered years). Office of Revisor of Statutes, 700 State Office Bldg., St. Paul, MN 55155. TEL 612-296-2868.

LAW

340 350 US ISSN 0146-7751
KFM5436
MINNESOTA STATE REGISTER. 1976. 2/w. $140 for Monday edition; with Monday and Thurs. mid-week contract supplement $195. Department of Administration, Print Communications Division, 117 University Ave., St. Paul, MN 55155. TEL 612-296-0931. Ed. Robin PanLener. index, cum.index; circ. 1,250. (also avail. in microfiche; back issues avail.)
   Description: Focuses on the administrative rules of state government, official notices, state contracts for commodities, printing, and professional, technical, and consulting services.

348 US ISSN 0191-1562
KFM5429
MINNESOTA STATUTES. 1941. biennial. $165. Office of Revisor of Statutes, 700 State Office Bldg., St. Paul, MN 55155. TEL 612-296-2868. circ. 4,500.

348 US ISSN 0094-1727
KFM5431
MINNESOTA STATUTES. SUPPLEMENT. 1973. biennial. Office of Revisor of Statutes, 700 State Office Bldg., St. Paul, MN 55155. TEL 612-296-2868. circ. 2,800.

348 US
MINNESOTA STATUTES ON C D - R O M. 1989. a. $205. Office of Revisor of Statutes, 700 State Office Bldg., St. Paul, MN 55155. TEL 612-296-2868. circ. 100.
●Available only on CD-ROM.

MINNESOTA TAX APPEALS. see *BUSINESS AND ECONOMICS — Public Finance, Taxation*

MINZHU YU FAZHI/DEMOCRACY & LEGAL SYSTEMS. see *POLITICAL SCIENCE*

340 IS
MISHPATIM. 1971. 3/yr. IS.60($40) Hebrew University of Jerusalem, Faculty of Law, P.O. Box 24100, Jerusalem, Israel. TEL 02-882550. Eds. A. Aberman, A. Well. bk.rev.; circ. 1,500.

340 US ISSN 0277-1152
K13
MISSISSIPPI COLLEGE LAW REVIEW. 1978. s-a. $12. (Mississippi College of Law) Mississippi College Law Review, 151 E. Griffith St., Jackson, MS 39201. TEL 601-944-1950. Ed. Denise Schreiber. adv.; bk.rev.; index, cum.index; circ. 650. (also avail. in microfilm from WSH; back issues avail.; reprint service avail. from WSH) **Indexed:** Abstr.Bk.Rev.Curr.Leg.Per., C.L.I., L.R.I., Leg.Per.
●Also available online. Vendor(s): WESTLAW.

340 US ISSN 0026-6280
K13
MISSISSIPPI LAW JOURNAL. 1928. 3/yr. $35. (University of Mississippi Law School) Mississippi Law Journal, Box 849, University, MS 38677. TEL 601-232-7361. FAX 601-232-7731. Ed. Louis H. Watson, Jr. adv.; bk.rev.; index, cum.index every 10 yrs.; circ. 1,100. (also avail. in microfilm from RRI; reprint service avail. from RRI) **Indexed:** C.C.L.P., C.L.I., Curr.Cont., L.R.I., Leg.Per., SSCI.
●Also available online. Vendor(s): WESTLAW.
—BLDSC shelfmark: 5828.927000.

340 US
MISSOURI COURT RULES HANDBOOK; local rules of the forty-four Judicial Circuit Courts in Missouri. 1989. base vol. (plus q. suppl.). $135. Butterworth Legal Publishers (Salem) (Subsidiary of: Reed International PLC), 90 Stiles Rd., Salem, NH 03079. TEL 800-548-4001. FAX 603-898-9858. Ed.Bd. (looseleaf format)

340 US ISSN 1054-6375
▼**MISSOURI EMPLOYMENT LAW LETTER.** 1991. 12/yr. $127. M. Lee Smith Publishers & Printers, 162 Fourth Ave. N., Box 2678, Nashville, TN 37219. TEL 615-252-7395. FAX 615-256-6601. (Co-sponsor: Lashly & Baer) Eds. Robert A. Kaiser, Vance D. Miller.
   Description: Reports the latest Missouri employment law developments that affect Missouri employers.

340 US
▼**MISSOURI ENVIRONMENTAL LAW LETTER.** 1991. 12/yr. $137. M. Lee Smith Publishers & Printers, 162 4th Ave. N., Box 2678, Nashville, TN 37219. TEL 615-242-7385. FAX 615-256-6601. Ed. George M. von Stamitz.

340 US ISSN 0026-6604
K13
MISSOURI LAW REVIEW. 1936. q. $25. University of Missouri, Columbia, School of Law, Columbia, MO 65211. TEL 314-882-7055. FAX 314-882-7055. Ed. Brian Forbes. adv.; bk.rev.; index, cum.index every 10 yrs.; circ. 1,350. (tabloid format; also avail. in microfilm from WSH; reprint service avail. from WSH) **Indexed:** C.L.I., L.R.I., Leg.Cont., Leg.Per., P.A.I.S.
●Also available online. Vendor(s): WESTLAW.
—BLDSC shelfmark: 5829.075000.

340 US
MISSOURI NOTARY LAW PRIMER. a. $9.95. National Notary Association, 8236 Remmet Ave., Box 7184, Canoga Park, CA 91304-7184. TEL 818-713-4000. FAX 818-713-9061. Ed. Charles N. Faerber. (reprint service avail. from UMI)

340 GW ISSN 0723-5984
DIE MITBESTIMMUNG. 1954. m. DM.55. Hans-Boeckler-Stiftung, Bertha-von-Sultner-Platz 3, 4000 Duesseldorf 1, Germany. TEL 0211-7778149. FAX 0211-7778120. TELEX 8584-404-HBS-D. bk.rev.; circ. 16,500.
—BLDSC shelfmark: 5829.599600.

MITTEILUNGEN DER DEUTSCHEN PATENTANWAELTE. see *PATENTS, TRADEMARKS AND COPYRIGHTS*

347.016 GW
MITTEILUNGEN DES BAYERISCHEN NOTARVEREINS, DER NOTARKASSE UND DER LANDESNOTARKAMMER BAYERN. 1864. bi-m. DM.50. Landesnotarkammer Bayern, Ottostr. 10, 8000 Munich 2, Germany. TEL 089-55166-0. FAX 089-55166-304. bk.rev.; index; circ. 2,700. (back issues avail.)

348 CE
MODERN LAW REPORTS, EMBODYING CASES DECIDED BY THE SUPREME COURT OF THE REPUBLIC OF SRI LANKA.* (Text in English or Sinhalese) 1975. w. Rs.2.50. (Sresthadikaranaya) C.L. Perera, 29-12 Visaka Rd., Colombo 4, Sri Lanka.

340 UK ISSN 0026-7961
K13
MODERN LAW REVIEW. 1937. 6/yr. £45($79.50) Basil Blackwell Ltd., 108 Cowley Rd., Oxford OX4 1JF, England. Ed. Simon Roberts. adv.; bk.rev.; index; circ. 3,100. **Indexed:** Abstr.Bk.Rev.Curr.Leg.Per., Br.Hum.Ind., C.L.I., L.R.I., Leg.Cont., Leg.Per., RICS.
—BLDSC shelfmark: 5887.900000.

340 AT ISSN 0311-3140
K13
MONASH UNIVERSITY LAW REVIEW. 1974. s-a. Aus.$30 (effective 1991-1992). Monash University, Faculty of Law, Clayton, Vic. 3168, Australia. FAX 03-565-3374. Ed.Bd. adv.; bk.rev.; circ. 1,200. (also avail. in microform from UMI) **Indexed:** Aus.P.A.I.S., C.L.I., L.R.I., Leg.Per.
—BLDSC shelfmark: 5901.594000.

340 GW ISSN 0340-1812
K13
MONATSSCHRIFT FUER DEUTSCHES RECHT. 1947. m. DM.180 (students DM.126.50). Verlag Dr. Otto Schmidt KG, Unter den Ulmen 96-98, 5000 Cologne 51, Germany. TEL 0221-3498-0. FAX 0221-3498-181. TELEX 8883381. Ed. E. Paterna. adv.; bk.rev.; circ. 6,000. **Indexed:** Dok.Str.
—BLDSC shelfmark: 5906.320000.

340 SP ISSN 0077-0442
MONOGRAFIAS DE FILOSOFIA JURIDICA Y SOCIAL/MONOGRAPHS OF SOCIAL AND LEGAL PHILOSOPHY.* 1967. a. 70 ptas.($1) Universidad de Granada, Facultad de Derecho, Granada, Spain.

340 US ISSN 0026-9972
MONTANA LAW REVIEW. 1940. s-a. $10 (foreign $12). University of Montana, Students of School of Law, Missoula, MT 59812. TEL 406-243-2023. adv.; bk.rev.; cum.index; vols. 1-39; circ. 2,300. (also avail. in microfilm from UMI; microfiche from WSH; microfilm from WSH) **Indexed:** C.L.I., L.R.I., Leg.Cont., Leg.Per., SSCI.
—BLDSC shelfmark: 5928.006500.

MONTHLY PRESCRIBING REFERENCE. see *MEDICAL SCIENCES*

MOREANA; time trieth truth. see *HISTORY — History Of Europe*

349 RU ISSN 0027-1357
MOSKOVSKII UNIVERSITET. VESTNIK. SERIYA 12: PRAVO. 1960. bi-m. 13.50 Rub. Moskovskii Universitet, Ul. Gertsena 5-7, 103009 Moscow, Russia. (Dist. by: Mezhdunarodnaya Kniga, Moscow, G-200, Russia) bk.rev.; index.

340 AG
MUNDO JUSTICIALISTA. 1983. m. Billinghurst 527, Piso 6, Buenos Aires, Argentina. Dir. Hugo Cesar Luna.

MUNICIPAL AND PLANNING LAW REPORTS (2ND SERIES). see *HOUSING AND URBAN PLANNING*

340 US ISSN 0027-3449
K13
MUNICIPAL ATTORNEY. 1959. bi-m. membership only. National Institute of Municipal Law Officers, 1000 Connecticut Ave., N.W., Ste. 902, Washington, DC 20036. TEL 202-466-5424. FAX 202-785-0152. Ed. Benjamin L. Brown. circ. 2,500 (controlled). **Indexed:** C.L.I., L.R.I.
   Incorporates (1941-1991): Municipal Law Court Decisions (ISSN 0027-3503); (1947-1991): Municipal Ordinance Review (ISSN 0027-3538) Municipal Law Journal; (1985-1991): Municipalities in the United States Supreme Court; (1986-1991): N I M L O'S Congressional News; (1977-1991): Municipal Law Docket (ISSN 0148-3366); Which incorporated: Municipal Attorneys' Opinions (ISSN 0277-6294).
   Description: Articles on legal issues affecting cities, case digests, ordinances, summaries of federal and state regulations, opinions and reviews.

340 II ISSN 0377-757X
LAW
MUNICIPALITIES AND CORPORATION CASES; a monthly law reporter. (Text in English) m. Rs.120. International Law Book Co., Nijhawan Bldg., 1562 Church Rd., Kashmere Gate, Delhi 6, India. Ed. Mrs. Swarn Bhati Nijhawan.

N A A W S GRAPEVINE NEWSLETTER. (North American Association of Wardens and Superintendents) see *CRIMINOLOGY AND LAW ENFORCEMENT*

N A I C NEWSLETTER. (National Association of Insurance Commissioners) see *INSURANCE*

340 US
N A L P BULLETIN. 1971. m. $60 to non-members. National Association for Law Placement, 1666 Connecticut Ave., Ste. 450, Washington, DC 20009. TEL 202-667-1666. Ed. Honora A. Mara. bk.rev.; index; circ. 1,100. (back issues avail.)
   Formerly: N A L P Notes.
   Description: Articles on legal career development.

340 US
N A L S DOCKET. 1952. 6/yr. $14. National Association of Legal Secretaries, 2250 E. 73rd, No. 550, Tulsa, OK 74136-6864. FAX 918-493-5784. Ed. Ellen Sue Blakey. adv.; bk.rev.; circ. 18,000. **Indexed:** Law Ofc.Info.Svc.
   Description: For legal secretaries and other non-attorney support personnel. Addresses trends and emerging issues in the legal field. Provides information that helps to achieve proficiency in the performance of legal services, and offers techniques for career growth and development.

N A P F PENSIONS LEGISLATION SERVICE. see *INSURANCE*

N A R F LEGAL REVIEW. (Native American Rights Fund) see *ETHNIC INTERESTS*

N A S D NOTICES TO MEMBERS. see *BUSINESS AND ECONOMICS — Investments*

N A S D REGULATORY AND COMPLIANCE ALERT. (National Association of Securities Dealers, Inc.) see *BUSINESS AND ECONOMICS — Investments*

N A S S P LEGAL MEMORANDUM. (National Association of Secondary School Principals) see *EDUCATION — School Organization And Administration*

LAW

351.26 US
N A W J COUNTERBALANCE. 1980. 3/yr. $10. National Association of Women Judges, c/o Secretariat Services, National Center for State Courts, 300 Newport Ave., Williamsburg, VA 23187-8798. TEL 804-253-2000. FAX 804-220-0449. Ed. Katherine Gearin. circ. 1,200.
  Formerly: N A W J News and Announcements.

N C A M P'S TECHNICAL REPORT. (National Coalition Against the Misuse of Pesticides) see *ENVIRONMENTAL STUDIES*

346.066 640.73 US ISSN 1054-3775
KF1507
N C L C REPORTS: BANKRUPTCY & FORECLOSURES. 1982. bi-m. $30. National Consumer Law Center, 11 Beacon St., Ste. 821, Boston, MA 02108. TEL 617-523-8010. FAX 671-523-7398. Ed. Kathleen Keest. index; circ. 2,000. (looseleaf format; back issues avail.)
  Formerly: N C L C Reports: Consumer Bankruptcy and Foreclosures Edition (ISSN 0890-2623)
  Description: Covers latest developments in the practice of consumer law, with emphasis on bankruptcy and foreclosures.

346.066 640.73 US ISSN 0890-2615
KF1039.A15
N C L C REPORTS: CONSUMER CREDIT & USURY. 1982. bi-m. $30. National Consumer Law Center, 11 Beacon St., Ste. 821, Boston, MA 02108. TEL 617-523-8010. Ed. Kathleen Keest. index; circ. 2,000. (looseleaf format; back issues avail.)
  Description: Covers latest developments and new ideas in the practice of consumer law, with emphasis on consumer credit and usury.

346.066 640.73 US ISSN 0890-2607
KF1024.A15
N C L C REPORTS: DEBT COLLECTION & REPOSESSIONS. 1982. bi-m. $30. National Consumer Law Center, 11 Beacon St., Ste. 821, Boston, MA 02108. TEL 617-523-8010. Ed. Kathleen Keest. index; circ. 2,000. (looseleaf format; back issues avail.)
  Description: Covers latest developments and new ideas in the practice of consumer law, with emphasis on debt collection and repossessions.

346.066 640.73 US ISSN 0890-0973
KF1602
N C L C REPORTS: DECEPTIVE ACTS & WARRANTIES. 1982. bi-m. $30. National Consumer Law Center, 11 Beacon St., Ste. 821, Boston, MA 02108. TEL 617-523-8010. Ed. Kathleen Keest. index; circ. 2,000. (looseleaf format; back issues avail.)
  Description: Covers latest developments and new ideas in the practice of consumer law, with emphasis on deceptive acts and warranties.

N F R A NEWSLETTER. (National Forest Recreation Association) see *CONSERVATION*

340 GW ISSN 0179-4043
KK40
N J W - RECHTSPRECHUNGS-REPORT ZIVILRECHT. 1986. s-m. DM.464. C.H. Beck'sche Verlagsbuchhandlung, Wilhelmstr. 9, 8000 Munich 40, Germany. TEL 089-38189-338. FAX 089-38189-398. TELEX 5215085-BECK-D. Ed.Bd. circ. 5,000.

340 US
N L A D A CORNERSTONE. 1980. 4/yr. $20. National Legal Aid and Defender Association, 1625 K St. N.W., 8th Fl., Washington, DC 20006. TEL 202-452-0620. FAX 202-872-1031. tr.lit.; circ. 4,000. (back issues avail.; reprint service avail. from UMI)
  Formerly: N L A D A Washington Memo.
  Description: Technical information for public defenders, legal services attorneys, pro bono attorneys and clients.

346.066 US
N L R B CASE HANDLING MANUAL. 1976. irreg. $225. (U.S. National Labor Relations Board) Commerce Clearing House, Inc., 4925 W. Peterson Ave., Chicago, IL 60646. TEL 312-583-8500. Ed. D. Newquist.

N O L P E NOTES. (National Organization on Legal Problems of Education) see *EDUCATION — School Organization And Administration*

340 370 US ISSN 1059-4094
KF4114
N O L P E SCHOOL LAW REPORTER. 1961. m. $75. National Organization on Legal Problems of Education, 3601 S.W. 29th, Ste. 223, Topeka, KS 66614. TEL 913-273-3550. Eds. Patricia First, Lawrence Rossow. cum.index; circ. 2,800. (looseleaf format) **Indexed:** Educ.Admin.Abstr.

799.202 364.4 US
N R A ACTION. 1974. m. $20. National Rifle Association of America, Institute for Legislative Action, 1600 Rhode Island Ave., N.W., Washington, DC 20036. TEL 202-828-6326. FAX 202-833-4323. Ed. T.C. Wyld. circ. 340,000. (tabloid format; back issues avail.)
  Former titles: N R A Monitor; N R A Institute for Legislative Action. Reports from Washington; N R A Unified Sportsmen of America. Reports from Washington.
  Description: Covers legislative initiatives and Second Amendment issues, including relevant discussions of constitutional law and criminology, as well as hunting, wildlife conservation and the animal rights movement.

343 US ISSN 0362-8833
KF2125.A15
N R E C A - A P P A LEGAL REPORTING SERVICE. 1975. m. $90. National Rural Electric Cooperative Association, Management Services Department, 1800 Massachusetts Ave., N.W., Washington, DC 20036. TEL 202-857-9500. (Co-sponsor: American Public Power Association)
  Formerly: N R E C A Legal Reporting Service (ISSN 0547-8847)

340 GW ISSN 0934-8603
N V W Z RECHTSPRECHUNGS REPORT VERWALTUNGSRECHT. 1988. m. DM.340. C.H. Beck'sche Verlagsbuchhandlung, Wilhelmstr. 9, 8000 Munich 40, Germany. TEL 089-38189-1. FAX 089-38189398. TELEX 5215085-BECK-D. adv.; index. (back issues avail.)

340 US
N.Y. COUNTY LAWYER. 1970. 10/yr. membership. New York County Lawyers' Association, 14 Vesey St., New York, NY 10007. TEL 212-267-6646. FAX 212-285-4482. Ed. Steve Bookbinder. adv.; circ. 10,500.
  Formerly (until 1981): Vesey Street Letter (ISSN 0049-6030)

340 CN
NADIN-DAVIS CANADIAN SENTENCING DIGEST. 1980. irreg.(4-6/yr.). Can.$408. Carswell Publications, 2330 Midland Ave., Agincourt, Ont. M1S 1P7, Canada. TEL 416-291-8421. FAX 416-291-3426. Ed. Bob Stonehouse. (looseleaf format)

340 KE
THE NAIROBI LAW MONTHLY. (Text in English) m. Tumaini House, P.O. Box 53234, Nkrumah Ave., 4th Fl., Nairobi, Kenya. TEL 728978. Ed. Gitobu I. Imanyara.

363.2 US
NARC OFFICER. 1985. m. $35 (foreign $70). International Narcotic Enforcement Officers Association, 112 State St., Ste. 1200, Albany, NY 12207. TEL 518-463-6232. Ed. Celeste Morga. adv.; illus.; circ. 10,000.
  Incorporates (in Sept. 1985): International Narcotic Enforcement Officers Association. Annual Conference Report (ISSN 0538-8821)

350.765 US ISSN 8755-8289
KF3890.A59
NARCOTICS LAW BULLETIN. 1974. m. $50.75. Quinlan Publishing Co., Inc., 23 Drydock Ave., Boston, MA 02210-2307. TEL 617-542-0048. FAX 617-345-9646. Ed. M. Quinlan. (looseleaf format; also avail. in microform from UMI; reprint service avail. from UMI) **Indexed:** CJPI.

349 CI ISSN 0027-8165
K30
NASA ZAKONITOST; periodical for law theory and practice. (Text in Serbo-Croatian) 1947. m. 2000 din. to individuals; institutions 4000 din. Savez Drustava Pravnika Hrvatske, Savska 41, P.O. Box 684, 41000 Zagreb, Croatia. (Subscr. to: "Mladost" Export Import, Ilica 30, 41000 Zagreb, Croatia) (Co-sponsors: Udruzenje za Upravne Znanosti i Praksu Hrvatske; Republicki Zavod za Javnu Upravu Sr Hrvatske) Ed. Ilija Bekic. adv.; bk.rev.; circ. 4,000.

340 US ISSN 0047-8695
K14
NASSAU LAWYER. 1943. 10/yr. $15. (Nassau County Bar Association) Anton Community Newspapers, 15th and West Sts., Mineola, NY 11501. TEL 516-747-4070. FAX 516-747-4147. Ed.Bd. adv.; bk.rev.; illus.; tr.lit.; circ. 6,500.

340 SA
NATAL UNIVERSITY LAW AND SOCIETY REVIEW. 1972. a. $10. University of Natal, Howard College School of Law, King George V Ave., Durban, Natal 4001, South Africa. TEL 031-816-2558. Ed. D.J. McQuoid-Mason. adv.; bk.rev.; circ. 700. (back issues avail.) **Indexed:** Foreign.Leg.Per., Ind.S.A.Per.
  Formerly: Natal University Law Review.

NATIONAL ADOPTION REPORTS. see *SOCIAL SERVICES AND WELFARE*

NATIONAL AND FEDERAL LEGAL EMPLOYMENT REPORT. see *BUSINESS AND ECONOMICS — Personnel Management*

NATIONAL ASSOCIATION OF INSURANCE COMMISSIONERS. COMPILATION OF REPORTS. see *INSURANCE*

NATIONAL ASSOCIATION OF INSURANCE COMMISSIONERS. LIFE AND HEALTH ACTUARIAL REPORT. see *INSURANCE*

NATIONAL ASSOCIATION OF INSURANCE COMMISSIONERS. LISTING OF COMPANIES. see *INSURANCE*

NATIONAL ASSOCIATION OF INSURANCE COMMISSIONERS. PROCEEDINGS. see *INSURANCE*

NATIONAL BANKING LAW REVIEW; banking business and the law. see *BUSINESS AND ECONOMICS — Banking And Finance*

340 US
NATIONAL BLACK LAW JOURNAL. 1971. 3/yr. $18 to individuals; institutions $25; students $12.50. University of California, Los Angeles, School of Law, 405 Hilgard Ave., Los Angeles, CA 90024. TEL 213-825-7941. adv.; bk.rev.; circ. 5,000. (tabloid format; also avail. in microform from UMI,WSH,PMC; reprint service avail. from UMI,WSH) **Indexed:** Abstr.Bk.Rev.Curr.Leg.Per., C.L.I., L.R.I., Leg.Per.
  Formerly: Black Law Journal (ISSN 0896-0194)

NATIONAL COAL ASSOCIATION. LETTER OF THE LAW. see *MINES AND MINING INDUSTRY*

340 US
NATIONAL CONFERENCE OF COMMISSIONERS ON UNIFORM STATE LAWS. HANDBOOK AND PROCEEDINGS. 1892. a. price varies. (National Conference of Commissioners on Uniform State Laws) William S. Hein & Co., Inc., 1285 Main St., Buffalo, NY 14209. TEL 800-828-7571. FAX 617-883-8100. TELEX 91-209 WU 7 HEIN BUF. Ed. Edith Davies. circ. 800. (also avail. in microfiche from WSH; reprint service avail. from RRI) **Indexed:** C.L.I., Leg.Per.

NATIONAL COUNCIL OF SAVINGS INSTITUTIONS. OPERATIONS LETTER. see *BUSINESS AND ECONOMICS — Banking And Finance*

NATIONAL COUNCIL OF SAVINGS INSTITUTIONS. REGULATORY UPDATE. see *BUSINESS AND ECONOMICS — Banking And Finance*

NATIONAL COUNCIL OF SAVINGS INSTITUTIONS. TRUSTEES & DIRECTORS LETTER. see *BUSINESS AND ECONOMICS — Banking And Finance*

340 US
NATIONAL COUNCIL OF UNITED STATES MAGISTRATES. BULLETIN. 1972. q. free. National Council of United States Magistrates, c/o Ralph J. Geffen, Ed., U.S. Courthouse, Los Angeles, CA 90012. TEL 213-688-3698. circ. 400 (controlled).

651 US
NATIONAL COURT REPORTERS ASSOCIATION. a. **PROCEEDINGS OF THE ANNUAL CONVENTION.** a. National Court Reporters Association, 8224 Old Courthouse Rd., Vienna, VA 22182-3808. circ. 500.
Formerly: National Shorthand Reporters Association. Proceedings of the Annual Convention (ISSN 0077-572X)

NATIONAL CREDITOR - DEBTOR REVIEW; a journal of creditor-debtor relations. see BUSINESS AND ECONOMICS — Banking And Finance

340 350 JA ISSN 0034-2912
H8
NATIONAL DIET LIBRARY. REFERENCE/KOKURITSU KOKKAI TOSHOKAN. REFARENSU. (Text in English, Japanese) 1951. m. 9480 Yen. National Diet Library - Kokuritsu Kokkai Toshokan, 1-10-1 Nagata-cho, Chiyoda-ku, Tokyo 100, Japan. TEL 03-3581-2331. TELEX 2225393. bk.rev.; abstr.; charts; illus.; stat.; index, cum.index; circ. 1,600.
—BLDSC shelfmark: 7331.880000.

NATIONAL FIRE AND ARSON REPORT. see FIRE PREVENTION

NATIONAL FUTURES ASSOCIATION MANUAL. see BUSINESS AND ECONOMICS — Investments

NATIONAL GROUND WATER ASSOCIATION. BRIEFINGS. see EARTH SCIENCES — Hydrology

NATIONAL INSOLVENCY REVIEW. see BUSINESS AND ECONOMICS — Banking And Finance

344.022 US ISSN 0743-7927
K14
NATIONAL INSURANCE LAW REVIEW. 1984. q. $85. N I L S Publishing Company, 21625 Prairie St., Box 2507th, Chatworth, CA 91311. TEL 818-998-8830. Ed.Bd. (back issues avail.)
Description: Disseminates articles on insurance from law reviews of schools and universities.

340 US ISSN 0162-7325
K14
NATIONAL LAW JOURNAL; the weekly newspaper for the profession. 1978. w. $88. New York Law Publishing Co., 111 Eighth Ave., New York, NY 10011. TEL 212-741-8300. (Subscr. to: P.O. Box 50316, Belvedere, CO 80321-0316) Ed. Doreen Weisenhaus. adv.; circ. 45,000. (tabloid format; also avail. in microfiche from NYL) Indexed: Bank.Lit.Ind., C.L.I., CAD CAM Abstr., Environ.Abstr., Hlth.Ind., L.R.I., Law Ofc.Info.Svc., Leg.Info.Manage.Ind., Tel.Abstr., Telegen.
●Also available online. Vendor(s): Mead Data Central.
—BLDSC shelfmark: 6026.164000.
Description: News and analyses of latest trends and developments in all areas of the law.

340 US ISSN 0148-0588
KF200
NATIONAL LAWYERS GUILD. GUILD NOTES. 1972. q. $50 to institutions; free to members. National Lawyers Guild, 55 Sixth Ave., New York, NY 10013-1601. TEL 212-966-5000. Ed. Tim Ledwith. adv.; bk.rev.; cum.index: 1937-1970; circ. 10,000. (back issues avail.) Indexed: Alt.Press Ind., Chic.Per.Ind.

340 US ISSN 0730-532X
NATIONAL LAWYERS GUILD PRACTITIONER. 1937. q. $10 to students; others $15. National Lawyers Guild (Berkeley), 1715 Francisco St., Berkeley, CA 94701. TEL 415-848-0599. Ed.Bd. adv.; bk.rev.; circ. 700. (also avail. in microfilm from RRI; reprint service avail. from RRI) Indexed: C.L.I., HR Rep., L.R.I., Leg.Per., P.A.I.S.
—BLDSC shelfmark: 4230.140000.
Formerly (until 1981): Guild Practitioner (ISSN 0017-5390); Which was formed by the merger of: Law in Transition; Lawyers Guild Review; Which incorporates (in 1943): International Juridical Association. Monthly Bulletin (ISSN 0098-7700); (in 1940): National Lawyers Guild Querterly.

340 US
NATIONAL LAWYERS GUILD REFERRAL DIRECTORY. 1986. triennial. $15. National Lawyers Guild, 55 Sixth Ave., New York, NY 10013-1601. TEL 212-966-5000.
Description: Lists guild attorneys by state and city, with their areas of practice.

347.016 US
NATIONAL NOTARY. 1957. bi-m. $26. National Notary Association, 8236 Remmet Ave., Box 7184, Canoga Park, CA 91304-7184. TEL 818-713-4000. FAX 818-713-9061. Ed. Charles N. Faerber. adv.; bk.rev.; index; circ. 80,000. (also avail. in microfilm; back issues avail.; reprint service avail. from UMI)

347.016 US ISSN 0894-7872
NATIONAL NOTARY YEARBOOK. 1977. a. $26 (foreign $30). National Notary Association, 8236 Remmet Ave., Box 7184, Canoga Park, CA 91304-7184. TEL 818-713-4000. FAX 818-713-9061. Ed. Charles N. Faerber. charts; illus.; index; circ. 80,000. (also avail. in microfilm; back issues avail.)
Description: Articles, lists and directories of interest to notaries and to government officials regulating notaries.

340 331.1 US
NATIONAL PARALEGAL EMPLOYMENT & SALARY SURVEY. (9 regional editions avail.) 1984. a. $50 to non-members (members $30). National Paralegal Association, Box 406, Solebury, PA 18963. TEL 215-297-8333. FAX 215-297-8358. Ed. H. Jeffrey Valentine.
Description: Regional and national compilation of paralegal jobs, salaries, work environment, and benefits.

NATIONAL PARALEGAL REPORTER. see WOMEN'S INTERESTS

346 US ISSN 0363-8340
KF567.8
NATIONAL PROPERTY LAW DIGESTS. m. $360. National Property Law Digests, Inc., 7200 Wisconsin Ave., Ste. 314, Bethesda, MD 20814-4811. TEL 301-654-8004. FAX 301-654-8894. circ. 1,000.

NATIONAL PUBLIC EMPLOYMENT REPORTER. see BUSINESS AND ECONOMICS — Labor And Industrial Relations

340 CN
NATIONAL REPORTER. (Text in English; occasionally in French) irreg. (6 vols. per year). Can.$79 per vol. Maritime Law Book Ltd., Box 302, Fredericton, N.B. E3B 4Y9, Canada. TEL 506-454-9921. Ed. Eric B. Appleby. (back issues avail.)
●Also available online. Vendor(s): QL Systems Ltd..

340 US
NATIONAL REPORTER ON LEGAL ETHICS AND PROFESSIONAL RESPONSIBILITY. 1982. 10/yr. $695. University Publications of America (Subsidiary of: Congressional Information Service), 4520 East-West Hwy. Ste. 800, Bethesda, MD 20814-3389. TEL 301-657-3200. FAX 301-657-3203. Ed. David Luban. abstr.; bibl.; index. (looseleaf format)
Description: Full texts of federal and state court cases and ethics opinions from state bar associations.

340 US
KF4850.A15
NATIONAL SECURITY LAW REPORT. 1979. m. free. American Bar Association, Standing Committee on Law and National Security, 1501 Trombone Court, Vienna, VA 22182. Ed. James Arnold Miller. bk.rev.; circ. 2,600.
Formerly (until 1991): Intelligence Report (Washington) (ISSN 0736-2773)
Description: Cases, articles, legislation, regulations, and other materials concerning law and national security.

340 362.6 US ISSN 0277-7460
NATIONAL SENIOR CITIZENS LAW CENTER WEEKLY. 1974. w. $150. National Senior Citizens Law Center, 1815 H St., N.W., Ste. 700, Washington, DC 20006. TEL 202-887-5280. FAX 202-785-6702. Ed. Rita E. Johnson. bk.rev.; circ. 1,700.

NATIONAL TRADE AND TARIFF SERVICE. see BUSINESS AND ECONOMICS — Public Finance, Taxation

340 US ISSN 0094-1875
KF2231.A59
NATIONAL TRAFFIC LAW NEWS.* 1974. m. $103. Donald M. Wallace, Ed. & Pub., 7429 Madison, Kansas City, MO 64114. index; circ. 500. (looseleaf format)

340 US
NATIONAL TRIAL AND DEPOSITION DIRECTORY.* 1980. a. $35 to reporters. Richard Tackman, 421 W. Franklin St., Boise, ID 83702-4516. adv.

347.91 US ISSN 1049-684X
NATIONAL TRIAL LAWYER. 1989. bi-m. $25. Trial Lawyer Publications, Inc., Box 1217, 212 E. Vine St., Millville, NJ 08332-8217. TEL 609-825-9099. FAX 609-825-5959. adv.; bk.rev.; circ. 9,500.
Description: Independent forum for the exchange of professional information, news and opinions.

NATIONAL TRUCK EQUIPMENT ASSOCIATION. LEGISLATIVE REPORT. see TRANSPORTATION — Trucks And Trucking

NATIONAL TRUCK EQUIPMENT ASSOCIATION. REGULATIONS REPORT. see TRANSPORTATION — Trucks And Trucking

NATIONAL WETLANDS NEWSLETTER. see ENVIRONMENTAL STUDIES

NATURAL GAS POLICY ACT NOTICES OF DETERMINATION (F E R C FORM 121). see PETROLEUM AND GAS

NATURAL RESOURCES & ENVIRONMENT. see CONSERVATION

NATURAL RESOURCES JOURNAL. see CONSERVATION

NATURAL RESOURCES LAW NEWSLETTER. see CONSERVATION

NATURAL RIGHTS. see ENVIRONMENTAL STUDIES

NATURAL RIGHTS CENTER ANNUAL REPORT. see ENVIRONMENTAL STUDIES

344 US
NAVAL LAW REVIEW. 1947. a. price varies. Naval Justice School, Naval Education and Training Center, Newport, RI 02841. FAX 401-841-3985. Ed. Frank V. Russo. bk.rev.; illus.; index, cum.index every 4 yrs.; circ. 12,200. (also avail. in microfilm from UMI; reprint service avail. from UMI) Indexed: C.L.I., Ind.U.S.Gov.Per., L.R.I., Leg.Per., Mar.Aff.Bibl., P.A.I.S.
●Also available online. Vendor(s): WESTLAW.
Formerly (until vol.33): J A G Journal (ISSN 0021-3519)
Description: Addresses legislative, administrative, and judicial developments in military and related fields of law.

340 US ISSN 0047-9209
K14
NEBRASKA LAW REVIEW. 1922. q. $24. University of Nebraska, Lincoln, College of Law, Nebraska Law Review, Lincoln, NE 68583-0903. TEL 402-472-1267. adv.; bk.rev.; bibl.; index; circ. 2,000. (also avail. in microform from WSH; reprint service avail. from WSH) Indexed: C.L.I., Crim.Just.Abstr., L.R.I., Leg.Cont., Leg.Per., Sel.Water Res.Abstr.
●Also available online. Vendor(s): WESTLAW.
—BLDSC shelfmark: 6068.250000.

340 US
NEBRASKA LIMITATIONS MANUAL. 2nd ed., 1990. base vol. (plus suppl.). $50. Butterworth Legal Publishers (Salem) (Subsidiary of: Reed International PLC), 90 Stiles Rd., Salem, NH 03079. TEL 800-548-4001. FAX 603-898-9858. Ed.Bd. (looseleaf format)
Description: Quick reference to Nebraska statutes and rules of court that set time limitations.

NEBRASKA LIVESTOCK BRAND BOOK. see AGRICULTURE — Poultry And Livestock

340 US
NEBRASKA TRANSCRIPT. 1966. q. free to qualified personnel. University of Nebraska, Lincoln, College of Law, Lincoln, NE 68583-0902. TEL 402-472-2161. Ed. Sharon Bartter. bk.rev.; illus.; circ. 4,500.

2658 LAW

340   NP
NEPAL MISCELLANEOUS SERIES. (Text in English) 1964. irreg. Rs.900($50) per year. Regmi Research (Pvt.) Ltd., Lazimpat, Kathmandu, Nepal. TEL 4-11927. Ed. Mahesh C. Regmi. (also avail. in microfilm from LCP)
    Formerly: Nepal Law Translation Series (ISSN 0077-6572)
    Description: Texts of laws and regulations, periodically revised to incorporate amendments and additions.

418.02   NP
NEPAL RECORDER. (Text in English) 1957. irreg. (2-3/mo.). Rs.900($50) Nepal Press Digest (Pvt) Ltd., Lazimpat, Kathmandu, Nepal. Ed. Mahesh C. Regmi. index. (also avail. in microfilm from LCP)
    Formerly: Nepal Gazette Translation Service (ISSN 0028-2707)

340   NP
NEPALA KANUNA PARICARCA/NEPAL LAW REVIEW. (Text in English and Nepali) 1977. q. Rs.4. Tribhuvan University, Institute of Law, Box 1247, Kathmandu, Nepal. Ed. Tope Bahadur Singh. bk.rev.; circ. 1,000.

347.9   NE
NETHERLANDS. CENTRAAL BUREAU VOOR DE STATISTIEK. CIVIL AND ADMINISTRATIVE JURISDICTION. BURGERLIJKE EN ADMINISTRATIEVE RECHTSPRAAK. (Text in Dutch and English) 1951. a. Centraal Bureau voor de Statistiek, Prinses Beatrixlaan 428, 2270 AZ Voorburg, Netherlands. TEL 070-694341. (Orders to: SDU - Publishers, Christoffel Plantijnstraat, The Hague, Netherlands)
    Formerly: Netherlands. Centraal Bureau voor de Statistiek. Justitiele Statistiek. Judicial Statistics.

340   NE
NETHERLANDS. CENTRAAL BUREAU VOOR DE STATISTIEK. KWARTAALBERICHT RECHTSBESCHERMING EN VEILIGHEID/QUARTERLY BULLETIN ON JUSTICE AND SECURITY STATISTICS. (Text in Dutch and English) q. Centraal Bureau voor de Statistiek, Prinses Beatrixlaan 428, Postbus 959, 2270 AZ Voorburg, Netherlands. TEL 070-694341. (Orders to: SDU - Publishers, P.O. Box 20014, 2500 EA The Hague, Netherlands)
    Formerly: Netherlands. Centraal Bureau voor de Statistiek. Maandstatistiek Rechtsbescherming en Veiligheid - Monthly Bulletin on Justice and Security Statistics.

342.085   NE   ISSN 0169-3441
NETHERLANDS QUARTERLY OF HUMAN RIGHTS. NEWSLETTER. (Text in English) 1983. q. fl.50. Netherlands Institute of Human Rights - Studie- en Informatiecentrum Mensenrechten, Janskerhof 16, 3512 BM Utrecht, Netherlands. TEL 31-30394033. FAX 31-30393028. Eds. Leo Zwaak, Jacqueline Smith. circ. 700.

340   GW   ISSN 0341-1915
NEUE JURISTISCHE WOCHENSCHRIFT. 1947. w. DM.276 (microfiche edition (1947-70) DM.898). (Deutscher Anwaltverein) C.H. Beck'sche Verlagsbuchhandlung, Wilhelmstr. 9, 8000 Munich 40, Germany. TEL 089-38189-338. FAX 089-38189-398. TELEX 5215085-BECK-D. (Co-sponsor: Bundesrechtsanwaltskammer) Ed.Bd. adv.; cum.index; circ. 57,000. (also avail. in microfiche) **Indexed:** Dok.Str.

349   GW   ISSN 0028-3231
LAW
NEUE JUSTIZ; Zeitschrift fuer sozialistisches Recht und Gesetzlichkeit. 1947. s-m. DM.72. (Ministerium fuer Justiz) Staatsverlag der DDR, Otto-Grotewohl-Str. 17, 1086 Berlin, Germany. adv.; bk.rev.; charts; index; circ. 40,000.
    —BLDSC shelfmark: 6077.580000.

NEUE WIRTSCHAFTS-BRIEFE; Zeitschrift fuer Steuer- und Wirtschaftsrecht. see *BUSINESS AND ECONOMICS — Public Finance, Taxation*

340   GW   ISSN 0176-3814
NEUE ZEITSCHRIFT FUER ARBEITS- UND SOZIALRECHT. 1981. s-m. DM.302. C.H. Beck'sche Verlagsbuchhandlung, Wilhelmstr. 9, 8000 Munich 40, Germany. TEL 089-38189-338. FAX 089-38189-398. TELEX 5215085-BECK-D. Ed.Bd. adv.; circ. 4,800.
    —BLDSC shelfmark: 6077.826800.

340   GW   ISSN 0720-1753
NEUE ZEITSCHRIFT FUER STRAFRECHT. 1981. m. DM.224. C.H. Beck'sche Verlagsbuchhandlung, Wilhelmstr. 9, 8000 Munich 40, Germany. TEL 089-38189-338. FAX 089-38189-398. TELEX 5215085-BECK-D. Ed.Bd. adv.; circ. 4,400.

NEUE ZEITSCHRIFT FUER VERKEHRSRECHT. see *TRANSPORTATION*

340   GW   ISSN 0721-880X
KK5571.2
NEUE ZEITSCHRIFT FUER VERWALTUNGSRECHT. 1949. m. DM.564. C.H. Beck'sche Verlagsbuchhandlung, Wilhelmstr. 9, 8000 Munich 40, Germany. TEL 089-38189-338. FAX 089-38189-398. TELEX 5215085-BECK-D. Ed.Bd. adv.; circ. 4,200.
    —BLDSC shelfmark: 6077.827750.
    Formerly (until Dec. 1981): Verwaltungsprechsprechung in Deutschland (ISSN 0342-2534)

349   GW   ISSN 0028-3525
NEUE ZEITSCHRIFT FUER WEHRRECHT. 1959. 6/yr. DM.144. J. Schweitzer Verlag, Heddesdorfer Str. 31, Postfach 1780, 5450 Neuwied, Germany. TEL 02631-8010. FAX 02631-801210. Ed. Klaus Dau. adv.; bk.rev.; index. (reprint service avail. from UMI)

NEUES STEUERRECHT VON A BIS Z; Kommentar-Zeitschrift fuer das gesamte Steuerrecht. see *BUSINESS AND ECONOMICS — Public Finance, Taxation*

340   CN
NEW BRUNSWICK REPORTS. 1968. irreg. Can.$86 per vol. Maritime Law Book Ltd., Box 302, Fredericton, N.B. E3B 4Y9, Canada. TEL 506-454-9921. (back issues avail.)
    ●Also available online. Vendor(s): QL Systems Ltd..

340   US   ISSN 0740-8994
NEW ENGLAND JOURNAL ON CRIMINAL AND CIVIL CONFINEMENT. 1973. s-a. $20 (foreign $22). New England School of Law, 154 Stuart St., Boston, MA 02116-5687. TEL 617-451-0010. FAX 617-482-6634. Ed. Paul R. Robinson. bk.rev.; circ. 500. (also avail. in microfilm from RRI; reprint service avail. from RRI) **Indexed:** Abstr.Bk.Rev.Curr.Leg.Per., C.C.L.P., C.L.I., Crim.Just.Abstr., L.R.I., Leg.Cont., Leg.Per.
    Formerly: New England Journal on Prison Law (ISSN 0095-7364)
    Description: Covers current trends and future proposals for correctional law and the prison community. Includes criminal, juvenile and civil confinement law and discrimination.

340   US   ISSN 0028-4823
NEW ENGLAND LAW REVIEW. 1965. q. $20. New England School of Law, New England Law Review, 154 Stuart St., Boston, MA 02116. TEL 617-451-0010. Ed. Leonard DePasquale. bk.rev.; cum.index: 1965-1975; circ. 750. (also avail. in microfilm from UMI,WSH; reprint service avail. from WSH) **Indexed:** C.L.I., L.R.I., Leg.Cont., Leg.Per.
    —BLDSC shelfmark: 6084.010000.
    Formerly: Portia Law Journal.
    Description: Provides the legal community with well-researched, reasoned analyses of important issues. Includes articles by members of the judiciary, legal educators and practicing attorneys.

343   US   ISSN 1051-4023
KF200
NEW HAMPSHIRE BAR NEWS. 1974. fortn. $50 to non-members (effective 1992). New Hampshire Bar Association, 112 Pleasant St., Concord, NH 03301. TEL 603-224-6942. FAX 603-224-2910. Ed. Ellen V. Barial. adv.; bk.rev.; abstr.; charts; illus.; stat.; index; circ. 4,200. (back issues avail.) **Indexed:** C.L.I., L.R.I.
    Formerly (until 1990): New Hampshire Law Weekly (ISSN 0362-1073)

NEW HAMPSHIRE CODE OF ADMINISTRATIVE RULES ANNOTATED. see *PUBLIC ADMINISTRATION*

340   US
NEW HAMPSHIRE COURT RULES ANNOTATED. 1979. 2 base vols. (plus a. suppl.). $98. Butterworth Legal Publishers (Salem) (Subsidiary of: Reed International PLC), 90 Stiles Rd., Salem, NH 03079. TEL 800-548-4001. FAX 603-898-9858. Ed.Bd. (looseleaf format)
    Description: Contains the rules for the New Hampshire courts plus those for the US Court of Appeals and the US District Court.

340   US
NEW HAMPSHIRE FISH AND GAME LAWS. a. $19. Butterworth Legal Publishers (Salem) (Subsidiary of: Reed International PLC), 90 Stiles Rd., Salem, NH 03079. TEL 800-548-4001. FAX 603-898-9858. Ed.Bd.
    Description: For attorneys, law enforcement agencies, environmentalists, sportsmen and students.

340   US
NEW HAMPSHIRE MOTOR VEHICLE AND BOATING LAWS. (In 2 vols.) q. $30. Butterworth Legal Publishers (Salem) (Subsidiary of: Reed International PLC), 90 Stiles Rd., Salem, NH 03079. TEL 800-548-4001. FAX 603-898-9858. Ed.Bd. charts.

340   US
NEW HAMPSHIRE PRACTICE SERIES. VOLS. 8 AND 9: PERSONAL INJURY - TORT AND INSURANCE PRACTICE. (Series consists of 14 vols.; Vols. 1 and 2: Criminal Practice and Procedure; Vol. 3: Family Law; Vols. 4, 5 and 6: Civil Practice and Procedure; Vol. 7: Wills, Trusts and Gifts; Vols. 8 and 9: Personal Injury - Tort and Insurance Practice; Vol. 10, 11 and 12: Probate Law and Procedure; Vol. 13 and 14: Local Government Law) 1988. 2 base vols. (plus suppl.). $110 (14-vol. set $575). Butterworth Legal Publishers (Salem) (Subsidiary of: Reed International PLC), 90 Stiles Rd., Salem, NH 03079. TEL 800-548-4001. FAX 603-898-9858. Ed. Richard B. McNamara.
    Description: Analysis of the law involved in personal injury actions along with a discussion of the procedural aspects in resolving a claim.

340   US
▼**NEW HAMPSHIRE PRACTICE SERIES. VOLS. 10, 11 AND 12: PROBATE LAW AND PROCEDURE.** (Series consists of 14 vols.; Vols. 1 and 2: Criminal Practice and Procedure; Vol. 3: Family Law; Vols. 4, 5 and 6: Civil Practice and Procedure; Vol. 7: Wills, Trusts and Gifts; Vols. 8 and 9: Personal Injury - Tort and Insurance Practice; Vols. 10, 11 and 12: Probate Law and Procedure; Vols. 13 and 14: Local Government Law) 1990. 3 base vols. (plus a. suppl.). $165 (14-vol. set $525). Butterworth Legal Publishers (Salem) (Subsidiary of: Reed International PLC), 90 Stiles Rd., Salem, NH 03079. TEL 800-548-4001. FAX 603-898-9858. Eds. Charles A. DeGrandpre, Kathleen M. Robinson. (looseleaf format)
    Description: Contains practical advice, analysis of current law, checklists and completed forms used in probate proceedings.

NEW HAMPSHIRE PRACTICE SERIES. VOLS. 13 AND 14: LOCAL GOVERNMENT LAW. see *PUBLIC ADMINISTRATION — Municipal Government*

340   US
NEW HAMPSHIRE REPORTS. irreg. (4-6/yr. in 1-2 vols./yr.) $38 per vol. Butterworth Legal Publishers (Salem) (Subsidiary of: Reed International PLC), 90 Stiles Rd., Salem, NH 03079. TEL 800-548-4001. FAX 603-898-9858.

340   US
NEW HAMPSHIRE REVISED STATUTES ANNOTATED. 23 base vols. (plus a. suppl.). $928. Butterworth Legal Publishers (Salem) (Subsidiary of: Reed International PLC), 90 Stiles Rd., Salem, NH 03079. TEL 800-548-4001. FAX 603-898-9858. Ed.Bd.

340   US
NEW HAMPSHIRE RULE OF EVIDENCE MANUAL. 1986. base vol. (plus suppl.). $45. Butterworth Legal Publishers (Salem) (Subsidiary of: Reed International PLC), 90 Stiles Rd., Salem, NH 03079. TEL 800-548-4001. FAX 603-898-9858. Ed. Charles G. Douglas, III.

340 US
NEW HAMPSHIRE RULES OF EVIDENCE. a. $13. Butterworth Legal Publishers (Salem) (Subsidiary of: Reed International PLC), 90 Stiles Rd., Salem, NH 03079. TEL 800-548-4001. FAX 603-898-9858. Ed.Bd.

340 US
NEW HAMPSHIRE STATUTES RELATING TO SURVEYING AND BOUNDARIES. a. $19.50. Butterworth Legal Publishers (Salem) (Subsidiary of: Reed International PLC), 90 Stiles Rd., Salem, NH 03079. TEL 800-548-4001. FAX 603-898-9858. Ed.Bd.

NEW JERSEY EDUCATION LAW REPORT; the authority on labor relations in New Jersey schools. see *EDUCATION*

340 US
▼**NEW JERSEY ENVIRONMENTAL LAW LETTER.** 1992. 12/yr. $137. M. Lee Smith Publishers & Printers, 162 4th Ave. N., Box 2678, Nashville, TN 37219. TEL 615-242-7385. FAX 615-256-6601. Ed. Gail H. Allyn.

340 US ISSN 0028-5803
LAW
NEW JERSEY LAW JOURNAL. 1878. w. $215. American Lawyer Media, L.P. (Newark), 238 Mulberry St., Newark, NJ 07102. TEL 201-642-0075. FAX 201-642-0920. Ed. Tim O'Brien. adv.; bk.rev.; abstr.; s-a index; circ. 11,800. (also avail. in microfilm from MCA) **Indexed:** C.L.I., Hlth.Ind., L.R.I.

340 US ISSN 0195-0983
KF200
NEW JERSEY LAWYER. 1957. w. $99 includes membership. New Jersey Lawyer, Inc. (Subsidiary of: New Jersey State Bar Association), 2825 Woodbridge Ave., Edison, NJ 08817. TEL 908-549-4800. Ed. Ron Ostroff. adv.: B&W page $1700. bk.rev.; illus.; index; circ. 20,000. (tabloid format; also avail. in microfiche from WSH; microfilm from WSH) **Indexed:** C.L.I., L.R.I., Leg.Per.
●Also available online. Vendor(s): WESTLAW.
Former titles: Bar Journal (Trenton) (ISSN 0162-1211); New Jersey State Bar Journal (ISSN 0028-5951)
Description: Discusses substantive law, with a mix of theme and general practice issues.

340 US
NEW JERSEY STATE BAR ADVOCATE. 1974. irreg. (8-10/yr.). membership. New Jersey State Bar Association, 1 Constitution Sq., New Brunswick, NJ 08901-1587. TEL 201-249-5000. Ed. Angela C. Scheck. circ. 17,300. (tabloid format)
Description: Covers activities of the association.

347.91 US
NEW JERSEY TRIAL LAWYER. 1987. bi-m. $25. Trial Lawyer Publications, Inc., Box 1217, 212 E. Vine St., Millville, NJ 08332-8217. TEL 609-825-9099. FAX 609-825-5959. adv.; circ. 3,504.
Description: Independent, open forum for the free exchange of information, ideas, and opinions.

340 US ISSN 0890-2941
KF1
NEW LAW BOOKS REVIEWER.* 1986. bi-m. $90. Huddleston Brown Publishers, Inc., 60 Madison Ave., Ste. 1201, New York, NY 10010. Ed. Gerome Leone. bk.rev.; circ. 120.

NEW LAW FOR SURVEYORS. see *REAL ESTATE*

340 UK ISSN 0306-6479
K14
NEW LAW JOURNAL. 1980. w. £49($297) Butterworth & Co. (Publishers) Ltd. (Subsidiary of: Reed International PLC), 88 Kingsway, London WC2B 6AB, England. TEL 71-405-6900. FAX 71-405-1332. TELEX 95678. (US addr.: Butterworth Legal Publishers, 90 Stiles Rd., Salem, NH 03079. TEL 800-548-4001) Ed. Patricia Wynn Davies. adv.; circ. 8,500. **Indexed:** ASSIA, C.L.I., L.R.I., Lang.& Lang.Behav.Abstr., Leg.Per.
●Also available online. Vendor(s): Mead Data Central.
—BLDSC shelfmark: 6084.350000.
Incorporates: Law Times; Law Journal.
Description: For lawyers and students of law.

340 US
NEW MEXICO APPELLATE PRACTICE MANUAL. 1978. base vol. (plus a. suppl.). $115. Butterworth Legal Publishers (Salem) (Subsidiary of: Reed International PLC), 90 Stiles Rd., Salem, NH 03079. TEL 800-548-4001. FAX 603-898-9858. Ed. Michael Schwarz. (looseleaf format)

340 US
NEW MEXICO CONSTRUCTION LAW. 1987. base vol. (plus suppl.). $120. Butterworth Legal Publishers (Salem) (Subsidiary of: Reed International PLC), 90 Stiles Rd., Salem, NH 03079. TEL 800-548-4001. FAX 603-898-9858. Ed. Timothy M. Sheehan. (looseleaf format)

340 US
NEW MEXICO CREDITOR - DEBTOR LAW. 1989. base vol. (plus suppl. 1-2/yr.). $115. Butterworth Legal Publishers (Salem) (Subsidiary of: Reed International PLC), 90 Stiles Rd., Salem, NH 03079. TEL 800-548-4001. FAX 603-898-9858. Ed. Marian Matthews. (looseleaf format)
Formerly: New Mexico Collections Manual.
Description: Practical analysis of New Mexico law and procedure governing the most common forms of action to obtain payment in the event of default on various obligations.

340 US ISSN 0028-6214
K14
NEW MEXICO LAW REVIEW. 1971. 3/yr. $20. University of New Mexico, School of Law, 1117 Stanford, N.E., Albuquerque, NM 87131. TEL 505-277-2146. Ed. Frederick M. Hart. adv.; bk.rev.; index, cum.index every 10 yrs.; circ. 1,000. (also avail. in microfiche from WSH; microfilm from WSH) **Indexed:** C.L.I., L.R.I., Leg.Cont., Leg.Per.
—BLDSC shelfmark: 6084.650000.

NEW MEXICO LOCAL AND FEDERAL RULES HANDBOOK. see *PUBLIC ADMINISTRATION*

340 US
NEW MEXICO PROBATE MANUAL. 1978. base vol. (plus suppl.). $120. Butterworth Legal Publishers (Salem) (Subsidiary of: Reed International PLC), 90 Stiles Rd., Salem, NH 03079. TEL 800-548-4001. FAX 603-898-9858. Ed. William N. Henderson. (looseleaf format)
Description: Practical guide to New Mexico estate administration that includes attorney's checklists, legal assistant instructions, master information list, Key Probate Code, forms, and a glossary.

340 US
NEW MEXICO RULES OF EVIDENCE. (Revised ed., 1991) 1983. base vol. (plus suppl.). $125. Butterworth Legal Publishers (Salem) (Subsidiary of: Reed International PLC), 90 Stiles Rd., Salem, NH 03079. TEL 800-548-4001. FAX 603-898-9858. Ed. Murl A. Larkin. (looseleaf format)
Description: Contains current case law and commentary on the construction and interpretation of the rules.

340 070.5 AT
NEW RELEASES PUBLICATIONS LIST. m. free. Law Printer, P.O. Box 203, North Melbourne, Vic. 3051, Australia. TEL 03-320-0100. FAX 03-328-1657.

340.3 AT ISSN 0085-400X
NEW SOUTH WALES. LAW REFORM COMMISSION. REPORT. 1966. irreg., no.67, 1991. price varies. Law Reform Commission, G.P.O. Box 5199, Sydney, N.S.W. 2001, Australia. FAX 02-247-1054.

347 336 AT
NEW SOUTH WALES CONVEYANCING LAW AND PRACTICE. (In 4 vols.: Vols.1 & 2: Commentary; Vol.3: New Developments, Cases and Index; vol.4: Legislation) 1980. 10/yr. C C H Australia Ltd., P.O. Box 230, North Ryde, N.S.W. 2113, Australia. TEL 888-2555. FAX 02-888-7324.

340 AT ISSN 0312-1674
LAW
NEW SOUTH WALES LAW REPORTS. 1971. irreg. (6-8/yr.). (Council of Law Reporting for New South Wales) Law Book Co. Ltd., 44-50 Waterloo Rd., North Ryde, N.S.W. 2113, Australia. TEL 02-887-0177. FAX 02-888-9706. TELEX ASBOOK 27995. index.
●Also available online.
Supersedes: New South Wales Weekly Notes (ISSN 0023-9232); New South Wales State Reports (ISSN 0085-6703)
Description: Authorized reports of state and federal cases decided in the Supreme Court.

340 AT ISSN 1031-7872
NEW SOUTH WALES STATUTES ANNOTATIONS. 2/yr. $98. Butterworths Pty. Ltd., 271-273 Lane Cove Rd., P.O. Box 345, N. Ryde, N.S.W. 2113, Australia. TEL 02-335-4444. FAX 02-335-4655.

340 AT
NEW SOUTH WALES STRATA AND COMMUNITY TITLES LAW. (In 2 vols.) 1979. q. C C H Australia Ltd., P.O. Box 230, North Ryde, N.S.W. 2113, Australia. TEL 02-888-2555. FAX 02-888-7324.
Formerly: New South Wales Strata Title Law.

340 364 US
NEW YORK (CITY). DEPARTMENT OF JUVENILE JUSTICE. ANNUAL REPORT. a. Department of Juvenile Justice, 365 Broadway, New York, NY 10013-3991. TEL 212-925-7779. Ed.Bd.

340 US
NEW YORK (CITY). OFFICE OF MIDTOWN ENFORCEMENT. ANNUAL REPORT. a. Office of Midtown Enforcement, 330 W. 42nd St., 26th Fl., New York, NY 10036. TEL 212-971-6865.

340 US
NEW YORK (STATE). OPINIONS OF THE ATTORNEY GENERAL. 1890. a. (plus bi-m. supplements). $66. (Department of Law, Office of the Attorney General) Lenz & Riecker, Inc., Legal Publishing Division, One Columbia Place, Albany, NY 12207. TEL 518-436-8647. FAX 518-436-0939. circ. 3,000. (looseleaf format; back issues avail.)
Description: Formal and informal opinions on legal questions concerning state and local government. Includes subject index, statutory reference table, and concise descriptions of recent judicial opinions.

340 352 US
NEW YORK (STATE). OPINIONS OF THE COMPTROLLER. 1979. m. $88. Lenz & Riecker, Inc., 1 Columbia Place, Albany, NY 12207. TEL 518-426-8647. FAX 518-436-0939. cum.index 1979-1990. (looseleaf format; back issues avail.)
Description: Contains official decisions of the comptroller.

340 US
▼**NEW YORK ACTIONS AND REMEDIES.** 1991. 5 base vols. (plus suppl.). $375. Butterworth Legal Publishers (Salem) (Subsidiary of: Reed International PLC), 90 Stiles Rd., Salem, NH 03079. TEL 800-548-4001. FAX 603-898-9858. Ed. Mark Rhodes. (looseleaf format)
Description: Topics covered include: torts, contracts, marriage, divorce, and real estate.

NEW YORK APARTMENT LAW INSIDER. see *REAL ESTATE*

NEW YORK BANKING LAW. see *BUSINESS AND ECONOMICS — Banking And Finance*

NEW YORK BUILDING LAWS MANUAL. see *BUILDING AND CONSTRUCTION*

340 US
NEW YORK CITY CHARTER: ADMINISTRATIVE CODE. 1948. biennial. price varies. New York Legal Publishing Corp., 6 Charles Park, Guilderland, NY 12084. TEL 800-541-2681. FAX 518-456-0828. index, cum.index. (back issues avail.)
Description: Certified and recodified charter for New York City.

NEW YORK EDUCATION LAW REPORT. see *EDUCATION*

NEW YORK EMPLOYER'S ALERT. see *BUSINESS AND ECONOMICS — Labor And Industrial Relations*

NEW YORK EMPLOYER'S GUIDE. see *BUSINESS AND ECONOMICS — Labor And Industrial Relations*

LAW

346 US
NEW YORK ESTATES - WILLS - TRUSTS. m. $870. Commerce Clearing House, Inc., 4025 W. Peterson Ave., Chicago, IL 60646. TEL 312-583-8500. (looseleaf format)

340 US
NEW YORK LAW JOURNAL. 1888. d. (5/wk.). $410. New York Law Publishing Co., 111 Eighth Ave., New York, NY 10011. TEL 212-741-8300. (also avail. in microfilm from NYL) **Indexed:** C.L.I., Hlth.Ind., L.R.I., Leg.Info.Manage.Ind.
●Also available online. Vendor(s): Mead Data Central, Wilsonline.
Description: Covers trends in the law and decisions of statewide and national interest. Provides commentary by experts in various specialties.

347.0 917.402 US
NEW YORK LAW JOURNAL DIGEST ANNOTATOR. 12/yr. (a. cum. vol. avail.). $370. New York Law Publishing Co., Marketing Dept., 111 Eighth Ave., New York, NY 10011. TEL 212-741-8300.
Description: A guide to Lower Court opinions in New York's First and Second Judicial Departments, and an index to the New York Law Journal.

340 US ISSN 0145-448X
K14
NEW YORK LAW SCHOOL LAW REVIEW. 1955. 4/yr. $30. New York Law School, 57 Worth St., New York, NY 10013-2960. TEL 212-431-2118. Ed. Jeffrey W. Berkman. adv.; bk.rev.; bibl.; charts; illus.; stat.; index, cum.index; circ. 1,500. (also avail. in microform from UMI,WSH; reprint service avail. from UMI,WSH) **Indexed:** Abstr.Bk.Rev.Curr.Leg.Per., C.L.I., L.R.I., Leg.Cont., Leg.Per., P.A.I.S.
—BLDSC shelfmark: 6089.341000.
Formerly: New York Law Forum (ISSN 0028-7318)
Description: Examines the complete range of topics available to scholars of law, from legal ethics to interpretations of SEC regulations.

NEW YORK LAW SCHOOL REPORTER. see *COLLEGE AND ALUMNI*

340 368 US
NEW YORK NO-FAULT ARBITRATION REPORTS. 1977. m. $85. American Arbitration Association, 140 W. 51st St., New York, NY 10020-1203. TEL 212-484-4013. FAX 212-765-4874. Ed. Richard Wentzler. s-a. cum.index; circ. 500. (looseleaf format; back issues avail.)
Description: Summarizes cases involving personal injuries caused by automobiles.

340 US
NEW YORK NOTARY LAW PRIMER. a. $9.95. National Notary Association, 8236 Remmet Ave., Box 7184, Canoga Park, CA 91304-7184. TEL 818-713-4000. FAX 818-713-9061. Ed. Charles N. Faerber. (reprint service avail. from UMI)

340 US ISSN 0028-7547
K14
NEW YORK STATE BAR JOURNAL. vol.41, 1969. m. $16. New York State Bar Association, One Marine Midland Plaza, Binghamton, NY 13902. FAX 607-772-6093. Ed. Eugene Gerhart. adv.; bk.rev.; charts; illus.; stat.; tr.lit.; circ. 59,000 (controlled). (also avail. in microform from UMI; microfiche from WSH; reprint service avail. from UMI) **Indexed:** C.L.I., L.R.I., Law Ofc.Info.Svc., Leg.Per., P.A.I.S.
●Also available online. Vendor(s): WESTLAW (NYSTBJ).

340 US
NEW YORK STATE COMMITTEE ON OPEN GOVERNMENT. ANNUAL REPORT. 1978. a. New York State Committee on Open Government, Department of State, 162 Washington Ave., Albany, NY 12231. TEL 518-474-2518. cum.index; circ. 1,000. (back issues avail.)

NEW YORK STATE SCHOOL BOARDS ASSOCIATION. LEGISLATIVE BULLETIN. see *EDUCATION — School Organization And Administration*

NEW YORK UNIVERSITY. INSTITUTE ON FEDERAL TAXATION. CONFERENCE ON CHARITABLE FOUNDATIONS. see *BUSINESS AND ECONOMICS — Public Finance, Taxation*

340 US ISSN 0028-7881
K14
NEW YORK UNIVERSITY LAW REVIEW. 1924. 6/yr. $30 (foreign $35). New York University, Law Review, 110 W. Third St., New York, NY 10012. TEL 212-998-6350. FAX 212-995-4032. adv.; bk.rev.; index; circ. 2,800. (also avail. in microfiche from WSH; microfilm from RRI,WSH; reprint service avail. from RRI) **Indexed:** Abstr.Bk.Rev.Curr.Leg.Per., Account.Ind. (1974-), C.L.I., Crim.Just.Abstr., Curr.Cont., HRIS, L.R.I., Leg.Cont., Leg.Per., P.A.I.S., SSCI.
●Also available online. Vendor(s): Mead Data Central, WESTLAW.
—BLDSC shelfmark: 6089.820000.

340 US ISSN 0894-3303
NEW YORK UNIVERSITY SCHOOL OF LAW. INGRAM DOCUMENTS IN AMERICAN LEGAL HISTORY. 1986. irreg. price varies. Oceana Publications, Inc., 75 Main St., Dobbs Ferry, NY 10522. TEL 914-693-1320. FAX 914-693-0402. (back issues avail.)
Description: Scholarly discussion of social justice issues in American legal history.

340 US ISSN 0894-329X
NEW YORK UNIVERSITY SCHOOL OF LAW. LINDEN STUDIES IN LEGAL HISTORY. 1984. irreg., latest 1991. price varies. Oceana Publications, Inc., 75 Main St., Dobbs Ferry, NY 10522. TEL 914-693-1320. FAX 914-693-0402. (back issues avail.)
Description: Scholarly treatment of issues in American legal history.

342.93 NZ ISSN 0110-1277
LAW
NEW ZEALAND ADMINISTRATIVE REPORTS. 1976. m. Butterworths of New Zealand Ltd., P.O. Box 472, 203-207 Victoria St., Wellington, New Zealand. TEL 04-385-1479. FAX 04-385-1598. Ed. John Cottle.
Description: Reproduces a selection of decisions of most administrative tribunals.

NEW ZEALAND BUSINESS BULLETIN. see *BUSINESS AND ECONOMICS*

NEW ZEALAND BUSINESS LAW GUIDE. see *BUSINESS AND ECONOMICS — Public Finance, Taxation*

340 NZ
NEW ZEALAND CONVEYANCING LAW AND PRACTICE. 1989. 8/yr. NZ.$479. C C H New Zealand Limited, P.O. Box 2378, Auckland, New Zealand. TEL 483-9179. FAX 483-4009. (looseleaf format)
Description: Includes full text of legislation, full text or extracts of cases, and information on new developments. Covers proposed legislation, reports and government statements.

347 336 NZ
NEW ZEALAND DUTIES GUIDE. 1974. 4/yr. NZ.$418. C C H New Zealand Limited, P.O. Box 2378, Auckland, New Zealand. TEL 483-9179. FAX 483-4009.
Former titles: New Zealand Duties and Sales Tax Guide; (until 1983): New Zealand Estate and Gift Duty Reporter.
Description: Commentary, text of legislation and other information on duties in New Zealand.

NEW ZEALAND EMPLOYERS HANDBOOK. see *BUSINESS AND ECONOMICS — Personnel Management*

NEW ZEALAND EMPLOYMENT LAW LIBRARY. see *BUSINESS AND ECONOMICS — Personnel Management*

340 NZ
▼**NEW ZEALAND FAMILY LAW COURT HANDBOOK.** 1990. 2-3/yr. NZ.$218. C C H New Zealand Limited, P.O. Box 2378, Auckland, New Zealand. TEL 483-9179. FAX 483-4009. (looseleaf format)
Description: A reference providing practitioners with the legislation and precedents most used in the Family Court. Includes practice notes, court sitting dates and information on legal aid.

340 NZ
NEW ZEALAND FORMS & PRECEDENTS. 3 base vols. (plus updates 3-4/yr.). Butterworths of New Zealand Ltd., 203-207 Victoria St., P.O. Box 472, Wellington, New Zealand. TEL 04-385-1479. FAX 04-385-1598. Ed. Christine O'Brien. (looseleaf format)
Description: Modern precedents library written specifically for New Zealand.

NEW ZEALAND GOODS AND SERVICES TAX GUIDE. see *BUSINESS AND ECONOMICS — Public Finance, Taxation*

NEW ZEALAND INCOME TAX LEGISLATION. see *BUSINESS AND ECONOMICS — Public Finance, Taxation*

NEW ZEALAND JOURNAL OF INDUSTRIAL RELATIONS. see *BUSINESS AND ECONOMICS — Labor And Industrial Relations*

340 NZ ISSN 0028-8373
NEW ZEALAND LAW JOURNAL. 1925; N.S.1962. m. Butterworths of New Zealand Ltd., P.O. Box 472, 203-207 Victoria St., Wellington, New Zealand. TEL 04-385-1479. FAX 04-385-1598. Ed. P.J. Downey. adv.; bk.rev.; index; circ. 1,750. (also avail. in microfiche from BHP) **Indexed:** C.L.I., L.R.I., Leg.Per., P.A.I.S.
—BLDSC shelfmark: 6095.500000.
Description: Current legal news, editorials and articles; comment on recent cases.

346 AT ISSN 0078-0081
LAW
NEW ZEALAND LAW REGISTER. 1950. a. Aus.$59. Law Book Co. Ltd., 44-50 Waterloo Rd., North Ryde, N.S.W. 2113, Australia. TEL 02-887-0177. FAX 02-888-9706. TELEX ASBOOK 27995. circ. 3,500.

340 NZ ISSN 0110-148X
NEW ZEALAND LAW REPORTS. 1861. m. (New Zealand Council of Law Reporting) Butterworths of New Zealand Ltd., P.O. Box 472, 203-207 Victoria St., Wellington, New Zealand. TEL 04-385-1479. FAX 04-385-1598. Ed. Christine O'Brien.
Description: The official report series on law in NZ.

NEW ZEALAND SUPERANNUATION GUIDE. see *BUSINESS AND ECONOMICS — Public Finance, Taxation*

NEW ZEALAND TAX CASES. see *BUSINESS AND ECONOMICS — Public Finance, Taxation*

NEW ZEALAND TAX REPORTS. see *BUSINESS AND ECONOMICS — Accounting*

340 NZ ISSN 0549-0618
LAW
NEW ZEALAND UNIVERSITIES LAW REVIEW. 1963. s-a. NZ.$75. Mallinson Rendel Publishers Ltd., P.O. Box 9409, Wellington, New Zealand. FAX 4-385-4235. Ed. Andrew Beck. adv.; bk.rev.; cum.index; circ. 700. (back issues avail.) **Indexed:** C.L.I., Leg.Per.
—BLDSC shelfmark: 6099.600000.

340 US
NEWBERG ON CLASS ACTIONS, 2-E. 1985. 5 base vols. (plus s-a. suppl.). $475 price varies. Shepard's - McGraw-Hill, Inc., Box 35300, Colorado Springs, CO 80935-3530. TEL 800-525-2474. Ed. Herbert Newberg. cum.index.
Description: Provides current class action decisions and rules at federal and state levels.

340 CN
NEWFOUNDLAND & PRINCE EDWARD ISLAND REPORTS. 1970. irreg. Can.$86 per vol. Maritime Law Book Ltd., Box 302, Fredericton, N.B. E3B 4Y9, Canada. TEL 506-454-9921. (back issues avail.)
●Also available online. Vendor(s): QL Systems Ltd..

NEWS MEDIA AND THE LAW. see *JOURNALISM*

347.7 NQ
NICARAGUA. CORTE SUPREMA DE JUSTICIA. BOLETIN JUDICIAL. irreg. Corte Suprema de Justicia, Managua, Nicaragua.

349 GW ISSN 0028-9787
NIEDERSAECHSISCHER STAATSANZEIGER. 1945. w. DM.65. (Ministerium der Justiz) Schluetersche Verlagsanstalt GmbH und Co., Georgswall 4, Postfach 5440, 3000 Hannover 1, Germany. TEL 0511-1236-0. adv.; bk.rev.; circ. 2,095.

340 NR ISSN 0189-207X
K14
NIGERIAN CURRENT LAW REVIEW. (Text in English) 1982. a. $80. Nigerian Institute of Advanced Legal Studies, University of Lagos Campus, P.M.B. 12820, Lagos, Nigeria. FAX 825558. TELEX 27506-NIALS-N. Ed. M.A. Ajomo. bk.rev.; circ. 2,000. (back issues avail.)

340 NR ISSN 0048-0401
NIGERIAN JOURNAL OF CONTEMPORARY LAW. 1970. 3/yr. EAs.21. University of Lagos, Faculty of Law, P.O. Box 12003, Lagos, Nigeria. Ed.Bd. bibl.

370.26 JA
NIHON KYOIKUHO GAKKAI NENPO. Added title: Educational Law Review. 1972. a. 1000 Yen. (Nihon Kyoikuho Gakkai - Japan Society for Education Law) Yuhikaku Publishing Co. Ltd., 2-17 Kanda Jimbocho, Chiyoda-ku, Tokyo 101, Japan. circ. 2,000.

340 NE
NIJHOFF LAW SPECIALS. (Text in English) 1984. irreg. price varies. Kluwer Academic Publishers, P.O. Box 17, 3300 AA Dordrecht, Netherlands. TEL 078-334267. FAX 078-334254. (Dist. by: Kluwer Academic Publishers, P.O. Box 322, 3300 AH Dordrecht, Netherlands; U.S. address: P.O. Box 358, Accord Station, Hingham, MA 02018-0358)

340 CE
NITI VIMAMSA. (Text in Sinhalese) a. Rs.12. Sri Lanka Nitivedi Shishya Sanvidhanaya, Sevana, Seeduwa North, Sri Lanka.

340 CE
NITIVIDYA. (Text in Sinhalese) q. Rs.3 per no. Nitividya Study Circle, 80 Sanchi Arachchige Watta, Colombo 12, Sri Lanka.

NOISE REGULATION REPORT. see *ENVIRONMENTAL STUDIES — Pollution*

303.50 US ISSN 0148-7957
KF3813.A73
NOISE REGULATION REPORTER. 1974. bi-w. $303.50. Business Publishers, Inc., 951 Pershing Dr., Silver Spring, MD 20910-4464. TEL 301-587-6300. FAX 301-587-1081. Ed. Mary R. Worobec. index. (looseleaf format; back issues avail.)
Formerly: B N A Noise Regulation Reporter.
Description: Notification and reference service covering federal and state noise control legislation, regulation, and litigation.

340 US ISSN 0890-2208
K14
NOLO NEWS; the legal self-help newspaper. 1980. q. $12 (foreign $20). Nolo Press, Inc., 950 Parker St., Berkeley, CA 94710. TEL 510-549-1976. FAX 510-548-5902. Ed. Mary Randolph. bk.rev.; circ. 100,000. (tabloid format)

340 GR
NOMIKO VIMA. 1953. m. Dr.7500. Athens Bar Association, Academia 60, 106 79 Athens, Greece. TEL 361-4289-290. FAX 36-10-537.

340 NO ISSN 0029-1315
NORDISK DOMSSAMLING; a collection of cases from the supreme courts of the Scandinavian countries. (Text in Scandinavian languages) 1958. q. $74. Universitetsforlaget, P.O. Box 2959-Toeyen, N-0608 Oslo 1, Norway. (U.S. addr.: Publications Expediting Inc., 200 Meacham Ave., Elmont, NY 11003) Ed. Jacob Walnum. adv.; circ. 1,000.

340 SW ISSN 0300-3094
DL1
NORDISK STATUTSAMLING. (Subseries of: Nordisk Utredningsserie) (Text in Danish, Finnish, Icelandic, Norwegian, or Swedish) 1970. a. Nordiska Raadet, Box 19506, S-104 32 Stockholm, Sweden.

340 NO ISSN 0085-4220
NORDISKE DOMME I SJOFARTSANLIGGENDER. 1900. irreg. NOK 80. Nordisk Skibsrederforening, Kristinelundvei 22, 0207 Oslo 2, Norway. adv.; index, cum.index every 10 yrs.; circ. 900. (tabloid format)

340 GW ISSN 0932-710X
NORDRHEIN-WESTFAELISCHE VERWALTUNGBLAETTER; Zeitschrift fuer Oeffentliches Recht und Oeffentliche Verwaltung. 1987. m. DM.213.60. Richard Boorberg Verlag (Stuttgart), Scharrstr. 2, 7000 Stuttgart 80, Germany. TEL 0711-73783-0. bibl.; index. (back issues avail.)

340 GW
NORDRHEIN-WESTFALEN. JUSTIZMINISTERIALBLATT. m. DM.60. Karl-Heinz Junge GmbH Druckerei u. Verlag, Sessenbergstr. 2, 4300 Essen 1, Germany.

349 NO ISSN 0029-2060
NORSK RETSTIDENDE. 1836. 23/yr. NOK 900. Advokatenes Servicekontor - Norwegian Bar Association, Kr. Augustsgt. 0164, 0153 Oslo 1, Norway. Ed. Hans Stenberg-Nilsen. adv.; index, cum.index.

340 US ISSN 1054-6359
▼**NORTH CAROLINA EMPLOYMENT LAW LETTER.** 1991. 12/yr. $127. M. Lee Smith Publishers & Printers, 162 Fourth Ave. N., Box 2678, Nashville, TN 37219. TEL 615-242-7395. FAX 615-256-6601. (Co-sponsor: Womble Carlyle Sandridge & Rice) Ed. Ann Anderson.
Description: Reports the latest North Carolina employment law developments that affect North Carolina employers.

340 614.7 US ISSN 1047-4633
▼**NORTH CAROLINA ENVIRONMENTAL LAW LETTER.** 1990. 12/yr. $147. M. Lee Smith Publishers & Printers, 162 Fourth Ave. N., Box 2678, Nashville, TN 37219. TEL 615-242-7385. FAX 615-256-6601. (Co-sponsor: Womble, Carlyle, Sandridge & Rice) Eds. R. Howard Grubbs, Keith W. Vaughn.
Description: Reports the latest North Carolina environmental law developments that affect North Carolina companies.

NORTH CAROLINA LAW MONITOR. see *PUBLIC ADMINISTRATION*

340 US ISSN 0029-2524
K14
NORTH CAROLINA LAW REVIEW. 1922. 6/yr. $28 (foreign $32). (North Carolina Law Review Association) University of North Carolina at Chapel Hill, School of Law, Chapel Hill, NC 27514. TEL 919-962-3926. adv.; bk.rev.; cum.index every 5 yrs.; circ. 2,300. (also avail. in microform from BHP; microfiche from WSH; microfilm from WSH) Indexed: C.L.I., L.R.I., Leg.Per., P.A.I.S.
●Also available online. Vendor(s): Mead Data Central, WESTLAW.
—BLDSC shelfmark: 6149.050000.

340 US
NORTH CAROLINA LAWYERS WEEKLY. 1988. w. Lawyers Weekly Publications, Inc., Box 27566, Raleigh, NC 27611-7566. TEL 919-829-9333. FAX 919-829-8088. adv.; circ. 2,893.
Description: Contains recent court opinions from local and state courts. Reports news of the legal community and issues relevant to the state.

340 US ISSN 0164-6850
KF200
NORTH CAROLINA STATE BAR QUARTERLY. 1954. q. $10. North Carolina State Bar, Box 25850, Raleigh, NC 27611. TEL 919-828-4620. Ed. Jennifer Eichenberger. adv.; bk.rev.; illus.; circ. 12,500. (also avail. in microform from UMI; reprint service avail. from UMI) Indexed: C.L.I., L.R.I., Leg.Per.
Formerly (until 1978): North Carolina Bar (ISSN 0048-0657)

340 US
NORTH DAKOTA. STATE BAR BOARD. DIRECTORY OF LAWYERS AND JUDGES. a. $8. State Bar Board, Judicial Wing, 1st Fl., 600 E. Boulevard Ave., Bismarck, ND 58505-0530. TEL 701-224-4201.
Former titles: North Dakota Directory of Lawyers and Judges; North Dakota Directory of Judges and Attorneys; Directory of North Dakota Lawyers.

340 US ISSN 0029-2745
NORTH DAKOTA LAW REVIEW. 1927. q. $18. (State Bar Association of North Dakota) University of North Dakota, School of Law, Grand Forks, ND 58201. TEL 701-777-2941. FAX 701-777-2217. Ed.Bd. adv.; bk.rev.; index; circ. 2,000. (also avail. in microfiche from WSH; microfilm from WSH; reprint service avail. from WSH) Indexed: C.L.I., L.R.I., Leg.Cont., Leg.Per., Sel.Water Res.Abstr.
●Also available online. Vendor(s): WESTLAW.
—BLDSC shelfmark: 6149.392000.

340 US ISSN 0734-1490
K14
NORTHERN ILLINOIS UNIVERSITY LAW REVIEW. 1980. 3/yr. $18. Northern Illinois University, College of Law, DeKalb, IL 60115. TEL 815-753-0619. bk.rev.; circ. 535. (also avail. in microform from WSH; reprint service avail. from WSH) Indexed: C.L.I., Crim.Just.Abstr., L.R.I., Leg.Cont., Leg.Per.
—BLDSC shelfmark: 6151.005900.

340 IE
NORTHERN IRELAND LAW REPORTS. 1925. q. £25. Incorporated Council of Law Reporting for Northern Ireland, Bar Library, Royal Courts of Justice, Belfast BT1 3JX, Northern Ireland. Ed. W.D. Trimble. circ. 700. (back issues avail.)

340 UK ISSN 0029-3105
K14
NORTHERN IRELAND LEGAL QUARTERLY. 1937. q. £42. S L S Legal Publications, School of Law, Belfast BT7 1NN, N. Ireland. TEL 0232-245133. Ed. D.S. Greer. adv.; index, cum.index: vols.1-14; circ. 700. Indexed: Abstr.Bk.Rev.Curr.Leg.Per., C.L.I., L.R.I., Leg.Per.
—BLDSC shelfmark: 6151.012000.

340 US ISSN 0198-8549
K14
NORTHERN KENTUCKY LAW REVIEW. 1973. 3/yr. $15. Northern Kentucky University, Salmon P. Chase College of Law, Highland Heights, KY 41076. TEL 606-572-5444. Ed. Candace Smith. adv.; bk.rev.; circ. 2,500. (also avail. in microform from UMI; reprint service avail. from UMI) Indexed: C.L.I., L.R.I., Leg.Cont., Leg.Per., P.A.I.S.
●Also available online. Vendor(s): WESTLAW.
—BLDSC shelfmark: 6151.013550.
Formerly: Northern Kentucky State Law Forum.

340 CN ISSN 0824-3433
NORTHWEST TERRITORIES REPORTS. 1983. 4/yr. (in 1 vol.). Can.$115. Carswell Publications, 800 Rocky Mountain Plaza, 615 MacLeod Trail S.E., Calgary, Alta. T2G 4T8, Canada. TEL 416-609-8000. FAX 416-298-5094. (Subscr. to: Carswell Publications, Corporate Plaza, 2075 Kennedy Rd., Scarborough, Ont. M1T 3V4, Canada) Ed.Bd. cum.index; circ. 300.

340 US ISSN 0029-3571
K14
NORTHWESTERN UNIVERSITY LAW REVIEW. 1906. q. $30 (foreign $33). Northwestern University, School of Law, 357 E. Chicago Ave., Chicago, IL 60611. TEL 312-503-8467. adv.; bk.rev.; charts; index; circ. 1,200. (also avail. in microfiche from WSH; microfilm from BHP,RRI,UMI,WSH; reprint service avail. from RRI) Indexed: A.B.C.Pol.Sci., Abstr.Bk.Rev.Curr.Leg.Per., BPIA, Bus.Ind., C.L.I., Crim.Just.Abstr., Curr.Cont., L.R.I., Lang.& Lang.Behav.Abstr., Leg.Per., P.A.I.S., Sage Pub.Admin.Abstr., SSCI.
●Also available online. Vendor(s): Mead Data Central, WESTLAW.
—BLDSC shelfmark: 6152.045000.
Formerly (until 1952): Illinois Law Review.

340 US
NORTON BANKRUPTCY LAW ADVISER. 1983. m. $120. Callaghan & Co., 155 Pfingsten Rd., Deerfield, IL 60015. TEL 800-323-1336. Ed. William L. Norton, Jr. (looseleaf format)
Description: Information on current court and legislative activity. Includes a practice guide.

349 IT ISSN 0029-3857
NOTARO; periodico quindicinale di libera discussione, organo della classe notarile. 1912. s-m. L.50000. Massime, Via Alberico II, 35, 00193 Rome, Italy. Ed. Massimo Pavnini Rosati. bk.rev.; bibl.; index; circ. 3,200. (tabloid format)

347.016   US
NOTARY PUBLIC PRACTICES & GLOSSARY. 1978. biennial. $17.95. National Notary Association, 8236 Remmet Ave., Box 7184, Canoga Park, CA 91304-7184. TEL 818-713-4000. FAX 818-713-9061. Ed. Charles N. Faerber. (reprint service avail. from UMI)
   Supersedes in part: Customs and Practices of Notaries Public and Digest of Notary Laws in the U.S.

347.016   US
NOTARY VIEWPOINT. 1973. bi-m. $26. National Notary Association, 8236 Remmet Ave., Box 7184, Canoga Park, CA 91304-7184. TEL 818-713-4000. FAX 818-713-9061. Ed. Charles N. Faerber. circ. 80,000. (also avail. in microfilm; reprint service avail. from UMI)

340   CN
NOTARY'S COMPENDIUM; B.C. statutes and regulations. base vol. (plus irreg. suppl.). Can.$135.50. Ministry of Attorney General, Parliament Bldgs., Victoria, B.C. V8V 1X4, Canada. (Subscr. to: Crown Publications, 546 Yates St., Victoria, B.C. V8W 1K8, Canada. TEL 604-386-4636) (looseleaf format; back issues avail.)
   Description: Contains statutes and regulations required by Notaries for their respective provincees.

340   US
NOTER UP; an updated service and semi-annual newsletter on legal research and legal bibliography. 1977. s-a. $65. William S. Hein & Co., Inc., 1285 Main St., Buffalo, NY 14209. TEL 800-828-7571. FAX 716-883-8100. TELEX 91-209 WU 7 HEIN BUF. Ed. Donald J. Dunn. illus.

NOTRE DAME JOURNAL OF LAW, ETHICS & PUBLIC POLICY. see *PUBLIC ADMINISTRATION*

340   US
NOTRE DAME LAW REVIEW. 1925. 5/yr. $28. University of Notre Dame, School of Law, Box 988, Notre Dame, IN 46556. TEL 219-239-7097. FAX 219-239-6371. (Dist. by: Darby Printing Company) adv.; bk.rev.; circ. 1,700. (also avail. in microfilm from RRI; reprint service avail. from WSH) **Indexed:** Abstr.Bk.Rev.Curr.Leg.Per., C.L.I., Cath.Ind., Curr.Cont., L.R.I., Leg.Cont., Leg.Per., P.A.I.S., SSCI.
   ●Also available online. Vendor(s): WESTLAW.
   Formerly (until 1982): Notre Dame Lawyer (ISSN 0029-4535)

340   US
NOTRE DAME STUDIES IN LAW AND CONTEMPORARY ISSUES. 1985. irreg., vol.3, 1990. price varies. University of Notre Dame Press, Notre Dame, IN 46556. TEL 219-239-6346.

349.41   UK   ISSN 0965-0660
K24
NOTTINGHAM LAW JOURNAL. 1992. a. £4. Nottingham Polytechnic, Nottingham Law School, Burton St., Nottingham NG1 4BU, England. TEL 0602-418418. FAX 0602-486489. Ed. Janet S. Ulph. adv.; bk.rev.; circ. 1,000. **Indexed:** C.L.I., L.R.I., Leg.Per.
   Supersedes (1977-1987): Trent Law Journal (ISSN 0309-8990)

331   US
NOVA LAW REVIEW. 1977. 3/yr. $20. Nova Law Review, 3100 S.W. 9th Ave., Fort Lauderdale, FL 33315. TEL 305-522-2300. Ed. Holiday Russell. adv.; bk.rev.; circ. 700. (also avail. in microform from WSH; back issues avail.; reprint service avail. from WSH) **Indexed:** C.L.I., Leg.Per.
   ●Also available online. Vendor(s): WESTLAW.
   Formerly: Nova Law Journal.

340   CN
NOVA SCOTIA BARRISTERS' SOCIETY. ANNUAL REPORT. a. Nova Scotia Barristers' Society, 1475 Hollis St., Halifax, N.S. B3J 3M4, Canada.
TEL 902-422-1491.

340   CN   ISSN 0316-6325
KE361.N6
NOVA SCOTIA LAW NEWS. 1974. bi-m. Can.$60. Nova Scotia Barristers' Society, 1475 Hollis St., Halifax, N.S. B3J 3M4, Canada. TEL 902-422-1491. Ed. Ruth Epstein. bk.rev.; index; circ. 1,800.
   Description: Digests of decisions of Nova Scotia's courts and Nova Scotia legislation, and articles.

340   CN   ISSN 0048-0983
LAW
NOVA SCOTIA REPORTS. 1970. 6/yr. Can.$86 per vol. Maritime Law Book Ltd., Box 302, Fredericton, N.B. E3B 4Y9, Canada. TEL 902-667-3889. Ed.Bd. (back issues avail.)
   ●Also available online. Vendor(s): QL Systems Ltd..

NOW HIRING; government jobs for lawyers. see *OCCUPATIONS AND CAREERS*

340   PL
NOWE PRAWO. 1945. m. $84. Wydawnictwo Prawnicze, Ul. Wisniowa 50, 02-520 Warsaw, Poland. (Dist. by: Ars Polona-Ruch, Krakowskie Przedmiescie 7, Warsaw, Poland)

NUCLEAR LAW BULLETIN. see *ENERGY — Nuclear Energy*

343   US   ISSN 0360-7690
KF2138.A6
NUCLEAR REGULATION REPORTS. 1975. w. $2420. Commerce Clearing House, Inc., 4025 W. Peterson Ave., Chicago, IL 60646. TEL 312-583-8500.
   Supersedes: Atomic Energy Law Reports.

340   IT
NUOVA GIURISPRUDENZA CIVILE COMMENTATA. 1985. bi-m. L.170000 (foreign L.210000)(effective 1991). Casa Editrice Dott. Antonio Milani, Via Jappelli 5, 35121 Padua, Italy. TEL 049-656677. FAX 049-8752900. Ed. Paolo Zatti.

340   IT
NUOVE LEGGI CIVILI COMMENTATE. 1978. bi-m. L.180000 (foreign L.210000)(effective 1991). Casa Editrice Dott. Antonio Milani, Via Jappelli 5, 35121 Padua, Italy. TEL 049-656677. FAX 049-8752900. Ed. Piero Schlesinger.

349   IT   ISSN 0029-6368
NUOVO DIRITTO; rassegna giuridica pratica. 1924. m. L.80000 (foreign L.110000)(typically set in Jan.). Via Antonio Labriola, 64, 00136 Rome, Italy. (Subscr. to: Casella Postale 11-171, 00141 Roma-Montesacro, Italy) Ed. Vittoria Maffuccini Visco. adv.; bk.rev. (back issues avail.)

THE NURSE, THE PATIENT AND THE LAW; the journal of nursing law & risk management. see *MEDICAL SCIENCES — Nurses And Nursing*

NUTRITION LEGISLATION NEWS; a twice-monthly report of United States government activities. see *NUTRITION AND DIETETICS*

340   BL
O A B - R J. REVISTA. 3/yr. Ordem dos Advogados do Brasil - Rio de Janeiro, Av. Mal. Camara, 210-6o, ZC-39 Rio de Janeiro, Brazil.

O P A S T C O ROUNDTABLE; the magazine of ideas for small telephone companies. (Organization for the Protection and Advancement of Small Telephone Companies) see *COMMUNICATIONS — Telephone And Telegraph*

340   NR
OBAFEMI AWOLOWO UNIVERSITY. FACULTY OF LAW. LAW REPORT. 1972. q. $50 per set. Obafemi Awolowo University Press, Ltd., Ile-Ife, Nigeria. Ed. M.A. Owoade. adv.; circ. 800.
   Formerly: University of Ife. Faculty of Law. Law Report.

340   NR
OBAFEMI AWOLOWO UNIVERSITY LAW JOURNAL. 1987. a. $25. Obafemi Awolowo University Press Ltd., Ile-Ife, Nigeria. Ed. J.O. Fabunmi. circ. 1,000.

340   SA
OBITER. (Text in Afrikaans and English) 1979. a. R.8. University of Port Elizabeth, Faculty of Law, Box 1600, Port Elizabeth 6000, South Africa. Ed. A.C. Cilliers. adv.; bk.rev.; circ. 600. **Indexed:** Ind.S.A.Per.

340   CN   ISSN 0029-7585
OBITER DICTA. 1927. 24/yr. Can.$25. York University, Osgoode Hall Law School, 4700 Keele St., Rm. 118D, Downsview, Ont. M5J 2R5, Canada. TEL 416-736-2100. adv.; abstr.; circ. 1,200. (tabloid format) **Indexed:** C.L.I., L.R.I., Leg.Info.Manage.Ind.

340   US
▼**OBJECTIONS AT TRIALS.** 1990. irreg. $29.95. Butterworth Legal Publishers (Salem) (Subsidiary of: Reed International PLC), 90 Stiles Rd., Salem, NH 03079. TEL 800-548-4001. FAX 603-898-9858. Eds. Ronald L. Carlson, Myron H. Bright.

340   US   ISSN 0195-1696
KF9444.A15
OBSCENITY LAW BULLETIN. 1977. bi-m. $10. National Obscenity Law Center, 475 Riverside Dr., New York, NY 10115. TEL 212-870-3232.
FAX 212-870-2765. Ed. Paul J. McGeady. circ. 1,000.
   Description: Report and commentary on current court decisions and legislation pertaining to obscenity and related matters.

950 340   US   ISSN 0730-0107
OCCASIONAL PAPERS - REPRINT SERIES IN CONTEMPORARY ASIAN STUDIES. 1977. bi-m. $18 (foreign $24). University of Maryland School of Law, 500 W. Baltimore St., Baltimore, MD 21201. TEL 301-328-7579. Ed. Hungdah Chiu. circ. 800.
   —BLDSC shelfmark: 6224.858700.

340   IT
OCCASIONI GIUDIZIARIE. 1978. bi-m. Via Anapo 29, 00199 Rome, Italy.

344.7 614   CN   ISSN 0706-5019
OCCUPATIONAL HEALTH AND SAFETY LAW. 1977. m. Can.$295. Business Law Reporting Limited, Box 908, Cobourg, Ont. K9A 4W4, Canada.
TEL 416-372-0253.

340   IS   ISSN 0792-3279
OD MEIDA. 1983. bi-m. free to members. Israel Bar Central Committee, 30 Ibn Givirol St., Tel Aviv 64078, Israel. TEL 03-6916108.
FAX 03-6916107. Ed. Yair Ben-David. adv.; circ. 13,000.

O'DWYER'S F A R A REPORT. see *ADVERTISING AND PUBLIC RELATIONS*

340 352   GW   ISSN 0029-8565
DER OEFFENTLICHE DIENST. m. DM.102. Carl Heymanns Verlag KG, Luxemburgerstr. 449, 5000 Cologne 41, Germany. TEL 0221-46010-0. FAX 0221-4601069.

DIE OEFFENTLICHE VERWALTUNG; Zeitschrift fuer oeffentliches Recht und Verwaltungswissenschaft. see *PUBLIC ADMINISTRATION*

340   AU   ISSN 0029-9251
OESTERREICHISCHE JURISTEN - ZEITUNG. 1946. s-m. S.1840. Manzsche Verlags- und Universitaetsbuchhandlung, Kohlmarkt 16, A-1014 Vienna, Austria. TEL 0222-531610.
FAX 0222-5316181. Ed. Herbert Loebenstein. adv.; bk.rev.; charts; index; circ. 3,800. (also avail. in microfilm; microfiche) **Indexed:** CERDIC.
   —BLDSC shelfmark: 6307.750000.
   Description: For Austrian lawyers on all aspects of law.

340   AU   ISSN 0029-9340
OESTERREICHISCHE NOTARIATS-ZEITUNG. 1859. m. S.720. (Oesterreichische Notariatskammer) Manzsche Verlags- und Universitaetsbuchhandlung, Kohlmarkt 16, A-1014 Vienna, Austria.
TEL 0222-531610. FAX 0222-5316181. Ed. Friedrich Stefan. bk.rev.; charts; index, cum.index: 1949-1973; circ. 1,700. (also avail. in microfilm; microfiche)
   Description: For the Austrian notary.

340   US   ISSN 0173-1718
OESTERREICHISCHE ZEITSCHRIFT FUER OEFFENTLICHES RECHT UND VOELKERRECHT. SUPPLEMENT. 1971. irreg. price varies. Springer-Verlag, 175 Fifth Ave., New York, NY 10010. TEL 212-460-1500. (Also: Berlin, Heidelberg, Vienna) (also avail. in microform from UMI; reprint service avail. from ISI)
   Formerly: Oesterreichische Zeitschrift fuer Oeffentliches Recht. Supplement (ISSN 0078-3552)

340   US   ISSN 0378-3073
K15   CODEN: OZORAA
OESTERREICHISCHE ZEITSCHRIFT FUER OEFFENTLICHES RECHT UND VOELKERRECHT/AUSTRIAN JOURNAL OF PUBLIC AND INTERNATIONAL LAW. (Text in German) 1914. q. DM.314($176) Springer-Verlag, Journals, 175 Fifth Ave., New York, NY 10010. TEL 212-460-1500. (Also: Berlin, Heidelberg, Tokyo and Vienna) Ed.Bd. adv.; bk.rev.; index. (also avail. in microform from UMI; back issues avail.; reprint service avail. from ISI)
  Formerly: Oesterreichische Zeitschrift fuer Oeffentliches Recht. Neue Folge (ISSN 0029-9634)

340   AU   ISSN 0029-9820
OESTERREICHISCHES ARCHIV FUER KIRCHENRECHT. 1896. 4/yr. $64. Verband der Wissenschaftlichen Gesellschaften Oesterreichs, Lindengasse 37, A-1070 Vienna, Austria. TEL 932166. (Co-sponsor: Universitaet Wien, Rechts- und Staatswissenschaftliche Fakultaet, Institut fuer Kirchenrecht) Ed. circ. 450. **Indexed:** CERDIC, Hist.Abstr. (until 1991).
—BLDSC shelfmark: 6311.700000.

OESTERREICHISCHES RECHT DER WIRTSCHAFT. see BUSINESS AND ECONOMICS

349   AU   ISSN 0029-9952
OESTERREICHISCHES STANDESAMT; Fachzeitschrift fuer Personenstands-, Ehe- und Staatsbuergerschaftsrecht. 1947. m. S.300. Fachverband der Oesterreichischen Standesbeamten, Habsburgergasse 5, A-1010 Vienna, Austria. Ed. Ferdinand Deschka. adv.; bk.rev.; index, cum.index; circ. 1,800. (tabloid format)

340 658   US   ISSN 0730-3815
KF300.A1
OF COUNSEL; the monthly legal practice report. s-m. $325. Prentice Hall Law & Business, 270 Sylvan Ave., Englewood Cliffs, NJ 07632-2513. TEL 201-894-8484. FAX 201-894-8666. Eds. Steven Nelson, Larry Smith. adv.; stat.; index; circ. 1,228. (back issues avail.)
  Description: Reports on all aspects of running a law office: practice development, technology, salaries.

OFFICE CENTRAL DES TRANSPORTS INTERNATIONAUX FERROVIAIRES. BULLETIN. see TRANSPORTATION — Railroads

OFFICIAL GUIDE TO U.S. LAW SCHOOLS. see EDUCATION — Higher Education

340   US
OHIO AGENT. m. $15. Professional Insurance Agents of Ohio, 929 Harrison Ave., Ste. 202, Columbus, OH 43215. TEL 614-294-8878. FAX 614-294-4831. Ed. Eric D. Wygle. adv.; circ. 2,300.

340   US   ISSN 0748-6170
LAW
OHIO ATTORNEY GENERAL OPINIONS. 1963. q. $95. (Office of the Attorney General) Banks - Baldwin Law Publishing Co., University Center, Box 1974, Cleveland, OH 44106. TEL 216-721-7373. FAX 216-721-8055.

OHIO CRIMINAL LAW HANDBOOK. see CRIMINOLOGY AND LAW ENFORCEMENT

340   US   ISSN 0274-7294
KF128.O36
OHIO DISTRICT COURT REVIEW. 1980. m. $225. Anadem Publishing, Inc., 3620 N. High St., Columbus, OH 43214. TEL 614-262-2539. index.
  Description: Summaries of unreported Court of Appeals cases in Ohio.

340   US   ISSN 1046-9206
▼**OHIO EMPLOYMENT LAW LETTER.** 1990. 12/yr. $127. M. Lee Smith Publishers & Printers, 162 Fourth Ave. N., Box 2678, Nashville, TN 37219. TEL 615-242-7395. FAX 615-256-6601. (Co-sponsor: Denlinger Rosenthal & Greenberg) Eds. Dean E. Denlinger, Gary L. Greenberg.
  Description: Reports the latest Ohio employment law developments that affect Ohio employers.

340 614.7   US   ISSN 1052-4355
▼**OHIO ENVIRONMENTAL LAW LETTER.** 1990. 12/yr. $147. M. Lee Smith Publishers & Printers, 162 Fourth Ave. N., Nashville, TN 37219. TEL 615-242-7395. FAX 615-256-6601. (Porter, Wright, Morris & Arthur) Ed. Martin S. Seltzer.
  Description: Reports the latest Ohio environmental law developments that affect Ohio companies.

340   US
OHIO LAWYER. 1987. bi-m. $24. Ohio State Bar Association, Box 16562, Columbus, OH 43216-6562. TEL 614-487-2050. Ed. Kate Hagan. circ. 22,500. (back issues avail.)

340   US   ISSN 0094-534X
K15
OHIO NORTHERN UNIVERSITY LAW REVIEW. 1973. q. $20. Ohio Northern University, Pettit College of Law, Box 153, Ada, OH 45810. TEL 419-772-2248. adv.; bk.rev.; circ. 1,400. (also avail. in microform from UMI; microfilm from WSH; reprint service avail. from WSH) **Indexed:** C.L.I., L.R.I., Leg.Per.
—BLDSC shelfmark: 6247.146000.

340   US   ISSN 0744-8376
KF200
OHIO STATE BAR ASSOCIATION REPORT. 1928. w. $135. Ohio State Bar Association, Box 16562, Columbus, OH 43216-6562. TEL 614-487-2050. Ed. Kate Hagan. adv.; index; circ. 20,000. **Indexed:** C.L.I., L.R.I.

340   US
OHIO STATE JOURNAL ON DISPUTE RESOLUTION. 1986. 2/yr. $15 (foreign $18). Ohio State University, College of Law, 1659 N. High St., Columbus, OH 43210-1391. TEL 614-292-7170. adv.; circ. 400. **Indexed:** C.L.I., Leg.Per.
  ●Also available online. Vendor(s): WESTLAW, Wilsonline.
  Description: A medium for the exchange of information between scholars and law practitioners concerning alternatives to traditional legal redress.

340   US   ISSN 0048-1572
K15
OHIO STATE LAW JOURNAL. 1935. 5/yr. $35 (foreign $40). Ohio State University, College of Law, 1659 North High St., Columbus, OH 43210-1391. TEL 614-292-6829. bk.rev.; circ. 1,800. (also avail. in microform from UMI; microfiche from WSH; microfilm from WSH; reprint service avail. from WSH) **Indexed:** Abstr.Bk.Rev.Curr.Leg.Per., C.C.L.P., C.L.I., L.R.I., Leg.Per., P.A.I.S., SSCI.
  ●Also available online. Vendor(s): Mead Data Central, WESTLAW, Wilsonline.
  Also available on CD-ROM.
—BLDSC shelfmark: 6247.280000.
  Description: General law topics with one issue per year focusing on an annual symposium on banking or insurance law; also includes articles devoted to judges and judging.

OHIO TAVERN NEWS. see BEVERAGES

OIL AND GAS REPORTER. see PETROLEUM AND GAS

340 665.5   US   ISSN 1055-9175
▼**OIL SPILL U S LAW REPORT;** legislation, litigation, regulations & enforcement actions. 1991. m. $667 (foreign $767). Cutter Information Corp., 37 Broadway, Arlington, MA 02174. TEL 617-648-8700. FAX 617-648-8707. TELEX 650 100 9891 MCI UW. Ed. Amy M. Stolls.
  Description: Provides analysis and commentary on the latest court decisions, regulations, statutes, and administrative.

340   UK
OKE'S MAGISTERIAL FORMULIST. (In 2 vols.) 3/yr. $450. Butterworth & Co. (Publishers) Ltd. (Subsidiary of: Reed International PLC), 88 Kingsway, London WC2B 6AB, England. TEL 71-405-6900. FAX 71-405-1332. TELEX 95678. (US addr.: Butterworth Legal Publishers, 90 Stiles Rd., Salem, NH 03079. TEL 800-548-4001) Eds. John E. Pearson, Stuart Baker. (looseleaf format)

LAW   2663

340   US   ISSN 0475-0926
KFO1640
OKLAHOMA. ATTORNEY GENERAL'S OFFICE. OPINIONS OF THE ATTORNEY GENERAL. 1968. a. price varies. Attorney General's Office, Rm. 112, State Capitol, Oklahoma City, OK 73105. TEL 405-521-3921. FAX 405-521-6246. circ. 1,000. (back issues avail.)

340   US
OKLAHOMA BAR JOURNAL. 1930. w. (except Aug.) $25. Oklahoma Bar Association, Box 53036, Oklahoma City, OK 73152. TEL 405-524-2365. FAX 405-524-1115. Ed.Bd. adv.; index, cum.index published irregularly; circ. 12,500. (also avail. in microform from UMI; microfiche from WSH; reprint service avail. from UMI) **Indexed:** C.L.I., L.R.I., Law Ofc.Info.Svc., Leg.Per.
  Formerly (until vol.50, Jan. 1979): Oklahoma Bar Association Journal (ISSN 0030-1655)

340   US
OKLAHOMA CITY UNIVERSITY LAW REVIEW. 1976. s-a. $18. Oklahoma City University, School of Law, 2501 N. Blackwelder, Oklahoma City, OK 73106. TEL 405-521-5280. Ed. A.C. Yardley. adv.; bk.rev.; circ. 1,000. (also avail. in microform from MIM; microfiche from WSH; back issues avail.; reprint service avail. from WSH) **Indexed:** C.L.I., L.R.I., Leg.Per.
  ●Also available online. Vendor(s): WESTLAW.

340   US
OKLAHOMA DISCOVERY PRACTICE MANUAL. 1987. base vol. (plus a. suppl.). $120. Butterworth Legal Publishers (Salem) (Subsidiary of: Reed International PLC), 90 Stiles Rd., Salem, NH 03079. TEL 800-548-4001. FAX 603-898-9858. Ed. Charles W. Adams. (looseleaf format)
  Description: Contains the text of the Oklahoma Discovery Code and the Federal Rules on which the Code is based, plus analysis of leading cases, practice commentary describing techniques for effective use of the Code.

340   US   ISSN 0030-1752
LAW
OKLAHOMA LAW REVIEW. 1948. q. $25. University of Oklahoma, College of Law, 300 Timberdell Rd., Norman, OK 73019. TEL 405-325-5191. Ed. Jay Johnson. adv.; bk.rev.; index; circ. 1,100. (also avail. in microform from MIM; microfiche from WSH; reprint service avail. from WSH) **Indexed:** Account.Ind. (1974-), C.L.I., Crim.Just.Abstr., L.R.I., Leg.Cont., Leg.Per.
  ●Also available online. Vendor(s): WESTLAW.
—BLDSC shelfmark: 6253.100000.
  Description: Articles and student notes on all areas of state and federal law.

340   US
OKLAHOMA LIEN LAWS; mechanic's and oil and gas liens and claims against Public Works. base vol. (plus a. suppl.). $120. Butterworth Legal Publishers (Salem) (Subsidiary of: Reed International PLC), 90 Stiles Rd., Salem, NH 03079. TEL 800-549-4001. FAX 603-898-9858. Ed. Charles W. Adams. (looseleaf format)
  Description: Covers all aspects of Oklahoma mechanic's lien laws from the perspective of subcontractors, contractors, property owners, lenders and sureties. Provides advice on how owners and contractors can manage construction projects so mechanic's liens may be avoided.

340   US   ISSN 0030-1728
J1
OKLAHOMA REGISTER (OKLAHOMA CITY). 1962. s-m. $150. Department of Libraries, Legislative Reference Division, 200 N.E. 18th, Oklahoma City, OK 73105. TEL 405-521-2502. FAX 405-525-7804. Ed. Peggy Coe. circ. 280.
  Description: State administrative rules, notification of rulemaking actions, and local project funding contract announcements by state entities.

340   US
OKLAHOMA WILLS AND INTERSTATE SUCCESSION. 1987. base vol. (plus suppl.). $95. Butterworth Legal Publishers (Salem) (Subsidiary of: Reed International PLC), 90 Stiles Rd., Salem, NH 03079. TEL 800-548-4001. FAX 603-898-9858. Ed. Nancy I. Kenderdine. (looseleaf format)

L

2664 LAW

340   CN   ISSN 0710-538X
K15
OMBUDSMAN JOURNAL. a. $40. International Ombudsman Institute, Faculty of Law, University of Alberta, Edmonton, Alta. T6G 2H5, Canada. TEL 403-492-3196.
Description: Articles of interest to ombudsmen and students in the area of ombudsmanship.

ON THE LINE. see *COMMUNICATIONS — Telephone And Telegraph*

340   CN
ONTARIO ANNUAL PRACTICE. a. Can.$63. Canada Law Book Inc., 240 Edward St., Aurora, Ont. L4G 3S9, Canada. TEL 416-841-6472.
Formerly: Chitty's Ontario Annual Practice (ISSN 0084-8751)

340   CN
ONTARIO APPEAL CASES. 1984. irreg. Can.$59 per vol. Maritime Law Book Ltd., Box 302, Fredericton, N.B. E3B 4Y9, Canada. TEL 506-454-9921.
●Also available online. Vendor(s): QL Systems Ltd..

340   CN
ONTARIO LEGISLATIVE DIGEST SERVICE. 1985. 40/yr. Can.$457. Carswell Publications, Corporate Plaza, 2075 Kennedy Rd., Scarborough, Ont. M1T 3V4, Canada. TEL 416-609-8000. FAX 416-298-5094.

340   CN
ONTARIO LIMITATION PERIODS. s-a. Can.$75. Butterworths Canada Ltd., 75 Clegg Rd., Markham, Ont. L6G 1A1, Canada. TEL 416-479-2665. FAX 416-479-2826. (looseleaf format)
Description: Guide to limitations of action and other statutory time limitations contained in the statutes of Ontario.

340   CN   ISSN 0318-7527
KEO866.4
ONTARIO MUNICIPAL BOARD REPORTS. 1972. bi-m. Can.$105. Canada Law Book Inc., 240 Edward St., Aurora, Ont. L4G 3S9, Canada. TEL 416-841-6472.

340   CN   ISSN 0030-3089
ONTARIO REPORTS. 1931. w. Can.$90. Butterworths Canada Ltd., 75 Clegg Rd., Markham, Ont. L6G 1A1, Canada. TEL 416-479-2665. FAX 416-479-2826. Ed. Bruce Dunlop. adv.; circ. 17,000.
●Also available online. Vendor(s): QL Systems Ltd..
Incorporates: Ontario Weekly Notes.

340   CN
ONTARIO SECURITIES LEGISLATION. irreg., 14th ed., 1988. Can.$17.95. C C H Canadian Ltd, 6 Garamond Court, Don Mills, Ont. M3C 1Z5, Canada. TEL 416-444-9011. FAX 800-461-4131.

340   CN   ISSN 0030-3127
ONTARIO STATUTE CITATOR. 4/yr. Can.$170. Canada Law Book Inc., 240 Edward St., Aurora, Ont. L4G 3S9, Canada. TEL 416-841-6472. Ed. L.R. MacTavish. (looseleaf format)

342   US   ISSN 0030-3429
OPEN FORUM.* 1923. bi-m. $20. American Civil Liberties Union (Southern California), 1616 Beverly Blvd., Los Angeles, CA 90026-5752. TEL 213-487-1720. FAX 213-480-3221. Ed. Rosa Martinez. adv.; illus.; circ. 25,000. (tabloid format)

340   US
OREGON APPELLATE MANUAL. 1986. base vol. (plus suppl.). $60. Butterworth Legal Publishers (Salem) (Subsidiary of: Reed International PLC), 90 Stiles Rd., Salem, NH 03079. TEL 800-548-4001. FAX 603-898-9858. Ed. George Kelly. (looseleaf format)
Description: Follows an imaginary case through the appellate process to illustrate the application of the hundred-plus rules that apply to appeals under Oregon law.

340   US
OREGON DEBTOR - CREDITOR LAW. 1986. base vol. (plus suppl.). $70. Butterworth Legal Publishers (Salem) (Subsidiary of: Reed International PLC), 90 Stiles Rd., Salem, NH 03079. TEL 800-548-4001. FAX 603-898-9858. Ed. Brian A. Blum.
Description: Covers Oregon law relating to attachment, claim and delivery, restraining orders, receivership, judgement by default and confession, judgement liens, enforcement of foreign judgements, execution, redemption, garnishment, liens and lien foreclosure, foreclosure of mortgages, tax liens, and fraudulent conveyances.

340   US
OREGON EVIDENCE. 1989. base vol. (plus a. suppl.). $80. Butterworth Legal Publishers (Salem) (Subsidiary of: Reed International PLC), 90 Stiles Rd., Salem, NH 03079. TEL 800-548-4001. FAX 603-898-9858. Ed. Laird C. Kirkpatrick.
Description: Contains current statutory amendments and current case law and provides thorough analysis of the rules of Oregon and federal cases interpreting them.

340   US   ISSN 0196-2043
K15
OREGON LAW REVIEW. 1921. 4/yr. $20. Christensen Inc. (Eugene), University of Oregon, School of Law, Eugene, OR 97403-1221. TEL 503-346-3844. FAX 503-346-3985. Ed. Andy Pharies. adv.; bk.rev.; index; circ. 1,100. (also avail. in microfilm from RRI,WSH; back issues avail.; reprint service avail. from RRI) Indexed: C.L.I., L.R.I., Leg.Cont., Leg.Per., Mar.Aff.Bibl., Ocean.Abstr., Pollut.Abstr.
●Also available online. Vendor(s): WESTLAW.
—BLDSC shelfmark: 6281.500000.

340   US
OREGON NOTARY LAW PRIMER. a. $9.95. National Notary Association, 8236 Remmet Ave., Box 7184, Canoga Park, CA 91304-7184. TEL 818-713-4000. FAX 818-713-9061. Ed. Charles N. Faerber. (reprint service avail. from UMI)

340   US
OREGON REVISED STATUTES ANNOTATED. (Supplement avail.: Comprehensive Index to Oregon Statutes (Year)) 1983. 52 base vols. (plus a. suppl.). $2400. Butterworth Legal Publishers (Salem) (Subsidiary of: Reed International PLC), 90 Stiles Rd., Salem, NH 03079. TEL 800-548-4001. FAX 603-898-9858. Ed.Bd.

340   US   ISSN 0030-4816
KF200
OREGON STATE BAR BULLETIN. 1935. m. (10/yr.). $35 includes For the Record. Oregon State Bar, Box 1689, Lake Oswego, OR 97035-0889. TEL 503-620-0222. FAX 503-684-1366. Ed. Paul Nickell. adv.; bk.rev.; circ. 11,000. (back issues avail.) Indexed: Law Ofc.Info.Svc.

340   US
OREGON UNIFORM COMMERCIAL CODE. 3 base vols. (plus suppl.). $225. Butterworth Legal Publishers (Salem) (Subsidiary of: Reed International PLC), 90 Stiles Rd., Salem, NH 03079. TEL 800-548-4001. FAX 603-898-9858. Ed. Henry J. Bailey, III.

ORGANISATION; Zeitschrift fuer Leitungs- und Verwaltungsorganisation der sozialistischen Staatsorgans. see *PUBLIC ADMINISTRATION*

340   UK
ORGANISATION AND MANAGEMENT OF A SOLICITORS PRACTICE. irreg. Longman Group UK Ltd., Professional and Business Communications Division, 21-27 Lambs Conduit St., London WC1N 3NJ, England. TEL 01-242 2548. (looseleaf format)
Description: Provides how-to information on efficiently organizing a solicitors' practices.

340   US
ORGANIZATION OF AMERICAN STATES. LEGAL NEWSLETTER.* 1982. q. $12. Organization of American States, Department of Legal Publications and Informatics, 1889 F St., N.W., Washington, DC 20006. Dir. Christian Garcia-Godoy. circ. 600.

340   PL
ORZECZNICTWO SADOW POLSKICH. 1957. m. $49.20. (Polska Akademia Nauk, Instytut Panstwa i Prawa) Panstwowe Wydawnictwo Naukowe, Miodowa 10, 00-251 Warsaw, Poland. (Dist. by: Ars Polona, Krakowskie Przedmiescie 7, 00-068 Warsaw, Poland) Ed. W. Czachorski. index; circ. 11,570.
Formerly (until 1990): Orzecznictwo Sadow Polskich i Komisji Arbitrazowych (ISSN 0030-6061)

340   CN   ISSN 0030-6185
K15
OSGOODE HALL LAW JOURNAL. 1958. 4/yr. Can.$30 to individuals; libraries Can.$40. York University, Osgoode Hall Law School, 4700 Keele St., Rm. 118D, Downsview, Ont. M5J 2R5, Canada. TEL 416-736-5354. adv.; bk.rev.; index; circ. 1,100. (also avail. in microfilm from WSH; back issues avail.; reprint service avail. from WSH) Indexed: C.L.I., Crim.Just.Abstr., Ind.Can.L.P.L., L.R.I., Leg.Cont., Leg.Per.
—BLDSC shelfmark: 6300.570000.

340   IT   ISSN 0030-6290
OSSERVATORE LEGALE:* periodico di informazione giuridico-forense. 1944. s-m. S. Migliarino, Via Canonico Rotolo, 90143 Palermo, Italy.

349   GW   ISSN 0030-6444
LAW
OSTEUROPA-RECHT. (Text in German; occasionally in English) 1955. q. DM.58.40 (students DM.44.40). (Deutsche Gesellschaft fuer Osteuropakunde) Deutsche Verlags-Anstalt GmbH, Neckarstr. 121, Postfach 106012, 7000 Stuttgart 10, Germany. TEL 0711-2631-0. FAX 0711-2631-292. Eds. D. Frenzke, A. Uschakow. adv.; bk.rev.; bibl.; index, cum.index; circ. 1,000.

340   GW
OSTEUROPA RECHT. q. DM.58.40 (students DM.44.40). Deutsche Verlags-Anstalt GmbH, Neckarstr. 121, Postfach 106012, 7000 Stuttgart 10, Germany. TEL 0711-7200591. FAX 0711-2631292.

340   NZ   ISSN 0078-6918
K15
OTAGO LAW REVIEW. 1965. a. NZ.$30. Otago Law Review Trust Board, c/o Faculty of Law, University of Otago, Dunedin, New Zealand. TEL 24-791-100. FAX 64-24-741-607. (Dist. in U.S. by: Wm. M. Gaunt & Sons, Inc., Gaunt Bldg., 3011 Gulf Dr., Holmes Beach, FL 33510) Eds. R. Ahdar, I. Williams. adv.; bk.rev.; circ. 1,200. Indexed: C.L.I., L.R.I., Leg.Cont., Leg.Per., Manage.Cont.
—BLDSC shelfmark: 6313.189400.
Description: Articles of general legal interest to the New Zealand law community.

340   CN   ISSN 0048-2331
K15
OTTAWA LAW REVIEW. (Text in English, French) 1967. 3/yr. Can.$30. University of Ottawa, Faculty of Law, Common Law Section, 57 rue Louis Pasteur, Ottawa, Ont. K1N 6N5, Canada. TEL 613-564-2919. FAX 613-564-9800. adv.; bk.rev.; bibl.; index; circ. 850. (also avail. in microfiche; microfilm from WSH; reprint service avail. from WSH) Indexed: Abstr.Bk.Rev.Curr.Leg.Per., C.L.I., Ind.Can.L.P.L., L.R.I., Leg.Per., P.A.I.S.
Description: Covers all fields of law with particular interest in recent developments in Canadian law and French-language common law jurisprudence.

341   UK   ISSN 0143-6503
K15
OXFORD JOURNAL OF LEGAL STUDIES. 1981. 4/yr. £58($125) Oxford University Press, Oxford Journals, Pinkhill House, Southfield Road, Eynsham, Oxford OX8 1JJ, England. TEL 0865-882283. FAX 0865-882890. TELEX 837330 OXPRES G. Ed. P.M. North. adv.; bk.rev.; index; circ. 950. Indexed: C.L.I., Leg.Per.
—BLDSC shelfmark: 6321.005850.
Description: Examines the theory and issues arising from the relationship of law to other disciplines, with an emphasis on legal philosophy and socio-legal matters.

OXY-FUEL NEWS. see *ENERGY*

340   CN   ISSN 0475-1671
OYEZ. 1970. irreg. University of Windsor, Faculty of Law, Student Law Society, Windsor, Ont. N9P 3P4, Canada. TEL 519-253-4232. illus.

340 CN
P L I A N NEWS. 1987. irreg. free. Public Legal Information Association of Newfoundland, P.O. Box 1064, Sta. C, St. John's, N.F. A1C 5M5, Canada. TEL 709-722-2643. FAX 709-722-0168. Ed. Peter Ringrose.

340 614.7   US   ISSN 0738-6206
K16
PACE ENVIRONMENTAL LAW REVIEW. 1983. s-a. $30. Pace University, School of Law, 78 N. Broadway, White Plains, NY 10603. Ed.Bd. bk.rev.; circ. 200. (also avail. in microform from WSH; back issues avail.; reprint service avail. from WSH) Indexed: C.L.I., Environ.Abstr., Ind.Per.Art.Relat.Law, Leg.Per.

340   US   ISSN 0272-2410
K16
PACE LAW REVIEW. 1979. 3/yr. $15. Pace University, School of Law, 78 N. Broadway, White Plains, NY 10603. adv.; bk.rev.; circ. 700. (also avail. in microfiche from WSH; microfilm from WSH; back issues avail.; reprint service avail. from WSH) Indexed: Abstr.Bk.Rev.Curr.Leg.Per., C.L.I., L.R.I., Leg.Cont., Leg.Per.
—BLDSC shelfmark: 6328.226000.

340   US   ISSN 0030-8757
LAW
PACIFIC LAW JOURNAL. 1970. q. $18. (University of the Pacific, McGeorge School of Law) Western Newspaper Publishing, Co., 3200 Fifth Ave., Sacramento, CA 95817. TEL 916-739-7171. adv.; bk.rev.; circ. 3,200. (tabloid format; also avail. in microfilm from RRI,WSH; reprint service avail. from RRI) Indexed: C.L.I., Crim.Just.Abstr., L.R.I., Leg.Cont., Leg.Per., Mar.Aff.Bibl.
●Also available online. Vendor(s): WESTLAW.
—BLDSC shelfmark: 6330.050000.

PAKISTAN. NATIONAL ASSEMBLY. DEBATES. OFFICIAL REPORT. see PUBLIC ADMINISTRATION

340   PK   ISSN 0078-785X
LAW
PAKISTAN ANNUAL LAW DIGEST. (Text in English) 1947. a. Rps.600($36) P.L.D. Publishers, Nabha Rd., Lahore 1, Pakistan. (reprint service avail. from UMI)

PAKISTAN CRIMINAL LAW JOURNAL; monthly reporter of criminal laws. see CRIMINOLOGY AND LAW ENFORCEMENT

340 331   PK   ISSN 0030-994X
LAW
PAKISTAN LABOUR CASES. 1960. m. Rs.500. P.L.D. Publishers, Nabha Rd., Lahore 1, Pakistan. Ed. Malik Muhammad Saeed. (reprint service avail. from UMI)

340   PK
PAKISTAN LAW JOURNAL. (Text in English, Urdu) 1973. m. Rs.480($30) Punjab Bar Council, 13 Fane Rd., Lahore, Pakistan. Ed. M. Bashir Chaudhri. adv.; circ. 4,200.
 Description: Judgements and decisions of the Superior Courts of Pakistan, and speeches of the judiciary.

340   PK
PAKISTAN SUPREME COURT CASES. (Text in English) 1982. m. R.120($20) Supreme Court, 1 Turner Rd., Lahore, Pakistan. Ed. Malik Muhammad Qayyum. index; circ. 2,000. (back issues avail.)

340   PL   ISSN 0031-0344
PALESTRA/BAR. m. $78. Wydawnictwo Prawnicze, Ul. Wisniowa 50, 02-520 Warsaw, Poland. (Dist. by: Ars Polona - Ruch, Krakowskie Przedmiescie 7, Warsaw, Poland)

340   II
PANJAB UNIVERSITY LAW REVIEW. (Text in English) 1951. s-a. Rs.50($10) Panjab University, Department of Laws, Chandigarh 160014, Union Territory, India. TEL 22577. Ed.Bd. adv.; bk.rev.; circ. 1,000.

340   PL   ISSN 0031-0980
LAW
PANSTWO I PRAWO. (Text in Polish; summaries in English, French, Russian) 1946. m. $30. (Polska Akademia Nauk, Instytut Panstwa i Prawa) Panstwowe Wydawnictwo Naukowe, Ul. Miodowa 10, 00-251 Warsaw, Poland. TEL 48-22-285330. (Dist. by: Ars Polona-Ruch, Krakowskie Przedmiescie 7, Warsaw, Poland) Ed. Leszek Kubicki. bk.rev.; index; circ. 5,600. Indexed: A.B.C.Pol.Sci., Hist.Abstr.

340   IO
PANTA-RHEI. 1975. irreg. University of North Sumatra, Faculty of Law - Universitas Sumatera Utara, Fakultas Hukum, Jalan Universitas 4, Medan, Indonesia.

340   US   ISSN 0011-8060
PAPER BOOK. 1913. 4/yr. $1. Delta Theta Phi Law Fraternity, International, 666 High St., Worthington, OH 43085. TEL 800-783-2600. FAX 614-888-7680. Ed. Gael Gallant. adv.; illus.; circ. 15,000.

340   AT   ISSN 0085-4689
PAPUA AND NEW GUINEA LAW REPORTS. 1963. a. Law Book Co. Ltd., 44-50 Waterloo Rd., North Ryde, N.S.W. 2112, Australia. TEL 02-887-0177. FAX 02-888-9706. TELEX ASBOOK 27995. Ed. Naida J. Haxton. index. (back issues avail.)
 Description: Reports of the Supreme Court of Justice and National Court of Justice of Papua New Guinea.

340   AT
PAPUA NEW GUINEA LABOUR LAW. 1988. irreg. (approx. 2/yr.) C C H Australia Ltd., P.O. Box 230, North Ryde, N.S.W. 2113, Australia. TEL 02-88-2555. FAX 02-888-7324.

340   US   ISSN 0739-3601
KF320.L4
PARALEGAL; the publication for the paralegal profession. 1983. irreg., (approx. 6/yr.). $30 (foreign $37.50). National Paralegal Association, Box 406, Solebury, PA 18963. TEL 215-297-8333. FAX 215-297-8358. Ed. William Cameron. adv.; bk.rev.; circ. 30,000. (reprint service avail. from WSH)

340 371.0025   US
PARALEGAL SCHOOL DIRECTORY. 1983. a. $7. National Paralegal Association, Box 406, Solebury, PA 18963. TEL 215-297-8333. FAX 215-297-8358. Ed. William Cameron.
 Description: Lists over 900 schools, colleges and institutions offering training in paralegal studies.

340   US
PARALEGAL UPDATE. 1973. s-w. $17.50. National Legal Assistant Conference Center, 2444 Wilshire Blvd., Ste. 301, Santa Monica, CA 90403. TEL 213-453-1941. Ed. Joseph E. Deering, Jr. circ. 1,000.

340   US   ISSN 0738-1247
KF8750.A15
PARASCOPE. 1979. q. $19. (American Bar Association, Committee of Appellate Staff Attorneys) A B A Press, 750 N. Lake Shore Dr., Chicago, IL 60611-4497. TEL 312-988-5700. Ed. Howie Zibel. bk.rev.; circ. 500.
 Description: Newsletter on matters concerning appellate courts.

345   US   ISSN 0196-6138
KF192.C3
PARKER DIRECTORY OF CALIFORNIA ATTORNEYS.* 1925. a. $25.45. Parker and Son Publications, Inc., Box 9040, Carlsbad, CA 92008-9040. Ed. Mary Redondo. adv.; circ. 60,000.
 Formerly: Parker Directory of Attorneys (ISSN 0079-0044)

346   UK   ISSN 0079-0095
PARLIAMENT HOUSE BOOK. 1824. 2/yr. (regular updating). W. Green, 21 Alva St., Edinburgh EH2 4PS, Scotland. Ed. P. Nicholson. (looseleaf format)

342 350.086   UK
PARLIAMENTARY HOUSING NEWS. w. £55 (foreign £75). (National Campaign for the Homeless) Shelter Publications, 88 Old St., London EC1V 9HU, England. TEL 071-253-0202. FAX 071-608-3325.
 Formerly: Parliamentary News.
 Description: Housing issues in Britain.

340   BE   ISSN 0031-2614
PASICRISIE BELGE. (Text in French) 1814. m. 16500 Fr. Etablissements Emile Bruylant, 67 rue de la Regence, B-1000 Brussels, Belgium. TEL 02-512-9845. index; circ. 1,000.

349   BE   ISSN 0031-2630
PASINOMIE. (Text in French) 1789. m. 22000 Fr. Etablissements Emile Bruylant, 67 rue de la Regence, B-1000 Brussels, Belgium. TEL 02-512-9845. index; circ. 500.

PATENTS AND THE FEDERAL CIRCUIT. see PATENTS, TRADEMARKS AND COPYRIGHTS

PATENTS AND THE FEDERAL CIRCUIT. SUPPLEMENT. see PATENTS, TRADEMARKS AND COPYRIGHTS

340   US   ISSN 0269-3658
PATERSON'S LICENSING ACTS. a. $240. Butterworth & Co. (Publishers) Ltd. (Subsidiary of: Reed International PLC), 88 Kingsway, London WC2B 6AB, England. TEL 71-405-6900. FAX 71-405-1332. TELEX 95678. (US addr.: Butterworth Legal Publishers, 90 Stiles Rd., Salem, NH 03079. TEL 800-548-4001) Ed. J.N. Martin.

340 658   US
PATIENT CARE LAW. bi-m. $275. Action Kit Publications, 1614 Fifth Ave., Pittsburgh, PA 15213. TEL 800-245-1205. Ed. John Horty. (looseleaf format)
 Description: Serves as a resource for nurse management and provides current legal analyses.

340   AT   ISSN 0728-3210
PAUL'S POLICE OFFENCES. 1981. 3/yr. Aus.$195. Law Book Co. Ltd., 44-50 Waterloo Rd., N. Ryde, N.S.W. 2113, Australia. TEL 02-887-0177. FAX 02-888-9706. TELEX ASBOOK 27995. Ed.Bd. circ. 574. (back issues avail.)
 Description: Contains a comprehensive annotation of the Penalties and Sentences Act 1985 and Regulations Summary Offences Act 1986 in Victoria.

PAY AND BENEFITS BULLETIN. see BUSINESS AND ECONOMICS — Labor And Industrial Relations

PAYROLL ADMINISTRATION GUIDE. see BUSINESS AND ECONOMICS — Labor And Industrial Relations

PELICAN FARM NEWS. see AGRICULTURE

PENNSYLVANIA CHAMBER OF BUSINESS AND INDUSTRY. CHECKLIST. see PUBLIC HEALTH AND SAFETY

340 350   US
PENNSYLVANIA CHAMBER OF BUSINESS AND INDUSTRY. LEGISLATIVE REPORTER. w. (in session). $250 to non-members; members $175. Pennsylvania Chamber of Business and Industry, 222 N. Third St., Harrisburg, PA 17101. TEL 800-326-3252. FAX 717-255-3298.
 Description: Provides detailed information about legislative activity, including new bills and committee activities, for a business audience.

PENNSYLVANIA CHAMBER OF BUSINESS AND INDUSTRY. TAX BULLETIN. see BUSINESS AND ECONOMICS — Public Finance, Taxation

PENNSYLVANIA EDUCATION LAW REPORT. see EDUCATION

340   US   ISSN 1052-4363
▼PENNSYLVANIA EMPLOYMENT LAW LETTER. 1990. 12/yr. $95. M. Lee Smith Publishers & Printers, 162 Fourth Ave. N., Box 2678, Nashville, TN 37219. TEL 615-242-7395. FAX 615-256-6601. Eds. John E. Krampf, Harry Reagan.
 Description: Reports the latest Pennsylvania employment law developments that affect Pennsylvania employers.

340 614.7   US   ISSN 1046-6568
KFP354.A15
PENNSYLVANIA ENVIRONMENTAL LAW LETTER. 1989. m. $150. Andrews Publications, 1646 West Chester Pike, Box 1000, Westtown, PA 19395. TEL 215-399-6600. FAX 215-399-6610. Ed. Maureen McGuire. bibl.; stat.; cum.index every 6 mos. (looseleaf format; back issues avail.)
 Description: Covers environmental disputes in federal and state courts in Pennsylvania, legislative developments and DER criminal proceedings impacting PA attorneys and their clients.

340 US
PENNSYLVANIA LAW JOURNAL REPORTER. 1977. w. (48/yr.) $150. Legal Communications, Ltd., 1617 JFK Blvd., Ste. 1245, Philadelphia, PA 19103. TEL 215-563-2700. Ed. Brian Harris. adv.; bk.rev.; charts; stat.; index; circ. 2,500. (tabloid format; also avail. in microfilm; back issues avail.) Indexed: C.L.I., Hlth.Ind., L.R.I.
  Formerly (until 1981): Pennsylvania Law Journal (ISSN 0160-8495)
  Description: Provides coverage of events and significant court decisions.

340 US
PENNSYLVANIA LAWYER. 1978. bi-m. $15. Pennsylvania Bar Association, 100 South St., Harrisburg, PA 17108. TEL 717-238-6715. (Subscr. to: Box 186, Harrisburg, PA 17108) Ed. Donald C. Sarvey. adv.; circ. 30,000 (controlled). (back issues avail.)
  Description: Covers legal trends of interest to practicing Pennsylvania attorneys.

340 US
▼**PENNSYLVANIA MECHANICS' LIENS.** 1990. base vol. (plus irreg. suppl.). $75. Butterworth Legal Publishers (Salem) (Subsidiary of: Reed International PLC), 90 Stiles Rd., Salem, NH 03079. TEL 800-548-4001. FAX 603-898-9858. Ed. Michael G. Walsh. (looseleaf format)
  Description: Presents detailed account and explanation of every aspect of a lien claim.

340 US
PENNY RESISTANCE; economic and tax resistance to the death penalty. 1984. s-a. free. 8319 Fulham Court, Richmond, VA 23227-1712. TEL 804-266-7400. Ed. Jerome D. Gorman. circ. 200.

340 US ISSN 1041-1941
PEOPLE AND PROGRAMS. 3/yr. free. American Bar Association, Resource Development Office, 750 N. Lake Shore Dr., Chicago, IL 60611. TEL 312-988-5000.
  Description: For donors and volunteers for the ABA Fund for Justice and Education, which supports over 150 public service and law-related education programs.

340.05 US ISSN 0092-430X
K16
PEPPERDINE LAW REVIEW. 1973. 4/yr. $20 (typically set in June). Pepperdine University, School of Law, Malibu, CA 90265. TEL 213-456-4694. FAX 213-456-4266. (Dist. by: Joe Christensen, Inc., 1540 Adams St., Lincoln, NE 68521) Ed. Selina Hewitt. adv.; bk.rev.; index; circ. 600. (also avail. in microfiche from WSH; microfilm from UMI,WSH; reprint service avail. from UMI) Indexed: C.L.I., Crim.Just.Abstr., L.R.I., Leg.Cont., Leg.Per., Mar.Aff.Bibl.
  ●Also available online. Vendor(s): WESTLAW.
  —BLDSC shelfmark: 6422.953200.

340 US
▼**THE PERFECT LAWYER.** 1990. m. $110. Shepard's - McGraw-Hill, Inc., Box 35300, Colorado Springs, CO 80935-3530. TEL 719-488-3000. Ed. Robert P. Wilkins.

340 SP ISSN 0211-4526
PERSONA Y DERECHO. 1975. 2/yr. 2800 ptas.($30) (Universidad de Navarra, Facultad de Derecho) Servicio de Publicaciones de la Universidad de Navarra, S.A., Apdo. 177, 31080 Pamplona, Spain. TEL 94 25 2700. Dir. Javier Hervada. bk.rev.

340 GW ISSN 0724-360X
DAS PERSONAL A B C; Arbeitsrecht - Lohnsteuer - Sozialversicherung. 1983. bi-m. DM.58. Wirtschaft Recht und Steuern Verlag, Fraunhoferstr. 5, Postfach 1363, 8033 Planegg-Munich, Germany. TEL 089-8577944. FAX 089-857-7990. (looseleaf format)

340 GW ISSN 0341-2792
PERSONAL-BUERO IN RECHT UND PRAXIS; Arbeitsrecht - Lohnsteuer - Sozialversicherung - Personalfuehrung - Organisation. 1969. m. DM.128. Rudolf Haufe Verlag GmbH & Co. KG, Hindenburgstr. 64, 7800 Freiburg im Breisgau, Germany. TEL 0761-3683-0. FAX 0761-3683-195. cum.index. (looseleaf format)

340 CN
PERSONAL INJURY DAMAGE ASSESSMENTS IN ALBERTA. q. Can.$135. Butterworths Canada Ltd., 75 Clegg Rd., Markham, Ont. L6G 1A1, Canada. TEL 416-479-2665. FAX 416-479-2826. (looseleaf format)
  Description: Catalogues Alberta's judicial awards in motor vehicle accident cases since 1969.

340 CN
PERSONAL INJURY DAMAGE ASSESSMENTS IN BRITISH COLUMBIA. q. Can.$160. Butterworths Canada Ltd., 75 Clegg Rd., Markham, Ont. L6G 1A1, Canada. TEL 416-479-2665. FAX 416-479-2826. (looseleaf format)
  Description: Catalogues British Columbia's judicial awards in motor vehicle accident cases since 1962.

348.73 US
PERSONAL INJURY NEWSLETTER. 1967. fortn. $150. Matthew Bender & Co., 11 Penn Plaza, New York, NY 10001. TEL 212-967-7707. (Subscr. to: 1275 Broadway, Box 989, Albany, NY 12201) Ed. David A. Kaplan. index; circ. 2,315. (looseleaf format; back issues avail.)
  Description: Covers personal injury law, with emphasis on case reports. Includes law review reports and lawyers' medical reports for lawyers and medical professionals.

340 610 US
PERSONAL INJURY REVIEW (YEAR). 1961. a. $90. Matthew Bender & Co., Inc., 11 Penn Plaza, New York, NY 10001. TEL 212-967-7707. Eds. Barry D. Denkensohn, Agnes A. Fliss. cum.index. (also avail. in microfilm from RRI; back issues avail.; reprint service avail. from RRI) Indexed: C.L.I., Hlth.Ind.
  Formerly (until 1986): Personal Injury Deskbook.
  Description: Covers personal injury and medical field with original articles, digests of medical articles and significant personal injury cases.

340 US ISSN 0031-5591
PERSONAL INJURY VALUATION HANDBOOKS; injury valuation & special research reports. 1959. m. $450. Jury Verdict Research, Inc., 30700 Bainbridge Rd., Ste. H, Solon, OH 44139. TEL 800-321-6910. TELEX 216-349-JURY. Ed. Virginia M. Hermann. (looseleaf format)
  Description: Information aided by the use of graphs and diagrams on injuries and liability in personal damage litigation.

PERSONAL INJURY VERDICT REVIEWS. see INSURANCE

PERSONNEL FORMS AND EMPLOYMENT CHECKLISTS. see BUSINESS AND ECONOMICS — Personnel Management

340 370 US
PERSPECTIVE (MADISON); the campus legal monthly. 1986. m. $135. Magna Publications, 2718 Dryden Dr., Madison, WI 53704. TEL 608-246-3580. FAX 608-249-0355. Ed. Dennis Black. circ. 1,300. (back issues avail.)
  Description: Focuses on legal issues for college and university administrators.

340 150 US
PERSPECTIVES IN LAW AND PSYCHOLOGY. 1977. irreg., vol.8, 1988. price varies. Plenum Publishing Corp., 233 Spring St., New York, NY 10013. TEL 212-620-8000. FAX 212-463-0742. TELEX 23-421139. Ed. Bruce Dennis Sales. bibl.
  Refereed Serial

340 364 AT ISSN 0158-2720
PETTY SESSIONS REVIEW. 1967. bi-m. Aus.$35. Petty Publishing Pty. Ltd., c/o Travelaw, 126 Phillip St., Level 7, Sydney, N.S.W., Australia. Ed. R.J. Bartley. adv.; cum.index; circ. 750. (back issues avail.)

340 US ISSN 0887-7815
KF1297.D7
PHARMACEUTICAL LITIGATION REPORTER; the national journal of record of pharmaceutical litigation. 1985. m. $700. Andrews Publications, 1646 West Chester Pike, Box 1000, Westtown, PA 19395. TEL 215-399-6600. FAX 215-399-6610. Ed. Robert Sullivan. abstr.; bibl.; stat.; cum.index every 6 mos. (looseleaf format; back issues avail.)

PHARMACY LAW DIGEST. see PHARMACY AND PHARMACOLOGY

340 US
PHILADELPHIA BAR ASSOCIATION. LEGAL DIRECTORY. 1880. a. $21.50. Winchell Co., 1617 John F. Kennedy Blvd., Ste. 1245, Philadelphia, PA 19103. TEL 215-563-2700. FAX 215-563-4911. adv.; circ. 27,500.
  Description: Lists attorneys, law firms, legal associations in the greater Philadelphia area.

340 CN
THE PHILANTHROPIST. 1972. q. Can.$40. (Canadian Bar Association, Ontario Branch) Agora Foundation, Publishing and Printing Services, 36 Bessemer Ct., No.3 Box 116, Concord, Ont. M4W 2C9, Canada. TEL 416-364-4609. FAX 416-925-8639. Ed. John Gregory. adv.; bk.rev.; circ. 1,000. (also avail. in microfilm from UMI; reprint service avail. from UMI) Indexed: Ind.Can.L.P.L.

340 PH ISSN 0031-7721
LAW
PHILIPPINE LAW JOURNAL. (Text in English) 1914. 4/yr. P.100($20) University of the Philippines, Law Publishing House, Diliman, Quezon City, Philippines. Ed. Eloisa D. Palazo. bk.rev.; index; circ. 821. (also avail. in microfilm from BHP,WSH; reprint service avail. from RRI,WSH) Indexed: C.L.I., Foreign Leg.Per., HR Rep., Ind.Phil.Per., Leg.Per.
  —BLDSC shelfmark: 6456.060000.

340 PH ISSN 0115-7205
PHILIPPINE LAW REPORT. (Text in English) 1974. m. P.45($12) University of the Philippines, Law Publishing House, Diliman, Quezon City, Philippines.

340 US
PIRSIG ON MINNESOTA PLEADING. 1987. 2 base vols. (plus suppl.), latest 5th ed., 1991. $175. Butterworth Legal Publishers (Salem) (Subsidiary of: Reed International PLC), 90 Stiles Rd., Salem, NH 03079. TEL 800-548-4001. FAX 603-898-9858. Ed. Maynard E. Pirsig.
  Description: Guide to pleading under the Minnesota Rules of Civil Procedure.

340 US ISSN 0032-0331
KFP52.P5
PITTSBURGH LEGAL JOURNAL. 1963. m. $70. Allegheny County Bar Association, 436 7th Ave., Ste. 400, Pittsburgh, PA 15219-1818. TEL 412-261-6161. FAX 412-261-3622. Ed.Bd. adv.; bk.rev.; index; circ. 6,300. Indexed: Law Ofc.Info.Svc.
  Description: Pittsburgh court opinions and announcements of importance to members of the association.

340 SZ
PLAEDOYER; das Magazin fuer Recht und Politik. (Text in French and German) 1976. bi-m. 89 Fr.($30) Swiss Association of Democratic Lawyers, Postfach 421, CH-8026 Zuerich, Switzerland. FAX 2910820. TELEX 3632321. Ed. Bennie Koprio. adv.; bk.rev.; circ. 3,000.
  Formerly (until 1983): Volk und Recht.

340 690 AT ISSN 0727-792X
PLANNING AND DEVELOPMENT SERVICE (NEW SOUTH WALES). 1980. 6/yr. Aus.$260. Law Book Co. Ltd., 44-50 Waterloo Rd., N. Ryde, N.S.W. 2113, Australia. TEL 02-887-0177. FAX 02-888-9706. TELEX ASBOOK 27995. Ed. S. White. (looseleaf format)
  Formerly (until 1989): Building, Planning and Development Service (New South Wales) (ISSN 0727-7911)
  Description: Covers land and environment court, land subdivision and building, environmental and planning law.

PLANNING & ENVIRONMENT LAW SERVICE - VICTORIA. see ENVIRONMENTAL STUDIES

347.91 UK
PLANNING APPEAL DECISIONS. 1986. bi-m. £190. Sweet & Maxwell, South Quay Plaza, 8th Fl., 183 Marsh Wall, London E14 9FT, England. TEL 071-538-8686. FAX 071-538-9508. Eds. Christopher Beaumont, W.G. Nutley.

PLANO DA SAFRA ACUCAR E ALCOOL. see AGRICULTURE — Crop Production And Soil

PLASTIC WASTE STRATEGIES. see PUBLIC HEALTH AND SAFETY

POLICE MISCONDUCT AND CIVIL RIGHTS LAW REPORT. see *CRIMINOLOGY AND LAW ENFORCEMENT*

340 364 US
POLICE PLAINTIFF. 1980. q. $35. North Publishing, Box 3132, Glen Ellyn, IL 60138-3132. TEL 312-469-3211. Ed. Kenneth E. North. index. (back issues avail.)
Description: Covers law suits brought by law enforcement personnel.

340 IT ISSN 0032-3063
POLITICA DEL DIRITTO. 1970. q. L.110000. Societa Editrice Il Mulino, Strada Maggiore, 37, 40125 Bologna, Italy. TEL 051-256011. FAX 051-256034. Ed. Stefano Rodota. adv.; cum.index; circ. 1,700. (tabloid format; back issues avail.) Indexed: P.A.I.S.For.Lang.Ind.
—BLDSC shelfmark: 6543.858000.

340 628.5 CN ISSN 0827-2123
POLLUTION LAW REPORTING SERVICE. 1972. m. Can.$250. Business Law Reporting Limited, Box 908, Cobourg, Ont. K9A 4W4, Canada. TEL 416-372-0253.

POLLUTION PREVENTION REVIEW. see *ENVIRONMENTAL STUDIES — Waste Management*

347.016 FR
POMPADOUR NOTARIAT 2000; revue independante d'animation et de promotion du notariat francais. 1956. m. 200 F. 19230 Pompadour, France. Ed. Louis Reillier. adv.; bk.rev.; illus.; stat.

340 US ISSN 0739-0203
PONTIAC - OAKLAND AND COUNTY LEGAL NEWS. 1927. w. $45. Pontiac-Oakland County Legal News Publishing Co., Inc., 500 W. Huron, Ste. 102, Box 430238, Pontiac, MI 48343-0238. TEL 313-338-4567. FAX 313-338-4240. Ed. Nancy L. Howarth. adv.; bk.rev.; circ. 1,500. (back issues avail.)

POPULAR GOVERNMENT. see *POLITICAL SCIENCE*

340 PO
PORTUGAL. MINISTERIO DA JUSTICIA. BOLETIM. no.241, 1974. a. Esc.19,000($120) Ministerio da Justica, Gabinete de Gestao Financeira, Of. Subdirector-Geral, Praca do Comercio, 1194 Lisbon Codex, Portugal. bk.rev.; bibl.; circ. 5,500.

POWER PLANT REPORT (E I A 759). (Energy Information Administration) see *ENERGY*

340 US
POYNTER CENTER NEWSLETTER. 1986. 2/yr. free. Poynter Center for the Study of Ethics and American Institutions, 410 N. Park Ave., Bloomington, IN 47405. TEL 812-855-0261. Ed. Judith A. Granbois. circ. 1,200.
Description: Reports center activities and projects.

340 PL ISSN 0138-0508
PRACE POPULARNONAUKOWE. BIBLIOTECZKA PRAWNICZA. (Subseries of: Prace Popularnonaukowe (ISSN 0079-4805)) 1982. irregr. no.4, 1988. price varies. Towarzystwo Naukowe w Toruniu, Ul. Wysoka 16, 87-100 Torun, Poland. TEL 48-56-239411. TELEX 552388 FSBH PL. circ. 6,500.

340 UK
PRACTICAL CONVEYANCING PRECEDENTS. irreg. £115. Longman Group UK Ltd., Law, Tax and Finance Division, 21-27 Lambs Conduit St., London WC1N 3NJ, England. TEL 071-242-2548. FAX 071-831-8119. Ed. Trevor Aldridge. (looseleaf format)
Description: Conveyancing forms and precedents.

340 AT ISSN 0048-508X
PRACTICAL FORMS AND PRECEDENTS. 1957-1987; resumed 1990. 4/yr. Aus.$275. Law Book Co. Ltd., 44-50 Waterloo Rd., North Ryde, N.S.W. 2113, Australia. TEL 02-887-0177. FAX 02-888-9706. TELEX ASBOOK 27995. Ed. Ian Salmon.
Description: Comprises a comprehensive set of precedents covering the entire range of commercial and property matters including revenue notes relevant to N.S.W.

340 610 US
PRACTICAL GUIDE TO PREVENTING LEGAL MALPRACTICE. 1983. base vol. (plus a. suppl.). $95. Shepard's - McGraw-Hill, Inc., Box 35300, Colorado Springs, CO 80935-3530. TEL 800-525-2474.
Description: Offers practical ideas that can be implemented in everyday practice to reduce and eliminate malpractice risk.

340 US ISSN 0032-6429
K16
THE PRACTICAL LAWYER. 1955. 8/yr. $35. American Law Institute, Committee on Continuing Professional Education, 4025 Chestnut St., Philadelphia, PA 19104. TEL 215-243-1604. FAX 215-243-1664. (Co-sponsor: American Bar Association) Ed. Mark T. Cornoll. adv.; bk.rev.; illus.; index, cum.index every 5 yrs.; circ. 10,275. (also avail. in microform from UMI; reprint service avail. from UMI) Indexed: Account.Ind. (1974-), Bank.Lit.Ind., C.L.I., L.I.I., L.R.I., Law Ofc.Info.Svc., Leg.Cont., Leg.Info.Manage.Ind., Leg.Per.
—BLDSC shelfmark: 6594.700000.
Description: Forms, checklists and practical articles for attorneys.

340 US
▼**THE PRACTICAL LITIGATOR.** 1990. 6/yr. $35. American Law Institute, Committee on Continuing Professional Education, 4025 Chestnut St., Philadelphia, PA 19104. TEL 215-243-1604. FAX 215-243-1664. (Co-sponsor: American Bar Association) Ed. Mark T. Carroll. adv.; illus.; index, cum.index every 5 yrs.; circ. 2,900.
Description: Practical articles for litigation attorneys.

340 336 US
THE PRACTICAL TAX LAWYER. 1986. q. $35 to non-members; members $27.50. American Law Institute, Committee on Continuing Professional Education, 4025 Chestnut St., Philadelphia, PA 19104. TEL 215-243-1604. FAX 215-243-1664. (Co-sponsor: American Bar Association) Ed. Mark T. Carroll. adv.; cum.index; circ. 3,643. Indexed: Account.Ind. (1986-), C.L.I., Leg.Per.
Description: Forms, checklists and practical articles for tax lawyers.

340 UK ISSN 0954-6421
PRACTITIONERS' CHILD LAW BULLETIN. 10/yr. £85. Longman Law, Tax and Finance, 21-27 Lamb's Conduit St., London WC1N 3NJ, England. TEL 0279-429655. (Subscr. to: Longman Group UK Ltd., Fourth Ave., Pinnacles, Harlow, Essex CM19 5AA, England) bk.rev.
—BLDSC shelfmark: 6598.074700.
Formerly: Practitioners' Child Law Journal.

340 US
▼**PRACTITIONER'S GUIDE TO THE OKLAHOMA UNIFORM CONSUMER CREDIT CODE.** 1990. base vol. (plus a. suppl.). $89.50. Butterworth Legal Publishers (Salem) (Subsidiary of: Reed International PLC), 90 Stiles Rd., Salem, NH 03079. TEL 800-548-4001. FAX 603-898-9858. Ed.Bd. (looseleaf format)
Description: Covers credit sales, loans and other consumer finance transactions governed by the UCCC, as well as rent-to-own deals, pawnshop transactions and other special purpose agreements.

349 IS ISSN 0017-7571
PRAKLIT. (Text in Hebrew) 1942. q. IS.0.25 to non-members. Israel Bar Association, Box 14152, Tel-Aviv, Israel. Ed. A. Gabrieli. adv.; bk.rev.; pat.; index; circ. 6,500. Indexed: Foreign Leg.Per., Ind.Heb.Per.
—BLDSC shelfmark: 4262.470000.

347 NE ISSN 0165-0025
PRAKTIJKGIDS. 1939. fortn. fl.0.38 per page. Gouda Quint B.V., P.O. Box 1148, 6801 MK Arnhem, Netherlands. TEL 3185-454762. FAX 3185-514509. adv. Indexed: Key to Econ.Sci.
Description: Decisions of the Dutch Magistrates Courts.

340 BU ISSN 0032-6968
PRAVNA MISAL. (Contents page in French, Russian) 1957. 6/yr. 1.10 lv. per no. (Bulgarska Akademiia na Naukite, Institut za Pravni Nauki) Publishing House of the Bulgarian Academy of Sciences, Acad. G. Bonchev St., Bldg. 6, 1113 Sofia, Bulgaria. (Dist. by: Hemus, 6, Rouski Blvd., 1000 Sofia, Bulgaria) Ed. Stefan Pavlov. bk.rev.; index; circ. 3,600. Indexed: BSL Econ.
—BLDSC shelfmark: 0131.100000.

340 CS ISSN 0079-4929
PRAVNEHISTORICKE STUDIE. (Text in Czech; summaries in French, German, Russian) 1955. irreg., vol.29, 1989. price varies. (Czechoslovak Academy of Sciences) Academia, Publishing House of the Czechoslovak Academy of Sciences, Vodickova 40, 112 29 Prague 1, Czechoslovakia. TEL 23-63-065. Indexed: Amer.Hist.& Life, CERDIC.

340 CS ISSN 0551-9039
PRAVNICKE STUDIE. (Text in Slovak; summaries in German and Russian; contents page in French, German, Russian and Slovak) 1953. a. fl.30 per no. (Slovenska Akademia Vied, Ustav Statu a Prava) Veda, Publishing House of the Slovak Academy of Sciences, Klemensova 19, 814 30 Bratislava, Czechoslovakia. (Dist. in Western countries by: John Benjamins B.V., Amsteldijk 44, Amsterdam (Z.), Netherlands) charts; stat. Indexed: Geo.Abstr.

340 CS ISSN 0324-7007
PRAVNIK/LAWYER. (Text in Czech; occasional summaries in English, French, German, Russian) 1961. m. DM.186. (Czechoslovak Academy of Sciences, Institute of State and Law) Academia, Publishing House of the Czechoslovak Academy of Sciences, Vodickova 40, 112 29 Prague 1, Czechoslovakia. TEL 20-16-20. (Dist. in Western countries by: Kubon & Sagner, P.O. Box 34 01 08, 8000 Munich 34, Germany) Ed. Miroslav Dolezal. bk.rev.; circ. 3,700. Indexed: CERDIC.

340 CS ISSN 0032-6984
PRAVNY OBZOR/LAW REVIEW. 1917. 10/yr. 120 Kcs.($24) (Slovenska Akademia Vied, Ustav Statu a Prava) Veda, Publishing House of the Slovak Academy of Sciences, Klemensova 19, 814 30 Bratislava, Czechoslovakia. (Dist. in Western countries by: John Benjamins B.V., Amsteldijk 44, Amsterdam (Z.), Netherlands) Ed. Jan Azud. bibl.; index; circ. 2,200. Indexed: Geo.Abstr., World Bibl.Soc.Sec.
Description: Covers actual problems of law theory and practice. Explores questions regarding all areas of law.

340 CS
PRAVO A ZAKONNOST; casopis pro pravni praxi. (Text in Czech or Slovak) 1952. 10/yr. 60 Kcs. Ministerstvo Spravedlnosti Ceske Republiky, Vysehradska 16, 128 10 Prague 2, Czechoslovakia. TEL 2-294545. FAX 2-531322. (Subscr. to: Artia, Ve Smeckach 30, 111 27 Prague 1, Czechoslovakia) Ed. Alena Winterova. bk.rev.; bibl.; circ. 7,100.
Formerly: Socialisticka Zakonnost (ISSN 0037-8305)

340 PL
PRAWO. (Text in Polish; summaries in English, French or Russian) 1961. irreg., no.138, 1989. price varies. Adam Mickiewicz University Press, Nowowiejskiego 55, 61-734 Poznan, Poland. TEL 527-380. FAX 61-526425. TELEX 413260 UAMPL. Indexed: Canon Law Abstr.
Formerly: Uniwersytet im. Adama Mickiewicza w Poznaniu. Wydzial Prawa. Prace (ISSN 0083-4262)
Description: Contains current research results of one author in the field of law, including Ph.D. works and monographs.

340 PL ISSN 0551-9101
PRAWO I ZYCIE. 1956. w. $6.50 for 3 mos. Oferta dla Kazdego, Spolka z o.o., Ul. Wiejska 12, 00-490 Warsaw, Poland. TEL 48-22-272466. FAX 48-22-2675. Ed. Andrzej Dobrzynski. adv.; bk.rev.; circ. 120,000. (looseleaf format; back issues avail.)

PRAXIS DES BUNDESGERICHTS. see *PUBLIC ADMINISTRATION*

340 200 FR ISSN 0758-802X
PRAXIS JURIDIQUE ET RELIGION. (Text in French; summaries in English, French) 1984. s-a. 250 F. (typically set in Jan.). (Universite de Strasbourg II) CERDIC Publications, 2 Rue Goethe, Palais Universitaire, F-67083 Strasbourg, France. TEL 88-22-97-09. Ed. Marie Zimmermann. adv.; circ. 1,000. (back issues avail.) Indexed: Bull.Signal., Cath.Ind., Rel.Ind.One.
—BLDSC shelfmark: 6603.171370.
Description: Research in the fields of Christian and non-Christian canon, ecclesiastical and religious law and theology.

LAW

340 US ISSN 0741-1162
KF287
PRE LAW JOURNAL. 1983. 3/yr. $9.75. Legal Institute, 3250 Wilshire Blvd., No. 1000, Los Angeles, CA 90010. TEL 213-487-6268. Ed. Herman B. Lancaster. circ. 300. **Indexed:** C.L.I.

340 CI
PREGLED SUDSKE PRAKSE. (Issued as Supplement to Nasa Zakonitost, by Ustavni Sud Hrvatske and Other Legislative Bodies) 1972. irreg. (Vrhovni Sud) Narodne Novine, Zagreb, Ratkajev Prolaz 4, Zagreb, Croatia. (Co-sponsors: Croatia. Ustavni Sud; Visi Privredni Sud u Zagrebu) Ed. Ivan Salinovic.

PRESERVATION LAW REPORTER. see *ENVIRONMENTAL STUDIES*

340 II
PREVENTION OF FOOD ADULTERATION CASES. (Text in English) 1972. m. Rs.120. International Law Book Co., Nijhawan Bldg., 1562 Church Rd., Kashmere Gate, Delhi 6, India. Ed. Swarn Bhatia Nijhawan. bibl.

340 US ISSN 0363-0048
KF4547.8
PREVIEW OF UNITED STATES SUPREME COURT CASES. 1963-1973; resumed 1982. irreg. (10-12/yr.). $120. American Bar Association, Public Education Division, 750 N. Lake Shore Dr., Chicago, IL 60611. TEL 312-988-5728. FAX 312-988-5494. Ed. Charles Williams. index; circ. 3,120.
● Also available online. Vendor(s): WESTLAW.
Description: Analyzes each case orally argued before the Supreme Court; published by the Public Education Division of the American Bar Association.

PRIMER OF LABOR RELATIONS. see *BUSINESS AND ECONOMICS — Labor And Industrial Relations*

340 323.4 US
PRIVACY LAW AND PRACTICE. (Issued in 3 vols. with supplements) 1987. irreg. Matthew Bender & Co., Inc., 11 Penn Plaza, New York, NY 10001. TEL 212-967-7707. Ed. George B. Trubow. (looseleaf format)
Description: Provides expert analysis of pertinent federal, state and constitutional law for a broad spectrum of privacy issues. Includes practical guidance and procedural considerations.

PRIVACY TIMES. see *POLITICAL SCIENCE — Civil Rights*

PRIVATE LETTER RULINGS. see *BUSINESS AND ECONOMICS — Public Finance, Taxation*

PRIVATE SECURITY CASE LAW REPORTER; the security professional's digest of state & federal court decisions. see *CRIMINOLOGY AND LAW ENFORCEMENT — Security*

340 YU ISSN 0032-9002
K16
PRIVREDNO PRAVNI PRIRUCNIK; za pravnu opstu i kadrovsku sluzbu privrednih i ostalih radnih organizacija. 1963. m. 5520000 din.($84.50) Skupstina Grada Beograd, Privredno Pravni Prirucnik, Cika Ljubina 16-I, 11000 Belgrade, Yugoslavia. TEL 636-609. Ed. Vojislav Kukoljac. adv.; circ. 3,600.
—BLDSC shelfmark: 6617.073000.

340 BE
PRO JUSTITIA; revue politique de droit. 1973. q. Foulek Ringelheim, Ed. & Pub., 62 rue Emile van Driessche, 1060 Brussels, Belgium.

333.33 US ISSN 0164-0372
KF566.A3
PROBATE & PROPERTY. 1959. 6/yr. $40 (foreign $52). American Bar Association, Real Property, Probate and Trust Law Section, 750 N. Lake Shore Dr., Chicago, IL 60611. TEL 312-988-5591. Ed. Ann E. Houle. adv.; bk.rev.; charts; illus.; circ. 37,500. **Indexed:** Account.Ind. (1988-), C.L.I., L.R.I., Leg.Per.
● Also available online. Vendor(s): WESTLAW.
Former titles (until 1987): Probate and Property Newsletter; American Bar Association. Section of Real Property, Probate and Trust Law. Newsletter (ISSN 0569-3357)
Description: Recent developments in estate, trust, and real property law.

340 US ISSN 0737-3112
K16
PROBATE LAW JOURNAL. 1982. 3/yr. $15. (National College of Probate Judges) Boston University, School of Law, 765 Commonwealth Ave., Boston, MA 02215. TEL 617-353-4797. Dir. Faye G. Yoffa Stone. circ. 1,000. **Indexed:** Leg.Per.

340 US ISSN 1050-5342
KFO144.A15
▼**PROBATE LAW JOURNAL OF OHIO.** 1990. bi-m. $150. Banks - Baldwin Law Publishing Co., University Center, Box 1974, Cleveland, OH 44106. TEL 216-721-7373. FAX 216-721-8055. Ed. Robert M. Brucken.
Description: Analysis of new legislation, rules, court decisions, developments in Ohio probate, estate planning, and juvenile law and practice.

340 US
PROBATE PRACTICE REPORTER. 1989. m. $235. Shepard's - McGraw-Hill, Inc., Box 35300, Colorado Springs, CO 80935-3530. TEL 719-475-7230. Ed. William Jordan.

343 US ISSN 0276-6965
KF9750.A59
PROBATION AND PAROLE LAW REPORTS. 1979. m. $98. Knehans-Miller Publications, Box 88, Warrensburg, MO 64093. TEL 816-429-1102. Ed. Dane C. Miller. index. (looseleaf format; back issues avail.)
Formerly: Probation and Parole Law Summaries.
Description: Summaries and verbatim excerpts of all Federal and State Appellate Court decisions relating to probation and parole. Indexed by subject and jurisdiction.

340 IT
PROCESSO LEGISLATIVO NEL PARLAMENTO ITALIANO. no.3, 1974. irreg. (Universita degli Studi di Firenze, Facolta di Scienze Politiche) Casa Editrice Dott. A. Giuffre, Via Busto Arsizio 40, 20151 Milan, Italy. TEL 02-38000905. FAX 02-3809582. Ed. Alberto Predieri.

349 LE ISSN 0032-9649
K16
PROCHE-ORIENT ETUDES JURIDIQUES. (Text in Arabic, French) 1967. a. £L120. Universite Saint Joseph, Faculte de Droit et des Sciences Politiques, Rue Huvelin, Box 293, Beirut, Lebanon. (Foreign subscr. addr.: Office du Livre, 14 bis rue Jean Ferrandi, 75006 Paris, France) Ed. I. Najjar. **Indexed:** Refug.Abstr.
Formerly: Etudes de Droit Libanais.

340 AT
PROCTOR. 1982. m. (11/yr.). Aus.$45 (foreign Aus.$55). Queensland Law Society, Inc., Law Society House, 179 Ann St., Brisbane, Qld. 4000, Australia. TEL 07-2335888. adv.; index; circ. 4,000.
Description: Law and legal practice in Queensland.

340 640.73 UK
PRODUCT LIABILITY & SAFETY ENCYCLOPEDIA. (In 2 vols.) irreg. (2-3/yr.) $435. Butterworth & Co. (Publishers) Ltd. (Subsidiary of: Reed International PLC), 88 Kingsway, London WC2B 6AB, England. TEL 71-405-6900. FAX 71-405-1332. TELEX 95678. (US addr.: Butterworth Legal Publishers, 90 Stiles Rd., Salem, NH 03079. TEL 800-548-4001) (looseleaf format)

PRODUCT LIABILITY LAW AND STRATEGY. see *BUSINESS AND ECONOMICS — Production Of Goods And Services*

340 US
PRODUCT LIABILITY LAW IN OKLAHOMA. base vol. (plus suppl.). $120. Butterworth Legal Publishers (Salem) (Subsidiary of: Reed International PLC), 90 Stiles Rd., Salem, NH 03079. TEL 800-548-4001. FAX 603-898-9858. Ed. Vicki Lawrence MacDougall. (looseleaf format)
Description: Analysis of Oklahoma law concerning products liability and related causes of action, highlighting advantages and disadvantages of each theory of recovery.

346.066 368 US ISSN 0164-9574
K953.A13
PRODUCT LIABILITY TRENDS; a monthly analysis of product liability developments. m. $195. National Legal Research Group, Inc., 2421 Ivy Rd., Box 7187, Charlottesville, VA 22906-7187. TEL 800-446-1870. FAX 804-295-4667. Ed. Jeremy Taylor.
Description: Analyses of recent cases and reports of legislative developments in product liability trends.

340 338 US
PRODUCTS LIABILITY. 1981. base vol. (plus a. suppl.). $95. Shepard's - McGraw-Hill, Inc., Box 35300, Colorado Springs, CO 80935-3530. TEL 800-525-2474.
Description: Covers traditional causes of action such as negligence, misrepresentation and warranty under the Uniform Commercial Code. Defines the outer boundaries of strict liability in tort.

340 338 US
PRODUCTS LIABILITY: DESIGN AND MANUFACTURING DEFECTS. 1986. base vol. (plus a. suppl.). $95. Shepard's - McGraw-Hill, Inc., Box 35300, Colorado Springs, CO 80935-3530. TEL 800-525-2474.
Description: Explores all factors of product liability, including manufacturer's responsibility, advertising material, packaging, instruction manuals, warnings and labels.

340 640.73 US
PRODUCTS LIABILITY LAW JOURNAL. 1989. q. $79.50. Butterworth Legal Publishers (Salem) (Subsidiary of: Reed International PLC), 90 Stiles Rd., Salem, NH 03079. TEL 603-898-9664. FAX 603-898-9858. Ed. Warren W. Eginton.
Description: Includes articles on current products liability problems and emerging areas of concern.

330 340 US ISSN 0162-122X
PRODUCTS LIABILITY REPORTER. 1963. fortn. $560. Commerce Clearing House, Inc., 4025 W. Peterson Ave., Chicago, IL 60646. TEL 312-583-8500. Ed. Daniel L. Newquist. circ. 2,414. (looseleaf format; also avail. in microfilm) **Indexed:** I.P.A.
● Also available online.

PROFESSIONAL APARTMENT MANAGEMENT. see *REAL ESTATE*

340 US ISSN 1042-5675
PROFESSIONAL LAWYER. q. free. American Bar Association, Center for Professional Responsibility, 750 N. Lake Shore Dr., Chicago, IL 60611. TEL 312-988-5000.
Description: Provides a forum for the exchange of views and ideas on professional issues for bar leaders, lawyers, law school educators, and others interested in fostering professionalism.

340 US
▼**PROFESSIONAL LIABILITY LITIGATION REPORTER.** 1991. m. $425. Andrews Publications, 1646 West Chester Pike, Box 1000, Westtown, PA 19395. TEL 215-399-6600. FAX 215-399-6610. Ed. Gary Crouse. bibl.; stat.; s-a. cum.index. (looseleaf format; back issues avail.)
Description: Focuses on lawsuits filed against accountants, attorneys, investment bankers, financial advisors, rating services and other financial professionals.

340 US ISSN 0145-3505
KF1289.A59
PROFESSIONAL LIABILITY REPORTER; recent decisions of national significance. 1976. m. $305. (Litigation Research Group) Shepard's - McGraw-Hill, Inc., Box 35300, Colorado Springs, CO 80935-3530. TEL 719-488-3000. Ed. William Jordan, Esq. bibl.; index. (looseleaf format; back issues avail.)
Description: Summarizes and analyzes reported and most unreported decisions pertaining to professional liability litigation.

PROFESSIONAL LIABILITY TODAY. see *INSURANCE*

340 US ISSN 1043-2051
PROFESSIONAL LICENSING REPORT. 1988. m. $156. Paxton Associates, 9904 Foxborough Cir., Rockville, MD 20850. TEL 301-869-4889. Ed. Anne Paxton. circ. 350.
Description: Covers legal and legislative issues affecting the licensing and regulation of professionals in all fields with news on state requirements, relevant court decisions, and discussions of professional ethics.

340   UK   ISSN 0267-078X
KD1978.A13
PROFESSIONAL NEGLIGENCE; a journal of liability, ethics and discipline. 1985. 4/yr. £95($155) Tolley Publishing Co. Ltd., Tolley House, 2 Addiscombe Rd., Croydon, Surrey CR9 5AF, England. Ed. David K. Allen. Indexed: C.L.I., Hlth.Ind.
—BLDSC shelfmark: 8863.686555.

PROFITABILITY BY LINE BY STATE. see INSURANCE — Abstracting, Bibliographies, Statistics

340 333.33   AT   ISSN 0727-6346
PROPERTY LAW AND PRACTICE IN QUEENSLAND. 1982. 3/yr. Aus.$175. Law Book Co. Ltd., 44-40 Waterloo Rd., N. Ryde, N.S.W. 2113, Australia. TEL 02-887-0177. Eds. W.D. Duncan, R.J. Vann. (looseleaf format)

346   UK   ISSN 0144-6517
PROPERTY LAW BULLETIN. 1980. 10/yr. £105($165) Longman Group UK Ltd., Law, Tax and Finance Division, 21-27 Lamb's Conduit St., London WC1N 3NJ, England. TEL 071-242-2548. FAX 071-831-8119. TELEX 295445. Ed. John M. Samson. bk.rev.; circ. 1,350.
—BLDSC shelfmark: 6927.308000.
Description: Information on all aspects of property law.

347   UK
KD826.A2
PROPERTY, PLANNING AND COMPENSATION REPORTS. 1950. 6/yr. (3 nos./vol., 2 vols./yr.). £146. Sweet & Maxwell, South Quay Plaza, 8th Floor, 183 Marsh Wall, London E14 9FT, England. TEL 071-538-8686. FAX 071-538-9508. Ed. Margaret Unwin. (reprint service avail. from RRI) Indexed: C.L.I., Leg.Per., RICS.
•Also available online. Vendor(s): Mead Data Central.
Former titles: Property and Compensation Reports (ISSN 0033-1295); Planning and Compensation Reports.

343   US   ISSN 0027-6383
K16
PROSECUTOR. 1965. q. membership. National District Attorneys Association, 1033N. Fairfax St. Ste. 200, Alexandria, VA 22314. TEL 703-549-9222. Ed. Jack E. Yelverton. adv.; bk.rev.; illus.; circ. 7,500. Indexed: C.L.I., Crim.Just.Abstr., L.R.I., Leg.Per.

340 640.73   US
PROTECTING CONSUMER RIGHTS. 1987. base vol. (plus a. suppl.). $95. Shepard's - McGraw-Hill, Inc., Box 35300, Colorado Springs, CO 80935-3530. TEL 800-525-2474.
Description: Pragmatic approach to solving consumer problems.

340   GW
PROZESSRECHTLICHE ABHANDLUNGEN. (Text in German) 1952. irreg. Carl Heymanns Verlag KG, Luxemburgerstr. 449, 5000 Cologne 41, Germany. TEL 0221-46010-0. Ed. Hanns Pruetting. circ. 500. (back issues avail.)

340 150   US
PSYCHIATRIC & PSYCHOLOGICAL EVIDENCE. 1986. base vol. (plus a. suppl.). $95. Shepard's - McGraw-Hill, Inc., Box 35300, Colorado Springs, CO 80935-3530. TEL 800-525-2474.
Description: Examines and evaluates evidence from psychiatrists and psychologists in civil and criminal proceedings to provide guidelines for admissibility.

PUBLIC AND LOCAL ACTS OF THE LEGISLATURE OF THE STATE OF MICHIGAN. see PUBLIC ADMINISTRATION — Municipal Government

PUBLIC ASSISTANCE REPORT. see SOCIAL SERVICES AND WELFARE

340   US   ISSN 0033-3441
K16
PUBLIC CONTRACT LAW JOURNAL. 1967. q. $30 to non-members. American Bar Association, Public Contract Law Section, 750 N. Lake Shore Dr., Chicago, IL 60611. TEL 312-988-5000. Ed. Matthew J. Simchak. (reprint service avail. from RRI) Indexed: C.L.I., L.R.I., Leg.Per.
•Also available online. Vendor(s): WESTLAW.
—BLDSC shelfmark: 6963.100000.
Description: Articles by leading authorities on all phases of federal, state, and local procurement and grant law.

340   US   ISSN 0569-3314
KF849.A1
PUBLIC CONTRACT NEWSLETTER. 1965. q. membership only. American Bar Association, Public Contract Law Section, 750 N. Lake Shore Dr., Chicago, IL 60611. TEL 312-988-5000. Ed. Martin J. Harty. Indexed: C.L.I., L.R.I.
Description: Covers current developments in federal grant law, recent developments in state and local public contract law, upcoming educational programs.

PUBLIC EYE (MADISON). see CONSUMER EDUCATION AND PROTECTION

340   US   ISSN 0742-5325
PUBLIC JUSTICE REPORT. 1977. bi-m. $12. Center for Public Justice, 321 8th St., N.E., Washington, DC 20002-6107. TEL 202-546-0489. Ed. James W. Skillen. bk.rev.; circ. 2,100. (looseleaf format; back issues avail.)
Description: Analysis and commentary of domestic and international affairs.

347.2   US   ISSN 0148-6489
K16
PUBLIC LAND & RESOURCES LAW DIGEST. 1962. s-a. $29.50. Rocky Mountain Mineral Law Foundation, Porter Administration Bldg., 7039 E. 18th Ave., Denver, CO 80220. TEL 303-321-8100. FAX 303-321-7657. Ed. Mark H. Holland. index; circ. 500. Indexed: Energy Ind., Energy Info.Abstr., Environ.Abstr., GeoRef., Mar.Aff.Bibl., P.A.I.S.
—BLDSC shelfmark: 6967.130000.
Formerly (until vol.8): Rocky Mountain Mineral Law Review (ISSN 0035-7618)
Description: Covers mining, oil, gas and water law.

342   UK   ISSN 0033-3565
K16
PUBLIC LAW; the constitutional and administrative law of the commonwealth. 1956. q. £75. Sweet & Maxwell, South Quay Plaza, 8th Floor, 183 Marsh Wall, London E14 9FT, England. TEL 071-538-8686. FAX 071-538-9508. Ed. A.W. Bradley. adv.; bk.rev.; index. (reprint service avail. from RRI) Indexed: Abstr.Bk.Rev.Curr.Leg.Per., ASSIA, C.L.I., Crim.Just.Abstr., L.R.I., Leg.Cont., Leg.Per.
—BLDSC shelfmark: 6967.150000.

342   JA
PUBLIC LAW REVIEW/KOHO KENKYU. 1949. q. (Japan Public Law Association - Nihon Koho Gakkai) Yuhikaku Publishing Co. Ltd., 2-17 Kanda Jimbo-cho, Chiyoda-ku, Tokyo 101, Japan.

340   AT   ISSN 1034-3024
PUBLIC LAW REVIEW. q. Aus.$175. Law Book Co. Ltd., 44-50 Waterloo Rd., North Ryde, N.S.W. 2113, Australia. TEL 02-887-0177. FAX 02-888-9706. TELEX ASBOOK 27995. Ed. Cheryl Sunders.
Description: Covers new and emerging developments in the law affecting government in Australia and New Zealand.

PUBLIC RADIO LEGAL HANDBOOK. see COMMUNICATIONS — Radio

340   AT
PUBLIC SERVICE NOTICES. fortn. Aus.$40. Law•Printer, P.O. Box 203, North Melbourne, Vic. 3051, Australia. TEL 03-320-0100. FAX 03-328-1657.

340 363.6   US   ISSN 0095-5086
KF2094.A1
PUBLIC UTILITIES LAW ANTHOLOGY. 1974. a. $149.95. International Library Law Book Publishers, Inc., 101 Lakeforest Blvd., Ste. 270, Bethesda, MD 20877. TEL 301-990-7755. FAX 301-990-7642. Ed. Donald J. Hoyes. bibl.; cum.index vols.1-14.
Description: Selected best U.S. law review articles, printed in their entirety, in the field of public utilities culled from over 900 U.S. law review journals.

THE PUNCH LIST. see BUSINESS AND ECONOMICS — Labor And Industrial Relations

340   II   ISSN 0033-4332
PUNJAB LAW REPORTER. (Text in English) 1900. fortn. Rs.150. 36 Sector 9-A, Chandigarh 19, India. Eds. Lalit Mohan Suri, Ravinder Mohan Suri. adv.; bk.rev.; index, cum.index every 5 yrs.

340 330   UA
QANOUN WAL IQTISAD/DROIT ET ECONOMIE POLITIQUE. (Text in Arabic, English) 1931. q. P.T.300. University of Cairo, Faculty of Law, Cairo, Egypt. Ed.Bd. bibl.; cum.index: 1931-1960, 1961-1970.

340.59 297   TS
AL-QISTAS/SCALES. (Text in Arabic) 1978. a. exchange basis. United Arab Emirates University, Faculty of Law and Islamic Jurisprudence, P.O. Box 15551, Al-Ain, United Arab Emirates. TEL 642500. TELEX 33521 JAMEAH EM. bk.rev.; circ. 500.
Description: Publishes legal studies and discussions of Islamic jurisprudence.

340   IT
QUADERNI FIORENTINI PER LA STORIA DEL PENSIERO GIURIDICO MODERNO. (Text in English, French, German, Italian and Spanish) 1972. a. (University of Florence, Centro di Studi per la Storia del Pensiero Giuridico Moderno) Casa Editrice Dott. A. Giuffre, Via Busto Arsizio 40, 20151 Milan, Italy. TEL 02-38000905. FAX 02-3809582.

340   IT
QUADERNI REGIONALI. 1982. q. L.90000 (foreign L.135000). Casa Editrice Dott. A. Giuffre, Via Busto Arsizio 40, 20151 Milan, Italy. TEL 02-38000905. FAX 02-3809582. Ed. Fausto Cuocolo. adv.; circ. 1,500.

340   IT
QUADRIMESTRE - RIVISTA DI DIRITTO PRIVATO. 1984. 3/yr. L.80000 (foreign L.120000). Casa Editrice Dott. A. Giuffre, Via Busto Arsizio 40, 20151 Milan, Italy. TEL 06-38000905. FAX 06-38009582.

QUALITY & RISK MANAGEMENT IN HEALTH CARE; an information service. see HOSPITALS

QUALITY ASSURANCE; good practice, regulation, and law. see BUSINESS AND ECONOMICS — Management

QUARTERLY LISTING OF ALIEN INSURERS. see INSURANCE

340   CN
QUEBEC (PROVINCE). COMMISSION DE PROTECTION DU TERRITOIRE AGRICOLE. DECISIONS. q. Can.$35. (Commission de Protection du Territoire Agricole) S O Q U I J, 276 St-Jacques ouest, Ste. 310, Montreal, Que. H2X 1N3, Canada. TEL 514-270-7172. (Subscr. to: Service Abonnements, 7 Chemin Bates, Outremont, Que. H2V 1V6, Canada)

354   CN   ISSN 0703-0762
KEQ180.A13
QUEBEC (PROVINCE). COMMISSION DES SERVICES JURIDIQUES. RAPPORT ANNUEL. 1973. a. Commission des Services Juridiques, C.P. 123, Succursale Desjardins, Montreal, Que. H5B 1B3, Canada. TEL 514-873-3562. FAX 514-873-8762. Ed. Jacques Lemaitre-Auger. circ. 1,600.

QUEBEC CORPORATION AND INCOME TAX LEGISLATION. see BUSINESS AND ECONOMICS — Public Finance, Taxation

340   US   ISSN 0048-6302
KF200
QUEENS BAR BULLETIN. 1936. 8/yr. $2.50. Queens County Bar Association, 90-35 148 St., Jamaica, NY 11435. TEL 718-291-4500. adv.; bibl.; charts; illus.; index; circ. 2,500.

342   CN   ISSN 0316-778X
K17
QUEEN'S LAW JOURNAL. 1968. 3/yr. $21 to individuals; institutions $39. Queen's University, Faculty of Law, Kingston, Ont. K7L 3N6, Canada. TEL 613-545-2220. FAX 613-545-6611. adv.; bk.rev.; circ. 900. Indexed: C.L.I., Ind.Can.L.P.L., Leg.Cont.

340   AT
QUEENSLAND CONVEYANCING LAW AND PRACTICE. (In 3 vols.) 1982. irreg. (approx. 10/yr.). C C H Australia Ltd., P.O. Box 230, North Ryde, N.S.W. 2113, Australia. TEL 02-888-2555. FAX 02-888-7324.

340   AT
QUEENSLAND DISTRICT COURTS PRACTICE. base vol. (plus updates 3/yr.). $265. Butterworths Pty. Ltd., 271-273 Lane Cove Rd., P.O. Box 345, North Ryde, N.S.W. 2113, Australia. TEL 02-887-3444. (looseleaf format)

340   AT   ISSN 0726-0784
QUEENSLAND LAW REPORTER. 1908. w. Aus.$105. Incorporated Council of Law Reporting, c/o Sec. Mrs. J.T. Mengel, P.O. Box 39, North Quay, Qld. 4002, Australia. TEL 07-227-4409. FAX 07-220-3782. circ. 1,040.

340   AT   ISSN 0313-4253
K17
QUEENSLAND LAW SOCIETY JOURNAL. 1971. 6/yr. Aus.$75 (foreign Aus.$100). Queensland Law Society, Inc., Law Society House, 179 Ann St., Brisbane, Qld. 4000, Australia. TEL 07-233-5888. FAX 07-233-5999. Ed. R.P.S. Smith. adv.; bk.rev.; index; circ. 4,000. (also avail. in microform from UMI) Indexed: C.L.I., L.R.I., Leg.Per.
Description: For Australian lawyers covering contract law, business and review law, criminal law and common law. Includes Queensland Law Society news and events.

340   AT   ISSN 0312-1658
LAW
QUEENSLAND LAWYER. 1907. bi-m. Law Book Co. Ltd., 44-50 Waterloo Rd., N. Ryde, N.S.W. 2113, Australia. TEL 02-887-0177. FAX 02-888-9706. TELEX ASBOOK 27995. Ed. Barnard Cains. bk.rev.; cum.index: 1907-1966. (tabloid format)
Formerly: Queensland Justice of the Peace and Reports (ISSN 0033-6181)
Description: Presents articles, comments and notes on recent developments and decisions. Reports on cases heard before the various courts of Australia.

340   AT
QUEENSLAND STATUTES ANNOTATIONS. base vol. (plus s-a. update). $150. Butterworths Pty. Ltd., 271-273 Lane Cove Rd., P.O. Box 345, North Ryde, N.S.W. 2113, Australia. TEL 02-335-4444. FAX 02-335-4655. (looseleaf format)

340   AT
QUEENSLAND UNIT & GROUP TITLES LAW AND PRACTICE. (In 2 vols.) 1980. irreg. (approx. 10/yr.) C C H Australia Ltd., P.O. Box 230, North Ryde, N.S.W. 2113, Australia. TEL 02-888-2555. FAX 02-888-7324.

340   AT   ISSN 1032-6693
QUEENSLAND UNIVERSITY OF TECHNOLOGY LAW JOURNAL. 1985. a. Aus.$15. Queensland University of Technology, Faculty of Law, George St., Brisbane, Qld. 4000, Australia. TEL 07-223-211. (Subscr. in U.S. to: Wm. W. Gaunt & Sons Inc., 3011 Gulf Dr., Holmes Beach, FL 34217-2199) circ. 500. (back issues avail.)
Formerly: Queensland Institute of Technology Law Journal.

340   IT
QUESTIONE GIUSTIZIA. 1982. N.S. q. L.85000 (foreign L.100000)(effective 1992). (Magistratura Democratica) Franco Angeli Editore, Viale Monza 106, 20127 Milan, Italy. TEL 02-28-27-651.

340   US
QUESTIONING TECHNIQUES AND TACTICS. 1982. base vol. (plus a. suppl.). $95. Shepard's - McGraw-Hill, Inc., Box 35300, Colorado Springs, CO 80935-3530. TEL 800-525-2474.
Description: Provides information on new techniques of cross-examination, innovative questioning tactics and proven methods of witness control to help deal with hostile witnesses and opposing counsel at both deposition and trial.

R I C O LAW REPORTER. (Racketeer Influenced and Corrupt Organizations) see COMPUTERS

340 332   BL
R T - INCOLA. 1971. 36/yr. (3/m.). $330. Editora Revista dos Tribunais, Rua Conde do Pinhal 78, 01501 Sao Paulo, Brazil. Ed. Arnaldo Malheiros. adv.; bk.rev.; index; circ. 11,000.
Formerly (until Jul. 1955): R T - Informa.

340   GW   ISSN 0723-0095
R W P. (Rechts- und Wirtschafts-Praxis); Blattei-Handbuch fuer das Steuer- und Wirtschaftsrecht. 1946. m. DM.313.80. Forkel-Verlag GmbH, Postfach 2120, 6200 Wiesbaden, Germany. TEL 0611-42785. FAX 0611-419545. Ed. Friedrich Vohl. adv.; bk.rev.; circ. 3,000. (looseleaf format)
Incorporates: R W P S Steuerrecht. Ausgabe A und B.
Description: Topical information and contributions on tax law and economic law.

RACHEL'S HAZARDOUS WASTE NEWS; providing news and resources to the movement for environmental justice. see ENVIRONMENTAL STUDIES

340   KR   ISSN 0132-1331
RADYANS'KE PRAVO; naukovo-praktychny zhurnal. (Text in Ukrainian) 1922. m. 8.40 Rub. (Ministerstvo Yustitsii Ukrainskoi S.S.R., Verkhovnyi Sud, Prokuratura) Izdatel'stvo Naukova Dumka, c/o Yu.A. Khramov, Dir, Ul. Repina, 3, Kiev 252 601, Ukraine. TEL 225-20-17. (Subscr. to: Mezhdunarodnaya Kniga, Moscow, G-200, Russia) (Co-sponsor: Akademiya Ukrainskoi S.S.R., Institut Derzhavy ta Prava) Ed. Y.G. Verbenko.
—BLDSC shelfmark: 0139.850000.

340   IT
RASSEGNA DI DIRITTO CIVILE. 1980. q. L.100000 to individuals; institutions L.160000; foreign L.190000(effective 1992). Edizioni Scientifiche Italiane S.p.A., Via Chiatamone, 7, 80121 Naples, Italy. TEL 081-7645768. FAX 081-7646477. Ed. Pietro Perlingieri. circ. 1,200.

340   IT   ISSN 0300-3485
RASSEGNA DI DIRITTO, LEGISLAZIONE E MEDICINA LEGALE VETERINARIA. (Text in Italian; summaries in English, French and Italian) 1967. q. L.40000 (foreign L.45000). Universita degli Studi di Milano, Istituto di Medicina Legale e Legislazione Veterinaria, Via Celoria 10, 20133 Milan, Italy. TEL 23-62-724. Ed. Pierluigi Canziani. adv.; bk.rev.; index; circ. 1,000.
—BLDSC shelfmark: 7294.132000.

340   IT   ISSN 0033-9512
RASSEGNA DI DIRITTO PUBBLICO. 1945. q. Via A. Falcone 249, 80127 Naples, Italy. Ed. Alfonso Tesauro. index; circ. 1,000.

340   IT
RASSEGNA FORENSE. 1989. q. L.60000 (foreign L.90000). Casa Editrice Dott. A. Giuffre, Via Busto Arsizio 40, 20151 Milan, Italy. TEL 06-38000905. FAX 06-38009582.

RASSEGNA GIURIDICA DELL'ENERGIA ELETTRICA. see ENGINEERING — Electrical Engineering

349   IT
RASSEGNA PARLAMENTARE. 1959. q. L.30000 (foreign L.60000). Istituto per la Ricerca Normativa, Palazzo Grazioli, Via del Plebiscito 102, Rome 00186, Italy. TEL 06-6793449.
Former titles: I S L E Rassegna Parlamentare (Istituto di Studi Legislativa); I S L E Rassegna Parlamentare Schedario Legislativo (ISSN 0033-9814)

340   UK   ISSN 0048-6817
RATING AND VALUATION REPORTER. 1924. 11/yr. £140. Rating Publishers Ltd., 4 Breams Bldg., London EC4A 1AQ, England. TEL 0483-234804. Ed. Christopher Lewsley. adv.; bk.rev.; index. (tabloid format) Indexed: RICS.
—BLDSC shelfmark: 7295.350000.

340 100   UK   ISSN 0952-1917
K18   CODEN: RAJUEQ
RATIO JURIS; an international journal of jurisprudence and philosophy law. 1988. 3/yr. £37.50($70) to individuals; institutions £75($150). Basil Blackwell Ltd., 108 Cowley Rd., Oxford, OX4 1JF, England. TEL 0865 791100. FAX 0865-791347. TELEX 837022-OXBOOK-G. Ed. Enrico Pattaro.
—BLDSC shelfmark: 7295.431000.
Description: International and transcultural forum for philosophical ideas about the legal issues.

340 301.45   US   ISSN 8755-8815
LA RAZA LAW JOURNAL. 1987. a. $16 (foreign $19). University of California Press, Journals Division, 2120 Berkeley Way, Berkeley, CA 94720. TEL 510-642-4191. FAX 510-643-7127. Ed.Bd. circ. 250. (back issues avail.; reprint service avail. from UMI)
Description: Provides a forum for the analysis of pressing social issues affecting the Latino community.
Refereed Serial

340   SA   ISSN 0250-0329
K18
DE REBUS; the S A attorneys' journal. (Text in Afrikaans, English) 1956. m. R.44 (foreign R.60). Association of Law Societies, P.O. Box 36626 Menlo Park, Pretoria 0102, South Africa. TEL 012-3423330. FAX 012-3423305. Ed. Philip van der Merwe. adv.; index; circ. 11,800. Indexed: Ind.S.A.Per.
Formerly (until 1979): De Rebus Procuratoriis (ISSN 0045-9755)
Description: Publishes articles on law and practice, finance and office administration, professional news and practical aids.

340 917.306   US
RECENT ETHICS OPINIONS. irreg. $28. American Bar Association, Center for Professional Responsibility, 750 N. Lake Shore Dr., Chicago, IL 60611. TEL 312-988-5555. (looseleaf format)
Description: Describes recent opinions on lawyer discipline and professional responsibility.

340   SZ   ISSN 0253-9810
RECHT; Zeitschrift fuer juristische Ausbildung und Praxis. 1983. 4/yr. 59 Fr. (students 39 Fr.). Staempfli und Cie AG, Postfach, CH-3001 Berne, Switzerland. FAX 031-276699. TELEX 911987. Ed. Wolfgang Wiegand. adv.; circ. 2,000.

RECHT & PSYCHIATRIE. see PSYCHOLOGY

340   GW   ISSN 0342-1945
RECHT DER ARBEIT; Zeitschrift fuer die Wissenschaft und Praxis des gesamten Arbeitsrechts. 1948. bi-m. DM.206. (Deutscher Arbeitsgerichtsverband e.V.) C.H. Beck'sche Verlagsbuchhandlung, Wilhelmstr. 9, 8000 Munich 40, Germany. TEL 089-38189-338. FAX 089-38189-398. TELEX 5215085-BECK-D. (Co-sponsor: Institut fuer Arbeits- und Wirtschaftsrecht der Univeristaet zu Koeln) Ed.Bd. adv.; circ. 1,800.
—BLDSC shelfmark: 7309.300000.

RECHT DER DATENVERARBEITUNG; Zeitschrift fuer Praxis und Wissenschaft. see COMPUTERS — Computer Security

RECHT DER SCHIFFAHRT/MARITIME LAW REVIEW; a card index periodical of the international shipping law. see TRANSPORTATION — Ships And Shipping

340 330   GW
DAS RECHT DER WIRTSCHAFT. (Supplement: Schriftenreihe Recht der Wirtschaft) 1948. s-m. DM.220.80. Richard Boorberg Verlag (Stuttgart), Scharrstr. 2, Postfach 800260, 7000 Stuttgart 80, Germany. Eds. Max D. Kleiner, Roderich Dohse. adv.
Former titles: Chef; Wichtigste fuer den Chef (ISSN 0043-5236); Rechtsarchiv der Wirtschaft (ISSN 0034-1355)

340   NE   ISSN 0165-7607
RECHT EN KRITIEK. 1975. 4/yr. fl.56.25. Stichting Ars Aequi, Postbus 1043, 6501 BA Nijmegen, Netherlands. TEL 080-223506. FAX 080-241108. adv.; bk.rev.; circ. 850.

340   GW   ISSN 0034-1339
RECHT IM AMT; Zeitschrift fuer Behoerden, Verwaltungen und oeffentliche Betriebe. 1954. bi-m. DM.144. Luchterand Verlag, Heddesdorfer Str. 31, Postfach 1780, 5450 Neuwied, Germany. TEL 02631-801-0. TELEX 867853-HLVN-D. Ed. Peter Stechele. adv.; bk.rev.; index; circ. 1,200.

340 GW ISSN 0344-7871
RECHT UND POLITIK; Vierteljahreshefte fuer Rechts- und Verwaltungspolitik. 1965. q. DM.35. Berlin Verlag Arno Spitz GmbH, Pacelliallee 5, 1000 Berlin 33, Germany. TEL 030-8326232. FAX 030-8316249. Eds. Gerhard Kunze, Rudolf Wassermann. adv.; bk.rev.; circ. 1,050.
—BLDSC shelfmark: 7309.376500.
Description: Deals with problems and background of administration and jurisdiction in politics and legal practice.

340 AU
RECHT-WIRTSCHAFT-AUSSENHANDEL SCHRIFTENREIHE. 1981. irreg., vol.15, 1991. price varies. Manzsche Verlags-und Universitaetsbuchhandlung, Kohlmarkt 16, A-1014 Vienna, Austria. TEL 0222-531610. FAX 0222-5316181. Eds. Helmut H. Haschek, Peter Doralt. circ. 1,500.

340 320 US ISSN 0080-0163
RECHTS- UND STAATSWISSENSCHAFTEN. 1947. irreg. price varies. Springer-Verlag, 175 Fifth Ave., New York, NY 10010. TEL 212-460-1500. (Also: Berlin, Heidelberg, Tokyo and Vienna) (reprint service avail. from ISI)

340.09 NE ISSN 0169-9032
RECHTSHISTORISCH INSTITUUT LEIDEN. SERIES 1. irreg., vol.6, 1988. price varies. E.J. Brill, P.O. Box 9000, 2300 PA Leiden, Netherlands. TEL 071-312624. FAX 071-317532. TELEX 39296 BRILL NL. (In N. America: E.J. Brill, 24 Hudson St., Kinderhook, NY 12106. TEL 800-962-4406)

RECHTSMEDIZIN. see *MEDICAL SCIENCES*

340 GW ISSN 0080-018X
RECHTSPFLEGE JAHRBUCH. 1954. a. Gieseking-Verlag, Deckerstr. 2-10, Postfach 42, 4813 Bielefeld-Bethel, Germany.

340 GW ISSN 0174-0156
RECHTSPFLEGER - STUDIENHEFTE. 1977. bi-m. DM.28. Bund Deutscher Rechtspfleger e.V., Zweibrueckenstr. 2, D-8000 Munich 2, Germany. (Subscr. to: Verlag Ernst und Werner Gieseking GmbH, Postfach 130 120, Deckertstr. 30, D-4800 Bielefeld 13, Germany) Ed. Hans-Joachim von Schuckmann. adv.; bk.rev.; bibl.; index; circ. 2,000. (back issues avail.)

340 GW ISSN 0034-1363
RECHTSPFLEGERBLATT. 1953. 6/yr. membership. Bund Deutscher Rechtspfleger, Postfach, D-8000 Munich 35, Germany. Ed. Peter Weber. adv.; bk.rev.; abstr.; stat.; circ. 11,000. (tabloid format)

340 GW ISSN 0931-6183
RECHTSPRECHUNG; Materialen und Studien. 1986. irreg., vol.3, 1991. price varies. (Max-Planck-Institut fuer Europaeische Rechtsgeschichte) Vittorio Klostermann, Frauenlobstr. 22, 6000 Frankfurt a.M. 90, Germany. TEL 069-774011. FAX 069-708038.

RECHTSSTAAT IN DER BEWAEHRUNG. see *LAW — International Law*

340 GW ISSN 0034-1398
K18
RECHTSTHEORIE; Zeitschrift fuer Logik, Methodenlehre, Kybernetik und Soziologie des Rechts. 1970. q. DM.164. Duncker und Humblot GmbH, Postfach 410329, 1000 Berlin 41, Germany. TEL 030-7900060. FAX 030-79000631. Ed.Bd. adv.; bk.rev.; index. **Indexed:** Phil.Ind.

340 320 AU
RECHTSWISSENSCHAFT UND SOZIALPOLITIK. 1966. irreg., vol.16, 1991. price varies. Manzsche Verlags- und Universitaetsbuchhandlung, Kohlmarkt 16, A-1014 Vienna, Austria. TEL 0222-531610. FAX 0222-5316181. Eds. H. Floretta, R. Strasser.
Description: On law and social policy.

333.7 340 US ISSN 0743-5649
KF5638.A59
RECREATION AND PARKS LAW REPORTER. 1984. q. $100 to non-members; members $50. National Recreation and Park Association, 3101 Park Center Dr., Alexandria, VA 22302. TEL 703-820-4940. FAX 703-671-6772. Ed. James C. Kozlowski. index; circ. 1,000. (back issues avail.) **Indexed:** Sportsearch (1987-).

342 BE
RECUEIL ANNUEL DE JURISPRUDENCE BELGE. 1950. a. price varies. Maison Ferdinand Larcier S.A., Rue des Minimes 39, 1000 Brussels, Belgium.

340 FR ISSN 0034-1835
KJV112
RECUEIL DALLOZ-SIREY. (Includes three sections: Chroniques, Jurisprudence, Legislation) 1845. w. 970 F. (foreign 1180 F.). Editions Dalloz, 11 rue Soufflot, 75240 Paris Cedex 05, France. (Subscr. to: 35, rue Tournefort, 75240 Paris Cedex 05, France. TEL 40-51-54-54) (Co-publisher: Editions Sirey) bk.rev.; bibl.; stat.; index, cum.index every 5 yrs.
Formerly: Recueil Dalloz.

340 FR ISSN 0249-7271
RECUEIL DES DECISIONS DU CONSEIL D'ETAT. 1821. bi-m. 500 F. (foreign 600 F.). Editions Sirey-Diffusion Dalloz, 11 rue Soufflot, 75240 Paris Cedex 05, France. TEL 40-51-54-54. FAX 45-87-37-48. TELEX 206446F. (Subscr. to: 35, rue Tournefort, 75240 Paris Cedex 05, France) (reprint service avail. from SCH)

349 368 FR ISSN 0034-1878
RECUEIL JURIDIQUE DE L'EST SECURITE SOCIALE; doctrine jurisprudence, documents administratifs. 1947. q. 275 F. Association Juridique de l'Est, 25 rue Jean Mieg, 68100 Mulhouse, France. Ed. R. Schwob. bibl.

340 FR
RECUEIL PERIODIQUE DES JURIS-CLASSEURS: DROIT CIVIL. q. Editions Techniques, 123, rue d'Alesia, 75014 Paris, France. TEL 45-39-22-91. FAX 45-42-81-55. TELEX EIDTEC 270737.
Formerly: Juris-Classeurs. Droit Civil.

340 AT ISSN 0313-153X
REFORM. 1976. q. Aus.$12. Law Reform Commission, G.P.O. Box 3708, Sydney, N.S.W. 2001, Australia. TEL 02-231-1733. FAX 02-223-1203. Ed. Barry Hunt. bk.rev.; circ. 1,800. (also avail. in microform from UMI; back issues avail.)
Description: Bulletin of law reform news, views and information.

346 UK
REFORM IN NORTHERN IRELAND. irreg. (approx. a.). H.M.S.O. (N. Ireland), Chichester House, Chichester St., Belfast BT1 4JY, N. Ireland. (reprint service avail. from UMI)

344.73 US
KF3827.E87
REFUSAL OF TREATMENT LEGISLATION (YEAR). (Supplement avail.) 1975. a. $100 to non-members; members $90. Choice in Dying, Inc., 200 Varick St., New York, NY 10013. TEL 212-246-6973. FAX 212-586-6248. Ed. Norma Silfen. (back issues avail.)
Former titles: Handbook of Living Will Laws (ISSN 0886-7402); Society for the Right to Die. Handbook (ISSN 0198-8786); Legislative Manual (ISSN 0193-550X)

340 362 US ISSN 0034-317X
REGAN REPORT ON HOSPITAL LAW. 1960. m. $48. Medica Press Inc., Westminster Sq. Bldg., Ste. 500, Providence, RI 02903. TEL 401-421-4747. FAX 401-421-1400. Ed. A. David Tammelleo, J.D. stat.; circ. 5,000. (also avail. in microform from UMI; reprint service avail. from UMI)

340 610 US ISSN 0034-3188
REGAN REPORT ON MEDICAL LAW. 1968. m. $48. Medica Press Inc., Westminster Sq. Bldg., Ste. 500, Providence, RI 02903. TEL 401-421-4747. FAX 401-421-1400. Ed. A. David Tammelleo, J.D. stat.; circ. 5,000. (also avail. in microform from UMI; reprint service avail. from UMI)

340 610.73 US ISSN 0034-3196
REGAN REPORT ON NURSING LAW. 1960. m. $48. Medica Press Inc., Westminster Sq. Bldg., Ste. 500, Providence, RI 02903. TEL 401-421-4747. FAX 401-421-1400. Ed. A. David Tammelleo, J.D. stat.; circ. 10,000. (also avail. in microform from UMI; reprint service avail. from UMI) **Indexed:** C.I.N.L., Int.Nurs.Ind.
—BLDSC shelfmark: 7336.435000.

340 NE ISSN 0920-8720
REGEL & RECHT NIEUWS. fortn. fl.90. Delwel Uitgeverij B.V., Postbus 19110, 2500 CC The Hague, Netherlands. TEL 070-3624800. FAX 070-3605606. Ed. J.M. Stevers.

REGIMEN LEGAL TRIBUTARIO. see *BUSINESS AND ECONOMICS — Public Finance, Taxation*

340 SA
REGIONAL LEVIES SERVICE. a. $51. Butterworth Publishers (Pty.) Ltd., 8 Walter Pl., Waterval Park, Durban 4000, South Africa. TEL 031-294247. FAX 031-283255.

340 IT ISSN 0391-7576
REGIONI; rivista bimestrale di documentazione giuridica. 1973. bi-m. L.140000. (Istituto di Studi Giuridici Regionali) Societa Editrice Il Mulino, Strada Maggiore, 37, 40125 Bologna, Italy. TEL 051-256011. FAX 051-256034. Ed. Umberto Pototschnig. adv.; index; circ. 1,500. (back issues avail.)

340 332.64 US
REGULATION OF THE COMMODITIES FUTURES AND OPTIONS MARKETS. 1983. 2 base vols. (plus a. suppl.). $195. Shepard's - McGraw-Hill, Inc., Box 35300, Colorado Springs, CO 80935-3530. TEL 800-525-2474. (looseleaf format)
Description: Discusses the Commodity Exchange Act and CFTC regulations. Provides examples of day-to-day issues, in-depth analyses of law and regulations related to exchanges and market participants and off-exchange instruments.

343 SZ
REIHE STRAFRECHT. 1976. irreg. Verlag Rueegger AG, Aemtlerstr. 201, CH-8004 Zuerich, Switzerland.

340 US
RELATIVE VALUES: DETERMINING ATTORNEYS' FEES. 1985. base vol. (plus a. suppl.). $95. Shepard's - McGraw-Hill, Inc., Box 35300, Colorado Springs, CO 80935-3530. TEL 800-525-2474. (looseleaf format)
Description: Guide to legal billing and management procedures.

RELAZIONI INDUSTRIALI. see *BUSINESS AND ECONOMICS — Labor And Industrial Relations*

RELIGIOUS FREEDOM REPORTER. see *POLITICAL SCIENCE — Civil Rights*

REMEDIATION; the journal of environmental cleanup costs, technologies & techniques. see *ENVIRONMENTAL STUDIES — Waste Management*

340 CC
RENMIN JIANCHA. (Text in Chinese) m. Zhongguo Jiancha Chubanshe, Beijing 100726, People's Republic of China. TEL 550831. Ed. Su Deyong.

347 II
RENT CASES; a monthly law reporter. m. Rs.48. International Law Book Co., Nijhawan Bldg., Church Rd., Kashmere Gate, Delhi 6, India. Ed. Swarn Bhatia Nkjhawan.

340 FR
REPERTOIRE DU NOTARIAT DEFRENOIS. 1884. bi-m. 260 F. 83, Avenue Denfert-Rochereau, 75014 Paris, France. adv.; bk.rev.; circ. 10,000.

340 SP
REPERTORIO ARANZADI DEL TRIBUNAL CONSTITUCIONAL. (Includes q. bound vols. with indexes.) 1981. irreg., (several/wk.). 43450 ptas. (effective 1991). Editorial Aranzadi, S.A., Avda. Carlos III, 34, Apdo. 111, 31080 Pamplona, Spain. TEL 948-331212. FAX 948-330919. bibl.; index, cum.index 1981-1990.

340 SP
REPERTORIO CRONOLOGICO DE LEGISLACION. (Includes bound vols. with indexes.) 1930. irreg., (several/wk.). 44096 ptas. (includes Indice Progresivo de Legislacion)(effective 1991). Editorial Aranzadi, S.A., Avda. Carlos III, 34, Apdo. 111, 31080 Pamplona, Spain. TEL 948-331212. FAX 948-330919. bibl.; index.
●Also available on CD-ROM.

2672 LAW

340   SP
REPERTORIO DE JURISPRUDENCIA. (Includes bound vols. and m. Indice Progresivo.) 1930. irreg., (several/wk.). 55000 ptas. (effective 1991). Editorial Aranzadi, S.A., Avda. Carlos III, 34, Apdo. 111, 31080 Pamplona, Spain. TEL 948-331212. FAX 948-330919. index.
●Also available on CD-ROM.

340   IT
REPERTORIO DEL FORO ITALIANO. 1876. a. L.1295000 (price varies). Zanichelli Editore, Via Irnerio 34, 40126 Bologna, Italy. TEL 051-293111. FAX 051-249782. abstr.; bibl.
●Available only on CD-ROM.

342   IT
REPERTORIO DELLE DECISIONI DELLA CORTE COSTITUZIONALE. 1956. biennial. price varies. Casa Editrice Dott. A. Giuffre, Via Busto Arsizio 40, 20151 Milan, Italy. TEL 02-38000905. FAX 02-3809582. Ed. Nicola Lipari.

347.9   IT
REPERTORIO DI GIURISPRUDENZA DEL LAVORO. 1968. biennial. price varies. Casa Editrice Dott. A. Giuffre, Via Busto Arsizio 40, 20151 Milan, Italy. TEL 02-38000905. FAX 02-3809582. Eds. Mario Pacifico, Enrico Pacifico.

340   AG
REPERTORIO GENERAL: LA LEY; fallos de la Corte Suprema Nacional y tribunales provinciales. m. plus s-a. cumulations. Arg.$160($320) Ley, S.A., Tucuman 1471, 1050 Buenos Aires, Argentina.

340 320   US   ISSN 0893-0708
REPORT FROM THE HILL. 6/yr. $10. League of Women Voters of the U S, 1730 M St., N.W., Washington, DC 20036. TEL 202-429-1965. FAX 202-429-0854. Ed. Karen Everhart Bedford. circ. 5,000. (tabloid format; back issues avail.)
Description: Legislative newsletter covering the league's issue priorities in Congress.

348   US   ISSN 0094-7148
KFN3645
REPORT OF CASES DETERMINED IN THE SUPREME COURT AND COURT OF APPEALS OF THE STATE OF NEW MEXICO. Spine title: New Mexico Reports. 1968. irreg. (Supreme Court) West Publishing Co., Box 64526, St. Paul, MN 55164-0526. TEL 800-328-9352.

340   EI   ISSN 0378-7591
LAW
REPORTS OF CASES BEFORE THE COURT OF JUSTICE OF THE EUROPEAN COMMUNITIES. (Editions in Danish, Dutch, English, French, German, Greek, Italian, Portuguese, Spanish)) irreg. (10-12/yr.). $165. Office for Official Publications of the European Communities, L-2985 Luxembourg, Luxembourg. (Dist. in the U.S. by: Unipub, 4611-F Assembly Dr., Lanham, MD 20706-4391. TEL 800-274-4888)
—BLDSC shelfmark: 7639.590000.
Formerly: Information on the Court of Justice of the European Communities.

REPRODUCTIVE FREEDOM. see POLITICAL SCIENCE — Civil Rights

REPRODUCTIVE RIGHTS UPDATE. see POLITICAL SCIENCE — Civil Rights

340   BE
RES ET JURA IMMOBILIA. q. 2200 Fr. Etablissements Emile Bruylant, 67 rue de la Regence, B-1000 Brussels, Belgium. TEL 02-512-9845.

340   US
RES IPSA LOQUITUR. 1939. 3/yr. Georgetown University Law Center, Office of Public Relations, 600 New Jersey Ave., N.W., Washington, DC 20001. TEL 202-662-9690. Ed. Adrienne Kuehneman. bk.rev.; circ. 19,000. (reprint service avail. from UMI)

RESEARCH IN LAW AND ECONOMICS; a research annual. see BUSINESS AND ECONOMICS

RESEARCH RECOMMENDATIONS; economics, political & tax advisory letter. see BUSINESS AND ECONOMICS — Small Business

RESOLUTION TRUST REPORTER. see REAL ESTATE

RESOLUTIONS, BELIEFS & POLICIES, CONSTITUTION AND BYLAWS. see EDUCATION — School Organization And Administration

340 531.64   CN   ISSN 0714-5918
RESOURCES. 1982. q. free. Canadian Institute of Resources Law, Rm. 430, Bio-Sciences Bldg., Faculty of Law, University of Calgary, Calgary, Alta. T2N 1N4, Canada. TEL 403-220-3200. FAX 403-282-6182. Ed. Nancy Money. circ. 6,200.
Description: Comments on current resources legal issues, with information on Institute publications and programs.

340   IT
RESPONSABILITA CIVILE E PREVIDENZA. 1930. bi-m. L.100000 (foreign L.150000). Casa Editrice Dott. A. Giuffre, Via Busto Arsizio 40, 20151 Milan, Italy. TEL 02-38000905. FAX 02-38009852. Eds. Gianguido Scalfi, Ugo Carnevali. adv.; circ. 5,500.

RESPONSIBILITIES OF INSURANCE AGENTS AND BROKERS. see INSURANCE

340   US
RESTATEMENT IN THE COURTS. POCKET PARTS. 1977. a. price varies. (American Law Institute) American Law Institute Publishers, Box 64526, 50 West Kellogg Blvd., St. Paul, MN 55164-0526. TEL 215-243-1650. (Subscr. to: 4025 Chestnut St., Philadelphia, PA 19104) Ed. Violet Meehan. circ. 2,400.
Formerly (until 1976): Restatement in the Courts. Supplements.

340   DK   ISSN 0105-1121
RETFAERD. (Text in Danish, Norwegian, Swedish) 1976. 4/yr. DKK 290. Akademisk Forlag, Store Kannikestraede 8, P.O. Box 54, 1002 Copenhagen K, Denmark. bk.rev.; circ. 900.

RETIREMENT AND BENEFIT PLANNING; strategy and design for businesses and tax-exempt organizations. see BUSINESS AND ECONOMICS — Personnel Management

340   NO   ISSN 0034-6187
RETTENS GANG. 1933. 22/yr. NOK 850. Advokatenes Servicekontor - Norwegian Bar Association, Kr.Augustsgt. 9, 0164 Oslo, Norway. Ed. Thor Jensen. index, cum.index.

340   GH   ISSN 0034-6578
K18
REVIEW OF GHANA LAW. 1969. a. $46.50. Council for Law Reporting, Box M.165, Accra, Ghana. Ed. S.Y. Bimpong-Buta. adv.; bk.rev.; index; circ. 2,000. (also avail. in microform from UMI; reprint service avail. from UMI)
—BLDSC shelfmark: 7790.767000.

340   US   ISSN 0048-7481
K14.E97
REVIEW OF LAW & SOCIAL CHANGE. 1971. 4/yr. $16 per vol. (foreign $22)(effective 1992). New York University, Review of Law & Social Change, 110 W. Third St., New York, NY 10012. TEL 212-998-6370. FAX 212-995-4032. adv.; bk.rev.; circ. 850. (processed; also avail. in microform from UMI; reprint service avail. from RRI,UMI) **Indexed:** C.L.I., Crim.Just.Abstr., L.R.I., Leg.Per., Psychol.Abstr.
—BLDSC shelfmark: 6089.820500.

340   US   ISSN 0734-4015
K18
REVIEW OF LITIGATION. 1981. 3/yr. $20 (foreign $23). University of Texas at Austin, School of Law Publications, 727 E. 26th St., Ste. 3.102A, Austin, TX 78705-3299. TEL 512-471-1106. FAX 512-471-6988. Ed. David Klinger. bk.rev.; circ. 800. (also avail. in microform from WSH; back issues avail.; reprint service avail. from WSH)
Description: Articles, comments and notes on current legal topics.

340 320.531   NE   ISSN 0165-0300
K18   CODEN: RSLAEY
REVIEW OF SOCIALIST LAW. 1975. q. $65.50 to individuals; institutions $131. (Rijksuniversiteit te Leiden, Documentation Office for East European Law - University of Leiden) Kluwer Academic Publishers, Postbus 17, 3300 AA Dordrecht, Netherlands. TEL 078-334911. FAX 078-334254. TELEX 29245. (Dist. by: Kluwer Academic Publishers Group, P.O. Box 322, 3300 AH Dordrecht, Netherlands; N. America dist. addr.: Box 358, Accord Station, Hingham, MA 02018-0358. TEL 617-871-6600) Ed. F.J.M Feldbrugge. **Indexed:** C.L.I., Leg.Per.
—BLDSC shelfmark: 7796.914000.
Formerly: Communist Law Journal.

340   CL
REVISTA CHILENA DE DERECHO. 1974. q. $50. Universidad Catolica de Chile, Facultad de Derecho, Casilla 114D, Santiago, Chile. Ed. Jose Luis Cea. bk.rev.; circ. 1,000.

340   CU   ISSN 0864-165X
REVISTA CUBANO DE DERECHO. (Text in Spanish; summaries in English, French, Russian) q. $15 in N. and S. America; Europe $16; elsewhere $18. (Comision de Estudios Juridicos) Ediciones Cubanas, Obispo No. 527, Apdo. 605, Havana, Cuba.
—BLDSC shelfmark: 7852.102000.
Description: Covers legal topics of interest to all members of the legal and judicial community.

340   AG   ISSN 0325-0601
REVISTA DE CIENCIAS JURIDICAS SOCIALES. 1922. irreg. exchange basis. Universidad Nacional del Litoral, Facultad de Ciencias Juridicas y Sociales, Candido Pujato 2751, 3000 Santa Fe, Argentina. bk.rev.; circ. 500.

340   BO   ISSN 0034-7868
REVISTA DE DERECHO.* q. Universidad Boliviana Mayor de San Andres, Facultad de Economia, Juridica y Ciencias Sociales, Departamento de Publicaciones, La Paz, Bolivia. Dir. Dr. Alipio Valencia Vega.

340   HO
REVISTA DE DERECHO. 1969. s-a. $7 per no. Universidad Nacional Autonoma de Honduras, Instituto de Investigacion Juridica, Bloque de Aulas, 2, Ciudad Universitaria, Tegucigalpa, D.C., Honduras. Ed. Jorge Omar Casco. bk.rev.

300 340   CL   ISSN 0303-9986
REVISTA DE DERECHO (CONCEPCION). vol.33, 1965. s-a. exchange basis. Universidad de Concepcion, Escuela de Derecho, Casilla 26C, Concepcion, Chile. FAX 222712. (Subscr. to: Biblioteca Central, Canje y Donacion, Casilla 1807, Concepcion, Chile) Dir. Hernan Troncoso Larronde. circ. 1,000.
Formerly: Revista de Derecho y Ciencias Sociales (ISSN 0034-7957)

340   CL
REVISTA DE DERECHO (VALPARAISO). 1977. a. $33. (Universidad Catolica de Valparaiso, Escuela de Derecho) Ediciones Universitarias de Valparaiso, Casilla 1415, Valparaiso, Chile. TEL 252900. FAX 032-272746. TELEX 230389 UCVAL CL. Dir. Alejandro Guzman Brito. circ. 300.

349   UY
REVISTA DE DERECHO COMERCIAL Y DE LA EMPRESA. 1977. q. $35. Fundacion de Cultura Universitaria, 25 de Mayo 568, Casilla de Correo No. 1155, Montevideo, Uruguay. TEL 961152. FAX 962540. Ed. Sagunto F. Perez Fontana. bk.rev.; bibl.; pat.; index.
Supersedes (1964-1973): Revista de Derecho Comercial (ISSN 0034-7876)

340   UY   ISSN 0034-7906
REVISTA DE DERECHO, JURISPRUDENCIA Y ADMINISTRACION. (Text in Spanish; occasionally in English, French, Portuguese) 1894. m. $18. c/o Prof. Horacio Cassinelli Munoz, 18 de Julio 1745, Montevideo, Uruguay. bk.rev.; bibl.; index, cum.index; circ. 2,000. (tabloid format)

340 331   AG
REVISTA DE DERECHO LABORAL. m. Calle Uruguay 115, Buenos Aires, Argentina.

343   UY
REVISTA DE DERECHO PENAL. 1981. irreg. $35. Fundacion de Cultura Universitaria, 25 de Mayo 568, Casilla de Correo No. 1155, Codigo Postal 11000, Montevideo, Uruguay. TEL 961152. FAX 005982-962540.

340   SP   ISSN 0034-7922
REVISTA DE DERECHO PRIVADO. 1913. 11/yr. 6000 ptas.($36) Editoriales de Derecho Reunidas, S.A., Valverde 32, 1o, 28004 Madrid, Spain. TEL 91-5210246. Dir. Manuel Albadalejo. adv.; bk.rev.; index, cum.index; circ. 4,500.
—BLDSC shelfmark: 7852.480000.

340   CL
REVISTA DE DERECHO PROCESAL. 1971. s-a. (Universidad de Chile, Facultad de Ciencias Juridicas y Sociales, Departamento de Derecho Procesal) Editorial Juridica de Chile, Avda. Ricardo Lyon 946, Casilla 4256, Santiago, Chile.

340   SP   ISSN 0210-2897
REVISTA DE DERECHO PUBLICO. q. 4000 ptas. Editoriales de Derecho Reunidas, S.A., Valverde 32, 1o, 28004 Madrid, Spain. TEL 91-5210246. Dir. Luis Sanchez Agesta.

340   AG
REVISTA DE DERECHO PUBLICO. 1950. irreg. Universidad Nacional de Tucuman, Instituto de Derecho Publico, Tucuman, Buenos Aires, Argentina.

342   VE
REVISTA DE DERECHO PUBLICO. q. Bs.350.00. Editorial Juridica Venezolana, Apdo. Postal No. 17598, Caracas, Venezuela.

340   PR   ISSN 0034-7930
LAW
REVISTA DE DERECHO PUERTORRIQUENO. 1961. q. $15. Universidad Catolica de Puerto Rico, School of Law, Ponce, PR 00732. Ed. Edna Santiago. bk.rev.; bibl.; circ. 1,000. **Indexed:** C.L.I., L.R.I., Leg.Per.

340   EC   ISSN 0484-6923
REVISTA DE DERECHO SOCIAL ECUATORIANO. 1952-1956; resumed 1958. irreg. Universidad Central del Ecuador, Box 2349, Quito, Ecuador. Ed. H. Valencia.

349   PE   ISSN 0034-7949
K19
REVISTA DE DERECHO Y CIENCIAS POLITICAS. 1936. 3/yr. S.300($10) Universidad Nacional Mayor de San Marcos, Facultad de Derecho, Apdo. 524, Lima, Peru. adv.; bk.rev.; bibl.; index, cum.index every 20 yrs. (1936-1956); circ. 4,500. (tabloid format)

340 630   VE
REVISTA DE DERECHO Y REFORMA AGRARIA. 1969. a. $7. (Universidad de los Andes, Instituto Iberoamericano de Derecho Agrario y Reforma Agraria) Talleres Graficos, Merida, Venezuela. FAX 074-404644. bk.rev.; bibl.; circ. 1,200.

630 340   BL
REVISTA DE DIREITO AGRARIO. 1973. s-a. free. Instituto Nacional de Colonizacao e Reforma Agraria, Procurador Geral, Palacio do Desenvolvimento, 21 andar, Setor Bancario Norte CEP 70437, Brasilia, DF, Brazil. Eds. Agnaldo Silva, Eliene Rodrigues da Costa Maia.

340   BL
REVISTA DE DIREITO CIVIL; imobiliario, agrario e empresarial. 1977. q. Cz.$800($80) Editora Revista dos Tribunais, Rua Conde do Pinhal 78, 01501 Sao Paulo, Brazil. Ed. R. Limongi Franca. adv.; bk.rev.; abstr.; bibl.; index; circ. 5,000.

340   BL
REVISTA DE DIREITO DO TRABALHO (PETROPOLIS).* 1973. irreg. Industrias Graficas Centrograf Ltd., Rua Alencar Lima, 35- Grupo 903-7, Petropolis, Brazil. **Indexed:** Int.Lab.Doc.

347.9 331   BL
REVISTA DE DIREITO DO TRABALHO (SAO PAULO). 1976. q. $60. Editora Revista dos Tribunais, Rua Conde do Pinhal 78, 01501 Sao Paulo, Brazil. Ed. Alvaro Malheiros. adv.; bk.rev.; abstr.; bibl.; index; circ. 5,000.

340   BL
REVISTA DE DIREITO MERCANTIL, INDUSTRIAL, ECONOMICO, E FINANCEIRO. 1951; N.S. 1971. q. $40. (Instituto Brasileiro de Direito Comercial Comparado) Editora Revista dos Tribunais, Rua Conde do Pinhal, 78-01501 Sao Paulo, SP, Brazil. (Co-sponsors: Biblioteca Tullio Ascarelli; Instituto de Direito Economico e Financeiro) Ed. Alvaro Malheiros. adv.; bk.rev.; bibl.; index; circ. 5,000.

340   BL   ISSN 0034-8015
K19
REVISTA DE DIREITO PUBLICO. 1967. q. $80. (Universidade de Sao Paulo, Instituto de Direito Publico) Editora Revista dos Tribunais, Rua Conde do Pinhal, 78, 01501 Sao Paulo, SP, Brazil. Ed. Dr. Alvaro Malheiros. adv.; bk.rev.; abstr.; bibl.; index; circ. 6,000.

340   BL
REVISTA DE DIREITO TRIBUTARIO. 1977. 2/yr. $80. Editora Revista dos Tribunais, Rua Conde do Pinhal 78, 01501 Sao Paulo, Brazil. Ed. Geraldo Ataliba. adv.; bk.rev.; bibl.; index; circ. 5,000.

340   AG
REVISTA DE ESTUDIOS PROCESALES. 1969. 2/yr. $30. Centro de Estudios Procesales, Dorrego No. 1748, 2000 Rosario, Argentina. Ed. Adolfo Alvarado Velloso. bk.rev.; abstr.; bibl.; charts; stat.; index, cum.index; circ. 1,500.

340   AG
REVISTA DE HISTORIA DE DERECHO. 1973. a. (Instituto de Investigaciones de Historia del Derecho) Librart s.r.l., Departamento de Publicaciones Cientificas Argentinas, Avda. Corrientes 127, Casilla Correo Central 5047, Buenos Aires, Argentina. Dir. Ricardo Zorraquin Becu.

340   BL   ISSN 0034-835X
CODEN: RINLE7
REVISTA DE INFORMACAO LEGISLATIVA. 1964. q. Cr.$4500. Senado Federal, Subsecretaria de Edicoes Tecnicas, Anexo 1, 22 andar, Praca dos Tres Poderes, 70160 Brasilia, D.F., Brazil. FAX 611156. TELEX 612025SEFE BR. Dir. Anna Maria Villela. cum.index: nos.1-100; circ. 5,000. (tabloid format) **Indexed:** P.A.I.S.For.Lang.Ind.

340   SP
REVISTA DE LA FACULTAD DE DERECHO. 3/yr. Universidad de Granada, Servicio de Publicaciones, Antiguo Colegio Maximo, Campus de Cartuja, 18071 Granada, Spain. TEL 281356. Ed. Jose M. Perez Prendes.

340   PO   ISSN 0870-8487
REVISTA DE LEGISLACAO E DE JURISPRUDENCIA. 1868. m. $14.20. Coimbra Editora Limitada, Rua do Arnado, P.O. Box 101, 3002 Coimbra, Portugal. TEL 25459. index; circ. 3,250.

340   AG   ISSN 0034-8481
LAW
REVISTA DE LEGISLACION ARGENTINA. 1966. a. (in 3 vols.). $100 per volume. Jurisprudencia Argentina S.A., Talcahuano 650, 1013 Buenos Aires, Argentina. TEL 40-0528. Dir. Ricardo Estevez Boero. adv.; charts; illus.; stat.

340 300   CL
REVISTA DE LEGISLACION Y DOCUMENTACION EN DERECHO Y CIENCIAS SOCIALES. 1976. 4/yr. free. Congreso Nacional, Biblioteca, Compania 1175, Clasificador 1199, Santiago, Chile. Ed. Neville Blanc-Renard. index; circ. 600. (back issues avail.)
Formed by the merger of: Boletin de Legislacion Nacional; Boletin de Autoridades; Boletin de Documentacion en Derecho y Ciencias Sociales.

340   BL
REVISTA DE PROCESSO. 1976. q. $85. Editora Revista dos Tribunais, Rua Conde do Pinhal 78, 01501 Sao Paulo, Brazil. Ed. Arruda Alvim. adv.; bk.rev.; abstr.; bibl.; index; circ. 6,000.

340 330   AG
REVISTA DEL DERECHO INDUSTRIAL. 1979. 3/yr. $80 (effective Jan. 1992). Ediciones Depalma S.r.l., Talcahuano No. 494, Buenos Aires, Argentina. FAX 054-40-6913. Ed. Carlos Correa. bk.rev.
Description: Provides updated information on economic law, intellectual property, communications and computer law, from a Latin American point of view.

349   BL   ISSN 0034-9275
REVISTA DOS TRIBUNAIS. 1912. m. $375. Editora Revista dos Tribunais, Rua Conde do Pinhal, 78, 01501 Sao Paulo SP, Brazil. Ed. Alvaro Malheiros. adv.; bk.rev.; abstr.; bibl.; cum.index; circ. 11,000.

344   SP   ISSN 0034-9399
REVISTA ESPANOLA DE DERECHO MILITAR. 1956. s-a. 300 ptas. per no. Instituto Francisco de Vitoria, Escuela de Estudios Juridicos del Ejercito, Calle Tambre No. 35, Madrid-2, Spain. bk.rev.; bibl.; charts; index, cum.index nos.1-6 (1956-1958); circ. 750.

340   BL   ISSN 0034-9739
REVISTA JURIDICA. 1977. irreg. (1-3/yr.) Cr.$30($7.) Av. Paris 72, ZC-24 Bonsucesso, 20000 Rio de Janeiro, Brazil. Eds. Angelito A. Aiquel, Jamil A. Aiquel. illus.; charts.

340   BO
REVISTA JURIDICA. 1938. q. Universidad Boliviana Mayor de "San Simon", Departamento de Derecho, Casilla 658, Cochambamba, Bolivia. bibl.

340   CU
REVISTA JURIDICA. q. $16 in N. America; S. America $18; Europe $21. (Ministerio de Justicia, Departamento de Divulgacion) Ediciones Cubanas, Obispo No. 527, Apdo. 605, Havana, Cuba. (And: O No. 261st 23 y 25, Vedado, Havana, Cuba)

340   SP   ISSN 0210-4296
REVISTA JURIDICA DE CATALUNA. 1895. q. Academia de Jurisprudencia y Legislacion, Colegio de Abogados de Barcelona, Mallorca 283, 08037 Barcelona, Spain. Ed.Bd. bk.rev.; bibl.; circ. 5,500.
—BLDSC shelfmark: 7862.501200.

340   PE
REVISTA JURIDICA DEL PERU. 1950. q. $100. Julio Ayasta Gonzalez, Ed. & Pub., Lampa 1115, Lima, Peru. TEL 277854. adv.; bk.rev.; circ. 2,000.

619 331   CL
REVISTA JURIDICA DEL TRABAJO. 1929. 9/yr. $180. (Sociedad Chilena de Derecho del Trabajo) Editorial Arbi Ltda., Avenida Bulnes 180, ofc. 80, Casilla 9447, Santiago, Chile. TEL 6967474. Ed. Mario Soto Venegas. bk.rev.; circ. 1,100. (back issues avail.)

340   DR
REVISTA JURIDICA DOMINICANA. 1939. q. (some double issues). (Secretaria de Estado de Justicia y Trabajo) Editoria del Caribe, Autopista Duarto Km. 7 1-2, Apdo. 416, Santo Domingo, Dominican Republic.

340   PE
REVISTA PERUANA DE DERECHO DE LA EMPRESA. 1984. q. $100. Revista Peruana de Derecho de la Empresa y Asesorandina, Av. Salaverry 674, OF 403 Jesus, Maria Casilla 11-0059, Peru. TEL 237730. adv.; bk.rev.; stat.; circ. 1,200.

REVISTA POLITICA COMPARADA. see POLITICAL SCIENCE

340   RM   ISSN 0035-0435
REVISTA ROMANA DE DREPT. 1945. m. 200 lei($25) Asociatia Juristilor din Republica Socialista Romania, B-Dul Magheru Nr. 22, Bucharest, Rumania. (Subscr. to: ILEXIM, Str. 13 Decembrie Nr. 3, P.O. Box 136-137, Bucharest, Rumania) Ed. Vasile Patulea. bibl.; index; circ. 8,000.

340   BL
REVISTA TRIMESTRAL DE JURISPRUDENCIA. 1964. q. price varies. Supremo Tribunal Federal, SIG-Quadra 6-Lote 800, 70604 Brasilia, D.F., Brazil. index; circ. 2,000 (controlled). (processed)
Former titles: Tribunal Federal de Recursos. Revista (ISSN 0041-2813); Ter Jurisprudencia.

340   UY
REVISTA URUGUAYA DE DERECHO PROCESAL. 1975. q. $35. Fundacion de Cultura Universitaria, 25 de Mayo no. 568, Casilla de Correo No. 1155, Montevideo, Uruguay. TEL 961152. FAX 962540.

340　　　　　　　US
▼REVOCABLE TRUSTS, 2-E. 1991. base vol. (plus a. suppl.). $95. Shepard's - McGraw-Hill, Inc., Box 35300, Colorado Springs, CO 80935-3530. TEL 800-525-2474.
　　Description: Provides a forum for the analysis of drafting techniques, using specific documents such as revocable trusts, pour-over wills and accompanying transfer documents.

340　　　　　　　BD
REVUE ADMINISTRATIVE ET JURIDIQUE DU BURUNDI. 1967. q. Association d'Etudes Administratives et Juridiques du Burundi, B.P. 1613, Bujumbura, Burundi.

340 320 340　　　AE
REVUE ALGERIENNE DES SCIENCES JURIDIQUES. 1964. q. 120 din. Universite d'Alger, Institut des Sciences Juridiques et Administratives, 11 Chemin Mokhtar Doudou ITFC, Ben-Aknoun, Algiers, Algeria. TEL 64-69-70. (Dist. in US by: African Imprint Library Service, Box 350, West Falmouth, MA 02574. TEL 508-540-5378) bk.rev.; bibl. Indexed: P.A.I.S.For.Lang.Ind., Rural Recreat.Tour.Abstr., World Agri.Econ.& Rural Sociol.Abstr.
　　Former titles: Revue Algerienne des Sciences Juridiques, Economiques et Politiques; (until 1968): Revue Algerienne des Sciences Juridiques, Politiques et Economiques (ISSN 0035-0699)

340　　　　BE　　ISSN 0035-0966
REVUE CRITIQUE DE JURISPRUDENCE BELGE. (Text in French) 1947. q. 5200 Fr. Etablissements Emile Bruylant, 67 rue de la Regence, B-1000 Brussels, Belgium. TEL 02-512-9845. index; circ. 1,250.
—BLDSC shelfmark: 7897.800000.

347.7　　　BE　　ISSN 0772-8050
REVUE DE DROIT COMMERCIAL BELGE/TIJDSCHRIFT VOOR BELGISCH HANDELSRECHT. (Text in Dutch, French) 1968. 12/yr. 2950 Fr. Palais de Justice, Place Poelaert, B-1000 Brussels, Belgium. TEL 02-508-62-45. FAX 02-358-4597. (Subscr. to: E. Story-Scientia, Bd. E. Bockstael 228, B-1020 Brussels, Belgium. TEL 11-68-68) Ed. I Verougstraete. bk.rev. (also avail. in microfiche)
　　Formerly: Jurisprudence Commerciale de Belgique. Refereed Serial

340 341　　　FR　　ISSN 0768-9659
REVUE DE DROIT FRANCAIS COMMERCIAL MARITIME ET FISCAL. (Text in French) 1924. q. 250 Fr. 28 bd. Peytral, F-13006 Marseille, France. TEL 9133-3829. Ed. Louis Scapel. index; circ. 300. (back issues avail.) Indexed: World Agri.Econ.& Rural Sociol.Abstr.

340　　　　FR　　ISSN 0180-9849
REVUE DE DROIT IMMOBILIER. 1979. q. 530 F. (foreign 650 F.). Editions Sirey-Diffusion Dalloz, 11 rue Soufflot, 75240 Paris Cedex 05, France. TEL 40-51-54-54. FAX 45-87-37-48. TELEX 206446F. (Subscr. to: 35, rue Tournefort, 75240 Paris Cedex 05, France) Ed. Philippe Malinvaud.

340　　　　BE　　ISSN 0035-1083
REVUE DE DROIT INTELLECTUEL L'INGENIEUR-CONSEIL. (Text in Dutch, French) 1911. bi-m. 4200 BEF. Bureau Vander Haeghen, 108A Rue Colonel Bourg, B-1040 Brussels, Belgium. TEL 02-736-3963. FAX 02-733-9809. Ed. Edouard Fobe. bk.rev.; index; circ. 625.
　　Description: Disseminates intellectual property law and practice through discussion of a variety of subjects, including patents, trademarks, copyright and competition.

REVUE DE DROIT INTERNATIONAL DE SCIENCES DIPLOMATIQUES ET POLITIQUES. see POLITICAL SCIENCE

REVUE DE DROIT INTERNATIONAL ET DE DROIT COMPARE. see LAW — International Law

340　　　　CN
REVUE DE DROIT JUDICIAIRE.* (Text in French) 1898. bi-m. Can.$125. Wilson et Lafleur Ltee., C.P. 24, Place d'Armees, Montreal, Que. H2Y 3L2, Canada. Ed. Mario Du Mesnil. circ. 1,250. Indexed: Ind.Can.L.P.L.
　　Supersedes: Rapports de Pratique de Quebec (ISSN 0384-6970)
　　Description: Covers law in the Quebec province.

340　　　　FR
REVUE DE DROIT RURAL. 1971. m. 770 F. Editions Techniques, 123, rue d'Alesia, 75014 Paris, France. adv.; bk.rev. Indexed: Geo.Abstr.

347.9　　　BE　　ISSN 0035-1113
REVUE DE DROIT SOCIAL/TIJDSCHRIFT VOOR SOCIAAL RECHT. (Text in Dutch, French) 1913. 6/yr. 3200 Fr. Maison Ferdinand Larcier S.A., Rue des Minimes 39, 1000 Brussels, Belgium. Ed. R. Geysen. bk.rev.; index, cum.index every 5 yrs. Indexed: P.A.I.S.For.Lang.Ind.
—BLDSC shelfmark: 7898.554000.

346　　　　FR　　ISSN 0048-7937
REVUE DE JURISPRUDENCE COMMERCIALE; journal des agrees. 1957. m. 800 F. 77 rue Royale, 78000 Versailles, France. TEL 30-50-44-97. FAX 39-49-52-13. adv.; bk.rev.

REVUE DE JURISPRUDENCE FISCALE. see PUBLIC ADMINISTRATION

REVUE DE SCIENCE CRIMINELLE ET DE DROIT PENAL COMPARE. see CRIMINOLOGY AND LAW ENFORCEMENT

340　　　　FR
REVUE DES CAHIERS DU BARREAU DE PARIS. q. 120 F. per no. Jurisprudence Generale Dalloz, 11, rue Soufflot, 75240 Paris Cedex 05, France. (Subscr. to: 35, rue Tournefort, 75240 Paris Cedex 05, France. TEL 40-51-54-54)

340　　　　FR
REVUE DES SOCIETES. s-a. 455 F. (foreign 530 F.). Editions Dalloz, 11 rue Soufflot, 75240 Paris Cedex 05, France. (Subscr. to: 35, rue Tournefort, 75240 Paris Cedex 05, France. TEL 40-51-54-54) (reprint service avail. from SCH)
　　Formerly: Revue des Societes - Journal des Societes; Which incorporates (in 1974): Journal des Societes.

340　　　　CN　　ISSN 0383-669X
REVUE DU BARREAU. (Text in English, French) 1941. 5/yr. Can.$30. (Barreau du Quebec) Editions Yvon Blais Inc., 445 bd. St-Laurent, Montreal, Que. H2Y 3T8, Canada. TEL 514-954-3400. FAX 514-954-3463. Ed.Bd. adv.; bk.rev.; bibl.; charts; illus.; stat.; index, cum.index.; circ. 14,000. Indexed: C.L.I., Ind.Can.L.P.L., L.R.I., Leg.Per., Pt.de Rep. (1983-).

340　　　　FR　　ISSN 0035-2578
JA11
REVUE DU DROIT PUBLIC ET DE LA SCIENCE POLITIQUE EN FRANCE ET A L'ETRANGER. 1894. bi-m. 540 F. (foreign 560 F.). (Librairie Generale de Droit et de Jurisprudence) Editions Juridiques Associees, 26 rue Vercingetorix, 75014 Paris, France. TEL 1-43-35-01-67. FAX 43-20-07-42. TELEX EJA 203 918 F. Eds. Jacques Robert, J.M. Auby. bk.rev.; abstr.; bibl.; index, cum.index: 1951-1964; circ. 3,800. (reprint service avail. from SCH) Indexed: P.A.I.S.For.Lang.Ind.
—BLDSC shelfmark: 7898.550000.

340　　　　CN　　ISSN 0035-2632
LAW
REVUE DU NOTARIAT. 1898. bi-m. (except July & Aug.). Can.$25($15) Chambre des Notaires du Quebec, C.P. 130, Outremont, Que. H2V 4M8, Canada. TEL 514-733-7540. Ed. Roger Comtois. adv.; bk.rev.; index; circ. 3,500. Indexed: C.L.I., Ind.Can.L.P.L., L.R.I., Leg.Per., Pt.de Rep. (1983-).

347.016　　　BE
REVUE DU NOTARIAT BELGE.* q. 2850 Fr. 535 Chaussee de Waterloo, bte 6, 1050 Brussels, Belgium.

346.066 330　　　FR
REVUE EUROPEENNE DE DROIT DE LA CONSOMMATION. q. 840 F. (effective 1991). Lamy S.A., 155, rue Legendre, 75850 Paris Cedex 17, France. TEL 46-27-28-90. FAX 46-27-28-90. TELEX 214 398.
　　Description: Analyzes the evolution and implications of the communal arrangement and national laws of distribution, competition and consumption in 17 European countries.

340　　　　FR
REVUE FRANCAISE DE DROIT ADMINISTRATIF. 6/yr. 575 F. (foreign 660 F.). Editions Sirey-Diffusion Dalloz, 11, rue Soufflot, 75240 Paris, France. TEL 40-51-54-54. FAX 45-87-37-48. TELEX 206446F. (Subscr. to: 35 rue Tournefort, 75240 Paris Cedex 05, France)

REVUE FRANCAISE DE DROIT AERIEN. see AERONAUTICS AND SPACE FLIGHT

340　　　　FR　　ISSN 0035-3280
REVUE HISTORIQUE DE DROIT FRANCAIS ET ETRANGER. 1855. 4/yr. 570 F. (foreign 640 F.). Editions Sirey-Diffusion Dalloz, 22 rue Soufflot, 75005 Paris, France. (Subscr. to: Diffusion Dalloz, 35 rue Tournefort, 75240 Paris Cedex 05, France) Ed.Bd. bk.rev.; bibl.; index. (reprint service avail. from SCH) Indexed: CERDIC, Hist.Abstr.
—BLDSC shelfmark: 7920.750000.

340　　　　BE
REVUE INTERDISCIPLINAIRE D'ETUDES JURIDIQUES. s-a. 600 Fr. to individuals (foreign 700 Fr.); institutions 900 Fr. (foreign 1000 Fr.). Universite de Saint Louis, Facultes des Seminaires Interdisciplinaire d'Etudes Juridiques, Boulevard du Jardin Botanique, 43, 1000 Brussels, Belgium. TEL 02-2117894. FAX 02-2117997.

340 330　　　BE
REVUE INTERNATIONALE DE DROIT ECONOMIQUE. Short title: R.I.D.E. (Text in French) 3/yr. 2900 Fr. De Boeck Wesmael, Serials Department, Av. Louise 203, Boite 1, B-1050 Brussels, Belgium. TEL 2-627-35-37. FAX 2-627-36-50. TELEX 65701-DBWES-B. (Dist. by: Acces Plus, Rue Fonds Jean Paques, 4, B-1348 Louvain-la-Neuve, Belgium.

340 940　　　BE　　ISSN 0556-7939
REVUE INTERNATIONALE DES DROITS DE L'ANTIQUITE. 1948. a. 1000 Fr. Office International des Periodiques, Kouterveld 14, B-1831 Diegem, Belgium. TEL 02-723-11-11. FAX 02-723-14-13. circ. 500. (back issues avail.)

REVUE INTERNATIONALE DU DROIT D'AUTEUR. see PATENTS, TRADEMARKS AND COPYRIGHTS

340　　　　IV　　ISSN 0048-816X
REVUE IVOIRIENNE DE DROIT. 1971. s-a. 120 F. Centre Ivoirien d'Etude et de Recherche Juridique, B.P. 3811, Abidjan, Ivory Coast. Ed.Bd. adv.; circ. 1,500.

REVUE JURIDIQUE DE L'ENVIRONNEMENT. see ENVIRONMENTAL STUDIES

340　　　　BD
REVUE JURIDIQUE DU BURUNDI.* 1980. q. 120 F. Ecole Nationale d'Administration, B.P. 1613, Bujumbura, Burundi.

REVUE JURIDIQUE DU RWANDA. see LAW — Judicial Systems

REVUE JURIDIQUE DU ZAIRE. see LAW — Judicial Systems

REVUE JURIDIQUE THEMIS. see LAW — Judicial Systems

340　　　　CN　　ISSN 0035-3604
REVUE LEGALE.* (Text in French) 1952. bi-m. Can.$100. Wilson et Lafleur Ltee., C.P. 24, Place d'Armes, Montreal, Que. H2Y 3L2, Canada. Ed. Mario Du Mesnil. adv.; circ. 1,000. Indexed: C.L.I., Leg.Per.
　　Description: Covers law in the Quebec province.

343　　　　FR　　ISSN 0035-3825
REVUE PENITENTIAIRE ET DE DROIT PENAL. 1877. q. 232 F. Societe Generale des Prisons et de Legislation Criminelle, 27 rue de Fleurus, 75006 Paris, France. Ed. M. Dutheillet Lamonthezie. Indexed: Excerp.Med.
—BLDSC shelfmark: 7942.200000.

340　　　　FR　　ISSN 0399-1148
REVUE PRATIQUE DE DROIT SOCIAL. 1944. m. 305 F. Vie Ouvriere, 33 rue Bouret, 75940 Paris cedex 19, France. Ed. Maurice Cohen. circ. 17,500.

301　　　　BE
REVUE PRATIQUE DES SOCIETES CIVILES ET COMMERCIALES. 1889. q. 2700 Fr. Etablissements Emile Bruylant, 67 rue de la Regence, B-1000 Brussels, Belgium. TEL 02-512-9845.

LAW

346 K21   FR   ISSN 0244-9358
REVUE TRIMESTRIELLE DE DROIT COMMERCIAL ET DU DROIT ECONOMIQUE. 1948. q. 485 F. (foreign 565 F.). Editions Sirey-Diffusion Dalloz, 11 rue Soufflot, 75240 Paris Cedex 05, France. TEL 40-51-54-54. FAX 45-87-37-48. TELEX 206446F. (Subscr. to: 35, rue Tournefort, 75240 Paris Cedex 05, France) bk.rev.; bibl. (reprint service avail. from SCH)
— BLDSC shelfmark: 7956.783000.
  Formerly: Revue Trimestrielle de Droit Commercial (ISSN 0048-8208)

340 K21   FR   ISSN 0035-4317
REVUE TRIMESTRIELLE DE DROIT EUROPEEN. 1965. q. 505 F. (foreign 645 F.). Editions Sirey-Diffusion Dalloz, 11 rue Soufflot, 75240 Paris Cedex 05, France. TEL 40-51-54-54. FAX 45-87-37-48. TELEX 206446F. bk.rev.; bibl.; index, cum.index. **Indexed:** P.A.I.S.For.Lang.Ind., Rural Recreat.Tour.Abstr., World Agri.Econ.& Rural Sociol.Abstr.
— BLDSC shelfmark: 7956.785000.

340   ZR
REVUE ZAIROISE DE DROIT.* 1971. s-a. $6. Office National de la Recherche et du Developpement, B.P. 16706, Kinshasa, Zaire. Ed.Bd. bibl.

340 LAW   US   ISSN 0556-8595
RHODE ISLAND BAR JOURNAL. 1952. m. (Oct.-June). $10. Rhode Island Bar Association, 115 Cedar St., Providence, RI 02903-1035. Ed.Bd. adv.; bk.rev.; bibl.; circ. 4,000. (also avail. in microfilm from WSH) **Indexed:** Abstr.Bk.Rev.Curr.Leg.Per., C.L.I., L.R.I., Leg.Per.

340 K22   US   ISSN 0279-0882
RHODE ISLAND LAWYERS WEEKLY. 1982. w. $195. Lawyers Weekly Publications, 30 Court Sq., Boston, MA 02108. TEL 617-227-6034. Ed. Danial Hackett. adv.; circ. 900.

340   US
▼**RHODE ISLAND RULES OF EVIDENCE.** 1990. base vol. (plus a. suppl.). $85.50. Butterworth Legal Publishers (Salem) (Subsidiary of: Reed International PLC), 90 Stiles Rd., Salem, NH 03079. TEL 800-548-4001. FAX 603-898-9858. Ed. Eric D. Green. (looseleaf format)

340   BL   ISSN 0101-1480
RIO GRANDE DO SUL, BRAZIL. PROCURADORIA GERAL DO ESTADO. REVISTA. 1971. irreg. free. (Instituto de Informatica Juridica) Procuradoria Geral do Estado, Av. Borges Medeiros 1501, 13th, Porto Alegre 90060, Brazil. FAX 0512-255496. circ. 1,500 (controlled).
  Formerly (until 1979): Rio Grande do Sul, Brazil. Consultoria-Geral. Revista.
  Description: Contains legal doctrine and procedure and the Attorney General's juridical reports.

RISK MANAGEMENT FOR EXECUTIVE WOMEN. see *INSURANCE*

RIVERS; studies in the science, environmental policy and law of instream flow. see *WATER RESOURCES*

340   IT   ISSN 0035-5763
RIVISTA AMMINISTRATIVA DELLA REPUBBLICA ITALIANA. 1850. m. Via Barnaba Tortolini 34, 00197 Rome, Italy. Ed. Leopoldo Piccardi.
— BLDSC shelfmark: 7980.750000.

340   IT
RIVISTA DEL CONSIGLIO. 1989. q. L.30000 (foreign L.60000). Casa Editrice Dott. A. Giuffre, Via Busto Arsizio 40, 20151 Milan, Italy. TEL 06-38000905. FAX 06-38009582.

340 600   IT
RIVISTA DEL CONSULENTE TECNICO. 1985; N.S. 1991. 3/yr. L.98000 (effective 1992). Maggioli Editore, Via Crimea, 1, Casella Postale 290, 47037 Rimini, Italy. TEL 0541-626777. FAX 0541-622020.

340   IT   ISSN 0035-5887
RIVISTA DEL DIRITTO COMMERCIALE E DEL DIRITTO GENERALE DELLE OBBLIGAZIONI. 1903. bi-m. L.100000($145) Piccin Nuova Libraria, Via Altinate 107, 35100 Padua, Italy. TEL 049-655566. FAX 039498750693. TELEX 432074 PICCIN I. Ed. Prof. Libonati. adv.; bk.rev.; index; circ. 2,000.
— BLDSC shelfmark: 7984.680000.

340   IT
RIVISTA DEL NOTARIATO. 1947. bi-m. L.110000 (foreign L.165000). Casa Editrice Dott. A. Giuffre, Via Busto Arsizio 40, 20151 Milan, Italy. TEL 02-38000905. FAX 02-38009582. Ed. M. Atlante. adv.; circ. 5,100.

340   IT
▼**RIVISTA DELL'ARBITRATO.** 1991. q. L.80000 (foreign L.120000). Casa Editrice Dott. A. Giuffre, Via Busto Arsizio 40, 20151 Milan, Italy. TEL 02-38000905. FAX 02-38009582.

340   IT   ISSN 0394-9028
RIVISTA DELLE CANCELLIERE; rassegna bimestrale dei servizi guidiziari. 1968. bi-m. L.63000($100) Edizioni Bucalo snc, Casella Postale, 51, 04100 Latina, Italy. FAX 773-623226. Dir. Angelo Cardillo. adv.; bk.rev.; bibl.; cum.index; circ. 5,500.

340   IT   ISSN 0035-6018
RIVISTA DELLE SOCIETA. (Text in French, Italian) 1956. bi-m. L.120000 (foreign L.180000). Casa Editrice Dott. A. Giuffre, Via Busto Arsizio 40, 20151 Milan, Italy. TEL 02-38000905. FAX 02-38009582. Ed. Giuseppe Auletta. adv.; bk.rev.; bibl.; charts; index; circ. 5,600. (back issues avail.)
— BLDSC shelfmark: 7992.826000.

340   IT
RIVISTA DI DIRITTO DELL'IMPRESA. 1982. 3/yr. L.75000 to individuals; institutions L.110000(effective 1992). Edizioni Scientifiche Italiane S.p.A., Via Chiatamone, 7, I-80121 Naples, Italy. Eds. Giuseppe Guarino, Natalino Irti. adv.; bk.rev.; circ. 5,000.

340   IT   ISSN 0035-6123
RIVISTA DI DIRITTO EUROPEO. 1961. q. L.60000. Via degli Spagnoli 29, 00186 Rome, Italy. Dir. Curti Gialdino Carlo. adv.; bk.rev.; bibl.; index; circ. 1,000.

RIVISTA DI DIRITTO FINANZIARIO E SCIENZA DELLE FINANZE. see *BUSINESS AND ECONOMICS — Banking And Finance*

340   IT   ISSN 0035-614X
RIVISTA DI DIRITTO INDUSTRIALE. 1952. q. L.80000 (foreign L.120000). Casa Editrice Dott. A. Giuffre, Via Busto Arsizio 40, Milan 20151, Italy. TEL 02-38000905. FAX 02-38009582. Ed. Remo Franceschelli. adv.; bk.rev.; abstr.; circ. 1,200.
— BLDSC shelfmark: 7984.850000.

RIVISTA DI DIRITTO SPORTIVO. see *SPORTS AND GAMES*

340   IT
▼**RIVISTA DI DIRITTO TRIBUTARIO.** 1991. m. L.150000 (foreign L.225000). Casa Editrice Dott. A. Giuffre, Via Busto Arsizio 40, 20151 Milan, Italy. TEL 02-38000905. FAX 02-38009582.

RIVISTA GIURIDICA DEL LAVORO E DELLA PREVIDENZA SOCIALE. DOTTRINA. see *LABOR UNIONS*

340   IT   ISSN 1120-9542
RIVISTA GIURIDICA DEL MEZZOGIORNO; trimestrale della SVIMEZ. 1987. q. L.140000. (Associazione per lo Sviluppo dell'Industria nel Mezzogiorno) Societa Editrice Il Mulino, Strada Maggiore, 37, 40125 Bologna, Italy. TEL 051-256011. FAX 051-256034. Ed. Massimo Annesi. adv.; circ. 1,100. (back issues avail.)

340   IT
▼**RIVISTA GIURIDICA DEL MOLISE E DEL SANNIO.** 1990. q. L.90000. Edizioni Scientifiche Italiane S.p.A., Via Chiatamone 7, 80121 Naples, Italy. TEL 081-7645768. FAX 081-7646477.

RIVISTA GIURIDICA DELL'AMBIENTE. see *ARCHITECTURE*

RIVISTA GIURIDICA DELL'EDILIZIA. see *BUILDING AND CONSTRUCTION*

349   IT   ISSN 0035-6700
RIVISTA GIURIDICA DELLA CIRCOLAZIONE E DEI TRASPORTI. 1947. bi-m. L.80000($120) (Automobile Club d'Italia) Editrice dell' Automobile s.r.l., Viale Regina Margherita 290, I-00198 Rome, Italy. TEL (06) 4402061. FAX 06-8840926. Ed. Sabino Cassese. bk.rev.; bibl.; circ. 10,000.

340   IT
RIVISTA GIURIDICA SARDA. 1986. 3/yr. L.80000 (foreign L.120000). Casa Editrice Dott. A. Giuffre, Via Busto Arsizio 40, 20151 Milan, Italy. TEL 02-38000902. FAX 02-38009582.

340 323.4   IT   ISSN 0394-6495
RIVISTA INTERNAZIONALE DEI DIRITTI DELL' UOMO. 1988. 3/yr. L.99000($76) (effective 1992). (Universita Cattolica del Sacro Cuore) Vita e Pensiero, Largo Gemelli, 1, 20123 Milan, Italy. TEL 02-8856-310. FAX 02-8856-260. Dir. Giovanni Maria Umbertazzi.
  Description: Covers the doctrine and science of jurisprudence. Covers the activities of organizations concerned with human rights.

341 K22   IT   ISSN 0035-6727
RIVISTA INTERNAZIONALE DI FILOSOFIA DEL DIRITTO. 1921. q. L.70000 (foreign L.105000). (Societa Italiana di Filosofia Giuridica e Politica) Casa Editrice Dott. A. Giuffre, Via Busto Arsizio 40, 20151 Milan, Italy. TEL 02-38000905. FAX 02-38009582. (Co-sponsor: Istituto di Filosofia del Diritto dell'Universita di Roma) Ed. Sergio Cotta. adv.; bk.rev.; bibl.; index; circ. 700.
— BLDSC shelfmark: 7987.130000.

340 331 K22   IT   ISSN 0393-2494
RIVISTA ITALIANA DI DIRITTO DEL LAVORO. (Text in Italian; summaries in English, French, German and Spanish) 1982. q. L.140000 (foreign L.210000). Casa Editrice Dott. A. Giuffre, Via Busto Arsizio 40, 20151 Milan, Italy. TEL 02-38000905. FAX 02-38009582. Ed. Giuseppe Pera. adv.; bk.rev.; bibl.; illus.; index; circ. 3,200.
— BLDSC shelfmark: 7987.296000.
  Supersedes: Rivista di Diritto del Lavoro (ISSN 0035-6107)

340   IT   ISSN 0557-1391
RIVISTA ITALIANA DI DIRITTO E PROCEDURA PENALE. 1958. q. L.130000 (foreign L.195000). Casa Editrice Dott. A. Giuffre, Via Busto Arsizio 40, 20151 Milan, Italy. TEL 02-38000905. FAX 02-38009582. Ed. Cesare Pedrazzi. adv.; circ. 3,500. **Indexed:** CERDIC.
— BLDSC shelfmark: 7987.295000.
  Formed by the merger of: Rivista Italiana di Diritto Penale & Rivista di Diritto Processuale Penale.

340   IT
▼**RIVISTA ITALIANA DI DIRITTO PUBBLICO COMUNITARIO.** 1991. q. L.100000 (foreign L.150000). Casa Editrice Dott. A. Giuffre, Via Busto Arsizio 40, 20151 Milan, Italy. TEL 02-38000905. FAX 02-38009582.

343   IT   ISSN 0035-7022
RIVISTA PENALE. 1874. m. L.90000 (foreign L.180000)(effective 1992). Casa Editrice la Tribuna, Via Don Minzoni 51, 29100 Piacenza, Italy. TEL 0523-759015. FAX 0523-757219. Ed. Paolo Appella. bk.rev.; index. (back issues avail.)

RIVISTA PENALE DELL'ECONOMIA. see *BUSINESS AND ECONOMICS*

340 330   IT
RIVISTA TRIMESTRALE DI DIRITTO PENALE DELL'ECONOMIA. 1988. q. L.150000 (foreign L.180000)(effective 1991). Casa Editrice Dott. Antonio Milani, Via Jappelli 5, 35121 Padua, Italy. TEL 049-656677. FAX 049-8752900. Ed. Giuseppe Zuccala.

340   IT   ISSN 0557-1464
RIVISTA TRIMESTRALE DI DIRITTO PUBBLICO. 1951. q. L.120000 (foreign L.180000). Casa Editrice Dott. A. Giuffre, Via Busto Arsizio 40, 20151 Milan, Italy. TEL 02-38000905. FAX 02-38009582. Eds. Giovanni Miele, Massimo Severo Giannini. adv.; circ. 2,200.
— BLDSC shelfmark: 7993.468000.

340   UK
ROAD LAW. 1985. 8/yr. £47.75. Barry Rose Law Periodicals, Little London, Chichester, W. Sussex PO19 1PG, England. TEL 0243-787841. FAX 0243-779278. Ed. Michael G. Jewell.
  Description: Topics covered include deregulation, road traffic regulations, competition, tachographs, European Community law, PSV operations and road law reports.

LAW

340 622   US
ROCKY MOUNTAIN MINERAL LAW FOUNDATION. NEWSLETTER. 1967. m. free. Rocky Mountain Mineral Law Foundation, Porter Administration Bldg., 7039 E. 18th Ave., Denver, CO 80220. TEL 303-321-8100. FAX 303-321-7657. bibl.; circ. 12,700.
Formerly: Rocky Mountain Mineral Law Newsletter (ISSN 0557-8051)

ROCKY MOUNTAIN MINERAL LAW INSTITUTE. PROCEEDINGS. see *MINES AND MINING INDUSTRY*

RODO HO/LABOUR LAW. see *BUSINESS AND ECONOMICS — Labor And Industrial Relations*

ROYAL NATIONAL INSTITUTE FOR THE BLIND. LAW NOTES. EXTRACTS. see *HANDICAPPED — Visually Impaired*

340   PL   ISSN 0035-9629
RUCH PRAWNICZY, EKONOMICZNY I SOCJOLOGICZNY. 1921. q. $48. (Akademia Ekonomiczna, Poznan) Adam Mickiewicz University Press, Nowowiejska 55, 61-734 Poznan, Poland. (Dist. by: Ars Polona, Krakowskie Przedmiescie 7, 00-068 Warsaw, Poland) (Co-sponsor: Akademia Ekonomiczna w Poznaniu) Ed. Z. Radwanski. adv.; bk.rev.; charts; index, cum.index; circ. 1,100.
—BLDSC shelfmark: 8047.400000.

340   UA
RUH AL-QAWANIN. 1989. a? Jami'at Tanta, Kulliyyat al-Huquq - Tanta University, Faculty of Law, Tanta, Egypt.

346.066   US
LAW
▼**RUSSIA AND COMMONWEALTH BUSINESS LAW REPORT**; monthly news and analysis. 1990. m. $970 (foreign $992). Buraff Publications (Subsidiary of: Millin Publications, Inc.), 1350 Connecticut Ave., N.W., Ste. 1000, Washington, DC 20036. TEL 202-862-0990. FAX 202-862-0999. Ed. Ted Stewart. (back issues avail.)
Formerly: Soviet Business Law Report (ISSN 1050-3730)

349   US
LAW
RUSSIAN POLITICS; a journal of translations. 1962. q. $260 to institutions. M.E. Sharpe, Inc., 80 Business Park Dr., Armonk, NY 10504. TEL 914-273-1800. FAX 914-273-2106. Ed. Nils H. Wessell. adv.; index. (also avail. in microfilm from WSH; reprint service avail. from WSH) **Indexed:** ASCA, C.L.I., Curr.Cont., Leg.Per., SSCI.
Formerly: Soviet Law and Government (ISSN 0038-5530)
Refereed Serial

340   US   ISSN 0277-318X
K22
RUTGERS LAW JOURNAL. 1969. q. $22.50 (foreign $27.50)(effective 1992). Rutgers University, School of Law - Camden, Fifth & Penn Sts., Camden, NJ 08102. TEL 609-757-6177. Ed. D. Matthew Jameson. adv.; B&W page $100. bk.rev.; charts; cum.index; circ. 1,200. (also avail. in microform from RRI; back issues avail.; reprint service avail. from RRI) **Indexed:** C.L.I., Crim.Just.Abstr., L.R.I., Leg.Cont., Leg.Per.
Formerly (until 1980): Rutgers-Camden Law Journal (ISSN 0036-0449)

340   US   ISSN 0036-0465
LAW
RUTGERS LAW REVIEW. 1936. q. $30 (foreign $35). Rutgers University, School of Law, Law Review, 15 Washington St., Newark, NJ 07102. TEL 201-648-5391. FAX 201-648-5391. adv.; bk.rev.; circ. 3,200. (reprint service avail. from RRI) **Indexed:** Abstr.Bk.Rev.Curr.Leg.Per., ASCA, Bank.Lit.Ind., C.L.I., Crim.Just.Abstr., Curr.Cont., L.R.I., Leg.Cont., Leg.Per., Sage Urb.Stud.Abstr., SSCI.
—BLDSC shelfmark: 8053.390000.
Formerly (until 1942): University of Newark Law Review.

S A E. (Sammlung Arbeitsrechtlicher Entscheidungen) see *BUSINESS AND ECONOMICS — Labor And Industrial Relations*

340 378   US
S A L T EQUALIZER. 1986. q. $35. Society of American Law Teachers, c/o Stuart Filler, Treas., University of Bridgeport, School of Law, Rm. 248, 303 University Ave., Bridgeport, CT 06601. TEL 203-576-4442. Ed. Michael Burns. circ. 550. (back issues avail.)

340   SA   ISSN 0258-6568
S A PUBLIEKREG/S A PUBLIC LAW. (Text in Afrikaans, English) 1986. 2/yr. $30 (effective 1992). University of South Africa, VerLoren van Themaat Centre for Public Law Studies, P.O. Box 392, Pretoria 0001, South Africa. TEL 012-429-8468. FAX 012-429-3321. Ed. D.H. van Wyk. circ. 350. (back issues avail.)

S C A D BULLETIN. (Systeme Communautaire d'Acces a la Documentation) see *BIBLIOGRAPHIES*

340 360   UK   ISSN 0264-8717
S C O L A G. 1975. 12/yr. £14 to individuals; institutions £21. Scottish Legal Action Group, The Old Schoolhouse, Coupar Angus, Perthshire PH13 9AP, Scotland. TEL 0828-27326. Ed. J. Black. adv.; bk.rev.; index; circ. 1,100. **Indexed:** ASSIA, C.L.I.
—BLDSC shelfmark: 8205.456000.

S E C COMPLIANCE: FINANCIAL REPORTING AND FORMS. see *BUSINESS AND ECONOMICS — Investments*

S E C GUIDELINES (YEAR); rules and regulations. (Security, Exchange and Commission) see *BUSINESS AND ECONOMICS — Investments*

340   US   ISSN 0894-3486
S E R B OFFICIAL REPORTER. (State Employment Relations Board) 1987. m. $180. Banks - Baldwin Law Publishing Co., University Center, Box 1974, Cleveland, OH 44106. TEL 216-721-7373. FAX 216-721-8055. charts.
Description: Includes the full text of SERB opinions: new court decisions; relevant statutes and rules; official forms, practice outlines; and research aids.

S I A WASHINGTON REPORT. (Securities Industry Association (Washington)) see *BUSINESS AND ECONOMICS — Investments*

SACRAMENTO NEWSLETTER. see *POLITICAL SCIENCE*

340   AT
SAFETY & INDUSTRY LAW SERVICE N S W. (In 2 volumes) q. (plus bulletins). $425. Butterworths Pty. Ltd., 271-273 Lane Cove Rd., P.O. Box 345, North Ryde, N.S.W. 2113, Australia. TEL 02-335-4444. FAX 02-335-4655. (looseleaf format)

SAILORMAN STAR MAGAZINE. see *SPORTS AND GAMES — Boats And Boating*

346.066   SZ
ST. GALLER STUDIEN ZUM PRIVAT-, HANDELS- UND WIRTSCHAFTSRECHT. 1982. irreg., vol.26, 1991. price varies. (Hochschule St. Gallen fuer Wirtschafts- und Sozialwissenschaften) Paul Haupt AG, Falkenplatz 14, CH-3001 Berne, Switzerland. TEL 031-232425.

340   US   ISSN 0036-2905
K23
ST. JOHN'S LAW REVIEW. 1926. q. $12. St. John's University, School of Law, Grand Central and Utopia Parkway, Jamaica, NY 11439. TEL 718-990-6600. bk.rev.; charts; stat.; index; circ. 3,000. (also avail. in microfiche from WSH; microfilm from WSH) **Indexed:** Account.Ind. (1974-), C.L.I., Cath.Ind., Crim.Just.Abstr., L.R.I., Leg.Cont., Leg.Per.
—BLDSC shelfmark: 8070.163000.

340   US
ST. LOUIS BAR JOURNAL. q. ADmore, Inc., 9701 Gravois Rd., St. Louis, MO 63123. TEL 800-451-0914. FAX 314-638-3880.

ST. LOUIS COUNTIAN. see *JOURNALISM*

340   US
ST. LOUIS DAILY RECORD. d. Legal Communications Corp., Box 88910, St. Louis, MO 63188-1910. TEL 314-421-1880. FAX 314-421-0436. Ed. Will Connaghan. circ. 1,219.

340   US
ST. LOUIS LAWYER. m. ADmore, Inc., 9701 Gravois Rd., St. Louis, MO 63123. TEL 800-451-0914. FAX 314-638-3880.

340   US   ISSN 0036-3030
LAW
SAINT LOUIS UNIVERSITY LAW JOURNAL. 1949. q. $20. St. Louis University School of Law, 3700 Lindell Blvd., St. Louis, MO 63108. TEL 314-658-3933. Ed.Bd. adv.; bk.rev.; charts; index; circ. 1,000. (also avail. in microfiche; microfilm from WSH; back issues avail.; reprint service avail. from WSH) **Indexed:** Abstr.Bk.Rev.Curr.Leg.Per., C.L.I., L.R.I., Leg.Cont., Leg.Per.
●Also available online. Vendor(s): WESTLAW.
—BLDSC shelfmark: 8070.180000.

340   US   ISSN 0898-8404
SAINT LOUIS UNIVERSITY PUBLIC LAW REVIEW. 1981. 3/yr. $20. Saint Louis University School of Law, 3700 Lindell Blvd., Saint Louis, MO 63108. TEL 314-658-3937. Ed. Norma Tamez Maret. adv.; bk.rev.; circ. 750. (reprint service avail. from WSH) **Indexed:** C.L.I., L.R.I., Leg.Per., P.A.I.S.
—BLDSC shelfmark: 8070.182000.
Formerly: Saint Louis University Public Law Forum (ISSN 0738-5390)
Description: Multi-disciplinary law review analyzing topical social issues and public policy legal issues.

340   US   ISSN 0581-3441
K23
ST. MARY'S LAW JOURNAL. 1969. 4/yr. $25. St. Mary's University School of Law, One Camino Santa Maria, San Antonio, TX 78228-8604. TEL 512-436-3439. FAX 512-436-3756. Ed.Bd. adv.; bk.rev.; circ. 1,600. (also avail. in microform from MIM,RRI; microfilm from WSH; reprint service avail. from RRI) **Indexed:** C.L.I., L.R.I., Leg.Cont., Leg.Per.

340   US
ST. PAUL LEGAL LEDGER. 1927. d. $90. Legal Ledger, Inc., 640 Minnesota Bldg., 46 E. 4th St., St. Paul, MN 55101-1163. TEL 612-222-0059. Ed. Samuel E. Lewis, Jr. adv.; circ. 700.

340   AT   ISSN 0310-6861
ST. THOMAS MORE SOCIETY. JOURNAL. 1971. irreg. St. Thomas More Society, Box 282 G.P.O., Sydney, N.S.W. 2001, Australia. Ed. John D. Traill.

346.066   US
▼**SALES OF A BUSINESS IN MINNESOTA.** 1990. base vol. (plus suppl.). $88. Butterworth Legal Publishers (Salem) (Subsidiary of: Reed International PLC), 90 Stiles Rd., Salem, NH 03079. TEL 800-548-4001. FAX 603-898-9858. Ed. George Gaffaney. (looseleaf format)
Description: Examines the basic types of sales and discusses related issues such as the tax consequences of a sale, minority interests, and how to investigate both buyers and sellers.

340   GW
SAMELBLATT FUER RECHTSVORSCHRIFTEN DES BUNDES UND DER LAENDER. 1947. bi-m. DM.248. Engel Verlag, Wilhelmstr. 42, Postfach 2229, D-6200 Wiesbaden, Germany. circ. 2,000.

340   AU
SAMMLUNG ARBEITSRECHTLICHER ENTSCHEIDUNGEN DER GERICHTE UND EINIGUNGSAEMTER. 1932. q. S.675. Manzsche Verlags- und Universitaetsbuchhandlung, Kohlmarkt 16, A-1014 Vienna, Austria. TEL 0222-531610. FAX 0222-5316181. Ed. Helmuth Tades. circ. 3,000.
Description: Collects cases concerning labor law.

340 320   GW   ISSN 0080-5823
SAMMLUNG GELTENDER STAATSANGEHOERIGKEITSGESETZE. 1949. irreg., vol.39, 1982. price varies. (Universitaet Hamburg, Institut fuer Internationale Angelegenheiten) Nomos Verlagsgesellschaft mbH und Co. KG, Waldseestr. 3-5, Postfach 610, 7570 Baden Baden, Germany.

340 664   GW   ISSN 0080-5831
SAMMLUNG LEBENSMITTELRECHTLICHER ENTSCHEIDUNGEN. 1959. irreg., vol.21, 1989. DM.890. Carl Heymanns Verlag KG, Luxemburgerstr. 449, 5000 Cologne 41, Germany. TEL 0221-46010-0. FAX 0221-4601069. Ed. Herbert Bens.

340 US ISSN 0036-4037
LAW
SAN DIEGO LAW REVIEW. 1964. 5/yr. $25. (San Diego Law Review Association, San Diego Law Review) University of San Diego, School of Law, Alcala Park, San Diego, CA 92110. TEL 619-260-4531. Ed. Lance Shea. adv.; index; circ. 2,000. (also avail. in microform from WSH; reprint service avail. from WSH) **Indexed:** ABI Inform., BPIA, C.L.I., Crim.Just.Abstr., Deep Sea Res.& Oceanogr.Abstr., L.R.I., Leg.Cont., Leg.Per., Ocean.Abstr., Pollut.Abstr., PSI, Sel.Water Res.Abstr.
—BLDSC shelfmark: 8072.870000.

340 US
SAN FRANCISCO ATTORNEY MAGAZINE. 6/yr. $21. Bar Association of San Francisco, 685 Market St., Ste. 700, San Francisco, CA 94105. Ed. James Hargarten. bk.rev.; circ. 8,500. **Indexed:** C.L.I., Leg.Per.
  Former titles: Brief - Case; In Re (ISSN 0046-8754)

340 US
SAN FRANCISCO BAY AREA REGISTER OF EXPERTS AND CONSULTANTS. a. $10 to non-members. Bar Association of San Francisco, 685 Market St., Ste. 700, San Francisco, CA 94105. circ. 15,000.
  Formerly: Forensic Register of Expert Consultants.
  Description: Lists expert witnesses and consultants in over 150 specialties who service the legal community.

340 US
SAN FRANCISCO DAILY JOURNAL. d. (Mon.-Fri.). $234. Daily Journal Corporation (San Francisco), 1390 Market St., Ste. 910, San Francisco, CA 94102-5402. TEL 415-558-9888. FAX 415-558-8469. Ed. Ray Reynolds. adv.; bk.rev.; circ. 5,512.

340 US ISSN 0036-4185
SAN JOSE POST-RECORD; daily legal, & commercial real estate & financial news. 1910. d. $59. Rose Publishing Co., Inc., 20 N. First St., No. A, San Jose, CA 95113-1201. Ed. Opal McLean. adv.; stat.; circ. 1,200. (tabloid format)

340 US
▼**SANCTIONS IN FEDERAL LITIGATION.** 1991. base vol. (plus a. suppl.) $95. Butterworth Legal Publishers (Salem) (Subsidiary of: Reed International PLC), 90 Stiles Rd., Salem, NH 03079. TEL 800-548-4001. FAX 603-898-9858. Ed.Bd. (looseleaf format)
  Description: Addresses statutory and case law and strategies for asking for or defending against a motion for sanctions.

340 IO ISSN 0303-321X
SANGKAKALA PERADILAN. Rps.450. Ikatan Hakim Indonesia, Tjabang Semarang, Jalan Siliwangi 151, Semarang, Indonesia. illus.

340 SZ
ST. GALLER STUDIEN ZUM WETTBEWERBS UND IMMATERIALGUETERRECHT. 1971. irreg. price varies. Verlag Ostschweiz, Oberer Graben 8, Postfach 716, CH-9001 St. Gallen, Switzerland. Ed. Mario M. Pedrazzini.

340 600 US
SANTA CLARA COMPUTER AND HIGH-TECHNOLOGY LAW JOURNAL. 1985. s-a. $40. Santa Clara University, School of Law, Santa Clara, CA 95053. TEL 408-554-4197. Ed.Bd. **Indexed:** C.L.I., Leg.Per.
  Formerly: Computer and Technology Law Journal.
  Description: For lawyers and laypersons interested in current issues and decisions in computer and technology law.

340 US ISSN 0146-0315
K23
SANTA CLARA LAW REVIEW. 1961. 4/yr. $25. Santa Clara University, School of Law, Santa Clara, CA 95053. TEL 408-554-4074. Ed. Michael Droke. adv.; bk.rev.; circ. 1,750. (also avail. in microfiche from WSH; microfilm from WSH) **Indexed:** Abstr.Bk.Rev.Curr.Leg.Per., C.L.I., L.R.I., Leg.Cont., Leg.Per., Sel.Water Res.Abstr.
●Also available online. Vendor(s): WESTLAW.
—BLDSC shelfmark: 8075.320000.
  Formerly (until vol.15, no.4, 1975): Santa Clara Lawyer (ISSN 0581-6106)

SAO PAULO, BRAZIL (STATE). SECRETARIA DA EDUCACAO. ATIVIDADES DESENVOLVIDAS. see *EDUCATION*

340 CN
SASKATCHEWAN DECISIONS CITATOR. (Includes: Statute Citator, Rules Citator, Regulations Table and Library News) 1981. m. Can.$120. Western Legal Publications, 301-1 Alexander St, Vancouver, B.C. V6A 1B2, Canada. TEL 604-687-5671. FAX 604-687-2796.
  Formerly: Saskatchewan Decisions - Rules and Statute Citator (ISSN 0824-7285)

340 CN ISSN 0319-7999
SASKATCHEWAN DECISIONS, CIVIL AND CRIMINAL CASES. 1975. m. Can.$265. Western Legal Publications, 301-1 Alexander St., Vancouver, B.C. V6A 1B2, Canada. TEL 604-687-5671. FAX 604-687-2796. (looseleaf format)
●Also available online.
  Description: Presents all available civil and criminal decisions from the Saskatchewan Court of Appeal, Court of Queen's Bench and selected decisions of the Provincial Court of Saskatchewan.

340 CN ISSN 0036-4894
CODEN: SAGAEU
SASKATCHEWAN GAZETTE. vol.69, 1973. w. Can.$115. Queen's Printer, Saskatchewan, 8th fl., 1874 Scarth St., Regina, Sask. S4P 3V7, Canada. TEL 306-787-6894. FAX 306-787-9111. Ed. Marilyn A. Lustig-McEwan. illus.; circ. 3,000. (also avail. in microfilm from UMI,KTO; reprint service avail. from UMI)

340 CN ISSN 0036-4916
SASKATCHEWAN LAW REVIEW. 1935. s-a. Can.$26. University of Saskatchewan, College of Law, Law Building, Saskatoon, Sask. S7N 0W0, Canada. TEL 306-966-5872. FAX 306-966-5900. adv.; bk.rev.; index, cum.index; circ. 1,800. (also avail. in microfiche from WSH; microfilm from WSH) **Indexed:** C.L.I., HR Rep., Ind.Can.L.P.L., L.R.I., Leg.Cont., Leg.Per.
—BLDSC shelfmark: 8076.537000.
  Formerly: Saskatchewan Bar Review.
  Refereed Serial

340 CN
SASKATCHEWAN REPORTS. 1979. irreg. Can.$84 per vol. Maritime Law Book Ltd., Box 302, Fredericton, N.B. E3B 4Y9, Canada. TEL 506-454-9921. (back issues avail.)
●Also available online. Vendor(s): QL Systems Ltd..

340 GW ISSN 0323-4045
SAVIGNY-STIFTUNG FUER RECHTSGESCHICHTE. ZEITSCHRIFT. GERMANTISCHE ABTEILUNG. a., vol.13, 1991. DM.248. Boehlau Verlag GmbH, Theodor-Heuss-Str. 76, 5000 Cologne 90, Germany. adv.; bk.rev.; bibl.; illus.; index; circ. 800. **Indexed:** Canon Law Abstr., Hist.Abstr.

340 GW ISSN 0323-4142
SAVIGNY-STIFTUNG FUER RECHTSGESCHICHTE. ZEITSCHRIFT. KANONISTISCHE ABTEILUNG. a., vol.8, 1991. DM.184. Boehlau Verlag GmbH, Theodor-Heuss-Str. 76, 5000 Cologne 90, Germany. Ed.Bd. bk.rev. **Indexed:** CERDIC.

340 GW ISSN 0323-4096
SAVIGNY-STIFTUNG FUER RECHTSGESCHICHTE. ZEITSCHRIFT. ROMANISTISCHE ABTEILUNG. a., vol.12, 1991. DM.296. Boehlau Verlag GmbH, Theodor-Heuss-Str. 76, 5000 Cologne 90, Germany.
—BLDSC shelfmark: 9485.770000.

340 YU ISSN 0036-5173
SAVREMENA PRAKSA; list za privredna i pravna pitanja radnih organizacija. 1966. w. 49000 din. Savremena Administracja, Knez Mihajlova 6-V, 11001 Belgrade, Yugoslavia. TEL 623-287. Ed. Stevan Petrovic. circ. 13,000.

340 CS ISSN 0036-522X
SBIRKA SOUDNICH ROZHODNUTI A STANOVISEK.* vol.23, 1971. 10/yr. 36 Kcs. Nejvyssi Soud, Nam. Hrdinu 1300, Prague 4, Czechoslovakia. Eds. Anna Vaskova, Karel Matys. index.
  Formerly: Sbirka Rozhodnuti a Sdeleni Soudu C S S R.
  Description: Collection of court decisions.

340 AT ISSN 0727-7903
SCALES OF COST QUEENSLAND. 1979. 8/yr. Aus.$125. Law Book Co. Ltd., 44-5- Waterloo Rd., North Ryde, N.S.W. 2113, Australia. TEL 02-887-0177. FAX 02-888-9706. TELEX ASBOOK 27995.
  Description: Scales of costs are provided from a wide range of services without commentary or precedent. Covers both Queensland and federal jurisdictions.

340 AT ISSN 0727-7881
SCALES OF COSTS, CHARGES AND FEES N.S.W. 1984. 12/yr. Aus.$325. Law Book Co. Ltd., 44-50 Waterloo Rd., North Ryde, N.S.W. 2113, Australia. TEL 02-887-0177. FAX 02-888-9706. TELEX ASBOOK 27995.
  Description: Provides information to assist practitioners in the preparation of bills of costs.

340 SW ISSN 0085-5944
SCANDINAVIAN STUDIES IN LAW. (Text in English) 1957. a. SEK 193. (Stockholms Universitet) Almqvist & Wiksell International, P.O. Box 638, S-101 28 Stockholm, Sweden. FAX 08-7912335. Ed. Anders Victorin. circ. 900.
—BLDSC shelfmark: 8087.685000.

340 323.4 350 GW ISSN 0342-7471
SCHIEDSMANNS ZEITUNG. 1926. m. DM.77. Carl Heymanns Verlag, Hahnenfussweg 70, 4630 Bochum, Germany. TEL 0221-46010-0. FAX 0221-4601069. TELEX 8881888. Ed. Lugwig Hans Serwe. circ. 4,500.
—BLDSC shelfmark: 8088.690000.

340 US ISSN 8755-8297
KF4114
SCHOOL LAW BULLETIN (BOSTON).* 1974. m. $37.10. Quinlan Publishing Co., Inc., 23 Drydock Ave., 2nd Fl., Boston, MA 02210-2307. Ed. M. Quinlan. (looseleaf format; also avail. in microform from UMI; reprint service avail. from UMI) **Indexed:** C.L.I., L.R.I.

340 370 US ISSN 0886-2508
SCHOOL LAW BULLETIN (CHAPEL HILL). 1970. q. $20. University of North Carolina at Chapel Hill, Institute of Government, CB No. 3330, Knapp Bldg., Chapel Hill, NC 27599-3330. TEL 919-966-4119. FAX 919-962-0654. Ed. Laurie L. Mesibov. (also avail. in microform from UMI; reprint service avail. from UMI) **Indexed:** C.I.J.E., C.L.I., L.R.I., P.A.I.S.
—BLDSC shelfmark: 8092.779000.

344.73 US ISSN 0164-3851
KF4150.A59
SCHOOLS AND THE COURTS; briefs of selected court cases involving secondary and elementary schools. 1975. q. $95.50. College Administration Publications, Inc., School Administration Publications, 21 Mt. Vernon Pl., Box 8492, Asheville, NC 28814. TEL 704-252-0883. Eds. D. Parker Young, Donald D. Gerhing. index; circ. 1,800.
  Formerly (until vol.5, no.1, Feb. 1979): School Student and the Courts (ISSN 0098-8952)
  Description: Lists of publications on legislative, policy, judicial, and procedural developments pertaining to the managerial activities and responsibilities of faculty and administrators in the field of higher education.

SCHRIFTENREIHE FINANZWIRTSCHAFT UND FINANZRECHT. see *BUSINESS AND ECONOMICS — Banking And Finance*

340 AU
SCHRIFTENREIHE: GESELLSCHAFT UND BETRIEB. 1974. irreg., vol.4, 1980. price varies. (Institut fuer Partnerschaftliche Betriebsverfassung) Manzsche Verlags- und Universitaetsbuchhandlung, Kohlmarkt 16, A-1014 Vienna, Austria. TEL 0222-531610. FAX 0222-5316181. circ. 1,800.
  Description: Collects articles on legal policy.

340 SZ ISSN 0036-7613
SCHWEIZERISCHE JURISTEN-ZEITUNG/REVUE SUISSE DE JURISPRUDENCE. (Text in French and German) 1904. s-m. 132 Fr. (students 95 Fr.). (Schweizerischer Anwaltsverband - Federation Suisse des Avocats) Schulthess Polygraphischer Verlag AG, Zwingliplatz 2, 8001 Zurich, Switzerland. TEL 01-2519336. Eds. P. Forstmoser, H. Aeppli. adv.; bk.rev.; bibl.; index, cum.index every 10 yrs.; vols.1-65 (1904-1969), vols.66-76 (1970-1979), vols.77-85 (1980-1989); circ. 4,000. **Indexed:** CERDIC.
—BLDSC shelfmark: 8117.350000.

LAW

340   PO   ISSN 0559-1422
SCIENTIA JURIDICA. 1951. bi-m. Esc.750($20) (Associacao Juridica) Livraria Cruz, Rua D. Diogo de Sousa 127-133, Braga, Portugal.
—BLDSC shelfmark: 8172.500000.

340   UK   ISSN 0036-908X
SCOTS LAW TIMES. 1893. w. £295. W. Green, 21 Alva St., Edinburgh EH2 4PS, Scotland. adv.; bk.rev.; index. (also avail. in microfiche from BHP) **Indexed:** C.L.I., RICS.

340   UK
SCOTS LAW TIMES CHRISTMAS CHARITY. SUPPLEMENT. a. W. Green, 21 Alva St., Edinburgh EH2 4PS, Scotland.

340   UK   ISSN 0265-6159
SCOTTISH CURRENT LAW YEAR BOOK. 1948. a. £85. W. Green, 21 Alva St., Edinburgh EH2 4PS, Scotland.

346   UK   ISSN 0080-8083
SCOTTISH LAW DIRECTORY. 1892. a. £29. T & T Clark, 59 George St., Edinburgh EH2 2LQ, Scotland. TEL 031-225-4703. FAX 031-220-4260. circ. 4,500.

340   UK   ISSN 0036-9314
SCOTTISH LAW GAZETTE. 1933. q. £15 to non-members; students £5. Scottish Law Agents Society, c/o R.M. Sinclair, Secy., 3 Albyn Place, Edinburgh EH2 4NQ, Scotland. TEL 031-225-7515. FAX 031-220-1083. adv.; bk.rev.; index; circ. 2,500.
—BLDSC shelfmark: 8210.670000.

343   US   ISSN 0037-0193
KF9630.A59
SEARCH AND SEIZURE BULLETIN.* 1964. m. $39.03. Quinlan Publishing Co., Inc., 23 Drydock Ave., 2nd Fl., Boston, MA 02210-2307. Ed. M. Quinlan. cum.index; circ. 3,500. (looseleaf format; also avail. in microform from UMI; back issues avail.; reprint service avail. from UMI) **Indexed:** CJPI.

340   US   ISSN 0095-1005
KF9630.A73
SEARCH AND SEIZURE LAW REPORT. 1973. 11/yr. $150. Clark - Boardman - Callaghan Company, Inc., 375 Hudson St., New York, NY 10014. TEL 212-929-7500. FAX 212-924-0460. Ed. Alan Weinstein. index. (looseleaf format; back issues avail.) **Indexed:** C.L.I., CJPI, L.R.I.

340   US
▼**SECURITIES ARBITRATION PROCEDURE MANUAL.** 1990. base vol. (plus a. suppl.). Butterworth Legal Publishers (Salem) (Subsidiary of: Reed International PLC), 90 Stiles Rd., Salem, NH 03079. TEL 800-548-4001. FAX 603-898-9858. (looseleaf format)
Description: Discusses issues encountered in a securities arbitration dispute, including evaluation of the merits of a case and its preparation and presentation to arbitration panels anywhere in the country.

340 332.64   US
SECURITIES FRAUD AND COMMODITIES FRAUD. 1980. 7 base vols. (plus a. suppl.). $490. Shepard's - McGraw-Hill, Inc., Box 35300, Colorado Springs, CO 80935-3530. TEL 800-525-2474.
Description: Covers misrepresentation, non-disclosure, manipulation, churning and insider trading.

340   US
SECURITIES INSIDER TRADING LITIGATION REPORTER; the national journal of record reporting litigation concerning insider trading and other securities law abuses which adversely affect market stability. 1987. s-m. $1250. Andrews Publications, 1646 West Chester Pike, Box 1000, Westtown, PA 19395. TEL 215-399-6600. FAX 215-399-6610. Ed. Barbara Murphy. bibl.; stat.; cum.index every 6 mos. (looseleaf format; back issues avail.)

340 332   US
SECURITIES INSTITUTE. a. $35 softcover. Continuing Education of the Bar - California, University of California Extension, 2300 Shattuck Ave., Berkeley, CA 94704. TEL 510-642-6211. FAX 800-642-3788. (Co-sponsor: State Bar of California)

SECURITIES LAW REVIEW. see BUSINESS AND ECONOMICS — Banking And Finance

340   US   ISSN 1053-0266
KF1436.3
▼**SECURITIES LITIGATION REPORTER.** 1990. s-m. $600. Andrews Publications, 1646 West Chester Pike, Box 1000, Westtown, PA 19395. TEL 215-399-6600. FAX 215-399-6610. Ed. Barbara Pizzirani. bibl.; stat.; cum.index every 6 mos. (looseleaf format; back issues avail.)
Description: Covers class action suits, RICO law and common law claims in securities-related litigation.

SECURITIES REGULATION. see BUSINESS AND ECONOMICS — Investments

340   US   ISSN 0037-0665
KF1439.A1
SECURITIES REGULATION & LAW REPORT. 1969. w. $870. The Bureau of National Affairs, Inc., 1231 25th St., N.W., Washington, DC 20037. TEL 202-452-4200. FAX 202-822-8092. TELEX 285656 BNAI WSH. (Subscr. to: 9435 Key West Ave., Rockville, MD 20850. TEL 800-372-1033) Ed. Susan Raleigh Jenkins. q. index. (looseleaf format; back issues avail.) **Indexed:** Leg.Per.
●Also available online. Vendor(s): Bureau of National Affairs, Mead Data Central (SECREG), WESTLAW (BNA-SRLR).
Description: Covers the latest securities and commodities activity at the federal and state levels, including developments from Congress, the Administration, SEC, CFTC, banking regulations, FASB, professional associations, the courts and industry. Contains full text of selected regulations, opinions and legislation.

SECURITIES REGULATION LAW JOURNAL. see BUSINESS AND ECONOMICS — Investments

942   UK
SELDEN SOCIETY, LONDON. HANDBOOK: PUBLICATIONS, LIST OF MEMBERS AND RULES. 1952. irreg. (every 4-5 yrs.). $10 to non-members. Selden Society, Queen Mary College, Faculty of Laws, Mile End Rd., London E1 4NS, England. TEL 071-975-5136. FAX 081-981-8733. TELEX 893750.
Description: List of publications and members of the Selden Society worldwide.

942   UK
SELDEN SOCIETY, LONDON. LECTURES. 1953. irreg. (every 2-3 yrs.). price varies. Selden Society, Queen Mary College, Faculty of Laws, Mile End Rd., London E1 4NS, England. TEL 071-975-5136. FAX 081-981-8733. TELEX 893750.
Description: Lectures on English legal history.

942   UK
SELDEN SOCIETY, LONDON. MAIN (ANNUAL) SERIES. (Text in English, French, Latin; summaries in English) 1887. a. $50 to individuals; libraries $65. Selden Society, Queen Mary College, Faculty of Laws, Mile End Road, London E1 4NS, England. TEL 071-975-5136. FAX 081-981-8733. TELEX 893750. bibl.; charts; illus.; cum.index: vols. 1-105; circ. 1,700. (also avail. in microfilm from BHP)
Description: Source material on the history of English law, legal institutions and the legal profession.

942   UK   ISSN 0582-4788
SELDEN SOCIETY, LONDON. SUPPLEMENTARY SERIES. 1965. irreg. price varies. Selden Society, Queen Mary College, Faculty of Laws, Mile End Rd., London E1 4NS, England. TEL 071-975-5136. FAX 081-981-8733. TELEX 893750.
Description: Compilations and reference works for the study of English legal history.

340   FR   ISSN 0049-0156
SEMAINE JURIDIQUE; juris-classeur periodique. (In three editions: Commerce et Industrie, Generale and Notariale) 1924. w. $120 for each edition. Editions Techniques, 12 rue d'Alesia, Paris 75014, France. TEL 45-39-22-91. FAX 45-42-81-55. TELEX EDITEC 270737 F. adv.; bibl.; index; circ. 15,000.

340   FR   ISSN 0223-4637
SEMAINE SOCIALE LAMY; l'actualite du droit social, de la gestion et des remunerations. w. 990 F. Lamy S.A., 115 rue Legendre, 75850 Paris Cedex 17, France. TEL 16-1-40-38-03-03. FAX 16-1-40-38-90-69. TELEX 214 398. (back issues avail.)
Description: Analyzes the diversity of social laws and their impact on the economy.

340   US   ISSN 1050-3250
SENIOR LAW REPORT. 1989. s-m. $197. (Community Development Services, Inc.) C D Publications, 5204 Fenton St., Silver Spring, MD 20910-2889. TEL 301-588-6380. FAX 301-588-6385. Ed. Herb Weiss. index. (back issues avail.)
Description: Covers current legislation, court rulings, and trends affecting the legal status of older Americans, including age discrimination, nursing homes regulations, Social Security, pension, and benefit policies.

340   CN
SENTENCES ARBITRALES DE LA FONCTION PUBLIQUE. m. Can.$95. Ministere des Communications, P.O. Box 1005, Quebec, Que. G1K 7B5, Canada. TEL 514-948-1222. (Subscr. to: Service Abonnements, CP1190, Outremont, Que. H2V 1V6, Canada)

340   SP   ISSN 0210-3427
SENTENCIAS EN APELACION DE LAS AUDIENCIAS PROVINCIALES; en materia civil y penal. 1969. a. 5300 ptas.($34) Ministerio de Justicia, Centro de Publicaciones, Secretaria General Tecnica, Gran Via, 76-8, 28013 Madrid, Spain. TEL 247 54 22. Ed.Bd. circ. 3,000. (back issues avail.)

340   US
SENTENCING IN WASHINGTON. 1985. irreg., latest ed. 1991. $120. Butterworth Legal Publishers (Salem) (Subsidiary of: Reed International PLC), 90 Stiles Rd., Salem, NH 03079. TEL 800-548-4001. FAX 603-898-9858. Ed. David Boerner. (looseleaf format)
Description: Covers all aspects of the Sentencing Reform Act of 1981.

347   II   ISSN 0304-100X
LAW
SERVICES LAW CASES; monthly law reporter dealing with law relating to promotion, discharge, dismissals, etc. containing recent judgments of all the high courts in the country and Supreme Court of India. (Text in English) m. Rs.60. International Law Book Co., Nijhawan Bldg., 1562 Church Rd., Kashmere Gate, Delhi 6, India. Ed. Mrs. Swarn Bhati Nijhawan.

340   UK   ISSN 0037-282X
SESSION CASES; the official Law Reports of Scotland. 1904. irreg. (approx. 3-4/yr.). £100. (Scottish Council of Law Reporting) T & T Clark Ltd., 59 George St., Edinburgh EH2 2LQ, Scotland. TEL 031-225-4703. FAX 031-220-4260. Ed. R.J. Hunter. index, cum.index; circ. 1,000.
Description: Official law reports of Scotland.

340   US
SETON HALL LEGISLATIVE JOURNAL. 1975. s-a. $10. (Seton Hall Legislative Bureau) Seton Hall University, Law Center, 1095 Raymond Blvd., Newark, NJ 07102. TEL 201-642-8500. bk.rev.; circ. 4,000. (also avail. in microform from WSH; reprint service avail. from WSH) **Indexed:** Abstr.Bk.Rev.Curr.Leg.Per., C.L.I., Crim.Just.Abstr., L.R.I., Leg.Cont., Leg.Per.

340   IT
SETTIMANA GIURIDICA. 1960. w. L.500000. Casa Editrice Italedi, Piazza Cavour 19, 00193 Rome, Italy. Ed. Ignazio Scotto. adv.; circ. 5,000.

340   CC
SHANDONG LUSHI/SHANDONG LAWYERS. (Text in Chinese) q. Shandong Lushi Xiehui - Shandong Lawyers Association, No. 9, Jing 10 Lu, Jinan, Shandong 250014, People's Republic of China. TEL 616138. Ed. Wang Weimin.

340   CC
SHANGHAI FAYUAN/SHANGHAI LEGAL WORLD. (Text in Chinese) m. Shanghai Shi Sifaju - Shanghai Municipal Bureau of Justice, No.3. Alley 112, Fenyang Lu, Shanghai 200031, People's Republic of China. TEL 4312801. Ed. Xu Qingzhen.

SHAREHOLDER REMEDIES IN CANADA. see BUSINESS AND ECONOMICS — Investments

340 US ISSN 0730-465X
SHEPARD'S CODE OF FEDERAL REGULATIONS CITATIONS. 1986. supplements 5/yr. plus a. cum. $336. Shepard's - McGraw-Hill, Inc., Box 35300, Colorado Springs, CO 80935-3530. TEL 800-525-2474.

340 US ISSN 0730-7039
SHEPARD'S FEDERAL CIRCUIT TABLE. 1981. 4/yr. $250. Shepard's - McGraw-Hill, Inc., Box 35300, Colorado Springs, CO 80935-3530. TEL 800-525-2474.

340 US ISSN 0730-4633
SHEPARD'S FEDERAL CITATIONS. 1981. 10/yr. (plus s-a. supplements to 24 base vols.). $2633. Shepard's - McGraw-Hill, Inc., Box 35300, Colorado Springs, CO 80935-3530. TEL 800-525-2474.

340 US ISSN 0746-312X
SHEPARD'S FEDERAL ENERGY LAW CITATIONS. 1982. 3 base vols. (plus q. suppl.). $435. Shepard's - McGraw-Hill, Inc., Box 35300, Colorado Springs, CO 80935-3530. TEL 800-525-2474.

340 US ISSN 0730-4684
SHEPARD'S FEDERAL LABOR LAW CITATIONS. 1959. 8 base vols. (plus s-a suppl.). $1305. Shepard's - McGraw-Hill, Inc., Box 35300, Colorado Springs, CO 80935-3530. TEL 800-525-2474.

348.7 US ISSN 0094-9531
KF105.2
SHEPARD'S FEDERAL LAW CITATIONS IN SELECTED LAW REVIEWS. 1974. 6/yr. $230. Shepard's - McGraw-Hill, Inc., Box 35300, Colorado Springs, CO 80935-3530. TEL 719-475-7230.

SHEPARD'S FEDERAL OCCUPATIONAL SAFETY AND HEALTH CITATIONS. see *BUSINESS AND ECONOMICS — Labor And Industrial Relations*

SHEPARD'S FEDERAL SECURITIES LAW CITATIONS. see *BUSINESS AND ECONOMICS — Investments*

340 US ISSN 0746-3138
SHEPARD'S IMMIGRATION AND NATURALIZATION CITATIONS. 1982. base vol. (plus q. suppl.). $240. Shepard's - McGraw-Hill, Inc., Box 35300, Colorado Springs, CO 80935-3530. TEL 800-525-2474.

340 US
SHEPARD'S INSURANCE LAW CITATIONS. 1987. 6 base vols. (plus q. suppl.). $660. Shepard's - McGraw-Hill, Inc., Box 35300, Colorado Springs, CO 80935-3530. TEL 800-525-2474.

340 US ISSN 0582-9887
SHEPARD'S LAW REVIEW CITATIONS. 1968. 3 base vols. (plus 6/yr suppl.). $430. Shepard's - McGraw-Hill, Inc., Box 35300, Colorado Springs, CO 80935-3530. TEL 800-525-2474.

340 US ISSN 8750-1112
SHEPARD'S PARTNERSHIP LAW CITATIONS. 1983. base vol. (plus q. suppl.). $210. Shepard's - McGraw-Hill, Inc., Box 35300, Colorado Springs, CO 80935-3530. TEL 800-525-2474.

340 US ISSN 8750-1139
SHEPARD'S PRODUCTS LIABILITY CITATIONS. 1983. 2 base vols. (plus q. suppl.). $300. Shepard's - McGraw-Hill, Inc., Box 35300, Colorado Springs, CO 80935-3530. TEL 800-525-2474.

340 US ISSN 0270-529X
KFT1259
SHEPARD'S TEXAS BRIEFCASE. 1979. base vol. (plus q. suppl.). $85. Shepard's - McGraw-Hill, Inc., Box 35300, Colorado Springs, CO 80935-3530. TEL 800-525-2474.

340 US ISSN 0745-5925
SHEPARD'S UNIFORM COMMERCIAL CODE CITATIONS. 1982. 2 base vols. (plus suppl. 6/yr). $390. Shepard's - McGraw-Hill, Inc., Box 35300, Colorado Springs, CO 80935-3530. TEL 800-525-2474.

340 US ISSN 0582-9909
SHEPARD'S UNITED STATES ADMINISTRATIVE CITATIONS. Variant title: Shepard's United States Administrative Law Citations. 1967. 5 base vols. (plus bi-m. suppl.). $540. Shepard's - McGraw-Hill, Inc., Box 35300, Colorado Springs, CO 80935-3530. TEL 800-525-2474.

340 US ISSN 0582-9917
SHEPARD'S UNITED STATES PATENTS AND TRADEMARKS CITATIONS. 1968. 9 base vols. (6/yr suppl.). $1044. Shepard's - McGraw-Hill, Inc., Box 35300, Colorado Springs, CO 80935-3530. TEL 800-525-2474.

340 CN
SHERIFF SERVICES SELECTED OPERATING PROCEDURES. base vol. (plus irreg. suppl.). Can.$28. Ministry of Attorney General, Parliament Bldgs., Victoria, B.C. V8V 1X4, Canada. (Subscr. to: Crown Publications, 546 Yates St., Victoria, B.C. V8W 1K8, Canada. TEL 604-386-4636) (looseleaf format; back issues avail.)
Description: A guide to the protocol, procedure, conduct and practice of the Office of the Sheriff.

340 320 JA ISSN 0583-0362
SHIMANE LAW REVIEW. (Text in Japanese) 1955. 3/yr. exchange basis. Shimane Daigaku, Hobungakubu - Shimane University, Faculty of Law and Literature, 1060 Nishi-Kawazu-machi, Matsue-shi, Shimane-ken 690, Japan. Eds. Yuzoh Fukao, Hobotake Nike.
bk.rev.

340 US ISSN 0037-444X
SI DE KA MAGAZINE. 1915. q. membership. Sigma Delta Kappa Law Foundation, Inc., Dixie Bldg., No.107, 2060 N. 14th St., Arlington, VA 22201. TEL 703-524-0220. adv.; charts; illus.; circ. 5,000.

SIGN CONTROL NEWS. see *ENVIRONMENTAL STUDIES*

340 SI ISSN 0218-2173
SINGAPORE JOURNAL OF LEGAL STUDIES. (Text in English) 1959. s-a. $32 (typically set in Jan.). National University of Singapore, Faculty of Law, 10 Kent Ridge Cres., Singapore 0511, Singapore. FAX 779-0979. TELEX RS 33943-UNISPO. Ed. K.L Koh. adv.; bk.rev.; circ. 1,850. (back issues avail.)
—BLDSC shelfmark: 8285.463750.
Formerly (until July 1990): Malaya Law Review (ISSN 0542-335X)

340 SI ISSN 0218-3161
SINGAPORE LAW REPORTS. 1992. fortn. S.$375 for Singapore and Brunei; Malaysia M.$605. Butterworths Asia (Subsidiary of: Reed International (Singapore) Pte. Ltd.), 3 Shenton Way, No. 14-03, Shenton House, Singapore 0106, Singapore. TEL 2203684. FAX 2255026. circ. 1,200.

349 SI ISSN 0080-9691
SINGAPORE LAW REVIEW. (Text in English) 1969. a. S.15. National University of Singapore Law Club, c/o Law Faculty, Kent Ridge Campus, Singapore 0511, Singapore. FAX 7790970. Ed. Ngeow Yuen Lian. adv.; circ. 1,350.
Supersedes (1958-1969): Me Judice.

SKATTERETT; journal on Norwegian tax law. see *BUSINESS AND ECONOMICS — Public Finance, Taxation*

340 CN
SMALL CLAIM MANUAL. base vol. (plus irreg. suppl.). Ministry of Attorney General, Parliament Bldgs., Victoria, B.C. V8V 1X4, Canada. (Subscr. to: Crown Publications, 546 Yates St., Victoria, B.C. V8W 1K8, Canada. TEL 604-386-4636) (looseleaf format)
Description: Corrects policies, practices and procedures for the small claim clerk.

SOCIAL ACTION AND THE LAW. see *PSYCHOLOGY*

SOCIAL AND LEGAL STUDIES. see *SOCIOLOGY*

SOCIAL RESPONSIBILITY: BUSINESS, JOURNALISM, LAW, MEDICINE. see *PHILOSOPHY*

340 UK
SOCIAL WELFARE LAW. irreg. £145. Longman Group UK Ltd., Law, Tax and Finance Division, 21-27 Lambs Conduit St., London WC1N 3NJ, England. TEL 071-242-2548. FAX 071-831-8119. TELEX 295445. Ed. David Pollard. (looseleaf format)
Description: Analysis of laws relating to the welfare system.

SOCIALFOERFATTNINGAR. see *SOCIAL SERVICES AND WELFARE*

340 SP ISSN 0213-0483
K3
SOCIEDAD DE ESTUDIOS VASCOS. CUADERNOS DE SECCION. DERECHO. 1984. irreg. Eusko Ikaskuntza, S.A., Legazpi, 10-1, 20004 Donostia-San Sebastian, Spain. TEL 425 111.

344 PE
SOCIEDAD Y DERECHO. q. Jiron Huancavelica No. 470-Of. 308, Lima, Peru.

SOCIEDADES POR ACOES. see *BUSINESS AND ECONOMICS*

340 FR ISSN 0081-0843
SOCIETE DES AUTEURS, COMPOSITEURS, EDITEURS POUR LA GERANCE DES DROITS DE REPRODUCTION MECANIQUE. BULLETIN. Variant title: A.C.E. Bulletin. irreg. price varies. Societe des Auteurs, Compositeurs, Editeurs pour la Gerance des Droits de Reproduction Mecanique, 62 rue Blanche, 75009 Paris, France.

SOCIETY OF MARITIME ARBITRATORS. AWARD SERVICE. see *TRANSPORTATION — Ships And Shipping*

344 IT
SOCIOLOGIA DEL DIRITTO. 1974; N.S. 3/yr. L.69000 (foreign L.80000)(effective 1992). (Centro Nazionale di Prevenzione e Difesa Sociale, Commissione Permanente di Sociologia del Diritto) Franco Angeli Editore, Viale Monza 106, 20127 Milan, Italy. TEL 02-28-27-651. Ed. Renato Treves.
Indexed: Lang.& Lang.Behav.Abstr., Sociol.Abstr.

340 BU ISSN 0081-1866
K7
SOFIISKI UNIVERSITET. JURIDIHESKI FAKULTET. GODISNIK. (Summaries in English, French, and German) irreg., vol.72, 1979. price varies. Publishing House of the Bulgarian Academy of Sciences, Acad. G. Bonchev St., Bldg. 6, 1113 Sofia, Bulgaria. Ed. G. Boychev. circ. 550. **Indexed:** BSL Econ.
—BLDSC shelfmark: 0051.190000.

SOFTWARE LAW BULLETIN; a compendium of current issues and cases involving software. see *COMPUTERS — Software*

SOFTWARE LAW JOURNAL. see *COMPUTERS — Software*

SOFTWARE PROTECTION; a journal on the legal, technical and practical aspects of protecting computer software. see *COMPUTERS — Software*

SOLAR LAW. see *ENERGY — Solar Energy*

340 UK
SOLICITORS' AND BARRISTERS' DIRECTORY. 1844. a. £38. M B C Information Services, Paulton House, 8 Shepherdess Walk, London N1 7LB, England. TEL 071-490-0049. FAX 071-490-2979. adv.; circ. 8,000.
●Also available online.
Supersedes in part: Solicitors' and Barristers' Directory and Diary; **Formerly:** Solicitors' Diary and Directory.
Description: Directory of solicitors and barristers in England and Wales arranged alphabetically, individually, and geographically by firm.

340 UK ISSN 0038-1047
K23
SOLICITORS' JOURNAL. 1857. w. £68($100) Longman Group UK Ltd., Law, Tax and Finance Division, 21-27 Lamb's Conduit St., London WC1N 3NJ, England. TEL 071-242-2548. FAX 071-831-8119. Ed. Julian Harris. (also avail. in microform from UMI,BHP; reprint service avail. from UMI) **Indexed:** Abstr.Bk.Rev.Curr.Leg.Per., C.L.I., L.R.I., Leg.Per., RICS.
—BLDSC shelfmark: 8327.270000.
Description: Information for practicing solicitors.

340 CN
SOLICITOR'S JOURNAL. (Text in English, French) 1985. q. Canadian Bar Association, New Brunswick Branch, 133 Regent St., Ste. 206, Fredericton, N.B. E3B 3Z2, Canada. TEL 506-458-8536. FAX 506-458-1076. Ed. Timothy Rattenburg. circ. 1,200. (looseleaf format)

2680 LAW

340   CH   ISSN 0259-3750
SOOCHOW LAW REVIEW. (Text in Chinese or English) 1976. s-a. $15 per no. Soochow University, Soochow University Library, Wai Shuang Hsi, Shih Lin, Taipei, Taiwan, Republic of China. FAX 886-02-8829310. (reprint service avail.) Key Title: Dongwu Falu Xuebao.
Description: Publication of the Soochow University School of Law.

340   RU   ISSN 0038-1691
SOTSIALISTICHESKAYA ZAKONNOST'. 1922. m. 12 Rub. Prokuratura S.S.S.R., Moscow, Russia. (Co-sponsor: U.S.S.R. Verkhovnyi Sud) index. **Indexed:** Curr.Dig.Sov.Press, World Bibl.Soc.Sec.

340 610   US
SOURCEBOOK ON ASBESTOS DISEASES. (Supplement avail.: Sourcebook on Asbestos Diseases Case Law Quarterly) 1980. 5 base vols. (plus suppl.) $400 for set. Butterworth Legal Publishers (Salem) (Subsidiary of: Reed International PLC), 90 Stiles Rd., Salem, NH 03079. TEL 800-548-4001. FAX 603-898-9858. Eds. George A. Peters, Barbara J. Peters.
Description: Contains information, insights, and data for trial attorneys and others involved in asbestos litigation or legal research.

340 610   US
SOURCEBOOK ON ASBESTOS DISEASES CASE LAW QUARTERLY. (Supplement to: Sourcebook on Asbestos Diseases) 1989. q. $85. Butterworth Legal Publishers (Salem) (Subsidiary of: Reed International PLC), 90 Stiles Rd., Salem, NH 03079. TEL 800-548-4001. FAX 603-898-9858.
Description: Provides summaries of recent asbestos cases organized by issue.

340   US
SOURCES OF CONNECTICUT LAW. 1987. base vol. (plus suppl.). $65. Butterworth Legal Publishers (Salem) (Subsidiary of: Reed International PLC), 90 Stiles Rd., Salem, NH 03079. TEL 800-548-4001. FAX 603-898-9858. Ed. Shirley Rassi Bysiewicz.
Description: Comprehensive citator to all sources of Connecticut law, from historical beginnings to the present.

SOUTH AFRICAN JOURNAL OF LABOUR RELATIONS. see BUSINESS AND ECONOMICS — Labor And Industrial Relations

SOUTH AFRICAN JOURNAL ON HUMAN RIGHTS. see POLITICAL SCIENCE — Civil Rights

340   SA   ISSN 0038-2388
K23
SOUTH AFRICAN LAW JOURNAL. 1884. q. R.115. Juta & Co. Ltd., P.O. Box 14373, Kenywn 7790, South Africa. TEL 021-797-5101. FAX 021-761-5010. Ed. Ellison Kahn. adv.; bk.rev.; index. (also avail. in microfiche from WSH) **Indexed:** Abstr.Bk.Rev.Curr.Leg.Per., C.L.I., Ind.S.A.Per., Leg.Per.
—BLDSC shelfmark: 8340.700000.
Description: Articles on Roman, Dutch and modern South African law.

340   SA   ISSN 0038-2396
SOUTH AFRICAN LAW REPORTS. (Text and summaries in Afrikaans, English) 1947. m. R.342. Butterworth Publishers (Pty.) Ltd., 8 Walter Pl., Waterval Park, Durban 4000, South Africa. TEL 031-294247. FAX 031-283255. Ed.Bd. index. (also avail. in microfiche from BHP)
Description: For the South African lawyer.

340   SA
SOUTH AFRICAN LAW REPORTS, INDEX & NOTER-UP. Variant title: Gracie's Index. a. Butterworth Publishers (Pty.) Ltd., 8 Walter Pl., Waterval Park, Durban 4000, South Africa. TEL 031-294247. FAX 031-283255.

346.066   SA   ISSN 1015-0099
SOUTH AFRICAN MERCANTILE LAW JOURNAL/SUID-AFRIKAANSE TYDSKRIF VIR HANDELSREG. (Text in Afrikaans and English) 1979. 3/yr. R.79. (University of South Africa, Faculty of Law, Department of Mercantile Law) Juta & Co. Ltd., P.O. Box 14373, Kenywn 7790, South Africa. TEL 021-761-5010. FAX 021-797-5101. (Editorial addr.: P.O. Box 392, Pretoria 0001, South Africa. TEL 012-429-8465) Ed.Bd. adv.; bk.rev.; circ. 1,000. **Indexed:** Ind.S.A.Per.
Supersedes (with vol.11, 1989): Modern Business Law - Moderne Besigheidreg.
Description: Concerned with the legal aspects of commerce and trade.

340   AT   ISSN 0049-1470
SOUTH AUSTRALIAN STATE REPORTS. 1866. m. Law Book Co. Ltd., 44-50 Waterloo Rd., N. Ryde, N.S.W. 2113, Australia. TEL 02-887-0177. FAX 02-888-9706. TELEX ASBOOK 27995. Ed. Victor Kline. cum.index. (back issues avail.)
Description: Reports on decisions and appeals of the South Australian Supreme Court.

340   US   ISSN 0743-2453
KFS1857
SOUTH CAROLINA APPELLATE DIGEST; bi-weekly case law review for South Carolina attorneys including up-to-date summaries of State and Federal cases from South Carolina. 1985. bi-w. $85. National Legal Research Group, Inc., 2421 Ivy Rd., Box 7187, Charlottesville, VA 22906-7187. TEL 800-446-1870. FAX 804-295-4667. Ed. Chris Hudson.
Description: For South Carolina attorneys. Contains summaries of recent opinions from South Carolina Supreme Court and Court of Appeals, U.S. Supreme Court and South Carolina Fourth Circuit.

340   US   ISSN 0038-3104
LAW
SOUTH CAROLINA LAW REVIEW. 1949. 4/yr. $20. University of South Carolina, School of Law, Columbia, SC 29208. TEL 803-777-5874. FAX 803-777-9405. Ed. Matthew J. Nortcn. adv.; bk.rev.; cum.index every 10 yrs.; circ. 3,000. (also avail. in microfiche from WSH; microfilm from WSH) **Indexed:** C.L.I., L.R.I., Leg.Cont., Leg.Per.
●Also available online. Vendor(s): WESTLAW.
—BLDSC shelfmark: 8350.100000.
Formerly: South Carolina Law Quarterly.

340   US   ISSN 1044-4238
K23
SOUTH CAROLINA LAWYER. 1989. bi-m. $18. South Carolina Bar, c/o Beth Littlejohn, Man. Ed., Box 608, Columbia, SC 29202. TEL 803-799-6653. FAX 803-799-4118. Ed. Robert Wilkins. adv.; circ. 8,000 (controlled). (also avail. in microform from UMI)
Description: Covers legal issues, court decisions, new rulings and changes in the law. University of South Carolina presents the latest cases and their significance.

SOUTH CAROLINA RULES AND REGULATIONS FOR HUNTING AND FISHING LICENSES. see SPORTS AND GAMES — Outdoor Life

340   US   ISSN 0038-3325
K23
SOUTH DAKOTA LAW REVIEW. 1956. 3/yr. $20. University of South Dakota, School of Law, Vermilion, SD 57069. TEL 605-677-5646. FAX 605-677-5417. Ed. Bruce Kness. adv.; bk.rev.; circ. 1,200. (also avail. in microfiche from WSH; microfilm from WSH) **Indexed:** C.L.I., L.R.I., Leg.Per., Sel.Water Res.Abstr.
●Also available online. Vendor(s): WESTLAW.
—BLDSC shelfmark: 8351.200000.

340   US
SOUTH TEXAS LAW REVIEW.* 1954. 3/yr. $30. (South Texas College of Law) South Texas Law Review, Inc., c/o Kibun, Kibun Products International, 5609 Departure Dr., Raleigh, NC 27604-1642. Ed. Robert S. Marsel. adv.; bk.rev.; cum.index; circ. 2,200. (also avail. in microform from WSH; reprint service avail. from WSH) **Indexed:** C.L.I., L.R.I., Leg.Cont., Leg.Per., Mar.Aff.Bibl.
●Also available online. Vendor(s): WESTLAW.
Formerly: South Texas Law Journal (ISSN 0038-3546)

340   US
SOUTHEAST LITIGATION GUIDE. (Issued in 12 base vols. with supplements) 1981. irreg. Matthew Bender & Co., Inc., 11 Penn Plaza, New York, NY 10001. TEL 212-967-7707. (looseleaf format)
Description: Prominent trial lawyers in Florida, Georgia and Alabama provide step-by-step guidance through every aspect of litigation practice.

340   US
SOUTHEAST TRANSACTION GUIDE. (Issued in 20 base vols. with supplements) 1976. irreg. Matthew Bender & Co., Inc., 11 Penn Plaza, New York, NY 10001. TEL 212-967-7707. (looseleaf format)
Description: For Florida, Georgia and Alabama practitioners. Covers a wide variety of business and legal transactions.

340   US   ISSN 0038-3910
K23
SOUTHERN CALIFORNIA LAW REVIEW. 1927. 6/yr. $30. University of Southern California, Law Center, Room 330, University Park, Los Angeles, CA 90089-0071. TEL 213-740-8475. FAX 213-743-6314. Ed. Peter Juzwiak. adv.; bk.rev.; abstr.; index; circ. 1,500. (also avail. in microfilm from WSH; reprint service avail. from WSH) **Indexed:** ASCA, BPIA, Bus.Ind., C.L.I., Crim.Just.Abstr., L.R.I., Leg.Cont., Leg.Per., Sage Pub.Admin.Abstr., Sage Urb.Stud.Abstr., SSCI.
—BLDSC shelfmark: 8352.930000.

340   US   ISSN 0145-3432
K23
SOUTHERN ILLINOIS UNIVERSITY LAW JOURNAL. 1976. q. $20. Southern Illinois University, Carbondale, School of Law, Lesar Law Bldg., Carbondale, IL 62901. TEL 618-536-7711. FAX 618-453-8769. Ed. Lyndon Sommer. adv.; bk.rev.; index; circ. 900. (also avail. in microform from UMI; reprint service avail. from RRI,UMI) **Indexed:** C.L.I., L.R.I., Leg.Per.
—BLDSC shelfmark: 8354.180000.
Description: Articles analyzing current legal issues with emphasis on topics of interest to Illinois attorneys, judges and legislators.

340   US   ISSN 0006-9965
SOUTHERN METHODIST UNIVERSITY SCHOOL OF LAW. BRIEF. 1965. a. Southern Methodist University School of Law, Dallas, TX 75275. TEL 214-692-4330. circ. 6,500.

344   US   ISSN 0361-0861
KF4114
SOUTHERN SCHOOL LAW DIGEST. 1974. m. $55. Louisiana School Boards Association, Drawer 80459, Baton Rouge, LA 70895. TEL 504-769-3191. Ed. Robert Hammomds.

340   US   ISSN 0099-1465
K12
SOUTHERN UNIVERSITY LAW REVIEW. 1974. s-a. $10. Southern Branch P.O., Baton Rouge, LA 70813. TEL 504-771-2552. Ed. Brian A. Jackson. adv.; bk.rev.; circ. 450. (back issues avail.) **Indexed:** C.L.I., L.R.I., Leg.Per., Mar.Aff.Bibl.

340   US   ISSN 0038-4836
K23
SOUTHWESTERN LAW JOURNAL. 1947. 4/yr. $33. Southern Methodist University School of Law, Dallas, TX 75275. TEL 214-692-2594. FAX 214-692-4330. bk.rev.; index. cum.index every 10 yrs.; circ. 1,800. (also avail. in microform from WSH; reprint service avail. from WSH) **Indexed:** Abstr.Bk.Rev.Curr.Leg.Per., C.L.I., L.R.I., Leg.Cont., Leg.Per.
●Also available online. Vendor(s): WESTLAW.
—BLDSC shelfmark: 8357.230000.

340 341   US   ISSN 0561-1784
SOUTHWESTERN LEGAL FOUNDATION. ANNUAL REPORT. 1955. a. free. Southwestern Legal Foundation, Box 830707, Richardson, TX 75083-0707. TEL 214-690-2370. TELEX 284522 SWLF UR. circ. 2,000. (back issues avail.)

340   RU   ISSN 0038-5115
SOVETSKAYA YUSTITSIYA. 1957. s-m. $13.20. Izdatel'stvo Kniga, 50, Gorky St., 125047 Moscow, Russia. bk.rev.; index. **Indexed:** Curr.Dig.Sov.Press.

340 RU ISSN 0038-5204
K23
SOVETSKOE GOSUDARSTVO I PRAVO. (Text in Russian; contents page in English and French; summaries in English) 1927. m. 32.40 Rub. (Akademiya Nauk S.S.S.R., Institut Gosudarstva i Prava) Izdatel'stvo Nauka, 90 Profsoyuznaya ul., 117864 Moscow, Russia. (Dist. by: Mezhdunarodnaya Kniga, ul. Dimitrova D.39, 113095 Moscow, Russia) Ed. M.I. Piskotin. bk.rev.; bibl.; index; circ. 52,250. (also avail. in microform from MIM) **Indexed:** Curr.Dig.Sov.Press, Hist.Abstr., Rural Recreat.Tour.Abstr., World Agri.Econ.& Rural Sociol.Abstr.

346.066 US
▼**SOVIET BUSINESS LAW;** institutions, principles and processes. 1991. 2 base vols. (plus a. suppl.). $180. Butterworth Legal Publishers (Salem) (Subsidiary of: Reed International PLC), 90 Stiles Rd., Salem, NH 03079. TEL 800-548-4001. FAX 603-898-9664. Ed. Christopher Osakwe. (looseleaf format)

340 US
SOVIET LAW. irreg., 2nd ed., 1988. $40. Butterworth Legal Publishers (Salem) (Subsidiary of: Reed International PLC), 90 Stiles Rd., Salem, NH 03079. TEL 800-548-4001. FAX 603-898-9858. Ed. W.E. Butler.

340 PL ISSN 0038-5956
SOVREMENNOE POLSKOE PRAVO. French edition: Droit Polonais Contemporain (ISSN 0070-7325) (Text in Russian) 1964. q. price varies. (Polska Akademia Nauk, Instytut Panstwa i Prawa) Ossolineum, Publishing House of the Polish Academy of Sciences, Rynek 9, Wroclaw, Poland. TELEX 0712771 OSS PL. (Dist. by: Ars Polona-Ruch, Krakowskie Przedmiescie 7, Warsaw, Poland) Ed. E. Letowska. bk.rev.; circ. 500. (also avail. in microfilm)
Description: Papers on all domains of Polish contemporary law and current legislative acts.

340 AU
SOZIALVERSICHERUNGSRECHTLICHE ENTSCHEIDUNGEN. 1953. a. price varies. Manzsche Verlags- und Universitaetsbuchhandlung, Kohlmarkt 16, A-1014 Vienna, Austria. TEL 0222-531610. FAX 0222-5316181. Ed. Hellmut Teschner. circ. 2,000.
Description: Collects cases on provisions of social welfare law.

370.26 SP
SPAIN. MINISTERIO DE EDUCACION Y CIENCIA. BOLETIN OFICIAL: COLECCION LEGISLATIVA. m. 2250 ptas. (foreign 3900 ptas.). Ministerio de Educacion y Ciencia, Centro de Publicaciones, Ciudad Universitaria, 28040 Madrid, Spain. TEL 549 77 00.

340 SP
SPAIN. MINISTERIO DE JUSTICIA. BOLETIN DE INFORMACION. (Supplements avail.) 34/yr. 4000 ptas. (foreign 5000 ptas.). Ministerio de Justicia, Centro de Publicaciones, Secretaria General Tecnica, Gran Via, 76-8, 28013 Madrid, Spain. TEL 247 54 22.

340 SP ISSN 0210-1165
SPAIN. MINISTERIO DE JUSTICIA. DICCIONARIOS INDICE DE JURISPRUDENCIA CIVIL. (Subseries of: Coleccion Legislativa de Espana) 1971. irreg., latest 1981-1987. 28000 ptas. Ministerio de Justicia, Centro de Publicaciones, Secretaria General Tecnica, Gran Via, 76-8, 28013 Madrid, Spain. TEL 247 54 22. Ed. Urbano Ruiz Gutierrez.

340 SP ISSN 0210-1157
SPAIN. MINISTERIO DE JUSTICIA. DICCIONARIOS INDICE DE JURISPRUDENCIA PENAL. (Subseries of: Coleccion Legislativa de Espana) 1957. irreg., latest 1983-1988. 10600 ptas. Ministerio de Justicia, Centro de Publicaciones, Gran Via, 76-8, 28013 Madrid, Spain. TEL 247 54 22.

340 SP ISSN 0210-3419
SPAIN. MINISTERIO DE JUSTICIA. SECRETARIA GENERAL TECNICA. DOCUMENTACION JURIDICA. 1974. q. 4700 ptas. (foreign 5350 ptas.). Ministerio de Justicia, Centro de Publicaciones, Secretaria General Tecnica, Gran Via, 76-8, 28013 Madrid, Spain. TEL 247 54 22. FAX 247-98-33. Ed.Bd. bk.rev.; circ. 1,200. (back issues avail.)
—BLDSC shelfmark: 3609.855000.
Supersedes: Spain. Ministerio de Justicia. Secretaria General Tecnica. Informacion Juridica (ISSN 0303-9927)

347 US
SPECIAL COURT NEWS. q. membership only. American Bar Association, National Conference of Special Court Judges, 750 N. Lake Shore Dr., Chicago, IL 60611. TEL 312-988-5555.
Description: Newsletter reporting current activities and plans of the conference.

340 US
SPECIALIZATION UPDATE. s-a. free. American Bar Association, Standing Committee on Specialization, 750 N. Lake Shore Dr., Chicago, IL 60611. TEL 312-988-5000.
Description: Compilation of current news briefs and articles.

340 US ISSN 0198-8778
KF3821.A59
SPECIALTY LAW DIGEST: HEALTH CARE. 1979. m. $330. Specialty Digest Publications, Inc., 10301 University Ave., N.E., Blaine, MN 55434. TEL 612-780-3157.
—BLDSC shelfmark: 8404.906000.

THE SPECTRUM (TOPEKA); newsletter of the Kansas commission on civil rights. see POLITICAL SCIENCE — Civil Rights

340 SA ISSN 0584-8652
SPECULUM JURIS. (Text in Afrikaans, English) a. R.5. (University of Fort Hare, Faculty of Law) Fort Hare University Press, Private Bag X1314, Alice, Republic of Ciskei, South Africa. FAX 0404-32011. TELEX 250863. Ed. J. Labuschagne. bibl. **Indexed:** A.I.C.P., Ind.S.A.Per.

SPILL REPORTING PROCEDURES GUIDE. see ENVIRONMENTAL STUDIES — Waste Management

340 617.1 US
SPORTS AND RECREATIONAL INJURIES. 1985. base vol. (plus a. suppl.). $95. Shepard's - McGraw-Hill, Inc., Box 35300, Colorado Springs, CO 80935-3530. TEL 800-525-2474.
Description: Discusses the liability of sporting goods manufacturers and retailers, governments, schools, commercial recreational facilities and insurance carriers in more than 40 different areas of sport.

SPORTS AND THE COURTS; physical education and sports law newletter. see SPORTS AND GAMES

340 617.1 US ISSN 1041-696X
KF2910.S653
SPORTS MEDICINE STANDARDS & MALPRACTICE REPORTER. q. $39.95. Professional Reports Corporation, 4571 Stephen Circle, N.W., Canton, OH 44718-3629. TEL 800-336-0083. FAX 216-499-6609. (looseleaf format)
Description: Covers legal issues of interest to sports medicine professionals, including current trends in liability, professional standards, drug screening, legal aspects of athletic programs, and more.

340 790.1 US ISSN 0893-8210
KF1290.S66
SPORTS, PARKS AND RECREATION LAW REPORTER. q. $39.95. Professional Reports Corporation, 4571 Stephen Circle, N.W., Canton, OH 44718-3629. TEL 800-336-0083. FAX 216-499-6609. (looseleaf format)
Description: Covers legal issues of interest to sports, parks and recreation professionals, including liability, releases and waivers, drug testing, professional standards, and more.

SPUREN UND MOTIVE; Informationsdienst fuer innere Sicherheit. see CRIMINOLOGY AND LAW ENFORCEMENT

347.91 II
SRINAGAR LAW JOURNAL. 6/yr. Rs.80. Court Rd., Srinagar, Kashmir 190001, India. Ed. Hakim Tshtiag Hussain.

DER STAAT; Zeitschrift fuer Staatslehre, Oeffentliches Recht und Verfassungsgeschichte. see POLITICAL SCIENCE

340 GW ISSN 0138-5208
STAATS- UND RECHTSTHEORETISCHE STUDIEN. 1976. irreg., vol.18, 1989. (Akademie der Wissenschaften) Akademie-Verlag Berlin, Leipziger Str. 3-4, 1086 Berlin, Germany. TELEX 114420-AVERL-DD.

340 GW ISSN 0724-7885
STAATSANZEIGER FUER DAS LAND HESSEN. 1946. w. DM.112.40. (Hessisches Ministerium des Innern) Verlag Kultur und Wissen GmbH, Wilhelmstr. 42, 6200 Wiesbaden, Germany. TEL 0611-36098-0. FAX 0611-301303. (back issues avail.)

STAMP DUTIES N.S.W. & A.C.T.. see BUSINESS AND ECONOMICS — Public Finance, Taxation

STANDARD & POOR'S REVIEW OF SECURITIES, COMMODITIES REGULATION; an analysis of current laws, regulations and court decisions affecting the securities industry. see BUSINESS AND ECONOMICS — Investments

340 SA
STANDARD TRUST INCOME TAX GUIDE. a. $24. Butterworth Publishers (Pty.) Ltd., 8 Walter Pl., Waterval Park, Durban 4000, South Africa. TEL 031-294247. FAX 031-283255.

340 GW
DAS STANDESAMT. 1877. m. DM.187. (Bundesverband der deutschen Standesbeamten e.V) Verlag fuer Standesamtswesen GmbH, Hanauer Landstr. 197, 6000 Frankfurt a.M. 1, Germany. TEL 069-405894-0. FAX 069-405894-99. Ed.Bd. **Incorporates (in Jan. 1979):** Bayerische Standesamt (ISSN 0005-7096) & Standesbeamte.

344.73 US ISSN 0892-7138
K23
STANFORD ENVIRONMENTAL LAW JOURNAL. 1978. a. $15. Stanford Environmental Law Society, Stanford Law School, Stanford, CA 94305. TEL 415-723-4421. bk.rev.; circ. 500. (also avail. in microform from WSH; reprint service avail. from WSH) **Indexed:** C.L.I., L.R.I., Leg.Per.
—BLDSC shelfmark: 8431.330000.
Formerly (until 1985): Stanford Environmental Law Annual (ISSN 0197-7873)

340 US ISSN 1044-4386
H97
STANFORD LAW AND POLICY REVIEW. 1989. a. $15 to individuals; institutions $35. Stanford Law School, Crown Quadrangle, Stanford, CA 94305-8610. TEL 415-725-7297. Ed. Will Needle. adv.; abstr.; circ. 5,000. (back issues avail.)
—BLDSC shelfmark: 8432.150000.
Description: Nonideological publication written for and distributed to the nation's policymakers. Each issue features a symposium on a current policy topic. Articles are written and edited to present new and innovative ideas to readers in an accessible form.

340 US ISSN 0038-9765
K23
STANFORD LAW REVIEW. 1948. 6/yr. $35 (foreign $40). Stanford University, Stanford Law School, Crown Quadrangle, Stanford, CA 94305-8610. TEL 415-723-3210. Ed. Tony West. adv.; bk.rev.; index. cum.index: vols.1-30. (also avail. in microfiche from RRI,WSH; microfilm from WSH; back issues avail.; reprint service avail. from RRI) **Indexed:** A.B.C.Pol.Sci., Abstr.Bk.Rev.Curr.Leg.Per., Account.Ind. (1974-), ASCA, BPIA, C.L.I., Crim.Just.Abstr., Curr.Cont., L.R.I., Leg.Cont., Leg.Per., P.A.I.S., SSCI.
●Also available online. Vendor(s): Mead Data Central, WESTLAW.
—BLDSC shelfmark: 8432.200000.
Formerly: Stanford Intramural Law Review.
Description: Articles and notes with conclusions on the interdisciplinary study of law.

LAW

340 320 US ISSN 0585-0576
STANFORD LAWYER. 1966. a. Stanford University, Stanford Law School, Stanford, CA 94305-8610. TEL 415-723-9301. Ed. Constance Hellyer. illus.; circ. 9,500. **Indexed:** C.L.I.
Description: Articles on law and legal studies, politics, history and government, along with news of Stanford Law School.

340.115 CS ISSN 0585-0967
STAT A PRAVO. 1956. irreg., vol.26, 1989. price varies. (Czechoslovak Academy of Sciences, Ustav Statu a Prava) Academia, Publishing House of the Czechoslovak Academy of Sciences, Vodickova 40, 112 29 Prague 1, Czechoslovakia. TEL 23-63-065.

340 US
STATE BAR OF NEW MEXICO. BAR BULLETIN. Variant title: New Mexico State Bar Bulletin & Advance Opinions. 1960. w. $45. State Bar of New Mexico, 1117 Stanford, N.E., Albuquerque, NM 87131. TEL 505-842-6132. FAX 505-843-8765. Ed. Cheryl Bruce. adv.; bk.rev.; index; circ. 4,000. (looseleaf format)
Former titles: State Bar of New Mexico. Bulletin and Advance Opinions; (until 1986): State Bar of New Mexico. News and Views (ISSN 0279-375X); State Bar of New Mexico. Bar Bulletin and Advance Opinions (ISSN 0039-0038)

340 US ISSN 0145-3076
KF8732.A15
STATE COURT JOURNAL. 1977. q. $24. National Center for State Courts, 300 Newport Ave., Williamsburg, VA 23187-8798. TEL 804-253-2000. FAX 804-220-0449. bibl.; illus.; stat. (also avail. in microform from UMI; microfiche from WSH; reprint service avail. from WSH) **Indexed:** C.L.I., CJPI, Crim.Just.Abstr., L.R.I., Law Ofc.Info.Svc., Leg.Per.

STATE HAZARDOUS WASTE REGULATION. see ENVIRONMENTAL STUDIES — Waste Management

STATE HEALTH NOTES. see PUBLIC HEALTH AND SAFETY

340 US ISSN 0276-7651
STATE LAWS AND PUBLISHED ORDINANCES, FIREARMS. a. U.S. Department of the Treasury, Bureau of Alcohol, Tobacco and Firearms, 15th and Pennsylvania Ave. N.W., Washington, DC 20224. TEL 202-566-7777.
Formerly: Firearms, State Laws and Published Ordinances.

340 350 US ISSN 0898-7297
JK2495
STATE LEGISLATIVE SOURCEBOOK; a resource guide to legislative information in the fifty states. 1985. a. $135 (effective 1992). Government Research Service, 701 Jackson, Topeka, KS 66603. TEL 913-232-7720. FAX 913-232-1615. Ed. Lynn Hellebust.
Description: Contains information on legislation in the 50 states, D.C. and Puerto Rico.

STATE REGULATION REPORT; toxic substances & hazardous waste. see ENVIRONMENTAL STUDIES — Waste Management

346 AT ISSN 0158-1996
STATE REPORTS W.A.. 1899. irreg. (with annual cumulation). price varies. Law Book Co. Ltd., 44-50 Waterloo Rd., N. Ryde, N.S.W. 2113, Australia. TEL 02-887-0177. FAX 02-888-9706. TELEX ASBOOK 27995.
Formerly (until 1984): Western Australian Reports (ISSN 0083-8764)
Description: Reports from Family Court, District Court, Workers Compensation Board, and Town Planning Tribunal of Western Australia.

STATISTICAL PROOF OF DISCRIMINATION. see POLITICAL SCIENCE — Civil Rights

340 UK ISSN 0144-3593
K23
STATUTE LAW REVIEW. 1980. 3/yr. £57($110) (Statute Law Society) Oxford University Press, Oxford Journals, Pinkhill House, Southfield Road, Eynsham, Oxford OX8 1JJ, England. TEL 0865-882283. FAX 0865-882890. TELEX 837330-OXPRES-G. Eds. J.N. Bates, Gavin Drewry. adv.; bk.rev.; circ. 550. (reprint service avail. from RRI) **Indexed:** C.L.I., L.R.I., Leg.Per.
—BLDSC shelfmark: 8458.558000.
Description: Provides a forum for the consideration of the legislative process, the use of legislation as an instrument of public policy, and the drafting and interpretation of legislation.

349 US
K23
STATUTES AND DECISIONS; a journal of translations. 1964. q. $294 to institutions. M.E. Sharpe, Inc., 80 Business Park Dr., Armonk, NY 10504. TEL 914-273-1800. FAX 914-273-2106. Ed. Serge Levitsky. adv.; index. (also avail. in microform from WSH; reprint service avail. from WSH) **Indexed:** C.L.I., Leg.Per., P.A.I.S.
Formerly: Soviet Statutes and Decisions (ISSN 0038-5840)
Refereed Serial

340 II ISSN 0039-0763
STATUTES AND NOTIFICATIONS. (Editions in Gujarat, Hamarastra) 1965. m. Rs.40. Chandrakant Chimanlal Vora, 57-2 Gandhi Rd., P.O. Box 163, Ahmedabad 380 001, Gujarat, India. index; circ. 500.

347.9 CN
STATUTES OF ALBERTA - JUDICIALLY CONSIDERED; case annotations. 1980. 3/yr. price varies. Carswell Publications, 800 Rocky Mountain Plaza, 615 Macleod Trail, S.E., Calgary, Alta. T2G 4T8, Canada. TEL 403-609-8000. FAX 416-298-5094. (Subscr. to: Carswell Publications, Corporate Plaza, 2075 Kennedy Rd., Scarborough, Ont. M1T 3V4, Canada) Ed. John Leeder.
Former titles: Alberta - Judicially Considered; Alberta Statutes and Rules of Court - Judicially Considered.

340 NZ
STATUTES OF NEW ZEALAND. a. NZ.$60. (Parliamentary Services Commission) Government Printing Office, Private Bag, Wellington, New Zealand. TEL 737-320. index. (back issues avail.)

340 CN
STATUTES OF NEWFOUNDLAND. (Text in English) a. price varies. Office of The Queen's Printer, Confederation Bldg., East Block, St. John's, Nfld. A1B 4J6, Canada. TEL 709-729-3649. FAX 709-729-1900. Ed. David C.B. Dawe. index; circ. 800. (back issues avail.)

340 US
STATUTORY TIME LIMITATIONS: COLORADO. 1981. base vol. (plus a. suppl.). $50. Butterworth Legal Publishers (Salem) (Subsidiary of: Reed International PLC), 90 Stiles Rd., Salem, NH 03079. TEL 800-548-4001. FAX 603-898-9858. (looseleaf format)

340 US
STATUTORY TIME LIMITATIONS: WASHINGTON STATE. 1981. base vol. (plus a. suppl.). $55. Butterworth Legal Publishers (Salem) (Subsidiary of: Reed International PLC), 90 Stiles Rd., Salem, NH 03079. TEL 800-548-4001. FAX 603-898-9858. Ed.Bd. (looseleaf format)
Description: Identifies limitation periods as found in the revised code of Washington, including the rules of court.

340 US
STEIN ON PROBATE; administration of decedents' estates under the Uniform Probate Code as enacted in Minnesota. (Second edition) 1986. 2 base vols. (plus suppl.). $225. Butterworth Legal Publishers (Salem) (Subsidiary of: Reed International PLC), 90 Stiles Rd., Salem, NH 03079. TEL 800-548-4001. FAX 603-898-9858. Ed. Robert A. Stein. (looseleaf format)

340 US
STETSON LAW JOURNAL. 2/yr. Stetson University College of Law, 1401 61st. St. S., St. Petersburg, FL 33707. Ed. Debra A. Lamm.
Description: Introduces a variety of topics for a broad readership including legal papers, columns from legal updates, and humor.

340 US
STETSON LAW REVIEW. 1970. 3/yr. $18. Stetson University, College of Law, 1401 61 St. So., St. Petersburg, FL 33707. TEL 813-345-1300. FAX 813-345-8973. Ed. Laura Belflower. adv.; circ. 9,000. (also avail. in microfilm from RRI; back issues avail.; reprint service avail. from RRI) **Indexed:** C.L.I., L.R.I., Leg.Per.
●Also available online. Vendor(s): WESTLAW.

346 GW ISSN 0170-6845
STEUER TRAINING. 1975. m. DM.170. Verlag Dr. Peter Deubner GmbH, Fuerst-Pueckler-Str. 30, Postfach 410268, 5000 Cologne 41, Germany. TEL 0221-403020.

340 336 GW
STEUER UND STUDIUM; Zeitschrift fuer die Aus- und Fortbildung im Steuerrecht. 1980. m. DM.120. Neue Wirtschafts Briefe Verlag, Eschstr. 22, 4690 Herne 1, Germany. TEL 02323-141-0. Ed.Bd. index; circ. 7,000. (back issues avail.)

340 SZ ISSN 0254-8992
KKW3546.3
STEUERENTSCHEID; Sammlung aktueller steuerrechtlicher Entscheidungen. 1983. 10/yr. 245 Fr. (Praxis in der Wissenschaft) Helbing und Lichtenhahn Verlag AG, Freie Str. 82, CH-4051 Basel, Switzerland. TEL 064-268626. FAX 064-245780. TELEX 981195-SAG-CH. adv.; index; circ. 1,500. (back issues avail.)

STICHTING TOT UITGAAF DER BRONNEN VAN HET OUD-VADERLAANDSE RECHT. 2 SERIES: WERKEN, AND VERSLAGEN EN MEDEDELINGEN. see HISTORY — History Of Europe

340 US ISSN 1042-5780
KF228.M33
STOCKHOLDERS AND CREDITORS NEWS SERVICE CONCERNING THE JOHNS-MANVILLE CORPORATION, ET AL; the national journal of record reporting details of the Johns-Manville Corporation bankruptcy proceedings. 1986. s-m. $1300. Andrews Publications, 1646 West Chester Pike, Box 1000, Westtown, PA 19395. TEL 215-399-6600. FAX 215-399-6610. Ed. Thomas Hennessey. (looseleaf format; back issues avail.)

340 US ISSN 1053-0223
KF228.F42
▼**STOCKHOLDERS & CREDITORS NEWS SERVICE RE: FEDERATED DEPARTMENT STORES, INC..** 1990. s-m. $800. Andrews Publications, 1646 West Chester Pike, Box 1000, Westtown, PA 19395. TEL 215-399-6600. FAX 215-399-6610. Ed. Harry Armstrong. bibl.; stat.; cum.index every 6 mos. (looseleaf format; back issues avail.)
Description: Covers federated bankruptcy proceedings; includes reproduction of key case documents.

340 US ISSN 1053-0215
KF228.H55
▼**STOCKHOLDERS & CREDITORS NEWS SERVICE RE: HILLSBOROUGH HOLDING CORP..** 1990. s-m. $750. Andrews Publications, 1646 West Chester Pike, Box 1000, Westtown, PA 19395. TEL 215-399-6600. FAX 215-399-6610. Ed. Michael Rinker. bibl.; stat.; cum.index every 6 mos. (looseleaf format; back issues avail.)
Description: Summaries of legal maneuvers, court actions in Hillsborough bankruptcy case; occasional comments; features on people; events related to this case.

340 UK ISSN 0269-3682
STONE'S JUSTICES' MANUAL. a. price varies. Butterworth & Co. (Publishers) Ltd. (Subsidiary of: Reed International PLC), 88 Kingsway, London WC2B 6AB, England. TEL 71-405-6900. FAX 71-405-1332. TELEX 95678. (US addr.: Butterworth Legal Publishers, 90 Stiles Rd., Salem, NH 03079. TEL 800-548-4001) Eds. S.J. Richman, A.T. Draycott.
Description: Compendium of legislation and case law affecting the administration of justice in the magistrates' courts of England and Wales.

343 GW ISSN 0720-1605
K23
STRAFVERTEIDIGER. 1980. m. DM.270. Alfred Metzner Verlag, Zeppelinallee 43, 6000 Frankfurt a.M. 97, Germany. TEL 069-793009-0. TELEX 4189621-KOMED. (reprint service avail. from SCH)

340 YU ISSN 0039-2138
STRANI PRAVNI ZIVOT. SERIJA D: TEORIJA, ZAKONODAVSTVO, PRAKSA. 1956. q. $30. Institut za Uporedno Pravo, Belgrade, Terazije 41, 11000 Belgrade, Yugoslavia. Ed. Vladimir Jovanovic. circ. 300.
  Description: Theory, legislation and practice of foreign law, translations and notes on important foreign statutes, and international regulation.

340 AT
STRATA TITLES (NSW). 1989. 3/yr. Aus.$175. Law Book Co. Ltd., 44-50 Waterloo Rd., North Ryde, N.S.W 2113, Australia. TEL 02-887-0177. FAX 02-888-9706. TELEX ASBOOK 27995.
  Description: Contains the full text of the Strata Titles Act 1973 and Strata Titles Regulations 1974, with commentary relating to the meaning ambit and application of each section.

STREETWIZE COMICS; youth rights comics. see CHILDREN AND YOUTH — For

340 333.33 NE
STRUCTURING FOREIGN INVESTMENT IN U.S. REAL ESTATE. (Text in English) 1982. base volume plus a. updates. fl.350($195) Kluwer Law and Taxation Publishers, P.O. Box 23, 7400 GA Deventer, Netherlands. TEL 31-5700-47261. FAX 31-5700-22244. TELEX 49295 KLUDV NL. (N. America dist. addr.: 6 Bigelow St., Cambridge, MA 02139. TEL 617-354-0140) Ed. W. Donald Knight.

STUDENT AID NEWS; the independent biweekly news service on student financial assistance programs. see EDUCATION — Higher Education

STUDENT GUIDE TO GRADUATE LAW STUDY PROGRAMS. see EDUCATION — Guides To Schools And Colleges

340.07 US ISSN 0197-6656
KF266
STUDENT GUIDE TO SUMMER LAW STUDY PROGRAMS. 1980. a. $17.50. Joint Committee on Law Study Programs, 154 Stuart St., Boston, MA 02116. TEL 617-451-0010. Eds. Ellen Wayne, Betsy McCombs.
  Formerly: Directory of Summer Law Programs.

340 US ISSN 0039-274X
K23
STUDENT LAWYER (CHICAGO). 1972. m. $21 to non-members. American Bar Association, Law Student Division, 750 N. Lake Shore Dr., Chicago, IL 60611. TEL 312-988-6048. Ed. Sarah Hoban. adv.; bk.rev.; illus.; index; circ. 37,283. (also avail. in microfiche; microfilm; back issues avail.; reprint service avail. from UMI) **Indexed:** C.L.I., L.R.I., Law Ofc.Info.Svc., Leg.Cont.
  Supersedes: Student Lawyer Journal.
  Description: For law students, featuring articles on legal, political and social issues, law school and the profession.

340 US ISSN 0160-3825
KF4165.A15
STUDENT PRESS LAW CENTER REPORT. vol.3, 1979. 3/yr. $15. Student Press Law Center, Inc., 1735 Eye St., N.W., Washington, DC 20006. TEL 202-466-5242. FAX 202-466-6326. circ. 2,700. (back issues avail.) **Indexed:** ERIC.

340 945 IT ISSN 0039-3010
STUDI SENESI. 1884. q. L.40000. Universita degli Studi di Siena, Facolta di Giurisprudenza, Siena, Italy. FAX 0577-298746. Ed. Paolo Nardi. adv.; bk.rev.; circ. 350.

340 IT ISSN 0039-307X
STUDI URBINATI. SERIE A: DIRITTO. N.S. 1950. s-a. L.7000. (Universita degli Studi di Urbino, Facolta di Giurisprudenza) Armando - Argalia Editore, N. Sauro 1, 61029 Urbino, Italy. Ed. Carlo Bo. bk.rev.; charts; illus.; index. **Indexed:** Chem.Abstr.

340 PL ISSN 0039-3126
STUDIA CYWILISTYCZNE. (Text in Polish; summaries in English, French, German, Russian) 1961. s-a. price varies. Panstwowe Wydawnictwo Naukowe, Miodowa 10, 00-251 Warsaw, Poland. (Dist. by: Ars Polona, Krakowskie Przedmiescie 7, 00-608 Warsaw, Poland) Ed. Stefan Grzybowski. charts; circ. 230.

STUDIA ET DOCUMENTA HISTORIAE ET IURIS. see HISTORY

340 PL ISSN 0081-6671
STUDIA IURIDICA. (Text in Polish; summaries in English, French, German) 1962. irreg., vol.18, no.3, 1991. price varies. Towarzystwo Naukowe w Toruniu, Ul. Wysoka 16, 87-100 Torun, Poland. TEL 48-56-23941. TELEX 552388 FSBH PL. Ed. Janusz Gilas. circ. 500.
  —BLDSC shelfmark: 8482.954000.

340 HU ISSN 0324-5934
STUDIA IURIDICA AUCTORITATE UNIVERSITATIS PECS PUBLICATA. (Text in Hungarian; summaries in English, French, German, Russian) 1958. irreg., no.121, 1992. exchange basis. Janus Pannonius Tudomanyegyetem, Allam- es Jogtudomanyi Karanak Tudomanyos Bizottsaga, 48-as ter 1, 7601 Pecs, Hungary. TELEX 12301. Ed. Antal Adam. circ. 400.

347.9 IT ISSN 0081-6698
STUDIA JURIDICA. 1964. irreg., no.84, 1988. price varies. L'Erma di Bretschneider, Via Cassiodoro, 19, 00193 Rome, Italy. TEL 06-687-41-27. FAX 06-687-41-29.

340 PL ISSN 0039-3312
LAW
STUDIA PRAWNICZE. 1962. q. $42. (Polska Akademia Nauk, Instytut Panstwa i Prawa) Ossolineum, Publishing House of the Polish Academy of Sciences, Rynek 9, Wroclaw, Poland. TELEX 0712771 OSS PL. (Dist. by: Ars Polona-Ruch, Krakowskie Przedmiescie 7, Warsaw, Poland) Ed. Jan Skupinski. abstr.; circ. 600. (cards)
  Description: Contemporary research on all domains of law.

340 PL ISSN 0081-6841
STUDIA PRAWNO-EKONOMICZNE. (Text in Polish; summaries in English) 1968. 2/yr. (Lodzkie Towarzystwo Naukowe) Ossolineum, Publishing House of the Polish Academy of Sciences, Rynek 9, Wroclaw, Poland. TELEX 0712771 OSS PL. (Dist. by: Ars Polona-Ruch, Krakowskie Przedmiescie 7, Warsaw, Poland) (Co-sponsor: Polska Akademia Nauk) Eds. Jerzy Wroblewski, Wladyslaw Welfe. bk.rev.; circ. 500.

340 RM ISSN 0578-5464
STUDIA UNIVERSITATIS "BABES-BOLYAI". IURISPRUDENTIA. (Text in Rumanian; summaries in English, French, German) 1958. s-a. exchange basis. Universitatea "Babes-Bolyai", Biblioteca Centrala Universitara, Str. Clinicilor nr. 2, Cluj-Napoca, Rumania. bk.rev.; cum.index: 1956-1963, 1964-1970.

340 AU
STUDIEN ZU POLITIK UND VERWALTUNG. 1982. s-a. price varies. Boehlau Verlag GmbH & Co.KG., Sachsenplatz 4-6, Postfach 87, A-1201 Vienna, Austria. TEL 0222-3302427. FAX 0222-3302432. TELEX 114-506-SPRIW-A. Ed.Bd.

900 340 330 AU
STUDIEN ZUR RECHTS-, WIRTSCHAFTS- UND KULTURGESCHICHTE. (Subseries of: Universitaet Innsbruck. Veroeffentlichungen) 1969. irreg., vol.10, 1974. price varies. (Universitaet Innsbruck) Oesterreichische Kommissionsbuchhandlung, Maximilianstr. 17, A-6020 Innsbruck, Austria. Ed. Nikolaus Grass.

340.1 301 US
STUDIES IN LAW, POLITICS, AND SOCIETY; a research annual. 1978. a. $63.50 to institutions. J·A·I Press Inc., 55 Old Post Rd., No. 2, Box 1678, Greenwich, CT 06836-1678. TEL 203-661-7602. (UK addr.: J A I Press Ltd., 3 Henrietta St., London WC2E 8LU, England) Eds. Susan S. Silbey, Austin Sarat. **Indexed:** C.L.I., L.R.I., Lang.& Lang.Behav.Abstr., Leg.Per.
  Formerly (until 1988): Research in Law, Deviance and Social Control.

340 US
STUDIES IN LEGAL HISTORY. 1973. irreg., latest 1991. price varies. (University of North Carolina at Chapel Hill, Department of English) University of North Carolina Press, Box 2288, Chapel Hill, NC 27515-2288. TEL 919-966-3561. FAX 919-966-3829. (Co-sponsor: American Society for Legal History) Ed. Stanley N. Katz.
  Refereed Serial

340 PL ISSN 0239-9997
K23
STUDIES IN THE THEORY AND PHILOSOPHY OF LAW. (Text in English) 1987. s-a. $28. (Polish Academy of Sciences, Lodz Section) Ossolineum, Publishing House of the Polish Academy of Sciences, Rynek 9, 50-106 Wroclaw, Poland. TEL 386-25. (Dist. by: Ars Polona, Krakowskie Przedmiescie 7, 00-068 Warsaw, Poland) Ed. Jerzy Wroblewski.
  —BLDSC shelfmark: 8491.792800.
  Description: Theoretical studies concerning contemporary law applications.

340 RM
STUDII DE DREPT ROMANESC. 1955. 4/yr. $56. (Academia Romana) Editura Academiei Romane, Calea Victoriei 125, 79717 Bucharest, Rumania. (Dist. by: Rompresfilatelia, Calea Grivitei 64-66, P.O. Box 12-201, 78104 Bucharest, Rumania) bk.rev.; index.
  Formerly: Studii si Cercetari Juridice (ISSN 0039-4041)

340 IT
STUDIO LEGALE. 1972. bi-m. Casa Editrice Dott. A. Giuffre, Via Busto Arsizio 40, 20151 Milan, Italy. TEL 02-38000905. FAX 02-38009582. Ed. Gaetano Giuffre. adv.; circ. 46,000.

343 US ISSN 0362-2983
KF6450.A7
STUDY OF FEDERAL TAX LAW. INCOME TAX VOLUME: BUSINESS ENTERPRISES. 1975. irreg. $52.50. Commerce Clearing House, Inc., 4025 W. Peterson Ave., Chicago, IL 60646. TEL 312-583-8500.
  Formerly: Study of Federal Tax Law. Income Tax Materials, Business Enterprises; Supersedes in part: Study of Federal Tax Law. Income Tax Volume.

343 US
STUDY OF FEDERAL TAX LAW. INCOME TAX VOLUME: INDIVIDUALS. 1976. irreg. $52.50. Commerce Clearing House, Inc., 4025 W. Peterson Ave., Chicago, IL 60646. TEL 312-583-8500.
  Supersedes in part: Study of Federal Tax Law. Income Tax Volume (ISSN 0362-5230)

340 SJ ISSN 0585-8631
SUDAN LAW JOURNAL AND REPORTS. 1956. a. Judiciary, Khartoum, Sudan.

SUEDDEUTSCHE EISEN- UND STAHL-BERUFSGENOSSENSCHAFT. MITTEILUNGEN. see OCCUPATIONAL HEALTH AND SAFETY

340 US ISSN 0886-2648
K23
SUFFOLK TRANSNATIONAL LAW JOURNAL. 1977. 2/yr. $18 (foreign $23). Suffolk University Law School, Suffolk Transnational Law Journal, 41 Temple St., Boston, MA 02114-4280. TEL 617-573-8610. bk.rev.; index every 5 yrs. (also avail. in microfilm from RRI; back issues avail.; reprint service avail. from RRI) **Indexed:** Abstr.Bk.Rev.Curr.Leg.Per., C.L.I., L.R.I., Leg.Cont., Leg.Per., Mar.Aff.Bibl.
  ●Also available online. Vendor(s): WESTLAW.
  Description: Covers international legal topics.

340 US ISSN 0039-4696
SUFFOLK UNIVERSITY LAW REVIEW. 1967. 4/yr. $18. Suffolk University Law School, Suffolk University Law Review, Beacon Hill, Boston, MA 02114. TEL 617-227-2854. bk.rev.; index. cum.index every 5 yrs.; circ. 1,000. (also avail. in microform from MIM,RRI; microfilm from WSH; back issues avail.; reprint service avail. from RRI) **Indexed:** Abstr.Bk.Rev.Curr.Leg.Per., C.L.I., L.R.I., Leg.Cont., Leg.Per.
  ●Also available online. Vendor(s): WESTLAW.
  —BLDSC shelfmark: 8509.870000.

340 US
SUMMARY OF ALASKA LEGISLATION. a. (for qualified personnel only). Legislative Affairs Agency, Box Y, State Capitol, Juneau, AK 99811. TEL 907-465-3800.

LAW

340 US ISSN 0039-5072
SUMMONS. 1921. q. membership. Tau Epsilon Rho Law Society, c/o Alan M. Tepper, 36 Kresson Rd., Suite E, Cherry Hill, NJ 08034. adv.; bk.rev.; circ. 4,000. (tabloid format)

340 AT
SUPERANNUATION & RETIREMENT BENEFITS IN AUSTRALIA. base vol. (plus bi-m. update). $380. Butterworths Pty. Ltd., 271-273 Lane Cove Rd., P.O. Box 345, North Ryde, N.S.W. 2113, Australia. TEL 02-335-4444. FAX 02-335-4655. (looseleaf format)

SUPERFUND. see *CONSERVATION*

340 CN ISSN 0228-0108
K23
SUPREME COURT LAW REVIEW. (Text in English) 1980. a. Can.$155. Butterworths Canada Ltd., 75 Clegg Rd., Markham, Ont. L6G 1A1, Canada. TEL 416-479-2665. FAX 416-479-2826. Eds. E.P. Belobaba, E. Gertner. Indexed: C.L.I., Ind.Can.L.P.L., L.R.I., Leg.Per.
  Description: Offers in-depth analysis of Supreme Court of Canada's key decisions and a critical examination of Court's performance in reaching them.

SURVEY OF PHARMACY LAW. see *PHARMACY AND PHARMACOLOGY*

347 AT ISSN 0082-0512
SYDNEY LAW REVIEW. 1953. q. Aus.$64. Law Book Co. Ltd., 44-50 Waterloo Rd., North Ryde, N.S.W. 2113, Australia. TEL 02-887-01776. FAX 02-888-9706. (U.S. subscr. to: Wm. Gaunt & Sons, Inc., 3011 Gulf Dr., Holmes Beach, FL 33510) adv.; bk.rev.; index; circ. 1,250. (also avail. in microform from UMI; reprint service avail. from UMI) Indexed: Aus.Leg.Mon.Dig., Aus.P.A.I.S., C.C.L.P., C.L.I., L.R.I., Leg.Cont., Leg.Per., SSCI.
  —BLDSC shelfmark: 8577.200000.

340 US
SYLLABUS. 1981. q. $15. American Bar Association, Legal Education and Admissions to the Bar Section, 750 N. Lake Shore Dr., Chicago, IL 60611. TEL 312-988-5581. FAX 317-988-4664. Ed. Susan K. Boyd. bk.rev.; circ. 10,000. (tabloid format) Indexed: Anbar, C.L.I., L.R.I.
  Formerly: Legal Education Newsletter.
  Description: Describes and comments on developments in legal education; also reports on the activities of the Section.

340 JO
SYNDICATE OF LAWYERS/NAKABAT UL-MUHAMIN. (Text in Arabic) 1952. m. 5 din. Jordan Bar Association, Box 588, Amman, Jordan. Ed. Omar Abul Ragheb. circ. 950.

SYNTHESIS (ASHEVILLE); law and policy in higher education. see *EDUCATION — Higher Education*

340 US ISSN 0039-7938
K23
SYRACUSE LAW REVIEW. 1949. q. $22. Syracuse University College of Law, Syracuse, NY 13210. TEL 315-423-3680. adv.; circ. 1,200. (also avail. in microfiche from WSH; microfilm from WSH) Indexed: ASCA, C.L.I., Crim.Just.Abstr., Curr.Cont., L.R.I., Leg.Cont., Leg.Per., SSCI.
  —BLDSC shelfmark: 8588.800000.

T M A GUIDE TO TOBACCO TAXES; summaries of key provisions of tobacco tax laws, all tobacco products, all states. (Tobacco Merchants Association of the United States, Inc.) see *TOBACCO*

T M A LEGISLATIVE BULLETIN. (Tobacco Merchants Association of the United States, Inc.) see *TOBACCO*

342 BE
TABLES CHRONOLOGIQUES ET ALPHABETIQUES DU MONITEUR BELGE. (Supplement to: Bulletin Legislatif Belge) m. 2500 Fr. Maison Ferdinand Larcier S.A., Rue des Minimes 39, 1000 Brussels, Belgium.

340 US
TAKING SIDES: CLASHING VIEWS ON CONTROVERSIAL LEGAL ISSUES. irreg., 4th ed., 1990. $11.95. Dushkin Publishing Group, Inc., Sluice Dock, Guilford, CT 06437-9989. TEL 203-453-4351. FAX 203-453-6000. Ed. M. Ethan Katsh. illus.

340 330 HU ISSN 0231-2522
H8
TARSADALOMKUTATAS. 1966. q. $12. (Magyar Tudomanyos Akademia) Akademiai Kiado, Publishing House of the Hungarian Academy of Sciences, P.O. Box 24, H-1363, Budapest, Hungary. Ed. K. Kulcsar. adv.; bk.rev. Indexed: World Agri.Econ.& Rural Sociol.Abstr.
  —BLDSC shelfmark: 8606.355000.
  Formerly: Gazdasag es Jogtudomany (ISSN 0580-4795)

340 AT ISSN 0085-7106
LAW
TASMANIAN REPORTS. 1897. a. Law Book Co. Ltd., 44-50 Waterloo Rd., North Ryde, N.S.W. 2112, Australia. TEL 02-887-0177. FAX 02-888-9706. TELEX ASBOOK 27995.
  ●Also available online.
  Description: Contains cases determined in the Supreme Court of Tasmania and other Superior Courts in the Island.

TAX LAW REVIEW. see *BUSINESS AND ECONOMICS — Public Finance, Taxation*

345 336.2 US ISSN 0040-005X
K24
TAX LAWYER. 1947. q. $53. American Bar Association, Taxation Section, 1800 M St., N.W., Washington, DC 20036. TEL 202-331-2231. FAX 202-331-2220. (Alt. addr.: 750 N. Lake Shore Dr., Chicago, IL 60611) Ed. Paul J. Sax. adv.; bk.rev.; circ. 32,000. (looseleaf format; also avail. in microform from RRI,UMI; microfilm from WSH; reprint service avail. from RRI) Indexed: ABI Inform, Account.Ind. (1974-), Bank.Lit.Ind., BPIA, C.L.I., L.I.I., L.R.I., Leg.Cont., Leg.Per., PSI.
  ●Also available online. Vendor(s): Mead Data Central, WESTLAW.
  —BLDSC shelfmark: 8611.606050.
  Description: Scholarly articles with student notes and comments on tax law.

TAX NOTES; the weekly tax service. see *BUSINESS AND ECONOMICS — Public Finance, Taxation*

TAXATION FOR LAWYERS. see *BUSINESS AND ECONOMICS — Public Finance, Taxation*

TEACHER RIGHTS NEWSLETTER. see *EDUCATION*

TEAM LICENSING BUSINESS. see *SPORTS AND GAMES*

340 IS
TEL AVIV UNIVERSITY. LAW REVIEW/IYUNEI MISHPAT. (Text in Hebrew; summaries in English) 1971. q. $21. Ramot, 32 University St., Ramat Aviv, Tel Aviv, Israel. Ed. Izhak Hadari. bk.rev.; index. Indexed: Ind.Heb.Per.

TELECOMMUNICATIONS REGULATORY MONITOR. see *COMMUNICATIONS — Telephone And Telegraph*

TELECOMMUNICATIONS REPORTER. see *COMMUNICATIONS — Telephone And Telegraph*

340 SP
TEMAS DE HISTORIA DEL DERECHO. irreg. Universidad de Sevilla, Servicio de Publicaciones, San Fernando, 4, 41004 Seville, Spain. TEL 954-22-8071. FAX 954-22-1315.

340 IT ISSN 0495-0658
TEMI ROMANA. 1952. s-a. L.50000 (foreign L.75000). Casa Editrice Dott. A. Giuffre, Via Busto Arsizio 40, 20151 Milan, Italy. TEL 02-38000905. FAX 02-38009582. Ed. M. Rossi. adv.; circ. 8,250.

340 US ISSN 0899-8086
K24
TEMPLE LAW REVIEW. 1927. q. $22 (foreign $23). Temple University School of Law, Philadelphia, PA 19122. TEL 215-787-7868. adv.; bk.rev.; bibl.; index; circ. 2,300. (also avail. in microfilm from WSH) Indexed: ASCA, C.L.I., Curr.Cont., L.R.I., Leg.Cont., Leg.Per., SSCI.
  ●Also available online. Vendor(s): WESTLAW.
  Formerly (until vol.60, 1988): Temple Law Quarterly (ISSN 0040-2974)

TENDENCIAS ECONOMICAS: LEGISLACION ECONOMICAS ARGENTINA/BUSINESS TRENDS: ARGENTINE ECONOMIC LEGISLATION. see *BUSINESS AND ECONOMICS*

340 US
TENNESSEE ATTORNEYS DIRECTORY AND BUYERS GUIDE. 1982. a. $39. M. Lee Smith Publishers & Printers, 162 Fourth Ave. N., Box 2678, Nashville, TN 37219. TEL 615-242-7395. FAX 615-256-6601. Ed. Joseph L. White.
  Description: Listing of all Tennessee attorneys and related vendors.

340 US
TENNESSEE ATTORNEYS MEMO, PERMANENT EDITION. 1975. w. $680. M. Lee Smith Publishers & Printers, 162 Fourth Ave. N., Box 2678, Nashville, TN 37219. TEL 615-242-7395. FAX 615-256-6601. Ed. Bradford N. Forrister. index; circ. 1,700. (back issues avail.)
  Formerly: Tennessee Attorneys Memo (ISSN 0194-1259)
  Description: Summarizes opinions of Tennessee appellate courts (published and unpublished), new General Assembly acts, selected opinions of Tennessee's Attorney General and of the Sixth Circuit Court of Appeals.

320 US ISSN 0497-2325
TENNESSEE BAR JOURNAL. 1952. 6/yr. $35. Tennessee Bar Association, 3622 West End Ave., Nashville, TN 37205-2403. Ed. Suzanne Craig Robertson. adv.; circ. 6,800. Indexed: C.L.I., L.R.I., Law Ofc.Info.Svc., Leg.Per.
  ●Also available online. Vendor(s): WESTLAW.
  Supersedes (in 1985): Tennessee Lawyer (ISSN 0495-1328)

340 331.11 US
TENNESSEE EMPLOYMENT LAW. (Suppl. avail.: Tennessee Employment Law Update) 1989. a. $89. John-Carroll Enterprises, Inc., Box 428, Chattanooga, TN 37401. TEL 615-821-8281. FAX 615-256-6601. (Dist. by: M. Lee Smith Publishers & Printers, 162 Fourth Ave. N., Box 2678, Nashville, TN 37219. TEL 615-242-7395) Ed. John P. Phillips, Jr.
  Description: Collects and analyzes all appellate decisions both published and unpublished in the area of employment law and employment legislation.

TENNESSEE EMPLOYMENT LAW UPDATE. see *BUSINESS AND ECONOMICS — Labor And Industrial Relations*

340 US ISSN 1042-3168
TENNESSEE ENVIRONMENTAL LAW LETTER. 1989. m. $167. M. Lee Smith Publishers & Printers, 162 Fourth Ave. N., Box 2678, Nashville, TN 37219. TEL 615-242-7395. FAX 615-256-6601. (Co-sponsor: Bass, Berry & Sims) Ed. J. Andrew Goddard. index.
  Description: Reports the latest Tennessee environmental law developments that affect Tennessee companies.

340 US
▼**TENNESSEE LAW OFFICE DESK BOOK.** 1990. a. $34. M. Lee Smith Publishers & Printers, 162 Fourth Ave. N., Box 2678, Nashville, TN 37219. TEL 615-242-7395. FAX -256-6601. Ed. Pamela D. Brooks.
  Description: Designed to assist the daily work of a law office by providing attorneys, legal secretaries, paralegals and legal assistants with information that is routinely needed.

340 US ISSN 0040-3288
K24
TENNESSEE LAW REVIEW. 1923. q. $24 (foreign $26). Tennessee Law Review Association, Inc., 1505 W. Cumberland Ave., Knoxville, TN 37996-1800. Ed.Bd. adv.; bk.rev.; index. cum.index; circ. 1,800. (also avail. in microfiche from BHP; microform from WSH; reprint service avail. from WSH) Indexed: C.L.I., L.R.I., Leg.Cont., Leg.Per.
  ●Also available online. Vendor(s): WESTLAW.
  —BLDSC shelfmark: 8790.730000.

346 US
TENNESSEE MEDICO-LEGAL REPORTER. 1983. m. $180. M. Lee Smith Publishers & Printers, 162 Fourth Ave. N., Box 2678, Nashville, TN 37219. TEL 615-242-7395. FAX 615-256-6601. Ed. Lewis L. Laska.
  Description: Reviews trial and appellate cases and developments of interest to Tennessee health care lawyers and managers.

TERMINATION OF EMPLOYMENT. see *BUSINESS AND ECONOMICS — Personnel Management*

LAW

340   US
TESTIMONIAL PRIVILEGES. 1983. base vol. (plus a. suppl.). $95. Shepard's - McGraw-Hill, Inc., Box 35300, Colorado Springs, CO 80935-3530. TEL 800-525-2474.
   Description: Provides advice on problems ranging from maintaining the confidentiality of office files to conducting complex intra-corporate investigations. Discussions explain the legal principles and precedents needed for successful assertion of privileges.

340   US   ISSN 0040-4187
K24
TEXAS BAR JOURNAL. 1938. m. (11/yr.). $12. State Bar of Texas, Box 12487, Capitol Sta., Austin, TX 78711. TEL 512-463-1522. Ed. Kelley Jones. adv.; bk.rev.; illus.; index; circ. 62,000. (also avail. in microform from UMI,BHP; microfiche from WSH; microfilm from WSH) **Indexed:** C.L.I., L.R.I., Law Ofc.Info.Svc., Leg.Per.
   —BLDSC shelfmark: 8798.673000.

340   US
TEXAS COMMERCIAL COLLECTIONS; forms and procedures for attorneys and legal assistants. 1989. base vol. (plus suppl. 1-2/yr.). $150. Butterworth Legal Publishers (Salem) (Subsidiary of: Reed International PLC), 90 Stiles Rd., Salem, NH 03079. TEL 800-548-4001. FAX 603-898-9858. (looseleaf format)

340   US
TEXAS DRUNK DRIVING LAW. 2nd ed. 1991. 2 base vols. (plus a. suppl.). $195. Butterworth Legal Publishers (Salem) (Subsidiary of: Reed International PLC), 90 Stiles Rd., Salem, NH 03079. TEL 800-548-4001. FAX 603-898-9858. Eds. J. Gray Trichter, W. Troy McKinney. (looseleaf format)
   Description: Provides a textual discussion and analysis of the current law; includes applicable statutes, codes, Department of Public Safety guidelines and regulations, and case law and literature, as well as pre-trial and courtroom mechanics of DWI prosecution and defense.

340   US   ISSN 1046-9214
TEXAS EMPLOYMENT LAW LETTER. 1989. 12/yr. $92. M. Lee Smith Publishers & Printers, 162 Fourth Ave., Box 2678, Nashville, TN 37219. TEL 615-242-7395. FAX 615-256-6601. Eds. David M. Ellis, Michael P. Maslanka.
   Description: Reports the latest Texas employment law developments that affect Texas employers.

340 614.7   US
▼**TEXAS ENVIRONMENTAL LAW LETTER.** 1991. 12/yr. $147. M. Lee Smith Publishers & Printers, 162 Fourth Ave. N., Box 2678, Nashville, TN 37219. TEL 615-242-7395. FAX 615-256-6601. Eds. Neil R. Mitchell, Rebecca A. Leigh.
   Description: Reports the latest Texas environmental law developments that affect Texas companies.

340   US   ISSN 0266-0814
KFT1740.A15
TEXAS EVIDENCE REPORTER. 1984. bi-m. $96. Butterworth Legal Publishers, Austin Division (Subsidiary of: Reed International PLC), Echelon II, Ste. 100, 9430 Research, Austin, TX 78759-6598. TEL 512-346-9686. FAX 512-346-9373. Ed. Richard J. Clarkson. index. (looseleaf format; back issues avail.)

340 610   US   ISSN 0266-0806
KFT1560.A15
TEXAS HEALTH LAW REPORTER. 1984. bi-m. $96. Butterworth Legal Publishers, Austin Division (Subsidiary of: Reed International PLC), Echelon II, Ste. 100, 9430 Research, Austin, TX 78759-6598. TEL 512-346-9686. FAX 512-346-9373. Eds. David M. Davis, Brian McElroy. index. (looseleaf format; back issues avail.)

340   US
TEXAS HOSPITAL LAW. 1988. base vol. (plus a. suppl.). $115. Butterworth Legal Publishers (Salem) (Subsidiary of: Reed International PLC), 90 Stiles Rd., Salem, NH 03079. TEL 800-548-4001. FAX 603-898-9858. Eds. Richard L. Griffith, Dewey M. Johnston. (looseleaf format)
   Description: Case analysis and examination of legal and administrative issues affecting the medical community in Texas.

340 368   US
KFT1385.A15
TEXAS INSURANCE LAW JOURNAL. 1983. q. $96. Butterworth Legal Publishers, Austin Division (Subsidiary of: Reed International PLC), Echelon II, Ste. 100, 9430 Research, Austin, TX 78759-6598. TEL 512-346-9686. FAX 512-346-9373. Ed.Bd. index. (looseleaf format; back issues avail.)
   Formerly (until 1991): Texas Insurance Law Reporter (ISSN 0264-6307)

340 323.4   US   ISSN 1058-5427
▼**TEXAS JOURNAL OF WOMEN AND THE LAW.** 1992. a. $25 (students $12.50). J. Christiansen, Publisher, 727 E. 26th St., Austin, TX 78705. TEL 512-471-3227. FAX 512-471-6988. Eds. Suzanne Tetzlass, Lynne Boswell. circ. 400.

340   US
TEXAS LAW OF OIL AND GAS. 1989. 3 base vols. (plus suppl.). $350. Butterworth Legal Publishers (Salem) (Subsidiary of: Reed International PLC), 90 Stiles Rd., Salem, NH 03079. TEL 800-548-4001. FAX 603-898-9858. Eds. Ernest E. Smith, Jacqueline Lang Weaver. (looseleaf format)

340   US   ISSN 0040-4411
K24
TEXAS LAW REVIEW. 1922. 6/yr. $32 (foreign $39). University of Texas at Austin, School of Law Publications, 727 E. 26th St., Ste. 3.102A, Austin, TX 78705-1106. TEL 512-471-3164. FAX 512-471-6988. Ed. J.R. Nichols. adv.; bk.rev.; index; circ. 2,100. (also avail. in microfiche from RRI,WSH; microfilm from WSH; back issues avail.; reprint service avail. from RRI) **Indexed:** A.B.C.Pol.Sci., ABI Inform, ASCA, C.L.I., Curr.Cont., L.R.I., Leg.Cont., Leg.Per., Mar.Aff.Bibl., SSCI.
●Also available online. Vendor(s): Mead Data Central.
   —BLDSC shelfmark: 8799.300000.
   Description: Examines current legal issues.

340   US   ISSN 0267-8306
K24
TEXAS LAWYER. 1985. w. $159. American Lawyer Media, L.P. (New York), 600 Third Ave., 3rd Fl., New York, NY 10016. TEL 212-973-2800. FAX 214-741-2325. (Subscr. to: 400 S. Record, Ste. 1400, Dallas, TX 75202. TEL 214-744-9300) Ed. Mark Obbie. adv.; index; circ. 10,400. (tabloid format; also avail. in microfiche; back issues avail.)
●Also available online.
   Description: Presents articles on law cases, firms and politics in Texas; includes court summaries.

340   US
TEXAS LIMITATIONS MANUAL. 1987. biennial. $85. Butterworth Legal Publishers (Salem) (Subsidiary of: Reed International PLC), 90 Stiles Rd., Salem, NH 03079. TEL 800-548-4001. FAX 603-898-9858. Ed. Jennifer Nosler Mellett. (looseleaf format)
   Description: Quick reference to statutes, codes and statewide rules of court that set time limitations.

340   US
TEXAS LITIGATOR'S HANDBOOK. 1989. base vol. (plus suppl.). $95. Butterworth Legal Publishers (Salem) (Subsidiary of: Reed International PLC), 90 Stiles Rd., Salem, NH 03079. TEL 800-548-4001. FAX 603-898-9858. Ed. Edward F. Butler. (looseleaf format)
   Description: Trial strategy guide designed for Texas attorneys when handling tort, contract and business litigation or divorce and custody suits.

TEXAS NATURAL RESOURCES REPORTER. see WATER RESOURCES

340   US
TEXAS NOTARY LAW PRIMER. a. $9.95. National Notary Association, 8236 Remmet Ave., Box 7184, Canoga Park, CA 91304-7184. TEL 818-713-4000. FAX 818-713-9061. Ed. Charles N. Faerber. (reprint service avail. from UMI)

340   US   ISSN 0950-3285
TEXAS OIL AND GAS LAW JOURNAL. 1986. bi-m. $96. Butterworth Legal Publishers, Austin Division (Subsidiary of: Reed International PLC), Echelon II, Ste. 100, 9430 Research, Austin, TX 78759-6598. TEL 512-346-9686. FAX 512-346-9373. Ed. Owen Anderson. (looseleaf format; back issues avail.)

340   US
TEXAS PERSONAL INJURY LAW. 1981. 3 base vols. (plus suppl. 1-2/yr.). $185. Butterworth Legal Publishers (Salem) (Subsidiary of: Reed International PLC), 90 Stiles Rd., Salem, NH 03079. TEL 800-548-4001. FAX 603-898-9858. (looseleaf format)
   Description: Analysis of the applicable statutes, rules and case law.

340   US   ISSN 0264-4770
KFT1397.P3
TEXAS PERSONAL INJURY LAW REPORTER. 1983. bi-m. $96. Butterworth Legal Publishers, Austin Division (Subsidiary of: Reed International PLC), Echelon II, Ste. 100, 9430 Research, Austin, TX 78759-6598. TEL 512-346-9686. FAX 512-346-9373. Ed. Frank R. Southers. index. (looseleaf format; back issues avail.)

340   US
TEXAS PROBATE CODE MANUAL. 1984. 2 base vols. (plus suppl. 1-2/yr.). $125. Butterworth Legal Publishers (Salem) (Subsidiary of: Reed International PLC), 90 Stiles Rd., Salem, NH 03079. TEL 800-548-4001. FAX 603-898-9858. (looseleaf format)

340   US
TEXAS PRODUCT LIABILITY LAW. 1986. base vol. (plus a. suppl.). $110. Butterworth Legal Publishers (Salem) (Subsidiary of: Reed International PLC), 90 Stiles Rd., Salem, NH 03079. TEL 800-548-4001. FAX 603-898-9858. Ed. William Powers, Jr. (looseleaf format)
   Description: Describes and analyzes current Texas products liability law, including all potential theories of recovery, the effects of recent tort reform legislation, and relevent Texas Supreme Court and Court of Appeals decisions through the prior calendar year.

TEXAS PUBLIC UTILITY NEWS. see ENERGY

340 333.33   US   ISSN 0267-8896
TEXAS REAL ESTATE LAW REPORTER. 1985. bi-m. $96. Butterworth Legal Publishers, Austin Division (Subsidiary of: Reed International PLC), Echelon II, Ste. 100, 9430 Research, Austin, TX 78759-6598. TEL 512-346-9686. FAX 512-346-9373. Ed. Charles J. Jacobus. index. (looseleaf format; back issues avail.)

348   US   ISSN 0362-4781
KFT1236
TEXAS REGISTER. 1976. s-w. $90. Secretary of State, Box 13684, TX 78711. TEL 512-463-5561. Ed. Dan Procter. circ. 4,500. (also avail. in microfilm; back issues avail.) **Indexed:** F.

TEXAS SCHOOL LAW BULLETIN. see EDUCATION — School Organization And Administration

340   US   ISSN 0564-6197
K24
TEXAS TECH LAW REVIEW. 1969. q. $32. Texas Tech University, School of Law, Lubbock, TX 79409. TEL 806-742-3791. FAX 806-742-1629. Ed. G. Douglas Welch. adv.; circ. 1,300. (also avail. in microfilm from WSH; reprint service avail. from WSH) **Indexed:** C.L.I., L.R.I., Leg.Cont., Leg.Per., Mar.Aff.Bibl.
●Also available online. Vendor(s): WESTLAW.

340   FR
TEXTES D'INTERET GENERAL. irreg. Direction des Journaux Officiels, 26 rue Desaix, 75727 Paris Cedex 15, France. TEL 1-45-78-61-44.

340   PH
THOMASIAN LAW UPDATE. (Text in English) 1985. s-a. P.50. University of Santo Tomas, Faculty of Civil Law, Sampalco St., Espana, Manila, Philippines. circ. 800.

340.05   US
K24
THURGOOD MARSHALL LAW REVIEW. 1975. 2/yr. $20. Texas Southern University, Thurgood Marshall School of Law, 3100 Cleburne, Houston, TX 77004. TEL 713-527-7246. FAX 713-639-1049. Ed. Lateefah Muhammad. adv.; bk.rev.; circ. 500. (also avail. in microform from UMI) **Indexed:** C.L.I., Leg.Per.
●Also available online. Vendor(s): WESTLAW.
   Formerly: Texas Southern University Law Review (ISSN 0092-3559)

LAW

TIDBITS. see EDUCATION

TIDE. see CONSERVATION

340 309   SW   ISSN 0281-2584
TIDSKRIFT FOER RAETTSSOCIOLOGI. (Text in Danish, English, Swedish; summaries in English) 1983. q. SEK 140($30) Humanistisk-Samhaellsvetenskapliga Forskningsradet, P.O. Box 6712, S-113 85 Stockholm, Sweden. TEL 08-151580. (Subscr. to: Bredgaten 4, S-221 21 Lund) Ed. Antoinette Hetzler. adv.; bk.rev.; charts; index; circ. 300. (back issues avail.)
—BLDSC shelfmark: 8821.755000.

349   DK   ISSN 0040-6880
TIDSSKRIFT FOR GROENLANDS RETSVAESEN. 1965. q. DKK 90. Danish Polar Center, Hauserkgade 3, 1128 Copenhagen K, Denmark. TEL 33-158666. FAX 33-134976. Ed. Agnete Weis Bentzon. adv.; bk.rev.; charts; stat.; index; index; circ. 500.

349   NO   ISSN 0040-7143
K24
TIDSSKRIFT FOR RETTSVITENSKAP; Scandinavian journal of law. Short title: T F R. (Text in Scandinavian languages) 1888. 5/yr. $64. Universitetsforlaget, P.O. Box 2959-Toeyen, N-0608 Oslo 1, Norway. (U.S. addr.: Publications Expediting Inc., 200 Meacham Ave., Elmont, NY 11003) Eds. Birger Stuevold Lassen, Magnus Aarbakke. adv.; bk.rev.; bibl.; cum.index; circ. 2,000. (back issues avail.)
—BLDSC shelfmark: 8828.040000.

340   NE   ISSN 0167-1359
TIJDSCHRIFT VOOR ARBITRAGE. 1980. bi-m. fl.91.50. (Stichting Tijdschrift Arbitrage) Kluwer Law and Taxation Publishers, Postbus 23, 7400 GA Deventer, Netherlands. TEL 05700-33155. FAX 0570-31419. TELEX 49295 KLUWDV NL. (Subscr. to: Libresso B.V., Postbus 23, 7400 GA Deventer, Netherlands) (Co-sponsors: T.M.C. Asser Instituut, Institut voor International Privaat- en Publiekrcht, Internationale Handelsarbitrage en Europees Recht) Ed. A.J. van den Berg. adv.; bk.rev.; circ. 900.

340   BE   ISSN 0040-7437
TIJDSCHRIFT VOOR BESTUURSWETENSCHAPPEN EN PUBLIEKRECHT. 1946. m. 3500 Fr. Hoger Instituut voor Bestuurswetenschappen, c/o P. Berckx, C. Mercatorlaan 28, B-1780 Wemmel, Belgium. Ed.Bd. adv.; bk.rev.; index; circ. 2,000.
Description: Focuses on Belgian and European law concerning administration, management, social regulations education and environment, with summaries and comments of judgments.

349   BE   ISSN 0082-4313
TIJDSCHRIFT VOOR PRIVAATRECHT. Short title: T P R. 1964. q. 4000 Fr. E. Story-Scientia, De Jamblinne de Meuxplein 34-34, B-1040 Brussels, Belgium. TEL 32-2-36-89-80. Ed. M. Storme. bk.rev.; circ. 1,200.
—BLDSC shelfmark: 8844.150000.

340 900   NE   ISSN 0040-7585
K24   CODEN: TIREES
TIJDSCHRIFT VOOR RECHTSGESCHIEDENIS/REVUE D'HISTOIRE DU DROIT/LEGAL HISTORY REVIEW. (Text in English, French, German, Italian, Latin and Spanish) 1918. q. $144. Kluwer Academic Publishers, Postbus 17, 3300 AA Dordrecht, Netherlands. TEL 078-334911. FAX 078-334254. TELEX 29245. (Dist. by: Kluwer Academic Publishers Group, Distribution Center, Postbus 322, 3300 AH Dordrecht, Netherlands; N. America dist. addr.: Box 358, Accord Station, Hingham, MA 02018-0358. TEL 617-871-6600) Ed.Bd. bk.rev. (back issues avail.) Indexed: Hist.Abstr.
—BLDSC shelfmark: 5181.325000.

TIME CHARTERS. see TRANSPORTATION — Ships And Shipping

340   UK   ISSN 0958-0441
▼TIMES LAW REPORTS. 1990. m. £75($135) (The Times) T & T Clark, 59 George St., Edinburgh EH2 2LQ, Scotland. TEL 031-225-4703. FAX 031-220-4260. Ed. Iain Sutherland. cum.index; circ. 2,000.
Description: Law cases of England and Wales, European courts.

340 333.33   US   ISSN 0738-6923
KF598.A15
TIMESHARING LAW REPORTER. 1980. bi-m. $195. Land Development Institute, Ltd., 1300 N St., N.W., Washington, DC 20005. TEL 202-545-2144. Eds. Stuart Marshall Bloch, William Ingersoll. circ. 250.
Description: Covers state and federal legislation, court and regulatory action relating to real estate timesharing, fractional interests and membership camp grounds.

TITLE AND REGISTRATION BOOK; summary of motor vehicle laws and regulations. see TRANSPORTATION — Automobiles

340   AT
TITLES OFFICE PRACTICE. 1986. 2/yr. Aus.$150. Law Book Co. Ltd., 44-50 Waterloo Rd., North Ryde, N.S.W. 2113, Australia. TEL 02-887-0177. FAX 02-888-9706. TELEX ASBOOK 27995. Ed. A.J.S. Byrne.
Description: Provides information regarding the practices, procedures and requirements of the Titles Office.

340   US   ISSN 0887-7831
KF1297.T63
TOBACCO INDUSTRY LITIGATION REPORTER; the national journal of record of litigation affecting the tobacco industry. 1985. m. $675. Andrews Publications, 1646 West Chester Pike, Box 1000, Westtown, PA 19395. TEL 215-399-6600. FAX 215-399-6610. Ed. Jay Steinberg. abstr.; bibl.; stat.; cum.index every 6 mos. (looseleaf format; back issues avail.)

657   US
TODAY'S LAWYER.* q. C P A Associates, 201 State Rte. 17, 4th fl., Rutherford, NJ 07070-2574. TEL 212-818-9700.
Description: Provides information on members' services to clients.

340   IT   ISSN 0040-8654
TOGA CALABRESE; rassegna di dottrina giurisprudenza-vita e varieta giudiziarie e forensi. 1932. bi-m. L.10000. Corso Mazzini 291, 88100 Catanzaro (Calabria), Italy. TEL 23700. Dir. Domenico Pittelli. adv.; bk.rev.; film rev.; charts; illus. (newspaper)
Description: Covers current events in law, politics and other various topics related to lawyers.

TOILETRIES, FRAGRANCES AND SKIN CARE: THE ROSE SHEET. see BEAUTY CULTURE — Perfumes And Cosmetics

TORONTO LEGAL DIRECTORY. see BUSINESS AND ECONOMICS — Trade And Industrial Directories

340 333.33   AT
TORRENS SYSTEM IN N.S.W.. 1985. 2/yr. Aus.$150. Law Book Co. Ltd., 44-50 Waterloo Rd., North Ryde, N.S.W 2113, Australia. TEL 02-887-0177. FAX 02-888-9706. TELEX ASBOOK 27995. Eds. R.A. Woodman, Kevin Nettle.
Description: Text provides both annotations and commentary to all provisions of the legislation and the Real Property Act 1990 and the Conveyancing Act, dealing with easements and covenants.

340   US   ISSN 0885-856X
K6
TORT & INSURANCE LAW JOURNAL. 1965. q. $23 (foreign $28). American Bar Association, Tort and Insurance Practice Section, 750 N. Lake Shore Dr., Chicago, IL 60611. TEL 312-988-5000. Ed. Jeffery Anne Tatum. abstr.; charts; illus.; stat.; tr.lit.; index; circ. 35,000. (also avail. in microform from UMI; microfilm from WSH; reprint service avail.) Indexed: C.L.I., INIS Atomind., L.R.I., Leg.Per.; Risk Abstr.
●Also available online. Vendor(s): Mead Data Central, WESTLAW.
—BLDSC shelfmark: 8869.702000.
Formerly: Forum (Chicago, 1965) (ISSN 0015-8356)
Description: Scholarly journal on current or emerging issues of national scope in the fields of tort and insurance law.

340   US
▼TORT LAW AND PERSONAL INJURY PRACTICE (RHODE ISLAND). 1990. 2 base vols. (plus a. suppl.). $145. Butterworth Legal Publishers (Salem) (Subsidiary of: Reed International PLC), 90 Stiles Rd., Salem, NH 03079. TEL 800-548-4001. FAX 603-898-9858. Ed. Ronald J. Resmini.
Description: Analyzes the statutes, common law and case law pertaining to torts, motor vehicles, insurance and arbitration.

340   US
TORT TRENDS NEWSLETTER. 1955. q. $38 to non-profit institutions, excluding libraries; profit institutions $68. Illinois State Bar Association, 424 S. Second St., Springfield, IL 62701. TEL 217-525-1760. Eds. Lester Foreman, Joseph R. Marconi. circ. 5,750.
Formerly: Illinois State Bar Association. Tort Trends (ISSN 0040-9626)

340   US   ISSN 8756-7326
K24
TOURO LAW REVIEW. s-a. $12. Darby Printing Co., 715 W. Whitehall St., S.W., Atlanta, GA 30310. TEL 404-755-4521.
—BLDSC shelfmark: 8870.941000.

340   FR
TOUT LYON; et le moniteur judiciaire reunis. 1895. s-w. 1295 F. Jean Matagrin, 40 rue du President-Edouard-Herriot, 69282 Lyon Cedex 01, France. Ed. Jean Matagrin. adv.; circ. 10,000.
Incorporates: Metropole.

340   US   ISSN 0737-8513
KF3958.A59
TOXIC CHEMICALS LITIGATION REPORTER; the national journal of record for litigation involving claims of personal injury and/or property damage from exposure to toxic chemicals. 1983. s-m. $850. Andrews Publications, 1646 West Chester Pike, Box 1000, Westtown, PA 19395. TEL 215-399-6600. FAX 215-399-6610. Ed. Edith McFall. bibl.; stat.; cum.index every 6 mos. (looseleaf format; back issues avail.)

340 604.7   US
TOXIC TORT LITIGATION. 1989. base vol. (plus s-a. suppl.). Maxwell Macmillan, Rosenfeld Launer, 910 Sylvan Ave., Englewood Cliffs, NJ 07632-3310. TEL 800-562-0245. FAX 201-816-3569. Eds. Edward Greer, Warren Freedman.

TOXICS LAW REPORTER. see ENVIRONMENTAL STUDIES — Waste Management

340 330   AT
TRADE PRACTICES LAW. 1989. 3/yr. Aus.$360. Law Book Co. Ltd., 44-50 Waterloo Rd., North Ryde, N.S.W. 2113, Australia. TEL 02-887-0177. FAX 02-888-9706. TELEX ASBOOK 27995. Ed. J.D. Heydon.
Description: Examines restrictive trade practices, deceptive conduct and consumer protection with enforcement and remedies, with a full reproduction of the 1974 Trade Practices Act.

340 341   US   ISSN 0731-5813
KF3176.A32
TRADEMARK LAW HANDBOOK. 1981. a. $65. (United States Trademark Association) Clark - Boardman - Callaghan Company, Ltd., 375 Hudson St., New York, NY 10014. TEL 212-929-7500. FAX 212-924-0460. Ed. Robert Bouchard.

340   UK   ISSN 0262-9240
TRADING LAW. 1982. q. £69.75. Barry Rose Law Periodicals, East Row, Little London, Chichester, West Sussex PO19 1PG, England. TEL 0243-787841. FAX 0243-779278. Ed. G. Stephenson.
—BLDSC shelfmark: 8881.051300.
Description: Details various aspects of consumer--trading law, competition, monopolies, mergers, international trade, credit trading and fair trading.

340   UK   ISSN 0268-9510
TRADING LAW REPORTS. 1985. 6/yr. £93.75. Barry Rose Law Periodicals, Little London, Chichester, West Sussex PO19 1PG, England. TEL 0243-787841. FAX 0243-779278. Ed. G. Stephenson.
Description: Contains all important trading law cases.

TRAFFIC LAW REPORTS. see *TRANSPORTATION — Automobiles*

340 US ISSN 1058-1006
K24
▼**TRANSNATIONAL LAW & CONTEMPORARY PROBLEMS.** 1991. 2/yr. (in 1 vol.). $15 (foreign $18). University of Iowa, College of Law, Boyd Law Bldg., Rm. 187, Iowa City, IA 52242. TEL 319-335-9736. FAX 319-335-9019.

TRANSPORT-DE-REGULATION REPORT. see *TRANSPORTATION*

346.73 US ISSN 0092-6175
KF195.T7
TRANSPORTATION AND PRODUCTS LEGAL DIRECTORY.* 1973. a. Spangler, Jennings, Spangler & Dougherty, 8396 Mississippi St., Merrillville, IN 46410.

340 388.324 US
KF2179.A2
TRANSPORTATION LAW INSTITUTE PAPERS AND PROCEEDINGS. 1971. a. Association of Transportation Practitioners, 1725 K St., N.W., Ste. 301, Washington, DC 20006-1401. TEL 202-466-2080.
Supersedes (in 1988): Eastern Transportation Law Seminar Papers and Proceedings (ISSN 0271-437X) & Western Transportation Law Seminar Papers and Proceedings (ISSN 0271-4396); Supersedes in part: Transportation Law Seminar. Papers and Proceedings (ISSN 0164-1689)

343.093 US ISSN 0049-450X
K24
TRANSPORTATION LAW JOURNAL. 1969. s-a. $15 (foreign $20). c/o Paul Stephen Dempsey, Ed., University of Denver, College of Law, 1900 Olive St., Denver, CO 80220. TEL 303-871-6269. FAX 303-871-6411. adv.; bk.rev.; circ. 2,000. (also avail. in microform from WSH; reprint service avail. from WSH) **Indexed:** BPIA, Bus.Ind., C.L.I., L.R.I., Leg.Cont., Leg.Per.

347.7 US ISSN 8756-9302
K24
TRANSPORTATION PRACTITIONERS JOURNAL. 1933. q. $55. Association of Transportation Practitioners, 1725 K St., N.W., Ste. 301, Washington, DC 20006-1401. TEL 202-466-2080. Ed. James F. Bromley. bk.rev.; charts; illus.; index; circ. 4,000. (also avail. in microform from WSH; reprint service avail. from WSH) **Indexed:** C.L.I., Hlth.Ind., L.R.I., Leg.Per.
Formerly: I C C Practitioners' Journal (ISSN 0018-8859)

240 US
TRANSPORTATION SAFETY LAW PRACTICE MANUAL. 1989. 2 base vols. (plus suppl.). $165. Butterworth Legal Publishers (Salem) (Subsidiary of: Reed International PLC), 90 Stiles Rd., Salem, NH 03079. TEL 800-548-4001. FAX 603-898-9858. Ed. William E. Kenworthy. (looseleaf format)
Description: Provides information enabling attorneys to establish or improve safety programs in transportation companies, and to ensure compliance with current regulations.

TREATMENT ISSUES; newsletter of experimental AIDS therapies. see *MEDICAL SCIENCES — Communicable Diseases*

340 US
TRESPASS TO TRY TITLE. 1988. base vol. (plus a. suppl.). $95. Butterworth Legal Publishers (Salem) (Subsidiary of: Reed International PLC), 90 Stiles Rd., Salem, NH 03079. TEL 800-548-4001. FAX 603-898-9858. Ed. Harold F. Thurow. (looseleaf format)
Description: Practitioner's guide to determine who has the right of possession to any interest or title in real estate.

TRIBUNA MEDICA HOSPITALES. see *HOSPITALS*

340 SP
TRIBUNAL. (Includes bound vols. with indexes). m. 46000 ptas. (effective 1991). Editorial Aranzadi, S.A., Avda. Carlos III, 34, Apdo. 111, 31080 Pamplona, Spain. TEL 948-331212. FAX 948-330919.

349 FR ISSN 0071-9129
TRIBUNAL DE COMMERCE, PARIS. ANNUAIRE.* 1969. a. price varies. Tribunal de Commerce de Paris, 1 Bd. du Palais, Paris, France.

340 BL ISSN 0041-2805
TRIBUNAL DE JUSTICA DO ESTADO DO RIO GRANDE DO SUL. REVISTA DE JURISPRUDENCIA;* doutrina, jurisprudencia, legislacao. 1966. bi-m. Cr.$90. Tribuna de Justica, Palacio da Justica, Porto Alegre, RS, Brazil. bk.rev.; cum.index.

340 CU
TRIBUNAL SUPREMO POPULAR. BOLETIN. a. Tribunal Supremo Popular, San Rafael No. 3, Habana 2, Havana, Cuba.

340 IT
TRIBUNALI AMMINISTRATIVI REGIONALI. 1974. m. L.440000. Casa Editrice Italedi, Piazza Cavour 19, 00192 Rome, Italy. Ed. Ignazio Scotto.

340 US
TRUST DEPARTMENT ADMINISTRATION AND OPERATIONS. (Issued in 2 base vols. with supplements) 1981. irreg. Matthew Bender & Co., Inc., 11 Penn Plaza, New York, NY 10001. TEL 212-967-7707. (looseleaf format)
Description: Covers every aspect of setting up a trust department, day-to-day administration, asset management, operations, marketing, and internal management.

346.066 UK
KD1480.A13
TRUST LAW INTERNATIONAL. 1986. 4/yr. £85($140) Tolley Publishing Co. Ltd., Tolley House, 2 Addiscombe Rd., Croydon, Surrey CR9 5AF, England. Ed.Bd. adv.; bk.rev.; index. (back issues avail.)
Formerly: Trust Law and Practice (ISSN 0269-5782)
Description: Offers extensive coverage of trust law both within the UK and internationally.

TRUSTS AND ESTATES. see *BUSINESS AND ECONOMICS — Investments*

340 GW ISSN 0082-6731
TUEBINGER RECHTSWISSENSCHAFTLICHE ABHANDLUNGEN. 1961. irreg. price varies. (Universitaet Tuebingen, Rechts- und Wirtschaftswissenschaftliche Fakultaet) Verlag J.C.B. Mohr (Paul Siebeck), Wilhelmstr. 18, Postfach 2040, 7400 Tuebingen, Germany. TEL 07071-26064. FAX 07071-51104. TELEX 7262872-MOHR-D.

340 US ISSN 0041-3992
K24
TULANE LAW REVIEW. 1929/30. 6/yr. $35. Tulane Law Review Association, Tulane University Sta., New Orleans, LA 70118. TEL 504-865-5969. Ed. Louis L. Plotkin. adv.; bk.rev.; index. cum.index: vols. 1-15; 16-35; 36-45; circ. 2,954. (also avail. in microform from RRI,UMI; microfilm from WSH; microfilm from WSH; reprint service avail. from RRI) **Indexed:** A.B.C.Pol.Sci., Amer.Bibl.Slavic & E.Eur.Stud, C.L.I., L.R.I., Leg. Cont., Leg.Per., Mar.Aff.Bibl., Sel.Water Res.Abstr.
●Also available online. Vendor(s): Mead Data Central, WESTLAW.
—BLDSC shelfmark: 9070.300000.

340 US ISSN 0041-4050
TULSA LAW JOURNAL. 1964. q. $23 (typically set in Sep.). University of Tulsa, College of Law, 3120 E. Fourth Pl., Tulsa, OK 74104. TEL 918-631-2408. FAX 918-631-3556. Ed. Ann Dooley. adv.; bk.rev.; index. cum.index every 5 yrs.; circ. 1,350. (tabloid format; also avail. in microform from UMI; reprint service avail. from RRI) **Indexed:** C.C.L.P., C.L.I., L.R.I., Leg.Per.
●Also available online. Vendor(s): WESTLAW.
—BLDSC shelfmark: 9070.450000.
Description: Provides articles on legal subjects of special concern in the Southwest, including oil and gas law, environmental law, and American Indian law, with many articles of broad national interest.

340 US ISSN 0041-4069
TULSA LAWYER. 1961. m. membership. Tulsa County Bar Association, 1446 S. Boston, Tulsa, OK 74119-3612. TEL 918-584-5243. FAX 918-592-0208. Ed. Delores Bedington. adv.; bk.rev.; charts; circ. 2,000.

346.066 US ISSN 0889-1699
TURNAROUNDS & WORKOUTS; news for people tracking distressed companies. 1986. s-m. $354. Beard Group, Inc., Box 9867, Washington, DC 20016. TEL 301-951-6400. FAX 301-951-3621. Ed. Maxim Kniazkon.

346.066 US
▼**TURNAROUNDS & WORKOUTS - SUPPLEMENT;** troubled companies data. 1990. m. $195. Beard Group, Inc., Box 9867, Washington, DC 20016. TEL 301-951-6400. FAX 301-951-3621. Ed. April Handison. adv.
Description: Contains data and statistics for professionals on troubled companies in the US and Canada.

346.066 US
▼**TURNAROUNDS & WORKOUTS - SURVEY;** bankruptcy & insolvency issues. 1991. m. $195. Beard Group, Inc., Box 9867, Washington, DC 20016. TEL 301-951-6400. FAX 301-551-3621. Ed. Maxim Kniazkov.

340 BE
TWEETALIGE LOSBLADIGE WETBOEKEN. 1965. irreg. price varies. E. Story-Scientia, De Jamblinne de Meuxplein 34-35, B-1040 Brussels, Belgium. TEL 32-3-36-89-80.

340 SA ISSN 0257-7747
TYDSKRIF VIR DIE SUID-AFRIKAANSE REG/JOURNAL OF SOUTH AFRICAN LAW. (Text in Afrikaans or English; summaries in English) 1976. q. R.100. Juta & Co. Ltd., P.O. Box 14373, Kenwyn 7790, South Africa. TEL 021-797-5101. FAX 021-761-5010. Ed. J.C. Sonnekus. adv.; bk.rev.; circ. 1,300. **Indexed:** Ind.S.A.Per.
Description: Covers all aspects of South African law.

340 SA
TYDSKRIF VIR HEDEDAAGSE ROMEINS-HOLLANDSE REG/JOURNAL OF CONTEMPORARY ROMAN DUTCH LAW. (Text in Afrikaans, English; summaries in English) 1939. q. R.62. Professional Publishers (Pty) Ltd., P.O. Box 792, Durban 4000, South Africa. TEL 031-294247. FAX 2731-286350. Ed. J. Neethling. adv.; bk.rev.; index; circ. 2,000.

340 US
TYLER REVIEW. 1980. m. Box 871, Tyler, TX 75710. TEL 903-592-1356. adv.; circ. 10,000.

340 368.4 FR
U C A N S S S. BULLETIN JURIDIQUE. 1947. w. Union des Caisses Nationales de Securite Sociale, Tour Maine Montparnasse, 33 av. du Maine, Boites 45 & 46, 75755 Paris Cedex 15, France. cum.index.

340 US ISSN 0197-4564
K3
U C DAVIS LAW REVIEW. 1966. q. $30. University of California, Davis, School of Law, Martin Luther King, Jr. Hall, Davis, CA 95616. TEL 916-752-2551. FAX 916-752-4704. adv.; bk.rev.; circ. 800. (also avail. in microform from RRI; back issues avail.; reprint service avail. from RRI) **Indexed:** C.L.I., Leg.Cont., Leg.Per.
●Also available online. Vendor(s): Wilsonline.
Also available on CD-ROM.
—BLDSC shelfmark: 9104.455000.

340 US ISSN 0733-401X
K25
U C L A JOURNAL OF ENVIRONMENTAL LAW AND POLICY. 1980. s-a. $15. University of California, Los Angeles, School of Law, 405 Hilgard Ave., Los Angeles, CA 90024. TEL 213-825-0314. adv. (back issues avail.) **Indexed:** C.L.I., Energy Rev., Environ.Per.Bibl., Leg.Per.

340 US ISSN 0041-5650
K25
U C L A LAW REVIEW. 1953. 6/yr. $24. University of California, Los Angeles, School of Law, 405 Hilgard Ave., Los Angeles, CA 90024. TEL 213-825-4841. adv.; bk.rev.; circ. 1,660. (also avail. in microfiche from RRI,WSH; microfilm from WSH; reprint service avail. from RRI) **Indexed:** ABI Inform, BPIA, Bus.Ind., C.C.L.P., C.L.I., Commun.Abstr., Crim.Just.Abstr., Curr.Cont., L.R.I., Leg. Cont., Leg.Per., P.A.I.S., SSCI.
●Also available online. Vendor(s): Mead Data Central.
—BLDSC shelfmark: 9079.640000.

LAW

340   SZ   ISSN 0003-9454
U F I T A. (Archiv fuer Urheber-, Film-, Funk- und Theaterrecht) (Text in English, French, German and Italian) 1928. 3/yr. 195 Fr. Staempfli und Cie AG, Postfach, CH-3001 Berne, Switzerland. TEL 031-276666. FAX 031-276699. Ed. Manfred Rehbinder. adv.; bk.rev.; charts; index; circ. 500.

340 341   MW
U M A STUDENTS LAW JOURNAL. 1978. a. K.4.00. University of Malawi, Students Law Society, Chancellor College, Box 280, Zomba, Malawi. TELEX 44742. adv.; bk.rev.

340   US   ISSN 0047-7575
K11
U M K C LAW REVIEW. 1932. 4/yr. $16. University of Missouri, Kansas City, School of Law, 5100 Rockhill Rd., Kansas City, MO 64110. TEL 816-276-1000. Ed.Bd. adv.; bibl.; circ. 1,200. (also avail. in microfiche from WSH; microfilm from WSH) **Indexed:** C.L.I., L.R.I., Leg.Cont., Leg.Per.

U S ENVIRONMENTAL LAWS. see *ENVIRONMENTAL STUDIES*

330   US   ISSN 1055-8276
▼**U S IMMIGRATION**. (Supplement avail.) 1991. a. $23.99. Publishing & Business Consultants, 951 S. Oxford, No. 109, Los Angeles, CA 90006. TEL 213-732-3477. (Subscr. to: Box 75392, Los Angeles, CA 90075) Ed. Atia Napoleon. adv.; circ. 100,000.
Description: Provides general information on visas and other immigration topics affecting foreign nationals in the US.

U S LABOR AND EMPLOYMENT LAW. see *BUSINESS AND ECONOMICS — Labor And Industrial Relations*

U S OIL WEEK; inside report on trends in petroleum marketing without the influence of advertising. see *PETROLEUM AND GAS*

340   BB
U W I STUDENTS' LAW REVIEW. 1976. a. B.$5($5) University of the West Indies, Faculty of Law, Student's Law Review Committee, Cave Hill Campus, P.O. Box 64, Bridgetown, Barbados, W.I. Ed. Rudolph Muir. adv.; bk.rev.

340   US   ISSN 0899-7446
K25
U W L A LAW REVIEW. 1967. a. $20. University of West Los Angeles, Law Review, 12201 Washington Pl., Los Angeles, CA 90066. TEL 213-313-1011. adv.; bk.rev.; circ. 1,000. (also avail. in microfilm from WSH; reprint service avail. from WSH) **Indexed:** C.L.I., L.R.I., Leg.Cont., Leg.Per.
Formerly (until 1981): University of West Los Angeles Law Review (ISSN 0083-4068)

340 657.6   DK
UGESKRIFT FOR RETSVAESEN. w. Danmarks Jurist- og Oekonomforbund, Gothersgade 133, 1123 Copenhagen K, Denmark. adv.; circ. 9,800.

UKRANIAN BUSINESS REPORT; a monthly report on the business environment in the Ukraine. see *BUSINESS AND ECONOMICS — Domestic Commerce*

340   US
UNCLAIMED PROPERTY LAW AND REPORTING FORMS. (Issued in 4 vols. with supplements) 1984. irreg. Matthew Bender & Co., Inc., 11 Penn Plaza, New York, NY 10001. TEL 212-967-7707. Ed.Bd. (looseleaf format)
Description: Comprehensive coverage of the escheat laws and unclaimed property requirements applicable in each state. Includes analysis of the Uniform Unclaimed Property Acts, relevant case law, and state statutes.

340 364   US
UNCLASSIFIED. 1989. q. $20. Association of National Security Alumni, 921 Pleasant St., Des Moines, IA 50309. TEL 515-283-2115. Ed. David MacMichael. bk.rev.; circ. 700.

UNIFORM COMMERCIAL CODE LAW LETTER. see *BUSINESS AND ECONOMICS — Domestic Commerce*

340   US
UNIFORM COMMERCIAL CODE REPORTING SERVICE. 1965. m. $782.50. Callaghan & Co., 155 Pfingsten Rd., Deerfield, IL 60015. TEL 800-323-8067. (back issues avail.)
Description: Official text of the code, focusing on sales of goods, leases, bankruptcy, secured transactions, product liabilities, warranties, consumer loans, debt collections, letters of credit, and damages.

UNION LABOR REPORT. see *BUSINESS AND ECONOMICS — Labor And Industrial Relations*

665.5   UK
UNITED KINGDOM OFFSHORE LEGISLATION GUIDE. 1980. a. £195 (renewal £130). Benn Technical Books, Tolley House, 2 Addiscombe Rd., Croydon, Surrey CR9 5AF, England. TEL 081-686-9141. FAX 081-686-3155. Ed. Fred Osliff. circ. 500. (looseleaf format)

UNITED NATIONS POPULATION FUND. ANNUAL REVIEW OF POPULATION LAW. see *POPULATION STUDIES*

341.13   II   ISSN 0503-4663
UNITED SCHOOLS INTERNATIONAL. DOCUMENTS OF THE BIENNIAL CONFERENCE. 1961. irreg. free. United Schools International, Uso House, Arya Samaj Rd., New Delhi 110 003, India. Ed. Jiya Lal Jain. circ. 500.

346.066   US   ISSN 0734-4074
U.S. CHAMBER WATCH ON SMALL BUSINESS LEGISLATION & REGULATION; an inside Washington report. 1988. 11/yr. $65 to non-members; members $49.50. U.S. Chamber of Commerce, Small Business Center, 1615 H St., N.W., Washington, DC 20062-2000. TEL 202-463-5503. Ed. Cheryl Nikos. circ. 1,000. (tabloid format; back issues avail.)
Formerly: Services Watch.
Description: Reports to the small business community about issues impacting the way they do business. Provides insight into priority small business legislation; includes how-to articles on small business persons on a variety of issues.

345   US   ISSN 0082-9943
U.S. DEPARTMENT OF JUSTICE. ANNUAL REPORT OF THE ATTORNEY GENERAL OF THE UNITED STATES. 1870. a. price varies. U.S. Department of Justice, Office of Legal Policy, Constitution Ave. & 10th St., N.W., Washington, DC 20530. TEL 202-633-4601. (Subscr. to: Supt. of Documents, Washington DC 20402.)

340   US
U.S. DEPARTMENT OF JUSTICE. OFFICE OF LEGAL COUNSEL. OPINIONS. 1977. a. $15. U.S. Department of Justice, Office of Legal Counsel, Washington, DC 20530. Ed. Margaret C. Love. circ. 800.

345   US   ISSN 0082-9951
U.S. DEPARTMENT OF JUSTICE. OPINIONS OF ATTORNEY GENERAL. 1789. irreg. price varies. U.S. Department of Justice, Office of Legal Counsel, Constitution Ave. & 10th St., N.W., Washington, DC 20530. TEL 202-633-2041. (Subscr. to: Supt. of Documents, Washington DC 20402.) Ed. Margaret C. Love. cum.indexes issued separately. (also avail. in microfiche)

U.S. DEPARTMENT OF THE INTERIOR. DECISIONS OF THE DEPARTMENT OF THE INTERIOR. see *PUBLIC ADMINISTRATION*

602.7   US   ISSN 0042-1219
U.S. FEDERAL REGISTER. (MICROFICHE EDITION). 1951. w. $487. William S. Hein & Co., Inc., 1285 Main St., Buffalo, NY 14209. TEL 716-882-2600. FAX 716-883-8100. TELEX 91-209 WU 7 HEIN BUF. (microfiche; back issues avail.) **Indexed:** Ocean.Abstr., Pollut.Abstr.

U.S. FEDERAL TRADE COMMISSION. COURT DECISIONS PERTAINING TO THE FEDERAL TRADE COMMISSION. see *BUSINESS AND ECONOMICS — Domestic Commerce*

U.S. FEDERAL TRADE COMMISSION. FEDERAL TRADE COMMISSION DECISIONS, FINDINGS, ORDERS AND STIPULATIONS. see *BUSINESS AND ECONOMICS — Domestic Commerce*

346   US   ISSN 0093-4631
KF5640
U.S. FISH AND WILDLIFE SERVICE. SELECTED LIST OF FEDERAL LAWS AND TREATIES RELATING TO SPORT FISH AND WILDLIFE. irreg. $1.75. U.S. Fish and Wildlife Service, Dept. of the Interior, Washington, DC 20240. TEL 202-343-1100. (Subscr. to: Supt. of Documents, Washington DC 20402.) (looseleaf format) Key Title: Selected List of Federal Laws and Treaties Relating to Sport Fish and Wildlife.

340   US
U.S. LIBRARY OF CONGRESS. CONGRESSIONAL RESEARCH SERVICE. DIGEST OF PUBLIC GENERAL BILLS AND RESOLUTIONS. 1936. irreg. U.S. Library of Congress, Congressional Research Service, Washington, DC 20540. TEL 202-707-5000. (Dist. by: Supt. of Documents, Washington DC 20402) Ed. Terry G. Guertin. abstr.; cum.index for session; circ. 5,000. (also avail. in microfiche from BHP)
Former titles: U.S. Library of Congress. Congressional Research Service. Digest of Public Bills and Resolutions (ISSN 0012-2785); U.S. Library of Congress. Legislative Reference Service. Digest of Public General Bills and Selected Resolutions (ISSN 0090-0125); U.S. Library of Congress. Legislative Reference Service. Digest of Public General Bills (ISSN 0090-0117)

U.S. NUCLEAR REGULATORY COMMISSION. INFORMATION REPORT ON STATE LEGISLATION. see *ENERGY — Nuclear Energy*

U.S. OCCUPATIONAL SAFETY AND HEALTH REVIEW COMMISSION. ADMINISTRATIVE LAW JUDGE AND COMMISSION DECISIONS. see *OCCUPATIONAL HEALTH AND SAFETY*

340   US   ISSN 0148-8139
LAW
UNITED STATES LAW WEEK; a national survey of current law. 1933. w. $668. The Bureau of National Affairs, Inc., 1231 25th St., N.W., Washington, DC 20037. TEL 202-452-4200. FAX 202-822-8092. TELEX 285656 BNAI WSH. (Subscr. to: 9435 Key West Ave., Rockville, MD 20850. TEL 800-372-1033) Ed. Gregory R. Pease. bk.rev.; abstr.; bibl.; index. (back issues avail.)
●Also available online. Vendor(s): Mead Data Central (USLW), WESTLAW.
Description: Notification and reference service providing current information about all significant court decisions, rulings, regulations, and interpretations in state and federal law.

340   US   ISSN 0190-5252
UNITED STATES LAW WEEK SUMMARY AND ANALYSIS. 1933. w. $312. The Bureau of National Affairs, Inc., 1231 25th St., N.W., Washington, DC 20037. TEL 202-452-4200. FAX 202-822-8092. TELEX 285656 BNAI WSH. (Subscr. to: 9435 Key West Ave. Rockville, MD 20850. TEL 800-372-1033) Ed. Gregory R. Pease. index. (back issues avail.)
Description: Summary of current legal developments, with an index and table of cases.

345   US   ISSN 0083-3401
UNITED STATES STATUTES AT LARGE. 1873. a. $132. U.S. Office of the Federal Register, National Archives and Records Administration, Washington, DC 20408. TEL 202-523-5240. (Orders to: Supt. of Documents, Box 371954, Pittsburgh, PA 15250-7954) (also avail. in microform from UMI,BHP)
Description: Cumulation of daily slip law prints and annotated pamphlets of public laws enacted by Congress.

UNITED STATES TAX COURT REPORTS. see *BUSINESS AND ECONOMICS — Public Finance, Taxation*

UNITS. see *HOUSING AND URBAN PLANNING*

340   VE
UNIVERSIDAD CENTRAL DE VENEZUELA. FACULTAD DE CIENCIAS JURIDICAS Y POLITICAS. REVISTA. 1954. q. price varies. Universidad Central de Venezuela, Facultad de Ciencias Juridicas y Politicas, Caracas, Venezuela. Ed.Bd. bk.rev.; bibl.; cum.index: nos. 1-50; circ. 2,000. **Indexed:** Foreign Leg.Per.
Formerly (until 1981?): Universidad Central de Venezuela. Facultad de Derecho. Revista (ISSN 0041-8293)

340   EC
UNIVERSIDAD CENTRAL DEL ECUADOR. INSTITUTO DE DERECHO COMPARADO. BOLETIN. 1951. s-a. Universidad Central del Ecuador, Instituto de Derecho Comparado, Editorial Universitaria, Quito, Ecuador. bibl.

340   SP   ISSN 0075-773X
UNIVERSIDAD DE LA LAGUNA. FACULTAD DE DERECHO. ANALES. 1963. a. 150 ptas. Universidad de la Laguna, Secretariado de Publicaciones, San Agustin, 30, 38201 La Laguna-Tenerife, Canary Islands, Spain. TEL 922-25-81-27. **Indexed:** Amer.Hist.& Life, Hist.Abstr.

347.9 320   VE
UNIVERSIDAD DE LOS ANDES. FACULTAD DE CIENCIAS JURIDICAS Y POLITICAS. ANUARIO. a. Universidad de los Andes, Facultad de Ciencias Juridicas y Politicas, Centro de Investigaciones Juridicas, Merida, Venezuela. Ed. Pedro Rincon Gutierrez. charts; stat.

340   VE   ISSN 0076-6550
UNIVERSIDAD DE LOS ANDES. FACULTAD DE DERECHO. ANUARIO.* 1970. irreg. Universidad de Los Andes, Facultad de Derecho, Centro de Investigaciones Juridicas, Via los Chorras, C.P. 5101, Merida, Venezuela. Ed.Bd. bibl.
 Supersedes (1955-19??): Universidad de Los Andes. Facultad de Derecho. Revista.

340   SP
UNIVERSIDAD DE MURCIA. DEPARTAMENTO DE DERECHO POLITICO. PUBLICACIONES. SERIE MONOGRAFIAS. 1977. irreg. Universidad de Murcia, Secretariado de Publicaciones e Intercambio Cientifico, Santo Cristo, 1, 30001 Murcia, Spain.

349   SP
UNIVERSIDAD DE NAVARRA. COLECCION MANUALES DE DERECHO. irreg., no.17, 1989. price varies. (Universidad de Navarra, Facultad de Derecho) Ediciones Universidad de Navarra, S.A., Apdo. 396, 31080 Pamplona, Spain. TEL 94 825 6850.
 Formerly: Universidad de Navarra. Manuales: Derecho Notarial Espanol (ISSN 0078-8767)

340 327   PN
UNIVERSIDAD DE PANAMA. FACULTAD DE DERECHO Y CIENCIAS POLITICAS. CUADERNOS. 1960. irreg. Universidad de Panama, Facultad de Derecho y Ciencias Politicas, Oficina de Informacion y Publicaciones, Panama, Panama.

340 658   SP   ISSN 0582-8929
UNIVERSIDAD DE SEVILLA. INSTITUTO GARCIA OVIEDO. PUBLICACIONES. irreg., latest no.52. price varies. Universidad de Sevilla, Instituto Garcia Oviedo, Servicio de Publicaciones, San Fernando, 4, 41004 Seville, Spain. TEL 954-22-8071. FAX 954-22-1315.

340   SP
UNIVERSIDAD DE SEVILLA. SERIE: DERECHO. irreg, latest no.53. price varies. Universidad de Sevilla, Servicio de Publicaciones, San Fernando, 4, 41004 Seville, Spain. TEL 954-22-8071. FAX 954-22-1315.
 Formerly (until 1967): Universidad Hispalense. Anales. Serie: Derecho (ISSN 0210-7686)

344.01   SP
UNIVERSIDAD DE VALENCIA. CATEDRA DE DERECHO DEL TRABAJO. CUADERNOS.* 1971. s-a. Universidad de Valencia, Nave 2, Valencia, Spain.

340   VE
UNIVERSIDAD DEL ZULIA. FACULTAD DE DERECHO. REVISTA. (Not published 1976) 1961. irreg; no.49, 1977. Bs.15($3.50) Universidad del Zulia, Facultad de Derecho, Apdo. 526, Maracaibo, Venezuela. Dir. Alice Adrianza Alvarez. circ. 2,500. **Indexed:** P.A.I.S.

340   MX
UNIVERSIDAD NACIONAL AUTONOMA DE MEXICO. FACULTAD DE DERECHO DE MEXICO. REVISTA. (Text mainly in Spanish) 1939. bi-m. Mex.$3000($50) Universidad Nacional Autonoma de Mexico, Facultad de Derecho, Ciudad Universitaria, 04510 Mexico, D.F., Mexico. Ed. Fernando Flores Garcia. abstr.; bibl.; cum.index: 1939-1950; circ. 3,000. (back issues avail.) **Indexed:** Hist.Abstr. (until 1988)

340   PE
UNIVERSIDAD NACIONAL FEDERICO VILLAREAL. FACULTAD DE DERECHO. REVISTA.* 1967. s-a. Universidad Nacional Federico Villareal, Facultad de Derecho, Av. Nicolas de Pierota 1128, Lima, Peru.

340   PO
UNIVERSIDADE DE LISBOA. FACULDADE DE DIREITO. REVISTA. 1944. a. Universidade de Lisboa, Faculdade de Direito, Lisbon, Portugal. bk.rev.

340   BL   ISSN 0080-6250
K23.
UNIVERSIDADE DE SAO PAULO. FACULDADE DE DIREITO. REVISTA. 1893. a. Cr.$2000. Universidade de Sao Paulo, Faculdade de Direito, Biblioteca Central, Largo de Sao Francisco, 95-1 Andar, 01005 Sao Paolo, Brazil. Ed. Antonio Augusto Machado de Campos. bk.rev.; circ. 1,500.

340   BL   ISSN 0102-1397
UNIVERSIDADE FEDERAL DE UBERLANDIA. CURSO DE DIREITO. REVISTA. 1972. a. free. Universidade Federal de Uberlandia, Curso de Direito, Campus Umuarama-Bloco E, Sala 2E25, 38400 Uberlandia, MG, Brazil. Eds. Jacy de Assis, Dinah Fernandes de Carvalho. bibl.; circ. 5,000.
 Formerly (until 1978): Universidade de Uberlandia. Faculdade de Direito. Revista.

340   IT   ISSN 0435-3048
UNIVERSITA DEGLI STUDI DI GENOVA. FACOLTA DI GIURISPRUDENZA. ANNALI. 1962. s-a. price varies. Casa Editrice Dott. A. Giuffre, Via Busto Arsizio 40, 20151 Milan, Italy. TEL 02-38000905. FAX 02-38009582. Ed. Enrico Zanelli.

340   CS
UNIVERSITAS COMENIANA: ACTA FACULTATIS IURIDICAE. (Text in Slovak; summaries in German, Russian) 1980. irreg. exchange basis. Univerzita Komenskeho, Pravnicka Fakulta, c/o Study and Information Center, Safarikovo nam. 6, 818 06 Bratislava, Czechoslovakia. Ed. Jordan Girasek. circ. 500.

340   RM   ISSN 0379-7872
UNIVERSITATEA "AL. I. CUZA" DIN IASI. ANALELE STIINTIFICE. SECTIUNEA 3D: STIINTE JURIDICE. (Text in Rumanian; summaries in foreign languages) 1955. a. 35 lei. Universitatea "Al. I. Cuza" din Iasi, Calea M. Eminescu 11, Jassy, Rumania. (Subscr. to: ILEXIM, Str. 13 Decembrie Nr. 3, P.O. Box 136-137, Bucharest, Rumania) Ed. I. Macovei. bk.rev.; abstr.; charts; illus.; circ. 250.
 Description: Theoretical and practical studies in civil law, criminal sciences and international law.

UNIVERSITATEA BUCURESTI. ANALELE. FILOZOFIE. ISTORIE. DREPT. see PHILOSOPHY

340   FR
UNIVERSITE DE CLERMONT-FERRAND I. FACULTE DE DROIT ET DE SCIENCE POLITIQUE. ANNALES. a. 220 F. (Universite de Clermont-Ferrand I, Faculte de Droit et de Science Politique) Editions Juridiques Associees, 26 rue Vercingetorix, 75014 Paris, France. TEL 1-43-35-01-67. FAX 43-20-07-42. TELEX EJA 203 918 F. (Co-sponsor: Librairie Generale de Droit et de Jurisprudence) (back issues avail.)

340 300
UNIVERSITE DE DROIT, ECONOMIE ET DE SCIENCES SOCIALES DE PARIS. TRAVAUX DU SEMINAIRE DE RECHERCHES SUR LES FAITS ELECTORAUX DE MONSIEUR LE PROFESSEUR ROBERT VILLERS. irreg. price varies. (Universite de Droit, Economie et de Sciences Sociales de Paris) Librarie Touzot, 38 rue Saint Sulpice, 75278 Paris Cedex 06, France.

340   CN   ISSN 0317-9656
K21
UNIVERSITE DE SHERBROOKE. REVUE DE DROIT. (Text in English and French) 1970. s-a. Can.$25($26) Universite de Sherbrooke, Faculte de Droit, Sherbrooke, Que. J1K 2R1, Canada. TEL 819-821-7508. FAX 819-821-7578. Ed. Claude Boisclair. adv.; bk.rev.; circ. 2,000. (also avail. in microfilm from UMI) **Indexed:** C.L.I., Ind.Can.L.P.L., Leg.Per., Pt.de Rep. (1983-).

340   FR
UNIVERSITE JEAN MOULIN. ANNALES. 1968. irreg. price varies. Editions Hermes, 31 Pasteur, 69007 Lyon, France. bk.rev.; circ. 500.
 Former titles (until 1975): Universite de Lyon III. Faculte de Droit. Annales (ISSN 0336-1357); Universite de Lyon. Faculte de Droit et des Sciences Economiques. Annales (ISSN 0076-1664)

340   BE
▼**UNIVERSITE LIBRE DE BRUXELLES. REVUE DE DROIT.** Short title: Revue de Droit de l'U L B. 1990. s-a. 1700 Fr. Etablissements Emile Bruylant, 67 rue de la Regence, B-1000 Brussels, Belgium. TEL 02-512-9845.

340   ZR
UNIVERSITE NATIONALE DU ZAIRE, KINSHASA. FACULTE DE DROIT. ANNALES. 1972. a. Universite Nationale du Zaire, Kinshasa, Faculte du Droit, B.P. 125, Kinshasa XI, Zaire.

340   US   ISSN 0162-8372
K25
UNIVERSITY OF ARKANSAS AT LITTLE ROCK LAW JOURNAL. 1978. q. $12. University of Arkansas at Little Rock, School of Law, 2801 S. University Ave., Little Rock, AR 72201. TEL 501-371-1144. adv.; bk.rev.; circ. 3,800. (also avail. in microform from WHS; reprint service avail. from WSH) **Indexed:** C.L.I., L.R.I., Leg.Cont., Leg.Per.
 —BLDSC shelfmark: 9104.040000.

340   US   ISSN 0091-5440
K2
UNIVERSITY OF BALTIMORE LAW REVIEW. 1971. 3/yr. $15 per vol. University of Baltimore School of Law, Business Editor, 1420 N. Charles St., Baltimore, MD 21201. TEL 301-625-3440. adv.; bk.rev.; circ. 2,000. (also avail. in microfilm from WSH; reprint service avail. from WSH) **Indexed:** C.L.I., L.R.I., Leg.Cont., Leg.Per.
 ●Also available online. Vendor(s): WESTLAW.
 —BLDSC shelfmark: 9104.150000.

340   US
UNIVERSITY OF BRIDGEPORT LAW REVIEW. 1980. s-a. $12. Bridgeport Law Review at Quinnipiac College, 303 University Ave., Bridgeport, CT 06601. Ed. J. Balleyr. bk.rev.; circ. 1,000. (also avail. in microfiche from WSH; microfilm from WSH; back issues avail.) **Indexed:** Leg.Cont.

346   CN   ISSN 0068-1849
LAW
UNIVERSITY OF BRITISH COLUMBIA LAW REVIEW. 1959. s-a. Can.$30($35) University of British Columbia Law Review Society, Faculty of Law, Vancouver, B.C. V6T 1Z1, Canada. TEL 604-822-3066. FAX 604-822-8108. adv.; bk.rev.; index: 1949-81; 1982-90; circ. 900. (also avail. in microform from WSH; back issues avail.; reprint service avail. from WSH) **Indexed:** Abstr.Bk.Rev.Curr.Leg.Per., C.L.I., Ind.Can.L.P.L., L.R.I., Leg.Cont., Leg.Per., P.A.I.S.
 —BLDSC shelfmark: 9104.313000.
 Description: Promotion of legal scholarship, with articles by judges, professors, practising lawyers.

340   US   ISSN 0041-9494
K25   CODEN: UCLRA2
UNIVERSITY OF CHICAGO LAW REVIEW. 1933. q. $30. University of Chicago Law School, 1111 E. 60th St., Chicago, IL 60637. TEL 312-702-9832. FAX 312-702-0730. adv.; bk.rev.; index; circ. 2,400. (also avail. in microfiche from RRI,WSH; microfilm from WSH; reprint service avail. from RRI) **Indexed:** A.B.C.Pol.Sci., ABI Inform, Bank.Lit.Ind., BPIA, Bus.Ind., C.L.I., Crim.Just.Abstr., Curr.Cont., L.R.I., Leg.Cont., Leg.Per., SSCI.
 ●Also available online. Vendor(s): Mead Data Central.
 —BLDSC shelfmark: 9106.500000.

340   US
UNIVERSITY OF CHICAGO LEGAL FORUM. 1986. a. $20. University of Chicago Law School, 1111 E. 60th St., Chicago, IL 60637. TEL 312-702-9832. FAX 312-702-0730. circ. 1,000.
 ●Also available online. Vendor(s): WESTLAW.
 Description: Focuses on noteworthy contemporary legal issues.

340   US   ISSN 0041-9516
K25
UNIVERSITY OF COLORADO LAW REVIEW. 1929. 4/yr. $25. University of Colorado Law Review, Inc., c/o Robert Davis, Bus. Sec., 290 Fleming Law Bldg., Campus Box 401, Boulder, CO 80309. TEL 303-492-6145. FAX 303-492-1200. adv.; bk.rev.; index; circ. 875. (also avail. in microfilm from RRI,WSH; reprint service avail.) **Indexed:** Abstr.Bk.Rev.Curr.Leg.Per., C.L.I., L.R.I., Leg.Cont., Leg.Per., Sel.Water Res.Abstr.
 —BLDSC shelfmark: 9106.990000.
 Formerly: Rocky Mountain Law Review.

340 K4 US ISSN 0162-9174
UNIVERSITY OF DAYTON LAW REVIEW. 1976. 3/yr. $17.50. University of Dayton, Law School, 300 College Park, Dayton, OH 45469. TEL 513-229-3642. Ed. Patrick Edward Beck. adv.; bk.rev.; circ. 750. (also avail. in microfiche from WSH; microfilm from WSH) **Indexed:** C.L.I., L.R.I., Leg.Cont., Leg.Per., M.L.A.
—BLDSC shelfmark: 9109.357000.
Formerly (until vol.2): University of Dayton Intramural Law Review (ISSN 0363-2148)

340 US
UNIVERSITY OF DETROIT LAW REVIEW. 1916. 4/yr. $17. University of Detroit, School of Law, 651 E. Jefferson Ave., Detroit, MI 48226. TEL 313-596-0237. adv.; bk.rev.; index. cum.index for vols.44-50, 1966-1973; circ. 700. (also avail. in microfiche from WSH; microfilm from WSH; reprint service avail. from ISI) **Indexed:** C.C.L.P., C.L.I., Cath.Ind., Curr.Cont., L.R.I., Leg.Cont., Leg.Per., Sage Pub.Admin.Abstr., Sage Urb.Stud.Abstr., SSCI.
Former titles (until vol.61, no.4, 1984): University of Detroit Journal of Urban Law (ISSN 0161-7095); Journal of Urban Law (ISSN 0041-9559); University of Detroit Law Journal.

340 BG
UNIVERSITY OF DHAKA. DEPARTMENT OF LAW. JOURNAL. (Text in Bengali or English) 1978. Tk.2.50. University of Dhaka, Department of Law, Dhaka 2, Bangladesh.

340 GH ISSN 0041-9605
UNIVERSITY OF GHANA LAW JOURNAL. 1964. s-a. $15. University of Ghana, Faculty of Law, Legon, Ghana. Ed.Bd. adv.; bk.rev.; index; circ. 500. **Indexed:** Leg.Per.

340 US
UNIVERSITY OF HAWAII LAW REVIEW. 1979. s-a. $16. William S. Richardson School of Law, Law Review, 2515 Dole St., Honolulu, HI 96822. FAX 808-956-6402. Ed. Katherine G. Leonard. adv.; bk.rev.; circ. 500. (back issues avail.) **Indexed:** C.L.I., Leg.Cont., Leg.Per.
Description: Focuses on cases and legal issues of particular interest in Hawaii and the Pacific region.

340 K25 US ISSN 0276-9948
UNIVERSITY OF ILLINOIS LAW REVIEW. 1949. q. $14. University of Illinois at Urbana-Champaign, College of Law, Champaign, IL 61820. TEL 217-333-1000. Ed. William R. Jung. adv.; bk.rev.; index; cum.index every 10 yrs.; circ. 2,100. (also avail. in microform from UMI) **Indexed:** Abstr.Bk.Rev.Curr.Leg.Per., C.L.I., Crim.Just.Abstr., L.R.I., Leg.Cont., Leg.Per., SSCI.
●Also available online. Vendor(s): WESTLAW.
—BLDSC shelfmark: 9110.663100.
Formerly: University of Illinois Law Forum (ISSN 0041-963X)

340 K25 US ISSN 0083-4025
UNIVERSITY OF KANSAS LAW REVIEW. 1952. q. $21. University of Kansas, School of Law, Rm. 510, Green Hall, Lawrence, KS 66045. TEL 913-864-3463. FAX 913-864-3680. Ed. Greg Ash. adv.; bk.rev.; index; cum.index every 5 yrs.; circ. 1,375. (also avail. in microfiche from WSH; microfilm from WSH; back issues avail.) **Indexed:** Abstr.Bk.Rev.Curr.Leg.Per., C.C.L.P., C.L.I., L.R.I., Leg.Cont., Leg.Per., Mar.Aff.Bibl.
●Also available online. Vendor(s): WESTLAW.
—BLDSC shelfmark: 9110.930000.

340 PH ISSN 0041-9796
UNIVERSITY OF MANILA LAW GAZETTE. 1951. s-a. free to law students. University of Manila, 546 Dr. M. V. de los Santos St., Sampaloc, Manila D-403, Philippines. Ed. Antonio A. Figueras. bk.rev.; abstr.; circ. 500 (controlled).

340 US ISSN 0041-9818
UNIVERSITY OF MIAMI LAW REVIEW. 1947. 5/yr. $18. University of Miami, School of Law, Coral Gables, FL 33124. TEL 305-284-2523. Ed. Tucker Ronzetti. adv.; index; circ. 1,400. (also avail. in microform from UMI; microfiche from WSH; microfilm from WSH) **Indexed:** Abstr.Bk.Rev.Curr.Leg.Per., Account.Ind. (1974-), C.L.I., Crim.Just.Abstr., L.R.I., Lang.& Lang.Behav.Abstr., Leg.Cont., Leg.Per., Mar.Aff.Bibl., P.A.I.S.
—BLDSC shelfmark: 9113.560000.

340 K16 US ISSN 0033-1546
UNIVERSITY OF MICHIGAN JOURNAL OF LAW REFORM. 1968. q. $28 (foreign $31). University of Michigan, S-324 Legal Research Bldg., Ann Arbor, MI 48109. TEL 313-763-2195. Ed. Valerie J. Wald. adv.; circ. 1,000. (also avail. in microform from WSH; reprint service avail. from WSH) **Indexed:** C.L.I., Crim.Just.Abstr., L.R.I., Leg.Cont., Leg.Per., P.A.I.S.
—BLDSC shelfmark: 9113.650000.
Formerly: Prospectus.

346 CN ISSN 0836-6632
UNIVERSITY OF NEW BRUNSWICK LAW JOURNAL. (Text in English, French) 1947. a. Can.$15. University of New Brunswick, Faculty of Law, P.O. Box 4400, Fredericton, N.B. E3B 5A3, Canada. TEL 506-453-4669. FAX 506-453-5186. (Subscr. to: Carswell, Thomson Professional Publishing, Corporate Plaza, 2075 Kennedy Rd., Scarborough, Ont. M1T 3V4, Canada) Ed. Eugene F. Derenyi. adv.; bk.rev.; cum.index: 1947-87; circ. 2,200. (also avail. in microform from UMI; microfiche from WSH; microfilm from WSH; reprint service avail. from UMI) **Indexed:** C.L.I., Ind.Can.L.P.L., L.R.I., Leg.Per.

340 AT ISSN 0811-7632
UNIVERSITY OF NEW SOUTH WALES. FACULTY HANDBOOKS: LAW. a? Aus.$5. University of New South Wales, P.O. Box 1, Kensington, N.S.W. 2033, Australia. TEL 02-697-2840. FAX 02-662-2163.

340 AT ISSN 0313-0096
UNIVERSITY OF NEW SOUTH WALES LAW JOURNAL. 1975. a. (in 2 vols.). Aus.$40. University of New South Wales, Faculty of Law, P.O. Box 1, Kensington, N.S.W. 2033, Australia. TEL 02-697-2237. FAX 02-313-7209. adv.; bk.rev.; index; circ. 1,500. (also avail. in microfiche; back issues avail) **Indexed:** C.L.I., Leg.Cont., Leg.Per.
—BLDSC shelfmark: 9116.183000.
Description: Legal periodical of comtemporary issues.

UNIVERSITY OF OSAKA PREFECTURE. BULLETIN. SERIES D: ECONOMICS, BUSINESS ADMINISTRATION AND LAW/OSAKA-FURITSU DAIGAKU KIYO, D. KEIZAIGAKU, KEIEIGAKU, HOGAKU. see *BUSINESS AND ECONOMICS*

340 K25 US ISSN 0041-9907
UNIVERSITY OF PENNSYLVANIA LAW REVIEW. 1852. 6/yr. $35 (foreign $40)(effective 1992). (University of Pennsylvania Law School) University of Pennsylvania Law Review, 3400 Chestnut St., Philadelphia, PA 19104. TEL 215-898-7060. FAX 215-573-2005. Ed. M. Mazen Anbari. adv. contact: Keith Eisner. bk.rev.; index; circ. 2,150. (also avail. in microfiche from RRI,WSH; microfilm from WSH; back issues avail.; reprint service avail. from RRI) **Indexed:** A.B.C.Pol.Sci., Abstr.Bk.Rev.Curr.Leg.Per., C.L.I., Crim.Just.Abstr., Curr.Cont., L.R.I., Leg.Cont., Leg.Per., P.A.I.S., SSCI.
●Also available online. Vendor(s): Mead Data Central.
—BLDSC shelfmark: 9116.380000.

340 K25 US ISSN 0041-9915
UNIVERSITY OF PITTSBURGH LAW REVIEW. 1935. q. $25 (foreign $30). University of Pittsburgh, School of Law, Pittsburgh, PA 15260. TEL 412-648-1354. Ed. Richard A. Halloran. adv.; bk.rev.; index. cum.index every 25 yrs.; circ. 1,500. (also avail. in microfilm from RRI,WSH; reprint service avail. from WSH) **Indexed:** Abstr.Bk.Rev.Curr.Leg.Per., C.L.I., Curr.Cont., L.R.I., Leg.Per., SSCI.
●Also available online. Vendor(s): Mead Data Central, WESTLAW.
—BLDSC shelfmark: 9116.385000.
Description: Provides scholarly legal articles on all areas and facets of the law.

340 K24 US ISSN 0161-0708
UNIVERSITY OF PUGET SOUND LAW REVIEW. 1977. 3/yr. $18. University of Puget Sound, School of Law, 950 Broadway Plaza, Tacoma, WA 98402. TEL 206-591-2995. bk.rev.; cum.index; circ. 3,000. (also avail. in microfilm from RRI; back issues avail.; reprint service avail. from RRI) **Indexed:** C.L.I., Leg.Per.
—BLDSC shelfmark: 9116.386700.

340 AT ISSN 0083-4041
UNIVERSITY OF QUEENSLAND LAW JOURNAL. 1948. a. Aus.$21($20) University of Queensland Press, P.O. Box 42, St. Lucia, Qld. 4067, Australia. TEL 07-377-2127. FAX 07-371-5896. TELEX UNIVQLD AA0315 PRESS. Eds. R. O'Hair, D. Gifford. adv.; bk.rev.; circ. 750. (also avail. in microform from UMI) **Indexed:** Aus.P.A.I.S., C.L.I., L.R.I., Leg.Per.
—BLDSC shelfmark: 9116.387000.

340 K25 US ISSN 0566-2389
UNIVERSITY OF RICHMOND LAW REVIEW. 1958. q. $30. University of Richmond, T. C. Williams School of Law, Richmond, VA 23173. TEL 804-289-8216. FAX 804-289-8683. Ed. Jeffery K. Mitchell. adv.; bk.rev.; circ. 1,200. (also avail. in microfilm from WSH; reprint service avail. from WSH) **Indexed:** Abstr.Bk.Rev.Curr.Leg.Per., C.C.L.P., C.L.I., L.R.I., Leg.Cont., Leg.Per.
●Also available online. Vendor(s): WESTLAW.
—BLDSC shelfmark: 9116.840000.
Formerly (until 1968): University of Richmond Law Notes.

340 LAW US ISSN 0042-0018
UNIVERSITY OF SAN FRANCISCO LAW REVIEW. 1966. 4/yr. $25 per vol. University of San Francisco, School of Law, Kendrick Hall, 2130 Fulton St., San Francisco, CA 94117. TEL 415-666-6154. FAX 415-666-6433. adv.; bk.rev.; index; circ. 1,000. (also avail. in microform from UMI; back issues avail.; reprint service avail. from RRI) **Indexed:** Abstr.Bk.Rev.Curr.Leg.Per., C.L.I., HR Rep., L.R.I., Leg.Cont., Leg.Per., Mar.Aff.Bibl.
●Also available online. Vendor(s): WESTLAW.
—BLDSC shelfmark: 9116.950000.

340 K25 AT ISSN 0082-2108
UNIVERSITY OF TASMANIA LAW REVIEW. Title varies: Tasmanian University Law Review. 1958. s-a. Aus.$15 (foreign Aus.$20) per issue. University of Tasmania Law Review, Box 252 C, Hobart, Tas. 7001, Australia. Ed. M. Tsamenyi. adv.; bk.rev.; index; circ. 450. (also avail. in microfilm from UMI; microform from WSH; reprint service avail. from WSH) **Indexed:** Aus. P.A.I.S., C.C.L.P., C.L.I., L.R.I., Leg.Per.
—BLDSC shelfmark: 9118.280000.
Description: Includes articles on all aspects of law throughout the world, not just in Tasmania and Australia.

340 375 AT ISSN 1036-0689
▼**UNIVERSITY OF TECHNOLOGY, SYDNEY. FACULTY OF LAW & LEGAL PRACTICE HANDBOOK.** 1990. a. Aus.$5 (foreign Aus.$10). University of Technology, Sydney, P.O. Box 123, City Camp, Broadway, N.S.W. 2007, Australia. TEL 02-330-1990. FAX 02-330-1551. circ. 3,000.

340 K24 US ISSN 0042-0190
UNIVERSITY OF TOLEDO LAW REVIEW. 1969. q. $16. University of Toledo, College of Law, Toledo, OH 43606. TEL 419-537-2962. index; circ. 900. (also avail. in microfilm from WSH; reprint service avail. from WSH) **Indexed:** C.L.I., L.R.I., Leg.Cont., Leg.Per., SSCI.
—BLDSC shelfmark: 9118.800000.

340 K24 CN ISSN 0381-1638
UNIVERSITY OF TORONTO. FACULTY OF LAW. REVIEW. 1942. 2/yr. Can.$28 per no. University of Toronto, Faculty of Law, Toronto, Ont. M5S 2C5, Canada. TEL 416-978-4399. FAX 416-978-7899. (Dist. by: Carswell Co., Ltd., 2075 Kennedy Rd., Scarborough, Ont. M4A 2V8, Canada) **Indexed:** Abstr.Bk.Rev.Curr.Leg.Per., C.L.I., Ind.Can.L.P.L., L.R.I., Leg.Cont., Leg.Per.
—BLDSC shelfmark: 9119.050000.

340   CN   ISSN 0042-0220
K25
UNIVERSITY OF TORONTO LAW JOURNAL. (Text in English, French) 1937. q. Can.$30 to individuals; institutions Can.$50; students Can.$20. University of Toronto Press, Journals Department, P.O. Box 1280, 1011 Sheppard Ave. W., Downsview, Ont. M3H 5V4, Canada. TEL 416-667-7782. Ed. S. Waddams. adv.; bk.rev.; index; circ. 1,000. (also avail. in microform from JAI,MML,UMI; reprint service avail. from WSH) **Indexed:** Abstr.Bk.Rev.Curr.Leg.Per., C.L.I., Ind.Can.L.P.L., L.R.I., Leg.Per., P.A.I.S., SSCI.
—BLDSC shelfmark: 9119.100000.

340   AT   ISSN 0042-0328
K25
UNIVERSITY OF WESTERN AUSTRALIA LAW REVIEW. 1948. s-a. Aus.$40 (foreign Aus.$45). University of Western Australia, Faculty of Law, Nedlands (Perth), W.A., Australia. FAX 380-1045. TELEX AA92992. Ed.Bd. adv.; bk.rev.; index; circ. 450. (reprint service avail. from WSH) **Indexed:** Aus.P.A.I.S., C.L.I., L.R.I., Leg.Per.
—BLDSC shelfmark: 9120.135000.

340 330.1 301   CI   ISSN 0350-2058
UNIVERZITET U ZAGREBU. PRAVNI FAKULTET. ZBORNIK. (Text in English, German, Italian and Serbo-Croatian) 1948. bi-m. 6000 din.($15) Univerzitet u Zagrebu, Pravni Fakultet, Trg Marsala Tita 14, 41000 Zagreb, Croatia. TEL 429-222. Ed. Stanko Petkovic. index; circ. 1,000. (back issuse avail.) **Indexed:** Leg.Per.

340   PL   ISSN 0208-4910
LAW
UNIWERSYTET GDANSKI. WYDZIAL PRAWA I ADMINISTRACJI. ZESZYTY NAUKOWE. PRAWO. (Text in Polish; summaries in English and Russian) 1972. irreg. price varies. Uniwersytet Gdanski, Wydzial Prawa i Administracji, c/o Biblioteka Glowna, Ul. Armii Krajowej 110, 81-824 Sopot, Poland. TEL 51-0061. TELEX 051-2247 BMOR PL. (Dist. by: Ars Polona-Ruch, Krakowskie Przedmiescie 7, 00-680 Warsaw, Poland) Ed. Marian Cieslak. circ. 250.
Description: Problems of criminal and civil law and procedures, evidence, public law, history of state, law and legal doctrines, chronicle of law.

340   PL
UNIWERSYTET GDANSKI. WYDZIAL PRAWA I ADMINISTRACJI. ZESZYTY NAUKOWE. PRACE Z ZAKRESU ADMINISTRACJI I ZARZADZANIA. (Text in Polish; summaries in English, Russian) 1976. irreg. price varies. Uniwersytet Gdanski, Wydzial Prawa i Administracji, c/o Biblioteka Glowna, Ul. Armii Krajowej 110, 81-824 Sopot, Poland. TEL 51-0061. TELEX 051 2247 BMOR PL. (Dist. by: Ars Polona-Ruch, Krakowskie Przedmiescie 7, 00-680 Warsaw, Poland) Ed. Zbigniew Jaskiewicz. circ. 250.
Formerly: Uniwersytet Gdanski. Wydzial Prawa i Administracji. Zeszyty Naukowe. Prace Instytutu Administracji i Zarzadzania (ISSN 0208-4929)
Description: Covers problems in the structure of governmental and economic administration and the role of public finances in the state and national economy.

340   PL   ISSN 0860-3731
UNIWERSYTET GDANSKI. WYDZIAL PRAWA I ADMINISTRACJI. ZESZYTY NAUKOWE. STUDIA PRAWNO-USTROJOWE. 1988. irreg. price varies. Uniwersytet Gdanski, Wydzial Prawa i Administracji, Biblioteka Glowna, Ul. Armii Krajowej 110, 81-824 Sopot, Poland. TEL 51-00-61. (Dist. by: Ars Polona-Ruch, Krakowskie Przedmiescie 7, Warsaw, Poland) Ed. Tomasz Langer. circ. 200.

349   PL   ISSN 0083-4394
UNIWERSYTET JAGIELLONSKI. ZESZYTY NAUKOWE. PRACE PRAWNICZE. (Text in Polish; summaries in English, Russian) 1955. irreg., no.110, 1984. price varies. Panstwowe Wydawnictwo Naukowe, Miodowa 10, 00-251 Warsaw, Poland. (Dist. by: Ars Polona, Krakowskie Przedmiescie 7, 00-068 Warsaw, Poland) Ed. W. Litewski. circ. 500.

343.093   PL   ISSN 0208-5518
UNIWERSYTET SLASKI W KATOWICACH. PRACE NAUKOWE. PROBLEMY PRAWA PRZEWOZOWEGO. (Text in Polish; summaries in English, German, Russian) 1979. irreg. price varies. Wydawnictwo Uniwersytetu Slaskiego, Ul. Bankowa 14, 40-007 Katowice, Poland. TEL 48-32-596-915. FAX 48-32-599-605. TELEX 0315584 USKPL. (Dist. by: CHS Ars Polona, P.O. Box 1001, 00-950 Warsaw, Poland) **Indexed:** Mar.Aff.Bibl.
Description: Theory of overland transport law, comprehended from the aspect of the practical needs of that law.

340 622   PL   ISSN 0208-5488
UNIWERSYTET SLASKI W KATOWICACH. PRACE NAUKOWE. PROBLEMY PRAWNE GORNICTWA. (Text in Polish; summaries in German and Russian) 1977. irreg. price varies. Wydawnictwo Uniwersytetu Slaskiego, Ul. Bankowa 14, 40-007 Katowice, Poland. TEL 48-32-596-915. FAX 48-32-599-605. TELEX 0315584 USKPL. (Dist. by: CHZ Ars Polona, P.O. Box 1001, 00-950 Warsaw, Poland)
Description: Legal problems of mining, especially the substance and nature of mining rights and environmental protection related to their exploitation.

346.066   PL   ISSN 0208-5496
UNIWERSYTET SLASKI W KATOWICACH. PRACE NAUKOWE. PROBLEMY PRAWNE HANDLU ZAGRANICZNEGO. (Text in Polish; summaries in English and Russian or French) 1977. irreg. price varies. Wydawnictwo Uniwersytetu Slaskiego, Ul. Bankowa 14, 40-007 Katowice, Poland. TEL 48-32-596-915. FAX 48-32-599-605. TELEX 0315584 USKPL. (Dist. by: CHZ Ars Polona, P.O. Box 1001, 00-950 Warsaw, Poland)
Description: Covers international private and commercial law and international procedure, international arbitration and comparative law of obligations.

347   PL   ISSN 0208-502X
UNIWERSYTET SLASKI W KATOWICACH. PRACE NAUKOWE. STUDIA IURIDICA SILESIANA. (Text in Polish; summaries in French, German, Russian) 1976. irreg. price varies. Wydawnictwo Uniwersytetu Slaskiego, Ul. Bankowa 14, 40-007 Katowice, Poland. TEL 48-32-596-915. FAX 48-32-599-605. TELEX 0315584 USKPTL. (Dist. by: CHZ Ars Polona, P.O. Box 1001, 00-950 Warsaw, Poland)
Description: Covers theoretical, historical and constitutional law.

340   PL   ISSN 0208-5003
UNIWERSYTET SLASKI W KATOWICACH. PRACE NAUKOWE. Z PROBLEMATYKI PRAWA PRACY I POLITYKI SOCJALNEJ. (Text in Polish; summaries in French and Russian) 1977. irreg. Wydawnictwo Uniwersytetu Slaskiego, Ul. Bankowa 14, 40-007 Katowice, Poland. TEL 48-32-596-915. FAX 48-32-599-605. TELEX 0315584 USKPL. (Dist. by: CHZ Ars Polona, P.O. Box 1001, 00-950 Warsaw, Poland)
Description: Covers problems of the labor laws (individual and collective) in the aspect of legal practice, legal legislation and teaching.

UNMARRIED PARENTS TODAY. see *SOCIAL SERVICES AND WELFARE*

340 375   US   ISSN 0147-8648
KF4208.5.L3
UPDATE ON LAW-RELATED EDUCATION. 3/yr. $14.95. American Bar Association, Youth Education for Citizenship, 750 N. Lake Shore Dr., Chicago, IL 60611. TEL 312-988-5735. Ed. Jack Wolowiec. adv. **Indexed:** A.D.& D., C.I.J.E., C.L.I., L.R.I.
—BLDSC shelfmark: 9121.956000.
Description: Provides articles on the law in clear, informal language; current legal developments, including Supreme Court previews and decisions; classroom strategies and reviews of current curriculum materials; practical law for teachers and their students.

340   US   ISSN 0042-0905
K25
URBAN LAWYER; the national quarterly on urban law. 1969. q. $36 (foreign $40.50). American Bar Association, Urban, State and Local Government Law Section, 750 N. Lake Shore Dr., Chicago, IL 60611. TEL 312-988-5000. FAX 312-988-6281. Ed. Robert H. Freilich. bk.rev.; index; circ. 6,600. (also avail. in microfiche from WSH; microfilm from WSH; back issues avail.) **Indexed:** Abstr.Bk.Rev.Curr.Leg.Per., C.L.I., Curr.Cont., Energy Ind., Energy Info.Abstr., Environ.Per.Bibl., L.R.I., Leg.Cont., Leg.Per., Sage Pub.Admin.Abstr., Sage Urb.Stud.Abstr., SSCI.
—BLDSC shelfmark: 9123.688500.
Description: Articles on various areas of urban, state, and local government law.

URBAN, STATE, AND LOCAL LAW NEWSLETTER. see *PUBLIC ADMINISTRATION — Municipal Government*

340   US   ISSN 0042-1448
K25
UTAH LAW REVIEW. 1949. q. $20. (Utah Law Review Society) University of Utah College of Law, Salt Lake City, UT 84112. TEL 801-581-6833. Ed. Kurt Holzer. adv.; bk.rev.; index; circ. 600. (also avail. in microform from UMI,WSH; reprint service avail. from WSH) **Indexed:** C.L.I., Crim.Just.Abstr., L.R.I., Leg.Cont., Leg.Per., Sel.Water Res.Abstr.
●Also available online. Vendor(s): WESTLAW.
—BLDSC shelfmark: 9135.180000.

340   US
UTAH NOTARY LAW PRIMER. irreg. $9.95. National Notary Association, 8236 Remmet Ave., Box 7184, Canoga Park, CA 91304-7184. TEL 818-713-4000. FAX 818-713-9061. Ed. Charles N. Faerber. (reprint service avail. from UMI)

340   US   ISSN 1053-0258
KF2089
UTILITIES INDUSTRY LITIGATION REPORTER; national coverage of the many types of litigation stemming from the transmission and distribution of energy by publicly and privately owned utilities. 1989. s-m. $650. Andrews Publications, 1646 West Chester Pike, Box 1000, Westtown, PA 19395. TEL 215-399-6600. FAX 215-399-6610. Ed. Ronald Baker. abstr.; bibl.; stat.; cum.index every 6 mos. (looseleaf format; back issues avail.)

340   NE
UTRECHT STUDIES IN AIR AND SPACE LAW. (Text in English) 1987. a. Kluwer Academic Publishers, P.O. Box 17, 3300 AA Dordrecht, Netherlands. TEL 078-334911. FAX 078-334254. (Dist. by: Kluwer Academic Publishers, P.O. Box 322, 3300 AH Dordrecht, Netherlands; U.S. addr.: Box 358, Accord Sta., Hingham, MA 02018-0358)

340   US   ISSN 0042-2363
K26
VALPARAISO UNIVERSITY LAW REVIEW. 1966. 3/yr. $18. Valparaiso University, School of Law, Valparaiso, IN 46383. TEL 219-465-7807. FAX 219-465-7872. adv.; bk.rev.; bibl.; index; circ. 750. (also avail. in microfilm from WSH; reprint service avail. from WSH) **Indexed:** Abstr.Bk.Rev.Curr.Leg.Per., C.L.I., L.R.I., Leg.Per., P.A.I.S.
—BLDSC shelfmark: 9141.720000.

340   US   ISSN 0042-2533
K26
VANDERBILT LAW REVIEW. 1947. 6/yr. $28 (foreign $30). Vanderbilt University School of Law, Nashville, TN 37240. TEL 615-322-4766. Ed. Michael Daneker. adv.; bk.rev.; bibl.; index; cum.index every 10 yrs.; circ. 1,600. (also avail. in microform from UMI; microfilm from WSH; reprint service avail. from UMI,WSH) **Indexed:** Abstr.Bk.Rev.Curr.Leg.Per., Account.Ind. (1974-), BPIA, Bus.Ind., C.L.I., Commun.Abstr., Crim.Just.Abstr., Curr.Cont., L.R.I., Leg.Cont., Leg.Per., SSCI.
●Also available online. Vendor(s): Mead Data Central, WESTLAW.
—BLDSC shelfmark: 9144.500000.

VERBRAUCHER UND RECHT. see *REAL ESTATE*

2692 LAW

240   US
VERDICT REVIEW. w. $375. Jury Verdict Research, Inc., 30700 Bainbridge Rd., Ste. H, Solon, OH 44139. TEL 216-248-7960. TELEX 216-349- JURY. index. (looseleaf format; back issues avail.)
  Formerly: Verdict Reports (ISSN 0092-2293)
  Description: Analysis of verdict trends.

340   US
VERDICTS, SETTLEMENTS & TACTICS. 1988. m. $340. Shepard's - McGraw-Hill, Inc., Box 35300, Colorado Springs, CO 80935-3530. TEL 800-525-2474. Ed. William Jordan.

VEREENIGING TOT UITGAAF DER BRONNEN VAN HET OUD-VADERLANDSE RECHT. WERKEN. see HISTORY

340   GW   ISSN 0506-7286
LAW
VERFASSUNG UND RECHT IN UEBERSEE; law and politics in Africa, Asia, and Latin America. (Text in English, French, German and Spanish; summaries in English) 1968. q. DM.108. Hamburger Gesellschaft fuer Voelkerrecht und Auswaertige Politik e.V., Rothenbaumchaussee 21-23, 2000 Hamburg 13, Germany. (Subscr. to: Nomos Verlag, Postfach 610, 7570 Baden-Baden, Germany) (Co-sponsor: Universitaet Hamburg. Institut fuer Internationale Angelegenheiten) Ed.Bd. adv.; bk.rev.; abstr.; index; circ. 500. (back issues avail.) Indexed: Foreign Leg.Per., Int.Polit.Sci.Abstr., P.A.I.S., P.A.I.S.For.Lang.Ind.
  —BLDSC shelfmark: 9155.900000.

VERFASSUNG UND VERFASSUNGSWIRKLICHKEIT. see POLITICAL SCIENCE

340   NE   ISSN 0042-398X
VERKEERSRECHT; juridical monthly for the road traffic, liability, damage and insurance. 1953. m. fl.217 to non-members. Koninklijke Nederlandse Toeristenbond ANWB - Royal Dutch Touring Club, Wassenaarseweg 220, Box 93200, 2509 BA The Hague, Netherlands. bk.rev.; index; circ. 2,400.

VERKEHRSRECHTLICHE MITTEILUNGEN. see TRANSPORTATION

340   RU
▼**VERKHOVNYI SUD S.S.S.R. VESTNIK.** 1991. m. 1 Rub. per issue. Verkhovnyi Sud S.S.S.R., Ul. Vorovskogo 15, 121260 Moscow, Russia. TEL 202-66-08. Ed. N.P. Zaikin. circ. 63,000.

340   US
VERMONT BAR JOURNAL AND LAW DIGEST. 1960. bi-m. $35 (effective Sep. 1990). Vermont Bar Association, Box 100, Montpelier, VT 05601. TEL 802-223-2020. FAX 802-223-1573. Ed. Phyllis A. Andrews. adv.; bk.rev.; circ. 2,000. (back issues avail.)

340   US
VERMONT FISH AND WILDLIFE REGULATIONS. 1985. base vol. (plus suppl.). $10.50. Butterworth Legal Publishers (Salem) (Subsidiary of: Reed International PLC), 90 Stiles Rd., Salem, NH 03079. TEL 800-548-4001. FAX 603-898-9858. Ed.Bd.
  Description: Contains recent amended laws and regulations covering Vermont fish and wildlife, together with historical notes, annotations and an index.

340   US
VERMONT REPORTS. irreg. (1-2 vols./yr.). $32 per vol. Butterworth Legal Publishers (Salem) (Subsidiary of: Reed International PLC), 90 Stiles Rd., Salem, NH 03079. TEL 800-548-4001. FAX 603-898-9858. Ed.Bd.
  Description: Contains current opinions with headnotes, table of cases reported arranged in alpha-county order.

340   US
VERMONT RULES OF EVIDENCE. a. $13. Butterworth Legal Publishers (Salem) (Subsidiary of: Reed International PLC), 90 Stiles Rd., Salem, NH 03079. TEL 800-548-4001. FAX 603-898-9858. Ed.Bd.

340   US
VERMONT STATUTES ANNOTATED. 25 base vols. (plus a. suppl.). $699. Butterworth Legal Publishers (Salem) (Subsidiary of: Reed International PLC), 90 Stiles Rd., Salem, NH 03079. TEL 800-548-4001. FAX 603-898-9858. Ed.Bd.
  Description: Official statutes of the state of Vermont, containing all the laws of a general and permanent nature.

340 943   GW
VEROEFFENTLICHUNGEN ZUR VERFASSUNGSGESCHICHTE VON BADEN-WUERTTEMBERG SEIT 1945. 1983. irreg. Kommission fuer geschichtliche Landeskunde in Baden-Wuerttemberg, Eugen-Str. 7, 7000 Stuttgart 1, Germany. circ. 1,000.
  Description: Sources of information about the constitutional development of southwest Germany after the Second World War.

340   GW   ISSN 0042-4501
VERWALTUNGSARCHIV; Zeitschrift fuer Verwaltungslehre, Verwaltungsrecht und Verwaltungspolitik. 1893. q. DM.110. Carl Heymanns Verlag KG, Luxemburgerstr. 41, 5000 Cologne 41, Germany. TEL 0221-46010-0. FAX 0221-4601069. Ed. C.H. Ule. adv.; bk.rev.; abstr.; charts; stat.; index; circ. 3,300. (reprint service avail. from SCH)

340   GW   ISSN 0342-5592
VERWALTUNGSRUNDSCHAU; Zeitschrift fuer Verwaltung in Praxis und Wissenschaft. m. DM.169. W. Kohlhammer GmbH, Hessbruehlstr. 69, Postfach 800430, 7000 Stuttgart 80, Germany. TEL 0711-7863-1.

340   GW   ISSN 0174-6162
DER VERWALTUNGSWIRT. bi-m. DM.44. R. v. Decker's Verlag, G. Schenck GmbH, Im Weiher 10, 6900 Heidelberg 1, Germany. TEL 06221-489281. FAX 06221-489279. TELEX 461727-HUEHD-D.

340   GW
VERZEICHNIS RHEINLAND-PFAELZISCHER RECHT- UND VERWALTUNGSVORSCHRIFTEN. 1981. a. DM.16. (Ministerium der Justiz) Nomos Verlagsgesellschaft mbH und Co. KG, Waldseestr. 3-5, D-7570 Baden-Baden, Germany.

VETERINARY MEDICINE GUIDANCE MANUAL. see PUBLIC HEALTH AND SAFETY

LA VETTA D'ITALIA; mensile di politica e di cultura dell'Alto Adige. see BIOGRAPHY

340   AT   ISSN 0506-8509
VICTORIA, AUSTRALIA. STATUTORY RULES. irreg. Aus.$900. Law Printer, P.O. Box 203, North Melbourne, Vic. 3051, Australia. TEL 03-320-0100. FAX 03-328-1657. index. (looseleaf format; back issues avail.)

340   NZ   ISSN 0042-5117
K26
VICTORIA UNIVERSITY OF WELLINGTON LAW REVIEW. 1955. 4/yr. NZ.$65 to Australia; elsewhere NZ$85. (Victoria University of Wellington, Law Faculty) Victoria University Press, P.O. Box 600, Wellington, New Zealand. (Subscr. in U.S. to: William W. Gaunt & Sons Inc., Gaunt Building, 3011 Gulf Dr., Holmes Beach, Fl. 33510-2199) Ed. A.H. Angelo. adv.; bk.rev.; circ. 600. (also avail. in microfiche; back issues avail.) Indexed: C.L.I., L.R.I., Leg.Cont., Leg.Per., Mar.Aff.Bibl.
  —BLDSC shelfmark: 9232.600000.
  Description: General Law Faculty review with special issues on treaties, land claims, constitutional, criminal and international issues.

340 331   AT
VICTORIAN ACCIDENT COMPENSATION PRACTICE GUIDE. (In 2 vols.) 1980. 6/yr. C C H Australia Ltd., P.O. Box 230, North Ryde, N.S.W. 2113, Australia. TEL 888-2555. FAX 02-888-7324.
  Formerly: Victorian Workers Compensation Practice Guide.

340 350   AT
VICTORIAN ADMINISTRATIVE LAW. 1986. 6/yr. Aus.$175. Law Book Co. Ltd., 44-50 Waterloo Rd., North Ryde, N.S.W. 2113, Australia. TEL 02-887-0177. FAX 02-888-9706. TELEX ASBOOK 27995. Ed. Emilios Kyrou.
  Incorporates: Victorian Administrative Reports.
  Description: Provides commentary on administrative law remedies and jurisdiction of the Administrative Appeals Tribunal.

340   AT
VICTORIAN BAR COUNCIL. ANNUAL REPORT. 1964. a. members only. Victorian Bar Council, Owen Dixon Chambers, 205 William St., Melbourne, Vic. 3000, Australia. TEL 608-7111. FAX 670-2959. Ed.Bd. circ. 1,800.

340 990   AT   ISSN 0159-3285
VICTORIAN BAR NEWS. 1971. q. free. Victorian Bar Council, Owen Dixon Chambers, 205 William St., Melbourne, Vic. 3000, Australia. TEL 03 608-7111. FAX 03-670-2959. Eds. Gerard Nash, Paul Elliott. bk.rev.; circ. 2,000. (back issues avail.)
  Description: Journal of the Victorian Bar, reporting law, movement in the profession of barristers, and general interest in the Bar of the State of Victoria, Australia.

340   AT
VICTORIAN CONVEYANCING LAW AND PRACTICE. (In 3 vols.) 10/yr. C C H Australia Ltd., P.O. Box 230, North Ryde, N.S.W. 2113, Australia. TEL 888-2555.
  Description: Reference on conveyancing law for the State of Victoria, Australia.

340   AT   ISSN 0042-5214
VICTORIAN REPORTS. 1966. m. $198. Butterworths Pty. Ltd., 271-273 Lane Cove Rd., North Ryde, N.S.W. 2113, Australia. TEL 02-335-4444. FAX 02-335-4655.
  ●Also available online.

340   AT   ISSN 0816-9799
VICTORIAN STATUTES - ANNOTATIONS. 3/yr. (plus 2 updates). Butterworths Pty. Ltd., 271-273 Lane Cove Rd., P.O. Box 345, North Ryde, N.S.W. 2113, Australia. TEL 02-335-4444. FAX 02-335-4655.

340   AT   ISSN 0314-5204
VICTORIAN STATUTES CUMULATIVE SUPPLEMENT. 1962. a. Law Book Co. Ltd., 44-50 Waterloo Rd., North Ryde, N.S.W. 2113, Australia. TEL 02-887-0177. FAX 02-888-9706. TELEX ASBOOK 27995.
  Description: Provides a legislative history of principal acts since the 1958 consolidation. Includes notes on administration of acts and references to relevant journals and periodicals.

368 344   GW   ISSN 0301-2999
K26
VIERTELJAHRESSCHRIFT FUER SOZIALRECHT.* (Text in German; summaries in English) 1973. q. DM.148. Carl Heymanns Verlag KG, Luxemburgerstr. 449, 5000 Cologne 41, Germany. TEL 0221-046010-0. FAX 0221-4601069. Ed.Bd. (reprint service avail. from UMI)

340   US   ISSN 0042-6229
K26
VILLANOVA LAW REVIEW. 1955. 5/yr. $25. Villanova University Law School, Villanova, PA 19085. TEL 215-645-7053. Ed. James King. adv.; bk.rev.; index; circ. 1,600. (also avail. in microfiche from WSH; microfilm from WSH; back issues avail.) Indexed: Abstr.Bk.Rev.Curr.Leg.Per., C.I.J.E., C.L.I., Crim.Just.Abstr., L.R.I., Lang.& Lang.Behav.Abstr., Leg.Cont., Leg.Per., Sociol.Abstr.
  ●Also available online. Vendor(s): WESTLAW.
  —BLDSC shelfmark: 9236.500000.

340   US
VIRGIN ISLANDS CODE ANNOTATED. 14 base vols. (plus suppl.). $600. Butterworth Legal Publishers (Salem) (Subsidiary of: Reed International PLC), 90 Stiles Rd., Salem, NH 03079. TEL 800-548-4001. FAX 603-898-9858. Ed.Bd.
  Description: Official statutes for the US Virgin Islands, containing all of the general and permanent laws of the Territory.

340 US ISSN 0360-3857
KF200
THE VIRGINIA BAR ASSOCIATION JOURNAL. 1975. q. $30 (effective Jan. 1992). Virginia Bar Association, 3849 W. Weyburn Rd., Richmond, VA 23235. TEL 804-644-0041. (Or: c/o Charles E. Friend, 322 Scotland St., Williamsburg, VA 23185) Ed.Bd. bk.rev.; illus.; circ. 3,800. **Indexed:** C.L.I., L.R.I., Leg.Per.

340 US
VIRGINIA CONDOMINIUM LAW. 1987. base vol. (plus suppl. 2-3/yr.). $50. Butterworth Legal Publishers (Salem) (Subsidiary of: Reed International PLC), 90 Stiles Rd., Salem, NH 03079. TEL 800-548-4001. FAX 603-898-9858. Ed. Douglas S. MacGregor. (looseleaf format)
Description: Includes an analysis of the current state Condominium Act and Regulations, the Uniform Act, and relevant federal legislation.

340 US ISSN 1042-461X
KFV2731.A15
VIRGINIA EMPLOYMENT LAW LETTER. 1989. m. $95. M. Lee Smith Publishers & Printers, 162 Fourth Ave. N., Box 2678, Nashville, TN 37219. TEL 615-242-7395. FAX 615-256-6601. Ed. James V. Meath.
Description: Survey of employment law developments in Virginia.

340 US ISSN 1045-5183
K26
VIRGINIA ENVIRONMENTAL LAW JOURNAL. 1980. s-a. $32 (foreign $48) (typically set in Nov.). Virginia Environmental Law Journal, University of Virginia, School of Law, Charlottesville, VA 22901. TEL 804-924-3683. FAX 804-924-7536. Ed. David Taffet. circ. 460. **Indexed:** C.L.I., Environ.Abstr., Leg.Per.
●Also available online. Vendor(s): WESTLAW.
—BLDSC shelfmark: 9238.460000.
Formerly (until 1988): Virginia Journal of Natural Resources Law (ISSN 0748-8122)

340 US ISSN 0042-6601
K26 CODEN: VLIBAD
VIRGINIA LAW REVIEW. 1913. 8/yr. $40. (Virginia Law Review Association) University of Virginia, School of Law, Charlottesville, VA 22901. TEL 804-924-3079. adv.; bk.rev.; index, cum.index; circ. 2,200. (also avail. in microfiche from RRI,WSH; microfilm from WSH; back issues avail.); reprint service avail. from RRI) **Indexed:** A.B.C.Pol.Sci., ABI Inform., Abstr.Bk.Rev.Curr.Leg.Per., Account.Ind. (1974-), BPIA, Bus.Ind., C.L.I., Chic.Per.Ind., Crim.Just.Abstr., L.R.I., Leg.Cont., Leg.Per., P.A.I.S., Pers.Lit., SSCI.
—BLDSC shelfmark: 9239.300000.
Description: General law publication.

340 US ISSN 0042-661X
VIRGINIA LAW WEEKLY. 1948. 28/yr. $25 (typically set in May). University of Virginia, School of Law, Charlottesville, VA 22901. TEL 804-924-3070. FAX 804-924-7536. Ed. Jonathan E. Perkel. adv.; bk.rev.; illus.; stat.; circ. 1,200. (newspaper)
Description: Student-run newspaper chronicling the events and opinions of the law school and the nation.

340 US
VIRGINIA LAWYER. Variant title: Virginia Lawyer Register. 1953. m. $18. Virginia State Bar, 801 E. Main St., Ste. 1000, Richmond, VA 23219. TEL 804-786-2061. FAX 804-786-3036. Ed. Cariline B. Bolte. adv.; bk.rev.; stat.; circ. 25,000. **Indexed:** Law Ofc.Info.Svc.
Formerly: Virginia Bar News.

340 US
VIRGINIA LAWYER'S WEEKLY. 1986. w. $195. Lawyer's Weekly Publications, 106 N. Eighth St., Richmond, VA 23219. TEL 804-783-0770. FAX 804-343-7365. Ed. Paul E. Fletcher. adv.; index; circ. 3,100. (tabloid format; back issues avail.)
Description: Contains summaries of current precedent setting cases from Virginia state and federal courts.

340 US
VIRGINIA PROBATE LAW. 1987. 2 base vols. (plus suppl. 2-3/yr.). $80. Butterworth Legal Publishers (Salem) (Subsidiary of: Reed International PLC), 90 Stiles Rd., Salem, NH 03079. TEL 800-548-4001. FAX 603-898-9858. Ed. Elizabeth Hapner. (looseleaf format)
Description: Practical analysis of the methods and problems of estate administration in Virginia.

340 333.33 US
▼**VIRGINIA RESIDENTIAL LANDLORD AND TENANT LAW.** 1991. base vol. (plus s-a. suppl.). $60. Butterworth Legal Publishers (Salem) (Subsidiary of: Reed International PLC), 90 Stiles Rd., Salem, NH 03079. TEL 800-548-4001. FAX 603-898-9664. Ed. Douglas S. MacGregor. (looseleaf format)

343 US ISSN 0364-2232
KF9602
VOICE FOR THE DEFENSE.* 1973. m. $36 to non-members; members $10. (Texas Criminal Defense Lawyers Association) Artforms, Inc., Box 1434, Round Rock, TX 78680-1434. TEL 512-451-3588. Ed. Kerry Fitzgerald. adv.; bk.rev.; charts; illus.; stat.; circ. 2,000.

W A D E EXCHANGE. (World Association of Document Examiners) see CRIMINOLOGY AND LAW ENFORCEMENT

347.9 CN ISSN 0509-5166
W.C.J. MEREDITH MEMORIAL LECTURES. 1961. a. $65. Les Editions Yvon Blais, 430 rue St. Pierre, Bureau 200, Montreal, Que. H2Y 2M5, Canada. TEL 514-842-3937. **Indexed:** Ind.Can.L.P.L.
Formerly: Lectures Bar Extension.

340 GW ISSN 0042-9678
K27
W G O - MONATSHEFTE FUER OSTEUROPAEISCHES RECHT. 1959. bi-m. DM.118. Universitaet Hamburg, Seminarabteilung fuer Ostrechtsforschung, Moorweidenstr. 7, D-2000 Hamburg 13, Germany. TEL 040-4123-2630. FAX 06221-489410. TELEX 461727-HUEHD. Eds. G. Tontsch, B. Bytomski. adv.; bk.rev.; abstr.; bibl.; charts; index; circ. 315.

346.013 US ISSN 0736-9433
KF477.A15
W L D F NEWS.* 1971. 3/yr. free. Women's Legal Defense Fund, 1875 Connecticut Ave N.W. No. 710, Washington, DC 20009-5728. Ed. Ann Parley. (back issues avail.)
Description: Covers activities in the areas of employment and family law, work and policy as they pertain to women.

346.066 GW
W M TEIL IV: ZEITSCHRIFT FUER WIRTSCHAFTS- UND BANKRECHT. w. DM.97.55. Herausgebergemeinschaft Wertpapier-Mitteilungen Keppler, Lehmann GmbH & Co., Duesseldorferstr. 16, Postfach 110932, 6000 Frankfurt a.M. 11, Germany. TEL 069-2732-0. FAX 069-232264. TELEX 412066-BZFFM. index. (back issues avail.)

347 NE ISSN 0165-8476
W P N R. (Weekblad voor Privaatrecht, Notariaat en Registratie) 1870. w. fl.195.75. Koninklijke Notariele Broederschap, Postbus 96827, 2509 JE The Hague, Netherlands. TEL 070-3307138. FAX 070-3453226. Ed. A.L. Moussault-Jeswiet. adv.; bk.rev.; index; circ. 4,500. **Indexed:** Key to Econ.Sci.
—BLDSC shelfmark: 9284.660000.
Incorporates: Maandblad voor het Notariaat;
Formerly: Weekblad voor Privaatrecht, Notariaat en Registratie.

340 US ISSN 0043-003X
K27
WAKE FOREST LAW REVIEW. vol.7, 1970. 4/yr. $21. Wake Forest Law Review Association, Inc., Wake Forest University, Winston-Salem, NC 27109. TEL 919-761-5439. FAX 919-759-6077. Ed. Martha Sewell. adv.; bk.rev.; cum.index; circ. 1,500 (controlled). (processed; also avail. in microfilm from RRI,WSH; reprint service avail. from RRI) **Indexed:** ABI Inform., C.L.I., L.R.I., Leg.Per., PSI.
—BLDSC shelfmark: 9261.430000.
Formerly: Wake Forest Intramural Law Review.

LAW 2693

340 US
WAKE FOREST UNIVERSITY SCHOOL OF LAW. CONTINUING LEGAL EDUCATION. ANNUAL REVIEW, NORTH CAROLINA. a. $80. Wake Forest University School of Law, Continuing Legal Education, Box 7206, Reynolds Sta., Winston-Salem, NC 27109. TEL 919-761-5560.

340 IQ
WAQAI AL-IRAQIYA; official gazette of the Republic of Iraq. 1924. w. ID.21 for Arabic edition; English edition ID.27. Ministry of Justice, Judicial Relations Department, Baghdad, Iraq. Dir. H.N. Jaafar. circ. 13,000 (12,000 Arabic ed.; 1,000 English ed.). (also avail. in microfilm from BHP)
Formerly: Iraq. Weekly Gazette of the Republic of Iraq.

340 US ISSN 0043-0420
K27
WASHBURN LAW JOURNAL. 1960. 3/yr. $10. Washburn University, School of Law, Topeka, KS 66621. TEL 913-295-6660. Ed. Denise Anderson. adv.; bk.rev.; charts; illus.; index, cum.index every 5 yrs.; circ. 2,100. (also avail. in microfilm from WSH; reprint service avail. from WSH) **Indexed:** C.L.I., Crim.Just.Abstr., L.R.I., Leg.Cont., Leg.Per.
—BLDSC shelfmark: 9263.125000.

WASHINGTON ADMINISTRATIVE LAW PRACTICE MANUAL. see PUBLIC ADMINISTRATION

340 US ISSN 0043-0463
K27
WASHINGTON & LEE LAW REVIEW.* 1939. 4/yr. $25. Washington and Lee University, School of Law, Lewis Hall, Lexington, VA 24450-1799. TEL 703-463-8566. FAX 703-463-8567. adv.; bk.rev.; index; circ. 1,600. (also avail. in microfilm from RRI,WSH; reprint service avail. from RRI) **Indexed:** Account.Ind. (1974-), Bank.Lit.Ind., C.L.I., L.R.I., Leg.Cont., Leg.Per., Mar.Aff.Bibl.
●Also available online. Vendor(s): WESTLAW.
—BLDSC shelfmark: 9263.127000.
Description: Provides a forum for discussion of legal problems.

340 US
WASHINGTON GUARDIANSHIP LAW; administration and litigation. 1988. base vol. (plus suppl.). $75. Butterworth Legal Publishers (Salem) (Subsidiary of: Reed International PLC), 90 Stiles Rd., Salem, NH 03079. TEL 800-548-4001. FAX 603-898-9858. Ed. Gerald B. Treacy, Jr. (looseleaf format)
Description: Describes the law of guardianship and related issues; explains how the law is applied and what to do.

340 US
WASHINGTON LAND USE AND ENVIRONMENTAL PRACTICE. 1983. irreg., latest 1991. $65. Butterworth Legal Publishers (Salem) (Subsidiary of: Reed International PLC), 90 Stiles Rd., Salem, NH 03079. TEL 800-548-4001. FAX 603-898-9858. Ed. Richard L. Settle.
Description: Provides a comprehensive description of the law and practical analysis of its application.

340 US ISSN 0043-0617
WASHINGTON LAW REVIEW. 1926. 4/yr. $24. Washington Law Review Association, Condon Hall, JB-20, 1100 N.E. Campus Pkwy., School of Law, University of Washington, WA 98105. TEL 206-543-6335. FAX 206-543-5671. adv.; bk.rev.; index; circ. 1,500. (also avail. in microfiche from RRI,WSH; microfilm from WSH; back issues avail.; reprint service avail. from RRI) **Indexed:** Account.Ind. (1979-), C.L.I., Curr.Cont., Leg.Per., Mar.Aff.Bibl, Ocean.Abstr., Risk Abstr., Sel.Water Res.Abstr., SSCI.
●Also available online. Vendor(s): Mead Data Central, WESTLAW.
—BLDSC shelfmark: 9263.165000.

340 US
WASHINGTON LAWYER. 1976. bi-m. $20. District of Columbia Bar, 1707 L St. N.W., Ste. 350, Washington, DC 20036-4201. TEL 202-331-7700. FAX 202-223-7726. Ed. Jane Ottenberg. adv.; illus.; circ. 56,000. (also avail. in microfilm from WSH) **Indexed:** C.L.I., L.R.I., Leg.Per.
Formerly: District Lawyer (ISSN 0147-7943)

L

LAW

340   US
WASHINGTON NOTARY LAW PRIMER. a. $9.95. National Notary Association, 8236 Remmet Ave., Box 7184, Canoga Park, CA 91304-7184. TEL 818-713-4000. FAX 818-713-9061. Ed. Charles N. Faerber. (reprint service avail. from UMI)

340   US
WASHINGTON STATE ENVIRONMENTAL POLICY ACT; a legal and policy analysis. 1987. base vol. (plus suppl.). $75. Butterworth Legal Publishers (Salem) (Subsidiary of: Reed International PLC), 90 Stiles Rd., Salem, NH 03079. TEL 800-548-4001. FAX 603-898-9858. Ed. Richard L. Settle. (looseleaf format)

WASHINGTON STATE PATROL. ANNUAL REPORT. see *CRIMINOLOGY AND LAW ENFORCEMENT*

WASHINGTON TROOPER. see *CRIMINOLOGY AND LAW ENFORCEMENT*

340   US   ISSN 0043-0862
K23
WASHINGTON UNIVERSITY LAW QUARTERLY. 1915. 4/yr. $20. Washington University, School of Law, St. Louis, MO 63130. TEL 314-889-6498. Ed. Kelly Riley. adv.; bk.rev.; index; circ. 800. (also avail. in microfiche from WSH; microfilm from RRI,WSH) **Indexed:** C.L.I., L.R.I., Leg.Cont., Leg.Per.
—BLDSC shelfmark: 9263.450000.
    Formerly: St. Louis Law Review (ISSN 0271-2849)

WASSERRECHT UND WASSERWIRTSCHAFT. see *WATER RESOURCES*

WASTE MINIMIZATION & RECYCLING REPORT; hazardous & solid waste. see *ENVIRONMENTAL STUDIES — Waste Management*

WASTELINE. see *ENVIRONMENTAL STUDIES — Waste Management*

340   US   ISSN 0043-1249
WATER LAW NEWSLETTER. 1965. 3/yr. $20. Rocky Mountain Mineral Law Foundation, Porter Administration Bldg., 7039 E. 18th Ave., Denver, CO 80220. TEL 303-321-8100. FAX 303-321-7657. Ed. George A. Gould. circ. 500. (looseleaf format)

340   US   ISSN 0043-1621
LAW
WAYNE LAW REVIEW. 1953. 4/yr. $28. Wayne State University Law School, 468 W. Ferry, Detroit, MI 48202. TEL 313-577-3939. FAX 313-577-5498. Ed. Jane Derse Quasarano. adv.; bk.rev.; abstr.; bibl.; charts; illus.; stat.; index, cum.index; circ. 2,000. (also avail. in microfiche from WSH; microfilm from WSH) **Indexed:** Abstr.Bk.Rev.Curr.Leg.Per., L.R.I., Leg.Cont., Leg.Per.
—BLDSC shelfmark: 9280.980000.

340   UK   ISSN 0264-3723
WEEKLY LAW DIGEST. 1958. w. £24.25. Justice of the Peace Ltd., Little London, Chichester, W. Sussex PO19 1PG, England. TEL 0243-783637. FAX 0243-779278. (back issues avail.)
—BLDSC shelfmark: 9284.940000.
    Description: Abbreviated summaries of cases, sentencing features and miscellaneous information.

340   UK   ISSN 0019-3518
WEEKLY LAW REPORTS. 1953. w. £148 (foreign £164). Incorporated Council of Law Reporting for England and Wales, 3 Stone Bldgs., Lincoln's Inn, London WC2A 3XN, England. TEL 071-242-6471. FAX 071-831-5247. Ed. R.C. Williams. **Indexed:** RICS.
●Also available online. Vendor(s): Mead Data Central.

340   JM   ISSN 0253-7370
K27
WEST INDIAN LAW JOURNAL. 1977. s-a. $20. Council of Legal Education, P.O. Box 231, Mona, Kingston, Jamaica, W.I. Ed. H. Aubrey Fraser. adv.; bk.rev.; circ. 1,000. **Indexed:** C.L.I., L.R.I., Leg.Per., Mar.Aff.Bibl.
—BLDSC shelfmark: 9299.075000.
    Supersedes: Jamaica Law Journal.

340   US   ISSN 0043-3268
K27
WEST VIRGINIA LAW REVIEW. 1894. 4/yr. $27. West Virginia University Law Center, Morgantown, WV 26506-6130. TEL 304-293-2301. FAX 304-293-6891. adv.; bk.rev.; abstr.; cum.index; circ. 1,200. (processed; also avail. in microform from UMI; microfiche from WSH; microfilm from WSH) **Indexed:** Abstr.Bk.Rev.Curr.Leg.Per., C.L.I., L.R.I., Leg.Cont., Leg.Per., SSCI.
—BLDSC shelfmark: 9300.030000.

340   US   ISSN 0049-7274
K27
WESTCHESTER LAW JOURNAL. 1936. w. $30. Westchester Law Journal Inc., 175 Main St., White Plains, NY 10601. TEL 914-948-0715. adv.; circ. 250.

350   AT
WESTERN AUSTRALIA. LAW REFORM COMMISSION. ANNUAL REPORT. 1973. a. free. Law Reform Commission, KPMG House, 214 St. Georges Terrace, Perth, W.A. 6000, Australia. FAX 09-481-4197. stat.; circ. 300(AP).

340   AT   ISSN 0085-8161
WESTERN AUSTRALIA LAW ALMANAC. 1913. a. Aus.$12.50. Crown Law Department, 38 Mourts Bay Rd., Perth, W.A. 6000, Australia. FAX 322-4713. Ed. Terry McAdam. circ. 1,500. (avail. on floppy disk)

340   AT
WESTERN AUSTRALIA REPORTS. 1960. bi-m. Law Book Co. Ltd., 44-50 Waterloo Rd., North Ryde, N.S.W. 2113, Australia. TEL 02-887-0177. FAX 02-888-9706. TELEX ASBOOK 27995.
●Also available online.
    Formerly (until 1983): West Australian Reports.
    Description: Authorized law reports of the Supreme Court of Western Australia.

347.9 979   US   ISSN 0896-2189
K27
WESTERN LEGAL HISTORY. 1988. s-a. $25. Ninth Judicial Circuit Historical Society, 620 S.W. Main St., Rm.703, Portland, OR 97205. TEL 503-326-3458. FAX 503-326-7788. Ed. Chet Orloff. adv.; bk.rev.; circ. 2,000. **Indexed:** Amer.Hist.& Life, Hist.Abstr.
    Description: Explores, analyzes, and presents the history of law, the legal profession, and the courts, particularly the federal courts in Alaska, Arizona, California, Hawaii, Idaho, Montana, Nevada, Oregon, Washington, Guam, and the Northern Mariana Islands.

340   US   ISSN 0190-6593
K27
WESTERN NEW ENGLAND LAW REVIEW. 1978. s-a. $10 (foreign $12). Western New England College, School of Law, 1215 Wilbraham Rd., Springfield, MA 01119. TEL 413-782-3111. (Subscr. to: William S. Hein & Co., Inc. 1285 Main St. Buffalo, New York 14209.) adv.; bk.rev.; index; circ. 2,000. (also avail. in microfiche from WSH; microfilm from WSH; back issues avail.) **Indexed:** Abstr.Bk.Rev.Curr.Leg.Per., C.L.I., L.R.I., Leg.Cont., Leg.Per.
—BLDSC shelfmark: 9301.432000.

340   CN   ISSN 0049-7525
WESTERN WEEKLY REPORTS. 1911. 48/yr. (in 6 vols.). Can.$115 per vol. Carswell Publications (Subsidiary of: Thompson Professional Publishing Canada), Corporate Plaza, 2075 Kennedy Rd., Scarborough, Ont. M1T 3V4, Canada. TEL 416-609-8000. FAX 416-298-5094. (Subscr. to: Carswell Publications, 2330 Midland Ave., Agincourt, Ont. M1S 1P7, Canada) cum.index; circ. 1,170.
●Also available online. Vendor(s): QL Systems Ltd..

340   344.07   US
WEST'S EDUCATION LAW REPORTER. 1984. bi-w. West Publishing Co., 50 W. Kellogg Blvd., Box 64526, St. Paul, MN 55164-0526. TEL 800-328-9352.

340   371.2   US
WEST'S LEGAL ALERT FOR EDUCATORS. 1984. bi-w. West Publishing Co., Box 64526, St. Paul, MN 55164-0526. TEL 800-328-9352.

346.066   GW   ISSN 0172-049X
KK6456.A13
WETTBEWERB IN RECHT UND PRAXIS. Short title: W R P. 1955. m. DM.542 (foreign DM.554). Deutscher Fachverlag GmbH, Mainzer Landstr. 251, Postfach 100606, 6000 Frankfurt a.M.1, Germany. circ. 2,000. (reprint service avail. from SCH)

340   US
WHAT'S HAPPENING (WASHINGTON). 1957. q. Federal Judicial Center, Division of Continuing Education and Training, 1520 H St., N.W., Washington, DC 20005. TEL 202-633-6332. Ed. Michael Eric Siegel.

340   AT   ISSN 0085-820X
WHITEACRE.* 1967. irreg. free. University of Sydney, Law Graduates Association, 173-175 Phillip St., Sydney, N.S.W. 2000, Australia.

340   US   ISSN 0162-7880
KF372
WHO'S WHO IN AMERICAN LAW. 1977. biennial, 7th ed. 1991. $229. Marquis Who's Who, A Reed Reference Publishing Company, Division of Reed Publishing (USA) Inc., 121 Chanlon Rd., New Providence, NJ 07974. TEL 800-521-8110. FAX 908-665-6688. TELEX 138 755. (Subscr. to: R.R. Bowker, Order Dept., Box 31, New Providence, NJ 07974) (also avail. in magnetic tape)
    Description: Includes more than 27,650 biographical sketches of leading attorneys, judges, educators, and other top professionals in the legal field. Entries contain principal occupation, fields of practice or interest, education, bar(s), civic and political activities, military service, professional memberships, and home, office addresses.

WICKEN'S THE LAW OF LIFE INSURANCE IN AUSTRALIA. see *INSURANCE*

340   AU   ISSN 0084-0025
WIENER RECHTSWISSENSCHAFTLICHE STUDIEN. 1964. irreg., no.20, 1990. price varies. (Universitaet Wien, Institut fuer Rechtsvergleichung) Manzsche Verlags- und Universitaetsbuchhandlung, Kohlmarkt 16, A-1014 Vienna, Austria. TEL 0222-531610. FAX 0222-5316181. (Co-sponsor: Oesterreichische Gesellschaft fuer Rechtsvergleichung) Ed. Fritz Schwind.
    Description: Legal doctoral theses.

340   UK   ISSN 0265-7937
KD2617.A13
WILKINSON'S ROAD TRAFFIC LAW BULLETIN. 1984. 10/yr. £70($112) Longman Group UK Ltd., Law, Tax and Finance Division, 21-27 Lambs Conduit St., London WC1N 3NJ, England. TEL 071-242-2548. FAX 071-831-8119. TELEX 295445. Ed. Paul Niekirk.
    Description: Information on all aspects of motoring and traffic law.

340   US   ISSN 0043-5589
K27
WILLIAM & MARY LAW REVIEW. 1957. q. $20. College of William and Mary, Williamsburg, VA 23185. TEL 804-253-4430. adv.; bk.rev.; circ. 1,200. (also avail. in microfiche from WSH) **Indexed:** C.L.I., Geo.Abstr., L.R.I., Leg.Per., Mar.Aff.Bibl., P.A.I.S.
—BLDSC shelfmark: 9318.909500.

340   US   ISSN 0270-272X
K27
WILLIAM MITCHELL LAW REVIEW. 1974. q. $24. William Mitchell College of Law, 875 Summit Ave., St. Paul, MN 55105. TEL 612-227-6305. circ. 2,100. (also avail. in microfiche from WSH; microfilm from WSH; reprint service avail. from WSH) **Indexed:** C.L.I., Crim.Just.Abstr., L.R.I., Leg.Cont., Leg.Per.
●Also available online. Vendor(s): WESTLAW.
—BLDSC shelfmark: 9318.918200.

340   CN
WILLISTON & ROLLS COURT FORMS. s-a. Can.$525. Butterworths Canada Ltd., 75 Clegg Rd., Markham, Ont. L6G 1A1, Canada. TEL 416-479-2665. FAX 416-479-2826. Ed. R.J. Rolls. (looseleaf format)
    Description: Every type of form used at civil action trials.

347.91   CN   ISSN 0710-0841
K27
WINDSOR YEARBOOK OF ACCESS TO JUSTICE/RECUEIL ANNUEL DE WINDSOR D'ACCES A LA JUSTICE. (Text in English, French) 1981. a. Can.$25. University of Windsor, Faculty of Law, Windsor, Ont. N9B 3P4, Canada. TEL 519-253-4232. FAX 519-973-7064. Ed.Bd. Indexed: C.L.I., Curr.Cont., Ind.Can.L.P.L., Leg.Per., PAIS, SSCI.
 —BLDSC shelfmark: 9319.371000.

WIRTSCHAFT UND RECHT; Zeitschrift fuer Wirtschaftspolitik und Wirtschaftsrecht mit Einschluss des Sozial- und Arbeitsrechtes. see *BUSINESS AND ECONOMICS*

WIRTSCHAFT UND WETTBEWERB; Zeitschrift fuer Kartellrecht, Wettbewerbsrecht und Marktorganisation. see *BUSINESS AND ECONOMICS — Production Of Goods And Services*

340   GW
WIRTSCHAFTSRECHT; Zeitschrift fuer Theorie und Praxis des sozialistischen Wirtschaftsrechts. 1957. q. DM.24. Staatsverlag der DDR, Otto-Grotewohl-Str. 17, 1086 Berlin, Germany.
 Formerly: Vertragssystem (ISSN 0042-4463)

WIRTSCHAFTSWISSENSCHAFTLICHE UND WIRTSCHAFTSRECHTLICHE UNTERSUCHUNGEN. see *BUSINESS AND ECONOMICS*

340   US   ISSN 0043-650X
K27
WISCONSIN LAW REVIEW. 1920. bi-m. $30. University of Wisconsin Law School, 975 Bascom Mall, Madison, WI 53706-1399. TEL 608-262-5815. Ed. Michael A. Lawrence. adv.; bk.rev.; cum.index; circ. 2,150. (also avail. in microform from UMI; microfiche from WSH; microfilm from WSH) Indexed: BPIA, Bus.Ind., C.L.I., Crim.Just.Abstr., Curr.Cont., L.R.I., Leg.Cont., Leg.Per., P.A.I.S., SSCI.
 ●Also available online. Vendor(s): Mead Data Central, WESTLAW.
 —BLDSC shelfmark: 9325.770000.
 Description: Forum for analysis and discussions of various subjects related to law.

340   US
WISCONSIN LAWYER. 1927. m. $42 to non-members; students $18. State Bar of Wisconsin, 402 W. Wilson St., Madison, WI 53703. TEL 608-257-3838. FAX 608-257-5502. Ed. Joyce R. Hastings. adv.; bk.rev.; index; circ. 14,200. (also avail. in microform from UMI; microfilm from WSH; reprint service avail. from UMI) Indexed: C.L.I., HRIS, L.R.I., Law Ofc.Info.Svc., Leg.Per.
 Formerly (until 1988): Wisconsin Bar Bulletin (ISSN 0043-6380)
 Description: Articles and columns on Wisconsin's legal systems, including offical notices from the Wisconsin Supreme Court.

340   US
WISCONSIN LEGISLATIVE COUNCIL RULES CLEARINGHOUSE. ANNUAL REPORT. 1980. a. Wisconsin Legislative Council, Box 2536, Madison, WI 53701-2536. TEL 608-266-1304. Ed. Ronald Sklansky. (back issues avail.)

340   US
WISCONSIN MISDEMEANORS AND MOVING TRAFFIC VIOLATIONS. irreg., 2nd ed., 1989. $88. Butterworth Legal Publishers (Salem) (Subsidiary of: Reed International PLC), 90 Stiles Rd., Salem, NH 03079. TEL 800-548-4001. FAX 603-898-9858. Ed. Clifford R. Steele. (looseleaf format)
 Description: Guide to prosecution and defense of misdemeanor cases in the circuit and municipal courts of Wisconsin.

340 346.013   US   ISSN 1052-3421
K27
WISCONSIN WOMEN'S LAW JOURNAL. 1985. a. $8 to individuals; institutions $15. University of Wisconsin-Madison, Law School, 975 Bascom Mall, Madison, WI 53706. TEL 608-262-8294. bk.rev.; circ. 500. (back issues avail.) Indexed: Leg.Per.

340   GW
WISSENSCHAFT UND GEGENWART. JURISTISCHE REIHE. 1970. irreg., no.6, 1973. price varies. Vittorio Klostermann, Frauenlobstr. 22, Postfach 900601, 6000 Frankfurt a.M. 90, Germany. TEL 069-774011. FAX 069-708038.

301 340   GW   ISSN 0084-0939
WISSENSCHAFTLICHE GESELLSCHAFT FUER PERSONENSTANDSWESEN UND VERWANDTE GEBIETE. SCHRIFTENREIHE. NEUE FOLGE. 1960. irreg., vol.37, 1991. price varies. Verlag fuer Standesamtswesen GmbH, Hanauer Landstr. 197, 6000 Frankfurt a.M. 1, Germany.
 TEL 069-405894-0. FAX 069-405894-99. Ed.Bd.

349   GW   ISSN 0043-6976
WISSENSCHAFTSRECHT, WISSENSCHAFTSVERWALTUNG, WISSENSCHAFTSFOERDERUNG. 1968. 3/yr. DM.150. Verlag J.C.B. Mohr (Paul Siebeck), Wilhelmstr. 18, Postfach 2040, 7400 Tuebingen, Germany. TEL 07071-26064. FAX 07071-51104. TELEX 7262872-MOHR-D. Ed.Bd. adv.; bk.rev.; bibl.; index, cum.index: 1968-1977, 1978-1987.
 —BLDSC shelfmark: 9340.270000.
 Description: Studies the legal and administrative problems of modern research and teaching at the university level.

DER WOHNUNGSEIGENTUEMER. see *BUILDING AND CONSTRUCTION*

340   GW
WOHNUNGSWIRTSCHAFT UND MIETRECHT. 1948. m. DM.96. (Deutscher Mieterbund e.V.) Verlagsgesellschaft des Deutschen Mieterbundes mbH, Aachenerstr. 313, 5000 Cologne 41, Germany. TEL 0221-40083-0. FAX 0221-4008322. Ed. Ulrich von Schoenebeck. adv.; bk.rev.; index; circ. 6,000.

WOMEN & GUNS. see *SPORTS AND GAMES*

340   US   ISSN 0043-7468
WOMEN LAWYERS JOURNAL. 1911. q. $16. National Association of Women Lawyers, 750 N. Lake Shore Dr., Chicago, IL 60611. TEL 312-988-6186. Ed. Linda Lengyel. adv.; bk.rev.; charts; illus.; index; circ. 1,312. (also avail. in microform from UMI; reprint service avail. from RRI) Indexed: C.L.I., L.R.I., Leg.Per.

WORD ON.... see *EDUCATION — School Organization And Administration*

347   US   ISSN 0074-0837
WORK ACCOMPLISHED BY THE INTER-AMERICAN JURIDICAL COMMITTEE DURING ITS MEETING. Spanish edition: Trabajos Realizados por el Comite Juridico Interamericano Durante el Periodo Ordinario de Sesiones. (Editions in Spanish, English, French and Portuguese) a. price varies. Organization of American States, Department of Publications, 1889 F St., N.W., Washington, DC 20006. TEL 703-789-3533. circ. 2,000.

WORKERS' COMPENSATION JOURNAL OF OHIO. see *PUBLIC ADMINISTRATION*

WORKER'S COMPENSATION LAW REVIEW. see *INSURANCE*

340 331   US   ISSN 0748-4135
KFC592.A29
WORKERS' COMPENSATION LAWS OF CALIFORNIA. 1961. a. Matthew Bender & Co., Inc., 11 Penn Plaza, New York, NY 10001. TEL 212-967-7707.
 Description: Covers California and federal statutes, administrative rules and regulations, tables and schedules for determining compensation payments and medical fees, and digests of relevant opinions from the California and federal court systems.

WORKERS COMPENSATION N S W. see *BUSINESS AND ECONOMICS — Labor And Industrial Relations*

346.066   US
WORKING GUIDE TO THE TENNESSEE BUSINESS CORPORATION ACT. 1988. a. $34. M. Lee Smith Publishers & Printers, 162 Fourth Ave. N., Box 2678, Nashville, TN 37219. TEL 615-242-7395. FAX 615-256-6601. Ed. Eric V. Youngquist.
 Description: Reference guide to the Tennessee Business Corporation Law for both company executives and attorneys.

346.066   UK   ISSN 0960-0949
▼**WORLD ARBITRATION & MEDIATION REPORT.** 1990. m. $422. B N A International, Inc. (Subsidiary of: The Bureau of National Affairs, Inc.), 17 Dartmouth St., London, SW1H 9BL, England. TEL 222-8831. FAX 222-0294. TELEX 262570 BNALDN G. (US addr.: 1231 25th St., N.W., Washington, DC 20037. TEL 202-452-4200) Ed. Joel S. Kolko. (back issues avail.)
 Description: Covers arbitration and other alternatives to litigation in international commercial disputes.

WORLD FOOD REGULATION REVIEW. see *FOOD AND FOOD INDUSTRIES*

340   US   ISSN 1053-0274
KF3471.A59
WRONGFUL DISCHARGE REPORT. 1987. m. $250. Andrews Publications, 1646 West Chester Pike, Box 1000, Westtown, PA 19395. TEL 215-399-6600. FAX 215-399-6610. Ed. Linda Coady. bibl.; stat.; cum.index: 1987-1988. (looseleaf format; back issues avail.)
 Formerly (until 1989): Wrongful Discharge Case Law Reporter (ISSN 0893-8458)
 Description: Provides coverage of employment-related litigation for attorneys and human resource executives.

340   CC   ISSN 1001-2397
XIANDAI FAXUE/MODERN LAW SCIENCE. (Text in Chinese; summaries in English) 1979. bi-m. (Xinan Zhengfa Xueyuan) Xiandai Faxue Zazhishe, Chongqing, Sichuan 630031, People's Republic of China. TEL 661671. Ed. Xu Jingcun. circ. 10,000 (paid); 50,000 (controlled).
 Description: Theoretical law journal.

340   CC
XUEXI YU FUDAO/STUDY AND GUIDANCE. (Text in Chinese) m. Zuigao Renmin Fayuan - Supreme Court, 27, Dongjiao Minxiang, Beijing 100745, People's Republic of China. TEL 548311. Ed. Hui Huming.

347 305.4   US   ISSN 1043-9366
K29
YALE JOURNAL OF LAW AND FEMINISM. 1989. s-a. $12 to individuals; institutions $25. Yale University, School of Law, 401A Yale Sta., New Haven, CT 06520. TEL 203-432-4056. FAX 203-432-2592. circ. 550. (back issues avail.)
 —BLDSC shelfmark: 9370.019000.
 Description: Forum for discussion of women's and feminist issues.

YALE JOURNAL OF LAW & THE HUMANITIES. see *HUMANITIES: COMPREHENSIVE WORKS*

346.006 363.6   US   ISSN 0741-9457
K29
YALE JOURNAL ON REGULATION. 1983. s-a. $16 to individuals (foreign $26); institutions $25 (foreign $35). Yale University, School of Law, Yale Journal on Regulation Staff, 401A Yale Sta., New Haven, CT 06520. TEL 203-432-4861. FAX 203-432-2592. adv.; bk.rev.; bibl.; charts; stat.; circ. 1,300. (also avail. in microfiche; back issues avail.) Indexed: Abstr.Health Care Manage.Stud., C.L.I., Energy Info.Abstr., Environ.Abstr., J.of Econ.Lit., Leg.Per., P.A.I.S., Tel.Abstr.
 ●Also available online. Vendor(s): WESTLAW.
 —BLDSC shelfmark: 9370.040000.
 Description: Forum for research and debate on regulatory policy and its impact on the public and private sectors.

340   US
YALE LAW & POLICY REVIEW. 1982. s-a. $16 to individuals; institutions $25. Yale University, School of Law, 401A Yale Sta., New Haven, CT 06520. TEL 203-432-4863. adv.; bk.rev.; circ. 500. (also avail. in microform from WSH; reprint service avail. from WSH) Indexed: Abstr.Health Care Manage.Stud., C.L.I., Leg.Per.

LAW

340   US   ISSN 0044-0094
K29
YALE LAW JOURNAL. 1891. 8/yr. $36. (Yale University, School of Law) Yale Law Journal Co., Inc., 401-A Yale Sta., New Haven, CT 06520. TEL 203-432-1666. FAX 203-432-2592. adv.; bk.rev.; index; circ. 4,500. (also avail. in microfiche from RRI,WSH; microfilm from WSH; reprint service avail. from ISI,RRI) Indexed: A.B.C.Pol.Sci., ABI Inform., Abstr.Bk.Rev.Curr.Leg.Per., Account.Ind. (1974-), Bank.Lit.Ind., Bk.Rev.Ind. (1981-), BPIA, C.L.I., Child.Bk.Rev.Ind. (1981-), Crim.Just.Abstr., Curr.Cont., Energy Ind., Energy Info.Abstr., J.of Econ.Lit., L.R.I., Leg.Cont., Leg.Per., P.A.I.S., Pers.lit., Risk Abstr., SSCI.
●Also available online. Vendor(s): Mead Data Central.
—BLDSC shelfmark: 9370.200000.

340   343.09   NE
YEARBOOK MARITIME LAW. 1987. a. price varies. Kluwer Law and Taxation Publishers, P.O. Box 23, 7400 GA Deventer, Netherlands. (Dist. by: Libresso Distribution Centre, P.O. Box 23, 7400 GA Deventer, Netherlands. TEL 31-5700-33155; N. America dist. addr.: 6 Bigelow St., Cambridge, MA 02139. TEL 617-354-0140)

340   US   ISSN 1049-0264
YEARBOOK OF EDUCATIONAL LAW. 1972. a. price varies. National Organization on Legal Problems of Education, 3601 S.W. 29th, Ste. 223, Topeka, KS 66614. TEL 913-273-3550. circ. 3,000. (also avail. in microform from UMI) Indexed: Educ.Ind.
—BLDSC shelfmark: 9411.677000.
Formerly: Yearbook of School Law.

YEARBOOK OF EUROPEAN STUDIES/ANNUAIRE D'ETUDES EUROPEENNES. see POLITICAL SCIENCE — International Relations

YEARBOOK OF LAW COMPUTERS AND TECHNOLOGY. see LAW — Computer Applications

YEARBOOK OF MARYLAND LEGISLATORS. see POLITICAL SCIENCE

YOU AND THE LAW; executive guide to legal problems. see BUSINESS AND ECONOMICS — Small Business

343   CN
YOUNG OFFENDERS SERVICE. q. Can.$355. Butterworths Canada Ltd., 75 Clegg Rd., Markham, Ont. L6G 1A1, Canada. TEL 416-479-2665. FAX 416-479-2826. Eds. Roman Komar, Priscilla Platt. (looseleaf format)
Description: Updates all judicial and statutory developments pertaining to youthful offenders.

340   US   ISSN 0882-8520
KF3731.A3
YOUTH LAW NEWS. 1982. bi-m. $40 to individuals; institutions $95. National Center for Youth Law, 114 Sansome St., Ste. 900, San Francisco, CA 94104. TEL 415-543-3307. Ed. Marcia Henry. bk.rev.; cum.index: 1982-1987; circ. 4,700. (back issues avail.)
Description: Provides current information to attorneys and other youth-serving professionals about legal issues affecting low-income children and youth.

340   YU   ISSN 0350-2252
K29
YUGOSLAV LAW/DROIT YOUGOSLAVE. (Text in English and French) 1975. 3/yr. $30. (Union of Jurists Associations of Yugoslavia) Institut za Uporedno Pravo, Belgrade, Terazije 41, 11000 Belgrade, Yugoslavia. Ed. Vladimir Jovanovic. bibl.; circ. 900. Indexed: P.A.I.S.
—BLDSC shelfmark: 9421.659600.
Formerly: New Yugoslav Law (ISSN 0028-7946)
Description: Contemporary issues, constitutional courts of justice and surveys of legislation in Yugoslavian law.

340   IO   ISSN 0215-840X
YURIDIKA; Majalah Fakultas Hukum Universitas Airlangga. (Text in English and Indonesian) 1981. bi-m. Rps.1750. Universitas Airlangga, Fakultas Hukum, Jalan Darmawangsa Dalam Selatan, Surabaya 60286, Indonesia. TEL 031-41228. (Subscr. to: Sari Agung PT, Jl. Tunjungan 5, Surabaya, Indonesia) Ed. S.S. Rangkuti. adv.; bk.rev.; circ. 750.
Formerly: Majalah Fakultas Hukum Universitas Airlangga.

Z F A. (Zeitschrift fuer Arbeitsrecht) see BUSINESS AND ECONOMICS — Labor And Industrial Relations

340   640   GW   ISSN 0342-3476
K30
Z L R - ZEITSCHRIFT FUER DAS GESAMTE LEBENSMITTELRECHT. 1974. q. DM.310 (foreign DM.322). Deutscher Fachverlag GmbH, Mainzer Landstr. 251, Postfach 100606, 6000 Frankfurt a.M. 1, Germany. Ed. Sabine Klamroth. circ. 800.

328.675   ZR
ZAIRE. CONSEIL LEGISLATIF NATIONAL. COMPTE RENDU ANALYTIQUE. 1972. irreg. Conseil Legislatif National, Kinshasa, Zaire.
Formerly: Zaire. Assemblee Nationale. Compte Rendu Analytique.

345.01   ZA
ZAMBIA. DEPARTMENT OF LEGAL AID. ANNUAL REPORT. (Text in English) a. K.30. Government Printer, Box 30136, Lusaka, Zambia.
Description: Covers legal aid for civil cases in the High Courts and Subordinate Courts of Zambia.

340   ZA
ZAMBIA. HIGH COURT. LAW DIRECTORY AND LEGAL CALENDAR. (Text in English) a. Government Printer, Box 30136, Lusaka, Zambia.
Description: Directory of barristers and judges in Zambia.

340   ZA
ZAMBIA LAW JOURNAL. (Text in English) 1969. a. K.100($15) University of Zambia, School of Law, P.O. Box 32379, Lusaka, Zambia. FAX 260-1-253952. TELEX 44370 UNZALU ZA. (Subscr. to: Dr. A. Milner, Law Reports International, Trinity College, Oxford OX1 3BH, England) Ed. Ngosa R. Simbyakula. adv.; bk.rev.; bibl.; circ. 300 (controlled).
Description: Articles on legal issues with particular reference to Africa. Occasional legislative and case commentaries.

348   ZA
ZAMBIA LAW REPORTS. 1963. a. K.15. Council of Law Reporting, Box 50067, Lusaka, Zambia. Ed. Margaret S. Sekaggya. cum.index; circ. 500.

340   SZ   ISSN 0044-2127
ZEITSCHRIFT DES BERNISCHEN JURISTENVEREINS. (Text in French and German) 1865. m. 65 Fr. Staempfli und Cie AG, Postfach, CH-3001 Berne, Switzerland. FAX 031-276699. TELEX 911987. Ed. Heinz Hausheer. adv.; bk.rev.; bibl.; charts; index; circ. 4,500.
—BLDSC shelfmark: 9441.850000.

347.9   AU   ISSN 0044-2321
ZEITSCHRIFT FUER ARBEITSRECHT UND SOZIALRECHT. 1966. bi-m. S.450. (Bundeskammer der Gewerblichen Wirtschaft) Manzsche Verlags- und Universitaetsbuchhandlung, Kohlmarkt 16, A-1014 Vienna, Austria. TEL 0222-531610. FAX 0222-5316181. Ed. Theodor Tomandl. bk.rev.; charts; index; circ. 2,700. (also avail. in microfilm; microfiche)
—BLDSC shelfmark: 9452.030000.
Description: Examines labor and social law.

340   GW   ISSN 0721-5746
ZEITSCHRIFT FUER AUSLAENDERRECHT UND AUSLAENDERPOLITIK. Short title: Z A R. q. DM.69. Nomos Verlagsgesellschaft mbH und Co. KG, Waldseestr. 3-5, D-7570 Baden-Baden, Germany. TEL 07221-2104-0. FAX 07221-210427. TELEX 051-93524. circ. 2,000.
—BLDSC shelfmark: 9426.775000.

347.9   GW   ISSN 0930-861X
ZEITSCHRIFT FUER AUSLAENDISCHES UND INTERNATIONALES ARBEITS- UND SOZIALRECHT. q. DM.260. C.F. Mueller Juristischer Verlag GmbH, Im Weiher 10, Postfach 102640, 6900 Heidelberg 1, Germany. TEL 06221-489281.
FAX 06221-489279. TELEX 461727-HUEHD-D.

340   351.1   GW   ISSN 0514-2571
ZEITSCHRIFT FUER BEAMTENRECHT. 1953. m. DM.158. W. Kohlhammer GmbH, Hessbruehlstr. 69, Postfach 800430, 7000 Stuttgart 80, Germany. TEL 0711-7863-1.

340   GW
ZEITSCHRIFT FUER BERGRECHT. 1860. q. Carl Heymanns Verlag KG, Luxemburgerstr. 449, 5000 Cologne 41, Germany. TEL 0221-46010-0. FAX 0221-46010-69.

340   GW   ISSN 0044-2410
ZEITSCHRIFT FUER DAS GESAMTE FAMILIENRECHT; Ehe und Familie im privaten und oeffentlichen Recht. 1954. m. DM.106.80. Gieseking-Verlag, Deckertstr. 2, 4813 Bielefeld-Bethel, Germany. Ed. F.W. Bosch. bk.rev.; bibl.; index; circ. 2,000. (tabloid format; reprint service avail. from SCH)
—BLDSC shelfmark: 9462.803000.

340   GW   ISSN 0044-2437
ZEITSCHRIFT FUER DAS GESAMTE HANDELSRECHT UND WIRTSCHAFTSRECHT. 1858. bi-m. DM.255. Verlag Recht und Wirtschaft GmbH, Haeusserstr. 14, Postfach 105960, 6900 Heidelberg 1, Germany. TEL 06221-906-1. Eds. K. Schmidt, P. Ulmer. adv.; bk.rev.; index per vol.; circ. 1,750. Indexed: SCIMP (1991-).

347.016   GW
ZEITSCHRIFT FUER DAS NOTARIAT IN BADEN-WUERTTEMBERG. m. Wuertt. Notaverein e.V., Kronenstr. 34, 7000 Stuttgart 1, Germany.

340   336   GW   ISSN 0044-247X
ZEITSCHRIFT FUER DEN LASTENAUSGLEICH. 1953. q. DM.60. Verlag Otto Schwartz und Co., Annastr. 7, 3400 Goettingen, Germany. TEL 0551-31051. FAX 0551-372812. Ed. Karl-Heinz Bernotat. adv.; bk.rev.; index.

343   GW   ISSN 0084-5310
K30
ZEITSCHRIFT FUER DIE GESAMTE STRAFRECHTSWISSENSCHAFT. 1881. 4/yr. $192. Walter de Gruyter und Co., Genthiner Str. 13, 1000 Berlin 30, Germany. TEL 030-26005-0. FAX 030-26005251. TELEX 184027. (U.S. addr.: Walter de Gruyter, Inc., 200 Saw Mill Rd., Hawthorne, NY 10532) Ed.Bd. adv.; bk.rev.; bibl.; index.

ZEITSCHRIFT FUER EVANGELISCHES KIRCHENRECHT. see RELIGIONS AND THEOLOGY — Protestant

340   GW   ISSN 0179-4051
K30
ZEITSCHRIFT FUER GESETZGEBUNG; Vierteljahresschrift fuer staatliche und kommunale Rechtsetzung. 1986. q. DM.194. C.H. Beck'sche Verlagsbuchhandlung, Wilhelmstr. 9, 8000 Munich 40, Germany. TEL 089-38189-338. FAX 089-38189-398. TELEX 5215085-BECK-D. Ed. J. Hensen. circ. 600.

ZEITSCHRIFT FUER MIET- UND RAUMRECHT. see REAL ESTATE

340   AU   ISSN 0250-6459
K30
ZEITSCHRIFT FUER NEUERE RECHTSGESCHICHTE. 1979. q. S.835. Manzsche Verlags- und Universitaetsbuchhandlung, Kohlmarkt 16, A-1014 Vienna, Austria. TEL 0222-531610. FAX 0222-5316181. Ed. Wilhelm Brauneder. circ. 800.

340   GW   ISSN 0514-6496
ZEITSCHRIFT FUER RECHTSPOLITIK. (Supplement to: Neue Juristische Wochenschrift) 1968. m. DM.83. C.H. Beck'sche Verlagsbuchhandlung, Wilhelmstr. 9, 8000 Munich 40, Germany. TEL 089-38189-338. FAX 089-38189-398. TELEX 5215085-BECK-D. Eds. R. Gerhardt, M. Kriele. circ. 56,700. Indexed: Refug.Abstr.

ZEITSCHRIFT FUER RECHTSSOZIOLOGIE. see SOCIOLOGY

340   AU
ZEITSCHRIFT FUER RECHTSVERGLEICHUNG, INTERNATIONALES PRIVATRECHT UND EUROPARECHT. 1960. bi-m. S.1470. (Universitaet Wien, Institut fuer Rechtsvergleichung) Manzsche Verlags- und Universitaetsbuchhandlung, Kohlmarkt 16, A-1014 Vienna, Austria. TEL 0222-531610. FAX 0222-5316181. (Co-sponsor: Oesterreichische Gesellschaft fuer Rechtsvergleichung) Ed.Bd. bk.rev.; circ. 800. (back issues avail.) Indexed: CERDIC.
Formerly: Zeitschrift fuer Rechtsvergleichung (ISSN 0514-275X)
Description: Covers comparative law; includes reports and judgements.

LAW — ABSTRACTING, BIBLIOGRAPHIES, STATISTICS

340   GW   ISSN 0173-0568
KK1610.A13
ZEITSCHRIFT FUER SCHADENSRECHT; monatliches Fachblatt fuer Schadens-, Versicherungs- und Verkehrsstrafrecht. Short title: Z F S. 1980. m. DM.198. Deutscher Anwaltverlag Gmbh, Bocholder Str. 259, 4300 Essen, Germany.
TEL 0201-611114. (back issues avail.)

340   SZ   ISSN 0254-945X
ZEITSCHRIFT FUER SCHWEIZERISCHES RECHT/REVUE DE DROIT SUISSE. (Text in German and French) 1860. 11/yr. 165 Fr. Helbing und Lichtenhahn Verlag AG, Freie Str. 82, CH-4051 Basel, Switzerland. TEL 064-268626. FAX 064-268626. TELEX 981195-SAG-CH. (Subscr. to: Sauerlaender AG, Postfach, CH-5001 Aarau, Switzerland) Ed.Bd. bk.rev.; index, cum.index every 10 yrs.

ZEITSCHRIFT FUER STRAFVOLLZUG UND STRAFFAELLIGENHILFE. see *CRIMINOLOGY AND LAW ENFORCEMENT*

340   GW   ISSN 0340-2479
ZEITSCHRIFT FUER UNTERNEHMENS- UND GESELLSCHAFTSRECHT. 1972. 4/yr. $157 (bound ed. $198). Walter de Gruyter und Co., Genthiner Str. 13, 1000 Berlin 30, Germany.
TEL 030-26005-0. FAX 030-26005251. TELEX 184027. (U.S. addr.: Walter de Gruyter, Inc., 200 Saw Mill Rd., Hawthorne, NY 10532) Ed.Bd. circ. 1,400. (back issues avail.)
—BLDSC shelfmark: 9487.470000.

340   GW
ZEITSCHRIFT FUER URHEBER- UND MEDIENRECHT; Film und Recht. 1957. m. DM.293. Institut fuer Urheber- und Medienrecht, Widenmayerstr. 32, 8000 Munich 22, Germany. TEL 089-2913474.
FAX 089-2913474. Dir. Manfred Rehbinder. adv.; bk.rev.; abstr.; bibl.; index.
Formerly: Film und Recht (ISSN 0015-1440)

340   AU   ISSN 0044-3662
ZEITSCHRIFT FUER VERKEHRSRECHT. (Includes irreg. supplement: Gesamtregister mit den Rechtssaetzen und Fundstellen der Zeitschrift fuer Verkehrsrecht) 1956. m. S.990. Manzsche Verlags- und Universitaetsbuchhandlung, Kohlmarkt 16, A-1014 Vienna, Austria. TEL 0222-531610.
FAX 0222-5316181. Ed. Robert Dittrich. adv.; bk.rev.; index; circ. 2,800. (also avail. in microfiche; microfilm)
—BLDSC shelfmark: 9488.600000.
Description: Covers traffic law, including treaties and judgments.

ZEITSCHRIFT FUER WASSERRECHT. see *WATER RESOURCES*

340 332   GW   ISSN 0723-9416
K9
ZEITSCHRIFT FUER WIRTSCHAFTSRECHT - Z I P. 1980. s-m. DM.558. Verlag Kommunikationsforum GmbH Recht Wirtschaft Steuern, Aachener Str. 217, 5000 Cologne 41, Germany. TEL 0221-40088-0.
FAX 0221-4008828. Ed. Bruno M. Kuebler. adv.; bk.rev. (back issues avail.)

340   GW   ISSN 0342-3468
ZEITSCHRIFT FUER ZIVILPROZESS. q. DM.192. Carl Heymanns Verlag KG, Luxemburgerstr. 449, 5000 Cologne 41, Germany. TEL 0221-46010-0.
FAX 0221-46010-69. adv.; bk.rev. (back issues avail.)

ZENTRALBLATT FUER JUGENDRECHT; Jugend und Familie - Jugendhilfe - Jugendgerichtshilfe. see *CHILDREN AND YOUTH — About*

ZENTRALBLATT FUER SOZIALVERSICHERUNG, SOZIALHILFE UND VERSORGUNG; Zeitschrift fuer das Recht der Sozialen Sicherheit. see *POLITICAL SCIENCE*

340   CC   ISSN 1000-0208
ZHENGFA LUNTAN/POLITICAL SCIENCE & LAW TRIBUNE; zhongguo zhengfa daxue xuebao. (Text in Chinese) bi-m. $30.60. Zhongguo Zhengfa Daxue, Zhengfa Luntan Bianjibu - China University of Political Science and Law, 41 Xueyuan Lu, Beijing 100088, People's Republic of China. TEL 2015577. (Dist. in US by: China Books & Periodicals, Inc., 2929 24th St., San Francisco, CA 94110. TEL 415-282-0994) Ed. Gao Chao.

340 320   CC
ZHENGZHI YU FALU/POLITICS AND LAW. (Text in Chinese) bi-m. Shanghai Shehui Kexueyuan, Faxue Yanjiusuo - Shanghai Academy of Social Sciences, Institute of Law, No.7, Alley 622, Huaihai Zhonglu, Shanghai 200020, People's Republic of China.
TEL 3271170. Ed. Qi Naikuan.

340   CC
ZHONGGUO FALU NIANJIAN/CHINA LAW YEARBOOK. (Text in Chinese) a. Zhongguo Faxuehui, Zhongguo Falu Nianjian Bianjibu, No. 23, Fuxing Lu, Beijing 100036, People's Republic of China. TEL 8317547. Ed. Gan Zhongdou.

340   CC
ZHONGGUO FAXUE/JURISPRUDENCE IN CHINA. (Text in Chinese) bi-m. $54. Zhongguo Faxuehui - China Jurisprudence Society, 23 Fuxing Lu, Haidian Qu, Beijing 100036, People's Republic of China.
TEL 447471. (Dist. in US by: China Books & Periodicals, Inc., 2929 24th St., San Francisco, CA 94110. TEL 415-282-2994) Ed. Song Shutao.

340   US
ZHONGGUO LUSHI/CHINESE LAWYERS. (Text in Chinese) bi-m. $20.70. China Books & Periodicals, Inc., 2929 24th St., San Francisco, CA 94110.
TEL 415-292-2994. FAX 415-282-0994.

ZHONGHUA RENMIN GONGHEGUO. ZUIGAO RENMIN JIANCHAYUAN GONGBAO/CHINA, PEOPLE'S REPUBLIC. SUPREME PEOPLE'S PROCURATE POST. see *PUBLIC ADMINISTRATION*

340   US
ZHONGHUA RENMIN GONGHEGUO ZUIGAO RENMIN FAYUAN GONGBAO/CHINA, PEOPLE'S REPUBLIC. PEOPLE'S SUPREME COURT. BULLETIN. (Text in Chinese) irreg. $9.80. (Zuigao Renmin Fayuan, CC) China Books & Periodicals, Inc., 2929 24th St., San Francisco, CA 94110. TEL 415-282-2994.
FAX 415-282-0994.

340   CC   ISSN 1000-5234
ZHONGNAN ZHENGFA XUEYUAN XUEBAO. (Text in Chinese) q. Zhongnan Zhengfa Xueyuan, No. 1, Zhengyuan Lu, Wuchang-qu, Wuhan, Hubei 430074, People's Republic of China. TEL 703001. Ed. Ding Huanchun.

340   RH
ZIMBABWE LAW REVIEW. 1985. a. Z.$40. University of Zimbabwe, Department of Law, Box MP 167, Harare, Zimbabwe. Ed. R.H.F. Austin. adv.; bk.rev.; circ. 600.

340   US   ISSN 0514-7905
LAW
ZONING BULLETIN.* 1954. m. $39.05. Quinlan Publishing Co., Inc., 23 Drydock Ave., 2nd Fl., Boston, MA 02210-2307. Ed. M. Quinlan. index. (looseleaf format; back issues avail.)

340   US   ISSN 0892-7308
KF112 11th.1
11TH CIRCUIT LAW LETTER. 1987. 26/yr. $157. M. Lee Smith Publishers & Printers, 162 Fourth Ave. N., Box 2678, Nashville, TN 37219.
TEL 615-242-7395. Ed. Elizabeth Lane. index.
Description: Summarizes all opinions of the 11th Circuit Court of Appeals.

LAW — Abstracting, Bibliographies, Statistics

A B C POL SCI; a bibliography of contents: political science and government. see *POLITICAL SCIENCE — Abstracting, Bibliographies, Statistics*

ABSTRACTS OF BULGARIAN SCIENTIFIC LITERATURE. ECONOMICS AND LAW. see *BUSINESS AND ECONOMICS — Abstracting, Bibliographies, Statistics*

347.788   US   ISSN 0094-7504
KFC1871
ANNUAL STATISTICAL REPORT OF THE COLORADO JUDICIARY. 1970. a. $7. State Judicial Department, Office of the Court Administrator, 1301 Pennsylvania St., No.300, Denver, CO 80203-2416. FAX 303-831-1814. Ed.Bd. circ. 1,100.

340   IT
ANNUARIO DI STATISTICHE GIUDIZIARIE - TOMO 2. a. L.38000. Istituto Centrale di Statistica, Via Cesare Balbo 16, 00100 Rome, Italy.

340 016   GW   ISSN 0300-0990
ARBEITSGEMEINSCHAFT FUER JURISTISCHES BIBLIOTHEKS- UND DOKUMENTATIONSWESEN. MITTEILUNGEN. 1971. 3/yr. DM.30. Arbeitsgemeinschaft fuer Juristisches Bibliotheks- und Dokumentationswesen, Memmingerstr. 6, 8900 Augsburg, Germany. Ed. Burkard Meyer. adv.; bk.rev.; index; circ. 350. Key Title: Mitteilungen der Arbeitsgemeinschaft fuer Juristisches Bibliotheks- und Dokumentationswesen.

346.066   AT
▼**AUSTRALIAN INDUSTRIAL LAW INDEX.** (Previously included in: Australian Labour Law Reporter) 1991. q. C C H Australian Ltd., P.O. Box 230, North Ryde, N.S.W. 2113, Australia. TEL 02-888-2555.
FAX 02-888-7324.
Description: Includes an alphabetical listing of subjects, an inventory of principles, precedents and sources in the field of industrial relations law and practice.

340   AU
AUSTRIA. STATISTISCHES ZENTRALAMT. STATISTIK DER RECHTSPFLEGE. a. S.380. Oesterreichische Staatsdruckerei, Rennweg 120, 1037 Vienna, Austria. TEL 0222-787631.

340   BE
BELGIUM. INSTITUT NATIONAL DE STATISTIQUE. STATISTIQUES JUDICIAIRES. irreg., no.5, 1989. 290 Fr. (foreign 690 Fr.). Institut National de Statistique, 44 rue de Louvain, B-1000 Brussels, Belgium. TEL 02-513-96-50. Indexed: P.A.I.S.For.Lang.Ind.
Incorporates: Statistique Criminelle de la Belgique; Which was formerly (until 1944): Statistique Judiciaire de la Belgique (ISSN 0081-5268)

340 016   US   ISSN 0360-2745
K38
BIBLIOGRAPHIC GUIDE TO LAW. 1975. a. $295 cloth (foreign $325). G.K. Hall & Co., 70 Lincoln St., Boston, MA 02111. TEL 617-423-3990.
FAX 617-423-3999. TELEX 94-0037.
Formerly: Law Book Guide (ISSN 0146-3861)
Description: Covers all aspects of law.

349 016   SZ
BIBLIOGRAPHIE DES SCHWEIZERISCHEN RECHTS. (Text in French, German, Italian) a. price varies. Helbing und Lichtenhahn Verlag AG, Freie Str. 82, CH-4051 Basel, Switzerland. (Subscr. to: Sauerlaender AG, Postfach, CH-5001 Aarau, Switzerland) bibl.; index, cum.index every 5 yrs.

340 016   FR
BIBLIOGRAPHIE EN LANGUE FRANCAISE D'HISTOIRE DU DROIT DE 987 A 1914. vol.13, 1975. a. (since 1962). price varies. Centre National de la Recherche Scientifique, c/o Mme. Boulet-Sautel, Universite de Paris II (Universite de Droit d'Economie et des Sciences Social), 12 pl. du Pantheon, 75005 Paris, France. Ed.Bd.
Formerly (until 1945): Bibliographie en la Langue Francaise d'Histoire du Droit de 987 a 1875 (ISSN 0067-6985)

340 016   GW
BIBLIOGRAPHIE RECHTSWISSENSCHAFT. 1963. s-m. DM.12. Hochschule fuer Recht und Verwaltung, Informationszentrum, August-Bebel-Str. 89, 1590 Potsdam, Germany. circ. 300.
Former titles: Bibliographie Staat und Recht; (until 1972): Rechtswissenschaftliche Dokumentation (ISSN 0138-1385)

340 320   US   ISSN 0742-6909
BIBLIOGRAPHIES AND INDEXES IN LAW AND POLITICAL SCIENCE. 1984. irreg., no.15, 1992. price varies. Greenwood Press, Inc. (Subsidiary of: Greenwood Publishing Group Inc.), 88 Post Rd. W., Box 5007, Westport, CT 06881-5007. TEL 203-226-3571. FAX 203-222-1502.

LAW — ABSTRACTING, BIBLIOGRAPHIES, STATISTICS

016   US   ISSN 0067-7329
K38
BIBLIOGRAPHY ON FOREIGN AND COMPARATIVE LAW: BOOKS AND ARTICLES IN ENGLISH. 1953. quinquennial with a. supplements. price varies. (Columbia University, Parker School of Foreign and Comparative Law) Oceana Publications, Inc., Dobbs Ferry, NY 10522. TEL 914-693-1320. FAX 914-693-0402. Ed. Vratislav Pechota. circ. 500.
   Description: Bibliography of books and articles in English that focus on foreign and comparative law.

340 011   BL   ISSN 0006-1662
BIBLIOTECA DO SEJUR. BOLETIM. (Text in Portuguese; summaries in English, French, Italian, Portuguese and Spanish) 1966. q. free. Petroleo Brasileiro S.A., Servico Juridico, Av. Republica do Chile, 65 S-2056, 20035 Rio de Janeiro, Brazil. (processed)

340   US   ISSN 0882-7052
BIO-BIBLIOGRAPHIES IN LAW AND POLITICAL SCIENCE. 1985. irreg. price varies. Greenwood Press, Inc. (Subsidiary of: Greenwood Publishing Group Inc.), 88 Post Rd. W., Box 5007, Westport, CT 06881-5007. TEL 203-226-3571. FAX 203-222-1502.

BIOETHICS LITERATURE REVIEW. see *MEDICAL SCIENCES — Abstracting, Bibliographies, Statistics*

BOWKER'S LAW BOOKS AND SERIALS IN PRINT; a multimedia sourcebook. see *BUSINESS AND ECONOMICS — Trade And Industrial Directories*

340 016   US   ISSN 0000-1031
KF1
BOWKER'S LAW BOOKS AND SERIALS IN PRINT SUPPLEMENT; materials on law and law related topics recently published and to be published. 1983. 3/yr. (avail. only with Bowker's Law Books and Serials in Print). R.R. Bowker, A Reed Reference Publishing Company, Division of Reed Publishing (USA) Inc., 121 Chanlon Rd., New Providence, NJ 07974. TEL 800-521-8110. FAX 908-665-6688. TELEX 138 755. (Subscr. to: Order Dept., Box 31, New Providence, NJ 07974)
   Former titles: Bowker's Law Books and Serials in Print Update (ISSN 0000-0760); Law Information Update (ISSN 0000-0728)
   Description: Lists new books and serials information received after publication of base volume. Cumulates previous issues. Books indexed by subject, author and title; includes publisher information.

C A SELECTS. FOOD, DRUGS, & COSMETICS - LEGISLATIVE & REGULATORY ASPECTS. see *FOOD AND FOOD INDUSTRIES — Abstracting, Bibliographies, Statistics*

CANADIAN INCOME TAX RESEARCH INDEX. see *BUSINESS AND ECONOMICS — Abstracting, Bibliographies, Statistics*

347.9   UK
CASE SEARCH MONTHLY. m. £200. Sweet & Maxwell, European Law Centre, South Quay Plaza, 183 Marsh Wall, London E14 9FT, England. TEL 0264-332424. (Subscr. to: c/o ITPS, North Way, Andover, Hampshire SP10 5BE, England) Ed. Neville March Hunnings.
   Description: Provides a running index of the case law of the European Court of Justice.

340   US   ISSN 0000-1058
KF70.A34
CODE OF FEDERAL REGULATIONS INDEX. 1988. a. $595. R.R. Bowker, A Reed Reference Publishing Company, Division of Reed Publishing (USA) Inc., 121 Chanlon Rd., New Providence, NJ 07974. TEL 800-521-8110. FAX 908-665-6688. TELEX 138 755. (Subscr. to: Order Dept., Box 31, New Providence, NJ 07974) Ed. Lucille Boorstein.
   Description: Organizes and cross-references CFR subjects by title and by subject.

341   US   ISSN 0886-6724
COLLECTION OF BIBLIOGRAPHIC AND RESEARCH RESOURCES. 1984. irreg. price varies. Oceana Publications, Inc., 75 Main St., Dobbs Ferry, NY 10522. TEL 914-693-1320. FAX 914-693-0402. Ed.Bd. circ. 150. (back issues avail.)
   Description: A series of bibliographies, primarily in international law and relations.

340 011   US
▼**COMPREHENSIVE INDEX TO OREGON STATUTES (YEAR).** (Suppl. to: Oregon Revised Statutes Annotated) 1991. biennial. $90. Butterworth Legal Publishers (Salem) (Subsidiary of: Reed International PLC), 90 Stiles Rd., Salem, NH 03079. TEL 800-548-4001. FAX 603-898-9858. Ed.Bd.

340   US
CONGRESSIONAL INDEX. 2 biennial vols. plus w. updates during session. $785. Commerce Clearing House, Inc., 4025 W. Peterson Ave., Chicago, IL 60646. TEL 312-583-8500.

340 016   FR
COUNCIL OF EUROPE. DOCUMENTATION SECTION. BIBLIO BULLETIN. SERIES: LEGAL AFFAIRS.. 1973. m. free. Council of Europe, Documentation Section, BP 431 R6, 67006 Strasbourg, France. TEL 88-41-20-00. FAX 88-36-70-57. TELEX EUR 870 943F. (Dist. in U.S. by: Manhattan Publishing Co., 225 Lafayette St., New York, NY 10012) circ. 250.
   Former titles: Council of Europe. Central Library. Biblio Bulletin. Series: Legal Affaires; Council of Europe. Documentation Section and Library. Bibliographical Bulletin. Series: Legal Affairs.
   Description: Index of periodical articles on law, lawyers and human rights.

016 340   AT   ISSN 0310-5415
CURRENT AUSTRALIAN AND NEW ZEALAND LEGAL LITERATURE INDEX. 1973. q. Law Book Co. Ltd., 44-50 Waterloo Rd., North Ryde, N.S.W. 2112, Australia. TEL 02-887-0177. FAX 02-888-9706. TELEX ASBOOK 27995. Ed. Gwenda Fischer. abstr.; bibl.
   Description: Contains notes, comments, reports published in Australian and New Zealand legal periodicals.

340   US   ISSN 0196-1780
K33
CURRENT LAW INDEX; multiple access to legal periodicals. m. (plus 3 q. and 1 a. cumulations). $395. Information Access Company, 362 Lakeside Dr., Foster City, CA 94404. TEL 800-227-8431. FAX 415-378-5499. (Co-sponsor: American Association of Law Libraries) Cheryl Ann Toliver.
   ●Also available online. Vendor(s): BRS, DIALOG, Mead Data Central, WESTLAW.
   Description: Timely guide to the legal periodicals of the United States, Canada, the UK, Australia and New Zealand.

340 016   US   ISSN 0011-3859
CURRENT PUBLICATIONS IN LEGAL AND RELATED FIELDS. 1953. m. (except June, July & Sep.; plus a. cum.). $125. (American Association of Law Libraries) Fred B. Rothman & Co., 10368 W. Centennial Rd., Littleton, CO 80127. TEL 303-979-5657. FAX 303-978-1457. index; circ. 500. (back issues avail.)

341.2   US   ISSN 0731-8189
JX236.5
CURRENT TREATY INDEX; a cumulative index to the United States slip treaties and agreements. 1982. s-a. $49.50. William S. Hein & Co., Inc., 1285 Main St., Buffalo, NY 14209. TEL 800-828-7571. FAX 716-883-8100. TELEX 91-209 WU 7 HEIN BUF. Eds. Igor I. Kavass, Adolf Sprudzs. circ. 400.
   Incorporates (in 1990): United States International Treaties Today; Which was formerly: Unpublished and Unnumbered Treaties Index (ISSN 0894-1564)

340   KU
DALIL AL-KUWAIT AL-YAWM. (Text in Arabic) 1975. a. K.3.50. Kuwait Information and Microfilm Centre, Ministry of Planning, P.O. Box 15 - Safat, 13001 Safat, Kuwait. TEL 965-24 20 331. FAX 00965-2430583. TELEX 22468 TAKHTEET. Ed. Abdulaziz A. Al-Askar. circ. 1,000. (also avail. in microfiche; back issues avail.)
   Description: An abstracting and indexing service to Kuwait Official Gazette. Provides a brief abstract, publishing and microfilming data of Kuwait laws, decrees and ministerial issues.

340   UK
DIGEST; annotated British, Commonwealth and European cases. 1919. 6/yr. £700($1232) Butterworth & Co. (Publishers) Ltd. (Subsidiary of: Reed International PLC), 88 Kingsway, London WC2B 6AB, England. TEL 71-405-6900. FAX 71-405-1332. TELEX 95678. (US addr.: Butterworth Legal Publishers, 90 Stiles Rd., Salem, NH 03079. TEL 800-548-4001) Ed. Peter Stickland. index, cum.index. (back issues avail.)
   Description: Digested case law with over 350,000 legal cases. All legal subjects covered with full annotations.

347.9   IT   ISSN 0419-4632
DIZIONARIO BIBLIOGRAFICO DELLE RIVISTE GIURIDICHE ITALIANE. 1956. a. price varies. Casa Editrice Dott. A. Giuffre, Via B. Arsizio 40, 20151 Milan, Italy. TEL 02-38000905. FAX 02-38009582. Ed. Vincenzo Napoletano.

665.5 016   BL   ISSN 0013-662X
EMENTARIO DA LEGISLACAO DO PETROLEO. 1968. s-a. free. Petroleo Brasileiro S.A., Servico Juridico, Setor de Documentacao, Av. Republica do Chile, 65 S-2056, 20035 Rio de Janeiro, Brazil. (processed)

318   PN   ISSN 0378-259X
HV7322   ●
ESTADISTICA PANAMENA. SITUACION POLITICA, ADMINISTRATIVA Y JUSTICIA. SECCION 631. JUSTICIA. 1964. a. Bl.0.75. Direccion de Estadistica y Censo, Contraloria General, Apartado 5213, Panama 5, Panama. FAX 63-9322. circ. 1,000.

340 016   FR   ISSN 0252-0648
LAW
EXCHANGE OF INFORMATION ON RESEARCH IN EUROPEAN LAW/ECHANGE D'INFORMATIONS SUR LES RECHERCHES EN DROIT EUROPEEN. (Text in English, French) 1971. a. $6. Council of Europe, Directorate of Legal Affairs - Conseil de l'Europe, Publications Section, 67006 Strasbourg, France. (Dist. in U.S. by: Manhattan Publishing Co., 80 Brook St., Box 650, Croton, NY 10520)
   —BLDSC shelfmark: 3836.199500.

331 340   GW   ISSN 0173-1688
FUNDHEFT FUER ARBEITS- UND SOZIALRECHT; systematischer Nachweis der deutschen Rechtsprechung, Zeitschriftenaufsaetze und selbstaendigen Schriften. 1945. a. price varies. C.H. Beck'sche Verlagsbuchhandlung, Wilhelmstr. 9, 8000 Munich 40, Germany. TEL 089-38189-338. FAX 089-38189-398. TELEX 5215085-BECK-D. Ed. Wolfgang Blomeyer. circ. 1,600.
   Formerly (until 1977): Fundheft fuer Arbeitsrecht (ISSN 0071-9900)

340 011   GW   ISSN 0071-9919
FUNDHEFT FUER OEFFENTLICHES RECHT; systematischer Nachweis der deutschen Rechtsprechung, Zeitschriftenaufsaetze und selbstaendigen Schriften. 1948. a. price varies. C.H. Beck'sche Verlagsbuchhandlung, Wilhelmstr. 9, 8000 Munich 40, Germany. TEL 089-38189-338. FAX 089-38189-398. TELEX 5215085-BECK-D. Ed. Otto Stroessenreuther. circ. 2,000.

340   GW   ISSN 0532-8632
FUNDHEFT FUER STEUERRECHT; Leitsaetze der Entscheidungen, Literaturuebersicht, Nachweis der Verwaltungsvorschriften. 1949. a. price varies. C.H. Beck'sche Verlagsbuchhandlung, Wilhelmstr. 9, D-8000 Munich 40, Germany. TEL 089-38189-1. circ. 2,400.

340 011   GW   ISSN 0071-9927
FUNDHEFT FUER ZIVILRECHT; systematischer Nachweis der deutschen Rechtsprechung und Zeitschriftenaufsaetze. 1948. a. price varies. C.H. Beck'sche Verlagsbuchhandlung, Wilhelmstr. 9, 8000 Munich 40, Germany. TEL 089-38189-338. FAX 089-38189-398. TELEX 5215085-BECK-D. Ed.Bd. circ. 2,800.

340   AU
GESAMTREGISTER MIT DEN RECHTSSAETZEN UND FUNDSTELLEN DER ENTSCHEIDUNGEN DER ZEITSCHRIFT FUER VERKEHRSRECHT. 1956. irreg. price varies. Manzsche Verlags- und Universitaetsbuchhandlung, Kohlmarkt 16, A-1014 Vienna, Austria. TEL 0222-531610. FAX 0222-5316181. Ed. Erika Veit. circ. 2,400.
   Description: Abstracts on traffic law.

LAW — ABSTRACTING, BIBLIOGRAPHIES, STATISTICS 2699

341.2   US   ISSN 0736-5713
JX236.5
GUIDE TO UNITED STATES TREATIES IN FORCE. 1982. s-a. $135. William S. Hein & Co., Inc., 1285 Main St., Buffalo, NY 14209. TEL 800-828-7571. FAX 716-883-8100. TELEX 91-209 WU 7 HEIN BUF. Eds. Igor I. Kavass, Adolf Sprudzs. circ. 400.
Description: Information on current treaties and other international acts published in slip form and not yet bound in the United States treaty index.

I C E L REFERENCES. (International Council on Environmental Law) see ENVIRONMENTAL STUDIES — Abstracting, Bibliographies, Statistics

341   UN
I C J BIBLIOGRAPHY. 1966. a. International Court of Justice, Peace Palace, 2517 KJ The Hague, Netherlands.

340   AU
INDEX DER RECHTSMITTELENTSCHEIDUNGEN UND DES SCHRIFTTUMS. 1947. a. price varies. Manzsche Verlags- und Universitaetsbuchhandlung, Kohlmarkt 16, A-1014 Vienna, Austria. TEL 0222-531610. FAX 0222-5316181. Ed. Rudolf Stohanzl. circ. 2,400.
Description: A general index of Austrian law.

340   CN   ISSN 0316-8891
LAW
INDEX TO CANADIAN LEGAL PERIODICAL LITERATURE. (Text in English and French) 1960. q. Can.$125. P.O. Box 386, N.D.G. Station, Montreal, Que. H4A 3P7, Canada. TEL 514-288-1893. bk.rev.; circ. 450.

340 016   CH   ISSN 0259-3793
INDEX TO CHINESE LEGAL PERIODICALS. 1963-1970; resumed 1972. a. $30. Soochow University, Library - Tung Wu Ta Hsueh T'u Shu Kuan, Wai Shuang Hsi, Taipei, Taiwan, Republic of China. FAX 886-02-8829310. (reprint service avail.) Key Title: Zhongwen Falu Lunwen Suoyin.

340 016   US   ISSN 0019-400X
LAW
INDEX TO FOREIGN LEGAL PERIODICALS. (Subject headings in English with translation into French, German and Spanish included in a. cumulation) 1960. q. (a. cumulations). $460 (foreign $472). (American Asscociation of Law Libraries, School of Law Library) University of California Press, Journals Division, 2120 Berkeley Way, Berkeley, CA 94720. TEL 510-642-4191. FAX 510-643-7127. Ed. T.H. Reynolds. index; circ. 600.
Description: Indexes legal and business periodicals from 59 countries. Includes legal essays.

340 016   II   ISSN 0019-4034
INDEX TO INDIAN LEGAL PERIODICALS. 1963. s-a. Rs.60. Indian Law Institute, Bhagwandass Rd., New Delhi 110001, India.

340 016   US   ISSN 0019-4077
K9
INDEX TO LEGAL PERIODICALS. 1908. m (plus q. & a. cum.). $210. H.W. Wilson Co., 950 University Ave., Bronx, NY 10452. TEL 800-367-6770. FAX 212-538-2716. TELEX 4990003HWILSON. Ed. Stephen Rosen. (also avail. in magnetic tape) Indexed: C.L.I.
●Also available online. Vendor(s): Mead Data Central, WESTLAW, Wilsonline (File ILP).
Also available on CD-ROM. Producer(s): H.W. Wilson (WILSONDISC).
—BLDSC shelfmark: 4380.800000.
Description: Author and subject index to legal periodicals published in the U.S., Canada, Great Britain, Ireland, Australia, and New Zealand. Includes a table of cases under both the plaintiff's and the defendant's name and a table of statutes by jurisdiction.

340 016   US   ISSN 0019-4093
INDEX TO PERIODICAL ARTICLES RELATED TO LAW. 1958. a. $65. Glanville Publishers, Inc., 75 Main St., Dobbs Ferry, NY 10522. TEL 914-693-5956. FAX 914-693-0402. Eds. Roy M. Mersky, J. Myron Jacobstein. cum.index: 1958-1988; circ. 250.
—BLDSC shelfmark: 4385.210000.
Description: Provides bibliographic information on law-related periodical articles not included in Current Law Index, Index to Foreign Legal Periodicals, Index to Legal Periodicals, Legal Resource Index or Legaltrac.

340   SP   ISSN 0213-4683
INDICE ESPANOL DE CIENCIAS SOCIALES. SERIES C: LAW. 1979. a. 5000 ptas. or exchange basis. Instituto de Informacion y Documentacion en Ciencias Sociales y Humanidades, Pinar, 25, 3, 28006 Madrid, Spain.
●Also available online.
Also available on CD-ROM.
Supersedes in part (in 1982): Indice Espanol de Ciencias Sociales (ISSN 0213-019X)

340 010   SP
INSTITUTO INTERNACIONAL DE HISTORIA DEL DERECHO INDIANO. ACTAS Y ESTUDIOS. a. 1500 ptas. Instituto Nacional de Estudios Juridicos, Duque de Medinaceli St., No. 8, Madrid, Spain.

INSURANCE REGULATORY INFORMATION SYSTEM RATIO RESULTS. see INSURANCE — Abstracting, Bibliographies, Statistics

347.9   IS   ISSN 0075-1030
ISRAEL. CENTRAL BUREAU OF STATISTICS. JUDICIAL STATISTICS. (Subseries of its Special Series) (Text in English, Hebrew) 1951. irreg., no.748, 1983. price varies. Central Bureau of Statistics, Box 13015, Jerusalem 91 130, Israel. TEL 02-21 12 11.

340   IT   ISSN 0392-7571
ISTITUTO PER LA DOCUMENTAZIONE GIURIDICA. BIBLIOGRAFIA. DIRITTO CIVILE. 1979. a. L.23000. Giuffre Editore, Via Busto Arsizio 40, 20151 Milan, Italy. Ed. Mario Ragona. circ. 400.

340   IT
ISTITUTO PER LA DOCUMENTAZIONE GIURIDICA. BIBLIOGRAFIA. DIRITTO INTERNAZIONALE; rassegna automatica di dottrina giuridica. a. Istituto per la Documentazione Giuridica, Via Panciatichi, 56-16, 50127 Florence, Italy. (Subscr. to: Casa Editrice Giuffre, Via Statuto, 2, 20121 Milan, Italy) Ed.Bd.

340   IT
ITALY. ISTITUTO CENTRALE DI STATISTICA. STATISTICHE GIUDIZIARIE. 1949. a. L.38000. Istituto Centrale di Statistica, Via Cesare Balbo 16, 00100 Rome, Italy. circ. 1,050.
Formerly (until 1962): Italy. Istituto Centrale di Statistica. Annuario di Statistiche Giudiziario (ISSN 0075-1715)

347.9   CN   ISSN 0715-271X
JURISTAT. irreg. Can.$78($94) (foreign $109). Statistics Canada, Publications Division, Ottawa, Ont. K1A 0T6, Canada. TEL 613-951-7277. FAX 613-951-1584.
Description: Provides readers with timely and succinct statistical information on a variety of justice related programs.

340 016   GW
JURISTISCHE NEUERSCHEINUNGEN. 1923. bi-m. DM.30.60. Theodor Oppermann Verlag, Ostfeldstr. 46, Postfach 710140, 3000 Hannover 71, Germany. Ed. E.W. Hennies. adv.; bibl.; circ. 6,800.

JUSTITIELE VERKENNINGEN. see CRIMINOLOGY AND LAW ENFORCEMENT — Abstracting, Bibliographies, Statistics

340 314   GW
JUSTIZ IN ZAHLEN. 1980. a. Justizministerium NW Duesseldorf, Martin-Luther-Platz 40, 4000 Duesseldorf 1, Germany. FAX 0211-8792456. TELEX 2114184. circ. 10,000.
Description: Data and figures on the criminal justice system in the German state of Northrhine-Westfalia.

340 016   GW   ISSN 0453-3283
K11
KARLSRUHER JURISTISCHE BIBLIOGRAPHIE; systematischer Nachweis neuer Buecher und Aufsaetze in monatlicher Folge aus Recht, Staat, Gesellschaft. 1965. m. DM.408. C.H. Beck'sche Verlagsbuchhandlung, Wilhelmstr. 9, 8000 Munich 40, Germany. TEL 089-38189-338. FAX 089-38189-398. TELEX 5215085-BECK-D. Ed.Bd. circ. 1,200. (reprint service avail. from SCH)

340 362.7   US   ISSN 0733-8937
K33
KINDEX; an index to legal periodical literature concerning children. 1976. a. $35. National Center for Juvenile Justice, 701 Forbes Ave., Pittsburgh, PA 15219. TEL 412-227-6950. Ed. Linda Szymanski. index; circ. 300. (back issues avail.)

340 016   US   ISSN 0886-0408
KF1
LAW BOOKS IN REVIEW; a quarterly journal of reviews of current publications in law and related fields. 1974. q. $55. Glanville Publishers, Inc., Dobbs Ferry, NY 10522. TEL 914-693-5956. FAX 914-693-0402. Ed. M.C. Susan DeMaio. cum.index: 1974-1979; circ. 400. (processed; back issues avail.) Indexed: Leg.Info.Manage.Ind.
Description: Features timely reviews of coretexts, audio and video cassettes, software packages and CD-ROMs on law and law-related subjects.

340 016   US   ISSN 0023-9240
KF1
LAW BOOKS PUBLISHED. (Supplement to: Law Books in Print) 1969. 2/yr. $140. Glanville Publishers, Inc., 75 Main St., Dobbs Ferry, NY 10522. TEL 914-693-5956. FAX 914-693-0402. Ed. Nicholas Triffin. circ. 700. (processed; back issues avail.)
Description: Provides bibliographic information on law books published in the English language in a given year.

340 016.658   US   ISSN 0164-5390
KF318.A1
LAW OFFICE INFORMATION SERVICE; a bibliography of material on law office economics. 1978. q. $85. Institute of Continuing Legal Education, 1020 Greene St., Ann Arbor, MI 48109-1444. TEL 313-764-0533. Eds. Austin G. Anderson, Barbara A. Concannon. circ. 500. Indexed: C.L.I., L.R.I.
Description: Bibliography of articles from journals covering law office economics.

340   US   ISSN 1049-7978
LAWYERS MONTHLY CATALOG. GOVERNMENT DOCUMENTS FROM OFFICIAL AND COMMERCIAL SOURCES. 1986. a. $285. William S. Hein & Co., Inc., 1285 Main St., Buffalo, NY 14209. TEL 800-828-7571. FAX 716-883-8100. TELEX 91-209 WU 7 HEIN BUF. Ed. Peter D. Ward.
Formerly: National Legal Bibliography. Part 2. Government Documents from Official and Commercial Sources (ISSN 0887-106X)

340   AT
LEGAL & COMMERCIAL LOOSELEAF SERVICES AVAILABLE IN AUSTRALIA. 1987. irreg. (2-3/yr.) Aus.$99. Noyce Publishing, G.P.O. Box 2222T, Melbourne, Vic. 3001, Australia. (back issues avail.)

340 016   US   ISSN 0883-1297
KF240
LEGAL INFORMATION ALERT; what's new in legal publications, databases and research techniques. 1981. 10/yr. $142. Alert Publications, Inc., 399 W. Fullerton Parkway, Chicago, IL 60614-9904. TEL 312-525-7594. FAX 312-525-7015. Ed. Donna Tuke Heroy. bk.rev. (reprint service avail.)
Formerly: U S Law Library Alert (ISSN 0278-5854)
Description: Designed to keep law librarians and legal researchers informed of new legal information products and research techniques.

340 020   US   ISSN 0747-9298
Z675.L2
LEGAL INFORMATION MANAGEMENT INDEX. 1984. bi-m. (plus a. cum.) $118 (foreign $140). Legal Information Services, Box 67, Newton Highlands, MA 02161-0067. TEL 508-443-4087. Ed. Elyse H. Fox.
Description: Provides broad subject coverage, including legal research and bibliography, law library management, automation, space planning, microforms, budgeting, online databases and many other topics.

340   UK
LEGAL JOURNALS INDEX. 1986. m. £560. Legal Information Resources Ltd., Elphin House, 1 New Rd., Mytholmroyd, Hebden Bridge, West Yorkshire HX7 5DZ, England. TEL 0422-886277. FAX 0422-886250. Ed.Bd. index. (also avail. in magnetic tape; back issues avail.)
Description: Covers over 200 legal journals.

2700　LAW — ABSTRACTING, BIBLIOGRAPHIES, STATISTICS

340 015　　US　ISSN 8755-416X
KF1
LEGAL NEWSLETTERS IN PRINT. 1985. a. $85. Infosources Publishing, 140 Norma Rd., Teaneck, NJ 07666. TEL 201-836-7072. Ed. Arlene L. Eis. adv.; circ. 1,000.
  Description: Bibliography of 2,100 legal newsletters with publisher and subject indexes.

340 016　　US
LEGAL PERIODICALS IN ENGLISH. (Set of 5 binders) 1976. irreg., latest 1991-2. $125 per update; whole set $525. Glanville Publishers, Inc., 75 Main St., Dobbs Ferry, NY 10522. TEL 914-693-5956. FAX 914-693-0402. Ed. Eugene M. Wypyski. (looseleaf format)

340　　US　ISSN 0272-9296
LEGAL RESOURCE INDEX. m. $3100. Information Access Company, 362 Lakeside Dr., Foster City, CA 94404. TEL 800-227-8431. FAX 415-378-5499. (Co-sponsor: American Association of Law Libraries) (also avail. in microfilm)
●Also available online. Vendor(s): BRS (LAWS), DIALOG (File no.150), Mead Data Central (LGLIND), WESTLAW (LRI).
Also available on CD-ROM.
  Description: Comprehensive guide to law journals, legal newspapers and articles selected from the general press.

340 350　　US　ISSN 0457-3633
LEGISLATIVE TRENDS; recent acquisitions received in the New York State Library. 1971. 9/yr. $9. New York State Library, Cultural Education Center, Empire State Plaza, Albany, NY 12230. TEL 518-474-3940. FAX 518-474-5786. Ed. Robert Allan Carter. index; circ. 900. (back issues avail.)

340 690　　AT　ISSN 0727-7989
LOCAL GOVERNMENT INDEX (NEW SOUTH WALES). 1975. 4/yr. Aus.$125. Law Book Co. Ltd., 44-50 Waterloo Rd., N. Ryde, N.S.W. 2113, Australia. TEL 02-887-0177. FAX 02-888-9706. TELEX ASBOOK 27995. Eds. W.A.C. Dale, S. White. (looseleaf format)
  Description: Covers local government law, building law, environmental planning and planning law in N.S.W.

340　　MH
MACAO. DIRECCAO DOS SERVICOS DE ESTATISTICA E CENSOS. ESTATISTICAS DA JUSTICA E DA CRIMINALIDADE/MACAO. CENSUS AND STATISTICS DEPARTMENT. STATISTICS OF JUSTICE AND CRIMINALITY. (Text in Portuguese) 1981. irreg. free. Direccao dos Servicos de Estatistica e Censos, P.O. Box 3022, Macao.

011 341　　US　ISSN 0226-8361
Z6464.M2
MARINE AFFAIRS BIBLIOGRAPHY; a comprehensive index to marine law and policy literature. (Text in French, German, Italian and Spanish) 1980. q. $95. University of Virginia, School of Law Library, Charlottesville, VA 22901. TEL 804-924-3384. Eds. Christian L. Wiktor, Larry B. Wenger. circ. 350.

347　　US　ISSN 0098-7875
KFM4271
MICHIGAN. STATE COURT ADMINISTRATOR. ANNUAL REPORT.. (Supplement avail.) 1961. a. $10 for annual report; supplement $15. State Court Administrative Office, Box 30048, Lansing, MI 48909. TEL 517-373-0130. FAX 517-373-8922. circ. 1,500 (controlled). Key Title: Judicial Statistics.

340 310　　AT
MONTHLY ACTS TABLES & TABLE OF UNREPEALED PRINCIPAL ACTS. m. Aus.$70. Law Printer, P.O. Box 203, North Melbourne, Vic. 3051, Australia. TEL 03-320-0100. FAX 03-328-1657.

340 310　　AT
MONTHLY STATUTORY RULES TABLES & TABLE OF UNREVOKED PRINCIPAL STATUTORY RULES. m. Aus.$70. Law Printer, P.O. Box 203, North Melbourne, Vic. 3051, Australia. TEL 03-320-0100. FAX 03-328-1657.

347.9　　US
NEW JERSEY. ADMINISTRATIVE OFFICE OF THE COURTS. COURT MANAGEMENT REPORT. m. Administrative Office of the Courts, RJH Justice Complex CN-037, Trenton, NJ 08625. TEL 609-292-9580.
  Description: Statistical summary of court workload.

347　　US
NORTH DAKOTA. JUDICIAL SYSTEM. ANNUAL REPORT. 1928. a. free. Judicial System, Office of State Court Administrator, State Capitol, Bismarck, ND 58505. TEL 701-224-4216. Ed. William G. Bohn. stat.; circ. 1,000 (controlled).
  Former titles: North Dakota. Judicial Conference. Annual Report; North Dakota. Judicial Council. Annual Report; North Dakota. Judicial Council. Statistical Compilation and Report (ISSN 0095-6120)

340 016　　CN
NOVA SCOTIA CURRENT LAW. every 4 weeks. Can.$70. Nova Scotia Barristers' Society, 1475 Hollis St., Halifax, N.S. B3J 3M4, Canada. TEL 902-422-1491. Ed. Ruth Epstein.
  Description: A cumulative index to Nova Scotia court decisions.

340 016　　RU　ISSN 0134-2843
NOVAYA INOSTRANNAYA LITERATURA PO OBSHCHESTVENNYM NAUKAM. GOSUDARSTVO I PRAVO; bibliograficheskii ukazatel' 1973. m. 9.60 Rub. Akademiya Nauk S.S.S.R., Institut Nauchnoi Informatsii po Obshchestvennym Naukam, Ul. Krasikova 28-21, 117418 Moscow V-418, Russia. Ed. L.S. Podkuychenko.
  Inostrannaya Literatura po Gosudarstvu i Pravu.

340 016　　RU
NOVAYA SOVETSKAYA LITERATURA PO GOSUDARSTVU I PRAVU. NOVAYA YURIDICHESKAYA LITERATURA V S.S.S.R.; bibliograficheskii byulleten' 1973. m. 0.10 Rub. per no. Akademiya Nauk S.S.S.R., Institut Nauchnoi Informatsii po Obshchestvennym Naukam, Ul. Krasikova 28-21, 117418 Moscow, Russia. (Subscr. to: Mezhdunarodnaya Kniga, Moscow 121200, U.S.S.R.)

340　　RU　ISSN 0134-2738
NOVAYA SOVETSKAYA LITERATURA PO OBSHCHESTVENNYM NAUKAM. GOSUDARSTVO I PRAVO; bibliograficheskii ukazatel' 1973. m. 7.20 Rub. Akademiya Nauk S.S.S.R., Institut Nauchnoi Informatsii po Obshchestvennym Naukam, Ul. Krasikova 28-21, 117418 Moscow V-418, Russia. Ed. B.L. Polunin.

340　　RU　ISSN 0202-2060
K15
OBSHCHESTVENNYE NAUKI V S.S.S.R. GOSUDARSTVO I PRAVO; referativnyi zhurnal. 1974. bi-m. 4.20 Rub. Akademiya Nauk S.S.S.R., Institut Nauchnoi Informatsii po Obshchestvennym Naukam, Ul. Krasikova 28-21, 117418 Moscow V-418, Russia. Ed. S.N. Bratus'.

340　　RU　ISSN 0202-2109
OBSHCHESTVENNYE NAUKI ZA RUBEZHOM. GOSUDARSTVO I PRAVO; referativnyi zhurnal. 1973. bi-m. 4.20 Rub. Akademiya Nauk S.S.S.R., Institut Nauchnoi Informatsii po Obshchestvennym Naukam, Ul. Krasikova 28-21, 117418 Moscow V-418, Russia. Ed. O.A. Zhidkov.

340 016　　US
PIMSLEUR'S CHECKLIST OF BASIC AMERICAN LEGAL PUBLICATIONS. irreg., latest 1988 (suppl. 1990). price varies. (American Association of Law Libraries) Fred B. Rothman & Co., 10368 W. Centennial Rd., Littleton, CO 80127. TEL 303-979-5657. FAX 303-978-1457. Ed. Marcia S. Zubrow. (looseleaf format)
  Formerly: Checklist of Basic American Legal Publications.

343　　GW　ISSN 0340-7349
Z6461　　CODEN: PILAEA
PUBLIC INTERNATIONAL LAW; a current bibliography of articles. (Text in English) 1975. 2/yr. DM.88($49) (Max-Planck Institute for Comparative Public Law and International Law) Springer-Verlag, Heidelberger Platz 3, D-1000 Berlin 33, Germany.
TEL 030-8207-1. (Also Heidelberg, Tokyo, Vienna, and New York) Ed. R. Bernhardt. bibl. (also avail. in microform from UMI; reprint service avail. from ISI)
Indexed: C.L.I., Leg.Per.

340 016 380　　US
K25　　CODEN: UCCLA7
QUINN'S UNIFORM COMMERCIAL CODE LAW JOURNAL. 1968. q. $145. Warren, Gorham and Lamont, One Penn Plaza, New York, NY 10119. TEL 800-950-1205. FAX 212-971-5240. (also avail. in microform from UMI; reprint service avail. from RRI) Indexed: ABI Inform., Bank.Lit.Ind., BPIA, Bus.Ind., C.L.I., L.R.I., Leg.Cont., Leg.Per., Manage.Cont., SSCI, Tr.& Indus.Ind.
  Formerly: Uniform Commercial Code Law Journal (ISSN 0041-672X)
  Description: Covers every aspect of business practice affected by the Uniform Commercial Code: commercial lending, secured transactions, consumer credit and negotiable instruments. Includes truth-in-lending and fair credit reporting.

016 340　　SZ　ISSN 0250-5940
RECHTSBIBLIOGRAPHIE/BIBLIOGRAPHIE JURIDIQUE/LAW BIBLIOGRAPHY. (In 2 vols.: Vol.1 Switzerland; Vol.2 Austria, Liechtenstein) 1978. a. 33 Fr. per vol. Studio Verlag, CH-8023 Zurich, Switzerland. Ed. N. Mario Cerutti. bk.rev.; circ. 5,000. (also avail. in microfiche)

REFUGEE ABSTRACTS. see *POPULATION STUDIES — Abstracting, Bibliographies, Statistics*

340　　GW
SCHWEITZER'S VADEMECUM RECHT. 1987. biennial. Schweitzer Sortiment, Lenbachplatz 1, Postfach 370104, 8000 Munich 37, Germany.
TEL 089-55134-0.

340　　GW
SCHWEITZER'S VADEMECUM STEUERRECHT, JAHRESABSCHLEISS UND WIRTSCHAFTSPRUEFUNG. 1986. biennial. Schweitzer Sortiment, Lenbachplatz 1, Postfach 370104, 8000 Munich 3737, Germany. TEL 089-55134-0.
  Formerly: Schweitzer's Vademecum Steuerrecht und Wirtschaftspruefung.

340 016　　GW　ISSN 0081-3680
KKA3
SPEZIALBIBLIOGRAPHIEN ZU FRAGEN DES STAATES UND DES RECHTS. 1963. irreg. price varies. Hochschule fuer Recht und Verwaltung, Informationszentrum, August-Bebel-Str. 89, 1590 Potsdam, Germany.

340 011　　US　ISSN 1057-0586
Z1223.5.A1
▼**STATE REFERENCE PUBLICATIONS;** a bibliographic guide to state blue books, legislative manuals and other general reference sources. 1990. a. $55 (typically set in June). Government Research Service, 701 Jackson, Ste. 304, Topeka, KS 66603. TEL 913-232-7720. FAX 913-232-1615. Ed. Lynn Hellebust.
  Formerly (until 1990): State Blue Books, Legislative Manuals and Reference Publications.
  Description: Covers all fifty states, D.C., and Puerto Rico. Entires includ the book's name, content, author & editor, publication date, frequency, price, address, telephone and fax numbers, plus the 800 number of the publishing agency or firm.

340　　US
STATISTICS IN LITIGATION: PRACTICE APPLICATIONS FOR LAWYERS. 1985. base vol. (plus a. suppl.). $95. Shepard's - McGraw-Hill, Inc., Box 35300, Colorado Springs, CO 80935-3530. TEL 800-525-2474.
  Description: Practice-oriented information on how to strengthen client's cases with statistics.

340 011　　CN
SUBJECT MATTER INDEX TO PUBLIC AND PRIVATE STATUES OF NEW BRUNSWICK. 1971. a. Can.$87. Maritime Law Book Ltd., Box 302, Fredericton, N.B. E3B 4Y9, Canada. TEL 506-454-9921.

340　　SW　ISSN 0082-0318
HV8440
SWEDEN. STATISTISKA CENTRALBYRAAN. STATISTISKA MEDDELANDEN. SUBGROUP R (JUDICIAL STATISTICS. LAW AND SOCIAL WELFARE). (Text in Swedish; table heads and summaries in English) 1963 N.S. irreg. SEK 700. Statistiska Centralbyraan, Publishing Unit, S-701 89 Oerebro, Sweden. circ. 1,400.

LAW — CIVIL LAW   2701

341.2   UN   ISSN 0252-5321
JX170
UNITED NATIONS. TREATY SERIES. CUMULATIVE INDEX.
French edition: Nations Unies. Recueil des Traites. Index Cumulatif (ISSN 0252-5461) 1957. irreg. United Nations Publications, Room DC2-0853, New York, NY 10017. TEL 212-963-8302. FAX 212-963-3489.

340   US
UNIVERSITY OF SOUTHERN CALIFORNIA. LAW CENTER. BIBLIOGRAPHY SERIES. irreg. University of Southern California, Law Center, Los Angeles, CA 90089-0072. TEL 213-740-6482. FAX 213-740-7179.

016 340   US   ISSN 0085-7092
UNIVERSITY OF TEXAS, AUSTIN. TARLTON LAW LIBRARY. LEGAL BIBLIOGRAPHY SERIES. 1970. irreg., no.33, 1989. price varies. University of Texas at Austin, Tarlton Law Library, 727 E. 26 St., Austin, TX 78705-5799. TEL 512-471-7726. FAX 512-471-6988. bibl. (processed)

340   US   ISSN 0886-0807
KF49
WASHINGTON SUMMARY. w. when Congress is in session. $50 to non-members; members $40. American Bar Association, Governmental Affairs Office, 1800 M St., N.W., Washington, DC 20036. TEL 202-331-2606. Ed. Julia C. Ross.
    Description: Abstracts from the Congressional Record and Federal Register items pertaining to legislation and federal agency activity of interest to the legal profession.

LAW — Civil Law

340.5   US   ISSN 0099-1244
KF8841
B A R - B R I BAR REVIEW. CIVIL PROCEDURE. a. $395. B A R - B R I Bar Review, 3280 Motor Ave., Los Angeles, CA 90034-3710. TEL 213-477-2542.

340.5   US
B N A CIVIL TRIAL MANUAL. (Subseries of: Trial Practice Series) 1985. fortn. $572. The Bureau of National Affairs, Inc., 1231 25th St., N.W., Washington, DC 20037. TEL 202-452-4200. FAX 202-822-8092. TELEX 285656 BNAI WSH. (Subscr. to: 9435 Key West Ave., Rockville, MD 20037. TEL 800-372-1033) Ed. Larry Ritchie. (looseleaf format; back issues avail.)
    Description: Notification and reference service covering the litigation process from initial client interview through trial. Newsletter covers decisions on civil procedure and evidence, verdicts and settlements, and new procedure and practice techniques.

340.5   GW
BAYERISCHEN OBERLANDESGERICHTE. ENTSCHEIDUNGEN IN ZIVILSACHEN. 1965. q. DM.142. C.H. Beck'sche Verlagsbuchhandlung, Wilhelmstr. 9, 8000 Munich 40, Germany. TEL 089-381890. Eds. Joachim Kuntze, Max Maerz.

340.5   CN   ISSN 0824-717X
BRITISH COLUMBIA DECISIONS - CIVIL CASES. 1972. fortn. Can.$415. Western Legal Publications, 301-1 Alexander St., Vancouver, B.C. V6A 1B2, Canada. TEL 604-681-5671. FAX 604-687-2796. m.index. (looseleaf format)
●Also available online.
    Description: Allows access to all available civil decisions from the British Columbia Court of Appeal, Supreme Courts of British Columbia and selected decisions of the British Columbia Provincial Courts.

340.5 345   US   ISSN 0741-5788
KF4742
BULWARK. irreg. (approx. q.). membership only. (N L G Foundation) National Lawyers Guild (Boston), Civil Liberties Committee, 14 Beacon St., Ste. 407, Boston, MA 02108.

340.5   NZ
BUTTERWORTHS DISTRICT COURTS PRACTICE - CIVIL. base vol. (plus q. update). NZ.$296. Butterworths of New Zealand Ltd., 203-207 Victoria St., P.O. Box 472, Wellington, New Zealand. TEL 04-385-1479. FAX 04-385-1598. (looseleaf format)
    Description: Guide to the workings of the District Court in its civil jurisdiction, including the annotated text of the District Courts Act.

340.5   US
CALIFORNIA CIVIL ACTIONS: PLEADING AND PRACTICE. 1983. 5 base vols. (plus irreg. supplements). Matthew Bender & Co., Inc., 11 Penn Plaza, New York, NY 10001. TEL 212-967-7707. (looseleaf format)
    Description: Practice guide for handling civil action and proceedings in California. Provides detailed textual analysis of all the important stages before, during and after trial.

340.5   US
CALIFORNIA DEPOSITION AND DISCOVERY PRACTICE. 1958. 3 base vols. (plus irreg. supplements). Matthew Bender & Co., Inc., 11 Penn Plaza, New York, NY 10001. TEL 212-967-7707. Eds. J.N. DeMeo, John F. DeMeo. (looseleaf format)
    Description: Complete guide, with law, text, annotated forms, and procedural checklists to every phase of discovery procedure in civil cases. Provides extensive discussion of privileges, motion procedures, and sanctions, as well as thorough coverage of all methods of obtaining discovery under the Civil Discovery Act of 1986.

340.5   US
CALIFORNIA TORTS. 1985. 6 base vols. (plus irreg. supplements). Matthew Bender & Co., Inc., 11 Penn Plaza, New York, NY 10001. TEL 212-967-7707. Ed.Bd. (looseleaf format)
    Description: Covers the well-established areas of civil tort liability, such as government tort liability, professional malpractice, and motor vehicle cases. Highlights the newly emerging areas as well.

340.5   US
CALIFORNIA TRIAL GUIDE. 1986. 5 base vols. (plus irreg. supplements). Matthew Bender & Co., Inc., 11 Penn Plaza, New York, NY 10001. TEL 212-967-7707. Ed. Earl Johnson. (looseleaf format)
    Description: Practice tool for civil practitioners, providing substantive and procedural guidance to the evidentiary issues encountered throughout the trial process.

340.5   US
CIVIL ACTIONS AGAINST STATE GOVERNMENT: ITS DIVISIONS, AGENCIES, AND OFFICES. 1982. base vol. (plus a. suppl.). $95. Shepard's - McGraw-Hill, Inc., Box 35300, Colorado Springs, CO 80935-3530. TEL 800-525-2474.
    Description: Information on bringing or defending a civil action suit against state or local governments in all 50 states. State and federal cases are examined as well as statutes and constitutional provisions.

CIVIL & MILITARY LAW JOURNAL. see *LAW — Military Law*

340.5   US
CIVIL COMMITMENT IN MINNESOTA. base vol. (plus irreg. suppl.), 2nd ed., 1991. $95. Butterworth Legal Publishers (Salem) (Subsidiary of: Reed International PLC), 90 Stiles Rd., Salem, NH 03079. TEL 800-548-4001. FAX 603-898-9858. Ed. Eric S. Janus. (looseleaf format)
    Description: Covers all the procedures from admissions and rights of patients to review and discharge.

340.5   CN
CIVIL DOCUMENT PROCESSING MANUAL. base vol. (plus irreg. suppl.). Can.$28. Ministry of Attorney General, Parliament Bldgs., Victoria, B.C. V8V 1X4, Canada. (Subscr. to: Crown Publications, 546 Yates St., Victoria, B.C. V8W 1K8, Canada. TEL 604-386-4636) (looseleaf format; back issues avail.)

340.5   UK
CIVIL JUSTICE QUARTERLY. 1982. q. £80. Sweet & Maxwell, South Quay Plaza, 8th Floor, 183 Marsh Wall, London E14 9FT, England. TEL 071-538-8686. FAX 071-538-9508. Ed. I.R. Scott. (reprint service avail. from RRI) Indexed: C.L.I., Leg.Per.

340.5   PK
CIVIL LAW CASES. (Text in English) 1979. m. Rps.500. P L D Publishers, Nabha Road, Lahore 1, Pakistan. Ed. Malik Muhammad Saeed. (also avail. in microfilm from UMI)

340.5   US   ISSN 0009-7934
CIVIL LIBERTIES REPORTER. vol.5, 1970. q. $20 includes membership. American Civil Liberties Union of New Jersey, 2 Washington Place, Newark, NJ 07102. TEL 201-642-2084. adv.; circ. 6,600 (controlled).

340.5   US   ISSN 0199-0802
KFC995.A1
CIVIL LITIGATION REPORTER. 1979. 8/yr. $175 (effective July 1991). Continuing Education of the Bar - California, University of California Extension, 2300 Shattuck Ave., Berkeley, CA 94704. TEL 510-642-0306. FAX 800-642-3788. (Co-sponsor: State Bar of California) Ed. Michael Woods. (tabloid format; back issues avail.)

340.5   AT
CIVIL PROCEDURE VICTORIA. 3 base vols. (plus updates 12/yr.). $565. Butterworths Pty. Ltd., 271-273 Lane Cove Rd., P.O. Box 345, North Ryde, N.S.W. 2113, Australia. TEL 02-335-4444. FAX 02-335-4655. (looseleaf format)

340.5 364   US
KF9375.A59
CIVIL R I C O LITIGATION REPORTER; the national journal of record of litigation brought under the Federal Racketeer Influenced Corrupt Organizations Act. 1984. m. $750. Andrews Publications, 1646 West Chester Pike, Box 1000, Westtown, PA 19395. TEL 215-399-6600. FAX 215-399-6610. Ed. Jay Steinberg. abstr.; bibl.; stat.; s-a. cum.index. (looseleaf format; back issues avail.)
    Formerly: Racketeering Litigation Reporter (ISSN 0887-7874)

340.5   US   ISSN 0884-0032
KF9375.A15
CIVIL R I C O REPORT; the weekly newsletter on civil litigation under the Racketeer Influenced and Corrupt Organization Act. 1985. w. $695 (foreign $717). Buraff Publications (Subsidiary of: Millin Publications, Inc.), 1350 Connecticut Ave. N.W., Ste. 1000, Washington, DC 20036. TEL 202-862-0990. FAX 202-822-0999. TELEX 285656 BNAI WSH. Ed. Rose Lally. (back issues avail.)
    Description: Covers civil litigation under the Racketeer Influenced and Corrupt Organizations Act: case summaries, new RICO suits being filed, new plaintiff strategies, defense tactics, and legislation.

340.5   US
CIVIL RIGHTS AND CIVIL LIBERTIES LITIGATION: THE LAW OF SECTION 1983, 3-E. 2 base vols. (plus a. suppl.). $165. Shepard's - McGraw-Hill, Inc., Box 35300, Colorado Springs, CO 80935-3530. TEL 800-525-2474.
    Description: Covers Section 1983 issues, from both the plaintiff's and the defendant's perspective. Includes the "new" due process, local government and supervisory liability, immunities, damages and injunctive relief, attorney's fees and advice on whom to sue.

340.5   US   ISSN 0887-1191
KF1325.C58
CIVIL RIGHTS LITIGATION AND ATTORNEY FEES ANNUAL HANDBOOK. 1985. a. $25. Clark Boardman - Callaghan, 375 Hudson St., New York, NY 10014. TEL 212-929-7500.

345   US   ISSN 0895-0016
K9
DEFENSE COUNSEL JOURNAL. 1934. q. $55. International Association of Defense Counsel, 20 N. Wacker Dr., Ste. 3100, Chicago, IL 60606. TEL 312-368-1494. FAX 312-368-1854. Ed. Mgr. Richard B. Allen. bk.rev.; index, cum.index every 5 yrs.; circ. 3,700. (also avail. in microform from UMI,WSH; reprint service avail. from UMI,WSH) Indexed: ABI Inform, BPIA, Bus.Ind., C.L.I., Geo.Abstr., INIS Atomind., L.R.I., Leg.Cont., Leg.Per., Mar.Aff.Bibl.
    Formerly (until vol. 53, 1987): Insurance Counsel Journal (ISSN 0020-465X)
    Description: For lawyers and insurance executives engaged in the defense of major civil litigation, provides commentary, analysis, and developments in insurance and tort and civil procedure law.

L

LAW — CIVIL LAW

340.5   US   ISSN 0011-7587
K4
DEFENSE LAW JOURNAL. 1957. 5/yr. $80. Michie Company, Box 7587, Charlottesville, VA 22906-7587. TEL 804-972-7600. Ed. Richard M. Patterson. index, cum.index. (also avail. in microform from UNM; reprint service avail. from UMI) **Indexed:** C.L.I., Curr.Cont., L.R.I., Leg.Per., SSCI.
—BLDSC shelfmark: 3546.220000.

340.5   US   ISSN 0191-877X
KF1307.A73
DEFENSE MANUAL. 1973. q. $89. (Americans for Effective Law Enforcement, Inc.) Legal Research Publications, Inc., 421 Ridgewood Ave., Ste. 100, Glen Ellyn, IL 60137-4900. TEL 708-858-6392. Ed. James P. Manak. adv.; bk.rev.; circ. 950. (also avail. in microform from UMI; back issues avail.) **Indexed:** CJPI.
Formerly: A.E.L.E. Law Enforcement Legal Defense Manual (ISSN 0092-2552)
Description: Covers civil litigation involving state, county and municipal law enforcement agencies.

340.5   US
FLORIDA CIVIL DISCOVERY MANUAL. 1979. base vol. (plus suppl. 2-3/yr.) $80. Butterworth Legal Publishers (Salem) (Subsidiary of: Reed International PLC), 90 Stiles Rd., Salem, NH 03079. TEL 800-548-4001. FAX 603-898-9858. (looseleaf format)

340.5   US
▼**FLORIDA CIVIL PROCEDURE.** 1990. 3 base vols. (plus irreg. suppl.). $120. Butterworth Legal Publishers (Salem) (Subsidiary of: Reed International PLC), 90 Stiles Rd., Salem, NH 03079. TEL 800-548-4001. FAX 603-898-9858. Ed. Elizabeth Hapner. (looseleaf format)
Description: Includes practical analysis of current law and developments, forms, checklists and applicable provisions of all relevant rules and statutes.

FREE SPEECH NEWSLETTER. see *POLITICAL SCIENCE — Civil Rights*

340.5   US   ISSN 0363-5783
KFC52.S8
THE GAVEL; jury verdicts on civil actions in California and Nevada Superior Courts. 1961. s-m. $260. California Jury Verdicts, 2100 Watt Ave., No. 165, Sacramento, CA 95825. TEL 916-485-4990. FAX 916-485-4917. Ed. John D. Hartney. adv.; bk.rev.; circ. 300. **Indexed:** C.L.I., Leg.Per.

340.5   US
GILBERT LAW SUMMARIES. CIVIL PROCEDURE. irreg., 14th ed., 1989. $15.95. Law Distributors (Subsidiary of: H B J Legal & Professional Publications Inc.), 14415 S. Main St., Gardena, CA 90248. TEL 800-421-1893. FAX 213-324-6381.

340.5   IT   ISSN 0017-0631
GIUSTIZIA CIVILE; rivista mensile di giurisprudenza. 1951. m. L.220000 (foreign L.330000). Casa Editrice Dott. A. Giuffre, Via Busto Arsizio 40, 20151 Milan, Italy. TEL 02-38000905. FAX 02-38009582. Ed. Mario Stella Richter. adv.; bk.rev.; bibl.; index, cum.index; circ. 9,700. (tabloid format)

340.5   IT
GIUSTIZIA CIVILE. REPERTORIO GENERALE ANNUALE. 1955. a. price varies. Casa Editrice Dott. A. Giuffre, Via Busto Arsizio 40, 20151 Milan, Italy. TEL 02-38000905. FAX 02-38009582. Ed. Angelo Jannuzzi.

340.5   US   ISSN 0017-8039
K8
HARVARD CIVIL RIGHTS - CIVIL LIBERTIES LAW REVIEW. 1966. 2/yr. $24 (foreign $28). Harvard University, Law School, Publications Center, Hastings Hall, Cambridge, MA 02138. TEL 617-495-3694. adv.; bk.rev.; circ. 1,300. (also avail. in microform from UMI,WSH; back issues avail.; reprint service avail. from UMI,WSH) **Indexed:** C.I.J.E., C.L.I., Crim.Just.Abstr., Curr.Cont., Human Resour.Abstr., L.R.I., Leg.Cont., Leg.Per., P.A.I.S., Refug.Abstr., Sage Urb.Stud.Abstr., SSCI.
●Also available online. Vendor(s): WESTLAW.
—BLDSC shelfmark: 4265.885000.

HARVARD HUMAN RIGHTS JOURNAL. see *POLITICAL SCIENCE — Civil Rights*

HARVARD HUMAN RIGHTS YEARBOOK. see *POLITICAL SCIENCE — Civil Rights*

HUMAN RIGHTS. see *POLITICAL SCIENCE — Civil Rights*

HUMAN RIGHTS QUARTERLY; a comparative and international journal of the social sciences, humanities and law. see *SOCIOLOGY*

340.5   UK
IMMIGRATION AND NATIONALITY LAW & PRACTICE. 1986. 4/yr. £85($140) Tolley Publishing Co. Ltd., Tolley House, 2 Addiscombe Rd., Croydon, Surrey CR9 5AF, England. Eds. Laurence Grant, David Pearl. adv.; bk.rev.; index. (back issues avail.)
Description: Covers immigration and nationality law and practice in the UK and overseas.

340.5 325.1   US   ISSN 0149-9807
K9
IMMIGRATION AND NATIONALITY LAW REVIEW. 1986. a. $65. William S. Hein & Co., Inc., 1285 Main St., Buffalo, NY 14209. TEL 716-882-2600. FAX 716-883-8100. TELEX 91-209 WU 7 HEIN BUF. Ed. Maurice A. Roberts. (reprint service avail. from WSH)
Refereed Serial

IMMIGRATION BRIEFINGS; practical, tight-knit analysis of U.S. immigration and nationality law. see *POPULATION STUDIES*

340.5   US   ISSN 0884-3244
KF4802
IMMIGRATION JOURNAL. 1968. q. $20 (foreign $30) per issue. American Immigration Lawyers Association, 1400 I St., N.W., Ste. 1200, Washington, DC 20005-2208. TEL 202-371-9377. Ed.Bd. adv.; bk.rev.; index; circ. 3,200. **Indexed:** C.L.I., L.R.I., Refug.Abstr.
Supersedes (1948-1968): Immigration Bar Bulletin (ISSN 0019-2775)

340.5 325.1   US   ISSN 0731-5767
KF4802
IMMIGRATION LAW REPORT. 1981. 11/yr. $150. (Fragomen, Del Rey & Bernsen) Clark - Boardman - Callaghan Company Ltd., 375 Hudson St., New York, NY 10014. TEL 212-929-7500. FAX 212-924-0460. index. (looseleaf format; back issues avail.) **Indexed:** HR Rep.

IMMIGRATION LAW REPORTER. SECOND SERIES. see *POPULATION STUDIES*

340.5 320   US
IMMIGRATION REPORT. 1979. m. $20. Federation for American Immigration Reform (FAIR), 1666 Connecticut Ave., N.W., Ste. 400, Washington, DC 20009. TEL 202-328-7004. FAX 202-387-3447. Ed. Dave Ray. bk.rev.; circ. 45,000. (back issues avail.)
Description: Presents news articles, reports on announcements dealing with the impact of legal and illegal immigration on the U.S.; also tracks immigration-related legislation.

INTERNATIONAL JOURNAL OF REFUGEE LAW. see *POLITICAL SCIENCE — International Relations*

340.5   AT   ISSN 0727-7954
JACKSON AND BYRON LOCAL COURTS (CIVIL CLAIMS) PRACTICE. 1980. 8/yr. Aus.$375. Law Book Co. Ltd., 44-50 Waterloo Rd., N. Ryde, N.S.W. 2113, Australia. TEL 02-887-0177. FAX 02-888-9706. TELEX ASBOOK 27995. Eds. H.R. Rustinand, M.F. Morahan. (looseleaf format)
Description: Covers court practice, local courts, civil claims, small debts and jurisdiction in New South Wales.

340.5   JA   ISSN 0075-4188
JOURNAL OF CIVIL PROCEDURE/MINJI SOSHO ZASSHI. (Text in Japanese; summaries in English or German) 1954. a. 1500 Yen. (Japan Association of Civil Procedure - Minji Soshoho Gakkai) Horitsu Bunka Sha, 71 Kamigamo-Iwagu-Kakiuchi-cho, Kita-ku, Kyoto, Japan. adv.; bk.rev.; circ. 1,500.

340 301.4157   US
JOURNAL OF SEXUAL LIBERTY. 1985. m. $10. Committee to Preserve Our Sexual & Civil Liberties, Box 422385, San Francisco, CA 94142-2385. Ed. Jerry Jansen. adv.; bk.rev.; circ. 100. (back issues avail.)
Description: Summary of recent happenings in the area of sex and civil liberties.

340.5   US
JURISDICTION IN CIVIL ACTIONS. 2 base vols. (plus a. suppl.), 2nd ed., 1991. $165. Butterworth Legal Publishers (Salem) (Subsidiary of: Reed International PLC), 90 Stiles Rd., Salem, NH 03079. TEL 800-548-4001. FAX 603-898-9858. Ed. Robert C. Casad.
Description: Provides treatment of civil jurisdiction in all state and federal courts.

340   US   ISSN 0271-5481
KF1307.A73
LIABILITY REPORTER. 1973. m. $138. Americans for Effective Law Enforcement, Inc., 5519 N. Cumberland Ave., Ste. 1008, Chicago, IL 60656-1498. TEL 312-763-2800. Ed.Bd. adv.; bk.rev.; bibl.; index; circ. 3,000. (looseleaf format; back issues avail.) **Indexed:** CJPI.
Formerly (until 1979): A E L E Law Enforcement Legal Liability Reporter (ISSN 0092-0940)
Description: Covers law regarding civil liability issues in law enforcement.

340.5   US
MAINE CIVIL REMEDIES. 1988. base vol. (plus suppl.). $90. Butterworth Legal Publishers (Salem) (Subsidiary of: Reed International PLC), 90 Stiles Rd., Salem, NH 03079. TEL 800-548-4001. FAX 603-898-9858. Ed.Bd. (looseleaf format)
Description: Analysis of remedies available to civil litigants in the Maine state courts including damages, injunctions and other equitable remedies, and declaratory judgement.

MANITOBA DECISIONS - CIVIL AND CRIMINAL CASES. see *LAW*

342   US   ISSN 0742-4647
KF3964.A73
MEALEY'S LITIGATION REPORT: ASBESTOS. 1984. s-m. $850. Mealey Publications, Inc., Box 446, Wayne, PA 19087. TEL 215-688-6566. FAX 215-688-7552. Ed. Pamela J. Craft.
Description: Editorial and document coverage of asbestos litigation nationwide, as well as related insurance litigation. Includes commentaries by principles on key subjects of interest.

340.5   US   ISSN 1040-0192
KF3964.A73
MEALEY'S LITIGATION REPORT: ASBESTOS PROPERTY ACTIONS. 1988. s-m. $750. Mealey Publications, Inc., Box 446, Wayne, PA 19087.
TEL 215-688-6566. FAX 215-688-7552. Ed. Pamela J. Craft.
Description: Covers asbestos in buildings. Includes litigation, insurance coverage, asbestos abatement regulations, training and certification programs.

340.5 340.5   US   ISSN 0893-1011
KF1301.5.I58
MEALEY'S LITIGATION REPORT: BAD FAITH. 1987. s-m. $650. Mealey Publications, Inc., Box 446, Wayne, PA 19087. TEL 215-688-6566.
FAX 215-688-7552. Ed. Karen Storey.
Description: Tracks bad faith insurance law in courts nationwide. Summaries and full texts of opinions, briefs and motions.

340.5 332   US   ISSN 1057-1000
KF1009.A15
▼**MEALEY'S LITIGATION REPORT: BANKING INSOLVENCY.** 1990. s-m. $550. Mealey Publications, Inc., Box 446, Wayne, PA 19087. TEL 215-688-6566. FAX 215-688-7552. Ed. John T. Hayes.
Former titles (until 1991): Mealey's Litigation Report: S and L Bailout (ISSN 1047-6385); Mealey's S and L Bailout Report.
Description: Focuses on litigation concerning the failure and attempted rescue of banks and thrift institutions.

342 US ISSN 8755-9005
KF1147
MEALEY'S LITIGATION REPORT: INSURANCE. 1984. 4/m. (48/yr.). $1275. Mealey Publications, Inc., Box 446, Wayne, PA 19087. TEL 215-688-6566. FAX 215-688-7552. Eds. Steven Bierstler, W. Thomas Hagy.
Description: Covers insurance disputes concerning latent property damage or personal injury from asbestos, toxic chemicals, hazardous wastes and pharmaceuticals.

340 368 US ISSN 1043-8416
KF1535.I58
MEALEY'S LITIGATION REPORT: INSURANCE INSOLVENCY. 1989. s-m. $650. Mealey Publications, Inc., Box 446, Wayne, PA 19087. TEL 215-688-6566. FAX 215-688-7552. Ed. Teresa Zink.
Description: Covers legal and financial implications of the growing number of insurer insolvencies across the country.

340.5 US
▼**MEALEY'S LITIGATION REPORT: LEAD.** 1991. fortn. $575. Mealey Publications, Inc., Box 446, Wayne, PA 19087. TEL 215-688-6566. FAX 215-688-7552. Ed. W. Thomas Hagy.
Description: Provides nationwide editorial and document coverage of litigation concerning lead.

340.5 US ISSN 1055-307X
KF1246.A3
MEALEY'S LITIGATION REPORT: PUNITIVE DAMAGES AND TORT REFORM. 1986. s-m. $650. Mealey Publications, Inc., Box 446, Wayne, PA 19087. TEL 215-688-6566. FAX 215-688-7552. Ed. Scott Jacobs.
Former titles (until 1991): Insurance Anti-Trust and Tort Reform Report (ISSN 0898-5170); Mealey's Litigation Report: National Tort Reform (ISSN 0888-3114)
Description: Covers punitive damages, initiatives to revise tort laws, anti-trust actions brought against the insurance industry, and precedent-setting civil litigation in product liability and personal injury cases.

340.5 368 US
KF1236.A15
▼**MEALEY'S LITIGATION REPORT: REINSURANCE.** 1990. s-m. $650. Mealey Publications, Inc., Box 446, Wayne, PA 19087. TEL 215-688-6566. FAX 215-688-7552. Eds. W. Thomas Nagy, Teresa Zink.
Formerly: Mealey's Reinsurance Report (ISSN 1049-5347)
Description: Focuses on the rapidly developing field of reinsurance law.

340.5 US ISSN 0897-3407
KF1299.H39
MEALEY'S LITIGATION REPORT: SUPERFUND. 1988. s-m. $750. Mealey Publications, Inc., Box 446, Wayne, PA 19087. TEL 215-688-6566. FAX 215-688-7552. Ed. Karen Storey.
Description: Covers events surrounding all sites on Superfund's national priority list. Includes litigation, insurance disputes, agency actions and awards.

340.6 US ISSN 0886-0122
KF1297.T63
MEALEY'S LITIGATION REPORT: TOBACCO. 1986. m. $550. Mealey Publications, Inc., Box 446, Wayne, PA 19087. TEL 215-688-6566. FAX 215-688-7552. Ed. Barbara Domanowski.
Description: Editorial and document coverage of tobacco litigation nationwide.

340.5 US ISSN 0199-1272
KF2905.3.A15
MEDICAL LIABILITY ADVISORY SERVICE. 1975. m. $142. Business Publishers, Inc., 951 Pershing Dr., Silver Spring, MD 20910-4464. TEL 301-587-6300. FAX 301-587-1081. Ed. Bryan Morris.

340 US ISSN 0199-1833
KF2905.3.A59
MEDICAL LIABILITY REPORTER; recent decisions of national significance. 1979. m. $295. (Litigation Research Group) Shepard's - McGraw-Hill, Inc., Box 35300, Colorado Springs, CO 80935-3530. TEL 719-488-3000. Ed. Kevin Bushnell. bibl.; index. (looseleaf format; back issues avail.)
Description: Summarizes and analyzes all reported and most unreported decisions related to health care law.

340.5 630 US
MEDICAL MALPRACTICE: BASES OF LIABILITY. 1985. base vol. (plus a. suppl.). $95. Shepard's - McGraw-Hill, Inc., Box 35300, Colorado Springs, CO 80935-3530. TEL 800-525-2474.
Description: Examines the elements of malpractice and their interpretations in the courts, as well as the frontier issues of constitutional law.

340 610 US
MEDICAL MALPRACTICE DEFENSE AND HEALTH CARE COUNSEL DIRECTORY. a. $12.45. Professional Reports Corporation, 4571 Stephen Circle, N.W., Canton, OH 44718-3629. TEL 800-336-0083. FAX 216-499-6609. index.
Formerly: Medical Malpractice Defense Attorney and Health Care Counsel Directory.
Description: For professionals in the health care fields. Lists medical malpractice defense firms, attorneys, and health care counsel.

340.5 610 US ISSN 0893-8229
KF2905.3.A15
MEDICAL MALPRACTICE DEFENSE REPORTER. q. $59.95. Professional Reports Corporation, 4561 Stephen Circle, N.W., Canton, OH 44718-3629. TEL 800-336-0083. FAX 216-499-6609. (looseleaf format)
Description: Provides current information on developments affecting medical malpractice defense attorneys, health care professionals, insurance adjusters and risk management professionals.

340.5 617.6 US
▼**MEDICAL MALPRACTICE: HANDLING DENTAL CASES,** 2-E. 1991. 2 base vols. (plus a. suppl.). $185. Shepard's - McGraw-Hill, Inc., Box 35300, Colorado Springs, CO 80935-3530. TEL 800-525-2474.
Description: Covers methods of investigating dental malpractice and provides tips on how to trap the defendant and structure the plaintiff's closing argument. Includes sample complaints and interrogations.

340.5 618 US
MEDICAL MALPRACTICE: HANDLING OBSTETRIC AND NEONATAL CASES. 1986. base vol. (plus a. suppl.). $95. Shepard's - McGraw-Hill, Inc., Box 35300, Colorado Springs, CO 80935-3530. TEL 800-525-2474.
Description: Helps to answer questions such as whether to accept a case, how to efficiently win a case, and what a case can be worth to your client and yourself.

340.5 610 US
MEDICAL MALPRACTICE LAW & STRATEGY. m. $165. New York Law Publishing Co., Marketing Dept., 111 Eighth Ave., New York, NY 10011. TEL 212-741-8300.
Description: Latest court developments, new negotiating techniques, presentation suggestions and changes in the law for malpractice lawyers.

340.5 610 US ISSN 1056-4098
KF2905.3.A59
MEDICAL MALPRACTICE - OB-GYN LITIGATION REPORTER; the monthly national journal of record reporting general medical malpractice, obstetrical and gynecological litigation. 1985. m. $800. Andrews Publications, 1646 West Chester Pike, Box 1000, Westtown, PA 19395. TEL 215-399-6600. FAX 215-399-6610. Ed. Kathy Knaub. abstr.; bibl.; stat.; cum.index every 6 mos.; circ. 92. (looseleaf format; back issues avail.)
Formerly (until 1991): Medical Malpractice Litigation Reporter (ISSN 0882-8555)

340.5 615 US
MEDICAL MALPRACTICE: PHARMACY LAW. 1986. base vol. (plus a. suppl.). $95. Shepard's - McGraw-Hill, Inc., Box 35300, Colorado Springs, CO 80935-3530. TEL 800-525-2474.
Description: Presents precedent-setting decisions and explains complicated issues in laymen's terms.

LAW — CIVIL LAW 2703

340.5 616.8 US
MEDICAL MALPRACTICE: PSYCHIATRIC CARE. 1986. base vol. (plus a. suppl.) $105. Shepard's - McGraw-Hill, Inc., Box 35300, Colorado Springs, CO 80935-3530. TEL 800-525-2474.
Description: Highlights developing trends in the law which have direct impact on the standards of care in psychiatric practice.

340.5 US
MEDICAL MALPRACTICE REPORTS. 1987. m. $180. Matthew Bender & Co., Inc., 11 Penn Plaza, New York, NY 10001. TEL 212-967-7707. Ed. Leonard J. Nelson.
Description: Provides medical malpractice news, abstracts of cases, including text and analysis of the decision, plus discussions of growing trends.

340.5 US ISSN 0888-658X
KF2905.3.A59
MEDICAL MALPRACTICE VERDICTS, SETTLEMENTS & EXPERTS. 1985. m. $247. 901 Church St., Nashville, TN 37203. TEL 615-255-6288. FAX 615-255-6289. Ed. Lewis L. Laska. adv.; index.
Description: Looks at the outcome of medical malpractice cases nationally.

MEDICAL RECORD RISKS: CLAIMS & LITIGATION. see INSURANCE

340.5 610 US
MEDICAL STAFF LAW MANUAL. m. $675. Action Kit Publishers, 1614 Fifth Ave., Pittsburgh, PA 15213. TEL 800-245-1205. Ed. John Horty. (looseleaf format)
Description: Helps hospital administrators understand what must be done to comply with the law and to limit liability.

340.5 610 US ISSN 0025-7591
MEDICAL TRIAL TECHNIQUE QUARTERLY. 1954. q. $102.50. Callaghan & Co., 155 Pfingston Rd., Deerfield, IL 60015. TEL 800-323-1336. Ed. Fred Lane. bk.rev.; bibl.; charts; index; circ. 2,500. (also avail. in microfiche from WSH; microfilm from WSH) Indexed: Abstr.Bk.Rev.Curr.Leg.Per., C.L.I., Hlth.Ind., L.R.I., Leg.Cont., Leg.Per.
—BLDSC shelfmark: 5532.045000.
Description: Presents articles on contemporary medico-legal issues confronting today's practitioner.

340 610 US ISSN 0899-0255
RA1001
MEDICO-LEGAL ADVISOR. 1985. m. $65. Health Law Research Group, Health-Law Plaza, 140 E. Division Rd., Ste. C3, Oak Ridge, TN 37830. TEL 615-482-6600. FAX 615-481-0264. Ed. Dr. Laurence R. Dry. circ. 1,000.
Formerly (until Apr. 1988): Attorney's Medical Advisory Letter (ISSN 0887-2015)
Description: Reviews the latest medico-legal developments in medicine and product liability.

344.041 AT ISSN 0047-6595
MEDICO-LEGAL SOCIETY OF VICTORIA. PROCEEDINGS. 1931. 5/yr. free. Medico-Legal Society of Victoria, 205 William St., Melbourne, Vic. 3000, Australia. Ed. D. Graham. circ. 600 (controlled).

340.5 610 GW ISSN 0340-9511
MEDIZIN IN RECHT UND ETHIK. 1976. irreg., latest vol.24, 1991. price varies. Ferdinand Enke Verlag, Postfach 101254, 7000 Stuttgart 10, Germany. TEL 0711-8931-0. FAX 0711-8931-419. TELEX 07252275-GTV-D. Eds. A. Eser, E. Seidler.

340.5 150 US ISSN 0883-7902
KF480.A15
MENTAL AND PHYSICAL DISABILITY LAW REPORTER; covers all aspects of handicapped law. 1976. bi-m. $180 to individuals; institutions $238. American Bar Association, Commission on the Mental & Physical Disability Law, 1800 M St., N.W., Washington, DC 20036. TEL 202-331-2240. FAX 202-331-2220. Ed. John Parry. bk.rev.; index; circ. 1,500. (back issues avail.) Indexed: Adol.Ment.Hlth.Abstr., C.L.I., Crim.Just.Abstr., Hlth.Ind., L.R.I., Leg.Cont., Leg.Per., Psychol.Abstr.
Formerly (until 1984): Mental Disability Law Reporter (ISSN 0147-3700)
Description: Articles on subjects of interest to practitioners and consumers. Indexes are available by case name and subject matter.

MENTAL CAPACITY: MEDICAL AND LEGAL ASPECTS OF THE AGING. see PSYCHOLOGY

LAW — CIVIL LAW

614.58 340 US ISSN 0889-017X
KF2910.P75
MENTAL HEALTH LAW NEWS. 1986. m. $79. Interwood Publications, 3 E. Interwood Pl., Box 20241, Cincinnati, OH 45220. TEL 513-221-3715. Ed. Frank J. Bardack. (looseleaf format)
 Description: Provides case law summaries on mental health malpractice, commitment, appropriate treatment, consent and patient danger to community.

614.58 340 US ISSN 0741-5141
KF480.A15
MENTAL HEALTH LAW REPORTER. 1983. m. $192.48. Business Publishers, Inc., 951 Pershing Dr., Silver Spring, MD 20910-4464. TEL 301-587-6300. FAX 301-585-9075. Ed. Bonita Becker. (looseleaf format; back issues avail.)
 ●Also available online. Vendor(s): NewsNet.
 Description: Covers the avoidance of mental health lawsuits for mental health professionals, advice on winning suits that are brought.

MICHIGAN CIVIL RIGHTS COMMISSION NEWSLETTER. see POLITICAL SCIENCE — Civil Rights

MICHIGAN COUNCIL FOR THE ARTS. LEGISLATIVE REPORT. see ART

340 614.7 US ISSN 1046-9192
▼**MICHIGAN ENVIRONMENTAL LAW LETTER.** 1990. 12/yr. $147. M. Lee Smith Publishers & Printers, 162 Fourth Ave. N., Box 2678, Nashville, TN 37219. TEL 615-242-7395. FAX 615-256-6601. (Co-sponsor: Honigman Miller Schwartz & Cohn) Ed. Joseph M. Polito.
 Description: Reports the latest Michigan environmental law developments that affect Michigan companies.

340.5 US
MINNESOTA CIVIL PRACTICE. 2nd ed., 1990. 4 base vols. (plus a. suppl.). $295. Butterworth Legal Publishers (Salem) (Subsidiary of: Reed International PLC), 90 Stiles Rd., Salem, NH 03079. TEL 800-548-4001. FAX 603-898-9858. Eds. Douglas D. McFarland, William J. Keppel.
 Description: Provides a practical step-by-step guide through all facets of civil practice, from the client interview to final judgement and appeal. Presents an analysis of the rules of civil procedure, with emphasis on pertinent and recent case law, books, journals, articles and statutes.

MONOGRAPHS ON INDUSTRIAL PROPERTY AND COPYRIGHT LAW. see PATENTS, TRADEMARKS AND COPYRIGHTS

340 US
▼**MOTIONS IN FEDERAL COURT: CIVIL PRACTICE, 2-E.** 1991. 3 base vols. (plus a. suppl.). $225. Shepard's - McGraw-Hill, Inc., Box 35300, Colorado Springs, CO 80935-3530. TEL 800-515-2474.
 Description: Supplies information on more than 125 of the most frequently used motions as provided by the Federal Rules of Civil Procedure and federal statutes.

340 AT
MOTOR & TRAFFIC LAW SERVICE - VICTORIA. 2 base vols. (plus updates 6/yr.). $395. Butterworths Pty. Ltd., 271-273 Lane Cove Rd., P.O. Box 345, N. Ryde, N.S.W. 2113, Australia. TEL 02-335-4444. FAX 02-335-4655. (looseleaf format)

340 AT
MOTOR VEHICLE LAW S.A.. 1983. 4/yr. Aus.$175. Law Book Co. Ltd., 44-50 Waterloo Rd., North Ryde, N.S.W. 2113, Australia. TEL 02-887-0177. FAX 02-888-9706. TELEX ASBOOK 27995. Ed. D.W. Bollen.
 Description: A manual for motor vehicle and traffic law in South Australia.

MOTOR VEHICLE REPORTS. see TRANSPORTATION

340 AT ISSN 0813-782X
MOTOR VEHICLE REPORTS. 1985. 6/yr. Aus.$175. Butterworths Pty. Ltd., P.O. Box 345, North Ryde, N.S.W. 2113, Australia. TEL 02-335-4444. FAX 02-335-4655.

340 US
NEW HAMPSHIRE CIVIL JURY INSTRUCTIONS. 1989. base vol. (plus suppl.). $45. Butterworth Legal Publishers (Salem) (Subsidiary of: Reed International PLC), 90 Stiles Rd., Salem, NH 03079. TEL 800-548-4001. FAX 603-898-9858. Ed.Bd.
 Description: Contains suggested instructions for use in drafting jury instructions in a particular case.

340.5 US
NEW HAMPSHIRE PRACTICE SERIES. VOL. 7: WILLS, TRUSTS AND GIFTS. (Series consists of 14 vols.; Vols. 1 and 2: Criminal Practice and Procedure; Vol. 3: Family Law; Vols. 4, 5 and 6: Civil Practice and Procedure; Vol. 7: Wills, Trusts and Gifts; Vols. 8 and 9: Personal Injury - Tort and Insurance; Vols. 10, 11 and 12: Probate Law and Procedure; Vols. 13 and 14: Local Government Law) 1986. base vol. (plus suppl.). $55 (14-vol. set $575). Butterworth Legal Publishers (Salem) (Subsidiary of: Reed International PLC), 90 Stiles Rd., Salem, NH 03079. TEL 800-548-4001. FAX 603-898-9858. Ed. Charles A. DeGrandpre.
 Description: Covers the requirements for and manner of execution of wills, trusts, and gifts.

340.5 US
NEW HAMPSHIRE PRACTICE SERIES. VOLS. 4, 5 AND 6: CIVIL PRACTICE AND PROCEDURE. (Series consists of 14 vols.; Vols. 1 and 2: Criminal Practice and Procedure; Vol. 3: Family Law; Vols. 4, 5 and 6: Civil Practice and Procedure; Vol. 7: Wills, Trusts and Gifts; Vols. 8 and 9: Personal Injury - Tort and Insurance Practice; Vols. 10, 11 and 12: Probate Law and Procedure; Vols. 13 and 14: Local Government Law) 1984. 3 base vols. (plus suppl.). $165 (14-vol. set $575). Butterworth Legal Publishers (Salem) (Subsidiary of: Reed International PLC), 90 Stiles Rd., Salem, NH 03079. TEL 800-548-4001. FAX 603-898-9858. Ed. Richard V. Wiebusch.
 Description: Provides analysis of arbitration, equity proceedings, and administrative agency proceedings as well as sample forms and pleadings.

340.5 AT
NEW SOUTH WALES LOCAL COURTS CIVIL PRACTICE. 1989. irreg. (approx. q.). C C H Australia Ltd., P.O. Box 230, North Ryde, N.S.W. 2113, Australia. TEL 02-888-2555. FAX 02-888-7324.

340.5 US ISSN 1047-5419
KFO530.A1
▼**OHIO CIVIL PRACTICE JOURNAL.** 1990. bi-m. $160. Banks - Baldwin Law Publishing Co., University Center, Box 1974, Cleveland, OH 44106. TEL 216-721-7373. FAX 216-721-8055. Ed. J. Patrick Browne.
 Description: Provides analysis of procedural issues and specific practical advice for Ohio litigators.

340.5 US
▼**OREGON RULES OF CIVIL PROCEDURE ANNOTATED (YEAR).** 1991. a. $35. Butterworth Legal Publishers (Salem) (Subsidiary of: Reed International PLC), 90 Stiles Rd., Salem, NH 03079. TEL 800-548-4001. FAX 603-898-9858. Ed.Bd.
 Description: Full text of each rule, accompanied by summaries of cases discussing the rules.

340.5 FR ISSN 0397-9873
K21
REVUE TRIMESTRIELLE DE DROIT CIVIL. 1902. q. 385 F. (foreign 492 F.). Editions Sirey-Diffusion Dalloz, 11 rue Soufflot, 75240 Paris Cedex 05, France. TEL 40-51-54-54. FAX 45-87-37-48. TELEX 206446F. (back issues avail.)
 —BLDSC shelfmark: 7956.770000.

340.5 US
RIGHTS AND LIABILITIES OF PUBLISHERS, BROADCASTERS, AND REPORTERS. 1982. 2 base vols. (plus a. suppl.). $195. Shepard's - McGraw-Hill, Inc., Box 35300, Colorado Springs, CO 80935-3530. TEL 800-525-2474. (looseleaf format)
 Description: Covers entire spectrum of media litigation: libel, privacy, compelled disclosure, media access, prior restraint, anti-trust law and commercial speech and advertising.

340.5 US
RIGHTS OF PHYSICALLY HANDICAPPED PERSONS. 1984. base vol. (plus a. suppl.). $95. Shepard's - McGraw-Hill, Inc., Box 35300, Colorado Springs, CO 80935-3530. TEL 800-525-2474.
 Description: Outlines both substantive and procedural provisions of federal laws and offers suggestions for remedial actions that can be pursued on behalf of handicapped clients.

340.5 IT ISSN 0035-6093
K22
RIVISTA DI DIRITTO CIVILE. 1955. bi-m. L.140000 (foreign L.170000)(effective 1991). Casa Editrice Dott. Antonio Milani, Via Jappelli 5, 35121 Padua, Italy. TEL 049-656677. FAX 049-8752900. Ed. Alberto Trabucchi. cum.index, 1955-1974. **Indexed:** World Agri.Econ.& Rural Sociol.Abstr.
 —BLDSC shelfmark: 7984.650000.

340.5 IT ISSN 0035-6182
RIVISTA DI DIRITTO PROCESSUALE. 1924. q. L.135000 (foreign L.175000)(effective 1991). Casa Editrice Dott. Antonio Milani, Via Jappelli 5, 35121 Padua, Italy. TEL 049-656677. FAX 049-8752900. Ed. G. Tarzia. bk.rev.; bibl.; index, cum.index 1946-1965; circ. 2,500.
 —BLDSC shelfmark: 7984.925000.
 Formerly (until 1943): Rivista di Diritto Processuale Civile.

340.5 IT
RIVISTA TRIMESTRALE DI DIRITTO E PROCEDURA CIVILE. 1947. q. L.110000 (foreign L.165000). Casa Editrice Dott. A. Giuffre, Via Busto Arsizio 40, 20151 Milan, Italy. TEL 02-38000905. FAX 02-38009582. Eds. Umberto Romagnoli, Federico Carpi. adv.; circ. 3,150.

340.5 AU ISSN 0379-4423
RUNDFUNKRECHT. 1977. q. Manzsche Verlags- und Universitaetsbuchhandlung, Kohlmarkt 16, A-1014 Vienna, Austria. TEL 0222-531610. FAX 0222-5316181. Ed. Robert Dittrich. circ. 900.
 Description: Concerns law on radio and television broadcasting.

340.5 UK ISSN 0951-0443
SCOTTISH CIVIL LAW REPORTS. 1987. 5/yr. £85. Law Society of Scotland, 26 Drumsheugh Gardens, Edinburgh EH3 7YR, Scotland. Ed. Sheriff A. Graham Johnston.

340 US
SHEPARD'S MEDICAL MALPRACTICE CITATIONS. 1987. base vol. (plus q. suppl.). $230. Shepard's - McGraw-Hill, Inc., Box 35300, Colorado Springs, CO 80935-3530. TEL 800-525-2474.

340.5 US
TEXAS RULES OF CIVIL PROCEDURE. 1984. base vol. (plus suppl.). $38.50. Butterworth Legal Publishers (Salem) (Subsidiary of: Reed International PLC), 90 Stiles Rd., Salem, NH 03079. TEL 800-548-4001. FAX 603-898-9858. Ed.Bd. (looseleaf format)

340 US
TULANE CIVIL LAW FORUM.* 1973-1977; N.S. 1987. q. $8. Tulane University School of Law, New Orleans, LA 70118. Ed. Alain A. Levasseur. circ. 250. (also avail. in microform from UMI,WSH; back issues avail.; reprint service avail. from WSH) **Indexed:** Leg.Per.

340.5 PH ISSN 0047-5734
K25
UNIVERSITY OF SANTO TOMAS. FACULTY OF CIVIL LAW. LAW REVIEW. (Text in English) 1950. s-a. P.60($7) University of Santo Tomas, Faculty of Civil Law, Espana St., Sampaloc, Metro Manila, Philippines. Ed. Liza A. Lopez. adv.; bk.rev.

340.5 CN ISSN 0827-4266
WEEKLY DIGEST OF CIVIL PROCEDURE (2ND SERIES). 1987. 40/yr. Can.$350. Carswell Publications, Corporate Plaza, 2075 Kennedy Rd., Scarborough, Ont. M1T 3V4, Canada. TEL 416-609-8000. FAX 416-298-5094.

340.5 II
YEARLY ALL INDIA CIVIL DIGEST. (Text in English) 1986. a. Rs.500. The Law Book Co. (P) Ltd., Sardar Patel Marg, P.B. 1-004, Allahabad 211 001, India. TEL 602415. Ed. Rakesh Bagga.
 Description: Contains digest of all civil judgements of the Supreme Court and of all the high courts of India.

LAW — Computer Applications

340 001.642 US
A B A - UNIX - GROUP NEWSLETTER. q. $50. American Bar Association, Law Practice Management Section, 750 N. Lake Shore Dr., Chicago, IL 60611. TEL 312-988-5000.
  Description: Provides readers with updates on the use of UNIX system computers, articles on hardware and software, software reviews, tips and tricks, and information on the UNIX User Group.

340 US
A M S ADVISOR. (Acquisition Management Service) 1981. m. $495. Information Strategies Group, 8000 Towers Crescent Dr., Ste. 1180, Vienna, VA 22182. TEL 703-893-0833. FAX 703-356-3111. Ed. Kay Carlson. circ. 250. (back issues avail.)
  Formerly (until Jan. 1990): P I M S Advisor.
  Description: Covers developments affecting the world of federal procurements and ADP acquisition policies.

340 US ISSN 0191-863X
KF318.A1
ALTMAN WEIL PENSA REPORT TO LEGAL MANAGEMENT. 1974. m. Can.$245($195) (foreign $220). Altman Weil Pensa Publications, Inc., Box 625, Newtown Sq., PA 19073. TEL 215-359-9900. FAX 215-359-0467. Ed. Linda Ianelli. bk.rev.; index; circ. 1,200. (back issues avail.)
  Description: Geared to the legal profession.

340 340 GW ISSN 0934-8778
COMPUTERREPORT DER NEUE JURISTISCHEN WOCHENSCHRIFT; Informationsmanagement und Bueroorganisation in der juristischen Praxis. Short title: N J W - Co R. 1988. bi-m. DM.58. C.H. Beck'sche Verlagsbuchhandlung, Wilhelmstr. 9, D-8000 Munich 40, Germany. adv.; bk.rev.; index. (back issues avail.)

340 026 FR
COUNCIL OF EUROPE. SYMPOSIUM ON LEGAL PROCESSING. PROCEEDINGS. no.5, 1979. irreg. price varies. Council of Europe, Publishing and Documentation Service, 67006 Strasbourg, France. (Dist. in U.S. by: Manhattan Publishing Co., 225 Lafayette St., New York, NY 10012)

340 001.642 US
DOCUMENT ASSEMBLY USER GROUP NEWS. q. $50. American Bar Association, Law Practice Management Section, 750 N. Lake Shore Dr., Chicago, IL 60611. TEL 312-988-5000.
  Description: Includes updates on the use of document assembly systems in law offices, "how to" articles about available systems, and news about the activities of the Document Assembly User Group.

340 US
I B M & COMPATIBLES USER GROUP NEWS. q. $50. American Bar Association, Law Practice Management Section, 750 N. Lake Shore Dr., Chicago, IL 60611. TEL 312-988-5000.
  Description: Includes updates on using IBM and compatible computers in law offices, MS-DOS hardware and software, and news about the user group's activities.

340 301 001.2 FR ISSN 0181-110X
INFORMATIQUE ET SCIENCES JURIDIQUES. 1974. 2/yr. 160 F. Institut de l'Information Scientifique et Technique, INIST - CNRS, 2 allee du Parc de Brabois, 54514 Vandoeuvre-les-Nancy Cedex, France. TEL 33-83-50-46-00. FAX 33-83-50-46-50.
  ●Also available online. Vendor(s): DIALOG, Telesystemes - Questel.

340 US ISSN 1055-128X
▼**LAW OFFICE COMPUTING.** 1991. bi-m. $39.95. James Publishing Group, Inc., 3520 Cadillac Ave., Costa Mesa, CA 92626. TEL 714-755-5450. adv.; circ. 5,000.
  Description: Contains practical solutions to law office computer problems, practical applications for small firms and how-to advice for both experienced users and beginners.

340 US ISSN 0458-8630
K12
LAW OFFICE ECONOMICS & MANAGEMENT. 1960. q. $55. Callaghan & Co., 155 Pfingsten Rd., Deerfield, IL 60015. TEL 800-323-1336. Ed. Paul Hoffman. bk.rev.; illus.; index. (also avail. in microfiche from UMI) **Indexed:** Account.Ind. (1974-), C.L.I., L.R.I., Law Ofc.Info.Svc., Leg.Cont., Leg.Per.
  Former titles: Law Office Economics and Management Manual (ISSN 0023-9313); Law Office Economics and Management.
  Description: For lawyers and office managers. Covers client relations, personnel, strategic planning and computers in the office.

340 US ISSN 1047-6482
KF320.A9
LAW OFFICE TECHNOLOGY REVIEW. 1989. m. $99.50. 2640 W. 183 St., Box 2577, Homewood, IL 60430. TEL 708-957-3322. FAX 708-957-3337. Ed.Bd. bk.rev.
  ●Also available online. Vendor(s): NewsNet.
  Description: Features hands-on reviews of computer software, add-ons, and systems for law office computer users.

340 510.78 US ISSN 0278-3916
K87 CODEN: LATEDT
LAW - TECHNOLOGY. 1968. q. $75. World Jurist Association, Section on Law & Computer Technology, 1000 Connecticut Ave., Ste. 202, Washington, DC 20036. TEL 202-466-5428. FAX 202-452-8540. TELEX 440456. bk.rev.; bibl.; charts; circ. 800. (processed; also avail. in microform from UMI) **Indexed:** C.L.I., Comput.Cont., Comput.Lit.Ind., L.R.I., Leg.Per., Sci.Abstr.
  —BLDSC shelfmark: 5161.447500.
  Formerly: Law and Computer Technology (ISSN 0023-9178)

340 621.381 US ISSN 0740-0942
KF320.A9
LAWYER'S P C. 1983. bi-m. $105. Shepard's - McGraw-Hill, Inc., Box 35300, Colorado Springs, CO 80935-3530. TEL 719-488-3000. Ed. Robert P. Wilkins. adv.; bk.rev. **Indexed:** Comput.Cont., Comput.Lit.Ind., Leg.Cont.
  Incorporates: Lawyer's Microcomputer (ISSN 0732-0922)
  Description: For lawyers using personal computers. Features articles about hardware and software--advances and applications. Also contains product and service announcements of interest in the legal field.

LEADER'S LEGAL TECH NEWSLETTER. see *LAW*

340 US
LITIGATION USER GROUP NEWS. q. $50. American Bar Association, Law Practice Management Section, 750 N. Lake Shore Dr., Chicago, IL 60611. TEL 312-988-5000.
  Description: Includes updates on computer use in litigation practice and news about the activities of the user group.

340 011 FR
REPERTOIRE INTERNATIONAL DES BANQUES DE DONNEES JURIDIQUE. 1988. a. 470 F. (Association pour le Developpement de l'Information Juridique) Editions F L A Consultants, 27 rue de la Vistule, 75013 Paris, France. TEL 1-45-82-75-75. FAX 1-45-82-46-04. TELEX 205 231 FLA.
  Description: A tool to better understand and use French and foreign law data bases.

340 330 US ISSN 0735-8938
K22 CODEN: RCTJDM
RUTGERS COMPUTER & TECHNOLOGY LAW JOURNAL. 1970. s-a. $32. Rutgers University, School of Law - Newark, 15 Washington St., Newark, NJ 07102. TEL 201-648-5549. adv.; bk.rev.; bibl.; charts; cum.index: vols.1-16 in vol.16; circ. 1,500. (also avail. in microfilm from UMI,WSH; reprint service avail. from UMI,WSH) **Indexed:** C.L.I., Comput.Cont., Comput.Lit.Ind., L.R.I., Leg.Cont., Leg.Per., Sci.Abstr.
  Former titles (until 1981): Rutgers Journal of Computers, Technology, and the Law (ISSN 0278-5633); (until 1978): Rutgers Journal of Computers and the Law (ISSN 0048-8844)

SANTA CLARA COMPUTER AND HIGH-TECHNOLOGY LAW JOURNAL. see *LAW*

340 025 US
TRENDS IN THE LAW LIBRARY MANAGEMENT AND TECHNOLOGY. 1987. 10/yr. $75. Fred B. Rothman & Co., 10368 W. Centennial Rd., Littleton, CO 80127. TEL 303-979-5657. FAX 303-978-1457. Ed. Dennis S. Stone. (back issues avail.)

340 US
WORD PROGRESS. q. $50. American Bar Association, Law Practice Management Section, 750 N. Lake Shore Dr., Chicago, IL 60611. TEL 312-988-5000.
  Description: Includes updates on word processing in the law office, "how to" articles on hardware and software, and news about the activities of the Word Processing User Group.

340 510.78 UK ISSN 0269-3712
K29
YEARBOOK OF LAW COMPUTERS AND TECHNOLOGY. 1984. a. $375. Butterworth & Co. (Publishers) Ltd. (Subsidiary of: Reed International PLC), 88 Kingsway, London WC2B 6AB, England. TEL 71-405-6900. FAX 71-405-1332. TELEX 95678. (US addr.: Butterworth Legal Publishers, 90 Stiles Rd., Salem, NH 03079. TEL 800-548-4001) Ed. Christopher Arnold. bk.rev.
  —BLDSC shelfmark: 9414.450000.

LAW — Constitutional Law

342 US ISSN 0098-7638
KF4550.Z9
B A R - B R I BAR REVIEW. CONSTITUTIONAL LAW. a. $395. B A R - B R I Bar Review, 3280 Motor Ave., Los Angeles, CA 90034-3710. TEL 213-477-2542.

342 US ISSN 0743-0310
KF4546.A3
BENCHMARK (RICHMOND); a quarterly review of the constitution and the courts. 1984. q. $18 to individuals; institutions $20. Center for Judicial Studies, Box 17248, Richmond, VA 23226. TEL 804-282-1798. Ed. James McClellan. adv.; bk.rev.; circ. 5,000. (also avail. in microform from WSH; back issues avail.; reprint service avail. from WSH)
  Description: Articles on the Constitution and the role of the courts.

342 US ISSN 0160-7731
KF4742
BILL OF RIGHTS IN ACTION. Short title: B R I A. 1971. q. free. Constitutional Rights Foundation, 601 S. Kingsley Dr., Los Angeles, CA 90005. TEL 213-487-5590. FAX 213-386-0459. Ed. Marshall Croddy. bk.rev.; circ. 40,000. (also avail. in microform from UMI; back issues avail.; reprint service avail. from UMI)
  Formerly: Bill of Rights Newsletter (ISSN 0006-2502)
  Description: Contains educational materials for grades 7-12.

342 350 IT
CAMERA DEI DEPUTATI. BOLLETTINO DI INFORMAZIONI COSTITUZIONALI E PARLAMENTARI. 1981. q. L.40000. Camera dei Deputati, Palazzo Montecitorio, Rome, Italy. TEL 06-67179328. FAX 06-6783082. Ed. Anton Paolo Tanda. circ. 200. (back issues avail.)
  Description: Examines original documents of parliamentary procedure and constitutional law.

342 US
CASES AND MATERIALS ON CONSTITUTIONAL LAW. irreg. price varies. Foundation Press, Inc., 615 Merrick Ave., Westbury, NY 11590-6607.

342 US
CONSTITUTIONAL COMMENTARIES. 1984. irreg. (approx. 2/yr.). $6. Center for Judicial Studies, Box 17248, Richmond, VA 23226. TEL 804-282-1798. Ed. James McClellan. circ. 1,500. (back issues avail.) **Indexed:** C.L.I.
  Description: Scholarly studies on the Constitution, constitutional law and the courts.

LAW — CORPORATE LAW

342 320 US ISSN 1043-4062
▼CONSTITUTIONAL POLITICAL ECONOMY. 1990. 3/yr. $27 to individuals (foreign $33); institutions $65 (foreign $71)(typically set in Jan.). George Mason University, Center for Study of Public Choice, George's Hall, Fairfax, VA 22030-4444. TEL 703-993-2329. FAX 703-993-2323. Eds. Viktor J. Vanberg, Richard E. Wagner. adv.; bk.rev.; circ. 532.
Description: Provides a forum for papers in the broad area of constitutional analysis. Integrates the institutional dimension (the study of legal, political and moral institutions) into economic analysis.

342 UK ISSN 0269-2511
CONSTITUTIONAL REFORM; the quarterly review. 1986. q. £12($30) Constitutional Reform Centre, 60 Chandos Pl., London WC2N 4H6, England. TEL 01-240-1719. Ed. Hilary Muggridge. index; circ. 1,000.

342 US
GILBERT LAW SUMMARIES. CONSTITUTIONAL LAW. irreg., 26th ed., 1990. $19.95. Law Distributors (Subsidiary of: H B J Legal & Professional Publications Inc.), 14415 S. Main St., Gardena, CA 90248. TEL 800-421-1893. FAX 213-324-6381.

342 IT
GIURISPRUDENZA COSTITUZIONALE. 1956. bi-m. L.220000 (foreign L.330000). Casa Editrice Dott. A. Giuffre, Via Busto Arsizio 40, 20151 Milan, Italy. TEL 02-38000905. FAX 02-38009582. Ed. Leopoldo Elia. adv.; bk.rev.; circ. 2,400.

342 US ISSN 0094-5617
K8
HASTINGS CONSTITUTIONAL LAW QUARTERLY. 1974. q. $20 (foreign $22). University of California, San Francisco, Hastings College of the Law, 200 McAllister St., San Francisco, CA 94102-4978. TEL 415-565-4726. FAX 415-565-4814. Ed. Nancy Schiff. adv.; bk.rev.; circ. 1,200. (tabloid format; also avail. in microfilm from WSH; back issues avail.; reprint service avail. from WSH) **Indexed:** C.C.L.P., C.L.I., Crim.Just.Abstr., L.R.I., Leg.Cont., Leg.Per.
●Also available online. Vendor(s): WESTLAW. Also available on CD-ROM.
—BLDSC shelfmark: 4273.030000.
Description: Legal scholarship on topics significant to current developments in constitutional law.

342 GW ISSN 0174-4704
K8
HUMAN RIGHTS LAW JOURNAL. (Text in English) 1980. m. DM.286($192) N.P. Engel Verlag, P.O. Box 1670, Gutenbergstr. 29, 7640 Kehl am Rhein, Germany. TEL 07851-2463. FAX 07851-4234. (U.S. addr.: N.P. Engel, Publisher, 3608 South 12th St., Arlington, VA 22204 Fax 703-920-3127) Ed. Erika Engel. adv.; cum.index: 1980-1988. **Indexed:** C.L.I., HR Rep., L.R.I., Leg.Per.
—BLDSC shelfmark: 4336.440500.
Incorporates: Human Rights Review.
Description: Articles, reports and documentation on constitutional and Supreme Court decisions. Includes information on pending proceedings.

342 II
INTRODUCTION TO THE CONSTITUTION OF INDIA. (Text in English) irreg., latest 13th ed. (National Research Professor of Constitutional Law) Prentice - Hall of India Pvt., Ltd., M-97, Connaught Circus, New Delhi 110 001, India. TEL 3321779. FAX 011-371-7179. TELEX 031-61808 PH IN.

342 GW ISSN 0075-2517
JF13
JAHRBUCH DES OEFFENTLICHEN RECHTS DER GEGENWART. N.S. 1951. a. price varies. Verlag J.C.B. Mohr (Paul Siebeck), Wilhelmstr. 18, Postfach 2040, 7400 Tuebingen, Germany. TEL 07071-26064. FAX 07071-51104. TELEX 7262872-MOHR-D. Ed. Peter Haeberle. **Indexed:** CERDIC.
Description: Developments in constitutional law in Europe and elsewhere.

342 US
LANDMARK BRIEFS AND ARGUMENTS OF THE SUPREME COURT OF THE UNITED STATES: CONSTITUTIONAL LAW. SUPPLEMENT. (Issued as 80 vol.set covering 1793-1973; annual supplements in several vols. cover each court term thereafter) 1974. a. $860 for current supplement. University Publications of America (Subsidiary of: Congressional Information Service), 4520 East-West Hwy., Ste. 800, Bethesda, MD 20814-3389. TEL 301-657-3200. FAX 301-657-3203. Eds. Philip B. Kurland, Gerhard Casper. (back issues avail.)

342 IT ISSN 0392-6664
QUADERNI COSTITUZIONALI. 1981. 3/yr. L.100000. Societa Editrice Il Mulino, Strada Maggiore, 37, 40125 Bologna, Italy. TEL 051-256011. FAX 051-256034. Ed. Livio Paladin. adv.; index; circ. 1,700. (back issues avail.) **Indexed:** P.A.I.S.For.Lang.Ind.

342 SP
REVISTA ESPANOLA DE DERECHO CONSTITUCIONAL. 3/yr. $40. (Centro de Estudios Constitucionales) Edisa, Lopez de Hoyos, 141, 28002 Madrid, Spain. TEL 415-97-12.

342 FR
▼REVUE FRANCAISE DE DROIT CONSTITUTIONNEL. 1990. 4/yr. 450 F. (foreign 510 F.). Presses Universitaires de France, Departement des Revues, 14 av. du Bois-de-l'Epine, B.P. 90, 91003 Evry Cedex, France. TEL 1-60-77-82-05. FAX 1-60-79-20-45. TELEX PUF 600 474 F. Eds. Louis Favoreu, Didier Maus.

342 PN
UNIVERSIDAD DE PANAMA. CENTRO DE INVESTIGACION JURIDICA. JURISPRUDENCIA CONSTITUTIONAL. 1968. irreg. price varies. Universidad de Panama, Centro de Investigacion Juridica, Estafeta Universitaria, Panama, Panama. Ed. Aura G. de Villalaz.

UNIWERSYTET SLASKI W KATOWICACH. PRACE NAUKOWE. STUDIA IURIDICA SILESIANA. see LAW

LAW — Corporate Law

346 330 340 US ISSN 0571-8279
KF297.A1
ATTORNEY - C P A. 1966. 5/yr. $30 to non-members; foreign $40. American Association of Attorney-Certified Public Accountants, Inc., 24196 Alicia Parkway, Ste. K, Mission Viejo, CA 92691. TEL 714-768-0336. Ed. Ronald M. DeVore. adv.; bk.rev.; circ. 1,600. (back issues avail.) **Indexed:** Account.Ind. (1974-).
Description: Technical information and updates on dual license regulation. Includes association news.

346 657 US
ATTORNEY'S HANDBOOK OF ACCOUNTING. 1965. base vol. (plus irreg. suppl.). Matthew Bender & Co., Inc., 11 Penn Plaza, New York, NY 10001. TEL 212-967-7007.
Formerly: Attorney's Practical Guide to Accounting.
Description: Covers accounting principles and practices, from financial statement analysis to accounting procedures for businesses and nonprofit organizations.

346 AT ISSN 0310-1053
K1 CODEN: ABRVDO
AUSTRALIAN BUSINESS LAW REVIEW. 1973. bi-m. Aus.$184. Law Book Co. Ltd., 44-50 Waterloo Rd., N. Ryde, N.S.W. 2113, Australia. TEL 02-887-0177. FAX 02-888-9706. TELEX ASBOOK 27995. bk.rev.; illus. **Indexed:** ABI Inform., Abstr.Bk.Rev.Curr.Leg.Per., Aus.P.A.I.S., BPIA, C.L.I., L.R.I., Leg.Cont.
—BLDSC shelfmark: 1798.095000.
Description: Contains leading articles on matters of topical interest and comments by regular contributors on legislative and case law developments affecting banking and investment.

346 AT
AUSTRALIAN COMPANY LAW CASES. 1971. 16/yr. (every 3 w.). C C H Australia Ltd, P.O. Box 230, North Ryde, N.S.W. 2113, Australia. TEL 888-2555. FAX 02-888-7324.

346 330 AT
AUSTRALIAN COMPANY SECRETARY'S BUSINESS LAW MANUAL. 1987. s-a. C C H Australia Ltd., P.O. Box 230, North Ryde, N.S.W. 2113, Australia. TEL 02-888-2555. FAX 02-888-7324.

346 336 AT ISSN 0729-1221
AUSTRALIAN COMPANY SECRETARY'S LETTER; a practical business review for corporate administrators. 1982. irreg. (approx. 3/w.). C C H Australia Ltd., P.O. Box 230, North Ryde, N.S.W. 2113, Australia. TEL 02-888-2555. FAX 02-888-7324.

346 AT
▼AUSTRALIAN CORPORATIONS & SECURITIES LAW REPORTER. (In 2 vols.) 1990. irreg. (approx. 3/yr.). C C H Australia Ltd., P.O. Box 230, North Ryde, N.S.W. 2113, Australia. TEL 02-888-2555. FAX 02-888-7324.

346 AT ISSN 1033-7466
LAW
AUSTRALIAN CORPORATIONS AND SECURITIES REPORTS; reports of leading cases in company law in Australia. 1977. 2/yr. (plus updates every 3 weeks). Aus.$235. Butterworths Pty. Ltd, 271-273 Lane Cove Rd., North Ryde, N.S.W. 2113, Australia. TEL 02-335-4444. FAX 02-335-4655. Ed. W.E. Paterson. circ. 1,608. (back issues avail.)
Formerly (until 1990): Australian Company Law Reports (ISSN 0313-8445)

346 331 AT
AUSTRALIAN EMPLOYMENT LAW GUIDE. 1984. 10/yr. C C H Australia Ltd., P.O. Box 230, North Ryde, N.S.W. 2113 Australia. TEL 02-888-2555. FAX 02-888-7324.

346 331 AT
AUSTRALIAN EMPLOYMENT LEGISLATION. (In 3 vols.) 1984. m. C C H Australia Ltd., P.O. Box 230, North Ryde, N.S.W. 2113, Australia. TEL 02-888-2555. FAX 02-888-7324.

346 336 AT
AUSTRALIAN FRINGE BENEFITS TAX GUIDE FOR EMPLOYERS. 1986. 8/yr. C C H Australia Ltd., P.O. Box 230, North Ryde, N.S.W. 2113, Australia. TEL 02-888-2555. FAX 02-888-7324.
Description: Provides practical commentary and full text legislation.

346 AT ISSN 0726-5883
AUSTRALIAN INDUSTRIAL LAW REVIEW. 1959. fortn. C C H Australia Ltd., Box 230, North Ryde, N.S.W. 2113, Australia. TEL 888-2555. FAX 02-888-7324.

346 331 AT ISSN 1030-7222
AUSTRALIAN JOURNAL OF LABOUR LAW. 1988. 3/yr. Aus.$115. Butterworths Pty. Ltd., 271-273 Lane Cove Rd., North Ryde, N.S.W. 2113, Australia. TEL 02-335-4444. FAX 02-335-4655. Ed. Richard Mitchell. bk.rev.; circ. 1,000.
Description: Articles, notes, comments and commentaries on recent cases, legislation on labor law and labor relations suited for academics and practitioners.

346 331 AT
AUSTRALIAN LABOUR LAW REPORTER. (In 3 vols.) 1977. m. C C H Australia Ltd., P.O. Box 230, North Ryde, N.S.W. 2113, Australia. TEL 888-2555. FAX 02-888-7324. charts.

346 AT
▼AUSTRALIAN SECURITIES COMMISSION RELEASES. 1991. irreg. C C H Australia Ltd., P.O. Box 230, North Ryde, N.S.W. 2113, Australia. TEL 02-888-2555. FAX 02-888-7324.

346 332.6 AT ISSN 0311-0265
AUSTRALIAN SECURITIES LAW REPORTER. (In 2 vols.) 1972. every 6 weeks. C C H Australia Ltd., P.O. Box 230, North Ryde, N.S.W. 2113, Australia. TEL 888-2555. FAX 02-888-7324.

346 US ISSN 0099-1236
KF1414.3
B A R - B R I BAR REVIEW. CORPORATIONS. a. $395. B A R - B R I Bar Review, 3280 Motor Ave., Los Angeles, CA 90034-3710. TEL 213-477-2542.

LAW — CORPORATE LAW

346 US
BALLANTINE AND STERLING CALIFORNIA CORPORATION LAWS. 1932. 6 base vols. (plus irreg. suppl.). Matthew Bender & Co., Inc., 11 Penn Plaza, New York, NY 10001. TEL 212-967-7707. (Co-publisher: Parker & Son)
  Description: Provides detailed analysis of both the general and non-profit corporation law of California, combined with procedural guides from incorporation to dissolution.

346 KF1519 US ISSN 0098-7336
BANKRUPTCY COURT DECISIONS. 1974. w. $685. L R P Publications, 747 Dresher Rd., Box 980, Horsham, PA 19044. TEL 215-784-0860. Ed. Joanne E. Fiore. bk.rev.; circ. 2,000. (back issues avail.)

346 US ISSN 0005-5530
BANKRUPTCY LAW REPORTS. fortn. $695. Commerce Clearing House, Inc., 4025 W. Peterson Ave., Chicago, IL 60646. TEL 312-583-8500. Ed. Martin Bernstein. bibl.; charts; stat.; index. (looseleaf format)

346 657 US
BANKRUPTCY LAW REVIEW. 1989. q. $125. Faulkner & Gray, Inc. (New York), 11 Penn Plaza, 17th Fl., New York, NY 10001. TEL 212-967-7155. Ed. Bob Murdich. *Indexed:* Account.Ind. (1989-).
  Description: Presents interpretations, analysis and news.

346 US
BANKRUPTCY PRACTICE DESKBOOK. 3 base vols. (plus a. suppl.). $285. Butterworth Legal Publishers (Salem) (Subsidiary of: Reed International PLC), 90 Stiles Rd., Salem, NH 03079. TEL 800-548-4001. FAX 603-898-9858. Eds. David D. Bird, Richard H.W. Maloy. (looseleaf format)
  Formerly: Bankruptcy Practice Manual.
  Description: Incorporates the ongoing changes in the Bankruptcy Code, Rules, and case law developments in all states.

346 US
BANKRUPTCY PRACTICE FOR THE GENERAL PRACTITIONER. 1980. 2 base vols. (plus s-a. suppl.). $195. Shepard's - McGraw-Hill, Inc., Box 35300, Colorado Springs, CO 80935-3530. TEL 800-525-2474. (looseleaf format)
  Description: Focuses on the procedural and substantive aspects of the Bankruptcy Code.

346 330 US
BANKRUPTCY SERVICE CURRENT AWARENESS ALERT. 1980. 12/yr. $125. Clark Boardman Callaghan, Aqueduct Bldg., 50 Broad St. E., Rochester, NY 14694. TEL 716-546-5530. FAX 716-258-3768. Ed. Larry E. Edmonson. (looseleaf format)
  Description: Places in context recent rulings on bankruptcy law and practice.

346 US
BASIC PATTERNS IN UNION CONTRACTS. irreg., 12th ed., 1989. $25. B N A Books (Subsidiary of: The Bureau of National Affairs, Inc.), 1231 25th St., N.W., Washington, DC 20037. TEL 201-225-1900. FAX 201-417-0482. (Subscr.to: BNA Books Distribution Center, 300 Raritan Center Parkway, Box 7816, Edison, NJ 08818-7816. TEL 800-372-1033) Ed.Bd.

346 GW ISSN 0005-9935
DER BETRIEB; Wochenzeitschrift fuer Betriebswirtschaft, Steuerrecht, Wirtschaftsrecht, Arbeitsrecht. 1948. w. DM.396. Handelsblatt GmbH, Kasernenstr. 67, Postfach 102717, 4000 Duesseldorf 1, Germany. TEL 0211-8870. Ed. G. Ackermann. adv.; bk.rev.; charts; illus.; stat.; index, cum.index; circ. 25,000. (reprint service avail. from UMI) *Indexed:* CERDIC, Dok.Arbeitsmed., INIS Atomind., SSCI.

346 331 CN
BRITISH COLUMBIA DECISIONS - INDUSTRIAL RELATIONS COUNCIL. m. Can.$250. Western Legal Publications, 301-1 Alexander St., Vancouver, B.C. V6A 1B2, Canada. TEL 604-687-5671. FAX 604-687-2796. index. (looseleaf format)
  ●Also available online.
  Formerly: British Columbia Decisions - Labour Relations Board Decisions (ISSN 0715-5808)
  Description: Provides full summaries of all written and letter decisions of the Industrial Relations Council of British Columbia.

346 640.73 CN
BUSINESS & EMPLOYMENT LAW NEWS. 1979. m. Can.$115. Dunhill Publishing Company, 6389 Coburg Rd., Halifax, N.S. B3H 2A5, Canada.
  Former titles: Business Law News; Dunhill Products Liability Law Report.

346 CN ISSN 0825-4982
BUSINESS & THE LAW. 1984. m. $205. Carswell Publications, Corporate Plaza, 2075 Kennedy Rd., Scarborough, Ont. M1T 3V4, Canada. TEL 416-609-8000. FAX 416-298-5094. *Indexed:* Ind.Can.L.P.L.

346 US
BUSINESS COUNSEL; a quarterly update of the litigation activities of the U.S. Chambers of Commerce. 1979. q. $15 to non-member legal libraries. National Chamber Litigation Center (NCLC), 1615 H St., N.W., Washington, DC 20062. TEL 202-463-5337. FAX 202-463-5836. Ed. Cam Esser. illus.; tr.lit.; circ. 1,000.
  Formerly: Business Advocate (ISSN 0193-4414); Supersedes (1979-1983): Washington Report (Washington, 1979) (ISSN 0043-0714)

346 330 US
BUSINESS ETHIC RESOURCE; a resource on ethics management for the CEO. 1987. q. $24. Reheven Consultants, 28 Marshal St., Ste. 3, Brookline, MA 02146. TEL 617-232-1820. Ed. Phyllis Nygard. bk.rev.; circ. 1,200.
  Description: Covers news of ethics related issues for the business community.

346 UK
BUSINESS LAW BRIEF. 1972. m. £295 (foreign £319). Financial Times Business Information Ltd., Tower House, Southampton St., London WC2E 7HA, England. TEL 071-240 9391. FAX 071-240-7946. TELEX 296926-BUSINF-G. Ed. A.H. Hermann. bk.rev.; index.
  ●Also available online. Vendor(s): Data-Star, Mead Data Central.
  Former titles (until Dec. 1983): European Law Letter & European Law Newsletter (ISSN 0300-2233)
  Description: Provides the latest information on judicial developments and judgements.

346 330 US
BUSINESS LAW MONOGRAPHS. 1984. 26 base vols. (plus q. updates). Matthew Bender & Co., Inc., 11 Penn Plaza, New York, NY 10001. TEL 212-967-7707. (looseleaf format)
  Description: Each monograph concentrates on a particular subject of interest to corporate counsel, explaining what the law requires and how counsel can handle common transactions and prevent or resolve common problems.

346 CN ISSN 0703-5551
KE915.8
BUSINESS LAW REPORTS (2ND SERIES). 1977. m. (4 vols./yr.). Can.$115. Carswell Publications, Corporate Plaza, 2075 Kennedy Rd., Scarborough, Ont. M1T 3V4, Canada. TEL 416-609-5094. FAX 416-298-5094. Ed. George C. Glover, Jr. (looseleaf format) *Indexed:* C.L.I., Ind.Can.L.P.L., L.R.I.

346 330 UK ISSN 0143-6295
BUSINESS LAW REVIEW. 1980. m. £210($370) Graham & Trotman Ltd. (Subsidiary of: Kluwer Academic Publishers Group), Sterling House, 66 Wilton Rd., London SW1V 1DE, England. (Dist. by: Kluwer Academic Publishers Group, P.O. Box 322, 3300 AH Dordrecht, Netherlands; N. America dist. addr.: Box 358, Accord Station, Hingham, MA 02018-0358. TEL 617-871-6600) Ed. Susan Nicholas. adv. *Indexed:* Bus.Ind., L.R.I.
—BLDSC shelfmark: 2934.122000.

346 381 UK
BUSINESS LAWS OF EGYPT. a. (plus s-a. supplements). £349($660) basic work; supplement service £210($399). Graham & Trotman Ltd., Sterling House, 66 Wilton Rd., London SW1V 1DE, England. (Dist. in U.S. and Canada by: Kluwer Inc., 101 Philip Dr., Assinippi Park, Norwell, MA 02061) Ed. N.H. Karam. (looseleaf format)

346 381 UK
BUSINESS LAWS OF IRAQ. a. (plus q. supplements). £349($660) basic work; supplement service £210($399). Graham & Trotman Ltd., Sterling House, 66 Wilton Rd., London SW1V 1DE, England. (Dist. in U.S. and Canada by: Kluwer Inc., 101 Philip Dr., Assinippi Park, Norwell, MA 02061) Ed. N.H. Karam. (looseleaf format)

346 381 UK
BUSINESS LAWS OF KUWAIT. a. (plus q. supplements). £349($660) basic work; supplement service £210($399). Graham & Trotman Ltd., Sterling House, 66 Wilton Rd., London SW1V 1DE, England. (Dist. in U.S. and Canada by: Kluwer Inc., 101 Philip Dr., Assinippi Park, Norwell, MA 02061) Ed. N.H. Karam. (looseleaf format)

346 381 UK
BUSINESS LAWS OF SAUDI ARABIA. a. (plus bi-m supplements). £340($660) basic work; supplement service £260($495). Graham & Trotman Ltd., Sterling House, 66 Wilton Rd., London SW1V 1DE, England. (Dist. in U.S. and Canada by: Kluwer Inc., 101 Philip Dr., Assinippi Park, Norwell, MA 02061) Ed. N.H. Karam. (looseleaf format)

346 381 UK
BUSINESS LAWS OF UNITED ARAB EMIRATES. a. (plus s-a. supplements). £349($660) to basic work; supplement service £210($399). Graham & Trotman Ltd., Sterling House, 66 Wilton Rd., London SW1V 1DE, England. (Dist. in U.S. and Canada by: Kluwer Inc., 101 Philip Dr., Assinippi Park, Norwell, MA 02061) Ed. M.J. Hall.

346 US ISSN 0007-6899
LAW
BUSINESS LAWYER. 1946. q. $28 to non-members (foreign $33). American Bar Association, Business Law Section, 750 N. Lake Shore Dr., Chicago, IL 60611. TEL 312-988-5588. Ed. George Freeman. adv.; bk.rev.; circ. 55,000. (also avail. in microfilm from MIM,RRI; reprint service avail. from RRI) *Indexed:* AAR, ABI Inform, Account.Ind. (1974-), BPIA, Bus.Ind., C.L.I., Curr.Cont., L.R.I., Law Ofc.Info.Svc., Leg.Per., P.A.I.S., SSCI, Tr.& Indus.Ind.
●Also available online. Vendor(s): Mead Data Central (BUSLAW), WESTLAW (BUSLAW).
—BLDSC shelfmark: 2934.170000.
  Description: Covers business and financial law, with articles on current legal topics and substantive section programs.

346 KF872 US ISSN 0884-1977
BUSINESS LAWYER UPDATE. 1980. bi-m. membership only. American Bar Association, Business Law Section, 750 N. Lake Shore Dr., Chicago, IL 60611. TEL 312-988-5588. Ed. Larry Scriggins. circ. 50,000.
  Formerly: Business Law Memo (ISSN 0271-9045)
  Description: Newsletter on Section activities and recent developments in business or banking law.

346 330 US
BUSINESS ORGANIZATIONS: CORPORATE ACQUISITIONS AND MERGERS. 1968. 4 base vols. (plus irreg. supplements). Matthew Bender & Co., Inc., 11 Penn Plaza, New York, NY 10001. TEL 212-967-7707. Eds. Byron E. Fox, Eleanor M. Fox.
  Description: Guide to the anti-trust, tax, corporate, securities and financial aspects of business combinations.

346 331 US
BUSINESS ORGANIZATIONS: PENSION AND PROFIT-SHARING PLANS. 1977. 5 base vols. (plus irreg. supplements) Matthew Bender & Co., Inc., 11 Penn Plaza, New York, NY 10001. TEL 212-967-7707. Ed. Sheldon Mike Young.
  Description: Covers the whole field of pension and profit-sharing plans. Provides detailed treatment of attributes, benefits, special plans, rights of participants, processing plan through the IRS and other agencies, integration with Social Security benefits, union negotiated plans and terminations.

BUSINESS ORGANIZATIONS: PROFESSIONAL CORPORATIONS AND ASSOCIATIONS. see *BUSINESS AND ECONOMICS*

LAW — CORPORATE LAW

346   US
BUSINESS TORT OF FRAUD & MISREPRESENTATION. 1989. 2 base vols. (plus suppl.). $180. Butterworth Legal Publishers (Salem) (Subsidiary of: Reed International PLC), 90 Stiles Rd., Salem, NH 03079. TEL 800-548-4001. FAX 603-898-9858. Ed. Warren Freedman. (looseleaf format)

346 330   US
BUSINESS TORTS. 1989. 4 base vols. (plus irreg. supplements). Matthew Bender & Co., Inc., 11 Penn Plaza, New York, NY 10001. TEL 212-967-7707. Ed. Joseph D. Zamore.
    Description: Covers a variety of important business torts.

346   SA   ISSN 0045-3668
BUSINESSMAN'S LAW. 1971. 8/yr. R.150. Juta & Co. Ltd., P.O. Box 14373, Kenwyn 7790, South Africa. TEL 021-797-5101. FAX 021-761-5010. Ed. M. Dendy. adv.; circ. 3,000. Indexed: Ind.S.A.Per.
—BLDSC shelfmark: 2934.960000.

346   NZ
BUTTERWORTHS COMMERCIAL SERVICE. 2 base vols. (plus updates 3/yr.). NZ.$296. Butterworths of New Zealand Ltd., 203-207 Victoria St., P.O. Box 472, Wellington, New Zealand. TEL 04-385-1479. FAX 04-385-1598. Ed. Stuart Coghill.
    Description: Full text of acts, regulations, orders and notices most frequently consulted in commercial practice.

346   UK   ISSN 0267-145X
BUTTERWORTHS COMPANY LAW CASES. 1983. bi-m. $375. Butterworth & Co. (Publishers) Ltd. (Subsidiary of: Reed International PLC), 88 Kingsway, London WC2B 6AB, England. TEL 071-405-6900. FAX 71-405-1332. (US addr.: Butterworth Legal Publishers, 90 Stiles Rd., Salem, NH 03079. TEL 800-548-4001) Eds. D.D. Prentice, M. Stokes. (looseleaf format)

346   UK
BUTTERWORTHS COMPANY LAW SERVICE; for UK use. 2 base vols. (plus 2-4 updates/yr. and bi-m. bulletin). $415. Butterworth & Co. (Publishers) Ltd. (Subsidiary of: Reed International PLC), 88 Kingsway, London WC2B 6AB, England. TEL 71-405-6900. FAX 71-405-1332. (US addr.: Butterworth Legal Publishers, 90 Stiles Rd., Salem, NH 03079. TEL 800-548-4001) (looseleaf format)

346   AT
C C H AUSTRALIAN COMPANIES AND SECURITIES LEGISLATION. (In 2 vols.) 1982. irreg. (as required for all legislative changes). C C H Australia Ltd., P.O. Box 230, North Ryde, N.S.W. 2113, Australia. TEL 02-888-2555. FAX 02-888-7324.

346   UK
C M L R ANTITRUST REPORTS. m. £185. Sweet & Maxwell, South Quay Plaza, 8th Fl., 183 Marsh Wall, London E14 9FT, England. TEL 071-538-8686. FAX 071-538-9508. Eds. Joe McDonald Hill, Neville Hunnings.

346   US   ISSN 0892-2349
CALIFORNIA BUSINESS LAW PRACTITIONER. 1986. 4/yr. $175 (effective July 1991). Continuing Education of the Bar - California, University of California Extension, 2300 Shattuck Ave., Berkeley, CA 94704. TEL 510-642-0306. FAX 800-642-3788. (Co-sponsor: State Bar of California) Ed. Hale Kronenberg. (back issues avail.)

346   US   ISSN 0199-669X
KFC337.A15
CALIFORNIA BUSINESS LAW REPORTER. 1980. 8/yr. $175 (effective July 1991). Continuing Education of the Bar - California, University of California Extension, 2300 Shattuck Ave., Berkeley, CA 94704. TEL 415-642-0306. FAX 415-800-3788. (Co-sponsor: State Bar of California) Ed. Hale Kronenberg. (tabloid format; back issues avail.)

346 381   US
CALIFORNIA CORPORATIONS CODE AND CORPORATE SECURITES RULES. 1972. a. $33. Matthew Bender & Co., Inc., 11 Penn Plaza, New York, NY 10001. TEL 212-967-7707. Ed.Bd.

346   CN   ISSN 0317-6649
CANADA BUSINESS CORPORATIONS ACT WITH REGULATIONS. vol.5, 1983. irreg. Can.$10.95. C C H Canadian Ltd., 6 Garamond Ct., Don Mills, Ont. M3C 1Z5, Canada. TEL 416-441-2992. FAX 416-445-9011. index.

346   CN
CANADA CORPORATIONS LAW REPORTER. m. Can.$500. C C H Canadian Ltd., 6 Garamond Ct., Don Mills, Ont. M3C 1Z5, Canada. TEL 416-441-2992. FAX 416-444-9011. index.
    Formerly: Dominion Companies Law Reports (ISSN 0046-0559)
    Description: Reports on federal legislation governing companies under federal charter.

346   CN
K18
CANADA - U S BUSINESS LAW REVIEW. 1988. base vol. (plus 3/yr. supplements). Can.$128($102) Carswell Publications, Corporate Plaza, 2075 Kennedy Rd., Scarborough, Ont. M1T 3V4, Canada. TEL 416-609-8000. FAX 416-298-5094. Ed. Errol P. Mendes. adv.; bk.rev. (also avail. in microform from WSH; reprint service avail. from WSH)
    Formerly: Review of International Business Law (ISSN 0835-2399)
    Description: Analysis and discussion of Canada - U S trade, securities and banking law, dispute settlement, foreign investment and taxation questions. Articles, updates on current issues, and case comments on significant decisions.

346   CN   ISSN 0319-3322
K3
CANADIAN BUSINESS LAW JOURNAL. 1976. q. Can.$116. Canada Law Book Inc., 240 Edward St., Aurora, Ont. L4G 3S9, Canada. TEL 416-841-6472. Indexed: ABI Inform, Abstr.Bk.Rev.Curr.Leg.Per., BPIA, Bus.Ind., C.L.I., Can.B.P.I., Ind.Can.L.P.L., L.R.I., Leg.Cont., Leg.Per.
—BLDSC shelfmark: 3018.255000.

346   CN
CANADIAN COMMERCIAL LAW GUIDE. 1967. m. Can.$495. C C H Canadian Ltd., 6 Garamond Ct., Don Mills, Ont. M3C 1Z5, Canada. TEL 416-441-2992. FAX 416-444-9011. index.
    Formerly: Canadian Sales and Credit Law Guide (ISSN 0045-5318)
    Description: Full texts of federal and provincial laws relating to sales contracts, conditional sales, installment sales, chattel mortgages and bills of sale.

346   CN
CANADIAN TRADE LAW REPORTER. 1989. m. Can.$395. C C H Canadian Ltd., 6 Garamond Ct., Don Mills, Ont. M3C 1Z5, Canada. TEL 416-441-2992. FAX 416-444-9011.
    Description: Explains and analyzes the Customs Act, Customs Tariff, Special Import Measures Act, Export and Import Permits Act, Canadian Charter of Rights and Freedoms and Access to Information Act.

346 336   US
CHAPTER 11: REORGANIZATIONS. 1983. base vol. (plus a. suppl.). $95. Shepard's - McGraw-Hill, Inc., Box 35300, Colorado Springs, CO 80935-3530. TEL 800-525-2474.
    Description: Explains reorganization law from the pragmatic viewpoint of a long-time practitioner, emphasizing examples of how the law works.

346   US   ISSN 1055-9477
▼**CHAPTER 11 UPDATE;** monitors all major developments in today's corporate bankruptcies and examines pertinent court decisions related to Chapter 11 filings. 1991. s-m. $350. Andrews Publications, 1646 West Chester Pike, Box 1000, Westtown, PA 19395. TEL 215-399-6600. FAX 215-399-6610. Eds. Mary Jeffers, Kathy Knaub. bibl.; stat. (looseleaf format; back issues avail.)

346   AT
▼**CHINA BUSINESS LAW GUIDE.** 1991. q. C C H Australia Ltd., P.O. Box 230, North Ryde, N.S.W. 2113, Australia. TEL 02-888-2555. FAX 02-888-7324.
    Description: Contains information of immediate importance to business people on every major area of China's business laws. Companion publication to CCH's China Laws for Foreign Business.

346 382   AT
CHINA LAWS FOR FOREIGN BUSINESS. (In 6 vols.) (Text in Chinese, English) 1985. irreg. (approx. 10/yr.). C H Australia Ltd., P.O. Box 230, North Ryde, N.S.W. 2113, Australia. TEL 02-888-2555. FAX 02-888-7324.

346   AT   ISSN 0729-2775
COMPANIES AND SECURITIES LAW JOURNAL. 1982. q. Aus.$210. Law Book Co. Ltd., 44-50 Waterloo Rd., North Ryde, N.S.W. 2113, Australia. TEL 02-887-0177. FAX 02-888-9706. TELEX ASBOOK 27995. Ed. S. Sievers. bk.rev.; index; circ. 509. (back issues avail.) Indexed: Leg.Per.
—BLDSC shelfmark: 3363.734700.
    Description: Examines a range of subjects including company law, takeovers and public securities, proprietary companies and insolvency.

346   UK   ISSN 0260-4620
COMPANY LAW DIGEST; every development in company law. 1979. q. £35. Tolley Publishing Co. Ltd., Tolley House, 2 Addiscombe Rd., Croydon, Surrey CR9 5AF, England. Ed. Linda Carter. adv.; bk.rev.; circ. 500.

346   II   ISSN 0045-7787
COMPANY LAW INSTITUTE OF INDIA. REPORTS OF COMPANY CASES INCLUDING BANKING & INSURANCE. (Text in English) 1931. fortn. Rs.405. Company Law Institute of India Pvt. Ltd., 88 Thayagaraya Rd., Madras 600017, India. Ed.Bd. index; circ. 5,000.

346   UK
K3
COMPANY LAWYER AND COMPANY LAWYER DIGEST. 1980. m £139($225) Longman Group UK Ltd., Law, Tax and Finance Division, 21-27 Lamb's Conduit St., London WC1N 3NJ, England. TEL 071-242-2548. FAX 071-242-2548. TELEX 295445. Eds. B. Rider, M. Khan. Indexed: C.L.I., L.R.I.
    Formerly: Company Lawyer (ISSN 0144-1027)
    Description: Information on changes and developments in business and company law.

346.066   US
CONNECTICUT CORPORATION STATUTES AND FORMS. a. $25. Connecticut Law Book Company, Box 575, Guilford, CT 06437. TEL 203-458-8000.
    Description: Compilation of the current statutes of this state that deal with corporations and of the official forms utilized by the office of the Connecticut Secretary of the State.

346.066   US
CORPORATE ACQUISITIONS, MERGERS AND DIVESTITURES. base vol. (plus m. Ideas Letter and updates). Walter, Gorham & Lamont, Inc., 210 South Street, Boston, MA 02111. TEL 617-423-2020. FAX 617-423-2926. Ed. Lewis D. Solomon. (looseleaf format)

346   AT   ISSN 1033-2405
CORPORATE AND BUSINESS LAW JOURNAL. 1988. s-a. $20. Corporate & Business Law Centre, c/o Department of Law, University of Adelaide, N. Terr., Adelaide, S.A. 5000, Australia. TEL 08-228-5063. FAX 08-232-4679. (Dist. in U.S. by: William S. Hein & Co., 1285 Main St., Buffalo, NY 14209)

346   US   ISSN 0743-0272
KF1477.A15
CORPORATE CONTROL ALERT; a report on current changes in corporate control. 1984. m. $1495. American Lawyer Media, L.P. (New York), 600 Third Ave., New York, NY 10016. TEL 212-986-0088. FAX 212-972-6258. Ed. Martha Sellers Klein. charts. (back issues avail.)
    Description: News on mergers and acquisitions.

346 658   US
CORPORATE COUNSELLOR. m. $210. New York Law Publishing Co., Marketing Dept., 111 Eighth Ave., New York, NY 10011. TEL 212-741-8300.
    Description: Provides reports on legal and regulatory issues faced in an in-house practice, as well as administrative, recruitment and financial issues involved in running an in-house firm.

346 628.4 US
▼**CORPORATE ENVIRONMENTAL DATA CLEARINGHOUSE REPORTS.** 1991. q. $1500 for 100 issues; single report $100. Council for Economic Priorities, 30 Irving Pl., New York, NY 10003-2386. TEL 212-420-1133. FAX 212-420-0988.
Description: Comprehensive reports analyzing corporate environmental compliance records, energy efficiency, hazardous waste disposal policies, and other important environmental issues. Each report covers all aspects of a single company and compares that company's performance to industry averages.

346 US
CORPORATE GOVERNANCE BULLETIN. 1981. bi-m. $275 (effective 1992). Investor Responsibility Research Center, Inc., 1755 Massachusetts Ave., N.W., Ste. 600, Washington, DC 20036-2102. TEL 202-234-7500. FAX 202-332-8570. Ed. Peg O'Hara. circ. 1,200.

346 US ISSN 0898-8390
HG4028.M4
CORPORATE GROWTH MAGAZINE. 1982. m. $325. Quality Services Company, 5290 Overpass Rd., Ste.126, Santa Barbara, CA 93111-9950. TEL 805-964-7841. Ed. Carmen Lodise. adv.; circ. 500. (also avail. in microform from UMI) **Indexed:** BPIA, P.A.I.S.
—BLDSC shelfmark: 3472.066300.
Former titles: Buyouts and Acquisitions Magazine; Journal of Buyouts and Acquisitions (ISSN 0736-5527)

346 UK ISSN 0141-4852
CORPORATE LEGAL LETTER. 1977. m. £135 (foreign £150). Monitor Press, Rectory Rd., Great Waldingfield, Sudbury, Suffolk CO10 0TL, England. TEL 0787-78607. FAX 0787-880201. (back issues avail.)
Description: Addresses the practical implications of all the major relevant cases, statutes and regulations, including those from the European Economic Community for company lawyers and senior management.

346 330 US
CORPORATE LEGAL TIMES. m. $95. Giant Steps Publishing Corporation, 420 W. Grand Ave., Chicago, IL 60610. TEL 312-644-4378. FAX 312-644-0765. Ed. Charles H. Carman. adv.; bk.rev.; circ. 50,000. (tabloid format)
Description: Contains news and analysis for general counsel and other in-house lawyers.

346 US ISSN 0887-7793
KF1423.A59
CORPORATE OFFICERS AND DIRECTORS LIABILITY LITIGATION REPORTER; the twice-monthly national journal of record of litigation based on fiduciary responsibility. 1985. s-m. $800. Andrews Publications, 1646 West Chester Pike, Box 1000, Westtown, PA 19395. TEL 215-399-6600. FAX 215-399-6610. Ed. Frank Reynolds. abstr.; bibl.; stat.; cum.index every 6 mos. (looseleaf format; back issues avail.)

346 US ISSN 0010-8995
LAW
CORPORATE PRACTICE COMMENTATOR. 1959. q. $105. Callaghan & Co., 155 Pfingsten Rd., Deerfield, IL 60015. TEL 800-323-1336. Ed. F. Hodge O'Neal. bk.rev.; abstr.; index. **Indexed:** Account.Ind. (1986-), C.L.I., L.R.I., Leg.Cont., Leg.Per., Tr.& Indus.Ind.

346 US ISSN 0162-5691
KF1397
CORPORATE PRACTICE SERIES. (Includes BNA's Corporate Counsel Weekly) 1978. w. $1190. The Bureau of National Affairs, Inc., 1231 25th St., N.W., Washington, DC 20037. TEL 202-452-4200. FAX 202-822-8092. TELEX 285656 BNAI WSH. (Subscr. to: 9435 Key West Ave., Rockville, MD 20850. TEL 800-372-1033) Ed. Larry Lempert. bibl.; charts; stat. (looseleaf format; back issues avail.)
Description: Corporate law reference service organized into a series of portfolios written by legal experts. Each portfolio covers a different legal subject with detailed analyses, working papers and a bibliography.

346 US
DELAWARE CORPORATE LAW REPORTER. 1985. m. $250. Delaware Law Monthly, Box 262, Wilmington, DE 19899. TEL 302-652-2050. Ed. Bette Meserlian. (back issues avail.)
Description: Studies corporate banking and law.

346.066 US ISSN 1042-5756
KFD213.A59
DELAWARE CORPORATE LITIGATION REPORTER; the journal reporting service of litigation concerning record of law in Delaware. s-m. $800. Andrews Publications, 1646 West Chester Pike, Box 1000, Westtown, PA 19395. TEL 215-399-6600. FAX 215-399-66107. Ed. Frank Reynolds. abstr.; bibl.; stat.; cum.index every 6 mos. (looseleaf format; back issues avail.)

346.066 US ISSN 0888-434X
KFD213.A59
DELAWARE CORPORATION LAW UPDATE. 1985. m. $375. Andrews Publications, 1646 West Chester Pike, Box 1000, Westtown, PA 19395. TEL 215-399-6600. FAX 215-399-6610. Ed. Frank Reynolds. bibl.; stat.; cum.index every 6 mos. (looseleaf format; back issues avail.)
Description: Analysis of every opinion, reported and unreported, issued by Delaware's courts involving corporate law issues. Also reports new suits filed in DE Chancery Court.

346.066 US ISSN 0364-9490
K4
DELAWARE JOURNAL OF CORPORATE LAW. 1976. 2/yr. $32 for 2 vols. Widener University, School of Law, Box 7286, Wilmington, DE 19803. TEL 302-477-2145. Ed. Joshua L. Cohen. adv.; bk.rev.; circ. 2,100. (also avail. in microform from RRI,UMI,WSH; reprint service avail. from UMI,WSH) **Indexed:** BPIA, Bus.Ind., C.L.I., L.R.I., Leg.Cont., Leg.Per.
●Also available online. Vendor(s): Mead Data Central, WESTLAW.

346 US
FLORIDA CORPORATIONS MANUAL. 1977. 5 base vols. (plus suppl. 2-3/yr.). $320. Butterworth Legal Publishers (Salem) (Subsidiary of: Reed International PLC), 90 Stiles Rd., Salem, NH 03079. TEL 800-548-4001. FAX 603-898-9858. (looseleaf format)

346 US
FLORIDA CREDITORS' RIGHTS MANUAL. 1975. 4 base vols. (plus suppl. 4-5/yr.). Butterworth Legal Publishers (Salem) (Subsidiary of: Reed International PLC), 90 Stiles Rd., Salem, NH 03079. TEL 800-548-4001. FAX 603-898-9858. (looseleaf format)

346 US
FLORIDA SECURITIES LAW. 1989. base vol. (plus a. suppl.). $60. Butterworth Legal Publishers (Salem) (Subsidiary of: Reed International PLC), 90 Stiles Rd., Salem, NH 03079. TEL 800-548-4001. FAX 603-898-9858. (looseleaf format)

346 331.1 658.3 US ISSN 0733-0324
FORDYCE LETTER; commentary and information provided exclusively for those involved in the personnel, search, employment, recruiting and outplacement professions. 1969. m. $96. Kimberly Organization, Box 31011, Des Peres, MO 63131. TEL 314-965-3883. FAX 314-965-8177. Ed. Paul A. Hawkinson. bk.rev.; circ. 8,500.

FOREIGN INVESTMENTS IN BRAZIL. LEGISLATION. see BUSINESS AND ECONOMICS — International Commerce

346 CN
FREE TRADE LAW REPORTER. 1989. q. Can.$310. C C H Canadian Ltd., 6 Garamond Ct., Don Mills, Ont. M3C 1Z5, Canada. TEL 416-441-2992. FAX 416-444-9011.
Description: Provides expert commentary on key trade issues like the elimination of customs duties, tariff exemptions for trade in goods and import-export restrictions.

GABLERS - MAGAZIN; Zeitschrift fuer innovative Fuehrungskraefte. see BUSINESS AND ECONOMICS — Management

346 AU ISSN 0250-6440
DER GESELLSCHAFTER. 1972. q. S.560. Manzsche Verlags- und Universitaetsbuchhandlung, Kohlmarkt 16, A-1014 Vienna, Austria. TEL 0222-531610. FAX 0222-5316181. Ed. Rudolf Jahn. adv.; circ. 1,500.
Description: Covers corporate and partnership law.

346 658.3 GW
GEWERBEARCHIV; Zeitschrift fuer Gewerbe- und Wirtschaftsverwaltungsrecht. 1955. m. DM.330 (foreign DM.340). Gildefachverlag GmbH & Co. KG, Postfach 1351, 3220 Alfeld, Germany. TEL 05181-80040. Ed. Ludwig Froehler. circ. 1,900. (back issues avail.; reprint service avail. from SCH) **Indexed:** INIS Atomind.

GILBERT LAW SUMMARIES. AGENCY AND PARTNERSHIP. irreg., 4th ed., 1982. $11.95. Law Distributors (Subsidiary of: H B J Legal & Professional Publications Inc.), 14415 S. Main St., Gardena, CA 90248. TEL 800-421-1893. FAX 213-324-6381.

346 US
GILBERT LAW SUMMARIES. ANTITRUST. irreg., 8th ed., 1983. $11.95. Law Distributors (Subsidiary of: H B J Legal & Professional Publications Inc.), 14415 S. Main St., Gardena, CA 90248. TEL 800-421-1893. FAX 213-324-6381.

346 US
GILBERT LAW SUMMARIES. BANKRUPTCY. 1989. irreg. $17.95. Law Distributors (Subsidiary of: H B J Legal & Professional Publications Inc.), 14415 S. Main St., Gardena, CA 90248. TEL 800-421-1893. FAX 213-324-6381.

346 657 US
GILBERT LAW SUMMARIES. BASIC ACCOUNTING FOR LAWYERS. 1984. irreg. $10.95. Law Distributors (Subsidiary of: H B J Legal & Professional Publications Inc.), 14415 S. Main St., Gardena, CA 90248. TEL 800-421-1893. FAX 213-324-6381.

346 US
GILBERT LAW SUMMARIES. BUSINESS LAW. irreg., 2nd ed., 1984. $10.95. Law Distributors (Subsidiary of: H B J Legal & Professional Publications Inc.), 14415 S. Main St., Gardena, CA 90248. TEL 800-421-1893. FAX 213-324-6381.

346 US
GILBERT LAW SUMMARIES. COMMERCIAL PAPER. irreg., 13th ed., 1988. $14.95. Law Distributors (Subsidiary of: H B J Legal & Professional Publications Inc.), 14415 S. Main St., Gardena, CA 90248. TEL 800-421-1893. FAX 213-324-6381.

346 US
GILBERT LAW SUMMARIES. CONTRACTS. irreg., 11th ed., 1984. $14.95. Law Distributors (Subsidiary of: H B J Legal & Professional Publications Inc.), 14415 S. Main St., Gardena, CA 90248. TEL 800-421-1893. FAX 213-324-6381.

346 US
GILBERT LAW SUMMARIES. CORPORATIONS. irreg., 13th ed., 1989. $15.95. Law Distributors (Subsidiary of: H B J Legal & Professional Publications Inc.), 14415 S. Main St., Gardena, CA 90248. TEL 800-421-1893. FAX 213-324-6381.

346 US
GILBERT LAW SUMMARIES. INCOME TAX 2 (CORPORATE). irreg., 11th ed., 1990. $14.95. Law Distributors (Subsidiary of: H B J Legal & Professional Publications Inc.), 14415 S. Main St., Gardena, CA 90248. TEL 800-421-1893. FAX 213-324-6381.

346 IT
GIURISPRUDENZA ANNOTATA DI DIRITTO INDUSTRIALE. (Issued in pts.) 1972. a. price varies. Casa Editrice Dott. A. Giuffre, Via B. Arsizio 40, 20151 Milan, Italy. TEL 02-38000905. FAX 02-38009582.

346 332 IT
GIURISPRUDENZA COMMERCIALE. 1974. bi-m. L.160000 (foreign L.240000). Casa Editrice Dott. A. Giuffre, Via Busto Arsizio 40, 20151 Milan, Italy. TEL 02-38000905. FAX 02-38009582. Ed. Pier Giusto Jaeger. adv.; bk.rev.; bibl.; circ. 5,800.
Formerly: Giurisprudenza Commerciale - Societa e Fallimento.

LAW — CORPORATE LAW

346 380.5 US
GOODS IN TRANSIT. (Issued in 3 base vols. with supplements) 1976. irreg. Matthew Bender & Co., Inc., 11 Penn Plaza, New York, NY 10001. TEL 212-967-7707. Ed. Saul Sorkin. (looseleaf format)
Description: Provides information on how to recover or avoid liability for lost, damaged or delayed goods shipped by air, sea, rail or truck anywhere in the world; plus practical coverage of the rights, obligations and remedies for losses, damages and delays.

346 GW ISSN 0533-3407
GRUNDLAGEN UND PRAXIS DES WIRTSCHAFTSRECHTS. 1964. irreg. Eric Schmidt Verlag GmbH & Co. (Berlin), Genthiner Str. 30 G, 1000 Berlin 30, Germany. TEL 030-2500850. (back issues avail.)

GUIDE TO EMPLOYMENT LAW AND REGULATION - O S H A. see *BUSINESS AND ECONOMICS — Labor And Industrial Relations*

346.066 US
HANDBOOK OF CONNECTICUT CORPORATION STATUTES. a. $25. Connecticut Law Book Company, Box 575, Guilford, CT 06437. TEL 203-458-8000.

346 AU
HANDELSRECHTLICHE ENTSCHEIDUNGEN. 1961. a. price varies. Manzsche Verlags- und Universitaetsbuchhandlung, Kohlmarkt 16, A-1014 Vienna, Austria. TEL 0222-531610. FAX 0222-5316181. Ed. Johannes Wolfgang Steiner. circ. 2,000.
Description: Collection of decisions on commercial law.

HARVEY ON INDUSTRIAL RELATIONS & EMPLOYMENT LAW. see *BUSINESS AND ECONOMICS — Labor And Industrial Relations*

HUMAN RESOURCES MANAGEMENT IN CANADA. see *BUSINESS AND ECONOMICS — Personnel Management*

346 NE
I C C A CONGRESS SERIES. 1983. irreg., no.4, 1989. price varies. (International Council for Commercial Arbitration) Kluwer Law and Taxation Publishers, P.O. Box 23, 7400 GA Deventer, Netherlands. TEL 31-5700-47261. FAX 31-5700-22244. TELEX 49295 KLUDV NL. (Dist. by: Libresso Distribution Centre, P.O. Box 23, 7400 GA Deventer, Netherlands. TEL 31-5700-33155; N. America dist addr.: 6 Bigelow St., Cambridge, MA 02139. TEL 617-354-0140) (Co-sponsor: T.M.C. Asser Institute for International and European Law) Ed. P. Sanders.

346 US ISSN 1060-5924
▼**I O M A'S REPORT ON CONTROLLING LAW FIRMS COSTS.** 1992. m. $175. Institute of Management and Administration, 29 W. 35th St., 5th Fl., New York, NY 10001-2299. TEL 212-244-0360. FAX 212-564-0465. Ed. Lee Rath.
Description: Covers staffing, equipment, production, record-keeping and other management techniques to get the most productivity.

I O M A'S REPORT ON MANAGING 401K PLANS. see *BUSINESS AND ECONOMICS — Banking And Finance*

346 US ISSN 1049-9385
▼**ILLINOIS EMPLOYMENT LAW LETTER.** 1990. 12/yr. $127. M. Lee Smith Publishers & Printers, 162 Fourth Ave. N., Box 2678, Nashville, TN 37219. TEL 615-242-7395. FAX 615-256-6601. (Co-sponsor: Matkov, Salzman, Madoff & Gunn) Ed. Eve Subrin.
Description: Reports the latest Illinois employment law developments that affect Illinois employers.

346 US ISSN 1053-6191
▼**INDIANA EMPLOYMENT LAW LETTER.** 1991. 12/yr. $127. M. Lee Smith Publishers & Printers, 162 Fourth Ave. N., Box 2678, Nashville, TN 37219. TEL 615-242-7395. FAX 615-256-6601. (Co-sponsor: Baker & Daniels) Eds. J.T. Neighbors, T.M. Nierman.
Description: Reports the latest Indiana employment law developments that affect Indiana employers.

346 UK ISSN 0306-2163
KD3040.A38
INDUSTRIAL CASES REPORTS. 1972. m. £163 (typically set in Aug.). Incorporated Council of Law Reporting for England and Wales, 3 Stone Bldgs., Lincoln's Inn, London WC2A 3XN, England. TEL 071-242 6471. FAX 071-831-5247. Ed. C.J. Ellis.
●Also available online. Vendor(s): Mead Data Central.
Incorporates: Restrictive Practices Reports (ISSN 0073-571X)

INDUSTRIAL COURT REPORTER. see *BUSINESS AND ECONOMICS — Labor And Industrial Relations*

346 AT
INDUSTRIAL LAW: FEDERAL. base vol. (plus updates 8/yr.). $405. Butterworths Pty. Ltd., 271-273 Lane Cove Rd., P.O. Box 345, North Ryde, N.S.W. 2113, Australia. TEL 02-335-4444. FAX 02-335-4655. (looseleaf format)
Formerly: Federal Industrial Law.

INDUSTRIAL LAW JOURNAL. see *BUSINESS AND ECONOMICS — Labor And Industrial Relations*

346 SA ISSN 0258-249X
INDUSTRIAL LAW JOURNAL. (Text in English) 1980. bi-m. R.300. Juta & Co. Ltd., P.O. Box 14373, Kenwyn 7790, South Africa. TEL 021-797-5101. FAX 021-761-5010. Ed.Bd. cum.index; circ. 2,200. (back issues avail.)

INDUSTRIAL RELATIONS LAW JOURNAL. see *BUSINESS AND ECONOMICS — Labor And Industrial Relations*

346 AT ISSN 0728-8417
LAW
INDUSTRIAL REPORTS. 1948. irreg. Law Book Co. Ltd., 44-50 Waterloo Rd., North Ryde, N.S.W. 2112, Australia. TEL 02-887-0177. FAX 02-888-9706. TELEX ASBOOK 27995. Ed.Bd.
Supersedes (in 1981): Industrial Arbitration Service (ISSN 0312-4029)

346 GW
INDUSTRIEGESELLSCHAFT UND RECHT.* 1974. irreg., vol.5, 1975. price varies. Gieseking-Verlag, Deckerstr. 2, Postfach 42, 4813 Bielefeld-Bethel, Germany. Eds. Manfred Rehbinder, Bernd Rebe.

INTERNATIONAL SECURITIES REGULATION REPORT. see *BUSINESS AND ECONOMICS — Investments*

INTERNATIONALE WIRTSCHAFTS-BRIEFE; Zeitschrift fuer internationales Steuer- und Wirtschaftsrecht, Euratom, OECD, Steuern und Zoelle im gemeinsamen Markt. see *BUSINESS AND ECONOMICS — Public Finance, Taxation*

INVESTMENT LIMITED PARTNERSHIPS HANDBOOK. see *BUSINESS AND ECONOMICS — Investments*

346 336 US ISSN 0893-1364
KF6415.A15
INVESTMENT LIMITED PARTNERSHIPS LAW REPORT. 1981. 10/yr. $235. Clark - Bordman - Callaghan Company Ltd., 375 Hudson St., New York, NY 10014. TEL 212-929-7500. FAX 212-924-0460. Eds. Robert J. Haft, Peter M. Fass. index. (looseleaf format; back issues avail.)
Formerly: Tax Sheltered Investments Law Report (ISSN 0731-5759)

346 US
IOWA BANKRUPTCY. 1984. base vol. (plus suppl.). $55. Butterworth Legal Publishers (Salem) (Subsidiary of: Reed International PLC), 90 Stiles Rd., Salem, NH 03079. TEL 800-548-4001. FAX 603-898-9858. Ed. Robert S. Oppold. (looseleaf format)
Description: Covers chapter 7 liquidation cases in Iowa.

JILIN CAIMAO XUEYUAN XUEBAO/JILIN INSTITUTE OF FINANCE AND TRADE. JOURNAL. see *BUSINESS AND ECONOMICS — Banking And Finance*

346 CC
JINGJI FAZHI. (Text in Chinese) m. Zhongguo Jingjifa Yanjiuhui - China Economic Law Research Society, No. 11, Wenjin Jie, Xicheng-qu, Beijing 100017, People's Republic of China. TEL 6016633. Ed. Gu Ming.

346 330 US
JOINT VENTURES: STRUCTURING ALTERNATIVES. 1988. base vol. (plus a. suppl.). $95. Shepard's - McGraw-Hill, Inc., Box 35300, Colorado Springs, CO 80935-3530. TEL 800-525-2474. (looseleaf format)
Description: Gives lawyers, accountants and anyone involved in business transactions more creative alternatives to reaching financial goals.

JOURNAL OF BANKING AND FINANCE - LAW AND PRACTICE. see *BUSINESS AND ECONOMICS — Banking And Finance*

346 UK ISSN 0021-9460
K10
JOURNAL OF BUSINESS LAW. 1957. 6/yr. £74. Sweet & Maxwell, South Quay Plaza, 8th Fl., 183 Marsh Wall, London E14 9FT, England. TEL 071-538-8686. FAX 071-538-9508. (Dist. in U.S. & Canada by: Carswell Co. Ltd., 233 Midland Ave., Agincourt, Ont., Canada) Ed. R. Merkin. adv.; bk.rev.; index. (reprint service avail. from RRI)
Indexed: BPIA, Bus.Ind., C.L.I., C.R.E.J., Cont.Pg.Manage., L.R.I., Leg.Cont, Leg.Per., Mar.Aff.Bibl., SCIMP (1979-), SSCI.
—BLDSC shelfmark: 4954.700000.

346 US ISSN 0360-795X
K10
JOURNAL OF CORPORATION LAW. 4/yr. $25. University of Iowa, College of Law, Iowa City, IA 52242. TEL 319-335-9061. bk.rev. (also avail. in microfilm from RRI; back issues avail.) **Indexed:** Account.Ind. (1975-), Bank.Lit.Ind., BPIA, Bus.Ind., C.L.I., Curr.Cont., L.R.I., Leg.Per., P.A.I.S.
●Also available online. Vendor(s): WESTLAW.

346 UK ISSN 0267-937X
K10
JOURNAL OF INTERNATIONAL BANKING LAW. 1986. m. £265. (E S C Publishing Ltd.) Sweet & Maxwell, South Quay Plaza, 8th Fl., 183 Marsh Wall, London E14 9FT, England. TEL 071-538-8686. FAX 071-538-8625. Ed. Graham Penn. bk.rev.; index. (back issues avail.)
—BLDSC shelfmark: 5007.583000.
Description: Legal information service on case law, new legislation and developments in the globalization of the banking regulatory system.

JOURNAL OF INTERNATIONAL FRANCHISING & DISTRIBUTION LAW. see *BUSINESS AND ECONOMICS*

346.066 US ISSN 0733-2491
K10
JOURNAL OF LAW & COMMERCE. 1980. 2/yr. $20. University of Pittsburgh, School of Law, 3900 Forbes Ave., Pittsburgh, PA 15260. TEL 412-648-1361. FAX 412-648-2649. adv.; bk.rev.; circ. 500. (also avail. in microform from WSH; back issues avail.; reprint service avail. from WSH) **Indexed:** C.L.I., Leg.Cont., Leg.Per.
●Also available online. Vendor(s): WESTLAW.
—BLDSC shelfmark: 5010.118000.
Description: Focuses on commercial law, providing scholarly and practical articles written by scholars, practitioners, and students that are of immediate interest to practitioners, academicians, and leaders in the legal and business community.

346.066 330 FR
LAMY DROIT COMMERCIAL. (Supplement avail.: Lamy Droit Commercial - Formulaire) a. 1390 F. (with supplement 1650 F.)(effective 1991). Lamy S.A., 155, rue Legendre, 75850 Paris Cedex 17, France. TEL 46-27-28-90. FAX 42-29-86-81. TELEX 214398. index.

346.066 330 FR
LAMY PROTECTION SOCIALE; regime general de securite sociale - salaires, regimes des non-salaries, retraites complementaires, regimes de retraite d'entreprise, prevoyance, aide sociale et action sociale. a. 1300 F. Lamy S.A., 155, rue Legendre, 75850 Paris, France. TEL 46-27-28-90. FAX 42-29-86-81. TELEX 214398. charts; index.
Description: Answers the daily questions faced by those who manage the benefits of a company.

LAW — CORPORATE LAW 2711

346.066 332 FR
LAMY SOCIETE COMMERCIALES. (Supplements avail.: Lamy Societes Commerciales - Formulaire S.A. a Conseil d'Administration; Lamy Societes Commerciales - Formulaire S.A. a Directoire; Lamy Societes Commerciales - Formulaire S.A.R.L; Lamy Societes Commerciales - Formulaire Autres que S.A.R.L. et S.A. Regroupements de Societes) a. 1460 F. Lamy S.A., 155, rue Legendre, 75840 Paris Cedex 17, France. TEL 46-27-28-90. FAX 42-29-86-81. TELEX 214398. charts; index.
Description: Analyzes the constitution, management, finances and benefits, competition and dissolution of commercial companies.

310 US
LAW & BUSINESS DIRECTORY OF CORPORATE COUNSEL. Short title: Directory of Corporate Counsel. a. $275. Law & Business, Inc. (Subsidiary of: Prentice Hall), 270 Sylvan Ave., Englewood Cliffs, NJ 07632. TEL 201-894-8484.
●Also available online. Vendor(s): WESTLAW.

346.066 UK ISSN 0954-2809
LAW FOR BUSINESS. 1988. 10/yr. £189($300) Wallace Publishing Ltd., 161 Chertsey Road, Twickenham, Mddx. TW1 1EP, England. TEL 01-891-3575. Ed. Jean Campbell. index; circ. 1,000. (back issues avail.)
—BLDSC shelfmark: 5161.368400.

LAW RELATING TO BANKER AND CUSTOMER IN AUSTRALIA. see LAW

LEGAL CONNECTION: CORPORATIONS AND LAW FIRMS; a directory of publicly-held corporations and their law firms. see LAW

LEGAL INSIGHTS FOR MANAGERS. see LAW

346.066 US ISSN 0162-5764
KF3145.A15 CODEN: LLBRDL
LICENSING LAW AND BUSINESS REPORT. 1978. bi-m. $195. Clark - Boardman - Callaghan Company, Ltd., 375 Hudson St., New York, NY 10014. TEL 212-929-7500. FAX 212-924-0460. index. (looseleaf format; back issues avail.) **Indexed:** C.L.I., L.R.I.
Description: Discusses legal aspects of business.

LLOYD'S LAW REPORTS. see LAW

346 US ISSN 1049-9377
KFM1534.A15
▼**MARYLAND EMPLOYMENT LAW LETTER.** 1990. 12/yr. $127. M. Lee Smith Publishers & Printers, 162 Fourth Ave. N., Box 2678, Nashville, TN 37219. TEL 615-242-7395. FAX 615-256-6601. (Co-sponsor: Venable, Baetjer & Howard) Eds. George W. Johnson, Patrick J. Stewart.
Description: Reports the latest Maryland employment law developments that affect Maryland employers.

MASSACHUSETTS DISCRIMINATION LAW REPORTER. see LAW

346 US ISSN 1049-2062
KFM2731.A15
▼**MASSACHUSETTS EMPLOYMENT LAW LETTER.** 1990. 12/yr. $127. M. Lee Smith Publishers & Printers, 162 Fourth Ave. N., Box 2678, Nashville, TN 37219. TEL 615-242-7395. FAX 615-256-6601. (Co-sponsor: Skoler, Abbot, Hayes & Presser) Eds. Ralph F. Abbott, Jr., Judith A. McDonald.
Description: Reports the latest Massachusetts employment law developments that affect Massachusetts employers.

340 US
MASSACHUSETTS WORKERS' COMPENSATION PRACTICE MANUAL. 1988. base vol. (plus a. suppl.), 2nd ed. $115. Butterworth Legal Publishers (Salem) (Subsidiary of: Reed International PLC), 90 Stiles Rd., Salem, NH 03079. TEL 800-548-4001. FAX 603-898-9858. Ed. Paul A. Gargano. (looseleaf format)

346 US
MASSACHUSETTS WORKERS' COMPENSATION REPORTS. 1988. 3 base vols. (plus a. suppl.). $75. Butterworth Legal Publishers (Salem) (Subsidiary of: Reed International PLC), 90 Stiles Rd., Salem, NH 03079. TEL 800-548-4001. FAX 603-898-9858. Ed. Paul A. Gargano.

346 US
MERGERS AND ACQUISITIONS LAW REPORTER. m. $1,200. Computer Law Reporter, Inc., 1519 Connecticut Ave., N.W., Ste. 200, Washington, DC 20036. TEL 202-462-5755. FAX 202-328-2430. Ed. Neil J. Cohen. (back issues avail.)

346 US ISSN 1046-9109
▼**MICHIGAN EMPLOYMENT LAW LETTER.** 1990. 12/yr. $127. M. Lee Smith Publishers & Printers, 162 Fourth Ave. N., Box 2678, Nashville, TN 37219. TEL 501-771-1775. FAX 501-771-1775. (Co-sponsor: Honigman Miller Schwartz & Cohn) Eds. Frank T. Mamat, A. David Mikesell.
Description: Reports the latest Michigan employment law developments that affect Michigan employers.

346 US
MINNESOTA CORPORATIONS PRACTICE MANUAL. 1986. base vol. (plus suppl.). $78. Butterworth Legal Publishers (Salem) (Subsidiary of: Reed International PLC), 90 Stiles Rd., Salem, NH 03079. TEL 800-548-4001. FAX 603-898-9858. Ed. Bert Black. (looseleaf format)
Description: Provides a complete analysis of corporate law in Minnesota by tracking the chronological "life" of a corporation from creation to dissolution.

346 US ISSN 1054-6367
▼**MINNESOTA EMPLOYMENT LAW LETTER.** 1991. 12/yr. $127. M. Lee Smith Publishers & Printers, 162 Fourth Ave. N., Box 2678, Nashville, TN 37219. TEL 615-242-7395. FAX 615-256-6601. (Co-sponsor: Felhaber, Larson, Fenlon & Vogt, P.A.) Eds. Edward J. Bohrer, Stephen J. Burton.
Description: Reports the latest Minnesota employment law developments that affect Minnesota employers.

346 NZ
MORISON'S COMPANY LAW REPORTS. 3 base vols. (plus m. update). Butterworths of New Zealand Ltd., 203-207 Victoria St., P.O. Box 472, Wellington, New Zealand. TEL 04-385-1479. FAX 04-385-1598. Ed. John Cottle.
Formerly (until June 1991): Butterworths Company Reports.
Description: Detailed coverage of High Court, Court of Appeal and Privy Council decisions pertaining to company law.

340 NZ
MORRISON'S COMPANY LAW IN NEW ZEALAND. 2 base vols. (plus q. update). NZ.$296. Butterworths of New Zealand Ltd., 203-207 Victoria St., P.O. Box 472, Wellington, New Zealand. TEL 04-385-1479. FAX 04-385-1598. Ed. John Cottle. (looseleaf format)
Description: Statutes and regulations followed by a treatise on company law and discussion on cases.

MUNICIPALITIES AND CORPORATION CASES; a monthly law reporter. see LAW

NEW HAMPSHIRE CORPORATIONS, PARTNERSHIPS AND ASSOCIATIONS. see BUSINESS AND ECONOMICS

346 US
NEW HAMPSHIRE WORKERS' COMPENSATION MANUAL. base vol. (plus suppl.). $45. Butterworth Legal Publishers (Salem) (Subsidiary of: Reed International PLC), 90 Stiles Rd., Salem, NH 03079. TEL 800-548-4001. FAX 603-898-9858. Ed. Richard Galway.
Description: Covers the history, statutory requirements, judicial interpretation, and procedure of workers' compensation law in New Hampshire.

346 NZ
NEW ZEALAND COMPANY LAW AND PRACTICE. 1979. 10/yr. NZ.$1358. C C H New Zealand Ltd., P.O. Box 2378, Auckland, New Zealand. TEL 483-9179. FAX 483-4009. (looseleaf format)
Formerly: New Zealand Company Secretary's Practice Manual and Company Law Service.
Description: Provides analysis of new developments in companies and securities law and their impact on professional and corporate practice. Includes full text legislation, and cases, and new developments covering legislative proposals, government reports and statements.

346 NZ
NEW ZEALAND COMPANY LAW AND PRACTICE MANUAL. 1979. 10/yr. NZ.$1358. C C H New Zealand Limited, P.O. Box 2378, Auckland, New Zealand. TEL 483-9179. FAX 483-4009.
Formerly: New Zealand Company Law Service.
Description: Practical analysis of the new developments in companies and securities law and the impact on professional and corporate practice.

346 657 NZ
NEW ZEALAND COMPANY SECRETARY'S GUIDE. 1987. 4/yr. NZ.$530. C C H New Zealand Limited, P.O. Box 2378, Auckland, New Zealand. TEL 483-9179. FAX 483-4009. (looseleaf format)
Description: Provides information on company law matters for company secretaries, accountants and business executives in commerce, and legal and accounting practitioners.

346 CN
ONTARIO CORPORATIONS LAW GUIDE. m. Can.$425. C H Canadian Ltd., 6 Garamond Ct., Don Mills, Ont. M3C 1Z5, Canada. TEL 416-441-2992. FAX 416-444-9011. index.
Formerly: Ontario Companies Law Guide (ISSN 0048-1750)
Description: Relevant Ontario statutes dealing with company law, editorial commentary, forms and precedents.

340 330 US
ORGANIZING CORPORATE AND OTHER BUSINESS ENTERPRISES. 1949. irreg. Matthew Bender & Co., Inc., 11 Penn Plaza, New York, NY 10001. TEL 212-967-7707.
Description: For the attorney who is advising proposed or existing small businesses. Acts as a guide to the legal and tax factors to be considered in selecting a form of business organization.

346 AT
PAPUA NEW GUINEA COMPANIES LEGISLATION. 1980. irreg., as required for legislative changes. C C H Australia Ltd., P.O. Box 230, N. Ryde, N.S.W. 2113, Australia. TEL 888-2555. FAX 02-888-7324.

346 US ISSN 0892-4805
PARTNER'S REPORT, A MONTHLY BRIEF FOR LAW FIRM OWNERS. m. $245. Institute of Management and Administration, 29 W. 35th St., 5th Fl., New York, NY 10001-2299. TEL 212-244-0360. FAX 212-564-0465. Ed. Rebecca Morrow. index. (back issues avail.)

346 331 US
PENSION AND PROFIT-SHARING PLANS COMPLIANCE GUIDE. 1986. in 5 base vols. with bi-m. supplements. Matthew Bender & Co., Inc., 11 Penn Plaza, New York, NY 10001. TEL 212-967-7707. Ed. Carmine V. Scudere. (looseleaf format)
Description: Provides step-by-step guidance and analysis on every aspect of pension and profit-sharing plan compliance.

346 331 US
PENSION AND PROFIT-SHARING PLANS: FORMS AND PRACTICE WITH TAX ANALYSIS. (Issued in 3 vols. with supplements) 1988. irreg. Matthew Bender & Co., Inc., 11 Penn Plaza, New York, NY 10001. TEL 212-967-7707. Ed. Harvey Frutkin. (looseleaf format)
Description: Provides commentary and tax analysis of pension or profit-sharing plans.

340 US ISSN 1052-9640
KF3512
▼**PENSION FUND LITIGATION REPORTER.** 1990. m. $550. Andrews Publications, 1646 West Chester Pike, Box 1000, Westtown, PA 19395. TEL 215-399-6600. FAX 215-399-6610. Ed. Barbara Pizzirani. bibl.; stat.; cum.index every 6 mos. (looseleaf format; back issues avail.)
Description: Presents record of lawsuits involving benefit plan fiduciaries.

346.092 US
PRACTICE UNDER THE CALIFORNIA CORPORATE SECURITIES LAWS. (Issued as 3 base vols. with supplements) 1972. irreg. Matthew Bender & Co., Inc., 11 Penn Plaza, New York, NY 10001. TEL 212-967-7707. Ed.Bd. (looseleaf format)

PRIMER ON EMPLOYEE RETIREMENT INCOME SECURITY ACT. see BUSINESS AND ECONOMICS — Labor And Industrial Relations

2712 LAW — CRIMINAL LAW

PUBLIC LAW; the constitutional and administrative law of the commonwealth. see *LAW*

346   CN   ISSN 0831-3482
KE1412
SECURITIES AND CORPORATE REGULATION REVIEW. m. Can.$195. Butterworths Canada Ltd., 75 Clegg Rd., Markham, Ont. L6G 1A1, Canada. TEL 800-668-6481. FAX 416-479-2826. Ed. Willian Jenkins. (back issues avail.)
Description: Covers recent cases, policy statements and legislative developments in matters affecting securities and corporate regulation.

345 346.066   US   ISSN 0273-0685
KF1432
SECURITIES AND FEDERAL CORPORATE LAW REPORT. 1979. 11/yr. $195. Clark - Boardman - Callaghan Company, Ltd., 375 Hudson St., New York, NY 10014. TEL 212-929-7500. FAX 212-924-0460. Ed. Harold S. Bloomenthal. index. (looseleaf format; back issues avail.) Indexed: C.L.I., L.R.I.

346   US   ISSN 8750-1104
SHEPARD'S CORPORATION LAW CITATIONS. 1983. 3 base vols. (plus q. suppl.). $480. Shepard's - McGraw-Hill, Inc., Box 35300, Colorado Springs, CO 80935-3530. TEL 800-525-2474.

TAX PLANNING FOR CORPORATE ACQUISITIONS. see *BUSINESS AND ECONOMICS — Public Finance, Taxation*

346   US
TEXAS CORPORATION LAW. 1981. 3 base vols. (plus a. suppl.). $175. Butterworth Legal Publishers (Salem) (Subsidiary of: Reed International PLC), 90 Stiles Rd., Salem, NH 03079. TEL 800-548-4001. FAX 603-898-9858. (looseleaf format)

346 332.04   US
TEXAS FORECLOSURE: LAW AND PRACTICE. 1984. base vol. (plus biennial suppl.). $95. Shepard's - McGraw-Hill, Inc., Box 35300, Colorado Springs, CO 80935-3530. TEL 800-525-2474.
Description: Covers issues such as bankruptcy considerations, sequestration, receivership, federal tax considerations, setoff, garnishment, sheriff's sales, landlord's liens, injunctions and property exemptions.

346.066   US
U C GUIDE (YEAR). (Unemployment Compensation) a. $70 to non-members; members $35. Pennsylvania Chamber of Business and Industry, 222 N. Third St., Harrisburg, PA 17101. TEL 800-326-3252. FAX 717-255-3298.
Description: Provides employers with information on unemployment compensation, including analysis of methods of cost reduction.

LAW — Criminal Law

see also Criminology and Law Enforcement

345   US   ISSN 0889-9312
B N A CRIMINAL PRACTICE MANUAL. (Subseries of: Trial Practice Series) 1987. fortn. $508. The Bureau of National Affairs, Inc., 1231 25th St., N.W., Washington, DC 20037. TEL 202-452-4200. FAX 202-822-8092. TELEX 285656 BNAI WSH. (Subscr. to: 9435 Key West Ave., Rockville, MD 20850. TEL 800-372-1033) Ed. Judith C. Mroczka. index. (looseleaf format; back issues avail.)
Description: Notification and reference service covering the entire court process from arrest through sentencing, and a newsletter covering developments in criminal law, evidence and procedures, and practice techniques.

345   CN
BRITISH COLUMBIA DECISIONS - CRIMINAL CONVICTION AND SENTENCE CASES. 1972. m. Can.$250. Western Legal Publications, 301-1 Alexander St., Vancouver, B.C. V6A 1B2, Canada. TEL 604-687-5671. FAX 604-687-2796. (looseleaf format)
●Also available online.
Formerly: British Columbia Decisions - Criminal Cases (ISSN 0824-7242)
Description: Digests all available criminal decisions from the British Columbia Court of Appeal, Supreme Courts of British Columbia, as well as selected decisions from its Provincial Courts.

BUERGERRECHTE & POLIZEI. see *CRIMINOLOGY AND LAW ENFORCEMENT*

BULWARK. see *LAW — Civil Law*

CALIFORNIA. OFFICE OF CRIMINAL JUSTICE PLANNING. RESEARCH UPDATE. see *CRIMINOLOGY AND LAW ENFORCEMENT*

345 364   US
CALIFORNIA CRIMINAL DEFENSE PRACTICE. 1981. 6 base vols. (plus irreg. supplements). Matthew Bender & Co., Inc., 11 Penn Plaza, New York, NY 10001. TEL 212-967-7707. Ed.Bd. (looseleaf format)
Description: Comprehensive exposition of California criminal law and procedure. Chapters are arranged chronologically, in topical order of criminal action, with discussion of substantive law and strategy and procedures available.

345 364   US
CALIFORNIA CRIMINAL DEFENSE REPORTER. (Complements California Criminal Defense Practice) 1981. base vol. (plus m. updates). $220. Matthew Bender & Co., Inc., 11 Penn Plaza, New York, NY 10001. TEL 212-967-7707. (looseleaf format)
Description: Summarizes all important new criminal cases and statutes each month.

345   CN
CANADA. LAW REFORM COMMISSION. CRIMINAL LAW SERIES. STUDY PAPERS. (Text in English, French) irreg. free. Law Reform Commission, 130 Albert St., Ottawa, Ont. K1A 0L6, Canada. TEL 613-996-7844. FAX 613-996-8599. (reprint service avail. from MML)
Description: Monographs on criminal law.

345   CN   ISSN 0008-3348
LAW
CANADIAN CRIMINAL CASES. 1898. w. Can.$114. Canada Law Book Inc., 240 Edward St., Aurora, Ont. L4G 3S9, Canada. TEL 416-841-6472. Ed. E.L. Greenspan. index.
●Also available online.

345   CN
CANADIAN PRISON LAW. s-a. Can.$245. Butterworths Canada Ltd., 75 Clegg Rd., Markham, Ont. L6G 1A1, Canada. TEL 416-479-2665. FAX 416-479-2826. Ed. J.S. Conroy. (looseleaf format)
Description: Federal statutes and regulations affecting inmates and authorities in Federal reformatories and penitentiaries.

345   AT
CARTER'S CRIMINAL LAW OF QUEENSLAND. 2 base vols. (plus updates 3-4/yr.). $355. Butterworths Pty. Ltd., 271-273 Lane Cove Rd., P.O. Box 345, North Ryde, N.S.W. 2113, Australia. TEL 02-335-4444. FAX 02-335-4655. (looseleaf format)

345   US   ISSN 0744-9488
KF9602
CHAMPION. 1975. m. (10/yr.). $25. National Association of Criminal Defense Lawyers, 1110 Vermont Ave. N.W., No. 1150, Washington, DC 20005. FAX 202-331-8269. Ed. James G. O'Haver. adv.; bk.rev.; circ. 5,000.

345 301   II
CRIME & SOCIETY. (Text in English) 1974. m. Rs.12($8) 305a, Hans Bhavan, Bahadur Shah Zafar Marg, New Delhi 110002, India. Ed. P.J. Koshy. adv.; circ. 5,000.
Formerly: Path.
Description: News and current affairs.

345   UK
CRIMINAL APPEAL REPORTS (SENTENCING). 1979. 4/yr. £130. Sweet & Maxwell, South Quay Plaza, 8th Fl., 183 Marsh Wall, London E14 9FT, England. TEL 071-538-8686. FAX 071-538-9508. Ed. David Thomas.

345   US   ISSN 0887-7785
KF9602
CRIMINAL JUSTICE (CHICAGO). 1986. q. $33 (foreign $38). American Bar Association, Criminal Justice Section, 750 N. Lake Shore Dr., Chicago, IL 60611. TEL 312-988-6076. FAX 312-988-6281. Eds. George M. Eberhart, Carole Smith. adv.; bk.rev.; circ. 11,500. (also avail. in microform from UMI)
—BLDSC shelfmark: 3487.347000.
Description: Provides practical treatment of aspects of the criminal justice system and reports on legislative, policy-making and educational activities of the section.

345   US   ISSN 0731-129X
HV7231
CRIMINAL JUSTICE ETHICS. 1982. s-a. $15 to individuals (foreign $20); institutions $30 (foreign $35). Institute for Criminal Justice Ethics, John Jay College, 899 10th Ave., New York, NY 10019. TEL 212-237-8033. FAX 212-237-8901. Ed. John Kleinig. bk.rev.; circ. 1,000. (also avail. in microform from UMI) Indexed: C.L.I., CJPI, Crim.Just.Abstr., Phil.Ind.
—BLDSC shelfmark: 3487.350100.

345   US
CRIMINAL JUSTICE JOURNAL (SAN DIEGO). 1976. 2/yr. $18. Western State University, College of Law, 2121 San Diego Ave., San Diego, CA 92110. TEL 619-298-3111. (also avail. in microform from WSH; back issues avail.; reprint service avail. from WSH) Indexed: C.L.I., Leg.Per.

345   US   ISSN 0734-0168
K3
CRIMINAL JUSTICE REVIEW. 1976. s-a. $25 to individuals; institutions $30. Georgia State University, College of Public and Urban Affairs, Box 4018, Atlanta, GA 30302-4018. TEL 404-651-3515. adv.; bk.rev.; bibl.; circ. 1,200. (also avail. in microfiche from UMI; microfilm from UMI; reprint service avail. from UMI) Indexed: Abstr.Bk.Rev.Curr.Leg.Per., C.L.I., CJPI, Crim.Just.Abstr., Leg.Per., Sage Pub.Admin.Abstr., Sage Urb.Stud.Abstr., SSCI.
—BLDSC shelfmark: 3487.351000.
Description: Dedicated to presenting a broad perspective of criminal justice issues, institutions, and processes. Articles focus on trends, problems, and research on the regional and national levels.

345   US
CRIMINAL LAW ADVOCACY REPORTER. 1982. 8/yr. $205. Matthew Bender & Co., Inc., 11 Penn Plaza, New York, NY 10001. TEL 212-967-7707.

345   US   ISSN 0011-1317
K3
CRIMINAL LAW BULLETIN. 1964. 6/yr. $115. Warren, Gorham and Lamont, One Penn Plaza, New York, NY 10119. TEL 800-950-1205. FAX 212-971-5240. Ed. Fred Cohen. abstr.; index. (also avail. in microform from UMI,MIM; reprint service avail. from RRI,UMI) Indexed: C.L.I., CJPI, Crim.Just.Abstr., L.R.I., Leg.Cont., Leg.Per.
—BLDSC shelfmark: 3487.352000.
Refereed Serial

345   AT   ISSN 0705-7377
HD9696.C63
CRIMINAL LAW IN NEW SOUTH WALES. VOLUME 1: INDICTABLE OFFENCES. 1971. irreg. (3-4/yr.). Law Book Co. Ltd., 44-50 Waterloo Rd., North Ryde, N.S.W. 2113, Australia. TEL 02-887-0177. FAX 02-888-9706. TELEX ASBOOK 27995. Eds. R. Watson, H. Purnell. circ. 2,100. (looseleaf format)
Description: Standard practical reference on criminal law in New South Wales.

345   AT   ISSN 0705-7385
CRIMINAL LAW IN NEW SOUTH WALES. VOLUME 2: SUMMARY OFFENCES. 1978. irreg. (3-4/yr.). Law Book Co. Ltd., 44-50 Waterloo Rd., North Ryde, N.S.W. 2113, Australia. TEL 02-887-0177. FAX 02-888-9706. TELEX ASBOOK 27995. Eds. R. Watson, R. Bartley. circ. 1,400. (looseleaf format; back issues avail.)
Description: Contains every summary offense listed by statutes in New South Wales.

345 II ISSN 0011-1325
CRIMINAL LAW JOURNAL; full reports of all reportable criminal cases of the High courts and the Supreme Court of India. 1904. m. Rs.288($96) All India Reporter Ltd., P.O. Box 209, Nagpur 440012, India. Ed. V.R. Manohar. adv.; bk.rev.; index; circ. 16,800. **Indexed:** C.L.I., L.R.I., Leg.Per.

345 AT ISSN 0314-1160
K3
CRIMINAL LAW JOURNAL. 1977. bi-m. Aus.$178. Law Book Co. Ltd., 44-50 Macleod Rd., North Ryde, N.S.W. 2112, Australia. TEL 02-887-0177. FAX 02-888-9706. TELEX ASBOOK 27995. **Indexed:** Aus.P.A.I.S., Leg.Cont.
—BLDSC shelfmark: 3487.354500.
Description: Caters to all those who have an interest in criminal law - whether as legal practitioners, police or academics. Features cases, comments and legislation reviews.

345 US ISSN 0145-7322
KF9210.3
CRIMINAL LAW OUTLINE. 1966. a. $12. National Judicial College, Judicial College Bldg., University of Nevada, Reno, NV 89557. TEL 702-784-6747. FAX 702-784-4234. Ed. William A. Grimes. circ. 5,000.

345 CN ISSN 0011-1333
CRIMINAL LAW QUARTERLY; a Canadian journal of criminal law for judges, magistrates, lawyers and police officers. 1958. q. Can.$107. Canada Law Book Inc., 240 Edward St., Aurora, Ont. L4G 3S9, Canada. TEL 416-841-6472. Ed. A.W. Mewett. bk.rev.; charts; illus.; index. **Indexed:** C.L.I., CJPI, Crim.Just.Abstr., Curr.Cont., Ind.Can.L.P.L., L.R.I., Leg.Per., SSCI.
—BLDSC shelfmark: 3487.356000.

345 US ISSN 0011-1341
KF9615
CRIMINAL LAW REPORTER. 1967. w. $590. The Bureau of National Affairs, Inc., 1231 25th St., N.W., Washington, DC 20037. TEL 202-452-4200. FAX 202-822-8092. TELEX 285656 BNAI WSH. (Subscr. to: 9435 Key West Ave., Rockville, MD 20850. TEL 800-372-1033) Ed. Robert L. Goebes. bk.rev.; index. (also avail. in microform; back issues avail.) **Indexed:** C.L.I., Chic.Per.Ind., L.R.I.
Description: Notification service covering court decisions, federal legislative activities, and administrative developments in the field of criminal law.

345 UK ISSN 0011-135X
K3
CRIMINAL LAW REVIEW. 1954. m. £85. Sweet & Maxwell, S. Quay Plaza, 8th Fl., 183 Marsh Wall, London E14 9FT, England. TEL 071-538-8686. FAX 071-538-9508. (Dist. in U.S. & Canada by: Carswell Co. Ltd., 233 Midland Ave., Agincourt, Ont., Canada) Ed. A. Ashworth. adv.; bk.rev.; abstr.; bibl. **Indexed:** Br.Hum.Ind., C.L.I., CJPI, Crim.Just.Abstr., Curr.Cont., L.R.I., Leg.Cont., Leg.Per., SSCI.
—BLDSC shelfmark: 3487.358000.

345 AT
CRIMINAL LAW VICTORIA. base vol. (plus updates 6/yr.). $315. Butterworths Pty. Ltd., 271-273 Lane Cove Rd., P.O. Box 345, North Ryde, N.S.W. 2113, Australia. TEL 02-335-4444. FAX 02-335-4655. (looseleaf format)

345 CN
CRIMINAL LAWYERS COMMONPLACE BOOK. s-a. Can.$145. Butterworths Canada Ltd., 75 Clegg Rd., Markham, Ont. L6G 1A1, Canada. TEL 416-479-2665. FAX 416-479-2826. Ed. Paul Richard Meyers. (looseleaf format)
Description: For reference on criminal practice.

345 AT
CRIMINAL PRACTICE & PROCEDURE N S W. 2 base vols. (plus updates 6/yr.). $390. Butterworths Pty. Ltd., 271-273 Lane Cove Rd., P.O. Box 345, North Ryde, N.S.W. 2113, Australia. TEL 02-335-4444. FAX 02-335-4655. (looseleaf format)
Formerly: Justices Act and Summary Offences N S W.

345 CN
CRIMINAL PROCEDURE; Canadian law and practice. a. Can.$195. Butterworths Canada Ltd., 75 Clegg Rd., Markham, Ont. L6G 1A1, Canada. TEL 416-479-2665. FAX 416-479-2826. Ed.Bd. (looseleaf format)
Description: Comprehensive review on all aspects of criminal law and criminal practice.

345 CN ISSN 0383-9494
CRIMINAL REPORTS (4TH SERIES). 1967. 24/yr. (in 8 vols.). Can.$100. Carswell Publications, 800 Rocky Mountain Plaza, 615 Macleod Trail S.E., Calgary, Alta. T2G 4T8, Canada. TEL 416-609-8000. FAX 416-298-5094. (Subscr. to: Carswell Publications, Corporate Plaza, 2075 Kennedy Rd., Scarborough, Ont. M1T 3V4, Canada) Ed. Don Stuart. adv.; cum.index. **Indexed:** C.L.I., Ind.Can.L.P.L., L.R.I.

345 CN
DEFENCE LAWYERS TRIAL BOOK. s-a. Can.$155. Butterworths Canada Ltd., 75 Clegg Rd., Markham, Ont. L6G 1A1, Canada. TEL 416-479-2665. FAX 416-479-2826. Eds. Julius Melnitzer, D. Fletcher Dawson. (looseleaf format)
Description: Digest of recent leading cases reflecting the structure of the criminal code on issues affecting the defense of an action at both the trial and appellate court stages.

345 US
DEFENDING D W IS IN WASHINGTON. 1987. base vol. (plus suppl.). $115. Butterworth Legal Publishers (Salem), 90 Stiles Rd., Salem, NH 03079. TEL 800-548-4001. FAX 603-898-9858. Eds. Douglas L. Cowan, Stephen W. Hayne. (looseleaf format)

345 US ISSN 1047-1758
DEFENSE CONTRACT LITIGATION REPORTER; covers defense procurement fraud litigation as well as False Claim Acts (Qui Tam) litigation. 1988. s-m. $755. Andrews Publications, 1646 West Chester Pike, Box 1000, Westtown, PA 19395. TEL 215-399-6600. FAX 215-399-6610. Ed. Gary Crouse. bibl.; stat.; cum.index every 6 mos. (looseleaf format; back issues avail.)

345 US
FLORIDA CRIMINAL DEFENSE TRIAL MANUAL. 1972. 5 base vols. (plus suppl. 5-6/yr.). $320. Butterworth Legal Publishers (Salem) (Subsidiary of: Reed International PLC), 90 Stiles Rd., Salem, NH 03079. TEL 800-548-4001. FAX 603-898-9858. (looseleaf format)

345 US
FLORIDA CRIMINAL DISCOVERY & PRETRIAL MOTIONS. 1979. base vol. (plus suppl. 2-3/yr.). $80. Butterworth Legal Publishers (Salem) (Subsidiary of: Reed International PLC), 90 Stiles Rd., Salem, NH 03079. TEL 800-548-4001. FAX 603-898-9858. (looseleaf format)

345 US
FLORIDA CRIMINAL PROCEDURE SERVICE. 1980. base vol. (plus a. suppl.). $80. Butterworth Legal Publishers (Salem) (Subsidiary of: Reed International PLC), 90 Stiles Rd., Salem, NH 03079. TEL 800-548-4001. FAX 603-898-9858. (looseleaf format)

345 US
FLORIDA CRIMINAL SENTENCING LAW. 1984. 2 base vols. (plus suppl. 2-3/yr.). $160. Butterworth Legal Publishers (Salem) (Subsidiary of: Reed International PLC), 90 Stiles Rd., Salem, NH 03079. TEL 800-548-4001. FAX 603-898-9858. (looseleaf format)

345 US
GILBERT LAW SUMMARIES. CRIMINAL LAW. irreg., 14th ed., 1988. $13.95. Law Distributors (Subsidiary of: H B J Legal & Professional Publications Inc.), 14415 S. Main St., Gardena, CA 90248. TEL 800-421-1893. FAX 213-324-6381.

345 US ISSN 0193-8010
KF9619.3
GILBERT LAW SUMMARIES. CRIMINAL PROCEDURE. 1968. irreg., 13th ed., 1987. $14.95. (Gilbert Law Summaries) Law Distributors (Subsidiary of: H B J Legal & Professional Publications Inc.), 14415 S. Main St., Gardena, CA 90248. TEL 800-421-1893. FAX 213-324-6381. Ed. Marcus Whitebread.
Formerly: Criminal Practices (ISSN 0193-922X)

345 AT ISSN 0727-7938
HANNAN'S LOCAL AND DISTRICT CRIMINAL COURTS PRACTICE. 1979. 3/yr. Aus.$195. Law Book Co. Ltd., 44-50 Waterloo Rd., North Ryde, N.S.W. 2113, Australia. TEL 02-887-0177. FAX 02-888-9706. TELEX ASBOOK-27995. Ed. R.W. Grubb.
Description: Covers the practice and procedure of the local courts in South Australia.

345 US
ILLINOIS CRIMINAL LAW; a survey of crimes and defenses. 1986. base vol. (plus suppl.). $110. Butterworth Legal Publishers (Salem) (Subsidiary of: Reed International PLC), 90 Stiles Rd., Salem, NH 03079. TEL 800-548-4001. FAX 603-898-9858. Ed. John F. Decker.

345 US
ILLINOIS CRIMINAL PROCEDURE. 1987. base vol. (plus suppl.). $95. Butterworth Legal Publishers (Salem) (Subsidiary of: Reed International PLC), 90 Stiles Rd., Salem, NH 03079. TEL 800-548-4001. FAX 603-898-9858. Ed. Ralph Ruebner.
Description: Analyzes procedural rules and studies the effect of state statutes, rules and case law on criminal procedure.

345 US
ILLINOIS CRIMINAL TRIAL EVIDENCE. 1986. base vol. (plus suppl.). $45. Butterworth Legal Publishers (Salem) (Subsidiary of: Reed International PLC), 90 Stiles Rd., Salem, NH 03079. TEL 800-548-4001. FAX 603-898-9858. Ed. Ralph Ruebner.
Description: Practical, analytical guide to the evidentiary rules applicable in Illinois criminal trials.

IOWA CRIMINAL LAW BULLETIN. see *CRIMINOLOGY AND LAW ENFORCEMENT*

345 IE ISSN 0791-539X
▼**IRISH CRIMINAL LAW JOURNAL.** 1991. s-a. I£32($60) Round Hall Press, Kill Lane, Blackrock, Co. Dublin, Ireland. TEL 2892922. FAX 2893072. Ed. Shane Murphy. circ. 350 (controlled).
Description: Articles, law reports and case references to the leading decisions in this area.

JAIL AND PRISONER LAW BULLETIN. see *CRIMINOLOGY AND LAW ENFORCEMENT*

345 JA ISSN 0022-0191
JOURNAL OF CRIMINAL LAW/KEIHO ZASSHI. (Text in Japanese; title and contents page in English) 1950. q. $28.75. Criminal Law Society of Japan - Nihon Keiho Gakkai, c/o Faculty of Law, University of Tokyo, Motofuji-cho, Bunkyo-ku, Tokyo, Japan. adv.; index; circ. 1,000. **Indexed:** C.L.I.
—BLDSC shelfmark: 4965.560000.

345 UK ISSN 0022-0183
LAW
JOURNAL OF CRIMINAL LAW. 1937. q. £26($110) Pageant Publishing, 5 Turners Wood, London NW11 6DT, England. TEL 081-455-3703. FAX 081-209-0726. (Dist. by: Baileys Management Services, 127,Sandgate Rd., Folkestone, Kent CT20 2BL, England) Ed. Neil McKittrick. adv.; bk.rev.; index; circ. 600. (reprint service avail. from KTO) **Indexed:** ASSIA, C.L.I., L.R.I.
—BLDSC shelfmark: 4965.580000.
Description: Notes and comments on recent cases dealing with the practice of criminal law.

JOURNAL OF CRIMINAL LAW & CRIMINOLOGY. see *CRIMINOLOGY AND LAW ENFORCEMENT*

345 CN
JUDICIAL INTERIM RELEASE: BAIL MANUAL. a. Can.$150. Butterworths Canada Ltd., 75 Clegg Rd., Markham, Ont. L6G 1A1, Canada. TEL 416-479-2665. FAX 416-479-2826. Ed. K.R. Hamilton. (looseleaf format)
Description: Complete coverage of bail in Canadian law; organized by section and subsection of the Criminal Code.

345 CN
THE JURY; a handbook of law and procedure. 1989. s-a. Can.$95. Butterworths Canada Ltd., 75 Clegg Rd., Markham, Ont. L6G 1A1, Canada. TEL 800-668-6481. FAX 416-479-2826. Ed. Balfour Q.H. Der. index; circ. 270. (looseleaf format)
Description: Examines the role of the jury in a criminal trial.

2714 LAW — ESTATE PLANNING

345   UK   ISSN 0141-5859
K10
JUSTICE OF THE PEACE. 1837. w. £115 including index. Justice of the Peace Ltd., Little London, Chichester, W. Sussex PO19 1PG, England. TEL 0243-787841. FAX 0243-779278. Ed. F. Davies. adv.; bk.rev.; stat.; index. (also avail. in microform from UMI; reprint service avail. from UMI) **Indexed:** ASSIA.
—BLDSC shelfmark: 5075.640000.
Description: Presents commentary on magisterial and criminal law.

345   US
MAINE CRIMINAL PRACTICE. 1985. 2 base vols. (plus a. suppl.). $185. Butterworth Legal Publishers (Salem) (Subsidiary of: Reed International PLC), 90 Stiles Rd., Salem, NH 03079. TEL 800-548-4001. FAX 603-898-9858. (looseleaf format)

MANITOBA DECISIONS - CIVIL AND CRIMINAL CASES. see *LAW*

345   CN   ISSN 0527-7892
MARTIN'S ANNUAL CRIMINAL CODE. a. Can.$59. Canada Law Book Inc., 240 Edward St., Aurora, Ont. L4G 3S9, Canada. TEL 416-841-6472. Ed. Edward L. Greenspan.

345 364   CN   ISSN 0710-1805
MARTIN'S RELATED CRIMINAL STATUTES. biennial. Can.$53. Canada Law Book Inc., 240 Edward St., Aurora, Ont. L4G 3S9, Canada. TEL 416-841-6472. Ed. Edward L. Greenspan.

345 364   US
▼**MASSACHUSETTS CRIMINAL DEFENSE.** 1990. 2 base vols. (plus a. suppl.). $130. Butterworth Legal Publishers (Salem) (Subsidiary of: Reed International PLC), 90 Stiles Rd., Salem, NH 03079. TEL 800-548-4001. FAX 603-898-9858. Ed. Eric D. Blumenson.

345   US
MINNESOTA CRIMINAL LAW DIGEST. 1982. 3 base vols. (plus suppl. 6/yr.). $190. Butterworth Legal Publishers (Salem) (Subsidiary of: Reed International PLC), 90 Stiles Rd., Salem, NH 03079. TEL 800-548-4001. FAX 603-898-9858. Ed.Bd. (looseleaf format)
Description: Covers state statutes, rules of criminal procedure and case law as well as federal court decisions.

340   US
NEW HAMPSHIRE CRIMINAL CODE. a. $20. Butterworth Legal Publishers (Salem) (Subsidiary of: Reed International PLC), 90 Stiles Rd., Salem, NH 03079. TEL 800-548-4001. FAX 603-898-9858. Ed.Bd.

345   US
NEW HAMPSHIRE PRACTICE SERIES. VOLS. 1 AND 2: CRIMINAL PRACTICE AND PROCEDURE. (Series consists of 14 vols.; Vols. 1 and 2: Criminal Practice and Procedure; Vol. 3: Family Law; Vols. 4, 5 and 6: Civil Practice and Procedure; Vol. 7: Wills, Trusts and Gifts; Vols. 8 and 9: Personal Injury - Tort and Insurance; Vols. 10, 11 and 12: Probate Law and Procedure; Vols. 13 and 14: Local Government Law) 1981. 2 base vols. (plus suppl.) $75 (14-vol. set $575). Butterworth Legal Publishers (Salem) (Subsidiary of: Reed International PLC), 90 Stiles Rd., Salem, NH 03079. TEL 800-548-4001. FAX 603-898-9858. Ed.Bd.
Description: Covers pre-arrest investigation, identification procedure, criminal proceedings, trial and sentencing approaches, and appeal and parole practices.

345 364.6   US
NEW YORK (STATE). DIVISION OF CRIMINAL JUSTICE SERVICES. FELONY PROCESSING QUARTERLY REPORT. 1974. q. free. Division of Criminal Justice Services, Executive Park Tower, Stuyvesant Plaza, Albany, NY 12203.

343   US   ISSN 0271-6283
KFN6155.A59
NEW YORK STATE CRIMINAL LAW REVIEW. 1976. m. Division of Criminal Justice Services, Bureau of Prosecution Services, Executive Park Tower, Stuyvesant Plaza, Albany, NY 12203. TEL 518-457-8413. FAX 518-457-2416. Eds. Valerie Friedlander, Darlene Van Sickle. adv.; circ. 10,000.
Description: Notes on various criminal cases recently before the New York courts and the United States Supreme Court.

345   US   ISSN 1049-2356
KF9240.A59
NOT GUILTY; the newsletter for criminal defense attorneys. 1989. m. $129 (foreign $139). Knehans-Miller Publications, Box 88, Warrensburg, MO 64093. TEL 816-429-1102. Ed. Michael J. McGreevy.

345   US
OKLAHOMA CRIMINAL PRACTICE MANUAL. 1987. base vol. (plus a. suppl.). $120. Butterworth Legal Publishers (Salem) (Subsidiary of: Reed International PLC), 90 Stiles Rd., Salem, NH 03079. TEL 800-548-4001. FAX 603-898-9858. Eds. Chris Blair, Charles L. Cantrell. (looseleaf format)
Description: Covers all the procedural steps in a criminal trial, from initial appearance and preliminary matters to post-conviction proceedings, arranged in chronological sequence.

343   CN
ONTARIO DECISIONS - CRIMINAL CONVICTION AND SENTENCE CASES. 1980. m. Can.$265. Western Legal Publications, 301-1 Alexander St., Vancouver, B.C. V6A 1B2, Canada. TEL 604-687-5671. FAX 604-687-2796. m.index. (looseleaf format)
Formerly: Ontarino Decisions - Criminal Cases (ISSN 0824-7269)
Description: Digests all available criminal decisions in conviction and sentence matters from the Ontario Court of Appeal, Ontario Courts of Justice as well as all decisions of the Supreme Court of Canada regarding Ontario criminal cases.

345   BE   ISSN 0035-4384
REVUE DE DROIT PENAL ET DE CRIMINOLOGIE. (Supplements avail.) 1907. m. (10/yr.). 3000 Fr. to non-members (foreign 3200 Fr.); members 2400 Fr.; students 2200 Fr. La Charte - Die Keure, Oude Gentweg 108, B-8000 Brugge, Belgium. FAX 050-34-37-68. bk.rev.; abstr.; bibl.; charts; index. (back issues avail.) **Indexed:** Refug.Abstr.
—BLDSC shelfmark: 7898.540000.
Description: Discusses criminology and penal law.

345   US
RHODE ISLAND CRIMINAL PROCEDURE. 1988. base vol. (plus suppl.). $125. Butterworth Legal Publishers (Salem) (Subsidiary of: Reed International PLC), 90 Stiles Rd., Salem, NH 03079. TEL 800-548-4001. FAX 603-898-9858. Eds. Barbara Hurst, John A. MacFadyen. (looseleaf format)
Description: Covers the mechanics of criminal litigation, including discussion of pleas at arraignment, discovery, the filing and grounds for pretrial motions, voir dire, objections to evidence, mid-trial motions, jury instructions and verdicts.

340   US
RHODE ISLAND SUPREME COURT AND THE LAW OF CRIMES. 1983. base vol. (plus suppl.). $60. Butterworth Legal Publishers (Salem) (Subsidiary of: Reed International PLC), 90 Stiles Rd., Salem, NH 03079. TEL 800-548-4001. FAX 603-898-9858. Ed. Bruce G. Pollock. (looseleaf format)
Description: Covers cases pertaining to homicide, assault, robbery and other offenses; includes evidence issues, exclusions and privileges.

455 364   US
RIGHTS OF PRISONERS. 1981. base vol. (plus a. suppl.). $95. Shepard's - McGraw-Hill, Inc., Box 35300, Colorado Springs, CO 80935-3530. TEL 800-525-2474.
Description: Analysis of appropriate caveats, qualifications and indications of potential or emerging trends. Covers both statutory and constitutional development.

345   US
SCIENTIFIC SLEUTHING REVIEW; forensic science in criminal law. 1976. q. $20 (foreign $25). c/o J.E. Starrs, Ed., George Washington University, National Law Center, Washington, DC 20052. TEL 202-994-6770. Ed. Patrick Zickler. adv.; bk.rev.; circ. 800. (looseleaf format; back issues avail.)
Former titles: Scientific Sleuthing Newsletter (ISSN 0749-1395); Science in Criminal Law Newsletter; Scientific Sleuthing Newsletter.

345   UK   ISSN 0263-2381
SCOTTISH CRIMINAL CASE REPORTS. 5/yr. £85. Law Society of Scotland, 26 Drumsheugh Gardens, Edinburgh EH3 7YR, Scotland. Ed. Sheriff Gerald H. Gordon.

SECURITY AND SPECIAL POLICE LEGAL UPDATE. see *CRIMINOLOGY AND LAW ENFORCEMENT — Security*

SECURITY LAW NEWSLETTER. see *CRIMINOLOGY AND LAW ENFORCEMENT — Security*

345   US   ISSN 0363-0978
KF9610.5
SHEPARD'S CRIMINAL JUSTICE CITATIONS. 1975. 4/yr. $144. Shepard's - McGraw-Hill, Inc., Box 35300, Colorado Springs, CO 80935-3530. TEL 800-525-2474.

345   II   ISSN 0253-6544
SUPREME COURT CASES (CRIMINAL). (Text in English) 1970. m. $41. Eastern Book Company, 34 Lalbagh, Lucknow 226 001, India. TEL 43171. FAX 0091-522-242061. TELEX 535 436 FAST IN. Ed. Surendra Malik. adv.; bk.rev.; circ. 3,000. (back issues avail.)

345   PL   ISSN 0208-5577
UNIWERSYTET SLASKI W KATOWICACH. PRACE NUKOWE. PROBLEMY PRAWA KARNEGO. (Text in Polish; summaries in German, Russian) 1975. irreg. price varies. Wydawnictwo Uniwersytetu Slaskiego, Ul. Bankowa 14, 40-007 Katowice, Poland. TEL 48-32-596-915. FAX 48-32-599-605. TELEX 0315584 USKPL. (Dist. by: CHS Ars Polona, P.O. Box 1001, 00-950 Warsaw, Poland)
Description: Covers criminal law, the law of criminal court proceedings, executive criminal law, criminology, crime detection law.

340 345   CN   ISSN 1180-0453
▼**VICTIMS OF VIOLENCE REPORT.** 1990. 5/yr. Can.$25($25) (effective 1991). Victims of Violence International, B150 151 Slater St., Ottawa, Ont. K1P 5H3, Canada. TEL 613-233-0052. FAX 613-233-2712. (Subscr. in US to: Box 1305, Ogdensburg, NY 13669) Ed. Gary Rosenfeldt. adv.; circ. 21,000. (back issues avail.)
Description: Covers crime victimization, child abuse, crime and punishment.

345   CN   ISSN 0703-1319
WEEKLY CRIMINAL BULLETIN. 1977. w. Can.$167. Canada Law Book Inc., 240 Edward St., Aurora, Ont. L4G 3S9, Canada. TEL 416-841-6472.
●Also available online.

345 305.4   US   ISSN 0897-4454
HV7231   CODEN: WCJUER
WOMEN & CRIMINAL JUSTICE. 1989. s-a. $24 to individuals; institutions $32; libraries $48. Haworth Press, Inc., 10 Alice St., Binghamton, NY 13904. TEL 800-342-9678. FAX 607-722-1424. TELEX 4932599. Ed. Clarice Feinman. adv.; bk.rev. (also avail. in microfiche from HAW; reprint service avail. from HAW) **Indexed:** Wom.Stud.Abstr. (1989-).
—BLDSC shelfmark: 9343.241000.
Description: Devoted specifically to interdisciplinary scholarly research dealing with all areas of women and criminal justice.
Refereed Serial

LAW — Estate Planning

332.04 333.33   US
AUDIO ESTATE PLANNER. 4/yr. $75. American Law Institute, Committee on Continuing Professional Education, 4025 Chestnut St., Philadelphia, PA 19104. TEL 215-243-1697. FAX 215-243-1664. (Co-sponsor: American Bar Association) Ed. William Stevens. circ. 350. (audio cassette)
Description: Articles of practical interest to the attorney specializing in estate planning and administration.

LAW — ESTATE PLANNING

332.04 US
B A R - B R I BAR REVIEW. WILLS. a. $395. B A R - B R I Bar Review, 3280 Motor Ave., Los Angeles, CA 90034-3710. TEL 213-477-2542.

332.040 US
DRAFTING WILLS AND TRUST AGREEMENTS. 1980. base vol. (plus m. supplements). $220. Shepard's - McGraw-Hill, Inc., Box 35300, Colorado Springs, CO 80935-3530. TEL 800-525-2474. (Co-sponsor: R.P.W. Publishing Corp.) Ed. Robert P. Wilkins. (looseleaf format)

332.04 US
ESTATE POWERS & TRUSTS LAW OF NEW YORK. 1988. a. $8.95 (effective 1992). Gould Publications (Binghamton), 199-300 State St., Binghamton, NY 13901. TEL 607-724-3000. FAX 607-723-4285. (looseleaf format)

332.04 CN
ESTATES AND TRUSTS JOURNAL. 1974. q. Can.$96. Canada Law Book Inc., 240 Edward St., Aurora, Ont. L4G 3S9, Canada. TEL 416-841-6472. Ed. Robert C. Dick. **Indexed:** BPIA, Bus.Ind., C.L.I., Ind.Can.L.P.L., L.R.I.
  Formerly: Estates and Trusts Quarterly (ISSN 0381-8888)

332.04 CN ISSN 0706-5655
ESTATES & TRUSTS REPORTS. 1977. 12/yr. (in 4 vols.). Can.$115. Carswell Publications, Corporate Plaza, 2075 Kennedy Rd., Scarborough, Ont. M1T 3V4, Canada. TEL 416-609-8000. FAX 416-298-5094. Ed. T.G. Youdan. **Indexed:** C.L.I., Ind.Can.L.P.L., L.R.I.

332.04 UK
ESTATES GAZETTE LAW REPORTS. s-a. price varies. Estates Gazette Ltd., 151 Wardour Street, London, W1V 4BN, England.
  Supersedes: Estates Gazette Digest of Land and Property Cases (ISSN 0071-1586)

332.04 US
FIDUCIARY STANDARDS IN PENSION AND TRUST FUND MANAGEMENT. 1989. base vol. (plus suppl.). $65. Butterworth Legal Publishers (Salem) (Subsidiary of: Reed International PLC), 90 Stiles Rd., Salem, NH 03079. TEL 800-548-4001. FAX 603-898-9858. Ed. Betty L. Krikorian.
  Description: Provides an explanation of the complex legal and business environment in which today's pension and trust fund fiduciaries work.

332.04 US
GILBERT LAW SUMMARIES. WILLS. irreg., 10th ed., 1986. $15.95. Law Distributors (Subsidiary of: H B J Legal & Professional Publications Inc.), 14415 S. Main St., Gardena, CA 90248. TEL 800-421-1893. FAX 213-324-6381.

332.04 US
▼**GUARDIANSHIP AND CONSERVATORSHIP IN MASSACHUSETTS.** 1991. base vol. (plus irreg. suppl.). $85. Butterworth Legal Publishers (Salem) (Subsidiary of: Reed International PLC), 90 Stiles Rd., Salem, NH 03079. TEL 800-548-4001. FAX 603-898-9858. Eds. Johh H. Cross, Robert D. Fleischner. (looseleaf format)
  Description: Provides information concerning procedures for the appointment of guardians and conservators for individuals with mental and physical disabilities.

332.04 US
MAINE PROBATE MANUAL. 1988. base vol. (plus suppl.). $95. Butterworth Legal Publishers (Salem) (Subsidiary of: Reed International PLC), 90 Stiles Rd., Salem, NH 03079. TEL 800-548-4001. FAX 603-898-9858. Ed. James E. Mitchell. (looseleaf format)
  Description: Contains the Maine Rules of Probate Procedure with notes and commentary.

332.04 US
MASSACHUSETTS CONDOMINIUM LAW. 1985. base vol. (plus suppl.). $125. Butterworth Legal Publishers (Salem) (Subsidiary of: Reed International PLC), 90 Stiles Rd., Salem, NH 03079. TEL 800-548-4001. FAX 603-898-9858. Eds. Barry Brown, Bernard V. Keenan. (looseleaf format)
  Description: Covers condominium law; provides advice on every step of the process, from creating the condominium to ongoing operations.

332.04 US
MECHANICS' AND CONSTRUCTION LIENS IN ALASKA, OREGON AND WASHINGTON. 1987. base vol. (plus suppl.). $70. Butterworth Legal Publishers (Salem) (Subsidiary of: Reed International PLC), 90 Stiles Rd., Salem, NH 03079. TEL 800-548-4001. FAX 603-898-9858. Ed. Brian A. Blum. (looseleaf format)

332.04 AU
MIETRECHTLICHE ENTSCHEIDUNGEN. Abbreviated title: MietSlg. 1951. irreg., vol.40, 1990. price varies. Manzsche Verlags- und Universitaetsbuchhandlung, Kohlmarkt 16, A-1014 Vienna, Austria. TEL 0222-531610. FAX 0222-5316181. Ed. Helmut Wuerth. (back issues avail.)
  Description: Collects decisions on landlord and tenant law.

332.04 US
MINNESOTA REAL ESTATE LAW JOURNAL. 1981. bi-m. $75. Butterworth Legal Publishers (St. Paul) (Subsidiary of: Reed International PLC), 289 E. 5th St., St. Paul, MN 55101. TEL 800-333-3839. Ed. Stephen Liebo. (back issues avail.)
  Description: Real estate law articles, case comments and court decisions.

332.04 US
▼**MINNESOTA RESIDENTIAL REAL ESTATE.** 1991. 2 base vols. (plus suppl.). $160. Butterworth Legal Publishers (Salem) (Subsidiary of: Reed International PLC), 90 Stiles Rd., Salem, NH 03079. TEL 800-548-4001. FAX 603-898-9858. Ed. James D. Olson. (looseleaf format)
  Description: Complete guide to the law of residential real estate transactions in Minnesota.

MOBILE HOMES AND MOBILE HOME PARKS. see HOUSING AND URBAN PLANNING

NATIONAL REAL PROPERTY REVIEW; monthly views on real estate. see REAL ESTATE

332.04 333.33 US
NEIGHBORING PROPERTY OWNERS. 1988. base vol. (plus a. suppl.). $95. Shepard's - McGraw-Hill, Inc., Box 35300, Colorado Springs, CO 80935-3530. TEL 800-525-2474.
  Description: Analyzes the full range of legal principles that define the legal rights and obligations of neighboring landowners.

340 332.04 US
NEW HAMPSHIRE LAND SALES DISCLOSURE AND CONDOMINIUM LAWS AND RULES. a. $15. Butterworth Legal Publishers (Salem) (Subsidiary of: Reed International PLC), 90 Stiles Rd., Salem, NH 03079. TEL 800-548-4001. FAX 603-898-9858. Ed.Bd.
  Description: For attorneys, real estate professionals, municipal boards and private developers; contains both the New Hampshire laws relating to land sales disclosure and the administrative rules.

332.04 US
NEW HAMPSHIRE LANDLORD AND TENANT LAW. a. $15. Butterworth Legal Publishers (Salem) (Subsidiary of: Reed International PLC), 90 Stiles Rd., Salem, NH 03079. TEL 800-548-4001. FAX 603-898-9858. Ed.Bd.
  Description: Covers landlord and tenant law as well as related laws dealing with manufactured housing and requirements of the New Hampshire Human Rights Commission.

332.04 352.7 US
NEW HAMPSHIRE PLANNING AND LAND USE REGULATION. a. $16. Butterworth Legal Publishers (Salem) (Subsidiary of: Reed International PLC), 90 Stiles Rd., Salem, NH 03079. TEL 800-548-4001. FAX 603-898-9858. Ed.Bd.

332.04 US ISSN 0951-547X
NEW MEXICO REAL ESTATE LAW REPORTER. 1987. q. $80. Butterworth Legal Publishers, Austin Division (Subsidiary of: Reed International PLC), Echelon II, Ste. 100, 9430 Research, Austin, TX 78759-6598. TEL 512-346-9686. FAX 512-346-9373. Ed.Bd. (looseleaf format; back issues avail.)

332.04 US
NEW YORK REAL ESTATE REPORTER. 1986. m. $185. New York Law Publishing Co., 111 Eighth Ave., New York, NY 10011. TEL 212-741-8300.
  Description: Roundup of New York's real estate cases, with commentary on what impacts real estate practices. Also covers current developments affecting the real estate industry.

332.04 NZ ISSN 0110-1390
NEW ZEALAND TOWN PLANNING APPEALS. 1956. 10/yr. Butterworths of New Zealand Ltd., P.O. Box 472, 205-207 Victoria St., Wellington, New Zealand. TEL 04-385-1479. FAX 04-385-1598. Ed. Peter Haig.
  Description: Selected decisions of the Planning Tribunal, High Court and Court of Appeal on town planning, environmental, and local government issues.

333.33 332.04 CN ISSN 0382-5906
ONTARIO REAL ESTATE LAW GUIDE. m. Can.$495. C C H Canadian Ltd., 6 Garamond Ct., Don Mills, Ont. M3C 1Z5, Canada. TEL 416-441-2992. FAX 416-444-9011. index.
  Description: Complete coverage of laws governing real estate transactions in Ontario. Texts of over 55 statutes and regulations.

340 US
OREGON RULES OF CIVIL PROCEDURE HANDBOOK (YEAR). biennial. $29.50. Butterworth Legal Publishers (Salem) (Subsidiary of: Reed International PLC), 90 Stiles Rd., Salem, NH 03079. TEL 800-548-4001. FAX 603-898-9858. Ed. Frederic R. Merrill.

332.04 US
THE PRACTICAL REAL ESTATE LAWYER. 1985. bi-m. $35. American Law Institute, Committee on Continuing Professional Education, 4025 Chestnut St., Philadelphia, PA 19104. TEL 215-243-1604. FAX 215-243-1664. (Co-sponsor: American Bar Association) Ed. Mark T. Carroll. adv.; cum.index; circ. 6,432. **Indexed:** C.L.I., Leg.Per.
  Description: Forms, checklists and practical articles for real estate lawyers.

332.04 343.05 US
▼**PRESERVING LANDS: LEGAL ISSUES.** 1990. q. $35. Preserving Family Lands, Box 146, W. Peterborough, NH 03468. TEL 617-244-7553. FAX 617-728-9797. Ed. Stephen J. Small.
  Description: News and legal developments concerning tax issues in land ownership, including estate planning, environmental and conservation easements, and wildlife preservation strategies.

332.04 US ISSN 1046-9966
KF1298.A15
REAL ESTATE - ENVIRONMENTAL LIABILITY NEWS; the bi-weekly report on litigation, regulation, and industry practice. 1989. fortn. $497 (foreign $519). (Subsidiary of: Millin Publications, Inc.), 1350 Connecticut Ave., N.W., Ste. 1000, Washington, DC 20036. TEL 800-333-1291. FAX 202-862-0999. Ed. Susan Winchurch. (back issues avail.)

332.04 US
REAL ESTATE LAW DIGEST (SUPPLEMENT). two base vols. (plus s-a. supplements). $115 for base volumes and supplements. Warren, Gorham and Lamont, One Penn Plaza, New York, NY 10119. TEL 800-950-1205. FAX 212-971-5240. (also avail. in microform from UMI; reprint service avail. from UMI)

LAW — FAMILY AND MATRIMONIAL LAW

332.04 US ISSN 0048-6868
K18
REAL ESTATE LAW JOURNAL. 1972. q. $115. Warren, Gorham and Lamont, One Penn Plaza, New York, NY 10119. TEL 800-950-1205. FAX 212-971-5240. Ed. Jerome G. Rose. bk.rev.; bibl. (also avail. in microform from UMI; reprint service avail. from RRI,UMI) Indexed: ABI Inform., Abstr.Bk.Rev.Curr.Leg.Per., Bank.Lit.Ind., BPIA, Bus.Ind., C.L.I., L.R.I., Leg.Cont., Leg.Per., P.A.I.S., SSCI.
—BLDSC shelfmark: 7303.280900.
Description: Draws upon the expertise of leading real estate attorneys, tax specialists, financial experts, and government officials. Covers joint venture agreements, leasebacks, real estate tax shelters, real estate investment trusts, zoning, option agreements, landlords' responsibilities and new financing methods.
Refereed Serial

332.04 US ISSN 0162-752X
KF570
REAL ESTATE LAW REPORT. 1971. m. $98. Warren, Gorham and Lamont, One Penn Plaza, New York, NY 10119. TEL 800-950-1205. FAX 212-971-5240. Ed.Bd. (looseleaf format; also avail. in microform from UMI)
Description: Presents case histories in a jargon-free style so that real estate professionals as well as attorneys can keep up with the legal developments in the real estate field. Follows each history with an editorial observation.

332.04 US
REAL ESTATE SECURITIES & CAPITAL MARKETS. m. $185. New York Law Publishing Co., Marketing Dept., 111 Eighth Ave., New York, NY 10011. TEL 212-741-8300.
Formerly: Real Estate Syndicator Newsletter.
Description: Provides legal, regulatory, business and financial information in real estate.

333.33 332.04 US
REAL PROPERTY INSTITUTE; troubled projects: workout techniques and litigation strategies. a. $42 softcover. Continuing Education of the Bar - California, University of California Extension, 2300 Shattuck Ave., Berkeley, CA 94704. TEL 510-642-6211. FAX 800-642-3788. (Co-sponsor: State Bar of California)

332.04 US
REAL PROPERTY LAW COMMUNICATOR. q. Chicago Bar Association, 321 S. Plymouth Court, Chicago, IL 60604. TEL 312-554-2000. FAX 312-554-2054. Ed. Janet Johnson.

332.04 US ISSN 0898-1698
KFC140.A15
REAL PROPERTY LAW REPORTER. 1977. 8/yr. $175. Continuing Education of the Bar - California, University of California Extension, 2300 Shattuck Ave., Berkeley, CA 94704. TEL 510-642-0306. FAX 800-642-3788. (Co-sponsor: State Bar of California) Ed. Jo Sherlin.

332.04 US ISSN 0034-0855
K18
REAL PROPERTY, PROBATE AND TRUST JOURNAL. 1966. q. $22 (foreign $27). American Bar Association, Real Property, Probate and Trust Law Section, 750 N. Lake Shore Dr., Chicago, IL 60611. TEL 312-988-6083. Ed. S. Alan Medlin. bk.rev.; circ. 37,970. (also avail. in microform from RRI,UMI; reprint service avail. from RRI,UMI) Indexed: Abstr.Bk.Rev.Curr.Leg.Per., Account.Ind. (1974-), BPIA, Bus.Ind., C.L.I., Curr.Cont., L.I.I., L.R.I., Leg.Cont., Leg.Per., SSCI.
●Also available online. Vendor(s): WESTLAW.
—BLDSC shelfmark: 7303.282570.
Description: Scholarly articles in the fields of estate planning, trust law, and real property law.

332.04 AT
REGULATION OF BUILDING STANDARDS N S W. base vol. (plus q. update). $195. Butterworths Pty. Ltd., 271-273 Lane Cove Rd., P.O. Box 345, North Ryde, N.S.W. 2113, Australia. TEL 02-335-4444. FAX 02-335-4655. (looseleaf format)

332.04 AT
REGULATION OF BUILDING STANDARDS QUEENSLAND. base vol. (plus q. update). $175. Butterworths Pty. Ltd., 271-273 Lane Cove Rd., P.O. Box 345, North Ryde, N.S.W. 2113, Australia. TEL 02-335-4444. FAX 02-335-4655. (looseleaf format)

RIVISTA TRIMESTRALE DEGLI APPALTI; rivista di dottrina-legislazione-giurisprudenza. see *BUILDING AND CONSTRUCTION*

332.04 352.7 UK ISSN 0144-8196
KDC446.A13
SCOTTISH PLANNING LAW & PRACTICE. 1980. 3/yr. £17. Law Society of Scotland, 26 Drumsheugh Gardens, Edinburgh EH3 7YR, Scotland. Ed.Bd. (back issues avail.) Indexed: Geo.Abstr.
—BLDSC shelfmark: 8211.062000.
Description: For planners, surveyors, lawyers, architects, councillors and others: all aspects of planning law in Scotland.

332.04 US
SUCCESSFUL ESTATE PLANNING: IDEAS AND METHODS. 2 base vols. (plus s-m. updates). Maxwell Macmillan, Professional and Business Reference Publishing, 910 Sylvan Ave., Englewood Cliffs, NJ 07632-3310. TEL 800-562-0245. FAX 201-816-3569. (looseleaf format)

332.04 US
TENNESSEE REAL ESTATE LAW LETTER. 1983. 12/yr. $93. M. Lee Smith Publishers & Printers, 162 Fourth Ave. N., Box 2678, Nashville, TN 37219. TEL 615-242-7395. FAX 615-256-6601. Ed. C. Dewees Berry IV.
Description: Surveys Tennessee and federal real estate law developments.

332.04 US
TEXAS CONDOMINIUM LAW MANUAL. 1983. base vol. (plus suppl. 1-2/yr.). $95. Butterworth Legal Publishers (Salem) (Subsidiary of: Reed International PLC), 90 Stiles Rd., Salem, NH 03079. TEL 800-548-4001. FAX 603-898-9858. (looseleaf format)

332.04 690 US
TEXAS CONSTRUCTION LAW MANUAL. 1981. base vol. (plus a. suppl.). $95. Shepard's - McGraw-Hill, Inc., Box 35300, Colorado Springs, CO 80935-3530. TEL 800-525-2474.
Description: Designed to guide attorneys and contractors working in Texas through the complexities and the legal considerations of the construction business.

TEXAS FORECLOSURE: LAW AND PRACTICE. see *LAW — Corporate Law*

332.04 US
TEXAS MUNICIPAL ZONING LAW. 1985. base vol. (plus a. suppl.). $110. Butterworth Legal Publishers (Salem) (Subsidiary of: Reed International PLC), 90 Stiles Rd., Salem, NH 03079. TEL 800-548-4001. FAX 603-898-9858. Ed. John Mixon. (looseleaf format)
Description: Analysis of Texas case law and procedure governing the creation, enforcement and modification of local zoning.

332.04 US
TEXAS RESIDENTIAL LANDLORD - TENANT LAW. 1986. 2 base vols. (plus suppl. 2-3/yr.). $125. Butterworth Legal Publishers (Salem) (Subsidiary of: Reed International PLC), 90 Stiles Rd., Salem, NH 03079. TEL 800-548-4001. FAX 603-898-9858. Ed.Bd. (looseleaf format)
Description: Practical guide to using Texas statutes, rules and court decisions in handling landlord-tenant disputes.

332.04 352 AT
TOWN PLANNING LAW AND PRACTICE. 1987. 8/yr. Law Book Co. Ltd., 44-50 Waterloo Rd., North Ryde, N.S.W. 2113, Australia. TEL 02-887-0177. FAX 02-888-9706. TELEX ASBOOK 27995. Eds. D.J. Gifford, K.H. Gifford.
Description: Coverage of decision made in all courts in town planning law and practice in Australia.

332.04 US ISSN 0537-9768
UNIVERSITY OF MIAMI, CORAL GABLES. LAW CENTER. ANNUAL INSTITUTE ON ESTATE PLANNING. 1967. a. $105. Matthew Bender & Co., Inc., 11 Penn Plaza, New York, NY 10001. TEL 212-967-7707. Ed. Philip Heckerling. (also avail. in microfilm from RRI; back issues avail.; reprint service avail. from RRI)

332.04 AT
WILLS, PROBATE & ADMINISTRATION SERVICE N S W. base vol. (plus q. update). $385. Butterworths Pty. Ltd., 271-273 Lane Cove Rd., P.O. Box 345, North Ryde, N.S.W. 2113, Australia. TEL 02-335-4444. FAX 02-335-4655. (looseleaf format)

332.04 US
▼**WILLS, TRUSTS AND GIFTS - RHODE ISLAND.** 1991. base vol. (plus a. suppl.). $90. Butterworth Legal Publishers (Salem) (Subsidiary of: Reed International PLC), 90 Stiles Rd., Salem, NH 03079. TEL 800-548-4001. FAX 603-898-9858. Ed. David T. Riedel.
Description: Contains the cases and statutes in Rhode Island relating to wills, trusts and gifts complete with summaries and analysis.

LAW — Family And Matrimonial Law

346.01 AT
AUSTRALIAN FAMILY LAW & PRACTICE. (In 3 vols.) 1975. every 3 weeks. C C H Australia Ltd., P.O. Box 230, North Ryde, N.S.W. 2113, Australia. TEL 888-2555. charts.
Description: Includes family law cases.

346.01 AT
AUSTRALIAN FAMILY LAW - COURT HANDBOOK. 1989. bi-m. C C H Australia Ltd., P.O. Box 230, North Ryde, N.S.W. 2113, Australia. TEL 02-888-2555. FAX 02-888-7324.

346.01 AT
AUSTRALIAN FAMILY LAW SERVICE. base vols. (plus m. updates). $715. Butterworths Pty. Ltd., 271-273 Lane Cove Rd., P.O. Box 345, North Ryde, N.S.W. 2113, Australia. TEL 02-335-4444. FAX 02-335-4655.

346.01 AT ISSN 0817-623X
K1
AUSTRALIAN JOURNAL OF FAMILY LAW. 1986. 3/yr. Aus.$97. Butterworths Pty. Ltd., P.O. Box 345, North Ryde, N.S.W. 2113, Australia. TEL 02-335-4444. FAX 02-335-4655.

346.01 CN ISSN 0824-7196
BRITISH COLUMBIA DECISIONS - FAMILY LAW CASES. 1980. m. Can.$120. Western Legal Publications, 301-1 Alexander St., Vancouver, B.C. V6A 1B2, Canada. TEL 604-687-5671. FAX 604-687-2796. m.index. (looseleaf format)
●Also available online.

346.01 CN
BRITISH COLUMBIA FAMILY LAW. m. Can.$195. Butterworths Canada Ltd., 75 Clegg Rd., Markham, Ont. L6G 1A1, Canada. TEL 416-479-2665. FAX 416-479-2826.
Description: Provides family lawyers with a guide to the legislation and case law on family law practice in British Columbia.

346.01 NZ
BUTTERWORTHS FAMILY LAW BULLETIN. 1985. 8/w. NZ.$90. Butterworths of New Zealand Ltd., P.O. Box 472, 203-207 Victoria St., Wellington, New Zealand. TEL 04-385-1479. FAX 04-385-1598. Ed. Hellen Papadopoulos.
Formerly: New Zealand Family Law Bulletin (ISSN 0112-6261)
Description: Articles plus notes on all developments of relevance to family law in New Zealand.

346.01 NZ
BUTTERWORTHS FAMILY LAW REPORTS. 1981. m. Butterworths of New Zealand Ltd., P.O. Box 472, 203-207 Victoria St., Wellington, New Zealand. TEL 04-385-1479. FAX 04-385-1598. Ed. Hellen Papadopoulos.
Formerly: New Zealand Family Law Reports (ISSN 0111-8358)
Description: Full text of latest decisions from Family Courts, the High Court and Court of Appeal.

346.01 NZ
BUTTERWORTHS FAMILY LAW SERVICE; for New Zealand use. 2 base vols. (plus q. update). NZ.$296. Butterworths of New Zealand Ltd., 203-207 Victoria St., P.O. Box 472, Wellington, New Zealand. TEL 04-385-1479. FAX 04-385-1598. (looseleaf format)
Description: Legislation and commentary for those involved in proceedings before the Family Court and in matters concerning the family generally.

LAW — FAMILY AND MATRIMONIAL LAW

346.01   UK
BUTTERWORTHS FAMILY LAW SERVICE; for UK use. 6/yr. (plus m. updates). Butterworth & Co. (Publishers) Ltd. (Subsidiary of: Reed International PLC), 88 Kingsway, London WC2B 6AB, England. TEL 71-405-6900. FAX 71-405-1332. (US addr.: Butterworth Legal Publishers, 90 Stiles Rd., Salem, NH 03079. TEL 800-548-4001) (looseleaf format)

346.01 360   US
CALIFORNIA FAMILY LAW MONTHLY. 1984. m. $235. Matthew Bender & Co., Inc., 11 Penn Plaza, New York, NY 10001. TEL 212-967-7707. Ed.Bd.

346.01   US
CALIFORNIA FAMILY LAW: PRACTICE AND PROCEDURE. 1978. 7 base vols. (plus irreg. supplements). Matthew Bender & Co., Inc., 11 Penn Plaza, New York, NY 10001. TEL 212-967-7707. Ed. Hon. Christian E. Markey, Jr. (looseleaf format)
Description: Covers law and procedure for contemporary family law problems, on issues arising in cases of dissolution, as well as those related to ongoing family situations.

346.01   CN
CANADIAN FAMILY LAW GUIDE. 1976. m. Can.$525. C H Canadian Ltd., 6 Garamond Ct., Don Mills, Ont. M3C 1Z5, Canada. TEL 416-441-2992. FAX 416-444-9011.
Description: Text of more than 175 federal, provincial and territorial statutes on family law in Canada, commentary and court decisions concerning marriage and annulment of marriage, custody and access to children, status of children, guardianship, adoption and children in need of protection.

346.01   CN   ISSN 0832-6983
K3
CANADIAN FAMILY LAW QUARTERLY; a journal for practitioners. 1986. q. (plus bound vol.). Can.$128($102) Carswell Publications, Corporate Plaza, 2075 Kennedy Rd., Scarborough, Ont. M1T 3V4, Canada. TEL 416-609-8000. FAX 416-298-5094. Ed. James G. McLeod. adv.; bk.rev. Indexed: C.L.I.
Description: Focuses on topics of practical interest to family law practitioners.

346.01   US
CONNECTICUT FAMILY LAW CITATIONS. 1980. s-a. $25 per no. Butterworth Legal Publishers (Salem) (Subsidiary of: Reed International PLC), 90 Stiles Rd., Salem, NH 03079. TEL 800-548-4001. FAX 603-603-898-9858. Ed. Cynthia C. George.
Description: Contains case names and citations accumulated from all reported and unreported cases from 1979 to date.

346.01 301.42   US
DISSOLUTION OF MARRIAGE. 1986. base vol. (plus a. suppl.). $70. Shepard's - McGraw-Hill, Inc., Box 35300, Colorado Springs, CO 80935-3530. TEL 800-525-2474.
Description: Reviews current national trends in family law and their historical roots. Focuses on significant changes in state legislation, federal legislation and case law with complete documentation.

346.01   US   ISSN 1042-5934
DOMESTIC RELATIONS JOURNAL OF OHIO. 1989. bi-m. $125. Banks - Baldwin Law Publishing Co., University Center, Box 1974, Cleveland, OH 44106. TEL 216-721-7373. FAX 216-721-8055. Ed. Stanley Morganstern.
Description: Commentary on developments in domestic relations law and practice on topics such as marital asset valuation and visitation rights. Includes current case analysis, recent legislative actions, and court rule changes.

346.01   US
DOMESTIC RELATIONS: THE SUBSTANTIVE LAW. 1984. base vol. (plus suppl.). $50. Butterworth Legal Publishers (Salem) (Subsidiary of: Reed International PLC), 90 Stiles Rd., Salem, NH 03079. TEL 800-548-4001. FAX 603-898-9858. Ed. Ernest I. Rotenberg. (looseleaf format)

346.01   US   ISSN 0163-710X
KF501.A3
FAMILY ADVOCATE. 1978. q. $37 (foreign $42). American Bar Association, Family Law Section, 750 N. Lake Shore Dr., Chicago, IL 60611. TEL 312-988-6069. Ed. Deborah Eisel. adv.; bk.rev.; circ. 17,000. (also avail. in microfilm from WSH) Indexed: Adol.Ment.Hlth.Abstr., C.L.I., L.R.I., Leg.Per.
●Also available online. Vendor(s): WESTLAW (FAMADVO).
—BLDSC shelfmark: 3865.557000.
Formerly: Family Law Newsletter (ISSN 0427-9638)
Description: Pratical advice for attorneys practicing family law.

346.01 360   US   ISSN 1047-5699
K3   CODEN: FCCREY
FAMILY AND CONCILIATION COURTS REVIEW. 1963. q. $40 to individuals; institutions $85. (Association of Family and Conciliation Courts) Sage Publications, Inc., 2455 Teller Rd., Newbury Park, CA 91320. TEL 805-499-0721. FAX 805-499-0871. Eds. Stanley Cohen, Hugh McIsaac. cum.index; circ. 1,800. (back issues avail.) Indexed: Psychol.Abstr.
—BLDSC shelfmark: 3865.558700.
Formerly: Conciliation Courts Review.
Description: International communication forum to develop and improve the practice of conciliation counseling as a complement to judicial procedures.

346.01   UK   ISSN 0952-8199
KD750
FAMILY COURT REPORTER. 1987. w. £45. Justice of the Peace Ltd., Little London, Chichester, W. Sussex PO19 1PG, England. TEL 0243-787841. FAX 0243-779278. Ed. C.T. Latham.
Description: Provides law report news and commentary.

346.01   UK   ISSN 0014-7281
K6
FAMILY LAW; every development in UK family law. 1971. 12/yr. £65. Jordan & Sons Ltd., 21 St. Thomas St., Bristol BS1 6JS, England. TEL 0272-230600. FAX 0272-230063. TELEX 449119. Ed. Elizabeth Walsh. bk.rev.; stat.; index; circ. 5,000. Indexed: Adol.Ment.Hlth.Abstr., ASSIA, C.L.I., L.R.I., Stud.Wom.Abstr.
—BLDSC shelfmark: 3865.565100.

346.01   US
FAMILY LAW GUIDEBOOK; a handbook with forms. 1985. base vol. (plus suppl.). $50. Butterworth Legal Publishers (Salem) (Subsidiary of: Reed International PLC), 90 Stiles Rd., Salem, NH 03079. TEL 800-548-4001. FAX 603-898-9858. Ed. Edward M. Ginsburg. (looseleaf format)

346.01   US   ISSN 0014-729X
FAMILY LAW QUARTERLY. 1967. q. $34 to non-members. American Bar Association, Family Law Section, 750 N. Lake Shore Dr., Chicago, IL 60611. TEL 312-988-6068. Ed. Timothy B. Walker. adv.; bk.rev.; abstr.; charts; index; circ. 16,000. (also avail. in microfiche from WSH; microfilm from UMI,WSH) Indexed: Adol.Ment.Hlth.Abstr., C.L.I., Crim.Just.Abstr., Curr.Cont., L.R.I., Leg.Cont., Leg.Per., SSCI, SSCI.
●Also available online. Vendor(s): WESTLAW (FAMLQ).
—BLDSC shelfmark: 3865.566000.
Description: Scholarly journal on judicial decisions, legislation, taxation, and summaries of state and local bar association projects.

346.01   US   ISSN 0148-7922
KF501.A3
FAMILY LAW REPORTER. 1974. w. $520. The Bureau of National Affairs, Inc., 1231 25th St., N.W., Washington, DC 20037. TEL 202-452-4200. FAX 202-822-8092. TELEX 285656 BNAI WSH. (Subscr. to: 9435 Key West Ave., Rockville, MD 20850. TEL 800-372-1033) Ed. Randy P. Auerbach. (looseleaf format; back issues avail.) Indexed: CJPI.
Description: Notification and reference service dealing with all significant state and federal developments in the field of family law.

345.05   UK   ISSN 0261-4375
FAMILY LAW REPORTS. 1980. 12/yr. £120. Jordan & Sons Ltd., 21 St. Thomas St., Bristol BS1 6JS, England. TEL 0272-230600. FAX 0272-230063. TELEX 449119. Eds. Nigel Lowe, Elizabeth Walsh. circ. 1,500.
●Also available online. Vendor(s): Mead Data Central.

346.05   AT   ISSN 0706-7666
F1086
FAMILY LAW REPORTS. 1976. m. Aus.$90. Butterworth Pty. Ltd., P.O. Box 345, North Ryde, N.S.W. 2113, Australia. TEL 02-335-4444. FAX 02-335-4655. circ. 800. (back issues avail.)

346.05   SA
FAMILY LAW SERVICE. s-a. $245. Butterworth Publishers (Pty.) Ltd., 8 Walter Pl., Waterval Park, Durban 4000, South Africa. TEL 031-294247. FAX 031-283255. (looseleaf format)

346.05   US
FAMILY LAW TAX GUIDE. 1985. m. $445. Commerce Clearing House, Inc., 4025 W. Peterson Ave., Chicago, IL 60646. TEL 312-583-8500.

346.05   US
FAMILY MATTERS. 1989. q. $20. Center for Law and Social Policy, 1616 "P" St. N.W., Ste.450, Washington, DC 20036. TEL 202-328-5140. FAX 202-328-5195. circ. 250. (back issues avail.)

346.01   US
FLORIDA FAMILY LAW PRACTICE. 1976. 4 base vols. (plus suppl. 4-5/yr.). $280. Butterworth Legal Publishers (Salem) (Subsidiary of: Reed International PLC), 90 Stiles Rd., Salem, NH 03079. TEL 800-548-4001. FAX 603-898-9858. (looseleaf format)

346.01   US
FLORIDA JUVENILE PROCEDURE. 1985. base vol. (plus suppl. 2-3/yr.). $80. Butterworth Legal Publishers (Salem) (Subsidiary of: Reed International PLC), 90 Stiles Rd., Salem, NH 03079. TEL 800-548-4001. FAX 603-898-9858. (looseleaf format)

346.01   US
GEORGIA FAMILY LAW MANUAL. 1985. 2 base vols. (plus suppl. 2-3/yr.). $80. Butterworth Legal Publishers (Salem) (Subsidiary of: Reed International PLC), 90 Stiles Rd., Salem, NH 03079. TEL 800-548-4001. FAX 603-898-9858. (looseleaf format)

346.01   US
▼**GITLIN ON DIVORCE**; a guide to Illinois matrimonial law. 1991. 2 base vols. (plus a. suppl.). $160. Butterworth Legal Publishers (Salem) (Subsidiary of: Reed International PLC), 90 Stiles Rd., Salem, NH 03079. TEL 800-548-4001. FAX 603-898-9858. Ed. H. Joseph Gitlin. (looseleaf format)
Description: Analyzes all areas of Illinois law from jurisdiction and venue to grounds and post-judgement proceedings.

346.01 301.4   US
HANDLING CHILD CUSTODY CASES. 1983. base vol. (plus a. suppl.). $70. Shepard's - McGraw-Hill, Inc., Box 35300, Colorado Springs, CO 80935-3530. TEL 800-525-2474.
Description: Covers representation of parents, grandparents, adopting parents and children, as well as the intricacies of state and federal child custody laws.

346.01 613.9   US
HANDLING PREGNANCY AND BIRTH CASES. 1983. base vol. (plus a. suppl.). $70. Shepard's - McGraw-Hill, Inc., Box 35300, Colorado Springs, CO 80935-3530. TEL 800-525-2474.
Description: Discusses surgical sterilizations, wrongful conception, wrongful pregnancy, artificial insemination, in vitro fertilization, surrogate motherhood, abortion, and prenatal injury actions.

INCOME TAX AND FAMILY LAW HANDBOOK. see *BUSINESS AND ECONOMICS — Public Finance, Taxation*

346.01   UK   ISSN 0950-4109
K9   CODEN: IJLFEN
INTERNATIONAL JOURNAL OF LAW AND THE FAMILY. 1987. 3/yr. £51($105) Oxford University Press, Oxford Journals, Pinkhill House, Southfield Road, Eynsham, Oxford OX8 1JJ, England. TEL 0865-882283. FAX 0865-882890. TELEX 837330 OXPRES G. Eds. Robert Dingwall, John Eekelaar. adv.; bk.rev.; circ. 600. Indexed: ASSIA.
—BLDSC shelfmark: 4542.312350.
Description: Theoretical analyses of family law.

LAW — FAMILY AND MATRIMONIAL LAW

346.01 US
IOWA MATRIMONIAL LAW. 1986. base vol. (plus suppl.). $88. Butterworth Legal Publishers (Salem) (Subsidiary of: Reed International PLC), 90 Stiles Rd., Salem, NH 03079. TEL 800-548-4001. FAX 603-898-9858. Ed. Daniel L. Bray. (looseleaf format)

346.01 UK ISSN 0955-4475
JOURNAL OF CHILD LAW. 1988. 4/yr. £60($95) Tolley Publishing Co. Ltd., Tolley House, 2 Addiscombe Rd., Croydon, Surrey CR9 5AF, England. Ed. Michael Bryan. adv.; bk.rev.; index. (back issues avail.)
—BLDSC shelfmark: 4957.610000.
Description: Aimed at practitioners in child law.

346.01 US ISSN 0022-1066
K10
JOURNAL OF FAMILY LAW. 1961. q. $20. University of Louisville, School of Law, Louisville, KY 40292. TEL 502-588-6396. adv.; bk.rev.; abstr.; circ. 1,200. (also avail. in microform from UMI; reprint service avail. from RRI) **Indexed:** Abstr.Soc.Work., Adol.Ment.Hlth.Abstr., C.L.I., Crim.Just.Abstr., Curr.Cont., L.R.I., Leg.Cont., Leg.Per., Psychol.Abstr., Soc.Work Res.& Abstr., Sociol.Abstr., SSCI.
—BLDSC shelfmark: 4983.700000.

346.01 360 UK
K10
JOURNAL OF SOCIAL WELFARE AND FAMILY LAW. 1978. bi-m. £69. Sweet & Maxwell, South Quay Plaza, 8th Fl., 183 Marsh Wall, London E14 9FT, England. TEL 071-538-8686. FAX 071-538-9508. **Indexed:** Adol.Ment.Hlth.Abstr., ASSIA, C.L.I., CJPI, Hlth.Ind., L.R.I., Leg.Cont., Sage Urb.Stud.Abstr., Stud.Wom.Abstr.
Former titles: Journal of Family and Social Welfare Law; Journal of Social Welfare Law (ISSN 0141-8033)

346.01 US ISSN 0161-7109
K10 CODEN: JFCJD6
JUVENILE AND FAMILY COURT JOURNAL. 1949. q. $40 (foreign $46). National Council of Juvenile and Family Court Judges, Box 8978, University of Nevada, Reno, NV 89507. TEL 702-784-6012. Ed. Marie Mildon. bk.rev.; cum.index: 1974-1984; circ. 2,700. (also avail. in microform from UMI; back issues avail.; reprint service avail. from RRI,UMI) **Indexed:** Adol.Ment.Hlth.Abstr., C.L.I., CJPI, Crim.Just.Abstr., Curr.Cont., L.R.I., Leg.Per., Soc.Work Res.& Abstr., SSCI.
—BLDSC shelfmark: 5077.290000.
Former titles: Journal of Juvenile and Family Courts (ISSN 0162-0525); Juvenile Justice (ISSN 0093-7231); (until 1972): Juvenile Court Judges Journal (ISSN 0022-7153)
Description: Compendium of articles centering on a variety of juvenile justice issues, occasionally exploring a single topic of current interest to juvenile justice professionals.

346.09 US ISSN 0162-9859
KF9772
JUVENILE AND FAMILY COURT NEWSLETTER. 6/yr. $16. National Council of Juvenile and Family Court Judges, Box 8970, University of Nevada, Reno, NV 89507. TEL 702-784-6012. Ed. Verita Black. circ. 2,500.
Description: News for members of the council's officers, educational programs, and results of studies in the field of juvenile justice.

364.36 US ISSN 0279-2257
KF9776.3
JUVENILE AND FAMILY LAW DIGEST. 1967. m. $120 (foreign $130). National Council of Juvenile and Family Court Judges, Box 8978, University of Nevada, Reno, NV 89507. TEL 702-784-6012. Ed. Lindsay G. Arthur. circ. 2,700. (also avail. in microform from UMI; back issues avail.; reprint service avail. from RRI,UMI) **Indexed:** Abstr.Crim.& Pen., C.L.I., CJPI, Leg.Per.
Former titles: Juvenile Law Digest (ISSN 0162-5055); Juvenile Court Digest (ISSN 0085-2430)
Description: Digest of current juvenile and family law court cases from state level to Supreme Court.

346.01 US ISSN 0276-9603
JUVENILE LAW REPORTS. 1979. m. $98. Knehans-Miller Publications, Box 88, Warrensburg, MO 64093. TEL 816-429-1102. Ed. Dane C. Miller. index. (looseleaf format; back issues avail.)
Description: Summaries and verbatim excerpts of all Federal and State Appellate Court decisions involving juveniles. Indexed by subject and jurisdiction.

346.01 UK ISSN 0265-1211
LAW REPORTS: CHANCERY AND FAMILY DIVISION. m. £51 (typically set in Aug.). Incorporated Council of Law Reporting for England and Wales, 3 Stone Bldgs., Lincoln's Inn, London WC2A 3XN, England. TEL 071-242 6471. FAX 07-831-5247. (also avail. in microfiche from BHP)

346.01 301.42 US
MARRIAGE AND FAMILY LAW AGREEMENTS. 1984. base vol. (plus a. suppl.). $70. Shepard's - McGraw-Hill, Inc., Box 35300, Colorado Springs, CO 80935-3530. TEL 800-525-2474.
Description: Covers antenuptial agreements, nonmarital cohabitation agreements, separation and property settlement agreements and surrogate motherhood contracts.

346.01 US
MASSACHUSETTS FAMILY LAW JOURNAL. 1983. 6/yr. $75. Butterworth Legal Publishers (Salem) (Subsidiary of: Reed International PLC), 90 Stiles Rd., Salem, NH 03079. TEL 800-548-4001. FAX 603-898-9858. cum.index. (looseleaf format; back issues avail.)
Description: Family law articles, case comments, and Massachusetts Probate Court decisions.

346.01 II
MATRIMONIAL LAW REPORTER. (Text in English) 1977. m. Rs.70. G.R. Arora, 33-34 Gokhale Market, Delhi 110054, India. Ed. Shiv Narayan. adv.; bk.rev.; circ. 3,000.

346.01 US
MATRIMONIAL STRATEGIST. m. $145. New York Law Publishing Co., Marketing Dept., 111 Eighth Ave., New York, NY 10011. TEL 212-741-8300.
Description: Reports on taxation, valuation, discovery, trial, appeal, ethical dilemmas, fee arrangements and other topics for matrimonial lawyers.

346.01 US
MINNESOTA FAMILY LAW JOURNAL. 1981. bi-m. $75. Butterworth Legal Publishers (St. Paul) (Subsidiary of: Reed International PLC), 289 E. Fifth St., St. Paul, MN 55101. TEL 800-333-3839. Ed. Stephen Liebo. (back issues avail.)
Description: Family law articles, case comments and court decisions.

346.01 US
MINNESOTA FAMILY LAW PRACTICE MANUAL. base vol. (plus suppl. 6/yr.) $95. Butterworth Legal Publishers (Salem) (Subsidiary of: Reed International PLC), 90 Stiles Rd., Salem, NH 03079. TEL 800-548-4001. FAX 603-898-9858. Ed. Cathy E. Gorlin. (looseleaf format)

NATIONAL COUNCIL FOR ADOPTION. LEGAL NOTES. see *SOCIAL SERVICES AND WELFARE*

NATIONAL COUNCIL FOR ADOPTION. MEMO. see *SOCIAL SERVICES AND WELFARE*

340 US
NEW HAMPSHIRE PRACTICE SERIES. VOL. 3: FAMILY LAW. (Series consists of 14 vols.; Vols. 1 and 2: Criminal Practice and Procedure; Vol. 3: Family Law; Vols. 4, 5 and 6: Civil Practice and Procedure; Vol. 7: Wills, Trust and Gifts; Vol. 8 and 9: Personal Injury - Tort and Insurance Practice; Vols. 10, 11 and 12: Probate Law and Procedure; Vols. 13 and 14: Local Government Law) 1982. base vol. (plus suppl.) $41 (14-vol. set $575). Butterworth Legal Publishers (Salem) (Subsidiary of: Reed International PLC), 90 Stiles Rd., Salem, NH 03079. TEL 800-548-4001. FAX 603-898-9858. Ed. Charles D. Douglas, III.
Description: Detailed treatment of the substantive law relating to the family.

346.01 CN
ONTARIO ANNOTATED FAMILY LAW SERVICE. q. Can.$275. Butterworths Canada Ltd., 75 Clegg Rd., Markham, Ont. L6G 1A1, Canada. TEL 416-479-2665. FAX 416-479-2826. (looseleaf format)
Description: Practical reference for the practitioner of Ontario family law.

346.01 301.4 CN
ONTARIO FAMILY LAW QUANTUM SERVICE. q. Can.$170. Butterworths Canada Ltd., 75 Clegg Rd., Markham, Ont. L6G 1A1, Canada. TEL 416-479-2665. FAX 416-479-2826. (looseleaf format)
Description: Reference on facts relevant to the amounts awarded in quantum service in Ontario.

346.01 CN
ONTARIO FAMILY LAW REFORM ACT MANUAL. 5/yr. Can.$128. Canada Law Book Inc., 240 Edward St., Aurora, Ont. L4G 3S9, Canada. TEL 416-841-6472. (looseleaf format)

346.01 CN ISSN 0835-636X
ONTARIO FAMILY LAW REPORTER. 1987. m. $170. Butterworths Canada Ltd., 75 Clegg Rd., Markham, Ont. L6G 1A1, Canada. TEL 800-668-6481. FAX 416-479-2826. Eds. Malcolm C. Kronby, Jeffery Wilson. cum.index; circ. 330. (back issues avail.)
Description: Deals with unreported cases.

346.01 UK
RAYDEN & JACKSON ON DIVORCE & FAMILY MATTERS. (In 2 vols.) irreg., latest 16th ed. $930. Butterworth & Co. (Publishers) Ltd. (Subsidiary of: Reed International PLC), 80 Kingsway, London WC2B 6AB, England. TEL 71-409-6900. FAX 71-405-1332. TELEX 95678. (US addr.: Butterworth Legal Publishers, 90 Stiles Rd., Salem, NH 03079. TEL 800-548-4001) (looseleaf format)

346.01 CN ISSN 0317-4859
LAW
REPORTS OF FAMILY LAW (3RD SERIES). 1970. 24/yr. (in 6 vols.). Can.$115. Carswell Publications, 800 Rocky Mountain Plaza, 615 MacLeod Trail S.E., Calgary, Alta. T2G 4T8, Canada. TEL 416-609-8000. FAX 416-298-5094. (Subscr. to: Carswell Publications, Corporate Plaza, 2075 Kennedy Rd., Scarborough, Ont. M1T 3V4, Canada) Ed. James G. McLeod. cum.index. **Indexed:** C.L.I., Ind.Can.L.P.L., L.R.I.

346.01 BE
REVUE TRIMESTRIELLE DE DROIT FAMILIAL. Short title: R.T.D.F. (Text in French) q. 3000 Fr. De Boeck Wesmael, Serials Department, Av. Louise 203 Boite 1, B-1050 Brussels, Belgium. TEL 2-627-35-37. FAX 2-627-36-50. TELEX 65701-DBWES-B. (Dist. by: Acces Plus, Rue Fonds Jean Paques, 4, B-1348 Louvain-la-Neuve, Belgium) index.

346.01 US ISSN 0890-5355
KFT94.A59
TENNESSEE FAMILY LAW LETTER. 1986. m. $80. M. Lee Smith Publishers & Printers, 162 Fourth Ave. N., Box 2678, Nashville, TN 37219. TEL 615-242-7395. FAX 615-256-6601. Ed. W. Walton Garrett.
Description: Digest of Tennessee family law developments.

346.01 305.31 US
TODAY'S DADS. 1988. m. $20. Wisconsin Fathers for Equal Justice, Inc., Box 1741, Madison, WI 53701-1741. Ed. William N. Fetzner. circ. 800.
Description: Offers information regarding father's relationship with children; custody; child support; divorce; paternity; equal rights to parent; equal justice.

346.01 US
▼**VIRGINIA FAMILY LAW.** 1991. base vol. (plus s-a. suppl.). $80. Butterworth Legal Publishers (Salem) (Subsidiary of: Reed International PLC), 90 Stiles Rd., Salem, NH 03079. TEL 800-548-4001. FAX 603-898-9858. Ed. Anita Butler. (looseleaf format)
Description: Addresses issues which practitioners need to be aware of in handling family law cases in Virginia.

346.01   CN   ISSN 0713-7907
WEEKLY DIGEST OF FAMILY LAW. 1982. w. (50/yr.). Can.$395. Carswell Publications (Subsidiary of: Thompson Professional Publishing Canada), Corporate Plaza, 2075 Kennedy Rd., Scarborough, Ont. M1T 3V4, Canada. TEL 416-609-8000. FAX 416-298-5094. (Subscr. to: Carswell Publications, 2330 Midland Ave., Agincourt, Ont. M1S 1P7, Canada) adv.; cum.index; circ. 240. (back issues avail.)

LAW — International Law

341   GW   ISSN 0581-9792
A D A C HANDBUCH: SCHMERZENSGELD-BETRAEGE. biennial. DM.58. (Allgemeiner Deutscher Automobil-Club e.V.) A D A C Verlag GmbH, Am Westpark 8, Postfach 700126, 8000 Munich 70, Germany. TEL 089-7676-0.
Formerly: Schmerzensgeld-Betraege.

341   NE   ISSN 0001-401X
JX74
ACADEMIE DE DROIT INTERNATIONAL DE LA HAYE. RECUEIL DES COURS/HAGUE ACADEMY OF INTERNATIONAL LAW. COLLECTED COURSES. (Text in English, French) 1923. 5/yr. $120 per no. Kluwer Academic Publishers, Postbus 17, 3300 AA Dordrecht, Netherlands. TEL 078-334911. FAX 078-334254. TELEX 29245. (Dist. by: Kluwer Academic Publishers Group, P.O. Box 322, 3300 AH Dordrecht, Netherlands; N. America dist. addr.: Box 358, Accord Station, Hingham, MA 02018-0358. TEL 617-871-6600) index, cum.index. **Indexed:** Foreign Leg.Per.

ALMANAC OF CHINA'S FOREIGN ECONOMIC RELATIONS AND TRADE. see BUSINESS AND ECONOMICS — International Development And Assistance

340.5   US   ISSN 0002-919X
K1
AMERICAN JOURNAL OF COMPARATIVE LAW. 1952. q. $20. American Association for the Comparative Study of Law, 394 Boalt Hall, University of California, Berkeley, CA 94720. FAX 415-643-6171. Ed. Richard M Buxbaum. adv.; bk.rev.; bibl.; index, cum.index: 1952-1961, 1962-1967, 1968-1977; circ. 2,100. (also avail. in microform from UMI; reprint service avail. from ISI,RRI,UMI) **Indexed:** A.B.C.Pol.Sci., Abstr.Rev.Curr.Leg.Per., Amer.Bibl.Slavic & E.Eur.Stud., Bibl.Ind., C.L.I., Crim.Just.Abstr., Curr.Cont., Foreign Leg.Per., Int.Lab.Doc., L.R.I., Leg.Cont., Leg.Per., P.A.I.S., SSCI.
—BLDSC shelfmark: 0824.100000.

341   US   ISSN 0002-9300
JX1
AMERICAN JOURNAL OF INTERNATIONAL LAW. 1907. 4/yr. $100. American Society of International Law, 2223 Massachusetts Ave., N.W., Washington, DC 20008-2864. TEL 202-265-4313. FAX 202-797-7133. Ed. Thomas M. Franck. adv. contact: Rachel de la Vega. bk.rev.; bibl.; index, cum.index thru vol.84, 1990; circ. 7,000. (also avail. in microfilm from UMI,PMC; back issues avail.; reprint service avail. from RRI) **Indexed:** A.B.C.Pol.Sci., Amer.Bibl.Slavic & E.Eur.Stud., C.L.I., Curr.Cont., Deep Sea Res.& Oceanogr.Abstr., Hist.Abstr., HR Rep., Int.Lab.Doc., L.R.I., Leg.Cont., Leg.Info.Manage.Ind., Leg.Per., Mar.Aff.Bibl., Mid.East: Abstr.& Ind., P.A.I.S., Peace Res.Abstr., Refug.Abstr., Sel.Water Res.Abstr., So.Pac.Per.Ind., Soc.Sci.Ind., SSCI.
●Also available online. Vendor(s): Mead Data Central. Also available on CD-ROM. Producer(s): University Microfilms International.
—BLDSC shelfmark: 0826.800000.
Description: Articles on developments and judicial decisions in international law.

341 382   US
▼**AMERICAN REVIEW OF INTERNATIONAL ARBITRATION.** 1990. 4/yr. $120. (Columbia University, Parker School of Foreign and Comparative Law) Transnational Juris Publications, Inc., Box 7282, Ardsley-on-Hudson, NY 10503. TEL 914-693-0089. FAX 914-693-8776. Ed.Bd. bk.rev.; bibl.
Description: Provides comprehensive coverage of developments in international commercial arbitration, including analysis of recent cases and arbitration awards.

341   US   ISSN 0066-0639
AMERICAN SOCIETY OF INTERNATIONAL LAW. NEWSLETTER. 1961. 5/yr. American Society of International Law, 2223 Massachusetts Ave., N.W., Washington, DC 20008-2864. TEL 202-265-4313. FAX 202-797-7133.
Formerly: American Society of International Law. Letter to Members.
Description: Newsletter for society members.

341   US   ISSN 0272-5045
AMERICAN SOCIETY OF INTERNATIONAL LAW. PROCEEDINGS OF THE ANNUAL MEETING. 1907. a. $60. American Society of International Law, 2223 Massachusetts Ave. N.W., Washington, DC 20008-2864. TEL 202-265-4313. FAX 202-797-7133. Ed. John Lawrence Hargrove. adv. contact: Rachel de la Vega. index, cum.index: 1907-1920, 1921-1940, 1941-1960, 1961-1970, 1971-1980; circ. 2,000. (also avail. in microform from UMI,WSH; back issues avail.; reprint service avail. from KTO,WSH) **Indexed:** Amer.Hist.& Life, C.L.I., Deep Sea Res.& Oceanogr.Abstr., Hist.Abstr., L.R.I., Leg.Per., Mar.Aff.Bibl.
Formerly (until 1974): American Society of International Law. Proceedings (ISSN 0066-0647)
Description: Digest of the annual meeting.

341 323.4   FR   ISSN 0570-1937
DT30
ANNEE AFRICAINE. 1963. a. price varies. Editions A. Pedone, 13 rue Soufflot, 75005 Paris, France. Ed. A. Pedone.

341   FR   ISSN 0066-3085
JX21
ANNUAIRE FRANCAIS DE DROIT INTERNATIONAL. 1955. a. price varies. (Academie de Droit International de la Haye, Groupe Francais des Anciens Auditeurs, NE) Editions du C N R S, 1 Place Aristide Briand, 92195 Meudon Cedex, France. TEL 1-45-34-75-50. FAX 1-42-26-28-49. TELEX LABOBEL 204 135 F. (Subscr. to: Presses du C N R S, 20-22, rue Saint Amand, 75015 Paris, France. TEL 1-45-33-16-00) adv.; bk.rev.; index; circ. 1,500 (controlled). **Indexed:** Int.Lab.Doc.
—BLDSC shelfmark: 1069.500000.

ANNUAL ON TERRORISM (YEAR). see CRIMINOLOGY AND LAW ENFORCEMENT

341   SP
ANUARIO DE DERECHO INTERNACIONAL. 1975. a. 3000 ptas.($36) (Universidad de Navarra, Departamento de Derecho Internacional) Servicio de Publicaciones de la Universidad de Navarra, S.A., Apdo. 177, 31080 Pamplona, Spain. TEL 94 25 2700. Dir. Jose Antonio Corriente Cordoba. bk.rev.

341   EC   ISSN 0570-4251
ANUARIO ECUATORIANO DE DERECHO INTERNACIONAL. 1964. a. $24. Universidad Central del Ecuador, Instituto de Investigaciones Internationales, Apdo. 17-07-9078, Quito, Ecuador. FAX 5932-234392. Ed. Mario A. Gomez de la Torre. bk.rev.; circ. 2,000.

341   US
ANUARIO INTERAMERICANO DE DERECHOS HUMANOS/INTER-AMERICAN YEARBOOK ON HUMAN RIGHTS. (Text in English and Spanish) biennial. $15. Organization of American States, Inter-American Commission on Human Rights, 1889 F. St. NW, Washington, DC 20006-4499. TEL 202-458-3527. FAX 202-458-3534. (Distr. by: Center for Promotion and Distribution of Publications, Box 66398, Washington, DC, 20035)

341   UK   ISSN 0268-0556
K1   CODEN: ALQUEJ
ARAB LAW QUARTERLY. 1986. q. £125($250) (Society of Arab Comparative and International Law) Graham & Trotman Ltd. (Subsidiary of: Kluwer Academic Publishers Group), Sterling House, 66 Wilton Rd., London SW1V 1DE, England. (Dist. by: Kluwer Academic Publishers Group, P.O. Box 322, 3300 AH Dordrecht, Netherlands; N. America dist. addr.: Box 358, Accord Station, Hingham, MA 02018-0358. TEL 617-871-6600) Ed. Mark S.W. Hoyle.
—BLDSC shelfmark: 1583.239850.
Description: Articles on legal developments throughout the 20 countries of the Arab world.

ARBITRATION MATERIALS. see BUSINESS AND ECONOMICS — International Commerce

341.18   FR   ISSN 0083-8853
JN94
ASSEMBLY OF WESTERN EUROPEAN UNION. PROCEEDINGS. French edition: Assemblee de l'Union de l'Europe Occidentale. Actes Officiels. (In four parts) (Editions in English, French) 1955. s-a. price varies. Assembly of Western European Union, 43 av. du President Wilson, 75775 Paris Cedex 16, France. (Dist. in the U.S. by: Manhattan Publishing Co., P.O. Box 650, Croton on Hudson, NY 10520. TEL 914-271-5194)
Description: Contains all documents submitted for discussion in the assembly: reports, motions for recommendation, resolutions, amendments. Also contains verbatim report of the sittings of the corresponding part-session.

341   NE   ISSN 0066-8923
ASSOCIATION OF ATTENDERS AND ALUMNI OF THE HAGUE ACADEMY OF INTERNATIONAL LAW. YEARBOOK. 1925. a. price varies. Kluwer Academic Publishers, Postbus 17, 3300 AA Dordrecht, Netherlands. TEL 078-334911. (U.S. addr.: P.O. Box 358, Accord Sta., Hingham, MA 02018-0358)

341   SZ
ASYL; Schweizerische Zeitschrift fuer Asylrecht und -praxis. (Supplement avail.) (Text in French and German) 1986. q. 40 Fr. (foreign 45 Fr.). Schweizerische Zentralstelle fuer Fluechtlingshilfe, Kinkelstr. 2, Postfach 279, CH-8035 Zurich, Switzerland. TEL 01-3619640. FAX 01-3628710. Ed. Walter Stoeckli. adv.; bk.rev.; stat.; circ. 1,600.
Description: Articles on asylum law and policy and administrative decisions concerning refugees in Switzerland. Includes list of events and new publications.

ATMA JAYA RESEARCH CENTRE. INTERNATIONAL CONTRACT LABOUR. see BUSINESS AND ECONOMICS — Labor And Industrial Relations

341   AT   ISSN 0811-9260
AUSTRALIAN INTERNATIONAL LAW NEWS. 1984. s-a. Aus.$20. J. Lilamand, Ed. & Pub., 3 Powder Works Rd. North, Narrabeen, N.S.W. 2101, Australia. TEL 02-9138742. circ. 500.
Description: Updates recent developments of legal interest in the international scene.

341.2   AT
AUSTRALIAN TREATY SERIES. irreg. price varies. Australian Government Publishing Service, G.P.O. Box 84, Canberra, A.C.T. 2601, Australia.
Formerly: Australian Treaty List.

BAILRIGG PAPERS ON INTERNATIONAL SECURITY. see POLITICAL SCIENCE — International Relations

340   BG
BANGLADESH IN INTERNATIONAL AFFAIRS. (Text in English) 1978. m. $6.50. Bangladesh Institute of Law and International Affairs, 501 Dhanmondi Residential Area, Rd. No. 7, Dhaka 5, Bangladesh. (Dist. by: Karim International, 3 Padmalochon Roy Lane, Mahttuly, Dhaka 1, Bangladesh) Ed.Bd. circ. 3,000.

341 338.47   US
BASIC OIL LAWS & CONCESSION CONTRACTS: ASIA & AUSTRALASIA. q. $6100 first year; thereafter $1350. Barrows Co., Inc., 116 E. 66th St., New York, NY 10021. TEL 212-772-1199. FAX 212-288-7242. TELEX 4971238 BARROWS. Eds. Gordon H. Barrow, Marta Guerra.
Formerly: Far East Oil Laws and Concession Contracts.
Description: Contains the complete texts, in English translation, of oil laws, contracts and concessions in Asian and Australasian countries.

341 338.47   US
BASIC OIL LAWS & CONCESSION CONTRACTS: CENTRAL AMERICA & CARIBBEAN. q. $6100 first year; thereafter $1350. Barrows Co., Inc., 116 E. 66th St., New York, NY 10021. TEL 212-772-1199. FAX 212-288-7242. TELEX 4971238 BARROWS. Eds. Gordon H. Barrow, Marta Guerra.
Description: Contains the complete texts, in English translation, of oil laws, contracts, and concessions in all Central American and Caribbean countries.

LAW — INTERNATIONAL LAW

341 338.47   US   ISSN 0093-5018
LAW
BASIC OIL LAWS & CONCESSION CONTRACTS: EUROPE. q. $6100 first year; thereafter $1350. Barrows Co., Inc., 116 E. 66th St., New York, NY 10021. TEL 212-772-1199. FAX 212-288-7242. TELEX 4971238 BARROWS. Eds. Gordon H. Barrows, Martha Guerra.
Description: Contains the complete texts, in English translation, of oil laws, contracts, and concessions in all European countries.

341 338.47   US
BASIC OIL LAWS & CONCESSION CONTRACTS: MIDDLE EAST. q. $6100 first year; thereafter $1350. Barrows Co., Inc., 116 E. 66th St., New York, NY 10021. TEL 212-772-1199. FAX 212-288-7242. TELEX 4971238 BARROWS.
Description: Contains the complete texts, in English translation, of oil laws, contracts and concessions in all Middle Eastern countries.

341 338.47   US
BASIC OIL LAWS & CONCESSION CONTRACTS: NORTH AFRICA. q. $6100 first year; thereafter $1350. Barrows Co., Inc., 116 E. 66th St., New York, NY 10021. TEL 212-772-1199. FAX 212-288-7242. TELEX 4971238 BARROWS. Eds. Gordon H. Barrows, Marta Guerra.
Description: Contains the complete texts, in English translation, of oil laws, contracts, and concessions in all North African countries.

341 338.47   US
BASIC OIL LAWS & CONCESSION CONTRACTS: SOUTH AMERICA. q. $6100 first year; thereafter $1350. Barrows Co., Inc., 116 E. 66th St., New York, NY 10021. TEL 212-772-1199. FAX 212-288-7242. TELEX 4971238 BARROWS. Eds. Gordon H. Barrows, Marta Guerra.
Description: Contains the complete texts, in English translation, of oil laws, contracts, and concessions in all South American countries.

341 338.47   US
BASIC OIL LAWS & CONCESSION CONTRACTS: SOUTH & CENTRAL AFRICA. q. $6100 first year; thereafter $1350. Barrows Co., Inc., 116 E. 66th St., New York, NY 10021. TEL 212-772-1199. FAX 212-288-7242. TELEX 4971238 BARROWS. Eds. Gordon H. Barrows, Marta Guerra.
Description: Contains the complete texts, in English translation, of oil laws, contracts, and concessions in all South and Central African countries.

341   US   ISSN 0172-4770
BEITRAEGE ZUM AUSLAENDISCHEN OEFFENTLICHEN RECHT UND VOELKERRECHT. (Text mainly in German) vol.86, 1984. irreg., vol.99 1989. price varies. Springer-Verlag, 175 Fifth Ave., New York, NY 10010. TEL 212-460-1500. (Also Berlin, Heidelberg, Tokyo and Vienna) (reprint service avail. from ISI)

341.87 387   US
BENEDICT ON ADMIRALTY. (Issued in 23 base vols. with supplements) irreg. Matthew Bender & Co., Inc., 11 Penn Plaza, New York, NY 10001. TEL 212-967-7707. (looseleaf format)
Description: Covers all aspects of the American law of the sea and shipping.

341   SP
BOLETIN DE LEGISLACION EXTRANJERA. q. 7540 ptas. Congreso de los Diputados, C. Floridablanca s-n., 28014 Madrid, Spain.

341   US   ISSN 0277-5778
K2
BOSTON COLLEGE INTERNATIONAL AND COMPARATIVE LAW REVIEW. 1977. s-a. $10. Boston College, School of Law, 885 Centre St., Newton, MA 02159. TEL 617-552-8554. circ. 600. (also avail. in microfilm from WSH,PMC; reprint service avail. from WSH) **Indexed:** A.B.C.Pol.Sci., Abstr.Bk.Rev.Curr.Leg.Per., Amer.Bibl.Slavic & E.Eur.Stud., C.L.I., L.R.I., Leg.Cont., Leg.Per., Mar.Aff.Bibl., P.A.I.S.
—BLDSC shelfmark: 2251.812200.
Formerly: Boston College International and Comparative Law Journal (ISSN 0161-2832)
Description: Indexed journal covering international law.

341 950   US   ISSN 0276-3583
K2
BOSTON THIRD WORLD LAW JOURNAL. 1980. s-a. $10 (foreign $11). Boston College, School of Law, 885 Centre St., Newton, MA 02159. TEL 617-969-0100. Ed. Peter S. Michaels. bk.rev.; circ. 1,000. (also avail. in microform from WSH; back issues avail.; reprint service avail. from WSH)
—BLDSC shelfmark: 2251.813400.
Description: Covers legal issues in Third World countries, and civil, human and minority rights issues throughout the world.

341   US   ISSN 0737-8947
K2
BOSTON UNIVERSITY INTERNATIONAL LAW JOURNAL. 1981. s-a. $20. Boston University, School of Law, 765 Commonwealth Ave., Boston, MA 02215. TEL 617-353-3157. Ed. Elisabeth L. Gibbs. circ. 450. (back issues avail.) **Indexed:** C.L.I., Leg.Per.
—BLDSC shelfmark: 2251.838000.

341   UK
BRITISH INSTITUTE OF INTERNATIONAL AND COMPARATIVE LAW. QUARTERLY NEWSLETTER. 1973. q. British Institute of International and Comparative Law, 17 Russell Square, London WC1B 5DR, England. TEL 071-636-5802. FAX 071-323-2016.

341.058   UK   ISSN 0068-2691
JX21
BRITISH YEAR BOOK OF INTERNATIONAL LAW. 1920? a. varies. (Royal Institute of International Affairs) Oxford University Press, Walton St., Oxford OX2 6DP, England. TEL 0865-56767. FAX 0865-56646. TELEX 837330 OXPRES G. (U.S. addr.: 200 Madison Ave., New York, NY 10016) Eds. D.W. Bowett, I. Brownlie. adv.; bk.rev.; index. (also avail. in microfilm from RRI; reprint service avail. from RRI) **Indexed:** C.L.I., L.R.I., Leg.Per.
—BLDSC shelfmark: 2348.200000.

341.05   US   ISSN 0740-4824
JX1
BROOKLYN JOURNAL OF INTERNATIONAL LAW. 1975. 3/yr. $15. Brooklyn Law School, 250 Joralemon, Brooklyn, NY 11201. TEL 718-780-7971. bk.rev.; index. (also avail. in microfilm from WSH,PMC; back issues avail.; reprint service avail. from WSH) **Indexed:** Abstr.Bk.Rev.Curr.Leg.Per., C.C.L.P., C.L.I., L.R.I., Leg.Cont., Leg.Per., So.Pac.Per.Ind.
●Also available online. Vendor(s): WESTLAW.
—BLDSC shelfmark: 2350.140000.

341 382   US
▼**BULLETIN ON SOVIET AND EAST EUROPEAN LAW.** Short title: S E E L. 1990. 10/yr. $255. (Columbia University, Parker School of Foreign and Comparative Law) Transnational Juris Publications, Inc., Box 7282, Ardsley-on-Hudson, NY 10503. TEL 914-693-0089. FAX 914-693-8776. Ed. Vratislav Pechota.
Description: Covers new developments affecting investment and trade in the Soviet Union and Eastern Europe, with analysis of legislative changes.

341   UK
BUTTERWORTHS INTERNATIONAL LAW DIRECTORY. a. £42. Reed Information Services Ltd., Specialist Publications, Windsor Court, E. Grinstead House, E. Grinstead, W. Sussex RH19 1XA, England. TEL 0342-326972. FAX 0342-317422.

BUYER. see BUSINESS AND ECONOMICS — International Commerce

341   FR
C E E INTERNATIONAL. DROIT ET AFFAIRES.* a. Communaute Economique Europeenne - European Communities, 2 Rue Dufrenoy, 75116 Paris, France.

341.7   NE
CAHIERS DE DROIT FISCAL INTERNATIONAL. 1939. a. membership. International Fiscal Association, World Trade Center, Beursplein 37, Postbus 30215, 3001 DE Rotterdam, Netherlands. TEL 01-4052990. FAX 01-4055031. TELEX 23229 BEURS NL. (Dist. by: Kluwer Law and Taxation Publishers, Box 23, 7400 GA Deventer, Netherlands; In N. America: 6 Bigelow St., Cambridge, MA 02139) (reprint service avail. from SWZ)

341   US   ISSN 0886-3210
JX1
CALIFORNIA WESTERN INTERNATIONAL LAW JOURNAL. 1970. 2/yr. $15 (foreign $17). California Western School of Law, 350 Cedar St., San Diego, CA 92101. TEL 619-239-0391. FAX 619-696-9999. Ed.Bd. adv.; bk.rev.; bibl.; circ. 1,300. (also avail. in microfilm from RRI; back issues avail.; reprint service avail. from RRI) **Indexed:** Abstr.Bk.Rev.Curr.Leg.Per., Amer.Bibl.Slavic & E.Eur.Stud., C.L.I., L.R.I., Leg.Per., Mar.Aff.Bibl., Peace Res.Abstr.

341 323.4   CN
CANADA. INFORMATION COMMISSIONER. ANNUAL REPORT. (Text in English, French) 1983. a. free. Information Commissioner, 112 Kent St., Ottawa, Ont K1A 1H3, Canada. TEL 613-995-2410. FAX 613-995-1501. stat.; circ. 5,000. (back issues avail.)

CANADA. PRIVACY COMMISSIONER. ANNUAL REPORT. see COMPUTERS — Computer Security

341   US   ISSN 0163-6391
K3
CANADA - UNITED STATES LAW JOURNAL.* (Text in English and French) 1978. a. $6. Case Western Reserve University, School of Law, 2040 Adelbert, Cleveland, OH 44106. TEL 216-368-2000. adv.; bk.rev.; circ. 650. (also avail. in microfilm from WSH,PMC) **Indexed:** Abstr.Bk.Rev.Curr.Leg.Per., C.L.I., Foreign Leg.Per., Ind.Can.L.P.L., L.R.I., Leg.Cont., Leg.Per., P.A.I.S.

CANADIAN R & D DIRECTORY. see BUSINESS AND ECONOMICS — International Commerce

341   CN   ISSN 0382-8662
CANADIAN WORLD FEDERALIST/FEDERALISTE MONDIAL DU CANADA. (Text in English, French) 1961. 5/yr. Can.$8. World Federalist Foundation, 145 Spruce St., Ste. 207, Ottawa, Ont. K1R 6P1, Canada. TEL 613-232-0647. FAX 613-563-0017. Ed. Fergus Watt. bk.rev.; circ. 3,000. (tabloid format; back issues avail.)

341   CN   ISSN 0069-0058
JX21
CANADIAN YEARBOOK OF INTERNATIONAL LAW. French edition: Annuaire Canadien de Droit International. (Editions in English and French) 1963. a. price varies. University of British Columbia Press, 6344 Memorial Rd., Vancouver, B.C. V6T 1Z2, Canada. TEL 604-822-3259. FAX 604-822-6083. Ed. C.B. Bourne. bk.rev. (also avail. in microfilm from RRI) **Indexed:** Amer.Bibl.Slavic & E.Eur.Stud, C.L.I., Can.Per.Ind., Foreign Leg.Per., Ind.Can.L.P.L., L.R.I., Leg.Per., Mar.Aff.Bibl.
—BLDSC shelfmark: 3046.180000.
Description: Articles on international law, Canadian practice in international law, and a digest of Canadian cases in public international law and conflict of law.

341   US
CASES AND MATERIALS ON THE LAW OF THE EUROPEAN COMMUNITIES. irreg., 2nd ed., 1990. $54. Butterworth Legal Publishers (Salem) (Subsidiary of: Reed International PLC), 90 Stiles Rd., Salem, NH 03079. TEL 800-548-4001. FAX 603-898-9858. Ed. Richard Plender.

341   US
CHINA LAW REPORTER. 1983. q. $43 (foreign $53). American Bar Association, International Law and Practice Section, 750 N. Lake Shore Dr., Chicago, IL 60611. TEL 312-988-5555. Eds. Thomas J. Rasmussen; Tao Tai Hsia. **Indexed:** C.L.I., L.R.I., Leg.Per.
Description: Issues facing lawyers and scholars who deal with business law in the People's Republic of China.

COLLECTION OF BIBLIOGRAPHIC AND RESEARCH RESOURCES. see LAW — Abstracting, Bibliographies, Statistics

341.11   BE   ISSN 0503-2407
COLLECTION OF DOCUMENTS FOR THE STUDY OF INTERNATIONAL NON-GOVERNMENTAL RELATIONS. Alternate title: Union of International Associations. Documents. (Text in English or French) 1956. irreg. Union of International Associations, c/o Robert Fenaux, Rue Washington 40, 1050 Brussels, Belgium.

COLLOQUIUM ON THE LAW OF OUTER SPACE. PROCEEDINGS. see AERONAUTICS AND SPACE FLIGHT

341 614.7 US ISSN 1050-0391
K3
▼COLORADO JOURNAL OF INTERNATIONAL ENVIRONMENTAL LAW AND POLICY. 1990. s-a. $25. (University of Colorado, School of Law) University Press of Colorado, Box 849, Niwot, CO 80544. Ed.Bd. Indexed: Environ.Abstr.
 Description: Examines environmental issues with international implications, such as global climate change, and the legal and policy ramifications of international environmental concerns.

341 US ISSN 0010-1931
LAW
COLUMBIA JOURNAL OF TRANSNATIONAL LAW. 1961. 3/yr. $30 (foreign $33). (Columbia University, School of Law) Columbia Journal of Transnational Law Association, 435 W. 116th St., New York, NY 10027. TEL 212-854-3742. adv.; bk.rev.; cum.index; circ. 1,000. (also avail. in microfilm from WSH; back issues avail.; reprint service avail. from WSH) Indexed: A.B.C.Pol.Sci., Abstr.Bk.Rev.Curr.Leg.Per., Amer.Bibl.Slavic & E.Eur.Stud., Amer.Hist.& Life, C.L.I., Curr.Cont., Hist.Abstr., L.R.I., Leg.Cont., Leg.Per., SSCI.
●Also available online. Vendor(s): WESTLAW.
—BLDSC shelfmark: 3323.100000.

341.57 II
COMMERCIAL LAW GAZETTE. (Text in English) 1978. fortn. Rs.75. Commercial Law Publications, E-157, Kamla Nagar, Delhi 110007, India. Ed. S.N. Gupta. adv.; bk.rev.; index; circ. 5,000.

COMMISSION OF THE EUROPEAN COMMUNITIES. COLLECTION OF AGREEMENTS. see BUSINESS AND ECONOMICS — International Commerce

341.18 BE ISSN 0590-6563
COMMISSION OF THE EUROPEAN COMMUNITIES. COMMUNITY LAW. (Editions also in Dutch, French, German, Italian) 1968. a. free. Commission of the European Communities, Service de Renseignement et de Diffusion des Documents, 200 rue de la Loi, B-1049 Brussels, Belgium.
 Description: Reports on activities of the EEC.

341.11 EI ISSN 0591-1745
HC240.A1
COMMISSION OF THE EUROPEAN COMMUNITIES, DIRECTORY. (Text in English, French) 1968. a. $105. Office for Official Publications of the European Communities, L-2985 Luxembourg, Luxembourg. FAX 301-923-0056. (Dist. in the U.S. by: Unipub, 4611-F Assembly Dr., Lanham, MD 20706-4391)

341 NE ISSN 0165-0750
LAW CODEN: CMLRDD
COMMON MARKET LAW REVIEW. 1963. q. $263. (British Institute of International and Comparative Law, UK) Kluwer Academic Publishers, Postbus 17, 3300 AA Dordrecht, Netherlands. TEL 078-334911. FAX 078-334254. TELEX 29245. (N. America distr. addr.: Box 358, Accord Station, Hingham, MA 02018-0358. TEL 617-871-6600) (Co-sponsor: University of Leiden, Europa Institute) Ed. Henry G. Schermers. adv.; bk.rev.; index; circ. 1,700. Indexed: Abstr.Bk.Rev.Curr.Leg.Per., C.L.I., C.R.E.J., Curr.Cont., Foreign Leg.Per., Int.Lab.Doc., L.R.I., Leg.Per., Mar.Aff.Bibl., RICS, SCIMP, SSCI, World Bank.Abstr.
—BLDSC shelfmark: 3339.270000.

341 US
COMMONWEALTH INTERNATIONAL LAW CASES. 1964. irreg., vol.11, 1985. price varies. (International Law Fund) Oceana Publications, Inc., Dobbs Ferry, NY 10522. TEL 914-693-1320. FAX 914-693-0402. (Co-sponsor: British Institute of Foreign and Comparative Law) Eds. C. Parry, J.A. Hopkins. (back issues avail.)
 Supersedes (in 1974): British International Law Cases (ISSN 0068-2195)
 Description: Annotated decisions of British and Commonwealth courts on points of international law.

341 SA ISSN 0010-4051
K3
COMPARATIVE AND INTERNATIONAL LAW JOURNAL OF SOUTHERN AFRICA. (Text in English; occasionally in Afrikaans, French, German, Portuguese; summaries in English) 1968. 3/yr. R.30($30.) University of South Africa, Institute of Foreign and Comparative Law, P.O. Box 392, Pretoria 0001, South Africa. FAX 012-4292925. TELEX 9-350068. Ed. J.J. Joubert Ballb. adv.; bk.rev.; index; circ. 900. (also avail. in microfiche from WSH; microfilm from WSH; back issues avail.) Indexed: Abstr.Bk.Rev.Curr.Leg.Per., C.L.I., Curr.Cont.Africa, Ind.S.A.Per., Leg.Per., Mar.Aff.Bibl.
—BLDSC shelfmark: 3363.746000.
 Description: Comprehensive coverage of international law and comparative law contributions in South Africa.

341 UK ISSN 0141-769X
COMPETITION LAW IN THE EUROPEAN COMMUNITIES. 1977. 12/yr. £245($455) Monitor Press, Rectory Rd., Great Waldingfield, Sudbury, Suffolk CO10 OTL, England. TEL 0787-78607. FAX 0787-880201. index. (back issues avail.)
—BLDSC shelfmark: 3363.993000.
 Description: For the specialist lawyer or legal advisor in companies or organizations needing to be informed about the complex decisions and regulations emanating from the common market.

341.57 NE
COMPETITION LAW IN WESTERN EUROPE AND THE U S A. (Text in English) 1974. base vol. (plus m. updates). fl.1500($800) Kluwer Law and Taxation Publishers, P.O. Box 23, 7400 GA Deventer, Netherlands. TEL 31-5700-47261. FAX 31-5700-22244. TELEX 48285 KLUDV VL. (Dist. by: Libresso Distribution Centre, P.O. Box 23, 7400 GA Deventer, Netherlands. TEL 31-5700-33155; N. America dist. addr.: 6 Bigelow St., Cambridge, MA 02139. TEL 617-354-0140) Ed. D.J. Gijlstra.
 Formerly: Competition Law.

341 UK
COMPLETING THE INTERNAL MARKET OF THE EUROPEAN COMMUNITY: 1992 LEGISLATION - BUSINESS. (Complete set consists of 6 sectors in 14 vols.) a. (plus q. supplement). £155($295) basic work; supplement service £60($115). (Commission of the European Communities) Graham & Trotman Ltd. (Subsidiary of: Kluwer Academic Publishers Group), Sterling House, 66 Wilton Rd., London SW1V 1DE, England. TEL 0524-68765. FAX 0524-63232. TELEX 65212 SCITEC. (Order from: Kluwer Academic Publishers Group, Customer Service Dept., Falcon House, Queen Sq., Lancaster LA1 1RN, England) Eds. Mark Brealey, Conor Quigley. (looseleaf format)
 Description: Covers legislation as it affects different sectors of business, commerce and industry.

341 UK
COMPLETING THE INTERNAL MARKET OF THE EUROPEAN COMMUNITY: 1992 LEGISLATION - FINANCIAL SERVICES AND CAPITAL MOVEMENTS. (Complete set consists of 6 sectors in 14 vols.) a. (plus q. supplement). £155($295) basic work; supplement service £60($115). (Commission of the European Communities) Graham & Trotman Ltd. (Subsidiary of: Kluwer Academic Publishers Group), Sterling House, 66 Wilton Rd., London SW1V 1DE, England. TEL 0524-68765. FAX 0524-63232. TELEX 65212 SCITEC G. (Order from: Kluwer Academic Publishers Group, Customer Service Dept., Falcon House, Queen Sta., Lancaster LA1 1RN, England) Eds. Mark Brealey, Conor Quigley. (looseleaf format)
 Description: Covers the legislation as it affects financial services and capital movements.

341 UK
COMPLETING THE INTERNAL MARKET OF THE EUROPEAN COMMUNITY: 1992 LEGISLATION. (Complete set consists of 6 sectors in 14 vols.) a. (plus q. supplement). £465($880) basic work; supplement service £160($300). (Commission of the European Communities) Graham & Trotman Ltd. (Subsidiary of: Kluwer Academic Publishers Group), Sterling House, 66 Wilton Rd., London SW1V 1DE, England. TEL 0524-68765. FAX 0524-63232. TELEX 65212 SCITEC G. (Order from: Kluwer Academic Publishers Group, Customer Service Dept., Falcon House, Queen Sq., Lancaster LA1 1RN, England) Eds. Mark Brealey, Conor Quigley. (looseleaf format)
 Description: Covers the European Economic Community laws and proposals that form the 1992 legislative programe.

341 UK
COMPLETING THE INTERNAL MARKET OF THE EUROPEAN COMMUNITY: 1992 LEGISLATION - TRANSPORT, CUSTOMS & TRAVEL. (Complete set consists of 6 sectors in 14 vols.) a. (plus q. supplement). £155($295) basic work; supplement service £60($115). (Commission of the European Communities) Graham & Trotman Ltd. (Subsidiary of: Kluwer Academic Publishers Group), Sterling House, 66 Wilton Rd., London SW1V 1DE, England. TEL 0524-68765. FAX 0524-63232. TELEX 65212 SCITEC G. (Order from: Kluwer Academic Publishers Group, Customer Service Dept., Falcon House, Queen Sq., Lancaster LA1 1RN, England) Eds. Mark Brealey, Conor Quigley. (looseleaf format)
 Description: Covers the legislation as it affects transport, customs and travel.

341 UK
COMPLETING THE INTERNAL MARKET OF THE EUROPEAN COMMUNITY: 1992 LEGISLATION - TECHNICAL STANDARDS. (Complete set consists of 6 sectors in 14 vols.) a. (plus q. supplement). £155($295) basic work; supplement service £60($115). (Commission of the European Communities) Graham & Trotman Ltd. (Subsidiary of: Kluwer Academic Publishers Group), Sterling House, 66 Wilton Rd., London SW1V 1DE, England. TEL 0524-68765. FAX 0524-63232. TELEX 65212 SCITEC G. (Order from: Kluwer Academic Publishers Group, Customer Service Dept., Falcon House, Queen Sq., Lancaster LA1 1RN, England) Eds. Mark Brealey, Conor Quigley. (looseleaf format)
 Description: Covers legislation as it affects technical standards.

341 636.089 UK
COMPLETING THE INTERNAL MARKET OF THE EUROPEAN COMMUNITY: 1992 LEGISLATION - VETERINARY & PHYTOSANITARY CONTROLS. (Complete set consists of 6 sectors in 14 vols.) a. (plus q. supplement). £155($295) basic work; supplement service £60($115). (Commission of the European Communities) Graham & Trotman Ltd. (Subsidiary of: Kluwer Academic Publishers Group), Sterling House, 66 Wilton Rd., London SW1V 1DE, England. TEL 0524-68765. FAX 0524-63232. TELEX 65212 SCITEC G. (Order from: Kluwer Academic Publishers Group, Customer Service Dept., Falcon House, Queen Sq., Lancaster LA1 1RN, England) Eds. Mark Brealey, Conor Quigley. (looseleaf format)
 Description: Covers the legislation as it affects veterinary and phytosanitary controls.

COMUNITA INTERNAZIONALE. see POLITICAL SCIENCE — International Relations

341.2 US ISSN 1059-8561
▼CONSOLIDATED TREATIES & INTERNATIONAL AGREEMENTS: EUROPEAN COMMUNITY DOCUMENT SERVICE. 1991. 4/yr. $500. Oceana Publications, Inc., 75 Main St., Dobbs Ferry, NY 10522. TEL 914-693-8100. FAX 914-693-0402. Ed. Brian H.W. Hill. (back issues avail.)
●Also available on CD-ROM.
 Description: Current information and full texts of all agreeements entered into by the EC with other countries and international organizations.

LAW — INTERNATIONAL LAW

341.2 US ISSN 1053-9905
JX236 1990
▼CONSOLIDATED TREATIES & INTERNATIONAL AGREEMENTS: UNITED STATES CURRENT DOCUMENT SERVICE. 1990. 4/yr. $500. Oceana Publications, Inc., 75 Main St., Dobbs Ferry, NY 10522. TEL 914-693-8100. FAX 914-693-0402. Ed. Erwin C. Surrency. (back issues avail.)
●Also available on CD-ROM.
Description: Full text of all current international agreements to which the U.S. is signatory, with subject index and cross-references to treaties cited.

341 US ISSN 0010-8812
JX1
CORNELL INTERNATIONAL LAW JOURNAL. 1968. 3/yr. $20 (foreign $23). Cornell University, Law School, Myron Taylor Hall, Ithaca, NY 14853. TEL 607-255-9666. Ed.Bd. adv.; bk.rev.; bibl.; index; circ. 1,000. (also avail. in microform from MIM,RRI; back issues avail.; reprint service avail. from RRI,UMI) **Indexed:** Abstr.Bk.Rev.Curr.Leg.Per., C.L.I., Foreign Leg.Per., L.R.I., Leg.Cont., Leg.Per., P.A.I.S., SSCI.
●Also available online. Vendor(s): WESTLAW.
—BLDSC shelfmark: 3470.950500.

341.18 FR ISSN 0070-105X
COUNCIL OF EUROPE. EUROPEAN TREATY SERIES. (Text in English, French) 1949. irreg., no.135, 1989. $8.60. Council of Europe, Publishing and Documentation Service, Strasbourg, France. (Dist. in U.S. by: Manhattan Publishing Co., One Croton Point Ave., Box 650, Croton-on-Hudson, NY 10520)
—BLDSC shelfmark: 3830.330000.

341.18 FR ISSN 0252-0656
JN22
COUNCIL OF EUROPE. PARLIAMENTARY ASSEMBLY. DOCUMENTS: WORKING PAPERS. (Text in English, French) 1949. a. $26 per vol. Council of Europe, Parliamentary Assembly, Publications Section, F 67004 Strasbourg, France. (Dist. in U.S. by: Manhattan Publishing Co., Box 650, Croton-on-Hudson, NY 10520) (also avail. in microfiche from BHP)
—BLDSC shelfmark: 3608.805000.
Supersedes (since vol.26, pt.3, 1974): Council of Europe. Consultative Assembly. Documents: Working Papers (ISSN 0070-1009)

341.8 FR ISSN 0252-0664
JN22
COUNCIL OF EUROPE. PARLIAMENTARY ASSEMBLY. OFFICIAL REPORT OF DEBATES.. (Text in English or French) 1949. a. (in 3 vols.). $26 per vol. Council of Europe, Parliamentary Assembly, Publications Section, F 67006 Strasbourg, France. (Dist. in U.S. by: Manhattan Publishing Co., 80 Brook St., Box 650, Croton-on-Hudson, NY 10520)
—BLDSC shelfmark: 6242.670000.

341.18 FR ISSN 0377-1962
JN22
COUNCIL OF EUROPE. PARLIAMENTARY ASSEMBLY. ORDERS OF THE DAY, MINUTES OF PROCEEDINGS. (Text in English, French) 1949. 3/yr. $14.40. Council of Europe, Publishing and Documentation Service, Strasbourg, France. (Dist in U.S. by: Manhattan Publishing Co., One Croton Point Ave., Box 650, Croton-on-Hudson, NY 10520)
Supersedes (in 1974): Council of Europe. Consultative Assembly. Orders of the Day, Minutes of Proceedings (ISSN 0070-1017)

341.18 FR ISSN 0377-6093
JN22
COUNCIL OF EUROPE. PARLIAMENTARY ASSEMBLY. TEXTS ADOPTED BY THE ASSEMBLY. (Text in English, French) 1949. a. (in 3 vols.). $7.50 per vol. Council of Europe, Parliamentary Assembly, Publications Section, F 67006 Strasbourg, France. (Dist. in U.S. by: Manhattan Publishing Co., 80 Brook St., Box 650, Croton-on-Hudson, NY 10520)
—BLDSC shelfmark: 8813.777000.
Supersedes (in 1974): Council of Europe. Consultative Assembly. Texts Adopted by the Assembly (ISSN 0070-1033)

341 EI
COURT OF JUSTICE OF THE EUROPEAN COMMUNITIES. REPORT OF CASES OF THE COURT. (Text in Dutch, English, French, German, Italian) 1954. a. price varies. Office for Official Publications of the European Communities, L-2985 Luxembourg, Luxembourg. (Dist. in the U.S. by: Unipub, 4611-F Assembly Dr., Lanham, MD 20706-4391)
Formerly: Court of Justice of the European Communities. Recueil de la Jurisprudence (ISSN 0070-1386)

CRIMINAL LAW FORUM; an international journal. see **CRIMINOLOGY AND LAW ENFORCEMENT**

341 UY
CUADERNOS DE DERECHO INTERNACIONAL PRIVADO. 1975. irreg. Fundacion de Cultura Universitaria, 25 de Mayo no. 568, Casilla de Correo No. 1155, Montevideo, Uruguay. TEL 961152. FAX 962540.

CURRENT TREATY INDEX; a cumulative index to the United States slip treaties and agreements. see **LAW — Abstracting, Bibliographies, Statistics**

341 GW
D A J V - NEWSLETTER. (Text in English and German) 1975. q. DM.90 membership to individuals; law libraries DM.50. Deutsch-Amerikanische Juristen-Vereinigung, Loebestr. 1, Postfach 200442, 5300 Bonn 2, Germany. TEL 0228-361376. bk.rev.; circ. 2,700.
Description: Comparative studies of American and European law.

341.18 330 EI ISSN 0071-3015
DEBATES OF THE EUROPEAN PARLIAMENT. (Text in Danish, Dutch, English, French, German, Greek, Italian, Portugese, Spanish) 1958. irreg. $165. (European Parliament) Office for Official Publications of the European Communities, L-2985 Luxembourg, Luxembourg. (Dist. in the U.S. by: Unipub, 4611-F Assembly Dr., Lanham, MD 20706-4391) (microfiche)

341 US ISSN 0196-2035
JX1
DENVER JOURNAL OF INTERNATIONAL LAW AND POLICY. 1971. 3/yr. $23 (foreign $25). University of Denver, College of Law, 7039 E. 18th Ave., Ste. 235, Denver, CO 80220. TEL 303-871-6170. Ed. Debra Asimus. bk.rev.; cum.index every 10 yrs; circ. 700. (also avail. in microform from UMI; microfiche from WSH; microfilm from WSH; back issues avail.; reprint service avail. from UMI) **Indexed:** Abstr.Bk.Rev.Curr.Leg.Per., Amer.Bibl.Slavic & E.Eur.Stud., C.L.I., Environ.Abstr., Environ.Ind., Foreign Leg.Per., Int.Polit.Sci.Abstr., L.R.I., Leg.Cont., Leg.Per., P.A.I.S., Sel.Water Res.Abstr., So.Pac.Per.Ind.
●Also available online. Vendor(s): WESTLAW.
—BLDSC shelfmark: 3553.564000.

341 NE
DEVELOPMENTS IN INTERNATIONAL LAW. (Text in English) 1979. irreg. price varies. Kluwer Academic Publishers, P.O. Box 17, 3300 AA Dordrecht, Netherlands. (Dist. by: Kluwer Academic Publishers, P.O. Box 322, 3300 AH Dordrecht; U.S. addr.: P.O. Box 358, Accord Sta., Hingham, MA 02018-0358)

341 327 US ISSN 0887-283X
K4
DICKINSON JOURNAL OF INTERNATIONAL LAW. 1982. 3/yr. $25. Dickinson School of Law, 150 S. College St., Carlisle, PA 17013. TEL 717-243-4611. FAX 717-243-4443. Ed. Kimberly Cicci. circ. 250. (also avail. in microform from WSH; back issues avail.; reprint service avail. from WSH) **Indexed:** C.L.I., Leg.Per.
—BLDSC shelfmark: 3580.260000.
Formerly: Dickinson International Law Annual.

DICTIONNAIRE JOLY PRATIQUE DES CONTRATS INTERNATIONAUX. see **BUSINESS AND ECONOMICS — International Commerce**

341 FR
DICTIONNAIRE PERMANENT DROIT EUROPEEN DES AFFAIRES. m. 1225.59 F. Editions Legislatives et Administratives, 80, ave. de la Marne, 92546 Montrouge Cedex, France. TEL 1-40-92-68-68. FAX 1-46-56-00-15. TELEX 632 855 F. (looseleaf format)
Description: Addresses the evolution of European common law, and studies how it will affect France in particular.

341.57 382 US ISSN 0419-1285
DIGEST OF COMMERCIAL LAWS OF THE WORLD. 1968. irreg. $850 (includes forms of commercial agreements). (National Association of Credit Management) Oceana Publications, Inc., Dobbs Ferry, NY 10522. TEL 914-693-1320. FAX 914-693-0402. Ed. Lester Nelson. bibl.; circ. 500. (looseleaf format)
Description: Compilation of commercial laws for countries of the world.

341 UY
DOCUMENTACION INTERNACIONAL. 1987. irreg. Fundacion de Cultura Universitaria, Montevideo, Uruguay. TEL 961152. FAX 962540.

341.2 FR
DOCUMENTS D'ACTUALITE INTERNATIONALE. 1972. fortn. 460 F. (Ministere des Relations Exterieurs) Documentation Francaise, 29-31 Quai Voltaire, 75340 Paris Cedex 07, France. TEL 1-40-15-70-00. bibl. (also avail. in microfiche)
Description: Lists treaty agreements.

DOYLES DISPUTE RESOLUTION PRACTICE - ASIA PACIFIC. see **LAW**

DOYLES DISPUTE RESOLUTION PRACTICE - NORTH AMERICA. see **LAW**

341 FR ISSN 0335-5047
K4
DROIT ET PRATIQUE DU COMMERCE INTERNATIONAL/INTERNATIONAL TRADE LAW AND PRACTICE. (Text in English, French) 1975. q. $210 (typically set in Jan.). Masson, 120 bd. St. Germain, 75280 Paris Cedex 06, France. TEL 1-46-34-21-60. FAX 1-45-87-29-99. TELEX 202 671 F. Ed. P. Juillard. adv.; bk.rev.; index; circ. 1,600. (also avail. in microform from UMI; reprint service avail. from ISI,SCH) **Indexed:** P.A.I.S.For.Lang.Ind., P.A.I.S.
—BLDSC shelfmark: 3627.359300.

341 FR
DROIT INTERNATIONAL PRIVE. a. price varies. Editions du C N R S, 1 Place Aristide Briand, 92195 Meudon Cedex, France. TEL 1-45-34-75-50. FAX 1-46-26-28-49. TELEX LABOBEL 204 135 F. (Subscr. to: Presses du C N R S, 20-22, rue Saint Amand, 75015 Paris, France. TEL 1-45-33-16-00) adv.; bk.rev.; index; circ. 1,500 (controlled).

341.57 NE
▼**E E C NEWSLETTER;** review of current legal developments in the E E C. (Text in English) 1990. 5/yr. fl.200($100) Kluwer Law and Taxation Publishers, P.O. Box 23, 7400 GA Deventer, Netherlands. TEL 31-5700-47261. FAX 31-57000-22244. (Dist. by: Libresso Distribution Center, P.O. Box 23, 7400 GA Deventer, Netherlands. TEL 31-57000-33155; N. America dist. addr.: 6 Bigelow St., Cambridge, MA 02139. TEL 617-354-0140) Ed.Bd.
Description: Highlights new developments in European case law, legislation and administrative decisions.

341.18 EI ISSN 0250-5754
E P NEWS. (Issued in relation to Parliament's sessions.) (Editions in Danish, Dutch, French, German, Greek, Italian, Portuguese, Spanish) 1967. m. (except Aug.). free. European Parliament, Secretariat, Centre Europeen, Case Postale 1601, L-2929 Luxembourg, Luxembourg. FAX 43-70-09. Ed. R. Worsley. bk.rev.; circ. 150,000.
—BLDSC shelfmark: 3793.200000.
Formerly (until 1979): European Parliament News (ISSN 0531-4321)

341.4 UA ISSN 0080-259X
JX3
EGYPTIAN REVIEW OF INTERNATIONAL LAW/REVUE EGYPTIENNE DE DROIT INTERNATIONAL. (Text in Arabic, English, French) 1945. a. $45. Egyptian Society of International Law, 16 Rameses St., Cairo, Egypt. Ed. Salah Amer. bk.rev.; cum.index: 1945-49. **Indexed:** A.B.C.Pol.Sci., Mar.Aff.Bibl.

ELECTION ARCHIVES AND INTERNATIONAL POLITICS. see **POLITICAL SCIENCE**

EUROFOOD MONITOR. see **FOOD AND FOOD INDUSTRIES**

LAW — INTERNATIONAL LAW

341   IT
L'EUROPA DELLA C E E. (Comunita Europea Economica) 1988. m. L.100000($77) Pirola Editore S.p.A., Via Comelico 24, Casella Postale 10444, 20110 Milan, Italy. Ed.Bd. bk.rev.; circ. 1,200.

341   GW   ISSN 0531-2485
EUROPARECHT. 1966. q. DM.125. (Wissenschaftliche Gesellschaft fuer Europarecht) Nomos Verlagsgesellschaft mbH und Co. KG, Waldseestr. 3, Postfach 610, 7570 Baden Baden, Germany.
Indexed: INIS Atomind.

341.1   FR   ISSN 0589-9575
EUROPEAN CO-OPERATION. irreg. Council of Europe, Publishing and Documentation Service, 67000 Strasbourg, France. (Dist. in U.S. by: Manhattan Publishing Co., Box 650, Croton-on-Hudson, NY 10520)

341   UK
EUROPEAN COMMUNITY LAW SERIES. 1990. irreg. (approx. 1-2/yr.) £45. Athlone Press Ltd., 1 Park Dr., London NW11 7SG, England. TEL 081-458-0888. (Subscr. to: B M S, Merlin Way, N. Weald Industrial Estate, N. Weald, Epping, Essex CM16 6MR, England) Ed. D. Lasok. bk.rev.; bibl.; index. (back issues avail.)
Description: Examines copyright and company law in the UK and EC, transport laws and the legalities of drug control in the EC.

341   GW   ISSN 0938-5428
K5
▼**EUROPEAN JOURNAL OF INTERNATIONAL LAW.** 1990. s-a. DM.86. C.H. Beck'sche Verlagsbuchhandlung, Wilhelmstr. 9, 8000 Munich 40, Germany. TEL 089-38189-338. FAX 089-38189-398. TELEX 5215085-BECK-D. Ed.Bd.
—BLDSC shelfmark: 3829.730850.

341.18   EI
EUROPEAN PARLIAMENT. WORKING DOCUMENTS. 1958. irreg. price varies. Office for Official Publications of the European Communities, L-2985 Luxembourg, Luxembourg. (Dist. in the U.S. by: Unipub, 4611-F Assembly Dr., Lenham, MD 20706-4391) (microfiche)
Formerly: European Parliament. Documents de Seance (ISSN 0071-3023)

EUROPEAN PATENT OFFICE REPORTS. see *PATENTS, TRADEMARKS AND COPYRIGHTS*

EUROPEAN TRANSPORT LAW/DROIT EUROPEEN DES TRANSPORTS/EUROPAEISCHES TRANSPORTRECHT/DIRITTO EUROPEO DEI TRASPORTI/EUROPEES VERVOERRECHT. see *TRANSPORTATION*

FLETCHER FORUM OF WORLD AFFAIRS. see *POLITICAL SCIENCE — International Relations*

341   US   ISSN 0882-6420
K6
FLORIDA INTERNATIONAL LAW JOURNAL. 1984. 3/yr. $21 (foreign $25). University of Florida, College of Law, Holland Law Center, Gainesville, FL 32611. TEL 904-392-4980. circ. 250. (reprint service avail. from WSH) **Indexed:** C.L.I., Leg.Per.
—BLDSC shelfmark: 3956.050000.

341   US   ISSN 0426-7230
FONTES IURIS GENTIUM. SECTION 2. (Text in English, French and German) irreg. price varies. Springer-Verlag, 175 Fifth Ave., New York, NY 10010. TEL 212-460-1500. (Also Berlin, Heidelberg, Tokyo and Vienna) Eds. H. Mosler, R. Bernhardt. (reprint service avail. from ISI)
Supersedes in part: Fontes Iuris Gentium (ISSN 0428-903X)

FOREIGN INVESTMENT IN CANADA. see *BUSINESS AND ECONOMICS — Investments*

341 382   US
▼**FOREIGN INVESTMENT IN CENTRAL AND EASTERN EUROPE.** 1990. irreg. $185. (Columbia University, Parker School of Foreign and Comparative Law) Transnational Juris Publications, Inc., Box 7282, Ardsley-on-Hudson, NY 10503. TEL 914-693-0089. FAX 914-693-8776. Ed. Vratislav Pechota. (looseleaf format)
Description: Presents comprehensive information on doing business in Central and Eastern Europe.

341   US
▼**FOREIGN STATE IMMUNITY IN COMMERCIAL TRANSACTIONS.** 1991. base vol. (plus a. suppl.). $100. Butterworth Legal Publishers (Salem) (Subsidiary of: Reed International PLC), 90 Stiles Rd., Salem, NH 03079. TEL 800-548-4001. FAX 603-898-9858. Ed. Michael Wallace Gordon. (looseleaf format)
Description: Covers the Foreign Sovereign Immunities Act of 1976 (US) and the State Immunity Act of 1978 (UK).

346.066   US
FOREIGN TRADE AND INVESTMENT. 2nd ed., 1991. base vol. (plus a. suppl.). $95. Butterworth Legal Publishers (Salem) (Subsidiary of: Reed International PLC), 90 Stiles Rd., Salem, NH 03079. TEL 800-548-4001. FAX 603-898-9858. Ed. Thomas F. Clasen. (looseleaf format)
Description: Guide to foreign trade and investment principles of international law.

341   FR   ISSN 0071-8971
FRANCE. SECRETARIAT D'ETAT AUX AFFAIRES ETRANGERES CHARGE DE LA COOPERATION. RECUEIL DES TRAITES ET ACCORDS DE LA FRANCE. 1961. a. price varies. Secretariat d'Etat aux Affaires Etrangeres Charge de la Cooperation, Direction de l'Aide au Developpement, 37, Quai d'Orsay, 75700 Paris, France.

341   GW   ISSN 0340-0255
JX1903
DIE FRIEDENS - WARTE; Blaetter fuer internationale Verstaendigung und zwischenstaatliche Organisation. 1899. s-a. DM.50. Berlin Verlag Arno Spitz GmbH, Pacelliallee 5, 1000 Berlin 33, Germany. TEL 030-8326232. FAX 030-8316249. Ed. Ferenc Majoros. adv.; bk.rev.; circ. 500.
Description: Forum for the discussion of contemporary theoretical and practical problems of international law and peace studies.

341 382   US
G A T T LEGAL SYSTEM AND WORLD TRADE DIPLOMACY. (General Agreement on Tariffs and Trade) irreg., 2nd ed., 1990. $85. Butterworth Legal Publishers (Salem) (Subsidiary of: Reed International PLC), 90 Stiles Rd., Salem, NH 03079. TEL 800-548-4001. FAX 603-898-9858. Eds. Robert E. Hudec, Melvin C. Steen.
Description: Examines the historical development of the GATT legal system, from the negotiation of the GATT Agreement in 1946-1948 to the beginning of the Tokyo Round in 1975.

341   GW
DAS GELTENDE SEEVOELKERRECHT IN EINZELDARSTELLUNGEN. 1970. irreg., vol.11, 1979. price varies. (Universitaet Hamburg, Institut fuer Internationale Angelegenheiten) Nomos Verlagsgesellschaft mbH und Co. KG, Walderstr. 3-5, Postfach 610, 7570 Baden-Baden, Germany.
Formerly: Geltende Seekriegsrecht in Einzeldarstellungen (ISSN 0435-1924)

341   US
GEORGE WASHINGTON JOURNAL OF INTERNATIONAL LAW AND ECONOMICS. 1966. 3/yr. $22 (foreign $24). George Washington University, National Law Center, Burns Library, Rm. B433, 716 20th St., N.W., Washington, DC 20052. TEL 202-994-7164. Ed.Bd. adv.; bk.rev.; circ. 1,250. (also avail. in microform from UMI,WSH; reprint service avail. from UMI,WSH) **Indexed:** ABI Inform., Abstr.Bk.Rev.Curr.Leg.Per., Amer.Bibl.Slavic & E.Eur.Stud., BPIA, Bus.Ind., C.L.I., Curr.Cont., Foreign Leg.Per., L.R.I., Leg.Cont., Leg.Per., Mar.Aff.Bibl., P.A.I.S., SSCI.
●Also available online. Vendor(s): WESTLAW.
Formerly: Journal of International Law and Economics (ISSN 0022-2003)

341 340.2   US   ISSN 0046-578X
K7
GEORGIA JOURNAL OF INTERNATIONAL AND COMPARATIVE LAW. 1970. 3/yr. $15. Georgia Journal of International and Comparative Law, Inc., University of Georgia, School of Law, Athens, GA 30602. TEL 404-542-7289. Ed.Bd. adv.; bk.rev.; index; circ. 900. (also avail. in microfilm from UMI; microfiche from UMI; reprint service avail. from RRI,UMI) **Indexed:** Abstr.Bk.Rev.Curr.Leg.Per., C.C.L.P., C.L.I., Foreign Leg.Per., L.R.I., Leg.Cont., Leg.Per., P.A.I.S.
—BLDSC shelfmark: 4158.420000.

341   GW   ISSN 0344-3094
JX21
GERMAN YEARBOOK OF INTERNATIONAL LAW. 1948. a. DM.220. (Universitaet Kiel, Institut fuer Internationales Recht) Duncker und Humblot GmbH, Postfach 410329, 1000 Berlin 41, Germany. TEL 030-7900060. FAX 030-79000631. **Indexed:** Amer.Hist.& Life (until 1989), Hist.Abstr. (until 1989).
Formerly: Jahrbuch fuer Internationales Recht (ISSN 0021-3993)

341 340   GW
GOETTINGER RECHTSWISSENSCHAFTLICHE STUDIEN. 1951. irreg. (2-3/yr.). price varies. Verlag Otto Schwartz und Co., Annastr. 7, 3400 Goettingen, Germany. TEL 0551-31051. FAX 0551-372812.

341 382   US
GUIDE TO INTERNATIONAL ARBITRATION AND ARBITRATORS (YEAR). 1989. a., latest 2nd ed. 1992. $250. (Columbia University, Parker School of Foreign and Comparative Law) Transnational Juris Publications, Inc., Box 7282, Ardsley-on-Hudson, NY 10503. TEL 914-693-0089. FAX 914-693-8776. Ed.Bd.
Description: Includes data on more than 500 commercial arbitrators, including nationality, qualifications, specializations, addresses.

341.57 382   US
GUIDE TO INTERNATIONAL COMMERCE LAW. 1982. 2 base vols. (plus a. suppl.). $195. Shepard's - McGraw-Hill, Inc., Box 35300, Colorado Springs, CO 80935-3530. TEL 800-525-2474. (looseleaf format)
Description: Discusses laws relating to import and export of products and technology, distribution in the U.S. and abroad and foreign investment, with emphasis on transactions and contracts between U.S. and foreign firms.

GUIDE TO UNITED STATES TREATIES IN FORCE. see *LAW — Abstracting, Bibliographies, Statistics*

341   NE   ISSN 0072-9272
HAGUE CONFERENCE ON PRIVATE INTERNATIONAL LAW. ACTES ET DOCUMENTS/HAGUE CONFERENCE ON PRIVATE INTERNATIONAL LAW. DOCUMENTS AND PROCEEDINGS. (Text in English and French) 1893. quadrennial, latest 1988. price varies. Hague Conference on Private International Law, Permanent Bureau, Scheveningseweg 6, 2517 KT The Hague, Netherlands. FAX 070-360-4867. TELEX 33383 NL. circ. 1,000. (also avail. in microfiche)

341   US   ISSN 0017-8063
JX1
HARVARD INTERNATIONAL LAW JOURNAL. 1959. 2/yr. $24 (foreign $28). Harvard University, Law School, Publications Center, Hastings Hall, Cambridge, MA 02138. TEL 617-495-3694. bk.rev.; cum.index; circ. 1,200. (also avail. in microform from UMI; back issues avail.; reprint service avail. from RRI,UMI) **Indexed:** A.B.C.Pol.Sci., Abstr.Bk.Rev.Curr.Leg.Per., Amer.Bibl.Slavic & E.Eur.Stud., C.L.I., HR Rep., L.R.I., Leg.Cont., Leg.Per., P.A.I.S., So.Pac.Per.Ind.
●Also available online. Vendor(s): WESTLAW.
—BLDSC shelfmark: 4267.200000.
Formerly: Harvard International Law Club Journal.
Description: Publishes articles and comments on varied topics of interest to international lawyers and scholars.

HARVARD INTERNATIONAL REVIEW. see *POLITICAL SCIENCE — International Relations*

341   US   ISSN 0149-9246
K8
HASTINGS INTERNATIONAL AND COMPARATIVE LAW REVIEW. 1977. q. $20 (foreign $22). University of California, San Francisco, Hastings College of the Law, 200 McAllister St., San Francisco, CA 94102-4978. TEL 415-565-4730. FAX 415-565-4825. Ed. Valerie Karno. adv.; bk.rev.; bibl.; cum.index every 5 yrs.; circ. 1,200. (tabloid format; also avail. in microfilm from RRI; back issues avail.; reprint service avail. from WSH) **Indexed:** A.B.C.Pol.Sci., Abstr.Bk.Rev.Curr.Leg.Per., Amer.Bibl.Slavic & E.Eur.Stud., C.L.I., L.R.I., Leg.Per., P.A.I.S., Peace Res.Abstr.
●Also available online. Vendor(s): WESTLAW.
Description: Articles by law professors and practitioners addressing timely issues in public and private international law.

LAW — INTERNATIONAL LAW

I C J BIBLIOGRAPHY. (International Court of Justice) see LAW — Abstracting, Bibliographies, Statistics

341   NE
I F A SEMINAR SERIES. 1976. a. price varies. International Fiscal Association, World Trade Center, Beursplein 37, Postbus 30215, 3001 DE Rotterdam, Netherlands. TEL 01-4052990. FAX 01-4055031. TELEX 23229 BEURS NL. (Dist. by: Kluwer Law and Taxation Publishers, P.O. Box 23, 7400 GA Deventer, Netherlands; In N. AMerica: 6 Bigelow St., Cambridge, MA 02139)

341   US   ISSN 0190-5821
I L A NEWSLETTER. 1974. bi-m. membership. International Law Association, American Branch, c/o P. Nicholas Kourides, Chase Manhattan Bank, N.A., One Chase Manhattan Plaza, 29th Fl., New York, NY 10081. circ. 700.

341   US
I L A PRACTITIONER'S NOTEBOOK. 1978. q. $20 to non-members. International Law Association, American Branch, c/o P. Nicholas Kourides, Chase Manhattan Bank, N.A., One Chase Manhattan Plaza, 29th Fl., New York, NY 10081. Eds. Howard Hill, Ved Nanda. circ. 850.

341   US   ISSN 0145-3416
JV6001.A1
IMMIGRATION NEWSLETTER. 1972. q. $40 to individuals; institutions and libraries $50. National Lawyers Guild (Boston), National Immigration Project, 14 Beacon St., Ste. 506, Boston, MA 02108. FAX 617-227-5495. Ed. Dan Kesselbrenner. bk.rev.; circ. 600. **Indexed:** HR Rep.
Description: Includes legal analysis and political comment of interest to immigration practitioners.

341   II   ISSN 0019-5294
JX18
INDIAN JOURNAL OF INTERNATIONAL LAW. (Text in English) 1960. q. $35. Indian Society of International Law, 7-8 Scindia House, Kasturba Gandhi Marg, New Delhi 110001, India. Ed. Rahmatullah Khan. adv.; bk.rev.; bibl.; circ. 1,500. **Indexed:** C.L.I., HR Rep., Leg.Per., Refug.Abstr.

341   II   ISSN 0073-6678
INDIAN SOCIETY OF INTERNATIONAL LAW. PUBLICATIONS. 1960. q. $35. Indian Society of International Law, 7-8 Scindia House, Kasturba Gandhi Marg, New Delhi 110001, India. Ed. Rahmatullah Khan. adv.; bk.rev.; circ. 1,500.

341   GW   ISSN 0174-2108
KK6050.A13
INFORMATIONSBRIEF AUSLAENDERRECHT. 1979. 10/yr. DM.152. Alfred Metzner Verlag, Zeppelinallee 43, 6000 Frankfurt a.M. 97, Germany. TEL 069-793009-0. TELEX 4189621-KOMED. Ed.Bd. adv.; bk.rev.; circ. 2,600.

341   SZ
INSTITUT FUER INTERNATIONALES RECHT UND INTERNATIONALE BEZIEHUNGEN. SCHRIFTENREIHE. (Text mainly in German; occasionally in English or French) 1939. irreg. price varies. Helbing und Lichtenhahn Verlag AG, Freie Str. 82, CH-4051 Basel, Switzerland. (Subscr. to: Sauerlaender AG, Postfach, CH-5001 Aarau, Switzerland)

341   CI   ISSN 0351-2800
INSTITUTE OF INTERNATIONAL LAW AND INTERNATIONAL RELATIONS. CONTRIBUTIONS TO THE STUDY OF COMPARATIVE AND INTERNATIONAL LAW/PRINOSI ZA POREDBENO PROUCAVANJE PRAVA I MEDUNARODNO PRAVO. (Text in English, German and Serbo-Croatian; summaries English, French, German and Serbo-Croatian) 1968. s-a. free. University of Zagreb, Faculty of Law, Institute of International Law and International Relations, Cirilometodska 4, 41000 Zagreb, Croatia. Ed. Kresimir Sajko. bk.rev.; circ. 500. (back issues avail.)

INTELLECTUAL PROPERTY DECISIONS. see BUSINESS AND ECONOMICS — International Commerce

341.57   UK   ISSN 0955-2197
INTELLECTUAL PROPERTY IN BUSINESS (BRIEFING AND REVIEW). 1989. 10/yr.(Briefing); bi-m.(Review). £180 (foreign £200). Eclipse Publications Ltd., 18-20 Highbury Place, London N5 1QP, England. TEL 071-354-5858. FAX 071-359-4000. Ed. Anthony Korn. circ. 400. (back issues avail.)
Description: Covers national and international intellectual property law: legal, commercial and regulatory developments affecting the management, protection and marketing of innovation.

INTELLECTUAL PROPERTY NEWSLETTER. see BUSINESS AND ECONOMICS — International Commerce

341   US
▼**INTELLECTUAL PROPERTY PROTECTION IN ASIA.** 1991. base vol. (plus a. suppl.). $125. Butterworth Legal Publishers (Salem) (Subsidiary of: Reed International PLC), 90 Stiles Rd., Salem, NH 03079. TEL 800-548-4001. FAX 603-898-9858. Ed. Arthur Wineburg. (looseleaf format)
Description: Provides attorneys and their clients with information and methods to determine where, when, and how to establish and exercise the right to their intellectual property.

341   US
INTER-AMERICAN LAW REVIEW. 1969. 3/yr. $20. University of Miami, School of Law, Box 248087, Coral Gables, FL 33124. TEL 305-284-2523. (Co-sponsor: Inter-American Bar Association) adv.; bk.rev.; index; circ. 800. (tabloid format; also avail. in microfilm from WSH; reprint service avail. from RRI,WSH) **Indexed:** C.L.I., L.R.I., Leg.Per., Ocean.Abstr., Pollut.Abstr.
●Also available online. Vendor(s): WESTLAW.
Formerly (until 1984): Lawyer of the Americas (ISSN 0023-9445)

341   US
INTER-AMERICAN LEGAL MATERIALS. q. $71 (foreign $81). American Bar Association, International Law and Practice Section, 750 N. Lake Shore Dr., Chicago, IL 60611. TEL 312-988-5000.
Description: Designed to increase understanding and communication between US lawyers and their collegues in Latin America and the Caribbean.

346.066   US
▼**INTERNATIONAL AGENCY AND DISTRIBUTION AGREEMENTS.** (Vol. 1: Analysis and Forms; Vol. 2: Europe; Vol. 3: Middle East, Africa, Asia, Pacific; Vol. 4: North America, South America) 1991. 4 base vols. (plus a. suppl.). $425 for set. Butterworth Legal Publishers (Salem) (Subsidiary of: Reed International PLC), 90 Stiles Rd., Salem, NH 03079. TEL 800-548-4001. FAX 603-898-9858. Ed. Thomas F. Clasen. (looseleaf format)
Description: Provides US and foreign practitioners with information needed to prepare and review foreign sales agency and distribution agreements.

341   UK   ISSN 0020-5893
LAW
INTERNATIONAL AND COMPARATIVE LAW QUARTERLY. 1952. q. £55($105) British Institute of International and Comparative Law, 17 Russell Square, London WC1B 5DR, England. TEL 071-636-5802. FAX 071-323-2016. Ed. Hazel Fox. adv.; bk.rev.; bibl.; index; circ. 2,500. (reprint service avail. from KTO) **Indexed:** A.B.C.Pol.Sci., Abstr.Bk.Rev.Curr.Leg.Per., C.L.I., Foreign Leg.Per., HRIS, Int.Lab.Doc., L.R.I., Leg.Info.Manage.Ind., Leg.Per., Mar.Aff.Bibl., P.A.I.S., SSCI.
—BLDSC shelfmark: 4535.700000.

341 382   US   ISSN 0886-0114
K2400.A13
INTERNATIONAL ARBITRATION REPORT. 1986. m. $350. Mealey Publications, Inc., Box 446, Wayne, PA 19087. TEL 215-688-6566. FAX 215-688-7552. Ed. Edie Scott.
Description: Covers court and arbitration panel opinions worldwide concerning international arbitration.

341   UK   ISSN 0143-7453
K110.I47
INTERNATIONAL BAR NEWS. 1970. q. membership only. International Bar Association, 2 Harewood Place, Hanover Sq., London W1R 9HB, England. Ed. Ruth Eldon. adv.; bk.rev.; bibl.; circ. 12,500. (also avail. in microfiche from WSH) **Indexed:** C.L.I., Leg.Per.
Formerly (until 1980): International Bar Journal (ISSN 0047-0589)

INTERNATIONAL BOUNDARY STUDY. see GEOGRAPHY

346.07   UK   ISSN 0309-7676
K9
INTERNATIONAL BUSINESS LAWYER. 1973. 11/yr. £115. International Bar Association, 2 Harewood Place, Hanover Sq., London W1R 9HB, England. Ed. Ruth Eldon. adv.; bk.rev.; cum.index; circ. 10,500. (also avail. in microfiche from WSH) **Indexed:** C.L.I., L.R.I., Leg.Per.
—BLDSC shelfmark: 4538.370000.

INTERNATIONAL CENTRE FOR SETTLEMENT OF INVESTMENT DISPUTES. ANNUAL REPORT. see BUSINESS AND ECONOMICS — Investments

341   SZ   ISSN 0020-6393
K9
INTERNATIONAL COMMISSION OF JURISTS. REVIEW. 1969. s-a. 20 Fr. International Commission of Jurists, 109 Route de Chene, 1224 Chene-Bougeries, Geneva, Switzerland. FAX 4122-493145. Ed. Adama Dieng. bk.rev.; bibl.; circ. 7,000. (also avail. in microform from JAI,MIM; back issues avail.) **Indexed:** C.L.I., L.R.I., Mid.East: Abstr.& Ind., P.A.I.S.
—BLDSC shelfmark: 7786.180000.
Formed by the merger of: International Commission of Jurists. Bulletin (ISSN 0534-8242) & International Commission of Jurists. Journal (ISSN 0047-0678)
Description: Non-governmental organization concerned with the legal protection of human rights.

341   UK   ISSN 0958-5214
▼**INTERNATIONAL COMPANY AND COMMERCIAL LAW REVIEW.** 1990. m. £250. E S C Publishing Ltd., Mill St., Oxford OX2 0JU, England. TEL 0865-249248. FAX 0865-792301.
—BLDSC shelfmark: 4538.724100.
Description: Provides insight into worldwide developments in case law and changes in legislation which affect company and commercial lawyers.

341 690   UK   ISSN 0265-1416
INTERNATIONAL CONSTRUCTION LAW REVIEW. 1983. q. $295. Lloyd's of London Press Ltd., Sheepen Place, Colchester, Essex CO3 3LP, England. TEL 0206-772277. FAX 0260-46273. (In US, subscr. to: 611 Broadway, Ste. 308, New York, NY 10012. TEL 212-529-9500) Eds. Humphrey Lloyd, David Wightman. bk.rev.; index; circ. 400.
—BLDSC shelfmark: 4539.410000.
Description: Covers legal and commercial aspects on international construction. Contains case notes from all parts of the world, correspondents' reports on current developments and articles on a wide range of topics.

341   UN   ISSN 0074-445X
JX1971.6
INTERNATIONAL COURT OF JUSTICE. YEARBOOK. French edition: Cour Internationale de Justice. Annuaire (ISSN 0251-0669) (Editions in English and French) 1946. a. price varies. United Nations Publications, Room DC2-853, New York, NY 10017. TEL 212-963-8300. FAX 212-963-3489. TELEX 32323. (And: Peace Palace, 2517 KJ The Hague, Netherlands; Distribution and Sales Section, Palais des Nations, CH-12 Geneva, Switzerland) Ed.Bd. circ. 2,000.

341 332.4   UK   ISSN 0262-6969
K9
INTERNATIONAL FINANCIAL LAW REVIEW. 1982. m. Euromoney Publications PLC, Nestor House, Playhouse Yard, London EC4V 5EX, England. Ed. Josephine Carr. **Indexed:** ABI Inform., Bank.Lit.Ind., BPIA, Cont.Pg.Manage., Leg.Cont., World Bank.Abstr.
—BLDSC shelfmark: 4540.189700.

341.7   NE
INTERNATIONAL FISCAL ASSOCIATION. YEARBOOK. a. membership only. International Fiscal Association, World Trade Center, Beursplein 37, Postbus 30215, 3001 DE Rotterdam, Netherlands. TEL 10-4052990. FAX 010-4055031. TELEX 23229 BEURS NL.

LAW — INTERNATIONAL LAW   2725

341   UK   ISSN 0950-365X
INTERNATIONAL FRANCHISING AND DISTRIBUTION LAW.
1986. 4/yr. £85($140) Tolley Publishing Co. Ltd., Tolley House, 2 Addiscombe Rd., Croydon, Surrey CR9 5AF, England. Ed. Martin Mendelsohn. adv.; bk.rev.
—BLDSC shelfmark: 5007.662000.
Description: Covers all aspects of international franchising and distribution law.

INTERNATIONAL GENEVA YEARBOOK. see *POLITICAL SCIENCE — International Relations*

341.57   NE
INTERNATIONAL HANDBOOK ON COMMERCIAL ARBITRATION. (Text in English) 1984. base vol. (plus q. updates). fl.520($277) Kluwer Law and Taxation Publishers, P.O. Box 23, 7400 GA Deventer, Netherlands. TEL 31-5700-47261. FAX 31-5700-22244. TELEX 49295 KLUWDV NL. (Dist. by: Libresso Distribution Centre, P.O. Box 23, 7400 GA Deventer, Netherlands. TEL 31-5700-33155; N. America dist. addr.: 6 Bigelow St., Cambridge, MA 02139. TEL 617-354-0140)
Formerly: Handbook Commercial Law.

INTERNATIONAL INCOME TAX RULES OF THE UNITED STATES. see *BUSINESS AND ECONOMICS — Public Finance, Taxation*

341   UK   ISSN 0268-0106
K9   CODEN: IJELE6
INTERNATIONAL JOURNAL OF ESTUARINE AND COASTAL LAW. 1986. q. fl.470($240) Graham & Trotman Ltd. (Subsidiary of: Kluwer Academic Publishers Group), Sterling House, 66 Wilton Rd., London SW1V 1DE, England. (Dist. by: Kluwer Academic Publishers Group, P.O. Box 322, 3300 AH Dordrecht, Netherlands; N. America dist. addr.: Box 358, Accord Station, Hingham, MA 02018-0358. TEL 617-871-6600) Ed. Freestone. adv. **Indexed:** C.L.I., Deep Sea Res.& Oceanogr.Abstr., Environ.Per.Bibl.
—BLDSC shelfmark: 4542.244300.

340   US
INTERNATIONAL LAW AND TRADE PERSPECTIVE. 1975. m. $150. Box 27495, Washington, DC 20038-7495. Ed.Bd. bk.rev.; abstr.; circ. 250.
Formed by the July 1987 merger of: International Law Perspective & International Trade Perspective (ISSN 0098-7719)
Description: Reviews and sumarizes significant and interesting developments in the Congress, the courts, the legal periodicals, as well as other sources, pertaining to international law and trade.

341   US
INTERNATIONAL LAW ASSOCIATION. AMERICAN BRANCH. PROCEEDINGS. biennial. $35. International Law Association, American Branch, c/o P. Nicholas Kourides, Chase Manhattan Bank, N.A., One Chase Manhattan Plaza, 29th Fl., New York, NY 10081. Ed. Theordore Giuttari. bibl.; circ. 650.

341   UK   ISSN 0074-6738
INTERNATIONAL LAW ASSOCIATION. REPORTS OF CONFERENCES. (Text in English; some papers in French) 1875. biennial; 63rd, 1988, Warsaw. price varies. International Law Association, 3 Paper Bldgs., The Temple, London EC4Y 7EU, England. TEL 01-353-2904. cum.index: 1873-1972; circ. 4,000. **Indexed:** C.L.I., Leg.Per.
Formerly: Association Internationale du Droit Commercial. Et du Droit Affaires. Groupe Francais. Travaux (ISSN 0571-5873)

341   US   ISSN 0047-0813
JX1
INTERNATIONAL LAW NEWS. 1972. q. membership only. American Bar Association, International Law and Practice Section, 750 N. Lake Shore Dr., Chicago, IL 60611. TEL 312-988-5555. Ed. Robert S. Rendell. circ. 12,400. **Indexed:** C.L.I., L.R.I.
Description: Newsletter reports on committee activities and other current matters of interest to Section members.

341   US   ISSN 1041-3405
K1001.2
INTERNATIONAL LAW PRACTICUM; practicing the law of the world from New York. 1988. s-a. $65 includes New York International Law Review (free to qualified personnel). New York State Bar Association, International Law and Practice Section, One Elk St., Albany, NY 12207-1096. TEL 518-463-3200. Ed. Ingrid Sapona.
Description: Articles relating to the practical needs of attorneys in an international setting, emphasizing clinical matters as opposed to academic, exploring the application of the law for the generalist rather than theoretical discussions for the expert.
Refereed Serial

341   II   ISSN 0300-4058
INTERNATIONAL LAW REPORTER. (Text in English) 1970. m. Rs.45($15) Intlaw Publishers Corporation, P.O. Box 3528, New Delhi 110024, India. Ed. R.S. Butalia. adv.; bk.rev.; index.

341 327   UK
INTERNATIONAL LAW REPORTS. 1932. q. $127 per no. (University of Cambridge, Research Centre for International Law) Grotius Publications Ltd., P.O. Box 115, Cambridge CB3 9BP, England.
FAX 0223-313545. Ed. E. Lauterpacht. cum.index. (back issues avail.)

341   US   ISSN 0020-7810
JX1
INTERNATIONAL LAWYER. 1966. q. $31 to non-members. American Bar Association, International Law and Practice Section, 750 N. Lake Shore Dr., Chicago, IL 60611. TEL 312-988-6067. Ed. Joseph J. Norton. adv.; bk.rev.; abstr.; bibl.; charts; index; circ. 13,000. (also avail. in microfilm from RRI,WSH; reprint service avail. from RRI)
Indexed: Abstr.Bk.Rev.Curr.Leg.Per., Amer.Bibl.Slavic & E.Eur.Stud., C.L.I., Int.Lab.Doc., L.R.I., Leg.Per., Mar.Aff.Bibl., Sel.Water Res.Abstr., SSCI.
●Also available online. Vendor(s): Mead Data Central, WESTLAW.
—BLDSC shelfmark: 4542.840000.
Formerly: American Bar Association. Section of International and Comparative Law. Journal and Proceedings.
Description: Articles directed at lawyers with an interest in the fields of international business transactions, public international law and comparative law.

341   US   ISSN 0020-7829
JX68
INTERNATIONAL LEGAL MATERIALS. 1962. bi-m. $150 to non-members. American Society of International Law, 2223 Massachusetts Ave., N.W., Washington, DC 20008-2864. TEL 202-265-4313. FAX 202-797-7133. Ed. Marilou M. Righini. adv. contact: Rachael de la Vega. index, cum.index: 1962-1969, 1970-1979, 1980-1989; circ. 2,600. (also avail. in microfiche from WSH; back issues avail.; reprint service avail. from WSH) **Indexed:** A.B.C.Pol.Sci., C.L.I., Deep Sea Res.& Oceanogr.Abstr. L.R.I., Leg.Per., Mar.Aff.Bibl., Mid.East: Abstr.& Ind., P.A.I.S.
●Also available online. Vendor(s): Mead Data Central.
—BLDSC shelfmark: 4542.860000.

341   UK   ISSN 0309-7684
K110.I47
INTERNATIONAL LEGAL PRACTITIONER. 1976. q. £65. International Bar Association, 2 Harewood Place, Hanover Sq., London W1R 9HB, England. Ed. Ruth Eldon. adv.; bk.rev.; index; circ. 2,800.
—BLDSC shelfmark: 4542.870000.

341   UK
▼**INTERNATIONAL LITIGATION PROCEDURE.** 1990. bi-m. £220. (European Law Centre) Sweet & Maxwell, South Quay Plaza, 8th floor, 183 Marsh Wall, London E14 9FT, England.
TEL 071-538-8686. FAX 071-538-9508. Ed. Marina Milmo. (back issues avail.)

341   UK   ISSN 0263-6395
INTERNATIONAL MEDIA LAW; bulletin on rights, clearances and legal practice. 1982. m. £160($280) Longman Group UK Ltd., Law, Tax and Finance Division, 21-27 Lamb's Conduit St., London WC1N 3NJ, England. TEL 071-242-2548. FAX 071-831-8119. TELEX 295445. Ed. Clive Fisher.
—BLDSC shelfmark: 4544.008300.
Description: Analysis of laws relating to broadcasting, publishing, film, video, music and live performance.

341.57 382   US   ISSN 1053-4660
▼**INTERNATIONAL MERGER LAW: EVENTS AND COMMENTARY.** 1990. m. $600. Washington Regulatory Reporting Associates, Box 2220, Springfield, VA 22152. TEL 703-690-8240. Eds. Robert Skitol, Bruce Stewart.
●Also available online. Vendor(s): NewsNet.

INTERNATIONAL PROBLEMS; society and politics. see *POLITICAL SCIENCE — International Relations*

341 361.77   SZ   ISSN 0020-8604
INTERNATIONAL REVIEW OF THE RED CROSS. French edition: Revue Internationale de la Croix Rouge (ISSN 0035-3361); Spanish edition: Revista Internacional de la Cruz Roja (ISSN 0250-569X) 1961 (English ed.); 1869 (French ed.); 1976 (Spanish ed.); 1988 (Arabic ed.). bi-m. 30 Fr.($18) International Committee of the Red Cross, 19 Avenue de la Paix, 1202 Geneva, Switzerland. Ed. Dr. J. Meurant. stat. **Indexed:** HR Rep.
—BLDSC shelfmark: 4545.840000.

341 336   US   ISSN 0741-4269
K9
INTERNATIONAL TAX AND BUSINESS LAWYER. 1983. s-a. $43 (foreign $47). University of California Press, Journals Division, 2120 Berkeley Way, Berkeley, CA 94720. TEL 510-642-6221. FAX 510-643-7127. Ed. Jogn E. Somorjai. adv.; index; circ. 500. (also avail. in microfiche from WSH; back issues avail.) **Indexed:** C.L.I., Foreign Leg.Per., L.R.I., Leg.Cont., Leg.Per., P.A.I.S.
—BLDSC shelfmark: 4550.392000.
Description: Information on all legal aspects of international tax and business transactions.
Refereed Serial

341 336   US   ISSN 0892-1032
K4473
INTERNATIONAL TAX TREATIES OF ALL NATIONS. SERIES A. 1975. irreg., vol.13, 1986. $50 per vol. Oceana Publications, Inc., 75 Main St., Dobbs Ferry, NY 10522. TEL 914-693-1320. FAX 914-693-0402. Eds. Walter H. Diamond, Dorothy B. Diamond. cum.index; circ. 300. (back issues avail.)
Description: Provides English language texts of all tax treaties in force between two or more nations.

341 336   US   ISSN 0892-1040
K4473
INTERNATIONAL TAX TREATIES OF ALL NATIONS. SERIES B. 1975. irreg., vol.23, 1989. price varies. Oceana Publications, Inc., 75 Main St., Dobbs Ferry, NY 10522. TEL 914-693-1320. FAX 914-693-0402. Eds. Walter H. Diamond, Dorothy B. Diamond. cum.index; circ. 300. (back issues avail.)
Description: Tax treaties in force between two or more nations not yet published by the U.N.

INTERNATIONAL TAXATION SERIES. see *BUSINESS AND ECONOMICS — Public Finance, Taxation*

INTERNATIONAL TRADE REPORTER DECISIONS. see *BUSINESS AND ECONOMICS — International Commerce*

LAW — INTERNATIONAL LAW

341 338.91 NE ISSN 0020-9317
D839 CODEN: ISPCET
INTERNATIONALE SPECTATOR; maandblad voor internationale politiek. (Text in Dutch; occasionally in English; summaries in English) 1947. m. fl.85 in Europe; students fl.70; elsewhere fl.120. Nederlands Instituut voor Internationale Betrekkingen - Netherlands Institute of International Relations, Clingendael 7, 2597 VH The Hague, Netherlands. TEL 070-245384. FAX 070-282002. (Subscr. to: Administratie Internationale Spectator, Antwoordnummer 1823, 2500 VB The Hague, Netherlands) Ed. H.J. Neuman. adv.; bk.rev.; index; circ. 4,500. **Indexed:** Amer.Hist.& Life, Hist.Abstr., Key to Econ.Sci., Rural Recreat.Tour.Abstr., World Agri.Econ.& Rural Sociol.Abstr.
—BLDSC shelfmark: 4554.700000.
Description: Examines developments in international relations, politics and international law.

341 US ISSN 0277-2922
JX238.I7
IRANIAN ASSETS LITIGATION REPORTER. 1980. s-m. $2300. Andrews Publications, 1646 West Chester Pike, Box 1000, PA 19395. TEL 215-399-6600. FAX 215-399-6610. Ed. Edith F. McFall. abstr.; bibl.; stat.; s-a. index. (looseleaf format; back issues avail.)
Description: Covers events in the U.S. and foreign countries regarding the attachment of Iranian assets and the complicated litigation and international arbitration that has resulted.

341 IT
ITALIA E L'EUROPA. q. Centro Italiano di Studi Europei, Piazza SS Apostoli 80, 00187 Rome, Italy. Ed. Gian Pero Orsello.

341 IT
ITALIAN YEARBOOK OF INTERNATIONAL LAW. 1975. a. $25. Casa Editrice Dott. A. Guiffre, Via Busto Arsizio 40, 20151 Milan, Italy. **Indexed:** Mar.Aff.Bibl.

341 382 US
JOINT VENTURES IN THE SOVIET UNION; a legal treatise with forms and commentary. irreg. $165. (Columbia University, Parker School of Foreign and Comparative Law) Transnational Juris Publications, Inc., Box 7282, Ardsley-on-Hudson, NY 10503. TEL 914-693-0089. FAX 914-693-8776. Ed. Kaj Hober. (looseleaf format)
Description: Provides comprehensive discussion of legal aspects of doing business in the Soviet Union, including foreign exchange laws, property rights, dispute resolution, and negotiating techniques.

341 382 US
JOINT VENTURES WITH INTERNATIONAL PARTNERS. 1989. base vol. (plus a. suppl.). $105. Butterworth Legal Publishers (Salem) (Subsidiary of: Reed International PLC), 90 Stiles Rd., Salem, NH 03079. TEL 800-548-4001. FAX 603-898-9644. Eds. Jeffrey A. Burt, James A. Dobkin. (looseleaf format)
Description: Technical and legal examination of joint venture laws and practices; provides the "ins" and "outs" of forming joint ventures with overseas business entities.

346.066 US
▼**JOINT VENTURES WITH THE SOVIET UNION**; law and practice. 1990. base vol. (plus a. suppl.). $125. Butterworth Legal Publishers (Salem) (Subsidiary of: Reed International PLC), 90 Stiles Rd., Salem, NH 03079. TEL 800-548-4001. FAX 603-898-9858. Ed. Christopher Osakwe. (looseleaf format)

341 FR ISSN 0021-8170
JX6002
JOURNAL DU DROIT INTERNATIONAL. 1874. q. $110. Editions Techniques, 123 rue d'Alesia, 75014 Paris Cedex 14, France. TEL 45-39-22-91. FAX 45-42-81-55. TELEX EDITEC 270737 F. bk.rev.; abstr.; charts; index, cum.index; circ. 2,000. (reprint service avail. from SCH) **Indexed:** Mar.Aff.Bibl., P.A.I.S.For.Lang.Ind., P.A.I.S.
—BLDSC shelfmark: 4970.500000.

341 US ISSN 1053-6735
K4
▼**JOURNAL OF COMPARATIVE AND INTERNATIONAL LAW.** 1991. s-a. $20 (foreign $23). Duke University, School of Law, Rm. 006, Durham, CT 27706-2580. TEL 919-684-5966. FAX 919-684-3417.

341 SZ ISSN 0255-8106
K10
JOURNAL OF INTERNATIONAL ARBITRATION. 1984. q. 250 Fr.($195) Werner Publishing Co. Ltd., P.O. Box 93, 1211 Geneva 11, Switzerland. TEL 022-283422. FAX 022-214592. **Indexed:** Leg.Per.
—BLDSC shelfmark: 5007.581500.

341 332.6 IT ISSN 0394-3933
HC307.S69
JOURNAL OF REGIONAL POLICY; mezzogiorno d'Europa. (Text in English) 1981. q. Institute for the Economic Development of Southern Italy, Via Alcide De Gasperi, 71, 801333 Naples, Italy. TEL 081-7853640. (Subscr. to: Via San Giacomo, 19, 80133 Naples, Italy) index. (back issues avail.) **Indexed:** World Agri.Econ.& Rural Sociol.Abstr.
Formerly: Mezzogiorno d'Europa.
Description: Covers regional and European economics and law.

629.1 340 US ISSN 0095-7577
JX1
JOURNAL OF SPACE LAW. 1973. s-a. $65 (foreign $75). (University of Mississippi, School of Law) Journal of Space Law, University, MS 38677. TEL 601-232-7361. FAX 601-232-7731. Ed.Bd. adv.; bk.rev.; index; circ. 900. (also avail. in microform from MIM; microfilm from WSH; back issues avail.; reprint service avail. from WSH) **Indexed:** C.L.I., Int.Aerosp.Abstr., L.R.I., Leg.Cont., Leg.Per.
Description: Covers legal problems arising out of human activities in outer space.

341.57 382 SZ ISSN 0022-5444
K10
JOURNAL OF WORLD TRADE. 1967. bi-m. 330 Fr.($245) Werner Publishing Co. Ltd., P.O. Box 93, 1211 Geneva 11, Switzerland. TEL 022-283422. FAX 022-214592. Ed. Jacques Werner. adv.; bk.rev.; index. **Indexed:** ABI Inform, Abstr.Bk.Rev.Curr.Leg.Per., Amer.Hist.& Life, BPIA, Br.Hum.Ind., Bus.Ind., C.L.I., C.R.E.J., Cont.Pg.Manage., Curr.Cont., Hist.Abstr., Int.Lab.Doc., J.of Econ.Lit., Key to Econ.Sci., L.R.I., Leg.Per., Mar.Aff.Bibl., P.A.I.S., Risk Abstr., Rural Recreat.Tour.Abstr., SCIMP (1978-), SSCI, Tr.& Indus.Ind., World Agri.Econ.& Rural Sociol.Abstr., World Bank.Abstr.

341 YU ISSN 0022-6084
JX18
JUGOSLOVENSKA REVIJA ZA MEDJUNARODNO PRAVO. (Text in Serbo-Croatian; summaries in English and French) 1954. 3/yr. Jugoslovensko Udruzenje za Medjunarodno Pravo, Makedonska 25, Belgrade, Yugoslavia. Ed. B. Babovic. bk.rev.; bibl.; index; circ. 1,200.

341 327 IT ISSN 0022-6963
JUS GENTIUM; diritto delle relazioni internazionali. (Consists of two issues not available separately: Part A, Theoretical Elaborations (Ratio and Lectio); Part B, Positive Applications (Ars and Jura).) (Text in English, French and Italian) 1950. s-a. L.80000. Corso Vittorio Emanuele 142, I-00186 Rome, Italy. (Subscr. to: Casella Postale 410 (Centro), I-00100 Rome, Italy) Ed. Giovanni Scarangella. bk.rev.; index; circ. 1,000.
—BLDSC shelfmark: 5075.615000.

341 JA ISSN 0023-2866
KOKUSAIHO GAIKO ZASSHI/JOURNAL OF INTERNATIONAL LAW AND DIPLOMACY. (Text in Japanese; table of contents and summaries in English) 1903. bi-m. 7200 Yen to non-members. Kokusaiho Gakkai - Japanese Association of International Law, c/o Faculty of Law, University of Tokyo, 3-1, Hongo 7-chome, Bunkyo-ku, Tokyo, Japan. (Subscr. to: Yuhikaku, 2-17 Jinbo-cho, Kanda, Chiyoda-ku, Tokyo, Japan) Ed.Bd. bk.rev.; circ. 800 (controlled). **Indexed:** Amer.Hist.& Life, Hist.Abstr.
—BLDSC shelfmark: 5007.670000.
Description: Public and private international law and diplomacy.

341 KO ISSN 0023-3994
KOREAN JOURNAL OF INTERNATIONAL LAW. (Text in Korean; summaries in English or other languages) 1956. 2/yr. $200. Korean Association of International Law, 37 Suhsomoon-Dong, Suhdaimoon-Ky, Seoul, S. Korea. adv.; bk.rev.; cum.index; circ. 500. (back issues avail.)

LAMY CONTRATS INTERNATIONAUX. see BUSINESS AND ECONOMICS — International Commerce

341.57 380.5 FR
LAMY TRANSPORT TOME 1; route. a. 820 F. Lamy S.A., 155, rue Legendre, 75850 Paris Cedex 17, France. TEL 1-46-27-28-90. FAX 42-29-86-81. TELEX 214 398. index.
Description: Covers responsibilities and obligations of the transporter, contract types, legislation, insurance, regulations.

341.57 380.5 FR
LAMY TRANSPORT TOME 2; douane, commissionnaires de transport, transports maritimes, transports par chemin de fer, transports aeriens, lexique. a. 630 F. (effective 1991). Lamy S.A., 155, rue Legendre, 75850 Paris Cedex 17, France. TEL 1-46-27-28-90. FAX 42-29-86-81. TELEX 214 398. index.
Description: Covers regulations, responsibilities and privileges of the transporter, customs regulations, international sales, air and sea insurance.

341.57 380.5 FR
LAMY TRANSPORT TOME 3; marchandises dangereuses. (Includes supplement: Nomenclatures des matieres) a. 875 F. (effective 1991). Lamy S.A., 155, rue Legendre, 75850 Paris Cedex 17, France. TEL 1-46-27-28-90. FAX 42-29-86-81. TELEX 214 398. index.
Description: Covers regulations concerning the national and international transport of hazardous materials.

341 US ISSN 0023-9208
K12
LAW AND POLICY IN INTERNATIONAL BUSINESS. 1969. 4/yr. $30 (foreign $35). Georgetown University Law Center, 600 New Jersey Ave., N.W., Washington, DC 20001. TEL 202-662-9468. Ed. Gil Bonwitt. adv.; bk.rev.; index; circ. 1,183. (also avail. in microform from UMI; microfiche from WSH; reprint service avail. from UMI) **Indexed:** ABI Inform, Abstr.Bk.Rev.Curr.Leg.Per., Amer.Bibl.Slavic & E.Eur.Stud, BPIA, Bus.Ind., C.L.I., Foreign Leg.Per, Geo.Abstr., L.R.I., Leg.Cont., Leg.Per, P.A.I.S., Tr.& Indus.Ind.
●Also available online. Vendor(s): WESTLAW.
—BLDSC shelfmark: 5161.363000.

341 GW ISSN 0341-6151
K12
LAW AND STATE; a biannual collection of recent German contributions to these fields. 1970. s-a. exchange basis. Institute for Scientific Co-operation with Developing Countries, Landhausstr. 18, 7400 Tuebingen, Germany. TEL 07071-5066. Ed. K.-H.W. Bechtold. circ. 3,000. **Indexed:** HR Rep., Refug.Abstr.

340 NE ISSN 0075-823X
KJC510.A15
LAW IN EASTERN EUROPE. (Text in English) 1958. irreg., no.30, 1985. price varies. (Rijksuniversiteit te Leiden, Documentation Office for East European Law) Kluwer Academic Publishers, Postbus 17, 3300 AA Dordrecht, Netherlands. TEL 078-334911. FAX 078-334254. (Dist. by: Kluwer Academic Publishers Group, P.O. Box 322, 3300 AH Dordrecht, Netherlands; U.S. addr.: P.O. Box 358, Accord Sta., Hingham, MA 02018-0358) Ed. F.J. Feldbrugge. index; circ. 900.

LAW REPRINTS: TRADE REGULATION SERIES. see BUSINESS AND ECONOMICS — International Commerce

340 AT ISSN 0047-4207
LAWASIA. 1969. a. Aus.$22. University of Technology, Sydney, P.O. Box 123, City Campus, Haymarket, N.S.W. 2007, Australia. TEL 02-330-3412. FAX 02-330-3421. Ed. G.F. Payne. adv.; bk.rev.; bibl.; circ. 2,000. **Indexed:** Abstr.Bk.Rev.Curr.Leg.Per., C.L.I., Leg.Per., So.Pac.Per.Ind.
Description: Covers legal issues and developments which have a bearing on countries in the Asian and Pacific regions.

LECCIONES Y ENSAYOS. see LAW

341 NE
LEGAL ASPECTS OF INTERNATIONAL ORGANIZATION. 1983. irreg. Kluwer Academic Publishers, Distribution Center, P.O. Box 322, 3300 AH Dordrecht, Netherlands.

LAW — INTERNATIONAL LAW 2727

341.57 NE
LEGAL ISSUES OF EUROPEAN INTEGRATION. (Text in English) 1974. s-a. price varies. (Universiteit van Amsterdam, Europa Instituut) Kluwer Law and Taxation Publishers, P.O. Box 23, 7400 GA Deventer, Netherlands. TEL 31-5700-47261. FAX 31-5700-22244. TELEX 49295 KLUDV NL. (Dist. by: Libresso Distribution Centre, P.O. Box 23, 7400 GA Deventer, Netherlands. TEL 31-5700-33155; N. America dist. addr.: 6 Bigelow St., Cambridge, MA 02139. TEL 617-354-0140) Ed.Bd. (back issues avail.) Indexed: Key to Econ.Sci.
Formerly: Legal Issues.

341 DK ISSN 0106-8474
LOVTIDENDE C FOR KONGERIGET DANMARK. 1936. irreg. DKK 325. Justitsministeriet, Sekretariatet for Retsinformation, Axeltorv 6, 5. sal, D-1609 Copenhagen V, Denmark. TEL 33-32-52-22. FAX 33-91-28-01. index; circ. 760.
●Also available online.
Description: Official organ for promulgating international treaties and agreements in accordance with Danish law.

MAGHREB, MACHREK, MONDE ARABE. see *POLITICAL SCIENCE*

341.2 MW ISSN 0076-3357
MALAWI TREATY SERIES. (Text in English) a. K.0.60. Government Printer, P.O. Box 37, Zomba, Malawi. Ed. James S. Friedlander. cum.index 1964-1969.

341 382 US
MARYLAND JOURNAL OF INTERNATIONAL LAW AND TRADE. 1975. s-a. $12 (foreign $14). University of Maryland School of Law, 500 W. Baltimore St., Baltimore, MD 21201. Ed. Peggy A. Rodgers. circ. 500. (also avail. in microfilm from RRI; back issues avail.; reprint service avail. from RRI) Indexed: C.L.I., Leg.Per.

341 610
MEDICOLEGAL LIBRARY. 1984. irreg. price varies. Springer-Verlag, 175 Fifth Ave., New York, NY 10010. TEL 212-460-1500. (Also Berlin, Heidelberg, Tokyo, Vienna) (reprint service avail. from ISI)

MEDIEN UND RECHT INTERNATIONAL; Zeitschrift fuer das Recht der Medien und der Werbung. see *LAW*

341 SZ
MENSCH UND RECHT. 1981. q. 18.50 Fr. Schweizerische Gesellschaft fuer die Europaeische Menschenrechtskonvention, Postfach 10, CH-8127 Forch, Switzerland. TEL 411-9800454. TELEX 817585159 COM CH. Ed. Ludwig A. Minelli. circ. 11,500. (back issues avail.)
Description: Provides information on human rights in Europe.

340 364 US
MICHIGAN JOURNAL OF INTERNATIONAL LAW. 1979. q. $30 (foreign $35). University of Michigan, Hutchins Hall, Ann Arbor, MI 48109-1215. TEL 313-763-2050. FAX 313-764-8309. bk.rev.; bibl.; index. (reprint service avail. from WSH) Indexed: C.L.I., L.R.I., Leg.Per.
Formerly: Michigan Yearbook of International Legal Studies (ISSN 8756-0615)

341.57 622 US
MINING LEGISLATION: AFRICA. base vols. (plus q. supplements). $3400 first year; thereafter $1300. Barrows Co., Inc., 116 E. 66th St., New York, NY 10021. TEL 212-772-1199. FAX 212-288-7242. TELEX 4971238 BARROWS.
Description: Contains the complete text, in English translation, of mining laws in African countries.

341.57 622
MINING LEGISLATION: CENTRAL AMERICA & CARIBBEAN. base vols. (plus q. supplements). $3400 first year; thereafter $1300. Barrows Co., Inc., 116 E. 66th St., New York, NY 10021. TEL 212-772-1199. FAX 212-288-7242. TELEX 4971238 BARROWS.
Description: Contains the complete texts, in English translation, of mining laws in Central American and Caribbean countries.

341.57 622 US
MINING LEGISLATION: EUROPE. base vols. (plus q. supplements). $3400 first year; thereafter $1300. Barrows Co., Inc., 116 E. 66th St., New York, NY 10021. TEL 212-772-1199. FAX 212-288-7242. TELEX 4971238 BARROWS.
Description: Contains the complete texts, in English translation, of the mining laws in European countries.

341.57 622 US
MINING LEGISLATION: FAR EAST. base vols. (plus q. supplements). $3400 first year; thereafter $1300. Barrows Co., Inc., 116 E. 66th St., New York, NY 10021. TEL 212-772-1199. FAX 212-288-7242. TELEX 4971238 BARROWS.
Description: Contains the complete texts, in English translation, of mining laws in Far Eastern countries.

341.57 622 US
MINING LEGISLATION: MIDDLE EAST. base vols. (plus q. supplements). $3400 first year; thereafter $1300. Barrows Co., Inc., 116 E. 66th St., New York, NY 10021. TEL 212-772-1199. FAX 212-288-7242. TELEX 4971238 BARROWS.
Description: Contains the complete texts, in English translation, of mining laws in Middle Eastern countries.

341.57 622 US
MINING LEGISLATION: SOUTH AMERICA. base vols. (plus q. supplements). $3400 first year; thereafter $1300. Barrows Co., Inc., 116 E. 66th St., New York, NY 10021. TEL 212-772-1199. FAX 212-288-7242. TELEX 4971238 BARROWS.
Description: Contains the complete texts, in English translation, of mining laws in South American countries.

MONTHLY IMPORT DETENTION LIST. see *PUBLIC HEALTH AND SAFETY*

341 NE ISSN 0165-070X
JX18 CODEN: NILRE5
NETHERLANDS INTERNATIONAL LAW REVIEW. 1953. q. $186. (T.M.C. Asser Institute) Kluwer Academic Publishers, Postbus 17, 3300 AA Dordrecht, Netherlands. (Dist. by: Kluwer Academic Publishers Group, P.O. Box 322, 3300 AH Dordrecht, Netherlands; N. America dist. addr.: Box 358, Accord Sta., Hingham, MA 02018-0358. TEL 617-871-6600) Ed. P. Morris. adv.; bk.rev.; index; circ. 800. (reprint service avail. from SWZ) Indexed: Foreign Leg.Per., Int.Lab.Doc., Key to Econ.Sci., Mar.Aff.Bibl.
Formerly: Nederlands Tijdschrift voor Internationaal Recht - Netherlands International Law Review (ISSN 0028-2138)

341 NE
NETHERLANDS YEARBOOK OF INTERNATIONAL LAW. (Text in English) 1970. a. (T.M.C. Asser Institute) Kluwer Academic Publishers, Postbus 17, 3300 AA Dordrecht, Netherlands. TEL 078-334267. FAX 078-334254. (Dist. by: Kluwer Academic Publishers Group, P.O. Box 322, 3300 AH Dordrecht, Netherlands; U.S. addr.: P.O. Box 358, Accord Sta., Hingham, MA 02018-0358) Ed. Ko Swan Sik. bk.rev.; bibl.; circ. 750. (reprint service avail. from SWZ) Indexed: Foreign Leg.Per., Mar.Aff.Bibl.

341 NE ISSN 0738-2812
NEW HAVEN STUDIES IN INTERNATIONAL LAW AND WORLD PUBLIC ORDER. (Text in English) 1987. irreg. price varies. (New Haven Press) Kluwer Academic Publishers, P.O. Box 17, 3300 AA Dordrecht, Netherlands. TEL 078-334267. FAX 078-334254. (Dist. by: Kluwer Academic Publishers, P.O. Box 322, 3300 AH Dordrecht, Netherlands; U.S. addr.: P.O. Box 358, Accord Sta., Hingham, MA 02018-0358)

341 US ISSN 1050-9453
K14
NEW YORK INTERNATIONAL LAW REVIEW; views of the law of the world from New York. 1988. s-a. $65 includes International Law Practicum (free to qualified personnel). New York State Bar Association, International Law and Practice Section, One Elk St., Albany, NY 12207-1096. TEL 518-463-3200. Ed. Monica McCabe.
Refereed Serial

341 US ISSN 0736-4075
K14
NEW YORK LAW SCHOOL JOURNAL OF INTERNATIONAL AND COMPARATIVE LAW. vol.12, 1991. 3/yr. $22 (foreign $27). New York Law School, 57 Worth St., New York, NY 10013-2960. TEL 212-431-2113. adv.; circ. 1,000. (reprint service avail. from RRI)

341 US ISSN 0028-7873
JX1
NEW YORK UNIVERSITY JOURNAL OF INTERNATIONAL LAW AND POLITICS. 1968. 4/yr. $22 (foreign $25). New York University, Law Publications, 110 W. Third St., New York, NY 10012. TEL 212-998-6520. FAX 212-995-4032. Ed.Bd. adv.; bk.rev.; abstr.; bibl.; index; circ. 1,200. (also avail. in microfilm from RRI; back issues avail.; reprint service avail. from RRI) Indexed: A.B.C.Pol.Sci., Abstr.Bk.Rev.Curr.Leg.Per., Amer.Bibl.Slavic & E.Eur.Stud, Amer.Hist.& Life, C.L.I., Foreign Leg.Per., Hist.Abstr., L.R.I., Leg.Cont., Leg.Per., P.A.I.S.
—BLDSC shelfmark: 6089.810000.
Description: Addresses current international topics that impinge upon the legal and non-legal communities.

341 US ISSN 0743-1759
K10
NORTH CAROLINA JOURNAL OF INTERNATIONAL LAW AND COMMERCIAL REGULATION. 1976. 3/yr. $20 (foreign $24). University of North Carolina at Chapel Hill, School of Law, Chapel Hill, NC 27599-3380. TEL 919-962-4402. FAX 914-962-1277. Ed. William P. Janvier. adv.; bk.rev.; index, cum.index; circ. 1,150. (back issues avail.) Indexed: Abstr.Bk.Rev.Curr.Leg.Per., C.L.I., L.R.I., Leg.Per.
●Also available online. Vendor(s): Wilsonline.
—BLDSC shelfmark: 6149.045000.

NORTHERN IRELAND NEWS SERVICE; NINS NewsBreak. see *POLITICAL SCIENCE*

341 US ISSN 0196-3228
K14
NORTHWESTERN JOURNAL OF INTERNATIONAL LAW & BUSINESS. Short title: J I L B. 1979. 3/yr. $25 (foreign $28). Northwestern University, School of Law, 357 E. Chicago Ave., Chicago, IL 60611. TEL 312-503-8467. circ. 500. (also avail. in microfilm from RRI,UMI; reprint service avail. from RRI) Indexed: C.L.I., Chic.Per.Ind., L.R.I., Leg.Per., P.A.I.S.
●Also available online. Vendor(s): WESTLAW.
—BLDSC shelfmark: 6152.025000.

OCEAN DEVELOPMENT AND INTERNATIONAL LAW; the journal of marine affairs. see *EARTH SCIENCES — Oceanography*

OESTERREICHISCHE ZEITSCHRIFT FUER OEFFENTLICHES RECHT UND VOELKERRECHT/AUSTRIAN JOURNAL OF PUBLIC AND INTERNATIONAL LAW. see *LAW*

OESTERREICHISCHE ZEITSCHRIFT FUER WIRTSCHAFTSRECHT. see *BUSINESS AND ECONOMICS — Public Finance, Taxation*

ORGANIZATION OF AMERICAN STATES. PERMANENT COUNCIL. DECISIONS TAKEN AT MEETINGS (CUMULATED EDITION). see *HISTORY — History Of North And South America*

341 664 UK
OVERSEAS FOOD LEGISLATION MANUAL. 1971. 3/yr. £480 for base vol.; updates £235. Leatherhead Food Research Association, Randalls Rd., Leatherhead, Surrey KT22 7RY, England. TEL 0372-376761. FAX 0372-386228. (looseleaf format; back issues avail.)

341 CY
PALESTINE YEARBOOK OF INTERNATIONAL LAW. (Text in English) 1984. a. $55. Al-Shaybani Society of International Law Ltd., P.O. Box 4247, Nicosia, Cyprus. Ed. Anis F. Kassim. bk.rev.; circ. 500. (back issues avail.)
Description: Dedicated to the rule of law, justice and equality in Palestine.

341.57 665.5 US
PETROLEUM CONCESSION HANDBOOK. base vols. (plus q. supplements). $4200 (renewal $1350). Barrows Co., Inc., 116 E. 66th St., New York, NY 10021. TEL 212-772-1199. FAX 212-288-7242. TELEX 4971238 BARROWS.
Description: Contains a summary of concession contracts worldwide.

L

LAW — INTERNATIONAL LAW

341.57 665.5   US
PETROLEUM LEGISLATION. base vols. (plus q. supplements). $4500 first year; thereafter $1200. Barrows Co., Inc., 116 E. 66th St., New York, NY 10021. TEL 212-772-1199. FAX 212-288-7242. TELEX 4971238 BARROWS.
Description: Presents an overview of oil and gas regulation, with a summary and analysis by country.

341   PH
PHILIPPINE YEARBOOK OF INTERNATIONAL LAW. vol.3, 1974. a. P.18($7) Philippine Society of International Law, University of the Philippines, College of Law, Diliman, Quezon City, Philippines. Ed. Esteban B. Bautista. bibl.; stat. **Indexed:** C.L.I., Ind.Phil.Per., Leg.Per., Mar.Aff.Bibl.

341   PL   ISSN 0554-498X
JX21
POLISH YEARBOOK OF INTERNATIONAL LAW/ANNUAIRE POLONAIS DE DROIT INTERNATIONAL. (Text in English and French) 1966. a. price varies. (Polska Akademia Nauk, Instytut Nauk Prawnych) Ossolineum, Publishing House of the Polish Academy of Sciences, Rynek 9, Wroclaw, Poland. TELEX 0712771 OSS PL. (Dist. by: Ars Polona-Ruch, Krakowskie Przedmiescie 7, Warsaw, Poland) Ed. Andrzey Wasilkowski.
—BLDSC shelfmark: 6543.835000.
Description: Publications on international law by Polish authors.

PRINCETON UNIVERSITY. CENTER OF INTERNATIONAL STUDIES. MONOGRAPH SERIES. see POLITICAL SCIENCE — International Relations

PRINCETON UNIVERSITY. CENTER OF INTERNATIONAL STUDIES. PROGRAM ON U S - JAPAN RELATIONS. MONOGRAPH SERIES. see POLITICAL SCIENCE — International Relations

PRIVATE INVESTMENTS ABROAD; problems and solutions in international business. see BUSINESS AND ECONOMICS — Investments

341   NE
PROBLEMS IN PRIVATE INTERNATIONAL LAW. 1977. irreg., vol.3, 1982. price varies. Elsevier Science Publishers B.V., Books Division, P.O. Box 211, 1000 AE Amsterdam, Netherlands. TEL 020-5803911. FAX 020-5803705. TELEX 18582 ESPA NL. (Subscr. in U.S. and Canada to: Elsevier Science Publishing Co., Inc., Box 882, Madison Sq. Sta., New York, NY 10159. TEL 212-989-5800)
Refereed Serial

PUBLIC INTERNATIONAL LAW; a current bibliography of articles. see LAW — Abstracting, Bibliographies, Statistics

341   GW   ISSN 0033-7250
K1
RABELS ZEITSCHRIFT FUER AUSLAENDISCHES UND INTERNATIONALES PRIVATRECHT. (Text in English and German) 1927. q. DM.214. (Max-Planck-Institut fuer Auslaendisches und Internationales Privatrecht) Verlag J.C.B. Mohr (Paul Siebeck), Wilhelmstr. 18, Postfach 2040, 7400 Tuebingen, Germany. TEL 07071-26064. FAX 07071-51104. TELEX 7262872-MOHR-D. Eds. U. Drobnig, H. Koetz, E-J. Mestmaecker. adv.; bk.rev.; charts; cum.index: vols.1-44, 1927-1980.
—BLDSC shelfmark: 7225.815000.
Description: Studies comparative law and foreign law, law of international transactions and the unification of law, including the law of the European Community.

382 341   GW   ISSN 0340-7926
K1
RECHT DER INTERNATIONALEN WIRTSCHAFT; Betriebs-Berater International. 1954. m. DM.547.20. Verlag Recht und Wirtschaft GmbH, Haeusserstr. 14, Postfach 105960, 6900 Heidelberg 1, Germany. TEL 06221-906-1. FAX 06221-906-259. Ed.Bd. adv.; bk.rev.; abstr.; tr.lit.; index; circ. 3,000. **Indexed:** Dairy Sci.Abstr., Key to Econ.Sci.
—BLDSC shelfmark: 7309.330000.
Formerly: Aussenwirtschaftsdienst des Betriebs-Berater (ISSN 0004-8232)

341   GW
RECHT IN OST UND WEST; Zeitschrift fuer Ostrecht und Rechtsvergleichung. 1957. m. DM.128. Berlin Verlag Arno Spitz GmbH, Pacelliallee 5, 1000 Berlin 33, Germany. TEL 030-8326232. FAX 030-8316249. Ed. H-D. Kittke. adv.; bk.rev.; circ. 1,000. **Indexed:** Hist.Abstr.
Description: Analyzes and comments on legal development and jurisdiction in Middle East and East European countries in the fields of public law, civil and criminal law, economic law and property regulations.

341.57   GW   ISSN 0343-9771
K18
RECHT UND SCHADEN; Monatliche Informationsschrift fuer Schadenversicherung und Schadenersatz. 1974. m. DM.163.80. Verlag Information Ambs GmbH, Obere Hauptstr. 13, Postfach 208, 7634 Kippenheim, Germany. TEL 07825-7114. adv.; bk.rev.; circ. 2,600.

340 341   GW
RECHTSSTAAT IN DER BEWAEHRUNG. 1975. irreg. price varies. C.F. Mueller Juristischer Verlag GmbH, Im Weiher 10, Postfach 102640, 6900 Heidelberg 1, Germany. TEL 06221-489281. FAX 06221-489279.

341   UK
REGISTER OF LAWS OF THE ARABIAN GULF. 1986. q. £580($1,230) Graham & Trotman Ltd., Sterling House, 66 Wilton Rd., London SW1V 1DE, England. Ed. W. Ballantyne.

346.066   US
▼**REGULATION OF FOREIGN BANKS;** United States and international. 1991. base vol. (plus a. suppl.). $125. Butterworth Legal Publishers (Salem) (Subsidiary of: Reed International PLC), 90 Stiles Rd., Salem, NH 03079. TEL 800-548-4001. FAX 603-898-9858. Eds. Micheal Gruson, Ralph Reisner.
Description: Provides a comprehensive and practical resource for banking law practitioners, managers of internationally orientated financial institutions, and bank regulators. Details analysis of the laws governing the regulation of foreign banks in the US and in other money center countries.

REVIEW OF EUROPEAN COMMUNITY AND INTERNATIONAL ENVIRONMENTAL LAW. see BUSINESS AND ECONOMICS — Management

341   AG   ISSN 0034-7892
REVISTA DE DERECHO INTERNACIONAL Y CIENCIAS DIPLOMATICAS.* 1949. s-a. Arg.$14($3.50) Universidad Nacional de Rosario, Instituto de Derecho Internacional, Cordoba 1814, 2000 Rosario, Argentina. Ed. Prof. Dr. Werner Goldschmidt. adv.; bk.rev.; abstr.; bibl.; circ. 1,750. **Indexed:** Geo.Abstr.

341   SP   ISSN 0034-9380
JX9
REVISTA ESPANOLA DE DERECHO INTERNACIONAL. 1948-1978; resumed 1985. s-a. 3300 ptas. (foreign 4950 ptas.). Consejo Superior de Investigaciones Cientificas (C.S.I.C.), Departamento de Derecho Internacional "Francisco de Vitoria", Vitruvio, 8, 28006 Madrid, Spain. bk.rev.; bibl.; index.
—BLDSC shelfmark: 7853.935000.
Description: Covers international law, both public and private, Spanish jurisprudence and law practice in Spain.

341   PE   ISSN 0035-0370
REVISTA PERUANA DE DERECHO INTERNACIONAL. 1941. s-a. $4 per. no. Sociedad Peruana de Derecho Internacional, Box 686, Lima, Peru. Ed.Bd. bk.rev.; index; circ. 600. **Indexed:** P.A.I.S.For.Lang.Ind.

341   BE   ISSN 0035-0788
JX3
REVUE BELGE DE DROIT INTERNATIONAL/BELGIAN REVIEW OF INTERNATIONAL LAW. (Text in Dutch, English and French) 1965. s-a. 3042 Fr. (Societe Belge de Droit International) Etablissements Emile Bruylant, 67 rue de la Regence, B-1000 Brussels, Belgium. TEL 02-512-9845. Dir. J.A. Salmon. bk.rev.; index. **Indexed:** Mar.Aff.Bibl., P.A.I.S., P.A.I.S.For.Lang.Ind.
—BLDSC shelfmark: 7891.700000.

341   FR   ISSN 0035-0958
K21
REVUE CRITIQUE DE DROIT INTERNATIONAL PRIVE. 1905. q. 590 F. (foreign 670 F.). Editions Sirey, 22 rue Soufflot, 75240 Paris Cedex 05, France. TEL 40-51-54-54. FAX 45-87-37-48. TELEX 206446F. (Subscr. to: Dalloz, 35 rue Tournefort, 75240 Paris Cedex 05, France. TEL 1-40-51-54-54) Dir. Henri Batiffol. bk.rev.; abstr.; index, cum.index every 25 yrs. (reprint service avail. from SCH)
—BLDSC shelfmark: 7897.700000.

REVUE DE DROIT FRANCAIS COMMERCIAL MARITIME ET FISCAL. see LAW

REVUE DE DROIT INTERNATIONAL DE SCIENCES DIPLOMATIQUES ET POLITIQUES. see POLITICAL SCIENCE

341   BE   ISSN 0035-1105
K21
REVUE DE DROIT INTERNATIONAL ET DE DROIT COMPARE. 1908. q. 3425 Fr. (Institut Belge de Droit Compare) Etablissements Emile Bruylant, 67 rue de la Regence, B-1000 Brussels, Belgium. TEL 02-512-9845. index.

341   FR   ISSN 1152-9172
REVUE DES AFFAIRES EUROPEENNES. q. 920 F. (foreign 940 F.). (Librairie Generale de Droit et de Jurisprudence) Editions Juridiques Associees, 26 rue Vercingertorix, 75014 Paris, France. TEL 1-43-35-01-67. FAX 43-20-07-42. TELEX EJA 203 918 F. Ed. Charles-Etienne Gudin. bibl.
—BLDSC shelfmark: 7882.928000.

341   FR   ISSN 0035-3094
REVUE GENERALE DE DROIT INTERNATIONAL PUBLIC; droit des gens, histoire diplomatique, droit penal, droit fiscal, droit administratif. 1894. q. 780 F. Editions A. Pedone, 13 rue Soufflot, 75005 Paris, France. Ed. Charles Rousseau. adv.; bk.rev.; bibl.; index; circ. 1,200. (reprint service avail. from SCH) **Indexed:** CERDIC, Int.Lab.Doc., Mar.Aff.Bibl.

341   GR   ISSN 0035-3256
REVUE HELLENIQUE DE DROIT INTERNATIONAL. (Text in English, French German and Italian) 1948. q. $35. Hellenic Institute of International and Foreign Law - Institut Hellenique de Droit International et Etranger, 73 Solonos St., Athens, Greece. TEL 30-1-3615646. FAX 30-1-3619777. bk.rev.; bibl.; index; circ. 2,000. (reprint service avail. from SCH)

341   FR   ISSN 0035-3337
K21
REVUE INTERNATIONALE DE DROIT COMPARE. 1949. q. 625 F. Societe de Legislation Comparee, 28 rue Saint Guillaume, 75007 Paris, France. TEL 45-44-44-67. FAX 19-1-45-49-41-65. adv.; bk.rev.; bibl.; cum.index: 1949-1973; 1974-1988; circ. 1,600. **Indexed:** A.B.C.Pol.Sci., Foreign Leg.Per.
Description: Sole review of comparative law published in France.

341   CN   ISSN 0828-9999
K21
REVUE QUEBECOIS DE DROIT INTERNATIONAL. 1984. a. Can.$45($35) (Societe Quebecoise de Droit International) Editions Themis, University of Montreal, Faculte de Droit, C.P. 6128, Succ. A, Montreal, Que. H3C 3J7. TEL 514-343-3446. cum.index (every 5 yrs.); circ. 500. (back issues avail.) **Indexed:** Ind.Can.L.P.L., Leg.Per.

REVUE ROUMAINE D'ETUDES INTERNATIONALES. see POLITICAL SCIENCE — International Relations

341   IT   ISSN 0035-6158
RIVISTA DI DIRITTO INTERNAZIONALE. (Text in English, French and Italian) 1906. q. L.90000 (foreign L.135000). Casa Editrice Dott. A. Giuffre, Via Busto Arsizio 40, 20151 Milan, Italy. TEL 02-38000905. FAX 02-38009582. Ed. Giorgio Gaja. adv.; bk.rev.; abstr.; bibl.; index; circ. 900. **Indexed:** Mar.Aff.Bibl.
—BLDSC shelfmark: 7984.900000.

341 331   IT   ISSN 0035-6166
RIVISTA DI DIRITTO INTERNAZIONALE E COMPARATO DEL LAVORO. (Text in several languages) 1961. 3/yr. L.16000. Casa Editrice Dott. Antonio Milani, Via Jappelli 5, Padua, Italy. bk.rev.; abstr.; bibl.; index.

LAW — INTERNATIONAL LAW

341   IT   ISSN 0035-6174
RIVISTA DI DIRITTO INTERNAZIONALE PRIVATO E PROCESSUALE. (Text in English, French, Italian and Spanish) 1965. q. L.130000 (foreign L.170000)(effective 1991). Casa Editrice Dott. Antonio Milani, Via Jappelli 5, 35121 Padua, Italy. TEL 049-656677. FAX 049-8752900. Ed. F. Pocar. bk.rev.; bibl.; cum.index 1965-1974.
—BLDSC shelfmark: 7984.920000.

340 382   IT   ISSN 0392-8748
RIVISTA DI DIRITTO VALUTARIO E DI ECONOMIA INTERNAZIONALE/REVIEW OF CURRENCY LAW AND INTERNATIONAL ECONOMICS; legislazione internazionale - ricerche - giurisprudenza - documenti. 1979. q. L.270000. Edizioni Giuridico Scientifiche s.r.l., Via Donizette 37, 20122 Milan, Italy. TEL 02-795700. FAX 76110744. TELEX 323319 EGS MIZ I. Ed. Ennio Alessio Mizzau. adv.; bk.rev.; circ. 3,500.
Formerly: Rivista di Diritto ed Economia Valutaria.

341   GW
SCHRIFTEN ZUM STAATS- UND VOELKERRECHT. 1975. irreg., vol.43, 1991. Verlag Peter Lang GmbH, Eschborner Landstr. 42-50, 6000 Frankfurt a.M 90, Germany. TEL 069-7807050. FAX 069-785893. Ed. Dieter Blumenwitz.
Formerly: Augsburger Schriften zum Staats- und Voelkerrecht.

SOCIAL JUSTICE; a journal of crime, conflict and world order. see CRIMINOLOGY AND LAW ENFORCEMENT

341   BL
SOCIEDADE BRASILEIRA DE DIREITO INTERNACIONAL. BOLETIM. 1945. 2/yr. Sociedade Brasileira de Direito Internacional, Palacio Itamaraty, Rio de Janeiro, Brazil.

341   SA   ISSN 0379-8895
JX21
SOUTH AFRICAN YEARBOOK OF INTERNATIONAL LAW/SUID-AFRIKAANSE JAARBOEK VIR VOLKEREG. 1975. a. $45. University of South Africa, VerLoren van Themaat Centre for Public Law Studies, P.O. Box 392, Pretoria 0001, South Africa. TEL 012-429-8468. FAX 012-429-3321. Eds. D.H. Van Wyk, M. Wiechers. adv.; bk.rev.; circ. 500.
Indexed: Ind.S.A.Per.
—BLDSC shelfmark: 8348.424000.

SOUTHWESTERN LEGAL FOUNDATION. ANNUAL REPORT. see LAW

SOVIET & EASTERN EUROPEAN REPORT; the monthly newsletter on developments in business, law & finance. see BUSINESS AND ECONOMICS — International Development And Assistance

341   US   ISSN 0731-5082
JX1
STANFORD JOURNAL OF INTERNATIONAL LAW. 1966. s-a. $22 (foreign $28). Stanford University, Stanford Law School, Stanford, CA 94305-8610. TEL 415-723-1375. adv.; bk.rev.; circ. 600. (reprint service avail. from RRI) Indexed: A.B.C.Pol.Sci., ASCA, C.L.I., Ind.Per.Art.Relat.Law, L.R.I., Leg.Cont., Leg.Per., Mar.Aff.Bibl., Mid.East: Abstr.& Ind., P.A.I.S., SSCI.
●Also available online. Vendor(s): WESTLAW.
—BLDSC shelfmark: 8432.080000.
Formerly: Stanford Journal of International Studies (ISSN 0081-4326)

STUDI PARLAMENTARI E DI POLITICA; costituzionale. see ENVIRONMENTAL STUDIES

341.7   NE
STUDIES IN TRANSNATIONAL ECONOMIC LAW. 1980. irreg., no.6, 1989. price varies. Kluwer Law and Taxation Publishers, P.O. Box 23, 7400 GA Deventer, Netherlands. TEL 31-5700-47261. FAX 31-5700-22244. TELEX 49295 KLUDV NL. (Dist. by: Libresso Distribution Centre, P.O. Box 23, 7400 GA Deventer, Netherlands. TEL 31-5700-33155; N. America dist. addr.: 6 Bigelow St., Cambridge, MA 02139. TEL 617-354-0140) Ed. Norbert Horn. bibl.

340   US   ISSN 1057-0551
STUDIES IN TRANSNATIONAL LEGAL POLICY. Variant title: American Society of International Law. Occasional Papers. irreg., latest no.22. price varies. American Society of International Law, 2223 Massachusetts Ave, N.W., Washington, DC 20008-2864. TEL 202-265-4313.
FAX 202-797-7133. Indexed: Deep Sea Res.& Oceanogr.Abstr.

341 332.6   US
SYMPOSIUM ON PRIVATE INVESTMENTS ABROAD. 1967. a. $90. Southwestern Legal Foundation, Box 830707, Richardson, TX 75083-0707.
TEL 214-690-2370. Ed. Carol Holgren.

341 382   US   ISSN 0093-0709
JX1
SYRACUSE JOURNAL OF INTERNATIONAL LAW & COMMERCE. 1972. a. $10 (foreign $13). (Syracuse University, College of Law) Joe Christensen, Inc. (Syracuse), E I White Hall, Ste. 0041, Syracuse, NY 13244-1030. TEL 315-443-2056. adv.; bk.rev.; circ. 500. (reprint service avail. from RRI) Indexed: ABI Inform, BPIA, C.L.I., L.R.I., Leg.Cont., Leg.Per., Mar.Aff.Bibl., Refug.Abstr., Sel.Water Res.Abstr.
●Also available online. Vendor(s): WESTLAW.
Description: Publishes articles prepared by scholars and practitioners in the field of public and private international law.

341   US   ISSN 0163-7479
JX1
TEXAS INTERNATIONAL LAW JOURNAL. 1964. 3/yr. $20 (foreign $23). University of Texas at Austin, School of Law Publications, 727 E. 26th St., Ste. 3.102A, Austin, TX 78705-3299.
TEL 512-471-1106. FAX 512-471-6988. Ed. Martin Lutz. adv.; bk.rev.; index, cum.index every 5 yrs.; circ. 850. (also avail. in microform from UMI; microfilm from WSH; back issues avail.; reprint service avail. from WSH) Indexed: Amer.Bibl.Slavic & E.Eur.Stud., C.L.I., L.R.I., Leg.Cont., Leg.Per., Mar.Aff.Bibl.
—BLDSC shelfmark: 8798.892000.
Formerly: Texas International Law Forum (ISSN 0040-4381)

341 338.91   US   ISSN 0895-5018
THIRD WORLD LEGAL STUDIES (YEAR). 1982. a. $20. International Third World Legal Studies Association, c/o Valparaiso University, School of Law, Valparaiso, IN 46383. TEL 219-465-7829.
FAX 219-465-7872. Ed. Samuel O. Gyandoh Jr. circ. 500. Indexed: C.L.I.
Description: Examines legal problems in the development of Third World countries.

THIRD WORLD WITHOUT SUPERPOWERS: COLLECTED DOCUMENTS OF THE GROUP OF 77. see POLITICAL SCIENCE — International Relations

THIRD WORLD WITHOUT SUPERPOWERS: COLLECTED DOCUMENTS OF THE NON-ALIGNED COUNTRIES. see POLITICAL SCIENCE — International Relations

TOLLEY'S TAXATION IN THE REPUBLIC OF IRELAND (YEAR). see BUSINESS AND ECONOMICS — Public Finance, Taxation

TRADEMARK LAW HANDBOOK. see LAW

341   US
▼**TURNAROUNDS & WORKOUTS - EUROPE.** 1991. q. $195. Beard Group, Inc., Box 9867, Washington, DC 20016. TEL 301-951-6400.
FAX 301-951-3621. Ed. Maxim Kniazkov. adv.
Description: Covers current developments in bankruptcy and insolvency in Europe.

U M A STUDENTS LAW JOURNAL. (University of Malawi) see LAW

U N I D I R NEWSLETTER/LETTRE DE L'U N I D I R. (United Nations Institute for Disarmament Research) see POLITICAL SCIENCE — International Relations

341 382   US
U S INTERNATIONAL TRADE LAWS. 1988. irreg., latest 1989 ed. $48. B N A Books, 1231 25th St., N.W., Washington, DC 20037. TEL 908-225-1900.
FAX 908-417-0482. (Subscr. to: BNA Books Distribution Center, 300 Raritan Center Parkway, Box 7816, Edison, NJ 08818-7816. TEL 800-372-1033) Ed. Alan M. Stowell.

341 382   US
▼**U S S R & CENTRAL AND EASTERN EUROPEAN LEGAL MATERIALS.** (In 3 vols.) 1990. irreg. $725. (Columbia University, Parker School of Foreign and Comparative Law) Transnational Juris Publications, Inc., Box 7282, Ardsley-on-Hudson, NY 10503. TEL 914-693-0089. FAX 914-693-8776. Ed. Vratislav Pechota. (looseleaf format)
Description: Consists of English translations of Central and Eastern European business and investment laws.

341   US
UNIFORM LAW REVIEW. 1973. s-a. $25. (Unidroit - International Institute for the Unification of Private Law) Oceana Publications, Inc., 75 Main St., Dobbs Ferry, NY 10522. TEL 914-693-1320.
FAX 914-693-0402. circ. 150.
Formed by the merger of: Uniform Law Cases & Unidroit Yearbook.

341   UN   ISSN 0082-8289
JX1261
UNITED NATIONS. INTERNATIONAL LAW COMMISSION YEARBOOK. French edition: Nations Unies. Commission de Droit International. Annuaire (ISSN 0497-9877); Russian edition: Organizatsiya Ob'edinennykh Natsii. Komissiya Mezhdunarodnogo Prava. Ezhegodnik (ISSN 0251-771X); Spanish edition: Naciones Unidas. Comision de Derecho Internacional. Anuario (ISSN 0497-9885) (Issued in 2 vols.) (Text in English) 1949. a. price varies. United Nations Publications, Room DC2-853, New York, NY 10017. TEL 212-963-8302.
FAX 212-963-3489. (And: Distribution and Sales Section, Palais des Nations, CH-1211 Geneva 10, Switzerland) (also avail. in microfiche; reprint service avail. from KTO)

341.2   UN   ISSN 0255-724X
UNITED NATIONS. MULTILATERAL TREATIES DEPOSITED WITH THE SECRETARY-GENERAL. French edition: Nations Unies. Traites Mulitnationaux Deposes aupres de Secretaire General (ISSN 0255-7258) (Text in English and French) 1967. irreg. $70. United Nations Publications, Room DC2-853, New York, NY 10017. TEL 212-963-8302.
FAX 212-963-3489. (And: Distribution and Sales Section, Palais des Nations, CH-1211 Geneva 10, Switzerland) (also avail. in microfiche)
Formerly (until 1980): United Nations. Multilateral Treaties in Respect of Which the Secretary-General Performs Depository Functions (ISSN 0082-8319)

341.2   UN   ISSN 0379-8267
JX170
UNITED NATIONS. TREATY SERIES. (Text in English and French) 1947. irreg. United Nations Publications, Rm. DC2-853, New York, NY 10017.
TEL 212-963-8302. FAX 212-963-3489.

UNITED NATIONS. TREATY SERIES. CUMULATIVE INDEX. see LAW — Abstracting, Bibliographies, Statistics

UNITED NATIONS ASSOCIATION IN CANADA. QUARTERLY BULLETIN. see POLITICAL SCIENCE — International Relations

341.7   UN
UNITED NATIONS COMMISSION ON INTERNATIONAL TRADE LAW. REPORT ON THE WORK OF ITS SESSION. (Subseries of: United Nations. General Assembly. Official Records. Supplement no.17) 1968. a. United Nations Commission on International Trade Law (UNCITRAL), Vienna International Centre, P.O. Box 500, A-1400 Vienna, Austria. TEL 2631-4060. (Dist. by: Distribution and Sales Section, Palais des Nations, CH-1211 Geneva 10, Switzerland; and United Nations Publications, Room DC2-853, New York, N.Y. 10017, U.S.A.) Sec. Gerold Herrmann.

341 382   UN   ISSN 0251-4265
K1004.5
UNITED NATIONS COMMISSION ON INTERNATIONAL TRADE LAW. YEARBOOK. (Editions in English, French, Russian and Spanish) irreg. (approx. a.), vol.18, 1987. price varies. United Nations Commission on International Trade Law (UNCITRAL), Vienna International Centre, P.O. Box 500, A-1400 Vienna, Austria. (Dist. by: Distribution and Sales Section, Palais des Nations, CH-1211 Geneva 10, Switzerland; and United Nations Publications, Rm. DC2-853, New York, N.Y. 10017) Sec. Gerold Herrmann. bibl.

LAW — INTERNATIONAL LAW

341   UN   ISSN 0082-8297
JX1977.A1
UNITED NATIONS JURIDICAL YEARBOOK. French edition: Nations Unies Annuaire Juridique (ISSN 0251-7558); Russian edition: Organizatziya Ob'edinennykh Natsii. Yuridicheskiy Ezhegodnik (ISSN 0251-7574); Spanish edition: Naciones Unidas Anuario Juridico (ISSN 0251-7566) 1962. a. price varies. United Nations Publications, Room DC2-853, New York, NY 10017. TEL 212-963-8302. FAX 212-963-3489. (Or: Distribution and Sales Section, CH-1211 Geneva 10, Switzerland) (also avail. in microfiche)
—BLDSC shelfmark: 9097.010000.

341   US   ISSN 0886-6686
JX1977.A3155
UNITED NATIONS RESOLUTIONS. SERIES 1. RESOLUTIONS ADOPTED BY THE GENERAL ASSEMBLY. 1972. irreg., vol.24, 1988. price varies. (United Nations, General Assembly) Oceana Publications, Inc., 75 Main St., Dobbs Ferry, NY 10522. TEL 914-693-1320. FAX 914-693-0402. Ed. Dusan Djonovich. cum.index; circ. 375. (back issues avail.)
Description: Presents resolutions of the United Nations for the General Assembly.

341   US   ISSN 0898-2929
JX1977
UNITED NATIONS RESOLUTIONS. SERIES 2. RESOLUTIONS AND DECISIONS OF THE SECURITY COUNCIL. (Text in English, French) 1988. irreg., vol.9, 1990. $65 per vol. (United Nations, General Assembly) Oceana Publications, Inc., 75 Main St., Dobbs Ferry, NY 10522. TEL 914-693-1320. FAX 914-693-0402. Ed. Dusan J. Djonovich. circ. 400.
Description: Contains resolutions and decisions of the United Nations Security Council, with a topical index, clarifying documents, and country-by-country voting records.

UNITED NATIONS REVIEW. see POLITICAL SCIENCE — International Relations

327 341.2   US   ISSN 0083-0186
JX235.9
U.S. DEPARTMENT OF STATE. TREATIES AND OTHER INTERNATIONAL ACTS SERIES. (Texts of individual treaties collected and issued in bound form as United States Treaties and Other International Agreements: ISSN 0083-3487) 1946. irreg., vol.32, pt.5, 1979-80. $9 price varies. U.S. Department of State, Office of the Legal Adviser, 2201 C St., N.W., Washington, DC 20520. TEL 202-647-2044. (Dist. by: Supt. of Documents, Washington, DC 20402-9371)

341.2   US   ISSN 0083-0194
U.S. DEPARTMENT OF STATE. TREATIES IN FORCE. 1956. a. price varies. U.S. Department of State, Office of the Legal Adviser, 2201 C St., N.W., Washington, DC 20520. TEL 202-647-2044. (Dist. by: Supt. of Documents, Washington, DC 20402)

327 341.2   US   ISSN 0083-3487
JX231
UNITED STATES TREATIES AND OTHER INTERNATIONAL AGREEMENTS. 1950. a. price varies. U.S. Department of State, Office of the Legal Adviser, 2201 C St., N.W., Washington, DC 20520. TEL 202-647-2044. (Dist. by: Supt. of Documents, Washington, DC 20402)

341 327   GW   ISSN 0341-3241
UNIVERSITAET HAMBURG. INSTITUT FUER INTERNATIONALE ANGELEGENHEITEN. WERKHEFTE. 1965. irreg., vol.38, 1982. price varies. Nomos Verlagsgesellschaft mbH und Co. KG, Waldseestr. 3-5, Postfach 610, 7570 Baden Baden, Germany. (Co-sponsor: Deutscher Verein fuer Internationales Seerecht)
Formerly: Forschungstelle fuer Voelkerrecht und Auslaendisches Oeffentliches Recht. Werkhefte (ISSN 0072-9493)

341.57   US   ISSN 0891-9895
K10
UNIVERSITY OF PENNSYLVANIA JOURNAL OF INTERNATIONAL BUSINESS LAW. (Continues numbering of Journal of Comparative Business and Capital Market Law) (Text in English) 1978. q. $27.50 (foreign $37.50). University of Pennsylvania, Law School, 3400 Chestnut St., Philadelphia, PA 19104-6204. TEL 215-898-6869. FAX 215-898-6619. Ed.Bd. adv.; bk.rev.; index; circ. 500. (also avail. in microform from UMI; reprint service avail. from UMI, WSH) **Indexed:** BPIA, C.L.I., L.R.I., Leg.Per.
—BLDSC shelfmark: 9116.375000.
Supersedes (as of vol.9, 1987): Journal of Comparative Business and Capital Market Law; (until 1983): Journal of Comparative Corporate Law and Securities Regulation (ISSN 0165-0165)
Description: Covers all areas of international business law, including securities, taxation, corporate and tort issues.

UTRECHT STUDIES IN AIR AND SPACE LAW. see LAW

341   US   ISSN 0090-2594
JX1
VANDERBILT JOURNAL OF TRANSNATIONAL LAW. 1967. 5/yr. $20 (foreign $21). Vanderbilt University School of Law, Nashville, TN 37240. TEL 615-322-2284. Ed. John C. Herman. adv.; bk.rev.; circ. 1,100. (also avail. in microfilm from UMI,WSH; reprint service avail. from WSH) **Indexed:** Abstr.Bk.Rev.Curr.Leg.Per., Amer.Bibl.Slavic & E.Eur.Stud., C.L.I., L.R.I., Leg.Cont., Leg.Per., Mar.Aff.Bibl., P.A.I.S., Refug.Abstr.
●Also available online. Vendor(s): WESTLAW.
—BLDSC shelfmark: 9144.300000.
Formerly: Vanderbilt International (ISSN 0042-2525)

341   US   ISSN 0042-6571
JX1
VIRGINIA JOURNAL OF INTERNATIONAL LAW. 1960. q. $28 (foreign $33). (Virginia Journal of International Law Association) University of Virginia, School of Law, Charlottesville, VA 22901. TEL 804-924-3415. adv.; bk.rev.; stat.; index, cum.index; circ. 1,000. (also avail. in microfilm from RRI,WSH; back issues avail.; reprint service avail. from RRI) **Indexed:** A.B.C.Pol.Sci., Abstr.Bk.Rev.Curr.Leg.Per., Amer.Bibl.Slavic & E.Eur.Stud., C.L.I., Deep Sea Res.& Oceanogr.Abstr., L.R.I., Leg.Cont., Leg.Per., Mar.Aff.Bibl., Mid.East: Abstr.& Ind., Refug.Abstr., Sel.Water Res.Abstr., So.Pac.Per.Ind., SSCI.
●Also available online. Vendor(s): WESTLAW.
—BLDSC shelfmark: 9238.950000.

341.57 382   US   ISSN 0276-8275
WASHINGTON TARIFF & TRADE LETTER; a weekly report for business executives on U.S. international trade policies, legislation, opportunities and restrictions. 1981. 50/yr. $447 (foreign $477). Gilston Communications Group, Box 467, Washington, DC 20044. TEL 301-570-4544. FAX 301-570-4545. Ed. Samuel M. Gilston. (back issues avail.)

WIENER RECHTSWISSENSCHAFTLICHE STUDIEN. see LAW

341   US   ISSN 0743-7951
K27
WISCONSIN INTERNATIONAL LAW JOURNAL. 1983. 2/yr. $18. University of Wisconsin-Madison, Law School, 975 Bascom Mall, Madison, WI 53706. TEL 608-262-2240. Ed. Ward W. McCarragher. circ. 1,000. (back issues avail.) **Indexed:** C.L.I., Leg.Per.
—BLDSC shelfmark: 9325.735000.
Description: Forum for analysis and discussion of international law.

341 327   US
WORLD CITIZEN NEWS. 1975. m. $12. (World Service Authority) N W O Publications, 113 Church St., Burlington, VT 05401. TEL 802-864-4656. FAX 802-864-6878. Ed. Kevin Kelley. circ. 5,000. (back issues avail.)
Description: Covers world citizenship news, world government news, world law news, human rights news, and world service authority news.

341   SZ   ISSN 1011-4548
K21
WORLD COMPETITION; law and economics review. (Text in English) 4/yr. 250 Fr.($195) Werner Publishing Co. Ltd., P.O. Box 93, 1211 Geneva 11, Switzerland. TEL 022-283422. FAX 022-214592. **Indexed:** P.A.I.S.
—BLDSC shelfmark: 9353.255500.
Formerly: Swiss Review of International Competition Law (ISSN 0255-8246)

341   UN
WORLD DIRECTORY OF TEACHING AND RESEARCH INSTITUTIONS IN INTERNATIONAL LAW. irreg., 2nd ed., 1990. $22. Unesco, 7-9 Place de Fontenoy, 75700 Paris, France.

341   US
WORLD JURIST. 1964. bi-m. $75. World Jurist Association, 1000 Connecticut Ave., N.W., Ste. 202, Washington, DC 20036. TEL 202-466-5428. bibl.; circ. 6,000.

341.57 665.5   US
WORLD L N G - GAS CONTRACTS. base vols. (plus q. supplements). $1750 first year; thereafter $1100. Barrows Co., Inc., 116 E. 66th St., New York, NY 10021. TEL 212-772-1199. FAX 212-288-7242. TELEX 4971238 BARROWS.
Description: Contains text, in English translations, of contracts for production, liquefaction, and transport of liquefied natural gas (LNG) in all countries.

241.57 665.5   US
WORLD NATIONAL OIL COMPANY STATUTES. base vols. (plus q. supplements). $1500 first year; thereafter $700. Barrows Co., Inc., 116 E. 66th St., New York, NY 10021. TEL 212-772-1199. FAX 212-288-7242. TELEX 4971238 BARROWS.
Description: Contains texts, in English translation, of statutes, by-laws, and related statutes of national oil companies for over 85 countries.

WORLDWIDE FINANCIAL REGULATIONS. see BUSINESS AND ECONOMICS — International Commerce

341   US   ISSN 0889-7743
JX1
YALE JOURNAL OF INTERNATIONAL LAW. s-a. $25 to institutions. Yale University, School of Law, 401A Yale Sta., New Haven, CT 06520. TEL 203-432-4884. FAX 203-432-2592. circ. 450. (also avail. in microform from WSH; reprint service avail. from WSH)
Description: Discusses current topics relating to international law.

341.57   NE
YEARBOOK COMMERCIAL ARBITRATION. (Text in English) 1976. a. price varies. (International Council for Commercial Arbitration) Kluwer Law and Taxation Publishers, P.O. Box 23, 7400 GA Deventer, Netherlands. TEL 31-5700-47261. FAX 31-5700-22244. TELEX 49295 KLUDV NL. (Dist. by: Libresso Distribution Centre, P.O. Box 23, 7400 GA Deventer, Netherlands. TEL 31-5700-33155; N. America dist. addr.: 6 Bigelow St., Cambridge, MA 02139. TEL 617-354-0140) (Co-sponsor: T.M.C. Asser Institute for International and European Law) Ed. A.J. van den Berg. (back issues avail.)

341   UK   ISSN 0266-7223
YEARBOOK OF EUROPEAN LAW. 1981. a. £55. Oxford University Press, Walton St., Oxford OX2 6DP, England. TEL 0865-56767. Ed. F. Jacobs.

341   GW   ISSN 0044-2348
K30
ZEITSCHRIFT FUER AUSLAENDISCHES OEFFENTLICHES RECHT UND VOELKERRECHT. (Text in English, French or German; summaries in English) 1929. q. DM.274. (Max-Planck-Institut fuer Voelkerrecht) W. Kohlhammer GmbH, Hessbruehlstr. 69, Postfach 800430, 7000 Stuttgart 80, Germany. TEL 0711-7863-1. adv.; bk.rev.; abstr.; bibl.; index; circ. 1,000. **Indexed:** A.B.C.Pol.Sci, Mar.Aff.Bibl, P.A.I.S.For.Lang.Ind.
—BLDSC shelfmark: 9453.270000.

LAW — JUDICIAL SYSTEMS 2731

341.57 GW ISSN 0340-8329
K30
ZEITSCHRIFT FUER LUFT- UND WELTRAUMRECHT. 1952. q. DM.168. (Universitaet zu Koeln, Institut fuer Luft- und Weltraumrecht) Carl Heymanns Verlag KG, Luxemburgerstr. 449, 5000 Cologne 41, Germany. TEL 0221-46010-0. FAX 0221-4601069. Ed. Prof. Dr. Alex Meyer. adv.; bk.rev.; bibl.; tr.lit.; circ. 600. **Indexed:** Int.Aerosp.Abstr.
 Formerly: Zeitschrift fuer Luftrecht und Weltraumrechtsfragen (ISSN 0044-3034)

341 GW ISSN 0044-3638
K30
ZEITSCHRIFT FUER VERGLEICHENDE RECHTSWISSENSCHAFT; Archiv fuer Internationales Wirtschaftsrecht. 1878. q. DM.178. Verlag Recht und Wirtschaft GmbH, Haeusserstr. 14, Postfach 105960, 6900 Heidelberg 1, Germany. TEL 06221-906-1. adv.; bk.rev.; circ. 400. **Indexed:** A.I.C.P.

LAW — Judicial Systems

347 UK
CAMBRIDGE STUDIES IN ENGLISH LEGAL HISTORY. irreg. price varies. Cambridge University Press, Edinburgh Bldg., Shaftesbury Rd., Cambridge CB2 2RU, England. TEL 0223-312393. FAX 0223-315052. TELEX 851817256. Ed. J.H. Baker.

347 BL ISSN 0530-0657
COLECAO DE ESTUDOS JURIDICOS. 1956. irreg., latest 1982. Fundacao Casa de Rui Barbosa, Rua Sao Clemente 134, Botafogo 22260, Rio de Janeiro, RJ, Brazil. FAX 5371114. Dir. Agnello Uchoa Bittencourt.

347 SP ISSN 0069-5122
COLECCION JURIDICA. 1954. irreg., no.101, 1990. price varies. (Universidad de Navarra, Facultad de Derecho) Ediciones Universidad de Navarra, S.A., Apdo. 396, 31080 Pamplona, Spain. TEL 94 825 6850. index vols.1-6.

347 SP
COLECCION JURISPRUDENCIA Y TEXTOS LEGALES. 1973. irreg., no.6, 1984. price varies. (Universidad de Navarra, Facultad de Derecho) Ediciones Universidad de Navarra, S.A., Apdo. 396, 31080 Pamplona, Spain. TEL 94 825 6850.

347 AT
COMMONWEALTH STATUTES ANNOTATIONS. a. Law Book Co. Ltd., 44-50 Waterloo Rd., North Ryde, N.S.W. 2113, Australia. TEL 02-887-0177. FAX 02-888-9706. TELEX ASBOOK 27995.
 Formerly: Commonwealth Statutes Cumulative Supplement.

347 US
THE CONNECTICUT LAW REPORTER; reporting Connecticut Superior Court decisions. vol.5, no.11, 1991. w. $275. Connecticut Law Book Company, Box 575, Guilford, CT 06437. TEL 203-458-8000.

347 US
THE CONNECTICUT LAW REPORTER, BOUND SERIES. s-a. $95. Connecticut Law Book Company, Box 575, Guilford, CT 06437. TEL 203-458-8000.

347 US
COURT EXCELLENCE. 1987. q. $50. Council for Court Excellence, 1025 Vermont Ave. N.W., Ste.510, Washington, DC 20005. TEL 202-783-7736. FAX 202-783-7697. Ed. Samuel F. Harahan. circ. 2,000. (back issues avail.)
 Description: News of civic public interest group working to improve the administration of justice.

347 AT
COURT FORMS, PRECEDENTS & PLEADINGS - N S W. 3 base vols. (plus q. updates). Aus.$475. Butterworths Pty. Ltd., 271-273 Lane Cove Rd., P.O. Box 345, North Ryde, N.S.W. 2113, Australia. TEL 02-335-4444. FAX 02-335-4655.

347 AT
COURT FORMS, PRECEDENTS & PLEADINGS - QUEENSLAND. 3 base vols. (plus q. updates). Aus.$335. Butterworths Pty. Ltd., 271-273 Lane Cove Rd., P.O. Box 345, North Ryde, N.S.W. 2113, Australia. TEL 02-335-4444. FAX 02-335-4655.

347 US
▼COURT MANAGEMENT & ADMINISTRATIVE REPORT; newsletter for professionals in justice systems management. 1990. 11/yr. $135. G P Subscription Publications (Subsidiary of: Greenwood Publishing Group Inc.), 88 Post Rd., W., Box 5007, Westport, CT 06881-5007. TEL 203-226-3571. FAX 203-685-0285. Ed. Clifford Kirsch. (reprint service avail.)

347 US
COURT MANAGER. 1973. q. $25. National Association for Court Management, National Center for State Courts, 300 Newport Ave., Williamsburg, VA 23187. TEL 804-253-2000. FAX 804-253-0449. Ed. Anne Kelly. adv.; illus.; circ. 1,800.
 Formerly: Court Crier (ISSN 0098-8871)

347 US
COURT NEWS.* 1927. bi-m. free. Judicial Council of California, Administrative Office of the California Courts, 303 Second St., San Francisco, CA 94107-1366. FAX 415-396-9349. Dir. William E. Davis. circ. 3,600.
 Formerly (until 1990): A O C Newsletter.

347 US ISSN 0011-0647
K3
COURT REVIEW. 1961. q. $25 to non-members. (American Judges Association) National Center for State Courts, 300 Newport Ave., Williamsburg, VA 23187-8798. TEL 804-253-2000. FAX 804-220-0449. Ed. Martin Kravarik. adv.; bk.rev.; illus.; circ. 2,800. **Indexed:** Crim.Just.Abstr.
 Formerly: Municipal Court Review.

347 US
COURTROOM CURRENTS. m. 83 Calvert St., Harrison, NY 10528-3212. TEL 914-835-3110. FAX 914-835-5098. Ed. J. Jerome Olitt. circ. 1,500.

347 US
COURT'S CHARGE REPORTER. a. $175. Butterworth Legal Publishers (Salem) (Subsidiary of: Reed International PLC), 90 Stiles Rd., Salem, NH 03079. TEL 800-548-4001. FAX 603-898-9858. Ed. Will G. Barber. (looseleaf format)
 Description: Contains condensed transcripts of actual charges from Texas civil jury cases.

347 US
DELAWARE COURT REPORTER. m. Delaware Law Monthly, Box 262, Wilmington, DE 19899. TEL 215-563-2700.

347 US
ELECTED AND APPOINTED BLACK JUDGES IN THE UNITED STATES. biennial. $10. Joint Center for Political Studies, Inc., 1301 Pennsylvania Ave., N.W., Ste. 400, Washington, DC 20004. TEL 202-626-3500. (Co-sponsor: Judicial Council of the National Bar Association)

FEDERAL AND STATE JUDICIAL CLERKSHIP DIRECTORY. see *BUSINESS AND ECONOMICS — Trade And Industrial Directories*

347 CN ISSN 0227-0390
FEDERAL COURT OF APPEAL DECISIONS. 1981. m. Can.$145. Western Legal Publications, 301-1 Alexander St., Vancouver, BC V6A 1B2, Canada. TEL 604-687-5671. FAX 604-687-2796. index, cum.index. (looseleaf format)
 ●Also available online.
 Description: Digests of all current Federal Court of Appeal decisions.

347 CN
FEDERAL COURT OF CANADA SERVICE. q. Can.$350. Butterworths Canada Ltd., 75 Clegg Rd., Markham, Ont. L6G 1A1, Canada. TEL 416-479-2665. FAX 416-479-2826. Ed. Roger T. Hughes. (looseleaf format)
 Description: Coverage of the Federal Court Act, includes courtroom procedure and selected sections of the Income Tax Act.

347 AT
FEDERAL COURT PRACTICE. 1989. 4/yr. Aus.$195. Law Book Co. Ltd., 44-50 Waterloo Rd., North Ryde, N.S.W. 2113, Australia. TEL 02-887-0177. FAX 02-888-9706. TELEX ASBOOK 27995. Ed. Geoffrey Flick.
 Description: Comprehensive guide to practice in the Federal Court of Australia.

330.9 US ISSN 0734-9513
KF845.A2
FEDERAL COURT PROCUREMENT DECISIONS. m. $347. Federal Publications, Inc., 1120 20th St., N.W., Ste. 500 S., Washington, DC 20036. TEL 202-377-7000. FAX 202-223-0755.
 Description: Reports on government contracts.

347 AT
FEDERAL COURT REPORTER (SYDNEY). 1982. 20/yr. Aus.$295. Law Press of Australia, G.P.O. Box 3793, Sydney, N.S.W. 2001, Australia. TEL 02-360-7788. FAX 02-360-7838. Ed. Richard Ackland. bk.rev. (back issues avail.)

347 AT ISSN 0813-7803
FEDERAL COURT REPORTS (NORTH RYDE). 1984. irreg. Law Book Co. Ltd., 44-50 Waterloo Rd., North Ryde, N.S.W. 2113, Australia. TEL 02-887-0177. FAX 02-888-9706. TELEX ASBOOK 27995. Ed. V. Kline. cum.index. (back issues avail.)
 Description: Contains full text of all reportable decisions of the Full Court of single judges.

347 US
FEDERAL LOCAL COURT RULES. 1964. bi-m. $261. Callaghan & Co., 155 Pfingsten Rd., Deerfield, IL 60015. TEL 800-323-8067.
 Description: Compilation of U.S. federal district court and court of appeals local rules pertaining to civil procedures in all U.S. jurisdictions, for the legal practitioner.

347 US
GEORGIA STATE RULES OF COURT. 1986. base vol. (plus suppl.). $50. Butterworth Legal Publishers (Salem) (Subsidiary of: Reed International PLC), 90 Stiles Rd., Salem, NH 03079. TEL 800-548-4001. FAX 603-898-9858. Ed.Bd. (looseleaf format)
 Description: Tracks all the latest changes in the uniform rules for the probate, juvenile and magistrate, superior and state courts as well as the Rules of the Supreme Court and the Court of Appeals of Georgia.

347 US
GILBERT LAW SUMMARIES. FEDERAL COURTS. 1987. irreg. $15.95. Law Distributors (Subsidiary of: H B J Legal & Professional Publications Inc.), 14415 S. Main St., Gardena, CA 90248. TEL 800-421-1893. FAX 213-324-6381.

347 UK ISSN 0308-4388
KD310
HALSBURY'S LAWS OF ENGLAND ANNUAL ABRIDGMENT. Short title: Laws of England Annual Abridgment. 1974. a. $218. Butterworth & Co. (Publishers) Ltd. (Subsidiary of: Reed International PLC), 88 Kingsway, London WC2B 6AB, England. TEL 71-405-6900. FAX 71-405-1332. TELEX 95678. (US addr.: Butterworth Legal Publishers, 90 Stiles Rd., Salem, NH 03079. TEL 800-548-4001)

347 UK ISSN 0307-9821
HALSBURY'S LAWS OF ENGLAND MONTHLY REVIEW. 1973. m. £35 avail. only with subscr. to Halsbury's Laws of England Annual. Butterworth & Co. (Publishers) Ltd. (Subsidiary of: Reed International PLC), 88 Kingsway, London WC2B 6AB, England. TEL 71-405-6900. FAX 71-405-1332. TELEX 95678. (US addr.: Butterworth Legal Publishers, 90 Stiles Rd., Salem, NH 03079. TEL 800-548-4001) Ed. Kenneth Mugford. circ. 10,000.

347 297 TS
AL-HAQQ - SHARI'AH WA QANUN. (Text in Arabic) 1982. a. exchange basis. Jam'iyat al-Huquqiyyin - Jurisprudents' Society, P.O. Box 2233, Sharjah, United Arab Emirates. TEL 371166. circ. 1,000.
 Description: Focuses on Islamic jurisprudence and legal research, court rulings, and society activities.

347 HK
HONG KONG. LAW REFORM COMMISSION. REPORT. (Editions in Chinese, English) irreg., latest no.17. price varies. Government Publication Centre, G.P.O. Bldg., Ground Fl., Connaught Place, Hong Kong, Hong Kong. TEL 842-8801. (Subscr. to: Director of Information Services, Information Services Dept., 1 Battery Path, G-F, Central, Hong Kong) Ed.Bd.

LAW — JUDICIAL SYSTEMS

347   US
IOWA LIMITATIONS MANUAL. 1989. base vol. (plus suppl.). $50. Butterworth Legal Publishers (Salem) (Subsidiary of: Reed International PLC), 90 Stiles Rd., Salem, NH 03079. TEL 800-548-4001. FAX 603-898-9858. Ed.Bd. (looseleaf format)
Description: Reference to Iowa statutes and rules of court that set time limitations within which certain actions must or should be taken.

347   US   ISSN 0047-2972
K10
JUDGES' JOURNAL. vol.10, 1971. q. $25 to non-members. American Bar Association, Judicial Administration Division, 750 N. Lake Shore Dr., Chicago, IL 60611. TEL 312-988-6077. Ed. Frederic G. Melcher. bk.rev.; illus.; index; circ. 8,600. *Indexed:* C.L.I., Crim.Just.Abstr., L.R.I., Leg.Per.
—BLDSC shelfmark: 5073.829400.
Formerly: Trial Judges Journal.
Description: Created to help judges and lawyers improve the administration of justice. Includes articles on successful court innovations and major jurisprudential issues.

340   UY
JUDICATURA. 1975. m. Avda. Libertador Brig. Gral. Lavalleja 1464, Montevideo, Uruguay. Ed.Bd. circ. 5,000.

347 300   US   ISSN 0022-5800
K10
JUDICATURE. 1917. bi-m. $48. American Judicature Society, 25 E. Washington, Ste. 1600, Chicago, IL 60602-1805. adv.; bk.rev.; charts; illus.; index, cum.index every 20 yrs.; circ. 20,000. (also avail. in microform from UMI; reprint service avail. from ISI,RRI,UMI) *Indexed:* C.L.I., CJPI, Crim.Just.Abstr., Curr.Cont., L.R.I., Law Ofc.Info.Svc., Leg.Cont., Leg.Per., P.A.I.S., SSCI.
●Also available online. Vendor(s): WESTLAW.
—BLDSC shelfmark: 5073.830000.
Formerly: American Judicature Society Journal.
Description: Discusses all aspects of the administration of justice and its improvement.
Refereed Serial

347.91   US   ISSN 0193-7367
KF8779.A15
JUDICIAL CONDUCT REPORTER. 1979. q. $12. American Judicature Society, Center for Judicial Conduct Organizations, 25 E. Washington, Ste. 1600, Chicago, IL 60602. TEL 312-558-6900. FAX 312-558-9175. Ed. Anne Lawton. adv.; bk.rev.; index; circ. 6,000.
●Also available online. Vendor(s): WESTLAW.
Description: Developments in judicial discipline and disability law.

347   IT   ISSN 0076-5163
MATERIALI PER UNA STORIA DELLA CULTURA GIURIDICA. 1979. 2/yr. L.100000. (Universita degli Studi di Genova, Istituto di Filosofia del Diritto) Societa Editrice Il Mulino, Strada Maggiore, 37, 40125 Bologna, Italy. TEL 051-256011. FAX 051-256034. Ed.Bd. adv.; index; circ. 800. (back issues avail.)

347   MF
MAURITIUS. JUDICIAL DEPARTMENT. ANNUAL REPORT. (Text in English) a. Government Printing Office, Elizabeth II Ave., Port Louis, Mauritius.

347   US
MODERN COURTS. 1984. q. free. Fund for Modern Courts, Inc., 36 W. 44th St., Ste. 310, New York, NY 10036-8181. TEL 212-575-1577. FAX 212-869-1133. Ed. Robert M. Fabricant. bk.rev.; circ. 10,000. (back issues avail.)
Description: Covers judicial issues, court reform, merit selection of judges, court merger, and jury service.

347   CN   ISSN 0828-4989
K13
MONDE JURIDIQUE. 1984. 6/yr. $34 (effective Jan. 1991). Agence Quebec Nouvelles Inc., 381 Richelieu Bvd., Saint-Basile-le-Grand, Que. J3N 1M4, Canada. TEL 514-658-5983. Ed. Andre Gagnon. adv.; circ. 10,000. *Indexed:* Ind.Can.L.P.L.
Description: Information about lawyers, their professional life, profiles and trends in French Canada.

347   IT
MONDO GIUDIZIARIO. 1946. w. L.43000. (Associazione del Mondo Giudiziario) Edizioni del Mondo Giudiziario, Viale Angelico 90, 00195 Rome, Italy. adv.

347   AT   ISSN 0705-3886
NASH ON MAGISTRATES' COURTS - VICTORIA. 1975. 5/yr. Aus.$325. Law Book Co. Ltd., 44-50 Waterloo Rd., N. Ryde, N.S.W. 2113, Australia. TEL 02-887-0177. FAX 02-888-9706. TELEX ASBOOK 27995. Ed. G. Nash. (looseleaf format)
Description: Covers court practice, magistrates courts, juvenile courts and coroners jurisdiction in Victoria.

347   US
NATIONAL CENTER FOR STATE COURTS. PUBLICATIONS. irreg. National Center for State Courts, 300 Newport Ave., Williamsburg, VA 23187-8798. TEL 804-253-2000. FAX 804-220-0449.

347   US   ISSN 0195-5241
KF8736.A15
NATIONAL CENTER FOR STATE COURTS. REPORT. 1974. m. $12 (includes Master Calendar). National Center for State Courts, 300 Newport Ave., Williamsburg, VA 23187-8798. TEL 804-253-2000. FAX 804-220-0449. circ. 300. (looseleaf format; back issues avail.)

347 380 020   US   ISSN 1054-9471
KF8700.A19
▼**NATIONAL DIRECTORY OF COURTS OF LAW.** 1991. biennial. $90 (effective Mar.1991). Information Resources Press, 1110 N. Glebe Rd., Ste. 550, Arlington, VA 22201. TEL 703-558-8270. FAX 703-558-4979. Ed. Mark A. Yannone. (back issues avail.)
Description: Encompasses every indentifiable US, federal, state, county, local, territorial, tribal and specialized agency officially designated or functioning as a court of law. Contains 20,130 entries.

347   US
NEW JERSEY. ADMINISTRATIVE OFFICE OF THE COURTS. ANNUAL REPORT OF THE NEW JERSEY JUDICIARY. 1949. a. free. Administrative Office of the Courts, RJH Justice Complex CN-037, Trenton, NJ 08625. TEL 609-292-9580. illus.; circ. 2,000.
Formerly: New Jersey. Administrative Office of the Courts. Annual Report of the Administrative Director of the Courts.
Description: Annual compendium of statistical and programmatic information on the operation of the courts.

347   US   ISSN 0748-3430
NEW YORK JURY VERDICT REPORTER. 1981. w. $300. 577 Main St., Box 310, Islip, NY 11751. TEL 516-581-1930. FAX 516-581-8937. Ed. Lynda A. Moran. adv.; circ. 1,000. (looseleaf format; back issues avail.)
Description: Covers both city and state verdicts.

347   FR   ISSN 0338-1552
NOUVEAU POUVOIR JUDICIAIRE. 1975. m. 75 F. Union Syndicale des Magistrats, 33 rue du Four, 75006 Paris, France. adv.; illus.
Supersedes: Pouvoir Judiciaire.

347   US
OREGON UNIFORM TRIAL COURT RULES AND SUPPLEMENTARY LOCAL RULES. 1985. base vol. (plus suppl.). $50. Butterworth Legal Publishers (Salem) (Subsidiary of: Reed International PLC), 90 Stiles Rd., Salem, NH 03079. TEL 800-548-4001. FAX 603-898-9858. Ed.Bd. (looseleaf format)

347   AT   ISSN 0727-8063
QUEENSLAND MAGISTRATES COURTS. 1982. 5/yr. Aus.$250. Law Book Co. Ltd., 44-50 Waterloo Rd., N. Ryde, N.S.W. 2113, Australia. TEL 02-887-0177. FAX 02-888-9706. TELEX ASBOOK 27995. Eds. M.G. Morley, G. Marth. (looseleaf format; back issues avail.)
Description: Covers magistrate, land and environment courts, industrial tribunals, and court practice. Includes summary jurisdiction.

347   AT   ISSN 0726-3759
QUEENSLAND REPORTS. 1908. m. Aus.$225. Incorporated Council of Law Reporting, c/o Mrs. J.T. Mengel, Sec., P.O. Box 39, N. Quay, Qld. 4002, Australia. TEL 07-227-4409. FAX 07-229-3782. adv.; circ. 1,700.
Description: Reports of the Supreme Court of Queensland; includes Full and Appeal Courts.

347   AT
QUEENSLAND SUPREME COURT PRACTICE. 2 base vols. (plus q. update). $445. Butterworths Pty. Ltd., 271-273 Lane Cove Rd., P.O. Box 345, North Ryde, N.S.W. 2113, Australia. TEL 02-335-4444. FAX 02-335-4655. (looseleaf format)

347   CL
REVISTA DE ESTUDIOS HISTORICO JURIDICO. 1976. a. $38. (Universidad Catolica de Valparaiso, Escuela de Derecho) Ediciones Universitarias de Valparaiso, Casilla 1415, Valparaiso, Chile. TEL 252900. FAX 032-212746. TELEX 230389 UCVAL CL. Dir. Alejandro Guzman B. bk.rev.; circ. 300. *Indexed:* Hist.Abstr.

347 340   RW   ISSN 1010-8238
REVUE JURIDIQUE DU RWANDA. (Text in French, Kinyarwanda) 1977. q. $50. Ministere de la Justice, Faculte de Droit, B.P. 1690, Kigali, Rwanda. Ed. James Bucyana. bk.rev. (back issues avail.)

347   ZR
REVUE JURIDIQUE DU ZAIRE. 1924. 3/yr. (Societe d'Etudes Juridiques du Zaire) Universite du Lubumbashi, B.P. 510, Lubumbashi, Zaire.
Supersedes: Revue Juridique du Congo.

347   CN   ISSN 0556-7963
K21
REVUE JURIDIQUE THEMIS. Running title: Themis. (Text in English and French) 1953. a. Can.$32. Editions Themis, C.P. 6128, Succursale A, Montreal, Que. H3C 3J7, Canada. TEL 514-739-9945. adv.; bk.rev.; bibl.; index; circ. 1,700. (also avail. in microfilm from WSH; reprint service avail. from WSH) *Indexed:* C.L.I., Ind.Can.L.P.L., L.R.I., Leg.Cont., Leg.Per., Mar.Aff.Bibl., Pt.de Rep. (1982-).
—BLDSC shelfmark: 7926.260000.
Supersedes: Revue Juridique Themis de l'Universite de Montreal.

347   RM
REVUE ROUMAINE DE SCIENCES JURIDIQUES. 1956. 2/yr. 80 lei($45) (Academia Romana) Editura Academiei Romane, Calea Victoriei 125, 79717 Bucharest, Rumania. (Dist. by: Rompresfilatelia, Calea Grivitei 64-66, P.O. Box 12-201, 78104 Bucharest, Rumania) *Indexed:* P.A.I.S.For.Lang.Ind.
Formerly: Revue Roumaine des Sciences Sociales. Serie de Sciences Juridiques (ISSN 0035-4023)

347   US
RHODE ISLAND APPELLATE PRACTICE. 1985. base vol. (plus suppl.). $50. Butterworth Legal Publishers (Salem) (Subsidiary of: Reed International PLC), 90 Stiles Rd., Salem, NH 03079. TEL 800-548-4001. FAX 603-898-9858. Ed. Joseph R. Weisberger. (looseleaf format)
Description: Rules and statutes affecting appellate practice and procedure with commentary.

347   CN
RULES OF COURT AND RELATED ENACTMENTS. base vol. (plus irreg. suppl.). Can.$58. Ministry of Attorney General, Parliament Bldgs., Victoria, B.C. V8V 1X4, Canada. (Subscr. to: Crown Publications, 546 Yates St., Victoria, B.C. V8W 1K8, Canada. TEL 604-386-4636) (looseleaf format; back issues avail.)
Description: Consists of the procedural rules by which the affairs of the BC Supreme and County Courts and the Court of Appeal are conducted.

347   UK   ISSN 0264-312X
SHAW'S DIRECTORY OF COURTS IN THE UNITED KINGDOM. 1970. a. £20. Shaw & Sons Ltd., Shaway House, 21 Bourne Park, Bourne Road, Crayford, Kent DA1 4BZ, England. TEL 0322-550676. FAX 0322-550553. Ed. Gordon Morris. adv.; bk.rev.; circ. 3,000.
Former titles (until 1983): Shaw's Directory of Courts in England and Wales (ISSN 0085-6061); Shaw's Directory of Magistrates' Courts and Crown Courts; Directory of Magistrates Courts.

LAW — JUDICIAL SYSTEMS   2733

347 US ISSN 0730-6229
KF308.A535
SHEPARD'S PROFESSIONAL AND JUDICIAL CONDUCT CITATIONS. 1980. base vol. (plus q. suppl.). $100. Shepard's - McGraw-Hill, Inc., Box 35300, Colorado Springs, CO 80935-3530. TEL 800-525-2474.

347 NZ
SIM & CAIN: PRACTICE & PROCEDURE OF THE HIGH COURT OF APPEAL OF NEW ZEALAND. (12th ed.) base vol. (plus updates 5/yr.). NZ.$296. Butterworths of New Zealand Ltd., 203-207 Victoria St., P.O. Box 472, Wellington, New Zealand. TEL 04-385-1479. FAX 04-385-1598. Ed. Stuart Coghill. (looseleaf format)
Description: Full text of statutes and rules plus commentary on law relating to the practice of the High Court and Court of Appeal.

347 ISSN 0199-5030
SUPREME COURT BULLETIN. 1979. w. during U.S. Supreme Court session. $29. Armstrong Graphics, Box 628, Windham, NH 03087. TEL 603-889-7231. adv.; index; circ. 4,000. (back issues avail.)

347 II ISSN 0039-5951
SUPREME COURT CASES. (Text in English) 1969. fortn. $97. Eastern Book Company, 34 Lalbagh, Lucknow 226 001, India. TEL 43171. FAX 0091-522-242061. TELEX 535 436 FAST IN. Ed. Surendra Malik. adv.; bk.rev.; index; circ. 6,000. (back issues avail.)

SUPREME COURT CASES (CRIMINAL). see *LAW — Criminal Law*

347 II ISSN 0253-6552
SUPREME COURT CASES (LABOUR AND SERVICES). (Text in English) 1973. m. $41. Eastern Book Company, 34 Lalbagh, Lucknow 226 001, India. TEL 43171. FAX 0091-522-242061. TELEX 535 436 FAST IN. Ed. Surendra Malik. adv.; bk.rev.; index; circ. 2,200. (back issues avail.)

347 US ISSN 0736-9921
K23
SUPREME COURT ECONOMIC REVIEW. 1983. a. $23.95. (Emory University, Law and Economics Center) Macmillan Publishing Company, 866 Third Ave., New York, NY 10022. Ed. Peter H. Aranson.

347 US ISSN 0362-5249
KF8741.A15
SUPREME COURT HISTORICAL SOCIETY. YEARBOOK.* 1976. a. $15 hardcover; softcover $10. Supreme Court Historical Society, 111 Second St., N.E., Washington, DC 20002. Ed. William Swindler. illus.; circ. 2,850. **Indexed:** C.L.I., Hist.Abstr., L.R.I., Leg.Per. Key Title: Yearbook - Supreme Court Historical Society.
—BLDSC shelfmark: 9403.850000.

349 PK ISSN 0585-9794
SUPREME COURT MONTHLY REVIEW. (Text in English) 1968. m. Rs.500. P.L.D. Publishers, Nabha Rd., Lahore 1, Pakistan. Ed. Malik Muhammad Saeed. (reprint service avail. from UMI)

340 II ISSN 0039-596X
LAW
SUPREME COURT NOTES. (Text in English) 1959. fortn. Rs.60. Supreme Court, New Delhi, D-8 Nizamuddin East, New Delhi 13, India. Ed. Saroja Gopalakrishnan. circ. 1,200. (back issues avail.)

347 CN
SUPREME COURT OF CANADA DECISIONS.. 1978. m. Can.$100. Western Legal Publications, 301-1 Alexander St., Vancouver, B.C. V6A 1B2, Canada. TEL 604-687-5671. FAX 604-687-2796. index. (looseleaf format)
●Also available online.
Formerly: Supreme Court of Canada Decisions. Civil and Criminal (ISSN 0709-5600)

347 CN
SUPREME COURT OF CANADA REPORTS SERVICE. 5/yr. Can.$240. Butterworths Canada Ltd., 75 Clegg Rd., Markham, Ont. L6G 1A1, Canada. TEL 416-479-2665. FAX 416-479-2826. (looseleaf format)
Description: Indexes and digests recent judgments of the Canadian Supreme Court.

347 AT
SUPREME COURT PROCEDURE N S W. 2 base vols. (plus m. update). $465. Butterworths Pty. Ltd., 271-273 Lane Cove Rd., P.O. Box 345, North Ryde, N.S.W. 2113, Australia. TEL 02-335-4444. FAX 02-335-4655. (looseleaf format)

347 US ISSN 0081-9557
KF4546
SUPREME COURT REVIEW. 1960. a. University of Chicago Press, Journals Division, 5720 S. Woodlawn Ave., Chicago, IL 60637. TEL 312-702-7600. FAX 312-702-0694. TELEX 25-4603. (Subscr. to: Box 37005, Chicago, IL 60637) Ed.Bd. (also avail. in microform from UMI; reprint service avail. from UMI,ISI) **Indexed:** A.B.C.Pol.Sci., ASCA, C.L.I., L.R.I., Leg.Per., SSCI.
—BLDSC shelfmark: 8547.650000.
Description: Essays by scholars with a wide range of expertise, presenting informed analyses of court opinions and examining important legal issues that have come under the court's consideration.
Refereed Serial

347 US
SURVEY OF JUDICIAL SALARIES. 1976. s-a. $12. National Center for State Courts, 300 Newport Ave., Williamsburg, VA 23187-8798. TEL 804-253-2000. FAX 804-220-0449. Ed. Dixie Knoebel. stat.; circ. 2,500.
Former titles: Survey of Judicial Salaries in State Court Systems (ISSN 0196-7304); Quarterly Survey of Judicial Salaries in State Court Systems (ISSN 0098-9061)

347 SW ISSN 0039-6591
SVENSK JURISTTIDNING. 1916. 10/yr. SEK 100. Norstedts Tryckeri AB, Box 2080, 103 12 Stockholm, Sweden. Ed. Hans Danelius. adv.; bk.rev.; index, cum.index every 10 yrs.; circ. 6,000.
—BLDSC shelfmark: 8560.200000.

347 US
TEXAS RULES OF APPELLATE PROCEDURE. 1986. base vol. (plus suppl.). $40. Butterworth Legal Publishers (Salem) (Subsidiary of: Reed International PLC), 90 Stiles Rd., Salem, NH 03079. TEL 800-548-4001. FAX 603-898-9858. Ed.Bd. (looseleaf format)
Description: Compilation of the complete text of the new rules governing appellate procedure in civil cases and posttrial, appellate and review procedures in criminal cases, promulgated by the Texas Supreme Court and the Texas Court of Criminal Appeals.

347 US ISSN 0040-6120
KF8700.A16
THIRD BRANCH; a bulletin of the federal courts. 1968. m. free. United States Courts, Administrative Office, 811 Vermont Ave., N.W., Washington, DC 20544. TEL 202-633-6040. FAX 202-786-6018. Eds. Martha Kendall, David Sellers. illus.; index; circ. 12,000. **Indexed:** C.L.I., Leg.Per.

347 US
THIS WEEK IN COURT; summaries of Mississippi Supreme Court opinions. 1977. w. $30. Mississippi College Law Review, 151 E. Griffith, Jackson, MS 39201. TEL 601-944-1950. Ed. Denise Schreiber. circ. 225. (tabloid format)

347.91 US ISSN 0041-2538
KF8911.A3
TRIAL. 1965. m. $48. Association of Trial Lawyers of America, 1050 31st St., N.W., Washington, DC 20007. TEL 202-965-3500. Ed. Elizabeth Yeary. adv.; bk.rev.; abstr.; circ. 70,000. (also avail. in microfilm from UMI) **Indexed:** Abstr.Bk.Rev.Curr.Leg.Per., ASCA, C.L.I., Chic.Per.Ind., CJPI, Crim.Just.Abstr., Curr.Cont., Hlth.Ind., HRIS, L.R.I., Law Ofc.Info.Svc., Leg.Info.Manage.Ind., Leg.Per., Risk Abstr., Soc.Sci.Ind., SSCI.
—BLDSC shelfmark: 9050.050000.
Formerly: National Legal Magazine (ISSN 0027-9625)

347 US ISSN 0743-412X
KFF538.A1
TRIAL ADVOCATE QUARTERLY. 1981. q. $30. (Florida Defense Lawyers Association) Fred B. Rothman & Co., 10368 W. Centennial Rd., Littleton, CO 80127. TEL 303-979-5657. FAX 303-978-1457. Ed. Michael L. Richmond. (back issues avail.) **Indexed:** C.L.I.

347 US
TRIAL COMMUNICATION SKILLS. 1986. base vol. (plus a. suppl.). $95. Shepard's - McGraw-Hill, Inc., Box 35300, Colorado Springs, CO 80935-3530. TEL 800-525-2474.
Description: Covers the art of persuasion and effective communication and its specific applications in the courtroom.

347.91 US ISSN 0160-7308
KF8911.A3
TRIAL DIPLOMACY JOURNAL. 1978. bi-m. $96 (foreign $112). John Wiley & Sons, Inc., 605 Third Ave., New York, NY 10158-0012. TEL 212-850-6000. FAX 212-850-6088. Eds. J. Romano, R. Romano. adv.; bk.rev.; illus.; circ. 3,000. (reprint service avail. from UMI) **Indexed:** C.L.I., CJPI, L.R.I., Leg.Per.
—BLDSC shelfmark: 9050.055000.
Description: Articles and interviews targeted to trial attorneys.

347 US
TRIAL JUDGES NEWS. 1981. q. $13. American Bar Association, National Conference of State Trial Judges, 750 N. Lake Shore Dr., Chicago, IL 60611. TEL 312-988-5691. FAX 312-988-6281. Ed. Kenneth L. Gillis. circ. 2,250.
Description: Reports activities and programs of the conference.

347.91 US ISSN 0041-2546
K24.R46
TRIAL LAWYER'S GUIDE. 1957. q. $100. Callaghan & Co., 155 Pfingsten Rd., Deerfield, IL 60015. TEL 800-323-1336. Ed. John J. Kennelly. bk.rev.; index. (also avail. in microfiche from WSH; microfilm from WSH) **Indexed:** C.L.I., L.R.I., Leg.Per.

347 US
TRIAL LAWYERS MARKETING BRIEFS. m. Trial Lawyers Marketing Association, One Boston Pl., Boston, MA 02108-4401. TEL 617-742-0696. Ed. Fran Senner-Hurley.

347.91 US ISSN 0041-2554
K24
TRIAL LAWYERS QUARTERLY. 1959. q. $25. New York State Trial Lawyers Association, 132 Nassau St., Ste. 200, New York, NY 10038. TEL 212-349-5890. Ed.Bd. adv.; bk.rev.; circ. 5,000. (reprint service avail. from. UMI) **Indexed:** C.L.I., L.R.I., Leg.Per.
—BLDSC shelfmark: 9050.070000.

347.91 US
▼**TRIALS DIGEST.** 1991. m. $495. Amicus Information Services, 1300 Clay St., Ste. 600, Oakland, CA 94612. TEL 415-956-5643. FAX 415-268-4013. adv.; circ. 10,000.
Description: Gives California civil trial results.

347 US
U S SUPREME COURT BULLETIN. 1936. w. $580. Commerce Clearing House, Inc., 4025 W. Peterson Ave., Chicago, IL 60646. TEL 312-583-8500. Ed. D. Newquist. (looseleaf format)

347 US ISSN 0097-7977
KF9670
U.S. ADMINISTRATIVE OFFICE OF THE UNITED STATES COURTS. REPORT ON APPLICATIONS FOR ORDERS AUTHORIZING OR APPROVING THE INTERCEPTION OF WIRE OR ORAL COMMUNICATIONS. 1972. a. since 1977. free. Administrative Office of the United States Courts, Washington, DC 20544. TEL 202-633-6036. Key Title: Report on Applications for Orders Authorizing or Approving the Interception of Wire or Oral Communications.

347 US ISSN 0094-2553
KF105.1
UNITED STATES JUDICIAL REPORTER. m. $35. Box 541, Harrisburg, PA 17108.

347 PN
UNIVERSIDAD DE PANAMA. CENTRO DE INVESTIGACION JURIDICA. ANUARIO. a. price varies. Universidad de Panama, Centro de Investigacion Juridica, Estafeta Universitaria, Panama, Panama.

347 PN
UNIVERSIDAD DE PANAMA. CENTRO DE INVESTIGACION JURIDICA. BOLETIN DE INFORMACION JURIDICA. s-a. $1. Universidad de Panama, Centro de Investigacion Juridica, Estafeta Universitaria, Panama, Panama. Dir. Aura G. de Villalaz.

LAW — Legal Aid

347   PN
UNIVERSIDAD DE PANAMA. CENTRO DE INVESTIGACION JURIDICA. LEGISLACION PANAMENA. INDICES CRONOLOGICOS Y ANALITICO DE LEYES (0 DECRETOS EJECUTIVOS). 1958. quinquennial. price varies. Universidad de Panama, Centro de Investigacion Juridica, Estafeta Universitaria, Panama, Panama. Dir. Aura G. de Villalaz.

347   PR
LAW
UNIVERSIDAD DE PUERTO RICO. REVISTA JURIDICA. (Text in English, Spanish) 1932. 4/yr. $34. Universidad de Puerto Rico, Escuela de Derecho, Apdo. 23349, Estacion U.P.R., Rio Piedras, PR 00931-3349. TEL 809-764-0000. Ed. Teresa Medina. adv.; bk.rev.; index. cum.index: vols.1-30, vols.31-48; circ. 1,000. (also avail. in microform from WSH; back issues avail.) **Indexed:** C.L.I., L.R.I., Leg.Per.
Formerly: Universidad de Puerto Rico. Escuela de Derecho. Revista Juridica (ISSN 0041-851X)
Description: Puerto Rican juridical problems and solutions.

347   US   ISSN 0187-0203
K3
UNIVERSIDAD NACIONAL AUTONOMA DE MEXICO. INSTITUTO DE INVESTIGACIONES JURIDICAS. CUADERNOS. 1987. 3/yr. Mex.$18000($42) Universidad Nacional Autonoma de Mexico, Instituto de Investigaciones Juridicas, Ciudad Universitaria, 04510 Mexico, D.F., Mexico. FAX 5481501. Ed. Jorge Madrazo. charts; stat.; circ. 2,000.
Description: Comprehensive coverage of judicial systems.

347   CK   ISSN 0041-9060
AS82
UNIVERSITAS; ciencias juridicas y socio-economicas. 1951. s-a. Col.$80($12) Pontificia Universidad Javeriana, Facultad de Ciencias Juridicas y Socioeconomicas, Departamento de Publicaciones, Carrera 7, No. 40-62, Bogota DE, Colombia. Ed. Gabriel Giraldo, S.J. adv.; abstr.; index; circ. 1,500. **Indexed:** Int.Lab.Doc.
—BLDSC shelfmark: 9101.341000.

347   US
VERMONT COURT RULES ANNOTATED. 1981. 2 base vols. (plus a. suppl.). $85. Butterworth Legal Publishers (Salem) (Subsidiary of: Reed International PLC), 90 Stiles Rd., Salem, NH 03079. TEL 800-548-4001. FAX 603-898-9858. Ed.Bd. (looseleaf format)
Description: Contains the rules of procedure for all civil and criminal trial and appellate courts in Vermont.

347   AT
VICTORIA COURT PRACTICE. (In 2 vols.) 1987. q. C C H Australia Ltd., P.O. Box 230, North Ryde, N.S.W. 2113, Australia. TEL 02-888-2555. FAX 02-888-7324.

347   FR   ISSN 0042-5567
VIE JUDICIAIRE; informations judiciaires et juridiques. 1901. w. 200 F. Vie Judiciaire, 41 rue de Richelieu, 75001 Paris, France. TEL 42-96-23-54. FAX 42-96-91-39. Ed. Roland Ferrari. adv.; bk.rev.; bibl.; illus.; circ. 17,000.
Description: News for professionals on law history, judicial cases, professions, schedules of events, summaries of legal information and reflections of law and justice.

WANT'S FEDERAL - STATE COURT DIRECTORY (YEAR). see *BUSINESS AND ECONOMICS — Trade And Industrial Directories*

347   II
YEARLY SUPREME COURT DIGEST. (Supplement to: Shree Krishan Agarwal's "Twenty-One Years Supreme Court Digest, 1950-1970") (Text in English) 1966. a. Rs.200. The Law Book Co. (P) Ltd., Sardar Patel Marg, P.B. 1-004, Allahabad 211 001, India. TEL 602415. Ed. Rakesh Bagga. circ. 2,000. (back issues avail.)
Description: Contains digest of all the judgements of the Supreme Court of India.

LAW — Legal Aid

362.5 368.4   US
ATTORNEY'S GUIDE TO SOCIAL SECURITY DISABILITY CLAIMS. 1986. base vol. (plus a. suppl.). $95. Shepard's - McGraw-Hill, Inc., Box 35300, Colorado Springs, CO 80935-3530. TEL 800-525-2474.
Description: Discusses the Disability Reform Act of 1984, its ramifications and the mental impairment regulations. Provides a listing of impairments now in effect.

362.5   AU
AUSTRIA. ENTSCHEIDUNGEN DES OBERSTEN GERICHTSHOFES IN SOZIALRECHTSSACHEN (SSV-NF).. 1961. a. price varies. Manzsche Verlags- und Universitaetsbuchhandlung, Kohlmarkt 16, A-1014 Vienna, Austria. TEL 0222-531610. FAX 0222-5316181. Eds. Wilhelm Resch, Peter Bauer. circ. 2,000.
Formerly (until 1988): Austria. Oberlandesgericht Wien im Leistungsstreitverfahren Zweiter Instanz der Sozialversicherung (SSV). Entscheidungen.
Description: Collects decisions on legal aspects of social welfare.

362.5   US
▼**B N A'S AMERICANS WITH DISABILITIES ACT MANUAL.** 1992. m. $355. The Bureau of National Affairs, Inc., 1231 25th St., N.W., Washington, DC 20037. TEL 202-452-4200. FAX 202-822-8092. TELEX 285656 BANI WSH. (Subscr. to: 9435 Key West Ave., Rockville, MD 20850. TEL 800-372-1033) Ed. Susan Sala. (looseleaf format; back issues avail.)
Description: Reference service providing guidance on the provisions of the Americans with Disabilities Act which concern employers, employment and public accomodations.

362.5 658.3   US   ISSN 0897-7992
K2
BENEFITS LAW JOURNAL. 1988. 4/yr. $168 (foreign $218)(effective 1992). Executive Enterprises Publications Co., Inc., 22 W. 21st St., New York, NY 10010-6904. TEL 212-645-7880. FAX 212-645-117- Ed. Jane G. Bensahel. (also avail. in microform from WSH; reprint service avail. from UMI,WSH) **Indexed:** Account.Ind. (1988-).
Description: Provides coverage of welfare benefits field, including new types, delivery methods and legal requirements.

347   AT
HEARSAY. 1980. q. free. Legal Aid Commission of Western Australia, 105 St. George's Terrace, Perth, W.A. 6000, Australia. FAX 09-321-8785. Ed. J.R. Armitage. circ. 3,000.
Description: Legal aid newsletter for the community.

362.5   US   ISSN 0730-7624
KF3675.Z95
HIGHLIGHTS OF STATE UNEMPLOYMENT COMPENSATIONS LAWS. 1981. a. $15. National Foundation for Unemployment Compensation & Workers' Compensation, c/o U B A Inc., 820 First St., N.E., Ste. 400, Washington, DC 20002-4205. TEL 202-484-3346. circ. 3,000.

LAW AND LEGAL INFORMATION DIRECTORY. see *LAW*

347.01   CN   ISSN 0381-2049
LAW
LEGAL AID NEW BRUNSWICK ANNUAL REPORT/AIDE JURIDIQUE NOUVEAU BRUNSWICK RAPPORT ANNUEL. (Text in English and French) 1972. a. Law Society of New Brunswick, 1133 Regent St., Suite 305, Fredericton, N.B. E3B 3Z2, Canada. TEL 506-458-8540. FAX 506-458-1076. circ. 1,500.
Description: Reports on the activities of New Brunswick's legal aid program.

362.5 350   US
LEGAL ISSUES, GOVERNMENT PROGRAMS & THE ELDERLY (FLORIDA); a handbook for the advocates. 1987. base vol. (plus suppl.). $50. (Center for Governmental Responsibility, Gainesville) Butterworth Legal Publishers (Salem) (Subsidiary of: Reed International PLC), 90 Stiles Rd., Salem, NH 03079. TEL 800-548-4001. FAX 603-898-9858. (looseleaf format)
Description: Designed to help Florida attorneys, social workers and other professionals who act as advocates, conduct research and prepare for litigation, recognize problems for which legal assistance should be sought, recognize services or benefits available under various government programs and know where to obtain further assistance and information.

347   US
OHIO LEGAL RIGHTS SERVICE. ANNUAL REPORT. 1976. a. $1. Ohio Legal Rights Service, Atlas Bldg., 8 E. Long St., Columbus, OH 43215. TEL 614-466-7264. Ed. David E. Merry. circ. 300.

347   US   ISSN 0737-7630
KF298
PASSPORT TO LEGAL UNDERSTANDING; the newsletter on public education programs and materials. 1983. s-a. free. American Bar Association, Commission on Public Understanding About the Law, 541 N. Fairbanks, Chicago, IL 60611. FAX 312-988-5032. Ed. Cynthia Canary. adv.; bk.rev.; circ. 10,000. (back issues avail.)

PHILADELPHIA BAR ASSOCIATION. LEGAL DIRECTORY. see *LAW*

362.5 614.7 350   US
PUBLIC INTEREST BRIEFS. 1971. 2/yr. membership. Center for Law in the Public Interest, 5750 Wilshire Blvd., Ste. 561, Los Angeles, CA 90036-3697. TEL 213-470-3000. FAX 213-474-7083. Ed. Jack Nicholl. bk.rev.; circ. 2,000.
Description: Provides free legal services on a broad range of important issues: civil rights, free speech, affordable housing, the homeless, fair elections, environmental protection, land use, corporate and governmental accountability.

LAW — Maritime Law

COASTAL MANAGEMENT; an international journal of marine environment, resources, law and society. see *EARTH SCIENCES — Oceanography*

347   AT   ISSN 0069-7133
LAW
COMMONWEALTH LAW REPORTS. 1901. irreg. (approx. 10/yr.). Law Book Co. Ltd., 44-50 Waterloo Rd., North Ryde, N.S.W. 2112, Australia. TEL 02-887-0177. FAX 02-888-9706. TELEX ASBOOK 27995. index, cum.index: vols.1-150; 151-171. **Indexed:** C.L.I., Curr.Aus.N.Z.Leg.Lit.Ind., Leg.Per.
●Also available online.
Description: Contains authorized reports of the High Court of Australia.

347   UK   ISSN 0307-6539
COMMONWEALTH MAGISTRATES' CONFERENCE. REPORT. 1972. irreg., 9th, 1991, Australia. £25. Commonwealth Magistrates' and Judges' Association, 28 Fitzroy Sq., London W1P 6DD, England. FAX 01-383-0757. circ. 500.

341.7 340   US
COURT CASE DIGEST. 1981. m. $440. Maritime Advisory Services Inc., 10 Signal Rd., Stamford, CT 06902. TEL 203-975-7070. FAX 203-975-7002. circ. 185. (back issues avail.)
Description: Reviews all major American and Canadian court decisions.

343.09   FR   ISSN 0012-642X
DROIT MARITIME FRANCAIS. 1923. m. 1355 F. (foreign 1470 F.). Moreux, 190 bd. Haussmann, 75008 Paris, France. TEL 45-63-11-55. TELEX 290 131. bk.rev.; bibl.; charts; stat.; circ. 12,000. **Indexed:** Mar.Aff.Bibl.

343.09 387   US
FEDERAL MARITIME COMMISSION SERVICE. 1970. irreg. (10-12/yr.). $260. Hawkins Publishing Co., Inc., Box 480, Mayo, MD 21106-0480. TEL 301-798-1677. Ed. Carl R. Eyler. (looseleaf format)

341.7 387　　　US　　ISSN 0022-2410
K10
JOURNAL OF MARITIME LAW AND COMMERCE. 1969. q. $65 (foreign $75). Anderson Publishing Co., 2035 Reading Rd., Cincinnati, OH 45202. TEL 513-421-4142. FAX 513-562-8116. Ed. Nicholas J. Healy. adv.; bk.rev.; bibl.; circ. 2,500. (back issues avail.; reprint service avail. from UMI) **Indexed:** Abstr.Bk.Rev.Curr.Leg.Per., BMT, C.L.I., C.R.E.J., Deep Sea Res.& Oceanogr.Abstr., L.R.I., Leg.Cont., Leg.Per., Mar.Aff.Bibl., Ocean.Abstr., P.A.I.S., Pollut.Abstr., Sel.Water Res.Abstr., SSCI.
—BLDSC shelfmark: 5012.070000.

343.09　　　BE　　ISSN 0022-6831
JURISPRUDENCE DU PORT D'ANVERS. (Text in Dutch, French) 1856. bi-m. 4500 Fr. Lloyd Anversois S.A., Eiermarkt 23, B-2000 Antwerp, Belgium. TEL 03-234-0550. FAX 03-234-0850. TELEX 31446. Ed. G. Dubois. index; circ. 750.
Description: Verbatim reports of important judicial decisions affecting maritime cases.

LAMY TRANSPORT TOME 1; route. see *LAW — International Law*

LAMY TRANSPORT TOME 2; douane, commissionnaires de transport, transports maritime, transports par chemin de fer, transports aeriens, lexique. see *LAW — International Law*

LAMY TRANSPORT TOME 3; marchandises dangereuses. see *LAW — International Law*

LAND AND WATER LAW REVIEW. see *LAW*

341.44　　　US　　ISSN 0092-6426
JX4131
LIMITS IN THE SEAS. irreg., no.101, 1984. free. U.S. Department of State, Office of Ocean Law and Policy, c/o Bureau of Oceans and Environmental Science, 2201 C St., N.W., Washington, DC 20520. TEL 202-647-2250.

LLOYD'S LAW REPORTS. see *LAW*

340 341.7　　UK　　ISSN 0306-2945
K12
LLOYD'S MARITIME & COMMERCIAL LAW QUARTERLY. 1974. q. $195. Lloyd's of London Press Ltd., Sheepen Place, Colchester, Essex CO3 3LP, England. TEL 0206-772277. FAX 0206-46273. TELEX 987321 LLOYDS G. (US subscr. to: 611 Broadway, Ste. 308, New York, NY 10012. TEL 212-529-9500) bk.rev. (also avail. in microfilm from WSH; reprint service avail. from WSH) **Indexed:** Abstr.Bk.Rev.Curr.Leg.Per., C.L.I., L.R.I., Leg.Per., Mar.Aff.Bibl.
—BLDSC shelfmark: 5287.270000.
Description: Covers commercial and shipping law on an international scale. Provides general information noting international developments in the law, notable meetings and seminars.

340　　　UK　　ISSN 0268-0696
LLOYD'S MARITIME LAW NEWSLETTER. 1979. fortn. $343.09 (foreign $530). Lloyd's of London Press Ltd., Sheepen Place, Colchester, Essex CO3 3LP, England. TEL 0206-772277. FAX 0206-46273. TELEX 987321 LLOYDS G. (US subscr. to: 611 Broadway, Ste. 308, New York, NY 10012. TEL 212-529-9500) Ed. Joseph Sweeney.

LOUISIANA COASTAL LAW REPORT; coastal zone management, marine resource law, and environmental law related to coastal and marine issues. see *LAW*

343.09 551.46　　US
MARINE LAWS; navigation and safety. 1985. 3 base vols. (plus a. suppl.), 3rd ed. $135. Butterworth Legal Publishers (Salem) (Subsidiary of: Reed International PLC), 90 Stiles Rd., Salem, NH 03079. TEL 800-548-4001. FAX 603-898-9858.
Description: Contains the principal laws relating to navigational and safety aspects of commercial shipping, supplemented by selected laws and international agreements and conventions on related subjects.

MARINE POLICY. see *EARTH SCIENCES — Oceanography*

MARITIME ADVISOR ARBITRATION AWARD DIGEST. see *TRANSPORTATION — Ships And Shipping*

MARITIME ADVISOR MARINE OPERATIONS REPORTER. see *TRANSPORTATION — Ships And Shipping*

347.75　　　US
MARITIME LAW REPORTER. 1987. bi-m. $185. Butterworth Legal Publishers (Salem) (Subsidiary of: Reed International PLC), 90 Stiles Rd., Salem, NH 03079. TEL 800-548-4001. FAX 603-898-9858. (looseleaf format)

MARITIME PERSONAL INJURY REPORT. see *TRANSPORTATION — Ships And Shipping*

343.09　　　US　　ISSN 1052-6730
JX4419
OCEAN AND COASTAL LAW MEMO. 1973. irreg., no.33, 1989. free. University of Oregon, School of Law, Ocean and Coastal Law Center, Eugene, OR 97403-1221. TEL 503-346-3845. FAX 503-346-3985. Eds. Richard G. Hildreth, Jon L. Jacobson. circ. 1,500. (back issues avail.)
Formerly (until no.32, 1989): Ocean Law Memo (ISSN 0361-2473)
Description: Analyzes a current issue in ocean and coastal law in each number.

343.09　　　US
OCEANA'S LEGAL ALMANACS, SECOND SERIES. 1952; N.S. 1991. irreg. price varies. Oceana Publications Inc., Dobbs Ferry, NY 10522. TEL 914-693-1320. FAX 914-693-0402. Ed. Irving J. Sloan. (back issues avail.)
Supersedes (in 1991): Legal Almanac Series (ISSN 0075-8582)
Description: Monographs on popular legal matters for a non-specialist audience.

341 614.7　　　US
OCEANS POLICY NEWS. 1983. m. price varies. Council on Ocean Law, 1709 New York Ave., N.W., Ste. 700, Washington, DC 20006. TEL 202-347-3766. FAX 202-638-0036. circ. 1,000. (back issues avail.)
Description: For ocean law and policy specialists.

343.09　　　US
▼**TERRITORIAL SEA JOURNAL**; legal and policy journal on U.S. coastal law. 1990. s-a. (University of Maine, School of Law) Marine Law Institute, 246 Deering Ave., Portland, ME 04102. TEL 207-780-4474. FAX 207-780-4913. Ed. Allison Rieser. circ. 300.

343.09　　　US　　ISSN 1048-3748
K13　　　　　　　　CODEN: TMLJE7
TULANE MARITIME LAW JOURNAL. 1975. s-a. $20 (foreign $25) (effective Oct. 1991). Tulane University, School of Law, New Orleans, LA 70118. TEL 504-865-5959. FAX 504-865-6748. Ed. R. Brett Kelly. adv.; bk.rev.; circ. 1,000. (also avail. in microfilm from RRI; reprint service avail. from RRI) **Indexed:** C.L.I., L.R.I., Leg.Per., Mar.Aff.Bibl.
●Also available online. Vendor(s): Mead Data Central, WESTLAW.
—BLDSC shelfmark: 9070.330000.
Formerly: Maritime Lawyer.

343.09　　　PL　　ISSN 0860-374X
UNIWERSYTET GDANSKI. WYDZIAL PRAWA I ADMINISTRACJI. ZESZYTY NAUKOWE. STUDIA IURIDICA MARITIMA. 1989. irreg. price varies. Uniwersytet Gdanski, Wydzial Prawa i Administracji, c/o Biblioteka Glowna, Ul. Armii Krajowej 110, 81-824 Sopot, Poland. TEL 51-00-61. (Dist. by: Ars Polona-Ruch, Krakowskie Przedmiescie 7, Warsaw, Poland) Ed. Wladyslaw Mogilski. circ. 200.

YEARBOOK MARITIME LAW. see *LAW*

LAW — Military Law

343　　　Il　　ISSN 0045-7043
CIVIL & MILITARY LAW JOURNAL. (Text in English) 1965. q. Rs.150($40) Defence Employees Welfare Council, New Delhi, D-1-24, Rajouri Garden, New Delhi 110 027, India. TEL 504498. Ed. H.S. Bhatin. adv.; bk.rev.; circ. 1,050.
Description: Covers Indian rule of law, military jurisprudence and legal aid for defense personnel.

341.57 380.5　　Il　　ISSN 0377-0494
LAW
JOURNAL OF SHIPPING, CUSTOMS, AND TRANSPORT LAW. (Text in English) 1974. m. Rs.100. Milan Law Publishers, Box 4591, 15-2 Navjivan, Bombay 400008, India. Ed. A.B. Gandhi. adv.; bk.rev.; bibl.; circ. 500.

LEATHER AND FUR INDUSTRIES　　2735

343　　　UK
MANUAL OF AIR FORCE LAW - AMENDMENTS. irreg. price varies. H.M.S.O., P.O. Box 276, London SW8 5DT, England. circ. 4,650.

343　　　UK
MANUAL OF MILITARY LAW - AMENDMENTS. irreg. price varies. H.M.S.O., P.O. Box 276, London SW8 5DT, England. circ. 13,000.

343　　　US　　ISSN 0193-3906
MILITARY LAW REPORTER. 1973. 6/yr. $350 (effective 1992). Public Law Education Institute, 1601 Connecticut Ave. N.W., Ste. 450, Washington, DC 20009-1035. TEL 202-232-1400. Eds. Thomas Alder, Lawrence Baskir. bk.rev.; abstr.; bibl.; circ. 1,000. (looseleaf format)
Supersedes (in 1974): Selective Service Law Reporter (ISSN 0049-0113)

343　　　US　　ISSN 0026-4040
K13
MILITARY LAW REVIEW. 1958. q. $12 (foreign $15). U.S. Army, Judge Advocate Generals School, Charlottesville, VA 22903-1781. TEL 804-293-4382. (Subscr. to: Supt. of Documents, Washington D.C. 20402) Ed. Daniel P. Shaver. bk.rev.; bibl.; index; circ. 8,000. (also avail. in microform from MIM,UMI; back issues avail.) **Indexed:** A.B.C.Pol.Sci., Abstr.Bk.Rev.Curr.Leg.Per., C.L.I., Curr.Cont., Ind.U.S.Gov.Per., L.R.I., Leg.Cont., Leg.Per., Mid.East: Abstr.& Ind., P.A.I.S., Pers.Lit., SSCI.
●Also available online. Vendor(s): Mead Data Central.
—BLDSC shelfmark: 5768.100000.

343　　　US　　ISSN 0163-1101
SHEPARD'S MILITARY JUSTICE CITATIONS. 1978. base vol. (plus bi-m suppl.). $220. Shepard's - McGraw-Hill, Inc., Box 35300, Colorado Springs, CO 80935-3530. TEL 800-525-2474.

U.S. ARMS CONTROL AND DISARMAMENT AGENCY. ANNUAL REPORT TO CONGRESS. see *MILITARY*

LEATHER AND FUR INDUSTRIES

see also Clothing Trade; Shoes and Boots

685 639.9　　　US
AMERICAN FUR INDUSTRY. NEWSLETTER. q. membership only. American Fur Industry, 363 Seventh Ave., 7th fl., New York, NY 10001. TEL 212-564-5133. circ. 3,000.
Description: Covers association and industry developments. Promotes fur and the conservation of fur-bearing animals.

675.2 660　　　US　　ISSN 0002-9726
TS940　　　　　　　　CODEN: JALCAQ
AMERICAN LEATHER CHEMISTS ASSOCIATION. JOURNAL. 1906. m. $85 to non-members. American Leather Chemists Association, Campus Sta., Location 14, Cincinnati, OH 45221. TEL 513-556-1197. Ed. Stephen Feairheller. adv.; bk.rev.; abstr.; bibl.; charts; illus.; pat.; index; circ. 1,083. (also avail. in microform from UMI,PMC; reprint service avail. from UMI) **Indexed:** Biol.Abstr., C.I.S. Abstr., Chem.Abstr., Curr.Cont., Curr.Leather Lit., Eng.Ind., Ind.Vet., Soils & Fert., Vet.Bull.
—BLDSC shelfmark: 4688.000000.
Description: Publishes original research reports on technological advancements in the leather and tanning industry, as well as patents issues and research articles from other publications are covered in abstract form.
Refereed Serial

AMERICAN SHOEMAKING. see *SHOES AND BOOTS*

639.1　　　US
AMERICAN TRAPPER. bi-m. National Trappers Association, P.O. Box 513, Riverton, WY 82501-0513. TEL 307-856-3830. FAX 307-856-4000. Ed. Tom Krause. bk.rev.; circ. 20,000.

685　　　FR　　ISSN 0066-2526
ANNUAIRE DE LA CHAUSSURE ET DES CUIRS. 1905. a. 545 F. Editions Louis Johanet, 68 rue Boursault, 75017 Paris, France.

LEATHER AND FUR INDUSTRIES

685   IT   ISSN 1120-2777
ARPEL; fashion review on Italian and international leathergoods, luggage, leather garments. (Text in English, French, German, Italian and Spanish) 1964. 4/yr. $282. Editrice Arpel s.r.l., Via I. Nievo 33, 20145 Milan, Italy. circ. 50,000.

685.2 659.152   IT   ISSN 1120-3501
ARPEL FUR; fashion review on Italian and international furs and leather garments. (Text in English, French, German, Italian, Spanish) 1982. 6/yr. $303. Editrice Arpel S.r.l., Via I. Nievo 33, 20145 Milan, Italy. Ed. Laura Muggiani.

685 646.3   IT   ISSN 1120-2785
ARS WEEK; fashion and economy news on footwear and leather field. (Text in English, Italian) w. $220. Editrice Arpel S.r.l., Via I. Nievo 33, 20145 Milan, Italy. FAX 0039-2-3493558. adv.

685   SP
ARTEPIEL; moda y comercio de la piel en Espana. 2/yr. 4000 ptas. Pedeca Sociedad Cooperativa Ltda., Maria Auxiliadora 5, 28040 Madrid, Spain. TEL 459 60 00.

675.2   NE   ISSN 0067-4834
BEDRIJFSCHAP VOOR DE LEDERWARENINDUSTRIE. JAARVERSLAG. 1957. a. fl.35($18) Bedrijfschap voor de Lederwarenindustrie, Postbus 90154, 5000 LG Tilburg, Netherlands. TEL 013-654390. FAX 013-686872. Ed. G. van der Werf. circ. 400.
Description: Includes complete statistics of turnover, number of workers, imports, and exports.

636.088   US
BLUE BOOK OF FUR FARMING. 1943. a. $20. Communications Marketing, Inc., 9995 W. 69th St., Eden Prairie, MN 55344-3408. TEL 612-941-5820. FAX 612-941-6746. adv.; circ. 2,100.

675 685   HU   ISSN 0006-7652
CODEN: BOPCAM
BOR- ES CIPOTECHNIKA. (Text in Hungarian; contents page in English, German, Russian) 1951. m. $40.50. (Bor- es Cipoipari Tarsasag) Lapkiado Vallalat, Lenin korut 9-11, 1073 Budapest 7, Hungary. TEL 222-408. (Subscr. to: Kultura, P.O. Box 149, H-1389 Budapest, Hungary) Ed. E. Vermes. adv.; bk.rev.; charts; illus.; stat.; circ. 690. **Indexed**: Chem.Abstr.

675.3   GW   ISSN 0007-2664
CODEN: BRULDU
BRUEHL; Fachzeitschrift fuer Rauchwarenhandel, Pelzkleidung, Rauchwarenveredlung und Pelztierzucht. (Text in German; summaries in English, French, Russian) 1960. 6/yr. DM.36 (foreign DM.46.20). Fachbuchverlag, Karl-Heine-Str. 16, 7031 Leipzig, Germany. adv.; bk.rev.; charts; illus.; tr.lit.; index. **Indexed**: Chem.Abstr, Nutr.Abstr.
Description: Trade publication for the fur industry. Covers fur trade, market, farming, and fashions, reports and announcements of events, auctions. Includes new publications, bibliographies.

CANADIAN FOOTWEAR & LEATHER DIRECTORY. see *BUSINESS AND ECONOMICS — Trade And Industrial Directories*

CANADIAN FOOTWEAR JOURNAL. see *SHOES AND BOOTS*

CANADIAN LEATHERCRAFT. see *ARTS AND HANDICRAFTS*

639.11   CN   ISSN 0317-0756
CANADIAN TRAPPER. (Text in English and French) q. Can.$10 to non-members. Ontario Trappers Association, 1971 Bond St., P.O. Box 705, North Bay, Ont. P1B 8J8, Canada. TEL 705-476-8777. Ed. Florence Friel. circ. 25,000.

685   FR   ISSN 0247-7181
CHAUSSER. 1946. m. (11/yr.) 415 F. (foreign 950 F.). Societe des Publications le Cuir, 175, Av. Achille Peretti, 92200 Neuilly Seine, France. TEL 47-38-11-07. FAX 46-24-99-24. TELEX 610 672 F. Ed. Nathalie Bailleux. adv.; illus.

636 338.1   US   ISSN 0009-3521
CHICAGO DAILY HIDE AND TALLOW BULLETIN; the first daily hide market service established in America. d. $225. Jacobsen Publishing Co., 300 W. Adams St., Chicago, IL 60606. TEL 312-726-6600. adv.; charts; mkt.; stat. (processed)

685   AG   ISSN 0009-8728
CLEO EN LA MODA. English edition: Cleo Internacional. 1966. bi-m. Arg.$4000($10) Ediciones Ariadna, 472 Suipacha, Buenos Aires, Argentina. Ed. Alvaro D'Elia. adv.; tr.lit.; circ. 5,000. (tabloid format)

675.2   FR   ISSN 0011-2690
LE CUIR PARIS. (Text in English, French) 1908. w. 760 F. (foreign 945 F.). Societe des Publications le Cuir, 175, Av. Achille Peretti, 92200 Neuilly Seine, France. TEL 47-38-11-07. FAX 46-24-99-24. TELEX 610 672F. Ed. Frederic Taddei. adv.; stat. (tabloid format)

675.2 685.31   IT   ISSN 0011-3034
CODEN: CPMAAJ
CUOIO PELLI MATERIE CONCIANTI. (Special issues avail.) 1923. bi-m. L.40000 (foreign L.60000). Stazione Sperimentale per l'Industria delle Pelli e delle Materie Concianti, Via Poggioreale 39, 80143 Naples, Italy. FAX 265574. TELEX STSPNA 721160 I. adv.; bk.rev.; abstr.; bibl.; charts; illus. circ. 2,000. **Indexed**: C.I.S. Abstr., Chem.Abstr., Curr.Leather Lit.
—BLDSC shelfmark: 3493.000000.

675.3   DK   ISSN 0011-6424
DANSK PELSDYRAVL. 1938. m. DKK 300 to non-members. Dansk Pelsdyravlerforening - Danish Fur Breeders Association, Langagervej 60, DK-2600 Glostrup, Denmark. TEL 43-434400. FAX 42-452546. TELEX 33171. Ed. Helge Olsen. adv.; bk.rev.; circ. 8,000. **Indexed**: Anim.Breed.Abstr., Chem.Abstr., Nutr.Abstr.
—BLDSC shelfmark: 3526.920000.
Formerly: Dansk Pelsdyrblad (ISSN 0105-0834)

675.3   GW   ISSN 0012-0553
DER DEUTSCHE PELZTIERZUECHTER. 1926. 6/yr. DM.60. Animal - Verlag GmbH, Peiner Weg 84, 3167 Burgdorf, Germany. Ed. Reinhard Scheelje. adv.; bk.rev.; charts; illus.; index; circ. 3,000. **Indexed**: Anim.Breed.Abstr., Ind.Vet., Nutr.Abstr.
—BLDSC shelfmark: 3573.225000.

636.088   US   ISSN 0013-6905
SF405.C45
EMPRESS CHINCHILLA BREEDER. 1945. m. $20 to libraries (foreign $25). Empress Chinchilla Breeders Cooperative, Inc., 575 Union Blvd., Ste. 209, Lakewood, CO 80228-1242. Ed. Gail V. Sanden. adv.; bk.rev.; charts; illus.; stat.; circ. 1,687.

FASHION EXTRAS. see *CLOTHING TRADE — Fashions*

636.088   FI   ISSN 0430-5817
FINSK PALSTIDSKRIFT. 1928. m. FIM 340. Finlands Palsdjursuppfodares Forbund r.f., Postbox 5, 01601 Vanda 60, Finland. FAX 90-8498217. TELEX 124786 FUR. Ed. Kalevi Pesso. adv.; circ. 1,900. **Indexed**: Anim.Breed.Abstr., Nutr.Abstr.

FOOTWEAR INDUSTRIES OF AMERICA. EXECUTIVE DIGEST. see *SHOES AND BOOTS*

675.3   US   ISSN 0016-2884
FUR AGE WEEKLY.* 1918. w. $42. Fur Vogue Publishing Co. Inc., Box 868, Glenwood Landing, NY 11547-0703. TEL 212-239-4983. Ed. E.R. Harrowe. adv.; bk.rev.; circ. 5,000. (tabloid format)
Incorporating: Fur Age Monthly.
Description: Covers all aspects of the fur industry.

636.088   US   ISSN 0744-7701
FUR RANCHER. 1922. m. $20 (includes Blue Book of Fur Farming). Communications Marketing, Inc., 9995 W. 69th St., Eden Prairie, MN 55344-3408. TEL 612-941-5820. FAX 612-941-6746. Ed. Bruce W. Smith. adv.; bk.rev.; charts; illus.; mkt.; stat.; tr.lit.; index; charts. circ. 2,100. **Indexed**: Agri.Ind.
Formerly (until 1978): U S Fur Rancher (ISSN 0041-7653)

636.088   US   ISSN 0016-2965
FUR TAKER JOURNAL.* 1968. m. $15. Fur Takers of America, Inc., 1541 Shannon Dr., New Haven, IN 46774-2318. adv.; bk.rev.; charts; illus.; circ. 10,000.

675.3   UK   ISSN 0016-2981
FUR WEEKLY NEWS. 1933. w. L.3. Fur Weekly News Ltd., 122 Lea Bride Rd., London E5 9RB, England. Ed. A. Coster. adv.; bk.rev.

675.2   FR   ISSN 0399-5461
HEBDOCUIR. 1977. w. 425 F. (foreign 560 F.). Promotion Press Internationale, 7 ter, Cour des Petites-Ecuires, 75010 Paris, France. TEL 42-47-12-05. FAX 47-70-33-94. Ed. Patrick Horde. circ. 7,000.
Formed by the merger of: Independant Chaussure; Halle aux Cuirs.

685.31   US   ISSN 0018-1293
HIDE AND LEATHER BULLETIN; for the tanning and shoe manufacturing industry. d. $225. Jacobsen Publishing Co., 300 W. Adams St., Chicago, IL 60606. TEL 312-726-6600. adv.; stat. (processed)

675.2   UK   ISSN 0142-1891
HD9778.A1
HIDES AND SKINS. 1978. 2/yr. £25. Commonwealth Secretariat, Publications Division, Marlborough House, Pall Mall, London SW1Y 5HX, England. charts; illus.; stat. **Indexed**: IIS.

675.2   GW   ISSN 0178-5052
IN LEDER. 1922. m. DM.153. Umschau Verlag Breidenstein GmbH, Stuttgarter Str. 18-24, 6000 Frankfurt a.M. 1, Germany. TEL 069-2600-0. FAX 069-2600-609. TELEX 411964. Ed. Gerhard Franz. adv.; bk.rev.; illus.; pat.; stat.; tr.lit.; circ. 6,600. **Indexed**: Key to Econ.Sci.
Formerly: Lederwaren-Zeitung (ISSN 0047-4312)

675.2   II   ISSN 0019-574X
INDIAN LEATHER. (Text in English) 1967. m. $100. Indian Leather, 120 Vepery High Rd., Periamet, Madras 600 003, India. TEL 586566. Ed. S. Sankaran. adv.; bk.rev.; circ. 1,000. **Indexed**: Curr.Leather Lit.
—BLDSC shelfmark: 4422.240000.

675.2   II   ISSN 0019-5758
INDIAN LEATHER TECHNOLOGISTS' ASSOCIATION. JOURNAL. (Text in English) 1952. m. Rs.100($45) Indian Leather Technologists' Association, Mercantile Bldgs., 1st Fl., E. Gate, Lalbazar St., Calcutta 700 001, India. TEL 20-7472. Ed. Ashish Chakraborty. adv.; bk.rev.; charts; illus.; index; circ. 1,100. **Indexed**: Chem.Abstr.

685.2   FR   ISSN 0980-1367
CODEN: INCUEH
INDUSTRIE DU CUIR. Short title: I D C. (Text in English, French, Spanish) m. (10/yr.). 645 F. (foreign 945 F.). Societe de Publications le Cuir, 175, Av. Achille Peretti, 92200 Neuilly Seine, France. TEL 47-38-11-07. FAX 46-24-99-24. TELEX 610672 F.
—BLDSC shelfmark: 4467.270000.
Incorporates: Revue Technique des Industries du Cuir (ISSN 0004-5462)

INSTITUTUL POLITEHNIC "GHEORGHE ASACHI" DIN IASI. BULETINUL. SECTIA VII: TEXTILE, PIELARIE. see *TEXTILE INDUSTRIES AND FABRICS*

685   CN   ISSN 0823-6976
INTERNATIONAL FUR FASHION REVIEW.* 1982. 6/yr. $50 in Canada and U.S.; elsewhere $65. Fashion Mode Communications, Inc., 310 Victoria Ave., Westmount, Que. H3Z 2M9, Canada. TEL 514-844-9326. Ed. Marsha Ross. adv.; circ. 10,000.
Description: Trade magazine covering the fur and leather industry in Canada.

675.2   UK   ISSN 0955-5080
TS945
INTERNATIONAL LEATHER GUIDE. 1970. a. £72 (foreign £85). Benn Business Information Services Ltd., P.O. Box 20, Sovereign Way, Tonbridge, Kent TN9 1RQ, England. TEL 0732-362666. FAX 0732-770483. TELEX 95162-BENTON-G. Ed. Pat Bryant. adv.; index; circ. 1,850.
—BLDSC shelfmark: 4542.859500.
Former titles: Leather Guide (ISSN 0140-413X); European Leather Guide (ISSN 0071-2906)
Description: International buyer's guide for tanners and merchants, hide and skin suppliers, and machinery manufacturers. Includes a five language glossary.

685   II   ISSN 0047-0988
INTERNATIONAL PRESS CUTTING SERVICE: LEATHER - HIDES - SKIN - FOOTWEAR. 1967. w. $65. International Press Cutting Service, P.O. Box 63, Allahabad 211001, India. Ed. N. Khanna. bk.rev.; index; circ. 1,200. (processed)

LEATHER AND FUR INDUSTRIES

685 685.31 JA
KAWA TO HAKIMONO/LEATHER & FOOTWEARS. (Text in Japanese) 1972. q. free. Tokyo-to Sangyo Rodo Kaikan - Tokyo Industrial and Vocational Center, 1-6 Hashiba 1-chome, Taito-ku, Tokyo, Japan. TEL 03-3876-2961. charts; illus.; stat.; circ. 3,000.

675.2 CS ISSN 0023-4338
TS940 CODEN: KOZAAT
KOZARSTVI/LEATHER INDUSTRY; odborny casopis pro prumysl kozedelny, obuvnicky a gumove obuvi. (Text in Czech; summaries in English, German, Russian) 1950. m. $44. Nakladatelstvi Technicke Literatury, Spalena 51, 113 02 Prague 1, Czechoslovakia. (Dist. by: Artia, Ve Smeckach 30, 111 27 Prague 1, Czechoslovakia) Ed. Josef Cundrle. **Indexed:** Art & Archaeol.Tech.Abstr., C.I.S. Abstr., Chem.Abstr.

675 685.3 BU
KOZHARSKA I OBUVNA PROMISHLENOST. (Text in Bulgarian; summaries in English, German and Russian) 1960. 8/yr. $7. Ministerstvo na Lekata Promishlenost, Sofia, Bulgaria. (Dist. by: Hemus 6, Rouski Blvd., 1000 Sofia, Bulgaria) circ. 1,588. **Indexed:** Chem.Abstr.

KOZHEVENNO-OBUVNAYA PROMYSHLENNOST. see SHOES AND BOOTS

675.2 SA
L I R I QUARTERLY REVIEW. 1941. q. (Rhodes University, Leather Industries Research Institute) L I R I Technologies, P.O. Box 185, Grahamstown 6140, South Africa. FAX 0461-26517. illus.; stat.; index; circ. 1,200.
Formerly: L I R I Monthly Circular (ISSN 0023-9755)

675 SA ISSN 0085-2724
L I R I RESEARCH BULLETIN. 1942. irreg. (approx. 20/yr.). price varies. (Rhodes University, Leather Industries Research Institute) L I R I Technologies, P.O. Box 185, Grahamstown 6140, South Africa. FAX 0461-26517. charts; illus.

675 SA
L I R I TECHNICAL BULLETIN. 1975. irreg. (approx. 10/yr.). (Rhodes University, Leather Industries Research Institute) L I R I Technologies, P.O. Box 185, Grahamstown 6140, South Africa. FAX 0461-26517.

675.3 GW ISSN 0048-3176
L P T JOURNAL. (Leder Pelz Textil) 1905. m. DM.132. C B Verlag Carl Boldt, Baseler Str. 80, 1000 Berlin 45, Germany. TEL 030-8337087. FAX 030-8339125. Ed. J. Sartorius. adv.; bk.rev.; circ. 5,500.
Formerly: Pelzwirtschaft (ISSN 0048-3176); Incorporates (1948-1989): Pelzspiegel.

685 GW ISSN 0024-0192
TS940 CODEN: LSLEBB
L S L (Leder, Schuhe, Lederwaren); Fachzeitschrift fuer die Leder-, Kunstleder-, Schuh- und Lederwarenindustrie; das Schuhmacher-, Sottler- und Taeschnerhandwerk sowie den Fachhandel. (Text in German; index in English and Russian) 1966. 6/yr. DM.27 (foreign DM.37.20). Fachbuchverlag, Karl-Heine-Str. 16, 7031 Leipzig, Germany. illus.; pat. **Indexed:** Chem.Abstr.
Description: Trade publication for the leathergoods industry, featuring shoe and handbag fashions, technology, materials, synthetic leather, schooling, and reports of events.

675.2 UK ISSN 0023-9739
TS940
LEATHER. 1867. m. £56 (foreign £75). Benn Publications Ltd., Sovereign Way, Tonbridge, Kent TN9 1RW, England. TEL 0732-364422. Ed. Shelagh Davy. adv.; bk.rev.; illus.; mkt.; tr.lit.; circ. 4,000. (also avail. in microform from UMI) **Indexed:** Key to Econ.Sci.
—BLDSC shelfmark: 5179.332000.

675.2 JA ISSN 0018-1811
LEATHER CHEMISTRY/HIKAKU KAGAKU. (Text in Japanese; summaries in English) 1955. q. 2500 Yen. Japanese Association of Leather Technology - Nihon Hikaku Gijutsu Kyokai, c/o Scleroprotein and Leather Research Institute, Tokyo Noko University, 3-5-8 Saiwai-cho, Fuchu-shi, Tokyo 183, Japan. Ed.Bd. adv.; index; circ. 900. **Indexed:** Chem.Abstr., Curr.Leather Lit.
—BLDSC shelfmark: 4312.500000.

LEATHER CRAFTERS JOURNAL. see ARTS AND HANDICRAFTS

685 PK
▼**LEATHER GOODS INTERNATIONAL.** (Text in English) 1991. m. $4 per no. Press Corporation of Pakistan, P.O. Box 3138, Karachi 75400, Pakistan. TEL 21-455-3703. FAX 21-7736198. Ed. Saeed Hafeez. circ. 5,000.

675.23 US
LEATHER INDUSTRIES OF AMERICA. NEWSBREAK. 1933. every 3 wks. membership. Leather Industries of America, 1000 Thomas Jefferson St., N.W., Ste. 515, Washington, DC 20007. TEL 202-342-8086. FAX 202-342-9063. Ed. Jean Ann Firestone. stat.; circ. 1,000.
Former titles: Tanner's Council of America. Newsbreak; Tanners' Council of America. Council News (ISSN 0010-9932)
Description: Information on government regulation, leather statistics, environmental concerns, business productivity.

685 US
LEATHER: LATIN AMERICAN INDUSTRIAL REPORT. (Avail. for each of 22 Latin American countries) 1985. a. $435 per country report. Aquino Productions, Box 15760, Stamford, CT 06901. TEL 203-325-3138. Ed. Andres C. Aquino.

675.23 US ISSN 0023-9763
CODEN: LEMAA7
LEATHER MANUFACTURER. 1883. m. $33. Shoe Trades Publishing Co., Box 198, Cambridge, MA 02140. TEL 617-648-8160. Ed. J.D. Sutton. adv.; illus.; mkt.; stat.; index. **Indexed:** Chem.Abstr.

LEATHER MANUFACTURER'S DIRECTORY. see BUSINESS AND ECONOMICS — Trade And Industrial Directories

675.2 II ISSN 0023-9771
TS940
LEATHER SCIENCE. 1954. m. Rs.50($25) Central Leather Research Institute, Adyar, Madras 600020, India. TEL 412616. (Affiliate: Council of Scientific and Industrial Research) Ed. G. Thyagarajn. adv.; bk.rev.; abstr.; charts; illus.; pat.; tr.mk.; index; circ. 500. **Indexed:** Chem.Abstr., Irr.& Drain.Abstr., Soils & Fert., Sorghum & Millets Abstr.
—BLDSC shelfmark: 5179.398000.

675.2 JA ISSN 0018-1803
LEATHER TECHNOLOGY/HIKAKU GIJUTSU. (Text in Japanese) 1960. s-a. 3000 Yen. Japanese Association of Leather Technology - Nihon Hikaku Gijutsu Kyokai, c/o Scleroprotein and Leather Research Institute, Tokyo Noko University, 3-5-8 Saiwai-cho, Fuchu-shi, Tokyo 183, Japan. Ed.Bd. adv.; illus.; circ. 900. **Indexed:** Chem.Abstr.

338 US ISSN 0884-660X
LEATHER TODAY. Issued with: Outerwear. 1985. m. $80. Fur Publishing Plus, Inc., 19 W. 21st St., Ste. 403, New York, NY 10010. TEL 212-727-1210. Ed. Richard Harrow. adv.; bk.rev.; circ. 13,500 (controlled).

675.2 382 II ISSN 0023-9828
HD9780.I62
LEATHERS. (Text in English) 1957. bi-m. Rs.100($40) Council for Leather Exports, 53 Sydenhams Rd., Periamet, Madras 600 003, India. TEL 589098. TELEX 41-7354 CLE IN. Ed. S. Manoharan. adv.; bk.rev.; charts; mkt.; stat.; circ. 4,000.
Description: Covers the leather industry.

675.2 GW ISSN 0024-0176
TS940 CODEN: LEDEA8
DAS LEDER; Fachzeitschrift fuer die Chemie und Technologie der Lederherstellung. (Summaries in English, French and Spanish) 1950. m. DM.102. (Verein fuer Gerberei-Chemie und Technik e.V.) Eduard Roether Verlag, Berliner Allee 56, 6100 Darmstadt 1, Germany. TEL 06151-3001-17. Ed. E. Heidemann. adv.; bk.rev.; abstr.; bibl.; charts; illus.; pat.; circ. 2,500. (also avail. in microform from UMI) **Indexed:** Biol.Abstr., Chem.Abstr.

675.2 GW ISSN 0024-0184
LEDER ECHO. 1949. m. DM.10 to non-members. Gewerkschaft Leder, Will-Bleicher-Str. 20, 7000 Stuttgart 1, Germany. FAX 0711-293345. Ed. Doerte Hautmann. adv.; bk.rev.; film rev.; play rev.; bibl.; illus.; stat.; circ. 42,000 (controlled).

685 GW ISSN 0342-7641
LEDER- UND HAEUTEMARKT. 36/yr. DM.282.60. Umschau Verlag Breidenstein GmbH, Stuttgarterstr. 18-24, 6000 Frankfurt a.M. 1, Germany. TEL 069-2600-0. FAX 069-2700-609. illus.

685 GW ISSN 0024-0214
LEDERWAREN-REPORT. 1958. m. DM.214. Verlag Otto Sternefeld GmbH, Postfach 11 12 49, Oberkasseler Str.100, 4000 Duesseldorf 11, Germany. Ed. C. Foecking. circ. 5,050. (processed)

685 II
LEXPORT. vol.11, 1974. a. Export Promotion Council for Finished Leather & Leather Manufacturers, 15-46 Civil Lines, P.O. Box 198, Kanpur 208001, India.

LIVING AMONG NATURE DARINGLY!; how to for trappers, farmers, and homesteaders. see GARDENING AND HORTICULTURE

685 CN ISSN 0836-3862
LUGGAGE, LEATHERGOODS & ACCESSORIES. Short title: L L A. 4/yr. Can.$25.70($70) Laurentian Media Inc., 501 Oakdale Rd., Downsview, Ont. M3N 1W7, Canada. TEL 416-746-7360. FAX 416-746-1421. Ed. Virginia Hutton. adv.; circ. 5,200.
Formerly (until Dec. 1987): Luggage and Leathergoods News.
Description: Trade journal covering the luggage and leathergoods industries.

636.088 CC ISSN 1000-7407
MAOPI DONGWU SIYANG/BREEDING OF FUR-BEARING ANIMALS. (Text in Chinese) q. Jilin Nongye Daxue - Jilin University of Agriculture, Donghuan Lunan, Changchun, Jilin 130118, People's Republic of China. TEL 42112. Ed. Chen Qiren.

685 SP
MARROQUINERIA ESPANOLA. 1972. s-a. 2400 ptas. Prensa Tecnica, S.A., Caspe 118-120, Barcelona 13, Spain. Ed. F. Canet Tomas. adv.; illus.; circ. 5,000.

685 SP
MECANIPEL; revista de informacion general y tecnica de la piel y sus manufacturas. 11/yr. 5000 ptas. Pedeca Sociedad Cooperativa Ltda., Maria Auxiliadora 5, 28040 Madrid, Spain. TEL 459 60 00.

MUSEUM OF THE FUR TRADE QUARTERLY. see HISTORY — History Of North And South America

636.088 CN ISSN 0027-8963
NATIONAL CHINCHILLA BREEDERS OF CANADA. BULLETIN. (Text in English and French) 1946. m. $30. National Chinchilla Breeders of Canada, R.R. 10, Brampton, Ont. L6V 3N2, Canada. TEL 416-451-8736. FAX 416-457-5326. Ed. T. Riedstra. adv.; stat.; circ. 600. (processed)
Description: Technically oriented trade magazine providing education for the chinchilla rancher.

636.088 NO ISSN 0369-5255
NORSK PELSDYRBLAD. 1926. m. NOK 200. Norges Pelsdyralslag, P.O. Box 145, Okern, 0509 Oslo 5, Norway. FAX 02-643591. Ed. Einar Storsul. adv.; circ. 5,500. **Indexed:** Anim.Breed.Abstr., Nutr.Abstr.
—BLDSC shelfmark: 6144.500000.

685 333.7 CN ISSN 0705-4831
NOVA SCOTIA TRAPPERS NEWSLETTER. 1964. a. free. Nova Scotia Lands and Forests, P.O. Box 68, Truro, N.S. B2N 5B8, Canada. TEL 902-893-5660. FAX 902-893-6102. bk.rev.; circ. 6,800.
Description: Conservation, management and trapping statistics for trappers and managers.

675 PK
PAKISTAN LEATHER TRADE JOURNAL. (Text in English) 1974. q. $35. (Pakistan Society of Leather Technologists) Alam Ara Jamil, 132-A Block 2, P.E.C.H.S., P.O. Box 7821, Mahmood Ghaznavi Road, Karachi 75400, Pakistan. TEL 431900. TELEX 23364 KHLIL PK. Ed. M. Jamil Khan. adv.; bk.rev.; circ. 1,000.

PARFYME OG PORTEFOELJE. see BEAUTY CULTURE — Perfumes And Cosmetics

685 AU
PELZ UND LEDER. m. S.360. Johann L. Bondi und Sohn, Industriestr. 2, A-2380 Perchtoldsdorf, Austria. adv.; circ. 1,000.

LEATHER AND FUR INDUSTRIES — ABSTRACTING, BIBLIOGRAPHIES, STATISTICS

685   PH   ISSN 0115-6608
PHILIPPINES FOOTWEAR LEATHERGOODS & ACCESORIES JOURNAL. 6/yr. Essence Publications & Communication Arts, Cynthia Marie Bldg., 6E New York St. cnr Rodriquz, Cubao, Quezon City, Philippines. TEL 7210821.

PLASTICS, RUBBER AND LEATHER INDUSTRIES JOURNAL. see *PLASTICS*

PREVISIONS GLISSANTES DETAILLEES EN PERSPECTIVES SECTORIELLES (VOL.3): TEXTILE - HABILLEMENT - CUIR. see *BUSINESS AND ECONOMICS — Economic Situation And Conditions*

685   PL   ISSN 0370-1743
TS940   CODEN: PRZKAX
PRZEGLAD SKORZANY. (Text in Polish; summaries in English, German, Russian) 1946. m. $61. (Polska Izba Przemyslu Skorzanego) Wydawnictwo Czasopism i Ksiazek Technicznych SIGMA - NOT, Ul. Biala 1, 1004 Warsaw, Poland. (Dist. by: SIGMA NOT Ltd., Ul. Bartycka 20, 00-716 Warsaw, Poland) adv.; bk.rev.; circ. 930. **Indexed:** Chem.Abstr.

338.7   II   ISSN 0302-4881
TS959.I4
RAJASTHAN STATE TANNERIES LIMITED. ANNUAL REPORT. (Text in English) 1973. a. Rajasthan State Tanneries Limited, P-6 Tilak Marg, C Scheme, Jaipur, India. Key Title: Annual Report - Rajasthan State Tanneries Limited.

639.11   CN
SASKATCHEWAN, ALBERTA, YUKON TRAPPER. 1986. q. Can.$10. McIntosh Publishing Co. Ltd., P.O. Box 430, N. Battleford, Sask. S9A 2Y5, Canada. TEL 306-445-4401. Ed. C. Irwin McIntosh. circ. 9,800.
     Formerly: Saskatchewan Trapper.

SCHOENWERELD. see *SHOES AND BOOTS*

SCHUH-ZEITUNG. see *SHOES AND BOOTS*

SCHUHMARKT. see *SHOES AND BOOTS*

SHOE AND LEATHER NEWS. see *SHOES AND BOOTS*

SHOW REPORTER. see *SHOES AND BOOTS*

SKO. see *SHOES AND BOOTS*

675.2 660   UK   ISSN 0144-0322
                         CODEN: JSLTBY
SOCIETY OF LEATHER TECHNOLOGISTS AND CHEMISTS. JOURNAL. 1917. bi-m. £35 to non-members. Society of Leather Technologists and Chemists, 1 Edges Court, Moulton, Northampton NN3 1UJ, England. Ed. M.K. Leafe. adv.; bk.rev.; abstr.; bibl.; charts; illus.; pat.; index; circ. 1,500. **Indexed:** Anal.Abstr., Br.Tech.Ind., Chem.Abstr., Chem.Eng.Abstr., Curr.Cont., Curr.Leather Lit., W.R.C.Inf.
     —BLDSC shelfmark: 4889.900000.
     Formerly: Society of Leather Trades' Chemists. Journal (ISSN 0037-9921)

SOUTH AFRICAN SHOEMAKER AND LEATHER REVIEW. see *SHOES AND BOOTS*

675.23   II   ISSN 0039-9442
TANNER.* (Text in English) 1946. m. Rs.21($6) S. Raja, 32-2 Aga Abbas Ali Rd., 3rd Cross, Bangalore 560 042, India. Ed. Mrs. L.S. Raja. adv.; bk.rev.; charts; illus.; mkt.; tr.lit. (reprint service avail. from UMI) **Indexed:** Chem.Abstr.

685   BL   ISSN 0101-1138
TECNICOURO. (Abstracts in English and Portuguese) 1979. 8/yr. Cz.$2085. Centro Tecnologico do Couro, Calcados e Afins, Rua Araxa, 750, Caixa Postal 450, 93300 Novo Hamburgo, RS, Brazil. TELEX 0512-897. Ed. Affonso Ritter. adv.; bk.rev.; circ. 10,000.

639.11   CN
TRAPPER. 1986. 6/yr. Can.$12.50($18) McIntosh Publishing Co. Ltd., P.O. Box 430, N. Battleford, Sask. S9A 2Y5, Canada. TEL 306-445-4401. FAX 306-445-1977. Ed. Bill McIntosh. adv.

685.5   US
TRAVELWARE. 9/yr. $28. Business Journals, 50 Day St., Box 5550, Norwalk, CT 06856. TEL 203-853-6015. Ed. Dana Carpenter. **Indexed:** Key to Econ.Sci.
     Former titles: Luggage and Travelware (ISSN 0193-0559); Luggage and Leather Goods.

TRAVELWARE RESOURCES DIRECTORY. see *BUSINESS AND ECONOMICS — Trade And Industrial Directories*

V W D - HAEUTE UND LEDER. (Vereinigte Wirtschaftsdienste GmbH) see *BUSINESS AND ECONOMICS — Investments*

636.088   SW   ISSN 0042-2703
VAARA PAELSDJUR/OUR FURRED ANIMALS. 1930. 8/yr. SEK 200 (typically set in Jan.). Sveriges Paelsdjursuppfoedares Riksfoerbund - Swedish Fur Breeders' Association, Box 8124, S-163 08 Spanga, Sweden. TEL 08-362770. FAX 08-7618169. TELEX 08-362770. Ed. Leif Sjoeblom. adv.; charts; illus.; index; circ. 1,150. **Indexed:** Vet.Bull.

VOGUE PELLE. see *CLOTHING TRADE — Fashions*

WIADOMOSCI PRODUKCYJNE: WLOKNO, ODZIEZ, SKORA. see *CLOTHING TRADE*

675.3   GW
WINCKELMANN PELZMARKET. 1969. w. DM.95. Winckelmann Verlag GmbH, Savignystr. 49, D-6000 Frankfurt 1, Germany.

WINCKELMANN SALES REPORT. see *CLOTHING TRADE*

675.2   US   ISSN 0894-3087
WORLD LEATHER. 1987. 6/yr. $45. 61 Massachusetts, Arlington, MA 02174. TEL 617-648-8160. FAX 617-492-0126. Iain Howie. adv.; circ. 5,000. (back issue avail)
     Description: For the leather tanning industry worldwide.

LEATHER AND FUR INDUSTRIES — Abstracting, Bibliographies, Statistics

636.088   CN   ISSN 0318-7888
CANADA. STATISTICS CANADA. REPORT ON FUR FARMS. (Catalogue 23-208) (Text in English and French) 1919. a. Can.$34($41) (foreign $48). Statistics Canada, Publications Sales and Services, Ottawa, Ont. K1A 0T6, Canada. TEL 613-951-7277. FAX 613-951-1584. (also avail. in microform from MML)
     Description: Contains supply and disposition of fox and mink on fur farms, by province, the number of farms classified by number and reported by province, number and value of mink pelts by color, type and province.

675 016   II
TS940
LEATHER SCIENCE ABSTRACTS. (Text in English) 1968. m. Rs.100($50) Central Leather Research Institute, Adyar, Madras 600020, India. TEL 412616. (Affiliate: Council of Scientific and Industrial Research) Ed. R. Vengan. index; circ. 500.
     Formerly (until 1988): Current Leather Literature (ISSN 0011-3638)

PLUIMVEE DOCUMENTATIE. see *AGRICULTURE — Abstracting, Bibliographies, Statistics*

LEGAL AID

see *Law–Legal Aid*

LEISURE AND RECREATION

see also *Hobbies; Sports and Games*

BARE IN MIND. see *PHYSICAL FITNESS AND HYGIENE*

BRITISH LEISURE & SWIMMING POOL DIRECTORY. see *BUSINESS AND ECONOMICS — Trade And Industrial Directories*

BRITISH LEISURE CENTRE DIRECTORY. see *BUSINESS AND ECONOMICS — Trade And Industrial Directories*

CAMPING & OUTDOOR LEISURE TRADER. see *SPORTS AND GAMES — Outdoor Life*

796 917.1   CN
CATALOGUE OF CANADIAN RECREATION AND LEISURE RESEARCH. 1973. irreg. (every 2-3/yrs.). price varies. Ontario Research Council on Leisure, 77 Bloor St. W., 8th Fl., Toronto, Ont. M7A 2R9, Canada. circ. 5,000.

CHARTERED INSTITUTE OF PUBLIC FINANCE AND ACCOUNTANCY. CHARGES FOR LEISURE SERVICES. ACTUALS. see *SPORTS AND GAMES — Abstracting, Bibliographies, Statistics*

CHARTERED INSTITUTE OF PUBLIC FINANCE AND ACCOUNTANCY. LEISURE AND RECREATION STATISTICS. ESTIMATES. see *SPORTS AND GAMES — Abstracting, Bibliographies, Statistics*

CHARTERED INSTITUTE OF PUBLIC FINANCE AND ACCOUNTANCY. LEISURE USAGE. ACTUALS. see *SPORTS AND GAMES — Abstracting, Bibliographies, Statistics*

268   US   ISSN 0191-4294
BV4596.S5
CHRISTIAN SINGLE. m. $17.75. Southern Baptist Convention, Sunday School Board, 127 Ninth Ave., N., Nashville, TN 37234. TEL 800-458-2772.

CONGRESS FOR RECREATION AND PARKS. SYMPOSIUM FOR LEISURE RESEARCH. ABSTRACTS. see *SPORTS AND GAMES — Abstracting, Bibliographies, Statistics*

051   US
DISNEY NEWS. 1965. q. $14.95 for 8 nos. Box 3310, Anaheim, CA 92803. Ed. Anne Okey. adv.; circ. 290,000.
     Description: Provides articles about Disneyland, Walt Disney World, Tokyo Disneyland, new program offerings from the Disney Channel, and latest movies from Walt Disney Pictures and Touchstone Films.

GAMES & LEISURE INC.. see *SPORTS AND GAMES*

HARPERS SPORTS & LEISURE. see *SPORTS AND GAMES — Outdoor Life*

JOURNAL OF HOSPITALITY & LEISURE MARKETING. see *HOTELS AND RESTAURANTS*

333.78   US   ISSN 0022-2216
GV1   CODEN: JLERA
JOURNAL OF LEISURE RESEARCH. 1968. q. $30 to non-members; members $20; institutions $50. National Recreation and Park Association, 3101 Park Center Dr., Alexandria, VA 22302. TEL 703-820-4940. FAX 703-671-6772. (Co-sponsor: University of North Texas) Ed. Peter A. Witt. adv.; bk.rev.; bibl.; charts; illus.; stat.; index. (also avail. in microform from UMI; reprint service avail. from UMI) **Indexed:** ASSIA, C.I.J.E., Commun.Abstr., Curr.Cont., Geo.Abstr., Lang.& Lang.Behav.Abstr., Mag.Ind., Phys.Ed.Ind., Psychol.Abstr., Rural Recreat.Tour.Abstr., Soc.Sci.Ind., Sportsearch (1974-), SSCI, World Agri.Econ.& Rural Sociol.Abstr.
     —BLDSC shelfmark: 5010.280000.

790.1   UK
L S A NEWSLETTER. (Supplement avail.) 1980. q. £22 to members; institutions £44. Leisure Studies Association, Leeds Polytechnic, Dept. of Leisure and Consumer Studies, Calverley St., Leeds LS1 3HE, England. TEL 0532-833111. FAX 0532-833113. Ed. David Leslie. adv.; bk.rev.; circ. 500. **Indexed:** Rural Recreat.Tour.Abstr., World Agri.Econ.& Rural Sociol.Abstr.
     Formerly: L S A Quarterly (ISSN 0260-6364)

790.1   UK
LEISURE AND FITNESS. 1982. a. £25. (Recreation Managers' Association of Great Britain) Millbank Publications Ltd., 25 Catherine St., London WC2B 5JW, England. TEL 071-379-3036. FAX 071-240-6840. circ. 2,500.
     Formerly (until 1989): Recreation Managers' Association of Great Britain Year Book (ISSN 0267-2103)

LEISURE ARTS. see *HOBBIES*

332 UK ISSN 0263-7774
LEISURE FUTURES. 1976. q. £975($1460) Henley Centre for Forecasting Ltd., 2 Tudor St., Blackfriars, London EC4Y 0AA, England. TEL 071-3535-9961. Ed. Kieron Culligan. charts; stat. (back issues avail.)
●Also available online.
—BLDSC shelfmark: 5182.240000.
Description: Analysis of free time activity patterns and associated spending in the UK.

790.1 US
LEISURE INDUSTRY REPORT. 1981. m. $65. Leisure Industry - Recreation News, Box 43563, Washington, DC 20010. TEL 202-232-7107. Ed. Marj Jensen. adv.; bk.rev. (back issues avail.)
Formerly: Leisure Industry Digest (ISSN 0276-0916)
Description: Compiles news reports from a wide range of sources into summary reviews of trends and developments on leisure and discretionary spending.

301 US
LEISURE INFORMATION QUARTERLY.* 1972. q. $14 to individuals (foreign $20) institutions $24 (foreign $30). New York University, School of Education, Health, Nursing and Arts Profession, 635 East Bldg., Washington Square, New York, NY 10003. Ed. Arnold Grossman. bk.rev.; bibl.; circ. 300. (back issues avail.) **Indexed:** Rural Recreat.Tour.Abstr., Sportsearch (1983-), World Agri.Econ.& Rural Sociol.Abstr.
Formerly: Leisure Information Newsletter.

052 UK
LEISURE INTELLIGENCE. 1983. q. £795. Mintel International Group Ltd., 18-19 Long Lane, London EC1A 9HE, England. TEL 071-606-4533. FAX 071-606-5159. Ed. Fenella McCarthy. (back issues avail.)
●Also available online.

333.78 US
LEISURE LINES; a monthly action report. vol.6, 1980. 8/yr. membership. California Park and Recreation Society, Inc., 3031 F St., Ste. 202, Box 161118, Sacramento, CA 95816. TEL 919-446-2777.

790.1 790.13 UK ISSN 0266-9102
LEISURE MANAGEMENT. 1981. m. £36($120) (Europe £45; elsewhere £60). Dicestar Ltd., 40 Bancroft, Hitchin, Herts S95 1LA, England. TEL 0462-431385. FAX 0462-422919. Ed. Liz Terry. adv.; bk.rev.; circ. 16,500. (back issues avail.)
—BLDSC shelfmark: 5182.266000.
Description: Documents and analyzes the leisure markets for policy makers, managers, developers and investors in and of leisure facilities.

333.78 790.1 UK ISSN 0267-3754
LEISURE MANAGER. 1936. m. £35. (Institute of Leisure and Amenity Management) John S. Turner & Associates Ltd., Victoria House, 25 High St., Over, Cambridge CB4 5NB, England. TEL 0954-30940. FAX 0954-31886. Ed. Judy Richardson. adv.; bk.rev.; illus.; index; circ. 7,500. **Indexed:** Curr.Adv.Ecol.Sci., Rural Recreat.Tour.Abstr., Sportsearch (1985-), World Agri.Econ.& Rural Sociol.Abstr.
—BLDSC shelfmark: 5182.266200.
Former titles (until Dec. 1984): I L A M Journal (ISSN 0265-6000); (until Jan. 1983): I L A M; Parks and Recreation (ISSN 0031-2223); Park Administration.

LEISURE, RECREATION AND TOURISM ABSTRACTS. see TRAVEL AND TOURISM — Abstracting, Bibliographies, Statistics

150 US ISSN 0149-0400
GV1 CODEN: LESCDC
LEISURE SCIENCES; an interdisciplinary journal. 1977. q. $99. Taylor & Francis, 1900 Frost Rd., Ste. 101, Bristol, PA 19007. TEL 215-785-5800. FAX 215-785-5515. Ed. Robert B. Ditton. adv.; bk.rev.; abstr.; index. **Indexed:** Commun.Abstr., Forest.Abstr., Geo.Abstr., Human Resour.Abstr., P.A.I.S., Psychol.Abstr., Rural Recreat.Tour.Abstr., Sage Pub.Admin.Abstr., Sage Urb.Stud.Abstr., Sportsearch (1977-).
—BLDSC shelfmark: 5182.270000.
Description: Presents scientific inquiries into the study of leisure, recreation, travel and their impact on the physical and social environment.
Refereed Serial

301 790.1 UK ISSN 0261-4367
LEISURE STUDIES. 1982. 3/yr. £50($90) to individuals; institutions £66($119). (Leisure Studies Association) E. & F.N. Spon, 2-6 Boundary Row, London SE1 8HN, England. TEL 071-865-0066. FAX 071-522-9623. (Dist. by: International Thomson Publishing Services, Ltd., N. Way, Andover, Hampshire SP10 5BE, England. TEL 0264-33-2424; U.S. addr.: Chapman & Hall, 29 W. 35th St., New York, NY 10001-2291. TEL 212-244-3336) Ed. Jonathan Long. bk.rev. (reprint service avail. from SWZ) **Indexed:** I D A, Psychol.Abstr., Sportsearch (1983-), Stud.Wom.Abstr.
—BLDSC shelfmark: 5182.272000.
Description: Covers all aspects of leisure and recreation: leisure behaviour in the arts, sports, cultural and informal activities, tourism, and urban and rural recreation.

910.202 CN
LEISURE WORLD. 1988. bi-m. Can.$15. Ontario Motorist Publishing Co., 1253 Ovellette Ave., Windsor, Ont. N8X 1J3, Canada. TEL 519-971-3208. FAX 519-977-1197. Ed. Douglas O'Neil. adv.; bk.rev.; film rev.; illus.; tr.lit.; circ. 270,000. (back issues avail.)
Formerly: Leisure Ontario (ISSN 0838-2913)
Description: Covers Canadian and international travel, destinations, automobiles and leisure time activities.

301 790.1 CN ISSN 0705-3436
GV14.45
LOISIR ET SOCIETE/SOCIETY AND LEISURE. (Text in English and French) 1978. s-a. Can.$20 to individuals; institutions Can.$35. Presses de l'Universite du Quebec, C.P. 250, Sillery, Que. G1T 2R1, Canada. TEL 418-657-3551. (In Europe subscr. to: Editions ESKA, 30 de Domremy, 75013 Paris, France) (Co-sponsor: International Sociological Association) Ed. Max D'Amours. bk.rev. (reprint service avail.) **Indexed:** Lang.& Lang.Behav.Abstr., Pt.de Rep. (1982-), Sportsearch (1978-).
—BLDSC shelfmark: 8319.191700.
Description: Humanities and social sciences journal devoted to the academic study of leisure in various societies.

790.1 BE
LOISIRAMA. q. Galerie Ravenstein, 27, 1000 Brussels, Belgium. **Indexed:** Sportsearch (1981-).

MOTORING & LEISURE. see TRANSPORTATION — Automobiles

OUTDOORS, RECREATION & LEISURE. see SPORTS AND GAMES — Outdoor Life

PROGRAMMING TRENDS IN THERAPEUTIC RECREATION. see EDUCATION — Special Education And Rehabilitation

790.1 613.7 CN ISSN 0031-2231
RECREATION CANADA. 1952. 5/yr. Can.$40($45) (typically set Oct.). Canadian Parks - Recreation Association, c/o Diane M. Smith, Exec.Dir., 1600 James Naismith Dr., Gloucester, Ont. K1B 5N4, Canada. TEL 613-748-5651. FAX 613-748-5706. adv.; bk.rev.; charts; illus.; index; circ. 3,000. (also avail. in microform from UMI) **Indexed:** Sportsearch (1972-).
Description: Covers current research and trends, innovative leisure programs and facilities, arts and culture, wellness - fitness for those who are interested in the parks - recreation - leisure industry.

790 US ISSN 0890-2194
RECREATION EXECUTIVE REPORT. 1973. m. $65. Leisure Industry - Recreation News, Box 43563, Washington, DC 20010. TEL 202-232-7107. Ed. Marj Jensen. adv.; bk.rev.; index; circ. 600.
Supersedes: Leisure Information Service. Fund Development and Revenue Source Report; Which was formerly: Leisure Information Service. Fund Development and Technical Assistance Report.
Description: Presents coverage of recreation issues, directed primarily to those involved in public recreation.

LIBRARY AND INFORMATION SCIENCES 2739

790.1 US
RECREATION RESOURCES; new products and services for professional recreation managers in parks, schools, clubs, resorts and other fitness and leisure facilities. 1981. 9/yr. $24 (foreign $50). Lakewood Publications, Inc. (Subsidiary of: Maclean Hunter Publishing Company), 50 S. Ninth, Minneapolis, MN 55402. TEL 612-333-0471. Ed. Galynn Nordstrom. circ. 51,000. (tabloid format; back issues avail.)
Formerly: Recreation, Sports and Leisure (ISSN 0277-707X)
Description: Product information for the managed recreation industry.

S B. (Sportstaettenbau und Baederanlagen - Sports Facilities and Swimming Pools) see BUILDING AND CONSTRUCTION

SOPHISTICATED LEISURE TRAVEL DIRECTORY. see TRAVEL AND TOURISM

SPORT & LEISURE (CARDIFF). see SPORTS AND GAMES

SPORT AND LEISURE (LONDON). see SPORTS AND GAMES

SPORTS & LEISURE NEWS. see SPORTS AND GAMES

SUID-AFRIKAANSE TYDSKRIF VIR NAVORSING IN SPORT, LIGGAAMLIKE OPVOEDKUNDE EN ONTSPANNING/SOUTH AFRICAN JOURNAL FOR RESEARCH IN SPORT, PHYSICAL EDUCATION AND RECREATION. see PHYSICAL FITNESS AND HYGIENE

TRAVEL & LEISURE. see TRAVEL AND TOURISM

790.01 028.5 CN ISSN 0380-9552
VANCOUVER MAGAZINE. 1968. m. Can.$18. Telemedia West, 300 Southeast Twr., 555 W. 12th Ave., Vancouver, B.C. V5Z 4L4, Canada. TEL 604-877-7732. FAX 604-877-4849. Ed. Scott Mowbray. adv.; bk.rev.; film rev.; play rev.; illus.; circ. 85,500.
Former titles: Vancouver's Leisure Magazine (ISSN 0380-9544); Dick Maclean's Leisure Magazine; Maclean's Leisure Magazine; Maclean's Guide (ISSN 0024-9254)

790.01 CC ISSN 1000-2928
WENHUA YULE/CULTURE & RECREATION. (Text in Chinese) 1980. m. Y12($36.80) (Zhejiang Sheng Qunzhong Yishu-guan - Zhejiang Provincial Popular Art Center) Wenhua Yule Bianjibu, 51 Wulin Lu, Hangzhou, Zhejiang 310006, People's Republic of China. TEL 778991. (Subscr. to: Nanjing City Post, Nanjing, Jiangsu, P.R.C.; Dist. in US by: China Books & Periodicals, Inc., 2929 24th St., San Francisco, CA 94110) Ed. Guo Jinkang. circ. 210,000.
Description: Contains popular literature, folklore, art, and information on recreation and culture.

790.01 CN
WORLD LEISURE AND RECREATION. 1958. q. $30 to individuals; institutions $50; students $15. World Leisure and Recreation Association, Box 309, Sharbot Lake, Ont. K0H 2P0, Canada. TEL 613-279-3172. FAX 613-279-3372. adv.; bk.rev.; abstr.; bibl.; illus.; circ. 3,000. **Indexed:** Rural Recreat.Tour.Abstr., Sportsearch (1984-), World Agri.Econ.& Rural Sociol.Abstr.
Former titles: World Leisure Review; (until 1984): W L R A Journal; W L R A Bulletin; International Recreation Association. Bulletin (ISSN 0441-9057)

LIBRARY AND INFORMATION SCIENCES

see also Bibliographies

020.6 CN
A A B C NEWSLETTER. 1981. q. membership. Archives Association of British Columbia, P.O. Box 78530, University Post Office, Vancouver, B.C. V6T 2E7, Canada. TEL 604-683-8588. FAX 604-683-8568. Ed. Anne Maclean. adv.; circ. 1,300.
Former titles: A I B C Newsletter (ISSN 0835-3859); Architectural Institute of British Columbia. News, Views and Reviews.
Description: Association news, news on members, industry news.

A A L L PUBLICATIONS SERIES. (American Association of Law Libraries) see LAW

LIBRARY AND INFORMATION SCIENCES

020   GW   ISSN 0720-6763
Z678.9.A1
A B I TECHNIK; Zeitschrift fuer Automation, Bau und Technik im Archiv, Bibliotheks- und Informationswesen. 1981. q. DM.108. Verlag Karlheinz Holz, Rheingaustr. 85, Postfach 3329, 6200 Wiesbaden 1, Germany. TEL 0611-23044. FAX 0611-261124. Ed. Berndt Dugall. adv.; bk.rev.; index; circ. 2,000. (back issues avail.) **Indexed:** LISA.
—BLDSC shelfmark: 0549.396000.
   Description: Covers information on automation, building and technology of libraries and information centers. Includes reports of events and exhibitions and new products.

020   AT   ISSN 0726-0644
Z674.83.A82
A B N NEWS. (Australian Bibliographic Network) 1982. bi-m. Aus.$33. National Library of Australia, Publications Section, Public Programs, Parkes Place, Canberra, A.C.T. 2600. **Indexed:** AESIS.

020   UK   ISSN 0263-6832
A C O L A M NEWSLETTER. 1980. s-a. free. Standing Conference of National and University Libraries (SCONUL), Advisory Committee on Latin American Materials, 102 Euston St., London NW1 2HA, England. FAX 071-388-5024. Ed. A. Biggins. circ. 130. (back issues avail.)
   Description: Reports Committee activities and news of library and information matters relating to Latin American Studies in the UK and elsewhere.

A D R I S NEWSLETTER. (Association for the Development of Religious Information Services) see *RELIGIONS AND THEOLOGY*

A F V A EVALUATIONS. (American Film & Video Association, Inc.) see *EDUCATION — Teaching Methods And Curriculum*

020 011   IT   ISSN 1120-2521
A I B NOTIZIE. 1988. m. L.50000. Associazione Italiana Biblioteche, Casella Postale 2461, 00100 Rome, Italy. Dir. Giovanni Solimine. circ. 3,000.

A I M NETWORK. (Association for Information Management) see *BUSINESS AND ECONOMICS — Management*

020 296   US   ISSN 0747-6175
A J L NEWSLETTER. 4/yr. $25 includes Judaica Librarianship. Association of Jewish Libraries, c/o National Foundation for Jewish Culture, 330 7th Ave., 21st Fl., New York, NY 10001-5010. TEL 513-221-1875. (Subscr. to: 3101 Clifton Ave., Cincinnati, OH 45220) Eds. Hazel Karp, Irene Levin. (back issues avail.)
   Description: Focuses on Judaica library-related activities. Includes media reviews, and job listings.

020.622   US   ISSN 0084-6406
Z673.A5
A L A HANDBOOK OF ORGANIZATION. a. $10 to non-members. American Library Association, 50 E. Huron St., Chicago, IL 60611. TEL 800-545-2433. FAX 312-440-9374. (reprint service avail. from UMI)
—BLDSC shelfmark: 0786.469000.
   Formerly: A L A Handbook of Organization and Membership Directory (ISSN 0273-4605)
   Description: Information on staff, officers and committees of the American Library Association.

020   US   ISSN 0001-1746
Z671
A L A WASHINGTON NEWSLETTER. 1949. 12/yr. $25 (foreign $30). American Library Association, Washington Office, 110 Maryland Ave., N.E., Washington, DC 20002. TEL 202-547-4440. Eds. Eileen D. Cooke, Carol C. Henderson. circ. 2,500. (processed; back issues avail.) **Indexed:** Lib.Lit.
   Description: Informs librarians and educators of the current status of all federal legislation that concerns libraries and librarians.

020.6   US   ISSN 1047-949X
Z688.5   CODEN: ALNWEA
A L C T S NEWSLETTER. 1976. 8/yr. $25 to non-members (foreign $35). American Library Association, Association for Library Collections and Technical Services, 50 E. Huron St., Chicago, IL 60611-2795. TEL 312-280-5035. FAX 312-280-3257. Ed. Ann Swartzell. circ. 8,200. (also avail. in microform from UMI; back issues avail.; reprint service avail. from UMI) **Indexed:** LHTN, Lib.Lit.
   Formerly: R T S D Newsletter (Resources and Technical Services Division) (ISSN 0360-5906)

020   PN
A L E B C I; BOLETIN INFORMATIVO. 1972. s-a. membership. Asociacion Latinoamericana de Escuelas de Bibliotecologia y Ciencias de la Informacion, Escuela de Bibliotecologia, Centro Regional de Veraguas, Santiago de Veraguas, Panama. FAX 984056. (Subscr. to: c/o Estela Morales Campos, Torre II de Humanidades, pisos 12 y 13, Ciudad Universitario, 04510 Mexico D.F., Mexico. TEL 550-5931) Ed. Carlos Ceballos Sosa. circ. 500 (controlled). (back issues avail.)

020 028.5   US   ISSN 0162-6612
A L S C NEWSLETTER. vol.5, 1973. 2/yr. membership. American Library Association, Association for Library Service to Children, Mid-Continent Public Library, 50 E. Huron St., Chicago, IL 60611. FAX 312-440-9374. Ed. Anitra T. Steele. circ. 4,000.

020   CN   ISSN 0827-0074
A M A NEWSLETTER. (Text in English, French) 1980. 4/yr. membership. Association of Manitoba Archivists, Box 27007, One Lombard Place, Winnipeg, Manitoba R3B 3K1, Canada. TEL 204-945-3971. bk.rev. (back issues avail.)
   Description: Articles related to archives in Manitoba and issues of interest to individuals working on Manitoba's archival community.

020   MX   ISSN 0001-186X
A M B A C NOTICIERO. 1966. q. $20 to non-members (effective 1991). Asociacion Mexicana de Bibliotecarios, A.C., Apdo. 27-651, Mexico, D.F. 06760, Mexico. Ed. Estela Morales Campos. adv.; bk.rev.; illus.; circ. 1,000.

020   US
A M S STUDIES IN LIBRARY AND INFORMATION SCIENCE. 1989. irreg. A M S Press, Inc., 56 E. 13th St., New York, NY 10003. TEL 212-777-4700. FAX 212-995-5413.
   Description: Numbered monographic series of library science information.

023   SP   ISSN 0210-4164
A N A B A D BOLETIN. 1950. q. 2500 ptas.($31) Asociacion Espanola de Archiveros Bibliotecarios, Museologos y Documentalistas, Paseo de Recoletos 20, Apdo. 14281, Madrid 1, Spain. Ed.Bd. bk.rev.; bibl.; stat.; circ. 3,000. **Indexed:** Amer.Hist.& Life, Hist.Abstr.
   Formerly (until 1977): A N A B A Boletin (ISSN 0044-9288)

029.7   CN
A N L A BULLETIN. 1983. q. Can.$10. Association of Newfoundland Labrador Archivists, c/o Colonial Bldg., Military Rd., St. John, N.F. A1C 2C9, Canada. TEL 709-729-3065. FAX 709-737-3118. Ed. Gail Weir. bk.rev.; bibl.; charts; illus.; circ. 110.
   Description: Outlines the activities of the archives and archivists in the province.

020   CN   ISSN 0001-2203
A P L A BULLETIN. (Text in English, French) 1936. 6/yr. Can.$25. Atlantic Provinces Library Association, c/o School of Library and Information Studies, Dalhousie University, Halifax, N.S. B3H 4H8, Canada. TEL 902-424-3656. FAX 506-364-2617. Ed. Bradd Burningham. adv.; illus.; circ. 550. (also avail. in microform from MIM,UMI; reprint service avail. from UMI) **Indexed:** Can.Per.Ind., CMI, Lib.Sci.Abstr., LISA.
   Supersedes (in 1958, vol.23): M L A Bulletin.

020 312   US   ISSN 0891-0847
A P L I C COMMUNICATOR. q. Association for Population - Family Planning Library & Information Center International, c/o Population Council Library, 1 Dag Hammarskjold Plaza, New York, NY 10017. circ. 200.

020   US   ISSN 1050-6098
Z671
A R L; a bimonthly newsletter of research libraries issues and actions. 1965. 6/yr. $40. Association of Research Libraries, 1527 New Hampshire Ave., N.W., Washington, DC 20036. TEL 202-232-2466. Ed. Jaia Barrett. circ. 1,000. (back issues avail.)
   Formerly (until 1990): A R L Newsletter (ISSN 0066-9652)

020.6   US   ISSN 0361-5669
Z682.3
A R L ANNUAL SALARY SURVEY. 1968. a. $60. Association of Research Libraries, 1527 New Hampshire Ave., N.W., Washington, DC 20036. TEL 202-232-2466. Ed. Sarah Pritchard. circ. 1,000. (back issues avail.) **Indexed:** SRI.

020   US   ISSN 0044-9652
Z673
A R L MINUTES. Variant title: Minutes of the Meetings. 1932. s-a. $60 to non-members. Association of Research Libraries, 1527 New Hampshire Ave., N.W., Washington, DC 20036. TEL 202-232-2466. Ed. Pamela Bixby. cum.index: 1932-1954, 1954-1969; circ. 500. (back issues avail.)
—BLDSC shelfmark: 5810.740000.

A R S C JOURNAL. (Association for Recorded Sound Collections, Inc.) see *SOUND RECORDING AND REPRODUCTION*

A R S C NEWSLETTER. (Association for Recorded Sound Collections, Inc.) see *SOUND RECORDING AND REPRODUCTION*

027   CN   ISSN 0835-8672
A RAYONS OUVERTS. 1967. q. free. Bibliotheque Nationale du Quebec, 1700 rue Saint-Denis, Montreal, Que. H2X 3K6, Canada. TEL 514-873-1100. FAX 514-873-9932. bibl.; circ. 1,200. (back issues avail.)
   Description: Information about the library, its documents and services, and news about exhibitions.

020   US
A S I D I C NEWSLETTER. 1969. s-a. $50. Association of Information and Dissemination Centers, Box 8105, Athens, GA 30603. TEL 404-542-6820. FAX 908-302-2067. Ed. Donald T. Hawkins. circ. 125. (also avail. in looseleaf format; back issues avail.)

029.7   US   ISSN 0066-0124
                      CODEN: AIHDC2
A S I S HANDBOOK AND DIRECTORY. a. $100 to non-members. American Society for Information Science, 8720 Georgia Ave., Ste. 501, Silver Spring, MD 20910. TEL 301-495-0900. adv.

020   US
A S I S KEY PAPERS SERIES. irreg., latest 1983. price varies. (American Society for Information Science) Greenwood Press, Inc. (Subsidiary of: Greenwood Publishing Group Inc.), 88 Post Rd. W., Box 5007, Westport, CT 06881-5007. TEL 203-226-3571. FAX 203-222-1502. **Indexed:** C.I.J.E.

020.6   US   ISSN 0515-0272
A S L A NEWSLETTER. 1961. 10/yr. membership. Arizona State Library Association, c/o Adrienne Sanden, Ed., 1227 N. 84th Place, Scottsdale, AZ 85257-4171. FAX 602-946-7475. adv.; B&W page $250; adv. contact: Adrienne Sanden. circ. 1,300.

026   PH   ISSN 0001-2548
A S L P BULLETIN. 1954. q. 30p.($15) membership. Association of Special Libraries of the Philippines, National Library Bldg., Rm. 301, T.M. Kalaw St., Manila 2801, Philippines. Ed. Angelica A. Cabanero. adv.; bk.rev.; illus.; index, cum.index; circ. 500.

027.4   CN
A S P L O NEWSLETTER. 1982. s-a. Can.$5. Association of Small Public Libraries of Ontario, 2 Library Lane, Tillsonburg, Ont. N4G 4S7, Canada. TEL 519-842-5571. Ed. Matthew Scholtz. circ. 110. (looseleaf format; back issues avail.)

LIBRARY AND INFORMATION SCIENCES

020   US   ISSN 0276-8291
ABBEY NEWSLETTER; bookbinding and conservation. 1975. 8/yr. $37 to individuals; institutions $45. Abbey Publications, Inc., 320 E. Center St., Provo, UT 84606. TEL 801-373-1598. FAX 801-375-4423. Ed. Ellen R. McCrady. bk.rev.; bibl.; charts; illus.; stat.; tr.lit.; index.; circ. 1,272. (back issues avail.) Indexed: Abstr.Bull.Inst.Pap.Chem., Art & Archaeol.Tech.Abstr., Graph.Arts Lit.Abstr.
—BLDSC shelfmark: 0537.724860.
Description: Covers bookbinding and conservation of book and paper materials.

020   US   ISSN 0278-2820
Z668
ABSTRACTS STRENGTHENING RESEARCH LIBRARY RESOURCES PROGRAM. 1978. a. free. U.S. Department of Education, Library Programs, Washington, DC 20208-5571. Ed. Louise Sutherland. circ. 1,000. (back issues avail.)
Description: Information on grants funded by Title II-C of the Higher Education Act under the Research Library Resources Program.

020   CU   ISSN 0138-7324
Z1007   CODEN: AITEEX
ACADEMIA DE CIENCIAS DE CUBA. INSTITUTO DE DOCUMENTACION E INFORMACION CIENTIFICA Y TECNICA. ACTUALIDADES DE LA INFORMACION CIENTIFICA Y TECNICA. 1968. bi-m. $23 in N. America; S. America $25; Europe $29. Ediciones Cubanas, Obispo No. 527, Apdo. 605, Havana, Cuba.
—BLDSC shelfmark: 0677.035000.

020   US
ACADEMIC LIBRARY BOOK REVIEW. 1985. bi-m. $36 (foreign $44). 290 Broadway, Ste. 354, Lynbrook, NY 11563. FAX 516-596-2911. Ed. Hannah Merker. adv.; bk.rev.; circ. 5,000(AP).

020   IT   ISSN 0001-4451
ACCADEMIE E BIBLIOTECHE D'ITALIA. 1927. q. L.50000. (Ministero per i Beni Culturali e Ambientali) Casa Editrice Fratelli Palombi, Via dei Gracchi 181-185, 00192 Rome, Italy. Dir. Renzo Frattarolo. illus.; index. **Indexed:** Lib.Lit., Lib.Sci.Abstr., LISA, M.L.A.
—BLDSC shelfmark: 0570.805000.
Description: Forum features bibliographies, initiatives and activities promoting cultural institutes.

020   AT   ISSN 1030-0155
ACCESS (ELIZABETH). 1964. q. Aus.$40 (foreign Aus.$48). Australian School Library Association, Inc., P.O. Box 140, Elizabeth, S.A. 5112, Australia. TEL 08-263-6244. FAX 08-263-6072. Ed. Andrew Perry. circ. 2,800. (back issues avail.)
—BLDSC shelfmark: 0570.819750.
Supersedes (in 1987): Australian School Librarian (ISSN 0005-0199)
Description: Provides a focus for those teachers and teacher-librarians concerned with co-operative planning and teaching.

029.7   BL
ACONTECEU. w. Cr.$300. (Centro Ecumenico de Documentacao e Informacao) Tempo e Presenca Editora, Ltda, Caixa Postal 16082, 22221 Rio de Janeiro, Brazil. Ed. Jose Ricardo Ramalho.

020   US   ISSN 0896-3576
Z689.A15   CODEN: AQLIER
ACQUISITIONS LIBRARIAN. 1989. s-a. $24 to individuals; institutions and libraries $75. Haworth Press, Inc., 10 Alice St., Binghamton, NY 13904. TEL 607-722-1695. FAX 607-722-1424. Ed. Bill Katz. adv.; bk.rev.; circ. 142. (also avail. in microfiche from HAW; reprint service avail. from HAW) **Indexed:** Chem.Abstr., LISA.
—BLDSC shelfmark: 0578.881170.
Description: Devoted to a single, broad, but well-defined and practical issue or topic of immediate concern to librarians and information professionals.
Refereed Serial

020   SW   ISSN 0065-1060
ACTA BIBLIOTHECAE REGIAE STOCKHOLMIENSIS. 1961. irreg. price varies. Kungliga Bibliotek, Box 5039, 102 41 Stockholm, Sweden. FAX 08-6116956. TELEX 19640-KBS-S.

020   SW   ISSN 0065-1079
ACTA BIBLIOTHECAE UNIVERSITATIS GOTHOBURGENSIS. 1941. irreg., no.25, 1991. price varies; also exchange basis. Goeteborgs Universitet, Universitetsbibliotek, Centralbiblioteket, Box 5096, S-402 22 Goeteborg, Sweden.
Formerly: Acta Bibliothecae Gothoburgensis.

010 020   HU   ISSN 0001-7175
ACTA UNIVERSITATIS SZEGEDIENSIS DE ATTILA JOZSEF NOMINATAE. ACTA BIBLIOTHECARIA. (Text in English, German or Hungarian; summaries in English, French, German or Russian) 1955. irreg. exchange basis. Attila Jozsef University, c/o E. Szabo, Exchange Librarian, Dugonics ter 13, P.O.B. 393, Szeged H-6701, Hungary. TEL 62-24-022. TELEX 82605 JATCK H. (Subscr. to: Kultura, Box 149, H-1389 Budapest, Hungary) Ed. Bela Karacsonyi. charts; circ. 500.
Description: Library science and cultural history with publishing history as secondary concern.

025   US   ISSN 0363-0250
ACTION FOR LIBRARIES. 1975. m. $10 to foreign libraries (free to US libraries). Bibliographical Center for Research, Rocky Mountain Region, Inc., 4500 Cherry Creek Dr. S., Ste. 206, Denver, CO 80222. TEL 303-691-0550. FAX 303-691-0112. Ed. Joyce Hillshafer. adv.; bk.rev.; circ. 2,000.
—BLDSC shelfmark: 0675.625000.

020   CN
ACTUALITES S D M. (Text and summaries in French) 1972. bi-m. free. Services Documentaires Multimedia, Inc., 1685 Est, Rue Fleury, Montreal, Que H2C 1T1, Canada. TEL 514-382-0895. FAX 514-384-9139. Ed. Francoise Bray. circ. 7,000. (looseleaf format)
Former titles: Actualites C B; (until 1987): Information C.B. (ISSN 0704-2728)

027.7   ET   ISSN 0017-6680
ADDIS ABABA UNIVERSITY. COLLEGE OF TECHNOLOGY. LIBRARY BULLETIN. (Name of issuing body varies: Haile Sellassie I University, University of Addis Ababa, National University) vol.10, 1977. q. free. Addis Ababa University, College of Technology, P.O. Box 518, Addis Ababa, Ethiopia. Ed. Befekadu Debela. bibl. (looseleaf format)

027.7   ET
ADDIS ABABA UNIVERSITY. LIBRARY. ANNUAL REPORT. a. Addis Ababa University, Library, University College, Addis Ababa, Ethiopia.

ADDRESS LIST, REGIONAL AND SUBREGIONAL LIBRARIES FOR THE BLIND AND PHYSICALLY HANDICAPPED. see *HANDICAPPED — Visually Impaired*

029   US   ISSN 0044-636X
Z671   CODEN: ATLBA
ADVANCED TECHNOLOGY LIBRARIES. Variant title: A T - L Newsletter. 1971. m. $89 (effective 1992). Macmillan Publishing Company, Macmillan Reference, 866 Third Ave., New York, NY 10022. TEL 212-702-4301. FAX 212-605-9368. adv.; bibl.; index. (also avail. in microform from UMI) **Indexed:** Info.Media & Tech., Leg.Info.Manage.Ind., Pers.Lit., PROMT, Tr.& Indus.Ind.
—BLDSC shelfmark: 0696.935000.
Description: Covers technical advances in library science: optical publishing, hardware and software, library services, bibliographic utilities, legislation and results of meetings.

020   US   ISSN 0065-2830
Z674   CODEN: AVLSA
ADVANCES IN LIBRARIANSHIP. 1970. irreg., vol.15, 1991. Academic Press, Inc., 1250 Sixth Ave., San Diego, CA 92101. TEL 619-230-0926. FAX 619-699-6715. Ed. Melvin J. Voigt. (reprint service avail. from ISI)
—BLDSC shelfmark: 0709.260000.

025   US   ISSN 0732-0671
Z678
ADVANCES IN LIBRARY ADMINISTRATION AND ORGANIZATION. 1982. a. $63.50 to institutions. J A I Press Inc., 55 Old Post Rd. No. 2, Box 1678, Greenwich, CT 06836-1678. TEL 203-661-7602. Ed.Bd.

020   US   ISSN 1040-4384
Z692.S5
ADVANCES IN SERIALS MANAGEMENT. 1986. irreg. $58.50 to institutions. J A I Press Inc., 55 Old Post Rd., Box 1678, Greenwich, CT 06836-1678. TEL 203-661-7602. Eds. Marcia Tuttle, Jean Cook.
—BLDSC shelfmark: 0711.383500.

020.6   NR   ISSN 0189-6709
AFRICAN JOURNAL OF ACADEMIC LIBRARIANSHIP. (Text in English; summaries in French) 1983. s-a. £N25($50) Standing Conference of African University Libraries (SCAUL), P.O. Box 46, University of Lagos, Akoka, Yaba, Lagos, Nigeria. Ed. E.B. Bankole. adv.; bk.rev.; circ. 200. **Indexed:** LISA.
—BLDSC shelfmark: 0732.514000.
Supersedes: S C A U L Newsletter (ISSN 0563-0924)

021   SA
AFRICAN LIBRARY ASSOCIATION OF S.A. NEWSLETTER.* (Text mainly in English; occasionally in Afrikaans) 1967. q. R.0.50. African Library Association of South Africa, c/o Mamelodi Branch Library, P.O. Mamelodi, Pretoria, South Africa.
Formerly: B L A S A Newsletter (ISSN 0006-4580)

AFRICANA JOURNAL; a bibliographic library journal and review annual. see *BIBLIOGRAPHIES*

026   US
AFRICANA LIBRARIES NEWSLETTER. 1975. q. free. c/o Joseph J. Lauer, Ed., Africana Bibliographer, Michigan State University Libraries, E. Lansing, MI 48824-1048. TEL 517-355-2366. FAX 517-336-1445. bibl.; circ. 600 (controlled). (looseleaf format; back issues avail.)
Former titles: Boston University Africana Libraries. Newsletter; Africana Libraries Newsletter (ISSN 0148-7868)

020   US   ISSN 1043-2094
Z689.5.U6
AGAINST THE GRAIN. 1989. 5/yr. $25. Katina Strauch, Ed. & Pub., Citadel Station, Charleston, SC 29409. TEL 803-792-8020. FAX 803-792-8019. adv.; bk.rev.; abstr.; circ. 500.
Description: Covers library-vendor relations, acquisition business, publisher profiles, prices and studies.

020 630   US   ISSN 0095-2699
Z675.A8
AGRICULTURAL LIBRARIES INFORMATION NOTES. 1975. m. free. U.S. Department of Agriculture, National Agricultural Library, 10301 Baltimore Blvd., Beltsville, MD 20705. TEL 301-344-3937. FAX 301-344-5472. Ed. Joseph N. Swab. adv.; bk.rev.; circ. 4,500.
—BLDSC shelfmark: 0750.240000.

029.7   PL   ISSN 0002-3787
AG500   CODEN: APDKAG
AKTUALNE PROBLEMY INFORMACJI I DOKUMENTACJI. (Text in Polish; summaries in English, French, Polish, Russian) 1950. bi-m. $33. Instytut Informacji Naukowej, Technicznej i Ekonomicznej, Al. Niepodleglosci 188, 00-931 Warsaw, Poland. (Dist. by: Ars Polona - Ruch, Krakowskie Przedmiescie 7, Warsaw, Poland) Ed. Mieczyslaw Derentowicz. bk.rev.; charts; illus.; index; circ. 2,000. **Indexed:** Bull.Signal., INIS Atomind., LISA, Ref.Zh., Sci.Abstr.
—BLDSC shelfmark: 0785.720000.

027.4   US
ALABAMA. PUBLIC LIBRARY SERVICE. ANNUAL REPORT. 1956. a. free to Alabama libraries. Public Library Service, 6030 Monticello Dr., Montgomery, AL 36130. TEL 205-277-7330. circ. 1,200. (also avail. in microform from EDR) **Indexed:** SRI.
Supersedes: Alabama. Public Library Service. Basic State Plan and Annual Program (ISSN 0095-361X)

027.7   US
ALABAMA JUNIOR COLLEGE LIBRARY ASSOCIATION NEWSLETTER. 1965. 3/yr. membership. (Alabama Junior College Library Association) George C. Wallace State Community College, Drawer 1049, Salem, AL 36702-1049. Ed. Ann B. Mobbs. cum.index: 1965-1975; circ. 200.
Formerly (until 1973): Alabama Junior College Librarian (ISSN 0002-4260)

LIBRARY AND INFORMATION SCIENCES

020 US ISSN 0002-4295
Z671
ALABAMA LIBRARIAN. 1949. 7/yr. $25 (foreign $55). Alabama Library Association, Inc., 400 S. Union St., Ste. 255, Montgomery, AL 36104. TEL 205-262-5210. Ed. Barbara Bishop. adv.; illus.; cum.index: vols. 1-7; circ. 1,400. (also avail. in microform from UMI) **Indexed:** Lib.Lit., Lib.Sci.Abstr.

070 US
ALABAMA PRESS ASSOCIATION. RATE AND DATA GUIDE. (Cover title: Alabama Rate and Data) a. $20. Alabama Press Association, Commerce Center, Ste. 1100, 2027 1st Ave., N., Birmingham, AL 35203. TEL 205-322-0380. FAX 205-322-0389. Ed. Mike Ryland. adv.; circ. 2,000.
Formerly: A P A Newspaper Directory (ISSN 0065-5643)

021 US
ALASKA LIBRARY DIRECTORY. 1973. a. $10. Alaska Library Association (Fairbanks), c/o Isabelle Mudd, Exec.Sec., Box 81084, Fairbanks, AK 99708. TEL 907-479-4522. circ. controlled.
Formerly: Alaska Libraries and Library Personnel Directory.
Description: Lists names and addresses of Alaskan libraries and their staffs.

027.7 CN ISSN 0829-4321
ALBERTA ASSOCIATION OF COLLEGE LIBRARIANS. NEWSLETTER. 1978. 2/yr. Can.$10. Alberta Association of College Librarians, Canadian Union College Library, Box 460, College Heights, Alta. TOC 0Z0, Canada. Ed. Keith Clouten. adv.; bk.rev.; circ. 100 (controlled).
Formerly: Alberta Council of College Librarians. Newsletter (ISSN 0707-7327)

020 CN ISSN 0707-0306
ALBERTA GOVERNMENT LIBRARIES' NEWSLETTER. 1974. m. (11/yr.). Can.$13.50. Alberta Legislature Library, Cooperative Government Library Service Sections, 902 Legislature Annex, 9718-107 St., Edmonton, Alta. T5K 1E4, Canada. TEL 403-427-3837. FAX 403-427-1623. Ed. Karen Powell. circ. 145.

020 IS ISSN 0334-4754
ALEI SEFER. s-a. $14 per no. Bar-Ilan University Press, Ramat Gan 52900, Israel. TEL 03-5318401. Ed. S.Z. Havlin. (back issues avail.)
Description: Innovative comprehensive journal devoted to the scientific examinations of bibliographies and to the study of the Hebrew book.

020 UK
ALEXANDRIA: JOURNAL OF NATIONAL & INTERNATIONAL LIBRARY & INFORMATION ISSUES. 1989. 3/yr. £75. Gower Publishing Co. Ltd., Gower House, Croft Rd., Aldershot, Hants GU11 3HR, England. TEL 0252-331551. **Indexed:** LISA.
Description: National library and international policy issues of interest to all in the library and information world.

020 US ISSN 8756-4173
Z673.W3
ALKI. 1985. 3/yr. $14. Washington Library Association, 1232 143rd Ave. S.E., Bellevue, WA 98007. TEL 206-747-6917. Ed. Lisa Wolfe. adv.; circ. 1,350. (also avail. in microform from UMI)
Description: Philosophical and substantive analyses of current and enduring issues for and about Washington State libraries.

020 808.8 CN
ALTERNATIVE ARCHIVIST. 1979. q. Can.$5. Federation of Alternative Libraries, Box 1294, Kitchener, Ont. N2G 4G8, Canada. adv.; bk.rev.; abstr.; bibl.; circ. 75. (looseleaf format)

020 US ISSN 0749-6885
Z716.4
ALTERNATIVE LIBRARY LITERATURE. 1984. biennial. $35. McFarland & Company, Inc., Box 611, Jefferson, NC 28640. Ed. Robert Franklin.
—BLDSC shelfmark: 0803.587500.
Description: Anthology on library issues and current topics. Includes essays and cartoons.

070.5 970 US ISSN 0569-2229
E172
AMERICAN ANTIQUARIAN SOCIETY. NEWS-LETTER. 1968. s-a. included in subscr. to its proceedings. American Antiquarian Society, 185 Salisbury St., Worcester, MA 01609. TEL 508-755-5221. Ed. Lynnette P. Sodha. illus.; circ. 1,525. (also avail. in microform from UMI; reprint service avail. from UMI)
Description: Contains information about programs, grants, and members and staff of the Society.

970 US ISSN 0044-751X
E172
AMERICAN ANTIQUARIAN SOCIETY. PROCEEDINGS. 1812. s-a. $45 (foreign $53). American Antiquarian Society, 185 Salisbury St., Worcester, MA 01609. TEL 508-755-5221. Ed. John B. Hench. bibl.; illus.; circ. 1,000. (also avail. in microfilm from UMI; reprint service avail. from KTO) **Indexed:** Amer.Hist.& Life, Art & Archaeol.Tech.Abstr., Arts & Hum.Cit.Ind., Bibl.Ind., Curr.Cont., RILA.
Description: Focuses on tools for scholarship-bibliographies, finding aids, and edited primary documents concerning American history and culture through 1876.

026 US ISSN 0572-4953
Z675.L2
AMERICAN ASSOCIATION OF LAW LIBRARIES. NEWSLETTER. (Supersedes the association's President's Newsletter) 1972. 10/yr. $50. American Association of Law Libraries, 53 W. Jackson Blvd., Ste. 940, Chicago, IL 60604. TEL 312-939-4764. FAX 312-431-1097. Ed. Mary Sworsky. circ. 4,700. **Indexed:** Leg.Info.Manage.Ind.

AMERICAN INDIAN LIBRARIES NEWSLETTER. see *ETHNIC INTERESTS*

011 IS
AMERICAN JEWISH COMMITTEE. RECENTLY ARRIVED IN THE LIBRARY; selected items. (Text in English) 1979. irreg. free. American Jewish Committee Library, 16 King George St., P.O. Box 1538, Jerusalem 91014, Israel. TEL 02-255281. FAX 02-254396. Ed. Ellen Infeld. circ. 500.

020 US ISSN 0002-9769
Z673.A5
AMERICAN LIBRARIES. 1907. m. (11/yr.). $60 (foreign $70). American Library Association, 50 E. Huron St., Chicago, IL 60611-2795. TEL 800-545-2433. FAX 312-440-9374. Ed. Thomas Gaughan. adv.; bk.rev.; illus.; index; circ. 53,300. (also avail. in microform from UMI,MIM; back issues avail.; reprint service avail. from UMI) **Indexed:** Access (1980-), Bk.Rev.Ind., C.I.J.E., Child.Bk.Rev.Ind. (1969-), Educ.Ind., Inform.Sci.Abstr., Leg.Info.Manage.Ind., LHTN, Lib.Lit, LISA, Mag.Ind., Media Rev.Dig., P.A.I.S., Pers.Lit., PROMT, R.G., Resour.Ctr.Ind.
●Also available online. Vendor(s): DIALOG.
—BLDSC shelfmark: 0840.730000.
Formerly: A L A Bulletin (ISSN 0364-4006)
Description: Provides current news and information concerning the library industry.

020 US
AMERICAN LIBRARY ASSOCIATION. ANNUAL CONFERENCE PROGRAM. a. $12. American Library Association, Conference Arrangements Office, 50 E. Huron St., Chicago, IL 60611. TEL 312-280-3218. FAX 312-280-3224. Ed. Pier A. London. adv.; circ. 16,000.

020 US ISSN 0065-910X
Z731
AMERICAN LIBRARY DIRECTORY. 1908. a. $215. R.R. Bowker, A Reed Reference Publishing Company, Division of Reed Publishing (USA) Inc., 121 Chanlon Rd., New Providence, NJ 07974. TEL 800-521-8110. FAX 908-665-6688. TELEX 138 755. (Subscr. to: Order Dept., Box 31, New Providence, NJ 07974)
●Also available online. Vendor(s): DIALOG (File no.460).
Also available on CD-ROM. Producer(s): R.R. Bowker.
—BLDSC shelfmark: 0840.750000.
Description: Lists all types of libraries and library-related organizations in U.S. and Canada.

021.7 US ISSN 0882-5351
AMERICAN MAGAZINE AND HISTORICAL CHRONICLE. 1943. s-a. free to qualified personnel. (Clements Library Associates) University of Michigan, William L. Clements Library of American History, Ann Arbor, MI 48109. TEL 313-764-2347. Eds. John Dann, John Harriman. circ. 900. (back issues avail.)
Supersedes (in 1984): Quarto (Ann Arbor).

026
AMERICAN MERCHANT MARINE LIBRARY ASSOCIATION. ANNUAL REPORT. 1921. a. free. American Merchant Marine Library Association, One World Trade Center, Ste. 2161, New York, NY 10048. TEL 212-775-1038. FAX 212-432-5492. TELEX 222146 UNS UR. Ed. Jeannine Russell. circ. 2,500.
Formerly: American Merchant Marine Library Association. Report (ISSN 0065-938X)

AMERICAN PETROLEUM INSTITUTE. CENTRAL ABSTRACTING & INFORMATION SERVICES. THESAURUS. see *PETROLEUM AND GAS — Abstracting, Bibliographies, Statistics*

020 US ISSN 0160-0044
Z1008 CODEN: PAISDQ
AMERICAN SOCIETY FOR INFORMATION SCIENCE. ANNUAL MEETING. PROCEEDINGS. 1964. a. $45 to non-members; members $36. (American Society for Information Science) Learned Information, Inc., 143 Old Marlton Pike, Medford, NJ 08055-8750. TEL 609-654-6266. FAX 609-654-4309. Ed. Jose-Marie Griffiths. illus.; index. (back issues avail.) **Indexed:** Biol.Abstr., C.I.J.E., Compumath, SSCI.
Formerly: American Society for Information Science. Proceedings (ISSN 0044-7870)

029.7 US ISSN 0095-4403
Z699.A1 CODEN: BASICR
AMERICAN SOCIETY FOR INFORMATION SCIENCE. BULLETIN. 1974. bi-m. $60 to non-members (foreign $70). American Society for Information Science, 8720 Georgia Ave, Ste. 501, Silver Spring, MD 20910. TEL 301-495-0900. Ed. Richard Hill. adv.; bibl.; circ. 4,500. (also avail. in microform from UMI; back issues avail.; reprint service avail. from UMI) **Indexed:** C.I.J.E., Curr.Cont., GeoRef., Inform.Sci.Abstr., Leg.Info.Manage.Ind., LHTN, Lib.Lit., LISA, Mag.Ind., Sci.Abstr., Soc.Work Res.& Abstr., SSCI.
—BLDSC shelfmark: 2392.805000.
Supersedes: A S I S Newsletter (ISSN 0001-2513) Former titles: American Documentation Institute. Newsletter; American Society for Information Science. Newsletter (ISSN 0190-5201).
Description: Offers news, opinions and analysis of happenings in the world of information.

029.7 016 US ISSN 0002-8231
Z1007 CODEN: AISJB6
AMERICAN SOCIETY FOR INFORMATION SCIENCE. JOURNAL. Short title: J A S I S. 1950. 10/yr. $295 to individuals (foreign $390). John Wiley & Sons, Inc., Journals, 605 Third Ave., New York, NY 10158-0012. TEL 212-850-6000. FAX 212-850-6088. Ed. Donald H. Kraft. adv.; bk.rev.; charts; illus.; index; circ. 5,200. (also avail. in microform from RPI; back issues avail.; reprint service avail. from KTO,RPI) **Indexed:** ABI Inform, Abstr.Bull.Inst.Pap.Chem., Amer.Hist.& Life, BPIA, Bus.Ind., Chem.Abstr., Compumath, Comput.Cont., Comput.Rev., Curr.Cont., Excerp.Med., GeoRef., Hist.Abstr., Inform.Sci.Abstr., Key to Econ.Sci., Lang.& Lang.Behav.Abstr., Leg.Info.Manage.Ind., LHTN, Lib.Lit., LISA, P.A.I.S., Sci.Abstr., Sci.Cit.Ind., Soc.Work Res.& Abstr., SSCI.
—BLDSC shelfmark: 4692.870000.
Formerly: American Documentation.
Description: Forum for discussion and experimentation in the theory and practice of communicating information. Articles cover operations research, automation applications, communications and computer technology.

020 CN ISSN 0318-9937
AMERICAN SOCIETY FOR INFORMATION SCIENCE. WESTERN CANADA CHAPTER. ANNUAL MEETING PROCEEDINGS. 1969. a. Can.$15 price varies. American Society for Information Science, Western Canada Chapter, c/o Margo Young, Ed., 1111-87 Ave., Ste. 702, Edmonton, Alta. T6G 0X9, Canada. TEL 403-432-2728. FAX 403-492-4327. Ed. M. Young. circ. 150. (back issues avail.) **Indexed:** Compumath.
—BLDSC shelfmark: 6841.279300.
Description: Papers presented at the annual conference.

LIBRARY AND INFORMATION SCIENCES

020　　　　　　　UK　　ISSN 0265-3389
AMERICAN STUDIES LIBRARY NEWSLETTER. 1978. 2/yr. free to qualified personnel. S.C.O.N.U.L. Advisory Committee on American Studies, c/o Liverpool School of Tropical Medicine, School Library, Permbroke Place, Liverpool L3 5QA, England. TEL 051-708-9393. FAX 051-708-8733. Ed. C.M. Deering. adv.; bk.rev.; circ. 400. **Indexed:** LISA.
—BLDSC shelfmark: 0857.677000.
 Formerly (until no.15, 1984): A.S.L.G. Newsletter (ISSN 0141-6383)

025　　　　　　　US　　ISSN 0066-0868
Z673
AMERICAN THEOLOGICAL LIBRARY ASSOCIATION. CONFERENCE. SUMMARY OF PROCEEDINGS. 1947. a. $20. American Theological Library Association, Office of the Executive Secretary, 820 Church St., Ste. 300, Evanston, IL 60201. TEL 708-869-7788. Ed. Betty O'Brien. cum.index every 40 yrs; circ. 700. (also avail. in microfilm) **Indexed:** Rel.Ind.One.
—BLDSC shelfmark: 8531.140000.

027.67　　　　　　US　　ISSN 0003-1399
Z675.T4
AMERICAN THEOLOGICAL LIBRARY ASSOCIATION. NEWSLETTER. 1953. q. $10. American Theological Library Association, Office of the Executive Secretary, 820 Church St., Ste. 300, Evanston, IL 60201. TEL 708-869-7788. Ed. Donn Michael Farris. cum.index every 5 yrs; circ. 700. (processed) **Indexed:** Lib.Lit.
—BLDSC shelfmark: 6106.338150.

020　　　　　　　UK　　ISSN 0260-3667
AMERICAN TRUST FOR THE BRITISH LIBRARY. NEWSLETTER. 1980. s-a. British Library, Humanities and Social Sciences, Great Russell St., London WC1B 3DG, England. TEL 071-323-7704. FAX 071-323-7736. TELEX 21462. Ed. Gill Ridgeley. illus.; circ. controlled.
—BLDSC shelfmark: 6106.338200.
 Description: Covers details of exhibitions, acquisitions and other interesting and important developments.

AMERIKAI MAGYAR LEVELESTAR/HUNGARIAN ARCHIVES OF AMERICA. see HISTORY — History Of Europe

AMICI. see RELIGIONS AND THEOLOGY — Roman Catholic

027.4 021.7　　　US　　ISSN 0003-195X
Z673
AMONG FRIENDS. 1945. s-a. $2 to non-members. Friends of the Detroit Public Library, Inc., 5201 Woodward Ave., Detroit, MI 48202. TEL 313-833-4048. Ed. Paul T. Scupholm. bk.rev.; illus.; circ. 4,500.

027.4　　　　　　US
ANALYSES OF NEW JERSEY PUBLIC LIBRARY STATISTICS FOR (YEAR). 1981. a. free. State Library, 185 W. State St., Trenton, NJ 08625-0520. Ed. Robert K. Fortenbaugh. circ. 675. **Indexed:** SRI.

ANDREWS ADVISOR; quarterly newsletter for law librarians. see LAW

020 001.539　　　II　　ISSN 0003-4835
Z671
ANNALS OF LIBRARY SCIENCE AND DOCUMENTATION. (Text in English) 1954. q. Rs.100($50) Indian National Scientific Documentation Centre, 14 Satsang Vihar Mag, Off SJS Sansanwal Marg, New Delhi 110 067, India. Ed. B. Guha. adv.; bk.rev.; bibl.; index; circ. 650. **Indexed:** Chem.Abstr., Lib.Lit., LISA.
—BLDSC shelfmark: 1041.810000.

ANNOTATED BIBLIOGRAPHIES OF SERIALS: A SUBJECT APPROACH. see BIBLIOGRAPHIES

ANNOTATION. see HISTORY — History Of North And South America

020　　　　　　　US
ANNUAL DIRECTORY OF OKLAHOMA LIBRARIES. 1984. a. Department of Libraries, 200 N.E. 18th St., Oklahoma City, OK 73105. TEL 405-521-2502. FAX 405-525-7804. circ. 250.
 Supersedes in part (1955-1984): Oklahoma. Department of Libraries. Annual Report and Directory of Libraries in Oklahoma (ISSN 0066-4065)

001.5　　　　　　NE　　ISSN 0066-4200
Z699.A1　　　　　　　　CODEN: ARISBC
ANNUAL REVIEW OF INFORMATION SCIENCE AND TECHNOLOGY. 1966. irreg., vol.25, 1990. price varies. (American Society for Information Science, Information & Business Division) Elsevier Science Publishers B.V., Books Division, P.O. Box 211, 1000 AE Amsterdam, Netherlands. TEL 020-5803911. FAX 020-5803705. TELEX 18582 ESPA NL. (Subscr. in U.S. and Canada to: Elsevier Science Publishing Co., Inc., Box 882, Madison Sq. Sta., New York, NY 10159. TEL 212-989-5800) Ed. Martha E. Williams. bibl.; index, cum.index: vols.1-10. (back issues avail.) **Indexed:** Biol.Abstr., Compumath, Curr.Cont., Sci.Abstr., SSCI.
—BLDSC shelfmark: 1522.570000.
 Description: Current reviews and analyses of the year's most important trends, innovations, and advances in the field of information science.
 Refereed Serial

020　　　　　　　US
ANSWERS; the information access digest. 1977. m. (except Jul. and Aug.). $45. Data and Research Technology Corp., 1102 McNeilly Ave., Pittsburgh, PA 15216. TEL 412-563-2212. Ed. K.K. McNulty, Sr. adv.; bk.rev.; bibl.; index; circ. 5,000. (also avail. in microfiche)
 Former titles: Information Access Digest & Information Access.

ANTHROPOS; revista de documentacion cientifica de la cultura. see HUMANITIES: COMPREHENSIVE WORKS

ANTHROPOS. DOCUMENTOS A; genealogia cientifica de la cultura. see HUMANITIES: COMPREHENSIVE WORKS

ANTHROPOS. SUPLEMENTOS. see HUMANITIES: COMPREHENSIVE WORKS

ANUARIO INTERAMERICANO DE ARCHIVOS. see HISTORY — History Of North And South America

020 410 053　　　GW
ARBEITSGEMEINSCHAFT DER BIBLIOTHEKEN UND DOKUMENTATIONSSTELLEN DER OST-, OSTMITTEL- UND SUEDOSTEUROPAFORSCHUNG. MITTEILUNGEN. (Text in English, German, Russian) 1981. q. free. Arbeitsgemeinschaft der Bibliotheken und Dokumentationsstellen der Ost-, Ostmittel- und Suedosteuropaforschung, c/o Martin-Opitz-Bibliothek, Berliner Platz 11, 4690 Herne 1, Germany. TEL 23230162805. Ed. W. Kessler. adv.; bk.rev.; abstr.; bibl.; circ. 400. (back issues avail.)
 Formerly: Arbeitsgemeinschaft der Bibliotheken und Dokumentationsstellen der Osteuropa-, Suedosteuropa- und DDR-Forschung. Mitteilungen (ISSN 0721-9105)
 Description: Information on German libraries and documentation centers concerned with Eastern, East Central and Southeastern Europe. Includes annual reports, events, statistics.

020　　　　　　　GW　　ISSN 0518-2220
ARBEITSGEMEINSCHAFT DER PARLAMENTS- UND BEHOERDENBIBLIOTHEKEN. ARBEITSHEFTE. 1958. a. DM.24. Arbeitsgemeinschaft der Parlaments- und Behoerdenbibliotheken, c/o Bibliothek des Deutschen Patentamtes, Zweibrueckenstr. 12, 8000 Munich 2, Germany. TEL 089-2195-2448. FAX 089-2195-2221. circ. 600.

020　　　　　　　GW　　ISSN 0170-5598
ARBEITSGEMEINSCHAFT DER PARLAMENTS- UND BEHOERDENBIBLIOTHEKEN. MITTEILUNGEN. 1958. s-a. DM.24. Arbeitsgemeinschaft der Parlaments- und Behoerdenbibliotheken, c/o Bibliothek des Deutschen Patentamts, Zweibrueckenstr. 12, 8000 Munich 2, Germany. TEL 089-2195-2448. FAX 089-2195-2221. circ. 600.
—BLDSC shelfmark: 5831.983000.

027.7　　　　　　GW　　ISSN 0177-8358
ARBEITSGEMEINSCHAFT KATHOLISCH-THEOLOGISCHER BIBLIOTHEKEN. MITTEILUNGSBLATT. 1952. a. DM.15. Arbeitsgemeinschaft Katholisch-Theologischer Bibliotheken (AKThB), Bibliothek des Priester Seminars, Jesuitenstr. 13, Postfach 1330, 5500 Trier, Germany. Ed. Michael Embrach. adv.; bk.rev.; cum.index; circ. 250.

020　　　　　　　SZ　　ISSN 0258-0764
Z673.V43
ARBIDO-B; offizielles Mitteilungsorgan-bulletin d'information officiel-bollettino d'informazioni officiale. (Text in French, German and Italian) 1925. 8/yr. 30 Fr. Vereinigung Schweizerischer Archivare - Association des Bibliothecaires Suisses (Associazione dei Bibliotecari Svizzeri); Association Suisse de Documentation (Associazione Svizzera di Documentazione), c/o Sekretariat REBUS, Sprengliweg 6, CH-3360 Herzbuchsee, Switzerland. Ed. C. Staudenmann. adv.; bk.rev.; charts; illus.; index; circ. 3,200. **Indexed:** Lib.Lit.
 Formerly (until 1984): Nachrichten V S B - S V D (ISSN 0042-3807)
 Description: Covers association news, information and reports. Includes budgets, reports and lists of events, and positions available.

020　　　　　　　SZ　　ISSN 0258-0772
Z837.A1
ARBIDO-R; Fachorgan-revue professionnelle-rivista professionale. (Text in French, German and Italian) 1986. 4/yr. 25 Fr. Association des Archivistes Suisses, c/o Institut d'Etudes Sociales, Ecole superieure d'information documentaire, Case Postale, CH-1211 Geneva 4, Switzerland. TEL 022-209311. FAX 022-207246. (Co-sponsors: Association des Bibliothecaires Suisses; Association Suisse de Documentation) Ed. Michel Gorin. adv.; bk.rev.; circ. 2,500. **Indexed:** Lib.Lit.
 Description: Provides information specialists with articles and reports in the fields of archives, library and documentation sciences.

020　　　　　　　AU　　ISSN 0253-7400
ARCHIV DER GESCHICHTE DER NATURWISSENSCHAFTEN. 1980. irreg. Verlagsbuchhandlung Brueder Hollinek und Co. GmbH, Feldgasse 13, A-1238 Vienna, Austria. TEL 0222-8893646. FAX 0222-889364724. Ed. R. Hink. bk.rev.; abstr.; index; circ. 1,000. (reprint service avail. from ISI)

026 974.4　　　　CN　　ISSN 0044-9423
ARCHIVES.* 1969. q. Can.$22. Association des Archivistes du Quebec, C.P. 423, Sillery, Que. G1T 2R8, Canada. TEL 418-652-2357. Ed. Louise Gagnon-Arguin. adv.; bk.rev.; bibl.; illus.; circ. 500. (also avail. in microfiche) **Indexed:** Arts & Hum.Cit.Ind., Curr.Cont., Pt.de Rep. (1982-), SSCI.

ARCHIVES; journal of the British Records Association. see HISTORY — History Of Europe

025.17　　　　　UK　　ISSN 0066-653X
ARCHIVES AND THE USER. 1970. irreg. price varies. British Records Association, 18 Padbury Court, London E2 7EH, England.

ARCHIVES ET BIBLIOTHEQUES DE BELGIQUE/ARCHIEF-EN BIBLIOTHEEKWEZEN IN BELGIE. see HISTORY — History Of Europe

025.17　　　　　GW　　ISSN 0004-038X
CD1373.A2
ARCHIVMITTEILUNGEN; Zeitschrift fuer Theorie und Praxis des Archivwesens. 1951. bi-m. DM.36. (Staatliche Archivverwaltung) Staatsverlag der DDR, Otto-Grotewohl-Str. 17, 1086 Berlin, Germany. adv.; bk.rev.; charts; illus.; index, cum.index; circ. 5,000. **Indexed:** Amer.Hist.& Life, Hist.Abstr.
—BLDSC shelfmark: 1649.050000.

025　　　　　　　CS　　ISSN 0004-0398
CD15
ARCHIVNI CASOPIS. 1951. q. 32 Kcs.($27.10) Archivni Sprava, Milady Horakove 133, 166 21 Prague 6, Czechoslovakia. (Dist. by: Artia, Ve Smeckach 30, 111 27 Prague 1, Czechoslovakia) Ed. Jana Prazakova. adv.; bk.rev.; cum.index: 1951-1965, 1966-1980. **Indexed:** Amer.Hist.& Life, Hist.Abstr.

930.25　　　　　AG　　ISSN 0325-2868
CD4020
ARCHIVO GENERAL DE LA NACION. REVISTA. 1971; suspended in 1975; resumed 1976. a. Archivo General de la Nacion, Leandro N. Alem 246, 1003 Buenos Aires, Argentina. Ed. Enrique M. Barba. bk.rev.; bibl.; circ. 1,000. **Indexed:** Hist.Abstr.

LIBRARY AND INFORMATION SCIENCES

020 972   UY   ISSN 0797-0129
Z907.U83
ARCHIVOS DE LA BIBLIOTECA NACIONAL. 1987. irreg. exchange basis. Biblioteca Nacional del Libro, Av. 18 de Julio, 1790, Casilla de Correo 452, Montevideo, Uruguay.

020   GW   ISSN 0066-6793
CD1
ARCHIVUM; international review on archives-revue internationale des archives. Every 4th year includes: International Congress on Archives. Proceedings. (Text in English, French, German, Italian, Spanish) 1951. a. price varies. (Conseil International des Archives, FR - International Council on Archives) K.G. Saur Verlag KG, Ortlerstr. 8, Postfach 701620, 8000 Munich 70, Germany. TEL 089-76902-0. FAX 089-76902150. Ed. Andre Vanrie. circ. 2,000. **Indexed:** A.B.C.Pol.Sci., Amer.Hist.& Life, Hist.Abstr.
—BLDSC shelfmark: 1658.400000.
Description: Monographs and studies on archive administration.

020   CN   ISSN 0828-3192
ARCHIVY. (Text in English) 1985. irreg. (3-4/yrs.). Can.$20. Southwestern Chapter Ontario Archivists Association, c/o Windsor Public Library, 850 Ouellette Ave., Windsor, Ont. N9Z 4M9, Canada. TEL 519-255-6782. Ed. Bob Buckie. illus.; circ. 50. (back issues avail.)
Description: Archival concerns of Essex, Kent and Lambton counties in Ontario.

020   CN   ISSN 0315-9930
Z673.C9533
ARGUS (MONTREAL). (Text in English, French) 1971. q. Can.$33($33) Corporation des Bibliothecaires Professionnels du Quebec - Corporation of Professional Librarians of Quebec, 307 rue Ste-Catherine Ouest, Ste.320, Montreal, Que. H2X 2A3, Canada. TEL 514-845-3327. FAX 514-845-1618. Ed. Pierre Meunier. adv.; bk.rev.; circ. 1,200. **Indexed:** Bull.Signal., Inform.Sci.Abstr., Lib.Lit., LISA, Pt.de Rep. (1983-), RADAR.
—BLDSC shelfmark: 1664.359000.

020   US   ISSN 0004-184X
Z732
ARKANSAS LIBRARIES. 1930. bi-m. membership. Arkansas Library Association, 1100 N. University, Ste. 109, Little Rock, AR 72207. TEL 501-661-1127. FAX 501-663-1218. Eds. Jan Hart, Mary Hawkes. adv.; bk.rev.; illus.; circ. 900. (also avail. in microfilm; reprint service avail. from UMI) **Indexed:** Lib.Lit.

ARKHIVY UKRAINY. see HISTORY — History Of Europe

ARKIV; tidsskrift for arkivforskning. see HISTORY

020   SW   ISSN 0349-0505
CD1830
ARKIV, SAMHAELLE OCH FORSKNING. 1953. a. SEK 100. Svenska Arkivsamfundet - Swedish Archival Association, Riksarkivet, Box 12541, S-10229 Stockholm, Sweden. Ed. Lars-Olof Welander. bk.rev.; circ. 500.
Formerly: Svenska Arkivsamfundets Skrifterie (ISSN 0562-7451)

700 020   US   ISSN 0743-040X
Z675.A85
ARLIS - N A UPDATE. 1984. bi-m. membership only. Art Libraries Society of North America, 3900 E. Timrod St., Tucson, AZ 85711. TEL 602-881-8479. FAX 602-322-6778. Eds. Pamela J. Parry, Judy Dyki. adv.; circ. 1,300. (back issues avail.)
Description: Covers professional and society news for art librarians and visual resources curators; includes job ads.

026 700   UK   ISSN 0308-809X
ARLIS NEWS-SHEET. 1976. 6/yr. £14 to individuals; institutions £38. Art Libraries Society (ARLIS UK & Eire), 18 College Rd., Bromsgrove, Worcs. B60 2NE, England. Ed. Judith Preece. circ. 400. (back issues avail.)
Description: Contains details of the Society's activities, information about new books, journals and audiovisual materials, reports of meetings, conferences and forthcoming events.

700 020   US   ISSN 0730-7187
Z5937
ART DOCUMENTATION. 1972. 4/yr. $55 to individuals; institutions $75. Art Libraries Society of North America, 3900 E. Timrod St., Tucson, AZ 85711. TEL 602-881-8479. FAX 602-322-6778. Eds. Beryl K. Smith, Judy Dyki. adv.; bk.rev.; circ. 1,300. (also avail. in microfilm from UMI; back issues avail.) **Indexed:** Artbibl.Mod., CALL, Curr.Cont., Lib.Lit., LISA, RILA.
—BLDSC shelfmark: 1733.395800.
Supersedes (in 1981): A R L I S - N A Newsletter (ISSN 0090-3515)
Description: Articles relevant to art librarianship and visual resources curatorship.
Refereed Serial

026 700   UK   ISSN 0307-4722
Z675.A85
ART LIBRARIES JOURNAL. 1976. q. £25. Art Libraries Society (ARLIS UK & Eire), 18 College Rd., Bromsgrove, Worcs. B60 2NE, England. Ed. Philip Pacey. adv.; bk.rev.; bibl.; index; circ. 600. (also avail. in microfiche; back issues avail.) **Indexed:** Artbibl.Mod., Avery Ind.Archit.Per., Br.Tech.Ind., Lib.Lit., LISA, RILA.
—BLDSC shelfmark: 1733.461500.
Formerly: A R L I S Newsletter (ISSN 0044-9032)
Description: Publishes articles on art librarianship and documentation, including conference papers.

700 020   US   ISSN 0730-7160
ART LIBRARIES SOCIETY OF NORTH AMERICA. OCCASIONAL PAPERS. 1982. irreg. price varies. Art Libraries Society of North America, 3900 E. Timrod St., Tucson, AZ 85711. TEL 602-881-8479. FAX 602-322-6778. bibl.; charts; illus. (back issues avail.)
Description: Professional monographs on a variety of topics of interest to art librarians and visual resources curators.

020   SA   ISSN 1011-8012
ARTES NATALES. (Text in Afrikaans, English) 1971. 11/yr. free to libraries in South Africa. Provincial Library Service, Private Bag 9016, Pietermaritzburg 3200, South Africa. TEL 0331-940-241. TELEX 643030. Ed. H.F. Rivers-Moore. bk.rev.; bibl.; circ. 700. (processed)
Formerly (until 1982): Libri Natales.
Description: Disseminates local news for non-urban librarians in Natal and acts as a medium for in-service training and information.

020   HK   ISSN 1017-6748
▼**ASIAN LIBRARIES.** (Text in English) 1991. 3/yr. $72 (effective 1992). Library Marketing Services Ltd., 11th Fl., Hophing Centre, 8 Hennessy Road, Hong Kong. TEL 66-2-2471032. FAX 66-2-2471033. (Subscr. to: GPO Box 701, Bangkok 10501, Thailand) Eds. Y.F.J. Yee, Andre McNicoll. adv.; circ. 1,000. (back issues avail.)
Description: Covers Asian information technology trends, information industry and products.
Refereed Serial

020   US   ISSN 1040-8517
ASIAN - PACIFIC AMERICAN LIBRARIANS ASSOCIATION NEWSLETTER. 1980. q. membership. Asian - Pacific American Librarians Association, c/o Dr. Jack T. Tsukamoto, Library, Ball State University, Muncie, IN 47306. TEL 317-285-5722. adv.; bk.rev.; circ. 300. (looseleaf format; back issue avail.)
Description: Designed specifically to meet the needs of Association members, professional growth, collection development, and needs of Asian communities.

020   UK
ASLIB ANNUAL REPORT. a. free. Aslib, Association for Information Management, Publications Department, Information House, 20-24 Old St., London EC1V 9AP, England. TEL 071-253-4488. FAX 071-430-0514.
Formerly: Work of Aslib: Annual Report (ISSN 0084-1285)

020   UK   ISSN 0305-0033
ASLIB INFORMATION. 1973. 10/yr. £55($110) to non-members; members £45. Aslib, Association for Information Management, Publications Department, Information House, 20-24 Old St., London EC1V 9AP, England. TEL 071-253-4488. FAX 071-430-0514. (Dist. in N. America by: Learned Information, Inc., 143 Old Marlton Pike, Medford, NJ 08055-8750) Ed. Moira Duncan. adv.; bibl.; circ. 2,700. **Indexed:** Br.Ceram.Abstr., Key to Econ.Sci., LISA.
—BLDSC shelfmark: 1744.000000.
Description: News and articles about the information profession and Aslib's activities.

020   UK   ISSN 0001-253X
Z673   CODEN: ASLPAO
ASLIB PROCEEDINGS. 1949. 10/yr. £110($220) to non-members; members £75. Aslib, Association for Information Management, Publications Department, Information House, 20-24 Old St., London EC1V 9AP, England. TEL 071-253-4488. FAX 071-430-0514. (Dist. in N. America by: Learned Informaton, Inc., 143 Old Marlton Pike, Medford, NJ 08055-8750. TEL 609-654-6266) Ed. Moira Duncan. adv.; charts; illus.; index; circ. 3,500. **Indexed:** Account.& Data Proc.Abstr., Br.Ceram.Abstr., Build.Manage.Abstr., Chem.Abstr., Compumath, Curr.Cont., Dairy Sci.Abstr., Excerp.Med., Forest.Abstr., Forest Prod.Abstr., Int.Lab.Doc., Key to Econ.Sci., LHTN, Lib.Lit., LISA, Res.High.Educ.Abstr., Sci.Abstr., SSCI, World Surf.Coat.
—BLDSC shelfmark: 1745.000000.
Description: Published papers from the Association's meetings and conferences with articles on new equipment, techniques and services for the information industry.

ASOCIACION ARCHIVISTICA ARGENTINA BOLETIN. see HISTORY — History Of North And South America

020   CR   ISSN 0004-4784
ASOCIACION COSTARRICENSE DE BIBLIOTECARIOS. BOLETIN. 1955. irreg. free. Asociacion Costarricense de Bibliotecarios, Apdo. 3308, San Jose, Costa Rica. circ. 500. **Indexed:** Lib.Sci.Abstr.

020.6   MX
ASOCIACION DE BIBLIOTECARIOS DE INSTITUCIONES DE ENSENANZA SUPERIOR E INVESTIGACION. ARCHIVOS.* 1976. irreg. Asociacion de Bibliotecarios de Instituciones de Ensenanza Superior e Investigaciones, Apartado Postal 20-671, Mexico 20, D.F., Mexico.

020.7   AG   ISSN 0004-4806
ASOCIACION DE EX-ALUMNOS DE LA ESCUELA NACIONAL DE BIBLIOTECARIOS. BOLETIN. 1965. q. free. Asociacion de Ex-Alumnos de la Escuela Nacional de Bibliotecarios, Mexico 564, Buenos Aires, Argentina. adv.; bk.rev.; bibl.; index, cum.index; circ. 1,000.

ASOCIACION INTERAMERICANA DE BIBLIOTECARIOS Y DOCUMENTALISTAS AGRICOLAS. BOLETIN ESPECIAL. see AGRICULTURE

020   CR   ISSN 0001-1495
ASOCIACION INTERAMERICANA DE BIBLIOTECARIOS Y DOCUMENTALISTAS AGRICOLAS. BOLETIN INFORMATIVO. 1966. 3/yr. $12 to non-members. Asociacion Interamericana de Bibliotecarios y Documentalistas Agricolas, Apdo. Postal 55, 2200 Coronado, Costa Rica. TEL 29-0222. FAX 506-294741. TELEX 2144 IICA. Ed. Ghislaine Poitevien. bk.rev.; illus.; circ. 900.
Description: Covers association activities, current news on library and information sciences, conferences and new publications.

020   VE   ISSN 0066-8591
ASOCIACION VENEZOLANA DE ARCHIVEROS. COLECCION DOCTRINA.* 1970. irreg. Asociacion Venezolana de Archiveros, Archivo General de la Nacion, Santa Capilla a Carmelitas 15, Av. Urdaneta, Caracas 100, Venezuela.

ASSISTANT EDITOR; original short articles, fillers, and clip art for library newsletter. see LITERATURE

LIBRARY AND INFORMATION SCIENCES

023 UK ISSN 0004-5152
Z671
ASSISTANT LIBRARIAN. 1898. m. £18 to non-members. Association of Assistant Librarians, Sherwood Library, Spondon Street, Mansfield Road, Nottingham NG5 4AB, England. TEL 0602-606680. FAX 0602-504207. (Subscr. to: West Glamorgan Library, West Glamorgan House, 12 Orchard Street, Swansea SA1 5AZ, England) Ed. Nigel Ward. adv.; bk.rev.; bibl.; illus.; index; circ. 14,500 (paid); 10,500 (controlled). (also avail. in microfilm from UMI) **Indexed:** Lib.Lit., Lib.Sci.Abstr., LISA.
—BLDSC shelfmark: 1746.661500.

020 BL ISSN 0004-5187
ASSOCIACAO BAHIANA DE BIBLIOTECARIOS. INFORMA.* q. free. Associacao Bahiana de Bibliotecarios, Biblioteca Central do Estado, Rua General Labatut 27, Barris Salvador, Bahia, Brazil. (processed)

020.6 PO ISSN 0251-4141
ASSOCIACAO PORTUGUESA DE BIBLIOTECARIOS ARQUIVISTAS E DOCUMENTALISTAS. NOTICIA. Short title: Noticia B A D. 1975. bi-m. free. Associacao Portuguesa de Bibliotecarios Arquivistas e Documentalistas, Edificio da Biblioteca Nacional, Campo Grande 83, 1751 Lisbon, Portugal. FAX 834697. Ed. Maria Ines Lopes. adv.; bk.rev.; bibl.; circ. 2,000. **Indexed:** Bull.Signal., LISA.

029.7 BE ISSN 0007-9804
Z1008
ASSOCIATION BELGE DE DOCUMENTATION. CAHIERS DE LA DOCUMENTATION. (Text in Dutch, English and French) 1947. q. 850 BEF. Association Belge de Documentation, Boulevard L. Schmidt 119, B3, B-1040 Brussels, Belgium. Ed. P. Hubot. adv.; circ. 360.
—BLDSC shelfmark: 2948.830000.

020 FR ISSN 0066-8877
ASSOCIATION DE L'ECOLE NATIONALE SUPERIEURE DES BIBLIOTHECAIRES. ANNUAIRE. 1969. biennial. 180 F. Association de l'Ecole Nationale Superieure des Bibliothecaires, 17-21 Bd. du 11 Novembre, 69100 Villeurbanne, France. adv.; circ. 1,200.

020 FR ISSN 0992-6801
ASSOCIATION DE L'ECOLE NATIONALE SUPERIEURE DES BIBLIOTHECAIRES. INFOS. q. 150 F. Association de l'Ecole Nationale Superieure des Bibliothecaires, 17-21, bd. du 11 Novembre, 69100 Villeurbanne, France.

020 FR ISSN 0066-8958
ASSOCIATION DES BIBLIOTHEQUES ECCLESIASTIQUES DE FRANCE. BULLETIN DE LIAISON. 1971. q. 120 F. Association des Bibliotheques Ecclesiastiques de France, 6 rue du Regard, 75006 Paris, France. Ed. M. Francoise Dupuy. bk.rev.; circ. 220.

026.95 US ISSN 0148-6225
Z688.E25
ASSOCIATION FOR ASIAN STUDIES. COMMITTEE ON EAST ASIAN LIBRARIES. BULLETIN. 3/yr. $15 to individuals; institutions $25. Association for Asian Studies, Inc., Committee on East Asian Libraries, c/o Maureen H. Donovan, Main Library, Rm.310, Ohio State University Libraries, 1858 Neil Ave. Mall, Columbus, OH 43210-1286. TEL 614-292-3502. FAX 614-292-7859. bk.rev.; illus.; circ. 300.
—BLDSC shelfmark: 2454.645000.
Formerly: Association for Asian Studies. Committee on East Asian Libraries. Newsletter (ISSN 0571-5520)

020 US ISSN 0748-5786
ASSOCIATION FOR LIBRARY AND INFORMATION SCIENCE EDUCATION. DIRECTORY. (Special annual edition of Journal of Education for Library and Information Science) a. $30. Association for Library and Information Science Education, 5623 Palm Aire Dr., Sarasota, FL 34243-3702. TEL 813-355-1795. Ed. Ilse Moon. circ. 2,000. (also avail. in microfilm from UMI)
Formerly: Association of American Library Schools Directory.

029.7 378 GH
ASSOCIATION OF AFRICAN UNIVERSITIES. NEW ACQUISITIONS LIST. irreg. free. Association of African Universities, Box 5744, Accra, Ghana.

020 200 100 UK ISSN 0305-781X
Z675.T4
ASSOCIATION OF BRITISH THEOLOGICAL AND PHILOSOPHICAL LIBRARIES. BULLETIN. N.S. 1974. 3/yr. £10($17.50) Association of British Theological and Philosophical Libraries, Philosophy & Religion Dept., Central Library, Birmingham B3 3HQ. FAX 021-472-8852. (Subscr. to: M.J. Walsh, Heythrop College Library, 11-13 Cavendish Square, London W1M 0AN, England) Ed. Alan Smith. adv.; bk.rev.; abstr.; bibl.; circ. 280. (back issues avail.) **Indexed:** LISA.
—BLDSC shelfmark: 2396.810000.
Description: Provides a forum for professional discussion and development with special emphasis on international aspects of theological and philosophical librarianship.

020.6 PR
ASSOCIATION OF CARIBBEAN UNIVERSITY RESEARCH AND INSTITUTIONAL LIBRARIES. CARTA INFORMATIVA DE A C U R I L/A C U R I L NEWSLETTER. (Text in English, Spanish) 1973. q. free to members. Association of Caribbean University Research and Institutional Libraries, Box S, Estacion de la Universidad, San Juan, PR 00931. Ed.Bd. bk.rev.; bibl.; illus.; circ. controlled. (back issues avail.)
Formerly: Association of Caribbean University and Research Libraries. Carta Informativa de ACURIL.

025 US
ASSOCIATION OF RESEARCH LIBRARIES. OFFICE OF MANAGEMENT STUDIES. OCCASIONAL PAPER. 1971. irreg., no.9, 1985. $20 per issue. Association of Research Libraries, Office of University Library Management Studies, 1527 New Hampshire Ave., N.W., Washington, DC 20036. TEL 202-232-8656. Ed. C. Brigid Welch.
Formerly: Association of Research Libraries. University Library Management Studies Office. Occasional Paper (ISSN 0091-4479)

020 CN ISSN 0316-0963
ASSOCIATION POUR L'AVANCEMENT DES SCIENCES ET DES TECHNIQUES DE LA DOCUMENTATION. NOUVELLES DE L'ASTED. 1974. 5/yr. membership. Association pour l'Avancement des Sciences et des Techniques de la Documentation, 1030 rue Cherrier, Bureau 505, Montreal, Que. H2L 1H9, Canada. TEL 514-522-7833. bk.rev.; circ. 700. **Indexed:** Can.Per.Ind.
Formerly (until 1974): Association Canadienne des Bibliothecaires de Langue Francaise. Nouvelles de l'ACBLF (ISSN 0044-9407)

020 CN ISSN 0316-0955
ASSOCIATION POUR L'AVANCEMENT DES SCIENCES ET DES TECHNIQUES DE LA DOCUMENTATION. RAPPORT ANNUEL. 1945. a. Association pour l'Avancement des Sciences et des Techniques de la Documentation, 1030 rue Cherrier, Bureau 505, Montreal, Que. H2L 1H9, Canada. TEL 514-522-7833. FAX 514-521-9561. circ. 2,000.
Formerly: Association Canadienne des Bibliothecaires de Langue Francaise. Rapport (ISSN 0066-8826)

020 011 IT ISSN 0004-5934
Z671
ASSOCIAZIONE ITALIANA BIBLIOTECHE. BOLLETTINO D'INFORMAZIONI. (Text in Italian; summaries in English) 1961. q. L.70000. Associazione Italiana Biblioteche, Casella Postale 2461, 00100 Rome, Italy. TEL 6-493532. Dir. Angela Vinay. adv.; bk.rev.; abstr.; bibl.; index; circ. 3,300. (also avail. in microform from UMI; back issues avail.; reprint service avail. from UMI) **Indexed:** Bull.Signal., Lib.Lit., LISA.
—BLDSC shelfmark: 2238.010000.

027.4 US
AT THE LIBRARY. 1965. q. $3. Public Library of Youngstown and Mahoning County, 305 Wick Ave., Youngstown, OH 44503. TEL 216-744-8636. FAX 216-744-2258. Ed. Janet S. Loew. bk.rev.; illus.; stat.; circ. 2,000. (processed)
Formerly (until 1991): Biblio-Files; **Supersedes (in 1980):** Public Library of Youngstown and Mahoning County. Staff Bulletin (ISSN 0033-3573)

020 IO ISSN 0126-1630
ATMA JAYA RESEARCH CENTRE. LIBRARY BULLETIN. (Text in Indonesian) 1978. m. Atma Jaya Research Centre - Pusat Penelitian Atma Jaya, Jalan Jenderal Sudirman 57, Box 2639, Jakarta 10001, Indonesia.

AUCHMUTY LIBRARY PUBLICATION. see BIBLIOGRAPHIES

020 UK ISSN 0302-3451
Z717
AUDIOVISUAL LIBRARIAN. 1973. q. £33 (foreign £39). c/o A.H. Thompson, Ed., Coach House Frongog, Llanbadarn Fawr, Aberystwyth SY23 3HN, Wales. FAX 0970-622190. adv.; bk.rev.; bibl.; index; circ. 3,000. (also avail. in microform from UMI) **Indexed:** CINAHL, Educ.Tech.Abstr., Lib.Lit., LISA.
—BLDSC shelfmark: 1789.020000.
Former titles: Library Association. Audiovisual Group. Bulletin; Aslib Audio-Visual Group Newsletter; Aslib Sound Recordings Group Newsletter.

025 CN ISSN 0714-7058
AURORA. 1981. bi-m. Northern Lights Library System, General Delivery, Elk Point, Alta. T0A 1A0, Canada. TEL 403-724-2596. FAX 403-724-2597. Ed. H. West. circ. 700. (also avail. in microfilm from MML; back issues avail.)

020 AT ISSN 1030-5033
Z870.A1
AUSTRALASIAN PUBLIC LIBRARIES AND INFORMATION SERVICES. 1988. q. Aus.$32 to individuals; institutions Aus.$38. Auslib Press, P.O. Box 622, Blackwood, S.A. 5051, Australia. TEL 08-278-4363. FAX 08-270-4000. TELEX AA88420. Ed. Alan Bundy. circ. 900. (back issues avail.) **Indexed:** Aus.Educ.Ind., LISA.
—BLDSC shelfmark: 1796.150000.
Description: Publishes articles and shorter items on public libraries and other publicly accessible information services in Australia, New Zealand and the South Pacific.

027.7 AT ISSN 0004-8623
Z675.U5
AUSTRALIAN ACADEMIC AND RESEARCH LIBRARIES. 1970. q. Aus.$40 (foreign Aus.$50)(effective 1992). Australian Library and Information Association, University College & Research Libraries Section, P.O. Box E411, Queen Victoria Terrace, A.C.T. 2600, Australia. TEL 06-285-1877. FAX 06-282-2249. Ed. J.I. Horacek. adv.; bk.rev.; bibl.; stat.; index; circ. 1,100. (also avail. in microform from MIM) **Indexed:** AESIS, Aus.P.A.I.S., Inform.Sci.Abstr., Lib.Lit., Lib.Sci.Abstr., Ref.Sour.
—BLDSC shelfmark: 1796.660000.
Supersedes: New Sheet.

020 US ISSN 0898-3283
Z692.S5 CODEN: ANZLEH
▼**AUSTRALIAN & NEW ZEALAND JOURNAL OF SERIALS LIBRARIANSHIP;** the serials journal of Australasia. 1990. q. $20 to individuals; institutions and libraries $32. Haworth Press, Inc., 10 Alice St., Binghamton, NY 13904. TEL 800-342-8678. FAX 607-722-1424. Ed. Toby Burrows. adv.; bk.rev. (also avail. in microfiche from HAW; reprint service avail. from HAW) **Indexed:** LISA.
—BLDSC shelfmark: 1796.895000.
Description: Presents reviews and news of serials in the area, in order to provide collection development tools for librarians interested in Australasian serials, and to deal with practical aspects of collection management.
Refereed Serial

AUSTRALIAN EDUCATION INDEX. see EDUCATION — Abstracting, Bibliographies, Statistics

020 AT ISSN 0311-5984
AUSTRALIAN LAW LIBRARIANS' GROUP. NEWSLETTER. 1973. bi-m. Aus.$35 (foreign Aus.$60). Australian Law Librarians' Group, P.O. Box 92, 367 Collins St., Melbourne, Vic. 3000, Australia. TEL 03-617-4853. FAX 03-617-4666. Ed. Fay O'Grady. adv.; bk.rev.; circ. 450. (back issues avail.) **Indexed:** Leg.Info.Manage.Ind.
Description: Details developments of legal information retrieval and sources of information.

LIBRARY AND INFORMATION SCIENCES

020   AT   ISSN 1031-5187
Z870.A1
AUSTRALIAN LIBRARIES: THE ESSENTIAL DIRECTORY.
biennial. Aus.$26 plus Aus.$4 postage. Auslib Press, P.O. Box 622, Blackwood, S.A. 5051, Australia. TEL 08 2784363. FAX 08-278-4000. TELEX AA88420. Eds. Alan and Judith Bundy. adv.; circ. 2,500.
Incorporates (in 1988): W A T Acronyms and Initialisms in Australian Library and Information Science.
Description: Contains brief details of all Australian academic, public and special libraries, publishers, consultants etc.

020   AT   ISSN 0004-9670
Z671
AUSTRALIAN LIBRARY JOURNAL. 1951. 4/yr. Aus.$40 (foreign Aus.$50)(effective 1992). Australian Library and Information Association, P.O. Box E411, Queen Victoria Terrace, A.C.T. 2600, Australia. TEL 06-285-1877. FAX 06-282-2249. adv.; bk.rev.; illus.; index, cum.index: 1951-1965; 1966-1970; circ. 7,000. **Indexed:** AESIS, Aus.P.A.I.S., Gdlns, LHTN, Lib.Lit., Lib.Sci.Abstr., LISA, Ref.Sour.
—BLDSC shelfmark: 1813.800000.
Description: Presents articles of interest to people working in library and information management.

020   AT   ISSN 1034-8042
AUSTRALIAN LIBRARY REVIEW. vol.7, 1990. 4/yr. Aus.$30. Charles Stuart University - Riverina, Centre for Information Studies, P.O. Box 588, Wagga Wagga, N.S.W. 2650, Australia. FAX 069-222-733. Ed.Bd. adv.; bk.rev.; circ. 250. **Indexed:** Aus.Educ.Ind., Aus.P.A.I.S., Lib.Lit., LISA.
—BLDSC shelfmark: 1813.832000.
Former titles: Riverina Library Review (ISSN 0812-7352) & Riv Lib File (ISSN 0157-650X)
Description: Covers current issues of importance to the library profession and includes an extensive book reviewing section on library and information science.

026   AT   ISSN 0005-027X
Z675.A2
AUSTRALIAN SPECIAL LIBRARY NEWS. 1967. q. Aus.$36 (foreign Aus.$42)(effective 1992). Australian Library and Information Association, P.O. Box E411, Queen Victoria Terrace, A.C.T. 2600, Australia. TEL 06-285-1877. FAX 06-282-2249. adv.; bk.rev.; bibl.; circ. 1,000. **Indexed:** AESIS, Aus.P.A.I.S., LISA.
Description: Covers a wide variety of articles of interest to special librarians.

029.7 510 400   US   ISSN 0005-1055
Z699.A1   CODEN: ADMLAE
AUTOMATIC DOCUMENTATION AND MATHEMATICAL LINGUISTICS. English Translation of: Nauchno-Tekhnicheskaya Informatsiya. Seriya 2. 1967. bi-m. $715. (Vsesoyuznyi Institut Nauchno-Tekhnicheskoi Informatsii (VINITI), UR) Allerton Press, Inc., 150 Fifth Ave., New York, NY 10011. TEL 212-924-3950. Ed. A.I. Mikhailov. charts. **Indexed:** Chem.Abstr., M.L.A., Math.R.
—BLDSC shelfmark: 0404.850000.
Description: Reports on the most recent advancements in the field of science concerned with the relationship between studies in linguistics and verbal behavior, and computer engineering and artificial intelligence.

020 070.5   UK   ISSN 0261-0302
AVERAGE PRICES OF BRITISH ACADEMIC BOOKS. 1974. s-a. £8. Loughborough University, Library and Information Statistics Unit, Loughborough, Leicestershire LE11 3TU, England. TEL 0509 223071. TELEX 34319. (Co-sponsor: British Library) Ed. Joan Sumsion. circ. 300.
—BLDSC shelfmark: 5276.223000.

020 070.5   UK   ISSN 0951-8975
AVERAGE PRICES OF U S A ACADEMIC BOOKS. 1986. s-a. £8. Loughborough University, Library and Information Statistics Unit, Department of Library and Information Studies, Loughborough, Leicestershire LE11 3TU, England. TEL 0509 223071. FAX 0509-223053. TELEX 34319. (Co-sponsor: British Library) Ed. John Sumsion.
—BLDSC shelfmark: 5276.227000.

020   CN   ISSN 0005-2876
B C L A REPORTER. 1957. 6/yr. Can.$25 to non-members. British Columbia Library Association, 6545 Bonsor Ave., Ste. 110, Burnaby, B.C. V5H 1H3, Canada. TEL 604-430-9633. Ed. Terry Dobroslavic. adv.; bk.rev.; bibl.; circ. 700. (reprint service avail. from UMI) **Indexed:** Lib.Lit.
—BLDSC shelfmark: 1871.384300.

029   SG
B L I B A D. (Bulletin de Liaison a l'Intention des Bibliothecaires, Archivistes et Documentalistes Africains) 3/yr. Universite de Dakar, Ecole des Bibliothecaires, Archivistes et Documentalistes, B.P. 3252, Dakar, Senegal. Ed. Salif Mane.

020   DK   ISSN 0905-4650
Z671
B 70. 1970. 22/yr. DKK 275 (typically set in Jan.). Bibliotekarforbundet - Union of Danish Librarians, Lindevangs Alle 2, 2000 Frederiksberg, Denmark. TEL 38-881770. FAX 38-883201. Ed. Per Nyeng. adv.; bk.rev.; illus.; index; circ. 6,067 (controlled). **Indexed:** Lib.Lit., Lib.Sci.Abstr., LISA.
—BLDSC shelfmark: 2942.910000.
Formerly: Bibliotek 70 (ISSN 0006-1824); **Supersedes:** Bibliotekaren.

020   IO   ISSN 0125-9008
Z671
BACA/READ; brief communication for information workers and information users in science and technology. 1974. bi-m. Rps.1000. Indonesian Institute of Sciences, Centre for Scientific Documentation and Information - Lembaga Ilmu Pengetahuan Indonesia, Pusat Dokumentasi dan Informasi Ilmiah, Jalan Jenderal Gatot Subroto 10, Box 269-JKSMG-88, Jakarta 12790, Indonesia. TEL 021-538465. TELEX 62875 IA. Ed. Kosam Rimbarawa. bk.rev.; circ. 1,000. **Indexed:** E.I., Ind.Child.Mag., LISA.
—BLDSC shelfmark: 1854.623000.

027   US   ISSN 0067-3412
Z881.C1522
BANCROFTIANA. 1950. 3/yr. membership. Friends of the Bancroft Library, University of California, Berkeley, Bancroft Library, Berkeley, CA 94720. TEL 415-642-3781. Ed. James D. Hart. cum.index: 1950-1966.; circ. 1,500.

020   BG
BANGLADESH LIBRARY SCIENCE NEWS BULLETIN.
Running title: B L S News Bulletin. (Text in English) 1975. bi-m. exchange basis. University of Dhaka, Department of Library Science, Ramna, Dhaka 2, Bangladesh. Ed. A.K.M. Shamsul Alam. (processed) **Indexed:** Lib.Lit., LISA.

020   FR   ISSN 0067-3951
PC2689
BANQUE DES MOTS. 2/yr. 200 F. Conseil International de la Langue Francaise, 142 bis, rue de Grenelle, 75007 Paris, France. TEL 47-05-07-93. FAX 45-55-41-16. (reprint service avail. from KTO) **Indexed:** Pt.de Rep. (1979-).

027.8   SW   ISSN 0037-6477
BARN OCH KULTUR/CHILDREN AND CULTURE. 1955. 6/yr. SEK 250. Bibliotekstjaenst AB, Box 200, 221 00 Lund, Sweden. TEL 46-180-000. Ed. Charlotte Brattstroem. adv.; bk.rev.; illus.; index, cum.index: 1955-1957, 1958-1960; circ. 2,400. **Indexed:** Child.Lit.Abstr., Lib.Lit.
Formerly: Skolbiblioteket.

BASE LINE. see GEOGRAPHY

020   US   ISSN 0005-6944
Z673.M4
BAY STATE LIBRARIAN. 1910. q. $15. Massachusetts Library Association, Country Side Offices, 707 Turnpike St., N. Andover, MA 01845. TEL 508-686-8543. adv.; circ. 2,000. (also avail. in microfilm from UMI) **Indexed:** Lib.Lit.
Formerly: Bay State Letter.

020   GW   ISSN 0342-0221
BAYERISCHE STAATSBIBLIOTHEK. JAHRESBERICHT. 1972. a. Bayerische Staatsbibliothek, Ludwigstr. 16, Postfach 340150, 8000 Munich 34, Germany. FAX 089-28638-293.

029.7   UK   ISSN 0308-8537
BECTIS BULLETIN. 1976. 10/yr. £15. Bell College of Technology, Almada St., Hamilton ML3 0JB, Scotland. FAX 0698-282131. Ed. J. O'Brien. adv.; bk.rev.; circ. 150.
Description: Covers courses, news items, film and government publication reviews, periodical abstracts and British Standards.

020   US   ISSN 0163-9269
Z675.S6   CODEN: BSSLDR
BEHAVIORAL & SOCIAL SCIENCES LIBRARIAN. 1979. s-a. $35 to individuals; institutions and libraries $75. Haworth Press, Inc., 10 Alice St., Binghamton, NY 13904. TEL 800-342-9678. FAX 607-722-1424. Ed. Michael F. Winter. adv.; bk.rev.; bibl.; circ. 437. (also avail. in microfiche from HAW; back issues avail.; reprint service avail. from HAW) **Indexed:** ASSIA, C.I.J.E., CINAHL, Comput.& Info.Sys., Curr.Cont., Excerp.Med., Inform.Sci.Abstr., Lib.Lit., LISA, P.A.I.S., Psychol.Abstr., Ref.Zh., Sci.Abstr., Soc.Work Res.& Abstr., SSCI, Stud.Wom.Abstr.
—BLDSC shelfmark: 1877.296000.
Description: Presents current research by librarians in the field. Focuses in detail on the day-to-day basics of the practice, from networking, on both formal and informal levels, to the pleasures and perils of automation.
Refereed Serial

020   GW   ISSN 0408-8107
BEITRAEGE ZUM BUCH- UND BIBLIOTHEKSWESEN. 1965. irreg., vol.32, 1991. price varies. Verlag Otto Harrassowitz, Taunusstr. 14, Postfach 2929, 6200 Wiesbaden 1, Germany. TEL 0611-530-0. FAX 0611-530570. TELEX 4186135. Ed. Max Pauer.

BEITRAEGE ZUR INKUNABELKUNDE. DRITTE FOLGE. see PUBLISHING AND BOOK TRADE

BENTLEY HISTORICAL LIBRARY. see HISTORY — History Of North And South America

027.7   US   ISSN 0362-6881
Z733.B476
BENTLEY HISTORICAL LIBRARY ANNUAL REPORT. 1935. a. free. University of Michigan, Bentley Historical Library, 1150 Beal Ave., Ann Arbor, MI 48109-2113. TEL 313-764-1817. Ed. William K. Wallach. circ. 500.
Description: Reports on annual accessions, processing activities, reference work, special projects, grants and essays on a variety of historical topics.

020 016   GW
BERGAKADEMIE FREIBERG. BIBLIOTHEK "GEORGIUS AGRICOLA". VEROEFFENTLICHUNGEN. 1964. irreg., no.120, 1990. exchange basis. Bergakademie Freiberg, Hochschulbibliothek, Agricolastr. 10, 9200 Freiberg, Germany. Ed. Hans-Henning Walter. **Indexed:** LISA.
Formerly: Bergakademie Freiberg. Wissenschaftliches Informationszentrum. Veroeffentlichungen.

020   IT   ISSN 0409-1132
LA BERIO; bollettino d'informazioni bibliografiche. 1961. 3/yr. free. Servizio Biblioteche del Comune di Genova, Piazza de Ferrari 5, 16121 Genova, Italy. TEL 587314. Ed. Laura Malfatto. bk.rev.; circ. 1,000.

020   HU
BERZSENYI DANIEL MEGYEI KONYVTAR. EVKONYVE. 1962. irreg. free. (Vas Megye Tanacsa) Berzsenyi Daniel Megyei Konyvtar, Petofi Sandor u. 43, 9700 Szombathely, Hungary. TEL 94-11-366. FAX 94-12-179. TELEX 37-398. Ed. Miklos Takacs. abstr.; bibl.; illus.; stat.; circ. 600. (back issues avail.)

020   GW   ISSN 0724-8164
BESPRECHUNGEN ANNOTATIONEN. 1949. m. DM.600. Einkaufszentrale fuer Oeffentliche Bibliotheken, Bismarckstr. 3, Postfach 1542, 7410 Reutlingen, Germany. Ed. Erich H. Wurster. index, cum.index; circ. 1,700.

020   US
BETA PHI MU MONOGRAPH SERIES. 1987. irreg. Greenwood Press, Inc. (Subsidiary of: Greenwood Publishing Group Inc.), 88 Post Rd. W., Box 5007, Westport, CT 06881-5007. TEL 203-226-3571. FAX 203-22-1502. Ed. Wayne A. Wiegand.

LIBRARY AND INFORMATION SCIENCES   2747

020.7   US   ISSN 1059-0757
BETA PHI MU NEWSLETTER. 1954. s-a. membership. Beta Phi Mu, International Library and Information Science Honor Society, c/o University of Pittsburgh, School of Library and Information Science, 135 N. Bellefield, Pittsburgh, PA 15260. TEL 412-624-9435. Ed. Charles A. Seavey. (processed)

011   VE   ISSN 0006-1085
Z1911
BIBLIOGRAFIA VENEZOLANA. (Text in Spanish) 1970. a. $20. Instituto Autonomo Biblioteca Nacional y de Servicios de Bibliotecas, Oficina de Information, Apdo. 6525, Caracas 1010A, Venezuela. TEL 5723623. bibl.; circ. 1,500. (processed)
● Also available online.
Formerly (until 1982): Bibliografia Venezuela Anuario.

020 949.7   YU   ISSN 0409-3739
BIBLIOGRAFSKI VJESNIK. 1961. 3/yr. 800 din. Centralna Narodna Biblioteka SR Crne Gore Djurdje Crnojevic Cetinje, Bulevar Lenjina 163, Cetinje, Montenegro, Yugoslavia. Ed. Dusan Martinovic. adv.; bibl.

BIBLIOGRAPHICAL SOCIETY OF AMERICA. PAPERS. see *PUBLISHING AND BOOK TRADE*

011 020   US   ISSN 0145-3084
Z1219
BIBLIOGRAPHY NEWSLETTER. Abbreviated title: BiN. 1973. q. $20. Walrus Press, 32 Trimountain Ave., P.O. Box 280, South Rage, MI 49963. Ed. Bryan R. Johnson. bk.rev.; illus.; index; circ. 800. (back issues avail.)
Description: Publishes articles, news and reviews on the history of books and printing.

BIBLIOTECA "JOSE ARTIGAS". BOLETIN. see *BIBLIOGRAPHIES*

020   IT
BIBLIOTECA MUNICIPALE A. PANIZZI. CONTRIBUTI. 1977. s-a. L.30000. Biblioteca Municipale "A. Panizzi", Via Farini 3, 42100 Reggio Emilia, Italy. Ed.Bd. adv.; bk.rev.; circ. 1,000.

020   BL   ISSN 0100-1922
BIBLIOTECA NACIONAL DE BRASIL. ANAIS. 1876. a. Biblioteca Nacional de Brasil, Av. Rio Branco 219, 20042 Rio de Janeiro, Brazil. TEL 021-240-8429. FAX 021-220-4173. TELEX 21-22941. circ. 1,000.
● Also available online.

020   PO   ISSN 0251-1711
Z946.L72
BIBLIOTECA NACIONAL DE PORTUGAL. REVISTA. 1981. s-a. Esc.360($10) Biblioteca Nacional de Portugal, Campo Grande 83, 1751 Lisbon, Portugal. circ. 2,500.

020   UY   ISSN 0544-9189
Z907
BIBLIOTECA NACIONAL DE URUGUAY. REVISTA. 1966. irreg. donation or exchange basis. Biblioteca Nacional de Uruguay, Av. 18 de Julio, 1790, Casilla de Correo 452, Montevideo, Uruguay. Ed. Alvaro Miranda. adv.; bk.rev.; circ. 750. **Indexed:** Hisp.Amer.Per.Ind.

020   PE   ISSN 0031-6067
Z907
BIBLIOTECA NACIONAL DEL PERU. BOLETIN. 1943. a. $20. Biblioteca Nacional del Peru, Digbine, Apdo. 2335, Lima, Peru. Ed. Isabel Miranda M. bk.rev.; abstr.; bibl.; illus.; circ. 500. **Indexed:** A.I.C.P.

020   IT
IL BIBLIOTECARIO. 1984. q. L.55000. Bulzoni Editore, Via dei Liburni n.14, 00185 Rome, Italy. TEL 06-4455207. FAX 06-4450355. Ed. Alfredo Serrai. **Indexed:** LISA.

021   CU   ISSN 0006-176X
BIBLIOTECAS. 1963. bi-m. free or exchange basis. Consejo Nacional de Cultura, Direccion Nacional de Bibliotecas, Biblioteca Nacional Jose Marti, Plaza de la Revolucion, Havana, Cuba. Ed.Bd. bk.rev.; bibl.; charts; circ. 800. **Indexed:** Amer.Hist.& Life, Hist.Abstr.

020 600 500   PO   ISSN 0870-0974
Z833.A1
BIBLIOTECAS, ARQUIVOS E MUSEUS.* 1985. s-a. $10. Instituto Portugues do Patrimonio Cultural, Rua Occidental ao Campo Grande 83-1o, 1799 Lisbon, Portugal. TEL 37 3741. Ed. Fernando Bandeira Ferreira. bk.rev.; circ. 2,000.

027.7   NQ
BIBLIOTECAS UNIVERSITARIAS. 1981. 1/yr. free to universities. Universidad Nacional Autonoma de Nicaragua, Biblioteca Central, Apartado 68, Leon CA, Nicaragua. Ed. Walterio Lopez Adaros.

027   IT   ISSN 0392-8586
Z809.A1
BIBLIOTECHE OGGI; rivista bimestrale di informazione ricerca e dibattito. 1983. bi-m. L.96000 (foreign L.148000). Editrice Bibliografica s.r.l., Viale Vittorio Veneto 24, 20124 Milan, Italy. TEL 02-6597950. Ed. Massimo Belotti. adv.; bk.rev.; circ. 3,000. **Indexed:** LISA.
—BLDSC shelfmark: 2016.567400.
Description: Library science review.

020   PY   ISSN 0258-6436
BIBLIOTECOLOGIA Y DOCUMENTACION PARAGUAYA. 1972. irreg. $5. Asociacion de Bibliotecarios del Paraguay, Casilla de Correo 1505, Asuncion, Paraguay. Eds. Sofia Mareski, Margarita Kallsen. circ. 200. (processed; also avail. in microform)

026.61 610   DK   ISSN 0006-1786
BIBLIOTEK FOR LAEGER. 1809. 4/yr. DKK 130. Almindelige Danske Laegeforening - Danish Medical Association, Trondhjemsgade 9, 2100 Copenhagen, Denmark. TEL 31 38 55 00. FAX 31-15-28-58. (Subscr. to: Laegeforeningens Forlag, Esplanaden 8A, DK-1263 Copenhagen K, Denmark) Eds. Povl Riis, Eskil Hohwy. adv.; circ. 1,100. **Indexed:** Biol.Abstr., Chem.Abstr., Excerp.Med.
—BLDSC shelfmark: 2016.630000.

020   UK
BIBLIOTEKA BULTENO. (Text in Esperanto) 3/yr. £5.50. Tutmonda Esperantista Biblioteka Asocio, 228 Capworth St., London E10 7HL, England. TEL 081-556-0984. Ed. Douglas Portmann. bk.rev.
Description: Covers the application of Esperanto in library work, comparative librarianship, and the use of library terminology in Esperanto.

020   PL   ISSN 0551-3790
BIBLIOTEKA KORNICKA. PAMIETNIK. (Text in Polish; summaries in English) 1929. irreg., vol.21, 1986. price varies. (Polska Akademia Nauk, Biblioteka Kornicka) Ossolineum, Publishing House of the Polish Academy of Sciences, Rynek 9, Wroclaw, Poland. TELEX 0712771 OSS PL. (Dist. by: Ars Polona-Ruch, Krakowskie Przedmiescie 7, Warsaw, Poland) Ed. H. Chlopocka. circ. 700. (also avail. in microfilm)
Description: Includes historical articles on various cultural sections, based on the rich collection of the Kornik Library.

020   BU   ISSN 0204-7438
BIBLIOTEKAR; spisanie za bibliotechno delo. (Contents page in Bulgarian, English and Russian) 1954. m. 36 lv.($25) Narodna Biblioteka Kiril i Metodii, 11, V. Levski Blvd., 1504 Sofia, Bulgaria. (Dist. by: Hemus; 6, Rouski Blvd., 1000 Sofia, Bulgaria) Ed. V. Stojanov. bk.rev.; bibl.; charts; illus.; index; circ. 3,700. **Indexed:** Lib.Sci.Abstr., LISA.
—BLDSC shelfmark: 0017.060000.

020   RU   ISSN 0006-1808
BIBLIOTEKAR'. 1923. m. 4.30 Rub. Izdatel'stvo Kniga, 50, Gorky St., 125047 Moscow, Russia. (Subscr. to: Mezhdunarodnaya Kniga, Moscow G-200, Russia) (Co-sponsor: Ministerstvo Kul'tury) Ed. G.I. Samsonov. index; circ. 203,324. **Indexed:** Lib.Lit.

020   YU   ISSN 0006-1816
Z671
BIBLIOTEKAR. 1948. bi-m. 60 din.($4.58) Drustvo Bibliotekara Srbije - Society of Librarians of Serbia, Skerliceva 1, 11000 Belgrade, Yugoslavia. Ed. Vlarimir Jokanovic. adv.; bk.rev.; circ. 1,000. **Indexed:** Lib.Lit., Lib.Sci.Abstr.
—BLDSC shelfmark: 0017.030000.

020   SW   ISSN 0345-1097
BIBLIOTEKARIESAMFUNDET MEDDELAR. 1971. 3/yr. SEK 200. Svenska Bibliotekariesamfundet, c/o Kerstin Assarsson-Rizzi, Vitterhetsakademiens Bibliotek, Box 5405, S-114 84 Stockholm, Sweden. FAX 46-8-663-3825. Ed. Kerstin Assarsson-Rizzi. adv.; bk.rev.; circ. 1,300.

020   BN   ISSN 0006-1832
BIBLIOTEKARSTVO/LIBRARIANSHIP. (Text in Serbo-Croatian; summaries in English, German) 1956. a. 100 din.($6.25) Drustvo Bibliotekara Bosne i Hercegovine - Library Association of Bosnia and Hercegovina, Vojvode Stepe Obala 42, 71000 Sarajevo, Bosnia Hercegovina. Ed. Tatjana Prastalo. adv.; bk.rev.; circ. 750.

020   PL   ISSN 0208-4333
Z671
BIBLIOTEKARZ. 1934. m. $36. Stowarzyszenie Bibliotekarzy Polskich, Konopczynskiego 5-7, 00-953 Warsaw, Poland. TEL 27 52 96. (Dist. by: Ars Polona-Ruch, Krakowskie Przedmiescie 7, 00-068 Warsaw, Poland) Ed. Jan Wolosz. bk.rev.; bibl.; circ. 6,600. **Indexed:** Lib.Lit., LISA.
—BLDSC shelfmark: 2017.000000.

020   PL   ISSN 0406-1578
BIBLIOTEKARZ ZACHODNIOPOMORSKI/LIBRARIAN OF WEST POMERANIA. 1959. q. price varies. Wojewodzka i Miejska Biblioteka Publiczna, Ksiaznica Szczecinska im. Stanislawa Staszica, Podgorna 15, 70-952 Szczecin, Poland. TEL 392-01. TELEX 422335. Ed. Stanislaw Krzywicki. bk.rev.; bibl.; illus.; stat.; circ. 500. (also avail. in microfilm)
Description: For librarians and library management students.

020   RU
BIBLIOTEKOVEDENIE, BIBLIOGRAFIYA I INFORMATIKA. 1974. irreg. 0.60 Rub. Moskovskii Gosudarstvennyi Institut Kul'tury, Moscow, Russia.

020   RU   ISSN 0519-9514
BIBLIOTEKOVEDENIE I BIBLIOGRAFIYA ZA RUBEZHOM. 1958. 5/yr. price varies. Gosudarstvennaya Biblioteka S.S.S.R. im. V.I. Lenina, Pr. Kalinina 3, 121019 Moscow, Russia. Ed. B.P. Kanevskii. cum.index: nos.1-50 (1958-1974); circ. 6,000. (also avail. in microfilm) **Indexed:** Lib.Sci.Abstr.

020   BU   ISSN 0861-4881
▼**BIBLIOTEKOZNANIE, BIBLIOGRAFIA, KNIGOZNANIE.** 1991. a. $35. Narodna Biblioteka Kiril i Metodii, 11, V. Levski Blvd., 1504 Sofia, Bulgaria. Ed. H. Hadjihristov. circ. 350.

020 016   BU   ISSN 0324-1858
BIBLIOTEKOZNANIE, BIBLIOGRAFIIA, KNIGOZNANIE, NAUCHNA INFORMATSIIA. 1969. a. price varies. Narodna Biblioteka Kiril i Metodii, 11, V. Levski, 1504 Sofia, Bulgaria. circ. 350. **Indexed:** LISA.

027   DK   ISSN 0084-957X
BIBLIOTEKSAARBOG. (In two parts: Statistik for Folke- og Forskningsbibliotekerne; Beretning fra Folke- og Forskningsbibliotekerne) 1939. a. DKK 428. Bibliotekscentralen, Tempovej 7-11, DK-2750 Ballerup, Denmark. TEL 42-97-50-00. FAX 42-65-53-10. (Co-sponsor: Statens Bibliotekstjeneste) circ. 4,800.
Description: Contains information from research libraries, public libraries, institutions and associations concerning libraries.

020 011   SW   ISSN 0006-1867
Z671
BIBLIOTEKSBLADET/LIBRARY JOURNAL. (Text in Scandinavian languages) 1916. 10/yr. SEK 300. Sveriges Allmaenna Biblioteksfoerening - Swedish Library Association, Box 3127, 103 62 Stockholm, Sweden. TEL 08-7230082. FAX 08-7230038. Ed. Ylva Mannerheim. adv.; bk.rev.; bibl.; illus.; circ. 5,206 (controlled). (also avail. in microform from UMI; reprint service avail. from UMI) **Indexed:** Lib.Lit., Lib.Sci.Abstr., Tr.& Indus.Ind.

020   DK   ISSN 0109-923X
BIBLIOTEKSHISTORIE. a. free for members. (Dansk Bibliothekshistorisk Selskab) Bibliotekscentralen, Tempovej 7-11, DK-2750 Ballerup, Denmark. TEL 2-974000. FAX 2-655310.

L

LIBRARY AND INFORMATION SCIENCES

027   DK
BIBLIOTEKSVEJVISER/GUIDE TO DANISH LIBRARIES.
(Subtitles and index in English) 1970. a.
DKK 325($35) Danmarks Biblioteksforening -
Danish Library Association, Trekronergade 15,
DK-2500 Valby, Denmark. FAX 36-308080. Ed.
Hanne Wiberg. circ. 2,200.
   Description: A list of research and public libraries in Denmark.

026   CN   ISSN 0707-3674
BIBLIOTHECA MEDICA CANADIANA. (Text in English, French) 1979. q. Can.$45 to members; non-members Can.$55; institutions Can.$65. Canadian Health Libraries Association - Association des Bibliotheques de la Sante du Canada, P.O. Box 434, Station "K", Toronto, Ont. M4P 2G9, Canada. TEL 416-485-0377. FAX 416-485-0377. Ed. Diane Jewkes. index; circ. 450. **Indexed:** LISA.
—BLDSC shelfmark: 2019.129420.
   Description: Vehicle to increase communication among health libraries and health science librarians in Canada.

020   BE
BIBLIOTHEEK- EN ARCHIEFGIDS. 1922. 5/yr. 1400 Fr. Vlaamse Vereniging voor Bibliotheek-, Archief- en Documentatiewezen v.z.w., Goudbloemstraat 10-12, B-2060 Antwerp, Belgium. FAX 03-232-42-94. Ed. Marc Storms. adv.; bk.rev.; bibl.; illus.; index; circ. 1,450. **Indexed:** Bull.Signal., Inform.Sci.Abstr., Lib.Lit., Lib.Sci.Abstr., LISA, Ref.Zh.
   Formerly (until 1983): Bibliotheekgids (ISSN 0006-1956)

020   NE   ISSN 0165-1048
Z671
BIBLIOTHEEK EN SAMENLEVING. 1973. 11/yr. fl.50.35. Nederlands Bibliotheek en Lektuur Centrum, Taco Scheltemastraat 5, Box 93054, 2509 AB The Hague, Netherlands. Ed.Bd. adv.; bk.rev.; illus.; index; circ. 5,000. **Indexed:** Key to Econ.Sci., LISA.
   Description: Professional journal for public librarians.

070   GW   ISSN 0340-8051
BIBLIOTHEK DES BUCHWESENS (B B). 1972. irreg., vol.10, 1992. price varies. Anton Hiersemann Verlag, Rosenbergstr. 113, Postfach 140155, 7000 Stuttgart 1, Germany. TEL 0711-638265. FAX 0711-6369010. Ed. R.W. Fuchs.

020   GW   ISSN 0341-4183
Z671
BIBLIOTHEK FORSCHUNG UND PRAXIS. 1977. 3/yr. DM.178. K.G. Saur Verlag KG, Ortlerstr. 8, Postfach 701620, 8000 Munich 70, Germany. TEL 089-76902-0. FAX 089-76902150. Ed.Bd. bk.rev.; bibl. **Indexed:** LISA.
—BLDSC shelfmark: 2020.162000.

026   GW   ISSN 0176-2397
BIBLIOTHEK FUER ALLE; Informationen ueber soziale Bibliotheksarbeit. 1984. q. DM.16. Deutsches Bibliotheksinstitut, Abt. 1-Publikationen, Bundesallee 184-185, 1000 Berlin 30, Germany. TEL 030-8505-0. bibl.; stat.; circ. 800. (back issues avail.)

020   GW   ISSN 0067-8236
BIBLIOTHEK UND WISSENSCHAFT. (Text in English, French, German and Italian) 1964. a., vol.24, 1990. price varies. Verlag Otto Harrassowitz, Taunusstr. 14, Postfach 2929, 6200 Wiesbaden 1, Germany. TEL 0611-530-0. FAX 0611-530570. TELEX 4186135. Ed.Bd. adv.; circ. 600. (back issues avail.)

020   GW   ISSN 0175-6796
BIBLIOTHEKEN DER BUNDESREPUBLIK DEUTSCHLAND. DATIERTE HANDSCHRIFTEN. 1984. irreg., vol.3, 1991. price varies. Anton Hiersemann Verlag, Rosenbergstr. 113, Postfach 140155, 7000 Stuttgart 1, Germany. TEL 0711-638265. FAX 0711-6369010. Ed. J. Autenrieth.

020   GW
BIBLIOTHEKS TASCHENBUCH. a. DM.9.80. Bock & Herchen Verlag, Reichenberger Str. 11e, 5340 Bad Honnef, Germany.

020   GW   ISSN 0006-1972
Z801.A1
BIBLIOTHEKSDIENST. 1966. m. DM.52. Deutsches Bibliotheksinstitut, Abt. 1-Publikationen, Bundesallee 184-185, 1000 Berlin 31, Germany. TEL 030-8505-0. FAX 030-8505-100. adv.; bk.rev.; circ. 4,000.
—BLDSC shelfmark: 2020.198000.
   Formerly: Buechereidienst.

020   GW   ISSN 0340-000X
Z801.B3
BIBLIOTHEKSFORUM BAYERN. Abbreviated title: B F B. 1973. 3/yr. DM.50. (Bayerischen Staatliche Bibliotheken, Munchen) K.G. Saur Verlag KG, Ortlerstr. 8, Postfach 701620, 8000 Munich 70, Germany. TEL 089-76902-0. FAX 089-76902150. (Dist. in North America by: R.R. Bowker, 121 Chanlon Rd., New Providence, NJ 07974, USA) Ed.Bd. adv.; bk.rev.; bibl.; charts; illus.; circ. 2,000.
—BLDSC shelfmark: 2020.240000.

020   GW   ISSN 0300-287X
BIBLIOTHEKSPRAXIS. irreg., vol.28, 1990. price varies. K.G. Saur Verlag KG, Ortlerstr. 8, Postfach 701620, 8000 Munich 70, Germany. TEL 089-76902-0. FAX 089-76902150. Ed.Bd.

020   FR   ISSN 0249-7344
Z927.P22
BIBLIOTHEQUE NATIONALE. REVUE. 1976. q. 278 F.($82) Bibliotheque Nationale, 58 rue Richelieu, 75084 Paris Cedex 02, France. TEL 47-03-81-07. FAX 42-96-84-47. (Dist. by: Armand Colin, B.P. 22, 41353 Vineuil Cedex, France) Ed. A. Fauve-Chamoux. adv.; bk.rev.; illus.; circ. 2,000.
   Formerly: Bibliotheque Nationale Bulletin (ISSN 0338-4446)

020   BE   ISSN 0770-4372
BIBLIOTHEQUE ROYAL ALBERT 1ER. BULLETIN TRIMESTRIEL D'INFORMATION. Dutch edition: Koninklijke Biblioteek Albert I. Driemaandelijks Informatie Bulletin (ISSN 0770-4429) bi-m. free to institutions. Bibliotheque Royale Albert 1er, 4 bd. de l'Empereur, 1000 Brussels, Belgium. illus.
   Former titles: Bibliotheque Royal Albert 1er. Bulletin Bimestriel d'Information; Bibliotheque Royal Albert 1er. Bulletin; Bibliotheque Royale de Belgique. Bulletin (ISSN 0524-7632)

020   BE   ISSN 0772-3776
BIBLIOTHEQUE ROYALE ALBERT 1ER. PUBLICATIONS ANNONCEES/KONINKLIJKE BIBLIOTHEEK ALBERT I. AANGEKONDIGDE PUBLIKATIES. 1983. 24/yr. 1000 BEF. Bibliotheque Royale Albert 1er - Koninklijke Bibliotheek Albert I, 4 bd. de l'Empereur, B-1000 Brussels, Belgium.

020   BE   ISSN 0770-4526
BIBLIOTHEQUE ROYALE ALBERT 1ER. RAPPORT ANNUEL. Dutch edition: Koninklijke Bibliotheek Albert I. Jaarverslag (ISSN 0770-447X) a. free to institutions. Bibliotheque Royale Albert 1er - Koninklijke Bibliotheek Albert I, 4 bd. de l'Empereur, B-1000 Brussels, Belgium. stat.
—BLDSC shelfmark: 7275.799000.
   Formerly: Bibliotheque Royale de Belgique. Rapport Annuel.

015 026   JA   ISSN 0006-2030
Z675.A2
BIBLOS/BIBUROSU; monthly report of special libraries. (Text in Japanese) 1950. m. 3360 Yen. National Diet Library - Kokuritsu Kokkai Toshokan, 1-10-1 Nagata-cho, Chiyoda-ku, Tokyo 100, Japan. TEL 03-3581-2331. TELEX 2225393. bibl.; charts; illus.; circ. 1,600. **Indexed:** LISA.
—BLDSC shelfmark: 2021.970000.

020   SW   ISSN 1100-3847
▼**BIBSAMNYTT.** (Text in Swedish) 1989. irreg. (3-4/yr.). free. BIBSAM - the Royal Library's Office for National Planning and Co-ordination, Royal Library, Box 5039, S-102 41 Stockholm, Sweden. TEL 468-679-5040. FAX 468-611-2570. TELEX 19640 KBS S. Ed. Ingrid Svensson. circ. 700.

020   BE   ISSN 0067-8538
BIJDRAGEN TOT DE BIBLIOTHEEKWETENSCHAP/ CONTRIBUTIONS TO LIBRARY SCIENCE. 1961. irreg. price varies. Rijksuniversiteit te Gent, Centrale Bibliotheek, Rozier 9, B-9000 Gent, Belgium.

020 012   YU   ISSN 0352-6437
BILTEN DOKUMENTACIJE. SERIJA I1. INFORMATIKA/BULLETIN OF DOCUMENTATION. SERIES I1. INFORMATICS. 1972. bi-m. $198. Jugoslovenski Centar za Tehnicku i Naucnu Dokumentaciju - Yugoslav Center for Technical and Scientific Documentation (YCTSD), Sl. Penezica-Krcuna 29-31, Box 724, 11000 Belgrade, Yugoslavia. Ed. Ljiljana Kojic-Bogdanovic.
   Former titles (until 1985): Bilten Dokumentacije. Serija I1, 1. Informatika (ISSN 0351-4056); (until 1980): Bilten Dokumentacije. Serija I1. Informatika (ISSN 0350-0357)

BIMONTHLY REVIEW OF LAW BOOKS. see *LAW*

021   PL   ISSN 0006-3983
BIULETYN INFORMACYJNY BIBLIOTEKI NARODOWEJ. (Text in Polish; contents page in English) 1956. q. 2100 Zl. Biblioteka Narodowa, Al. Niepodleglosci 213, 00-973 Warsaw, Poland. TEL 48-22-259271. FAX 48-22-255251. TELEX 813702 BN PL. (Dist. by: Ars Polona-Ruch, ul. Krakowskie Przedmiescie 7, 00-068 Warsaw, Poland) Ed. Waclaw Sznee. adv.; bibl.; illus.; index, cum.index; circ. 600.
   Description: Presents the library's activities, collections and cooperation with domestic and foreign libraries.

029   UK   ISSN 0520-2795
Z696.B59
BLISS CLASSIFICATION BULLETIN. 1954. a. membership. Bliss Classification Association, c/o Library, Fitzwilliam College, Huntingdon Rd., Cambridge CB3 ODG, England. FAX 0223-464162. Ed. A.G. Curwen. bk.rev.; circ. 200.
—BLDSC shelfmark: 2111.555000.

020   UK   ISSN 0067-9488
Z792.094
BODLEIAN LIBRARY RECORD. 1938. s-a. £7 per no. Bodleian Library, Oxford OX1 3BG, England. FAX 0865-277182. TELEX 83656. Ed. D.S. Porter. index; circ. 1,500. (also avail. in microform from UMI; reprint service avail. from UMI,KTO) **Indexed:** Abstr.Engl.Stud., Amer.Hist.& Life, Br.Hum.Ind., Hist.Abstr., M.L.A.
—BLDSC shelfmark: 2117.000000.
   Description: Articles based on Bodleian holdings, news of acquisitions.

BOERN OG BOEGER. see *PUBLISHING AND BOOK TRADE*

028   DK   ISSN 0006-5692
Z671
BOGENS VERDEN; tidsskrift for dansk biblioteksvaesen. 1918. 8/yr. DKK 390($39) for non-members. Danmarks Biblioteksforening - Danish Library Association, Trekronergade 15, DK-2500 Valby, Denmark. FAX 36-308080. Ed. Flemming Ettrup. circ. 3,000. (also avail. in microform from UMI; reprint service avail. from UMI) **Indexed:** Lib.Lit, Lib.Sci.Abstr., LISA.
   Description: Information of Danish literature and libraries.

021   NO   ISSN 0006-5811
Z671
BOK OG BIBLIOTEK. 1934. 8/yr. NOK 125. Statens Bibliotektilsyn, Postboks 8145, DEP 0033 Oslo 1, Norway. TEL 02-832585. FAX 02-83-1552. Ed. Mar't Boedtker. adv.; bk.rev.; charts; illus.; stat.; index; circ. 11,000. **Indexed:** Lib.Lit., M.L.A.
—BLDSC shelfmark: 2121.450000.

020   GW   ISSN 0068-0028
BONNER BEITRAEGE ZUR BIBLIOTHEKS- UND BUECHERKUNDE. 1954. irreg., vol.30, 1985. price varies. Bouvier Verlag Herbert Grundmann, Am Hof 32, Postfach 1268, 5300 Bonn 1, Germany. Eds. Hartwig Lohse, Irmgard Ooms.

020   US
BOOK MARKS. 1949. 6/yr. membership; $15 outside South Dakota. South Dakota Library Association, 610 Quincy, Rapid City, SD 57701-0045. TEL 605-394-4171. FAX 605-394-6626. Ed. Susan Braunstein. adv.; bk.rev.; circ. 800.
   Formerly: Catalyst (ISSN 0045-5954)
   Description: Covers regional library issues and provides features on library services.

LIBRARY AND INFORMATION SCIENCES

027.8 028.1   SA   ISSN 0258-7149
BOOK PARADE/BOEKPARADE. (Text in Afrikaans, English) 1976. q. free. Transvaal Provincial Library Service - Transvaalse Provinsiale Biblioteekdiens, Private Bag X288, Pretoria 0001, South Africa. TEL 012-201-3349. FAX 012-201-2445. Ed. Karin Kriel. bk.rev.; film rev.; circ. 1,100.
  Description: Contains general information on the Transvaal Provincial Library Service, as well as reviews of newly acquired books.

027.8   US   ISSN 0731-4388
Z675.S3
BOOK REPORT; journal for junior and senior high school librarians. 1982. bi-m. (during school yr.) $39. Linworth Publishing, Inc., 480 E. Wilson Bridge Road, Ste. L, Worthington, OH 43085. TEL 614-436-7107. FAX 614-436-9490. Ed. Carolyn Hamilton. adv.; bk.rev.; circ. 11,000. (also avail. in microfilm; microfiche from UMI; back issues avail.; reprint service avail. from UMI) **Indexed:** Bk.Rev.Ind. (1983-), Child. Bk.Rev.Ind. (1983-), Ind.Child.Mag., Jun.High.Mag.Abstr.
  —BLDSC shelfmark: 2248.187800.
  Description: Provides articles, tips and ideas for day-to-day school library management, as well as reviews of audio-visuals and software, all written by school librarians.

202 051   US   ISSN 0893-6471
Z732.P42
BOOKENDS. 1982. 6/yr. membership. Friends of the Reading-Berks Public Libraries, Box 227, Wernersville, PA 19565. TEL 215-678-6480. Ed. Chet Hagan. bk.rev.; circ. 2,000 (controlled).
  Description: News and informational articles on the activities, events, and holdings of the Friends of the Reading -Berks (Pennsylvania) public libraries, with profiles of resident authors and publishing executives.

BOOKLEGGER. see *PUBLISHING AND BOOK TRADE*

BOOKMARK. see *EDUCATION*

020   US   ISSN 0006-7407
                                        CODEN: BOKMA
BOOKMARK (ALBANY); news about library services. 1949. q. $15 (foreign $20); or exchange basis. New York State Library, Albany, NY 12230. FAX 518-474-5786. Ed. Joseph F. Shubert. bibl.; circ. 5,000. (also avail. in microform from UMI; reprint service avail. from UMI) **Indexed:** LHTN, Lib.Lit., P.A.I.S.
  —BLDSC shelfmark: 2250.099500.
  Formerly: J P S Bookmark (ISSN 0275-8539)
  Description: Articles on professional library issues with emphasis on New York State.

021.7   US   ISSN 0006-7393
BOOKMARK (CHAPEL HILL). 1944. irreg. membership. (Friends of the University of North Carolina Library) University of North Carolina, Academic Affairs Library, Rare Book Collection, CB 3936 Wilson Library, Chapel Hill, NC 27599-3900. TEL 919-962-1143. Ed. Charles B. McNamara. circ. 600.

027.7   US   ISSN 0735-0295
BOOKMARK (MOSCOW); a newsletter about the library for the University of Idaho community. 1948. q. free. University of Idaho Library, Moscow, ID 83843. TEL 208-885-6584. FAX 208-885-6817. Ed. R. Force, G. Pollastro. bk.rev.; circ. 1,100 (controlled). (also avail. in microfilm) **Indexed:** Lib.Lit.

027.7   US   ISSN 0006-7458
BOOKS AND LIBRARIES AT THE UNIVERSITY OF KANSAS. 1952. irreg. free. University of Kansas Libraries, Lawrence, KS 66045. TEL 913-864-4334. Ed. James Helyar. bibl.; illus.; circ. controlled.

021.7   US   ISSN 0006-7474
Z881 .I644
BOOKS AT IOWA. 1964. s-a. membership. Friends of the University of Iowa Libraries, University of Iowa, Iowa City, IA 52242. Ed. Robert A. McCown. illus.; cum.index every 5 yrs; circ. 1,130. **Indexed:** Abstr.Engl.Stud., M.L.A.

020   US   ISSN 0891-9615
BORGO CATALOGING GUIDES. 1987. irreg., no.6, 1992. price varies. Borgo Press, Box 2845, San Bernardino, CA 92406. TEL 714-884-5813. Ed. Michael Burgess.
  Description: Provides current surveys of cataloging practice and science in the Library of Congress classification scheme.

026   BS
BOTSWANA. NATIONAL ARCHIVES. REPORT ON THE NATIONAL ARCHIVES. 1975. a. free. National Archives, c/o T. Masisi Lekaukau, Director, Box 239, Gaborone, Botswana. FAX 313584. TELEX 2994 HOMES BD. circ. 200.
  Description: Records the activities of a given year for the information of the relevant authorities in the country, as well as the users.

021   BS
BOTSWANA. NATIONAL LIBRARY SERVICE. REPORT. (Text in English) irreg. National Library Service, Private Bag 0036, Gaborone, Botswana. illus.
  Description: A report of activities of the Botswana National Library Service over a specified period.

332 020   US   ISSN 0888-045X
Z683   CODEN: BOLIEO
BOTTOM LINE (NEW YORK); a financial magazine for librarians. q. $49.95 (Canada $60; elsewhere $65). Neal-Schuman Publishers, Inc., 100 Varick St., New York, NY 10013. TEL 212-925-8650. FAX 212-219-8916.
  —BLDSC shelfmark: 2264.020100.
  Description: Aimed at managers in all types of libraries. Provides practical information on planning, budgeting, managing cash, purchasing, investment, cost analysis, new technology, and other financial tools and techniques.

020 070.5   US   ISSN 0068-0540
Z731
THE BOWKER ANNUAL LIBRARY AND BOOK TRADE ALMANAC. Short title: Bowker Annual. 1955. a. $142. R.R. Bowker, A Reed Reference Publishing Company, Division of Reed Publishing (USA) Inc., 121 Chanlon Rd., New Providence, NJ 07974. TEL 800-521-8110. FAX 908-665-6688. TELEX 138 755. (Subscr. to: Order Dept., Box 31, New Providence, NJ 07974) stat.; cum. index: 1972-1976 in 1976 ed. (also avail. in magnetic tape; microfiche) **Indexed:** SRI.
  ●Also available online. Vendor(s): BRS, DIALOG, European Space Agency, Orbit Information Technologies.
  Also available on CD-ROM.
  —BLDSC shelfmark: 2265.049000.
  Description: Essays and reports reviewing book industry and library developments, with statistical information on pricing and expenditures, and funding and legislative changes.

BRAILLE BOOK REVIEW (LARGE PRINT EDITION). see *HANDICAPPED — Visually Impaired*

020   US
BRANCHING OUT. 1963. m. free. Baltimore County Public Library, 320 York Rd., Towson, MD 21204. TEL 301-296-8500. FAX 301-296-3139. Ed. Kenna Forsyth. circ. 1,000 (controlled). (looseleaf format)

020   BL
BRAZIL. INSTITUTO NACIONAL DO LIVRO. RELATORIO DE ATIVIDADES. 1974. a. Instituto Nacional do Livro, Brasilia, D.F., Brazil.

026.78   UK   ISSN 0007-0173
BRIO. 1964. s-a. £19.50($42.50) International Association of Music Libraries, Archives & Documentation Centres (U.K. Branch), Faculty of Music Lib., St. Aldate's, Oxford OX1 1DB, England. (Subscr. to: c/o Dr. A. Reed, Music Section, British Library, Boston Spa, Wetherby, W. Yorks. LS23 8BQ, England) Ed. John Wagstaff. adv.; bk.rev.; circ. 500. (reprint service avail. from UMI) **Indexed:** Lib.Lit., Lib.Sci.Abstr., LISA, Music Ind., RILM.
  —BLDSC shelfmark: 2284.400000.

020   UK   ISSN 0269-0497
Z675.U5
BRITISH JOURNAL OF ACADEMIC LIBRARIANSHIP. 1986. 3/yr. £53($103) Taylor Graham Publishing, 500 Chesham House, 150 Regent St., London W1R 5FA, England. Ed. Colin Harris. adv.; bk.rev. (back issues avail.) **Indexed:** Lib.Lit., LISA.
  —BLDSC shelfmark: 2303.760000.

020   UK
BRITISH LIBRARIANSHIP & INFORMATION WORK. (In two volumes) 1972. quinquiennial. price varies. Library Association Publishing Ltd., 7 Ridgmount St., London WC1E 7AE, England. TEL 071-636-7543. FAX 071-636-3627. TELEX 21897. Eds. D. Bromley, A. Allott. index.
  Former titles: British Librarianship and Information Science (ISSN 0071-5662) & Five Years Work in Librarianship.

027   UK   ISSN 0305-7887
Z792   CODEN: ARBLDQ
BRITISH LIBRARY. ANNUAL REPORT. 1974. a. £7. British Library, Publication Sales Unit, Boston Spa, Wetherby, West Yorkshire LS23 7BQ, England. FAX 0937-546236. **Indexed:** Apic.Abstr.
  —BLDSC shelfmark: 1125.900000.

020   UK   ISSN 0952-892X
                                       CODEN: BLDNEC
BRITISH LIBRARY. DOCUMENT SUPPLY CENTRE. DOCUMENT SUPPLY NEWS. 1985. q. free. British Library, Document Supply Centre, Boston Spa, Wetherby, W. Yorkshire LS23 7BQ, England. TEL 0937-843434. FAX 0937-546333. TELEX 557381. Ed. Katy King. circ. 15,000. **Indexed:** AESIS.
  —BLDSC shelfmark: 3609.193900.
  Former titles: British Library. Document Supply Centre. Newsletter (ISSN 0269-1175); (until 1986): British Library. Lending Division Newsletter (ISSN 0267-064X)
  Description: Provides information about BLDSC.

026   UK
BRITISH LIBRARY. NEWSPAPER LIBRARY. NEWSLETTER. 1980. s-a. free. British Library, Newspaper Library, Colindale Ave., London NW9 5HE, England. FAX 01-323-7379. TELEX 21462. Ed. J. Allbrooke. bk.rev.; circ. 2,500.
  Formerly: British Library. Reference Division Newspaper Library. Newsletter (ISSN 0144-9958)
  Description: Reports developments in the Library and in newspaper services in the UK and worldwide.

020   UK   ISSN 0305-5167
Z921.B854
BRITISH LIBRARY JOURNAL. 1975. s-a. £35 (foreign £40). British Library, Humanities and Social Sciences, Great Russell St., London WC1B 3DG, England. TEL 017-323-7704. FAX 071-323-7736. TELEX 21462. Ed. C. Wright. illus.; cum.index; circ. 900. **Indexed:** Amer.Hist.& Life, Arts & Hum.Cit.Ind., Br.Hum.Ind., Curr.Cont., Hist.Abstr., M.L.A., RILA.
  —BLDSC shelfmark: 2327.679000.

020.6   UK   ISSN 0307-9481
BRITISH LIBRARY NEWS. 1976. m. free. British Library, 96 Euston Rd., London NW1 2DB, England. (Subscr. to: British Library, Publications Sales Unit, Boston Spa, Wetherby, W. Yorkshire LS23 7BQ, England) bk.rev.; circ. 8,000. **Indexed:** Apic.Abstr, Br.Ceram.Abstr.
  —BLDSC shelfmark: 2327.679500.

020   UK   ISSN 0261-2178
BRITISH LIBRARY RESEARCH REVIEWS. 1981. irreg. price varies. British Library, Research and Development Department, 2 Sheraton St., London W1V 4BH, England. FAX 071-323-7251. TELEX 21462. (Dist. in U.S.: ALA Publishing Services, 50 East Huron St., Chicago, IL 60611)
  —BLDSC shelfmark: 7769.589300.
  Description: Each issue covers a particular topic in library and information science.

021   US   ISSN 0007-2397
BROOKLYN PUBLIC LIBRARY BULLETIN. 1952. q. free. Brooklyn Public Library, Grand Army Plaza, Brooklyn, NY 11238. TEL 718-780-7700. Ed. Ellen Rudley. charts; illus.; circ. 10,000.

027.4   US
BROOME COUNTY PUBLIC LIBRARY. ANNUAL REPORT. (Former name of issuing body: Binghamton Public Library) a. Broome County Public Library, 78 Exchange St., Binghamton, NY 13901. TEL 607-723-6457.
  Formerly: Binghamton Public Library. Annual Report.

LIBRARY AND INFORMATION SCIENCES

655   AU   ISSN 0007-3040
BUECHERSCHAU; Zeitschrift fuer Betriebs- und Gewerkschaftsbibliotheken. 1962. q. free. Oesterreichischer Gewerkschaftsbund, Hohenstaufengasse 10-12, A-1010 Vienna, Austria. Ed. Kurt Link. bk.rev.; mkt.; circ. 2,500.

021   US   ISSN 0020-966X
BUFFALO AND ERIE COUNTY PUBLIC LIBRARY BULLETIN. 1969. m. (except Jul.-Aug.). free. Buffalo and Erie County Public Library, Lafayette Sq., Buffalo, NY 14203. TEL 716-858-7181. FAX 716-858-6211. Ed. Michael C. Mahaney. bk.rev.; circ. 750. **Indexed:** Lib.Lit.
Supersedes: Interpreter.

020   FR   ISSN 0006-2006
Z671
BULLETIN DES BIBLIOTHEQUES DE FRANCE. 1956. 6/yr. 410 F. Ministere de l'Education Nationale, Sous-direction des Bibliotheques, 61-65 rue Dutot, 75732 Paris Cedex 15, France. TEL 40-65-63-78. FAX 40-65-60-93. (Subscr. to: Ecole Nationale Superieure de Bibliothecaires (ENSB), 17-21 bd. du 11 Novembre 1918, 69100 Villeurbanne, France) Ed.Bd. adv.; bk.rev.; abstr.; bibl.; charts; illus.; index; circ. 2,200. (back issues avail.) **Indexed:** Curr.Cont, Int.Lab.Doc., Lib.Lit., Lib.Sci.Abstr., LISA.
—BLDSC shelfmark: 2411.480000.

028.5   GW   ISSN 0045-351X
BULLETIN JUGEND UND LITERATUR. 1969. m. DM.105. (Eulenhof Institut) Eulenhof-Verlag, Hallerplatz 5, 2000 Hamburg 13, Germany. TEL 040-445373. FAX 040-445282. Ed. Ehrhardt Heinold. adv.; bk.rev.; film rev.; play rev.; bibl.; illus.; circ. 1,200. **Indexed:** Child.Lit.Abstr.
Description: Contains critical reviews of newly published children's and young adult books. Also includes literary information, articles about writers and library practice, events, readers' comments, and title index.

BULLETIN OF BIBLIOGRAPHY. see *BIBLIOGRAPHIES*

020   US
Z674.5.U5
BURWELL DIRECTORY OF INFORMATION BROKERS. 1978. a. $59.50. Burwell Enterprises, 3724 F.M. 1960 W., Ste. 214, Houston, TX 77068. TEL 713-537-9051. FAX 713-537-8332. Ed. Helen P. Burwell.
Formerly: Directory of Fee-Based Information Services (ISSN 0147-1678)
Description: Directory of companies and individuals worldwide who provide information for a fee.

020 330   UK
BUSINESS AND GOVERNMENT: A MONTHLY SURVEY OF OFFICIAL PUBLICATIONS FOR BUSINESS AND GOVERNMENT. 1981. m. £31.50. Key Facts, The Old Rectory, Northill, Bedfordshire SG18 9AH, England. **Indexed:** Br.Ceram.Abstr.

BUSINESS INFORMATION ALERT; what's new in business publications, databases and research techniques. see *BUSINESS AND ECONOMICS — Abstracting, Bibliographies, Statistics*

020   US   ISSN 0892-6034
BUSINESS INFORMATION FROM YOUR PUBLIC LIBRARY. 1973. 3/yr. $48 (minimum order: 100 copies). Administrator's Digest, Inc., Box 993, South San Francisco, CA 94080. TEL 415-573-5474. Ed. Robert S. Alvarez. circ. 34,000.

026   US   ISSN 0191-4006
BUSINESS LIBRARY NEWSLETTER. 1978. m. $52. Business Library Newsletter, Inc., 427-3 Amherst St., Ste. 305, Nashua, NH 03063. TEL 603-672-0705. Ed. Raymond T. Hubbard. adv.; bk.rev.; index; circ. 500. (back issues avail.)
Description: Publishes a review of 12-15 of the latest titles in business and related areas.

BUSINESS RESEARCH GUIDES. see *BUSINESS AND ECONOMICS — Management*

BUY BOOKS WHERE, SELL BOOKS WHERE; a directory of out of print book dealers and their author-subject specialties. see *PUBLISHING AND BOOK TRADE*

027.8   CN   ISSN 0829-254X
C A A T TRACKS. 1986. q. Can.$20. Ontario Colleges of Applied Arts and Technology, Committee on Learning Resources, St. Lawrence College, King and Portsmouth Avenues, Kingston, Ont. K7L 5A6, Canada. TEL 613-544-5400. FAX 613-545-3920. Eds. Barbara Carr, Barbara Love. bk.rev.; circ. 60. (back issues avail.)
Formerly: Com-O-Lib.
Description: Newsletter for and about Ontario Community Colleges libraries.

020   US   ISSN 0091-5270
Z666
C A L L. (Current Awareness - Library Literature) 1972. bi-m. $25. Goldstein Associates, 35 Whittemore Rd., Framingham, MA 01701. Ed. Samuel Goldstein. bk.rev.; abstr.; index.

C A M L NEWSLETTER/A C B M NOUVELLES. (Canadian Association of Music Libraries) see *MUSIC*

026   CN   ISSN 0821-3127
C A S L I S, CALGARY CHAPTER. NEWSLETTER. 1976. bi-m. Can.$20 (effective Jan. 1991). Canadian Library Association, Canadian Association of Special Libraries and Information Services, 401 9th Ave. S.W., P.O. Box 22152, Calgary, Alta. T2P 4J5, Canada. Ed. Jean Peterson. circ. 210. (back issues avail.)
Description: News of interest to regional professional librarians.

C & L APPLICATIONS; monthly information for libraries and information services. see *LIBRARY AND INFORMATION SCIENCES — Computer Applications*

025   US   ISSN 8755-5727
HD9697.P56   CODEN: CDDRED
C D DATA REPORT; a monthly newsletter covering the compact disc (CD-ROM) industry and related optical storage technologies. 1984. 12/yr. $395 in North America; foreign $495. Disc Company, 6609 Rosecroft Pl., Falls Church, VA 22043-1828. TEL 703-237-0682. FAX 703-532-5447. Ed. Linda W. Helgerson. bk.rev.; circ. 1,500.
—BLDSC shelfmark: 3096.250000.
Description: For the CD-ROM industry. Reports services, products, projects and applications, and provides information on what others are doing in CD-ROM.

020   JA   ISSN 0914-6601
C D N L A O NEWSLETTER. (Conference of Directors of National Libraries on Resource Sharing in Asia and Oceania) 3/yr. National Diet Library, International Cooperation Division - Kokuritsu Kokkai Toshokan, 1-10-1 Nagata-cho, Chiyoda-ku, Tokyo 100, Japan. TEL 03-3581-2331. TELEX 2225393. circ. 1,100.
Formerly: A O Newsletter.
Description: Forum for the exchange of information, views, and experiences among librarians in Asia and Oceania.

621.38   US   ISSN 0893-9934
Z681.3.067   CODEN: CDLIEQ
C D - R O M LIBRARIAN; the optical media review for information professionals. 1986. 11/yr. $82. Meckler Publishing Corporation, 11 Ferry Lane W., Westport, CT 06880-5808. TEL 203-226-6967. Ed. Norman Desmarais. **Indexed:** Compumath, Info.Media & Tech., Lib.Lit., LISA, Tr.& Indus.Ind.
●Also available online. Vendor(s): DIALOG, NewsNet.
—BLDSC shelfmark: 3096.303500.
Formerly (until 1987): Optical Information Systems Update: Library and Information Center Applications (ISSN 0886-019X)

020   US   ISSN 0895-2485
C D S CONNECTION. 1988. s-a. free. U.S. Library of Congress, Cataloging Distribution Service, Customer Services Section, Washington, DC 20541. TEL 202-707-6100. FAX 202-707-1334. Ed. Pat Gray. circ. 7,000.
Description: Reports on news, developments, and ideas for new products that will affect library professionals.

026 959   US
Z3001
C E A L DIRECTORY. biennial. $10. Association for Asian Studies, Inc., Committee on East Asian Libraries, c/o Maureen H. Donovan, Main Library, Rm.310, Ohio State University Libraries, 1858 Neil Ave. Mall, Columbus, OH 43210-1286. TEL 614-292-3502. FAX 614-292-7859.
Description: Directory of East Asian Collections in North American Libraries (ISSN 0148-0065)

021   US
C E F TRAILBLAZER. 1974. q. free. Clinton - Essex - Franklin Library System, 17 Oak St., Plattsburgh, NY 12901. TEL 518-563-5190. Ed. Mary Shaw Hopkins. bk.rev.; circ. 860.
Supersedes: C E F News (ISSN 0007-8212)

C E R L A L C: EL LIBRO EN AMERICA LATINA Y EL CARIBE. see *PUBLISHING AND BOOK TRADE*

C H R A PROGRESS NOTES. (Canadian College of Health Record Administrators, Canadian Health Record Association.) see *MEDICAL SCIENCES*

020   CN
C L A DIRECTORY. 1950. irreg., latest 1990. $25 to non-members. Canadian Library Association, 200 Elgin Street, Ste. 602, Ottawa, Ont. K2P 1L5, Canada. TEL 613-232-9625. FAX 613-563-9895.
Former titles: C L A Organization Handbook and Membership List (ISSN 0068-9130); Canadian Library Directory.

020   US
C L E N EXCHANGE NEWSLETTER. 1984. q. $20. (Continuing Library Education Network and Exchange Round Table) American Library Association, 50 E. Huron St., Chicago, IL 60611. TEL 312-944-6780. FAX 312-440-9374. Ed. Marie E. Bryan. circ. 450.

020   II   ISSN 0970-0943
Z665.2.I4
C L I S OBSERVER. 1984. q. Rs.200($40) Centre for Library and Information Study, C-30, Lajpat Nagar III, New Delhi 110 024, India. TEL 11-6836119. Ed. D.R. Kalia. adv.; bk.rev.; circ. 1,000.
Description: Research and development in library and information sciences.

020   US   ISSN 0892-0605
C L R REPORTS. 1957. irreg. free to qualified personnel. Council on Library Resources, Inc., 1785 Massachusetts Ave., N.W., Ste. 313, Washington, DC 20036. TEL 202-483-7474. FAX 202-483-6410. Ed. Ellen Timmer. circ. 4,000.
Supersedes (in 1986, vol.14, no.2): C L R Recent Developments (ISSN 0034-1169)

025   US
C L S I NEWSLETTER OF LIBRARY AUTOMATION. 1976. s-a. free. C L S I, Inc., 320 Nevada St., Newtonville, MA 02160. TEL 617-965-6310. FAX 617-969-1928. Ed. Trudy Kontoff. index; circ. 5,000.
Formerly: C L S I Newsletter (ISSN 0363-9479)
Description: Yearly articles about CLSI, its customers' automation activities, and the company's latest developments in product, personnel and technology.

020   CN
C M: A REVIEWING JOURNAL OF CANADIAN MATERIALS FOR YOUNG PEOPLE. 1971. 6/yr. Can.$42. Canadian Library Association, 200 Elgin St., Ste. 602, Ottawa, Ont. K2P 1L5, Canada. TEL 613-232-9625. FAX 613-563-9895. Ed. Elizabeth Morton. adv.; bk.rev.; film rev.; illus.; index; circ. 2,000. **Indexed:** Bk.Rev.Ind. (1988-), Child.Bk.Rev.Ind. (1988-), CMI, Media Rev.Dig.
Former titles: C M: Canadian Materials for Schools and Libraries (ISSN 0821-1450); Canadian Materials (ISSN 0317-4654)

LIBRARY AND INFORMATION SCIENCES 2751

027.8 370 US ISSN 0196-3309
Z675.S3
C M L E A JOURNAL. 1977. 2/yr. $15 to
non-members. California Media and Library
Educators Association, 1499 Old Bayshore Hwy.,
No. 142, Burlingame, CA 94010.
TEL 415-692-2350. Ed. Barbara Jeffus. adv.;
bk.rev.; illus.; circ. 2,000. (also avail. in microform
from UMI; reprint service avail. from UMI) **Indexed:**
Cal.Per.Ind. (1980-), Lib.Lit.
—BLDSC shelfmark: 3287.250000.
Former titles: Journal of Media and Technology;
California School Libraries (ISSN 0008-1523)
Description: Addresses current issues of interest to
school library media personnel.

020 JM ISSN 0378-1070
C O M L A NEWSLETTER. (Text in English) 1973. q.
$35. Commonwealth Library Association, P.O. Box
144, Kingston 7, Jamaica, W.I. TEL 809-927-2123.
FAX 809-927-1926. Eds. Norma Y. Amenu-Kpodo,
H. Brown. adv.; bk.rev.; bibl.; circ. 500. (back issues
avail) **Indexed:** LISA.
—BLDSC shelfmark: 3331.270000.

C P L NEWSLETTER. (Council of Planning Librarians)
see HOUSING AND URBAN PLANNING

025 US ISSN 0882-6846
C R I A R L NEWSLETTER. 1982. 3/yr. free to libraries.
Consortium of Rhode Island Academic and Research
Libraries, c/o Helena F. Rodrigues, Ed., Library,
Roger Williams University, One Old Ferry Rd., Bristol,
RI 02809-2921. TEL 401-254-3053. circ. 500.

020 PO ISSN 0007-9421
Z671
**CADERNOS DE BIBLIOTECONOMIA, ARQUIVISTICA E
DOCUMENTACAO.** Short title: Cadernos B A D. 1963.
s-a. Esc.1500. Associacao Portuguesa de
Bibliotecarios, Arquivistas e Documentalistas, Edificio
da Biblioteca Nacional, Campo Grande 83, 1751
Lisbon, Portugal. FAX 834697. Ed. Maria Luisa
Cabral. adv.; bk.rev.; abstr.; bibl.; charts; circ. 1,000.
Indexed: Bull.Signal.

001 020 FR ISSN 0339-3097
CODEN: CADODG
CAHIERS DE L'ANALYSE DES DONNEES. (Text in French;
summaries in Arabic, English, French) 1975. q.
585 F. (Association pour le Developpement et la
Diffusion de l'Analyse des Donnees) Dunod, 15 rue
Gossin, 92543 Montrouge Cedex, France.
TEL 33-1-40-92-65-00. FAX 33-1-40-92-65-97.
TELEX 270 004. (Subscr. to: Centrale des Revues,
11 rue Gossin, 92543 Montrouge Cedex, France.
TEL 33-1-46-56-52-66) Ed. J.P. Benzecri. adv.; circ.
750. (also avail. in microform from MIM) **Indexed:**
Br.Archaeol.Abstr., INIS Atomind.
—BLDSC shelfmark: 2948.618500.
Description: Features articles on statistics and data
processing from a teacher's point of view, listings,
programs of computation designed for techniques of
data analysis.

**CALENDAR OF CONFERENCES, MEETINGS AND
EXHIBITIONS TO BE HELD IN SOUTH AFRICA.** see
MEETINGS AND CONGRESSES

020 US ISSN 1056-1528
CALIFORNIA LIBRARIES. 1967. m. membership.
California Library Association, 717 K St., Ste. 300,
Sacramento, CA 95814. TEL 916-447-8541.
FAX 914-447-8394. Ed. Mary Sue Ferrell. adv.;
bk.rev.; circ. 3,600. (also avail. in microfilm)
Formerly: C L A Newsletter (ISSN 0007-8557)

979 020 US ISSN 0741-0344
Z733.C13
CALIFORNIA STATE LIBRARY FOUNDATION BULLETIN.
1982. q. $20. California State Library Foundation,
Box 942837, Sacramento, CA 94237-0001.
TEL 916-654-0174. Ed. Gary E. Strong. cum.index:
1982-1988; circ. 1,200. (back issues avail.)
Indexed: Lib.Lit.
Description: Provides a combination of
library-related news and information, as well as
coverage of topics relevant to California history and
library services.

020 US ISSN 0008-1744
CALL NUMBER. 1939. 3/yr. free to qualified personnel.
University of North Texas, School of Library and
Information Sciences, NT Box 13796, Denton, TX
76203. TEL 817-565-2445. FAX 817-565-3101.
Ed. Kenneth L. Ferstl. circ. 2,500.

029 BL ISSN 0101-6903
**CAMARA BRASILEIRA DO LIVRO. CENTRO DE
CATALOGACAO NA FONTE. OFICINA DE LIVROS:
NOVIDADES CATALOGADAS NA FONTE.** 1974. a.
Cr.$5250($50) Camara Brasileira do Livro, Centro
de Catalogacao na Fonte, Av. Ipiranga, 1267, 10
andar, Sao Paulo 01039, Brazil. FAX 229-7463.
TELEX 24788 VRLI. Ed. Zilpha Rizzo Piazza. bk.rev.;
bibl.; circ. 1,000.

020 UK
**CAMBRIDGE UNIVERSITY LIBRARY LIBRARIANSHIP
SERIES.** irreg. price varies. Cambridge University
Press, Edinburgh Bldg., Shaftesbury Rd., Cambridge
CB2 2RU, England. TEL 0223-312393.
FAX 0223-315052. TELEX 851817256.

026 UK
CAMBRIDGE UNIVERSITY MEDICAL LIBRARY BULLETIN.
1980. 4/yr. free. Cambridge University, Medical
Library, Addenbrooke's Hospital, Hills Rd.,
Cambridge CB2 2QQ, England. TEL 0223-336750.
FAX 0223-336709. circ. 380.
Former titles: Cambridge Medical Library Bulletin;
Medical Library Bulletin.
Description: Library accession list plus library
news.

020.6 340 CN ISSN 1180-176X
**CANADIAN LAW LIBRARIES/BIBLIOTHEQUES DE DROIT
CANADIENNES.** 1970. 5/yr. Can.$60. Canadian
Association of Law Libraries - Association
Canadienne des Bibliotheques de Droit, c/o York
University Law Library, 4700 Keele St., North York,
Ont. M3J 1P3, Canada. Ed. Vivienne Denton. adv.;
bk.rev.; bibl.; index; circ. 500.
—BLDSC shelfmark: 3037.315000.
Formerly: Canadian Association of Law Libraries.
Newsletter (ISSN 0319-5376)
Description: Publishes news, developments,
articles, reports of interest to its members.

020 CN ISSN 0008-4352
CODEN: CLIJBX
CANADIAN LIBRARY JOURNAL. 1944. bi-m. Can.$45 to
non-members. Canadian Library Association, 200
Elgin St., Ste. 602, Ottawa, Ont. K2P 1L5, Canada.
TEL 613-232-9625. FAX 613-563-9895. Ed.
Jacqueline Easby. adv.; bk.rev.; charts; illus.; stat.;
circ. 5,500. (also avail. in microform) **Indexed:**
Amer.Hist.& Life, C.I.J.E., Can.Per.Ind., CMI,
Curr.Cont., Hist.Abstr., LHTN, Lib.Lit., LISA,
Ref.Sour., Sci.Abstr., SSCI.
—BLDSC shelfmark: 3037.700000.
Formerly: Canadian Library.
Description: Provides a forum for the discussion,
analysis and evaluation of issues in librarianship.
Refereed Serial

020 CN ISSN 0225-1574
CANADIANA AUTHORITIES. (Text in English, French)
1976. q. base vol. plus bi-w. supplements.
Can.$107. National Library of Canada, Canadiana
Editorial Division, Aquisitions and Bibliographic
Services Branch, 395 Wellington St., Ottawa, Ont.
K1A 0N4, Canada. TEL 819-994-6918. (also avail.
in magnetic tape)

020 SA ISSN 0008-5790
CAPE LIBRARIAN/KAAPSE BIBLIOTEKARIS. (Text in
Afrikaans, English) 1957. m. (except July & Dec.).
R.50 free to affiliated public libraries or on exchange
basis. Cape Provincial Library Service, Box 2108,
Cape Town, South Africa. FAX 021-419-7541. Ed. I.
Oggel. bk.rev.; index; circ. 1,200. (also avail. in
microfilm from UMI; reprint service avail. from UMI)
Indexed: Lib.Lit., Lib.Sci.Abstr., LISA.
—BLDSC shelfmark: 3050.647000.
Description: Promotes the information function of
the Cape Provincial library.

**CARIBBEAN ARCHIVES/ARCHIVES
ANTILLAISES/ARCHIVOS DEL CARIBE.** see
HISTORY — History Of North And South America

021.7 US ISSN 0008-6894
Z881
CARRELL. 1960. a. $5. (Friends of the University of
Miami Library) University of Miami Library, Box
248214, Coral Gables, FL 33124.
TEL 305-284-4585. FAX 305-665-7352. Eds.
Ronald P. Naylor, Laurence Donovan. bibl.; illus.;
cum.index: vol.1-13, 1972; circ. 500. **Indexed:**
Bibl.Engl.Lang.& Lit., M.L.A., Numis.Lit.
Description: Poetry, literature, criticism and art by
the university's faculty and students.

CARTA DE ARCHIVO. see HISTORY — History Of North
And South America

CASSETTE BOOKS. see HANDICAPPED — Visually
Impaired

CATALOG OF CURRENT LAW TITLES; recent acquisitions
of major legal libraries. see LIBRARY AND
INFORMATION SCIENCES — Abstracting,
Bibliographies, Statistics

020 US ISSN 0163-9374
Z693.A15 CODEN: CCQUDB
CATALOGING & CLASSIFICATION QUARTERLY. 1980. q.
$40 to individuals; institutions $105. Haworth
Press, Inc., 10 Alice St., Binghamton, NY 13904.
TEL 800-342-9678. FAX 607-722-1424. TELEX
4932599 HAWORTH. Ed. Ruth Carter. adv.; bk.rev.
(also avail. in microfiche from HAW; back issues
avail.; reprint service avail. from HAW) **Indexed:**
Bull.Signal., C.I.J.E., Comput.& Info.Sys., Excerp.Med.,
Inform.Sci.Abstr., Lib.Lit., LISA, Ref.Zh., Sci.Abstr.
—BLDSC shelfmark: 3074.275000.
Description: Presents theoretical and applied
articles in the field of cataloging and classification.
Refereed Serial

020 AT ISSN 0312-4371
Z693.5.A8
CATALOGUING AUSTRALIA. q. Aus.$28 (foreign
Aus.$36)(effective 1992). Australian Library and
Information Association, P.O. Box E411, Queen
Victoria Terrace, A.C.T. 2600, Australia.
TEL 06-285-1877. FAX 06-282-2249. **Indexed:**
LISA.
—BLDSC shelfmark: 3090.414000.
Description: Materials of professional interest to
catalogers.

020 US ISSN 0730-711X
Z673
CATALYST (DES MOINES). 1948. bi-m. $25 to
non-members. Iowa Library Association, 823
Insurance Exchange Bldg., Des Moines, IA 50309.
TEL 515-243-2172. Ed. Naomi Stovall. adv.; bk.rev.;
circ. 1,800.
Formerly: I L A Catalyst (ISSN 0018-9944)

020 UK ISSN 0144-9931
CATALYST (LONDON); information from the University
of London Shared Automated Library Services.
1980; N.S. 1985. irreg. free. University of London,
Library Resources Co-ordinating Committee, Senate
House, Malet St., London WC1E 7HU, England. Ed.
Paul McLaughlin. **Indexed:** LISA.

020 282 US ISSN 0008-8161
**CATHOLIC LIBRARY ASSOCIATION. NORTHERN ILLINOIS
CHAPTER. NEWSLETTER.** 1957. 4/yr. $8. Catholic
Library Association, Northern Illinois Chapter, c/o Sr.
Lauretta McCusker, Oak Lawn Public Library, 9427
S. Raymond, Oak Laun, IL 60653. Ed. Kathleen
O'Learyr. bk.rev.; circ. 450. (processed)

020 282 US ISSN 0008-820X
Z671
CATHOLIC LIBRARY WORLD. 1929. 4/yr. $60. Catholic
Library Association, 461 W. Lancaster Ave.,
Haverford, PA 19041. TEL 215-649-5250. Ed.
Anthony Prete. adv.; bk.rev.; bibl.; index; circ. 3,000.
(also avail. in microfilm from UMI) **Indexed:**
Bk.Rev.Ind. (1965-), C.I.J.E., Cath.Ind.,
Child.Bk.Rev.Ind. (1965-), Lib.Lit., Lib.Sci.Abstr.,
Ref.Sour.
—BLDSC shelfmark: 3093.077000.

020 US
CENTENNIAL STATE LIBRARIES. 1968. bi-m. free to
Colorado institutions. State Library, Department of
Education, 201 E. Colfax Ave., Rm. 309, Denver, CO
80203. TEL 303-866-6881. FAX 303-830-0793.
Ed. Kim Luchau. circ. 3,000. (tabloid format)
Formerly: Colorado State Library Newsletter (ISSN
0010-1761); Supersedes: Capitol Hill Library Crier.

020 US
CENTER FOR RESEARCH LIBRARIES. HANDBOOK. irreg.
$15 to non-members. Center for Research Libraries,
6050 S. Kenwood Ave., Chicago, IL 60637.
TEL 312-955-4545. index.
Description: Descriptions of collections and access
to them.

LIBRARY AND INFORMATION SCIENCES

020   MX
CENTRO DE BIBLIOTECOLOGIA, ARCHIVOLOGIA E INFORMACION. ANUARIO. 1961. a. Universidad Nacional Autonoma de Mexico, Centro de Bibliotecologia, Archivologia e Informacion, Villa Obregon, Ciudad Universitaria, Mexico 20, D.F., Mexico. Ed. Alicia Perales de Mercado. bk.rev.; cum.index; circ. 1,000. (back issues avail)
Formerly: Anuario de Bibliotecologia, Archivologia e Informatica.

020   SP   ISSN 0210-9492
CENTRO DE INFORMACION DOCUMENTAL DE ARCHIVOS. BOLETIN DE INFORMACION. 1980. q. free. Centro de Informacion Documental de Archivos, Avda. Juan de Herrera 2, planta 4a, 28040 Madrid, Spain. TEL 543-70-48.

CERCLE BELGE DE LA LIBRAIRIE. ANNUAIRE. see *PUBLISHING AND BOOK TRADE*

020   CS
CESKOSLOVENSKA AKADEMIE VED. USTREDNI ARCHIV. ARCHIVNI ZPRAVY. 1970. 1-2/yr. free. Academia, Publishing House of the Czechoslovak Academy of Sciences, Vodickova 40, 112 29 Prague 1, Czechoslovakia. TEL 23-63-065. Ed. Jindrich Schwippel. bk.rev.; bibl.; circ. 500.

020   US   ISSN 0146-1095
CHANNEL D L S. 1966. m. (combined Jul.-Aug.). free. Department of Public Instruction, Division for Library Services, 125 S. Webster St., 5th Fl., Box 7841, Madison, WI 53707. TEL 608-266-9679. FAX 608-267-1052. Ed. Telise E.M. Johnsen. circ. 3,450 (controlled). (reprint service avail. from UMI)

020.4   US
CHAUTAUQUA - CATTARAUGUS LIBRARY SYSTEM NEWSLETTER. bi-m. Chautauqua - Cattaraugus Library System, 106 W. Fifth St., Jamestown, NY 14701. FAX 716-483-6880. circ. 700.

020   CN
CHECK IT OUT!. 1972. bi-m. free. Mississauga Library System, 301 Burnhamthorpe Rd. W., Mississauga, Ont. L5B 3Y3, Canada. TEL 416-615-3611. FAX 416-615-3615. Ed. Kelly Smith. adv.; bk.rev.; circ. 15,000.
Formerly (until vol.19, no.2, 1991): Link (Mississauga) (ISSN 0703-7007)
Description: Calendar of library events and services for the public.

020   US
CHICORY (BATON ROUGE). 1980. 3/yr. membership. Louisiana Library Association, Box 3058, Baton Rouge, LA 70821. TEL 504-342-4928. Ed. Sona Dombourian. circ. 450. (back issues avail.; reprint service avail. from UMI)

CHILDREN'S BOOK REVIEW SERVICE. see *PUBLISHING AND BOOK TRADE*

028.5   US   ISSN 0885-0429
PN1008.2
CHILDREN'S LITERATURE ASSOCIATION QUARTERLY. 1976. q. membership. Children's Literature Association, 22 Harvest Ln., Battle Creek, MI 49017-7938. Ed. Gillian Adams. adv.; bk.rev.; circ. 1,500. **Indexed:** Bk.Rev.Ind. (1986-), Child.Bk.Rev.Ind. (1986-), Child.Lit.Abstr., M.L.A.
Description: Editorials, articles, and announcements pertaining to scholarship and research in the field.

020   CH   ISSN 0034-5016
Z846.K864
CHINA, REPUBLIC. NATIONAL CENTRAL LIBRARY. NEWSLETTER. 1969. q. free. National Central Library, Bureau of International Exchange of Publications - Kuo Li Chung Yang T'u Shu Kuan, 20 Chung Shan S. Rd., Taipei, Taiwan 10040, Republic of China. FAX 02-311-0155. bibl.
—BLDSC shelfmark: 6021.511320.

026 280   US   ISSN 0412-3131
    CODEN: CHLIDJ
CHRISTIAN LIBRARIAN. 1957. q. $20 (foreign $24). Association of Christian Librarians Inc., Box 4, Cedarville, OH 45314. TEL 513-766-2211. FAX 513-766-2337. Ed. Ron Jordahl. adv.; bk.rev.; illus.; bibl.; circ. 450. (back issues avail.; reprint service avail. from UMI) **Indexed:** Child Lit.Abstr., Chr.Per.Ind., Inform.Sci.Abstr., Sci.Abstr.
—BLDSC shelfmark: 3181.831000.
Description: Vehicle for Christian interpretation of library science in institutions of higher learning.

020 266 200   UK   ISSN 0309-4170
CHRISTIAN LIBRARIAN. 1976. a. £1.90. Librarians' Christian Fellowship, c/o Graham Hedges, Ed., 34 Thurlestone Ave., Seven Kings, Ilford, Essex IG3 9DU, England. TEL 081-871 6351. adv.; bk.rev.; abstr.; circ. 500. (back issues avail.) **Indexed:** Chr.Per.Ind., Lib.Sci.Abstr.
Description: Articles on librarianship issues written from a Christian viewpoint.

026   US   ISSN 0009-6342
Z675.C5
CHURCH AND SYNAGOGUE LIBRARIES. 1967. bi-m. $18. Church & Synagogue Library Association, Box 19357, Portland, OR 97280-0357. TEL 503-244-6919. Ed. Lorraine E. Burson. adv.: B&W page $250; trim 8 1/2 x 11. bk.rev.; charts; illus.; index; circ. 3,400. (back issues avail.; reprint service avail. from UMI) **Indexed:** CERDIC, Chr.Per.Ind.
—BLDSC shelfmark: 3189.745000.
Formerly: Church and Synagogue Library Association. News Bulletin.
Description: News articles, announcements, and book reviews pertaining to the members and activities of the association.

020 286   US   ISSN 0884-6197
CHURCH MEDIA LIBRARY MAGAZINE. 1970. q. $13.75. Southern Baptist Convention, Sunday School Board, 127 Ninth Ave., N., Nashville, TN 37234. TEL 800-458-2772. bk.rev.; record rev.; bibl.; charts; illus.; index, cum.index; circ. 20,000. **Indexed:** South.Bap.Per.Ind.
Formerly: Media: Library Services Journal (ISSN 0009-6423); Supersedes: Church Library Magazine.

020   BL   ISSN 0100-1965
Z1007
CIENCIA DA INFORMACAO. (Text in Portuguese; summaries in English and Portuguese) 1972. 2/yr. Cr.$5000($40) Instituto Brasileiro de Informacao em Ciencia e Tecnologia, SAS Quadra 2, Lote 6, Bloco H, 70070 Brasilia, D.F., Brazil. TEL 2176161. FAX 2262677. Ed. Noris A. Bethonico Foresti. adv.; bk.rev.; abstr.; bibl.; charts; illus. **Indexed:** Bull.Signal., Inform.Sci.Abstr., Lib.Lit., LISA, P.A.I.S.For.Lang.Ind., P.A.I.S., Ref.Zh.
—BLDSC shelfmark: 3196.400000.

027   US   ISSN 0069-4215
CIRCUM-SPICE. 1965. s-a. free. City College of New York, Library, Convent Ave. & W. 135 St., New York, NY 10031. TEL 212-650-7601. FAX 212-650-7604. Eds. Martin W. Helgesen, Neil Jacobowitz. circ. 1,200.
Description: Newsletter reporting library events, professional activities of librarians.

020   US   ISSN 0009-885X
CLEVELAND PUBLIC LIBRARY STAFF ASSOCIATION. NEWS AND VIEWS. 1937. irreg. membership. Cleveland Public Library Staff Association, 325 Superior Ave., Cleveland, OH 44114. TEL 216-623-2800. bk.rev.; circ. 350. (processed)

020   US
CODE NAMES DICTIONARY. 1963. irreg. $55. Gale Research Inc., 835 Penobscot Bldg., Detroit, MI 48226. TEL 313-961-2242. FAX 313-961-6083. TELEX 810-221-7086. Eds. Frederick G. Ruffner, Robert C. Thomas.

090   AU   ISSN 0379-3621
CODICES MANUSCRIPTI; Zeitschrift fuer Handschriftenkunde. 1975. 4/yr. S.1200. Verlagsbuchhandlung Brueder Hollinek und Co. GmbH, Feldgasse 13, A-1238 Vienna, Austria. TEL 0222-8893646. FAX 0222-889364724. Eds. Otto Mazal, Eva Irblich. bk.rev. (reprint service avail. from ISI)

027.7   CK
COLEGIO MAYOR DE NUESTRA SENORA DEL ROSARIO. BIBLIOTECA. BOLETIN INFORMACION. 1975. m. Colegio Mayor de Nuestra Senora del Rosario, Biblioteca, Calle 14 no. 6-25, Bogota, Colombia.

027   IT
COLLANA DI MONOGRAFIE DELLE BIBLIOTECHE D'ITALIA. 1954. irreg., no. 8, 1983. price varies. Casa Editrice Leo S. Olschki, Casella Postale 66, 50100 Florence, Italy. TEL 055-6530684. FAX 055-6530214.

025.21   US   ISSN 0160-4953
Z689
COLLECTION BUILDING. 1978. 4/yr. $60.50 (Canada $63.50; elsewhere $65.50). Neal-Schuman Publishers, Inc., 100 Varick St., New York, NY 10013. TEL 212-925-8650. FAX 212-219-8916. Ed. Arthur Curley. **Indexed:** Leg.Info.Manage.Ind., Lib.Lit., LISA.
—BLDSC shelfmark: 3310.477400.

020   US   ISSN 0146-2679
Z703.6   CODEN: COMADF
COLLECTION MANAGEMENT; a quarterly journal devoted to the management of library collections. 1975. q. $45 to individuals; institutions $115. Haworth Press, Inc., 10 Alice St., Binghamton, NY 13904. TEL 800-342-9678. FAX 607-722-1424. Ed. Peter Gellatly. adv.; bk.rev.; abstr.; circ. 668. (also avail. in microfiche from HAW; reprint service avail. from HAW) **Indexed:** Behav.Abstr., Bull.Signal., CALL, Leg.Info.Manage.Ind., Lib.Lit., LISA.
—BLDSC shelfmark: 3310.588500.
Formerly (until 1978): De-Acquisitions Librarian (ISSN 0098-2121)
Description: Focuses on all aspects of collection management and development that affect college, university, and research libraries of all types.
Refereed Serial

027.7 026   US   ISSN 0010-0870
Z671
COLLEGE & RESEARCH LIBRARIES. Short title: C R L. (Supplement avail.: C & R L News) 1939. bi-m. $45 (Canada, Spain and other PUAS countries $50; elsewhere $55). (Association of College and Research Libraries) American Library Association, 50 E. Huron St., Chicago, IL 60611-2795. TEL 312-944-6780. FAX 312-440-9374. Ed. Gloriana St. Clair. adv.; bk.rev.; charts; index, cum.index every 5 yrs.; circ. 13,000. (also avail. in microfilm from UMI; back issues avail.; reprint service avail. from UMI,KTO) **Indexed:** Amer.Bibl.Slavic & E.Eur.Stud., Amer.Hist.& Life, Bk.Rev.Dig., Bk.Rev.Ind. (1965-), C.I.J.E., Chem.Abstr., Child.Bk.Rev.Ind. (1965-), Cont.Pg.Educ., Curr.Bk.Rev.Cit., Curr.Cont., Educ.Ind., High.Educ.Curr.Aware.Bull., Hist.Abstr., Inform.Sci.Abstr., Lib.Lit., Lib.Sci.Abstr., LISA, P.A.I.S., Pers.Lit., Ref.Sour., Sci.Cit.Ind., SSCI.
—BLDSC shelfmark: 3311.000000.
Description: Articles of interest to college and research libraries.

027.7   US   ISSN 0099-0086
COLLEGE & RESEARCH LIBRARIES NEWS. (Supplement to: College & Research Libraries) 1966. m. (11/yr.). $20 ($25 for Canada, Mexico, Spain; $30 for all other foreign countries). (Association of College and Research Libraries) American Library Association, 50 E. Huron St., Chicago, IL 60611-2795. TEL 800-545-2433. FAX 312-440-9374. Ed. Mary Ellen Kyger Davis. adv.; circ. 10,500. (back issues avail.; reprint service avail. from UMI) **Indexed:** Art & Archaeol.Tech.Abstr., C.I.J.E., Curr.Cont., Inform.Sci.Abstr., LHTN, Lib.Lit, LISA, Sci.Cit.Ind.
—BLDSC shelfmark: 3311.008000.

COLLEGE CATALOG COLLECTION ON MICROFICHE. see *EDUCATION*

020   US
Z732.C6
COLORADO EDUCATION & LIBRARY DIRECTORY. a. $15. Department of Education, Communications Center, 201 E. Colfax Ave., Denver, CO 80203. TEL 303-866-6646. adv.; circ. 8,000.
Formed by the 1990 merger of: Directory of Colorado Libraries (ISSN 0094-8403) & Colorado Education Directory.
Description: Lists the Dept. of Ed. offices, school districts, and libraries throughout the state.

LIBRARY AND INFORMATION SCIENCES 2753

020 US ISSN 0147-9733
COLORADO LIBRARIES. 1975. q. $25 to non-members; foreign $35. Colorado Library Association, Box 489, Pinecliffe, CO 80471-0489. TEL 303-642-0203. FAX 303-642-0201. Ed. Nancy Carter. adv.; bk.rev.; bibl.; stat.; circ. 1,000. (also avail. in microfiche; back issues avail.) **Indexed:** Lib.Lit.
—BLDSC shelfmark: 3321.550000.

020 US ISSN 0084-8905
COLORADO STATE UNIVERSITY LIBRARIES. PUBLICATION. 1966. irreg., no.22, 1979. free. Colorado State University, University Library, Fort Collins, CO 80523. TEL 303-491-5911. circ. 300.

021.7 US ISSN 0010-1966
Z671
COLUMBIA LIBRARY COLUMNS. 1951. 3/yr. $12. (Friends of Columbia Libraries, Butler Library) Columbia University Libraries, New York, NY 10027. TEL 212-854-2231. Ed. Kenneth A. Lohf. illus.; circ. 800. **Indexed:** Lib.Lit., M.L.A.

020 US ISSN 0192-5881
COMIC ART COLLECTION. 1979. q. exchange basis. (Russel B. Nye Popular Culture Collection) Michigan State University Libraries, Special Collections Division, East Lansing, MI 48824-1048. TEL 517-355-3770. Ed. Randall W. Scott. circ. 400. (back issues avail.)
 Description: Newsletter to facilitate communication about holdings at the Michigan State University Library and about public-comics collecting in general, with inventories.

027.7 US ISSN 0276-3915
Z675.J8 CODEN: CJCLDV
COMMUNITY & JUNIOR COLLEGE LIBRARIES; the journal for learning resources centers. 1982. s-a. $30 to individuals; institutions $50. Haworth Press, Inc., 10 Alice St., Binghamton, NY 13904. TEL 800-342-9678. FAX 607-722-1424. Eds. Joseph F. Borowski, Margaret Holleman. adv.; bk.rev.; circ. 447. (also avail. in microfiche from HAW; reprint service avail. from HAW) **Indexed:** C.I.J.E., Excerp.Med., Lib.Lit., LISA, Ref.Zh., Sci.Abstr.
—BLDSC shelfmark: 3363.588200.
 Description: Presents current profiles of LRCs around the country, news of special relevance, such as legislation, systems and development, and pertinent reviews.
 Refereed Serial

020 025 II
CONCEPTS IN COMMUNICATION INFORMATICS AND LIBRARIANSHIP. (Text in English) 1988. irreg. (approx. 4-5/yr.). price varies. Concept Publishing Company, A 15-16, Commercial Block, Mohan Garden, New Delhi 110 059, India. TEL 11-5554-042. Ed. Shri S.P. Agrawal. bibl.; stat.; index.
 Description: Covers communication, information technology, and librarianship for academics and professionals in related fields. Includes computer applications.

347 SI
CONFERENCE OF SOUTHEAST ASIAN LIBRARIANS. PROCEEDINGS. 1970. irreg. price varies. Chopmen Publishers, Katong Shopping Centre, Mountbatten Rd., No. 05-28, Singapore 1543, Singapore. TEL 3441495. FAX 340180.

020 US ISSN 0010-5821
Z881
CONGREGATIONAL LIBRARY. BULLETIN. 1949. 3/yr. $5. (American Congregational Association) Congregational Library, 14 Beacon St., Boston, MA 02108. TEL 617-523-0470. Ed. Harold F. Worthley. bk.rev.; bibl.; illus.; circ. 1,500.

020.6 SP
CONGRESO NACIONAL DE BIBLIOTECAS. PONENCIAS, COMUNICACIONES Y CRONICA. 1966. irreg., latest 1984. 1000 ptas. Asociacion Espanola de Archiveros, Bibliotecarios, Museologos y Documentalistas (A N A B A D), Paseo de Recoletos, 20, Madrid 1, Spain. bk.rev. (also avail. in microfilm)

021 US ISSN 0010-616X
CONNECTICUT LIBRARIES. 1958. 11/yr. $30 to non-members. Connecticut Library Association, Inc., 638 Prospect Ave., Hartford, CT 06106. TEL 203-232-4825. FAX 203-232-0819. Ed. David L. Kapp. circ. controlled. (also avail. in microform from UMI; reprint service avail. from UMI)
 Formerly: C L A News and Views.
 Description: News items and feature articles relating to Connecticut libraries and librarians.

020 US ISSN 0192-2912
CONSERVATION ADMINISTRATION NEWS; library and archival preservation. 1979. q. $24 (effective Jan. 1991). University of Tulsa, McFarlin Library, 600 S. College Ave., Tulsa, OK 74104. TEL 918-631-2864. FAX 918-631-3823. Ed. Robert H. Patterson. adv.; bk.rev.; bibl.; circ. 700. (also avail. in microfiche; back issues avail.) **Indexed:** Art & Archaeol.Tech.Abstr., Biodet.Abstr., Graph.Arts Lit.Abstr., LHTN, Lib.Lit., LISA.
—BLDSC shelfmark: 3417.960000.

025 US ISSN 0069-9136
CONSERVATION OF LIBRARY MATERIALS. (Subseries of: American Library Association. Library Technology Program. L T P Publications) 1967. irreg. American Library Association, Library Technology Program, 50 E. Huron St., Chicago, IL 60611. TEL 312-944-6780.

CONTINUO. see *MUSIC*

029.7 US ISSN 0084-9243
CONTRIBUTIONS IN LIBRARIANSHIP AND INFORMATION SCIENCE. 1972. irreg., no.72, 1992. price varies. Greenwood Press, Inc. (Subsidiary of: Greenwood Publishing Group Inc.), 88 Post Rd. W., Box 5007, Westport, CT 06881-5007. TEL 203-226-3571. FAX 203-222-1502. Ed. Paul Wasserman.
—BLDSC shelfmark: 3458.890000.

027 US ISSN 1041-343X
CORN BELT LIBRARY SYSTEM. SUM AND SUBSTANCE. 1967. m. free. Corn Belt Library System, 1809 W. Hovey Ave., Normal, IL 61761. TEL 309-452-4485. FAX 309-452-9192. Ed.Bd. bk.rev.; circ. 550. (processed)
 Description: For the Corn Belt Library System members and interested individuals and organizations. Provides information and stories of interest which relate to CBLS and its members.

020 CN ISSN 0843-140X
CORPO CLIP. 1975. 5/yr. Can.$6. Corporation of Professional Librarians of Quebec, 307 Ste-Catherine W., Ste. 320, Montreal, Que. H2X 2A3, Canada. TEL 514-845-3327. FAX 514-845-1618. Ed. Josee Saint-Marseille. circ. 1,000. (back issues avail.)
 Formerly: Bulletin Argus.
 Description: News about events in the field and information about the Corporation.

020 US ISSN 0196-8238
COTTONBOLL. 1979. bi-m. Public Library Service, 6030 Monticello Dr., Montgomery, AL 36130. TEL 205-277-7330. Ed. Julie Hare. circ. 2,700.

020 US
COUNCIL ON LIBRARY - MEDIA TECHNICAL ASSISTANTS. NEWSLETTER.* 1968. m. membership. Council on Library - Media Technical Assistants, c/o Margaret Barron, Cuyahoga Community College, 2900 Community College Ave., Cleveland, OH 44115. TEL 216-987-4621. Ed. Shirley Daniels. illus.; circ. 600.
 Formerly: Council of Library Technology. Newsletter (ISSN 0010-9983)

025 US
COUNCIL ON LIBRARY RESOURCES ANNUAL REPORT. 1957. a. free. Council on Library Resources, Inc., 1785 Massachusetts Ave., N.W., Ste. 313, Washington, DC 20036. TEL 202-483-7474. FAX 202-483-6410. circ. 4,000. (also avail. in microform from EDR) **Indexed:** ERIC.
 Formerly: Council on Library Resources Report (ISSN 0070-1181)

020 US ISSN 0300-7561
Z673.M393
CRAB. 1971. q. $15. Maryland Library Association, 400 Cathedral St., 3rd Fl., Baltimore, MD 21201. TEL 301-727-7422. Eds. Kathleen Reif, Lynne Degen. adv.; bibl.; circ. 1,300. (also avail. in microform from UMI; reprint service avail. from UMI) **Indexed:** Lib.Lit.
 Supersedes: Maryland Libraries.
 Description: Covers issues, information and personalities of interest to Maryland librarians.

020 800 CS ISSN 0011-2321
CTENAR; mesicnik pro praci s knihou. (Supplement avail.: Knihovnictvi a Bibliografie) (Text in Czech; contents page also in English, German and Russian) vol.19, 1967. m. 42 Kcs.($36) (Ministerstvo Kultury Ceske Republiky) Panorama, Halkova ul. 1, 120 72 Prague 2, Czechoslovakia. (Dist. by: Artia, Ve Smeckach 30, 111 27 Prague 1, Czechoslovakia) Ed. Vladimir Voznicka. bk.rev.; film rev.; bibl.; charts; illus.; circ. 7,300. **Indexed:** Lib.Sci.Abstr.
—BLDSC shelfmark: 3490.503000.

020 UK
CURRENT AWARENESS ABSTRACTS; a review of information management literature. 1973. 10/yr. £90($160) to non-members; members £80. Aslib, Association for Information Management, Publications Department, Information House, 20-24 Old St., London EC1V 9AP, England. TEL 071-253-4488. FAX 071-430-0514. (Dist. in N. America by: Learned Information, Inc., 143 Old Marlton Pike, Medford, NJ 08055-8750. TEL 609-654-6266) Ed. Monty Hyams. adv.; bibl.; circ. 700. **Indexed:** Print.Abstr.
 Formerly (until 1992): Current Awareness Bulletin (ISSN 0265-9271)
 Description: Abstracts of professional literature in the library and information fields.

020 UK ISSN 0263-9254
Z669.7
CURRENT RESEARCH IN LIBRARY & INFORMATION SCIENCE. 1974. q. £125($255) Bowker-Saur Abstracts & Indexes, 59-60 Grosvenor St., London WX1 9DA, England. TEL 071-493-5841. FAX 071-499-1590. (Subscr. to: Bailey Bros. and Swinfen Ltd., Warner House, Bowles Well Gardens, Folkestone, Kent CT19 6PH, England. TEL 0303-850501) Ed. Pirkko Elliott. adv.; index. (also avail. in magnetic tape)
 ●Also available online. Vendor(s): DIALOG (File no.61), Orbit Information Technologies.
—BLDSC shelfmark: 3501.963000.
 Formerly: R A D I A L S Bulletin (ISSN 0302-2706)
 Description: Covers current research in library and information science and related subjects.

025 US
CURRENT STUDIES IN LIBRARIANSHIP. 1977. irreg. (1-2/yr.). $10. Texas Woman's University, School of Library and Information Sciences, c/o Bernie Schlessinger, Box 22905, Denton, TX 76204. Ed. Shelly Karp. circ. 600. **Indexed:** Lib.Lit., LISA.

027.7 AT
CURTIN UNIVERSITY OF TECHNOLOGY. LIBRARY. ANNUAL REPORT. 1976. a. free. Curtin University of Technology, Library, Kent St., Bentley, W.A. 6102, Australia.
 Formerly: Western Australian Institute of Technology. Library. Annual Report.

010 AT
CURTIN UNIVERSITY OF TECHNOLOGY. LIBRARY. MONOGRAPH FICHE CATALOGUE. 1980. q. Aus.$123. Curtin University of Technology, Library, Kent St., Bentley, W.A. 6102, Australia. (microfiche)
 Formerly: Western Australian Institute of Technology. Library. Monograph Fiche Catalogue.

020 AT
CURTIN UNIVERSITY OF TECHNOLOGY. LIBRARY. WESTERN LIBRARY STUDIES. 1983. irreg. Curtin University of Technology, Library, Kent St., Bentley, W.A. 6102, Australia.
 Formerly: Western Australian Institute of Technology. Library. Western Library Studies (ISSN 0810-5030)

LIBRARY AND INFORMATION SCIENCES

L

021　　　　UK　　ISSN 0011-4421
CYLCHGRAWN LLYFRGELL GENEDLAETHOL CYMRU/NATIONAL LIBRARY OF WALES JOURNAL. (Text in English, Welsh) 1939. s-a. £8. National Library of Wales, Aberystwyth, Dyfed SY23 3BU, Wales. Ed. Brynley F. Roberts. charts; illus.; circ. 500. **Indexed:** Amer.Hist.& Life, Br.Archaeol.Abstr., Br.Hum.Ind., Hist.Abstr., M.L.A., RILA.
　—BLDSC shelfmark: 6026.640000.

020　　　　GW　　ISSN 0175-6893
D B I - PRESSESPIEGEL. 1981. m. DM.32. Deutsches Bibliotheksinstitut, Abt. 1-Publikationen, Bundesallee 184-185, 1000 Berlin 31, Germany. TEL 030-8505-0. FAX 030-8505-100. circ. 200.

029　　　　GW　　ISSN 0344-5372
D G D SCHRIFTENREIHE. irreg., latest 1990. price varies. (Deutsche Gesellschaft fuer Dokumentation e.V.) K.G. Saur Verlag KG, Ortlerstr. 8, Postfach 701620, 8000 Munich 70, Germany. TEL 089-76902-0. FAX 089-76902150.

020 410　　　US
D S N A NEWSLETTER. 1977. 3/yr. $6. Dictionary Society of North America, Cleveland State University, FT-1214, 1983 E. 24th St., Cleveland, OH 44115. TEL 216-687-4830. FAX 216-687-9366. Ed. Louis T. Milic. adv.; bk.rev.; bibl.; circ. 600. (tabloid format; back issues avail.)
　Description: Information on dictionaries and other word reference books.

020　　　　CN
DALHOUSIE UNIVERSITY. SCHOOL OF LIBRARY AND INFORMATION STUDIES. NEWSLETTER. 1971. a. Dalhousie University, School of Library and Information Studies, Halifax, N.S. B3H 4H8, Canada. TEL 902-494-3656. FAX 902-494-2319. TELEX 019-21863. Ed. Mary Dykstra. circ. 1,000.
　Formerly: Dalhousie University. School of Library Service. Newsletter (ISSN 0315-0054)

DALHOUSIE UNIVERSITY. SCHOOL OF LIBRARY AND INFORMATION STUDIES. OCCASIONAL PAPERS. see LIBRARY AND INFORMATION SCIENCES — Computer Applications

020　　　　CN
DALHOUSIE UNIVERSITY. SCHOOL OF LIBRARY AND INFORMATION STUDIES. Y-A HOTLINE; an alert to matters concerning young adults. 1977. irreg. Can.$10($12) for 4 nos. Dalhousie University, School of Library and Information Studies, Halifax, N.S. B3H 4H8, Canada. TEL 902-494-3656. FAX 902-494-2319. TELEX 019-21863. Ed. L.J. Amey. bk.rev.; circ. 310.
　Formerly: Dalhousie University. School of Library Service. Y-A Hotline (ISSN 0701-8894)
　Description: Devoted to library services for junior and senior high school-aged youth in schools, public libraries and institutions.

029.7　　　　CC
DANG'AN XUE YANJIU. (Text in Chinese) q. Zhongguo Dang'an Xuehui, 21, Fengsheng Hutong, Beijing 100032, People's Republic of China. TEL 6013970. Ed. Pei Tong.

025.171 900　　US　　ISSN 1000-4165
DANG'AN YU LISHI/ARCHIVES AND HISTORY. (Text in Chinese) 1985. q. $39.50. (Shanghai Shi Dang'anguan, CC - Shanghai City Archives) China Books & Periodicals, Inc., 2929 24th St., San Francisco, CA 94110. TEL 415-282-2994. FAX 415-282-0994.

025.171 900　　CC　　ISSN 1001-201X
DANG'ANXUE TONGXUN/ARCHIVES SCIENCE BULLETIN. (Text in Chinese; table of contents in English) bi-m. $6. Zhongguo Renmin Daxue - People's University of China, 3, Zhang Zizhong Lu, Beijing 100007, People's Republic of China. TEL 4035109. (Subscr. to: China International Book Trading Corporation, 21 Chegongzhuang Xilu, P.O. Box 399, Beijing, China. TEL 8413063) Ed. Chen Zhaowu. bk.rev.; circ. 39,000.

020　　　　DK　　ISSN 0069-9861
DANMARKS BIBLIOTEKSSKOLE. SKRIFTER. 1965. a. price varies. Danmarks Biblioteksskole, 6 Birketinget, 2300 Copenhagen S, Denmark. FAX 45-32-84-02-01. bk.rev.

020　　　　DK　　ISSN 0900-4645
DANMARKS TEKNISKE BIBLIOTEK. KATALOG. a. Danmarks Tekniske Bibliotek, Anker Engelunds Vej 1, DK-2800 Lyngby, Denmark.
●Available only online.

027.7　　　　US　　ISSN 0011-6750
DARTMOUTH COLLEGE LIBRARY BULLETIN. N.S. 1957. s-a. free to educational institutions & other libraries. Dartmouth College, Library, Hanover, NH 03755. TEL 603-646-2235. Eds. Lois A. Krieger, Virginia L. Close. charts; illus.; index every 3 yrs.; circ. 1,000. (also avail. in microfilm) **Indexed:** Lib.Lit.

020　　　　CC
DAXUE TUSHUGUAN XUEBAO/JOURNAL OF UNIVERSITY LIBRARIES. (Text in Chinese) bi-m. Quanguo Gaodeng Xuexiao Tushu Qingbao Gongzuo Weiyuanhui - National Committee on Higher Education Institution Library Affairs, Beijing Daxue, Hadian, Beijing 100871, People's Republic of China. TEL 2561166. Ed. Li Xiaoming.

DEAF NEWSLETTER. see HANDICAPPED — Hearing Impaired

020　　　　US　　ISSN 0011-7773
DELAWARE LIBRARY ASSOCIATION BULLETIN. 1947. 3/yr. $25 includes membership. Delaware Library Association, Box 1843, Wilmington, DE 19899. adv.; bk.rev.; circ. 650.

027　　　　DK　　ISSN 0069-9896
Z941
DENMARK. KONGELIGE BIBLIOTEK. FUND OG FORSKNING. (Text in Danish; summaries in English) 1954. a. price varies. Kongelige Bibliotek, Christians Brygge 8, DK-1219 Copenhagen K, Denmark. cum.index: 1954-73.
　Description: Findings and research in the collections of the Royal Library.

020　　　　DK　　ISSN 0905-555X
DENMARK. STATENS BIBLIOTEKSTJENESTE. RETNINGSLINIER. 1987. irreg. free. Statens Bibliotekstjeneste, Nyhavn 31 E, DK-1051 Copenhagen K, Denmark. TEL 45-33-93-46-93. FAX 45-33-93-60-93.
　Formerly (until 1988): Rigsbibliotekarembedet. Retningslinier (ISSN 0903-8302)

020　　　　US　　ISSN 0011-9156
DES MOINES. PUBLIC LIBRARY. MONTHLY MEMO; current business materials available at the Public Library of Des Moines. 1955. m. free. Public Library of Des Moines, 100 Locust St., Des Moines, IA 50308. TEL 515-283-4152. FAX 515-283-4503. Dir. Elaine G. Estes. bk.rev.; illus.; circ. 1,000 (controlled). (looseleaf format)

025.4　　　　US　　ISSN 0083-1573
Z696.D5
DEWEY DECIMAL CLASSIFICATION ADDITIONS, NOTES AND DECISIONS. Cover title: D C & 1959. irreg., vol.4, no.5. free to subscr. to LC Card Service, Purchasers of 19th ed. of Dewey Decimal Classification, and teachers of library science, upon request to: Forest Press, 85 Watervliet Ave., Albany, NY 12206. U.S. Library of Congress, Decimal Classification Division, Washington, DC 20540. Ed. John P. Comaromi.

020 410　　　US　　ISSN 0197-6745
P327　　　　　CODEN: DICTEQ
DICTIONARIES. (Text in English, French) 1979. a. $20 (foreign $25). Dictionary Society of North America, Cleveland State University, FT-1214, 1983 E. 24th St., Cleveland, OH 44115. TEL 216-687-4830. FAX 216-687-9366. Ed. William S. Chisholm. bk.rev.; circ. 500. (back issues avail.)
　—BLDSC shelfmark: 3580.285000.
　Description: Dictionary making, collection, use; dissemination of information and ideas on lexicography to editors, scholars and users.

020　　　　US　　ISSN 0363-5414
Z711.92.P5
DIKTA. 1976. s-a. $8. Southern Conference of Librarians for the Blind and Physically Handicapped, 420 Platt St., Daytona Beach, FL 32114-2804. (Subscr. to: c/o Joyce Smith, Box 443, Huntsville, AL 35804) Ed. Michael Gunde. bk.rev.; illus.; index; circ. 200. (back issues avail.)
　—BLDSC shelfmark: 3588.397950.

DIRECTIONS (BRIDGEWATER); monthly journal for academic & research libraries. see PUBLISHING AND BOOK TRADE

020　　　　US　　ISSN 0899-5877
DIRECTIONS FOR UTAH LIBRARIES. 1959. m. (except Jun.-Jul., Nov.-Dec., combined). free to qualified personnel. Department of Community and Economic Development, State Library Division, 2150 S. 300 W., Ste. 16, Salt Lake City, UT 84115. TEL 801-466-5888. FAX 801-533-4657. Ed. Chip Ward. bk.rev.; circ. 2,000 (controlled). (processed)
　Formerly (until vol.23, no.6, 1988): Horsefeathers (ISSN 0018-5205)
　Description: Focuses on service improvements, reading programs, public relations and audio-visual programs; includes calender of events.

026　　　　CK
DIRECTORIO COLOMBIANO DE UNIDADES DE INFORMACION. 1973. irreg; latest 1982. $50. Fondo Colombiano de Investigaciones Cientificas y Proyectos Especiales, Apdo. Aereo 051580, Bogota, Colombia. FAX 2744460. TELEX 44305. adv.; bk.rev.; circ. 10,000. (also avail. in microform from NTI)

020　　　　SP
DIRECTORIO DE ESPECIALISTAS IBEROAMERICANOS EN INFORMACION Y DOCUMENTACION/DIRECTORIO DE ESPECIALISTAS IBEROAMERICANOS EM INFORMACAO E DOCUMENTACAO; area educacion - area educacao. (Text in Portuguese, Spanish) 1989. biennial. 2000 ptas.($20) Organizacion de Estados IberoAmericanos para la Educacion, la Ciencia y la Cultura (OEI), C. Bravo Murillo 38a, 28015 Madrid, Spain. TEL 549-53-82. FAX 549-32-86. TELEX 48422 OEI E.
　Description: Lists education specialists in order to set up collaboration between schools and between specialists

027.7　　　　AT
Z870.A1
DIRECTORY OF AUSTRALIAN ACADEMIC AND RESEARCH LIBRARIES. 1978. irreg. (approx. 3/yr.). Aus.$40. Auslib Press, P.O. Box 622, Blackwood, S.A. 5051, Australia. TEL 08-2784363. FAX 08-278-4000. TELEX AA88420. Ed. Alan and Judith Bundy. adv.; circ. 1,200.
　Formerly (until 1989): Directory of Australian Academic Libraries (ISSN 0155-1027)

020　　　　AT　　ISSN 0729-4271
Z870.A1
DIRECTORY OF AUSTRALIAN PUBLIC LIBRARIES. 1982. irreg. (every 2-3 yrs.). Aus.$40. Auslib Press, P.O. Box 622, Blackwood, S.A. 5051, Australia. TEL 08-278-4363. FAX 08-370-4000. Eds. Alan and Judith Bundy. circ. 1,000. **Indexed:** LISA.
　Description: Comprehensive directory of Australian public lending libraries and state reference libraries.

DIRECTORY OF CANADIAN MAP COLLECTIONS. see GEOGRAPHY

023　　　　US
DIRECTORY OF CHINESE AMERICAN LIBRARIANS. (Text in Chinese, English) 1977. irreg., latest ed., 1986. $6. Chinese Culture Service, Box 444, Oak Park, IL 60303. Ed. Tze-chung Li. circ. 500.

027　　　　US　　ISSN 0070-5276
DIRECTORY OF COLLEGE AND UNIVERSITY LIBRARIES IN NEW YORK STATE. 1965. irreg. free to libraries in New York State; libraries elsewhere on exchange basis. New York State Library, Library Development, Albany, NY 12230. circ. 1,000.

DIRECTORY OF CONNECTICUT LIBRARIES AND MEDIA CENTERS. see BUSINESS AND ECONOMICS — Trade And Industrial Directories

020　　　　US　　ISSN 0276-959X
Z1223.Z7
DIRECTORY OF GOVERNMENT DOCUMENT COLLECTIONS AND LIBRARIANS. 1974. triennial. $45. Congressional Information Service, 4520 East-West Hwy., Bethesda, MD 20814. TEL 301-654-1550. FAX 301-654-4033. TELEX 292386 CIS UR. Ed. Barbara Kile. circ. 1,500.
　Description: Guide to federal, state, local, foreign and international documents collections in US, including collection specialties and contact names.

LIBRARY AND INFORMATION SCIENCES

020   JA
DIRECTORY OF INFORMATION SOURCES IN JAPAN. a. Intercontinental Marketing Corp., P.O. Box 5056, Tokyo 100-31, Japan. TEL 86-3-661-8373. FAX 81-3-667-9646.

DIRECTORY OF LAW LIBRARIES. see *LAW*

027   US
DIRECTORY OF LIBRARIES AND LIBRARY SYSTEMS IN THE SOUTH CENTRAL RESEARCH LIBRARY COUNCIL REGION. 1969. a. $25. South Central Research Library Council, DeWitt Bldg., 215 N. Cayuga St., Ithaca, NY 14850. TEL 607-273-9106. FAX 607-272-0740. Ed. Janet E. Steiner. circ. 1,100.
    Former titles: Directory of Libraries and Library Resources in the South Central Research Library Council Region; South Central Research Library Council. Library Directory (ISSN 0081-2722)
    Description: Information on all types of libraries in a fourteen county region.

020   CN
DIRECTORY OF LIBRARIES IN CANADA. a. Can.$100. Micromedia Ltd., 20 Victoria St., Toronto, Ont. M5C 2N8, Canada. TEL 416-362-5211. FAX 416-362-6161. Ed. Wendy Alexander. (also avail. in microform)
    Formerly (until 1991): Canadian Library Yearbook (ISSN 0827-3715); **Supersedes:** Canadian Library Handbook (ISSN 0707-9680)

021   CN   ISSN 0317-8536
Z735.M3
DIRECTORY OF LIBRARIES IN MANITOBA. 1973. biennial. Public Library Services, 1525 1st St., Unit 200, Brandon, Man. R7A 7A1, Canada. TEL 204-726-6590. FAX 204-726-6868.

020   US
DIRECTORY OF LIBRARY & INFORMATION PROFESSIONALS. 1988. irreg. $365. Gale Research Inc., 835 Penobscot Bldg., Detroit, MI 48226. TEL 800-223-4153. FAX 313-961-6815. TELEX 810-221-7086.
    Description: Lists over 43,000 library and information specialists currently working in North America.

027   US
DIRECTORY OF LIBRARY SYSTEMS IN NEW YORK STATE. 1976. a. free to libraries in New York State; libraries elsewhere on exchange basis. New York State Library, Library Development, Albany, NY 12230. (Co-sponsor: New York State Education Department) circ. 1,250.
    Formed by the merger of (1960-1975): Directory of New York State Public Library Systems (ISSN 0070-5950); (1967-1975): Directory of Reference and Research Library Resource Systems in New York State (ISSN 0070-6183)

DIRECTORY OF LONG ISLAND LIBRARIES AND MEDIA CENTERS. see *BUSINESS AND ECONOMICS — Trade And Industrial Directories*

027   US   ISSN 0070-5810
Z675.M4
DIRECTORY OF MEDICAL LIBRARIES IN NEW YORK STATE. 1967. irreg., 8th ed., 1985. free to libraries in New York State; libraries elsewhere on exchange basis. New York State Library, Library Development, Albany, NY 12230. FAX 518-474-5786. circ. 800.

027   US   ISSN 0092-4067
Z732.M82
DIRECTORY OF MISSOURI LIBRARIES; public, college, university & special libraries. 1965. a. free. State Library, Box 387, Jefferson City, MO 65102. TEL 314-751-3615. FAX 314-751-3612. stat.; circ. 750. (reprint service avail. from UMI) **Indexed:** SRI.
    Description: Statistics and information about Missouri libraries.

026   GH
DIRECTORY OF RESEARCH AND SPECIAL LIBRARIES IN GHANA. 1974. irreg. Council for Scientific and Industrial Research, Box M32, Accra, Ghana. Ed. L. Agyei-Gyane. circ. 500.
    Formerly: Directory of Special Libraries in Ghana.

DIRECTORY OF RESEARCH INSTITUTES IN ISRAEL. see *SCIENCES: COMPREHENSIVE WORKS*

026   TH   ISSN 0858-1630
DIRECTORY OF SCIENTIFIC AND TECHNICAL LIBRARIES IN THAILAND. 1973. irreg. Thailand Institute of Scientific and Technological Research, 196 Phahonyothin Rd., Chatuchak, Bangkok 10900, Thailand. TEL 579-4929. FAX 662-579-8594.
    Formerly: Directory of Scientific Libraries in Thailand.
    Description: Information on facilities and services of 119 libraries in Thailand.

DIRECTORY OF SOUTH AFRICAN PUBLISHERS; with addresses and ISBN identifiers. see *PUBLISHING AND BOOK TRADE*

027.4   SA
DIRECTORY OF SOUTHERN AFRICAN LIBRARIES. irreg., latest 1990. State Library, P.O. Box 397, Pretoria 0001, South Africa. TEL 012-21-8931. FAX 012-325-5984. TELEX 3-22171 SA.

026   US
DIRECTORY OF SPECIAL LIBRARIES AND INFORMATION CENTERS. (In 3 vols.) 1963. a. $399 vol.1; vol.2 $340; vol.3 $335. Gale Research Inc., 835 Penobscot Bldg., Detroit, MI 48226. TEL 313-961-2242. FAX 313-961-6083. TELEX 810-221-7086. Ed. Janice DeMaggio.
    Formerly: Directory of Special Libraries and Information Centers in the U S and Canada (ISSN 0731-633X)
    Description: Directory of libraries for specialized purposes in the U.S.

026   IO
DIRECTORY OF SPECIAL LIBRARIES AND INFORMATION SOURCES (YEAR). (Text in Indonesian, English) 1961. irreg., latest 1985. $15 per no. Indonesian National Scientific Documentation Center - Pusat Dokumentasi Ilmiah Nasional, Jalan Jenderal Gatot Subroto, Box 3065-Jkt., Jakarta, Indonesia. Eds. Sudaisman Dwinarto, Setya Iswanti. circ. 1,000. (also avail. in microfiche)
    Formerly: Directory of Special Libraries in Indonesia (ISSN 0376-8600)

026   IS   ISSN 0070-637X
DIRECTORY OF SPECIAL LIBRARIES IN ISRAEL. (Text in English and Hebrew) 1961. irreg., 6th ed., 1985. $50. National Center of Scientific and Technological Information, ATIDIM Scientific Park, Devorah Haneviah St., Tel Aviv 61430, Israel. TEL 03-492040. FAX 03-492033. TELEX C3-2332-IL. index.
    Description: Covers 330 special libraries in institutes of higher education, technical schools, local councils and government institutions.

020   CN   ISSN 0319-2563
DIRECTORY OF SPECIAL LIBRARIES IN THE MONTREAL AREA/REPERTOIRE DES BIBLIOTHEQUES SPECIALISEES DE LA REGION DE MONTREAL. (Text in English and French) biennial. Can.$75. Special Libraries Association, Eastern Canada Chapter, Box 1538, Station B, Montreal, Que. H3B 3L2, Canada. Ed. Anne M. Galler. circ. 350.
    Formerly: Directory of Special Libraries in Montreal (ISSN 0070-6396)
    Description: Includes keyword description of each library's specializations.

020 340   US
DIRITTO DELL'INFORMAZIONE E DELL'INFORMATICA. 1985. 3/yr. L.90000 (foreign L.135000). Casa Editrice Dott. A. Giuffre, Via Busto Arsizio 40, 20151 Milan, Italy. TEL 02-38000905. FAX 02-38009582.

020   US   ISSN 0070-6663
DISCOURSE UNITS IN HUMAN COMMUNICATION FOR LIBRARIANS. 1969. irreg., no.27, 1983. price varies. University of Pittsburgh, Communications Media Research Center, c/o Patrick R. Penland, Graduate School of Library and Information Science, 135 No. Bellefield, Pittsburgh, PA 15260. TEL 412-624-4469. Ed. Patrick R. Penland. (back issues avail.) **Indexed:** ERIC, Lib.Lit.

027.7   AT   ISSN 0728-6481
DIXSON LIBRARY REPORT. 1982. q. Aus.$9 (foreign Aus.$12). University of New England, Dixson Library, Armidale, N.S.W. 2351, Australia. TEL 067-732187. FAX 067-711602. TELEX 166050. Eds. Margaret Maticka, Karl G. Schmude. bibl.; circ. 600. (back issues avail.)
    Formerly: Current Developments (ISSN 0811-2045)
    Description: Information for users of the Library.

621.38   US   ISSN 1054-9692
TK5105   CODEN: DIATEG
DOCUMENT IMAGE AUTOMATION. 1981. bi-m. $125. Meckler Publishing Corporation, 11 Ferry Lane W., Westport, CT 06880-5808. TEL 203-226-6967. Ed. Judith Paris Roth. adv.; bk.rev. (also avail. in microform from UMI) **Indexed:** ABI Inform., C.I.J.E., Cab.Vid.Ind., Compumath, Comput.Cont., Comput.Dtbs., Educ.Tech.Abstr., Leg.Info.Manage.Ind., LHTN, Lib.Lit., LISA, Resour.Ctr.Ind., Sci.Abstr.
    Former titles: Optical Information Systems (ISSN 0886-5809); Videodisc and Optical Disk (ISSN 0742-5740); (until 1984): Videotex - Videotext (ISSN 0278-9183); (until vol.1, no.3): Videodisc - Teletext (ISSN 0198-9456)

DOCUMENT IMAGE AUTOMATION UPDATE. see *COMMUNICATIONS — Television And Cable*

029 020   FR   ISSN 0012-4508
Z1007   CODEN: DSINE6
DOCUMENTALISTE - SCIENCES DE L'INFORMATION. (Text in French; summaries in English) 1964. 5/yr. 480 F. (foreign 520 F.). Association Francaise des Documentalistes et des Bibliothecaires Specialises, 25 rue Claude Tillier, 75012 Paris, France. TEL 43-72-25-25. FAX 43-72-30-41. Ed. J.M. Rauzier. adv.; bk.rev.; abstr.; bibl.; charts; illus.; index; circ. 5,000. **Indexed:** Bull.Signal., Chem.Abstr., Inform.Sci.Abstr., Lib.Lit., LISA, Ref.Zh., Sci.Abstr.
    —BLDSC shelfmark: 3609.900000.
    Description: Devoted to techniques, professions, services and policies in the information and library fields, and to research in information sciences; with particular focus on European and French-speaking countries.

020   CN   ISSN 0315-2340
Z735.A1   CODEN: DCBBBO
DOCUMENTATION ET BIBLIOTHEQUES. 1955. q. Can.$42. Association pour l'Avancement des Sciences et des Techniques de la Documentation, 1030 rue Cherrier, Bureau 505, Montreal, Que. H2L 1H9, Canada. TEL 514-522-7833. FAX 514-521-9561. Ed. Jean-Remi Brault. adv.; bk.rev.; bibl.; charts; illus.; index, cum.index: 1955-1962; circ. 1,100. **Indexed:** Bull.Signal., Can.Per.Ind., Lib.Lit., LISA, Pt.de Rep. (1983-), Sci.Abstr.
    —BLDSC shelfmark: 3610.710000.
    Formerly (until 1973): Association Canadienne des Bibliothecaires de Langue Francaise. Bulletin (ISSN 0004-5314)

020   UN
DOCUMENTATION, LIBRARIES AND ARCHIVES: STUDIES AND RESEARCH. (Editions in English, French and Spanish) 1951. irreg. price varies. Unesco Press, 7 Place de Fontenoy, F-75700 Paris, France. (Dist. in U.S. by: Unipub, 4611-F Assembly Drive, Lanham MD, 20706-4391)
    Formerly (until 1972): Unesco Manuals for Libraries (ISSN 0082-7495)

020   US   ISSN 0738-8128
DOCUMENTATION NEWSLETTER. 1975. s-a. $3 (foreign $8.86). Cornell University Libraries, Department of Manuscripts and University Archives, 101 Olin Library, Ithaca, NY 14853-5301. TEL 607-255-3530. FAX 607-255-9346. Ed. Elaine Engst. adv.; circ. 700.
    Supersedes (in 1975): Cornell University Libraries. Collection of Regional History and University Archives. Report of the Curator; Cornell Program in Oral History. Newsletter; Cornell Program in Oral History. Bulletin (ISSN 0010-8871)

LIBRARY AND INFORMATION SCIENCES

020   US   ISSN 0091-2085
DOCUMENTS TO THE PEOPLE. Short title: D t t P. 1972. q. $20 (foreign $25). American Library Association, Government Documents Round Table, 50 E. Huron St., Chicago, IL 60611. TEL 312-944-6780. Ed. Mary Redmond. adv.; circ. 2,000. (also avail. in microfilm; back issues avil. from UMI) **Indexed:** Leg.Info.Manage.Ind.
—BLDSC shelfmark: 3630.517000.
Description: Information on librarianship, government publications and other information products on related governmental activities.

350   US   ISSN 0749-0356
DOCUMENTS TO THE PEOPLE OF NEW YORK STATE. 1980. q. $8. New York State Library Association, Government Documents Roundtable, 252 Hudson Ave., Albany, NY 12210-1802. Ed. Marilyn Moody. adv.; bk.rev.; circ. 85.
Description: Covers news pertaining to Federal and New York State documents of interest to member librarians.

DOKUMENTATION SPRACHWISSENSCHAFTLICHE FORSCHUNGSVORHABEN. see *LINGUISTICS*

020   GW   ISSN 0176-781X
Z666
DOKUMENTATIONSDIENST BIBLIOTHEKSWESEN. Short title: D O B I. 1984. s-a. DM.95. Deutsches Bibliotheksinstitut, Abt. 1-Publikationen, Bundesallee 184-185, 1000 Berlin 31, Germany. TEL 030-8505-0. FAX 030-8505-100. circ. 280.
Incorporates: Informationsdienst Bibliothekswesen (ISSN 0044-1457)

027   IE   ISSN 0332-0006
DUBLIN. NATIONAL LIBRARY OF IRELAND. COUNCIL OF TRUSTEES REPORT. 1901. a. price varies. Stationery Office, Bishop St., Dublin 8, Ireland. (Avail. from: Government Publications Postal Sales Office, St. Martin's House, Waterloo Rd., Dublin 4, Ireland) illus.; circ. 500.

020 370   US   ISSN 0895-4909
Z733
DUKE UNIVERSITY LIBRARIES. 1987. 3/yr. $15. Duke University, Library, 220 Perkins Library, Durham, NC 27706. TEL 919-684-2034. FAX 919-684-2855. Ed. Joline R. Ezzell. illus.; circ. 2,800. (back issues avail.)
Description: Descriptions of library collections, programs, and activities.

025   BA
DUNYA AL-MAKTABAT. (Text in Arabic) m. Ministry of Education, Manama Central Library, P.O. Box 43, Manama, Bahrain. TEL 258550. TELEX 9094.

027.4   SA
DURBAN MUNICIPAL LIBRARY. ANNUAL REPORT. (Text in English) 1854. a. free. Durban Municipal Library, P.O. Box 917, Durban 4000, South Africa. FAX 031-3006301. circ. 75.

029 015   UK   ISSN 0262-9216
E D C NEWSLETTER. (European Documentation Centre) 1980. 6/yr. £7.50 (Europe £15; elsewhere £20). Association of E D C Librarians, c/o Radcliffe Camera, Bodleian Library, Oxford OX1 3BG, England. Ed. Mike Cooper. bk.rev.; bibl.; circ. 150. **Indexed:** World Bank.Abstr.
Formerly: Northern E D C Newsletter.

027.7   UK
E L G NEWS. 1971. 3/yr. £3 to non-members. Library Association, Education Librarians Group, The Library, Whitefield Centre, Macdonald Rd., Walthamstow, London E17 4AZ, England. Ed. J. Henleyrds. adv.; bk.rev.; circ. 1,100.
Supersedes (in 1981): C I S E Newsletter.

027.5967   RH   ISSN 0376-4753
E S A R B I C A JOURNAL. 1973. a. $5.50 to non-members. International Council on Archives, Eastern and Southern Africa Regional Branch, c/o TechTop (pvt), Ltd., P.O. Box 4555, Harare, Zimbabwe. TEL 735607. TELEX 6444 ZW. (Subscr. to: c/o Mrs. M. Lekaukau, Treasurer, National Archives of Botswana, PO Box 239, Gaborone, Botswana) Ed. Peter C. Mazikana. circ. 100. (back issues avail.)
—BLDSC shelfmark: 3647.287000.
Description: Articles on various aspects of information science.

020   BG   ISSN 0012-8848
Z671
EASTERN LIBRARIAN. (Text in English) 1966. 3/yr. Tk.40($10) Library Association of Bangladesh, Bangladesh Univ. of Engineering & Technology Library, Dhaka 2, Bangladesh. Ed. Muhammad Siddiq Khan. adv.; bk.rev.; index; circ. 1,000. **Indexed:** Lib.Sci.Abstr.

020   US   ISSN 0012-8899
EASTERN MASSACHUSETTS REGIONAL LIBRARY SYSTEM. EASTERN REGION NEWS. 1966. 6/yr. free to qualified personnel. Eastern Massachusetts Regional Library System, Boston Public Library, Copley Square, Boston, MA 02117. TEL 617-536-4010. Ed. Edward J. Montana, Jr. bk.rev.; illus.; stat.; circ. 2,400 (controlled). (looseleaf format)

020   UK
EASTERNER. 1960. 4/yr. free. East Anglian Librarian's Consultative Committee, Central Library, St. Andrews St. North, Bury St. Edmunds IP33 1TZ, England. TEL 0284-701611. FAX 0284-705875. Ed. B. King. adv.; bk.rev.; circ. controlled. (processed)
Description: Newsletter to the East Anglians Librarians' Consultative Committee, which represents all members of the Library Association in East Anglia.

016.05 020   US   ISSN 0360-0637
Z6941
EBSCO BULLETIN OF SERIALS CHANGES. 1975. bi-m. $20. EBSCO Subscription Services, 5724 Highway 280 East, Birmingham, AL 35242-6818. TEL 205-991-6600. adv.; illus.; circ. 8,000.
—BLDSC shelfmark: 3647.168000.

027.4   CN   ISSN 0706-5205
L'ECHANGE. 1977. bi-m. Can.$20 (typically set in Jan.). Bibliotheque Centrale de Pret de l'Abitibi-Temiscamingue, 20 boul. Quebec, Rouyn-Noranda, Que. J9X 2E6, Canada. TEL 819-762-4305. FAX 819-797-1161. Ed. Norman Fink. adv.; bk.rev.; circ. 350.
Description: A brief survey of activities within the library system. Informative articles on library technologies, management, marketing. For library boards in small rural communities.

020   US
EDUCATION AND TRAINING IN INDEXING AND ABSTRACTING. 1977. irreg., latest 1991 ed. $20 to non-members; members $12. American Society of Indexers, Inc., Box 386, Port Aransas, TX 78373. TEL 512-749-6634.

020   NE   ISSN 0167-8329
EDUCATION FOR INFORMATION. (Text in English) 1983. q. fl.335($168) (effective 1991). I O S Press, Van Diemenstraat 94, 1013 CN Amsterdam, Netherlands. TEL 020-6382189. FAX 020-6203419. (In N. America: Box 10558, Burke, VA 22009-0558) Eds. R.F. Guy, J.A. Large. **Indexed:** ASCA, Cont.Pg.Educ., Educ.Tech.Abstr., Lib.Lit.
—BLDSC shelfmark: 3661.286500.
Description: For educators, librarians and information managers. Articles cover new technology and procedures utilized in the library and information science fields.

378   AT   ISSN 0813-4235
EDUCATION FOR LIBRARIANSHIP: AUSTRALIA. 1984. 3/yr. Aus.$30 (foreign Aus.$38). Australian Library and Information Association, Education for Librarianship and Information Services Section, P.O. Box E441, Queen Victoria Terrace, A.C.T. 2600, Australia. TEL 06-285-1877. FAX 06-282-2249. Eds. Kate Beattie, Pam Naylor. adv.; bk.rev.; cum.index; circ. 350. (back issues avail.)
—BLDSC shelfmark: 3661.291000.
Description: Information about education for librarianship and information management, library schools, training and current developments in the field.
Refereed Serial

027.8   CN   ISSN 0148-1061
Z675.P3
EDUCATION LIBRARIES. 1976. 3/yr. $15 to individuals; libraries $20; foreign $25 (effective 1992). Special Library Association, Education Division, c/o Concordia University, 7141 Sherbrooke St. W., TA 7079, Montreal, Que. H4B 1R6, Canada. TEL 514-848-2543. FAX 514-848-3492. Ed. Anne M. Galler. adv.; bk.rev.; bibl.; circ. 400. (also avail. in microform from UMI) **Indexed:** C.I.J.E.
—BLDSC shelfmark: 3661.291300.

026   UK   ISSN 0076-079X
EDUCATION LIBRARIES BULLETIN SUPPLEMENTS. 1958. irreg., no.24, 1987. price varies. University of London, Institute of Education Library, 20 Bedford Way, London WC1H 0AL, England. TEL 071-612-6060. FAX 071-612-6126. Ed. Claire E. Drinkwater. adv.; circ. 500. **Indexed:** Br.Educ.Ind., Lib.Sci.Abstr.
—BLDSC shelfmark: 3661.296000.
Description: Covers all aspects of libraries in education.

026   UK   ISSN 0957-9575
EDUCATION LIBRARIES JOURNAL. 1958. 3/yr. £10($20) University of London, Institute of Education Library, 20 Bedford Way, London WC1H 0AL, England. TEL 071-612-6060. FAX 071-612-6126. Ed. Claire E. Drinkwaker. bk.rev.; bibl.; index; circ. 400. (processed; also avail. in microfilm from UMI; reprint service avail. from UMI) **Indexed:** Br.Educ.Ind., Cont.Pg.Educ., Lib.Sci.Abstr., LISA.
—BLDSC shelfmark: 3661.296300.
Formerly: Education Libraries Bulletin (ISSN 0013-1407)
Description: Covers all aspects of libraries in education.

020   UA   ISSN 0531-6723
EGYPTIAN LIBRARY JOURNAL/SAHIFAT AL MAKTA-BAH. (Text in Arabic; summaries in English) 1969. q. P.T.300($9) Egyptian School Library Association, 35 al-Galaa St., Cairo, Egypt. TEL 753 001. Ed. Medhat Kazem. adv.; bk.rev.; bibl.

020 410   HU   ISSN 0230-1806
EGYUTT; Szolnok megyei konyvtarak hiradoja. 1970. 3/yr. 21 Ft. Verseghy Ferenc Megyei Konyvtar, Kossuth ter 4, 5000 Szolnok, Hungary. TEL 13-101. TELEX 23210. Ed. Papayne Kemenczey Judit. illus.; stat.; index; circ. 200. (back issues avail.)

020   SZ   ISSN 0514-0668
EIDGENOESSISCHE TECHNISCHE HOCHSCHULE ZUERICH. BIBLIOTHEK. SCHRIFTENREIHE. 1948. irreg. price varies. E T H - Bibliothek (Eidgenoessische Technische Hochschule), CH-8092 Zurich, Switzerland. circ. 100.

020   US
ELECTRIC QUARTERLY. 1979. q. $35 (includes membership). Bakken, 3537 Zenith Ave. S., Minneapolis, MN 55416. TEL 612-927-6508. FAX 612-927-7265. Ed. Elizabeth Ihrig. circ. 1,300. (back issues avail.)
Description: Covers the Bakken library activities, announcements, calendar of events (including music concerts), and news of recent acquisitions.

027.8 372.21   US
ELEMENTARY SCHOOL LIBRARY COLLECTION. 1965. biennial. $99.95. Brodart Co., 500 Arch St., Williamsport, PA 17705. TEL 800-233-8467. FAX 717-326-6769. Ed. Lauren Lee. bk.rev.; bibl.; circ. 10,000.
Description: Lists titles for core collections in elementary school libraries. Includes books, periodicals, audiovisuals, and microcomputer software.

LIBRARY AND INFORMATION SCIENCES

020 301.412 CN ISSN 0315-8888
EMERGENCY LIBRARIAN. (Text in English) 1973. 5/yr. Can.$45. Dyad Services, P.O. Box 46258, Station G, Vancouver, B.C. V6R 4G6, Canada. TEL 604-734-0255. FAX 604-734-0221. (U.S. subscr. to: Department 284, Box C34069, Seattle, WA 98124-1069) Ed. Michele Farguharson. adv.; bk.rev.; bibl.; circ. 10,000. (processed; also avail. in microfiche from UMI; reprint service avail. from UMI; back issues avail.) **Indexed:** Bk.Rev.Ind. (1981-), Can.Per.Ind., Chic.Per.Ind., Child.Bk.Rev.Ind. (1981-), Child.Lit.Abstr., CMI, Ind.Child.Mag., Lib.Lit., LISA, New Per.Ind.
—BLDSC shelfmark: 3733.184000.
Refereed Serial

EMPLOYMENT NEWS. see *LABOR UNIONS*

021 US ISSN 0013-8495
ENOCH PRATT FREE LIBRARY. STAFF REPORTER. 1933. s-m. $3. Enoch Pratt Free Library, 400 Cathedral St., Baltimore, MD 21201-4484. TEL 301-396-5494. FAX 301-396-5856. Ed. Averil Jordan Kadis. circ. 500. (processed)

020 US
ETC.. 1973-1975; resumed 1978. m. (except Jul.). free. King County Library System, 300 Eighth Ave., N., Seattle, WA 98109. TEL 206-684-6606. FAX 206-684-6690. Ed. Jeanne Thorsen. illus.; circ. 4,000. (also avail. in microform from UMI; reprint service avail. from UMI) **Indexed:** Arts & Hum.Cit.Ind., Curr.Cont., Hum.Ind.

020 ET ISSN 0014-1747
Z673.E85
ETHIOPIAN LIBRARY ASSOCIATION. BULLETIN. (Text in Amharic and English) 1969. 2/yr. $10. Ethiopian Library Association, Box 30530, Addis Ababa, Ethiopia. Ed. Kebreab W. Giorgis. bk.rev.; circ. 200.

020.6 UK ISSN 0261-2747
EUROPEAN INFORMATION SERVICE. 1978. 10/yr. £85 to individuals; institutions £170. Local Government International Bureau, 35 Gt. Smith St., London SW1P 3BJ, England. TEL 071-222-1636. FAX 071-233-2179. TELEX 21879 ATT IUL. Ed. H. Bell. bk.rev.; circ. 1,500.
—BLDSC shelfmark: 3829.720740.

020 US ISSN 1048-5287
EUROPEAN JOURNAL OF SERIALS LIBRARIANSHIP. 1989. q. $28 to individuals; institutions $36. Haworth Press, Inc., 10 Alice St., Binghamton, NY 13904. TEL 800-342-9678. FAX 607-722-1424. Ed. Claude Daris. adv.; bk.rev. (also avail. in microfiche from HAW; reprint service avail. from HAW)
Formerly (until 1991): British Journal of Serials Librarianship (ISSN 0896-0844)
Description: Reports on the practice of serials librarianship in the UK, with special attention to rapid innovations that are applicable in the US, Europe, and around the world.
Refereed Serial

020 GW
Z675.R45
EUROPEAN RESEARCH LIBRARY COOPERATION. 1978. q. DM.240. Ligue des Bibliotheques Europeennes de Recherche, c/o Prof. H.-A. Koch, Sec., Staats- und Universitaetsbibliothek, Postfach 33 01 60, 2800 Bremen, Germany. Ed. Heiner Schnelling. adv.; bk.rev. (back issues avail.)
Formerly: L I B E R News Sheet (ISSN 0721-6858); **Incorporates:** L I B E R Bulletin (ISSN 0304-0224)
Description: Promotes cooperation of European research libraries.

DER EVANGELISCHE BUCHBERATER. see *RELIGIONS AND THEOLOGY — Other Denominations And Sects*

027.4 US
EVANSVILLE - VANDERBURGH COUNTY PUBLIC LIBRARIES. STAFF NEWS BULLETIN. 1952. s-m. $3.50. Evansville - Vanderburgh County Public Libraries, 22 S.E. Fifth St., Evansville, IN 47708. TEL 812-428-8200. FAX 812-428-8215. Ed. Carol Young. cum.index: 1952-1990; circ. 60.
Former titles: Evansville - Vanderburgh County Public Library. Staff News Bulletin; Evansville Public Library and Vanderburgh County Public Library. Staff News Bulletin (ISSN 0014-3669)
Description: Contains calendar of events, minutes from staff meetings, departmental and agency news, and Library-related articles.

029 NE ISSN 0014-5424
EXTENSIONS AND CORRECTIONS TO THE U D C. (Text in English, French, German) 1950. a. £90 in E.E.C.; elsewhere $171(effective 1992). Federation Internationale d'Information et de Documentation - International Federation for Information and Documentation, Postbus 90402, 2509 LK The Hague, Netherlands. TEL 070-3140671. FAX 070-3140667. TELEX 34402 KB GV NL. (Subscr. to: Distribution Centre, Blackhorse Rd., Letchworth, Herts. SG6 1HN, United Kingdom) circ. 500.
—BLDSC shelfmark: 3853.000000.

029 GW
F I D - C R NEWS. (Included in: International Classification) 1973. 4/yr. (Federation Internationale d'Information et de Documentation - International Federation for Documentation) Indeks Verlag, Woogstr. 36a, 6000 Frankfurt a.M. 50, Germany. TEL 069-523690. Ed. Nancy Williamson. circ. 900.
Formerly: F I D - C R Newsletter.

029.7 NE ISSN 0379-3680
Z1008
F I D DIRECTORY. 1958. biennial. £27 in E.E.C.; elsewhere $46(effective 1992). Federation Internationale d'Information et de Documentation - International Federation for Information and Documentation, Postbus 90402, 2509 LK The Hague, Netherlands. TEL 070-3140671. FAX 070-3140667. TELEX 34402 KB GV NL. (Subscr. to: Distribution Centre, Blackhorse Rd., Letchworth, Herts. SG6 1HN, England) circ. 1,000.
—BLDSC shelfmark: 3918.765000.
Formerly: F I D Yearbook (ISSN 0074-5839)

029 NE ISSN 0014-5874
Z699.A1
F I D NEWS BULLETIN. (Includes Quarterly Document Delivery Reproduction Survey, Newsletter on Education and Training Programmes for Information Personnel, Research Reviews in Information and Documentation) (Text in English) 1951. 11/yr. £44 in E.E.C.; elsewhere $80(effective 1992). Federation Internationale d'Information et de Documentation - International Federation for Information and Documentation, Postbus 90402, 2509 LK The Hague, Netherlands. TEL 070-3140671. FAX 070-3140667. TELEX 34402 KB GV NL. (Subscr. to: Distribution Centre, Blackhorse Rd., Letchworth, Herts. SG6 1HN, United Kingdom.) Ed. Theresa Stanton. adv.; bk.rev.; bibl.; index, cum.index every 3 yrs.; circ. 2,000. (also avail. in microfilm from SWZ,UMI; reprint service avail. from UMI) **Indexed:** CALL, Inform.Sci.Abstr., Key to Econ.Sci., Lib.Lit., LISA, Ref.Zh.
—BLDSC shelfmark: 3918.800000.
Description: Covers members' news, meeting and publications announcements, committees and special interest groups, articles on new developments in information management, industrial, business and financial news and marketing of systems and services.

020 US ISSN 0882-908X
Z675.G7
F L I C C NEWSLETTER. 1965. q. free. U.S. Library of Congress, Federal Library and Information Center Committee, Washington, DC 20540. TEL 202-707-4828. FAX 202-707-4818. Ed. Darlene Dolan. bk.rev.; stat.; circ. controlled. (processed)
Formerly: F L C Newsletter (ISSN 0014-5939)

020 GW ISSN 0724-0775
FACHHOCHSCHULE FUER BIBLIOTHEKS- UND DOKUMENTATIONSWESEN IN KOELN. AMTLICHE MITTEILUNGEN. 1983. irreg. free. Fachhochschule fuer Biobliotheks- und Dokumentation in Koeln, Claudiusstr. 1, D-5000 Cologne 1, Germany. TEL (0221)8275-3374. index. (back issues avail.)
Description: Legal regulations of library and information education.

070.5 GW ISSN 0071-3627
FACHLITERATUR ZUM BUCH- UND BIBLIOTHEKSWESEN/INTERNATIONAL BIBLIOGRAPHY OF THE BOOK TRADE AND LIBRARIANSHIP. 1961. irreg., latest 1981. price varies. K.G. Saur Verlag KG, Ortlerstr. 8, Postfach 701620, 8000 Munich 70, Germany. TEL 089-76902-0. FAX 089-76902150. Eds. Helga Lengenfelder, Gitta Hausen. adv.
Formerly: Literature About the Book and Librarianship.

026 686.2 UK ISSN 0141-3635
FACTOTUM. 1978. irreg. (3-4/yr.). free. British Library, Humanities and Social Sciences, Great Russell St., London WC1B 3DG, England. TEL 071-323-7704. FAX 071-323-7746. TELEX 21462. Ed. J.L. Wood. bibl.; cum.index; circ. 2,000. (back issues avail.)
—BLDSC shelfmark: 3864.106000.
Description: News of the progress of the Eighteenth Century Short Title Catalogue.

023 US ISSN 0273-1061
FEDERAL LIBRARIAN. 1972. irreg. membership only. American Library Association, Federal Librarians Round Table, c/o Anne Heanue, 110 Maryland Ave., N.E., Washington, DC 20002. Ed. Gail Kohlhorst. circ. 500.
Supersedes (in 1986): F L I R T Newsletter (ISSN 0090-9661)

020 US
FEDERAL LIBRARY RESOURCES; a user's guide to research collections. irreg. $37.50. Science Associates International, Inc., 465 West End Ave., New York, NY 10024. TEL 212-873-0656. FAX 212-873-5587.

020 US ISSN 0737-4178
CODEN: FTENDE
FEDLINK TECHNICAL NOTES. 1983. m. free. U.S. Library of Congress, Federal Library and Information Center Committee, Washington, DC 20540. TEL 202-707-4828. FAX 202-707-4818. Ed. Darlene Dolan.
Description: Covers the technology and microcomputers, both hardware and software for the library and information sciences.

020 HU ISSN 0139-2115
FEJER MEGYEI KONYVTAROS. 1961. s-a. free. Vorosmarty Mihaly Megyei Konyvtar, Bartok Bala ter 1, 8000 Szekesfehervar, Hungary. TEL 22-12-684. FAX 22-11-634. TELEX 21351 VMKSZ H. Ed. Eva Hegedus. abstr.; bibl.; illus.; stat.; tr.lit.; circ. 300. (looseleaf format; back issues avail.)

020 CN ISSN 0014-9802
FELICITER. Variant title: C.L.A. Feliciter. 1956. 11/yr. Can.$65 or membership. Canadian Library Association, 200 Elgin Street, Ste. 602, Ottawa, Ont. K2P 1L5, Canada. TEL 613-232-9625. FAX 613-563-9895. Ed. Mary Moore. adv.; circ. 5,000. (tabloid format; also avail. in microfilm from CLA) **Indexed:** Can.Per.Ind., CMI, Lib.Lit., LISA.
—BLDSC shelfmark: 3905.113000.
Description: Contains news and opinions on issues in the Canadian library community, as well as association positions and proceedings.

028 PE ISSN 0015-0002
Z671
FENIX; revista. 1944. a. $30. Biblioteca Nacional del Peru, Digbine, Apartado 2335, Lima, Peru. Ed. Isabel Miranda M. bk.rev.; music rev.; bibl.; cum.index; circ. 500. **Indexed:** Amer.Hist.& Life, Hist.Abstr.

020 FJ
FIJI LIBRARY ASSOCIATION. JOURNAL. (Text in English) 1979. s-a. F.$7 per issue plus postage. Fiji Library Association, c/o Editor, Government Bldgs., Box 2292, Suva, Fiji. circ. 150. **Indexed:** So.Pac.Per.Ind.
Description: Articles and reviews relating to librarianship in Fiji and the South Pacific.

025 FJ
FIJI LIBRARY ASSOCIATION. NEWSLETTER. (Text in English) 1973. m. F.$0.50 per no. plus postage. Fiji Library Association, c/o Editor, FLA Newsletter, Government Buildings, Box 2292, Suva, Fiji. circ. 150. **Indexed:** So.Pac.Per.Ind.
Description: Brief articles and reviews regarding the activities of the Fiji Library Association.

020 FJ
FIJI LIBRARY DIRECTORY. irreg., latest 1981. F.$2.50 per no. plus postage. Fiji Library Association, Government Buildings, Box 2292, Suva, Fiji. circ. 55.
Description: Lists of school, public, governmental, special and academic libraries in Fiji.

FINANCIAL ASSISTANCE FOR LIBRARY EDUCATION. see *EDUCATION — Higher Education*

LIBRARY AND INFORMATION SCIENCES

020 659.1 US ISSN 0892-7367
Z684
FINDING. 1989. a. L D A Publishers, 42-36 209 St., Bayside, NY 11361. TEL 718-224-9484. FAX 718-224-9487. Ed. Margaret Riconda. adv.; circ. 3,500 (controlled).
Description: For library, information and media specialists, record managers, information brokers, and archivists.

020 US ISSN 0195-4016
FINGER LAKES LIBRARY SYSTEM. NEWSLETTER. 1979. bi-m. free. Finger Lakes Library System, 314 N. Cayuga St., Ithaca, NY 14850. TEL 607-273-4074. FAX 607-272-8111. Ed. Loretta Heimbuch. bk.rev.; film rev.; illus.; stat.; tr.lit.; circ. 450. (back issues avail.)

020 US
FLICKERTALE NEWSLETTER. 1969. bi-m. $12. North Dakota State Library, Capitol Grounds, 604 E. Boulevard Ave., Bismarck, ND 58505-0800. TEL 701-224-2490. FAX 701-224-2040. bk.rev.; bibl.; circ. 1,600.

020 US
FLORIDA STATE UNIVERSITY. SCHOOL OF LIBRARY AND INFORMATION STUDIES. ALUMNI NEWSLETTER. 1954. q. membership. Florida State University, School of Library and Information Studies Alumni Association, Shores Bldg., Tallahassee, FL 32306. TEL 904-644-2761. FAX 904-644-9763. Ed. Mary Alice Hunt. circ. 2,600. (back issues avail.)

020 CN
FOCUS (REGINA). 1954. irreg. (approx. 4/yr.). free to libraries. Saskatchewan Provincial Library, 1352 Winnipeg St., Regina, Sask. S4P 3V7, Canada. TEL 306-787-2977. Ed. Jim Oxman. bk.rev.; circ. 5,000.
Former titles: Focus on Saskatchewan Libraries (ISSN 0015-5179) & News Notes from the Provincial Library.

020 CN
FOCUS (TORONTO). 1962. 4/yr. Can.$35. Ontario Library Association, 100 Richmond St. E., Ste. 300, Toronto, Ont. M5C 2P9, Canada. TEL 416-363-3388. FAX 416-941-9581. Ed. Jefferson Gilbert. adv.; illus.; circ. 4,000. (back issues avail.)
Formerly: O L A Focus (ISSN 0318-0247); **Supersedes:** O L A Newsletter (ISSN 0474-2125)
Description: Issues and programs of concern to librarians and trustees in college, school, public and university libraries.

020 301.435
027.663 US ISSN 0740-4956
FOCUS: LIBRARY SERVICE TO OLDER ADULTS, PEOPLE WITH DISABILITIES. 1983. m. $12. Michael G. Gunde, Ed.& Pub., 216 N. Frederick Avenue, Daytona Beach, FL 32114. index; circ. 153. (back issues avail.)
Description: Newsletter of library resources and services pertaining to elderly persons and persons with disabilities.

020 US ISSN 0015-5152
Z732.I4
FOCUS ON INDIANA LIBRARIES. 1946. m. $15 for non-members. Indiana Library Association, 1500 N. Delaware St., Indianapolis, IN 46202. TEL 317-636-6613. (Co-sponsor: State Library) Ed. Susan E. Humphrey. adv.; bk.rev.; illus.; index; circ. 3,500. (also avail. in microfilm from UMI; reprint service avail. from UMI) **Indexed:** Lib.Lit.

020 UK ISSN 0305-8468
FOCUS ON INTERNATIONAL AND COMPARATIVE LIBRARIANSHIP. 1967. 3/yr. £10($21) Library Association, International & Comparative Librarianship Group, 7 Ridgmount St., London WC1E 7AE, England. TEL 0970-623181. TELEX 35391-CLW-G. Ed. Michael Wise. adv.; bk.rev.; bibl.; charts; cum.index; circ. 1,800. (tabloid format) **Indexed:** Inform.Sci.Abstr., LISA, Ref.Zh.
—BLDSC shelfmark: 3964.216000.

020 US ISSN 0275-4924
Z675.R45
FOCUS: ON THE CENTER FOR RESEARCH LIBRARIES. 1949. 6/yr. free. Center for Research Libraries, 6050 S. Kenwood, Chicago, IL 60637. TEL 312-955-4545. Ed. Linda Naru. bibl.; circ. 4,000. (tabloid format; back issues avail.)
—BLDSC shelfmark: 3964.186000.
Supersedes (in 1980): Center for Research Libraries. Newsletter (ISSN 0008-9087) And (in 1964): Midwest Inter-Library Center. Newsletter.
Description: News and feature articles on Center for Research Libraries activities and programs.

026 US
FOLGER NEWS. 1969. 3/yr. membership only. Folger Shakespeare Library, 201 E. Capitol St., S.E., Washington, DC 20003. TEL 202-544-4600. Ed. Ann Greer. circ. 3,000. (also avail. in microfilm from UMI)
Formerly: Folger Library Newsletter (ISSN 0015-5438)

026 664 US ISSN 0198-0246
FOOD FOR THOUGHT (LOS ANGELES). vol.7, 1975. bi-m. $10. Special Libraries Association, Food & Nutrition Division, c/o Lawry's Foods Inc., 570 W. Avenue 26, Los Angeles, CA 90065. Ed. Susan N. Newcomer. bk.rev.; bibl.; circ. 250.

020 US ISSN 0736-8879
FOOTNOTES (CHICAGO). 1970. q. membership. American Library Association, New Members Round Table, 50 E. Huron St., Chicago, IL 60611. TEL 312-944-6780. Ed. Darlene P. Nichols. adv.; bk.rev.; circ. 1,400. **Indexed:** Sportsearch.
Formerly: Junior Members Round Table. News Notes (ISSN 0022-6661)

020 US ISSN 0015-685X
FOR REFERENCE. 1966. m. $10. New York Metropolitan Reference & Research Library Agency (METRO), 57 E. 11th St., New York, NY 10003-4605. TEL 212-228-2320. circ. 2,000. (processed)

FOR THE RECORD (SPRINGFIELD). see HISTORY — History Of North And South America

023 US
FOR YOUR INFORMATION (BUFFALO). 1972. bi-m. free. Western New York Library Resources Council, 180 Oak St., Buffalo, NY 14203. TEL 716-852-3844. FAX 716-852-0276. Ed. Mary Ghikas. circ. 1,050. (back issues avail.)
Formerly: Western New York Library Resources Council Newsletter.

FORECAST (BRIDGEWATER); a prepublication announcement journal of hardcover and trade-paper titles (adult and children's) for public libraries. see PUBLISHING AND BOOK TRADE

020 378 US
FORUM (WASHINGTON, 1970). 1970. 2/yr. Catholic University of America, School of Library Science & Information, 620 Michigan Ave., N.E., Marist Hall, Rm. 228, Washington, DC 20064. TEL 202-635-5085. Ed. Andrea Rutledge. circ. 2,300.

020 US
FOUNDATIONS IN LIBRARY AND INFORMATION SCIENCE; a series of monographs, texts and treatises. 1980. irreg., vol.23, 1986. $58.50 to institutions. J A I Press Inc., 55 Old Post Rd., No. 2, Box 1678, Greenwich, CT 06836-1678. TEL 203-661-7602. Ed. Thomas Leonhart.
Description: Readings on information technology and information services.

FREE MAGAZINES FOR LIBRARIES. see PUBLISHING AND BOOK TRADE

020 SA ISSN 0016-0458
FREE STATE LIBRARIES/VRYSTAATSE BIBLIOTEKE. (Text in Afrikaans, English) 1958. q. exchange basis. Provincial Library Service, Private Bag X20606, Bloemfontein 9300, South Africa. FAX 051-304-958. Ed.Bd. bk.rev.; bibl.; circ. 500.

028.9 US ISSN 0046-5038
KF4774.A16
FREEDOM TO READ FOUNDATION NEWS. 1971. q. membership. Freedom to Read Foundation, 50 E. Huron St., Chicago, IL 60611. TEL 312-280-4223. FAX 312-440-9374. Ed. Judith F. Krug. circ. controlled.
Description: Covers legislative cases and judicial decisions that affect censorship in the United States. Provides information on the activities of the foundation.

020 US
FRIENDS OF LIBRARIES U S A NATIONAL NOTEBOOK. 1978. q. membership. American Library Association, Friends of Library U S A, 50 E. Huron St., Chicago, IL 60611. Ed. James A. Houck. circ. 1,500.
Formerly: Friends of the Library National Notebook (ISSN 0195-3419)

020 US
FRIENDS OF THE AMHERST COLLEGE LIBRARY. NEWSLETTER. 1972. a. free. Friends of the Amherst College Library, Box 2256, Amherst, MA 01002. TEL 413-542-2212. Ed. Richard Cody.
Description: Presents articles of literary interest, and news of the Friends of the Amherst College Library.

020 US
FRIENDS OF THE DARTMOUTH LIBRARY NEWSLETTER. 1976. s-a. Friends of the Dartmouth Library, Dartmouth College, 115 Baker Library, Hanover, NH 03755. TEL 603-646-2236. FAX 603-646-3702. circ. 1,000.

020 070 UK
FRIENDS OF THE NATIONAL LIBRARIES. ANNUAL REPORT. 1932. a. £10($22) to individuals; institutions £20($44) (effective Jan.). Friends of the National Libraries, British Library, Great Russell St., London WC1B 3DG, England. TEL 071-323-7559. Ed. J.F. Fuggles. circ. 900.

020 US ISSN 0192-5539
FRIENDSCRIPT. 1979. q. membership. University of Illinois at Urbana-Champaign, Library Friends, 227 Library, 1408 W. Gregory, Urbana, IL 61801. TEL 217-333-5682. Ed. Terry Maher. illus.; circ. 8,000. (looseleaf format)
Description: Information on new purchases, existing collections, services, and programs at the university library.

020 US
G P O. (Government Publications for Oklahoma) 1987. bi-m. free. Department of Libraries, 200 N.E. 18th St., Oklahoma City, OK 73105-3298. TEL 405-521-2502. FAX 405-525-7804. Ed. Steve Beleu. circ. 225.

020 PE ISSN 0433-0730
GACETA BIBLIOTECARIA DEL PERU. 1963. irreg. Biblioteca Nacional del Peru, Direccion General de Bibliotecas Publicas, Apdo. 2335, Lima, Peru. Ed. Carlos Puntriano. illus.; circ. 1,000.

GANZTAGSSCHULE. see EDUCATION — School Organization And Administration

020 GW ISSN 0724-6358
GEMEINSAME KOERPERSCHAFTSDATEI. 1980. a. Verlag Otto Harrassowitz, Taunusstr. 14, Postfach 2929, 6200 Wiesbaden 1, Germany. TEL 0611-530-0. FAX 0611-530570. TELEX 4186135. Ed. Bd. (microfiche)

GEOACTIVE. see GEOGRAPHY

020 US ISSN 0016-8319
Z732.G4
GEORGIA LIBRARIAN. 1964. q. $12.50 (foreign $20). Georgia Library Association, Box 39, Young Harris, GA 30582-0039. FAX 404-669-2705. Ed. Joanne Lincoln. adv.; bk.rev.; circ. 1,400. (also avail. in microform from UMI; reprint service avail. from UMI) **Indexed:** Lib.Lit.
—BLDSC shelfmark: 4158.435000.
Description: Features news and information of interest to Georgia librarians as well as articles of both state-wide or general interest in the field of librarianship.

LIBRARY AND INFORMATION SCIENCES

027.4   CN   ISSN 0380-8068
GEORGIAN BAY REGIONAL LIBRARY SYSTEM. DIRECTORY-MEMBER LIBRARIES. 1968. irreg. Georgian Bay Regional Library System, 30 Morrow Rd., Barrie, Ont. L4N 3V8, Canada. TEL 705-726-8251. circ. 100.

020   UK   ISSN 0951-2616
GERMAN STUDIES LIBRARY GROUP NEWSLETTER. 1987. 2/yr. free to members. German Studies Library Group, c/o D.K. Lowe, Cambridge University Library, West Rd., Cambridge CB3 9DR, England. TEL 0223-333094. FAX 0223-333160. circ. 100.
—BLDSC shelfmark: 4162.157380.
Description: Matters relating to library provision for the study of German-speaking countries and their cultures.

020   US   ISSN 0891-0553
Z733.G47
GEST LIBRARY JOURNAL. 1986. s-a. $25 to individuals and institutions; students and scholars $15. c/o Friends of the Gest Library, Jones Hall 211, Princeton University, Princeton, NJ 08544. Ed. H.L. Goodman. bk.rev.; circ. 200.
Description: Forum for scholarship, news, notes and reviews on East Asian libraries, particularly Princeton's Gest Oriental Library.

020   GH   ISSN 0016-9552
GHANA LIBRARY JOURNAL.* 1963. irreg. $5. Ghana Library Association, Box 5015, Accra, Ghana. Ed. D.E.M. Oddoye. adv.; bk.rev.; abstr.; charts; illus.; stat.; index, cum.index; circ. 500. (also avail. in microform) Indexed: Lib.Sci.Abstr.

020.6   MM
GHAQDA BIBLJOTEKARJI/LIBRARY ASSOCIATION NEWSLETTER. (Text in English) 1969. q. membership. Library Association, c/o Public Library, Beltissebh, Malta. Ed. William Zammit. bk.rev.; circ. 170 (controlled).
Formerly (until no.30, 1978): Malta Library Association Newsletter.
Description: Contains news items and coverage of association activities and local and international library and information developments.

020   US
GOLDA MEIR LIBRARY NEWSLETTER. 1974. irreg. free. University of Wisconsin-Milwaukee, Golda Meir Library, 2311 E. Hartford Ave., Box 604, Milwaukee, WI 53201. TEL 414-229-4786. FAX 414-229-4380. Ed. Jeane Knapp. circ. 4,000 (controlled).
Formerly: U W M Library Newsletter.
Description: Contains news of library activities, collections and services.

020   US   ISSN 0882-4746
GOOD STUFF. 1971. q. $10 to non-members. North Dakota Library Association, c/o Chester Fritz Library, University of North Dakota, Box 9000, Grand Forks, ND 58202. TEL 701-777-4636. FAX 701-777-3319. Ed. Michael Hurley. adv.; bk.rev.; circ. 500.
Description: Covers association activities, local and regional events and concerns.

020   US   ISSN 0890-3360
GOSSAGE REGAN MANAGER'S MEMO; trends & events in management & personnel for libraries/information centers. 1986. q. $25. (Gossage Regan Associates) Gordon Associates, 118 W. 74th St., Ste. 2B, New York, NY 10023. TEL 212-787-8930. Ed. Lucille Gordon. bk.rev.; circ. 1,200. (back issues avail.)
Description: Brief articles, and announcements on issues of interest to management and personnel in libraries and information centers.

020   US   ISSN 0740-624X
Z688.G6   CODEN: GIQUEU
GOVERNMENT INFORMATION QUARTERLY; an international journal of resources, services, policies, and practices. 1984. q. $45 to individuals; institutions $90. J A I Press Inc., 55 Old Post Rd., No. 2, Box 1678, Greenwich, CT 06836-1678. TEL 203-661-7602. Ed. Peter Hernon. Indexed: ASCA, Lib.Lit., P.A.I.S.
—BLDSC shelfmark: 4204.235000.

025   US
GRADUATE LIBRARY EDUCATION PROGRAMS; accredited by the American Library Association. s-a. free. American Library Association, Committee on Accreditation, 50 E. Huron St., Chicago, IL 60611. TEL 312-944-6780. FAX 312-440-9374.
Formerly: Graduate Library School Programs.

020   US   ISSN 0046-6301
GRANITE STATE LIBRARIES. 1965. bi-m. free to New Hampshire libraries, library organizations and qualified personnel. State Library, Department of Cultural Affairs, 20 Park St., Concord, NH 03301. TEL 603-271-2425. FAX 603-271-2205. Ed. Matthew J. Higgins. adv.; bk.rev.; bibl.; illus.; circ. 2,500 (controlled).
Formerly: Books and Libraries.
Description: Reports on matters of importance to all types of libraries.

020   II   ISSN 0017-324X
GRANTHAGAR. (Text in Bengali; summaries in English) 1937. m. Rs.36($8) Indian Association of Special Libraries and Information Centre, Bengal Library Association, P134 C.I.T. Scheme No. 52., Calcutta 700014, India. Ed. Ramkrishna Saha. adv.; bk.rev.; bibl.; charts; index; circ. 2,500. Indexed: LISA.

020   II
GRANTHALAYA VIJNANA. (Text in Hindi) 1970. s-a. Rs.125($25) P. Kaula Endowment for Library and Information Science, C-239 Indira Nagar, Lucknow 226 016, India. Ed. P.N. Kaula. adv.; bk.rev.; charts; illus.; index. Indexed: Indian Lib.Sci.Abstr.
Description: Covers library science in the Hindi language. Each issue has a specific theme.

GREATER NEW ORLEANS ARCHIVISTS NEWSLETTER. see HISTORY — History Of North And South America

GREEN LIBRARY JOURNAL; environmental topics in the information world. see ENVIRONMENTAL STUDIES

020   US   ISSN 0894-2986
GREENWOOD LIBRARY MANAGEMENT COLLECTION. 1988. irreg. price varies. Greenwood Press, Inc. (Subsidiary of: Greenwood Publishing Group Inc.), 88 Post Rd. W., Box 5007, Westport, CT 06881-5007. TEL 203-226-3571. FAX 203-222-1502.

GROWING POINT. see PUBLISHING AND BOOK TRADE

GUIDE TO MICROFORMS IN PRINT. AUTHOR - TITLE. see BIBLIOGRAPHIES

027.5   UN   ISSN 0072-8608
GUIDE TO NATIONAL BIBLIOGRAPHICAL INFORMATION CENTRES. (Text in English, French) 1962. irreg., 3rd ed., 1970. 23 F. Unesco, 7-9 Place de Fontenoy, 75700 Paris, France.

020   CC
GUJI ZHENGLI YANJIU XUEKAN. (Text in Chinese) bi-m. Dongbei Shifan Daxue - Northeast Normal University, 110, Stalin Street, Changchun, Jilin 130024, People's Republic of China. TEL 882320. Ed. Gao Zhenfeng.

020   GY
GUYANA LIBRARY ASSOCIATION BULLETIN. 1970. s-a. $20. Guyana Library Association, c/o National Library, Box 10240, 76-77 Main St, Georgetown, Guyana. Ed. Karen Sills. adv.; circ. 75. Indexed: LISA.
Description: Aimed at keeping interested persons informed on developments in library and information science in Guyana.

020   US
H C L AUTHORITY FILE (MICROFICHE EDITION). 1977. q. $15. Hennepin County Library, Technical Services Division, 12601 Ridgedale Dr., Minnetonka, MN 55343. TEL 612-541-8561. FAX 612-541-8600.
Description: Contains personal and corporate authors, added name entries (e.g., for joint authors, illustrators, translators, editors, government agencies, small presses) uniform title headings, author-title added entries, series forms, subject headings, and cross-references.

029   GW   ISSN 0340-1332
HANDBUCH DER INTERNATIONALEN DOKUMENTATION UND INFORMATION/HANDBOOK OF INTERNATIONAL DOCUMENTATION AND INFORMATION. irreg. price varies. K.G. Saur Verlag KG, Ortlerstr. 8, Postfach 701620, 8000 Munich 70, Germany. TEL 089-76902-0. FAX 089-76902150.
Formerly: Handbuch der Technischen Dokumentation und Bibliographie.
Description: Consists of a series of bibliographies, directories and guides to various aspects of documentation and information science.

020   GW   ISSN 0301-9225
Z801
HANDBUCH DER OEFFENTLICHEN BIBLIOTHEKEN. 1952. biennial. DM.64. Deutsches Bibliotheksinstitut, Abt. 1-Publikationen, Bundesallee 184-185, 1000 Berlin 31, Germany. TEL 030-8505-0. FAX 030-8505-100. stat.; circ. 1,200. (back issues avail.)

HANGKONG DANG'AN/AERONAUTICS ARCHIVES. see AERONAUTICS AND SPACE FLIGHT

020   CN   ISSN 0844-5753
HAPPENINGS. 1979. 3/yr. Calgary Public Library, 616 Macleod Tr. S.E., Calgary, Alta. T2G 2M2, Canada. TEL 403-260-2640. FAX 403-234-8763. Ed. Glenna Cross. adv.; circ. 265,000. (back issues avail.)
Description: Covers children's, young adult, adult programs.

HARVARD BUSINESS SCHOOL. BAKER LIBRARY. WORKING PAPERS IN BAKER LIBRARY; a quarterly checklist. see BUSINESS AND ECONOMICS

027   US   ISSN 0073-0564
Z881
HARVARD LIBRARIAN. 1957. 4/yr. free. Harvard University Library, Publications Office, 25 Mount Auburn St., Cambridge, MA 02138. TEL 617-495-7793. FAX 617-496-8344. Ed. Timothy Hanke. circ. 4,000. (reprint service avail. from UMI) Indexed: CALL.

027.7   US   ISSN 0017-8136
Z881
HARVARD LIBRARY BULLETIN. 1920-1988; N.S. 1990. q. $35. Harvard University Library, Publications Office, 25 Mount Auburn St., Cambridge, MA 02138. TEL 617-495-7793. FAX 617-496-8344. Ed. Kenneth E. Carpenter. bibl.; illus.; circ. 1,500. (also avail. in microform from JAI,MIM,UMI; reprint service avail. from UMI) Indexed: Abstr.Engl.Stud., Amer.Bibl.Slavic & E.Eur.Stud., Amer.Hist.& Life, Arts & Hum.Cit.Ind., CERDIC, Curr.Cont., Hist.Abstr., Lib.Lit., M.L.A., Mid.East: Abstr.& Ind.
—BLDSC shelfmark: 4268.000000.
Former titles (until 1942): Harvard University Library Notes (ISSN 1052-3685); (until 1940): Harvard Library Notes (ISSN 0363-7107)

510.78 410   US   ISSN 0073-0769
P307
HARVARD UNIVERSITY. COMPUTATION LABORATORY. MATHEMATICAL LINGUISTICS AND AUTOMATIC TRANSLATION; REPORT TO NATIONAL SCIENCE FOUNDATION. 1959. irreg., no.27, 1970. free. Harvard University, Aiken Computation Laboratory, Cambridge, MA 02138. (Subscr. to: National Technical Information Service, Operations Division, Springfield, VA 22151) Ed. Susumu Kuno.

027.7   US   ISSN 1050-2408
HARVARD UNIVERSITY LIBRARY NOTES. 1968. w. Harvard University Library, 25 Mount Auburn St., Cambridge, MA 02138. TEL 617-495-7793. FAX 617-496-8344.
Formerly (until 1990): H U L Notes (ISSN 0098-0919)

020   US
HAWAII. STATE PUBLIC LIBRARY SYSTEM. ANNUAL REPORT. 1962. a. free. State Public Library System, Office of Library Services, Kekuanaoa Bldg., Rm. B-1, 465 S. King St., Honolulu, HI 96813. TEL 808-548-5585.
Formerly: Hawaii. Department of Education. Office of Library Services. Annual Report.

LIBRARY AND INFORMATION SCIENCES

026   UK   ISSN 0305-9340
HEALTH AND WELFARE LIBRARIES QUARTERLY. 1965. q. L.3. Library Association, Hospital Libraries and Handicapped Readers Group, 50 Canadian Ave., Catford, London S.E.6., England. Ed. Antonia Bunch. adv. **Indexed:** Hosp.Abstr., LISA.
    Formerly: Book Trolley (ISSN 0045-2513)

026   HU   ISSN 0864-991X
▼**HEALTH INFORMATION AND LIBRARIES;** international journal for medical, health and welfare librarians and information officers. (Text in English) 1990. q. $45 to individuals; institutions $55; students $25(effective Jan. 1992). Orszagos Orvastudomanyi Informacios Intezet es Konyvtar - National Institute for Medical Information and Libraries, Szentkiralyi u. 21, Box 278, 1444 Budapest, Hungary. FAX 361-11-76-352. (Subscr. to: O.M.I.K.K., Technoinform, P.O. Box 12, H-1428 Budapest, Hungary) Ed. Maria Benda. bk.rev. **Indexed:** LISA.
   —BLDSC shelfmark: 4275.016900.
    Description: Attempts to help librarians and information specialists publish their scientific work based on their practical experience in the health field.

020   UK   ISSN 0265-6647
Z675.M4
HEALTH LIBRARIES REVIEW. 1984. q. £55 (foreign £60). (Library Association, Medical Health and Welfare Libraries Group) Blackwell Scientific Publications Ltd., Osney Mead, Oxford OX2 0EL, England. TEL 0865-240201. FAX 0865-721205. TELEX 83355-MEDBOK-G. Ed. S. Godbolt. adv.; bk.rev.; bk.; rev.; abstr.; bibl.; illus.; index.
   —BLDSC shelfmark: 4275.050650.

020   US
HEALTHDOCS. 1986. m. free. Department of Libraries, 200 N.E. 18th St., Oklahoma City, OK 73105-3298. TEL 405-521-2502. FAX 405-525-7804. Ed. Steve Beleu. circ. 61.

020   CC   ISSN 1001-5604
HEILONGJIANG TUSHUGUAN/HEILONGJIANG LIBRARY. (Text in Chinese) bi-m. Heilongjiang Sheng Tushuguan - Heilongjiang Provincial Library, 22, Wenchang Jie, Nangang-qu, Harbin, Heilongjiang 150001, People's Republic of China. TEL 224594. Ed. Wang Shengmao.

027   FI   ISSN 0355-1350
HELSINGIN YLIOPISTON KIRJASTON. JULKAISUJA/HELSINGFORS UNIVERSITETS BIBLIOTEKS SKRIFTER/HELSINKI UNIVERSITY LIBRARY. PUBLICATIONS. 1918. irreg., no.52, 1988. price varies. Helsingin Yliopiston Kirjasto - Helsinki University Library, P.O. Box 312, 00171 Helsinki, Finland. bibl.
    Description: Includes special bibliographies, studies on library and information science.

025.305   US   ISSN 0732-894X
Z693.A15
HENNEPIN COUNTY LIBRARY CATALOGING BULLETIN. 1973. bi-m. $6 to individuals; institutions $12. Hennepin County Library, Technical Services Division, 12601 Ridgedale Dr., Minnetonka, MN 55343. TEL 612-541-8561. FAX 612-541-8600. circ. 200. Key Title: Cataloging Bulletin (Edina).
    Description: Reports new or altered cross-references, DCC-numbers, and subject descriptors, citing authorities, precedents and applications.

020   II   ISSN 0018-0521
Z671   CODEN: HLBSAB
HERALD OF LIBRARY SCIENCE. (Special Numbers issued irregularly) 1962. q. Rs.250($68) P. Kaula Endowment for Library and Information Science, C-239 Indira Nagar, Lucknow 226 016, India. Ed. P.N. Kaula. adv.; bk.rev.; charts; illus.; index. (also avail. in microform from UMI; reprint service avail. from UMI) **Indexed:** Indian Lib.Sci.Abstr., Lib.Lit., LISA, Sci.Abstr.
   —BLDSC shelfmark: 4296.100000.
    Description: Articles, technical and information notes, book reviews, as well as reports on library science.

020   US
HIGH ROLLER. 1964. q. $20 to non-members. Nevada Library Association, c/o J.R. Dickinson Library, University of Nevada - Las Vegas, Las Vegas, NV 89154. TEL 702-739-3252. Ed. David P. Robrock. adv.; bk.rev.; illus.; stat.; circ. 400. (processed)
    Former titles: Highroller (ISSN 0197-6044); Nevada Libraries Highroller; Nevada Libraries (ISSN 0028-4068)

027.4   US
HITCHHIKER; for librarians in New Mexico. 1972. w. free to qualified personnel. State Library, 325 Don Gaspar, Santa Fe, NM 87503. TEL 505-827-3810. FAX 505-827-3888. (Co-sponsor: Office of Cultural Affairs) Ed. Robert Upton. circ. 1,200.
    Description: Covers news and events of New Mexico libraries. Includes information on job openings and workshops.

020   JA   ISSN 0018-3431
HOKKAIDO TOSHOKAN KENKYUKAI. KAIHO/HOKKAIDO LIBRARIANS STUDY CIRCLE. BULLETIN. (Text in Japanese) 1954. a. 1000 Yen. Hokkaido Toshokan Kenkyukai - Hokkaido Librarians Study Circle, c/o Sapporo Ika Daigaku Fuzoku Toshokan, Nishi-17-chome, Minami 1-jo, Sapporo, Japan. adv.; circ. 300.

020   HK   ISSN 0073-3237
HONG KONG LIBRARY ASSOCIATION. JOURNAL. (Text in Chinese, English) 1969. a. $30. Hong Kong Library Association, G.P.O. Box 10095, Hong Kong. FAX 7658274. Eds. K. Ladizesky, I. Shieh. adv.; bk.rev.; circ. 500.

HORIZONT; veszprem megyei kozmuvelodesi tajekoztato. see CLUBS

025   US
HOW TO DO IT MANUALS FOR LIBRARIANS. 1989. irreg. (approx 12/yr.). price varies. Neal-Schuman Publishers, Inc., 100 Varick St., New York, NY 10013. TEL 212-925-8650. FAX 212-219-8916. Ed. Bill Katz.
    Description: Focuses on specific technological, administrative and service-oriented aspects of librarianship, from computers and cataloguing to personnel, fundraising and community issues.

025   US
▼**HOW TO DO IT MANUALS FOR SCHOOL AND PUBLIC LIBRARIANS.** (Subseries of: How To Do It Manuals for Librarians) 1992. irreg. (approx. 10/yr). price varies. Neal-Schuman Publishers, Inc., 100 Varick St., New York, NY 10013. TEL 212-925-8650. FAX 212-219-8916. Ed. Barbara Stein.
    Description: For professionals working in public and school libraries.

020   GW   ISSN 0522-9898
HUMBOLDT - UNIVERSITAET ZU BERLIN. UNIVERSITAETSBIBLIOTHEK. SCHRIFTENREIHE. 1967. irreg., no.55, 1986. price varies. Humboldt-Universitaet zu Berlin, Universitaets-Bibliothek, Clara-Zetkin-Str. 27, PF 1236, 1086 Berlin, Germany. TELEX 0112757. Ed. Waltraud Irmscher.

020   US   ISSN 0257-3229
Z675.S3
I A S L CONFERENCE PROCEEDINGS. 1972. a. $25. International Association of School Librarianship, c/o Secretariate, Box 1486, Kalamazoo, MI 49005. TEL 616-343-5728. Ed. J. Lowrie. circ. 250. (looseleaf format; back issues avail.) **Indexed:** ERIC.

026   II   ISSN 0018-8441
Z671   CODEN: IASLA9
I A S L I C BULLETIN. (Text in English) 1956. q. Rs.160($30) Indian Association of Special Libraries and Information Centres, P-291 C.I.T. Scheme No. 6M, Kankurgachi, Calcutta 700 054, India. TEL 34-9651. adv.; bk.rev.; index; circ. 600. **Indexed:** Biol.Abstr., Lib.Lit., Lib.Sci.Abstr.
   —BLDSC shelfmark: 4359.543000.

026   II   ISSN 0018-845X
I A S L I C NEWSLETTER. 1966. m. membership. Indian Association of Special Libraries and Information Centres, P-291 C.I.T. Scheme No. 6M, Kankurgachi, Calcutta 700 054, India. TEL 34-9651. circ. 600.

026   II   ISSN 0073-6279
I A S L I C SPECIAL PUBLICATION; working papers of seminars and conferences. (Text in English) 1960. a. price varies. Indian Association of Special Libraries and Information Centres, P-291 C.I.T. Scheme No. 6M, Kankurgachi, Calcutta 700 054, India. TEL 34-9651.

026   II   ISSN 0073-6260
I A S L I C TECHNICAL PAMPHLETS. 1964. a. price varies. Indian Association of Special Libraries and Information Centres, P-291 C.I.T. Scheme No. 6M, Kankurgachi, Calcutta 700 054, India. TEL 34-9651.

020   US   ISSN 0085-2015
I A S L NEWSLETTER. 1971. q. $20. International Association of School Librarianship, c/o Secretariate, Box 1486, Kalamazoo, MI 49005. TEL 616-327-1390. Ed. Peter Genco. bk.rev.; circ. 950. (processed; back issues avail.)
    Description: Covers international programs in school library centers to publicize activities in the field.

020 310 025   US   ISSN 0739-1137
I A S S I S T QUARTERLY. 1974. q. $20 to individuals; institutions $35. International Association for Social Science Information Services and Technology, c/o Kay Worrell, Treas., IASSIST, Conference Board, 843 Third Ave., New York, NY 10022. TEL 212-339-0480. Ed. W. Piovesan. adv.; bk.rev.; circ. 400.
   —BLDSC shelfmark: 4359.546200.
    Formerly: I A S S I S T Newsletter.

020   UK   ISSN 0950-4117
Z675.T3   CODEN: IATQEX
I A T U L QUARTERLY. (International Association of Technological Universities Libraries) 1963. q. £40($83) Oxford University Press, Oxford Journals, Pinkhill House, Southfield Road, Eynsham, Oxford OX8 1JJ, England. TEL 0865-882283. FAX 0865-882890. TELEX 837330 OXPRES G. Ed. Joan Hardy. adv.; bk.rev.; bibl.; illus.; circ. 600. **Indexed:** Inform.Sci.Abstr., Lib.Lit., LISA, Sci.Abstr.
   —BLDSC shelfmark: 4359.610000.
    Supersedes: I A T U L Proceedings (ISSN 0018-8476); I A T U L Newsletter.
    Description: Forum for the exchange of views and ideas on common problems for librarians.

020   FR
▼**I C S T I FORUM.** (Text in English) 1990. q. free. International Council for Scientific and Technical Information - Conseil International pour l'Information Scientifique et Technique, 51 bd. de Montmorency, 75016 Paris, France. TEL 45-25-65-92. FAX 42-88-14-66. TELEX ICSU 645 554 F. bk.rev.; circ. 600.
    Description: Aims at increasing accessibility to, and awareness of, scientific and technical information.

I D. (Information Display) see LIBRARY AND INFORMATION SCIENCES — Computer Applications

020   GW   ISSN 0074-5987
I F L A ANNUAL; proceedings of the General Council Meetings. (Text in English) 1927. a. DM.98($60) (International Federation of Library Associations and Institutions) K.G. Saur Verlag KG, Ortlerstr. 8, Postfach 701620, 8000 Munich 70, Germany. TEL 089-76902-0. FAX 089-76902150. Eds. Willem R.H. Koops, Carol Henry.
    Description: Detailed summary of activities for the year and plans for the future. Lists conference participants and papers presented.

020   NE   ISSN 0074-6002
Z673
I F L A DIRECTORY. 1969. biennial. fl.75 to non-members; members free. International Federation of Library Associations and Institutions, Box 95312, 2509 CH The Hague, Netherlands. FAX 3834827. TELEX 34402 KB NL. Ed.Bd. circ. 2,000.
   —BLDSC shelfmark: 4363.300100.

020   GW   ISSN 0340-0352
Z672
I F L A JOURNAL. (Includes annual: I F L A Progress Report) (Text in English, French and German) 1975. q. DM.149($96) (International Federation of Library Associations and Institutions) K.G. Saur Verlag KG, Ortlerstr. 8, Postfach 701620, 8000 Munich 70, Germany. TEL 089-76902-0. FAX 089-76902150. Ed.Bd. adv.; bk.rev.; circ. 1,500. Indexed: Curr.Cont., Lib.Lit., So.Pac.Per.Ind., SSCI.
—BLDSC shelfmark: 4363.301400.
Supersedes: I F L A News (ISSN 0018-9685)
Description: Official journal of the organization.

025   GW   ISSN 0344-6891
I F L A PUBLICATIONS. (Text in English and French) 1974. irreg., vol.55, 1991. (International Federation of Library Associations and Institutions) K.G. Saur Verlag KG, Ortlerstr. 8, Postfach 701620, 8000 Munich 70, Germany. TEL 089-76902-0. FAX 089-76902150. Eds. Willem R. Koops, P. Havard-Williams. bibl.
Description: Consists of papers presented at various symposia, bibliographies, studies and monographs on aspects of library science.

020   US
I F R T REPORT. 1973. s-a. membership only. American Library Association, Intellectual Freedom Round Table, 50 E. Huron St., Chicago, IL 60611. TEL 312-280-4224. Ed. Paul Vermouth. circ. 1,500. (back issues avail.)
Description: Includes news about current censorship controversies, ALA conferences and the activities of the round table.

020   US   ISSN 0018-9979
I L A REPORTER. 1962. 10/yr. $25 (membership). Illinois Library Association, 33 W. Grand Ave No. 301, Chicago, IL 60610. TEL 312-644-1896. FAX 312-644-1899. adv.; illus.; circ. 4,400 (controlled).
Description: Professional association publication containing news about or of interest to all types of Illinois libraries, staff and trustees, including a statewide calendar of Illinois library events.

010   UN   ISSN 0047-0856
I N I S NEWSLETTER. 1972. 4/yr. free. International Atomic Energy Agency, Wagramer Str. 5, Box 100, A-1400 Vienna, Austria. circ. 1,500.
● Also available online. Vendor(s): STN International.
—BLDSC shelfmark: 4513.930000.

539   UN
I N I S REFERENCE SERIES. 1969. irreg. price varies. International Atomic Energy Agency, Wagramer Str. 5, Box 100, A-1400 Vienna, Austria. (Dist. in U.S. by: Unipub, 4611-F Assembly Dr., Lanhanm MD 20706-4391) (some issues also avail. in microfiche)

020   CI   ISSN 0351-0123
                 CODEN: IRBUD5
I R C I H E BULLETIN. (Text in English) 1975. q. 250 din.($24) International Referral Centre for Information Handling Equipment, c/o Institute for Information Sciences, P.O. Box 327, Trg. Marsala Tita 3, 41001 Zagreb, Croatia. TEL 38-41-427-866. FAX 38-41-427-903. TELEX 22686 RCSZ26 YU. Ed.Bd. adv.; circ. 600. (back issues avail.)
—BLDSC shelfmark: 4567.643000.

I S B N REVIEW. (International Standard Book Number) see PUBLISHING AND BOOK TRADE

I S C A QUARTERLY. (International Society of Copier Artists) see ART

026   IS   ISSN 0021-2318
                 CODEN: ISLBA2
I S L I C BULLETIN. (Text in Hebrew; summaries in English) 1966. 2/yr. $30 to individuals; institutions $50. Israel Society of Special Libraries and Information Centers, P.O. Box 43074, Tel Aviv 61430, Israel. Ed. Shoshana Langerman. adv.; bk.rev.; bibl.; index; circ. 1,000. (processed) Indexed: Ind.Heb.Per., LISA, Sci.Abstr.
—BLDSC shelfmark: 2593.470000.

I S O BULLETIN (ENGLISH EDITION). (International Organization for Standardization) see METROLOGY AND STANDARDIZATION

020   US
I U B LIBRARIES. FACULTY NEWSLETTER. 1989. irreg. Indiana University Libraries, c/o Jennifer Paustenbaugh, Ed., Library Administration, Library C-2, Bloomington, IN 47405. FAX 812-855-2576. circ. 2,500.
Description: Focuses on library issues of current concern to teaching faculty and administrators. News of new and noteworthy materials and exhibitions as well as research interests of library faculty are included.

021.7   US   ISSN 0360-8409
Z881.C25
ICARBS. 1973. irreg. $5 per vol. (2 issues). Friends of Morris Library, Southern Illinois University, Morris Library, Carbondale, IL 62901. TEL 618-453-2516. Eds. David V. Koch, Alan M. Cohn. adv.; circ. 600. (back issues avail.) Indexed: Abstr.Engl.Stud., Amer.Hum.Ind., M.L.A.
—BLDSC shelfmark: 4360.249000.
Description: Publishes research emanating from the special research collection of Morris Library.

027   IC
ICELAND. LANDSBOKASAFN ISLANDS. ARBOK. NYR FLOKKUR. N.S. 1976. a. ISK 800($13) Landsbokasafn Islands - National Library of Iceland, Safnahusinu, Hverfisgoetu 15, 101 Reykjavik, Iceland. Ed. Finnbogi Gudmundsson.
Supersedes in part: Iceland. Landsbokasafn Islands. Arbok.

020   US   ISSN 0019-1213
IDAHO LIBRARIAN. 1945. q. $15 to non-members. Idaho Library Association, Library, Univ. of Idaho, Moscow, ID 83843. FAX 208-858-6817. Ed. Mary K. Bolin. adv.; bk.rev.; bibl.; illus.; index; circ. 600. (also avail. in microform from UMI; reprint service avail. from UMI) Indexed: Lib.Lit., SRI.
—BLDSC shelfmark: 4362.258000.

610 026   JA   ISSN 0445-2429
                   CODEN: IGTODY
IGAKU TOSHOKAN. (Text in Japanese) 1954. q. 7000 Yen. Japan Medical Library Association - Nihon Igaku Toshokan Kyokai, 5-F, Gakkai Center Bldg., 2-4-16 Yayoi, Bunkyo-ku, Tokyo 113, Japan. FAX 03-3815-1608. Ed. Shigeaki Yamazaki. adv.; bk.rev.; circ. 1,650.
—BLDSC shelfmark: 4363.387000.

025 380   TS
AL-I'LAMIYYAH/INFORMATION. (Text in Arabic) 1985. q. exchange basis. United Arab Emirates University, Information Department, P.O. Box 15551, Al-Ain, United Arab Emirates. TEL 678333. TELEX 33521 JAMEAH EM. Ed. Tawfiq Yaqub. circ. 1,000.
Description: Social and cultural examination of the role of information and television in development.

020   US   ISSN 0019-2104
Z732.I2
ILLINOIS LIBRARIES. 1919. 6/yr. free. State Library, 300 S. Second St., Springfield, IL 62701. TEL 217-782-4287. Ed. Mrs. Irma Bostian. bibl.; illus.; stat.; circ. 9,000. (also avail. in microfilm from UMI; reprint service avail. from UMI) Indexed: Lib.Lit., Rehabil.Lit., SRI.
—BLDSC shelfmark: 4365.380000.

020   US
ILLINOIS NOTES. 1972. m. free. State Library, 300 S. Second St., Springfield, IL 62701. TEL 217-782-7846. Ed. Jim Bradley. circ. 3,900 (controlled). (back issues avail.)

020   US   ISSN 0732-2402
IMPULSE. 1913. w. $7. Fresno County Public Library, 2420 Mariposa St., Fresno, CA 93721. TEL 209-488-3223. FAX 209-488-1971. Ed. John Freitas. circ. 280.
Description: Staff newsletter of the Fresno County Public Library.

IN TOUCH (AUSTIN). see HANDICAPPED — Visually Impaired

020   AT   ISSN 0158-0876
Z673
INCITE. 1980. 20/yr. Aus.$80 (foreign Aus.$100)(effective 1992). Australian Library and Information Association, P.O. Box E411, Queen Victoria Terrace, A.C.T. 2600, Australia. TEL 06-285-1877. FAX 06-282-2249. adv.
—BLDSC shelfmark: 4374.970000.
Description: Information in the field of library and information management.

020   UK   ISSN 0073-6066
Z5055.G69
INDEX TO THESES ACCEPTED FOR HIGHER DEGREES IN THE UNIVERSITIES OF GREAT BRITAIN AND IRELAND. s-a. £165. Aslib, Association for Information Management, Publications Department, Information House, 20-24 Old St., London EC1V 9AP, England. TEL 071-253-4488. FAX 071-430-0514. (Dist. in N. America by: Learned Information, Inc., 143 Old Marlton Pike, Medford, NJ 08055-8750. TEL 609-654-6266) Eds. G.M. Paterson, Joan Hardy. (reprint service avail. from KTO) Indexed: Agri.Eng.Abstr., Anim.Breed.Abstr., Bio-Contr.News & Info., Cott.& Trop.Fibr.Abstr., Crop Physiol.Abstr., Dairy Sci.Abstr., Field Crop Abstr., Herb.Abstr., Ind.Vet., Pig News & Info., Plant Grow.Reg.Abstr., Poult.Abstr., Protozool.Abstr., Rural Devel.Abstr., Seed Abstr., Small Anim.Abstr., Triticale Abstr., Vet.Bull., Weed Abstr.
Description: Lists and abstracts all theses accepted for higher degrees in the universities of Great Britain and Ireland.

029.7   II   ISSN 0046-8975
INDIAN ARCHIVES. (Text in English) 1947. s-a. Rs.19($6.84) National Archives of India, Janpath, New Delhi 110001, India. Ed. R.K. Perti. bk.rev.; circ. 300. Indexed: Amer.Hist.& Life, Chem.Abstr., Hist.Abstr.
Description: Examines archival studies and the preservation of manuscripts. Features technical as well as general information on records administration, preparation and preservation of reference media as well as various documents and records of various bodies and institutions. Includes microfilming as well as other forms of documentary reproduction.

INDIAN BOOK REVIEW SUPPLEMENT. see PUBLISHING AND BOOK TRADE

020.6   II
INDIAN JOURNAL OF LIBRARY SCIENCE. (Text in English) 1975. q. Rs.20($3) Institute of Librarians (I.O.L.), c/o Sanskrit College, 1 Bankim Chatterjee St., Calcutta 700073, India. Ed. A K. Chakravorty. adv.; bk.rev.; circ. 300. (back issues avail.)

020   II   ISSN 0019-5782
Z671
INDIAN LIBRARY ASSOCIATION. BULLETIN. (Text in English) 1965. q. Rs.200($40) to non-members. Indian Library Association, A-40-41 Flat No.201 Ansal Buildings, Dr. Mukerjee Nagar, Delhi 110009, India. Ed. Krishan Kumar. adv.; bk.rev.; bibl.; illus.; circ. 2,000. (also avail. in microfilm from UMI) Indexed: Lib.Lit., Lib.Sci.Abstr.
Supersedes: Indian Library Association. Journal.

020   II   ISSN 0377-7367
Z845.I4
INDIAN LIBRARY MOVEMENT. (Text in Hindi) 1974. q. Rs.200($100) Model Town, Ambala City 134003, India. Ed. N.K. Bhagi. adv.; bk.rev.; bibl.; circ. 500.

020   II   ISSN 0067-3439
INDIAN STATISTICAL INSTITUTE. DOCUMENTATION RESEARCH AND TRAINING CENTRE. D R T C ANNUAL SEMINAR. 1963. a. price varies. Indian Statistical Institute, Documentation Research and Training Centre, 8th Mile, Mysore Road, Bangalore 560 059, India. TELEX 845-8376 ISIB IN. circ. 500. (also avail. in microfilm; microfiche) Indexed: Inform.Sci.Abstr., LISA.

020   II
INDIAN STATISTICAL INSTITUTE. DOCUMENTATION RESEARCH AND TRAINING CENTRE. D R T C REFRESHER SEMINAR. 1969. a. price varies. Indian Statistical Institute, Documentation Research and Training Centre, 8th Mile, Mysore Road, Bangalore 560 059, India. TELEX 845-8376 ISIB IN. circ. 500. (also avail. in microform) Indexed: Inform.Sci.Abstr., LISA.

LIBRARY AND INFORMATION SCIENCES

020 US ISSN 0275-777X
INDIANA LIBRARIES.* 1906. irreg. (2-4/yr.). $10. Indiana Library Association, 1500 N. Delavare St., Indianapolis, IN 46202-2419. TEL 317-636-6613. (Co-sponsors: Indiana State Library; Indiana Library Trustee Association) Ed. Dan Callison. bibl.; charts; illus.; circ. 2,000. (also avail. in microform from UMI; back issues avail.) Indexed: Lib.Lit.
Supersedes (in 1981): Library Occurrent (ISSN 0024-2454)

020 AG ISSN 0327-2915
INDICE DE CONTENIDOS - SERIE 1: CIENCIAS DE LA INFORMACION. (Text in English, French, Spanish) 1991. m. $15. Centro Argentino de Informacion Cientifica y Tecnologica, Moreno 431-33, piso 3, 1091 Buenos Aires, Argentina. TEL 34-1777. FAX 34-1777.

020 US
INFO ABOUT INFO. 4/yr. $6. Resources for Communication, 341 Mark West Station Rd., Windsor, CA 95492. Ed. Robert Cramer. illus.

INFO OUTLOOK (YEAR); a guide to trends and sources for the information commodity. see BUSINESS AND ECONOMICS — Management

020 US
INFOCUS (EMPORIA). 1973. s-a. free. (Emporia State University, School of Library and Information Management) Emporia State University Press, 1200 Commercial, Emporia, KS 66801-5087. TEL 316-341-5203. FAX 316-341-5997. Ed. Martha Hale. illus.; stat.; circ. 2,500. Indexed: Hist.Abstr.
Former titles (until 1987): Gleanings (Emporia); Library School Review Newsletter (ISSN 0277-8939); E S U Library School Newsletter.

020 NE ISSN 0169-2763
Z674.2 CODEN: IFMDES
INFOMEDIARY. (Text in English) 1987. q. fl.330($165) I O S Press, Van Diemenstraat 94, 1013 CN Amsterdam, Netherlands. TEL 020-6382189. FAX 020-6203419. (In N. America: Box 10558, Burke, VA 22009-0558) Ed.Bd. bk.rev.
—BLDSC shelfmark: 4478.879800.
Description: Covers information brokerage and consultancy developments in commercial and non-profit sectors. Includes survey articles, conference and project reports, professional services information and a calendar of events.
Refereed Serial

020 UK
INFORM. 10/yr. £25. Institute of Information Scientists, 44 Museum St., London WC1A 1LY, England. TEL 071-831-8003. circ. 2,900.
Description: Covers recent developments in the information world. Includes association news for members.

027.4 SA ISSN 0256-4106
INFORMAT. International edition (ISSN 1018-3310) (Text in Afrikaans, English) 1985. bi-m. free. State Library - Staatsbiblioteek, P.O. Box 397, Pretoria 0001, South Africa. TEL 012-21-8931. FAX 012-325-5984. TELEX 3-22171-SA. Ed. Hester van der Walt. bk.rev.; illus.; circ. 937.
Description: Discusses international and national conferences, quality control, board appointments and activities.

027.4 SA ISSN 1018-3310
▼**INFORMAT (INTERNATIONAL EDITION).** Bilingual National edition (ISSN 0256-4106) (Text in English) 1990. bi-m. free. State Library - Staatsbiblioteek, P.O. Box 397, Pretoria 0001, South Africa. TEL 012-21-8931. FAX 012-325-5984. TELEX 3-22171 SA. Ed. Hester van der Walt. bk.rev.; illus.; circ. 535.

029.9 340 IT
INFORMATICA E DIRITTO. (Text in English, Italian, and Spanish; summaries in English, French, Italian) 1975. q. L.95000($95) (effective 1991). (Istituto per la Documentazione Giuridica) Editoriale e Finanziaria Le Monnier, S.p.a., Via A. Meucci 2, Casella Postale 202, 50100 Florence, Italy. illus. Indexed: Sci.Abstr.
Description: Covers computer applications in law and sociology. Also looks at the theory and technology of computers.

020 001.539 GW ISSN 0019-9915
Q224.3.G3
INFORMATIK; Theorie und Praxis der wissenschaftlich-technischen Information. 1953. 6/yr. DM.80.40. Verlag Die Wirtschaft Berlin GmbH, Am Friedrichshain 22, 1055 Berlin, Germany. TEL 43870. FAX 4361249. Ed. Horst Christoph. adv.; bk.rev.; abstr.; bibl.; charts; illus.; stat.; upd. 25 91131. Indexed: Chem.Abstr., INIS Atomind., Sci.Abstr.
Formerly: Z I I D - Zeitschrift.
Description: Covers automated information systems, computer storage and retrieval, microcomputers, information processing, information systems, information centers, etc. Includes new publications.

029 004 YU ISSN 0019-9923
INFORMATIKA. (Text in Serbo-Croatian; summaries in English, Russian, Serbo-Croatian) 1967. q. $214. Jugoslovenski Centar za Tehnicku i Naucnu Dokumentaciju - Yugoslav Center for Technical and Scientific Documentation (YCTSD), Sl. Penezica-Krcuna 29-31, Box 724, 11000 Belgrade, Yugoslavia. Ed. Ljiljana Kojic-Bogdanovic.

020 500 HU ISSN 0230-4619
INFORMATIKA ES TUDOMANYELEMZES. (Text in English, Hungarian) 1981. irreg. price varies or exchange basis. Magyar Tudomanyos Akademia Konyvtara, Aranyjanos u.1, P.O. Box 7, 1361 Budapest 5, Hungary. Ed. T. Braun.
Description: Contains studies on information science and scientometrics, quantitative aspects of the science of science and science policy.

020 US
INFORMATION BROKER. 1978. 6/yr. $35. Burwell Enterprises, 3724 F.M. 1960 W., Ste. 214, Houston, TX 77068. TEL 713-537-9051. FAX 713-537-8332. Ed. Helen P. Burwell.
Formerly: Journal Fee-Based Information Services (ISSN 0190-2261)
Description: Newsletter for, by, and about the companies which dial in information for a fee.

020 AT ISSN 1037-6399
INFORMATION CENTRES IN THE NORTHERN TERRITORY. LIST. 1980. a. Aus.$10 to non-members (typically set in Dec.). Library Association of Australia, Northern Territory, G.P.O. Box 2786, Darwin, N.T. 0891, Australia. TEL 089-895279. FAX 089-814806. Ed. Murray Maynard. circ. 80. (back issues avail.)
Formerly: Libraries and Resources Centres in the Northern Territory. List (ISSN 0728-7429)

020 UK ISSN 0142-5471
INFORMATION DESIGN JOURNAL. 1979. 3/yr. £30($55) P.O. Box 185, Milton Keynes MK7 6BL, England. Ed. Robert Waller. bk.rev.; bibl.; charts; illus.; circ. 700. (also avail. in microfiche; back issues avail.) Indexed: Artbibl.Mod., Ergon.Abstr., LISA, Print.Abstr.
—BLDSC shelfmark: 4493.537000.

020 UK ISSN 0266-6669
Z672 CODEN: INDEE8
INFORMATION DEVELOPMENT; the international journal for librarians, archivists and information specialists. (Text in English, French, Portuguese, Spanish; summaries in English) 1985. q. £32.50($58.50) to individuals; institutions £65($117). Mansell Publishing Ltd., Villiers House, 41-47 Strand, London WC2N 5JE, England. TEL 071-839-4900. FAX 071-839-1804. TELEX 9413701-CASPUB-G. (Dist. by: Carfax Publishing Co., P.O. Box 25, Abingdon, Oxfordshire OX14 3UE, England) Ed. J. Stephen Parker. adv.; bk.rev.; circ. 500. (also avail. in microfiche; back issues avail.) Indexed: Info.Media & Tech., Lib.Lit., Rural Ext.Educ.& Tr.Abstr., World Agri.Econ.& Rural Sociol.Abstr.
—BLDSC shelfmark: 4493.538200.
Description: Contains articles, news, book reviews on current issues, problems and trends in information work throughout the world, with particular emphasis in the needs and concerns of developing countries.

INFORMATION DISPLAY. see LIBRARY AND INFORMATION SCIENCES — Computer Applications

029.7 US ISSN 0360-5817
Q223 CODEN: INHODN
INFORMATION HOTLINE. 1969. 10/yr. $150 (foreign $175). Science Associates International, Inc., 465 West End Ave., New York, NY 10024. TEL 212-873-0656. FAX 212-873-5587. Ed. Ivan Lyons. bk.rev.; bibl. (also avail. in microfilm from UMI; back issues avail.; reprint service avail. from UMI) Indexed: Comput.& Info.Sys., Inform.Sci.Abstr., Leg.Info.Manage.Ind., Lib.Lit., Lib.Sci.Abstr., PROMT, Resour.Ctr.Ind.
—BLDSC shelfmark: 4493.607300.
Former titles: Information News and Sources (ISSN 0360-5809); Information-Part 1-News, Sources, Profiles (ISSN 0036-8776); Scientific Information Notes.

070.5 020 US
INFORMATION INDUSTRY FACTBOOK. 1987. a. $195. Digital Information Group, 51 Bank St., Stamford, CT 06901. TEL 203-348-2751. stat.
Description: Covers trends and statistics about the information publishing business, including electronic and print publishing.

020 US
INFORMATION MANAGEMENT, POLICIES AND SERVICES. 1988. irreg. price varies. Ablex Publishing Corporation, 355 Chestnut St., Norwood, NJ 07648. TEL 201-767-8450. FAX 201-767-6717. TELEX 135-393. Eds. Charles R. McClure, Peter Hernon.

INFORMATION MANAGEMENT REPORT. see LIBRARY AND INFORMATION SCIENCES — Computer Applications

020 US
INFORMATION MANAGEMENT SOURCEBOOK. a. $79 (free to new members, $39 thereafter). Association for Information & Image Management, 1100 Wayne Ave., Ste. 1100, Siver Springs, MD 20910. TEL 301-587-8202. adv.; circ. 10,000.
Description: Annual directory of products, services, vendors and manufacturers of information and image management technologies and systems.

029.7 US ISSN 0306-4573
Z699.A1 CODEN: IPMADK
INFORMATION PROCESSING & MANAGEMENT; an international journal. (Text in English, French, German, Italian) 1963. 6/yr. £255 (effective 1992). Pergamon Press, Inc., Journals Division, 660 White Plains Rd., Tarrytown, NY 10591-5153. TEL 914-524-9200. FAX 914-333-2444. (And: Headington Hill Hall, Oxford OX3 0BW, England. TEL 0865-794141) Ed. Tefko Saracevic. adv.; bk.rev.; charts; illus.; index; circ. 2,000. (also avail. in microform from MIM,UMI; reprint service avail. from UMI) Indexed: ABI Inform, Biol.Abstr., BPIA, Commun.Abstr., Compumath, Comput.Abstr., Comput.Cont., Comput.Rev., Curr.Cont., Excerp.Med., Key to Econ.Sci., Leg.Info.Manage.Ind., LHTN, Lib.Lit., LISA, Math.R., Sci.Abstr., Soft.Abstr.Eng., SSCI, Tr.& Indus.Ind.
—BLDSC shelfmark: 4493.893000.
Formerly: Information Storage and Retrieval (ISSN 0020-0271)
Description: For library and information scientists, managers of information systems and communication networks, and researchers. Provides papers on research and development of non-traditional approaches to information management, electronic publishing, library and information systems and related fields.
Refereed Serial

020 UK
INFORMATION RESEARCH NEWS. 1976. 3/yr. £14. University of Sheffield, Department of Information Studies, Western Bank, Sheffield S10 2TN, England. TEL 0742-768555. FAX 0742-739826. TELEX 547216-UGSHEF-G. adv.; bk.rev.; circ. 1,100. Indexed: Curr.Cont., Lib.Sci.Abstr, LISA.
Formerly: C R U S News (ISSN 0140-4253)
Description: Disseminates recent research findings and the review of current information issues and concepts in library and information studies.

INFORMATION RESOURCES MANAGEMENT JOURNAL. see BUSINESS AND ECONOMICS — Management

LIBRARY AND INFORMATION SCIENCES 2763

020　　　　　　NE　ISSN 0167-5265
Z699.A1　　　　　　CODEN: ISUDX8
INFORMATION SERVICES & USE; an international journal. (Text in English) 1981. q. fl.362 (effective 1992). Elsevier Science Publishers B.V., P.O. Box 211, 1000 AE Amsterdam, Netherlands. TEL 020-5803911. FAX 020-5803598. TELEX 18582 ESPA NL. (Subscr. in U.S. and Canada to: Elsevier Science Publishing Co., Inc., Box 882, Madison Sq. Sta., New York, NY 10159. TEL 212-989-5800) Ed. A.W. Elias, T. Cawkell. adv.; bk.rev. (also avail. in microform from RPI) **Indexed:** AESIS, BPIA, Bus.Ind., Comput.Abstr., Comput.Cont., Comput.Lit.Ind., Fluidex, Key to Econ.Sci., Leg.Info.Manage.Ind., LHTN, Manage.Cont., Mgmt.& Market.Abstr., Sci.Abstr., Tr.& Indus.Ind.
—BLDSC shelfmark: 4495.950000.
　Description: Contains data on international developments in information management and its applications. Articles cover on-line systems, library automation, word processing, micrographics, videotex and telecommunications.
　Refereed Serial

INFORMATION SOLUTIONS; a newsletter of ideas and techniques about how to profit from information. see *BUSINESS AND ECONOMICS — Management*

INFORMATION STANDARDS QUARTERLY. see *PUBLISHING AND BOOK TRADE*

020　　　　　　UK　ISSN 0266-8513
INFORMATION TECHNOLOGY AND PUBLIC POLICY. 1982. 3/yr. £35($68) (foreign £40). (Parliamentary Information Technology Committee) Philip Virgo, 2 Eastbourne Ave., Acton, London W3 6JN, England. Ed. K. Norman. adv.; circ. 500. **Indexed:** CAD CAM Abstr., Cont.Pg.Manage., Sci.Abstr.
—BLDSC shelfmark: 4496.368740.
　Formerly: P I T C O M (ISSN 0263-614X)

INFORMATION TODAY; the newspaper for users and producers of electronic information services. see *LIBRARY AND INFORMATION SCIENCES — Computer Applications*

020　　　　　　CI
INFORMATOLOGIA. (Text and summaries in Croatian, English) 1969. s-a. $60 1000 CRD (effective 1992). Institut Informacijskih Znanosti - Institute for Information Sciences, Trg Marsala Tita 3, Box 327, 41001 Zagreb, Croatia. TEL 38-41-427-878. FAX 38-41-427-903. TELEX 22486 RCSZGH. Ed. Mario Plenkovic. bk.rev.; abstr.; charts; index; circ. 600. (back issues avail.) **Indexed:** Lib.Sci.Abstr., Ref.Zh., Sci.Abstr.
　Formerly (until vol.23, 1991): Informatologia Yugoslavica (ISSN 0046-9483)
　Description: Publishes original scientific papers, professional papers, short notes, preliminary communications, reports, recommendations and reviews in the field of librarianship and the documentation and information sciences.

INFOTERM SERIES. (International Information Centre for Terminology, Vienna) see *LINGUISTICS*

027.4　　　　US　ISSN 0020-1308
INGLEWOOD PUBLIC LIBRARY QUARTERLY REPORT. 1962. q. free. Inglewood Public Library, 101 W. Manchester Blvd., Inglewood, CA 90301-1771. TEL 310-412-5397. FAX 310-412-8848. Ed. John W. Perkins. stat.; circ. 200. (processed; also avail. in microfiche) **Indexed:** Ind.Curr.Urb.Doc.
　Description: Events and performance indicators during the quarter at the library.

020　　　　　　US
INLAND MESSENGER. 1969. bi-m. $25. Inland Library System, Box 468, Riverside, CA 92502. TEL 714-369-7995. Ed. Vaughn Simon. bk.rev.; illus.; circ. 480. (processed)

020 011　　　　EI　ISSN 0255-0806
　　　　　　　　　　CODEN: ITETEW
INNOVATION AND TECHNOLOGY TRANSFER. (Text in English) 1980. irreg., 5-6/yr. free. Commission of the European Communities, Directorate XIII-C Exploitation of Research and Technological Development, Technology Transfer and Innovation, Attn: Edward Phillips, DG XIII-C JMO B4-082, L-2920 Luxembourg, Luxembourg. TEL 342-4301-2916. FAX 352-4301-2084. TELEX 3423 COMEUR LU. bk.rev.; circ. 48,000. (back issues avail.)
—BLDSC shelfmark: 4515.480370.
　Former titles: New Technologies and Innovation Policy; New Technologies; D S T C Newsletter (ISSN 0251-2645)
　Description: Provides information on research and research-related activities of the commission, with particular emphasis on expoitation of research results.

020 001.539　　　UK
INSIDE INFORMATION. 1989. biennial. £35. T F P L Publishing, 22 Peters Lane, London EC1M 6DS, England. TEL 071-251-5522. FAX 071-251-8318.

027.7　　　　　US
INSIDE WAU. 1979. s-m. University of Washington Libraries, M171 Suzzallo Library, Seattle, WA 98195. TEL 206-543-1760. FAX 206-685-8049. Ed. Marie A. Spears. circ. controlled.

027.4　　　　　US
INSIGHT (AKRON). 1960. bi-m. $2 (free to libraries). Akron-Summit County Public Library, 55 S. Main St., Akron, OH 44326. TEL 216-762-7621. Ed. Patricia H. Latshaw. illus.; circ. 2,000 (controlled). (processed)
　Formerly (until 1986): Owlet (ISSN 0030-7602)
　Description: Aims to keep Summit County residents informed of library resources and services.

020　　　　　US
Z733
INSIGHTS (WASHINGTON, 1988). 1969. bi-m. membership. Library of Congress Professional Association, Library of Congress, Washington, DC 20540. TEL 202-707-3635. Eds. Sarah Rouse, Phil DeSellem. adv.; bk.rev.; circ. 2,000 (controlled). (processed)
　Formerly (until 1988): Library of Congress Professional Association. Newsletter (ISSN 0098-1648)

026　　　　　GW　ISSN 0019-0217
Z675.A2　　　　　　CODEN: INPLBI
INSPEL. (Text in English, French, German and Russian) 1975. q. DM.48. International Federation of Library Associations, European Patent Office, Erhardtstr. 27, D-8000 Munich 2, Germany. Ed. Gerhard Kruse. bk.rev.; index; circ. 400. **Indexed:** LHTN, Lib.Lit., Lib.Lit., LISA, Sci.Abstr.
—BLDSC shelfmark: 4518.660000.

INSTITUT PROVINCIAL D'ETUDES ET RECHERCHES BIBLIOTHECONOMIQUES. MEMOIRES. see *BIBLIOGRAPHIES*

020 300　　　　　JA　ISSN 0020-2827
INSTITUTE OF DEVELOPING ECONOMIES. LIBRARY BULLETIN/AJIA KEIZAI SHIRYO-GEPPO. (Text in English and Japanese) 1959. m. 7200 Yen. Institute of Developing Economies - Ajia Keizai Kenkyusho, 42 Ichigaya-Hommura-cho, Shinjuku-ku, Tokyo 162, Japan. bibl.; circ. 1,000. (also avail. in microform)

020　　　　　US　ISSN 0047-0414
Z732.D62
INTERCOM (WASHINGTON, 1971). 1971. m. (11/yr.). membership. District of Columbia Library Association, Box 14177, Benjamin Franklin Sta., Washington, DC 20044. Eds. Ann Benson, Jacque-Lynne Schulman. adv.; circ. 1,000. (processed)
　Supersedes: D.C. Libraries.
　Description: Lists courses, seminars and job opportunities.

026　　　　　US　ISSN 0270-6717
Z672
INTERFACE (CHICAGO). 1978. q. $15. American Library Association, Association of Specialized and Cooperative Library Agencies, 50 E. Huron St., Chicago, IL 60611-2795. TEL 312-944-6780. Ed. Thomas Dorst. adv.; bk.rev.; circ. 2,000. (also avail. in microform from UMI; back issues avail.; reprint service avail. from UMI) **Indexed:** API Abstr., Lib.Lit.
　Supersedes: A S L A President's Newsletter; H R L S D Journal; Which was formerly (nos.1-2, 1975): Health and Rehabilitative Library Services News (ISSN 0098-3462); Which superseded: Association of Hospital and Institution Libraries. Quarterly (ISSN 0090-3116) & A H I L Quarterly (ISSN 0001-1428)

020　　　　　UK　ISSN 0264-1615
Z921.B854　　　　　CODEN: IDSUDQ
INTERLENDING AND DOCUMENT SUPPLY. 1971. q. £31 (foreign £36). British Library, Document Supply Centre, Publishing Section, Boston Spa, Wetherby, W. Yorkshire LS23 7BQ, England. TEL 0937-843434. FAX 0937-546333. TELEX 557381. Ed. D.N. Wood. bibl.; index, cum.index: 1971-1975; circ. 1,200. (back issues avail.) **Indexed:** Br.Ceram.Abstr., Curr.Cont., Dairy Sci.Abstr., Field Crop Abstr., Herb.Abstr., Inform.Sci.Abstr., LHTN, Lib.Lit., LISA, Nutr.Abstr., Ref.Zh., Sci.Abstr., SSCI.
—BLDSC shelfmark: 4534.463000.
　Former titles (until 1983): Interlending Review: Journal of the British Library Lending Division (ISSN 0140-2773); (until 1978): B L L Review (ISSN 0305-6503); N L L Review (ISSN 0027-6790)

026　　　　　US
INTERNATIONAL ASSOCIATION OF LAW LIBRARIES. DIRECTORY. 1977. irreg., latest ed. 1988. $25. Institute for International Legal Information, c/o Dr. Ivan Sipkov, Box 5709, Washington, DC 20016-1309. adv.; bk.rev.; circ. 1,000. **Indexed:** C.L.I., Leg.Per.

INTERNATIONAL ASSOCIATION OF PERFORMING ARTS LIBRARIES AND MUSEUMS. CONGRESS PROCEEDINGS. see *ART*

026 266　　　　　US　ISSN 0272-6122
BV2350
INTERNATIONAL BULLETIN OF MISSIONARY RESEARCH. 1950; N.S. 1977. q. $18 (foreign $34). Overseas Ministries Study Center, 490 Prospect St., New Haven, CT 06511. TEL 203-624-6672. (Subscr. to: Box 3000, Denville, NJ 07834) Ed. Gerald H. Anderson. adv.; bk.rev.; bibl.; index, cum.index: 1977-80, 1981-84, 1985-88; circ. 7,000. (also avail. in microform from UMI; reprint service avail. from UMI) **Indexed:** CERDIC, Chr.Per.Ind., G.Soc.Sci.& Rel.Per.Lit., Rel.& Theol.Abstr. (1981-), Rel.Ind.One.
—BLDSC shelfmark: 4538.080000.
　Formed by the merger of: Gospel in Context (ISSN 0193-8320); Occasional Bulletin of Missionary Research (ISSN 0364-2178); Which was formerly (until 1977): Missionary Research Library. Occasional Bulletin (ISSN 0026-606X)

029　　　　　GW　ISSN 1011-8829
Z693.A15　　　　　　CODEN: ICBCEH
INTERNATIONAL CATALOGUING AND BIBLIOGRAPHIC CONTROL. 1972. q. £28($48) (International Federation of Library Associations, UBCIM Programme) Deutsche Bibliothek, Zeppelinallee 4-8, 6000 Frankfurt a.M. 1, Germany. FAX 069-7566476. (Subscr. to: Bailey Management Services, Warner House, Bowles Well Gardens, Folkestone, Kent CT19 6PH, England) Marie-France Plassard. bk.rev.; bibl. **Indexed:** Lib.Lit., LISA.
—BLDSC shelfmark: 4538.411000.
　Formerly: International Cataloguing (ISSN 0047-0635)

020　　　　　GW　ISSN 0340-0050
Z696　　　　　　　　CODEN: INCLDN
INTERNATIONAL CLASSIFICATION; a journal devoted to concept theory, organization of knowledge and data, and to systematic terminology. (Text in English, French, German) 1974. 4/yr. DM.97 to institutions. (International Society for Knowledge Organization) Indeks Verlag, Woogstr. 36a, 6000 Frankfurt a.M. 50, Germany. TEL 069-523690. FAX 069-520566. adv.; bk.rev.; abstr.; bibl.; circ. 1,000. (Reprint service avail. from UMI, ISI) **Indexed:** Bull.Signal., Curr.Cont., Lib.Lit., LISA, Sci.Abstr., SSCI.
—BLDSC shelfmark: 4538.668000.

LIBRARY AND INFORMATION SCIENCES

020   US   ISSN 0364-3670
CODEN: ICDIDA
INTERNATIONAL CODEN DIRECTORY. every 5 yrs. (plus a. supplements). $900 for base vol.; $240 for each supplement. Chemical Abstracts Service (Subsidiary of: American Chemical Society), 2540 Olentagy River Rd., Box 3012, Columbus, OH 43210. TEL 614-447-3600. FAX 614-447-3713. TELEX 6842086. (microfiche)
—BLDSC shelfmark: 4538.703000.

025.17   SP   ISSN 0255-3139
INTERNATIONAL COUNCIL ON ARCHIVES. COMMITTEE ON CONSERVATION AND RESTORATION. COMMITTEE ON ARCHIVAL REPROGRAPHY (BULLETIN). (Text in English; summaries in English, French, German, Italian, Spanish) 1972. a. free. (Ministerio de Cultura, FR) Archivo Historico Nacional, c/o Sra. Carmen Crespo Nogueira, Ed., Serrano 115, 28006 Madrid, Spain. illus.; circ. 2,350.
Formerly: International Council on Archives. Microfilm Committee. Bulletin.

026   BS
INTERNATIONAL COUNCIL ON ARCHIVES. EAST AND CENTRAL AFRICA REGIONAL BRANCH. GENERAL CONFERENCE PROCEEDINGS. 1969. a. $25. International Council on Archives, Eastern and Southern Africa Regional Branch, c/o Botswana National Archives and Records Services, Government Enclave, Khama Crescent, P.O. Box 239, Gaborone, Botswana. TEL 3601187. FAX 313584. Ed. R.J. Kukubo.
Description: Covers Biennial conference proceedings of the ESARBICA - various themes and sub-themes.

025   US   ISSN 0889-0919
INTERNATIONAL DIRECTORY OF NEWS LIBRARIES INCLUDING FINDING. 1985. irreg. $69.95. (Special Libraries Association, Newspaper Division) L D A Publishers, 42-36 209 St., Bayside, NY 11361. TEL 718-224-9484. FAX 718-224-9487. adv.; circ. 350.
Former titles: International Directory of News Libraries Including Buyers' Guide (Year); International Directory of News Libraries and Buyers' Guide (Year).
Description: Alphabetical listings by country and state with information on special collections, services to other new libraries, banners and access.

029   NE   ISSN 0378-7656
Z696
INTERNATIONAL FEDERATION FOR DOCUMENTATION. P-NOTES. 1931. irreg. (20-30/yr.). £21.50 in E.E.C.: elsewhere $41. Federation Internationale d'Information et de Documentation - International Federation for Information and Documentation, Postbus 90402, 2509 LK The Hague, Netherlands. TEL 070-3140671. FAX 070-3140667. TELEX 34402 KB GV NL. (Subscr. to: Distribution Centre, Blackhorse Rd., Letchworth, Herts. SG6 1HN, United Kingdom)

029.7   NE
INTERNATIONAL FEDERATION FOR INFORMATION AND DOCUMENTATION. PROCEEDINGS OF CONGRESS. 1895. biennial, latest 1989. price varies. Elsevier Science Publishers B.V., Books Division, P.O. Box 211, 1000 AE Amsterdam, Netherlands. TEL 020-5803911. FAX 020-5803705. TELEX 18582 ESPA NL. (Subscr. in U.S. and Canada to: Elsevier Science Publishing Co., Inc., Box 882, Madison Sq. Sta., New York, NY 10159. TEL 212-989-5800)
Formerly: International Federation for Documentation. Proceedings of Congress (ISSN 0074-5812)
Refereed Serial

020 700   NE   ISSN 0261-152X
INTERNATIONAL FEDERATION OF LIBRARY ASSOCIATIONS AND INSTITUTIONS. SECTION OF ART LIBRARIES. NEWSLETTER. 1981. 3/yr. membership. International Federation of Library Associations and Institutions, Section of Art Libraries, Postbus 95312, 2509 The Hague, Netherlands. Ed. Rossella Todros. circ. 900.
—BLDSC shelfmark: 6107.449000.
Formerly: Round Table of Art Librarians. Newshet.
Description: News about upcoming conferences and new art library literature.

020 029   RU   ISSN 0304-9701
Z1007   CODEN: IFIDD7
INTERNATIONAL FORUM ON INFORMATION AND DOCUMENTATION. (Editions in English, Russian) 1975. q. fl.100. Vsesoyuznyi Institut Nauchno-Tekhnicheskoi Informatsii (VINITI), Ul. Baltiiskaya 14, 125219 Moscow, Russia. (Subscr. to: F I D General Secretariat, P.O. Box 90402, 2509 LK The Hague, Netherlands) (Co-sponsor: International Federation for Documentation) Ed. A.I. Mikhailov. adv.; circ. 6,000. **Indexed:** Curr.Cont., Lib.Lit., Sci.Abstr., SSCI.
—BLDSC shelfmark: 4540.340000.

020   II   ISSN 0970-1850
Z671
INTERNATIONAL INFORMATION, COMMUNICATION AND EDUCATION. 1982. s-a. Rs.290($58) P. Kaula Endowment for Library and Information Science, C-239, Indira Nagar, Lucknow 226 016, India. Ed. P.N. Kaula. adv.; bk.rev.; charts; index. (also avail. in microform from UMI) **Indexed:** Curr.Cont., Inform.Sci.Abstr., LISA.
Description: Multidisciplinary journal on communication and information sciences within developing nations. Includes relevant computer applications.

020   UK   ISSN 0953-556X
Z671
INTERNATIONAL JOURNAL OF INFORMATION AND LIBRARY RESEARCH. 1989. 3/yr. £51($96) Taylor Graham Publishing, 500 Chesham House, 150 Regent St., London W1R 5FA, England. Ed. Stephen Roberts. adv.; bk.rev.
—BLDSC shelfmark: 4542.304800.
Description: Current research and development in information management and information technology.

INTERNATIONAL JOURNAL OF INFORMATION MANAGEMENT. see COMPUTERS — Information Science And Information Theory

INTERNATIONAL JOURNAL OF INFORMATION RESOURCE MANAGEMENT. see BUSINESS AND ECONOMICS — Management

026.34 340   US   ISSN 0731-1265
Z675.L2
INTERNATIONAL JOURNAL OF LEGAL INFORMATION. (Text in English) 1973. 3/yr. $55 to individuals; institutions $80. International Institute for Legal Information, Box 5709, Washington, DC 20016-1309. TEL 202-244-3386. Ed. Ivan Sipkov. adv.; bk.rev.; index; circ. 1,000. **Indexed:** C.L.I., Foreign Leg.Per., Int.Lab.Doc., L.R.I., Leg.Info.Manage.Ind., Leg.Per.
—BLDSC shelfmark: 4542.315000.
Formerly: International Journal of Law Libraries (ISSN 0340-045X); Which supersedes in part: International Association of Law Libraries. Bulletin (ISSN 0538-4524)

020 327   US   ISSN 0892-4546
Z672
INTERNATIONAL LEADS. 1957. q. $12. American Library Association, International Relations Round Table, 50 E. Huron St., Chicago, IL 60611. TEL 312-944-6780. FAX 312-440-9374. Ed. Leena M. Siitonen. bk.rev.; bibl.; circ. 800 (controlled). **Indexed:** Lib.Lit., LISA.
Former titles: Leads (ISSN 0458-8983); Leads: A Fact Sheet.

020   UK   ISSN 1057-2317
Z671
INTERNATIONAL LIBRARY AND INFORMATION REVIEW. 1969. q. $182. Academic Press Ltd., 24-28 Oval Rd., London NW1 7DX, England. TEL 071-267-4466. FAX 071-482-2293. TELEX 25775 ACPRES G. Eds. N. Moore, T. Carbo Bearman. **Indexed:** Amer.Hist.& Life, C.I.J.E., Comput.Rev., Curr.Cont., Hist.Abstr., Lib.Lit., So.Pac.Per.Ind., SSCI.
—BLDSC shelfmark: 4541.266000.
Formerly: International Library Review (ISSN 0020-7837)
Description: Addresses progress and research in international and comparative librarianship, documentation, and information retrieval for librarians worldwide.

025   II   ISSN 0970-0048
Z671
INTERNATIONAL LIBRARY MOVEMENT. (Text in English) 1974. q. Rs.350($120) Post Box No. 1, (G.P.O.), Model Town, Ambala City 134 003, India. Ed. N.K. Bhagi. adv.; bk.rev.; abstr.; bibl.; stat.; circ. 1,000.
—BLDSC shelfmark: 4542.930000.
Description: Examines the theory and practice of librarianship and information science with emphasis on the needs and problems of developing countries.

020   UK   ISSN 0269-0500
INTERNATIONAL REVIEW OF CHILDREN'S LITERATURE AND LIBRARIANSHIP. 1986. 3/yr. £46($88) Taylor Graham Publishing, 500 Chesham House, 150 Regent St., London W1R 5FA, England. Ed. Margaret Kinnell. adv.; bk.rev. (back issues avail.) **Indexed:** Lib.Lit., LISA.
—BLDSC shelfmark: 4546.343000.

020 025   US
INTERNATIONAL YEARBOOK OF SERIALS LIBRARIANSHIP. 1988. a. $34.95. Haworth Press, Inc., 10 Alice St., Binghamton, NY 13904. TEL 800-342-9678. FAX 607-722-1424. Ed. David P. Woodworth.
Refereed Serial

020   GW   ISSN 0000-0221
Z721
INTERNATIONALES BIBLIOTHEKS-HANDBUCH/WORLD GUIDE TO LIBRARIES. (Text in English and German) 1966. irreg., 10th ed., 1991. $325. K.G. Saur Verlag KG, Ortlerstr. 8, Postfach 701620, 8000 Munich 70, Germany. TEL 089-76902-0. FAX 089-76902150. (N. America subscr. to: K.G. Saur, A Reed Reference Publishing Company, 121 Chanlon Rd., New Providence, NJ 07974. TEL 908-665-3576) Ed.Bd. adv.
—BLDSC shelfmark: 9356.032000.
Description: Lists libraries in 167 countries, including national, federal, regional, academic, large public, and special libraries. Arranged by continent and country, plus an alphabetical index.

020   MX   ISSN 0187-358X
INVESTIGACION BIBLIOTECOLOGICA; archivonomia, bibliotecologia, e informacion. (Text in Spanish; abstracts in English) 1986. s-a. $12. Universidad Nacional Autonoma de Mexico, Centro Universitario de Investigaciones Bibliotecologicas, Torre II de Humanidades, pisos 12 y 13, Ciudad Universitaria, 04510 Mexico, D.F., Mexico. TEL 550-5931. FAX 550-74-61. Ed. Carlos Ceballos Sosa. adv.; abstr.; bibl.; circ. 1,000 (controlled). **Indexed:** LISA.

027.8   US
IOWA MEDIA MESSAGE. (Former name of issuing body: Audiovisual Education Association of Iowa) 1972. 4/yr. membership. Iowa Educational Media Association, A E A 7, 3712 Cedar Heights Dr., Cedar Falls, IA 50613. Ed. Bev Trost. adv.; bk.rev.; circ. 650.
Formerly: Iowa Association of School Librarians. Library Lines (ISSN 0021-0447)

026 025   IE
IRISH ARCHIVES. (Text in English, Gaelic) 1971. irreg. £4.50. Irish Society for Archives, c/o Mr. Brian Donnelly, National Archives, Four Courts, Dublin 7, Ireland. Ed. Ailsa C. Holland. bk.rev.; circ. 200. (back issues avail.)
Formerly: Irish Archives Bulletin.
Description: Contains material on archival practices and development inland and overseas.

020   AT   ISSN 0814-303X
ISSUES; for serials librarians. 1984. irreg. (2-3/yr.). free. I S A Australia, 5-2 Benson St., Toowong, Qld. 4066, Australia. TEL 07-371-7500. FAX 61-7-371-5206. (Subscr. to: P.O. Box 709, Toowong, Qld. 4066, Australia) Ed. Alfred J. Gans. adv.; bk.rev.; circ. 2,000. (back issues avail.)

LIBRARY AND INFORMATION SCIENCES

016   IT
ITALY. ISTITUTO DI STUDI SULLA RICERCA E DOCUMENTAZIONE SCIENTIFICA. NOTE DI BIBLIOGRAFIA E DOCUMENTAZIONE SCIENTIFICA. 1955. irreg., vol.52, 1989. price varies. Istituto di Studi sulla Ricerca e Documentazione Scientifica, Centro di Riferimento Italiano Diane, Via Cesare do Lollis 12, 00185 Rome, Italy. FAX 06-493836. TELEX 610076 CORICERC. Ed. Maria Pia Carosella. circ. 1,000.
Former titles: Italy. Laboratorio di Studi sulla Ricerca e sulla Documentazione. Note di Bibliografia e Documentazione Scientifica; Italy. Consiglio Nazionale delle Ricerche. Nota di Bibliografia e di Documentazione Scientifica (ISSN 0085-2309)

026   IT   ISSN 0036-9845
ITALY. SCUOLA DI GUERRA. BIBLIOTECA. BOLLETTINO. 1952. bi-m. Scuola di Guerra, Biblioteca, Civitavecchia, Italy.

ITIHAS; journal of the Andhra Pradesh archives. see HISTORY — History Of Asia

020 600   CS   ISSN 0862-9382
I'91. (Text in Czech or Slovak; summaries in English and Russian) 1957. m. $60. (Ministry for Economic Politics and Development of the Czech Republic) Central Office of Scientific, Technical and Economic Information (COSTEI), Konviktska 5, 113 57 Prague 1, Czechoslovakia. Ed. Jelena Hankova. adv.; bk.rev.; stat.; index. **Indexed:** LISA, Sci.Abstr.
Formed by the 1990 merger of: Ceskoslovenska Informatika (ISSN 0322-8509) & Technicka Knihovna (ISSN 0049-3171)
Description: Presents original papers on all aspects of librarianship and information science.

020.6   JM
J L A NEWS. q. Jamaica Library Association, P.O. Box 58, Kingston 5, Jamaica, W.I.
Description: News of current events in the libraries of Jamaica.

JAHRBUCH DER AUKTIONSPREISE FUER BUECHER, HANDSCHRIFTEN UND AUTOGRAPHEN; Ergebnisse der Auktionen in Deutschland, den Niederlanden, Oesterreich und der Schweiz. see MUSEUMS AND ART GALLERIES

020   GW   ISSN 0075-2215
Z801
JAHRBUCH DER BIBLIOTHEKEN, ARCHIVE UND INFORMATIONSEINRICHTUNGEN DER DEUTSCHEN DEMOKRATISCHEN REPUBLIK.* Title varies: Jahrbuch der Bibliotheken, Informationsstellen und Archive der D D R. 1959. triennial. Deutsche Buecherei Leipzig, Deutscher Platz, 7010 Leipzig, Germany. Eds. Heinz Gittig, Wolfgang Horscht. adv.; bk.rev.; circ. 3,500.
Description: Includes index of libraries, archives and information centers in East Germany, as well as organizations, government bodies, central catalogs, and statistics.

020   GW   ISSN 0075-2223
Z801
JAHRBUCH DER DEUTSCHEN BIBLIOTHEKEN. 1902. biennial, no.54, 1991. price varies. (Verein Deutscher Bibliothekare) Verlag Otto Harrassowitz, Taunusstr. 14, Postfach 2929, 6200 Wiesbaden 1, Germany. TEL 0611-530-0. FAX 0611-530570. TELEX 4186135. adv.; circ. 2,600.

020.6   JM
JAMAICA LIBRARY ASSOCIATION. BULLETIN. 1950. a. Jamaica Library Association, P.O. Box 58, Kingston 5, Jamaica, W.I.
Formerly: Jamaica Library Association. Annual Bulletin (ISSN 0448-2174)
Description: Reports on developments and issues affecting the library and information profession in Jamaica.

029.7   JA   ISSN 0913-3801
JAPAN. INFORMATION SCIENCE AND TECHNOLOGY ASSOCIATION. JOURNAL/JOHO NO KAGAKU TO GIJUTSU. 1950. m. 15450 Yen. Information Science and Technology Association, Sasaki Bldg., 2-5-7 Koisikawa, Bunkyo-ku, Tokyo 112, Japan. FAX 81-3-3813-3793. Ed. Hiroyuki Taya. adv.; bk.rev.; circ. 8,000. **Indexed:** INIS Atomind.
Formerly: Documentation Study (ISSN 0012-5180)

020   JA   ISSN 0040-9650
JAPAN SOCIETY OF LIBRARY SCIENCE. ANNALS/TOSHOKAN GAKKAI NENPO. (Text in Japanese; summaries in English) 1954. q. (plus a. supplement) 8000 Yen. Japan Society of Library Science - Nippon Toshokan Gakkai, c/o Office of Library and Information Science, Faculty of Sociology, Toyo University, 28-20 Hakusan 5-chome, Bunkyo-ku, Tokyo 112, Japan. Ed. Shojiro Maruyama. adv.; bk.rev.; charts; index; circ. 900.
—BLDSC shelfmark: 1028.380000.

020   CC
JIANGSU TUSHUGUAN XUEBAO/JIANGSU LIBRARY. JOURNAL. (Text in Chinese) bi-m. Jiangsu Tushuguan Xuehui - Jiangsu Library Association, Nanjing Tushuguan, 66 Chengxian Jie, Nanjing, Jiangsu 210018, People's Republic of China. TEL 637654. Ed. Lu Zibo.

020   CC
JIANGXI TUSHUGUAN XUEKAN/JIANGXI LIBRARY JOURNAL. (Text in Chinese) q. Jiangxi Sheng Tushuguan - Jiangxi Provincial Library, No. 65, Zhongshan Lu, Nanchang, Jiangxi 330008, People's Republic of China. TEL 62269. Ed. Zheng Jinhui.

020   CC
JINTU XUEKAN. (Text in Chinese) q. Shanxi Sheng Tushuguan Xuehui, Shanxi Daxue Tushuguan, Wucheng Lu, Taiyuan, Shanxi 030006, People's Republic of China. TEL 773441. Ed. Feng Jinsheng.

027.4   SA
JOHANNESBURG PUBLIC LIBRARY. ANNUAL REPORT. (Text in English) 1891. a. free. Johannesburg Public Library, Market Square, Johannesburg 2001, South Africa. TEL 011-836-3787. FAX 011-836-6607. (back issues avail.)

JOHN RYLANDS UNIVERSITY LIBRARY OF MANCHESTER. BULLETIN. see HUMANITIES: COMPREHENSIVE WORKS

JOKESMITH. see LITERARY AND POLITICAL REVIEWS

020   BE
JOURNAL DE LA LIBRAIRIE.* 1883. bi-m. 1325 Fr. Cercle Belge de la Librairie (CBL), 140 Blvd. Lanbermont, 1030 Brussels, Belgium. Ed. N. Mertens. adv.; bk.rev.

050   US   ISSN 0893-5386
Z6945
JOURNAL HOLDINGS IN THE NATIONAL CAPITAL AREA. 1969. biennial. $190. Interlibrary Users Association, c/o Macron Systems, Inc., 212 Elmhurst Circle, Evans City, PA 16033. Ed. Mary Lynn Kingston. charts; circ. 250 (controlled). (processed)
Formerly: Journal Holdings in the Washington-Baltimore Area (ISSN 0362-4544)

020   US   ISSN 0099-1333
Z671
JOURNAL OF ACADEMIC LIBRARIANSHIP; articles, features, and book reviews for the academic library professional. 1975. bi-m. $29 to individuals; institutions $52. Mountainside Publishing, Inc., 321 S. Main St., Box 8330, Ann Arbor, MI 48107. TEL 313-662-3925. FAX 313-662-4450. Ed. Richard M. Dougherty. adv.; bk.rev.; abstr.; bibl.; charts; illus.; index; circ. 3,000. (also avail. in microform from MIM,UMI; back issues avail.; reprint service avail. from UMI) **Indexed:** Bk.Rev.Ind. (1975-), C.I.J.E., CALL, Child.Bk.Rev.Ind. (1975-), Curr.Cont., Educ.Ind., Leg.Info.Manage.Ind., LHTN, Lib.Lit., LISA, PSI, Ref.Sour.; SSCI.
—BLDSC shelfmark: 4918.858000.
Description: Covers all aspects of academic librarianship plus offers an extensive review of the literature through its "Guide to the Professional Literature."
Refereed Serial

020 330   US   ISSN 0896-3568
Z675.B8   CODEN: JBFLEY
JOURNAL OF BUSINESS & FINANCE LIBRARIANSHIP. 1989. q. $24 to individuals; institutions $40. Haworth Press, Inc., 10 Alice St., Binghamton, NY 13904. TEL 800-342-9678. FAX 607-722-1424. Ed. William Fisher. adv.; bk.rev. (also avail. in microfiche from HAW; reprint service avail. from HAW)
—BLDSC shelfmark: 4954.661057.
Description: Provides articles to information professionals who are involved with, or have an interest in, the creation, organization, dissemination, retrieval, and use of business information.
Refereed Serial

JOURNAL OF CLASSIFICATION. see MATHEMATICS

029   UK   ISSN 0022-0418
Z1007   CODEN: JDOCAS
JOURNAL OF DOCUMENTATION; devoted to the recording, organization and dissemination of specialized knowledge. 1945. q. £90($180) to non-members; members £60. Aslib, Association for Information Management, Publications Department, Information House, 20-24 Old St., London EC1V 9AP, England. TEL 071-253-4488. FAX 071-430-0514. (Dist. in N. America by: Learned Information Inc., 143 Old Marlton Pike, Medford, NJ 08055-8750. TEL 609-654-6266) Ed. R.T. Kimber. adv.; bk.rev.; abstr.; bibl.; index; circ. 3,500. (reprint service avail. from KTO) **Indexed:** Abstr.Bull.Inst.Pap.Chem., Biol.Abstr., Br.Ceram.Abstr., C.I.J.E., Chem.Abstr., Compumath, Comput.Cont., Curr.Cont., Dairy Sci.Abstr., Deep Sea Res.& Oceanogr.Abstr., Excerp.Med., Fluidex, Ind.Sci.Rev., Ind.Vet., Int.Lab.Doc., Key to Econ.Sci., Lib.Lit., M.L.A., Mid.East: Abstr.& Ind., Sci.Abstr., Sci.Cit.Ind., SSCI, Vet.Bull., World Surf.Coat.
—BLDSC shelfmark: 4970.000000.
Description: Articles on documentation, librarianship and information science, both theoretical and practical.

020.7   US   ISSN 0748-5786
Z671
JOURNAL OF EDUCATION FOR LIBRARY AND INFORMATION SCIENCE. 1960. 5/yr. $50 (foreign $60). Association for Library and Information Science Education, 5623 Palm Aire Dr., Sarasota, FL 34243-3702. TEL 813-355-1795. Ed. Rosemary DuMont. bk.rev.; charts; cum.index: 1960-1975, 1975-1980; circ. 1,700. (also avail. in microfilm from UMI,ISI; back issues avail.; reprint service avail. from UMI) **Indexed:** C.I.J.E., Cont.Pg.Educ., Curr.Cont., Educ.Ind., Lib.Lit., Lib.Sci.Abstr., Res.High.Educ.Abstr., Sci.Abstr., SSCI.
—BLDSC shelfmark: 4973.150100.
Formerly (until 1984): Journal of Education for Librarianship (ISSN 0022-0604)
Refereed Serial

370 020   CH   ISSN 1013-090X
     CODEN: CYTHD5
JOURNAL OF EDUCATIONAL MEDIA AND LIBRARY SCIENCES. (Text in Chinese and English; summaries in English) 1970. q. NT.$360($30) Tamkang University, Graduate Institute of Educational Media and Library Sciences, Tamsui, Taipei, Taiwan 25137, Republic of China. FAX 02-622-6149. (Co-sponsor: Chueh Sheng Memorial Library) Ed. Shih-hsion Huang. adv.; bk.rev.; index; circ. 1,200. (back issues avail.; reprint service avail. from UMI) **Indexed:** C.I.J.E., Educ.Ind, Inform.Sci.Abstr, Lib.Lit, LISA, P.A.I.S. Key Title: Jiaoyu Ziliao yu Tushuguan Xue.
—BLDSC shelfmark: 4973.157500.
Formerly (until 1982): Journal of Educational Media Sciences (ISSN 0377-9890)

JOURNAL OF INFORMATION ETHICS. see LAW

029.7   JA   ISSN 0021-7298
     CODEN: JOKAAB
JOURNAL OF INFORMATION PROCESSING AND MANAGEMENTS/JOHO KANRI. (Text in Japanese) 1958. m. $126. Japan Information Center of Science and Technology - Nihon Kagaku Gijutsu Joho Senta, 5-2 Nagata-cho, 2-chome, Chiyoda-ku, Tokyo 100, Japan. TEL 03-3581-6411. FAX 03-3581-6446. TELEX 02223604 J. adv.; bk.rev.; charts; illus.; index; circ. 5,000. **Indexed:** Chem.Abstr., INIS Atomind., JTA, Math.R., Sci.Abstr.
—BLDSC shelfmark: 5006.772200.
Formerly: Information and Documentation.

LIBRARY AND INFORMATION SCIENCES

020 025   NE   ISSN 0165-5515
Z1007   CODEN: JISCDI
JOURNAL OF INFORMATION SCIENCE; principles and practice. (Text in English) 1979. bi-m. fl.346 (effective 1992). (Institute of Information Scientists, UK) Elsevier Science Publishers B.V., P.O. Box 211, 1000 AE Amsterdam, Netherlands.
TEL 020-5803911. FAX 020-5803598. TELEX 18582 ESPA NL. (Subscr. in U.S. and Canada to: Elsevier Science Publishing Co., inc., Box 882, Madison Sq. Sta., New York, NY 10159. TEL 212-989-5800) Ed. A. Gilchrist. adv.; illus.; index, cum.index; circ. 3,800. (also avail. in microform from RPI; back issues avail.; reprint service avail.) **Indexed:** AESIS, BPIA, Bus.Ind., Chem.Abstr., Compumath, Comput.Cont., Comput.Lit.Ind., Comput.Rev., Curr.Cont., Eng.Ind., ERIC, Fluidex, Inform.Sci.Abstr., INSPEC, Intl.Civil Eng.Abstr., LHTN, Lib.Lit., LISA, Manage.Cont., Ref.Zh., Sci.Abstr. Sci.Cit.Ind., Soft.Abstr.Eng., SSCI, Tr.& Indus.Ind., World Text.Abstr.
—BLDSC shelfmark: 5006.772800.
Supersedes: Information Scientist (ISSN 0020-0263)
Description: For information scientists and librarians. Reports developments and theories in mechanized information systems. Articles cover office-library automation, communications, technology transfer and innovations, writing, publishing and transmission, and filing and retrieval of data.
Refereed Serial

020   UK   ISSN 0268-3962
    CODEN: JINTEB
JOURNAL OF INFORMATION TECHNOLOGY. Variant title: J I T. q. £99 for EC (US & Canada $160). (Association for Information Technology) Chapman & Hall, 2-6 Boundary Row, London SE1 8HN, England. TEL 071-865-0066. FAX 071-522-9623. (US addr.: Chapman & Hall, 29 West 35th St., New York, NY 10001-2291. TEL 212-244-3336) Ed. Igor Aleksander. adv.; abstr. (back issues avail.)
—BLDSC shelfmark: 5006.790000.
Description: Views and opinions from the information technology community in Britain, Europe, the United States and Japan.

020   US   ISSN 1042-4458
Z713   CODEN: JILSEW
▼**JOURNAL OF INTERLIBRARY LOAN & INFORMATION SUPPLY.** 1990. q. $18 to individuals; institutions and libraries $24. Haworth Press, Inc., 10 Alice St., Binghamton, NY 13904. TEL 800-342-9678. FAX 607-722-1424. Ed. Leslie R. Morris. (also avail. in microfiche from HAW; reprint service avail. from HAW)
—BLDSC shelfmark: 5007.548600.
Description: Devoted to practice-oriented interlibrary loan problems and the basic expanding roles of interlibrary loan librarians.
Refereed Serial

020   UK   ISSN 0961-0006
Z671   CODEN: JLSCE6
JOURNAL OF LIBRARIANSHIP AND INFORMATION SCIENCE. 1969. q. £60($115) Bowker-Saur Ltd., 59-60 Grosvenor St., London W1X 9DA, England. TEL 071-493-5841. FAX 071-499-1590. (Subscr. to: Bailey Bros. and Swinfen Ltd., Warner House, Bowles Well Gardens, Folkestone, Kent CT19 6PH, England) Ed. David Stoker. bk.rev.; index; circ. 1,400. (reprint service avail. from SWZ) **Indexed:** Curr.Cont., Lib.Lit., LISA, Sci.Abstr, SSCI.
—BLDSC shelfmark: 5010.330100.
Formerly (until 1991): Journal of Librarianship (ISSN 0022-2232)
Description: Reports and reflects significant work and developments in all aspects of library and information science worldwide. Includes articles and critical reviews of new publications.

025   US   ISSN 0193-0826
Z678   CODEN: JLADEL
JOURNAL OF LIBRARY ADMINISTRATION. 1980. q. $40 to individuals; institutions $90. Haworth Press, Inc., 10 Alice St., Binghamton, NY 13904.
TEL 800-342-9678. FAX 607-722-1424. TELEX 4932599. Ed. Sul Lee. adv.; bk.rev.; charts; illus.; stat.; circ. 1,112. (also avail. in microfiche from HAW; reprint service avail. from HAW) **Indexed:** BPIA, Bull.Signal., C.I.J.E., Comput.& Info.Sys., Excerp.Med., Inform.Sci.Abstr., Leg.Info.Manage.Ind., Lib.Lit., LISA, Manage.Cont., P.A.I.S., Pers.Lit., Ref.Zh., Tr.& Indus.Ind.
—BLDSC shelfmark: 5010.333000.
Description: Provides information on all aspects of the effective management of libraries, with emphasis on practical applications.
Refereed Serial

020   CH   ISSN 0363-3640
Z671   CODEN: TSKHE4
JOURNAL OF LIBRARY & INFORMATION SCIENCE/TUSHUGUANXUE YU ZIXUN KEXUE. 1975. s-a. NT.$300($20) National Taiwan Normal University, Department of Social Education - Tai-wan Shih Fan Ta Hsueh, 162 Ho-ping E. Rd. Sec.1, Taipei, Taiwan 10610, Republic of China.
TEL 02-363-1097. FAX 02-363-6334. (Subscr. to: Student Book Co. Ltd., 198 Ho-ping E. Rd. Sec.1, Taipei, Taiwan 10610, Republic of China) (Co-sponsor: Chinese American Librarians Association) Ed.Bd. bk.rev.; circ. 1,000. **Indexed:** Inform.Sci.Abstr., Lib.Lit., LISA, P.A.I.S.
—BLDSC shelfmark: 5010.340000.
Description: Aims to serve as a forum for discussion of problems common to librarians and information scientists, to introduce new concepts, systems, and technology, to report leading events worldwide, and to promote the development of Chinese library and information services.

020   II   ISSN 0970-714X
Z671
JOURNAL OF LIBRARY AND INFORMATION SCIENCE. Variant title: J L I S. (Text in English) 1976. s-a. Rs.80($14) (typically set Jan.). University of Delhi, Department of Library and Information Science, Delhi 110 007, India. Ed. P. B. Mangla. adv.; bk.rev.; circ. 350. **Indexed:** Curr.Cont., Ind.Per.Lit., Inform.Sci.Abstr., LISA, P.A.I.S.
Description: Research journal with the objective to keep users informed about the latest developments in the field and to encourage research programs.

JOURNAL OF NEWSPAPER AND PERIODICAL HISTORY. see *PUBLISHING AND BOOK TRADE*

020   PH   ISSN 0022-359X
JOURNAL OF PHILIPPINE LIBRARIANSHIP. (Text in English) 1968-1971; resumed 1981. s-a. P.100($20) (effective 1992). University of the Philippines, Institute of Library Science, Diliman, Quezon City 1101, Philippines.
TEL 98-24-71-6249. Ed. Rosa M. Vallejo. **Indexed:** Ind.Phil.Per.
—BLDSC shelfmark: 5034.200000.

028.1   US   ISSN 0894-2498
Z718.1.A1
JOURNAL OF YOUTH SERVICES IN LIBRARIES. 1946. q. $40 (foreign $50). American Library Association, Association for Library Service to Children, and Young Adult, 50 E. Huron St., Chicago, IL 60611-2795. TEL 800-545-2433.
FAX 312-440-9374. Eds. Donald J. Kenney, Linda J. Wilson. adv.; bk.rev.; bibl.; illus.; index, cum.index: 1942-1963; circ. 9,500. (also avail. in microform from UMI; back issues avail.; reprint service avail. from UMI) **Indexed:** Bk.Rev.Ind. (1967-), C.I.J.E., Chic.Per.Ind., Child.Bk.Rev.Ind. (1967-), Child.Lit.Abstr., LHTN, Lib.Lit., LISA, Media Rev.Dig.
—BLDSC shelfmark: 5072.722000.
Formerly (until 1987): Top of the News (ISSN 0040-9286)
Description: News and articles of interest to children and young adult librarians.

026 296   US   ISSN 0739-5086
Z675.J4
JUDAICA LIBRARIANSHIP. 1983. s-a. $25 to individuals and institutions; students $18. Includes A J L Newsletter. Association of Jewish Libraries, c/o National Foundation for Jewish Culture, 330 7th Ave., 21st Fl., New York, NY 10001-5010.
TEL 513-221-1875. (Subscr. to: 3101 Clifton Ave., Cincinnati, OH 45220) Eds. Marcia Posner, Bella Weinberg. adv.; bk.rev.; charts; illus.; index. (back issues avail.) **Indexed:** Geneal.Per.Ind., Ind.Artic.Jew.Stud., Ind.Jew.Per., Inform.Sci.Abstr., Lib.Lit., Lib.Sci.Abstr., M.L.A., Ref.Sour.
—BLDSC shelfmark: 5073.824500.
Supersedes: Association of Jewish Libraries Bulletin.
Description: Covers the full spectrum of functions and types of Judaica libraries.

610 020   IR
JUNDI SHAPUR UNIVERSITY. FACULTY OF MEDICINE. LIBRARY BULLETIN/DANESHGAH-E JONDISHAPUR. DANESHKADE-YE PEZESAKI. BULTAN-E KETABKHANEH. (Text in Persian) 1972. q. free. Jundi Shapur University, Faculty of Medicine, Box 339, Ahvaz, Iran.

JUNIOR BOOKSHELF; a review of children's books. see *PUBLISHING AND BOOK TRADE*

020   US
JUNIOR HIGH SCHOOL LIBRARY CATALOG. 1965. quinquennial (plus a. supplement). $105. H.W. Wilson Co., 950 University Ave., Bronx, NY 10452. TEL 800-367-6770. FAX 212-538-2716. TELEX 4990003HWILSON. Ed. Juliette Yaakov.
Description: Classified list of books recommended for young people (grades 7-9), including fiction and story collections; with author, title, subject, and analytical index.

JUVENILE MISCELLANY. see *CHILDREN AND YOUTH — About*

020   KO   ISSN 0022-7358
K L A BULLETIN. 1960. 6/yr. $20. Korean Library Association, C.P.O. Box 2041, 100-177, 1-KA, Hoehyun-Dong, Choong-ku, Seoul, S. Korea. Ed. Dae Kwon Park. adv.; bk.rev.; circ. 5,000.

020.6   US
K L A NEWSLETTER. vol.10, 1983. 4/yr. membership. Kansas Library Association, c/o South Central Kansas Library System, 901 N. Main St., Hutchinson, KS 67501. TEL 316-663-2501. FAX 316-662-1215. Ed. Paul Hawkins. adv.; circ. 1,100.
Description: Covers association sponsored activities and news of interest to the Kansas library community.

020   II   ISSN 0022-9083
KARNATAK GRANTHALAYA. (Text in Kannada; contents page in English and Kannada) 1969. q. Rs.25. S. R. Gunjal, Ed. & Pub., Granthalaya Vijnana Prakashana, Gulbarga University, Gulbarga 585106, Karnatak, India. adv.; bk.rev.; bibl.; illus.

020.6 282   GW   ISSN 0931-4458
KATHOLISCHE OEFFENTLICHE BUECHEREI; Vierteljahreszeitschrift fuer Mitarbeiter der Katholischen Oeffentlichen Buechereien. Short title: K Oe B. 1957. q. DM.16. Erzbistum Koeln, Fachstelle fuer Buechereien, Marzellenstr. 32, 5000 Cologne 1, Germany. FAX 0221-1642-700. Ed. Siegmund Schramm. cum.index every 5 yrs.; circ. 5,300.
Formerly (until 1987): Unsere Sammlung.
Description: Covers library and literary subjects.

020   US   ISSN 0075-5311
KEEPSAKE (DAVIS). (Each issue also has a distinctive title) 1966. irreg., no.13, 1990. price varies. Library Associates, General Library, University of California, Davis, CA 95616. TEL 916-752-2110. FAX 916-752-6899. circ. 1,200.
Description: Each Keepsake addresses a unique and specialized subject area.

020   CC   ISSN 1000-4467
KEJI QINGBAO GONGZUO/SCIENCE AND TECHNOLOGY INFORMATION. (Text in Chinese) m. Zhongguo Kexue Jishu Qingbao Yanjiusuo - China Science and Technology Information Institute, 15 Fuxing Lu, Beijing 100038, People's Republic of China. TEL 8015544. Ed. Li Wenyun.

020   CC
KEJI QINGBAO SHICHANG/INFORMATION MARKET OF SCIENCE AND TECHNOLOGY. (Text in Chinese) m. Sichuansheng Kexue Jishu Qingbao Yanjiusuo - Sichuan Science and Technology Information Research Institute, 32 Dongfeng Lu Yiduan (Sec. 1), Chengdu, Sichuan 610016, People's Republic of China. TEL 22946-36.

020   US   ISSN 0732-5452
Z732.K37
KENTUCKY LIBRARIES. 1933. q. $18 for non-members (foreign $50). Kentucky Library Association, 1501 Twilight Trail, Frankfort, KY 40601. TEL 502-223-5322. adv.; bk.rev.; circ. 1,200. (also avail. in microform from UMI; reprint service avail. from UMI) Indexed: Lib.Lit.
—BLDSC shelfmark: 5089.646000.
  Formerly: K L A Bulletin (ISSN 0022-734X)
  Description: Keeps readers and members of the profession informed of new developments and thinking in the broad areas of librarianship and information science.

020   KE   ISSN 0075-5923
KENYA. NATIONAL LIBRARY SERVICE BOARD. ANNUAL AND AUDIT REPORT. 1967. a. available on exchange. National Library Services, P.O. Box 30573, Nairobi, Kenya. circ. 1,000.

020   US   ISSN 0277-0792
TS519
KEYNOTES (NEW ORLEANS). 1966. irreg. free to qualifed personnel. New Orleans Public Library, 219 Loyola Ave., New Orleans, LA 70140. TEL 504-596-2619. Ed. Germaine Age. circ. 200 (controlled).

KIDSTUFF. see CHILDREN AND YOUTH — For

020   FI   ISSN 0023-1843
Z673
KIRJASTOLEHTI. (Text in Finnish; summaries in English and Swedish) 1908. m. FIM 260. Suomen Kirjastoseura - Finnish Library Association, Museokatu 18 A 5, 00100 Helsinki 10, Finland. FAX 358-0-441345. Ed. Heleena Loennroth. adv.; bk.rev.; bibl.; illus.; stat.; index; circ. 7,015 (controlled). Indexed: Lib.Lit., LISA.

020   GW   ISSN 0232-346X
KLEINE NATURWISSENSCHAFTLICHE BIBLIOTHEK. 1962-1991. a. B.G. Teubner Verlagsgesellschaft mbH, Sternwartenstr. 8, 7010 Leipzig, Germany. TEL 293158.

020 943.7   CS   ISSN 0139-5335
KNIHOVNA. 1957. irreg. Statni Pedagogicke Nakladatelstvi, Ostrovni 30, 113 01 Prague 1, Czechoslovakia. (Subscr. to: c/o Dr. Blechova, Statni Knihovna CSR, Klementinum c.190, 110 00 Prague 1, Czechoslovakia)
—BLDSC shelfmark: 5099.900000.

020   CS   ISSN 0075-6369
KNIZNICNY ZBORNIK. (Text in Slovak; summaries in English, German and Russian) 1957. a. price varies. Matica Slovenska, Slovenska Narodna Kniznica, Ul. L. Novomeskeho 32, 036 52 Martin, Czechoslovakia. TEL 0842-313-71. FAX 0842-324-54. TELEX 075 331. Ed. Margita Buocikova. bk.rev.

020 010   XV   ISSN 0023-2424
Z671
KNJIZNICA; glasilo Zveze Bibliotekarskih Drustev Slovenije. (Text in Slovenian; summaries in English) 1957. q. $20. Zveza Bibliotekarskih Drustev Slovenije, Turjaska 1, Ljubljana, Slovenia. TEL 061-150-131. (Co-sponsors: Ministrstvo za Kulturo; Ministrstvo za Znanost in Tehnologijo) Ed. Jelka Gazvoda. adv.; bk.rev.; bibl.; circ. 1,300. Indexed: LISA.
●Also available on CD-ROM.

020   XV   ISSN 0353-9237
KNJIZNICARSKE NOVICE. 1975. m. Narodna in Univerzitetna Knjiznica, Turjaska 1, 61001 Ljubljana, Slovenia. TEL 061-150-141. FAX 38-611-150-134. TELEX 32285 NUK-LJB-SLO.
  Former titles (until 1991): Obvesila Republiske Maticne Sluzbe (ISSN 0350-3577); (until 1975): Obvestila Republiske Maticne Knniznice.

020   GW   ISSN 0721-7587
KOELNER ARBEITEN ZUM BIBLIOTHEKS- UND DOKUMENTATIONSWESEN. 1981. irreg., no.13, 1989. price varies. (Fachhochschule fuer Bibliotheks- und Dokumentationswesen in Koeln) Greven Verlag Koeln GmbH, Neue Weyerstr. 1-3, 5000 Cologne 1, Germany. TEL 0221-2033-0. FAX 0221-2033-162. circ. 700.
  Continues: Bibliothekar-Lehrinstitut des Landes Nordrhein-Westfalen. Arbeiten aus dem B L I (ISSN 0069-5858) & Bibliothekar-Lehrinstitut des Landes Nordrhein-Westfalen. Bibliographische Hefte (ISSN 0069-5866)

027   JA   ISSN 0027-9153
Z955.T585
KOKURITSU KOKKAI TOSHOKAN GEPPO/NATIONAL DIET LIBRARY. MONTHLY BULLETIN. (Text in Japanese; contents page in English) 1961. m. 3600 Yen. National Diet Library - Kokuritsu Kokkai Toshokan, 1-10-1 Nagata-cho, Chiyoda-ku, Tokyo 100, Japan. TEL 03-3581-2331. TELEX 2225393. bk.rev.; bibl.; charts; illus.; circ. 3,745.

027   JA   ISSN 0385-325X
KOKURITSU KOKKAI TOSHOKAN NENPO/NATIONAL DIET LIBRARY. ANNUAL REPORT. (Text in Japanese) 1948. a. 2742 Yen. National Diet Library - Kokuritsu Kokkai Toshokan, 1-10-1 Nagata-cho, Chiyoda-ku, Tokyo 100, Japan. TEL 03-581-2331. TELEX 2225393. circ. 1,925.

020   JA   ISSN 0385-3306
KOKUTRITSU KOKKAI TOSHOKAN. SANKO SHOSI KENKYU/NATIONAL DIET LIBRARY. REFERENCE SERVICE AND BIBLIOGRAPHY. (Text in Japanese) 1970. s-a. price varies. National Diet Library - Kokutritsu Kokkai Toshokan, 10-1 Nagata-cho 1-chome, Chiyoda-ku, Tokyo 100, Japan. TEL 03-3581-2331. TELEX 2225393. circ. 1,000.

020   DK
Z824.K65
KONGELIGE BIBLIOTEK. MAGASIN. 1986. 4/yr. free. Kongelige Bibliotek, Christians Brygge 8, 1219 Copenhagen K, Denmark. Ed. Lotte Philipson. circ. 3,000.
  Former titles: Kongelige Bibliotek og Universitetsbiblioteket. Magasin (ISSN 0901-7496) & Rigsbibliotekaren. Meddelelser (ISSN 0461-5298)

020   DK   ISSN 0105-3167
KONGELIGE BIBLIOTEK. PUBLIKUMSORIENTERINGER. 1974. irreg., latest no.21, 1990. Kongelige Bibliotek - Royal Library, Christians Brygge 8, DK-1219 Copenhagen K, Denmark.

020   HU   ISSN 0139-1305
KONYV ES KONYVTAR/BOOK AND LIBRARY. (Text in Hungarian; summaries in English, French, German and Russian) 1958. irreg., vol.16, 1991. $5 (effective 1991). Kossuth Lajos Tudomanyegyetem Konyvtara, Egyetem ter 1, 4010 Debrecen, Hungary. TEL 36-52-16-666. FAX 36-52-16-835. TELEX 72200. Ed. Olga Gomba. bk.rev.; illus.; circ. 400. (back issues avail.)
  Description: Concerned with the history of manuscripts, books, literature, libraries and printing offices. Includes articles on bibliography, reading habits and bibliophilism.

020   HU
KONYVTARI FIGYELO. UJ FOLYAM/LIBRARY REVIEW. NEW SERIES. (Text in Hungarian; summaries in English, German) 1955. q. 500 Ft.($24) or exchange basis. Orszagos Szechenyi Konyvtar, Konyvtartudomanyi es Modszertani Kozpont - Centre for Library Science and Methodology at the National Szechenyi Library, Budavari Palota F epulet, 1827 Budapest, Hungary. TEL 1750-686. TELEX 224226 BIBLN H. Ed. Ferenc Szente. bk.rev.; index; circ. 1,350. Indexed: Hung.Lib.& Info.Sci.Abstr., Lib.Sci.Abstr., LISA, Ref.Zh.
  Former titles (until 1990): Konyvtari Figyelo (ISSN 0023-3773); (until 1957): Konyvtari Tajekoztato (ISSN 0200-0202)
  Description: Contains essays related to the theory of librarianship and information science, a rich abstracting feature and review articles.

020   HU   ISSN 0865-1329
KONYVTARI LEVELEZO/LIBRARY POSTCARD. m. 300 Ft. or exchange basis. Orszagos Szechenyi Konyvtar, Konyvtartudomanyi es Modszertani Kospont - National Szechenyi Library, Center for Library Science and Methodology, Budavari Palota Fepulet, 1827 Budapest, Hungary. TEL 175-7533. TELEX 224226 BIBLN H. Ed. Gyula Gero. circ. 900.
—BLDSC shelfmark: 5113.242000.
  Supersedes (in 1989): Konyvtari Expressz (ISSN 0239-1333)
  Description: Contains general interest items for librarians.

023   HU
KONYVTAROS. 1951. m. $25. Frangepan u. 50-56, 1135 Budapest, Hungary. TEL 111-3279. Ed. Laszlo Bereczky. circ. 6,000. Indexed: Hung.Lib.& Info.Sci.Abstr.

020   DK   ISSN 0902-7270
KORT SAGT. 1987. 12/yr. DKK 420($55) Danmarks Biblioteksforenings Forlag - Danish Library Association Publishing, Trekronergade 15, DK-2500 Valby, Denmark. FAX 45-36-30-80-80. Ed.Bd. adv.; circ. 2,500.
  Description: Newsletter on library and information work, mainly in Denmark.

020   PL
KSIAZNICA SLASKA. 1956. irreg. free. Biblioteka Slaska, Ul. Francuska 12, 40-956 Katowice, Poland. TEL 48-32-156-49-53. TELEX 0312534 BSK PL. bk.rev.; bibl.; cum.index every 5 yrs.; circ. 350.
  Formerly (until 1980): Biblioteka Slaska. Biuletyn Informacyjny.

026   KO   ISSN 0027-8572
KUKHOE TOSOGWANBO/NATIONAL ASSEMBLY LIBRARY REVIEW. Variant spelling: Kuk Hoe Do So Kwan Bo. (Text in Korean) 1964. bi-m. free. National Assembly Library - Kukhoe Tosogwan, 1 Yoido-dong, Seoul, S. Korea. FAX 02-788-4194. bk.rev.; bibl.; charts; illus.; stat.; index; circ. 1,700. (processed)

026   UK
L A I G NEWS. irreg. membership. Library Association, Industrial Group, Bacon & Woodrow, St. Olaf House, London Bridge City, London SE1 2PE, England. TEL 071-357-7171. FAX 071-378-8428. TELEX 825477. Ed. J.P. Heath. bk.rev.; circ. 1,450.
  Formerly (until 1988): Library Association. Industrial Group Newsletter.

020   AT   ISSN 0047-3774
                              CODEN: IBLEAS
L A S I E. 1970. bi-m. Aus.$65 to institutional members. (Library Automated Systems Information Exchange) L A S I E Australia Company Ltd., P.O. Box K446, Haymarket, N.S.W. 2000, Australia. Ed. Carmel Maguire. adv.; bk.rev.; index; circ. 400. (also avail. in microfiche) Indexed: Aus.Educ.Ind., Aus.P.A.I.S., Lib.Lit., LISA, Sci.Abstr.
—BLDSC shelfmark: 5156.688000.

020   US
L A S L NEWSLETTER. 1980. 3/yr. membership. (Louisiana Association of School Librarians) Louisiana Library Association, Box 3058, Baton Rouge, LA 70821. TEL 504-342-4928. Ed. Terry Thibodeaux. circ. 500. (back issues avail.; back issues avail. from UMI)

020 398   US   ISSN 0736-4903
ML156.4.F5
L C FOLK ARCHIVE FINDING AID. 1983. irreg. free. U.S. Library of Congress, Archive of Folk Culture, American Folklife Center, 10 First St., S.E., Washington, DC 20540. TEL 202-707-5510. Ed. Joseph C. Hickerson. circ. 2,000.

020 398   US   ISSN 0736-4911
Z5982
L C FOLK ARCHIVE REFERENCE AID. irreg. free. U.S. Library of Congress, Archive of Folk Culture, 10 First St., S.E., Washington, DC 20540. TEL 202-707-5510. Ed. Joseph C. Hickerson. circ. 2,000.

900 020   US   ISSN 0737-4984
L H R T NEWSLETTER. 1979. s-a. membership. American Library Association, Library History Round Table, 50 E. Huron St., Chicago, IL 60611. TEL 312-280-2156. FAX 312-440-9374. circ. 390.
  Formerly: A L H R T Newsletter.

LIBRARY AND INFORMATION SCIENCES

020 US ISSN 0024-6867
Z673
L L A BULLETIN. 1937. q. $15 for out-of-state non-members. Louisiana Library Association, Box 3058, Baton Rouge, LA 70821. Ed. Florence Jumonville. adv.; bk.rev.; illus.; cum.index: 1937-1968; circ. 1,600. (also avail. in microfilm from UMI; reprint service avail. from UMI) **Indexed:** Lib.Lit.
—BLDSC shelfmark: 5285.548000.
Description: Articles concerning libraries, poetry, reviews and Association news.

LABORATORY INFORMATION MANAGEMENT. see MEDICAL SCIENCES — Experimental Medicine, Laboratory Technique

023 NR ISSN 0047-3901
LAGOS LIBRARIAN. 1966. irreg., vol.12, no.1 & 2, 1985. $20. Nigerian Library Association, Lagos Division, c/o University Library, University of Lagos, Yaba, Lagos, Nigeria. Ed. S.O. Olanlokun. adv.; bk.rev.; circ. 400.

020 340 GW ISSN 0175-6524
LANSKY: BIBLIOTHEKSRECHTLICHE VORSCHRIFTEN. irreg., 9th, 1991. DM.50. Vittorio Klostermann, Frauenlobstr. 22, Postfach 900601, 6000 Frankfurt a.M. 90, Germany. TEL 069-774011. FAX 069-708038.

027.7 US ISSN 0047-4053
LANTERN'S CORE. 1970. m. free. Northwestern University Library, Staff Association, 1935 Sheridan Rd., Evanston, IL 60208. TEL 312-491-7633. FAX 312-491-5685. Ed.Bd. bk.rev.; bibl.; stat.; circ. 650 (controlled).

LAURENTIUS. see PUBLISHING AND BOOK TRADE

LAURENTIUS SONDERHEFTE. see PUBLISHING AND BOOK TRADE

026 340 UK ISSN 0023-9275
Z675.L2 CODEN: LALIE2
LAW LIBRARIAN. 1970. 4/yr. £22 to non-members. Sweet & Maxwell, South Quay Plaza, 8th Fl., 183 Marsh Wall, London E14 9FT, England. TEL 071-538-8686. FAX 071-538-9508. (Dist. in U.S. & Canada by: Carswell Co. Ltd., 233 Midland Ave., Agincourt, Ont., Canada) Ed. Christine Miskin. adv.; bk.rev.; bibl.; cum.index. **Indexed:** C.L.I., L.R.I., Leg.Cont., Leg.Per., LHTN, Lib.Lit.
—BLDSC shelfmark: 5161.395000.

LAW LIBRARIAN'S BULLETIN BOARD. see LAW

026 US
LAW LIBRARY ASSOCIATION OF MARYLAND NEWS. 1981. q. $20. Law Library Association of Maryland, c/o Baltimore Bar Library, 618 Mitchell Courthouse, Baltimore, MD 21202. FAX 301-685-4791. (Subscr. to: Anne Deinlein c/o Piper & Marbury, 36 S. Charles St., Baltimore, MD 21201) Ed. Maxine Grosshans. adv.; circ. 130.
Description: Announcements of events and publication information pertaining to legal research management and documentation in the state.

LAW LIBRARY INFORMATION REPORTS. see LAW

026 340 US ISSN 0023-9283
K12
LAW LIBRARY JOURNAL. 1908. q. $50 (foreign $55). American Association of Law Libraries, 53 W. Jackson Blvd., Ste. 940, Chicago, IL 60604. TEL 312-939-4764. FAX 312-431-1097. Ed. Richard A. Dammer. adv.; bk.rev.; bibl.; stat.; index, cum.index: vols.1-50, 1908-1957; circ. 5,000. (reprint service avail. from RRI) **Indexed:** C.I.S. Abstr., C.L.I., Curr.Cont., L.R.I., Leg.Info.Manage.Ind., Leg.Per., LHTN, Lib.Lit., SSCI.
—BLDSC shelfmark: 5161.400000.

020 US
LAWDOCS. 1986. q. free. Department of Libraries, 200 N.E. 18th St., Oklahoma City, OK 73105-3298. TEL 405-521-2502. FAX 405-525-7804. Ed. Steve Beleu. circ. 40.

020 UK ISSN 0023-9542
Z671
AN LEABHARLANN/IRISH LIBRARY. 1972. q. £12. Library Association of Ireland and the Library Association, Northern Ireland Branch, c/o Main Library, Queen's University of Belfast, Belfast BT7 1NN, N. Ireland. TEL 0232-323340. FAX 0232-247895. Eds. N. Butterwick, L. Ronayne. adv.; bk.rev.; charts; illus.; index; circ. 1,000. **Indexed:** Lib.Lit., Lib.Sci.Abstr., So.Pac.Per.Ind.
—BLDSC shelfmark: 4572.840000.
Supersedes: Northern Ireland Libraries (ISSN 0029-3113)

020 US ISSN 0170-8643
LECTURE NOTES IN CONTROL AND INFORMATION SCIENCES. 1978. irreg. price varies. Springer-Verlag, 175 Fifth Ave., New York, NY 10010. TEL 212-460-1500. (Also Berlin, Heidelberg, Tokyo and Vienna) Eds. A.V. Balakrishnan, M. Thoma. (report service avail. from ISI) **Indexed:** CAD CAM Abstr., Compumath.

LEGAL INFORMATION ALERT; what's new in legal publications, databases and research techniques. see LAW — Abstracting, Bibliographies, Statistics

LEGAL INFORMATION MANAGEMENT INDEX. see LAW — Abstracting, Bibliographies, Statistics

LEGAL INFORMATION MANAGEMENT REPORTS. see LAW

020 340 US ISSN 0270-319X
K12 CODEN: LRSQD9
LEGAL REFERENCE SERVICES QUARTERLY. 1981. q. $36 to individuals; institutions $90. Haworth Press, Inc., 10 Alice St., Binghamton, NY 13904. TEL 800-342-9678. FAX 607-722-1424. TELEX 4932599. Ed. Robert C. Berring. adv.; bk.rev.; bibl.; charts; illus.; circ. 915. (also avail. in microfiche from HAW; back issues avail.; reprint service avail. from HAW) **Indexed:** C.L.I., Comput.& Info.Sys., Leg.Info.Manage.Ind., Leg.Per., Lib.Lit., LISA, Sci.Abstr.
—BLDSC shelfmark: 5181.377000.
Description: Directed towards the working reference librarian involved with legal research materials.
Refereed Serial

027 BW ISSN 0130-9218
Z2514.W5
LETOPIS' PECHATI B.S.S.R.. 1924. m. 50 Rub. Gosudarstvennaya Knizhnaya Palata B.S.S.R., Prospect Masherova, 11, 220600 Minsk, Byelarus. Ed. K.V. Bazarboyeva. circ. 380.
—BLDSC shelfmark: 0097.485000.

020.6 CN ISSN 0705-4890
LETTER OF THE L A A. 5/yr. membership. Library Association of Alberta, Box 64197, 5512-4 St. N.W., Calgary, Alta. T3K 6J1, Canada. TEL 403-228-0898. FAX 403-228-0929. Ed. Karen Labuik. circ. 500.

020 US
LETTER TO LIBRARIES. 1911-1988 (vol.77, no.3). 10/yr. $24. Oregon State Library, Salem, OR 97310-0640. TEL 503-378-4367. Ed. Wesley A. Doak. circ. 750. (processed)
Supersedes: Watermark (ISSN 0194-2999); Which superseded (in 1976): Letter to Libraries (ISSN 0024-1296)
Description: Information on statewide library activities and national library news for librarians.

020 266 200 UK ISSN 0308-5473
LIBRARIANS' CHRISTIAN FELLOWSHIP NEWSLETTER. 1974. 3/yr. £7. Librarians' Christian Fellowship, 34 Thurlestone Ave., Seven Kings, Ilford, Essex IG3 9DU, England. TEL 081-871 6351. Ed. Graham Hedges. adv.; bk.rev.; abstr.; circ. 450. (back issues avail.)
Description: Covers issues in librarianship from a Christian viewpoint.

020 UK
LIBRARIAN'S HANDBOOK. irreg., vol.2, 1980. price varies. Library Association Publishing Ltd., 7 Ridgmount St., London WC1E 7AE, England. Ed. L.J. Taylor.

020 070.5 US ISSN 0739-0297
LIBRARIAN'S WORLD. 1970. q. $15 (foreign $20). Evangelical Church Library Association, Box 353, Glen Ellyn, IL 60138. TEL 312-668-0519. Ed. Nancy Dick. adv.; bk.rev.; circ. 689. (back issues avail.)
Description: Presents promotional ideas for church librarians.

020 970 US ISSN 0894-8631
Z671
LIBRARIES & CULTURE. 1966. q. $24 to individuals; institutions $36. University of Texas Press, Box 7819, Austin, TX 78713. TEL 512-471-3821. Ed. Donald G. Davis, Jr. adv.; bk.rev.; abstr.; bibl.; charts; illus.; stat.; index, cum.index: 1966-1976; circ. 900. (also avail. in microfilm from UMI; reprint service avail. from UMI) **Indexed:** Amer.Bibl.Slavic & E.Eur.Stud., Amer.Hist.& Life, Bk.Rev.Ind. (1966-), CALL, Child.Bk.Rev.Ind. (1966-), Hist.Abstr., Lib.Lit., LISA, M.L.A., SSCI.
—BLDSC shelfmark: 5186.892520.
Former titles: Journal of Library History, Philosophy and Comparative Librarianship (ISSN 0275-3650); Journal of Library History. State Library History Bibliography Series.
Description: Explores collections of graphic records and their creators and users in the context of cultural history.

LIBRARIES DIRECTORY. see BUSINESS AND ECONOMICS — Trade And Industrial Directories

LIBRARIES IN THE UNITED KINGDOM & THE REPUBLIC OF IRELAND. see BUSINESS AND ECONOMICS — Trade And Industrial Directories

LIBRARIES OF MAINE; DIRECTORY AND STATISTICS. see BUSINESS AND ECONOMICS — Trade And Industrial Directories

020 JA
LIBRARIES TODAY/GENDAI NO TOSHOKAN. (Text in Japanese) 1963. q. 6000 Yen. Japan Library Association - Nihon Toshokan Kyokai, 1-1-10 Taishido, Setagaya-ku, Tokyo 154, Japan. FAX 81-3-3421-7588. Ed. Mieko Nagakura. bk.rev.; abstr.; charts; circ. 5,000.
Formerly: Contemporary Library Trends (ISSN 0016-6332)

027.4 US
LIBRARIES UNLIMITED NEWSLETTER. 1964. irreg. membership. Gloucester City Library, Gloucester City, NJ 08030. TEL 609-456-4181. Ed. Elizabeth Egan. bk.rev.; circ. 150.
Description: Serves South Jersey libraries. Provides information for library development and innovation.

020 UK ISSN 0024-2160
Z671
LIBRARY; a quarterly journal of bibliography. 1899. q. £50($104) (Bibliographical Society) Oxford University Press, Oxford Journals, Pinkhill House, Southfield Road, Eynsham, Oxford OX8 1JJ, England. TEL 0865-882283. FAX 0865-882890. TELEX 837330 OXPRES G. Ed. Mervyn Jannetta. adv.; bk.rev.; bibl.; illus.; index; circ. 500. (also avail. in microform) **Indexed:** Artbibl.Mod., Bk.Rev.Ind. (1967-), Child.Bk.Rev.Ind. (1967-), Curr.Cont., Hist.Abstr., Ind.Bk.Rev.Hum., Lib.Lit., Lib.Sci.Abstr., M.L.A., RILA.
—BLDSC shelfmark: 5186.950000.
Description: Official journal of the Bibliographical Society for the history of books, both manuscript and printed, covering the role of books in history.

LIBRARY AND INFORMATION SCIENCES 2769

020   US   ISSN 0364-6408
Z689   CODEN: LAPTDK
LIBRARY ACQUISITIONS: PRACTICE AND THEORY. 1977. 4/yr. £70 (effective 1992). Pergamon Press, Inc., Journals Division, 660 White Plains Rd., Tarrytown, NY 10591-5153. TEL 914-524-9200. FAX 914-333-2444. (And: Headington Hill Hall, Oxford OX3 0BW, England. TEL 0865-794141) Ed. Scott R. Bullard. adv.; circ. 5,300. (also avail. in microform from MIM,UMI; back issues avail.)
Indexed: Comput.& Info.Sys., Curr.Cont., Leg.Info.Manage.Ind., LHTN, Lib.Lit., LISA, Sci.Abstr., SSCI.
—BLDSC shelfmark: 5188.130000.
   Description: A forum for the exchange of ideas and experiences among members of library acquisitions, collections management and bookselling communities worldwide. Emphasizes practical experience as well as theoretical foundations of the profession.
Refereed Serial

020   US   ISSN 0888-4463
Z678
LIBRARY ADMINISTRATION AND MANAGEMENT. 1975. q. $45 (foreign $55). American Library Association, Library Administration and Management Association, 50 E. Huron St., Chicago, IL 60611-2795. TEL 312-944-6780. FAX 312-440-9374. Ed. Fred Heath. adv.; circ. 6,000. (also avail. in microform from UMI; back issues avail.; reprint service avail. from UMI) **Indexed:** C.I.J.E., Lib.Lit.
—BLDSC shelfmark: 5188.158000.
   Former titles (until 1986): L A M A Newsletter (Library Administration and Management Association) (ISSN 0193-0451); L A D Newsletter (Library Administration Division) (ISSN 0098-7972)

020   US   ISSN 0746-6129
LIBRARY ADMINISTRATOR'S DIGEST. 1965. m. (except Jul. & Aug.). $36. Administrator's Digest, Inc., Box 993, S. San Francisco, CA 94080. TEL 415-573-5474. Ed. Robert S. Alvarez. (also avail. in microfilm from UMI; reprint service avail. from UMI)
   Formerly (until 1983): Administrator's Digest (ISSN 0001-8422)

020   US   ISSN 0196-0075
Z679.6
LIBRARY & ARCHIVAL SECURITY. 1975. q. $36 to individuals; institutions $90. Haworth Press, Inc., 10 Alice St., Binghamton, NY 13904. TEL 800-342-9678. FAX 607-722-1424. TELEX 4932599. Eds. Alan Jay Lincoln, Carol Zall Lincoln. adv.; bk.rev.; abstr.; bibl.; index. (also avail. in microfiche from HAW; back issues avail.; reprint service avail. from HAW) **Indexed:** Comput.& Info.Sys., Inform.Sci.Abstr., Leg.Info.Manage.Ind., Lib.Lit., LISA.
—BLDSC shelfmark: 5188.250000.
   Formerly (until 1979): Library Security Newsletter (ISSN 0094-0216)
   Description: Provides information to librarians, scholars, and researchers concerned with security planning, policies, procedures, and strategies for libraries and archives.
Refereed Serial

020   UK
LIBRARY AND INFORMATION ACTIVISTS RECORD. 1987. 4/yr. £5. Hector & Ruffle Ltd., 11 Eaton Court, Eaton Road, Sutton, Surrey SM2 5DZ, England. circ. 750.
   Description: Covers library administration and operation, information science, and computer applications.

020.6   UK   ISSN 0957-7912
LIBRARY AND INFORMATION ASSISTANT. 1988. s-a. £7.50. Association for the Education and Training of Library Technicians and Assistants, c/o Donald Steele, Ed., Telford College, Crewe Toll, Edinburgh EH4 2NZ, Scotland. FAX 031-343-1218. adv.; bk.rev.; circ. 400.
   Description: Articles and news columns cover items of interest to junior library staff, with an emphasis on education, training and career enhancement.

020   UK
LIBRARY AND INFORMATION NEWS. 1972. m. £44. Wm. Dawson & Sons Ltd., Cannon House, Park Farm Rd., Folkestone CT19 5EE, England. TEL 0303-850101. FAX 0303-850440. TELEX 96392. Ed. John Cowley. adv.; bk.rev.; circ. 1,500.
   Description: News and articles about library and information service developments as well as those organizations who supply libraries with goods or services.

020   UK   ISSN 0141-6561
LIBRARY AND INFORMATION RESEARCH NEWS. 1978. 3/yr. £10 to individuals; institutions £25 (foreign £30). c/o British Library, Research and Development Dept., 2 Sheraton St., London W1V 4Bh, England. TEL 071-323-7049. FAX 071-323-7251. (Dist. by: Library Document Supply Centre, Boston Spa, Wetherby, W. Yorkshire LS23 7BQ) Ed. Ros Cotton. adv.; bk.rev.; circ. 350. **Indexed:** LISA.
—BLDSC shelfmark: 5188.550000.
   Description: Articles, news and reviews relating to research in librarianship and information science.

020   JA   ISSN 0373-4447
Z671   CODEN: LIFSBL
LIBRARY AND INFORMATION SCIENCE. (Text in English and Japanese) 1963. a. $20. Mita Society for Library and Information Science - Mita Toshokan Joho Gakkai, c/o Keio University, 2-15-45 Mita, Minato-ku, Tokyo 108, Japan. TEL 03-798-7480. bk.rev.; circ. 1,650. **Indexed:** Curr.Cont., Lib.Lit., Lib.Sci.Abstr., SSCI.
—BLDSC shelfmark: 5188.600000.

020   US   ISSN 0740-8188
Z671   CODEN: LISRDH
LIBRARY & INFORMATION SCIENCE RESEARCH; an international journal. 1979. q. $39.50 to individuals; institutions $85. Ablex Publishing Corporation, 355 Chestnut St., Norwood, NJ 07648. TEL 201-767-8450. FAX 201-767-6717. TELEX 135-393. Ed. Jane Robbins. adv.; bk.rev.; circ. 650. (back issues avail.; reprint service avail. from ISI) **Indexed:** ASCA, C.I.J.E., Curr.Cont., Lang.& Lang.Behav.Abstr., Lib.Lit., LISA, Res.High.Educ.Abstr., Sociol.Abstr.
   Formerly (until 1983): Library Research (ISSN 0164-0763)

020   AT
LIBRARY AND INFORMATION SERVICE OF WESTERN AUSTRALIA. NEWSLETTER. 1955. m. Aus.$20. Library and Information Service of Western Australia, Alexander Library Building, Perth Cultural Centre, Perth, W.A. 6000, Australia. circ. 700. (back issues avail.)
   Formerly: Library Service of Western Australia. Newsletter (ISSN 0159-7477)
   Description: Library service news from public libraries throughout Western Australia.

027.7   UK   ISSN 0144-056X
LIBRARY ASSOCIATION. UNIVERSITY, COLLEGE AND RESEARCH SECTION. NEWSLETTER. 1980. 3/yr. free to qualified personnel. Library Association, University College and Research Section, c/o Mrs. M.A. Watson, Dept. Information & Library Management, Newcastle-upon-Tyne Polytechnic, Newcastle-upon-Tyne NE1 8ST, England. TEL 091-232-6002. FAX 091-235-8572. adv.; bk.rev.; circ. 4,000.
—BLDSC shelfmark: 6108.423400.

020   UK   ISSN 0075-9066
LIBRARY ASSOCIATION. YEARBOOK. 1892. a. price varies. Library Association Publishing Ltd., 7 Ridgmount St., London WC1E 7AE, England. TEL 071-636-7543. FAX 071-636-3627. TELEX 21897.
—BLDSC shelfmark: 9389.000000.

020   CN
LIBRARY ASSOCIATION OF ALBERTA. NEWSLETTER. 1969. 5/yr. membership. Library Association of Alberta, Box 64197, 5512-4 St. N.W., Calgary, Alta. T3K 6J1, Canada. TEL 403-228-0898. FAX 403-228-0929. bk.rev.; circ. 700.
   Formerly: Library Association of Alberta. Occasional Papers (ISSN 0075-904X)

020.6   BB
LIBRARY ASSOCIATION OF BARBADOS. BULLETIN. 1968. irreg., no.12, 1985. $5. Library Association of Barbados, P.O. Box 827E, Bridgetown, Barbados, W.I.

020   CH   ISSN 0254-4784
LIBRARY ASSOCIATION OF CHINA. NEWSLETTER. 1954. a. NT.$400($15) Library Association of China, c/o National Central Library, 20 Chung Shan S. Rd., Taipei, Taiwan 10040, Republic of China. FAX 02-311-0155. Ed. Teresa Wang Chang. adv.; bk.rev.; circ. 2,000. Key Title: Zhongguo Tushuguan Xuehui Huiwu Tongxun.
   Description: Aims to improve the overall effectiveness of libraries and library management. Covers issues in data collection, library automation, calaloging, history and more.

020   TR   ISSN 0521-9590
LIBRARY ASSOCIATION OF TRINIDAD AND TOBAGO. BULLETIN. 1964. a. T.T.$20. Library Association of Trinidad and Tobago, P.O. Box 1275, Port of Spain, Trinidad, W.I. Ed.Bd. adv.; circ. 200.

020   UK   ISSN 0024-2195
Z671
LIBRARY ASSOCIATION RECORD. 1899. 12/yr. £64($157) (foreign £79)(typically set in Jan.). Library Association, 7 Ridgmount St., London WC1E 7AE, England. TEL 071-636 7543. FAX 071-323-6675. TELEX 21897 LALDN-G. Ed. Tony Mason. adv.; bk.rev.; bibl.; index; circ. 26,000. (also avail. in microfilm from UMI; reprint service avail. from KTO) **Indexed:** Bk.Rev.Ind. (1991-), Child.Bk.Rev.Ind. (1991), Child.Lit.Abstr., LHTN, Lib.Lit., LISA, Ref.Sour.
—BLDSC shelfmark: 5189.000000.
   Description: News briefs on current regulatory developments, profiles and feature articles pertaining to the administrative and operational aspects of library and information management, with announcements of conferences and seminars.

020   US   ISSN 0024-2241
Z881
LIBRARY CHRONICLE (AUSTIN). 1944; N.S. 1970. q. $30. University of Texas at Austin, Harry Ransom Humanities Research Center, Box 7219, Austin, TX 78713. TEL 512-471-8944. FAX 512-471-9646. Ed. Dave Oliphant. illus.; circ. 350. (also avail. in microform from UMI; reprint service avail. from UMI; back issues avail.) **Indexed:** Abstr.Engl.Stud., Amer.Hist.& Life, Amer.Hum.Ind., Arts & Hum.Cit.Ind., Curr.Cont., Hist.Abstr.
—BLDSC shelfmark: 5194.700000.

020.6   US   ISSN 0160-922X
Z733
LIBRARY COMPANY OF PHILADELPHIA. ANNUAL REPORT. a. free. Library Company of Philadelphia, 1314 Locust St., Philadelphia, PA 19107. bibl.; illus.; stat.

LIBRARY COMPANY OF PHILADELPHIA. OCCASIONAL MISCELLANY. see *HISTORY — History Of North And South America*

LIBRARY CONSERVATION NEWS. see *CONSERVATION*

020   US   ISSN 0741-4188
LIBRARY CURRENTS; your source for current library information. 1984. m. $42. Practical Perspectives, Inc., Box 202108, Austin, TX 78720-2108. TEL 512-218-8038. Ed. Edward Seidenberg. bk.rev.; circ. 1,000.

020   US   ISSN 0145-5397
Z732.T25
LIBRARY DEVELOPMENTS. 1974. bi-m. free. Texas State Library, Library Development Division, Box 12927, Austin, TX 78711. TEL 512-463-5465. FAX 512-463-5436. Eds. Anne Ramos, Vicky Crosson. circ. 1,000 (controlled).

020   US   ISSN 0269-963X
LIBRARY EQUIPMENT REPORT. 1986. 6/yr. £115($230) Headland Press, One Henry Smith's Terrace, Headland, Cleveland TS24 0PD, England. TEL 0429-231902. FAX 0429-860674.
—BLDSC shelfmark: 5198.685000.

020   CN   ISSN 0838-360X
LIBRARY FOOTNOTES. 1975. q. free. Newfoundland Public Libraries Board, Public Library Services, St. John's, Nfld. A1B 3A3, Canada. TEL 709-737-3966. Ed. Glenda Quinn. circ. 300.
   Former titles (until 1988): Newfoundland and Labrador Provincial Libraries. Newsletter (ISSN 0381-2022); Newfoundland and Labrador Regional Libraries. Newsletter (ISSN 0381-209X)

LIBRARY AND INFORMATION SCIENCES

020　　　　II　　ISSN 0024-2292
Z671
LIBRARY HERALD. (Text in English) 1958. q. Rs.70($25) Delhi Library Association, Box 1270, c/o Hardinge Public Library, Queen's Garden, Delhi 110006, India. Ed.Bd. adv.; abstr.; index; circ. 800. **Indexed:** Lib.Lit., Lib.Sci.Abstr.
　—BLDSC shelfmark: 5198.800000.

020　　　　UK　　ISSN 0024-2306
Z721
LIBRARY HISTORY. 1967. s-a. £11. Library Association, Library History Group, 7 Ridgmount St., London WC1E 7AE, England. Ed. K.A. Manley. adv.; bk.rev.; bibl.illus.; circ. 1,200. **Indexed:** Amer.Hist.& Life, Br.Hum.Ind., Hist.Abstr., Lib.Lit., LISA.
　—BLDSC shelfmark: 5198.915000.

020　　　　II　　ISSN 0378-7508
LIBRARY HISTORY REVIEW. (Text in English) 1974. q. Rs.360($45) (International Agency for Research in Library History) K.K. Roy (Private) Ltd., 55 Gariahat Rd., P.O. Box 10210, Calcutta 700 019, India. Ed. K.K. Roy. adv.; bk.rev.; index; circ. 1,650. **Indexed:** Amer.Hist.& Life, Hist.Abstr.
　—BLDSC shelfmark: 5198.920000.

020　　　　US　　ISSN 0740-736X
Z671
LIBRARY HOTLINE. 1972. w. (except last 2 weeks of yr.). $74 (foreign $91). Cahners Publishing Company (New York), Bowker Magazine Group, Cahners Magazine Division (Subsidiary of: Reed International PLC), Division of Reed Publishing (USA) Inc., 249 W. 17th St., New York, NY 10011. TEL 800-435-0715. FAX 212-242-6987. (Subscr. to: Box 445, Mt. Morris, IL 61054-9893) Ed. Susan S. DiMattia. adv. (looseleaf format; reprint service avail. from UMI)
　—BLDSC shelfmark: 5198.933000.
　Formerly (until 1983): L J - S L J Hot Line (Library Journal - School Library Journal) (ISSN 0000-0078)
　Description: Newsletter summarizing developments affecting libraries and librarians. Includes job postings.

027　　　　US　　ISSN 0197-5587
LIBRARY IMAGINATION PAPER. 1979. q. $26. Carol Bryan Imagines, 1000 Byus Dr., Charleston, WV 25311. TEL 304-345-2378. Ed. Carol Bryan. circ. 2,400. (tabloid format; back issues avail.)
　Description: Library promotional clip art articles, tips and help on public relations topics by field experts.

020　　　　US　　ISSN 0196-1977
LIBRARY INSIGHTS, PROMOTION & PROGRAMS. Short title: L I P P. 1976. 6/yr. $20 (Canada $25; elsewhere $26). Deja Vu, Box 431, LaGrange, IL 60525. Eds. Ann Montgomery, Dawn Heller. circ. 1,000.
　Description: Focuses on the varied aspects of public relations in library work, created by two practicing librarians.

027　　　　US　　ISSN 0734-3035
Z675.U5
LIBRARY ISSUES; briefings for faculty and administrators. bi-m. $35. Mountainside Publishing, Inc., 321 S. Main St., Box 8330, Ann Arbor, MI 48107. TEL 313-662-3925. FAX 313-662-4450. Ed. Richard M. Dougherty.
　Description: In layman's terms, explains academic library problems as they relate to faculty, administrators and the parent institution.

020　　　　US　　ISSN 0363-0277
Z671
LIBRARY JOURNAL. 1876. 20/yr. $74 (Canada $99; elsewhere $130). Cahners Publishing Company (New York), Bowker Magazine Group, Cahners Magazine Division (Subsidiary of: Reed International PLC), Division of Reed Publishing (USA) Inc., 249 W. 17th St., New York, NY 10011. TEL 800-669-1002. FAX 212-242-6987. (Subscr. to: Box 1977, Marion, OH 43305-1977) Ed. John N. Berry. adv.; bk.rev.; bibl.; illus.; index; circ. 24,145. (also avail. in microfilm from RPI; reprint service avail. from UMI) **Indexed:** Acad.Ind., Access (1980-), Bk.Rev.Dig., Bk.Rev.Ind. (1965-), Bus.Ind., C.I.J.E., Chic.Per.Ind., Child.Bk.Rev.Ind. (1965-), Curr.Cont., Educ.Ind., Gard.Lit. (1992-), Hlth.Ind., Leg.Info.Manage.Ind., LHTN, Lib.Lit., Lib.Sci.Abstr., Mag.Ind, Mid.East: Abstr.& Ind., P.A.I.S., Peace Res.Abstr., Pers.Lit., PMR, PROMT, Ref.Sour., Rehabil.Lit., So.Pac.Per.Ind., SRI, SSCI, Tel.Abstr., Tr.& Indus.Ind.
　—BLDSC shelfmark: 5199.000000.
　Description: News and events, articles identifying trends, and reviews of books and audiovisual materials.

020.6　　　　JA　　ISSN 0385-4000
Z671
LIBRARY JOURNAL/TOSHOKAN ZASSHI. (Text in Japanese) 1907. m. 12000 Yen. Japan Library Association - Nihon Toshokan Kyokai, 1-1-10 Taishido, Setagaya-ku, Tokyo 154, Japan. FAX 81-3-3421-7588.
　—BLDSC shelfmark: 5199.200000.

020　　　　NZ　　ISSN 0110-4373
Z673.N683
LIBRARY LIFE. 1956. 11/yr. NZ.$55 (effective 1992). New Zealand Library Association, P.O. Box 12-212, Wellington 1, New Zealand. TEL 04-473-5834. FAX 04-499-1480. adv.; circ. 2,200. (looseleaf format; also avail. in processed)
　Supersedes (in 1977): N Z L A Newsletter (ISSN 0027-7215)

026　　　　CN
LIBRARY LINES. 1975. 3/yr. membership. Church Library Association of Ontario, 1202 York Mills Rd., No. 1104, Don Mills, Ont. M3A 1Y2, Canada. TEL 416-449-4213. Ed. Emma Austin. bk.rev.; circ. 200.
　Description: News for church librarians.

020　　　　II
LIBRARY LITERATURE IN INDIA SERIES. no.2, 1975. irreg. price varies. Library Literature House, Chandigarh, India. illus.

020　　　　UK　　ISSN 0143-5124
Z678
LIBRARY MANAGEMENT. 1976. 6/yr. $1649.95. M C B University Press Ltd., 62 Toller Ln., Bradford, W. Yorks BD8 9BY, England. TEL 0274 499821. FAX 547143. TELEX 51317 MCBUNI G. Ed. Ken Bakewell. (reprint service avail. from SWZ) **Indexed:** ABI Inform., Anbar, Curr.Cont.
　—BLDSC shelfmark: 5200.415000.
　Formerly: Library Research Occasional Paper (ISSN 0309-2232)
　Description: Monitors the dynamic new techniques which are pushing forward the frontiers of the profession.

025　　　　US　　ISSN 0271-3306
Z675.A2
LIBRARY MANAGEMENT QUARTERLY. 1977. q. $25 (foreign $35). Special Libraries Association, Library Management Division, c/o Susan Warner, Ed., Wang Laboratories, One Industrial Ave, Lowell, MA 01851. TEL 508-967-6366. (Subscr. to: Jean Scanlan, Price Waterhouse, 160 Federal St., Boston, MA 02110. TEL 617-439-7412) adv.; bk.rev.; circ. 1,800.
　—BLDSC shelfmark: 5200.430000.
　Formerly (until 1985): Library Management Bulletin.

020　　　　US
LIBRARY MATERIALS GUIDE. s-a. $20 per no. Christian Schools International, 3350 E. Paris Ave., S.E., Grand Rapids, MI 49512. TEL 616-957-1070. Ed. Mark Boer. bk.rev.; circ. 400.
　Description: Includes reviews of approximately 500 new books for school libraries.

027.4　　　　US
LIBRARY MATTERS. 1969. q. free. Queens Borough Public Library, 89-11 Merrick Blvd., Jamaica, NY 11432. TEL 718-990-0705. FAX 718-291-8936. Ed. Himi Karen. charts; illus.; circ. 15,000.
　Formerly (until 1985): Queens Borough Public Library News.
　Description: Includes photos, news stories about library collections, services, and events.

020　　　　US　　ISSN 1054-9676
Z671
LIBRARY MOSAICS. 1989. bi-m. $20. Yenor, Inc., P.O. Box 5171, Culver City, CA 90231. TEL 213-410-1573. Ed Ed Martinez. adv.; bk.rev.
　Description: Focuses on library, media and information center support staff issues, trends and developments.

021.7　　　　US
LIBRARY NEWS (ATLANTA). m. Atlanta Public Library, One Margaret Mitchell Square, Atlanta, GA 30303. **Indexed:** Bibl.Cart.

020　　　　US
LIBRARY NEWS (CHICAGO). q. Mosby - Year Book, Inc., Continuity Division, 200 N. LaSalle St., Chicago, IL 60601. TEL 800-622-5410. (reprint service avail.)

020　579　　　　US
LIBRARY NEWS FOR ZOOS AND AQUARIUMS. 1982. s-a. free. Indianapolis Zoological Society, Inc., 1200 W. Washington St., Indianapolis, IA 46222. TEL 317-630-2040. FAX 317-630-5153. Ed. Suzanne K. Braun. bk.rev.; circ. 350. (back issues avail.)
　Description: Provides information for operation of zoo or aquarium library.

020　　　　US　　ISSN 0895-1179
Z711.92.A32
LIBRARY OUTREACH REPORTER. 1987. 6/yr. $21. Library Outreach Reporter, 148 Liberty St., Fords, NJ 08863-2042. TEL 908-738-5183. Ed. Allan M. Kleiman. adv.; bk.rev.; index; circ. 1,000. (back issues avail.)
　Description: Professional publication that provides information, analysis and evaluation of issues in Outreach special services.

025　　　　US　　ISSN 0164-9566
LIBRARY P R NEWS. 1978. bi-m. $26.95 in U.S.; Canada $28.95; elsewhere $37.95. (Library Educational Institute, Inc.) L E I, Inc., Rd. 1, Box 219, New Albany, PA 18833. TEL 717-746-1842. Ed. Phillip J. Bradbury. bk.rev.; circ. 5,000.
　Incorporates: Tips from C.L.I.P. (Coordinated Library Information Program).
　Description: For public, school, and academic libraries. Devoted to library public relations, programming, promotion exhibits and graphic arts.

023　　　　US　　ISSN 0891-2742
Z681.5
LIBRARY PERSONNEL NEWS. 1987. 6/yr. $20. American Library Association, Office for Library Personnel Resources, 50 E. Huron St., Chicago, IL 60611-2795. TEL 312-944-6780. FAX 312-280-3256. Eds. Margaret Myers, Jeniece Guy. circ. 1,000. (back issues avail.) **Indexed:** Lib.Lit.
　Description: Provides information for general adminstrative personnel, trends, practices, and legislative news.

020　　　　US
LIBRARY POINTES. 1982. q. free. Grosse Pointe Public Library, 10 Kercheval Ave., Grosse Pointe, MI 48236. TEL 313-343-2074. Eds. Helen Leonard, Carol Evans.
　Formerly (until 1984): Word.

020　　　　II　　ISSN 0970-1052
Z730
LIBRARY PROGRESS. 1981. 2/yr. Rs.40($8) to individuals; institutions Rs.80($12). Dr. A.K. Sharma, Ed. & Pub., P.O. Box 38, Modinagar 201 204, India. adv.; bk.rev.; circ. 300.

LIBRARY AND INFORMATION SCIENCES

020　　　　　US　　ISSN 0024-2519
Z671　　　　　　　　CODEN: LIBQAS
LIBRARY QUARTERLY; a journal of investigation and discussion in the field of library science. 1931. q. $23 to individuals; institutions $35; students $18. (University of Chicago Graduate Library School) University of Chicago Press, Journals Division, 5720 S. Woodlawn Ave., Chicago, IL 60637. TEL 312-753-3347. FAX 712-702-0694. TELEX 25-4603. (Subscr. to: Box 37005, Chicago, IL 60637) Ed. Stephen P. Harter. adv.; bk.rev.; charts; stat.; index; circ. 2,600. (also avail. in microform from MIM,UMI; reprint service avail. from UMI,ISI) **Indexed:** Amer.Bibl.Slavic & E.Eur.Stud., Amer.Hist.& Life, Bk.Rev.Dig., Bk.Rev.Ind. (1965-), C.I.J.E., Chem.Abstr., Child.Bk.Rev.Ind. (1965-), Child.Lit.Abstr., Curr.Cont., Hist.Abstr., Lib.Lit., Lib.Sci.Abstr., Mag.Ind., Mid.East: Abstr.& Ind., P.A.I.S., Ref.Sour., Res.High.Educ.Abstr., Sci.Abstr., SSCI.
— BLDSC shelfmark: 5202.000000.
Description: A general interest journal for scholars and professionals, covering a wide range of topics.
Refereed Serial

020 950　　　　　　AT
▼**LIBRARY RESEARCH IN ASIA, AFRICA & AUSTRALIA**. 1990. s-a. Aus.$156. Noyce Publishing, G.P.O. Box 2222T, Melbourne, Vic. 3001, Australia. bibl. (back issues avail.)

025　　　　　US　　ISSN 0024-2527
Z671　　　　　　　　CODEN: LRTSAH
LIBRARY RESOURCES & TECHNICAL SERVICES. 1957. q. $45 (foreign $55). American Library Association, Association for Library Collections and Technical Services, 50 E. Huron St., Chicago, IL 60611-2795. TEL 312-944-6780. FAX 312-440-9374. Ed. Richard Smiraglia. adv.; bk.rev.; bibl.; charts; index; circ. 9,600. (also avail. in microform from UMI; back issues avail.) **Indexed:** ASCA, Bk.Rev.Ind. (1965-), C.I.J.E., Child.Bk.Rev.Ind. (1965-), Curr.Cont., LHTN, Lib.Lit., LISA, Pers.Lit., Resour.Ctr.Ind., Sci.Abstr., SSCI, Tr.& Indus.Ind.
— BLDSC shelfmark: 5204.400000.
Formed by the merger of: Serial Slants (ISSN 0559-5258); Journal of Cataloging and Classification.
Description: Scholarly papers on bibliographic access and control, preservation, conservation and reproduction of library materials.

027　　　　　US　　ISSN 0364-1236
Z675.B6
LIBRARY RESOURCES FOR THE BLIND AND PHYSICALLY HANDICAPPED (LARGE PRINT EDITION). 1968. a. free to qualified individuals. U.S. Library of Congress, National Library Service for the Blind and Physically Handicapped, Washington, DC 20542. TEL 202-707-5100. (large print in 11 pt.) **Indexed:** ERIC.
Formerly: Directory of Library Resources for the Blind and Physically Handicapped (ISSN 0278-7857)

020　　　　　UK　　ISSN 0024-2535
Z671
LIBRARY REVIEW; a bimonthly devoted to information transfer, conservation and exploitation. 1927. 6/yr. $799.95. M C B University Press Ltd., 62 Toller Ln., Bradford, W. Yorks BD8 9BY, England. TEL 0274-499821. FAX 0274-547143. TELEX 51317 MCBUNI G. Ed. Stuart James. adv.; bk.rev.; index; circ. 1,000. (back issues avail.; reprint service avail. from SWZ,KTO) **Indexed:** Abstr.Engl.Stud., Amer.Hist.& Life, Bk.Rev.Ind. (1965-), Child.bk.Rev.Ind. (1965-), Hist.Abstr., Lib.Lit., LISA, Ref.Sour.
— BLDSC shelfmark: 5204.450000.
Description: Covers all topics of concern to librarians and information professionals combining scholarly and technical analysis with discussions of and opinion on current and future trends.

027.7　　　　　US　　ISSN 0041-9788
Z881 .L898
LIBRARY REVIEW. 1960. s-a. $15 includes membership. University of Louisville, Library Associates, University of Louisville Library, Louisville, KY 40292. TEL 502-588-6762. FAX 502-588-8753. Ed. George T. McWhorter. circ. 500. **Indexed:** Amer.Hum.Ind.

020　　　　　US　　ISSN 0024-2551
Z669.N5
LIBRARY SERVICE NEWS. 1929. 2/yr. $5. Columbia University, School of Library Service, Box 44, Butler Library, 535 W. 114th St., New York, NY 10027. TEL 212-280-2294. circ. 8,000.
Description: Contains organization news.

027.8　　　　　US　　ISSN 1043-237X
LIBRARY TALK; the magazine for elementary school libraries. 1988. bi-m. $35. Linworth Publishing, Inc., 480 E. Wilson Bridge Rd., Ste. L, Worthing, OH 43085. TEL 614-436-7107. FAX 614-436-9490. Ed. Carolyn Hamilton. adv.; bk.rev.; circ. 7,000. (also avail. in microform; back issues avail.; reprint service avail. from UMI) **Indexed:** Bk.Rev.Ind. (1989-), Child.Bk.Rev.Ind. (1989-).
Description: Provides articles, tips, and ideas for elementary school librarians.

020　　　　　US　　ISSN 0024-2586
Z684
LIBRARY TECHNOLOGY REPORTS; evaluative information on library systems, equipment and supplies. 1965. bi-m. $185 (foreign $215). American Library Association, 50 E. Huron St., Chicago, IL 60611-2795. TEL 800-545-2433. FAX 312-440-9374. Ed. Howard S. White. abstr.; charts; illus.; cum.index; circ. 1,900. (looseleaf format; back issues avail.; reprint service avail. from UMI) **Indexed:** Consum.Ind., Info.Media & Tech., Leg.Info.Manage.Ind., LHTN, Lib.Lit., Mag.Ind., Resour.Ctr.Ind.
— BLDSC shelfmark: 5205.700000.
Description: Evaluative information on library systems, equipment and supplies.

020　　　　　US　　ISSN 0743-4839
LIBRARY TIMES INTERNATIONAL; world news digest of library and information science. 1984. q. $18 to individuals (foreign $24); institutions $25 (foreign $31). Future World Publishing Company of Canada, India and the United States, Box 15661, Evansville, IN 47716. TEL 812-473-2420. Ed. R.N. Sharma. adv.; bk.rev.
— BLDSC shelfmark: 5205.770000.
Description: Aimed at librarians, library educators, information scientists. Includes: pertinent world news, information science update, special reports on conferences, calendar of national and international conferences, and more.

020　　　　　US　　ISSN 0024-2594
Z671　　　　　　　　CODEN: LIBTA3
LIBRARY TRENDS. 1952. q. $60 (foreign $65). University of Illinois at Urbana-Champaign, Graduate School of Library and Information Science, 249 Armory Bldg., 505 E. Armory St., Champaign, IL 61820. TEL 217-333-1359. (Subscr. to: University of Illinois Press, Journals Dept., 54 E. Gregory Dr., IL 61820) Ed. F.W. Lancaster. index; circ. 3,298. (also avail. in microform from MIM,UMI) **Indexed:** C.I.J.E., Curr.Cont., Leg.Info.Manage.Ind., Lib.Lit., LISA, Mag.Ind., Mid.East: Abstr.& Ind., P.A.I.S., Pers.Lit., Sci.Abstr, Sci.Cit.Ind., SSCI.
— BLDSC shelfmark: 5207.150000.

020　　　　　US　　ISSN 0047-4541
LIBRARY TRUSTEES FOUNDATION OF NEW YORK STATE. NEWSLETTER. 1971. q. $25. New York State Association of Library Boards, 71 W. 23rd St., Box 208, New York, NY 10010. Ed. Dr. Allan Boudreau. adv.; bk.rev.; illus.; circ. 4,500.
Description: Information on public library construction, aid, automation, standards and Association administrative matters.

020　　　　　US　　ISSN 0895-2248
LIBRARY VIDEO MAGAZINE. 1986. 3/yr. $169.95. American Library Association, 50 E. Huron St., Chicago, IL 60611-2795. TEL 800-545-2433. FAX 312-440-9374. Ed. Art. Plotnik. circ. 250. (video cassette; VHS, Beta, or 3-4 format; back issues avail.)
Description: Videotape coverage of news and events in the library community.

020.6　　　　　JA
LIBRARY YEARBOOK/TOSHOKAN NENKAN. 1982. a. 12360 Yen. Japan Library Association - Nihon Toshokan Kyokai, 1-1-10 Taishido, Setagaya-ku, Tokyo 154, Japan. FAX 81-3-3421-7588.

020　　　　　DK　　ISSN 0024-2667
Z671
LIBRI; international library review. (Text in English, French and German) 1951. q. DKK 965. Munksgaard International Publishers Ltd., 35 Noerre Soegade, P.O. Box 2148, DK-1016 Copenhagen K, Denmark. TEL 33-127030. FAX 33-129387. TELEX 19431-MUNKS-DK. Eds. Irene Wormel, Hans Peter Geh. adv.; bk.rev.; illus.; index; circ. 900. (also avail. in microform from ISI,SWZ; reprint service avail. from ISI,SWZ) **Indexed:** Curr.Cont., Lib.Lit., P.A.I.S.For.Lang.Ind., P.A.I.S., SSCI.
— BLDSC shelfmark: 5207.300000.

020　　　　　CN　　ISSN 0712-6115
LIBSAT. 1982. 2/yr. Can.$4($3) for four nos. Gananoque Public Library Board, 100 Park St., Gananoque, Ont. K7G 2Y5, Canada. Ed. John Love. circ. 50. (back issues avail.)

020　　　　　FR
LIEN INFORMATIQUE; magazine de detente de l'informaticien. 1977. m. 100 F. Manifestation S.A.R.L., 61 rue Falguiere, 75015 Paris, France. Ed. Joelle Daireaux Chapon. adv.

026　　　　　US　　ISSN 0024-3698
LINCOLN LIBRARY BULLETIN. 1942. m. (Sep.-Jun.). free. Lincoln Library, 326 S. 7th St., Springfield, IL 62701. TEL 217-753-4925. Ed. Corrine Frisch. adv.; bk.rev.; circ. 7,000.

027.4　　　　　US
LINKING LIBRARIES. 1981. bi-m. membership. Rochester Regional Library Council, 302 N. Goodman St. at Village Gate, Rochester, NY 14607. circ. 1,050 (controlled).
Formerly (until 1986): Local Data Record.

LISHI DANG'AN/HISTORICAL ARCHIVES. see *HISTORY — History Of Asia*

020　　　　　UK　　ISSN 0957-6053
Z678
LOGISTICS INFORMATION MANAGEMENT. 1981. 4/yr. $599.95. M C B University Press Ltd., 62 Toller Ln., Bradford, W. Yorks BD8 9BY, England. FAX 547143. TELEX 51317 MCBUNI G. (Dist. in N. America by: M C B University Press Ltd., Box 10812, Birmingham, AL 35201-0812. TEL 800-633-4931) Ed. Abby Day. adv.; bk.rev.; circ. 450. (reprint service avail. from SWZ) **Indexed:** ERIC, Leg.Info.Manage.Ind., LISA.
— BLDSC shelfmark: 5292.316000.
Former titles (until 1991): Information and Library Manager (ISSN 0260-6879); (until 1989): Logistics World (ISSN 0953-2137)
Description: Aims to increase awareness and understanding of the information professional's role. Presents a number of articles concerned with the changing face of the profession. Technology and systems are covered.

LOGOS; the professional journal for the book world. see *PUBLISHING AND BOOK TRADE*

029.7 976 929　　US
LOUISIANA ARCHIVES AND MANUSCRIPTS ASSOCIATION. NEWSLETTER. 1978. s-a. $10. Louisiana Archives and Manuscripts Association, Newsletter Editor, Manuscripts Dept., Howard - Tilton Library, Tulane University, New Orleans, LA 70118-5682. TEL 504-865-5685. FAX 504-865-6773. (Subscr. to: Box 51213, New Orleans, LA 70151-1213) Ed. Leon C. Miller. bibl.; circ. 400.
Formerly (until 1990): Friends of the Archives of Louisiana. Newsletter.
Description: Lists new accessions for state manuscript-archives repositories, and contains items of related interest.

027　　　　　US　　ISSN 0085-2759
Z671
LOUISIANA STATE UNIVERSITY. LIBRARY LECTURES. 1965. irreg., no.6, 1979. free. Louisiana State University, Library, Baton Rouge, LA 70803-7507. TEL 504-388-2217. Ed. Caroline Wire. circ. controlled. (also avail. in microform from EDR) **Indexed:** Inform.Sci.Abstr., Lib.Lit., LISA.
Description: Series of lectures sponsored by Louisiana State University and reproduced as articles pertaining to library management, facilities, technologies, and employment.

LIBRARY AND INFORMATION SCIENCES

020   II   ISSN 0024-7219
Z671
LUCKNOW LIBRARIAN. (Text in English) 1962. q. Rs.150($30) (£20). Uttar Pradesh Library Association, Lucknow Branch, U.P. Library Association, P.O. Box 446, Lucknow 226 001, India. Ed. S.N. Agarwal. adv.; bk.rev.; abstr.; bibl.; charts; illus.; index; circ. 1,000. **Indexed:** Art & Archaeol.Tech.Abstr., G. Indian Per.Lit., Indian Lib.Sci.Abstr., Lib.Lit., LISA.
●Also available on CD-ROM.
—BLDSC shelfmark: 5303.150000.

027.4   ZA
LUSAKA CITY LIBRARY. ANNUAL REPORT. 1977. a. free. Lusaka City Library, P.O. Box 31304, Katondo Rd., Lusaka, Zambia. TEL 227282. circ. 150. (processed)

020 284   US   ISSN 0024-7472
LUTHERAN LIBRARIES. 1958. q. $15 (bulk rates avail.). Lutheran Church Library Association, 122 W. Franklin Ave., Minneapolis, MN 55404. TEL 612-870-3623. Ed. Ron Klug. adv.; bk.rev.; audio rev.; video rev.; illus.; tr.lit.; circ. 9,000. (back issues avail.) **Indexed:** CERDIC.
Description: Provides news and promotional ideas for church librarians of the Lutheran Church Library Association.

020   US   ISSN 0741-0379
M A C NEWSLETTER. 1973. q. $16 to individuals; institutions $32. Midwest Archives Conference, Evangelical Lutheran Church, 8765 W. Higgins Rd., Chicago, IL 60631-4198. (Subscr. to: University Archives, Northwestern University Library, Evanston, IL 60208-2300) Ed. Thomas Rick. bibl.; circ. 1,100. (also avail. in microfilm)

025   CN   ISSN 0710-3417
M A L T NEWSLETTER. 1976. q. Can.$25 to individuals; students Can.$12.50. Manitoba Association of Library Technicians, P.O. Box 1872, Winnipeg, Man. R3C 3R1, Canada. circ. 100.

029.7   US
M A P S NEWSLETTER.* 1987. q. free. Mid-Atlantic Preservation Service, Nine S. Commerce Way, Bethlehem, PA 18017. TEL 215-758-8700. FAX 215-758-9700. Ed. C. Lee Jones.

020   US   ISSN 0364-2410
M E L A NOTES. 1973. 3/yr. $10 (foreign $15). Middle East Librarians Association, c/o Michael E. Hopper, Library, University of California, Santa Barbara, CA 93106. TEL 805-893-3369. FAX 805-893-4676. Ed. John A. Eilts. bibl.; circ. 200. (back issues avail.)

026   CN   ISSN 0848-9009
M H L A NEWS. 1979. 3/yr. membership. Manitoba Health Libraries Association, Box 232, Winnipeg, Man. R3M 3S7, Canada. FAX 204-231-0640. Ed. Charlie Pennell. bk.rev.; circ. 75.
Formerly (until 1989): M H L A Newsletter (ISSN 0821-1310).

023   US   ISSN 1049-0760
M H L S NEWS. 1974. q. free. Mid-Hudson Library System, 103 Market St., Poughkeepsie, NY 12601. TEL 914-471-6060. FAX 914-454-5940. Eds. Deborah Begley, Joshua Cohen. adv.; bk.rev.; circ. 1,100 (controlled).
Former titles: Mid-Hudson News; Mid-Hudson Library Systems Newsletter.
Description: News and announcements on issues of interest to trustees of public libraries throughout the New York State region.

M L A NEWS (CHICAGO). (Medical Library Association) see *MEDICAL SCIENCES*

020.6   US
M L A NEWSLETTER (MINNEAPOLIS). 1974. 10/yr. $20. Minnesota Library Association, 1315 Lowry Ave. N., Minneapolis, MN 55411. TEL 612-521-1735. Eds. Kristi Gibson, Janet Urbanowicz. circ. 1,000.

020 658   US   ISSN 0896-3908
M L S. (Marketing Library Services) 1987. 8/yr. $59 (foreign $70)(effective 1992). Learned Information, Inc., 143 Old Marlton Pike, Medford, NJ 08055-8750. TEL 609-654-6266. FAX 609-654-4309. Ed. Sharon La Rosa. bk.rev.; circ. 1,200.
—BLDSC shelfmark: 5381.648200.
Supersedes (1986-1987): P C Free.
Description: Provides information on designing and presenting plans for new services and acquiring new products.

020   US   ISSN 0145-6180
Z671
M P L A NEWSLETTER. 1956. bi-m. $17. Mountain Plains Library Association, c/o University of South Dakota Libraries, Vermillion, SD 57069. TEL 605-677-6082. Ed. Jim Dertien. adv.; bk.rev.; bibl.; charts; illus.; circ. 1,400. (also avail. in microform from UMI; back issues avail.) **Indexed:** Lib.Lit.
—BLDSC shelfmark: 5980.730700.
Incorporates (in 1965): Mountain-Plains in Books (ISSN 0580-0714); Which was formerly: Mountain-Plains Library Quarterly (ISSN 0027-2582)

020   US
M P L NOW!. 1970. m. free. Muncie Public Library, 301 E. Jackson St., Muncie, IN 47305. TEL 317-747-8200. FAX 317-747-8221. Ed. John Drumm. bk.rev.; circ. 500.

027.8   CN   ISSN 0315-9124
M S L A V A JOURNAL. (Includes supplement: M S L A V A Newsletter) 1968. 4/yr (plus 2 supplements). $20 to members. Manitoba School Library Audio Visual Association, c/o Manitoba Teachers' Society, 191 Harcourt St., Winnipeg, Man. R3J 3H2, Canada. TEL 204-888-7961. adv.; bk.rev.; illus.; index; circ. 400 (controlled). **Indexed:** Can.Per.Ind.
—BLDSC shelfmark: 5980.869500.
Formerly: Manitoba Association of School Librarians Newsletter (ISSN 0025-2204)

020   US
M S R R T NEWSLETTER. (Minnesota Social Responsibilities Round Table) 1988. 10/yr. Minnesota Library Association, 1315 Lowry Ave. N., Minneapolis, MN 55411. TEL 612-521-1735. Eds. Christopher Dodge, Jan DeSirey. bk.rev.; index; circ. 225.

MAGAZINES FOR LIBRARIES; for the general reader and school, junior college, university and public libraries. see *BIBLIOGRAPHIES*

MAGAZINES FOR YOUNG PEOPLE; a children's magazine guide. see *BIBLIOGRAPHIES*

MAGYAR KONYVSZEMLE/HUNGARIAN BOOK REVIEW; review of bookhistory, bibliography and documentation. see *PUBLISHING AND BOOK TRADE*

026.025   US   ISSN 0091-0759
Z732.M2
MAINE. STATE LIBRARY. SPECIAL SUBJECT RESOURCES IN MAINE. irreg., latest 1972. State Library, State House Sta. 64, Augusta, ME 04333. TEL 207-289-5600. Key Title: Special Subject Resources in Maine.

020   US
MAINE ENTRY. 1974. 4/yr. $25. Maine Library Association, c/o Maine Municipal Association, Community Dr., Augusta, ME 04330. TEL 207-623-1634. (Co-sponsor: Maine State Library) Ed.Bd. circ. 1,200.
Formerly: Downeast Libraries; Formed by the merger of: Downeast Newsletter; Maine Library Association. Bulletin.

020   US
MAINE MEMO. 1979. m. $25. Maine Library Association, Maine Municipal Association, Community Dr., Augusta, ME 04330. TEL 207-623-1634. (Co-sponsor: Maine State Library) Ed. Laura Juraska. circ. 1,500.
Formerly: Maine Library Association. Monthly Memo.

020   MY   ISSN 0126-7809
Z845.M3
MAJALLAH PERPUSTAKAAN MALAYSIA. (Text in English and Malay) 1972. a. M.8. Persatuan Perpustakaan Malaysia, Box 2545, Kuala Lumpur, Malaysia. Ed. Lim Hucktee. adv.; bk.rev.; circ. 500. **Indexed:** LISA.

025   XN   ISSN 0350-1728
MAKEDONSKI ARHIVIST. (Text in Macedonian; summaries in English, French, Russian) 1972. a. 350 din.($1.50) Sojuz na Drustvata na Arhivskite Rabotnici i Arhivite na R. Makedonija, Gligor Prlicev 3, P.O. Box 496, Skopje 91001, Macedonia. TEL 091-234-461. Ed. Violeta Gerasimova. bk.rev.; illus.

020   UG   ISSN 0075-4854
MAKERERE UNIVERSITY. LIBRARY. MAKERERE LIBRARY PUBLICATIONS. Short title: Makerere Library Publications. 1961. irreg. free. Makerere University, Library, Box 16002, Kampala, Uganda.

020   KE   ISSN 0070-7988
MAKTABA. (Text in English, Swahili) 1962. s-a. $25. Kenya Library Association, Box 46031, Nairobi, Kenya. Ed. Symphrose Ouma. adv.; bk.rev.
Incorporates: Kenya Library Association Chairman's Annual Report; Formerly: East African Library Association. Bulletin.

027.5689   MW
MALAWI. NATIONAL LIBRARY SERVICE BOARD. ANNUAL REPORT. 1969. a. free. National Library Service Board, Box 30314, Lilongwe 3, Malawi. FAX 730626. circ. controlled.
Formerly: Malawi. National Library. Annual Report (ISSN 0581-0906)

027.4   MW
MALAWI. NATIONAL LIBRARY SERVICE. BULLETIN. (Text in English) no.10, 1970. s-a. free. National Library Service, Box 30314, Lilongwe 3, Malawi. FAX 730626. circ. 700.

023   MW
MALAWI NATIONAL LIBRARY SERVICE BOARD. STAFF NEWSLETTER. 1982. biennial. free. National Library Service Board, P.O. Box 30314, Lilongwe 3, Milawi. FAX 365-730626. Dir. R.S. Mabomba. circ. controlled.
Description: Provides a forum for staff expression on various library themes and topics of general interest.

020   UK   ISSN 0260-8502
MANCHESTER POLYTECHNIC. DEPARTMENT OF LIBRARY AND INFORMATION STUDIES. OCCASIONAL PAPERS. 1980. irreg. price varies. Manchester Polytechnic, Department of Library and Information Studies, All Saints, Manchester M15 6BH, England. TEL 061-247-6144. circ. 200.

021   CN   ISSN 0706-7798
MANITOBA. PUBLIC LIBRARY SERVICES. NEWSLETTER. (Text in English and French) 1978. bi-m. free. Public Library Services, 1525 1st St., Unit 200, Brandon, Man. R7A 7A1, Canada. TEL 204-726-6590. FAX 204-726-6868. circ. 400.

020   CN   ISSN 0700-3684
MANITOBA LIBRARY ASSOCIATION. NEWSLINE. 12/yr. membership. Manitoba Library Association, Box 176, Winnipeg, Man. R3C 2G9, Canada. TEL 204-943-4567. Ed. Norma Godavari.
Incorporates (in 1991): Manitoba Library Association Bulletin.

MARIAN LIBRARY STUDIES. NEW SERIES. see *RELIGIONS AND THEOLOGY — Roman Catholic*

020   UK
MARITIME INFORMATION ASSOCIATION NEWSLETTER. 1970. 4/yr. membership. Maritime Information Association, 202 Lambeth Road, London SE1 7JW, England. (Co-sponsor: Marine Society)
Formerly: Marine Librarians' Association Newsletter.
Description: Covers matters relating to members of the association.

LIBRARY AND INFORMATION SCIENCES

020 US ISSN 0895-1799
MARKETING TREASURES. 1987. bi-m. $54 (Canada $59; elsewhere $66). Chris Olson & Associates, 857 Twin Harbor Dr., Arnold, MD 21012. TEL 301-647-6708. FAX 301-647-0415. Ed. Christine Olson. adv.; bk.rev.; circ. 1,000. (back issues avail.)
Description: Designed to help librarians promote the services of their libraries. Provides creative ideas, helpful hints and insights on how other libraries promote their services.

MARTIN & OSA JOHNSON SAFARI MUSEUM WAIT-A-BIT NEWS. see *MUSEUMS AND ART GALLERIES*

021 UK
MARX MEMORIAL LIBRARY BULLETIN. 1957. irreg. (2-3/yr.). £5($15) to non-members. Marx Memorial Library, 37a Clerkenwell Green, London EC1R 0DU, England. Ed. Mary Rosser. bk.rev.; circ. 1,400.
Formerly: Marx Memorial Library. Quarterly Bulletin (ISSN 0025-410X)

020 MF ISSN 0076-5481
MAURITIUS. ARCHIVES DEPARTMENT. ANNUAL REPORT. (Includes yearly supplement Bibliography of Mauritius) (Text in English; bibliographical supplement in English, French) 1950. a. Rs.15. Archives Department, Development Bank of Mauritius Complex, Petite Riviere, Beau-Bassin, Mauritius. (Subscr. to: Government Printing Office, Elizabeth II Ave., Port Louis, Mauritius)

027.8 SA ISSN 1016-8206
MEDIA FOCUS/MEDIAFOKUS. (Text in Afrikaans, English) 1969. s-a. R.30 to non-members (effective 1992). Transvaal School Media Association, c/o Transvaal Education Media Service, Private Bag X290, Pretoria 0001, South Africa. Ed.Bd. adv.; bk.rev.; circ. 2,300. **Indexed:** Child.Lit.Abstr.
Former titles (until 1988): School Media Centre; (until 1980): School Library (ISSN 0036-6617)
Description: Aims to heighten media awareness in South African schools.

MEDIAFILE. see *EDUCATION — Teaching Methods And Curriculum*

020 FR ISSN 0153-4270
MEDIATHEQUES PUBLIQUES. 1967. q. 45 F.($15) Association pour la Mediatheque Publique, 37 rue St. Georges, 59409 Cambrai, France. Ed. Michel Bouvy. adv.; bk.rev. **Indexed:** LISA.
Formerly: Lecture et Bibliotheques.

MEDICAL LIBRARY ASSOCIATION. BULLETIN. see *MEDICAL SCIENCES*

020 US ISSN 0276-3869
R118.2 CODEN: MRSQDK
MEDICAL REFERENCE SERVICES QUARTERLY. 1982. q. $36 to individuals; institutions $90. Haworth Press, Inc., 10 Alice St., Binghamton, NY 13904. TEL 800-342-9678. FAX 607-722-1424. TELEX 4932599. Ed. M. Sandra Wood. adv.; bk.rev.; abstr.; bibl.; circ. 1,038. (also avail. in microfiche from HAW; back issues avail.; reprint service avail. from HAW) **Indexed:** Abstr.Health Care Manage.Stud., Biol.Abstr., CINAHL, Excerp.Med., Hosp.Lit.Ind., Inform.Sci.Abstr., Leg.Info.Manage.Ind., Lib.Lit., LISA, Sci.Abstr.
—BLDSC shelfmark: 5531.593000.
Description: Specializes in practice-oriented articles relating to medical reference services, with an emphasis on online search services.
Refereed Serial

020 CN ISSN 0025-8377
MEDIUM. vol.18, 1977. 5/yr. Can.$36. (Saskatchewan Association of Educational Media Specialists) Saskatchewan Teachers' Federation, Box 1108, Saskatoon, Sask. S7K 3N3, Canada. TEL 306-525-0368. Ed. Susan McCutcheon. adv.; bk.rev.; bibl.; circ. 400 (controlled). (processed) **Indexed:** Can.Educ.Ind, Lang.Teach.& Ling.Abstr., Pt.de Rep.
Formerly: Saskatchewan Association of Media Specialists. Medium (ISSN 0025-8377)

020 NE
MEDIUM-TERM PROGRAMME (YEARS). (Editions in English, French, German, Russian, Spanish) 1981. quinquennial. fl.40($20) International Federation of Library Associations and Institutions, Headquarters, P.O. Box 95312, 2509 CH The Hague, Netherlands. TEL 70-3140884. FAX 70-3834827. TELEX 34402 KB NL. Ed.Bd. charts; illus.; stat.; circ. 2,000.

MERIDIAN. see *GEOGRAPHY*

020 JO ISSN 0257-7739
MESSAGE OF THE LIBRARY/RISALAT AL-MAKTABA. (Text in Arabic; summaries in English) 1965. q. $20. Jordan Library Association, P.O. Box 6289, Amman, Jordan. TEL 629-412. adv.; bk.rev.; index; circ. 1,200.
Description: Focuses on research and technology in the areas of library and information science.

026 US ISSN 0076-7018
METRO; NEW YORK METROPOLITAN REFERENCE AND RESEARCH LIBRARY AGENCY. METRO MISCELLANEOUS PUBLICATIONS SERIES. 1968. irreg., latest no.40. New York Metropolitan Reference & Research Library Agency (METRO), 57 E. 11th St., New York, NY 10003-4605. TEL 212-228-2320.

025 CN ISSN 0700-4532
METROPOLITAN TORONTO LIBRARY BOARD. ANNUAL REPORT. 1968. a. free. Metropolitan Toronto Library Board, Public Relations Office, 789 Yonge St., Toronto, Ont. M4W 2G8, Canada. TEL 416-393-7133. FAX 416-393-7229. TELEX 06-22232. Ed. Mario Bernardi. illus.; circ. 3,000.

023 CN ISSN 0842-9707
METROPOLITAN TORONTO REFERENCE LIBRARY. NEWS. 4/yr. Metropolitan Toronto Library Board, 789 Yonge St., Toronto, Ont. M4W 2G8, Canada. TEL 416-393-7160. Ed. Jytte Birnbaum.
Formerly: Metropolitan Toronto Library Board. News (ISSN 0318-9244)

027 US
MICHIE LIBRARY QUARTERLY. 1982. q. free. Michie Company, Box 7587, Charlottesville, VA 22906-7587. TEL 804-972-7600. Ed. Gretchen Notermann.

020 US
MICHIGAN LIBRARIAN. 1935. 10/yr. $40 (foreign $50). Michigan Library Association, 1000 Long Blvd., Ste. 1, Lansing, MI 48911-6857. TEL 517-694-6615. Ed. Marianne Gessner. adv.; circ. 1,800. (also avail. in microform from UMI; reprint service avail. from UMI) **Indexed:** Lib.Lit.
Former titles: Michigan Librarian Newsletter (ISSN 0149-435X); (until 1980): Michigan Librarian (ISSN 0026-2242)
Description: Covers the history of the Association. Provides information on the Association's fund raising activities and other administrative matters.

MICHIGAN LIBRARY DIRECTORY. see *BUSINESS AND ECONOMICS — Trade And Industrial Directories*

020 010 KO ISSN 0026-2536
MICRO-LIBRARY BULLETIN.* 1963. m. Won100($2.) Korean Micro-Library Association, Central National Library Bldg., 6 Sogong-Dong, Jung-Gu, Seoul, S. Korea. Ed. Dae-Sup Ohm. bk.rev.; bibl.; illus. (processed)

025 778 NE ISSN 0076-8480
Z265
MICROFICHE FOUNDATION. NEWSLETTER. 1963. 3/yr. $15. Microfiche Foundation, Delft Technological University Library, Doelenstraat 101, 2611 NS Delft, Netherlands. Ed. J.H.I. de Bruin. bk.rev.; illus.; circ. 1,000. (also avail. in microfiche)

778.1 GW ISSN 0362-0999
Z286.M5
MICROFORM MARKET PLACE; an international directory of micropublishing. Short title: M M P. 1974. biennial. $59.95. K.G. Saur Verlag KG, Ortlerstr. 8, Postfach 701620, 8000 Munich 70, Germany. TEL 089-76902-0. FAX 089-76902150. (N. America subscr. to: K.G. Saur, A Reed Reference Publishing Company, 121 Chanlon Rd., Box 31, New Providence, NJ 07974. TEL 908-665-3576) Ed. Barbara Hopkinson. adv.
Description: Provides information on the specialized world of microform publishing. Main entries furnish publisher name, address, telephone, fax and telex numbers, ISBN prefix, key personnel, major microform programs and micro-formats offered.

778.315 GW ISSN 0002-6530
Z265 CODEN: MFRVA
MICROFORM REVIEW. 1972. q. $125. K.G. Saur Verlag KG, Ortlerstr. 8, Postfach 701620, 8000 Munich 70, Germany. TEL 089-76902-0. FAX 089-76902150. (Dist. in US by: R.R. Bowker, 121 Chanlon Rd., New Providence, NJ 07974. TEL 908-665-6719) Ed. Susan Szasz. adv.; bk.rev.; index. (also avail. in microform) **Indexed:** C.I.J.E., Info.Media & Tech., Inform.Sci.Abstr., Leg.Info.Manage.Ind., LHTN, Lib.Lit., LISA., Resour.Ctr.Ind., Sci.Abstr.
—BLDSC shelfmark: 5759.120000.

020 US
MICROGRAPHICS AND OPTICAL STORAGE EQUIPMENT REVIEW. 1976. a. $185 (institutional price varies). Meckler Publishing Corporation, 11 Ferry Lane W., Westport, CT 06880-5808. TEL 203-226-6967. Ed. William Saffady. **Indexed:** Consum.Ind.
Supersedes: International File of Micrographics Equipment and Accessories. (ISSN 0148-5121) & Index to Micrographics Equipment Evaluations (ISSN 0733-9577); **Formerly (until 1985):** Micrographics Equipment Review (ISSN 0362-1006)

020 US ISSN 0738-9396
MID-ATLANTIC ARCHIVIST. 1972. 4/yr. $10. Mid-Atlantic Regional Archives Conference, University Archives, Gelman Library, George Washington University, Washington, DC 20052. TEL 202-994-7549. FAX 202-994-1340. (Subscr. to: Marsha Trimble, University of Virginia Law Library, Charlottesville, VA 22901) Ed. G. David Anderson. adv.; bk.rev.; circ. 1,000. (processed)
Description: Promotes the professional welfare of its members and cooperation among individuals concerned with the documentation of the human experience.

MIDDLE ATLANTIC PERSPECTIVE. see *MEDICAL SCIENCES*

MIDWESTERN ARCHIVIST. see *HISTORY*

020 IT
MILLELIBRI. 1987. m. L.58000. Giorgio Mondadori e Associati S.p.A., Via Cadore, 19, 20135 Milan, Italy. TEL 02-5456421. FAX 5469150. Ed. Renato Olivieri. circ. 62,039.

MINGUO DANG'AN/ARCHIVES OF THE REPUBLIC OF CHINA. see *HISTORY — History Of Asia*

027.4 US ISSN 0026-5438
MINNESOTA. DEPARTMENT OF EDUCATION. PUBLIC LIBRARY NEWSLETTER. 1970. m. free to public libraries in Minnesota. Department of Education, Office of Library Development and Services, 440 Capitol Square Bldg., 550 Cedar St., St. Paul, MN 55101. TEL 612-296-2821. Ed. Darlene M. Arnold. circ. 750. (processed; reprint service avail. from UMI)
Description: Includes brief summaries of library news and events.

LIBRARY AND INFORMATION SCIENCES

020 US ISSN 0026-5551
Z732
MINNESOTA LIBRARIES. 1904. q. free to libraries in Minnesota; on exchange basis to out-of-state and -nation libraries. Department of Education, Office of Library Development and Services, 440 Capitol Square Bldg., 550 Cedar St., St. Paul, MN 55101. TEL 612-296-2821. Ed. William G. Asp. stat.; index; circ. 1,968. (also avail. in microfilm from UMI; reprint service avail. from UMI) **Indexed:** Lib.Lit., Lib.Sci.Abstr., SRI.
Description: Covers state long range plan, and library development and services. Includes library statistics.

020 US ISSN 0194-388X
Z671
MISSISSIPPI LIBRARIES. 1936. q. $16 to non-members (foreign $24). Mississippi Library Association, c/o Sharon Buchanan, Box 20448, Jackson, MS 39289-1448. TEL 601-352-3917. Ed. Carol Cubberley. adv.; bk.rev.; bibl.; stat.; index; circ. 1,500. (also avail. in microfilm from UMI; reprint service avail. from UMI) **Indexed:** Lib.Lit.
—BLDSC shelfmark: 5810.393000.
Formerly (until vol.43, 1979): Mississippi Library News (ISSN 0026-6302)
Description: News, articles, book reviews, and announcements of interest to members of the Mississippi Library Association.

020 US ISSN 0899-6458
MISSOURI LIBRARIES. 1988. bi-m. free. State Library, Box 387, Jefferson City, MO 65102-0387. TEL 314-751-2680. FAX 314-751-3612. Ed. Madeline Matson. circ. 4,250 (controlled).
Description: News about the State Library and Missouri libraries.

MITTEILUNGEN FUER DIE ARCHIVPFLEGE IN BAYERN. see HISTORY

020 US ISSN 0884-2205
Z673
MO INFO. 1970. 6/yr. $6 to non-members. Missouri Library Association, 1015 E. Broadway, Ste. 215, Columbia, MO 65201. TEL 314-449-4627. Ed. J. McCartney. adv.; bk.rev.; circ. 1,500. (also avail. in microform from UMI; reprint service avail. from UMI)
Former titles (until 1985): M L A Newsletter (ISSN 0581-0205); M L A Quarterly.
Description: News, announcements, and issues of interest to members of the Missouri Library Association.

027.4 US
MOBILE PUBLIC LIBRARY TODAY. 1984. m. free. Mobile Public Library, 701 Government St., Mobile, AL 36602. FAX 205-434-7571. Ed. C. Bowersox. bk.rev.; circ. 5,200.
Description: News of the library, articles about library users and coverage of the organizational meetings.

021 US
Z732.M9
MONTANA LIBRARY DIRECTORY. a. State Library, 1515 E. 6th Ave., Helena, MT 59620. TEL 406-444-3115. FAX 406-444-5612. stat. **Indexed:** SRI.
Formerly: Montana Library Directory, with Statistics of Montana Public Libraries (ISSN 0094-873X)

020 US
MONTANA NEWSLETTER. 1965. 6/yr. free. State Library, 1515 E. 6th Ave., Helena, MT 59620. TEL 406-444-3115. FAX 406-444-5612. Ed. Cathy Stegner. bibl.; circ. controlled. (tabloid format; back issues avail.)
Description: Summary of Montana library news and issues.

020 US
MONTANA STATE LIBRARY NEWS. bi-m. free. Montana State Library, 1515 E. 6th., Helena, MT 59620. TEL 406-444-5353. FAX 406-444-5612. Ed. Cathy Siegner. bk.rev.; circ. 1,800. (back issues avail.)
Description: Covers news on the State Library and all libraries in Montana.

020 US
MONTANA STATE LIBRARY NEWS UPDATE. 1988. bi-m. free. Montana State Library, 1515 E. 6th Ave., Helena, MT 59620. TEL 406-444-3115. FAX 406-444-5612. Ed. Catherine A. Siegner. circ. 1,200. (controlled). (looseleaf format; back issues avail.)
Description: Presents an update of library-related news, construction projects, conferences, personnel changes, policy announcements, calendar.

020 SA ISSN 0027-2639
Z857.S7
MOUSAION; library science contributions. (Text in Afrikaans, English) 1955. 2/yr. R.13.20($15) University of South Africa, P.O. Box 392, Pretoria 0001, South Africa. FAX 012-429-2533. (Co-sponsor: University Library) illus.; circ. 1,000. (reprint service avail. from UMI) **Indexed:** Ind.S.A.Per., LHTN, Lib.Lit., Lib.Sci.Abstr.

MUNICIPAL REFERENCE LIBRARY BULLETIN/BULLETIN VAN DIE MUNISIPALE NASLAANBIBLIOTEEK. see PUBLIC ADMINISTRATION — Municipal Government

020 060 AU ISSN 0077-2208
MUSEION. 1957. irreg. price varies. (Oesterreichische Nationalbibliothek) Verlagsbuchhandlung Brueder Hollinek und Co. GmbH, Feldgasse 13, A-1238 Vienna, Austria. TEL 0222-8893646. FAX 0222-889364724. (reprint service avail. from ISI)

026 780 US ISSN 0027-4283
ML111
MUSIC CATALOGING BULLETIN. 1970. m. $18 (foreign $23). Music Library Association, Box 487, Canton, MA 02021. TEL 617-828-8450. Ed. Elizabeth Gamble. circ. 850.

MUSIC FILE. see EDUCATION — Teaching Methods And Curriculum

026 780 US ISSN 0027-4380
ML27.U5
MUSIC LIBRARY ASSOCIATION. NOTES. 1942. q. $45 to individuals; institutions $60. Music Library Association, P.O. Box 487, Canton, MA 02021. TEL 215-569-3948. Ed. Michael Ochs. adv.; bk.rev.; bibl.; music rev.; tr.lit.; index; circ. 2,900. (also avail. in microform from UMI) **Indexed:** Bk.Rev.Dig., Bk.Rev.Ind. (1966-), Child.Bk.Rev.Ind. (1966-), G.Perf.Arts, Hum.Ind., Lib.Lit., Lib.Sci.Abstr., Music Artic.Guide, Music Ind., Ref.Sour., RILM.
—BLDSC shelfmark: 6155.860000.

026 US ISSN 0094-5099
MUSIC LIBRARY ASSOCIATION. TECHNICAL REPORTS; information for music media specialists. 1973. irreg. price varies. Music Library Association, Box 487, Canton, MA 02021. TEL 617-828-8450. Ed. Michael Fling. circ. 150. **Indexed:** RILM.

020 US ISSN 0161-1704
MUSIC O C L C USERS GROUP. NEWSLETTER. (Includes membership directories) 1977. irreg. $10 to individuals; institutions $15; foreign $25. Music O C L C Users Group, c/o Ann Churukian, Treas., Music Library, Box 38, Vassar College, Poughkeepsie, NY 12601. TEL 914-437-7492. Ed. Karen Little. circ. 570. (back issues avail.)
Description: Contains summaries of annual meeting presentations, articles, and news relating to OCLC, Inc., its products, and the music library community.

020 780.7 US ISSN 1058-8167
▼**MUSIC REFERENCE SERVICES QUARTERLY.** 1992. q. Haworth Press, Inc., 10 Alice St., Binghamton, NY 13904. TEL 800-342-9678. FAX 607-722-1424. TELEX 4932599. Ed. William Studwell. adv.; bk.rev. (also avail. in microfiche from HAW; reprint service avail. from HAW)
Description: Covers administration, collection development, cataloguing, online services, and bibliographies.
Refereed Serial

780 DK ISSN 0109-0364
MUSIKALIER I DANSKE BIBLIOTEKER (QUARTERLY)/MUSIC IN DANISH LIBRARIES; accessionkatalog. (Text in Danish; summaries in Danish and English) 1971. q. DKK 5830. Bibliotekscentralen - Danish Library Bureau, Tempovej 7-11, 2750 Ballerup, Denmark. TEL 2-974000. FAX 2-655310. (microfilm; back issues avail.)
●Also available online.

020 HU ISSN 0027-3015
MUSZAKI EGYETEMI KONYVTAROS/TECHNICAL UNIVERSITY LIBRARIAN. 1964. s-a. free. Budapesti Muszaki Egyetem, Kozponti Konyvtar - Central Library of the Technical University of Budapest, Budafoki ut 4-6, 1111 Budapest XI, Hungary. TEL 166-4305. FAX 181-2753. TELEX 225931 MUEGY. Ed. Imre Lebovits. bk.rev.; bibl.; charts; circ. 400. (also avail. in microfilm)

020 GW ISSN 0340-9090
N A B D - MITTEILUNGEN. 1976. irreg. (approx 3/yr.). free. Normenausschuss Bibliotheks- und Dokumentationswesen, Burggrafenstr. 6, 1000 Berlin 30, Germany. TEL 030-2601318. FAX 030-2601231. TELEX 184273-DIN-D. Ed. Eva-Maria Baxmann-Krafft. circ. 420. (looseleaf format; back issues avail.)

027.7 US ISSN 0892-1733
CODEN: NASNE6
N A S I G NEWSLETTER. 1986. bi-m. $20 (foreign $30). North American Serials Interest Group, Wallace Library, Wheaton College, Norton, MA 02766. TEL 508-285-7722. FAX 508-285-6329. Ed. Jean Callaghan. circ. 800.
—BLDSC shelfmark: 6015.602300.
Description: Covers NASIG meetings and conferences. Includes pertinent news items and announcements.

025 II
N A S S D O C RESEARCH INFORMATION SERIES. ACQUISITION UPDATE. (Text in English) s-a. Rs.20. Indian Council of Social Science Research, National Social Science Documentation Centre, 35 Ferozshah Rd., New Delhi 110 001, India. TEL 11-384353. TELEX 31-61083-ISSR-IN. circ. 100.

020 UN
N A T I S - NEWS. (National Information System) French edition: N A T I S-Nouvelles. Spanish edition: N A T I S Noticias. (Text in English, French, Spanish) 1975. irreg. free. Unesco, 7-9 Place de Fontenoy, 75700 Paris, France. TEL 577-16-10. (Dist. in U.S. by: Unipub, 4611-F Assembly Dr., Lanhanm Dr., MD 20706-4391)
Description: Covers efforts by Unesco member states to implement a national information system.

027 NE ISSN 0165-2583
N B L C INFO BULLETIN. no.30, 1975. w. Nederlands Bibliotheek en Lektuur Centrum, Box 93054, 2509 AB The Hague, Netherlands. Ed. K. Schade van Westrum.
Description: Information on the activities of the NBLC, including news from local public libraries.

020 US
N C S U LIBRARIES FOCUS. 1964. q. free. North Carolina State University, Libraries, Box 7111, Raleigh, NC 27695-7111. TEL 919-515-2843. FAX 919-515-3628. Ed. Terrell A. Crow. circ. 4,000. (processed)
Formerly: D.H. Hill Library Focus.

025 US ISSN 0027-6448
Z673
N E L A NEWSLETTER. 1968. bi-m. $35. New England Library Association, Inc., Box 421, Wakefield, MA 01880-0921. TEL 617-438-7179. circ. 1,500.
Description: Covers Association news and events.

020 US ISSN 0028-5269
N H L A NEWSLETTER. vol.31, 1977. 6/yr. $4. New Hampshire Library Association, c/o Merrimack Public Library, 470 Daniel Webster Hwy., Merrimack, NH 03054. Ed. Diane Hathaway, Diane Arrato Gavrish. circ. 700. (processed)

LIBRARY AND INFORMATION SCIENCES

020　　　　　　TH　ISSN 0125-5606
N I D A BULLETIN. (Text in English, Thai) 1969. bi-m. $16. National Institute of Development Administration, Library and Information Center, Publication and Dissemination of Information Division, Klongjan, Bangkapi, Bangkok 10240, Thailand.

020　　　　　　　　　US
N M R T NEWSLETTER. (New Members Round Table) 1980. 3/yr. membership. Louisiana Library Association, Box 3058, Baton Rouge, LA 70821. TEL 504-342-4928. Eds. Debbie Legget, Betty Tucker. circ. 125. (back issues avail.)

020　　　　　　FI　ISSN 0358-7045
N O R D I N F O PUBLIKATION. 1981. irreg., no.21, 1991. price varies. Nordiska Samarbetsorganet för Vetenskaplig Information - Nordic Council for Scientific Information, c/o Helsinki University of Technology Library, Otnaesvaegen 9, SF-02150 Esbo, Finland. TEL 358-0-455-2633. FAX 358-0-455-2576. TELEX 12-1591-TKK-SF. circ. 2,500.
—BLDSC shelfmark: 6117.938000.
　Description: Information about the project activities of Nordinfo.

600　　　　　　　　　US
N T I S DIGEST. 1984. irreg. free. U.S. National Technical Information Service, 5285 Port Royal Rd., Springfield, VA 22161. TEL 703-487-4679. FAX 703-321-8547. TELEX 64617. **Indexed**: Concr.Abstr.

020　　　　　　　　　US
N T I S NEWSLINE. 1980. q. free. U.S. National Technical Information Service, 5285 Port Royal Rd., Springfield, VA 22161. TEL 703-487-4600. FAX 703-321-8547. TELEX 64617.

020　　　　　　US　ISSN 0027-7134
Z671
N Y L A BULLETIN. 1953. m. (Sep.-June). membership. New York Library Association, 252 Hudson Ave., Albany, NY 12210-1802. TEL 518-432-6952. FAX 518-427-1697. Ed. Gail Sacco. adv.; bk.rev.; illus.; circ. 3,500. (also avail. in microform from UMI; reprint service avail. from UMI) **Indexed**: ERIC, Lib.Lit.

020　　　　　　XV　ISSN 0350-3569
NARODNA IN UNIVERZITETNA KNJIZNICA. ZBORNIK. (Text in Slovenian; summaries in French and German) 1974. irreg. Narodna in Univerzitetna Knjiznica, Turjaska 1, 61001 Ljubljana, Slovenia. TEL 061-150-141. FAX 38-611-150-134. TELEX 32285 NUK-LJB-SLO. illus.

020　　　　　　CS　ISSN 0862-7487
Z795.A1
NARODNI KNIHOVNA. a? 10 Kcs. per issue. Narodni Knihovna v Praze, Klementium 190, 110 01 Prague 1, Czechoslovakia. TEL 22-59-93. FAX 261-775. TELEX 121207 STKN C. (Dist. by: Narodni Knihovna v Praze, Odd. Odbytu Publikaci, Liliova 5, 110 01 Prague 1, Czechoslovakia) circ. 300.
　Formerly (until 1990): Statni Knihovna C S R. Zpravodaj (ISSN 0139-6129)

020　　　　　　CS　ISSN 0036-5351
PG5000
NARODNI MUZEUM V PRAZE. SBORNIK. RADA C: LITERARNI HISTORIE/ACTA MUSEI NATIONALIS PRAGAE. (Text in Czech; summaries in English, French, German, Russian) 1955. q. 20 Kcs. Narodni Muzeum, Vaclavske nam. 68, 115 79 Prague 1, Czechoslovakia. TEL 269-451. (Dist. by: PNS - Ustredni Expedice a Dovoz Tisku Praha, Zavod 01, Administrace Vyvozu Tisku, Kafkova 19, 160 00 Prague 6, Czechoslovakia) Ed. Jaroslav Vrchotka. bibl.; illus.
—BLDSC shelfmark: 8083.100000.
　Formerly: Narodni Muzeum v Praze. Sbornik: Literarni Historie.

020　　　　　　UK　ISSN 0950-5326
NATIONAL ACQUISITIONS GROUP. NEWSLETTER. 1986. 4/yr. free. National Acquisitions Group, Westfield House, North Rd., Horsforth, Leeds LS18 5HG, England. TEL 0532-591447. adv.; circ. 400.
—BLDSC shelfmark: 6107.582950.
　Description: Covers the acquisition of library materials from book trade suppliers, topics in library collection development, bookselling and publishing.

025.17　　　　　ZA　ISSN 0084-4942
NATIONAL ARCHIVES OF ZAMBIA. ANNUAL REPORT. 1964. a. kip 50. National Archives, P.O. Box RW 50010, Ridgeway, Lusaka, Zambia.

020　　　　　　　　　CH
NATIONAL CENTRAL LIBRARY BULLETIN. (Text in Chinese) 1967. s-a. free. National Central Library, 20 Chung Shan S. Rd., Taipei, Taiwan 10040, Republic of China. FAX 02-311-0155. adv.; bk.rev.; bibl.; circ. 700.
　Formerly: National Central Library News Bulletin (ISSN 0251-4796)
　Description: Covers the affairs of the Library, theory and practice of library science. Includes the history of books and printing as well as other areas of history and literature.

020　　　　　　　　　NP
NATIONAL COUNCIL FOR SCIENCE & TECHNOLOGY. DIRECTORY; scientists and technologists of Nepal. (Text in English) 1977. a. $20. National Council for Science & Technology, Kirtipur, Kathmandu, Nepal. circ. 500.

027　　　　　　JA　ISSN 0027-9161
Z955.T585
NATIONAL DIET LIBRARY. NEWSLETTER. (Text in English) 1958. 3/yr. National Diet Library, Library Cooperation Department - Kokuritsu Kokkai Toshokan, 10-1 Nagata-cho 1-chome, Chiyoda-ku, Tokyo 100, Japan. TEL 03-3581-2331. TELEX 2225393. bk.rev.; bibl.; charts; illus.; stat.; circ. 1,000 (controlled).
—BLDSC shelfmark: 6021.875000.
　Description: Focuses on innovations in library science, staff activities and foreign language book acquisitions.

NATIONAL DIRECTORY OF BULLETIN BOARD SYSTEMS.
see *BUSINESS AND ECONOMICS — Trade And Industrial Directories*

NATIONAL INFORMATION CENTER FOR CHILDREN AND YOUTH WITH HANDICAPS. TRANSITION SUMMARY.
see *EDUCATION — Special Education And Rehabilitation*

020　　　　　　US　ISSN 1041-5653
NATIONAL INFORMATION STANDARDS SERIES. irreg. National Information Standards Organization (NISO), Box 1056, Bethesda, MD 20827. TEL 301-975-2814. FAX 301-869-8071. (Dist. by: Transaction Publishers, Department 3091, Rutgers University, New Brunswick, NJ 08903. TEL 908-932-2280)
　Description: Develops and promotes voluntary standards for information science, libraries, and related publishing practices.

020　　　　　　US　ISSN 0191-359X
NATIONAL LIBRARIAN; the N L A newsletter. 1976. q. $15. National Librarians Association, Box 486, Alma, MI 48801. TEL 517-463-7227. FAX 517-463-8694. Ed. Peter Dollard. adv.; bk.rev.; abstr.; bibl.; circ. 500. (back issues avail.)
—BLDSC shelfmark: 6026.241000.
　Formerly: N L A Newsletter.

020　　　　　　　　　RH
NATIONAL LIBRARY AND DOCUMENTATION SERVICE. ANNUAL REPORT. 1961. a. exchange basis. National Library and Documentation Service, P.O. Box 1773, Bulawayo, Zimbabwe. circ. 450.
　Former titles (until 1989): National Free Library of Zimbabwe. Annual Report; National Free Library Service. Annual Report; National Free Library of Rhodesia. Annual Report (ISSN 0068-3612)

020　　　　　　CN　ISSN 0027-9633
Z883.076
NATIONAL LIBRARY NEWS/BIBLIOTHEQUE NATIONALE. NOUVELLES. (Text in English and French) 1969. 10/yr. free. National Library of Canada, Publication and Marketing Services, 395 Wellington St., Ottawa, Ont. K1A 0N4, Canada. TEL 613-995-7969. FAX 613-996-7941. Ed.Bd. bibl.; illus.; circ. 5,000. **Indexed**: Can.Per.Ind., CMI.
●Also available online.
—BLDSC shelfmark: 6026.610000.
　Incorporates: Accessible (ISSN 0315-0003)
　Description: Information, news, and updates on activities and services of the Canadian National Library.

020　　　　　　AT　ISSN 0313-1971
NATIONAL LIBRARY OF AUSTRALIA. ANNUAL REPORT. 1961. a. Aus.$12.50. National Library of Australia, Publications Section, Public Programs, Parkes Place, Canberra, A.C.T. 2600, Australia. TEL 06-262-1365. FAX 06-273-4493. TELEX AA62100.
　Formerly: National Library of Australia. Annual Report of the Council (ISSN 0069-0082)

020　　　　　　AT　ISSN 1035-753X
▼**NATIONAL LIBRARY OF AUSTRALIA NEWS**. 1990. m. National Library of Australia, Publications Section, Public Programs, Parkes Place, Canberra, A.C.T 2600, Australia. TEL 06-262-1365. FAX 06-273-4493. Ed. Paul Hetherington. circ. 5,000.
　Description: Informative guide to library services.

027.571　　　　　CN　ISSN 0078-7000
NATIONAL LIBRARY OF CANADA. ANNUAL REPORT. (Text in English and French) 1953. a. free. National Library of Canada, Publications and Marketing Services, 395 Wellington St., Ottawa, Ont. K1A 0N4, Canada. TEL 613-995-7969. FAX 613-996-7941. circ. 4,500.

020　　　　　　US　ISSN 0093-0393
Z733
NATIONAL LIBRARY OF MEDICINE. PROGRAMS AND SERVICES. a. price varies. U.S. National Library of Medicine, 8600 Rockville Pike, Bethesda, MD 20894. TEL 301-496-6308. FAX 301-496-4450. (Subscr. to: NTIS, U.S. Dept. of Commerce, 5285 Port Royal Rd., Springfield, VA 22161) (reprint service avail. from UMI)
　Formerly (until 1972): U.S. National Library of Medicine. Annual Report (ISSN 0083-2243)

026 610　　　　US　ISSN 0027-965X
NATIONAL LIBRARY OF MEDICINE NEWS. 1945. m. free. U.S. National Library of Medicine, Office of Inquiries and Publications Management, 8600 Rockville Pike, Bethesda, MD 20894. TEL 301-496-6308. FAX 301-496-4450. (Subscr. to: University Microfilms, 330 N. Zeeb St., Ann Arbor, Michigan 48106. TEL 800-521-0600) Ed. Roger L. Gilkeson. illus.; circ. 6,000. (also avail. in microfilm from UMI; back issues avail.; reprint service avail. from UMI) **Indexed**: MEDOC.
—BLDSC shelfmark: 6102.600000.
　Description: Provides ongoing information about the world's largest medical library's people, programs, projects, and publications.

020　　　　　　UK　ISSN 0950-7086
NATIONAL LIBRARY OF SCOTLAND NEWS. 1986. 3/yr. free. National Library of Scotland, George IV Bridge, Edinburgh EH1 IEW, Scotland. TEL 031-226-4531. FAX 031-220-6662. Eds. Pauline Scott, Jackie Cromarty. circ. 4,500.
—BLDSC shelfmark: 6102.601000.
　Description: Discusses current activities and policies of the National Library of Scotland and the library community in Scotland.

NATIONAL ONLINE MEETING. PROCEEDINGS. see *MEETINGS AND CONGRESSES*

NATIONAL PRESERVATION OFFICE SEMINAR PAPERS. see *CONSERVATION*

020　　　　　　RU　ISSN 0548-0019
Z699.A1　　　　　　　　CODEN: NTOMAA
NAUCHNO-TEKHNICHESKAYA INFORMATSIYA. SERIYA 1. ORGANIZATSIYA I METODIKA INFORMATSIONNOI RABOTY. English translation: Scientific and Technical Information Processing (US ISSN 0147-6882) 1967. m. 15.6 Rub.($24) Vsesoyuznyi Institut Nauchno-Tekhnicheskoi Informatsii (VINITI), Baltiiskaya Ul., 14, Moscow A-219, Russia. bk.rev.; charts. **Indexed**: Chem.Abstr, Compumath, Curr.Cont., Lib.Lit., Sci.Abstr, SSCI.
—BLDSC shelfmark: 0121.090000.
　Formerly: Nauchno-Tekhnicheskaya Informatsiya (ISSN 0028-1131)

NEBRASKA LIBRARIES: A DIRECTORY. see *BUSINESS AND ECONOMICS — Trade And Industrial Directories*

LIBRARY AND INFORMATION SCIENCES

020 US ISSN 0028-1883
NEBRASKA LIBRARY ASSOCIATION QUARTERLY. 1970. q. $10 to non-members. Nebraska Library Association, c/o R. B. Means, Creighton University, 2500 California St., Omaha, NE 68178. TEL 402-280-2217. FAX 402-280-2435. Ed. Ron Norman. adv.; bk.rev.; circ. 900. **Indexed:** Lib.Lit.
—BLDSC shelfmark: 6068.260000.
Supersedes: Nebraska Library Association. Newsletter.

020 NE
NEDERLANDSE BIBLIOTHEEK- EN DOCUMENATIEGIDS; adresboek van in Nederland gevestigde bibliotheken en documentatieinstellingen. 1984. triennial. fl.125. (Federatie van Organistie op gebied van Bibliotheck-, Informatie-, en Documentatuewezen) Nederlands Bibliotheek en Lektuur Centrum, P.O.B. 93054, 2509 AB the Hague, Netherlands. adv.
Formerly: Venadam Bibliotheekgids.

020.6 UK
NEMCON. 1966. s-a. membership. Library Association, East-Midlands Division, Staveley Library, Hall Lane, Staveley, Chesterfield, Debbyshire S43 3TP, England. Ed. Ruth Kaye. bk.rev.; circ. 1,350.

020 011 GW ISSN 0028-3126
Z801
DIE NEUE BUECHEREI; Zeitschrift fuer die oeffentlichen Buechereien in Bayern. 1964. 5/yr. DM.30. Generaldirektion der Bayerischen Staatlichen Bibliotheken, Ludwigstr. 16, Postfach 340150, 8000 Munich 34, Germany. Eds. Helga Unger, Franz Kaessl. bk.rev.; charts, illus.; index, cum. index; circ. 1,500.

NEVADA LIBRARY DIRECTORY AND STATISTICS. see BUSINESS AND ECONOMICS — Trade And Industrial Directories

025 US ISSN 0887-3844
NEW DIRECTIONS IN INFORMATION MANAGEMENT. 1978. irreg., no.29, 1992. price varies. Greenwood Press, Inc. (Subsidiary of: Greenwood Publishing Group Inc.), 88 Post Rd. W., Box 5007, Westport, CT 06881-5007. TEL 203-226-3571. FAX 203-222-1502. Ed. Michael Buckland.
—BLDSC shelfmark: 6083.377000.
Formerly: New Directions in Librarianship (ISSN 0147-1090)

NEW ENGLAND SOUNDING LINE. see MEDICAL SCIENCES — Abstracting, Bibliographies, Statistics

020 US ISSN 0028-5811
Z732.N6
NEW JERSEY LIBRARIES. 1966; N.S. 1968. 4/yr. $12 to non-members. New Jersey Library Association, Box 1534, Trenton, NJ 08607. Ed. Eleanor Clarke. adv.; bibl.; circ. 1,900. (also avail. in microform from UMI; reprint service avail. from UMI) **Indexed:** Lib.Lit.

027.4 US
NEW JERSEY LIBRARIES NEWSLETTER. 1982. 11/yr. membership. New Jersey Library Association, Box 1534, Trenton, NJ 08607. Ed. Patricia A. Tumulty. circ. 1,900.

025.7 655 US ISSN 0735-8571
Z671
NEW LIBRARY SCENE.* 1953. bi-m. $18. Library Binding Institute, 7401 Metro Blvd., No. 325, Edina, MN 55439-3031. TEL 512-836-4141. FAX 512-836-4849. Ed. Sally Grauer. adv.; bk.rev.; charts; illus.; circ. 3,000. (also avail. in microfilm; back issues avail.; reprint service avail. from UMI) **Indexed:** Abstr.Engl.Stud., Graph.Arts Lit.Abstr., Leg.Info.Manage.Ind., LHTN, Lib.Lit.
—BLDSC shelfmark: 6084.454700.
Former titles (until 1982): Library Scene (ISSN 0090-8746); Library Binder (ISSN 0024-2209)
Description: Covers the library, binding preservation and conservation fields. Also addresses new technology, profiling individuals and achievements in the library binding fields.

020 UK ISSN 0307-4803
Z671
NEW LIBRARY WORLD. 1898. m. $759.95. M C B University Press Ltd., 62 Toller Ln., Bradford, W. Yorks BD8 9BY, England. TEL 0274-499821. FAX 0274-547143. TELEX 51317 MCBUNI G. Ed. Ian Pettman. adv.; bk.rev.; bibl.; illus.; index; circ. 1,000. (also avail. in microform from UMI; reprint service avail. from SWZ,UMI) **Indexed:** BMT, Educ.Tech.Abstr., LISA.
—BLDSC shelfmark: 6084.455000.
Formerly: Library World (ISSN 0024-2616)
Description: Covers news from America, commercial and technical news, research, community information, cuts and alerts.

020.6 US ISSN 0893-2956
NEW MEXICO LIBRARY ASSOCIATION NEWSLETTER.* 1972. 4/yr. membership. New Mexico Library Association, 4 Mariposa Eldorado, Santa Fe, NM 87505. TEL 505-277-6202. FAX 505-277-6019. Ed. Stefanie Wittenbach. adv.; bk.rev.; circ. 700.

026 US ISSN 0193-4287
NEW SPECIAL LIBRARIES. (Supplement to: Directory of Special Libraries and Information Centers) no.4, 1973. 2/yr. $335. Gale Research Inc., 835 Penobscot Bldg., Detroit, MI 48226. TEL 313-961-2242. FAX 313-961-6083. TELEX 810-221-7086. Ed. Janice A. DeMaggio.

027.4 US
NEW YORK PUBLIC LIBRARY NEWS. bi-m. $35 membership. New York Public Library, 455 Fifth Ave., New York, NY 10016. TEL 212-704-8600. FAX 212-768-7439. Ed. Esther Harriott. circ. 20,000.
Formerly: Library Lines.

027 US ISSN 0077-930X
KFN5675.A29
NEW YORK STATE LIBRARY, ALBANY. LIBRARY DEVELOPMENT. EXCERPTS FROM NEW YORK STATE EDUCATION LAW, RULES OF THE BOARD OF REGENTS, AND REGULATIONS OF THE COMMISSIONER OF EDUCATION PERTAINING TO PUBLIC AND FREE ASSOCIATION LIBRARIES, LIBRARY SYSTEMS, TRUSTEES AND LIBRARIANS. 1959. irreg. free to libraries in New York State; libraries elsewhere on exchange basis. New York State Library, Library Development, Albany, NY 12230. circ. 1,500.

020 NZ ISSN 0028-8381
Z671
NEW ZEALAND LIBRARIES. 1937. q. NZ.$55 (effective 1992). New Zealand Library Association, P.O. Box 12-212, Wellington 1, New Zealand. TEL 04-473-5834. FAX 04-499-1480. Ed. P. Calvert. adv.; bk.rev.; illus.; index. cum.index: vols. 1-20; 21-33; circ. 2,220. (also avail. in microfilm from UMI; reprint service avail. from UMI) **Indexed:** Lib.Lit., Lib.Sci.Abstr.
—BLDSC shelfmark: 6096.000000.

020 070.5 US
NEWBERRY NEWSLETTER. 1973. 4/yr. membership only. Newberry Library, 60 W. Walton St., Chicago, IL 60610. TEL 312-943-9090. Ed. Mary Patricia Mauro. illus.; circ. 5,500.

NEWS ABOUT LIBRARY SERVICES FOR THE BLIND AND PHYSICALLY HANDICAPPED. see HANDICAPPED

NEWS ABOUT THE A - V SCENE. see MOTION PICTURES

020 US ISSN 0730-1618
NEWS & CLUES. 1959. m. $25. San Joaquin Valley Library System, 2420 Mariposa St., Fresno, CA 93721. TEL 209-488-3229. FAX 209-488-2965. Ed. David DeLaurant. bk.rev.; circ. 275. (back issues avail.)
Description: Newsletter for cooperative library system.

020 US ISSN 0146-1842
Z732.S72
NEWS FOR SOUTH CAROLINA LIBRARIES. 1957. m. free. South Carolina State Library, 1500 Senate St., Box 11469, Columbia, SC 29211. TEL 803-734-8666. FAX 803-734-8676. Ed. Angela Cook. bibl.; circ. 1,800 (controlled). (processed)

020 US ISSN 1047-417X
NEWS LIBRARY NEWS. 1978. q. $30. Special Libraries Association, News Division, c/o Newsday Library, 235 Pinelawn Rd., Melville, NY 11747. TEL 516-454-2338. FAX 516-454-2323. (Subscr. to: Jan Summers, Box 798, News Library, Columbia Daily Tribune, Columbia, MO 65205) Ed. Elizabeth Whisnant. adv.; bk.rev.; index; circ. 750.
Description: Gives information services and technology for news researchers and professionals.

020 323.4 US ISSN 0028-9485
Z671
NEWSLETTER ON INTELLECTUAL FREEDOM. 1952. bi-m. $30 (foreign $40). American Library Association, Intellectual Freedom Committee, 50 E. Huron St., Chicago, IL 60611-2795. TEL 800-545-2433. FAX 312-440-9374. Ed. Judith F. Krug. bk.rev.; bibl.; index, cum.index: 1952-65 (in 2 vols.), 1966-72 (in 7 vols.), 1973-84 (in 4 vols.); circ. 3,200. (also avail. in microform from UMI; back issues avail.; reprint service avail. from UMI) **Indexed:** Curr.Lit.Fam.Plan., Lib.Lit.
Description: Report on threats to First Amendment rights.

020 US ISSN 1046-3410
NEWSLETTER ON SERIALS PRICING ISSUES. 1989; N.S. 1991. irreg. free. Marcia Tuttle, Ed. & Pub., Serials Department, C.B. 3938, Davis Library, University of North Carolina, Chapel Hill, NC 27599-3938. TEL 919-962-1067. FAX 919-962-0484. circ. 800. (electronic format; back issues avail.)
●Also available online.
Description: Scope includes trends in pricing for library serials, specific examples of price increases - decreases, libraries' strategies for coping with increasing prices of serials. Audience includes librarians, publishers, subscription agents, faculty members, and other scholars.

025 GW ISSN 0072-4866
NIEDERSAECHSISCHE STAATS- UND UNIVERSITAETSBIBLIOTHEK, GOETTINGEN. ARBEITEN. 1954. irreg., no.20, 1986. price varies. (Niedersaechsische Staats- und Universitaetsbibliothek) Vandenhoeck und Ruprecht, Robert-Bosch-Breite 6, 3400 Goettingen, Germany. TEL 0551-6959-0. FAX 0551-695917.

020 NR ISSN 0794-3865
NIGERIA PERIODICALS REVIEW. 1986. q. Abic Books & Equipment Ltd., 18 Kenyatta St., P.O. Box 13740, Enugu, Nigeria. TEL 042-331827. Ed. C.N.C. Asomugha. bk.rev.; abstr.; bibl. (back issues avail.)
—BLDSC shelfmark: 6112.147000.

020 655 NR ISSN 0029-0122
Z673.N698
NIGERIAN LIBRARIES. (Text in English) 1963. 3/yr. $6. (Nigerian Library Association) Ibadan University Press, University of Ibadan, Dept. of Library Studies, Ibadan, Nigeria. (Orders to: Business Manager, c/o University of Ibadan Library, Ibadan, Nigeria or P.M.B. 12655, Lagos, Nigeria) Ed. E. Bejide Bankole. adv.; bk.rev.; charts; illus.; stat.; index; circ. 500. (tabloid format) **Indexed:** Lib.Lit., Lib.Sci.Abstr.

020 NR ISSN 0189-4412
Z857.N5
NIGERIAN LIBRARY AND INFORMATION SCIENCE REVIEW. 1983. s-w. £N50($35) Nigerian Library Association, Oyo State Chapter, P.O. Box 20672, U.I. Post Office, Ibadan, Nigeria. Ed. B.C. Nzotta. adv.; bk.rev.; circ. 1,000. (back issues avail.)
—BLDSC shelfmark: 6112.142000.
Description: Publishes results of empirical research in library and information science, especially in Nigeria and Africa.

020 070.5 CC
NONGYE TUSHU QINGBAO XUEKAN/AGRICULTURAL BOOKS INFORMATION JOURNAL. (Text in Chinese) bi-m. Zhongguo Nongye Tushuguan Xiehui, 30, Baishiqiao Lu, Beijing 100081, People's Republic of China. TEL 8314433. Ed. Wang Yonghou.

020 FI ISSN 0356-9624
NORDINFO-NYTT. (Text in Danish, Norwegian, Swedish) 1978. 4/yr. free. Nordiska Samarbetsorganet for Vetenskaplig Information - Nordic Council for Scientific Inormation, c/o Helsinki University of Technology Library, Otnaesvaegen 9, SF-02150 Esbo, Finland. TEL 358-0-455-2633. FAX 358-0-455-2576. TELEX 12-1591-TKK-SF.
Description: Information about the project activities and working program of Nordinfo.

LIBRARY AND INFORMATION SCIENCES 2777

NORDISK TIDSKRIFT FOER BOK- OCH BIBLIOTEKSVAESEN/SCANDINAVIAN JOURNAL OF LIBRARIES. see *PUBLISHING AND BOOK TRADE*

026   NO
NORSKE VITENSKAPELIGE OG FAGLIGE BIBLIOTEKER; en haandbok. (Text in Norwegian; contents and subject index in English) 1963. irreg., no.7, 1991. price varies. Riksbibliotektjenesten, Box 2439, Solli, 0201 Oslo, Norway. TEL 02-430880. FAX 02-560981. (Dist. by: A-L Biblioteksentralen, Malerhaugveien 20, 0661 Oslo 6, Norway) Ed. Libena Vokac. bk.rev.
  Description: Detailed information about 380 academic and special libraries.

020   US   ISSN 0029-2540
Z671
NORTH CAROLINA LIBRARIES. 1942. q. $32 to non-members; foreign $50. North Carolina Library Association, Joyner Library, East Carolina University, Greenville, NC 27858. Ed. Frances Bryant Bradburn. adv.; bk.rev.; index; circ. 2,000. (also avail. in microform from UMI; reprint service avail. from UMI) **Indexed:** Lib.Lit., Lib.Sci.Abstr.
  —BLDSC shelfmark: 6149.055000.

027.7   CN   ISSN 0048-0754
NORTHERN AIR. 1969. s-a. free. Wapiti Regional Library, 145-12 St. E., Prince Albert, Sask. S6V 0K7, Canada. Ed. Karen Labuik. bk.rev.; circ. 200.

020   UK
NORTHERN EASTERN EDUCATION LIBRARY BOARD. LIBRARY BULLETIN. 1974. 3/yr. free. Northern Eastern Education Library Board, Area Library, Demesne Ave., Ballymena, Co. Antrim BT43 7BG, England. TEL 0266-41531.
  Formerly: Antrim County Library Quarterly Newssheet.

020   UK
NORTHERN LIBRARIAN. 1979. 6/yr. free. c/o Dorothy Procter, Denton Park Library, West Denton Way, Newscastle Upon Tyne NE5 2QZ, England. TEL 091-267-7922. circ. 1,300.
  Formerly: East Libraries Bulletin.
  Description: Information and comments about professional activities in the Library Association's northern branch area.

020   NO   ISSN 0800-4153
NORWAY. RIKSBIBLIOTEKTJENESTEN. AARSMELDING. a. free. Riksbibliotektjenesten, Box 2439, Solli, 0201 Oslo, Norway. TEL 02-430880. FAX 02-560981.
  Description: National Office for Research and Special Libraries' annual report.

020   NO   ISSN 0800-4129
NORWAY. RIKSBIBLIOTEKTJENESTEN. SKRIFTER. (Text in Norwegian) irreg. free. Riksbibliotektjenesten, Box 2439, Solli, 0201 Oslo, Norway. TEL 02-430880. FAX 02-560981.
  —BLDSC shelfmark: 8306.600000.
  Description: Committee reports and library studies.

NOTES AND QUERIES; for readers and writers, collectors and librarians. see *LITERATURE*

020   US
NOTES AND TRACINGS. 1980. 3/yr. membership. Louisiana Library Association, Box 3058, Baton Rouge, LA 70821. TEL 504-342-4928. Ed. Ada Jarred. circ. 450. (back issues avail.)

020   NR   ISSN 0331-1481
Z858.U465
NSUKKA LIBRARY NOTES. 1975. a. £N20($10) University of Nigeria, Library, Nsukka, Nigeria. TELEX ULIONS 51496. Ed. M.W. Anyakoha. adv.; circ. 400. (back issues avail.) **Indexed:** Lib.Lit.

020   DK   ISSN 0903-6342
NYT FRA NYHAVN. 1968. 4/yr. free. Statens Biblotektjeneste, Nyhavn 31E, DK-1051 Copenhagen K, Denmark. FAX 45-33-93-60-93. Ed. Peter Heise.
  Formerly (until 1988): Information for Forskningsbiblioteker (ISSN 0105-2616)
  Description: Official news and information from the Danish National Library Authority.

021.6   US   ISSN 0730-5125
Z732.05
O C L C ANNUAL REPORT. a. free. Online Computer Library Center, Inc., 6565 Frantz Rd., Dublin, OH 43017. TEL 614-764-6000. FAX 614-764-6096.
  —BLDSC shelfmark: 1382.160000.
  Formerly: Ohio College Library Center. Annual Report (ISSN 0090-8673)

020 378   US   ISSN 0163-898X
Z674.82.015
O C L C NEWSLETTER. 1967. m. free to qualified persons. Online Computer Library Center, Inc., 6565 Frantz Rd., Dublin, OH 43017. TEL 614-764-6000. Ed. Philip Schieber. bibl.; circ. 13,850.
  —BLDSC shelfmark: 6235.137000.

020   US
O D L ARCHIVES. 1984. 4/yr. free. Department of Libraries, 200 N.E. 18th St., Oklahoma City, OK 73105. TEL 405-521-2502. FAX 405-525-7804. Ed. Gary Harrington. circ. 100.
  Description: Information on state archives.

020   US
O D L RECORD. 1982. 4/yr. free. Department of Libraries, 200 N.E. 18th St., Oklahoma City, OK 73105-3298. TEL 405-521-2502. FAX 405-525-7804. Ed. Judith McCune. circ. 400.
  Description: Information to Oklahoma State Government Agencies on records management issues, workshops, helpful tips and more.

020   US   ISSN 0193-3086
O D L SOURCE. 1976. m. free. Department of Libraries, 200 N.E. 18th St., Oklahoma City, OK 73105. TEL 405-521-2502. FAX 405-525-7804. Eds. Marilyn Vesely, William R. Young. circ. 3,800.
  Description: Agency newsletter on news and events for Oklahoma's library community.

026   CN
O H L A NEWSLINE. 1986. q. Can.$50. Ontario Hospital Libraries Association, c/o Library, Ontario Hospital Assoc, 150 Ferrand Dr., Don Mills, Ont. M3C 1H6, Canada. TEL 416-429-2661. FAX 416-429-1363. Ed. Mary Conchelos. bk.rev.; circ. 200. (back issues avail.)
  Formerly: O H L A Newsletter (ISSN 0843-5901)

020   US
O I F MEMORANDUM. 1968. m. $20. American Library Association, Office for Intellectual Freedom, 50 E. Huron St., Chicago, IL 60611. FAX 312-440-9374. Eds. Judith F. Krug, Anne E. Levinson. bk.rev.; circ. 700.
  Formerly: American Library Association. Memorandum (ISSN 0734-3086)
  Description: Communication link between ALA Office for Intellectual Freedom and Intellectual Freedom Committees of the state library associations. Includes information on legislation, trends in censorship, and suggestions for programs through which librarians and the public can understand the importance of protecting intellectual freedom.

O I O C NEWSLETTER. (Oriental and India Office Collections) see *ORIENTAL STUDIES*

020   US   ISSN 0739-1153
O L A C NEWSLETTER. 1981. q. $10 to individuals; institutions $16 (foreign $18). Online Audiovisual Catalogers, Inc., Dartmouth College Library, Hanover, NH 03755. (Subscr. to: Bobby Ferguson, Treas., 285 Sharp Rd., Baton Rouge, LA 70815) Ed. Cecilia Piccolo Tittemore. bk.rev.; cum.index: 1981-1990; circ. 650.
  —BLDSC shelfmark: 6253.750000.
  Description: For catalogers of audiovisual media in an online environment.

020   US   ISSN 0278-4882
Z673.M64
OCCASIONAL PAPERS IN MIDDLE EASTERN LIBRARIANSHIP. 1981. irreg. $10 (foreign $15). Middle East Librarians' Association, c/o Michael E. Hopper, Library, University of California, Santa Barbara, CA 93106. TEL 805-893-3369. FAX 805-893-4676. Ed. David H. Partington. circ. 175.

352   NE   ISSN 0923-6600
OD. 1947. m. fl.56. (Vereniging voor Documentaire Informatievoorziening en Administratieve Organisatie) V N G Uitgeverij, P.O. Box 30435, 2500 GK The Hague, Netherlands. TEL 070-3738888. FAX 070-3651826. Ed.Bd. adv.; bk.rev.; illus.; index; circ. 3,300. **Indexed:** Key to Econ.Sci.
  Formerly (until 1989): Overheidsdocumentatie (ISSN 0166-9028)

026 016   AU
OESTERREICHISCHES STAATSARCHIV. PUBLIKATIONEN; Inventare oesterreichischer staatlicher Archive. 1909. irreg., vol.36, 1984. price varies. Verlag Ferdinand Berger und Soehne GmbH, Wienerstr. 21-23, A-3580 Horn, Austria. TEL 02982-2317-0.

OFFICIAL DIRECTORY OF NEW JERSEY LIBRARIES AND MEDIA CENTERS. see *BUSINESS AND ECONOMICS — Trade And Industrial Directories*

027   US
OHIO. STATE LIBRARY. ANNUAL REPORT. 1972. a. free. State Library Board, 65 S. Front St., Columbus, OH 43266-0334. TEL 614-644-6875. Ed. Jane M. Byrnes. charts; illus.; stat.
  Formerly: Ohio. State Library. State Library Review.

029   US   ISSN 1047-5400
OHIO ARCHIVIST. 1970. s-a. $10 to individuals; institutions $15; students $5. Society of Ohio Archivists, c/o Cleveland Clinic Archives, E-20, 9500 Euclid Ave., Cleveland, OH 44195. TEL 216-444-2929. FAX 216-444-5446. Ed. Frederick Lautzenheiser. adv.; bk.rev.; charts; illus.; circ. 500.
  Formerly: Society of Ohio Archivists Newsletter (ISSN 0030-0780)
  Description: Includes articles of interest to archives and manuscripts collections, news from Ohio archival and manuscripts collections and announcements and reports of meetings.

020   US   ISSN 1046-4336
                              CODEN: OHLIEG
OHIO LIBRARIES. 1988. 6/yr. $30. Ohio Library Association, 67 Jefferson Ave., Columbus, OH 43215. TEL 614-221-9057. FAX 614-221-6234. Ed. George Needham. adv.; bk.rev.; circ. 5,000. (also avail. in microform from UMI; reprint service avail. from UMI) **Indexed:** Lib.Lit.
  Formed by the 1988 merger of: O L A Bulletin (ISSN 0029-7135) & Ohio Libraries Newsletter & Ohio Library Trustee (ISSN 0030-0977)
  Description: Contains articles of current interest, historical significance, or literary value concerning all aspects of librarianship, especially items pertinent to Ohio, and includes official statements of the Association.

027.8   US   ISSN 0192-6942
Z675.S3
OHIO MEDIA SPECTRUM. 1976. q. $30. Ohio Educational Library Media Association, 67 Jefferson Ave., Columbus, OH 43215-3840. TEL 614-221-9057. Ed. Edward F. Newren. adv.; bk.rev.; cum.index; circ. 1,300. (also avail. in microfilm from UMI; reprint service avail. from UMI) **Indexed:** Lib.Lit.
  —BLDSC shelfmark: 6247.105000.
  Formed by the 1976 merger of: Ohio Association of School Librarians' Bulletin (ISSN 0030-0799); Educational Media in Ohio.
  Description: Provides news of Association activities and discussions of issues in librarianship.

OHIOANA QUARTERLY. see *LITERATURE*

020   JA
OKINAWA TOSHOKAN KYOKAI SHI/OKINAWA LIBRARY ASSOCIATION. ANNALS. 1964. a. 500 Yen. Okinawa Toshokan Kyokai - Okinawa Library Association, c/o Okinawa Prefectural Library, 2-16 Yorimiya 1-chome, Naha, Okinawa, Japan. adv.; bk.rev.; circ. 1,000.

LIBRARY AND INFORMATION SCIENCES

027 US
OKLAHOMA DEPARTMENT OF LIBRARIES. ANNUAL REPORT; Oklahoma Public Library Service in communites and state institutions. 1984. a. free. Department of Libraries, 200 N.E. 18th St., Oklahoma City, OK 73105. TEL 405-521-2502. FAX 405-525-7804. Ed. Beverly Jones. circ. 400.
  Supersedes in part (1955-1984): Oklahoma. Department of Libraries. Annual Report and Directory of Libraries in Oklahoma (ISSN 0066-4065)
  Description: Oklahoma library statistics.

OKLAHOMA GOVERNMENT PUBLICATIONS; a checklist. see PUBLIC ADMINISTRATION

020 US ISSN 0030-1760
Z732
OKLAHOMA LIBRARIAN. 1950. bi-m. $15 (foreign $20). Oklahoma Library Association, 300 Hardy Dr., Edmond, OK 73013. TEL 405-348-0506. Eds. Karen Morris, Jennifer Paustenbaugh. adv.; bk.rev.; bibl.; illus.; cum.index: 1950-1965; circ. 1,100. (also avail. in microform from UMI; reprint service avail. from UMI)

OMNIBUS. see BIBLIOGRAPHIES

023 US ISSN 0748-8831
ONE-PERSON LIBRARY; a newsletter for librarians & management. 1984. m. $70 (foreign $80). O P L Resources, Ltd., Murray Hill Sta., Box 948, New York, NY 10156-0614. TEL 212-683-6285. Ed. Andrew Berner. bk.rev.; index; circ. 2,000. (looseleaf format; back issues avail.)

ONLINE BUSINESS SOURCEBOOK. see BUSINESS AND ECONOMICS

026 CN ISSN 0826-7871
ONTARIO GOVERNMENT LIBRARIES COUNCIL. EXCHANGE. 1971. q. free. Ontario Government Libraries Council, Ministry of Government Services, 77 Wellesley St., W., 4th Fl., Ferguson Block, Toronto, Ont. M7A 1N3, Canada. TEL 416-327-2535. FAX 416-327-2530. circ. 100. (looseleaf format)
  Description: News and issues of interest to Ontario government libraries.

020 NE ISSN 0030-3372
CODEN: OPNNBQ
OPEN; vaktijdschrift voor bibliothecarissen, literatuuronderzoekers en documentalisten. (Text mainly in Dutch; occasionally in English; summaries in English) 1969. 11/yr. fl.95. c/o C. Van Schendel, Keizersgracht 802III, 1017 ED Amsterdam, Netherlands. TEL 020-6224322. FAX 020-6384860. (Subscr. to: Stichting Vaktydschrift, Postbus 572, 2600 AN Delft, Netherlands. TEL 015-562073) adv.; bk.rev.; abstr.; bibl.; charts; illus.; index; circ. 4,500. (also avail. in microform from UMI; reprint service avail. from UMI) **Indexed:** Key to Econ.Sci., Lib.Lit., Sci.Abstr.
  —BLDSC shelfmark: 6265.945000.

023 UK ISSN 0048-1904
OPEN ACCESS; a magazine for West Midland librarians. vol.22, 1978. 2/yr. £7. Library Association, West Midland Branch, c/o Book Purchase Dept., Birmingham Central Library, Chamberlain Square, Birmingham B3 3HQ, England. FAX 021-233-4458. Ed. Martin Underwood. adv.; circ. 1,650.
  —BLDSC shelfmark: 6265.950000.

020.6 US
OPERATIONS UPDATE (MOUNTAIN VIEW). q. Research Libraries Group, Inc., 1200 Villa St., Mountain View, CA 94041-1100. TEL 415-691-2207. FAX 415-964-0943.

027.625 AT
ORANA; journal for school and children's librarians. 1965. q. Aus.$25 (foreign Aus.$32)(effective 1992). Australian Library and Information Association, P.O. Box E411, Queen Victoria Terrace, A.C.T. 2600, Australia. TEL 06-285-1877. FAX 06-282-2249. Ed. Mrs. Val Watson. adv.; bk.rev.; circ. 3,700. **Indexed:** Aus.Educ.Ind., Aus.P.A.I.S., Child.Lit.Abstr.
  Formerly: Children's Libraries Newsletter (ISSN 0045-6705)

020 US
ORANGE SEED TECHNICAL BULLETIN. 1973. m. free to qualified personnel. Department of State, Division of Library and Information Services, R.A. Gray Bldg., Tallahassee, FL 32399-0250. TEL 904-487-2651. Ed. Lawrence Webster. bk.rev.; film rev.; circ. 500 (controlled).
  Formerly: Orange Seed; Incorporates (1970-1989): Intercom Technical Bulletin; (1968-1988): Keystone (ISSN 0741-918X)
  Description: News from the State Library on all library related news, resources, new publications, events, and fundraising throughout the state. Includes information on the activities of Firends of Libraries groups throughout the state, and articles for librarians in special libraries.

020 US ISSN 0030-4735
OREGON LIBRARY NEWS. 1952. m. $15. Oregon Library Association, c/o Carolyn Peake, Pres., 6 Adams Ct., Lake Oswego, OR 97034. Ed. Wayne L. Suggs. adv.; circ. 750. (processed)

020 US ISSN 0078-6381
ORGANIZATION OF AMERICAN STATES. DEPARTMENT OF CULTURAL AFFAIRS. MANUALES DEL BIBLIOTECARIO. 1961. irreg., latest no.9. $15. Organization of American States, 1889 F St., N.W., Washington, DC 20006. TEL 703-941-1617. circ. 2,000.

ORO MADRE. see LITERATURE

020 HU ISSN 0524-8868
ORSZAGOS SZECHENYI KONYVTAR EVKONYVE. (Text in Hungarian; summaries in English, French, German, Russian) 1958. a. 170 Ft. Orszagos Szechenyi Konyvtar - National Szechenyi Library, Budavari Palota F epulet, 1827 Budapest, Hungary. TEL 175-7533. FAX 202-0804. TELEX 224226 BIBLN H. Ed. Ilona Kovacs. circ. 800.
  Description: Yearbook containing reports and essays on the history and activity of the National Szechenyi Library, as well as studies on the history of bibliography and culture.

026 HU ISSN 0030-6010
Z675.M4
ORVOSI KONYVTAROS/MEDICAL LIBRARIAN. (Text in Hungarian; summaries in English) 1961. q. 240 Ft.($17.50) Orszagos Orvostudomanyi Informacios Intezet es Konyvtar - National Institute for Medical Information and Library of Medicine, Szentkiralyi u. 21, 1088 Budapest, Hungary. TEL 361-117-6352. Eds. Dr. Maria Benda, Dr. Tibor Koltay. bk.rev.; index; circ. 350.
  —BLDSC shelfmark: 6296.504000.
  Description: Directed at continuing education of medical librarians.

026 610 CN ISSN 0085-4557
OSLER LIBRARY NEWSLETTER. 1969. 3/yr. free. McGill University, Osler Library, 3655 Drummond St., Montreal, Que. H3G 1Y6, Canada. TEL 514-398-4720. FAX 514-398-5747. Ed. F.E. Wallis. circ. 1,400.

020 US ISSN 0030-7319
OUTRIDER. 1968. m. free. State Library, Supreme Court Bldg., Cheyenne, WY 82002. TEL 307-777-7281. Ed. Linn Rounds. bk.rev.; circ. 1,550. (processed)

020 DK ISSN 0904-3853
OVER BROEN. 1970. m. DKK 40. Danmarks Biblioteksskole, Birketinget 6, 2300 Copenhagen S, Denmark. Ed.Bd. bibl.; illus.; circ. 500.
  Formerly (until 1988): Biblioten.

020 US ISSN 0161-1828
HV1571
OVERSEAS OUTLOOK (LARGE PRINT EDITION). 1977. s-a. free to qualified individuals. U.S. Library of Congress, National Library Service for the Blind and Physically Handicapped, Washington, DC 20542. TEL 202-707-5100. (large print in 18 pt.)

020 US ISSN 0149-5011
OVERTONES. m. Library Commission, 1420 P St., Lincoln, NE 68508. TEL 402-471-2045. circ. 2,000.
  Formerly: Overtones from the Underground.
  Description: News and feature articles concerning Nebraska libraries.

020 FJ ISSN 1011-5080
P I C NEWSLETTER. 1980. q. free. Pacific Information Centre, University of the South Pacific, G.P.O. Box 1168, Suva, Fiji. TEL 313900. FAX 300830.
  Supersedes: R B C Newsletter.

020 PK ISSN 0048-2714
P L A NEWSLETTER.* (Text in English) 1970. m. Rs.12. Pakistan Library Association, c/o Pakistan Institute of Development Economics, P.O.B. 1091, Islamabad, Pakistan. Ed. Syed Mubarak Ali. adv.; charts; circ. 1,000. (processed; also avail. in microform from UMI; reprint service avail. from UMI) **Indexed:** Lib.Lit.

027.4 PP
P N G L A NIUS.* 1980. s-a. (included in subscr. to: Tok Tok Bilong Haus Buk). Papua New Guinea Library Association, c/o National Library Service, Boroko 5770, Boroko, N.S.C., Papua New Guinea. Ed.Bd.

020 US ISSN 0030-8188
Z673.P11
P N L A QUARTERLY. 1936. q. price varies. Pacific Northwest Library Association, 1631 E. 24th Ave., Eugene, OR 97403-1718. FAX 503-346-3023. Ed. Katherine G. Eaton. adv.; bk.rev.; bibl.; illus.; index; circ. 1,000. (also avail. in microform from UMI; reprint service avail. from UMI) **Indexed:** Curr.Cont., Lib.Lit., Lib.Sci.Abstr.
  —BLDSC shelfmark: 6541.130000.

P R ACTIVITY REPORT. see ADVERTISING AND PUBLIC RELATIONS

020 US ISSN 0195-9646
PACKET; newsletter of the Mississippi Library Commission. 1968. m. free. Library Commission, Box 10700, Jackson, MS 39289-0700. TEL 601-359-1036. FAX 601-354-4181. Ed. Lisa W. Ruble. adv.; bk.rev.; circ. 2,400. (reprint service avail. from UMI)

020 CR ISSN 0257-0114
PAGINAS DE CONTENIDO: CIENCIAS DE LA INFORMACION. 1979. 3/yr. $12 to non-members. Asociacion Interamericana de Bibliotecarios y Documentalistas Agricolas, Apdo. Postal 55, 2200 Coronado, Costa Rica. TEL 29-0222. FAX 506-294741. TELEX 2144 IICA. Ed. Ghislaine Poitevien.
  Description: Reproduction of table of contents of library and information science journals available at cooperating libraries.

020 PK ISSN 0030-9966
Z845.P28
PAKISTAN LIBRARY BULLETIN. (International ed. in English; domestic ed. in English and Urdu) 1966. q. Rs.80($80) per no. Library Promotion Bureau, P.O. Box 8421, University of Karachi, Karachi 75270, Pakistan. Ed.Bd. adv.; bk.rev.; charts; index; circ. 500. **Indexed:** Hist.Abstr., Lib.Lit., Lib.Sci.Abstr, R.G.
  —BLDSC shelfmark: 6343.029000.

PAKISTAN'S BOOKS & LIBRARIES; the only monthly magazine of its kind. see PUBLISHING AND BOOK TRADE

020.6 DR
PAPIRO. 1976. q. $5. Asociacion Dominicana de Bibliotecarios, Biblioteca Nacional, Plaza de la Cultura, Santo Domingo, Dominican Republic. Dir. Miriam Michel de Campusano. adv.; bk.rev.; bibl.; circ. 500.

020 AT
PARAPHERNALIA. 1978. q. Aus.$15 to non-members. Australian Library and Information Association, Norther Territory Branch, P.O. Box 41303, Casuarina, N.T. 0811, Australia. FAX 089-228208. Eds. Ann Alderslade, Lucinda Steuart. adv.; circ. 120.
  Formerly (until 1989): N T Newsletter (ISSN 0157-2229)
  Description: Information for and about libraries in the Northern Territory.

020 282 US
PARISH AND COMMUNITY LIBRARIES NEWS. 1960. bi-m. membership. Catholic Library Association, Parish Section, Box 16321, St. Paul, MN 55116. FAX 612-690-2131. Ed. Betty Hammargren. adv.; bk.rev.; bibl.; circ. 350 (controlled). (processed)
  Formerly: Parish and Lending Library News (ISSN 0008-8188)

020　　　　　　　　IT　　ISSN 0031-2371
PAROLA E IL LIBRO;* the word and the book. 1917. m. L.1200. Ente Nazionale per le Biblioteche Popolari e Scholastiche, Via Michele Mercati 4, 00153 Rome, Italy. Dir. Ettore Apollonj. bk.rev.; illus.; index; circ. 25,000. Indexed: Lib.Sci.Abstr.

020　　　　　　　　US　　ISSN 0197-9299
Z673.P395
PENNSYLVANIA LIBRARY ASSOCIATION. BULLETIN. Short title: P L A Bulletin. 1945. 8/yr. $25 to non-members. Pennsylvania Library Association, 3107 N. Front St., Harrisburg, PA 17110-1203. FAX 717-233-3121. Ed. Margaret Bauer. adv.; bk.rev.; illus.; stat.; index. cum.index: 1945-1958; circ. 2,000. (looseleaf format; also avail. in microfilm from UMI; back issues avail.; reprint service avail. from UMI) **Indexed:** Lib.Lit, Lib.Sci.Abstr, LISA.

020　　　　　　　　US　　ISSN 0079-0656
PENNSYLVANIA STATE UNIVERSITY. LIBRARIES. BIBLIOGRAPHICAL SERIES. 1969. irreg., latest no.11. price varies. Pennsylvania State University, University Libraries, University Park, PA 16802. TEL 814-865-0401. FAX 814-865-3665. Ed. Jillian Stevenson. circ. 500.

025　　　　　　　　UK
PERGAMON JOURNALS BULLETIN. m. free. Pergamon Press plc, Headington Hill Hall, Oxford OX3 0BW, England. TEL 0865-794141. FAX 0865-743911. TELEX 83177 PERGAP. (And: 660 White Plains Rd., Tarrytown, NY 10591-5153. TEL 914-524-9200)
Description: Lists dispatch dates for all currently published journals, with news of forthcoming volumes, title changes, cessations and new publications available from Pergamon.

020　　　　　　　　UK
PERSONNEL, TRAINING AND EDUCATION; a journal for library and information workers. 1983. 3/yr. £35. British Library of Political and Economic Science, London School of Economics, 10 Portugal St., London WC2A 2HD, England. (Co-sponsor: Library Association, Personnel, Training & Education Group) Ed. H. Nicholson. adv.; bk.rev.; circ. 1,050. **Indexed:** C.I.J.E., Cont.Pg.Educ., Inform.Sci.Abstr., Lib.Lit., Lib.Sci.Abstr., Ref.Zh.
Formerly: Training and Education (ISSN 0264-8466)

PERSONS TO CONTACT FOR VISITING SCHOOL LIBRARY MEDIA PROGRAMS. see *EDUCATION — International Education Programs*

027.4　　　　　　　MY
PERUTUSAN RATU DARUL EHSAN. 1989. a. Selangor Public Library Corporation, Perpustakaan Raja Tun Uda, Persiaran Perdagangan, 40572 Shah Alam, Malaysia. FAX 03-559-6045. circ. 1,000.
Description: Newsletter of the library.

020　　　　　　　　HU　　ISSN 0209-6145
PEST MEGYEI KONYVTAROS. 1955. q. free. Pest Megyei Konyvtar, Engels u. 7, 2001 Szentendre, Hungary. TEL 10-870. FAX 10-320. TELEX 22-4712 PMKK H. Ed. Biczak Peter. bk.rev.; circ. 500. (back issues avail.)

026　　　　　　　　JA　　ISSN 0386-2062
Z675.P48　　　　　　　　　CODEN: YATODW
PHARMACEUTICAL LIBRARY BULLETIN/YAKUGAKU TOSHOKAN. (Text in Japanese) 1956. q. 6000 Yen. Japan Pharmaceutical Library Association - Nihon Yakugaku Toshokan Kyogikai, University of Tokyo, Faculty of Pharmaceutical Science, 7-3-1 Hongo, Bunkyo-ku, Tokyo 113, Japan. Ed. S. Takada. adv.; bk.rev.; circ. 1,200. **Indexed:** Chem.Abstr.
—BLDSC shelfmark: 6444.007000.

020　　　　　　　　PH
PHILIPPINE LIBRARY ASSOCIATION. BULLETIN. (Text in English) vol.8, 1973. a. P.10($6) Philippine Library Association, c/o National Library, T.M. Kalaw St., Manila, Philippines. Ed. Angelica A. Cabanero. adv.; bk.rev.; circ. 1,000. (back issues avail.) **Indexed:** Ind.Phil.Per.

020　　　　　　　　PH　　ISSN 0115-7167
PHILIPPINES. NATIONAL LIBRARY. T N L NEWS. (The National Library) q. National Library, T.M. Kalaw St., Manila, Philippines.
Description: Official newsletter of the Philippine National Library.

PHILIPPINES. NATIONAL PRINTING OFFICE. ITEMIZATION OF PERSONAL SERVICES AND ORGANIZATIONAL CHARTS. see *PUBLIC ADMINISTRATION*

027　　　　　　　　US　　ISSN 0196-6707
PITTSBURGH REGIONAL LIBRARY CENTER. NEWSLETTER. 1967. 4/yr. $25 (foreign $50). Pittsburgh Regional Library Center, 103 Yost Blvd., Pittsburgh, PA 15221. TEL 412-825-0600. FAX 412-825-0762. Ed. H.E. Broadbent, III. adv.; circ. 600.

PLAN DE CLASSEMENT P A S C A L. (Programme Applique a la Selection et la Compilation Automatique de la Literature) see *LIBRARY AND INFORMATION SCIENCES — Computer Applications*

020　　　　　　　　CN　　ISSN 0704-0628
PLUG-IN. 1977. q. free. Ontario Library Services Centre, 141 Dearborn Place, Waterloo, Ont. N2J 4N5, Canada. TEL 519-746-4420. FAX 519-746-4425. Ed. Bill Zambusi. circ. 250.

020　　　　　　　　US
POINTS NORTH. 1968. 10/yr. membership. North Country Reference & Research Resources Council, Box 568, Canton, NY 13617. TEL 315-386-4569. FAX 315-379-9553. Ed. Bridget Doyle. stat.; circ. 200 (controlled). (processed)
Formerly (until 1988): North Country Reference and Research Resources Council. Newsletter (ISSN 0029-2699)

020　　　　　　　　US
POINTS NORTHWEST. 1972. 4/yr. $5 to non-members. American Society for Information Science, Pacific Northwest Chapter, c/o Peg Walter, Ed., City University Library, 4030 86th Ave., S.E., Mercer Island, WA 98040. TEL 206-232-1745. adv.; bk.rev.; circ. 120.
Description: Includes references to articles of current interest, information about the Society, the PNW Chapter and its meetings.

026 060　　　　　　PL　　ISSN 0079-3140
Z818.P62
POLSKA AKADEMIA NAUK. BIBLIOTEKA, KRAKOW. ROCZNIK. (Text in Polish; summaries in English and Russian) 1955. a. price varies. Ossolineum, Publishing House of the Polish Academy of Sciences, Rynek 9, 50-106 Wroclaw, Poland. TELEX 0712771 OSS PL. (Dist. by: Ars Polona-Ruch, Krakowskie Przedmiescie 7, Warsaw, Poland) Ed. Krystyna Stachowska. index.
Description: Articles and source materials related to the history of science, culture and recordmaking of the library collection in Krakow and Krakow region.

020　　　　　　　　CN　　ISSN 1183-0824
LE PONT. 1984. 5/yr. Can.$25. Biblio-Regions de Quebec et Chaudiere-Appalaches, 3189 Rue Albert-Demers, Charny, Que. G6X 3A1, Canada. FAX 418-832-6168. adv.; circ. 550.
Formerly (until 1990): L'Agent 03 (ISSN 0829-0938)

020　　　　　　　　US　　ISSN 1053-8747
　　　　　　　　　　　　　　CODEN: PCLIEQ
▼**POPULAR CULTURE IN LIBRARIES.** 1992. q. $18 to individuals; institutions and libraries $24. Haworth Press, Inc., 10 Alice St., Binghamton, NY 13904-1580. TEL 800-342-9678. FAX 607-722-1424. TELEX 4932599. Ed. Frank Hoffman. (also avail. in microfiche from HAW; reprint service avail. from HAW)
Description: Deals with the selection, acquisition, evaluation, organization, and utilization of popular culture materials and concepts for libraries, special collections, and archives.
Refereed Serial

020　　　　　　　　PL　　ISSN 0032-4752
Z671
PORADNIK BIBLIOTEKARZA. 1949. m. $45. Stowarzyszenie Bibliotekarzy Polskich, Konopczynskiego 5-7, 00-953 Warsaw, Poland. TEL 27 52 96. (Dist. by: Ars Polona-Ruch, Krakowskie Przedmiescie 7, 00-068 Warsaw, Poland) Ed. Wladyslawa Wasilewska. bk.rev.; bibl.; illus.; index; circ. 23,341. **Indexed:** LISA.
—BLDSC shelfmark: 6553.800000.

020 800　　　　　　US　　ISSN 0899-9821
Z666
PREVIEW (ANN ARBOR); professional and reference literature review. 1988. m. $25 (foreign $35). Mountainside Publishing, Inc., 321 S. Main St., Ste. 300, Box 8330, Ann Arbor, MI 48107. TEL 313-662-3925. FAX 313-662-4450. Ed. Christy Havens. adv.; bk.rev.; cum.index; circ. 2,500. (back issues avail.)
—BLDSC shelfmark: 6612.810000.
Description: Notice and evaluations of new publications in library and information science, allied fields, and new reference titles. Includes original reviews, annotations, and summaries of reviews from over 100 journals; reviews of software for library applications; new editions; children's reference materials.

029.7 976 333.7　　US　　ISSN 0741-6563
THE PRIMARY SOURCE. 1979. q. $7.50 to individuals. Society of Mississippi Archivists, Box 1151, Jackson, MS 39215-1151. TEL 601-359-6868. FAX 601-359-6905. Ed. Sandra E. Boyd. bk.rev.; circ. 200. (looseleaf format; back issues avail.)
Description: Compilation of meeting reports and publications, accessions from state repositories, and news for those interested in archives and history.

020　　　　　　　　US　　ISSN 1042-8216
Z688.A2
PRIMARY SOURCES & ORIGINAL WORKS. 1981. q. $25 to individuals; institutions and libraries $45. Haworth Press, Inc., 10 Alice St., Binghamton, NY 13904. TEL 800-342-9678. FAX 607-722-1424. TELEX 4932599. Ed. Lee Ash. adv.; bk.rev.; bibl.; circ. 236. (also avail. in microfiche from HAW; back issues avail.; reprint service avail. from HAW) **Indexed:** Inform.Sci.Abstr., Lib.Lit., LISA, Sci.Abstr.
Formerly (until vol.4, no.2, 1990): Special Collections (ISSN 0270-3157)
Description: Provides guide to and description of collections in a specific subject field.
Refereed Serial

027.1　　　　　　　UK　　ISSN 0032-8898
Z990
PRIVATE LIBRARY. 1957. q. £20($40) Private Libraries Association, Ravelston, South View Road, Pinner, Middlesex HA5 3YD, England. (US address: c/o William A. Klutts, 145 East Jackson, Box 289, Ripley, TN 38063) Ed. David Chambers. adv.; bk.rev.; illus.; circ. 1,000. **Indexed:** Abstr.Engl.Stud., Artbibl.Mod., Ind.Bk.Rev.Hum., Lib.Lit., Lib.Sci.Abstr.
—BLDSC shelfmark: 6617.066000.
Description: Essays concerned with book collecting.

029.7　　　　　　　RM　　ISSN 0018-9111
PROBLEME DE INFORMARE SI DOCUMENTARE. (Text in English, Rumanian) 1967. q. $111 or exchange basis. Institutul National de Informare si Documentare, Str. Cosmonautilor 27-29, 70141 Bucharest, Rumania. TEL 134010. TELEX 11247 INIDR. (Dist. by: Rompresfilatelia, Export-Import Presa, Calea Grivitei nr.64-66, 78104 Bucharest 12, Rumania) bk.rev.; bibl.; charts; illus.; circ. 1,500. **Indexed:** Chem.Abstr., Ref.Zh., Sci.Abstr.
—BLDSC shelfmark: 6617.560000.
Formerly: Probleme de Documentare si Informare.
Description: Contains studies, news, and technical notes in the field of information science and librarianship.

029　　　　　　　　US　　ISSN 8755-0253
PROFESSIONAL DOCUMENT RETRIEVAL.* 1985. q. $15. Information Store, Inc., 500 Sansome St., K No.400, San Francisco, CA 94111-3219. TEL 415-543-4636. Ed. Keith Emerson. circ. 1,500.
—BLDSC shelfmark: 6857.740000.

PROGRESS IN COMMUNICATION SCIENCES. see *COMMUNICATIONS*

PROVENANCE. see *HISTORY — History Of North And South America*

LIBRARY AND INFORMATION SCIENCES

020   PL   ISSN 0033-202X
Z671
PRZEGLAD BIBLIOTECZNY. (Supplement avail.: Bibliografia Analityczna Bibliotekoznawstwa i Informacji Naukowej) (Text in Polish; summaries in English) 1927. q. $32. (Polska Akademia Nauk, Biblioteka, Palac Kultury i Nauki) Ossolineum, Publishing House of the Polish Academy of Sciences, Rynek 9, Wroclaw, Poland. TELEX 0712771 OSS PL. (Dist. by: Ars Polona-Ruch, Krakowskie Przedmiescie 7, Warsaw, Poland) (Co-sponsor: Stowarzyszenie Bibliotekarzy Polskich) Ed. Barbara Sordylowa. bk.rev.; charts; illus.; index; cum.index: 1927-1976; circ. 5,000. (also avail. in microform from UMI; reprint service avail. from UMI) **Indexed:** Lib.Lit., Lib.Sci.Abstr., LISA.
—BLDSC shelfmark: 6939.000000.

020   659.1   UK   ISSN 0268-0149
PUBLIC EYE. 1984. 4/yr. £8. Library Association, Publicity and P R Group, c/o Princes Risborough Library, Bell St., Princes Risborough, Buckinghamshire, England. TEL 08444-3559. Ed. Alec Kennedy. bk.rev.; illus.; circ. 1,350. (back issues avail.)
—BLDSC shelfmark: 6963.396000.
Description: Covers library publicity and promotion, PR, marketing, design and print.

027.4   US   ISSN 0163-5506
Z731
PUBLIC LIBRARIES. 1970. 6/yr. $45 (foreign $55). (Public Library Association) American Library Association, 50 E. Huron St., Chicago, IL 60611-2795. TEL 800-545-2433. FAX 312-440-9374. Ed. Sandra Garrison. adv.; circ. 5,781. (also avail. in microform from UMI; back issues avail.; reprint service avail. from UMI) **Indexed:** Lib.Lit.
—BLDSC shelfmark: 6967.185000.
Former titles: P L A Newsletter (ISSN 0022-6998); Just Between Ourselves.
Description: News and articles of interest to public libraries.

020   UG
PUBLIC LIBRARIES BOARD. NEWSLETTER. 2/yr. Public Libraries Board, P.O. Box 4262, Kampala, Uganda.
Description: Contains news of events happening on the library scene at the Public Libraries Board and in Uganda; includes feature articles.

025   UK   ISSN 0268-893X
          CODEN: PLJOET
PUBLIC LIBRARY JOURNAL. 1986. bi-m. £36. Library Association - Public Library Group, 7 Ridgmount St., London WC1E 7AE, England. FAX 081-508-5041. (Subscr. to: Woodspring Central Library, Boulevard, Weston-S-Mare, Avon BS23 1PL, England) Ed. Rob Froud. adv.; bk.rev.; illus.; bibl.; index; circ. 7,000. (back issues avail.) **Indexed:** Lib.Lit., Lib.Sci.Abstr., LISA.
—BLDSC shelfmark: 6967.241800.

020   US   ISSN 0161-6846
Z671
PUBLIC LIBRARY QUARTERLY. 1979. q. $36 to individuals; institutions $85. Haworth Press, Inc., 10 Alice St., Binghamton, NY 13904. TEL 800-342-9678. FAX 607-722-1424. TELEX 4932599. Ed. Richard L. Waters. adv.; bk.rev.; circ. 475. (also avail. in microfiche from HAW; back issues avail.; reprint service avail. from HAW) **Indexed:** Comput.& Info.Sys., Excerp.Med., Inform.Sci.Abstr., LHTN, Lib.Lit., LISA.
—BLDSC shelfmark: 6967.242000.
Description: Addresses the major administrative challenges and opportunities that face the nation's public libraries.
Refereed Serial

PUBLISHERS' CATALOGS ANNUAL. see *BIBLIOGRAPHIES*

025   CE
PUSTAKALA PRAVRTTI. (Text in Sinhalese) 1973. q. Rs.20. National Library Services Board, Independence Ave., Colombo 7, Sri Lanka. Ed. M.S.U. Amarasiri. adv.; bk.rev.; circ. 1,200.

020   II   ISSN 0033-4693
PUSTAKALAYA. (Text in Gujarati) 1925. m. Rs.20. Gujarat Pustakalaya Sahayak Sahakari Mandal Ltd., Raopura, Box 10, Baroda, Gujarat, India. Ed. Avinash B. Maniar. adv.; bk.rev.; abstr.; illus.; circ. 2,500.

020   CN   ISSN 0380-7150
Q L A BULLETIN/BULLETIN A B Q. (Text in English and French) 3/yr. membership. Quebec Library Association, Box 2216, Dorval, Que. H9S 5J4, Canada. TEL 514-630-4875. Ed. Karen Russell. adv.; bk.rev.; circ. 300. **Indexed:** LISA.
—BLDSC shelfmark: 7163.735000.
Description: Articles cover developments in local library services, new library technology, upcoming provincial events and workshops.

QINGBAO KEXUE/INFORMATION SCIENCE. see *COMPUTERS — Information Science And Information Theory*

020   CC   ISSN 1000-7490
QINGBAO LILUN YU SHIJIAN/INFORMATION SCIENCE: THEORY AND APPLICATION. (Text in Chinese) 1964. bi-m. $50. Qingbao Lilun yu Shijian Zazhishe, P.O. Box 2413, Beijing 100081, People's Republic of China. TEL 8414477. FAX 8413642. TELEX 22558 NISTI CN. Ed. Zhang Lizhi. bk.rev.; bibl.; illus.; index.
—BLDSC shelfmark: 4494.224000.

020   CC   ISSN 1000-0135
QINGBAO XUEBAO/CHINESE SOCIETY FOR SCIENTIFIC AND TECHNICAL INFORMATION. JOURNAL. (Text in Chinese; abstracts in English) bi-m. Y2.80 per no. (Zhongguo Kexue Jishu Qingbao Xuehui - Chinese Society for Scientific and Technical Information) Kexue Jishu Wenxian Chubanshe, 15 Fuxing Lu, Beijing 100038, People's Republic of China. TEL 8014035. FAX 8014025. TELEX 20079 ISTIC CN. (Dist. outside China by: Guoji Shudian - China International Book Trading Corp., P.O. Box 399, Beijing, P.R.C.. TEL 8413036) Ed. Xu Zengqi.
—BLDSC shelfmark: 4729.219150.

020   CC
QINGBAO XUEKAN. (Text in Chinese) bi-m. Sichuansheng Kexue Jishu Qingbao Yanjiusuo - Sichuan Science and Technology Information Research Institute, 32 Dongfeng Lu Yiduan (Sec. 1), Chengdu, Sichuan 610016, People's Republic of China. TEL 22946-93.

020   CC
QINGBAO ZILIAO GONGZUO. (Text in Chinese) bi-m. Zhongguo Shehui Kexue Qingbao Xuehui - China Social Science Information Society, No. 3, Zhangzizhong Lu, Beijing 100007, People's Republic of China. TEL 4014455. (Co-sponsor: Zhongguo Renmin Daxue) Ed. Kou Entian.

020   CN
QUEBEC (PROVINCE) SERVICES DOCUMENTATION MULTIMEDIA. CHOIX JEUNESSE: DOCUMENTATION IMPRIMEE. (Text in French) 1978. 10/yr. Can.$38($47) Services Documentaires Multimedia Inc., 1685 Est, rue Fleury, Montreal, Que. H2C 1T1, Canada. TEL 514-382-0895. FAX 514-384-9139. (also avail. in microfiche)
Formerly: Quebec (Province) Centrale des Bibliotheques. Choix Jeunesse: Documentation Imprimee (ISSN 0706-2265)

020   374   US   ISSN 0198-8344
R A S D UPDATE. 1980. q. $15 to non-members (foreign $25). American Library Association, Reference and Adult Services Division, 50 E. Huron St., Chicago, IL 60611-2795. TEL 312-280-4398. FAX 312-280-3257. Ed. Jane Kleiner. circ. 5,500. (also avail. in microform from UMI; back issues avail.)
Description: News about RASD committee, section and discussion group activities, RASD conference programs, RASD Board actions, state and regional events.

R I C S LIBRARY INFORMATION SERVICE. WEEKLY BRIEFING; a digest of news selected from the press. (Royal Institution of Chartered Surveyors) see *ENGINEERING — Civil Engineering*

020   II
R I L I S A R BULLETIN. 1982. q. Rs.24($20) Ranganathan Institute of Library and Information Science for Applied Research, 59-12, IV Main Road, Gandhi Nagar, Adyar, Madras 600 020, India. TEL 412074. Ed. Abbas Ibrahim.

026   CN   ISSN 0824-5665
R M S NEWS. 1981. 10/yr. Can.$8.56. Metropolitan Toronto Reference Library, Language & Literature Department, 789 Yonge Street, Toronto, Ont. M4W 2G8, Canada. TEL 416-393-7007. FAX 416-393-7229. TELEX 06-22232. Eds. Jaswinder Gundara, Ted Uranowski. bk.rev.; bibl.; circ. 720.
Description: Aimed at ethnic groups; provides information on multicultural literature, ESL classes, programs and library services.

020   US   ISSN 0033-7072
Z671
R Q. (Reference Quarterly) 1960. q. $42 (foreign $52); effective Fall 1991. American Library Association, 50 E. Huron St., Chicago, IL 60611-2795. TEL 800-545-2433. FAX 312-440-9374. Eds. Connie Van Fleet, Danny P. Wallace. adv.; bk.rev.; index; cum.index: 1960-1965; circ. 6,000. (also avail. in microform from UMI; back issues avail.; reprint service avail. from UMI) **Indexed:** Bibl.Ind., Bk.Rev.Ind. (1969-), C.I.J.E., Chic.Per.Ind., Child.Bk.Rev.Ind. (1969-), Curr.Cont., Hist.Abstr., Inform.Sci.Abstr., Leg.Info.Manage.Ind., Lib.Lit., Lib.Sci.Abstr., Mag.Ind., P.A.I.S., PMR, Ref.Sour., Tr.& Indus.Ind.
—BLDSC shelfmark: 8036.500000.
Refereed Serial

020   US   ISSN 0884-450X
Z688.R3
RARE BOOKS AND MANUSCRIPTS LIBRARIANSHIP. 1986. 2/yr. $25 to individuals; institutions $30; foreign $40. American Library Association, 50 E. Huron St., Chicago, IL 60611-2795. TEL 800-545-2433. FAX 312-440-9374. (Co-sponsor: Association of College and Research Libraries) Ed. Alice D. Schreyer. circ. 450. (back issues avail.; reprint service avail. from UMI)
—BLDSC shelfmark: 7291.797240.
Description: News and articles on rare books librarianship and archives management.

025.171   UK   ISSN 0959-1656
Z1029
RARE BOOKS NEWSLETTER. 1974. 4/yr. £8 (foreign £10; free to members). Library Association, Rare Books Group, The Dower House, Morville Hall, Bridgnorth, Shropshire WV16 5NB, England. TEL 074-631-407. (Subscr. to: c/o Mrs. P.C. Williams, Language & Literature Dept., City of Birmingham Public Libraries, Central Library, Birmingham B3 3HQ, England) Ed. Katherine Swift. adv.; bk.rev.; circ. 1,400.
—BLDSC shelfmark: 7291.797270.
Formerly (until no.34, 1989): Library Association. Rare Books Group. Newsletter (ISSN 0307-5826)

READ, AMERICA!; a quarterly newsletter for reading coordinators. see *EDUCATION — Teaching Methods And Curriculum*

370   020   US
READ, SEE AND HEAR. 1950. bi-m. Newark Board of Education, Office of Educational Media Services, 2 Cedar St., Newark, NJ 07102. Ed. Binnie B. McIntosh. circ. 180.
Description: News of educational materials acquired by the library of the Newark Board of Education.

020   US
READING IN INDIANAPOLIS. 1973. bi-m. free to library patrons. Indianapolis - Marion County Public Library, Box 211, Indianapolis, IN 46206. TEL 317-269-1732. FAX 317-269-1768. Ed.Bd. bk.rev.; film rev.; circ. 18,500.

025   US   ISSN 0277-5948
Z1035.1
RECOMMENDED REFERENCE BOOKS FOR SMALL & MEDIUM-SIZED LIBRARIES AND MEDIA CENTERS. 1981. a. $38.50. Libraries Unlimited, Inc., Box 3988, Englewood, CO 80155-3988. TEL 800-237-6124. FAX 303-220-8843. Ed. Bohdan S. Wynar. bk.rev.
Description: Contains price, scope, and coverage of reference books in any subject area. Arranged by subject and coded for application to college, public, or school libraries.

RECORDS & RETRIEVAL REPORT; the newsletter for professional information managers. see *BUSINESS AND ECONOMICS — Office Equipment And Services*

LIBRARY AND INFORMATION SCIENCES

020   US   ISSN 1050-2343
HF5736   CODEN: RMGQAB
RECORDS MANAGEMENT QUARTERLY. (Association formed by 1975 merger of American Records Management Association and Association of Records Executives and Administrators) 1967. q. $50 to non-members (foreign $60); libraries and institutions $43. Association of Records Managers and Administrators, 4200 Somerset Dr., Ste. 215, Box 8540, Prairie Village, KS 66208. TEL 913-341-3808. Ed. Ira A. Penn. adv.; bk.rev.; bibl.; charts; illus.; stat.; cum.index; circ. 10,500. (also avail. in microform from UMI; back issues avail., reprint service avail. from UMI) **Indexed:** ABI Inform, Account.& Data Proc.Abstr., B.P.I., BPIA, Bus.Educ.Ind., Bus.Educ.Ind., Comput.Cont., Manage.Cont., PSI, Sci.Abstr, Tr.& Indus.Ind.
Formerly (until Jan. 1990): A R M A Records Management Quarterly (ISSN 0191-1503)
Description: Technical methods on all levels for those interested in records and information management.

020   UK   ISSN 0144-2384
Z711
REFER. 1980. 3/yr. £12 (foreign £14). Library Association, Information Services Group, School of Information Studies, Birmingham Polytechnic, Perry Barr, Birmingham B42 2SU, England. TEL 021-331-5624. (Subscr. to: ISG Publications Officer, Wall Heath, Kingswinford, West Midlands DY6 0HX) Ed. David Butcher. adv.; bk.rev.; circ. 5,200. **Indexed:** LISA.
—BLDSC shelfmark: 7331.570000.
Description: Covers all aspects of reference and information work, with reviews of new reference works, listings of official British and European Communities publications.

REFERENCE AND RESEARCH BOOK NEWS; annotations and reviews of new books for libraries. see *BIBLIOGRAPHIES*

023   US   ISSN 0276-3877
Z711   CODEN: RELBD6
REFERENCE LIBRARIAN. 1981. s-a. $40 to individuals; institutions and libraries $95. Haworth Press, Inc., 10 Alice St., Binghamton, NY 13904. TEL 800-342-9678. FAX 607-722-1424. TELEX 4932599. Ed. Bill Katz. adv.; bk.rev.; circ. 631. (also avail. in microfiche from HAW; back issues avail.; reprint service avail. from HAW) **Indexed:** C.I.J.E., Comput.& Info.Sys., Excerp.Med., Inform.Sci.Abstr., Leg.Info.Manage.Ind., Lib.Lit., LISA, Ref.Zh., Sci.Abstr.
—BLDSC shelfmark: 7331.913700.
Description: Each issue focuses on a topic of current concern, interest, or practical value to the reference librarian.
Refereed Serial

020   UK   ISSN 0950-4125
Z1035.1
REFERENCE REVIEWS. 1987. q. £56. Longman Group UK Ltd., Promotions Department, Longman House, Burnt Mill, Harlow, Essex CM20 2JE, England. Ed. Nick Moore. adv.; bk.rev.; circ. 100.
—BLDSC shelfmark: 7331.919030.
Description: Presents independent critiques of new reference works, all written by librarians.

020   CN   ISSN 0384-0697
REFLECTIONS (NORTH BATTLEFORD). 1973. 3/yr. Lakeland Library Region, 10023 Thatcher Ave., P.O. Box 813, North Battleford, Sask. S9A 2Z3, Canada. TEL 306-445-6108. Ed. Jane Zhang. bk.rev.; circ. 170.

026   US   ISSN 0891-8880
REFORMA NEWSLETTER. 1971. q. $20 (effective Dec. 1991). Reforma: National Association to Promote Library Services to the Spanish Speaking, Box 9441, Washington, DC 20016. TEL 202-473-4050. (Subscr. to: Box 3887, Santa Fe Springs, CA 90670. TEL 714-773-2975) Ed. Francisco Garcia-Ayvens. adv.; bk.rev.; bibl.; circ. 1,000. (back issues avail.)
Description: News and information of interest to librarians, including discussion of minority recruitment issues and local chapter items.

020   US
REGIONAL PLAN ASSOCIATION SELECTED LIBRARY ACQUISITIONS. 1961. s-a. membership. Regional Plan Association, Inc., 1040 Ave. of the Americas, New York, NY 10018. TEL 212-398-1140. Ed. Peter Haskel. (processed)
Former titles: Regional Plan Association Library Acquisitions (ISSN 0300-6441); Regional Plan Association Library Accessions.

029   US   ISSN 0149-4694
REGISTER OF INDEXERS. 1974. a. $15. American Society of Indexers, Inc., Box 386, Port Aransas, TX 78373. TEL 512-749-6634. circ. 1,000.

020   JA   ISSN 0914-2045
REJISUMEITO. (Text in Japanese) irreg. National Diet Library - Kokuritsu Kokkai Toshokan, 1-10-1 Nagata-cho, Chiyoda-ku, Tokyo 100, Japan. TEL 03-3581-2331. TELEX 2225393. circ. 2,100.
Description: Intended for Diet members, their staff and people working closely with them. Each issue carries a variety of current information to help readers better utilize the services provided by the library.

029 370   SP   ISSN 1010-2973
REPERTORIO DE SERVICIOS IBEROAMERICANOS DE DOCUMENTACION E INFORMACION EDUCATIVA/REPERTORIO DE SERVICOS IBEROAMERICANOS DE DOCUMENTACAO E INFORMACAO EDUCATIVAS. (Text in Portuguese and Spanish) 1982. biennial. 2500 ptas.($25) Organizacion de Estados IberoAmericanos para la Educacion, la Ciencia y la Cultura (OEI), C. Bravo Murillo 38, 28015 Madrid, Spain. TEL 549-43-82. FAX 549-32-86. TELEX 48422 OEI E.
Formerly: Repertorio de Servicios de Documentacion e Informacion Educativa IberoAmericanos.
Description: For education specialists, lists services and groups interested in collaboration between institutions.

020.6   US   ISSN 0196-173X
Z674.82.R47
RESEARCH LIBRARIES GROUP NEWS. 1980. 3/yr. free. Research Libraries Group, Inc., 1200 Villa St., Mountain View, CA 94041-1100. TEL 415-691-2207. FAX 415-964-0943. illus.
—BLDSC shelfmark: 7741.855000.
Supersedes (in 1991): R G L in (Year) (ISSN 0147-3158); Which was formerly (1975-1983): Research Libraries Group. Annual Report (ISSN 0270-5311); Supersedes (1977-1979): Research Libraries Group. Newsletter (ISSN 0147-3158) Which was formed by the merger of: Ballots Newsletter (ISSN 0360-1579); R L I N Newsletter (Research Libraries Information Network) (ISSN 0163-2388).
Description: Provides an overview of the activities of the Research Libraries Group

020   US   ISSN 0734-3310
Z675.U5
RESEARCH STRATEGIES; a journal of library concepts and instruction. 1983. q. $28 to individuals (foreign $33); institutions $40 (foreign $45). Mountainside Publishing, Inc., 321 S. Main St., Box 8330, Ann Arbor, MI 48107. TEL 313-662-3925. FAX 313-662-4450. Ed. Barbara Wittkopf. adv.; bk.rev.; circ. 800. (also avail. in microfilm from UMI; back issues avail.; reprint service avail. from UMI) **Indexed:** C.I.J.E., LHTN, Lib.Lit., Lib.Sci.Abstr.
—BLDSC shelfmark: 7770.950000.
Description: Covers all aspects of bibliographic instruction, teaching library use, and how to research a topic in the library.

020   US
RESEARCH UPDATE. 1985. s-a. University Microfilms International, Research Information Services (Subsidiary of: Bell & Howell Company), 300 N. Zeeb Rd., Box 34, Ann Arbor, MI 48106-1346. TEL 800-521-0600. Ed. Tina Creguer.
Formerly: Addendum.
Description: Keeps librarians informed of new collections, dissertation titles, and library issues.

020   US   ISSN 0737-7797
Z672
RESOURCE SHARING & INFORMATION NETWORKS. 1981. s-a. $32 to individuals; institutions $85. Haworth Press, Inc., 10 Alice St., Binghamton, NY 13904. TEL 800-342-9678. FAX 607-722-1424. TELEX 4932599. Ed. Robert P. Holley. adv.; bk.rev.; circ. 350. (also avail. in microfiche from HAW; back issues avail.; reprint service avail. from HAW) **Indexed:** Biol.Abstr., Comput.& Info.Sys., Excerp.Med., Inform.Sci.Abstr, Leg.Info.Manage.Ind., LHTN, Lib.Lit., LISA, Sci.Abstr.
—BLDSC shelfmark: 7777.605430.
Former titles (until 1983): Resource Sharing and Library Networks (ISSN 0270-3173); Network Librarian.
Description: Provides a forum for ideas on the basic theoretical and practical problems faced by planners, practitioners, and users of network services.
Refereed Serial

020   DK   ISSN 0034-5806
Z701   CODEN: RESTBP
RESTAURATOR; international journal for the preservation of library and archival material. (Text in English, French, German) 1969. 4/yr. DKK 690. Munksgaard International Publishers Ltd., 35 Noerre Soegade, P.O. Box 2148, DK-1016 Copenhagen K, Denmark. TEL 33-127030. FAX 33-129387. TELEX 19431-MUNKS-DK. Ed. Helmut Bansa. illus.; index; circ. 800. (reprint service avail. from ISI) **Indexed:** Abstr.Bull.Inst.Pap.Chem., Art & Archaeol.Tech.Abstr., Br.Archaeol.Abstr., C.I.J.E., Chem.Abstr, Curr.Cont., Lib.Lit., Lib.Sci.Abstr., Sci.Cit.Ind., SSCI.
—BLDSC shelfmark: 7777.800000.

020 630   CR   ISSN 0250-3190
   CODEN: REVADJ
REVISTA A I B D A. (Text in English, Portuguese or Spanish) 1980. s-a. $20 to non-members; institutions $30; members $12. Asociacion Interamericana de Bibliotecarios y Documentalistas Agricolas, Apdo. Postal 55, 2200 Coronado, Costa Rica. TEL 29-0222. FAX 506-294741. TELEX 2144 IICA. Ed. Ghislaine Poitevien. bk.rev.; circ. 800. **Indexed:** Sci.Abstr.
—BLDSC shelfmark: 7802.500000.
Description: Articles on library and information sciences, documents presented to technical conferences and meetings, case studies, and current awareness notes.

REVISTA ARHIVELOR. see *HISTORY — History Of Europe*

020   BL
REVISTA BRASILEIRA DE BIBLIOTECONOMIA E DOCUMENTACAO. 1973. s-a. $35. Federacao Brasileira de Associacoes de Bibliotecarios, 40 Rua Avanhandava, Conj. 110, CEP 01306 Sao Paulo, Brazil. Ed. Carminda Nogueira de Castro Ferreira. adv.; bk.rev.; circ. 2,000. **Indexed:** Lib.Lit., LISA.

020   CK   ISSN 0121-0203
Z673.A629
REVISTA DE ASCOLBI; publicacion oficial de la asociacion colombiana de bibliotecologos y documentalistas. q. Col.$3,000 to individuals (foreign $40); institutions Col.$4,000 (foreign $40). (Asociacion Colombiana de Bibliotecologos y Documentalistas (ASCOLBI)) Rojas Eberhard Editores, Ltda., Carrera 6 No. 51-21, Apdo. Aereo 34270, Bogota, D.E., Colombia. TEL 285 17 79. FAX 274-44-60. TELEX 44305. (Alt. Addr.: Apdo. aereo 55674, Bogota, Colombia) Ed. Isabel Forero de Moreno. illus.; charts.

020   BL   ISSN 0100-7157
Z769.A1
REVISTA DE BIBLIOTECONOMIA DE BRASILIA. (Text in Portugese; occasionally in Spanish; summaries in English) 1973. s-a. $25. Universidade de Brasilia, Departamento de Biblioteconomia, Caixa Postal 15-3011, Brasilia, Brazil. (Co-sponsor: Associacao dos Bibliotecarios do Distrito Federal) Ed. Suzana P.M. Mueller. adv.; bk.rev.; circ. 2,000. **Indexed:** Bull.Signal., Lib.Lit., Lib.Sci.Abstr., LISA, Ref.Zh.

REVISTA DE LIBRERIA ANTIQUARIA. see *HISTORY — History Of Europe*

LIBRARY AND INFORMATION SCIENCES

020 SP ISSN 0210-0614
Z695.1.S3 CODEN: REDCD3
REVISTA ESPANOLA DE DOCUMENTACION CIENTIFICA.
1977. q. 3710 ptas. Instituto de Informacion y Documentacion en Ciencia y Tecnologia, Joaquin Costa 22, 28002 Madrid, Spain. TEL 91-5635482. FAX 91-5642644. TELEX 22628. adv.; abstr.; charts; stat.; circ. 2,000. Indexed: Sci.Abstr.
●Also available online.
Also available on CD-ROM.
—BLDSC shelfmark: 7853.945000.
Formerly (until no.451, 1976): Ciencia y Tecnica en el Mundo.

020 CK ISSN 0120-0976
Z738.A1
REVISTA INTERAMERICANA DE BIBLIOTECOLOGIA. (Text in Spanish; summaries in English and Spanish) 1978. 2/yr. Col.1800($50) Universidad de Antioquia, Escuela Interamericana de Bibliotecologia, Apdo. Aereo 1307, Medellin, Colombia. FAX 263-8282. Ed. Marta Alicia Perez. adv.; bk.rev.; abstr.; charts; stat.; circ. 500. Indexed: Lib.Lit., LISA, Ref.Zh.
—BLDSC shelfmark: 7861.450000.
Description: Presents findings and knowledge in the fields of library studies and information sciences that support their progress and enrichment.

REVUE DES LIVRES POUR ENFANTS. see *PUBLISHING AND BOOK TRADE*

020 FR ISSN 0037-9212
Z119
REVUE FRANCAISE D'HISTOIRE DU LIVRE. 1971. q. 250 F. Societe des Bibliophiles de Guyenne, c/o Bibliotheque de Bordeaux, 7 rue du Corps-Franc-Pommies, 33075 Bordeaux Cedex, France. Ed. M. Raymond Darricau. adv.; bk.rev.; bibl.; charts; illus.

020 US ISSN 0035-4597
RHODE ISLAND. DEPARTMENT OF STATE LIBRARY SERVICES. NEWSLETTER. 1964. bi-m. free. Department of State Library Services, 300 Richmond St., Providence, RI 02903-4222. TEL 401-277-2726. FAX 401-831-1311. Ed. Frank P. Iacono. circ. 800 (controlled). (processed)
Description: News pertaining to Rhode Island libraries and librarianship.

020 US ISSN 0146-8685
RHODE ISLAND LIBRARY ASSOCIATION. BULLETIN. 1907. m. (10/yr.). $15 (foreign $20). Rhode Island Library Association, c/o John Fay, 197 Indiana Ave., Providence, RI 02905. TEL 401-277-2473. adv.; circ. 500. (back issues avail.)
Description: Covers library activities, personalities and issues for the state.

020 SW ISSN 0280-3046
RIKSARKIVETS RAPPORTER. 1981. irreg. price varies. Riksarkivet, Box 12541, S-102 29 Stockholm, Sweden.

020 BL
RIO DE JANEIRO, BRAZIL (CITY). ARQUIVO GERAL DA CIDADE DO RIO DE JANEIRO. BOLETIM INFORMATIVO. 1979. 3/yr. Arquivo Geral da Cidade do Rio de Janeiro, Rio de Janeiro, Brazil. bk.rev.; circ. 2,000.

027 US ISSN 0080-3227
RIVER BEND LIBRARY SYSTEM. REPORT OF THE DIRECTOR. Variant Title--Annual Report. 1966. a. free. River Bend Library System, Box 125, Coal Valley, IL 61240. TEL 309-799-3155. Ed. Robert W. McKay. (back issues avail.) Indexed: Lib.Lit.

020 US
RIVER CITY LIBRARY TIMES. 1977. m. free. Evansville - Vanderburgh County Public Libraries, 22 S.E. 5th St., Evansville, IN 47708. TEL 812-428-8204. FAX 812-428-8215. Ed. Nancy Allee. circ. 1,500. (back issues avail.)

020 US
ROCKEFELLER COLLEGE. SCHOOL OF INFORMATION SCIENCE AND POLICY. BULLETIN. 1967. biennial. free. Rockefeller College, School of Information Science and Policy, 135 Western Ave., Albany, NY 12222. TEL 518-455-6288. FAX 212-251-3003. Ed. Richard S. Halsey. illus.; circ. 3,000.
Formerly: State University of New York at Albany. School of Library and Information Science. Bulletin.

020 PL ISSN 0083-7261
Z674
ROCZNIK BIBLIOTEKI NARODOWEJ/NATIONAL LIBRARY YEAR-BOOK. (List of contents in English, French, German, Russian; summaries in English) 1964. a. 11000 Zl.($11) Biblioteka Narodowa, Al. Niepodleglosci 213, 00-973 Warsaw, Poland. FAX 48-22-255251. TELEX 813702 BN PL. (Dist. by: Ars Polona-Ruch, Ul. Krakowskie Przedmiescie 7, 00-068 Warsaw, Poland) Ed. Stanislaw Czajka. bk.rev.; circ. 750.

026 PL ISSN 0080-3626
ROCZNIKI BIBLIOTECZNE. (Text in Polish; summaries in English, French, German and Russian) 1957. s-a. price varies. (Ministerstwo Edukacji Narodowey) Panstwowe Wydawnictwo Naukowe, Miodowa 10, 00-251 Warsaw, Poland. (Dist. by: Ars Polona, Krakowskie Przedmiescie 7, 00-068 Warsaw, Poland) Ed. K. Maleczynska. bk.rev.; circ. 670.
—BLDSC shelfmark: 8008.600000.

020 DK ISSN 0105-564X
ROSKILDE UNIVERSITETSBIBLIOTEK. SKRIFTSERIE. 1977. irreg., latest no.17. free. Roskilde Universitetsbibliotek - Roskilde University Library, P.O. Box 258, DK-4000 Roskilde, Denmark. FAX 45-46756102. TELEX 43158. circ. 500. (back issues avail.)

027.7 GW
RUNDSCHREIBEN. 1951. q. membership. Verein der Diplom-Bibliothekare an Wissenschaftlichen Bibliotheken, e.V., c/o Nieders. Staats- und Universitaetsbibliothek, Prinzenstr. 1, Postfach 2932, 3400 Goettingen, Germany. FAX 0421-2183631. adv.; bk.rev.; circ. 4,500.

RUSSELL: THE JOURNAL OF THE BERTRAND RUSSELL ARCHIVES. see *PHILOSOPHY*

027.7 US ISSN 0036-0473
Z733
RUTGERS UNIVERSITY. LIBRARIES. JOURNAL. 1937. s-a. $25 or membership. Rutgers University Libraries, Alexander Library, New Brunswick, NJ 08903. TEL 201-932-7509. FAX 908-932-6916. Ed. Pamela Spence Richards. bk.rev.; illus.; cum.index every 5 yrs.: vols.1-33, Dec.1937-1970; circ. 750. Indexed: Amer.Hist.& Life, Bibl.Engl.Lang.& Lit., Hist.Abstr., M.L.A.
Description: Covers topics pertaining to the history of libraries, Rutgers University history, and New Jerseyana.

020 SA ISSN 0256-6710
S A I L I S NEWSLETTER/S A I B I NUUSBRIEF. (Text in Afrikaans, English) 1981. m. R.30. South African Institute for Librarianship and Information Science, Box 36575, Menlo Park, Pretoria 0102, South Africa. TEL 012-429-6071. FAX 012-469-4967. TELEX 350068. Ed. T.B. van der Walt. adv.; bk.rev.; circ. 2,900.
Supersedes (1947-1981): S A L A Newsletter - S A B V Nuusbrief (ISSN 0036-0783)
Description: Current news on South African libraries, librarians, information work and workers and products.

S A L A L M NEWSLETTER. (Seminar on the Acquisition of Latin American Library Materials) see *BIBLIOGRAPHIES*

020 616.86 US
S A L I S DIRECTORY. 1981. triennial. $35 in U.S., Can. & Mex; foreign $38. Substance Abuse Librarians and Information Specialists, c/o Andrea L. Mitchell, Ed., Alcohol Research Group, Box 9513, Berkeley, CA 94709-0513. TEL 510-642-5208. FAX 510-642-7175.
Description: International listing of nearly 200 alcohol and other drug specific libraries, clearing houses, resource and information centers.

020 157.6 US
S A L I S NEWS. 1981. q. $20 in U.S., Can. & Mex; elsewhere $25. Substance Abuse Librarians and Information Specialists, c/o Andrea L. Mitchell, Ed., Alcohol Research Group, Box 9513, Berkeley, CA 94709-0513. TEL 510-642-5208. FAX 510-642-7175. Ed. Andrea L. Mitchell. bk.rev.; circ. 300. (back issues avail.)
Description: Linkage and networking of relevant information sources.

020 US
S A L S IN BRIEF. 1960. q. free. Southern Adirondack Library System, 22 Whitney Place, Saratoga Springs, NY 12866. TEL 518-584-7300. circ. 425 (controlled). (processed; reprint service avail. from UMI)
Formerly: Proof Sheet (ISSN 0033-1228)

620 025.33 US
S H E. (Subject Headings for Engineering) 1972. irreg., latest 1987. $45. Engineering Information, Inc., Castle Point on the Hudson, Hoboken, NJ 07030. TEL 800-221-1044. FAX 201-216-8532. (U.K. and Western Europe subscr. to: Thompson, Henry Ltd., London Rd., Sunningdale, Berks. SL5 OEP, England)
Description: Alphabetical listing of the controlled vocabulary subject terms used in the indexing of EI's products.

026 023 US
S L A TRIENNIAL SALARY SURVEY. 1964. triennial. $25. Special Libraries Association, 1700 Eighteenth St., N.W., Washington, DC 20009. TEL 202-234-4700. (reprint service avail. from UMI) Indexed: SRI.

020 GW ISSN 0863-0682
Z803.S23
S L B KURIER; Nachrichten aus der Saechsischen Landesbibliothek. 1987. 4/yr. DM.3. Saechsische Landesbibliothek, Marienalle 12, 8060 Dresden, Germany. Ed. L. Koch.

020 US
S O R T BULLETIN. 1938. s-a. membership. American Library Association, Staff Organizations Round Table, 8905 Chatwood Dr., Houston, TX 77078. Ed. Gwendolyn Potier Richard. bk.rev.; circ. 550 (controlled). (looseleaf format)

025 US ISSN 0160-3582
CODEN: SPKIE9
S P E C KIT. 1973. 10/yr. (combined Jul.-Aug., Nov.-Dec.). $210 (foreign $325). (Systems and Procedures Exchange Center) Association of Research Libraries, Office of Management Services, 1527 New Hampshire Ave., N.W., Washington, DC 20036. TEL 202-232-8656. FAX 202-462-7849. Ed. C. Brigid Welch. circ. 475. (back issues avail.) Indexed: ERIC.
—BLDSC shelfmark: 8361.875200.
Formerly: S P E C Flyer (ISSN 0160-3574)

020 070.5 UK ISSN 0951-4635
S R I S NEWSLETTER. 1977. irreg. (3-4/yr.). free. Science Reference and Information Service, 25 Southampton Bldgs., Chancery Lane WC2A 1AW, England. TEL 071-323-7959. FAX 071-323-7947. TELEX 266959-SCIFREF-G. Ed. Christine Wise. adv.; circ. 8,500.
—BLDSC shelfmark: 6108.282000.
Formerly (until 1986): S R L News (ISSN 0306-428X)

S R R T NEWSLETTER. (Social Responsibilities Round Table) see *LITERARY AND POLITICAL REVIEWS*

020 US ISSN 0731-7883
S U N Y L A NEWSLETTER. 1968. 4/yr. membership. State University of New York Librarians Association, c/o James M. Milne Library, State University of New York at Oneonta, Oneonta, NY 13820-4041. TEL 607-431-2453. FAX 607-431-3081. Eds. Arleen Benedict, Kathryn Franco. bibl.; circ. 400.

032 023 GW
SAECHSISCHE LANDESBIBLIOTHEK. NEUERWERBUNGEN. m. Saechsische Landesbibliothek, Marienalle 12, 8060 Dresden, Germany. Ed. C. Zuehlke.
Formerly: Saechsische Landesbibliothek. Neuewerbungen und Nachrichten (ISSN 0233-1098)

020 US
SAN BERNARDINO COUNTY LIBRARY. NEWSLETTER. 1962. m. free. San Bernardino County Library, 104 W. 4th St., San Bernardino, CA 92415. TEL 714-383-2134. FAX 714-387-5724. Ed. John Grimm. bk.rev.; circ. 1,500.

020 CN ISSN 0831-3016
SASKATCHEWAN LIBRARY ASSOCIATION. FORUM. 5/yr. Can.$25 (free to members). Saskatchewan Library Association, Box 3388, Regina, Sask. S4P 3H1, Canada. TEL 306-586-3089. FAX 306-347-7500. adv.; bk.rev.; circ. 200.

LIBRARY AND INFORMATION SCIENCES

025 943.7   CS   ISSN 0036-5246
CD1150
SBORNIK ARCHIVNICH PRACI. (Text in Czech; summaries in German) 1951. s-a. 64 Kcs.($30.90) Archivni Sprava, Milady Horakove 133, 166 21 Prague 6, Czechoslovakia. (Dist. by: Artia, Ve Smeckach 30, 111 27 Prague 1, Czechoslovakia) Ed. Borivoj Indra. cum.index: 1951-1970. **Indexed:** CERDIC, Hist.Abstr., Numis.Lit.
—BLDSC shelfmark: 8086.900000.

027.4   SW   ISSN 0036-5602
Z822
SCANDINAVIAN PUBLIC LIBRARY QUARTERLY. 1968. q. SEK 160. National Council for Cultural Affairs, P.O. Box 7843, S-10398 Stockholm, Sweden. TEL 46-8-247260. FAX 46-8-211349. Ed. Elisabeth Nilsson. circ. 1,000. **Indexed:** Lib.Lit., LISA.
—BLDSC shelfmark: 8087.573000.
Formerly: Reol.

025   US
SCARECROW LIBRARY ADMINISTRATION SERIES. irreg., latest no.2. Scarecrow Press, Inc., 52 Library St., Box 4167, Metuchen, NJ 08840. TEL 800-537-7107.

027.8   UK   ISSN 0036-6595
Z675.S3
SCHOOL LIBRARIAN. 1937. 4/yr. £40 to non-members. School Library Association, Liden Library, Barrington Close, Liden, Swindon SN3 6HF, England. TEL 0793-617838. Ed. Sheila Ray. adv.; bk.rev.; bibl.; index; circ. 4,000. **Indexed:** Bk.Rev.Ind. (1979-), Br.Educ.Ind., Child.Bk.Rev.Ind. (1979-), Child.Lit.Abstr., Cont.Pg.Educ., Lib.Lit., Lib.Sci.Abstr.
—BLDSC shelfmark: 8092.790000.
Formerly: School Librarian and School Library Review.
Description: Developments, book reviews and other information for school librarians in primary and secondary schools.

020   US   ISSN 0271-3667
SCHOOL LIBRARIAN'S WORKSHOP. 1980. m. (except Jul.-Aug.). $40. Library Learning Resources, Inc., 61 Greenbriar Dr., Box 87, Berkeley Heights, NJ 07922. TEL 201-635-1833. FAX 201-635-2614. Eds. Ruth Toor, Hilda K. Weisburg. bk.rev.; bibl.; index; circ. 7,800. (back issues avail.)
Description: For school librarians grades K-12. Contains teaching units, professional development concerns, bulletin boards, reference questions, pencil games, and annual survey.

027.8   NR   ISSN 0331-8109
SCHOOL LIBRARIES BULLETIN. 1965. s-a. $20. Anambra State School Libraries Association, c/o Enugu Campus Library, University of Nigeria, Enugu, Nigeria. Eds. Virginia W. Dike, Dorothy S. Obi. adv.; bk.rev. 250 (controlled). (processed) **Indexed:** Child.Lit.Abstr., LISA.
Former titles (until 1976): E C S School Libraries Bulletin; Eastern Nigerian School Libraries Association. Bulletin (ISSN 0424-1851)
Description: Scientific journal intended to heighten the standard of education and awareness of resources available in Nigerian libraries. For teacher-librarians.

020   UK   ISSN 0261-1678
SCHOOL LIBRARIES GROUP NEWS. 1980. s-a. £2 to non-members. Library Association, School Libraries Group, c/o The Librarian, Solihull VIth Form College, Widney Manor Rd., Solihull, W. Midlands B91 3JG, England. TEL 021-704-2581. circ. 2,300.
—BLDSC shelfmark: 6102.559000.
Description: Covers school librarianship. Examines the professional aspects, including management, computers, and education.

020   CN   ISSN 0227-3780
SCHOOL LIBRARIES IN CANADA. vol.17, 1974. 3/yr. Can.$35($35) Canadian School Library Association, Canadian Library Association, 602-200 Elgin St., Ottawa, Ont. K2P 1L5, Canada. TEL 613-232-9625. FAX 604-321-2153. Ed. Leslie Aitken. adv.; bk.rev.; circ. 1,000. (also avail. in microfilm) **Indexed:** Can.Educ.Ind., Can.Per.Ind., Child.Lit.Abstr., CMI, Lib.Lit.
—BLDSC shelfmark: 8092.805200.
Formerly (until 1980): Moccasin Telegraph (ISSN 0076-9878)
Description: Covers recent developments in the field of school librarianship. Includes information on the activities and news of the Association.

027.8   US   ISSN 0362-8930
Z675.S3
SCHOOL LIBRARY JOURNAL; the magazine of children, young adults & school librarians. (Supplement avail.: Star Track) 1954. 12/yr. $63 (Canada $86; elsewhere $104). Cahners Publishing Company (New York), Bowker Magazine Group, Cahners Magazine Division (Subsidiary of: Reed International PLC), Division of Reed Publishing (USA) Inc., 249 W. 17th St., New York, NY 10011. TEL 800-669-1002. FAX 212-242-6987. (Subscr. to: Box 1978, Marion, OH 43305-1978) Ed. Lillian N. Gerhardt. adv.; bk.rev.; bibl.; charts; illus.; stat.; tr.lit.; circ. 41,265. (also avail. in microform from UMI; reprint service avail. from UMI) **Indexed:** Access (1980-), Bk.Rev.Dig., Bk.Rev.Ind. (1975-), Bus.Ind., C.I.J.E., Child.Bk.Rev.Ind. (1975-), Child.Lit.Abstr., Cont.Pg.Educ., Educ.Ind., Ind.Child.Mag., Jun.High.Mag.Abstr., LHTN, Lib.Lit., Lib.Sci.Abstr., Mag.Ind., PMR, Tr.& Indus.Ind. Key Title: S L J, School Library Journal.
—BLDSC shelfmark: 8092.810000.
Description: For librarians serving children and young adults in schools and public libraries.

020 371.3   US   ISSN 0889-9371
SCHOOL LIBRARY MEDIA ACTIVITIES MONTHLY. 1984. m. (10/yr.). $44. L M S Associates, 17 E. Henrietta St., Baltimore, MD 21230. TEL 301-685-8621. Eds. Paula Montgomery, H. Thomas Walker. adv.; bk.rev.; index; circ. 11,000. (back issues avail.)
Description: For school library media specialists (K-8), focusing on teaching library media skills.

020   US   ISSN 0739-7712
Z675.S3
SCHOOL LIBRARY MEDIA ANNUAL. 1982. a. $34.50. Libraries Unlimited, Inc., Box 3988, Englewood, CO 80155-3988. TEL 800-237-6124. FAX 303-220-8843. Ed. Jane Bandy Smith.
—BLDSC shelfmark: 8092.813000.
Description: Provides fundamental background and current professional information at every level. Covers new materials, equipment, development practices, as well as implications of legal decisions.

027.8   US   ISSN 0278-4823
Z675.S3
SCHOOL LIBRARY MEDIA QUARTERLY. 1952. 4/yr $40 to non-members (foreign $50). (American Association of School Librarians) American Library Association, 50 E. Huron St., Chicago, IL 60611-2795. TEL 800-545-2433. FAX 312-440-9374. Ed.Bd. adv.; bk.rev.; illus.; cum.index every 5 yrs.; circ. 7,400. (also avail. in microform from UMI; back issues avail.) reprint service avail. from UMI) **Indexed:** Bk.Rev.Ind. (1965-), C.I.J.E., Child.Bk.Rev.Ind. (1965-), Child.Lit.Abstr., Curr.Cont., Educ.Ind., Except.Child.Educ.Abstr., Lib.Lit., Ref.Sour.
—BLDSC shelfmark: 8092.813500.
Former titles (until 1981): School Media Quarterly (ISSN 0361-1647); School Libraries (ISSN 0036-6609)
Description: News and articles of interest to school library media specialists from kindergarten to twelfth grade.

020   US   ISSN 1050-8147
SCHOOL OF LIBRARY AND INFORMATION SCIENCE. OCCASIONAL PAPERS SERIES. 1989. irreg., approx. 4/yr. $23. University of Wisconsin - Milwaukee, School of Library and Information Science, Enderis Hall, Box 413, Milwaukee, WI 53201. TEL 414-229-4704. FAX 414-229-4848. TELEX 4909991372 ALAUI. Ed. Mohammed M. Aman. circ. 600. (back issues avail.)
—BLDSC shelfmark: 6224.967750.
Description: Includes timely papers of interest to librarians and information professionals.

020   GW   ISSN 0341-471X
SCHULBIBLIOTHEK AKTUELL. 1975. q. DM.32. Deutsches Bibliotheksinstitut, Abt. 1-Publikationen, Bundesallee 184-185, 1000 Berlin 31, Germany. TEL 030-8505-0. FAX 030-8505-100. adv.; bk.rev.; abstr.; circ. 600. (back issues avail.)

020   SZ
SCHWEIZERISCHE BIBLIOTHEKEN/BIBLIOTHEQUES SUISSES. (Text in French and German) 1959. a. 5 Fr. Bundesamt fuer Statistik, Hallwylstr. 15, CH-3003 Bern, Switzerland. TEL 031-618836. FAX 031-617856.

026   US   ISSN 0194-262X
Z675.T3   CODEN: STELDF
SCIENCE & TECHNOLOGY LIBRARIES. 1980. q. $36 to individuals; institutions $105. Haworth Press, Inc., 10 Alice St., Binghamton, NY 13904. TEL 800-342-9678. FAX 607-722-1424. TELEX 4932599. Ed. Cynthia Steinke. adv.; bk.rev.; circ. 661. (also avail. in microfiche from HAW; back issues avail.; reprint service avail. from HAW) **Indexed:** Biol.Abstr., Bull.Signal., Chem.Abstr., Comput.& Info.Sys., Eng.Ind., Excerp.Med., Inform.Sci.Abstr., Lib.Lit., LISA, P.A.I.S., Ref.Zh., Sci.Abstr.
—BLDSC shelfmark: 8134.275000.
Description: Provides a variety of instructive material prepared specifically for the science and technology librarian.
Refereed Serial

020   FR
SCIENCES DE L'INFORMATION. LEXIQUE. (Text in English, French, Spanish) 1978. a. 330 F.($280) Centre National de la Recherche Scientifique, Institut de l'Information Scientifique et Technique, Chateau du Montet, 54514 Vandoeuvre-les-Nancy, France. (Subscr. to: Service des Abonnements, 26 rue Boyer, 75971 Paris cedex 20, France)

020   US   ISSN 0147-6882
Z699.A1   CODEN: STIPDD
SCIENTIFIC AND TECHNICAL INFORMATION PROCESSING. English translation of: Nauchno-Tekhnicheskaya Informatsiya. Seriya 1 (RU ISSN 0548-0019) 1974. bi-m. $640. (Vsesoyuznyi Institut Nauchno Tekhnicheskoi Informatsii (VINITI), RU) Allerton Press, Inc., 150 Fifth Ave., New York, NY 10011. TEL 212-924-3950. Ed. A.I. Mikhailov. charts. **Indexed:** Biol.Abstr., Excerp.Med.
—BLDSC shelfmark: 0420.793500.
Description: For librarians and professionals involved with information processing. Presents reports on developments in manual and machine methods for storing and retrieving data.

SCIENTIFIC MEETINGS. see *MEETINGS AND CONGRESSES*

020   UK
SCOTTISH ACADEMIC LIBRARIES NEWSLETTER. 1988. 6/yr. £5. c/o David Scott, Ed., Dundee College of Further Education Library, Old Glamis Rd., Dundee DD3 8LE, Scotland. TEL 0382-21125.
Description: Short items of interest to Scottish academic librarians.

SCOTTISH BOOK COLLECTOR. see *PUBLISHING AND BOOK TRADE*

020   UK   ISSN 0950-0189
SCOTTISH LIBRARIES. 1950. bi-m. £21 to non-members (foreign £23). Scottish Library Association, Motherwell Business Centre, Coursington Rd., Motherwell ML1 1PW, Scotland. TEL 0698-52526. FAX 0698-52057. Eds. C. Dakers, G.A. Campbell. adv.; bk.rev.; circ. 2,500. (also avail. in microform from UMI; back issues avail.; reprint service avail. from UMI) **Indexed:** Lib.Lit., Lib.Sci.Abstr., LISA.
—BLDSC shelfmark: 8210.676200.
Formerly: S L A News (ISSN 0048-9786)

021   UK   ISSN 0267-1425
SCOTTISH LIBRARY AND INFORMATION RESOURCES. 1984. irreg. £25. Scottish Library Association, Motherwell Business Centre, Coursington Rd., Motherwell ML1 1PW, Scotland.
—BLDSC shelfmark: 8210.678000.
Formerly: Library Resources in Scotland.

020   AU
SCRINIUM. 1969. s-a. S.300. Verband Oesterreichischer Archivare, Postfach 164, A-1014 Vienna, Austria. Ed.Bd. adv.; circ. controlled. (back issues avail.) **Indexed:** Hist.Abstr.

020   IT
SCUOLA SPECIALE PER ARCHIVISTI E BIBLIOTECARI. NUOVA ANNALI. 1986. a. L.54000 (foreign L.65000). Casa Editrice Leo S. Olschki, Casella Postale 66, 50100 Florence, Italy. TEL 055-5630684. FAX 055-6530214. Ed. Alessandro Pratesi.

LIBRARY AND INFORMATION SCIENCES

020 US
SEARCH TOOLS: THE GUIDE TO U M I - DATA COURIER ONLINE. 1983. biennial. $75 (effective 1992). University Microfilms International, Data Courier, 620 S. Third St., Louisville, KY 40202-2475. TEL 800-626-2823. FAX 502-589-5572. (looseleaf format)
Formerly (until 1991): Search Inform.

020 US
SEARCHING DIALOG: THE COMPLETE GUIDE. 1987. irreg. Dialog Information Services, Inc., 3460 Hillview Ave., Palo Alto, CA 94304. TEL 415-858-3785. FAX 415-858-7069. (looseleaf format)
Formerly: Guide to Dialog Searching.

027.4 MY
SELANGOR PUBLIC LIBRARY CORPORATION. ANNUAL REPORT/PERBADANAN PERPUSTAKAAN AWAM SELANGOR. LAPURAN TAHUNAN. 1972. a. Selangor Public Library Corporation, Perpustakaan Raja Tun Uda, Persiaran Perdagangan, 40572 Shah Alam, Malaysia. FAX 03-559-6045. stat.; circ. 1,000.
Formerly: Selangor Public Library. Annual Report.

020 UK
SELECT: NATIONAL BIBLIOGRAPHIC SERVICE NEWSLETTER. 1976. 3/yr. free. British Library, Bibliographic Services, 2 Sheraton St., London W1V 4BH, England. TEL 01-323-7077. circ. 4,000.
Indexed: LISA.
Former titles: British Library. Bibliographic Services. Newsletter (ISSN 0268-9707); British Library. Bibliographic Services Division. Newsletter (ISSN 0308-230X)
Description: Contains articles of interest to all users of the division's products and services, and details of future plans and policy.

070 980 US ISSN 0080-8857
SEMINAR ON THE ACQUISITION OF LATIN AMERICAN LIBRARY MATERIALS. MICROFILMING PROJECTS NEWSLETTER. 1964. a. $3. Seminar on the Acquisition of Latin American Library Materials, General Library, University of New Mexico, Albuquerque, NM 87131. TEL 505-277-5102. Ed. Basil Malish. cum.index: nos.1-20; circ. 325. (processed; back issues avail.) Indexed: Lib.Lit.
Description: Lists original microreproduction projects in Latin American or Iberian subjects.

025 US
SEMINAR ON THE ACQUISITION OF LATIN AMERICAN LIBRARY MATERIALS. PAPERS. (Text in English, Portuguese, Spanish; summaries in English, Spanish) 1956. a. membership; price varies for individual nos. Seminar on the Acquisition of Latin American Library Materials, General Library, University of New Mexico, Albuquerque, NM 87131. TEL 505-277-5702. bibl.; charts; stat.; cum.index: nos.1-29. (also avail. in microfiche from BHP; back issues avail.) Indexed: Lib.Lit.
Former titles: Seminar on the Acquisition of Latin American Library Materials. Final Report and Working Papers (ISSN 0080-8849); Seminar on the Acquistion of Latin American Library Materials. Working Papers.

026 SG ISSN 0850-010X
SENEGAL. ARCHIVES DU SENEGAL. RAPPORT ANNUEL. 1976. a. exchange basis. Archives du Senegal, Immeuble Administratif, Av. Roume, Dakar, Senegal. Ed. Saliou Mbaye.

020 US
SENIOR HIGH SCHOOL LIBRARY CATALOG. quinquennial (with a. supplement). price varies. H.W. Wilson Co., 950 University Ave., Bronx, New York, NY 10452-9978. TEL 800-367-6770. FAX 212-538-2716. TELEX 4990003HWILSON. Ed. Juliette Yaakov. bk.rev.
Description: Classified list of books recommended for secondary school students (grades 9-12), including fiction and story collection; with author, title, subject, and analytical index.

026 JA ISSN 0385-0188
SENMON TOSHOKAN/SPECIAL LIBRARIES ASSOCIATION, JAPAN. BULLETIN. (Text in Japanese; summaries in English) 1960. 5/yr. 7000 Yen. Senmon Toshokan Kyogikai - Japan Special Libraries Association, c/o National Diet Library, 10-1 Nagata-cho 1-chome, Chiyoda-ku, Tokyo 100, Japan. Ed. Isao Tanaka. adv.; bk.rev.; circ. 2,000. Indexed: Comput.Cont., Jap.Per.Ind., LISA, Mag.Ind.
—BLDSC shelfmark: 2593.872000.
Formerly: Senmon Toshokan Kyogikai Kaiho.

020 UK ISSN 0953-0460
Z692.S5 CODEN: SERIEZ
SERIALS; the journal of the UK Serials Group. 1988. 3/yr. £46.34 membership only. United Kingdom Serials Group, c/o Mrs. Jill Tolson, Administrator, 114 Woodstock Rd., Witney, Oxon OX8 6DY, England. TEL 0993-703466. FAX 0993-778879. adv.; bk.rev.
—BLDSC shelfmark: 8242.737300.
Description: Provides a forum for the interchange of information, ideas, suggestions and solution of problems concerning serials and associated areas, between all interested parties in the information industry, both nationally and internationally.

SERIALS IN THE BRITISH LIBRARY. see BIBLIOGRAPHIES

020 US ISSN 0361-526X
Z692.S5 CODEN: SELID4
SERIALS LIBRARIAN; the international quarterly journal of serials management. 1976. q. $40 to individuals; institutions and libraries $95. Haworth Press, Inc., 10 Alice St., Binghamton, NY 13904. TEL 800-342-9678. FAX 607-722-1424. TELEX 4932599. Ed. Peter Gellatly. adv.; bk.rev.; index; circ. 931. (also avail. in microfiche from HAW; back issues avail.; reprint service avail. from HAW)
Indexed: Amer.Hist.& Life, ASCA, Bull.Signal, Chem.Abstr., Comput.& Info.Sys., Curr.Cont., Excerp.Med., Inform.Sci.Abstr., L.I.S.A., Leg.Info.Manage.Ind., LHTN, Lib.Lit., SSCI.
—BLDSC shelfmark: 8242.740000.
Description: Serials management for librarians. Coverage includes serials selection and acquisition, bibliographic control, cataloging, staffing and department management, serials control systems, subscription agencies, publishers, and computerization problems.
Refereed Serial

020 US ISSN 0747-5411
SERIALS PERSPECTIVE. 1984. 2/yr. free. University Microfilms International, Serials Publishing, c/o Carol Bamford, Mktg. Mgr., 300 N. Zeeb Rd., Ann Arbor, MI 48106. TEL 800-521-0600. FAX 313-665-5022. Ed. Steven Koch. circ. 15,000.
Description: Special interest articles and University Microfilms International product information for serials librarians.

020 US ISSN 0098-7913
PN4832
SERIALS REVIEW. 1975. q. $40 to individuals; institutions $65. Pierian Press, Box 1808, Ann Arbor, MI 48106. TEL 313-434-5530. FAX 313-434-6409. Ed. Cindy Hepfer. adv. (back issues avail.) Indexed: Bibl.Ind., Bk.Rev.Ind. (1977-), Child.Bk.Rev.Ind. (1977-), Inform.Sci.Abstr., Leg.Info.Manage.Ind., LHTN, Lib.Lit.
—BLDSC shelfmark: 8242.760000.
Description: Contains practical information on the management and administration of serial publications.
Refereed Serial

025 UK ISSN 0306-0942
SERVICE POINT. 1972. q. £20 (foreign £30). Library Association, Branch and Mobile Libraries Group, 176 Haigh Moor Rd., Tingley, Wakefield WF3 1EJ, England. Ed. Ian Stringer. adv.; bk.rev.; circ. 1,550.
Indexed: LISA.
—BLDSC shelfmark: 8251.870000.
Description: Presents articles on branch and mobile library service, library group meetings, and library sponsored courses.

SHIJIE TUSHU/WORLD BOOKS. see PUBLISHING AND BOOK TRADE

SHIXUE JIKAN/COLLECTION OF HISTORICAL MATERIALS. see HISTORY

020 US ISSN 0037-4326
Z671
SHOW-ME LIBRARIES. 1949. q. $10 (foreign $20). State Library, Box 387, Jefferson City, MO 65102. TEL 314-751-2680. Ed. Madeline Matson. bk.rev.; bibl.; charts; illus.; stat.; circ. 2,350. (processed; also avail. in microform from UMI; back issues avail.; reprint service avail. from UMI) Indexed: CALL, LHTN, Lib.Lit.
—BLDSC shelfmark: 8270.094900.
Description: Articles pertaining to Missouri libraries and librarians.

020 CC
SHU PIN. (Text in Chinese) q. Zhonghua Shuju, No. 36, Wangfujing Dajie, Beijing 100710, People's Republic of China. TEL 554504. Ed. Zhao Shouyan.

SICHUAN DANG'AN/SICHUAN ARCHIVES. see HISTORY — History Of Asia

020 CC
SICHUAN TUSHUGUAN XUEBAO/SICHUAN JOURNAL OF LIBRARY SCIENCE. (Text in Chinese) bi-m. Sichuan Tushuguan Xuehui - Sichuan Libraries Society, 31 Banbianqiao Beijie, Chengdu, Sichuan 610015, People's Republic of China. TEL 667333. Ed. Wang Enlai.

020 SL ISSN 0583-2268
SIERRA LEONE. LIBRARY BOARD. REPORT. 1961. a. Library Board, Box 326, Freetown, Sierra Leone. (back issues avail.)

020 SL
SIERRA LEONE LIBRARY JOURNAL. (Text in English) 1974. s-a. Le.1.50. Sierra Leone Library Association, c/o Mrs. A.M. Thomas, Ed., Milton Margai Teachers College, Private Mail Bag, Goderich near Freetown, Sierra Leone. adv.; bk.rev.; bibl.; circ. 200. Indexed: Lib.Sci.Abstr.

020 FI ISSN 0355-0036
SIGNUM. (Text in Finnish and Swedish) 1968. 8/yr. FIM 250. Suomen Tieteellinen Kirjastoseura - Finnish Research Library Association, P.O. Box 387 Valmet Area, 33101 Tampere, Finland. Ed. Liisa Niinikangas. adv.; bk.rev.; abstr.; bibl.; circ. 1,100. Indexed: CERDIC.
—BLDSC shelfmark: 8276.326500.

020 366 US
SIMMONS LIBRARIAN. 2/yr. free. Simmons College, Graduate School of Library and Information Science, Attn: Em Claire Knowles, Asst. Dean, 300 The Fenway, Boston, MA 02115-5898. TEL 617-738-2222. Ed. Kate Jones - Randall. circ. 7,000.
Description: For alumni, to apprise them of alumni and faculty accomplishments and activities.

020 SI ISSN 0217-1546
Z846
SINGAPORE. NATIONAL LIBRARY. ANNUAL REPORT. 1963. a. exchange basis. National Library, Stamford Rd., Singapore 0617, Singapore. TEL 3377355. FAX 3309611. TELEX RS-26620-NATLIB. circ. 1,500.

027 SI ISSN 0085-6118
Z845.S5
SINGAPORE LIBRARIES. (Text mainly in English; occasionally in Chinese, Malay and Tamil) 1971. a. S.$18($15) Library Association of Singapore, c/o Bukit Merah Branch Library, Bukit Merah Central, Singapore 0315, Singapore. Ed. Idris Rashid. adv.; bk.rev.; circ. 600. Indexed: Lib.Lit., LISA.

020 US ISSN 0037-5837
SIPAPU. 1970. 2/yr. $8. Noel Peattie, Ed. & Pub., 23311 County Rd. 88, Winters, CA 95694-9008. TEL 916-622-3364. bk.rev.; illus.; cum.index every 5 yrs.; circ. 350. (processed) Indexed: Alt.Press Ind.
—BLDSC shelfmark: 8285.980000.
Description: Newsletter for librarians, collectors and others interested in the alternative press, which includes small and "underground" presses, Third World, dissent, feminist, peace, and other types of publishing.

027.8 DK ISSN 0105-9556
SKOLEBIBLIOTEKET. 1972. 9/yr. DKK 280. Danmarks Skolebibliotekarforening, Mariavej 1, Sdr. Bjert, DK-6091 Bjert, Denmark. TEL 75-57-71-01. Ed. Bent Rasmussen. adv.; bk.rev.; circ. 3,000.

020 SW ISSN 0346-8488
SKRIFTER UTGIVNA AV SVENSKA RIKSARKIVET. 1931. irreg. price varies. Riksarkivet, Box 12541, S-102 29 Stockholm, Sweden.

020 AT
SOCIAL CHANGE AND INFORMATION SYSTEMS. 1972. 3/yr. Aus.$198. Noyce Publishing, G.P.O. Box 2222T, Melbourne, Vic. 3001, Australia. adv.; bk.rev.; abstr.; bibl.; illus.; cum.index; circ. 400. (back issues avail.) Indexed: LISA.
Formerly (until 1985): Librarians for Social Change (ISSN 0305-165X)

LIBRARY AND INFORMATION SCIENCES 2785

SOCIETY FOR INFORMATION DISPLAY. SEMINAR LECTURE NOTES. see *LIBRARY AND INFORMATION SCIENCES — Computer Applications*

025.17   UK   ISSN 0037-9816
CD23.S6
SOCIETY OF ARCHIVISTS. JOURNAL. 1955. q. £12($23) Society of Archivists, c/o C.C. Webb, Ed., Borthwick Institute of Historical Research, University of York, St. Anthony's Hall, Peasholme Green, York YO1 2PW, England. (Subscr. to: Dr. P. Durrant, Berkshire Record Office, Shire Hall, Shinfield Park, Reading, Berks. RG2 9XD, England) adv.; bk.rev.; cum. index; circ. 1,600. (also avail. in microfilm from UMI; reprint service avail. from UMI (vols.1-3)) **Indexed:** Amer.Hist.& Life, Arts & Hum.Cit.Ind., Br.Archaeol.Abstr., Br.Hum.Ind., Curr.Cont., Hist.Abstr., LISA.
—BLDSC shelfmark: 4880.780000.

891.8 070.5   UK   ISSN 0038-0903
DJK36.G7
SOLANUS. 1966; N.S. 1987. a. £7. Standing Conference of National and University Libraries, c/o Dr. C. Thomas, Ed., The British Library, Great Russell St., London WC1B 3DG, England. TEL 01-323-7587. FAX 01-323-7736. TELEX 21462. adv.; bk.rev.; circ. 150. (back issues avail.) **Indexed:** A.I.C.P., LISA.
—BLDSC shelfmark: 8327.170000.
Description: Presents bibliographic, library and publishing studies in the USSR, and Eastern Europe. Includes research papers, documentary material, reference lists.

020.6   US
SOLINET. ANNUAL REPORT. 1973. a. free. Southeastern Library Network, Inc., 1438 W. Peachtree St., N.W., Atlanta, GA 30309-2955. TEL 404-892-0943. FAX 404-892-7879. Ed. Liz Hornsby. charts; stat.; circ. 1,500.
Formerly: Southeastern Library Network. Annual Report (ISSN 0099-085X)

020   US   ISSN 0038-1853
Z881.C1579
SOUNDINGS (SANTA BARBARA); collections of the University Library. 1969. a. $4 to non-members. University of California, Santa Barbara, University Library, Santa Barbara, CA 93106. TEL 805-893-3014. FAX 805-961-4676. Ed. Donald E. Fitch. bibl.; illus.; circ. 650. **Indexed:** Hist.Abstr., M.L.A.

SOURCES FOR THE STUDY OF RELIGION IN MALAWI. see *RELIGIONS AND THEOLOGY*

020   US   ISSN 0002-4570
SOURDOUGH. 1962. q. $15 (foreign $20). Alaska Library Association (Fairbanks), Box 81084, Fairbank, AK 99708. TEL 907-479-4522. Ed. Bill Galbraith. adv.; bk.rev.; illus.; circ. 550. **Indexed:** Lib.Lit.
—BLDSC shelfmark: 8330.740000.
Formerly: Alaska State Library Association. Newsletter.
Description: Articles by, for, of interest and of use to Alaskan libraries and librarians.

027.568   SA
SOUTH AFRICA. STATE LIBRARY COUNCIL. ANNUAL REPORT. (Text in Afrikaans, English) 1910. a. free. State Library, P.O. Box 397, Pretoria 0001, South Africa. TEL 012-218931. FAX 012-325-5984. TELEX 3-22171 SA. illus.; circ. 857.

020   SA   ISSN 0256-8861
Z671   CODEN: SALSE7
SOUTH AFRICAN JOURNAL OF LIBRARY AND INFORMATION SCIENCE. (Text in Afrikaans, English) 1933. q. R.72($45) (South African Institute for Librarianship and Information Science) Bureau for Scientific Publications, P.O. Box 1758, Pretoria 0001, South Africa. TEL 012-322-6422. Ed. J. Bekker. bk.rev.; illus.; circ. 2,500. **Indexed:** Comput.& Contr.Abstr, Ind.S.A.Per., Lib.Lit., Lib.Sci.Abstr., Sci.Abstr.
—BLDSC shelfmark: 8338.954000.
Former titles (until 1983): South African Journal for Librarianship and Information Science; South African Libraries - Suid-Afrikaanse Biblioteke (ISSN 0038-240X)

900   SA   ISSN 0038-2418
Z965
SOUTH AFRICAN LIBRARY. QUARTERLY BULLETIN/SUID-AFRIKAANSE BIBLIOTEEK. KWARTAALBLAD. (Text in Afrikaans, English; summaries in English) 1946. q. $30. South African Library, P.O. Box 496, Cape Town 8000, South Africa. TEL 021-246320. FAX 021-244848. Ed. P.E. Westra. adv.; bibl.; illus.; index; circ. 1,000. (also avail. in microform from UMI) **Indexed:** Hist.Abstr., Ind.S.A.Per., Lib.Lit.
—BLDSC shelfmark: 7177.000000.
Description: Covers the socio-cultural history of Southern Africa, with emphasis on the Cape.

025   AT   ISSN 0081-2633
SOUTH AUSTRALIA. LIBRARIES BOARD. ANNUAL REPORT. 1884. a. free. Libraries Board of South Australia, Box 419 G.P.O., Adelaide 5001, Australia. circ. 350.

027   US   ISSN 0361-6479
Z733
SOUTH CAROLINA STATE LIBRARY. ANNUAL REPORT. 1943. a. free. South Carolina State Library, 1500 Senate St., Box 11469, Columbia, SC 29211. TEL 803-734-8666. FAX 803-734-8676. Ed. James B. Johnson, Jr. circ. 500 (controlled). **Indexed:** ERIC, SRI.

027   US   ISSN 0361-7122
SOUTH CENTRAL RESEARCH LIBRARY COUNCIL. REPORTS. Short title: S C R L C Reports. 1968. m. $25. South Central Research Library Council, DeWitt Bldg., 215 N. Cayuga St., Ithaca, NY 14850. TEL 607-273-9106. FAX 607-272-0740. circ. 1,100.
Description: Newsletter of a library network serving 82 libraries.

020 950   UK   ISSN 0308-4035
SOUTH EAST ASIA LIBRARY GROUP NEWSLETTER. 1968. irreg. (approx. 2/yr.). £7.50($15) for 2 nos. South East Asia Library Group, c/o Anabel Gallop, Oriental and India Office Collections, The British Library, 197 Blackfriars Rd., London SE1 8NG, England. FAX 071-412-7858. TELEX 83656. Ed. M. Smyth. adv.; bk.rev.; bibl.; circ. 200. **Indexed:** A.I.C.P., E.I.
—BLDSC shelfmark: 6108.380000.
Description: Newsletter of a West European group of libraries concerned with Southeast Asia.

020   US   ISSN 0038-3686
Z673
SOUTHEASTERN LIBRARIAN. 1951. q. $35 to non-members. Southeastern Library Association, Inc., Box 987, Tucker, GA 30085-0987. TEL 404-939-5080. Ed. Elizabeth Curry. adv.; index; circ. 2,200. (also avail. in microform from UMI; reprint service avail. from UMI) **Indexed:** Lib.Lit., LISA.
—BLDSC shelfmark: 8352.460000.
Description: Includes articles which address professional concerns of the library community, announcements, and news of professional interest to librarians in the Southeast.

020   US
SOUTHEASTERN NEWSLINE. 1982. bi-w. free. Southeastern New York Library Resources Council, Box 879, Highland, NY 12528-0879. Ed. Ellen A. Parravano. bk.rev.; circ. 500.
Formerly (until 1986): S E News.

020   US
SOUTHERN EXPOSURE (CARBONDALE); the newsletter of the Southern Illinois University at Carbondale Library. 1955. w. Southern Illinois University at Carbondale, Library, Carbondale, IL 62901. TEL 618-453-2818. Ed. Jody Bales Foote. circ. 275 (controlled). (processed)
Formerly: Southern Exposure Library Staff Bulletin (ISSN 0038-4089)

020   US
SOUTHERN ILLINOIS UNIVERSITY AT CARBONDALE. LIBRARY. LIBRARY PROGRESS. 1955. s-a. Southern Illinois University at Carbondale, Library, Carbondale, IL 62901. TEL 618-453-2683. Ed. Mark Watson. circ. 1,800.
Formerly: Southern Illinois University, Carbondale. University Libraries. Library Progress.

SOUTHWEST BOOK REVIEW. see *LITERARY AND POLITICAL REVIEWS*

026   US   ISSN 0038-6723
Z671   CODEN: SPLBAN
SPECIAL LIBRARIES. 1910. 4/yr. $95 (foreign $100) (subscr. includes m. SpeciaList newsletter and membership directory). Special Libraries Association, 1700 Eighteenth St., N.W., Washington, DC 20009. TEL 202-234-4700. Ed. Maria Barry. adv.; bk.rev.; bibl.; charts; illus.; index, cum.index; circ. 13,000. (also avail. in microform from UMI; reprint service avail. from KTO,UMI) **Indexed:** ASCA, B.P.I., Bibl.Cart., Bk.Rev.Ind. (1965-), Bus.Ind., C.I.J.E., Child.Bk.Rev.Ind. (1965-), CINAHL, Comput.Cont., Comput.Lit.Ind., Curr.Cont., Hist.Abstr., Hosp.Lit.Ind., Inform.Sci.Abstr., Intl.Civil Eng.Abstr., Key to Econ.Sci., Leg.Info.Manage.Ind., LHTN, Lib.Lit., Lib.Sci.Abstr, Mag.Ind., Manage.Abstr., P.A.I.S., Sci.Abstr., Sci.Cit.Ind., Soft.Abstr.Eng., SSCI.
—BLDSC shelfmark: 8367.000000.
Description: Discusses administration, organization and operations. Includes reports on research, technology and professional standards.

020   CN   ISSN 0824-7749
SPECIAL LIBRARIES ASSOCIATION. EASTERN CANADA CHAPTER. BULLETIN. 1956. q. membership. Special Libraries Association, Eastern Canada Chapter, Box 1538, Sta. B, Montreal, Que. H3B 3L2, Canada. Ed. Linda Ordogh. adv.; bk.rev.; circ. 375 (controlled).
Former titles: Special Libraries Association. Montreal Chapter. Bulletin (ISSN 0381-9833); Montreal Special Libraries Association. Bulletin (ISSN 0381-9825)
Description: Provides members with information on activities.

026 900   US   ISSN 0036-1607
Z673   CODEN: SGBUB2
SPECIAL LIBRARIES ASSOCIATION. GEOGRAPHY AND MAP DIVISION. BULLETIN. 1947. q. $25 (foreign $30). Special Libraries Association, Geography and Map Division, c/o Anita T. Sprankle, Bus. Mrg., 406 E. Smith St., Topton, PA 19562-1121. TEL 215-683-4480. FAX 215-683-4483. Ed. Joanne Perry. bk.rev.; bibl.; illus.; index, cum.index: nos.1-70, 1947-1967; nos. 71-102, 1968-1975; circ. 950. (also avail. in microform from UMI; reprint service avail. from KTO,UMI) **Indexed:** Bibl.& Ind.Geol., Bibl.Cart., Geo.Abstr., LHTN, Lib.Lit., LISA, Ref.Sour.
—BLDSC shelfmark: 2763.094000.

020.6   US
SPECIAL LIBRARIES ASSOCIATION. SOCIAL SCIENCE DIVISION. BULLETIN. 3/yr. membership only. Special Libraries Association, Social Science Division, 2000 15th St., N., Ste. 701, Arlington, VA 22201-2617. TEL 202-625-8400. FAX 202-625-8404. Ed. Olivia Pickett. adv.; bk.rev.; circ. 800.
Description: Covers the division's activities and news on health and human services, international and urban affairs, international dispute, municipal reference libraries, independent sector, law and public policy.

020   US
SPECIAL LIBRARIES ASSOCIATION. UPSTATE NEW YORK CHAPTER. BULLETIN. vol.42, 1986. 4/yr. $10 to non-members. Special Libraries Association, Upstate New York Chapter, Library Division, The Saratogian, 20 Lake Ave., Saratoga Springs, NY 12866. Ed. Ellie Brower. adv.; bk.rev.; tr.lit.; circ. 315.

026   US   ISSN 0739-7097
SPECIAL LIBRARIES ASSOCIATION. WASHINGTON D.C. CHAPTER. CHAPTER NOTES. 1968. 10/yr. $10 to non-members. Special Libraries Association, Washington D.C. Chapter, Box 287, Benjamin Franklin Sta., Washington, DC 20044. TEL 202-707-8723. FAX 202-707-1832. Eds. Mary Nell Bryant, Penny Heavner. adv.; circ. 1,000.

020 070 051   US   ISSN 0883-282X
D839
SPECTRUM (OLATHE); a guide to the independent press and informative organizations. 1973. a. $24.95 per no. Laird Wilcox, Box 2047, Olathe, KS 66061. TEL 913-829-0609. FAX 913-829-0609. circ. 5,000. **Indexed:** Hist.Abstr.
Former titles: Censored (ISSN 0163-2280); Some Hard-to-Locate Sources of Information on Current Affairs.
Description: Provides a listing of little known sources of news, factual background and analysis of current affairs, and controversial issues.

SPORT AND RECREATION INFORMATION GROUP BULLETIN. see *SPORTS AND GAMES*

LIBRARY AND INFORMATION SCIENCES

027.4   US
SPOTLIGHT ON YOUR LIBRARY. 1955. bi-m. free. Dayton & Montgomery County Public Library, 215 E. Third St., Dayton, OH 45402. TEL 513-227-9500. Ed. Mark Willis. circ. 8,000. (processed)
    Formerly: This Month in Your Library (ISSN 0040-6252)
    Description: Record and promotion of library activities, community involvement and new services.

020   US   ISSN 0720-678X
SPRINGER SERIES IN INFORMATION SCIENCES. 1980. irreg. price varies. Springer-Verlag, 175 Fifth Ave., New York, NY 10010. TEL 212-460-1500. (Also Berlin, Heidelberg, Tokyo and Vienna) Eds. K.S. Fu, T.S. Huang. (reprint service avail. from ISI) **Indexed:** Sci.Abstr.

020   CE
Z845.C4
SRI LANKA LIBRARY REVIEW. (Text in English or Sinhalese) 1967. biennial. Rs.40($7) per copy. Sri Lanka Library Association, 275-75 Bauddhaloka Mawatha, Colombo 7, Sri Lanka. adv.; bk.rev.; circ. 300.
    Formerly (1973): Ceylon Library Review.

026   GW   ISSN 0340-0700
STAATSBIBLIOTHEK PREUSSISCHER KULTURBESITZ. AUSSTELLUNGSKATALOGE. 1970. irreg. price varies. Staatsbibliothek Preussischer Kulturbesitz, Potsdamer Str. 33, Postfach 1407, 1000 Berlin 30, Germany. TEL 030-266-1. FAX 030-266-2814. TELEX 183-160-STAAB-D. (Order from: Dr. Ludwig Reichert Verlag, Tauernstr. 11, 6200 Wiesbaden, Germany)
    Description: Exhibition catalogues of important items from the holdings of the Staatsbibliothek.

026   GW   ISSN 0340-2274
STAATSBIBLIOTHEK PREUSSISCHER KULTURBESITZ. JAHRESBERICHT. 1950. irreg. Staatsbibliothek Preussischer Kulturbesitz, Potsdamer Str. 33, Postfach 1407, 1000 Berlin 30, Germany. TEL 030-266-1. FAX 030-266-2814. TELEX 183160-STAAB-D. stat. (back issues avail.)
    Description: Bulletin on the work of the Staatsbibliothek and its departments.

020   GW   ISSN 0038-8866
Z929.B625
STAATSBIBLIOTHEK PREUSSISCHER KULTURBESITZ. MITTEILUNGEN. 1969. 2/yr. Staatsbibliothek Preussischer Kulturbesitz, Potsdamer Str. 33, Postfach 1407, 1000 Berlin 30, Germany. TEL 030-266-1. FAX 030-266-2814. TELEX 183160-STAAB-D. Ed. Siegfried Detemple.
—BLDSC shelfmark: 5868.300000.
    Description: Bulletin reporting on the current work of the Staatsbibliothek with articles on subjects relating to the work and collections of the library.

026   UK
STANDARDS AND TECHNOLOGY BULLETIN. (Former name of issuing body: Machine Tool Industry Research Association) (Text in Dutch, English, French, German, Italian) 1968. m. £25. Advanced Manufacturing Technology Research Institute, Hulley Rd., Macclesfield, Cheshire SK10 2NE, England. TEL 0625-25421. FAX 0625-34964. Ed. K. Gowing. circ. 250.
    Former titles (until 1991): A M T R I Library Bulletin; (until 1986): M T I R A Library Bulletin.
    Description: Lists articles from journals, reports, proceedings and translations relevant to the manufacturing industry. Includes news on standards and safety topics.

027.7   US
STANFORD UNIVERSITY LIBRARIES. LIBRARY BULLETIN. 1948. m. free. Stanford University Libraries, Attn.: Lisa Carlson, Green Library, Stanford, CA 94305. TEL 415-723-0461. FAX 415-725-6874. Ed. Thomas Holt. circ. 625.
    Description: Information for and by the staff of the libraries.

027.8   US
▼**STAR TRACK.** (Supplement to: School Library Journal) 1990. s-a. free with subscr. to: School Library Journal. Cahners Publishing Company (New York), Bowker Magazine Group, Cahners Magazine Division (Subsidiary of: Reed International PLC), Division of Reed Publishing (USA) Inc., 249 W. 17th St., New York, NY 10011. TEL 800-669-1002. FAX 212-242-6987. TELEX 138 755. (Subscr. to: Box 1978, Marion, OH 43305-1978)
    Description: Reviews all starred titles in School Library Journal.

020   UK   ISSN 0305-9189
Z675.G7
STATE LIBRARIAN. 1948. 3/yr. £6($20) to non-members. Circle of State Librarians, c/o Marie Jackson, The British Library, Gt. Russel St., London WC1B 3DG, England. adv.; bk.rev.; circ. 700. **Indexed:** Lib.Lit., LISA.
—BLDSC shelfmark: 8438.260000.
    Formerly: Circle of State Librarians. Bulletin.

020   IT
STRUMENTI BIBLIOGRAFICI. 1974. irreg., latest no.4. price varies. Angelo Longo Editore, Via Paolo Costa 33, P.O. Box 431, 48100 Ravenna, Italy. TEL 0544-217026. Ed. Enzo Esposito. circ. 2,000.

020 070.5   PL   ISSN 0137-3404
STUDIA O KSIAZCE. (Text in Polish; summaries in French and Russian) 1970. a. price varies. (Uniwersytet Wroclawski) Ossolineum, Publishing House of the Polish Academy of Sciences, Rynek 9, Wroclaw, Poland. TELEX 0712771 OSS PL. Ed. Krzysztof Migon. bk.rev.; bibl.
—BLDSC shelfmark: 8482.957500.
    Description: Articles devoted to sources for studies of book history, printing, editorial work.

020   AU
STUDIEN ZUR BIBLIOTHEKSGESCHICHTE. 1973. irreg. price varies. Akademische Druck- und Verlagsanstalt Dr. Paul Struzl, Schoenaugasse 6, A-8010 Graz, Austria. TEL 813460.

025   UK   ISSN 0307-0808
STUDIES IN LIBRARY MANAGEMENT. 1972. irreg. price varies. Clive Bingley Ltd., 7 Ridgmount St., London WC1E 7AE, England. TEL 01-636-7543. FAX 01-636-3627. TELEX 21897-LALDN-G. Ed. Anthony Vaughan. circ. 1,500. **Indexed:** LISA.

026   US   ISSN 0732-927X
Z675.A2
SUBJECT DIRECTORY OF SPECIAL LIBRARIES AND INFORMATION CENTERS. 1975. a. $695 for 3-vol. set; $250 per vol. Gale Research Inc., 835 Penobscot Bldg., Detroit, MI 48226. TEL 800-877-4253. FAX 313-961-6083. TELEX 810-221-7086. Ed. Janice DeMaggio.
    Description: Irregularly updated guide to non-general libraries in the U.S.

020
SUBJECT SPECIALISTS SECTION NEWSLETTER. 1980. irreg. membership. Louisiana Library Association, Box 3058, Baton Rouge, LA 70821. TEL 504-342-4928. Ed. Charlotte Mattmiller. circ. 100. (back issues avail.)

027   SJ
SUDAN. NATIONAL COUNCIL FOR RESEARCH. NATIONAL DOCUMENTATION CENTRE. LIBRARY INFORMATION BULLETIN. (Text in English) m. National Council for Research, National Documentation Centre, Box 2404, Khartoum, Sudan.

020   SA   ISSN 1012-2796
SUID-AFRIKAANSE ARGIEFBLAD/SOUTH AFRICAN ARCHIVES JOURNAL. (Text and summaries in Afrikaans, English) 1959. a. R.20 (typically set in Apr.). South African Society of Archivists, c/o Treasurer, State Archives, Private Bag X236, Pretoria 0001, South Africa. TEL 012-323-5300. FAX 012-323-5287. Eds. A. Nel., V.S. Harris. adv.; bk.rev.; bibl.; circ. 300. (back issues avail.)
    Description: Articles on archival matters, reviews, society notices, select list of publications.

SVENSKA BARNBOKSINSTITUTET. SKRIFTER/SWEDISH INSTITUTE FOR CHILDREN'S BOOKS. STUDIES. see CHILDREN AND YOUTH — For

SWARBICA JOURNAL. see HISTORY — History Of Asia

020   US   ISSN 0095-0874
Z881.U49
SYMBOLS OF AMERICAN LIBRARIES. 1932. irreg. $13. U.S. Library of Congress, Enhanced Cataloging Division, Washington, DC 20540. TEL 202-707-6100. (Subscr. to: Cataloging Distribution Service, Washington, DC 20541) Ed. William W. Palmer. circ. 2,500.

020   NO   ISSN 0332-656X
Z671
SYNOPSIS; informasjon om informasjon. (Text in Norwegian; summaries in English) 1970. bi-m. free. Riksbibliotektjenesten, Bygdoe Alle 21, P.O. Box 2439, Solli, 0201 Oslo, Norway. TEL 02-43-08-80. FAX 02-56-09-81. Ed. Kjellaug Scheie. abstr.; bibl.; index. (back issues avail.)
—BLDSC shelfmark: 8586.109000.
    Description: News reports and articles of interest to professional librarians.

020   CN   ISSN 0039-8470
T.P.L. NEWS. 1971. m. free. Toronto Public Library, 281 Front St.E., Toronto, Ont. M5A 4L2, Canada. TEL 416-393-7565. FAX 416-393-7782. Ed. Dora Auramis. bk.rev.; film rev.; circ. 900 (controlled).

TALKING BOOK TOPICS (LARGE PRINT EDITION). see HANDICAPPED — Visually Impaired

020   CN   ISSN 0380-2973
TALKING BOOKS IN THE PUBLIC LIBRARY SYSTEMS OF METROPOLITAN TORONTO. 1974. irreg. Can.$35. Metropolitan Toronto Library Board, 789 Yonge St., Toronto, Ont. M4W 2G8, Canada. TEL 416-393-7160. bibl.

020   TZ   ISSN 0856-1621
TANZANIA LIBRARY SERVICE. OCCASIONAL PAPER. irreg. price varies. Library Services Board, Box 9283, Dar es Salaam, Tanzania.

TANZANIA NATIONAL BIBLIOGRAPHY. see BIBLIOGRAPHIES

020   US   ISSN 0193-4309
TAR HEEL LIBRARIES. 1977. bi-m. membership. Department of Cultural Resources, Division of State Library, 109 E. Jones St., Raleigh, NC 27611. TEL 919-733-2570. FAX 919-733-8748. TELEX EASYLINK 62953578. Ed. Diana D. Young. illus.; stat.; circ. 5,000 (controlled).
    Former titles (until 1976): Library Reporter; North Carolina State Library Newsletter (ISSN 0549-7728)

020   NZ   ISSN 0114-1090
TE PUNA MATAURANGA. 1988. q. free. National Library of New Zealand, National Librarian, P.O. Box 1467, Wellington, New Zealand. TEL 04-743-000. FAX 04-743-035. Ed. Bill Davidson. circ. 2,000.
—BLDSC shelfmark: 8612.593750.

027.8   AT   ISSN 0049-3090
TEACHER AND LIBRARIAN. 1965. q. Aus.$30. School Library Association of New South Wales, P.O. Box 187, Rozelle, N.S.W. 2039, Australia. circ. 900. **Indexed:** Aus.Educ.Ind.

020   CN
Z675.S3
TEACHING LIBRARIAN. 1974. 4/yr. Can.$36. (Ontario School Library Association) Ontario Library Association, 100 Richmond St. E., Suite 300, Toronto, Ont. M5C 2P9, Canada. TEL 416-363-3388. Ed. Judy Tye. adv.; bk.rev.; illus.; index; circ. 1,300.
    Formerly: Reviewing Librarian (ISSN 0318-0948)
    Description: Articles and reviews of new materials for teachers and librarians with emphasis on applications to learning, teaching styles and curriculum.

LIBRARY AND INFORMATION SCIENCES

020 US ISSN 0731-7131
Z688.5
TECHNICAL SERVICES QUARTERLY. 1983. q. $36 to individuals; institutions and libraries $95. Haworth Press, Inc., 10 Alice St., Binghamton, NY 13904. TEL 800-342-9678. FAX 607-722-1424. TELEX 4932599. Ed. Gary Pitkin. adv.; bk.rev.; circ. 515. (also avail. in microfiche from HAW; back issues avail.; reprint service avail. from HAW) **Indexed:** C.I.J.E., Comput.Cont., Inform.Sci.Abstr., Leg.Info.Manage.Ind., Lib.Lit., LISA, Ref.Zh., Sci.Abstr.
—BLDSC shelfmark: 8726.665000.
Description: Devoted to new trends in computer automation and advanced technologies in the technical operation of libraries and information centers.
Refereed Serial

020.5 US ISSN 0272-0884
Z671
TECHNICALITIES. 1980. m. $47. Media Periodicals (Subsidiary of: Westport Publishers, Inc.), 2444 O St., Ste. 202, Lincoln, NE 68510. TEL 402-474-2676. Ed. Brian Alley. adv.; bk.rev.; index; circ. 750. (also avail. in microfilm from UMI; microfiche; back issues avail.) **Indexed:** LHTN, Lib.Lit., LISA.
—BLDSC shelfmark: 8732.405000.
Description: Professional publication updating librarians in library and information service usage, with special emphasis on computer applications.

TECHNISCHE UNIVERSITAET BRAUNSCHWEIG. UNIVERSITAETSBIBLIOTHEK. VEROEFFENTLICHUNGEN. see *EDUCATION — Higher Education*

TECHNOLOGY TRANSFER DIRECTORY. see *BUSINESS AND ECONOMICS — Trade And Industrial Directories*

020 US ISSN 0162-1564
Z671
TENNESSEE LIBRARIAN.* N.S. 1948. q. $10. Tennessee Library Association, Box 158417, Nashville, TN 37215-8417. TEL 615-297-8316. Ed. Sue Klipsch. adv.; bk.rev.; illus.; circ. 1,600. (also avail. in microform from UMI; reprint service avail. from UMI) **Indexed:** Lib.Lit.
—BLDSC shelfmark: 8790.733000.
Formerly: T L - Tennessee Librarian (ISSN 0040-3296)

027.7 US ISSN 0040-4136
TEXAS A & M UNIVERSITY LIBRARY NOTES. 1965. bi-m. (except Aug.). free. Texas A & M University Library, College Sta., TX 77843. TEL 409-845-5741. Ed. Candace R. Benefiel. circ. 3,000.
Description: Covers current events within the Library.

020 US ISSN 0040-4438
Z671
TEXAS LIBRARIES. 1906. q. free to libraries and qualified personnel. Texas State Library and Archives Commission, Box 12927, Austin, TX 78711. TEL 512-463-5492. FAX 512-463-5436. Ed. Susan Hildebrand. bk.rev.; bibl.; illus.; index; circ. 1,400 (controlled). (also avail. in microform from UMI) **Indexed:** Child.Lit.Abstr., Lib.Lit.
Description: Features articles on Texas, the library and information science fields and publishing.

020 US ISSN 0040-4446
TEXAS LIBRARY JOURNAL. 1924. q. $20 (foreign $25). Texas Library Association, 3355 Beecave Rd., Ste. 603, Austin, TX 78746. TEL 512-328-1518. FAX 512-328-8852. Ed. Josette Lyders. adv.; illus.; index; circ. 5,300. (also avail. in microfilm) **Indexed:** Lib.Lit.
—BLDSC shelfmark: 8799.450000.

TEXAS WOMAN'S UNIVERSITY. SCHOOL OF LIBRARY AND INFORMATION STUDIES. ALUMNAE NEWSLETTER. see *COLLEGE AND ALUMNI*

THESAURUS OF E R I C DESCRIPTORS. (Educational Resources Information Center) see *EDUCATION*

020 US
THIRD INDICATOR. 1985. bi-m. $25 (free to qualified personnel). Bibliographical Center for Research, 4500 Cherry Creek Dr. S., Ste. 206, Denver, CO 80222. TEL 303-691-0550. FAX 303-691-0112. Ed. Rosario Garza. circ. 500. (looseleaf format; back issues avail.)

020 338.91 US ISSN 1052-3049
Z730
▼**THIRD WORLD LIBRARIES;** an international journal focusing on libraries and socio-economic development. 1990. s-a. $15 in developing countries ($35 to N. America, Europe, Japan, Australia, New Zealand. Rosary College, Graduate School of Library and Information Science, 7900 W. Division, River Forest, IL 60305. TEL 708-366-2490. FAX 703-366-5360. Ed. Guy A. Marco. bk.rev.; index; circ. 390.
—BLDSC shelfmark: 8820.145190.
Description: Covers issues pertaining to libraries and their role in development.

029 SW ISSN 0040-6872
CODEN: TDDKA5
TIDSKRIFT FOER DOKUMENTATION/NORDIC JOURNAL OF DOCUMENTATION. (Text in Swedish; occasionally in English; summaries in English) 1945. q. SEK 180. Tekniska Litteratursaellskapet, c/o Ingenjoersvetenskapsakademien, Box 5073, S-102 42 Stockholm 5, Sweden. Eds. Gunnar Lager, Birgitta Levin. adv.; bk.rev.; bibl.; illus.; index; circ. 1,000. **Indexed:** Biol.Abstr., Lib.Lit., Lib.Sci.Abstr, Sci.Abstr.
—BLDSC shelfmark: 8821.000000.

020 II ISSN 0563-5489
TIMELESS FELLOWSHIP; annual journal of comparative librarianship. (Text in English) 1964. a. Rs.40($9) Karnatak University Library Association, Karnatak University, Pavat Nagar, Dharwad 580 003, Karnataka, India. Eds. K.S. Deshpande, M.R. Kumbhar. adv.; bk.rev.; circ. 500. **Indexed:** LISA.

027.4 PP ISSN 0310-463X
TOK TOK BILONG HAUS BUK.* 1972. s-a. 20 n.($23) Papua New Guinea Library Association, c/o National Library Service, Box 5770, Boroko, N.C.D., Papua New Guinea. Ed.Bd. adv.; bk.rev.; circ. 500. **Indexed:** LISA, So.Pac.Per.Ind.

020 HU ISSN 0133-8358
TOLNAI KONYVTAROS. 1970. s-a. free. Tolna Megyei Konyvtar - Public Library of the County Tolna, Szechenyi ut 51, H-7100 Szekszard, Hungary. TEL 11-834. Ed. Maria Elekes. adv.; bk.rev.; bibl.; illus.; stat.; cum.index: 1970-1985; circ. 300. (back issues avail.)

020 UK ISSN 0268-9928
TOP 3,000 DIRECTORIES AND ANNUALS: A GUIDE TO THE MAJOR TITLES USED IN BRITISH LIBRARIES. 1980. a. £43. Wm. Dawson & Sons Ltd., Cannon House, Park Farm Rd., Folkestone CT19 5EE, England. TEL 0303-850101. FAX 0303-850440. TELEX 96392.
—BLDSC shelfmark: 8867.374330.
Formerly: Top 2,000 Directories and Annuals: A Guide to the Major Titles Used in British Libraries (ISSN 0262-0219)

020 JA ISSN 0454-1960
TOSHOKAN KENKYU SIRIZU/N.D.L. LIBRARY SCIENCE SERIES. (Text in Japanese) 1960. a. price varies. National Diet Library - Kokuritsu Kokkai Toshokan, 10-1 Nagata-cho 1-chome, Chiyada-ku, Tokyo 100, Japan. TEL 03-3581-2331. TELEX 2225393. circ. 950.
—BLDSC shelfmark: 6067.848000.

020 JA
TOSHOKAN KYORYOKU TSUSHIN/LIBRARY COOPERATION NEWS. (Text in Japanese) 1987. bi-m. National Diet Library - Kokuritsu Kokkai Toshokan, 1-10-1 Nagata-cho, Chiyoda-ku, Tokyo 100, Japan. TEL 03-3581-2331. TELEX 2225393. circ. 4,000.
Description: Provides information about interlibrary loans, photocopying, and reference services that will be of interest to user libraries. Also reports on seminars and workshops organized by the NDL.

020 KO
TOSOGUAN HAK. 1970. a. 400 Won($1) Korean Library Science Society, Yonsei University Library, 134 Sinchon-Dong, Seodaemoon-Ku, Seoul 120, S. Korea.

029 UK
TREND MONITOR REPORTS; computing, communications, media and socio-technology. 6/yr. (in 2 vols., 3 nos./vol.). £105 per no. Aslib, Association for Information Management, Publications Department, Information House, 20-24 Old St., London EC1V 9AP, England. TEL 071-253-4488. FAX 071-430-0574. Ed. Jan Wyllie.
Formerly: Trend Monitor (ISSN 0954-7479)

020 IE ISSN 0790-388X
TRINITY COLLEGE. FRIENDS OF THE LIBRARY. NEWSLETTER. 1984. 3/yr. £6. Trinity College, Friends of the Library, College St., Dublin 2, Ireland. FAX 719003. TELEX 93782. Ed. P.K. Fox. circ. 500. (back issues avail.)

027.7 AT
LA TROBE UNIVERSITY LIBRARY NEWS. irreg. (2-4/yr.). free. La Trobe University, University Library, Bundoora, Vic. 3085, Australia. TEL 479-2920. FAX 03-471-0993.
Description: News sheet directed at academic staff of the University. Covers library developments.

TURNBULL LIBRARY RECORD. see *HISTORY — History Of Australasia And Other Areas*

020 060 FI ISSN 0082-7010
TURUN YLIOPISTO. KIRJASTO. JULKAISUJA. (Text in English, Finnish, French; summaries in English, French, German) 1948. irreg., no.12, 1983. price varies. Turun Yliopisto, Kirjasto - Turku University Library, Kirjasto, SF-20500 Turku 50, Finland. FAX 358-21-6335050. TELEX 62123 TYK SF. circ. 300.

020 CC ISSN 0252-3116
Z671
TUSHU QINGBAO GONGZUO/LIBRARY AND INFORMATION SERVICE. (Text in Chinese) 1980. bi-m. $8.20 (foreign $41.90). (Chinese Academy of Sciences, Documentation and Information Center) Science Press, Marketing and Sales Department, 16 Donghuangchenggen Beijie, Beijing 100707, People's Republic of China. TEL 4010642. FAX 4012180. TELEX 210247-SPBJ-CN. Ed. Xin Ximeng. adv.; circ. 32,000.
—BLDSC shelfmark: 5188.815000.
Description: Devoted to the study and exploration of library and information work, as well as the theories and methods helpful to the modernization of these services. Reports and comments on the development of these services in China and abroad.

020 CC
TUSHU QINGBAO ZHISHI/BOOK INFORMATION KNOWLEDGE. (Text in Chinese) q. Wuhan Daxue - Wuhan University, Luojiashan, Wuchang-qu, Wuhan, Hubei 430072, People's Republic of China. TEL 812712. Ed. Huang Zongzhong.

020 CC
TUSHUGUAN GONGZUO YU YANJIU. (Text in Chinese) q. Tianjin Tushuguan - Tianjin Library, 12 Chengde Dao, Heping Qu, Tianjin, People's Republic of China. TEL 393561. Ed. Dong Changxu.

020 CC
TUSHUGUAN JIE/LIBRARY CIRCLE. (Text in Chinese) q. Guangxi Tushuguan - 28138, 22 Minzhu Dadao, Nanning, Guangxi 530022, People's Republic of China. TEL 28138. Ed. He Shanxiang.

020 CC
TUSHUGUAN XUEKAN/LIBRARY JOURNAL. (Text in Chinese) bi-m. Liaoning Sheng Tushuguan - Liaoning Provicial Library, 48 Shaoshuaifu Xiang, Chaoyang Jie, Shenyang, Liaoning 110011, People's Republic of China. TEL 443150. Ed. Zhu Yupei.

020 CC
TUSHUGUAN YUAN/LIBRARIANS. (Text in Chinese) bi-m. Sichuan Sheng Tushuguan - Sichuan Provincial Library, 6 Zongfu Jie, Chengdu, Sichuan 610016, People's Republic of China. TEL 29350.

020 CC ISSN 0494-1225
TUSHUGUANXUE TONGXUN/BULLETIN OF LIBRARY SCIENCE. (Text in Chinese) bi-m. $24.30. Society of Library Science, 7 Wenjing Jie, Beijing 100802, People's Republic of China. TEL 6016633. (Dist. in US by: China Books & Periodicals, Inc., 2929 24th St., San Francisco, CA 94110. TEL 415-282-2994) Huang Jungui.

LIBRARY AND INFORMATION SCIENCES

020   UK   ISSN 0264-2441
U A P NEWSLETTER. (Universal Availability of Publications) Spanish edition: Boletin D U P. 1983. irreg. free. International Federation of Library Association and Institutions, International Programme for UAP, c/o British Library Document Supply Centre, Boston Spa, Wetherby, West Yorkshire LS23 7BQ, England. TEL 0937-546124. FAX 0937-546236. TELEX 557381. (Spanish edition avail. from: c/o E.M. Guerrero, A. Postal 21-094, Coyoacan, 04000 Mexico Df, Mexico) Ed. Graham Cornish. bk.rev.; circ. 1,750 Eng.ed.; 1,000 Span.ed.

020   GW   ISSN 1012-327X
U B C I M OCCASIONAL PAPER. (International Federation of Library Associations and Instituions - Universal Bibliographic Control and International Marc Programme) 1989. irreg. I F L A I - U B C I M Programme, c/o Deutsche Bibliothek, Zeppelinallee 4 - 8, 6000 Frankfurt am Main 1, Germany. TEL 49-69-741-0906. FAX 49-69-756-6476. TELEX 416-643 DEU BI. (Dist. by: K.G. Saur, Division of R.R. Bowker, 245 W. 17th St., New York, NY 10011. TEL 212-337-7023) Eds. Hana Komorous, Robert B. Harriman. circ. 500.
—BLDSC shelfmark: 9078.175000.

027.7   CN   ISSN 0382-0661
U B C LIBRARY NEWS. 1968. q. free. University of British Columbia, Main Library, Vancouver, B.C. V6T 1Y3, Canada. Ed. Julie Stevens. circ. 3,200.

020   CN   ISSN 1010-9501
U D T NEWSLETTER/BULLETIN DE L'U D T. (Text in English, French) 1987. 3/yr. free. (I F L A International Office for U D T) National Library of Canada, 395 Wellington St., Ottawa, Ont. K1A 0N4, Canada. TEL 819-994-6963. FAX 819-994-6835. circ. 2,500.
—BLDSC shelfmark: 9079.712000.

020   BL   ISSN 0100-0829
Z671
U F M G. ESCOLA DE BIBLIOTECONOMIA. REVISTA. (Text in Portuguese; summaries in English) 1972. s-a. $35 (typically set in Oct.). Universidade Federal de Minas Gerais, Escola de Biblioteconomia, Caixa Postal 1906, 30161 Belo Horizonte MG, Brazil. TEL 441-1131. FAX 031-441-9354. Ed. Ana Maria Cardoso de Andrade. adv.; bk.rev.; abstr.; bibl.; charts; stat.; cum.index: 1972-1986; circ. 800 (controlled). (back issues avail.) Indexed: Inform.Sci.Abstr., Lib.Lit., LISA.
—BLDSC shelfmark: 7805.520000.
Description: Devoted to research and other contributions in library and information science.

020   UK   ISSN 0963-7354
▼**U K O L N NEWSLETTER.** (U K Office for Library Networking) 1991. s-a. University of Bath Library, Centre for Bibliographic Management, Claverton Down, Bath BA2 7AY, England. TEL 0225-826580. FAX 0225-826229. Ed. Philip Bryant. circ. 600.

020   MX
U N A M DIRECTORIO DE BIBLIOTECAS. 1976. biennial. $8 (or exchange). Universidad Nacional Autonoma de Mexico, Direccion General de Bibliotecas, Ciudad Universitaria, Mexico 20, D.F., Mexico.

029.7   UN   ISSN 0304-0062
U N I S I S T BOLETIN DE INFORMACION. (Unesco Programme of International Cooperation in Scientific and Technological Information) (Spanish ed. of UNISIST Newsletter; also available in English, French, Russian eds.) vol.3 1975. q. free. Unesco, Division of Scientific and Technological Documentation and Information, 7-9 Place de Fontenoy, 75700 Paris, France. (back issues avail.) Indexed: LISA.

020   UN   ISSN 0300-2519
Q223
U N I S I S T NEWSLETTER. (Unesco Programme of International Cooperation in Scientific and Technological Information) Russian edition (ISSN 0304-0070) (Editions in English, French, Russian and Spanish) 1973. irreg. (4-6/yr.); (q. Russian ed.). free. Unesco, Division of Scientific and Technological Information and Documentation, 7-9 Place de Fontenoy, 75700 Paris, France. Indexed: Field Crop Abstr., Herb.Abstr., Nutr.Abstr.

020   UN   ISSN 0379-2218
Q223
U N I S I S T NEWSLETTER - GENERAL INFORMATION PROGRAMME. (Editions in English, French, Spanish and Russian) 1979. q. free. Unesco, 7 Place de Fontenoy, 75700 Paris, France. bk.rev.; index, cum.index; circ. 9,000. (back issues avail.)
—BLDSC shelfmark: 9090.784000.
Formerly: Unisist Newsletter.

020   US   ISSN 0364-5215
Z690
U S B E NEWS.* 1949. m. $75 to non-members. Universal Serials and Book Exchange, Universal Serials, 3335 V St., N.E., Washington, DC 20018. TEL 202-636-USBE. Ed. Mary W. Ghikas. circ. 1,800. (processed)
Formerly (until 1976): United States Book Exchange Newsletter (ISSN 0041-753X)

UMBRELLA. see ART

020   US   ISSN 0049-514X
Z671
UNABASHED LIBRARIAN; the "how I run my library good" letter. 1971. 4/yr. $30 (foreign $36). Box 2631, New York, NY 10116. Ed. Marvin H. Scilken. bk.rev.; bibl. (back issues avail.) **Indexed:** Lib.Lit.
—BLDSC shelfmark: 9083.900000.

020 025   US   ISSN 0083-1565
Z733
U.S. LIBRARY OF CONGRESS. ANNUAL REPORT OF THE LIBRARIAN OF CONGRESS. 1866. a. price varies; free to libraries upon request to LC Central Services Division. U.S. Library of Congress, Washington, DC 20540. TEL 202-707-5000.

025.3   US   ISSN 0160-8029
Z693.A15   CODEN: CSBUDE
U.S. LIBRARY OF CONGRESS. CATALOGING SERVICE BULLETIN. 1978. q. $19. U.S. Library of Congress, Processing Services, Washington, DC 20540. TEL 202-707-6100. (Dist. by: Cataloging Distribution Service, Library of Congress, Washington, DC 20541) Key Title: Cataloging Service Bulletin.
—BLDSC shelfmark: 3074.300000.
Supersedes (1945-1978): U.S. Library of Congress. Cataloging Service (ISSN 0041-7890)

020   US   ISSN 0041-7904
Z733.U57
U.S. LIBRARY OF CONGRESS. INFORMATION BULLETIN. 1942. bi-w. free to libraries and institutions. U.S. Library of Congress, Washington, DC 20540. index; circ. 6,000. (also avail. in microform from LCP,MIM) **Indexed:** Amer.Bibl.Slavic & E.Eur.Stud, Art & Archaeol.Tech.Abstr., Ind.U.S.Gov.Per., Lib.Lit., LISA. Key Title: Information Bulletin - Library of Congress.
—BLDSC shelfmark: 5198.200000.

025.3   US   ISSN 0041-7912
Z696   CODEN: LCCCAH
U.S. LIBRARY OF CONGRESS. L.C. CLASSIFICATION - ADDITIONS AND CHANGES. 1928. q. $55. U.S. Library of Congress, Subject Cataloging Division, Washington, DC 20540. TEL 202-707-6100. (Dist by: Cataloging Distribution Service Divsion, Library of Congress, Washington, DC 20541) Ed. Emma E. Curtis. circ. 1,500.

U.S. LIBRARY OF CONGRESS. NATIONAL LIBRARY SERVICE FOR THE BLIND AND PHYSICALLY HANDICAPPED. NEWS. see HANDICAPPED — Visually Impaired

UNITED STATES BOARD ON BOOKS FOR YOUNG PEOPLE. NEWSLETTER. see PUBLISHING AND BOOK TRADE

020   SP   ISSN 0078-8740
UNIVERSIDAD DE NAVARRA. ESCUELA DE BIBLIOTECARIAS. COLECCION BIBLIOTECARIAS. 1969. irreg., no.4, 1977. price varies. Ediciones Universidad de Navarra, S.A., Apdo. 396, 31080 Pamplona, Spain. TEL 94 825 6850.
Formerly: Universidad de Navarra. Escuela de Bibliotecarias. Manuales: Bibliotecarias.

020.7   PN
UNIVERSIDAD DE PANAMA. DEPARTAMENTO DE BIBLIOTECOLOGIA. BOLETIN. 1968. q. Bl.12. Universidad de Panama, Departamento de Bibliotecologia, Estafeta Universitaria, Panama, Panama. adv.; bk.rev.; bibl.; circ. 350.
Formerly: Universidad de Panama. Escuela de Bibliotecologia. Boletin (ISSN 0014-0422)

020   MX   ISSN 0185-0067
UNIVERSIDAD NACIONAL AUTONOMA DE MEXICO. INSTITUTO DE INVESTIGACIONES BIBLIOGRAFICA. INSTRUMENTA BIBLIOGRAPHICA; catalogo de seudonimos, anagramas, iniciales otros alias usados por escritores Mexicanos y extranjeros que han publicado en Mexico. 1973. irreg., latest 1985. $10. Universidad Nacional Autonoma de Mexico, Instituto de Investigaciones Bibliograficas, Ciudad Universitaria, Coyoacan, Mexico 04510, D.F., Mexico. (Co-sponsor: Biblioteca Nacional) Ed. Ignacio Osorio Romero. (back issues avail.)

020   PY
UNIVERSIDAD NACIONAL DE ASUNCION. ESCUELA DE BIBLIOTECOLOGIA. INFORMACIONES. 1972. a. $5. Universidad Nacional de Asuncion, Escuela de Bibliotecologia, Espana 1098, Casilla de Correo 1408, Asuncion, Paraguay. Ed.Bd. bk.rev.; circ. 200.

020   PO
UNIVERSIDADE DE COIMBRA. ARQUIVO. BOLETIM. 1973. a. Esc.2000. Universidade de Coimbra, Arquivo, R.S. Pedro, 2, Coimbra, Portugal. FAX 039-20987. Ed. Manuel Augusto Rodriguez. circ. 3,000.

020   GW   ISSN 0438-4415
UNIVERSITAETS- UND LANDESBIBLIOTHEK SACHSEN-ANHALT. ARBEITEN. 1952. irreg., vol.36, 1990. price varies. Universitaets- und Landesbibliothek Sachsen-Anhalt, August-Bebel-Str. 13, 4010 Halle (Saale) 1, Germany. TELEX 4252-ULB-HAL-DD.

027   GW   ISSN 0072-4483
UNIVERSITAETSBIBLIOTHEK GIESSEN. BERICHTE UND ARBEITEN. 1962. irreg. price varies. Universitaetsbibliothek Giessen, Otto-Behaghel-Str. 8, 6300 Giessen, Germany. TEL 0641-702-2330. FAX 0641-46406. circ. 500.
Description: Bibliographies and studies about the library, the history of the University and the history of printing in Giessen.

UNIVERSITAT DE BARCELONA. BIBLIOTECA. see BIBLIOGRAPHIES

020   SP
UNIVERSITAT DE BARCELONA. BIBLIOTECA. MEMORIA ANUAL. 1969. a. free. Universitat de Barcelona, Biblioteca, Gran via de les Corts Catalanes, 585, 08007 Barcelona, Spain. illus.; circ. controlled.

027.7   NO   ISSN 0802-2836
UNIVERSITETSBIBLIOTEKET I TRONDHEIM. RAPPORT. 1971. irreg. price varies. Universitetsbiblioteket i Trondheim, Erling Skakkes gt. 47C, N-7013 Trondheim, Norway. FAX 07-592202. TELEX 55384 BIBL. circ. 200. (also avail. in microfilm) **Indexed:** LISA.
Formerly: Universitetet i Trondheim. Biblioteket. Avdeling B. Rapport.

027.7   UK
UNIVERSITY OF BATH. CENTRE FOR BIBLIOGRAPHIC MANAGEMENT. NEWSLETTER. 1979-1989; 1991-? 2/yr. free. University of Bath Library, Centre for Bibliographic Management, Claverton Down, Bath BA2 7AY, England. TEL 0225-826580. FAX 0225-826229. TELEX 449097. Ed. Philip Bryant. circ. 700.
Formerly (until 1987): University of Bath. Centre for Catalogue Research. Newsletter (ISSN 0144-5073)

027   NR
UNIVERSITY OF BENIN. LIBRARY. ANNUAL REPORT. (Title varies slightly) 1970. a. University of Benin, Library, P.M.B. 1154, Eken Wan Rd., Benin City, Nigeria. stat.

020   US   ISSN 0069-3375
UNIVERSITY OF CHICAGO STUDIES IN LIBRARY SCIENCE. 1939. irreg., latest 1984. price varies. University of Chicago Press, 5801 S. Ellis Ave., Chicago, IL 60637. TEL 312-702-7899. Ed. Don R. Swanson. (back issues avail.; reprint service avail. from UMI,ISI)
Refereed Serial

LIBRARY AND INFORMATION SCIENCES

027.4 CN ISSN 0226-3300
UNIVERSITY OF GUELPH LIBRARY. COLLECTION UPDATE. 1979. a. Can.$6.50 per no. University of Guelph Library, Guelph, Ont. N1G 2W1, Canada. Ed. Carol Goodger-Hill. bibl.; illus.; cum.index: 1979-1989; circ. 200. (back issues avail.)
Description: Aims to increase awareness within the University community and among the public, of the diverse materials available at the University Library.

027 NR ISSN 0073-4322
Z858
UNIVERSITY OF IBADAN. LIBRARY. ANNUAL REPORT. 1948. a. free. University of Ibadan, Library, Ibadan, Nigeria. bk.rev.; circ. 500.

027.7 NR ISSN 0046-8436
UNIVERSITY OF IBADAN. LIBRARY. LIBRARY RECORD. 1949. m. free. University of Ibadan, Library, Ibadan, Nigeria. bk.rev.; bibl.; circ. 80. (processed; back issues avail.)

025 US ISSN 0069-4789
Z678.9.A1
UNIVERSITY OF ILLINOIS AT URBANA-CHAMPAIGN. CLINIC ON LIBRARY APPLICATIONS OF DATA PROCESSING. PROCEEDINGS. 1963. a. $20. University of Illinois at Urbana-Champaign, Graduate School of Library and Information Science, 249 Armory Bldg., 505 E. Armory St., Champaign, IL 61820. TEL 217-333-1359. index. (also avail. in microfiche; back issues avail.)
—BLDSC shelfmark: 6842.865000.

020 US
UNIVERSITY OF ILLINOIS AT URBANA-CHAMPAIGN. GRADUATE SCHOOL OF LIBRARY AND INFORMATION SCIENCE. ALLERTON PARK INSTITUTE. PAPERS. 1954. a. $20. University of Illinois at Urbana-Champaign, Graduate School of Library and Information Science, 249 Armory Bldg., 505 E. Armory St., Champaign, IL 61820. TEL 217-333-1359. index.
Formerly: University of Illinois at Urbana-Champaign. Graduate School of Library Science. Allerton Park Institute. Papers (ISSN 0536-4604)

020 US
UNIVERSITY OF ILLINOIS AT URBANA-CHAMPAIGN. GRADUATE SCHOOL OF LIBRARY AND INFORMATION SCIENCE. MONOGRAPH SERIES. 1963. irregg. price varies. University of Illinois at Urbana-Champaign, Graduate School of Library and Information Science, 249 Armory Bldg., 505 E. Armory St., Champaign, IL 61820. TEL 217-333-1359.
Formerly: University of Illinois at Urbana-Champaign. Graduate School of Library Science. Monograph Series. (ISSN 0073-5302)

020 US ISSN 0276-1769
UNIVERSITY OF ILLINOIS AT URBANA-CHAMPAIGN. GRADUATE SCHOOL OF LIBRARY AND INFORMATION SCIENCE. OCCASIONAL PAPERS. 1949. irreg. University of Illinois at Urbana-Champaign, Graduate School of Library and Information Science, 249 Armory Bldg., 505 E. Armory St., Champaign, IL 61820. TEL 217-333-1359. Ed. Donald W. Krummel. circ. 500. (back issues avail.) **Indexed:** Biol.Abstr.
—BLDSC shelfmark: 6223.870000.
Formerly: University of Illinois at Urbana-Champaign. Graduate School of Library Science. Occasional Papers.

027.7 US ISSN 0047-1402
UNIVERSITY OF IOWA. LIBRARIES. NEWSLETTER. 1972. 2/yr. free. (Friends of the University of Iowa Libraries) University of Iowa Libraries, Iowa City, IA 52242. TEL 319-353-4490. Ed. Jeffery Dodd. bibl.; circ. 2,500.

020 US
UNIVERSITY OF IOWA. SCHOOL OF LIBRARY AND INFORMATION SCIENCE. NEWSLETTER. 1966. a. free. University of Iowa, School of Library and Information Science, 3087 Library, Iowa City, IA 52242. TEL 319-335-5707. Ed. Ethel Bloesch. bibl.; circ. 3,000. (back issues avail.)
Formerly: University of Iowa. School of Library Science. Newsletter (ISSN 0041-9648)

020 US ISSN 0075-5001
UNIVERSITY OF KANSAS LIBRARIES. LIBRARY SERIES.. 1935. irreg. price varies. University of Kansas Libraries, Lawrence, KS 66045. TEL 913-864-4334. Ed. James Helyar.

020 US ISSN 0743-8915
UNIVERSITY OF KENTUCKY LIBRARIES. OCCASIONAL PAPERS. 1980. irreg., no.4, 1983. price varies. University of Kentucky Library, University of Kentucky, Lexington, KY 40506. Ed. Terry L. Birdwhistell. circ. 300.

027.7 SJ
UNIVERSITY OF KHARTOUM. LIBRARY BULLETIN. (Text in Arabic or English) 1977. a. University of Khartoum, Library, Box 321, Khartoum, Sudan.

020 NR ISSN 0075-7705
UNIVERSITY OF LAGOS. LIBRARY. ANNUAL REPORT. 1962. a. free. (University of Lagos, Library) Lagos University Press, P.O. Box 132, Akoka, Yaba, Lagos, Nigeria. Ed. E.B. Bankole. circ. 1,000.

UNIVERSITY OF LONDON. SCHOOL OF SLAVONIC AND EAST EUROPEAN STUDIES. LIBRARY. BIBLIOGRAPHICAL GUIDES. see *BIBLIOGRAPHIES*

027.7 MW
UNIVERSITY OF MALAWI. LIBRARY. BULLETIN. (Text in English) 1977. 2/yr. free. University of Malawi, Library, Box 280, Zomba, Malawi. Ed. Foster G. Howse. circ. 200.

027 MW ISSN 0085-3038
UNIVERSITY OF MALAWI LIBRARIES. REPORT TO THE SENATE ON THE UNIVERSITY LIBRARIES. 1965. a. free. University of Malawi Libraries, Central Library Services, Box 280, Zomba, Malawi. TEL 265-522-222-135. FAX 265-523-225. TELEX 4742 CHANCOL MI. Ed. Steve S. Mwiyeriwa. circ. 200. (processed)
Description: Report on the activities and progress of five units of the University of Malawi Library System.

020 US ISSN 0076-4841
UNIVERSITY OF MARYLAND. COLLEGE OF LIBRARY AND INFORMATION SERVICES. STUDENT CONTRIBUTION SERIES. 1967. irreg., no.10, 1977. price varies. University of Maryland, College of Library and Information Services, c/o Esther Herman, Director of Publications, College Park, MD 20742. TEL 301-405-2064. **Indexed:** Lib.Lit.

027.7 US
UNIVERSITY OF MISSOURI, COLUMBIA. LIBRARY SERIES. 1908. irreg., no.29, 1985. exchange basis. University of Missouri, Columbia, Ellis Library, Columbia, MO 65201. TEL 314-882-4701. circ. 500.

020 US
UNIVERSITY OF MISSOURI - KANSAS CITY. FRIENDS OF THE LIBRARY. PUBLICATION SERIES. 1980. irreg. price varies. University of Missouri - Kansas City, Friends of the Library, Kansas City, MO 64110. TEL 816-235-1531. FAX 816-333-5584.

020 AT ISSN 0313-427X
UNIVERSITY OF NEW SOUTH WALES. LIBRARY. ANNUAL REPORT. 1975. a. free. University of New South Wales, Library, Box 1, Kensington, N.S.W. 2033, Australia. circ. 500.

020 AT
UNIVERSITY OF NEW SOUTH WALES. LIBRARY. STAFF PAPERS. 1966. irreg. University of New South Wales Library, P.O. Box 1, Kensington, N.S.W. 2033, Australia. circ. 100.

020 US
UNIVERSITY OF RHODE ISLAND. LIBRARY. LIBRARY LETTER. 1967. a. free to qualified personnel. University of Rhode Island, Association of Friends of the Library, Kingston, RI 02881. Ed. Kevin Logan. bk.rev./ circ. (controlled)

026 610 US
UNIVERSITY OF ROCHESTER. SCHOOL OF MEDICINE AND DENTISTRY. EDWARD G. MINER LIBRARY. BULLETIN. 1964. m. free. University of Rochester, School of Medicine and Dentistry. Edward G. Miner Library, 601 Elmwood Ave., Rochester, NY 14642. TEL 716-275-3364. FAX 716-275-4799. Ed. Lucretia McClure. circ. 350. (looseleaf format)

027.7 US ISSN 0041-9974
UNIVERSITY OF ROCHESTER LIBRARY BULLETIN. 1945. irreg. (approx. 1-2/yr.). membership. University of Rochester, Rush Rhees Library, Rochester, NY 14627-0055. TEL 716-275-4437. Ed. Margaret Becket. illus.; circ. 1,000. (back issues avail.)
Indexed: Lib.Lit.
Description: Contains articles of literary, bibliographic and historical interest based on the Libraries' own collections and those of other collectors in the area and beyond.

020 IR ISSN 0497-1000
UNIVERSITY OF TEHERAN. CENTRAL LIBRARY. LIBRARY BULLETIN/DANESHGAH-E TEHRAN. KETABKHANE-YE MARKAZI. NASHRIYE-YE KETABKHANEH. (Text in Persian) 1966. irreg. price varies. University of Teheran, Central Library, Enghelabi Ave., Teheran, Iran. Ed. Iraj Afshar. bk.rev.

610 020 IR
UNIVERSITY OF TEHERAN. FACULTY OF MEDICINE. LIBRARY BULLETIN/DANESHGAH-E TEHRAN. DANESHKADE-YE PEZESHKI. NASHRIYE-YE KETABKHANEH. (Text in Persian) 1971. m. University of Teheran, Faculty of Medicine, Enghelab Ave., Teheran, Iran. bk.rev.

020 US ISSN 0277-450X
UNIVERSITY OF TEXAS AT AUSTIN. GENERAL LIBRARIES. LIBRARY BULLETIN. 1972. w. free. University of Texas at Austin, General Libraries, Box P, Austin, TX 78713-7330. TEL 512-495-4350. FAX 512-495-4347. Ed. Carole Cable. circ. 970.
Description: Staff communication newsletter.

020 US ISSN 0362-854X
UNIVERSITY OF TEXAS AT AUSTIN. GENERAL LIBRARIES. NEWSLETTER. 1974. irreg. free. University of Texas at Austin, General Libraries, Austin, TX 78713-7330. TEL 512-495-4350. FAX 512-495-4347. Ed. Carole Cable. bibl.; circ. 3,500.
Description: Focuses on the work programs of the General Libraries of the University.

020 378 US
UNIVERSITY OF TEXAS AT AUSTIN. GRADUATE SCHOOL OF LIBRARY AND INFORMATION SCIENCE. ALUMNI NEWS. 1969. s-a. free. University of Texas at Austin, Graduate School of Library and Information Science, EDB 564, University of Texas at Austin, Austin, TX 78712-1276. TEL 512-471-3821. FAX 512-471-3971. Ed. Mel Boggins. circ. 2,400. (back issues avail.)

020 PH ISSN 0300-3612
UNIVERSITY OF THE PHILIPPINES. INSTITUTE OF LIBRARY SCIENCE. NEWSLETTER. (Text in English) 1965. q. free. University of the Philippines, Institute of Library Science, Diliman, Quezon City 1101, Philippines. TEL 98-24-71-6249. Ed. Rosa M. Vallejo. circ. 900 (controlled).

027.7 SA
UNIVERSITY OF THE WITWATERSRAND, JOHANNESBURG. LIBRARY. AFRICANA SERIES. 1985. irreg. price varies. University of Witwatersrand, Johannesburg, Library, Private Bag XI, Wits 2050, South Africa. TEL 011-716-2330. FAX 011-403-1421. TELEX 4-20765 JUILL. Ed. R. Musiker.
Description: Focuses on the unique Africana collections of the University Library.

027 SA ISSN 0075-3807
UNIVERSITY OF THE WITWATERSRAND, JOHANNESBURG. LIBRARY. ANNUAL REPORT OF THE UNIVERSITY LIBRARIAN. 1932. a. free. University of the Witwatersrand, Johannesburg, Library, Private Bag XI, Wits 2050, South Africa. FAX 339-7559. TELEX 4-20765 JUILL.

027.7 SA
UNIVERSITY OF THE WITWATERSRAND, JOHANNESBURG. LIBRARY. ARCHIVAL SERIES. irreg., no.14, 1987. University of the Witwatersrand, Johannesburg, Library, Private Bag XI, Wits 2050, South Africa. FAX 339-7559. TELEX 4-20765 JUILL.

027.7 SA
UNIVERSITY OF THE WITWATERSRAND, JOHANNESBURG. LIBRARY. OCCASIONAL PUBLICATIONS. 1976. irreg., no.12, 1986. University of the Witwatersrand, Johannesburg, Library, Private Bag XI, Wits 2050, South Africa. FAX 339-7559. TELEX 4-20765 JUILL.

LIBRARY AND INFORMATION SCIENCES

020 900   UK
UNIVERSITY OF WARWICK LIBRARY. OCCASIONAL PUBLICATIONS.. 1971. irreg. price varies. University of Warwick Library, Coventry, Warwickshire, CV4 7AL, England. FAX 0203-524211. TELEX 31406-COVLIB-G. Ed. Dr. J.A. Henshall. circ. controlled. (processed)

020   CN   ISSN 0076-0595
UNIVERSITY OF WESTERN ONTARIO. D.B. WELDON LIBRARY. LIBRARY BULLETIN. 1941. irreg., no.9, 1976. free. University of Western Ontario, D.B. Weldon Library, London, Ont., Canada. TEL 519-885-1211. Ed. Edward Phelps. circ. 500.

020
UNIVERZITA KOMENSKEHO. FILOZOFICKA FAKULTA. ZBORNIK: INFORMATIKA. (Text in Slovak; summaries in English, German and Russian) 1973. irreg. exchange basis. Univerzita Komenskeho, Filozoficka Fakulta, c/o Ustrenda Kniznica Filozofickej Fakulty, Gondova 2, 818 01 Bratislava, Czechoslovakia. Ed. Marta Cabrunova. circ. 600.

020.6   BB
UPDATE (BRIDGETOWN); occasional newsletter of the Library Association of Barbados. 1974. irreg., no.9, 1986. membership. Library Association of Barbados, Box 827E, Bridgetown, Barbados, W.I.
Formerly: Library Association of Barbados. Occasional Newsletter.

UPDATE (WASHINGTON). see *HANDICAPPED — Visually Impaired*

020   US
UPDATE C S L. 1988. bi-m. Connecticut State Library, 231 Capitol Ave., Hartford, CT 06106. TEL 203-566-2441. FAX 203-566-8940. Ed. Mike Beringer. circ. 2,500.

020   US   ISSN 0276-9298
Z668
URBAN ACADEMIC LIBRARIAN. 1972. s-a. $10 to individuals; institutions $12; (foreign $15). Library Association of the City University of New York, Hunter College Library, 695 Park Ave., New York, NY 10021. Ed.Bd. adv.; bk.rev.; bibl.; illus.; circ. 500. **Indexed:** LHTN, Lib.Lit.
Supersedes (after vol.5, no.2): L A C U N Y Journal (ISSN 0094-615X)

020   US
URBAN LIBRARIES EXCHANGE. 1984. m. $25. Urban Libraries Council, 500 E. Marylyn Ave., Ste. D50, State College, PA 19801-6269. TEL 814-237-0194. Ed. Roy H. Millenson. circ. 230. (back issues avail.)
Description: Provides information of interest to large urban public libraries.

UT DE SMIDTE FAN DE FRYSKE AKADEMY. see *PUBLISHING AND BOOK TRADE*

020.6   US
UTAH LIBRARY - NEWS. 1981. bi-m. $8. Utah Library Association, 2150 S. 300 W., Salt Lake City, UT 84115. Ed. Dale Swensen. adv.; bk.rev.; circ. 650.
Formerly (until Jun. 1986): Hatu.

020   RU   ISSN 0042-188X
V MIRE KNIG. 1961. m. 22.20 Rub. (Komitet po Pechati Soveta Ministrov) Izdatel'stvo Kniga, 50, Gorky St., 125047 Moscow, Russia. Ed. P.I. Fedotov. adv.; charts; index, cum.index. (also avail. in microform)

020.6 026   BE   ISSN 0777-6306
V R B - INFORMATIE. (Text in Flemish, French) 1971. q. 250 BEF. Vereniging van Religieus - Wetenschappelijke Bibliothecarissen - Association of Scientific - Religious Librarians, Minderbroedersstraat 5, 3800 Sint-Truiden, Belgium. Ed. K. van de Casteele. bk.rev.; bibl.; circ. 100.

027.4   CN   ISSN 0380-1691
VANCOUVER ISLAND REGIONAL LIBRARY NEWSLETTER. 1960. q. free. Vancouver Island Regional Library, Box 3333, 6250 Hammond Bay Road, Namaimo, B.C. V9R 5N3, Canada. TEL 604-758-4697. FAX 604-758-2482. Ed. Laurene Miller. circ. 389 (controlled). (looseleaf format; back issues avail.)
Description: In-house publication: activities, developments in the Regional Library.

020   HU   ISSN 0133-7351
VAS MEGYEI KONYVTARAK ERTESITOJE. 1971. 3/yr. free. (Vas Megyei Pedagogiai Intezet) Berzsenyi Daniel Megyei Konyvtar, Petofi Sandor u. 43, 9700 Szombathely, Hungary. TEL 94-11-366. FAX 94-12-179. TELEX 37-398. adv.; bk.rev.; bibl.; illus.; stat.; circ. 500.

020.6   AU   ISSN 0042-3793
VEREINIGUNG OESTERREICHISCHER BIBLIOTHEKARE. MITTEILUNGEN. 1948. q. S.410. Vereinigung Oesterreichischer Bibliothekare, Josefsplatz 1, A-1014 Vienna 1, Austria. FAX 0222-53410280. TELEX 112624-OENB-A. Ed. Marianne Jobst-Rieder. adv.; bk.rev.; circ. 1,400.
—BLDSC shelfmark: 5872.850000.

020   US
VERY OCCASIONAL PAPERS. irreg. membership. Louisiana Library Association, Box 3058, Baton Rouge, LA 70821. TEL 504-342-4928. Ed. Charlene Cain. circ. 100.

VETERAN CAR. see *TRANSPORTATION — Automobiles*

020   US
VIBRATIONS. 1968. s-a. free. Indiana University, Alumni Association, Bloomington, IN 47402-4822. TEL 812-855-4822. Ed. Marian Armstrong. illus.; circ. 3,800 (controlled).
Former titles: Indiana University. School of Library and Information Science. Alumni Newsletter; Indiana University. Graduate Library School Alumni Newsletter (ISSN 0019-6827)

020   US   ISSN 0887-6851
Z692.V52
VIDEO LIBRARIAN. 1986. m. (combined Jul.-Aug.). $35 (Canada $40; elsewhere $57). Box 2725, Bremerton, WA 98310-0351. Ed. Randy Pitman. bk.rev.; film rev.; circ. 764. (back issues avail.)
Description: Articles, news, and reviews on the subject of video in public and school libraries.

020 384.554   US   ISSN 1045-3393
Z692.V52
▼**VIDEO RATING GUIDE FOR LIBRARIES.** 1990. q. $89.50. A B C-Clio, 130 Cremona, Box 1911, Santa Barbara, CA 93116-1911. TEL 805-968-1911. FAX 805-685-9685.
Description: Reviews and rates special-interest, informational, and children's video cassettes for all types of libraries.

020   US
VIRGINIA LIBRARIAN. 1953. q. Virginia Library Association, Box 298, Alexandria, VA 22313. TEL 703-370-6020. FAX 703-370-3371. Ed. Jennilou Groutevant. adv.; illus.; circ. 1,500. (also avail. in microform from UMI) **Indexed:** Lib.Lit.
Former titles: Virginia Librarian Newsletter (ISSN 0273-3951); Virginia Librarian.

VISUAL RESOURCES ASSOCIATION BULLETIN. see *ART*

020   GR
VIVLIOGRAPHIKA. 1972. Vivliographike Hetaireia tes Hellados, 3, Vamva St., T. T. 138, Athens, Greece.

020   CI   ISSN 0507-1925
Z671
VJESNIK BIBLIOTEKARA HRVATSKE. (Text in Serbo-Croatian) 1950. q. $30. Hrvatsko Bibliotekarsko Drustvo, Nacionalna i Sveucilisna Biblioteka, Marulicev trg. 21, 41000 Zagreb, Croatia. Ed. Dubravka Kunstek. adv.; bk.rev.; bibl.; circ. 1,000. **Indexed:** Bull.Signal., LISA.

VOICE OF YOUTH ADVOCATES. see *CHILDREN AND YOUTH — About*

027.1   US
THE VOLUNTEER LIBRARIAN. 1975. irreg. Association of Private Libraries, c/o Sophie Mitrisin, 66 Frankfort St., Apt. 2G, New York, NY 10038-1622. adv.; bk.rev.; circ. controlled. (looseleaf format)
Formerly (until Oct. 1989): T L C Gossip (The Library Club).

020   US   ISSN 0043-6518
W L A NEWSLETTER. 1945. bi-m. $20. Wisconsin Library Association, 4785 Hayes Rd., Madison, WI 53704-7364. TEL 608-242-2040. FAX 608-242-2050. Ed. James A. Gollata. circ. 2,000.
Formerly: Wisconsin Library Association. President's Newsletter (ISSN 0032-7778)
Description: Reflects the purposes and responsibilities of the Association and reports the activities and developments of the library profession.

020   US   ISSN 0272-1996
Z682.4.W65
W L W JOURNAL; news, views, reviews for women and libraries. 1975. q. $18 (foreign $22). (Women Library Workers) McFarland and Company, Inc., Box 611, Jefferson, NC 28640. TEL 919-246-4460. Ed. Audrey Eaglen. adv.; bk.rev.; film rev.; index; circ. 500. (back issues avail.) **Indexed:** Chic.Per.Ind., Lib.Lit.
—BLDSC shelfmark: 9341.557000.
Formerly (until vol.5, Jan.-Feb., 1980): Women Library Workers Newsletter.

020   US   ISSN 0278-4858
WASHINGTON STATE LIBRARY NEWS. 1982. 6/yr. Washington State Library, Olympia, WA 98504. TEL 206-753-2114. Ed. Karen Goettling.

WENXIAN/DOCUMENTS. see *BIBLIOGRAPHIES*

020   US   ISSN 0043-3276
Z673
WEST VIRGINIA LIBRARIES. 1947. bi-m. $15. West Virginia Library Association, Box 884, Morgantown, WV 26505. TEL 304-255-0511. FAX 302-722-4245. Ed. Yvonne Farley. adv.; bk.rev.; circ. 1,000. (also avail. in microform from UMI)
—BLDSC shelfmark: 9300.040000.

020   US
WEST VIRGINIA LIBRARY COMMISSION. NEWSLETTER. 1972. irreg., latest 1988. free. West Virginia Library Commission, Cultural Center, Charleston, WV 25305. TEL 304-348-2041. FAX 304-248-2044. Ed. Shirley A. Smith. circ. 1,500.

526.8   US   ISSN 0049-7282
WESTERN ASSOCIATION OF MAP LIBRARIES. INFORMATION BULLETIN. 1969. 3/yr. $25 (Canada $28; elsewhere $30). Western Association of Map Libraries, c/o Richard E. Soares, Bus. Mgr., Box 1667, Provo, UT 84603-1667. TEL 801-378-6179. Ed. Mary Larsgaard. bk.rev.; bibl.; index, cum.index: vols. 1-10; circ. 425. (processed) **Indexed:** Bibl.Cart., Geo.Abstr., Lib.Lit., LISA.
—BLDSC shelfmark: 4485.342000.

020   US
WESTERN ASSOCIATION OF MAP LIBRARIES. OCCASIONAL PAPERS. 1973. irreg., no.12, 1990. price varies. Western Association of Map Libraries, c/o Richard Soares, Bus. Mgr., Box 1667, Provo, UT 84603-1667. TEL 801-378-6179. **Indexed:** Geo.Abstr., GeoRef.

027.7   US   ISSN 0734-4503
WESTERN EUROPEAN SPECIALISTS SECTION NEWSLETTER. q. (Association of College and Research Libraries, Western European Specialists Section) American Library Association, 50 E. Huron St., Chicago, IL 60611-2795. TEL 800-545-2433. FAX 312-440-9374.

020   US   ISSN 0043-4051
WESTERN PLAINS LIBRARY SYSTEM NEWSLETTER. 1966. bi-m. free. Western Plains Library System, Service Center, 605 Avant-Box 1027, Clinton, OK 73601. TEL 405-323-0974. Ed. Dee Ann Ray. bk.rev.; circ. 1,700. (processed)
Formerly: Custer-Washita Newsletter.

027.4   US
WHAT'S LINE. 1979. q. Public Library Service, Division for the Blind & Physically Handicapped, 6030 Monticello Dr., Montgomery, AL 36130. TEL 205-277-7330. circ. 6,500.

LIBRARY AND INFORMATION SCIENCES   2791

027.7 US ISSN 0363-1028
WHISTLE STOP; Harry S. Truman Library Institute newsletter. 1973. q. membership. Harry S. Truman Library Institute for National and International Affairs, Harry S. Truman Library, US Hwy. 24 and Delaware St., Independence, MO 64050.
TEL 816-833-1400. Ed. Benedict K. Zobrist. bibl.; circ. 4,000. (processed)
Formerly: Harry S. Truman Library Institute Research Newsletter (ISSN 0017-7954)

WHO KNOWS ABOUT INDUSTRIES AND MARKETS. see BUSINESS AND ECONOMICS

026 US ISSN 0278-842X
Z673
WHO'S WHO IN SPECIAL LIBRARIES. 1981. a. $35 non-members $50. Special Libraries Association, 1700 Eighteenth St., N.W., Washington, DC 20009. TEL 202-234-4700. Ed. Maria Barry. circ. 13,000.
—BLDSC shelfmark: 9312.546600.
Description: Provides a complete alphabetical listing of members, their addresses and telephone numbers. Includes indexes for Chapter and Divisiion affiliates and a business index.

020 920 UK
▼**WHO'S WHO IN THE U K INFORMATION WORLD.** 1991. a. £57. T F P L Publishing, 22 Peters Lane, London EC1M 6DS, England. TEL 071-251-5522. FAX 071-251-8318.

020 US ISSN 0043-5651
Z1217
WILSON LIBRARY BULLETIN. 1914. m. (Sept.-Jun.). $50 (foreign $56). H.W. Wilson Co., 950 University Ave., Bronx, NY 10452. TEL 800-367-6770. FAX 212-538-2716. TELEX 4990003HWILSON. Ed. Mary Jo Godwin. adv.; bk.rev.; bibl.; illus. (also avail. in microform from UMI) Indexed: Acad.Ind., Access (1980-), Amer.Hist.& Life, Bk.Rev.Ind. (1965-), C.I.J.E., Child.Bk.Rev.Ind. (1965-), Child.Lit.Abstr., CINAHL, Curr.Bk.Rev.Cit., Curr.Cont., Educ.Ind., Gard.Lit. (1992-), Hist.Abstr., Leg.Info.Manage.Ind., LHTN, Lib.Lit., LISA, Mag.Ind., PMR, Pop.Per.Ind., PSI, SSCI, TOM.
—BLDSC shelfmark: 9319.080000.

025.5 US ISSN 0361-2848
L216
WISCONSIN LIBRARY SERVICE RECORD. (Subseries of: Wisconsin. Department of Public Instruction. Bulletin) 1973. a. free. Department of Public Instruction, Division for Library Services, 125 S. Webster St., 3rd Fl., Box 7848, Madison, WI 53707.
TEL 608-266-2205. FAX 608-267-1052. (reprint service avail. from UMI) Indexed: SRI.

027.7 SA
WITS JOURNAL OF LIBRARIANSHIP AND INFORMATION SCIENCE. 1982. a. R.10. University of the Witwatersrand, Johannesburg, Library, Private Bag XI, Wits 2050, South Africa. FAX 339-7559. TELEX 4-20765 JUILL. Ed. Reuben Musiker. Indexed: Ind.S.A.Per., Lib.Lit.

WOLFENBUETTELER BIBLIOTHEKS - INFORMATIONEN. see HISTORY

020 GW ISSN 0300-2012
WOLFENBUETTLER BEITRAEGE. 1972. irreg., vol.8, 1988. price varies. (Herzog-August-Bibliothek, Wolfenbuettel) Vittorio Klostermann, Frauenlobstr. 22, 6000 Frankfurt a.M. 90, Germany.
TEL 069-774011. FAX 069-708038. Ed. Paul Raabe. cum.index. (back issues avail.)

020.6 301.412 US
WOMEN IN LIBRARIES. 1971. 5/yr. $5 to individuals; institutions $8. American Library Association, Social Responsibilities Round Table, Feminist Task Force, 50 E. Huron St., Chicago, IL 60611.
TEL 312-944-6780. FAX 312-440-9374. Ed. Madeleine Tainton. bk.rev.; cum.index; circ. 400. (processed; back issues avail.)

WOMEN'S INFORMATION UPDATES. see WOMEN'S INTERESTS

025 US
WORCESTER PUBLIC LIBRARY STAFF NEWSLETTER. 1941. m. Worcester Public Library, Salem Sq., Worcester, MA 01608. TEL 508-799-1655. Ed. E. Glenn Musser, Jr. circ. 230. (looseleaf format)
Description: For the staff of the Worcester Public Library.

029 US
WORLD GUIDE TO ABBREVIATIONS OF ORGANIZATIONS. 5th ed., 1974. irreg., 9th ed., 1991. $140. Gale Research Inc., 835 Penobscot Bldg., Detroit, MI 48226. TEL 313-961-2242. FAX 313-961-6083. TELEX 810-221-7086. Ed. F.A. Buttress.
Description: Guide to organizational title abbreviations.

020 PL
WYZSZA SZKOLA PEDAGOGICZNA IM. KOMISJI EDUKACJI NARODOWEJ W KRAKOWIE. ROCZNIK NAUKOWO-DYDAKTYCZNY. PRACE BIBLIOTEKOZNAWCZE. 1982. irreg., no.6, 1991. price varies. Wydawnictwo Naukowe W S P, Ul. Karmelicka 41, 31-128 Krakow, Poland.
TEL 33-78-20. (Co-sponsor: Ministerstwo Edukacji Narodowej)

020 CC ISSN 1001-0297
XINXI SHIJIE/INFORMATION WORLD. (Text in Chinese) m. Zhongguo Xinjishu Chuangye Gongsi - China New Technology Pioneering Enterprise, Building No.6, State Science Commission - Guojia Kexue Weiyuanhui, Weigongcun, Beijing 100081, People's Republic of China. TEL 891537.

020 IS ISSN 0334-200X
YAD LAKORE/READER'S AID; Israel journal for libraries and archives. (Text in Hebrew; summaries in English) 1946. q. $30. Center for Public Libraries, P.O. Box 242, Jerusalem 91002, Israel.
TEL 02-247392. FAX 02-250620. Ed. Carole Pfeffer. bk.rev.; circ. 1,500. (back issues avail.)
Indexed: Ind.Heb.Per., LISA.
Description: Covers all aspects of library, archive and information studies throughout the world, with emphasis on Israel and Judaica.

027.7 US ISSN 0044-0175
Z733
YALE UNIVERSITY LIBRARY GAZETTE. 1926. s-a. $20. Yale University Library, New Haven, CT 06520. TEL 203-432-2967. FAX 203-432-4047. Ed. Stephen Parks. bibl.; index, cum.index: vols.1-45; circ. 1,500. **Indexed:** Curr.Cont., Hist.Abstr., Lib.Lit., M.L.A., Mid.East: Abstr.& Ind.
—BLDSC shelfmark: 9370.930000.

020 UK ISSN 0307-2509
YORKSHIRE LIBRARY NEWS. 1974. 4/yr. free to members. Library Association, Yorkshire and Humberside Branch, c/o Ray Prytherch, Lomond, Scotland Ln., Horsforth, Leeds LS18 5SE, England. TEL 0532-580681. circ. 1,500.
—BLDSC shelfmark: 9421.235300.
Formerly: Yorkshire Librarian.

021.7 US
YOUR LIBRARY. 1981. m. $5. Worcester Public Library, Salem Sq., Worcester, MA 01608.
TEL 508-799-1655. Ed. Christine C. Kardokas. circ. 2,300.
Description: Published for the use of library patrons and Friends of the Worcester Public Library.

027.7 JA
YUIN. (Text in Japanese) 1967. q. free. Hokkaido University Library - Hokkaido Daigaku Toshokan, Kita-8, Nishi-5, Kita-ku, Sapporo-shi, Hokkaido 060, Japan. FAX 011-747-2855. Ed. Hirozumi Uno. bk.rev.; circ. 2,000.

026 PL ISSN 0137-5172
Z817.A1
Z BADAN NAD POLSKIMI KSIEGOZBIORAMI HISTORYCZNYMI. 1975. irreg., vol.13, 1992. 15000 Zl. per no. Uniwersytet Warszawski, Instytut Bibliotekoznawstwa i Informacji Naukowej, Krakowskie Przedmiescie 26-28, 00-325 Warsaw, Poland. FAX 267520. TELEX 815439 UWPL. Ed. Barbara Bienkowska. index; circ. 350.
Description: Devoted to the history and research of rare book collections.

029.7 PL ISSN 0324-8194
ZAGADNIENIA INFORMACJI NAUKOWEJ. (Text in Polish; summaries in English and Russian) 1962. s-a. free. (Polska Akademia Nauk, Osrodek Informacji Naukowej - Polish Academy of Sciences, Center of Scientific Information) Ossolineum, Publishing House of the Polish Academy of Sciences, Rynek 9, 50-106 Wroclaw, Poland. (Dist. by: Ars Polona, Krakowskie Przedmiescie 7, 00-068 Warsaw, Poland) Ed. Bronislaw Lugowski. bk.rev.; bibl.; charts; circ. 700. (also avail. in microform)
—BLDSC shelfmark: 9425.504000.
Formerly: Polska Akademia Nauk. Osrodek Dokumentacji i Informacji Naukowej. Biuletyn (ISSN 0030-6282)
Description: Papers on various practical aspects and theories of the development of modern sciences.

ZAMBIA. MINISTRY OF LEGAL AFFAIRS. ANNUAL REPORT. see BUSINESS AND ECONOMICS

020 ZA ISSN 0049-853X
Z857.Z3
ZAMBIA LIBRARY ASSOCIATION. JOURNAL. 1969. q. K.10 to institutions. Zambia Library Association, P.O. Box 2839, Lusaka, Zambia. Ed. W.D. Sweeney. adv.; bk.rev.; bibl.; index, cum.index: vols.1-4; circ. 200. (also avail. in microfilm)

020.6 ZA
ZAMBIA LIBRARY ASSOCIATION. NEWSLETTER. (Text in English) 1979. bi-m. Zambia Library Association, P.O. Box 32839, Lusaka, Zambia.

020 GW ISSN 0044-2380
Z671
ZEITSCHRIFT FUER BIBLIOTHEKSWESEN UND BIBLIOGRAPHIE. 1953. bi-m. DM.94. (Verein Deutscher Bibliothekare) Vittorio Klostermann, Frauenlobstr. 22, 6000 Frankfurt a.M. 90, Germany. TEL 069-774011. FAX 069-708038. Ed. Klaus-Dieter Lehmann. adv.; bk.rev.; bibl.; charts; stat.; in; circ. 2,200. (reprint service avail. from KTO) **Indexed:** Curr.Cont., Lib.Lit., LISA, P.A.I.S.For.Lang.Ind., SSCI.
—BLDSC shelfmark: 9454.000000.
Incorporates (in 1991): Zentralblatt fuer Bibliothekswesen (ISSN 0044-4081)

020 GW ISSN 0514-6364
ZEITSCHRIFT FUER BIBLIOTHEKSWESEN UND BIBLIOGRAPHIE. SONDERHEFTE. 1963. irreg., vol.54, 1991. price varies. Vittorio Klostermann, Frauenlobstr. 22, Postfach 900601, 6000 Frankfurt a.M. 90, Germany. TEL 069-774011. FAX 069-708038.

020 GW ISSN 0171-8932
ZEITSCHRIFTEN - DATENBANK (Z D B). 1973. s-a. DM.340. Deutsches Bibliotheksinstitut, Bundesallee 184-5, 1000 Berlin 31, Germany.
TEL 030-8505130. Eds. G. Franzmeier, P. Gruber. circ. 400. (microfiche)
●Also available online.
Supersedes (in 1979): Gesamtverzeichnis der Zeitschriften und Serien in Bibliotheken der Bundesrepublik Deutschland Einschliesslich Berlin (West) (ISSN 0302-0657)

029.7 630 CS ISSN 0862-2086
ZEMEDELSKA INFORMATIKA/INFORMATION SCIENCES FOR AGRICULTURE; metodicky zpravodaj. (Text in Czech or Slovak; table of contents in English, Russian) 1961. bi-m. $16. Ustav Vedeckotechnickych Informaci pro Zemedelstvi, Slezska 7, 120 56 Prague 2, Czechoslovakia.
TEL 257541. Ed. D. Lenzova. bk.rev.; abstr.; bibl.; charts; illus.; mkt.; index; circ. 500.

020 CC ISSN 1003-9082
ZHONGWEN XINXI/CHINESE INFORMATION PROCESSING. (Text in Chinese) q. Y18. Zhongguo Zhongwen Xinxi Xuehui - Chinese Society for Chinese Language Information, Chengdu Keji Daxue - Chengdu University of Science and Technology, Chengdu, Sichuan 610065, People's Republic of China. TEL 581554-473.

020 RH
ZIMBABWE LIBRARIAN. 1969. s-a. Z.$15($20) Zimbabwe Library Association, P.O. Box 3133, Harare, Zimbabwe. Ed. E.R.T. Chiware. adv.; bk.rev.; index; circ. 420. **Indexed:** Ind.S.A.Per., Lib.Sci.Abstr., LISA.
Former titles: Rhodesian Librarian (ISSN 0035-4848); Rhodesia and Nyasaland Library Association. Newsletter.

L

LIBRARY AND INFORMATION SCIENCES — Abstracting, Bibliographies, Statistics

011 RM ISSN 1220-3092
A B S I - ABSTRACTE IN BIBLIOLOGIE SI STIINTA INFORMARII. 1960. m. 756 lei (effective 1992). Biblioteca Nationala a Romaniei, Str. Ion Ghica 4, 79708 Bucharest, Rumania. abstr.; index; circ. 1,000.
Formerly: Buletin de Informare in Bibliologie (ISSN 0007-3784)

020 029.7 AT ISSN 0810-9265
A L I S A. (Australian Library and Information Science Abstracts) 1982. a. Aus.$45. Australian Clearing House for Library & Information Science, Library, S.A.C.A.E., Lorne Ave., Magill, S. Aust. 5072, Australia. TEL 08 3339457. FAX 61-8-3326122. (Co-sponsor: South Australian College of Advanced Education Library) Ed. B. Blacoe. circ. 150. (back issues avail.)
●Also available online. Vendor(s): AUSINET.
Also available on CD-ROM.

027 US ISSN 0147-2135
Z675.U5
A R L STATISTICS. 1964. a. $60. Association of Research Libraries, 1527 New Hampshire Ave., N.W., Washington, DC 20036. TEL 202-232-2466. Ed. Sarah Pritchard. circ. 1,400. (back issues avail.)
Indexed: SRI.
—BLDSC shelfmark: 1682.110000.
Formerly: Academic Library Statistics (ISSN 0571-6519)

020 AT ISSN 0725-0037
Z870.A1
ACQUISITION, BIBLIOGRAPHY, CATALOGUING NEWS. 1981. q. Aus.$25. National Library of Australia, Publications Section, Public Programs, Parkes Place, Canberra, A.C.T. 2600, Australia. FAX 062-571703. Ed.Bd. circ. 865. (back issues avail.)
Formerly: R O D News.

020 CN ISSN 0080-1569
ALBERTA RESEARCH COUNCIL. LIST OF PUBLICATIONS. 1968. a. free. Alberta Research Council, Publications Dept., P.O. Box 8330, Sta. F, Edmonton, Alta. T6H 5X2, Canada. TEL 403-450-5390. FAX 403-461-2651. TELEX 037-2147.
Description: Bibliography of reports by the Alberta Research Council.

020 US ISSN 0733-3048
CODEN: NEAIEV
AMERICAN SOCIETY OF INDEXERS. NEWSLETTER. 1970. 6/yr. $30 to non-members. American Society of Indexers, Inc., Box 386, Port Aransas, TX 78373. TEL 805-434-2330. Ed. Anne Leach. cum.index: 1970-1983; circ. 900. (back issues avail.)

973 015 US ISSN 0003-6625
APPALACHIAN OUTLOOK; new sources of regional information. (Supplement to: Appalachian Bibliography) 1964. 3/yr. $6 to individuals; institutions $10 (effective 1992). West Virginia University Library, Main Office, Box 6069, Morgantown, WV 26506-6069.
TEL 304-293-3640. Ed. Jo Baily Brown. circ. 130. (processed)

ARCHITECTURAL PERIODICALS INDEX. see ARCHITECTURE — Abstracting, Bibliographies, Statistics

011 020 070.5 AT ISSN 0314-3767
AUSTRALIAN SOCIETY OF INDEXERS NEWSLETTER. 1977. 11/yr. (except Jan.). Aus.$25 (Metropolitan Aus.$30; foreign Aus.$35). Australian Society of Indexers, G.P.O. Box 1251L, Melbourne, Vic. 3001, Australia. TEL 61-03-418-7320.
FAX 61-03-329-6185. Ed. Helen Kinniburgh. adv.; bk.rev.; circ. 270. (back issues avail.)

BECTIS BULLETIN. see LIBRARY AND INFORMATION SCIENCES

020 011 JA ISSN 0006-0860
BIBLIA. (Text in Japanese) 1949. 2/yr.
3500 Yen($25) per no. Tenri University Press, Tenri Central Library, Tenri-shi, Nara 632, Japan. TEL 07436-3-1515. FAX 07436-2-1965. Ed. Rev. Hidetsugu Ueda. bk.rev.; bibl.; circ. 1,000. (also avail. in microform; back issues avail.)

020 011 PL ISSN 0033-233X
BIBLIOGRAFIA ANALITYCZNA BIBLIOTEKOZNAWSTWA I INFORMACJI NAUKOWEJ. (Supplement to: Przeglad Biblioteczny) 1951. q. 20000 Zl. (price changes every quarter). Biblioteka Narodowa, Al. Niepodleglosci 213, 00-973 Warsaw, Poland.
TEL 48-22-259271. FAX 48-22-255251. (Dist. by: Ars Polona Centrala Handlu Zagranicznego, Krakowskie Przedmiescie 7, 00-068 Warsaw, Poland) Ed. Barbara Eychler. bk.rev.; abstr.; index; circ. 2,300.
Formerly: Przeglad Pismiennictwa o Ksiazce.

020 016 AG ISSN 0067-656X
BIBLIOGRAFIA BIBLIOTECOLOGICA ARGENTINA. 1963. irreg. price varies. (Universidad Nacional del Sur) Centro de Documentacion e Informacion Educativa, Paraguay 1657-ler. piso, 1062-Capital Federal, Argentina. bk.rev.; index; circ. 300.
Description: Argentine bibliography on library science.

015 BL
BIBLIOGRAFIA BRASILEIRA. 1918. q. Biblioteca Nacional de Brasil, Av. Rio Branco, 219, 20042 Rio de Janeiro, Brazil. TEL 021-240-8429.
FAX 021-220-4173. TELEX 21-22941. circ. 2,000.
●Also available online.
Formerly: Biblioteca Nacional de Brasil. Boletim Bibliografico (ISSN 0100-1876)

029.7 010 AT ISSN 0084-7852
BIBLIOGRAPHICAL SOCIETY OF AUSTRALIA AND NEW ZEALAND. BULLETIN. 1970. q. Aus.$30 to individuals (foreign Aus.$32); institutions Aus.$40 (foreign Aus.$48). Bibliographical Society of Australia & New Zealand, c/o Graduate Dept. of Librarianship, Archives and Records, Monash University, Clayton, Vic. 3168, Australia.
FAX 61-3-565-2952. Ed. Ross Harvey. adv.; bk.rev.; circ. 300. Indexed: Aus.P.A.I.S.
—BLDSC shelfmark: 2411.370000.

BIBLIOGRAPHIE DER ANTIQUARIATS-, AUKTIONS- UND KUNSTKATALOGE. see ART — Abstracting, Bibliographies, Statistics

020 GW ISSN 0723-3590
BIBLIOGRAPHIE DER BUCH- UND BIBLIOTHEKSGESCHICHTE. 1982. a. DM.110. Bibliographischer Verlag Dr. Horst Meyer, Muehlenstr. 47, 4505 Bad Iburg, Germany.
TEL 05403-2527. circ. 800. (back issues avail.)

020 US ISSN 0742-6879
BIBLIOGRAPHIES AND INDEXES IN LIBRARY AND INFORMATION SCIENCE. 1987. irreg. price varies. Greenwood Press, Inc. (Subsidiary of: Greenwood Publishing Group Inc.), 88 Post Rd. W., Box 5007, Westport, CT 06881-5007. TEL 203-226-3571. FAX 203-222-1502.
—BLDSC shelfmark: 1993.097420.

BIBLIOGRAPHY OF EDUCATION THESES IN AUSTRALIA. see EDUCATION — Abstracting, Bibliographies, Statistics

BIBLIOTECA DO SEJUR. BOLETIM. see LAW — Abstracting, Bibliographies, Statistics

020 011 RM ISSN 1220-3076
BIBLIOTECONOMIE. CULEGERE DE TRADUCERI PRELUCRATE. 1965. q. 120 lei. Biblioteca Nationala a Romaniei, Str. Ion Ghica 4, 79708 Bucharest, Rumania. abstr.; bibl.; circ. 620.
Formerly: Revista de Referate in Bibliologie (ISSN 0034-8783)

BIBLOS; oesterreichische Zeitschrift fuer Buch- und Bibliothekswesen, Dokumentation, Bibliographie und Bibliophilie. see PUBLISHING AND BOOK TRADE — Abstracting, Bibliographies, Statistics

020 PO ISSN 0253-343X
BOLETIM DE BIBLIOGRAFIA PORTUGUESA. DOCUMENTOS NAO TEXTUAIS. 1981. a. Biblioteca Nacional de Portugal, Campo Grande 83, 1751 Lisbon Codex, Portugal. index; circ. 750.
Supersedes in part (1935-1980): Boletim de Bibliografia Portuguesa (ISSN 0006-5897)

015 PO ISSN 0253-3413
Z2715
BOLETIM DE BIBLIOGRAFIA PORTUGUESA. MONOGRAFIAS. 1981. q. Biblioteca Nacional de Portugal, Campo Grande 83, 1751 Lisbon Codex, Portugal. index; circ. 750.
Supersedes in part (1935-1980): Boletim de Bibliografia Portuguesa (ISSN 0006-5897)

020 PO ISSN 0253-3421
Z6956.P8
BOLETIM DE BIBLIOGRAFIA PORTUGUESA. PUBLICACOES EM SERIE. 1981. a. Biblioteca Nacional de Portugal, Campo grande 83, 1751 Lisbon Codex, Portugal. index; circ. 750.
Supersedes in part (1935-1980): Boletim de Bibliografia Portuguesa (ISSN 0006-5897)

028.5 US ISSN 0068-0192
Z1037
BOOKS FOR THE TEEN AGE. 1929. a. $7. New York Public Library, Office of Young Adult Services, 455 Fifth Ave., New York, NY 10016.
TEL 212-340-0907. Ed. Marilee Foglesong. index; circ. 10,000.
Description: Lists approximately 1,250 titles on subjects of special interest and appeal to adolescents.

020 US
BOOKS IN LIBRARY AND INFORMATION SCIENCE SERIES. 1973. irreg., vol.54, 1991. price varies. Marcel Dekker, Inc., 270 Madison Ave., New York, NY 10016. TEL 212-696-9000. FAX 212-685-4540. TELEX 421419. Ed. A. Kent.
Refereed Serial

027 CN
BRITISH COLUMBIA PUBLIC LIBRARIES, STATISTICS. 1965. a. free. Ministry of Municipal Affairs, Recreation and Culture, Library Services Branch, Parliament Bldgs., Victoria, B.C. V8V 1X4, Canada. FAX 604-387-4048. stat.; circ. 750.
Formerly: British Columbia. Library Development Commission. Public Libraries, Statistics (ISSN 0084-8034)

020 UK
BRITISH LIBRARY. NAME AUTHORITY LIST. 1981. m. £170 (foreign £205). British Library, Bibliographic Services, 2 Sheraton St., London W1V 4BH, England. TEL 01-323 7077. (microfiche)

C P L BIBLIOGRAPHIES. (Council of Planning Librarians) see HOUSING AND URBAN PLANNING — Abstracting, Bibliographies, Statistics

016.051 020 CN ISSN 0000-0345
Z6954.C2
CANADIAN SERIALS DIRECTORY/REPERTOIRE DES PUBLICATIONS SERIEES CANADIENNES. (Text in English and French) 1976. biennial. $45. Reference Press, P.O. Box 70, Teeswater, Ont. N0G 2S0, Canada. TEL 519-392-6634. Ed. Gordon Ripley. bibl.; circ. 1,000.

026 340 US ISSN 1049-796X
KF4
CATALOG OF CURRENT LAW TITLES; recent acquisitions of major legal libraries. 1984. a. $275. William S. Hein & Co., Inc., 1285 Main St., Buffalo, NY 14209. TEL 800-828-7571. FAX 716-883-8100. TELEX 91-209 WU 7 HEIN BUF. Eds. Margaret A. Goldblatt, Peter D. Ward. circ. 250.
Formerly: National Legal Bibliography (ISSN 0739-1951)

020 UK ISSN 0008-7629
Z695
CATALOGUE & INDEX. 1966. q. £10($12) to non-members. Library Association, Cataloguing and Indexing Group, c/o C.J. Koster, 18 Apple Grove, Enfield, Middx. EN1 3DD, England. Ed. R. Brunt. bk.rev.; cum.index: 1966-67, 1968-69; circ. 3,500. (also avail. in microfilm) Indexed: Lib.Lit., Lib.Sci.Abstr., LISA.
—BLDSC shelfmark: 3086.028000.

020 US ISSN 0084-6902
CENTER FOR CHINESE RESEARCH MATERIALS. BIBLIOGRAPHICAL SERIES. 1968. irreg. price varies. Center for Chinese Research Materials, Box 3090, Oakton, VA 22124. TEL 703-281-7731. Ed. Pingfeng Chi.

LIBRARY AND INFORMATION SCIENCES — ABSTRACTING, BIBLIOGRAPHIES, STATISTICS

310   UK   ISSN 0309-6629
Z791.A1
CHARTERED INSTITUTE OF PUBLIC FINANCE AND ACCOUNTANCY. PUBLIC LIBRARY STATISTICS. ACTUALS. 1957. a. £55. Chartered Institute of Public Finance and Accountancy, 3 Robert St., London WC2N 6BH, England. stat. (back issues avail.)

310   UK   ISSN 0307-0522
Z791.A1
CHARTERED INSTITUTE OF PUBLIC FINANCE AND ACCOUNTANCY. PUBLIC LIBRARY STATISTICS. ESTIMATES. 1974. a. £35. Chartered Institute of Public Finance and Accountancy, 3 Robert St., London WC2N 6BH, England. TEL 071-895-8823. FAX 071-895-8825. (back issues avail.)

015   UK   ISSN 0084-8085
Z2009
CHECKLIST OF BRITISH OFFICIAL SERIAL PUBLICATIONS. 1967. irreg. (approx. biennial). £10($15) British Library, Humanities and Social Sciences, Great Russell St., London WC1B 3DG, England. TEL 071-323-7704. FAX 071-323-7736. TELEX 21462. Ed. Hazel Finnie.

020 016   CH   ISSN 0301-5165
Z3111
CHINESE NATIONAL BIBLIOGRAPHY. (Text mainly in Chinese; occasionally in English) 1960. m. $53. National Central Library, Bureau of International Exchange of Publications, 20 Chung Shan S. Rd., Taipei, Taiwan 10040, Republic of China. FAX 02-311-0155. bibl. Key Title: Zhonghua Minguo Chuban Tushumulu.
    Formerly (until 1970): Hsin Shu Chien Pao.

011 020   US
COLLEGE READING ASSOCIATION. MONOGRAPHS. irreg. College Reading Association, c/o Dr. E. Sutton Flynt, Dept. Curriculum and Instruction, Pittsburg State University, Pittsburg, KS 66762. TEL 316-235-4494. (reprint service avail. from UMI)

025 011   US
COMPUTER LIBRARY'S COMPUTER PERIODICALS DATABASE. 1988. m. $765. Ziff Communications, One Park Ave., New York, NY 10016. TEL 212-503-4400. FAX 212-503-4414. bk.rev.
● Also available online.
Also available on CD-ROM.
    Formerly: Computer Library.
    Description: For information center managers, PC coordinators, MIS directors, product planners, developers and marketers, purchasing agents, systems integrators, journalists and industry analysts. Serves as a comprehensive desktop reference for anyone needing to access and manage large amounts of timely information about the computer industry.

020   UK
COUNCIL OF POLYTECHNIC LIBRARIANS. ANNUAL STATISTICS. a. £8.50. Council of Polytechnic Librarians, c/o Christine Moon, Brighton Polytechnic, Watts Building, Moulsecoomb, Brighton BN2 4GJ, England.

CURRENT RESEARCH IN BRITAIN. BIOLOGICAL SCIENCES. see *BIOLOGY — Abstracting, Bibliographies, Statistics*

CURRENT RESEARCH IN BRITAIN. PHYSICAL SCIENCES. see *SCIENCES: COMPREHENSIVE WORKS — Abstracting, Bibliographies, Statistics*

CURRENT RESEARCH IN BRITAIN. SOCIAL SCIENCES. see *SOCIAL SCIENCES: COMPREHENSIVE WORKS — Abstracting, Bibliographies, Statistics*

310   GW
DEUTSCHE BIBLIOTHEKSSTATISTIK TEIL A: OEFFENTLICHE BIBLIOTHEKEN. 1979. a. DM.36. Deutsches Bibliotheksinstitut, Abt. 1-Publikationen, Bundesallee 184-185, 1000 Berlin 31, Germany. TEL 030-8505-0. FAX 030-8505-100. circ. 630.

310   GW   ISSN 0720-969X
DEUTSCHE BIBLIOTHEKSSTATISTIK TEIL B: WISSENSCHAFTLICHE BIBLIOTHEKEN. 1979. a. DM.36. Deutsches Bibliotheksinstitut, Abt. 1-Publikationen, Bundesallee 184-185, 1000 Berlin 31, Germany. TEL 030-8505-0. circ. 450.

020   US   ISSN 0162-0290
Z732.08
DIRECTORY AND STATISTICS OF OREGON LIBRARIES. 1913. a. $10. Oregon State Library, Salem, OR 97310-0640. TEL 503-378-2112. FAX 503-588-7119. circ. 650.
    Formerly: Directory of Oregon Libraries.
    Description: Provides directory and statistical information for public, academic and special libraries in Oregon.

010 020   UN
DOCUMENTATION, LIBRARIES AND ARCHIVES: BIBLIOGRAPHIES AND REFERENCE WORKS. 1972. irreg. price varies. Unesco, 7-9 Place de Fontenoy, F-75700 Paris, France.
    Formerly: Unesco Bibliographical Handbooks (ISSN 0082-7460)

550 910   US   ISSN 0743-7250
GOLDTHWAIT POLAR LIBRARY ACCESSIONS LIST. irreg. free. Ohio State University, Byrd Polar Research Center, Goldthwait Polar Library, 125 S. Oval Mall, Columbus, OH 43210-1308. TEL 614-292-6715. FAX 614-292-4697. TELEX 4945696 OSUPOLAR. (looseleaf format; back issues avail.)
    Formerly (until 1977): I P S Accessions List.
    Description: Listings of new acquisitions in the Goldthwait Polar Library.

029 011   SA
GREY BIBLIOGRAPHIES. 1946. irreg., no.17, 1989. price varies. South African Library, P.O. Box 496, Cape Town 8000, South Africa. TEL 021-246320. FAX 021-244848. TELEX 5-22604 SA.
    Description: Bibliographies of subjects of South African interest.

028.1 011   US   ISSN 0017-5269
Z881.C57
GUIDE POST. 1926. 10/yr. free to qualified personnel. Public Library of Cincinnati and Hamilton County, 800 Vine St., Cincinnati, OH 45202. TEL 513-369-6960. Ed. Anne B. Keller. bk.rev.; circ. 3,000.
    Description: Notes and comments about new materials in the collections of the Public Library at Cincinnati and Hamilton County.

027.8   US
GUIDE TO REFERENCE BOOKS FOR SCHOOL MEDIA CENTERS. irreg. $36. Libraries Unlimited, Inc., Box 3988, Englewood, CO 80155-3988. TEL 800-237-6124. FAX 303-220-8843. Ed. Christine Genrt Wynar.
    Description: Comprehensive guide to current reference materials for school media centers; covers a wide range of subjects, of age and reading levels, depths of information and prices.

011   AT   ISSN 0156-6717
GUIDELINES; a subject guide for Australian libraries. (Also avail. on floppy disk.) 1969. 9/yr. (plus a cumulation). Aus.$76. Bibliographic Services, P.O. Box 2, Mount Waverley, Vic. 3149, Australia. Ed. Keith S. Darling. adv.; circ. 1,800. (also avail. in microfiche)
    Description: Subject index to Australian and selected overseas periodicals chosen for secondary schools.

020   AT
HOW AND WHERE DIRECTORY; an index to sources of information. irreg. Aus.$10. School Library Association of New South Wales, P.O. Box 187, Rozelle, N.S.W. 2039, Australia. circ. 1,000.
    Description: Lists sources of school library materials.

020 016   HU   ISSN 0046-8304
Z671
HUNGARIAN LIBRARY AND INFORMATION SCIENCE ABSTRACTS. (Text in English) 1971. s-a. exchange basis. Orszagos Szechenyi Konyvtar, Konyvtartudomanyi es Modszertani Kozpont - Centre for Library Science and Methodology at the National Szechenyi Library, Budavari Palota F epulet, 1827 Budapest, Hungary. TEL 1750-686. TELEX 224226 BIBLN H. Ed. Agnes Feimer. index; circ. 420. (back issues avail.)
    —BLDSC shelfmark: 4337.032300.
    Description: Lists books and periodical articles in the field that may be of interest to foreign colleagues.

020.6   NE   ISSN 0109-5366
Z666
I F L A COMMUNICATIONS; bibliography of IFLA conference papers. 1984. a. fl.22. International Federation of Library Associations and Institutions, Bibliotheek Centraal - Federation Internationale des Associations de Bibliothecaires et des Bibliotheques, P.O.B. 95312, 2509 CH The Hague, Netherlands. TEL 070-140884. FAX 070-834827. TELEX 34402 KB NL. Ed. Mona Madsen. circ. 100.

600 016   US   ISSN 0019-0136
I N F O. 1965. bi-m. free. Tulsa City-County Library System, Business and Technology Dept., 400 Civic Center, Tulsa, OK 74103. TEL 918-596-7988. FAX 918-596-7895. Ed. Karen S. Curtis. adv.; bk.rev.; bibl.; circ. 1,400 (controlled). (processed)
    Description: Informs the community about government documents, on-line data bases, books, plus programs and services available at the library.

015   BL   ISSN 0019-0276
I P A S E BIBLIOTECA INFORMA.* 1965. q. free. Instituto de Previdencia e Assistencia dos Servidores do Estado, Divisao de Relacoes Publicas, Biblioteca, Rua Pedro Lessa 36, 13 Andar, Rio de Janeiro, G B, Brazil. circ. 400 (controlled). (microform)

020   UK
INDEX LIBRARY. 1888. irreg. £15 to individuals; institutions £25. British Record Society, Stone Barn Farm, Sutherland Rd., Longsdon, Stoke-On-Trent ST9 9QD, England. TEL 0538-385024. (also avail. in microfiche; reprint service avail. from KTO)
    Description: Indexes to testamentary material.

020   UN   ISSN 0073-6074
Z6514.T7
INDEX TRANSLATIONUM. (Text in English and French) 1950. a. $80. Unesco, 7-9 Place de Fontenoy, 75700 Paris, France. TEL 577-16-10. (Dist. in U.S. by: Unipub, 4611-F Assembly Dr., Lanham, MD 20706-4391) (reprint service avail. from KTO)

020   II
INDIAN LIBRARY AND INFORMATION SCIENCE INDEXES SERIES. irreg. Gina House Publishers, 71 Sector 27-A, Chandigarh 160019, India.

020 016   II   ISSN 0019-5790
INDIAN LIBRARY SCIENCE ABSTRACTS. (Text in English) 1967. a. Rs.100($20) Indian Association of Special Libraries and Information Centres, P-291 C.I.T. Scheme No. 6M, Kankurgachi, Calcutta 700 054, India. TEL 34-9651. Ed.Bd.
    —BLDSC shelfmark: 4422.270000.

INDICE ESPANOL DE CIENCIAS SOCIALES. SERIES D: SCIENCE AND SCIENTIFIC INFORMATION. see *SCIENCES: COMPREHENSIVE WORKS — Abstracting, Bibliographies, Statistics*

020   US   ISSN 0360-0971
Z699.A1   CODEN: INRBDY
INFORMATION REPORTS AND BIBLIOGRAPHIES. 1972. 6/yr. $95 (foreign $125). Science Associates International, Inc., 465 West End Ave., New York, NY 10024. TEL 212-873-0656. FAX 212-873-5587. Ed. Ivan Lyons. (reprint service avail. from UMI)
    Indexed: LHTN, Lib.Lit.
    Formerly: Information-Part 2-Reports - Bibliographies (ISSN 0046-9378)

029.7 651.8 016   US   ISSN 0020-0239
Z699.A1
INFORMATION SCIENCE ABSTRACTS. 1965. m. $485 (foreign $565). (American Society for Information Science) I F I - Plenum (Subsidiary of: Plenum Publishing Corp.), 233 Spring St., New York, NY 10013. TEL 212-620-8000. FAX 212-463-0742. TELEX 23-421139. (Co-sponsors: Special Libraries Association; American Chemical Society, Division of Chemical Information; American Society of Indexers; Medical Library Association; Association of Library and Information Science Education) Eds. Harry Allcock, Anne Meagher. adv.; bk.rev.; index. (also avail. in microfilm from JSC; back issues avail.)
● Also available online. Vendor(s): DIALOG (File no.202).
    —BLDSC shelfmark: 4494.230000.
    Formerly: Documentation Abstracts.

LIBRARY AND INFORMATION SCIENCES — ABSTRACTING, BIBLIOGRAPHIES, STATISTICS

020   SI   ISSN 0217-0914
INSTITUTE OF SOUTHEAST ASIAN STUDIES. LIBRARY BULLETIN. (Text in English) 1971. irreg., no.18, 1989. price varies. Institute of Southeast Asian Studies, Heng Mui Keng Terrace, Pasir Panjang, Singapore 0511, Singapore. TEL 7780955. FAX 7781735. TELEX RS 37068 ISEAS.
—BLDSC shelfmark: 5191.620000.
    Description: Bibliographies on Southeast Asia.

INTERNATIONAL ASSOCIATION OF AGRICULTURAL INFORMATION SPECIALISTS. QUARTERLY BULLETIN. see *AGRICULTURE — Abstracting, Bibliographies, Statistics*

020   US
TR835
INTERNATIONAL IMAGING SOURCE BOOK. 1972. biennial. $97.50. Microfilm Publishing, Inc., Box 950, Larchmont, NY 10538-0950. TEL 914-834-3044. FAX 914-834-3993. Ed. Mitchell M. Badler. adv.; bk.rev.; illus.; stat.; circ. 3,500.
    Former titles: International Micrographics Source Book (ISSN 0272-0310) & International Microfilm Source Book (ISSN 0362-4498); Microfilm Source Book (ISSN 0090-2861)

020 016   IT   ISSN 0075-0026
INVENTARI DEI MANOSCRITTI DELLE BIBLIOTECHE D'ITALIA. 1890. irreg., vol.106, 1990. price varies. Casa Editrice Leo S. Olschki, Casella Postale 66, 50100 Florence, Italy. TEL 055-6530684. FAX 055-6530214. Eds. A. Sorbelli, L. Ferrari. cum.index; circ. 1,000.

020 011   IC   ISSN 0254-1378
Z2590.A3
ISLENSK BOKASKRA/ICELANDIC NATIONAL BIBLIOGRAPHY. (Supplement avail.: Islensk Hljodritaskra) 1974. a. ISK 1500($27) Landsbokasafn Islands - National Library of Iceland, Safnahusinu, Hverfisgoetu 15, P.O. Box 1210, 121 Reykjavik, Iceland. Ed. Hildur G. Eythorsdottir.
    Supersedes in part: Iceland. Landsbokasafn Islands. Arbok.

050 015   II
JOURNAL OF INDEXING & REFERENCE WORK. (Text in English) 1966. m. Rs.15($6) Mukherjee Library, 1 Gopi Mohan Dutta Lane, Calcutta 700003, India. Ed. Amitabha Chatterjee. adv.; bk.rev.; bibl.; index; circ. 200.
    Formerly: Indian Periodicals Record (ISSN 0019-6088)

KAGAKU GIJUTSU BUNKEN TOYAMA/TOYAMA SCIENCE AND TECHNICAL DOCUMENTS. see *TECHNOLOGY: COMPREHENSIVE WORKS — Abstracting, Bibliographies, Statistics*

500 016   PL   ISSN 0022-9172
KARTY DOKUMENTACYJNE/DOCUMENTATION CARDS. 1956. s-m. price varies. Instytut Informacji Naukowej, Technicznej i Ekonomicznej, Al. Niepodleglosci 188, 00931 Warsaw, Poland. (cards)

020   KE
KENYA NATIONAL BIBLIOGRAPHY. (Text in English) 1980. a. EAs.95($15.50) Kenya National Library Services, P.O. Box 30573, Nairobi, Kenya. Ed. Patrick Wanyama. circ. 500. (back issues avail.)

020   KE
KENYA NATIONAL LIBRARY SERVICES. CLASSIFIED ACCESSION LIST OF BOOKS ADDED TO STOCK. (Text in English) 1975. q. free. Kenya National Library Services, P.O. Box 30573, Nairobi, Kenya. circ. 50.
    Supersedes (since 1975): Kenya National Library Services. A Brief Selection of Recent Additions.

020   KE
KENYAN PERIODICALS DIRECTORY. (Text in English) 1984. biennial. EAs.75($9.50) Kenya National Library Services, National Reference and Bibliographic Department, P.O. Box 30573, Nairobi, Kenya. Ed. Clement W. Kabiru. circ. 1,000.

029 011   UK   ISSN 0143-9553
KEYWORD INDEX TO SERIAL TITLES. 1980. q. £289 (foreign £294). British Library, Document Supply Centre, Publishing Section, Boston Spa, Wetherby, W. Yorkshire LS23 7BQ, England. TEL 0937-843434. FAX 0937-546333. TELEX 557381. (microfiche)

KNJIZNICA; glasilo Zveze Bibliotekarskih Drustev Slovenije. see *LIBRARY AND INFORMATION SCIENCES*

LEGAL INFORMATION MANAGEMENT INDEX. see *LAW — Abstracting, Bibliographies, Statistics*

020   US   ISSN 0093-1888
LIBRARIANS' HANDBOOK. 1971. a. free to qualified personnel. EBSCO Subscription Services, Title Information Department, Box 1431, Birmingham, AL 35201-1943. FAX 205-995-1518. TELEX 78-2661. Ed. Mary Beth Vanderpoorten. adv.; circ. 25,000.
—BLDSC shelfmark: 5186.856750.

020 029.7 016   UK   ISSN 0024-2179
Z671
LIBRARY & INFORMATION SCIENCE ABSTRACTS. 1969. m. (plus a. cum. index). £264($498) Bowker-Saur Ltd., 59-60 Grosvenor St., London W1X 9DA, England. TEL 071-493-5841. FAX 071-499-1590. (Subscr. to: Bailey Bros. and Swinfen Ltd., Warner House, Bowles Well Gardens, Folkestone, Kent CT19 6PH, England) Ed. N. Moore. index, cum.index; circ. 2,500. (also avail. in magnetic tape; reprint service avail. from KTO) **Indexed:** AESIS.
● Also available online. Vendor(s): BRS (LISA), DIALOG (File no.61/LISA), Orbit Information Technologies (LISA).
Also available on CD-ROM.
—BLDSC shelfmark: 5188.700000.
    Supersedes: Library Science Abstracts.

020   US
LIBRARY AND INFORMATION SCIENCE EDUCATION STATISTICAL REPORT. a. $30. Association for Library and Information Science Education, 5623 Palm Aire Dr., Sarasota, FL 34243-3702. TEL 813-355-1795. Ed. Timothy W. Sineath. (also avail. in microfiche from CIS; back issues avail.)
    Formerly: A L I S E Statistics Report (ISSN 0739-506X)

020   CN   ISSN 0820-0521
LIBRARY AND INFORMATION SCIENCE UPDATE. 1976. m. Can.$24($48) University of Toronto, Library and Information Science Library, 140 St. George Street, Toronto, Ont. M5S 1A1, Canada. TEL 416-978-7060. FAX 416-978-5762. Ed. K. Lavin. circ. 200. (back issues avail.)
—BLDSC shelfmark: 5188.803000.
    Description: Geared to the needs of information professionals: abstracts of current periodical articles in the fields of library and information science.

020   US   ISSN 0085-2767
Z671
LIBRARY LIT. 1971. a. price varies. Scarecrow Press, Inc., 52 Liberty St., Metuchen, NJ 08840. TEL 800-537-7107. Ed. Jane Anne Hannigan. circ. 1,500.

020 029 016   US   ISSN 0024-2373
Z666
LIBRARY LITERATURE; an index to library and information science publications. 1921. bi-m. (a. cumulations). service basis. H.W. Wilson Co., 950 University Ave., Bronx, NY 10452. TEL 800-367-6770. FAX 212-538-2716. TELEX 4990003HWILSON. Ed. Cathy Rentschler. (also avail. in magnetic tape)
● Also available online. Vendor(s): BRS, BRS/Saunders Colleague, Wilsonline (File LIB). Also available on CD-ROM. Producer(s): H.W. Wilson (WILSONDISC).
—BLDSC shelfmark: 5200.250000.

020   US
LIBRARY OF CONGRESS CLASSIFICATION SCHEDULES: A CUMULATION OF ADDITIONS AND CHANGES. 1971. irreg., latest 1992. $2,810 (microfiche ed. $1,570). Gale Research Inc., 835 Penobscot Bldg., Detroit, MI 48226. TEL 313-961-2242. FAX 313-961-6083. TELEX 810-221-7086. Eds. Kathy Droste, Rita Runchock. (also avail. in microfiche)
    Description: Lists changes in Library of Congress classification schedules.

020 011   IE   ISSN 0024-631X
LONG ROOM. 1970. a. £10. Trinity College, Friends of the Library, College St., Dublin 2, Ireland. FAX 719003. TELEX 93782. Ed. W. E. Mackey. adv.; bibl.; illus.; circ. 700. (back issues avail.) **Indexed:** Br.Hum.Ind.
—BLDSC shelfmark: 5294.225000.

020 016   HU   ISSN 0133-736X
MAGYAR KONYVTARI SZAKIRODALOM BIBLIOGRAFIAJA/HUNGARIAN LIBRARY LITERATURE. 1965. q. $30. Orszagos Szechenyi Konyvtar, Konyvtartudomanyi es Modszertani Kozpont - Centre for Library Science and Methodology at the National Szechenyi Library, Budavari Palota F epulet, 1827 Budapest, Hungary. TEL 1750-686. TELEX 224226 LIBLN H. (Subscr. to: Kultura, Box 149, 1376 Budapest, Hungary) Ed. Ferencne Javori. circ. 700. (back issues avail.)
    Formerly: Gyorstajekoztato a Magyar Konyvtartudomanyi Irodalomrol (ISSN 0017-6052)

MAGYAR TUDOMANYOS AKADEMIA KONVYTARANAK KOZLEMENYEI. see *SCIENCES: COMPREHENSIVE WORKS — Abstracting, Bibliographies, Statistics*

020 610   UG
MAKERERE UNIVERSITY. ALBERT COOK LIBRARY. LIBRARY BULLETIN AND ACCESSION LIST. irreg., no.2, 1977. free. Makerere University, Albert Cook Library, Makerere Medical School, Box 7072, Kampala, Uganda. Ed. Maria Gioretti Musoke. circ. controlled. (processed; back issues avail.)
    Description: Each issue consists of hundreds of bibliographic entries pertaining to monographs only.

MATERIAL MATTERS. see *CHILDREN AND YOUTH — Abstracting, Bibliographies, Statistics*

020   UK   ISSN 0266-4879
MICROINDEXER. 1983. irreg. £15 to non-members. Society of Indexers (Kent), c/o The Secretary, 16 Green Road, Birchington, Kent CT7 9JZ, England. TEL 0843-41115. Eds. I. and P. McLean. adv.; bk.rev.; circ. 1,000.
—BLDSC shelfmark: 5759.148000.
    Description: Information on indexing by micro-computers and word processors.

027.4   US   ISSN 0164-0496
Z6945
MISSOURI UNION LIST OF SERIAL PUBLICATIONS. 1975. a. $50. St. Louis Public Library, Board of Directors, 1301 Olive St., St. Louis, MO 63103. FAX 314-241-3840. (also avail. in microfiche; avail. only in microfiche)
● Also available on CD-ROM.
    Description: Contains serial and periodical holdings for approximately 125 libraries throughout Missouri and adjacent states.

021   US
MONTANA PUBLIC LIBRARY STATISTICS. 1989. a. State Library, 1515 E. Sixth Ave., Helena, MT 59620. TEL 406-444-3115. FAX 406-444-5612.

MUSIC, BOOKS ON MUSIC AND SOUND RECORDINGS. see *MUSIC — Abstracting, Bibliographies, Statistics*

020   II
N A S S D O C RESEARCH INFORMATION SERIES. PAGING PERIODICAL; preview of contents. (Text in English) 1986. bi-m. Indian Council of Social Science Research, National Social Science Documentation Centre, 35, Ferozshah Rd., New Delhi 110 001, India. TEL 385959. TELEX 31-61083-ISSR-IN. Eds. K.G. Tyagi, Meena Walia.
    Description: Offers indexed names, title words, and publishers directory of journals in the social, library, and information sciences.

020 016   US
N T I S ALERTS: LIBRARY & INFORMATION SCIENCES. w. $125 (foreign $175). U.S. National Technical Information Service, 5285 Port Royal Rd., Springfield, VA 22161. TEL 703-487-4630. FAX 703-321-8547. TELEX 64617. index. (back issues avail.)
    Former titles: Abstract Newsletter: Library and Information Sciences; Weekly Abstract Newsletter: Library and Information Sciences; Weekly Government Abstracts. Library and Information Sciences (ISSN 0364-6467)

NATIONAL UNION CATALOG. AUDIOVISUAL MATERIALS. see *MOTION PICTURES — Abstracting, Bibliographies, Statistics*

LIBRARY AND INFORMATION SCIENCES — ABSTRACTING, BIBLIOGRAPHIES, STATISTICS

020 655 011   US   ISSN 0734-7650
NATIONAL UNION CATALOG. BOOKS. 1956. m. $610 to N. American libraries; foreign libraries $695. (U.S. Library of COngress) Advanced Libray Systems, Inc., 100 Brickstone Sq., Box 246, Andover, MA 01810. TEL 508-470-0610. FAX 508-475-1072. circ. 2,093. (also avail. in microfiche from ALS)
   Formerly (until 1983): National Union Catalog (ISSN 0028-0348)

027.4   NE   ISSN 0168-3462
Z815.A1
NETHERLANDS. CENTRAAL BUREAU VOOR DE STATISTIEK. STATISTIEK VAN DE OPENBARE BIBLIOTHEKEN. a. Centraal Bureau voor de Statistiek, Prinses Beatrixlaan 428, Voorburg, Netherlands. (Dist. by: SDU - Publishers, Christoffel Plantijnstraat, The Hague, Netherlands)

020 310   US
NEW JERSEY PUBLIC LIBRARY STATISTICS FOR (YEAR). 1958. a. free. State Library, 185 W. State St., Trenton, NJ 08625-0520. TEL 609-292-7854. Ed. Robert K. Fortenbaugh. circ. 675. **Indexed:** SRI.
   Formerly: New Jersey Public Libraries. Statistics (ISSN 0093-1098)

027   US   ISSN 0077-9318
NEW YORK STATE LIBRARY, ALBANY. LIBRARY DEVELOPMENT. INSTITUTION LIBRARIES STATISTICS. 1954. a. free to libraries in New York State; libraries elsewhere on exchange basis. New York State Library, Library Development, Albany, NY 12230. circ. 1,000.

027   US   ISSN 0077-9326
Z732.N7
NEW YORK STATE LIBRARY, ALBANY. LIBRARY DEVELOPMENT. PUBLIC AND ASSOCIATION LIBRARIES STATISTICS. Title varies: 1950-1955: Statistics of Public and Association Libraries. 1950. a. free to libraries in New York State; libraries elsewhere on exchange basis. New York State Library, Library Development, Albany, NY 12230. circ. 1,250.

029   NR   ISSN 0794-6406
NIGERIAN PERIODICALS INDEX. 1986. s-a. £N80($50) Committee of University Librarians of Nigerian Universities, c/o Dr. H.I. Said, The Library, Bayero University, Kano, Nigeria. Ed. B.U. Nwafor. circ. 500. (back issues avail.)
   Description: Author-subject index with the entries filing in one alphabetical sequence, word-by-word, following ALA filing rules.

021 027.7   US
NORTH DAKOTA LIBRARY STATISTICS. a. $5. North Dakota State Library, Capitol Grounds, 604 E. Boulevard Ave., Bismarck, ND 58505-0800. TEL 701-224-2490. FAX 701-224-2040. **Indexed:** SRI.
   Formerly: North Dakota Academic Library Statistics. (ISSN 0094-5455)

020 016   CS   ISSN 0139-5459
NOVINKY LITERATURY: NOVINKY KNIHOVNICKE LITERATURY. 1958. 5/yr. 30 Kcs.($30) Narodni Knihovna v Praze - National Library Prague, Klementinum 190, 110 01 Prague 1, Czechoslovakia. TEL 26-65-41. FAX 42-2-261775. TELEX 121207 STKN C. (Dist. by: Narodni Knihovna v Praze, Oddeleni Odbytu Publikaci, Liliova 5, 110 01 Prague 1, Czechoslovakia. TEL 22-59-93) Ed. Jaroslav Skolek. bk.rev.; abstr.; index; circ. 500.
   Description: Abstracts from foreign library and information science journals

020   AT   ISSN 0816-956X
ONLINE CURRENTS. 1986. 10/yr. Aus.$126 (typically set Aug.-Sep.). Enterprise Information Management Pty. Ltd., P.O. Box 471, Roseville, N.S.W. 2069, Australia. TEL 02 46 5290. FAX 02-423-1710. TELEX KEYD AA100200. Ed. Katie Blake. adv.; bk.rev.; index; circ. 450. (back issues avail.)
   Description: Information about the online industry and optical publishing industry. Contains both Australian and overseas news.

POLITISCHE DOKUMENTATION; Referatedienst. see POLITICAL SCIENCE — Abstracting, Bibliographies, Statistics

500 016   PL
PRZEGLAD DOKUMENTACYJNY INFORMACJI NAUKOWEJ. (Contents page in English, Polish, Russian) 1962. bi-m. $42. Instytut Informacji Naukowej Technicznej i Ekonomicznej, St. Jasna 14-16, 00-041 Warsaw, Poland. (Dist. by: Ars Polona - Ruch, Krakowskie Przedmiescie 7, Warsaw, Poland) Ed.Bd. bk.rev.; circ. 830.
   Formerly (until 1980): Przeglad Pismiennictwa Zagadnien Informacji (ISSN 0033-2348)

PSYCINFO NEWS. see PSYCHOLOGY — Abstracting, Bibliographies, Statistics

020   AT   ISSN 0729-199X
PUBLIC LIBRARIES IN WESTERN AUSTRALIA. STATISTICAL BULLETIN. 1981. a. Aus.$12. Library & Information Service of Western Australia, Alexander Library Bldg., Perth Cultural Center, Perth, W.A. 6000, Australia. TEL 09-427-3111. circ. 300. (back issues avail.)
   Description: Compares statistics of all public library operations and stock holdings in Western Australia.

020   US
PUBLIC LIBRARY CATALOG. quinquennial (with a. supplements). price varies. H.W. Wilson Co., 950 University Ave., Bronx, NY 10452. TEL 800-367-6770. FAX 212-538-2716. TELEX 4990003HWILSON. Ed. Juliett Yaakov. bk.rev.
   Formerly: Standard Catalog for Public Libraries.
   Description: Classified list of nonfiction English-language books recommended for adults; with author, title, subject, and analytical index.

020   UK   ISSN 0951-8983
PUBLIC LIBRARY STATISTICS; a ten year trend analysis. 1985. a. £11. Loughborough University, Library and Information Statistics Unit, Loughborough, Leics. LE11 3TU, England. TEL 0509 223071. FAX 0509-231983. (Co-sponsor: British Library) Ed. Joan Sumsion. circ. 240.
   —BLDSC shelfmark: 5276.225000.

020   CN   ISSN 0075-6113
QUEEN'S UNIVERSITY AT KINGSTON. DOUGLAS LIBRARY. OCCASIONAL PAPERS. 1969. irreg., latest 1987. price varies. Queen's University, Douglas Library, Kingston, Ont. K7L 5C4, Canada. TEL 613-545-2528. FAX 613-545-6819. TELEX 230961000. circ. 300. (also avail. in microfilm)

020 016   US
READERS ADVISORY SERVICE. 1974. irreg. $115. Science Associates International, Inc., 465 West End Ave., New York, NY 10024. TEL 212-873-0656. Ed. Leonard Cohan. (reprint service avail. from UMI)

020 016   RU   ISSN 0486-235X
REFERATIVNYI ZHURNAL. INFORMATIKA. English edition: Informatics Abstracts (ISSN 0203-3054) (English edition without index available) 1963. m. 65 Rub. Vsesoyuznyi Institut Nauchno-Tekhnicheskoi Informatsii (VINITI), Baltiiskaya ul., 14, Moscow A-219, Russia. (Subscr. to: Mezhdunarodnaya Kniga, Dimitrova ul. 39, 113095 Moscow, Russia)

011 020   SA
S A JOINT CATALOGUE OF MONOGRAPHS ON MICROFICHE, SERIES 3, UNICAT. Short title: S A UNICAT. 1971. 2/yr. R210. State Library, P.O. Box 397, Pretoria 0001, South Africa. index.
   Supersedes in part: S A Joint Catalogue of Monographs.
   Description: Listing of monographs in Southern African libraries by ISBN number.

026   US
S A L A L M BIBLIOGRAPHY AND REFERENCE SERIES. (Text in English, French, Portuguese, Spanish) 1969. irreg. (approx. s-a.). price varies. Seminar on the Acquisition of Latin American Library Materials, General Library, University of New Mexico, Albuquerque, NM 87131. TEL 505-277-5102.
   Incorporates: Seminar on the Acquisition of Latin American Library Materials. Report on Bibliographic Activities; Formerly: S A L A L M Bibliography Series (ISSN 0586-9781)

020 011   UK   ISSN 0307-1456
S A L G NEWSLETTER. 1973. a. £4. South Asia Library Group, c/o Oriental and India Office Collections, The British Library, 197 Blackfriars Rd., London SE1 8NG, England. TEL 071-412-7834. FAX 071-412-7857. Ed. John Sims. bk.rev.; circ. 70. (back issues avail.)
   —BLDSC shelfmark: 8070.790000.

011   CH   ISSN 0006-1581
SHU MO CHI KAN/BIBLIOGRAPHY QUARTERLY. (Text in Chinese) 1966. q. $32. Student Book Co., Ltd., 198 Ho-Ping E. Rd., Sec. 1, Taipei, Taiwan, Republic of China. FAX 02-3636334. Ed. Ting Wen-Tsu. adv.; bk.rev.; abstr.; bibl.; circ. 2,500.

011 029   SL
SIERRA LEONE PUBLICATIONS. 1964. q. $6. Library Board, Box 326, Freetown, Sierra Leone. (back issues avail.)

027   BU   ISSN 0204-4684
STATISTICESKI DANNI ZA BIBLIOTEKITE V BULGARIA/STATISTICAL DATA ON LIBRARIES IN BULGARIA. 1966. a. $15. Narodna Biblioteka Kiril i Metodii, 11, V. Levski Blvd., 1504 Sofia, Bulgaria. Ed. H. Hadjihzistov. charts; stat.; circ. 600. (processed)

027   US   ISSN 0081-5152
Z732.I6
STATISTICS OF INDIANA LIBRARIES.* 1890. a. $3. Indiana Library Association, 1500 N. Delaware St., Indianapolis, IN 46202-2419. TEL 317-232-3697. (Co-sponsor: Indiana State Library) circ. 300.
   Description: Contains tables of statistics representing a compilation and analysis of date reported by public, academic, institutional and special libraries.

020   US
STATISTICS OF SOUTHERN COLLEGE AND UNIVERSITY LIBRARIES. 1929. a. free. Louisiana State University, Baton Rouge, LA 70803. TEL 504-388-2217. Ed. D.W. Schneider. circ. controlled. **Indexed:** SRI.
   Description: Lists broken down by number of volumes, periodicals, and microfilm units; expenditures by library and institution, staff positions, and enrollment figures.

027.4   US   ISSN 0731-8464
Z732.V8
STATISTICS OF VIRGINIA PUBLIC LIBRARIES AND INSTITUTIONAL LIBRARIES. 1923. a. free. Virginia State Library, Public Library Development Division, Richmond, VA 23219. TEL 804-225-3892. FAX 804-225-4608. Ed. Peggy D. Rudd. circ. 3,800. **Indexed:** SRI.
   Formerly: Statistics of Virginia Public Libraries (ISSN 0095-3490)

010   US   ISSN 0081-7600
STUDIES IN BIBLIOGRAPHY. 1948. a. $30. (Bibliographical Society of the University of Virginia) University Press of Virginia, Box 3608 University Station, Charlottesville, VA 22903. TEL 804-924-3468. FAX 804-982-2655. Ed. D. Vander Meulen. circ. 2,000. **Indexed:** M.L.A.
   —BLDSC shelfmark: 8489.650000.
   Description: Scholarly articles on bibliographic studies.

026   US   ISSN 0000-0140
SUBJECT COLLECTIONS; a guide to special book collections and subject emphasis in libraries. 1958. irreg., 7th ed., 1992. $275. R.R. Bowker, A Reed Reference Publishing Company, Division of Reed Publishing (USA) Inc., 121 Chanlon Rd., New Providence, NJ 07974. TEL 800-521-8110. FAX 908-665-6688. TELEX 138 755. (Subscr. to: Order Dept., Box 31, New Providence, NJ 07974) Eds. Lee Ash, William G. Miller. index.
   Description: Locates significant US and Canadian library collections on any subject. Entries for more than 18,000 collections in over 11,000 academic, public, special libraries and museums are indexed and cross-referenced under 37,000 LC subject headings; and provides full contact and descriptive information.

027.4   US   ISSN 0363-7158
Z732.T18
TENNESSEE PUBLIC LIBRARY STATISTICS. 1965? a. free. State Library and Archives, Planning and Development Section, Office of Secretary of State, Nashville, TN 37243-0312. TEL 615-741-3158. FAX 615-741-6471. circ. 1,500.

027   US   ISSN 0082-3120
Z732.T25
TEXAS PUBLIC LIBRARY STATISTICS. 1965. a. free. Texas State Library, Library Development Division, Box 12927, Austin, TX 78711. TEL 512-463-5465. Ed. Edward Seidenber. circ. 1,650. **Indexed:** SRI.

LIBRARY AND INFORMATION SCIENCES — ABSTRACTING, BIBLIOGRAPHIES, STATISTICS

029   HU   ISSN 0041-3917
Q4   CODEN: TMTAAG
TUDOMANYOS ES MUSZAKI TAJEKOZTATAS/SCIENTIFIC AND TECHNICAL INFORMATION. (Text in Hungarian; summaries in English, German and Russian) 1953. m. 1680 Ft.($41) Orszagos Muszaki Informacios Kozpont es Konyvtar (O.M.I.K.K.) - National Technical Information Centre and Library, Muzeum u. 17, Box 12, 1428 Budapest, Hungary. TEL 0138-2300. (Subscr. to: OMIKK Technoinform, Box 12, H-1428 Budapest, Hungary) Ed. P. Szanto. bk.rev.; abstr.; bibl.; index; circ. 1,200. **Indexed:** AESIS, Bull.Signal., Chem.Abstr., Hung.Lib.& Info.Sci.Abstr., Inform.Sci.Abstr., LISA, Ref.Zh., Sci.Abstr.
—BLDSC shelfmark: 9068.500000.
Formerly (until 1962): Muszaki Konyvtarosok Tajekoztatoja.

026 011   US
U.S. DEPARTMENT OF STATE. LIBRARY. COMMERCIAL LIBRARY PROGRAM. PUBLICATIONS LIST. 1978. irreg. U.S. Department of State, 2201 C St., N.W., Washington, DC 20520. (Orders to: Supt. of Documents, Washington, DC 20402)

020 016   US   ISSN 0083-1603
Z733.U57
U.S. LIBRARY OF CONGRESS. LIBRARY OF CONGRESS PUBLICATIONS IN PRINT. 1935. a. free. U.S. Library of Congress, Washington, DC 20540. TEL 202-707-5000. circ. 10,000.

020   UK   ISSN 0268-3539
UNIVERSITY LIBRARY EXPENDITURE STATISTICS. 1981. a. £12.50. Standing Conference of National & University Libraries (SCONUL), 102 Euston St., London NW1 2HA, England. FAX 071-383-3197. stat.; circ. 250. (looseleaf format)
—BLDSC shelfmark: 9111.819550.

020   US   ISSN 0037-1300
UNIVERSITY OF CALIFORNIA, BERKELEY. LIBRARY SCHOOL LIBRARY. SELECTED ADDITIONS TO THE LIBRARY SCHOOL LIBRARY COLLECTION. 1947-1990. bi-m. free. University of California, Berkeley, Library School Library, Berkeley, CA 94720. TEL 415-642-2253. Ed. Dorothy Koenig. (processed)

027.7   SA   ISSN 0576-6885
UNIVERSITY OF CAPE TOWN. LIBRARIES. STATISTICAL REPORT. a. free. University of Cape Town, Libraries, Rondebosch 7700, South Africa. TEL 021-650-3097. FAX 021-650-3714. TELEX 52-0327.
Description: Statistical record of both Technical Services and User Services divisions of UCT Libraries.

027.7 011   SU
UNIVERSITY OF RIYADH. CENTRAL LIBRARY. ACCESSION LIST. (Text in English and Arabic) q. University of Riyadh, Central Library, Riyadh, Saudi Arabia.

020   CN   ISSN 0829-948X
UNIVERSITY OF WATERLOO BIBLIOGRAPHY SERIES. 1978. irreg. price varies. University of Waterloo, Library, Waterloo, Ont. N2L 3G1, Canada. TEL 519-885-1211. FAX 519-747-4606. Ed. Bruce MacNeil. (back issues avail.)
—BLDSC shelfmark: 1998.950000.

020   AT   ISSN 1035-4832
VICTORIAN PUBLIC LIBRARIES. ANNUAL SURVEY. 1969. a. Aus.$12. Victorian Ministry for the Arts, Library Services, Level 3, 176 Wellingotn Parade, E. Melbourne, Vic. 3005, Australia. TEL 03-649-8888. FAX 03-614-6186. Ed. Ross Gibbs. circ. 500.
●Also available online.
Supersedes (in 1989): Public Libraries of Victoria. Annual Statistical Bulletin (ISSN 0156-4374).

700 015   ISSN 0733-2149
YEAR'S WORK IN COMIC INDEXING. 1978. a. exchange basis. (Amateur Press Alliance for Indexing) Michigan State University Libraries, Special Collections Division, East Lansing, MI 48824-1048. Ed. Randall W. Scott. circ. 75.
Description: Annual index of all contributions to the Amateur Press Alliance in Indexing by mailing number, item number, name of indexer, and title of work.

LIBRARY AND INFORMATION SCIENCES — Computer Applications

025   US   ISSN 1056-6694
▼**A L C T S NETWORK NEWS.** 1990. irreg. free. American Library Association, Association for Library Collections & Technical Services, 50 E. Huron St., Chicago, IL 60611-2759. TEL 312-280-5035. FAX 312-280-3257. Ed. Karen Muller.
●Available only online.

025 621.381
001.642   US   ISSN 1055-4769
Z678.9.A1   CODEN: ALICER
ACADEMIC AND LIBRARY COMPUTING. 1984. m. (combined Jul.-Aug.). $95. Meckler Publishing Corporation, 11 Ferry Lane W., Westport, CT 06880-5808. TEL 203-226-6967. FAX 203-454-5840. Eds. Michael Schuyler, Edward Valauskas. circ. 1,500. (also avail. in microfilm) **Indexed:** Comput.Dtbs., Microcomp.Ind.
—BLDSC shelfmark: 0570.510400.
Former titles (until 1991): Library Workstation Report (ISSN 1041-7923); (until 1989): Library Workstation and P C Report (ISSN 0894-9158); (until vol.4, no.7, 1987): M300 and P C Report (ISSN 0743-7633)
Description: Covers the use of campus-wide information systems, the use of computer networks on campus and online public access catalogs.

025 621.381   US   ISSN 0887-2716
APPLE LIBRARY USERS GROUP NEWSLETTER. 1983. q. free. Apple Computer, Inc., 10381 Bandley Dr., Cupertino, CA 95014. TEL 408-974-2552. Ed. Monica Ertel. bk.rev.; circ. 16,000. (back issues avail.)
Description: For people interested in using Apple and Macintosh computers in libraries and information centers.

025   US   ISSN 1042-1459
ARCHIVES AND MUSEUM INFORMATICS TECHNICAL REPORT. 1987. irreg. price varies. Archives and Museum Informatics, 5600 Northumberland St., Pittsburgh, PA 15217. FAX 412-421-1915. Ed. David Bearman.
—BLDSC shelfmark: 1631.160000.
Formerly: Archival Informatics Technical Report.
Description: Monographs on information management issues and technologies in archives and museums.

B R S BULLETIN. see COMPUTERS — Information Science And Information Theory

350   BE   ISSN 0250-9725
BIBLIOTEEK VOOR HEDENDAAGSE DOKUMENTATIE. BULLETIN. (Text in English) 1973. m. $10. Biblioteek voor Hedendaagse Dokumentatie, Parklaan 2, B-9100 St. Niklaas Waas, Belgium. TEL 32-3-776-5063. FAX 32-3-778-0785. Ed. Yvan van Garsse. circ. 500. (also avail. in microfiche)

BIOSCENE. see BIOLOGY — Abstracting, Bibliographies, Statistics

020   UK   ISSN 0957-4085
   CODEN: CLAPEE
C & L APPLICATIONS; monthly information for libraries and information services. 1987. 10/yr. £40 (foreign £45). Information Partnership, 140 Tabernacle St., Ste. 4-2, London EC2A 4SD, England. FAX 071-253-0607. Ed. Peter Gillman. adv.; bk.rev.; circ. 200.
—BLDSC shelfmark: 2943.175130.
Formerly: Computers and Libraries (ISSN 0950-8392)

025   US   ISSN 0897-3296
C D - R O M DATABASES. (Compact Disc - Read Only Memory) 1988. m. $150 (foreign $190). Worldwide Videotex, Box 138, Babson Park, Boston, MA 02157. TEL 617-449-1603. Ed. Mark Wright. bk.rev.
●Also available online. Vendor(s): DIALOG, NewsNet.
Description: Lists all databases currently being marketed on CD-ROMs. Provides titles, prices, categories and vendors of CD-ROMs and whether or not they are for use on Macintosh or IBM computers.

025   US   ISSN 1042-8623
TA1635
C D - R O M ENDUSER. 1989. m. free to qualified personnel. Disc Company, 6609 Rosecroft Pl., Falls Church, VA 22043-1828. TEL 703-237-0682. FAX 703-532-5447. Ed. Linda W. Helgerson.
—BLDSC shelfmark: 3096.303461.
Description: For buyers and users of CD-ROM products and services.

025   US   ISSN 1049-0833
TA1635   CODEN: CRPFEX
C D - R O M PROFESSIONAL. 1988. bi-m. $86 (foreign $121). Pemberton Press Inc., 11 Tannery Ln., Weston, CT 06883. TEL 800-248-8466. FAX 203-222-0122. Ed. Nancy K. Herther. adv.; bk.rev.; circ. 5,400. (also avail. in microform from UMI) **Indexed:** ABI Inform., Lib.Lit., LISA, Tr.& Indus.Ind.
●Also available online. Vendor(s): DIALOG (File no.170).
—BLDSC shelfmark: 3096.303980.
Formerly (until May 1990): Laserdisk Professional.
Description: Assists publishers, librarians and other information professionals in the selection, evaluation, purchase, and operation of CD-ROM systems.

015   US
▼**C D - R O M PROFESSIONAL INSIDE NEWS**; the newsletter for CD-ROM industry executives. 1992. m. $295. Pemberton Press Inc., 462 Danbury Rd., Wilton, CT 06897-2126. TEL 800-248-8466.

025   US   ISSN 1048-406X
HD9696.067
▼**C D - R O M SHOPPERS GUIDE.** 1990. q. $19.95 (foreign $29.95). Disc Company, 6609 Rosecroft Pl., Falls Church, VA 22043-1828. TEL 703-237-0682. Ed. Linda W. Helgerson.
Description: Provides with up-to-date listings of commercially available CD-ROM titles and CD-ROM drives.

025   US
C D - R O M SOURCEBOOK. a. Disc Company, 6609 Rosecroft Pl., Falls Church, VA 22043-1828. TEL 703-237-0682. FAX 703-532-5447.
●Also available on CD-ROM.

001.6   CL   ISSN 0716-4858
COMPUTACION PERSONAL. m. Publicaciones en Computacion, Avda. Pedro de Valdivia 2103, Santiago, Chile. TEL 2232616. Ed. Soledad Amenabar Matte.

COMPUTER ABSTRACTS ON MICROFICHE. see COMPUTERS — Abstracting, Bibliographies, Statistics

COMPUTER LIBRARY'S COMPUTER PERIODICALS DATABASE. see LIBRARY AND INFORMATION SCIENCES — Abstracting, Bibliographies, Statistics

COMPUTERS IN LIBRARIES. see COMPUTERS — Microcomputers

COMPUTERS IN LIBRARIES: BUYERS GUIDE & CONSULTANT DIRECTORY. see COMPUTERS — Personal Computers

025   AT
CONCATENATION. q. free. Ferntree Information, P.O. Box 42, Clayton, Vic. 3168, Australia. TEL 03-541-5600. Ed. Robert Grundy. circ. 1,500.
Formerly (until Aug. 1990): Ausinet Newsletter.
Description: Newsletter to clients of the Ferntree Information. Covers computer applications to online databases and library and information sciences.

CONCEPTS IN COMMUNICATION INFORMATICS AND LIBRARIANSHIP. see LIBRARY AND INFORMATION SCIENCES

025   US   ISSN 0272-037X
D L A BULLETIN. 1981. irreg. University of California, Division of Library Automation, 300 Lakeside Dr., 8th Fl., Oakland, CA 94612-3550. TEL 415-987-0564. Ed. Mary Jean Moore. bk.rev.; circ. 2,500.
●Also available online.
—BLDSC shelfmark: 3605.635000.
Description: Library automation and library telecommunication networking news from the University of California.

LIBRARY AND INFORMATION SCIENCES — COMPUTER APPLICATIONS

020 001.6   CN
DALHOUSIE UNIVERSITY. SCHOOL OF LIBRARY AND INFORMATION STUDIES. OCCASIONAL PAPERS. irreg. price varies. Dalhousie University, School of Library and Information Studies, Halifax, N.S. B3H 4H8, Canada. TEL 902-494-3656. FAX 902-494-2319. TELEX 019-21863. Ed. Mary Dykstra. **Indexed:** LISA.
Former titles: Dalhousie University. University Libraries and School of Library Service. Occasional Papers; Dalhousie University. School of Library Service. Occasional Papers (ISSN 0318-7403)
Description: Forum for the dissemination of refereed scholarly papers, bibliographies, checklists and symposia proceedings on topics of interest to librarians and other information professionals.
Refereed Serial

340   US   ISSN 1042-2595
CODEN: DARVEH
DATABASE REVIEW. 1989. bi-m. $95 (foreign $115). DataBase Associates, P.O. Box 215, Morgan Hill, CA 95038-0215. TEL 408-779-0436. FAX 408-779-3274. Ed. Colin J. white. (back issues avail.)
—BLDSC shelfmark: 3535.803575.
Description: Looks at key developments in the database marketplace.

025   US   ISSN 1052-4053
TA1635
▼**DISC MAGAZINE.** 1991. m. $44.95 in North America; foreign $64.95. Disc Company, 6609 Rosecroft Pl., Falls Church, VA 22043-1828. TEL 702-237-5447. FAX 703-532-5447. Ed. Linda W. Helgerson.
●Also available on CD-ROM.
Description: Technical publication for producers and suppliers of CD-ROM products and services.

025   US   ISSN 8756-2294
DYNIX DATALINE. 1984. q. free. Dynix, Inc., 151 East 1700 South, Provo, UT 84606. TEL 801-375-2770. FAX 801-373-1889. circ. 4,700.

020 600   US
E R I C - I R UPDATE. (Educational Resources Information Center - Information Resources) 1977. 2/yr. free. E R I C Clearinghouse on Information Resources, 030 Huntington Hall, Syracuse University, Syracuse, NY 13244-2340. TEL 315-443-3640. FAX 315-443-5732. Ed. Jane K. Janis. bk.rev.; circ. 4,200.
Description: Includes publications, practitioner information, and trends and issues in the area of library and information science and education technology.

025 629.13   NE
E S A - I R S NEWS & VIEWS. (Information Retrieval Systems) q. free. European Space Agency, Publications Division, Keplerlaan 1, 22000 AG Noordwijk, Netherlands. TEL 01719-86555. FAX 01719-85433. TELEX 39098. Ed. N. Longdon. illus.; circ. 12,000.

EDUCATIONAL I R M QUARTERLY. see *EDUCATION — Teaching Methods And Curriculum*

025   US   ISSN 0264-0473
Z678.9
ELECTRONIC LIBRARY. 1983. bi-m. $99. Learned Information, Inc., 143 Old Marlton Pike, Medford, NJ 08055-8750. TEL 609-654-4888. FAX 609-654-4309. (And: Managing Editor, Learned Information Ltd., Woodside, Hinksey Hill, Oxford OX1 5AV, England) Ed. David Raitt. adv.; bk.rev.; bibl.; circ. 2,000. **Indexed:** ASCA, BMT, CINAHL, Comput.Cont., Curr.Cont., Info.Media & Tech., Leg.Info.Manage.Ind., Lib.Lit., SSCI, Tr.& Indus.Ind.
—BLDSC shelfmark: 3702.580500.
Description: For librarians and information center managers interested in microcomputers and library automation. Features include industry news and product announcements.

025   US   ISSN 1057-834X
▼**ELECTRONIC PUBLIC INFORMATION NEWSLETTER.** 1991. 24/yr. $249 to individuals; libraries $130. E P I N Publishing, Box 21001, Washington, DC 20009. TEL 703-237-9501. FAX 703-237-7923. Eds. James McDonough, Vigdor Schreibman. q. index; circ. 60. (back issues avail.)
Description: Covers transformation of public information into electronic form, policy issues and practice; for information resource management personnel, information science specialist, librarians, and the information industry.

ESPIAL CANADIAN DATA BASE DIRECTORY; a guide to current Canadian information contained in national and international databases and data banks. see *COMPUTERS — Abstracting, Bibliographies, Statistics*

025   US   ISSN 1055-1743
F Y I - I M. (For Your Information and Image Management); the A I I M newsletter. 1985. s-m. membership only. Association for Information & Image Management, 1100 Wayne Ave., Ste. 1100, Silver Spring, MD 20910-5699. TEL 301-587-8202. FAX 301-587-2711. Ed. Katharine J. Brophy. adv.; circ. 9,000. (looseleaf format; back issues avail.)
Description: Designed for end users of systems and manufacturers, consultants, and service companies. Covers news of the information and image management industry, including association news, business news, industry trends, and technology.

025   US
Z681.3.067
FAXON GUIDE TO C D - R O M. 1988. a. $12 (free to qualified personnel). Faxon Company, Inc., 15 Southwest Park, Westwood, MA 02090. TEL 617-329-3350. FAX 617-461-1862. TELEX 681-7238. Ed. Michael Ault. adv.; circ. 10,000.
Formerly: Access Faxon (ISSN 0897-6139)
Description: Directory of CD-ROM information. Includes a comprehensive listing of CD-ROM discs available through Faxon.

I A S S I S T QUARTERLY. (International Association for Social Science Information Services and Technology) see *LIBRARY AND INFORMATION SCIENCES*

651.8 001.53   US
I D. (Information Display) a. $70 (foreign $75). (Society for Information Display) Palisades Institute for Research Services, Attn: Jay Morreale, 201 Varick St., 11th Fl., New York, NY 10014. TEL 212-305-1502.

025   US   ISSN 0019-0012
TR835   CODEN: IMGCB7
I M C JOURNAL. 1967. 6/yr. $90 (foreign $115). International Information Management Congress, 345 Woodcliff Dr., Fairport, NY 14450-4201. TEL 716-383-8330. FAX 716-383-8442. Ed. William McArthur. adv.; bk.rev.; abstr.; bibl.; charts; illus.; stat.; circ. 30,000. (also avail. in microform from UMI; reprint service avail. from UMI) **Indexed:** ABI Inform, Account.& Data Proc.Abstr., Bus.Educ.Ind., Bus.Ind., Comput.Cont., Comput.Lit.Ind., Info.Media & Tech., Leg.Info.Manage.Ind., LHTN, Resour.Ctr.Ind., Sci.Abstr.
—BLDSC shelfmark: 4369.070000.
Formerly: I M C Newsletter (ISSN 0739-4268)
Description: Covers electronic information and records management trends, computer-assisted retrieval and indexing, micrographics, microfilms, office automation and word processing.

001.6 621.381   FR   ISSN 0754-1996
INDUSTRIE DE L'INFORMATION; lettre quotidienne internationale des systems d'information automatises. (Text in French) 1982. d. 6000 F. A Jour, 11 rue du Marche St. Honore, 75001 Paris, France. TEL 42-96-67-22. FAX 40-20-07-75. TELEX TELEXEL 615887. Ed. Dominique Le Cleach.

001.6   US
INFORMATICA. (Text in Spanish) m. Publicaciones en Computacion, c/o C W Communications, 375 Cochituate Rd., Framingham, MA 01701. TEL 617-879-0700. adv.; circ. 1,000.

621.381 001.539   CL   ISSN 0716-0658
INFORMATICA; revista de computacion y sistemas. 1980. m. $82. C I I S A, Avda. Pedro de Valdivia 2103, Santiago, Chile. TEL 2232616. FAX 562-223-1066. Ed. Oscar Barros. adv.; circ. 2,000.

001.6 621.381   NE   ISSN 0019-9907
INFORMATIE. 1958. m. fl.160. Kluwer Bedrijfswetenschappen B.V., Postbus 23, 7400 GA Deventer, Netherlands. TEL 05700-48999. FAX 05700-11504. (Co-sponsors: Nederlands Genootschap voor Informatica, Belgisch Studiecentrum voor Automatische Informatieverwerking, Nederlands Opleidings Instituut voor Informatica) Ed.Bd. adv.; bk.rev.; bibl.; charts; illus.; index; circ. 13,000. (also avail. in microform from UMI; reprint service avail. from UMI) **Indexed:** Account.& Data Proc.Abstr., Cyb.Abstr., Ref.Zh., Sci.Abstr.
—BLDSC shelfmark: 4481.300000.
Description: Contains information and scientific articles on computer science, systems development, and EDP management.

001.6 621.381   GW   ISSN 0170-6012
QA75.5
INFORMATIK-SPEKTRUM; archive of applied mechanics. (Text mainly in German) 1978. 6/yr. DM.248($154) (Gesellschaft fuer Informatik e.V.) Springer-Verlag, Heidelberger Platz 3, D-1000 Berlin 33, Germany. TEL 030-8207-1. (Also Heidelberg, Tokyo, Vienna, and New York) Ed. Dr. W. Brauer. adv. (also avail. in microform from UMI; reprint service avail. from ISI) **Indexed:** INIS Atomind., Sci.Abstr.
—BLDSC shelfmark: 4481.367000.

001.53 651.8   US   ISSN 0020-0042
TK7882.I6   CODEN: INFDAB
INFORMATION DISPLAY. 1963. m. $36 (foreign $72). (Society for Information Display) Palisades Institute for Research Services, Attn.: Jay Morreale, 201 Varick St., 11th Fl., New York, NY 10014. Ed. Joseph A. MacDonald. adv.; bk.rev.; charts; illus.; tr.lit.; circ. 10,000. (reprint service avail. UMI) **Indexed:** Comput.Cont., Sci.Abstr.
Formerly: S I D Journal.

025 380.3   UK   ISSN 0961-7612
CODEN: IMRPE2
INFORMATION MANAGEMENT REPORT. 1991. m. £182 (effective 1992). Elsevier Science Publishers Ltd., Crown House, Linton Rd., Barking, Essex IG11 8JU, England. TEL 081-594-7272. FAX 081-594-5942. TELEX 896950 APPSCI G. (Subscr. in U.S. and Canada to: Elsevier Science Publishing Co., Inc., Box 882, Madison Sq. Sta., New York, NY 10159. TEL 212-989-5800) Eds. R. Prytherch, J. Meyer. bk.rev.; charts; illus.; stat. (back issues avail.) **Indexed:** Comput.Lit.Ind., LISA, Print.Abstr., PROMT.
●Also available online. Vendor(s): Data-Star (PTBN), DIALOG (File no.636).
—BLDSC shelfmark: 4493.687155.
Incoporates (1979-1991): Outlook on Research Libraries (ISSN 0165-2818); (1979-1991); Advanced Information Report (ISSN 0953-8712); Which was formerly: Communication Technology Impact (ISSN 0142-5854)
Description: Provides comprehensive coverage of new developments in the information world, with analysis of the implications of new technology, and other news for information professionals and librarians.

INFORMATION PROCESSING ASSOCIATION OF ISRAEL. NATIONAL CONFERENCE ON DATA PROCESSING. PROCEEDINGS. see *COMPUTERS — Information Science And Information Theory*

LIBRARY AND INFORMATION SCIENCES — COMPUTER APPLICATIONS

029 US
INFORMATION RETRIEVAL & LIBRARY AUTOMATION. 1965. m. $66 (foreign $79.50). Lomond Publications, Inc., Box 88, Mt. Airy, MD 21771. TEL 301-829-1496. Ed. Susan W. Johnson. bk.rev.; index; circ. 1,160. (also avail. in microfiche from UMI; back issues avail.; reprint service avail. from UMI) **Indexed:** Bk.Rev.Ind. (1981-), Child.Bk.Rev.Ind. (1981-), Comput.Cont., Comput.Lit.Ind., Graph.Arts Lit.Abstr., Intl.Civil Eng.Abstr., Leg.Info.Manage.Ind., Pers.Lit., Soft.Abstr.Eng.
  Former titles: Information Retrieval and Library Automation Newsletter (ISSN 0020-0220); Information Retrieval Letter.
  Description: News, articles, and announcements on new techniques, equipment, and software in information services for both the public and private sectors.

INFORMATION SEARCHER. see EDUCATION — Computer Applications

INFORMATION SOCIETY; an international journal. see COMPUTERS — Information Science And Information Theory

029 001.6 US ISSN 0306-4379
QA76.9.D3 CODEN: INSYD6
INFORMATION SYSTEMS (TARRYTOWN); data base: their creation, management and utilization. 1975. 6/yr. £285 (effective 1992). Pergamon Press, Inc., Journals Division, 660 WHite Plains Rd., Tarrytown, NY 10591-5153. TEL 914-524-9200. FAX 914-333-2444. (And: Headington Hill Hall, Oxford OX3 0BW, England. TEL 0865-794141) Ed. Hans Jochen Schneider. adv.; bk.rev.; circ. 1,200. (also avail. in microform from MIM,UMI; reprint service avail. from UMI) **Indexed:** Biol.Abstr., Compumath, Comput.Cont., Comput.Lit.Ind., Comput.Rev., Curr.Cont., Excerp.Med., Sci.Abstr.
  —BLDSC shelfmark: 4496.367300.
  Refereed Serial

029.7 US ISSN 0730-9295
Z678.9.A1 CODEN: ITLBDC
INFORMATION TECHNOLOGY AND LIBRARIES. 1968. q. $45 (foreign $50). (Library and Information Technology Association) American Library Association, 50 E. Huron St, Chicago, IL 60611-2795. TEL 312-944-6780. FAX 312-440-9374. Ed. Thomas W. Leonhardt. adv.; bk.rev.; charts; illus.; index; circ. 6,800. (also avail. in microform from UMI; back issues avail.; reprint service avail. from UMI) **Indexed:** A.I.Abstr., ABI Inform., Bus.Ind., C.I.J.E., Chem.Abstr., Compumath, Comput.Cont., Comput.Lit.Ind., Comput.Rev., Curr.Cont., Educ.Ind., Inform.Sci.Abstr., Leg.Info.Manage.Ind., LHTN, Lib.Lit., LISA, Mag.Ind., Pers.Lit., PMR, Ref.Sour., Ref.Zh., Sci.Abstr., Soft.Abstr.Eng., Tr.& Indus.Ind.
  —BLDSC shelfmark: 4496.368710.
  Formerly (until 1982): Journal of Library Automation (ISSN 0022-2240)
  Description: Articles on library automation, communication technology, cable systems, computerized information processing and video technologies.
  Refereed Serial

025 US ISSN 0959-3845
INFORMATION TECHNOLOGY AND PEOPLE. 1982-1989; resumed 1992. q. $135 (foreign $155)(effective 1992). Box 500, 19363 Willamette Dr., W. Linn, OR 97068. TEL 503-656-7108. Ed. Eleanor H. Wynn. adv. **Indexed:** Account.& Data Proc.Abstr., BPIA, Comput.Cont., Cont.Pg.Manage., Mgmt.& Market.Abstr., Sci.Abstr.
  Former titles (until vol.6, no.1, 1992): Technology and People (ISSN 0956-5388); Office - Technology and People (ISSN 0167-5710)
  Description: Provides interdisciplinary international coverage of social and organizational issues in the design and use of information technology. For academics and practitioners in the fields of information system management and computer systems design and management.

001.6 301.16 070.5
340 US
INFORMATION TIMES. 1974. q. membership. Information Industry Association, 555 New Jersey Ave., N.W., Ste. 800, Washington, DC 20001. TEL 202-639-8262. Ed. Kevin A. Siegel. adv.; bibl.; illus. **Indexed:** Comput.Lit.Ind., PROMT, Tel.Abstr., Telegen.
  Former titles: New Information Times (ISSN 8756-0941); Information Times (ISSN 0095-8131)

001.6 621.3 US ISSN 8755-6286
INFORMATION TODAY; the newspaper for users and producers of electronic information services. 1983. 11/yr. $39.95. Learned Information, Inc., 143 Old Marlton Pike, Medford, NJ 08055. TEL 609-654-6266. FAX 609-654-4309. Ed. Patricia Lane. bk.rev. (also avail. in microform from UMI) **Indexed:** ABI Inform., CAD CAM Abstr., Comput.Bus., Leg.Info.Manage.Ind., Microcomp.Ind., PCR2, PROMT, PSI, Tr.& Indus.Ind.
  ●Also available online. Vendor(s): Mead Data Central.
  Description: Geared toward users and producers of electronic information services. Offers articles and news about the industry, calendar of events and product information.

025 US
INTEGRATED ONLINE LIBRARY SYSTEMS. MEETING PROCEEDINGS. 1983. a. $30. Learned Information, Inc., 143 Old Marlton Pike, Medford, NJ 08055-8750. TEL 609-654-4888. FAX 609-654-4309. Ed. David C. Genaway.

020 070.5 US ISSN 0958-9961
Z265 CODEN: IMOTEX
INTERNATIONAL JOURNAL OF MICROGRAPHICS & OPTICAL TECHNOLOGY; including all aspects of electronic information transfer. 1982. q. £110 (effective 1992). Pergamon Press, Inc., Journals Division, 660 White Plains Rd., Tarrytown, NY 10591-5153. TEL 914-524-9200. FAX 914-333-2444. (And: Headington Hill Hall, Oxford OX3 0BW, England. TEL 0865-794141) Ed. Don M. Avedon. adv.; circ. 1,000. (also avail. in microform from MIM,UMI; reprint service avail. from UMI) **Indexed:** Account.& Data Proc.Abstr., Br.Archaeol.Abstr., Comput.Cont., Deep Sea Res.& Oceanogr.Abstr., Leg.Info.Manage.Ind., Sci.Abstr.
  —BLDSC shelfmark: 4542.354300.
  Formerly: International Journal of Micrographics and Video Technology (ISSN 0743-9636); Incorporates: Microdoc; Which was formerly (until 1982): Micropublishing of Current Periodicals (ISSN 0364-3999)
  Refereed Serial

INTERNATIONAL YEARBOOK OF SERIALS LIBRARIANSHIP. see LIBRARY AND INFORMATION SCIENCES

JOURNAL OF INFORMATION SCIENCE; principles and practice. see LIBRARY AND INFORMATION SCIENCES

025 US ISSN 0739-9014
T58.6 CODEN: JISMEF
JOURNAL OF INFORMATION SYSTEMS MANAGEMENT. 1983. q. $98. Auerbach Publishers (Subsidiary of: Warren, Gorham & Lamont), One Penn Plaza, New York, NY 10119. TEL 212-971-5000. FAX 617-423-2026. (Subscr. to: 210 South St., Boston, MA 02111-9990. TEL 800-950-1218) Ed. Robert E. Umbaugh. circ. 5,155. (reprint service avail. from SCH) **Indexed:** ABI Inform., Account.Ind. (1984-), B.P.I., Comput.Lit.Ind., Cont.Pg.Manage., Mgmt.& Market.Abstr.
  Description: Provides MIS and DP managers with information in the following areas: consultants' experiences, corporate issues, data center operations, data communications, data management, economic and financial issues, end-user computing.

029.7 US ISSN 0196-1799
Z678.9.A1
LITA NEWSLETTER. 1980. q. $25 to non-members (foreign $40). (Library and Information Technology Association) American Library Association, 50 E. Huron St., Chicago, IL 60611-2795. TEL 312-280-4270. FAX 312-280-3257. Ed. Walt Crawford. illus.; circ. 5,000. (back issues avail.)

025 US ISSN 1059-3195
▼**LETTER TO LIBRARIES ONLINE.** Short title: L T L O. 1991. 12/yr. free. Oregon State Library, Salem, OR 97310-0640. TEL 503-378-2112. FAX 503-588-7119. circ. 1,000.
  ●Available only online.
  Description: Provides information on the State Library and statewide library issues and activities.

025 621.381 US
LIBRARY COMPUTER SYSTEMS & EQUIPMENT REVIEW. 1979. s-a. $225 to individuals; institutional price varies. Meckler Publishing Corporation, 11 Ferry Lane W., Westport, CT 06880-5808. TEL 203-226-6967. Ed. William Saffady. **Indexed:** Comput.Cont., Consum.Ind., Intl.Civil Eng.Abstr., Leg.Info.Manage.Ind., Lib.Lit., Sci.Abstr, Soft.Abstr.Eng.
  Former titles: Computer Equipment Review (ISSN 0278-260X); Library Computer Equipment Review (ISSN 0191-1295)
  Description: Features articles on automated systems for office applications. Each issue focuses on a specific topic.

025 US ISSN 1040-4333
Z666
LIBRARY HI TECH BIBLIOGRAPHY. 1986. a. $45. Pierian Press, Box 1808, Ann Arbor, MI 48106. TEL 313-434-5530. FAX 313-434-6409.
  —BLDSC shelfmark: 5198.880000.

025 US ISSN 0737-8831
Z671
LIBRARY HI TECH JOURNAL. 1983. q. $40 to individuals; institutions $65. Pierian Press, Box 1808, Ann Arbor, MI 48106. TEL 313-434-5530. FAX 313-434-6409. Ed. C. Edward Wall. adv.; bk.rev.; circ. 5,000. (also avail. in microform from UMI; back issues avail.) **Indexed:** Bibl.Ind., Bk.Rev.Ind. (1984-), Bus.Educ.Ind., C.I.J.E., Child.Bk.Rev.Ind. (1984-), Comput.Cont., Comput.Lit.Ind., Consum.Ind., Int.Lab.Doc., Leg.Info.Manage.Ind., LHTN, Lib.Lit., LISA, Microcomp.Ind., Pers.Lit., Ref.Zh.
  —BLDSC shelfmark: 5198.870000.
  Description: A comprehensive guide to forthcoming and available technologies applicable to libraries and information centers. Concentrates on reporting on the selection, installation, maintenance and integration of systems and hardware.
  Refereed Serial

025 US ISSN 0741-9058
Z678.9.A1
LIBRARY HI TECH NEWS. 1984. 10/yr. $70 to individuals; institutions $95. Pierian Press, Box 1808, Ann Arbor, MI 48106. TEL 313-434-5530. FAX 313-434-6409. Ed. C. Edward Wall. adv.; circ. 5,000. **Indexed:** Bk.Rev.Ind. (1984-), Child.Bk.Rev.Ind. (1984-), Comput.Dtbs., Comput.Lit.Ind., LHTN.
  —BLDSC shelfmark: 5198.875000.
  Description: News about all aspects of technology related to library operations for professionals in the information management-sciences field.

020 029 II ISSN 0024-2543
Z671 CODEN: LSSDA8
LIBRARY SCIENCE WITH A SLANT TO DOCUMENTATION AND INFORMATION STUDIES. (Text in English) 1964. q. Rs.400($75) Sarada Ranganathan Endowment for Library Science, Bangalore, 432, 10th Cross, 18th Main Rd., Second Phase, J.P. Nagar, Bangalore 560 078, India. Ed. A. Neelameghan. bk.rev.; charts; illus.; index; circ. 500. **Indexed:** Chem.Abstr., Comput.Cont., Curr.Cont., Inform.Sci.Abstr., Lib.Lit., Lib.Sci.Abstr.
  Formerly (until 1988): Library Science with a Slant to Documentation.

LIBRARY SOFTWARE REVIEW. see COMPUTERS — Software

020 US ISSN 0277-0288
LIBRARY SYSTEMS NEWSLETTER. 1981. m. $40 (foreign $50). American Library Association, Library Technology Reports, 50 E. Huron St., Chicago, IL 60611-2795. TEL 312-944-6780. FAX 312-440-9374. Ed. Howard S. White. circ. 1,500. (tabloid format; back issues avail.) **Indexed:** Leg.Info.Manage.Ind., LHTN.
  —BLDSC shelfmark: 5205.660000.
  Description: Features articles and news briefs covering all aspects of library automation and the application of information technologies in libraries.

025 621.381 UK ISSN 0964-7627
LIBRARY TECHNOLOGY NEWS. 1984. 5/yr. £25 (foreign £35). Library Information Technology Centre, South Bank Techno Park, 90 London Rd., London SE1 6LN, England. TEL 071-334-3260. FAX 071-261-1865. Ed. Caroline Moore. circ. 500. **Indexed:** Sci.Abstr.
Formerly (until 1991): Library Micromation News (ISSN 0262-7841)
Description: News of library automaiton developments in Europe.

621.381 US
MICROCOMPUTERS FOR INFORMATION MANAGEMENT; an international journal for library and information services. 1984. q. $39.50 to individuals; institutions $90. Ablex Publishing Corporation, 355 Chestnut St., Norwood, NJ 07648. TEL 201-767-8450. FAX 201-767-6717. TELEX 135-393. Ed. Ching-chih Chen. adv.; abstr.; bibl.; illus.; circ. 850. (back issues avail.; reprint service avail.) **Indexed:** C.I.J.E., Curr.Cont., ERIC, Lib.Lit., LISA, Microcomp.Ind., Sci.Abstr.
Description: For librarians and information specialists. Features articles on the applications of microcomputers in information processing, organization and dissemination as well as information on microcomputer hardware and software.

025 US ISSN 0743-0302
MICROCOMPUTERS FOR LIBRARIES; product review and procurement guide. 1984. irreg. (base vol. plus q. updates). $115 (renewal $60). James E. Rush Associates, Inc., 673 Old Eagle School Rd., Wayne, PA 19087-2042. TEL 215-386-4214. Ed. James E. Rush. adv.; bibl.; circ. 500.
Description: Information on hardware and software for libraries and information service applications.

500 GW ISSN 0172-732X
O L B G - INFO; Mitteilungsblatt der Online-Benutzergruppe in der D G D. irreg. (approx. 4/yr.). DM.60 to non-members. Deutsche Gesellschaft fuer Dokumentation e.V., Hanauerlandstr. 126-128, 6000 Frankfurt, Germany. TEL 069-740805. (back issues avail.)
Formerly: Online Info.
Description: News on all areas of available online information, including new technologies in the field of information and documentation, calendar of events, and seminars.

025 US
Z678.9.A1 CODEN: IIOMEI
ONLINE LIBRARIES AND MICROCOMPUTERS. 1983. 10/yr. $43.75 to individuals; institutions $62.50; students $25 (combined rates avail.). Information Intelligence, Inc., Box 31098, Phoenix, AZ 85046. TEL 800-228-9982. Ed. George S. Machovec. bk.rev.; index. (looseleaf format; back issues avail.) **Indexed:** LISA, Microcomp.Ind., Ref.Zh.
● Also available online. Vendor(s): Data-Star, DIALOG, NewsNet.
Also available on CD-ROM.
Formerly: Information Intelligence Online Libraries and Microcomputers (ISSN 0737-7770)
Description: Aimed at library and information center developments and applications throughout North America. Features articles covering new online library and automation applications using a wide variety of microcomputers and software.

025 CN ISSN 0827-4932
ONLINE - ONWARD. 1978. irreg. (approx. 8/yr.). Can.$20. Vacouver Online Users Group, P.O. Box 798, Station "A", Vancouver, B.C. V6C 2N6, Canada. circ. 100.
Description: Events and information of interest to local librarians and others who work with computerized information retrieval and database management systems.

025 US
ORBIT SEARCHLIGHT. 1978. m. free. Maxwell Online, Inc., 8000 Westpark Dr., McLean, VA 22102. TEL 703-442-0900. FAX 703-893-4632. Ed. Wayne Jackson. adv.; index; circ. 11,000. (back issues avail.)
Description: To acquaint Orbit Search Service users with new databases available, changes in current database files, price changes, online information searching, tips, techniques and announcements.

025 US ISSN 0278-9469
PALINET NEWS. 1974. m. $25 to non-members. PaLiNet, 3401 Market St., Ste. 262, Philadelphia, PA 19104. TEL 215-382-7031. FAX 215-382-0022. Ed. Jean M. Dorrian. circ. 1,200. (back issues avail.)
Description: Contains information about services, training programs, workshops and products available through the Network. Focuses on library technology and its applications.

025 029 FR ISSN 0992-5996
PLAN DE CLASSEMENT P A S C A L. (Programme Applique a la Selection et la Compilation Automatique de la Literature) a. free. Centre National de la Recherche Scientifique, Institut de l'Information Scientifique et Technique, B.P. 54, 54514 Vandoeuvre-Les-Nancy Cedex, France. (also avail. in magnetic tape)

PLUS; plus system newsletter. see PUBLISHING AND BOOK TRADE — Computer Applications

020 029 UK ISSN 0033-0337
Z678.9.A1 CODEN: PRGRDU
PROGRAM; automated library and information systems. 1966. q. £95($190) to non-members; members £75. Aslib, Association for Information Management, Publications Department, Information House, 20-24 Old St., London EC1V 9AP, England. TEL 071-253-4488. FAX 071-430-0514. (Dist. in N. America by: Learned Information, Inc., 143 Old Marlton Pike, Medford, NJ 08055-8750. TEL 609-654-6266) Ed. Lucy Tedd. adv.; bk.rev.; index; circ. 1,000. **Indexed:** Account.& Data Proc.Abstr., Anbar, Comput.Abstr., Comput.Cont., Curr.Cont., Fluidex, Intl.Civil Eng.Abstr., Lib.Lit., Sci.Abstr., Soft.Abstr.Eng.
—BLDSC shelfmark: 6864.320000.
Description: Computer applications to library and information services.

026 621.381 US ISSN 0273-2351
Z674.82.015
RESEARCH LIBRARIES IN O C L C: A QUARTERLY. 1981. q. free to qualified personnel. Online Computer Library Center, Inc., 6565 Frantz Rd., Dublin, OH 43017-0702. TEL 614-764-6144. Ed. Philip Schieber. circ. 6,700. (back issues avail.)
—BLDSC shelfmark: 7741.857000.

025 US ISSN 0193-273X
S O L I N E W S. 1973. q. free. Southeastern Library Network, Inc., 1438 W. Peachtree St., N.W., Atlanta, GA 30309-2955. TEL 404-892-0943. FAX 404-892-7879. Ed.Bd. circ. 1,500. (back issues avail.)

651.8 001.53 US
SOCIETY FOR INFORMATION DISPLAY. SEMINAR LECTURE NOTES. a. $50 (foreign $55). (Society for Information Display) Palisades Institute for Research Services, Attn: Jay Morreale, 201 Varick St., 11th Fl., New York, NY 10014. TEL 213-305-1502.

020 001.6 US ISSN 0273-9399
SPECIALIST. 1978. m. $95 (foreign $100) (includes Special Libraries). Special Libraries Association, 1700 Eighteenth St., N.W., Washington, DC 20009. TEL 202-234-4700. Ed. Maria Barry. adv.; bk.rev.; circ. 16,000. (looseleaf format; back issues avail.; reprint service avail. from UMI) **Indexed:** Fluidex, PROMT.
—BLDSC shelfmark: 8404.764000.
Description: Examines current activities in the area of computer applications in the library and information sciences.

025 US
STATE DATA AND DATABASE FINDER. 1989. a. $145 (diskette $345). Information U S A, Inc., Box E, Kensington, MD 20895-0418. TEL 301-942-6303. FAX 301-929-8907. Ed. Andrew Naprawa.
Description: Identifies databases and data sources which are maintained by state governments. Provides data on general business management, as well as data on specific vertical markets.

TRENDS IN THE LAW LIBRARY MANAGEMENT AND TECHNOLOGY. see LAW — Computer Applications

LINGUISTICS 2799

025 UK ISSN 0305-5728
CODEN: VINEDT
VINE. 1971. 4/yr. £50 (foreign £60). Library Information Technology Centre, South Bank Techno Park, 90 London Rd., London SE1 6LNN, England. TEL 071-334-3260. FAX 071-261-1865. circ. 800.
—BLDSC shelfmark: 9236.855000.
Description: Covers the application of technology in libraries with special emphasis on management systems.

025 US ISSN 0884-593X
WIRED LIBRARIAN'S NEWSLETTER. 1983. irreg. (approx. m.). $15. c/o Eric Anderson, Ed., 292 Hammertown Rd., Jackson, OH 45640-2058. bk.rev.; software rev.; circ. 800.

LINGUISTICS

see also Classical Studies; Oriental Studies

410 US
A A A LETTER. 1979. 3/yr. membership. American Association for Applied Linguistics, Box 24083, Oklahoma City, OK 73124. TEL 405-843-5113. Ed. Donna Christian. bk.rev.; circ. 600. (back issues avail.)
Description: Presents research in applied linguistics. Includes information on annual meetings and conferences.

A A T A NEWSLETTER. (American Association of Teachers of Arabic (Provo)) see EDUCATION — Teaching Methods And Curriculum

440 375.4 US
A A T F NATIONAL BULLETIN. (Text in English, French) 1975. q. membership. American Association of Teachers of French, c/o Fred M. Jenkins, Exec. Dir., University of Illinois, 57 E. Armory Ave., Champaign, IL 61820. TEL 217-333-2842. Ed. Jane B. Goepper. bk.rev.; bibl.; illus.; stat.; tr.lit.; circ. 11,200. (back issues avail.)
Description: Newsletter for U.S. teachers and professors of French; calendar of forthcoming meetings.

430.07 370 US ISSN 0001-0243
A A T G NEWSLETTER. 1970. 4/yr. $10 to non-members. American Association of Teachers of German, Inc., 112 Haddontowne Ct., Ste. 104, Cherry Hill, NJ 08034. TEL 609-795-5553. FAX 609-795-9398. Ed. Helene Zimmer-Loew. circ. 7,500.
Description: Includes announcements and articles of current interest to members.

491 370 US ISSN 0001-0251
A A T S E E L NEWSLETTER. (Text in English and Russian) 1958. 6/yr. $15 to non-members. American Association of Teachers of Slavic and East European Languages, c/o Prof. George Gutsche, Russian - Modern Languages 340, University of Arizona, Tucson, AZ 85721. TEL 602-621-1615. adv.; bk.rev.; abstr.; bibl.; illus.; circ. 2,000. (also avail. in microfilm from UMI)

407 US ISSN 0148-7639
P57.U7
A D F L BULLETIN. 1969. 3/yr. $15 to individuals; libraries $30. Association of Departments of Foreign Languages, 10 Astor Pl., New York, NY 10003. TEL 212-614-6319. FAX 212-477-9863. (Affiliate: Modern Language Association) adv.; bk.rev.; bibl.; tr.lit.; circ. 1,700. (also avail. in microfilm from UMI; microfiche from EDR; reprint service avail. from UMI) **Indexed:** C.I.J.E., ERIC, M.L.A., PSI.
—BLDSC shelfmark: 0680.470000.
Formerly: Association of Departments of Foreign Languages. Bulletin (ISSN 0148-8066)

410 FI ISSN 0356-8156
A FIN L A YEARBOOK. (Text in English) 1977. a. FIM 75. Association Finlandaise de Linguistique Appliquee, Department of Linguistics, University of Jyvaeskylae, SF-40100 Jyvaeskylae, Finland. TEL 931-156-856. circ. 600.

418 IT ISSN 0044-9490
A I L A BULLETIN. (Text in English, French, German, Spanish) 1970. q. membership. Association Internationale de Linguistique Appliquee, 27 via Cuppari, I-56100 Pisa, Italy. Ed. Antonio Zampolli. adv. **Indexed:** Lang.Teach.& Ling.Abstr.

2800 LINGUISTICS

418.02 US
A L T A NEWSLETTER. 1979. irreg. (3-4/yr.). $30 includes membership. American Literary Translators Association, University of Texas at Dallas, Box 830688, Richardson, TX 75083-0688. TEL 214-690-2093. Ed. Elizabeth Gamble Miller. circ. 1,000.

400 US
A N S BULLETIN. 1954. irreg. (2-3/yr.). American Name Society, c/o Wayne H. Finke, Ed., Department of Modern Languages, Baruch College, Box 340, 17 Lexington Ave., New York, NY 10010. (Alt. addr.: c/o Thomas J. Gasque, Department of English, University of South Dakota, Vermillion, SD 57069) circ. 950.

410 DK ISSN 0106-441X
A R K; sproginstitutternes arbejdspapirer. vol.9, 1981. irreg. Handelshoejskolen i Koebenhavn, Erhvervssproglige Fakultet, Dalgas Have 15, DK-2000 Copenhagen F, Denmark. Ed. Lita Lundquist. circ. 200.
   Description: Contains articles on language use in business as well as general linguistics.

418.02 US
A T A CHRONICLE. 1972. m. $35. American Translators Association, 109 Croton Ave., Ossining, NY 10562. TEL 914-941-1500. FAX 914-941-1330. Ed. Jane Morgan Zorrilla. adv.; bk.rev.; circ. 3,600.
   Description: Contains association news, short articles of interest to linguists, and dictionary reviews.

410 800 AT
A U L L A; journal of literary criticism, philology & linguistics. (Text in English, French and German) 1951. s-a. Aus.$18($16) Australian Universities Language and Literature Association, University of Sydney, Dept. of French, Sydney, NSW 2006, Australia. Ed. J. Hay. adv.; bk.rev.; cum.index; circ. 950. (back issues avail.)

410 DK ISSN 0902-9958
AALBORG UNIVERSITETSCENTER. INSTITUT FOR SPROG OG INTERNATIONALE KULTURSTUDIER. ARBEIJDSPAPIRER. English edition: Aalborg University. Papers on Language and Intercultural Studies (ISSN 0903-8892); German edition: Universitaet Aalborg. Arbeitspapiere des Instituts fuer Sprache und Interkulturelle Studien. 1987. irreg. $7 per no. Aalborg University, Department of Languages and Cultural Studies, P.O. Box 159, DK-9100 Aalborg, Denmark. TEL 45-98158522. FAX 45-98157303.
   Formerly (until 1985): Serie om Fremmedsprog (ISSN 0106-1992)

460 DK ISSN 0107-6531
CB226
AARHUS UNIVERSITET. ROMANSK INSTITUT. SPANSK AFDELINGEN. INFORMATION. 1975. irreg., no.36, 1983. DKK 15 per no. Aarhus University, 8000 Aarhus C, Denmark. TEL 06-19-70-33. illus.

800 AG ISSN 0001-3757
AS78
ACADEMIA ARGENTINA DE LETRAS. BOLETIN. 1932. 2/yr. Arg.$20($25) Academia Argentina de Letras, Sanchez de Bustamante 2663, Buenos Aires 1425, Argentina. **Indexed:** Amer.Hist.& Life, Hist.Abstr.

460 BO
ACADEMIA BOLIVIANA DE LA LENGUA. ANALES. 1985. a. Academia Boliviana de la Lengua, Casilla de Correos 4154, La Paz, Bolivia. Dir. Carlos Castanon Barrientos. bk.rev.; circ. 400.

400 CK ISSN 0001-3773
AS82
ACADEMIA COLOMBIANA. BOLETIN. 1936; N.S. 1956. q. $20. Academia Colombiana de la Lengua, Carrera 3-A, Numero 17-34, Bogota, Colombia. Ed. Manuel Jose Forero. bk.rev.; bibl.; index, cum.index; circ. 1,000. **Indexed:** Amer.Hist.& Life, Hist.Abstr., Lang.& Lang.Behav.Abstr., M.L.A.

400 060 HO ISSN 0065-0471
AS64.A3
ACADEMIA HONDURENA DE LA LENGUA. BOLETIN. 1957. a. $10. Academia Hondurena de la Lengua, Apdo. Postal 38, Tegucigalpa, Honduras. Ed. Jorge Fidel Duron. bk.rev.; circ. 500. (back issues avail.)

ACADEMIA PAULISTA DE LETRAS. REVISTA. see *LITERATURE*

ACADEMIA SCIENTIARUM HUNGARICA. ACTA ANTIQUA. see *CLASSICAL STUDIES*

410 HU ISSN 0001-5946
P25
ACADEMIA SCIENTIARUM HUNGARICA. ACTA LINGUISTICA. (Text in English, French, German, Russian) 1951. q. $62. (Magyar Tudomanyos Akademia) Akademiai Kiado, Publishing House of the Hungarian Academy of Sciences, P.O. Box 24, H-1363 Budapest, Hungary. Eds. J. Herman, F. Kiefer. adv.; bk.rev.; charts; illus.; index. **Indexed:** Arts & Hum.Cit.Ind., Curr.Cont., Lang.& Lang.Behav.Abstr. (1972-), Lang.Teach.& Ling.Abstr., M.L.A.
   —BLDSC shelfmark: 0629.400000.

ACADEMIA SINICA. INSTITUTE OF HISTORY AND PHILOLOGY. BULLETIN. see *HISTORY — History Of Asia*

460 375.4 VE
ACADEMIA VENEZOLANA DE LA LENGUA. CORRESPONDIENTE DE LA ESPANOLA. BOLETIN. * vol. 39, 1971. s-a. Academia Venezolana de la Lengua, Bolsa a San Francisco, Caracas 1010, Venezuela. Ed.Bd. adv.; bk.rev.; bibl. **Indexed:** Amer.Hist.& Life, Hist.Abstr.

400 840 FR ISSN 0065-0544
ACADEMIE DES INSCRIPTIONS ET BELLES-LETTRES. ETUDES ET COMMENTAIRES. 1946. irreg. price varies. Editions Klincksieck, 11 rue de Lille, 75007 Paris, France. (also avail. in microfiche)

840 BE ISSN 0567-6584
ACADEMIE ROYALE DE LANGUE ET DE LITTERATURE FRANCAISES. ANNUAIRES. a. price changes. Academie Royale de Langue et de Litterature Francaises, Palais des Academies, 1 rue Ducale, Brussels, Belgium. Ed. Thomas Owen. bibl.

440 840 BE
ACADEMIE ROYALE DE LANGUE ET DE LITTERATURE FRANCAISES. BULLETIN. 1922. 3/yr. Academie Royale de Langue et de Litterature Francaises, Palais des Academies, 1 rue Ducale, Brussels, Belgium. Ed. Thomas Owen. **Indexed:** M.L.A.

492.4 IS ISSN 0065-0692
ACADEMY OF THE HEBREW LANGUAGE. SPECIALIZED DICTIONARIES. irreg. Academy of the Hebrew Language, P.O. Box 3449, 91034 Jerusalem, Israel.

492.4 IS
ACADEMY OF THE HEBREW LANGUAGE. TEXTS & STUDIES. irreg. Academy of the Hebrew Language, P.O. Box 3449, Jerusalem 91034, Israel.
   Formerly: Academy of the Hebrew Language. Linguistic Studies (ISSN 0075-9643)

423.1 US ISSN 0270-4404
P365
ACRONYMS, INITIALISMS AND ABBREVIATIONS DICTIONARY; a guide to alphabetic designations, contractions, acronyms, initialisms, and similar condensed appellations. 1960. a. $225. Gale Research Inc., 835 Penobscot Bldg., Detroit, MI 48226. TEL 800-877-4253. FAX 313-961-6083. TELEX 810-221-7086. Ed. Jennifer Mossman.
   —BLDSC shelfmark: 0578.886800.
   Formerly (until 1976): Acronyms and Initialisms Dictionary (ISSN 0065-0889)
   Description: Over 520,000 acronyms, initialisms and abbreviations, and the words and phrases they represent.

480 BE
ACTA COLLOQUII DIDACTICI CLASSICI; didactica classica gandensia. (Text in Dutch, English, French, German and Latin) 1963. a. 350 BEF. International Bureau for the Study of the Problems in the Teaching of Greek and Latin, Blandijnberg 2, B-9000 Ghent, Belgium. Eds. J. Veremans, F. Decreus.

430 GW ISSN 0065-1273
PF3010
ACTA GERMANICA. (Text in English, French and German) 1966. a. DM.42. (Suedafrikanischer Germanistenverband, SA - Association for German Studies in Southern Africa) Verlag Peter Lang GmbH, Eschborner Landstr. 42-50, 6000 Frankfurt a.M. 90, Germany. FAX 069-785893. Ed. Walter Koeppe. bk.rev.; circ. 400. (back issues avail.) **Indexed:** M.L.A.

410 DK ISSN 0374-0463
P2
ACTA LINGUISTICA HAFNIENSIA; international journal of general linguistics. (Text in English, French or German) 1939. irreg., vol.19, no.1-2, 1985. DKK 250. (Institute of Linguistics) C A Reitzel A-S, Noerregade 20, 1165 Copenhagen K, Denmark. Ed.Bd. bk.rev.; bibl.; circ. 600. (reprint service avail. from ISI) **Indexed:** Curr.Cont., Lang.& Lang.Behav.Abstr. (1973-), M.L.A., Mid.East: Abstr.& Ind.
   —BLDSC shelfmark: 0629.420000.
   Formerly: Acta Linguistica (ISSN 0105-001X)

057 XV ISSN 0567-784X
PN1
ACTA NEOPHILOLOGICA. (Text in various languages) 1968. a. $6. Univerza v Ljubljani, Filozofska Fakulteta, Askerceva 12, 61000 Ljubljana, Slovenia. TEL 061-150-001. FAX 061-159-337. Ed. Janez Stanonik. bk.rev.; bibl.; circ. 400. **Indexed:** M.L.A.

459 IT ISSN 0065-1516
ACTA PHILOLOGICA. (Contributions in English, French, German, Italian, Rumanian and Spanish) 1958. irreg. price varies. Societa Accademica Romena, Foro Traiano 1a, 00187 Rome, Italy.

410 PL ISSN 0065-1524
ACTA PHILOLOGICA. (Text in English, French, German and Polish) 1968. irreg., vol.17, 1989. price varies. (Uniwersytet Warszawski, Wydzial Neofilologii) Wydawnictwa Uniwersytetu Warszawskiego, Ul. Obozna 8, 00-032 Warsaw, Poland. (Dist. by: Ars Polona-Ruch, Krakowskie Przedmiescie 7, 00-068 Warsaw, Poland) Eds. J. Reychman, Witold Tyloch. circ. 400.

489 AU ISSN 0065-1532
ACTA PHILOLOGICA AENIPONTANA. 1962. irreg., vol.5, 1987. price varies. (Gesellschaft fuer Klassische Philologie in Innsbruck) Universitaetsverlag Wagner, Andreas-Hofer-Str. 13, Postfach 165, A-6010 Innsbruck, Austria. FAX 0512-582209. Ed. Robert Muth. circ. 600.

ACTA REGIAE SOCIETATITIS HUMANIORUM LITTERATUM LUNDENSIS. see *ARCHAEOLOGY*

440 840 HU ISSN 0567-8099
ACTA UNIVERSITATIS DE ATTILA JOZSEF NOMINATAE. ACTA ROMANICA. (Text in French and Italian) 1964; N.S. 1972. a. exchange basis. Attila Jozsef University, c/o E. Szabo, Exchange Librarian, Dugonics ter 13, P.O.B. 393, Szeged H-6701, Hungary. (Subscr. to: Kultura, P.O. Box 149, H-1389 Budapest, Hungary) Ed. Bd. circ. 250.
   Description: Journal of French and Italian studies focusing on language, literature and the history of civilization.

420 810 820 HU ISSN 0230-2780
PE9
ACTA UNIVERSITATIS DE ATTILA JOZSEF NOMINATAE. PAPERS IN ENGLISH AND AMERICAN STUDIES. (Text in English) 1980. irreg. exchange basis. Attila Jozsef University, c/o E. Szabo, Exchange Librarian, Dugonics ter 13, P.O.B. 393, Szeged H-6701, Hungary. (Subscr. to: Kultura, Box 149, H-1389 Budapest, Hungary) Ed. B. Rozsnyai. circ. 400. **Indexed:** M.L.A.
   Description: English and American studies with special attention paid to literary studies, generative grammar and teaching English as a foreign language.

410 370 PL ISSN 0208-6077
P1.A1
ACTA UNIVERSITATIS LODZIENSIS: FOLIA LINGUISTICA. (Text in Polish; summaries in various languages) 1955-1974; N.S. 1981. irreg. Wydawnictwo Uniwersytetu Lodzkiego, Ul. Jaracza 34, Lodz, Poland. (Dist. by: Ars Polona-Ruch, Krakowskie Przedmiescie 7, Warsaw, Poland)
   —BLDSC shelfmark: 0585.207350.
   Supersedes in part: Uniwersytet Lodzki. Zeszyty Naukowe. Seria 1: Nauki Humanistyczno-Spoleczne (ISSN 0076-0358)
   Description: Devoted to linguistics, mainly Polish, but also English, German, French and Russian.

430   PL   ISSN 0208-5259
ACTA UNIVERSITATIS NICOLAI COPERNICI. FILOLOGIA GERMANSKA. 1974. irreg. price varies. Uniwersytet Mikolaja Kopernika, Fosa Staromiejska 3, Torun, Poland. (Dist. by: Osrodek Rozpowszechniania Wydawnictw Naukowych PAN, Palac Kultury i Nauki, 00-901 Warsaw, Poland)

491.85   PL   ISSN 0208-5321
PG6014
ACTA UNIVERSITATIS NICOLAI COPERNICI. FILOLOGIA POLSKA. 1959. irreg. price varies. Uniwersytet Mikolaja Kopernika, Fosa Staromiejska 3, Torun, Poland. (Dist. by: Osrodek Rozpowszechniania Wydawnictw Naukowych PAN, Palac Kultury i Nauki, 00-901 Warsaw, Poland)
 Formerly: Uniwersytet Mikolaja Kopernika, Torun. Nauki Humanistyczno-Spoleczne. Filologia Polska (ISSN 0083-4483)

430 375.4   HU   ISSN 0238-079X
PF3009
ACTA UNIVERSITATIS SZEGEDIENSIS DE ATTILA JOZSEF NOMINATAE. ACTA GERMANISTICA. (Text in German) 1961-1972; resumed 1987. biennial. exchange basis. Attila Jozsef University, c/o E. Szabo, Exchange Librarian, Dugonics ter 13, P.O. Box 393, H-6701 Szeged, Hungary. (Subscr. to: Kultura, P.O. Box 149, H-1389 Budapest, Hungary) Eds. Janos Marvany, Miklos Salyamossy. circ. 350.
 Supersedes (until 1971): Acta Universitatis Szegediensis de Attila Jozsef Nominatae. Acta Germanica et Romanica; (until 1966): Acta Universitatis Szegediensis de Attila Jozsef Nominatae. Acta Romanica et Germanica; (until 1964): Acta Universitatis Szegedeinsis. Section Scientiarum Philologiae Germanicae.
 Description: A journal on the history of German literature and language.

491.7 891.7   HU
ACTA UNIVERSITATIS SZEGEDIENSIS DE ATTILA JOZSEF NOMINATAE. DISSERTATIONES SLAVICAE. SECTIO LINGUISTICA. (Supplement avail. at irreg. intervals) (Text in Russian) 1962. a. exchange basis. Attila Jozsef University, c/o E. Szabo, Exchange Librarian, Dugonics ter 13, P.O. Box 393, Szeged H-6701, Hungary. (Subscr. to: Kultura, P.O. Box 149, H-1389 Budapest, Hungary) Ed. Imre H. Toth. bk.rev.; circ. 350.
 Supersedes in part (in 1982): Acta Universitatis Szegediensis de Attila Jozsef Nominatae. Dissertationes Slavicae (ISSN 0586-3732)
 Description: Journal of Russian descriptive linguistics and of Old Slavonic historical and comparative studies.

494.511   HU   ISSN 0209-9543
ACTA UNIVERSITATIS SZEGEDIENSIS DE ATTILA JOZSEF NOMINATAE. SECTIO ETHNOGRAPHICA ET LINGUISTICA/NEPRAJZ ES NYELVTUDOMANY. (Summaries in English, French, German and Russian) 1957. a. exchange basis. Attila Jozsef University, c/o E. Szabo, Exchange Librarian, Dugonics ter 13, P.O.B. 393, Szeged H-6701, Hungary. (Subscr. to: Kultura, Box 149, H-1389 Budapest, Hungary) Ed.Bd. bk.rev.; circ. 500. **Indexed:** M.L.A.
 Description: Hungarian, Finno-Ugrian and universal linguistics and ethnographic studies.

410   US   ISSN 0761-022X
ACTES SEMIOTIQUES. (Text and summaries in French) 1985. irreg., vol.6, 1988. price varies. John Benjamins Publishing Co. (Subsidiary of: John Benjamins Publishing Co.), 821 Bethlehem Pike, Philadelphia, PA 19118. TEL 215-836-1200. FAX 215-836-1204. (And: Amsteldijk 44, P.O. Box 75577, 1007 AN Amsterdam, Netherlands. TEL 020-6738156) Ed.Bd.

499.993   DK   ISSN 0901-2273
ACTUALITATES DE INTERLINGUA. (Text in Danish, Interlingua and Swedish) 1960. 4/yr. DKK 20. Dansk Interlingua Union, Ellegaardspark 79, DK-3520 Farum, Denmark. TEL 45 42 95 41 32. (Subscr. to: Union Danese pror Interlingua, Juvelvej 25, DK-5210 Odense NV, Denmark) Ed. Joergen Kofod-Jensen. bk.rev.
 Formerly: Actualitates (ISSN 0106-4819)

418.02   CN   ISSN 0001-7779
ACTUALITE TERMINOLOGIQUE/TERMINOLOGY UPDATE. (Catalog no. S52-1) 1968. 6/yr. Can.$14.95 (foreign $17.95). Canada Communication Group, Publishing Division, Ottawa, Ont. K1A 0S9, Canada. TEL 819-997-2560.

410   US
ADVANCES IN DISCOURSE PROCESSES. 1977. irreg., vol.42, 1990. price varies. Ablex Publishing Corporation, 355 Chestnut St., Norwood, NJ 07648. TEL 201-767-8450. FAX 201-767-6717. TELEX 135-393. Ed. Roy O. Freedle. (reprint service avail. from ISI)

ADYATAN. see *ORIENTAL STUDIES*

400   IT   ISSN 0001-9593
AP37
AEVUM; rassegna di scienze storiche, linguistiche e filologiche. 1927. 3/yr. L.139000($107) (effective 1992). (Universita Cattolica del Sacro Cuore) Vita e Pensiero, Largo Gemelli 1, 20123 Milan, Italy. TEL 02-8856310. FAX 02-8856260. TELEX 321033 UCTMI 1. Ed. Raffaele de Cesare. adv.; bk.rev.; bibl.; index. **Indexed:** Amer.Hist.& Life, Hist.Abstr., M.L.A., Old Test.Abstr.
 Description: Covers historic, literary, philosophical and linguistic areas on the national, as well as the international level.

AFGHANISTAN. see *HISTORY — History Of Asia*

496   UK   ISSN 0954-416X
PL8000   CODEN: ALCUEH
AFRICAN LANGUAGES AND CULTURES. 1988. s-a. £10($25) University of London, School of Oriental and African Studies, Thornhaugh St., Russell Sq., London WC1H 0XG, England. TEL 071-637-2388. FAX 071-436-3844. adv.; bk.rev.; bibl.; circ. 120.
—BLDSC shelfmark: 0732.596300.
 Description: Covers comparative African linguistics, including language classification, cultural studies and language literatures.

AFRICAN STUDIES; a biannual journal devoted to the study of African anthropology, history, sociology, and languages. see *ANTHROPOLOGY*

AFRICANA MARBURGENSIA. see *ETHNIC INTERESTS*

496 896   GW   ISSN 0002-0427
PL8000
AFRIKA UND UEBERSEE; Sprachen, Kulturen. (Text in English, French and German) 1910. 2/yr. DM.124. (Universitaet Hamburg) Dietrich Reimer Verlag, Unter den Eichen 57, 1000 Berlin 45, Germany. TEL 030-8314081. Ed. J. Zwernemann. bk.rev.; abstr.; bibl.; index. (reprint service avail. from KTO) **Indexed:** A.I.C.P., Curr.Cont.Africa, M.L.A.

492   US   ISSN 0732-6416
AFROASIATIC DIALECTS. 1977. irreg., no.4, 1983. price varies. Undena Publications, Box 97, Malibu, CA 90265. TEL 805-746-5870. FAX 805-746-2728. (Dist. by: Crescent Academic Services, 29528 Madera Ave., Shafter, CA 93263) Ed. Thomas Penchoen. bibl.; charts; illus. (back issues avail.) **Indexed:** Lang.& Lang.Behav.Abstr.
 Description: Data-oriented series which seeks to provide concise descriptions of individual languages which belong to the Afroasiatic language family.

492   US   ISSN 0362-3637
PJ991
AFROASIATIC LINGUISTICS. (Subseries of: Monographic Journals of the Near East) 1974. irreg., latest vol.9, no.3. price varies. Undena Publications, Box 97, Malibu, CA 90265. TEL 805-746-5870. FAX 805-746-2728. (Dist. by: Crescent Academic Services, 29528 Madera Ave., Shafter, CA 93263) Ed. Russell Schuh. bibl.; charts; illus. (back issues avail.) **Indexed:** Curr.Cont.Africa, Lang.& Lang.Behav.Abstr., M.L.A., Old Test.Abstr.
—BLDSC shelfmark: 0735.537000.
 Description: Articles of general, theoretical interest using Afroasiatic material. Includes descriptive, historical and comparative studies in Afroasiatic (Hamito-Semitic) languages.

400 900   GW   ISSN 0065-5287
P3
AKADEMIE DER WISSENSCHAFTEN IN GOETTINGEN. NACHRICHTEN 1. PHILOLOGISCH-HISTORISCHE KLASSE. (Text in English, German, occasionally French) 1893. irreg. price varies. Vandenhoeck und Ruprecht, Robert-Bosch-Breite 6, Postfach 37 53, 3400 Goettingen, Germany. TEL 0551-6959-0. FAX 0551-695917. index. (reprint service avail. from KTO) **Indexed:** Amer.Hist.& Life, Hist.Abstr.

AKADEMIJA NAUKA I UMJETNOSTI BOSNE I HERCEGOVINE. ODJELJENJE DRUSTVENIH NAUKA. DJELA. see *HISTORY — History Of Europe*

LINGUISTICS 2801

400 800   AJ   ISSN 0002-3132
PL311
AKADEMIYA NAUK AZERBAIDZHANSKOI S.S.R. IZVESTIYA. SERIYA YAZYKOZNANIE, LITERATURA I ISKUSSTVO. 1967. q. 15 Rub. Izdatel'stvo Elm, Ul. Narimanova, 31, Baku 370073, Azerbaijan. bk.rev.; index.

400   RU
AKADEMIYA NAUK KAZAKHSKOI S.S.R. IZVESTIYA. SERIYA FILOLOGICHESKAYA. 1974. q. 2.40 Rub. Izdatel'stvo Nauka, 90 Profsoyuznaya ul.,.117864 Moscow, Russia. TEL 234-05-84.

430.07 370   UK   ISSN 0959-5740
AKTUELL. (Text in German) 1963. 6/yr. (during school year). Mary Glasgow Publications Ltd., Avenue House, 131-133 Holland Park Ave., London W11 4UT, England. TEL 071-603-4688. FAX 071-602-5197. TELEX 311890-MGPUBS. (U.S. subscr. to: Delta Systems, 570 Rock Rd. Dr., Dundee, IL 60118-9992) charts; illus.; circ. 16,000. (also avail. in microform from UMI; reprint service avail. from UMI)
 Former titles: Aktuell Auf Deutsch; Roller (ISSN 0035-7901)
 Description: German language magazine for advanced level students.

410   CC
ALABO SHIJIE/ARAB WORLD. (Text in Chinese) q. Shanghai Waiguoyu Xueyuan, Alabo Yu Xi - Shanghai Foreign Language Institute, Arabic Department, 1550 Dalian Xilu, Shanghai 200083, People's Republic of China. TEL 5420900. Ed. Li Qilie.

497 572   US   ISSN 0883-8526
                          CODEN: ANLPER
ALASKA NATIVE LANGUAGE CENTER RESEARCH PAPERS. 1979. irreg., no.8, 1990. price varies. University of Alaska, Alaska Native Language Center, Fairbanks, AK 99775-0120. TEL 907-474-7874. FAX 907-474-6586. Ed. Michael Krauss. circ. 200. **Indexed:** Lang.& Lang.Behav.Abstr. (1979-).

410   GW   ISSN 0722-0332
ALEMANNISCH DUNKT UES GUET. (Text in Alemannisch and German) 1967. s-a. membership. Muettersproch - Gsellschaft, Am Hofacker 15, 7801 Buchenbach - Unteribental, Germany. TEL 07661-1236. Ed. Klaus Poppen. bk.rev.; circ. 4,200.
 Description: Promotes use of Alemannisch, the dialect of south-west Germany.

400 800   BL   ISSN 0002-5216
PN9   CODEN: ALFA D5
ALFA; revista de linguistica. (Text in Portuguese; summaries in English and Portuguese) 1962-1977; resumed 1980. a. $30 or exchange basis. Universidade Estadual Paulista, Av. Vicente Ferreira, 1278, Caixa Postal 603, 17500 Marilia, SP, Brazil. TEL 0144-33-1844. FAX 0144-22-2504. TELEX 111-9016 UJME BR. Ed.Bd. bk.rev.; bibl.; index; circ. 1,000. **Indexed:** Lang.& Lang.Behav.Abstr. (1980-), M.L.A., Sociol.Abstr.

497.3   CN   ISSN 0711-382X
ALGONQUIAN AND IROQUOIAN LINGUISTICS. 1972. q. Can.$8($8) c/o J.D. Nichols, Ed., Native Languages Programme, 532 Fletcher Argue University of Manitoba, Winnipeg, Man. R3T 2N2, Canada. bk.rev.; bibl.; circ. 300. **Indexed:** M.L.A.
 Description: Research papers and news relating to the languages of the Algonquin and Iroquoian families

ALGONQUIAN CONFERENCE. PAPERS. see *ANTHROPOLOGY*

400   II
ALL-INDIA CONFERENCE OF LINGUISTS. PROCEEDINGS. (Text in English) 1970. a. price varies. Linguistic Society of India, c/o Deccan College Postgraduate and Research Institute, Poona 411006, India. Ed. R.V. Dhongde.

400   II
ALL-INDIA CONFERENCE OF LINGUISTS. SOUVENIR. 1970. irreg. $2. Linguistic Society of India, c/o Deccan College Postgraduate and Research Institute, Poona 411006, India. Ed. R.V. Dhongde. adv.

440.370   UK   ISSN 0957-6215
ALLONS. (Text in French) 1966. 6/yr. (during school year). Mary Glasgow Publications Ltd., Avenue House, 131-133 Holland Park Ave., London W11 4UT, England. TEL 071-603 4688. FAX 071-602-5197. TELEX 311890-MGPUBS. (U.S. subscr. to: Delta Systems, Co. Inc., Rock Rd. Dr., Dundee, IL 60118-9992) illus.; circ. 53,000.
Formerly: Boum (ISSN 0032-0471)
Description: French language magazine for beginners.

410   GW   ISSN 0179-387X
DIE ALTEN SPRACHEN IM UNTERRICHT. 1953. q. DM.19.80. (Altphilologische Fachgruppe im Bayerischen Philologenverband) C.C. Buchners Verlag, Laubanger 8, 8600 Bamberg, Germany. TEL 0951-65202. FAX 0951-61774. adv.; bk.rev.; circ. 1,700.

430   GW
ALTHOCHDEUTSCHES WOERTERBUCH. 1952. a. (Saechsische Akademie der Wissenschaften zu Leipzig) Akademie-Verlag Berlin, Leipziger Str. 3-4, 1086 Berlin, Germany. Ed. Rudolf Grosse.
Description: Dictionary of Old High German.

489 371   GW   ISSN 0002-6670
DER ALTSPRACHLICHE UNTERRICHT; Arbeitshefte zu seiner wissenschaftlichen Begruendung und praktischen Gestalt. 1958. 6/yr. DM.93.10 (foreign DM.99.40). Erhard Friedrich Verlag GmbH, Im Brande 15, Postfach 100150, 3016 Seelze-Velber, Germany. TEL 0511-40004-0. index: vols. 1-15; circ. 4,800.
—BLDSC shelfmark: 0803.903000.

400   US
AMERICAN ASSOCIATION OF LANGUAGE SPECIALISTS. YEARBOOK. a. American Association of Language Specialists, 1000 Connecticut Ave., N.W., Washington, DC 20036. TEL 301-986-1542. Ed. H.T. Willett. circ. 750.

AMERICAN ASSOCIATION OF TEACHERS OF ESPERANTO QUARTERLY BULLETIN/AMERIKA ASOCIO DE INSTRUISTOJ DE ESPERANTO KVARONJARA BULTENO. see *EDUCATION — Teaching Methods And Curriculum*

480   US   ISSN 0278-5943
AMERICAN CLASSICAL STUDIES. no.18, 1988. irreg. (American Philological Association) Scholars Press, Box 15399, Atlanta, GA 30333-0399. TEL 404-636-4757. FAX 404-636-8301. Ed. Matthew Santirocco.

427   US   ISSN 0002-8193
PE2801
AMERICAN DIALECT SOCIETY. NEWSLETTER. 1969. 3/yr. $25 (includes subscr. to P A D S and American Speech). American Dialect Society, c/o Allan Metcalf, Ed., English Department, MacMurray College, Jacksonville, IL 62650. TEL 217-479-7049. FAX 217-245-5214. adv.; bk.rev.; abstr.; bibl.; circ. 925. (back issues avail.) Indexed: Lang.& Lang.Behav.Abstr., Res.Educ.
Description: Contains news of American Dialect Society meetings, committees, and publications.

427   US   ISSN 0002-8207
PE1702
AMERICAN DIALECT SOCIETY. PUBLICATIONS. Abbreviated title: P A D S. 1944. irreg. price varies. (American Dialect Society) University of Alabama Press, Box 870380, Tuscaloosa, AL 35487-0380. TEL 205-348-5180. circ. 800. Indexed: Lang.& Lang.Behav.Abstr.

430 375.4   US   ISSN 1040-8207
AMERICAN JOURNAL OF GERMANIC LINGUISTICS AND LITERATURES. 1989. s-a. $25 to members; students and retired $15. Society for Germanic Philology, Box 020225, Brooklyn, NY 11202-0005. TEL 718-997-5587. Ed. Richard K. Seymour. bk.rev.; circ. 200.
—BLDSC shelfmark: 0824.660000.
Description: For professionals in Germanic linguistics.
Refereed Serial

420   US   ISSN 0002-9475
P1
AMERICAN JOURNAL OF PHILOLOGY. 1880. q. $27 to individuals (foreign $30); institutions $64 (foreign $67). Johns Hopkins University Press, Journals Publishing Division, 701 W. 40th St., Ste. 275, Baltimore, MD 21211. TEL 410-516-6987. FAX 410-516-6998. Ed. George Kennedy. adv.; bk.rev.; index; circ. 1,407. (also avail. in microform from UMI,PMC; back issues avail.; reprint service avail. from SWZ,UMI) Indexed: Arts & Hum.Cit.Ind., Bk.Rev.Ind. (1965-), Child.Bk.Rev.Ind. (1965-), Curr.Cont., Hum.Ind., Ind.Bk.Rev.Hum., Lang.& Lang.Behav.Abstr, Numis.Lit, Phil.Ind., Soc.Sci.Ind.
—BLDSC shelfmark: 0831.500000.
Description: Presents articles concerned with literary interpretation and history, textual criticism, historical investigation, epigraphy, religion, linguistics, and philosophy.

400   US   ISSN 0044-779X
P11
AMERICAN PHILOLOGICAL ASSOCIATION. DIRECTORY OF MEMBERS. 1970. irreg. (approx. biennial). price varies. (American Philological Association) Scholars Press, Box 15399, Atlanta, GA 30333-0399. TEL 404-636-4757. FAX 404-636-8301. circ. 3,000.
Description: Directory of members of the American Philological Association.

406   US   ISSN 0360-5949
P11   CODEN: TAPAEI
AMERICAN PHILOLOGICAL ASSOCIATION. TRANSACTIONS. 1870. a. $45. (American Philological Association) Scholars Press, Box 15399, Atlanta, GA 30333-0399. TEL 404-636-4757. FAX 404-636-8301. Ed. Ruth Scodel. cum.index (1869-1969); circ. 3,000. (also avail. in microform from PMC) Indexed: Curr.Cont.
—BLDSC shelfmark: 8893.950000.
Supersedes in part: American Philological Association. Transactions and Proceedings (ISSN 0065-9711)
Description: Academic papers on Greek, Roman and classical literature and civilizations.

428   US   ISSN 0003-1283
PE2801
AMERICAN SPEECH; a quarterly of linguistic usage. 1926. q. $20 to individuals; institutions $25. (American Dialect Society) University of Alabama Press, Box 870380, Tuscaloosa, AL 35487-0380. TEL 205-348-5180. FAX 205-348-9201. Ed. Ronald Butters. adv.; bk.rev.; bibl.; index; circ. 1,800. (also avail. in microform from UMI,SCH) Indexed: Abstr.Engl.Stud., Amer.Hist.& Life, Curr.Cont., Hist.Abstr., Hum.Ind., Ind.Bk.Rev.Hum., Lang.& Lang.Behav.Abstr. (1968-), Lang.Teach.& Ling.Abstr., M.L.A.
—BLDSC shelfmark: 0857.550000.

418.02   US
AMERICAN TRANSLATORS ASSOCIATION. ANNUAL CONFERENCE PROCEEDINGS. a. $50. Learned Information, Inc., 143 Marlton Pike, Medford, NJ 08055-8750. TEL 609-654-4888. FAX 609-654-4309. Ed. A. Leslie Willson.
Description: Explores new areas of the language-oriented professions.

430 374.4 833.91   US   ISSN 0721-1392
AMERICAN UNIVERSITY STUDIES. SERIES 1. GERMANIC LANGUAGES AND LITERATURE. 1981. irreg. Peter Lang Publishing, Inc., 62 W. 45th St., 4th Fl., New York, NY 10036. TEL 212-302-6740. Ed. Michael Flamini.

410 495.1   US   ISSN 0739-6406
AMERICAN UNIVERSITY STUDIES. SERIES 6. FOREIGN LANGUAGE INSTRUCTION. 1983. irreg. Peter Lang Publishing, Inc., 62 W. 45th St., 4th Fl., New York, NY 10036. TEL 212-302-6740. Ed. Kathryn Earle.

891.733   US   ISSN 0740-0497
AMERICAN UNIVERSITY STUDIES. SERIES 12. SLAVIC LANGUAGES AND LITERATURE. 1983. irreg. Peter Lang Publishing, Inc., 62 W. 45th St., 4th Fl., New York, NY 10036. TEL 212-302-6740. Ed. Kathryn Earle.

447   US   ISSN 0740-4557
AMERICAN UNIVERSITY STUDIES. SERIES 13. LINGUISTICS. 1984. irreg. Peter Lang Publishing, Inc., 62 W. 45th St., 4th Fl., New York, NY 10036. TEL 212-302-6740. Ed. Michael Flamini.

420 440 375.4   CS
L'AMITIE/FRIENDSHIP. (Text in English and French) 1967. 10/yr. 30 Kcs. (Ministerstvo Skolstvo Slovenskej Republiky) Slovenske Pedagogicke Nakladatelstvo, Sasinkova 5, 815 60 Bratislava, Czechoslovakia. (Subscr. to: Slovart, Gottwaldovo nam. 6, 805-32 Bratislava, Czechoslovakia) Ed. Jozef Blaho. circ. 55,000.
Description: English and French study and teaching.

410 150   US   ISSN 0165-716X
AMSTERDAM STUDIES IN THE THEORY AND HISTORY OF LINGUISTIC SCIENCE. SERIES 2: CLASSICS IN PSYCHOLINGUISTICS. Short title: C I P L. (Text in English and German) 1978. irreg., vol.5, 1991. price varies. John Benjamins Publishing Co., 821 Bethlehem Pike, Philadelphia, PA 19118. TEL 215-836-1200. FAX 215-836-1204. (And: Amsteldijk 44, P.O. Box 75577, 1070 AN Amsterdam, Netherlands. TEL 020-6738156) Ed. E.F.Konard Koerner. Indexed: M.L.A.
Description: New editions of seminal works from the nineteenth and twentieth century in the area of psycholinguistics.

410   US   ISSN 0304-0720
AMSTERDAM STUDIES IN THE THEORY AND HISTORY OF LINGUISTIC SCIENCE. SERIES 3: STUDIES IN THE HISTORY OF THE LANGUAGE SCIENCES. Variant title: Amsterdam Studies in the Theory and History of the Linguistic Science. Series 3: Studies in the History of Linguistics. Short title: S I H O L S. 1973. irreg., vol.58, 1990. price varies. John Benjamins Publishing Co., 821 Bethlehem Pike, Philadelphia, PA 19118. TEL 215-836-1200. FAX 215-836-1204. (And: Amsteldijk 44, P.O. Box 75577, 1070 AN Amsterdam, Netherlands. TEL 020-6762325) Ed. E.F.K. Koerner. Indexed: M.L.A.
—BLDSC shelfmark: 0859.603000.
Description: Information concerning the heritage of linguistic ideas of more than two millennia.

410   US   ISSN 0304-0763
AMSTERDAM STUDIES IN THE THEORY AND HISTORY OF LINGUISTIC SCIENCE. SERIES 4: CURRENT ISSUES IN LINGUISTIC THEORY. Short title: C I L T. (Text in English) 1975. irreg., vol.81, 1991. price varies. John Benjamins Publishing Co., 821 Bethlehem Pike, Philadelphia, PA 19118. TEL 215-836-1200. FAX 215-836-1204. (And: Amsteldijk 44, P.O. Box 75577, 1070 AN Amsterdam, Netherlands. TEL 020-6762325) Ed. E.F.K. Koerner. Indexed: M.L.A.
—BLDSC shelfmark: 0859.604000.
Description: Forum for discussion of unorthodox ideas in the field of linguistics.

430   NE   ISSN 0169-0221
AMSTERDAMER PUBLIKATIONEN ZUR SPRACHE UND LITERATUR. 1972. irreg. (approx. 20/yr.). price varies. Editions Rodopi B.V., Keizersgracht 302-304, 1016 EX Amsterdam, Netherlands. TEL 020-6227507. FAX 020-6380948. (US and Canada subscr. to: 233 Peachtree St. N.E., Ste. 404, Atlanta GA 30303-1504. TEL 800-225-3998) Ed. H.A. Quak. circ. 700. Indexed: M.L.A.
Description: Covers Germanic languages and literature.

440 840   GW   ISSN 0569-986X
ANALECTA ROMANICA. (Beihefte zu den Romanischen Forschungen) 1955. irreg., vol.51, 1986. price varies. Vittorio Klostermann, Frauenlobstr. 22, Postfach 900601, 6000 Frankfurt a.M. 90, Germany. TEL 069-774011. FAX 069-708038. Ed. Wido Hempel.

460 375.4   SP   ISSN 0569-9878
ANALES CERVANTINOS. a. 2000 ptas. (foreign 3000 ptas.). Consejo Superior de Investigaciones Cientificas (C.S.I.C.), Instituto de Filologia, Duque de Medinaceli, 6, 28014 Madrid, Spain. Dir. Alberto Sanchez Sanchez. (reprint service avail. from SWZ)

420　　　　　GW　　ISSN 0003-3251
ANGLIA; Zeitschrift fuer englische Philologie. (Text in English and German) 1878. s-a. DM.186. Max Niemeyer Verlag, Postfach 2140, 7400 Tuebingen 1, Germany. TEL 07071-81104. FAX 07071-87419. Ed.Bd. adv.; bk.rev.; charts; index; circ. 800. (back issues avail.; reprint service avail. from SCH) **Indexed**: Abstr.Engl.Stud., Arts & Hum.Cit.Ind., Can.Rev.Comp.Lit, Curr.Cont., Ind.Bk.Rev.Hum., Lang.& Lang.Behav.Abstr., M.L.A.
—BLDSC shelfmark: 0902.760000.
Description: Essays and reviews of English and American language and literature.

420　　　　　JA　　ISSN 0003-326X
ANGLICA; journal of English philology. (Text in English and Japanese) 1951. s-a. 360 Yen($1) Meicho Fukyukai, 1-16-6 Taira-cho Meguroku, Tokyo 152, Japan. Ed. Tadao Yamamoto. bibl.; circ. 900.

420　　　　　DK　　ISSN 0105-9963
ANGLICA ET AMERICANA. vol.14, 1981. irreg., vol.23, 1988. price varies. Koebenhavns Universitet, Department of English, Njalsgade 84-96, 2300 Copenhagen S, Denmark. FAX 32-96-37-77. (Dist. by: Atheneum Booksellers, 6 Norregade, DK-1165 Copenhagen K, Denmark) Ed.Bd. bk.rev.; circ. 600.

430 792　　　　　UK
ANGLICA GERMANICA: SERIES 2. irreg. price varies. Cambridge University Press, Edinburgh Bldg., Shaftesbury Rd., Cambridge CB2 2RU, England. TEL 0223-312393. FAX 0223-315052. TELEX 851817256. (N. American addr.: Cambridge University Press, Journals Dept., 40 W. 20th St., New York, NY 10011. TEL 212-924-3900) Ed.Bd.

ANGLO-AMERICAN FORUM. see *LITERATURE*

ANNALES AEQUATORIA. see *ANTHROPOLOGY*

ANNALES DU MIDI; revue de la France Meridionale. see *ARCHAEOLOGY*

400　　　　　PL　　ISSN 0239-426X
PB5
ANNALES UNIVERSITATIS MARIAE CURIE-SKLODOWSKA. SECTIO FF. PHILOLOGIAE. (Text in English, French, German, Polish and Russian; summaries in English, French, Polish) 1983. a. price varies. Uniwersytet Marii Curie-Sklodowskiej, Wydwnictwo, Pl. M. Curie-Sklodowskiej 5, 20-031 Lublin, Poland. TEL 48-81-375304. FAX 48-81-336699. TELEX 0643223. Ed. Alina Aleksandrowicz. circ. 550.
—BLDSC shelfmark: 0961.000000.

470　　　　　FR　　ISSN 0066-2348
ANNEE EPIGRAPHIQUE; REVUE DES PUBLICATIONS EPIGRAPHIQUES RELATIVES A L'ANTIQUITE ROMAINE. 1962. a. 315 F. (foreign 390 F.). Presses Universitaires de France, Departement des Revues, 14 Avenue du Bois-de-l'Epine, B.P. 90, 91003 Evry Cedex, France. TEL 1-60-77-82-05. FAX 1-60-79-50-45. TELEX PUF 600 474 F. (reprint service avail. from KTO) **Indexed**: Br.Archaeol.Abstr.

491.992　　　　　US　　ISSN 0271-9800
PK8001
ANNUAL OF ARMENIAN LINGUISTICS. (Text in English, French, German, Italian) 1980. a. $20 to individuals; institutions $30 (for 2 yrs). c/o John A.C. Greppin, Ed., Cleveland State University, Cleveland, OH 44115. TEL 216-687-3967. FAX 216-687-9366. TELEX 810-421-8252 CSU CLV. adv.; bk.rev.; bibl.; circ. 225. (back issues avail.) **Indexed**: Amer.Bibl.Slavic & E.Eur.Stud, Lang.& Lang.Behav.Abstr. (1986-), M.L.A.

418　　　　　UK　　ISSN 0267-1905
P129
ANNUAL REVIEW OF APPLIED LINGUISTICS. a. $26 to individuals; institutions $46. Cambridge University Press, Edinburgh Bldg., Shaftesbury Rd., Cambridge CB2 2RU, England. TEL 0223-312393. FAX 0223-315052. TELEX 851817256. (N. American addr.: Cambridge University Press, 40th W. 20th St., New York, NY 10011. TEL 212-924-3900) Ed. Robert B. Kaplan. adv.; bk.rev. (also avail. in microform from UMI) **Indexed**: Lang.& Lang.Behav.Abstr. (1984-).
—BLDSC shelfmark: 1520.474500.
Description: Covers bilingualism, psycholinguistics, computer-assisted instruction, sociolinguistics and lexicography.

410 306.4　　　　　US　　ISSN 0003-5483
ANTHROPOLOGICAL LINGUISTICS. 1959. 4/yr. $20 to individuals; institutions $40. Indiana University, Department of Anthropology, Rawles Hall 108, Bloomington, IN 47405. TEL 812-335-1472. Ed. Martha B. Kendall. adv.; bk.rev.; charts; circ. 1,200. (also avail. in microform from JAI,KTO,MIM) **Indexed**: A.I.C.P., Abstr.Anthropol., Curr.Cont., E.I., Lang.& Lang.Behav.Abstr. (1972-), M.L.A., Mid.East: Abstr.& Ind., SSCI.
—BLDSC shelfmark: 1542.880000.
Description: Theoretical and methodological papers on the use of language in its social setting, particularly focused on ethnolinguistics, ethnography of communication, psycholinguistics and sociolinguistics.

ANTHROPOS; revue internationale d'ethnologie et de linguistique. see *ANTHROPOLOGY*

ANTICHITA CLASSICA E CRISTIANA. see *HISTORY*

400 800　　　　　SP　　ISSN 0210-1343
P1.A1
ANUARIO DE FILOLOGIA. (Yearly volume consists of six separate nos., one for each language covered.) (Text in various European languages) 1975. a. 9000 ptas.($120) Universidad de Barcelona, Facultad de Filologia, Gran Via de les Corts Catalanes 585, 08007 Barcelona, Spain. Ed. Fernando Diaz Esteban. adv.; bk.rev.; cum.index; circ. 600. (back issues avail.) **Indexed**: Old Test.Abstr.
Formerly: Universidad de Barcelona. Facultad de Filologia. Anuario.

460 375.4　　　　　SP　　ISSN 0213-053X
ANUARIO DE LINGUISTICA HISPANICA. 1985. irreg., vol.5, 1990. 3000 ptas. Universidad de Valladolid, Secretariado de Publicaciones, Avda. Ramon y Cajal, 7, 47005 Valladolid, Spain. TEL 983-423000. FAX 983-423003. TELEX 26357.

ANUARIO L L. (Literatura Linguistica) see *LITERATURE*

418.02　　　　　II　　ISSN 0003-6218
ANUVAD/TRANSLATION; a quarterly on theoretical and practical aspects of translation. (Text in English and Hindi) 1964. q. Rs.35. Translators' Association of India, 203 Asha Deep, 9 Hailey Rd., New Delhi 110 001, India. TEL 11-3714838. FAX 3329916. Ed. Gargi Gupta. adv.; bk.rev.; charts; illus.; index; circ. 1,500.

491.8　　　　　AU　　ISSN 0066-5282
ANZEIGER FUER SLAVISCHE PHILOLOGIE. 1966. irreg., vol.20, 1991. Akademische Druck- und Verlagsanstalt Dr. Paul Struzl, Schoenaugasse 6, 8010 Graz, Styria, Austria. TEL 4153-42158.

410 572　　　　　FR　　ISSN 0755-9291
APPLICATIONS ET TRANSFERTS DE LA S E L A F. 1982. irreg. price varies. Societe d'Etudes Linguistiques et Anthropologiques de France (SELAF), 5 rue de Marseille, 75010 Paris, France.

418　　　　　UK　　ISSN 0142-6001
P129
APPLIED LINGUISTICS. 1980. 4/yr. £58($115) Oxford University Press, Oxford Journals, Pinkhill House, Southfield Road, Eynsham, Oxford OX8 1JJ, England. TEL 0865-882283. FAX 0865-882890. TELEX 837330-OXPRES-G. (U.S. addr.: 200 Madison Ave., New York, NY 10016) Eds. Alan Davies, Elaine Tarone. adv.; bk.rev.; circ. 1,400. (also avail. in microform) **Indexed**: Cont.Pg.Educ., Lang.& Lang.Behav.Abstr. (1980-), Lang.Teach.& Ling.Abstr., Sp.Ed.Needs Abstr., SSCI.
—BLDSC shelfmark: 1573.260000.
Description: Studies the relationship between theoretical and practical aspects of language education.

418 401 616.8　　　　　UK　　ISSN 0142-7164
P37　　　　　CODEN: APPSDZ
APPLIED PSYCHOLINGUISTICS; psychological studies of language processes. 1980. q. $42 to individuals; institutions $82. Cambridge University Press, Edinburgh Bldg. Shaftesbury Rd., Cambridge CB2 2RU, England. TEL 0223-312393. FAX 0223-315052. TELEX 851817256. (N. American addr.: Cambridge University Press, 40 W. 20th St., New York, NY 10011. TEL 212-924-3900) Eds. Catherine E. Snow, John L. Locke. adv.; bk.rev.; cum.index. (also avail. in microform from UMI; back issues avail.) **Indexed**: ASCA, C.I.J.E., Child Devel.Abstr., Curr.Cont., Lang.& Lang.Behav.Abstr. (1980-), Lang.Teach.& Ling.Abstr., M.L.A., Psychol.Abstr., Sociol.Abstr., Sp.Ed.Needs Abstr., SSCI.
—BLDSC shelfmark: 1576.545000.
Description: Papers on the psychological processes in language. Articles address the nature, acquisition and impairments of language expression and comprehension, including writing and reading.

401 150　　　　　US
APPLIED PSYCHOLINGUISTICS AND COMMUNICATION DISORDERS. 1979. irreg., latest 1991. price varies. Plenum Publishing Corp., 233 Spring St., New York, NY 10013-1578. TEL 212-620-8000. FAX 212-463-0742. TELEX 23-421139. Ed. R.W. Rieber. **Indexed**: SSCI.
Formerly: Studies in Applied Psycholinguistics.
Refereed Serial

492.7　　　　　SJ
ARAB JOURNAL OF LANGUAGE STUDIES. (Text in Arabic, English) 1982. s-a. £S30($25) (Arab League Educational, Cultural and Scientific Organization) Khartoum International Institute for Arabic Language, P.O. Box 26, Eastern Deims, Khartoum, Sudan. Ed. Awan Asharif Qasim.
Description: Focuses on the teaching of Arabic to non-native speakers.

492.7 370　　　　　US　　ISSN 0889-8731
PJ6001
AL-ARABIYYA. (Text in Arabic and English) 1967. irreg. (1-2/yr.). $25 to individuals; institutions $25; students $10. American Association of Teachers of Arabic, University of Utah, Bldg. 113, Middle East Center, Salt Lake City, UT 84112. TEL 801-581-6181. FAX 801-581-6183. Ed. Mushira Eid. adv.; bk.rev.; bibl.; circ. 300. (processed; back issues avail.) **Indexed**: C.I.J.E., ERIC, Ind.Islam., M.L.A., Sociol.Abstr.
—BLDSC shelfmark: 2943.175230.
Formerly (until vol. 8): Al-Nashra (ISSN 0003-2387)
Description: Publishes scholarly, pedagogical articles and reviews which contributes to the advancement of study, research, criticism, and teaching in the fields of Arabic language, literature and linguistics.

ARBEITEN AUS ANGLISTIK UND AMERIKANISTIK. see *LITERATURE*

ARBEITSGEMEINSCHAFT DER BIBLIOTHEKEN UND DOKUMENTATIONSSTELLEN DER OST-, OSTMITTEL- UND SUEDOSTEUROPAFORSCHUNG. MITTEILUNGEN. see *LIBRARY AND INFORMATION SCIENCES*

400 800　　　　　GW　　ISSN 0003-8970
ARCHIV FUER DAS STUDIUM DER NEUEREN SPRACHEN UND LITERATUREN. (Text in English, French, German, Italian or Spanish) 1846. 2/yr. DM.120. Erich Schmidt Verlag GmbH & Co. (Berlin), Genthiner Str. 30G, 1000 Berlin 30, Germany. TEL 030-2500850. FAX 030-25008521. Ed.Bd. bk.rev.; index; circ. 800. (reprint service avail. from SCH,KTO) **Indexed**: Arts & Hum.Cit.Ind., Can.Rev.Comp.Lit, Curr.Cont., Ind.Bk.Rev.Hum., Lang.& Lang.Behav.Abstr., M.L.A.
—BLDSC shelfmark: 1623.970000.

450　　　　　IT　　ISSN 0004-0207
PC4
ARCHIVIO GLOTTOLOGICO ITALIANO. 1873. s-a. L.90000($90) (effective 1992). Editoriale e Finanziaria Le Monnier, S.p.a., Via A. Meucci 2, Casella Postale 202, 50100 Florence, Italy. Dir. C.A. Mastrelli. adv.; bk.rev.; bibl.; index. (also avail. in microfiche from BHP) **Indexed**: Lang.& Lang.Behav.Abstr., M.L.A.
Description: Looks at general methological and historical research in Indo-European, Romance and Italian linguistics.

LINGUISTICS

450   IT   ISSN 0066-6696
ARCHIVIO LINGUISTICO VENETO. QUADERNI. 1962. irreg., no.5, 1969. price varies. (Fondazione Giorgio Cini) Casa Editrice Leo S. Olschki, Casella Postale 66, 50100 Florence, Italy. TEL 055 6530684. FAX 055-6530214. circ. 1,000.

410 709 880   IT
ARCHIVIO PER L'ALTO ADIGE; rivista di studi alpini. 1906. a. L.50000. Istituto di Studi per l'Alto Adige, Via Cesare Battisti 4, 50122 Florence, Italy. circ. 150. **Indexed:** M.L.A.

407   GW   ISSN 0721-0442
ARCHIVUM CALDERONIANUM. (Text in Spanish) 1982. irreg., vol.6, 1991. price varies. Franz Steiner Verlag Wiesbaden GmbH, Birkenwaldstr. 44, Postfach 101526, 7000 Stuttgart 1, Germany. TEL 0711-2582-0. FAX 0711-2582290. TELEX 723636-DAZD. Ed. Hans Flasche.
—BLDSC shelfmark: 1659.000000.

450   IT   ISSN 0066-6815
ARCHIVUM ROMANICUM. BIBLIOTECA. SERIE 2: LINGUISTICA. (Text in French, German or Italian) 1921. irreg., no.48, 1990. price varies. Casa Editrice Leo S. Olschki, Casella Postale 66, 50100 Florence, Italy. TEL 055-6530684. FAX 055-6530214. circ. 1,500. (also avail. in microfiche from BHP)

480 470   PL   ISSN 0066-6866
ARCHIWUM FILOLOGICZNE. (Vols. are not issued in chronological order) (Text in French, German, Latin and Polish; summaries in French) 1958. irreg., vol.41, 1984. price varies. (Polska Akademia Nauk, Komitet Nauk o Kulturze Antycznej) Ossolineum, Publishing House of the Polish Academy of Sciences, Rynek 9, Wroclaw, Poland. TELEX 0712771 OSS PL. (Dist. by: Ars Polona-Ruch, Krakowskie Przedmiescie 7, Warsaw, Poland) Ed. J. Wolski. circ. 500-1,000.
Description: Dissertations and monographical papers on literature, history, archaeology and culture in ancient world.

491.85 891.85   PL   ISSN 0208-7596
ARCHIWUM TLUMACZEN Z TEORII LITERATURY I METODOLOGII BADAN LITERACKICH. 1966. irreg. price varies. Katolicki Uniwersytet Lubelski, Katedra Teorii Literatury, Al. Raclawickie 14, 20-950 Lublin, Poland. Ed. Jozef Japola. index; circ. 225.

ARCTOS; ACTA PHILOLOGICA FENNICA. see *CLASSICAL STUDIES*

ARGUMENTATION; an international journal on reasoning. see *PHILOSOPHY*

400   GR
ARISTOTLE UNIVERSITY OF THESSALONIKI. SCHOOL OF PHILOSOPHY. PHILOLOGY DEPARTMENT. SCIENTIFIC YEARBOOK. resumed 1990. a. Aristotle University of Thessaloniki, School of Philosophy, Philology Department, 540 06 Thessaloniki, Greece. TEL 031-9911. FAX 206138. TELEX 041-2181. Ed. A.-Ph. Christides.

ARIZONA ENGLISH BULLETIN. see *EDUCATION — Teaching Methods And Curriculum*

410   US
ARKANSAS PHILOLOGICAL ASSOCIATION. PUBLICATIONS. 1974. 2/yr. $25. University of Central Arkansas Press, Box 4933, Conway, AR 72035. TEL 501-450-5118. Ed. Bob Lowrey. bk.rev. (also avail. in microfilm)

439   SW   ISSN 0066-7668
PD1503
ARKIV FOR NORDISK FILOLOGI/ARCHIVES FOR SCANDINAVIAN PHILOLOGY. (Text in Danish, English, French, German, Norwegian, Swedish) 1882. a. price varies. Lund University Press, P.O. Box 141, S-221 00 Lund, Sweden. TEL 46-46-312000. FAX 46-305338. Eds. Bengt Pamp, Christer Platzack. bk.rev.; circ. 470. **Indexed:** M.L.A., NAA.

ARNAMAGNAEAN INSTITUTE AND DICTIONARY. BULLETIN. see *LITERATURE*

ARS LYRICA: JOURNAL OF LYRICA. see *MUSIC*

408   UK   ISSN 0587-3584
ART - LANGUAGE. irreg. £6. Art & Language Press, 13 Milverton Crescent, Leamington Spa, Warwickshire, England. **Indexed:** Artbibl.Mod.

410   CK
ARTICULOS EN LINGUISTICA Y CAMPOS AFINES. 1974. irreg., latest 1985. $3.50 per no. Instituto Linguistico de Verano, Departamento de Estudios Tecnicos, Apdo. Aereo 100602, Bogota, Colombia. FAX 2590093. circ. 500. **Indexed:** Lang.& Lang.Behav.Abstr. (1974-), Sociol.Abstr.
Description: Studies on South American Indian languages.

ARYANA. see *HISTORY — History Of Asia*

400   KO
ASIAN AND PACIFIC QUARTERLY; of cultural and social affairs. (Text in English) 1969. q. free. Cultural and Social Centre for the Asian and Pacific Region, C.P.O. Box 3129, Seoul, S. Korea. TEL 02-679-5651. FAX 02-679-5653. Ed. Lien-Kong Tsai. bk.rev.; illus.; circ. 500. (reprint service avail. from UMI) **Indexed:** Amer.Hist.& Life, Hist.Abstr.
Former titles: Asian Pacific Quarterly of Cultural and Social Affairs; A S P A C Quarterly of Cultural and Social Affairs (ISSN 0001-2599)
Description: Emphasizes language, history, and literature of Korea and China.

410   FR   ISSN 0224-2680
ASIE DU SUD-EST ET MONDE INSULINDIEN. 1976. irreg. price varies. Societe d'Etudes Linguistiques et Anthropologiques de France (SELAF), 5 rue de Marseille, 75010 Paris, France. TEL 42-08-83-93. **Indexed:** E.I.

ASOCIACION DE HISPANISTAS DE LAS AMERICAS. COLECCION MONOGRAFIAS. see *LITERATURE — Poetry*

100   CN   ISSN 0381-5781
ASSOCIATION DES TRADUCTEURS ET INTERPRETES DE L'ONTARIO. INFORMATIO/ASSOCIATION OF TRANSLATORS AND INTERPRETERS OF ONTARIO. INFORMATIO. (Text in English and French) 1971. 4/yr. Can.$20. Association des Traducteurs et Interpretes de l'Ontario, 1 Nicholas, Ste.1402, Ottawa, Ont. K1N 7B7, Canada. TEL 613-233-6395. FAX 613-233-7473. circ. 1,000.

400   CN   ISSN 0066-9016
ASSOCIATION DES TRADUCTEURS ET INTERPRETES DE L'ONTARIO. REPERTOIRE/ASSOCIATION OF TRANSLATORS AND INTERPRETERS OF ONTARIO. DIRECTORY. (Text in English, French) 1970. a. Can.$25. Association des Traducteurs et Interpretes de l'Ontario, 1 Nicholas, Ste.1402, Ottawa, Ont. K1N 7B7, Canada. TEL 613-233-6395. FAX 613-233-7473. Ed.Bd. adv.; circ. 1,500.

ASSOCIATION FOR COMMONWEALTH LITERATURE AND LANGUAGE STUDIES. BULLETIN. see *LITERATURE*

840   FR   ISSN 0004-5527
ASSOCIATION GUILLAUME BUDE. BULLETIN. 1923. q. 120 F. Societe d'Edition les Belles Lettres, 95 Bd. Raspail, 75006 Paris, France. Ed. M. Michel. adv.; bk.rev. **Indexed:** M.L.A.

495.6 370   US   ISSN 0885-9884
PL501
ASSOCIATION OF TEACHERS OF JAPANESE. JOURNAL. 1963. s-a. $25. Association of Teachers of Japanese, c/o University of Pittsburgh, East Asian Languages & Literatures, Pittsburgh, PA 15260. TEL 412-624-5568. FAX 412-624-4419. (Alt. addr.: c/o Japanese Program, Middlebury College, Middlebury, VT 05753. TEL 802-388-3711) Ed.Bd. adv.; bk.rev.; bibl.; index; circ. 1,300. (tabloid format; also avail. in microform from UMI; back issues avail., reprint service avail. from UMI) **Indexed:** C.I.J.E.
Formerly: Association of Teachers of Japanese. Journal-Newsletter (ISSN 0004-5810)
Description: Explores Japanese literature, linguistics and language pedagogy.

491.7 375.4   UK   ISSN 0306-7432
ASSOCIATION OF TEACHERS OF RUSSIAN. NEWSLETTER. 1975. s-a. Association of Teachers of Russian, c/o Philip Hood, 7 Bringhurst, Orton, Goldhay, Peterborough PE20 ORS, England. bk.rev.; bibl.
Description: For teachers of Russian in schools, colleges and universities.

410   US   ISSN 0066-9903
ASSYRIOLOGICAL STUDIES. 1931. irreg., vol.25, 1991. price varies. University of Chicago, Oriental Institute, 1155 E. 58th St., Chicago, IL 60637. TEL 312-702-9508. FAX 312-702-9853.

ASTRADO; revue bilingue de Provence. see *LITERATURE*

ATHENIAN; Greece's English language monthly. see *TRAVEL AND TOURISM*

410   CN   ISSN 0820-8204
ATLANTIC PROVINCES LINGUISTIC ASSOCIATION. ANNUAL MEETING. PAPERS. (Text in English, French) 1977. a. Can.$15 (includes Atlantic Provinces Linguistic Association Journal). Atlantic Provinces Linguistic Association, Linguistics Department, Memorial University, St. John's, Nfld. A1B 3X9, Canada. TEL 709-737-8134. circ. 150.

410   CN   ISSN 0706-6910
P1
ATLANTIC PROVINCES LINGUISTIC ASSOCIATION JOURNAL. 1978. a. Can.$15($15) Atlantic Provinces Linguistic Association, c/o J. Black, Memorial University, Linguistics Department, St. John's, Nfld. A1B 3X9, Canada. TEL 709-737-8134. FAX 709-737-4000. TELEX 016-4101. bk.rev.; circ. 200. **Indexed:** Lang.& Lang.Behav.Abstr. (1985-), Sociol.Abstr.
Description: Covers all areas of descriptive and theoretical linguistics.

410   AT   ISSN 0312-5467
AUSTRALIA. WORKING PAPERS IN LANGUAGE AND LINGUISTICS. 1975. s-a. Aus.$6 to individuals; institutions Aus.$10. Tasmanian State Institute of Technology, P.O. Box 1214, Launceston, Tas. 7250, Australia. TEL (003) 260245. Eds. Thao Le, Mike McCausland. circ. 100. (back issues avail.) **Indexed:** Aus.Educ.Ind., Aus.P.A.I.S., Lang.& Lang.Behav.Abstr. (1986-).

AUSTRALIAN AND NEW ZEALAND STUDIES IN GERMAN LANGUAGE AND LITERATURE. see *LITERATURE*

410 499   AT
AUSTRALIAN ESPERANTIST. (Text in Esperanto) 1940. bi-m. Aus.$25. Australian Esperanto Association, 46 Great Eastern Hwy., Bakers Hill, W.A. 6562, Australia. TEL 09-574-1307. (Subscr. to: c/o Owen Loneragan, 16 Deverell Way, S. Bentley, W.A. 6102, Australia) Ed. Donald Broadribb. bk.rev.; circ. 250.
Formerly: Rondo.
Description: Includes short stories, poems, basic Esperanto news events, columns on language usage.

AUSTRALIAN JOURNAL OF FRENCH STUDIES. see *LITERATURE*

410   AT   ISSN 0726-8602
P1
AUSTRALIAN JOURNAL OF LINGUISTICS. 1981. s-a. $53. (Australian Linguistic Society) La Trobe University Press, Bundoora, Vic. 3085, Australia. TELEX 851817256. Eds. David Bradley, Roland Sussex. **Indexed:** Lang.& Lang.Behav.Abstr. (1981-).
—BLDSC shelfmark: 1809.160000.

491.7 891.7   AT   ISSN 0818-8149
AUSTRALIAN SLAVONIC AND EAST EUROPEAN STUDIES. (Text in English and Russian) 1967. s-a. Aus.$25. University of Melbourne, Department of Russian, Parkville, Vic. 3052, Australia. TEL 03-344-5193. FAX 03-344-7821. Ed. Paul Cubberley. adv.; bk.rev.; circ. 150. (also avail. in microfilm from UMI) **Indexed:** M.L.A.
—BLDSC shelfmark: 1820.330000.
Formerly: Melbourne Slavonic Studies (ISSN 0076-6267)
Description: Publishes scholarly articles, review articles and short reviews on all aspects of Slovonic and East European studies, in particular language, literature, history and political science; also art and social science.

AUTOMATIC DOCUMENTATION AND MATHEMATICAL LINGUISTICS. see *LIBRARY AND INFORMATION SCIENCES*

BABEL. see *EDUCATION — Teaching Methods And Curriculum*

LINGUISTICS 2805

400 800   NE   ISSN 0521-9744
PN241.A1
BABEL; revue internationale de la traduction - international journal of translation. (Text in English and French, occasionally in other languages) 1955. q. fl.118($62) (International Federation of Translators, BE - Federation Internationale des Traducteurs) John Benjamins Publishing Co., Amsteldijk 44, P.O. Box 75577, 1070 AN Amsterdam, Netherlands. TEL 020-6738156. FAX 020-6739797. (In N. America: 821 Bethlehem Pike, Philadelphia, PA 19118. TEL 215-836-1200) (Co-sponsor: Unesco) Ed. Rene Haeseryn. (reprint service avail. from SWZ) Indexed: C.I.J.E., Lang.Teach.& Ling.Abstr.
—BLDSC shelfmark: 1854.500000.
  Description: Covers news and events related to the Federation.

BAHANA. see LITERATURE

430 375.4   GW   ISSN 0170-8007
PC603
BALKAN-ARCHIV NEUE FOLGE. 1976. irreg., no.11, 1986. price varies. Helmut Buske Verlag Hamburg, Friedrichsgaber Weg 138, P.O. Box 1249, D-2000 Norderstedt, Germany. Eds. Johannes Kramer, Wolfgang Dahmen.

430   GW   ISSN 0720-0994
BALKAN-ARCHIV NEUE FOLGE BEIHEFT. (Supplement to Balkan-Archiv Neuye Folge) 1981. irreg. price varies. Helmut Buske Verlag Hamburg, Friedrichsgaber Weg 138, Postfach 1249, D-2000 Norderstedt, Germany.

491.9   LI   ISSN 0132-6503
PG8001
BALTISTICA; studies in Baltic linguistics. (Text in English, French, German, Latvian, Lithuanian and Russian) 1965. 2/yr. price varies. (Ministry of Culture and Education) Leidykla Mokslas, Zvaigzdziu 23, Vilnius 2050, Lithuania. TEL 45-85-26. TELEX 261107 LMOKSU. (Co-sponsor: Vilnius University) Ed. Vytautas Maziulis. bk.rev.; abstr.; charts; illus.; circ. 500. Indexed: M.L.A.
—BLDSC shelfmark: 1861.400000.
  Description: Traces the history of Baltic languages and considers the relations between Baltic and Slavonic languages and other problems of comparative linguistics.

BAMLA EKADEMI GABESHANA PATRIKA. see LITERATURE

430 375.4   GW   ISSN 0342-8036
BARGFELDER BOTE; Materialien zum Werk Arno Schmidts. 1972. irreg. DM.42 for 6 nos. Edition Text und Kritik Verlag, Levelingstr. 6a, 8000 Munich 80, Germany. TEL 089-432929. FAX 089-433997.

410   US   ISSN 0736-1122
PE1630
BARNHART DICTIONARY COMPANION; a quarterly to update general dictionaries. 1982. q. $60 to institutions. (Lexik House Publishers) Springer-Verlag, Journals, 175 Fifth Ave., New York, NY 10010. TEL 212-460-1500. TELEX 23 22 35. Ed. Clarence L. Barnhart. bk.rev.; index; circ. 1,000.
  Description: Update to general dictionaries providing definitions of new and unrecorded words and meanings that reflect changes occuring in the English language.

BASLER STUDIEN ZUR DEUTSCHEN SPRACHE UND LITERATUR. see LITERATURE

430   GW
BAUSTEINE ZUR SPRACHGESCHICHTE DES NEUHOCHDEUTSCHEN. 1970. irreg., vol.65, 1988. price varies. (Akademie der Wissenschaften der DDR, Zentralinstitut fuer Sprachwissenschaft) Akademie-Verlag Berlin, Leipziger Strasse 3-4, 1086 Berlin, Germany.
  Formerly: Bausteine zur Geschichte des Neuhochdeutschen (ISSN 0067-463X)

BAYERISCHE STAATSBIBLIOTHEK. NEW CONTENTS SLAVISTICS. INHALTSVERZEICHNISSE SLAVISTISCHER ZEITSCHRIFTEN - ISZ. see BIBLIOGRAPHIES

430 375.4   GW   ISSN 0721-4383
BAYREUTHER BEITRAEGE ZUR SPRACHWISSENSCHAFT. 1978. irreg., vol.9, 1988. price varies. Helmut Buske Verlag Hamburg, Friedrichsgaber Weg 138, Postfach 1249, D-2000 Norderstedt, Germany. Eds. Hans-Werner Eroms, Robert Hinderling.

410   GW   ISSN 0721-8923
BAYREUTHER BEITRAEGE ZUR SPRACHWISSENSCHAFT. DIALEKTOLOGIE. 1980. irreg. price varies. Helmut Buske Verlag Hamburg, Friedrichsgaber Weg 138, Postfach 1249, D-2000 Norderstedt, Germany.

BAZMAVEP. see HISTORY — History Of The Near East

420 370   GW   ISSN 0005-7347
BEACON; the English student's own magazine. (Text in English and German) 1949. 11/yr. DM.16.50. Beacon-Verlag Koerber oHG, Birkental 13, Postfach 1420, 6702 Bad Duerkheim, Germany. Ed. Ortrun Scheumann. adv.; circ. 6,000. (tabloid format)

BEACON (GEORGIA). see EDUCATION

420 370   GW   ISSN 0005-7363
BEACONETTE; the beginner's English magazine. (Text in English and German) 1952. 11/yr. DM.7.70. Beacon-Verlag Koerber oHG, Birkental 13, Postfach 1420, 6702 Bad Duerkheim, Germany. Ed. Ortrun Scheumann. illus.; circ. 5,000. (tabloid format)

439.2   NE   ISSN 0005-738X
AS243
BEAKEN. (Text in Dutch, English, French, Frisian and German) 1938. q. fl.42.50. Fryske Akademy, Doelestrjitte 8, 8911 DX Ljouwert-Leeuwarden, Netherlands. TEL 058-131414. FAX 058-131409. Ed.Bd. bk.rev.; charts; illus.; stat.; index, cum.index; circ. 2,500. Indexed: M.L.A.
  Description: Studies on Frisian language and culture.

430 375.4   GW
BEITRAEGE ZUR DEUTSCHEN PHILOLOGIE. 1962. irreg. price varies. Wilhelm Schmitz Verlag, Staufenbergerweg 22, 6304 Lollar, Germany. TEL 06406-2324. Ed.Bd. circ. 100. Indexed: M.L.A.

430 830   GW   ISSN 0005-8076
BEITRAEGE ZUR GESCHICHTE DER DEUTSCHEN SPRACHE UND LITERATUR. (Text in English, French or German) 1874. 3/yr. DM.164. Max Niemeyer Verlag, Postfach 2140, 7400 Tuebingen 1, Germany. TEL 07071-81104. FAX 07071-87419. Ed.Bd. adv.; bk.rev.; charts; circ. 700. (back issues avail.; reprint service avail. from SCH) Indexed: Arts & Hum.Cit.Ind., Curr.Cont., M.L.A.
  Incorporates: Beitraege zur Erforschung der Deutschen Sprache (ISSN 0232-2714)
  Description: Essays and reviews on Old High German and Middle High German language and literature up to 1500.

480   GW
BEITRAEGE ZUR KLASSISCHEN PHILOLOGIE. 1960. irreg., no.173, 1985. price varies. Verlag Anton Hain GmbH, Savignystr. 53, 6000 Frankfurt a.M. 1, Germany. Ed.Bd.

409   LU
BEITRAEGE ZUR LUXEMBURGISCHEN SPRACH- UND VOLKSKUNDE. (Text in French, German) 1925. irreg. price varies. Institut Grand-Ducal de Luxembourg, Section de Linguistique, de Folklore et de Toponymie, 5 rue Large, Luxembourg, Luxembourg. circ. 750. (back issues avail.)

400   GW   ISSN 0005-8114
P769
BEITRAEGE ZUR NAMENFORSCHUNG. 1950. 4/yr. DM.150 (students DM.110). Carl Winter Universitaetsverlag GmbH, Lutherstr. 59, 6900 Heidelberg, Germany. Ed.Bd. adv.; bk.rev.; index; circ. 440. (reprint service avail. from KTO) Indexed: M.L.A.

410   GW   ISSN 0178-1723
BEITRAEGE ZUR PHONETIK UND LINGUISTIK. (Text in English, French, German) 1972. irreg., no.59, 1988. price varies. Helmut Buske Verlag Hamburg, Friedrichsgaber Weg 138, Postfach 1249, D-2000 Norderstedt, Germany.
  Formerly: Hamburger Phonetische Beitraege (ISSN 0341-3187)

BEITRAEGE ZUR ROMANISCHEN PHILOLOGIE DES MITTELALTERS. see LITERATURE

430 375.4   AU   ISSN 0259-0662
BEITRAEGE ZUR SPRACHINSELFORSCHUNG. 1981. irreg., no.8, 1990. price varies. Verband der Wissenschaftlichen Gesellschaften Oesterreichs, Lindengasse 37, A-1070 Vienna, Austria. TEL 932166. Ed. Maria Hornung.

491.799   BW   ISSN 0320-7552
PG2831
BELARUSSKAYA LINHVISTIKA. (Text in Byelorussian; contents in English) 1972. s-a. 1 Rub. Akademiya Navuk Belarusskai S.S.R., Institut Movaznaustva im. Yakuba Kolasa, Skoryna 25, 220600 Minsk, Byelarus. Ed. A.J. Padluzhnyy. adv.; bk.rev.; circ. 700. (also avail. in microform)
—BLDSC shelfmark: 0015.118000.

BELMONDA LETERO. see RELIGIONS AND THEOLOGY — Other Denominations And Sects

410   PO
BEM LINGUA PORTUGUESA. no. 25, 1974. bi-m. Esc.300. Sociedade de Lingua Portuguesa, Rua de S. Jose 41, 20 Lisbon, Portugal. Eds. Guilherme Matos, Aldina de Araujo Oliveira. adv.; bk.rev.

BERGOMUN; studi di letteratura, storia ed arte. see HISTORY — History Of Europe

410   US   ISSN 0893-6935
BERKELEY INSIGHTS IN LINGUISTICS AND SEMIOTICS. (Text in English and other European languages.) 1988. irreg. Peter Lang Publishing, Inc., 62 W. 45th St., 4th Fl., New York, NY 10036. TEL 212-302-6740. Ed. Irmengard Rauch.
—BLDSC shelfmark: 1940.339000.

BEYOND WORDS. see RELIGIONS AND THEOLOGY

491.1 294.1   II
BHAU VISHNU ASHETAR VEDIC RESEARCH SERIES. (Text in English, Sanskrit) 1965. irreg. price varies. University of Poona, Centre of Advanced Study in Sanskrit, Ganeshkhind, Poona 411 007, India. TEL 54220. (Subscr. to: Section Officer, Publication Branch, University of Poona, Poona 411 007) Ed. V.N. Jha.

407   GW
BIBLIOGRAPHIE MODERNER FREMDSPRACHENUNTERRICHT.. (Text in various languages) 1970. q. DM.78. (Informationszentrum fuer Fremdsprachenforschung Marburg) Max Hueber Verlag, Max-Hueber-Str. 4, 8045 Ismaning, Germany. TEL 089-9602-0. FAX 089-9602-358. TELEX 523613-HUEBD. abstr.; bibl.

BIBLIOGRAPHY OF MEDIAEVAL LATIN LEXICOLOGY. see BIBLIOGRAPHIES

460 375.4   SP
BIBLIOTECA DE LINGUISTICA. irreg., no.5, 1983. Editorial Anagrama, S.A., Calle Pedro de la Creu, 58, 08034 Barcelona, Spain.

499.94   IT   ISSN 0067-7450
BIBLIOTECA DI STUDI ETRUSCI. 1963. irreg., vol.22, 1991. price varies. (Istituto di Studi Etruschi, Florence) Casa Editrice Leo S. Olschki, Casella Postale 66, 50100 Florence, Italy. TEL 055-6530684. FAX 055-6530214. circ. 1,000.

410   SP
BIBLIOTECA FILOLOGICA. ENSAYOS. irreg. Editorial Bello, Barcas 5, Valencia, Spain.

410   SP
BIBLIOTECA FILOLOGICA. MANUALES. no.4, 1977. irreg. Editorial Bello, Barcas 5, Valencia, Spain.

BIBLIOTEKA BULTENO. see LIBRARY AND INFORMATION SCIENCES

493   US   ISSN 0742-1117
BIBLIOTHECA AFROASIATICA. 1982. irreg., no.3, 1986. price varies. Undena Publications, Box 97, Malibu, CA 90265. TEL 805-746-5870. FAX 805-746-7228. (Dist. in U.S. by: Crescent Academic Services, 29528 Madera Ave., Shafter, CA 93263) Ed.Bd. Indexed: M.L.A.

LINGUISTICS

439.6 839.6   DK   ISSN 0067-7841
PT7113
BIBLIOTHECA ARNAMAGNAEANA; a Jon Helgason condita, auspiciis praesidii Arnamagnaeani. (Text in Danish, English, German, Icelandic, Norwegian, and Swedish) 1941. irreg. price varies. Arnamagnaean Commission, Njalsgade 76, DK-2300 Copenhagen S, Denmark. TEL 31-542211. (Dist. by: C.A. Reitzels Boghandel A-S, Noerregade 20, DK-1165 Copenhagen K, Denmark) **Indexed:** M.L.A.
—BLDSC shelfmark: 2017.932000.
   Description: Presents editions, articles and monographs primarily in the area of Old Norse-Icelandic philology and literature.

439.6 439.6   DK   ISSN 0067-785X
BIBLIOTHECA ARNAMAGNAEANA. SUPPLEMENTUM.
1956. irreg. price varies. Arnamagnaean Commission, Njalsgade 76, DK-2300 Copenhagen S, Denmark. TEL 31-542211. (Dist. by: C.A. Reitzels Boghandel A-S, Noerregade 20, DK-1165 Copenhagen K, Denmark)
   Description: Presents editions, articles and monographs primarily in the area of Old Norse-Icelandic philology and literature.

450   IT   ISSN 0067-7868
BIBLIOTHECA ATHENA. 1965. irreg., no.25, 1983. price varies. (Universita degli Studi di Roma, Scuola di Filologia Classica) Edizioni dell' Anteneo S.P.A., P.O. Box 7216, 00100 Rome, Italy. Ed. Scevola Mariotti. circ. 2,500.

430 324   SZ   ISSN 0067-7477
BIBLIOTHECA GERMANICA. HANDBUECHER, TEXTE UND MONOGRAPHIEN AUS DEM GEBIETE DER GERMANISCHEN PHILOLOGIE. 1951. irreg., vol.28, 1985. price varies. Francke Verlag, Postfach 1445, CH-3001 Berne, Switzerland. TEL 031-221715. Ed.Bd.

410   US   ISSN 0342-4871
BIBLIOTHECA NOSTRATICA. 1977. irreg. price varies. Eurolingua, Box 101, Bloomington, IN 47402-0101. TEL 812-332-8918.
   Description: Monographs on interphyletic linguistics, language origins, preproto-linguistics, global and intercontinental language studies.

430 440   GW   ISSN 0067-7515
BIBLIOTHECA ROMANICA. (Text in French, German or Italian) 1945. irreg., vol.13, 1977. price varies. K.G. Saur Verlag KG, Ortlerstr. 8, 8000 Munich 70, Germany. TEL 089-76902-0. FAX 089-76902150.

800   GW   ISSN 0341-3217
BIBLIOTHECA RUSSICA. 1979. irreg., no.3, 1983. price varies. Helmut Buske Verlag Hamburg, Friedrichsgaber Weg 138, Postfach 1249, D-2000 Norderstedt, Germany. Ed. Irene Nowikowa.

491 943   FR   ISSN 0067-8325
BIBLIOTHEQUE D'ETUDES BALKANIQUES. 1925. irreg., vol.8, 1965. price varies. Institut d'Etudes Slaves, 9 rue Michelet, F 75006 Paris, France.

BIBLIOTHEQUE DE L'ECOLE DES CHARTES; revue d'erudition. see *HISTORY*

496   FR   ISSN 0081-1238
BIBLIOTHEQUE DE LA S E L A F. 1967. 6/yr. 160 F. Societe d'Etudes Linguistiques et Anthropologiques de France (SELAF), 5 rue de Marseille, 75010 Paris, France.
   Formerly (until 1969): Societe pour l'Etude des Langues Africaines. Bulletin.

440   FR   ISSN 0067-8341
BIBLIOTHEQUE FRANCAISE ET ROMANE. SERIE A: MANUELS ET ETUDES LINGUISTIQUES. 1960. irreg. price varies. (Universite de Strasbourg II, Centre de Philologie et de Litteratures Romanes) Editions Klincksieck, 11 rue de Lille, 75007 Paris, France. Ed. Georges Straka.

800 479   FR   ISSN 0067-8384
BIBLIOTHEQUE FRANCAISE ET ROMANE. SERIE E: LANGUE ET LITTERATURE FRANCAISES AU CANADA. 1966. irreg., no.8, 1973. price varies. (Universite de Strasbourg II, Centre de Philologie et de Litteratures Romanes) Editions Klincksieck, 11 rue de Lille, 75005 Paris, France. Ed. Georges Straka.

BIBLOS. see *LITERATURE*

430 375.4   GW   ISSN 0172-3510
BIELEFELDER BEITRAEGE ZUR SPRACHLEHRFORSCHUNG. (Text in English, French and German) 1980. s-a. DM.58($10) E. Keimer Verlag, Postfach 1463, 5340 Bad Honnef am Rhein, Germany. Ed. Manfred Sprissler. adv.; bk.rev.
   Indexed: Lang.Teach.& Ling.Abstr.

BIJDRAGEN TOT DE TAAL-, LAND- EN VOLKENKUNDE. see *ANTHROPOLOGY*

410 914.2   UK
BILINGUAL FAMILY NEWSLETTER. 1984. q. £5($12.50) Multilingual Matters Ltd., Bank House, 8A Hill Rd., Clevedon, Avon BS21 7HH, England. TEL 0272-876 519. FAX 0272-343096. adv.; bk.rev. (back issues avail.)
   Description: Features articles on language, learning, linguistics, and biculturalism; a communication liaison between bilingual families throughout the world.

460   US   ISSN 0094-5366
P115
BILINGUAL REVIEW/REVISTA BILINGUE. 1974. 3/yr. $16 to individuals; institutions $28. Bilingual Review Press, Hispanic Research Center, Arizona State University, Tempe, AZ 85287-2702. TEL 602-965-3867. FAX 602-965-8309. Ed. Gary D. Keller. adv.; bk.rev.; circ. 1,000. (also avail. in microform from UMI; reprint service avail. from UMI) **Indexed:** Arts & Hum.Cit.Ind., C.I.J.E., Chic.Per.Ind., Curr.Cont., Educ.Ind., Hisp.Amer.Per.Ind., Lang.& Lang.Behav.Abstr., M.L.A., Mid.East: Abstr.& Ind.
—BLDSC shelfmark: 2059.900000.
   Description: Devoted to the linguistics and literature of bilingualism and bilingual education, primarily Spanish-English, in the United States.

410   US   ISSN 1045-4365
BILINGUALISM TODAY. irreg. Peter Lang Publishing, Inc., 62 W. 45th St., 4th Fl., New York, NY 10036. TEL 212-302-6740. FAX 212-302-7574. Ed. Dennis J. Bixler-Marquez.
   Description: Encompasses theoretical and applied research on societal and cognitive aspects of bilingualism and biculturalism.

375.4   IS   ISSN 0334-9985
BITON LEMORIM LE'ARAVIT. (Text in Arabic, Hebrew) 1987. 3/yr. free. Institute for Arabic Studies, Givat Haviva, M.P. Menasche 37 850, Israel. TEL 06-378944. FAX 06-373335. Eds. Hanna Amit-Kohavi, Sarah Ozacky-Lazar. bk.rev.; circ. 1,300.
   Description: Covers the teaching of Arabic as a foreign language.

400 800   PL   ISSN 0067-902X
BIULETYN POLONISTYCZNY. 1958. q. $25. (Polska Akademia Nauk, Instytut Badan Literackich) Ossolineum, Publishing House of the Polish Academy of Sciences, Rynek 9, 50-106 Wroclaw, Poland. TELEX 0712771 OSS PL. (Dist. by: Ars Polona-Ruch, Krakowskie Przedmiescie 7, Warsaw, Poland) Ed. Krystyna Sierocka. abstr.; circ. 1,500.
—BLDSC shelfmark: 2105.470000.
   Description: A survey of research results and activities of the Polish philologists in Poland and in the world.

420 422   GW   ISSN 0172-0872
BLAETTER FUER OBERDEUTSCHE NAMENFORSCHUNG. (Text mainly in German; occasionally in English, Greek, Italian and Latin) 1958. a. DM.16. Verband fuer Orts- und Flurnamenforschung, Leonrodstr. 57, 8000 Munich 19, Germany. Ed. Wolf-Armin von Reitzenstein. circ. 700.

407 371.3   US
BLUEGRASS BULLETIN.* 1973. s-a. Kentucky Council on the Teaching of Foreign Languages, c/o Dr. David R. Hume, Ed., Department of Modern Languages, University of Louisville, Louisville, KY 40208. bk.rev.

BOARD OF CELTIC STUDIES. BULLETIN. see *LITERATURE*

400   PO
BOLETIM DE FILOLOGIA.* vol. 23, 1974. q. Centro de Estudos Filologicos, Av. Cinco de Octubro 85, 50 Lisbon 2, Portugal. Ed.Bd. bk.rev. **Indexed:** M.L.A.

400   CL   ISSN 0067-9674
P25
BOLETIN DE FILOLOGIA. (Text in English, French, German, Spanish) 1934. a. $14. Universidad de Chile, Departamento de Linguistica, Facultad de Filosofia, Humanidades y Educacion, Casilla 10136, Correo Central, Santiago, Chile. Ed. Luis Prieto Vera. adv.; bk.rev.; cum.index; circ. 1,000. **Indexed:** Amer.Hist.& Life, Hist.Abstr., M.L.A.

410   IT
BOLLETTINO DELL'ATLANTE LINGUISTICO ITALIANO. 1976. a. L.10000. Istituto dell' Atlante Linguistico Italiano, Via Sant' Ottavio, 20, 10124 Turin, Italy. TEL 011-874848. Ed.Bd. bk.rev.; circ. 250. (back issues avail.) **Indexed:** M.L.A.

499.992   SA   ISSN 0006-7024
BONA ESPERO. (Text in Esperanto) 1964. s-a. R.15. Esperanto Association of Southern Africa, 75 Bronkhorst St., Groenkloof, Pretoria 0181, South Africa. Ed. H. von Blottnitz. bk.rev.; circ. 120.

440   UK   ISSN 0006-7121
BONJOUR. (Text in French) 1963. 6/yr. (during school year). Mary Glasgow Publications Ltd., Avenue House, 131-133 Holland Park Ave., London W11 4UT, England. TEL 071-603-4688. FAX 071-602-5197. TELEX 311890-MGPUBS. (U.S. subscr. to: Delta Systems Co. Inc., 570 Rock Rd. Dr., Dundee, IL 60118-9992) illus.; circ. 54,000. (also avail. in microform from UMI; reprint service avail. from UMI)
   Description: French language magazine for older beginners.

400   GW   ISSN 0170-821X
BONNER ROMANISTISCHE ARBEITEN. 1977. irreg. Universitaet Bonn, Romanisches Seminar, Am Hof 1, 5300 Bonn 1, Germany. Ed.Bd. (back issues avail.) **Indexed:** M.L.A.

BORE DA. see *CHILDREN AND YOUTH* — For

BRAIN AND LANGUAGE. see *PSYCHOLOGY*

437   GW
BRANDENBURG - BERLINISCHES WOERTERBUCH. 1968. a. (Saechsische Akademie der Wissenschaften zu Leipzig) Akademie-Verlag Berlin, Leipziger Str. 3-4, 1086 Berlin, Germany.
   Description: Dictionary of regional German from the Brandenburg-Berlin area.

410   BL   ISSN 0101-0530
BRAZIL. MUSEU DO INDIO. BOLETIM. LINGUISTICA. 1980. irreg. Museu do Indio, Biblioteca Marechal Rondon, Rua das Palmeiras 55, Botafogo, CEP 22270 Rio de Janeiro, Brazil.

499.992   UK   ISSN 0007-067X
LA BRITA ESPERANTISTO. (Text in English and Esperanto) 1905. bi-m. 12 to non-members (foreign £10). Esperanto-Asocio de Britujo, 140 Holland Park Ave., London W11 4UF, England. TEL 4471-727-7821. Ed. William Auld. adv.; bk.rev.; illus.; index; circ. 1,300.
   Incorporates: Esperanto News (ISSN 0306-5693)
   Description: The organ of the British Esperanto movement, with literary items plus news of British and international interest to Esperanto speakers.

BRITISH COLUMBIA ENGLISH TEACHERS' ASSOCIATION. JOURNAL. see *EDUCATION — Teaching Methods And Curriculum*

499.27   HU
BUDAPEST STUDIES IN ARABIC. irreg. Eotvos Lorand University, Chair for Arabic Studies, 1364 Budapest, Hungary. (Co-sponsor: Csoma de Koros Society, Section of Islamic Studies)

491.81   BU   ISSN 0068-3787
BULGARSKA AKADEMIIA NA NAUKITE. INSTITUT ZA BULGARSKI EZIK. IZVESTIIA. (Text in Bulgarian; summaries in various languages) vol.19, 1970. irreg. 4.68 lv. per no. Publishing House of the Bulgarian Academy of Sciences, Acad. G. Bonchev St., Bldg. 6, 1113 Sofia, Bulgaria. (Dist. by: Hemus, 6, Rouski Blvd., 1000 Sofia, Bulgaria) circ. 577.

LINGUISTICS

491.81 BU ISSN 0005-4283
PG801
BULGARSKI EZIK. 1951. 6/yr. 1.20 lv. per no. (Bulgarska Akademiia na Naukite, Institut za Bulgarski Ezik) Publishing House of the Bulgarian Academy of Sciences, Acad. G. Bonchev St., Bldg. 6, 1113 Sofia, Bulgaria. (Dist. by: Hemus, 6, Rouski Blvd., 1000 Sofia, Bulgaria) Ed. L. Andreichin. circ. 2,200. **Indexed:** M.L.A.
—BLDSC shelfmark: 0018.632000.

440 375.4 FR ISSN 0007-408X
BULLETIN ANALYTIQUE DE LINGUISTIQUE FRANCAISE. 1969. 4/yr. $54. Editions Klinscksieck, 11 rue de Lille, 75007 Paris, France. Ed. Annie Becquer. circ. 600. (also avail. in microform from UMI)
—BLDSC shelfmark: 2828.610000.
Supersedes: Bulletin Analytique de Lexicologie.
Description: French language study and teaching.

418 SZ ISSN 0251-7256
P51
BULLETIN C I L A. (Text in English, French, German, Italian) 1966. s-a. 20 SFr. to individuals (foreign 25 SFr.); institutions 40 SFr. Commission Interuniversitaire Suisse de Linguistique Appliquee, Universite de Neuchatel, Institut de Linguistique, CH-2000 Neuchatel, Switzerland. TEL 038.038834. Ed. Gerard Merkt. bk.rev.; circ. 750. (also avail. in microfiche) **Indexed:** ERIC, Lang. & Lang.Behav.Abstr. (1971-), Lang.Teach.& Ling.Abstr., M.L.A.
—BLDSC shelfmark: 2838.485000.

BULLETIN HISPANIQUE. see HISTORY — History Of Europe

410 572 LU ISSN 0068-4066
BULLETIN LINGUISTIQUE ET ETHNOLOGIQUE. (Text in French, German, Luxembourgeois) 1953. irreg. price varies. Institut Grand-Ducal de Luxembourg, Section de Linguistique, de Folklore et de Toponymie, 5 rue Large, Luxembourg, Luxembourg. circ. 500. (back issues avail.)
—BLDSC shelfmark: 2866.041000.

BULLETIN OF HISPANIC STUDIES. see LITERATURE

400 800 PL ISSN 0068-4570
BYDGOSKIE TOWARZYSTWO NAUKOWE. WYDZIAL NAUK HUMANISTYCZNYCH. PRACE. SERIA B (JEZYK I LITERATURA). 1965. irreg. price varies. Bydgoskie Towarzystwo Naukowe, Jezuicka 4, Bydgoszcz, Poland. (Dist. by: Ars Polona-Ruch, Krakowskie Przedmiescie 7, Warsaw, Poland)

489 889 UK ISSN 0307-0131
DF541
BYZANTINE AND MODERN GREEK STUDIES. (Text in English; quotations in Greek) 1975. a. £17($40) to individuals; institutions £25($55). c/o Prof. Anthony Bryer, Centre for Byzantine, Ottoman and Modern Greek Studies, University of Birmingham, P.O. Box 363, Birmingham B15 2TT, England. TEL 021-414-5775. FAX 021-414-3656. Ed. J.F. Haldon. adv.; circ. 300. **Indexed:** Amer.Bibl.Slavic & E.Eur.Stud., Amer.Hist.& Life, Curr.Cont., Hist.Abstr., M.L.A.
—BLDSC shelfmark: 2941.950000.
Description: Welcomes research, criticism, contributions on theory and method in the form of articles, critical studies and short notes.

BYZANTION NEA HELLAS. see HUMANITIES: COMPREHENSIVE WORKS

C C A I; the journal for the integrated study of artificial intelligence, cognitive science and applied epistemology. see COMMUNICATIONS

410 800 UK ISSN 0261-314X
C E C T A L CONFERENCE PAPERS SERIES. 1981. irreg. price varies. University of Sheffield, Centre for English Cultural Tradition and Language, Sheffield S10 2TN, England. Ed. J.D.A. Widdowson.
—BLDSC shelfmark: 3096.946000.

410 TI ISSN 0564-7975
P2
C E R E S CAHIERS. SERIE LINGUISTIQUE.* 1970. q. Universite de Tunis, Centre d'Etudes et de Recherches Economiques et Sociales, 23 rue d'Espagne, Tunis, Tunisia. bibl.; charts; illus.

491.1 375.4 II
C I I L. BILINGUAL HINDI SERIES. (Text in English, Hindi) 1976. irreg. Ministry of Human Resource Development, Central Institute of Indian Languages, Manasagangotri, Mysore 570 006, India. bibl.

491.1 375.4 II
C I I L. GRAMMAR SERIES. 1975. irreg., latest 1987. Rs.10. Ministry of Human Resource Development, Central Institute of Indian Languages, Manasagangotri, Mysore 570 006, India. bibl.

491.1 375.4 II
C I I L. OCCASIONAL MONOGRAPH SERIES. 1971. irreg., latest 1987. price varies. Ministry of Human Resource Development, Central Institute of Indian Languages, Manasagangotri, Mysore 570 006, India.

491.1 375.4 II
C I I L BILINGUAL EDUCATION SERIES. 1976. irreg., latest 1987. price varies. Ministry of Human Resource Development, Central Institute of Indian Languages, Manasagangotri, Mysore 570 006, India. Ed.Bd.

491.1 375.4 II
C I I L COMMON VOCABULARY SERIES. 1975. irreg., latest 1980. price varies. Ministry of Human Resource Development, Central Institute of Indian Languages, Manasagangotri, Mysore 570 006, India. Ed.Bd.

491.1 375.4 II
C I I L DOCUMENTATION SERIES. 1972. irreg., latest 1984. price varies. Ministry of Human Resource Development, Central Institute of Indian Languages, Manasagangotri, Mysore 570 006, India. Ed.Bd.

491.1 375.4 II
C I I L INTENSIVE COURSE SERIES. 1979. irreg., latest 1987. price varies. Ministry of Human Resource Development, Central Institute of Indian Languages, Manasagangotri, Mysore 570 006, India. Ed.Bd.

491.1 375.4 II
C I I L- K V S. MOTHER TONGUE SERIES - APNI BOLI. 1969. irreg. price varies. Ministry of Human Resource Development, Central Institute of Indian Languages, Manasagangotri, Mysore 570 006, India. Ed.Bd.

491.1 375.4 II
C I I L OCCASIONAL BULLETIN SERIES. 1979. irreg., latest 1985. price varies. Ministry of Human Resource Development, Central Institute of Indian Languages, Manasagangotri, Mysore 570 006, India. Ed.Bd.

491.1 375.4 II
C I I L PHONETIC READER SERIES. 1972. irreg., latest 1986. price varies. Ministry of Human Resource Development, Central Institute of Indian Languages, Manasagangotri, Mysore 570 006, India. Ed.Bd.

491.1 375.4 II
C I I L PICTORIAL GLOSSARY SERIES. 1986. irreg., latest 1987. price varies. Ministry of Human Resource Development, Central Institute of Indian Languages, Manasagangotri, Mysore 570 006, India. Ed.Bd.

491.1 375.5 II
C I I L READING SERIES. 1974. irreg., latest 1978. price varies. Ministry of Human Resource Development, Central Institute of Indian Languages, Manasagangotri, Mysore 570 006, India. Ed.Bd.

491.1 375.4 II
C I I L SECOND LANGUAGE TEXTBOOK SERIES. 1973. irreg., latest 1986. price varies. Ministry of Human Resource Development, Central Institute of Indian Languages, Manasagangotri, Mysore 570 006, India. Ed.Bd.

491.1 375.4 II
C I I L SOCIOLINGUISTICS SERIES. 1974. irreg., latest 1986. price varies. Ministry of Human Resource Development, Central Institute of Indian Languages, Manasagangotri, Mysore 570 006, India. Ed.Bd.

406 US ISSN 0007-8549
P1.A1
C L A JOURNAL. (Text in various languages) 1957. q. $35. College Language Association, c/o Cason L. Hill, Ed., Morehouse College, Atlanta, GA 30314. TEL 404-681-2800. adv.; bk.rev.; index; circ. 1,500. **Indexed:** Abstr.Engl.Stud., Amer.Bibl.Slavic & E.Eur.Stud., Arts & Hum.Cit.Ind., Curr.Cont., Hum.Ind., Ind.Bk.Rev.Hum., M.L.A.
—BLDSC shelfmark: 3274.280000.
Description: Scholarly articles on language and literature.

407 FR ISSN 0765-1937
C R E D I F BULLETIN BIBLIOGRAPHIQUE. 1972. 7/yr. 140 F. (foreign 215 F.). Ecole Normale Superieure de Fontenay Saint Cloud, Centre de Recherche et d'Etude pour la Diffusion du Francais, Parc de St. Cloud, Grille d'Honneur, 92211 St. Cloud Cedex, France. TEL 47-71-91-11. FAX 46-02-39-11. TELEX ENSCLOU 206937 F. Eds. Rosine Adda, Catherine Robine. **Indexed:** M.L.A.
Description: Reviews recent publications on the art of teaching languages, particularly French as a foreign language.

410 US
C U N Y FORUM; working papers in linguistics. 1976. a. $7.50. City University of New York, Ph.D. Program in Linguistics, Graduate Center, 33 W. 42nd St., New York, NY 10036-8099. TEL 212-642-2154. Ed. Robert Hollander. circ. 125. **Indexed:** ERIC.

440 371.3 UK ISSN 0007-9243
CA VA. (Text in French) 1963. 6/yr. (during school year). Mary Glasgow Publications Ltd., Avenue House, 131-133 Holland Park Ave., London W11 4UT, England. TEL 071-603-4688. FAX 071-602-5197. TELEX 311890-MGPUBS. (U.S. subscr. to: Delta Systems Co. Inc., 570 Rock Rd., Dundee, IL 60118-9992) charts; illus.; circ. 45,500. (also avail. in microform from UMI; reprint service avail. from UMI)
Description: French language magazine for intermediate level students.

410 BL ISSN 0102-5767
CADERNOS DE ESTUDOS LINGUISTICOS. 1978. s-a. Cz.$500($25) or exchange basis. Universidade Estadual de Campinas, Instituto de Estudos da Linguagem, Departamento de Linguistica, Caixa Postal 6045, 13081 Campinas SP, Brazil. FAX 55-192-391501. Dir. Eduardo Roberto Junqueira Guimaraes. bibl.; charts. **Indexed:** Lang.& Lang.Behav.Abstr. (1981-).
—BLDSC shelfmark: 2947.120000.
Description: Presents studies in linguistics.

487 FR
CAHIERS BALKANIQUES. 1981. 2/yr. price varies. Institut National des Langues et Civilisation Orientales, Centre d'Etudes Balkaniques, 2 rue de Lille, 75343 Paris Cedex 07, France. TEL 49-26-42-74.
Description: Publishes research works by members.

CAHIERS D'ETUDES ARABES. see ORIENTAL STUDIES

CAHIERS D'ETUDES CHINOISE. see ORIENTAL STUDIES

CAHIERS DE L'ASIE DU SUD-EST. see ORIENTAL STUDIES

428 375.4 FR ISSN 0759-8661
CAHIERS DE L'I L S E R. s-a. Universite de Montpellier III (Universite Paul Valery), Institut de Langues de Specialite Enseignement et Recherche, B.P. 5043, 34032 Montpellier Cedex 1, France. TEL 67-14-20-00. Dir. Tony Lattes.
Description: Situated on the wide and as yet undefined boundary between English for Specific Purposes (E.S.P.) and linguistic studies.

CAHIERS DE L'INSTITUT D'ETUDES GERMANIQUES. see LITERATURE

418.005 FR ISSN 0007-9871
CAHIERS DE LEXICOLOGIE. 1960. s-a. $28. Didier Erudition, 6 rue de la Sorbonne, 75005 Paris, France. (U.S. Subscr. to: Didier Erudition, N. American Fullfillment Office, Box 830350, Birmingham, AL 35283-0350) Ed. D.B. Quemada. **Indexed:** Lang.& Lang.Behav.Abstr. (1972-), Lang.Teach.& Ling.Abstr., M.L.A.
—BLDSC shelfmark: 2949.620000.

L

LINGUISTICS

495.1 FR ISSN 0153-3320
CAHIERS DE LINGUISTIQUE ASIE ORIENTALE. 1977. s-a. 180 F. Centre de Recherches Linguistiques sur l'Asie Orientale, 54 bd. Raspail, 75006 Paris, France. adv.; bk.rev.; circ. 300. **Indexed:** Lang.& Lang.Behav.Abstr. (1986-), M.L.A.

410 FR
CAHIERS DE LINGUISTIQUE HISPANIQUE MEDIEVALE. 1976. irreg., no.8, 1983. (Universite de Paris XIII) Editions Klincksieck, 11 rue de Lille, 75005 Paris, France.

418 RM
CAHIERS DE LINGUISTIQUE THEORIQUE ET APPLIQUEE. (Subseries of: Revue Roumaine de Linguistique) 1963. 2/yr. 70 lei($48) (Academia Romana) Editura Academiei Romane, Calea Victoriei 125, 79717 Bucharest, Rumania. (Dist. by: Rompresfilatelia, Calea Grivitei 64-66, P.O. Box 12-201, 78104 Bucharest, Rumania) **Indexed:** M.L.A.

419 FR
CAHIERS DE LITTERATURE ORALE. 2/yr. price varies. Institut National des Langues et Civilisations Orientales, Centre de Recherche sur l'Oralite, 2 rue de Lille, 75343 Paris Cedex 07, France. TEL 49-26-42-74. (back issues avail.)
Description: Studies texts transmitted orally.

400 FR ISSN 0153-5048
CAHIERS DE PHILOLOGIE. (Includes supplements) 1976. irreg. (Universite de Lille III, Centre de Recherche Philologique) Presses Universitaires de Lille, Rue du Barreau, B.P. 199, 59654 Villeneuve d'Ascq Cedex, France. Dir. Jean Bollack.

440 301 FR ISSN 0765-4944
CAHIERS DE PRAXEMATIQUE. s-a. Universite de Montpellier (Universite Paul Valery), B.P. 5043, 34032 Montpellier Cedex 1, France. TEL 67-14-20-00. Ed. M. Paul Siblot.
Description: Contains both theoretical studies and analyses of discursive practices using a linguistic model that accounts for the conditions governing the production and circulation of meaning.

400 CN ISSN 0068-5070
CAHIERS DE PSYCHOMECANIQUE DE LANGAGE. irreg. price varies. (Universite Laval, Department de Langues et linguistique) Presses de l'Universite Laval, Cite Universitaire, Quebec, Que. G1K 7P4, Canada. TEL 418-656-2590. FAX 418-656-2600.
Formerly: Cahiers de Linguistique Structurale.

418.02 CN
CAHIERS DE TRADUCTOLOGIE. 1979. irreg. University of Ottawa Press, 603 Cumberland, Ottawa. Ont. K1N 6N5, Canada. TEL 613-564-2270.
Description: Books in English and French on various aspects of translation.

410 FR ISSN 0045-3773
CAHIERS DU BILINGUISME/LAND UN SPROCH. (Text in French, German) 1971. q. 80 F. Cercle Rene Schickele, 31 rue Oberlin, 67000 Strasbourg, France. Ed. R. Greib. adv.; bk.rev.; bibl.; circ. 3,000.

410 306.4 BE ISSN 0994-7736
CAHIERS DU L A C I T O - REVUE D'ETHNOLINGUISTIQUE. Short title: Revue d'Ethnolinguistique. (Text in English, French) vol.4, 1989. a. 1200 BEF. (Laboratoire de Langues et de Civilisations a Traditions Orales, FR) Editions Peeters s.p.r.l., Bondgenotenlaan 153, B-3000 Leuven, Belgium. TEL 016-235170. FAX 016-228500. Ed.Bd. adv.; bk.rev. (back issues avail.)
Description: Publishes multidisciplinary papers in ethnolinguistics at the intersection of linguistics, ethnology and the natural sciences.

410 SZ ISSN 0068-516X
P25
CAHIERS FERDINAND DE SAUSSURE; review de linguistique general. 1941. irreg., no.44, 1990. 50 F. (Cercle Ferdinand de Saussure) Librairie Droz S.A., 11, rue Massot, CH-1211 Geneva 12, Switzerland. TEL 022-466666. FAX 022-472391. bk.rev.; circ. 1,000. (back issues avail.) **Indexed:** Lang.Teach.& Ling.Abstr., M.L.A.

410 CN ISSN 0315-3967
P1.A1
CAHIERS LINGUISTIQUES D'OTTAWA. (Text in English and French) 1972. s-a. Can.$8 per no. University of Ottawa, Department of Linguistics, Ottawa, Ont. K1N 6N5, Canada. TEL 613-231-4207. FAX 613-564-9067. Ed. Moussa Ndaiye. bk.rev.; circ. 300. **Indexed:** Lang.& Lang.Behav.Abstr. (1973-), Lang.Teach.& Ling.Abstr., M.L.A., Sociol. Abstr.
—BLDSC shelfmark: 2949.675000.

CALIFORNIA ENGLISH. see EDUCATION — Teaching Methods And Curriculum

470 870 UK
CAMBRIDGE LATIN TEXTS. irreg. price varies. Cambridge University Press, Edinburgh Bldg., Shaftesbury Rd., Cambridge CB2 2RU, England. TEL 0223-312393. FAX 0223-315052. TELEX 851817256.

CAMBRIDGE MEDIEVAL CELTIC STUDIES. see HISTORY — History Of Europe

CAMBRIDGE PHILOLOGICAL SOCIETY. PROCEEDINGS. see CLASSICAL STUDIES

CAMBRIDGE PHILOLOGICAL SOCIETY. PROCEEDINGS. SUPPLEMENT. see CLASSICAL STUDIES

400 UK ISSN 0068-676X
CAMBRIDGE STUDIES IN LINGUISTICS. 1969. irreg., no.48, 1987. price varies. Cambridge University Press, Edinburgh Bldg., Shaftesbury Rd., Cambridge CB2 2RU, England. TEL 0223-312393. FAX 0223-315052. TELEX 851817256. Ed.Bd.
Indexed: M.L.A.

CANADIAN ASSOCIATION OF SLAVISTS NEWSLETTER. see HUMANITIES: COMPREHENSIVE WORKS

CANADIAN COUNCIL OF TEACHERS OF ENGLISH. NEWSLETTER. see EDUCATION — Teaching Methods And Curriculum

400 CN ISSN 0008-4131
P1
CANADIAN JOURNAL OF LINGUISTICS/REVUE CANADIENNE DE LINGUISTIQUE. (Text in English and French) 1954. q. Can.$40. Association Canadienne de Linguistique, University of Toronto, Experimental Phonetics Lab, Toronto, Ont. M5S 1A1, Canada. TEL 416-599-0973. Ed. William Cowan. adv.; bk.rev.; cum.index: 1954-1980; circ. 750. (also avail. in microform from UMI; back issues avail.; reprint service avail. from SWZ,UMI) **Indexed:** Abstr.Anthropol., Arts & Hum.Cit.Ind., Curr.Cont., Ind.Bk.Rev.Hum., Lang.& Lang. Behav.Abstr. (1972-), Lang.Teach.& Ling.Abstr., M.L.A., SSCI.
—BLDSC shelfmark: 3031.800000.

400 CN ISSN 0008-4506
PB5
CANADIAN MODERN LANGUAGE REVIEW. (Text in English, French, German, Italian, Spanish) 1944. q. Can.$25($25) to individuals; institutions Can.$35($35). 237 Hellems Avenue, Welland, Ont. L3B 3B8, Canada. TEL 416-734-3640. FAX 416-734-3640. Eds. Sally Rehorick, Viviane Edwards. adv.; bk.rev.; charts; illus.; circ. 2,400. (also avail. in microform from UMI; reprint service avail. from UMI) **Indexed:** Amer.Bibl.Slavic & E.Eur.Stud, C.I.J.E., Can.Educ.Ind., Can.Per.Ind., Chic.Per.Ind., Curr.Cont., Educ.Ind., Lang.& Lang.Behav.Abstr., Lang.Teach.& Ling.Abstr., M.L.A., Sp.Ed.Needs Abstr., SSCI.
—BLDSC shelfmark: 3042.600000.
Description: Presents linguistic and pedagogical articles of interest to teachers of French, German, Italian, Russian, Spanish and English as a second language.

CANADIAN SLAVONIC PAPERS/REVUE CANADIENNE DES SLAVISTES. see HUMANITIES: COMPREHENSIVE WORKS

420 375.4 AT ISSN 0311-4627
CANBERRA LINGUIST. (Text in English, French, German and Asian languages; summaries in English) 1974. s-a. Aus.$20. Modern Language Teachers Association of the A.C.T., G.P.O. Box 989, Canberra, A.C.T. 2601, Australia. FAX 069-880073. Ed. Gerda Smith. bk.rev.; circ. 150. (back issues avail.)

400 SP
CAPLLETRA. s-a. 1400 ptas. (Institut de Filologia Valenciana) Publicacions de l' Abadia de Montserrat, Ausias March 92-98, 08013 Barcelona, Spain.

491.66 UK ISSN 0263-0362
PB2101
CARDIFF WORKING PAPERS IN WELSH LINGUISTICS/PAPURAU GWAITH IEITHYDDOL CYMRAEG CAERDYDD. (Text in English or Welsh; summary in English) 1981. biennial. £2.75. Department of Welsh, University of Wales College of Cardiff, Cathays Park, Cardiff CF1 3NP, Wales. charts; illus. (back issues avail.)
—BLDSC shelfmark: 3051.175000.

407 CN ISSN 0824-7714
PB35
CARLETON PAPERS IN APPLIED LANGUAGE STUDIES. 1984. a. Can.$8($8) Carleton University, Centre for Applied Language Studies, Ottawa, Ont. K1S 5B6, Canada. FAX 613-788-6641. TELEX 053-4232. Ed. James H. Morrison. circ. 200. (also avail. in microfilm from UMI; reprint service avail. from UMI)
—BLDSC shelfmark: 3053.416600.

410 US ISSN 0739-3474
PM7801
CARRIER PIDGIN. 1973. 3/yr. $7.50 to individuals; institutions $15 (effective Jan. 1992). c/o Department of English as a Second Language, 1890 East-West Rd., University of Hawaii at Manoa, HI 96822. TEL 808-956-2786. FAX 808-956-2802. adv.; bk.rev.; bibl.; circ. 500.
—BLDSC shelfmark: 3055.464000.
Description: Studies Creole and Pidgin languages.

491.7 891.7 NE ISSN 0862-8459
CASOPIS PRO MODERNI FILOLOGII. (Previously issued (until 1991) as sub-section of: Philologia Pragensia) (Text in Czech and Russian; summaries in Russian) vol.73, 1991. 2/yr. fl.93($48) (effective 1992). (Czechoslovak Academy of Sciences, Institute for Czech Language, CS) John Benjamins Publishing Co., Amsteldijk 44, P.O. Box 75577, 1070 AN Amsterdam, Netherlands. TEL 020-6738156. FAX 020-6739773. (In N. America: 821 Bethlehem Pike, Philadelphia, PA 19118. TEL 215-836-1200) Ed. H. Belicova. bk.rev.; illus.; index; circ. 1,350. (back issues avail.) **Indexed:** M.L.A.
Supersedes in part (1956-1991): Ceskoslovenska Rusistika (ISSN 0009-0638)

450 375.4 IT
CE FASTU?. (Text in Friulian, Italian) 1919. s-a. L.40000($33) (Regione Fiuli - Venezia - Giulia) GEAP Pordenone, Via Malignani 41, 33080 Fiume Veneto, Italy. TEL 0432-501598. FAX 0432-511766. (Subscr. to: Societa Filologica Friulana, Via Manin 18, 33100 Udine, Italy) bk.rev.; circ. 3,800. (back issues avail.)

407 DK
CEBAL. (Text and summaries in English, French, German) 1970. biennial. price varies. Nyt Nordisk Forlag-Arnold Busck A-S, Koebmagergade 49, 1150 Copenhagen K, Denmark. TEL 45-33-11-11-03. FAX 45-33-93-44-90. Ed. Niels Davidsen-Nielsen. bk.rev.; circ. 500. (back issues avail.)

CENTRAL ASIATIC JOURNAL; international periodical for the languages, literatures, history and archaeology of Central Asia. see ORIENTAL STUDIES

407 US
CENTRAL STATES CONFERENCE ON THE TEACHING OF FOREIGN LANGUAGES. EDUCATION SERIES. 1972. a. $10.95. (Central States Conference on the Teaching of Foreign Languages) National Textbook Co., 4255 W. Touhy Ave., Lincolnwood, IL 60646. TEL 708-679-5500. Ed. Maurice W. Conner.

410 306.4 ZR
CENTRE D'ETUDES ETHNOLOGIQUES. PUBLICATIONS. SERIE 3: TRAVAUX LINGUISTIQUES. 1972. irreg., no.16, 1989. C E E B A Publications, B.P. 246, Bandundu, Zaire. circ. 700.

410 FR
CENTRE INTERNATIONAL DE DOCUMENTATION OCCITANE. BIBLIOTHEQUE. CATALOGUE. (Text in French and Occitan) 1976. irreg. Centre International de Documentation Occitane, Boite Postale 4202, 34325 Beziers Cedex, France.

410 RM
CERCETARI DE LINGVISTICA. (Text in Rumanian; summaries in English, French) 1956. 2/yr. 70 lei($45) (Academia Romana) Editura Academiei Romane, Calea Victoriei 125, 79717 Bucharest, Rumania. (Subscr. to: Rompresfilatelia, Calea Grivitei 64-66, P.O. Box 12-201, 78104 Bucharest, Rumania) Ed. Ioan Patrut. bk.rev.; bibl.; illus. **Indexed:** Lang.& Lang.Behav.Abstr., M.L.A.

CESKOSLOVENSKA AKADEMIE VED. USTAV PRO JAZYK CESKY. ONOMASTICKY ZPRAVODAJ. see *HISTORY — History Of Europe*

CESKY JAZYK A LITERATURA; casopis pro metodiku. see *EDUCATION*

407 FR
▼**CHAMPS DU SIGNE;** cahiers de stylistique. 1991. a. 70 F. (effective 1992). (Universite de Toulouse II (le Mirail)) Presses Universitaires du Mirail, 56 rue du Taur, 31069 Toulouse Cedex, France. TEL 61-22-58-31. FAX 61-21-84-20. Ed. Francois-Charles Gaudard.

CHASQUI. see *LITERATURE*

440 370 UK ISSN 0009-3424
CHEZ NOUS. (Text in French) 1963. 6/yr. (during school year). Mary Glasgow Publications Ltd., Avenue House, 131-133 Holland Park Ave., London W11 4UT, England. TEL 071-603 4688. FAX 071-602-5197. TELEX 311890-MGPUBS. (U.S. subscr. to: Delta Systems Co. Inc., 570 Rock Rd. Dr., Dundee, IL 60118-9992) illus.; play rev.; circ. 35,000. (tabloid format; also avail. in microform from UMI; reprint service avail. from BLH, UMI)
Description: French language magazine for advanced level students.

410 US ISSN 0577-7240
P21
CHICAGO LINGUISTIC SOCIETY. PAPERS FROM THE REGIONAL MEETINGS. 1965. a. price varies. Chicago Linguistic Society, University of Chicago, Classics 314A, 1050 E. 59th St., Chicago, IL 60637. Ed.Bd. circ. 1,500. (back issues avail.) **Indexed:** Lang.& Lang.Behav.Abstr. (1974-).
Former titles: Parasession: Non-Declarative Sentences; Parasession: Interplay of Phonology, Morphology and Syntax.

410 US ISSN 0163-2809
P118
CHILDREN'S LANGUAGE. 1978. irreg., vol.7, 1990. $49.95 cloth. Lawrence Erlbaum Associates, Inc., 365 Broadway, Hillsdale, NJ 07642. TEL 201-666-4110. FAX 201-666-2394. (back issues avail.)
—BLDSC shelfmark: 3172.990300.
Refereed Serial

495.1 370 US ISSN 0009-4595
PL1065
CHINESE LANGUAGE TEACHERS ASSOCIATION. JOURNAL. (Text in Chinese and English) 1966. 3/yr. $40. Chinese Language Teachers Association, c/o Kalamazoo College, 1200 Academy St., Kalamazoo, MI 49006. Ed. James Tai. adv.; bk.rev.; circ. 900. (also avail. in microform from MIM,UMI; reprint service avail. from UMI) **Indexed:** Bk.Rev.Ind., C.I.J.E., ERIC, Hum.Ind., Lang.& Lang.Behav.Abstr., Sociol.Abstr.
—BLDSC shelfmark: 4729.320000.

495.13 CC ISSN 1000-6125
CISHU YANJIU/JOURNAL OF LEXICOGRAPHICAL STUDIES. (Text in Chinese) 1979. bi-m. $7.20. Shanghai Cishu Chubanshe, 457 Shaanxi Beilu, Shanghai 200040, People's Republic of China. TEL 2472088. FAX 2475370. (Overseas subscr. to: Guoji Shudian - China International Book Trading Corp., P.O. Box 399, P.R.C.) Ed.Bd.
Description: Covers the theory and practice of compiling dictionaries published in China.

450 IT ISSN 0069-4339
CIVILTA VENEZIANA. DIZIONARI DIALETTALI E STUDI LINGUISTICI. 1960. irreg., no.5, 1976. price varies. (Fondazione Giorgio Cini) Casa Editrice Leo S. Olschki, Casella Postale 66, 50100 Florence, Italy. TEL 055-6530684. FAX 055-6530214. circ. 1,000.

CIZI JAZYKY; casopis pro vyucovani cizim jazykum - zejmena anglictine, nemcine, francouzstine, spanelstine, rustine a latine. see *EDUCATION*

CLASSICAL PHILOLOGY; devoted to research in the languages, literatures, history and life of classical antiquity. see *CLASSICAL STUDIES*

CLASSICS AND TODAY'S WORLD. see *LITERATURE*

CLASSICUM. see *CLASSICAL STUDIES*

375.4 UK ISSN 0142-1042
CLICK. 6/yr. (during school year). Mary Glasgow Publications Ltd., Avenue House, 131-133 Holland Park Ave., London W11 4UT, England. TEL 071-603 4688. FAX 071-602-5197. TELEX 311890-MGPUBS. illus.; circ. 75,100.
Description: For complete beginners learning English.

CLINICAL LINGUISTICS & PHONETICS. see *MEDICAL SCIENCES — Psychiatry And Neurology*

CLOCKWORK. see *EDUCATION*

CLUB. see *EDUCATION*

440 SZ ISSN 0008-0128
CLUB DE LA GRAMMAIRE. CAHIERS.* 1969. q. 8 Fr. Club de la Grammaire, c/o M.J. Degiorgis, 6 Ch. Betems, Geneva, Switzerland. (processed)

401 US
COGNITION AND LANGUAGE; a series in psycholinguistics. 1979. irreg., latest 1991. price varies. Plenum Publishing Corp., 233 Spring St., New York, NY 10013-1578. TEL 212-620-8000. FAX 212-463-0742. TELEX 23-421139. Ed. R.W. Rieber. (back issues avail.)
Refereed Serial

410 GW ISSN 0936-5907
P37 CODEN: COGLEJ
▼**COGNITIVE LINGUISTICS.** 1990. 9/yr. $86. Mouton de Gruyter, Genthiner Str. 13, 1000 Berlin 30, Germany. TEL 030-26005-0. FAX 030-26005-251. (U.S. Addr.: 200 Saw Mill Rd., Hawthorne, NY 10532) Ed. Dirk Geeraerts. circ. 500.
—BLDSC shelfmark: 3292.878000.
Description: Covers high-quality research on language from a cognitive perspective: as an instrument for organizing, processing, and conveying information.

COGNITIVE SCIENCE; a multidisciplinary journal of artificial intelligence, psychology, and language. see *PSYCHOLOGY*

COGNITIVE SYSTEMS. see *PSYCHOLOGY*

400 BL ISSN 0587-6435
COLECAO DE ESTUDOS FILOLOGICOS. 1956. irreg. Fundacao Casa de Rui Barbosa, Rua Sao Clemente 134, Botafogo 22260, Rio de Janeiro, RJ, Brazil. FAX 5371114. Dir. Agnello Uchoa Bittencourt.

410 FR ISSN 0220-746X
COLLECTION ORALITES-DOCUMENTS. 1978. irreg. Societe d'Etudes Linguistiques et Anthropologiques de France (SELAF), 5 rue de Marseille, 75010 Paris, France. TEL 42-08-83-93.

430 SZ ISSN 0010-1338
PF3001
COLLOQUIA GERMANICA; an international journal for Germanic philology and literary criticism. (Text in English and German) 1967. 4/yr. 96 SFr. (University of Kentucky, Department of Germanic and Classical Languages, US) Francke Verlag, Postfach 1445, CH-3001 Berne, Switzerland. TEL 031-221715. Ed. Bernd Kratz. adv.; bk.rev.; index; circ. 1,000. **Indexed:** Arts & Hum.Cit.Ind., Can.Rev.Comp.Lit, Curr.Cont., Ind.Bk.Rev.Hum., M.L.A.
—BLDSC shelfmark: 3315.230000.

400 JA ISSN 0069-598X
F2510
COLOQUIO DE ESTUDOS LUSO BRASILEIROS. ANAIS. (Text in Portuguese) 1967. a. 3500 Yen. Associacao Japoneza de Estudos Luso-Brasileiros, Brazilian Center, Sophia University, 7-1 Kioicho, Chiyoda-Ku, Tokyo 102, Japan. Ed. Vendelino Lorscheiter. bk.rev.; bibl.; index; circ. 220. (back issues avail.)

420 375.4 US
COLUMBIA UNIVERSITY. AMERICAN LANGUAGE PROGRAM. BULLETIN; instruction in English as a foreign language. 1953. biennial. free. Columbia University, School of General Studies, American Language Program, 505 Lewisohn Hall, New York, NY 10027. TEL 212-280-3768. Ed. Louis Levi. circ. 6,000.

400 BE ISSN 0774-8396
COMMISSION ROYALE DE TOPONYMIE ET DE DIALECTOLOGIE. BULLETIN/KONINKLIJKE COMMISSIE VOOR TOPONYMIE EN DIALECTOLOGIE. HANDELINGEN. (Editions in Dutch, French) 1927. a. 500 BEF. Commission Royale de Toponymie et de Dialectologie - Koninklijke Commissie voor Toponymie en Dialectologie, c/o Frans Debrabandere, Keizer Karelstraat 83, B-8000 Bruges, Belgium. TEL 050-31-73-66. circ. 500.

COMMUNICATION AND COGNITION. see *COMMUNICATIONS*

COMMUNICATION MONOGRAPHS. see *EDUCATION*

410 US ISSN 1050-3293
P87 CODEN: CNTHEV
▼**COMMUNICATION THEORY.** 1991. q. $30 to individuals; institutions $60. (International Communication Association) Guilford Publications, Inc., 72 Spring St., 4th Fl., New York, NY 10012. TEL 212-431-9800. FAX 212-966-6708. Ed. Robert T. Craig. adv.
—BLDSC shelfmark: 3363.459000.
Description: Contributes to the theoretical development and integration of communications. Covers transcending methodological provinces, geographical boundaries and media specializations.
Refereed Serial

COMMUNITY STUDIES SERIES. see *SOCIAL SCIENCES: COMPREHENSIVE WORKS*

COMPARATIVE LITERATURE. see *LITERATURE*

COMPARATIVE LITERATURE STUDIES. see *LITERATURE*

440 US ISSN 0010-4167
PC1
COMPARATIVE ROMANCE LINGUISTICS NEWSLETTER. 1951. 2/yr. $8 to individuals; institutions $10. Modern Language Association of America, Comparative Romance Linguistics Section, University of Florida, Department of Romance Languages, Gainesville, FL 32611. Ed. David A. Pharies. bk.rev.; bibl.; circ. 120. (processed) **Indexed:** M.L.A.

CONNECTICUT ENGLISH JOURNAL. see *EDUCATION*

410.5 BL
CONSTRUCTURA. (Text in Portuguese; summaries in English) 1973. q. $6. (Universidade Catolica do Parana, Departamento de Letras) Editora F T D, C.P. 30402, Rua do Lavapes 1023, Sao Paulo, Brazil. bibl.

440 375.4 CN ISSN 0714-3192
CODEN: CNTAEA
CONTACT; Canadian revue for French teachers. (Text in English, French) 1982. q. Can.$15 to individuals; institutions Can.$25. Simon Fraser University, Faculty of Education, Burnaby, B.C. V5A 1S6, Canada. TEL 604-291-3143. FAX 604-291-3143. Ed. Andre A. Obadia. adv.; bk.rev.; cum.index; circ. 1,000. (also avail. in microfilm; back issues avail.) **Indexed:** Pt.de Rep. (1988-).
Description: Covers French teacher training, research, practical methodology on French as a second language and mother tongue, supervision and administration of French programs.

407 FR ISSN 0247-915X
CONTRASTES. (Text in English, French) 1981. s-a. 260 F. to individuals; institutions 300 F. Z'Editions, 15 rue Alberti, 06047 Nice Cedex, France. FAX 93-13-41-29. Ed. Anne-Marie Laurian. adv.; bk.rev. (back issues avail.) **Indexed:** Lang.& Lang.Behav.Abstr. (1981-), Lang.Teach.& Ling.Abstr., M.L.A.
—BLDSC shelfmark: 3426.352000.
Description: Deals with contrastive linguistics that concerns all those interested in the confrontation of languages and cultures.

LINGUISTICS

492.4 NE ISSN 0169-7846
CONTRIBUTIONS TO THE SOCIOLOGY OF JEWISH LANGUAGES. (Text in English) 1985. irreg., vol.3, 1988. price varies. E.J. Brill, P.O. Box 9000, 2300 PA Leiden, Netherlands. TEL 071-312624. FAX 071-317532. TELEX 39296 BRILL NL. (In N. America: E.J. Brill, 24 Hudson St., Kinderhook, NY 12106. TEL 800-962-4406) Ed. J.A. Fishman.
—BLDSC shelfmark: 3461.448000.

440 430 SZ ISSN 0010-8170
CONVERSATION ET TRADUCTION; franzoesisch-deutsche Sprach- und Unterhaltungszeitschrift. (Text in French and German) 1948. m. 45 SFr. Emmentaler Druck AG, Dorfstr. 5, CH-3550 Langnau, Switzerland. adv.; bk.rev.; illus.; circ. 4,500.

410 NE ISSN 0169-779X
CORNELL LINGUISTIC CONTRIBUTIONS. (Text in English) 1977. irreg., vol.5, 1986. price varies. (Cornell University, US) E.J. Brill, P.O. Box 9000, 2300 PA Leiden, Netherlands. TEL 071-312624. FAX 071-317532. TELEX 39296 BRILL NL. (In N. America: E.J. Brill, 24 Hudson St., Kinderhook, NY 12106. TEL 800-962-4406) Eds. Frans van Coetsem, Linda R. Waugh.

860 US ISSN 0193-3892
PC4001
CORONICA;* Spanish medieval language and literature newsletter. (Text and summaries in English and Spanish) 1972. s-a. $10 to individuals; institutions $25. Modern Language Association of America, Division of Spanish Medieval Language and Literature, c/o Maier, Phillips Acad., 180 Main St., Andover, MA 01810-4166. Eds. Constance and Heanon Wilkins. bk.rev.; abstr.; bibl.; charts; illus.; circ. 300. (back issues avail.) **Indexed:** M.L.A.
—BLDSC shelfmark: 3472.058000.

420 810 820 US ISSN 0165-9618
PE1
COSTERUS; essays in English and American language and literature. (Text in English) 1972. irreg., vol.7 1990. price varies. Humanities Press, 165 First Ave., Atlantic Highlands, NJ 07716-1289. TEL 908-872-1441. FAX 908-872-0717. (Co-publisher: Editions Rodopi B.V., NE) Ed. James L.W. West, III. adv.; bk.rev.; illus.; circ. 500. **Indexed:** Lang.& Lang.Behav.Abstr., M.L.A.

410 US ISSN 0920-9026
CREOLE LANGUAGE LIBRARY. Abbreviated title: C L L. 1986. irreg., vol.9, 1991. price varies. John Benjamins Publishing Co., 821 Bethlehem Pike, Philadelphia, PA 19118. TEL 215-836-1200. FAX 215-836-1204. (And: Amsteldijk 44, P.O. Box 75577, 1070 AN Amsterdam, Netherlands. TEL 020-6762325) Eds. Pieter Muysken, John Singler.
—BLDSC shelfmark: 3487.299500.
Description: Descriptive and theoretical studies on Pidgin and Creole languages.

400 800 IT
CRITICA LETTERARIA. 1973. q. L.7000. Loffredo Editore S.p.A., Via Consalvo, 99-H, 80126 Naples, Italy. Ed. P. Giannantonio. bk.rev.; circ. 3,000. **Indexed:** Arts & Hum.Cit.Ind., Can.Rev.Comp.Lit, Curr.Cont.
Supersedes: Filologia e Letteratura (ISSN 0015-1777)

410 US ISSN 0920-3060
CRITICAL THEORY. Abbreviated title: C T. 1985. irreg., vol.8, 1988. price varies. John Benjamins Publishing Co., 821 Bethlehem Pike, Philadelphia, PA 19118. TEL 215-836-1200. FAX 215-836-1204. (And: Amsteldijk 44, P.O. Box 75577, 1070 AN Amsterdam, Netherlands. TEL 020-6762325) Eds. Miriam Diaz-Diocaretz, Iris Zavala.
—BLDSC shelfmark: 3487.488640.
Description: Addresses the interdisciplinary approach to language discourse and ideology.

CROSS CURRENTS; a journal of language teaching and cross-cultural communication. see EDUCATION — Teaching Methods And Curriculum

CROWN. see EDUCATION

400 SP
CUADERNOS DE FILOLOGIA. (Text in French, German or Spanish) 1971. s-a. Universidad de Valencia, Departamento Literatura Espanola, Avda. Blasco Ibanez, 2, Valencia-10, Spain. bk.rev.; bibl.; illus. **Indexed:** M.L.A.

489 SP ISSN 0210-0746
CUADERNOS DE FILOLOGIA CLASICA. (Text in Spanish and other languages) 1971. s-a. 500 ptas. Universidad Complutense de Madrid, Facultad de Filologia, Ciudad Universitaria, Madrid 3, Spain. Ed. Antonio Ruiz De Elvira. bk.rev.; circ. 700.

460 800 SP ISSN 0211-0547
P1.A1
CUADERNOS DE INVESTIGACION FILOLOGICA. 1975. s-a. 1500 ptas. (foreign 1800 ptas.). Colegio Universitario de la Rioja, Servicio de Publicaciones, Obispo Bustamante, 3, 26001 Logrono, Spain. TEL 43-41-231699. Ed. Pedro Santana. circ. 500. (also avail. in microform; reprint service avail.) **Indexed:** M.L.A., Sociol.Abstr.
Description: Includes essays on general linguistics theory of literature and critism applied to classical and modern philological fields such as Greek, Latin, English, French and Spanish.

410 MX
CUADERNOS DE LINGUISTICA. 1975. irreg. price varies. Universidad Nacional Autonoma de Mexico, Instituto de Investigaciones Filologicas, Circuito Mano de la Cueva, Villa Obregau, Ciudad Universitaria, 04510 Mexico 20, D.F., Mexico. Ed. Juan M. Lope Blanch.

460 375.4 SP ISSN 0212-0550
P306.A1
CUADERNOS DE TRADUCCION E INTERPRETACION. 1982. 2/yr. 1500 ptas.($14) Universidad Autonoma de Barcelona, Servicio de Publicaciones e Intercambios, Bellaterra-Barcelona, Spain. FAX 5812004. Ed. Fernando Valls. adv.; bk.rev.; circ. 1,000.
—BLDSC shelfmark: 3490.807000.

CURRENT. see EDUCATION — Teaching Methods And Curriculum

CURRENTS IN COMPARATIVE ROMANCE LANGUAGES AND LITERATURES. see LITERATURE

D S L'S PRAESENTATIONSHAEFTE. (Danske Sprog- og Litteraturselskab) see LITERATURE

D S N A NEWSLETTER. (Dictionary Society of North America) see LIBRARY AND INFORMATION SCIENCES

840 440 GW
DACOROMANIA; Jahrbuch fuer oestliche Latinitaet. 1973. a. Karl Alber GmbH, Hermann-Herder-Str. 4, 7800 Freiburg, Germany. Ed. Paul Miron.

DANCE NOTATION BUREAU NEWSLETTER. see DANCE

DECCAN COLLEGE. POSTGRADUATE & RESEARCH INSTITUTE. BULLETIN. see SOCIAL SCIENCES: COMPREHENSIVE WORKS

400 100 BE ISSN 0770-8378
DEGRES; revue de synthese a orientation semiologique. 1973. q. 1250 BEF. A.S.B.L. Degres, 2 Place Constantin Meunier, Bte. 13, 1180 Brussels, Belgium. Ed. Andre Helbo. adv.; bk.rev. **Indexed:** Can.Rev.Comp.Lit, Curr.Cont., Lang.& Lang.Behav.Abstr., M.L.A.

407 US
DELAWARE SYMPOSIUM ON LANGUAGE STUDIES SERIES. 1985. irreg., vol.7, 1990. price varies. Ablex Publishing Corporation, 355 Chestnut St., Norwood, NJ 07648. TEL 201-767-8450. FAX 201-767-6717. TELEX 135-393. Ed. Robert Di Pietro.
Formerly: Delaware Symposia Series.

430 370 GW ISSN 0011-9741
DEUTSCH ALS FREMDSPRACHE; Zeitschrift fuer Theorie und Praxis des Deutschunterrichts fuer Auslaender. 1964. bi-m. DM.38. (Universitaet Leipzig, Herder Institut) Verlag Langenscheidt KG, Crellestr. 28-30, 1000 Berlin 62, Germany. FAX 030-780002-15. TELEX 183175 EKGBL. bk.rev.; bibl.; charts; illus.; index. (also avail. in microform from UMI; reprint service avail. from UMI) **Indexed:** M.L.A.
—BLDSC shelfmark: 3561.650000.

430 375.4 GW ISSN 0178-0417
DEUTSCH - BETRIFFT UNS. 1985. 6/yr. DM.63. Bergmoser und Hoeller Verlag GmbH, Karl-Friedrich Str. 76, 5100 Aachen, Germany. TEL 0241-17309-25. FAX 0241-1730934. circ. 2,900. (looseleaf format; back issues avail.)

DEUTSCH LERNEN; Zeitschrift fuer den Sprachunterricht mit auslaendischen Arbeitnehmern. see EDUCATION — Adult Education

DEUTSCH-SLAWISCHE FORSCHUNGEN ZUR NAMENKUNDE UND SIEDLUNGSGESCHICHTE. see HISTORY — History Of Europe

410 GW ISSN 0070-3923
PF3013
DEUTSCHE AKADEMIE FUER SPRACHE UND DICHTUNG. JAHRBUCH. 1953. a. DM.26. Luchterhand Verlag, Heddesdorferstr. 31, Postfach 1780, 5450 Neuwied, Germany. Ed. Marieluise Huebscher-Bitter. **Indexed:** M.L.A.

410 GW ISSN 0179-3233
PF5003
DEUTSCHE DIALEKTGEOGRAPHIE. (Text in English, German) 1908. irreg. price varies. N.G. Elwert Verlag, Reitgasse 7-9, Postfach 1128, 3550 Marburg, Germany. Ed. Reiner Hildebrandt. **Indexed:** M.L.A.

430 375.4 GW ISSN 0418-8802
DER DEUTSCHE LEHRER IM AUSLAND. 1953. 9/yr. DM.52. Schroedel Schulbuchverlag GmbH, Hildesheimer Str. 202-206, Postfach 810555, 3000 Hannover 81, Germany. TEL 0511-8388-0. TELEX 9-23527-HSVHAD. (Subscr. to: Oeding Druck GmbH, Wilhelmstr. 1, 3300 Braunschweig, Germany) Ed.Bd. adv.; bk.rev.; circ. 2,600.
—BLDSC shelfmark: 3572.100000.
Incorporates: Mitteilungen Meinungen Materialien.

410 GW ISSN 0340-9341
PF3003
DEUTSCHE SPRACHE; Zeitschrift fuer Theorie, Praxis und Dokumentation. 1972. q. DM.119 (students DM.103). (Institut fuer Deutsche Sprache) Erich Schmidt Verlag GmbH & Co. (Bielefeld), Viktoriastr. 44A, Postfach 7330, 4800 Bielefeld 1, Germany. Ed. H. Steger. adv.; bibl. **Indexed:** Lang.& Lang.Behav.Abstr., Lang.Teach.& Ling.Abstr., M.L.A.
—BLDSC shelfmark: 3573.630000.

430 375.4 GW ISSN 0170-3153
DEUTSCHE SPRACHE IN EUROPA UND UEBERSEE. irreg., vol.14, 1991. price varies. (Institut fuer Deutsche Sprache, Mannheim) Franz Steiner Verlag Wiesbaden GmbH, Birkenwaldstr. 44, Postfach 101526, 7000 Stuttgart 1, Germany. TEL 0711-2582-0. FAX 0711-2582290. TELEX 723636-DAZD. Ed.Bd. **Indexed:** Lang.& Lang.Behav.Abstr.

DEUTSCHER ALTPHILOLOGEN-VERBAND. MITTEILUNGSBLATT. see CLASSICAL STUDIES

430 GW ISSN 0418-9426
DEUTSCHER GERMANISTEN-VERBAND. MITTEILUNGEN. 1954. DM.48. Verlag Moritz Diesterweg, Waechtersbacher Str. 89, 6000 Frankfurt a.M. 1, Germany. TEL 069-42081-0. FAX 069-1301-100. TELEX 413234-MDD. Ed. Dr. Franz R. Franke. adv.; bk.rev.; bibl.; circ. 3,250.

430 370 SA ISSN 1016-4367
DEUTSCHUNTERRICHT IM SUEDLICHEN AFRIKA. (Text mainly in German) 1970. s-a. R.10. Sudafrikanischer Germanistenverband - South African Association for German Studies, University of the Western Cape, German Department, Private Bag X17, Bellville 7535, South Africa. FAX 021-9592376. Ed. Klaus Menck. adv.; bk.rev.; circ. 650.
Formerly (until 1990): Deutschunterricht in Suedafrika (ISSN 0012-1487)
Description: Presents German language study and teaching.

430 375.4 CC
DEYU XUEXI/LEARNING GERMAN. (Text in Chinese and German) bi-m. $14.40. Beijing Foreign Language Institute, German Department, Suzhou Jie, Haidian Qu, Beijing 100081, People's Republic of China. TEL 899791. (Dist. in US by: China Books & Periodicals, Inc., 2929 24th St., San Francisco, CA 94110. TEL 415-282-2994) Ed. Zhu Yan.

DIA REGNO/DIVINE KINGDOM: CHRISTIAN ESPERANTO MAGAZINE; Kristana Esperanto-Gazeto. see RELIGIONS AND THEOLOGY

410   NE   ISSN 0176-4225
P140
DIACHRONICA; international journal for historical linguistics. (Text in English, French, German) 1984. s-a. fl.150($80) (effective 1992). John Benjamins Publishing Co., Amsteldijk 44, P.O. Box 75577, 1070 AN Amsterdam, Netherlands. TEL 020-6738156. FAX 020-6739773. (In N. America: 821 Bethlehem Pike, Philadelphia, PA 19118. TEL 215-836-1200) Ed.Bd. bk.rev.; bibl. (back issues avail.) **Indexed:** Lang.& Lang.Behav.Abstr. (1984-).
—BLDSC shelfmark: 3579.615850.
  Description: Provides a forum for exchanging and synthsizing information concernig historical linguistics in all language families.

447.9   BE   ISSN 0773-7688
PC3041
DIALECTES DE WALLONIE. Spine title: D W. (Text in French) 1972. a. 500 Fr. Societe de Langue et de Litterature Wallonnes, Place du Vingt-Aout 7, B-4000 Liege, Belgium. TEL 041-231960. Ed. Jean Lechanteur. bk.rev.; bibl.; illus.; circ. 600. **Indexed:** M.L.A.
  Description: Covers dialectology, onomastics and ethnography.

DIALETTI D'ITALIA. see LITERATURE

460   NE
DIALOGOS HISPANICOS DE AMSTERDAM. (Text in Spanish) 1980. irreg. price varies. Editions Rodopi B.V., Keizersgracht 302-304, 1016 EX Amsterdam, Netherlands. TEL 020-6227507. FAX 020-6380948. (US and Canada susbcr. to: 233 Peachtree St. N.E., Ste. 404, Atlanta GA 30303-1504. TEL 800-225-3998) Ed.Bd. circ. 750. (back issues avail.) **Indexed:** M.L.A.

440 375.4   FR   ISSN 0226-6881
DIALOGUES ET CULTURES. 1970. a. 60 F. Federation Internationale des Professeurs de Francais, 1 av. Leon Journault, F-92310 Sevres, France. FAX 46-26-81-69. adv.; bk.rev.; circ. 1,500. **Indexed:** Lang.Teach.& Ling.Abstr.
—BLDSC shelfmark: 3579.775730.
  Former titles: Dialogues; Federation Internationale des Professeurs de Francais. Bulletin.
  Description: Contains selected acts of the World Congresses of French teachers.

440   FR   ISSN 0399-7081
DICO - PLUS. Variant title: Cahiers des Amis du Lexique Francais. 1977. 4/yr. 72 F. Amis du Lexique Francais, 81 bis rue Lauriston, 75016 Paris, France. Dir. Albert Doillon. bk.rev.; circ. 160. (processed)

DICTIONARIES. see LIBRARY AND INFORMATION SCIENCES

DICTIONARY OF CONTEMPORARY QUOTATIONS. see LITERATURE

429.3   CN   ISSN 0826-8134
DICTIONARY OF OLD ENGLISH. PUBLICATIONS. irreg. (Dictionary of Old English) Pontifical Insitute of Mediaeval Studies, 59 Queen's Park Cres. E., Toronto, Ont. M5S 2C4, Canada. TEL 416-926-7144. FAX 416-926-7276.

DIMENSION: LANGUAGES (YEAR); proceedings of the Southern Conference on Language Teaching. see EDUCATION — Teaching Methods And Curriculum

DIRECTORY OF PERIODICALS PUBLISHING ARTICLES ON ENGLISH AND AMERICAN LITERATURE AND LANGUAGE. see LITERATURE

410   US
DIRECTORY OF PROGRAMS IN LINGUISTICS; in the United States and Canada. 1962. triennial. $20. Linguistic Society of America, 1325 18th St., N.W., Ste. 211, Washington, DC 20036-6501. TEL 202-835-1714. adv.
  Former titles: Guide to Programs in Linguistics; University Resources in the United States and Canada for the Study of Linguistics; University Resources in the United States for Linguistics and the Teaching of English as a Foreign Language (ISSN 0511-3040)

428   UK   ISSN 0307-1006
DISCOURSE ANALYSIS MONOGRAPHS. 1976. irreg. no.16, 1990. price varies. University of Birmingham, English Language Research, P.O. Box 363, Birmingham B15 2TT, England. Ed.Bd. circ. 400. (also avail. in microfiche)
—BLDSC shelfmark: 3595.800000.

150   US   ISSN 0163-853X
P302   CODEN: DIPRDG
DISCOURSE PROCESSES; a multidisciplinary journal. 1978. q. $40 to individuals; institutions $100. Ablex Publishing Corporation, 355 Chestnut St., Norwood, NJ 07648. TEL 201-767-8450. FAX 201-767-6717. TELEX 135-393. Ed. Roy O. Freedle. bk.rev.; index; circ. 700. (back issues avail.; reprint service avail. from ISI) **Indexed:** Biol.Abstr., C.I.J.E., Curr.Cont., ERIC, Lang.& Lang.Behav.Abstr. (1978-), Lang.Teach.& Ling.Abstr., M.L.A., Psychol.Abstr., Sociol.Abstr., SSCI.
—BLDSC shelfmark: 3595.860000.

430 375.4   GW   ISSN 0342-1589
DISKUSSION DEUTSCH; Zeitschrift fuer Deutschlehrer aller Schulformen in Ausbildung und Praxis. 1970. bi-m. DM.54. Verlag Moritz Diesterweg, Waechtersbacher Str. 89, 6000 Frankfurt a.M. 1, Germany. TEL 069-42081-0. FAX 069-1301-100. TELEX 413234-MDD. index; circ. 9,000.
—BLDSC shelfmark: 3598.430000.

DISTRIBUTED LANGUAGE TRANSLATION. see LINGUISTICS — Computer Applications

410   BL   ISSN 0102-4450
P1.A1
DOCUMENTACAO DE ESTUDOS EM LINGUISTICA TEORICA E APLICADA. Short title: D.E.L.T.A. (Text in Portuguese, English, French) 1985. s-a. $15 to individuals; institutions $30. (Asociacao Brasileira de Linguistica) Editora da Pontificia Universidade Catolica de Sao Paulo, Departamento de Linguistica, Rua Monte Alegre, 984, 05014 Sao Paulo S.P., Brazil. TEL 62-0280. Ed. Mary Aizawa Kato. bk.rev.; circ. 1,000. (back issues avail.)

DOITSU BUNGAKU. see LITERATURE

410 378 020   GW   ISSN 0724-4320
DOKUMENTATION SPRACHWISSENSCHAFTLICHE FORSCHUNGSVORHABEN. 1983. biennial. DM.29. Institut fuer Deutsche Sprache, Friedrich-Karl-Strasse 12, 6800 Mannheim 1, Germany. TEL 0621-4401243. Ed. Konrad Plastwich. cum.index; circ. 300. (back issues avail.)
  Description: Biennial publication of the Institut fuer Deutsche Sprache.

DOSHISHA LITERATURE; journal of English literature and philology. see LITERATURE

420 430 440   NE   ISSN 0012-6187
DRIE TALEN; maandblad voor de studie van Frans, Duits en Engels. 1884. 10/yr. fl.78. Wolters-Noordhoff B.V., Damspart 157, 9728 PS Groningen, Netherlands. TEL (050)226922. (Subscr. to: Postbus 58, 9700 MB Groningen, Netherlands) adv.; bk.rev.

410   CS
DRUZBA. (Text in Russian) 1951. 10/yr. 10 Kcs. (Ministerstvo Skolstvo Slovenskej Republiky) Slovenske Pedagogicke Nakladatelstvo, Sasinkova 5, 815 60 Bratislava, Czechoslovakia. (Subscr. to: Slovart, Gottwaldovo nam. 6, 805-32 Bratislava, Czechoslovakia) Ed. Viera Labuzova. circ. 240,000.

499.992   AU
LA DUA JARCENTO. INFORMILO. (Text in Esperanto) 1950. q. membership. Internacia Esperanto-Muzeo en Wien - Internationales Esperanto-Museum in Wien, Hofburg, A-1015 Vienna, Austria. Ed. Herbert Mayer. bk.rev.; abstr.; bibl.; circ. 500.
  Formerly: Internacia Esperanto-Muzeo en Wien. Informilo (ISSN 0020-5710)

400 800   US
DUQUESNE STUDIES. LANGUAGE AND LITERATURE SERIES. 1960. irreg. price varies. Duquesne University Press, 600 Forbes Ave., Pittsburgh, PA 15282. TEL 412-434-6610. Ed. Albert Labriola. **Indexed:** M.L.A.
  Formerly: (until vol.17): Duquesne Studies. Philological Series (ISSN 0070-7694)

LINGUISTICS   2811

496 419   TZ
E A C R O T A N A L INFORMATION. (Text in English and French) 1979. a. $3.50 per no. Eastern African Centre for Research on Oral Traditions and African National Languages, P.O. Box 600, Zanzibar, Tanzania. Ed. Didier Rapanoel. bk.rev.; bibl. (back issues avail.)

496 419   TZ
E A C R O T A N A L STUDIES & DOCUMENTS. (Text in English, French) 1980. a. $4. Eastern African Centre for Research on Oral Traditions and African National Languages, Box 600, Zanzibar, Tanzania. Ed. Didier Rapanoel. (back issues avail)

420   US
E S C O L PROCEEDINGS. (Eastern States Conference on Linguistics) 1984. a. $10 to individuals; institutions $12. Ohio State University, Department of Linguistics, 222 Oxley Hall, 1712 Neil Ave., Columbus, OH 43210-1298. TEL 614-292-4052. FAX 614-292-4273.

EDITIONES ARNAMAGNAEANAE. SERIES A. see LITERATURE

EDITIONES ARNAMAGNAEANAE. SERIES B. see LITERATURE

EDITOR'S REVENGE. see JOURNALISM

410   US   ISSN 0163-3848
EDWARD SAPIR MONOGRAPH SERIES IN LANGUAGE, CULTURE, AND COGNITION. (Supplement to: Forum Linguisticum) 1977. irreg. (approx. 2/yr.). price varies. (Linguistic Association of Canada and the United States) Jupiter Press, Box 101, Lake Bluff, IL 60044. TEL 312-234-3997. Ed. Adam Makkai. circ. 1,000. (back issues avail.) **Indexed:** M.L.A.

EGYUTT; Szolnok megyei konyvtarak hiradoja. see LIBRARY AND INFORMATION SCIENCES

491.62 891.62   IE   ISSN 0013-2608
EIGSE; a journal of Irish studies. 1939. a. (in one vol.). £12. National University of Ireland, 49 Merrion Square, Dublin 2, Ireland. TEL 767246. FAX 619665. Ed. Padraig Breatnach. bk.rev.; circ. 400. **Indexed:** Arts & Hum.Cit.Ind., Curr.Cont., M.L.A.

400   SP   ISSN 0013-6662
PA9
EMERITA; revista de linguistica y filologia clasica. (Text in Spanish; summaries in English) 1933. s-a. 3300 ptas. (foreign 4950 ptas.). Consejo Superior de Investigaciones Cientificas (C.S.I.C.), Instituto de Filologia, Duque de Medinaceli, 6, 28014 Madrid, Spain. bk.rev.; charts; illus.; index, cum.index; circ. 400. (reprint service avail. from SCH) **Indexed:** M.L.A.
—BLDSC shelfmark: 3733.450000.

493.1   GW   ISSN 0340-627X
ENCHORIA; Zeitschrift fuer Demotistik und Koptologie. (Text in English, French, German and Italian) 1971. a. price varies. Verlag Otto Harrassowitz, Taunusstr. 14, Postfach 2929, 6200 Wiesbaden 1, Germany. TEL 0611-530-0. FAX 0611-530570. TELEX 4186135. Ed.Bd. bk.rev.; circ. 400. (back issues avail.)
—BLDSC shelfmark: 3738.480000.

420 370   GW   ISSN 0013-8185
ENGLISCH; eine Zeitschrift fuer Englischlehrerinnen und Englischlehrer. (Supplement avail.) (Text mainly in German; occasionally in English) 1966. q. DM.26.80. Cornelsen Verlag GmbH und Co., Mecklenburgische Str. 53, 1000 Berlin 33, Germany. TEL 030-82996-285. FAX 030-82996-233. Ed.Bd. adv.; bk.rev.; illus.; tr.lit.; index; circ. 8,500. **Indexed:** Lang.& Lang.Behav.Abstr., Lang.Teach.& Ling.Abstr.
—BLDSC shelfmark: 3772.570000.

400   GW   ISSN 0071-0490
ENGLISH AND AMERICAN STUDIES IN GERMAN; summaries of theses and monographs. (Supplement to: Anglia - Zeitschrift fuer Englische Philologie) (Text in English) 1969. a. price varies. (German Congress of Scholars of English) Max Niemeyer Verlag, Postfach 2140, 7400 Tuebingen 1, Germany. TEL 07071-81104. FAX 07071-87419. Ed. Horst Weinstock. (back issues avail.)
—BLDSC shelfmark: 3772.830000.
  Description: Summaries of theses and monographs on English and American language and literature, (originally written in German).

L

LINGUISTICS

ENGLISH EDUCATION. see *EDUCATION*

ENGLISH FOR SPECIFIC PURPOSES; an international journal of English for specific purposes. see *EDUCATION — Teaching Methods And Curriculum*

420 820   AT   ISSN 0046-208X
ENGLISH IN AUSTRALIA. 1965. 4/yr. Aus.$15. Australian Association for the Teaching of English, P.O. Box 203, Norwood, S.A. 5067, Australia. Ed. W. Corcoran. **Indexed:** Aus.Educ.Ind., Aus.P.A.I.S., C.I.J.E., Child.Lit.Abstr.
   Description: Contains articles of academic interest, and teacher resource materials in the field of English.

ENGLISH IN EDUCATION. see *EDUCATION — Teaching Methods And Curriculum*

420   AG
ENGLISH LANGUAGE JOURNAL/REVISTA DE LA LENGUA INGLESA; for the Latin American teacher of English. (Text in English & Spanish) 1970. q. $30. c/o Aldo O. Blanco, 224 Parana, 1st Fl., 1017 Buenos Aires, Argentina. adv.; bk.rev.; bibl.; circ. 500. **Indexed:** Lang.& Lang.Behav.Abstr., Lang.Teach.& Ling.Abstr.

420 375.4   UK
ENGLISH LANGUAGE RESEARCH JOURNAL. 1980. a. £6. University of Birmingham, English Language Research, P.O. Box 363, Birmingham B15 2TT, England. TEL 021-414 5696. Ed. C.J. Kennedy. **Indexed:** Lang.Teach.& Ling.Abstr.

420.07 370   UK   ISSN 0307-8337
PE1128.A2   CODEN: ELTJEB
ENGLISH LANGUAGE TEACHING JOURNAL. 1946. q. £30($55) (British Council) Oxford University Press, Oxford Journals, Pinkhill House, Southfield Road, Eynsham, Oxford OX8 1JJ, England. TEL 0865-882283. FAX 0865-882890. TELEX 837330 OXPRES G. Ed. N. Whitney. adv.; bk.rev.; cum.index every 2 yrs.; circ. 8,500. (also avail. in microform from UMI; reprint service avail. from UMI) **Indexed:** Br.Educ.Ind., C.I.J.E., Educ.Ind., Lang.& Lang.Behav.Abstr., Lang.Teach.& Ling.Abstr.
   —BLDSC shelfmark: 3732.462000.
   Formerly: English Language Teaching (ISSN 0013-8290)
   Description: Directed to teachers of English as second language. Includes practical help on procedure and techniques; discusses methods of teaching; reports on new ideas and systems of teaching; covers different uses of the English language.

ENGLISH LEADERSHIP QUARTERLY. see *EDUCATION — Teaching Methods And Curriculum*

420 422   UK   ISSN 0071-0636
ENGLISH PLACE-NAME SOCIETY. 1922. a. $50 (non-members $70). English Place-Name Society, c/o Mrs. M.D. Pattison, Department of English Studies, University of Nottingham, Nottingham NG7 2RD, England. Ed. Kenneth Cameron. index; circ. 740. **Indexed:** Br.Archaeol.Abstr., Geo.Abstr., NAA.

420 375.4   UK   ISSN 0955-8950
▼**ENGLISH REVIEW.** 1990. q. £17.50 (foreign £19). Philip Allan Publishers Ltd., Deddington, Oxfordshire OX15 0SE, England. TEL 0869-38652. FAX 0869-38803. (also avail. in microform from KTO)

420 820   NE   ISSN 0013-838X
PE1
ENGLISH STUDIES; a journal of English language and literature. 1919. bi-m. $143 to individuals; institutions $190. Swets Publishing Service (Subsidiary of: Swets en Zeitlinger B.V.), Heereweg 347, 2161 CA Lisse, Netherlands. TEL 31-2521-35111. FAX 31-2521-15888. TELEX 41325. (Dist. in N. America by: Swets & Zeitlinger, Box 517, Berwyn, PA 19312. TEL 215-644-4944) Ed. T.A. Birrell, J.M. Blom. adv.; bk.rev.; bibl.; index, cum.index: vols.1-40, 1919-1959; circ. 2,000. (also avail. in microform from SWZ; reprint service avail. from SWZ) **Indexed:** Abstr.Engl.Stud., Acad.Ind., Arts & Hum.Cit.Ind., Curr.Cont., Hum.Ind., Ind.Bk.Rev.Hum., Lang.& Lang.Behav.Abstr., Lang.Teach.& Ling.Abstr., M.L.A., Soc.Sci.Ind.
   —BLDSC shelfmark: 3775.117000.

410   UK   ISSN 0266-0784
PE1001
ENGLISH TODAY; the international review of the English language. q. $29 to individuals; institutions $63. Cambridge University Press, Edinburgh Bldg., Shaftesbury Rd., Cambridge CB2 2RU, England. TEL 0223-312393. FAX 0223-315052. TELEX 851817256. (N. American orders to: Cambridge University Press, 40 W. 20th St., New York, NY 10011) Eds. Tom McArthur, David Crystal. (also avail. in microform from UMI) **Indexed:** Lang.Teach.& Ling.Abstr.
   —BLDSC shelfmark: 3775.155800.
   Description: Focuses on the uses and speakers or teachers of English worldwide.

428   SA   ISSN 0046-2098
PE3452.S64
ENGLISH USAGE IN SOUTHERN AFRICA. 1970. a. R.13.20($8) University of South Africa, Department of English, P.O. Box 392, Pretoria 0001, South Africa. FAX 012-429-3221. TELEX 350068. Ed.Bd. bk.rev.; abstr.; circ. 400. **Indexed:** Ind.S.A.Per.

420 375.4   NE   ISSN 0172-8865
ENGLISH WORLD WIDE; a journal of varieties of English. Short title: E W W. 1980. s-a. fl.222($121) (effective 1992). John Benjamins Publishing Co., Amsteldijk 44, P.O. Box 75577, 1070 AN Amsterdam, Netherlands. TEL 020-6738156. FAX 020-6739773. (In N. America: 821 Bethlehem Pike, Philadelphia, PA 19118. TEL 215-836-1200) Ed. Manfred Goerlach. adv.; bk.rev.; circ. 600. (back issues avail.) **Indexed:** Lang.& Lang.Behav.Abstr. (1980-), M.L.A.
   —BLDSC shelfmark: 3775.161500.
   Description: Studies regional and social variations of English around the world.

410   BL
ENSAIOS LINGUISTICOS. 1978. irreg. price varies. Summer Institute of Linguistics, Departamento de Estudos Tecnicos, SAI-NO Lote D, Bloco 3, 70770 Brasilia DF, Brazil.
   Description: Contains sketches of grammar, lexicon and phonology concerning hthe indiginous languages of Brazil.

ENSEIGNEMENT DU RUSSE. see *LITERATURE*

400   PL   ISSN 0012-7825
P1.A1
EOS; commentarii societatis philologae polonorum. (Text in French, German, Latin and Polish) 1894. s-a. $32. (Polskie Towarzystwo Filologiczne) Ossolineum, Publishing House of the Polish Academy of Sciences, Rynek 9, Wroclaw, Poland. TELEX 0712771 OSS PL. (Dist. by: Ars Polona-Ruch, Krakowskie Przedmiescie 7, Warsaw, Poland) (Co-sponsor: Polska Akademia Nauk) Eds. Andrzej Wojcik, Sylwester Dworacki. bk.rev.; bibl.; charts; illus.; index; cum.index: 1894-1959; circ. 450. **Indexed:** M.L.A.
   Description: Contains papers on ancient philology, history, philosophy and classical culture (Latin-Greek) in later centuries.

EPIGRAPHIC SOCIETY. OCCASIONAL PAPERS. see *ARCHAEOLOGY*

418.02   BE
EQUIVALENCES. (Text mainly in French; occasionally in Dutch, English, French, German, Italian, Spanish) 1970. 2/yr. 500 BEF. Institut Superieur de Traducteurs et Interpretes de la Communaute francaise de Belgique, 34, rue Hazard, 1180 Brussels, Belgium. TEL 02-3440080. (Co-sponsor: Association pour la Promotion de l'Etude des Langues Modernes) Ed. J. M. van der Meerschen. adv.; bk.rev.; circ. 500. **Indexed:** M.L.A.

400   SW   ISSN 0013-9947
PA9
ERANOS; acta philologica suecana. (Text in English and German) 1896. 2/yr. SEK 285($38) Almqvist & Wiksell Periodical Company, Box 638, S-101 28 Stockholm, Sweden. Ed. Stig Y. Rudberg. adv.; index, cum.index every 50 yrs.; circ. 850. **Indexed:** M.L.A., Rel.Ind.Two.
   —BLDSC shelfmark: 3794.903000.

410 330   DK   ISSN 0107-9166
ERHVERSSPROG.* 1979. q. free. Erhvervssprogligt Forbund og Arbejdsloeshedskasse, Jydeholmen 15, DK-2720 Vanloese, Denmark. Ed. Jorgen Nielsen. adv.; bk.rev.; circ. 4,000.

460 375.4   SP   ISSN 0425-2772
PC4008
ESPANOL ACTUAL. 1963. s-a. 2200 ptas.($40) Instituto de Cooperacion Iberoamericana, Avenida los Reyes Catolicos, 4, 28040 Madrid, Spain. TEL 415-36-87. FAX 415-36-07. (Dist. by: Arco-Libros, S.A., Juan Bautista de Toledo 28, 28002 Madrid, Spain) **Indexed:** Lang.Teach.& Ling.Abstr., M.L.A.

469 375.4   BL   ISSN 0102-7077
ESPECIALIST. (Text in English, French, Portuguese, Spanish) 1981. 2/yr. $20 (effective 1992). (Centro de Pesquisas, Recursos e Informacao em Leitura) Editora da Pontificia Universidade Catolica de Sao Paulo, Rua Monte Alegre 984, 05014 Sao Paulo, SP, Brazil. TEL 62-0280. FAX 62-4920. (Co-sponsor: Conselho Nacional de Pesquisa) Ed. Maria Antonieta Alba Celani. bk.rev.

499.992   NE   ISSN 0014-0635
ESPERANTO. (Text in Esperanto) 1905. m. fl.55.12($27) Universala Esperanto-Asocio, Nieuwe Binnenweg 176, 3015 BJ Rotterdam, Netherlands. TEL 010-4361044. FAX 010-4361751. TELEX 23721 UEA NL. Ed. Istvan Ertl. adv.; bk.rev.; illus.; index; circ. 8,000. (back issues avail.) **Indexed:** M.L.A.

410   US   ISSN 0165-2575
ESPERANTO DOCUMENTS. N.S. 1976. 10/yr. $15. Universal Esperanto Association, Box 1129, El Cerrito, CA 94530. (European addr.: Universala Esperanto-Asocio, Nieuwe Binnenweg 176, 3015 BJ Rotterdam, Netherlands) (Co-sponsor: Center for Research and Documentation of the World Language Problem) Ed.Bd. adv. **Indexed:** Lang.& Lang.Behav.Abstr.

410   NE   ISSN 0165-2524
ESPERANTO-DOKUMENTOJ. NOVA SERIO. English edition: Esperanto Documents. New Series (ISSN 0165-2575); French edition: Documents sur l'Esperanto. Nouvelle Serie (ISSN 0165-2621) (Text in Esperanto) 1976. irreg. fl.46.65($22.50) for 10 nos. Universala Esperanto-Asocio - Universal Esperanto Association, Nieuwe Binnenweg 176, 3015 BJ Rotterdam, Netherlands. TEL 010-4361044. FAX 010-4361751. TELEX 23721 UEA NL. Ed. Thomas Bormann. circ. 550.

499.992   UK   ISSN 0014-0643
ESPERANTO EN SKOTLANDO. (Text in Esperanto) 1947. q. £2. Skota Federacio Esperantista - Scottish Esperanto Federation, 16 Woodlands Dr., Coatbridge ML5 1LE, Scotland. Ed. Dr. Albert Goodheir. bk.rev.; circ. 250.

499.992   FR   ISSN 0046-2500
ESPERANTO - INTERLANGUE UNIVERSELLE. (Text in Esperanto and French) q. 5 F. Editions Nova, 24 Ave de Riedisheim, F-68 Mulhouse, France.

499.992   FR   ISSN 0014-066X
ESPERANTO - LINGVO INTERNACIA. (Text in Esperanto and French) 1925. q. 4 F.($1) Esperanto-Editions, 24 Ave de Riedisheim, F-68100 Mulhouse, France. TEL 89-44-75-21. Ed. Albert Lienhardt. bk.rev.; bibl.
   Formerly: Tribune de l'Esperanto.

410 371.3   NO   ISSN 0802-0442
ESPERANTO - NYTT. 1959. 3/yr. NOK 20. Norvega - Esperantista Ligo - Norsk Esperanto - Forbund, Olaf Schous vei 18, 0572 Oslo 5, Norway. circ. 2,000.

410   UK   ISSN 0046-2527
ESPERANTO TEACHER. (Text in English and Esperanto) 1939. 3/yr. £7.50. Esperanto Teachers Association, 140 Holland Park Ave., London W11 4UF, England. Ed. Arnold Pitt. adv.; bk.rev.; play rev.; bibl.; illus.; circ. 500. (processed)

499.992   US
ESPERANTO - U S A; news of the language problem and Esperanto as a solution. (Text in English, Esperanto) 1952. bi-m. (plus occasional supplements). $15 to institutions. Universal Esperanto Association, Box 1129, El Cerrito, CA 94530. TEL 510-653-0998. Ed. D. Harlow. adv.; bk.rev.; illus.; circ. 1,200.
   Formerly: E L N A Newsletter (ISSN 0030-5065); Incorporates: E L N A Bulteno (ISSN 0012-771X); J E N - Bulteno (Junularo Esperantista de Nord-Amerikо) (ISSN 0021-5848); Supersedes: Organization of Esperanto-Speaking Young Americans. Newsletter.

499.992 SW ISSN 0014-0694
ESPERO; Svenska Esperantotidningen. (Text in Esperanto & Swedish) 1906. 6/yr. SEK 135. Svenska Esperantofoerbundet, Brunnsgatan 21, S-111 38 Stockholm, Sweden. Ed. Leif Nordenstorm. adv.; bk.rev.; circ. 2,000.
  Description: Provides information about the Swedish Esperanto movement; presents readings in Esperanto.

410 NE
ESSAIS DE DIALECTOLOGIE INTERLINGUALE. 1978. irreg. price varies. Van Gorcum en Co. B.V., P.O. Box 43, 9400 AA Assen, Netherlands. TEL 05920-46846. FAX 05920-72064.

ESTRENO; journal on the contemporary Spanish theater. see *THEATER*

480 375.4 SP
ESTUDIOS DE FILOLOGIA GRIEGA. 1985. a. 765 ptas. Universidad de Granada, Servicio de Publicaciones, Antiguo Colegio Maximo, Campus de Cartuja, 18071 Granada, Spain. TEL 281356.

400 SP ISSN 0210-7953
ESTUDIOS DE FILOLOGIA INGLESA. 1976. 2/yr. price varies. Universidad de Granada, Servicio de Publicaciones, Antiguo Colegio Maximo, Campus de Cartuja, 18071 Granada, Spain. TEL 281356. Ed. Rafael Fente Gomez.

470 375.4 SP
ESTUDIOS DE FILOLOGIA LATINA. 1980. irreg., no.4, 1984. 1750 ptas. Universidad de Granada, Servicio de Publicaciones, Antiguo Colegio Maximo, Campus de Cartuja, 18071 Granada, Spain. TEL 281356.

400 800 CL ISSN 0071-1713
P25
ESTUDIOS FILOLOGICOS. 1965. a. Esc.1300($13.27) in Latin America; elsewhere $17.70. Universidad Austral de Chile, Facultad de Filosofia y Humanidades, Casilla 142, Valdivia, Chile. Ed. Claudio Wagner. adv.; bk.rev.; circ. 700. **Indexed**: Amer.Hist.& Life, Arts & Hum.Cit.Ind., Curr.Cont., Hist.Abstr., M.L.A.

412 US ISSN 0014-164X
B840
ETC; a review of general semantics. Cover title: Et Cetera. 1943. 4/yr. $30. International Society for General Semantics, Box 728, Concord, CA 94522. TEL 510-798-0311. Ed. Jeremy Klein. adv.; bk.rev.; circ. 2,500. (also avail. in microform from MIM,UMI) **Indexed**: Amer.Hist.& Life, Hum.Ind., M.L.A., Mid.East: Abstr.& Ind., Psychol.Abstr., SSCI.
  Description: Reviews general semantics; devoted to how symbols influence human behavior: how uses of language and other media share thought, direct actions and determine the success or failure of communication.

ETUDES AEQUATORIA. see *ANTHROPOLOGY*

ETUDES BALKANIQUES. see *HISTORY — History Of Europe*

491.6 FR ISSN 0373-1928
ETUDES CELTIQUES. (Text in English and French) a. price varies. (Centre National de la Recherche Scientifique) Editions du C N R S, 1 Place Aristide Briand, 92195 Meudon Cedex, France. TEL 1-45-34-75-50. FAX 1-46-26-28-49. TELEX LABOBEL 204 135 F. (Subscr. to: Presses du C N R S, 20-22, rue St. Amand, 75015 Paris, France. TEL 1-45-33-16-00) Ed. Edward Bachellery. adv.; bk.rev.; bibl.; illus.; cum.index; circ. 1,250 (controlled). (reprint service avail. from KTO) **Indexed**: Br.Archaeol.Abstr., M.L.A.
  Description: Presents studies on archeology and linguistics, especially the ancient and modern Celtic languages. Contains original research.

447 CN ISSN 0708-2398
PM7851
ETUDES CREOLES; culture, langue, societe. 1978. s-a. Can.$30. Association des Universites Partiellement Ou Entierement de Langue Francaise, Universite de Montreal, B.P. 6128, Montreal, Que. H3C 3J7, Canada. TEL 514-343-6630. (Co-sponsor: Comite International des Etudes Creoles) bk.rev.; circ. 600. **Indexed**: M.L.A.
  —BLDSC shelfmark: 3817.300000.

418.005 FR ISSN 0071-190X
P1.A1
ETUDES DE LINGUISTIQUE APPLIQUEE. 1962. q. $64. Didier Erudition, 6 rue de la Sorbonne, 75005 Paris, France. (U.S. Subscr. to: Didier Erudition, N. American Fullfillment Office, Box 830350, Birmingham, AL 35283-0350) Ed. R. Galisson. illus. **Indexed**: Lang.& Lang.Behav.Abstr. (1972-), Lang.Teach.& Ling.Abstr., M.L.A.

400 BE ISSN 0071-1926
ETUDES DE PHILOLOGIE, D'ARCHEOLOGIE ET D'HISTOIRE ANCIENNE. 1934. irreg., vol.26, 1989. price varies. (Institut Historique Belge de Rome) N.V. Brepols I.G.P., Steenweg op Tielen 68, 2300 Turnhout, Belgium. TEL 014-41-54-63. FAX 014-42-89-19. TELEX 34 182. circ. controlled.
  Description: Studies classical philology and art history emphasizing excavation reports of Belgian missions in Italy.

410 GW ISSN 0176-7879
ETUDES DE PHONOLOGIE, PHONETIQUE ET LINGUISTIQUE DESCRIPTIVE DU FRANCAIS/STUDIEN ZUR PHONOLOGIE, PHONETIK UND LINGUISTIK DES FRANZOESISCHEN. 1984. irreg., vol.3, 1987. price varies. Helmut Buske Verlag Hamburg, Friedrichsgaber Weg 138, Postfach 1249, D-2000 Norderstedt, Germany.

492.7 306.4 FR ISSN 0757-7699
ETUDES ETHNO-LINGUISTIQUES MAGHREB-SAHARA. 1982. irreg. price varies. Societe d'Etudes Linguistiques et Anthropologiques de France (SELAF), 5 rue de Marseille, 75010 Paris, France. TEL 42-08-83-93.

494.5 894.5 FR ISSN 0071-2051
ETUDES FINNO-OUGRIENNES. 1964. irreg. price varies. (Centre d'Etudes Finno-Ougriennes) Editions Klincksieck, 11 rue de Lille, 75005 Paris, France. bk.rev.

400 FR ISSN 0071-2124
ETUDES LINGUISTIQUES. 1962. irreg. price varies. Editions Klincksieck, 11 rue de Lille, 75005 Paris, France. **Indexed**: Lang.& Lang.Behav.Abstr., M.L.A.

ETUDES MONGOLES ET SIBERIENNES. see *ANTHROPOLOGY*

499.3 306.4 FR
ETUDES OCEAN INDIEN. 1982. irreg., latest no.12. price varies. Institut National des Langues et Civilisations Orientales, Centre de Recherche de l'Ocean Indien Occidental, 2 rue de Lille, 75343 Paris Cedex 07, France. TEL 49-26-42-74.
  Description: Studies the linguistics, ethnology and archeology of the Indian Ocean countries.

410 SW ISSN 0347-0822
ETUDES ROMANES DE LUND. (Text in French) 1940. irreg. price varies. Lund University Press, P.O. Box 141, S-221 00 Lund, Sweden. TEL 46-46-31-20-00. FAX 46-46-30-53-38. Ed. L. Lindvall.

491 US ISSN 0898-0454
EURASIAN LANGUAGE ARCHIVES. 1988. irreg. Eurolingua, Box 101, Bloomington, IN 47402-0101. TEL 812-332-8918.
  Description: Focuses on synchronic and diachronic description concerning languages in Northern Eurasia between Japan and Germany.

410 IT
EUROASIATICA; journal of neohistorical linguistics. (Text in various European languages) 1970. irreg., vol.4, 1978. price varies. Giardini Editori e Stampatori, Via Santa Bibbiana 28, 56100 Pisa, Italy. TEL 050 502531. Ed. Nullo Minissi.

410 572 FR ISSN 0755-9313
EUROPE DE TRADITION ORALE. 1982. irreg. price varies. Societe d'Etudes Linguistiques et Anthropologiques de France (SELAF), 5 rue de Marseille, 75010 Paris, France. TEL 42-08-83-93. Ed. Fanny de Sivers. adv.; bk.rev.; circ. 250.

460 375.4 MX
LA EVOLUCION FONOLOGICA DEL PROTOVALTUAT. irreg., no.2, 1982. Universidad Nacional Autonoma de Mexico, Instituto de Investigaciones Filologicas, Ciudad Universitaria, Coyoacan 04510, Mexico, D.F., Mexico.
  Formerly: Coleccion Linguistica Indigena.

420 PK ISSN 0014-4975
P1
EXPLORATIONS. (Text in English) 1969. s-a. Rs.50($6) per no. Government College, Department of English Language and Literature, Lahore, Pakistan. Ed. A. R. Anjum. bk.rev.; circ. 900. **Indexed**: M.L.A.

491.7 375.4 CC
EYU XUEXI/LEARNING RUSSIAN. (Text in Chinese and Russian) bi-m. $14.40. Beijing Foreign Language Institute, Russian Department, Suzhou Jie, Haidian Qu, Beijing 100081, People's Republic of China. TEL 890351. (Dist. in US by: China Books & Periodicals, Inc., 2929 24th St., San Francisco, CA 94110. TEL 415-282-2994) Ed. Jiang Xiuwen.

F I P L V WORLD NEWS. (Federation Internationale des Professeurs de Langues Vivantes) see *EDUCATION*

418.02 BE
F I T NEWSLETTER/NOUVELLES DE LA F I T. (Text in various languages) 1968. q. 700 BEF (outside Europe 900 BEF). Federation Internationale des Traducteurs - International Federation of Translators, Heiveldstraat 245, B-9040 Gent, St. Amandsberg, Belgium. TEL 91-28-39-71. (Co-sponsor: Unesco) Ed. R. Haeseryn. adv.; bk.rev.; circ. 1,100.
  Description: Reports on activities of the International Federation of Translators as well as general news of interest to those in the field. Includes articles on translation, interpretation, and comparative linguistics.

407 AU
FACHSPRACHE; international journal of LSP. (Text in English, French, German) 1979. s-a. S.610. Universitaets Verlagsbuchhandlung GmbH, Servitengasse 5, A-1092 Vienna, Austria. TEL 0222-348124. Ed.Bd. adv.; bk.rev.; abstr.; bibl.; charts; illus. (back issues avail.)
  Description: Contains didactics and research for teachers, translators, journalists.

FAGUO YANJIU/ETUDES FRANCAISES. see *SOCIAL SCIENCES: COMPREHENSIVE WORKS*

495.1 CC ISSN 0257-0203
FANGYAN/DIALECT. (Text in Chinese; table of contents in English) 1979. q. Y6.80($21.90) Shehui Kexue Zazhishe, A-158 Gulou Xidajie, Beijing 100720, People's Republic of China. (Dist. outside China by: China International Book Trading Corp., P.O. Box 2820, Beijing, P.R.C.; Dist. in US by: China Books & Periodicals, Inc., 2929 24th St., San Francisco, CA 94110. TEL 415-282-2994)
  Description: Contains linguistic studies on Chinese dialects.

450 GW ISSN 0014-8555
IL FARO; Eine Monatszeitschrift zur Weiterbildung im Italienischen. (Text in German, Italian) 1955. 6/yr. DM.13.20. Beacon-Verlag Koerber oHG, Birkental 13, Postfach 1161, 6702 Bad Duerkheim, Germany. illus.; circ. 2,000. (tabloid format)

430 375.4 AU
FAUSTCHEN. 1973. irreg. Oesterreichische Hochschuelerschaft, S T R V Germanistik, Universitaetsstr. 7, A-1010 Vienna, Austria. Ed.Bd. bk.rev.; bibl.; circ. 1,000.
  Formerly (until 1980): Beitraege zum Deutschstudium.

440 375.4 CC
FAYU XUEXI/LEARNING FRENCH. (Text in Chinese and French) q. $9.90. Beijing Foreign Language Institute, French Department, Suzhou Jie, Haidian Qu, Beijing 100081, People's Republic of China. TEL 890351. (Dist. in US by: China Books & Periodicals, Inc., 2929 24th St., San Francisco, CA 94110. TEL 415-282-2994) Ed. Chen Zhenxiao.

LA FENICE. see *HISTORY*

490 GW ISSN 0341-311X
FENNO-UGRICA. 1973. irreg., no.11, 1989. price varies. Helmut Buske Verlag Hamburg, Friedrichsgaber Weg 138, Postfach 1249, D-2000 Norderstedt, Germany. Eds. Harald Haarmann, Janos Pusztay.

LINGUISTICS

499.992   NE   ISSN 0921-2302
FENOMENO. (Text in Dutch, Esperanto) 1969. m. fl.30. Federatie van Esperanto-Organisaties in Nederland - Federacio de Esperanto-Organizoj en Nederlando, Populierendreef 7, 2272 RA Voorburg, Netherlands. TEL 070-3866653. Ed. S.P. Smits. adv.; bk.rev.; circ. 1,200. (also avail. in Braille)
    Former titles: Komuna Esperanto-Gazeto (ISSN 0023-317X); Nederlanda Esperantisto; Laboratista Esperanto.

400 860   AG   ISSN 0071-495X
FILOLOGIA. 1949. a. $35 or exchange basis. Instituto de Filologia y Literaturas Hispanicas "Dr. Amado Alonso", 25 de Mayo 217, Buenos Aires 1002, Argentina. TEL 302733. (Subscr. to: Oficina de Venta de Publicaciones de la Facultad de Filosofia y Letras, Puan 470, Buenos Aires 1406, Argentina) Ed. Ana Maria Barrenechea. adv.; bk.rev.; circ. 1,000. **Indexed:** Amer.Hist.& Life, Hist.Abstr., M.L.A.

420   PL   ISSN 0554-8144
FILOLOGIA ANGIELSKA. (Text in English, Polish; summaries in English) 1972. irreg., no.22, 1988. price varies. Adam Mickiewicz University Press, Nowowiejskigo 55, 61-734 Poznan, Poland. TEL 527-380. FAX 61-526425. TELEX 413260 UAMPL.
    Formerly: Uniwersytet im. Adama Mickiewicza w Poznaniu. Wydzial Filologiczny. Seria Filologia Angielska.
    Description: Contains current research results of the university's students and professors of English, their Ph.D. works and monographs. Each volume contains monographs (thesis) of one author.

480 880   PL   ISSN 0554-8160
FILOLOGIA KLASYCZNA. (Text in Polish; summaries in various languages) 1966. irreg., lastest no.12. price varies. Adam Mickiewicz University Press, Nowowiejskiego 55, 61-734 Poznan, Poland. TEL 527-380. FAX 61-526425. TELEX 413260 UAMPL.
    —BLDSC shelfmark: 9120.455000.
    Formerly: Uniwersytet im. Adama Mickiewicza w Poznaniu. Wydzial Filologiczny. Seria Filologia Klasyczna.
    Description: Contains current research results of the university's scholars, their Ph.D. thesis and monographs. Each volume contains the work of one author.

400   SP
FILOLOGIA MODERNA. (Text in English, French, German, Italian, and Spanish) 1960. 150 ptas.($5) Universidad Complutense de Madrid, Facultad de Filologia, Cuidad Universitaria, Madrid-3, Spain. Ed. Hans Juretschke. (processed) **Indexed:** Ind.Bk.Rev.Hum.
    Formerly: Revista Filologia Moderna (ISSN 0046-3841)

400   IT
FILOLOGIA MODERNA. 1978. a. L.65000 (effective 1992). Pacini Editore s.r.l., Via della Gherardesca 1, 56014 Ospedaletto (Pisa), Italy. TEL 050-982439. FAX 050-983906. TELEX 501628 PACINI I. Ed.Bd.

491.85   PL   ISSN 0554-8179
FILOLOGIA POLSKA. (Text in Polish; summaries in English) 1961. irreg. prices varies. (Adam Mickiewicz University) Adam Mickiewicz University Press, Nowowiejskiego 55, 61-734 Poznan, Poland. TEL 527-380. TELEX 413260 UAM PL. circ. 800.

400   HU   ISSN 0015-1785
FILOLOGIAI KOZLONY/PHILOLOGICAL REVIEW. 1955. q. $26.50. (Magyar Tudomanyos Akademia) Akademiai Kiado, Publishing House of the Hungarian Academy of Sciences, P.O. Box 24, H-1363 Budapest, Hungary. Ed. M. Horanyi. adv.; bk.rev.; illus.; index. **Indexed:** M.L.A.

400   RU   ISSN 0028-1212
FILOLOGICHESKIE NAUKI. 1958. bi-m. $15. Izdatel'stvo Vysshaya Shkola, Prospekt Marksa 18, 103009 Moscow K-9, Russia. (Co-sponsor: Ministerstvo Vysshego i Spetsial'nogo Obrazovaniya S.S.S.R.) index; circ. 1,915. **Indexed:** Lang.& Lang.Behav.Abstr., M.L.A.

400   CK   ISSN 0071-4976
FILOLOGOS COLOMBIANOS. 1954. irreg., no.9, 1979. price varies. Instituto Caro y Cuervo, Seccion de Publicaciones, Apdo. Aereo 51502, Bogota, Colombia.

491   XN   ISSN 0352-3055
FILOLOSKI FAKULTET. KATEDRA ZA ISTOCNOSLOVENSKI I ZAPADNOSLOVENSKI JAZICI I KNIZEUNOSTI. SLAVISTICKI STUDII. (Text in all Slavic languages; summaries in English) 1976. biennial. 100 din. Filoloski Fakultet, Katedra za Istocnoslovenski i Zapadnoslovenski Jazici i Knizeunosti, 91000 Skopje, Macedonia. Eds. Boris Markov, Milan Gjurchinov. bk.rev.; circ. 300.

410 800   CI   ISSN 0350-3623
P9
FILOZOFSKI FAKULTET - ZADAR. RAZDIO FILOLOSKIH ZNANOSTI. RADOVI. (Text in Croatian, English, French, German, Italian; summaries in English) 1960. a. $20. Filozofski Fakultet u Zadru, Obala Marsala Tita 2, 57000 Zadar, Croatia. TEL 057-436-623. TELEX 25-882. (Co-sponsor: Samoupravna Interesna Zajednica Znanosti SR Hrvatske) Ed. Vjekoslav Cosic. index, cum.index: nos.1-15; circ. 800. (back issues avail.)

494   FI   ISSN 0355-1253
PH1
FINNISCH-UGRISCHE FORSCHUNGEN; Zeitschrift fuer Finnisch-Ugrische Sprach- und Volkskunde. (Text in English, French and German) 1902. irreg. FIM 140 per no. Suomalais-Ugrilainen Seura, PL 320, 00171 Helsinki 17, Finland. (Dist. by: Tiedekirja, Kirkkokatu 14, 00170 Helsinki, Finland) bk.rev.; index; circ. 350. (back issues avail.) **Indexed:** M.L.A.

494 894   GW   ISSN 0341-7816
PH1
FINNISCH-UGRISCHE MITTEILUNGEN. (Text in English, French, German) 1977. a. price varies. Helmut Buske Verlag Hamburg, Friedrichsgaber Weg 138, Postfach 1249, D-2000 Norderstedt, Germany. Eds. Istvan Futaky, Wolfgang Veenker. index; circ. 400. **Indexed:** Lang.& Lang.Behav.Abstr.

410   UK   ISSN 0142-7237
FIRST LANGUAGE. 1980. 3/yr. £40($85) Alpha Academic (Subsidiary of: Richard Sadler Ltd.), Halfpenny Furze, Mill Lane, Chalfont St. Giles, Bucks HP8 4NR, England. TEL 02407-2509. Ed. Kevin Durkin. adv.; bk.rev.; index. (back issues avail.) **Indexed:** Child Devel.Abstr., Lang.& Lang.Behav.Abstr. (1983-), Lang.Teach.& Ling.Abstr., Psychol.Abstr., Sp.Ed.Needs Abstr., SSCI.
    —BLDSC shelfmark: 3934.465000.
    Description: Empirical, theoretical and review papers in all areas of child language development.

FOCUS: TEACHING ENGLISH LANGUAGE ARTS. see EDUCATION — Teaching Methods And Curriculum

FODOR'S THREE-IN-ONE: FRANCE; guidebook, language cassette and phrase book. see TRAVEL AND TOURISM

FODOR'S THREE-IN-ONE: GERMANY; guidebook, language cassette and phrase book. see TRAVEL AND TOURISM

FODOR'S THREE-IN-ONE: ITALY; guidebook, language cassette and phrase book. see TRAVEL AND TOURISM

FODOR'S THREE-IN-ONE: MEXICO; guidebook, language cassette and phrase book. see TRAVEL AND TOURISM

FODOR'S THREE-IN-ONE: SPAIN; guidebook, language cassette and phrase book. see TRAVEL AND TOURISM

400   GW   ISSN 0165-4004
FOLIA LINGUISTICA; acta societatis linguisticae Europaeae. 1967. 4/yr. DM.235($145) (European Society of Linguistics) Mouton de Gruyter, Genthinerstr. 13, Postfach 110240, Germany. TEL 030-260-05235. circ. 1,500. **Indexed:** Amer.Bibl.Slavic & E.Eur.Stud, Amer.Hist.& Life, Hist.Abstr., Lang.& Lang.Behav.Abstr. (1971-), Lang.Teach.& Ling.Abstr., M.L.A., Mid.East: Abstr.& Ind.
    —BLDSC shelfmark: 3971.200000.
    Description: Treats the scientific study of language in all its aspects.

499.92   SP   ISSN 0046-435X
FONTES LINGUAE VASCONUM. 1969. 2/yr. 1800 ptas. Gobierno de Navarra, Fondo de Publicaciones, Navas de Tolosa, 21, 31002 Pamplona, Spain. TEL 10-71-21. FAX 22-76-73. bk.rev.; bibl.; charts.

407 370   US   ISSN 0015-718X
PB1
FOREIGN LANGUAGE ANNALS. 1967. 6/yr. $65 to individuals; libraries $55 (foreign $60). American Council on the Teaching of Foreign Languages, 6 Executive Plaza, Yonkers, NY 10701-6801. TEL 914-963-8830. FAX 914-963-1275. Ed. Frank Grittner. adv.; bk.rev.; abstr.; charts; index; circ. 6,000. (also avail. in microform from MIM,UMI; reprint service avail. from UMI,KTO) **Indexed:** C.I.J.E., Cont.Pg.Educ., Curr.Cont., Educ.Ind., Lang.& Lang.Behav.Abstr., Lang.Teach.& Ling.Abstr., Mid.East: Abstr.& Ind., SSCI.
    —BLDSC shelfmark: 3987.038000.
    Incorporates (after 1975, vol.5, no.4): Accent on A C T F L.
    Description: Presents study and teaching methods.

400   CK   ISSN 0120-338X
P9   CODEN: FOFUE6
FORMA Y FUNCION. 1981. s-a. Universidad Nacional de Colombia, Facultad de Ciencias Humanas, Departamento de Filologia e Idiomas, Ciudad Universitaria, Bogota, Colombia. **Indexed:** Lang.& Lang.Behav.Abstr. (1988-).

400   IT
LE FORME E LA STORIA; rivista di filologia moderna. 1989. s-a. L.80000. Rubbettino Editore, Viale dei Pini, 88049 Soveria Mannelli, Italy. Eds. Nicolo Mineo, Sergio Romangnoli. circ. 1,000. (back issues avail.)

FORUM (WASHINGTON, 1978). see EDUCATION — Teaching Methods And Curriculum

420 375.4   US
FORUM (WASHINGTON, 1980). 1963-1978; resumed 1980? q. $14. U.S. Information Agency, 301 4th St., S.W., Washington, DC 20547. (Orders to: Supt. of Documents, Washington, DC 20402) Ed. Anne C. Newton. illus.; index; circ. 110,000. **Indexed:** Cont.Pg.Educ., Ind.U.S.Gov.Per., Lang.Teach.& Ling.Abstr.
    Formerly: English Teaching Forum.

FORUM DER LETTEREN; tijdschrift voor taal- en letterkunde. see LITERATURE

400 800   UK   ISSN 0015-8518
PB1   CODEN: FMLSEG
FORUM FOR MODERN LANGUAGE STUDIES. 1965. q. £50($98) (University of St. Andrews) Oxford University Press, Oxford Journals, Pinkhill House, Southfield Road, Eynsham, Oxford OX8 1JJ, England. TEL 0865-882283. FAX 0865-882890. TELEX 837330-OXPRES-G. Ed.Bd. adv.; bk.rev.; index; circ. 450. (back issues avail.) **Indexed:** Arts & Hum.Cit.Ind., Can.Rev.Comp.Lit, Curr.Cont., M.L.A., Mid.East: Abstr.& Ind.
    —BLDSC shelfmark: 4024.093000.
    Description: Studies in the field of European language and literature, including English and American, from the Middle Ages to the present.

410   US   ISSN 0163-0768
FORUM LINGUISTICUM. (Supplement avail.: Edward Sapir Monograph Series in Language, Culture, and Cognition) 1976. 3/yr. $20 to individuals; students $16; institutions $30. (Linguistic Association of Canada and the United States) Jupiter Press, Box 101, Lake Bluff, IL 60044. TEL 312-234-3997. Ed. Adam Makkai. adv.; bk.rev.; circ. 1,000. (back issues avail.) **Indexed:** Lang.Teach.& Ling.Abstr., M.L.A.

410   GW
FORUM LINGUISTICUM. (Text in English and German; summaries in English) 1974. irreg., no.33, 1991. price varies. Verlag Peter Lang GmbH, Eschborner Landstr. 42-50, 6000 Frankfurt a.M. 90, Germany. TEL 069-7807050. FAX 069-785893. Ed. Christoph Gutknecht. bk.rev.; abstr.; bibl.; circ. 400 (controlled). (back issues avail.) **Indexed:** M.L.A.

410   GW   ISSN 0341-3144
FORUM PHONETICUM. 1973. irreg., no.46, 1989. price varies. Helmut Buske Verlag Hamburg, Friedrichsgaber Weg 138, Postfach 1249, D-2000 Norderstedt, Germany. Ed.Bd.

401   US   ISSN 0168-2555
FOUNDATIONS OF SEMIOTICS. Abbreviated title: F O S. (Text in English, French, German; summaries in English, French) 1983. irreg., vol.25, 1990. price varies. John Benjamins Publishing Co., 821 Bethlehem Pike, Philadelphia, PA 19118. TEL 215-836-1200. FAX 215-836-1204. (And: Amsteldijk 44, P.O. Box 75577, 1070 AN Amsterdam, Netherlands. TEL 020-6762325) Ed. Achim Eschbach.
  Description: Provides fundamental research in semiotics with contributions to the theory of signs.

400 800   SL
FOURAH BAY STUDIES IN LANGUAGE AND LITERATURE. (Text in English) 1980. a. L.30. University of Sierra Leone, Fourah Bay College, Freetown, Sierra Leone. Ed.Bd. circ. 150.

440 370   NR   ISSN 0015-9387
FRANCAIS AU NIGERIA. (Text in English and French) 1965. q. £N3. Nigerian Association of French Teachers, c/o A. Iwara, Ed., Department of Modern Languages, University of Ibadan, Ibadan, Nigeria. adv.; bk.rev.; cum.index every 2 yrs.; circ. 500. (back issues avail) **Indexed:** M.L.A.
  Description: Presents language study and teaching methods.

440   FR   ISSN 0015-9409
PC2002
FRANCAIS MODERNE; revue de linguistique francaise. 1933. q. 170 F. Conseil International de la Langue Francaise, 142 bis, rue de Grenelle, 75007 Paris, France. TEL 47-05-07-93. FAX 45-55-41-16. adv.; bk.rev.; abstr.; bibl.; index. **Indexed:** Arts & Hum.Cit.Ind., Curr.Cont., Ind.Bk.Rev.Hum., Lang.& Lang.Behav.Abstr., Lang.Teach.& Ling.Abstr., M.L.A.
  —BLDSC shelfmark: 4032.155000.

440 375.4 840   US
FRANCITE. (Text in French) 1973. s-a. $2 per copy. c/o Anne-Marie de Moret, Ed., 221 Northgrand St., St. Louis, MO 63103. bk.rev.; bibl.; circ. 750.
  Description: Contains articles about French language and literature.

440 375.4   UK   ISSN 0957-1744
▼**FRANCOPHONIE.** 1990. 2/yr. £20($40) (foreign £21). Association for Language Learning, 16 Regent Place, Rugby, Warwickshire CV21 2PN, England. TEL 0788-546443. FAX 0788-544149. Ed. Alan Smalley. adv.; bk.rev.; film rev.; play rev.; abstr.; bibl.; charts; illus.; stat.; index; circ. 4,000.
  Description: Contains articles and information of interest to teachers and students of French.

FRANKFURTER BEITRAEGE ZUR GERMANISTIK. see LITERATURE

FRANZOESISCH HEUTE; Informationsblaetter fuer Franzoesischlehrer in Schule und Hochschule. see EDUCATION — Teaching Methods And Curriculum

491.8 914.96   GW   ISSN 0170-1533
FREIE UNIVERSITAET BERLIN. OSTEUROPA-INSTITUT. BALKANOLOGISCHE VEROEFFENTLICHUNGEN. 1979. irreg., vol.19, 1991. price varies. (Freie Universitaet Berlin, Osteuropa-Institut) Verlag Otto Harrassowitz, Taunusstr. 14, Postfach 2929, 6200 Wiesbaden, Germany. TEL 0611-530-0. FAX 0611-530570. TELEX 4186135. Ed. Norbert Reiter. circ. 500.

FREIE UNIVERSITAET BERLIN. OSTEUROPA-INSTITUT. SLAVISTISCHE VEROEFFENTLICHUNGEN. see LITERATURE

400   GW   ISSN 0016-0970
FREMDSPRACHEN; Zeitschrift fuer Theorie und Praxis der Sprachmittlung. (Text in English, French, German, Russian and Spanish) 1957. 4/yr. DM.48. Verlag Alexandre Hatier GmbH, Oranienburgerstr. 13-14, 1020 Berlin, Germany. adv.; bk.rev.; circ. 5,000. **Indexed:** Lang.& Lang.Behav.Abstr., M.L.A.
  —BLDSC shelfmark: 4033.680000.
  Description: Devoted to the translation of German into Russian, English, French, and Spanish.

407   GW
FREMDSPRACHEN LEHREN UND LERNER; zur Theorie und Praxis des Sprachunterrichts an Hochschulen. 1971. a. DM.58. E. Keimer Verlag, Postfach 1463, 5340 Bad Honnef am Rhein, Germany.

370   GW
FREMDSPRACHENUNTERRICHT. 1957. 8/yr. DM.38.40. Volk und Wissen Verlag GmbH, Lindenstr. 54A, 1086 Berlin, Germany. TEL 0372-20343-0. **Indexed:** Lang.Teach.& Ling.Abstr.

407 371   GW   ISSN 0340-2207
PB35
DER FREMDSPRACHLICHE UNTERRICHT; textarbeit, landeskunde, sprachpraxis und methodenfragen. (Editions in English and French) 1967. 4/yr. DM.59. Erhard Friedrich Verlag GmbH, Im Brande 15, Postfach 100150, 3016 Seelze-Velber, Germany. TEL 0511-40004-0. cum.index: 1967-1981; circ. 5,600. **Indexed:** Lang.Teach.& Ling.Abstr.

FRENCH FORUM. see LITERARY AND POLITICAL REVIEWS

FRENCH REVIEW. see EDUCATION

439.2   NE
FRYSKE NAMMEN. (Text in Frisian) 1978. irreg. Fryske Akademy, Doelestrijtte 8, 8911 DX Ljouwert-Leeuwarden, Netherlands. TEL 058-131414. FAX 058-131409. Ed.Bd.

FU JEN STUDIES; literature & linguistics. see LITERATURE

420 375.4   CC
FUJIAN WAIYU/FOREIGN LANGUAGES IN FUJIAN. (Text in Chinese) 1984. q. Y4. Fujian Normal University, Foreign Language Department, Fuzhou, Fujian 350007, People's Republic of China. FAX 591-542840. TELEX 92269 FTUFO CN. (Dist. overseas by: Jiangsu Publications Import & Export Corp., 56 Gao Yun Ling, Nanjing, Jiangsu, P.R.C.) bk.rev.; circ. 1,500.
  Description: Discusses issues in the teaching of foreign languages, with a focus on English. Also covers Russian, Japanese and other foreign languages.

410   US
FUNCTIONAL GRAMMAR SERIES.* (Text in English) 1985. irreg., no.13, 1990. Walter de Gruyter, Inc., 200 Saw Mill River Rd., Hawthorne, NY 10532. TEL 914-747-0110. FAX 914-747-1326. Ed.Bd.

410   GW   ISSN 0175-2103
G A L - BULLETIN. (Text in English and German) 1983. s-a. DM.20($10) Gesellschaft fuer Angewandte Linguistik e.V., Universitaet Duisburg, Postfach 101503, 4100 Duisburg 1, Germany. TEL 0203-379-2064. FAX 0203-3793333. TELEX 855793-UNI-DU-D. Ed. Bernd Spillner. adv.; bk.rev.; bibl.; circ. 900.

499.992 370.196   GW
G E J - GAZETO. (Text in Esperanto and German) 1979. bi-m. DM.20. Deutsche Esperanto-Jugend, Rheinweg 15, 5300 Bonn 1, Germany. TEL 0228-235898. FAX 0228-232764. Ed. Ulrich Goertz. circ. 2,000.
  Description: Information on Esperanto meetings and international youth activities.

410   DK   ISSN 0106-0872
PF3025
G I P. (Germansk Instituts Publikationer) 1977. irreg., no.56, 1991. free. Odense Universitet, Institut for Germansk Filologi, Campusvej 55, DK-5230 Odense M, Denmark. TEL 66-15-86-00. FAX 66-15-84-28. Eds. Flemming Talbo Stubkjaer, Helge Nielsen. circ. 200.
  Description: Presents the teaching and research activity at the institute.

491.6 375.4   UK
GAELIC SOCIETY OF INVERNESS. TRANSACTIONS. (Text in English, Gaelic) 1872. biennial. Gaelic Society of Inverness, The Granary, Ness-side, Dores Rd., Inverness, Scotland. circ. 500.

410   SP   ISSN 0213-4403
GAVAGAI. 1985. s-a. $30 to individuals; libraries and institutions $35. Universidad de La Laguna, Asociacion Canaria de Filosofia del Lenguaje y de la Ciencia, Secretariado de Publicaciones, San Agustin, 30, 38201 La Laguna-Tenerife, Islas Canarias, Spain. TEL 922-25-81-27. adv.
  Description: Devoted to the philosophy of language and science.

410   PL   ISSN 0860-3456
PG6004
GDANSKIE STUDIA JEZYKOZNAWCZE. 1975. irreg., vol.3, 1983. price varies. (Gdansk Scientific Society) Ossolineum, Publishing House of the Polish Academy of Sciences, Rynek 9, 50-106 Wroclaw, Poland. TEL 386-25. (Dist. by: Ars Polona, Krakowskie Przedmiescie 7, 00-068 Warsaw, Poland) Ed. Boguslaw Kreja.
  Description: Linguistic studies by authors from the region of Gdansk Pomerania.

423.1   UK   ISSN 0072-0542
GEIRIADUR PRIFYSGOL CYMRU. (Text in English and Welsh) 1953. a. £3 per part. (Board of Celtic Studies) University of Wales Press, 6 Gwennyth St., Cathays, Cardiff CF2 4YD, Wales. TEL 0222-31919. FAX 0222-230908. Ed. G. A. Bevan. circ. 1,500.
  Description: Dictionary of the Welsh language.

400 300   US   ISSN 0016-6553
GENERAL LINGUISTICS; covering the field of linguistics, psycholinguistics, and sociolinguistics. 1955. q. $25 to individuals (foreign $32.50); institutions $35 (foreign $40). Medieval & Renaissance Texts and Studies, LNG 99, SUNY - Binghamton, Binghamton, NY 13902-6000. TEL 607-777-6758. Eds. Ernst Ebbinghaus, Saul Levin. adv.; bk.rev.; bibl.; circ. 800. (tabloid format; also avail. in microform from MIM,UMI; reprint service avail. from UMI) **Indexed:** Abstr.Anthropol., Amer.Bibl.Slavic & E.Eur.Stud., Arts & Hum.Cit.Ind., Curr.Cont., Ind.Bk.Rev.Hum., Lang.& Lang.Behav.Abstr. (1972-), Lang.Teach.& Ling.Abstr., M.L.A., Mid.East: Abstr.& Ind., SSCI.
  —BLDSC shelfmark: 4104.550000.

412   US   ISSN 0072-0771
B820
GENERAL SEMANTICS BULLETIN. 1950. a. $15. Institute of General Semantics, 163 Engle St., Englewood, NJ 07631. TEL 201-568-0551. Ed. Stuart Mayper. adv.; bk.rev.; cum.index: vols.1-37; circ. 600. (also avail. in microform from UMI; reprint service avail. from UMI) **Indexed:** Lang.& Lang.Behav.Abstr., Sociol.Abstr.
  —BLDSC shelfmark: 4111.200000.

GENRE (NORMAN). see LITERATURE

400   US   ISSN 0196-7207
P53
GEORGETOWN UNIVERSITY ROUND TABLE ON LANGUAGES AND LINGUISTICS. 1951. a. price varies. (Georgetown University, School of Languages and Linguistics) Georgetown University Press, Intercultural Center, Rm. 111, Washington, DC 20057. TEL 202-687-6063. FAX 202-687-5712. circ. 2,000. **Indexed:** Lang.& Lang.Behav.Abstr. (1972-), M.L.A.
  Former titles: Georgetown University. Institute of Languages and Linguistics. Report of the Annual Round Table Meeting on Linguistics and Language Studies (ISSN 0072-1212); Monograph Series on Languages and Linguistics (ISSN 0077-0612)
  Description: Provides a forum for internationally known scholars to focus on different aspects of linguistics and language teaching.

430.07 370   US   ISSN 0016-8831
PF3001
GERMAN QUARTERLY. (Text in English and German) 1928. 4/yr. $35 (foreign $45). American Association of Teachers of German, Inc., 112 Haddontowne Ct., Ste. 104, Cherry Hill, NJ 08034. TEL 609-795-5553. FAX 609-795-9398. Ed. Reinhold Grimm. adv.; bk.rev.; index; circ. 5,000. (also avail. in microform from UMI; reprint service avail. from UMI) **Indexed:** Amer.Bibl.Slavic & E.Eur.Stud., Arts & Hum.Cit.Ind., Bk.Rev.Ind. (1975-), Child.Bk.Rev.Ind. (1975-), Curr.Cont., Educ.Ind., Ind.Bk.Rev.Hum., Lang.& Lang.Behav.Abstr., Lang.Teach.& Ling.Abstr., M.L.A.
  —BLDSC shelfmark: 4162.151000.
  Description: Presents literary and philological articles.

GERMAN STUDIES LIBRARY GROUP NEWSLETTER. see LIBRARY AND INFORMATION SCIENCES

LINGUISTICS

430 375   UK   ISSN 0953-4822
GERMAN TEACHING. (Text in English and German) 1969. 2/yr. £20($40) (foreign £40). Association for Language Learning, 16 Regent Place, Rugby, Warwickshire CV21 2PN, England. TEL 0788-546443. FAX 0788-544149. Ed. Glyn Hatherall. adv.; bk.rev.; abstr.; bibl.; charts; film rev.; illus.; mkt.; play rev.; record rev.; stat.; index; circ. 3,000. **Indexed:** Cont.Pg.Educ., Lang.Teach.& Ling.Abstr.
    Formerly: Treffpunkt.
    Description: Contains articles and information of interest to teachers and students of German.

430 375.4   US
PD1
GERMANIC NOTES AND REVIEWS. (Text in English, German) 1970. q. $10 (effective 1992). Department of Modern and Classical Languages, Bemidji State University, Bemidji, MN 56601. Ed. Richard F. Krummel. adv.; bk.rev.; abstr.; bibl.; circ. 500. (also avail. in microform from GMC; back issues avail.) **Indexed:** Arts & Hum.Cit.Ind., Curr.Cont., M.L.A.
    Formerly (until vol.23, Jan. 1992): Germanic Notes (ISSN 0016-8882)

430   US   ISSN 0016-8890
PD1
GERMANIC REVIEW; devoted to studies dealing with the Germanic languages and literatures. 1926. q. $28 to individuals; institutions $55. (Helen Dwight Reid Educational Foundation) Heldref Publications, 1319 Eighteenth St., N.W., Washington, DC 20036-1802. TEL 202-296-6267. FAX 202-296-5149. Ed. James King. adv.; bk.rev.; bibl.; index; circ. 1,000. (also avail. in microform; reprint service avail. from KTO) **Indexed:** Acad.Ind., Amer.Bibl.Slavic & E.Eur.Stud, Arts & Hum.Cit.Ind., Can.Rev.Comp.Lit., Curr.Cont., Hum.Ind., Int.Z.Bibelwiss, Lang.& Lang.Behav.Abstr., M.L.A.
    —BLDSC shelfmark: 4162.160000.
    Refereed Serial

430   GW   ISSN 0072-1492
PF3025
GERMANISTISCHE LINGUISTIK. 1969. irreg.(4-6 /yr.). price varies. (Forschunginstitut fuer Deutsche Sprache, Marburg) Georg Olms Verlag, Hagentorwall 7, 3200 Hildesheim, Germany. FAX 05121-32007. TELEX 927454-OLMS-D. (Dist. in U.S. by: Hy Cohen, Literary Agency Ltd., 111 West 57 St., New York, NY 10019) Ed.Bd. adv.; bk.rev.; index; circ. 700. **Indexed:** Lang.Teach.& Ling.Abstr.

430 375.4   BE   ISSN 0344-5909
GERMANISTISCHE MITTEILUNGEN; Zeitschrift fuer deutsche Sprache, Literatur und Kultur in Wissenschaft und Praxis. 1975. s-a. DM.27. Belgischer Germanisten- und Deutschlehrerverband, Vrijheidslaan 17, B-1000 Brussels, Belgium. FAX 02-4124200. (Subscr. to: F. Duemmler Verlag, Postfach 1480, D-5200 Bonn, Germany) Eds. Peter Nelde, Rudolf Kern. adv.; bk.rev.; illus.; index; circ. 1,200. (back issues avail.) **Indexed:** Lang.& Lang.Behav.Abstr., M.L.A.

450 100   IT   ISSN 0017-0461
GIORNALE ITALIANO DI FILOLOGIA; rivista di cultura. 1948; N.S. 1970? s-a. L.70000. Herder Editrice e Libreria s.r.l., Piazza Montecitorio 120, 00186 Rome, Italy. TEL 67 94 628. FAX 678-47-51. TELEX 621427 NATEL. Ed. N. Scivoletto. bk.rev.; abstr.; index; circ. 800. (back issues avail.) **Indexed:** M.L.A.
    —BLDSC shelfmark: 4178.216000.

410   AA
GJUHA JONE. 3/yr. Akademia e Shkencave e RPSSH, Instituti i Gjuhesise dhe i Letersise, Tirana, Albania. Ed. Ali Dhiro.

410   NE   ISSN 0166-5790
GLOT; tijdschrift voor taalwetenschap. 1978. 3/yr. fl.90 to individuals; institutions fl.120. I C G Publications, P.O. Box 509, 3300 AM Dordrecht, Netherlands. TEL 078-510454. FAX 078-510972. Ed.Bd. bk.rev. (back issues avail.) **Indexed:** Lang.& Lang.Behav.Abstr. (1983-).
    Description: Discusses linguistics; especially theoretical developments in the field.

418   PL   ISSN 0072-4769
GLOTTODIDACTICA; an international journal of applied liguistics. (Text in English, French, German, and Russian) 1966. irreg., vol.20, 1990. price varies. Adam Mickiewicz University Press, Nowowiejskiego 55, 61-734 Poznan, Poland. TEL 527-380. FAX 61-526425. TELEX 413260 UAMPL. Ed. Waldemar Pfeiffer. bk.rev.; circ. 1,500. **Indexed:** Lang.& Lang.Behav.Abstr. (1972-), Lang.Teach.& Ling.Abstr., M.L.A.
    —BLDSC shelfmark: 4195.860000.
    Description: Contains current research results done by university students and professors of English, German, French, Russian etc., with emphasis on theoretical issues in the field of applied linguistics related to language learning and language teaching.

430 830   SW   ISSN 0072-4793
GOETEBORGER GERMANISTISCHE FORSCHUNGEN. (Subseries of Acta Universitatis Gothoburgensis) (Text in German) 1955. irreg., no.32, 1991. price varies; also exchange basis. Acta Universitatis Gothoburgensis, P.O. Box 5096, S-402 22 Goeteborg, Sweden. Ed. Sven-Gunnar Andersson.

430   GW
GOETHE-INSTITUT ZUR PFLEGE DER DEUTSCHEN SPRACHE IM AUSLAND UND ZUR FOERDERUNG DER INTERNATIONALEN KULTURELLEN ZUSAMMENARBEIT. JAHRBUCH. 1965. a. DM.11. Goethe-Institut zur Pflege der Deutschen Sprache im Ausland und zur Foederung der Internationalen Kulturellen Zusammenarbeit, Balanstr. 57, 8000 Munich 90, Germany. TEL 089-41868248. FAX 089-41868414. Ed. Uwe Schmelter. circ. 7,000.
    Formerly: Goethe-Institut zur Pflege Deutscher Sprache und Kultur im Ausland. Jahrbuch (ISSN 0072-4858)

400 800   GW   ISSN 0017-1549
GOETTINGISCHE GELEHRTE ANZEIGEN. 1739. s-a. DM.76. (Akademie der Wissenschaften, Goettingen) Vandenhoeck und Ruprecht, Robert-Bosch-Breite 6, Postfach 3753, 3400 Goettingen, Germany. TEL 0551-6959-22. FAX 0551-695917. Eds. U. Schindel, H. Boockmann. adv.; bk.rev.; index; circ. 600.

400 830   SW   ISSN 0072-503X
GOTHENBURG STUDIES IN ENGLISH. (Subseries of Acta Universitatis Gothoburgensis) 1952. irreg., no.63, 1991. price varies; also exchange basis. Acta Universitatis Gothoburgensis, PO Box 5096, S-402 22 Goeteborg, Sweden. **Indexed:** M.L.A.
    —BLDSC shelfmark: 4203.170000.

410   AU
GRAZER LINGUISTISCHE STUDIEN. (Text in English, French, German, Italian and Spanish) 1975. 2/yr. price varies. Universitaet Graz, Institut fuer Allgemeine und Angewandte Sprachwissenschaft, Mozartgasse 8, A-8010 Graz, Austria. FAX 0316-382130. Ed.Bd. adv.; bk.rev.; circ. 200. **Indexed:** Lang.& Lang.Behav.Abstr. (1983-), M.L.A.

GRIECHISCHEN CHRISTLICHEN SCHRIFTSTELLER DER ERSTEN JAHRHUNDERTE. see *RELIGIONS AND THEOLOGY*

410   US
GRONINGEN - AMSTERDAM STUDIES IN SEMANTICS.* (Text in English) 1983. irreg., no.12, 1990. Walter de Gruyter, Inc., 200 Saw Mill River Rd., Hawthorne, NY 10532. TEL 914-747-0110. FAX 914-747-1326. Ed.Bd.
    Description: Contains monographs and collections on the semantics of natural languages.

492   FR
GROUPE LINGUISTIQUE D'ETUDES CHAMITO-SEMITIQUES. COMPTES RENDUS. (Suspended publication 1940-1945) 1934. irreg. (Groupe Linguistique d'Etudes Chamito-Semitiques) Librarie Orientaliste Paul Geuthner, 12 rue Vavin, 75006 Paris, France. TEL 33-1-46-34-71-30. FAX 33-1-43-29-75-64. TELEX 250 303 PUBLIC PARIS.

430   GW
GRUNDLAGEN DER GERMANISTIK. irreg., vol.30, 1989. Erich Schmidt Verlag GmbH & Co. (Bielefeld), Viktoriastr. 44a, 4800 Bielefeld 1, Germany. TEL 0521-583080. Eds. Werner Besch, Hartmut Steinecke. (back issues avail.) **Indexed:** M.L.A.

420 375.4   US
GUIDE TO GRANTS AND FELLOWSHIPS IN LINGUISTICS. 1982. triennial. $6.50. Linguistic Society of America, 1325 18th St., N.W., Ste. 211, Washington, DC 20036-6501. TEL 202-835-1714.

410   GW   ISSN 0344-242X
AS181
GULLIVER; German-English Yearbook. (Text in English, German; summaries in English) 1976. s-a. DM.33 (students DM.27). Argument-Verlag GmbH, Rentzelstr. 1, 2000 Hamburg 13, Germany. TEL 040-456018. (back issues avail.)

410 370   CC
GUOWAI WAIYU JIAOXUE/FOREIGN LANGUAGE TEACHING IN FOREIGN COUNTRIES. (Text in Chinese) q. Huadong Shifan Daxue, Waiyu Xi - East China Normal University, Foreign Language Department, 3663 Zhongshan Beilu, Shanghai 200062, People's Republic of China. TEL 2577577. Ed. Zhu Zhizhong.

410 378   US
GUOWAI YUYANXUE. (Text in Chinese) q. $12.30. China Books & Periodicals, Inc., 2929 24th St., San Francisco, CA 94110. TEL 415-282-2994. FAX 415-282-0994.
    Description: Covers the field of linguistics outside of China.

GYPSY LORE SOCIETY. NEWSLETTER. see *ANTHROPOLOGY*

GYPSY LORE SOCIETY. PUBLICATIONS. see *ANTHROPOLOGY*

480   GW   ISSN 0072-9191
HABELTS DISSERTATIONSDRUCKE. REIHE KLASSISCHE PHILOLOGIE. 1953. irreg., no.38, 1988. price varies. Dr. Rudolf Habelt GmbH, Am Buchenhang 1, 5300 Bonn 1, Germany. Eds. W. Schetter, W. Schmid.

491.7   GW   ISSN 0072-9515
HAMBURGER BEITRAEGE FUER RUSSISCHLEHRER. 1964. irreg., no.37, 1989. price varies. Helmut Buske Verlag Hamburg, Friedrichsgaber Weg 138, Postfach 1249, D-2000 Norderstedt, Germany. Ed. Irene Nowikowa.

430   GW   ISSN 0072-9582
HAMBURGER PHILOLOGISCHE STUDIEN. 1966. irreg., no.60, 1984. price varies. Helmut Buske Verlag Hamburg, Friedrichsgaber Weg 138, Postfach 1248, D-2000 Norderstedt, Germany. **Indexed:** M.L.A.

HANDBUCH DER ORIENTALISTIK. 8. ABTEILUNG. HANDBOOK OF URALIC STUDIES. see *ORIENTAL STUDIES*

491.54   AU   ISSN 0017-7377
HANDES AMSORYA; Zeitschrift fuer Armenische Philologie. (Text in Armenian; index in Armenian and German) 1887. a. $100. Mechitharisten-Congregation in Wien, Mechitharistengasse 4, A-1070 Vienna, Austria. TEL 936417. Ed. P. Szekulian. bk.rev.; charts; circ. 400. **Indexed:** Numis.Lit.

495.1 375.4   CC
HANYU XUEXI/STUDYING CHINESE. (Text in Chinese) bi-m. Yanbian Daxue Chubanshe, 105 Gongyuan Lu, Yanji, Jilin 133002, People's Republic of China. TEL 515921. Ed. Wu Chang.

496   NR
HARSUNAN NIJERIYA. (Text in English and Hausa) 1971. a. $3. Bayero University, Kano, Centre for the Study of Nigerian Languages, P.M.B. 3011, Kano, Nigeria. Ed. Horahim Yaro Yahayh. circ. 500. (processed)

410 890 940   US
HARVARD CELTIC COLLOQUIUM. PROCEEDINGS.* (Text in Breton, English, Irish Gaelic and Welsh) 1981. a. $16. (Harvard University, Department of Celtic Languages and Literature) Quinlin, Campbell Publishers, Box 651, Allston, MA 02134. TEL 617-787-0178. Eds. Paul Jefferiss, William Mahon. circ. 250.
    Description: Highlights articles of scholarly and general interest on the literature, language, and history of the Celtic-speaking regions worldwide.

HARVARD ENGLISH STUDIES. see *LITERATURE*

492 220　　　　　　US　　ISSN 0073-0637
HARVARD SEMITIC MONOGRAPHS. 1968. irreg., no.6, 1973. price varies. Scholars Press, Box 15399, Atlanta, GA 30333-0399. TEL 404-636-4757. FAX 404-636-8301.
　　Description: Papers on Semitic language and civilization.

489　　　　　　　US　　ISSN 0073-0688
PA25
HARVARD STUDIES IN CLASSICAL PHILOLOGY. 1890. a. latest vol.94, 1992. price varies. Harvard University Press, 79 Garden St., Cambridge, MA 02138. TEL 617-495-2600. FAX 617-495-5898. (reprint service avail. from SCH)
　—BLDSC shelfmark: 4270.200000.
　　Refereed Serial

HARVARD - YENCHING INSTITUTE. MONOGRAPH SERIES. see *HISTORY — History Of Asia*

HAUTES ETUDES DU MONDE GRECO-ROMAIN. see *CLASSICAL STUDIES*

492.4　　　　　　IS　　ISSN 0792-3252
HEBREW COMPUTATIONAL LINGUISTICS. (Text in English, Hebrew) 1969. s-a. $26. (Bar-Ilan University, Department of Hebrew and Semitic Languages) Bar-Ilan University Press, Ramat Gan 52900, Israel. Ed. Maya Fruchtman. (back issues avail.) **Indexed:** Lang.& Lang.Behav.Abstr. (1972-), M.L.A.

492 296　　　　　　US　　ISSN 0146-4094
PJ4501
HEBREW STUDIES; a journal devoted to Hebrew language and literature of all periods. vol.16, 1975. a. $25. National Association of Professors of Hebrew, 1346 Van Hise Hall, 1220 Linden Dr., University of Wisconsin-Madison, Madison, WI 53706. TEL 608-262-2089. Ed. Michael V. Fox. adv.; bk.rev.; circ. 600. (also avail. in microform from UMI) **Indexed:** Mid.East: Abstr.& Ind., Old Test.Abstr., Rel.& Theol.Abstr. (1988-), Rel.Ind.One.
　Formerly (until vol. 17, 1976): Hebrew Abstracts (ISSN 0438-895X)
　　Refereed Serial

HEFTE FUER OSTASIATISCHE LITERATUR. see *LITERATURE*

400 100　　　　　　IT
HENOCH. (Text in English, French, German and Italian) 1979. 3/yr. $100. Herder Editrice e Libreria s.r.l., Piazza Montecitorio 120, 00186 Rome, Italy. TEL 67 94 628. FAX 678-47-51. TELEX 621427 NATEL. Ed. Paolo Sacchi. **Indexed:** New Test.Abstr., Old Test.Abstr.

480　　　　　　　GW　　ISSN 0018-0777
PA3
HERMES; Zeitschrift fuer klassische Philologie. (Text in English, French, German and Italian) 1866. q. DM.168 (supplements priced individually). Franz Steiner Verlag Wiesbaden GmbH, Birkenwaldstr. 44, Postfach 101526, 7000 Stuttgart 1, Germany. TEL 0711-2582-0. FAX 0711-2582290. TELEX 723636-DAZD. Ed.Bd. adv.; index; circ. 900. (back issues avail.; reprint service avail. from KTO) **Indexed:** Arts & Hum.Cit.Ind., Curr.Cont., M.L.A.

480　　　　　　　GW　　ISSN 0341-0064
HERMES - EINZELSCHRIFTEN. (Supplement to: Hermes) (Text in English and German) irreg., vol.57, 1991. price varies. Franz Steiner Verlag Wiesbaden GmbH, Birkenwaldstr. 44, Postfach 101526, 7000 Stuttgart 1, Germany. TEL 0711-2582-0. FAX 0711-2582290. TELEX 723636-DAZD. Ed.Bd.
　—BLDSC shelfmark: 4300.079200.

HERON; essays on language & literature. see *LITERATURE*

440　　　　　　　GW
HI HELLO SALUT. 1990. DM.12. Volk und Wissen Verlag GmbH, Lindenstr. 54 A, 1086 Berlin, Germany. TEL 0372-20343-0. circ. 50,000.

HIAKA KHRONIKA. see *HISTORY — History Of Europe*

491.43　　　　　　II　　ISSN 0378-3928
HINDUSTANI ZABAN. (Text in Hindi and Urdu) 1969. q. Rs.50. Mahatma Gandhi Memorial Research Centre and Library, Mahatma Gandhi Memorial Bldg., Netaji Subhash Rd, Bombay 400002, India. Ed. Dr. Abdussattar Dalvi. bk.rev.; circ. 500.

460 469 370　　　　US　　ISSN 0018-2133
PC4001
HISPANIA; a journal devoted to the interests of the teaching of Spanish and Portuguese. (Text in English, Portuguese, Spanish) 1918. q. $30. American Association of Teachers of Spanish and Portuguese, Inc., University of Southern California, Dept. of Spanish & Portuguese, Los Angeles, CA 90089-0358. TEL 617-832-3779. Ed. Theodore A. Sackett. adv.; bk.rev.; film rev.; charts; tr.lit.; index. cum.index; circ. 13,000. (also avail. in microform from UMI; reprint service avail. from UMI,KTO) **Indexed:** Arts & Hum.Cit.Ind., Bk.Rev.Ind. (1965-), C.I.J.E., Child.Bk.Rev.Ind. (1965-), Educ.Ind., Hisp.Amer.Per.Ind., Ind.Bk.Rev.Hum., Lang.& Lang.Behav.Abstr., Lang.Teach.& Ling.Abstr., M.L.A.
　—BLDSC shelfmark: 4315.760000.

460　　　　　　　US　　ISSN 0018-2176
PQ6001
HISPANIC REVIEW; a quarterly journal devoted to research in the Hispanic languages and literatures. (Text in English and Spanish) 1933. q. $22.50 to individuals; institutions $32.50. University of Pennsylvania, Romance Languages Department, Philadelphia, PA 19104-6305. TEL 215-898-7420. Ed. Russell P. Sebold. adv.; bk.rev.; index; circ. 1,600. (also avail. in microform from MIM; reprint service avail. from SCH) **Indexed:** Amer.Hist.& Life, Arts & Hum.Cit.Ind., Curr.Cont., Hisp.Amer.Per.Ind., Hist.Abstr., Hum.Ind., Ind.Bk.Rev.Hum., Lang.& Lang.Behav.Abstr., M.L.A.
　—BLDSC shelfmark: 4315.780000.

460 375.4　　　　　UK
HISPANIC TEXTS. 1957. irreg. price varies. Manchester University Press, Oxford Rd., Manchester M13 9PL, England. TEL 061-273-5539. FAX 061-274-3346. TELEX 666517-UNIMAN. Ed. Herbert Ramsden.
　Formerly: Spanish Texts.

HISPANORAMA. see *LITERATURE*

410 900　　　　　　NE　　ISSN 0302-5160
P61
HISTORIOGRAPHIA LINGUISTICA; international journal for the history of the language sciences. (Text in English, French, German, Italian, Spanish) 1974. 3/yr. fl.300($160) (effective 1992). John Benjamins Publishing Co., Amsteldijk 44, P.O. Box 75577, 1070 AN Amsterdam. TEL 020-6738156. FAX 020-6739773. (In N. America: 821 Bethlehem Pike, Philadelphia, PA 19118. TEL 215-836-1200) Ed. E.F.Konrad Koerner. bk.rev.; bibl.; index; cum.index; circ. 600. (back issues avail.) **Indexed:** Arts & Hum.Cit.Ind., Curr.Cont., Lang.& Lang.Behav.Abstr. (1974-), Lang.Teach.& Ling.Abstr., M.L.A.
　—BLDSC shelfmark: 4317.320000.
　　Description: Discussion of the epistemological and methodological foundations of a historiography of linguistic thought.

418　　　　　　　GW　　ISSN 0935-3518
P501　　　　　　　　　　CODEN: HISPE2
HISTORISCHE SPRACHFORSCHUNG/HISTORICAL LINGUISTICS. (Text partly in English and French) 1852. s-a. DM.96 price varies. Vandenhoeck und Ruprecht, Theaterstr. 13, Postfach 3753, 3400 Goettingen, Germany. TEL 0551-6959-22. FAX 0551-695917. Eds. A. Bammesberger, Guenter Neumann. adv.; circ. 420. (reprint service avail. from SCH) **Indexed:** Lang.& Lang.Behav.Abstr. (1988-), M.L.A.
　—BLDSC shelfmark: 4317.384000.
　　Formerly: Zeitschrift fuer Vergleichende Sprachforschung (ISSN 0044-3646)

HISTORY AND APPLIED LINGUISTICS. see *HISTORY*

460.07 370　　　　　UK　　ISSN 0018-6856
HOY DIA. (Text in Spanish) 1963. 6/yr. (during school year). Mary Glasgow Publications Ltd., Avenue House, 131-133 Holland Park Ave., London W11 4UT, England. TEL 071-603 4688. FAX 071-602-5197. TELEX 311890-MGPUBS. (U.S. subscr. to: Delta Systems Co. Inc., 570 Rock Rd., Dundee, IL 60118-9992) charts; illus.; circ. 14,500. (also avail. in microform from UMI; reprint service avail. from UMI)
　　Description: Spanish language magazine for advanced level students.

HUMAN COMMUNICATION AND ITS DISORDERS; a review. see *EDUCATION — Special Education And Rehabilitation*

HUMAN COMMUNICATION RESEARCH. see *COMMUNICATIONS*

410 800　　　　　　US　　ISSN 0194-164X
DB901
HUNGARIAN STUDIES NEWSLETTER. 1973. 3/yr. $9. American Hungarian Foundation, Box 1084, New Brunswick, NJ 08903. TEL 908-846-5777. Ed. August J. Molnar. adv.; bk.rev.; circ. 2,500. **Indexed:** Amer.Bibl.Slavic & E.Eur.Stud.

I F E F, AUSTRIA SEKCIO. BULTENO. (Federacio Esperantista Fervojista) see *TRANSPORTATION — Railroads*

410　　　　　　　II　　ISSN 0378-2484
PL4601
I J D L. (International Journal of Dravidian Linguistics) 1972. s-a. Rs.50($10) Dravidian Linguistics Association, Kerala Paanini Buildings Kunnumpuram, Trivandrum 695 001, Kerala, India. Ed. V.I. Subramoniam. adv.; bk.rev.; bibl.; charts; circ. 400. **Indexed:** M.L.A.

410　　　　　　　NE　　ISSN 0921-2566
I P O ANNUAL PROGRESS REPORT. (Text in English) 1966. a. free. Institute for Perception Research, P.O. Box 513, Eindhoven 5600 MB, Netherlands. TEL 040-773873. FAX 040-773876. TELEX 35000 PHCT NL. Ed.Bd. circ. 1,500. **Indexed:** Ergon.Abstr., Lang.& Lang. Behav.Abstr., Psychol.Abstr.

418 370　　　　　　GW　　ISSN 0019-042X
P1.A1　　　　　　　　　　CODEN: IRALA4
I R A L. (International Review of Applied Linguistics in Language Teaching) (Text in English, French and German) 1963. q. DM.98 to individuals; institutions DM.160. Julius Groos Verlag, Hertzstr. 6, 6900 Heidelberg 1, Germany. TEL 06221-303621. (Dist. by: Oxford University Press, Walton St., Oxford OX2 6DP, England) Eds. B. Malmberg, G. Nickel. adv.; bk.rev.; bibl.; index; circ. 900. (also avail. in microform from UMI; microfiche from UMI; reprint service avail. from UMI) **Indexed:** C.I.J.E., Cont.Pg.Educ., Curr.Cont., Educ.Ind., Ind.Bk.Rev.Hum., Lang.& Lang.Behav.Abstr. (1972-), Lang.Teach.& Ling.Abstr., M.L.A., Mid.East: Abstr.& Ind., Psychol.Abstr., SSCI.
　—BLDSC shelfmark: 4567.522000.

418　　　　　　　BE　　ISSN 0019-0829
P123
I T L REVIEW OF APPLIED LINGUISTICS. (Text in Dutch, English, French, German) 1968. q. 1000 BEF (foreign 1200 BEF). Universite Catholique de Louvain - Institute of Applied Linguistics, Blijde Inkomstraat 21, B-3000 Leuven, Belgium. FAX 16-285025. Ed. N. Delbecque. bk.rev.; bibl.; charts; illus.; stat.; circ. 600. (back issues avail.) **Indexed:** Ind.Bk.Rev.Hum., Lang.& Lang.Behav.Abstr. (1972-), Lang.Teach.& Ling.Abstr., M.L.A.
　—BLDSC shelfmark: 4588.670000.

479 879　　　　　　GW　　ISSN 0019-0993
PC4001　　　　　　　　　　CODEN: IBERE2
IBERO-ROMANIA; Zeitschrift fuer die iberoromanischen Sprachen und Literaturen in Europa und Amerika. (Text in English, German and Spanish) s-a. DM.86. Max Niemayer Verlag, Postfach 2140, 7400 Tuebingen 1, Germany. TEL 07071-81104. FAX 07071-87419. Ed.Bd. adv.; bk.rev. **Indexed:** Arts & Hum.Cit.Ind.

IBEROAMERICANA; Lateinamerika-Spanien-Portugal. see *LITERARY AND POLITICAL REVIEWS*

IDIOM. see *EDUCATION — Teaching Methods And Curriculum*

410　　　　　　　US
IDIOMS AND PHRASES INDEX. 1983. irreg. $230. Gale Research Inc., 835 Penobscot Bldg., Detroit, MI 48226. TEL 800-877-4253. FAX 313-961-6083. TELEX 810-221-7086. Ed. Laurence Urdang.
　　Description: Guide to idioms and phrases in English.

LINGUISTICS

410 UK
IDO-VIVO. 1930. 3/yr. $10. International Language (IDO) Society of Great Britain, 2 Bentham Way, Staincross, Barnsley, S. Yorkshire S75 5QA, England. TEL 0226-384533. Ed. Tom Lang. bk.rev.; circ. 150.
Formerly (until Jan. 1983): Ido-Letro.
Description: Official magazine of the International Language (IDO) Society of Great Britain. Contains articles, puzzles, short stories in English and IDO.

420 375.4 US
ILLINOIS T E S O L - B E NEWSLETTER. vol.7, 1979. 5/yr. membership. Illinois Teachers of English to Speakers of Other Languages - Bilingual Education, c/o G. Henllan-Jones, Amundsen High School, 5110 N. Damen, Chicago, IL 60625. TEL 312-989-3520. Ed. G. Henllan-Jones. adv.; bk.rev.; circ. 600.
Description: Includes articles and announcements for teachers of ESL and bilingual education.

IN OTHER WORDS. see RELIGIONS AND THEOLOGY

410 IT
INCONTRI LINGUISTICI. 1974. a. L.12000($14) (Universita degli Studi di Udine e Trieste) Editori e Stampatori Giardini, Via di Santa Bibbiana 28, 56100 Pisa, Italy. Ed.Bd. adv.; bk.rev.; circ. 3,000. Indexed: Lang.& Lang.Behav.Abstr., M.L.A.

418 II ISSN 0379-0037
PK101
INDIAN JOURNAL OF APPLIED LINGUISTICS. (Text in English) 1975. s-a. Rs.200($40) Bahri Publications, 997-A, St. No. 9, Gobindpuri, Kalkaji, New Delhi 110 019, India. TEL 644-5710. Ed. Ujjal Singh Bahri. adv.; bk.rev.; bibl. Indexed: Lang.& Lang.Behav.Abstr. (1987-), Lang.Teach.& Ling.Abstr.
—BLDSC shelfmark: 4410.220000.
Description: Research and theoretical work in applied linguistics.

410 II ISSN 0378-0759
PK1501
INDIAN LINGUISTICS; journal of the Linguistic Society of India. (Supplement avail.) (Text in English) 1931. q. Rs.100($20) Linguistic Society of India, c/o Deccan College Postgraduate and Research Institute, Poona 411006, India. Ed. R.V. Dhongde. adv.; bk.rev.; circ. 800. Indexed: Ind.Bk.Rev.Hum., Lang.& Lang.Behav.Abstr. (1972-), M.L.A.

491 II ISSN 0073-6589
INDIAN LINGUISTICS MONOGRAPH SERIES. (Text in English) 1958. irreg. price varies. Linguistic Society of India, c/o Deccan College Postgraduate and Research Institute, Poona 411006, India. Ed. R.V. Dhongde.

INDIANA ENGLISH. see LITERATURE

494 US ISSN 0073-7097
INDIANA UNIVERSITY. RESEARCH INSTITUTE FOR INNER ASIAN STUDIES. URALIC AND ALTAIC SERIES.. Short title: Uralic and Altaic Series. (Text in English unless reprint) 1960. irreg., no.154, 1990. price varies. Indiana University, Research Institute for Inner Asian Studies, Goodbody Hall 344, Bloomington, IN 47405. TEL 812-885-1605. FAX 812-855-7500. TELEX 272279 INDIANA U BLOM. Ed. Denis Sinor. Indexed: M.L.A.

494.2 951.7 HU ISSN 0073-7194
INDICES VERBORUM LINGUAE MONGOLIAE MONUMENTIS TRADITORUM. (Text in Mongolian with romanization; introduction in French) 1970. irreg. price varies. (Magyar Tudomanyos Akademia) Akademiai Kiado, Publishing House of the Hungarian Academy of Sciences, P.O. Box 24, H-1363 Budapest, Hungary. Ed. L. Ligeti.

INDO-IRANIAN JOURNAL. see ORIENTAL STUDIES

430 GW ISSN 0019-7262
INDOGERMANISCHE FORSCHUNGEN; Zeitschrift fuer Indogermanistik und allgemeine Sprachwissenschaft. (Text in English, French, German and Italian) 1891. a. $117. Walter de Gruyter und Co., Mouton Publishers, Genthlner Str. 13, 1000 Berlin 30, Germany. TEL 030-26005-0. FAX 030-26005-251. TELEX 184027. (U.S. addr.: Walter de Gruyter, Inc., 200 Saw Mill Rd., Hawthorne, NY 10532) Ed. Wolfgang P. Schmid. adv.; bk.rev.; charts; illus.; index. Indexed: Arts & Hum.Cit.Ind., Curr.Cont., Ind.Bk.Rev.Hum., Lang.& Lang.Behav.Abstr., M.L.A.

INDOLOGICAL STUDIES. see LITERATURE

375.4 440 CN ISSN 0822-5109
INFORM-ACTION; educateurs franco-manitobains. (Text in French) 1968. 3/yr. Can.$5 to non-members (typically set in Sep.). Manitoba Teachers Society, 191 Harcourt St., Winnipeg, Man. R3J 3H2, Canada. TEL 204-888-7961. FAX 204-831-0877. Ed. Paul Shurwood. circ. 1,800 (controlled).
Description: Professional journal for teachers of French and French immersion schools.

INFORMATIONEN DEUTSCH ALS FREMDSPRACHE. see EDUCATION — Higher Education

INFORMATIONEN ZUR DEUTSCHDIDAKTIK; Zeitschrift fuer den Deutschunterricht in Wissenschaft und Schule. see EDUCATION

418 025 GW
INFOTERM SERIES. irreg. price varies. (International Information Centre for Terminology, Vienna, AU) K.G. Saur Verlag KG, Ortlerstr. 8, Postfach 701620, 8000 Munich 70, Germany. TEL 089-76902-0. FAX 089-76902150.
Description: Consists of bibliographies, guides, and conference proceedings discussing theoretical and practical problems in terminology.

400 FR ISSN 0073-8018
INITIATION A LA LINGUISTIQUE. SERIE A. LECTURES. 1970. irreg. price varies. Editions Klincksieck, 11 rue de Lille, 75005 Paris, France. Eds. Pierre Guiraud, Alain Rey. Indexed: M.L.A.

400 FR ISSN 0073-8026
INITIATION A LA LINGUISTIQUE. SERIE B. PROBLEMES ET METHODES. 1970. irreg. price varies. Editions Klincksieck, 11 rue de Lille, 75005 Paris, France. Eds. Pierre Guiraud, Alain Rey.

410 KR ISSN 0320-2372
P9
INOZEMNA FILOLOHIJA. (Text in Ukrainian; summaries in English, French, German, Russian, Spanish) 1964. q. Izdatel'stvo Vysshaya Shkola, L'vovskoe Otdelenie, Ul. Universitetska 1, 290 000 Lvov, Ukraine. (Co-sponsor: Ministerstvo Vysshego i Srednego Spetsial'nogo Obrazovaniya) Ed. B.M. Zadorozhny. circ. 1,000.

491 FR ISSN 0078-9984
INSTITUT D'ETUDES SLAVES, PARIS. COLLECTION DE GRAMMAIRES. 1921. irreg., vol.7, 1980. price varies. Institut d'Etudes Slaves, 9 rue Michelet, 75006 Paris, France.

491 943 FR ISSN 0078-9992
INSTITUT D'ETUDES SLAVES, PARIS. COLLECTION DE MANUELS. 1923. irreg., vol.7, 1976. price varies. Institut d'Etudes Slaves, 9 rue Michelet, 75006 Paris, France.

375.4 FR ISSN 0300-2594
INSTITUT D'ETUDES SLAVES, PARIS. DOCUMENTS PEDAGOGIQUES. 1970. irreg., vol.31, 1989. price varies. Institut d'Etudes Slaves, 9 rue Michelet, 75006 Paris, France.
—BLDSC shelfmark: 3609.125000.

410 FR ISSN 0154-0157
INSTITUT D'ETUDES SLAVES, PARIS. LEXIQUES. 1978. irreg., vol.7, 1984. price varies. Institut d'Etudes Slaves, 9 rue Michelet, 75006 Paris, France.

INSTITUT D'ETUDES SLAVES, PARIS. TRAVAUX. see LITERATURE

400 BE
INSTITUT DE LINGUISTIQUE DE LOUVAIN. BIBLIOTHEQUE DES C I L L. (Supplement to: Cahiers de l'Institut de Linguistique de Louvain) (Text in English, French, German, Italian) 1976. irreg. Editions Peeters s.p.r.l., Bondgenotenlaan 153, B-3000 Leuven, Belgium. TEL 016-235170. FAX 016-228500. TELEX 65981 PULB.

400 BE ISSN 0771-6524
INSTITUT DE LINGUISTIQUE DE LOUVAIN. CAHIERS. Short title: C I L L. (Supplement avail.: Institut de Linguistique de Louvain. Bibliotheque des C I L L) (Text in Dutch, English, French, German, Spanish) 1972. s-a. 1200 BEF. Editions Peeters s.p.r.l., Bondgenotenlaan 153, B-3000 Leuven, Belgium. TEL 016-235170. FAX 016-228500. Eds. Y. Duhoux, G. Jucquois. adv.; bk.rev.; abstr.; bibl.; illus.; circ. 500. (back issues avail.) Indexed: Bull.Signal, Lang.Teach.& Ling.Abstr., M.L.A., Sociol.Abstr. Key Title: Cahiers de l'Institut de Linguistique de Louvain.
Formerly (until 1975): Universite Catholique de Louvain. Institut de Linguistique. Cahiers (ISSN 0303-3880)

410 SW
INSTITUT DE LINGUISTIQUE DE LUND. TRAVAUX. (Text in English, French or German) 1959. irreg., no.19, 1983. price varies. Liber Forlag, S-205 10, Malmo, Sweden. Eds. Eva Gaarding, Bengt Sigurd.

496 FR
INSTITUT NATIONAL DES LANGUES ET CIVILISATIONS ORIENTALES. BULLETIN DES ETUDES AFRICAINES. s-a. price varies. Institut National des Langues et Civilisations Orientales, Centre d'Etudes et de Recherche Africaines, 2 rue de Lille, 75343 Paris Cedex 07, France. TEL 49-26-42-74.
Description: Studies African languages and cultures.

410 CK
INSTITUTO CARO Y CUERVO. SEMINARIO ANDRES BELLO. CUADERNOS. 1978. irreg., no.4, 1990. Instituto Caro y Cuervo, Seccion de Publicaciones, Apdo. Aereo 51502, Bogota, Colombia.

INSTITUTO CARO Y CUERVO. SERIE MINOR. see LITERATURE

INSTITUTO DE ESTUDIOS ASTURIANOS. BOLETIN. see HISTORY — History Of Europe

INSTITUTO DE ESTUDIOS PERUANOS. DOCUMENTOS DE TRABAJO. see ANTHROPOLOGY

460 306.4 PE
INSTITUTO LINGUISTICO DE VERANO. DOCUMENTOS DE TRABAJO. 1973. irreg., no.21, 1989. price varies. Instituto Linguistico de Verano, Departamento de Estudios Etno-Linguisticos, Casilla 2492, Lima 100, Peru. FAX 5114-629-629. (Subscr. to: E. Iturriaga y Cia., Jiron Ica 441, Ofc. 202-203, Casilla 4640, Lima, Peru) Ed. Mary Ruth Wise. (also avail. in microfiche; back issues avail.)

460 375.4 PO
INSTITUTO NACIONAL DE INVESTIGACAO CIENTIFICA. TEXTOS DE LINGUISTICA. 1980. irreg., no.6, 1982. (Instituto Nacional de Investigacao Cientifica, Centro de Linguistica) Universidad de Coimbra, Centro de Estudos Classicos y Humanisticos, Faculdade de Letras, Coimbra, Portugal. circ. 25,000.

410 RM
INSTITUTUL DE SUBINGINERI ORADEA. LUCRARI STIINTIFICE: SERIA LINGVISTICA. (Text in Rumanian, occasionally in English or French; summaries in English, French, German or Rumanian) a. Institutul de Subingineri Oradea, Calea Armatei Rosii Nr. 5, 3700 Oradea, Rumania.
Formerly: Institutul Pedagogic Oradea. Lucrari Stiintifice: Seria Lingvistica; which continues in part (in 1973): Institutul Pedagogic Oradea. Lucrari Stiintifice: Seria Filologie; which superseded in part (in 1971): Institutul Pedagogic Oradea. Lucrari Stiintifice: Seria A and Seria B; which was formerly (until 1969): Institutul Pedagogic Oradea. Lucrari Stiintifice.

410 301 US
INTERCULTURAL STUDIES. irreg. price varies. Peter Lang Publishing, Inc., 62 W. 45th St., 4th Fl., New York, NY 10036. TEL 212-302-6740. FAX 212-302-7475. Ed. Thomas Vesce.
Description: Explores sociolinguistic issues in an intercultural aspect.

420 370.15 610
300   US
INTERFACES: LINGUISTICS, PSYCHOLOGY AND HEALTH THERAPEUTICS; an international journal of research, notes and commentary. 1973. 3/yr. $10. Providence College Press, Providence, RI 02918. Eds. Robert E. Haskell, Elaine Chiaka. bk.rev.; abstr.; bibl.; charts; stat.; tr.lit.; circ. 500. (back issues avail.) **Indexed:** ERIC, Lang.& Lang.Behav.Abstr., Psychol.Abstr., Sociol.Educ.Abstr.
Refereed Serial

410.5   JA
P1.A1
INTERNATIONAL CHRISTIAN UNIVERSITY. LANGUAGE RESEARCH BULLETIN. (Subseries of the university's publication 6-A) (Text in English) 1961. a. 2000 Yen. International Christian University, Division of Languages - Kokusai Kirisutokyo Daigaku, 3-10-2 Osawa, Mitaka, Tokyo 181, Japan. Ed.Bd. bibl.; circ. 500. **Indexed:** Lang.& Lang.Behav.Abstr. (1986-).
Formerly: Descriptive and Applied Linguistics. Annual Reports; Supersedes: Summer Institute in Linguistics. Studies in Descriptive and Applied Linguistics (ISSN 0385-8960)

410   BE   ISSN 0074-2791
INTERNATIONAL COMMITTEE OF ONOMASTIC SCIENCES. CONGRESS PROCEEDINGS. (Proceedings edited and published in country hosting the congress.) 1938. triennial, 15th, 1984, Leipzig. price varies. International Centre of Onomastics, Blijde-Inkomststr. 21, B-3000 Louvain, Belgium.

410   NE   ISSN 0074-3755
INTERNATIONAL CONGRESS OF LINGUISTS. PROCEEDINGS. (Published in host country) 1928. quinquennial, 14th, 1987, Berlin; 15th, 1992, Quebec. price varies. Permanent International Committee of Linguists, c/o E. M. Uhlenbeck, Dr. Kuyperlaan 11, 2215 NE Voorhout, Netherlands. circ. 1,700.

INTERNATIONAL JOURNAL FOR THE SEMIOTICS OF LAW; semiotic, linguistic, discursive approach to law. see *LAW*

497   US   ISSN 0020-7071
PM101
INTERNATIONAL JOURNAL OF AMERICAN LINGUISTICS. 1917. q. $36 to individuals; institutions $75; students $26. University of Chicago Press, Journals Division, 5720 S. Woodlawn Ave., Chicago, IL 60637. TEL 312-753-3347. (Orders to: Box 37005, Chicago, IL 60637) Ed. David S. Rood. adv.; bk.rev.; abstr.; index, cum.index every 10 yrs.: vols. 1-32, 1917-1966; circ. 1,600. (also avail. in microform from UMI; reprint service avail. from UMI,ISI,KTO) **Indexed:** A.I.C.P., Abstr.Anthropol., C.I.J.E., Curr.Cont., Hisp.Amer.Per.Ind., Hum.Ind., Ind.Bk.Rev.Hum., Lang.& Lang.Behav.Abstr. (1972-), Lang.Teach.& Ling.Abstr., M.L.A., Mid.East: Abstr.& Ind., SSCI.
—BLDSC shelfmark: 4542.050000.
Description: Scholarly journal devoted to the native languages of the Americas.
Refereed Serial

410   UK   ISSN 0950-3846
P327
INTERNATIONAL JOURNAL OF LEXICOGRAPHY. 1988. q. £46($90) Oxford University Press, Oxford Journals, Pinkhill House, Southfield Road, Enysham, Oxford OX8 1JJ, England. TEL 0865-882283. FAX 0865-882890. TELEX 837330 OXPRES G. Ed. Robert Ilson. adv.; bk.rev.; illus.; circ. 1,100. **Indexed:** Lang.& Lang.Behav.Abstr. (1988-).
—BLDSC shelfmark: 4542.319500.
Description: Covers theoretical, practical, diachronic and synchronic aspects of lexicography. Related disciplines such as lexicology, terminology, semantics, pragmatics, are also included.

419 371.912   UK   ISSN 0959-6402
INTERNATIONAL JOURNAL OF SIGN LINGUISTICS. 2/yr. £18($38) institutions £52($110); students £10($21). Multilingual Matters Ltd., Bank House, 8a Hill Rd., Clevedon, Avon BS21 7HH, England. TEL 0272-876519. FAX 0272-343096. bk.rev.; circ. 300.
Description: Promotes linguistic study of sign language.

491 891   US   ISSN 0538-8228
PG1
INTERNATIONAL JOURNAL OF SLAVIC LINGUISTICS AND POETICS. (Text in English, French, German and all Slavic languages) 1959-1976; resumed 1981. s-a. $20 to individuals; institutions and libraries $40. Slavica Publishers, Inc., Box 14388, Columbus, OH 43214. Ed.Bd. adv.; bk.rev.; charts; illus.; circ. 400. (reprint service avail. from SWZ) **Indexed:** Ind.Bk.Rev.Hum., M.L.A.
—BLDSC shelfmark: 4542.550000.

410 301   GW   ISSN 0165-2516
P40   CODEN: ISLGAH
INTERNATIONAL JOURNAL OF THE SOCIOLOGY OF LANGUAGE. (Text in English) 1974. bi-m. $54.50 to individuals; institutions $176. Mouton de Gruyter, Postfach 110240, 1000 Berlin 11, Germany. Ed. J.A. Fishman. adv.; bk.rev.; bibl.; circ. 900 (controlled). (back issues avail.) **Indexed:** Curr.Cont., E.I., Lang.& Lang.Behav.Abstr. (1974-), Lang.Teach.& Ling.Abstr., M.L.A., Mid.East: Abstr.& Ind., Psychol.Abstr., Sociol.Abstr. (1974-), SSCI.
—BLDSC shelfmark: 4542.573000.

418.02   II   ISSN 0970-9819
INTERNATIONAL JOURNAL OF TRANSLATION. (Text in English) 1989. s-a. Rs.150($40) Bahri Publications, 997-A, Street No. 9, Gobindpuri, Kalkaji, New Delhi 110 019, India. TEL 644-5710. Ed. R.K. Agnihotri. adv.; bk.rev.
—BLDSC shelfmark: 4542.695950.

400   US   ISSN 0074-6797
INTERNATIONAL LINGUISTIC ASSOCIATION. MONOGRAPH. (Supplement to: Word) 1951. irreg. International Linguistic Association, c/o Dr. Theodore S. Beardsley, Jr., Treas., Hispanic Society of America, 613 W. 155th St., New York, NY 10032. (reprint service avail. from UMI)

400   US   ISSN 0074-6800
INTERNATIONAL LINGUISTIC ASSOCIATION. SPECIAL PUBLICATIONS. 1964. irreg. price varies. International Linguistic Association, c/o Dr. Theodore S. Beardsley, Jr., Treas., Hispanic Society of America, 613 W. 155th St., New York, NY 10032. (reprint service avail. from UMI)

414   UK   ISSN 0025-1003
P215
INTERNATIONAL PHONETIC ASSOCIATION. JOURNAL. 1886. s-a. £25($45) International Phonetic Association, Dept. of Linguistics & Phonetics, University of Leeds, Leeds LS2 9JT, England. FAX 0532-333566. Ed. Ian Maddieson. adv.; bk.rev.; charts; circ. 800. (also avail. in microform from UMI; reprint service avail. from SWZ,UMI) **Indexed:** Lang.& Lang.Behav.Abstr. (1972-), Lang.Teach. & Ling.Abstr., Mid.East: Abstr.& Ind., Sociol.Abstr.
—BLDSC shelfmark: 4802.350000.
Formerly: Maitre Phonetique.
Description: Concerned with all aspects of the theory, description and use of phonetics and phonology.

418.02   SZ   ISSN 0047-1291
INTERPRETE. 1945. q. 15 SFr. Association d'Interpretes et de Traducteurs, Case Stand 388, 1211 Geneva 11, Switzerland. Ed. M. Wanstall-Sauty. adv.; bk.rev.; abstr.; circ. 600.

407   US   ISSN 0742-4876
QH541.2
INTERPRETER (SACRAMENTO); Western Interpreters Association journal for environmental communicators. 1969. q. membership. National Association of Interpretation, Box 1892, Fort Collins, CO 80522. (Co-sponsor: Association of Interpretive Naturalists) Ed. Greg Starypan. adv.; circ. 1,600. **Indexed:** Comput.Lit.Ind.

INTERSPECIES NEWSLETTER. see *BIOLOGY — Zoology*

IRIAN: BULLETIN OF IRIAN JAYA. see *ANTHROPOLOGY*

410 370   US
ISSUES IN LANGUAGE EDUCATION. 1988. irreg., no.3, 1989. $4 per no. Boston University, African Studies Center, 270 Bay State Rd., Boston, MA 02215. TEL 617-353-7306. FAX 617-353-4975. TELEX 9103501947 BUASC.

480 375.4   IT
ISTITUTO DI FILOLOGIA GRECA. BOLLETTINO. 1974. irreg., vol.5, 1980. L.35000. L'Erma di Bretschneider, Via Cassiodoro 19, 00193 Rome, Italy. TEL 06-687-41-27. FAX 06-687-41-29. Dir. Oddone Longo. circ. 500.

480 375.4   IT
ISTITUTO DI FILOLOGIA GRECA. BOLLETTINO. SUPPLEMENTI. 1977. irreg., no.10, 1990. price varies. L'Erma di Bretschneider, Via Cassiodoro 19, 00193 Rome, Italy. TEL 06-687-41-27. FAX 06-687-41-29. Dir. Oddone Longo.

ISTITUTO UNIVERSITARIO ORIENTALE. ANNALI; studi Nederlandesi, studi Nordici. see *ETHNIC INTERESTS*

ISTITUTO UNIVERSITARIO ORIENTALE DI NAPOLI. ANNALI. SEZIONE ROMANZA. see *LITERATURE*

410 800   IT
ISTITUTO UNIVERSITARIO ORIENTALE DI NAPOLI. DIPARTIMENTO DI STUDI LETTERARI E LINGUISTICI DELL' OCCIDENTE. ANNALI: FILIOGIA GERMANICA. (Text in English and German) 1974. a. $30. (Istituto Universitario Orientale di Napoli, Dipartimento di Studi Letterari e Linguistici dell' Occidente) Herder Editrice e Libreria s.r.l., Piazza Montecitorio 117-121, 00186 Rome, Italy. Ed. Anna Maria Guerrieri. charts; illus.; stat.
Description: Features articles on scholarly study in Germanic philology.

ISTITUTO UNIVERSITARIO ORIENTALE DI NAPOLI. DIPARTIMENTO DI STUDI LETTERARI E LINGUISTICI DELL' OCCIDENTE. ANNUALI: STUDI DI ANGLISTICA. see *LITERATURE*

ISTITUTO UNIVERSITARIO ORIENTALE DI NAPOLI. DIPARTIMENTO DI STUDI LETTERARI E LINGUISTICI DELL' OCCIDENTE. ANNUALI: STUDI TEDESCHI. see *LITERATURE*

457   IT   ISSN 0085-2295
L'ITALIA DIALETTALE; rivista di Dialettologia Italiana. 1925. a. L.95000. (Universita degli Studi di Pisa, Istituto di Glottologia) Giardini Editori e Stampatori, Via Santa Bibbiana 28, 56100 Pisa, Italy. TEL 050 502531. Ed. Tristano Bolelli. bk.rev. **Indexed:** M.L.A.

ITALIAN PRIVATE ENGLISH LANGUAGE SCHOOLS & ITALIAN LANGUAGE SCHOOLS FOR OVERSEAS & ITALY. see *EDUCATION — Guides To Schools And Colleges*

ITALICA (MADISON). see *LITERATURE*

450 375.4   GW   ISSN 0171-4996
ITALIENISCH; Zeitschrift fuer Italienische Sprache und Literatur in Wissenschaft und Unterricht. 1979. 2/yr. (May, Nov.). DM.25 (students DM.18). Verlag Moritz Diesterweg, Waechtersbacher Str. 89, 6000 Frankfurt a.M. 61, Germany. TEL 069-42081-0. FAX 069-1301-100. TELEX 413234-MDD. **Indexed:** M.L.A.

ITALIENISCHE STUDIEN. see *LITERATURE*

420 430   US   ISSN 0363-6941
PD1
J E G P: JOURNAL OF ENGLISH AND GERMANIC PHILOLOGY. 1897. q. $22 to individuals; institutions $45. (University of Illinois at Urbana-Champaign) University of Illinois Press, 54 E. Gregory Dr., Champaign, IL 61820. TEL 217-333-0950. FAX 217-244-8082. Ed.Bd. adv.; bk.rev.; circ. 1,600. (also avail. in microform from MIM,UMI; reprint service avail. from UMI,SCH) **Indexed:** Abstr.Engl.Stud., Arts & Hum.Cit.Ind., Bk.Rev.Ind. (1965-), Child.Bk.Rev.Ind. (1965-), Curr.Cont., Hum.Ind., Ind.Bk.Rev.Hum., M.L.A.
—BLDSC shelfmark: 4979.250000.
Former titles: Journal of English and Germanic Philology (ISSN 0022-0868); Journal of Germanic Philology (ISSN 0364-2968)
Refereed Serial

418.02   II   ISSN 0253-8776
J I S T A. (Journal of the Indian Scientific Translators Association) (Text in English and other languages) 1972. s-a. Rs.30($8) Indian Scientific Translators Association, c/o Indian National Scientific Documentation Centre, 14 Satsang Vihar Marg, New Delhi 110067, India. Ed. Hem Chandra Pande. adv.; bk.rev.; bibl.; charts; circ. 400.

LINGUISTICS

JAHRBUCH DER DEUTSCHDIDAKTIK. see *LITERATURE*

430 375.4   GW   ISSN 0083-5617
PF5601
JAHRBUCH DES VEREINS FUER NIEDERDEUTSCHE SPRACHFORSCHUNG. (Text in English, German) 1875. a. DM.40. Karl Wachholtz Verlag, Postfach 2769, 2350 Neumunster, Germany. TEL 04321-567-20. FAX 04321-56778. Ed. Hermann Niebaum. circ. 800. (back issues avail.)

JAHRBUCH DEUTSCH ALS FREMDSPRACHE. see *EDUCATION — Higher Education*

492.7   UA
JAMI'AT AL-AZHAR. KULLIYYAT AL-LUGHAH AL-ARABIYYAH BIL-MANSURAH. MAJALLAH/AL-AZHAR UNIVERSITY. ARABIC LANGUAGE FACULTY IN MANSOURA. JOURNAL. (Text in Arabic) irreg., no.8, 1987. Al-Azhar University, Arabic Language Faculty in Mansoura, Mansoura, Egypt.

492.7   UA
JAMI'AT AL-AZHAR. KULLIYYAT AL-LUGHAH AL-ARABIYYAH BIL-MANUFIYYAH. MAJALLAH/AL-AZHAR UNIVERSITY. ARABIC LANGUAGE FACULTY IN MENOUFIA. JOURNAL. (Text in Arabic) 1982. a. Al-Azhar University, Arabic Language Faculty in Menoufia, Menoufia, Egypt. circ. 300.
Description: Reviews Arabic linguistics, literature, literary criticism and Islamic studies.

492.7   UA
JAMI'AT AL-AZHAR. KULLIYYAT AL-LUGHAH AL-ARABIYYAH BIL-ZAGAZIG. MAJALLAH/AL-AZHAR UNIVERSITY. ARABIC LANGUAGE FACULTY IN ZAGAZIG. JOURNAL. (Text in Arabic) 1983. q. free. Jami'at al-Azhar, Kulliyyat al-Lughah al-Arabiyyah bil-Zagazig - Al-Azhar University, Arabic Language Faculty in Zagazig, Zagazig, Egypt. TEL 02-055-3302040. circ. controlled.

492.7   SU
JAMI'AT UMM AL-QURA. KULLIYYAT AL-LUGHAH AL-ARABIYYAH. MUHADARAT AL-MAWSIM AL-THAQAFI. Cover title: Muhadarat al-Mawsim al-Thaqafi li-Kulliyyat al-Lughah al-Arabiyyah. (Text in Arabic) 1983. a. Umm al-Qura University, Arabic Language Faculty - Jami'at Umm al-Qura, Kulliyat al-Lughah al-Arabiyyah, P.O. Box 407-715, Mecca, Saudi Arabia. TEL 02-5564770. TELEX 440026.

410   JA   ISSN 0389-1186
DJK1
JAPANESE SLAVIC & EAST EUROPEAN STUDIES. a. Japanese Society for Slavic & East European Studies, Sakyo-ku, Kyoto 606, Japan. TEL 075-7512111. (Subscr. to: Lavis Marketing, 73 Lime Walk, Headington, Oxford OX3 7AD, England) Ed. Iwao Yamaguchi.
—BLDSC shelfmark: 4662.045000.

JAPANESE STUDIES IN GERMAN LANGUAGE AND LITERATURE/JAPANISCHE STUDIEN ZUR DEUTSCHEN SPRACHE UND LITERATUR. see *LITERATURE*

499.992   NE   ISSN 0075-3491
JARLIBRO. (Text in Esperanto) 1908. a. fl.36($18) Universala Esperanto Asocio, Nieuwe Binnenweg 176, 3015 BJ Rotterdam, Netherlands. TEL 010-4361044. FAX 010-4361751. TELEX 23721 UEA NL. Ed. F. Javier Moleon. adv.; index; circ. 7,000. (back issues avail.)
Description: Includes specialist organizations and a network of more than 2,500 representatives of the Esperanto movement.

430 800   II   ISSN 0377-0648
P1
JAWAHARAL NEHRU UNIVERSITY. SCHOOL OF LANGUAGES. JOURNAL. Abbreviated title: J S L. (Text in English) 1973. s-a. $30. (Jawaharal Nehru University, School of Languages) Wiley Eastern Ltd., 4835-24 Ansari Rd., Darya Ganj, New Delhi - 110 002, India. Ed.Bd. adv.; bk.rev.; circ. 1,000.

400 491.87   CS   ISSN 0448-9241
PG5201
JAZYKOVEDNE STUDIE. (Text in Slovak; summaries in German and Russian) irreg., vol.13, 1976. fl.25 per no. (Slovenska Akademia Vied, Jazykovedny Ustav L. Stura) Veda, Publishing House of the Slovak Academy of Sciences, Klemensova 19, 814 30 Bratislava, Czechoslovakia. (Dist. in Western countries by: John Benjamins B.V., Amsteldijk 44, P.O. Box 75577, 1070 AN Amsterdam, Netherlands. TEL 020-6762325)

400   CS   ISSN 0021-5597
P9
JAZYKOVEDNY CASOPIS. (Text in Slovak; summaries in English, German, Russian) 1946. s-a. 30 Kcs.($13) (Slovenska Akademia Vied, Jazykovedny Ustav L. Stura) Veda, Publishing House of the Slovak Academy of Sciences, Klemensova 19, 814 30 Bratislava, Czechoslovakia. (Dist. in Western countries by: John Benjamins B.V., Amsteldijk 44, P.O. Box 75577, 1070 AN Amsterdam, Netherlands. TEL 020-6762325) Ed. Jan Horecky. bk.rev.; abstr.; charts; index; circ. 1,000. **Indexed:** Lang.& Lang.Behav.Abstr. (1972-).

492.4 296   US   ISSN 0333-8347
PJ5061
JEWISH LANGUAGE REVIEW. (Text mainly in English, occasionally in French and Hebrew) 1981. a. price varies. Association for the Study of Jewish Languages, 67-07 215th St., Oakland Gardens, NY 11364-2523. Ed. David L. Gold. adv.; bk.rev.; bibl. (back issues avail) **Indexed:** Arts & Hum.Cit.Ind., Bull.Signal., Curr.Cont., Lang.& Lang.Behav.Abstr., M.L.A., Sociol.Abstr.
Description: Devoted to all aspects of the inner and outer linguistic history of the Jewish people and related groups.

492.4 296   US   ISSN 0792-559X
▼**JEWISH LINGUISTIC STUDIES.** 1990. a. $24. Association for the Study of Jewish Languages, 67-07 215th St., Oakland Gardens, NY 11364-2523.

491.82   CI   ISSN 0021-6925
PG1201
JEZIK; casopis za kulturu hrvatskoga knjizevnog jezika. (Text in Croatian) 1952. bi-m. DM.25. Hrvatsko Filolosko Drustvo, Djure Salaja 3, 41000 Zagreb, Croatia. TEL 041 513-155. Ed. Stjepan Babic. **Indexed:** M.L.A.

491.84 890   XV   ISSN 0021-6933
PG1801
JEZIK IN SLOVSTVO. (Text in Slovenian) 1955. 8/yr. $12. Slavisticno Drustvo Slovenije, Askerceva 12, 61000 Ljubljana, Slovenia. TEL 061-150-001. FAX 061-159-337. Ed. Alenka Sivic-Dular. bk.rev.; bibl.; charts; index; circ. 2,400. **Indexed:** Lang.& Lang.Behav.Abstr., M.L.A.

491.85   PL   ISSN 0021-6941
PG6001
JEZYK POLSKI. 1913-1939; resumed 1945. 5/yr. 50000 Zl.($28) Towarzystwo Milosnikow Jezyka Polskiego, Straszewskiego 27, 31-113 Krakow, Poland. TEL 22-26-99. (Dist. by: Ars Polona- Ruch, Krakowskie Przemieście 7, Warsaw, Poland) Ed. Stanislaw Urbanczyk. adv.; bk.rev.; index; circ. 7,000. **Indexed:** M.L.A.
Description: Focuses on the history, and dialectology of the Polish language.

JEZYKI OBCE W SZKOLE. see *EDUCATION*

418   PL   ISSN 0137-1444
JEZYKOZNAWSTWO STOSOWANE/APPLIED LINGUISTICS. (Monograph series) 1975. irreg. price varies. Adam Mickiewica University Press, Marchlewskiego 128, 61-874 Poznan, Poland.

437.897   GW   ISSN 0720-6666
JIDISCHE SCHTUDIES. 1981. irreg. price varies. Helmut Buske Verlag Hamburg, Friedrichsgaber Weg 138, Postfach 1248, D-2000 Norderstedt, Germany. Ed. Walter Roll.

496   US   ISSN 0167-6164
PL8000
JOURNAL OF AFRICAN LANGUAGES AND LINGUISTICS.* (Text in English) 1979. 2/yr. fl.55 to individuals; institutions fl.110. (Rijksuniversiteit te Leiden, Department of African Linguistics, NE) Walter de Gruyter, Inc., 200 Saw Mill River Rd., Hawthorne, NY 10532. TEL 914-747-0110. FAX 914-747-1326. Ed. Thilo C. Schadeberg. bk.rev. (back issues avail.; reprint service avail. from SWZ) **Indexed:** Lang.& Lang.Behav.Abstr. (1979-), M.L.A.
—BLDSC shelfmark: 4919.993000.
Description: International academic journal in the African language field.

492   NE   ISSN 0894-9824
PJ990
▼**JOURNAL OF AFROASIATIC LANGUAGES.** 1990. 3/yr. fl.89.50($52) to individuals; institutions fl.125.50 ($71.75)(effective 1992). E.J. Brill, P.O. Box 9000, 2300 PA Leiden, Netherlands. TEL 071-312624. FAX 071-317532. TELEX 39296 BRILL NL. (In N. America: E.J. Brill, 24 Hudson St., Kinderhook, NY 12106. TEL 800-962-4406) Ed. R. Hetzron.

JOURNAL OF ASIAN PACIFIC COMMUNICATION. see *COMMUNICATIONS*

491.66   UK   ISSN 0962-1377
▼**JOURNAL OF CELTIC LINGUISTICS.** 1991. a. £10. University of Wales Press, 6 Gwennyth St., Cathays, Cardiff CF2 4YD, Wales. TEL 0222-231919. FAX 0222-230908. Ed. Martin Ball. adv.; bk.rev.; circ. 750.
—BLDSC shelfmark: 4955.053000.

495.1   US   ISSN 0091-3723
PL1001
JOURNAL OF CHINESE LINGUISTICS. 1973. s-a. $25 to individuals; institutions $35. Project on Linguistic Analysis, 2222 Piedmont Ave., Berkeley, CA 94720. TEL 510-642-5939. Ed. William S.-Y. Wang. adv.; bk.rev.; bibl.; cum.index every 5 yrs.; circ. 450. **Indexed:** C.I.J.E., Curr.Cont., Lang.& Lang.Behav.Abstr. (1973-), M.L.A.
—BLDSC shelfmark: 4958.100000.
Description: Publishes articles on all aspects of the Chinese language, including relevant contributions on neighboring languages.
Refereed Serial

495.1   US
JOURNAL OF CHINESE LINGUISTICS MONOGRAPH SERIES. 1982. irreg., no.4, 1991. price varies. Project on Linguistic Analysis, 2222 Piedmont Ave., Berkeley, CA 94720. TEL 510-642-5939. Ed. William S.-Y. Wang. (back issues avail.)
Description: Contributions on all aspects of Chinese, including related and neighboring languages.
Refereed Serial

370 407   US   ISSN 0891-2521
PB36
JOURNAL OF EDUCATIONAL TECHNIQUES AND TECHNOLOGIES; practices and products for language learning. (Text in English, French, German) 1968. 3/yr. $25. International Association of Learning Laboratories, c/o Language Laboratories, 304C Moore College Bldg., University of Georgia, Athens, GA 30602. TEL 404-542-5143. Ed. Suzanne E. Lindenau. adv.; bk.rev.; bibl.; illus.; circ. 2,000. (reprint service avail.) **Indexed:** C.I.J.E., ERIC, Lang.& Lang. Behav.Abstr., Lang.Teach.& Ling.Abstr.
Former titles (until 1984): N A L L D Journal (ISSN 0027-5905); N A L L D Newsletter (New Advances in Learning Laboratory Developments).

420   US   ISSN 0075-4242
PE1001
JOURNAL OF ENGLISH LINGUISTICS. 1967. s-a. $15 to individuals; institutions $20. c/o University of Georgia, Athens, GA 30602. TEL 404-542-2246. Ed. William A. Kretzschmar, Jr. adv.; bk.rev.; circ. 600. (back issues avail.) **Indexed:** Arts & Hum.Cit.Ind., Curr.Cont., Ind.Bk.Rev.Hum., Lang.& Lang.Behav.Abstr. (1973-), M.L.A.
—BLDSC shelfmark: 4979.280000.
Description: Articles on the modern and historical periods of the English language.

420 375.4   NR   ISSN 0189-6652
JOURNAL OF ENGLISH STUDIES. 1984. a. £N15($10) (Ademiya College of Education, Department of English) Ife Oluwa Ent. (Nigeria) Ltd., Ife Oluwa St., Ondo - Ore Ring Rd., P.O. Box 304, Ondo, Nigeria. TEL 034-610677. (Subscr. to: Adeyemi College of Education, c/o Business Mngr., P.M.B. 520, Ondo, Ondo State, Nigeria) Ed. Yemi Aboderin. adv.; bk.rev.; abstr.; circ. 1,000. (back issues avail.)
 Description: Disseminates empirical and non-empirical research reports in the field of English studies.

440 375.4   UK   ISSN 0959-2695
PC2001   CODEN: JFSLEP
▼**JOURNAL OF FRENCH LANGUAGE STUDIES.** 1991. s-a. $45 to individuals; institutions $69. Cambridge University Press, Edinburgh Bldg., Shaftesbury Rd., Cambridge CB2 2RU, England. TEL 0223-312393. FAX 0223-315052. Ed.Bd. bk.rev.
—BLDSC shelfmark: 4986.535000.
 Description: French language and linguistics, including sociolinguistics and discourse studies.

JOURNAL OF HELLENIC STUDIES. see *CLASSICAL STUDIES*

JOURNAL OF HISPANIC PHILOLOGY. see *LITERATURE*

420 375.4   US   ISSN 0899-885X
PE1128.A2   CODEN: JENGEC
JOURNAL OF INTENSIVE ENGLISH STUDIES. 1982. a. $15 (foreign $20). University of Arizona, Center for English as a Second Language, CESL 100, Tuscon, AZ 85721. TEL 602-621-1362. FAX 602-621-9180. Ed. Frank Pialorsi. adv.; circ. 500. (also avail. in microform from UMI; back issues avail.) **Indexed:** Lang.& Lang.Behav.Abstr.
 Formerly: American Language Journal (ISSN 0734-7545)

400   UK   ISSN 0022-2267
P1
JOURNAL OF LINGUISTICS. (Text mainly in English; also in French, German, Russian; Greek, Cyrillic and IPA types where necessary) 1965. s-a. $52 to individuals; institutions $79. (Linguistics Association of Great Britain) Cambridge University Press, Edinburgh Bldg., Shaftesbury Rd., Cambridge CB2 2RU, England. TEL 0223-312393. FAX 0223-315052. TELEX 851817256. (N. American addr.: Cambridge University Press, 40 W. 20th St., New York, NY 10011) Ed. Nigel Vincent. adv.; bk.rev.; index. (also avail. in microform from UMI; reprint service avail. from SWZ) **Indexed:** Abstr.Anthropol., Arts & Hum.Cit.Ind., C.I.J.E., Curr.Cont., Hum.Ind., Ind.Bk.Rev.Hum., Lang.& Lang.Behav.Abstr. (1972-), Lang.Teach.& Ling.Abstr., M.L.A., Mass Spectr.Bull., Mid.East: Abstr.& Ind., Sociol.Abstr, SSCI.
—BLDSC shelfmark: 5010.480000.
 Description: Studies all branches of theoretical linguistics including phonetics.

410 800   GW   ISSN 0341-7638
PN54
JOURNAL OF LITERARY SEMANTICS. 1972. 3/yr. DM.68 to individuals; institutions DM.74. Julius Groos Verlag, Hertzstr. 6, Postfach 102423, 6900 Heidelberg 1, Germany. TEL 06221-303621. Ed. Trevor Eaton. adv.; bk.rev.; circ. 800. **Indexed:** Arts & Hum.Cit.Ind., Curr.Cont., Ind.Bk.Rev.Hum., Lang.& Lang.Behav.Abstr. (1974-), Lang.Teach.& Ling.Abstr., M.L.A.
—BLDSC shelfmark: 5010.520000.

410   US   ISSN 0195-475X
PM3961
JOURNAL OF MAYAN LINGUISTICS. (Text in English, Mayan) 1978. irreg. $12 to individual; students $8. (Louisiana State University, Department of Geography and Anthropology) Geoscience Publications, Box 16010, Baton Rouge, LA 70893-6010. TEL 504-388-6245. FAX 504-388-2912. Ed. M. Jill Brody. adv.; bk.rev.; circ. 200. **Indexed:** Lang.& Lang.Behav.Abstr. (1984-).
 Description: Scholarly journal on Mayan linguistics, language and culture, and linguistics in the Mayan heiroglyphs.

410 301   UK   ISSN 0143-4632
P115
JOURNAL OF MULTILINGUAL & MULTICULTURAL DEVELOPMENT. 1980. bi-m. £23($29) to individuals; libraries £68 ($143); students £13 ($27). Multilingual Matters Ltd., Bank House, 8A Hill Rd., Clevedon, Avon BS21 7HH, England. TEL 0272-876519. FAX 0272-343096. Ed. Derrick Sharp. adv.; bk.rev.; index; circ. 800. (back issues avail.) **Indexed:** C.I.J.E., Chic.Per.Ind., Cont.Pg.Educ., Lang.& Lang.Behav.Abstr., Lang.Teach.& Ling.Abstr., M.L.A., Sp.Ed.Needs Abstr.
—BLDSC shelfmark: 5021.060000.
 Description: Publishes research studies about mulitculturalism and multilingualism in education, psychology, sociology, second language learning, and bilingualism.

JOURNAL OF NEAR EASTERN STUDIES. see *ARCHAEOLOGY*

JOURNAL OF NEUROLINGUISTICS. see *MEDICAL SCIENCES — Psychiatry And Neurology*

JOURNAL OF ONE-NAME STUDIES. see *GENEALOGY AND HERALDRY*

410   UK   ISSN 0095-4470
P221   CODEN: JPHNB9
JOURNAL OF PHONETICS. 1973. q. $210. Academic Press Ltd., 24-28 Oval Rd., London NW1 7DX, England. TEL 071-267-4466. FAX 071-482-2293. TELEX 25775 ACPRES G. Ed. M.E. Beckman. bk.rev.; bibl.; charts; index. **Indexed:** Abstr.Anthropol., Curr.Cont., Lang.& Lang.Behav.Abstr. (1982-), Lang.Teach.& Ling.Abstr., M.L.A., Psychol.Abstr., SSCI.
—BLDSC shelfmark: 5034.550000.
 Description: Contains papers of an experimental or theoretical nature that deal with phonetic aspects of language and linguistic communication processes.

410   NE   ISSN 0920-9034
PM7831
JOURNAL OF PIDGIN AND CREOLE LANGUAGES. (Text in English) 1986. 2/yr. fl.188($107) (effective 1992). John Benjamins Publishing Co., Amsteldijk 44, P.O. Box 75577, 1070 AN Amsterdam, Netherlands. TEL 020-6738156. FAX 020-6739773. (In N. America: 821 Bethlehem Pike, Philadelphia, PA 19118. TEL 215-836-1200) Ed. Glenn Gilbert. bk.rev.; circ. 650. (back issues avail.) **Indexed:** Lang.& Lang.Behav.Abstr. (1986-).
 Description: Presents descriptive and theoretical research into pidgin and creole languages, and its application to language planning, education, and social reform.

410   NE   ISSN 0378-2166
P99.4.P72
JOURNAL OF PRAGMATICS; an interdisciplinary monthly of language studies. (Text in English, French, German) 1977. 12/yr.(in 2 vols.; 6 nos./vol.). fl.598 (effective 1992). North-Holland (Subsidiary of: Elsevier Science Publishers B.V.), P.O. Box 211, 1000 AE Amsterdam, Netherlands. TEL 020-5803911. FAX 020-5803598. TELEX 18582 ESPA NL. (Subscr. in U.S. and Canada to: Elsevier Science Publishing Co., Inc., Box 882, Madison Sq. Sta., New York, NY 10159. TEL 212-989-5800) Ed. Jacob L. Mey. adv.; bk.rev.; bibl.; index. (also avail. in microform from RPI; back issues avail., reprint service avail. SWZ) **Indexed:** Art.Int.Abstr., Curr.Cont., Lang.& Lang.Behav.Abstr. (1977-), Lang.Teach.& Ling.Abstr., M.L.A., Phil.Ind., Sociol.Abstr., SSCI.
—BLDSC shelfmark: 5041.900000.
 Description: Directed to linguists, sociologists, anthropologists and artificial intelligence professionals; covers all aspects of pragmatic studies of language; includes applications in the information sciences, artificial intelligence, person-machine interaction and psychiatry.
 Refereed Serial

401   US   ISSN 0090-6905
P106   CODEN: JPLRB7
JOURNAL OF PSYCHOLINGUISTIC RESEARCH. 1971. bi-m. $320 (foreign $375)(effective 1992). Plenum Publishing Corp., 233 Spring St., New York, NY 10013-1578. TEL 212-620-8000. FAX 212-463-0742. TELEX 23-421139. Ed. R.W. Rieber. adv.; bibl.; charts; illus.; stat. (also avail. in microfilm from JSC; back issues avail.) **Indexed:** Abstr.Anthropol., Biol.Abstr., Child Devel.Abstr., Commun.Abstr., Curr.Cont., Ind.Med., Lang.& Lang.Behav.Abstr. (1973-), Lang.Teach.& Ling.Abstr., M.L.A., Mid.East: Abstr.& Ind., Psychol.Abstr., Ref.Zh., Sociol.Abstr., SSCI, Stud.Wom.Abstr.
—BLDSC shelfmark: 5043.285000.
 Refereed Serial

375.4 420   US   ISSN 0022-4111
LB1050   CODEN: JRBEAX
JOURNAL OF READING BEHAVIOR. 1969. q. $50 (foreign $60). National Reading Conference, Inc., 11 E. Hubbard St., Ste. 200, Chicago, IL 60611. TEL 312-329-2512. Ed. John Readence. adv.; bk.rev.; index; circ. 2,000. (also avail. in microform from MIM,UMI; reprint service avail. from UMI) **Indexed:** C.I.J.E., Commun.Abstr., Cont.Pg.Educ., Curr.Cont., Educ.Ind., ERIC, Lang.& Lang.Behav.Abstr., Psychol.Abstr., SSCI.
—BLDSC shelfmark: 5047.600000.

JOURNAL OF READING, WRITING, AND LEARNING DISABILITIES INTERNATIONAL. see *EDUCATION — Special Education And Rehabilitation*

410   UK   ISSN 0167-5133
P325   CODEN: JOSEEX
JOURNAL OF SEMANTICS. 1982. 4/yr. £55($110) Oxford University Press, Oxford Journals, Pinkhill House, Southfield Road, Eynsham, Oxford OX8 1JJ, England. TEL 0865-882283. FAX 0865-882890. TELEX 837330 OXPRES G. Ed. P. Bosch. adv.; bk.rev.; circ. 500. (reprint service avail. from SWZ) **Indexed:** Lang.& Lang.Behav.Abstr. (1984-), Lang.Teach.& Ling.Abstr.
—BLDSC shelfmark: 5063.380000.
 Description: Aims at an integration of philosophical, psychological and linguistic semantics as well as work done in artificial intelligence.

JOURNAL OF SEMITIC STUDIES. see *RELIGIONS AND THEOLOGY — Judaic*

JOURNAL OF SPEECH LANGUAGE PATHOLOGY AND AUDIOLOGY/REVUE D'ORTHOPHONIE ET D'AUDIOLOGIE. see *EDUCATION — Special Education And Rehabilitation*

494 894   II   ISSN 0022-4855
PL4758.A2
JOURNAL OF TAMIL STUDIES. (Text in English) 1969. s-a. Rs.35($12) International Institute of Tamil Studies, C.P.T. Campus, T.T.T.I. Post, Madras 600113, Tamil Nadu, India. Ed. A.N. Perumal. adv.; bk.rev.; bibl.; charts; stat.; circ. 2,000. **Indexed:** M.L.A.

407 220 378   US
JOURNAL OF TRANSLATION AND TEXTLINGUISTICS. Short title: J O T T. 1987. 4/yr. price varies. Summer Institute of Linguistics, Inc., Academic Publications, 7500 W. Camp Wisdom Rd., Dallas, TX 75236. TEL 214-709-2403. Ed. Robert L. Longacre.
 Formerly (unitl vol.5, 1991): Translation and Textlinguistics. Occasional Papers (ISSN 0890-7749)

496   US   ISSN 0022-5401
PL8017
JOURNAL OF WEST AFRICAN LANGUAGES. (Text in English and French) 1964. s-a. $30. West African Linguisitic Society, 7500 W. Camp Wisdom Rd., Dallas, TX 75236. FAX 214-709-2433. Ed. John Bendor-Samuel. adv.; bk.rev.; bibl.; charts; illus.; circ. 410. (also avail. in microform; back issues avail. **Indexed:** Abstr.Anthropol., Lang.& Lang.Behav.Abstr. (1985-), M.L.A., Sociol.Abstr.
—BLDSC shelfmark: 5072.580000.

499.992   YU   ISSN 0022-6025
JUGOSLAVIA FERVOJISTO. (Text in Esperanto) vol.11, 1956. bi-m. 200 din. Savez Zeleznicara Esperantista Jugoslavije, Nemanjina 6, Belgrade, Yugoslavia. TEL 38-681-286. FAX 641-352. TELEX 11166. Ed. Gvozden Sredic. adv.; bk.rev.

407   YU   ISSN 0350-185X
PG1
JUZNOSLOVENSKI FILOLOG. (Text in Slavic languages, English, French, German) 1913. a. 500 din.($17) Srpska Akademija Nauka i Umetnosti, Institut za Srpskohrvatski Jezik - Serbian Academy of Science and Arts, Knez Mihailova 35, 11000 Belgrade, Serbia, Yugoslavia. TEL 011-635-590. Ed. Milka Ivic. bk.rev.; circ. 800. (back issues avail.)
    Description: Contains papers about Serbo-Croatian language, Slavic linguistics and general linguistics.

375.4   GW   ISSN 0939-9275
K L A G E. (Koelner Linguistische Arbeiten - Germanistik) 1979. irreg. price varies. Gabel Verlag, Juelichstr. 7, 5030 Huerth-Efferen, Germany. TEL 02233-63550. Ed. Heinz Vater. circ. 300.

491.92   LI   ISSN 0022-7900
KALBOS KULTURA. 1961. s-a. exchange basis. Lietuvos Mokslu Akademija, Lietuviu Kalbos Institutas - Lithuanian Academy of Sciences, Institute of Lithuanian Language, Antakalnio g., 6, Vilnius, Lithuania. TEL 62-98-25. Ed. K. Ulvydas. bk.rev.; bibl.

410   LI   ISSN 0202-330X
PG8501
KALBOTYRA/LINGUISTICS. (Text in English, German, Lithuanian, Russian) 1958. 3/yr. price varies. (Ministry of Culture and Education) Leidykla Mokslas, Zvaigzdziu 23, Vilnius 2050, Lithuania. TEL 45-85-26. TELEX 261107 LMOKSU. (Co-sponsor: Vilnius University) Ed. A. Steponavicius.
—BLDSC shelfmark: 5081.970000.
    Description: Considers problems of Lithuanian, Russian, Germanic-Romance, and classical linguistics.

KATOLICKI UNIWERSYTET LUBELSKI. WYDZIAL HISTORYCZNO-FILOLOGICZNY. ROZPRAWY. see *HISTORY*

400 800   ER   ISSN 0131-1441
PH601
KEEL JA KIRJANDUS. 1958. m. $38. (Estonian Academy of Sciences) Kirjastus Perioodika, Parnu mnt. 8, 200090 Tallinn, Estonia.
TEL 0142-441-262. FAX 0142-442-484. (U.S. subscr. addr.: Imported Publications, Inc., 320 W. Ohio St., Chicago, IL 60610) (Co-sponsor: Estonian Writers' Union) Ed. Axel Tamm. bk.rev.; bibl.; charts; illus.; circ. 2,000. Indexed: M.L.A.
—BLDSC shelfmark: 5088.330000.

KEILSCHRIFTTEXTE AUS BOGHAZKOI. see *ARCHAEOLOGY*

410 511   JA   ISSN 0453-4611
KEIRYO KOKUGOGAKU/MATHEMATICAL LINGUISTICS. (Text mainly in Japanese; occasionally in English, French, German) 1957. q. 4400 Yen. Keiryo Kokugo Gakkai - Mathematical Linguistic Society of Japan, c/o Tokyo Joshi Daigaku, 6-1, Zenpukuji 2-chome, Suginami-ku, Tokyo 167, Japan. TEL 03-95-1211. Ed. Hisao Isii. bk.rev.; index; circ. 570. Indexed: M.L.A.
—BLDSC shelfmark: 5402.400000.
    Description: Covers quantitative mathematical and computational linguistics.

420 375.4 500   CC
KEJI YINGYU XUEXI/LEARNING ENGLISH FOR SCIENCE & TECHNOLOGY. (Text in Chinese and English) m. $19.70. Shanghai Jiaotong Daxue, Keji Yingyu Xuexi Bianjibu, 1954, Huashan Lu, Shanghai 200030. TEL 310310. (Dist. in US by: China Books & Periodicals, Inc., 2929 24th San Francisco, CA 94110. TEL 415-282-2994) Ed. Wu Yingeng.

420   US   ISSN 0023-0197
KENTUCKY ENGLISH BULLETIN. 1951. 3/yr. $10 (foreign $12). Kentucky Council of Teachers of English - Language Arts, Western Kentucky University, Dept. of English, Bowling Green, KY 42101. Ed. John Hagaman. bk.rev.; circ. 800. (also avail. in microform from MIM) Indexed: Lang.& Lang.Behav.Abstr.
—BLDSC shelfmark: 5089.622000.
    Description: Articles and essays. Each issue focuses on a single topic relevant to English grammar, composition, writing, linguistics, curricula, or literature.

491   KR
KHAR'KOVSKII GOSUDARSTVENNYI UNIVERSITET. FILOLOGIYA. (Subseries of: Khar'kovskii Gosudarstvennyi Universitet. Vestnik) 1964. a. 1.30 Rub. (Khar'kovskii Gosudarstvennyi Universitet) Izdatel'stvo Vysshaya Shkola, Khar'kovskoe Otdelenie, Ul. Universitetskaya 16, Khar'kov 310003, Ukraine. circ. 500.

418   FI
KIELIKESKUSUUTISIA/LANUAGE CENTRE NEWS. m. membership. Association Finlandaise de Linguistique Appliquee, Department of English, University of Jyvaeskylae, SF-40100 Jyvaeskylae, Finland. TEL 931-156-853.

496.392 896.392   TZ   ISSN 0856-048X
PL8701
KISWAHILI. (Text in English, Swahili) a. $15. University of Dar es Salaam, Institute of Kiswahili Research, P.O. Box 35110, Dar es Salaam, Tanzania.
FAX 010-255-5148274. Eds. E. Wesana-Chemi, H.J. Mwansoke. Indexed: M.L.A.

410 800   GW   ISSN 0453-9842
PT4848.G7
KLAUS GROTH GESELLSCHAFT. JAHRESGABEN. 1964. a. price varies. Westholsteinische Verlagsanstalt Boyens und Co., Am Wulf-Isebrand-Platz, Postfach 1880, 2240 Heide, Germany. TEL 0481-691-0. Ed.Bd. illus. Indexed: M.L.A.

491 891   YU
KNJIZEVNOST I JEZIK. (Text in Serbo-Croatian) 1954. q. 30 din. Drustvo za Srpskohrvatski Jezik i Knjizevnost Srbije, Knez Mihailova 35, Belgrade, Serbia, Yugoslavia. (Co-sponsor: Drustvo za Srpskohrvatski Jezik i Knjizevnost Crne Gore) Ed. Radoje Simic. Indexed: M.L.A.
    Formerly: Knjizevnost i Jezik u Skoli.

410 510   DK   ISSN 0106-8563
KOEBENHAVNS UNIVERSITET. INSTITUT FOR ANVENDT OG MATEMATISK LINGVISTIK. SKRIFTER. 1974. irreg. free. Koebenhavns Universitet, Institut for Anvendt og Matematisk Lingvistik, Njalsgade 96, Copenhagen S, Denmark. Ed.Bd. circ. 300.

410   DK   ISSN 0107-3265
KOEBENHAVNS UNIVERSITETS SLAVISKE INSTITUT. RAPPORTER. 1984. a. DKK 45.75. Koebenhavns Universitet, Norregade 10, DK-1165 Copenhagen K, Denmark.

410 800   BE   ISSN 0770-7762
KONINKLIJKE ACADEMIE VOOR NEDERLANDSE TAAL- EN LETTERKUNDE. JAARBOEK. 1887. a. price varies. Koninklijke Academie voor Nederlandse Taal- en Letterkunde, Koningstraat 18, B-9000 Ghent, Belgium. FAX 091-23-27-18.

KONINKLIJKE ACADEMIE VOOR NEDERLANDSE TAAL- EN LETTERKUNDE. VERSLAGEN EN MEDEDELINGEN. see *LITERATURE*

KONTAKTO. see *CHILDREN AND YOUTH — For*

KONTEKSTEN; publikatiereeks over taal, tekst en vertoog. see *SOCIOLOGY*

KOROSI CSOMA KISKONYVTAR. see *HISTORY — History Of Asia*

430   GW   ISSN 0023-4567
P501
KRATYLOS; kritisches Berichts- und Rezensionsorgan fuer indogermanische und allgemeine Sprachwissenschaft. (Text in English, French, German and Italian) 1956. a. DM.64. Dr. Ludwig Reichert Verlag, Tauernstr. 11, 6200 Wiesbaden, Germany. FAX 0611-468613. Ed. Ruediger Schmitt. adv.; bk.rev.; circ. 700.

430 375.4   GW   ISSN 0720-9983
KREOLISCHE BIBLIOTHEK. 1981. irreg., vol.9, 1988. price varies. Verlag Helmut Buske, Friedrichsgaber Weg 138, Postfach 1249, D-2000 Norderstedt, Germany. Ed. Annegret Bollee.

430 800   GW   ISSN 0340-9767
KRITIKON LITTERARUM; international book review for American, English, Romance and Slavic studies and for linguistics. (Text in English, German, French or Spanish) 1972. q. DM.298. Thesen Verlag, 3, place de la Gare, 6674 Mertert, Luxembourg.
TEL 00352-748715. Ed.Bd. adv.; bk.rev.; bibl.; index.

491.86 491.87   CS   ISSN 0023-5202
PG5201
KULTURA SLOVA/CULTURE OF THE WORD. (Text in Slovak) 1966. 10/yr. 30 Kcs.($14) (Linguistic Institute of L'udovit Stur) Veda, Publishing House of the Slovak Academy of Sciences, Klemensova 19, 814 30 Bratislava, Czechoslovakia. (Dist. in Western countries by: John Benjamins B.V., Amsteldijk 44, P.O. Box 75577, 1070 AN Amsterdam, Netherlands. TEL 020-6762325) Ed. Jan Kacala. bk.rev.; bibl.; illus.; index.
    Formerly: Ceskoslovensky Terminologicky Casopis.
    Description: Covers the theoretical problems of language culture as well as practical problems of language practice and stylistical appropriateness.

KUNAPIPI. see *LITERATURE*

400   SW   ISSN 0083-6745
P17
KUNGLIGA VITTERHETS HISTORIE OCH ANTIKVITETS AKADEMIEN. FILOLOGISKT ARKIV. (Text in English, French, German, Spanish or Swedish) 1955. irreg., no.35, 1988. price varies. Kungliga Vitterhets Historie och Antikvitets Akademien - Royal Academy of Letters, History and Antiquities, P.O. Box 5622, S-114 86 Stockholm, Sweden. (Dist. by: Almqvist & Wiksell International, P.O. Box 4627, S-116 91 Stockholm, Sweden) index.

400 100   SW   ISSN 0083-677X
AS284
KUNGLIGA VITTERHETS HISTORIE OCH ANTIKVITETS AKADEMIEN. HANDLINGAR. FILOLOGISK-FILOSOFISKA SERIEN/ROYAL ACADEMY OF LETTERS, HISTORY AND ANTIQUITIES. PROCEEDINGS. PHILOLOGICAL-PHILOSOPHICAL SERIES. (Text in English, French, German and Swedish) 1954. irreg., no.20, 1983. price varies. Kungliga Vitterhets Historie, och Antikvitets Akademien, P.O. Box 5622, S-114 86 Stockholm, Sweden. (Dist. by: Almqvist & Wiksell International, P.O. Box 4627, S-11691, Stockholm, Sweden) index.

410   GW   ISSN 0721-4340
KUSCHITISCHE SPRACHSTUDIEN/CUSHITIC LANGUAGE STUDIES. 1982. irreg., vol.6, 1987. price varies. Helmut Buske Verlag Hamburg, Friedrichsgaber Weg 1249, Postfach 1249, D-2000 Norderstedt, Germany. Eds. H.-J. Sasse.

400   PL   ISSN 0023-5911
PB5
KWARTALNIK NEOFILOLOGICZNY. (Text and summaries in various languages) 1954. q. $25. (Polska Akademia Nauk, Komitet Neofilologiczny) Panstwowe Wydawnictwo Naukowe, Ul. Miodowa 10, 00-251 Warsaw, Poland. (Dist. by: Ars Polona, Krakowskie Przedmiescie 7, 00-068 Warsaw, Poland) Ed. F. Grucza. bk.rev.; charts; index; circ. 600. Indexed: Abstr.Engl.Stud., Lang.& Lang.Behav.Abstr., M.L.A.

KYOIKU KENKYU/EDUCATIONAL STUDIES. see *EDUCATION*

410   US   ISSN 0195-377X
P21
L A C U S FORUM. 1974. a. $25. (Linguistic Association of Canada and the United States) L A C U S, PO Box 101, Lake Bluff, IL 60044.
TEL 312-234-3997. Ed. Valerie Makkai. circ. 1,000.
    Description: Contains proceedings of the annual meeting of the association.

L AE S. (Litteratur, Aestetik, Sprog) see *LITERATURE*

400 370   SW   ISSN 0023-6330
L M S - LINGUA. 1966. q. SEK 160. Riksfoereningen foer Laerarna i Moderna Spraak - Modern Language Teachers Association of Sweden, P.O. Box 41, S-425 02 Hisings-Kaerra, Sweden. Ed. Sverker Bengtsson. adv.; circ. 4,800.
    Description: Contains articles on languages and language teaching.

406   US   ISSN 0023-6365
P11
L S A BULLETIN. no.43, 1970. q. membership. Linguistic Society of America, 1325 18th St., N.W., Ste. 211, Washington, DC 20036-6501.
TEL 202-835-1714. Ed.Bd.; bibl.; circ. 7,000. (reprint service avail. from KTO)
—BLDSC shelfmark: 5300.390000.

492.4 296　　US
LA-MATHIL (AMERICAN EDITION); a voweled Hebrew newspaper. 1954. fortn. $12. World Zionist Organization - American Section Inc., 110 E. 59th St., New York, NY 10022. TEL 212-339-6000. Ed. Hayim Jacobson. illus.; circ. 5,000.

410 572　　FR　　ISSN 0754-2445
LACITO DOCUMENTS AFRIQUE. 1978. irreg. price varies. Societe d'Etudes Linguistiques et Anthropologiques de France (SELAF), 5 rue de Marseille, 75010 Paris, France. TEL 42-08-83-93.

410 572　　FR　　ISSN 0751-4875
LACITO DOCUMENTS ASIE - AUSTRONESIE. 1977. irreg. price varies. Societe d'Etudes Linguistiques et Anthropologiques de France (SELAF), 5 rue de Marseille, 75010 Paris, France. TEL 42-08-83-93.

410 572　　FR　　ISSN 0751-4883
LACITO DOCUMENTS EURASIE. 1978. irreg. price varies. Societe d'Etudes Linguistiques et Anthropologiques de France (SELAF), 5 rue de Marseille, 75010 Paris, France. TEL 42-08-83-93.

427　　UK
LAKELAND DIALECT. 1939. a. £3. Lakeland Dialect Society, c/o James T. Relph, Holly Cottage, Crosby Ravensworth, Penrith, Cumbria, CA10 3JP, England. TEL 09315-359. Ed. Ted Relph. bk.rev.; circ. 600.
　Formerly: Lakeland Dialect Society. Journal (ISSN 0307-9341)
　Description: Contains stories, poems and articles by members, in the dialects of the former counties of Cumberland, Westmoreland and "Lancashire North of the Sands". Includes news of the society's activities.

492.4　　IS　　ISSN 0333-9688
LAMED LESHONKHA. bi-m. $7. Academy of the Hebrew Language, PO Box 3449, 91 034 Jerusalem, Israel. circ. 15,000.

427　　UK　　ISSN 0075-7799
PE1946
LANCASHIRE DIALECT SOCIETY. JOURNAL. 1951. a. £3.50. Lancashire Dialect Society, c/o Dr. Peter Wright, Sec., Modern Languages Dept., University, Salford, England. TEL 061-745-5000. Ed. John Levitt. bk.rev.; cum.index: nos.1-14, 1951-1965; nos.15-35, 1966-1986; circ. 300.

LANGAGE ET SOCIETE. see *SOCIOLOGY*

400　　FR
LANGAGES; semiotiques textuelles. 1966. q. 310 F. Larousse, 17, rue du Montparnasse, 75280 Paris Cedex 06, France. (Dist. by: Gauthier-Villars, Centrale des Revues, 11 rue Gossin, 92543 Montrouge Cedex, France. TEL 1-46-56-52-66) circ. 4,000. (reprint service avail. from SWZ) **Indexed:** Lang.& Lang.Behav.Abstr, Lang.Teach.& Ling.Abstr., M.L.A.

370　　GW　　ISSN 0023-8252
LANGENSCHEIDTS SPRACH-ILLUSTRIERTE; a German language journal. (Text in German; summaries in English, French, Spanish) 1954. 4/yr. DM.12. Verlag Langenscheidt KG, Crellestr. 28-30, 1000 Berlin 62, Germany. FAX 030-780002-15. TELEX 183175 EKGBL. illus.; circ. 11,500.

400　　US　　ISSN 0097-8507
P1
LANGUAGE (BALTIMORE). 1925. q. $45 to individuals; students $15; institutions $75. Linguistic Society of America, 1325 18th St., N.W., Ste. 211, Washington, DC 20036-6501. Ed. Sarah Thomason. adv.; bk.rev.; charts; illus.; index; circ. 7,000. (also avail. in microfilm; back issues avail.; reprint service avail. from KTO) **Indexed:** A.I.C.P., Chic.Per.Ind., Hum.Ind., Ind.Bk.Rev.Hum., Lang.& Lang.Behav.Abstr. (1972-), Lang.Teach.& Ling.Abstr., Psychol.Abstr., SSCI.
　—BLDSC shelfmark: 5155.690000.

410　　US　　ISSN 1048-9223
▼**LANGUAGE ACQUISITION;** a journal of developmental linguistics. 1990. q. $25 to individuals (foreign $50); institutions $75 (foreign $100). Lawrence Erlbaum Associates, Inc., 365 Broadway, Hillsdale, NJ 07642. TEL 201-666-4110. FAX 201-666-2394. Ed.Bd.
　—BLDSC shelfmark: 5155.692000.
　Description: Provides a forum for the integration of studies over a wide range of topics related to fundamental questions about how language is learned.
　Refereed Serial

410　　UK　　ISSN 0169-0965
　　　　CODEN: LCPRET
LANGUAGE AND COGNITIVE PROCESSES. 1985? 4/yr. £27.50($52) to individuals; institutions £82.50(£157). Lawrence Erlbaum Associates Ltd., 27 Palmeira Mansions, Church Rd., Hove, E. Sussex BN3 2FA, England. TEL 0273-207411. FAX 0273-205612. (Co-publisher: V.S.P.) Ed. Lorraine K. Tyler. adv. **Indexed:** Lang.& Lang.Behav.Abstr.
　—BLDSC shelfmark: 5155.693600.
　Description: Provides an international forum for the publication of theoretical and experimental research into the mental processes and representations involved in language use.
　Refereed Serial

410 301.16　　US　　ISSN 0271-5309
P87　　　　CODEN: LACOD8
LANGUAGE & COMMUNICATION. 1981. 4/yr. £115 (effective 1992). Pergamon Press, Inc., Journals Division, 660 White Plains Rd., Tarrytown, NY 10591-5153. TEL 914-524-9200. FAX 914-333-2444. (And: Headington Hill Hall, Oxford O3 0BW, England. TEL 0865-794141) Eds. R. Harris, T. Taylor. (also avail. in microform from MIM,UMI) **Indexed:** Art.Int.Abstr., Lang.& Lang.Behav.Abstr. (1981-), Lang.Teach.& Ling.Abstr., M.L.A., Psychol.Abstr., Sci.Abstr, SSCI.
　—BLDSC shelfmark: 5155.693700.
　Refereed Serial

408 301.2　　JA
LANGUAGE AND CULTURE. (Text in English, French, German, or Japanese) 1982. s-a. Hokkaido University, Institute of Language and Culture Studies, Nishi 8, Kita 17, Kita-ku, Sapporo 060, Japan. circ. 200. **Indexed:** M.L.A.
　Supersedes: Essays in Foreign Languages and Literature.

407　　UK　　ISSN 0950-0782
LANGUAGE AND EDUCATION; an international journal. 1987. q. £22($46) to individuals; libraries £63 (£137); students £12 (£26). Multilingual Matters Ltd., Bank House, 8A Hill Rd., Clevedon, Avon BS21 7HH, England. TEL 0272-876519. FAX 0272-343096. Ed. David Corson.
　—BLDSC shelfmark: 5155.694450.
　Description: Studies the educational implications of research in all aspects of linguistics.

LANGUAGE AND EDUCATIONAL PROCESSES. see *EDUCATION — Teaching Methods And Curriculum*

LANGUAGE AND IDEOLOGY. see *POLITICAL SCIENCE*

410 800　　US　　ISSN 1057-6037
LANGUAGE AND LITERATURE. 1975. a. $25 to individuals; institutions $30. (Trinity University) Pitman Press, P.O. Box 791786, San Antonio, TX 78279-1786. TEL 512-736-7369. Ed. Bates L. Hoffer. bk.rev.; bibl.; illus.; circ. 150. **Indexed:** M.L.A.
　Formerly: Linguistics in Literature (ISSN 0147-0906)

410　　UK　　ISSN 0023-8309
P1
LANGUAGE AND SPEECH. 1958. q. £100($180) Kingston Press Services Ltd., 43 Derwent Rd., Whitton, Twickenham, Middlesex TW2 7HQ, England. TEL 081-893-3015. Ed. Bruno H. Repp. adv.; bk.rev.; bibl.; charts; illus.; index; circ. 1,000. (also avail. in microform from MIM; reprint service avail. from SCH) **Indexed:** C.I.J.E., Commun.Abstr., Curr.Cont., Dent.Ind., DSH Abstr., Ind.Med., Lang.& Lang.Behav.Abstr. (1972-), Lang.Teach.& Ling.Abstr., M.L.A., Mid.East: Abstr.& Ind., Psychol.Abstr., SSCI.
　—BLDSC shelfmark: 5155.700000.
　Description: Speech transmission and reception.

400　　US　　ISSN 0023-8317
PN203
LANGUAGE AND STYLE; an international journal. (Text in English, French, German) 1968. q. $16 to individuals (foreign $18); institutions $22 (foreign $25). (City University of New York, Queens College, Department of English) Queens College Press, c/o John Cassidy, Kiely 1309, Flushing, NY 11367. TEL 718-520-7773. Ed. Edmund L. Epstein. bk.rev.; charts; stat.; index; circ. 700. (back issues avail.) **Indexed:** Abstr.Engl.Stud., Amer.Hum.Ind., Arts & Hum.Cit.Ind., Can.Rev.Comp.Lit, Curr.Cont., Ind.Bk.Rev.Hum., Lang.& Lang.Behav.Abstr., M.L.A., Mid.East: Abstr.& Ind.
　—BLDSC shelfmark: 5155.705000.

054.1　　KE
LANGUAGE ASSOCIATION OF EASTERN AFRICA. JOURNAL. 2/yr. (Language Association of Eastern Africa) Ministry of Information & Broadcasting, P.O. Box 30571, Nairobi, Kenya. TEL 28411. TELEX 22244. Ed. T.P. Gorman.

407　　UK　　ISSN 0790-8318
LANGUAGE, CULTURE AND CURRICULUM. 1988. 3/yr. £18($38) to individuals; libraries £52 ($11); students £10 ($21). (Linguistic Institute of Ireland) Multilingual Matters Ltd., Bank House, 8a Hill Rd., Clevedon, Avon BS21 7HH, England. TEL 0272-876519. FAX 0272-343096. Ed. Eoghan MacAogain. circ. 400. **Indexed:** Lang.& Lang.Behav.Abstr. (1988-).
　—BLDSC shelfmark: 5155.708370.
　Description: Covers bilingualism, multiculturalism, language contact, lesser-used languages, cultural studies.
　Refereed Serial

491.1　　II　　ISSN 0253-9071
P1.A1
LANGUAGE FORUM. (Text in English) 1975. s-a. Rs.150($40) Bahri Publications, 997-A, St. No. 9, Gobindpuri, Kalkaji, New Delhi 110 019, India. TEL 644-5710. Ed. Ujjal Singh Bahri. adv.; bk.rev.
　Description: Contians articles on current trends in Indian literature; emphasizes curriculum planning, linguistic analyses of Indian languages, dialects and comparative literature.

410　　II　　ISSN 0254-0207
LANGUAGE FORUM MONOGRAPH SERIES. 1978. irreg. price varies. Bahri Publications, 997-A, Street No.9, Gobindpuri, Kalkaji, New Delhi 110 019, India. TEL 6448606. Ed. Ujjal Singh Bahri.
　Description: Focuses on a single theme connected to language, linguistics or literature in each issue.

400　　UK　　ISSN 0047-4045
P41　　　　CODEN: LGSCBO
LANGUAGE IN SOCIETY. 1972. q. $44 to individuals; institutions $88. Cambridge University Press, Edinburgh Bldg., Shaftesbury Rd., Cambridge CB2 2RU, England. TEL 0223-312393. FAX 0223-315052. TELEX 851817256. (N. American orders to: Cambridge University Press, 40 W. 20th., New York, NY 10011) Ed. Dell Hymes. adv.; bk.rev. (also avail. in microform from UMI; reprint service avail. from SWZ) **Indexed:** Abstr.Anthropol., ASSIA, Bk.Rev.Ind. (1984-), C.I.J.E., Chic.Per.Ind., Child.Bk.Rev.Ind. (1984-), Commun.Abstr., Curr.Cont., E.I., Ind.Bk.Rev.Hum., Lang.& Lang.Behav.Abstr. (1972-), Lang.Teach.& Ling.Abstr., M.L.A., Mid.East: Abstr.& Ind., Psychol.Abstr., Sociol.Abstr., Sp.Ed.Needs Abstr., SSCI.
　—BLDSC shelfmark: 5155.711800.
　Description: Covers sociolinguistics (speech and language as aspects of social life).

410　　NE　　ISSN 0923-182X
P106　　　　CODEN: LAINE2
LANGUAGE INTERNATIONAL; the magazine for language professionals. 1989. bi-m. fl.160($91) (effective 1992). John Benjamins Publishing Co., Amsteldijk 44, P.O. Box 75577, 1070 AN Amsterdam, Netherlands. TEL 020-6738156. FAX 020-6739773. (In N. America: 821 Bethlehem Pike, Philadelphia, PA 19118. TEL 215-836-1200) Ed. Geoffrey Kingscott. index; circ. 2,500.
　—BLDSC shelfmark: 5155.709680.
　Description: Provides an international forum in which language professionals can exchange the latest information related to their work and research.
　Refereed Serial

LINGUISTICS

418 370   US   ISSN 0023-8333
P1
LANGUAGE LEARNING; a journal of applied linguistics. 1948. q. $36 to individuals; institutions $60. Research Club in Language Learning, 178 Henry S. Frieze Bldg., 105 S. State St., Ann Arbor, MI 48109-1285. TEL 313-763-9216. Ed. John A. Upshur. bk.rev.; charts; stat.; circ. 2,000. (also avail. in microform from UMI) **Indexed:** C.I.J.E., Cont.Pg.Educ., Curr.Cont., E.I., Educ.Ind., Ind.Bk.Rev.Hum., Lang.& Lang.Behav.Abstr. (1972-), Lang.Teach.& Ling.Abstr., M.L.A., SSCI.

400 371.33   UK   ISSN 0957-1736
LB1633   CODEN: LLEJED
LANGUAGE LEARNING JOURNAL. (Text mainly in English; occasionally in French, German, Russian and Spanish) 1962. 2/yr. £30($60) (foreign £33). Association for Language Learning, 16 Regent Place, Rugby, Warwickshire CV21 2NP, England. TEL 0788-546443. FAX 0788-544149. Ed. C.A. Wringe. adv.; bk.rev.; film rev.; play rev.; abstr.; bibl.; charts; illus.; mkt.; stat.; index; circ. 5,500. (reprint service avail. from SWZ) **Indexed:** C.I.J.E., Cont.Pg.Educ., Curr.Cont., Educ.Tech.Abstr., Lang.& Lang.Behav.Abstr., Lang.Teach.& Ling.Abstr., Media Rev.Dig., Sp.Ed.Needs Abstr.
—BLDSC shelfmark: 5155.710200.
Formed by the merger of: Modern Languages (ISSN 0026-7945) & British Journal of Language Teaching (ISSN 0144-0888); Which was formerly: Audio-Visual Language Journal (ISSN 0004-7589)
Description: Contains articles about teaching and learning languages; applied linguistics, language policy, current issues; ideas for practical classroom teaching.

418   US
▼**LANGUAGE MAINTENANCE**; a word user's manual. 1990. bi-m. $16. Language Maintenance, 2745 Winnetka Ave., New Hope, MN 55427. TEL 612-533-2427. Ed. Patricia Maynard. circ. 181.
Description: Focuses on the use and misuse of the English language.

499.992   NE   ISSN 0272-2690
P40.5.L35
LANGUAGE PROBLEMS AND LANGUAGE PLANNING. 1969. 3/yr. fl.60($35) to individuals; institutions fl.125($66)(effective 1992). (Center for Research and Documentation on World Language Problems) John Benjamins Publishing Co., Amsteldijk 44, P.O. Box 75577, 1070 AN Amsterdam, Netherlands. TEL 020-6738156. FAX 020-6739773. (In N. America: 821 Bethlehem Pike, Philadelphia, PA 19118. TEL 215-836-1200) Ed. Humphrey Tonkin. adv.; bk.rev.; bibl.; index; circ. 750. (also avail. in microform from MIM,UMI; back issues avail.) **Indexed:** Amer.Bibl.Slavic & E.Eur.Stud, C.I.J.E., ERIC, Int.Polit.Sci.Abstr., Lang.& Lang.Behav.Abstr. (1977-), Lang.Teach.& Ling.Abstr., M.L.A.
—BLDSC shelfmark: 5155.710700.
Former titles: Lingvaj Problemoj Kaj Lingvo-Planado (ISSN 0165-2672); Mondo Lingvo Problemo (ISSN 0026-9344)
Description: Examines political, social, economic and cultural policies related to language and language use.

400 370 800   US
LANGUAGE QUARTERLY. (Not published during 1989) (Text in English, French, German, Spanish) 1962. s-a. $12. University of South Florida, Division of Language, 4202 E. Fowler Ave., Tampa, FL 33620. TEL 813-974-5618. Ed. Roger W. Cole. bk.rev.; charts; cum.index every 5 yrs.; circ. 600. (also avail. in microform from UMI; reprint service avail. from UMI) **Indexed:** ERIC, Lang.& Lang.Behav.Abstr., M.L.A.
Formerly: University of South Florida Language Quarterly (ISSN 0042-0077)
Description: Concentrates on study of linguistics and language teaching.

410   KO   ISSN 0254-4474
P9
LANGUAGE RESEARCH/OHAK YON'GU. (Text in English and Korean; summaries in English) 1965. q. $35. Language Research Institute, Seoul National University, San 56-1, Sinlim-dong, Kwanak-ku, Seoul 151-742, S. Korea. FAX 82-2-880-6907. Ed. Sang-Oak Lee. adv.; bk.rev.; circ. 800. **Indexed:** Lang.& Lang.Behav.Abstr., M.L.A., Sociol.Abstr. Key Title: Nehag Nyengu.
—BLDSC shelfmark: 5155.711300.

410   UK   ISSN 0388-0001
P1
LANGUAGE SCIENCES; a world journal of the sciences of language. (Includes supplements) (Text in English) 1978. q. £120 (effective 1992). Pergamon Press plc, Headington Hill Hall, Oxford OX3 0BW, England. TEL 0865-794141. FAX 0865-743911. TELEX 83177 PERGAP. (And: 660 White Plains Rd., Tarrytown, NY 10591-5153. TEL 914-524-9200) Ed.Bd. adv.; bk.rev.; abstr.; bibl.; charts; illus.; stat.; index; circ. 500. (also avail. in microfilm from UMI; back issues avail.) **Indexed:** Lang.& Lang.Behav.Abstr., Sociol.Abstr.
—BLDSC shelfmark: 5155.711700.
Description: Provides an international, multidisciplinary forum for exchanging information and ideas in sociolinguistics, pragmatics, child language and sign studies; topics in behavioral linguistics (phonology, morphology, syntax, semantics, historical linguistics, and dialectology) may also be treated.
Refereed Serial

407 370   UK
LANGUAGE TEACHER. 2/yr. £6($13) to individuals and students; libraries £11 ($24). Multilingual Matters Ltd., Bank House, 8a Hill Rd., Clevedon, Avon BS21 7HH, England. TEL 0272-876519. FAX 0272-343096.
Description: Aims to provide useful information for the language class; also covers current language issues in teaching.

410   UK   ISSN 0265-5322
P53.4
LANGUAGE TESTING. 1984. 2/yr. £32($57) to individuals; institutions £49($784). Edward Arnold (Subsidiary of: Hodder & Stoughton), Mill Road, Dunton Green, Sevenoaks, Kent TN13 2YA, England. TEL 0732-450111. FAX 0732-461321. (Distr. in U.S. and Canada by: Cambridge University Press, 40 E. 20th St., New York, NY 10011) adv.; bk.rev. **Indexed:** Lang.& Lang.Behav.Abstr. (1985-), Lang.Teach.& Ling.Abstr.
—BLDSC shelfmark: 5155.712910.
Description: Provides a forum for work in the field of linguistic testing and assessment.

410   UK   ISSN 0954-3945
P120.V37   CODEN: LVCHEX
LANGUAGE VARIATION AND CHANGE. 3/yr. $27 individuals; institutions $52. Cambridge University Press, Edinburgh Bldg., Shaftesbury Rd., Cambridge CB2 2RU, England. (N. American addr.: Cambridge University Press, 40 W. 20th St., New York, NY 10011) Ed.Bd. adv.; bk.rev. (also avail. in microform from UMI) **Indexed:** Lang.& Lang.Behav.Abstr. (1989-).
—BLDSC shelfmark: 5155.712975.
Description: Studies linguistic variations, with emphasis on sytematic and inherent variation in synchronic and diachronic linguistics.

410   SZ   ISSN 0085-2678
LANGUE ET CULTURES; etudes et documents. (Text and summaries in English and French) 1971. irreg, no.24, 1991. price varies. Librairie Droz S.A., 11, rue Massot, CH-1211 Geneva 12, Switzerland. TEL 022-466666. FAX 022-472391. circ. 800.
Description: Presents works of contemporary linguistics and classic texts plus philosophies relating to the nature and function of language. Includes the writings of Descartes, Liebnitz, Bopp and Saussure.

440   FR   ISSN 0023-8368
PC2002
LANGUE FRANCAISE. 1969. q. 270 F. Larousse, 17 rue du Montparnasse, 75280 Paris Cedex 06, France. (Dist. by: Gauthier-Villars, Centrale des Revues, 11 rue Gossin, 92543 Montrouge Cedex, France. TEL 1-46-56-52-66) Ed. J.Cl. Chevalier. adv.; bk.rev.; bibl.; circ. 5,000. (also avail. in microform from SWZ; reprint service avail. from SWZ) **Indexed:** Arts & Hum.Cit.Ind., Curr.Cont., Lang.& Lang.Behav.Abstr., Lang.Teach.& Ling.Abstr., M.L.A.
—BLDSC shelfmark: 5155.714000.

410   CM
LANGUES DU CAMEROUN. irreg., no.5, 1976. B.P. 5351, Douala, Cameroun.

410 301.2   FR   ISSN 0240-2041
LANGUES ET CIVILISATIONS A TRADITION ORALE. 1972. irreg. Societe d'Etudes Linguistiques et Anthropologiques de France (SELAF), 5 rue de Marseille, 75010 Paris, France. TEL 42-08-83-93.

496 572   FR   ISSN 0755-9305
LANGUES ET CULTURES AFRICAINES. 1982. irreg. price varies. Societe d'Etudes Linguistiques et Anthropologiques de France (SELAF), 5 rue de Marseille, 75010 Paris, France. TEL 42-08-83-93.

499 572   FR   ISSN 0750-2036
LANGUES ET CULTURES DU PACIFIQUE. 1982. irreg. price varies. Societe d'Etudes Linguistiques et Anthropologiques de France (SELAF), 5 rue de Marseille, 75010 Paris, France. TEL 42-08-83-93. adv.; bk.rev.; circ. 250.

LANGUES ET STYLES. see *LITERATURE*

400   FR   ISSN 0023-8376
PB2
LANGUES MODERNES. (Text in French) 1903. 4/yr. 290 F. Association des Professeurs de Langues Vivantes de l'Enseignement Public, 19 rue de la Glaciere, 75013 Paris, France. Ed. Christian Puren. adv.; bk.rev.; charts; index; circ. 5,000. **Indexed:** Lang.& Lang.Behav.Abstr., Lang.Teach.& Ling.Abstr.
—BLDSC shelfmark: 5155.715000.
Description: Deals with foreign language teaching; research, experiments and institutional changes.

490   BE   ISSN 0987-7738
LANGUES ORIENTALES ANCIENNES PHILOLOGIE ET LINGUISTIQUE. SHort title: L O A P L. 1988. a. 1500 Fr. Éditions Peeters s.p.r.l., Bondgenotenlaan 153, B-3000 Leuven, Belgium. TEL 016-235170. FAX 016-228500. Eds. G. Bohas, G. Roquet. bk.rev. (back issues avail.)

470 870   VC   ISSN 0023-883X
PA2009
LATINITAS; commentarii linguae latinae excolendae. (Text in Latin) 1953. q. L.45000($40) (Fondazione Latinitas) Libreria Editrice Vaticana, 00120 Vatican City (Rome), State of the Vatican City. TEL 0039-6-698-3532. FAX 0039-6-698-4716. adv.; bk.rev.; index; circ. 1,500.
Description: Periodical of cultural actuality and classical linguistics.

420.07 370   US   ISSN 0023-964X
LB1631
LEAFLET (LEXINGTON). 1902. 3/yr. (during school year). $25 (includes N E A T E Newsletter). New England Association of Teachers of English, Box 234, Lexington, MA 02173. TEL 617-646-2575. adv.; cum.index: 1969-1980; circ. 950. (back issues avail.) **Indexed:** Rev.Appl.Entomol.
Formerly: English Leaflet.
Description: Presents study and teaching methods.

400   GW   ISSN 0023-9909
PB5
LEBENDE SPRACHEN; Zeitschrift fuer fremde Sprachen in Wissenschaft und Praxis. (Text in English, French, German, Italian, Spanish) 1956. 4/yr. DM.82. Verlag Langenscheidt KG, Crellestr. 28-30, 1000 Berlin 62, Germany. FAX 030-780002-15. TELEX 183175 EKGBL. adv.; bk.rev.; bibl.; tr.lit.; cum.index every 2 yrs.; circ. 3,250. **Indexed:** Key to Econ.Sci., Lang.& Lang.Behav.Abstr., Lang.Teach.& Ling.Abstr., M.L.A.
—BLDSC shelfmark: 5179.622000.

LECTOR. see *PUBLISHING AND BOOK TRADE*

410 378 371.3   US   ISSN 0325-8637
LB1049.9
LECTURA Y VIDA; revista latinoamericana de lectura. 1980. q. $38 in U.S. Latin America $19. International Reading Association, Inc., 800 Barksdale Rd., Box 8139, Newark, DE 19714-8139. TEL 302-731-1600. FAX 032-731-1057. TELEX 5106002813 READING. Ed. Maria Elena Rodriguez. adv.; bk.rev.; bibl.; index; circ. 1,400. (also avail. in microform from UMI; reprint service avail. from UMI)
Description: Covers the teaching and learning of reading comprehension of written language.

LEEDS STUDIES IN ENGLISH. see *LITERATURE*

LEEDS TEXTS AND MONOGRAPHS. NEW SERIES. see *LITERATURE*

| 479 879 | NE | ISSN 0169-8656 |

LEIDSE ROMANISTISCHE REEKS. (Text in French, Italian and Spanish) 1954. irreg., vol.24, 1990. price varies. E.J. Brill, P.O. Box 9000, 2300 PA Leiden, Netherlands. TEL 071-312624. FAX 071-317532. TELEX 39296 BRILL NL. (N. America dist. addr.: E.J. Brill, 24 Hudson St., Kinderhook, NY 12106. TEL 800-962-4406) (Co-publisher: Leiden University Press)

LEMOUZI; revue franco-limousine. see *HISTORY — History Of Europe*

| 401 | FR | ISSN 0153-0313 |
| PC3371 | | |

LENGAS; revue de sociolinguistique. s-a. 85 F. Universite de Montpellier (Universite Paul Valery), B.P. 5043, 34032 Montpellier Cedex 1, France. TEL 67-14-20-00.
 Description: Examines the socio-linguistics of the Occitan public and individuals or groups involved with the Occitan culture. Includes critical studies of research in the field as well as theoretical articles on the problems and methods of sociolinguistics.

| 460 375.4 | PE | |

LENGUA Y SOCIEDAD. 1974. irreg., no.12, 1990. price varies. (Instituto de Estudios Peruanos) I E P Ediciones, Horacio Urteaga 694 (Campo de Marte), Lima 11, Peru. TEL 32-3070. FAX 324981. (back issues avail.)

| 410 | CK | ISSN 0120-3479 |

LENGUAJE. 1972. irreg. Col.$110($5) Universidad del Valle, Division de Humanidades, Departamento de Idiomas, Apdo. Aereo 25360, Cali, Colombia. Ed. Samuel Estrada. circ. 1,000. **Indexed:** Lang.& Lang.Behav.Abstr. (1973-), M.L.A.

| 400 500 | PE | ISSN 0024-0796 |
| P1.A1 | | |

LENGUAJE Y CIENCIAS. (Text in English, French, German, Spanish; summaries in English) 1961. s-a. $15. Universidad Nacional de Trujillo, Departamento de Idiomas y Linguistica, Trujillo, Peru. Ed. Ernesto Zierer. adv.; bk.rev.; charts; illus.; circ. 800. **Indexed:** ERIC, Hisp.Amer.Per.Ind., Lang.& Lang.Behav.Abstr. (1972-), Lang.Teach.& Ling.Abstr., M.L.A.
 —BLDSC shelfmark: 5182.390000.

| 410 | AG | |

LENGUAJES;* revista de linguistica y semiologia. 1974. 3/yr. Asociacion Argentina de Semiotica, Tucuman 3748, Buenos Aires, Argentina. Ed. Juan Carlos Indart. bk.rev.; bibl.

LENINGRADSKII UNIVERSITET. VESTNIK. SERIYA ISTORIYA, YAZYK I LITERATURA. see *HISTORY*

| 492.4 | IS | ISSN 0334-3626 |

LESHONENU. q. $35. Academy of the Hebrew Language, P.O. Box 3449, 91034 Jerusalem, Israel. **Indexed:** Ind.Heb.Per., Rel.& Theol.Abstr. (1969-).

| 492.4 | IS | ISSN 0024-1091 |

LESHONENU LA'AM. (Text in Hebrew) 10/yr. $23. Academy of the Hebrew Language, P.O. Box 3449, 91034 Jerusalem, Israel. Eds. Eli Eytan, Meir Medan. circ. 3,000. **Indexed:** Ind.Heb.Per., M.L.A., Rel.& Theol.Abstr.

| 450 | IT | ISSN 0075-8825 |

LESSICO INTELLETTUALE EUROPEO. 1969. irreg., no.50, 1990. price varies. Edizioni dell' Ateneo S.p.A., P.O. Box 7216, 00100 Rome, Italy. circ. 1,500.

| 410 | VE | |

LETRAS (CARACAS). 1958. s-a. Bs.200($10) Instituto Universitario Pedagogico de Caracas, Centro de Investigaciones Linguisticas y Literarias Andres Bello, Avda. J.A. Paez, El Paraiso, Caracas, Venezuela. (Orders to: Venezuelan Book Service, Apdo. Postal 25092, Caracas 1023-A, Venezuela) Dir. Luis Alvarez. bk.rev.; bibl.; circ. 2,000. (back issues avail.) **Indexed:** M.L.A.

| 469 | BL | ISSN 0047-4428 |
| P25 | | |

LETRAS DE HOJE; estudo e debate de assuntos da lingua Portuguesa. 1967. 4/yr. Cz.$800($10) (Pontificia Universidade Catolica do Rio Grande do Sul, Centro de Estudos de Lingua Portuguesa) Editora da P U C R S, c/o Antoninho M. Naime, Caixa Postal 12001, 90620 Porto Alegre RS, Brazil. Ed. Elvo Clemente. bk.rev./ circ. 1,000. **Indexed:** Lang.& Lang.Behav.Abstr.

| 430 | BE | ISSN 0024-1482 |

LEUVENSE BIJDRAGEN; tijdschrift voor Germaanse Filologie. (Text in Dutch, English, French, German) 1896. q. 600 BEF($21) Katholieke Universiteit te Leuven - Universite Catholique de Louvain, Blijde-Inkomststraat 21, B-3000 Leuven, Belgium. Ed. G. Geerts. adv.; bk.rev.; charts, illus.; index, cum.index; circ. 594. (reprint service avail. from SWZ) **Indexed:** Lang.& Lang.Behav.Abstr., M.L.A.
 —BLDSC shelfmark: 5185.400000.

| 410 | GW | ISSN 0175-6206 |

LEXICOGRAPHICA; international annual for lexicography. (Text and summaries in English, French, German) 1985. a. DM.156. Max Niemeyer Verlag, Postfach 2140, 7400 Tuebingen 1, Germany. TEL 07071-81104. FAX 07071-87419. Ed. Antonin Kucera. (back issues avail.)
 Description: Essays and reviews on lexicography/lexicology (German, English, French, etc., bi- and monolingual dictionaries).

| 410 860 | PE | ISSN 0254-9239 |
| P9 | | |

LEXIS; revista de linguistica y literatura. 1977. s-a. $16. Pontificia Universidad Catolica del Peru, Departamento de Humanidades, Fondo Editorial, Apdo. 1761, Lima 100, Peru. Ed. Jose L. Rivarola.
 —BLDSC shelfmark: 5185.770000.

| 491.92 | LI | ISSN 0130-0172 |
| PG8501 | | |

LIETUVIU KALBOTYROS KLAUSIMAI/PROBLEMS OF LITHUANIAN LINGUISTICS. (Text in Lithuanian or Russian; summaries in English, German, Lithuanian or Russian) 1957. a. price varies. (Lithuanian Academy of Sciences, Institute of Lithuanian Language) Leidykla Mokslas, Zvaigzdziu 23, Vilnius 2050, Lithuania. TEL 45-85-26. TELEX 278128 LIE SU. Ed. K. Gaivenis. **Indexed:** M.L.A.
 —BLDSC shelfmark: 5208.530000.
 Description: Treats problems of Lithuanian linguistics, terminology, and social linguistics.

| 400 800 | GW | ISSN 0049-8653 |
| P3 | | |

LILI. (Zeitschrift fuer Literaturwissenschaft und Linguistik) 1971. q. DM.78. Vandenhoeck und Ruprecht, Theaterstr. 13, Postfach 3753, 3400 Goettingen, Germany. TEL 0551-6959-22. FAX 0551-695917. Ed. Helmut Kreuzer. adv.; bk.rev.; bibl.; charts; circ. 680. **Indexed:** Arts & Hum.Cit.Ind., Curr.Cont., Lang.Teach.& Ling.Abstr., M.L.A.

| 400 800 | GW | |

LILI. BEIHEFTE. (Zeitschrift fuer Literaturwissenschaft und Linguistik) 1975. irreg., no.15, 1988. price varies. Vandenhoeck und Ruprecht, Theaterstr. 13, Postfach 3753, 3400 Goettingen, Germany. TEL 0551-6959-22. FAX 0551-695917. **Indexed:** Can.Rev.Comp.Lit.

| 459 | RM | ISSN 0024-3523 |
| PC601 | | |

LIMBA ROMANA/ROMANIAN LANGUAGE. 1952. 6/yr. 120 lei($48) (Academia Romana) Editura Academiei Romane, Calea Victoriei 125, 79717 Bucharest, Rumania. (Dist. by: Rompresfilatelia, Calea Grivitei 64-66, P.O. Box 12-201, 78104 Bucharest, Rumania) Ed. I. Coteanu. bk.rev.; bibl.; charts; index; circ. 5,000. (back issues avail) **Indexed:** Lang.& Lang.Behav.Abstr. (1973-), M.L.A.

| 400 | RM | ISSN 0583-8045 |

LIMBA SI LITERATURA. 1955. 4/yr. $40 (effective Jan. 1991). Societatea de Stiinte Filologice din Romania, Bd. Schitul Magureanu nr.1, Bucharest, cod 79664, sector 5, Rumania. TEL 15-171-92. bk.rev.; bibl.; circ. 3,000.
 Supersedes: Societatea de Stiinte Istorice si Filologice din R.P.R. Limba si Literatura.
 Description: Covers linguistics, stylistics, literary history, criticism and theory, texts and documents, text analysis, folklore, didactics and education history.

| 400 | NE | ISSN 0024-3841 |
| P9 | | |

LINGUA; international review of general linguistics. (Text in English, French, German) 1947. 12/yr.(in 3 vols.; 4 nos./vol.) fl.903 (effective 1992). North-Holland (Subsidiary of: Elsevier Science Publishers B.V.), P.O. Box 211, 1000 AE Amsterdam, Netherlands. TEL 020-5803911. FAX 020-5803598. TELEX 18582 ESPA NL. (Subscr. in U.S. and Canada to: Elsevier Science Publishing Co., Inc., Box 882, Madison Sq. Sta., New York, NY 10159. TEL 212-989-5800) Ed. T. Hoekstra. adv.; bk.rev.; bibl.; index, cum.index; circ. 1,078. (also avail. in microform from RPI; back issues avail.; reprint service avail. from SWZ) **Indexed:** Abstr.Anthropol., Arts & Hum.Cit.Ind., Chic.Per.Ind., Curr.Cont., DSH Abstr., E.I., Ind.Bk.Rev.Hum., Lang.& Lang.Behav.Abstr. (1971-), Lang.Teach.& Ling.Abstr., M.L.A., Mid.East: Abstr.& Ind., Sociol.Abstr., SSCI.
 —BLDSC shelfmark: 5221.155000.
 Description: Directed to people who are involved in linguistic studies.
 Refereed Serial

| 056.9 | PO | ISSN 0047-4703 |
| P9 | | |

LINGUA E CULTURA. 1971. 3/yr. Esc.200. Sociedade de Lingua Portuguesa, Rua de S. Jose 41, 2 Lisbon, Portugal. Ed. Jose Neves Henriques. adv.; bk.rev.; circ. 1,000.

| 400 800 | BL | ISSN 0047-4711 |

LINGUA E LITERATURA. (Text in various languages) 1972. a. $15. Universidade de Sao Paulo, Faculdade de Filosofia, Letras e Ciencias Humanas, Se͜cao de Publicacoes, C.P. 8105, CEP 05508, Sao Paulo, Brazil. TEL 011-813-3222. Eds. Aida Costa, Carlos Drumond, Paulo Vizioli. bk.rev.; charts; illus.; bibl.; circ. 1,000. **Indexed:** Hisp.Amer.Per.Ind.

| 400 810 | IT | ISSN 0024-385X |
| P9 | | |

LINGUA E STILE. (Text in French and Italian; summaries in English and Russian) 1966. q. L.120000. (Universita degli Studi di Bologna, Istituto di Glottologia) Societa Editrice Il Mulino, Strada Maggiore, 37, 40125 Bologna, Italy. TEL 051-256011. FAX 051-256034. Eds. Bruno Basile, Luigi Rosiello, Giorgio Sandri. adv.; bk.rev.; bibl.; index; circ. 1,600. (back issues avail.) **Indexed:** Arts & Hum.Cit.Ind., Can.Rev.Comp.Lit, Curr.Cont., Lang.Teach.& Ling.Abstr., M.L.A.

| 499.99 | UK | |

LINGUA E VITA. 1969. 3/yr. £3.50. British Interlingua Society, 14 Ventnor Court, Wostenholm Rd., Sheffield S7 1LB, England. TEL 0742-582931. (Subscr. address: c/o P. Berwick, 15 Barnton Park Gardens, Edinburgh EH4 6HL, Scotland; U.S. subscr.: Interlingua Institute, 496a Hudson St., G.34, New York 10014) Ed. B.C. Sexton. adv.; bk.rev.; circ. 180.
 Incorporates: Interlingua Institute Newsletter.

| 450 | IT | ISSN 0024-3868 |
| PC1001 | | |

LINGUA NOSTRA. 1939. q. L.80000. Casa Editrice G.C. Sansoni Editore Nuova S.p.A., Via Benedetto Varchi 47, 50132 Florence, Italy. Eds. G. Folena, G. Ghinassi. bk.rev.; abstr.index; circ. 1,500. **Indexed:** Arts & Hum.Cit.Ind., Curr.Cont., Lang.& Lang.Behav.Abstr., Lang.Teach.& Ling.Abstr., M.L.A.

| 491.85 | PL | ISSN 0079-4740 |
| P25 | | |

LINGUA POSNANIENSIS. (Text in various languages) 1949. a. price varies. (Poznanskie Towarzystwo Przyjaciol Nauk) Panstwowe Wydawnictwo Naukowe, Ul.Miodowa 10, Warsaw, Poland. (Dist. by: Ars Polona-Ruch, Krakowskie Przedmiescie 7, Warsaw, Poland) Ed. Jerzy Banczerowski. **Indexed:** Ind.Bk.Rev.Hum., Lang.& Lang.Behav.Abstr. (1972-), M.L.A.

| 410 900 | GW | ISSN 0341-3225 |

LINGUARUM MINORUM DOCUMENTA HISTORIOGRAPHICA. 1977. irreg., no.5, 1983. price varies. Helmut Buske Verlag Hamburg, Friedrichsgaber Weg 138, Postfach 1249, D-2000 Hamburg, Germany. Ed. H. Haarmann.

LINGUISTICS

400   IT   ISSN 0024-3876
LINGUE DEL MONDO; unica rivista Italiana di cultura linguistica. (Text in English, French, German, Italian, Rumanian, Russian, Spanish; summaries in Italian) 1934. bi-m. L.42000($35) Valmartina Editore, Via L. Dottesio, 1, 335138 Padua, Italy. Ed. Gabriele Pasquinelli. adv.; bk.rev.; bibl.; illus.; index; circ. 27,000. **Indexed:** Lang.& Lang.Behav.Abstr. (1985-).

400   IT
LINGUE E ISCRIZIONI DELL'ITALIA ANTICA. 1977. irreg., no.5, 1985. Casa Editrice Leo S. Olschki, Viuzzo del Pozzetto, Casella Postale 66, 50100 Florence, Italy. TEL 055-6530684. FAX 055-6530214. Dir. Aldo Prosdocimi. circ. 1,000.

410   IT   ISSN 0391-3228
LE LINGUE E LE CIVILTA STRANIERE MODERNE. 1981. irreg., no.8, 1989. price varies. Liguori Editore s.r.l., Via Mezzocanone 19, 80134 Naples, Italy. TEL 081-5227139. Ed. Elio Chinol.

400   UK   ISSN 0268-5965
P1
LINGUIST. 1962. bi-m. £15.50. Institute of Linguists, 24a Highbury Grove, London N5 2EA, England. TEL 01-359 7445. FAX 01-354-0202. Ed. J.L. Kettle-Williams. adv.; bk.rev.; index; circ. 6,000. **Indexed:** BMT, Lang.& Lang.Behav.Abstr., Lang.Teach.& Ling.Abstr., M.L.A., Mid.East: Abstr.& Ind., Sociol.Abstr.
—BLDSC shelfmark: 5221.220000.
Formerly (until 1986): Incorporated Linguist (ISSN 0019-3534)

400   BE
LINGUISTE/TAALKUNDIGE. (Text in Dutch, French) 1955. q. 500 BEF. (Chambre Belge des Traducteurs, Interpretes et Philologues - Belgische Kamer van Vertalers Tolken en Filologen) F. Lepeer, Ed. & Pub., 110 ave. De Heyn, B-1090 Brussels, Belgium. adv.; bk.rev.; circ. 1,000.

410   US   ISSN 0098-9053
P123
LINGUISTIC ANALYSIS. 1975-1986; resumed 1988. 4/yr. $52.50 to individuals; institutions $105. c/o Michael K. Brame, Ed., University of Washington, Department of Linguistics GN-40, Seattle, WA 98195. TEL 206-463-3451. FAX 206-463-3451. (Subscr. to: Linguistic Analysis, Box 95679, Seattle, WA 98145-2679) adv.; bk.rev.; circ. 1,000. **Indexed:** Abstr.Anthropol., Amer.Bibl.Slavic & E.Eur.Stud, Arts & Hum.Cit.Ind., Comput.Rev., Curr.Cont., Lang.& Lang.Behav.Abstr., Lang.Teach.& Ling.Abstr., M.L.A., Mid.East: Abstr.& Ind., SSCI.
Description: Focuses on formal syntax, semantics, and phonology.

410 800   US   ISSN 0165-7712
LINGUISTIC & LITERARY STUDIES IN EASTERN EUROPE. Short title: L L S E E. 1979. irreg., vol.35, 1991. price varies. John Benjamins Publishing Co., 821 Bethlehem Pike, Philadelphia, PA 19118. TEL 215-836-1200. FAX 215-836-1204. (And: Amsteldijk 44, P.O. Box 75577, 1070 AN Amsterdam, Netherlands. TEL 020-6762325) Ed. Philip Luelsdorff. **Indexed:** M.L.A., Math.R.
Description: Contains recent developments in linguistic and literary research in Eastern Europe.

400   NE
LINGUISTIC CALCULATION. (Text in English, French and German) 1961. a. price varies. Kluwer Academic Publishers, Spuiboulevard 50, P.O. Box 17, 3300 AA Dordrecht, Netherlands. TEL 078-334911. FAX 078-334254. TELEX 29245. (Dist. by: Kluwer Academic Publishers Group, P.O. Box 322, 3300 AH Dordrecht, Netherlands; U.S. addr.: Box 358, Accord Sta., Hingham, MA 02018-0358) Ed. Hans Karlgren. **Indexed:** M.L.A., SSCI.
Former titles: S M I L Quarterly Journal of Linguistic Calculus; (until 1977): Statistical Methods in Linguistics (ISSN 0039-0437)

410   US   ISSN 0075-9597
LINGUISTIC CIRCLE OF MANITOBA AND NORTH DAKOTA. PROCEEDINGS. 1959. a. $10. University of North Dakota, Department of Philosophy and Religion, Box 8258, Grand Forks, ND 58202. FAX 701-777-3650. (Co-sponsors: University of Winnipeg; University of Manitoba; Minot State University; North Dakota State University) Ed. Theodore Messenger. adv.; circ. 500 (controlled).

400   US   ISSN 0024-3892
P1
LINGUISTIC INQUIRY. 1970. q. $48 to individuals (foreign $59); institutions $90 (foreign $99); students or retired $30 (foreign $44). M I T Press, 55 Hayward St., Cambridge, MA 02142. TEL 617-253-2889. FAX 617-258-6779. TELEX 921473. (Editorial addr.: M I T Bldg. 20D-213, Cambridge, MA 02139) Ed. Samuel Jay Keyser. adv.; bk.rev.; index; circ. 3,000. (also avail. in microform from MIM,UMI; back issues avail.; reprint service avail. from ISI,SCH,UMI) **Indexed:** Abstr.Anthropol., Amer.Bibl.Slavic & E.Eur.Stud, Arts & Hum.Cit.Ind., Curr.Cont., Lang.& Lang.Behav.Abstr. (1972-), Lang.Teach.& Ling.Abstr., M.L.A., Mid.East: Abstr.& Ind., SSCI.
●Also available online.
—BLDSC shelfmark: 5221.280000.
Description: Provides information about new theoretical developments in phonology, syntax, semantics and morphology.
Refereed Serial

410   US
LINGUISTIC MODELS.* (Text in English) 1982. irreg., no.14, 1989. Walter de Gruyter, Inc., 200 Saw Mill River Rd., Hawthorne, NY 10532. TEL 914-747-0110. FAX 914-747-1326. Eds. Teun Hoekstra, Harry van der Hulst.
Description: Addresses the development of formal methods in the study of language.

410   US   ISSN 0737-4720
                CODEN: LNLJES
LINGUISTIC NOTES FROM LA JOLLA. no.5, 1973. irreg. $7 to individuals (foreign $8); institutions $9 (foreign $10). University of California, San Diego, Department of Linguistics, C-008, La Jolla, CA 92093. TEL 619-452-3600. charts; circ. 75. **Indexed:** Lang.& Lang.Behav.Abstr. (1988-).

410   US   ISSN 0167-6318
LINGUISTIC REVIEW.* 1981. 4/yr. fl.99 to individuals; institutions fl.190. Walter de Gruyter, Inc., 200 Saw Mill River Rd., Hawthorne, NY 10532. TEL 914-747-0110. FAX 914-747-1326. Ed.Bd. (back issues avail.; reprint service avail. from SWZ) **Indexed:** Curr.Cont., Lang.& Lang.Behav.Abstr. (1981-), Lang.Teach.& Ling.Abstr.
—BLDSC shelfmark: 5221.298000.
Description: Contributes original insights to the theory of formal grammar within the framework of generative grammar or related approaches.

400   US   ISSN 0075-9600
LINGUISTIC SOCIETY OF AMERICA. MEETING HANDBOOKS. 1965. a. free to qualified personnel. Linguistic Society of America, 1325 18th St., N.W., Ste. 211, Washington, DC 20036-6501. adv.; circ. 1,000. (back issues avail.)

491   II   ISSN 0075-9627
LINGUISTIC SOCIETY OF INDIA. BULLETIN. 1958. irreg., no.3, 1970. included with subscription to Indian Linguistics. Linguistic Society of India, c/o Deccan College Postgraduate and Research Institute, Poona 411006, India. Ed. R.V. Dhongde.

400   JA   ISSN 0024-3914
LINGUISTIC SOCIETY OF JAPAN. JOURNAL/GENGO KENKYU. (Text in English and Japanese) 1939. s-a. $27. Linguistic Society of Japan - Nihon Gengogakkai, c/o Sanseido Co., Ltd., 2-22-14 Misaki-cho, Chiyoda-ku, Tokyo 101, Japan. Ed. Katsumi Matsumoto. bk.rev.; circ. 1,000. **Indexed:** Lang.& Lang.Behav.Abstr., M.L.A.
—BLDSC shelfmark: 4814.500000.

400   XV   ISSN 0024-3922
P25
LINGUISTICA. (Text in various languages) 1955. a. $10. Univerza v Ljubljani, Filozofska Fakulteta, Askerceva 12, 61000 Ljubljana, Slovenia. TEL 061-150-001. FAX 061-159-337. Ed. Mitja Skubic. circ. 600. **Indexed:** Lang.& Lang.Behav.Abstr. (1972-), M.L.A.

220 400   GW   ISSN 0342-0884
BL65.L2
LINGUISTICA BIBLICA; Interdisziplinaere Zeitschrift fuer Theologie, Semiotik und Linguistik. (Text in German, English, French; summaries in English) 1970. 2/yr. DM.46. Verlag Linguistica Biblica, Postfach 130154, 5300 Bonn 1, Germany. FAX 02225-18474. Ed. Erhardt Guettgemanns. adv.; bk.rev.; abstr.; bibl.; illus.; index; circ. 500. **Indexed:** Arts & Hum.Cit.Ind., CERDIC, Curr.Cont., Lang.& Lang.Behav.Abstr. (1972-), M.L.A., New Test.Abstr., Old Test.Abstr., Rel.& Theol.Abstr. (1973-).

410 850   IT
LINGUISTICA E LETTERATURA. s-a. L.130000. Giardini Editori e Stampatori, Via Santa Bibbiana 28, 56100 Pisa, Italy. TEL 050 502531. Ed.Bd.

410   SP
LINGUISTICA ESPANOLA ACTUAL. 1979. s-a. 2700 ptas.($45) Instituto de Cooperacion Iberoamericana, Avenida los Reyes Catolicos, 4, 28040 Madrid, Spain. TEL 415-36-87. FAX 415-36-07. (Subscr. to: Arco-Libros, S.A., Juan Bautista de Toledo 28, 28002 Madrid, Spain)

400 800   NE
P1.A1
LINGUISTICA PRAGENSIA. (Text in English, French, German, Spanish) 1958. 2/yr. fl.96($49) (effective 1992). (Czechoslovak Academy of Sciences, Institute for Czech and World Literature, CS) John Benjamins Publishing Co., Amsteldijk 44, P.O. Box 75577, 1070 AN Amsterdam, Netherlands. TEL 020-6738156. FAX 020-6739773. (In N. America: 821 Bethlehem Pike, Philadelphia, PA 19118. TEL 215-836-1200) Ed.Bd. bk.rev.; index; circ. 1,000. **Indexed:** Lang.& Lang.Behav.Abstr., Lang.Teach.& Ling.Abstr., M.L.A.
Supersedes in part (in 1991): Philologica Pragensia (ISSN 0048-3885)
Description: Covers modern philology, linguistics, and literature.

410   PL   ISSN 0208-4228
P9
LINGUISTICA SILESIANA. (Text in English, French or Russian; summaries in Polish, Russian) 1975. irreg. price varies. Ossolineum, Publishing House of the Polish Academy of Sciences, Rynek 9, 50-106 Wroclaw, Poland. TEL 386-25. TELEX 0712771 OSS PL. (Dist. by: Ars Polona-Ruch, Krakowskie Przedmiescie 7, Warsaw, Poland) Ed. Kzimerz Polanski.
—BLDSC shelfmark: 5221.366000.

491   ER
LINGUISTICA URALICA. (Text in Finno-Ugrian and Samoyedic languages) 1965. q. $128. (Akademiya Nauk Estonii) Izdatel'stvo Perioodika, Parnu mnt. 8; pk.107, 200090 Tallinn, Estonia. (Subscr. to: Akateeminen Kirjakauppa, 128 SF 00101, Helsinki, Finland; or to: Bibliotekstjanst AB 200, S 22100 Lund, Sweden) Ed. P. Ariste. bk.rev.; bibl.; index; circ. 920.
Formerly (until 1989): Sovetskoe Finnougrovedenie (ISSN 0038-5182)

410   CK   ISSN 0120-5587
P9
LINGUISTICA Y LITERATURA. 1979. s-a. Col.3000($30) (effective 1992). Universidad de Antioquia, Departamento de Linguistica y Literatura, Facultad de Comunicaciones, Apdo. Aereo 1226, Medellin, Colombia. TEL 574-2630011. FAX 574-2638282. Ed. Oscar Castro Garcia. bk.rev.; film rev.; circ. 280.
Description: Publishes works in linguistics and literature by the department.

400   GW   ISSN 0024-3949
P1.A1
LINGUISTICS; an interdisciplinary journal of the language sciences. (Text in English, French, German) 1963. bi-m. $304. Walter de Gruyter und Co., Mouton Publishers, Postfach 110240, 1000 Berlin 11, Germany. TEL 030-26005-0. FAX 030-26005251. TELEX 184027. (U.S. addr.: Mouton de Gruyter, division of Walter de Gruyter, Inc., 200 Saw Mill River Road, Hawthorne, NY 10532) Ed. Wolfgang Klein. adv.; bk.rev.; charts; illus.; circ. 1,200. (also avail. in microform from UMI; reprint service avail. from SWZ) **Indexed:** Abstr.Anthropol., Arts & Hum.Cit.Ind., Curr.Cont., Hum.Ind., Ind.Bk.Rev.Hum., Lang.& Lang.Behav.Abstr. (1972-), Mid.East: Abstr.& Ind., SSCI.
—BLDSC shelfmark: 5221.375000.

LINGUISTICS ABSTRACTS. see *LINGUISTICS — Abstracting, Bibliographies, Statistics*

410 370   US   ISSN 0898-5898
P40.8
LINGUISTICS AND EDUCATION; an international research journal. 1988. q. $39.50 to individuals; institutions $85. Ablex Publishing Corporation, 355 Chestnut St., Norwood, NJ 07648. TEL 201-767-8450. FAX 201-767-6717. TELEX 1350393. Ed. David Bloome. index; circ. 400. (back issues avail.) **Indexed:** Lang.& Lang.Behav.Abstr. (1988-).
—BLDSC shelfmark: 5221.375600.
Description: Provides a forum for researchers from linguistic perspectives to share and discuss their inquiries into educational processes both in and outside of school.

LINGUISTICS AND PHILOSOPHY; a journal of natural language syntax, semantics, logic, pragmatics, and processing. see *PHILOSOPHY*

495.4   US   ISSN 0731-3500
PL3551
LINGUISTICS OF THE TIBETO-BURMAN AREA. 1974. s-a. $15 per no. University of California, Berkeley, Center for Southeast Asian Studies, Berkeley, CA 94720. FAX 914156435045. Ed. James A. Matisoff. bk.rev.; circ. 150. **Indexed:** M.L.A.

410   US   ISSN 0166-0829
LINGUISTIK AKTUELL; Amsterdamer Arbeiten zur theoretischen und angewandten Linguistik. 1980. irreg., vol.6, 1989. price varies. John Benjamins Publishing Co., 821 Bethlehem Pike, Philadelphia, PA 19118. TEL 215-836-1200. FAX 215-836-1204. (And: Amsteldijk 44, P.O. Box 75577, 1070 AN Amsterdam, Netherlands. TEL 020-6762325) Ed. Werner Abraham. **Indexed:** M.L.A.
Description: Contains interdisciplinary studies in linguistics and communication sciences, concentrating on studies in Germanic languages.

400   FR   ISSN 0024-3957
P2
LINGUISTIQUE. 1965. s-a. 250 F. (foreign 340 F.). Presses Universitaires de France, Departement des Revues, 14 Avenue du Bois-de-l'Epine, B.P.90, 91003 Evry Cedex, France. TEL 1-60-77-82-05. FAX 1-60-79-20-45. TELEX PUF 600 474 F. Dir. Andre Martinet. (reprint service avail. from KTO) **Indexed:** Arts & Hum.Cit.Ind., Curr.Cont., Lang.& Lang.Behav.Abstr. (1972-), Lang.Teach.& Ling.Abstr., M.L.A.
Description: Covers general linguistics, pure and applied.

491.8   BU   ISSN 0324-1653
P381.B3
LINGUISTIQUE BALKANIQUE/BALKANSKO IZIKOZNANIE. (Text in English, French, German, Russian) 1975. q. 7 lv. (Bulgarska Akademiia na Naukite) Publishing House of the Bulgarian Academy of Sciences, Acad. G. Bonchev St., Bldg. 6, 1113 Sofia, Bulgaria. (Dist. by: Hemus, 6, Rouski Blvd., 1000 Sofia, Bulgaria) Ed. Vladimir Georgiev. circ. 530. (back issues avail.) **Indexed:** Lang.& Lang.Behav.Abstr. (1985-), M.L.A.
—BLDSC shelfmark: 0014.400000.

410 375.4   MG
LINGUISTIQUE ET ENSEIGNEMENT. (Text in French or Malagasy) 1971. irreg. (approx. s-a). Universite de Madagascar, Institut de Linguistique Appliquee, B.P. 4099, Antananarivo, Malagasy Republic.

440 375.4   SZ
LINGUISTIQUE FRANCAISE. CAHIERS DE. (Text in French) no. 11, 1990. irreg. price varies. (Universite de Geneva, Unite de Linguistique Francaise) Librairie Droz S.A., 11 rue Massot, CH-1211 Geneva 12, Switzerland. TEL 022-466666. (Subscr. to: Base Postale 389, CH-1211 Geneva 12, Switzerland) Ed.Bd.

410   GW   ISSN 0344-6727
LINGUISTISCHE ARBEITEN. 1973. irreg. no.272, 1991. price varies. Max Niemeyer Verlag, Postfach 2140, 7400 Tuebingen 1, Germany. TEL 07071-81104. FAX 07071-87419. (back issues avail.)
Description: Monographs and collections of essays in all fields of linguistics, especially theoretical linguistics.

400   GW   ISSN 0024-3930
P1.A1
LINGUISTISCHE BERICHTE. (Text in English, French and German; abstracts in English) 1968. bi-m. DM.128 (students DM.72). Westdeutscher Verlag GmbH, Postfach 5829, 6200 Wiesbaden 1, Germany. TEL 0611-160230. FAX 0611-160229. TELEX 4186928-VWV-D. Eds. H.G. Grewendorf, A. Von Stechow. adv.; bk.rev.; index. (back issues avail.; reprint service avail. from SWZ) **Indexed:** Lang.& Lang.Behav.Abstr.
—BLDSC shelfmark: 5221.460000.

410 440   NE   ISSN 0378-4169
P1.A1
LINGVISTICAE INVESTIGATIONES; revue internationale de linguistique francaise et de linguistique generale. (Supplement avail.) (Text in English, French) 1977. 2/yr. fl.300($160) (effective 1991). (Universite de Paris VIII (Paris-Vincennes), Departement de Linguistique, FR) John Benjamins Publishing Co., Amsteldijk 44, P.O. Box 75577, 1070 AN Amsterdam, Netherlands. TEL 020-6738156. FAX 020-6739773. (In N. America: 821 Bethlehem Pike, Philadelphia, PA 19118. TEL 215-836-1200) (Co-sponsor: Centre National de la Recherche Scientifique, Laboratoire d'Automatique Documentaire et Linguistique, FR) Ed.Bd. adv.; bk.rev.; bibl.; index; circ. 600. (back issues avail.) **Indexed:** Lang.& Lang.Behav.Abstr. (1979-), Lang.Teach.& Ling.Abstr., M.L.A.
Description: Contans articles on all languages, with emphasis on French.

410 440   US   ISSN 0165-7569
LINGVISTICAE INVESTIGATIONES: SUPPLEMENTA; studies in French and general linguistics/etudes en linguistique francaise et generale. 1979. irreg., vol.16, 1988. price varies. (Universite de Paris VIII (Paris-Vincennes), Departement de Linguistique, FR) John Benjamins Publishing Co., 821 Bethlehem Pike, Philadelphia, PA 19118. TEL 215-836-1200. FAX 215-836-1204. (And: John Benjamins B.V., P.O. Box 75577, Amsteldijk 44, 1070 AN Amsterdam, Netherlands. TEL 020-738156) (Co-sponsor: Centre National de la Recherche Scientifique, Laboratoire d'Automatique Documentaire et Linguistique) Ed.Bd. **Indexed:** M.L.A.
—BLDSC shelfmark: 5221.465100.
Description: Contains French and general linguistics, modeern linguistic theory and fundamental descriptive studies.

410   RU   ISSN 0301-6900
P25
LINGVISTICHESKIE ISSLEDOVANIYA. irreg. 0.96 Rub. (Akademiya Nauk S.S.S.R., Institut Yazykoznaniya) Izdatel'stvo Nauka, 90 Profsoyuznaya ul., 117864 Moscow, Russia. TEL 234-05-84.

410   CS
LINGVISTICKE CITANKY/READINGS IN LINGUISTICS. 1970. irreg. 10 Kcs. Universita Karlova, Filosoficka Fakulta, Nam. Krasnoarmejcu 1, 116 38 Prague 1, Czechoslovakia. Ed. Bohumil Palek. circ. 500.

400   NE   ISSN 0024-4457
PA9
LISTY FILOLOGICKE/JOURNAL OF PHILOLOGY. (Text and summaries in Czech, English, French, German, Latin, Russian, Slovak) 1874. q. fl.202($110) (effective 1992). (Czechoslovak Academy of Sciences, Institute of Greek, Roman and Latin Studies, CS) John Benjamins Publishing Co., Amsteldijk 44, P.O. Box 75577, 1070 AN Amsterdam, Netherlands. TEL 020-6738156. FAX 020-6739773. (In N. America: 821 Bethlehem Pike, Philadelphia, PA 19118. TEL 215-836-1200) Ed. Helena Kurzova. bk.rev.; abstr.; bibl.; charts; illus.; index; circ. 700. **Indexed:** Amer.Hist.& Life, Hist.Abstr., M.L.A., Numis.Lit.
Description: Focuses on classical philology, archeology, medieval Latin and humanistic studies, and Old Czech language and literature.

410 800   SA   ISSN 0258-2279
LITERATOR; journal of literary criticism and linguistics. (Text in Afrikaans, English, French, German; summaries in English) 1980. 3/yr. R.25. Literator Society - Literatorvereniging van Suid-Afrika, Potchefstroom University, Potchefstroom 2520, South Africa. TEL 0148-991769. FAX 0148-99-1562. TELEX 346019 SA. Ed. D.H. Steenberg. adv.; bk.rev.; circ. 500.
Description: Studies of criticism, linguistics and comparative literature.

LITERATUR IN BAYERN. see *LITERATURE*

LITERATURA KAJERO; monata kultura kajero en esperanto. see *LITERATURE*

LITTERARIA PRAGENSIA. see *LITERATURE*

491   FR
LO GAI SABER. (Text in Catalan, French, Occitan) 1919. q. 80 F. (foreign 90 F.). Escola Occitana, Les Dames, Aureville, 31320 Castanet-Tolosan, France. TEL 61-73-08-70. Ed. Philippe Carbonne. bk.rev.; circ. 600. **Indexed:** M.L.A.
  Former titles (until 1985): Gai Saber; (until 1973): Lo Gai Saber (ISSN 0047-4916)

400   PL   ISSN 0076-0390
P19.L6
LODZKIE TOWARZYSTWO NAUKOWE. ROZPRAWY KOMISJI JEZYKOWEJ. 1954. irreg., vol.31, 1985. price varies. Ossolineum, Publishing House of the Polish Academy of Sciences, Rynek 9, 50-106 Wroclaw, Poland. TELEX 0712771 OSS PL. (Dist. by: Ars Polona-Ruch, Krakowskie Przedmiescie 7, 00-068 Warsaw, Poland) (Co-sponsor: Polska Akademia Nauk) Ed. Karol Dejna. circ. 500.

410   UK   ISSN 0309-6270
LOGOPHILE;* The Cambridge Journal of Words and Language. 1977. q. £5($12) to individuals; libraries and institutions £10($24). ATS Journal, Garden Flat, 17 Palmerston Rd., Dublin 6, Ireland. Ed. D. McFarlan. adv.; bk.rev.; illus.; index; circ. 2,000. (back issues avail.) **Indexed:** M.L.A.

410 398 572   UK   ISSN 0307-7144
GR140
LORE AND LANGUAGE. 1969. s-a. £16.50 to individuals; institutions £50. (Centre for English Cultural Tradition and Language) Sheffield Academic Press, 343 Fulwood Road, Sheffield S10 3BP, England. FAX 0742-610044. Ed. J.D.A. Widdowson. adv.; bk.rev.; charts; illus.; cum.index; circ. 700. (back issues avail.) **Indexed:** Lang.& Lang.Behav.Abstr., M.L.A., Sociol.Abstr.
—BLDSC shelfmark: 5294.586000.
Description: Addresses interdisciplinary issues regarding all aspects of language and cultural tradition.

420 375.4   US   ISSN 0456-7463
LOUISIANA ENGLISH JOURNAL. s-a. membership. Louisiana Council of Teachers of English, c/o Mari Ann Pritchett, State Department of Education, P.O. Box 44064, Baton Rouge, LA 70804. TEL 504-342-4411. Eds. John Cooke, Elizabeth F. Penfield. circ. 1,400.

496   TZ   ISSN 0047-5165
LUGHA YETU. (Text in Swahili) 1969. 2/yr. Sh.25 per. no. National Swahili Council, P.O. Box 4766, Dar es Salaam, Tanzania. Ed. M. M. Kumbuka. adv.; bk.rev.; circ. 5,000.

420   SW   ISSN 0076-1451
CODEN: LSENE6
LUND STUDIES IN ENGLISH. 1933. irreg., no.73, 1985. price varies. Liber Forlag, S-205 10, Malmo, Sweden. Eds. Claes Schaar, Jan Svartvik. (reprint service avail. from KTO) **Indexed:** M.L.A.
—BLDSC shelfmark: 5304.980000.

LUOJI YU YUYAN XUEXI/LOGIC AND LANGUAGE STUDIES. see *PHILOSOPHY*

M L A INTERNATIONAL BIBLIOGRAPHY OF BOOKS AND ARTICLES ON THE MODERN LANGUAGES AND LITERATURES. (Modern Language Association of America) see *BIBLIOGRAPHIES*

M L A JOB INFORMATION LISTS. (Modern Language Association of America) see *OCCUPATIONS AND CAREERS*

400 800   US   ISSN 0160-5720
M L A NEWSLETTER (NEW YORK). 1969. 4/yr. $6 to non-members (effective 1993). Modern Language Association of America, 10 Astor Pl., New York, NY 10003. TEL 212-475-9500. FAX 212-477-9863. Ed. Phyllis P. Franklin. adv.; circ. 32,000. (reprint service avail. from UMI)
Description: Information about the activities of the Modern Language Association, deadlines for fellowships and grants, and news of the language and literature profession.

LINGUISTICS

400 US ISSN 0026-7910
PB1
M L N. (Modern Language Notes) (Text in English, French, German, Italian, Spanish) 1886. 5/yr. $29 to individuals (foreign $42); institutions $72 (foreign $85). Johns Hopkins University Press, Journals Publishing Division, 701 W. 40th St., Ste. 275, Baltimore, MD 21211. TEL 410-516-6987. FAX 410-516-6998. Ed. Eduardo Saccone. adv.; bk.rev.; index, cum.index: vols.1-50, vols.51-60; circ. 1,637. (also avail. in microform from UMI; reprint service avail. from UMI,SCH,KTO) **Indexed:** Abstr.Engl.Stud., Acad.Ind., Amer.Bibl.Slavic & E.Eur.Stud., Arts & Hum.Cit.Ind., Bk.Rev.Ind. (1986-), Child.Bk.Rev.Ind. (1986-), Curr.Cont., Hum.Ind., Ind.Bk.Rev.Hum., Lang.& Lang.Behav.Abstr., Mid.East: Abstr.& Ind.
—BLDSC shelfmark: 5879.750000.
Description: Presents articles and notes on the theory, interpretation, and history of languages.

407 AT ISSN 0310-9674
M L T A NEWS. 1973. irreg. Modern Language Teachers' Association of New South Wales, c/o School of Modern Languages, Macquarie University, N. Ryde, NSW 2113, Australia. Ed. K.A.B. Strong. circ. 650 (controlled).

407 AT
M L T A V NEWSLETTER. 1965. 7/yr. Aus.$2 per no. Modern Language Teachers'Association of Victoria, P.O. Box 22, Ringwood, Vic. 3134, Australia. FAX 03-871-9267. Ed. Sue Ryan. adv.; bk.rev.; circ. 600.
Formerly: M L Newsletter.

406 US
MA F L A NEWSLETTER. 1956. 5/yr. $20 to non-members. Massachusetts Foreign Language Association, 41 Glenn Dr., Wilbraham, MA 01095-1439. TEL 617-861-6189. (Subscr. to: Patrick Loconto, 182 Marcy St., Southbridge, MA 01550) Ed. Ronie Webster. adv.; bk.rev.; circ. 2,000. (processed)
Supersedes (in 1979): Massachusetts Foreign Language Bulletin; **Formerly:** Bay State F L Bulletin (ISSN 0005-6936)

410 940 DK
MAL & MAELE. 1974. q. DKK 128. C.B.L. Tryk, P.O. Box 3072, DK-6710 Esbjerg V, Denmark. FAX 32-96-34-74. Ed.Bd. adv.; bk.rev.; bibl.; charts; circ. 2,000.

439 839 NO ISSN 0024-855X
PD2601
MAAL OG MINNE. 1909. s-a. DKK 160 to individuals; institutions DKK 210. (Norges Almenvitenskapelige Forskningsraad - Norwegian Research Council for Science and the Humanities) Norske Samlaget, Boks 4672 Sofienberg, 0506 Oslo 5, Norway. TEL 02-687600. FAX 02-687502. Eds. B. Fidjestoel, E. Lundeby. bk.rev.; index; circ. 550. **Indexed:** M.L.A.
Description: Scholarly publication on linguistics, mostly Scandinavian languages.

492 892 US ISSN 0149-5712
PJ3001
MAARAV; a journal for the study of the northwest semitic languages and literatures. 1978. s-a. $40 (Canada $43; foreign $46) (effective 1992). Western Academic Press, 12 Empty Saddle Rd., Rolling Hills Estates, CA 90274. TEL 213-541-4573. FAX 213-541-2361. Ed. Bruce Zuckerman. adv.; bk.rev.; circ. 750. (back issues avail.) **Indexed:** Curr.Cont., New Test.Abstr., Old Test.Abstr., Rel.& Theol.Abstr. (1981-), Rel.Ind.One.
—BLDSC shelfmark: 5319.740000.

440 370 AT ISSN 0815-7138
MACQUARIE UNIVERSITY FRENCH MONOGRAPHS. 1967-1972; N.S. 1973. irreg. Aus.$3 per no. Macquarie University, School of Modern Languages, North Ryde, N.S.W. 2109, Australia. Eds. Angus Martin, K.R. Dutton. circ. 250.
Supersedes: Monographs for Teachers of French (ISSN 0047-7907)

494.51 HU ISSN 0025-0228
PH2001
MAGYAR NYELV/HUNGARIAN LANGUAGE. 1905. q. $28. (Magyar Tudomanyos Akademia, Nyelvtudomanyi Intezet) Akademiai Kiado, Publishing House of the Hungarian Academy of Sciences, P.O. Box 24, H-1363 Budapest, Hungary. Ed. L. Benko. adv.; bk.rev.; index. **Indexed:** Lang.& Lang.Behav.Abstr., M.L.A.

494.51 HU ISSN 0025-0236
MAGYAR NYELVOR/HUNGARIAN PURIST. 1872. q. $18.50. (Magyar Tudomanyos Akademia, Nyelvtudomanyi Intezet) Akademiai Kiado, Publishing House of the Hungarian Academy of Sciences, P.O. Box 24, H-1363 Budapest, Hungary. Ed. L. Lorincze. adv.; bk.rev.; index. **Indexed:** Lang.& Lang.Behav.Abstr., M.L.A.

400 GW ISSN 0542-1551
MAINZER ROMANISTISCHE ARBEITEN. (Text in English, French, and German) irreg., vol.11, 1976. price varies. Franz Steiner Verlag Wiesbaden GmbH, Birkenwaldstr. 44, Postfach 101526, 7000 Stuttgart 1, Germany. TEL 0711-2582-0. FAX 0711-2582290. TELEX 723636-DAZD. Eds. W.T. Elwert, H. Kroell.

MAINZER STUDIEN ZUR AMERIKANISTIK. see LITERATURE

400 GW ISSN 0170-3560
MAINZER STUDIEN ZUR SPRACH- UND VOLKSFORSCHUNG. irreg., vol.17, 1989. price varies. (Universitaet Mainz, Institut fuer Geschichtliche Landeskunde) Franz Steiner Verlag Wiesbaden GmbH, Birkenwaldstr. 44, Postfach 101526, 7000 Stuttgart 1, Germany. TEL 0711-2582-0. FAX 0711-2582290. TELEX 723636-DAZD. Ed.Bd.

491.55 IR ISSN 0259-9082
MAJALLAH-I ZABANSHINASI/IRANIAN JOURNAL OF LINGUISTICS. (Text in Farsi) 1984. s-a. Rs.350 per no. Markaz-i Nashr-i Danishgahi, 85 Park St., Dr. Bihishti Ave., Teheran, Iran.

MAJMA' AL-LUGHAH AL-ARABIYYAH. MAJALLAH/ARAB LANGUAGE ACADEMY. JOURNAL. see LITERATURE

MAKEDONIKA. see HISTORY — History Of Europe

410 890 XN ISSN 0350-1914
MAKEDONSKA AKADEMIJA NA NAUKITE I UMETNOSTITE. ODDELENIE ZA LINGVISTIKA I LITERATURNA NAUKA. PRILOZI/MACEDONIAN ACADEMY OF SCIENCES AND ARTS. SECTION OF LINGUISTICS AND LITERARY SCIENCES. CONTRIBUTIONS. 1976. s-a. Makedonska Akademija na Naukite i Umetnostite, Oddelenie za Lingvistika i Literaturna Nauka, Bulevar Krste Misrkov bb, P.O. Box 428, 91000 Skopje, Macedonia. TEL 235-506. Ed. Bozidar Vidoeski.
Description: Linguistics and literary science topics, concentrating on Southern Slavic languages.

491.81 XN ISSN 0025-1089
PG1161
MAKEDONSKI JAZIK. (Text in Macedonian and other languages) 1950. a. Institut za Makedonski Jazik, Skopje - Institute of Macedonian Language, P.O. Box 434, 91000 Skopje, Macedonia. (Co-sponsor: Republicka Zaednica za Naucni Dejnosti) Ed. Bozidar Vidoeski. bk.rev.; circ. 1,000 (controlled). **Indexed:** M.L.A.

418.02 US ISSN 0363-3659
P409
MALEDICTA; the international journal of verbal aggression. 1977. biennial. $22 to individuals; institutions $26. (International Maledicta Society) Maledicta Press, Box 14123, Santa Rosa, CA 95402-6123. Ed. Reinhold Aman. bk.rev.; bibl.; index; circ. 4,000. (back issues avail.) **Indexed:** Lang.& Lang.Behav.Abstr., M.L.A., Sociol.Abstr.
—BLDSC shelfmark: 5356.085000.
Description: Contains essays and glossaries of verbal abuse, insults, curses, slurs, blasphemies, and obscenities in many languages.

418.02 US ISSN 1041-8504
MALEDICTA MONITOR. 4/yr. $8 (foreign $9.50). Maledicta Press, Box 14123, Santa Rosa, CA 95402-6123. TEL 707-523-4761. Ed. Reinhold Aman. bibl.
Description: Lists current usage of insults, curses, censorship and new slang.

418.02 US ISSN 0363-9037
MALEDICTA PRESS PUBLICATIONS. 1976. irreg., vol.5, 1979. price varies. Maledicta Press, Box 14123, Santa Rosa, CA 95402-6123. Ed. Reinhold Aman. circ. 4,000.
Description: Dictionaries and glossaries of verbal abuse of any kind and in many languages. Contains originals and reprints.

479.1 BE ISSN 0542-6669
PC2
MARCHE ROMANE. 1951. q. 1000 BEF. Universite de Liege, Association des Romanistes, 3 Place Cockerill, 4000 Liege, Belgium. bk.rev.; circ. 500. **Indexed:** M.L.A.
—BLDSC shelfmark: 5369.740000.

MARI ANNALES DE RECHERCHES INTERDISCIPLINAIRES. see ARCHAEOLOGY

MARTIN-LUTHER-UNIVERSITAET HALLE-WITTENBERG. WISSENSCHAFTLICHE ZEITSCHRIFT; Gesellschafts- und Sprachwissenschaftliche Reihe. see SOCIOLOGY

410 491.8 CS
P19
MASARYKOVA UNIVERZITA. FILOZOFICKA FAKULTA. SBORNIK PRACI. A: RADA JAZYKOVEDNA. 1952. irreg. (approx. a.). price varies. Masarykova Univerzita, Filozoficka Fakulta, A. Novaka 1, 660 88 Brno, Czechoslovakia.
Formerly: Univerzita J.E. Purkyne. Filozoficka Fakulta. Sbornik Praci. A: Rada Jazykovedna (ISSN 0231-7567)
Description: Covers problems of general linguistics, as well as Indo-European linguistics and phonetics, Slavonic languages syntax with focus on Czech and Russian languages.

420 430 CS
MASARYKOVA UNIVERZITA. FILOZOFICKA FAKULTA. SBORNIK PRACI. K: RADA GERMANISTICKO - ANGLISTICKA. (Text in English or German) 1959. irreg. (approx. a.). price varies. Masarykova Univerzita, Filozoficka Fakulta, A. Novaka 1, 660 88 Brno, Czechoslovakia.
Formerly: Univerzita J.E. Purkyne. Filozoficka Fakulta. Sbornik Praci. K: Rada Germanisticko - Anglisticka (ISSN 0231-5351)
Description: Covers English and German linguistics and literature.

440 809.02 CS
MASARYKOVA UNIVERZITA. FILOZOFICKA FAKULTA. SBORNIK PRACI. L: RADA ROMANISTICKA. 1965. irreg. (approx. a.). price varies. Masarykova Univerzita, Filozoficka Fakulta, A. Novaka 1, 660 88 Brno, Czechoslovakia.
Formerly: Univerzita J.E. Purkyne. Filozoficka Fakulta. Sbornik Praci. L: Rada Romanisticka (ISSN 0231-7532)
Description: Romanistic Series publishes studies and reviews concerning Romance linguistics (including phonetics) and literature.

410 AT
MATERIALS IN LANGUAGES OF INDONESIA. 1981. irreg. price varies. Australian National University, Research School of Pacific Studies, Pacific Linguistics, Dept. of Linguistics, G.P.O. Box 4, Canberra, A.C.T. 2601, Australia. Ed. W.A.L. Stokhof.

491.7 RU
MATERIALY I ISSLEDOVANIYA PO SIBIRSKOI DIALEKTOLOGII. 1974. a. 1.10 Rub. Krasnoyarskii Gosudarstvennyi Pedagogicheskii Institut, Krasnoyarsk, Russia. Ed. N. Tsomakion. circ. 1,000. (reprint service avail. from KTO)

410 FR ISSN 0293-7107
MATERIAUX POUR L'ETUDE DE L'ASIE ORIENTALE MODERNE ET CONTEMPORAINE. 1966. irreg., latest 1991. price varies. Editions de l' Ecole des Hautes Etudes en Sciences Sociales, 131 bd. St-Michel, 75005 Paris, France. TEL 43-54-47-15. FAX 43-54-80-73. (Dist. by: Centre Interinstitutionnel pour la Diffusion de Publications en Sciences Humaines, 131 bd. St-Michel, 75005 Paris, France)

MEANDER; miesiecznik poswiecony kulturze swiata starozytnego. see CLASSICAL STUDIES

437 GW
MECKLENBURGISCHES WOERTERBUCH. 1955. a. (Saechsische Akademie der Wissenschaften zu Leipzig) Akademie-Verlag Berlin, Leipziger Str. 3-4, 1086 Berlin, Germany. TELEX 114420-AVERL-DD.
  Description: Contains the dictionary of the Mecklenburg dialect.

MEDIAEVAL AND MODERN BRETON SERIES. see HISTORY — History Of Europe

400 IT ISSN 0390-0711
PC4
MEDIOEVO ROMANZO. 1974. 3/yr. L.110000. Societa Editrice Il Mulino, Strada Maggiore, 37, 40125 Bologna, Italy. TEL 051-2560111. FAX 051-256034. Ed.Bd. adv.; bibl.; index; circ. 600. (back issues avail.) **Indexed:** Ind.Bk.Rev.Hum., M.L.A.
  —BLDSC shelfmark: 5534.350000.

MEDITERRANEAN LANGUAGE AND CULTURE MONOGRAPH SERIES. see CLASSICAL STUDIES

MEDITERRANEAN LANGUAGE REVIEW. see CLASSICAL STUDIES

MEDIUM AEVUM. see LITERATURE

410 SW ISSN 0348-7741
PD5571
MEIJERBERGS ARKIV FOR SVENSK ORDFORSKNING. 1937. irreg. price varies. Meijerbergs Institut, Institutionen for Nordiska Spraak, S-412 98 Gothenburg, Sweden. TEL 031-634-662. Ed. Bo Ralph. (back issues avail.)

418.02 CN ISSN 0026-0452
P306.A1
META. (Text in English, French) 1956. q. Can.$27 to individuals; Can.$47 to institutions. Presses de l'Universite de Montreal, C.P. 6128, Succ. A, Montreal, Que. H3C 3J7, Canada. TEL 514-343-6933. Dir. M. Andre Clas. adv.; bk.rev.; bibl.; cum.index: 1955-1980; circ. 3,700. (also avail. in microform from UMI; reprint service avail. from UMI) **Indexed:** Lang.& Lang.Behav.Abstr., NAA, Pt.de Rep. (1983-).
  —BLDSC shelfmark: 5683.130000.
  Formerly: Journal des Traducteurs.

375.4 800 US ISSN 0885-7253
PN228.M4
METAPHOR AND SYMBOLIC ACTIVITY. 1986. q. $35 to individuals (foreign $57.50); institutions $125 (foreign $150). Lawrence Erlbaum Associates, Inc., 365 Broadway, Hillside, NJ 07642. TEL 201-666-4110. FAX 201-666-2394. Ed. Howard R. Pollio. (back volumes avail.) **Indexed:** Psychol.Abstr.
  —BLDSC shelfmark: 5701.650000.
  Description: Covers the study of figurative language from a wide variety of perspectives.
  Refereed Serial

450 156 IT ISSN 1120-3854
METHODOLOGIA; penseiro linguaggio modelli - thought language models. (Text in English, French, Italian) q. L.100000($150) to individuals; institutions L.150000($250). (Societa di Cultura Metodologico - Operativa - Society of Methodological - Operative Culture) Espansione s.r.l., Via Guinizelli 56, 00152 Rome, Italy. TEL 02-55-181630. FAX 02-5451692. (Editorial addr.: Via Senato 45, 20121 Milan, Italy) Ed. Felice Accame. bk.rev.; abstr.; bibl.

430 830 US ISSN 0098-8030
PD1
MICHIGAN GERMANIC STUDIES. (Text in English, German) 1975. s-a. $15 to individuals; institutions $25. University of Michigan, Department of Germanic Languages & Literatures, Ann Arbor, MI 48109-1275. TEL 313-764-8018. FAX 313-764-3521. Ed. Roy C. Cowen. adv.; bk.rev.; circ. 300. **Indexed:** Arts & Hum.Cit.Ind., Curr.Cont., Lang.& Lang.Behav.Abstr., M.L.A., Sociol.Abstr.
  —BLDSC shelfmark: 5755.070000.
  Description: Interdisciplinary journal that brings together scholarly studies of the histories, cultures, languages, and literatures of the peoples of Central Europe.

MICHIGAN SLAVIC MATERIALS. see LITERATURE

419.7 800 US ISSN 0888-8752
MIDDLEBURY STUDIES IN RUSSIAN LANGUAGE AND LITERATURE. irreg. Peter Lang Publishing, Inc., 62 W. 45th St., 4th Fl., New York, NY 10036. TEL 212-302-6740. FAX 212-302-7574. Ed. Thomas R. Beyer, Jr.
  Description: Covers the latest developments in linguistics, literary and pedagogical scholarship devoted to Russian language and literature. Includes analyses of texts and authors, translations of literary and scholarly works, and writings on theoretical and applied linguistics with special attention to new methods for the teaching of Russian language and literature.

480 SP ISSN 0213-9634
PA9
MINERVA: REVISTA DE FILOLOGIA CLASICA. 1987. a. 2800 ptas. Universidad de Valladolid, Secretariado de Publicaciones, Avda. Ramon y Cajal, 7, 47005 Valladolid, Spain. TEL 983-423000. FAX 983-423003. TELEX 26357.

400 809.4 CC ISSN 0257-5779
MINZU YUWEN/LINGUISTICS - NATIONAL MINORITIES. (Text mainly in Chinese) 1980. bi-m. $22.50. Zhongguo Shehui Kexueyuan, Minzu Yanjiusuo - Chinese Academy of Social Science, National Minorities Institute, 22 Baishiqiao Lu, Beijing 100081, People's Republic of China. TEL 8022288. (Dist. in US by: China Books & Periodicals, Inc., 2929 24th St., San Francisco, CA 94110. TEL 415-282-2994) Ed. Zhao Na Si Tu.
  Description: Covers the languages of China's national minorities.

296.68 US
LA-MISHPAHA. 1963. m. $12. Histadruth Ivrith of America, Inc., 47 W. 34th St., Rm. 609, New York, NY 10001-3012. TEL 212-629-9443. Ed. Hanita Brand. adv.; bk.rev.; circ. 6,500. (back issues avail.)

400 800 US ISSN 0026-6272
MISSISSIPPI LANGUAGE CRUSADER. 1953. 3/yr. $10. Mississippi Foreign Language Association, Univ. of Mississippi, Modern Languages Dept., University, MS 38677. TEL 601-232-7298. Ed. Hans-Juergen Gaycken. adv.; bk.rev.; circ. 350. **Indexed:** ERIC.

491.2 II ISSN 0026-6787
MITHILA INSTITUTE OF POST GRADUATE STUDIES AND RESEARCH IN SANSKRIT LEARNING. BULLETIN.* (Text in English and Sanskrit) vol.3, 1967. s-a. Rs.10. Mithila Research Institute, Darbhanga, Bihar, India. Ed. S. Bagchi. bk.rev.; bibl.

410 FR ISSN 0249-6267
MODELES LINGUISTIQUES. 1979. s-a. 160 F. (foreign 130 F.). Universite de Lille III, Rue du Barreau, B.P. 143, 59653 Villeneuve d'Ascq Cedex, France. Dirs. Andre Joly, Richard Lilly. **Indexed:** M.L.A.
  —BLDSC shelfmark: 5883.523000.

410 US ISSN 0736-5268
MODELS OF SCIENTIFIC THOUGHT; a series of monographs and tracts. price varies. irreg., latest vol.4, 1987. Harwood Academic Publishers, 270 Eighth Ave., New York, NY 10011. TEL 212-206-8900. FAX 212-645-2459. TELEX 236735 GOPUB UR. (Subscr. to: Box 786, Cooper Sta., New York, NY 10276. TEL 800-545-8398; UK subscr. to: Box 90, Reading, Berkshire RG1 8JL, England. TEL 0734-560-080) (also avail. in microform)
  —BLDSC shelfmark: 5883.541000.
  Refereed Serial

420 375.4 UK ISSN 0308-0587
MODERN ENGLISH TEACHER;* a magazine of practical suggestions for improving the teaching of English as a foreign language. 1973. q. £8.50. Modern English Publications Ltd., Brunel Rd., Houndsmills, Basingstoke, Hants. RG21 2XS, England. Ed. Susan Holden. adv.; bk.rev.; illus.; index; circ. 6,000. **Indexed:** Cont.Pg.Educ., Lang.Teach.& Ling.Abstr.
  —BLDSC shelfmark: 5886.440000.
  Description: Presents study and teaching methods.

410 HU ISSN 0076-9967
MODERN FILOLOGIAI FUZETEK. 1966. irreg., vol.46, 1989. price varies. (Magyar Tudomanyos Akademia) Akademiai Kiado, Publishing House of the Hungarian Academy of Sciences, PO Box 24, H-1363 Budapest, Hungary.

MODERN GREEK STUDIES ASSOCIATION BULLETIN. see HISTORY — History Of Europe

LINGUISTICS 2829

400 371.3 US ISSN 0026-7902
PB1   CODEN: MOLJA8
MODERN LANGUAGE JOURNAL. (Text in various languages) 1916. q. $17.50 to individuals; institutions $35. (National Federation of Modern Language Teachers Associations) University of Wisconsin Press, Journal Division, 114 N. Murray St., Madison, WI 53715. TEL 608-262-4925. FAX 608-262-7560. Ed. David P. Benseler. adv.; bk.rev.; abstr.; charts; film rev.; illus.; stat.; index; circ. 7,000. (also avail. in microform from UMI,MIM; back issues avail.; reprint service avail. from UMI) **Indexed:** Amer.Bibl.Slavic & E.Eur.Stud., Bk.Rev.Ind. (1965-), C.I.J.E., Chic.Per.Ind., Child.Bk.Rev.Ind. (1965-), Cont.Pg.Educ., Curr.Cont., Educ.Ind., Ind.Bk.Rev.Hum., Lang.& Lang.Behav.Abstr., Lang.Teach.& Ling.Abstr., M.L.A., Media Rev.Dig., Mid.East: Abstr.& Ind., Psychol.Abstr., SSCI.
  —BLDSC shelfmark: 5887.500000.

MODERN LANGUAGE QUARTERLY. see LITERATURE

MODERN LANGUAGE REVIEW. see LITERATURE

MODERN LANGUAGE STUDIES. see LITERATURE

400 US ISSN 0026-8232
PB1
MODERN PHILOLOGY; a journal devoted to research in medieval and modern literature. 1903. q. $25 to individuals; institutions $45; students $15. University of Chicago Press, Journals Division, 5720 S. Woodlawn Ave., Chicago, IL 60637. TEL 312-753-3347. FAX 312-702-0694. TELEX 25-4603. (Orders to: Box 37005, Chicago, IL 60637) Ed. Janel Mueller. adv.; bk.rev.; index; circ. 1,800. (also avail. in microform from MIM,UMI; reprint service avail. from UMI,ISI, SCH) **Indexed:** Abstr.Engl.Stud., Acad.Ind., Arts & Hum.Cit.Ind., Bk.Rev.Dig., Bk.Rev.Ind. (1965-), Child.Bk.Rev.Ind. (1965-), Curr.Cont., Hum.Ind., Ind.Bk.Rev.Hum., LCR, M.L.A.
  —BLDSC shelfmark: 5890.780000.
  Refereed Serial

400 370 SW ISSN 0026-8577
PB5
MODERNA SPRAAK. (Text in several languages) 1906. 2/yr. DKK 185. Riksfoereningen foer Laerarna i Moderna Spraak - Modern Language Teachers Association of Sweden, Aengen, S-56034 Visingsoe, Sweden. Claus Ohrt. adv.; bk.rev.; index; circ. 2,000. **Indexed:** Arts & Hum.Cit.Ind., Curr.Cont., Lang.& Lang.Behav.Abstr., Lang.Teach.& Ling.Abstr., M.L.A.
  —BLDSC shelfmark: 5900.027000.

410 DK ISSN 0107-2390
MODERSMAAL SELSKABET. AARBOG. 1980. a. DKK 122. Modersmaal Selskabet, c/o Grethe F. Rostboell, Ryslinge Hoejskole, 5856 Ryslinge, Denmark.
  Description: Contains articles on the Danish language.

MOKO. see LITERATURE

495.93 US ISSN 0147-5207
PL4301   CODEN: MKSTEF
MON-KHMER STUDIES; a journal of Austroasiatic philology. (Text in English, French and German) 1972? irreg. price varies. University of Hawaii Press, Journals Department, 2840 Kolowalu St., Honolulu, HI 96822. TEL 808-956-8833. FAX 808-988-6052. TELEX 6712668. Ed. Stephen O'Harrow. **Indexed:** M.L.A.
  —BLDSC shelfmark: 5909.370000.
  Description: Focuses on Southeast Asian languages as keys to understanding the past.
  Refereed Serial

430 371.3 US
MONATSHEFTE. (Text in English, German) 1899. q. $22 to individuals; institutions $53. (University of Wisconsin, Department of German) University of Wisconsin Press, Journal Division, 114 N. Murray St., Madison, WI 53715. TEL 608-262-4952. FAX 608-262-7560. Ed. Valters Nollendorfs. adv.; bk.rev.; bibl.; index; circ. 1,350. (also avail. in microform from MIM,UMI; back issues avail.; reprint service avail. from UMI) **Indexed:** Ind.Bk.Rev.Hum., M.L.A.
  Formerly: Monatshefte fuer Deutschen Unterricht (ISSN 0026-9271)
  Description: Presents study and teaching methods.

410 800   UK
MONOGRAPHS IN MODERN LANGUAGES. (Text in all modern languages except English) 1966. irreg. price varies. Hull University Press, Hull HU6 7RX, England. TEL 0482-46311. FAX 0482-465936. TELEX 592592-KHMAIL-G FAO HULIB 375. Ed. P.A. Holmes. **Indexed:** M.L.A.
Formerly: Occasional Papers in Modern Languages (ISSN 0078-3099)

894.2 494.2   HU   ISSN 0230-8452
MONUMENTA LINGUAE MONGOLICAE COLLECTA. (Text in Mongolian with transcriptions in Roman letters and introduction in French) 1971. irreg. price varies. (Magyar Tudomanyos Akademia) Akademiai Kiado, Publishing House of the Hungarian Academy of Sciences, P.O. Box 24, H-1363 Budapest, Hungary. Ed. L. Ligeti.
Supersedes: Mongol Nyelvemlektar (ISSN 0540-6471)

410   RU
MOSKOVSKII UNIVERSITET. VESTNIK. SERIYA 10: FILOLOGIYA. (Text in Russian; contents page in English) bi-m. 13.50 Rub. Moskovskii Universitet, Ul. Gertsena 5-7, 103009 Moscow, Russia. bk.rev.; bibl.; index.

418 800   YU   ISSN 0350-6525
MOSTOVI. (Text in Serbian in Cyrillic alphabet) 1970. q. $60. Udruzenje Knjizevnih Prevodilaca Srbije, Francuska 7, Belgrade, Serbia, Yugolsavia. Ed. Jovan Janicijevic. circ. 1,000. **Indexed:** M.L.A.

400   KR   ISSN 0027-2833
MOVOZNAVSTVO; naukovo-teoretychny zhurnal. 1967. bi-m. 3.30 Rub.($7.20) (Akademiya Nauk Ukrainskoi S.S.R.) Izdatel'stvo Naukova Dumka, c/o Yu.A. Khramov, Dir, Ul. Repina, 3, Kiev 252 601, Ukraine. TEL 228-43-83. Ed. V.M. Rusanivs'kii. bk.rev.; bibl. **Indexed:** Lang.& Lang.Behav.Abstr. (1972-), M.L.A.

LE MOYEN AGE. see HISTORY — History Of Europe

400   GW   ISSN 0077-1910
P25
MUENCHENER STUDIEN ZUR SPRACHWISSENSCHAFT. (Text in English, French and German) 1954. irreg. (1-2/yr.). price varies. J.H. Roell, Wuerzburgerstr. 16, 8716 Dettelbach, Germany. TEL 09324-1429. Eds. Bernhard Forssman, Johanna Narten. **Indexed:** Lang.& Lang.Behav.Abstr. (1973-).

MUENCHNER GERMANISTISCHE BEITRAEGE. see LITERATURE

496.396 896.396   TZ   ISSN 0856-0129
MULIKA. 1971. a. $5. University of Dar es Salaam, Institute of Kiswahili Research, P.O. Box 35110, Dar es Salaam, Tanzania. Eds. A.M. Khamisi, S.D. Kiange.

410   GW   ISSN 0167-8507
CODEN: MULTDF
MULTILINGUA; journal of cross-cultural and interlanguage communication. 1982. 4/yr. $41.25 to individuals; institutions $108. Mouton de Gruyter, Postfach 110240, 1000 Berlin 11, Germany. FAX 030-260-05251. TELEX 184027-WDG-D. (And: Mouton Publishers, division of Walter de Gruyter Inc., 200 Saw Mill River Rd., Hawthorne, NY 10532, U S A) Ed. Richard J. Watts. adv.; bk.rev.; circ. 550. **Indexed:** Lang.Teach.& Ling.Abstr., M.L.A., Sci.Abstr.
—BLDSC shelfmark: 5983.136000.

406   AU   ISSN 0027-3228
MUNDARTFREUNDE OESTERREICHS. MITTEILUNGEN. 1947. s-a. membership. Mundartfreunde Oesterreichs, Postgasse 7-9, A-1010 Vienna, Austria. Ed. Dr. Isolde Hausner. bk.rev.; abstr.; bibl.; circ. 300.

407   KN
MUNHWAO HAKSUP/STUDY OF KOREAN LANGUAGE. (Text in Korean) q. Publishing House of the Academy of Social Sciences, Pyongyang, N. Korea.

MUSEUM HELVETICUM; Schweizerische Zeitschrift fuer klassische Altertumswissenschaft. see CLASSICAL STUDIES

430   GW   ISSN 0027-514X
PF3003
MUTTERSPRACHE; Zeitschrift zur Pflege und Erforschung der deutschen Sprache. 1886. q. DM.120 (students DM.75). Gesellschaft fuer deutsche Sprache e.V., Taunusstr. 11, Postfach 2669, 6200 Wiesbaden 1, Germany. TEL 0611-520031. FAX 0611-51313. Ed. Gerhard Mueller. adv.; bk.rev.; bibl.; index; circ. 1,400. (reprint service avail. from SCH) **Indexed:** Arts & Hum.Cit.Ind., Curr.Cont., Lang.& Lang.Behav.Abstr., M.L.A.
—BLDSC shelfmark: 5992.130000.

MYND. see CHILDREN AND YOUTH — For

480   SP   ISSN 0213-7674
MYRTIA: REVISTA DE FILOLOGIA CLASICA. 1986. irreg. Universidad de Murcia, Secretariado de Publicaciones e Intercambio Cientifico, Santo Cristo, 1, 30001 Murcia, Spain. TEL 968-239450. FAX 968-247936.

410 200   US
N A O S; notes and materials for the linguistic study of the sacred. (Text in English) 1985. a. $10 to individuals; institutions $20. University of Pittsburgh, Department of Hispanic Languages and Literatures, Names of the Sacred Project, 1309 Cathedral of Learning, Pittsburgh, PA 15260. TEL 412-624-5225. Ed. Juan Adolfo Vazquez. bk.rev.; circ. 500. (back issues avail.)

663   US
N E A T E NEWSLETTER. 4/yr. $25 (includes Leaflet). New England Association of Teachers of English, P.O. Box 234, Lexington, MA 02173. TEL 617-646-2575.

400   UK   ISSN 0143-859X
PB1
N I M L A. 1978. s-a. £6. (Modern Language Association of Northern Ireland) University of Ulster, Department of Modern Languages and European Studies, Coleraine BT52 1SA, N. Ireland. FAX 0265-40903. Ed. Michael R. Jones. adv.; bk.rev.; circ. 500. **Indexed:** ERIC, Lang.Teach.& Ling.Abstr.
—BLDSC shelfmark: 6113.184000.

410   DK   ISSN 0108-8416
N O W E L E. (North-Western European Language Evolution) (Supplement avail.: N O W E L E (ISSN 0900-8675)) 1983. s-a. DKK 90. Odense University Press, Campusvej 55, DK-5230 Odense M, Denmark. TEL 66-157999.
—BLDSC shelfmark: 6180.474000.

418   BE   ISSN 0167-5257
NAAMKUNDE. (Text mainly in Dutch; occasionally in English, German) 1925. 4/yr. 950 BEF. (Katholieke Universiteit te Leuven, Instituut voor Naamkunde) Editions Peeters s.p.r.l., Bondgenotenlaan 153, B-3000 Leuven, Belgium. TEL 016-235170. FAX 016-228500. (Co-sponsor: Commissie voor Naamkunde en Nederzettingsgeschiedenis te Amsterdam, NE) Ed.Bd. bk.rev.; bibl.; charts; index. **Indexed:** Lang.& Lang.Behav.Abstr. (1978-), M.L.A.
Formerly (until 1969): Vereiniging voor Naamkunde. Mededelingen (ISSN 0042-3866)

410 830   GW   ISSN 0936-5761
NACHBARSPRACHE NIEDERLAENDISCH. (Text in Dutch, German) 1986. s-a. DM.40. Fachvereinigung Niederlaendisch e.V., Stolbergstr. 17, 4400 Muenster, Germany. TEL 0251-42860. Eds. Heinz Eickmans, Paul Wolfgang Jaegers. adv.; bk.rev.; bibl.; index; circ. 600. (back issues avail.)
Description: Studies Dutch language and literature.

400   CN   ISSN 0700-9445
NAME GLEANER/GLANURE DES NOMS. (Text in English; occasionally in French) 1977. irreg. (3-4/yr.) free to qualified personnel. York University, S. 561 Ross Bldg., 4700 Keele St., N. York, Ont. M3J 1P3, Canada. (Co-sponsor: Canadian Society for the Study of Names) circ. 120 (controlled). (processed; back issues avail.)
Description: In-house newsletter containing general news items, newspaper clippings, some book notices, and reviews as they are related to names.

410   GW
NAMENKUNDLICHE INFORMATIONEN. (Supplement avail.) 1964. s-a. DM.6 per no. Universitaet Leipzig, Sektion Theoretische und Angewandte Sprachwissenschaft, Wissenschaftsbereich Namenforschung, Augustusplatz 9, 7010 Leipzig, Germany. TEL 0719-2973. Ed.Bd. bk.rev.; circ. 400.
Description: Devoted to the study of names, such as topographical names and personal names. Covers German as well as English and Slavic names.

400   US   ISSN 0027-7738
P769
NAMES. 1953. q. $25 to individuals (foreign $30); institutions $35 (foreign $40). American Name Society, c/o Wayne H. Finke, Department of Modern Languages, Baruch College, Box 340, 17 Lexington Ave., New York, NY 10010. TEL 212-505-2177. FAX 212-370-1591. (Alt. addr.: c/o Thomas J. Gasque, Department of English, University of South Dakota, Vermillion, SD 57069) adv.; bk.rev.; bibl.; index; circ. 950. **Indexed:** Amer.Bibl.Slavic & E.Eur.Stud, Amer.Hist.& Life, Bull.Signal, Geo.Abstr., Hist.Abstr., Ind.Bk.Rev.Hum., Lang.& Lang.Behav.Abstr. (1987-), Mid.East: Abstr.& Ind.
—BLDSC shelfmark: 6015.331000.

410   SW   ISSN 0077-2704
DL1
NAMN OCH BYGD; journal for Nordic place-name research. (Text in English, German and Scandinavian Languages; summaries in English) 1913. a. SEK 135($14) Kungliga Gustav Adolfs Akademien - Royal Gustavus Adolphus Academy, Klostergatan 2, S-75321 Uppsala, Sweden. TEL 018-18 12 89. (Dist. by: Almqvist & Wiksell International, P.O. Box 638, S-104 30 Stockholm, Sweden) Ed. Thorsten Andersson. bk.rev.; circ. 500. (back issues avail.)
—BLDSC shelfmark: 6015.332400.

400   NO   ISSN 0800-4684
NAMN OG NEMNE/NAMES AND DENOMINATIONS. (Text in Norwegian; occasionally in English or German) 1984. a. NOK 130. Norsk Namnelag, Sydnes Plass 9, N-5007, Bergen, Norway. TEL 05-212-403. FAX 05-328-585. Ed. Oddvar Nes. bk.rev.; circ. 300. (back issues avail.)

491.8   YU   ISSN 0027-8084
PG1201
NAS JEZIK. 1933. 5/yr. 50 din. Institut za Srpskohrvatski Jezik, Knez Mihajlova 35, Belgrade, Serbia, Yugoslavia. TEL 011 63-55-90. Ed. Mitar Pesikan. bk.rev.; index; circ. 1,500. **Indexed:** M.L.A.

491.86   CS   ISSN 0027-8203
PG4004
NASE REC/OUR LANGUAGE. 1917. 5/yr. DM.95. (Czechoslovak Academy of Sciences, Institute for Czech Language) Academia, Publishing House of the Czechoslovak Academy of Sciences, Vodickova 40, 112 29 Prague 1, Czechoslovakia. TEL 53-93-51. (Dist. in Western countries by: Kubon & Sagner, P.O. Box 34 01 08, D-8000 Munich 34, Germany) Ed. Jan Petr. bk.rev.; index; circ. 2,500.
—BLDSC shelfmark: 6015.595000.
Description: Deals with problems of Czech language and language culture in general. Contains articles on the structure of Czech, on its stylistic variants and on the norm of codification of the standard literary language.

NATIONAL ASSOCIATION FOR THE TEACHING OF ENGLISH. NEWSLETTER. see EDUCATION — Teaching Methods And Curriculum

400   JA
NATIONAL LANGUAGE RESEARCH INSTITUTE. ANNUAL REPORT/KOKURITSU KOKUGO KENKYUJO NENPO.*
1951. a. National Language Research Institute - Kokuritsu Kokugo Kenkyujo, 9-14 Nishi-Gaoka 3-chome, Kita-ku, Tokyo 115, Japan.

410	NE	ISSN 0167-806X
P1		CODEN: NLLTDV

NATURAL LANGUAGE AND LINGUISTIC THEORY. 1983. q. $163 (effective 1992). Kluwer Academic Publishers, Postbus 17, 3300 AA Dordrecht, Netherlands. TEL 078-334911. FAX 078-334254. TELEX 29245. (Dist. by: Kluwer Academic Publishers Group, P.O. Box 322, 3300 AH Dordrecht, Netherlands; N. America dist. addr.: Box 358, Accord Station, Hingham, MA 02018-0358. TEL 617-871-6600) Ed. Joan Maling. adv.; bk.rev.; index. (reprint service avail. from SWZ) **Indexed:** Arts & Hum.Cit.Ind., Curr.Cont., Lang.& Lang.Behav.Abstr. (1983-), Lang.Teach.& Ling.Abstr., M.L.A., SSCI.
—BLDSC shelfmark: 6040.728000.
Description: Provides a forum for discussion of theoretical research that pays close attention to natural language data, providing a channel of communication between researchers of diverse points of view.

410	YU	

NAUCNI SASTANAK SLAVISTA U VUKOVE DANE. REFERATI I SAOPSTENJA. 1971. a. Medjunarodni Slavisticki Centar SR Srbije, Studetski trg 3-1, Belgrade, Yugoslvaia. illus. **Indexed:** M.L.A.

400	NE	ISSN 0028-2677
PB5		

NEOPHILOLOGUS; an international journal, devoted to the study of modern and mediaeval literature, including general linguistics, literary theory and comparative literature. (Text in English, French, German, Italian, Portuguese, Spanish) 1916. q. fl.230 (students fl.103). Wolters-Noordhoff B.V., Damsport 157, 9728 PS Groningen, Netherlands. TEL 050-226922. (Box 58, 9700 MB Groningen, Netherlands) Ed.Bd. adv.; abstr.; bibl.; index; circ. 900. (reprint service avail. from SCH,SWZ) **Indexed:** Abstr.Engl.Stud., Arts & Hum.Cit.Ind., Can.Rev.Comp.Lit, Curr.Cont., Lang.& Lang.Behav.Abstr., M.L.A., Mid.East: Abstr.& Ind.
—BLDSC shelfmark: 6075.627000.

NESTOR. see *ARCHAEOLOGY*

410	US	

NETHERLANDS PHONETIC ARCHIVES.* (Text in English) irreg., no.7, 1986. Walter de Gruyter, Inc., 200 Saw Mill River Rd., Hawthorne, NY 10532. TEL 914-747-0110. FAX 914-747-1326. Ed. Marcel P.R. van den Broecke, Vincent J. van Heuven.
Description: Reports recent advances in the field of linguistics and experimental phonology.

400	GW	ISSN 0342-3816

DIE NEUEREN SPRACHEN; Zeitschrift fuer Forschung, Unterricht und Kontaktstudium auf dem Fachgebiet der modernen Fremdsprachen. (Text in English, French, German, Italian, Spanish) 1952. bi-m. DM.54. Verlag Moritz Diesterweg, Waechtersbacher Str. 89, 6000 Frankfurt a.M. 61, Germany. TEL 069-42081-0. FAX 069-1301-100. TELEX 413234-MDD. Ed.Bd. adv.; bk.rev.; index, cum.index; circ. 5,100. (reprint service avail. from KTO) **Indexed:** Lang.& Lang.Behav.Abstr., Lang.Teach.& Ling.Abstr., M.L.A.
—BLDSC shelfmark: 6077.829000.
Formerly: Neuphilologische Zeitschrift.

490 350	GW	ISSN 0340-6385

NEUINDISCHE STUDIEN. 1970. irreg., vol.11, 1990. price varies. Verlag Otto Harrassowitz, Taunusstr. 14, Postfach 2929, 6200 Wiesbaden 1, Germany. TEL 0611-530-0. FAX 0611-530570. TELEX 4186135. Ed.Bd.
—BLDSC shelfmark: 6080.850000.

400	FI	ISSN 0028-3754
PB10		

NEUPHILOLOGISCHE MITTEILUNGEN. (Text in English, French, German, Italian, Spanish) 1899. q. $42. Uusfilologinen Yhdistys - Modern Language Society, Porthania, Helsinki University, 00100 Helsinki, Finland. Ed.Bd. adv.; abstr.; index; circ. 1,200. (also avail. in microform from SWZ; reprint service avail. from SWZ) **Indexed:** Arts & Hum.Cit.Ind., Can.Rev.Comp.Lit, Curr.Cont., Ind.Bk.Rev.Hum., Lang.& Lang.Behav.Abstr., Sociol.Abstr.
—BLDSC shelfmark: 6081.270000.

400	GW	ISSN 0028-3983
PB3		

NEUSPRACHLICHE MITTEILUNGEN AUS WISSENSCHAFT UND PRAXIS. (Text in English, French, German) 1948. q. DM.55. (Fachverband Moderne Fremdsprachen) Cornelsen Verlag GmbH und Co., Mecklenburgische Str. 53, 1000 Berlin 33, Germany. TEL 030-82996-285. FAX 030-82996-233. Ed. Michael Bludau. adv.; bk.rev.; index; circ. 5,000. (tabloid format; also avail. in microform from UMI; reprint service avail. from UMI) **Indexed:** Lang.& Lang.Behav.Abstr., M.L.A.
—BLDSC shelfmark: 6081.590000.

423.1	US	ISSN 0148-866X

NEW ACRONYMS, INITIALISMS AND ABBREVIATIONS. (Supplement to Acronyms, Initialisms and Abbreviations Dictionary) a. $199. Gale Research Inc., 835 Penobscot Bldg., Detroit, MI 48226. TEL 313-961-2242. FAX 313-961-6083. TELEX 810-221-7086. Ed. Jennifer Mossman.
Formerly (until 1976): New Acronyms and Initialisms (ISSN 0077-7986)
Description: Directory of acronyms and abbreviations.

NEW CEYLON WRITING; creative and critical writing of Sri Lanka. see *LITERATURE*

NEW ERA IN EDUCATION. see *EDUCATION*

NEW GERMAN REVIEW; a journal of Germanic studies. see *LITERATURE*

400 371.3	US	ISSN 0028-5293

NEW HAMPSHIRE POLYGLOT. (Text in English, French, German, Latin, Russian, Spanish) 1962. q. $15. New Hampshire Association for Teaching of Foreign Languages, Box 1128, Nashua, NH 03061. bk.rev.; circ. 850. (processed)
Description: Presents study and teaching methods.

439	GW	ISSN 0078-0545
PF5601		

NIEDERDEUTSCHES WORT; Beitraege zur niederdeutschen Philologie. 1960. irreg. price varies. Aschendorffsche Verlagsbuchhandlung, Soesterstr. 13, 4400 Muenster, Germany. TEL 0251-690-0. FAX 0251-690405. Ed. Jan Goossens. **Indexed:** M.L.A.

400	NE	ISSN 0028-9922
PF4		

NIEUWE TAALGIDS; tijdschrift voor neerlandici. 1907. 6/yr. fl.61. Wolters-Noordhoff B.V., Damsport 157, 9728 PS Groningen, Netherlands. TEL 050-226922. (Subscr. to: Postbus 58, 9700 MB Groningen, Netherlands) Ed.Bd. adv.; bk.rev.; abstr.; bibl. **Indexed:** Lang.& Lang.Behav.Abstr., M.L.A.
—BLDSC shelfmark: 6111.090000.

420.07 371.3	NR	ISSN 0029-0009

NIGERIA ENGLISH STUDIES ASSOCIATION JOURNAL.* 1967. s-a. £N3($6.) Nigeria English Studies Association, c/o University of Ibadan, Ibadan, Nigeria. Ed. Ebo Ubahakwe. adv.; bk.rev.; circ. 2,000.
Description: Presents study and teaching methods.

410	JA	

NIHONGO MAGAZINE. 4/yr. $55. Intercontinental Marketing Corp., I.P.O. Box 5056, Tokyo 100-31, Japan. FAX 03-667-9646.

420	UK	ISSN 0141-6340
DA645		

NOMINA; a journal of name studies relating to Great Britain and Ireland. 1977. a. £10 (foreign £12). Council for Name Studies in Great Britain and Ireland, c/o Anderson, 13 Church St., Chesterton, Cambridge CB4 1DT, England. TEL 0223-357585. Ed.Bd. adv.; bk.rev.; bibl.; circ. 250. (back issues avail.) **Indexed:** Br.Archaeol.Abstr., M.L.A.
—BLDSC shelfmark: 6116.740000.

410	SA	ISSN 1012-0254

NOMINA AFRICANA/NAMES OF AFRICA. (Text in Afrikaans and English; summaries in Afrikaans, Dutch, English, French, German) 1987. s-a. R.50. (Names Society of Southern Africa) Human Sciences Research Council, Onomastic Research Centre, c/o Dr. Lucie A. Moeller, Private Bag X41, Pretoria 0001, South Africa. TEL 012-202-2164. Ed.Bd. bk.rev.; index; circ. 180. (back issues avail.)
Description: Contains placenames, personal names, literary and general onomastics.

LINGUISTICS 2831

400	NO	ISSN 0332-5865
P1.A1		

NORDIC JOURNAL OF LINGUISTICS. (Text in English) 1972? s-a. $54. (Nordic Associations of Linguistics) Universitetsforlaget, P.O. Box 2959-Toeyen, N-0608 Oslo 1, Norway. (U.S. addr.: Publications Expediting Inc., 200 Meacham Ave., Elmont, NY 11003) Ed. Thorstein Fretheim. bk.rev.; illus.; index; circ. 600. (also avail. in microform from UMI; back issues avail.; reprint service avail. from ISI) **Indexed:** Lang.& Lang.Behav.Abstr. (1972-), M.L.A., Psychol.Abstr.
—BLDSC shelfmark: 6117.927000.
Supersedes (1928-1977): Norwegian Journal of Linguistics.

439	SW	ISSN 0078-1134

NORDISTICA GOTHOBURGENSIA. (Subseries of Acta Universitatis Gothoburgensis) (Text in Swedish; summaries in English and German) 1965. irreg., no.13, 1990. price varies; also exchange basis. Acta Universitatis Gothoburgensis, PO Box 5096, S-402 22 Goeteborg, Sweden. Ed. Bo Ralph.

410	SW	ISSN 0346-6728

NORNA - RAPPORTER. (Text in English, German, and Scandinavian languages) 1973. irreg. price varies. Norna-Foerlaget, Sankt Johannesgatan 11, S-753 12 Uppsala, Sweden. bk.rev.; charts; circ. 400.
Description: Contains proceedings of conferences within the field of onomastics, annual reports of Scandinavian onomastic research; lists of Scandinavian onomastic scholars.

400	US	

NORTH CENTRAL NAME SOCIETY. JOURNAL. 1987. a. free to NCNS members. Northern Illinois University, English Department, DeKalb, IL 60115. TEL 815-753-6627. FAX 815-753-1824. Ed. Edward Callary. circ. 100. (back issues avail.)
Description: Focuses on all aspects of onomastics.

400	NE	ISSN 0078-1592

NORTH-HOLLAND LINGUISTIC SERIES. 1970. irreg., vol.54, 1989. price varies. Elsevier Science Publishers B.V., Books Division, P.O. Box 211, 1000 AE Amsterdam, Netherlands. TEL 020-5803911. FAX 020-5803705. TELEX 18582 ESPA NL. (Subscr. in U.S. and Canada to: Elsevier Science Publishing Co., Inc., Box 882, Madison Sq. Sta., New York, NY 10159. TEL 212-989-5800) **Indexed:** M.L.A.
—BLDSC shelfmark: 6150.003000.
Refereed Serial

410 948	DK	ISSN 0900-8675

NORTH WESTERN EUROPEAN LANGUAGE EVOLUTION. (Supplement to: N O W E L E (ISSN 0108-8416)) a. price varies. Odense University Press, Campusvej 55, DK-5230 Odense M, Denmark. TEL 66-157999.
—BLDSC shelfmark: 6180.474200.
Description: Devoted to the study of history and prehistory of a locally determined group of languages, and to the study of purely theoretical questions concerning historical language development.

499.992	NO	ISSN 0029-361X

NORVEGA ESPERANTISTO; Esperantobladet. (Text in Esperanto) 1909. bi-m. NOK 70. Norvega Esperantista Ligo - Norsk Esperanto-Forbund, Olaf Schous vei 18, 0572 Oslo 5, Norway. adv.; bk.rev.; circ. 600.

410	BO	

NOTAS Y NOTICIAS LINGUISTICAS. 1978. m. Bol.$200($12) Instituto Boliviano de Cultura, Instituto Nacional de Estudios Linguisticos, Casilla 8877, La Paz, Bolivia. Ed.Bd. (looseleaf format; back issues avail.)

410	US	ISSN 0736-0673
P1		

NOTES ON LINGUISTICS. 1977. q. price varies. Summer Institute of Linguistics, Inc., Academic Publications, 7500 W. Camp Wisdom Rd., Dallas, TX 75236. TEL 214-709-2403. Ed. Eugene Loos. **Indexed:** Lang.& Lang.Behav.Abstr. (1987-).
—BLDSC shelfmark: 6167.542500.
Description: Provides researchers with practical, theoretical and administrative data regarding the field.

LINGUISTICS

410 US ISSN 0737-6707
NOTES ON LITERACY. no. 3, 1968. q. price varies. Summer Institute of Linguistics, Inc., Academic Publications, 7500 W. Camp Wisdom Rd., Dallas, TX 75236. TEL 214-709-2400. Ed. Olive A. Shell. circ. 1,000.

407 220 US
NOTES ON SCRIPTURE IN USE AND LANGUAGE PROGRAMS. 1981. q. price varies. Summer Institute of Linguistics, Inc., Academic Publications, 7500 W. Camp Rd., Dallas, TX 75236. TEL 214-709-2400. Ed. Thomas H. Crowell. circ. 900. (also avail. in microfiche)
Formerly (until 1989): Notes on Scripture in Use.

051 371.3 US ISSN 0163-7088
PE68.U5
NOTES ON TEACHING ENGLISH. 1973. s-a. $5. (Georgia-South Carolina College English Association) Valdosta State College, English Department, Valdosta, GA 31698. TEL 912-333-5946. Eds. Byron Brown, Barbara Stevenson. bk.rev.; circ. 400.

418 US ISSN 0734-0788
BS449
NOTES ON TRANSLATION. q. price varies. Summer Institute of Linguistics, Inc., Academic Publications, 7500 W. Camp Wisdom Rd., Dallas, TX 75236. TEL 214-709-2400. Ed. Ronald D. Olson. circ. 1,200.

NOTES PLUS; a quarterly of practical teaching ideas. see EDUCATION — Teaching Methods And Curriculum

400 FR ISSN 0755-7752
NOUVELLE REVUE D'ONOMASTIQUE/JOURNAL OF ONOMASTIC STUDIES. (Text in French; occasionally in Italian, Portuguese or Spanish) 1982. a. 290 F. Societe Francaise d'Onomastique, 87 rue Vielle-du-Temple, 75003 Paris, France. Ed. Pierre-Henri Billy. adv.; bk.rev.; circ. 260. (back issues avail.)
Description: Includes placenames, personal names, divine names, animal names, literary and general onomastics, and methodology.
Refereed Serial

400 IT
NOVANTIQUA; biblioteca di filologia, curiosita e dialettologia. 1977. irreg., no.13, 1984. price varies. Societa Editrice Napoletana s.r.l., Corso Umberto I 34, Naples, Italy. Ed. Antonio Altamura.

460 MX ISSN 0185-0121
PC4008
NUEVA REVISTA DE FILOLOGIA HISPANICA. 1947. s-a. Mex.$5500($75) to individuals (foreign $90); institutions $90 (foreign $96). Colegio de Mexico, A.C., Departamento de Publicaciones, Camino al Ajusco 20, Codigo Postal 01000, Mexico, D.F., Mexico. TEL 568-6033. FAX 652-6233. TELEX 1777585 COLME. Ed. Antonio Alatorre. bk.rev.; bibl.; index; circ. 1,500. (back issues avail.; reprint service avail. from SWZ) Indexed: Hisp.Amer.Per.Ind., Ind.Bk.Rev.Hum., M.L.A.
—BLDSC shelfmark: 6184.400000.

410 400 800 CL ISSN 0716-6346
NUEVA REVISTA DEL PACIFICO. (Text occasionally in English) 1976. s-a. $15 or exchange basis. Universidad de Playa Ancha de Ciencias de la Educacion, Facultad de Humanidades, Casilla 34-V, Valparaiso, Chile. TEL 281108. FAX 271136. bk.rev.; bibl.; charts; circ. 250. Indexed: M.L.A.
Incorporates: Alpha.
Description: Studies in language and literature.

410 IO ISSN 0126-2874
PL5051
NUSA; linguistic studies of Indonesian and other languages in Indonesia. (Text in English) 1975. irreg. (approx. 3/yr.). $32.50. Universitas Katolik Indonesia Atma Jaya, Lembaga Bahasa, P.O. Box 2639, Jakarta 10001, Indonesia. FAX 021-584-352. Ed.Bd. adv.; bk.rev.; circ. 450. (back issues avail.)

410 DK
NYDANSKE STUDIER OG ALMEN KOMMUNIKATIONSTEORI. 1971. irreg. price varies. Akademisk Forlag, Store Kannikestraede 8, P.O. Box 54, 1002 Copenhagen K, Denmark.

410 859 RM
NYELV- ES IRODALOMTUDOMANYI KOZLEMENYEK. vol.24, 1980. 2/yr. 70 lei($42) (Academia Romana) Editura Academiei Romane, Calea Victoriei 125, 71021 Bucharest, Rumania. (Dist. by: Rompresfilatelia, Calea Grivitei 64-66, P.O. Box 12-201, 78104 Bucharest, Rumania) Ed. Szabo Zoltan. bk.rev. Indexed: Lang.& Lang.Behav.Abstr., M.L.A.

410 HU ISSN 0078-2858
NYELVESZETI TANULMANYOK. 1951. irreg., vol.29, 1986. price varies. (Magyar Tudomanyos Akademia) Akademiai Kiado, Publishing House of the Hungarian Academy of Sciences, P.O. Box 24, H-1363 Budapest, Hungary.

410 HU ISSN 0078-2866
NYELVTUDOMANYI ERTEKEZESEK. 1953. irreg., vol.127, 1989. price varies. (Magyar Tudomanyos Akademia, Nyelvtudomanyi Intezet) Akademiai Kiado, Publishing House of the Hungarian Academy of Sciences, PO Box 24, H-1363 Budapest, Hungary.

400 HU ISSN 0029-6791
AS142
NYELVTUDOMANYI KOZLEMENYEK/LINGUISTIC STUDIES. 1862. s-a. $19.50. (Magyar Tudomanyos Akademia, Nyelvtudomanyi Intezet) Akademiai Kiado, Publishing House of the Hungarian Academy of Sciences, P.O. Box 24, H-1363 Budapest, Hungary. Eds. L. Honti, M. Bakro-Nagy. adv.; bk.rev.; charts; illus.; index. Indexed: Lang.& Lang.Behav.Abstr. (1972-), M.L.A.

439.7 SW ISSN 0345-8768
PD5004
NYSVENSKA STUDIER; tidskrift foer svensk stil och spraakforskning. 1921. a. SEK 130. Adolf Noreen-Saellskapet Institutionen for Nordiska Spraak, PO Box 513, 75120 Uppsala, Sweden. FAX 46-18-181272. Eds. Lennart Elmevik, Mats Thelander. circ. 600.
Description: Articles on stylistic and linguistic subjects related to modern Swedish: from the 1520's to the present.

O S L A NEWSLETTER. (Ontario Association of Speech - Language Pathologists and Audiologists) see HANDICAPPED — Hearing Impaired

OCCASIONAL PAPERS IN GERMAN STUDIES. see LITERATURE

410 UK ISSN 0308-2075
OCCASIONAL PAPERS IN LINGUISTICS AND LANGUAGE LEARNING. 1976. irreg. price varies. University of Ulster, Linguistics Panel, Coleraine BT52 1SA, N. Ireland. Ed. R. Thelwall. bibl.; circ. 175. Indexed: M.L.A.

OCCASIONAL PAPERS IN SLAVIC LANGUAGES AND LITERATURE. see LITERATURE

497 US
OCCASIONAL PAPERS ON LINGUISTICS. 1978. irreg., vol.15, 1990. price varies. Southern Illinois University, Carbondale, Department of Linguistics, Carbondale, IL 62901. TEL 618-536-3385. FAX 618-453-6527. Ed. James E. Redden. bibl.; charts; illus.; circ. 200.
Description: Covers primarily American Indian languages: theoretical, descriptive and applied linguistics.

499 US ISSN 0029-8115
PL5001
OCEANIC LINGUISTICS. 1962. s-a. $15 to individuals (foreign $16); institutions $20 (foreign $23). University of Hawaii Press, Journals Department, 2840 Kolowalu St., Honolulu, HI 96822. TEL 808-956-8833. FAX 808-988-6052. TELEX 6712668. Ed. Byrm W. Bender. adv.; bk.rev.; bibl.; charts; illus.; index; circ. 400. (also avail. in microfilm from UMI; back issues avail.; reprint service avail. from UMI,ISI) Indexed: E.I., Lang.& Lang.Behav.Abstr. (1971-), M.L.A.
—BLDSC shelfmark: 6231.480000.
Description: Focuses on the study of indigenous languages of Oceanic areas.
Refereed Serial

499 US ISSN 0078-3188
OCEANIC LINGUISTICS. SPECIAL PUBLICATIONS. 1966. irreg., no.22, 1988. price varies. (University of Hawaii, Social Science Research Institute) University of Hawaii Press, 2840 Kolowalu St., Honolulu, HI 96822. TEL 808-956-8697. FAX 808-988-6052. TELEX 6712668. Ed. George W. Grace. (reprint service avail. from UMI, ISI) Indexed: M.L.A.
—BLDSC shelfmark: 6231.483000.
Description: Presents studies of the languages used in the Pacific region.

410 DK ISSN 0078-3277
ODENSE UNIVERSITY SLAVIC STUDIES. (Text in English and Russian) 1970. irreg., latest 1986. price varies. Odense University Press, Campusvej 55, DK-5230 Odense M, Denmark. TEL 66-157999. (back issues avail.)

420 DK ISSN 0078-3293
ODENSE UNIVERSITY STUDIES IN ENGLISH. (Text in English) 1969. irreg. price varies. Odense University Press, Campusvej 55, DK-5230 Odense M, Denmark. TEL 66-157999. (back issues avail.) Indexed: M.L.A.
—BLDSC shelfmark: 6235.173600.

400 DK ISSN 0078-3315
ODENSE UNIVERSITY STUDIES IN LINGUISTICS. 1968. irreg. price varies. Odense University Press, Campusvej 55, DK-5230 Odense M, Denmark. TEL 66-157999. (back issues avail.) Indexed: Lang.& Lang.Behav.Abstr. (1968-).
—BLDSC shelfmark: 6235.175000.

439.5 839.5 DK ISSN 0078-3331
ODENSE UNIVERSITY STUDIES IN SCANDINAVIAN LANGUAGES AND LITERATURES. (Text in Danish) 1968. irreg. price varies. Odense University Press, Campusvej 55, DK-5230 Odense M, Denmark. TEL 66-157999. (back issues avail.)

OESTERREICHISCHE AKADEMIE DER WISSENSCHAFTEN. IRANISCHE KOMMISSION. VEROEFFENTLICHUNGEN. see HISTORY — History Of The Near East

410 401 AU
OESTERREICHISCHE AKADEMIE DER WISSENSCHAFTEN. KOMMISSION FUER LINGUISTIK UND KOMMUNIKATIONSFORSCHUNG. VEROEFFENTLICHUNGEN. (Subseries of: Oesterreichische Akademie der Wissenschaften. Philosophisch-Historische Klasse. Sitzungsberichte) 1973. irreg. Verlag der Oesterreichischen Akademie der Wissenschaften, Dr. Ignaz-Seipel-Platz 2, A-1010 Vienna, Austria. FAX 0222-5139541.

420 US ISSN 0473-9604
OHIO STATE UNIVERSITY. WORKING PAPERS IN LINGUISTICS. 1968. irreg. (2-3/yr.). $10 per nos. Ohio State University, Department of Linguistics, 222 Oxley Hall, 1712 Neil Ave., Columbus, OH 43210-1298. TEL 614-292-4052. FAX 614-292-4273. circ. 400. (back issues avail.) Indexed: ERIC, Lang.& Lang.Behav.Abstr. (1971-), M.L.A., Sociol.Abstr.
—BLDSC shelfmark: 9350.630000.

410 US
OHIO UNIVERSITY. WORKING PAPERS IN LINGUISTICS AND LANGUAGE TEACHING. 1974. irreg. price varies. Ohio University, Department of Linguistics, 103 Gordy, Athens, OH 45701. TEL 614-593-4564. FAX 614-593-4577. abstr.; bibl.; charts; illus.; circ. 250.
Formerly: Working Papers in Applied Linguistics (ISSN 0163-0016)

OLD ENGLISH NEWSLETTER. see LITERATURE

400 US
OLOGIES AND ISMS; a thematic dictionary. 1979. irreg., 3rd ed., 1986. $97. Gale Research Inc., 835 Penobscot Bldg., Detroit, MI 48226. TEL 313-961-2242. FAX 313-961-6083. TELEX 810-221-7086. Ed.Bd.
Description: Irregularly published guides to systems of belief and action.

410 BE ISSN 0078-463X
P323
ONOMA; bibliographical and information bulletin. (Text in English) 1950. a. 1500 BEF($75) (International Committee of Onomastic Sciences) International Centre of Onomastics, Blijde-Inkomststraat 21, B-3000 Leuven, Belgium. FAX 016-285025. (Orders to: Editions Peeters s.p.r.l., Bondgenotenlaan 153, B-3000 Leuven, Belgium. TEL 016-235170) Ed. W. van Langendonck. bk.rev. (back issues avail.) **Indexed:** Br.Archaeol.Abstr., M.L.A.
—BLDSC shelfmark: 6260.940000.

491.79 PL ISSN 0078-4648
G104
ONOMASTICA; pismo poswiecone nazewnictwu geograficznemu i osobowemu. (Summaries in French) 1955. a. price varies. (Polska Akademia Nauk, Komitet Jezykoznawstwa) Ossolineum, Publishing House of the Polish Academy of Sciences, Rynek 9, 50-106 Wroclaw, Poland. TELEX 0712771 OSS PL. (Dist. by: Ars Polona-Ruch, Krakowskie Przedmiescie 7, Warsaw, Poland) Ed. Kazimierz Rymut.
Description: Devoted to personal and geographical onomastics.

410 CN ISSN 0078-4656
F1004
ONOMASTICA CANADIANA. (Subseries of: Onomastica) (Text and summaries in English, French) 1959. s-a. Can.$20($18) Canadian Society for the Study of Names, Dept. of Languages, Literatures and Linguistics, York Univesity, 4700 Keele St., North York, Ont. M3J 1P3, Canada. TEL 416-736-5016. Ed. Frank R. Hamlin. bk.rev.; index; circ. 150. (back issues avail.) **Indexed:** Can.Per.Ind., M.L.A.
Description: Scholarly study of place and personal names in Canada and abroad.
Refereed Serial

400 SA
ONOMASTICS RESEARCH CENTER. ONOMASTICS SERIES. (Text in Afrikaans, English) 1972. irreg., no.10, 1980. price varies. Human Sciences Research Council, Onomastics Research Centre, c/o Dr. Lucie A. Moeller, Private Bag X41, Pretoria 0001, South Africa. TEL 012-202-2164.

491.7 891.7 GW
OPERA SLAVICA. NEUE FOLGE. 1961. irreg., vol.21, 1990. price varies. Verlag Otto Harrassowitz, Taunusstr. 14, Postfach 2929, 6200 Wiesbaden 1, Germany. TEL 0611-530-0. FAX 0611-530570. TELEX 4186135. Ed. Reinhard Lauer.
Formerly (until 1981): Opera Slavica (ISSN 0085-4514)

400 BE ISSN 0030-4379
P2
ORBIS; bulletin international de documentation linguistique. (Text in English, French, German, Italian, Russian, Spanish) 1952. a. 2000 BEF. (Universite Catholique de Louvain, Centre International de Dialectologie Generale) Editions Peeters s.p.r.l., Bondgenotenlaan 153, B-3000 Leuven, Belgium. TEL 016-235170. FAX 016-228500. Ed. R. Bosteels. adv.; bk.rev.; bibl.; charts; illus. (back issues avail.) **Indexed:** Hum.Ind., Mid.East: Abstr.& Ind., Soc.Sci.Ind.

439 800 DK ISSN 0108-8025
ORD & SAG. 1981. a. free. Aarhus Universitet, Institut for Jysk Sprog- og Kulturforskning, Niels Juels Gade 84, 8200 Aarhus N., Denmark. Ed. Viggo Soerensen. illus.; circ. 1,500.

ORIENS EXTREMUS; Zeitschrift fuer Sprache, Kunst und Kultur der Laender des fernen Ostens. see *ORIENTAL STUDIES*

410 IT
ORIENTAMENTI LINGUISTICI. 1977. irreg. price varies. (Universita degli Studi di Pisa, Istituto di Glottologia) Giardini Editori e Stampatori, Via Santa Bibbiana 28, 56100 Pisa, Italy. TEL 050-502531. Ed. Tristano Bolelli.

418.02 SW ISSN 0473-4351
ORTNAMNSSALLSKAPET I UPPSALA. AARSSKRIFT. (Text in English, German and Swedish; summaries in English) 1936. a. SEK 55($9) Ortnamnssallskapet i Uppsala - Place-Name Society of Uppsala, St. Johannesgatan 11, 753 12 Uppsala, Sweden. Ed. Karl I. Sandred. bk.rev.; circ. 1,000. (back issues avail.)

410 II ISSN 0970-0277
P1
OSMANIA PAPERS IN LINGUISTICS. (Text in English) 1975. a. Rs.15($3) Osmania University, Department of Linguistics, Hyderabad 500 007, Andhra Pradesh, India. adv.; bk.rev.; circ. 500. **Indexed:** Lang.& Lang.Behav.Abstr.

OUR HERITAGE. see *ORIENTAL STUDIES*

OXFORD GERMAN STUDIES. see *LITERATURE*

P A S A A JOURNAL. see *EDUCATION — Teaching Methods And Curriculum*

491.1 II
P.D. GUNE MEMORIAL LECTURE SERIES. (Text in English, Sanskrit) 1960. irreg. price varies. University of Poona, Centre of Advanced Study in Sanskrit, Ganeshkhind, Poona 411 007, India. TEL 54220. (Subscr. to: Section Officer, Publications Branch, University of Poona, Poona 411 007) Ed. V.N. Jha.

P M L A. see *LITERATURE*

410 GW ISSN 0343-4133
P Z L - PAPIERE ZUR LINGUISTIK. (Text in English, German) 1979. 2/yr. DM.68. Gunter Narr Verlag, Postfach 2567, 7400 Tuebingen, Germany. TEL 07071-78091. FAX 07071-75288.

PACIFIC COAST PHILOLOGY. see *LITERATURE*

499 AT ISSN 0078-7531
P11
PACIFIC LINGUISTICS. SERIES A: OCCASIONAL PAPERS. 1963. irreg. price varies. Australian National University, Research School of Pacific Studies, Pacific Linguistics, Dept. of Linguistics, G.P.O. Box 4, Canberra, A.C.T. 2601, Australia.

499 AT ISSN 0078-754X
PACIFIC LINGUISTICS. SERIES B: MONOGRAPHS. 1963. irreg. price varies. Australian National University, Research School of Pacific Studies, Pacific Linguistics, Dept. of Linguistics, G.P.O. Box 4, Canberra, A.C.T. 2601, Australia.
—BLDSC shelfmark: 6330.075000.

499 AT ISSN 0078-7558
PACIFIC LINGUISTICS. SERIES C: BOOKS. 1965. irreg. price varies. Australian National University, Research School of Pacific Studies, Pacific Linguistics, Dept. of Linguistics, G.P.O. Box 4, Canberra, A.C.T. 2601, Australia.
—BLDSC shelfmark: 6330.100000.

499 AT ISSN 0078-7566
PACIFIC LINGUISTICS. SERIES D: SPECIAL PUBLICATIONS. 1964. irreg. price varies. Australian National University, Research School of Pacific Studies, Pacific Linguistics, Dept. of Linguistics, G.P.O. Box 4, Canberra, A.C.T. 2601, Australia.
—BLDSC shelfmark: 6330.101000.

410 II
PAKHA SANJAM. (Text in English or Punjabi) 1968. s-a. Punjabi University, Department of Linguistics, Patiala 4, Punjab, India. Ed. Harjeet Singh Gill. adv.; bk.rev.; circ. 500.

491.8 PL ISSN 0078-866X
D377
PAMIETNIK SLOWIANSKI. 1950. a. $13.50. (Polska Akademia Nauk, Komitet Slowianoznawstwa) Ossolineum, Publishing House of the Polish Academy of Sciences, Rynek 9, 50-106 Wroclaw, Poland. TELEX 0712771 OSS PL. (Dist. by: Ars Polona-Ruch, Krakowskie Przedmiescie 7, Warsaw, Poland) Ed. Halina Janaczek-Ivanickova.
Description: Contains Slavonic studies devoted to literature, linguistics and culture of Slavonic countries and nations.

400 IT
PAN; studi dell'Istituto di Filologia Latina. 1973. a. exchange basis. Universita degli Studi, Istituto di Filologia Latina, Viale delle Scienze, 90134 Palermo, Italy.

LINGUISTICS 2833

495.1 MY ISSN 0553-0644
PAN T'AI HSUEH PAO/MAJALLAH PANTAI/UNIVERSITY OF MALAYA. CHINESE LANGUAGE SOCIETY. JOURNAL.* (Text in Chinese, English, Malay) irreg. University of Malaya, Chinese Language Society, Lembah Pantai, 59100 Kuala Lumpur, Malaysia. illus.

410 US
PAPERS AND REPORTS ON CHILD LANGUAGE DEVELOPMENT. 1970. a. $15. Stanford University, Department of Linguistics, Stanford, CA 94305. TEL 415-723-4284. FAX 415-723-3235. (Subscr. to: E R I C, National Institute of Education, U.S. Dept. of H.H.S., Washington DC 20208) Ed. E.V. Clark. circ. 200. **Indexed:** Lang.& Lang.Behav.Abstr. (1974-), Lang.Teach.& Ling.Abstr.
Description: Presents forum proceedings and some working papers on Stanford's current research concerning child language development.

410 PL ISSN 0137-2459
P134
PAPERS AND STUDIES IN CONTRASTIVE LINGUISTICS. (Text in English) 1973. irreg., vol.26, 1991. price varies. Adam Mickiewicz University Press, Nowowiejskiego 55, 61-734 Poznan, Poland. TEL 527-380. FAX 61-523130. TELEX 413260 UAM PL. Ed. Jacek Fisiak. adv.; bk.rev.; circ. 2,000. (reprint service avail. from EDR) **Indexed:** Lang.& Lang.Behav.Abstr. (1973-), M.L.A.
Description: Addresses contrastive and comparative linguisitcs studies; contains contributions from Poland and abroad.

499 AT ISSN 0078-9062
P11
PAPERS IN AUSTRALIAN LINGUISTICS. (Subseries of Pacific Linguistics. Series A: Occasional Papers) 1967. irreg. price varies. Australian National University, Research School of Pacific Studies, Pacific Linguistics, Dept. of Linguistics, G.P.O. Box 4, Canberra, A.C.T. 2601, Australia. **Indexed:** M.L.A.

495.6 375.4 JA
PAPERS IN JAPANESE LINGUISTICS. (Text in English) 1972. a. 4,650 Yen. Kurosio Shuppan Co., Ltd., 3-24, Kanda Ogawa-machi, Chiyoda-ku, Tokyo 101, Japan. Ed. Masayoshi Shibatani. bk.rev.; circ. 300.

410 AT ISSN 0811-0026
P11
PAPERS IN PIDGIN AND CREOLE LINGUISTICS. 1978. irreg. price varies. Australian National University, Research School of Pacific Studies, Pacific Linguistics, Dept. of Linguistics, G.P.O. Box 4, Canberra, A.C.T. 2601, Australia.

495 AT ISSN 0078-9178
P11
PAPERS IN SOUTH EAST ASIAN LINGUISTICS. (Subseries of Pacific Linguistics. Series A: Occasional Papers) 1967. irreg. price varies. Australian National University, Research School of Pacific Studies, Pacific Linguistics, Dept. of Linguistics, G.P.O. Box 4, Canberra, A.C.T. 2601, Australia. **Indexed:** M.L.A.

400 GW ISSN 0341-3195
PAPIERE ZUR TEXTLINGUISTIK/PAPERS IN TEXT LINGUISTICS. irreg., no.62, 1988. price varies. (Universitaet Bielefeld) Helmut Buske Verlag Hamburg, Friedrichsgaber Weg 138, Postfach 1249, D-2000 Norderstedt, Germany. Ed.Bd. **Indexed:** M.L.A.

400 II
PARKH. (Text in English and Punjabi) 1964. s-a. Rs.4. Panjab University, Publication Bureau, Chandigarh 160014, Union Territory, India. bk.rev.; bibl.; charts; circ. 500-1,000.

PARLANGHE. see *LITERATURE*

PARNASSOS; an annual literary journal. see *HUMANITIES: COMPREHENSIVE WORKS*

891.59 AF
PASHTU QUARTERLY. (Text in Pashtu) q. Afghanistan Academy of Sciences, Sher Alikhan St., Kabul, Afghanistan.

PATRISTICS. see *RELIGIONS AND THEOLOGY*

LINGUISTICS

491.86   CS
PEDAGOGICKA FAKULTA V USTI NAD LABEM. SBORNIK: RADA BOHEMISTICKA. (Text in Czech; summaries in English, German, Russian) irrge. 16 Kcs. Statni Pedagogicke Nakladatelstvi, Ostrovni 30, 113 01 Prague 1, Czechoslovakia.

PERITIA. see *HISTORY — History Of Europe*

PERSPECTIVES IN NEUROLINGUISTICS, NEUROPSYCHOLOGY, AND PSYCHOLINGUISTICS; a series of monographs and treatises. see *MEDICAL SCIENCES — Psychiatry And Neurology*

PERSPECTIVES UNIVERSITAIRES; la nouvelle revue de l'AUPELF. see *EDUCATION — Higher Education*

440 375.4   GW
LE PHARE. 1954. 6/yr. DM.13.20. Beacon-Verlag Koerber oHG, Birkental 13, Postfach 1161, 6702 Bad Duerkheim, Germany. circ. 1,000. (tabloid format)

479   US
PHI SIGMA IOTA FORUM. (Text and summaries in English and foreign languages) 1922. q. $5 to non-members. Phi Sigma Iota Honor Society, Department of Foreign Languages, University of Nevada, Las Vegas, NV 89154. TEL 800-769-7100. (Subscr. to: Prof. Santiago Vilas, 5211 Essen La., Ste. 2, Baton Rouge, LA 70809) adv.; bk.rev.; play rev.; abstr.; circ. 20,000. (tabloid format)
   Former titles: Phi Sigma Iota Newsletter (ISSN 0048-3699); Phi Sigma Iota News Notes (ISSN 0085-4867)

499.211   PH   ISSN 0048-3796
P1
PHILIPPINE JOURNAL OF LINGUISTICS. (Text in English and Pilipino) 1970. s-a. P.50($20) Linguistic Society of the Philippines, Box 3819, Manila, Philippines. TEL 02-504-611. FAX 02-522-3661. Ed. Andrew B. Gonzalez. bk.rev.; bibl.; charts; illus.; stat.; circ. 346. **Indexed:** E.I., Lang.& Lang.Behav.Abstr. (1970-), M.L.A.
  —BLDSC shelfmark: 6455.610000.
  Description: Presents original studies in descriptive, comparative, historical, and areal linguistics as well as papers on the application of theory to language teaching.

410   GW   ISSN 0079-1598
PHILOLOGEN-JAHRBUCH. a. DM.20. Verlag Jahrbuch der Lehrer der Hoeheren Schulen, Richard Wagner Str. 1, 5000 Cologne 10, Germany. Ed. K. Mueller.

439   NE
PHILOLOGIA FRISICA. (Text in Dutch, English, French, Frisian and German) 1956. triennial. Fryske Akademy, Doelestrjitte 8, 8911 DX Ljouwert-Leeuwarden, Netherlands. TEL 058-131414. FAX 058-131409.

401   US   ISSN 0079-1628
PHILOLOGICAL MONOGRAPHS. 1931. irreg., no.36, 1988. price varies. (American Philological Association) Scholars Press, Box 15399, Atlanta, GA 30333-0399. TEL 404-636-4757. FAX 404-636-8301. Ed. Matthew Santirocco. circ. 1,000.
  Description: Presents papers on classical literature and civilization.

400   US   ISSN 0031-7977
P1
PHILOLOGICAL QUARTERLY; devoted to scholarly investigation of the classical and modern languages and literatures. 1922. q. $15 to individuals; institutions $25. University of Iowa, Iowa City, IA 52242. TEL 319-335-0435. Ed. William Kupersmith. bk.rev.; bibl.; circ. 2,250. (also avail. in microform from MIM,UMI; reprint service avail. from UMI) **Indexed:** Abstr.Engl.Stud., Arts & Hum.Cit.Ind., Bk.Rev.Ind. (1965-), Child.Bk.Rev.Ind. (1965-), Curr.Cont., Hum.Ind., Lang.& Lang.Behav.Abstr.
  —BLDSC shelfmark: 6461.430000.

400   UK   ISSN 0079-1636
P11
PHILOLOGICAL SOCIETY TRANSACTIONS. 1842. a. £39.50($81) to individuals; institutions £68($133.50). Basil Blackwell Ltd., 108 Cowley Rd., Oxford OX4 1JF, England. TEL 0865-791100. FAX 0865-791347. TELEX 837022-OXBOOK-G. Ed. J.H.W. Penney. index. (also avail. in microform from SWZ; reprint service avail. from SWZ) **Indexed:** Lang.Teach.& Ling.Abstr.

PHILOSOPHY AND RHETORIC. see *PHILOSOPHY*

410 371.9   JA   ISSN 0911-0402
PL541
PHONETIC SOCIETY OF JAPAN. BULLETIN. (Text in English, French, Japanese) 1926. 3/yr. 6000 Yen. Phonetic Society of Japan, 5th Fl., Soyosha Bldg., 3-25-6, Higashi-Ueno, Taito-ku, Tokyo 110, Japan. TEL 03-3839-3957. Ed. Teruo Hirayama. adv.; circ. 1,100. (reprint service avail.) **Indexed:** Lang.& Lang.Behav.Abstr. (1972-).
  —BLDSC shelfmark: 2683.900000.

414   SZ   ISSN 0031-8388
P215   CODEN: PHNTAW
PHONETICA; international journal of speech science. (Text in English, French, German; summaries in English) 1957. q. 321 Fr.($214) S. Karger AG, Allschwilerstr. 10, P.O. Box, CH-4009 Basel, Switzerland. TEL 061-3061111. FAX 061-3061234. TELEX CH 962652. Ed. K. Kohler. adv.; bk.rev.; bibl.; charts; illus.; index; circ. 1,150. (also avail. in microform from RPI; reprint service avail. from SWZ) **Indexed:** Biol.Abstr., Curr.Cont., Dent.Ind., Excerp.Med., Ind.Med., Lang.& Lang.Behav.Abstr., Lang.Teach.& Ling.Abstr., M.L.A., SSCI.
  —BLDSC shelfmark: 6465.130000.

407   US   ISSN 0741-6164
PHONETICIAN. (Text in English; occasionally French, German) 1963. 3/yr. $20. International Society of Phonetic Sciences, Institute for Advanced Study of the Communication Process, University of Florida, 50 Dauer Hall, Gainesville, FL 32611. Ed. Harry Hollien. bk.rev.; circ. 1,500.

410   US
PHONETICS AND PHONOLOGY. 1989. irreg. Academic Press, Inc., 1250 Sixth Ave., San Diego, CA 92101. TEL 619-231-6616. FAX 619-699-6715. Eds. Stephen R. Anderson, Patricia A. Keating.
  Description: For graduate and research level.

410   UK   ISSN 0952-6757
P215
PHONOLOGY. s-a. $46 to individuals; institutions $79. Cambridge University Press, Edinburgh Bldg., Shaftesbury Rd., Cambridge CB2 2RU, England. TEL 0223-312393. FAX 0223-315052. TELEX 851817256. (North American addr.: Cambridge University Press, 40 W. 20th St., New York, NY 10011) Eds. John Anderson, Colin Ewen. (also avail. in microform from UMI; reprint service avail. from SWZ) **Indexed:** Lang.& Lang.Behav.Abstr. (1984-).
  —BLDSC shelfmark: 6465.172000.
  Formerly (until 1988): Phonology Yearbook (ISSN 0265-8062)
  Description: Combines theoretical and empirical interests to represent the diversity of opinion in the field.

450 055.1   DK   ISSN 0108-9935
PIRANESI; Italienske studier. 1983. a. DKK 109. University of Copenhagen, Museum Tusculanum Press, Njalsgade 94, DK-2300 Copenhagen S, Denmark. illus.
  Description: Contains articles on various facets of Italian linguistics.

PLANET; the Welsh internationalist. see *LITERATURE*

410   BE
PLURILINGUA. (Text in English, French, German) 1983. irreg., latest vol.12, 1991. DM.68. Research Centre on Multilingualism, Vrijheidslaan 17, B-1080 Brussels, Belgium. TEL 02-4124211. FAX 02-4124200. (Subscr. to: F. Dummler Verlag, Postfach 1480, D-5200 Bonn, Germany) Ed. Peter Hans Nelde. adv.; circ. 600.

410 371   GW
PO SVETU/PO SWIECIE/PO SVETE. (Text in Czech, Polish and Russian) 1948. 6/yr. DM.12. Volk und Wissen Verlag GmbH, Lindenstr. 54A, 1086 Berlin, Germany. TEL 0372-20343-0. illus.; circ. 135,000.
  Former titles: Around the World - A Travers le Monde - Po Svetu (ISSN 0323-830X); Durch die Welt.

POETICA; Zeitschrift fuer Sprach- und Literaturwissenschaft. see *LITERATURE*

410 800   JA
POETICA; an international journal of linguistic-literary studies. 1974. s-a. $50. Shubun International Co., Ltd., 12-7, 4-chome Komagome, Toshima-ku, Tokyo 170, Japan. TEL 03-915-8290. (Distr. by: Japan Publications Trading Co. Ltd., P.O. Box 5030, Tokyo, Japan) Ed. Shinsuke Ando. **Indexed:** Lang.Teach.& Ling.Abstr.

410   DK   ISSN 0109-2820
POETICA ET ANALYTICA. 1984. irreg. DKK 40. Aarhus University Press, Aarhus University, Bldg. 170, DK-8000 Aarhus, Denmark. FAX 45086-19-84-33.
  Formerly: Matieres (ISSN 0107-4946)

499.992   PL   ISSN 0032-2431
POLA ESPERANTISTO/ESPERANTIST'S MAGAZINE; socio-cultural review. 1906. m. £22. Polski Zwiazek Esperantystow, Krucza 38-42, 00-512 Warsaw, Poland. TEL 21-51-33. (Distr. by: Ars Polona-Ruch, Krakowskie Przedmiescie 7, Warsaw, Poland) Ed. Pawel Wimmer. adv.; bk.rev.; circ. 1,000.

407   PL
POLITECHNIKA WROCLAWSKA. STUDIUM NAUKI JEZYKOW OBCYCH. PRACE NAUKOWE. MONOGRAFIE. 1980. irreg., no.4, 1988. price varies. Politechnika Wroclawska, Wybrzeze Wyspianskiego 27, 50-370 Wroclaw, Poland. FAX 22-36-64. TELEX 712559 PWRPL. (Distr. by: Ars Polona-Ruch, Krakowskie Przedmiescie 7, Warsaw, Poland)
  Formerly: Politechnika Wroclawska. Studium Praktycznej Nauki Jezykow Obcych. Prace Naukowe. Monografie (ISSN 0208-8371)

407   PL   ISSN 0137-6349
POLITECHNIKA WROCLAWSKA. STUDIUM PRAKTYCZNEJ NAUKI JEZYKOW OBCYCH. PRACE NAUKOWE. STUDIA I MATERIALY. (Text in German, Polish, Russian; summaries in English) 1974. irreg., no.22, 1988. price varies. Politechnika Wroclawska, Wybrzeze Wyspianskiego 27, 50-370 Wroclaw, Poland. FAX 22-36-64. TELEX 712559 PWRPL. (Distr. by: Ars Polona-Ruch, Krakowskie Przedmiescie 7, Warsaw, Poland) circ. 380.

491.8   PL   ISSN 0137-9712
POLONICA. (Text in Polish; summaries in English) 1975. a. price varies. (Polska Akademia Nauk, Instytut Jezyka Polskiego) Ossolineum, Publishing House of the Polish Academy of Sciences, Rynek 9, 50-106 Wroclaw, Poland. TELEX 0712771 OSS PL. Ed. S. Urbanczyk.

POLONISTYKA. see *LITERATURE*

057 943.8   PL   ISSN 0208-4058
POLSKA AKADEMIA NAUK. INSTYTUT SLAWISTIKI. PRACE SLAWISTYCZNE. (Text in Polish; summaries in Russian) irreg., vol.64, 1987. price varies. Ossolineum, Publishing House of the Polish Academy of Sciences, Rynek 9, 50-106 Wroclaw, Poland. TEL 386-25. (Distr. by: Ars Polona, Krakowskie Przedmiescie 7, 00-068 Warsaw, Poland)
  Description: Monographs on Slavonic linguistics, literatures, history, ethnography.

400   PL   ISSN 0079-3272
POLSKA AKADEMIA NAUK. ODDZIAL W KRAKOWIE. KOMISJA FILOLOGII KLASYCZNEJ. PRACE. (Text in English, French, German, Latin and Polish; summaries in English and French) 1960. irreg., no.21, 1987. price varies. Ossolineum, Publishing House of the Polish Academy of Sciences, Rynek 9, Wroclaw, Poland. TELEX 0712771 OSS PL. (Distr. by: Ars Polona-Ruch, Krakowskie Przedmiescie 7, Warsaw, Poland) Ed. Marian Plezia.
  Description: Covers classical philology, ancient history, archeology of the mediterranean world, and the medieval and modern heritage of Poland.

400   PL   ISSN 0079-3310
POLSKA AKADEMIA NAUK. ODDZIAL W KRAKOWIE. KOMISJA JEZYKOZNAWSTWA. PRACE. (Text in Polish, Latin, French; occasionally in English and German) 1964. irreg., no.55, 1988. price varies. Ossolineum, Publishing House of the Polish Academy of Sciences, Rynek 9, 50-106 Wroclaw, Poland. TELEX 0712771 OSS PL. (Dist. by: Ars Polona-Ruch, Krakowskie Przedmiescie 7, Warsaw, Poland) Ed. Franciszek Slawski.
   Description: Problems of general Indo-European and Slavic linguistics.

400   PL   ISSN 0079-3329
POLSKA AKADEMIA NAUK. ODDZIAL W KRAKOWIE. KOMISJA JEZYKOZNAWSTWA. WYDAWNICTWA ZRODLOWE. (Text in Polish; summaries in English) irreg. price varies. Ossolineum, Publishing House of the Polish Academy of Sciences, Rynek 9, 50-106 Wroclaw, Poland. TELEX 0712771 OSS PL. (Dist. by: Ars Polona-Ruch, Krakowskie Przedmiescie 7, Warsaw, Poland) Indexed: M.L.A.

410   PL   ISSN 0032-3802
P19.P6
POLSKIE TOWARZYSTWO JEZYKOZNAWCZE. BIULETYN. (Text in English, German and Polish) irreg., vol.40, 1986. price varies. Ossolineum, Publishing House of the Polish Academy of Sciences, Rynek 9, Wroclaw, Poland. TELEX 0712771 OSS PL. (Dist. by: Ars Polona-Ruch, Krakowskie Przedmiescie 7, Warsaw, Poland) Ed. K. Polanski.

410   GW
POLYBIOS-LEXICON. (Text in Greek) 1968. irreg., latest 1975. (Akademie der Wissenschaften der DDR) Akademie-Verlag Berlin, Leipziger Str. 3-4, 1086 Berlin, Germany. TELEX 114420-AVERL-DD.

410 800   US
▼**POLYLINGUA;** a college journal of foreign languages. 1990. 3/yr. $20. Michigan Technological University, Department of Humanities, Houghton, MI 49931. TEL 906-487-2447. Ed. Francis Lide.
   Description: Devoted to the language component of foreign language studies.

437   GW
POMORANISCHES WOERTERBUCH. (Text in German and Pomoran) 1958. irreg., latest 1983. (Akademie der Wissenschaften der DDR) Akademie-Verlag Berlin, Leipziger Str. 3-4, 1086 Berlin, Germany.

439.2   NE   ISSN 0032-4205
POMPEBLEDEN; tydskrift foar Fryske Studzje. (Text in Frisian) 1928. 6/yr. fl.25. Stichting Algemiene Fryske Underrjoch Komisje, P.B. 53, 8900 AB Leeuwarden, Netherlands. FAX 058-159475. adv.; bk.rev.; index; circ. 550.

495   GW   ISSN 0554-7342
PORTA LINGUARUM ORIENTALIUM. 1965. irreg., vol.18, 1989. price varies. Verlag Otto Harrassowitz, Taunusstr. 14, Postfach 2929, 6200 Wiesbaden 1, Germany. TEL 0611-530-0. FAX 0611-530570. TELEX 4186135. Ed.Bd.

410   PL   ISSN 0079-4678
POZNANSKIE TOWARZYSTWO PRZYJACIOL NAUK. KOMISJA JEZYKOZNAWCZA. PRACE. (Text in English, German or Polish; summaries in English, French, German) 1962. irreg., vol.13, 1981. price varies. Panstwowe Wydawnictwo Naukowe, Ul. Miodowa 10, Warsaw, Poland. (Dist. by: Ars Polona-Ruch, Krakowskie Przedmiescie 7, Warsaw, Poland) Ed. Jerzy Wislocki. Indexed: Lang. & Lang.Behav.Abstr.

400   PL   ISSN 0079-3485
PRACE JEZYKOZNAWCZE. (Text in French and Polish) 1954. irreg., vol.110, 1986. price varies. (Polska Akademia Nauk, Komitet Jezykoznawstwa) Ossolineum, Publishing House of the Polish Academy of Sciences, Rynek 9, 50-106 Wroclaw, Poland. TELEX 0712771 OSS PL. (Dist. by: Ars Polona-Ruch, Krakowskie Przedmiescie 7, Warsaw, Poland)

491.8   PL   ISSN 0079-4775
PRACE ONOMASTYCZNE. (Text in Polish; summaries in English, French and German) 1955. irreg., vol.31, 1987. price varies. (Polska Akademia Nauk, Komitet Jezykoznawstwa) Ossolineum, Publishing House of the Polish Academy of Sciences, Rynek 9, 50-106 Wroclaw, Poland. TELEX 0712771 OSS PL. (Dist. by: Ars Polona-Ruch, Krakowskie Przedmiescie 7, Warsaw, Poland)

PRACTICAL ENGLISH TEACHING; for teachers of English as a foreign language. see EDUCATION — Teaching Methods And Curriculum

400 220   US   ISSN 0260-0943
PRACTICAL PAPERS FOR THE BIBLE TRANSLATOR. 1950. s-a. $6 ($12 including Technical Papers for the Bible Translator). United Bible Societies, Traslation Services Coordinator, 1865 Broadway, New York, NY 10023. FAX 212-582-7245. TELEX 23 62384. Ed. Rev. Euan Fry. adv.; bk.rev.; index, cum.index; circ. 3,000. (also avail. in microform from UMI; microfiche; reprint service avail. from UMI) Indexed: Chr.Per.Ind., New Test.Abstr., Old Test.Abstr., Rel.& Theol.Abstr. (1968-), Rel.Ind.One.
   Supersedes in part (since 1972): Bible Translator (ISSN 0006-0844)
   Description: Contains practical biblical and linguistic information.

430   US   ISSN 0922-842X
PRAGMATICS AND BEYOND NEW SERIES. 1985; N.S. 1988. irreg., vol.18, 1991. price varies. John Benjamins Publishing Co., 821 Bethlehem Pike, Philadelphia, PA 19118. TEL 215-836-1200. FAX 215-836-1204. (And: Amsteldijk 44, P.O. Box 75577, 1070 AN Amsterdam, Netherlands. TEL 020-6762325) Ed.Bd. (back issues avail.)
   —BLDSC shelfmark: 6598.516200.
   Supersedes (in 1988): Pragmatics and Beyond Companion Series (ISSN 0920-3079); **Incorporates (in 1988):** Pragmatics and Beyond (ISSN 0166-6258)
   Description: Comprehensive, interdisciplinary research in linguistic phenomena.

PRAGMATICS & COGNITION. see LINGUISTICS — Computer Applications

410 100   US
PRAGMATICS AND DISCOURSE ANALYSIS.* (Text and summaries in English) 1984. irreg., no.9, 1991. Walter de Gruyter, Inc., 200 Saw Mill River Rd., Hawthorne, NY 10532. TEL 914-747-0110. FAX 914-747-1326. Eds. Frans H. van Eemeren, Rob Grootendorst.
   Description: Contains research on argumentation and speech communication by linguists, philosophers, logicians and cognitive psychologists.

PRAKRIT TEXT SOCIETY. PUBLICATIONS. see LITERATURE

491.7 375.4   GW   ISSN 0179-7298
PRAKTIKA; Forum fuer den Russischunterricht. 1986. q. DM.48. Puschkin Buchhandelsgesellschaft mbH, Bonnerstr. 20, 5000 Cologne 1, Germany. TEL 0221-321353. FAX 0221-325952. Ed. Lutz Loescher. circ. 1,000.

491.86   CS   ISSN 0079-4902
PRAMENY CESKE A SLOVENSKE LINGVISTIKY. RADA CESKA. 1970. irreg. price varies. (Ceskoslovenska Akademie Ved) Academia, Publishing House of the Czechoslovak Academy of Sciences, Vodickova 40, 112 29 Prague 1, Czechoslovakia. TEL 23-63-065. Ed. Josef Vachek.

400 371.3   GW   ISSN 0032-7085
PRAXIS DES NEUSPRACHLICHEN UNTERRICHTS. (Text in English, French, German) 1953. q. DM.39. Verlag Lambert Lensing GmbH, Westenhellweg 67, Postfach 105051, 4600 Dortmund 1, Germany. TEL 0231-147008. FAX 0231-147284. Eds. R. Freudenstein, K. Hinz. adv.; bk.rev.; bibl.; circ. 6,500. (tabloid format; also avail. in microform from UMI; reprint service avail. from UMI,KTO) Indexed: Lang.& Lang.Behav.Abstr., Lang.Teach.& Ling.Abstr.
   Description: Directed to instructors of French and English in German schools. Covers special problems, new techniques in instruction and methods of teaching.

430 375.4   GW   ISSN 0721-8400
G72
PRAXIS DEUTSCH. bi-m. DM.82. Erhard Friedrich Verlag GmbH, Im Brande 15, Postfach 100150, 3016 Seelze-Velber, Germany. TEL 0511-40004-0. Ed. Uwe Brinkmann.

407   US   ISSN 0731-0714
P301
PRE-TEXT; a journal of rhetorical theory. 1980. q. $15 to individuals; institutions $45. Victor J. Vitanza, Pub. & Ed., c/o University of Texas, Dept. of English, Box 19035, Arlington, TX 76019-0035. adv.; bk.rev.; index; circ. 600. (back issues avail.) Indexed: M.L.A., Sociol.Abstr.
   —BLDSC shelfmark: 6603.630000.

440 840   DK   ISSN 0900-9507
PREPUBLICATIONS. (Text in Danish, English, French, Italian, Spanish) 1973. 7/yr. DKK 30. Universite d'Aarhus, Institut d'Etudes Romanes, Niels Juels gade 84, 8200 Aarhus N, Denmark. TEL 86-136-711. FAX 86-10-46-80. Ed.Bd. index; circ. 300. (back issues avail.) Indexed: M.L.A.

410 407   YU   ISSN 0351-8892
PREVODILAC; casopis Udruzenja Naucnih i Strucnih Prevodilaca Srbije. (Text in Serbo-Croatian) 1982. q. 10000 din.($50) Udruzenje Naucnih i Strucnih Prevodilaca, Kecevska 9, 11000 Belgrade, Serbia, Yugoslavia. TEL 011-444-2997. Ed. Zoran Jovanovic. circ. 2,000.

407   CS
PRIATEL'. (Text in Slovak) 1969. 10/yr. 15 Kcs. (Ministerstvo Skolstvo Slovenskej Republiky) Slovenske Pedagogicke Nakladatelstvo, Sasinkova 5, 815 60 Bratislava, Czechoslovakia. (Subscr. to: Slovart, Gottwaldovo nam. 6, 805-32 Bratislava, Czechoslovakia) Ed. Peter Aich. circ. 16,000.

808 949   YU   ISSN 0350-6673
PG560
PRILOZI ZA KNJIZEVNOST, JEZIK, ISTORIJU I FOLKLOR. (Text in Serbo-Croatian in Cyrillic alphabet) 1921. s-a. 33.60 din. Univerzitet u Beogradu, Filoloski Fakultet, Katedra za Jugoslovenske Knjizevnosti, Studentski trg 3-I, 1100 Belgrade, Serbia, Yugoslavia. FAX 011-630-039. (Subscr. to: Jugoslovenska Knjiga, Trg Republike 5-VIII, 11000 Belgrade, Serbia, Yugoslavia) (Co-sponsors: Fond za Nauku SR Srbije, Vukova Zaduzbina, Geobanka, Investbanka, Institut za Robni Promet) Ed. Miroslav Pantic. circ. 1,000. Indexed: M.L.A.
   Description: Articles and notes about Yugoslavian literature, languages, history and folkore.

430 375.4   CN   ISSN 0380-8815
PRISMA. 1975. s-a? Can.$10. (Saskatchewan Association of Teachers of German) Saskatchewan Teachers' Federation, Box 1108, Saskatoon, Sask. S7K 3N3, Canada. Ed. Rubi Rubrecht.

410   US   ISSN 0921-4771
PC1   CODEN: PRUSE2
PROBUS.* 1989. 3/yr. fl.72 to individuals; institutions fl.164. Walter de Gruyter, Inc., 200 Saw Mill River Rd., Hawthorne, NY 10532. TEL 914-747-0110. FAX 914-747-1326. Ed. W. Leo Wetzels. Indexed: Lang.& Lang.Behav.Abstr. (1989-).
   —BLDSC shelfmark: 6617.969000.
   Description: Discussion of historical and synchronic research in the field of Latin and Romance linguistics, with special emphasis on phonology, morphology, syntax, lexicon and sociolinguistics.

410   US   ISSN 0740-6959
P57.U7
PROFESSION. 1977. a. $7.50. Modern Language Association of America, 10 Astor Pl., New York, NY 10053. TEL 212-475-9500. FAX 212-477-9863. Ed. Phyllis Franklin. circ. 32,000. (back issues avail.; reprint service avail. from UMI)
   Description: Essays on the current state of the modern language profession and on aspects of the study of teaching of the modern languages and their literatures.

418.02   UK   ISSN 0955-615X
PROFESSIONAL TRANSLATOR AND INTERPRETER. 1986. 3/yr. £25($50) Institute of Translation and Interpreting, 318a Finchley Rd., London NW3 5HT, England. TEL 071-794-9931. FAX 071-435-2105. (Co-sponsor: Translators Association of the Society of Authors) Ed. M.J. Shields. adv.; bk.rev.; circ. 2,000.
   —BLDSC shelfmark: 6864.222500.
   Formerly: I T I News.

499.992   BE   ISSN 0048-5489
PROGRESO. (Text in Ido) no.230, 1972. 3/yr. 500 BEF. Uniono Por la Linguo Internaciona Ido (Reformed Esperanto), Ed. Franz Regnier, 27 Ville du Bois, B-6690 Vielsalm, Belgium. adv.; bk.rev.; bibl.

LINGUISTICS

PROSPECT; a journal of Australian TESOL. see *EDUCATION — Adult Education*

407   PL   ISSN 0137-544X
PRZEGLAD GLOTTODYDAKTYCZNY. (Text in Polish; summaries in English, Russian) 1978. a. price varies. Panstwowe Wydawnictwo Naukowe, Miodowa 10, 00-251 Warsaw, Poland. Ed. F. Grucza. circ. 400.

410 150   II   ISSN 0377-3132
P1.A1
PSYCHO-LINGUA; a biannual research journal devoted to communicative behavior. (Text in English) 1971. s-a. Rs.100. Psycholinguistic Association of India, c/o Institute of Psychological Services and Behavioural Research, 725, Shanti Vihar Colony, Dagnia, Raipur 492 001, India. (Dist. by: National Psychological Corporation, 4-230 Kacheri Ghat, Agra 282 004, India) Ed. V.P. Sharma. adv.; bk.rev.; abstr.; bibl.; circ. 250. Indexed: Lang.& Lang.Behav.Abstr., Psychol.Abstr.

410   US
PUBLICATIONS IN AFRICAN LANGUAGES AND LINGUISTICS.* 1983. irreg., no.10, 1989. Walter de Gruyter, Inc., 200 Saw Mill River Rd., Hawthorne, NY 10532. TEL 914-747-0110. FAX 914-747-1326. Eds. George N. Clements, Didier L. Goyvaerts.

410   NE
PUBLICATIONS IN LANGUAGE SERIES. 1981. irreg., no.36, 1991. Foris Publications, P.O. Box 509, 3300 AM Dordrecht, Netherlands.
TEL 078-510454. FAX 078-510972. (U.S. address: Box 5904, Providence, RI 02903. TEL 401-333-0044) Ed.Bd.
Description: Monographs and collections on topics in theoretical linguistics.

PUBLICATIONS OF THE NEW SOCIETY OF LETTERS AT LUND. see *ART*

PUBLICATIONS ROMANES ET FRANCAISES. see *LITERATURE*

410 840   US   ISSN 0165-8743
PURDUE UNIVERSITY MONOGRAPHS IN ROMANCE LANGUAGE. Short title: P U M R L. 1980. irreg., vol.34, 1991. price varies. John Benjamins Publishing Co., 821 Bethlehem Pike, Philadelphia, PA 19118. TEL 215-836-1200.
FAX 215-836-1204. (And: Amsteldijk 44, P.O. Box 75577, 1070 AN Amsterdam, Netherlands. TEL 020-6762325) Ed.Bd. Indexed: M.L.A.
Description: Critical studies in all aspects of romance languages and literature.

410 800   PK   ISSN 0555-8158
PUSHTO. Cover title: Pashto. (Text in Pushto) N.S. 1969. m. Rs.10. University of Peshawar, Pashto Academy, Peshawar, Pakistan. Ed. Syed Khayat Bokhan. bk.rev.; circ. 1,000.

400   SP   ISSN 0211-3589
DP102
AL QANTARA; revista de estudios arabes. s-a. 3300 ptas. (foreign 4950 ptas.). Consejo Superior de Investigaciones Cientificas (C.S.I.C.), Instituto de Filologia, Duque de Medinaceli, 6, 28014 Madrid, Spain. Dir. Manuela Marin.
—BLDSC shelfmark: 7163.581000.

QUADERNI DI LINGUE E LETTERATURE. see *LITERATURE*

410   IT   ISSN 0393-1226
QUADERNI DI SEMANTICA; rivista internazionale di semantica teorica e applicata. 1980. s-a. L.115000. Societa Editrice il Mulino, Strada Maggiore, 37, 40125 Bologna, Italy. TEL 051-256011.
FAX 051-256034. Ed. Mario Alinei. adv.; index; circ. 500. (back issues avail.) Indexed: M.L.A.

410 800   IT   ISSN 0033-4960
F1401
QUADERNI IBERO-AMERICANI; attualita culturale Penisola Iberica America-Latina. (Text in English, Italian, Portuguese and Spanish) 1948. irreg. L.35000($30) (Associazione Studi Iberici (ASI)) Bulzoni Editore, Via dei Liburni 14, 00185 Rome, Italy. TEL 06-4455207. FAX 06-4450355. Dir. Giovanni Maria Bertini. adv.; bk.rev.; cum.index; circ. 800. (back issues avail.)

410   IT
QUADERNI PATAVINI DI LINGUISTICA. (Text in English, French, German and Italian) 1979. a. L.15000($20) (Universita di Padova, Dipartimento di Linguistica) C.L.E.S.P., Via Seminario 12, 35122 Padua, Italy. circ. 100. (back issues avail.) Indexed: Lang.& Lang.Behav.Abstr. (1985-).

469   IT
QUADERNI PORTOGHESI. 1977. s-a. L.40000($40) Giardini Editori e Stampatori, Via Santa Bibbiana 28, 56100 Pisa, Italy. TEL 050-502531. Ed.Bd. Indexed: M.L.A.

QUADRANT. see *LITERATURE*

420 375.4   NE
QUADS; magazine for English language teaching. 5/yr. fl.7. Wolters-Noordhoff B.V., Damsport 157, 9728 PS Groningen, Netherlands. TEL (050)226922. (And Postbus 58, 9700 MB Groningen, Netherlands)

410   CC
QUANGUO ZHONGXUE YOUXIU ZUOWEN XUAN/SELECTED EXCELLENT COMPOSITIONS FROM NATION-WIDE MIDDLE SCHOOLS. (Text in Chinese) m. Jiangsu Jiaoyu Chubanshe, 165 Zhongyang Lu, Nanjing, Jiangsu 210009, People's Republic of China. TEL 631836.

420   US   ISSN 0735-5920
PE1460.A2
QUARTERLY REVIEW OF DOUBLESPEAK. 1973. q. $8. National Council of Teachers of English, Committee on Public Doublespeak, 1111 Kenyon Rd., Urbana, IL 61801. TEL 217-328-3870.
FAX 217-328-9645. Ed. William Lutz. bk.rev.; circ. 5,000. Indexed: Lang.& Lang.Behav.Abstr.
Formerly: Public Doublespeak Newsletter.

460 370   UK   ISSN 0033-5940
QUE TAL. (Text in Spanish) 1963. 6/yr. (during school year). Mary Glasgow Publications Ltd., Avenue House, 131-133 Holland Park Ave., London W11 4UT, England. TEL 071-603 4688.
FAX 071-602-5197. TELEX 311890-MGPUBS. (U.S. subscr. to: Delta Systems Co. Inc., 570 Rock Rd. Dr., Dundee, IL 60118-9992) illus.; circ. 39,000. (also avail. in microform from UMI; reprint service avail. from BLH, UMI)
Description: Spanish language magazine for beginners.

440   CN
QUEBEC (PROVINCE). OFFICE DE LA LANGUE FRANCAISE. RAPPORT D'ACTIVITES. a. Can.$2. (Office de la Langue Francaise) Publications du Quebec, C.P. 1005, Quebec, Que. G1K 7B5, Canada. TEL 800-463-2100. FAX 418-643-6177.

QUELLEN UND UNTERSUCHUNGEN ZUR LATEINISCHEN PHILOLOGIE DES MITTELALTERS. see *CLASSICAL STUDIES*

410 430   GW   ISSN 0170-7558
QUICKBORN; Zeitschrift fuer plattdeutsche Sprache und Dichtung. 1907. q. DM.38 (free to members). Quickborn Vereinigung fuer Niederdeutsche Sprache und Literatur e.V., Alexanderstr. 16, 2000 Hamburg 1, Germany. TEL 040-240809. Ed. F.W. Michelsen. bk.rev.; film rev.; play rev.; index; circ. 1,000. (back issues avail.)
Description: Reports on low-German language and literature, theatre, radio.

QUICKBORN BUECHER. see *LITERATURE*

410 800   UK   ISSN 0140-3397
QUINQUEREME; new studies in modern languages. 1978. s-a. £10($24) Claverton Down Bath Quinquereme, School of Modern Languages, The University, Bath BA2 7AY, England. Eds. Peter Wagstaff, David Head. adv.; bk.rev.; circ. 400. (also avail. in microfiche; back issues avail.) Indexed: Arts & Hum.Cit.Ind., Curr.Cont., Lang.& Lang.Behav.Abstr.

410   US   ISSN 0033-6602
QUINTO LINGO; the multi-lingual magazine. (Text in several languages) 1964-1980; resumed 1982. 6/yr. $27 for 6 nos. American National Heritage Association, Inc., Box 9340, Alexandria, VA 22304-0340. Ed. E. Peedo. adv.; circ. 30,000. (also avail. in microform from UMI; audio cassette from UMI; reprint service avail. from UMI)

420   SI   ISSN 0129-7716
PE1128.A2
R E L C ANNUAL REPORT. (Text in English) 1968. a. $12. Southeast Asian Ministers of Education Organization, Regional Language Centre, 30 Orange Grove Rd., Singapore 1025, Singapore.
TEL 737-9044. FAX 734-2753. TELEX RS 55598. charts; stat.; circ. 400. (back issues avail.)

407   SI   ISSN 0129-7767
R E L C GUIDELINES; magazine for language teachers. 1979. s-a. $14. Southeast Asian Ministers of Education Organization, Regional Language Centre, 30 Orange Grove Rd., Singapore 1025, Singapore. TEL 737-9044. FAX 734-2753. TELEX RS 55598. (back issues avail.)
—BLDSC shelfmark: 4230.026800.

406 370   SI   ISSN 0033-6882
PE1068.A7
R E L C JOURNAL; a journal of language teaching and research in Southeast Asia. 1970. s-a. $18. Southeast Asian Ministers of Education Organization, Regional Language Centre, 30 Orange Grove Rd., Singapore 1025, Singapore. TEL 737-9044.
FAX 734-2753. TELEX RS 55598. adv.; bk.rev.; circ. 1,000. (also avail. in microform from UMI; reprint service avail. from UMI) Indexed: C.I.J.E., Lang.& Lang.Behav.Abstr., Lang.Teach.& Ling.Abstr., M.L.A., Res.Educ.

407   SI   ISSN 0217-3077
R E L C NEWSLETTER. s-a. free. Southeast Asian Ministers of Education Organization, Regional Language Centre, 30 Orange Grove Rd., Singapore 1025, Singapore. TEL 737-9044. FAX 7342753. TELEX RS 55598. circ. 3,500.

407   SI   ISSN 0129-8844
R E L C OCCASIONAL PAPERS. irreg. $8. Southeast Asian Ministers of Education Organization, Regional Language Centre, 30 Orange Grove Rd., Singapore 1025, Singapore. TEL 737-9044. FAX 7342753. TELEX RS 55598. (back issues avail.)

407   SI
R E L C SEMINAR REPORT. 1970. a. $13. Southeast Asian Ministers of Education Organization, Regional Language Centre, 30 Orange Grove Rd., Singapore 1025, Singapore. TEL 737-9044. FAX 734-2753. TELEX RS 55598. (back issues avail.)

418   CL   ISSN 0033-698X
P9
R L A; revista de linguistica teorica y aplicada. (Text in Spanish; occasionally in English, French; abstracts in English) 1963. a. $9. Universidad de Concepcion, Facultad de Educacion, Humanidades y Artes, Casilla 2307, Concepcion, Chile. TELEX 260004 TEUCO CL. Ed. Max S. Echeverria. adv.; bk.rev.; charts; circ. 700. Indexed: Bull.Signal., Lang.& Lang.Behav.Abstr. (1970-), Lang.Teach.& Ling.Abstr.
—BLDSC shelfmark: 7863.633000.
Description: Covers the theory and application of linguistics.

410   CN   ISSN 0229-8651
P99
R S S I. (Recherches Semiotiques - Semiotic Inquiry) (Text and summaries in English and French) 1981. 2/yr. Can.$40 (foreign Can.$22). Universite du Quebec a Montreal, Departement d'Etudes Litteraire, C.P. 8888, succ. A, Montreal, Que. H3C 3P8, Canada. TEL 514-987-8404. Ed. Pierre Ouellet. adv.; bk.rev.; bibl.; circ. 500. (also avail. in microform from MML,UMI; reprint service avail. from MML)
—BLDSC shelfmark: 7309.185000.
Supersedes: Canadian Journal of Research in Semiotics (ISSN 0316-7917)
Description: Devoted to the empirical and theoretical study of signs, sign systems and processes of signification in all the domains of social and cultural praxis.

430.07 370   UK   ISSN 0033-7455
DAS RAD. (Text in German) 1964. 6/yr. (during school year). Mary Glasgow Publications Ltd., Avenue House, 131-133 Holland Park Ave., London W11 4UT, England. TEL 071-603 4688.
FAX 071-602-5197. TELEX 311890-MGPUBS. (U.S. subscr. to: Delta Systems Co. Inc., 570 Rock Rd. Dr., Dundee, IL 60118-9992) charts; illus.; circ. 45,000. (also avail. in microform from UMI; reprint service avail. from UMI)
Description: German language magazine for beginners.

410 809   IT   ISSN 0047-4401
RAGIONI CRITICHE; rivista di studi lingustici e letterari. 1974; N.S. 1980. q. L.10000. Aldo Marino Editore, Via Vecchia Ognina 90, 95129 Catania, Italy. Ed. Ermanno Scuderi. adv.; bk.rev.; illus.; cum.index. Indexed: M.L.A.

RAJASTHAN UNIVERSITY STUDIES IN ENGLISH. see *LITERATURE*

410 800   US   ISSN 0272-2747
RAM'S HORN. 1980. irreg. (approx a.). $10. Rassias Foundation, Dartmouth College, 6071 Wentworth Hall, Hanover, NH 03755-3526. TEL 603-646-3719. FAX 603-646-3838.

418   IT   ISSN 0033-9725
RASSEGNA ITALIANA DI LINGUISTICA APPLICATA. 1969. 3/yr. L.43000. (Centro Italiano di Linguistica Applicata) Bulzoni Editore, Via Liburni 14, 00185 Rome, Italy. TEL 06-4455207. FAX 06-4450355. Ed. Renzo Titone. adv.; bk.rev.; bibl.; circ. 2,000. Indexed: C.I.J.E., Lang.& Lang.Behav.Abstr. (1972-), Lang.Teach.& Ling.Abstr., M.L.A.
—BLDSC shelfmark: 7294.310000.

410   NE   ISSN 0922-4777
BF456.R2   CODEN: REWRE8
READING AND WRITING; an interdisciplinary journal. 1989. q. $66 to individuals; institutions $151. Kluwer Academic Publishers, Postbus 17, 3300 AA Dordrecht, Netherlands. TEL 078-334911. FAX 078-334254. TELEX 29245. (Dist. by: Kluwer Academic Publishers Group, P.O. Box 322, 3300 AH Dordrecht, Netherlands; N. America dist. addr.: Box 358, Accord Station, Hingham, MA 02018-0358. TEL 617-871-6600) Ed. R. Malatesha Joshi. (reprint service avail. from SWZ)
—BLDSC shelfmark: 7300.875000.
Description: Focuses on the interaction among various fields such as linguistics, information processing, neuropsychology, cognitive psychology, speech and hearing sciences, and education.

READING AROUND. see *EDUCATION — Teaching Methods And Curriculum*

410   UK   ISSN 0264-2425
READING IN A FOREIGN LANGUAGE. 1983. s-a. £12. International Education Centre, College of St. Mark & St. John, Derriford Rd., Plymouth PL6 8BH, England. FAX 0752-786622. TELEX 45789. Ed. A.H. Urquhart. adv.; bk.rev.; circ. 350. (back issues avail.) Indexed: Cont.Pg.Educ., Lang.Teach.& Ling.Abstr.
—BLDSC shelfmark: 7300.940000.

410   PR
READINGS IN SPANISH-ENGLISH CONTRASTIVE LINGUISTICS. (Text in English, Spanish) 1973. irreg. Universidad Interamericana de Puerto Rico, San German Campus, Call Box 5100, San German, PR 00753. TEL 809-892-1095. (reprint service avail. from UMI)

410   SP   ISSN 0210-4822
AS302
REAL ACADEMIA ESPANOLA. BOLETIN. 1914. 3/yr. 17000 ptas.($55.55) per no. Real Academia Espanola, Felipe IV 4, Madrid 14, Spain. Indexed: Amer.Hist.& Life, Hist.Abstr., M.L.A.

418.02   FR
RECHERCHES EN LINGUISTIQUE ETRANGERE. Variant title: Universite de Besancon. Annales Litteraires. 1973. irreg. (Universite de Besancon, Faculte des Lettres et Sciences Humaines) Societe d'Edition les Belles Lettres, 95 Bd. Raspail, Paris 75006, France.

RECHERCHES GERMANIQUES. see *LITERATURE*

410   FR
RECHERCHES LINQUISTIQUES. 1975. irreg. price varies. Universite de Metz, Centre d'Analyse Syntaxique, Metz, France. (Subscr. to: Librairie Klincksieck, 11 rue de Lille, 75007 Paris, France)

REGENSBURGER BEITRAEGE ZUR DEUTSCHEN SPRACH- UND LITERATURWISSENSCHAFT. REIHE A: QUELLEN. see *LITERATURE*

REGENSBURGER BEITRAEGE ZUR DEUTSCHEN SPRACH- UND LITERATURWISSENSCAHFT. REIHE B: UNTERSUCHUNGEN. see *LITERATURE*

400   CN
REGIONAL LANGUAGE STUDIES - NEWFOUNDLAND. 1968. irreg. free to qualified personnel. Memorial University of Newfoundland, Department of English, St. John's, Nfld. A1B 3X9, Canada. TEL 709-737-8000. FAX 709-737-4000. Ed. Graham Shorrocks. bk.rev.; circ. 370. Indexed: Lang.& Lang.Behav.Abstr., M.L.A.
Formerly: R L S: Regional Language Studies - Newfoundland (ISSN 0079-9335)

400   DK   ISSN 0900-3339
RETORIK. 1985. s-a. membership. Koebenhavn Universitet, Institut for Retorik, Klerkegade 2, 1308 Copenhagen K, Denmark. illus.

400   US   ISSN 0270-4390
REVERSE ACRONYMS, INITIALISMS AND ABBREVIATIONS DICTIONARY. 1972. irreg., 17th ed., 1992. $260. Gale Research Inc., 835 Penobscot Bldg., Detroit, MI 48226. TEL 313-961-2242. FAX 313-961-6083. TELEX 810-221-7086. Ed. Jennifer Mossman.
Formerly (until 1976): Reverse Acronyms and Initialisms Dictionary.

REVIEW (CHARLOTTESVILLE). see *LITERATURE*

REVIEW OF ENGLISH STUDIES; a quarterly journal of English literature and the English language. see *LITERATURE*

440   US
REVISTA AMERICANA DE ESTUDIOS SEMIOTICOS Y CULTURALES/AMERICAN JOURNAL OF SEMIOTIC AND CULTURAL STUDIES. (Text in English and Spanish) 1976. 3/yr. $25 to institutions; students $10; faculty $15. University of Michigan, Department of Romance Languages, Ann Arbor, MI 48109-1275. TEL 313-747-2383. FAX 313-764-3521. Ed. Walter Mignolo. adv.; bk.rev.; index; circ. 1,100. Indexed: Amer.Bibl.Slavic & E.Eur.Stud, Arts & Hum.Cit.Ind., Curr.Cont., M.L.A., RILA.
Former titles: Disposito - Teoria, Discursu, Produccion; Dispositio: Revista Hispanica de Semiotica Literaria (ISSN 0734-0591)

460 375   AG   ISSN 0326-6400
REVISTA ARGENTINA DE LINGUISTICA. (Text in Spanish; summaries in English.) 1985. 2/yr. Arg.$14 to individuals; institutions $28 (foreign $45). Casilla de Correo 45, 5511 Gral. Gutierrez, Mendoza, Argentina. TEL 061-978716. Eds. Victor M. Castel, Cesar E. Quiroga Salcedo. adv.; bk.rev.; abstr.; bibl.; charts; stat.; circ. 200. (back issues avail.) Indexed: Lang.& Lang.Behav.Abstr. (1985-), M.L.A.
Description: Covers study of linguistics. Includes theory, descriptive sociolinguistics, psycholinguistics, historical linguistics and computational linguistics.

420 375.4   SP   ISSN 0211-5913
PE9
REVISTA CANARIA DE ESTUDIOS INGLESES. 1980. s-a. $25 to individuals; institutions $30. Universidad de La Laguna, Facultad de Filologia. Departamento de Ingles, Secretariado de Publicaciones, San Agustin, 30, 38201 La Laguna-Tenerife, Islas Canarias, Spain. TEL 922-25-81-27. adv.
●Also available online.
—BLDSC shelfmark: 7847.270000.
Description: Devoted to the English language and literature of the English speaking countries. Includes software reviews.

REVISTA DE COMUNICACAO E LINGUAGENS. see *COMMUNICATIONS*

417 398   SP   ISSN 0034-7981
GR1
REVISTA DE DIALECTOLOGIA Y TRADICIONES POPULARES. 1944. q. 2000 ptas. (foreign 3000 ptas.). Consejo Superior de Investigaciones Cientificas (C.S.I.C.), Instituto de Filologia, Duque de Medinaceli, 6, 28014 Madrid, Spain. TEL 429 20 17. Dir. Julio Caro Baroja. bk.rev.; bibl.; charts; illus.; index; circ. 600. Indexed: A.I.C.P., Arts & Hum.Cit.Ind., Hist.Abstr., M.L.A.
Description: Covers the Spanish language in Iberia, and its dialects in America and Europe.

REVISTA DE ESTUDIOS HISPANICOS. see *LITERATURE*

410 056   SP   ISSN 0212-4130
REVISTA DE FILOLOGIA. 1981. a. $20 to individuals; institutions $30. Universidad de La Laguna, Facultad de Filologia, Seretariado de Publicaciones, San Agustin, 30, 38201 La Laguna-Tenerife, Islas Canarias, Spain. adv.
Description: Devoted to the Spanish and classical languages and literature.

400   SP   ISSN 0210-9174
PQ6001
REVISTA DE FILOLOGIA ESPANOLA. q. 3300 ptas. (foreign 4950 ptas.). Consejo Superior de Investigaciones Cientificas (C.S.I.C.), Instituto de Filologia, Duque de Medinaceli, 6, 28014 Madrid, Spain. Dir. Manuel Alvar. (also avail. in microform from BHP; microfilm from KTO; reprint service avail. from SCH)
—BLDSC shelfmark: 7854.650000.

400 410   CR   ISSN 0377-628X
REVISTA DE FILOLOGIA Y LINGUISTICA. 1975. s-a. $20. Editorial de la Universidad de Costa Rica, Apdo. 75-2060, Ciudad Universitaria Rodrigo Facio, 2050 San Pedro de Montes de Oca, San Jose, Costa Rica. TEL 506-25-3133. FAX 506-24-9367. TELEX UNICORI 2544.

410   SP   ISSN 0210-1874
P9
REVISTA ESPANOLA DE LINGUISTICA. 1971. s-a. 2075 ptas. (Sociedad Espanola de Linguistica) Editorial Gredos, S.A., Sanchez Pacheco 81, 28002 Madrid, Spain. FAX 341-5192033. Ed.Bd. Indexed: Lang.Teach.& Ling.Abstr.

410 306.4   PE
REVISTA LATINOAMERICANA DE ESTUDIOS ETNOLINGUISTICOS. (Text in Portuguese and Spanish) 1981. irreg., no.6, 1991. $12. Instituto Linguistico de Verano, Jiron Cusco 484, Lima 1, Peru. Ed. Ignacio Prado Pastor.
Description: Covers various topics in Latin American indigenous languages. Includes morphology and syntax, phonology and comparative linguistic studies.

REVISTA LETRAS. see *LITERATURE*

469   PO   ISSN 0080-2433
REVISTA PORTUGUESA DE FILOLOGIA. 1978. 2/yr. Esc.800. Universidade de Coimbra, Instituto de Estudos Romanicos, Casa do Castelo, Rua da Sofia 47, Coimbra, Portugal. Ed. Manuel de Paiva Boleo. Indexed: M.L.A.

REVISTA SIGNOS DE VALPARAISO; estudios de lengua y literatura. see *LITERATURE*

REVUE BELGE DE PHILOLOGIE ET D'HISTOIRE. see *HISTORY*

REVUE DE BIBLIOLOGIE. see *LITERATURE*

479   FR   ISSN 0035-1458
PC2
REVUE DE LINGUISTIQUE ROMANE. (Text in French, Italian, Spanish) 1925. s-a. 440 F. to non-members. Societe de Linguistique Romane, 44 av. de la Liberation, Case officielle 3310, 54014 Nancy Cedex, France. adv.; bk.rev.; bibl.; charts; index; circ. 700. Indexed: Arts & Hum.Cit.Ind., Ind.Bk.Rev.Hum., Lang.Teach.& Ling.Abstr., M.L.A.
—BLDSC shelfmark: 7926.600000.

REVUE DE PHILOLOGIE, DE LITTERATURE ET D'HISTOIRE ANCIENNES. see *CLASSICAL STUDIES*

414   FR   ISSN 0035-1660
P1
REVUE DE PHONETIQUE APPLIQUEE. (Text mainly in French; occasionally in English, German) 1965. 4/yr. $42. Didier Erudition, 6 rue de la Sorbonne, 75005 Paris, France. (Subscr. to: Didier Erudition, North American Fullfillment Office, P.O. Box 830350, Birmingham, AL-35283-0350) Ed. R. Renard. bk.rev.; abstr.; bibl.; charts; circ. 100. (also avail. in microform from UMI; reprint service avail. from UMI) Indexed: Lang.& Lang.Behav.Abstr. (1976-), Lang.Teach.& Ling.Abstr., M.L.A.
—BLDSC shelfmark: 7942.380000.

450 FR ISSN 0035-2047
PQ4001
REVUE DES ETUDES ITALIENNES. 1936. q. 200 F. Societe des Etudes Italiennes (Paris), Grand Palais-Perron Alexander III, Cours la Reine, 75008 Paris, France. Ed. M. Bec. adv.; bk.rev.; bibl.; index. **Indexed:** Arts & Hum.Cit.Ind., Can.Rev.Comp.Lit, Curr.Cont., Hist.Abstr., M.L.A.

REVUE DES ETUDES LATINES. see *CLASSICAL STUDIES*

REVUE DES ETUDES SLAVES. see *LITERATURE*

440 840 FR
REVUE DES LANGUES ROMANES. 1870. s-a. 185 F. Universite de Montpellier III (Universite Paul Valery), B.P. 5043, 34032 Montpellier Cedex 1, France. TEL 67-14-20-00. bk.rev.; bibl.; illus.; circ. 1,000. (reprint service avail. from KTO) **Indexed:** Arts & Hum.Cit.Ind., Curr.Cont., M.L.A.
Description: Main themes are the philology of Romance languages and Occitan literary texts.

499.992 FR ISSN 0988-6729
REVUE FRANCAISE D'ESPERANTO; Franca Esperantisto. 1908. bi-m. 155 F. Union Francaise pour l'Esperanto, 4 bis, rue de la Cerisaie, 75004 Paris, France. Ed. Herve Gonin. adv.; bk.rev.; circ. 2,000.
Incorporates: Esperanto-Actualites.

410 CN ISSN 0710-0167
REVUE QUEBECOISE DE LINGUISTIQUE; theorique et appliquee. 1971. 4/yr. Can.$30. Association Quebecoise de Linguistique Inc., C.P. 95, Trois-Rivieres, Que. G9A 5E3, Canada. Ed. Henri Wittmann. adv.; bk.rev.; circ. 600. (back issues avail.) **Indexed:** Lang.& Lang.Behav.Abstr. (1984-), Lang.Teach.& Ling.Abstr., M.L.A., Pt.de Rep. (1983-), Sociol.Abstr.
—BLDSC shelfmark: 7944.850000.
Formerly (until Apr. 1981): Cahier de Linguistique (ISSN 0315-4025)

479 DK ISSN 0035-3906
REVUE ROMANE. (Text in French, Italian, Spanish) 1966. s-a. DKK 325 (students DKK 162.50). (Koebenhavns Universitet, Institut d'Etudes Romanes - University of Copenhagen) Munksgaard International Publishers Ltd., 35 Noerre Soegade, P.O. Box 2148, DK-1016 Copenhagen K, Denmark. TEL 33-127030. FAX 33-129387. TELEX 19431-MUNKS-DK. Ed. Hans Peter Lund. bk.rev.; index; circ. 500. **Indexed:** Arts & Hum.Cit.Ind., Curr.Cont., Lang.& Lang.Behav.Abstr., M.L.A.
—BLDSC shelfmark: 7946.030000.

400 RM ISSN 0035-3957
P1.A1
REVUE ROUMAINE DE LINGUISTIQUE. (Text in English, French, German, Russian, Spanish) 1956. 6/yr. 210 lei($68) (Academia Romana) Editura Academiei Romane, Calea Victoriei 125, 79717 Bucharest, Rumania. (Dist. by: Rompresfilatelia, Calea Grivitei 64-66, P.O. Box 12-201, 78104 Bucharest, Rumania) bk.rev.; index. **Indexed:** Lang.& Lang.Behav.Abstr. (1972-), Lang.Teach.& Ling.Abstr., M.L.A.
Formerly: Revue de Linguistique.

499.992 JA ISSN 0035-4406
LA REVUO ORIENTA. (Text in Esperanto, Japanese) 1920. m. 3600 Yen. Japana Esperanto Instituto, 12-3, Waseda-machi, Shinjuku-ku, Tokyo 162, Japan. TEL 03-3203-4581. FAX 03-3203-4582. Ed. Satio Ikawa. adv.; bk.rev.; illus.; circ. 2,300. **Indexed:** Lang.& Lang.Behav.Abstr.

400 480 470 GW ISSN 0035-449X
PA3
RHEINISCHES MUSEUM FUER PHILOLOGIE. (Text mainly in German, partly in English, Greek, Latin) 1842. q. DM.174. J.D. Sauerlaender's Verlag, Finkenhofstr. 21, 6000 Frankfurt, Germany. Ed.Bd. illus.; index; circ. 600. (reprint service avil. from SCH) **Indexed:** M.L.A.
Description: Scholarly publication devoted to studies in the literature and history of ancient Greece and Rome.

RHETORIC REVIEW. see *EDUCATION — Higher Education*

410 US ISSN 0734-8584
PN183
RHETORICA; a journal of the history of rhetoric. 1983. q. $30 to individuals; institutions $50. (International Society for the History of Rhetoric) University of California Press, Journals Division, 2120 Berkeley Way, Berkeley, CA 94720. TEL 510-642-4191. FAX 510-643-7127. Ed. Michael Leff. adv.; bk.rev.; circ. 850. (back issues avail.) **Indexed:** Arts & Hum.Cit.Ind., Curr.Cont.
—BLDSC shelfmark: 7960.610300.
Description: Examines the theory, practice, and cultural context of rhetoric.
Refereed Serial

450 IT ISSN 0080-293X
RICERCHE DI STORIA DELLA LINGUA LATINA. 1967. irreg., no.19, 1985. price varies. Edizioni dell' Ateneo S.p.A., Box 7216, 00100 Rome, Italy. Ed. Alfonso Traina. circ. 1,000.

420 375.4 US ISSN 0892-581X
RIGHTING WORDS; the journal of language and editing. 1987. bi-m. $24. Righting Words Corp., Drawer 9808, Knoxville, TN 37904. Ed. Jonathan Kaufman. adv.; bk.rev.; circ. 1,500. (back issues avail.)
Description: Covers all phases of English, including professional editing.

RIJKSUNIVERSITEIT TE GRONINGEN. NEDERSAKSISCH INSTITUUT. DRIEMAANDELIJKSE BLADEN; taal en volksleven in het oosten van Nederland. see *LITERATURE*

410 SP
RILCE. 1985. 2/yr. 3000 ptas.($37) (Universidad de Navarra, Instituto de Lengua y Cultura Espanolas) Servicio de Publicaciones de la Universidad de Navarra, S.A., Apdo. 177, 31080 Pamplona, Spain. TEL 94 25 2700. Dir. Jesus Canedo.

480 IT ISSN 0035-6220
RIVISTA DI FILOLOGIA CLASSICA. 1872. q. (foreign L.122000)(effective 1992). Editore Loescher, Via Vittorio Amedeo II, 18, 10121 Turin, Italy. TEL 549-333. Ed.Bd. bk.rev.; bibl.; index; circ. 1,000. (reprint service avail. from KTO)

410 IT
RIVISTA DI GRAMMATICA GENERATIVA. (Text in English, French and Italian) L.15000($15) C.L.E.S.P., Via Seminario 12, 35122 Padua, Italy. (back issues avail.)

450 375.4 IT ISSN 1120-2726
RIVISTA DI LINGUISTICA. (Text in English) 1989. 2/yr. L.65000 (Europe L.75000; elsewhere L.95000). Rosenberg & Sellier, Via Andrea Doria, 14, 10123 Turin, Italy. TEL 011-561-39-07. FAX 011-532188. Ed. PierMarco Bertinetto.

450 375.4 IT
RIVISTA ITALIANA DI DIALETTOLOGIA; scuola societa territorio. Short title: R I D. 1977. s-a. L.10000($20) (Universita degli Studi di Bologna, Facolta di Lettere e Filosofia, Istituto di Glottologia) Cooperativa Libraria Universitaria Editrice Bologna, Via Marsala 24, 40126 Bologna, Italy. Ed.Bd. **Indexed:** Lang.& Lang.Behav.Abstr.

495.6 US
RIYU XUEXI/LEARNING JAPANESE. (Text in Chinese and Japanese) bi-m. $18.50. China Books & Periodicals, Inc., 2929 24th St., San Francisco, CA 94110. TEL 415-282-2994. FAX 415-282-0994.

495.6 CC
RIYU XUEXI YU YANJIU/STUDIES OF JAPANESE LANGUAGE. (Text in Chinese and Japanese) bi-m. $30.60. Duwai Jingji Maoyi Daxue - Foreign Economics and Trade University, Andingmenwai Xiaoguan, Chaoyang Qu, Beijing 100029, People's Republic of China. TEL 4212161. (Dist. in US by: China Books & Periodicals, Inc., 2929 24th St., San Francisco, CA 94110. TEL 415-282-2994) Ed. Leng Tiezheng.

495.6 375.4 CC
RIYU ZHISHI/JAPANESE LANGUAGE. (Text in Chinese and Japanese) 1983. m. $24.20. Dalian Waiguoyu Xueyuan, Riyu Xi - Dalian Foreign Language Institute, Japanese Department, Nanshan Lu, Zhongshan Qu, Dalian, Liaoning 116001, People's Republic of China. (Dist. outside China by: China International Book Trading Corp., P.O. Box 2820, Beijing, P.R.C.; Dist. in US by: China Books & Periodicals, Inc., 2929 24th St., San Francisco, CA 94110. TEL 415-282-2994)
Description: Assists in the study of basic Japanese: vocabulary, grammar, and writing. Helps the reader build listening, speaking, reading, writing, and translating skills. Also introduces Japanese society, culture, history, and customs, and contains short stories in Japanese with Chinese translation.

ROCKY MOUNTAIN REVIEW OF LANGUAGE AND LITERATURE. see *LITERATURE*

491.8 PL ISSN 0080-3588
PG1
ROCZNIK SLAWISTYCZNY. (Text in French, German and Polish) 1908. a. price varies. (Polska Akademia Nauk, Komitet Slowianoznawstwa) Ossolineum, Publishing House of the Polish Academy of Sciences, Rynek 9, 50-106 Wroclaw, Poland. TELEX 0712771 OSS PL. (Dist. by: Ars Polona-Ruch, Krakowskie Przedmiescie 7, Warsaw, Poland) Ed. F. Slawski. **Indexed:** M.L.A.
Description: Dissertations on Slavonic studies, bibliographies of published works.

479 US ISSN 0035-8002
PC1
ROMANCE PHILOLOGY. (Text in several languages) 1947. q. $27 to individuals (foreign $33); institutions $54 (foreign $60); students $15 (foreign $21). University of California Press, Journals Division, Berkeley, CA 94720. TEL 510-642-4191. FAX 510-643-7127. Ed.Bd. adv.; bk.rev.; index; circ. 1,150. (also avail. in microfilm from UMI; back issues avail.; reprint service avail. from UMI) **Indexed:** Arts & Hum.Cit.Ind., Curr.Cont., Hum.Ind., Ind.Bk.Rev.Hum., Lang.& Lang.Behav.Abstr., M.L.A.
—BLDSC shelfmark: 8019.470000.
Description: Contains articles on topics of linguistic and literary theory.
Refereed Serial

459 859 940 FR ISSN 0035-8029
PC2
ROMANIA; revue consacree a l'etude des langues et des litteratures romanes. (Text in English, French, Italian, Spanish) 1872. q. $60 to individuals; libraries & societies $60. Societe des Amis de la Romania, 19 Rue de la Sorbonne, 75005 Paris, France. Ed. Jacques Monfrin. bk.rev.; index, cum.index. (also avail. in microfilm from BHP; reprint service avail. from KTO) **Indexed:** Arts & Hum.Cit.Ind., Curr.Cont., Ind.Bk.Rev.Hum.

479.1 BE ISSN 0080-3855
ROMANICA GANDENSIA. 1953. irreg. price varies. Rijksuniversiteit te Gent, Section de Philologie Romane, Blandijnberg 2, B-9000 Gent, Belgium. TEL 91-64-4045. FAX 91-64-4195. circ. 600. **Indexed:** M.L.A.

430 830 SW ISSN 0080-3863
ROMANICA GOTHOBURGENSIA. (Subseries of Acta Universitatis Gothoburgensis) 1955. irreg., no.41, 1992. price varies; also exchange basis. Acta Universitatis Gothoburgensis, Box 5096, S-402 22 Goeteborg, Sweden.

400 SZ ISSN 0080-3871
ROMANICA HELVETICA. (Text in French, German, or Italian) 1935. irreg., vol.101, 1986. price varies. (Collegium Romanicum Helvetiorum a Curatoribus Vocis Romanicae) Francke Verlag, Postfach 1445, CH-3001 Berne, Switzerland. TEL 031-221715.

410 IT ISSN 0391-1950
ROMANICA NEAPOLITANA. 1969. irreg., no.25, 1990. price varies. Liguori Editore s.r.l., Via Mezzocannone 19, 80134 Naples, Italy. TEL 081-5227139. Eds. Francesco Bruni, Alberto Varvaro.

410   GW   ISSN 0344-676X
ROMANISTISCHE ARBEITSHEFTE. 1973. irreg., no.35, 1991. price varies. Max Niemeyer Verlag, Postfach 2140, 7400 Tuebingen 1, Germany. TEL 07071-81104. FAX 07071-87419. (back issues avail.)
Description: University course books on Romance languages.

400 870   GW   ISSN 0080-3898
PC3
ROMANISTISCHES JAHRBUCH. 1947. irreg., vol.42, 1991. price varies. (Universitaet Hamburg, Ibero-Amerikanisches Forschungsinstitut) Walter de Gruyter und Co., Genthiner Str. 13, 1000 Berlin 30, Germany. TEL 030-26005-0. FAX 030-26005251. TELEX 184027. (U.S. addr.: Walter de Gruyter, Inc., 200 Saw Mill Rd., Hawthorne, N.Y. 10532) bk.rev. **Indexed:** Can.Rev.Comp.Lit, M.L.A.
—BLDSC shelfmark: 8019.870000.

410   DK   ISSN 0106-0821
ROSKILDE UNIVERSITETSCENTER. LINGVISTGRUPPEN. ROLIG-PAPIR. 1974. irreg. free. Roskilde Universitetscenter, Lingvistgruppen, Postboks 260, 4000 Roskilde, Denmark. FAX 46-757401. TELEX 43158-RUBIBL-DK. Eds. Karen Risager, Hartmut Haberland. circ. 350.

491.7 891.7   CS
ROSSICA OLOMUCENSIA. (Text in Czech or Russian; summaries in Russian) 1968. a. free. Univerzita Palackeho, Filozoficka Fakulta, Katedra Rusistiky, Krizkovskeho 10, 771 80 Olomouc, Czechoslovakia. Ed. Jaroslav Reska. circ. 350.

491   II   ISSN 0035-9424
RTAM. (Text in English, Hindi, Sanskrit) 1969. s-a. Rs.20($5.) Akhila Bharatiya Sanskrit Parishad, c/o Dr. J.P. Sinha, Ed., Mahatma Gandhi Marg, Hazratganj, Lucknow-226 001, Uttar Pradesh, India. bk.rev.; index; circ. 200.

947 891.7   UK   ISSN 0957-1760
CODEN: RUSIE5
RUSISTIKA. 1959. 2/yr. £20($40) (foreign £21). Association for Language Learning, 16 Regent Place, Rugby, Warwickshire CV21 2PN, England. TEL 0788-546443. FAX 0788-544149. Ed. Margaret Tejerizo. adv.; bk.rev.; film rev.; play rev.; rec.rev.; abstr.; bibl.; charts; illus.; mkt.; stat.; index; circ. 1,000. (also avail. in microform from UMI; reprint service avail. from UMI) **Indexed:** Br.Educ.Ind., Br.Hum.Ind., Cont.Pg.Educ., Educ.Ind., Forest.Abstr., Lang.& Lang.Behav.Abstr., Lang.Teach.& Ling.Abstr., M.L.A.
—BLDSC shelfmark: 8052.647590.
Formerly (until 1990): Journal of Russian Studies (ISSN 0047-276X)
Description: Directed to teachers of Russian in schools, colleges and universities, with articles on language, literature, teaching methodology and history.

RUSKY JAZYK VE SKOLE; casopis pro vyucovani rustine na ceskoslovenskych skolach. see EDUCATION

491.7 370   US   ISSN 0036-0252
RUSSIAN LANGUAGE JOURNAL. (Text in English, Russian) 1947. 3/yr. $20 to individuals; institutions $25. Russian Language Journal Consortium, c/o Prof. Munir Sendich, A-601 Wells Hall, Department of Linguistics and Language, Michigan State University, E. Lansing, MI 48824-1027. TEL 517-355-5079. (Co-sponsors: Brown University; Ohio State University; Purdue University) Ed. Munir Sendich. adv.; bk.rev.; bibl.; stat.; cum.index: 1947-1965; circ. 500. (also avail. in microform from UMI; reprint service avail. from UMI) **Indexed:** Amer.Bibl.Slavic & E.Eur.Stud., C.I.J.E., Can.Rev.Comp.Lit., Ind.Bk.Rev.Hum., Lang.& Lang.Behav.Abstr., Lang.Teach.& Ling.Abstr., M.L.A.
Formerly: Guide to Teachers of the Russian Language in America.

491.7   NE   ISSN 0304-3487
PG2001
RUSSIAN LINGUISTICS; international journal for the study of the Russian language. (Text in English, Russian) 1974. 3/yr. $175. Kluwer Academic Publishers, Postbus 17, 3300 AA Dordrecht, Netherlands. TEL 078-334911. FAX 078-334254. TELEX 29245. (Dist. by: Kluwer Academic Publishers Group, P.O. Box 322, 3300 AH Dordrecht, Netherlands; N. America dist. addr.: Box 358, Accord Station, Hingham, MA 02018-0358. TEL 617-871-6600) Ed.Bd. adv.; bk.rev. (reprint service avail. from SWZ) **Indexed:** Curr.Cont., Ind.Bk.Rev.Hum., Lang.& Lang.Behav.Abstr. (1975-), Lang.Teach.& Ling.Abstr., M.L.A., Sociol.Abstr.
—BLDSC shelfmark: 8052.735000.

RUSSIAN POETICS IN TRANSLATION. see LITERATURE

375.4   DK   ISSN 0108-2442
RUSSISKLAERERFORENINGEN. MEDDELELSER. 1979. q. membership. Kastanie Alle 3, DK-6000 Kolding, Denmark. Ed. Anne Bryld. adv.; bk.rev.; illus.; circ. 250.

491.7   RU   ISSN 0036-0368
RUSSKAYA RECH'. 1967. bi-m. 8.10 Rub. (Akademiya Nauk S.S.S.R., Institut Russkogo Yazyka) Izdatel'stvo Nauka, 90 Profsoyuznaya ul., 117864 Moscow, Russia. (Dist. by: Mezhdunarodnaya Kniga, ul. Dimitrova D.39, 113095 Moscow, Russia) Ed. V.V. Ivanov. bk.rev.; bibl.; index. (also avail. in microform from MIM)

491.7   RU
PG2065   CODEN: RINSBP
RUSSKII YAZYK V S.S.S.R.. 1957. m. 0.70 Rub. per issue. Akademiya Pedagogicheskikh Nauk S.S.S.R., Smolenskii bul'var, 4, 119034 Moscow, Russia. TEL 971-15-63. Ed. M.I. Isaev. circ. 13,710.
Formerly (until 1991): Russkii Yazyk v Natsional'noi Shkole (ISSN 0131-6133)

491.7 370   RU   ISSN 0131-6141
RUSSKII YAZYK V SHKOLE. 1914. bi-m. 2.70 Rub. (Ministerstvo Prosveshcheniya) Izdatel'stvo Prosveshchenie, 3-i Proezd Mar'inoi Roshchi, 41, Moscow, Russia. TEL 289-42-24. TELEX 111999 PARK. (Co-sponsor: Ministerstvo Narodnogo Obrazovaniya R.S.F.S.R.) Ed. N.M. Shanskii. bk.rev.; bibl.; index; circ. 255,300. **Indexed:** Lang.& Lang.Behav.Abstr.
Description: Aimed at high school and college teachers of Russian language. Publishes articles on methodology, as well as practical advice and recommendations on conducting the lessons.

491.7 370   RU   ISSN 0036-0384
RUSSKII YAZYK ZA RUBEZHOM/RUSSIAN ABROAD. 1967. bi-m. 15 Rub. (effective 1991). Institut Russkogo Yazika im. Pushkina - Pushkin Russian Language Institute, Ul. Volgina 6, Moscow 117485, Russia. Ed. A.V. Abramovich. (also avail. in microform from MIM)

491.7 375.4   CS
RUSTINAR. (Text in Russian) 10/yr. $24. (Svaz Ceskoslovensko-Sovetskeho Pratelstvi - Union of Czechoslovak-Soviet Friendship) Obzor, Ceskoslovenskej Armady 35, 815 85 Bratislava, Czechoslovakia. (Co-sponsor: House of Czechoslovak-Soviet in Bratislava)

410   SI   ISSN 0129-8895
S E A M E O REGIONAL LANGUAGE CENTRE. ANTHOLOGY SERIES. (Text in English) irreg. $18. Southeast Asian Ministers of Education Organization, Regional Language Centre, 30 Orange Grove Rd., Singapore 1025, Singapore. TEL 7379044. FAX 7342753. TELEX RS 55598. circ. 1,000.

S E M A. (Semiotic Abstracts) see LINGUISTICS — Abstracting, Bibliographies, Statistics

407 371.3   AT   ISSN 1036-1243
S I L - A A I B OCCASIONAL PAPERS. 1978. irreg. price varies. Summer Institute of Linguistics, Australian Aborigines and Islanders Branch, P.O. Berrimah, N.T. 0828, Australia. TEL 089-844488. FAX 089-844321. Ed. Susanne K. Hargrave. (back issues avail.)
Formed by the 1990 merger of: Summer Institute of Linguistics. Australian Aborigines and Islanders Branch. Work Papers. Series A (ISSN 1030-9853) & Summer Institute of Linguistics. Australian Aborigines and Islanders Branch. Work Papers. Series B (ISSN 1030-9861)
Description: Presents linguistic and cultural data and analyses, language resource materials, and practical applications in communication and translation resulting from research in Australian Aboriginal and Islander languages.

400 900   GW   ISSN 0080-5297
SAECHSISCHE AKADEMIE DER WISSENSCHAFTEN, LEIPZIG. PHILOLOGISCH-HISTORISCHE KLASSE. ABHANDLUNGEN. 1896. irreg., vol.71, 1988. price varies. Akademie-Verlag Berlin, Leipziger Str. 3-4, 1086 Berlin, Germany. TELEX 114420-AVERL-DD.

410 900   GW   ISSN 0138-3957
AS182
SAECHSISCHE AKADEMIE DER WISSENSCHAFTEN, LEIPZIG. PHILOLOGISCH-HISTORISCHE KLASSE. SITZUNGSBERICHTE. irreg., vol.129, 1989. price varies. Akademie-Verlag Berlin, Leipziger Str. 3-4, 1086 Berlin, Germany. TELEX 114420-AVERL-DD.

SAGA OCH SED. see FOLKLORE

491.8   GW
SAGNERS SLAVISTISCHE SAMMLUNG. 1974. irreg., vol.10, 1986. price varies. Verlag Otto Sagner, Postfach 340108, 8000 Munich 34, Germany. TEL 089-522027. TELEX 5216711-KUSAD. Ed. Peter Rehder. circ. 250.

SAMMLUNG GROOS. see EDUCATION — Higher Education

430 375.4   GW
SAMMLUNG KURZER GRAMMATIKEN GERMANISCHER DIALEKTE. 1880. irreg. price varies. Max Niemeyer Verlag, Postfach 2140, 7400 Tuebingen 1, Germany. TEL 07071-81104. FAX 07071-87419. Ed.Bd. (back issues avail.)
Description: Scientific grammars on Germanic languages including Old and Middle High German, Gothic, Saxon, Old English and Middle English.

894.541   FI
SANANJALKA. (Text in Finnish; abstracts in English or German) 1959. a. FIM 160. Suomen Kielen Seura - Finnish Language Society, Fennicum, Henrikinkatu 3, 20500 Turku, Finland. Ed. Aimo Hakanen. adv.; bk.rev.; abstr.; circ. 700. (back issues avail.)
Formerly: Suomen Kielen Seuran Vuosikirja (ISSN 0558-4639)
Description: Focuses on Finnish ethnology, language, literature, folklore and religion.

SARGASSO; theater, film, poetry, performance, criticism. see LITERARY AND POLITICAL REVIEWS

410   MY   ISSN 0127-2721
PL5101
SARI. (Text in English and Malay-Indo) 1983. s-a. $15 per no. Penerbit Universiti Kebangsaan Malaysia, 43600 UKM Bangi, Selangor, Malaysia.
Description: Publishes research results in Malay studies. Includes language, linguistics, dialects, traditional and modern literary studies.

440 375.4   CN
SASKATCHEWAN ASSOCIATION OF TEACHERS OF FRENCH. BULLETIN DE SERVICE. irreg. (3-4/yr.). Can.$15. Saskatchewan Teachers' Federation, Box 1108, Saskatoon, Sask. S7K 3N3, Canada. Ed. Raymond C. Anderson.

440 375.4   RU
SBORNIK STATEI PO FRANTSUZSKOI LINGVISTIKE I METODIKE PREPODAVANIYA INOSTRANNOGO YAZIKA V V U ZE. vol.3, 1971. irreg. 0.35 Rub. Moskovskii Gosudarstvennyi Pedagogicheskii Institut Inostrannykh Yazykov, Rostokinskii pr., 13, Moscow B-14, Russia. bibl.
Description: Presents articles on French language study and teaching.

LINGUISTICS

439 839　　　US　　ISSN 0036-5637
PD1505
SCANDINAVIAN STUDIES (EUGENE). 1911. q. $40 (foreign $45). Society for the Advancement of Scandinavian Study, c/o Prof. Virpi Zuck, Dept. of Germanic Languages and Literatures, University of Oregon, Eugene, OR 97403. TEL 503-346-4054. FAX 503-346-3660. Ed. Steven Sondrup. adv.; bk.rev.; bibl.; circ. 1,000. (also avail. in microform from UMI; reprint service avail. from UMI) **Indexed:** Arts & Hum.Cit.Ind., Curr.Cont., Hist.Abstr., Hum.Ind., Ind.Bk.Rev.Hum., M.L.A.
—BLDSC shelfmark: 8087.650000.
Description: Examines scholarly articles on philological and linguistic problems of medieval and modern Scandinavian languages; the literatures of Denmark, the Faeroes, Finland (Finno-Swedish and Finnish), Iceland, Norway, and Sweden; the history, society and culture of the North.

491.8 891.8　　DK　　ISSN 0080-6765
PG1
SCANDO-SLAVICA. (Text in English, French, German, Italian or Russian) 1955. a. DKK 436. (Association of Scandinavian Slavicists and Baltologists) Munksgaard International Publishers Ltd., 35 Noerre Soegade, P.O. Box 2148, DK-1016 Copenhagen K, Denmark. TEL 33-127030. FAX 33-129387. TELEX 19431-MUNKS-DK. Ed. Gunnar Jacobsson. bk.rev.; index; circ. 600. (reprint service avail. from ISI) **Indexed:** Curr.Cont., M.L.A.
—BLDSC shelfmark: 8087.695000.

430.8 375.4　　US　　ISSN 0740-1965
SCHATZKAMMER; der deutschen Sprache, Dichtung und Geschichte. 1984. bi-a. $15. c/o Werner Kitzler, Mg. Ed., Department of Modern Languages, Univ. of S. Dakota, 414 E. Clark St., Vermillion, SD 57069. TEL 605-677-5401. FAX 605-677-5073. Ed. Pamela Saur. adv.; bk.rev.; circ. 1,000. **Indexed:** Lang.& Lang.Behav.Abstr.
Description: Provides teachers with practical information, especially with regard to classroom application; feature articles, reports, and news items on language, pedagogy, and "Landeskunde" of the German-speaking countries. Includes poems, short works in creative prose, translations by German-American and reference materials.

491.62　　　IE　　ISSN 0790-9853
SCHOOL OF CELTIC STUDIES. NEWSLETTER/SCEALA SCOIL AN LEINN CHEILTIGH. (Text in English and Gaelic) 1987. a. free. Dublin Institute for Advanced Studies, 10 Burlington Rd., Dublin 4, Ireland. TEL 680748. FAX 680561.

SCHOOLS; a guide to private English language schools in the U.K. for foreign students. see EDUCATION — Guides To Schools And Colleges

410　　　GW　　ISSN 0558-9274
SCHRIFTEN ZUR PHONETIK, SPRACHWISSENSCHAFT UND KOMMUNIKATIONSFORSCHUNG. 1960. irreg., vol.7, 1987. Akademie-Verlag Berlin, Leipziger Str. 3-4, 1086 Berlin, Germany. TELEX 114420-AVERL-DD.

430 375　　　UK　　ISSN 0048-9492
SCHUSS. (Text in German) 1963. 6/yr. (during school year). Mary Glasgow Publications Ltd., Avenue House, 131-133 Holland Park Ave., London W11 4UT, England. TEL 071-603 4688. FAX 071-602-5197. TELEX 311890-MGPUBS. (U.S. subscr. to: Delta Systems Co. Inc., 570 Rock Rd. Dr., Dundee, IL 60118-9992) circ. 28,000. (also avail. in microform from UMI; reprint service avail. from UMI, BLH)
Description: Directed to intermediate students of German.

437　　　GW　　ISSN 0933-7024
SCHWAEDDS. 1980. s-a. DM.25. Schwaedds Verlag, Seestr. 11, 7445 Bempflingen 2, Germany. TEL 07123-35409. Ed. Wilhelm Koenig. adv.; bk.rev.; circ. 2,000. (back issues avail.)
Description: Essays, poetry and fiction on German dialects.

400 800　　　GW　　ISSN 0080-7214
SCHWEIZER ANGLISTISCHE ARBEITEN/SWISS STUDIES IN ENGLISH. (Text in German or English) 1935. irreg., no. 115, 1988. price varies. K.G. Saur Verlag KG, Ortlerstr. 8, 8000 Munich 70, Germany. TEL 089-769020. FAX 089-76902150. Ed.Bd. **Indexed:** M.L.A.

439.69 839.69　　SW　　ISSN 0582-3234
DL301
SCRIPTA ISLANDICA. (Text in English and Scandinavian languages) 1949. a. SEK 75. (Islaendska Saellskapet) Almqvist & Wiksell Periodical Company, P.O. Box 638, S-101 28 Stockholm, Sweden. (Co-sponsor: Swedish Council for Research in the Humanities and Social Sciences) Ed. Claes Aaneman. bk.rev.; index; circ. 250.

410　　　US
▼**SECOND LANGUAGE LEARNING.** 1991. irreg. price varies. Ablex Publishing Corporation, 355 Chestnut St., Norwood, NJ 07648. TEL 201-767-8450. FAX 201-767-6717. TELEX 135-393. Ed. Robert J. DiPietro.

410　　　UK　　ISSN 0267-6583
SECOND LANGUAGE RESEARCH. 1985. 3/yr. £33($57) to individuals; institutions £55($88). Edward Arnold (Subsidiary of: Hodder & Stoughton), Mill Road, Dunton Green, Sevenoaks, Kent TN13 2YA, England. TEL 0732-450111. FAX 0732-461321. **Indexed:** Lang.& Lang.Behav.Abstr. (1985-), Lang.Teach.& Ling.Abstr.
—BLDSC shelfmark: 8216.150050.
Supersedes: Interlanguage Studies Bulletin.
Description: Provides a forum for investigators in non-native language learning; seeks to promote interdisciplinary research which links aquisition studies to neighbouring theoretical and experimental disciplines.

SEFARAD; revista de estudios Hebraicos, Sefardies y de Oriente Proximo. see HISTORY — History Of The Near East

410　　　US　　ISSN 0277-0598
PB11
SELECTA (CORVALLIS). (Text in English, French, German, Italian and Spanish) 1950. a. $12. Pacific Northwest Council on Foreign Languages, c/o Foreign Languages & Literatures, Oregon State Univ., Kidd 210, Corvallis, OR 97331-4603. TEL 503-737-3936. Ed. Guy H. Wood. adv.; circ. 750. (also avail. in microfiche) **Indexed:** Amer.Bibl.Slavic & E.Eur.Stud, M.L.A.
—BLDSC shelfmark: 8230.840000.
Former titles: Pacific Northwest Council on Foreign Languages. Proceedings (ISSN 0363-8391); Pacific Northwest Conference on Foreign Languages. Proceedings (ISSN 0078-7612) Pacific Northwest Conference of Foreign Language Teachers. Proceedings.
Description: For language professionals at all levels in Alaska, Alberta, British Columbia, Hawaii, Idaho, Montana, Nevada, Oregon, Utah, Washington, and Wyoming.

439　　　DK　　ISSN 0108-822X
PD1506
SELSKAB FOR NORDISK FILOLOGI. AARSBERETNING. 1934. biennial. DKK 65. Selskab for Nordisk Filologi, Institut for Dansk Dialektforskning, Njalsgde 80, 2300 Copenhagen S, Denmark. Ed. Britta Olrik Frederiksen. circ. 300.

499.992　　　DK　　ISSN 0108-3759
SEMAJNA BULTENO; Europa semajna Esperanto gazeto. (Text in Esperanto) 1976. irreg. (20-25/yr.). DKK 200. Esperanto Domo, Haslevangsvej 30, DK-8210 Aarhus V, Denmark. Ed. Bent Holm. adv.; bk.rev.; illus.
Formerly: Centra Bulteno (ISSN 0108-450X)

SEMEIA; an experimental journal for biblical criticism. see RELIGIONS AND THEOLOGY

SEMINAR; a journal of Germanic studies. see LITERATURE

494.8　　　II
SEMINAR ON DRAVIDIAN LINGUISTICS. PROCEEDINGS. irreg., 5th, 1975. Rs.25($5) Annamalai University, Publications Division, Annamalainagar P.O., Tamil Nadu, India. Eds. S. Agesthialingom, P.S. Subrahmanyam. bibl.; circ. 1,000.

499.92　　　SP　　ISSN 0582-6152
SEMINARIO DE FILOLOGIA VASCA JULIO DE URQUIJO. ANUARIO; international journal of Basque linguistics and philology. (Supplement avail.) (Text in English, French, Spanish) 1967. 3/yr. 2000 ptas. to individuals (foreign 3000 ptas.); institutions 4000 ptas. (foreign 5000 ptas.). Seminario de Filologia Vasca Julio de Urquijo, Palacio de la Diputacion de Guipuzcoa, Apdo. 1792, 20080 San Sebastian (Guipuzcoa), Spain. bk.rev.

499.92　　　SP
SEMINARIO DE FILOLOGIA VASCA JULIO DE URQUIJO. ANUARIO. SUPLEMENTO. 1955. irreg., no. 18, 1990. price varies. Seminario de Filologia Vasca Julio de Urquijo, Palacio de la Diputacion de Guipuzcoa, Apdo. 1792, 20080 San Sebastian, Spain.

SEMIOTEXT(E). see HUMANITIES: COMPREHENSIVE WORKS

410　　　US　　ISSN 0922-5072
SEMIOTIC CROSSROADS. Short title: S C. 1988. irreg., no.3, 1989. price varies. John Benjamins Publishing Co., 821 Bethlehem Pike, Philadelphia, PA 19118. TEL 215-836-1200. FAX 215-836-1204. (And: Amsteldijk 44, P.O. Box 75577, 1070 AN Amsterdam, Netherlands. TEL 020-6762325) Ed.Bd.
—BLDSC shelfmark: 8239.497300.
Description: Covers current semiotic research in France and abroad.

400　　　GW　　ISSN 0037-1998
B820
SEMIOTICA. (Text mainly in English and French; occasionally in German and Russian) 1969. 10/yr. $178 to members; institutions $437. (International Association for Semiotic Studies) Walter de Gruyter und Co., Mouton Publishers, Postfach 110240, 1000 Berlin 11, Germany. TEL 030-26005-0. FAX 030-26005251. TELEX 184027. (U.S. addr.: Mouton de Gruyter, Division of Walter de Gruyter, Inc., 200 Saw Mill River Rd., Hawthorne, NY 10532) Ed. Thomas A. Sebeok. adv.; bk.rev.; cum.index: vols. 1-50; circ. 850. **Indexed:** Arts & Hum.Cit.Ind., Commun.Abstr., Curr.Cont., Film Lit.Ind. (1990-), Ind.Bk.Rev.Hum., Psychol.Abstr., RILA.
—BLDSC shelfmark: 8239.500000.

410　　　US　　ISSN 1054-8386
SEMIOTICS AND THE HUMAN SCIENCES. irreg. price varies. Peter Lang Publishing, Inc., 62 W. 45th St., 4th Fl., New York, NY 10036. TEL 212-302-6740. Ed. Roberta Kevelson.

SEMIOTIQUE ET BIBLE. see RELIGIONS AND THEOLOGY

492　　　GW　　ISSN 0931-2811
SEMITICA VIVA. 1987. irreg., vol.7, 1991. price varies. Verlag Otto Harrassowitz, Taunusstr. 14, Postfach 2929, 6200 Wiesbaden 1, Germany. TEL 0611-530-0. FAX 0611-530570. TELEX 4186135. Ed. Otto Jastrow.

492　　　GW
SEMITICA VIVA - SERIES DIDACTICA. 1989. irreg. price varies. Verlag Otto Harrassowitz, Taunusstr. 14, Postfach 2929, 6200 Wiesbaden 1, Germany. TEL 0611-530-0. FAX 0611-530570. Ed. Otto Jastrow.

460 572 914.6 398　　US
SERIE DE VOCABULARIOS Y DICCIONARIOS INDIGENAS "MARIANO SILVA Y ACEVES". (Text in Spanish) 1959. irreg., no.30, 1987. price varies. Summer Institute of Linguistics, Inc., Academic Publications, 7500 W. Camp Wisdom Rd., Dallas, TX 75236. (Or: Box 8987 CRB, Tucson, AZ 85738) Eds. Doris Bartholmew, Louise Schoenhals. bibl.; circ. 1,000. (also avail. in microform; back issues avail.)

410　　　PE
SERIE LINGUISTICA PERUANA. 1963. irreg., no.29, 1988. price varies. Instituto Linguistico de Verano, Departamento de Estudios Etno-Linguisticos, Casilla 2492, Lima 100, Peru. FAX 5114-629-629. (Subscr. to: E. Iturriaga y Cia., Jiron Ica 441, Ofc. 202-203, Casilla 4640, Lima, Peru) Ed. Mary Ruth Wise. charts. (also avail. in microfiche; back issues avail.) **Indexed:** Lang.& Lang.Behav.Abstr. (1986-), M.L.A.
Description: Covers in depth, various topics in linguistics. Includes morphology, syntax, phonology and comparative linguistics studies.

SERIES IN ENGLISH LANGUAGE AND LITERATURE. see *LITERATURE*

407 II
SERIES IN INDIAN LANGUAGES AND LINGUISTICS. 1972. irreg. price varies. Bahri Publications, 997-A, Street No. 9, Gondpuri, Kalkaji, New Delhi 110 019, India. TEL 644-5710. Ed. Ujjal Shingh Bahri.
   Description: Historical and comparative analyses of Indian languages and literature. Includes teaching materials on Indian languages and scripts.

410 II
▼**SERIES IN INDIAN STUDIES IN THEORETICAL AND APPLIED LINGUISTICS.** (Text in English) 1991. irreg. Bahri Publications, 997-A, Gobindpuri, Kalkaji, P.O. Box 4453, New Delhi 110 019, India. TEL 644-8606. FAX 91-11-64601796. Ed. Rajendra Singh.

410 II
SERIES IN SEMIOTICS AND LINGUISTICS. (Text in English) 1989. irreg. price varies. Bahri Publications, 997-A, Street No. 9, Gobindpuri, Kalkaji, P.O. Box 4453, New Delhi 110 019, India. TEL 644-5710. FAX 91-11-64601796. Ed. Ujjal Singh Bahri.

495.1 375.4 CC
SHIJIE HANYU JIAOXUE/CHINESE TEACHING IN THE WORLD. (Text in Chinese) 1987. q. $24. Beijing Yuyan Xueyuan Chubanshe - Beijing Language Institute Press, Beijing Yuyan Xueyuan, Beijing, People's Republic of China. (Dist. in US by: China Books & Periodicals, Inc., 2929 24th St., San Francisco, CA 94110. TEL 415-282-2994) Ed. Zhu Dexi.

410 CC
SHUOXIE YUEKAN/SPEAKING AND WRITING MONTHLY. (Text in Chinese) m. Beijing Shifan Xueyuan - Beijing Normal Institute, 18 Baiguang Lu, Xuanwu-qu, Beijing 100053, People's Republic of China. TEL 3014150. Ed. Gao Yuan.

410 FR ISSN 0223-0100
P2
SIGMA (AIX-EN-PROVENCE). 1976. a. 98 F. Publications de l'Universite de Provence, 29, av. Robert Schumann, 13621 Aix-en-Provence Cedex 1, France. TEL 42-20-09-16. Ed. Rene Rivara. adv.; bk.rev.; circ. 300.
   —BLDSC shelfmark: 8275.360000.
   Description: Devoted to research in linguistics, especially in the English language.

420 375.4 FR
SIGMA (MONTPELLIER). a. Universite de Montpellier III (Universite Paul Valery), Centre d'Etudes Linguistiques d'Aix-Montpellier, B.P. 5043, 34032 Montpellier Cedex 1, France. TEL 67-14-20-00.
   Description: Features articles contributed by research workers belonging to the English department of the universities, dealing with linguistics, and related subjects.

419 572 US ISSN 0302-1475
HV2350
SIGN LANGUAGE STUDIES. 1972. q. $40 to individuals; institutions $50 (foreign $55). Linstok Press, Inc., 4020 Blackburn Lane, Burtonsville, MD 20865-1167. Ed. William C. Stokoe. adv.; bk.rev.; circ. 485. **Indexed:** A.I.C.P., C.I.J.E., DSH Abstr., ERIC, Except.Child.Educ.Abstr., Lang.Teach.& Ling.Abstr., M.L.A.
   —BLDSC shelfmark: 8275.650000.
   Description: Covers anthropology, linguistics, psychology, sociology as they are related to sign languages and the deaf population.

469 FR
SILLAGES. (Text in French and Portuguese; summaries in English) 1972. a. 15 F.($4.50) Universite de Poitiers, Departement d'Etudes Portugaises et Bresiliennes, 95 Avenue du Recteur Pineau, 86022 Poitiers, France. Ed. R.A. Lawton. circ. 750.
   Description: Presents articles regarding Portuguese language study and teaching.

428 UK ISSN 0950-9585
SIMPLIFIED SPELLING SOCIETY. JOURNAL. 1985. 3/yr. $20. Simplified Spelling Society, 61 Valentine Rd., Birmingham B14 7AJ, England. FAX 021-359-2725. Ed. Christopher Upward. bk.rev.; circ. 200. **Indexed:** Lang.Teach.& Ling.Abstr.
   —BLDSC shelfmark: 4876.350000.
   Former titles (until 1987): Simplified Spelling Society Newsletter (ISSN 0268-5655); Reading and Spelling.
   Description: Contains research on spelling and campaigns for its reform.

SINO-PLATONIC PAPERS. see *HISTORY — History Of Asia*

SISTEMI INTELLIGENTI; rivista quadrimestrale di scienze cognitive e intelligenza artificiale. see *PSYCHOLOGY*

420 375.4 CN
SKYLARK (SASKATOON). 1964. irreg. Can.$15 to non-members. (Saskatchewan English Teachers' Association) Saskatchewan Teachers' Federation, Box 1108, Saskatoon, Sask. S7K 3N3, Canada. TEL 306-565-6291. Eds. Al Forrie, Paddy O'Rourke. bk.rev.; bibl.; circ. 500.
   Description: Covers English language study and teaching.

491 CS ISSN 0037-6736
SLAVIA; casopis pro slovanskou filologii. (Text in English, French, German, Slavic languages) 1922. q. DM.191. (Czechoslovak Academy of Sciences, Institute of Czech and World Literature) Academia, Publishing House of the Czechoslovak Academy of Sciences, Vodickova 40, 112 29 Prague 1, Czechoslovakia. TEL 53-83-69. (Dist. in Western countries by: Kubon & Sagner, P.O. Box 34 01 08, 8000 Munich 34, Germany) Ed. Slavomir Wollman. (also avail. in microfiche from BHP) **Indexed:** Lang.& Lang.Behav.Abstr.
   Description: Comparative Slavonic philology, i.e. comparative Slavonic linguistics and literature (history and poetics). Modern methods of linguistic theory, general literature, poetics and stylistics; documents and information.

490 PL ISSN 0081-0002
SLAVIA OCCIDENTALIS. (Text in Czech, Polish, Russian; summaries in French) 1922. irreg., vol.37, 1980. price varies. (Poznanskie Towarzystwo Przyjaciol Nauk) Panstwowe Wydawnictwo Naukowe, Ul. Miodowa 10, Warsaw, Poland. (Dist. by: Ars Polona-Ruch, Krakowskie Przedmiescie 7, Warsaw, Poland) Ed. Wladyslaw Kuraszkiewicz. **Indexed:** Lang.& Lang.Behav.Abstr.

491 PL ISSN 0037-6744
SLAVIA ORIENTALIS. (Contents page in English and Russian) 1952. q. $32. (Polska Akademia Nauk, Komitet Slowianoznawstwa) Panstwowe Wydawnictwo Naukowe, Ul. Miodowa 10, 00-251 Warsaw, Poland. (Dist. by: Ars Polona-Ruch, Krakowskie Przedmiescie 7, Warsaw, Poland) Ed. Bazyli Bialokozowic. bk.rev.; index; circ. 580. **Indexed:** Hist.Abstr., M.L.A.

410 375 US ISSN 0037-6752
SLAVIC AND EAST EUROPEAN JOURNAL. Abbreviated title: S E E J. 1957. q. $20 to members. American Association of Teachers of Slavic and East European Languages, c/o Prof. George Gutsche, Russian - Modern Languages 340, University of Arizona, Tucson, AZ 85721. TEL 602-621-1615. Ed. Ernest Scatton. adv.; bk.rev.; index; circ. 2,100. (also avail. in microform from UMI; back issues avail.) **Indexed:** Amer.Bibl.Slavic & E.Eur.Stud, Arts & Hum.Cit.Ind., C.I.J.E., Curr.Cont., Hum.Ind., Ind.Bk.Rev.Hum., Lang.& Lang.Behav.Abstr., Lang.Teach.& Ling.Abstr., M.L.A.
   —BLDSC shelfmark: 8309.383000.

400 800 SW ISSN 0081-0010
SLAVICA GOTHOBURGENSIA. (Subseries of Acta Universitatis Gothoburgensis) 1958. irreg., no.7, 1980. price varies; also exchange basis. Acta Universitatis Gothoburgensis, Box 5096, S-402 22 Goeteborg, Sweden. Ed. Gunnar Jacobsson.
   —BLDSC shelfmark: 8309.387500.

491.8 891.8 SW ISSN 0346-8712
SLAVICA LUNDENSIA. (Text in English, German, Slavic and Swedish; summaries in English and Russian) 1973. a. price varies. Lunds Universitet, Slaviska Institutionen, Finngatan 13, S-223 62 Lund, Sweden. Ed. Lubomir Durovic. circ. 400. (also avail. in microfilm from UMI; back issues avail.)

LINGUISTICS 2841

491 DK ISSN 0106-1313
PG1
SLAVICA OTHINIENSIA. (Text in English, French, German or Russian) 1978. a. free. Odense Universitet, Slaviske Institut, Odense, Denmark. FAX 66-15-84-28. Ed.Bd. bk.rev.

491 891 CS ISSN 0037-6787
SLAVICA SLOVACA. (Text in Slavic languages and in English, French or German; summaries in French, German, Russian) 1966. q. 60 Kcs.($18) (Slovenska Akademia Vied, Jazykovedny Ustav) Veda, Publishing House of the Slovak Academy of Sciences, Klemensova 19, 814 30 Bratislava, Czechoslovakia. (Dist. in Western countries by: John Benjamins B.V., Amsteldijk 44, P.O. Box 75577, 1070 AN Amsterdam, Netherlands. TEL 020-6762325) Ed. Jozef Ruricka. **Indexed:** Can.Rev.Comp.Lit.
   Description: Covers literary and linguistic problems. For scientists in the field of Slavistics, Slovak language theachers at secondary school.

491 890 XV ISSN 0350-6894
SLAVISTICNA REVIJA; journal for linguistics and literary sciences. (Text in Slovenian; summaries in English, German) 1948. q. $8. Slavisticno Drustvo Slovenije, c/o Filozofska Fakulteta, Askerceva 12, YU-61000 Ljubljana, Slovenia. TEL 061-150-337. FAX 061-159-337. Ed. Franc Zadravec. bk.rev.; bibl.; circ. 1,200. **Indexed:** M.L.A., Sociol.Abstr.

SLAVISTISCHE BEITRAEGE. see *LITERATURE*

491.8 GW ISSN 0583-5445
SLAVISTISCHE STUDIENBUECHER. NEUE FOLGE. 1984. irreg., vol.3, 1989. price varies. Verlag Otto Harrassowitz, Taunusstr. 14, Postfach 2929, 6200 Wiesbaden 1, Germany. TEL 0611-530-0. FAX 0611-530570. TELEX 4186135. Ed.Bd.

490 RU
SLAVYANSKAYA FILOLOGIYA. 1964. irreg. 0.72 Rub. Leningradskii Universitet, Universitetskaya nab. 7-9, St. Petersburg B-164, Russia. bibl.

SLOVACI V ZAHRANICI. see *HISTORY — History Of Europe*

SLOVENE STUDIES. see *HISTORY — History Of Europe*

491.87 891.87 CS ISSN 0037-6981
PG5201
SLOVENSKA REC/SLOVAK LANGUAGE; casopis pre vyskum a kulturu slovenskeho jazyka. 1933. bi-m. 48 Kcs.($16) (Slovenska Akademia Vied, Jazykovedny Ustav L. Stura) Veda, Publishing House of the Slovak Academy of Sciences, Klemensova 19, 814 30 Bratislava, Czechoslovakia. (Dist. in Western countries by: John Benjamins B.V., Amsteldijk 44, P.O. Box 75577, 1070 AN Amsterdam, Netherlands. TEL 020-676-2325) Ed. Frantisek Kocis. bk.rev.; index; circ. 3,000. **Indexed:** Lang.& Lang.Behav.Abstr., M.L.A.
   Description: Devoted to the research of Slovak literary language, correct pronunciation, grammatical structure, word stock and stylistic problems.

400 CS
SLOVENSKY JAZYK A LITERATURA V SKOLE. 10/yr. 20 Kcs. (Ministerstvo Skolstva Slovenskej Republiky) Slovenske Pedagogicke Nakladatelstvo, Sasinkova 5, 815 60 Bratislava, Czechoslovakia. Ed. Juraj Koutun. circ. 4,500.

491.8 CS ISSN 0037-7031
SLOVO A SLOVESNOST/WORD AND WRITING; casopis pro otazky teorie a kultury jazyka. (Text mainly in Czech; summaries in English, French, German, Russian) 1935. q. DM.124. (Czechoslovak Academy of Sciences, Institute for Czech Language) Academia, Publishing House of the Czechoslovak Academy of Sciences, Vodickova 40, 112 29 Prague 1, Czechoslovakia. TEL 53-93-51. (Dist. in Western countries by: Kubon & Sagner, P.O. Box 34 01 08, 8000 Munich 34, Germany) Ed. Marie Tesitelova. bk.rev.; bibl.; charts; illus.; stat.; index, cum.index; circ. 1,400. **Indexed:** M.L.A.
   —BLDSC shelfmark: 8309.890000.
   Description: Problems at the grammatical, lexical, phonemic and phonetic levels; problems of stylistics, semantics and semiotics, of text theory and communication theory, problems of translation and theory of verse.

LINGUISTICS

491.79 CN ISSN 0583-6263
SLOVO NA STOROZHI/WORD ON GUARD. 1964. a. Can.$6($6) Ukrainian Language Association, 911 Carling Ave., Ottawa, Ont., Canada. TEL 613-225-4447. Ed. J.B. Rudnyckyj. adv.; bk.rev.; circ. 500. (back issues avail.) **Indexed:** M.L.A.

SOCIEDAD DE ESTUDIOS VASCOS. CUADERNOS DE SECCION. LENGUA Y LITERATURA. see *LITERATURE*

469 PO ISSN 0049-1039
SOCIEDADE DE LINGUA PORTUGUESA. BOLETIM. vol.26, 1975. bi-m. Esc.300. Sociedade de Lingua Portuguesa, Rua S. Jose 41-2, Lisbon, Portugal. Eds. Guilherme Matos, Aldina de Araujo Oliveira. adv.; bk.rev.; abstr.; bibl.; circ. 7,000.

490 GW ISSN 0340-6423
SOCIETAS URALO-ALTAICA. VEROEFFENTLICHUNGEN. 1969. irreg., vol.34, 1991. price varies. Verlag Otto Harrassowitz, Taunusstr. 14, Postfach 2929, 6200 Wiesbaden 1, Germany. TEL 0611-530-0. FAX 0611-530570. TELEX 4186135. Eds. A.V. Gabain, W. Veenker.

475 SP ISSN 0213-4098
SOCIETAT D'ONOMASTICA. BUTLLETI INTERIOR. (Text in Catalan; occasionally in French or Spanish) 1980. q. membership. Societat d'Onomastica, Enric Granados 26-28 (6-6), 08008 Barcelona, Spain. TEL 93-218-5034. Ed. E. Moreu Rey. bk.rev.
Description: Lists the works and research projects of the society's members in the field of onomastics.

410 301.2 FR ISSN 0249-7069
SOCIETE D'ETUDES LINGUISTIQUES ET ANTHROPOLOGIQUES DE FRANCE. NUMEROS SPECIAUX. 1971. irreg. price varies. Societe d'Etudes Linguistiques et Anthropologiques de France (SELAF), 5 rue de Marseille, 75010 Paris, France. TEL 42-08-83-93.

SOCIETE DE BIBLIOLOGIE ET DE SCHEMATISATION. ALMANACH. see *LITERATURE*

406 FR ISSN 0037-9069
P12
SOCIETE DE LINGUISTIQUE DE PARIS. BULLETIN. (Text in English and French) 1865. s-a. price varies. Editions Klincksieck, 11 rue de Lille, 75005 Paris, France. bk.rev.; abstr.; charts; index; circ. 1,200. (also avail. in microform from BHP) **Indexed:** M.L.A.

SOCIETE DES AMERICANISTES. JOURNAL. see *ANTHROPOLOGY*

SOCIETE FINNO-OUGRIENNE. MEMOIRES/SUOMALAIS-UGRILAISEN SEURAN. TOIMITUKSIA. see *ANTHROPOLOGY*

400 FI ISSN 0355-0192
PB10
SOCIETE NEOPHILOLOGIQUE DE HELSINKI. MEMOIRES. (Text in English, French, German) 1893. irreg. price varies. Modern Language Society of Helsinki, Hallituskatu 11-13, 00100 Helsinki, Finland. Ed.Bd. cum.index; circ. 500. (back issues avail.)

SOCIETY FOR SLOVENE STUDIES. DOCUMENTATION SERIES. see *HISTORY — History Of Europe*

410 US
SOCIETY OF FEDERAL LINGUISTS. NEWSLETTER. 1946. irreg., approx. 9/yr. membership. Society of Federal Linguists, Inc., Box 7765, Washington, DC 20044. Ed. E.E. Larson. bk.rev.; circ. 150 (controlled).

410 572 FR
SOCIOLINGUISTIQUE; systemes de langues et interactions sociales et culturelles. 1984. irreg. price varies. Societe d'Etudes Linguistiques et Anthropologiques de France (SELAF), 5 rue de Marseille, 75010 Paris, France. TEL 42-08-83-93. Ed. Jean Pierre Caprile. adv.; bk.rev.; circ. 500.

410 PL ISSN 0208-6808
SOCJOLINGWISTYKA. (Text in Polish; summaries in English, Russian) 1977. a. price varies. (Polish Academy of Science, Institute of Polish Language) Ossolineum, Publishing House of the Polish Academy of Sciences, Rynek 9, 50-106 Wroclaw, Poland. TEL 386025. TELEX 0712771 OSS PL. (Dist. by: Ars Polona, Krakowskie Przedmiescie 7, 00-068 Warsaw, Poland) Ed. Wladyslaw Lubas.
Description: Studies on social aspects on linguistics and verbal communications.

410 BU
SOFIISKI UNIVERSITET. FAKULTET PO KLASICESKI I NOVI FILOLOGII. GODISNIK/UNIVERSITE DE SOFIA. FACULTE DES LETTRES CLASSIQUES ET MODERNES. ANNUAIRE. (Text in various languages) irreg., vol.71, 1976. price varies. Publishing House of the Bulgarian Academy of Sciences, Acad. G. Bonchev St., Bldg. 6, 1113 Sofia, Bulgaria. bibl.; circ. 550.
Formerly: Sofiiski Universitet. Fakultet po Zapadni Filologii. Godisnik (ISSN 0584-0252)

491 BU ISSN 0081-1831
PG1
SOFIISKI UNIVERSITET. FAKULTET PO SLAVIANSKA FILOLOGIIA. GODISHNIK. (Text in various languages) irreg., vol.63, 1970. price varies. Publishing House of the Bulgarian Academy of Sciences, Acad. G. Bonchev St., Bldg. 6, 1113 Sofia, Bulgaria. Ed. I. Duridanov. bibl.; circ. 550.

460.07 370 UK ISSN 0038-0849
EL SOL. (Text in Spanish) 1963. 6/yr. (during school year). Mary Glasgow Publications Ltd., Avenue House, 131-133 Holland Park Ave., London W11 4UT, England. TEL 071-603 4688. FAX 071-602-5197. TELEX 311890-MGPUBS. (U.S. subscr. to: Delta Systems Co. Inc., 570 Rock Rd. Dr., Dundee, IL 60118-9992) charts; illus.; circ. 28,000. (also avail. in microfilm from UMI; reprint service avail. from UMI)
Description: Spanish language magazine for intermediate level students.

410 CH ISSN 0259-3777
P9
SOOCHOW JOURNAL OF FOREIGN LANGUAGES AND LITERATURES. (Text in Chinese, English, German, and Japanese) 1985. a. $15. Soochow University, Soochow University Library, Wai Shuang Hsi, Shih Lin, Taipei, Taiwan, Republic of China. FAX 886-02-8829310. (reprint service avail.) Key Title: Dongwu Waiyu Xuebao.

440 375.4 US
SOUND AND MEANING; the Roman Jakobson series in linguistics and poetry. 1989. irreg. Duke University, 6697 College Station, Durham, NC 27708. TEL 919-684-2173. FAX 919-684-8644. Ed. C.H. Van Schooneveld.

496 896 SA ISSN 0257-2117
CODEN: SAJLEA
SOUTH AFRICAN JOURNAL OF AFRICAN LANGUAGES. (Text in English) 1981. q. R.48($35) (African Languages Association of Southern Africa) Bureau for Scientific Publications, P.O. Box 1758, Pretoria 0001, South Africa. TEL 12-322-6422. Ed. L.J. Louwrens. circ. 620. **Indexed:** Ind.S.A.Per., Sp.Ed.Needs Abstr.

439.3 420 SA ISSN 1011-8063
SOUTH AFRICAN JOURNAL OF LINGUISTICS/SUID-AFRIKANNSE TYDSKRIF VIR TAALKUNDE. (Text and summaries in Afrikaans, English) 1983. q. R.48($35) (Linguistics Association of South Africa) Bureau for Scientific Publications, P.O. Box 1758, Pretoria 0001, South Africa. TEL 012-322-6422. Ed. G.J. van Jaarsveld. adv.; bk.rev.; circ. 300. (back issues avail.)
Formerly: Taalfassette.
Description: Aims to propriate the study of research into Afrikaans, English and Dutch linguistics in South Africa.

SOUTH ASIAN REVIEW. see *LITERATURE*

406 US ISSN 0277-335X
PB1
SOUTH ATLANTIC REVIEW. 1935. 4/yr. $15 to individuals; institutions $45; libraries $30. South Atlantic Modern Language Association, Drawer 6109, Univ. Sta., Tuscaloosa, AL 35486-6109. FAX 205-348-9642. Ed. Robert F. Bell. adv.; bk.rev.; bibl.; index; circ. 4,300. (also avail. in microform from UMI; reprint service avail. from ISI,UMI) **Indexed:** Abstr.Engl.Stud., Amer.Bibl.Slavic & E.Eur.Stud, Amer.Hum.Ind., Arts & Hum.Cit.Ind., Curr.Cont., M.L.A.
—BLDSC shelfmark: 8348.672000.
Formerly (until 1981): South Atlantic Bulletin.

428.3 US
PN4071
SOUTHERN COMMUNICATION JOURNAL. 1935. q. $15. Southern States Communication Association, c/o Susan A. Siltanen, Exec. Sec., Box 5131, Univ. of So. Mississippi, Hatttiesburg, MS 39406. Ed. Keith Erickson. adv.; bk.rev.; illus.; index; circ. 2,500. (also avail. in microform from KTO,UMI; reprint service avail. from KTO) **Indexed:** Abstr.Engl.Stud., C.I.J.E., Commun.Abstr., Hist.Abstr., Ind.Bk.Rev.Hum., Lang.& Lang.Behav.Abstr.
Former titles: Southern States Communication Journal (ISSN 1041-794X); Southern Speech Communication Journal (ISSN 0361-8269); Southern Speech Journal (ISSN 0038-4585)

410 US ISSN 0737-4143
P1
SOUTHWEST JOURNAL OF LINGUISTICS. (With occasional supplemental issues) 1975. a. $9.50 per no. University of North Texas and Linguistics Association of the Southwest, University of North Texas, Department of English, Denton, TX 76203-3827. TEL 817-565-2147. (Subscr. to: Donald E. Hardy, LASSO, Dept. of English, U of N. Texas, Denton, TX 76203-3827) Ed. Heather Hardy. adv.; bk.rev.; circ. 300. **Indexed:** Abstr.Anthropol., Lang.& Lang.Behav.Abstr. (1975-), M.L.A.
Formerly: Linguistic Association of the Southwest. Journal.
Description: Covers articles on all areas of linguistics.

SPANISH STUDIES; modern literature, history and politics. see *LITERATURE*

460 US ISSN 0049-1802
SPANISH TODAY. (Text in English and Spanish) 1968. bi-m. $15. Cruzada Spanish Publications, Box 650909, Miami, FL 33265. Ed. Andres Rivero. adv.; bk.rev.; charts; illus.; tr.lit.; circ. 10,000. (also avail. in microform from UMI; reprint service avail. from UMI)

460 DK ISSN 0109-307X
SPANSKLAERERFORENINGEN. INFORMATIONER. no.6, 1981. q. membership. Spansklaererforeningen, c/o Birgit Christiansen, Overgaden oven Vandet 102l, 1415 Copenhagen K, Denmark. adv.; illus.; circ. 250.
Description: Covers Spanish language study and teaching.

407 US
SPEAKOUT. 1973. m. membership. National Speakers Association, 1500 S. Priest Dr., Tempe, AZ 85281-6203. TEL 602-968-2552. Ed. Evangeline Ysmael. adv.; bk.rev.; circ. 3,800.
Description: Information, trends and ideas on professional speaking.

491.7 890 GW ISSN 0170-1320
SPECIMINA PHILOLOGIAE SLAVICAE. (Text in English, German, Russian and other Slavic languages) 1972. irreg. price varies. Verlag Otto Sagner, Postfach 340108, 8000 Munich 34, Germany. TEL 089-522027. TELEX 5216711-KUSAD. Eds. Olexa Horbatsch, Gerd Freihof. circ. 100. (back issues avail.)

440 FR
SPICAE; cahiers de l'atelier Vincent de Beauvais. 1978. irreg. price varies. (Universite de Nancy II, Centre de Recherches et d'Applications Linguistiques) Editions du C N R S, 1 Place Aristide Briand, 92195 Meudon Cedex, France. TEL 1-45-34-75-50. FAX 1-46-26-28-49. TELEX LABOBEL 204 315 F. (Subscr. to: Presses du C N R S, 20-22, rue Saint Amand, 75015 Paris, France. TEL 1-45-33-16-00) (Co-sponsor: Institut de Recherche et d'Histoire des Textes) Eds. Helene Nais, Jean Schneider. adv.; bk.rev.; index; circ. 1,500 (controlled).

420.07 370 UK ISSN 0038-772X
LB1576.A1 CODEN: SPEGE7
SPOKEN ENGLISH; ideas and developments in oral education. 1968. 3/yr. £14. English Speaking Board (International) Ltd., 26a Princes Street, Southport, Merseyside PR8 1EQ, England. TEL 0704-501730. Ed. Margaret Edwards. adv.; bk.rev.; bibl.; charts; cum.index every 5 yrs.; circ. 1,200. **Indexed:** Lang.Teach.& Ling.Abstr.
—BLDSC shelfmark: 8417.600000.
Description: Covers English language study and teaching, ideas and developments in oral education, and training in oral communication.

418.02   BU   ISSN 0204-8701
PG831
S'POSTAVITELNO EZIKOZNANIE/CONTRASTIVE LINGUISTICS. (Text in Bulgarian, English, French, German, Russian) 1976. 6/yr. $24. Sofiiski Universitet Kliment Ohridski, 15 Ruski Blvd., Sofia 1040, Bulgaria. (Dist. by: Hemus, Foreign Trade Organization, 6 Levski Str., 1000 Sofia, Bulgaria) Ed. Zivko Bojadziev. adv.; bk.rev.; bibl.; circ. 1,000. **Indexed:** Lang.& Lang.Behav.Abstr. (1978-), M.L.A. —BLDSC shelfmark: 0166.573000.
    Description: Publishes articles, review-articles and news-items in the fields of contrastive linguistics, the theory and practice of translation and history of linguistics.

410   NO   ISSN 0333-3825
SPRAAKNYTT. 1973. q. free. Norsk Spraakraad - Norwegian Language Council, Postboks 8107 Dep, 0032 Oslo 1, Norway. TEL 02-42-40-20. FAX 02-42-76-76. Eds. Egil Pettersen, Kjell Venaas. bk.rev.; circ. 18,000.
    Description: Presents articles about Norway's two official languages (Nynorsk and Bokmaal); information about new words and approved spellings, and readers' questions.

400   SW   ISSN 0038-8440
PD5004
SPRAAKVAARD. (Text in Danish, Norwegian, Swedish) 1965. q. SEK 90 (typically set in Jan.). Svenska Spraaknaemnden, Lundagatan 42, S-117 27 Stockholm, Sweden. TEL 46-8-720-6805. FAX 46-8-720-6805. TELEX 46-8-668-0150. Ed. Margareta Westman. bk.rev.; cum.index; circ. 5,000. (back issues avail.)
    Description: Treats the changes and the evaluation of changes in modern Swedish.

400   GW   ISSN 0038-8459
SPRACHDIENST. 1957. bi-m. DM.60. Gesellschaft fuer deutsche Sprache e.V., Taunusstr. 11, Postfach 2669, 6200 Wiesbaden 1, Germany. TEL 0611-520031. FAX 0611-51313. Ed. H. Walther. adv.; bk.rev.; index, cum.index: 1957-1972; circ. 3,200. **Indexed:** M.L.A.

400   GW   ISSN 0038-8467
DIE SPRACHE; Zeitschrift fuer Sprachwissenschaft. (Text in English, French, German) 1949. 2/yr. price varies. Verlag Otto Harrassowitz, Taunusstr. 14, Postfach 2929, 6200 Wiesbaden 1, Germany. TEL 0611-530-0. FAX 0611-530570. TELEX 4186135. Eds. Jochem Schindler, Martin Peters. adv.; bk.rev.; charts; illus.; index; circ. 450. (reprint service avail. from SWZ) **Indexed:** Lang.& Lang.Behav.Abstr. (1972-), Numis.Lit.

400   SZ   ISSN 0081-3826
SPRACHE UND DICHTUNG. NEUE FOLGE. 1956. irreg., vol.41, 1990. price varies. Paul Haupt AG, Falkenplatz 14, 3001 Berne, Switzerland. TEL 031-232425. Ed.Bd. **Indexed:** M.L.A.

496   GW   ISSN 0170-5946
PL8000
SPRACHE UND GESCHICHTE IN AFRIKA. Short title: S U G I A. (Text in English, French, German) 1979. irreg., approx. a. price varies. (Universitaet Bayreuth, Koeln, Institut fuer Afrikanistik) Helmut Buske Verlag Hamburg, Friedrichsgaber Weg 138, Postfach 1249, 2000 Norderstedt, Germany.

400 943   GW   ISSN 0138-5852
SPRACHE UND GESELLSCHAFT. 1974. irreg., vol.20, 1987. price varies. (Akademie der Wissenschaften, Zentralinstitut fuer Sprachwissenschaft) Akademie-Verlag Berlin, Leipziger Str. 3-4, 1086 Berlin, Germany. TELEX 114420-AVERL-DD. adv.
    Formerly: Akademie der Wissenschaften, Berlin. Zentralinstitut fuer Sprachwissenschaft. Schriften (ISSN 0065-5260)

410   GW   ISSN 0047-472X
P51
SPRACHE UND LITERATUR IN WISSENSCHAFT. 1970. s-a. DM.40. Ferdinand Schoeningh, Juehenplatz 1-3, 4790 Paderborn, Germany. TEL 05251-29010. FAX 05251-2901-35. TELEX 936929-FS-PB. Ed. Annamaria Rucktaeschel. adv.; bk.rev.; bibl. **Indexed:** Lang.& Lang.Behav.Abstr., Lang.Teach.& Ling.Abstr., M.L.A.
    Formerly (until 1978): Linguistik und Didaktik (Paderborn)
    Description: Publication devoted to studies in language and linguistics, including language interpretation and use of speech.

430 830   GW
SPRACHE UND LITERATUR IN WISSENSCHAFT UND UNTERRICHT. s-a. DM.40. Wilhelm Fink Verlag, Ohmstr. 5, 8000 Munich 40, Germany. (Co-publisher: Ferdinand Schoeningh Verlag) Ed.Bd. index; circ. 2,000. (back issues avail.) **Indexed:** Can.Rev.Comp.Lit.
    Formerly: Linguistik und Didaktik (Munich) (ISSN 0724-9713)

400   GW   ISSN 0038-8505
PB38.G39
DER SPRACHMITTLER; Informationshefte des Sprachendienstes der Bundeswehr. 1963. q. free. Bundesministerium der Verteidigung, S III 4, Postfach 1328, 5300 Bonn, Germany. Ed.Bd. bk.rev.; bibl.; charts; circ. 2,200. **Indexed:** Lang.Teach.& Ling.Abstr.
    —BLDSC shelfmark: 8419.880000.

SPRACHPRAXIS; Arbeitsmaterial fuer Deutsch lernende Auslaender. see EDUCATION — Adult Education

430   GW   ISSN 0178-644X
SPRACHREPORT; Informationen und Meinungen zur deutschen Sprache. 1986. q. DM.16. Institut fuer Deutsche Sprache, Mannheim, Postfach 101621, 6800 Mannheim, Germany. TEL 0621-44010. FAX 0621-4401200. bk.rev.; circ. 2,000. (back issues avail.)
    Description: Information about German language, communication and linguistics for non-linguists.

430   SZ   ISSN 0038-8513
PF3003
SPRACHSPIEGEL; Schweizerische Zeitschrift fuer die deutsche Muttersprache. 1945. bi-m. 45 SFr. Deutschschweizerischer Sprachverein, Alpenstr. 7, CH-6004 Lucerne, Switzerland. Ed. Werner Frick. adv.; bk.rev.; index; circ. 1,400. **Indexed:** M.L.A.

410   GW
SPRACHWISSENSCHAFT. 1977. q. DM.135 (student price DM.110). Carl Winter Universitaetsverlag GmbH, Lutherstr. 59, 6900 Heidelberg, Germany. Ed.Bd. **Indexed:** Arts & Hum.Cit.Ind., M.L.A.

410   US   ISSN 0172-620X
SPRINGER SERIES IN LANGUAGE AND COMMUNICATION. 1978. irreg. price varies. Springer-Verlag, 175 Fifth Ave., New York, NY 10010. TEL 212-460-1500. (Also Berlin, Heidelberg, Tokyo and Vienna) Ed. W.J.M. Levelt. (reprint service avail. from ISI)

407   DK
SPROG OG ERHVERV.* 1975. 12/yr. free. Erhvervssprogligt Forbund, Jydeholmen 15, DK-2720 Vanloese, Denmark. Ed. Jorgen Nielsen. adv.; bk.rev.; circ. 4,000.

410   DK   ISSN 0108-433X
SPROG OG SAMFUND. 1983. q. DKK 50. Modersmaal Selskabet, c/o Grethe Rostboell, Ryslinge Hoejskole, DK-5856 Ryslinge, Denmark. Ed. Rasmus Bjoergmose. bk.rev.
    Description: Articles, news, reviews relating to the activities of the Mothertongue Society and the Danish language in general.

410   DK
SPROGFORENINGENS ALMANAK. 1984. a. DKK 38. (Sprogforeningen) Dy-Po Bogforlag, Soenderborg, Denmark. (Dist. by: Boghendlers Kommissionsanstalt, Siljangade 6, 2300 Copenhagen S, Denmark)

491.1 891.1   II   ISSN 0081-3915
SRI VENKATESWARA UNIVERSITY. DEPARTMENT OF SANSKRIT. SYMPOSIUM. (Text in Sanskrit and English) 1962. irreg., no.4, 1967. Rs.4. Sri Venkateswara University, Department of Sanskrit, Tirupati, Andhra Pradesh, India. Ed. E.R. Sreekrishna Sarma.

SRI VENKATESWARA UNIVERSITY. ORIENTAL JOURNAL. see HISTORY — History Of Asia

400   YU   ISSN 0081-3958
SRPSKA AKADEMIJA NAUKA I UMETNOSTI. ODELJENJE JEZIKA I KNJIZEVNOSTI. GLAS. (Text in Serbo-Croatian; summaries in French, English, German or Russian) N.S. 1951. irreg. price varies. Srpska Akademija Nauka i Umetnosti, Knez Mihailova 35, 11001 Belgrade, Serbia, Yugoslavia. FAX 38-11-182-825. TELEX 72593 SANU YU. (Dist. by: Prosveta, Terazije 16, Belgrade, Serbia, Yugoslavia) circ. 1,000. **Indexed:** Amer.Hist.& Life, Hist.Abstr.

SRPSKA AKADEMIJA NAUKA I UMETNOSTI. ODELJENJE JEZIKA I KNJIZEVNOSTI. POSEBNA IZDANJA. see LITERATURE

407   YU   ISSN 0350-1906
SRPSKI DIJALEKTOLOSKI ZBORNIK. (Text in Serbo-Croatian, English, French, German, Russian) 1905. a. 1000 din.($34) Srpska Akademija Nauka i Umetnosti, Institut za Srpskohrvatski Jezik - Serbian Academy of Sciences and Arts, Knez Mihailova 35, 11000 Belgrade, Serbia, Yugoslavia. TEL 011-636-590. Ed. Pavle Ivic. bk.rev.; circ. 800. (back issues avail.)
    Description: Papers about Serbo-Croatian languages, other languages spoken in Yugoslavia, Slavic linguistics and general linguistics.

STIPENDIEN FUER SPRACHKURSE. see CHILDREN AND YOUTH — For

420   SW
STOCKHOLM STUDIES IN ENGLISH. (Subseries of Acta Universitatis Stockholmiensis) (Text in English) 1937. irreg., vol.76, 1988. price varies. (Stockholms Universitet) Almqvist & Wiksell International, Box 638, S-101 28 Stockholm, Sweden. Eds. Alarik Rynell, Lennart A. Bjork. (back issues avail.) **Indexed:** M.L.A.

400   CI
STRANI JEZICI. 1972. q. 240 din. (Hrvatsko Filolosko Drustvo, Institut za Lingvistiku) Skolska Knjiga, Masarykova 28, Zagreb, Croatia. TEL 41 458-511. Ed. Mirjana Vilke. adv.; bk.rev.; illus.; index; circ. 2,600. **Indexed:** Lang.Teach.& Ling.Abstr.

410 800   UK   ISSN 0261-099X
STRATHCLYDE MODERN LANGUAGE STUDIES. 1981. a. £3.50. University of Strathclyde, Department of Modern Languages, 26 Richmond St., Livingstone Tower, Glasgow G1 1XH, Scotland. TEL 041-552-4400. FAX 041-552-0775. Eds. D. Johnston, G. Martin. cum.index; circ. 150. (back issues avail.)
    —BLDSC shelfmark: 8474.047860.
    Description: Articles on European and American literature, languages and culture, and linguistics. Partly based on research seminars.

410   IT   ISSN 0391-1942
STRUMENTI LINGUISTICI. 1975. irreg., no.16, 1988. price varies. Liguori Editore s.r.l., Via Mezzocannone 19, 80134 Naples, Italy. TEL 081-5227139. Ed. Gianfranco Folena.

491.9 891.9   IT   ISSN 0081-6116
STUDI ALBANESI. STUDI E TESTI. 1965. irreg., no.6, 1986. price varies. (Universita degli Studi di Roma, Istituto Studi Albanesi) Casa Editrice Leo S. Olschki, Casella Postale 66, 50100 Florence, Italy. TEL 055-6530684. FAX 055-6530214. Ed. Ernesto Koliqi. circ. 1,000.

410   IT
STUDI DI FILOLOGIA ITALIANA. 1927. a., vol.45, 1987. L.40,000 (foreign L.60000). (Accademia della Crusca) Licosa S.p.A, Via Lamarmora 45, 50121 Florence, Italy.

410   IT
STUDI DI GRAMMATICA ITALIANA. 1971. a., vol.12, 1983. L.35,000 (foreign L.50000). (Accademia della Crusca) Licosa S.p.A, Via Lamarmora 45, 50121 Florence, Italy. **Indexed:** Lang.& Lang.Behav.Abstr. (1977-).

410   IT
STUDI DI LESSICOGRAFIA ITALIANA. 1979. a. L.42000 (foreign L.60000). (Accademia della Crusca) Licosa S.p.A, Via Lamarmora 45, 50121 Florence, Italy.

LINGUISTICS

450   IT   ISSN 0049-2361
P47
STUDI E PROBLEMI DI CRITICA TESTUALE. 1970. s-a. L.18000. Via Castiglione 8, 40124 Bologna, Italy. Ed. R. Raffaele Spongano. adv.; bk.rev.; bibl.; circ. 600. **Indexed:** Arts & Hum.Cit.Ind., Curr.Cont., M.L.A.

410   IT   ISSN 0085-6827
STUDI E SAGGI LINGUISTICI; supplemento alla rivista l'Italia dialettale. (Text in Italian; summaries in English) 1961. a. L.10000. (Universita degli Studi di Pisa, Istituto di Glottologia) Giardini Editori e Stampatori, Via Santa Bibbiana 28, Pisa, Italy. TEL 050 502531. Ed. Tristano Bolelli. index; circ. 350. **Indexed:** M.L.A.

440   IT   ISSN 0039-2944
PQ5
STUDI FRANCESI; cultura e civilta letteraria della Francia. (Text in English, French, Italian) 1957. 3/yr. L.104000 (Europe L.134000; elsewhere L.184000). (Universita degli Studi di Torino, Facolta di Lettere e Filosofia, Istituto di Lingua e Letteratura Francese) Rosenberg & Sellier, Via Andrea Doria 14, 10123 Turin, Italy. TEL 011-561-39-07. FAX 011-532188. Ed. Giorgio Calcagno. bk.rev.; abstr.; circ. 1,250. (back issues avail.) **Indexed:** Arts & Hum.Cit.Ind., CERDIC, Curr.Cont., M.L.A.
Description: Covers French civilization and culture. Includes historic studies, French literature and research.

450   IT   ISSN 0039-2987
PA9
STUDI ITALIANI DI FILOLOGIA CLASSICA. 1893; N.S. 1920. s-a. L.35000($95) (effective 1992). Editoriale e Finanziaria Le Monnier, S.p.a., Via A. Meucci 2, Casella Postale 202, 50100 Florence, Italy. Dirs. Umberto Albini, Marcello Gigante. index. (also avail. in microform from SWZ; reprint service avail. from SWZ)
Description: Covers Classical studies; evaluates how the classical period is related historically to the present.

450   IT   ISSN 0390-6809
STUDI ITALIANI DI LINGUISTICA TEORICA ED APPLICATA. (Text in English, French or Italian) 1972. 3/yr. L.65000. (Universita degli Studi di Bologna, Centro Interfacolta de Linguistica Teorica e Applicata) Liviana Editrice s.r.l., Via Luigi Dottesio 1, 35100 Padua, Italy. TEL 049-8710099. FAX 049-8710261. Ed. Enrico Arcaini. bk.rev.; bibl.; circ. 1,500. **Indexed:** Lang.& Lang.Behav.Abstr. (1972-), Lang.Teach.& Ling.Abstr., M.L.A.

400   IT
STUDI LATINI E ITALIANI. 1986. a. $50. (Universita di Roma "La Sapienza", Facolta di Magistero) Herder Editrice e Libreria s.r.l., Piazza Montecitorio, 120, 00186 Rome, Italy. TEL 67-94628. FAX 678-47-51. TELEX 66784751. Ed. V. Ussani. circ. 500.

450   IT
STUDI LINGUISTICI SALENTINI.* 1965. Associazione Linguistica Salentina, Villa Sebaste, Via per Campi, 73051, Novoli (Lecce), Italy. illus.

410   IT
STUDI MEDIOLATINI E VOLGARI. 1955? a. L.75000 (foreign L.85000)(effective 1992). Pacini Editore s.r.l., Via della Gherardesca 1, 56014 Ospedaletto (Pisa), Italy. TEL 050-982439. FAX 050-983906. TELEX 501628 PACINI I. Ed.Bd.

420   PL   ISSN 0081-6272
PE1
STUDIA ANGLICA POSNANIENSIA; international review of English Studies. (Text in English) 1969. irreg., vol.19, 1988. price varies. Adam Mickiewicz University Press, Nowowiejskiego 55, 61-734 Poznan, Poland. TEL 527-380. FAX 61-526425. TELEX 413260 UAMPL. Ed. Jacek Fisiak. adv.; bk.rev.; circ. 1,300. **Indexed:** Lang.& Lang.Behav.Abstr., Lang.Teach.& Ling.Abstr., M.L.A.
—BLDSC shelfmark: 8482.361000.
Description: Carries original articles and papers about English linguistics; studies American and English literature.

420   SW   ISSN 0562-2719
STUDIA ANGLISTICA UPSALIENSES. (Subseries of Acta Universitatis Upsaliensis) 1963. irreg., no.63, 1988. price varies. Almqvist & Wiksell International, Box 638, S-101 28 Stockholm, Sweden. Ed.Bd. (back issues avail.) **Indexed:** Abstr.Engl.Stud.

410 929   SW   ISSN 0280-8633
STUDIA ANTHROPONYMICA SCANDINAVICA; tidskrift foer nordisk personnamnsforskning. (Text in English, German, Scandinavian languages; summaries in English) 1983. a. SEK 135. Studia Anthroponymica Scandinavica, St. Johannesgatan 11, S-753 12 Uppsala, Sweden. TEL 018-18 12 89. Eds. Thorsten Andersson, Lena Peterson. bk.rev.; charts; illus.; circ. 400. (back issues avail.)
—BLDSC shelfmark: 8482.362500.
Description: Publishes articles in the field of Scandinavian personal name research. Presents studies dealing with the etymology, phonology, morphology, semantics, history, sociology and stylistics of names.

499.96   BE   ISSN 0081-6345
DK511.C1
STUDIA CAUCASICA. 1963. irreg., vol.9, 1989. 1000 BEF. Editions Peeters s.p.r.l., Bondgenotenlaan 153, B-3000 Leuven, Belgium. TEL 016-235170. FAX 016-228500. Ed. A.H. Kuipers. adv.; bk.rev.; illus.; charts; circ. 150. (back issues avail.) **Indexed:** M.L.A.

491.6   UK   ISSN 0081-6353
PB1001
STUDIA CELTICA. (Text in English and Welsh; occasionally in French and German) 1966. biennial. £20 per double vol. (University of Wales, Board of Celtic Studies) University of Wales Press, 6 Gwennyth St., Cathays, Cardiff CF2 4YD, Wales. TEL 0222-231919. FAX 0222-230908. Ed. J.E. Caerwyn Williams. adv.; bk.rev.; circ. 200. (reprint service avail. from UMI) **Indexed:** Br.Archaeol.Abstr., M.L.A.
Description: Covers Indo-European philology, continental and insular Celtic.

494 306.4   FI   ISSN 0085-6835
PH107
STUDIA FENNICA; review of Finnish linguistics and ethnology. (Text in English or German) 1933. a. FIM 150. Suomalaisen Kirjallisuuden Seura - Finnish Literature Society, Hallituskatu 1, P.O. Box 259, 00170 Helsinki 17, Finland. TEL 358-0-131237. adv.; bibl.; circ. 1,000. **Indexed:** A.I.C.P., M.L.A.
Description: Devoted to linguistics, folkloristics, and ethnology. Includes bibliographies of Finnish publications covering folklore and folklife research.

439   BE   ISSN 0081-6442
STUDIA GERMANICA GANDENSIA. (Text in Dutch, English, German) 1959. a. 300 BEF. Rijksuniversiteit te Ghent, Faculteit der Letteren en Wijsbegeerte, Blandijnberg 2, B-9000 Ghent, Belgium. Ed. G.A.R. De Smet. index; circ. 150. **Indexed:** M.L.A.

430   GW   ISSN 0081-6469
STUDIA GRAMMATICA. 1962. irreg., vol.30, 1989. price varies. (Akademie der Wissenschaften, Zentralinstitut fuer Sprachwissenschaft) Akademie-Verlag Berlin, Leipziger Str. 3-4, 1086 Berlin, Germany. TELEX 114420-AVERL-DD. **Indexed:** Lang.& Lang.Behav.Abstr., M.L.A.

400   IT
STUDIA HISTORICA ET PHILOGIA: SECTIO ROMANICA. 1974. irreg. L.10000. Licosa S.p.A., Via Lamarmora 45, 50121 Florence, Italy. Ed. R. Picchio. circ. 2,000.

400   IT
STUDIA HISTORICA ET PHILOGICA: SECTIO SLAVICA. irreg. price varies. Licosa S.p.A., Via Lamarmora 45, 50121 Florence, Italy.

400   IT
STUDIA HISTORICA ET PHILOGICA: SECTIO SLAVO-ROMANICA. irreg. price varies. Licosa S.p.A., Via Lamarmora 45, 50121 Florence, Italy. Ed. Riccardo Picchio.

410   PL   ISSN 0208-8665
PG6004
STUDIA JEZYKOZNAWCZE. a. price varies. (Polish Academy of Sciences, Linguistic Commission) Ossolineum, Publishing House of the Polish Academy of Sciences, Rynek 9, 50-106 Wroclaw, Poland. TEL 386-25. (Dist. by: Ars Poland, Krakowskie Przedmiescie 7, 00-068 Warsaw, Poland) Ed. W. Borys.
Description: Summaries of doctoral dissertations.

400   SW   ISSN 0039-3193
P9
STUDIA LINGUISTICA; revue de linguistique generale et comparee. (Text in English, French, German, Spanish) 1947. s-a. SEK 185. Almqvist & Wiksell International, P.O. Box 638, S-101 28 Stockholm, Sweden. Ed. Bengt Sigurd. adv.; bk.rev.; index. **Indexed:** Abstr.Anthropol., Arts & Hum.Cit.Ind., Ind.Bk.Rev.Hum., Lang.& Lang.Behav.Abstr. (1972-), Lang.Teach.& Ling.Abstr., M.L.A.
—BLDSC shelfmark: 8482.970000.

407   US
STUDIA LINGUISTICA ET PHILOLOGICA. 1975. irreg. $37.50 per vol. Anma Libri, Box 876, Saratoga, CA 95071. TEL 408-741-1522. **Indexed:** M.L.A.
Description: Linguistic and philological studies.

400   SW   ISSN 0039-3274
PB5
STUDIA NEOPHILOLOGICA; a journal of Germanic and Romance philology. (Text in English, French, German) 1928. 2/yr. SEK 325. Almqvist & Wiksell Periodical Company, Box 638, S-101 28 Stockholm, Sweden. Ed. Lars Hermodsson. bk.rev.; cum.index: vols.1-30; circ. 800. (tabloid format; reprint service avail. from SWZ) **Indexed:** Abstr.Engl.Stud., Arts & Hum.Cit.Ind., Curr.Cont., Ind.Bk.Rev.Hum., Lang.& Lang.Behav.Abstr., M.L.A.
—BLDSC shelfmark: 8483.080000.

490   NE   ISSN 0281-4528
STUDIA ORIENTALIA LUNDENSIA. 1983. irreg., vol.4, 1990. price varies. E.J. Brill, P.O. Box 9000, 2300 PA Leiden, Netherlands. TEL 071-312624. FAX 071-317532. TELEX 39296 BRILL NL. (In N. America: E.J. Brill, 24 Hudson St., Kinderhook, NY 12106. TEL 800-962-4406) Ed. Gosta Vitesta.

410   SW   ISSN 0081-6809
STUDIA PHILOLOGIAE SCANDINAVICAE UPSALIENSIA. (Subseries of Acta Universitatis Upsaliensis) 1961. irreg., vol.18, 1987. price varies; exchange avail. (Uppsala Universitet) Almqvist & Wiksell International, Box 638, S-101 28 Stockholm, Sweden. Ed.Bd.

400   FI   ISSN 0585-5462
STUDIA PHILOLOGICA JYVASKYLAENSIA. (Text in English, Finnish, French, German and Swedish) 1966. irreg. price varies. Jyvaskylan Yliopisto - University of Jyvaskyla, PL 35, 40351 Jyvaskyla, Finland. Eds. Raija Markkanen, Ellen Sakari. circ. 450.

410   PL   ISSN 0860-2085
STUDIA PHONETICA POSNANIENSIA; an international journal for linguistics and phonetics. (Text in English and Polish; abstracts in English) 1987. biennial. 280 Zl.($300) (Adam Mickiewicz University, Institute of Linguistics) Adam Mickiewicz University Press, Nowowiejskiego 55, 61-734 Poznan, Poland. TEL 527-380. Eds. Maria Steffen-Botog, Wieslaw Awedyk. bk.rev.; abstr.; circ. 500. (back issues avail.)

400   JA   ISSN 0300-1067
P215
STUDIA PHONOLOGICA/ONSEI KAGAKU KENKYU. (Text in English, German or Japanese) 1961. a. free. Kyoto University, Institution for Phonetic Sciences - Kyoto Daigaku Onsei Kagaku Sogo Kenkyu Bukai, Yoshida, Sakyo-ku, Kyoto 606, Japan. FAX 81-75-753-5977. Ed. Shuji Doshita. illus.; circ. 1,000. **Indexed:** Lang.& Lang.Behav.Abstr. (1971-).
—BLDSC shelfmark: 8483.130000.

STUDIA POETICA. see *LITERATURE*

400   PL   ISSN 0137-4370
STUDIA POLONISTYCZNE. (Text in Polish; summaries in English, French, German or Russian) 1973. irreg., vol.14-15, 1986-87. price varies. Adam Mickiewicz University Press, Nowowiejskiego 55, 61-734 Poznan, Poland. TEL 527-380. FAX 61-526425. TELEX 413260 UAMPL. Eds. Wladyslaw Kuraszkiewicz, Tadeusz Witczak. **Indexed:** Lang.& Lang.Behav.Abstr.
Description: Contains papers connected with the linguistic, literature and theory of literature problems.

LINGUISTICS 2845

479 420　　　　CI　ISSN 0039-3339
STUDIA ROMANICA ET ANGLICA ZAGRABIENSIA.
(Editions in English, French, Italian, Spanish) 1956. s-a. 100 din.($20) per no. Sveuciliste u Zagrebu, Filozofski Fakultet, Dure Salaja 3, 41000 Zagreb, Croatia. Ed. Ivo Vidan. **Indexed:** Lang.& Lang.Behav.Abstr., Lang.Teach.& Ling.Abstr.
  Description: Discusses linguistics and the creation of literature from an academic view.

410　　　　SW　ISSN 0562-3022
STUDIA ROMANICA UPSALIENSIA. (Text in French, Italian and Spanish; summaries in English or French) 1961. irreg. (Uppsala University, Acta Universitatis Upsaliensis) Almqvist & Wiksell International, Box 638, S-101 28 Stockholm, Sweden. Ed. Lennart Carlsson. circ. 600. (back issues avail.) **Indexed:** M.L.A.

410　　　　PL　ISSN 0137-6608
STUDIA SEMIOTYCZNE. a. price varies. (Polskie Towarzystwo Semiotyczne) Ossolineum, Publishing House of the Polish Academy of Sciences, Rynek 9, Wroclaw, Poland. TELEX 0712771 OSS PL. (Dist. by: Ars Polona-Ruch, Krakowskie Przedmiescie 7, Warsaw, Poland) Ed. Jerzy Pelc.

491　　　　HU　ISSN 0039-3363
PG1
STUDIA SLAVICA ACADEMIAE SCIENTIARUM HUNGARICAE. (Text in English, French, German or Slavic languages) 1955. q. $62. (Magyar Tudomanyos Akademia) Akademiai Kiado, Publishing House of the Hungarian Academy of Sciences, P.O. Box 24, H-1363 Budapest, Hungary. Eds. F. Papp, A. Hollos. adv.; bk.rev.; bibl.; charts; illus.; index. **Indexed:** Lang.& Lang.Behav.Abstr., M.L.A.

400 080　　　　NE　ISSN 0081-6957
STUDIA THEODISCA. (Summaries occasionally in English, French and German) 1965. irreg., no.13, 1974. price varies. Van Gorcum en Co. B.V., P.O. Box 43, 9400 AA Assen, Netherlands. TEL 05920-46864. FAX 05920-72064.

400 859　　　　RM　ISSN 0039-3444
P19
STUDIA UNIVERSITATIS "BABES-BOLYAI". PHILOLOGIA. (Text in English, French, German, Italian, Rumanian) 1956. q. exchange basis. Universitatea "Babes Bolyai", Biblioteca Centrala Universitara, Str. Clinicilor Nr. 2, Cluj-Napoca, Rumania. bk.rev.; charts; illus.; index.

494　　　　SW　ISSN 0081-7015
STUDIA URALICA ET ALTAICA UPSALIENSIA. (Subseries of Acta Universitatis Upsaliensis) (Text in English and Swedish) 1964. irreg., vol.18, 1987. price varies. (Uppsala Universitet) Almqvist & Wiksell International, Box 638, S-101 28 Stockholm, Sweden. Ed. Bo Wickman. bibl.; charts.

494 894　　　　US　ISSN 0133-4239
STUDIA URALO-ALTAICA. (Text in English, German, Russian) 1973. irreg., vol.31, 1989. price varies. John Benjamins Publishing Co., 821 Bethlehem Pike, Philadelphia, PA 19118. TEL 215-836-1200. FAX 215-836-1204. (And: Amsteldijk 44, P.O. Box 75577, 1070 AN Amsterdam, Netherlands. TEL 020-6762325) Eds. P. Hajdu, A. Rona-Tas. (back issues avail.)
  Description: Monographs on Uralo-Altaic studies.

491.8　　　　PL　ISSN 0081-7090
STUDIA Z FILOLOGII POLSKIEJ I SLOWIANSKIEJ. (Text in Polish; papers and summaries in Slavonic languages) 1955. irreg., vol.22, 1984. price varies. (Polska Akademia Nauk, Komitet Slowianoznawstwa) Panstwowe Wydawnictwo Naukowe, Miodowa 10, 00-251 Warsaw, Poland. (Dist. by: Ars Polona, Krakowskie Przedmiescie 7, 00-068 Warsaw, Poland) Ed. J. Siatkowski. circ. 500.

494.3　　　　GW　ISSN 0585-5853
P945
STUDIEN ZU DEN BOGAZKOEY-TEXTEN. 1965. irreg., vol.31, 1991. irreg. price varies. (Akademie der Wissenschaften und der Literatur, Kommission fuer den Alten Orient) Verlag Otto Harrassowitz, Taunusstr. 14, Postfach 2929, 6200 Wiesbaden, Germany. TEL 0611-530570. FAX 0611-530570. TELEX 4186135. **Indexed:** M.L.A.

430　　　　GW
STUDIEN ZUM KLEINEN DEUTSCHEN SPRACHATLAS. 1982. irreg. Max Niemeyer Verlag, Postfach 2140, 7400 Tuebingen 1, Germany. TEL 07071-81104. FAX 07071-87419. Eds. Werner H. Veith, Wolfgang Putschke. circ. 500. (back issues avail.)
  Description: Monographs and collections of essays on dialectological atlases, especially the "Kleiner deutscher Sprachatlas".

420 820　　　　GW　ISSN 0081-7244
STUDIEN ZUR ENGLISCHEN PHILOLOGIE, NEUE FOLGE. (Text in English or German) 1963. irreg., no.28, 1991. price varies. Max Niemeyer Verlag, Postfach 2140, 7400 Tuebingen 1, Germany. TEL 07071-81104. FAX 07071-87419. Ed.Bd. (back issues avail.) **Indexed:** M.L.A.
  Description: Monographs on English and American Literature from the Middle Ages to present.

STUDIEN ZUR INDOLOGIE UND IRANISTIK. see HISTORY — History Of Asia

400　　　　SW
STUDIER I MODERN SPRAAKVETENSKAP/STOCKHOLM STUDIES IN MODERN PHILOLOGY. (Text in English, French and German) 1898. irreg., no.8, 1987. (Humanistisk-Samhaellsvetenskapliga Forskning Raadet) Almqvist & Wiksell International, Box 638, 101 28 Stockholm, Sweden. Ed.Bd.

496　　　　US　ISSN 0039-3533
PL8000
STUDIES IN AFRICAN LINGUISTICS. 1970. 3/yr. $12 to individuals; institutions $20. University of California, Los Angeles, African Studies Center, Los Angeles, CA 90024. TEL 310-825-3686. (Co-sponsor: U.C.L.A. Department of Linguistics) Ed.Bd. bibl.; charts; circ. 350. (back issues avail.) **Indexed:** Abstr.Anthropol., Curr.Cont.Africa, Lang.& Lang.Behav.Abstr. (1970-), M.L.A.
  —BLDSC shelfmark: 8488.945000.
  Description: Descriptive or theoretical articles on linguistics and African languages.

410 375.4　　　　GW　ISSN 0171-6794
STUDIES IN DESCRIPTIVE LINGUISTICS. (Text in English; summaries in French, German) 1978. irreg. price varies. Julius Groos Verlag, Hertzstr. 6, Postfach 102423, 6900 Heidelberg 1, Germany. TEL 06221-303621. Ed. D. Nehls. circ. 1,000. (back issues avail.) **Indexed:** Lang.& Lang.Behav.Abstr. (1978-).

STUDIES IN ENGLISH LITERATURE/EIBUNGAKU KENKYU. see LITERATURE

415　　　　US
STUDIES IN GENERATIVE GRAMMAR.* irreg., no.36, 1990. price varies. Walter de Gruyter, Inc., 200 Saw Mill River Rd., Hawthorne, NY 10532. TEL 914-747-0110. FAX 914-747-1326. Eds. Jan Koster, Henk van Riemsdijk.

410　　　　US
STUDIES IN GENERATIVE LINGUISTIC ANALYSIS. 1979. irreg., vol.4, 1986. price varies. John Benjamins Publishing Co., 821 Bethlehem Pike, Philadelphia, PA 19118. TEL 215-836-1200. FAX 215-836-1204. (And: Amsteldijk 44, P.O. Box 75577, 1070 AN Amsterdam, Netherlands. TEL 020-6762325) Ed. D.L. Goyvaerts. (back issues avail.)
  Description: Contains monographs in generative linguistics.

485 475　　　　NE
STUDIES IN GREEK AND LATIN LINGUISTICS. 1980. irreg. price varies. Van Gorcum en Co. B.V., P.O. Box 43, 9400 AA Assen, Netherlands. TEL 05920-46864. FAX 05920-72064.

411
STUDIES IN INDIAN EPIGRAPHY/BHARATIYA PURABHILEKHA PATRIKA. 1975. a. Epigraphical Society of India, University Buildings, Mysore 570005, India. Eds. Z.A. Desai, Ajay Mitra Shastri. illus.

410　　　　II
STUDIES IN INDIAN PLACE NAMES/BHARATIYA STHALANAMA PATRIKA. (Text in English) 1980. a. (Place Names Society of India) Geetha Book House, K.R. Circle, Mysore 570 001, India. Ed. Mandhav N. Katti.

410 100　　　　NE　ISSN 0378-4177
P1.A1
STUDIES IN LANGUAGE. (Text in English, French, German) 1977. s-a. fl.340($185) (effective 1992). John Benjamins Publishing Co., Amsteldijk 44, P.O. Box 75577, 1070 AN Amsterdam, Netherlands. TEL 020-6738156. FAX 020-6739773. (In N. America: 821 Bethlehem Pike, Philadelphia, PA 19118. TEL 215-836-1200) Ed.Bd. adv.; bk.rev.; bibl.; index; circ. 800. (back issues avail.; reprint service avail from SWZ) **Indexed:** Abstr.Anthropol., Arts & Hum.Cit.Ind., Ind.Bk.Rev.Hum., Lang.& Lang.Behav.Abstr. (1977-), M.L.A., Math.R.
  Supersedes: Foundations of Language (ISSN 0015-900X)
  Description: Covers subjects basic to contemporary linguistics and philosophy, focusing on the foundations of language.

410 800　　　　US　ISSN 0165-7763
STUDIES IN LANGUAGE COMPANION SERIES. Short title: S L C S. (Supplement to: Studies in Language) 1978. irreg., vol.22, 1990. price varies. John Benjamins Publishing Co., 821 Bethlehem Pike, Philadelphia, PA 19118. TEL 215-836-1200. FAX 215-836-1204. (And: Amsteldijk 44, P.O. Box 75577, 1070 AN Amsterdam, Netherlands. TEL 020-6762325) Eds. John W.M. Verhaar, Werner Abraham. **Indexed:** M.L.A., Math.R.

410　　　　US
STUDIES IN LANGUAGE LEARNING; an interdisciplinary review of language acquisition, language pedagogy, stylistics, and language planning. 1975. irreg. (1-2/yr.). price varies. University of Illinois at Urbana-Champaign, Language Learning Laboratory, G70 Foreign Languages Bldg., 707 S. Mathews Ave., Urbana, IL 61801. TEL 217-333-9776. Ed. Bd. bk.rev.; circ. 300. (also avail. in microfiche) **Indexed:** ERIC, Lang.& Lang.Behav.Abstr. (1976-), Lang.Teach.& Ling.Abstr., Sociol.Abstr.

STUDIES IN LINGUISTICS AND PHILOSOPHY. see PSYCHOLOGY

400　　　　HU
STUDIES IN MODERN PHILOLOGY. (Text in English) 1984. irreg., vol.6, 1989. price varies. Akademiai Kiado, Publishing House of the Hungarian Academy of Sciences, P.O. Box 24, H-1363 Budapest, Hungary. TEL 181-2134. (Subscr. to: Kultura, P.O. Box 149, H-1389 Budapest, Hungary) Eds. Karoly Manherz, Janos Szavai.

410　　　　NE
STUDIES IN NATURAL LANGUAGE AND LINGUISTIC THEORY. (Text in English) 1985. irreg. price varies. Kluwer Academic Publishers, Spuiboulevard 50, P.O. Box 17, 3300 AA Dordrecht, Netherlands. TEL 078-334911. FAX 078-334254. TELEX 29245. (Dist. by: Kluwer Academic Publishers Group, P.O. Box 322, 3300 AH Dordrecht; U.S. address: P.O. Box 358, Accord Station, Hingham, MA 02018-0358) Eds. Frank Heny, Joan Maling.

430 800　　　　US　ISSN 0899-9872
STUDIES IN OLD GERMANIC LANGUAGES AND LITERATURES. irreg. Peter Lang Publishing, Inc., 62 W. 45th St., 4th Fl., New York NY 10036. TEL 212-302-6740. FAX 212-302-7574. Ed. Ernst A. Ebbinghaus.
  Description: Presents monographic studies in Old Germanic dialects (Gothic, Old English, Old Saxon, Old Norse, Old High German), including grammar and text editions; also includes comparative linguistic and literary studies emphasizing the Germanic languages.

499.21　　　　PH　ISSN 0116-0516
PL5501
STUDIES IN PHILIPPINE LINGUISTICS. (Text in English) 1977. a. $6. Summer Institute of Linguistics, Philippine Branch, P.O. Box 2270 CPO, 1099 Manila, Philippines. (Co-sponsor: Linguistic Society of the Philippines) Eds. Fe T. Otanes, Hazel Wrigglesworth. circ. 150. (also avail. in microfiche) **Indexed:** ERIC, Ind.Phil.Per.

LINGUISTICS

400   US   ISSN 0039-3738
P25
STUDIES IN PHILOLOGY. 1906. 4/yr. $18 to individuals (foreign $24); institutions $24 (foreign $30). (University of North Carolina at Chapel Hill, Department of English) University of North Carolina Press, Box 2288, Chapel Hill, NC 27515-2288. TEL 919-966-3561. FAX 919-966-3829. Ed. Jerry Mills. adv.; index every 10 yrs.; circ. 1,600. (also avail. in microform from MIM,UMI; reprint service avail. from UMI) **Indexed:** Abstr.Engl.Stud., Arts & Hum.Cit.Ind., Curr.Cont., Hum.Ind., LCR, M.L.A.
—BLDSC shelfmark: 8491.210000.
Refereed Serial

407   UK   ISSN 0272-2631
P118
STUDIES IN SECOND LANGUAGE ACQUISITION. 1977. q. $39 to individuals; institutions $73. Cambridge University Press, Edinburgh Bldg., Shaftesbury Rd., Cambridge CB2 2RU, England. TEL 0223-312393. FAX 0223-315052. TELEX 851817256. (North American addr. to: Cambridge University Press, 40 W. 20th St., New York, NY 10011) A. Valdman. adv.; bk.rev. (also avail. in microform from UMI; reprint service avail. from UMI) **Indexed:** C.I.J.E., Lang.& Lang.Behav.Abstr. (1985-), Lang.Teach.& Ling.Abstr.
—BLDSC shelfmark: 8491.571000.
Description: Deals with the acquisition of a second language or languages whether by formal learning or by assimilation.

410 890   II
STUDIES IN SEMIOTICS AND LITERATURE. 1979. irreg. price varies. Bahri Publications, 997-A, Street No. 9, Gobindpuri, Kalkaji, New Delhi 110 019, India. TEL 644-5710. Ed. Ujjal Singh Bahri.
Description: Semiotic studies of literature, emphasis on Indian literature.

492   NE   ISSN 0081-8461
STUDIES IN SEMITIC LANGUAGES AND LINGUISTICS. 1967. irreg., vol.18, 1992. price varies. E. J. Brill, P.O. Box 9000, 2300 PA Leiden, Netherlands. TEL 071-312624. FAX 071-317532. TELEX 39296 BRILL NL. (In N. America: E.J. Brill, 24 Hudson St., Kinderhook, NY 12106. TEL 800-962-4406)
—BLDSC shelfmark: 8491.575000.
Description: Scholarly monographs on topics in Semitic languages and linguistics, living and dead, including Arabic and Hebrew regional dialects.

491 410   NE   ISSN 0169-0124
PG1
STUDIES IN SLAVIC AND GENERAL LINGUISTICS. (Text in English, German, Polish or Russian) 1980. irreg. price varies. Editions Rodopi B.V., Keizersgracht 302-304, 1016 EX Amsterdam, Netherlands. TEL 020-6227507. FAX 020-6380948. (US and Canada subscr. to: 233 Peachtree St. N.E., Ste. 404, Atlanta GA 30303-1504. TEL 800-225-3998) Ed.Bd. adv.; circ. 500. **Indexed:** M.L.A.

410   US
STUDIES IN THE LINGUISTIC SCIENCES. 1971. s-a. $9.50 per issue. University of Illinois at Urbana-Champaign, Department of Linguistics, 707 S. Mathews, 4088 Foreign Language Bldg, Urbana, IL 61801. TEL 217-333-3563. Ed. Hans Hinrich Hock. bk.rev.; bibl.; circ. controlled. (back issues avail.) **Indexed:** Lang.& Lang.Behav.Abstr. (1971-), M.L.A., Sociol.Abstr.
Formerly: University of Illinois. Department of Linguistics. Working Papers (ISSN 0049-2388)

410   US
STUDIES IN THE SCIENCES OF LANGUAGE SERIES. 1975. irreg., vol.8, 1991. price varies. John Benjamins Publishing Co., 821 Bethlehem Pike, Philadelphia, PA 19118. TEL 215-836-1200. FAX 215-836-1204. (And: Amsteldijk 44, P.O. Box 75577, 1070 AN Amsterdam, Netherlands. TEL 020-6762325) Ed. D.L. Goyvaerts. (back issues avail.)
Description: Monographs and interdisciplinary studies in linguistics.

410 150   NE
STUDIES IN THEORETICAL PSYCHOLINGUISTICS. 1983. irreg. price varies. Kluwer Academic Publishers, Spuiboulevard 50, P.O. Box 17, 3300 AA Dordrecht, Netherlands. TEL 078-334911. FAX 078-334254. TELEX 29245. (Dist. by: Kluwer Academic Publishers Group, P.O. Box 322, 3300 AH Dordrecht, Netherlands) Eds. T. Roeper, K. Wexler.

STUDIES OF WORLD LITERATURE IN ENGLISH. see *LITERATURE*

410   US
STUDIES ON LANGUAGE ACQUISITION.* (Text in English) 1985. irreg., no.9, 1989. Walter de Gruyter, Inc., 200 Saw Mill River Rd., Hawthorne, NY 10532. TEL 914-747-0110. FAX 914-747-1326. Ed.Bd.
Description: Focuses on first language acquisition, second/foreign language acquisition, bilingualism, language loss, and language acquisiton in educational settings.

410   RM   ISSN 0039-405X
STUDII SI CERCETARI LINGVISTICE. 1950. 6/yr. 180 lei($60) (Academia Romana) Editura Academiei Romane, Calea Victoriei 125, 79717 Bucharest, Rumania. (Dist. by: Rompresfilatelia, Calea Grivitei 64-66, P.O. Box 12-201, 78104 Bucharest, Rumania) Ed. I. Coteanu. bk.rev.; charts; index. **Indexed:** Lang.& Lang.Behav.Abstr. (1972-), M.L.A.

SUBTLE JOURNAL OF RAW COINAGE. see *LITERATURE*

SUECANA EXTRANEA; books on Sweden and Swedish literature in foreign languages. see *BIBLIOGRAPHIES*

SUGIA; Sprache und Geschichte in Afrika. see *HISTORY — History Of Africa*

418   US   ISSN 1040-4406
SUMMER INSTITUTE OF LINGUISTICS. LANGUAGE DATA. AFRICA SERIES. 1971. irreg., no.21, 1981. price varies. Summer Institute of Linguistics, Inc., Academic Publications, 7500 W. Camp Wisdom Rd., Dallas, TX 75236. TEL 214-709-2403. Ed. Pamela Bendor-Samuel. (also avail. in microfiche)

410   US   ISSN 1040-1113
SUMMER INSTITUTE OF LINGUISTICS. LANGUAGE DATA. AMERINDIAN SERIES. 1973. irreg., no.7, 1979. price varies. Summer Institute of Linguistics, Inc., Academic Publications, 7500 W. Camp Wisdom Rd., Dallas, TX 75236. TEL 214-709-2403. Ed. Viola Waterhouse. bibl.; charts. (also avail. in microfiche)

499   US   ISSN 1040-4414
SUMMER INSTITUTE OF LINGUISTICS. LANGUAGE DATA. ASIA-PACIFIC SERIES. 1971. irreg., no.13, 1981. price varies. Summer Institute of Linguistics, Inc., Academic Publications, 7500 W. Camp Wisdom Rd., Dallas, TX 75236. TEL 214-709-2403. Ed.Bd. (also avail. in microfiche)

498   BL   ISSN 0102-6526
PM5151
SUMMER INSTITUTE OF LINGUISTICS. SERIE LINGUISTICA. 1973? irreg. price varies. Summer Institute of Linguistics, Departamento de Estudos Tecnicos, SAI-NO Lote D, Bloco 3, 70770 Brasilia DF, Brazil. circ. 300. **Indexed:** Lang.& Lang.Behav.Abstr. (1973-).
Description: Monographs on Brazilian indian languages.

410   US
SUMMER INSTITUTE OF LINGUISTICS. UNIVERSITY OF NORTH DAKOTA SESSION. WORK PAPERS. vol.25, 1991. a. price varies. Summer Institute of Linguistics, Inc., Academic Publications, 7500 W. Camp Wisdom Rd., Dallas, TX 75236. TEL 214-709-2404. Eds. Robert A. Douley, Stephen Quackenbush. (also avail. in microfiche)

499   US
SUMMER INSTITUTE OF LINGUISTICS AND THE UNIVERSITY OF TEXAS AT ARLINGTON PUBLICATIONS IN LINGUISTICS. 1958. irreg. price varies. Summer Institute of Linguistics, Inc., Academic Publications, 7500 W. Camp Wisdom Rd., Dallas, TX 75236. TEL 214-709-2403. Ed. William R. Merrifield.
Former titles: S I L Publications in Linguistics (ISSN 1040-0850); S I L Publications on Linguistics and Related Fields (ISSN 0079-7669)
Description: Theory applied to ethnic-Indian languages around the world as a result of linguistic research.

SUOMALAIS-UGRILAISEN SEURAN. AIKAKAUSKIRJA/SOCIETE FINNO-OUGRIENNE. JOURNAL. see *ANTHROPOLOGY*

491   CI
SUVREMENA METODIKA NASTAVE HRVATSKOG ILI SRPSKOG JEZIKA. 1976. q. 200 din. Skolska Knjiga, Masarykova 28, Zagreb, Croatia. TEL 41 429 111. Ed. Z. Diklic. bk.rev.; film rev.; play rev.; circ. 3,000.

SVENSKA LITTERATURSAELLSKAPET I FINLAND. SKRIFTER. see *HISTORY*

SVET LITERATURY/WORLD OF LITERATURE. see *LITERATURE*

499.992   SZ
SVISA ESPERANTO REVUO;* eldonita de svisa esperanto-societo. (Text in Esperanto) 1903. 9/yr. 30 SFr. Svisa Esperanto-Societo, Zumhofstr. 22, CH-6010 Kriens, Switzerland. TEL 022-44-09-85. Ed. Andres Bickel. adv.; bk.rev.; illus.; circ. 600.
Formerly: Svisa Espero (ISSN 0039-7148)

SVOBODNA SKOLA/FREE THINKING SCHOOL. see *LITERATURE*

400   SW   ISSN 0302-8348
SYDSVENSKA ORTNAMNSSAELLSKAPET. AARSSKRIFT/SOUTH SWEDISH PLACENAME SOCIETY. JOURNAL. (Text in Danish, English, German, Norwegian, Swedish; summaries in English) 1925. a. £40. South Swedish Placename Society, Institute of Dialect and Placename Research, Helgonabacken 14, S-223 62 Lund, Sweden. FAX 46-46-152381. Ed. Goeran Hallberg. bk.rev.; index; circ. 500.

870 410   BE
SYMBOLAE. SERIES C. LINGUISTICA. (Text in Dutch, English, French) 1986. irreg., vol.6, 1989. price varies. Leuven University Press, Krakenstraat 3, B-3000 Leuven, Belgium. TEL 016-284175. FAX 016-284176. Ed.Bd.

410   US   ISSN 0092-4563
P1
SYNTAX AND SEMANTICS. 1972. irreg., vol.24, 1990. Academic Press, Inc., 1250 Sixth Ave., San Diego, CA 92101. TEL 619-231-0926. FAX 619-699-6715. Ed. Stephen R. Anderson. (reprint service avail. from ISI) **Indexed:** ASCA, M.L.A.

SYSTEM; an international journal of educational technology and applied linguistics. see *EDUCATION — Teaching Methods And Curriculum*

410 371.3   CS
SZOCIALISTA NEVELES. (Text in Hungarian) 1954. 10/yr. 20 Kcs. (Ministry of Education of the Slovak Socialist Republic) Slovenske Pedagogicke Nakladatelstvo, Sasinkova 5, 815 60 Bratislava, Czechoslovakia. (Subscr. to: Slovart, Gottwaldovo nam. 6, 805-32 Bratislava, Czechoslovakia) Ed. Alexander Fibi. circ. 3,000.

410   FR   ISSN 0066-9776
T A DOCUMENTS. (Traduction Automatique) 1966. irreg. price varies. Editions Klincksieck, 11 rue de Lille, 75005 Paris, France. (Dist. by: University of Alabama Press, Drawer 2877, University, AL 35486, U.S.A.)

499.992   NE
T E J O - TUTMONDE. (Text in Esperanto) 1983. bi-m. fl.17($9) (Tutmonda Esperantista Junulara Organizo) Universala Esperanto-Asocio, Nieuwe Binnenweg 176, 3015 BJ Rotterdam, Netherlands. TEL 010-4361044. FAX 010-436-1751. TELEX 23721 UEA NL. (And: Zumhofstr. 22, CH-6010 Kriens Lu, Switzerland) Ed. Klaus Dahmann. bk.rev.; circ. 1,000.

LINGUISTICS

407 011 371.3   US   ISSN 1051-8886
PE1011   CODEN: TESMET
T E S O L MATTERS. 1967. bi-m. membership.
Teachers of English to Speakers of Other Languages, 1600 Cameron St., Ste. 300, Alexandria, VA 22314-2751. TEL 703-836-0774.
FAX 703-836-7864. Ed. Helen Kornblum. adv.; bk.rev.; circ. 21,000. (tabloid format; also avail. in microfilm)
—BLDSC shelfmark: 8796.321300.
Supersedes (in 1991): T E S O L Newsletter (ISSN 0496-9987)
Description: Offers organizational news and articles about classroom concerns, as well as conference announcements.
Refereed Serial

406 370   US   ISSN 0039-8322
PE1128.A2
T E S O L QUARTERLY; a journal for teachers of English to speakers of other languages and of standard English as a second dialect. 1967. q. membership. Teachers of English to Speakers of Other Languages, 1600 Cameron St., Ste. 300, Alexandria, VA 22314-2751. TEL 703-836-0774.
FAX 703-836-7864. Ed. Sandra Silberstein. adv.; bk.rev.; bibl.; cum.index; circ. 21,000. (also avail. in microfilm from UMI; reprint service avail. from UMI)
Indexed: ASCA, C.I.J.E., Cont.Pg.Educ., Curr.Cont., Educ.Ind., Hum.Ind., Ind.Bk.Rev.Hum., Lang.& Lang.Behav.Abstr., Lang.Teach.& Ling.Abstr., M.L.A., Mid.East: Abstr.& Ind., Res.High.Educ.Abstr., Soc.Sci.Ind., Sp.Ed.Needs Abstr., SSCI.
—BLDSC shelfmark: 8796.323000.
Description: Represents cross-disciplinary interests, both theoretical and practical. Features testing, evaluation, professional preparation, bilingual and adult education and language learning.

406 370   SW   ISSN 0039-8438
T N C - AKTUELLT. 1959. 3-4/yr. free. Tekniska Nomenklaturcentralen - Swedish Centre for Technical Terminology, Vaestra vaegen 9 C, 171 46 Solna, Sweden. TEL 45-08-735 85 25.
FAX 45-08-27-32-86. Ed.Bd. (processed)
—BLDSC shelfmark: 8859.447000.

410   NE   ISSN 0167-4773
T T T INTERDISCIPLINAIR TIJDSCHRIFT VOOR TAAL- EN TEKSTWETENSCHAP. 1981. 4/yr. fl.79.50 to individuals; institutions fl.121.97. I C G Publications, P.O. Box 509, 3300 AM Dordrecht, Netherlands. TEL 078-510454. FAX 078-510972. adv.; bk.rev.; circ. 2,000.
—BLDSC shelfmark: 4533.356230.
Formerly: Interdisciplinair Tijdschrift voor Taal en Tekstwetenschap.
Description: Discusses linguistics, argumentation, phonetics, semantics, pragmatics, language philosophy and communication.

439.3   BE   ISSN 0039-8691
PF701
TAAL EN TONGVAL; tijdschrift voor dialectologie. 1949. 3/yr. 650 BEF (effective 1992). Seminarie Vlaamse Dialektologie te Gent, Blandijnberg 2, B-9000 Gent, Belgium. FAX 091-644195. (Co-sponsors: Zuidnederlandse Dialektcentrale te Leuven; Dialectencommissie te Amsterdam) Ed. G. DeSchutter. adv.; bk.rev.; bibl.; circ. 375. **Indexed:** M.L.A.
Description: Presents articles on studies on Dutch dialects.

439.36   SA   ISSN 0039-8705
TAALGENOOT. (Text in Afrikaans) 1931. m. R.12.
Afrikaanse Taal en Kultuurvereniging, P.O. Box 4585, Johannesburg 2000, South Africa.
FAX 011-725-1527. Ed. F.J. Kok. adv.; bk.rev.; circ. 35,500. **Indexed:** Ind.S.A.Per.

TAMIL KALAI; research journal on Tamilology. see *HISTORY — History Of Asia*

418.02   NE   ISSN 0924-1884
TARGET; international periodical of translation studies. (Text in English, French, German) 1989. s-a. fl.130($69) John Benjamins Publishing Co., Amsteldijk 44, P.O. Box 75577, 1070 AN Amsterdam, Netherlands. TEL 020-6738156.
FAX 020-6739773. (In N. America: 821 Bethlehem Pike, Philadelphia, PA 19118. TEL 215-836-1200) Eds. Gideon Toury, Jose Lambert. circ. 650. (back issues avail.)
—BLDSC shelfmark: 8606.100000.
Description: Studies theoretical, methodological, and descriptive nature of translation. Also reports on current publications and research.

410   NZ   ISSN 0494-8440
P11
TE REO. (Text in English, French) 1958. a. NZ.$18 to individuals; institutions NZ$ 28. Linguistic Society of New Zealand, c/o Romance Languages, University, Private Bag 92019, Auckland 1, New Zealand.
TEL 64-9-737917. FAX 64-9-733429. Ed. R. Harlow. adv.; bk.rev.; bibl.; circ. 350. **Indexed:** Bull.Signal., E.I., Lang.Teach.& Ling.Abstr., M.L.A.
—BLDSC shelfmark: 8612.594000.
Description: Covers descriptive and theoretical linguistics, emphasizes research in indigenous and introduced languages of the South Pacific.
Refereed Serial

428 375.4   PH   ISSN 0116-8037
TEACHING ENGLISH FOR SPECIFIC PURPOSES JOURNAL. (Text in English) 1985. a. P.45($6.50) (De La Salle University, Center for English for Specific Purposes, Language Department) De La Salle University Press, 2401 Taft Ave., Manila, Philippines. TEL 2-595177. Ed. Casilda E. Luzares. adv.; bk.rev.; circ. 300.
Description: Deals with the teaching of writing, principles of testing, criteria for evaluating student performance, and language program evaluation. Includes short articles describing specific and practical principles.

TEACHING ENGLISH TO DEAF AND SECOND LANGUAGE STUDENTS. see *EDUCATION — Special Education And Rehabilitation*

220 400   US   ISSN 0260-0935
                                        CODEN: BTRAEV
TECHNICAL PAPERS FOR THE BIBLE TRANSLATOR. 1950. s-a. $6 ($12 including Practical Papers for the Bible Translator). United Bible Societies, 1865 Broadway, New York, NY 10023.
TEL 212-408-1468. FAX 212-582-7245. TELEX 23-62384. Ed. Paul Ellingworth. bk.rev.; index, cum.index every 10 yrs.; circ. 2,800. (also avail. in microfilm; microfiche; reprint service avail.) **Indexed:** Chr.Per.Ind., New Test.Abstr., Old Test.Abstr., Rel.& Theol.Abstr. (1968-), Rel.Ind.One.
Supersedes in part (since 1972): Bible Translator (ISSN 0006-0844)
Description: Contains technical biblical and linguistic information.

490   II
TELUGU AKADEMI LANGUAGE MONOGRAPH SERIES. 1974. irreg. Rs.16.25($8) Telugu Akademi, Hyderabad 500029, India.

491.7 375.4   CN   ISSN 0381-9582
TEMA. (Text in English and Ukrainian) 1968. q. Can.$15. (Saskatchewan Teachers of Ukranian) Saskatchewan Teachers' Federation, Box 1108, Saskatoon, Sask. S7K 3N3, Canada.
TEL 306-525-0368. Eds. Vera Labach, Nadia Prokopchuk. bk.rev.; film rev.; bibl.; illus.; stat.; circ. 200.

418.02   CN   ISSN 0225-3194
TERMINOGRAMME; bulletin d'information terminologique et linguistique. 4/yr. Can.$30. (Office de la Langue Francaise) Publications du Quebec, C.P. 1005, Quebec, Que. G1K 7B5, Canada. TEL 800-463-2100. FAX 418-643-6177. (Subscr. to: Service Abonnements, CP 1190, Outremont, Que. H2V 4S7, Canada) Ed.Bd.

410   CN
TERMINOLOGIE. 1968. q. free. Universite Laval, Comite Consultif de la Normalisation et de la Qualite du Francais, Pavillon des Sciences de l'Education, Quebec City, Que. G1K 7P4, Canada.
TEL 418-656-2131. Ed.Bd. circ. 22,000.
Former titles: Comite Consultif de la Normalisation et de la Qualite du Francais a l'Universite Laval. Bulletin; Comite de Terminologie. Bulletin.
Description: Covers university related terminology.

418   EI
TERMINOLOGIE ET TRADUCTION. (Text in Danish, Dutch, English, French, German, Greek, Italian) 1964. 3/yr. $28. Commission of the European Communities, Translation Service, Terminology Unit, Batiment Jean Monnet A2-100, L-2920 Luxembourg, Luxembourg. FAX 4301-4309. TELEX 3423 COMEUR LU. (Subscr. to: Office for Official Publications of the European Communities, L-2985 Luxembourg, Luxembourg) Ed. Wolfgang Osterheld. bk.rev.; circ. 1,100.
Formerly: Commission of the European Communities. Terminology and Computer Applications. Translation and Terminology Bulletin (ISSN 0256-7873); Supersedes (in 1984): Commission of the European Communities. Terminology Bureau. Terminology Bulletin - Bulletin de Terminologie.

TEXAS SPEECH COMMUNICATION JOURNAL. see *COMMUNICATIONS*

TEXAS STUDIES IN LITERATURE AND LANGUAGE; a journal of the humanities. see *LITERATURE*

TEXT; an interdisciplinary journal for the study of discourse. see *HUMANITIES: COMPREHENSIVE WORKS*

418.02   GW   ISSN 0179-6844
                                        CODEN: TCNTEB
TEXTCONTEXT; Translation, Theorie-Didaktik-Praxis. 1986. q. DM.72. Julius Groos Verlag, Hertzstr. 6, 6900 Heidelberg 1, Germany. TEL 06221-303621. Ed.Bd. circ. 400. (reprint service avail. from UMI, back issues avail.)
—BLDSC shelfmark: 8800.634700.

TEXTE ET L'IDEE. see *LITERATURE*

410   PO   ISSN 0120-5455
AS82.A1
TEXTO E CONTEXTO. 1982. q. Esc.1600. Circulo Eros Editora, Rua Infantaria 8, 360, 4700 Braga, Portugal. Ed. Jose Lorite Mena. bk.rev.

410   US
▼**THEMATIC STUDIES IN SECOND LANGUAGE LEARNING AND ACQUISITION.** 1990. irreg. price varies. Ablex Publishing Corporation, 355 Chestnut St., Norwood, NJ 07648. TEL 201-767-8450.
FAX 201-767-6717. TELEX 135-393. Ed. Robert J. DiPietro.

410   GW   ISSN 0301-4428
P1
THEORETICAL LINGUISTICS. 1974. 3/yr. $98. Walter de Gruyter und Co., Genthiner Str. 13, 1000 Berlin 30, Germany. TEL 030-26005-0.
FAX 030-26005251. TELEX 184027. (U.S. addr.: Walter de Gruyter, Inc. 200 Saw Mill Rd., Hawthorne, NY 10532) Ed. Helmut Schnelle. adv.; bk.rev.
Indexed: Arts & Hum.Cit.Ind., Lang.& Lang.Behav.Abstr., Lang.Teach.& Ling.Abstr. (1974-), Lang.Teach.& Ling.Abstr., Math.R.
—BLDSC shelfmark: 8814.560000.

410   US   ISSN 1051-6670
THEORETICAL STUDIES IN SECOND LANGUAGE ACQUISITION. irreg. Peter Lang Publishing, Inc., 62 W. 45th St., 4th Fl., New York, NY 10036.
TEL 212-302-6740. FAX 212-302-7574. Ed. Simon Belasco.
Description: Brings together research conducted in "naturalistic" as well as classroom acquisition. Focuses on the acquisition of pragmatic (extralinguistic) knowledge and the acquisition of grammatical (linguistic) knowledge.

400   CK   ISSN 0040-604X
THESAURUS. Variant title: Instituto Caro y Cuervo. Boletin. 1945. 3/yr. Col.$5000($25) Instituto Caro y Cuervo, Seccion de Publicaciones, Apdo. Aereo 51502, Bogota, Colombia. Ed. Jose Manuel Rivas Sacconi. bk.rev.; abstr.; charts; illus.; index, cum.index: vols.1-25, 1945-1970; vols.26-41, 1971-1986; circ. 2,400. **Indexed:** Hisp.Amer.Per.Ind, Lang.Teach.& Ling.Abstr., M.L.A.

TIJDSCHRIFT VOOR NEDERLANDSE TAAL- EN LETTERKUNDE. see *LITERATURE*

LINGUISTICS

439   NE
TIJDSCHRIFT VOOR TAALBEHEERSING. 1978. 4/yr. fl.90 to individuals; institutions fl.103; students fl.63. Wolters-Noordhoff B.V., Damsport 157, 9728 PS Groningen, Netherlands. TEL (050)226922. (And: Postbus 58, 9700 MB Groningen, Netherlands) Ed.Bd. adv.; bk.rev.

410 375.9   GW
TIRO. (Text in German and Latin) 1954. 6/yr. DM.7.20. Beacon-Verlag Koerber oHG, Birkental 13, Postfach 1420, 6702 Bad Duerkheim, Germany.

490 375.4   GW
TITO; locosa, lucunda, Seria. 1954. 6/yr. DM.9.60. Beacon Verlag Koerber oHG, Birkental 13, Postfach 1161, 6702 Bad Duerkheim, Germany. circ. 2,500. (tabloid format)

TOHOKU GAKUIN UNIVERSITY REVIEW; essays and studies in English language and literature. see *LITERATURE*

410   JA   ISSN 0389-3081
PB5
TOKAI DAIGAKU KIYO. GAIKOKUGO KYOIKU SENTA/TOKAI UNIVERSITY. FOREIGN LANGUAGE CENTER. BULLETIN. (Text mainly in Japanese; contents page in various languages) 1981. a. free. Tokai Daigaku, Gaikokugo Kyoiku Senta - Tokai University, Foreign Language Center, 1117 Kitakaname, Hiratsuka-shi, Kanagawa-ken 259-12, Japan. circ. 700.
Description: Contains articles on languages, literature, and related subjects. Emphasizes articles concerned with psychological insights into literature.

410   US
TOPICS IN SOCIOLINGUISTICS.* (Text in English) 1982. irreg., no.9, 1990. Walter de Gruyter, Inc., 200 Saw Mill River Rd., Hawthorne, NY 10532. TEL 914-747-0110. FAX 914-747-1326. Ed. Marinel Gerritsen.

TORONTO OLD ENGLISH SERIES. see *LITERATURE*

410   PR   ISSN 0040-9588
AS74.A1
LA TORRE. 1953. q. $16 to individuals (foreign $18); institutions $28 (foreign $30); students $8. University of Puerto Rico (Rio Piedras Campus), c/o Yudit de Ferdinandy, Ed., P.O. Box 23322, University of Puerto Rico Sta., San Juan, PR 00931-3322. TEL 809 758-0148. FAX 809-753-9116. Ed. Arturo Echavarria. bk.rev.; bibl.; index; circ. 1,000. **Indexed:** Hist.Abstr.
Description: Dedicated to literary and linguistic studies with emphasis on Latin American, Caribbean and Spanish literature.

418   BL   ISSN 0103-1813
TRABALHOS EM LINGUISTICA APLICADA. 1983. s-a. $25. Universidade Estadual de Campinas, Instituto de Estudos da Linguagem, Caixa Postal 6045, 13081 Campinas SP, Brazil. FAX 55-192-391501.
Description: Presents studies in applied linguistics.

418.02   FR   ISSN 0395-773X
P306.A1
TRADUIRE. (Includes yearbook) 1953. q. 230 F. Societe Francaise des Traducteurs, B.P. 295-09, 75425 Paris Cedex 09, France. TEL 1-48-78-43-32. Ed. Caroline Mandron. adv.; bk.rev.; bibl.; circ. 2,000. (tabloid format) **Indexed:** Lang.& Lang.Behav.Abstr. (1979-).
Description: Features general interest articles on different aspects of translation in the literary, scientific and technical fields, reviews of works, analyses of specialized magazines and technical glossaries.

TRANSLATION (NEW YORK, 1972). see *LITERATURE*

418.02   US
TRANSLATION (NEW YORK, 1977); a quarterly samizdat journal of materials for a history of American translation. 1977. q. Translation Index, 175 W. 87th St., No. 24A, New York, NY 10024.

418.02 028.1   US   ISSN 0737-4836
PN241.A1
TRANSLATION REVIEW. 1978. 3/yr. $30 to individuals; institutions $25. American Literary Translators Association, University of Texas at Dallas, Box 830688, Richardson, TX 75083-0688. TEL 214-690-2093. Ed. Rainer Schulte. circ. 1,000. (back issues avail.) **Indexed:** Amer.Bibl.Slavic & E.Eur.Stud, Arts & Hum.Cit.Ind., Curr.Cont., M.L.A.
—BLDSC shelfmark: 9024.908000.

418.02   DK   ISSN 0041-1264
TRANSLATOEREN. (Text in Danish, English, French, German, Norwegian, Swedish) 1939. 6/yr. DKK 300. Translatoerforeningen - Association of Danish Sworn Translators, Bornholmsgade 1, DK-1266 Copenhagen K, Denmark. FAX 45-31-42-11-31. adv.; bk.rev.; bibl.; cum.index: 1939-1960; 1961-1964; circ. 500.

440 375.4   FR   ISSN 0765-1635
TRAVAUX DE DIDACTIQUE DU FRANCAISE LANGUE ETRANGERE. 1979. s-a. 70 F. (foreign 90 F.). Universite de Montpellier (Universite Paul Valery), Centre de Formation Pedagogique pour l'Enseignement du Francais a l'Etranger, B.P. 5043, 34032 Montpellier Cedex 1, France. TEL 67-14-23-26. circ. 300.
Description: Aims to bring together teacher-trainers, both in France and abroad, and to keep teachers and future teachers informed about the latest research and its applications in the field of teaching French as a foreign-language.

440   SW   ISSN 0347-2558
TRAVAUX DE L'INSTITUTE DE LINGUISTIQUE DE LUND. (Text in English, French, German and Swedish) 1959. irreg. price varies. Lund University Press, P.O. Box 141, S-221 00 Lund, Sweden. TEL 46-46-31-20-00. FAX 46-46-30-53-38. Eds. G. Bruce, B. Sigurd.
—BLDSC shelfmark: 9031.590000.

410   BE   ISSN 0082-6049
TRAVAUX DE LINGUISTIQUE. (Text in French) 1969. s-a. 1950 BEF. (Rijksuniversiteit te Gent, Dienst voor Franse Linguistiek - State University of Ghent, Department of French Linguistics) Editions Duculot S.A., Av. de Lauzelle 65, B-1348 Louvain-la-Neuve, Belgium. TEL 10-471911. FAX 10-471925. Ed.Bd. adv.; bk.rev. **Indexed:** Lang.& Lang.Behav.Abstr. (1979-).
Description: Periodical of French and general linguistics.

400   FR   ISSN 0082-6057
PC2
TRAVAUX DE LINGUISTIQUE ET DE LITTERATURE. 1963. 2 vols. per yr. price varies. (Universite de Strasbourg II, Centre de Philologie et de Litteratures Romanes) Editions Klincksieck, 11 rue de Lille, 75007 Paris, France. Ed. George Straka. **Indexed:** Lang.& Lang.Behav.Abstr., M.L.A.

495.6   FR
TRAVAUX DE LINGUISTIQUE JAPONAISE. 1974. irreg. Universite de Paris VII, Groupe de Linguistique Japonaise, 2 Place Jussieu, 75005 Paris, France. Ed. Andre Wlodarczyk.
Formerly: Universite de Paris VII. Groupe de Linguistique Japonaise. Travaux (ISSN 0339-8811)

410   GW
TUDUV-STUDIE. REIHE SPRACH- UND LITERATURWISSENSCHAFTEN. 1975. irreg. price varies. Tuduv Verlagsgesellschaft mbH, Gabelsbergerstr. 15, 8000 Munich 2, Germany.

494   BE   ISSN 0082-6847
DR401
TURCICA; REVUE D'ETUDES TURQUES. (Supplement avail.: Cahiers Turcica) (Text in English, French, German) 1969. a. 2000 BEF. (Universite des Sciences Humaines de Strasbourg, Association pour le Developpement des Etudes Turques, FR) Editions Peeters s.p.r.l., Bondgenotenlaan 153, B-3000 Leuven, Belgium. TEL 016-235170. FAX 016-228500. (Co-sponsors: Institut Francais d'Etudes Anatoliennes a Istanbul, TU; Universite de Paris, Institut des Etudes Turques, FR) Ed. I. Melikoff. adv.; bk.rev.; index. **Indexed:** Hist.Abstr.
—BLDSC shelfmark: 9071.840000.

TURK DILI. see *LITERATURE*

450 370   UK   ISSN 0957-1752
▼**TUTTITALIA.** 1990. s-a. £20($40) (foreign £21). Association for Language Learning, Marton, Rugby CV23 9RY, England. TEL 0788-546443. FAX 0788-544149. Ed. Pam Williams. film rev.; play rev.; record rev.; abstr.; bibl.; charts; illus.; stat.; index; circ. 1,000.
—BLDSC shelfmark: 9076.178300.
Formerly: Association of Teachers of Italian. Journal.
Description: Contains articles and information for teachers and students of Italian.

400   US   ISSN 0167-7373
TYPOLOGICAL STUDIES IN LANGUAGE. 1982. irreg., vol.20, 1990. price varies. John Benjamins Publishing Co., 821 Bethlehem Pike, Philadelphia, PA 19118. TEL 215-836-1200. FAX 215-836-1204. (And: Amsteldijk 44, P.O. Box 75577, 1070 AN Amsterdam, Netherlands. TEL 020-6762325) Ed.Bd. (back issues avail.)
—BLDSC shelfmark: 9077.630000.
Description: Collects data from a wide variety of languages and language typologies.

400   CN
LE TYPONYME. (Text in French) 1983. 2/yr. free. Commission de Typonymie, 1245 Chemin, St. Foy, Que. G1S 42P, Canada. TEL 418-643-8660. circ. 4,500.

410   US
U C L A. OCCASIONAL PAPERS IN LINGUISTICS. 1972. irreg., no.8, 1989. price varies. University of California, Los Angeles, Department of Linguistics, 405 Hilgard Ave., Los Angeles, CA 90024. TEL 213-825-0634. (back issues avail.) **Indexed:** Lang.& Lang.Behav.Abstr. (1984-).

410   UK
U E A PAPERS IN LINGUISTICS. 1976? 3/yr. £12. University of East Anglia, Library, University Plain, Norwich NR4 7TJ, England. Ed. J.Hutchins. circ. 200. (back issues avail.) **Indexed:** Lang.& Lang. Behav.Abstr. (1961-), Lang.Teach.& Ling.Abstr.

491.79   KR   ISSN 0041-6096
UKRAINS'KA MOVA I LITERATURA V SHKOLI; metodychnyi zhurnal. 1951. m. 13.80 Rub. Ministerstvo Osvity, Yuriya Kotzyubyns'koho 5, Kiev 1, Ukraine. Ed. P.D. Mysnyk. bk.rev.; bibl.; index; circ. 45,950.

420 422   UK   ISSN 0953-461X
ULSTER PLACE-NAME SOCIETY. BULLETIN. 1986. irreg. (approx. a.) $9. Ulster Place-Name Society, Department of Celtic, Queen's University of Belfast, Belfast BT7 1NN, N. Ireland. TEL 245133. maps; circ. 350.
—BLDSC shelfmark: 0773.304000.

478 499   GW
▼**UNITARIO;** zurnalo poliglotte de latino moderne. (Text in German and Unitario) 1990. q. DM.16. European Center for the Promotion of Unitario, Postfach 1825, 6140 Bensheim, Germany.

410   SP   ISSN 0212-8047
UNIVERSIDAD DE LA LAGUNA. ANUARIOS; ciencias humanas. 1980. a. $15 to individuals; institutions $20. Universidad de La Laguna, Secretariado de Publicaciones, San Agustin, 30, 38201 La Laguana-Tenerife, Islas Canarias, Spain. TEL 922-25-81-27. bk.rev.

410   UY   ISSN 0250-6548
UNIVERSIDAD DE LA REPUBLICA. FACULTAD DE HUMANIDADES Y CIENCIAS. REVISTA. SERIE LINGUISTICA. N.S. 1979. irreg. exchange basis. Universidad de la Republica, Facultad de Humanidades y Ciencias, Seccion Revista, Tristan Narvaja 1674, Montevideo, Uruguay. Dir. Beatriz Martinez Osorio.
Supersedes in part: Universidad de la Republica. Facultad de Humanidades y Ciencias. Revista.

410 860   SP   ISSN 0210-4911
UNIVERSIDAD DE MURCIA. ESTUDIOS ROMANICOS. 1978. irreg., vol.3, 1986. $700. Universidad de Murcia, Secretariado de Publicaciones e Intercambio Cientifico, Santo Cristo 1, 30001 Murcia, Spain.

LINGUISTICS

410   SP
UNIVERSIDAD DE NAVARRA. COLECCION I.L.C.E. 1976. irreg. price varies. (Instituto de Lengua y Cultura Espanola) Ediciones Universidad de Navarra, S.A., Apdo. 396, 31080 Pamplona, Spain. TEL 94 825 6850.

UNIVERSIDAD NACIONAL AUTONOMA DE MEXICO. INSTITUTO DE INVESTIGACIONES FILOSOFICAS. CUADERNOS. see *PHILOSOPHY*

410 860   MX   ISSN 0185-0830
PQ7081.A1
UNIVERSIDAD VERACRUZANA. CENTRO DE INVESTIGACIONES LINGUISTICO-LITERARIAS. TEXTO-CRITICO. 1975. s-a. Mex.$20,000($25) Universidad Veracruzana, Centro de Investigaciones Linguistico-Literarias, Apdo. Postal 369, 91000 Xalapa, Veracruz, Mexico. Ed. Sixto Rodriguez. adv.; bk.rev.; cum.index; circ. 2,000. **Indexed:** Hisp.Amer.Per.Ind.

410   BL
UNIVERSIDADE DE SAO PAULO. CENTRO DE ESTUDOS PORTUGUESES. BOLETIM INFORMATIVO. 1975. 2/yr. Universidade de Sao Paulo, Centro de Estudos Portugueses, Cidade Universitaria "Armando de Salles Oliveira", C.P. 8105, 05508 Sao Paulo, Brazil. Ed. Carlos Felipe Moises. bk.rev.; circ. 1,500.

489   IT   ISSN 0072-0852
UNIVERSITA DEGLI STUDI DI GENOVA. ISTITUTO DI FILOLOGIA CLASSICA E MEDIEVALE. PUBBLICAZIONI. 1952. irreg. price varies. Universita degli Studi di Genova, Istituto di Filologia Classica e Medievale, Genoa, Italy. Ed. Francesco Della Corte.

UNIVERSITA DEGLI STUDI DI MACERATA. FACOLTA DI LETTERE E FILOSOFIA. ANNALI. see *ARCHAEOLOGY*

491.7 891.7   CS
UNIVERSITA PALACKEHO. PEDAGOGICKA FAKULTA. SBORNIK PRACI: RUSKY JAZYK A LITERATURA. (Text in Czech or Russian; summaries in Czech, English, German, and Russian.) 1972. irreg. price varies. Statni Pedagogicke Nakladatelstvi, Ostr. vni 30, 113 01 Prague 1, Czechoslovakia. Ed. Ljubov Ordeltova. bibl.; circ. 300. Key Title: Rusky Jazyk a Literatura.

410   RM   ISSN 0379-7880
UNIVERSITATEA "AL. I. CUZA" DIN IASI. ANALELE STIINTIFICE. SECTIUNEA 3E: LINGVISTICA. (Text in English, French, German, Rumanian, Russian, Spanish) 1955. a. 35 lei. Universitatea "Al. I. Cuza" din Iasi, Calea M. Eminescu 11, Jassy, Rumania. (Subscr. to: ILEXIM, Str. 13 Decembrie Nr. 3, Box 136-137, Bucharest, Rumania) Ed. D. Irimia. bk.rev.; abstr.; charts; illus.; circ. 300.
Description: Studies on the general theory of language, linguistics, stylistics and poetics.

410   RM
UNIVERSITATEA BUCURESTI. ANALELE. FILOLOGIE. (Text in English, French, Italian, Rumanian; summaries in Russian) a. $10. Universitatea Bucuresti, Bd. Gh. Gheorghiu-Dej Nr. 64, Bucharest, Rumania.

400   RM   ISSN 0082-4461
UNIVERSITATEA DIN TIMISOARA. ANALELE. STIINTE FILOLOGICE. 1962. a. $30. Universitatea din Timisoara, Faculty of Philology - University of Timisoara, Bd. Vasile Parvan nr.4, 1900 Timisoara, Romania. (Subscr. to: ILEXIM, Calea Grivitei 64-66, Box 136-137, Bucharest, Romania) (Co-sponsor: Ministry of Education) Ed. Simion Mioc. bk.rev.; circ. 250. **Indexed:** Lang.& Lang.Behav.Abstr. (1971-).

400   HU   ISSN 0583-5356
UNIVERSITATIS DEBRECENIENSIS DE LUDOVICO KOSSUTH NOMINATAE. INSTITUTI PHILOLOGIAE SLAVICAE. ANNALES. SLAVICA. (Text in several languages) 1961. irreg., vol.24, 1990. $10. Kossuth Lajos Tudomanyegyetem, Szlav Filologiai Intezet - Kossuth University, Department of Slavic Languages, Egyetem Ter 1, P.O. Box 53, 4010 Debrecen, Hungary. FAX 36-52-10-936. TELEX 72-200 UNIV K H. Ed. Zoltan Hajnady. adv.; bk.rev.; bibl.; circ. 700.

410   BE   ISSN 0577-1765
UNIVERSITE CATHOLIQUE DE LOUVAIN. CENTRE INTERNATIONAL DE DIALECTOLOGIE GENERALE. TRAVAUX. 1955. a. price varies. Universite Catholique de Louvain, Centre International de Dialectologie Generale, Blijde Inkomststraat 21, 6e, B-3000 Louvain, Belgium.

UNIVERSITE CATHOLIQUE DE LOUVAIN. FACULTE DE PHILOSOPHIE ET LETTRES. TRAVAUX. see *HUMANITIES: COMPREHENSIVE WORKS*

400   BE   ISSN 0076-1249
UNIVERSITE CATHOLIQUE DE LOUVAIN. INSTITUT DES LANGUES VIVANTES. CAHIERS. (Text in various languages) 1967. irreg., no.30, 1986. Universite Catholique de Louvain, Institut des Langues Vivantes, B-3000 Leuven, Belgium.

400 900   BE   ISSN 0076-1311
UNIVERSITE CATHOLIQUE DE LOUVAIN. RECUEIL DE TRAVAUX D'HISTOIRE ET DE PHILOLOGIE. (Text in Dutch, English, French) 1904. irreg., 6th series, no.31, 1985. price varies. Editions Peeters s.p.r.l., Bondgenotenlaan 153, B-3000 Leuven, Belgium. TEL 016-235170. FAX 016-228500. TELEX 65981 PULB.

440 840   DK   ISSN 0107-7392
UNIVERSITE D'ODENSE. ETUDES ROMANES. (Text in Danish, English and French) 1971. irreg. price varies. Odense University Press, Campusvej 55, DK-5230 Odense M, Denmark. TEL 66-157999. (back issues avail.)

414   FR
UNIVERSITE DE GRENOBLE III. INSTITUT DE PHONETIQUE. BULLETIN. 1972. a. 25 F. Universite de Grenoble III (Universite des Langues et Lettres), Institut de Phonetique, Domaine Universitaire de Saint-Martin-d'Heres, B. P. 25-X, 38040 Grenoble Cedex, France. TEL (76) 44.82.18. **Indexed:** Lang.Teach.& Ling.Abstr., M.L.A.

410   FR
UNIVERSITE DE GRENOBLE III. INSTITUT DE PHONETIQUE. TRAVAUX. SERIE A: MANUALS. irreg. price varies. Universite de Grenoble III (Universite des Langues et Lettres), Institut de Phonetique, Domaine Universitaire de Saint-Martin-d'Heres, Boite Postale 25-X, 38040 Grenoble Cedex, France. TEL (76) 44.82.18.
Formerly: Universite de Grenoble. Institut de Phonetique. Manuels. Serie A (ISSN 0085-1264)

410   FR   ISSN 0085-1272
UNIVERSITE DE GRENOBLE III. INSTITUT DE PHONETIQUE. TRAVAUX. SERIE B: ETUDES LINGUISTIQUES. 1967. irreg. price varies. Universite de Grenoble III (Universite des Langues et Lettres), Institut de Phonetique, Domaine Universitaire de Saint-Martin-d'Heres, Boite Postal 25-X, 38040 Grenoble Cedex, France. TEL (76) 44.82.18.

410   FR   ISSN 0756-7138
                                          CODEN: LXIQE2
UNIVERSITE DE LILLE III. LEXIQUE. 1982. a. (University de Lille III) Presses Universitaires de Lille, B.P. 199, 59654 Villeneuve d'Ascq Cedex, France. Ed. Pierre Corbin.

410   ZR
UNIVERSITE DE LUBUMBASHI. CENTRE DE LINGUISTIQUE THEORIQUE ET APPLIQUEE AFRICANISTIQUE. irreg., no.18, 1988. Universite de Lubumbashi, Centre de Linguistique Theorique et Appliquee, B.P. 1607, Lubumbashi, Zaire. **Indexed:** Lang.& Lang..Behav.Abstr. (1975-).
Formerly: Universite Nationale du Zaire, Lubumbashi. Centre de Linguistique Theorique et Appliquee Africanistique.
Description: Publishes articles related to Africa especially in the areas of literary and educational linguistics.

410   ZR
UNIVERSITE DE LUBUMBASHI. CENTRE DE LINGUISTIQUE THEORIQUE ET APPLIQUEE. BULLETIN DE LIAISON, ENSEIGNMENT DES LANGUES. 1974. irreg., no.14. $10. Universite de Lubumbashi, Centre de Linguistique Theorique et Appliquee, B.P. 1607, Lubumbashi, Zaire.
Former titles: Universite National de Zaire, Lubumbashi. Centre de Linguistique Theorique et Applique. Bulletin de Liaison, Enseignment des Langues; Universite Nationale du Zaire, Lubumbashi. Centre de Linguistique Theorique et Appliquee. Bulletin de Liaison.

410   ZR
UNIVERSITE DE LUBUMBASHI. CENTRE DE LINGUISTIQUE THEORIQUE ET APPLIQUEE. LINGUISTIQUE ET SCIENCES HUMAINES. BULLETIN D'INFORMATION. irreg., no.27, 1986. Universite de Lubumbashi, Centre de Linguistique Theorique et Appliquee, B.P. 1607, Lubumbashi, Zaire.
Former titles: Universite Nationale du Zaire, Lubumbashi. Centre de Linguistique Theorique et Appliquee. Linguistique et Sciences Humaines. Bulletin d'Information; Universite Nationale du Zaire, Lubumbashi. Centre de Linguistique Theorique et Appliquee. Bulletin d'Information.
Description: Publishes articles on the interaction of languages in Africa as well as African society in general.

UNIVERSITE DE NANCY II. CENTRE DE RECHERCHES ET D'APPLICATIONS PEDAGOGIQUES EN LANGUES. MELANGES. see *EDUCATION — Teaching Methods And Curriculum*

479   FR   ISSN 0081-5918
UNIVERSITE DE STRASBOURG II. CENTRE DE PHILOLOGIE ET LITTERATURES ROMANES. ACTES ET COLLOQUES. 1963. irreg. price varies. (Universite de Strasbourg II, Centre de Philologie et de Litteratures Romanes) Editions Klincksieck, 11 rue de Lille, 75007 Paris, France.

400   FR   ISSN 0081-5934
UNIVERSITE DE STRASBOURG II. INSTITUT DE PHONETIQUE. TRAVAUX. 1970. a. exchange basis. Universite de Strasbourg II, Institut de Phonetique, 22 rue Descartes, 67084 Strasbourg Cedex, France. FAX 88-41-73-54. circ. 600.

UNIVERSITE DE TUNIS. ECOLE NORMALE SUPERIEURE. SECTION A: LETTRES ET SCIENCES HUMAINES. SERIE 1: LANGUE ET LITTERATURE. see *LITERATURE*

UNIVERSITE SAINT-JOSEPH. FACULTE DES LETTRES ET DES SCIENCES HUMAINES. RECHERCHES. SERIE A: LANGUE ARABE ET PENSEE ISLAMIQUE. see *RELIGIONS AND THEOLOGY — Islamic*

410   NE
UNIVERSITEIT VAN AMSTERDAM. INSTITUUT VOOR ALGEMENE TAALWETENSCHAP. PUBLIKATIES. (Text in English and Dutch) 1971. irreg., vol.58, 1991. price varies. Universiteit van Amsterdam, Instituut voor Algemene Taalwetenschap, Spuistr. 210, 1012 VT Amsterdam, Netherlands. TEL 020-5253864. FAX 020-5253052. Ed. Hans den Besten. bk.rev.; circ. 150.

491.8 375.4 891.8   NO   ISSN 0803-2505
UNIVERSITETET I OSLO. SLAVISK-BALTISK AVDELING. MEDDELELSER. (Text in Norwegian, Russian and English) 1972. irreg. (3-5/yr.). price varies. Universitetet i Oslo, Slavisk-Baltisk Avdeling, P.O. Box 1030, N-0315 Oslo, Norway. FAX 47-2-85-43-10. Ed. Kjetil Ra Hauge. circ. 400.
Formerly: Universitetet i Oslo. Slavisk-Baltisk Institutt. Meddelelser.

400   US   ISSN 0068-6484
UNIVERSITY OF CALIFORNIA PUBLICATIONS IN LINGUISTICS. 1945. irreg. price varies. University of California Press, 2120 Berkeley Way, Berkeley, CA 94720. FAX 415-643-7127. Ed.Bd. (reprint service avail. from KTO)
Refereed Serial

400   US   ISSN 0068-6492
PB13
UNIVERSITY OF CALIFORNIA PUBLICATIONS IN MODERN PHILOLOGY. 1909. irreg. price varies. University of California Press, 2120 Berkeley Way, Berkeley, CA 94720. TEL 415-642-4247. FAX 415-643-7127. Ed.Bd.
—BLDSC shelfmark: 9105.600000.
Refereed Serial

410   DK   ISSN 0589-6681
P215
UNIVERSITY OF COPENHAGEN. INSTITUTE OF PHONETICS. ANNUAL REPORT. 1967. a. free. University of Copenhagen, Institute of Phonetics, Njalsgade 96, DK-2300 Copenhagen, Denmark. Ed. Joergen Rishel. circ. 350. (back issues avail.) **Indexed:** M.L.A.

2850 LINGUISTICS

410   GH
UNIVERSITY OF GHANA. INSTITUTE OF AFRICAN STUDIES. COLLECTED LANGUAGE NOTES. no.13, 1972. irreg., latest no.18, 1981. price varies. University of Ghana, Institute of African Studies, Box 73, Legon, Ghana.

496   NR   ISSN 0041-9613
P11
UNIVERSITY OF IBADAN. DEPARTMENT OF LINGUISTICS AND NIGERIAN LANGUAGES. RESEARCH NOTES.* 1967. irreg. University of Ibadan, Department of Linguistics and Nigerian Languages, Ibadan, Nigeria.

494   II
UNIVERSITY OF KERALA. DEPARTMENT OF TAMIL. RESEARCH PAPERS. (Text in English or Tamil) 1970. a. Rs.30. University of Kerala, Department of Tamil, Kariavattom, Thiruvananthapuram 695 581, Kerala, India. TEL 8419. (Subscr. to: Director of Publications, University of Kerala, Thiruvananthapuram 695 581) Ed. L. Gloria Sundramathy. bk.rev.
    Formerly (until 1974): University of Kerala. Department of Tamil. Journal.

410   SZ   ISSN 0256-1565
P1.A1
UNIVERSITY OF LAUSANNE. DEPARTEMENT DES LANGUES ET DES SCIENCES DU LANGAGE. CAHIERS. Short title: Cahiers du DLSL. 1984. s-a. 10 Fr. University of Lausanne, Departement des Langues et des Sciences du Langage, Faculty of Letters, Batiment des Facultes de Sciences Humaines, CH-1015 Lausanne, Switzerland. TEL 021-46 11 11. Ed. G. Peter Winnington. circ. 500.
    Description: Prints lectures & papers presented in interdisciplinary seminars organized by the DLSL, psychology and neurology departments of the University of Lausanne.

490   II   ISSN 0076-2237
UNIVERSITY OF MADRAS. KANNADA SERIES.* irreg. University of Madras, Chepauk, Triplicane, Madras 600005, Tamil Nadu, India.

490   II   ISSN 0076-2245
UNIVERSITY OF MADRAS. MALAYALAM SERIES.* irreg. University of Madras, Chepauk, Triplicane, Madras 600005, Tamil Nadu, India.

490   II   ISSN 0076-2261
UNIVERSITY OF MADRAS. SANSKRIT SERIES.* irreg. University of Madras, Chepauk, Triplicane, Madras 600005, Tamil Nadu, India.

490   II   ISSN 0076-227X
UNIVERSITY OF MADRAS. TAMIL SERIES.* irreg. University of Madras, Chepauk, Triplicane, Madras 600005, Tamil Nadu, India.

490   II   ISSN 0076-2288
UNIVERSITY OF MADRAS. TELUGU SERIES.* irreg. University of Madras, Chepauk, Triplicane, Madras 600005, Tamil Nadu, India.

490   II   ISSN 0076-2296
UNIVERSITY OF MADRAS. URDU SERIES.* irreg. University of Madras, Chepauk, Triplicane, Madras 600005, Tamil Nadu, India.

UNIVERSITY OF MANITOBA ANTHROPOLOGY PAPERS. see *ANTHROPOLOGY*

410   US   ISSN 0085-123X
UNIVERSITY OF NORTHERN COLORADO. MUSEUM OF ANTHROPOLOGY. OCCASIONAL PUBLICATIONS IN ANTHROPOLOGY. LINGUISTICS SERIES. 1970. irreg. price varies. University of Northern Colorado, Museum of Anthropology, Attn. George E. Fay, Ed., Greeley, CO 80639. TEL 303-351-1890. circ. 300. (processed)

491.1   II
UNIVERSITY OF POONA. CENTRE OF ADVANCED STUDY IN SANSKRIT. DOCTORAL THESES AND OTHER SANSKRIT & PRAKRIT PUBLICATIONS. (Text in English, Prakrit, Sanskrit) 1961. irreg. price varies. University of Poona, Centre of Advanced Study in Sanskrit, Ganeshkhind, Poona 411 007, India. TEL 54220. (Subscr. to: Section Officer, Publications Branch, University of Poona, Poona 411 007, India) Ed. V.N. Jha.

491.1   II   ISSN 0079-3809
UNIVERSITY OF POONA. CENTRE OF ADVANCED STUDY IN SANSKRIT. PUBLICATIONS. (Consists of series: Classes A through G.) (Text in English and Sanskrit) 1965. irreg. price varies. University of Poona, Centre of Advanced Study in Sanskrit, Ganeshkhind, Poona 411 007, India. TEL 54220. (Subscr. to: Section Officer, Publications Branch, University of Poona, Poona 411 007, India) Ed. V.N. Jha.

491.1   II
UNIVERSITY OF POONA. CENTRE OF ADVANCED STUDY IN SANSKRIT. SANSKRIT AND PRAKRIT STUDIES. (Text in English, Prakrit, Sanskrit) 1959. irreg. price varies. University of Poona, Centre of Advanced Study in Sanskrit, Ganeshkhind, Poona 411 007, India. TEL 54220. (Subscr. to: Section Officer, Publications Branch, University of Poona, Poona 411 007, India) Ed. V.N. Jha.

UNIVERSITY OF RAJASTHAN. STUDIES IN SANSKRIT AND HINDI. see *LITERATURE*

410   SW
UNIVERSITY OF STOCKHOLM. INSTITUTE OF LINGUISTICS. MONOGRAPHS. Abbreviated title: M I L U S. (Text in English) 1974. irreg., no.5, 1979. SEK 25. Stockholms Universitet, Institute of Linguistics, Drottninggatan 116, Box 6801, S-106 91 Stockholm, Sweden. Eds. Benny Brodda, Bjoern Lindblom.

UNIVERSITY OF THE NORTH. COMMUNIQUE. see *EDUCATION*

UNIVERSITY OF TORONTO ROMANCE SERIES. see *LITERATURE*

410   CS   ISSN 0083-4173
PG5203
UNIVERZITA KOMENSKEHO. FILOZOFICKA FAKULTA. ZBORNIK: PHILOLOGICA. (Text of each volume in a different language: i.e. English, French, German, Hungarian, Slovak, Spanish) 1949. a. exchange basis. Univerzita Komenskeho, Filozoficka Fakulta, c/o Ustredna Kniznica Filozofickej Fakulty, Gondova 2, 818 01 Bratislava, Czechoslovakia. illus.; maps; circ. 600.

491.86 891.86   CS
UNIVERZITA PALACKEHO. PEDAGOGICKA FAKULTA. SBORNIK PRACI: CESKY JAZYK A LITERATURA. (Text in Czech; summaries and contents page in Czech, German and Russian) irreg, vol.2, 1973. 28 Kcs. Statni Pedagogicke Nakladatelstvi, Ostrovni 30, 113 01 Prague 1, Czechoslovakia. Eds. Eva Doupalova, Miloslav Krbec. charts.

420 375.4   PL   ISSN 0208-5240
P1
UNIWERSYTET GDANSKI. WYDZIAL HUMANISTYCZNY. ZESZYTY NAUKOWE. FILOLOGIA ANGIELSKA. (Text in English) 1979. irreg. price varies. Uniwersytet Gdanski, Wydzial Humanistyczny, c/o Biblioteka Glowna, Ul. Armii Krajowej 110, 81-824 Sopot, Poland. TEL 51-0061. TELEX 051-2247 BMOR PL. (Dist. by: Ars Polona-Ruch, Krakowskie Przedmiescie 7, 00-680 Warsaw, Poland)
    Description: Contains studies on English and American fiction, poetry and drama, on linguistics and English language teaching.

400   PL   ISSN 0302-2315
UNIWERSYTET GDANSKI. WYDZIAL HUMANISTYCZNY. ZESZYTY NAUKOWE. FILOLOGIA POLSKA. PRACE JEZYKOZNAWCZE. 1973. irreg. price varies. Uniwersytet Gdanski, Wydzial Humanistyczny, c/o Biblioteka Glowna, Ul. Armii Krajowej 110, 81-824 Sopot, Poland. TEL 51-0061. TELEX 051 2247 BMOR PL. (Dist. by: Ars Polona-Ruch, Krakowskie Przedmiescie 7, 00-680 Warsaw, Poland) Ed. Edward Breza. circ. 250.
    Description: Covers onomastics, stylistics, morphology, dialectics, phraseology, statistical description, and computer translation.

491.7 375.4   PL   ISSN 0208-4678
UNIWERSYTET GDANSKI. WYDZIAL HUMANISTYCZNY. ZESZYTY NAUKOWE. FILOLOGIA ROSYJSKA. (Text in Polish and Russian) 1971. irreg. price varies. Uniwersytet Gdanski, Wydzial Humanistyczny, c/o Biblioteka Glowna, Ul. Armii Krajowej 110, 81-824 Sopot, Poland. TEL 51-0061. TELEX 051 2247 BMOR PL. (Dist. by Ars Polona-Ruch, Krakowskie Przedmiescie 7, 00-680 Warsaw, Poland) circ. 250.
    Description: Linguistics of the contemporary and historical Russian. Studies in the history of Russian and Soviet literature.

410   PL   ISSN 0138-063X
UNIWERSYTET GDANSKI. WYDZIAL HUMANISTYCZNY. ZESZYTY NAUKOWE. STUDIA SCANDINAVICA. (Text in English, German, Polish and Scandinavia languages) 1978. irreg. price varies. Uniwersytet Gdanski, Wydzial Humanistyczny, c/o Biblioteka Glowna, Ul. Armii Krajowej 110, 81-824 Sopot, Poland. TEL 51-0061. TELEX 051-2247 BMOR PL. (Dist. by: Ars Polona-Ruch, Krakowskie Przedmiescie 7, 00-680 Warsaw, Poland) Ed. Zenon Ciesielski. circ. 250.
    Description: Includes articles and conference proceedings on literature, culture, linguistics, history, socio-political and economic problems of Scandinavian countries.

375   PL   ISSN 0324-8895
UNIWERSYTET GDANSKI. WYDZIAL HUMANYSTYCZNY. ZESZYTY NAUKOWE. STUDIUM PRAKTYCZNEJ NAUKI JEZYKOW OBCYCH. (Text in English, French, German, Russian and Polish; summaries in German and English) 1976. irreg. price varies. Uniwersytet Gdanski, Wydzial Humanistyczny, c/o Biblioteka Glowna, Ul. Armii Krajowej 110, 81-824 Sopot, Poland. TEL 51-0061. TELEX 051 2247 BMOR PL. (Dist. by: Ars Polona-Ruch, Krakowskie Przedmiescie 7, 00-680 Warsaw, Poland) circ. 250.
    Formerly: Uniwersytet Gdanski. Zeszyty Naukowe Studium Jezykow Obcych.
    Description: Contains theoretical and practical essays on developing speaking skills, professionally guided conversation (on different levels of language acquisition), and all types of studies

410   PL   ISSN 0083-4378
PG6014
UNIWERSYTET JAGIELLONSKI. ZESZYTY NAUKOWE. PRACE JEZYKOZNAWCZE. (Vol. 3- called also vol. 6-, continuing the volume numbering of Seria Nauk Spolecznych, Filologia, which it supersedes) (Text in Polish; summaries in French) 1956. irreg., 1984. price varies. Panstwowe Wydawnictwo Naukowe, Miodowa 10, 00-251 Warsaw, Poland. (Dist. by: Ars Polona, Krakowskie Przedmiescie 7, 00-068 Warsaw, Poland) Ed. A. Heinz. circ. 550.
—BLDSC shelfmark: 9512.455000.

491.85   PL   ISSN 0209-3731
UNIWERSYTET SLASKI W KATOWICACH. PRACE NAUKOWE. JEZYK ARTYSTYCZNY. (Text in Polish; summaries in English and Russian) 1978. irreg. price varies. Wydawnictwo Uniwersytetu Slaskiego, Ul. Bankowa 14, 40-007 Katowice, Poland. TEL 48-32-596-915. FAX 48-32-599-605. TELEX 0315584 USKPL. (Dist. by: CHZ Ars Polona, P.O. Box 1001, 00-950 Warsaw, Poland)
    Description: Covers: theory of text, linguistic theory of style, structure of narrative text, figurative language, semantics, semiotics and onomastics.

410   PL   ISSN 0208-5550
PB5
UNIWERSYTET SLASKI W KATOWICACH. PRACE NAUKOWE. NEOPHILOLOGICA. (Text in French; summaries in Polish and Russian) 1980. irreg. Wydawnictwo Uniwersytetu Slaskiego, Ul. Bankowa 14, 40-007 Katowice, Poland. TEL 48-32-596-915. FAX 48-32-599-605. TELEX 0315584 USKPL. (Dist. by: CHS Ars Polona, P.O. Box 1001, 00-950 Warsaw, Poland)
    Description: Covers French linguistics, particularly syntax and semantics.

491.47　　　　PL　　ISSN 0208-5445
UNIWERSYTET SLASKI W KATOWICACH. PRACE NAUKOWE. PRACE JEZYKOZNAWCZE. (Text in Polish and Russian; summaries in English, Polish and Russian) 1969. irreg. price varies. Wydawnictwo Uniwersytetu Slaskiego, Ul. Bankowa 14, 40-007 Katowice, Poland. TEL 48-32-596-915. FAX 48-32-599-605. TELEX 0315584 USKPL. (Dist. by: CHZ Ars Polona, P.O. Box 1001, 00-950 Warsaw, Poland)
 Description: Presents results of synchronus and diachronus studies on the Polish language and Slavonic language studies, principally Russian.

491.85　　　　PL　　ISSN 0208-5011
PG6065
UNIWERSYTET SLASKI W KATOWICACH. PRACE NAUKOWE. Z TEORII I PRAKTYKI DYDAKTYCZNEJ JEZYKA POLSKIEGO. (Text in Polish; summaries in English and Russian) 1977. irreg. Wydawnictwo Uniwersytetu Slaskiego, Ul. Bankowa 14, 40-007 Katowice, Poland. TEL 48-32-596-915. FAX 48-32-599-605. TELEX 0315584 USKPL. (Dist. by: CHZ Ars Polona, P.O. Box 1001, 00-950 Warsaw, Poland)
 Description: Theoretical problems of teaching Polish language and literature.

430 370　　　US　　ISSN 0042-062X
PF3065
UNTERRICHTSPRAXIS. (Text in English and German) 1967. s-a. $20 (foreign $30). American Association of Teachers of German, Inc., 112 Haddontowne Ct., Ste. 104, Cherry Hill, NJ 08034. TEL 609-795-5553. FAX 609-795-9398. Ed. George Peters. adv.; bk.rev.; bibl.; charts; illus.; circ. 5,000. (also avail. in microfiche; reprint service avail. from UMI) **Indexed:** C.I.J.E., Educ.Ind., Lang.& Lang.Behav.Abstr., Lang.Teach.& Ling.Abstr., M.L.A.
—BLDSC shelfmark: 9121.320000.
 Description: Presents articles on language study and teaching methods.

479　　　　GW　　ISSN 0083-4580
UNTERSUCHUNGEN ZUR SPRACH- UND LITERATURGESCHICHTE DER ROMANISCHEN VOELKER. 1959. irreg., vol.11, 1986. price varies. (Akademie der Wissenschaften und der Literatur, Mainz, Kommission fuer Romanische Philologie) Franz Steiner Verlag Wiesbaden GmbH, Birkenwaldstr. 44, Postfach 101526, 7000 Stuttgart 1, Germany. TEL 0711-2582-0. FAX 0711-2582290. TELEX 723636-DAZD.

491.7 375.4　　GW　　ISSN 0174-0652
URAL-ALTAISCHE JAHRBUECHER. NEUE FOLGE. 1981. a. price varies. Verlag Otto Harrassowitz, Taunusstr. 14, Postfach 2929, 6200 Wiesbaden 1, Germany. TEL 0611-530-0. FAX 0611-530570. TELEX 4186135. Ed.Bd. bk.rev.; circ. 400. **Indexed:** M.L.A.

439.2　　　　NE　　ISSN 0042-1235
PF1401
US WURK; tydskrift foar Frisistyk. (Text mainly in Dutch, English, French, Frisian, German) 1952. q. fl.25. Rijksuniversiteit te Groningen, Stifting Freonen Frysk Ynstitut, Oude Kijk in 't Jatstraat 26, 9712 EK Groningen, Netherlands. FAX 050-635603. TELEX 53410 RUGRO NL. Ed.Bd. charts; index; circ. 500. **Indexed:** Lang.& Lang.Behav.Abstr., M.L.A.
 Description: Scholarly journal on the Frisian language and literature.

UTAH STUDIES IN LITERATURE AND LINGUISTICS. see *LITERATURE*

410　　　　IT
V S; quaderni di studi semiotici. 1971. 3/yr. L.36000. Gruppo Editoriale Fabbri SPA, Divisione Periodici, Via Mecenate 91, 20138 Milan, Italy. Ed. Umberto Eco. adv.; bk.rev.

407　　　　NE　　ISSN 0165-9030
VAN TAAL TOT TAAL. (Text in Dutch, English, French and German) 1956. q. fl.37.50. Nederlands Genootschap van Vertalers, Prinsessestraat 2, 2012 LR Haarlem, Netherlands. TEL 23-321298. FAX 23-310097. Ed. Frederick J.A. Mostert. adv.; bk.rev.; index; circ. 1,500. **Indexed:** Lang.& Lang.Behav.Abstr.
—BLDSC shelfmark: 9143.525000.
 Description: Features articles and glossaries as well as related subjects for professional translators and interpreters.

410　　　　US　　ISSN 0172-7362
VARIETIES OF ENGLISH AROUND THE WORLD. 1979. irreg., vol.10, 1991. price varies. John Benjamins Publishing Co., 821 Bethlehem Pike, Philadelphia, PA 19118. TEL 215-836-1200. FAX 215-836-1204. (And: Amsteldijk 44, P.O. Box 75577, 1070 AN Amsterdam, Netherlands. TEL 020-6762325) (back issues avail.)
—BLDSC shelfmark: 9146.530000.
 Description: Irregularly published monographs on the English language world-wide.

420 820　　　PK　　ISSN 0042-3483
VENTURE; bi-annual review of English language and literature. (Text in English) 1960. s-a. Rs.10($3.50) University of Karachi, Department of English, University Rd., Karachi 32, Pakistan. Ed. S.A. Ashraf. bk.rev.; bibl.; index; circ. 500.

460 375.4　　　SP　　ISSN 0210-377X
VERBA; anuario galego de filoloxia. 1974. a. 4500 ptas. (effective 1992). Universidade de Santiago, Servicio de Publicacions e Intercambio Cientifico, Campus Universitario, 15706 Santiago de Compostela, Spain. TEL 81-59-35-00. FAX 81-59-39-53. bk.rev.; charts; index; cum.index; circ. 700. (back issues avail.) **Indexed:** Lang.& Lang.Behav.Abstr. (1981-).

410　　　　US　　ISSN 0162-0932
PE1001
VERBATIM; the language quarterly. 1974. q. $16.50. 4 Laurel Heights, Old Lyme, CT 06371. TEL 203-434-2104. (Subscr. to: Verbatim, P.O. Box 78008, Indianapolis, IN 46278) Ed. Laurence Urdang. adv.; bk.rev.; bibl.; circ. 8,000. **Indexed:** Arts & Hum.Cit.Ind., Curr.Cont., Lang.& Lang.Behav.Abstr., M.L.A.
—BLDSC shelfmark: 9155.756000.

410　　　　FR　　ISSN 0182-5887
VERBUM; revue de linguistique. 1978. q. 220 F. (foreign 270 F.). Presses Universitaires de Nancy, 25 rue Baron Louis, B.P. 454, 54001 Nancy Cedex, France. Dir. Jean Marie Bonnet. circ. 500.
—BLDSC shelfmark: 9155.806500.

430　　　　GW　　ISSN 0342-0752
PF5601
VEREIN FUER NIEDERDEUTSCHE SPRACHFORSCHUNG. KORRESPONDENZBLATT.. 1875. a. DM.10. Karl Wachholtz Verlag, Gaensemarkt 1-3, Postfach 2769, 2350 Neumuenster, Germany. TEL 04321-56720. FAX 04321-56778. Ed. Hermann Niebaum. bk.rev.; bibl.; index; circ. 800. (back issues avail.)

460 370　　　UK　　ISSN 0308-4957
　　　　　　　　　　　　CODEN: VIHIEC
▼**VIDA HISPANICA.** (Text in English, Portuguese, Spanish) 1990. 2/yr. £20($40) (foreign £21). Association for Language Learning, 16 Regent Place, Rugby, Warwickshire CV21 2PN, England. TEL 0788-546443. FAX 0788-544149. Ed. Derek Utley. adv.; bk.rev.; film rev.; play rev.; record rev.; abstr.; bibl.; charts; illus.; mkt.; stat.; index; circ. 1,500.
—BLDSC shelfmark: 9232.860000.
 Description: Contains articles and information for teachers and students of Spanish and Portugese.

VIENNESE HERITAGE/WIENER ERBE. see *LITERATURE*

494.541　　　FI　　ISSN 0042-6806
PH101
VIRITTAAJAA. (Text in Finnish; summaries in English or German) 1897. q. Fmk.230. Kotikielen Seura - Mother Tongue Society, Fabianinkatu 33, 00170 Helsinki, Finland. Ed. Matti Larjavaara. adv.; bk.rev.; charts; illus.; index. cum.index: 1897-1946; 1947-1956; 1957-1971; 1972-1986; circ. 1,000. (also avail. in microform from UMI) **Indexed:** Lang.& Lang.Behav.Abstr., M.L.A.

491 954　　　II　　ISSN 0083-6621
VISHVESHVARANAND INDOLOGICAL SERIES. (Text in English and Sanskrit) 1950. irreg., vol.73, 1982. price varies. Vishveshvarand Vedic Research Institute, Sadhu Ashram, Hoshiarpur 146021, Punjab, India. Ed. S. Bhaskaran Nair.

VISIBLE LANGUAGE; the quarterly concerned with all that is involved in our being literate. see *COMMUNICATIONS*

470　　　　FR　　ISSN 0042-7306
VITA LATINA. (Text in Latin) 1957. 4/yr. 120 F. (Association pour la Diffusion et l'Usage de la Langue Latine) Editions Aubanel, 7 place St. Pierre, 84057 Avignon Cedex, France. Ed. Marie-Dominique Joffre. adv.; bk.rev.; circ. 800.
 Description: Covers study and teaching of Latin language.

VOORZETTEN. see *LITERATURE*

491.7　　　　RU
VOPROSY RUSSKOGO YAZYKOZNANIYA. 1976. irreg. 1.21 Rub. per issue. Moskovskii Universitet, Pr. Gertsena 5-7, 103009 Moscow, Russia. Ed. K. Gorshkova. circ. 4,760.

400　　　　RU　　ISSN 0042-8868
VOPROSY YAZYKOZNANIYA. 1952. bi-m. 32.10 Rub. (Akademiya Nauk S.S.S.R., Institut Yazykoznaniya) Izdatel'stvo Nauka, 90 Profsoyuznaya ul., 117864 Moscow, Russia. TEL 234-05-84. (Dist. by: Mezhdunarodnaya Kniga, ul. Dimitrova D.39, 113095 Moscow, Russia) Ed. F.P. Filin. bk.rev.; bibl.; charts; index; circ. 6,725. **Indexed:** Lang.& Lang.Behav.Abstr. (1972-).

479　　　　GW　　ISSN 0042-899X
PC1.A1
VOX ROMANICA; annales helvetici explorandis linguis romanicis destinati. (Text in English, French, German, Italian or Spanish) 1936. s-a. 92 Fr. K.G. Saur Verlag KG, Ortlerstr. 8, 8000 Munich 70, Germany. TEL 089-76902-0. FAX 089-76902150. bk.rev.; bibl.; cum.index; circ. 550. **Indexed:** Lang.& Lang.Behav.Abstr., M.L.A.
—BLDSC shelfmark: 9258.600000.

VRIJE FRIES. see *HISTORY — History Of Europe*

400 375.4　　　CC
WAIGUOYU/JOURNAL OF FOREIGN LANGUAGE. (Text in Chinese) 1979. bi-m. $31.50. (Shanghai International Studies University) Shanghai Foreign Language Education Press, 550 Dalian Xilu, Shanghai 200083, People's Republic of China. TEL 5420358. (Dist. in US by: China Books & Periodicals, Inc. 2929 24th St., San Francisco, CA 94110. TEL 415-282-2994) adv.; bk.rev.

400 375.4　　　CC
WAIYU JIAOXUE YU YANJIU/FOREIGN LANGUAGE TEACHING & RESEARCH. (Text in Chinese) q. $18.30. Beijing Foreign Language Institute, Suzhou Jie, Haidian Qu, Beijing 100081, People's Republic of China. TEL 890351. (Dist. in US by: China Books & Periodicals, Inc., 2929 24th St., San Francisco, CA 94110. TEL 415-282-2994) Ed. Xu guozhang.

400　　　　CC　　ISSN 1000-0100
WAIYU XUEKAN/JOURNAL OF FOREIGN LANGUAGES. (Text in Chinese) q. $24.30. Heilongjiang Daxue, Waiyu Xi - Heilongjiang University, Foreign Language Department, Xuefu Lu, Harbin, Heilongjiang 150080, People's Republic of China. TEL 64941. (Dist. in US by: China Books & Periodicals, Inc., 2929 24th St., San Francisco, CA 94110. TEL 415-282-2994)

420 375.4　　　UK　　ISSN 0960-877X
▼**WATCHWORDS G C S E ENGLISH REVIEW.** 1991. q. £12.50 (foreign £24.50). Philip Allan Publishers Ltd., Deddington, Oxfordshire OX15 OSE, England. TEL 0869-38652. FAX 0869-38803.

WELSH JOURNAL OF EDUCATION. see *EDUCATION*

DIE WELT DER SLAVEN. see *LITERATURE*

410　　　　NR　　ISSN 0331-0531
WEST AFRICAN JOURNAL OF MODERN LANGUAGES/REVUE OUEST AFRICAINE DES LANGUES VIVANTES. 1976. a. $20. West African Modern Languages Association, c/o University of Maiduguri, Department of Languages and Linguistics, Borno State, Nigeria. Ed. C.M.B. Brann. adv.; bk.rev.; circ. 1,000. **Indexed:** M.L.A.

LINGUISTICS

428.3 301   US   ISSN 1057-0314
PN4071
WESTERN JOURNAL OF COMMUNICATION. 1937. q. $24. Western States Communication Association, c/o Dennis Alexander, Dept. of Communication, University of Utah, Salt Lake City, UT 84112. Ed. Peter A. Andersen. adv.; cum.index; circ. 2,400. (also avail. in microform from UMI; back issues avail.; reprint service avail. from UMI) **Indexed:** C.I.J.E., Commun.Abstr., ERIC, Hist.Abstr., Lang.& Lang.Behav.Abstr., Psychol.Abstr., Sage Pub.Admin.Abstr.
Former titles: Western Journal of Speech Communication (ISSN 0193-6700); Western Speech Communication; Western Speech (ISSN 0043-4205)

420 820   AU   ISSN 0083-9914
PR13
WIENER BEITRAEGE ZUR ENGLISCHEN PHILOLOGIE. (Text in English, German) 1895. irreg., vol.79, 1983. price varies. Wilhelm Braumueller, Universitaets-Verlagsbuchhandlung GmbH, Servitengasse 5, A-1092 Vienna, Austria. TEL 0222-348124. FAX 0222-310-2805. Ed. Siegfried Korninger. index; circ. 600. **Indexed:** M.L.A.

400   AU   ISSN 0083-9922
WIENER BEITRAEGE ZUR KULTURGESCHICHTE UND LINGUISTIK. 1930. irreg., vol.20, 1981. price varies. (Universitaet Wien, Institut fuer Voelkerkunde) Verlag Ferdinand Berger und Soehne GmbH, Wienerstr. 21-23, A-3580 Horn, Austria. TEL 02982-2317-0.

400 800   AU   ISSN 0084-0033
WIENER ROMANISTISCHE ARBEITEN. (Text in French, German) 1962. a. price varies. Universitaets Verlagsbuchhandlung GmbH, Servitengasse 5, A-1092 Vienna, Austria. TEL 0222-348124. FAX 0222-310-2805. Ed. Georg Kremnitz. index; circ. 600.

491.7   AU   ISSN 0084-0041
PG1
WIENER SLAVISTISCHES JAHRBUCH/VIENNESE SLAVONIC YEARBOOK. (Text in English, French, German, Polish and Russian) 1950. a. price varies. (Universitaet Wien, Institut fuer Slavische Philologie) Verlag der Oesterreichischen Akademie der Wissenschaften, Dr. Ignaz-Seipel-Platz 2, A-1010 Vienna, Austria. FAX 0222-5139541. Ed.Bd. adv.; bk.rev.; bibl.; illus. **Indexed:** Arts & Hum.Cit.Ind., Can.Rev.Comp.Lit., M.L.A.

400 890   AU   ISSN 0258-6819
PG1
WIENER SLAWISTISCHER ALMANACH. (Text in Slavic and other European languages) 1978. 2/yr. S.300($24) Gesellschaft zur Foerderung Slawistischer Studien Wien, Teschnergasse 4-17, A-1180 Vienna, Austria. (Subscr. to: Buchvertrieb A. Neimanis, Hans-Sachs-Str. 10, 8000 Munich 5, Germany) Ed.Bd. bk.rev.; circ. 300. (back issues avail.) **Indexed:** M.L.A.

400   AU   ISSN 0084-005X
PA3
WIENER STUDIEN. ZEITSCHRIFT FUER KLASSISCHE PHILOLOGIE UND PATRISTIK. (Text in Ancient Greek, English, German and Latin) 1897. a. price varies. (Universitaet Wien, Institut fuer Klassische Philologie) Verlag der Oesterreichischen Akademie der Wissenschaften, Dr. Ignaz-Seipel-Platz 2, A-1010 Vienna, Austria. FAX 0222-5139541. Ed.Bd. adv.; bk.rev.; bibl.; illus. (reprint service avail. from KTO)

370 440   GW   ISSN 0043-6089
PF3003
WIRKENDES WORT; deutsche Sprache und Literatur in Forschung und Lehre. 1950. q. DM.90. Bouvier Verlag, Fuerstenstr. 3, 5300 Bonn 1, Germany. TEL 0228-7290141. FAX 0228-7290179. Ed. Heinz Roelleke. adv.; bk.rev.; index; circ. 3,500. **Indexed:** Can.Rev.Comp.Lit., M.L.A.

410 305.4   US   ISSN 8755-4550
P120.W66
WOMEN AND LANGUAGE. 1976. s-a. $10 to individuals (Canada $13; elsewhere $18); institutions $15 (Canada $18; elsewhere $20); members $8 (effective 1991). George Mason University, Communication Department, 4400 University Dr., Fairfax, VA 22030-4444. TEL 703-764-6127. (Co-sponsor: Organization for the Study of Communication Language and Gender) Ed. Anita Taylor. bk.rev.; bibl.; circ. 400. (back issues avail.) **Indexed:** Wom.Stud.Abstr. (1976-).
—BLDSC shelfmark: 9343.268000.
Description: Features news items and short articles related to women, communication and language.

400   US   ISSN 0043-7956
P1
WORD. 1945. 3/yr. $35 to individuals; students $25; institutions $55. International Linguistic Association, c/o Dr. Theodore S. Beardsley, Jr., Treas., Hispanic Society of America, 613 W. 155th St., New York, NY 10032. bk.rev.; bibl.; charts; index. (also avail. in microform from UMI; reprint service avail. from UMI) **Indexed:** A.I.C.P., Ind.Bk.Rev.Hum., Lang.& Lang.Behav.Abstr. (1970-), Lang.Teach.& Ling.Abstr.
—BLDSC shelfmark: 9347.750000.

410   US   ISSN 0043-7980
GV1507.W8
WORD WAYS; journal of recreational linguistics. 1968. q. $17. A. Ross Eckler, Ed.& Pub., Spring Valley Rd., Morristown, NJ 07960. TEL 201-538-4584. adv.; bk.rev.; circ. 500. (also avail. in microform from UMI; reprint service avail. from UMI) **Indexed:** Lang.& Lang.Behav.Abstr., M.L.A.
—BLDSC shelfmark: 9347.950000.
Description: Presents short (500-5000 words) expository articles on wordplay (anagrams, palindromes, word squares, pangrams, word ladders). Writing under literary constraint (lipograms, acrostics). Fictional and poetic treatment of wordplay subjects.

350   US   ISSN 0731-9290
WORDWATCHING. 1977. 10/yr. $10. American College, 270 Bryn Mawr Ave., Bryn Mawr, PA 19010. TEL 215-526-1313. Ed. Kay Powell. bk.rev.; index; circ. 1,000. (looseleaf format)

370 420   US   ISSN 0883-2919
PE1128.A2
WORLD ENGLISHES; journal of English as an international and intranational language. 1982. 3/yr. £110 (effective 1992). Pergamon Press, Inc., Journals Division, 660 White Plains Rd., Tarrytown, NY 10591-5153. TEL 914-524-9200. FAX 914-333-2444. (And: Headington Hill Hall, Oxford OX3 0BW, England. TEL 0865-794141) Ed. Braj B. Kachru. (also avail. in microform) **Indexed:** Cont.Pg.Educ., Lang.& Lang.Behav.Abstr. (1986-), Lang.Teach.& Ling.Abstr., Sociol.Abstr.
—BLDSC shelfmark: 9354.825500.
Formerly (until vol.4, no.2, 1985): World Language English (ISSN 0278-4335)
Description: Devoted to the study of global varieties of English in their distinctive cultural and sociolinguistic contexts.
Refereed Serial

WRITING RIGHT. see *PUBLISHING AND BOOK TRADE*

491.85   PL   ISSN 0084-2990
WROCLAWSKIE TOWARZYSTWO NAUKOWE. KOMISJA JEZYKOWA. ROZPRAWY. (Text in English, German and Polish) 1957. irreg., vol.14, 1986. price varies. Ossolineum, Publishing House of the Polish Academy of Sciences, Rynek 9, Wroclaw, Poland. TELEX 0712771 OSS PL. (Dist. by Ars Polona-Ruch, Krakowskie Przedmiescie 7, Warsaw, Poland)
—BLDSC shelfmark: 8036.060000.
Description: Papers on Polish and Indo-European linguistics and dialectology.

400 870 880   GW
WUERZBURGER JAHRBUECHER FUER DIE ALTERTUMSWISSENSCHAFT. 1975. a. DM.80. F. Schoenigh Kommissionsverlag, Franziskaner Platz 4, Postfach 129, 8700 Wuerzburg, Germany. Ed. Joachim Latacz, Guenter Neumann. circ. 600.

490   PL   ISSN 0860-5629
WYZSZA SZKOLA PEDAGOGICZNA IM. KOMISJI EDUKACJI NARODOWEJ W KRAKOWIE. ROCZNIK NAUKOWO-DYDAKTYCZNY. PRACE JEZYKOZNAWCZE. 1970. irreg., no.6, 1991. price varies. Wydawnictwo Naukowe W S P, Ul. Karmelicka 41, 31-129 Krakow, Poland. TEL 33-79-20. (Co-sponsor: Ministerstwo Edukacji Narodowej) Ed. Eugeniusz Pawlowski. illus.

840   PL   ISSN 0239-6556
WYZSZA SZKOLA PEDAGOGICZNA IM. KOMISJI EDUKACJI NARODOWEJ W KRAKOWIE. ROCZNIK NAUKOWO-DYDAKTYCZNY. PRACE ROMANISTYCZNE. 1983. irreg., no.3, 1991. price varies. Wydawnictwo Naukowe W S P, Ul. Karmelicka 41, 31-128 Krakow, Poland. TEL 33-78-20. (Co-sponsor: Ministerstwo Edukacji Narodowej)

WYZSZA SZKOLA PEDAGOGICZNA IM. KOMISJI EDUKACJI NARODOWEJ W KRAKOWIE. ROCZNIK NAUKOWO-DYDAKTYCZNY. PRACE RUSYCYSTYCZNE. see *LITERATURE*

491.85 891.85   PL   ISSN 0239-6025
WYZSZA SZKOLA PEDAGOGICZNA IM. KOMISJI EDUKACJI NARODOWEJ W KRAKOWIE. ROCZNIK NAUKOWO-DYDAKTYCZNY. PRACE Z DYDAKTYKI LITERATURY I JEZYKA POLSKIEGO. 1964. irreg., no.4, 1990. price varies. Wydawnictwo Naukowe W S P, Ul. Karmelicka 41, 31-128 Krakow, Poland. TEL 33-78-20. (Co-sponsor: Ministerstwo Edukacji Narodowej)

420 375.4   PL   ISSN 0860-2328
PE1
WYZSZA SZKOLA PEDAGOGICZNA, OPOLE. ZESZYTY NAUKOWE. SERIA A. FILOGOGIA ANGIELSKA. (Text and summaries in English and Polish) 1986. irreg., vol.3, 1987. price varies, avail. on exchange basis. Wyzsza Szkola Pedagogiczna, Opole, Oleska 48, 45-951 Opole, Poland. TEL 48-77-383-87. (Dist. by: Ars Polona-Ruch, Krakowskie Przedmiescie 7, Warsaw, Poland)
—BLDSC shelfmark: 9512.478960.

WYZSZA SZKOLA PEDAGOGICZNA, OPOLE. ZESZYTY NAUKOWE. SERIA A. FILOLOGIA ROSYJSKA. see *LITERATURE*

410   PL   ISSN 0078-5423
WYZSZA SZKOLA PEDAGOGICZNA, OPOLE. ZESZYTY NAUKOWE. SERIA A. JEZYKOZNAWSTWO. (Text in Polish) 1957. irreg., no.12, 1990. avail. on exchange; price varies. Wyzsza Szkola Pedagogiczna, Opole, Oleska 48, 45-951 Opole, Poland. TEL 48 77 383-87. (Dist. by: Ars Polona-Ruch, Krakowskie Przedmiescie 7, Warsaw, Poland)
—BLDSC shelfmark: 9512.478978.

495.1 375.4   CC
XIAOXUE YUWEN JIAOSHI/TEACHING CHINESE IN ELEMENTARY SCHOOL. (Text in Chinese) bi-m. $17.60. Shanghai Jiaoyu Chubanshe - Shanghai Education Publishers, 123 Yongfu Road, Shanghai 200031, People's Republic of China. TEL 4373213. (Dist. in US by: China Books & Periodicals, Inc., 2929 24th St., San Francisco, CA 94110. TEL 415-282-2994) Ed. Cao Yuzhang.

XIAOXUE YUWEN JIAOXUE/ELEMENTARY SCHOOL CHINESE TEACHING. see *EDUCATION — Teaching Methods And Curriculum*

410   CC
XIAOXUESHENG YUWEN XUEXI/CHINESE STUDIES FOR PUPILS. (Text in Chinese) m. Jiangsu Jiaoyu Chubanshe, 165 Zhongyang Lu, Nanjing, Jiangsu 210009, People's Republic of China. TEL 631836. Ed. Yuan Weizi.

410   US
XINYA. (Text written in romanized Mandarin Chinese) 1982. q. $15 to individuals; institutions $15. Institute for Advanced Communication, Box 254, Swarthmore, PA 19081. TEL 215-543-6286. Ed. Victor H. Mair. adv.; bk.rev.; circ. 1,000. (back issues avail.)
Former titles (until 1991): Xin Tang - New China (ISSN 0731-0897); Xin Talng; (until 1984): Shin Talng.
Description: Includes stories, poems, essays, illustrated narratives, and articles on language reform.

495.1 375.4   CC
XUE HANYU/LEARNING CHINESE. (Text in Chinese) bi-m. $18.50. Beijing Yuyan Xueyuan - Beijing Language Institute, 15 Xueyuan Lu, Beijing 100083, People's Republic of China. (Dist. in US by: China Books & Periodicals, Inc., 2929 24th St., San Francisco, CA 94110. TEL 415-282-2994) Ed. Sun Junzheng.
Formerly: Hanyu Xuexi.

400   US
YALE LANGUAGE SERIES. 1963. irreg., latest 1989. Yale University Press, 92A Yale Sta., New Haven, CT 06520. TEL 203-432-0940.
Formerly: Yale Linguistic Series (ISSN 0513-4412)

410   BO
YATINATAKI; boletin informativo trilingue. (Text in Aymara, Quechua, Spanish) 1974. m. Bol.$140($8) Instituto Boliviano de Cultura, Instituto Nacional de Estudios Linguisticos, Casilla 8877, La Paz, Bolivia. Ed.Bd. (looseleaf format; back issues avail.)

492.49   US   ISSN 0044-0442
PJ5111
YIDISHE SHPRAKH/YIDDISH LANGUAGE. (Text in Yiddish) 1941. irreg. $5. Y I V O Institute for Jewish Research, 1048 Fifth Ave., New York, NY 10028. TEL 212-535-6700. Ed. Mordkhe Schaechter. bk.rev.; circ. 1,000. (also avail. in microform)
Indexed: M.L.A.

420   CC
YINGYU SHIJIE/WORLD OF ENGLISH. (Text in Chinese and English) bi-m. $22.10. Shangwu Yinshu Guan, P.O. Box 1504, Beijing 100005, People's Republic of China. TEL 557190. (Dist. in US by: China Books & Periodicals, Inc., 2929 24th St., San Francisco, CA 94110. TEL 415-282-2994) Chen Yulun.

420   CC
YINGYU XUEXI/ENGLISH LANGUAGE LEARNING. (Text in Chinese and English) m. $26. Beijing Foreign Language Institute, English Department, Suzhou Jie, Haidian Qu, Beijing 100081, People's Republic of China. (Dist. in US by: China Books & Periodicals, Inc., 2929 24th St., San Francisco, CA 94110. TEL 415-282-2994) Ed. Liu Shimu.

420 375.4   CC
YINGYU ZIXUE/ENGLISH SELF-STUDY. (Text in Chinese, English) m. Shanghai Waiguoyu Xueyuan, Yingyu Xi - Shanghai International Studies University, English Department, 119 Xi Tiyuhui Lu, Shanghai 200083, People's Republic of China. TEL 5420900. Ed. Yang Xiaoshi.

410   UK   ISSN 0513-2762
YORKSHIRE DIALECT SOCIETY. SUMMER BULLETIN. 1953. a. £4 (with Transactions). Yorkshire Dialect Society, c/o Librarian, School of English, University of Leeds, Leeds LS2 9JT, England. Ed. M. Shackleton. bk.rev.; circ. 650.

410   UK
YORKSHIRE DIALECT SOCIETY TRANSACTIONS. 1897. a. £5 (with Summer Bulletin)(effective 1992). Yorkshire Dialect Society, c/o Librarian, School of English, University of Leeds, Leeds LS2 9JT, England. Ed. A. Kellett. circ. 650.

410 810 960   NR
YORUBA. (Text in English and Yoruba) 1973. s-a. £N2.50($5.50) (Yoruba Studies Association of Nigeria) Onibon-Oje Press and Book Company, Box 3109, Ibadan, Nigeria. Ed. Wande Abimbola. adv.; bk.rev.; circ. 2,000.

410   CI
YUGOSLAV SERBO-CROATIAN-ENGLISH CONTRASTIVE PROJECT. SERIES B: STUDIES. (Text in English) 1969. irreg. 50 din. Institute of Linguistics, Zagreb, Djure Salaja 3, 41000 Zagreb, Croatia. Ed. Rudolf Filipovic. circ. 500. Indexed: Sociol.Abstr.

495.1   CC
YUWEN JIANSHE/CHINESE LANGUAGE CONSTRUCTION. (Text in Chinese) bi-m. $16.20. Guojia Yuyian Wenzi Gongzu Weiyuanhui - National Language Affairs Committee, 51 Nanxiajie, Chaoyangmennei, Beijing 100010, People's Republic of China. TEL 554621. (Dist. in US by: China Books & Periodicals, Inc., 2929 24th St., San Francisco, CA 94110. TEL 415-282-0994) Ed. Wang Jun.

495.1 375.4   CC
YUWEN JIAOXUE TONGXUN/BULLETIN OF CHINESE LANGUAGE TEACHING. (Text in Chinese) m. Y15.60($44) Yuwen Bao She, Shanxi Shifan Daxue, Linfen, Shanxi 041004, People's Republic of China. (Dist. outside China by: China International Book Trading Corp., P.O. Box 399, Beijing, P.R.C.; Dist. in US by: China Books & Periodicals, Inc., 2929 24th St., San Francisco, CA 94110) Eds. Sun Quansheng, Jin Baotai.

495.1   CC
YUWEN XUEXI/CHINESE LANGUAGE LEARNING. (Text in Chinese) m. Y11.04($36.80) Shanghai Jiaoyu Chubanshe - Shanghai Education Publishers, 123 Yongfu Road, Shanghai 200031, People's Republic of China. TEL 4377165. (Dist. outside China by: China International Book Trading Corp., P.O. Box 339, Beijing, P.R.C.; Dist. in US by: China Books & Periodicals, Inc., 2929 24th St., San Francisco, CA 94110) Eds. Cao Yuzhang, Fan Shougang.

495.1   CC   ISSN 1000-2979
PL1004
YUWEN YANJIU/CHINESE LANGUAGE RESEARCH. (Text in Chinese) 1980. q. $22.80. (Shanxi Sheng Shehui Kexueyuan) Yuwen Chubanshe, Chaonei Nanxiaojie 51, Beijing. (Dist. in US by: China Books & Periodicals, Inc., 2929 24th St., San Francisco, CA 94110. TEL 415-282-2994)

495.1   CC
YUWEN YUEKAN. (Text in Chinese) m. Y10.80($32.30) Huanan Shifan Daxue, Zhongwen Xi - South China Normal University, Chinese Department, Shipai, Guangzhou, Guangdong 510631, People's Republic of China. (Dist. outside China by: China International Book Trading Corp., P.O. Box 399, Beijing, P.R.C.; Dist. in US by: China Books & Periodicals, Inc., 2929 24th St., San Francisco, CA 94110. TEL 415-282-2994) Ed. Huang Jizhuang.
Description: Covers all aspects of Chinese linguistics.

400 375.4   CC   ISSN 0257-9448
YUYAN JIAOXUE YU YANJIU/LANGUAGE TEACHING & STUDIES. (Text in Chinese) 1979. q. $16.50. Beijing Yuyan Xueyuan - Beijing Language Institute, 15 Xueyuan Lu, Haidian Qu, Beijing 100083, People's Republic of China. TEL 2017531. (Dist. outside China by: China International Book Trading Corp., P.O. Box 399, Beijing, P.R.C.; Dist. in US by: China Books & Periodicals, Inc., 2929 24th St., San Francisco, CA 94110. TEL 415-282-2994)
—BLDSC shelfmark: 5155.712600.

495.1   CC   ISSN 1001-3261
YUYAN WENZI XUE. (Subseries of: Fuyin Baokan Ziliao) (Text in Chinese) m. Y39.90. Zhongguo Renmin Daxue, Shubao Ziliao Zhongxin - China People's University, Book & Newspaper Information Center, P.O. Box 1122, Beijing 100007, People's Republic of China. TEL 441792.
Description: Contains reprints of papers and articles on language and linguistics.

410 890   YU   ISSN 0454-4617
ZA CASOPIS: KOVCEZIC. (Text in English, German, Russian and Serbian) 1958. biennial. 4000 din.($4) Vukov i Dositejev Muzej, 9 Jevremova 21, Belgrade, Yugoslavia. TEL 625-161. Ed. J. Saulic. circ. 500.

ZAMBIA MUSEUMS JOURNAL. see *ANTHROPOLOGY*

410   CI
PG1201
ZAVOD ZA HRVATSKI JEZIK. RASPRAVE. (Text in Serbo-Croatian; summaries in English, French, German, Russian) 1968. a. $8. Hrvatski Filoloski Institut, Zavod za Hrvatski Jazik, Strossmayerov Trg 2, 41000 Zagreb, Croatia. TEL 276-007. Ed. Mijo Loncaric. circ. 400. Indexed: Lang.& Lang.Behav.Abstr.
Formerly: Zavod za Jezik. Rasprave (ISSN 0351-434X)

891.59   AF
ZAYRAY. (Text in Pashtu) 1938. w. Afghanistan Academy of Sciences, Sher Alikhan St., Kabul, Afghanistan.

491   YU   ISSN 0350-0470
PG13
ZBORNIK ZA SLAVISTIKU/REVIEW OF SLAVIC STUDIES. s-a. Matica Srpska, Matice Srpske 1, Novi Sad, Vojvodina, Yugoslavia. Ed. Milorad Zivancevic. Indexed: M.L.A.

LINGUISTICS   2853

491   CI
ZBORNIK ZAGREBACKE SLAVISTICKE SKOLE. 1973. irreg. Medjunarodni Slavisticki Centar SR Hrvatske, Djure Salaja 3, Zagreb, Croatia. (Co-sponsor: Sveucilista u Zagrebu, Filozofski Fakultet) Eds. Franjo Grcevic, Mladen Kuzmanovic.

ZEITSCHRIFT FUER AEGYPTISCHE SPRACHE UND ALTERTUMSKUNDE. see *ORIENTAL STUDIES*

410   GW   ISSN 0932-4461
PJ4501
ZEITSCHRIFT FUER ALTHEBRAISTIK. (Text in English, French, German) 1988. s-a. DM.149. W. Kohlhammer GmbH, Hessbruehlstr. 69, Postfach 800430, 7000 Stuttgart 80, Germany. TEL 0711-7863-0. (back issues avail.) Indexed: Rel.& Theol.Abstr. (1988-).

ZEITSCHRIFT FUER ANGLISTIK UND AMERIKANISTIK. see *LITERATURE*

410   GW   ISSN 0170-026X
ZEITSCHRIFT FUER ARABISCHE LINGUISTIK/JOURNAL OF ARABIC LINGUISTICS/JOURNAL DE LINGUISTIQUE ARABE. (Text in English, French, German) 1978. irreg., vol.23, 1991. price varies. Verlag Otto Harrassowitz, Taunusstr. 14, Postfach 2929, 6200 Wiesbaden 1, Germany. TEL 0611-530-0. FAX 0611-530570. TELEX 4186135. Eds. H. Bobzin, O. Jastrow. adv.; bk.rev.; circ. 360. (back issues avail.) Indexed: Lang.& Lang.Behav.Abstr. (1985-), M.L.A.
—BLDSC shelfmark: 4947.165000.

491.6   GW   ISSN 0084-5302
ZEITSCHRIFT FUER CELTISCHE PHILOLOGIE. (Text in English, French, German or Irish) 1904; no issues published between 1944 and 1952. irreg. varies. Max Niemeyer Verlag, Postfach 2140, 7400 Tuebingen 1, Germany. TEL 07071-81104. FAX 07071-87419. (back issues avail.) Indexed: Arts & Hum.Cit.Ind., M.L.A.
Description: Essays and reviews on Celtic languages and literature.

430   GW   ISSN 0044-2496
PF3003
ZEITSCHRIFT FUER DEUTSCHE PHILOLOGIE. 1883. q. DM.208 (students DM.188). Erich Schmidt Verlag GmbH & Co. (Berlin), Genthiner Str. 30 G, 1000 Berlin 30, Germany. Ed.Bd. adv.; bk.rev.; bibl.; charts; illus.; index; circ. 1,300. (reprint service avail. from SWZ) Indexed: Curr.Cont., Ind.Bk.Rev.Hum., Lang.& Lang.Behav.Abstr., M.L.A.

430 830   GW   ISSN 0044-2518
ZEITSCHRIFT FUER DEUTSCHES ALTERTUM UND DEUTSCHE LITERATUR. 1841. 4/yr. DM.180. Franz Steiner Verlag Wiesbaden GmbH, Birkenwaldstr. 44, Postfach 101526, 7000 Stuttgart 1, Germany. TEL 0711-2582-0. FAX 0711-2582290. TELEX 723636-DAZD. Ed. Franz-Josef Worstbrock. adv.; bk.rev.; bibl.; index; circ. 800. (back issues avail.) Indexed: Arts & Hum.Cit.Ind., Curr.Cont., Ind.Bk.Rev.Hum., M.L.A.

400   GW   ISSN 0044-1449
PF5001
ZEITSCHRIFT FUER DIALEKTOLOGIE UND LINGUISTIK. (Text in English and German) 1924. 3/yr. DM.120 (supplements priced individually). Franz Steiner Verlag Wiesbaden GmbH, Birkenwaldstr. 44, Postfach 101526, 7000 Stuttgart 1, Germany. TEL 0711-2582-0. FAX 0711-2582290. TELEX 723636-DAZD. Ed. Joachim Goeschel. adv.; bk.rev.; abstr.; bibl.; charts; index; circ. 600. (back issues avail.; reprint service avail. from KTO) Indexed: Arts & Hum.Cit.Ind., Ind.Bk.Rev.Hum., Lang.& Lang.Behav.Abstr., M.L.A.
—BLDSC shelfmark: 9457.680000.
Formerly: Zeitschrift fuer Mundartforschung.

400   GW   ISSN 0341-0838
ZEITSCHRIFT FUER DIALEKTOLOGIE UND LINGUISTIK. BEIHEFTE. irreg., vol.71, 1991. price varies. Franz Steiner Verlag Wiesbaden GmbH, Birkenwaldstr. 44, Postfach 101526, 7000 Stuttgart 1, Germany. TEL 0711-2582-0. FAX 0711-2582290. TELEX 723636-DAZD. Ed. Joachim Goeschel.

2854 LINGUISTICS — ABSTRACTING, BIBLIOGRAPHIES, STATISTICS

440 GW ISSN 0044-2747
ZEITSCHRIFT FUER FRANZOESISCHE SPRACHE UND LITERATUR. (Text in English, French, German) 1879. 3/yr. DM.108 (supplements priced individually). Franz Steiner Verlag Wiesbaden GmbH, Birkenwaldstr. 44, Postfach 101526, 7000 Stuttgart 1, Germany. TEL 0711-2582-0. FAX 0711-2582290. TELEX 723636-DAZD. Eds. Peter Blumenthal, Klaus W. Hempfer. adv.; bk.rev.; bibl.; illus.; index; circ. 500. (back issues avail.; reprint service avail. from SWZ) **Indexed:** Curr.Cont., M.L.A.
—BLDSC shelfmark: 9462.100000.

440 GW ISSN 0341-0811
ZEITSCHRIFT FUER FRANZOESISCHE SPRACHE UND LITERATUR. BEIHEFTE. NEUE FOLGE. irreg., vol.19, 1991. price varies. Franz Steiner Verlag Wiesbaden GmbH, Birkenwaldstr. 44, Postfach 101526, 7000 Stuttgart 1, Germany. TEL 0711-2582-0. FAX 0711-2582290. TELEX 723636-DAZD. Eds. Klaus W. Hempfer, Peter Blumenthal.

430 GW ISSN 0301-3294
PF3003
ZEITSCHRIFT FUER GERMANISTISCHE LINGUISTIK. 1973. 3/yr. $105. Walter de Gruyter und Co., Genthiner Str. 13, 1000 Berlin 30, Germany. TEL 030-26005-0. FAX 030-26005251. TELEX 184027. (U.S. addr.: Walter de Gruyter, Inc., 200 Saw Mill Rd., Hawthorne, NY 10532) Ed.Bd. adv.; bk.rev.; abstr.; bibl.; index; circ. 2,000. (back issues avail.) **Indexed:** Arts & Hum.Cit.Ind., Curr.Cont., Ind.Bk.Rev.Hum., Lang.& Lang.Behav.Abstr. (1989-).

400 GW ISSN 0044-331X
ZEITSCHRIFT FUER PHONETIK, SPRACHWISSENSCHAFT UND KOMMUNIKATIONSFORSCHUNG. (Text in English, French, German, Russian) 1948. bi-m. M.226.80. (Akademie der Wissenschaften der DDR, Zentralinstitut fuer Sprachwissenschaft) Akademie-Verlag Berlin, Leipziger Str. 3-4, 1086 Berlin, Germany. TELEX 114420-AVERL-DD. Ed. W. Neumann. bk.rev.; bibl.; charts; illus.; index. **Indexed:** Ind.Bk.Rev.Hum., Lang.Teach.& Ling.Abstr., M.L.A.
—BLDSC shelfmark: 9480.800000.

479 GW ISSN 0049-8661
PC3
ZEITSCHRIFT FUER ROMANISCHE PHILOLOGIE. (Supplement: Romanische Bibliographie) (Text in French, German, Italian, Spanish) 1877. 3/yr. DM.296. Max Niemeyer Verlag, Postfach 2140, 7400 Tuebingen 1, Germany. TEL 07071-81104. FAX 07071-87419. Ed. Max Pfister. adv.; bk.rev. (also avail. in microfiche from BHP; back issues avail.; reprint service avail. from SCH) **Indexed:** Arts & Hum.Cit.Ind., Curr.Cont., Lang.& Lang.Behav.Abstr., M.L.A.
Description: Contains esays and reviews concerning Romance languages and literature, especially before the 16th century.

400 830 GW ISSN 0084-5396
ZEITSCHRIFT FUER ROMANISCHE PHILOLOGIE. BEIHEFTE. (Text in English, French, German, Italian and Spanish) 1906. irreg., no.240, 1991. Max Niemeyer Verlag, Postfach 2140, 7400 Tuebingen 1, Germany. TEL 07071-81104. FAX 07071-87419. Ed. Max Pfister. (also avail. in microfilm from BHP; back issues avail.)
Description: Monographs about Romance literature; critical editions of texts until the 15th century; Romance languages.

ZEITSCHRIFT FUER SEMIOTIK. see *PHILOSOPHY*

491 GW ISSN 0044-3492
PG1
ZEITSCHRIFT FUER SLAVISCHE PHILOLOGIE. vol.21, 1951. s-a. DM.200 (student DM.150). Carl Winter Universitaetsverlag GmbH, Lutherstr. 59, 6900 Heidelberg, Germany. Eds. H. Braeuer, P. Brang. bk.rev. (reprint service avail. from KTO) **Indexed:** Arts & Hum.Cit.Ind., Curr.Cont., Ind.Bk.Rev.Hum., Lang.& Lang.Behav.Abstr., M.L.A.

491 891 GW ISSN 0044-3506
PG1
ZEITSCHRIFT FUER SLAWISTIK. (Text in German and Russian) 1956. bi-m. M.178.80. (Akademie der Wissenschaften der DDR, Zentralinstitut fuer Literaturgeschichte und Sprachwissenschaft) Akademie-Verlag Berlin, Leipziger Str. 3-4, 1086 Berlin, Germany. TELEX 114410-AVERL-DD. Ed. G. Ziegengeist. bk.rev.; abstr.; bibl.; charts; illus.; index; cum.index(1956-60 only). **Indexed:** Arts & Hum.Cit.Ind., Curr.Cont., Lang.& Lang.Behav.Abstr., M.L.A.
—BLDSC shelfmark: 9486.350000.

430 375.4 GW ISSN 0721-9067
P3
ZEITSCHRIFT FUER SPRACHWISSENSCHAFT. 1982. s-a. DM.74. Vandenhoeck und Ruprecht, Theaterstr. 13, Postfach 3753, 3400 Goettingen, Germany. TEL 0551-6959-22. FAX 0551-695917. Ed.Bd. index; circ. 570.
—BLDSC shelfmark: 9486.401000.

491.7 375.4 CC
ZHONGGUO E YU JIAOXUE/CHINESE JOURNAL OF RUSSIAN TEACHING. (Text in Russian) q. Beijing Waiguoyu Xueyuan - Beijing Foreign Language Institute, Suzhou Jie, Haidian, Beijing 100081, People's Republic of China. TEL 890351. Ed. Wu Fuxiang.

418.02 CC ISSN 1000-873X
ZHONGGUO FANYI/CHINESE TRANSLATORS JOURNAL. (Text mainly in Chinese; table of contents in English) bi-m. Y6($18.50) (Zhongguo Fanyi Gongzuozhe Xiehui - Translators' Association of China) Waiwen Chuban Faxing Ju - Foreign Languages Publishing and Distribution Administration, 24 Baiwanzhuang Lu, Fuwai, Beijing 100037, People's Republic of China. TEL 8315599. (Dist. outside China by: China International Book Trading Corp., P.O. Box 399, Beijing, P.R.C.; Dist. in US by: China Books & Periodicals, Inc., 2929 24th St., San Francisco, CA 94110. TEL 415-282-2994) (Co-sponsor: Zhongguo Duiwai Chuban Gongsi - China Translation and Publishing Corporation) Ed. Ye Junjian.
—BLDSC shelfmark: 3181.122360.
Formerly: Translators' Notes.
Description: Aims to promote the theory and study of translation, exchange of translating experience, and provide commentary on translated works. Includes practice excercises.

495.1 CC ISSN 0578-1949
ZHONGGUO YUWEN. (Text and summaries in Chinese; table of contents in English) 1952. bi-m. Y10.20($32.90) (Zhongguo Shehui Kexueyuan, Yuwen Yanjiusuo - Chinese Academy of Social Sciences, Language Institute) Shehui Kexue Zazhishe, A-158 Gulou Xidajie, Beijing 100720, People's Republic of China. (Dist. outside China by: China International Book Trading Corp., P.O. Box 399, Beijing, P.R.C.; Dist. in US by: China Books & Periodicals, Inc., 2929 24th St., San Francisco, CA 94110. TEL 415-282-2994) bibl.
Description: Contains linguistic studies on the Chinese language.

410 370 CC ISSN 1000-7245
ZHONGWEN ZIXIU/CHINESE SELF-STUDY. (Text in Chinese) m. Shanghai Jiaoyu Xuehui - Shanghai Society of Education, 1045 Huaihai Zhonglu, Shanghai 200031, People's Republic of China. TEL 4375550. Ed. Chen Bixiang.

410 370 CC
ZHONGWEN ZIXUE ZHIDAO/GUIDE TO TEACHING YOURSELF CHINESE. (Text in Chinese) m. Huadong Shifan Daxue, Zhongwen Xi - East China Normal University, Chinese Department, 3663 Zhongshan Beilu, Shanghai 200062, People's Republic of China. TEL 2577577. Ed. Xu Zhongyu.

410 370 CC
ZHONGXIAOXUE YINGYU JIAOXUE YU YANJIU/ENGLISH TEACHING AND RESEARCH FOR ELEMENTARY AND SECONDARY SCHOOLS. (Text in Chinese) bi-m. Huadong Shifan Daxue, Waiyu Xi - East China Normal University, Foreign Language Department, 3663 Zhongshan Beilu, Shanghai 200062, People's Republic of China. TEL 2577577. Ed. Zhang Jianzhong.

410 CC ISSN 1000-419X
ZHONGXUE YUWEN/MIDDLE SCHOOL CHINESE. (Text in Chinese) m. Hubei Daxue, Zhongwen Xi - Hubei University, Department of Chinese, Baoji'an, Wuchang-qu, Wuhan, Hubei 430062, People's Republic of China. TEL 874753. Ed. Deng Xianzheng.

495.1 375.4 US ISSN 1001-280X
ZHONGXUE YUWEN JIAOXUE/LANGUAGE TEACHING IN MIDDLE SCHOOL. (Text in Chinese) m. $35.90. China Books & Periodicals, Inc., 2929 24th St., San Francisco, CA 94110. TEL 415-282-2994. FAX 415-282-0994.

430 370 GW ISSN 0341-5864
ZIELSPRACHE DEUTSCH; Zeitschrift fuer Unterrichtsmethodik und angewandte Sprachwissenschaft. 1951. 4/yr. DM.34. Max Hueber Verlag, Max-Hueber-Str.4, 8045 Ismaning, Germany. TEL 089-9602-0. FAX 089-9602-358. TELEX 523613-HUEBD. Ed. Elmar Winters-Ohle. adv.; bk.rev.; circ. 2,500. (also avail. in microform from SWZ; reprint service avail. from SWZ) **Indexed:** Lang.& Lang.Behav.Abstr., Lang.Teach.& Ling.Abstr., M.L.A.
Formerly: Deutschunterricht fuer Auslaender.
Description: Focuses on new developments and results in the various fields of applied linguistics and conveys suggestions as to teaching German as a foreign language.

420 374 GW ISSN 0342-6173
PE1001
ZIELSPRACHE ENGLISCH; Zeitschrift fuer den Englischunterricht in der Erwachsenbildung. (Text in English and German) 1961. 4/yr. DM.34. Max Hueber Verlag, Max-Hueber-Str.4, 8045 Ismaning, Germany. TEL 089-9602-0. FAX 089-9602-358. Ed. A. Schmitz. adv.; bk.rev.; circ. 2,800. **Indexed:** Lang.& Lang.Behav.Abstr., Lang.Teach.& Ling.Abstr.
—BLDSC shelfmark: 9513.132000.
Formerly: Englisch an Volkshochschulen (ISSN 0013-8193)
Description: Covers English study and teaching, including didactics, organization, language, cultural background studies and specialized literature.

440 375.4 GW ISSN 0342-6203
ZIELSPRACHE FRANZOESISCH; Zeitschrift fuer den Franzoesischunterricht in der Erwachsenbildung. (Text in French and German) 1971. 4/yr. DM.34. (Deutscher Volkshochschulverband, Paedagogische Arbeitsstelle) Max Hueber Verlag, Max-Hueber-Str.4, 8045 Ismaning, Germany. TEL 089-9602-0. FAX 089-9602-358. TELEX 523613-HUEBD. Ed. Albert Raasch. circ. 2,500.
Description: Covers the organization of study courses, advanced training, methodical, psychological and sociological problems.

491.7 GW ISSN 0173-9522
ZIELSPRACHE RUSSISCH; Zeitschrift fuer den Russischunterricht. (Text in German, Russian) 1967. q. DM.36. Max Hueber Verlag, Max-Hueber-Str. 4, 8045 Ismaning, Germany. TEL 089-9602-0. FAX 089-9602-358. TELEX 523613-HUEBD. Ed. R.-D. Keil. adv.; bk.rev.; index; circ. 1,000. (also avail. in microform from UMI; reprint service avail. from UMI) **Indexed:** Lang.& Lang.Behav.Abstr.
Formerly (1967-1980): Russisch (ISSN 0036-035X)
Description: Directed at those who study or teach Russian. Deals with modern teaching methods, practical information, relevant periodicals and new publications.

LINGUISTICS — Abstracting, Bibliographies, Statistics

400 800 016 BU ISSN 0861-0843
ABSTRACTS OF BULGARIAN SCIENTIFIC LITERATURE. LINGUISTICS AND LITERATURE. Russian edition (ISSN 0204-6245) (Editions in English and Russian) 1958. q. 20 lv. Bulgarska Akademiia na Naukite, 7 Noemvri St. 1, 1040 Sofia, Bulgaria. (Dist. by: RP, Klokotnica St., No.2A, 1202 Sofia, Bulgaria) Ed.Bd. abstr.; circ. 200.
Supersedes French edition: Bulletin d'Analyses de la Litterature Scientifique Bulgare. Linguistique et Litterature (ISSN 0204-7667)

410   GW   ISSN 0721-2488
AFRICAN LINGUISTIC BIBLIOGRAPHIES. 1981. irreg., vol.4, 1989. price varies. Helmut Buske Verlag Hamburg, Friedrichsgaber Weg 138, Postfach 1249, D-2000 Norderstedt, Germany. Eds. Franz Rottland, Rainer Vossen.

016 410   US   ISSN 0165-7267
AMSTERDAM STUDIES IN THE THEORY AND HISTORY OF LINGUISTIC SCIENCE. SERIES 5: LIBRARY AND INFORMATION SOURCES IN LINGUISTICS. Short title: L I S L. (Text in English) 1977. irreg., vol.20, 1990. price varies. John Benjamins Publishing Co., 821 Bethlehem Pike, Philadelphia, PA 19118. TEL 215-836-1200. FAX 215-836-1204. (And: Amsteldijk 44, P.O. Box 75577, 1070 AN Amsterdam, Netherlands. TEL 020-6762325) Ed. E.F.K. Koerner. **Indexed:** M.L.A.
—BLDSC shelfmark: 0859.604200.
  Description: Contains bibliographies, biographies and other reference works concerning linguisitcs.

410 016   NE   ISSN 0044-8176
Z7003
ANALECTA LINGUISTICA; informational bulletin of linguistics. 1971. 2/yr. fl.270($148) (effective 1992). (Hungarian Academy of Sciences, Linguistic Section, HU) John Benjamins Publishing Co., Amstejdijk 44, P.O. Box 75577, 1070 AN Amsterdam, Netherlands. TEL 020-6738156. FAX 020-6739773. (In N. America: 821 Bethlehem Pike, Philadelphia, PA 19118. TEL 215-836-1200) Ed. A. Rona-Tas. abstr.; bibl. (back issues avail.) **Indexed:** M.L.A.
  Description: Examines a variety of literature on liguistics.

ANNEE PHILOLOGIQUE; bibliographie critique et analytique de l'antiquite greco-latine. see *CLASSICAL STUDIES — Abstracting, Bibliographies, Statistics*

811 011   US   ISSN 0196-2221
PN6099.6
ANTHOLOGY OF MAGAZINE VERSE AND YEARBOOK OF AMERICAN POETRY. 1980. a. $37.50. Monitor Book Co., Inc., 610 N. Ave. Caballeros, Box 9078, Palm Springs, CA 92263. TEL 619-323-2270. Ed. Alan F. Pater. **Indexed:** Child.Auth.& Illus.
  Formerly: Anthology of Magazine Verse (ISSN 0270-3904)
  Description: Preserves the choicest poetry of the year selected from magazines across the United States and Canada.

439.3 016   NE   ISSN 0045-186X
BIBLIOGRAFIE VAN DE NEDERLANDSE TAAL- EN LITERATUUR WETENSCHAP.* 1970. a. fl.55. Koninklijke Nederlandse Akademie van Wetenschappen, Bureau voor de Bibliografie van de Neerlandistiek, Keizersgracht 569-571, 1017 DR Amsterdam, Netherlands. Ed.Bd. 5-yr cum. 1975.
●Also available online.

410   NE   ISSN 0920-7104
BIBLIOGRAPHIA DE INTERLINGUA. (Text in Interlingua) 1973. a. Servicio de Libros U M I, Zonnegloren 30, 7361 TL Beekbergen, Netherlands.
  Description: Recent publications in the international language, Interlingua.

430 015   GW   ISSN 0323-3154
BIBLIOGRAPHIE FREMDSPRACHIGER GERMANICA.* 1972. q. DM.12. Deutsche Buecherei Leipzig, Deutscher Platz, 7010 Leipzig, Germany. Ed. Erika Jesche.
  Description: Bibliography of books concerning Germany in languages other than German covering a large variety of fields and subjects.

BIBLIOGRAPHIE LINGUISTISCHER LITERATUR; bibliography of general linguistics and of English, German and Romance linguistics. see *LITERATURE — Abstracting, Bibliographies, Statistics*

400 016   FR   ISSN 0007-5590
P2
BULLETIN SIGNALETIQUE. PART 524: SCIENCES DU LANGAGE. 1947. q. 410 F. Centre National de la Recherche Scientifique, Institut de l'Information Scientifique et Technique, 54 bd. Raspail, 75270 Paris Cedex 06, France. FAX 45487015. TELEX MSH 203104 F. cum.index.
●Also available online. Vendor(s): Telesystemes - Questel.

410 016   US
CURRENT ESPERANTO BOOK LIST. (Text in English and Esperanto) 1964. s-a. $2. Esperanto League for North America, Box 1129, El Cerrito, CA 94530. TEL 510-653-0998. bk.rev.; bibl.; stat.; circ. 2,000.
  Description: Lists and descriptions of titles in Esperanto and relating to it.

440 840   UK
CURRENT RESEARCH IN FRENCH STUDIES AT UNIVERSITIES AND POLYTECHNICS IN THE UNITED KINGDOM AND IRELAND. (Text in English, French) 1969. biennial. £6. Society for French Studies, c/o Dr. John Harris, Ed., University of Bath, Secretary & Registrar's Dept., England. index; circ. 400. (back issues avail.)
  Former titles: Current Research in French Studies at Universities and Polytechnics in the United Kindom & Current Research in French Studies at Universities and University Colleges in the United Kingdom (ISSN 0263-4538)

400 016   US
DICTIONARIES, ENCYCLOPEDIAS, AND OTHER WORD-RELATED BOOKS. irreg., 4th ed., 1987. $520. Gale Research Inc., 835 Penobscot Bldg., Detroit, MI 48226. TEL 313-961-2242. FAX 313-961-6083. TELEX 810-221-7086. Ed. Annie M. Brewer.
  Description: Bibliography of word-related reference books.

E I. (Excerpta Indonesica) see *ANTHROPOLOGY — Abstracting, Bibliographies, Statistics*

440 016   CN   ISSN 0712-7561
ETUDES STRATEGIQUES ET MILITAIRES (COLLECTION). (Text in English, French) 1981. a. Can.$18. Centre Quebecois de Relations Internationales, Faculte des Sciences Sociales, Universite Laval, Quebec, Que. G1K 7P4, Canada. TEL 418-656-7530. Ed. Claude Basset. circ. 500. **Indexed:** A.B.C.Pol.Sci.
  Formerly (until 1981): Communautes Francophones: Bibliographie, Chroniques.

016 840   US   ISSN 0085-0888
Z2173
FRENCH 20 BIBLIOGRAPHY; critical and biographical references for the study of French literature since 1885. 1949. a. $78. (Susquehanna University Press) Associated University Presses, 440 Forsgate Dr., Cranbury, NJ 08512. TEL 609-655-4770. FAX 609-655-8366. Ed. Douglas W. Alden. circ. 700.
  Supersedes: French 7 Bibliography, Critical and Biographical References for the Study of Contemporary French Literature.

GERMANISTIK; internationales Referatenorgan mit bibliographischen Hinweisen. see *LITERATURE — Abstracting, Bibliographies, Statistics*

410 869   SP   ISSN 1130-1163
Z7003
INDICE ESPANOL DE HUMANIDADES. SERIES C: LINGUISTICS AND LITERATURE. 1978. a. 5000 ptas. or exchange basis. Instituto de Informacion y Documentacion en Ciencias Sociales y Humanidades, Pinar 25, 3, 28006 Madrid, Spain.
●Also available online.
Also available on CD-ROM.
  Supersedes in part (in 1989): Indice Espanol de Humanidades (ISSN 0210-8488)

410   CK
INSTITUTO LINGUISTICO DE VERANO EN COLOMBIA. BIBLIOGRAFIA. 1975. irreg., latest 1990. free. Instituto Linguistico de Verano, Departamento de Estudios Tecnicos, Apdo. Aereo 100602, Bogota, Colombia. FAX 2590093. circ. 1,000.

410 572 016   NE   ISSN 0074-0462
KONINKLIJK INSTITUUT VOOR TAAL-, LAND- EN VOLKENKUNDE. BIBLIOGRAPHICAL SERIES. (Text mainly in English; occasionally in Dutch, French) 1965. irreg., latest no. 16, 1987. price varies. P.O. Box 9515, 2300 RA Leiden, Netherlands.

400 370 016   UK   ISSN 0261-4448
PB35
LANGUAGE TEACHING. 1968. q. $42 to individuals; institutions $83. Cambridge University Press, Edinburgh Bldg., Shaftesbury Rd., Cambridge CB2 2RU, England. TEL 0223-312393. FAX 0223-315052. TELEX 851817756. (N. American addr.: Cambridge University Press, 40 W. 20th St., New York, NY 10011-4211, USA. TEL 800-431-1580) Ed. Valerie Kinsella. adv.; bk.rev.; abstr.; bibl.; index. cum.index. (also avail. in microform from UMI; reprint serivce avail. from SWZ)
—BLDSC shelfmark: 5155.711970.
  Former titles (until 1982): Language Teaching and Linguistics Abstracts (ISSN 0306-6304); (until 1975): Language-Teaching Abstracts (ISSN 0023-8279); English Teaching Abstracts.

016 410   NE   ISSN 0378-4592
LINGUISTIC BIBLIOGRAPHY/BIBLIOGRAPHIE LINGUISTIQUE. (Text in English and French) 1949. a. price varies. (Unesco International Permanent Committee of Linguists, UN) Kluwer Academic Publishers, Postbus 17, 3300 AA Dordrecht, Netherlands. TEL 078-334911. FAX 078-334254. TELEX 29245. (Dist. by: Kluwer Academic Publishers Group, Postbus 322, 3300 AH Dordrecht, Netherlands; N. America dist. addr: Kluwer Academic Publishers, Box 358, Accord Station, Hingham, MA 02018-0358. TEL 617-871-6600) Eds. Mark Janse, Sijmen Tol.
  Description: Contains information on publications in all fields of linguistics, classified by language and subject, with and author index.

410   UK   ISSN 0267-5498
P1
LINGUISTICS ABSTRACTS. 1985. q. £27.50($56) to individuals; institutions £81($160). Basil Blackwell Ltd., 108 Cowley Rd., Oxford OX4 1JF, England. TEL 0865-791100. FAX 0865-791347. TELEX 837022-OXBOOK-G. Ed. David Crystal. adv.; circ. 700. (also avail. in microform)

400 016   US   ISSN 0888-8027
                        CODEN: LLBAAZ
LINGUISTICS AND LANGUAGE BEHAVIOR ABSTRACTS. Short title: L L B A. 1967. q. $200 ($255 including annual index). Sociological Abstracts, Inc., Box 22206, San Diego, CA 92192. TEL 619-695-8803. FAX 619-695-0416. adv.; abstr.; bibl.; index. cum.index; circ. 900. (back issues avail.)
●Also available online. Vendor(s): BRS (LLBA), DIALOG (File no.36/LLBA).
—BLDSC shelfmark: 5221.375800.
  Incorporates as of vol.12, 1989: Reading Abstracts (ISSN 0361-6118); **Formerly (until 1985):** Language and Language Behavior Abstracts (ISSN 0023-8295)

M L A DIRECTORY OF PERIODICALS; a guide to journals and series in languages and literatures. (Modern Language Association of America) see *LITERATURE — Abstracting, Bibliographies, Statistics*

NOTE US; news from Sociological Abstracts, Linguistics and Language Behavior Abstracts, and Social Planning-Policy & Development Abstracts. see *ABSTRACTING AND INDEXING SERVICES*

410 011   RU   ISSN 0134-2819
NOVAYA INOSTRANNAYA LITERATURA PO OBSHCHESTVENNYM NAUKAM. YAZYKOZNANIE; bibliograficheskii ukazatel' 1953. m. 7.20 Rub. Akademiya Nauk S.S.S.R., Institut Nauchnoi Informatsii po Obshchestvennym Naukam, Ul. Krasikova 28-21, 117418 Moscow V-418, Russia. Ed. R.I. Rozina.

410 011   RU   ISSN 0134-2762
NOVAYA SOVETSKAYA LITERATURA PO OBSHCHESTVENNYM NAUKAM. YAZYKOZNANIE; bibliograficheskii ukazatel' 1954. m. 7.20 Rub. Akademiya Nauk S.S.S.R., Institut Nauchnoi Informatsii po Obshchestvennym Naukam, Ul. Krasikova 28-21, 117418 Moscow V-418, Russia. Ed. G.S. Antonyuk.

410   RU   ISSN 0202-2087
OBSHCHESTVENNYE NAUKI V S.S.S.R. YAZYKOZNANIE; referativnyi zhurnal. 1973. bi-m. 4.20 Rub. Akademiya Nauk S.S.S.R., Institut Nauchnoi Informatsii po Obshchestvennym Naukam, Ul. Krasikova 28-21, 117418 Moscow V-418, Russia. Ed. F.M. Berezin.

410   RU   ISSN 0202-2133
OBSHCHESTVENNYE NAUKI ZA RUBEZHOM. YAZYKOZNANIE; referativnyi zhurnal. 1973. bi-m. 4.20 Rub. Akademiya Nauk S.S.S.R., Institut Nauchnoi Informatsii po Obshchestvennym Naukam, Ul. Krasikova 28-21, 117418 Moscow V-418, Russia. Ed. F.M. Berezin.

410 800   GW   ISSN 0930-021X
PLATTDEUTSCHE BIBLIOGRAPHIE; laufendes Verzeichnis der Neuerscheinungen und Neuauflagen auf dem Gebiet der Plattdeutschen Sprache und Literatur. 1974. s-a. DM.12. Institut fuer Niederdeutsche Sprache e.V., Schnoor 41, 2800 Bremen 1, Germany. TEL 0421-324535. Ed. Friedrich W. Michelsen. circ. 500. (back issues avail.)
Description: Covers new literary and linguistic publications in the Low-German dialect (Plattdeutsch).

ROCZNIK SLAWISTYCZNY. see *LINGUISTICS*

479 016   GW   ISSN 0080-388X
ROMANISCHE BIBLIOGRAPHIE/BIBLIOGRAPHIE ROMANE/ROMANCE BIBLIOGRAPHY. (Supplement to: Zeitschrift fuer Romanische Philologie) (Text in German, French and English) 1965. a. price varies. Max Niemeyer Verlag, Postfach 2140, 7400 Tuebingen 1, Germany. TEL 07071-81104. FAX 07071-87419. Ed. Gustav Ineichen. (back issues avail.)
Description: Bibliography listing reviewed Romance language monographs and essays on literature.

410   NE
▼**S E M A**. (Semiotic Abstracts) 1990. 2/yr. fl.170($85) John Benjamins Publishing Co., Amsteldijk 44, P.O. Box 75577, 1070 AN Amsterdam, Netherlands. TEL 020-6738156. FAX 020-6739773. (In N. America: 821 Bethlehem Pike, Philadelphia, PA 19118. TEL 215-836-1200) Eds. Achim Eschback, Walter Schmitz.
Description: Summaries of articles, monographs, proceedings and dissertations in semiotics.

310   AT   ISSN 1031-5020
S I L - A A I B BIBLIOGRAPHY. (In 3 sections: Technical Works, Vernacular-Secular Works, Vernacular-Religious Works) 1972. irreg. Summer Institute of Linguistics, Australian Aborigines and Islanders Branch, P.O. Berrimah, N.T. 0828, Australia. TEL 089-84-4021. FAX 089-844321.
Formerly (until Oct., 1987): S I L - A A B Bibliography.
Description: Section 1 consists of articles, monographs on linguistics, anthropology, literacy, education; Section 2 consists of severalcategories of works in Australian languages; Section 3 consists of Bible stories, Scripture portions, complete books of the Bible, Old Testament, summaries and all of New Testament in Australian languages.

410   GW   ISSN 0933-1883
P40.45.E85
SOCIOLINGUISTICA; internationales Jahrbuch fuer Europaeische Soziolinguistik. (Text in English, French and German) 1987. a. price varies. Max Niemeyer Verlag, Postfach 2140, 7400 Tuebingen 1, Germany. TEL 07071-81104. FAX 07071-87419. Ed.Bd. adv.; bk.rev.; bibl. (back issues avail.)
—BLDSC shelfmark: 8319.579300.
Description: Covers essays in the field of sociolinguistics of the European languages; includes an updated bibliography.

808.5 371.9   US   ISSN 0081-3656
SPEECH INDEX; an index to 259 collections of orations and speeches for various occasions. 1935. irreg., 1966, 4th ed., supp. 1982. price varies. Scarecrow Press, Inc., 52 Liberty St., Box 4167, Metuchen, NJ 08840. TEL 800-537-7107. Ed. Charity Mitchell. circ. 3,000.

400 016   US
SUMMER INSTITUTE OF LINGUISTICS. PUBLICATIONS CATALOG. 1968. biennial. price varies. Summer Institute of Linguistics, Inc., Academic Publications, 7500 W. Camp Wisdom Rd., Dallas, TX 75236. TEL 214-709-2403. circ. 10,000.

410   US
TRANSLATION SERVICES DIRECTORY. 1965. biennial, 8th ed., 1991. $45 to non-members; members $35. American Translators Association, 109 Croton Ave., Ossining, NY 10562. TEL 914-941-1500. FAX 914-941-1330.
Formerly: A T A Professional Services Directory (ISSN 0567-4263)
Description: Focuses on ATA members who accept translating or interpreting assignments; indexed by subject area, source and target languages.

405   UK   ISSN 0084-4152
PB1
YEAR'S WORK IN MODERN LANGUAGE STUDIES. 1929-30. a. $174. Modern Humanities Research Association, King's College, London WC2, England. (Vols. 1-29 avail. from: Wm. Dawson & Sons Ltd., Cannon House, Folkstone, Kent, England) Ed. D.A. Wells. index; circ. 850. **Indexed:** Br.Hum.Ind., M.L.A.
Description: Critical bibliography of language and literature (modern and Medieval) for all European languages except English.

LINGUISTICS — Computer Applications

410   UK
COMPENDIA; computer generated aids to literary and linguistic research. 1968. irreg. price varies. W.S. Maney & Son Ltd., Hudson Rd., Leeds LS9 7DL, England. Ed. R.A. Wisbey. stat. (back issues avail.) **Indexed:** M.L.A.

410 800   US
COMPUTATIONAL AND LINGUISTIC APPROACHES TO LITERATURE. irreg. Peter Lang Publishing, Inc., 62 W. 45th St., 4th Fl., New York, NY 10036. TEL 212-302-6740. FAX 212-302-7574. Ed. David Chisholm.
Description: Publishes computationally and linguistically based empirical studies of literature that demonstrates how new methodological approaches can enhance our understanding of the various stylistic levels of literary works of art.

410 651.8   US   ISSN 0891-2017
P98   CODEN: AJCLD9
COMPUTATIONAL LINGUISTICS. 1974. q. $75 (foreign $89). (Association for Computational Linguistics) M I T Press, 55 Hayward St., Cambridge, MA 02142. TEL 617-253-2889. FAX 617-258-6779. TELEX 921473. (Subscr. to: c/o Dr. Donald E. Walker, Sec.-Treas., Bellcore, MRE 2A379, 445 South St., Box 1910, Morristown, NJ 07960-1910) Ed. James F. Allen. bk.rev.; abstr.; bibl.; stat.; index; circ. 2,500. (also avail. in microfilm; back issues avail.; reprint service avail. from UMI) **Indexed:** A.I.Abstr., Comput.Abstr., Comput.Cont., Comput.Rev., Ind.Med., Lang.& Lang.Behav.Abstr. (1974-), Sci.Abstr.
Formerly: American Journal of Computational Linguistics (ISSN 0362-613X); **Supersedes:** Finite String (ISSN 0015-2366)
Description: Covers the design and analysis of natural language processing systems. Encompasses research in language, linguistics, and the psychology of language processing and performance.
Refereed Serial

410 370   US
▼**COMPUTER ASSISTED LANGUAGE LEARNING.** 1990. 3/yr. $45 to individuals; institutions $90. Ablex Publishing Corporation, 355 Chestnut St., Norwood, NJ 07648. TEL 201-767-8450. FAX 201-767-6717. Ed. Keith Cameron. circ. 300.
Description: Covers pedagogical principles and applications to computer-assisted language learning.

410   US
DISTRIBUTED LANGUAGE TRANSLATION.* (Text in English) 1986. irreg., no.6, 1989. Walter de Gruyter, Inc., 200 Saw Mill River Rd., Hawthorne, NY 10532. TEL 914-747-0110. FAX 914-747-1326. Ed. Toon Witkam.
Description: Topics in computational linguistics and machine translation.

410   FR   ISSN 0085-4786
DOCUMENTS DE LINGUISTIQUE QUANTITATIVE. 1969. irreg. price varies. (Association Jean-Favard pour le Developpement de la Linguistique Quantitative) Editions Jean Favard, 37 rue du Four a Chaux, 91910 St. Sulpice de Favieres, France. Ed. Daniel J. Herault. circ. 850. **Indexed:** Bull.Signal.

410   US
I E E E COMPUTER SOCIETY WORKSHOP ON VISUAL LANGUAGES. 1984. biennial. price varies. (Institute of Electrical and Electronics Engineers, Inc.) I E E E Computer Society Press, 10662 Los Vaqueros Circle, Los Alamitos, CA 90720-1264. TEL 202-371-0101. FAX 202-728-9614. (Subscr. to: 345 E. 47th St., New York, NY 10017-2394)
Description: Examines the importance of visual information essential in the communication between personnel, the user and the system.

410   UK   ISSN 1045-926X
▼**JOURNAL OF VISUAL LANGUAGES AND COMPUTING.** 1990. 4/yr. $140. Academic Press Ltd., 24-28 Oval Rd., London NW1 7DX, England. TEL 071-267-4466. FAX 071-482-2293. TELEX 25775-ACPRES-G. Eds. S-K. Chang, S. Levialdi.
—BLDSC shelfmark: 5072.495200.
Description: Directed to researchers, practitioners, and developers to exchange ideas and results for the advancement of visual languages and their implication on the art of computing.

410   NE
LANGUAGE AND COMPUTERS; studies in practical linguistics. (Text in English) 1988. irreg. price varies. Editions Rodopi B.V., Keizersgracht 302-304, 1016 EX Amsterdam, Netherlands. TEL 020-6227507. FAX 020-6380948. (US and Canada subscr. to: Humanities Press International Inc., 171 First Ave., Atlantic Highlands, NJ 07716) (Co-publisher: Humanities Press International Inc.)
Description: Discusses practical applications of linguistic theory.

410 700   NE   ISSN 0927-3034
▼**LANGUAGES OF DESIGN**; formalisms for word, images and sound. (Text in English) 1992. 4/yr. fl.347 (effective 1992). Elsevier Science Publishers B.V., P.O. Box 211, 1000 AE Amsterdam, Netherlands. TEL 020-5803911. FAX 020-5803598. TELEX 18582 ESPA NL. (Subscr. in U.S. and Canada to: Elsevier Science Publishing Co., Inc., Box 882, Madison Sq. Sta., New York, NY 10159. TEL 212-989-5800) Ed. R.G. Lauzanna. (also avail. in microform)
Description: Interdisciplinary journal devoted to research in formal languages and their use for the generation and analysis of words, images and sound in both literary works and "nonliterary texts," music and visual art, as well as applications of computational methods in visual, audio and textual analyses.
Refereed Serial

001.6 410 800   UK   ISSN 0951-1474
P98   CODEN: ALLCB5
LITERARY AND LINGUISTIC COMPUTING. 1986. 4/yr. £44($83) (Association for Literary and Linguistic Computing) Oxford University Press, Oxford Journals, Pinkhill House, Southfield Road, Eynsham, Oxford OX8 1JJ, England. TEL 0865-882283. FAX 0865-882890. TELEX 387330 OXPRES G. Ed. Gordon Dixon. adv.; bk.rev.; bibl.; illus.; index; circ. 1,200. **Indexed:** Comput.Abstr., Comput.Cont., Comput.Rev., Lang.& Lang.Behav.Abstr. (1986-), Lang.Teach.& Ling.Abstr., M.L.A., Sci.Abstr, Sociol.Abstr.
Incorporates (1973-1986): A L L C Bulletin (ISSN 0305-9855); (1980-1986): A L L C Journal (ISSN 0143-3385)
Description: Covers all aspects of computing applied to literature and language.

410   NE   ISSN 0922-6567
P307   CODEN: MACTEZ
MACHINE TRANSLATION. 1986. q. $55 to individuals; institutions $157. Kluwer Academic Publishers, Postbus 17, 3300 AA Dordrecht, Netherlands. TEL 078-334911. FAX 078-334254. TELEX 29245. (Dist. by Kluwer Academic Publishers Group, P.O. Box 322, 3300 AH Dordrecht, Netherlands; N. America dist. addr.: Box 358, Accord Station, Hingham, MA 02018-0358. TEL 617-871-6600) Ed. Sergei Nirenburg. adv.; bk.rev.; charts; illus.; circ. 500. (back issues avail.; reprint service avail. from SWZ) **Indexed:** Art.Int.Abstr., Comput.Abstr., Comput.Lit.Ind., Sci.Abstr.
—BLDSC shelfmark: 5326.515000.
Formerly: Computers and Translation (ISSN 0884-0709)

410 US ISSN 0887-9206
P98
NOTES ON COMPUTING; a newsletter for academic computing in SIL. 1983. bi-m. $12. Summer Institute of Linguistics, Inc., JAARS Division, Box 248, Waxhaw, NC 28173. TEL 704-843-6000. Ed. Don Horneman. bk.rev.; cum.index; circ. 1,000. (also avail. in microfiche)

410 NE
▼PRAGMATICS & COGNITION. (Text in English) 1992. 2/yr. fl.200($100) John Benjamins Publishing Co., Amsteldijk 44, P.O. Box 75577, 1070 AN Amsterdam, Netherlands. TEL 020-6738156. FAX 020-6739773. (In N. America: 821 Bethlehem Pike, Philadelphia, PA 19118. TEL 215-836-1200) Ed. Marcelo Dascal.
   Description: Interdisciplinary journal exploring relations between semiotic systems used by humans, animals and machines, including neurological and biological bases, modeling and simulation, social and cultural variations.
   Refereed Serial

400 510 CS ISSN 0032-6585
CODEN: PBMLAT
PRAGUE BULLETIN OF MATHEMATICAL LINGUISTICS. (Text in English, German or Russian; summaries in English and Russian) 1964. s-a. 10 Kcs.($2) Universita Karlova, Fakulta Matematiky a Fysiky, Ovocny Trh 5, Prague 1, Czechoslovakia. Ed. E. Hajicova. bk.rev.; stat.; cum.index (1964-1973); circ. 800. Indexed: Lang.& Lang.Behav.Abstr. (1972-), M.L.A., Math.R., Sci.Abstr.

439 NE
RANDGEBIEDEN; een interdisciplinaire serie. vol.4, 1982. irreg. price varies. Dick Coutinho B.V., P.O. Box 10, 1399 ZG Muiderberg, Netherlands. TEL 02942-1888. bibl.

410 NE ISSN 0167-6393
CODEN: SCOMDH
SPEECH COMMUNICATION. 1982. 6/yr. fl.471 (effective 1992). (European Association for Signal Processing) North-Holland (Subsidiary of: Elsevier Science Publishers B.V.), P.O. Box 211, 1000 AE Amsterdam, Netherlands. TEL 020-5803911. FAX 020-5803598. TELEX 18582 ESPA NL. (Subscr. in U.S. and Canada to: Elsevier Science Publishing Co., Inc., Box 882, Madison Sq. Sta., New York, NY 10159. TEL 212-989-5800) (Co-sponsor: European Speech Communication Association) Ed. Max Wajskop. (back issues avail.) Indexed: Lang.& Lang.Behav.Abstr., Lang.Teach.& Ling.Abstr., Psychol.Abstr., Sci.Abstr., SSCI, Tel.Abstr.
   —BLDSC shelfmark: 8411.196000.
   Description: Covers all theoretical and experimental aspects of speech communication processes. Details speech production, transmission and perception, person to machine communication, phonetics, linguistics, as well as speech and hearing defects and aids.
   Refereed Serial

410 GW ISSN 0724-3103
SPRACHWISSENSCHAFT - COMPUTERLINGUISTIK. (Text in English, French and German) 1977. irreg. A Q-Verlag, Weinbergweg 16, 6600 Saarbruecken, Germany. TEL 0681-551185.
   —BLDSC shelfmark: 8419.891100.

029.756 400 FR ISSN 0039-8217
T.A. INFORMATIONS; revue internationale des applications de l'automatisme au langage. 1965. s-a. price varies. (Association pour la Traduction Automatique et la Linguistique Appliquee) Editions Klincksieck, 11 rue de Lille, 75005 Paris, France. bk.rev.; abstr.; charts; illus.; circ. 600. (also avail. in microform from SWZ)
   —BLDSC shelfmark: 8595.890000.
   Formerly: Traduction Automatique.

LITERARY AND POLITICAL REVIEWS

700 IT ISSN 0001-1584
A I L A. 1960. w. (Agenzia Internazionale Letteraria Artistica) Francesco Boneschi, Ed. & Pub., Via Gioliti 202, Rome, Italy. bk.rev.; film rev.; music rev.; play rev.; circ. 1,200.

800 UK
▼A I R. (Alternative Information Record) 1990. 5/yr. £6 to individuals; institutions £10. Librarians Within the Peace Movement, c/o 6 Endsleigh St., London WC1, England. circ. 150. (back issues avail.)

323.4 US
A IS A; writings on freedom and individualism. 1971. irreg. $4 for 12 issues. Mega, 9730 Hyne Rd., Brighton, MI 48116. Ed. Dale Haviland. adv.; bk.rev.; play rev.; illus.; circ. 500. (back issues avail.)
   Formerly: A Is A Newsletter (ISSN 0044-569X)

056 PO
A REVISTA. 1983. m. Esc.550($35) Gabinete 1, Imprensa, Promocao e Relacoes Publicas, Ltd., Rua de Sao Bento, 311, 3o Esq., 1200 Lisbon, Portugal. TEL 01-3961771. FAX 01-305688. Ed. Ilidio Francisco Alves. adv.; circ. 50,500. (microform; back issues avail.)
   Supersedes in part: Eles e Elas - a Revista (ISSN 0870-8932)

ABHANDLUNGEN ZUR KUNST-, MUSIK- UND LITERATURWISSENSCHAFT. see ART

055 IT
ABSTRACTA; curiosita della cultura e cultura delle curiosita. m. Stile Regina Editrice, Via Belluno 16, 00161 Rome, Italy. Ed. Roberto Scaramuzza.

053.1 AU
ACADEMIA; Zeitschrift fuer Politik und Kultur. 1949. bi-m. S.150. Oesterreichischer Cartell-Verband, Lerchenfelderstr. 14, A-1080 Vienna, Austria. FAX 0222-42162233. Ed. C.M. Auer. bk.rev.; film rev.; charts; illus.; stat.; circ. 20,000 (controlled).

ACADEMIE ROYALE DE LANGUE ET DE LITTERATURE FRANCAISES. ANNUAIRES. see LINGUISTICS

056 AG
ACCION; en defensa del cooperativismo y del pais. 1966. fortn. Arg.$8000. Instituto Movilizador de Fondos Cooperativos, Rivadavia 1944, 1033 Buenos Aires, Argentina. Ed.Bd. illus.

059.92 MR ISSN 0001-4869
ACHAAB/PEOPLE; serving the people, the throne, Arabism and Islam. 1952. s-w. DH.120($24.) Achaab Publishing, 12 rue Pormentier, Avenue Temara, Rabat, Morocco. Ed. El Hassan Arbii. adv.; bk.rev.; illus.; circ. 2,500. (tabloid format)

056.1 US
ACTIVA. 1976. fortn. Editorial America, S.A., Vanidades Continental Bldg., 6355 N.W. 36th St., Virginia Gardens, FL 33166. TEL 305-871-6400. FAX 305-871-8769. Ed. Elvira Mendoza. adv.; circ. 160,000.

808.8 US
THE ACTS THE SHELFLIFE.* 1980. a. $5. Xexoxial Euitions, RR 1 Box 131, La Farge, WI 54639-9601. circ. 500.

052 II ISSN 0044-6181
ADAM AND EVE. (Text in English) vol.5, 1972. m. Rs.10. A & P Publications, 3 Krishnier St., Nungambakkam, Madras 34, India. Ed. Amarlal Nichani. adv.; film rev.; charts; illus.

052 AT ISSN 0815-5992
ADELAIDE REVIEW. 1984. m. Aus.$15($25) Adelaide Review, 1 Dequetteville TCF, Kent Town, S.A. 5067, Australia. TEL 08-362-7699. FAX 08-362-7878. Ed. Christopher Pearson. adv.; bk.rev.; illus.; circ. 38,500. (back issues avail.)

052 II
ADMINISTRATION. (Text in English) 1973. m. Linge Gowda Detective & Security Chambers, Mysugar Bldg., J.C. Rd., Bangalore 560 002, India. Ed. D. Linge Gowda. adv.; illus.; circ. 1,000. Indexed: Mid.East: Abstr.& Ind.

051 US
ADVOCATE (PROVIDENCE). 1973. m. $0.50 per copy. 160 Chace Ave., Providence, RI 02906. Ed. Irwin N. Becker. bibl.; illus.; circ. 500.

AERIAL. see LITERATURE — Poetry

059.159 AF
AFGHANISTAN TODAY. (Text in Dari, Pashtu) 1985. bi-m. Block 106, Ansari Wat, Kabul, Afghanistan. Ed. Karim Huquq. circ. 10,500.

AFRICAN INTERPRETER; journal on African and Arab affairs. see BUSINESS AND ECONOMICS

059.927 UA
AHALI. (Text in Arabic) w. (National Progressive Unionist Party) Muassasat al- Ahali, 23 Sharia Abd el-Khaliq Tharwat, Cairo, Egypt. TEL 02-759114. Ed. Mahmoud al-Maragi.

059.927 QA
AL-AHD. (Text in Arabic) 1974. w. Al-Ahd Establishment for Journalism, Printing and Publications Ltd., P.O. Box 2531, Doha, Qatar. TEL 601506. TELEX 4920. Ed. Khalifa al-Hussaini. circ. 13,000.

053 GW
DIE AKTION; Zeitschrift fuer Politik, Literatur, Kunst. 1981. 4/yr. DM.48. Edition Nautilus Verlag Lutz Schulenburg, Hassestr. 22, 2050 Hamburg 80, Germany. TEL 040-7213536. Ed. Lutz Schulenburg. adv.; bk.rev.; film rev.; circ. 3,000. (also avail. in microfilm from KTO)

808.8 US ISSN 0890-1554
PS558.A5
ALABAMA LITERARY REVIEW. 1987. s-a. $9. Troy State University, 253 Smith Hall, Troy State University, Troy, AL 36082. TEL 205-670-3826. Ed. Theron Montgomery. bk.rev.; circ. 850.
   Description: Presents fiction, poetry, interviews, essays, photographs, graphic art and short drama.

051 US
ALABAMA MAGAZINE. 1936. m. $19.95. Drawer 6161, Montgomery, AL 36106. TEL 205-264-1981. Ed. Wayne Greenhaw. circ. 20,000.

056.1 MX
ALARMA. 1963. w. Mex.$4 per no. Publicaciones Llergo, Avda. Ceylan 517, 02300 Mexico D.F., Mexico. TEL 5-587-3855. Ed. Raymundo Medellin R. adv.; circ. 1,199,750.

800 US
▼ALASKA WOMEN. 1990. 4/yr. $30. Attn: G.R. Gardner, Ed., HCR 64, Box 453, Seward, AK 99664. TEL 907-288-3168. adv.; bk.rev.; illus.
   Description: Includes poetry, articles, art, photos, cartoons, interviews, criticism, reviews, non-fiction.

808.81 700 US ISSN 0895-559X
ALBANY REVIEW. Short title: A R. 1987. 10/yr. $15. Albany Review Associates, Inc., 4 Central Ave., Albany, NY 12210. TEL 518-436-5787. Ed. Theodore Bouloukos II. adv.; bk.rev.; circ. 25,000.
   Description: Cross-cultural monthly of the arts, literature and people.

056.1 CK ISSN 0120-0216
AP63
ALEPH. 1966. 4/yr. $100. Carlos Enrique Ruiz, Ed. & Pub., Apdo. Aereo 1080, Manizales, Colombia. bk.rev.; circ. 2,000.

052 AT
ALEXANDRA & EILDON STANDARD. 1886. w. Aus.$45. 49 Grant St., Alexadra, Vic. 3714, Australia. TEL 057 721002. FAX 057-721603. Ed. Geoffrey Heyes. circ. 2,150.

052 II
ALIVE. (Text in English) 1940. fortn. Rs.265($6.66) Delhi Press Patra Prakashan Ltd., Delhi Press Bldg., E-3 Jhandewala Estate, New Delhi 110 055, India. Ed. Vishwa Nath. adv.; bk.rev.; illus.; circ. 20,000.
   Formerly: Caravan (ISSN 0008-6150)
   Description: Covers social, political, and business topics.

ALL AREA. see ART

ALLIED ARTS NEWSLETTER. see PUBLIC ADMINISTRATION — Municipal Government

ALLMENDE. see LITERATURE — Poetry

056 AG
ALTERNATIVA CULTURA. m. Arg.$90. Editorial Surcos de Cultura S.R.L., Bustamante 1048, 1832 Lomas de Zamora, Buenos Aires, Argentina. Ed. Claudio Gustavo Basile.

ALTERNATIVE ARCHIVIST. see LIBRARY AND INFORMATION SCIENCES

LITERARY AND POLITICAL REVIEWS

808.8 301   CN
ALTERNATIVE RESEARCH NEWSLETTER. 1979. q. Can.$1. Alternative Research, Box 1294, Kitchener, Ont. N2G 4G8, Canada. Ed.Bd. adv.; bk.rev.; abstr.; bibl.; index.

051   US
ALTERNATIVES (HAMILTON).* 1987. 8/yr. $12 to individuals; institutions $20. Analysis and Policy Press, RR 1, Box 234A, Hamilton, NY 13346. Ed. Joan D. Mandle.

055.1   IT
ALTRI TERMINI.* 1972. 3/yr. L.35000. Societa Editrice Napoletana s.r.l., Corso Umberto I, 34, 80138 Naples, Italy. Ed. G. Battista Nazzaro.

AM ERKER; Zeitschrift fuer Literatur. see *LITERATURE*

056.1   MX
AMERICA DESDE MEXICO. 1958. m. Mex.$4($.50) per no. Gomez Farias 12, Mexico 21, D.F., Mexico. Dir. Esperanza Gutierrez. adv.

800 001.3   US   ISSN 0149-9408
AMERICAN BOOK REVIEW. 1977. bi-m. $24 to individuals; institutions $30. Writers Review, Inc., c/o Publications Center, English Dept., Box 494, Univ. of Colorado, Boulder, CO 80309. TEL 303-492-8947. FAX 303-492-5105. Ed. Don Laing. adv.; bk.rev.; illus.; circ. 15,000. (tabloid format; back issues avail.) **Indexed:** Arts & Hum.Cit.Ind., Bk.Rev.Ind. (1978-), Chic.Per.Ind., Child.Bk.Rev.Ind. (1978-), Curr.Cont.
Description: Guide to current books of literary interest published by the small, large, university, regional, ethnic, women's and other presses.

808.8   US
AMERICAN FORUM;* for the opinionated. 1984. w. $9.95. Vincent F. Palazzolo, Ed. & Pub., 27 Rainbow Ave., Staten Island, NY 10302-2141. TEL 718-720-2153. circ. 3,000. (looseleaf format)

AMERICAN IMAGO; a psychoanalytic journal for culture, science and the arts. see *MEDICAL SCIENCES — Psychiatry And Neurology*

378   US   ISSN 0003-0295
LH1.O8
AMERICAN OXONIAN. 1907. 4/yr. $25. Association of American Rhodes Scholars, Box 1027, Claremont, CA 91711-1027. Ed. John Funari. bk.rev.; bibl.; index; circ. 2,350.

300 378   US   ISSN 0003-0937
AP2
AMERICAN SCHOLAR. 1932. q. $21. Phi Beta Kappa Society, 1811 Q St., N.W., Washington, DC 20009. TEL 202-265-3808. Ed. Joseph Epstein. adv.; bk.rev.; illus.; index; circ. 26,000. (also avail. in microform from UMI,MIM,PMC) **Indexed:** A.I.P.P., Abstr.Engl.Stud., Acad.Ind., Amer.Bibl.Slavic & E.Eur.Stud., Amer.Hist.& Life, Arts Hum.Cit.Ind., Biog.Ind., Bk.Rev.Dig., Bk.Rev.Ind. (1965-), C.I.J.E., Chic.Per.Ind., Child.Bk.Rev.Ind. (1965-), Curr.Cont., Film Lit.Ind. (1973-), G.Soc.Sci.& Rel.Per.Lit., Hist.Abstr., Hum.Ind., Ind.Bk.Rev.Hum., Lang.& Lang.Behav.Abstr., M.L.A., Mag.Ind., Mid.East: Abstr.& Ind., P.A.I.S., PMR, PSI, Psychol.Abstr., R.G., Soc.Work Res.& Abstr., SSCI.
—BLDSC shelfmark: 0856.400000.

051   US   ISSN 0148-8414
AP2
AMERICAN SPECTATOR. 1967. m. $35 to individuals; students $17.50. 2020 N. 14th St., Ste. 750, Box 549, Arlington, VA 22216. TEL 703-243-3733. FAX 703-243-6814. Ed. R. Emmett Tyrrell, Jr. adv.; bk.rev.; film rev.; play rev.; illus.; index; circ. 32,000. (also avail. in microfiche from UMI,BHP; back issues avail.; reprint service avail. from ISI) **Indexed:** Access, Bk.Rev.Ind. (1980-), Chic.Per.Ind., Child.Bk.Rev.Ind. (1980-), Mag.Ind., Mid.East: Abstr.& Ind., P.A.I.S., Pop.Per.Ind., Sage Urb.Stud.Abstr.
●Also available online. Vendor(s): Information Access Company.
Also available on CD-ROM.
—BLDSC shelfmark: 0857.540000.
Former titles (until 1976): Alternative; an American Spectator; Alternative (ISSN 0044-7382)
Description: National magazine of politics and culture.

060   FR   ISSN 0003-178X
AMIS DE HAN RYNER. CAHIERS. 1939. N.S. 1946. q. 130 F. Societe des Amis de Han Ryner, 20 Allee du Rendez-vous, Pavillons-Sous-Bois 93320, France. Ed. Andre Simon. bk.rev.; bibl.; index; circ. 1,000.

341.1   JA   ISSN 0003-2026
AMPO; Japan-Asia quarterly review. (Text in English) 1969. q. $28 to individuals; institutions $40. Pacific Asia Resource Center, Box 5250, Tokyo International, Tokyo, Japan. TEL 03-3291-5901. FAX 03-3295-9453. adv.; bk.rev.; bibl.; illus. (also avail. in microfilm from UMI) **Indexed:** HR Rep.
Description: Contains cross-cultural articles about politics, ecomonics, and peoples' movements concerning Japan.

ANALYTICAL PSYCHOLOGY CLUB OF NEW YORK. BULLETIN. see *PSYCHOLOGY*

ANDERSCHUME - KONTIKI; das Schweizer Magazin fuer den schwulen Mann. see *HOMOSEXUALITY*

059.91   II   ISSN 0003-5203
ANNRINYA. (Text in Bengali) 1969. m. Rs.1.50($1) per copy. S. K. Poddar, Ed. & Pub., 50-8A Gouri Bari Ln., Calcutta 4, India. adv.; bk.rev.; bibl.; charts; film rev.; illus.; stat.; index; circ. 2,500.
Description: Contains literary and cultural items.

057.8   XV   ISSN 0003-536X
ANTENA. (Text in Slovenian) 1965. w. $90. Pavliha, Kardeljeva 4, 61000 Ljubljana, Slovenia. Ed. Aleksander Lucu.
Formerly: Horoskop.

055   IT   ISSN 0393-2664
ANTEPRIMA LIBRI. 1984. m. Casa Editrice Fratelli Palombi, Via dei Gracchi 181/185, 00192 Rome, Italy. Dir. Tiziana Sabuzi Giuliani. illus.

052   TR
ANTILIA. 1984. 2/yr. University of the West Indies, Faculty of Arts and General Studies, St. Augustine, Trinidad, West Indies. Ed.Bd.

810 300   US   ISSN 0003-5769
AP2
ANTIOCH REVIEW. 1941. q. $25 to individuals; institutions $36. (Antioch College) Antioch Review, Inc., Box 148, Yellow Springs, OH 45387. TEL 513-767-6389. Ed. Robert S. Fogarty. adv.; bk.rev.; index; circ. 4,500. (also avail. in microform from UMI,MIM,PMC; reprint service avail. from UMI, AMS; back issues avail.) **Indexed:** Abstr.Engl.Stud., Amer.Bibl.Slavic & E.Eur.Stud., Amer.Hist.& Life, Arts & Hum.Cit.Ind., Biog.Ind., Bk.Rev.Ind. (9165-), Child.Bk.Rev.Ind. (1965-), Curr.Cont., Film Lit.Ind. (1973-), Hist.Abstr., Hum.Ind., Ind.Amer.Per.Verse, Ind.Bk.Rev.Hum., Lang.& Lang.Behav.Abstr., M.L.A., Mag.Ind., P.A.I.S., Phil.Ind., Sage Fam.Stud.Abstr., Sociol.Abstr., SSCI.
—BLDSC shelfmark: 1549.450000.

056.1   AG   ISSN 0003-6137
AP63
ANTROPOS.* 1969. q. Rodriguez Pena 557, Buenos Aires, Argentina. Ed. Horacio G. Trejo. bk.rev.; illus.
Indexed: Psychol.Abstr.

808.8   II
ANUSTUP. (Text in Bengali) 1966. q. Rs.15($1.60) Anustup Prakashani, P-55B, C I T Rd, Calcutta 700010, India. Ed. Anil Acharya. bk.rev.; film rev.; play rev.; abstr.; circ. 2,100.

800   US
APOCALYPSO.* 1984. a. $3.50. Apocalypso Fourth World Ltd., 476 9th Ave., Ste. 1, New York, NY 10018-5603. TEL 212-247-8609. Ed. Oliver Trager. circ. 2,500. (back issues avail.)

AQLAM JOURNAL/PEN. see *LITERATURE*

051   US
AQUARIAN WEEKLY.* 1969. w. $60. Aquarian Publishing Co., 151 First Ave., New York, NY 10003-2947. Ed. James Rensenbrink. adv.; bk.rev.; film rev.; illus.; tr.lit.; circ. 40,000. (tabloid format; also avail. in microfilm)
Formerly: Aquarian.

054   FR   ISSN 0755-883X
AR FALZ; revue d'action culturelle. q. 100 F. Editions Skol Vreizh, 20 rue de Kerscoff, 29600 Morlaix, France. TEL 98-62-17-20.

ARAB BOOK WORLD. see *HISTORY — History Of The Near East*

ARBEITSGEMEINSCHAFT DER BIBLIOTHEKEN UND DOKUMENTATIONSSTELLEN DER OST-, OSTMITTEL- UND SUEDOSTEUROPAFORSCHUNG. MITTEILUNGEN. see *LIBRARY AND INFORMATION SCIENCES*

320   SW
ARBETAREN; veckotidning for frihetlig politik ekonomi och kultur. vol.69, 1922. w. SEK 370. Sveriges Arbetares Centralorganisation, P.O. Box 6507, S-113 83 Stockholm, Sweden. TEL 08-16-08-90. FAX 08-673-03-45. Ed. Martin Nilsson. adv.; bk.rev.; charts; illus. (tabloid format; also avail. in microform)

053 800 011   GW   ISSN 0723-2977
CODEN: ARBTEH
ARBITRIUM; Zeitschrift fuer Rezensionen zur germanistischen Literaturwissenschaft. (Text in English, German) 1983. 3/yr. DM.98. Max Niemeyer Verlag, Postfach 2140, 7400 Tuebingen 1, Germany. TEL 07071-81104. FAX 07071-87419. Eds. W. Fruehwald, Wolfgang Harms. bk.rev.; bibl.; index; circ. 700. (back issues avail.)
Description: Covers reviews of scholarly books on Germanic literature.

808.8   MP
ARDYN ARMI/PEOPLE'S ARMY. (Text in Mongolian) 1928. bi-m. Ulan Bator, Mongolia. Ed. B. Chantuu.

055.1   IT
AREOPAGO CIRALS. 1975. m. L.20000($27) Piazza Anco Marzio 13, 00122 Rome, Italy. circ. 3,000.

059.919 916.206   UA
AREV. (Text in Armenian) 1915. d. Armenian Liberal Democratic Party, 3 Sharia Soliman Halaby, Cairo, Egypt. TEL 754703. Ed. Avedis Yapoudjian.

ARGUMENTATION; an international journal on reasoning. see *PHILOSOPHY*

810   US   ISSN 0004-1610
AP2
ARIZONA QUARTERLY; a journal of American literature, culture and theory. 1945. q. $12 to individuals($16); institutions $16($20). University of Arizona, Main Library, Rm. B541, Tucson, AZ 85721. TEL 602-621-6396. Ed. Edgar A. Dryden. adv.; bk.rev.; bibl.; index; circ. 800. (also avail. in microfilm from UMI; back issues avail.; reprint service avail. from KTO) **Indexed:** A.I.P.P., Abstr.Engl.Stud., Amer.Hist.& Life, Amer.Hum.Ind., Chic.Per.Ind., Hist.Abstr., Ind.Bk.Rev.Hum., Ind.Little Mag., M.L.A.
—BLDSC shelfmark: 1668.490000.

808.8   US
ARK (TIBURON). 1973. w. $28. Ark Publishing Co., Box 1054, Tiburon, CA 94920. TEL 415-435-2652. FAX 415-435-0849. Eds. Marilyn Kessler, Barbara Gnoss. adv.; bk.rev.; illus.; circ. 3,200. (processed; also avail. in microform from UMI; reprint service avail. from UMI) **Indexed:** Ind.Amer.Per.Verse.
Former titles: Bleb - The Ark; (until no.13, 1978): Bleb (ISSN 0006-467X)
Description: Contains articles of local interest.

059.91   US   ISSN 0004-2366
AP2
ARMENIAN REVIEW. 1948. q. $25 to individuals (foreign $30); institutions $35 (foreign $40). Armenian Review, Inc., 80 Bigelow Ave., Watertown, MA 02172-2012. TEL 617-926-4037. FAX 617-926-1750. Ed. Tatul Sonentz-Papazian. adv.; bk.rev.; illus.; stat.; circ. 1,200. (also avail. in microfilm from UMI; reprint service avail. from UMI) **Indexed:** Amer.Bibl.Slavic & E.Eur.Stud., Amer.Hist.& Life, Hist.Abstr., Mid.East: Abstr.& Ind., P.A.I.S.
—BLDSC shelfmark: 1683.030000.
Description: Multidisciplinary journal publishing scholarly articles on the history, culture, society, economy of Armenia, its neighbors and Armenian communities abroad.

700   IT
ARS-UOMO; mensile di vita artistica e culturale. 1975. m. L.10000. Bulzoni Editore, Via dei Liburni 14, 00185 Rome, Italy. Ed. Giordana Canti. bk.rev.

059.91   US   ISSN 0004-4229
ASBAREZ. (Text in Armenian and English) 1908. 5/wk. $75 (Bilinguals ed. $30). (Armenian Revolutionary Federation) Asbarez Publishing Co., 419 W. Colorado St., Glendale, CA 91204-1537. Ed.Bd. adv.; bk.rev.; illus.; circ. 13,000. (tabloid format; also avail. in microfilm)

ASLAN. see *RELIGIONS AND THEOLOGY*

055.91   RM   ISSN 0004-6108
ASTRA. 1966. m. 5 lei($2.42) Comitetul de Cultura si Educatie Socialista al Judetului Brasov, Str. Mihail Sadoveanu Nr. 3, 2200 Brasov, Rumania. TEL 43179. (Subscr. to: Rompresfilatelia, Calea Grivitei no. 64-66, P.O. Box 12-201, Bucharest, Rumania) Ed. Aurel Ion Brumaru. adv.; bk.rev.; play rev.; illus.; circ. 15,000.

ASYLUM. see *LITERATURE — Poetry*

378.1   PR   ISSN 0044-9849
ATENEA. (Text in English, French, Italian, Spanish) 1962. s-a. (free to libraries and universities). Universidad de Puerto Rico, Faculty of Arts and Sciences, Mayaguez Campus, Mayaguez, PR 00681. FAX 809-834-3031. Eds. Hilda M. Rodriguez, Lilia Dapaz Strout. bk.rev.; circ. 800 (controlled). **Indexed:** Amer.Hist.& Life, Hist.Abstr., M.L.A.

056.1   ES
ATENEO DE EL SALVADOR. REVISTA. 1912. 3/yr. Ateneo de El Salvador, 13a Calle Poniente, Centro de Gobierno, San Salvador, El Salvador. TEL 22-9686.

055.1   IT
ATHENA MEDITERRANEA; periodico trimestrale di lettere, storia, arte e cultura varia. 1975. q. L.5000. Piazza Municipio 22, 81031 Aversa, Italy. Ed. Enzo di Grazia.

808.8   UK   ISSN 0262-5113
ATHOLL & BREADALBANE COMMUNITY COMMENT. 1981. 6/yr. £1.20. A B C Comment, Dunkeld St., Aberfeldy, Tayside, Scotland. Ed.Bd. adv.; bk.rev.; illus.; circ. 1,000.

051 300 700   US   ISSN 0276-9077
AP2   CODEN: ATLAEO
THE ATLANTIC. 1857. m. $15.94. Atlantic Monthly Co., 745 Boylston, Boston, MA 02116. TEL 617-536-9500. (Subscr. to: Box 2547, Boulder, CO 80322) Ed. William Whitworth. adv.; bk.rev.; index; circ. 457,343. (also avail. in microform from UMI,MIM,PMC; microfilm from KTO) **Indexed:** Abr.R.G., Amer.Hist.& Life, Amer.Bibl.Slavic & E.Eur.Stud., Amer.Hist.& Life, Bk.Rev.Dig., Bk.Rev.Ind. (1965-), Child.Bk.Rev.Ind. (1965-), Film Lit.Ind. (1973-), Fut.Surv., Hist.Abstr., Ind.Bk.Rev.Hum., Mag.Ind., Peace Res.Abstr., PROMT, R.G., TOM. —BLDSC shelfmark: 1765.897000. **Former titles (until 1981):** Atlantic Monthly (ISSN 0004-6795); (until 1971): Atlantic (ISSN 0160-6506); (until 1932): Atlantic Monthly (ISSN 0160-6514)

808.87   US
THE ATROCITY. 1979. m. $10. Absurd Sig, 2419 Greensburg Pike, Pittsburgh, PA 15221. Ed. Hank Roll. adv.; circ. 250. (back issues avail.)

056   AG
AUNARTE. Variant title: Revista Aunarte. 1980. m. Sociedad Cooperativa de Trabajo Artistico Ltda. (e.f.), Mercedes 153, 1047 Buenos Aires, Argentina. Ed. Ruben de Lorenzo.

808.8   US   ISSN 0889-7433
AURA LITERARY ARTS REVIEW. 1974. s-a. $6. University of Alabama at Birmingham, Box 76, University Center, Birmingham, AL 35294-1150. TEL 205-934-3216. Ed. Nan Smith. adv.; bk.rev.; circ. 600.

051   AT   ISSN 0313-9727
AUSTRALIA - ISRAEL REVIEW. 1975. fortn. Aus.$49($66) Australia-Israel Publications, 584 St. Kilda Rd., Melbourne, Vic. 3004, Australia. TEL 03-529-5022. FAX 03-5298-573. TELEX AA100200. Ed. Michael Danby. adv.; bk.rev.; circ. 4,600. (back issues avail.) **Description:** Regional newsletter on Israel and the Middle East including matters of Australian and regional concern.

052   AT   ISSN 0729-8595
HN841
AUSTRALIAN SOCIETY; the independent national monthly. 1982. m. Aus.$40 to individuals; institutions Aus.$60. Australian Modern Times Pty. Ltd., P.O. Box 274, Fitzroy, Vic. 3065, Australia. FAX 613-416-0903. Ed. Peter Browne. adv.; bk.rev.; illus.; stat.; index; circ. 10,000. (back issues avail.) **Indexed:** Aus.Educ.Ind., Aus.P.A.I.S., World Bibl.Soc.Sec.

AUT AUT; rivista di filosofia e di cultura. see *PHILOSOPHY*

320.5   IT   ISSN 0045-1118
AUTONOMI; resistenza, democrazia, Europa unita, periodico di fatti ed opinioni. (Includes supplement) vol.33 No.2. s-a. L.8000 (foreign L.16000). (Associazione Volontari della Liberta e del Circolo-Europa Libera del Piemonte) Autonomi Editore, Torino, Piazza Carignano 8, 10123 Turin, Italy. TEL 541505. Ed. Giuseppe Anacar. adv.; bk.rev.; illus.; circ. 3,000. **Description:** Acts as a forum for a variety of political issues.

054.1   FR
AP20
AUTRE JOURNAL.* 1922. m. 140 F. 10 rue Saint-Antoine, 75004 Paris, France. Dir. Michel Butelon. adv.; bk.rev.; film rev.; music rev.; play rev.; tele.rev.; illus.; circ. 220,000. **Formerly (until 1984):** Nouvelles Littéraires, Arts, Sciences, Spectacles (ISSN 0029-4942) **Description:** Covers literature, medicine, science, technology and news.

051   US   ISSN 0005-1918
AP2
AVANT GARDE. 1967. q. $7.50. Avant-Garde Media, Inc., 80 Central Park W., Ste. 16B, New York, NY 10023. TEL 212-581-2000. adv.; bk.rev.; illus.; circ. 250,000. (also avail. in microform from UMI)

001.3   IT
AVATAR; testimonianza culturale. 1978. m. L.12000. (Associazione Cultura e Umanita, SZ) Associazione Avatar, Via Bellinzona 181, Casella Postale 23, Ponte Chiasso, 22100 Como, Italy. Ed. Giuseppe Antonio Anzelmo.

AXE FACTORY REVIEW. see *LITERATURE*

054   FR
AXE SUD. 4/yr. 25 F. Axe Sud, 11 Place de la Daurade, 31000 Toulouse, France.

059.927   TS
AL-AYYAM. (Text in Arabic) 1969. w. Mu'assasat Dar al- Ayyam for Journalism, Printing, Publishing, P.O. Box 2788, Abu Dhabi, United Arab Emirates. TEL 477184. Ed. Yusuf al-Umran. circ. 10,000. **Description:** Covers cultural and political developments in the U.A.E.

800   SW   ISSN 0005-3198
AP48
B L M. (Bonniers Litteraera Magasin) 1932. 6/yr. SEK 280. Albert Bonniers Foerlag AB, Box 3159, 103 63 Stockholm 3, Sweden. TEL 08-22-91-20. FAX 08-20-84-51. (Subscr. to: Pressdata, Box 3263, 10365 Stockholm, Sweden) Ed. Maria Schottenius. adv.; bk.rev.; bibl.; illus.; index; circ. 4,000. **Indexed:** Arts & Hum.Cit.Ind., Curr.Cont., M.L.A.

800   US
BACK BAY VIEW; a literary and arts magazine. 1977. s-a. $5 for 4 nos. Back Bay View, Inc., c/o Charlotte A. Boehm, Ed., 33 Karen Dr., Randolph, MA 02368. TEL 617-986-5704. Ed.Bd. circ. 1,000.

820   UK
BACONIANA. 1885. a. £1. Francis Bacon Society Inc., Canonbury Tower, Islington, London N.1, England. Ed.Bd. bk.rev.; bibl.; index; circ. 200.

BAD HAIRCUT. see *POLITICAL SCIENCE*

051   US
THE BAFFLER. 1988. a. $10 for two issues. Box 378293, Chicago, IL 60637. TEL 312-324-3306. Ed. Thomas Frank. circ. 1,000.

BAGDALA; mesecni list za knjizevnost, umetnost i kulturu. see *LITERATURE*

052   AT
BAIRNSDALE ADVERTISER. 1877. s-w. Aus.$36. James Yeates and Sons Pty. Ltd., Cnr. Macleod and Bailey St., Bairnsdale, Vic. 3875, Australia. TEL 051-521117. Ed. Robert D. Yeates. circ. 7,500.

054.1   FR   ISSN 0378-469X
DT470
BALAFON; pour la connaissance de l'Afrique Noire. (Text in French; summaries in English) 1965-1988; resumed. bi-m. 155 F. Air Afrique, 71 rue Desnouettes, 75015 Paris, France. TEL 48-28-40-58. Ed. Guy Leger. adv.; bk.rev.; illus.; circ. 100,000.

800.055 914.706   IT   ISSN 0392-7660
BALCANICA; storia, cultura, politica. 1982. q. L.50000 (foreign L.100000). Via Conca d'Oro 238, 00141 Rome, Italy. TEL 06-8101700. Ed. Antonio Jerkov. bk.rev.; illus. (back issues avail.) **Indexed:** Amer.Hist.& Life, Hist.Abstr.

059.951   CC
BAN YUE TAN/SEMI-MONTHLY TRIBUNE. (Editions in Chinese and Uighur) 1980. s-m. Y27.50($91.80) (Xinhua News Agency) Ban Yue Tan Zazhishe, No.57, Xuanwumen Xidajie, Beijing 100803, People's Republic of China. TEL 3074433. (Dist. in US by: China Books & Periodicals, Inc., 2929 24th St., San Francisco, CA 94110. TEL 415-282-2994) Ed. Min Fanlu. adv.; circ. 5,380,000.

BANASTHALI PATRIKA. see *LITERATURE*

808.8   US
BARNEY; modern stone-age magazine. 1981. s-a. $12. Fred & Barney Press, 1140 1-2 Nowita Pl., Venice, CA 90291. TEL 213-392-2886. Ed. Jack Skelley.

808.8   US
BARNWOOD.* 1980. irreg. (3-4/yr.). $2.50 for 4 nos. (Barnwood Press Cooperative, Inc.) Barnwood Press, Box 146, Selma, IN 47383-0146. bk.rev.; circ. 500.

053   GW   ISSN 0178-000X
BATERIA; Zeitschrift fuer Kunstlerischen Ausdruck. 1982. a. DM.14($10) Wilhelm-Busch-Str. 21, 8500 Nuremberg 90, Germany. Ed. Manfred Rothenberger. adv.; circ. 1,500. (back issues avail.)

055.1   IT   ISSN 0005-6332
BATTAGLIA LETTERARIA;* bimestrale di letteratura e attualita. 1951. bi-m. L.3000. Luigi Vita, Ed. & Pub., Via Garibaldi 349, 98100 Messina, Italy. bk.rev.; index; circ. 2,000.

808.87   US
BAWL STREET JOURNAL; annual lampoon of the financial community. a. $3. Box 445, Wall St. Sta., New York, NY 10005. **Description:** Contains financial wit and humor.

055.1   IT   ISSN 0005-8351
AP37
BELFAGOR; rassegna di varia umanita. 1946. bi-m. L.55000 (foreign L.85000). Casa Editrice Leo S. Olschki, Casella Postale 66, 50100 Florence, Italy. TEL 055-6530684. FAX 055-6530214. Ed. Carlo F. Russo. adv.; bk.rev.; circ. 3,500. (back issues avail.) **Indexed:** Amer.Hist.& Life, Arts & Hum.Cit.Ind., Can.Rev.Comp.Lit., Curr.Cont., Hist.Abstr., M.L.A.

055   IT
BENI CULTURALI E AMBIENTE. m. L.50000. Audiovisivi e Periodici s.r.l., Via Taranto, 21, 00182 Rome, Italy. (Distr. by: Periodici Angelo Patuzzi Spa, Via Zuretti, 25, 20123 Milan, Italy) Ed. Sergio Trasatti.

052   NR
BENIN REVIEW. 1974. s-a. £N3($6) ($7.50 for libraries). Ethiope Publishing Corporation, 34 Murtala Mohammed St., PMB 1192, Benin City, Nigeria. Eds. Abio Ia Irele, Pius Oleghe. **Indexed:** M.L.A.

057   KR
BEREZIL; literaturno-khudozhnii ta hromads'ko-politychnyi zhurnal. 1956. m. 17.40 Rub. (Spilka Pys'mennykiv Ukrainy) Vydavnytstvo Radyanskii Pismennik, Chkalova, 52, Kiev, Ukraine. Ed. Yu. Stadnychenko. bk.rev.; bibl.; illus.; circ. 16,000. **Indexed:** M.L.A. **Formerly (until 1991):** Prapor (ISSN 0130-1608)

LITERARY AND POLITICAL REVIEWS

808.8 US
BERKELEY MONTHLY. 1970. m. $10. c/o Karen Klaber, Pub., 1301 59th St., Emeryville, CA 94608-2115. FAX 415-658-9902. Ed. Teresa Cirolia. adv.; bk.rev.; film.rev.; circ. 75,000.

053.1 GW ISSN 0005-9307
BERLINER LIBERALE ZEITUNG. 1962. fortn. DM.16. (Freie Demokratische Partei, Landesverband Berlin) D.A.V.I.D. GmbH, Im Dol 2-6, 1000 Berlin 33, Germany. TEL 030-8313071. Ed. Josef H. Mayer. adv.; bk.rev.; circ. 40,000.

741.5 808.87 US ISSN 0091-2220
E839.5
BEST EDITORIAL CARTOONS OF THE YEAR. 1973. a. $14.95 hardcover; $11.95 paperback. (Association of American Editorial Cartoonists) Pelican Publishing Co., 1101 Monroe St., Gretna, LA 70053. TEL 504-368-1175. FAX 504-368-1195. Ed. Charles Brooks. circ. 6,000. (back issues avail.)
—BLDSC shelfmark: 1942.325700.
Description: Offers a selection of national and international cartoons from members of the association.

800 US
BEST OF AMERICAN LITERATURE. 1987. irreg. price varies. Duke University Press, 6697 College Station, Durham, NC 27708. TEL 919-684-2173. FAX 919-684-8644. Eds. Louis Budd, Edwin Cady.

057 YU
BIBLIOGRAFIJA RECENZIJA IZ DOMACIH LISTOVA I CASOPISA. (Text in Macedonian, Serbo-Croatian, Slovenian) 1979. g. free. Biblioteka Grada Geograda, Knez Mihajlova 56, 11000 Belgrade, Yugoslavia. TEL 186313. circ. 100.
Formerly: Bilten Recenzija iz Damacih Listova i Casopisa.

808.8 809 830 SP ISSN 0006-1646
AS302
BIBLIOTECA DE MENENDEZ PELAYO. BOLETIN. 1919. a. 3000 ptas.($30) Sociedad "Menendez Pelayo", Santander, Spain. Ed. Manuel Revuelta Sanudo. bk.rev.; index. cum.index: 1919-1960; circ. 600. **Indexed:** Hist.Abstr, M.L.A.
—BLDSC shelfmark: 2161.440000.

808.8 US
BIG SCREAM. 1974. irreg., (2-3/yr.). $8. Nada, 2782 Dixie, SW, Grandville, MI 49418. TEL 616-531-1442. Eds. David Cope, Susan Cope. circ. 100.

808.87 US
BIGGEST GREATEST CRACKED ANNUAL. a. $1.50. Globe Communications Corp. (New York), 441 Lexington Ave., New York, NY 10017. TEL 800-472-7744. circ. 425,000.
Description: Contains humorous articles.

808.8 US
BIKINI GIRL; a serial anthology of unconventional literature and graphics. 1976. irreg. $10. Vortex Publications, Box 371, Midwood Sta., Brooklyn, NY 11230-0371. FAX 718-788-0620. (P.O. Box 319, Peter Stuyvesant Station, New York, NY 10009-0319) Ed. Keith Rahmmings. bk.rev.; abstr.; film rev.; illus.; circ. 1,500. (also avail. in video cassette; back issues avail.)
Formerly (until vol.2, no.2, 1981): Blank Tape.

053.1 AU
BILDUNGS-KURIER. 1948. q. S.40. Sozialistische Partei Oberoesterreichs, Landesorganisation, Landstr. 36, A-4020 Linz, Austria. Ed. Max Lotteraner. adv.; bk.rev.; bibl.; circ. 4,000.

808.8 US
BIRD EFFORT. 1975. a. $5 to individuals; institutions $6. Bird Effort Press, 25 Mudford Ave., Easthampton, NY 11937. Eds. Robert Long, Josh Dayton. adv.; bk.rev.; circ. 500. **Indexed:** Ind.Amer.Per.Verse.

808.81 US ISSN 0897-9057
BIRTH OF TRAGEDY MAGAZINE;* the fear issue, the God issue, the power issue, the love issue, the sex issue. (Text in English, Korean, Spanish, Swedish) 1981. a. $2. C.F.Y., Box 6271, Stanford, CA 94309. TEL 415-324-9483. Ed. Eugene S. Robinson. adv.; circ. 2,000. (tabloid format; back issues avail.)
Description: Philosophical inquiry into the darker side of life, love, and death.

059.92 US
BITZARON: A QUARTERLY OF HEBREW LETTERS. (Text in Hebrew; summaries in English) 1939. q. $18 (foreign $17). (Hebrew Literary Foundation) Bitzaron, Inc., Box 623, Cooper Sta., New York, NY 10003. (Co-sponsor: Institute of Hebrew Culture and Education) Ed. Hayim Leaf. adv.; bk.rev.; play rev.; illus.; stat.; index; circ. 18,800. (also avail. in microfilm from AJP; back issues avail.) **Indexed:** Amer.Hist.& Life, Hist.Abstr., Ind.Heb.Per., M.L.A.
Supersedes (1939-1978): Bitzaron: The Hebrew Monthly of America (ISSN 0006-3932)

057.8 CI ISSN 0006-4068
BJELOVARSKI LIST. 1946. w. 100 din. Socijalisticki Savez Radnog Naroda Opcine Bjelovar, Trg Jedinstva 11, Bjelovar, Croatia. Ed. Ivan Matunci.

808 US ISSN 0896-3517
BLACK MOUNTAIN REVIEW. 1987-1988; resumed 1990. a. $10. Lorien House, Box 1112, Black Mountain, NC 28711-1112. TEL 704-669-6211. Ed. David A. Wilson. bk.rev.; circ. 300. (back issues avail.)
Description: Articles and essays on social, ethical, cultural, and intellectual issues and topics.

808.87 IE ISSN 0332-253X
BLAZES; Ireland's humour monthly. 1981. m. 20 Essex St., Dublin 2, Ireland. illus.

059 II
BOMSEL; fortnightly of Bihar. (Text in English) vol.7, 1975. fortn. Rs.11. Nawal Kishore, Ed. & Pub., Paras Kothi Nayatola, Patna 4, India. adv.; illus.

BOOKENDS. see LIBRARY AND INFORMATION SCIENCES

BRAILLE MIRROR; a current topic magazine. see HANDICAPPED — Visually Impaired

808.8 US
BRASIL - BRAZIL; a journal of Brazilian literature. (Text in English, Portuguese) 1988. s-a. $15 to individuals; institutions $40. Brown University, Center for Portuguese and Brazilian Studies, Box O, Providence, RI 02912. Eds. Nelson H. Vieira, Regina Zilberman. adv.

051 CN ISSN 0382-8565
Z1035.A1
BRICK; a literary journal. 1977. 3/yr. $10 to individuals; institutions $14. Brick, P.O. Box 537, Sta. Q, Toronto, Ont. M4T 2M5, Canada. Ed. Linda Spalding. bk.rev.; illus.; index; circ. 1,200. (back issues avail.) **Indexed:** Br.Ceram.Abstr., Can.Lit.Ind.

052 UK
BRIGHTON VOICE. m. £12. Brighton Voice, Prior House, Tilbury Place, Carlton Hill, Brighton, England. Ed.Bd. adv.; bk.rev.; circ. 10,000. (tabloid format)

053 GW ISSN 0937-9509
BRUCKER SZENE; Infos fuer Kunst & Kultur. 1984. m. free. Thomtom Verlag, Schlehdornweg 23, 8080 Fuerstenfeldbruck, Germany. TEL 08141-26246-0. Ed. Thomas Himmler. adv.; bk.rev.; circ. 10,000. (back issues avail.)

052 AU
DIE BRUECKE; Kaerntner Kulturzeitschrift. 1975. q. S.230. Amt der Kaerntner Landesregierung, Abteilung 5 - Kultur, Paradeisergasse 7, A-9021 Klagenfurt, Austria. Ed. Ernst Gayer. adv.; bk.rev.; circ. 2,300.

053.1 GW
BUECHERKARREN. 4/yr. Verlag Volk und Welt, Otto-Nuschke-Str. 10-11, 1086 Berlin, Germany. TEL 030-203650211. Ed. H.D. Tschoertner. bk.rev.

808.8 US
BUG TAR. 1977. 4/yr. $5. Bug Tar Press, Box 1534, San Jose, CA 95109. Ed. Scott Mace. circ. 100.

052 820 AT ISSN 0157-3705
C R N L E REVIEWS JOURNAL. 1979. s-a. Aus.$25 to individuals; institutions Aus.$30. Flinders University of South Australia, Centre for Research in the New Literatures in English, School of Humanities, Bedford Park, S.A. 5042, Australia. TEL 08-201-2053. FAX 08-201-2556. TELEX AA 89624 FLINDU. Ed.Bd. adv.; bk.rev.; circ. 350. (back issues avail.) **Indexed:** Can.Lit.Ind.
—BLDSC shelfmark: 3487.496000.

808.87 SG
CAFARD LIBERE. 1987. w. 10 rue Tolbiac x autoroute, 3e etage, Dakar, Senegal. TEL 22-84-43. Ed. Laye Bamba Diallo. circ. 10,000.

054.1 FR ISSN 0222-5956
CAHIERS CONFRONTATION. 1979. s-a. 400 F. for 4 nos. Editions Aubier Montaigne, 13 Quai de Conti, 75006 Paris, France. Ed. Rene Major. adv.; circ. 2,500. **Indexed:** M.L.A.

054.1 BE
CAHIERS WALLONS. (Text in French, Walloon) 1937. 10/yr. 500 Fr. Relis Namurwes A.S.B.L., 31 rue Godart, B-5002 Namur, Belgium. TEL 081-733428. adv.; bk.rev.; bibl.; circ. 800.
Description: Promotes literature in the Walloon dialect in the area centered around Namur.

700 CU
CAIMAN BARBUDO. 1966. m. $20 in N. America; S. America $26; Europe $29; others $41. Ediciones Cubanas, Obispo No. 527, Aptdo. 605, Havana, Cuba. Dir. Alex Pausides. circ. 47,000.

051 CN ISSN 0381-856X
CALEDONIAN. vol.8, 1978. irreg. free. College of New Caledonia, 3330 22nd Ave., Prince George, B.C. V2N 1P8, Canada. TEL 604-562-2131. Ed. Hans Allgaier. bk.rev.; circ. 300. **Indexed:** Can.Per.Ind.

800 US
▼**CALENDAR OF LITERARY FACTS.** 1990. irreg. $45. Gale Research Inc., 835 Penobscot Bldg., Detroit, MI 48226. TEL 800-877-4253. FAX 313-961-6083. TELEX 810-221-7086. Ed. Samuel J. Rogal.
Description: Provides views of literary history anywhere, including a wide range of international facts and information on many popular writers.

817 US ISSN 0008-1361
CALIFORNIA PELICAN. 1903. s-a. $6. Associated Students of the University of California, University of California, Berkeley, 700 Eshleman Hall, Berkeley, CA 94720. TEL 415-642-3311. Ed. Seth Sutel. adv.; bk.rev.; illus.; circ. 2,500.
Formerly: Berkeleyan and California Pelican.
Description: Emphasis is on wit and humor.

320.532 CE ISSN 0045-401X
CALL. (Editions in English and French) 1971. q. Afro Asian Writers Bureau, 73 Castle St., Colombo 8, Sri Lanka. Ed.Bd. bk.rev.; bibl.; charts; illus.

056.1 SP
CAMBIO 16. 1972. w. 50 ptas. per no. Informacion y Revistas S.A., Hermanos Garcia Noblejas 41, 28037 Madrid, Spain. TEL 91-4072700. FAX 91-4070400. Ed. Federico Ysart. adv.; charts.

300 UK ISSN 0008-2007
CAMBRIDGE REVIEW; a journal of university life and thought. 1879. q. $28 to individuals; institutions $62. Cambridge University Press, Edinburgh Bldg., Shaftesbury Rd., Cambridge CB2 2RU, England. TEL 0223-312393. FAX 0223-315052. TELEX 851817256. (N. American addr.: Cambridge University Press, 40 W. 20th St., New York, NY 10011-4211, USA. TEL 212-924-3900) Eds. Ruth Morse, Stefan Collini. adv.; bk.rev.; film rev.; music rev.; play rev.; index. (also avail. in microform from UMI; back issues avail.)
—BLDSC shelfmark: 3015.990000.
Description: University life and thought: poetry, essays, articles.

055.1 IT ISSN 0008-2279
CAMMINO ECONOMICO; information bollettin. m. Via G. Verdi 13, 82100 Benevento, Italy. Ed. Esposito Antonio.

CAMPAIGN AUSTRALIA. see HOMOSEXUALITY

809 PO
CAMPO GRANDE. 1984. m. Faculdade de Letras de Lisboa, Associacao de Estudantes, Alameda da Universidade, 1699 Lisbon Codex, Portugal. Ed.Bd.

847 FR ISSN 0008-5405
CANARD ENCHAINE; journal satirique paraissant le Mercredi. 1915. w. 287 F. (foreign 410 F.). Editions Marechal, 173 rue St. Honore, 75001 Paris, France. TEL 1-42-60-31-36. FAX 16-14-92-79-787. Dir. A. Ribaud. bk.rev.; film rev.; illus.; circ. 450,000. (newspaper)

LITERARY AND POLITICAL REVIEWS 2861

052 UK
CANDOUR. 1953. m. £10 (foreign £12). Candour Publishing Co., Forest House, Liss Forest, Hampshire GU33 7DD, England. Ed. Rosine de Bouneviale. adv.; bk.rev.; circ. 2,500.
Description: British "views-letter" covering the role international finance plays in the defense of the sovereignty of Great Britain.

808.87 AT ISSN 0155-7157
CANE TOAD TIMES; Australia's humour magazine. 1983. q. Aus.$15. Studio 2, Level 2, McWhirters Artspace, Cnr Brunswick & Wickham Sts., Fortitude Valley, Qld. 4006. TEL 07-854-1511. FAX 07-854-1622. Ed.Bd. adv.; film rev.; illus.; circ. 15,000. (back issues avail.)
Description: Humorous look at Australian society using political satire and cartoons.

056 SP ISSN 0213-0467
CANELOBRE. irreg. 1800 ptas. for 4 nos. Instituto de Cultura "Juan Gil-Albert", Departamento de Cultura y Publicaciones, Diputacion Provincial, Alicante, Spain.

808.87 US
CAPITOL COMEDY. 1988. m. $105. Box 25605, Washington, DC 20007-8605. TEL 202-966-0264. FAX 202-966-0297. Ed. Elaine Bole. circ. 750.
Description: Contains topical political humor.

791.4 CN ISSN 0317-6193
CAPTAIN GEORGE'S PENNY DREADFUL. 1968. w. Can.$5. Vast Whizzbang Organization, Memory Ln., 594 Markham St., Toronto, Ont., Canada. Ed. Peter Harris. adv.; bk.rev.; film rev.; illus.; circ. 2,000.

052 TR ISSN 1011-5765
F2155
CARIBBEAN AFFAIRS. 1988. q. T.T.$100($45) (Caribbean $40, Europe $60, Canada $50). Trinidad Express Newspaper Ltd., P.O. Box 1252, Port-of-Spain, Trinidad & Tobago, W.I. TEL 809-623-1711. FAX 809-627-1451. (Co-publisher: Inprint Caribbean Ltd.) Ed. Owen Baptiste. adv.; bk.rev.; circ. 1,030.
—BLDSC shelfmark: 3052.595000.
Description: Features information, issues and events in the Caribbean Basin - from Brazil, Surinam and the Guianas in the South, to Mexico, the Bahamas and Cuba in the North. Written and edited exclusively by Caribbean people.

051 056.1 PR ISSN 0576-7598
F2183
CARIBBEAN MONTHLY BULLETIN. (Text in English, Spanish) 1963. m. $12 to individuals; institutions $16. Universidad de Puerto Rico, Institute of Caribbean Studies, P.O. Box BM, University Sta., Rio Piedras, PR 00931. Ed. Dale Mathews. bibl.; circ. 1,500.

051 JM ISSN 0008-6495
CARIBBEAN QUARTERLY. 1949. q. Jam.$90($30) University of the West Indies, Department of Extra-Mural Studies, Box 42, Kingston 7, Jamaica, W.I. Ed. Rex Nettleford. adv.; bk.rev.; index; circ. 1,500. (also avail. in microfilm from UMI; back issues avail.; reprint service avail. from KTO)
Indexed: Abstr.Engl.Stud., Amer.Hist.& Life, Hisp.Amer.Per.Ind., Hist.Abstr., Rural Recreat.Tour.Abstr., World Agri.Econ.& Rural Sociol.Abstr.
—BLDSC shelfmark: 3053.127000.

972.9 800 US ISSN 0008-6525
AP6
CARIBBEAN REVIEW; a quarterly dedicated to the Caribbean, Latin America and their emigrant groups. 1969. q. $20. Caribbean Review, Inc., 9700 S.W. 67th Ave., Miami, FL 33156. TEL 305-284-8466. FAX 305-284-1019. Ed. Barry B. Levine. adv.; bk.rev.; abstr.; bibl.; circ. 5,000. (also avail. in microform from UMI; reprint service avail. from UMI) Indexed: Amer.Hist.& Life, Curr.Cont., Hisp.Amer.Per.Ind., Hist.Abstr., HR Rep., I D A, Int.Polit.Sci.Abstr., New Per.Ind., P.A.I.S.
—BLDSC shelfmark: 3053.128300.
Supersedes: San Juan Review.

CARILLON. see COLLEGE AND ALUMNI

CARTOON WORLD. see ART

056.1 CU ISSN 0008-7157
PN6
CASA DE LAS AMERICAS. 6/yr. $15 in N. America; S. America $19; Europe $21; others $30. Ediciones Cubanas, Obispo No. 527, Apdo. 605, Havana, Cuba. bk.rev.; illus.; play rev. Indexed: Amer.Hist.& Life, Hisp.Amer.Per.Ind., Hist.Abstr., M.L.A.
Description: Contains letters and ideas, articles, essays, fiction, poetry, literary criticism, interviews, art criticism and cultural news from the Latin American and Caribbean countries.

800 700 NE ISSN 0008-7556
AP64
CASTRUM PEREGRINI; deutschsprachige Zeitschrift fuer Literatur-, Kunst- und Geistesgeschichte. (Text in German) 1950. 5/yr. fl.80 (DM.80). Stichting Castrum Peregrini - Castrum Peregrini Presse, P.O. Box 645, 1000 AP Amsterdam, Netherlands. FAX 20-624-7096. Ed. M.R. Goldschmidt. adv.; bk.rev.; abstr.; illus.; s-a index. (reprint service avail.) Indexed: M.L.A.

808.8 266 US
CAUSA - U S A REPORT. 1985. m. $18. Causa - U S A, One Penn Plaza, Ste. 100, New York, NY 10119. TEL 212-967-2400. (Subscr. to: Box 449, Greenbelt, MD 20770) Ed. Mary E. Rand. bk.rev.; circ. 50,000.
Description: News, commentary, and legislative reviews pertaining to CAUSA, which seeks to effect positive social change through responsible leadership and citizen involvement based on a belief in God, a commitment to freedom, and an opposition to communism.

056.1 CR ISSN 0034-9828
CENIT/ZENITH; revista literaria internacional. no.266, 1974. m. free. Academia Hispano Americana Zenith, Apdo. 40, Heredia, Costa Rica. Ed. Amando Cespedes Marin. adv.; illus.; circ. 2,000. (processed)

054.1 055.1 SZ ISSN 0008-896X
CENOBIO; rivista di cultura. (Text mainly in Italian; occasionally in French) 1952. q. 50 SFr. Edizioni Cenobio, Via Streccia 4, P.O. Box 174, CH-6903 Lugano 3, Switzerland. TEL 091-581048. FAX 091-565156. Ed. Riccardo Frigeri. adv.; bk.rev.; bibl.; charts; film rev.; illus.; play rev.; index; circ. 10,000. (back issues avail.) Indexed: M.L.A.
Description: Articles on a wide variety of topics dealing with customs and traditions, history and religion. Contains interviews and poetry.

847 FR ISSN 0045-6047
CENT BLAGUES.* 1962. m. 90 F. Editions E.G.E., B.P. 7085, 69007 Lyon, France.
Description: Emphasizes humor.

800 US ISSN 0273-3323
CENTRAL PARK. 1980. 2/yr. $9.50. (Central Park Trust Fund) Neword Productions, Inc., Box 1446, New York, NY 10023. TEL 212-362-9151. Ed.Bd. adv.; bk.rev.; film rev.; play rev.; illus.; circ. 500. (back issues avail.)

CHERRY. see MEN'S INTERESTS

CHIRICU. see LITERATURE

700 800 FR ISSN 0009-5001
CHOIX ARTISTIQUE ET LITTERAIRE. 1958. q. free. Editions Flammes Vives, 22 rue du Docteur-Benasson, 95410 Groslay, France. Ed. Jean Aubert. bk.rev.

800 200 US ISSN 0148-3331
PN49
CHRISTIANITY AND LITERATURE. 1951. q. $15 to individuals; institutions $20. Conference on Christianity and Literature, Seattle Pacific University, Seattle, WA 98119. Ed. Robert Snyder. adv.; bk.rev.; circ. 1,400. (back issues avail.) Indexed: Abstr.Engl.Stud., Amer.Bibl.Slavic & E.Eur.Stud., Arts & Hum.Cit.Ind., CERDIC, Chr.Per.Ind., Curr.Cont., LCR, M.L.A., Rel.& Theol.Abstr. (1989-), Rel.Ind.One.
—BLDSC shelfmark: 3181.954000.
Formerly: Conference on Christianity and Literature. Newsletter.
Description: Articles pertaining to the relationship between Christianity and the creation, study, and teaching of literature.

051 301.4157 US ISSN 0146-7921
HQ75
CHRISTOPHER STREET. 1976. m. $27. That New Magazine Inc., 28 W. 25th St., 4th Fl., New York, NY 10010. TEL 212-627-2120. FAX 212-727-9321. Ed. Thomas Steele. adv.; bk.rev.; film rev.; play rev.; illus.; tr.lit.

059 GR
CHRONICO. (Text in Greek) 1970. a. $20. Athens Cultural Center "ORA", 7 Xenofondos St., Athens 10557, Greece. Ed. A. Baharian. bk.rev.; film rev.; index; circ. 1,000. (back issues avail.)
Description: Covers all the intellectual and artistic activities of Greeks inside and outside of Greece.

056.9 BL
CIENCIAS HUMANAS. 1977. q. $25. Universidade Gama Filho, Rua Manoel Vitorino, CEP 625-Rio de Janeiro, Brazil. Ed. Beneval de Oliveira. adv.; bk.rev.; circ. 10,000.

320.9 IT ISSN 0045-6977
CITTA FUTURA.* (Supplement: Debate) vol.3, 1971. m. L.1500. Via della Vite 13, 00187 Rome, Italy. Ed. Ugu Moretti. adv.; bk.rev.; bibl.; circ. 4,500.

CITY LIGHTS REVIEW. see LITERATURE — Poetry

CIVILTA CATTOLICA. see RELIGIONS AND THEOLOGY — Roman Catholic

053.1 055.1 054.1 SZ
CIVITAS; Monatsschrift fuer Politik und Kultur - revue mensuelle politique et culturelle - mensile di politica e culture. (Text in French, German, Italian) 1856. m. 30 Fr. (foreign 35 Fr.). Schweizerischer Studentenverein, Alte Simplonstr. 10, CH-3900 Brig, Switzerland. TEL 028-236200. adv.; bk.rev.; circ. 10,000. (back issues avail.) Indexed: Amer.Hist.& Life, CERDIC, Hist.Abstr., P.A.I.S.

800 SA
CLASSIC; magazine of creative writing and art. (Text in Afrikaans and English) 1982. biennial. R.1.50($3) (African Writers Association (AWA)) Skotaville Publishers, P.O. Box 32483, Braamfontein, Johannesburg 2017, South Africa. Ed. Jaki Seroke. film rev.; illus.; play rev.; circ. 3,000. (back issues avail.) Indexed: Ind.S.A.Per.

800 US ISSN 0090-1237
PQ2605.L2
CLAUDEL STUDIES. 1972. s-a. $15 to individuals; libraries and institutions $20; foreign $20. University of Dallas, Claudel Studies, c/o Moses M. Nagy, Ed., Box 464, Irving, TX 75062-4799. TEL 214-721-5229. Ed. Moses M. Nagy. bk.rev.; bibl.; circ. 500. Indexed: Arts & Hum.Cit.Ind., Curr.Cont., M.L.A.

056 BL
COLECAO ENCANTO RADICAL. Short title: Encanto Radical. no.33, 1983. irreg. Editora Brasiliense S.A., 01416 Rua da Consolacao, 2697, Sao Paulo, Brazil.

056 BL
COLECAO POLEMICAS DO NOSSO TIEMPO. no.5, 1983. irreg. (Livraria Ltda.) Cortez Editora, Rua Bartira, 387, 05009 Sao Paulo, SP, Brazil.

056 BL
COLECAO PRIMEIROS PASSOS. no.98 1983. irreg., latest no.224. Editora Brasiliense S.A., Rua da Consolacao, 2697, 01416 Sao Paulo, Brazil.

COLECCAO N'GOLA. see HISTORY — History Of Africa

056.1 AG
COLECCION ENSAYOS. no.16, 1976. irreg. Editorial Plus Ultra, Viamonte 1755, 1055 Buenos Aires, Argentina.

056.1 SP
COLECCION PUNTO Y LINEA. m. price varies. Editorial Gustavo Gili S.A., Rosellon 87-89, Apdo. de Correos 35.149, Barcelona 29, Spain.

808.8 US
COLONNADES. 1937. a. free. c/o R. Hashell, Faculty Adviser, Box 2237, Elon College, NC 27244. circ. 2,500.

LITERARY AND POLITICAL REVIEWS

808.8   US   ISSN 1046-3348
COLORADO REVIEW; a journal of contemporary literature. 1955-1969; resumed 1977. s-a. $12.50. Colorado State University, English Department, 359 Eddy Bldg., Fort Collins, CO 80523. TEL 303-491-6428. Ed. Bill Tremblay. adv.; bk.rev.; circ. 1,450.
   Formerly (until 1965): Colorado State Review.
   Description: Short fiction, poetry, translations, articles by or interviews with contemporary poets and writers. Includes reviews of recent works of the literary imagination.

COLUMBIA REVIEW (NEW YORK). see LITERATURE

051   US
COLUMBUS FREE PRESS. 1970. m. $10. Columbus Institute for Contemporary Journalism, 1066 N. High St., Columbus, OH 43201. TEL 614-294-9200. Ed. Mary Jo Kilroy. adv.; bk.rev.; illus.; circ. 15,000. (tabloid format; also avail. in microfilm from BLH; reprint service avail. from UMI)

808.87   US
COMEDY BUYERS BULLETIN. a. $9. Robert Makinson, Ed. & Pub., Box 023304, Brooklyn, NY 11202-0066. TEL 718-855-5057.

051   US
COMEUNITY; * an alternative, independent journal. 1971. irreg. $5. ComeUnity, Margo J. Yazell, Ed., 1000 49th St. N., no.203, Saint Petersburg, FL 33710-6640. adv.; bk.rev.; circ. 2,000. (tabloid format; also avail. in microfilm from BLH; back issues avail.)
   Description: A non-profit, independent, alternative journal dedicated to the preservation and enhancement of human rights (civil, political, economic, social and cultural).

059.91   IE   ISSN 0010-2369
COMHAR. (Text in Irish) 1942. m. £18. 5 Rae Mhuirfean, Ath Cliath, Ireland. Ed. Tomas Ma Stomoin. adv.; bk.rev.; charts; illus.; index. cum.index: 1942-1981; circ. 2,500.

808.87   US
COMIC READER. 1961. m. $12. Box 255, Monomonee Falls, WI 53051-0255. TEL 414-251-6933. adv.; circ. 7,000.

296   US   ISSN 0010-2601
DS101
COMMENTARY; journal of significant thought and opinion on contemporary issues. 1945. m. $39. American Jewish Committee, 165 E. 56th St., New York, NY 10022. TEL 212-751-4000. FAX 212-751-1174. Ed. Norman Podhoretz. adv.; bk.rev.; index; circ. 45,000. (also avail. in microform from UMI,ISI,KMI,MIM; microform from NCR,KTO; reprint service avail. from UMI) **Indexed:** A.B.C.Pol.Sci., Acad.Ind., Amer.Bibl.Slavic & E.Eur.Stud., Amer.Hist.& Life, Bk.Rev.Dig., Bk.Rev.Ind. (1965-), Chic.Per.Ind., Child.Bk.Rev.Ind. (1965-), Curr.Cont.M.E., Film Lit.Ind. (1973-), Fut.Surv., G.Soc.Sci.& Rel.Per.Lit., Hist.Abstr., Hist.Abstr., HR Rep., Hum.Ind., Ind.Bk.Rev.Hum., Ind.Jew.Per., M.L.A., Mag.Ind., Media Rev.Dig., Mid.East: Abstr.& Ind., P.A.I.S., PMR, PROMT, R.G., Rel.Ind.One, RILA, SSCI.
—BLDSC shelfmark: 3333.600000.

052   SI   ISSN 0084-8956
DS501
COMMENTARY. 1968-1971; N.S. 1972. irreg. $10. National University of Singapore Society, 9 Kent Ridge Dr., 0511 Singapore, Singapore. FAX 778-8095. Ed. Zaibun Siraj. bk.rev.; circ. 6,000. **Indexed:** Acad.Ind., E.I., G.Soc.Sci.& Rel.Per.Lit., RILA, SSCI.

051 300   US   ISSN 0010-3330
AP2
COMMONWEAL. 1924. bi-w. $36. Commonweal Foundation, 15 Dutch St., New York, NY 10038. TEL 212-732-0800. Ed. Margaret O'Brien Steinfels. adv.; bk.rev.; film rev.; play rev.; index; circ. 18,000. (also avail. in microform from UMI,MIM; reprint service avail. from UMI) **Indexed:** A.I.P.P., Acad.Ind., Amer.Bibl.Slavic & E.Eur.Stud., Amer.Hist.& Life, Bk.Rev.Dig., Bk.Rev.Ind. (1965-), Cath.Ind., CERDIC, Child.Bk.Rev.Ind. (1965-), Curr.Lit.Fam.Plan., Film Lit.Ind. (1973-), G.Soc.Sci.& Rel.Per.Lit., Hist.Abstr., M.L.A., Mag.Ind., Media Rev.Dig., Mid.East: Abstr.& Ind., Old Test.Abstr., PMR, R.G.
—BLDSC shelfmark: 3339.340000.

329.9   CN   ISSN 0010-3357
COMMONWEALTH. 1937. m. Can.$12. Service Printing Co. Ltd., 1122 Saskatchewan Dr., Regina, Sask. S4P OC4, Canada. FAX 306-569-1363. Ed. Leslie Quennell. adv.; bk.rev.; illus.; circ. 10,000. (also avail. in microfilm) **Indexed:** So.Pac.Per.Ind.
   Description: News on democratic socialist politics in Saskatchewan and across Canada.

800   FR   ISSN 0395-6989
COMMONWEALTH; essays and studies. (Text in English, French) 1975. 2/yr. 130 F. Societe d'Etude des Pays du Commonwealth, Faculte de Langues, 2 Boulevard Gabriel, 21000 Dijon, France. FAX 80-39-56-48. Ed. J.P. Durix. adv.; bk.rev.; circ. 600.
—BLDSC shelfmark: 3339.348000.
   Description: Devoted to the study of post-colonial anglophone literatures of the world.

COMMONWEALTH NOVEL IN ENGLISH. see LITERATURE

055   IT   ISSN 1120-7094
COMPARATISTICA. 1989. a. L.39000 (foreign L.48000). Casa Editrice Leo S. Olschki, Casella Postale 66, 50100 Florence, Italy. TEL 055-6530684. FAX 055-6530214. Ed. E. Caramaschi.

055.1   FR   ISSN 0010-4418
COMPRENDRE; revue de politique de la culture. (Text in French) 1950. irreg. L.65000($53) for 4 nos. Societe Europeenne de Culture, Dorsoduro 909, 30123 Venice, Italy. TEL 041-52-30210. FAX 041-52-31033. Ed. Guiseppe Galasso. bk.rev.; illus.; index; circ. 2,500.
—BLDSC shelfmark: 3366.393000.

059.92   LE   ISSN 0010-5589
CONFERENCES DU CENACLE. * (Text in Arabic) vol.20, 1966. m. Box 1145, Beirut, Lebanon. Ed. Michel Asmar. charts; stat.

056.1   PE   ISSN 0010-5600
CONFERENCIAS; * conferencias, discursos, reportajes, articulos, tesis, notas culturales. (Text in English, French, Spanish) 1955. m. S/360.($12) Mario Herrera Gray, Ed. & Pub., Calle Mariano Carranza 306, Lima, Peru. adv.; bk.rev.; charts; illus.; index; circ. 1,000.

051 320   CN   ISSN 0227-1311
D839
CONFLICT QUARTERLY. 1980. q. Can.$15($15) University of New Brunswick, Centre for Conflict Studies, Fredericton, N.B. E3B 5A3, Canada. TEL 506-453-4587. Ed. Deborah Stapleford. bk.rev.; cum.index; circ. 500. **Indexed:** Abstr.Mil.Bibl., P.A.I.S.
—BLDSC shelfmark: 3410.654800.

051   US
CONNECTION (ALEXANDRIA); libertarian open forum. 1968-1979; resumed after 6 mos. 8/yr. $20. Erwin S. "Filthy Pierre" Strauss, Ed. & Pub., Box 3343, Fairfax, VA 22038-3343. adv.; bk.rev.; circ. 100.
   Formerly: Libertarian Connection (ISSN 0024-2012)

CONTACT 2; a poetry review. see LITERATURE — Poetry

808.8   US   ISSN 0732-7455
CB427
CONTEMPORARY ISSUES CRITICISM. 1982. irreg., vol.2, 1984. $108. Gale Research Inc., 835 Penobscot Bldg., Detroit, MI 48226. TEL 313-961-2242. FAX 313-961-6083. TELEX 810-221-7086. Ed. Robert L. Brubaker.
—BLDSC shelfmark: 3425.184170.

052   UK   ISSN 0010-7565
AP4
CONTEMPORARY REVIEW. 1866. m. £29($130) Contemporary Review Co. Ltd., 61 Carey St., London WC2 2JG, England. TEL 041-831-4491. Dir. Leonard Skipp. adv.; bk.rev.; film rev.; s-a. rev.; circ. 2,500. (also avail. in microform from UMI) **Indexed:** Amer.Bibl.Slavic & E.Eur.Stud., Br.Hum.Ind., Child.Bk.Rev.Ind. (1967-), Film Lit.Ind. (1973-), Hist.Abstr., Hum.Ind., M.L.A., Mid.East: Abstr.& Ind.
—BLDSC shelfmark: 3425.300000.
   Incorporates: Fortnightly.
   Description: Includes home affairs and politics, literature and the arts, history, travel and religion.

059.927   UA
CONTEMPORARY THOUGHT. (Text in Arabic) q. Cairo University, Orman, Giza, Cairo, Egypt. Ed. Z.N. Mahmoud.

CONTEMPORARY VERSE TWO; a magazine of Canadian poetry and criticism. see LITERATURE — Poetry

054.1   FR   ISSN 0010-7964
CONTREPOINT. (Text in French) 1970. q. 50 F. 4 rue Stockholm, 75008 Paris, France. adv.; bk.rev.; circ. 5,000.

COOLIBRI; Kultur Freizeit Programm im Ruhrgebiet. see MUSEUMS AND ART GALLERIES

808.87   US
CORNELL LUNATIC. 1978. q. $9. Cornell Lunatic, Inc., Box 56, Willard Straight Hall, Cornell University, Ithaca, NY 14853. Ed. P. Christopher Schoaff. adv.; circ. 3,000.

055.1   IT   ISSN 0589-8366
CORRIERE AFRICANO. 1964. m. Via XX Settembre 49, 00187 Rome, Italy. Ed. Antonio Acone.

055.1   IT
CORRISPONDENZA MERIDIONALE; rassegna di politica, economia, cultura, attualita. m. L.20000. Editrice Pellegrini, Via Roma 74, Casella Postale 158, 87100 Cosenza, Italy.
   Formerly: Incontri Meridionali (ISSN 0019-3488)

051   CN   ISSN 0383-6436
COUNTDOWN. 1972. q. Can.$5. Box 278, Postal Sta. K., Toronto, Ont. M4P 2G5, Canada. TEL 416-277-1218. Ed. F. Paul Fromm. adv.; bk.rev.; illus.; circ. 2,000.

808.87   US
CRACKED. 1957. 8/yr. $10.00. Globe Communications Corp. (New York), 441 Lexington Ave., New York, NY 10017. (And: 5401 N.W. Broken Sound Blvd., Boca Raton, FL 33431) Ed. Robert C. Sproul. illus.; circ. 750,000.
   Description: Contains wit and humour.

808.87   US
CRACKED COLLECTORS EDITION. bi-m. $1.35 per no. Globe Communications Corp. (New York), 441 Lexington Ave., New York, NY 10017. TEL 800-472-7744. illus.; circ. 450,000.
   Description: Contains humorous articles.

808.87   US
CRACKED DIGEST. q. $2 per no. Globe Communications Corp. (New York), 441 Lexington Ave., New York, NY 10017. TEL 800-472-7744.

054.1   FR
CRAPOUILLOT; * magazine non conformiste. 1915. 6/yr. 115 F. Societe les Editions Parisiennes, 4 rue Charles-Divry, 75014 Paris, France.

052   UK   ISSN 0260-8278
CREATIVE MIND; alternative directory Merseyside. 1978. q. £3.80. Lark Lane Community Association, 80 Lark Lane, Liverpool L17 8UU, England. Ed. Helen Prescott. adv.; bk.rev.; film rev.; play rev.; illus.; circ. 1,000. (back issues avail.)
   Incorporates: Alternatives.

810 700 300   US   ISSN 0011-1198
AP2
CRESSET; a review of literature, the arts and public affairs. 1937. m. (Sep.-May). $8.50 to individuals; students $4. (Valparaiso University) Valparaiso University Press, Valparaiso, IN 46383. TEL 219-464-5274. Ed. Gail McGrew Eifrig. bk.rev.; film rev.; record rev.; illus.; circ. 4,800. **Indexed:** Amer.Hum.Ind., Bk.Rev.Ind. (1965-), Child.Bk.Rev.Ind. (1965-).

056.1   AG   ISSN 0011-1473
AP63
CRITERIO. 1928. fortn. $60. Kriterion S.A., Junin 627, 1026 Buenos Aires, Argentina. Ed.Bd. adv.; bk.rev.; film rev.; play rev.; index; circ. 10,000.

051   US   ISSN 0093-1896
NX1
CRITICAL INQUIRY. 1974. q. $31 to individuals; institutions $68; students $22. University of Chicago Press, Journals Division, 5720 S. Woodlawn Ave., Chicago, IL 60637. TEL 312-753-3347. FAX 312-702-0694. TELEX 25-4603. (Orders to: Box 37005, Chicago IL 60637) Ed. W.J.T. Mitchell. adv.; circ. 3,400. (also avail. in microform from UMI; reprint service avail. from UMI,ISI) **Indexed:** Abstr.Engl.Stud., Amer.Hist.& Life, Amer.Hum.Ind., Artbibl.Mod., Arts & Hum.Cit.Ind., Can.Rev.Comp.Lit., Curr.Cont., Film Lit.Ind. (1975-), Hist.Abstr., Hum.Ind., Lang.& Lang.Behav.Abstr., LCR, M.L.A., Mid.East: Abstr.& Ind., Music Artic.Guide, RILA.
—BLDSC shelfmark: 3487.454000.
Description: Debates on a variety of topics about literature, art, architecture, film, history, philosophy, and music.
Refereed Serial

CRITICAL QUARTERLY. see *LITERATURE*

800 028   US   ISSN 0891-3811
JC599.U5   CODEN: CTRVE3
CRITICAL REVIEW; an interdisciplinary journal. 1987. q. $29 to individuals (foreign $35); institutions $49 (foreign $55). Center for Independent Thought, 942 Howard St., San Francisco, CA 94103. Ed. Jeffrey Friedman. adv.; bk.rev.; index; circ. 2,000. (back issues avail.) **Indexed:** Left Ind. (1990-).
—BLDSC shelfmark: 3487.464000.
Description: Contains research and essay-length book reviews on modern authors. Develops and critiques classical liberal theory with an emphasis on political philosophy, economics, sociology, and history.

301   US   ISSN 0896-9205
HM1
CRITICAL SOCIOLOGY. 1969. 3/yr. $15 to individuals; institutions $30. Critical Sociology, University of Oregon, Dept. of Sociology, Eugene, OR 97403. TEL 503-686-5039. adv.; bk.rev.; illus.; cum.index; circ. 1,500. (also avail. in microform from UMI) **Indexed:** Abstr.Mil.Bibl., Alt.Press Ind., E.I., Lang.& Lang.Behav.Abstr., Left Ind. (1982-), Mid.East: Abstr.& Ind., Polit.Sci.Abstr., Sociol.Abstr. (1971-), Stud.Wom.Abstr.
—BLDSC shelfmark: 3487.485800.
Formerly: Insurgent Sociologist (ISSN 0047-0384)

800 700   UK   ISSN 0011-1570
PN2
CRITICAL SURVEY. 1989. 3/yr. £25($52) Oxford University Press, Oxford Journals, Pinkhill House, Southfield Road, Eynsham, Oxford OX8 1JJ, England. TEL 0865-882283. FAX 0865-882890. TELEX 837330 OXPRES G. Ed. Bryan Loughrey. adv.; bk.rev.; circ. 900.
—BLDSC shelfmark: 3487.488510.
Description: Covers literary and cultural studies. Publishes detailed readings on individual texts, wide ranging debates in the nature of critical practice, discussions of current educational issues, original short stories and poetry.

809   US   ISSN 0730-2304
PN2
CRITICAL TEXTS: A REVIEW OF THEORY AND CRITICISM. 1982. 3/yr. $9 to individuals; institutions $15; foreign $20. Department of English and Comparative Literature, 602 Philosophy Hall, Columbia University, New York, NY 10027. TEL 212-749-6956. Ed. Joseph W. Childers. adv.; bk.rev.; bibl.; circ. 850. **Indexed:** Amer.Hum.Ind., Artbibl.Mod., M.L.A., Phil.Ind.
Formerly: Critical Texts: A Newsletter in Critical Theory and the History of Criticism.

053.1   GW   ISSN 0011-1597
CRITICON; konservative Zeitschrift. 1970. bi-m. DM.63. Criticon Verlag GmbH, Knoebelstr. 36, 8000 Munich 22, Germany. TEL 089-299885. Ed. Caspar Von Schrenck-Notzing. bk.rev.; abstr.; bibl. **Indexed:** M.L.A.

CRITIQUE (WEST VANCOUVER); the juicy embrace between information and transformation. see *NEW AGE PUBLICATIONS*

055.1   IT   ISSN 0390-1807
CRONORAMA. 1973. s-a. L.15000. Universita Popolare di Ragusa, Via Leonardo da Vinci 8-10, 97100 Ragusa, Sicily, Italy. TEL 21677 45327. circ. 1,000.

CROSS-BIAS; the newsletter of the friends of Bemerton honoring George Herbert 1593-1633. see *LITERATURE — Poetry*

CROSSCURRENTS. see *SOCIOLOGY*

051   US
CROW; your guide to alternate culture. Variant title: Bill Dale Marcinko's A F T A. 1978. bi-m. $18.95. A F T A Press, Inc., 47 Crater Ave., Wharton, NJ 07885-2023. TEL 201-828-5467. (Alt. addr.: Box A, Wharton, NJ 07885) Ed. Bill Dale Marcinko. adv.; bk.rev.; film rev.; illus.; circ. 25,000. (back issues avail.)
Formerly: A F T A (ISSN 0193-7782)

056.1   SP   ISSN 0572-2969
CUADERNO LITERARIO AZOR;* literatura, poesia, arte, historia, etc., del ambito de la hispanidad. 1974. q. 4000 ptas.($10) Ediciones Rondas, Peligro 8, 08012 Barcelona, Spain. Ed. Jose Jurado Morales. bk.rev.; bibl.; illus.
Supersedes: Azor (ISSN 0045-1258)

056.1   MX   ISSN 0185-156X
AP63
CUADERNOS AMERICANOS. 1942; N.S. 1987? bi-m. Mex.$62000($115) (effective 1992). Universidad Nacional Autonoma de Mexico, Apdo. Postal 965, 06000 Mexico, D.F., Mexico. TEL 5489662. FAX 5489662. (Or: Torre I de Humanidades, 2o piso, Ciudad Universitaria, 04510 Mexico D.F., Mexico) Dir. Leopoldo Zea. adv.; bk.rev.; bibl.; illus.; index. cum.index: 1942-1971; circ. 2,500. (also avail. in microfilm from BHP) **Indexed:** Amer.Hist.& Life, Hisp.Amer.Per.Ind., Hist.Abstr., M.L.A.

056.1   AG   ISSN 0011-2380
CUADERNOS DE CRITICA.* 1965. q. Charcas 4767, 20 "A" Buenos Aires, Argentina. Ed. Jorge C. Caballero. adv.; bk.rev.

CUADERNOS DE CRITICA (MEXICO). see *PHILOSOPHY*

808.8 320   CU
CUADERNOS DE NUESTRA AMERICA. s-a. $6 in N. America; S. America $7; Europe $8; elsewhere $10. (Centro de Estudio Sobre America) Ediciones Cubanas, Obispo No. 527, Apdo. 605, Havana, Cuba. TEL 32-5556-60.

056.1   AG
CUADERNOS DEL CAMINO. 1978. m. (Instituto Goethe Buenos Aires) Agencia Periodistica CID, Av. de Mayo 666, Buenos Aires, Argentina. Ed. Juan C. Paz.

946 980   SP   ISSN 0011-250X
AP63
CUADERNOS HISPANOAMERICANOS; revista mensual de cultura hispanica. 1948. m. 4500 ptas.($45) Instituto de Cooperacion Iberoamericana, Avda. de los Reyes Catolicos 4, Ciudad Universitaria, Madrid 28040, Spain. TEL 244-06-00. Dir. Jose Antonio Maravall. bk.rev.; bibl.; illus.; index.; circ. 2,000. (reprint service avail. from KTO) **Indexed:** Amer.Hist.& Life, Arts & Hum.Cit.Ind., Curr.Cont., Hisp.Amer.Per.Ind., Hist.Abstr., M.L.A.

056.1   CU
CUBA SOCIALISTA. (Summaries in English, French, Spanish) 1966. m. $12 in N. America; S. America $14; Europe $15; elsewhre $21. (Partido Comunista de Cuba, Comite Central) Ediciones Cubanas, Obispo No. 527, Apdo. 605, Havana, Cuba. TEL 22-5895-22-5892. (Subscr. to: Oficina Municipal de Prensa, Dragones No. 456, Havana, Cuba) bk.rev.
Formerly (until 1981): Pensamiento Critico.

056.1   ES   ISSN 0011-2755
AP63
CULTURA. 1955. q. free. Ministerio de Cultura y Comunicaciones, Direccion de Publicaciones e Impresos, 17 Avda. sur 430, San Salvador, El Salvador. bk.rev.; bibl.; illus.; index; cum.index 1961-1963; circ. 3,000. **Indexed:** Amer.Hist.& Life, Hist.Abstr., M.L.A.
Formerly (until 1974): Nueva Cultura (ISSN 0048-1076)

984   BO   ISSN 0011-2763
CULTURA BOLIVIANA.* 1964. m. Bol.$12.($1) Universidad Boliviana Tecnica de Oruro, Departamento de Extension Cultural, Oruro, Bolivia. Dir. Jorge Fajardo. bk.rev.; dance rev.; film rev.; illus.; play rev.; record rev.; index.

800   US   ISSN 0882-3049
CULTURA LUDENS. 1985. irreg. vol.4, 1991. price varies. John Benjamins Publishing Co., 821 Bethlehem Pike, Philadelphia, PA 19118. TEL 215-836-1200. FAX 215-836-1204. (And: Amsteldijk 44, P.O. Box 75577, 1070 AN Amsterdam, Netherlands. TEL 020-6762325) Eds. Mihai Spariosu, Giuseppe Mazzotta. (back issues avail.)
—BLDSC shelfmark: 3491.656050.

810   US
CULTURAL CORRESPONDENCE. 1976. q. $10. 505 West End Ave., New York, NY 10024. TEL 212-787-1784. Ed. Jim Murray. bk.rev.; bibl.; circ. 4,000. **Indexed:** Alt.Press Ind.

800.051   US   ISSN 0730-9503
CULTURAL DEMOCRACY. 1980. s-a. $25 to individuals; organizations $50. Alliance for Cultural Democracy, c/o Tripp Mikiah, 1326 Shotwell St., San Francisco, CA 94110. TEL 415-821-9652. FAX 415-546-0578. (Subscr. to: Box 7591, Minneapolis, MN 55407) adv.; bk.rev.; circ. 2,000. (back issues avail.)
Description: Provides a forum for promoting an understanding of the need for integrating cultural, political, and economic democracy in the US.

CULTURAL STUDIES. see *SOCIOLOGY*

300   US
CULTURAL WATCHDOG NEWSLETTER. 1977. m. $15. Ehrenkrantz Enterprises, 33 Baraud Rd., Scarsdale, NY 10583. Ed. Louis Ehrenkrantz. bk.rev.; circ. 7,800.

059   BD
CULTURE ET SOCIETE. (Text in French) 1978. q. $4. Ministere de la Jeunesse, des Sports et de la Culture, Centre de Civilisation Burundaise, B.P. 1400, Bujumbura, Burundi. Ed.Bd.

055   RM
CURIERUL ROMANESC. 1972. s-m. 168 lei($30) Fundatia Culturala Romana, Alleea Alexandru, no.38, Sector 1, Bucharest 63, Rumania. TEL 797510. FAX 127559. Ed. Ilie Traian. adv.; bk.rev.; circ. 15,100. (back issues avail.)
Supersedes (in 1989): Tribuna Romaniei.

052 800   FR   ISSN 0992-1893
CYCNOS. (Text in English, French) 1985. irreg. 40 F. for 3 nos. Centre de Recherche sur les Ecritures de Langue Anglaise, Universite de Nice, Dept. d'Etudes Anglophones, 98 Bvd Edouard Herriot, B.P. 369, 06007 Nice Cedex, France. Ed. Andre Viola.

942   UK   ISSN 0024-6204
CYMRO LLUNDAIN/LONDON WELSHMAN. (Text in English, Welsh) 1896. m. 85p. London Welsh Association, 157-163 Gray's Inn Rd., London W.C.1, England. Ed. Raymond Howell. adv.; bk.rev.; charts; illus.; play rev.; circ. 3,500.

819 300   CN   ISSN 0011-5827
DALHOUSIE REVIEW; a Canadian quarterly of literature and opinion. 1921. q. Can.$19. Dalhousie University Press, Sir James Dunn Bldg., Ste. 314, Halifax, N.S. B3H 3J5, Canada. TEL 902-494-2541. FAX 902-494-2319. TELEX 019-21863-DALUNIV-HFX. Ed. Alan Andrews. adv.; bk.rev.; index; circ. 1,000. (also avail. in microfilm from MML; reprint service avail. from MML) **Indexed:** Abstr.Engl.Stud., Amer.Hist.& Life, Arts & Hum.Cit.Ind., Bk.Rev.Ind. (1988-), Can.Lit.Ind., Can.Per.Ind., Child.Bk.Rev.Ind. (1988-), CMI, Curr.Cont., Hist.Abstr., Ind.Bk.Rev.Hum., M.L.A., Mid.East: Abstr.& Ind., P.A.I.S.
—BLDSC shelfmark: 3517.750000.

057.8   CI
DANAS/TODAY; informativno politicki tjednik. 1982. w. 14040 din.($23) Avenija Bratstva i Jedinstva 4, 41000 Zagreb, Croatia. TEL 041-333-333. Ed. Gojko Marinkovic. circ. 56,000. (back issues avail.)

895.1   CC
DANGDAI WENTAN BAO. (Text in Chinese) m. Zhongguo Zuojia Xiehui, Guangdong Fenhui - China Writers' Association, Guangdong Chapter, No. 75, Wende Lu, Guangzhou, Guangdong 510030, People's Republic of China. TEL 331851. Ed. Huang Shusen.

LITERARY AND POLITICAL REVIEWS

059.91   UK   ISSN 0011-6718
DARPON;* the independent and impartial Bengali quarterly. (Text in Bengali, English) 1968. q. $2. Darpon Publications, 1 Adelaide Villas, Copse Rd., St. Johns, Woking, Surrey, England. Ed. M. Sultan. adv.; bk.rev.; illus.; circ. 5,000. (processed)

057.8   CI
DARUVARSKI LIST; glasilo OKSSRN Daruvar. 1975. s-m. 780 din. Narodno Sveuciliste, Informativni Centar Daruvar, Strosmajerova 32A, 43500 Daruvar, Croatia. Ed. Damir Valdgoni.
     Formerly (until 1985): Vjesnik Komune (ISSN 0042-7624)

296   AG   ISSN 0011-703X
DAVAR; revista literaria. vol.124, 1970. 4/yr. $8. Sociedad Hebraica Argentina, Sarmiento 2233, Buenos Aires, Argentina. Dir. Bernardo Ezequiel Koremblit. bk.rev.; illus.; circ. 1,500.

322.4   IE   ISSN 0332-4281
DAWN TRAIN. 1982. 2/yr. £2. Dawn Editorial Collective, 16 Ravensdene Park, Belfast 6, Northern Ireland.

052   UK   ISSN 0011-7080
DAY BY DAY; news commentary and digest of national and international affairs and review of the arts, poems. 1963. m. $17. (Fellowship Party) Loverseed Press, Woolacombe House, 141 Woolacombe Rd., Blackheath, London SE3, England. TEL 01-856-6249. Ed. Ronald Mallone. adv.; bk.rev.; film rev.; music rev.; play rev.; circ. 23,000.

056   PE
DEBATE. 1979. bi-m. $40. Apoyo, S.A., Apdo. Postal 671, Lima 100, Peru. FAX 5114-455946. Ed. Augusto Alvarez-Rodrich. adv.; bk.rev.; circ. 10,000. **Indexed:** Hisp.Amer.Per.Ind.

052   II
DEBONAIR; Diwana parody. (Text in English) 1972. m. Rs.1.50 per copy. Debonair Publications Private Ltd., 41A Dr E. Moses Rd., Bombay 400 018, India. TEL 22-4941601. Ed. Amrita Shah. circ. 87,500.

059.91   YU   ISSN 0011-7935
AP56
DELO; mesecni knjizevni casopis. (Text in Serbo-Croatian) 1955. m. 5000 din. Nolit, Terazije 27-II, Belgrade, Yugoslavia. Ed. Jovica Acin. adv.; bk.rev.; index; circ. 1,600. (also avail. in microfilm from NRP) **Indexed:** M.L.A.

DEMOCRAZIA E DIRITTO/DEMOCRACY AND LAW. see LAW

057.1   RU
▼**DEN'.** 1991. w.? 0.20 Rub. per issue. Soyuz Pisatelei S.S.S.R., Tsvetnoi bul'var 30, 103662 Moscow, Russia. TEL 200-24-21. Ed. Aleksandr Prokhanov. (newspaper)

056.1   UY
DESTABANDA. 1977. irreg. Mario A. Aiello, Ed. & Pub., Gaboto 1918, Montevideo, Uruguay.

DEUTSCHLAND-MAGAZIN. see POLITICAL SCIENCE

053   GW
DIABOLO; Magazin aus Oldenburg. 1984. m. DM.24. Diabolo-Verlag, Bahnhofstr. 10a, 2900 Oldenburg, Germany. TEL 0441-25491. FAX 0441-13761. Ed. J. Pregla. circ. 4,250. (back issues avail.)

057.8   XV   ISSN 0012-2068
AP58.S55
DIALOGI. (Text in Slovenian) 1965. m. 60 din.($5.90) Zveza Kulturnih Delavcev v Mariboru, Rotovski trg 1, Maribor, Slovenia. Ed. Janez Svajncer. **Indexed:** M.L.A.

DIALOGUE ON LIBERTY. see POLITICAL SCIENCE

055.1   IT   ISSN 0012-2335
DIANA (MARCIANISE);* rassegna di politica e di cultura. 1953. bi-m. L.3000($10.) Via Raffaele Musone 175, 81025-Marcianise (Caserta), Italy. illus.

830 700   BE   ISSN 0012-2645
AP15
DIETSCHE WARANDE EN BELFORT; tijdschrift voor letterkunde en geestesleven. (Text in Dutch) 1855. 6/yr. 1750 Fr. Editions Peeters s.p.r.l., Bongenotenlaan 153, B-3000 Leuven, Belgium. TEL 016-235170. FAX 016-228500. Ed. Marcel Janssens. adv.; bk.rev.; index; circ. 3,000. (back issues avail.) **Indexed:** M.L.A.

A DIFFERENT LIGHT REVIEW; a catalog of gay and lesbian literature. see HOMOSEXUALITY

808.8   US
DIFFICULTIES.* 1979. s-a. $7 per no. 596 Marilyn St., Kent, OH 44240-3222. TEL 216-673-9282. Ed. Tom Beckett. circ. 300.

808.87   CS   ISSN 0012-284X
AP52
DIKOBRAZ; satiricky tydenik. 1945. w. 76 Kcs.($33) Rude Pravo, Na Porici 30, 112 86 Prague 1, Czechoslovakia. (Subscr. to: Artia, Ve Smeckach 30, 111 27 Prague 1, Czechoslovakia) Ed. Jindrich Besta. illus.; circ. 470,000.
     Description: Emphasis is on wit and humor.

378.1   PH   ISSN 0012-2858
DILIMAN REVIEW. 1953. q. P.120($65) University of the Philippines, Colleges of Science, Arts and Letters, and Social Sciences and Philosophy, Palma Hall Annex, Diliman, Quezon City 1101, Philippines. Ed. Eddie E. Escultura. bk.rev.; index. **Indexed:** Ind.Phil.Per., M.L.A.

055.1   IT   ISSN 0012-2904
DIMENSIONI; rivista abruzzese di cultura e d'arte. 1957. bi-m. L.2000.($5) Via Bendetto Croce 172, 65100 Pescara, Italy. Ed.Bd. adv.; bk.rev.; bibl.; charts; illus.; index.

055   IT   ISSN 0394-2473
DIORAMA LETTERARIO; mensile di attualita culturali e metapolitiche. 1976. m. L.30000($25) Casella Postale 1364, 50122 Florence, Italy. TEL 055-23-40-714. Ed. Marco Tarchi. bk.rev.; bibl.; circ. 2,000. (back issues avail.)

DIRECTORY OF HUMOR MAGAZINES & HUMOR ORGANIZATIONS IN AMERICA (AND CANADA). see BIBLIOGRAPHIES

800   IT   ISSN 0012-3668
DISCRETIO. 1962. irreg. Via F. M. Penna 20, 97018 Sicily, Italy. Ed. Dr. Giovanni Rossino. circ. 1,000. (tabloid format)
     Description: Translations from modern and classical languages.

057.91   KR   ISSN 0012-4354
DNIPRO; literaturno-khudozhnii ta hromads'ko-politychnyi zhurnal. 1927. m. 15.60 Rub. (Soyuz Molodezhnikh Organizatsii Ukrainy) Izdatel'stvo Molod, 38-42-Parkhomenko St., Kiev, Ukraine. TEL 213-9879. Ed. Mykola Lukiv. bk.rev.; bibl.; illus.; circ. 67,500. **Indexed:** M.L.A.

057.1   RU   ISSN 0012-5393
DON; literaturno-khudozhestvennyi i obshchestvenno-politicheskii zhurnal. 1957. m. 24 Rub. Soyuz Pisatelei Rossiiskoi S.F.S.R., Rostovskoe Oblastnoe Otdelenie, Krasnoarmeiskaya 23, Rostov-na-Donu, GSP-6, Russia. Ed. M.D. Sokolov. bk.rev.; illus.; circ. 60,000.

DOSTOEVSKY STUDIES. see LITERATURE

DOVETAIL. see RELIGIONS AND THEOLOGY

890   AA
DRITA. 1960. w. $16. Lidhja e Shkrimtareve dhe e Artisteve te Shqiperise - Union of Writers and Artists of Albania, Baboci 37z, Tirana, Albania. Ed. Zija Cela. bk.rev.; film rev.; illus. (also avail. in microfilm from NRP)

320.5   GW   ISSN 0012-6268
DER DRITTE WEG; freisoziale Alternative zu Kapitalismus und Kommunismus. 1970. m. DM.42. Freisoziale Union, Demokratische Mitte, Feldstr. 46, 2000 Hamburg 36, Germany. TEL 040-4399717. FAX 02054-84955. Ed. Hans-Bernhard Zill. bk.rev.; circ. 3,000.
     Description: Covers capitalism, socialism, and communism and their role in economics, finance, politics, and international politics.

057.1   RU   ISSN 0012-6756
DRUZHBA NARODOV. 1938. m. 27.60 Rub. (Soyuz Pisatelei S.S.S.R.) Izdatel'stvo Izvestiya, Pl. Pushkina, 5, 103798 Moscow, Russia. Ed. S. Baruzdin. bk.rev.; bibl.; illus.; index; circ. 33,300. **Indexed:** Curr.Dig.Sov.Press, M.L.A.
     —BLDSC shelfmark: 0056.250000.

057.8   CI   ISSN 0012-690X
DUBROVACKI VJESNIK; list Socijalistickog saveza radnog naroda opoine Dubrovnik. 1950. w. 150 din. Socijalisticki Savez Radnog Naroda Opcine Dubrovnik, Frana Bulica 6, 50101 Dubrovnik, Croatia. Ed. Miho Milic.

808.8   US
DUCK SOUP. 1978. a. free. North Lake College, 5001 N. MacArthur Blvd., Irving, TX 75062. TEL 214-659-5270. Ed. Nancy Jones. circ. 3,000.
     Description: Serves students, faculty and staff of the college.

895   CC   ISSN 1003-5702
DUFU YANJIU XUEKAN/JOURNAL OF DUFU STUDIES. (Text in Chinese) 1981. q. Y12. Chengdu Dufu Yanjiu Xuehui - Chengdu Society of Dufu Studies, Dufu Caotang Bowuguan Nei, Chengdu, Sichuan 610072, People's Republic of China. TEL 769687. (Subscr. to: Sichuan Sheng Xinhua Shudian, Chengdu, Sichuan 610017, P.R.C.) (Co-sponsor: Dufu Caotang Museum)
     Formerly (until 1988): Caotang - Dufu Yanjiu Xuekan.
     Description: Studies the life and poems of Dufu, a famous ancient poet in China.

057.1   KR
DZVIN; literaturno-mystetz'kyi ta hromads'kopolitychnyi zhurnal. 1940. m. $12. (Soyuz Pisatelei Ukrainskoi S.S.R.) Vydavnyctvo Kamenyar, Ul. Vatutina 6, Lvov, Ukraine. TEL 72-36-20. Ed. Roman Fedoriv. bk.rev.; illus.; circ. 107,100.
     Formerly (until 1990): Zhovten' (ISSN 0044-4499)

052   NZ
EARWIG. 1969. s-a. NZ.$2 for 5 nos. Earwig Graphics, 10 Norfolk St., Auckland 2, New Zealand. illus.; circ. 4,000.

052   IE
EAST CORK NEWS. (Text in English) 1981. w. £32.76. Waterford News & Star, Michael St., Waterford, Ireland. TEL 051-74951. FAX 051-55281. Ed. Peter Doyle. circ. 18,645. (newspaper)

051   FR
EASY SPEAKEASY. 1980. 5/yr. 35 F. Librairie Fernand Nathan, 9 rue Mechain, 75014 Paris, France. Ed. Rosalie Gomes.

054   FR   ISSN 0337-8659
ECLATS DE RIRE.* 1964. q. 99 F. Editions E.G.E., B.P. 7085, 69007 Lyon, France. Ed. J. Deschavanne. adv.; circ. 51,000.
     Description: Contains humorous articles.

056.1   PE
ECOS. 1962. m. Jose A. Valencia - Arenas, Apdo. 3758, Lima, Peru. illus.; circ. 5,000.

ECRITS DU CANADA FRANCAIS. see LITERATURE

056.9   BL
EDICOES CADERNOS CULTURAIS;* uma revista de cultura do nordeste para o Brasil. irreg. Cr.$10 per no. Universidade Federal de Pernambuco, Cidade Universitaria, 5000 Recife, PE, Brazil. illus.

941   UK   ISSN 0267-6672
EDINBURGH REVIEW. 1969. q. £4.95($9.50) per no. Edinburgh University Press, 22 George Sq., Edinburgh EH8 9LF, Scotland. FAX 031-662-0053. TELEX UNIVED G 727442. Ed. Murdo Macdonald. adv.; bk.rev.; film rev.; bibl.; illus.; circ. 1,500. (also avail. in microform from UMI; microfilm from KTO; reprint service avail. from UMI)
     —BLDSC shelfmark: 3661.022500.
     Formerly (until 1985): New Edinburgh Review (ISSN 0028-4645)
     Description: Features articles on all aspects of culture (literature, art, philosophy, education).

052   PK   ISSN 0013-2020
EDUCATOR.* (Text in English) 1965. m. Rs.9($3.) G. Rabbani Mirza, Ed. & Pub., 2 McLeod Rd., Lahore, Pakistan. bk.rev.; circ. 1,000.

LITERARY AND POLITICAL REVIEWS

811 US
EIGHTIES;* a magazine of poetry and opinion. (Text in Danish, French, German and Swedish) 1958; N.S. 1987. irreg. $10 for 4 nos. Eighties Press, 1783 Irving Ave. S., Minneapolis, MN 55403-2820. (Subscr. to: 2940 Seventh St., Berkeley, CA 94710) Ed. Robert Bly. bk.rev.; circ. 3,000. (also avail. in microfilm from UMI; back issues avail.; reprint service avail. from UMI)
Former titles: Seventies (ISSN 0037-5969); Sixties (ISSN 0583-4570)

059.89 CY
ELEFTHEROTYPIA TIS DEFTERAS/MONDAY'S FREE PRESS. (Text in Greek) 1980. w. Demoktatiko Komma (DIKO), Hasjisavvas Bldg., Eleftheria Sq., POB 3821, Nicosia, Cyprus.
Description: Greek-Cypriot right-of-center political review.

ELEMENTS. see ART

808.8 HU ISSN 0424-8848
ELET ES IRODALOM; irodalmi es politikai hetilap. 1957. w. 360 Ft.($43.50) Lapkiado Vallalat, Lenin krt. 9-11, Budapest 7, Hungary. (Subscr. to: Kultura, P.O. Box 149, H-1389 Budapest, Hungary) Ed. Imre Bata. film rev.; play rev.; illus.; circ. 60,000. (looseleaf format)

847 HU ISSN 0133-4751
ELETUNK. 1963. m. $24. (Vas Megye Tanacsa) Kultura, P.O. Box 149, 1389 Budapest 62, Hungary. Ed. Gyorgy Pete. bk.rev.; circ. 2,150.

059.89 CY
EMBROS (CYPRUS)/FORWARD. (Text in Greek) 1987. w. Ananeotiko Demokratiko Socialistiko Kinema (AIDSOK), 19 Nikitara St., Ag. Omoloyitae, POB 3739, Nicosia, Cyprus. Ed. P. Polydorides. circ. 2,500.
Description: Left-wing political review.

808 808.87 US
EMERALD CITY COMIX & STORIES; fiction, poetry, news, reviews, humor. 1987. bi-m. $12. Wonder Comix, Box 95402, Seattle, WA 98145-2402. TEL 206-527-2598. Ed. Nils Osmar. adv.; bk.rev.; circ. 12,000. (tabloid format; back issues avail.)
Description: Presents short stories and other "word pieces", poetry, cartoons and comics, graphics, news.

EMIGRE; non-stop design - the magazine that ignores boundaries. see ART

700 US ISSN 0193-5798
ENCLITIC; the timely taken seriously. 1977. 4/yr. $16 to individuals (foreign $18); institutions $36 (foreign $40). Box 36098, Los Angeles, CA 90036-0098. TEL 213-931-6623. Ed. John O'Kane. adv.; bk.rev.; circ. 7,500. **Indexed:** Amer.Hum.Ind., Film Lit.Ind. (1982-), Intl.Ind.TV, M.L.A., Sociol.Abstr.
—BLDSC shelfmark: 3738.516000.
Description: Writing on contemporary politics, ideas and cultural life.

052 300 UK ISSN 0013-7073
AP4
ENCOUNTER (LONDON, 1953).* 1953. m. (except Aug. & Sep.). £22($45) Encounter Ltd., 59 St. Martin's Lane, London WC2N 4JS, England. TEL 01-434-3063. Eds. Melvin J. Lasky, Richard Mayne. adv.; bk.rev.; s-a. index; circ. 18,000. (also avail. in microform) **Indexed:** Acad.Ind., Amer.Hist.& Life, Arts & Hum.Cit.Ind., Bk.Rev.Dig., Br.Hum.Ind., Film Lit.Ind. (1973-), Fut.Surv., G.Soc.Sci.& Rel.Per.Lit., Hist.Abstr., Hum.Ind., Ind.Bk.Rev.Hum., P.A.I.S.
Description: Focuses on current affairs, literature and the arts. Includes new poetry and short stories.

500 375.4 820 SA ISSN 0376-8902
ENGLISH IN AFRICA. 1974. s-a. R.16.50 to individuals; institutions R.27.50; outside Africa £15($20)(typically set in Jan.). Rhodes University, Institute for the Study of English in Africa, P.O. Box 94, Grahamstown 6140, South Africa. FAX 0461-25642. Ed. Gareth Cornwell. adv.; bk.rev.; circ. 500. **Indexed:** Curr.Cont.Africa, Ind.S.A.Per., M.L.A.

808.8 320 CU
ENIGMA; revista de literatura policiaca. q. $12 in N. and S. America; Europe $13; elsewhere $14. (Asociacion Internacional de Escritores Policiacos) Ediciones Cubanas, Obispo No. 527, Apdo. 605, Havana, Cuba. TEL 32-5556-60.

056.9 BL
ENSAIOS DE OPINIAO; revista mensal de cultura. 1975. m. Cr.$300. Editora Paz e Terra, Rua Sao Jose 90, Centro, Rio de Janeiro, Brazil.

055.1 800 IT ISSN 0046-2403
ERA; bimestrale di lettere ed arti. 1971; N.S. 1976. bi-m. L.2500. Via A. Volta 27, 56025 Pontedera (Pisa), Italy. Ed. Salvatore Amodel. bk.rev.; bibl.; illus.

800 US
ERGO!; the bumbershoot literary magazine. 1986. a. $6. Bumbershoot Festival Commission, Box 9750, Seattle, WA 98109-0750. TEL 206-622-5123. FAX 206-622-5154. TELEX 292-992 REEL UR. Ed. Judith Roche. adv.; bk.rev.; circ. 1,500. (back issues avail.)

808.8 AG
ESCARABAJO DE ORO.* 1972. m. Arg.$3000. c/o Abelardo Castillo, Liliana Heker, Eds., Puyerred 578, Buenos Aires, Argentina. adv.; bk.rev.; bibl.

ESPERANTO. see LINGUISTICS

055.1 IT
ESPERIENZE LETTERARIE; rivista trimestrale di critica e di cultura. 1976. q. L.40000. Societa Editrice Napoletana s.r.l., Corso Umberto I 34, 80138 Naples, Italy. Ed. M. Santoro. **Indexed:** M.L.A.

054.1 FR ISSN 0014-0759
AP20
ESPRIT. 1932. m. 200 F.($45) 212 rue Saint Martin, 75003 Paris, France. TEL 1-48-04-92-90. Ed. Olivier Mongin. adv.; bk.rev.; index; circ. 10,000. **Indexed:** Amer.Hist.& Life, Arts & Hum.Cit.Ind., CERDIC, Film Lit.Ind. (1985-), Hist.Abstr., Ind.Bk.Rev.Hum., M.L.A., Pt.de Rep. (1979-).

808.8 US
ESSENCE (WAYNE). 1963. a. free. William Paterson College, 300 Pomton Rd., Wayne, NJ 07570. TEL 201-595-2000. Ed. Graham Sailor. adv.; illus.; circ. 1,625.

800 FR
L'ESTAMPILLE - L'OBJET D'ART; art antiquites et artisanat. 1969. m. (11/yr.). 395 F. (foreign 545 F.). Archeologia S.A., 25 rue Berbisey, 2100 Dijon, France. (Subscr. to: BP 90, 21800 Quetigny, France. TEL 80-70-93-46) Ed. Louis Faton. adv.; bk.rev.; circ. 50,000.
Formerly: Estampille.

054.1 FR ISSN 0014-1941
ETUDES. 1856. m. 410 F. (foreign 490 F.). Assas Editions, 14 rue d'Assas, 75006 Paris, France. TEL 44-39-48-48. FAX 40-49-01-92. Ed. Jean-Yves Calvez. adv.; bk.rev.; abstr.; bibl.; index, cum.index: 1961-1978, 1979-1990; circ. 15,000. **Indexed:** Amer.Hist.& Life, Cath.Ind., CERDIC, Hist.Abstr., Int.Lab.Doc., M.L.A., New Test.Abstr., Phil.Ind., Pt.de Rep. (1979-).
—BLDSC shelfmark: 3816.555000.

808.87 GW ISSN 0423-5975
EULENSPIEGEL; Wochenzeitung fuer Satire und Humor. 1946. w. DM.20.40. Berliner Verlag, Karl-Liebknecht-Str. 29, 1026 Berlin, Germany. circ. 490,000.
Formerly (until 1954): Frischer Wind.

050 070.43 FR ISSN 0180-7897
EUROP. (Supplement avail.) (Text in English, French) 1978. q. 180 F. (foreign 220 F.)(typically set in Jan.). La Fondation Journalistes en Europe, 33 rue du Louvre, 75002 Paris, France. TEL 45-08-86-71. FAX 45-08-15-58. TELEX 240 586. Ed. Gerald Long. adv.; charts; illus.; stat.; circ. 1,900.
Description: Provides an insight into the Europe of tomorrow, undistorted by national preoccupations.

940 FR ISSN 0014-2751
AP20
EUROPE; revue litteraire mensuel. 1923. m. 450 F. (foreign 550 F.). Messidor Europe, 146 rue du Fbg. Poissonniere, 75010 Paris, France. TEL 1-42-81-91-03. FAX 48-74-19-99. Ed. Pierre Gamarra. adv.; bk.rev.; bibl.; film rev.; illus.; music rev.; index; circ. 16,000. (back issues avail.) **Indexed:** Curr.Cont., World Text.Abstr.
—BLDSC shelfmark: 3829.455000.

054.1 320 BE
EUROPE-MAGAZINE. (Text in French) 1944. w. 2400 Fr. Compagnie Internationale d'Editions et de Promotion, Rue Dekens 5, B-1040 Brussels, Belgium. Ed. Maurice Brebart. adv.; bk.rev.; illus.; circ. 30,000.
Former titles: Nouvel Europe-Magazine; Europe-Magazine.

052 NE
EUROPEAN AFFAIRS.* (Text in English) 1987. q. $53. B.V. Uitgeversmaatschaapij Bonaventura, Hoogoorddreef 60, 1101 BE Amsterdam, Netherlands. TEL 20-5674911. FAX 20-5674629. TELEX 14013 BONAV NL. Ed. Ferry A. Hoogendijk. circ. 18,000. **Indexed:** SCIMP (1990-), World Agri.Econ.& Rural Sociol.Abstr.

052 CH
EVENSONGS/YEH KO. (Text in Chinese or English) irreg., no.25, 1981. (Evensongs Association) Tamkang University, English Department Evening School, Tamsui, Taipei Hsien, Taiwan 25137, Republic of China. Ed. Chang-Fang Chen. adv.; bk.rev.; illus.; circ. 3,000.

052 UK
EVENT SOUTH WEST. 1986. m. £6. Printwest Ltd., 1 Parliament St., Exeter, England. Ed. Rupert Loydell.
Description: Features event listings, art reviews, sports and interviews.

052 UK
EXETER FLYING POST; the campaigning community newspaper. 1976. m. £5. Printwest Ltd., 1 Parliament St., 3rd Fl., Exeter, England. Ed. Patrick Cunningham. adv.; bk.rev.; film rev.; play rev.; circ. 1,500. (looseleaf format; back issues avail.)

053 GW ISSN 0721-6742
EXIL; Forschung Erkenntnisse Ergebnisse 1933-1945. 1981. 2/yr. DM.39($21) Goethestr. 122, 6457 Maintal 2, Germany. TEL 06109-65786. Ed. Edita Koch. adv.; bk.rev.; index; circ. 600. (back issues avail.)
—BLDSC shelfmark: 3836.337500.

EXILE. see LITERATURE

EXIT 13 MAGAZINE. see LITERATURE

057 CS
EXPRES. w. (Communist Party of Slovakia, Central Committee) Pravda, Volgogradska 8, 893 39 Bratislava, Czechoslovakia.

054.1 FR ISSN 0014-5270
AP20
EXPRESS. 1953. w. Groupe Express S.A., 61 av. Hoche, 75008 Paris, France. TEL 1-40-54-99-72. FAX 42-67-72-93. TELEX 650009. Ed. Yann de l'Ecotais. adv.; bk.rev.; circ. 600,000. **Indexed:** CERDIC, Pt.de Rep. (1979-).

051 US ISSN 0740-7815
EXQUISITE CORPSE; a journal of books & ideas. 1981. 6/yr. $20. Illinois State University, Publication Center, Research Services Bldg., Rm. 61, English Dept., Normal, IL 61761-6901. (Ed. addr.: Box 25051, Baton Rouge, LA 70894) Ed. Andrei Codrescu. bk.rev.; film rev.; illus.; circ. 3,000. (back issues avail.)
Description: Iconoclastic cultural, political and philosophical commentary on life and the arts, with poetry, fiction and bureau reports from around the world.

808.87 US
EXTRA SPECIAL CRACKED. a. $1.75. Globe Communications Corp. (New York), 441 Lexington Ave., New York, NY 10017. TEL 800-472-7744. illus.; circ. 400,000.
Description: Contains humorous articles.

LITERARY AND POLITICAL REVIEWS

058   DK   ISSN 0108-9870
FACET. 1983. m. DKK 160. (Dansk Alrussisk Venskabsforening) Forlaget REX, Box 2016, 1012 Copenhagen K, Denmark. TEL 01-108872. Ed. Lise-Lotte Hartvig. adv.; bk.rev.; illus.; circ. 1,000.

054.1   FR   ISSN 0339-3070
FAIRE.* 1975. m. 170 F. 47 av. Lena, 75016 Paris, France. Ed.Bd. adv.; bk.rev.; illus.

FAITH AND FORM. see *ARCHITECTURE*

FAITH TODAY; Canada's evangelical news-feature magazine. see *RELIGIONS AND THEOLOGY — Protestant*

057.85   PL
FAKTY (YEAR); tygodniowy magazyn kulturalny. 1973. w. $23. Wydawnictwo Wspolczesne R S W "Prasa-Ksiazka-Ruch", Ul. Wiejska 12, 00-420 Warsaw, Poland. TEL 48-22-285330. (Dist. by: Ars Polona-Ruch, Krakowskie Przedmiescie 7, Warsaw, Poland)
   Supersedes: Magazyn Pomorze, Fakty 1.

053   GW   ISSN 0176-9146
FAMILIENPOLITISCHE INFORMATIONEN. 1962. bi-m. DM.10. Evangelische Aktionsgemeinschaft fuer Familienfragen, Meckenheimer Allee 162, 5300 Bonn 1, Germany. Ed. Gabriele Conen. bk.rev.; index; circ. 2,900. (back issues avail.)

808.8 052   UK
FANATIC; a paper of passion. 1977. irreg. price varies. Open Head Press, 2 Blenheim Cresc., London W11 1NN, England. (back issues avail.)

059.91   UK
Y FANER. (Text in Welsh) 1847. w. $40. Gwasg Y Sir, Bala, Gwynedd, Wales. Ed. Hafina Clwyd. adv.; bk.rev.; illus.; play rev.; stat.; circ. 6,290.
   Formerly: Baner Ac Amserau Cymru (ISSN 0005-4976)

800   NE   ISSN 0167-9392
FAUX TITRE. (Text in English and French) 1980. irreg. Editions Rodopi B.V., Keizergracht 302-304, 1016 EX Amsterdam, Netherlands. TEL 020-6227507. FAX 020-6380948. (US and Canada subscr. to: 233 Peachtree St N.E., Ste. 404, Atlanta GA 30303-1504. TEL 800-225-3998) Ed. Keith Busby. circ. 500. **Indexed:** M.L.A.
   Formerly: Degre Second.

322.4   CH
FEN TOU/STRUGGLE. (Text in Chinese) no.43; 1975. m. Cultural Bldg., 5th Fl., Hsin-yi Rd. Sec. 1, Taipei, Taiwan, Republic of China.

055.1   IT   ISSN 0014-9969
FENARETE-LETTURE D'ITALIA;* Italian cultural and literary periodical. 1949. bi-m. L.22000. Editoriale Fenarete, Via Beruto 7, 20131 Milan, Italy. Ed. Alberto Pivi. adv.; illus.; circ. 57,800.

808.87   US
FENGCI YU YOUMO/SATIRE & HUMOR. (Text in Chinese) s-m. $15.60. China Books & Periodicals, Inc., 2929 24th St., San Francisco, CA 94110. TEL 415-282-2994. FAX 415-282-0994. (newspaper)

808   IT
FESTA.* 1978. m. L.18000 for 10 nos. Citta Armoniosa, Via Spallanzani 3, 42100 Reggio Emilia, Italy. Ed. Giovanni Riva. illus.

051   US   ISSN 8750-3530
FESTIVAL QUARTERLY.* 1974. 4/yr. $9.90. Main St., Box 419, Intercourse, PA 17534-0419. TEL 717-768-7171. adv.; circ. 4,000.

056.1   UY
FICCIONES; revista de cultura. 1977. bi-m. Almiron 5532, Montevideo, Uruguay. Ed. Elena Taboada.

051   US   ISSN 0015-0800
FIFTH ESTATE. 1965. q. $6 to individuals (foreign $8); libraries $10; corporate or government $50. Fifth Estate Newspaper, 4632 Second Ave., Detroit, MI 48201. TEL 313-831-6800. adv.; bk.rev.; film rev.; play rev.; circ. 10,000. (tabloid format; also avail. in microform from UMI; reprint service avail. from UMI; back issues avail.) **Indexed:** Alt.Press Ind.
   Description: Anti-capitalist, pro-anarchist, radical environmental, anti-civilization.

059.92   GW   ISSN 0015-0932
FIKRUN WA FANN. (Text in Arabic; occasionally in German) 1963. s-a. free. Inter Nationes e.V., Kennedy-Allee 91-103, 5300 Bonn 2, Germany. TEL 0228-880-0. FAX 0228-880457. TELEX 17228308. bk.rev.; illus.; circ. 6,000.

808.87   US
FILLMORE BUNGLE. 1975. irreg. $10. Society for the Preservation & Enhancement of the Recognition of Millard Fillmore, Last of the Whigs, Box 712, Cascade, CO 80809. TEL 719-684-2102. Ed. Phil Arkow. circ. 300. (back issues avail.)
   Description: Presents an irreverent look at mediocrity in American life as epitomized by Millard Fillmore, the thirteenth president of the United States.

FINE MADNESS. see *LITERATURE — Poetry*

054.1   FR   ISSN 0015-3486
FLAMMES VIVES. 1948. q. 100 F.($3.60) Editions Flammes Vives, 22 rue du Docteur-Benasson, 95410 Groslay, France. Ed. Jean Aubert. bk.rev.; bibl.; illus.; circ. 1,200.

808.8   US   ISSN 0742-2466
FLORIDA REVIEW. 1972. s-a. $7. Department of English, University of Central Florida, Orlando, FL 32816. TEL 407-823-2038. Ed. Russ Kessler. circ. 750.
   Description: Contains short stories, poetry and essays.

301 808.8   SL
FOCUS;* a Sierra Leonean international socio-economic political quarterly. vol.3, 1976. q. Jamawu Publications, P.O. Box 862, Freetown, Sierra Leone. Ed. Fred Awata-Coker. adv.; illus.

FOI ET VIE. see *RELIGIONS AND THEOLOGY*

058.81   DK   ISSN 0015-5845
FOLKEVIRKE; social, kulturel og polistisk oplysning. 1945. q. DKK 80. Folkevirke, Solsortvej 1, 2000 Frederiksberg, Denmark. FAX 4553510151. Ed. Annemarie Balle. adv.; bk.rev.; illus.; stat.; circ. 2,500 (controlled).

052   UK   ISSN 0952-3979
FOOLSCAP. 1987. q. £6($16) 78 Friars Road, East Ham, London E6 1LL, England. TEL 081-470-7680. Ed. Judi Benson. circ. 200. (back issues avail.)
   Description: Poetry and prose from well and little-known writers.

051   US   ISSN 0893-5599
FORCED EXPOSURE. 1982. 4/yr. $14. Forced Exposure, Inc., Box 9102, Waltham, MA 02254. TEL 617-562-0507. FAX 617-562-0533. Ed. James Johnson. adv.; bk.rev.; circ. 15,000. (back issues avail.)

LA FORGE. see *POLITICAL SCIENCE*

052   UK   ISSN 0141-7762
FORTNIGHT. 1970. m. £17 (Europe £20; elsewhere £29). Fortnight Publications Ltd., 7 Lower Crescent, Belfast BT7 1NR, N. Ireland. TEL 0232-232353. FAX 0232-232650. Ed. Robin Wilson. adv.; bk.rev.; cum.index vols.1-250; circ. 7,000.
   Description: An independent review of politics and the arms.

057.85   PL   ISSN 0015-8402
AS539.5
FORUM. 1965. w. $37. Ul. Sniadeckich 10, 00-656 Warsaw, Poland. TEL 48-22-256150. (Dist. by: Ars Polona-Ruch, Krakowskie Przedmiescie 7, Warsaw, Poland) Ed. Bohdan Herbich. circ. 53,400. **Indexed:** Hist.Abstr., Leg.Per.
   Description: Contains reprinted articles from foreign periodicals.

FORUM. see *LITERATURE*

301   US
FORUM (LORENTON).* 1976. q. free. Social Concern Committee of Springfield Gardens, Inc., 226-18 Merrick Blvd., Lorenton, NY 11413. TEL 718-978-3700. Ed. E. Cynthia Jenkins. circ. 6,000. **Indexed:** Excerp.Med.

FORUM LIBERAL; liberale Zeitung. see *POLITICAL SCIENCE*

053.1   AU
FORVM; International Zeitschrift fuer kulturelle Freiheit. 1954. 6/yr. DM.26. Gerhard Oberschlick Ed. & Pub., Museumstr. 5, A-1070 Vienna, Austria. FAX 938368. adv.; bk.rev.; film rev.; illus.; play rev.; index; circ. 25,000 (controlled). **Indexed:** Amer.Hist.& Life, CERDIC, Hist.Abstr.
   Former titles (until 1980): Neues Forvm (ISSN 0028-3622); (until 1965): Forvm.

378.1   PH   ISSN 0015-8984
FOUNDATION TIME. vol.20, 1968. m. Foundation University, Dumaguete City 6501, Philippines. Ed. Reuben M. Tadena. charts.

378.1   US   ISSN 0015-9107
AP2
FOUR QUARTERS. 1951; N.S. 1987. 2/yr. $13 for 2 yrs. La Salle University, 1900 W. Olney Ave., Philadelphia, PA 19141. TEL 215-951-1145. FAX 215-951-1892. Ed. John Keenan. bk.rev.; cum.index vols.1-20; circ. 1,000. (also avail. in microform from UMI; reprint service avail. from UMI) **Indexed:** Amer.Hum.Ind., Arts & Hum.Cit.Ind., Curr.Cont., Ind.Amer.Per.Verse, Ind.Little Mag.
   —BLDSC shelfmark: 4028.054000.
   Description: Includes fiction, poetry, and essays for the college-educated reader.

FOURTH ESTATE; Canada's national press journal. see *JOURNALISM*

052 700   FR   ISSN 0738-9299
PN771
FRANK; an international journal of contemporary writing and art. (Text in English) 1983. s-a. 150 F.($30) to individuals; institutions 300 F. ($60) for 4 issues. Frank Books, B.P. 29, F-94301 Vincennes Cedex, France. TEL 43-65-64-05. FAX 43-65-33-02. Ed. David Applefield. adv.; bk.rev.; illus.; circ. 4,000.
   Description: Publishes literary and visual art from contemporary writers and artists around the world, both established and emerging, in a broad range of innovative styles, forms, voices, visions, and cultures. Includes interviews and foreign dossiers.

FREE RADICAL. see *POLITICAL SCIENCE*

FREEDOMWAYS; a quarterly review of the Freedom Movement. see *ETHNIC INTERESTS*

800 410   US   ISSN 0098-9355
PQ1
FRENCH FORUM. (Text in English, French) 1976. 3/yr. $15 to individuals; institutions $35. French Forum Publishers Inc., Box 130, Nicholasville, KY 40430. TEL 606-885-1446. Eds. Raymond C. La Charite, Virginia A. La Charite. adv.; bk.rev.; bibl.; circ. 500. **Indexed:** Arts & Hum.Cit.Ind., Curr.Cont., Ind.Bk.Rev.Hum., M.L.A.
   —BLDSC shelfmark: 4034.260000.
   Description: Contains literary criticism.

052   UK   ISSN 0046-5062
FRENDZ.* bi-w. £3.50($14.40) Echidna Epics Co. Ltd., 301 Portobello Rd., London W10 5TR, England. adv.; bk.rev.; film rev.; play rev.; charts; illus.; circ. 15,000. (tabloid format)

052   UK
FRIENDSHIP BOOK OF FRANCIS GAY. 1939. a. £2.25. D.C. Thomson and Co. Ltd., 185 Fleet St., London EC4A 2HS, England. (Subscr. to: Subscribers Dept., 9-12 Bank St., Dundee DD1 9HU, Scotland) Ed. Maurice Fleming.

055.1   IT   ISSN 0016-2132
FRONTIERA; rivista mensile illustrata della Sardegna. 1968. m. L.10000. Editrice Cagliari, Via Col della Porretta 14, Rome, Italy. Ed. Remo Branca. adv.; bk.rev.; bibl.; illus.; circ. 3,000.
   Formerly: Frontiera-Sardegna.

FRONTLINE. see *ETHNIC INTERESTS*

808.8   US
FROZEN WAFFLES.* 1976. irreg. $4.50 per no. Frozen Waffles Press & Tapes, c/o Dave Wade, 329 W. First St., Apt. 5, Bloomington, IN 47401. Eds. Bro Dimitrios, David Wade. circ. 300.

700   IT
FUCK. q. L.10000. Vittorio Baccelli, Ed. & Pub., C.P. 132, 55100 Lucca, Italy. circ. 1,000. (tabloid format)

LITERARY AND POLITICAL REVIEWS

055.1 IT ISSN 0016-2876
FUOCO; rassegna di cultura e d'arte. 1953. bi-m. L.15000. (Studium Christi) Edizioni Il Fuoco, Via Giacinto Carini 28, 00152 Rome, Italy. TEL 06-5810969. Ed. Pasquale Magni. bk.rev.; bibl.; illus.; index; circ. 2,000.

053.1 AU ISSN 0016-299X
DIE FURCHE; freie kulturpolitische Wochenschrift. 1945. w. S.760. Die Furche Zeitschriften-Betriebsgesellschaft mbH und Co. KG, Singerstr. 7-VI, A-1010 Vienna, Austria. Ed. Hannes Schopf. adv.; bk.rev.; film rev.; music.rev.; play rev.; rec.rev.; charts; illus.; index; circ. 20,000. **Indexed:** Amer.Hist.& Life, Hist.Abstr.

053 NE ISSN 0144-6355
G D R MONITOR. 1979. s-a. fl.40. Editions Rodopi B.V., Keizersgracht 302-304, 1016 EX Amsterdam, Netherlands. TEL 020-6227507. FAX 020-6380948. (US and Canada subscr. to: 233 Peachtree St. N.E., Ste. 404, Atlanta GA 30303-1504. TEL 800-225-3998) Ed. Ian Wallace. adv.; bk.rev.; circ. 500. (back issues avail.)

056.1 MX ISSN 0016-3716
GACETA. 1954. m. Mex.$40000($60) Fondo de Cultura Economica, Av. de la Universidad 975, 03100 Mexico, D.F., Mexico. Ed. Adolfo Castanon Moran. adv.; bk.rev.; abstr.; bibl.; charts; illus.

378.1 UY ISSN 0016-3759
GACETA DE LA UNIVERSIDAD. 1957. q. Universidad de la Republica, 18 de Julio 1824, Montevideo, Uruguay.

GAG RECAP. see *ART*

051 VE
GALAXIA 71. (Summaries in Portuguese and Spanish) 1971. 3/yr. (with suppl.). $10. Grupo Escritores de Venezuela, Apdo. 4023, Carmelitas 101, Caracas, Venezuela. Ed. Modesto Vargas Lopez. bk.rev.; illus.; circ. 5,000 (controlled). (back issues avail.)

052 800 CN ISSN 0713-3545
AP5
GAMUT. 1982. q. $10. Artscorp, 238 Davenport Rd., Ste. 171, Toronto, Ont. M5R 1J6, Canada. Eds. Haygo Demir, Alfredo Romano. adv.; bk.rev.; illus.; circ. 3,000.

320 700 UY
GARIBALDI. (Text mainly in Spanish; occasionally in French, Italian, Portuguese) 1986. a. Asociacion Cultural Garibaldina de Montevideo, Florencio Sanchez, 2724, Montevideo, Uruguay. Ed. Carlos Novello. bibl.; illus.

058 NO
GATEAVISA. (Text in Danish, Norwegian, Swedish) 1970. bi-m. NOK 190($30) (Arbeidskollektivet) Futurum Forlag A-S, Hjelmsgate 3, 0355 Oslo 3, Norway. TEL 02-691284. Ed. A. Engh. adv.; bk.rev.; illus.; circ. 8,000.
Former titles (until 1988): Glasnost; Gateavisa.
Description: Anarchistic look at social and political subjects.

808.8 US ISSN 1047-4463
▼**GAUNTLET**; exploring the limits of free expression. 1990. a. $14.95. Gauntlet, Inc., 309 Powell Rd., Springfield, PA 19064. TEL 215-328-5476. FAX 215-328-9949. Ed. Barry Hoffman. adv.; bk.rev.; illus.; circ. 10,000.
Description: Covers key issues in censorship in literature, journalism, art and movies, reprinting censored writing and art, with critical essays, author and artist interviews, and an annual summary of pro- and anti-censorship activities, focusing on the US and Canada.

808.838 AT ISSN 0310-9968
GEGENSCHEIN. 1971. irreg., no.62, 1991. Aus.$1 for 2 nos.; US$1 for 1 no. c/o Eric B. Lindsay, Ed., 6 Hillcrest Ave., Faulconbridge, N.S.W. 2776, Australia. bk.rev.; circ. 245.

051 AU
DER GEISTIG SCHAFFENDE. 1949. m. membership. Verband der Geistig Schaffenden Oesterreichs, Kaerntnerstr. 51, A-1010 Vienna, Austria. Ed. Karl Lengheimer. adv.

658 808 US ISSN 8756-2898
GELOSOPHIST. 1985. irreg. (3-6/yr.). Lone Star Publications of Humor, Box 29000, Ste. 103, San Antonio, TX 78229. Ed. Lauren I. Barnett. bk.rev.; film rev.; play rev.; abstr.; illus.; stat. (looseleaf format; back issues avail.)

053 GW
GEMEINDE-NACHRICHTEN. 1952. w. DM.18. (Gemeinde Sandhausen) Mera-Druck GmbH & Co., Wingertstr. 7, 6902 Sandhausen, Germany. Ed.Bd. adv.; bk.rev.; bibl.; play rev.; stat.; circ. 3,500. (looseleaf format)

800 US ISSN 1048-0870
AP2
▼**GENERALIST PAPERS**. 1990. 6/yr. $12 (Canada and Mexico $15; elsewhere $20). (Generalist Association, Inc.) Harry Smith, Ed. & Pub., 69 Joralemon St., Brooklyn, NY 11201. bk.rev.; circ. 2,200.

052 CN ISSN 0533-7291
GENERATION (WINDSOR); creative work by the students of the University of Windsor. 1963. s-a. University of Windsor, Windsor, Ont. N9B 3P4, Canada. TEL 519-253-4232. illus.
Description: Contains poetry, short stories and line drawings.

052 011 US
GEORGE ELIOT - GEORGE HENRY LEWES STUDIES. 1982. s-a. £3($6) Dr. W. Baker, Ed. & Pub., Department of English, Northern Illinois University, Dekalb, IL 60115. TEL 815-753-1857. FAX 815-753-2003. adv.; bk.rev.; circ. 300. (back issues avail.)
Formerly (until 1992): George Eliot - George Henry Lewes Newsletter (ISSN 0953-0754)

GESHER. see *RELIGIONS AND THEOLOGY — Judaic*

808.87 US
GIANT CRACKED. a. $2.75. Globe Communications Corp. (New York), 441 Lexington Ave., New York, NY 10017. TEL 800-472-7744. illus.; circ. 475,000.
Description: Contains humorous articles.

053.931 NE ISSN 0016-9730
AP15
GIDS. 1837. m. fl.105 to individuals; students fl.84.50. (Stichting de Gids) Meulenhoff Nederland B.V., Postbus 100, 1000 AC Amsterdam, Netherlands. Ed. Theodor Duquesnoy. adv.; bk.rev.; index; circ. 2,500. **Indexed:** Amer.Hist.& Life, Hist.Abstr., Key to Econ.Sci., M.L.A.

055.1 IT ISSN 0017-0526
GIOVANE CRITICA. no.19, 1968. irreg. (5-6/yr.). Via della Trinita dei Pellegrini 19, 00186 Rome, Italy. Ed. Giampiero Mughini. bk.rev.; play rev.

057.8 CI ISSN 0017-0771
GLAS ISTRE. 1943. w. 20 din. (Socijalisticki Savez Radnog Naroda Istre, Hrvatskog primorja i Gorskog kotara) Glas Istre, Obala Marsala Tita 10, Pula, Croatia. Ed. Santo Kranjac.

057.8 CI ISSN 0017-0801
GLAS PODRAVINE. 1946. q. 160 din. Socijalisticki Savez Radnog Naroda Opcine Koprivnica, Oruzanska 25, Koprivnica, Croatia. Ed. Vladimir Kuzel.

949.7 BN ISSN 0017-0828
GLAS TREBINJA; list Socijalistickog saveza radnog naroda opstine Trebinje. 1952. m. 15 din. Socijalisticki Savez Radnog Naroda Opstine Trebinje, Mija Zupcevica 9, Trebinje, Bosnia Hercegovina. Ed. Miso Tica.

055 IT ISSN 0394-395X
IL GOLFO; periodico di informazione democratica. m? Viale 2 Giugno No. 40, 58023 Follonica, Italy. Ed. Rino Magagnini. illus.; circ. 1,000.

808.87 US
GOOFUS OFFICE GAZETTE. 1983. irreg. $15. Goofus Office, 8 Franklin Ave., Apt. 2, Box 259, Pearl River, NY 10965. TEL 914-620-1416. Ed. Samuel T. Godfrey. circ. 250. (back issues avail.)

808.8 CN
GRAMMATEION; the St. Michael's Journal of the Arts. 1975. a. Can.$5. St. Michael's College, Box 1, 81 St. Mary St., Toronto, Ont. M55 1J4, Canada. TEL 416-926-1300. adv.; circ. 1,500.
Description: Contains prose, poetry, interviews, short drama and art work.

055.1 IT
IL GRANDEVETRO. 1977. m. L.25000. Coop "I Segni", Via Provinciale Francesca Sud 6, Santa Croce sull'Arno Pisa, Italy. TEL 0571-49614.

054.1 FR ISSN 0182-0346
GRANDS REPORTAGES. 1978. 11/yr. 230 F. (foreign 310F.). Editions Mondiales, 2 rue des Italiens, 75440 Paris Cedex 09, France. TEL 48-24-46-21. FAX 42-47-14-13. TELEX 643 932. Ed. Jean Weiss. adv.; circ. 82,000. **Indexed:** Pt.de Rep. (1989-).

052 UK ISSN 0017-3231
PN2
GRANTA. 1979. q. £19.95($29.95) Granta Publications Ltd., 2-3 Hanover Yard, Noel Road, Islington, London N1 8BE, England. TEL 071-704-9776. FAX 071-704-0474. (Dist. addr. in U.S.: Granta, Ste. 1316, 250 W. 57th St. New York, NY 10107. TEL 212-246-1313) Ed. Bill Buford. adv.; bk.rev.; charts; illus.; circ. 90,000. (also avail. in microform from UMI)
—BLDSC shelfmark: 4210.900000.
Description: Features new fiction, travel and reportage by international writers.

059 UK
GREEK INSTITUTE REVIEW. (Text in English and Greek) 1972. q. £12($20) Greek Institute, 34 Bush Hill Rd., London N21 2DS, England. Ed. Kypros Tofallis. adv.; bk.rev.; bibl.; tr.lit.; circ. 1,000.
Formerly: Greek Review (ISSN 0307-4536)

808.8 614.7
GREEN SYNTHESIS (SAN PEDRO); a newsletter and journal for social ecology, deepecology, bioregionalism, eco feminism, and the green movement. 1975. 4/yr. $7.50 to individuals; institutions $13.50 for 10 nos. League for Ecological Democracy, Box 1858, San Pedro, CA 90733. TEL 213-833-2633. Ed.Bd. bk.rev.; circ. 8,000. (back issues avail.)
Formerly: Synthesis (San Pedro).

053 GW
GRENZFRIEDENSHEFTE. 1953. q. DM.24. Grenzfriedensbund e.V., Hafendamm 15, 2390 Flensburg, Germany. TEL 0461-26708. bk.rev. (back issues avail.)

808.8 US ISSN 0533-2869
PN2
GREYFRIAR-SIENA STUDIES IN LITERATURE. 1960. a. free. Siena College, Department of English, Loudonville, NY 12211. TEL 518-783-2300. FAX 518-783-2468. Ed. A.F. Gulliver. bibl.; circ. 1,200. **Indexed:** Abstr.Engl.Stud., M.L.A.

053.931 NE ISSN 0017-4483
DE GROENE AMSTERDAMMER; onafhankelijk weekblad. 1877. w. fl.163.50. N.V. Weekblad de Groene Amsterdammer, Westeinde 16, Box 353, 1000 AJ Amsterdam, Netherlands. adv.; bk.rev.; circ. 17,000. **Indexed:** Key to Econ.Sci.

051 CN ISSN 0017-453X
GRONK.* 1967. irreg. Can.$12 for 6 nos. Ganglia Press, c/o The Village Bookstore, 239 Queen St. W., Toronto, Ont. M5V 1Z4, Canada. Ed. B.P. Nichol. circ. 200.
Formerly: Ganglia.

058.7 SW ISSN 0017-4548
GRONKOPINGS VECKOBLAD. m. (10/yr). SEK 52. Norstedts Tryckeri AB, Box 2080, S-103 12 Stockholm, Sweden. Ed. Gunnar Ljusterdal. adv.; illus.; circ. 17,000. (tabloid format)

GYPSY; literary magazine. see *LITERATURE*

296 US ISSN 0017-6524
DS101
HADOAR. 1921. bi-w. $36 (effective Sep. 1990). (Histadruth Ivrith of America) Hadoar Association, Inc., 47 W. 34th St., Rm. 609, New York, NY 10001-3012. TEL 212-629-9443. FAX 212-629-9472. Ed. Yael Feldman. adv.; bk.rev.; charts; illus.; index; circ. 3,500. (also avail. in microfilm from AJP)

LITERARY AND POLITICAL REVIEWS

HAIKU ZASSHI ZO. see *LITERATURE — Poetry*

059.91   US   ISSN 0017-677X
HAIRENIK. (Text in Armenian) 1899. w. $50. Hairenik Association, Inc., 80 Bieglow Ave., Watertown, MA 02172. TEL 617-926-3974. Ed. Vatche Proudian. adv.; bk.rev.; illus.

059   MG
HAITENY, HAISORATA, HAIRAHA. 1978. irreg. Academie Malgache, Section 1, B.P. 6217, Tsimbazaza, Antananarivo, Malagasy Republic. circ. 300.

053   GW
HANNOVER VORSCHAU; Veranstaltungen. 1951. m. DM.24. Verkehrsverein Hannover E.V., Friedrichswall 5, 3000 Hannover 1, Germany. circ. 10,000.
    Formerly: Vorschau Hannover.

HARMONY (SAN FRANCISCO); voices for a just future. see *POLITICAL SCIENCE — Civil Rights*

808.8   US   ISSN 0896-114X
HARRIMAN INSTITUTE FORUM. 1988. m. $30 (foreign $40)(effective Aug. 1990). Columbia University, Harriman Institute, 420 W. 118th St., New York, NY 10027. TEL 212-854-6218. FAX 212-666-3481. Ed. Ronald Meyer. circ. 1,000. (back issues avail.)
    —BLDSC shelfmark: 4264.975200.

810   US   ISSN 0095-2427
LH1.H3
HARVARD MAGAZINE. 1898. bi-m. $27. Harvard Magazine, Inc., 7 Ware St., Cambridge, MA 02138. FAX 617-495-0324. Ed. John T. Bethell. adv.; bk.rev.; circ. 200,000. **Indexed:** Access (1981-), CAD CAM Abstr., Robomat.
    —BLDSC shelfmark: 4268.200000.
    Formerly (until 1973): Harvard Bulletin.

053.931   NE   ISSN 0017-8519
HAVENLOODS. 1951. s-w. free. Prins Hendrikkade 14, Rotterdam-3001, Netherlands. adv.; bk.rev.; play rev.; abstr.; circ. 266,100.

052   UK
HAWKFRENDZ. 1972. s-a. $3. Zephyr Magazines & Records, P.O. Box 6, Wallasey, Merseyside L45 4SJ, England. Ed. Trevor Hughes. adv.; bk.rev.; rec.rev.; illus.; circ. 500.
    Former titles: Zephyr; Hawkfriends.

327   AI
HAYRENIKY DZAYN. 1965. w. 2.65 Rub. Committee for Cultural Relations with Armenians Abroad, Alaverdian St. 37, Erevan, Armenia. (Subscr. addr.: Soyzpechat', Casian St. 6, Erevan, Armenia) Ed. Levon Zakarian. adv.; bk.rev.; charts; film rev.; illus.; play rev.; stat.; circ. 27,000.
    Formerly: Areiniki Dzain (ISSN 0017-8705)

051 808.838   US
HEARTLAND CRITIQUES. 1980. m. $50. 759 Allen Rd., Independence, MO 64050. TEL 816-254-1868. Ed. Julie Meisinger. bk.rev.; circ. 250.
    Formerly: Barbra Critiques.
    Description: Reviews of 150 romance novels for use by stores, libraries and individuals in the early selection of reading material.

900 700   DR
HELIOS.* 1973. q. Fondo Cultural de la Cuna de America, Jose Reyes 50, Santo Domingo, Dominican Republic. Ed.Bd. adv.; illus. **Indexed:** Arts & Hum.Cit.Ind., Curr.Cont., Fluidex.

HENDERSON COMMUNITY COLLEGE LITERARY MAGAZINE. see *LITERATURE — Poetry*

058   DK   ISSN 0903-9295
HENRY - D R U NYTT; magasin for kultur. 1983. 8/yr. DKK 40. Danmarks Retsforbunds Ungdom, Lyngbyvej 42, 2100 Copenhagen OE, Denmark. TEL 01-204488. Ed. Jette Lehrmann Madsen. illus.; circ. 300.
    Former titles (until 1987): D R U Nytt; Druiden (ISSN 0109-0119)

808.87   FR
HERISSON. 1936. w. 120 F. Publications Georges Ventillard, 2 a 12 rue de Bellevue, 75019 Paris, France. Ed. Philippe Carpentier. illus.; circ. 270,000. (tabloid format)

HISPAMERICA; revista de literatura. see *LITERATURE*

HISPANOFILA. see *LITERATURE*

HISPANORAMA. see *LITERATURE*

HISTORIA. see *HISTORY — History Of North And South America*

HISTORICA; rivista trimestrale di cultura. see *HISTORY*

HISTORY TODAY. see *HISTORY*

830   GW   ISSN 0441-6813
PT2617.O47
HOFMANNSTHAL-BLAETTER. 1968. 2/yr. DM.50 membership. Hugo von Hofmannstahl-Gesellschaft, c/o Dr. Gisela Baerbel Schmid, Am Flossgraben 4, D-7800 Freiburg, Germany. Ed.Bd. bk.rev.; bibl.

830   GW
HOFMANNSTHAL-FORSCHUNGEN. a. price varies. Hugo von Hofmannsthal-Gesellschaft, c/o Dr. Gisela Baerbel Schmid, Am Flossgraben 4, 7800 Freiburg, Germany.

808.87   MP
▼**HOH INEED/IRONIC LAUGH.** (Text in Mongolian) 1990. m. P.O. 46, Box 971, Ulan Bator, Mongolia. TEL 21425. Ed. J. Chimedtseren.
    Description: Features satirical jokes.

837   AU   ISSN 0018-3245
HOHE BRUECKE. 1953. m. S.50. Glueckstelle Mihalovits, Wipplingerstr. 21, A-1013 Vienna, Austria. Ed. Dr. Heinrich Bohn. adv.; illus.
    Description: Contains humorous articles.

949.2   NE   ISSN 0018-3601
HOLLANDS MAANDBLAD.* 1959. m. fl.87.50. Stichting Hollands Maandblad, Herengracht 464, 1017 CA Amsterdam, Netherlands. Ed. K.L. Poll. adv.; bk.rev.; illus.; play rev.; index; circ. 2,000.

378.1   US   ISSN 0018-3644
PS1
HOLLINS CRITIC. 1964. 5/yr. $6 (foreign $7.50). Hollins College, Box 9538, Hollins College, VA 24020. TEL 703-362-6317. Ed. John R. Moore. bk.rev.; bibl.; index; circ. 545. (also avail. in microform from UMI; back issues avail.; reprint service avail. from UMI) **Indexed:** A.I.P.P., Abstr.Engl.Stud., Ind.Amer.Per.Verse, LCR, M.L.A.
    —BLDSC shelfmark: 4322.402000.

808.8 053   GW
HOLZAUGE. 1975. irreg., no.33, 1992. DM.1.50 per no. Schuelerzeitung Holzauge, Remstalgymnasium, 7056 Weinstadt, Germany. TEL 07151-61469. Ed.Bd. adv.; bk.rev.; circ. 350.

HONEST ULSTERMAN. see *LITERATURE*

059   FR   ISSN 0769-0088
PB2801
HOR YEZH. (Text in Breton) 1954. irreg. 80 F. for 4 nos. c/o P. Denis, Le Ris, Ploare, 29100 Douarnenez, Brittany, France. **Indexed:** M.L.A.

056.1   PE
HORA DEL HOMBRE. 1943. m. Casilla 2378, Lima 1, Peru. TEL 14-220208. Ed. Jorge Falcon. illus.

970 300   US   ISSN 0018-4977
AP2
HORIZON (TUSCALOOSA).* 1958. 10/yr. $21.95. Horizon Publishers, Inc., Drawer 30, Tuscaloosa, AL 35402. Ed. Gray D. Boone. adv.; bk.rev.; illus.; circ. 65,000. (also avail. in microform from UMI; reprint service avail. from UMI) **Indexed:** Bk.Rev.Ind. (1985-), R.G.

051   CS
HORIZONT. m. $30. (Union of Czechoslovak - Soviet Friendship) Obzor, Ceskoslovenskej Armady 35, 815 85 Bratislava, Czechoslovakia.

808.8   US   ISSN 0896-9965
HORNS OF PLENTY.* Malcolm Cowley and his generation. 1988. a. $15 to individuals; institutions $20. P.O. Box 65, Crete, IL 60417. TEL 312-728-4671. Eds. Yolanda Butts, William Butts. bk.rev.; circ. 300. (back issues avail.) **Indexed:** Hum.Ind., M.L.A.
    Description: Looks at the works of critic - poet Malcolm Cowley and his generation of writers.

056.1   CL   ISSN 0716-3460
AP63
HOY. 1977. w. $200. Empresa Editora Araucaria Ltda., Monsenor Miller 74, Santiago, Chile. TEL 2236102. FAX 2516191. Dir. Abraham Santibanez. adv.; bk.rev.; illus.; circ. 30,000.
    Description: Includes articles, opinions and humor on the politics, economy and culture of Chile and the rest of the world.

059.91   SP   ISSN 0018-6902
HRVATSKA REVIJA. (Text mainly in Croatian) 1951. q. $80. Vinko Nikolic, Ed., Apdo. Correos 14030, 08017 Barcelona, Spain. bk.rev.; illus.; music rev.; cum.index: 1951-1988; circ. 1,300.

HUAN QIU/GLOBE. see *POLITICAL SCIENCE — International Relations*

810 700   US   ISSN 0018-702X
AP2
HUDSON REVIEW; a magazine of literature and the arts. 1948. q. $20 (foreign $24). Hudson Review, Inc., 684 Park Ave., New York, NY 10021. TEL 212-650-0020. Eds. Paula Deitz, Frederick Morgan. adv.; bk.rev.; film rev.; music rev.; play rev.; index; circ. 4,500. (also avail. in microform from UMI,MIM; reprint service avail. from UMI) **Indexed:** Abstr.Engl.Stud., Acad.Ind., Amer.Bibl.Slavic & E.Eur.Stud., Amer.Hum.Ind., Arts & Hum.Cit.Ind., Bk.Rev.Ind. (1965-), Can.Rev.Comp.Lit., Child.Bk.Rev.Ind. (1965-), Curr.Cont.; Film Lit.Ind. (1973-), Hum.Ind., Ind.Amer.Per.Verse, Ind.Bk.Rev.Hum., Lang.& Lang.Behav.Abstr., M.L.A., Soc.Sci.Ind.

059   DK   ISSN 0106-4959
HUG! 1974. bi-m. DKK 360. Tiderne Skrifter Forlag A-S, Skindergade 14,3, DK-1159 Copenhagen K, Denmark. TEL 33-124284. FAX 33-144205. Ed.Bd. bk.rev.; film rev.; illus.; circ. 2,000.

HUMANIST. see *PHILOSOPHY*

055.1   IT   ISSN 0018-7461
HUMANITAS;* rivista di cultura. 1946; N.S. 1977. bi-m. L.14400($14) Editrice Morcelliana S.p.A., Via Gabriele Rosa 71, 25100 Brescia, Italy. TEL 030-46451. Ed. Stefano Minelli. adv.; bk.rev.; bibl.; film rev.; illus.; play rev.; index; circ. 2,500. **Indexed:** CERDIC.

056.9   GW   ISSN 0018-7623
AP1
HUMBOLDT (PORTUGUESE EDITION); revista para o mondo Luso-Brasileiro. 1961. s-a. free. Inter Nationes e.V., Kennedy-Allee 91-103, 5300 Bonn 2, Germany. bk.rev.; illus.; circ. 5,300.

053.1 056.1   GW   ISSN 0018-7615
HUMBOLDT (SPANISH EDITION). (Text in Spanish) 1960. 3/yr. free. Inter Nationes e.V., Kennedy-Allee 91-103, 5300 Bonn 2, Germany. TEL 0228-880-0. FAX 0228-880457. TELEX 17228308. bk.rev.; illus.; circ. 13,400. **Indexed:** Hisp.Amer.Per.Ind.
    Description: Contains Spanish articles about German and Spanish culture. Includes cultural notices of events in Spanish speaking countries.

056   AG
HUMOR. 1978. s-m. $120. Ediciones de la Urraca, Venezuela 842, 1095 Buenos Aires, Argentina. TEL 334-5400. FAX 11-2700. TELEX 9072. Ed. Andres Cascioli. circ. 140,000.

808.87   US
HUMOR EVENTS & POSSIBILITIES. Short title: H E P. 1976. q. $25 in DC; elsewhere $20. Workshop Library on World Humor, Box 23334, Washington, DC 20026. TEL 202-484-4949. Ed. Barbara Cummings. bk.rev.; circ. 2,000.

808.87   IT
HUMOR GRAPHIC. q. Museo Internazionale dell'Umorismo, Via Arzaga 28, 20146 Milan, Italy. Ed. Luciano Consigli.

053 GW ISSN 0342-1864
F1408.3
IBEROAMERICANA; Lateinamerika-Spanien-Portugal. (Text in German, Portuguese, Spanish) 1977. 3/yr. DM.50($32) students DM.40($25). Vervuert Verlag GmbH, Wielandstr. 40, 6000 Frankfurt a.M. 1, Germany. TEL 069-599615. FAX 069-5978743. Ed.Bd. adv.; bk.rev.; circ. 1,000. (back issues avail.)
 Description: Contains information about the societies, history, culture, language and literature of Latin-America, Spain and Portugal.

808.8 US ISSN 1054-1381
▼**ICARUS (NEW YORK).** 1991. q. Rosen Publishing Group, Inc., 29 E. 21st St., New York, NY 10010. TEL 212-777-3017. Eds. Roger Rosen, Patra McSharry. (back issues avail.)

808.8 282 US
IDEA INK;* the national Catholic opinion quarterly. 1982. q. (I.D.E.A., Inc.) Fiore Companies, Box 2537, Madison, WI 53701-2537. TEL 608-273-0330. Ed. Fr. Charles Fiore, O.P. adv.; circ. 70,000.

059 JO
IDEAS/AFKAR.* (Text in Arabic) 1966. bi-m. Ministry of Culture and Information, Department of Culture & Arts, P.O. Box 88, Amman, Jordan. Ed. Mahmoud Saif Ul-Din Al-Irani.

052 UK ISSN 0264-4940
IDEAS AND PRODUCTIONS; a journal in the history of ideas. 1983. s-a. £6 to individuals; institutions £12. Cambridgeshire College of Arts and Technology (C.C.A.T.), East Rd., Cambridge CB1 1PT, England. TEL 0223 63271. Ed. Edward J. Esche. bk.rev.; illus. (back issues avail.)
 Description: Dedicated to exploring the range of theoretical radicalisms which developed during the 1970s. Each issue considers a particular area of inquiry using new methodologies.

057.8 XV ISSN 0019-1523
IDRIJSKI RAZGLEDI. (Text in Slovenian) 1956. 2/yr. 90 din.($8.20) Mestni Muzej v Idrii, Idrija, Slovenia. Ed. Joze Car. circ. 1,000.

808 US ISSN 0733-9526
ILLINOIS WRITERS REVIEW. 1975. 2/yr. $15 to individuals; institutions $20. Illinois Writers, Inc., Dept. of English, Illinois State University, Normal, IL 61701-6901. TEL 309-438-7705. Eds. Jim Elledge, Kevin Stein. adv.; bk.rev.; circ. 500. (back issues avail.)
 Description: Reviews of and by Illinois and national authors, with emphasis on those published by small presses. Contains essays and commentary on pressing issues in contemporary writing.

052 UK ISSN 0046-8703
IMPACT (LONDON). 1971. s-m. £23.50($39) News & Media Ltd., 33 Stroud Green Rd., London N4 3EF, England. TEL 01-263 1417. Ed.Bd. adv.; bk.rev.
 —BLDSC shelfmark: 4370.810000.

055.1 IT ISSN 0046-8711
IMPEGNO SETTANTA;* rassegna di politica, cultura e attualita. 1971. q. L.3000. Corso Umberto 22, 91026 Mazara del Vallo (Trapani), Italy. Ed.Bd. bk.rev.; bibl.; illus.

IMPETUS. see ART

INDEPENDENT (ARLINGTON); a monthly notice of small press periodicals, books and ideas. see PUBLISHING AND BOOK TRADE

051 US
INDEPENDENT REVIEW.* 1986. 4/yr. $16. Box F, Warrensburg, MO 64093-0890. TEL 816-429-4425. Ed. Rosemarie Kinder. circ. 250. (back issues avail.)
 Description: Designed as a vehicle for the publication of prize winning poetry and short stories.

052 UK ISSN 0306-4220
K9
INDEX ON CENSORSHIP. 1972. 10/yr. £23($39) (foreign £26)(effective Jan. 1992). Writers & Scholars International Ltd., 39c Highbury Place, London N5 1QP, England. TEL 071-359-0161. FAX 071-354-8665. Ed. Andrew Graham-Yooll. adv.; bk.rev.; bibl.; index, cum.index: 1972-1988; circ. 6,000. (also avail. in microform; reprint service avail. from ISI) **Indexed:** Alt.Press Ind., Arts & Hum.Cit.Ind., Curr.Cont., HR Rep., M.L.A., Mid.East: Abstr.& Ind., P.A.I.S., Sociol.Abstr.
 —BLDSC shelfmark: 4377.380000.
 Description: Reports denials of free speech throughout the world, publishes commentaries on their effects, and prints examples of banned literature.

052 II ISSN 0019-4379
INDIAN AND FOREIGN REVIEW. (Text in English) 1963. fortn. $6. Ministry of Information & Broadcasting, Publications Division, Patiala House, Tilak Marg, New Delhi 110001, India. (U.S. subscr. address: M-S Inter Culture Associates, Thompson, CT 06277) Ed. Shyam Ratna Gupta. adv.; bk.rev.; index; circ. 22,500. (also avail. in microfilm from UMI) **Indexed:** M.L.A.

052 II ISSN 0019-6304
AP8
INDIAN REVIEW; devoted to the discussion of all topics of interest. (Text in English) 1900. m. Rs.10($5) Manian Natesan, 2-A Cathedral Rd., Madras 600086, India. Ed. M.C. Subhramanyam. bk.rev. **Indexed:** Amer.Hist.& Life, Hist.Abstr.

059 II ISSN 0300-4007
INDRANIL. (Text in Bengali; summaries in Hindi and English) 1971. m. Rs.8.80($40) P. Ghosh, 5 Dhakuria Kalibari Ln., Calcutta 700031, India. Ed. C.S.D. Chaklader. adv.; bk.rev.; index; circ. 1,000.

054 FR
INFINI. 1983. 4/yr. 315 F. Gallimard, 5, rue Sebastien Boltin, 75007 Paris, France. TEL 33-1-46-59-89-00. Ed. Philippe Sollers. **Indexed:** Arts & Hum.Cit.Ind., Curr.Cont., M.L.A.

052 AT ISSN 0725-5489
INFOCAB. 1979. m. Aus.$40. Victorian Association of Citizens Advice Bureaux, 10th Fl., 176 Wellington, Parade, East Melbourne, Vic. 3002, Australia. TEL 03-419-9866. FAX 03-416-3392. Ed. Annette Ryan. bk.rev.; circ. 200. (back issues avail.)
 Description: New and updated community information covering the state of Victoria.

320.531 FR
INFORMATION OUVRIERES. 1958. w. 250 F. Mouvement pour un Parti des Travailleurs (MPPT), 87, rue Faubourg-Saint-Denis, 75010 Paris, France. TEL 42-47-13-34. FAX 40-22-01-96. Ed. Jean Pierre Raffi. charts; illus.; circ. 20,000.
 Formerly (until 1977): Jeune Revolutionnaire (ISSN 0021-6100)

054 CN
INFORMATION PROCHE-ORIENT. 1981. 6/yr. Can.$12($10) Comite Canada - Israel, 1310 Avenue Greene, Ste. 710, Montreal, Que. H3Z 2B2, Canada. TEL 514-934-0771. FAX 514-933-8211. Ed. Gilbert Lemieux. adv.; circ. 1,000.
 Formerly: Revue Jonathan (ISSN 0711-026X)

053.1 GW
▼**INITIAL;** Zeitschrift fuer Sozialwissenschaftlichen Diskurs. 1990. 6/yr. Verlag Volk und Welt, Otto-Nuschke-Str. 10-11, 1086 Berlin, Germany. TEL 030-203650211.

INKSTONE; a magazine of haiku. see LITERATURE — Poetry

059 NE ISSN 0167-3696
PR9091
INS AND OUTS; a magazine of awareness. (Text in English) 1978. irreg. $30 for 6 issues. Ins & Outs Press, Box 3759, Amsterdam, Netherlands. Ed. Edward Woods. bk.rev.; circ. 2,500.

INSIDE SAN FRANCISCO STATE UNIVERSITY. see COLLEGE AND ALUMNI

808.8 US
INSTEAD OF A MAGAZINE. 1980. q. $8 to individuals; institutions $17.50. Lysander Spooner Society, Box 433, Willimantic, CT 06226. TEL 203-456-9005. Ed. Michael Ziesing. adv.; bk.rev.; circ. 500.

378 ISSN 0020-5249
AP2
INTERCOLLEGIATE REVIEW;* a journal of scholarship and opinion. 1965. irreg. (2-4/yr.). $18 for 8 nos. Young America's Foundation, 110 Elden St., Herndon, VA 22070. TEL 703-318-9608. Ed. Dana Peringer. adv.; bk.rev.; illus.; index; circ. 35,000. (also avail. in microform from UMI,MIM; back issues avail.) **Indexed:** Curr.Cont., P.A.I.S.
 —BLDSC shelfmark: 4533.200000.
 Incorporates: Academic Reviewer.
 Description: Provides critical commentary on a wide variety of topics related to scholarship and culture.

INTERMEDIAIRE DES CHERCHEURS ET CURIEUX; de questions et responses historiques, litteraires, artistiques et sur toutes autres curiosites. see HISTORY

052 320 UK
INTERNATIONAL SOCIALISM. 1961. q. £12($20) to individuals; institutions £20($33). Socialist Workers Party, P.O. Box 82, London E3 3HL, England. TEL 071-538-1626. FAX 071-538-0018. Ed. John Rees. adv.; bk.rev.; circ. 5,500. (also avail. in microfiche) **Indexed:** Acad.Ind., Alt.Press Ind., ASCA, Curr.Cont.
 Former titles: Socialist Worker Review; Socialist Review (ISSN 0141-2442); (until 1978): International Socialism (ISSN 0020-8736)

808.87 UV
INTRUS. 1986. w. Ouagadougou, Burkina Faso.
 Description: Contains satirical humor.

INVISIBLE CITY. see LITERATURE — Poetry

IRAQ. MINISTRY OF EDUCATION. AL-MU'ALLEM AL-JADID. see EDUCATION

IRIS: A JOURNAL ABOUT WOMEN. see WOMEN'S INTERESTS

052 UK
IRISH POST. 1970. w. £49. Irish Post Ltd., Lex House, 77 South Rd., Southall, Middx. UB1 1SQ, England. TEL 081-574-2058. FAX 081-571-5884. Ed. Donal Mooney. adv.; bk.rev.; circ. 78,000.

052 059.916 UK ISSN 0790-7850
DA925
IRISH REVIEW. 1987. s-a. £10($25) Institute of Irish Studies, Queen's University of Belfast, 8 Fitzwilliam St., Belfast BT9 6AW, N. Ireland. Ed.Bd. adv.; bk.rev.; circ. 750.
 —BLDSC shelfmark: 4574.721000.

ISLAM CAGRISI. see RELIGIONS AND THEOLOGY — Islamic

ISLAMI BAYRLAYK. see RELIGIONS AND THEOLOGY — Islamic

051 960 US ISSN 0047-1607
DT1
ISSUE; a quarterly journal of opinion. 1972. 2/yr. membership. African Studies Association, Credit Union Bldg., Emory University, GA 30322. TEL 404-329-6410. Ed. Harvey Glickman. adv.; bibl.; circ. 3,000. (also avail. in microfilm) **Indexed:** Amer.Hist.& Life, Hist.Abstr., HR Rep.

059.91 CI ISSN 0021-2415
ISTARSKI MOZAIK; casopis za drustvena, knjizevna i umjetnicka pitanja Istre. (Text in Serbocroatian) 1963. q. 12 din.($6.25) Glas Istre, Obala Marsala Tita 10, Pula, Croatia. Ed. Marijan Grakalic.

054.1 FR ISSN 0021-3187
BX802
ITINERAIRES;* chroniques et documents. 1955. m. 75 F.($16) 4 rue Garanciere, 75006 Paris, France. Dir. Jean Madiran.

808.8 II
JANASUDHA DAILY. (Text in Coloqual) 1978. d. Rs.36. Mahendra Enterprises, Mahendra Nagar, Gollapudi-521225, Vijayawada, India. Ed. Naralasetti Venkateswarl-u. film rev.; circ. 5,000.

LITERARY AND POLITICAL REVIEWS

808.8 II
JANASUDHA MONTHLY. (Text in Coloqual) 1978. m. Rs.36. Mahendra Enterprises, Mahendra Nagar, Gollapudi-521225, Vijayawada, India. Ed. Narasetti Enkateswarl-u. film rev.; illus.; circ. 10,000. (also avail. in talking book)

808.8 II
JANASUDHA WEEKLY. (Text in Coloqual) 1978. w. Rs.36. Mahendra Enterprises, Mahendra Nagar, Gollapudi-521225, Vijayawada, India. Ed. Naralasetti Enkateswarl-u. film rev.; illus.; circ. 15,000. (also avail. in talking book)

059.91 II ISSN 0021-423X
JANTANTRA. (Text and summaries in Hindi) 1951. w. Rs.10($2.) N. Jaiswal, Ed. & Pub., Gonda City, Uttar Pradesh, India. film rev.; circ. 5,000.

952 JA ISSN 0021-4590
DS801
JAPAN QUARTERLY. (Text in English) 1954. q. $30. Asahi Shimbunsha - Asahi Shimbun Publishing Co., 3-2, Tsukiji 5-chome, Chuo-ku, Tokyo 104-11, Japan. TEL 03-3545-0131. FAX 03-3544-1428. (Orders for export to: Japan Publications Trading Co., Ltd., Box 5030, Tokyo International, Tokyo, Japan) Ed. Yuji Oishi. adv.; bk.rev.; illus. (also avail. in microform from UMI; back issues avail.; reprint service avail. from UMI) Indexed: Acad.Ind., Amer.Hist.& Life, Curr.Cont., Hist.Abstr., M.L.A., Mid.East: Abstr.& Ind., P.A.I.S., Soc.Sci.Ind., SSCI.

JAWAHARAL NEHRU UNIVERSITY. SCHOOL OF LANGUAGES. JOURNAL. see *LINGUISTICS*

808.8 HU ISSN 0447-6425
JELENKOR; irodalmi es muveszeti folyoirat. 1958. m. $20. Jelenkor Irodalmi es Muveszeti Kiado, Szechenyi ter 17, 7621 Pecs, Hungary. (Subscr. to: Hirlapelofizetesi es Lapellatasi Iroda, Lehel u.10A, 1900 Budapest, Hungary) Ed. Istvan Csuhai. bk.rev.; film rev.; music rev.; play rev.; illus.; index; circ. 2,600. (back issues avail.)
Description: Publishes fine writing and poetry in Hungarian, studies on aesthetics and modern theories of literature, and reviews on modern Hungarian art and Rumanian and Yugoslavian literature.

056.1 MX
JET SET; revista del gran mundo. 1975. m. Mex.$350($41) Corporacion Editorial S.A., Lucio Blanco 435, Col. San Juan Tlihuaca, 02400 Mexico D.F., Mexico. TEL 5-352-0771. Ed. Javier Ortiz Camorlinga. circ. 67,000.

JEWISH AFFAIRS. see *ETHNIC INTERESTS*

808.8 US
JEWISH BOOK WORLD. 1982. q. free. J W B Jewish Book Council, 15 E. 26 St., New York, NY 10010-1579. TEL 212-532-4949. Ed. William Wollheim. adv.; bk.rev.; circ. 3,500.

296 UK ISSN 0021-633X
JEWISH CHRONICLE; the world's leading Jewish newspaper. 1841. w. $142.80. Jewish Chronicle Publications Ltd., 25 Furnival St., London EC4A 1JT, England. FAX 071-405-9040. TELEX 940-11415. Ed. Ned Temko. adv.; bk.rev.; film rev.; illus.; cum.index; circ. 50,000. (also avail. in microform from RPI)

296 US
JEWISH CHRONICLE (YONKERS); serving Southern Westchester. 1968. 13/yr. $15. Jewish Council of Yonkers, 584 N. Broadway, Yonkers, NY 10701. TEL 914-423-5009. FAX 914-423-5077. Ed. Marilyn Shebshaievitz. adv.; bk.rev.; film rev.; circ. 6,000. (back issues avail.)

JEWISH QUARTERLY. see *ETHNIC INTERESTS*

296 UK ISSN 0021-6801
JEWISH VANGUARD. 1948. q. £1.20. Poale Zion - Labour Zionists, 48 College Rd., Wembley, Middlesex HA9 8RJ, England. TEL 081-904-8483. FAX 081-908-1936. Ed. Reginald Freeson. adv.; bk.rev.; film rev.; play rev.; record rev.; illus.; circ. 5,000.

891.8 YU ISSN 0021-6917
AP115
JEZ.* 1935. w. 520 din. Jez, Nusiceva 6, Belgrade, Yugoslavia. Ed. Radivoje Ivanovic.
Description: Contains humorous articles.

059.915 IR
JIHAD. (Text in Farsi) 1989. w. Sada-yi Inqilab-i Islami-i Afghanistan, P.O. Box 91460-172, Meshed, Iran. illus.

974 301.16 US ISSN 0749-4351
JOKESMITH. 1984. q. $40. Edward C. McManus, Ed. & Pub., 44 Queensview Rd., Marlborough, MA 01752. TEL 508-481-0979. FAX 508-481-0979. bk.rev.; circ. 800. (looseleaf format; back issues avail.)
Description: Directed to business and professional speakers with roast lines, presentation remarks, jokes, skits, stories and openers.

056.9 BL ISSN 0047-2093
AP66
JORNAL DE LETRAS. 1949. 11/yr. Cz.$900($100) Departamento de Assuntos Internacionais, Caixa Postal 44069, CEP. 22062, Rio de Janeiro, Brazil. TEL 236-0727. Ed. Claudia Agarez. adv.; bk.rev.; bibl.; illus.; circ. 20,000. (also avail. in microfilm)
Description: Covers the literature and writers of Brazil, with emphasis on contemporary works and authors.

700 BL
JOSE; literatura-critica-arte. 1976. m. Cr.$100. Editora Fontana Ltda, Rua Visconde de Piraja 430, Ipanema, ZC 37 Rio de Janeiro, Brazil. (Dist. by: Superbancas Ltda. Rua Ubaldino do Amaral 42, Rio de Janeiro, Brazil) Ed. Gastao de Holanda. bk.rev.; bibl.; illus.

JOURNAL OF CROATIAN STUDIES; annual review. see *HISTORY — History Of Europe*

JOURNAL OF LITERARY STUDIES/TYDSKRIF VIR LITERATUURWETENSKAP. see *LITERATURE*

JOURNAL OF REGIONAL CRITICISM. see *ART*

051 US
JOURNAL OF THE FANTASTIC IN THE ARTS. 1988. q. $24 (£12.50 in UK). (International Association for the Fantastic in the Arts) Orion Publishing, 3959 Rte. 31, Ste. 210, Liverpool, NY 13090. TEL 315-451-0605. (Subscr. in UK to: Chris Reed, NSFA, P.O. Box 625, Sheffield S1 3GY, England) Ed. Carl Yoke. adv.; bk.rev.; illus.; circ. 3,500.
Description: Publishes critical review articles on popular culture and the arts.

JUDAISM; a quarterly journal of Jewish life and thought. see *RELIGIONS AND THEOLOGY — Judaic*

053 GW ISSN 0932-660X
JUNGE FREIHEIT; Deutsche Zeitung fuer Politik und Kultur. 1986. m. DM.36 (foreign DM.42). Unitas Germanica e.V., Postfach 1872, 7900 Ulm, Germany. TEL 07661-5653. (Subscr. to: Junge Freiheit Verlag, Postfach 147, 7801 Stegen, Germany) Ed. Dieter Stein. adv.; bk.rev.; circ. 35,000.

296 YU ISSN 0022-748X
KADIMA. (Text in Serbo-Croatian) 1959. m. Savez Jevrejskih Opstina Jugoslavije - Federation of Jewish Communities in Yugoslavia, 7. Jula 71a, Belgrade, Yugoslavia. Ed. David Albahari. circ. 2,500.
Description: Literary and informative data for Jewish youth.

053.1 952 GW
KAGAMI; Japanischer Zeitschriftenspiegel. 1974. 3/yr. DM.30. Gesellschaft fuer Natur- und Voelkerkunde Ostasiens e.V., Japanisches Seminar, Von Melle-Park 6-VII, 2000 Hamburg 13, Germany. Ed.Bd. bk.rev.; circ. 500.
Description: German translations of Japanese essays on political, social and literary current affairs.

808.8 US
KAIMANA; literary arts Hawaii. 1974. q. $12. Literary Arts Hawaii, Box 11213, Honolulu, HI 96828. Ed. Tony Quagliano. adv.; bk.rev.; circ. 1,000.
Former titles: Literary Arts Hawaii; Hawaii Literary Arts Council Newsletter.
Description: Features fiction, poetry and literary essays.

700 TR
KAIRI. 1976. a. 22 Fitt St., Woodbrook, Port-of-Spain, Trinidad. Ed. Christopher Laird. bk.rev.; bibl.; illus.

051 US ISSN 0277-710X
PN2
KAIROS. 1981. s-a. $6 per no. Hermes House (KAIROS), Box 199, Hartsdale, NY 10530-0199. FAX 914-948-6206. Ed. Alan Mandell. adv.; bk.rev.; film rev.; illus.; circ. 500. (back issues avail.)
Indexed: New Test.Abstr.
Description: Journal of social-cultural criticism.

059 II
KALAPATRA. (Text in Hindi) m. Rs.8. F-1422 Krishnanagar, Delhi 110051, India.

070.448 CH ISSN 1016-4162
KALEIDOSCOPE. (Text in Chinese) 1967. m. NT.$1000 in ROC; Hong Kong $50; elsewhere $55. Wang Cheng-Sheng, Ed. & Pub., 108, Lungkiang Rd., Taipei, Taiwan, Republic of China. TEL 02-506-5311. FAX 02-506-6037. (Order in US to: World Journal Bookstore, 141-07 20th Ave., Whitestone, NY 11357. TEL 718-746-8889) adv.; illus. Key Title: Zhongwai Zazhi.

051 YE
AL-KALIMA; majallat al-muthaqqafiyn al-yamaniyiyn. irreg. 2 rials. Box 1109, Sana'a, Republic of Yemen. Ed. Ibrahim al-Maqhafi. adv.; bk.rev.

059.945 FI
KALTIO. 1945. bi-m. FIM 160. Mystintie 21 E, 90230 Oulu, Finland. adv.; circ. 1,300.

059.94 FI ISSN 0355-0303
AP80
KANAVA. 1932. 9/yr. FIM 249. Yhtyneet Kuvalehdet Oy, Maistraatinportti 1, 00240 Helsinki, Finland. TEL 0-15661. FAX 0-1566505. TELEX 121364. Ed. Seikko Eskola. adv.; bk.rev.; index; circ. 6,248.
Indexed: M.L.A.
Formerly: Aika (ISSN 0002-2098)

052 AT ISSN 1036-3262
KANGAROO. (Supplement to: Neucleus) 1980. a. University of New England, Armidale Students' Association, Armidale, N.S.W. 2351, Australia. TEL 067-732851. FAX 067-727633.

057.8 CI ISSN 0022-9059
KARLOVACKI TJEDNIK. 1953. w. 100 din. Socialisticki Savez Radnog Naroda Karlovca, Mihovilceva 2, Karlovac, Croatia. Ed. Jovica Radojcic.

808.87 PL
KARUZELA. 1957. fortn. Ul. Sienkiewicza 3-5, 90-113 Lodz, Poland. TEL 48-42-331432. TELEX 886265. Ed. Dariusz Dorozynski. circ. 100,000.

KAYHAN (TURKISH EDITION). see *ETHNIC INTERESTS*

KAYHAN ARABI. see *ETHNIC INTERESTS*

059.915 IR
KAYHAN FARHANGI/WORLD OF CULTURE. (Text in Farsi) 1984. m. Kayhan Publications, Ferdowsi Ave., P.O. Box 11365-9631, Teheran, Iran. TEL 021-310251. TELEX 212467.

KAYHAN-I HAVA'I. see *ETHNIC INTERESTS*

052 IR ISSN 0885-8160
KAYHAN INTERNATIONAL. (Text in English) 1959. d. Kayhan Publications, Ferdowsi Ave., P.O. Box 11365-9631, Teheran, Iran. TEL 021-310251. TELEX 212467. Ed. Hossein Raghfar. (newspaper)

KEVREN. see *POLITICAL SCIENCE*

059.915 IR
▼**KHAVARAN.** 1990. m. H. Mir'nizhad, P.O. Box 91735-1497, Meshed, Iran.

059.915 IR
KHURASAN. 1948. d. S.A. Musaviyan, P.O. Box 91735-511, Meshed, Iran.

052 II ISSN 0023-1282
KICK TO CORRUPTION. (Text in English) 1969. m. Red Rd., Hoshiarpur, India. Ed. S.K. Kapur. adv.; charts; illus.

057.91 KR ISSN 0208-0710
KIIV; literaturno-khudozhnii ta hromads'kopolitychnyi zhurnal. 1983. m. 20.40 Rub. (Spika Pys'mennykiv Ukrainy) Vedavnytstvo Radyanskii Pismennik, Chkalova, 52, Kiev, Ukraine. Ed. P.M. Perebyinis. circ. 30,000.

808.87   US
KING SIZED CRACKED. a. $14.40. Globe Communications Corp. (New York), 441 Lexington Ave., New York, NY 10017. TEL 800-472-7744. FAX 212-286-0072. Ed. Lou Silverstone. circ. 500,000.
  Description: Consists of humorous articles.

800   II
KINTU. (Text in Punjabi) 1971. q. Rs.25($5) Agandoot Parkashan, Sahit Sabha, Tapa 148108, India. Ed. Cee Markanda. circ. 5,000. (back issues avail.)

KIRKE OG KULTUR. see RELIGIONS AND THEOLOGY

053.1   GW   ISSN 0023-2211
AS181
KLUETER BLAETTER; Monatshefte fuer Kultur und Zeitgeschichte. 1949. m. DM.74. Tuermer Verlag Dr. Gert Sudholt, Kreuzanger 8, 8137 Berg 3, Germany. Ed. Gert Sudholt. adv.; bk.rev.; circ. 4,000.

053.9   BE
KNACK. (Text in Dutch) 1971. w. 4690 BEF. N.V. Roularta Media Group, Meiboomlaan 33, B-8800 Roeselare, Belgium. TEL 02-7366040. FAX 02-7356857. Ed. Frans Verleyen. adv.; bk.rev.; circ. 125,000.

057.8   YU   ISSN 0023-2416
AP56
KNJIZEVNE NOVINE; list za knjizevnost i kulturu. (Text in Serbo-Croatian) 1949. fortn. 120 din. Knjizevne Novine, Francuska 7, Belgrade, Yugoslavia. Ed. Dragan M. Jeremic. **Indexed:** M.L.A.

KNJIZEVNOST. see LITERATURE

051   US   ISSN 0738-8640
KNOWLEDGE; dedicated to the dissemination of knowledge for the happiness, health, security, and survival of humankind. 1976. 4/yr. $30. Knowledge, Inc., Knowledge Park, 3863 S.W. Loop 820, Ste. 100, Ft.Worth, TX 76133-2063. TEL 817-292-4270. FAX 817-294-2893. Ed. O.A. Battista. adv.; bk.rev.; circ. 1,500. **Indexed:** Curr.Cont., E.I.
  Description: Intellectual, speculative discourses, essays, and articles in pursuit of the enhancement of humankind's physical, emotional, and intellectual lives.

KOMPOST. see CHILDREN AND YOUTH — For

320.5   IO   ISSN 0023-3188
KOMUNIKASI;* demokrasi, persatuan dan pembangunan berdasarkan pantjasila. 1969. s-m. Rps.600($2.) Yayasan Komunikasi, Matramanx Raya 10 A, Jakarta, Indonesia. Ed. Sabam Sirait.

KOREAN STAMPS. see PHILATELY

059.94   HU   ISSN 0023-415X
PH3144
KORTARS. 1957. m. $19. (Magyar Irok Szovetsege) Lapkiado Vallalat, Lenin korut 9-11, 1073 Budapest 7, Hungary. TEL 222-408. (Subscr. to: Kultura, Box 149, H-1389 Budapest, Hungary) Ed. Arpad Thiery. adv.; bk.rev.; circ. 7,000.

059   MY
KRITIK. 1975. bi-m. M.$5.50. Pustaka Zakry Abadi, 89A Jalan Raja Muda, Kuala Lumpur, Malaysia.

891.7   RU   ISSN 0023-4877
KROKODIL. 1922. 3/m. 24 Rub. Bumazhny pr. 14, 101455 Moscow, Russia. TEL 095-250-1086. Ed. A.S. Pyanov. illus.; circ. 2,200,000. **Indexed:** Curr.Dig.Sov.Press.
  Description: Consists of satire and humor.

057.85   FR   ISSN 0023-5148
AP54
KULTURA; szkice, opowiadania, sprawozdania. (Text in Polish) 1947. m. 550 F.($106) Institut Litteraire, 91 Av. de Poissy, Le Mesnil-le-Roi, 78600 Maisons-Laffitte, France. TEL 1-39-62-19-04. FAX 33-1-39-62-57-52. Ed. Jerzy Giedroyc. adv.; bk.rev.; index; circ. 9,500. **Indexed:** Hist.Abstr.
  —BLDSC shelfmark: 5121.170000.

057.85   PL   ISSN 0023-5156
AP54
KULTURA; tygodnik spoleczno-kulturalny. 1963. w. $23. Wydawnictwo Wspolczesne R S W "Prasa-Ksiazka-Ruch", Ul. Wiejska 12, 00-420 Warsaw, Poland. (Dist. by: Ars Polona-Ruch, Krakowskie Przedmiescie 7, Warsaw, Poland) Ed. Dominik Horodynski. bk.rev.; abstr.; illus.; index; circ. 108,000.

057.85   PL   ISSN 0023-5172
AS261
KULTURA I SPOLECZENSTWO. (Text in Polish; tables of contents in English, Russian) q. $32. (Polska Akademia Nauk, Komitet Nauk Socjologicznych) Panstwowe Wydawnictwo Naukowe, Ul. Miodowa 10, 00-251 Warsaw, Poland. (Dist. by: Ars Polona, Krakowskie Przedmiescie 7, 00-068 Warsaw, Poland) Ed. A. Kloskowska. bk.rev.; index; circ. 2,060. **Indexed:** Amer.Hist.& Life, Hist.Abstr., Lang.& Lang.Behav.Abstr.

057.91   KR   ISSN 0023-5180
KULTURA I ZHYTTYA. (Text in Ukrainian) 1955. s-w. $6. Ministerstvo Kul'tury, Kiev, Ukraine. adv.; bk.rev.; abstr.; bibl.; illus.
  Formerly: Radyans'ka Kul'tura.

057.81   XN   ISSN 0047-3731
KULTUREN ZIVOT/CULTURAL LIFE; kultura, umetnost, opstestveni prasanja. (Text in Macedonian) 1956. m. $25 (effective Jan. 1991). Kulturen Zivot, Ruzveltova, 6, P.O. Box 85, 91001 Skopje, Macedonia. Ed. Boris Vishinski. illus. (tabloid format; avail. on records; reprint service avail. from UMI)

053   GW
KULTURPOLITIK. 1972. q. DM.24 (foreign DM.38). Bundesverband Bildender Kunstler, Meckenheimer Allee 85, 5300 Bonn 1, Germany. TEL 0228-630406. FAX 0228-696994. Ed.Bd. adv.; bk.rev.; circ. 15,000.
  Description: Information on the professional interests of artists.

055.1   IT
L.G. ARGOMENTI. (Letteratura Giovanile Argomenti) 1965. bi-m. L.25000. Comune di Genova, Civiche Biblioteche, Via Archimede, 44, 16142 Genoa, Italy. TEL 509181. bk.rev.; index, cum.index every 5 yrs.; circ. 1,500.
  Formerly (until 1977): Minuzzolo (ISSN 0026-5748)

051   US
L I O N.* (Living in the Ozarks Newsletter) 1973. m. $18 to individuals; institutions $24. First Ozark Press, Box 310, Omaha, AR 72662-0310. adv.; bibl.; illus.

808.8 051   US   ISSN 0887-4492
LAKE EFFECT. 1986. q. $7. Lake County Writers Group, Oswego Art Center, Box 59, Oswego, NY 13126. TEL 315-635-5714. Ed. Jean O'Connor Fuller. adv.; bk.rev.; illus.; circ. 10,000. (tabloid format; back issues avail.)

059   MR
LAMALIF; revue economique, sociale et culturelle. 1966. m. DH.77($15) (foreign 200 F.). Loghlam Presse, 6 bis, Rue Defly-Dieude, Casablanca, Morocco. Ed. Mohamed Loghlam. adv.; bk.rev.; film rev.; bibl.; illus.; stat.; circ. 16,000.

LAMBDA BOOK REPORT; a review of contemporary gay and lesbian literature. see HOMOSEXUALITY

051   US
LANCASTER INDEPENDENT PRESS. 1969. m. $10. Lancaster Independent Press, Inc., Box 275, Lancaster, PA 17603-0275. Ed. Frank J. Pitz. adv.; bk.rev.; film rev.; circ. 1,000. (tabloid format; reprint service avail.)
  Description: Covers local politics and national issues.

LANCE. see COLLEGE AND ALUMNI

052   NZ   ISSN 0023-7930
AP7
LANDFALL; a New Zealand literary magazine. 1947. q. NZ.$46. Caxton Press, 113 Victoria St., Christchurch, New Zealand. FAX 064-3-657840. Ed.Bd. adv.; bk.rev.; illus.; cum.index every 5 yrs.; circ. 1,850. **Indexed:** Abstr.Engl.Stud., Amer.Hist.& Life, Arts & Hum.Cit.Ind., Br.Hum.Ind., Curr.Cont., Hist.Abstr., M.L.A., So.Pac.Per.Ind.
  —BLDSC shelfmark: 5151.550000.

808.8   CE
LANKA GUARDIAN. (Text in English) 1978. s-m. Rs.60. (South Asia Media Representatives) Lanka Guardian Publishers, 246 Union Place, Colombo 2, Sri Lanka.

808.87   US   ISSN 0887-6991
LATEST JOKES. 1974. m. $24. Robert Makinson, Ed. & Pub., Box 023304, Brooklyn, NY 11202-0066. TEL 718-855-5057. circ. 250. (back issues avail.)
  Description: Covers short jokes about current events.

808.87   US
LAUGH FACTORY. 1981. m. $15. Fell Great Publishing Co., 1370 Windsor Rd., Teaneck, NJ 07666. TEL 201-833-0068. Ed. Vince Donato.

808.8   IT
IL LECCIO; rassegna letteraria ed artistica. 1953. irreg. free. Mario Cesare Guidi, Ed. & Pub., Via di Cammori 54, 50145 Florence, Italy. TEL 055-317647. adv.; bk.rev.; illus.; circ. 1,500. (reprint service avail. from UMI,ISI)
  Formerly: Leccio - Literature - Poetry - Art (Tales).

052   UK   ISSN 0024-0303
LEFT.* m. Brewster Printing Co., Rochester, Kent, England. Ed. Carl Gilleard. adv.; bk.rev.; circ. 7,000. (reprint service avail. from KTO)
  Formerly: Focus.

700   US   ISSN 0160-1857
NX180.R45
LEFT CURVE. 1974. irreg. $20 for 3 nos. to individuals; institutions $30. Left Curve Publications, Box 472, Oakland, CA 94604. TEL 510-763-7193. Ed. Csaba Polony. adv.; bk.rev.; film rev.; play rev.; illus.; circ. 1,200. (also avail. in microform from UMI; back issues avail.) **Indexed:** Alt.Press Ind., Artbibl.Mod., Left Ind. (1984-).
  —BLDSC shelfmark: 5181.307800.
  Description: Published by artists confronting the crises of modernity independent of the control of dominant institutions. All cultural forms considered.

LEGAL STUDIES FORUM; an interdisciplinary journal. see LAW

053 301.2   GW   ISSN 0170-3803
LENDEMAINS; etudes comparees sur la France - vergleichende Frankreichforschung. (Text in German and French) 1975. q. DM.48.60. Dr. Wolfram Hitzeroth Verlag, Franz-Tuczek-Weg 1, 3550 Marburg, Germany. TEL 06421-409261. FAX 06421-409199. Ed.Bd. circ. 950.

056.9   BL   ISSN 0047-441X
LETRAS DA PROVINCIA. 1948. bi-m. Empresa Grafica Editorial Paulista, Rue Dr. Trajano 572, Caixa Postal 109, Limeira, Estado de Sao Paulo, Brazil. Dir. Joao Baptista Petrelli. bk.rev.; bibl.; circ. 10,000.

055.1   IT   ISSN 0024-130X
LETTERATO; di varia cultura. 1952. m. L.40000. Editrice Pellegrini, Via Roma 74, Casella Postale 158, 87100 Cosenza, Italy. Ed. Luigi Pellegrini. adv.; bk.rev.; bibl.; illus.

809   YU   ISSN 0350-4158
LETUNK; tarsadalom, tudomany, kultura. (Text in English, Hungarian, Serbo-Croatian) 1971. bi-m. 250 din. Nisro Forum, Trg. Slobode 1-2, 24000 Subotica, Vojvodina, Yugoslavia. TEL 38-24-26-819. FAX 38-21-56-699. Ed. Dr. Tibor Varady. bk.rev.; index; circ. 240,000.

800   FR
LIBER. (Supplement to: Frankfurter Allgemeine Zeitung, L'Indice, Le Monde, El Pais, The Times Literary Supplement) bi-m. 52 rue du Cardinal Lemoine, 75005 Paris, France. FAX 47-53-77-69. Ed.Bd.

LITERARY AND POLITICAL REVIEWS

322.44   NE
LIBERAAL REVEIL. 1959. 4/yr. fl.35 to individuals; students fl.25. Stichting Liberaal Reveil, Prins Hendrikplein 4, 2518 JA The Hague, Netherlands. Ed.Bd. bk.rev.; circ. 1,350.

320.9   UK   ISSN 0024-1903
LIBERATION NEWS SERVICE.* 1968. w. free. Liberation News Services, 30 Holland Park Gardens, London W.14, England. Ed. Joseph M. Von Haag. bk.rev.; film rev.; play rev.; abstr.; charts; illus.; stat.; circ. 1,000. (processed)
   Description: Underground literature.

320.9   II   ISSN 0047-4495
DS401
LIBERATION WAR. (Text in English) 1971. m. Rs.12. 23 Lansdowne Pl., Calcutta 29, India. Ed. Asit Sen. bk.rev.

808.8   US   ISSN 0272-5959
JC571
LIBERTARIAN DIGEST. 1981. 6/yr. $10 (effective Apr. 1992; typically set in Jan.). 132 Roberts Ln., Ste. 301, Alexandria, VA 22314-4669. TEL 703-683-7769. Ed. Fred Foldvary. adv.; bk.rev.; circ. 200. (also avail. in microform)

320   US
LIBERTAS REVIEW; a journal of peace and liberty. 1973. q. $5. Society for Libertarian Life, California State University, UC2-43, Box 59, Fullerton, CA 92634. TEL 714-535-5798. bk.rev.; stat.; circ. 3,200. (tabloid format; back issues avail.)
   Formerly: New Libertarian Horizon.

LIBERTE. see LITERATURE — Poetry

330.1 320 100   US   ISSN 0894-1408
LIBERTY (PORT TOWNSEND). 1987. bi-m. $19.50. Liberty Publishing, Box 1167, Port Townsend, WA 98368. TEL 206-385-5097. FAX 206-385-3704. Ed. R.W. Bradford. adv.; bk.rev.; film rev.; circ. 4,500. (back issues avail.)
   Description: Review of culture, politics and the arts from a libertarian or classical-liberal perspective.

808.8   US   ISSN 0894-251X
LIBERTY AND THE PUBLICK GOOD. 1985. q. $50. Institute for Global Action, Inc., Box 677, Bath, OH 44210-0677. TEL 216-666-2815. adv.; bk.rev.; circ. 2,000. (tabloid format; back issues avail.)

051   US
LIBERTY REPORT.* m. Liberty Federation, Box 190, Forest, VA 24551. Ed. Martin Mawyer.
   Formerly: Moral Majority Report.

055.1   IT
LIBRIPER. 1978. bi-m. L.4000. Cooperativa Promozione Culturale s.r.l., Via Marruvio 4, 00183 Rome, Italy. Ed. Umberto Amadigi. adv.; circ. 10,000.

057.8   CI   ISSN 0350-2562
Z2953
LICKI VJESNIK. 1953. fortn. 50 din.($2) (Socijalisticki Savez Radnog Naroda Zajednice Opcina Gospic) Novinsko Informativna Ustanova u Osnivanju, Seste Licke Divizije 3, Gospic, Croatia. Ed. Stjepan Mazar.
   Formerly (until 1977): Licke Novine (ISSN 0024-2888)

059.951   CH
LIEN HO YUEH K'AN. (Text in Chinese) m. NT.$850 in ROC; Hong Kong $32; Asia $54; elsewhere $60. 555 Chung Hsiao E. Rd. Sec. 4, Taipei, Taiwan, Republic of China. TEL 02-768-0091. Ed. Yang Hsi-han. adv.

056.1   AG
LINEA DURA. 1973. m. $60. Alvar Nunez 179, Buenos Aires, Argentina. Ed. Alberto Hermida. illus.

800   UK   ISSN 0266-1500
LINEN HALL REVIEW. 1984. q. £3.50 (foreign £5). Linen Hall Library, 17 Donegall Sq., N. Belfast BT1 5GO, Northern Ireland. FAX 0232-321707. FAX 0232-438586. Eds. John Gray, Paul Campbell. adv.; bk.rev.; index; circ. 6,000.
   —BLDSC shelfmark: 5221.126000.
   Incorporates: Irish Booklore - New Series.
   Description: A Northern view of the world of Irish books.

808.8   CN
LINK (MONTREAL). 1936. 2/wk. Can.$20. Link Publication Society, Concordia Univ., Sir George Williams Campus, 1455 de Maisonneuve St. West, Montreal, Que. H3G 1M8, Canada. TEL 514-848-7405. Eds. Frances Lodico, Andy Riga. adv.; bk.rev.; charts; illus.; circ. 16,500. (tabloid format)
   Formed by merger of: Loyola News (ISSN 0024-7073) & Georgian (ISSN 0016-8467)

808.87   IT
LINUS. m. L.30000. Rizzoli Editore-Corriere della Sera, Via A. Rizzoli 2, 20132 Milan, Italy. Ed. F. Serra. adv.

800   US   ISSN 0147-2593
PN1009.A1
LION & THE UNICORN; a critical journal of children's literature. 1977. a. $18 to individuals (foreign $20.50); institutions $32 (foreign $34.50). Johns Hopkins University Press, Journals Publishing Division, 701 W. 40th St., Ste. 275, Baltimore, MD 21211. TEL 410-516-6987. FAX 410-516-6998. Eds. Geraldine DeLuca, Roni Natov. adv.; bk.rev.; bibl.; circ. 750. (reprint service avail. from ISI)
   Indexed: Abstr.Engl.Stud., Arts & Hum.Cit.Ind., Curr.Cont., M.L.A.
   —BLDSC shelfmark: 5221.742000.
   Description: Discusses literature for children.

808.87   CS
LISIAK. m. $24. Obzor, Ceskoslovenskej Armady 35, 815 85 Bratislava, Czechoslovakia.
   Description: Includes humorous articles.

053   GW
LITERARISCHER WEIHNACHTSKATALOG. 1877. a. DM.1.90. K.F. Koehler Verlag GmbH, Postfach 800569, 7000 Stuttgart 80, Germany. FAX 0711-7892-132. adv.; bk.rev. (back issues avail.)

052   II   ISSN 0024-452X
PR1
LITERARY CRITERION. (Text in English) 1952. q. Rs.60($15) c/o English Dept., Bangalore University, Jnana Bharathi, Bangalore 560 056, India. TEL 355299. Eds. C.D. Narasimhaiah, C.N. Srinath. adv.; bk.rev.; circ. 800.

800   US
▼**LITERARY GAZETTE INTERNATIONAL.*** Selected English translation of: Literaturnaya Gazeta (UR ISSN 0024-4848) 1990. bi-w. $59.99. Sun World Corporation, 900 Magoffin Ave., El Paso, TX 79901-1520. TEL 915-778-0015. FAX 915-778-0153. TELEX 377 8721. (Subscr. to: 6989 Commerce St., El Paso, TX 79915) film rev.; play rev.; abstr.; circ. 60,000. (tabloid format; also avail. in microfilm from BHP; back issues avail.)
   Description: Literary and political forum for Soviet writers.

800   UK   ISSN 0144-4360
NX645
LITERARY REVIEW AND QUARTO. 1979. m. $54. Namara Group, 51 Beak St., London W1R 3LF, England. Ed. Auberon Waugh. adv.; bk.rev.; circ. 15,000.
   —BLDSC shelfmark: 5276.654800.
   Formerly (until 1982): Literary Review.

LITERARY STUDIES; a quarterly review of literature and criticism from the Panjab. see LITERATURE

809   GW   ISSN 0024-4643
PN4
LITERATUR IN WISSENSCHAFT UND UNTERRICHT. 1968. q. DM.34.80. Universitaet Kiel, Englisches Seminar, Olshausenstr. 40-60, Haus 15, D-2300 Kiel, Germany. FAX 0431-880-2072. TELEX 292656-CAUKI-D. Ed. Walter T. Rix. adv.; bk.rev.; bibl.; circ. 1,700. **Indexed:** Abstr.Engl.Stud., Bibl.Engl.Lang. & Lit., M.L.A.
   Description: Devoted to textual interpretation and close reading of literature in the English and German languages, reviews.

808.8   GW   ISSN 0930-2778
LITERATUR-TELEGRAMM; das aktuelle Kulturmagazin. (Text in English, French, German, Italian) 1986. irreg. DM.17.80. Hofmann-Druck Augsburg, Zugspitzstr. 183, 8890 Augsburg 41, Germany. TEL 0821-791022. (Subscr. to: Anna Gross, Ernst-Moritz-Arndt Str. 19, 8900 Augsburg, Germany) Ed. Benno Griebel. bk.rev.; circ. 500.
   Description: Contemporary discussion about cultural development.

800   LI
LITERATURA IR MENAS. 1946. w. Writers' Union, Universiteto 4, 232600 Vilnius, Lithuania. TEL (0122) 612-586. Ed. Vytautas Rubavicius.

891.79   KR   ISSN 0024-4821
LITERATURNA UKRAYINA. (Text in Ukrainian) 1927. w. $15. (Spilka Pys'mennykiv Ukrainy) Vydavnytstvo Radyanskii Pismennik, Chkalova Str. 52, Kiev, Ukraine. Ed. B. Rogoza. (also avail. in microform from MIM)

891.992   AI   ISSN 0024-483X
LITERATURNAYA ARMENIYA. 1958. m. 15 Rub. Soyuz Pisatelei Armyanskoi S.S.R., Erevan, Armenia. index.

800   RU   ISSN 0024-4848
LITERATURNAYA GAZETA. English translation: Literary Gazette International. 1929. w. $16.80. Kostyanskii pereulok 13, Moscow 103654, Russia. TEL (095) 200-24-17. FAX 095-200-02-38. TELEX 411294. (Subscr. to: Mezhdunarodnaya Kniga, Moscow, G-200, Russia) Ed. A. Chakovskii. bk.rev.; film rev.; play rev.; abstr.; circ. 2,500,000. (newspaper; also avail. in microform from MIM; microfilm from KTO)
   Indexed: Curr.Dig.Sov.Press.

059   RU   ISSN 0132-1986
LITERATURNAYA OSETIYA. LITERATURNO-KHUDOZHESTVENNYI I OBSHCHESTVENNO-POLITICHESKII ZHURNAL. 1948. q. (Soyuz Pisatelei Severo-Osetinskoi A.S.S.R.) Izdatel'stvo I R, 362040 Ordzhonikidze, Ossetinian A.R., Russia. Ed. Sergey Kabaloev. circ. 1,000.
   Description: Prose and poetry on culture, history and society.

891.7   RU   ISSN 0024-4856
LITERATURNAYA ROSSIYA. 1958. w. $12. Soyuz Pisatelei Rossiiskoi S.F.S.R., Tsvetnoi bul. 30, 103662 Moscow, Russia. TEL (095) 200-40-05. FAX 095-200-27-55. (Co-sponsor: Moskovskaya Pisatel'skaya Organizatsiya) Ed. Ernst Safonov. bk.rev.; illus.; index. (also avail. in microform from MIM) **Indexed:** Curr.Dig.Sov.Press.

800   UK   ISSN 0263-4635
LITMUS. 1974-1985; resumed 1986. 3/yr. £6. Stukeley Press, The City Lt., Stukeley St., Drury Lane, London WC2B 5LJ, England. Ed. Laurie Smith. adv.; bk.rev.; circ. 500. (back issues avail.)
   Former titles (until 1982): Limestone Literary Magazine (ISSN 0308-4787); Limestone.

053   GW
LIVE SAAR. 1983. m. DM.15. H und P Verlag, Neumarkt 2, 6600 Saarbruecken, Germany. TEL 0681-5847394. Ed. Andreas Hoyer. adv.; bk.rev.; circ. 31,500.

850   IT
LIVORNOCRONACA - IL VERNACOLIERE; periodico politico satirico. 1961. m. L.25000. Mario Cardinali Editore s.r.l., Scali del Corso, 5, 57123 Livorno, Italy. TEL 880226. adv.; illus.; tr.lit.; circ. 16,000. (looseleaf format)
   Formerly: Livornocronaca (ISSN 0024-5321)

052 821   UK
LOBBY PRESS NEWSLETTER. (Text mainly in English; occasionally in German and Italian) 1978. bi-m. £1. Lobby Press, 17 Warkworth St., Cambridge CB1 1EG, England. adv.; bk.rev.; circ. 300. (looseleaf format)

053   CN   ISSN 0047-4967
LOGBERG-HEIMSKRINGLA. (Text in English, Icelandic) 1886. w. Can.$30. Logberg-Heimskringla Inc., 699 Carter, Winnipeg, Man. R3M 2C3, Canada. TEL 204-284-5686. Ed. H.K. Danielsdottir. adv.; bk.rev.; circ. 1,900. (tabloid format; also avail. in microfilm from CML)

942 UK ISSN 0024-6085
PR1
LONDON MAGAZINE. 1954. bi-m. £28.50($67) London Magazine Ltd., 30 Thurloe Pl., London S.W.7, England. Ed. Alan Ross. adv.; bk.rev.; circ. 4,000. (reprint service avail. from KTO) Indexed: Br.Hum.Ind.; Film Lit.Ind. (1973-), Ind.Bk.Rev.Hum.
—BLDSC shelfmark: 5293.854000.
Description: Features architecture, painting, films, art, fiction, poetry, and memoirs.

808.8 UK ISSN 0260-9592
LONDON REVIEW OF BOOKS. 1979. fortn. $48. L R B Ltd., Tavistock House South, Tavistock Sq., London WC1H 9JZ, England. TEL 071-388-6751. FAX 071-383-4792. Eds. Karl Miller, Mary-Kay Wilmers. adv.; bk.rev.; index; circ. 18,000. (also avail. in microfilm from UMI; reprint service avail. from UMI) Indexed: Bk.Rev.Ind. (1982-), Child.Bk.Rev.Ind. (1982-), RILA.
—BLDSC shelfmark: 5294.094000.

808.87 US
LONE STAR COMEDY SERVICE; a humor service for the professional comedian, public speakers, and broadcasters. 1984. m. Lone Star Publications of Humor, Box 29000, Ste. 103, San Antonio, TX 78229. Ed. Lauren Barnett. (looseleaf format)
Formerly: Lone Star Comedy Monthly.

808.57 US
LONE STAR HUMOR. 1983. irreg. (4-6/yr.). Lone Star Publications of Humor, Box 29000, Ste. 103, San Antonio, TX 78229. Ed. Lauren I. Barnett. adv.; bk.rev.; film rev.; play rev.; charts; illus.; tr.lit.; circ. 1,000. (back issues avail.)
Formerly: Lone Star (ISSN 0735-1623)

059.91 ER ISSN 0134-4536
LOOMING. (Text in Estonian) 1923. m. $71 (effective 1992). (Estonian Writers Union) Kirjastus Perioodika, Parnu mnt. 8, 200090 Tallinn, Estonia. TEL 0142-441-262. FAX 0142-442-484. Ed. Andres Langemets. bk.rev.; illus.; index; circ. 25,650. Indexed: M.L.A.

800 US
LOST AND FOUND TIMES. (Text in English or Spanish) 1975. s-a. $14 for 5 nos. Luna Bisonte Prods, 137 Leland Ave., Columbus, OH 43214. TEL 614-846-4126. Ed. John M. Bennett. adv.; bk.rev.; circ. 300. (back issues avail.) Indexed: A.I.P.P.
Description: Avant-garde poetry, verse, and drawings.

051 US
LOUISIANA POLITICAL REVIEW. bi-m. Box 80779, Baton Rouge, LA 70898. TEL 504-388-9520. Ed. John Maginnis.

059.945 HU
LUDAS MATYI. w. $34.50. Gyulai Pal u. 14, 1077 Budapest, Hungary. TEL 133-5718. Ed. Jozsef Arkus. circ. 352,000.

053 GW
LUEBECKER WOCHENSPIEGEL. 1978. w. free. Luebecker Nachrichten GmbH, P.O. Box 2238, Konigstr. 55, 2400 Lubeck 1, Germany. Ed. Jorg Loose. circ. 187,000.

056.9 US ISSN 0024-7413
DP501
LUSO - BRAZILIAN REVIEW; devoted to the culture of the Portuguese speaking world. (Text in English, Portuguese, Spanish) 1963. s-a. $25 to individuals; institutions $68. University of Wisconsin Press, 114 N. Murray St., Madison, WI 53715. TEL 608-262-4952. FAX 608-262-7560. Eds. Mary L. Daniel, Stanley Payne. adv.; bk.rev.; bibl.; cum.index every 2 yrs.; circ. 650. (also avail. in microform from UMI; back issues avail. in microform; reprint service avail. from UMI,KTO) Indexed: Amer.Hist.& Life, Hisp.Amer.Per.Ind., Hist.Abstr., M.L.A.
—BLDSC shelfmark: 5307.550000.

LUST & GRATIE; lesbisch cultureel universeel tijdschrift. see HOMOSEXUALITY

320.531 CN ISSN 0701-8746
LUTTE OUVRIERE. (Text in French) 1980. q. Can.$17($17) (effective Oct. 1990). Societe d'Editions A.G.P.P. Inc., C.P. 340, Succ. R., Montreal, Que. H2S 3M2, Canada. TEL 514-278-1743. FAX 514-278-1836. Ed. Michel Prarie. charts; illus.; circ. 1,500. (also avail. in microfilm; back issues avail.)
Incorporating: Jeune Garde (ISSN 0021-5759)
Description: A socialist review defending the interests of working people internationally.

296 AG ISSN 0024-7693
LUZ; la revista Israelita para toda Sudamerica. 1931. fortn. Pasteur 359, Buenos Aires, Argentina. Ed. Nissim Elnecave. bk.rev.; bibl.; illus.; circ. 25,000.

808.81 US ISSN 0897-6716
LYRA. (Text in English, French, Italian, Spanish) 1988. q. $15. Lyra Society for the Arts, Inc., 317 77th St., N. Bergen, NJ 07047. TEL 201-861-1941. (Subscr. to: Box 3188, Guttenberg, NJ 07093) Eds. Lourdes Gil, Iraida Iturralde. adv.; bk.rev.; film rev.; circ. 700. (back issues avail.)
Description: Multicultural approach to the study of world literature, creative writing and criticism.

M I S INFORMATION. see COMPUTERS

053.9 NE
MAATSTAF. vol.22, 1974. 10/yr. fl.82.50. B.V. de Arbeiderspers, Singel 262, 1016 AC Amsterdam, Netherlands. Ed. Bd. adv.; bibl.; circ. 4,500. Indexed: Arts & Hum.Cit.Ind., Curr.Cont., M.L.A.

052 AT
MACARTHUR ADVERTISER. 1935. w. Fairfax Community Newspapers Pty. Ltd., 317 Queen St., Campbelltown, N.S.W. 2560, Australia. FAX 046-284155. Ed. Lisa Harbormann. adv.; bk.rev.; circ. 44,300. (tabloid format)

052 CN
MACEDONIA. (Text in English, Macedonian) 1984. m. Can.$20. Macedonian Publishing Co., P.O.B. 291, West Hill Stn., Scarborough, Ont. M1E 4R6, Canada. Ed. Tanas Jovanovski. circ. 2,000. (tabloid format; back issues avail.)

808.87 UK
MAC'S YEAR (YEAR). 1988? a. £2.50. Chapmans Publishers, 141-143 Drury Lane, London WC2B 5TB, England. TEL 01-497-1199.
Description: Emphasis is on humor.

808.87 US ISSN 0024-9319
MAD. 1952. m. (8/yr.). $13.75. E.C. Publications, Inc., 485 Madison Ave., New York, NY 10022. TEL 212-752-7685. Eds. Nick Meglin, John Ficarra. illus.; circ. 800,000.

053.1 GW
MAGAZIN FUER MITARBEITER - WERK UND LEBEN. 1951. fortn. DM.35.33. Werkschriften-Verlag GmbH, Bachstr. 14-16, 6900 Heidelberg 1, Germany. Ed. Dieter Neumann. adv.; bk.rev.; circ. 120,000. (tabloid format)
Former titles: Magazin fuer Arbeitnehmer - Werk und Leben; Werk und Leben (ISSN 0049-7142)

052 AT
MAGGIE'S FARM.* 1979. q. Aus.$8. Maggie's Farm Media Centre, P.O. Falconbridge, Blue Mountain, N.S.W., Australia. Ed. Paul White. adv.; bk.rev.; circ. 30,000.

052 UK
MAGIC INK.* no.18, 1975. q. Underground Alternative Press Service - Europe, 22 Dane Rd., Margate, Kent, England. Ed. Ian King. bibl.

808.87 US
MAINEIAC EXPRESS. a. Dog Ear Press, 132 Water St., Gardiner, ME 04345. TEL 207-737-8116.

508 IR
MAJALLE-YE DANESH-E RUZ. 1973. q. Rs.200. Arak College of Science, Shahpur Ave., Arak, Iran. Ed. Abdolkarim Qarib.

052 IE ISSN 0791-0770
MAKING SENSE. m. 30 Gardiner Place, Dublin 1, Ireland. TEL 01-741045. Ed. Paddy Gillan.

LITERARY AND POLITICAL REVIEWS 2873

057.99 BW ISSN 0025-1208
MALADOSTS'; literaturno-khudozhestvennyi i obshchestvenno-politicheski zhurnal Ts.K. V.L.K.S.M. Belorussiyi. 1953. m. $8.40. (Leninskii Kommunisticheskii Soyuz Molodezhi Belorusskoi S.S.R.) Izdatel'stvo Zvyazda, Minsk, Byelarus.

800
MALAYALAM LITERARY SURVEY. (Text in English) 1977. q. Rs.20. Kerala Sahitya Akademi, Town Hall Rd., Trichur 680020, India. Ed. Erumeli Parameswarsan Pillai. adv.; bk.rev.; circ. 1,000.

052 UK ISSN 0306-5030
MANCHESTER FREE PRESS.* 1971. m. 95p.($4) Moss Side Press, 136 Withington Rd., Manchester 16, England. bk.rev.; film rev.; circ. 3,000.

MANCHESTER GUARDIAN WEEKLY. see GENERAL INTEREST PERIODICALS — Great Britain

059.927 SU
AL-MANHAL. (Text in Arabic) 1937. m. P.O. Box 2925, Jeddah, Saudi Arabia. Ed. Abd al-Qudous Ansari.

808.87 US
▼**MANHATTAN COMIC NEWS;** the news in cartoons. 1990. m. $15. M C N Inc., 250 Mercer St., Ste. 264, New York, NY 10013. TEL 212-517-0250. FAX 212-473-6296. adv.; circ. 21,000.

MANIPULATOR. see ART

059 II
MANORAMA WEEKLY. (Text in Malayalam) 1937. w. $29. Malayala Manorama Co. Ltd., P.O. Box 26, Kottayam 686 001, Kerala, India. TEL 481-3615. FAX 481-2479. TELEX 0888-201-MNR-IN. Ed. Mammen Varghese. circ. 1,169,023.

800 700 UK ISSN 0950-5091
NX456
MARGIN; at the edge of literature & ideas. 1986. q. £12($20) Common Margins Ltd., Square Inch, Lower Granco St., Dunning PH2 0SQ, Scotland. (U.S. addr.: 1430 Massachusetts Ave., No. 306-17, Cambridge, MA 02138) Eds. Robin Magowan, Walter Perrie. circ. 2,000. (back issues avail.)
Description: Publishes those who write from the margins of society.

800 GW ISSN 0025-2948
MARGINALIEN; Zeitschrift fuer Buchkunst und Bibliophilie. 1948. q. DM.72. Aufbau-Verlag Berlin und Weimar, Franzoesische Str. 32, 1086 Berlin, Germany. TEL 030-2202421. FAX 030-2298637. Ed. Lothar Lang. bibl.; illus. Indexed: M.L.A.

808.87 FR
MARIUS. 1977. a. Publications Georges Ventillard, 2 a 12, rue de Bellevue, 75940 Paris Cedex 19, France. adv.; circ. 175,000.

800 US ISSN 0735-1240
MARK. 1977. a. $3. University of Toledo, Graduate Student Association, 2514 Student Union, Toledo, OH 43606. Ed. Brenda J. Wyatt. adv.; bk.rev.; circ. 4,000.

059.927 BA
AL-MASIRAH. 1977. w. Al- Masirah Journalism, Printing and Publishing House, P.O. Box 5981, Manama, Bahrain. TEL 258882. FAX 276178. TELEX 7421. Ed. Khalifa Hasan Qassim.

810 300 700 US ISSN 0025-4878
AS30.M3
MASSACHUSETTS REVIEW; a quarterly of literature, arts and public affairs. 1959. q. $15 to individuals; libraries $20. Massachusetts Review, Inc., Memorial Hall, University of Massachusetts, Amherst, MA 01003. TEL 413-545-2689. Eds. Mary Heath, Paul Jenkins. adv.; bk.rev.; illus.; index; circ. 1,500. (also avail. in microfilm from UMI; reprint service avail. from UMI) Indexed: A.I.P.P., Abstr.Engl.Stud., Acad.Ind., Amer.Hist.& Life, Arts & Hum.Cit.Ind., Curr.Cont., Film Lit.Ind. (1990-), Hist.Abstr., Hum.Ind., Ind.Bk.Rev.Hum., Ind.Little Mag., Lang.& Lang.Behav.Abstr., M.L.A., Soc.Sci.Ind., Sociol.Abstr.
—BLDSC shelfmark: 5388.690000.

MASSIS. see RELIGIONS AND THEOLOGY — Other Denominations And Sects

MATATU; journal for African culture. see LITERATURE

2874 LITERARY AND POLITICAL REVIEWS

820 300 700   AT   ISSN 0815-953X
AP7
MEANJIN; a magazine of literature, art and discussion. 1940. q. Aus.$28 (foreign Aus.$32). Meanjin Company Ltd., 211 Grattan St., Parkville, Vic. 3052, Australia. TEL 03-344-6950. FAX 03-347-5104. Ed. J. Lee. adv.; bk.rev.; index; circ. 3,200. (also avail. in microform) **Indexed:** Abstr.Engl.Stud., Arts & Hum.Cit.Ind., Aus.P.A.I.S., Bk.Rev.Ind. (1988-), Child.Bk.Rev.Ind. (1988-), Curr.Cont., Gdlns., Ind.Bk.Rev.Hum., Lang.& Lang.Behav.Abstr., M.L.A., So.Pac.Per.Ind.
   Formerly: Meanjin Quarterly (ISSN 0025-6293)

057.8   CI   ISSN 0025-8229
MEDJIMURJE. 1952. w. 150 din. Socijalisticki Savez Radnog Naroda Opstine Cakovec, Uska Ul. 66, Cakovec, Croatia. Ed. Zika Dordevic.

800   SZ
MEMOPRESS AUSGABE D; Dokumentation ueber Informationen aus Politik, Wirtschaft und Religion. (Text in German) 1966. 16/yr. (in 2 vols., 8 nos./vol.). 12.50 Fr. (foreign DM.15). Memopress-Verlag, CH-8215 Hallau, Switzerland. TEL 053-61-31-44. FAX 053-61-40-14. Ed. Emil Rahm. circ. 4,000.
   Supersedes in part: Memo Press: Aktuelle Presse- und Literatur Hinweise mit Kommentar.

800   SZ
MEMOPRESS AUSGABE K; Kurzgefasste Informationen aus Politik, Wirtschaft und Religion mit Kommentar. (Text in German) 1989. 4/yr. 7.50 Fr. Memopress-Verlag, CH-8215 Hallau, Switzerland. TEL 053-61-31-44. FAX 053-61-40-14. Ed. Emil Rahm. adv.; bk.rev.; illus.; circ. 50,000.
   Supersedes in part: Memo Press: Aktuelle Presse- und Literatur Hinweise mit Kommentar.

053.1   GW   ISSN 0026-0096
AP30
MERKUR; Deutsche Zeitschrift fuer europaeisches Denken. 1947. m. DM.156. Verlag Klett-Cotta, Rotebuehlstr. 77, Postfach 10 60 16, 7000 Stuttgart 10, Germany. FAX 0711-6672505. Ed. Karl-Heinz Bohrer. adv.; bk.rev.; film rev.; illus.; index; circ. 5,800. **Indexed:** Abstr.Engl.Stud., Amer.Hist.& Life, Curr.Cont., Hist.Abstr., Ind.Bk.Rev.Hum., Phil.Ind.
   —BLDSC shelfmark: 5682.245000.

052 791.43   AT   ISSN 0814-8805
METAPHYSICAL REVIEW. 1984. irreg. (approx. 4/yr.). Aus.$35($25) Bruce Gillespie, Ed. & Pub., G.P.O. Box 5195AA, Melbourne, Vic. 3001, Australia. adv.; bk.rev.; circ. 200. (back issues avail.)
   Description: Reviews, criticism and discussion of science fiction, fantasy, music, cinema and literature.

MIBIFNIM/FROM WITHIN. see AGRICULTURE — *Agricultural Economics*

301.415   US
MICHAEL'S THING.* 1970. w. $20. Box 1708, New York, NY 10023-1708. Ed. Frank Schmitt. adv.; bk.rev.; film rev.; circ. 35,000.

MICHIGAN HISTORICAL REVIEW (MT. PLEASANT). see HISTORY — *History Of North And South America*

810 300   US   ISSN 0026-2420
AS30
MICHIGAN QUARTERLY REVIEW. 1962. q. $13 (foreign $17). University of Michigan, 3032 Rackham Bldg., Ann Arbor, MI 48109-1070. TEL 313-764-9265. Ed. Laurence Goldstein. adv.; bk.rev.; illus.; index; circ. 2,000. (also avail. in microform from UMI; back issues avail.; reprint service avail. from UMI) **Indexed:** Abstr.Engl.Stud., Amer.Bibl.Slavic & E.Eur.Stud., Amer.Hist.& Life, Amer.Hum.Ind., Arts & Hum.Cit.Ind., Bibl.Engl.Lang.& Lit., Bk.Rev.Ind. (1989-), Child.Bk.Rev.Ind. (1989-), Curr.Cont., Film Lit.Ind. (1986-), Hist.Abstr., Hum.Ind., Ind.Amer.Per.Verse, Ind.Bk.Rev.Hum., LCR, M.L.A., Mich.Mag.Ind., Mid.East: Abstr.& Ind., P.A.I.S.
   —BLDSC shelfmark: 5755.620000.
   Description: Presents fiction, poetry, essays, and interviews.

808.8   US   ISSN 0747-8216
MICROCOSM - LYRICAL WAYS. 1981. a. $5. Quixsilver Press, c/o Robert Randolph Medcalf, Jr., Ed., 144 N. Main St., Biglerville, PA 17307. circ. 100.
   Formerly: Apogee - Lyrical Ways.

808.8   US   ISSN 0747-8895
PS501
MID-AMERICAN REVIEW. 1976. s-a. $8. Bowling Green State University, Department of English, c/o George Looney, Ed., Bowling Green University, Bowling Green, OH 43403. TEL 419-372-2725. (Co-sponsors: Ohio Arts Council; National Endowment for the Arts) adv.; bk.rev.; circ. 1,000 (controlled). **Indexed:** Amer.Hum.Ind., Lang.& Lang.Behav.Abstr., M.L.A.
   Supersedes: Itinerary (Bowling Green).
   Description: Seeks essays and criticism of current literary trends which focus on contemporary authors.

053   GW
MID-ZEITSCHRIFT FUER LITERATUR- & ZEITKRITIK. m. DM.50($30) Verlag Herbert D. Debes, Marktstr. 125, 6000 Frankfurt 60, Germany. TEL 06109-22612. FAX 06109-22113. Ed. Herbert M. Debes. adv.; bk.rev.; circ. 30,000. (back issues avail.)

MIDAMERICA. see LITERATURE

052   UK   ISSN 0305-0734
HC410.7.A1
THE MIDDLE EAST. 1974. m. £30($80) I.C. Publications Ltd., Box 261, Carlton House, 69 Gt. Queen St., London WC2B 5BN, England. TEL 071-404-4333. FAX 071-404-5336. TELEX 8811757-ARABY-G. Ed. Grahan Benton. adv.; bk.rev.; illus.; stat.; circ. 14,382. (back issues avail.) **Indexed:** Curr.Cont.M.E., Key to Econ.Sci., Mid.East: Abstr.& Ind., PROMT.
   ●Also available online.
   Description: Covers all major political, economic and cultural events.

296   US   ISSN 0026-332X
DS149
MIDSTREAM; a monthly Jewish review. 1955. m. $21. Theodor Herzl Foundation, 110 E. 59th St., New York, NY 10022. TEL 212-339-6000. Ed. Joel Carmichael. adv.; bk.rev.; circ. 800,000. (also avail. in microform from AJP,UMI; reprint service avail. from UMI) **Indexed:** A.I.P.P., Abstr.Engl.Stud., Amer.Bibl.Slavic & E.Eur.Stud., Amer.Hist.& Life, Amer.Hum.Ind., CERDIC, Curr.Cont.M.E., Film Lit.Ind (1973-), G.Soc.Sci.& Rel.Per.Lit., Hist.Abstr., HR Rep., Ind.Artic.Jew.Stud., Ind.Bk.Rev.Hum., Mid.East: Abstr.& Ind., P.A.I.S.
   —BLDSC shelfmark: 5761.435800.

808   US   ISSN 0892-5267
MILDRED.* 1987. 2/yr. $12. Mildred Publishing, 961 Birchwood Ln., Schenectady, NY 12309-3118. TEL 518-374-5410. Eds. Ellen Biss, Kathryn Poppino. bk.rev.; circ. 350. (back issues avail.)
   Description: Features poetry, short stories, reviews, art and photography with a psychological focus.

059.951   HK
MING PAO MONTHLY. (Text in Chinese) m. HK.$130 in Hong Kong; Macao HK.$160; elsewhere HK.$200($26). Ming Pao Tsa Chih Co., 651 King's Rd., 5th Fl., North Point, Hong Kong. TEL 565-3194. FAX 880-9310. Ed. Poon Yiu Ming.

808.87   US
MINNE HA! HA!; the Twin Cities' sorely needed humor magazine. 1978. bi-m. $16. Box 14009, Minneapolis, MN 55414. TEL 612-491-1818. Ed. Lance Anger. adv.; bk.rev.; film rev.; play rev.; illus.; circ. 25,000. (tabloid format; back issues avail.)
   Description: Urban humor magazine.

954   II   ISSN 0026-5780
MIRA; a monthly journal of Indian culture. (Text in English) 1933. m. (10/yr.) $2.50. 10 Sadhu Vaswani Rd., Poona 1, India. Ed. Gangaram Sajandas. bk.rev.; illus.

810 300 700   US   ISSN 0026-637X
AS30.M58
MISSISSIPPI QUARTERLY; the journal of Southern culture. 1947. q. $12 (foreign $16). Mississippi State University, College of Arts and Sciences, Box 5272, Mississippi State, MS 39762. TEL 601-325-3069. FAX 601-325-3299. TELEX 785-045. (Subscr. to: Box 5272, Mississippi State, MS 39762) Ed. Robert L. Phillips, Jr. adv.; bk.rev.; bibl.; index; circ. 850. (also avail. in microform from UMI; reprint service avail. from UMI,ISI) **Indexed:** Abstr.Engl.Stud., Amer.Hist.& Life, Amer.Hum.Ind., Arts & Hum.Cit.Ind., Curr.Cont., Hist.Abstr., Hum.Ind., Ind.Bk.Rev.Hum., Lang.& Lang.Behav.Abstr., M.L.A., Sociol.Abstr.
   —BLDSC shelfmark: 5828.928000.
   Description: Publishes contributions in the humanities and the social sciences dealing with the South, past and present.

808.8   CN
MITRE; students' literary magazine. (Text in English) 1893. a. Can.$2.50($2.50) Bishop's University, Student's Representative Council, Lennoxville, Que. J1M 1Z7, Canada. TEL 819-569-9551. Ed. Eric Tartift. adv.; bk.rev.; illus.; circ. controlled. (tabloid format)
   Former titles: New Mitre; Mitre.
   Description: Short stories, photo essays, poetry and illustrations from the student body of Bishop's University.

947   GW   ISSN 0026-6833
MITTEILUNGEN AUS BALTISCHEM LEBEN. 1955. q. DM.40. Baltische Gesellschaft in Deutschland e.V., Lessingstr. 5, 8000 Munich 2, Germany. adv.; bk.rev.; charts; illus.; index; circ. 1,000.

057   PL   ISSN 0866-9791
MLODA POLSKA; tygodnik katolicki. 1989. w. $60. Societas Amicorum Catholicae Juventutis Poloniae, c/o Wieslaw Walendziak, Ed., Ul. Targ Drzewny 3-7, 80-886 Gdansk, Poland. TEL 31-17-51. TELEX 0512858 GWP PL. (Subscr. addr. in U.S.: Witold Balaban, P.S.C. 176 Java St., Brooklyn, N.Y. 11222) adv.; circ. 30,000.
   Description: Presents article on the political and economic situation in Poland from the Catholic and the conservative point of view.

051   US
MOBILE BAY MONTHLY. 1986. m. $15. Box 66200, Mobile, AL 36660. TEL 205-473-6269. FAX 205-479-8822. Ed. Chris McFadyen. adv.; circ. 15,000.

051 327   US   ISSN 0026-7457
AP2
MODERN AGE.* 1957. q. $15. Young America's Foundation, 110 Eledn St., Herndon, VA 22070. TEL 703-318-9608. Ed. George A. Panichas. adv.; bk.rev.; index; circ. 5,000. (also avail. in microform from UMI,KTO,MIM; back issues avail.) **Indexed:** Acad.Ind., Amer.Bibl.Slavic & E.Eur.Stud., Amer.Hist.& Life, Bk.Rev.Ind. (1965-), CERDIC, Child.Bk.Rev.Ind. (1965-), Hist.Abstr., Hum.Ind., Ind.Bk.Rev.Hum., Int.Polit.Sci.Abstr., M.L.A., Mid.East: Abstr.& Ind., P.A.I.S., Soc.Sci.Ind.
   —BLDSC shelfmark: 5883.560000.

MODERN AND CONTEMPORARY FRANCE. see HISTORY — *History Of Europe*

059.951   CH
MODERN CHINA/CHIN TAI CHUNG-KUO. (Text in Chinese; table of contents in English) bi-m. Modern China, Inc., 11 Chung Shan S. Rd., Taipei, Taiwan, Republic of China. TEL 02-937-3860. (Or: P.O. Box 20, Yangmingshan Post Office, Taipei, Taiwan, ROC) adv.; bk.rev.; illus.
   Description: Covers arts, politics, and events in the Republic of China.

808.8   UK   ISSN 0964-2323
▼**THE MODERN REVIEW**. 1991. q. £6($20) 6 Hopgood St., London W12 7JU, England. TEL 081-749-0593. Ed. Toby Young. adv.; bk.rev.; film rev.; bibl.; circ. 15,000. (tabloid format; back issues avail.)
   Description: Highbrow treatment of popular culture.

LITERARY AND POLITICAL REVIEWS

859.7 RM
MOFTUL ROMAN. 1949. m. 336 lei($46) Ministerul Culturii, Piata Presei Libere 1, Sector 1, Bucharest, Rumania. (Subscr. to: Calea Grivitei 66-68, Box 12201, Bucharest, Rumania) Ed. Mihai Ispirescu. illus.; circ. 225,000.
Formerly: Urzica (ISSN 0042-1200)

053 GW
MOIN; illustrierte Herdezeitung. 1981. m. DM.30. Uebermoin e.V., Auf dem Meere 41, D-2120 Lueneburg, Germany. Ed.Bd. circ. 3,000. (back issues avail.)

057.1 RU ISSN 0131-2251
CODEN: VMEZA4
MOLODAYA GVARDIYA. 1922. m. 28.80 Rub.($60.50) (Vsesoyuznyi Leninskii Kommunisticheskii Soyuz Molodezhi, Tsentral'nyi Komitet) Izdatel'stvo Molodaya Gvardiya, Novodmitrovskaya ul. 5A, 125015 Moscow, Russia. TEL 095-285-8858. (Dist. by: Mezhdunarodnaya Kniga, ul. Dimitrova D.39, 113095 Moscow, Russia) Ed. A. Ivanov. adv.; bk.rev.; film rev.; play rev.; bibl.; illus.; circ. 640,000. Indexed: Curr.Dig.Sov.Press.

054.1 320 FR ISSN 0026-9360
LE MONDE. (Supplement avail.: Liber) 1950. w. 370 F. (effective Oct. 1990). Le Monde s.a.r.l., 15, rue Falguieres, 75501 Paris Cedex 15, France. TEL 40-65-25-25. FAX 40-65-25-99. TELEX 206 806F. Ed. Andre Fontaine. adv.; bk.rev.; circ. 23,524. (newspaper) Indexed: Key to Econ.Sci., Pt.de Rep. (1988-).

MONDE LIBERTAIRE. see POLITICAL SCIENCE

808.8 US
MONEY MAKING MAGIC.* 1980. bi-m. $12. Le Tono Publishing Co., 900 N.W. Mawcrest, No. 204, Gresham, OR 97030. TEL 503-666-5824. Ed. Leo B. Minton.

056.1 PE
MONOS Y MONADAS. 1981. fortn. Camana 615, Ofc. 104, Lima, Peru. Ed. Nicolas Yerovi. circ. 17,000.

954 II ISSN 0027-1543
MOTHER INDIA; review of culture. (Text in English) 1949. m. $16. Sri Aurobindo Ashram Trust, Pondicherry 605002, India. Ed. K.D. Sethna. adv.; bk.rev.; circ. 1,500.

370 US ISSN 0362-8841
AP2
MOTHER JONES. 1976. 6/yr. $18 (foreign $28)(effective Jan. 1992). Foundation for National Progress, 1663 Mission St., 2nd Fl., San Francisco, CA 94103. TEL 415-558-8881. FAX 415-863-5136. (Subscr. to: Box 2606, Boulder, CO 80322) Ed. Douglas Foster. adv.; bk.rev.; circ. 110,000. (also avail. in microform from UMI; magnetic tape; reprint service avail. from UMI, IAC; back issues avail.) Indexed: Abstr.Pop.Cult., Acad.Ind., Access, Alt.Press Ind., Bk.Rev.Ind. (1988-), Chic.Per.Ind., Child.Bk.Rev.Ind. (1988-), Curr.Lit.Fam.Plan., Energy Info.Abstr., Environ.Abstr., Fut.Surv., Left Ind. (1982-), Mag.Ind., Media Rev.Dig., New Per.Ind., P.A.I.S., PMR, Pop.Per.Ind., PSI, Wom.Stud.Abstr.
Description: Progressive periodical featuring cultural reviews, news of current controversies, and high quality investigative reporting.

800 US
MOUNTAIN CALL; for the mountains, their people, their culture. 1973. m. $6 to individuals; institutions $10. Mountain Call, Inc., Box 611, Kermit, WV 25674. Ed.Bd. adv.; bk.rev.; charts; illus.; tr.lit.

808.8 US
MSS. (Manuscripts) 1981. 3/yr. $10 to individuals; institutions $15. State University of New York at Binghamton, Binghamton, NY 13901. TEL 607-777-2404. Ed. L.M. Rosenberg. illus.; circ. 1,000.

028.5 II ISSN 0027-3104
MUKTA. 1961. fortn. Rs.225. Delhi Press Patra Prakashan Ltd., Delhi Press Bldg., E-3 Jhandewala Estate, New Delhi 110 055, India. Ed. Vishwa Nath. adv.; bk.rev.; film rev.; illus.; circ. 45,000.
Description: Contains fiction and self-improvement articles for youth.

055.1 IT ISSN 0027-3120
AP37
MULINO; rivista trimestrale di cultura e politica. 1951. bi-m. L.110000. Societa Editrice Il Mulino, Strada Maggiore, 37, 40125 Bologna, Italy. TEL 051-256011. FAX 051-256034. Ed. Giovanni Evangelisti. adv.; bk.rev.; index, cum.index: 1951-1981; circ. 9,000. (tabloid format; back issues avail.) Indexed: CERDIC, Lang.& Lang.Behav.Abstr.

327 AG ISSN 0027-3333
MUNDO NUEVO.* 1966. m. Arg.$6($8.) Instituto Latinoamericano de Relacionas Internacionales, Montevideo 666, Of. 101, Buenos Aires, Argentina. (Alternate address: Horacio Daniel Rodriguez, Montevideo 666, Of. 101, Buenos Aires, Argentina) Ed. Horacio Daniel Rodriguez. adv.; bk.rev.; bibl.; cum.index; circ. 10,000.

052 AT
MURRAY PIONEER. 1892. s-w. Aus.$80. Murray Pioneer Pty. Ltd., Box 832, Renmark, S.A. 5341, Australia. FAX 085-865638. Ed. Peter G. Read. adv.; circ. 6,915. (back issues avail.)

808.8 US
MUSCADINE; a seniors' literary magazine. 1977. bi-m. $6. Boulder Senior Citizens Center, c/o Lucille Cyphers, 1940 Walnut St., No. 418, Boulder, CO 80302-4459. TEL 303-443-9748. Ed. Milanda Janborn. circ. 400.

MUSIC TEACHERS LIBRARY. see MUSIC

MUSLIM WORLD; a journal devoted to the study of Islam and of Christian-Muslim relationships past and present. see RELIGIONS AND THEOLOGY — Islamic

MWENDO. see LITERATURE

057.85 UK ISSN 0027-5581
MYSL POLSKA/POLISH THOUGHT; dwutygodnik poswiecony zyciu i kulturze narodu. (Text in Polish) 1942. fortn. $30. Trustees of the Polish National Democratic Party, 8 Alma Terrace, Allen St., London W8 6QY, England. TEL 937-1797. Ed. A. Dargas. adv.; bk.rev.; play rev.; circ. 2,000.

053 GW
N H Z. (Neue Hanauer Zeitung); Regionalmagazin Main Kinzig Osthessen. 1982. 8/yr. DM.24. Verlag am Freiheitsplatz, Am Freiheitsplatz, 6450 Hanau 1, Germany. TEL 06181-28180. adv.; bk.rev.; circ. 1,200. (back issues avail.)

NAPJAINK. see LITERATURE

057.8 CI ISSN 0027-7975
NARODNI LIST. 1862. w. $50. Narodni List, Lenjinovo Setaliste 4, Zadar, Croatia. Ed. Danijel Vucenovic. adv.; bk.rev.; circ. 8,500.

057.8 BN ISSN 0027-8106
NAS SVIJET. 1965. m. 40 din.($3) Matica Iseljenika Bosne i Hercegovine, Omladinska 5, Sarajevo, Bosnia Hercegovina. Ed. Petar Alfirevic. adv.

320.9 051 US ISSN 0027-8378
AP2
NATION. 1865. w. (except the first week in Jan.; bi-w in July & Aug.). $44. Nation Company, Inc., 72 Fifth Ave., New York, NY 10011. TEL 212-242-8400. FAX 212-463-9712. (Subscr. to: Box 10763, Des Moines, IA 50340-0763) Ed. Victor Navasky. adv.; bk.rev.; film rev.; music rev.; play rev.; index every 6 mos.; circ. 95,000. (also avail. in microfilm from UMI; back issues avail.; reprint service avail. from UMI) Indexed: Acad.Ind., Alt.Press Ind., Amer.Bibl Slavic & E.Eur.Stud., Bk.Rev.Dig., Bk.Rev.Ind. (1965-), Chic.Per.Ind., Child.Bk.Rev.Ind. (1965-), Energy Rev., Film Lit.Ind. (1973-), Fut.Surv., Hlth.Ind., HR Rep., Mag.Ind., Media Rev.Dig., Mid.East: Abstr.& Ind., P.A.I.S., R.G., SSCI.
—BLDSC shelfmark: 6015.675000.

338 GW ISSN 0027-8408
D1050
NATION EUROPA; Monatsschrift im Dienst der europaeischen Erneuerung. 1951. m. DM.100. Nation Europa Verlag GmbH, Postfach 2554, 8630 Coburg, Germany. TEL 09561-94596. FAX 09561-99574. adv.; bk.rev.; illus.; maps; index; circ. 7,500.

052 AT ISSN 0156-8221
NATION REVIEW. 1958. m. Aus.$15. General Magazine Company (Australia) Pty. Ltd., P.O. Box 1024, Richmonth North, Vic. 3121, Australia. TEL 03-429-5599. FAX 03-427-0332. Ed. Geoffey M. Gold. bk.rev.; film rev.; play rev.; circ. 46,000. (tabloid format) Indexed: Aus.P.A.I.S.
Formerly: Nation (ISSN 0027-836X)
Description: Covers national current affairs and arts criticism.

808.87 US ISSN 0027-9587
AP2
NATIONAL LAMPOON; the humor magazine for adults. 1970. bi-m. $13.95. J 2 Communications - National Lampoon, 10850 Wilshire Blvd., Ste. 1000, Los Angeles, CA 90024. TEL 310-474-5252. circ. 250,000. (also avail. in microfiche from UMI,KTO)
Description: Contains political and social satire.

059 II 0300-3809
NATUN THIKANA. 1972. q. 71-4 Dr. Nilmani Sarkar St., Calcutta 50, India. Eds. Premanshu Bardhan, Anil De. bk.rev.; film rev.; play rev.; circ. controlled.

800 CY
NEA EPOCHI/NEW EPOCH. (Text in Greek) 1959. bi-m. POB 1581, Nicosia, Cyprus. Ed. Achilleas Pyliotis. circ. 1,500.
Description: Greek-Cypriot literary review.

NEA HESTIA. see LITERATURE

808.87 SZ ISSN 0028-1786
NEBELSPALTER; die satirische schweizer Zeitschrift. 1875. w. 112 SFr. (foreign 128 SFr.). E. Loepfe-Benz AG, CH-9400 Rorschach, Switzerland. TEL 071-414341. FAX 071-414313. Ed.Bd. adv. contact: Benno Caviezel. bk.rev.; illus.; circ. 41,216.

054 CI
NEDELJNA DALMACIJA. 1971. w. 144 din. Slobodna Dalmacija, Splitskog odreda 4, Split, Croatia. Ed. Miro Jajcanin.

053 NE ISSN 0166-0586
HET NEDERLANDSE BOEK. 1852. 6/yr. fl.15. Het Nederlandse Boek, Prinsengracht 1065, 1017 JG Amsterdam, Netherlands. TEL 020-233187. Ed. Wim J. Simons. adv.; bk.rev.; circ. 20,000.

808 US ISSN 0277-5166
NEGATIVE CAPABILITY. 1981. 3/yr. $12 to individuals; institutions $16. Negative Capability Press, 62 Ridgelawn Dr. E., Mobile, AL 36608-2465. Ed. Sue Brannan Walker. adv.; bk.rev.; circ. 1,000. Indexed: Ind.Amer.Per.Verse.

800 US
NEIHARDT FOUNDATION NEWSLETTER. 1970. 2/yr. $10 membership. John G. Neihardt Foundation, Inc., Bancroft, NE 68004. TEL 402-648-7971. Eds. Lori Utechtm, Hilda Neihardt. bk.rev.; circ. 350.

057.1 BW ISSN 0130-7517
NEMAN. (Text in Russian) 1952. m. 9.60 Rub. (Sayuz Pismennikaw Belarusskai S.S.R. - Soyuz Pisatelei Belorusskoi S.S.R.) Izdatel'stvo Polymya, Ul. Zakharova 19, Minsk, Byelarus. TEL 33-1072. Ed. A.P. Kudravets. circ. 90,000.

320 GW ISSN 0028-2626
NEMZETOR. German edition: Donau Bote. (Text in Hungarian) 1956. m.(Hungarian); bi-m.(others). price varies. Foerderer Verein "Nemzetor", Ferchenbach Str. 88, 8000 Munich 50, Germany. FAX 089-3615610. Ed. Tibor Kecskesi-Tollas. adv.; bk.rev.; bibl.; charts; film rev.; illus.; circ. 7,000 (Hungarian ed.); 3,000 (German ed.).

800 700 AA ISSN 0548-1600
NENTORI; revue litteraire et artistique. 1954. m. $20. Lidhja e Shkrimtareve dhe e Artisteve te Shqiperise - Union des Exrivains et Artistes d'Albanie, Baboci 37z, Tirana, Albania. Ed. Kico Blushi.

057 CS
NEPMUVELES. (Text in Hungarian) m. $18. (Cultural Institute in Bratislava) Obzor, Ceskoslovenskej Armady 35, 815 85 Bratislava, Czechoslovakia.

051 AU
NEUE ORDNUNG. 1949. m. S.220. Wappenverlag, Postfach 256, A-1015-Vienna, Austria. Ed. Franz Frank. adv.; circ. 4,500. Indexed: CERDIC.

LITERARY AND POLITICAL REVIEWS

053.1 GW ISSN 0028-3347
AP30
NEUE RUNDSCHAU. 1890. q. DM.15. S. Fischer Verlag GmbH, Hedderichtstr. 114, Postfach 700335, 6000 Frankfurt a.M. 70, Germany. FAX 069-6062-319. TELEX 412410. Eds. Guenther Busch, Uwe Wittstock. adv.; bk.rev.; bibl.; index; circ. 7,000. (also avail. in microfilm from BHP) **Indexed:** Arts & Hum.Cit.Ind., Curr.Cont., M.L.A.
—BLDSC shelfmark: 6077.740000.
 Description: Literary and political essays.

NEUE SAMMLUNG; Vierteljahres-Zeitschrift fuer Erziehung und Gesellschaft. see *EDUCATION*

053 GW
NEUE SOLIDARITAET; internationale Wochenzeitung fuer Politik Wirtschaft, Wissenschaft und Kunst. 1973. w. DM.100. Dr. Boettiger Verlags GmbH, Dotzheimerstr. 166, 6200 Wiesbaden, Germany. TEL 06121-806955. Ed. Gabriele Liebig. circ. 20,000.

053 GW ISSN 0138-5011
NEUE ZEIT. 1945. d. DM.4 for one month. (Christlich-Demokratischen Union Deutschlands) Verlag Neue Zeit, Mittelstr. 2-4, 1086 Berlin, Germany. TELEX 112536. Ed. Dieter Eberle. (also avail. in microfilm from BHP,KTO)

057.1 RU ISSN 0028-4009
NEVA. 1955. m. 24 Rub. Sankt Piterburgskii Soyuz Pisatelei, Nevskii pr. 3, 20, 191065 St. Petersburg, Russia. TEL (812) 312-65-37. (Subscr. to: Mezhdunarodnaya Kniga, Moscow, G-200, Russia) Ed. B. Nikol'skii. bk.rev.; film rev.; play rev.; bibl.; charts; illus.; circ. 292,000. (also avail. in microfilm from MIM) **Indexed:** Curr.Dig.Sov.Press, M.L.A.

808.8 US ISSN 1040-4392
NEW BLOOD. 1986. q. $13 (foreign $25). c/o Chris Lacher, Ed., 540 W. Foothill Blvd., Ste. 3730, Glendora, CA 91740. adv.; bk.rev.; film rev.; illus.; circ. 20,000. (back issues avail.)
 Description: Features horror fiction considered too strong for other periodicals.

051 CN
NEW BREED. 1970. m. Can.$24. Native Communications (Wehtamatowin) Co., 173 Second Ave., S., 3rd Fl., Saskatoon, Sask. S7K 1K6, Canada. TEL 306-653-2253. FAX 306-653-3384. Ed. Gary Laplante. adv.; bk.rev.; circ. 10,000. (tabloid format; back issues avail.)

NEW CANADIAN REVIEW. see *LITERATURE*

808.8 US ISSN 0734-0222
NX503
NEW CRITERION. 1982. m. (10/yr.). $36 (effective Sep. 1991). Foundation for Cultural Review, 850 Seventh Ave., New York, NY 10019. TEL 212-247-6980. Ed. Hilton Kramer. adv.; bk.rev.; circ. 12,000. (also avail. in microform from UMI) **Indexed:** Amer.Hum.Ind., Artbibl.Mod., M.L.A., RILA.
—BLDSC shelfmark: 6082.993000.

800 US ISSN 1050-415X
NEW DELTA REVIEW. s-a. $7. English Department, Louisiana State University, Baton Rouge, LA 70803-5001. TEL 504-388-4079. Ed. Janet Wondra. adv.; bk.rev.; circ. 500. (back issues avail.)
 Description: Features fiction and poetry of rising writers, essays and interviews.

808.8 792 US ISSN 0893-8563
NEW DOG. 1986. s-a. $7. A.W. Baker Publishing Company, Inc., 605 W. Poplar Rd., Sterling, VA 22170. (Subscr. to: 3138 N. Southport, 2R, Chicago, IL 60657) Ed. Scott Baker. circ. 1,000. (back issues avail.)

NEW ENGLAND QUARTERLY; a historical review of New England life and letters. see *LITERATURE*

051 UK ISSN 0950-2378
NEW FORMATIONS. 1987. 3/yr. £22($42) to individuals; institutions £38.50($63). Routledge, 11 New Fetter Lane, London EC4P 4EE, England. TEL 01-583 9855. Ed. James Donald. adv.; bk.rev.; circ. 500. **Indexed:** Hist.Abstr. (until 1991).
—BLDSC shelfmark: 6084:189000.
 Description: Tackles questions of culture, politics and ideology both through the critical analysis of cultural practices, products and institutions and also by questioning the assumptions of contemporary theory. Engages in a variety of debates: about meaning and power, sexual and cultural difference, modernity and post-modernism, psychoanalysis and post-structuralism, democracy and civil society, aesthetics and style.

NEW HOPE INTERNATIONAL REVIEW. see *LITERATURE — Poetry*

943.9 808.8 HU ISSN 0028-5390
DB901
NEW HUNGARIAN QUARTERLY. (Text in English) 1960. q. 900 Ft.($24) to individuals; institutions $35. Magyar Tavirati Iroda, Kiado Hivatel - Hungarian News Agency, Publishing Office, Pl. Naphegy No.7-8, 1016 Budapest, Hungary. TEL 175-6722. FAX 118-8291. (Co-sponsor: Ministry of Culture) Ed. Miklos Vajda. adv.; bk.rev.; film rev.; play rev.; illus.; circ. 3,500. **Indexed:** Amer.Hist.& Life, Arts & Hum.Cit.Ind., Curr.Cont., Hist.Abstr., IBR, Int.Polit.Sci.Abstr., Key to Econ.Sci., M.L.A., Mid.East: Abstr.& Ind., Music Ind., Rural Recreat.Tour.Abstr., World Agri.Econ.& Rural Sociol.Abstr.
—BLDSC shelfmark: 6084.248000.
 Description: Includes modern prose and poetry as well as articles on literature, history, sociology, economics, current affairs, the arts, and other aspects of Hungarian life.

051 US
NEW INDICATOR. 1966. bi-w. $8. University of California, San Diego, New Indicator Collective, Student Center B-023, La Jolla, CA 92093. TEL 619-534-2016. Ed.Bd. adv.; bk.rev.; circ. 8,500. (tabloid format)

320.5 UK ISSN 0028-6060
HX3
NEW LEFT REVIEW. 1960. 6/yr. $35 to individuals; institutions $64. New Left Review Ltd., 6 Meard St., London W1V 3HR, England. TEL 071-734-8830. FAX 071-734-0059. Ed. Robin Blackburn. adv.; bk.rev.; circ. 16,000. (also avail. in microfiche) **Indexed:** Alt.Press Ind., Amer.Hist.& Life, ASSIA, Br.Hum.Ind., Hist.Abstr., Left Ind. (1982-), Mid.East: Abstr.& Ind., P.A.I.S., Soc.Sci.Ind., SSCI, Stud.Wom.Abstr., World Agri.Econ.& Rural Sociol.Abstr.
—BLDSC shelfmark: 6084.450000.

320.5 800 CN ISSN 0702-7532
NEW LITERATURE AND IDEOLOGY. French edition: Nouvelle Litterature et Ideologie (ISSN 0703-8011) 1969. irreg. Can.$6 for 4 nos. Canadian Cultural Workers Committee, Box 727, Adelaide Station, Toronto, Ont. M5C 2J8, Canada. (Subscr. to: National Publications Centre, Box 727, Adelaide Station, Toronto, Ont., Canada) bk.rev.; circ. 5,000. **Indexed:** Abstr.Engl.Stud., Mid.East: Abstr.& Ind.
 Incorporates: Literature and Ideology (ISSN 0024-4740)

052 CN
NEW MARITIMES; an independent, regional bi-monthly. (Text in English) 1982. 6/yr. Can.$17($25) New Maritimes Editorial Council Society, 6106 Lawrence St., Halifax, N.S. B3L 1J6, Canada. TEL 902-425-6622. Ed. Scott Milsom. adv.; bk.rev.; charts; illus.; circ. 1,400. (also avail. in microfilm from MML; back issues avail.) **Indexed:** Alt. Press Ind., Can.Per.Ind., CMI.
●Also available online.

320 US ISSN 0890-1619
NEW OPTIONS; new values, new politics. 1984. 11/yr. $25. New Options, Inc., Box 19324, Washington, DC 20036. TEL 202-745-7460. Ed. Mark Satin. bk.rev.; circ. 12,000. (looseleaf format; also avail. in microform from UMI; back issues avail.)
 Description: Investigates new ideas beyond those of the traditional left and right. Each issue reinterprets national and international news, and looks critically at "social change groups." Includes a forum section in which readers debate "post-liberal" and "post-socialist" ideas.

808.8 II ISSN 0258-0381
AP8
NEW QUEST. (Text in English) 1977. 6/yr. to individuals; institutions Rs.40 (foreign $10). Indian Association for Cultural Freedom, Aboli, 850-8A Shivajinagar, Poona 411 004, India. TEL 55744. Eds. M.P. Rege, M.V. Namjoshi. adv.; bk.rev.; circ. 1,500. **Indexed:** C.I.J.E., Lang.& Lang.Behav.Abstr., M.L.A.
 Supersedes: Quest.
 Description: Aims to promote a free exchange of ideas and contribute to the development of a free culture in India regardless of caste, creed, or sex through creative writing and criticism.

320.9 051 US ISSN 0028-6583
AP2
NEW REPUBLIC; a journal of opinion. 1914. w. (48/yr. in 2 vols.). $69.97 (effective 1992). 1220 19th St., N.W., Washington, DC 20036. TEL 202-331-7494. FAX 202-331-0275. (Subscr. to: Box 56515, Boulder, CO 80322. TEL 800-274-6686) Ed.Bd. adv.; bk.rev.; film rev.; music rev.; play rev.; s-a. index; circ. 95,000. (also avail. in microform from BLH,UMI; reprint service avail. from UMI) **Indexed:** Acad.Ind., Amer.Hist.& Life, Biog.Ind., Bk.Rev.Dig., Bk.Rev.Ind. (1965-), Chic.Per.Ind., Child.Bk.Rev.Ind. (1965-), Environ.Abstr., Film Lit.Ind. (1973-), Fut.Surv., Hist.Abstr., Hlth.Ind., HR Rep., Lang.& Lang.Behav.Abstr., Mag.Ind., Media Rev.Dig., Mid.East: Abstr.& Ind., Pers.Lit., PMR, R.G., SSCI, Tel.Abstr., Telegen, TOM.
●Also available online. Vendor(s): DIALOG.
—BLDSC shelfmark: 6087.740000.

800 910.03 US
NEW SENSE; the literary quarterly of African American students. 1974. s-a. membership. Northwestern University, African American Students, 1914 Sheridan Rd., Evanston, IL 60201. TEL 312-492-3741. Ed. Paula Edwards. bk.rev.; play rev.; film rev.; illus.; circ. 1,000. (looseleaf format)

320.9 052 UK ISSN 0954-2361
AP4 CODEN: NESSEF
NEW STATESMAN & SOCIETY; an independent political and literary review. 1913. w. $120. Statesman and Nation Publishing Co., Foundation House, Perseverance Works, 38 Kingsland Road, London E2 8DQ, England. TEL 071-739-3211. FAX 071-739-9307. TELEX 28449. Ed. Steve Platt. adv.; bk.rev.; film rev.; play rev.; record rev.; index every 6 mos.; circ. 39,874. (also avail. in microform from UMI; back issues avail.) **Indexed:** Abstr.Engl.Stud., Acad.Ind., ASSIA, Bk.Rev.Dig., Bk.Rev.Ind. (1965-), Br.Hum.Ind., Child.Bk.Rev.Ind. (1965-), Film Lit.Ind. (1973-), Gdlns., High.Educ.Curr.Aware.Bull., Hlth.Ind., HRIS, Key to Econ.Sci., Mag.Ind., Media Rev.Dig., Mid.East: Abstr.& Ind., PSI, Soc.Sci.Ind., Stud.Wom.Abstr.
—BLDSC shelfmark: 6088.760500.
 Formed by the 1988 merger of: New Statesman (ISSN 0028-6842); (1962-1988): New Society (ISSN 0028-6729)

051 US
NEW STUDIES ON THE LEFT. 1973. q. $10 to individuals; institutions $20. Saxifrage Publications Group, 1484 Wicklow St., Boulder, CO 80303. Ed. Ward Churchill. adv.; bk.rev.; bibl.; circ. 1,000. (also avail. in microform from UMI; reprint service avail. from UMI) **Indexed:** Alt.Press Ind., Psychol.Abstr.
 Formerly: Issues in Radical Therapy; **Supersedes:** State and Mind (ISSN 0161-1089) & Issues in Cooperation and Power; Former titles (until 1981): Issues in Radical Therapy and Cooperative Power; Issues in Radical Therapy. R T, A Journal of Radical Therapy; Rough Times; Radical Therapist.

051 US ISSN 0273-9836
NEW TIMES WEEKLY.* 1970. w. $8. New Times, Inc. (Phoenix), Box 2510, Phoenix, AZ 85002. TEL 602-271-0040. Ed. Michael Lacey. adv.; bk.rev.; film rev.; play rev.; illus.; circ. 40,000. (tabloid format; also avail. in microform from UMI; reprint service avail. from UMI)
 Former titles: New Times (Phoenix) (ISSN 0047-9942) & Arizona Times.

LITERARY AND POLITICAL REVIEWS

052 UK ISSN 0954-2116
NEW WELSH REVIEW. 1988. q. £15. Welsh Academy and University of Wales, Association for the Study of Welsh Writing in English, c/o Robin Reeves, Ed., 49 Park Place, Cardiff CF1 4AH, Wales. TEL 0222-665529. adv.; bk.rev.; film rev.; circ. 1,400. (back issues avail.) Indexed: M.L.A.
—BLDSC shelfmark: 6089.194300.
Description: Covers poetry, prose, literary criticism, with special emphasis on Welsh literature.

NEW YORK MAGAZINE. see *GENERAL INTEREST PERIODICALS — United States*

NEW YORK REVIEW OF BOOKS. see *PUBLISHING AND BOOK TRADE*

810 700 US ISSN 0028-792X
AP2
THE NEW YORKER. 1925. w. $32. New Yorker Magazine, Inc., 20 W. 43rd St., New York, NY 10036-7440. TEL 212-840-3800. adv.; bk.rev.; film rev.; music rev.; play rev.; illus.; circ. 615,260. (also avail. in microform from UMI) Indexed: A.I.P.P., Abstr.Engl.Stud., Acad.Ind., Bk.Rev.Dig., Bk.Rev.Ind. (1965-), Chic.Per.Ind., Child.Bk.Rev.Ind. (1965-), Deep Sea Res.& Oceanogr.Abstr., Film Lit.Ind. (1973-), GeoRef., Ind.Bk.Rev.Hum., Mag.Ind., Media Rev.Dig., Music Ind., PMR, R.G., RILA, TOM.
—BLDSC shelfmark: 6089.821000.
Description: Contains fiction, poetry, cartoons, longer articles and profiles for readers interested in cultural issues.

NEWEST REVIEW; a journal of culture and current events in the West. see *PUBLISHING AND BOOK TRADE*

808.8 GW ISSN 0720-6542
NIESPULVER. 1967. irreg. DM.2.50. Satire-Verlag, P.O. Box 210 207, 3000 Hannover, Germany. Ed. Hans Firzlaff. adv.; bk.rev.; illus.; circ. 20,000.
Former titles: Hannover Extra; Satire (Magazine); Steintor.

800 NR
NIGERIA. WORK IN PROGRESS. (Text in English) 1972. a. £N15. Ahmadu Bello University, Department of English, Zaria, Nigeria. Ed.Bd. adv.; bk.rev.; circ. 500.

NIGHTSUN; a journal of poetry, fiction, and interviews. see *LITERATURE*

059.91 US ISSN 0029-1161
NOR OR. (Text in Armenian) vol.48, 1970. s-w. $30. (Armenian Democratic Liberal Organization) Nor Or Publishing Co., 1901 N. Allen Ave., Altadena, CA 91001-3421. FAX 818-797-3050. Ed. Sarkis Minassian. adv.; bk.rev.; illus.; circ. 2,000.

055.1 IT
NORD;* settimanale indipendente d'informazione. 1964. w. L.5000. Gianni Cerutti, Ed. & Pub., Via Gen. G. Fara 5, 28100 Novara, Italy. adv.; bk.rev.; film rev.; play rev.; illus.; circ. 15,000. (looseleaf format)

056.1 AG ISSN 0029-1242
NORDESTE. 1960. irreg. Universidad Nacional del Nordeste, Facultad de Humanidades, Av. Las Heras 727, Corrientes, Resistencia, Argentina. Ed.Bd. bk.rev.; charts; illus.; circ. 2,400.

053 GW ISSN 0029-1196
NORDFRIESLAND (BREDSTEDT); Kultur, Politik, Wirtschaft. (Text in German and Frisian) 1965. q. DM.16. Nordfriisk Instituut, Süderstr. 30, 2257 Bredstedt, Germany. TEL 04671-2081. FAX 04671-1333. adv.; bk.rev.; bibl.; charts; illus.; index; circ. 1,200.

058 DK ISSN 0109-3967
NORDICA; tidsskrift for nordisk teksthistorie og aestetik. (Text in Danish, Norwegian and Swedish) 1984. a. DKK 100. Odense Universitet, Nordisk Institut) Odense University Press, Campusvej 55, DK-5230 Odense M, Denmark. TEL 66-157999.

058 SW ISSN 0029-1501
AP48
NORDISK TIDSKRIFT FOR VETENSKAP, KONST OCH INDUSTRI. (Text in Danish, Norwegian and Swedish) 1878. 6/yr. SEK 150. Letterstedtska Foereningen Nordisk Tidskrift, P.O. Box 34037, S-100 26 Stockholm, Sweden. TEL 08-6567570. FAX 08-6567570. Ed. Claes Wiklund. bk.rev.; illus.; index, cum.index: 1925-1974, 1975-1984; circ. 2,750.

058.82 NO ISSN 0029-1846
DL401
NORSEMAN; a review of current events. (Text in English and Norwegian) 1943. 6/yr. NOK 200($30) Nordmanns-Forbundet - Norsemen's Federation, Raadhusgt. 23 B, 0158 Oslo 1, Norway. TEL 47-2-333226. FAX 47-2-333226. Ed. Johan F. Heyerdahl. adv.; bk.rev.; illus.; index; circ. 15,000.
Incorporates: Nordmanns-Forbundet.

051 US ISSN 0029-2397
AP2
NORTH AMERICAN REVIEW. 1815. bi-m. $18 (effective 1992). c/o Robley Wilson, Ed., University of Northern Iowa, Cedar Falls, IA 50614. TEL 319-273-6455. FAX 319-273-3509. adv.; bk.rev.; illus.; index; circ. 4,700. (also avail. in microform from UMI; reprint service avail. from UMI) Indexed: A.I.P.P., Arts & Hum.Cit.Ind., Bibl.Engl.Lang.& Lit., Bk.Rev.Ind. (1976-), Child.Bk.Rev.Ind. (1976-), Curr.Cont., Hum.Ind., Ind.Little Mag.
—BLDSC shelfmark: 6148.250000.

052 UK ISSN 0265-7295
NORTH WIND. 1982. a. £6($15) George MacDonald Society, The Library, King's College, Strand, London WC2R 2LS, England. FAX 071-872-0207. (Subscr. to: c/o R. Johnson, 97 Hykeham Rd., Lincoln LN6 8AD, England) Ed. W. Raeper. adv.; bk.rev.; circ. 100.

808.8 811 US ISSN 0899-708X
NORTHLAND QUARTERLY.* 1988. q. $20. Northland Press (Mesa), 600 S. Dobson Rd., No. 196, Mesa, AZ 85202-1823. Ed. Jody Wallace. adv.; bk.rev.; film rev.; circ. 750. (back issues avail.)

054.1 FR ISSN 0048-0967
AP20
NOUVELLE ECOLE. 1968. q. 240 F. (students 200 F.). Editions du Labyrinthe, 41 rue Barrault, 75013 Paris, France. Ed. Alain de Benoist. adv.; bk.rev.; bibl.; charts; illus.; circ. 10,000.
—BLDSC shelfmark: 6176.770000.

971 CN ISSN 0029-4756
NOUVELLE FRANCE;* revue du Canada francais. 1957. q. Can.$4. Associes de Neuve-France, 6463 St. Dominique, Montreal, Que., Canada. Ed. Dir. Henri Alain. adv. (also avail. in microfiche from BHP)

054.1 FR ISSN 0029-4802
NOUVELLE REVUE FRANCAISE. 1953. m. 450 F. Editions Gallimard, 5 rue Sebastien-Bottin, 75007 Paris, France. TEL 33-1-46-59-89-00. TELEX 204 121. Ed. Jacques Redad. bk.rev. (reprint service avail. from KTO) Indexed: Arts & Hum.Cit.Ind., Curr.Cont., Ind.Bk.Rev.Hum., M.L.A.
—BLDSC shelfmark: 6176.798000.

NOUVELLE TOUR DE FEU; revue de creation poetique. see *LITERATURE — Poetry*

057 CI ISSN 0353-8052
DR301
NOVA MATICA. (Text in Croatian and English) 1951. m. 900 din.($30) Hrvatska Matica Iseljenika, Trnjanska bb, Zagreb, Croatia. TEL 530-002. FAX 38-41-539-111. TELEX MIH YU 22499. Ed. Boris Maruna. adv.; bk.rev.; circ. 7,500.
Formerly: Matica (ISSN 0025-5920)
Description: Devoted to preserving Croatian culture for emigrants all over the world.

053.1 SZ
AP30
NOVALIS; Zeitschrift fuer europaeisches Denken. 1946. m. 81 SFr. Verlag die Kommenden AG, Steigstr. 59, CH-8201 Schauffhausen, Switzerland. TEL 053-250023. FAX 053-833404. adv.; bk.rev.; illus.; index; circ. 10,000.
Formerly: Die Kommenden (ISSN 0023-3005)

NOVAYA GAZETA. see *CHILDREN AND YOUTH — For*

057 CS
NOVE SLOVO. w. (Communist Party of Slovakia, Central Committee) Pravda, Volgogradska 8, 893 39 Bratislava, Czechoslovakia.

057.1 RU ISSN 0029-5329
NOVYI MIR; literaturno-khudozhestvennyi i obshchestvenno-politicheski zhurnal. 1925. m. 30 Rub. (Soyuz Pisatelei S.S.S.R.) Izdatel'stvo Izvestiya, Pl. Pushkina, 5, 103798 Moscow, Russia. Ed. Sergei Narovchatov. bk.rev.; bibl.; index; circ. 160,000. (also avail. in microform from MIM,UMI; microfilm from KTO; reprint service avail. from UMI) Indexed: Arts & Hum.Cit.Ind., Curr.Cont., Curr.Dig.Sov.Press, Lang.& Lang.Behav.Abstr., M.L.A.

NOVYI ZHURNAL/NEW REVIEW. see *ETHNIC INTERESTS*

056.1 AG ISSN 0325-4453
NUDOS EN LA CULTURA ARGENTINA. 1977-1985 (no.15); resumed. 3/yr. $30. Parana 63, 1erpiso, 1017 Buenos Aires, Argentina. TEL 38-3313. Ed. Jorge Reinaldo Brega. adv.; bk.rev.; circ. 3,000.
Supersedes (since 1978): Posta de Arte y Literatura.

056.1 SP ISSN 0029-5795
NUESTRO TIEMPO; revista mensual de cuestiones actuales. 1954. m. 6000 ptas.($70) Servicio de Publicaciones de la Universidad de Navarra, S.A., Apdo. 177, 31080 Pamplona, Spain. TEL 94 25 2700. Ed. Juan Antonio Giner Junquera. adv.; bk.rev.; bibl.; s-a. index; circ. 10,000. Indexed: Hist.Abstr.
—BLDSC shelfmark: 6184.320000.

860 PH
NUEVA HORIZONTE.* (Text in Spanish) w. P.0.30 per no. Sociedad de Escritores Hispano-Filipinos, Herald Building, 61 Muralla, Intramuros, Manila, Philippines. Ed. Francisco C. Palisoc. adv.; illus. (tabloid format)

NUIT BLANCHE; l'actualite du livre. see *LITERATURE*

808.8 055 IT
NUOVA ANTOLOGIA. 1866. q. L.95000($95) (effective 1992). Fondazione Spadolini Nuova Antologia, Via A. Meucci 6, 50015 Grassina, Florence, Italy. adv.; bk.rev.; circ. 8,000. Indexed: Abstr.Engl.Stud., Hist.Abstr., RILA.

055.1 IT ISSN 0029-6201
NUOVA RASSEGNA; periodico di attualita-lettere-arti-cinema-teatro. vol.5, 1970. bi-m. L.40000. Editrice Pellegrini, Via Roma 74, Casella Postale 158, 87100 Consenza, Italy. Ed. Luigi Pellegrini-Cosenza. adv.; bk.rev.; film rev.; play rev.; charts; illus.

055.1 IT
NUOVA RIVISTA EUROPEA. 1977. bi-m. L.40000. Editrice Rapporti Europei s.r.l., Via Dietro le Mura B, No. 11, 38100 Trento, Italy. Ed. Giancarlo Vigorelli. bk.rev.

NUOVA RIVISTA INTERNAZIONALE/NEW INTERNATIONAL REVIEW; problemi della pace e del socialismo. see *POLITICAL SCIENCE — International Relations*

055.1 IT ISSN 0029-6295
AP37
NUOVI ARGOMENTI. 1953. q. L.48000 (foreign L.55200). Arnoldo Mondadori Editore S.p.A., Via Sicilia, 137, 00187 Rome, Italy. TEL 06-47497376. Ed.Bd. adv.; bk.rev.; index; circ. 2,046. Indexed: M.L.A.

055.1 IT
NUOVI ORIENTAMENTI. 1974. 6/yr. L.12000. Editrice Nuovi Orientamenti, Via B. Tricarico 11, 13014 Gallipoli, Italy. Ed. Luigi Carlo Fontana. illus.; circ. 1,500.

055.1 IT ISSN 0029-6309
NUOVO AGORA OMAGGIO.* vol.3, 1967. q. L.1500. Villa Benia Rapallo, Genoa, Italy. Ed. Vincenzo Mastrangeli. adv.; bk.rev.; charts; illus.

059.94 FI ISSN 0027-7126
NYA ARGUS.* 1908. 20/yr. Fmk.17. Postbox 100, 00251 Helsinki 25, Finland. Eds. Nils-Borje Stormbom, Jerker A. Eriksson.

LITERARY AND POLITICAL REVIEWS

370   CU   ISSN 0029-6961
LA543.7
O C L A E REVISTA. 1967. m. $20 in N. America; S. America $26; Europe $29; elsewhere $41. (Organizacion Continental Latino Americana de Estudiantes - Latin American Continental Students Organization) Ediciones Cubanas, Obispo No. 527, Apdo. 605, Havana, Cuba. Ed. Carlos Font Fernandez. charts; illus.; circ. 10,000.

056   UY
O DOS. bi-m. $8. c/o N.N. Arganarz, Ed., Miguelete 1669, Montevideo, Uruguay.

OBEROESTERREICH; Kulturzeitschrift. see *ART*

057.8   XV   ISSN 0029-7860
OBZORNIK; mesecna ljudska revija Presernove druzbe. (Text in Slovenian) 1953. m. $25. Presernova Druzba, Opekarska 4a, 61000 Ljubljana, Slovenia. TEL 061-218-909. Ed. Emil Cesar. adv.; bk.rev.; circ. 3,900. **Indexed:** GeoRef.

OCTOBER. see *ART*

057.8   BN   ISSN 0029-8387
ODJEK; revija za umjetnost nauku i drustvena pitanja. 1948. fortn. 400 din.($14.60) Kulturno-Prosvjetna Zajednica Bosne i Hercegovine, Otokara Kersovanija 13, Sarajevo, Bosnia Hercegovina. Ed. Cedo Kisic.

057.1   RU   ISSN 0030-0721
OGONEK. 1923. w. Bumazhny per. 14, 101456 Moscow, Russia. TEL 095-212-2337. FAX 095-943-0070. Ed. Lev Gushchin. adv.; charts; stat.; circ. 3,200,000. **Indexed:** Curr.Dig.Sov.Press.

700   US
EL OJITO. 1976. a. $3. New Mexico State University, Department of English, Box 3E, Las Cruces, NM 88003. TEL 505-646-3931. adv.; circ. 1,000. (back issues avail.)
Formerly (until 1987): Ojito Review.

057.1   RU   ISSN 0030-1957
OKTYABR'. 1924. m. 24 Rub. (Soyuz Pisatelei Rossiiskoi S.F.S.R.) Izdatel'stvo Pravda, Ul. Pravdy, 24, Moscow 125047, Russia. Ed. V. Kochetov. bk.rev.; index; circ. 195,000. (also avail. in microfilm from KTO) **Indexed:** Curr.Dig.Sov.Press.

052   AT   ISSN 0810-820X
ON THE BEACH. 1983. s-a. Aus.$8. 5-186 Glenmore Rd., Paddington, N.S.W. 2021, Australia. TEL 332 3548. Eds. Catherine Lumby, David Messer. adv.; cum.index; circ. 1,000. (back issues avail.) —BLDSC shelfmark: 6256.673000.
Description: Journal of contemporary arts, culture and philosophy.

056.1   PE   ISSN 0472-948X
ONDAS. 1959. m. Jose A. Valencia - Arenas, Apdo. 3758, Lima, Peru. circ. 5,000.

OPCION; revista de ciencias humanas y sociales. see *SOCIAL SCIENCES: COMPREHENSIVE WORKS*

055   IT
GLI ORATORI DEL GIORNO. 1927. bi-m. Via dei Colli dell Farnesina, 144, Rome 00194, Italy. FAX 3276774. Ed. N. Madia.

ORD & SAG. see *LINGUISTICS*

790   YU
OSMEH; humoristicki magazin. 1974. m. 120 din. Dnevnik, Bulevar 23. Oktobra 31, Novi Sad, Yugoslavia. Ed. Ivan Balenovic.

055.1   IT   ISSN 0030-6304
AP37
OSSERVATORE POLITICO LETTERARIO.* 1955. m. L.25500. Corso di Porta Nuova 34, 20121 Milan, Italy. Ed. Giuseppe Longo. adv.; bk.rev.; index; circ. 4,000. **Indexed:** M.L.A.

891.8   XN   ISSN 0030-6363
OSTEN; satiricno-humoristicen vesnik. (Text in Macedonian) 1945. fortn. 60 din. Nova Makedonija, Bulevar Jugoslavenske Narodne Armije 68, Skopje, Macedonia. Ed. Vlado Jocik.

808.8 070.4836   US
OSTENTATIOUS MIND. 1986. s-a. $5 (foreign $10). (L B and L N Society) Thursday Press, c/o Patricia D. Coscia, 224 82nd St., Brooklyn, NY 11209. TEL 718-680-3899. adv.; bk.rev.; illus.; index; circ. 200. (looseleaf format; back issues avail.)
Description: Discusses politics, society and the psyche.

051   US
OTTERBEIN MISCELLANY. (Text in English, French and German) 1965-1987; resumed 1991. a. $5. Otterbein College, Westerville, OH 43081. TEL 614-890-3000. Ed. James Bailey. bk.rev.; circ. 300 (controlled).
Description: Forum for Otterbein faculty and staff. Publishes essays, reviews, poetry and short fiction.

059 919 720   IS   ISSN 0333-6271
OUT OF JERUSALEM. 1970. q. free. Jerusalem Committee, 36 Keren Hayesod, P.O.B. 1312, Jerusalem, Israel. FAX 972-2-668374. TELEX 26210-SHALMIL. Ed. Daniel Furman. bk.rev.; circ. 2,500. **Indexed:** Avery Ind.Archit.Per.
Description: Research reports, press clippings, photo reports on urban planning and cultural and political coexistence in Jerusalem.

052   AT   ISSN 0030-7416
AP7
OVERLAND. 1954. q. Aus.$26($40) to individuals; pensioners & students Aus.$20; foreign Aus.$50. The Overland Society, c/o Barrett Reid, Ed., P.O. Box 14146, Melbourne, Vic. 3000, Australia. TEL 03-850-4347. FAX 03-852-0527. adv.; bk.rev.; film rev.; play rev.; illus.; index every 2 yrs.; circ. 2,500. (also avail. in microfilm from UMI; reprint service avail. from UMI; back issues avail.) **Indexed:** Arts & Hum.Cit.Ind., Aus.P.A.I.S., Curr.Cont., M.L.A.
Description: Covers current creative writing in fiction, poetry, literary criticism, history and social comment.

808 792   US
OVERSIGHT. 1989. every 9 m. (Angels Gate Cultural Center) Oversight, Box 29292, Los Angeles, CA 90029-0292. TEL 213-665-5328. Ed. Franklin Odel. adv.; bk.rev.; illus.; circ. 2,000. (tabloid format; back issues avail.)
Description: Features artists who work through community arts organizations, including photography, fine arts, fiction, music, film, and news of the Los Angeles art scene.

051   US
OVERTHROW. 1979. m. $10. Youth International Party Information Service, 9 Bleeker St., New York, NY 10012. TEL 212-533-5028. Ed. Alice Torbusch. adv.; bk.rev.; illus.; tr.lit.; circ. 15,000. (tabloid format; also avail. in microfilm from UMI) **Indexed:** Alt.Press Ind.
Supersedes (1973-1978): Yipster Times.

808.8   US
OVERTONE SERIES. 1973. q. $8. Overtone Press, c/o Otis Brown, 8517 Thouron St., Philadelphia, PA 19150. TEL 215-386-4279. Eds. Otis Brown, Beth Brown. circ. 2,500.

052   UK   ISSN 0030-7645
LH5
OXFORD. 1932. s-a. membership. Oxford Society, 8 Wellington Sq., Oxford OX1 2HY, England. FAX 0865-270708. Ed. H.A. Hurren. adv.; bk.rev.; illus.; circ. 30,000.

OXFORD MAGAZINE. see *LITERATURE*

P N REVIEW. see *LITERATURE — Poetry*

808.8 800   DK   ISSN 0109-4831
P S; tidsskrift for spontan satire, fjollet filosofi, funny fiction and lojerlig ligegyldighed. 1981. irreg. (3-4/yr.). DKK 54. Kreativ Filosofi Forening, Aakjaersvej 3, 6600 Vejen, Denmark. Ed. Bjarne Poulsen. adv.; bk.rev.; illus.; circ. 200.
Formerly: Philosophus (ISSN 0108-7460)

808.81   US
PACIFIC REVIEW; a magazine for poetry and prose. 1983. a. $4. California State University, San Bernardino, 5500 University Pkwy., San Bernardino, CA 92407. TEL 714-880-5894. Ed. James Brown. adv.; bk.rev.; film rev.; play rev.; illus.; circ. 750. (back issues avail.)

055   IT
PAGINE DELLA DANTE. q. Piazza Firenze, 27, Rome, Italy. Ed. E.G. di Giura.

059.951   HK
PAI SHING SEMI-MONTHLY. (Text in Chinese) 1981. s-m. HK.$15 (effective Apr. 1991). Pai Shing Cultural Enterprise Ltd., Block F, Haven Court, 5-F, 128 Leighton Rd., Hong Kong, Hong Kong. TEL 5770232. FAX 852-8956184. Ed.Bd. adv.; illus.

PAIDEIA; rivista letteraria di informazione bibliografica. see *PUBLISHING AND BOOK TRADE*

056.1   CU   ISSN 0552-9395
PALANTE. 1966. w. $50 in N. America; S. America $72; Europe $82; elsewhere $85. Ediciones Cubanas, Obispo No. 527, Apdo. 605, Havana, Cuba. TEL 7-3-5098. Dir. Rosendo Gutierrez Roman. illus.; circ. 235,000.

808.8 700   II
PANDULIPI. (Text in Bengali) 1969. q. Rs.6. Pandulipi Club, 5-1 D.T.N. Chatterji St., Calcutta 50, India. Ed. Debdas Bhattacharya. adv.; bk.rev.; bibl.; circ. 2,000.

PANEUROPA DEUTSCHLAND. see *POLITICAL SCIENCE — International Relations*

059.95   HK
PANORAMA MAGAZINE/TA CH'ENG. (Text in Chinese) m. HK.$130 (foreign HK.$170($22)). 1207 Loon Kee Bldg., 267 Des Voeux Rd., Central, Hong Kong. TEL 5532432. adv.

059   LE
PANORAMA OF EVENTS (HALIYYAT). 1977. q. $160. Publishing and Marketing House S.A.L., P.O. Box 70-285, Antelias, Lebanon. Ed. Viktor El-Kik. adv.; bk.rev.; circ. 3,000.

PANURGE. see *LITERATURE*

808.8   US
PAPER NEWS. 1980. irreg. Vanity Press, 160 6th Ave., New York, NY 10013. TEL 212-925-3823. Ed. Tuli Kupferberg. circ. 500.

059.91   II   ISSN 0031-1553
PARABAS. (Text in Bengali) 1970. m. Rs.2.50. 21-B, Quarter-6D, Chittaranjan, West Bengal, India. Ed. Aroon Kumar Chatterjee. bk.rev.; play rev.; circ. controlled.

051   US
PARAMETERS (PORTLAND); an occasional newsletter of critical issues. irreg. Circle Forum, Box 176, Portland, OR 97207. **Indexed:** Air Un.Lib.Ind., Amer.Bibl.Slavic & E.Eur.Stud., PROMT.

837   GW   ISSN 0031-1855
PARDON;* die Deutsche satirische Monatsschrift. 1962. m. DM.48. Pardon Verlagsgesellschaft mbH, Am Urselback 6, 6000 Frankfurt, Germany. Ed. Hans A. Nikel. adv.; bk.rev.; illus.; circ. 220,000.

054.1   FR   ISSN 0223-5765
PARLEMENTS ET FRANCOPHONIE. 1969. q. 150 F.($2) Assemblee Internationale des Parlementaires de Langue Francaise, 235 bd. St. Germain, 75007 Paris, France. TEL 47-05-26-87. TELEX AIPLF 202562. adv.; bk.rev.; charts; illus.; stat.; circ. 2,000.
Formerly: Revue des Parlementaires de Langue Francaise.

057   CS
PARTELET. m. $16. (Central Committee of Czechoslovakia) Rude Pravo, Na Porici 30, 112 86 Prague 1, Czechoslovakia.

LITERARY AND POLITICAL REVIEWS

810 US ISSN 0031-2525
HX1
PARTISAN REVIEW. 1934. q. $18. (Boston University) Partisan Review, Inc., 236 Bay State Rd., Boston, MA 02215. TEL 617-353-4260. (Subscr. to: Boston University Scholarly Publications, Subscr. Dept., 985 Commonwealth Ave., Rm. 230, Boston, MA 02215. TEL 617-353-4106) Ed. William Phillips. adv.; bk.rev.; film rev.; play rev.; index; circ. 10,000. (also avail. in microform from MIM,UMI; reprint service avail. from UMI) **Indexed:** A.I.P.P., Abstr.Engl.Stud., Acad.Ind., Amer.Bibl.Slavic & E.Eur.Stud., Arts & Hum.Cit.Ind., Bk.Rev.Ind. (1965-), Child.Bk.Rev.Ind. (1965-), Curr.Cont., Film Lit.Ind. (1990-), Hist.Abstr., Hum.Ind., Ind.Bk.Rev.Hum., Lang.& Lang.Behav.Abstr., M.L.A., Mag.Ind., Mid.East: Abstr.& Ind.

PASSAGES. see *ETHNIC INTERESTS*

808.8 US ISSN 0731-4663
PASSAIC REVIEW. 1979. s-a. $6. Forstmann Library, 195 Gregory Ave., Passaic, NJ 07055. Ed. Richard P. Quatrone. adv.; bk.rev.; circ. 1,000.

808.87 GO
PATRIOTE. irreg. Libreville, Gabon.

322.44 FR
PATRIOTE GUADELOUPEEN.* vol.5, 1974. m. 20 F. Association Generale des Etudiants Guadeloupeens, 85 rue Beaubourg, 75003 Paris, France. Ed. Frantz Succab. bk.rev.; illus.

810 US ISSN 0031-3262
PN2
PAUNCH. 1963. 2/yr. $7 to individuals; institutions $40; students $5. State University of New York at Buffalo, Department of English, 123 Woodward Ave., Buffalo, NY 14214. TEL 716-831-2000. Ed. Arthur Efron. bk.rev.; cum.index; circ. 200. **Indexed:** A.I.P.P., Abstr.Engl.Stud., Ind.Amer.Per.Verse, M.L.A.
—BLDSC shelfmark: 6412.989000.

891.8 XV ISSN 0031-3289
PAVLIHA. (Text in Slovenian) 1944. w. $50. Pavliha, Kardeljeva 4, Ljubljana, Slovenia. Ed. Joze Petelin.

051 US
PEACE PRESS. 1980. 10/yr. $15. Peace Press Collective, 540 Pacific Ave., Santa Rosa, CA 95404. TEL 707-575-8902. Ed.Bd. bk.rev.; circ. 2,500.
Formerly (until 1986): Nuke Notes Solidaridad; Formed by the merger of: Peace Network News; Nuke Notes; Solidaridad.
Description: Covers peace, justice and environmental issues in Sonoma County and the rest of the world. Includes a calendar of events.

052 UK
PEACEMAKER. 1973. bi-m. c/o Guy Otten, Ed., 168 Hamilton Rd., Longsight, Manchester M13 OPG, England. bk.rev.; circ. 400.

820 SZ ISSN 1013-1191
PEAKE STUDIES; dedicated to the life and work of Mervyn Peake (1911-1968). (Text in English) 1988. s-a. varies. c/o G. Peter Winnington, Ed. & Pub., Les 3 Chasseurs, CH-1413 Orzens, Switzerland. FAX 21-8877976. adv.; bk.rev.; play rev.; illus. (back issues avail.)

951 HK ISSN 0031-4110
PEKING INFORMERS. 1960. s-m. HK.$800($100) Continental Research Institute, G.P.O. Box 5699, Hong Kong, Hong Kong. Ed. Chow Ching-Wen. (back issues avail.)

810 US ISSN 0097-496X
PS1
PEMBROKE MAGAZINE. 1969. a. $5. (North Carolina Arts Council) Pembroke State University, Box 60, Pembroke, NC 28372. TEL 919-521-4214. Ed. Shelby Stephenson. adv.; bk.rev.; illus.; cum.index: 1969-73; circ. 600. (also avail. in microform from UMI; reprint service avail. from UMI) **Indexed:** A.I.P.P., Amer.Hum.Ind.

PEN IN HAND. see *JOURNALISM*

320.531 IT
PENSARE FAENZA/THINKING ABOUT FAENZA. 1904-1924; 1946-1958; resumed 1966. s-m. L.12000. Unione Comunale Partito Socialista Italiano di Faenza, Via 20 Settembre 29, Faenza, Italy. TEL 0546 21055. Ed. Renato Cavina. adv.; circ. 4,000. (tabloid format)
Formerly (until 1987): Socialista (ISSN 0037-8275)

055 809 IT
PENSIERO ED ARTE. q. Via Calefati, 379, Bari, Italy. Ed. G. Spinelli de'Santelena.

051 US ISSN 0048-332X
PEOPLE UNITED TO SAVE HUMANITY.
P.U.S.H.-OPERATION PUSH. 1970. m. $3. 930 E. 50th St., Chicago, IL 60615. TEL 312-373-3366. adv.; charts; illus.

808.87 KR ISSN 0031-5176
PERETS. (Text in Ukrainian) 1927. fortn. $4.20. Vul P. Nesterova 4, 252009 Kiev, Ukraine. TEL 044-441-8214. illus.; circ. 1,946,900.

800 FR ISSN 0181-4087
DT348
PEUPLES NOIRS, PEUPLES AFRICAINS. 1978. q. 250 F.($8) Editions des Peuples Noirs, 82, Av. de la Porte-des-Champs, 76000 Rouen, France. TEL 35-89-31-97. bk.rev.; circ. 1,500. (back issues avail.) **Indexed:** Curr.Cont.Africa.

PHOEBE. see *LITERATURE*

052 DK
PHYSIOGNOMY. (Text in English) 1970. 3/yr. DKK 30($6) Danish Centre for Renewable Energy, c/o David Gould, Ed., Asgard, Sdr. Ydby, DK-7760 Hurup Thy, Denmark. adv.; circ. 500.

052 CN ISSN 0710-3034
PIG PAPER. 1975. s-a. $5. Pig Productions, 70 Cotton Drive, Mississauga, Ont. L5G 1Z9, Canada. TEL 416-278-6594. Ed. Gary Pig Gold. adv.; bk.rev.; film rev.; circ. 1,000. (back issues avail.)
Description: Humorous overview of the mass media.

PIRANESI; Italienske studier. see *LINGUISTICS*

051 US
PLAGUE WATCH. (Also avail. on diskette) bi-m. $23.50. DeMigalt Media Group, P.O. Box 1287, Houston, TX 77251-1287. TEL 713-863-0244. FAX 713-864-2607. Ed. John Brisbin. film rev.; bibl.; illus.; stat.; circ. 2,500. (tabloid format; back issues avail.)
Formerly (until 1991): Journal of Ad-Jective Contagion.

PLAINSONG. see *LITERATURE — Poetry*

057.8 BU ISSN 0032-0528
AP58.B8
PLAMUK; spisanje za literatura, izkustvo i publitsistika. 1924. m. 6 lv.($8) Suiuz na Bulgarski Pisateli, 5, Ul. Angel Kanchev, Sofia, Bulgaria. (Dist. by: Hemus, 6, Rouski Blvd., 1000 Sofia, Bulgaria) bk.rev.; illus.; circ. 11,000. **Indexed:** M.L.A.

051 US
PLEIADES MAGAZINE. 1984. s-a. $9. Pleiades Productions, 6677 W. Colfax Ave., Ste. D, Box 357, Lakewood, CO 80214. Ed. John L. Moravec. bk.rev.; circ. 10,000.

056.1 CK
PLUMA; politica, economia, literatura, arte. 1975. m. Col.$250. Fundacion Pluma, Apdo. Aereo 12190, Bogota D.E., Colombia. Ed. Jorge Valencia Jaramillo. adv.; bk.rev.; film rev.; illus.; circ. 70,000.

056.1 AG
PLUMA Y PINCEL; para la difusion del arte y la cultura latinoamericanos. 1976. irreg. Editorial Arte y Letras de America, Nicaragua 5925, Buenos Aires, Argentina. Ed. Romeo Medina.

800 CY
PNEUMATIKI KYPROS/CULTURAL CYPRUS. (Text in Greek) 1960. m. Nicosia, Cyprus. TEL 02-659001. Ed. Kypros Chrysanthis.
Description: Explores a variety of original literature.

POET NEWS. see *LITERATURE — Poetry*

800 808 US ISSN 0731-5236
PN1042
POETICS JOURNAL. 1982. irreg. $10 per no. 2639 Russell St., Berkeley, CA 94705. TEL 510-548-1817. Eds. Lyn Hejinian, Barrett Watten. bk.rev.; circ. 750.
Description: Essays on contemporary poetic theory written by poets and other artists.

800 US ISSN 0333-5372
PN1039
POETICS TODAY; an international journal for theory and analysis of literature and communication. (Text in English) 1979. q. $28 to individuals (foreign $36); institutions $56 (foreign $64); students $14 (foreign $22). (Porter Institute for Poetics and Semiotics) Duke University Press, 6697 College Station, Durham, NC 27708. TEL 919-684-2173. FAX 919-684-8644. Ed. Itamar Even-Zohar. adv.; bk.rev.; index; circ. 800. **Indexed:** Arts & Hum.Cit.Ind., Bk.Rev.Ind. (1984-), Can.Rev.Comp.Lit., Child.Bk.Rev.Ind. (1984-), Curr.Cont., Film Lit.Ind. (1990-), Ind.Bk.Rev.Hum., Lang.& Lang.Behav.Abstr., M.L.A.
—BLDSC shelfmark: 6541.745000.
Refereed Serial

811 FR ISSN 0032-2024
PN3
POETIQUE; revue de theorie et d'analyse litteraires. 1970. q. 330 F. (foreign 360 F.) Editions du Seuil, 27 rue Jacob, 75261 Paris Cedex 06, France. TEL 1-40-46-50-50. FAX 1-40-46-51-43. TELEX 270 024. (Subscr. to: B.S.I., 49 rue de la Vanne, 92120 Montrouge, France) Ed.Bd. adv.; bk.rev.; bibl. **Indexed:** Arts & Hum.Cit.Ind., Can.Rev.Comp.Lit., Curr.Cont., M.L.A.

051 YU ISSN 0353-3832
DR2043
POGLEDI (KRAGUJEVAC)/VIEWS. (Text in Serbian) 1980. fortn. 480 din.($60) N I P "Pogledi", 27 Mart 14, 34000 Kragujevac, Serbia, Yugoslavia. TEL 034 49-031. Ed. Miloslav Samardzic. adv.; bk.rev.; circ. 90,000.

057.8 XN ISSN 0032-2245
POGLEDI (SKOPJE); spisanie za opstestveni prasanja. (Text in Macedonian) 1963. bi-m. $9.10. Makedonsko Izdanie na Komunist, Box 313, Skopje, Macedonia. Ed. Dusko Popovski.

808.8 US
POISONED PEN. 1978. q. $20. c/o Jeffrey Meyerson, 8801 Shore Rd., Apt. 6A East, Brooklyn, NY 11209-5409. bk.rev.; circ. 350.

943.8 PL ISSN 0032-2962
DK401
POLISH PERSPECTIVES. French edition: Perspectives Polonaises. German edition: Polnische Perspektiven. (Text in English) 1958. m. $14.30. Polski Instytut Spraw Miedzynarodowych, Warecka 1a, 00-950 Warsaw, Poland. (Dist. by: Ars Polona-Ruch, Krakowskie Przedmiescie 7, Warsaw, Poland) Ed. Artur Starewicz. adv.; bk.rev.; abstr.; bibl.; charts; illus.; stat.; index. (also avail. in microfilm from UMI; reprint service avail. from UMI) **Indexed:** Key to Econ.Sci., M.L.A., Mid.East: Abstr.& Ind.

059 IS
POLITICA. 1985. bi-m. $38 (in N. America $47). Politica Association, P.O. Box 23075, Tel Aviv, Israel. TEL 03-5101529. FAX 03-510008. Ed. Gideon Samet. adv.; bk.rev.
Description: Focuses on Israeli social, political and cultural concerns.

POLITICA ED ECONOMIA/POLITICS AND ECONOMICS. see *POLITICAL SCIENCE*

055 IT
POLITICA POPOLARE; rassegna di ispirazione sturziana. 1954. m. Via Costantinopoli 84, 80138 Naples, Italy. TEL 091 45-99-49. circ. 2,000.

056 EC
POLITICA Y SOCIEDAD. 1984. bi-m. $50. (Archivo de Historia Social Contemporanea) I N F O C, Casilla 235-B, Quito, Ecuador. Eds. Nelson Argones, Alexei Paez.

808.87 SG ISSN 0850-1807
POLITICIEN. 1977. w. $300. Consortium Africain de Documentation & Presse, Zone B, Villa N: 22B, B.P. 11018, Dakar, Senegal. TEL 24-43-24. Ed. Mam Less Dia.

LITERARY AND POLITICAL REVIEWS

808 AG
POLITICON; ni a la izquierda, ni a la derecha, ni al centro, arriba. 1986. fortn. Editories Asociados S.A., Maipu 942, 2 piso, Buenos Aires, Argentina. TEL 312-5743.

320.9 YU ISSN 0032-3381
POLITIKA-EKSPRES; nedeljna revija. 1963. d. 972 din. Politika, Makedonska 29, Belgrade, Yugoslavia. Ed. Bozidar Bogdanovic. (also avail. in microform from MIM)

058 DK
POLITIKEN WEEKLY. 1915. w. DKK 8($1) Dagbladet Politiken Ltd., Raadhuspladsen 37, 1585 Copenhagen V, Denmark. TELEX 16029. Ed. J. Falcon. adv.; circ. 8,000. (newspaper)

791 YU ISSN 0032-339X
POLITIKIN ZABAVNIK. 1940. w. 336 din.($23.50) Politika, Makedonska 29, Belgrade, Yugoslavia. Ed. Z. Stojanovic. adv.; circ. 330,000.

057.8 YU ISSN 0032-3578
POLJA; casopis za kulturu, umetnost i drustvena pitanja. 1955. m. 100 din. (Savez Socijalisticke Omladine Vojvodine, Pokrajinska Konferencija) Tribuna Mladih, Katolicka Porta 5, Box 190, 21000 Novi Sad, Yugoslavia. Ed. Jovan Zivlak. circ. 2,100.

621.32 IT ISSN 0032-423X
AP37
PONTE; rivista di politica e letteratura. 1945. m. Vallecchi Editore S.p.A., Via A. Giacomini 8, 50132 Florence, Italy. TEL 055-473964. Ed. Marcello Rossi. adv.; bk.rev.; index. **Indexed:** Amer.Hist.& Life, CERDIC, Curr.Cont., M.L.A., P.A.I.S.

058.82 NO
POPULIST. 1975. q. NOK 28. Norges Unge Venstre - Young Liberals of Norway, Mollergt. 16, Oslo 1, Norway. Ed. Leif Stavik. adv.; bk.rev.; illus.
Supersedes: Liberalt Perspektiv (ISSN 0047-4479)

052 AT
PORT STEPHENS EXAMINER. 1893. w. Port Stephens Publishers, 10 William St., Raymond Terrace, N.S.W. 2324, Australia. TEL 049-871411. (Subscr. to: P.O. Box 180, Nelson Bay, N.S.W. 3215, Australia) Ed. Don Comppell. circ. 14,712.

805 PE
POSIBLE. 1986. bi-m. $35. Instituto del Sur para la Cooperacion Democratica, Av. Santa Cruz 971, Miraflores, Lima, Peru. TEL 456792. Ed. Pablo Cateriano. adv.; bk.rev.; circ. 8,000.
Description: Political reviews on economic development and trends, emphasizing liberal ideas. Includes literary reviews and matters of national interest.

808.8 CN ISSN 0703-7139
F1051
POSSIBLES. 1976. q. Can.$18 to individuals; institutions Can.$30. Box 114 Succ. Cote-des-Neiges, Montreal, Que. H3S 2S4, Canada. TEL 514-495-7139. adv.; bk.rev.; circ. 2,500. **Indexed:** Lang.& Lang.Behav.Abstr., Pt.de Rep. (1983-).

808.87 US
POSSUM COUNTY NEWS. 1984. q. $11.88 for 12 nos. Poor Ol' George, Box 2572, Owensboro, KY 42302. circ. 12,000.
Description: Presents humorous and witty anecdotes.

POTATO EYES; Appalachian voices. see *LITERATURE — Poetry*

808.8 CN ISSN 0228-3344
POTBOILER MAGAZINE. (Text in English) 1978. s-a. Can.$5($4) Panda Press, Richard's Rd., Roberts Creek, B.C. VON 2W0, Canada. Ed. L.R. Davidson. adv.; bk.rev.; illus.; circ. 275. (back issues avail.)

808 US
POULTRY; a magazine of voice. 1980. irreg. (2-3/yr.). $2 per no. Poultry, Inc., Box 4413, Springfield, MA 01101. Ed.Bd. bk.rev.; circ. 1,000. (tabloid format; back issues avail.)
Description: Includes parodies, satire and send-ups of contemporary literature, especially poetry.

056.1 SP
PREGON; revista grafica Navarra. vol.34, 1976. q. 50 ptas. per no. Conde Oliveto, 5, Pamplona, Spain. Ed. Faustino Corella Estella. adv.; illus. **Indexed:** Amer.Hist.& Life.

960 FR ISSN 0032-7638
GN645
PRESENCE AFRICAINE; revue culturelle du monde noir. (Text in English, French) 1947. q. 330 F.($82.50) Societe Nouvelle Presence Africaine, 25 bis, rue des Ecoles, 75005 Paris, France. TEL 43-54-13-74. TELEX AFRISAC 200891F. Ed. Yande Christiane Diop. bk.rev.; circ. 2,000. **Indexed:** CERDIC, Curr.Cont.Africa, M.L.A., Rural Ext.Educ.& Tr.Abstr., Rural Recreat.Tour.Abstr., World Agri.Econ.& Rural Sociol.Abstr.
—BLDSC shelfmark: 6609.710000.

320 658 NR
PRESIDENT. 1976. m. £N48. New Breed Organisation Ltd., 35 Ogunlana Dr., Box 5414, Lagos, Nigeria. Ed. Chris Okolie.

057.8 YU ISSN 0350-5723
PRIMORSKA SRECANJA; revija za druzboslovje, gospodarstvo in kulturo. 1977. 6/yr. $10. Revija Primorska Srecanja, 65000 Nova Gorica, Slovenia. TEL 065 22 556. bk.rev.; illus.

827 UK ISSN 0032-888X
AP4
PRIVATE EYE. 1961. fortn. £21. Pressdram Ltd., 6 Carlisle St., London W.1., England. FAX 437-4017. Ed. Ian Hilop. adv.; bk.rev.; index; circ. 230,000. (tabloid format)

057.8 CI
PRIVLACICA. (Text in Croatian) 1980. bi-m. 1600 din.($4) Cultural Information Center, M. Tita 127, 56251 Privlaka, Croatia. TEL 056 75-449. (also avail. in talking book)

100 055 IT ISSN 0032-9339
PROBLEMI; periodico quadrimestrale di cultura. 1967. 3/yr. L.84000. G. B. Palumbo & C. Editore S.p.A., Via Ricasoli 59, 90139 Palermo, Italy. Ed. Giuseppe Petronio. adv.; bk.rev.; abstr.; bibl.

055 IT
PROCELLARIA. q. Via de Nova, 21c, Reggio, Calabria, Italy. Ed. F. Fiumara.

056.1 EC
PROFESIONAL. 1972. m. Calle Oriente 725, Quito, Ecuador. Ed. Wilson Almeida Munoz. circ. 3,000.

051 US ISSN 0889-2202
E876
PROGRESSIVE REVIEW. 1966. 9/yr. $14. 1739 Connecticut Ave., N.W., Washington, DC 20009. TEL 202-232-5544. FAX 202-234-6222. Ed. Sam Smith. bk.rev.; illus.; cum.index: 1969-1972, 1984-1988; circ. 1,500. (also avail. in microform from UMI; back issues avail.; reprint service avail. from UMI) **Indexed:** Alt.Press Ind. **Former titles** (until 1985): D.C. Gazette (ISSN 0011-7153); Capitol East Gazette.
Description: Newsletter of progressive politics.

059.91 II ISSN 0033-1201
PRONAB. (Text in Bengali) 1927. m. Rs.16. Swami Nirmalananda, Bharat Sevasram Sangha, 211 Rash Behari Ave., Calcutta 700 019, India. Ed. Swami Atmananda. adv.; bk.rev.; circ. 8,500.

808.8 US
PROOF ROCK. 1982. s-a. $5. Proof Rock Press, Box 607, Halifax, VA 24558. Ed. Serena Fusek. adv.; bk.rev.; circ. 300.

052 AT
PROSERPINE GUARDIAN. 1904. w. Aus.$36. Whitsunday Printing & Publishing Co., 16 Chapman St., Proserpine, Qld., Australia. TEL 079 451600. FAX 079-452-997. Ed. B.J. Lewis. adv.; bk.rev.; circ. 3,030. (back issues avail.)

PROSPETTIVE CULTURALI CALABRESI. see *LITERATURE — Poetry*

057.1 KZ ISSN 0131-5587
PROSTOR; literaturno-khudozhestvennyi i obshchestvennopoliticheskii illyustrirovannyi zhurnal. 1933. m. 18 Rub. Soyuz Pisatelei Kazakhskoi S.S.R., Alma-Ata, Kazakhstan. Ed. G.L. Tolmachev. adv.; bk.rev.; bibl.; illus.; circ. 135,000.

055 IT
PROTAGORA. s-a. Via Franco Lucchini, 33, Rome, Italy. Ed. B. Widmar.

054 FR ISSN 0758-7686
PROXIMA.* 1984. q. 30 F. Andromede, B.P. 42, 59009 Lille, France.

800 IT
PUBBLICO; rassegna annuale di fatti letterari. 1977. a. L.10000. Milano Libri Edizioni s.r.l., Via A. Rizzoli 2, 20137 Milan, Italy. Ed. Vittorio Spinazzola. circ. 4,500.

800 001.3 US ISSN 0899-2363
NX180.S6 CODEN: PUCUE7
PUBLIC CULTURE. 1988. s-a. $10 to individuals; institutions $20. University of Pennsylvania, Center for Transnational Cultural Studies, University Museum, University of Pennsylvania, 33rd & Spruce Sts., Philadelphia, PA 19104-6324. TEL 215-898-4054. FAX 215-898-0657. Ed. Carol A. Breckenridge. adv.; bk.rev.; illus.; circ. 1,100. (back issues avail.) **Indexed:** Film Lit.Ind. (1989-).
—BLDSC shelfmark: 6963.140000.
Description: Studies political, economic and social aspects of cultural commodity exchange in the postmodern world.
Refereed Serial

PUNCH BOWL. see *EDUCATION — Higher Education*

055.1 IT ISSN 0033-4294
PUNGOLO VERDE; arti-science e lettere. 1947. m. L.10000. Box 54, 86100 Campobasso, Italy. Ed. Guido Massarelli. adv.; bk.rev.; illus.; circ. 10,000.

320.9 PK ISSN 0048-6027
PUNJAB PUNCH;* a views weekly. (Text in English) 1971. w. Rs.30. 1 McLeod Rd., Lahore, Pakistan. Ed. Pervez Tahir. adv.; bk.rev.; illus.

059 UK
PUNJABI SAHITYA; magazine of Punjabi life and letters. (Text in Punjabi) 1942. q. £5. c/o H. S. Kalra, Ed., 254 Rowley Gardens, Woodberry Grove, London N4 1HW, England. adv.; bk.rev.; film rev.; play rev.; abstr.; bibl.; charts; illus.; pat.; stat.; tr.lit.; cum.index; circ. 4,000 (controlled).

320 IT
QUADERNI BIANCHI; rivista di cultura politica. 1979. bi-m. L.12000. Piazza S. Ambrogio 21, 20123 Milan, Italy. Ed.Bd.

052 AT ISSN 0033-5002
AP7
QUADRANT. 1956. 10/yr. Aus.$45 (foreign $54). (Australian Association for Cultural Freedom) Quadrant Magazine Co. Ltd., P.O. Box 1495, Collingwood, Vic. 3066, Australia. TEL 03-4176855. FAX 03-4162980. Ed. Rogert Manne. adv.; bk.rev.; circ. 5,500. (also avail. in microform; reprint service avail. from KTO) **Indexed:** Aus.P.A.I.S., Child.Lit.Abstr., Gdlns., M.L.A.
—BLDSC shelfmark: 7168.030000.
Description: Conservative reviews on politics, literature, economics, education, current affairs.

808.87 US
QUAGMIRE; livellafotoorehtsitnemnrevog. 1981. biennial. $25. (National Organization Taunting Safety and Fairness Everywhere) N O T - S A F E, Box 5743 PD, Santa Barbara, CA 93150. TEL 805-969-6217. Ed. Dale Lowdermilk. stat.; circ. 1,250. (tabloid format)

810 US ISSN 0736-4628
PS501
QUARRY WEST; a journal of literature & the arts. 1972. s-a. $12. University of California, Santa Cruz, Porter College, Santa Cruz, CA 95064. TEL 408-429-2155. Ed. Ken Weisner. bk.rev.; circ. 750. (back issues avail.)
Formerly (until 1977): Quarry.

054.1 FR ISSN 0033-5878
QUATRE VERITES. 1973. m. 600 F. Club des Quatre, 40 rue Jean Jaures, 93170 Bagnolet, France. Ed.Bd. bk.rev.; film rev.; play rev.; charts; illus.; tr.lit.; circ. 10,000.

351 920   US   ISSN 1049-5452
E840.8.Q28
▼QUAYLE QUARTERLY; a watchful eye on the vice-presidency. 1990. q. $14.95. Quayle Quarterly, Box 8593, Brewster Station, Bridgeport, CT 06605. TEL 203-333-9399. Ed. Deborah Werksman. adv.; circ. 14,000. (back issues avail.)
  Description: Covers the words and deeds of US Vice President Dan Quayle.

QUEST: MANHATTAN PROPERTIES & COUNTRY ESTATES. see REAL ESTATE

800   FR
QUESTIONS CLEFS. 1981. q. E.D.I., 29 rue Descartes, Paris 75005, France.

800   II
QUILL. (Text in English) 1974. m. Rs.10. Tulika Prakashan-Quill, 5C-14 New Rohtak Road, New Delhi, India. Ed. M.C. Bhandari. adv.; bk.rev.; film rev.

QUINQUEREME; new studies in modern languages. see LINGUISTICS

808.8   US
QUIXOTE, QUIXOTL.* q. $20. (Marxist Semi-International) Quixote Press, Inc., 2407 Watts St., Houston, TX 77030-1829. TEL 713-667-6639. Ed. Morris Edelson.
  Description: Political satire as an attack on bourgeois decadence.

059.951   CC
QUN YAN/POPULAR TRIBUNE. (Text in Chinese) m. $35.90. (Central Committee of the Chinese Democratice League) Qun Yan Zazhishe, No.1, Dongchang Hutong Beixiang, Dongcheng Qu, Beijing 100006, People's Republic of China. TEL 5127774. (Dist. in US by: China Books & Periodicals, Inc., 2929 24th St., San Francisco, CA 94110. TEL 415-282-0994) Ed. Tao Dayong.
  Description: Covers politics, economics, current events, and general interest topics.

QUNZHONG WENHUA/MASS CULTURE; wenhua yishu zonghexing yuekan. see GENERAL INTEREST PERIODICALS — China

R F D; a country journal for gay men everywhere. see HOMOSEXUALITY

059   UK
RACHNA. 1981. 12/yr. Rachna Publishers, 367 Katherine Rd., London E7 8LT, England. TEL 01-472-2406.
  Description: Political and literary articles, poetry and stories concerning immigrants from the Indian subcontinent.

RADICAL BOOKSELLER. see PUBLISHING AND BOOK TRADE

808.8   US   ISSN 0742-2768
RAG MAG. 1982. s-a. $10 to individuals; institutions $15. Box 12, Goodhue, MN 55027. TEL 612-923-4590. Ed. Beverly Voldseth. adv.; bk.rev.; circ. 500. Indexed: Amer.Hum.Ind.
  Formerly (until 1983): Underground Rag Mag.
  Description: Eclectic literary magazine of art, poetry and prose.

808.8   US   ISSN 0278-7016
RAISE THE STAKES; the Planet Drum review. 1979. 2/yr. $20 membership; $25 outside N. America. Planet Drum Foundation, Box 31251, San Francisco, CA 94131. TEL 415-285-6556. Ed.Bd. bk.rev.; circ. 3,000.

320   US
RAMPART INDIVIDUALIST; a journal of free market libertarian scholarship. 1981. s-a. $18. Rampart Institute, Inc., Box 22231, Carmel, CA 93922-0231. Ed. Lawrence Samuels. bk.rev.

808.8   US
RASPBERRY PRESS.* 1974. a. $2. Rte. 1, Box 81, Puposky, MN 56667. Ed. Susan Hauser. circ. 300.

055.1   IT   ISSN 0033-9482
RASSEGNA DI CULTURA E VITA SCOLASTICA. vol.22, 1968. m. L.2000. Via Giosue Borsi 3, 00197 Rome, Italy. Ed. Paola Di Marcantonio. bk.rev.; abstr.; bibl.; charts; illus.

052   UK   ISSN 0962-225X
RAVI; Asian newspaper. 1974. w. £20. Ravi Newspapers Ltd., 123 Grattan Rd., Bradford BD1 2JA, England. FAX 0274-721227. Ed. Farida Sheikh. adv.; bk.rev.; circ. 8,000. (tabloid format; back issues avail.)

RAW. see ART

810   US   ISSN 0742-9681
READER (HOUGHTON); essay in reader-oriented theory, criticism, and pedagogy. s-a. $8 to individuals (foreign $10); institutions $10 (foreign $12). Michigan Technological University, Department of Humanities, Houghton, MI 49931. TEL 906-487-2447. Ed. Elizabeth A. Flynn.
  —BLDSC shelfmark: 7300.640000.

051   US
READER (SAN DIEGO). 1972. w. $165. Box 85803, San Diego, CA 92138. TEL 619-235-3000. FAX 619-231-0489. Ed. James E. Holman. adv.; bk.rev.; film rev.; play rev.; circ. 131,000 (controlled). (tabloid format)

817   US   ISSN 0034-091X
THE REALIST. 1958-1974; resumed 1985. q. $23 for 12 nos. Box 1230, Venice, CA 90294. TEL 213-392-5848. Ed. Paul Krassner. circ. 2,500.
  Description: Social and political satire.

320.51   SA   ISSN 0034-0979
DT1
REALITY; a journal of liberal opinion. 1969. bi-m. $18. Reality Publications, P.O. Box 1104, Pietermaritzburg 3200, South Africa. Ed. I.M. Wyllie. bk.rev.; circ. 800. Indexed: Ind.S.A.Per.
  Supersedes: Transkei Liberal News.

052   CN
REALITY NOW; for defense of life on Earth. 1983. s-a. Can.$8. R N Publishers, P.O. Box 6326, Station "A", Toronto, Ont. M5W 1P7, Canada. bk.rev.; circ. 3,000. (back issues avail.)

800   US
RECORDING & PUBLISHING NEWS. 1988. 5/yr. $12.99. Anterior Bitewing Ltd., 7735 Brand Ave., Normandy, MO 63135. Ed. Tom Bergeron. bk.rev.; music rev.

800 700   US   ISSN 0883-0126
RED BASS. 1981. biennial. $20 for 2 nos. to individuals; institutions and foreign $35. Red Bass Productions, Inc., 216 Chartres St., New Orleans, LA 70130. TEL 504-522-7758. Ed. Jay Murphy. adv.; bk.rev.; circ. 3,000. Indexed: Alt.Press Ind., Amer.Hum.Ind., Ind.Amer.Per.Verse.
  Description: Explores the interface bewtween art and politics. Presents experimental, innovative and political art and literature, often featuring special themes.

800 320   UK   ISSN 0308-6852
RED LETTERS; a review of cultural politics. 1976. q. £6 to individuals (foreign £7); institutions £10 (foreign £11). 6 Cynthia St., London N1 9JF, England. Ed.Bd. adv.; bk.rev.; circ. 1,500. Indexed: Alt.Press Ind., M.L.A.
  —BLDSC shelfmark: 7331.261500.

808.8 320.531   CN
RED MENACE; a libertarian socialist newsletter. 1975. s-a. Can.$12. Libertarian Socialist Collective, Box 171, Sta. D, Toronto, Ont. M6P 3J8, Canada. Ed. Ulli Diemer. bk.rev.; circ. 1,000. (tabloid format) Indexed: Alt.Press Ind.

053.931   NE   ISSN 0034-3749
REKENSCHAP; humanistisch tijdschrift voor wetenschap en cultuur. 1954. q. fl.45. Humanistische Stichting Socrates, Oudkerkhof 11, Postbus 114, 3500 AC Utrecht, Netherlands. TEL 030-318145. FAX 030-361704. Ed.Bd. adv.; bk.rev.; illus.; circ. 1,500. Indexed: Excerp.Med.

REMARK (NEW YORK); a journal of essays and reviews. see LITERATURE

056.1   AG
REPERTORIO LATINO AMERICANO. 1975. q. $10. Repertorio Latinoamericano S.A., c/o Francisco R. Bello, Ed., Montevideo 524, Buenos Aires 1019, Argentina. adv.; bk.rev.; illus.; circ. 12,000. (tabloid format) Indexed: Hisp.Amer.Per.Ind.

055.1   IT   ISSN 0034-4745
REPORTAGE; quindicinale d'informazione e attualita. 1962. fortn. L.30000 (foreign L.60000). Via Belvedere 11, 88046 Lamezia Terme (Catanzaro), Italy. TEL 0968-21719. Ed. Rosario Arcuri. adv.; bk.rev.; abstr.; bibl.; charts; illus.; stat.; circ. 20,000. (tabloid format)
  Description: Political forum featuring news on various topics.

RESPONSABILITA DEL SAPERE. see LITERATURE

RETI - PRATICHE E SAPERI DI DONNE. see POLITICAL SCIENCE

700 301   LB
REVELATION;* social, political, economic and cultural monthly. (Text in English) 1973. m. $0.75 per no. University of Liberia, P.O. Box 9020, Monrovia, Liberia. adv.; bk.rev.

057.8   CI   ISSN 0034-6888
REVIJA (OSIJEK); casopis za knjizevnost, kulturu i drustvena pitanja. (Text in Serbo-Croatian) 1961. bi-m. 50 din. Narodno Sveuciliste "Bozidar Maslaric", Centar za Kulturu i Umjetnost, Kuhaceva 29, Osijek 54000, Croatia. Ed. Dejan Rebic.

053.931   NE   ISSN 0302-8852
PT5460
REVISOR. 1974. bi-m. fl.77.50 (foreign fl.92). Querido B.V., Singel 262, 1016 AC Amsterdam, Netherlands. TEL 020-273626. Ed.Bd. adv.; bk.rev.; bibl.; circ. 6,000. Indexed: M.L.A.

056.9   PO   ISSN 0034-6977
REVISTA ALENTEJANA. 1935. m. Esc.80. Casa do Alentejo, Rua das Portas de Santo Antao 58, Lisbon 2, Portugal. Eds. Vitor Santos, Fausto Goncalves. adv.; bk.rev.; film rev.; play rev.; abstr.; bibl.; illus.; tr.lit.; circ. 3,000 (controlled). (tabloid format)

808.8   SP
REVISTA DE MENORCA. 1888. q. 2800 ptas.($5) Ateneo de Mahon, Menorca, Baleares, Spain. Ed.Bd. bk.rev.; bibl.

056.1   SP.   ISSN 0034-8635
AP60
REVISTA DE OCCIDENTE. 1923; N.S. 1963, 1975, 1980. m. (11/yr.). 7600 ptas.($102) (elsewhere 9700 ptas.)(effective Mar. 1992). Fundacion Jose Ortega y Gasset, Fortuny, 53, 28010 Madrid, Spain. TEL 410-44-121. FAX 308-4007. Ed. Magdalena Mora. adv.: B&W page 125000 ptas.; color page 160000 ptas.; adv. contact: Belen Nieto. bk.rev.; illus.; index, cum.index: nos.1-50 in 1985; circ. 20,000. (also avail. in microform; reprint service avail. from KTO) Indexed: Abstr.Engl.Stud., Arts & Hum.Cit.Ind., Hist.Abstr.
  —BLDSC shelfmark: 7869.030000.
  Description: Covers social sciences and humanities. Includes a literary section by Spanish and Spanish American authors.

REVISTA DEL PENSAMIENTO CENTROAMERICANO. see POLITICAL SCIENCE

986.1   CK   ISSN 0034-9852
REVISTA MANIZALES; al servicio de la cultura colombiana y americana. 1940. m. $6. Apdo. Aereo 14-61, Manizales, Caldas, Colombia. Ed. J.B. Jaramillo Meza. adv.; bk.rev.; index.

800   SZ   ISSN 0035-1016
LA REVUE DE BELLES-LETTRES. (Text in French) 1877. q. 55 SFr. (foreign 85 SFr.). (Societe de Belles Lettres de Lausanne et Geneve) Editions Medecine et Hygiene, Case Postale 456, CH-1211 Geneva 4, Switzerland. TEL 022-469355. FAX 022-475610. Ed. Olivier Beetschen. adv.; bk.rev.; abstr.; bibl.; illus.; circ. 1,400.

327   FR   ISSN 0750-9278
AP20
REVUE DES DEUX MONDES: LITTERATURE, HISTOIRE, ARTS ET SCIENCES. 1829. m. 510 F. (foreign 975 F.). Societe de la Revue des Deux Mondes, 170 rue de Grenelle, 75007 Paris, France. TEL 1-47-53-71-10. FAX 1-47-05-66-74. Ed. Jean-Michel Place. adv.; bk.rev.; film rev.; play rev.; record rev.; index; circ. 20,000. (also avail. in microform from UMI; reprint service avail. from KTO,UMI) Indexed: Hist.Abstr.
  —BLDSC shelfmark: 7898.300000.
  Former titles: Nouvelle Revue des Mondes; Revue des Deux Mondes (ISSN 0035-1962)

LITERARY AND POLITICAL REVIEWS

054.1   FR   ISSN 0035-3310
REVUE INDEPENDANTE. 1912. bi-m. 90 F. Syndicat des Journalistes et Ecrivains, 206, rue Edouard-Branly, 93100 Montreuil-sous-Bois, France. Ed. Bernard Drupt. bk.rev.; dance rev.; film rev.; play rev.; rec.rev.; illus.; circ. 1,500.

057   GW
REVUE SLOWAKEI. a. DM.30. Slowakisches Matus-Cernak-Institut, Kulturelles Zentrum der Slowaken in Deutschland, D-8019 Glonn-Zinneberg 1, Germany. bk.rev.

957   CS
REVUE SVETOVEJ LITERATURY. 7/yr. $68. (Slovak Literary Fund) Vydavatel'stvo Slovensky Spisovatel', Laurinska 2, 813 67 Bratislava, Czechoslovakia. bk.rev.
   Description: Publishes translations of the works of contemporary authors and classics, not yet published in book form in this country, as well as critical articles, reviews of book translations, and profiles of the foremost Slovak translators.

808.8   US   ISSN 0891-1231
RIDGE REVIEW. 1981. q. $10. Ridge Times Press, Box 90, Mendocino, CA 95460. TEL 707-964-8465. Ed.Bd. adv.; bk.rev.; charts; illus.; circ. 3,500. (back issues avail.)
   Description: Covers themes concerning the Northern California coastal ridges.

RIFORMA DELLA SCUOLA/SCHOOL REFORM. see *EDUCATION*

322.4   CN
RIKKA. 1974. 2/yr. Can.$15 to individuals; institutions Can.$20. Plowshare Press, RR1, Little Current, Manitoulin Island, Ont. POP 1KO, Canada. TEL 705-368-3847. Ed. George Yamada. circ. 500. (back issues avail.)
   Description: Cross-cultural, trans-ethnic educational journal concerned with community (local and universal context) in a decentralized, bioregional network.

054.1   FR
RIMBAUD VIVANT. 1973. q. 40 F. Amis de Rimbaud, c/o Mme. Suzanne Briet, 24 rue Gutenberg, 92100 Boulogne, France. Ed. Pierre Petitfils. bk.rev.; bibl.
   Supersedes: Etudes Rimbaudiennes.

053.1   SZ
RING-POST; Ausblick vom Hauenstein. 1945. m. 15 Fr. Hauenstein-Verlag, Niedergrund 15, CH-4600 Olten 3, Switzerland. bk.rev.
   Formerly: Hauenstein Verlag. Mitteilungsblatt (ISSN 0017-839X)

800   US   ISSN 0149-8851
PS501
RIVER STYX. 1975. 3/yr. $20 to individuals; institutions $28. Big River Association, 14 S. Euclid, St. Louis, MO 63108. TEL 314-361-0043. Ed. Lee Schreiner. adv.; circ. 1,200. (back issues avail.)
   Indexed: A.I.P.P.
   Description: Multi-cultural publication of literature and art.

808.8   US
RIVERFRONT. 1980. s-a. Metropolitan Technical Community College, Box 3777, Omaha, NE 68103. TEL 402-449-8322. Ed. Jules DeSalvo. circ. 750.

RIVISTA DALMATICA. see *HISTORY — History Of Europe*

RIVISTA STORICA CALABRESE. see *HISTORY — History Of Europe*

808.8   US
ROAR; tapebook series. 1979. irreg. $15 for 2 nos. Ranger International Productions, Lion Publishing - Roar Recording, Box 71231, Shorewood Sta., Milwaukee, WI 53211-7331. TEL 414-332-7474. Ed. Martin J. Rosenblum. bk.rev.; circ. 100. (audio cassette)

ROCKY MOUNTAIN REVIEW OF LANGUAGE AND LITERATURE. see *LITERATURE*

057   CS
RODINA. bi-m. (Communist Party of Slovakia) Pravda, Volgogradska 8, 893 39 Bratislava, Czechoslovakia.

057   CS
ROHAC. w. (Communist Party of Slovakia) Pravda, Volgogradska 8, 893 39 Bratislava, Czechoslovakia.

800   US   ISSN 0886-2249
ROLLING STOCK. 1981. 3/yr. $9 to individuals; institutions $12. University of Colorado, c/o Univ. of Colorado, Campus Box 226, Boulder, CO 80309. TEL 303-442-7631. FAX 303-492-7272. Ed. Jennifer Dunbar Dorn. adv.; bk.rev.; circ. 3,000.
   Description: Features essays, columns, stories, interviews, poetry, and art by a diverse group of well-known writers. Serves up serious political comment lightly salted with literary adventure.

055.91   RM   ISSN 0035-8088
DR201
ROMANIAN REVIEW. French edition (ISSN 0251-3528); German edition (ISSN 1220-3327); Russian edition (ISSN 1220-5060) (Text in English) 1946. m. 360 lei($36) Foreign Languages Press Group, Piata Presei Libere Nr. 1, P.O. Box 33-28, 71341 Bucharest, Rumania. TEL 173836. TELEX 11272. Ed. Nicolae Saramei. adv.; bk.rev.; illus.; circ. 6,000.
   Indexed: Arts & Hum.Cit.Ind., Curr.Cont., M.L.A.

057   CS
ROMBOID. m. $58. (Asociacia Slovenskych Spisovatelov - Association of Slovak Writers) Vydavatel'stvo Slovensky Spisovatel', Laurinska 2, 813 67 Bratislava, Czechoslovakia.
   Description: Features original literary-scientific articles, critiques, reviews, shorter pieces and poems.

059.927   UA
ROSE AL-YUSUF. (Text in Arabic) 1925. w. 89A Sharia Qasr el-Aini, Cairo, Egypt. Ed. Muhammad Tuhami. circ. 35,000.

055.1   IT
IL ROSONE; periodico Pugliese di cultura e informazioni. 1978. bi-m. L.50000($45) Edizioni del Rosone, Via Zingarelli 10, 71100 Foggia, Italy. TEL 0881-87659. Ed. Franco Marasca. adv.; bk.rev.; circ. 10,000. (back issues avail.)

054.1   FR   ISSN 0035-970X
LA RUE; revue culturelle et litteraire d'expression anarchiste. 1968. q. 50 F.($10.) Association Culturelle Louise Michel, 24 rue Paul Albert, 75018 Paris, France. Dir. Maurice Joyeux. bk.rev.; bibl.

057.8   YU   ISSN 0035-9793
RUKOVET; casopis za knjizevnost, umetnost i drustvena pitanja. (Text in Serbo-Croatian) 1955. m. $20. (Opstinski Fond Kulture Subotica) N I P "Suboticke Novine", 8 Maksim Gorki St., 24000 Subotica, Yugoslavia. Ed. Milovan Mikovic.
   Description: Includes literary, arts and social issues. Contains original works of literature and translations from foreign languages.

056.1   PE
RUNA. 1977. m. S/150 per no. Instituto Nacional de Cultura, Casilla 5247, Lima, Peru. Ed. Mario Razzeto. illus.; circ. 10,000.

050   US
RYDER. 1979. m. $12. Out to Lunch Publications, 104 1-2 E. Kirkwood, Apt. 26, Bloomington, IN 47401. TEL 812-339-2001. Ed. Peter Lopilato. adv.; bk.rev.; film rev.; circ. 10,000. (also avail. in microfilm)

810   US   ISSN 0038-2876
AP2
S A Q: THE SOUTH ATLANTIC QUARTERLY. 1902. q. $20 to individuals (foreign $28); institutions $40 (foreign $48). Duke University Press, 6697 College Station, Durham, NC 27708. TEL 919-684-2173. FAX 919-684-8644. Ed. Frank Lentricchia. adv.; bk.rev.; circ. 1,800. (also avail. in microform from MIM,UMI; reprint service avail. from ISI,UMI) **Indexed:** Abstr.Engl.Stud., Acad.Ind., Amer.Bibl.Slavic & E.Eur.Stud., Amer.Hist.& Life, Arts & Hum.Cit.Ind., Bk.Rev.Ind. (1965-), CERDIC, Child.Bk.Rev.Ind. (1965-), Curr.Cont., Hist.Abstr., Hum.Ind., Ind.Bk.Rev.Hum., LCR, M.L.A., Mid.East: Abstr.& Ind., P.A.I.S.
   —BLDSC shelfmark: 8348.670000.
   Refereed Serial

052   UK   ISSN 0261-1953
S O A P. 1980. 6/yr. £0.60. Selly Oak Alternative Paper, c/o Ms. B. Fay, 64 Oak Tree La., Selly Oak, Birmingham, England. illus.

808.8   US   ISSN 0749-1670
Z716.4
S R R T NEWSLETTER. 1969. 4/yr. $10 to non-members; institutions $20. American Library Association, Social Responsibilities Round Table, 50 E. Huron St., Chicago, IL 60611. TEL 312-944-6780. FAX 312-440-9374. Ed. Thomas Wilding. bk.rev.; bibl.; illus.; circ. 1,290.
   Formerly: A L A Social Responsibilities Round Table Newsletter (ISSN 0065-9096)
   Description: information on underground library periodicals.

053.1   GW   ISSN 0036-2115
DD801.S13
SAARBRUECKER HEFTE. 1955. s-a. DM.14.50. Ottweiler Druckerei und Verlag GmbH, Sauermilchstr. 14, 6682 Ottweiler, Germany. Ed.Bd. bk.rev.; illus.; index.

808.87   UA
SABAH AL-KHAIR. w. 18 Sharia Muhammad Said Pasha, Cairo, Egypt. Ed. Mofeed Fawzi. circ. 70,000.
   Description: Humor and entertainment.

808.8   BG
SACHITRA SANDHANI. (Text in Bengali) 1978. w. Tk.2. 68-2 Purana Paltan, Dhaka, Bangladesh. TEL 2-409680. Ed. Gazi Shahabuddin Mahmud. circ. 13,000.

ST. LOUIS REVIEW. see *RELIGIONS AND THEOLOGY — Roman Catholic*

809   JA
SAITAMA UNIVERSITY. COLLEGE OF LIBERAL ARTS. JOURNAL. (Text in English) vol.26, 1978. irreg. free. Saitama Daigaku, Bungakubu - Saitama University, College of Liberal Arts, 1255 Shimookubo, Urawa-shi, Saitama-ken 338, Japan. circ. 500.

052   II
SAJIT MONTHLY. (Text in English) 1974. m. Rs.1.25 per no. Sajit Print, 2 F Dilkusha St., Calcutta 17, India. Ed. M.M. John.

056.1   MX   ISSN 0300-3388
SALAMANDRA;* revista de cultura. 1969. 3/yr. $60. Editorial "Alfonso Reyes", Adolfo Prieto 2407 Oriente, Monterrey, N.L., Mexico. adv.; bk.rev.; film rev.; bibl.; illus.; circ. controlled. (processed) **Indexed:** Biol.Abstr.

052   UK   ISSN 0265-4881
SALISBURY REVIEW; a quarterly magazine of conservative thought. q. £10($19) Sherwood Press, 88 Twlney Rd., London E7, England. Ed. Roger Scruton. adv.; bk.rev.; circ. 1,000. (back issues avail.) **Indexed:** ASSIA.
   —BLDSC shelfmark: 8070.921000.

055.1   IT
SALVO IMPREVISTI; quadrimestrale di poesia. 1974. 3/yr. L.20000. Salvo Imprevisti, c/o Mariella Bettarini, Ed., Borgo SS. Apostoli 4, 50123 Florence, Italy. TEL 055-289569. adv.; bk.rev.; bibl.

058.82   NO   ISSN 0036-3928
AP45
SAMTIDEN; tidsskrift for politikk, litteratur og samfunnsspoersmaal. 1890. bi-m. NOK 280 to individuals; libraries Kr.320 (typically set in Jan.). H. Aschehoug & Co. (W. Nygaard) A-S, Sehestedsgt 3, Oslo 1, Norway. FAX 02-206395. (Subscr. to: Forlagsentralen, Box 150 Furuset, 1001 Oslo 10, Norway) Ed.Bd. adv.; bk.rev.; circ. 5,500. (back issues avail.) **Indexed:** Hist.Abstr. (until 1990), M.L.A.

378.1   CU   ISSN 0048-9115
AS71.A1
SANTIAGO. 1971. q. $10 in N. and S. America; Europe $12; others $14. (Universidad de Oriente, Departamento de Extension Universitaria) Ediciones Cubanas, Obispo No. 527, Apdo. 605, Havana, Cuba. Ed. Nils Castro. bk.rev.; illus. **Indexed:** Hist.Abstr.

808.8   US
SAPIENS.* 1983. s-a. $10. Sapiens Press, 213 Deland Ave., Cherry Hill, NJ 08034-2043. Eds. Bonnie Gordon, Edward Kaplan. circ. 200.

LITERARY AND POLITICAL REVIEWS 2883

800 US
SAPPHO'S ISLE. 1988. m. $15. Sappho's Isle, Inc., 960 Willis Ave., Albertson, NY 11507. TEL 516-747-5417. FAX 516-747-5417. adv.; bk.rev.; circ. 10,000. (tabloid format; back issues avail.)

808.8 BG
SAPTAHIKA BICITRA. (Text in Bengali) 1972. w. Tk.6 per. no. Dainik Bangla Group of Publications, 1, DIT Avenue, Dhaka 2, Bangladesh. Ed. Shahadat Chowdhury. adv.; bk.rev.; circ. 53,000.

810 US
SARAH LAWRENCE REVIEW. 1957. a. free. Sarah Lawrence College, Writing Department, c/o Thomas Lux, Bronxville, NY 10708. TEL 914-337-0700. circ. 1,500 (controlled).
  Former titles: Sarah Lawrence Literary Review; S.L. Literary Review (ISSN 0036-4746)

808.87 US
SARCASTICS ANONYMOUS AND LAUGH LOVERS NEWS. 1981. q. $10. (Sarcastics Anonymous) Stoneridge Publishing, Box 1495, 7953 Stonehurst Pl., Pleasanton, CA 94566. TEL 415-462-3470. Ed. Virginia Tooper. circ. 600. (looseleaf format; back issues avail.)
  Formerly: Laugh Lovers News.
  Description: Explores the positive and negative uses of humor with a light approach.

808.8 410 PR
SARGASSO; theater, film, poetry, performance, criticism. 1984. s-a. $9 to individuals; institutions $18. Td Imag, Inc., Box 22831, University Sta., Rio Piedras, PR 00931-2831. (Co-sponsor: University of Puerto Rico) Ed. Lowell Fiet. circ. 300. (back issues avail.)

SARMATIAN REVIEW. see ETHNIC INTERESTS

055 IT
SATIRA.* 1980. m. Kaos Edizione, Viale Abruzzi 58, 20131 Milan, Italy. Ed. Domenico Nodari.

055.1 IT ISSN 0036-5742
SCENA ILLUSTRATA; politica, turismo, attualita, arte, cultura. 1865. m. L.35000. Via Cernaia 43, Rome, Italy. Dir. Italo Carlo Sesti. bk.rev.; illus.; circ. 24,100.

378 US ISSN 0048-931X
SCENE (NORTHRIDGE). 1971. 4/yr. free. California State University, Northridge, Department of Journalism, 335 Faculty Office Bldg., Northridge, CA 91330. TEL 818-885-3135. Ed. Maureen Rubin. illus.; circ. 8,000.

053.1 SZ ISSN 0036-7400
AP32
SCHWEIZER MONATSHEFTE; Zeitschrift fuer Politik, Wirtschaft, Kultur. (Text in German; occasionally in French) 1921. m. 60 Fr. (Gesellschaft Schweizer Monatshefte) Schulthess Polygraphisher, Zwingliplatz 2, 8022 Zurich, Switzerland. Ed.Bd. adv.; bk.rev.; abstr.; index; circ. 2,500. (tabloid format; also avail. in microform from UMI; reprint service avail. from UMI) Indexed: Hist.Abstr.
  —BLDSC shelfmark: 8112.350000.

052 UK
THE SCILLONIAN. 1925. s-a. £7 (foreign £8). Scillonian, c/o C.T. Mumford, Ed., St. Mary's, Isles of Scilly, Cornwall, England. circ. 2,500. (back issues avail.)

052 GW ISSN 0265-5543
SCORPION. 1981. s-m. $15. Scorpion Press, Schnellweiderstr. 50, 5000 Cologne 80, Germany. Ed. Michael Walker. adv.; bk.rev.; film rev.; play rev.; bibl.; illus.; circ. 2,000. (back issues avail.)

051 US ISSN 0360-2672
SCREE. 1973. 5/yr. $8.50 individuals; institutions $10. Duck Down Press, Box 1047, Fallon, NV 89406. Ed. Kirk Robertson. bk.rev.; illus.; circ. 1,000. Indexed: Access.

051 US ISSN 0036-9624
SCREW. 1968. w. $56. Milky Way Productions Inc., 116 W. 14th St., Box 432, Old Chelsea Sta., New York, NY 10011. TEL 212-989-8001. FAX 212-924-8154. Ed. Manny Neuhaus. adv.; bk.rev.; film rev.; play rev.; illus.; stat.; circ. 175,000. (tabloid format; also avail. in microfilm)
  Description: Covers adult literature, political, and social humor.

052 UK ISSN 0048-9905
SEAR.* no. 46, 1971. m. 75p. Manchester Mensa, c/o Andrew White, 212 Buxton Rd., Davenport, Stockport, Ches, England. Ed.Bd. illus. (processed)

056.1 MX
SEMANA POLITICA. 1955. m. Mex.$35. Antonio Caso 31-1, Mexico 4, D.F., Mexico. Ed. Francisco Arreola, Jr. adv.; circ. 21,400.

808.87 CU
SEMINARIA PA'LANTE. w. $50. (Instituto Cubano del Libro) Ediciones Cubanas, Departamento de Exportacion, Obispo No. 461, Apdo. 605, Havana, Cuba. illus.; circ. 50,000. (tabloid format)
  Description: Satirical humor magazine with caricatures, photos and text of a humorous nature on the current national and international political, economic, cultural and sport scenes.

808.8 US
SENSOR. 1976. a. $5. c/o George M. Rawlins, Box 16074, San Diego, CA 92116. adv.; circ. 700. Indexed: Forest Prod.Abstr.
  Formerly: Antenna.

378.1 US ISSN 0037-2420
PS508.C6
SEQUOIA (STANFORD). 1887. 2/yr. $10. Stanford University, Associated Students, Storke Publications Building, Stanford, CA 94305. TEL 415-497-4331. Eds. Carlos Rodriguez, Mark Clevenger. adv.; bk.rev.; illus.; circ. 500. Indexed: A.I.P.P.
  Description: Presents poetry, fiction, drama, and art.

052 UK
Y SEREN. 1948. bi-w. (during college term only). free. (University College of North Wales, Bangor Students' Union) Copycat, High St., Bangor, Gwynedd, Wales. Ed. Ingrid Mader. adv.; bk.rev.; film rev.; play rev.; circ. 2,000. (tabloid format)
  Former titles: Vox; Graffiti; Forecast (ISSN 0015-7074)

056.1 SP ISSN 0037-2501
DP302.C57
SERRA D'OR. 1959. m. (July-Aug. combined). 4250 ptas.($62) Publicacions de l' Abadia de Montserrat, Ausias March 92-98, Apdo. 244, 08013 Barcelona, Spain. TEL 93-2450303. Ed. Maur M. Boix. adv.; bk.rev.; film rev.; play rev.; bibl.; illus.; index; circ. 15,000. Indexed: Hist.Abstr.

SEWANEE REVIEW. see LITERATURE

057.1 RU
▼**SHANS.** 1990. m. 1.90 Rub. Soyuz Predprinimatelei i Arendatorov Urala, Ul. Gor'kogo 10 "A", 45007 Chelyabinsk, Russia. TEL 77-24-04. Ed. A.V. Lobashev. circ. 60,000.

AL-SHARQ. see ART

810 US ISSN 0037-3583
AP2
SHENANDOAH: THE WASHINGTON AND LEE UNIVERSITY REVIEW. 1950. q. $11. Washington and Lee University, Shenandoah, Box 722, Lexington, VA 24450. TEL 703-463-8765. FAX 703-463-8945. Eds. Lynn Williams, Dabney Stuart. adv.; bk.rev.; index; circ. 1,400. (also avail. in microform from UMI; back issues avail.; reprint service avail. from UMI) Indexed: Abstr.Engl.Stud., Amer.Hum.Ind., Arts & Hum.Cit.Ind., Ind.Amer.Per.Verse, Ind.Bk.Rev.Hum., LCR, M.L.A.
  —BLDSC shelfmark: 8256.375000.
  Description: Publishes award-winning fiction, poetry, essays and interviews.

SHEPHERD EXPRESS; Milwaukee's weekly alternative newspaper. see GENERAL INTEREST PERIODICALS — United States

059 JA
SHOKUN. 1969. m. 8280 Yen. Bungei Shunju Ltd., 3-23, Kioi-cho, Chiyoda-ku, Tokyo, Japan. FAX 03-3265-4878. Ed. Kouji Shirakawa.
  Description: Opinion magazine for intellectuals.

800 US ISSN 1052-648X
SHORT STORY. 1989. s-a. $7. T S C - U T Brownsville, Department of English, 80 Fort Brown, Brownsville, TX 78520. TEL 512-544-8239. (Co-sponsor: University of Northern Iowa) Eds. Mary Rohrberger, Farhat Iftekharuddin. adv.; bk.rev.; circ. 800. (back issues avail.)
  Description: Publishes original short stories, critical essays, and interviews.

052 AA
SHQIPERIA E RE. English edition: New Albania. 1947. m. (Albanian ed.); bi-m. (Arabic, English, French, German, Russian, Spanish editions). $3.60. Committee for Foreign Cultural Relations, Rruga Asim Vokshi 2, Tirana, Albania. Ed. Ymer Minxhozi. illus.; circ. 170,000.
  Description: Presents party directives and decisions. Includes speeches of political figures and features on Albanian industry, agriculture, history, science, education, literature, and art.

949.65 AA
SHQIPERIA SOT/ALBANIE AUJOURD'HUI. English edition: Albania Today (ISSN 0044-7072); French edition: Albanie Aujourd'hui (ISSN 0252-919X) (Editions in English, French, German, Italian, Spanish) 1971. bi-m. $3.60. Partia e Punes e Shqiperise, Tirana, Albania. Ed. Dhimiter Verli. charts; illus.

808.8 US ISSN 1059-2210
▼**SIDEWALKS**; a magazine for emerging and published writers. 1991. s-a. $8. Sidewalks, Box 321, Champlin, MN 55316. Ed. Tom Heie. circ. 500.

056.1 MX
SIEMPRE!. 1953. w. Vallarta 20, Apdo. 4-033, 06470 Mexico D.F., Mexico. TEL 5-566-9355. FAX 5-546-5130. Ed. Beatriz Pages Rebollas. circ. 185,000.

051 US ISSN 0891-6926
SIGN OF THE TIMES; a chronicle of decadence in the atomic age. 1981. s-a. $7.50. Studio 403, 3819 NE 15th St, Portland, OR 97212. TEL 206-323-6764. Ed. Mark Souder. circ. 750. (back issues avail.)

700 800 US ISSN 1040-4724
THE SIGNAL (EMMETT); network international. 1987. s-a. $10. Box 67, Emmett, ID 83617. TEL 208-365-5812. bk.rev.; circ. 500. (back issues avail.)
  Description: Concerned mainly with art and literature. Explores worldwide issues and human and planetary concerns.

055.1 IT ISSN 0037-5179
SILARUS; rassegna bimestrale di cultura. (Text in Italian, Latin; summaries in Italian) 1965. bi-m. L.15000. Italo Rocco, Ed. & Pub.; Via B. Buozzi 317, Casella Postale 317, 84091 Battipaglia, Salerno, Italy. adv.; bk.rev.; play rev.; abstr.; bibl.; illus.; circ. 2,000. Indexed: M.L.A.

052 CN ISSN 0037-5217
SILHOUETTE. 1930. w. Can.$40. (McMaster University, Students Union) M S U, Rm. 405, Hamilton Hall, 1280 Main St. W., Hamilton, Ont. L8S 4K1. TEL 416-525-9140. FAX 416-527-0100. Ed. Scott Humphrey. adv.; bk.rev.; film rev.; play rev.; circ. 12,000.
  Description: Covers university, community, national and international events from a student perspective.

891.553 IR
▼**SIMURGH.** 1990. m. Rs.350 per no. M.A. Biramabad, Ed. & Pub., P.O. Box 13145-844, Teheran, Iran.
  Description: Covers literary and Islamic affairs.

700 800 US
▼**SIREN MAGAZINE.** 1990. m. $18. Box 66099, Houston, TX 77266-6099. TEL 713-526-1262. FAX 713-771-6849. adv.; bk.rev.; circ. 15,000. (controlled).
  Formerly: Blonde on Blonde.
  Description: Covers fashion, fiction, music and art.

LITERARY AND POLITICAL REVIEWS

700 US
SKETCH. 1935. s-a. $3. Iowa State University, Government of the Student Body, Memorial Union, 203 Ross Hall, Ames, IA 50010. TEL 515-232-2477. circ. 3,000.
Description: Features the poetry, prose, photography and artwork of the Iowa State University student population.

808.87 GW
SLAPSTICK.* 1978. irreg.? DM.2.60 per no. Pardon Verlagsgesellschaft mbH, AM Urselback 6, 6000 Frankfurt, Germany. Ed. Hans A. Nikel.

052 UK
SLIGHTLY SOILED. 6/yr. £8. c/o Turret Bookshop, 42 Lambs Conduit St., London WC1N 3IJ, England. Eds. David Crystal, Timothy Cumming. illus.

057 CS
SLOBODA. w. $55. (Strana Slobody - Party of Liberty) Obzor, Ceskoslovenskej Armady 35, 815 85 Bratislava, Czechoslovakia.

059 GW
SLOBODNE SLOVENSKO/FREE SLOVAKIA; newspaper of the Slovaks abroad. (Text in Slovak) 1962. bi-m. DM.30. Slowakisches Matus-Cernak-Institut, Kulturelles Zentrum der Slowaken in Deutschland, D-8019 Glonn-Zinneberg 1, Germany. Ed. Kristof Greiner. bk.rev.; circ. 1,500.
Formerly: Cernakov Odkaz (ISSN 0009-0395)

057 CS
SLOVENSKE KUPELE. q. $20. (Slovakofarma) Obzor, Ceskoslovenskej Armady 35, 815 85 Bratislava, Czechoslovakia. Ed.Bd.

057.8 XV ISSN 0350-4697
SLOVENSKI CEBELAR. (Text in Slovenian; summaries in English) 1898. m. 250 din.($32) Zveza Cebelarskih Drustev Slovenije, Cankarjeva 3, 61000 Ljubljana, Slovenia. TEL 061-210-992. Ed. Janez Mihelic. adv.; bk.rev.; index; circ. 7,000. (back issues avail.)

943.7 GW ISSN 0037-7058
SLOWAKEI/SLOVAKIA; kulturpolitische Revue. 1963. a. DM.6. Matus-Cernak-Institut, Kulturelles Zentrum der Slowaken in Deutschland, Postfach 100924, 5000 Cologne 1, Germany. Ed. Alba Greiner. bk.rev.; circ. 1,500.

808.8 US
SNARF.* 1972. s-a. Kitchen Sink Press, Inc., Rt. 1, Box 329, Princeton, WI 54968. TEL 414-295-6922. FAX 414-295-6878. Ed. Denis Kitchen. circ. 7,000.
Description: Contains contributions by top cartoonists: Robert Crumb, Howard Cruse, Drew Friedman and Will Elder.

SNOECK'S: LITERATUUR KUNST FILM TONEEL MODE REIZEN. see *HUMANITIES: COMPREHENSIVE WORKS*

051 US ISSN 0196-4801
HX821
SOCIAL ANARCHISM; a journal of practice & theory. 1980. s-a. $14 for 4 nos. 2743 Maryland Ave., Baltimore, MD 21218. TEL 301-243-6987. Ed. H.J. Ehrlich. adv.; bk.rev.; circ. 1,200. Indexed: Alt.Press Ind.
Description: Essays, reviews interviews, poetry and graphics concerning anarchism, feminism, political ecology, and community.

320 US
SOCIALIST REPUBLIC. 1973. 4/yr. $3. Industrial Union Party, Box 80, Madison Square Station, New York, NY 10159. TEL 212-563-8100. (Or: Industrial Union Party, Box 711, Red Bank, NJ 07701) Eds. Murray Block, Walter Petrovich. adv.; bk.rev.; bibl.; circ. 2,000.

054.1 FR
SOCIETE J.K. HUYSMANS. BULLETIN. 1927. irreg., approx. 2/yr. 100 F. membership. Societe J.K. Huysmans, 22 rue Guynemer, 75006 Paris, France. adv.; bk.rev.; circ. 600 (controlled).

054.1 FR
SOCIETE LITTERAIRE DES P.T.T. BULLETIN. 1946. q. membership. 6 Impasse Bonne Nouvelle, 75010 Paris, France. Ed. Andre Darrigrand. adv.; bk.rev.; bibl.; circ. 6,000.

057.8 XV ISSN 0038-0482
AP58.S55
SODOBNOST. (Text in Slovenian) 1953. m. 120 din.($6.85) (Republiska Konferenca Delovnego Ljudstva Slovenije) Drzavna Zalozba Slovenije, Stritarjeva 3-11, Box 50-1, Ljubljana, Slovenia. Ed. Ciril Zlobec. circ. 1,400. Indexed: M.L.A.

914.7 LI
SOGLASIE. (Text in Russian) 1988. w. Zygimantu 26, Vilnius 232600, Lithuania. TEL (0122) 226-206. Ed. Liuba Ciornaya.

808.8 US
SOLID GROUND: A NEW WORLD JOURNAL.* 1981. q. $9. Go-For-What-You-Know, Inc., 371 Second St., No. 2, Brooklyn, NY 11215-2403. Ed. Kofi Natambu.

051 800 US
SOMA; left coast cultural. 1986. q. $10. SOMA Publications, 285 9th St., San Francisco, CA 94103. TEL 415-558-8974. Eds. Ali Ghanbarian, Jon Batchelor. adv.; bk.rev.; film rev.; play rev.; illus.; circ. 30,000. (back issues avail.)
Description: Provides a cultural overview of the San Francisco Bay area, with a focus on arts activities in the section south of Market St.

053.1 GW ISSN 0038-1411
AP30
SONNTAG; kulturpolitische Wochenzeitung. 1946. w. DM.15.60 (foreign DM.26). Kulturbund der DDR, Otto-Nuscke-Str. 1, 1080 Berlin, Germany. adv.; bk.rev.; dance rev.; film rev.; play rev.; illus.
Description: Covers theatre, literature, art, architecture, music, film, travel and more. Includes reports and announcements of events in Eastern part of Germany, and international news.

055 IT
IL SOSPIRO DEL TIFOSO; perodico vicentino di sport e cultura. 1964. bi-w. L.15000($12) Pino Dato, Via V. Veneto 13, 36100 Vicenza, Italy. adv.; circ. 2,000. (tabloid format; back issues avail.)

850 398 IT ISSN 0038-1659
SOT LA NAPE; filologje, leterature, folclor. (Text in Friulian, Italian) 1949. q. L.40000($33) membership. (Regione Friuli - Venezia - Giulia) GEAP Pordenone, Via Malignani 41, 33080 Fiume Veneto (PN), Italy. TEL 0432-501598. FAX 0432-511766. (Subscr. to: Societa Filologica Friulana, Via Manin 18, 33100 Udine, Italy) Ed. Giuseppe Bergamini. adv.; bk.rev.; illus.; index; circ. 3,800. (back issues avail.) Indexed: Numis.Lit.

057.91 KR ISSN 0038-1705
SOTSIALISTYCHNA KUL'TURA. (Text in Ukrainian) m. $6. Ministerstvo Kul'tury, Kiev, Ukraine. Ed. A.P. Varlamov. circ. 47,100.

057.1 RU ISSN 0868-8230
▼**SOTSIUM.** 1991. m. 1.30 Rub. Bol'shaya Pochtovaya 7, 107082 Moscow, Russia. TEL 261-33-59. Ed. Aleksandr Zolotarev.

SOUND MONEY INVESTOR. see *BUSINESS AND ECONOMICS — Investments*

296.67 IS ISSN 0082-4585
SOURCES OF CONTEMPORARY JEWISH THOUGHT/MEKEVOT. Title varies: To the Source - El Ha'ayin. (Text in English, French, Spanish, Hebrew) 1968. irreg., no.6, 1975. price varies. World Zionist Organization, Department for Torah Education and Culture in the Diaspora, P.O. Box 92, Jerusalem 91920, Israel. TEL 02-527156. FAX 02-533542. (Subscr. to: Jewish Agency, Publication Service, 515 Park Ave., New York, NY 10022) Ed.Bd.

051 US ISSN 0038-3430
THE SOUTH END. vol.7, 1973. d. $70. Wayne State University, Detroit, MI 48202. TEL 313-577-3494. FAX 313-577-6546. Ed. Rena K. Schneider. adv.; bk.rev.; charts; illus.; tr.lit.; circ. 10,000. (also avail. in microfiche)
Description: Gannett News Service wire copy and graphics.

052 659.1 AT
SOUTH EAST MAGAZINE. 1976. w. Queanbeyan Publishing Co., 210 Crawford St., Queanbeyan, N.S.W. 2620, Australia. FAX 06-2-97-6201. Ed. R.J. Woods. adv.; bk.rev.; circ. 40,000.
Description: Supplement to 18 local newspapers covering the south east region of New South Wales.

051 US ISSN 0146-809X
F206
SOUTHERN EXPOSURE (DURHAM). 1973. q. $24. Institute for Southern Studies, Box 531, Durham, NC 27702. TEL 919-688-8167. Ed. Eric Bates. adv.; bk.rev.; bibl.; charts; illus.; stat.; s-a. index; circ. 7,500. (also avail. in microfilm from UMI; back issues avail.; reprint service avail. from UMI) Indexed: Access (1977-), Alt.Press Ind., Hist.Abstr., Hum.Ind., Lang.& Lang.Behav.Abstr., Sociol.Abstr.
Description: Covers innovative design, investigative journalism, oral history and profiles.

051 020 US
SOUTHWEST BOOK REVIEW.* 1987. m. $15. 604 Arbor Cir., Austin, TX 78745-3030. TEL 512-443-6618. Ed. Julie Gomoll. adv.; bk.rev.; circ. 5,000. (back issues avail.)
Description: Intended for librarians.

810 US ISSN 0038-4712
AP2
SOUTHWEST REVIEW. 1915. q. $20 to individuals; institutions $25. Southern Methodist University, 307 Foudren Library West, Box 4374, Dallas, TX 75275. TEL 214-373-7440. Ed. Willard Spiegelman. adv.; index. cum.index: vols.10-29 (1924-1944), vols.30-60 (1945-1970); circ. 1,400. (also avail. in microform from UMI; reprint service avail. from UMI) Indexed: A.I.P.P., Abstr.Engl.Stud., Abstr.Pop.Cult., Amer.Hum.Ind., Bibl.Engl.Lang.& Lit., Bk.Rev.Ind. (1965-), Child.Bk.Rev.Ind. (1965-), Hist.Abstr., Hum.Ind., Ind.Amer.Per.Verse, Ind.Bk.Rev.Hum., M.L.A.
—BLDSC shelfmark: 8356.900000.
Description: Presents the work of writers and scholars from the surrounding states and offers analyses of problems and themes that are distinctly southwestern. Publishes works of good writers regardless of their locales.

059 RU
SOVIETISH HEIMLAND/SOVETSKAYA RODINA. (Text in Yiddish; summaries in English, Russian) 1961. bi-m. 9.60 Rub.($12.50) Soyuz Pisatelei S.S.S.R. - U.S.S.R. Union of Writers, Ul. Vorovskaya 11, Moscow, Russia. (Dist. by: Mezhdunarodnaya Kniga, Dimitrov Str. 39, Moscow 113095, Russia) Ed. Aron Vergelis. play rev.; bibl.; illus.; stat. (back issues avail.)

052 820 821 UK
SOW'S EAR. (Text in English) 1982. s-a. £1.40($5) per no. 1 Small Lane, Eccleshall, Stafford ST21 6AD, England. Ed. R.J. Ellis. circ. 250. (back issues avail.)
Supersedes: Strange Lime Fruit Stone.
Description: Poetry with features on a single author per issue.

052 700 UK ISSN 0584-8067
SPANNER (LONDON, 1974). 1974. irreg. £12 for 3 issues to institutions. 14 Hopton Rd., Hereford HR1 1BE, England. Ed. Allen Fisher. adv.; bk.rev.

059 LO
SPARK.* 1977. bi-m. National University of Lesotho, PO Rome 80, Maseru, Lesotho. Ed. N. Theko.

051 FR
SPEAKEASY; English through the news. (Text in English) 1979. 5/yr. 114 F. Librairie Fernand Nathan, 9 rue Mechain, 75680 Paris cedex 14, France. Ed. Michelle Sommers.

054.1 FR
AP20
SPECTACLE DU MONDE - REALITES - PERSPECTIVES. 1962. m. 576 F. (foreign 665 F.). Valmonde & Cie, 54 rue Martre, 92586 Clichy Cedex, France. TEL 49-68-18-18. FAX 1-47-35-85-00. Ed. Francois d'Orcival. adv.; bk.rev.; abstr.; bibl.; charts; illus.; stat.; index; circ. 140,000.
Former titles: Spectacle du Monde - Spectacle - Perspectives; Spectacle du Monde (ISSN 0038-6944); Incorporates (as of 1980): Realites.

LITERARY AND POLITICAL REVIEWS

827 UK ISSN 0038-6952
AP4
SPECTATOR. 1828. w. $110. Spectator (1828) Ltd., 56 Doughty St., London WC1N 2LL, England. FAX 242-0603. TELEX 27124. (Subscr. to: P.O. Box 14, Harold Hill, Romford, Essex RM3 8E0, England) Ed. D. Lawson. adv.; bk.rev.; film rev.; music rev.; play rev.; index; circ. 40,000. (also avail. in microform from UMI; reprint service avail. from UMI) **Indexed:** Bk.Rev.Ind. (1965-), Br.Hum.Ind., Child.Bk.Rev.Ind. (1965-).
—BLDSC shelfmark: 8408.600000.

378.1 UK ISSN 0038-7428
SPHINX; the student magazine for Liverpool. 1892. 4/yr. £4 per no. Liverpool Guild of Undergraduates, Student Union, 2 Bedford St. N., Liverpool 7, England. Ed. Claire Coombis. adv.; bk.rev.; circ. 5,000.

055.1 IT
SPIRALI;* giornale internazionale di cultura. 1978. m. L.20000. Spirali s.r.l., Via Victor Hugo 1, 21125 Milan, Italy. Ed. Annalisa Scalco. adv.; circ. 55,840.

057.8 XV ISSN 0038-8777
SRECANJA. (Text in Slovenian) 1948. bi-m. 200 din. Franciskanska Prokuratura, Presernov trg 4, Ljubljana, Slovenia. Ed. Mihael Vovk. circ. 3,000.

055.1 IT ISSN 0049-2051
STAMPA SUD. 1960? w. L.7000. Piazzetta Matilde Serao, N.7, 80132 Naples, Italy. Ed. Volturno Morani. adv.; bk.rev.; film rev.; illus.

STAND MAGAZINE. see LITERATURE

STANFORD CHAPARRAL. see COLLEGE AND ALUMNI

STANFORD ITALIAN REVIEW. see LITERATURE

057.8 CI ISSN 0352-2873
START; magazin modernog covjeka. 1969. bi-m. $32. Vjesnik, Avenija Bratstva i Jedinstva 4, 4100 Zagreb, Croatia. Ed. Mladen Plese.

STEAUA. see LITERATURE

053.1 IS
DIE STIMME. (Text in German) 1944. m. $50. World Association of Bukowinean Jews, P.O. Box 1356, Tel Aviv 61013, Israel. Ed. Meir Faerber. adv.; bk.rev.; play rev.; circ. 1,200.

057.1 RU ISSN 0868-698X
▼**STOLITSA.** 1990. w. 1 Rub.($2.98) per issue. Petrovka 22, 101425 Moscow K-51, Russia. TEL 928-23-49. FAX 095-921-2955. TELEX 413739 SU. (Subscr. to: Econews, Box 535, Lausanne 1001, Switzerland. TEL 41-21-311-4505) Ed. Andrei Mal'gin. illus.; circ. 300,000.

051 US
STONE'S JOURNAL. 1979. m? Double L, Inc., c/o J.W. Mondesire, Ed., 6715 Lincoln Dr., Philadelphia, PA 19119.

809 US ISSN 0146-2067
STONY HILLS; news and reviews of the small press. 1977. 3/yr. $4 to individuals; institutions $5. Diane Kruchkow, Ed. & Pub., Weeks Mills, New Sharon, ME 04955. (Or: Kilgour, Inc., Box 725, Newburyport, MA 01950) adv.; bk.rev.; cum.index: 1977-1981; circ. 3,000. (tabloid format; also avail. in microfilm; back issues avail.) **Indexed:** Access, Bk.Rev.Ind. (1981-1983), Child.Bk.Rev.Ind. (1981-1983).
Formerly: New England Small Press Review.

808.8 US
STORM; a journal for free spirits. 1976. irreg. (approx. 1-2/yr.). $4 per no. Mackay Society, Box 131, Ansonia Sta., New York, NY 10023. TEL 212-595-1669. Ed.Bd. adv.; bk.rev.; circ. 300. (back issues avail.)

055 IT
LO STRADONE; il giornale di Corato. 1979. m. L.17000 (foreign L.43000). Lo Stradone, Via Andria 44, 70033 Corato (Bari), Italy. TEL 080-8724205. FAX 8724205. Ed. Emilio D'Angelo. adv.; bk.rev.; circ. 3,500. (looseleaf format; back issues avail.) **Description:** Focuses on news, sports, politics and local history of Corato, Italy.

052 UK
STREETLIFE. 1985. s-a. free. London Borough of Hammersmith and Fulham, Town Hall, King St., London W6 9JU, England. FAX 741-2685. Ed. Carol Todd. adv.; stat.; circ. 86,000.
Formerly: London Borough of Hammersmith and Fulham. Review.

059.91 XN ISSN 0039-2294
STREMEZ; spisanie za literatura, umetnost i kultura. (Text in Macedonian) 1957. 10/yr. 40 din. Interesna Zaednica na Kulturata, Prilep, Joska Jordanoski 2, Prilep, Macedonia. Ed. Branko Ilievski. circ. 1,500.

053 NE ISSN 0165-6759
STUDENT; landelijk maandblad voor studenten. 1963. m. fl.18.25. De Studenten Uitgeverij, Smidstraat 12, 8746 NG Schraard, Netherlands. TEL 05175-1583. Ed. P.I. Bakker. adv.; bk.rev.; circ. 65,000.

320 UK ISSN 0260-2563
STUDENT NATIONALIST; the paper for the independent-minded Scot. 1979? irreg. contributions. Federation of Student Nationalists, c/o Student Union, Aberdeen University, Upper Kirkgate, Aberdeen, Scotland. Ed. Eric Herring. illus.; circ. 5,000.
Formerly: Nor'-easter.

STUDI STORICI/HISTORICAL STUDIES. see HISTORY

808.87 US ISSN 0095-280X
PS430
STUDIES IN AMERICAN HUMOR. 1974. 4/yr. $10 to individuals; institutions $15. American Humor Publications, Inc., Southwest Texas State University, Department of English, San Marcos, TX 78666. TEL 512-245-2163. Ed. John O. Rosenbalm. adv.; bk.rev.; circ. 500. **Indexed:** Abstr.Engl.Stud., M.L.A.
—BLDSC shelfmark: 8489.070000.
Incorporates (1974-1984): American Humor (ISSN 0193-7146)

808.87 US ISSN 0163-4143
PN6149.S2
STUDIES IN CONTEMPORARY SATIRE. 1973. a. $3. Clarion University, English Department, Clarion, PA 16214. Ed. C. Darrel Sheraw. adv.; bk.rev.; circ. 350. (back issues avail.) **Indexed:** Abstr.Engl.Stud., Amer.Bibl.Slavic & E.Eur.Stud., M.L.A.
—BLDSC shelfmark: 8490.307240.

055.1 IT ISSN 0039-4130
STUDIUM; rivista bimestrale di cultura. 1904. bi-m. L.48000 (foreign L.70000)(effective Jan. 1992). Edizioni Studium, Via Cassiodoro 14, 00193 Rome, Italy. (Subscr. to: C.P. 30100, 00100 Rome 47, Italy) adv.; bk.rev.; bibl.; index; circ. 3,000. (back issues avail.) **Indexed:** Hist.Abstr., M.L.A., RILA.
Description: Covers expressions of a working community in a creative and direct way, avoiding criticism. Faces the most significant cultural issues with passages, notes, summaries and reviews.

057.8 YU ISSN 0039-422X
STVARANJE; casopis za knjizevnost i kulturu. 1946. m. 200 din. Pobjeda, Bulevar Revolucije 11, Box 37, 81000 Titograd, Yugoslavia. Ed.Bd. bk.rev.; index; circ. 2,100. **Indexed:** M.L.A.
—BLDSC shelfmark: 0168.496000.

810 910.03 US
STYLUS LITERARY REPORT. 6/yr. 1046 Sterling Pl., Brooklyn, NY 11213. Ed. Erica Williams.
Description: Reviews African-American books.

SUBTERRANEAN SOCIOLOGY NEWSLETTER. see SOCIOLOGY

053.1 AU ISSN 0039-4629
SUEDTIROL IN WORT UND BILD. 1957. q. S.158. Suedtirol Verlag, Defreggerstr. 23, A-6020 Innsbruck, Austria. Ed. Herbert Neuner. adv.; bk.rev.; bibl.; illus.; circ. 15,000.

SULFUR; a literary bi-annual of the whole art. see LITERATURE

808.8 US ISSN 0744-9666
AP2
SUN (CHAPEL HILL); a magazine of ideas. 1974. m. $30. Sun Publishing Company, Inc., 107 N. Roberson St., Chapel Hill, NC 27516. TEL 919-942-5282. Ed. Sy Safransky. circ. 11,000. (also avail. in microform from UMI; back issues avail.) **Indexed:** Alt.Press Ind.

808.0 UK ISSN 0955-9647
SUNK ISLAND REVIEW. 1989. s-a. £6.80($15) Sunk Island Publishing, P.O. Box 74, Lincoln LN1 1QG, England. TEL 0522-520-645. Ed. Michael Blackburn. adv.; bk.rev. (back issues avail.)

808.87
SUPER CRACKED. q. $1.50 per no. Globe Communications Corp. (New York), 441 Lexington Ave., New York, NY 10017. TEL 800-472-7744. circ. 400,000.

860 CU
SUPLEMENTO LITERARIO DE REVOLUCION Y CULTURA. 4/yr. Ministerio de Cultura, Direccion de Literature, Calle 4, No.205, entre 11 y Linea Vedado, Havana, Cuba.

800 PK
SURAJ MUKHI. (Text in Panjabi) 1978. m. Rs.20. 129-17 Zaildar Rd, Ichhra, Lahore, Pakistan.

800 II
SURGE INTERNATIONAL. (Text in English) 1976. m. Rs.50. B-90, Defence Colony, New Delhi 110024, India. (U.S. dist. addr.: c/o Indrani Rahman, 314 W. 56th St., Apt. 1C, New York, NY 10019) Ed. Uma Vasudev. adv.; bk.rev.

SURPLUS; tijdschrift over literatuur van vrouwen (women's review of books). see LITERATURE

058.7 SW ISSN 0039-677X
AP48
SVENSK TIDSKRIFT. 1911. 7/yr. SEK 192. Foerlags AB Svensk Tidskrift, Linnegatan 28-30, IV, 114 47 Stockholm, Sweden. FAX 08-6673241. Ed. Rargaretha af Ugglas. adv.; illus.; index; circ. 3,500. **Indexed:** Hist.Abstr.
—BLDSC shelfmark: 8562.340000.

057.8 YU ISSN 0039-7059
SVETLOST. 1935. w. 104 din. Svetlost, 21 Oktobra 66, Kragujevac, Yugoslavia. Ed. Miodrag Stojinovic.

057.8 CI ISSN 0039-7113
SVIJET (ZAGREB); jugoslavenska zenska revija. 1958. bi-m. $16. Vjesnik, Avenija Bratstva i Jedinstva 4, 41000 Zagreb, Croatia. Ed. Vesna BluemImihaljevic.

057.1 RU
▼**SVOBODNYI KURS;** nezavisimaya gazeta. 1991. 26/yr. 0.40 Rub. (Altaiiskaya Regional'naya Assotsiatsiya Ekonomicheskogo Sotrudnichestva) Altaiiskaya Pravda, Ul. Korolenko 105, 656099 Barnaul, Russia. Ed. Vladimir Ovchinnikov. (newspaper)

800 US
SYMPOSIUM SERIES. 1974. irreg., latest no.31. $39.95 per no. Edwin Mellen Press, 240 Portage Rd., Box 450, Lewiston, NY 14092. TEL 716-754-8566. FAX 716-754-4335. **Indexed:** Ind.Sci.Rev.

058.82 NO ISSN 0039-7717
AP45
SYN OG SEGN. 1894. 4/yr. NOK 190 to individuals; institutions NOK 245. Det Norske Samlaget, Box 4672 Sofienberg, 0506 Oslo 5, Norway. TEL 02-687600. FAX 02-687502. Ed. Borghild Gramstad. adv.; bk.rev.; illus.; index, cum.index every 25 yrs.; circ. 5,000. **Indexed:** M.L.A.
Description: Essays and interviews about the modern and historical trends of Norwegian and international society; cultural development and conflicts.

290 US
SYNAPSE (BOSTON). 1983. 2/yr. free. Young Religious Unitarian Universalists, 25 Beacon St., Boston, MA 02108. adv.; bk.rev.; circ. 10,000. (tabloid format; back issues avail.)
Formerly: People Soup (ISSN 0360-8247)

051 US ISSN 0740-2619
SYNAPSE (SAN FRANCISCO). 1955. w. $25. University of California, San Francisco, Synapse Publication Board, Box 0234, San Francisco, CA 94143. TEL 415-476-2211. FAX 415-476-7295. Ed. Fred Gardner. adv.; bk.rev.; illus.; circ. 5,000. (tabloid format)

LITERARY AND POLITICAL REVIEWS

051   US
SYRACUSE NEW TIMES. 1969. w. $24.95 free. A. Zimmer Ltd., 1415 W. Genesee St., Syracuse, NY 13204. TEL 315-422-7011. FAX 315-422-1721. Ed. Mike Greenstein. adv.; bk.rev.; circ. 45,000 (paid); 45,000 (controlled). (tabloid format; also avail. in microfilm; back issues avail.)
    Description: News and arts magazine for central New York State.

057.85   PL   ISSN 0039-8152
SZPILKI; illustrated satirical weekly. 1935. w. $23. Pl. Trzech Krzyzy 16A, 00-499 Warsaw, Poland. TEL 48-22-280429. (Dist. by: Ars Polona-Ruch, Krakowskie Przedmiescie 7, Warsaw, Poland) illus.; circ. 78,800.

057   CS
T E T. (Termeszet es Tarsadalom) (Text in Hungarian) m. $26. (Socialist Academy of the Slovak Socialist Republic) Obzor, Ceskoslovenskej Armady 35, 815 85 Bratislava, Czechoslovakia.

053   GW
T M. (Trans Media); das medien-kritische Magazin. 1986. m. DM.48. (Buerger Frangen Journalisten) T M Verlags GmbH, Sonnenstr. 4, 8520 Erlangen, Germany. TEL 09131-604030. FAX 09131-604446. Ed. Herbert Eder. adv.; bk.rev.; illus.; stat.; tr.lit.; circ. 18,000. (back issues avail.)
    Formerly (until 1990): Trans Media.
    Description: Media critique, politics and culture.

TABLET. see *RELIGIONS AND THEOLOGY*

053   GW   ISSN 0933-6168
TABULA RASA; Trierer Regionalmagazin fuer Politik und Kultur. 1982. m. DM.30. A G Bildung und Information e.V., Postfach 1901, 5500 Trier, Germany. TEL 0€51-41199. Ed. Rudolf Mueller. film rev.; play rev.; circ. 15,000. (back issues avail.)

059.89 916.206   UA
TACHYDROMOS - EGYPTOS/EGYPTIAN POST. (Text in Greek) 1879. d. 4 Sharia Zangarol, Alexandria, Egypt. TEL 35650. Ed. Demos Coutsoumis. circ. 2,000. (newspaper)

TAI SHENG/VOICE OF TAIWAN. see *ETHNIC INTERESTS*

808.8   FR
TAKE IT EASY. 1982. 6/yr. 60 F. Librairie Fernand Nathan, 9 rue Mechain, 75014 Paris, France. Ed. Michelle Somme.

052   UK   ISSN 0049-2884
TALIESIN. 1962. q. £8. Yr. Academi Gymreig - Welsh Language Section, Mount Stuart House, Mount Stuart Sq., Cardiff CF1 6DQ, Wales. TEL 0222-492064. Eds. R. Gerallt Jones, B. Lewis Jones. bk.rev.; circ. 800. (back issues avail.)

056.1   CU
TALLER. LITERARIO.* no.22, 1971. q. Universidad de Oriente, Escuela de Letras, Avda. Patricio Lumumba s-n, Santiago de Cuba, Oriente, Cuba. Ed.Bd.

808.8   US
TAMAQUA. 1989. s-a. $10. Parkland College, Humanities Department, 2400 W. Bradley Ave., Champaign, IL 61821-1899. Ed. James McGowan. illus.

056.1 800   SP   ISSN 0049-2922
TAMBOR.* vol.13, 1971. m. 125 ptas. Sociedad Cultural Amigos del Arte de Baena, Plaza G. Cascajo 5, Baena, Spain. Ed.Bd. bk.rev.; illus.; circ. 700.

059.951   US
T'AN SO/QUEST. Variant title: Tansuo. (Text in Chinese) m. $24. Box 300742, Brooklyn, NY 11230-0011.

059   TR
TAPIA. 1969. w. T.T.$12($30) (Trinidad and Tobago Institute of the West Indies) Tapia House Publishing Co. Ltd., 91 Tunapuna Road, Tunapuna, Trinidad & Tobago, W.I. Ed. Allan Harris. adv.; bk.rev.; play rev.; circ. 5,000. (tabloid format)

TAPROOT. see *LITERATURE*

800 320   US
TARGET (WAYNE); the political cartoon quarterly. 1981. q. $15. 461 Sharon Dr., Wayne, PA 19087. Ed. Richard Samuel West. adv.; bk.rev.; illus.; circ. 500.

057.8   XV   ISSN 0040-1978
TEDNIK. (Text in Slovenian) 1948. w. 1100 SLT. Radio-Tednik, Raiceva 6, Ptuj, Slovenia. TEL 062 771 226. FAX 062-771-223. Ed. Ludvik Kotar. adv.; circ. 11,000.

200   FR   ISSN 0244-1462
TEMOIGNAGE CHRETIEN. 1941. w. 600 F. Societe de Presse et d'Edition, 49 rue du Faubourg Poissonniere, 75009 Paris, France. TEL 42-46-37-50. FAX 48-24-33-67. TELEX 290562. (Subscr. to: B.P. 63, F-77932 Perthes Cedex, France. TEL 1-64-38-01-55) Ed. Georges Montaron. adv.; bk.rev.; film rev.; play rev.; tele.rev.; circ. 80,000. (tabloid format; also avail. in microform) **Indexed:** CERDIC.
    Description: Covers politics, economics, society, culture and religion.

055   IT
TEMPO NUOVO. q. Via Francesco Feo, 34, Naples, Italy. Ed. L. Santucci.

055   IT
TEMPO PRESENTE; rivista mensile di cultura. 1980. m. L.42000. Tempo Presente, Via Virgilio, No. 11, 00193 Rome, Italy. TEL 06 687.3048. Ed.Bd. adv.; bk.rev.

800   US   ISSN 1055-7644
TEMPORARY CULTURE. 1988. irreg. approx 2/yr., no.7, 1992. $5 per no. Box 43072, Upper Montclair, NJ 07043. Ed. H. Wessells. bk.rev.; illus.; cum.index: nos.1-7 in no.7; circ. controlled. (back issues avail.)
    Formerly (until 1991): Newsletter of Temporary Culture.
    Description: Publishes original artwork, experimental poetry, essays and fiction extending the boundaries of language and meaning, and mapping the ideological landscapes of the post-industrial environment and culture.
    Refereed Serial

054.1   FR   ISSN 0040-3075
AP20
TEMPS MODERNES. 1945. m. 200 F. Presses d'Aujourd'hui, 4 rue Ferou, 75006 Paris, France. TEL 1-43-29-08-47. bk.rev.; film rev.; illus. **Indexed:** Arts & Hum.Cit.Ind., Curr.Cont., M.L.A., Pt.de Rep. (1980-).
    —BLDSC shelfmark: 8790.300000.

800   NE   ISSN 0921-2523
TEORIA LITERARIA: TEXTO Y TEORIA. (Text in Spanish) 1987. irreg. price varies. Editions Rodopi B.V., Keizersgracht 302-304, 1016 EX Amsterdam, Netherlands. TEL 020-6227507. FAX 020-6380948. (US and Canada subscr. to: 233 Peachtree St. N.E., Ste. 404, Atlanta GA 30303-1504. TEL 800-225-3998) Ed. Iris Zavala. circ. 500.

055.1   IT
TERZA PAGINA; antigruppo siciliano. (Text in English, Italian and Sicilian) 1950. w. L.25000($50) (Cooperativa Trapani Nuova) Cooperativa Editrice Antigruppo Siciliano, Via Argentaria Km. 4, Trapani, Sicily, Italy. TEL 0923-38681. (Co-sponsor: Cross Cultural Communications) Ed. Nat Scammacca. adv.; bk.rev.; play rev.; illus.; circ. 5,000. (tabloid format; back issues avail.)
    Formerly: Trapani Nuova (ISSN 0041-1779)
    Description: Creative writings and literary essays, including the latest poetic theories and information regarding the poetic movement.

055.1   IT   ISSN 0040-3989
TESTIMONIANZE; quaderni mensili. 1957. 10/yr. L.50000. Associazione Culturale Amici di Testimonianze, Via dei Roccettini 11, 50016 S. Domenico, Fiesole, Italy. TEL 055-597080. Dir. Lodovico Grassi. adv.; bk.rev.; illus.; index; circ. 7,000. **Indexed:** CERDIC, Old Test.Abstr.
    —BLDSC shelfmark: 8796.598000.

059   LV
TEVZEMES AVIZE. 1958. w. 20 Kop. per issue. Kulturas Sakaru Komiteja, Valdenbauma iela 11a, Riga 226047, Latvia. TELEX 161150 LETTO SU. Ed. V. Hermanis. adv.; circ. 33,300.
    Formerly (until 1990): Dzimtenes Balss.

THEATERZEITSCHRIFT. see *THEATER*

800 700   AT   ISSN 0816-5157
THIRD DEGREE; Australian mythological sights. 1985. a. Third Degree, P.O. Box 123, Broadway, N.S.W. 2007, Australia. TEL 02-3009-674. Ed. Kurt Brereton. circ. 1,500. (back issues avail.)

810   US   ISSN 0741-5958
THIRD RAIL; international arts & literature. 1975. a. $30 for 4 nos. to individuals; libraries $48; foreign $60. Box 46127, Los Angeles, CA 90046. TEL 213-850-7548. Ed. Uri Hertz. adv.; bk.rev.; circ. 12,000. (back issues avail.)
    Description: Explores new currents in the arts and literary avant-garde traditions.

800   US
THUNDER & HONEY; a publication for creative thought. 1983. q. $5. Kummunity Press, Box 11386, Atlanta, GA 30310. TEL 404-688-3376. Ed. Akbar Imhotep.

053.932   BE   ISSN 0040-764X
TIJDSPIEGEL; cultureel blad voor Limburg. 1946. m. 200 Fr. Opperstraat 60-Wijer, 3821 Kozen, Belgium. Ed. Ludo Rolskin. adv.; illus.; index; circ. 1,500.

808.87   GW
TITANIC; das endgueltige Satiremagazin. 1979. m. DM.62. Titanic Verlag Georg Buechner Verlagsbuchhandlung GmbH und Co. KG, Oranienstr. 25, Postfach 360440, 1000 Berlin 36, Germany. TEL 030-65005150. FAX 030-65005299. Ed. Hans Zippert. adv.; circ. 65,000.

808   US
TOOK. 1988. irreg. $20. Norton Coker Press, Box 640543, San Francisco, CA 94164-0543. TEL 415-922-0395. Ed. Edward Mycue. bk.rev.; film rev.; play rev.; bibl.; illus.; circ. 150. (back issues avail.)
    Description: Includes poetry, plays, stories, criticism, music, art, dance, film, psychology, travel, history, and food.

808   US
TOPSY TURVY-PATAS ARRIBAS. 1979. m. $6. 7060 Calle del Sol, Tucson, AZ 85710. TEL 602-747-9352. Ed. Jane Eppinga. circ. 250.

800   CN   ISSN 0714-3508
PK101
TORONTO SOUTH ASIAN REVIEW. 1982. 3/yr. Can.$15($15) Toronto South Asian Review, Box 6996, Sta. A, Toronto, Ont. M5W 1X7, Canada. TEL 416-483-7191. FAX 416-483-7191. Ed. M.G. Vassanji. bk.rev.; index; circ. 500. (also avail. in microform from MML; back issues avail. from Micromedia Ltd.) **Indexed:** Can.Lit.Ind.
    Description: Provides literary and political reviews

055.1   IT
TORRE. 1953. fortn. L.3000. Via Colombo 24, 92024 Canicatti, Italy. Ed. Giuseppe Alaimo. adv.; bk.rev.

056.9   BL
TOTEM.* q. Faculdade de Filosofia, Ciencias e Letras de Cataguases, Praca Santa Rita 340, Cataguases (MG) 36770, Brazil. Eds. Joaquim Branco, Ronald Werneck. adv.; bk.rev.; film rev.; illus.

TOUCHSTONE (HOUSTON); literary journal. see *LITERATURE — Poetry*

TRADE JOURNAL RECAP. see *BUSINESS AND ECONOMICS — Marketing And Purchasing*

053   GW   ISSN 0177-1361
TRAFIK; internationales Journal zur libertaeren Kultur und Politik. 1981. 2/yr. DM.20($12) Peterson - Trafik, Eduardstr. 40, 4330 Muelheim, Germany. TEL 0208-383086. Ed. Peter Peterson. adv.; bk.rev.; circ. 1,200.

LITERARY AND POLITICAL REVIEWS 2887

323.4 US
TRANSITION (NEW YORK). 1961-1977; resumed, no.51, 1991. q. $24 to individuals; institutions $48. Oxford University Press, Journals, 200 Madison Ave., New York, NY 10016. TEL 212-679-7300. FAX 212-725-2972. TELEX 6859654. (Subscr. to: Journals Fulfillment, 2001 Evans Rd., Cary, NC 25713. TEL 919-677-0977) Eds. Kwame Anthony Appiah, Henry Louis Gates, Jr. adv.; bk.rev.; illus.; circ. 800. (also avail. in microform from UMI) **Indexed:** Curr.Cont.Africa.
Former titles (until 1977): Ch'indaba (ISSN 0564-108X); (until no.50, 1975): Transition (ISSN 0041-1191)
Description: A literary, political and cultural review of modern Africa and the post-colonial world, focusing on Africans and members of the African diaspora.

057.8 XN ISSN 0041-266X
TRIBINA; vesnik za selo vo SR Makedonija. (Text in Macedonian) 1946. w. 100 din. Nasa Knjiga, Skopje, Partizanski Odredi 17, 91000 Skopje, Macedonia. Ed. Vasko Anastasov.

891.4 II ISSN 0041-2708
TRIBRITTA; news & literary monthly. (Text in Bengali) 1969. w. Rs.0.50 per copy. Saswati Deb, Ed.& Pub., 3, Tribritta Sarani, Cooch Behar - 736101, West Bengal, India. adv.; bk.rev.; tr.lit.; circ. 5,000.

022 IT
TRIMESTRE. s-a. Via Nicola Fabrizi, 82, Pescara, Italy. Ed. L. Iachini-Bellisarii. **Indexed:** M.L.A.

810 300 378 US ISSN 0041-3097
PS508.C6
TRIQUARTERLY. 1964. 3/yr. $18 to individuals; institutions $30. Northwestern University, College of Arts and Sciences, 2020 Ridge Ave., Evanston, IL 60208. TEL 708-491-3490. Ed. Reginald Gibbons. adv.; bk.rev.; film rev.; play rev.; illus.; cum.index; circ. 5,000. (also avail. in microfilm from UMI; back issues avail.; reprint service avail. from KTO) **Indexed:** A.I.P.P., Acad.Ind., Amer.Bibl.Slavic & E.Eur.Stud., Amer.Hum.Ind., Arts & Hum.Cit.Ind., Bk.Rev.Ind. (1986-), Child.Bk.Rev.Ind. (1986-), Curr.Cont., Hist.Abstr., Hum.Ind., LCR, M.L.A. —BLDSC shelfmark: 9050.692000.
Description: International journal of writing, art, and cultural inquiry.

051 301.412 US ISSN 0736-928X
HQ1402
TRIVIA; a journal of ideas. 1982. 2/yr. $14 to individuals; institutions $20. Box 606, N. Amherst, MA 01059. TEL 413-367-2254. Eds. Erin Rice, Kay Parkhurst. adv.; bk.rev.; circ. 2,000. **Indexed:** Alt.Press Ind., Left Ind. (1983-), Stud.Wom.Abstr. —BLDSC shelfmark: 9050.777500.
Description: Publishes writing that puts women in the center and is especially interested in forms that grow out of this intention; includes essays, interviews, and experimental forms of literature that combine rigorous thinking without compromising the feminist vision.

808.87 UK ISSN 0269-4824
TUBA. 1976. s-a. £0.50 per no. Tuba Press, Tunley Cottage, Tunley, Nr. Cirencester, Glos GL7 6LW, England. TEL 028576-424. Ed. Charlie Hamm. adv.; bk.rev.; circ. 500. (back issues avail.)

700 US ISSN 0742-0692
TUCSON WEEKLY. 1984. w. $25. Tucson Weekly, Inc., Box 2429, Tucson, AZ 85702. TEL 602-792-3630. Ed. Douglas Biggers. adv.; bk.rev.; circ. 34,000.

059.94 SW ISSN 0041-4034
AP95.E4
TULIMULD; eesti kirjanduse ja kultuuri ajakiri. (Text in Estonian) 1950. q. $45. Bernard Kangro, Ed.& Pub., Skoerdevaegen 1, 222 38 Lund, Sweden. adv.; bk.rev.; illus.; index; circ. 1,000. **Indexed:** M.L.A.

055 IT
TUSCAN SCENE. q. L.30000. Toscana '90, Villa Il Ventaglio, Via Delle Forbici 26, 50100 Florence, Italy. Ed. Giuseppe Mammarella.

057.85 PL ISSN 0041-4727
PG7001
TWORCZOSC. 1945. m. $9.90. Wydawnictwo Wspolczesne R S W "Prasa-Ksiazka-Ruch", Ul. Wiejska 12, 00-420 Warsaw, Poland. (Dist. by: Ars Polona-Ruch, Krakowskie Przedmiescie 7, Warsaw, Poland) Ed. Jerzy Lisowski. bk.rev.; index; circ. 38,014. **Indexed:** M.L.A.

800 SA ISSN 0041-476X
TYDSKRIF VIR LETTERKUNDE. 1951. q. R.15. Afrikaanse Skrywerskring, Posbus 1758, Pretoria 0001, South Africa. TEL 012-322-6404. Ed. E. Botha. bk.rev.; bibl.; illus.; circ. 2,000. **Indexed:** Ind.S.A.Per., M.L.A.

057.85 PL
▼**TYGODNIK WSPOLCZESNY.** 1990. w. 1500 Zl. per issue. Fundacja Solidarnosci Regionu Srodkowo-Wschodniego, Zaklad Gospodarczy, c/o Redakcja, U. Krolewska 3, 20-109 Lublin, Poland. TEL 207-96. Ed. Cezary Listowski.

808.8 US
U J Q. (Uncle Jam Quarterly) 1973. 4/yr. $10 (effective Dec. 1990). Fragments West, Box 670, Lompoc, CA 93438-0670. TEL 805-735-5134. Ed. Edmond Gauthier. adv.; bk.rev.; circ. 50,000. (tabloid format)
Formerly: Uncle Jam.
Description: Covers the arts, books, health and travel humor. Includes exclusive interviews.

U K Z - ZEITSCHRIFT VON UND FUER LESBEN. see HOMOSEXUALITY

056.1 CK
U N A U L A. 1968. s-a. Universidad Autonoma Latinoamericana, Carrera 55 No. 49-51, Apdo. Aereo 3455, Medellin, Colombia.

UGANDA JOURNAL. see HISTORY — History Of Africa

053 GW
ULTIMO (MUENSTER); Muensters Stadtmagazin. 1983. bi-w. DM.55. Ultimo Verlag, Hafenweg 18-20, 4400 Muenster, Germany. TEL 0251-60302.
Description: Information about cultural life in Muenster and its environs.

UMBRUCH; Zeitschrift fuer Kultur. see ART

800 US ISSN 0279-0815
UNCLE SAM. q. $10. Avant-Garde, Inc., 1780 Broadway, Ste. 811, New York, NY 10019. TEL 212-581-2000. adv.; bk.rev.; circ. 230,000.

819 CN
UNDERGROUND. 1969. w. free. Scarborough College Student Press, 1265 Military Trail, West Hill, Ont. M1C 1A4, Canada. TEL 416-978-2011. Ed. Eric Cohen. adv.; bk.rev.; film rev.; illus.; circ. 6,000.
Formerly (until Mar. 1982): Balcony Square (ISSN 0005-4267)

808.8 US ISSN 1045-3660
UNDERGROUND FOREST - SELVA SUBTERRANEA. (Text in English, Spanish) 1986. a. $12. 1701 Bluebell Ave., Boulder, CO 80302. Eds. Joseph Richey, Anne Becher. adv.; bk.rev.; circ. 5,000 (paid); 5,000 (controlled).
Formerly: Underground Forest.
Description: Contains reprints from small press and alternative magazines; original works including investigative articles, politics, literary criticism and non-fiction poems.

808.8 US
UNDERGROUND SURREALIST MAGAZINE; Boston's premiere cartoon. 1987. s-a. $6. Underground Surrealist Magazine, Box 2565, Cambridge, MA 02238. TEL 617-787-9513. Ed. Mick Cusimano. circ. 250.

800 DK ISSN 0905-1503
UNG OG FRI. 1982. bi-m. DKK 120. Venstres Ungdom, Oesterbrogade 132, 2100 Copenhagen OE, Denmark. Ed. Jesper Beinov. adv.; bk.rev.; circ. 5,000.
Former titles (until 1989): Liberal Debat (ISSN 0108-8874); Standpunkt (ISSN 0108-8866)

059.951 CH
UNITAS/LIEN HO WEN HSUEH; a literary monthly. (Text in Chinese) m. 7F, 180 Keelung Rd. Sec. 1, Taipei, Taiwan, Republic of China. TEL 02-766-5131. (Dist. in US by: World Journal Bookstore, 377 Broadway, New York, NY 10013. TEL 212-226-5131) Ed. Cheng Chou-yu. adv.

378.1 CL ISSN 0041-8374
CODEN: BOUCAD
UNIVERSIDAD DE CHILE. BOLETIN. 1959. 9/yr. Universidad de Chile, Avda. Bernardo O'Higgins 1058, Casilla 10 D, Santiago, Chile. Ed. Enrique Bello. adv.; bk.rev.; play rev.; bibl.; charts; illus.; maps; stat.; index; circ. 3,000. **Indexed:** Amer.Hist.& Life, Biol.Abstr., Hist.Abstr.

378.1 EC ISSN 0041-8390
UNIVERSIDAD DE CUENCA. ANALES. 1940. q. free. Universidad de Cuenca, Apdo. 168, Ciudad Universitaria, Cuenca, Ecuador. Dir. Agustin Cuera Tamariz. index; circ. 1,000. **Indexed:** Biol.Abstr.

UNIVERSIDADE DE LISBOA. FACULDADE DE LETRAS. REVISTA. see LITERATURE

800 UK ISSN 0001-320X
LH5
UNIVERSITY OF ABERDEEN REVIEW. 1913. s-a. £2.05. University of Aberdeen, Alumnus Association, 18 Bon-Accord Square, Aberdeen, AB9 1YE, Scotland. Ed. Eric E. Morrison. adv.; bk.rev.; bibl.; illus.; index; circ. 1,300.

378.1 US ISSN 0041-9524
AS30
UNIVERSITY OF DAYTON REVIEW. 1964. irreg. (approx. 3/yr.). free. (University of Dayton) University of Dayton Press, 300 College Park Ave., Dayton, OH 45469. TEL 513-229-0123. FAX 513-339-3433. Ed. Robert C. Conard. charts; illus.; index; circ. 1,500. **Indexed:** Abstr.Engl.Stud., Amer.Bibl.Slavic & E.Eur.Stud., Amer.Hum.Ind., M.L.A.

960 GH ISSN 0020-2703
UNIVERSITY OF GHANA. INSTITUTE OF AFRICAN STUDIES. RESEARCH REVIEW. (Text in English) 1965. 2/yr. $10. University of Ghana, Institute of African Studies, Box 73, Legon, Ghana. Ed. K. Arhin. bk.rev.; charts; illus.; circ. 500.

378.1 CN ISSN 0042-0352
AS42.W5
UNIVERSITY OF WINDSOR REVIEW. (Text in English, French) 1965. s-a. Can.$12. University of Windsor, Windsor, Ont. N9B 3P4, Canada. TEL 519-253-4232. FAX 519-973-7050. Ed. Joseph Quinn. adv.; bk.rev.; bibl.; charts; illus.; index; circ. 500. (also avail. in microform from MIM,UMI; reprint service avail. from UMI) **Indexed:** Abstr.Engl.Stud., Amer.Hum.Ind., Can.Lit.Ind., Can.Per.Ind., CMI, Curr.Cont., Hist.Abstr., Ind.Bk.Rev.Hum., M.L.A. —BLDSC shelfmark: 9120.144000.
Description: Contains fiction, poetry and criticism devoted to the arts.

UNMUZZLED OX. see LITERATURE — Poetry

296 US ISSN 0042-0506
UNSER TSAIT. (Text in Yiddish) 1941. 10/yr $15. Jewish Labor Bund, Coordinating Committee, Atran Center, 25 E. 21st St., 3rd Fl., New York, NY 10010. TEL 212-475-0059. **Indexed:** M.L.A.

055.1 IT ISSN 0042-0654
PQ4001
UOMINI E LIBRI. 1965. bi-m. L.40000 (foreign L.100000). Edizioni Effe Emme, Viale. E. Caldara 8, 20122 Milan, Italy. Eds. Mario Miccinesi, Fiora Vincenti. adv.; bk.rev.; bibl.; illus.; circ. 7,500. **Indexed:** M.L.A.

UPSTREAM; the Literary Center quarterly. see LITERATURE — Poetry

055.1 IT ISSN 0042-1030
URBE. 1936. bi-m. L.45000. Casa Editrice Fratelli Palombi, Via dei Gracchi 181-185, 00192 Rome, Italy. Dir. Manlio Barberito. adv.; bk.rev.; charts; illus.; index. Avery Ind.Archit.Per., M.L.A.
Description: Forum of history, literature, art, treasures of beauty and important figures in politics.

800   US   ISSN 8750-0256
PN4784.U53
UTNE READER;* the best of the alternative press. 1984. bi-m. $18. Lens Publishing Co., Inc., 1624 Harmon Pl., Suite 330, Minneapolis, MN 55403. TEL 612-338-5040. (Subscr. to: Utne Reader, Box 1974, Marion, OH 43306-1974) Ed. Jay Walljasper. adv.; bk.rev.; circ. 250,000. (also avail. in microform from UMI) **Indexed:** Acad.Ind., Alt.Press Ind., Bk.Rev.Ind. (1989-), Child.Bk.Rev.Ind. (1989-), Energy Rev., Mag.Ind.
  Description: Covers over 1,000 independent, small-circulation magazines, journals and newsletters.

800   US   ISSN 0167-8175
UTRECHT PUBLICATIONS IN COMPARATIVE LITERATURE. 1983. irreg., vol.28, 1991. price varies. John Benjamins Publishing Co., 821 Bethlehem Pike, Philadelphia, PA 19118. TEL 215-836-1200. FAX 215-836-1204. (And: Amsteldijk 44, P.O. Box 75577, 1070 AN Amsterdam, Netherlands. TEL 020-6762325) (back issues avail.)
—BLDSC shelfmark: 9135.518300.
  Description: Irregularly published monographs in comparative literature.

320   SW   ISSN 0346-3788
UTSIKT. 1956. q. SEK 50. Folkpartiet Liberalernas Riksorganisation - Swedish Liberal Party, Box 6508, 113 83 Stockholm, Sweden. FAX 08-349591. Ed. Anette Britalk. adv.; bk.rev.; illus.; circ. 65,000.

V O, VIE OUVRIERE. see *GENERAL INTEREST PERIODICALS — Canada*

055.1   IT   ISSN 0300-3175
VALORI UMANI; bimestrale di educazione letteraria scientifica, artistica e di costume. 1967. bi-m. L.15000 (foreign L.30000) suggested donation. Valori Umani, Via Alessandro Longo 11, 80127 Vomero, Naples, Italy. TEL 5799277. Ed. Pasquale De Orsi. bk.rev.; illus.
  Description: Features literary, scientific and artistic articles on customs and traditions of various countries. Articles reflect views of individual authors.

808.8   US
VANISHING CAB. 1976. a. $15 to individuals; institutions $20. 1152 Jackson, No. 8, San Francisco, CA 94133. TEL 415-771-9925. Ed. Jerry Estrin. circ. 815.

808.8   US   ISSN 0733-8899
AP2
VANITY FAIR. 1983. m. $15 (foreign $31). Conde Nast Publications Inc., Vanity Fair Magazine, 350 Madison Ave., New York, NY 10017. TEL 800-365-0635. FAX 212-880-8289. adv.; circ. 750,000. **Indexed:** Access (1984-1991), Music Ind., R.G.
  Description: Articles, interviews, and reviews of current trends, ideas, people, and writing.

057.8   CI   ISSN 0042-2711
VARAZDINSKE VIJESTI. 1946. w. 150 din.($4.) Socijalisticki Savez Radnog Naroda Varazdin, Opcinske Konferencije SSRN Varadzin, Marsala Tita 66, Varazdin, Croatia. Ed. Stjepan Jalusic. adv.; bk.rev.; abstr.; illus.; circ. 10,000.

059   RM
VATRA; lunar social-cultural. 1894; N.S. 1971. m. 180 lei($20) Uniunea Scriitorilor din Romania, Inspectoratul pentru Cultura al Judetului Mures, Str. Primariei, Nr. 1, 4300 Tirgu-Mures, Rumania. TEL 954-35005. FAX 954-35005. (Subscr. to: Str. Calea Victoriei nr. 133, P.O. Box BCR, Tirgu-Mures 45-10-6-100, Rumania) Ed. Cornel Moraru. adv.; bk.rev.; film rev.; play rev.; illus.; index; circ. 4,000. (back issues avail.)

057.8   CI   ISSN 0042-322X
VELIKOGORICKI LIST. 1963. fortn. 72 din. Narodno Sveuciliste Juraj Kokot, Zagrebacka 37, Velika Gorica, Kokot, Croatia. Ed. Ivan Zupetic.

945   IT   ISSN 0042-3254
AP37
VELTRO; rivista della civilta italiana. 1957. bi-m. L.80000. Veltro Editrice, Via S. Nicola De' Cesarini 3, 00186 Rome, Italy. Ed. Vincenzo Cappelletti. adv.; bk.rev.; charts; illus.; index, cum.index; circ. 6,000. **Indexed:** Can.Rev.Comp.Lit., Hist.Abstr., M.L.A.

322.4   CU   ISSN 0506-6913
AP63
VERDE OLIVO. 1960. m. $21 in N. America; S. America $27; Europe $30; elsewhere $42. (Fuerzas Armadas Revolucionarias) Ediciones Cubanas, Obispo No. 527, Apdo. 605, Havana, Cuba. TEL 7-79-8373. Dir. Eugenio Suarez Perez. charts; illus.; circ. 100,000.

808.8   US
▼**VERSION 90.** 1990. bi-m. $18. P M S Cafe Press, 107 Brighton Ave., Allston, MA 02134. Ed.Bd. adv.; bk.rev.

056.9   PO   ISSN 0042-4447
AP66
VERTICE; revista de cultura e arte. 1942; N.S. 1988. m. $30. Editorial Caminho, S.A., Alameda de St. Antonio dos Cpuchos, 6-B, 1100 Lisbon, Portugal. TEL 1-542683. FAX 1-534346. TELEX 65792-CAMIN-P. Ed. Francisco Melo. adv.; bk.rev.; charts; illus.; index. **Indexed:** M.L.A.

057.8   XV   ISSN 0042-4587
VESTNIK; glasilo obcinskih konferencs ZDL Murska Sobota, Gornja Radgona, Lendava in Ljutomer. (Text in Slovenian) 1949. w. 470 din.($10.) Zavod za Casopisno in Radijsko Dejavnost Murska Sobota, Titova 29-I, Murska Sobota, Slovenia. Ed. Stefan Dravec. adv.; circ. 20,000.

055.1   IT   ISSN 0042-5079
VICHIANA. 1964. s-a. $45. Loffredo Editore S.p.A., Via Conselvo, 99 H, 80138 Naples, Italy. FAX 081-636953. bk.rev.

055   IT
IL VIEUSSEUX. 1966. q. L.40000. Gabinetto G. P. Vieusseux, Piazza e Palazzo Strozzi, Florence 50123, Italy. TEL 055-2396743. Ed. Paolo Bagnoli. bk.rev.
  Formerly (until 1988): Antologia Vieusseux.

051   US   ISSN 0042-6180
AP2
VILLAGE VOICE. (Supplement avail: V L S) 1955. w. $44.95 in Metro NYC; elsewhere $47.95. V V Publishing Corporation, 36 Cooper Sq., New York, NY 10003. TEL 212-475-3300. FAX 212-615-9416. (Subscr. to: Box 1905, Marion, OH 43302. TEL 800-336-0686) Ed. Jonathan Larsen. adv.; bk.rev.; film rev.; play rev.; illus.; circ. 150,000. (tabloid format; also avail. in microform from UMI) **Indexed:** Access (1975-), Bk.Rev.Ind. (1970-), Child.Bk.Rev.Ind. (1970-), Film Lit.Ind. (1973-), Media Rev.Dig., Music Ind., New Per.Ind.

810 300 378   US   ISSN 0042-675X
AP2
VIRGINIA QUARTERLY REVIEW; a national journal of literature and discussion. 1925. q. $15. University of Virginia, 1 West Range, Charlottesville, VA 22903. TEL 804-924-3124. Ed. Staige Blackford. adv.; bk.rev.; index. (also avail. in microform from UMI; reprint service avail. from KTO) **Indexed:** Abstr.Engl.Stud., Acad.Ind., Amer.Bibl.Slavic & E.Eur.Stud., Arts & Hum.Cit.Ind., Bk.Rev.Ind. (1965-), Child.Bk.Rev.Ind. (1965-), Curr.Cont., Fut.Surv., Hist.Abstr., Hum.Ind., Ind.Bk.Rev.Hum., P.A.I.S.
—BLDSC shelfmark: 9240.130000.

056.1   MX
VISION; revista latinoamericana. 1950. 24/yr. $52. Editorial Vision, S.A., Arquimedes 199, 6o y 7o, 11570 Mexico, D.F., Mexico. TEL 5-203-6091. (Subscr. to: Vision, 13 E. 75th St., New York, NY 10021) Ed. Mariano Grondona. adv.; illus.; circ. 189,000.

322.4   US   ISSN 0042-7004
VISNYK/HERALD; suspil'no-politychnyi misiachnyk. 1947. m. (except July-Aug.). $8. Organization for Defense of Four Freedoms for Ukraine Inc., Box 304, Cooper Sta., New York, NY 10003. Ed. Viachslav Davydenko. adv.; bk.rev.; bibl.; index; circ. 2,000.

059.91   II   ISSN 0042-7195
AP8
VISVA - BHARATI QUARTERLY. (Text in English) 1923. q. Rs.80($20) Visva - Bharati, P.O. Santiniketan District, Birbhum, West Bengal, India. Ed. Shyamal Kumar Sarkar. adv.; bk.rev.; bibl.; illus.; index; circ. 1,000. (also avail. in microform from UMI) **Indexed:** G.Indian Per.Lit.

055.1   IT   ISSN 0042-725X
VITA E PENSIERO; rassegna italiana di cultura. 1914. m. (11/yr). L.58000($44) (effective 1992). (Universita Cattolica del Sacro Cuore) Vita e Pensiero, Largo Gemelli 1, 20123 Milan, Italy. TEL 02-8856310. FAX 02-8856260. TELEX 321033 UCATMI 1. Ed. Adriano Bausola. adv.; bk.rev.; bibl.; index. **Indexed:** M.L.A.
  Description: Focuses attention on the awareness of religion and the roles it plays in life.

057.91   KR   ISSN 0042-7470
VITCHYZNA; literaturno-khudozhnii ta hromads'kopolitychnyi misyachnyk. 1932. m. 24 Rub. (Spilka Pys'mennykiv Ukrainy) Vydavnytstvo Radyanskii Pismennik, Chkalova, 52, Kiev, Ukraine. Ed. O. Glushko. bk.rev.; bibl.; illus.; circ. 30,000. **Indexed:** M.L.A.

053.1   SZ
VIVA.* no.16, 1974. bi-m. 12 Fr. Linke Alternative, Postfach 701, 7002 Chur, Switzerland. adv.

053.932   BE   ISSN 0042-7675
VLAAMSE GIDS. 1905. bi-m. 600 Fr. to individuals (foreign 900 Fr.); students 350 Fr. Uitgeverij J. Hoste N.V., Leopoldstraat 10, 2000 Antwerp, Belgium. TEL 03-231-9680. Ed. F. Strieleman. adv.; bk.rev.; circ. 9,000. **Indexed:** M.L.A.

055.1   IT   ISSN 0042-7802
VOCE BRUZIA; indipendente politico letterario. 1961. m. (14/yr.). L.5000. Ed. Ruggiero Magliocchi, Via Nicola Serra 80, Cosenza, Italy. adv.; bk.rev.; film rev.; play rev.; illus.; circ. 2,000. (newspaper)

052   AT   ISSN 1036-1561
▼**VOICES.** 1991. q. Aus.$44 (foreign Aus.$56). National Library of Australia, Publications Section, Public Programs, Parkes Place, Canberra, A.C.T. 2600, Australia. TEL 06-262-1365. FAX 06-273-4493. Ed. P. Hetherington. circ. 1,000.

808 808.81   US   ISSN 1052-8814
AP2
▼**VOX MAGAZINE.*** 1990. bi-m. $14. Vox Publishing Inc., 306 Mott St., No. 3C, New York, NY 10012-2801. TEL 212-249-3892. Ed. Dana Groseclose. adv.; bk.rev.; film rev.; rec.rev.; illus.; circ. 30,000.
  Description: Literary and arts magazine featuring established and emerging writers.

320   PO
VOZ DO OPERARIO. 1879. m. Esc.1200. Sociedade de Instrucao e Beneficiencia a Voz do Operario, R. da Voz do Operario, 13, Lisbon-1100, Portugal. TEL 862155. adv.; bk.rev.; illus.; circ. 10,000.

057.91   KR   ISSN 0320-8370
VSESVIT; literaturno-khudozhnii ta hromads 'kopolitychnyi zhurnal. 1925. m. 24 Rub. (Silka Pys'mennykiv Ukrainy) Vydavnytstvo Radyanskii Pismennik, Chkalova, 52, Kiev, Ukraine. TEL 293-13-18. Ed. Oleg Mikitenko. bk.rev.; illus.; circ. 55,000. **Indexed:** M.L.A.

057.1   RU
▼**VSKHODY.** 1990. m.? Novosibirskii Oblastnoi Profsoyuz "Solidarnost"', c/o Vitalii D. Shapran, Ed., Mikroraion "A", dom 56, kv. 53, Berdsk, 633190 Novosibirskaya obl., Russia. TEL 4-00-56. circ. 10,000.

057.91   UK   ISSN 0042-9422
AP58.U5
▼**VYZVOL'NYI SHLYAKH/LIBERATION PATH;** Ukrainian political, social, scientific & literary magazine. 1954. m. $65. Ukranian Publishers Ltd., 200 Liverpool Rd., London N1 1LF, England. TEL 607 6266. Ed. I. Dmytriw. bk.rev.; bibl.; charts; stat.; index; circ. 2,800.

059   PK
W U F A. (Text in English) q. Rs.100($30) to individuals; institutions Rs.200($40). Writers Union of Free Afghanistan, P.O. Box 867, Peshawar University, Peshawar, Pakistan. Ed. A. Rasul Amin.

053   GW
WAGE; Magazin fuer Lippe, Kultur und Politik. 1982. m. DM.20. Detmolder Wage e.V., Postfach 1424, 4930 Detmold, Germany. TEL 05231-32396. adv.; bk.rev.; circ. 2,000. (back issues avail.)

LITERARY AND POLITICAL REVIEWS 2889

942 UK ISSN 0043-0056
WALES;* the national magazine of literature, the arts and Welsh affairs. 1937. q. 10s. Wales Publications Ltd., 40 Heath St., London N.W.3, England. Ed. Keidrych Rhys. bk.rev.; illus.

053 808.7 GW
WAS LEFFT; Erlanger Stadtzeitung. 1976. bi-m. DM.10($10) Verein zur Foerderung Alternativer Medien e.V., Postfach 3543, 8520 Erlangen, Germany. adv.; bk.rev.; circ. 2,500. (microfiche; back issues avail.)

WASCANA REVIEW. see *LITERATURE*

WASHINGTON MONTHLY. see *POLITICAL SCIENCE*

052 IE
WATERFORD NEWS & STAR. (Text in English) 1848. w. £43.16. Waterford News & Star, Michael St., Waterford, Ireland. TEL 051-74951. FAX 051-55281. Ed. Peter Doyle. circ. 18,645.
  Description: Devoted to the coverage of Waterford City and Waterford County.

WAY OF ST. FRANCIS. see *RELIGIONS AND THEOLOGY — Roman Catholic*

059 II
THE WEEK. (Text in English) 1982. w. Rs.800($42) Malayala Manorama Co. Ltd., P.O. Box 26, Kottayam 686 001, Kerala, India. FAX 481-2479. TELEX 0888-201-MNR-IN. Ed. Mammen Mathew. circ. 51,569.

808.8 US
WEIRDO. 1981. a. $5 per no. Last Gasp of San Francisco, 2180 Bryant St., San Francisco, CA 94110. TEL 415-824-6636. FAX 415-824-1836. Ed. Aline Kominski. bk.rev.; circ. 10,000. (back issues avail.)
  Description: Contains adult humor and satire.

053.1 GW ISSN 0043-2598
AP30
DIE WELTBUEHNE; Wochenschrift fuer Politik - Kunst - Wirtschaft. 1905. w. DM.100. Verlag der Weltbuehne, Oberwasserstr. 12, Postfach 1437, 1080 Berlin, Germany. TEL 2071435. FAX 2071519. (Subscr. to: Weltbuehne Leserservice, Postfach 103245, 2000 Hamburg 1, Germany) Ed. Helmut Reinhardt. adv.; bk.rev.; circ. 25,000.

808.8 US
WELTER. 1967. a. $2 per no. University of Baltimore Publications, English Department, University of Baltimore, Baltimore, MD 21201. TEL 301-659-3284. Eds. Daniel Tessitore, Alan Payne. circ. 500.

895.1 CC
WENHUI YUEKAN/ENCOUNTER MONTHLY. (Text in Chinese) m. Y21.60($67.50) Wenhui Bao She, 149, Yuanmingyuan Lu, Shanghai, People's Republic of China. TEL 3211410. (Dist. outside China by: China International Book Trading Corp., P.O. Box 2820, Beijing, P.R.C.; Dist. in US by: China Books & Periodicals, Inc., 2929 24th St., San Francisco, CA 94110. TEL 415-282-2994) illus.

895.1 CC
WENLUN YUEKAN/CRITICISM MONTHLY. (Text in Chinese) m. Hebeisheng Wenlian - Hebei Cultural Workers Association, 2 Shizhuang Lu, Shijiazhuang, Hebei 050000, People's Republic of China. TEL 744870. Ed. Yang Zhenxi.

800 CC
WENXUE ZIYOU TAN/ON LITERARY FREEDOM. (Text in Chinese) q. Tianjin Shi Wenlian, 237 Xinhua Lu, Tianjin 300040, People's Republic of China. TEL 395034. Ed. Feng Jicai.

895.1 CC
WENYI PINGLUN/LITERARY AND ART REVIEW. (Text in Chinese) bi-m. Heilongjiang Sheng Wenlian, 16, Yaojing Jie, Nangang-qu, Harbin, Heilongjiang 150006, People's Republic of China. TEL 34317. Ed. Li Fucai.

895.1 CC
WENYI PINGLUN JIA. (Text in Chinese) q. Jiangxi Sheng Wenxue Yishu Yanjiusuo, No. 89, Beijing Xilu, Nanchang, Jiangxi 330046, People's Republic of China. TEL 332920. Ed. Yu Yue.

700 CC
WENYI PINGLUN YU PIPING/ART REVIEW AND CRITICISM. (Text in Chinese) bi-m. Zhongguo Yishu Yanjiuyuan - Chinese Academy of Arts, 17 Qianhai Xijie, Beijing 100009, People's Republic of China. TEL 651128. Ed. Chen Yong.

895.1 CC
WENYI ZHENGMING. (Text in Chinese) m. Jilin Sheng Wenlian, Fu 111, Stalin Street, Changchun, Jilin 130021, People's Republic of China. TEL 884956. Ed. Yang Yinlong.

808.87 US ISSN 1045-0491
WE'RE LIVING IN FUNNY TIMES. Short title: Funny Times. 1985. m. $17.50. Susan Wolper & Raymond Lesser, Eds. & Pubs., Box 18530, Cleveland Heights, OH 44118. TEL 216-371-8600. illus.
  Description: Contains a collection of America's best cartoons, comics, and funny stoires.

WEST COAST LINE; a journal of contemporary writing and criticism. see *LITERATURE*

809 US
WESTERN WRITERS SERIES. 1972. 5/yr. $3.95 per no. Boise State University, Department of English, 1910 University Dr., Boise, ID 83725. TEL 208-385-1246. Ed. J. Maguire. bibl.; circ. 750.
  Indexed: M.L.A.
  Formerly: Discard.

800 700 US
WIDE OPEN MAGAZINE. 1984. q. $24. Wide Open Press, 116 Lincoln St., Santa Rosa, CA 95401. TEL 707-545-3821. Eds. Clif Simms, Lynn L. Simms. adv.; bk.rev.; circ. 700. (back issues avail.)
  Formerly: Wide Open Magazine of Poetry.
  Description: Examines solutions to wide-spread social problems.

057.8 PL ISSN 0043-5244
WIDNOKREGI. 1950. m. $6.60. Wydawnicto Wspolczesne R S W "Prasa-Ksiazka-Ruch", Ul. Wiejska 12, 00-420 Warsaw, Poland. TEL 48-22-285330. (Dist. by: Ars Polona-Ruch, Krakowskie Przedmiescie 7, Warsaw, Poland) Ed. Henryk Kurta. adv.; bk.rev.; illus.; stat.; circ. 82,000.

053.1 AU
WIENER KULTURKREIS. MITTEILUNGEN. 1975. bi-m. S.30. Wiener Kulturkreis, Prinz-Eugen Str. 3, A-1030 Vienna, Austria. Ed. Aurel Wolfram.

808.0 CS
WILD SHARKAAAH. (Text in English) no.2, 1990. irreg. Na Cihadle 55, 16000 Prague 6, Czechoslovakia. Ed. Eva Hauser.
  Description: Discusses literary and political issues pertaining to science fiction, feminism and environmentalism.

051 US ISSN 0363-3276
AS36.W79
WILSON QUARTERLY. 1976. 4/yr. $24. Woodrow Wilson International Center for Scholars, 370 L'Enfant Promenade S.W., Ste. 704, Washington, DC 20024-2518. TEL 800-876-8828. (Subscr. to: Box 2956, Boulder, CO 80322) Ed. Jay Tolson. adv.; bk.rev.; bibl.; charts; illus.; stat.; cum.index every 2 yrs.; circ. 110,000. (also avail. in microform from UMI) **Indexed:** Amer.Bibl.Slavic & E.Eur.Stud., Amer.Hum.Ind., Bk.Rev.Ind. (1980-), Child.Bk.Rev.Ind. (1980-), Hist.Abstr., Mid.East: Abstr.& Ind., P.A.I.S., Soc.Sci.Ind.
  —BLDSC shelfmark: 9319.082000.

WITNESS (FARMINGTON HILLS). see *LITERATURE — Poetry*

DER WOHLFAHRTSDIENST; Monatsschrift fuer Fragen der Wirtschaft und des Sozialen Lebens. see *SOCIOLOGY*

830 809 GW ISSN 0340-6318
WOLFENBUETTELER BAROCK - NACHRICHTEN. 1974. 2/yr. DM.64. (Herzog August Bibliothek Wolfenbuettel) Verlag Otto Harrassowitz, Taunusstr. 14, Postfach 2929, 6200 Wiesbaden 1, Germany. TEL 0611-530-0. FAX 0611-530570. TELEX 4186135. Ed. Martin Bircher. bk.rev.; bibl.; circ. 750. (back issues avail.) **Indexed:** M.L.A.

808.8 305.4 US ISSN 0738-1433
HQ1101
WOMEN'S REVIEW OF BOOKS. 1983. m. (except Aug.). $17 to individuals; institutions $30. (Wellesley College, Center for Research on Women) Women's Review, Inc., Wellesley, MA 02181. TEL 617-283-3645. FAX 617-283-2500. Ed. Linda Gardiner. adv.; bk.rev.; illus.; circ. 12,000. (also avail. in microform from UMI) **Indexed:** Alt.Press Ind., Amer.Hum.Ind., Bk.Rev.Ind. (1983-), Child.Bk.Rev.Ind. (1983-), Left Ind. (1986-), Stud.Wom.Abstr., Wom.Stud.Abstr. (1983-).
  —BLDSC shelfmark: 9343.420000.
  Description: Reviews from a feminist perspective; current scholarly and trade books by and about women.

800 UK ISSN 0266-6286
NX1
WORD & IMAGE; a journal of verbal/visual enquiry. 1985. q. £113($194) Taylor & Francis Ltd., Rankine Rd., Basingstoke, Hants RG24 0PR, England. TEL 0256-840366. FAX 0256-479438. TELEX 858540. Ed. John Dixon Hunt. adv.; bk.rev.; film rev.; illus.; circ. 750. (back issues avail.)
  Indexed: Artbibl.Mod., Arts & Hum.Cit.Ind., Curr.Cont., Hist.Abstr.
  —BLDSC shelfmark: 9347.837100.
  Description: Intended for literary critics, art historians and critics, linguisticians, cultural and social historians, philosophers and psychologists, as well as the academic departments of literature, art history and media and communications studies.
  Refereed Serial

052 UK ISSN 0143-2745
WORKER WRITER.* 1979. q. £1($2) Federation of Worker Writers & Community Publishers, c/o 76 Carysfort Rd., London N.16, England. bk.rev.; play rev.; circ. 1,000. (back issues avail.)

808.8 US ISSN 0886-8484
WORKING CLASSICS. 1981. q. $10. Red Wheelbarrow Press, 298 Ninth Ave., San Francisco, CA 94118. TEL 415-387-3412. Ed. David Joseph. adv.; bk.rev.; circ. 1,000.

051 327 US ISSN 0195-8895
AP2
WORLD PRESS REVIEW; news and views from around the world. 1961. m. $24.97. Stanley Foundation (New York), 200 Madison Ave., Ste. 2104, New York, NY 10016. TEL 212-889-5155. FAX 212-889-5634. TELEX WPRNY62342. (Subscr. to: Box 1997, Marion, OH 43305) Ed. Linda Rogers. adv.; bk.rev.; illus.; tr.lit.; cum.index: 1961-1972, 1974-1985; circ. 76,016. (also avail. in microform from UMI; reprint services avail. from UMI) **Indexed:** Acad.Ind., Energy Rev., Hum.Ind., Mag.Ind., P.A.I.S., Peace Res.Abstr., PMR, R.G., Soc.Sci.Ind.
  —BLDSC shelfmark: 9358.380000.
  Former titles (until 1980): Atlas World Press Review (ISSN 0161-6528); (until 1972): Atlas (ISSN 0004-6930)

WORMWOOD REVIEW. see *LITERATURE — Poetry*

052 AT
WORONI. 1948. fortn. Aus.$5($10) Australian National University, Students' Association, Canberra, A.C.T. 2600, Australia. FAX 062-489-062. Ed.Bd. adv.; bk.rev.; circ. 2,000.

WRITERS NEWS. see *LITERATURE*

053.1 GW ISSN 0043-9614
WUERZBURG-HEUTE; Zeitschrift fuer Kultur und Wirtschaft. 1966. s-a. DM.6. (Universitaetsbund Wuerzburg) Echter Wuerzburg Verlag GmbH, Juliuspromenade 64, Postfach 5560, 8700 Wuerzburg 1, Germany. adv. (back issues avail.)

WYZSZA SZKOLA PEDAGOGICZNA, OPOLE. ZESZYTY NAUKOWE. SERIA A. FILOGOGIA ANGIELSKA. see *LINGUISTICS*

056.1 MX ISSN 0043-986X
XALOC. (Text in Catalan) 1964. bi-m. Mex.$200. Ave. Uruguay 40-202, Mexico 1 D.F., Mexico. Ed. Ramon Fabregat. adv.; bk.rev.; illus.

L

2890 LITERARY AND POLITICAL REVIEWS — ABSTRACTING, BIBLIOGRAPHIES, STATISTICS

808.8 US
XIZQUIL; a place where social consciousness and creative speculation meet. no.5, 1991. irreg. $10 for 3 nos. Uncle River, Box 285, Reserve, NM 87830.
Description: Publishes wild imaginative fiction and poetry.

YALE FRENCH STUDIES. see LITERATURE

378.1 US ISSN 0044-0124
AP2
YALE REVIEW. 1911. q. $20 to individuals (foreign $30); institutions $40 (foreign $45). Basil Blackwell Inc., 3 Cambridge Center, Cambridge, MA 02142. TEL 617-225-0430. FAX 617-494-1437. Ed. J.D. McClatchy. bk.rev.; rec.rev.; index; circ. 3,000. (also avail. in microform from MIM,UMI; back issues avail.; reprint service avail. from ISI,SCH,UMI) Indexed: A.I.P.P., Abstr.Engl.Stud., Acad.Ind., Amer.Bibl.Slavic & E.Eur.Stud., Arts & Hum.Cit.Ind., Bk.Rev.Dig., Bk.Rev.Ind. (1965-), Child.Bk.Rev.Ind. (1965-), Curr.Cont., Film Lit.Ind. (1973-), Hum.Ind., Ind.Amer.Per.Verse, Ind.Bk.Rev.Hum., LCR, M.L.A., Mag.Ind., Mid.East: Abstr.& Ind., P.A.I.S., R.G.

800 US
YALE VERNACULAR; an undergraduate publication. 1987. 4/yr. $20. c/o Dean of Student's Office, 1604 A Yale Station, New Haven, CT 06520. Ed. Polly La Barre. adv.; bk.rev.; illus.; circ. 5,000.
Description: Presents undergraduate literature and art, and interviews with artists and writers.

051 YE
YAMAN AL-JADIYD; a monthly cultural journal. (Text in Arabic) 1971. m. 1.50 din. Ministry of Information and Culture, Sana'a, Republic of Yemen. Ed. 'Abd al-Wudud Sayf.

808.81 US ISSN 0278-9442
YET ANOTHER SMALL MAGAZINE. 1982. a. $2. Andrew Mountain Press, Box 14353, Hartford, CT 06114. TEL 203-549-6723. Ed. Candace C. Hall.

YOUNG SOCIALIST. see POLITICAL SCIENCE

808.8 US
YOUR TIMES EXPRESS.* 12/yr. $6. Foss Ronn, HCR 3 Box 40, Birch Tree, MO 55438-9807. adv.; illus.

057.1 RU ISSN 0021-3233
YUNOST. 1955. m. 18 Rub. (Soyuz Pisatelei S.S.S.R.) Yunost', Ul. Tverskaya 32-1, Moscow, Russia. Ed. A. Dementev. bk.rev.; film rev.; bibl.; charts; illus.; stat.; circ. 3,300,000. Indexed: Curr.Dig.Sov.Press.

057.8 CI ISSN 0044-1589
ZADARSKA REVIJA. 1952. bi-m. 300 din.($6.25) Narodni List, Zagrebacka 1, Zadar, Croatia. TEL 057-24070. Ed. Ante Franic. adv.; bk.rev.; circ. 1,000. Indexed: M.L.A.

ZANGO/FORUM; Zambian journal of contemporary issues. see GENERAL INTEREST PERIODICALS — Zambia

059 917.106 CN ISSN 0226-3068
AP53
ZAPAD/WEST. (Text in Czech and Slovak; occasionally in English) 1979. bi-m. $22. Collegium Bohemicum, P.O. Box 9021, Terminal P.O., Ottawa, Ont. K1G 3T8, Canada. TEL 613-824-7439. Ed. Milo Suchma. adv.; bk.rev.; film rev.; play rev.; illus.; circ. 3,500. (back issues avail.)

057 CI
ZAVOD ZA KNJIZEVNOST I TEATROLOGIJU. KRONIKA. (Text in Croatian; summaries in German) 1975. biennial. Zavod za Knizevnost i Teatrologiju, Opaticka 18, Zagreb, Croatia. circ. 500.

808.87 CC
ZAWEN JIE. (Text in Chinese) bi-m. Hebei Zawen Xuehui, 12 Hongjun Lu, Shijiazhuang, Hebei 050071, People's Republic of China. TEL 743153. Ed. Du Fangyuan.

057.8 XV ISSN 0350-8498
ZBORNIK OBCINE GROSUPLJE. (Text in Slovenian; summaries in English, German) 1969. biennial. 500 SLT($10) Obcina Grosuplje, P.O. Box 11, 61290 Grosuplje, Slovenia. FAX 61-783-232. Ed. Mihael Glavan. adv.; bk.rev.; circ. 1,000. (back issues avail.)

DIE ZEIT IM BUCH. see PUBLISHING AND BOOK TRADE

051 364 US
ZERO HOUR; where culture meets crime. 1988. 2/yr. $12. Zero Hour Publishing, Box 766, Seattle, WA 98111. TEL 206-632-8949. Ed. Jim Jones. adv.; bk.rev.; circ. 3,000.
Description: Examines specific aspects of contemporary society: cults, addiction, pornography.

056.1 VE
ZETA. 1974. w. Pinto a Santa Rosalia, 44, Apdo. 14067, La Candelaria, Caracas, Venezuela. Dir. Rafael Poleo.

057.1 RU ISSN 0044-4898
ZNAMYA; literaturno-khudozhestvennyi i obshchestvenno-politicheskii zhurnal. 1931. m. 24 Rub. Soyuz Pisatelei S.S.S.R., Ul. Vorovskovo 52, 121069 Moscow, Russia. Ed. Marianne Murphy. adv.; bk.rev.; index; circ. 130,000. Indexed: Curr.Dig.Sov.Press.

ZONE (NEW YORK). see LITERATURE

ZUID - AFRIKA; onafhankelijk maandblad, uitgegeven door Z A S M in Amsterdam. see POLITICAL SCIENCE

320.531 AU ISSN 0044-5452
H5
ZUKUNFT; Sozialistische Zeitschrift fuer Politik, Wirtschaft und Kultur. 1946. m. S.420. (Sozialistische Partei Oesterreichs) Zukunft-Verlagsgesellschaft mbH, Loewstr. 18, A-1014 Vienna, Austria. Ed.Bd. adv.; bk.rev.; film rev.; play rev.; illus.; circ. 10,000. (tabloid format) Indexed: M.L.A.
—BLDSC shelfmark: 9538.080000.

296 US ISSN 0044-5460
ZUKUNFT. (Text in Yiddish) 1892. 6/yr. $25. Congress of Jewish Culture, 25 E. 21st St., New York, NY 10010. Ed.Bd. adv.; bk.rev.; circ. 1,500. (also avail. in microfilm from AJP)

057.1 RU ISSN 0039-7105
ZVEZDA; literaturno-khudozhestvennyi i obshchestvenno-politicheskii zhurnal. 1924. m. 24 Rub. (Soyuz Pisatelei S.S.S.R.) Izdatel'stvo Khudozhestvennaya Literatura, Leningradskoe Otdelenie, Ul. Mokhovaya 20, St. Petersburg D-28, Russia. Ed. G.K. Kholopov. bk.rev.; bibl.; circ. 113,000. Indexed: Curr.Dig.Sov.Press, M.L.A.

057.8 PL ISSN 0591-2369
AP54
ZYCIE LITERACKIE. 1951. w. $23. Wydawnictwo Wspolczesne R S W "Prasa-Ksiazka-Ruch", Ul. Wiejska 12, 00-420 Warsaw, Poland. (Dist. by: Ars Polona - Ruch, Krakowskie Przedmiescie 7, Warsaw, Poland) bk.rev.; abstr.; illus.; stat.; index; circ. 75,000.

968 SA ISSN 0013-2578
1860 SETTLER. 1962. bi-m. $15 per no. S.R. Pather, Ed.& Pub, Box 1233, Durban, Natal, South Africa. Indexed: Ind.S.A.Per.

053 GW ISSN 0930-9977
HN1
1999; Zeitschrift fuer Sozialgeschichte des 20 und 21 Jahrhunderts. 1986. q. DM.60. Hamburger Stiftung fuer Sozialgeschichte des 20. Jahrhunderts, Schanzenstr. 75-77, 2000 Hamburg 36, Germany. TEL 040-437098. FAX 040-4392228. Ed. Angelika Ebbinghaus. adv.; bk.rev.

LITERARY AND POLITICAL REVIEWS — Abstracting, Bibliographies, Statistics

011 020 016 US ISSN 0002-662X
AI3
ALTERNATIVE PRESS INDEX; an index to alternative and radical publications. 1969. q. $30 to individuals; institutions $125. Alternative Press Center, Inc., Box 33109, Baltimore, MD 21218. TEL 410-243-2471. Ed.Bd. bk.rev.; circ. 550. (back issues avail.)
—BLDSC shelfmark: 0803.590000.
Description: Chronicles progressive articles through its exhaustive efforts at indexing and cross-referencing such journalism.

811 US
BOTTOM LINE PUBLICATIONS. 1988. m. $25. Star Route, Box 21AA, Artemas, PA 17211. TEL 814-458-3102. circ. 100.
Description: Market listing for poets and writers.

FRENCH 17; an annual descriptive bibliography of French seventeenth century studies. see HISTORY — Abstracting, Bibliographies, Statistics

GUIDE TO ALTERNATIVE PERIODICALS. see SOCIAL SCIENCES: COMPREHENSIVE WORKS — Abstracting, Bibliographies, Statistics

891.1 II
INDIAN LITERARY INDEX; documentation list of creative and critical writings and literary news. (Text in English) 1988. s-a. Rs.80($20) Sahitya Akademi, Rabindra Bhavan, Ferozeshah Rd., New Dehli 110 001, India. Ed. K.C. Dutt.

011 800 UK
LIGHT'S LIST OF LITERARY MAGAZINES (YEAR). a. (with irreg. updates). £1($2) per no. Photon Press, 29 Longfield Rd., Tring HP23 4DG, England.
Description: Lists more than 200 British literary magazines of all types, with addresses and descriptions of content and focus for each publication.

800 US
OLDERR'S FICTION INDEX FOR (YEAR). a. $50. St. James Press, 845 Penobscot Bldg., 645 Groswold St., Detroit, MI 48226-4232. TEL 800-345-0392. Ed. Stephen Olderr. abstr.; bibl.
Description: Includes publishers' addresses and phone numbers as well as citations, bibliographies of library press reviews and ratings.

OLDERR'S YOUNG ADULT FICTION INDEX FOR (YEAR). see CHILDREN AND YOUTH — Abstracting, Bibliographies, Statistics

700 800 016 SP ISSN 0038-6456
DP1
SPANISH CULTURAL INDEX.* (Text in English, French, German and Spanish) 1946. m. Ministerio Espanol de Asuntos Exteriores, Cultural Relations Dept., Palacio de Santa Cruz, Madrid, Spain. bk.rev.; abstr.; bibl.

STATE LIBRARY OF NEW SOUTH WALES. LIBRARY DEPOSIT LIST. see BIBLIOGRAPHIES

808.8 016 CN
WINTERGREEN; a directory of progressive periodicals. 1979. a. Can.$5($6) Alternative Research, Box 1294, Kitchener, Ont. N2G 4G8, Canada. Ed.Bd. circ. 1,500.

WORKBOOK. see ENVIRONMENTAL STUDIES — Abstracting, Bibliographies, Statistics

LITERATURE

see also Literature–Adventure and Romance; Literature–Mystery and Detective; Literature–Poetry; Literature–Science Fiction, Fantasy, Horror; Publishing and Book Trade

420.07 370 US ISSN 0001-0898
NA11
A D E BULLETIN. 1964. 3/yr. $15 to individuals; institutions $30. Association of Departments of English, 10 Astor Place, New York, NY 10003-6981. TEL 212-614-6317. FAX 212-477-9863. (Affiliate: Modern Language Association of America) Ed. David Laurence. adv.; bk.rev.; charts; stat.; circ. 2,000. (also avail. in microform from MIM,UMI; reprint service avail. from UMI) Indexed: C.I.J.E.
—BLDSC shelfmark: 0680.250000.
Description: Presents articles and surveys dealing with professional, pedagogical, curricular, and departmental issues.

891.92   US   ISSN 0003-7583
AP2
A G B U ARARAT; quarterly journal of Armenian literature, history and the arts. 1960. q. $24. Armenian General Benevolent Union, 585 Saddle River Rd., Saddle Brook, NJ 07662. TEL 201-797-7600. Ed. Leo Hamalian. adv.; bk.rev.; film rev.; bibl.; illus.; index; circ. 1,200. (also avail. in microfilm; back issues avail.) **Indexed:** Amer.Bibl.Slavic & E.Eur.Stud.
  Formerly: Ararat.
  Description: Fiction, poetry, and prose related to Armenian history and culture.

A L A N REVIEW. (Assembly on Literature for Adolescents) see EDUCATION — Teaching Methods And Curriculum

800   US   ISSN 0270-2983
A M S STUDIES IN MODERN LITERATURE. 1973. irreg., no.19, 1989. price varies. A M S Press, Inc., 56 E. 13th St., New York, NY 10003. TEL 212-777-4700. FAX 212-995-5413. (back issues avail.)
  —BLDSC shelfmark: 0859.554500.
  Description: Monographs, reference works and bibliographies focusing on various topics and writers of twentieth-century literature, drama and poetry.

800   US   ISSN 0196-6561
A M S STUDIES IN THE EIGHTEENTH CENTURY. 1970. irreg., no.17, 1990. price varies. A M S Press, Inc., 56 E. 13th St., New York, NY 10003. TEL 212-777-4700. FAX 212-995-5413. (back issues avail.) **Indexed:** M.L.A.
  —BLDSC shelfmark: 0859.552000.
  Description: Monographs, reference works and bibliographies on various writers and topics of study in eighteenth-century literature.

A M S STUDIES IN THE MIDDLE AGES. see HISTORY

800   US   ISSN 0196-657X
A M S STUDIES IN THE NINETEENTH CENTURY. 1980. irreg., no.10, 1990. A M S Press, Inc., 56 E. 13th St., New York, NY 10003. TEL 212-777-4700. FAX 212-995-5413. (back issues avail.)
  —BLDSC shelfmark: 0859.555000.
  Description: Monographs and reference works on various writers and topics of study in nineteenth-century literature.

800 792.02   US   ISSN 0195-8011
A M S STUDIES IN THE RENAISSANCE. 1976. irreg., no.29, 1990. price varies. A M S Press, Inc., 56 E. 13th St., New York, NY 10003. TEL 212-777-4700. FAX 212-995-5413. (back issues avail.)
  —BLDSC shelfmark: 0859.556000.
  Description: Monographs, reference works and bibliographies on various writers and topics of study in Renaissance literature and drama.

809   US   ISSN 0731-2342
A M S STUDIES IN THE SEVENTEENTH CENTURY. 1986. irreg., no.3, 1988. price varies. (Abrahams Magazine Service) A M S Press, Inc., 56 E. 13th St., New York, NY 10003. TEL 212-777-4700. FAX 212-995-5413.
  —BLDSC shelfmark: 0859.556500.
  Description: Monographs and reference works on various writers and topics of study in seventeenth-century literature, drama and poetry.

810   US   ISSN 0895-769X
PE1
A N Q: A QUARTERLY JOURNAL OF SHORT ARTICLES, NOTES AND REVIEWS. 1988. q. $14 to individuals; institutions $18; foreign $20. University Press of Kentucky, 663 S. Limestone St., Lexington, KY 40508-4008. TEL 606-257-2951. Ed. Arthur Wrobel. bk.rev.; bibl.; index, cum.index; circ. 600. (also avail. in microfilm from UMI; reprint service avail. from KTO,UMI) **Indexed:** Abstr.Engl.Stud., Abstr.Folk.Stud., Amer.Hum.Ind., Arts & Hum.Cit.Ind., Bk.Rev.Ind. (1965-), Child.Bk.Rev.Ind. (1965-), Curr.Cont., Hum.Ind., M.L.A.
  —BLDSC shelfmark: 1541.824000.
  Supersedes (1962-1986): American Notes and Queries (ISSN 0003-0171)
  Description: Contains scholarly articles on all aspects of British and American literature.
  Refereed Serial

A P U PRESS ALASKANA BOOK SERIES. (Alaska Pacific University Press) see HISTORY — History Of North And South America

820   CN   ISSN 0004-1327
PR1
A R I E L. (A Review of International English Literature) 1970. q. Can.$17 to individuals; institutions $25; students Can.$10. (Department of English) University of Calgary Press, 2500 University Dr. N.W., Calgary, Alta., Canada. TEL 403-220-4657. FAX 403-284-0848. TELEX 03-821545. Ed. Victor J. Ramraj. adv.; bk.rev.; bibl.; index; circ. 1,000. (back issues avail.) **Indexed:** Arts & Hum.Cit.Ind., Br.Hum.Ind., Can.Lit.Ind., Hum.Ind., Ind.Bk.Rev.Hum., M.L.A.
  —BLDSC shelfmark: 1668.349000.
  Formerly: Review of English Literature.
  Description: Provides critical and scholarly perspectives on literatures in English around the world.

A R P A CAHIERS DE RECHERCHE POETIQUE. (Association de Recherche Poetique en Auvergne) see LITERATURE — Poetry

A S C A P BIOGRAPHICAL DICTIONARY. (American Society of Composers, Authors and Publishers) see MUSIC

A U L L A; journal of literary criticism, philology & linguistics. (Australian Universities Language and Literature Association) see LINGUISTICS

800   GW
AACHENER BEITRAEGE ZUR KOMPARATISTIK. 1977. irreg., no.6, 1981. price varies. Bouvier Verlag Herbert Grundmann, Am Hof 32, Postfach 1268, 5300 Bonn 1, Germany. Ed. Hugo Dyserinck. **Indexed:** M.L.A.

AALBORG UNIVERSITETSCENTER. INSTITUT FOR SPROG OG INTERNATIONALE KULTURSTUDIER. ARBEIJDSPAPIRER. see LINGUISTICS

895.65   JA
ABIKO QUARTERLY RAG. (Text in English, Japanese) 1989. q. 8-1-1 Namiki, Abiko-shi, Chiba-ken 270-11, Japan. TEL 0471-84-7904. Ed. Vincent Broderick. circ. 300.

869   BL
ACADEMIA AMAZONENSE DE LETRAS. REVISTA. 1918. Cr.$30. Academia Amazonense de Letras, Rua Ramos Ferreira 1009, Manaus, Amazonas, Brazil. Dir. Mario Ypiranga Monteiro.

ACADEMIA ARGENTINA DE LETRAS. BOLETIN. see LINGUISTICS

898   BL
ACADEMIA BRASILEIRA DE LITERATURA. REVISTA. 1985. irreg. exchange basis. Academia Brasileira de Literatura, Rua Marques de Abrantes, 127-Apt.904, CEP 22230 Flamengo, Rio de Janeiro, Brazil. Dir. Leodegario A. de Azevedo Filho.

869   BL   ISSN 0065-0447
ACADEMIA CAMPINENSE DE LETRAS. PUBLICACOES. 1958. irreg., no.48, 1991. Cr.$50 or exchange basis. Academia Campinense de Letras, Rua Marechal Deodoro, 525, 13020 Campinas SP, Brazil. Ed. Lycurgo de Castro Santos Filho. circ. 200 (controlled).

ACADEMIA COLOMBIANA. BOLETIN. see LINGUISTICS

800   SP   ISSN 0065-0455
ACADEMIA ESPANOLA, MADRID. ANEJOS DEL BOLETIN. 1959. irreg., latest no.49. price varies. Real Academia Espanola, Calle de Felipe IV No. 4, Madrid 14, Spain.

860   US
ACADEMIA NORTEAMERICANA DE LA LENGUA ESPANOLA. BOLETIN. (Text in Spanish) 1976. irreg. $8 to individuals; institutions $12. Academia Norteamericana de la Lengua Espanola, Box 7, F.D.R. Post Office, New York, NY 10022. (Subscr. to: Odon Betanzos, 125 Queen St., Staten Island, NY 10314) Ed. Eugenio Chang-Rodriguez. bk.rev.; illus.; circ. 3,000. **Indexed:** M.L.A.

800   BL   ISSN 0001-3846
AS80
ACADEMIA PAULISTA DE LETRAS. REVISTA. 1937. irreg. free. Academia Paulista de Letras, Largo do Arouche 312, Sao Paulo, Brazil. Ed. Leonardo Arroyo. bibl.; circ. 1,500. **Indexed:** Hisp.Amer.Per.Ind.

860   BL
ACADEMIA PERNAMBUCANA DE LETRAS. REVISTA. 1901. irreg. Academia Pernambucana de Letras, Av. Rui Barbosa, 1596, Recife, Brazil. illus.

800   HU   ISSN 0567-7661
PN1
ACADEMIA SCIENTIARUM HUNGARICA. ACTA LITTERARIA. (Text in English, French, German, Russian) 1957. q. $56. (Magyar Tudomanyos Akademia) Akademiai Kiado, Publishing House of the Hungarian Academy of Sciences, P.O. Box 24, H-1363 Budapest, Hungary. Ed. G. Tolnai. adv.; bk.rev. **Indexed:** M.L.A.

840   FR   ISSN 0065-0587
ACADEMIE FRANCAISE. ANNUAIRE; documents et notices sur les membres de l'Academie. 1966. a. 50 F. Academie Francaise, 23 Quai de Conti, 75006 Paris, France. FAX 43-29-47-45.

ACADEMIE ROYALE DE LANGUE ET DE LITTERATURE FRANCAISES. BULLETIN. see LINGUISTICS

850 851   IT
L'ACERBA; periodico di tecnica (artistica, letteraria, libraria) culturale. bi-m. L.3000 per no. Corso Mazzini, 137, 63100 Ascoli Piceno, Italy. Dir. Angelo M. Guacci.

800 100   IT   ISSN 0001-494X
ACME. 1948. 3/yr. L.15000. Universita degli Studi di Milano, Facolta di Lettere e Filosofia., Via Festa del Perdono 7, Milan, Italy. Ed. Guido Bezzola. index; circ. 750. **Indexed:** Amer.Hist.& Life, Bibl.Engl.Lang.& Lit., Hist.Abstr.

860   CL   ISSN 0716-0909
PN1
ACTA LITERARIA. 1975. a. $9. Universidad de Concepcion, Facultade de Educacion, Humanidades y Arte, Departamento Espanol, Casilla 2307, Concepcion, Chile. Dir. Luis Munoz G. bk.rev.; circ. 600. **Indexed:** M.L.A.
  —BLDSC shelfmark: 0629.422000.
  Description: Theoretical approach to the study of literature, with emphasis on Hispanic literature.

ACTA NEOPHILOLOGICA. see LINGUISTICS

894.511   HU   ISSN 0586-3708
ACTA UNIVERSITATIS DE ATTILA JOZSEF NOMINATAE. ACTA HISTORIAE LITTERARUM HUNGARICARUM. (Text in Hungarian; summaries in English, French, German or Russian) 1961. a. exchange basis. Attila Jozsef University, c/o E. Szabo, Exchange Librarian, Dugonics ter 13, P.O.B. 393, Szeged H-6701, Hungary. (Subscr. to: Kultura, Box 149, H-1389 Budapest, Hungary) Eds. Ferenc Grezsa, Lajos Csetri. circ. 500. **Indexed:** M.L.A.
  Description: Journal of Hungarian literary criticism from the beginnings to present.

ACTA UNIVERSITATIS DE ATTILA JOZSEF NOMINATAE. ACTA ROMANICA. see LINGUISTICS

ACTA UNIVERSITATIS DE ATTILA JOZSEF NOMINATAE. PAPERS IN ENGLISH AND AMERICAN STUDIES. see LINGUISTICS

800 370   PL   ISSN 0208-6085
PN9
ACTA UNIVERSITATIS LODZIENSIS: FOLIA LITTERARIA. (Text in Polish; summaries in various languages) 1955-1974; N.S. 1981. irreg. Wydawnictwo Uniwersytetu Lodzkiego, Ul. Jaracz 34, Lodz, Poland. (Dist. by: Ars Polona-Ruch, Krakowskie Przedmiescie 7, Warsaw, Poland)
  —BLDSC shelfmark: 0585.207400.
  Supersedes in part: Uniwersytet Lodzki. Zeszyty Naukowe. Seria 1: Nauki Humanistyczno-Spoleczne (ISSN 0076-0358)
  Description: Studies in the history of literature, literary epochs and problems. Gives young writers a chance to publish their works.

LITERATURE

891.7 100   HU
ACTA UNIVERSITATIS SZEGEDIENSIS DE ATTILA JOZSEF NOMINATAE. DISSERTATIONES SLAVICAE. SECTIO HISTORIAE LITTERARUM. a. Attila Jozsef University, c/o E. Szabo, Exchange Librarian, Dugonics ter 13, P.O. Box 393, Szeged H-6701, Hungary. Ed. Adam Fejer. bk.rev.; circ. 350.
   Supersedes in part (in 1982): Acta Universitatis Szegediensis de Attila Jozsef Nominatae. Dissertationes Slavicae (ISSN 0586-3732)
   Description: Focuses on Russian literature and history of ideas in the nineteenth and twentieth centuries.

ACTA UNIVERSITATIS SZEGEDIENSIS DE ATTILA JOZSEF NOMINATAE. DISSERTATIONES SLAVICAE. SECTIO LINGUISTICA. see *LINGUISTICS*

890   SW   ISSN 0440-9078
ACTA UNIVERSITATIS UPSALIENSIS. HISTORIA LITTERARUM. (Text in English, French, German and Swedish; summaries in French, English and German) 1962. irreg. price varies. (Uppsala University, Historia Litterarum) Almqvist & Wiksell International, Box 638, S-101 28 Stockholm, Sweden. circ. 400. **Indexed:** M.L.A.

830   SW
ACTA UNIVERSITATIS UPSALIENSIS. STUDIA GERMANISTISCA UPSALIENSIS. (Text in German) 1964. irreg., latest no.29 1988. Almqvist & Wiksell International, Box 638, S-101 28 Stockholm, Sweden. Ed. John Evert Haerd. **Indexed:** M.L.A.

800   CN
ACTA VICTORIANA. 1876. s-a. Can.$9($15) 150 Charles St. W., Toronto, Ont. M5S 1K9, Canada. TEL 416-585-4473. Ed. Emma Thom. illus.; circ. 1,800. (back issues avail.)
   Description: Literary journal includes: poetry, short fiction, photography, drama, and interviews.

800   VE   ISSN 0001-7639
ACTUAL. 1968-1971; N.S. 1976-1983; N.S. 1983. irreg., no.20, 1991. Universidad de los Andes, Direccion General de Cultura y Extension, Avda. Tulio Febres Cordero, Edificio Administrativo, 4o piso, C.P. 5101, Merida, Venezuela. FAX 074-402655. Ed. Julio Tallaferro. bk.rev.; charts; illus.

891.553   IR
▼**ADABISTAN.** 1990. m. Rs.250 per no. Ettela'at Publications, Khayyam Ave., Teheran 11144, Iran. TEL 021-311071. TELEX 212336.

830   AU   ISSN 0001-799X
PT2525.Z4
ADALBERT-STIFTER-INSTITUT DES LANDES OBEROESTERREICH. VIERTELJAHRESSCHRIFT. 1952. s-a. S.140. (Amt der Oberoesterreichischen Landesregierung) Adalbert-Stifter-Institut des Landes Oberoesterreich, Adalbert-Stifter-Platz 1, A-4020 Linz, Austria. TEL 0732-2720-1295. Ed. Johann Lachinger. bk.rev.; bibl.; charts; illus.; index every 3 yrs.; circ. 750. **Indexed:** M.L.A.
   Description: Discusses work and background of Adalbert Stifter, literature of Upper Austria.

ADAM AND EVE. see *LITERARY AND POLITICAL REVIEWS*

700   UK   ISSN 0001-8015
AP1
ADAM INTERNATIONAL REVIEW. (Text in English and French) 1941. q. £6($10) 28 Emperors Gate, London SW7, England. Ed. Miron Grindea. adv.; bk.rev.; circ. 1,250. (back issues avail.) **Indexed:** Br.Hum.Ind., M.L.A.

800   US   ISSN 0065-1877
ADAPTATIONS SERIES. 1970. irreg., no.5, 1980. price varies. Proscenium Press, Box 361, Newark, DE 19711. TEL 302-737-5803. Ed. Robert Hogan. (reprint service avail. from UMI)

891.4   II   ISSN 0001-8228
ADHUNA SAHITYA.* (Text in Bengali) 1965. q. Rs.2.50($0.50) R.N. Nandy, 2 Bazarpara Main Rd., Halisahar, Parganas 24, West Bengal, India. Ed. S. Mukherjee.
   Formerly: Adhuna.

059.915   IR
ADINAH. bi-m. Rs.600 per no. G.H. Zakiri, P.O. Box 14185-345, Teheran, Iran.

800 914.1   US   ISSN 0736-4970
ADRIFT; writings: Irish, Irish-American and ... 1983. s-a. $8. Adrift Editions, 239 E. Fifth St., Apt. 4D, New York, NY 10003. Ed. Thomas McGonigle. adv.; bk.rev.; circ. 1,000. (back issues avail.)

808   US   ISSN 8756-1271
P211
ADVANCES IN WRITING RESEARCH. 1985. irreg., vol.2, 1988. price varies. Ablex Publishing Corporation, 355 Chestnut St., Norwood, NJ 07648. TEL 201-767-8450. FAX 201-767-6717. TELEX 135-393. Ed. Marcia Farr.
—BLDSC shelfmark: 0712.175000.

808   US   ISSN 1049-1740
ADVOCATE (PRATTSVILLE). 1987. bi-m. $10.50 ($22 to Canada; elsewhere $42.60. P K A Publications, 301A Rolling Hills Park, Prattsville, NY 12468. TEL 518-299-3103. Ed. Remington Wright. adv.; bk.rev.; circ. 12,000.
   Formerly (until 1988): Student Advocate.
   Description: Promotes careers in writing. Publishes works by new writers.

810   US
AEGEAN REVIEW: GREEK ARTS AND LETTERS. 1986. s-a. $10. Wire Press, 220 W. 19th St., Ste. 2A, New York, NY 10011. Ed. Dino Siotis. adv.; bk.rev.; illus.; circ. 5,000.
   Formerly: Aegean Review: Contemporary Greek Arts and Letters (ISSN 0891-7213); Which supersedes (1975-1984, no.13): Coffee House: Contemporary Greek Arts and Letters.

808   US
AFFINITIES.* 1981. s-a. Latitudes Press, Box 613, Mansfield, TX 76063-0613. Ed. Robert Bonazzi.

806 910.03   FR   ISSN 0243-7090
AFRAM NEWSLETTER. 1975. s-a. free. Universite de Paris III (Sorbonne Nouvelle), Centre d'Etudes Afro-Americaines et des Nouvelles Litteratures en Anglais, 5 rue de l'Ecole de Medecine, 75006 Paris, France. FAX 43-25-74-71. Ed. Michel Fabre. adv.; bk.rev.; circ. 350. (processed) **Indexed:** Can.Lit.Ind.

AFRICA; rivista trimestrale di studi e documentazione. see *HISTORY — History Of Africa*

AFRICAN ARTS. see *ART*

AFRICAN LANGUAGES AND CULTURES. see *LINGUISTICS*

800   CN
AFRICAN LITERATURE ASSOCIATION. BULLETIN. 1974. q. price varies. African Literature Association, Comparative Literature Department, University of Alberta, Edmonton, Alta. T6G 2E6, Canada. TEL 403-492-5535. FAX 403-492-0692. Ed. Stephen H. Arnold. adv.; bk.rev.; bibl.; circ. 850.
   Formerly: African Literature Association Newsletter (ISSN 0146-4965)

896   FR
AFRIQUE LITTERAIRE. 1968. q. 150 F. Societe Afrique Litteraire, 2 rue Cretet, 75009 Paris, France. adv.; bk.rev.; bibl.; illus.; index; circ. 2,500. **Indexed:** Curr.Cont.
   Formerly: Afrique Litteraire et Artistique (ISSN 0002-0508)

800   NR
AFRO IMAGE.* 1972. m. £N8. African Cultures Publications Ltd., Mile 2 Ubulunor Rd., Box 20, Ogwashi Uku, Nigeria.

AGADA; an illustrated Jewish literary magazine. see *ETHNIC INTERESTS*

990   US   ISSN 0884-5816
PR3532
AGE OF JOHNSON; a scholarly annual. 1987. a. $50. A M S Press, Inc., 56 E. 13th St., New York, NY 10003. TEL 212-777-4700. FAX 212-995-5413. Ed. Paul J. Korshin. bk.rev.; index. (back issues avail.)
—BLDSC shelfmark: 0736.094500.
   Description: Annual collection of scholarly articles and reviews pertaining to English literature, history and culture during the period of Samuel Johnson's life and circle.

810   US
AGNI. 1972. 2/yr. $12 to individuals; institutions $24. (Boston University, Creative Writing Program) Agni Review, Inc., 236 Bay State Rd., CRP, Boston, MA 02215-1403. TEL 617-353-5389. Ed. Askold Melnyczck. adv.; bk.rev.; circ. 1,500. (back issues avail.) **Indexed:** A.I.P.P., Amer.Hum.Ind., Ind.Amer.Per.Verse.
   Formerly: Agni Review (ISSN 0191-3352)
   Description: Includes fiction, poetry, essays and reviews by established and emerging writers.

AGORA; an alternative journal of Romanian culture. see *ETHNIC INTERESTS*

AHIJUNA. see *HISTORY — History Of North And South America*

800   FR   ISSN 0065-4787
AILLEURS ET DEMAIN; CLASSIQUES.* 1970. irreg. price varies. Editions R. Laffont, 6 Place Saint-Sulpice, Paris 6e, France.

889   GR
AIOLIKA GRAMMATA. 1971. bi-mg. Dr.40. Hodos Nireos 41, Palaion Phaliron, Athens, Greece. TEL 3600142. circ. 2,000. **Indexed:** M.L.A.

820 821   UK   ISSN 0261-0124
AIREINGS. 1980. s-a. £10. Aireings Publications, 24 Brudenell Rd., Leeds, West Yorkshire LS6 1BD, England. TEL 0532-785893. Ed. Jean Barker. bk.rev.; circ. 300.

800   GW   ISSN 0002-2985
PN504
AKADEMIE DER WISSENSCHAFTEN UND DER LITERATUR, MAINZ. KLASSE DER LITERATUR. ABHANDLUNGEN. 1950. irreg. price varies. Franz Steiner Verlag Wiesbaden GmbH, Birkenwaldstr. 44, Postfach 101526, 7000 Stuttgart 1, Germany. TEL 0711-2582-0. FAX 0711-2582290. TELEX 723636-DAZD. index.

AKADEMIYA NAUK AZERBAIDZHANSKOI S.S.R. IZVESTIYA. SERIYA YAZYKOZNANIE, LITERATURA I ISKUSSTVO. see *LINGUISTICS*

891.7   RU
AKADEMIYA NAUK S.S.S.R. IZVESTIYA. SERIYA LITERATURY I YAZYKA. 1940. bi-m. 25.20 Rub. Izdatel'stvo Nauka, 90 Profsoyuznaya ul., 117864 Moscow, Russia. TEL 234-05-84. (Dist. by: Mezhdunarodnaju Kniga, ul. Dimitrova D.39, 113095 Moscow, Russia) Ed. G.V. Stepanov.

890   II
AKS.* (Text in Panjabi) 1950. m. Rs.84. 22-83 W. Patel Nagar, New Delhi 110008, India. TEL 583740. adv.; bk.rev.; circ. 27,333.

810   US
AKWEKON; a national native American literary & arts journal. 1984. 4/yr. $20 to individuals (foreign $25); institutions $25 (foreign $30). Akwesasne Notes, Box 223, Hogansburg, NY 13655. TEL 518-358-9531. circ. 1,000.

810   US
AKWEKON LITERARY JOURNAL. 1984. 4/yr. $20. Akwesasne Notes, Box 223, Hagansburg, NY 13655. TEL 518-358-9531. Ed. Karoniakatie Doug George. circ. 1,000.

860   US   ISSN 0044-7064
ALALUZ; revista de poesia y narracion. 1969. s-a. $40. University of California, Riverside, Department of Literature & Language, Riverside, CA 92502. TEL 714-787-3406. (Or: Valdevarnes 13, 5 D, Madrid 28039, Spain) Ed. Ana Maria Fagundo. bk.rev.; bibl.; circ. 700.

800   US   ISSN 0737-268X
PN2
ALASKA QUARTERLY REVIEW. 1982. s-a. $8 to individuals; institutions $10. University of Alaska, College of Arts and Sciences, 3221 Providence Dr., Anchorage, AK 99508. TEL 907-786-1731. Ed.Bd. circ. 1,000. (back issues avail.)
   Description: Contains short stories, novel excerpts, interviews and essays.

800   CN   ISSN 0384-8523
ALCHEMIST. 1974. irreg. Can.$12. Marco Fraticelli, Ed.& Pub., Box 123, Lasalle, Que. H8R 3T7, Canada. Ed. Marco Fraticelli. illus.; circ. 500.

800   IS   ISSN 0334-4827
ALEI SIACH; literary conversation. 1974. irreg. IS.24. Brit Takam, Rehov Dobnov 10, Tel Aviv 64 732, Israel. Ed. Yadidiya Yitzhaki. bk.rev.; circ. 1,500.
  Description: Contemporary literature and literary research.

860   AG
ALEJANDRIA. bi-m. Arg.$90($25) Alejandria S.R.L., Larrea 716, Buenos Aires, Argentina. Ed. Jorge Montgomery.

800 300   GT
ALERO. 1973. bi-m. Q.3.50. Universidad de San Carlos de Guatemala, Ciudad Universitaria, Guatemala 12, Guatemala. Ed. Rafael Cuevas del Cid. illus.

800   CN   ISSN 0065-616X
ALEXANDER LECTURES. 1929. irreg. price varies. (University of Toronto, University College) University of Toronto Press, 5201 Dufferin St., Downsview, Ont. M3H 5T8, Canada. TEL 416-667-7791. FAX 416-667-7832. (U.S. address: 340 Nagel Drive, Cheektowaga, NY 14225)

ALFA; revista de linguistica. see *LINGUISTICS*

800 82   HU   ISSN 0401-3174
AP82
ALFOLD. 1950. m. 350 Ft.($23) Hajdu Megyei Lapkiado Vallalat, Tothfalusi ter. 10, 4024 Debrecen, Hungary. Ed. Thomas Koch. bk.rev.; circ. 1,800. Indexed: M.L.A.
  Description: Literary, cultural and critical periodical.

ALIF; journal of comparative poetics. see *LITERATURE — Poetry*

820   II   ISSN 0258-0365
PR1
ALIGARH JOURNAL OF ENGLISH STUDIES. (Text in English) 1976. s-a. Rs.30($6) Aligarh Muslim University, Department of English, Aligarh, Uttar Pradesh, India. Ed. S.M. Jafar Zaki. bk.rev.; circ. 350. Indexed: M.L.A.

895.65   JA
ALL YOMIMONO. (Text in Japanese) 1930. m. Bungei-Shunju Ltd., 3-23, Kioicho, Chiyoda-ku, Tokyo 102, Japan. TEL 03-3265-1211. Ed. Kenichi Fujino. circ. 122,000.

700 500   IT   ISSN 0002-5631
ALLA BOTTEGA; rivista di cultura ed arte. 1963. bi-m. L.50000 (foreign L.100000). Via Plinio 38, Milan, Italy. Ed. Giuseppe Lucano. adv.; bk.rev.; play rev.; bibl.; illus.; cum.index; circ. 4,000. Indexed: M.L.A.

800   US   ISSN 0742-096X
ALLEGHENY REVIEW; a national journal of undergraduate literature. 1983. a. $3.50. Allegheny College, Box 32, Meadville, PA 16335. TEL 814-724-6553. Eds. R. Scott Huth, Katherine Burkett. circ. 1,200. (back issues avail.)

800   IT
ALLEGORIA; per uno studio materialistico della letteratura. 1989. 3/yr. L.53000 (foreign L.70000)(effective 1992). Franco Angeli Editore, Casella Postale 17175, 20100 Milan, Italy. TEL 02-2895762. Ed. Romano Luperini.
  Formerly: Ombra d'Argo.

830 770   GW
ALLTAG; die Sensationen des Gewoehnlichen. 1978. q. DM.64($42) Alltag - Scalo Verlag, Potsdamerstr. 93, 1000 Berlin 30, Germany. TEL 030-2628813. Ed. Walter Keller. adv.; bk.rev.; circ. 5,000. (back issues avail.)

800 700   CN
ALPHA. 1976. irreg. (2-4/yr.). Can.$3. (Acadia University Students Unions) Either Or Publications, Acadia University, Wolfville, N.S. B0P 1X0, Canada. TEL 902-542-2201. Ed. Sian Morris Ross. adv.; bk.rev.; film rev.; play rev.; illus. (back issues avail.) Indexed: Can.Lit.Ind.

800   US   ISSN 0838-391X
ALPHA BEAT SOUP. 1987. s-a. $10. Alpha Beat Press, 12 N. Union St., Lambertville, NJ 08530. Ed. David Christy. bk.rev.; circ. 500. (back issues avail.)
  Description: Reviews and articles on the Beat generation and modern culture, its literature and poetry.

830   GW   ISSN 0065-6607
ALTDEUTSCHE TEXTBIBLIOTHEK. ERGAENZUNGSREIHE. 1963. irreg., no.106, 1991. price varies. Max Niemeyer Verlag, Postfach 2140, 7400 Tuebingen 1, Germany. TEL 07071-81104. FAX 07071-87419. (back issues avail.) Indexed: M.L.A.
  Description: Critical editions of Old High German and Middle High German manuscripts.

809   GW
ALTE ABENTEUERLICHE REISEBERICHTE. 1966. irreg. price varies. K. Thienemanns Verlag, Blumenstr. 36, 7000 Stuttgart 1, Germany. TEL 0711-21055-0. FAX 0711-21055-39. TELEX 723933-THLE-D. circ. 4,000.

L'ALTRA EUROPA. see *ART*

850   IT
▼**ALTROQUANDO**. 1990. irreg. price varies. Ligouri Editrice s.r.l., Via Mezzocannone 19, 80134 Naples, Italy. TEL 081-5227139. Ed. Sergio Brancato.

800   GW   ISSN 0721-0493
AM ERKER; Zeitschrift fuer Literatur. 1977. s-a. DM.24 for 4 nos. Verlag Am Erker, Dahlweg 64, 4400 Muenster, Germany. TEL 0251-793939. Ed.Bd. adv.; bk.rev.; circ. 1,000. (back issues avail.)
  Description: Explores experimental literature.

AMACADMY. see *ART*

800   II
AMAR CHITRA KATHA. (Text in English, Hindi) 1967. m. Rs.180. India Book House Pvt. Ltd., Mahalaxmi Chambers, 1st Fl., 22 Bhulabhai Desai Road, Bombay 400 026, India. TEL 4920253. TELEX 011-6297-DANI. (Subscr. to: Partha Books Division, Navprabhat Chambers, Ranade Road, Dadar, Bombay 400 028) Ed. Anant Pai. circ. 30,000.
  Description: Stories from Indian mythology, history, folktales and legends in a comic strip format.

860   AG
AMARU. m. Casilla de Correo 33, 1824 Sucural Lanus (O), Buenos Aires, Argentina. Ed. Juan C. Gimenez.

810   US
AMATEUR WRITER'S JOURNAL. 1967. q. $7.50. R.V. Gill Publishing Co., 3653 Harrison St., Bellaire, OH 43906-1142. Ed. Rosalind V. Gill. adv.; bibl.; circ. 1,500.
  Incorporates: Four Seasons.

800   GW   ISSN 0179-4922
AMBACHER SCHRIFTEN. 1986. irreg., vol.6, 1991. Verlag Otto Harrassowitz, Taunusstr. 14, Postfach 2929, 6200 Wiesbaden, Germany. TEL 0611-530-0. FAX 0611-530-570. TELEX 4186135. Ed. Rose-Marie Bonsels.

800 700   US   ISSN 1044-2006
AMBERGRIS. 1987. a. $8 for 2 nos. Ambergris Foundation, c/o Mark Kissling, Ed., Box 29919, Cincinnati, OH 45229. adv.; circ. 900.
  Description: Publishes art and fiction.

800   UK   ISSN 0002-6972
PR1098
AMBIT; a quarterly of poems, short stories, drawings and criticism. 1959. q. $30. 17 Priory Gardens, London N.6, England. Ed. M.C.O. Bax. adv.; bk.rev.; illus.; circ. 2,000. (also avail. in microfilm from UMI)
  —BLDSC shelfmark: 0808.970000.

810   US   ISSN 0743-2755
AMELIA. 1984. q. $25. Amelia, 329 "E" St., Bakersfield, CA 93304. TEL 805-323-4064. Eds. Frederick A. Raborg, Jr., Eileen M. Raborg. bk.rev.; circ. 1,236. Indexed: Amer.Hum.Ind., Ind.Amer.Per.Verse.
  Description: For the eclectic reader of fiction, poetry, essays, reviews, fine art and sophisticated cartoons.

AMERICAN BENEDICTINE REVIEW. see *RELIGIONS AND THEOLOGY — Roman Catholic*

AMERICAN CLASSICAL REVIEW. see *CLASSICAL STUDIES*

LITERATURE   2893

810   US   ISSN 0891-3277
AMERICAN COMPARATIVE LITERATURE ASSOCIATION NEWSLETTER. 1975. s-a. $6 to non-members. American Comparative Literature Association, Brigham Young University, 3010 JKHB, Provo, UT 84602. TEL 801-378-5529. FAX 801-378-4649. Ed. Larry H. Peer. circ. 800.
  Incorporates: Heliconian; Formerly (until 1975): American Comparative Literature Association Newsletter (ISSN 0002-8053)

800   US
AMERICAN FARMER SERIES. (In 2 vols.) 1985. bienniel. $12. Seven Buffaloes Press, Box 249, Big Timber, MT 59011. TEL 406-932-4168. Ed. Art Cuelho. circ. 750. (back issues avail.)
  Description: Contemporary short stories and poetry on farmer and rancher lifestyles, with emphasis on farms in trouble.

AMERICAN IMAGO; a psychoanalytic journal for culture, science and the arts. see *MEDICAL SCIENCES — Psychiatry And Neurology*

AMERICAN JOURNAL OF GERMANIC LINGUISTICS AND LITERATURES. see *LINGUISTICS*

800   US   ISSN 0896-7148
PS1
AMERICAN LITERARY HISTORY. 1989. 4/yr. $27 to individuals; institutions $62. Oxford University Press, Journals, 200 Madison Ave., New York, NY 10016. TEL 212-679-7300. FAX 212-725-2972. TELEX 6859654. (Subscr. to: Journals Fulfillment, 2001 Evans Rd., Cary, NC 27513. TEL 919-677-0977) Ed. Gordon Hutner. adv.; bk.rev.
  —BLDSC shelfmark: 0840.757500.
  Description: Covers the study of American literature from the colonial period through the present.

814.008   US   ISSN 0065-9142
PS3
AMERICAN LITERARY SCHOLARSHIP; an annual. 1963. a. price varies. Duke University Press, 6697 College Station, Durham, NC 27708. TEL 919-684-2173. FAX 919-684-8644. Eds. J. Albert Robbins, Warren G. French. (reprint service avail. from ISI,UMI) Indexed: M.L.A.
  —BLDSC shelfmark: 0840.770000.

810   US   ISSN 0002-9831
PS1
AMERICAN LITERATURE; a journal of literary history, criticism, and bibliography. 1929. q. $24 to individuals and secondary schools (foreign $36); institutions $44 (foreign $52); students $12 (foreign $20). Duke University Press, 6697 College Station, Durham, NC 27708. TEL 919-684-2173. FAX 919-684-8644. Ed. Cathy N. Davidson. adv.; bk.rev.; bibl.; index, cum.index; circ. 5,500. (also avail. in microform from MIM,UMI; reprint service avail. from ISI,UMI,KTO) Indexed: Abstr.Engl.Stud., Acad.Ind., Amer.Hist.& Life, Arts & Hum.Cit.Ind., Bk.Rev.Dig., Bk.Rev.Ind. (1965-), Chic.Per.Ind., Child.Bk.Rev.Ind. (1965-), Curr.Bk.Rev.Cit., Curr.Cont., Hist.Abstr., Hum.Ind., Ind.Bk.Rev.Hum., LCR, M.L.A., Ref.Sour., So.Pac.Per.Ind.
  —BLDSC shelfmark: 0840.780000.
  Refereed Serial

AMERICAN PHILOLOGICAL ASSOCIATION. DIRECTORY OF MEMBERS. see *LINGUISTICS*

AMERICAN REVIEW. see *ART*

800   US   ISSN 1051-4813
PS648.S5
▼**AMERICAN SHORT FICTION**. 1991. q. $24 to individuals; institutions $36. University of Texas Press, Box 7819, Austin, TX 78713-7819. TEL 512-471-4531. FAX 512-320-0668. TELEX 776453 UTEXPRES AUS. Ed. Laura Furman. circ. 110.
  Description: Offers original fiction from both the famous and the up-and-coming writers of today.

800   US   ISSN 0740-9257
AMERICAN UNIVERSITY STUDIES. SERIES 2. ROMANCE LANGUAGES AND LITERATURE. 1982. irreg. Peter Lang Publishing, Inc., 62 W. 45th St., 4th Fl., New York, NY 10036. TEL 212-302-6740. Ed. Kathryn Earle.

LITERATURE

808.1 US ISSN 0724-1445
AMERICAN UNIVERSITY STUDIES. SERIES 3. COMPARATIVE LITERATURE. 1982. irreg. Peter Lang Publishing, Inc., 62 W. 45th St., 4th Fl., New York, NY 10036. TEL 212-302-6740. Ed. Michael Flamini.
—BLDSC shelfmark: 0858.077970.

800 US ISSN 0741-0700
AMERICAN UNIVERSITY STUDIES. SERIES 4. ENGLISH LANGUAGE AND LITERATURE. 1983. irreg. Peter Lang Publishing, Inc., 62 W. 45th St., 4th Fl., New York, NY 10036. TEL 212-302-6740. Ed. Michael Flamini.
—BLDSC shelfmark: 0858.077980.
  Formerly: American University Studies (ISSN 0724-1453)

AMERICAN UNIVERSITY STUDIES. SERIES 17. CLASSICAL LANGUAGE AND LITERATURE. see *CLASSICAL STUDIES*

896 US ISSN 0742-1923
AMERICAN UNIVERSITY STUDIES. SERIES 18. AFRICAN LITERATURE. 1984. irreg. Peter Lang Publishing, Inc., 62 W. 45th St., 4th Fl., New York, NY 10036. TEL 212-302-6740. Ed. Michael Flamini.

810.9 US ISSN 0743-6645
AMERICAN UNIVERSITY STUDIES. SERIES 19. GENERAL LITERATURE. 1984. irreg. Peter Lang Publishing, Inc., 62 W. 45th St., 4th Fl., New York, NY 10036. TEL 212-302-6740. Ed. Kathryn Earle.

800 US ISSN 0895-0512
AMERICAN UNIVERSITY STUDIES. SERIES 24. AMERICAN LITERATURE. (Text in English and other West European languages.) 1988. irreg. Peter Lang Publishing, Inc., 62 W. 45th St., 4th Fl., New York, NY 10036. TEL 212-302-6740. Ed. Kathryn Earle.

800 US ISSN 0884-4356
PS501
THE AMERICAN VOICE. 1985. q. $12. Kentucky Foundation for Women, Inc., 332 W. Broadway, Ste. 1215, Louisville, KY 40202. TEL 502-562-0045. Ed. Frederick Smock. adv.; bk.rev.; circ. 2,000. (back issues avail.) **Indexed:** Abstr.Engl.Stud., Amer.Hum.Ind., Ind.Amer.Per.Verse.
  Description: Covers modern Panamerican literature.

800 US ISSN 1049-815X
PS5436.2
▼**AMERICAN WRITING.** 1990. s-a. $8 to individuals; institutions $15. Nierika Editions, 4343 Manayunk Ave., Philadelphia, PA 19128. TEL 215-483-7051. Ed. Alexandra Grilikhes. circ. 1,300,350. (back issues avail.)
  Description: Publishes writing that takes risks.

800 US ISSN 1042-6213
PS508.M4
THE AMERICA'S REVIEW;* a review of Hispanic literature and art of the U S A. (Text in English and Spanish) 1973. 3/yr. $15 to individuals; institutions $20. Arte Publico Press, University of Houston, Houston, TX 77204-2090. TEL 713-749-4768. Ed. Julian Olivares. adv.; bk.rev.; play rev.; circ. 1,000. (back issues avail.) **Indexed:** Abstr.Pop.Cult., Bk.Rev.Ind. (1990-), Chic.Per.Ind., Child.Bk.Rev.Ind. (1990-), Hisp.Amer.Per.Ind., M.L.A.
  Formerly: Revista Chicano - Riquena (ISSN 0360-7860)
  Description: Publishes new poems by Hispanic writers in the United States in their original English or Spanish.

860 MX
AMETRIAS; escritura de creacion. s-a? Universidad de Guadalajara, Apdo. Postal 4-010, 44430 Guadalajara, Jalisco, Mexico.

840 FR ISSN 0044-8133
PQ2613.I2
AMIS D'ANDRE GIDE. BULLETIN. 1968. q. 160 F.($32) Universite de Lyon II, Centre d'Etudes Gidiennes, 18 Quai Claude Bernard, F-69365 Lyon Cedex 07, France. Ed. M. Claude Martin. adv.; bk.rev.; bibl.; circ. 1,200. **Indexed:** M.L.A.

891.857 FR ISSN 0003-181X
AMIS DE MILOSZ. 1967. m. 120 F. Editions Andre Silvaire, 20 rue Domat, 75005 Paris, France. illus.

800 920 FR ISSN 0293-0773
AMIS DE RAMUZ. BULLETIN. 1981. a. 200 F. Les Amis du Ramuz, Universite Francois Rabelais, 3 rue des Tanneurs, F-37000 Tours, France. Ed. J.L. Pierre. adv.; bk.rev.; circ. 250. (back issues avail.)

840 FR ISSN 0180-8567
PQ2631.E25
AMITIE CHARLES PEGUY. BULLETIN D'INFORMATIONS ET DE RECHERCHES. 1978. q. 135 F. Amitie Charles Peguy, Chez Francoise Gerbod, 12 rue Notre Dame des Champs, 75006 Paris, France.
TEL 45-44-80-38. Ed.Bd. bk.rev.; circ. 700. **Indexed:** M.L.A.
  Formerly: Amitie Charles Peguy. Feuillets.
  Description: Articles covering the works of Charles Peguy and his counterparts.

800 UK ISSN 0306-8781
AMON HEN. bi-m. £15. Tolkien Society, 357 High St., Flat 5, Cheltenham, Glos. GL50 3HT, England.
TEL 0242-577232. **Indexed:** Child.Lit.Abstr.
  Description: News, reviews, letters, art work and short articles concerning the works of J.R.R. Tolkien.

830 943 NE ISSN 0165-7305
AMSTERDAMER BEITRAEGE ZUR AELTEREN GERMANISTIK. irreg. price varies. Editions Rodopi B.V., Keizersgracht 302-304, 1016 EX Amsterdam, Netherlands. TEL 020-6227507.
FAX 020-6380948. (In N. America: 233 Peachtree St. N.E., Ste. 404, Atlanta, GA 30303-1504. TEL 800-225-3998)

830 943 NE ISSN 0304-6257
PT9
AMSTERDAMER BEITRAEGE ZUR NEUEREN GERMANISTIK. 1972. irreg. price varies. Editions Rodopi B.V., Keizersgracht 302-304, 1016 EX Amsterdam, Netherlands. TEL 020-6227507.
FAX 020-6380948. (US and Canada subscr. to: 233 Peachtree St. N.E., Ste.404, Atlanta GA 30303-1504. TEL 800-225-3998) Ed. Gerd Labroisse. circ. 700. **Indexed:** M.L.A.
  Description: Covers various aspects of German literature.

AMSTERDAMER PUBLIKATIONEN ZUR SPRACHE UND LITERATUR. see *LINGUISTICS*

821 IE
▼**AN SEARUD.** (Text in English, Gaelic) 1990. irreg. free. Sunburst Press, 25 Newton Avenue, Blackrock, Co. Dublin, Ireland. Ed. Rudi Holzapfel. circ. 300.

808.8 US
ANAIS; an international journal. 1983. a. $7.50 (foreign $8.50)(effective Jan. 1991). Anais Nin Foundation, Box 276, Becket, MA 01223. (Subscr. to: 2335 Hidalgo Ave., Los Angeles, CA 90039) Ed. Gunther Stuhlmann. bk.rev.; circ. 1,250. **Indexed:** Amer.Hum.Ind.
  Description: Contains biographical and critical material on Anais Nin and her circle (H. Miller, O. Rank et al).

ANALECTA CARTUSIANA; review for Carthusian history and spirituality. see *RELIGIONS AND THEOLOGY*

ANALECTA ROMANICA. see *LINGUISTICS*

860 US ISSN 0272-1635
PQ6144
ANALES DE LA LITERATURA ESPANOLA CONTEMPORANEA. (Text and summaries in English and Spanish) 1973. 3/yr. $18 to individuals; institutions $45. (Twentieth Century Spanish Association of America) Society of Spanish and Spanish-American Studies, Department of Spanish and Portuguese, University of Colorado, Campus Box 278, Boulder, CO 80309-0278.
TEL 303-492-7308. FAX 303-492-3699. Ed. Luis Gonzalez-del-Valle. adv.; bk.rev.; a. index; circ. 1,000. (also avail. in microform from UMI; back issues avail.) **Indexed:** Arts & Hum.Cit.Ind., Curr.Cont., M.L.A.
—BLDSC shelfmark: 0889.850000.
  Formed by the 1981 merger of: Anales de la Narrativa Espanola Contemporanea (ISSN 0270-6334); Journal of Spanish Studies: Twentieth Century (ISSN 0092-1807); Formerly (1976-1979): Anales de la Novela de Posguerra (ISSN 0145-2363)

860 SP ISSN 0210-4547
ANALES DE LITERATURA HISPANOAMERICANA. 1972. a. 900 ptas.($14) Universidad Complutense de Madrid, Departamento de Literature Hispanoamericana, Facultad de Estomatologia, Ciudad Universitaria, 28040 Madrid, Spain. (Co-sponsor: Instituto de Cultura Hispanica) bk.rev.; bibl.

860 US
ANALES GALDOSIANOS. (Text in English, Spanish) 1966. a. $15. International Association of Galdos Scholars, Cornell University, Department of Romance Studies, Goldwin Smith Hill, Ithaca, NY 14853. Ed. John Kronik. bk.rev.; circ. 375. **Indexed:** M.L.A.

800 IT
ANALYSIS: QUADERNI DI ANGLISTICA. (Text in English and Italian) 1983. a. L.16.000($13) Editrice Tecnico Scientifica, Piazza Torricelli 4, I-56100 Pisa, Italy. Ed. Anthony L. Johnson. circ. 500. (back issues avail.) **Indexed:** Lang.Teach.& Ling.Abstr.

ANALYTICAL & ENUMERATIVE BIBLIOGRAPHY. see *BIBLIOGRAPHIES*

ANANDA ACHARYA UNIVERSAL SERIES. see *PHILOSOPHY*

800 II
ANANDA VIKATAN. (Text in English, Tamil) 1924. w. Rs.156 (foreign RS.990). Vasan Publications Pvt. Ltd., 757, Anna Salai, Madras 600 002, India. TEL 864054. FAX 91-44-867619. TELEX 041-7358 VASN IN. Ed. S. Balasubramanian. circ. 250,000.

809 IR ISSN 0517-8045
ANCIENT IRANIAN CULTURAL SOCIETY. PUBLICATION/ANJOMAN-E FARHANG-E IRAN-E BASTAN. NASHRIYEH.* (Text in Farsi) 1962. irreg., latest vol.17, 1979. Rs.30 per no. Ancient Iranian Cultural Society, Jomhorie Eslamie Ave., Shahrokh St., Teheran, Iran. Dir. A. Qoreishi. circ. 1,500.

800 DK ISSN 0084-6465
ANDERSENIANA. (Text in Danish; occasionally in English and German; summaries in Danish, English, French, German) 1933. a. DKK 90. Hans Christian Andersen Museum, Hans Jenssensstraede 39-43, DK-5000 Odense C, Denmark.
TEL 45-66-13-13-72. FAX 45-65-90-86-00. Ed. Niels Oxenvad. adv.; bk.rev.; abstr.; bibl.; illus.; cum.index; circ. 1,000. **Indexed:** Biog.Ind.

890 II
ANDHRA SACHITRA VARA PATRIKA. (Text in Telugu) 1908. w. Rs.226. Andhra Patrika, 14-14-21 Mallikarjuna Rao St., Gandhinagar, Vijayawada 520 003, India. TEL 61247. Ed. S. Radhakrishna. adv.; bk.rev.; illus.; circ. 48,276.

840 FR ISSN 0180-9350
ANDRE GIDE; la revue des lettres modernes. 1970. irreg., latest no.9, 1991. price varies. Lettres Modernes, 73 rue du Cardinal Lemoine, 75005 Paris, France. TEL 1-43-54-46-09. Ed. Claude Martin. bk.rev. (back issues avail.)

807 CL
ANDRES BELLO BIBLIOTECA. COLECCION. 1979. m? Editorial Andres Bello, Av. Ricardo Lyon 946, Casilla 4256, Santiago, Chile. FAX 2253600. TELEX 240901 EDJUR CL. Ed. Mercedes Gaju Valles. circ. 10,000.

ANEMONE. see *ART*

800 100 AG
ANFORA; revista cuatrimestral de literatura y filosofia. (Text in Greek, Latin, Spanish) 1987. q. Arg.$750. (Estudio de Abogacia-Dozo Moreno) Agencia Periodistica CID, Avenida de Mayo 666, Capital Federal, Argentina. TEL 30-2471. (Subscr. to: Rodriguez Pena, 545 Capital Federal, Argentina) Ed. Sebastian Dozo Labat. illus.; circ. 2,000. (back issues avail.)
  Description: Covers literature, philosophy and the distribution of works by certain contemporary writers.

820   UK
ANGELA THIRKELL SOCIETY. JOURNAL. 1981. a. £5. Angela Thirkell Society, c/o Mrs. V. Ramsden, 14 Stanhope Ave., Hosforth, Leeds LS1 5AR, England. (Subscr. addr.: c/o A. Ellis, 32 Carlton Walk, Bath, Avon BA2 4QQ, England) bk.rev.; circ. 200. (back issues avail.)

700 800   US
ANGELTREAD;* The lyrian ruse. 1984. q. $8. c/o Tina W. Phillips, Ed., 2100 Madison Ave., Ste. 10H, Charleston, IL 61920-2393. TEL 512-965-4842.

ANGLIA; Zeitschrift fuer englische Philologie. see *LINGUISTICS*

ANGLICA ET AMERICANA. see *LINGUISTICS*

820   DK   ISSN 0066-1805
ANGLISTICA. 1953. irreg. price varies. Rosenkilde og Bagger Ltd., 3 Kron-Prinsens-Gade, P.O.B. 2184, DK-1017, Denmark. Ed. T.J.B. Spencer. circ. 900. **Indexed:** Arts & Hum.Cit.Ind., Curr.Cont.

809   GW
ANGLISTISCHE FORSCHUNGEN. 1901. irreg. price varies. Carl Winter Universitaetsverlag GmbH, Lutherstr. 59, 6900 Heidelberg, Germany. (also avail. in microfiche from BHP; reprint service avail. from SWZ) **Indexed:** M.L.A.

940 820 410   GW
ANGLO-AMERICAN FORUM. (Text in English and German; summaries in English) 1975. irreg. price varies. Verlag Peter Lang GmbH, Eschborner Landstr. 42-50, 6000 Frankfurt a.M. 90, Germany. TEL 069-7807050. FAX 069-785893. Ed. Christoph Gutknecht. bk.rev.; abstr.; bibl.; circ. 400 (controlled). (back issues avail.) **Indexed:** M.L.A.

800   FR   ISSN 0003-391X
ANNALES DE BRETAGNE ET DES PAYS DE L'OUEST (ANJOU, MAINE, TOURAINE). 1886. q. 220 F. Association pour la Publication des Annales de Bretagne et des Pays de l'Ouest, Universite de Haute Bretagne, 6 av. Gaston Berger, 35043 Rennes, France. index. **Indexed:** Arts & Hum.Cit.Ind., Br.Archaeol.Abstr., Curr.Cont., M.L.A.
—BLDSC shelfmark: 0969.380000.
Formerly (until vol. 81, 1974): Annales de Bretagne.

850   IT
ANNALI ALFIERIANI. irreg. Centro Nazionale di Studi Alfieriani, Via Gaudenzi Ferrari, 9, I-14100 Asti, Italy.

850   US   ISSN 0741-7527
PQ4001
ANNALI D'ITALIANISTICA. 1983. a. $12 to individuals; students $8; institutions $19; foreign (excluding Can.) $21. (University of North Carolina, Chapel Hill, Romance Languages and Literatures) Annali d'Italianistica, Inc., 141 Dey Hall, CB 3170, University of North Carolina, Chapel Hill, NC 27599-3170. Ed. Dino S. Cervigni. adv.; bk.rev.; circ. 700. (back issues avail.) **Indexed:** M.L.A.
—BLDSC shelfmark: 1014.600000.

843   FR   ISSN 0084-6473
PQ2177.A2
ANNÉE BALZACIENNE. 1960. a. 85 F. (Groupe d'Etudes Balzaciennes) Presses Universitaires de France, Departement des Revues, 14 av. du Bois-de-l'Epine, 91003 Evry Cedex, France. TEL 1-60-77-82-05. FAX 1-60-79-20-45. TELEX PUF 600 474 F. (Subscr. to: Maison de Balzac, 47 rue Raynouard, 75016 Paris, France). **Indexed:** M.L.A.

840   FR   ISSN 0066-3387
ANNUAIRE NATIONAL DES LETTRES. 1948. biennial. Editions Dany Thibaud, 52 rue Labrouste, 75015 Paris, France.

900 800   UK   ISSN 0066-3832
ANNUAL BULLETIN OF HISTORICAL LITERATURE. 1911. a. £35($64) to non-members. (Historical Association) Basil Blackwell Ltd., 108 Cowley Rd., Oxford OX4 1JF, England. TEL 0865-79100. (Subscr. addr.: c/o Marston Book Services, P.O. Box 87, Oxford OX2 0DT, England) Ed. J. Smith. bk.rev.; index. (back issues avail.; reprint service avail. from UMI) **Indexed:** Br.Archaeol.Abstr.

810   US
ANON NINE. irreg. Street Fiction Press, 130 Touro St., Box 625, Newport, RI 01840. TEL 401-847-1067.

810   US   ISSN 0272-4359
PS580
ANOTHER CHICAGO MAGAZINE. Short title: A C M. 1977. s-a. $15. Left Field Press, 3709 N. Kenmore, Chicago, IL 60613. TEL 312-248-7665. Ed. Barry Silesky. adv.; bk.rev.; circ. 1,200. (back issues avail.) **Indexed:** Ind.Amer.Per.Verse.

820   US   ISSN 0003-5319
PR1098
ANTAEUS. 1970. s-a. $30 for 4 nos. Ecco Press Ltd., 100 W. Broad St., Hopewell, NJ 08525. TEL 609-466-4748. FAX 609-466-4706. Ed. Daniel Halpern. adv.; cum.index: nos.1-20, 21, 22-28, 59; circ. 5,000. (back issues avail.) **Indexed:** Amer.Bibl.Slavic & E.Eur.Stud., Amer.Hum.Ind., Arts & Hum.Cit.Ind., Curr.Cont., M.L.A.
—BLDSC shelfmark: 1542.080000.

800   IT
ANTEREM; semestrale di ricerca letteraria. 1976. s-a. $10. Edizioni Anterem, Via Cantarane 10, 37129 Verona, Italy. Eds. Flavio Ermini, Silvano Martini. circ. 2,000.

378.198 800   US
ANTHEON. 1982. s-a. free. City University of New York, Kingsborough Community College, 2001 Oriental Blvd., Brooklyn, NY 11235. TEL 718-934-5603. circ. 500. (back issues avail.)

800   US
ANTIETAM REVIEW. 1982. s-a. $5. Washington County Arts Council, 82 W. Washington St., Hagerstown, MD 21740. TEL 301-791-3132. Ed. Susanne Kass. circ. 1,600. (back issues avail.)
Description: Literary journal carrying short fiction, poetry, photography from writers and artists.

800   CN   ISSN 0003-5661
PN2
ANTIGONISH REVIEW. 1970. q. Can.$18. St. Francis Xavier University, Box 135, Antigonish, N.S. B2G 1C0, Canada. TEL 902-867-3962. Ed. George Sanderson. adv.; bk.rev.; illus.; index; circ. 900. (also avail. in microfiche from MML) **Indexed:** Abstr.Engl.Stud., Arts & Hum.Cit.Ind., Can.Lit.Ind., Can.Per.Ind., CMI, Curr.Cont., M.L.A.
—BLDSC shelfmark: 1547.530000.
Description: Literary quarterly that publishes poetry, fiction, reviews and articles with an emphasis on liveliness.

869   CK
ANTIOQUIA. SECRETARIA DE EDUCACION Y CULTURA. REVISTA CULTURA. 1976. q. Secretaria de Educacion y Cultura, Medellin, Antioquia, Colombia. illus.

820   US   ISSN 0893-5580
ANTIPODES; a North American journal of Australian literature. 1987. s-a. $20 to individuals (foreign $27); institutions $35 (foreign $42). American Association of Australian Literary Studies, 190 Sixth Ave., Brooklyn, NY 11217. TEL 718-789-5826. FAX 718-482-5599. Ed. Robert Ross. adv.; bk.rev.; film rev.; play rev.; bibl.; illus.; circ. 500. (back issues avail.) **Indexed:** Film Lit.Ind. (1988-).
Description: Presents both fiction and poetry, and articles about Australian literature for the literary scholar and the general public.

800   AG
ANTOLOGIA; revista literaria. 1974. q. Arg.$800. Ediciones Figaro, Av. Ceballos 274, C.C. 206, 6620 Chivilcoy (BA), Argentina. Ed. Diego B. Rositto. bk.rev.; circ. 2,000.

ANUARIO DE FILOLOGIA. see *LINGUISTICS*

860   MX   ISSN 0543-758X
ANUARIO DE LETRAS. 1961. a. Mex.$7000. Universidad Nacional Autonoma de Mexico, Instituto de Investigaciones Filologicas, Ciudad Universitaria, C.P. 04510, Mexico 21 DF, Mexico. **Indexed:** Amer.Hist.& Life, Hisp.Amer.Per.Ind., Hist.Abstr.

800   CU
ANUARIO L L. (Literatura Linguistica) a. $6 in N. America; S. America $7; Europe $9; others $10. (Academia de Ciencias de Cuba, Instituto de Literatura y Linguistica) Ediciones Cubanas, Obispo No. 527, Apdo. 605, Havana, Cuba. TEL 32-5556-60.

LITERATURE   2895

800 700   US
L'APACHE;* an international journal of literature and art. 1986. 4/yr. (2 nos. in one). $18 (foreign $25). Box 71, Wheeler, OR 97147. TEL 619-376-3634. Ed. Kathryn Vilips. bk.rev.; illus.; circ. 7,500.
Description: Focuses on short fiction, articles and poetry on the Indians or other ethnic groups.

800   US   ISSN 0890-6408
APALACHEE QUARTERLY. 1973. q. $15 to individuals; institutions $20; foreign $25. Apalachee Press, Box 20106, Tallahassee, FL 32316. Ed.Bd. adv.; bk.rev.; index, cum.index; circ. 500. **Indexed:** Access, Amer.Hum.Ind.

800   IS   ISSN 0334-0899
APEREYON. 1983. 4/yr. $20. P.O. Box 1861, Ramat Gan 1861, Israel. TEL 03-734144. Ed. Erez Biton. adv.; bk.rev.; circ. 800.
Description: Examines Mediterranean trends in Israeli culture, in relation to Jewish legacy and literature and poetry.

APPALACHIAN JOURNAL; a regional studies review. see *HISTORY — History Of North And South America*

891.7   RU
APPARAT UPRAVLENIYA SOTSIALISTICHESKOGO GOSUDARSTVA. (In 2 parts) 1976. irreg. (Akademiya Nauk S.S.S.R., Institut Gosudarstva i Prava) Izdatel'stvo Yuridicheskaya Literatura, Moscow, Russia. Ed.Bd.

810   US
APPEARANCES. 1977. a. $5. 165 W. 26th St., New York, NY 10001. TEL 212-675-3026. Ed.Bd. circ. 900.

800 792   US
APPLAUSE THEATRE BOOK REVIEW & CATALOG. 1989. a. $10. Applause Theatre Book Publishers, 211 W. 71st St., New York, NY 10023. TEL 212-595-4735. FAX 212-721-2856. Ed. Glenn Young. adv.; bk.rev.; circ. 50,000.

890   IQ   ISSN 0570-507X
AQLAM JOURNAL/PEN.* (Text in Arabic) 1964. m. ID.1.50($6) Ministry of Culture and Information, Nr au-Husor Sq., Fitruly Qasr as-Salaam Bldg., Baghdad, Iraq. Ed. Sami Mahdi. bk.rev.; bibl.; film rev, play rev.; index; circ. 15,000.

860   UY   ISSN 0066-5606
AQUI. 1983. w. Editorial Arca, Zabala 1322, Esc. 102, Montevideo, Uruguay. Dir. Francisco Jose O'Honelli.

ARAB BOOK GUIDE INTERNATIONAL. see *PUBLISHING AND BOOK TRADE*

AL-ARABIYYA. see *LINGUISTICS*

810 820 410   GW   ISSN 0171-5410
PE3
ARBEITEN AUS ANGLISTIK UND AMERIKANISTIK. (Text in English and German) 1976. 2/yr. DM.84. Gunter Narr Verlag, Dischingerweg 5, 7400 Tuebingen 5-Hirschau, Germany. TEL 07071-78091. FAX 07071-75288. Ed. Bernhard Kettemann. adv.; bk.rev.; circ. 200. (back issues avail.) **Indexed:** Bibl.Engl.Lang.& Lit., Curr.Cont., M.L.A.
—BLDSC shelfmark: 1585.808500.

800   GW   ISSN 0173-2307
ARBEITEN UND TEXT ZUR SLAVISTIK. (Text mainly in Russian) 1973. irreg. price varies. Verlag Otto Sagner, Postfach 340108, 8000 Munich 34, Germany. TEL 089-522027. TELEX 5216711-KUSAD. Ed. Wolfgang Kasack. circ. 200. (back issues avail.)

ARBITRIUM; Zeitschrift fuer Rezensionen zur germanistischen Literaturwissenschaft. see *LITERARY AND POLITICAL REVIEWS*

890   IS
ARC. (Text in English) 1982. a. IS.7($10) to N. America. Israel Association of Writers in English, P.O. Box 39385, Ramat Aviv, Tel Aviv 61393, Israel. Ed. Riva Rubin. circ. 1,500.

LITERATURE

830   GW   ISSN 0003-7982
PN851
ARCADIA; Zeitschrift fuer vergleichende Literaturwissenschaft. (Text mainly in German; occasionally in English, French, Italian and Spanish) 1966. 3/yr. $90. Walter de Gruyter und Co., Genthinerstr. 13, 1000 Berlin 30, Germany. TEL 030-26005-0. FAX 030-26005251. TELEX 184027. (U.S. addr.: Walter de Gruyter, Inc., 200 Saw Mill Rd., Hawthorne, NY 10532) Ed. Horst Ruediger. adv.; bk.rev.; bibl. **Indexed:** Arts & Hum.Cit.Ind., Can.Rev.Comp.Lit., Curr.Cont., Ind.Bk.Rev.Hum., M.L.A., RILA.

ARCHIV FUER DAS STUDIUM DER NEUEREN SPRACHEN UND LITERATUREN. see *LINGUISTICS*

ARCHIVE FOR REFORMATION HISTORY. LITERATURE REVIEW/ARCHIV FUER REFORMATIONSGESCHICHTE. LITERATURBERICHT. see *RELIGIONS AND THEOLOGY*

840   FR   ISSN 0066-6556
ARCHIVES CLAUDELIENNES; archives des lettres modernes. (Subseries of: Archives des Lettres Modernes) 1958. irreg. price varies. Lettres Modernes, 73 rue du Cardinal-Lemoine, 75005 Paris, France. TEL 1-43-54-46-09.

800   CN   ISSN 0066-6572
ARCHIVES DES LETTRES CANADIENNES. 1961. irreg. price varies. (University of Ottawa, Centre de Recherches de Litterature Canadienne-Francaise) Editions Fides, 165, rue Deslauriers, Ville St.-Laurent, Que. H4N 2S4, Canada. TEL 514-745-4290. FAX 514-745-4299. **Indexed:** RADAR.

809   FR   ISSN 0003-9675
ARCHIVES DES LETTRES MODERNES; etudes de critique et d'histoire litteraire. 1957. irreg. (6-10/yr.), latest no.252, 1991. 570 F. for 60 "cahiers". Lettres Modernes, 73 rue du Cardinal Lemoine, 75005 Paris, France. TEL 1-43-54-46-09. Ed. Michel J. Minard. **Indexed:** M.L.A.

860   CK   ISSN 0066-6734
ARCHIVO EPISTOLAR COLOMBIANO. 1965. irreg., latest no.20, 1990. price varies. Instituto Caro y Cuervo, Seccion de Publicaciones, Apdo. Aereo 51502, Bogota, Colombia.

809   IT   ISSN 0066-6807
ARCHIVUM ROMANICUM. BIBLIOTECA. SERIE 1: STORIA LETTERATURA PALEOGRAFIA. (Text in English, French, German, Italian) 1921. irreg., vol.244, 1991. price varies. Casa Editrice Leo S. Olschki, Casella Postale 66, 50100 Florence, Italy. TEL 055-6530684. FAX 055-6530214. circ. 1,000.

800   PL   ISSN 0066-6904
ARCHIWUM LITERACKIE. (Text in Polish) 1956. irreg., vol.25, 1982. price varies. (Polska Akademia Nauk, Instytut Badan Literackich) Ossolineum, Publishing House of the Polish Academy of Sciences, Rynek 9, Wroclaw, Poland. TELEX 0712771 OSS PL. (Dist. by: Ars Polona-Ruch, Krakowskie Przedmiescie 7, Warsaw, Poland) circ. 1,500.

ARCHIWUM TLUMACZEN Z TEORII LITERATURY I METODOLOGII BADAN LITERACKICH. see *LINGUISTICS*

ARIEL; a review of arts and letters in Israel. see *HUMANITIES: COMPREHENSIVE WORKS*

820   PK   ISSN 0254-3028
ARIEL. (Text in English) 1962. a. Rs.25($1.50) University of Sindh, Department of English, Jamshoro, Sindh, Pakistan. TEL 71251. Ed. K.M. Larik. bk.rev.; cum.index; circ. 500. **Indexed:** Arts & Hum.Cit.Ind., Curr.Cont., Hum.Ind.

ARISTOS; devoted to the preservation and advancement of traditional values (as opposed to modernism and post-modernism) in the arts. see *ART*

ARIZONA QUARTERLY; a journal of American literature, culture and theory. see *LITERARY AND POLITICAL REVIEWS*

ARIZONA STATE UNIVERSITY. CENTER FOR ASIAN STUDIES. MONOGRAPH SERIES. see *ORIENTAL STUDIES*

955 059.915   IR   ISSN 0378-2883
ARMAGHAN. 1910. m. Muhammad Vahid-Dastgerdi, Ed. & Pub., Baghe Saba, 127 Salim St., Teheran 16137, Iran. TEL 021-750698. circ. 3,000.

839 439   DK   ISSN 0107-1475
ARNAMAGNAEAN INSTITUTE AND DICTIONARY. BULLETIN. 1964. biennial. free. Arnamagnaean Institute and Arnamagnaean Dictionary, Njalsgade 76, DK-2300 Copenhagen S, Denmark. TEL 45-31-54-22-11.
Formerly (until 1975): Arnamagnaean Institute. Bulletin (ISSN 0066-7765)

800   US   ISSN 1043-5778
ARS INTERPRETANDI/ART OF INTERPRETATION. irreg. Peter Lang Publishing, Inc., 62 W. 45th St., 4th Fl., New York, NY 10036. TEL 212-302-6740. FAX 212-302-7574. Ed. Raymond Gay-Crosier.

800 851   IT   ISSN 0393-8263
ARSENALE; trimestrale di letteratura. 1984. q. L.20000($17.50) Edizioni Il Labirinto, Via Leonori 67, 00147 Rome, Italy. Ed. Gianfranco Palmery. adv.; bk.rev.; circ. 3,000. (back issues avail.)

ART AND CULTURE. see *ART*

ART INTERNATIONAL. see *ART*

810   US
ART - LIFE. 1981. 11/yr. $450. Art - Life Limited Editions, Box 23020, Ventura, CA 93002. TEL 805-648-4331. Ed. Gayle Jansen Beede. circ. 800.
Description: Publishes well-crafted poems and short prose.

ARTES. see *ART*

800   US   ISSN 0196-691X
ARTFUL DODGE. 1979. a. $10 to individuals; institutions $16. Artful Dodge Publications, Department of English, The College of Wooster, Wooster, OH 44691. TEL 216-262-8353. Eds. Daniel Bourne, Karen Kovacik. adv.; bk.rev.; illus.; circ. 1,000. (back issues avail.) **Indexed:** Amer.Hum.Ind.
Description: Publishes new American fiction and poetry, and translations from Eastern Europe and the Third World. Includes interviews.

840   FR   ISSN 0180-9385
ARTHUR RIMBAUD. 1972. a. Lettres Moderne, 73 rue du Cardinal Lemoine, 75005 Paris, France. Ed. Louis Forrestier. bk.rev. (back issues avail.)

800   US   ISSN 0890-4944
ARTHURIAN INTERPRETATIONS. 1968. 2/yr. $10 (foreign $12.50). Memphis State University, Department of English, Memphis, TN 38152. TEL 901-678-4591. Ed. Henry H. Peyton III. adv.; bk.rev.; circ. 500. (back issues avail.) **Indexed:** M.L.A.
Supersedes (in 1986): Interpretations (ISSN 0196-903X)
Description: Multi-disciplinary journal of Arthurian studies from the beginning to the twentieth century.

ARTPAPER. see *ART*

890   II
ARUN. (Text in Hindi) 1972. m. Rs.8. Arun Group of Publications, Box 27, Civil Lines, Moradabad, India. adv.; illus.

820.9   GH
ASEMKA. (Text in English or French) 1974. a. $10. University of Cape Coast, Cape Coast, Ghana. Ed. Y.S. Boafo. adv.; bk.rev.; circ. 1,000. **Indexed:** M.L.A.

811   US
ASSEMBLING ANNUAL. 1970. a. $30. (Participation Projects Foundation) Assembling Press, P.O. Box 1967, Brooklyn, NY 11202. Ed. Charles Doria. illus.; circ. 200. (also avail. in microfilm from UMI; back issues avail.)
Formerly: Assembling (ISSN 0161-8318)
Description: Publishes poems.

020   US   ISSN 1051-3299
▼**ASSISTANT EDITOR**; original short articles, fillers, and clip art for library newsletter. 1991. q. $75 (Canada $78; elsewhere $90). Chris Olson & Associates, 857 Twin Harbor Dr., Arnold, MD 21012. TEL 301-647-6708. FAX 301-647-0415. (also avail. on diskette)

808   US
ASSOCIATED WRITING PROGRAMS AWARD FOR CREATIVE NONFICTION. 1986. a. price varies. University of Georgia Press, Athens, GA 30602. TEL 404-542-2830. FAX 404-542-0601.

840   FR   ISSN 0066-8893
ASSOCIATION DES AMIS D'ALFRED DE VIGNY. BULLETIN. 1968. a. 96 F. membership. Association des Amis d'Alfred de Vigny, 6 av. Constant-Coquelin, 75007 Paris, France. TEL 42-73-12-86. Eds. Andre Jarry, C. Lefranc. adv.; bk.rev.; circ. 500. (also avail. in microfiche)

800   II   ISSN 0066-9083
ASSOCIATION FOR COMMONWEALTH LITERATURE AND LANGUAGE STUDIES. BULLETIN. 1967. s-a. Association for Commonwealth Literature and Language Studies, Indian Branch, Department of English, University of Mysore, Manasagangotri, Mysore 570006, India.
Formerly: A C L A L S Newsheet.

ASSOCIATION INTERNATIONALE D'ETUDES DU SUD-EST EUROPEEN. BULLETIN. see *HISTORY — History Of Europe*

944   FR   ISSN 0004-6116
ASTRADO; revue bilingue de Provence. (Text in French, Provencal) 1965. a. 120 F.($30) per no.(effective 1988). Astrado Prouvencalo, 7 rue des Fauvettes, 13130 Berre L'Etang, France. Ed. M. Courty. bk.rev.; illus.; circ. 1,000. **Indexed:** M.L.A.
Description: Centers on one theme every year and includes poems, short-stories, scholarly studies and papers in anthropology, linguistics, literature and history.

ASWAMEDHAM; the front runner. see *ADVERTISING AND PUBLIC RELATIONS*

800   IT
ATALANTA. 1976. irreg., no.2, 1977. price varies. Giardini Editori e Stampatori, Via Santa Bibbiana 28, 56100 Pisa, Italy. TEL 050-502531. Eds. S.G. Mancini, M. Pagnini. **Indexed:** Biol.Abstr.

869   BL
ATENEU ANGRENSE DE LETRAS E ARTES. REVISTA. 1973. q. Cz.$1200. Ateneu Angrense de Letras e Artes, Caixa Postal 03, Travesa Santa Luzia, 91 Sobrado, 23900 Angra dos Reis, Rio de Janeiro, Brazil. Dir. Alipio Mendes. adv.; bk.rev.; bibl.; charts; illus.; index; circ. 5,000. (back issues avail.)

ATHANOR. see *ART*

052   NR   ISSN 0004-7007
ATOKA; Yoruba photoplay series. (Text in Yoruba) 1967. s-m. 17.50 n. West African Book Publishers Ltd., Box 3445, Lagos, Nigeria. Ed. Eniola Adeyemi. adv.; illus.; circ. 83,000.

860   BL
ATRAVES. 1976. irreg. Livraria Duas Cidades, Rua Bento Freitas 158, 01220 Sao Paulo SP, Brazil. Ed.Bd. illus.

806   US
AUGUST DERLETH SOCIETY. NEWSLETTER. 1977. irreg. $5 membership. August Derleth Society, 61 Teecomwas Dr., Uncasville, CT 06382. TEL 203-848-0636. (Subscr. to: Herb Attix, 3333 Westview Ln., Madison, WI 53713. TEL 608-273-0520) Ed. Richard H. Fawcett. adv.; bk.rev.; circ. 200.
Description: Covers the life and writings of August Derleth, and artists and writers associated with him.

AULA. see *SOCIAL SCIENCES: COMPREHENSIVE WORKS*

AUM NAMO NARAYANAY. see *PHILOSOPHY*

830 709   GW   ISSN 0341-1230
AURORA; Jahrbuch der Eichendorff-Gesellschaft. (Text in German; summaries in English and German) 1953. a. price varies. Jan Thorbecke Verlag GmbH und Co., Postfach 546, 7480 Sigmaringen, Germany. TEL 07571-728-100. FAX 07571-728-280. Ed.Bd. bk.rev.; bibl.; illus.; index; circ. 1,000. (reprint service avail. from KTO) **Indexed:** M.L.A.

800 US
AURORA (RICHMOND). 1935. a. $1. Eastern Kentucky University, Richmond, KY 40475. TEL 606-622-0111. circ. 400. (back issues avail.)

830 709 GW ISSN 0171-6530
AURORA-BUCHREIHE. 1974. irreg. price varies. Jan Thorbecke Verlag GmbH und Co., Postfach 546, 7480 Sigmaringen, Germany. TEL 07571-728-100. FAX 07571-728-280. Ed.Bd. circ. 1,000.

809 700 GW
AUSGABE; ein Literatur- und Kunstmagazin. 1976. a. DM.20. Armin Hundertmark Ed.& Pub., Bruesselerstr. 29, 5000 Cologne 1, Germany. TEL 0221-237944. FAX 0221-249146. adv.

800 CN ISSN 0843-5049
PR9600
AUSTRALIAN AND NEW ZEALAND STUDIES IN CANADA. 1989. s-a. $15. University of Western Ontario, Department of English, London, Ont. N6A 3K7, Canada. TEL 519-679-2111. FAX 519-661-3292. Ed. Thomas E. Tausky. adv.; circ. 150.
 Description: Devoted to the study of literature and the related arts in Australia and New Zealand.

830 430 SZ
AUSTRALIAN AND NEW ZEALAND STUDIES IN GERMAN LANGUAGE AND LITERATURE. (Text in English and German) 1971. irreg. Verlag Peter Lang AG, Jupiterstr. 15, CH-3015 Bern, Switzerland. TEL 031-321122. FAX 031-321131. TELEX 912651-PELA-CH. Ed. G. Schulz. circ. 400. (back issues avail.)

820 AT ISSN 1034-0785
AUSTRALIAN BOOK COLLECTOR. 1987. m. Aus.$38 (foreign Aus.$50). Ross Burnet, Ed. & Pub., P.O. Box 2, Uralla, N.S.W. 2358, Australia. TEL 067-78-4682. FAX 067-78-4516. adv.; bk.rev.; bibl.; illus.; circ. 1,000. (back issues avail.)
 Former titles (until 1989): Bookman's Monthly (ISSN 1031-1556) & Book Market.
 Description: For the antiquarian trade and collectors.

840 440 AT ISSN 0004-9468
PQ1
AUSTRALIAN JOURNAL OF FRENCH STUDIES. (Text in English, French) 1964. 3/yr. Aus.$35($35) Monash University, Department of Romance Languages, Clayton, Vic. 3168, Australia. FAX 61-3-565-4007. TELEX AA32691. Ed. Dr. Wallace Kirsop. bk.rev.; bibl.; stat.; index; circ. 530. Indexed: Amer.Hist.& Life, Arts & Hum.Cit.Ind., Aus.P.A.I.S., Br.Hum.Ind., Can.Rev.Comp.Lit, Curr.Cont., Hist.Abstr., M.L.A.
—BLDSC shelfmark: 1808.200000.

820 AT ISSN 0004-9697
PR9400
AUSTRALIAN LITERARY STUDIES. 1963. s-a. Aus.$25 to individuals (foreign Aus.$30); institutions Aus.$35 (foreign Aus.$40); students Aus.$18. University of Queensland, Department of English, P.O. Box 88, St. Lucia, Qld. 4073, Australia. TEL 07-3651442. FAX 07-3652799. Ed. L.T. Hergenhan. adv.; bk.rev.; bibl.; cum.index every 2 yrs.; circ. 1,000. (also avail. in microform from UMI; reprint service avail from UMI) Indexed: Abstr.Engl.Stud., Arts & Hum.Cit.Ind., Aus.P.A.I.S., Curr.Cont., Gdlns., Ind.Bk.Rev.Hum., M.L.A., So.Pac.Per.Ind.
—BLDSC shelfmark: 1813.900000.

800 920 NE
AUSTRALIAN PLAYWRIGHTS; a series of monographs and video programmes. irreg. Editions Rodopi B.V., Keizersgracht 302-304, 1016 EX Amsterdam, Netherlands. TEL 020-6227507. FAX 020-6380948. (US and Canada subscr. to: Humanities Press International Inc., 171 First Ave., Atlantic Highlands, NJ 07716) (Co-publisher: Humanities Press International Inc.) Ed. Otrum Zuber-Skerritt. play rev.; bibl.
 Description: Promotes a better understanding of Australian drama through overviews of particular playwrights and their works. Most include videos of interviews with the playwrights.

800 AT ISSN 0810-4468
AUSTRALIAN SHORT STORIES. 1982. q. Aus.$30($38) Pascoe Publishing Pty. Ltd., P.O. Box 42, Apolb Bay, Vic. 3233, Australia. FAX 03-376-559. Eds. Bruce Pascoe, Lyn Harwood. adv.; circ. 12,000. (back issues avail.)
 Description: Contemporary stories from Australia and the world.

AUSTRALIAN SLAVONIC AND EAST EUROPEAN STUDIES. see LINGUISTICS

800 US ISSN 1054-058X
AUSTRIAN LITERATURE. (Text in English, German) irreg. Peter Lang Publishing, Inc., 62 W. 45th St., 4th Fl., New York, NY 10036. TEL 212-302-6704. FAX 212-302-7574. Ed. Harry Zohn.
 Description: Provides critical evaluations of Austrian authors, works, currents, or figures from the Middle Ages to the present.

070 800 UK ISSN 0005-0628
PN101
AUTHOR. 1890. q. £10 non-members. Society of Authors, 84 Drayton Gardens, London SW10 9SB, England. Ed. Derek Parker. adv.; bk.rev.; circ. 6,000. (also avail. in microfilm from UMI; reprint service avail. from UMI) Indexed: Br.Hum.Ind.
—BLDSC shelfmark: 1825.460000.

800 340 US
AUTHORS GUILD BULLETIN. 1914. q. membership only. Authors Guild, 330 W. 42nd St., 29th Fl., New York, NY 10036-6902. FAX 212-564-8363. Ed. Hugh Rawson. bk.rev.; circ. 6,500.
 Description: Covers business and legal matters of interest to authors.

070 800 US ISSN 0005-0660
AUTHORSHIP. 1943. bi-m. $18. National Writers Club, 1450 S. Havana, Ste. 620, Aurora, CO 80012. TEL 303-751-7844. Ed. Sandy WHelchel. adv.; bk.rev.; charts; circ. 4,000.
 Description: Discusses creative and compositional techniques.

869 BL
AUTORES AFRICANOS. 1982. irreg. Editora Atica, S.A., Rua Barao de Iguape, 110, Caixa Postal 8656, Sao Paulo, Brazil.

800 900 028.5 US ISSN 0741-1790
AVALON TO CAMELOT;* issued quarterly on matters Arthurian. 1983. q. $20. Avalon to Camelot, Inc., 2562 W. Winnemac-Lambides, Ste. 2, Chicago, IL 60625. Ed. Alan C. Lupack. adv.; bk.rev.; film rev.; bibl.; charts; illus.; circ. 2,000. (back issues avail.) Indexed: M.L.A.

800 700 NE
AVANT GARDE; revue interdisciplinaire et internationale des arts et litteratures du XXe siecle. (Text in English, French, German) 1988. 3/yr. fl.35 to individuals; institutions fl.100. Editions Rodopi B.V., Keizersgracht 302-304, 1016 EX Amsterdam, Netherlands. TEL 020-6227507. FAX 020-6380948. (US and Canada subscr. to: 233 Peachtree St., N.E., Ste. 404, Atlanta, GA 30303-1504. TEL 800-225-3998) Ed. Fernand Drijkoningen.
 Description: Includes information on research in avant-garde modernism and post-modernism in literature and other arts.

840 FR ISSN 0067-2610
AVANT-SIECLE. 1967. irreg., no.15, 1978. Lettres Modernes, 73, Rue du Cardinal-Lemoine, 75005 Paris, France. TEL 022-466666. FAX 022-472391. (Dist. outside France by: Librairie Droz S.A., 11, rue Massot, CH-1211 Geneva 12, Switzerland) Ed. Louis Forestier.
 Description: Presents modern literature of Western and Eastern Europe. From the "Editions 'Lettres Modernes'."

808 US ISSN 0899-3750
AVEC; a journal of writing. 1988. s-a. $12. Syntax Projects for the Arts, P.O. Box 1059, Penngrove, CA 94951. TEL 707-762-2370. FAX 707-769-0880. Ed. Cydney Chadwick. adv.; circ. 1,000. (back issues avail.)
 Description: Focuses on experimental poetry and ficiton from around the world.

800 UY ISSN 0067-2637
AVES DEL ARCA.* irreg. Editorial Arca, Colonia 1263, Montevideo, Uruguay.

059.927 TS
AWRAQ. 1983. w. Al- Waraqun Printing, Publishing and Distribution, P.O. Box 5015, Abu Dhabi, United Arab Emirates. TEL 47700. TELEX 22453 EM. Ed. Hallah Hamid Matouq. circ. 5,000.
 Description: Publishes cultural and literary news, stories, poetry, and analysis of Gulf and Arab world events.

808 700 778.534 US
AXE FACTORY REVIEW. 1985. a. $5. (Axe Factory Center for the Arts) Axe Factory Publications, Box 11186, Philadelphia, PA 19136. TEL 215-331-7389. Eds. Louis McKee, Joesph Farley. adv.; bk.rev.; circ. 600.

810 US
AZOREAN EXPRESS. 1985. s-a. $5. Seven Buffaloes Press, Box 249, Big Timber, MT 59011. Ed. Art Cuelho. circ. 500.

810 811 US ISSN 0897-5515
PS580
B-CITY. 1983. a. $5. B-City Press, Inc., 619 W. Surf St., No.2, Chicago, IL 60657. TEL 312-871-6175. Ed. Connie Deanovich. circ. 250. (back issues avail.)
 Description: Presents modern American poetry and literature.

B L A C. (Black Literature and Arts Congress) see ETHNIC INTERESTS

B U M. (Boerne og Ungdoms-Litteratur Magasinet) see CHILDREN AND YOUTH — For

BABEL; revue internationale de la traduction - international journal of translation. see LINGUISTICS

BACK BRAIN RECLUSE; new speculative fiction. see LITERATURE — Science Fiction, Fantasy, Horror

800 700 YU ISSN 0005-3880
BAGDALA; mesecni list za knjizevnost, umetnost i kulturu. (Text in Serbo-Croatian) 1959. m. 100 din. Zakiceva 3, Krusevac, Yugoslavia. TEL 037-33-409. Ed. Milos Petrovic. bk.rev.; circ. 1,000.

400 800 BX ISSN 0005-3988
PL5101
BAHANA. 1966. m. B.$1.50($0.75) Ministry of Culture, Youth and Sports, Language and Literature Bureau - Dewan Bahasa dan Pustaka, Jalan Elizabeth II, Bandar Seri Begawan 2604, Brunei Darussalam. FAX 02-241817. TELEX BU-2774. Ed.Bd. adv.; bk.rev.; illus.; circ. 3,000.

895.1 CC
BAIHUA YUAN. (Text in Chinese) m. Zhengzhou Shi Wenlian, No. 12, Yihe Lu, Zhengzhou, Henan 450007, People's Republic of China. TEL 449795. Ed. Wang Baomin.

895.1 CC
BAIHUA ZHOU. (Text in Chinese) bi-m. Baihua Zhou Wenyi Chubanshe, No.5, Xinwei Lu, Nanchang, Jiangxi 330002, People's Republic of China. TEL 333180. Ed. Lan Lisheng.

BAIJIA ZUOWEN ZHIDAO. see EDUCATION

BAKER STREET JOURNAL; an irregular quarterly of Sherlockiana. see LITERATURE — Mystery And Detective

BALSA DE LA MEDUSA. see ART

800 US ISSN 0733-0308
BAMBOO RIDGE; the Hawaii writers' quarterly. 1978. q. $12 to individuals; institutions $16. Bamboo Ridge Press, Box 61781, Honolulu, HI 96839-1781. Eds. Eric Chock, Darrell Lum. adv.; bk.rev.; circ. 1,000. (back issues avail.) Indexed: Amer.Hum.Ind.

491.1 891.1 BG
BAMLA EKADEMI GABESHANA PATRIKA. (Former name of issuing body: Bengali Academy) (Text in Bengali) 1957. q. Bangla Academy, Burdwan House, Dhaka 1000, Bangladesh. TEL 2-500131. Indexed: Apic.Abstr.
 Supersedes (1972): Patrika (ISSN 0522-8980)
 Description: Covers Bengali literature and culture.

LITERATURE

820 890 II
BANASTHALI PATRIKA. (Alternate issues in English and Hindi) vol.6, 1971. q. Rs.25($8) Banasthali-Vidyapith, Jaipur, Rajasthan, India. Ed. Rameshwar Gupta. bk.rev.; bibl.; circ. 1,000.
Indexed: Bibl.Engl.Lang.& Lit., M.L.A.

820 UK ISSN 0306-8404
BANDERSNATCH. 1973. irreg. membership. Lewis Carroll Society, 69 Ashby Rd., Woodville, Burton-on-Trent, Staffs, England. (Subscr. addr.: c/o Roger E. Allen, 35 Crown St., Harrow, Middlesex, HA2 OHX, England) Ed. Alfreda Blanchard. bk.rev.; circ. 350 (controlled).

820 BG
BANGLA ACADEMY JOURNAL. (Text in English) vol.4, 1973. s-a. Tk.4($2) Bangla Academy, Burdwan House, Dhaka 1000, Bangladesh. TEL 2-500131. Ed. Mazharul Islam. bk.rev.
  Supersedes: Bengali Academy Journal.
  Description: Discusses literary and cultural topics.

BAOGAO WENXUE/REPORTAGE LITERATURE. see *JOURNALISM*

850 IT
BARATARIA. 1989. irreg., no.5, 1990. price varies. Liguori Editore s.r.l., Via Mezzocannone, 19, 80134 Naples, Italy. TEL 081-5527139. Eds. Mario DiPinto, Laura Dolfi.

840 700 FR
BARBACANE; revue des pierres et des hommes. vol.11, 1975. a. 40 F. Cercle Culturel et Artisanal de Bonaguil, Chateau de Bonaguil, Saint Front sur Lemance, 47500 Fumel, France. Ed. Max Pons. adv.; bk.rev.; circ. 500.

BARCELONA. METROPOLIS MEDITERRANIA. see *HOUSING AND URBAN PLANNING*

820 UK ISSN 0307-3408
BARD. 1975. s-a. £3($6) Shakespearean Authorship Trust, 11 Old Square, Lincoln's Inn, London WC2A 3TS, England. Ed.Bd. adv.; bk.rev.; bibl.; circ. 400.
  Supersedes: Shakespearean Authorship Review.

371 028.5 AU ISSN 0067-4206
DIE BARKE; Lehrer-Jahrbuch. 1956. a. Oesterreichischer Buchklub der Jugend, Mayerhofgasse 6, A-1040 Vienna, Austria.

BARNBOKEN. see *PUBLISHING AND BOOK TRADE*

800 FR ISSN 0067-4222
BAROQUE; revue internationale. 1963. irreg., latest vol.12, 1985. 180 Fr. (Centre International de Synthese du Baroque) Editions Cocagne, 30 rue de la Banque, 82 000 Montauban, France. TEL 63-63-05-67. (back issues avail.) Indexed: M.L.A.
  Former titles (until 1966): Journees Internationales d'Etude du Baroque. Actes; (until 1965): Journees Internationales d'Etudes du Baroque.

BASIS; majalah bulanan kebudayaan umum/monthly for culture in general. see *ART*

830 430 GW ISSN 0067-4508
BASLER STUDIEN ZUR DEUTSCHEN SPRACHE UND LITERATUR. 1954. irreg., vol.59, 1983. price varies. K.G. Saur Verlag KG, Ortlerstr. 8, 8000 Munich 70, Germany. TEL 089-76902-0. FAX 089-76902150. Ed.Bd.

813 US ISSN 0005-6677
PS3503.A923
BAUM BUGLE. 1957. 3/yr. $10. International Wizard of Oz Club, Inc., 220 N. 11th St., Escanaba, MI 49829. bk.rev.; bibl.; illus. Indexed: M.L.A.
  Description: Focuses on the Land of Oz, L. Frank Baum and its other creators, books, films, etc..

800 296 IS ISSN 0302-8178
PJ5161.A1
BAY ZIKH.* 1972. Komitet far Yidisher Kultur in Yisroel, 228 Bnei Ephraim St., Tel Aviv, Israel.

BAYERISCHE STAATSBIBLIOTHEK. NEW CONTENTS SLAVISTICS. INHALTSVERZEICHNISSE SLAVISTISCHER ZEITSCHRIFTEN - ISZ. see *BIBLIOGRAPHIES*

BAZMAVEP. see *HISTORY — History Of The Near East*

BEAKEN. see *LINGUISTICS*

800 920 US ISSN 0882-4428
BEAN HOME NEWSLETTER. 1984. q. $12 for two yrs. Friends of Freddy, 1-F Northway Rd., Greenbelt, MD 20770. TEL 213-285-1085. FAX 213-278-3387. (And: 750 N. Vista St., Los Angeles, CA 90046) Ed. Michael Cart. circ. 300. (back issues avail.)
  Description: Contains news of the Friends of Freddy and critical evaluations of the writing of Walter R. Brooks.

BEBOP DRAWING CLUB BOOK. see *ART*

806 US ISSN 0732-2224
PR6003.E282
BECKETT CIRCLE/CERCLE DE BECKETT. 1978. bi-m. $12. Samuel Beckett Society, c/o Karen Laughlin, Ed., Dept. of English, Tallahassee, FL 32306. FAX 904-644-8817. adv.; bk.rev.; play rev.; bibl.; circ. 350. (back issues avail.)

891.4 II ISSN 0005-769X
BEDUIN. (Text in Bengali) 1966. a. Rs.12. Rani Suhasini Roy, Tamluk Raj House, Tamluk, Midnapore, West Bengal, India. Ed. Bhabanee Mukhopadhyay.

800 IS ISSN 0334-973X
BE'EMMET; a miscellany of studies, teaching and research in children's literature. 1987. s-a. IS.25($12.50) Beit Berl College, Yemima Center 44905, Israel. TEL 052-25151. FAX 052-25426. Ed. Shlomo Har-el. bk.rev.; circ. 1,000.

LE BEFFROI; revue philosophique et litteraire. see *PHILOSOPHY*

840 BE
LE BEGUE; la premiere revue facultaire. irreg. (7-8/yr.). 350 Fr. Maison de Droit de Louvain la Neuve, Place Montesquieu, 2 Bte. 45, 1348 Louvain La Neuve, Belgium. TEL 010-47-46-42. Ed. Benoit De Nayer.

895.1 CC ISSN 0476-031X
BEIFANG WENXUE/NORTHERN LITERATURE. (Text in Chinese) 1958. m. Y18($61.20) 16, Yaojing Jie, Nangang, Harbin, Heilongjiang 150006, People's Republic of China. (Dist. outside China by: China International Book Trading Corp., P.O. Box 399, Beijing, P.R.C.; Dist. in US by: China Books & Periodicals, Inc., 2929 24th St., San Francisco, CA 94110. TEL 415-282-2994) Eds. Han Mengjie, Li Fuliang.

895.1 CC
BEIJI GUANG/NORTHERN LIGHTS. (Text in Chinese) bi-m. Beiji Guang Bianjibu - Beiji Guang Magazine, Shengli Lu, Jia Ge Da Qi, Heilongjiang 165000, People's Republic of China. TEL 3968. (Dist. outside China by: China Publications Foreign Trade Corp., P.O. Box 782, Beijing, P.R.C.) Ed. Zhang Lianrong.

895.1 CC ISSN 0257-0262
BEIJING WENXUE/BEIJING LITERATURE. (Text in Chinese) m. $61.20. Beijing Wenxue Yuekanshe, Beijing, People's Republic of China. (Dist. in US by: China Books & Periodicals, Inc., 2929 24th St., San Francisco, CA 94110. TEL 415-282-2994)

BEITRAEGE ZUR DEUTSCHEN PHILOLOGIE. see *LINGUISTICS*

BEITRAEGE ZUR GESCHICHTE DER DEUTSCHEN SPRACHE UND LITERATUR. see *LINGUISTICS*

809 GW ISSN 0170-3315
BEITRAEGE ZUR LITERATUR DES 15.-18. JAHRHUNDERTS. (Text in English and German) irreg., vol.6, 1974. price varies. Franz Steiner Verlag Wiesbaden GmbH, Birkenwaldstr. 44, Postfach 101526, 7000 Stuttgart 1, Germany. TEL 0711-2582-0. FAX 0711-2582290. TELEX 723636-DAZD. Ed. Hans-Gert Roloff.

479 GW ISSN 0067-5202
BEITRAEGE ZUR ROMANISCHEN PHILOLOGIE DES MITTELALTERS. 1968. irreg. price varies. Wilhelm Fink Verlag, Ohmstr. 5, 8000 Munich 40, Germany. Eds. Hans-Wilhelm Klein, Ernstpeter Ruhe. Indexed: Arts & Hum.Cit.Ind., Curr.Cont., M.L.A.

895.1 CC
BEIYUE FENG. (Text in Chinese) bi-m. Beiyue Wenyi Chubanshe, 46 Jiefang Lu, Taiyuan, Shanxi 030002, People's Republic of China. TEL 224323. Ed. Yang Wenbin.

800 305.4 070.5 US ISSN 0884-2957
PN471
BELLES LETTRES; a review of books by women. 1985. q. $20 to individuals; students $15; institutions $40. 11151 Captain's Walk Ct., N. Potomac, MD 20878. TEL 301-294-0278. (Subscr. to: 785 Verbenia Dr., Satellite Beach, FL 32937) Ed. Janet Mullaney. adv.; bk.rev.; index; circ. 5,000. (also avail. in microform; back issues avail.) Indexed: Alt.Press Ind., Bk.Rev.Ind. (1988-), Child.Bk.Rev.Ind. (1988-), Wom.Stud.Abstr. (1985-).
  —BLDSC shelfmark: 1890.357000.
  Description: Founded to preserve, promote, and celebrate women's writing. Reviews scholarly and popular titles and includes interviews, rediscoveries, and retrospectives.

810 US ISSN 0734-2934
PS501
BELLINGHAM REVIEW. 1977. 2/yr. $5. Signpost Press, Inc., 1007 Queen St., Bellingham, WA 98226. Ed. Susan Hilton. adv.; bk.rev.; illus.; circ. 800. Indexed: A.I.P.P.
  Description: Covers the literary arts. Includes poetry, short fiction and drama, drawing and photographs.

800 US ISSN 0887-4115
BELLOWING ARK; a literary tabloid. 1984. bi-m. $15. Bellowing Ark Society, Box 45637, Seattle, WA 98145. TEL 206-545-8302. Ed. Robert R. Ward. circ. 1,000. (tabloid format; back issues avail.) Indexed: Ind.Amer.Per.Verse.
  Description: Covers material which portrays the human condition as a positive process.

800 US ISSN 0883-9131
BELOIT FICTION JOURNAL. 1985. 2/yr. $9. Box 11, Beloit College, Beloit, WI 53511. TEL 608-363-2308. Ed. Clint McCown. circ. 750. (back issues avail.)
  Description: Contains contemporary short stories on any theme or subject, up to fifty pages in length.

895.1 US
BEN LIU/TORRENT. (Text in Chinese) m. $54. China Books & Periodicals, Inc., 2929 24th St., San Francisco, CA 94110. TEL 415-282-2994. FAX 415-282-0994.

891.4 II ISSN 0005-8815
BENGALI LITERATURE.* vol.4, 1970. q. Rs.8($2) 53 Bidhan Palli, Jadavpur, Calcutta 32, India. Ed. Ashis Sanyal. adv.; bk.rev.; bibl.; film rev.; play rev.; index; circ. 2,100.

800 CN ISSN 0067-5733
BENT. (Text in English) 1969. irreg., no.7, 1971. Can.$0.25. 1111 Bewdley Avenue, Victoria, B. C., Canada. Ed. Byrd Lukinuk. adv.; circ. 300.

BERKELEY REVIEW OF BOOKS. see *PUBLISHING AND BOOK TRADE*

800 US
BERN PORTER INTERNATIONAL. 1911. w. $12.50. (Institute of Advanced Thinking) Bern Porter Books, 22 Salmond Rd., Belfast, ME 04915. Ed. Bern Porter. adv.; bk.rev.; film rev.; play rev.; bibl.; circ. 265,000. (also avail. in microform from UMI)

890 JA
BESSATSU BUNGEI SHUNJU; a quarterly on popular novels. 1946. q. 4240 Yen. Bungei Shunju Ltd., 3-23, Kioi-cho, Chiyoda-ku, Tokyo, Japan. FAX 03-3265-4878. Ed. Kazukiyo Takahashi.

810 US ISSN 0888-3742
PS688
BEST AMERICAN ESSAYS. 1986. a. $16.95. Ticknor & Fields, 215 Park Ave. S., New York, NY 10003. TEL 212-420-5800. Ed. Robert Atwan.

813.08 US ISSN 0067-6233
PZ1
BEST AMERICAN SHORT STORIES. 1915. a. price varies. Houghton Mifflin Co., One Beacon St., Boston, MA 02107. TEL 617-725-5000.

| 813.01 | CN | ISSN 0703-9476 |

PZ1
BEST CANADIAN STORIES. 1971. a. $29.95 (clothbound); $15.95 (paperback). Oberon Press, 400-350 Sparks St., Ottawa, Ont. K1R 7S8, Canada. TEL 613-238-3275. Eds. David Helwig, Maggie Helwig. adv.; bk.rev.; circ. 2,500.
   Supersedes: New Canadian Stories (ISSN 0316-7518)
   Description: Collection of the best Canadian stories published during the year.

| 800 | US |

BEST OF LAFAYETTE: THE SOUTHERN WRITER AND ARTIST. bi-m. Amie Lewis, Ed. & Pub., c/o Sew it Seams, 333 11th Pl., Kirkland, WA 98033.

| 812.5 | US | ISSN 0067-6284 |

PN6111
BEST SHORT PLAYS. 1969. a. $10.95. Applause Theatre Book Publishers, 211 W. 71st St., New York, NY 10023. TEL 212-595-4735. FAX 212-721-2856. Eds. Howard Stein, Glenn Young. circ. 10,000.
   Description: Presents 10-12 short plays which represent the range of style and ambition of the current season.

| 891.4 | II | ISSN 0006-050X |

BHARATI TE VIDESHI SAHITA. (Text in Punjabi) 1968. s-a. Punjabi University, Patiala 4, Punjab, India. Ed. Dr. Gurden Singh. bk.rev.

| 052 | | ISSN 0006-0518 |

BHAVAN'S JOURNAL. 1954. fortn. Rs.156. Bharatiya Vidya Bhavan, Kulapati K.M. Munshi Marg, Bombay 400007, India. Ed. S. Ramakrishnan. adv.; bk.rev.; circ. 40,000.

BIBLIOGRAPHIEN ZUR DEUTSCHEN LITERATUR DES MITTELALTERS. see *LITERATURE — Abstracting, Bibliographies, Statistics*

BIBLIOLOGIA. see *PUBLISHING AND BOOK TRADE*

| 860 | CK | |

BIBLIOTECA COLOMBIANA. 1970. irreg., latest no.33, 1990. price varies. Instituto Caro y Cuervo, Seccion de Publicaciones, Apdo. Aereo 51502, Bogota, Colombia. (back issues avail.)

| 860 | SP | |

BIBLIOTECA DE AUTORES ESPANOLES. PUBLICACION. irreg., no.5, 1983. Editorial Trieste, Villanueva, 14, Madrid 1, Spain.

BIBLIOTECA DE MENENDEZ PELAYO. BOLETIN. see *LITERARY AND POLITICAL REVIEWS*

| 860 | MX | ISSN 0188-476X |

▼**BIBLIOTECA DE MEXICO.** 1991. bi-m. Consejo Nacional para la Cultura y las Artes, Plaza de la Ciudadela 4, Centro Historico, Mexico D.F., Mexico. TEL 512-09-27. FAX 510-41-85. illus.

| 800 | IT | |

BIBLIOTECA DI LETTERATURA E ARTE. 1975. irreg. price varies. Giardini Editori e Stampatori, Via Santa Bibbiana 28, 56100 Pisa, Italy. TEL 050-502531.

| 860 | SP | |

BIBLIOTECA ROMANICA HISPANICA. 1950. irreg. Editorial Gredos, S.A., Sanchez Pacheco 81, 28002 Madrid, Spain. FAX 341-5192033.
   Formerly: Biblioteca Romanica Hispanica. Estudios y Ensayos (ISSN 0519-7201)

| 891.85 | PL | ISSN 0519-8631 |

BIBLIOTEKA PISARZOW POLSKICH. SERIA A. 1953. irreg. price varies. (Polska Akademia Nauk, Instytut Badan Literackich) Ossolineum, Publishing House of the Polish Academy of Sciences, Rynek 9, Wroclaw, Poland. TELEX 0712771 OSS PL. (Dist. by: Ars Polona-Ruch, Krakowskie Przedmiescie 7, Warsaw, Poland) Ed. Jerzy Woronczak. circ. 1,500.
   Formerly: Biblioteka Pisarzow Polskich (ISSN 0067-7736)

BIBLIOTHECA ARNAMAGNAEANA; a Jon Helgason condita, auspiciis praesidii Arnamagnaeani. see *LINGUISTICS*

BIBLIOTHECA ARNAMAGNAEANA. SUPPLEMENTUM. see *LINGUISTICS*

BIBLIOTHECA RUSSICA. see *LINGUISTICS*

BIBLIOTHEQUE D'ETUDES BALKANIQUES. see *LINGUISTICS*

BIBLIOTHEQUE D'HUMANISME ET RENAISSANCE; travaux et documents. see *HISTORY — History Of Europe*

| 840 | FR | ISSN 0067-835X |

BIBLIOTHEQUE FRANCAISE ET ROMANE. SERIE B: EDITIONS CRITIQUES DE TEXTES. 1962. irreg. price varies. (Universite de Strasbourg II, Centre de Philologie et de Litteratures Romanes) Editions Klincksieck, 11 rue de Lille, 75005 Paris, France. Ed. Georges Straka.

| 840 | FR | ISSN 0067-8368 |

BIBLIOTHEQUE FRANCAISE ET ROMANE. SERIE C: ETUDES LITTERAIRES. 1960. irreg. price varies. (Universite de Strasbourg II, Centre de Philologie et de Litteratures Romanes) Editions Klincksieck, 11 rue de Lille, 75005 Paris, France. Ed. Paul Vernois.

| 840 | FR | ISSN 0067-8376 |

BIBLIOTHEQUE FRANCAISE ET ROMANE. SERIE D: INITIATION, TEXTES ET DOCUMENTS. 1964. irreg. price varies. (Universite de Strasbourg II, Centre de Philologie et de Litteratures Romanes) Editions Klincksieck, 11 rue de Lille, 75005 Paris, France. Ed. Georges Straka.

BIBLIOTHEQUE FRANCAISE ET ROMANE. SERIE E: LANGUE ET LITTERATURE FRANCAISES AU CANADA. see *LINGUISTICS*

| 840 | FR | ISSN 0067-8422 |

BIBLIOTHEQUE INTROUVABLE. (Supplement avail.: Oeuvres Complementaires.) 1966. irreg., latest no. 16, 1990. Lettres Modernes, 73 rue du Cardinal Lemoine, 75005 Paris, France. TEL 022-466666. FAX 022-472391. (Dist. outside France by: Librairie Droz S.A., 11, rue Massot, CH-1211 Geneva 12, Switzerland.)
   Description: From the series "Editions 'Lettres Modernes'."

| 800 | PO | ISSN 0870-4112 |

BIBLOS. 1925. a. $30. Universidade de Coimbra, Faculdade de Letras, 3049 Coimbra Codex, Portugal. FAX 039-36733. bk.rev.; circ. 500.

| 800 | US | ISSN 1043-9978 |

▼**BIG ALLIS.** 1989. s-a. 139 Thompson St., Apt. 2, New York, NY 10012. (Dist. by: Segue, 303 E. 8th St., New York, NY 10009; Small Press Distribution, 1814 San Pablo Ave., Berkeley, CA 94702) Eds. Jessica Grim, Melanie Neilson.

BIJDRAGEN TOT DE TAAL-, LAND- EN VOLKENKUNDE. see *ANTHROPOLOGY*

| 800 | PP | |

BIKMAUS. 1980. q. K.10. National Research Institute, Cultural Studies Division, P.O. Box 5854, Boroko, NCD, Papua New Guinea. TEL 675-25-3200. FAX 675-25-3042. TELEX NE 22381. Ed. Jack Lahui. adv.; bk.rev.; illus.; circ. 3,000. **Indexed:** Abstr.Anthropol., So.Pac.Per.Ind.
   Supersedes: Papua New Guinea Writing.

BIKORET VEPARSHANUT/CRITICISM AND INTERPRETATION; journal for literature, linguistics, history and aesthetics. see *HUMANITIES: COMPREHENSIVE WORKS*

BILINGUAL REVIEW/REVISTA BILINGUE. see *LINGUISTICS*

| 800 | AT | |

BILLY BLUE; Sydney, best address on earth. 1968. q. Cogente Pty. Ltd., P.O. Box 728, N. Sydney, N.S.W. 2059, Australia. TEL 2-957-2844. Ed. Ross Renwick. circ. 30,000.

| 820 | BB | ISSN 0006-2766 |

AP6
BIM. 1943. irreg., vol.19, no.73, 1991. B.$8. Ferney, Atlantic Shores, Christ Church, Barbados, W.I. Ed.Bd. adv.; bk.rev.; play rev.; illus.; circ. 1,000. (reprint service avail. from KTO)

BIULETYN POLONISTYCZNY. see *LINGUISTICS*

BIZA NEIRA (BISE NOIRE); sur l'Auvergne et la civilisation Auvergnate. see *HISTORY — History Of Europe*

BLACK AMERICAN LITERATURE FORUM. see *ETHNIC INTERESTS*

BLACK AUTHORS & PUBLISHED WRITERS DIRECTORY. see *BIOGRAPHY*

| 800 | US | ISSN 0736-9271 |

BLACK FLY REVIEW. 1979. a. $3. University of Maine at Fort Kent, Fort Kent, MA 04743. Eds. Roland Burns, Wendy Kindred. circ. 700.

| 810 | US | ISSN 1047-515X |

BLACK ICE. 1984. a. $14. English Department, Publications Center, University of Colorado, Box 494, Boulder, CO 80309. Ed. Ronald Sukenick. adv.; circ. 500.

BLACK MOUNTAIN REVIEW. see *LITERARY AND POLITICAL REVIEWS*

| 896 910.3 | NR | ISSN 0067-9100 |

PL8000
BLACK ORPHEUS; journal of African and Afro-American literature. 1957. s-a. £N20($25) (University of Lagos) Lagos University Press, Publishing Division, P.O. Box 132, Akoka, Yaba, Lagos, Nigeria. Ed. T. Vincent. adv.; bk.rev.; circ. 2,000. (reprint service avail. from KTO) **Indexed:** Curr.Cont., M.L.A.
   Description: African literature, music, sculpture and other African art forms.

| 800 | US | ISSN 0193-6301 |

PS1
BLACK WARRIOR REVIEW. 1974. s-a. $9 to individuals; institutions $14. (University of Alabama) Black Warrior Review, Box 2936, Tuscaloosa, AL 35486. TEL 205-348-4518. Ed. Glenn Mott. adv.; bk.rev.; circ. 1,800. **Indexed:** Amer.Hum.Ind., Bk.Rev.Ind. (1982), Child.Bk.Rev.Ind. (1982), Hum.Ind., M.L.A.

BLACK WRITER. see *ETHNIC INTERESTS*

| 896 | SA | |

BLACK WRITERS SERIES. 1935. irreg. price varies. Witwatersrand University Press, Wits 2050, South Africa. FAX 011-339-3559. TELEX 4-27125 SA. (Dist. by: Hodder and Stoughton Educational Southern Africa, P.O. Box 359, Bergvlei 2012, South Africa.)
   Formerly: Bantu Treasury (ISSN 0067-4044)
   Description: Drama, poetry, and essays in African languages.

| 830 | GW | ISSN 1010-3597 |

BLAETTER DER RILKE-GESELLSCHAFT. (Text in English, French and German) 1972. a. (Rilke-Gesellschaft) Jan Thorbecke Verlag Gmbh und Co., Karlstr. 10, Postfach 546, 7480 Sigmaringen, Germany. TEL 07571-728-100. FAX 07571-728-280. Ed.Bd. adv.; bk.rev.; circ. 1,000. (back issues avail.)

| 830 | AU | ISSN 0006-4483 |

BLAETTER FUER VOLKSLITERATUR. 1962. q. S.100 or membership. Verein der Freunde der Volksliteratur, Lenneisgasse 11-13, A-1140 Vienna, Austria. Ed. Otto Braun. bk.rev.; circ. 2,200. (also avail. in microform from AMS)

| 820 | US | ISSN 0160-628X |

PR4147
BLAKE: AN ILLUSTRATED QUARTERLY. 1967. q. $20 individuals (foreign $26); institutions $40 (foreign $46). c/o Morris Eaves, Ed., English Dept., Univ. of Rochester, Rochester, NY 14627. TEL 716-275-3820. FAX 716-442-5769. Eds. Morris Eaves, Morton D. Paley. adv.; bk.rev.; illus.; index; circ. 650. (back issues avail.) **Indexed:** Abstr.Engl.Stud., Amer.Hum.Ind., Arts & Hum.Cit.Ind., Curr.Cont., Ind.Bk.Rev.Hum., M.L.A., RILA.
   Formerly (until vol.11, 1977): Blake Newsletter (ISSN 0006-453X)

| 808 | US | ISSN 0276-1564 |

BLOOMSBURY REVIEW. 1980. 8/yr. $18. Owaissa Communications Company, Inc., Box 8928, Denver, CO 80201. TEL 303-892-0620. FAX 303-892-5620. Ed. Tom Auer. adv.; bk.rev.; circ. 50,000. **Indexed:** Bk.Rev.Ind. (1988-), Chic.Per.Ind., Child.Bk.Rev.Ind. (1988-).
   Description: Features interviews, reviews and essays.

| 800 | US | |

BLUE HORSE. 1966. irreg. Box 6061, Augusta, GA 30906. Ed.Bd. bk.rev.

2900 LITERATURE

800   US   ISSN 1046-0012
PN6071.S33
BLUE LIGHT RED LIGHT; a periodical of speculative fiction and the arts. 1988. a. $15. 496A Hudson St., Ste. F-42, New York, NY 10014. TEL 212-423-3245. Ed. Alma Rodriguez. adv.; bk.rev.; illus.; circ. 1,200. (back issues avail.)
   Description: Fuses mainstream writing, magic realism and surrealism together with speculative fiction.

810   US
BLUE LIGHT REVIEW. 1983. irreg. $7 to individuals; institutions $12. Box 1621, Pueblo, CO 81002-1621. Ed. Paul Dilsaver. bk.rev.; circ. 200.

800 398   US
BLUE SMOKE.* 1984. s-a. $3 per no. c/o Bill De Noyelles, Ed., 600 Montview Ave., Apt. D, Rivervale, NJ 07675. TEL 201-391-0336. Eds. Bill De Noyelles, Phil Goon. circ. 300. (back issues avail.)

810   US   ISSN 0198-9901
BLUELINE. 1979. a. $6. Potsdam College, English Department, Potsdam, NY 13676. TEL 315-267-2005. Ed. Anthony Tyler. bk.rev.; illus.; circ. 500. (back issues avail.) **Indexed:** Ind.Amer.Per.Verse.

820   CN
BLUENOSE RAMBLER. 1969. q. contributions. Box 32, Western Shore, N.S. B0J 3MU, Canada. Ed. Blanche Fralic. circ. 450.

808.8   US
▼**BLUFF CITY.** 1990. 2/yr. $9. Box 7697, Elgin, IL 60121. Ed.Bd. circ. 400.
   Description: Publishes short fiction and innovative verse.

800 491.66 940   UK   ISSN 0142-3363
PB2101
BOARD OF CELTIC STUDIES. BULLETIN. (Text in English and Welsh) a. £20. (University of Wales, Board of Celtic Studies) University of Wales Press, 6 Gwennyth St., Cathays, Cardiff CF2 4YD, Wales. TEL 0222-231919. FAX 0222-230908. Ed.Bd. circ. 400. (also avail. in microform from UMI; reprint service avail. from UMI) **Indexed:** Abstr.Engl.Stud., Amer.Hist.& Life, Art & Archaeol.Tech.Abstr., Arts & Hum.Cit.Ind., Br.Archaeol.Abstr., Curr.Cont., Geo.Abstr., Hist.Abstr., M.L.A.
   —BLDSC shelfmark: 2411.720000.
   Description: Explores language and literature, archeology and art, history and law in Celtic studies.

820   NE   ISSN 0169-6165
BOCHUMER ANGLISTISCHE STUDIEN/BOCHUM STUDIES IN ENGLISH. 1975. irreg. price varies. John Benjamins Publishing Co., Amsteldijk 44, P.O. Box 75577, 1070 AN Amsterdam, Netherlands. TEL 020-6738156. FAX 020-6739773. (In N. America: 821 Bethlehem Pike, Philadelphia PA 19118. TEL 215-836-1200) Ed. Ulrich Suerbaum. **Indexed:** M.L.A.
   Description: Historical and critical studies in English and American literature.

BODENSEE HEFTE; Zeitschrift der Euro-Region Bodensee. see GEOGRAPHY

BOGENS VERDEN; tidsskrift for dansk biblioteksvaesen. see LIBRARY AND INFORMATION SCIENCES

BOGG; a journal of North American and British poetry, prose poems, reviews, and essays on small press publishing. see LITERATURE — Poetry

895.1   CC   ISSN 1000-4173
BOLAN QUNSHU. (Text in Chinese) 1985. m. Y13.20($35) Guangming Ribao Chubanshe, 106, Yong'an Lu, Beijing 100050, People's Republic of China. (Dist. outside China by: China International Book Trading Corp., P.O. Box 399, Beijing, P.R.C.; Dist. in US by: China Books & Periodicals, Inc., 2929 24th St., San Francisco, CA 94110. TEL 415-282-2994) adv.; bk.rev.
   Description: Contains book reviews, news and articles about books.

867   SP   ISSN 0214-9117
BOLETIN GALEGO DE LITERATURA; estudios de orientacion universitaria. 1989. s-a. Universidade de Santigao de Compostela, Servicio de Publicacions e Intercambio Cientifico, Campus Universitario, 15706 Santiago de Compostela, Spain. TEL 81-59-35-00. FAX 81-59-39-53.

800 080   UY   ISSN 0067-9909
BOLSILIBROS.* irreg. Editorial Arca, Colonia 1263, Montevideo, Uruguay.

BOMB; artists, writers, actors, directors. see ART

830   GW   ISSN 0068-001X
BONNER ARBEITEN ZUR DEUTSCHEN LITERATUR. 1961. irreg., no.44, 1986. price varies. Bouvier Verlag Herbert Grundmann, Am Hof 32, Postfach 1268, 5300 Bonn 1, Germany. Ed. Benno von Wiese. **Indexed:** M.L.A.

BOOK FORUM. see PUBLISHING AND BOOK TRADE

820   SZ   ISSN 0256-159X
BOOK PEOPLE. (Text in English) 1983. 2/yr. 7 Fr. c/o G. Peter Winnington, Ed. & Pub., Les 3 Chasseurs, CH-1413 Orzens, Switzerland. TEL 21-8877721. FAX 21-8877976. Ed. Keith Hewlett. adv.; bk.rev.; circ. 10,000.
   Description: Promotes contemporary literature in English through reviews and author profiles.

800   UK   ISSN 0260-0315
BOOKMARK. 1978. a. £2. College of Education, Language Studies, Moray House, Holyrood Rd., Edinburgh EH8 8AQ, Scotland. TEL 031-556-8455. FAX 031-557-3458. Ed. J. Aldridge. bk.rev.; illus.; circ. 400. **Indexed:** Child.Lit.Abstr.

800   UK   ISSN 0266-4208
BOOKNEWS.* 1975. q. membership. Book Trust, Book House, 45 East Hill, Wandsworth, London SW18 2QZ, England. Ed. Christine Shaw. adv.; bk.rev.; abstr.; circ. 3,500. **Indexed:** Child.Lit.Abstr.
   Formerly: Books (ISSN 0045-253X)

808.8   US
BOOKS ARE EVERYTHING. 1988. q. $25 (foreign $36)(effective 1992). R.C. Holland, Ed. & Pub., 302 Martin Dr., Richmond, KY 40475. TEL 606-624-9176. bibl.; illus.
   Description: Covers vintage paperback collecting, focusing on books from 1938-1965, with features on individual authors, news of interest to collectors, and reproductions of book covers.

808.8 301.4157   US
BOOKS BOHEMIAN. 1977. s-a. free. Box 17218, Los Angeles, CA 90017. TEL 213-385-6761. Ed. Robert J. Manners. circ. 900. (back issues avail.)

BORGO BIOVIEWS. see BIOGRAPHY

800   US   ISSN 0891-9623
▼**BORGO LITERARY GUIDES.** 1991. irreg., no.10, 1992. price varies. Borgo Press, Box 2845, San Bernardino, CA 92406. TEL 714-884-5813. Ed. Boden Clarke. index.
   Description: Reference guides to literary topics, including awards, bibliographies, directories, cyclopedias, and catalogues.

BORGO POLITICAL SCENARIOS. see POLITICAL SCIENCE

BORGO REFERENCE GUIDES. see HISTORY

810   US
BOSTON LITERARY REVIEW. 1984. 2/yr. $6. Box 357, West Somerville, MA 02144. Ed. Gloria Mindock. circ. 500.

BOSTON REVIEW. see PUBLISHING AND BOOK TRADE

810   US
BOTTOMFISH. 1976. a. $4. (De Anza College, Language Arts Department) Bottomfish Press, 21250 Stevens Creek Blvd., Cupertino, CA 95014. TEL 408-864-8538. Ed. Robert Scott. circ. 500.

800   US   ISSN 0885-9337
BOULEVARD; journal of contemporary writing. 1986. irreg. (approx. 1/yr.). $12. Opojaz, Inc., 2400 Chestnut St., Ste. 2208, Philadelphia, PA 19103. TEL 215-561-1723. Eds. David Brezovec, Richard Burgin. circ. 2,500. **Indexed:** Ind.Amer.Per.Verse.

800   UK   ISSN 0955-3819
BOUND SPIRAL. 1988. s-a. £4 (foreign £6) (effective through 1991). 72 First Ave., Bush Hill Park, Enfield, Middlesex EN1 1BW, England. Ed. M. Petrucci. adv.; circ. 150. (back issues avail.)

800   US   ISSN 0190-3659
PN2
BOUNDARY 2; an international journal of literature and culture. 1972. 3/yr. $20 to individuals; institutions $40. Duke University Press, 6697 College Station, Durham, NC 27708. TEL 919-684-2173. FAX 919-684-8644. Ed. Paul A. Bove. adv.; bk.rev.; illus.; index; circ. 800. **Indexed:** Abstr.Engl.Stud., Abstr.Pop.Cult., Amer.Hum.Ind., Arts & Hum.Cit.Ind., Curr.Cont., Film Lit.Ind. (1990-), Ind.Amer.Per.Verse, Ind.Bk.Rev.Hum., M.L.A.
   —BLDSC shelfmark: 2264.273000.
   Refereed Serial

800   FR
BOUTEILLE A LA MER. irreg. price varies. c/o Ed. Marc Beigbeder, 8 rue Theo-Renaudot, 75015 Paris, France.

800   UK   ISSN 0261-0353
BRADFORD OCCASIONAL PAPERS; essays in language, literature and area studies. 1980. a. £8. University of Bradford, Modern Languages Department, West Yorks BD7 1DP, England. TEL 0274-733466. FAX 0274-305340. TELEX 51809-UNIBFD-G. Ed.Bd. bk.rev.; circ. 200.
   —BLDSC shelfmark: 2265.947000.

830   AU
BRAGI; Vierteljahresschrift fuer Literatur. 1982. q. S.100. Otto R. Braun, Ed. & Pub., Lenneisg. 11 13-5-5, A-1140 Vienna, Austria. circ. 500.

BRAILLE BOOK REVIEW (LARGE PRINT EDITION). see HANDICAPPED — Visually Impaired

808   AT   ISSN 0725-5543
BRAVE NEW WORD;* contemporary Australian short stories and poetry. 1981. s-a. Aus.$12 (foreign Aus.$16). Brave New Word Publishing, 582 Rae St., North Fitzroy, Vic. 3068, Australia. TEL 03-482-2530. Ed. Helen Murname. circ. 500.

700   IT   ISSN 0006-968X
BREVE, IL GRUPPO, LA CULTURA, L'IDEE.* 1950. m. L.1000. Traversa Merbellina 24, Naples, Italy. Ed. Ettore Capuano. adv.; bk.rev.; abstr.

BRITISH AMATEUR JOURNALIST. see JOURNALISM

800   UK
BRITISH AND IRISH AUTHORS: INTRODUCTORY CRITICAL STUDIES. 1967. irreg., latest 1986. price varies. Cambridge University Press, Edinburgh Bldg., Shaftesbury Rd., Cambridge CB2 2RU, England. TEL 0223-312393. FAX 0223-315052. TELEX 851817256. Ed. Robin Mayhead. index.
   Formerly: British Authors Series (ISSN 0068-1334)

806   US
BRONTE NEWSLETTER. a. membership. Bronte Society, American Branch, 335 Grove St., Oradell, NJ 07649. Ed. Katherine M. Reise.

820   UK   ISSN 0309-7765
PR4168
BRONTE SOCIETY TRANSACTIONS. 1893. s-a. £6 (foreign £10). Bronte Society Inc., Bronte Parsonage, Haworth, Keighley, West Yorks BD22 8DR, England. TEL 0535-642323. FAX 0535-647131. Ed. Prof. M.R.D. Seaward. adv.; bk.rev.; bibl.; illus.; cum.index; circ. 3,500. (also avail. in microform **Indexed:** Abstr.Engl.Stud., Br.Hum.Ind.
   —BLDSC shelfmark: 8908.080000.

810   US
BROWNS MILLS REVIEW.* 1980. a. $4. David Vajda, Ed. & Pub., Box 908, Browns Mills, NJ 08015. (back issues avail.)

BROWNSTONE MYSTERY GUIDES. see LITERATURE — Mystery And Detective

891.6   FR   ISSN 0399-7014
PB2801
BRUD NEVEZ. (Text in Breton) 1954. m. 200 F. 6 rue Beaumarchais, 29200 Brest, Brittany, France. Ed.Bd. adv.; bk.rev.; charts; illus.; index; circ. 500.
   Formerly: Brud ar Yez hag ar Vro (ISSN 0007-2567)

BRULOT. see POLITICAL SCIENCE — Civil Rights

830 GW
BRUNNEN JOURNAL. 1988. q. DM.4. Brunnen Verlag GmbH, Postfach 5205, 6300 Giessen 1, Germany. TEL 0641-6059-0. FAX 0641-6059-40. TELEX 17-6419037. Ed. Ralf Tibusek. bk.rev.

830 GW ISSN 0178-7241
BUCHJOURNAL. 1985. q. DM.21. (Boersenverein des Deutschen Buchhandels e.V.) Buchhaendler-Vereinigung GmbH, Grosser Hirschgraben 17-21, 6000 Frankfurt a.M. 1, Germany. TEL 069-1306383. FAX 069-1306201. adv.; bk.rev.

800 GW ISSN 0176-8220
BUCHREPORT. 1970. w. DM.605.40. Harenberg Kommunikation Verlags- und Medien-GmbH & Co. KG, Westfalendamm 67, Postfach 101852-62, 4600 Dortmund 1, Germany. TEL 0231-4344-0. FAX 0231-4344221. Ed. Bodo Harenberg. adv.; bk.rev.; circ. 4,000. (back issues avail.)

841 US ISSN 0007-4128
PQ2191.Z5
BULLETIN BAUDELAIRIEN. (Text in French) 1965. 2/yr. $10 (foreign $14). Vanderbilt University, W. T. Bandy Center for Baudelaire Studies, Box 6325, Sta. B, Nashville, TN 37235. TEL 615-343-0372. bibl.; cum.index vols.1-20; circ. 200. **Indexed:** M.L.A.
—BLDSC shelfmark: 2834.400000.
Description: Biographical, bibliographical and documentary articles on Baudelaire and his literary milieu.

840 BE ISSN 0252-1121
BULLETIN CELINIEN. 1982. m. 500 Fr. Bulletin Celinien, B.P. 70, 1000 Brussels 22, Belgium. Ed. Marc Laudelout. adv.; bk.rev.; circ. 500.

846 FR ISSN 0338-0548
PQ2631.R63
BULLETIN D'INFORMATIONS PROUSTIENNES. 1975. a. 121 F. Presses de l'Ecole Normale Superieure, 48 bd. Jourdan, 75690 Paris Cedex 14, France. (Co-sponsors: Centre National de la Recherche Scientifique; Institut des Textes et Manuscrits Modernes) Ed. Bernard Brun. adv.; bk.rev.; circ. 500.
—BLDSC shelfmark: 2864.384000.

840 801 FR ISSN 0335-508X
BULLETIN DES ETUDES VALERYENNES. 1974. irreg. (2-3/yr.). Universite de Montpellier (Universite Paul Valery), B.P. 5043, 34032 Montpellier Cedex 1, France. TEL 67-14-20-00.
Description: Contains all relevant information concerning research on Valery in France and abroad.

BULLETIN HISPANIQUE. see HISTORY — History Of Europe

809 BE
BULLETIN JEAN RAY. (Text in Dutch, English and French) 1970. a. 350 Fr. Amis de Jean Ray, 4 rue Vautier, Brussels, Belgium. Ed. Emile Van Balberghe. bk.rev.; bibl.; circ. 400.
Formerly: Cahier Jean Ray.

860 UK ISSN 0007-490X
PC4008
BULLETIN OF HISPANIC STUDIES. (Text mainly in English, Spanish; occasionally in Catalan, French, Portuguese) 1923. q. £21($45) to individuals; institutions £54($120). Liverpool University Press, Box 147, Liverpool L69 3BX, England. TEL 051-794-2235. FAX 051-708-6502. TELEX 627095-UNIPL-G. Eds. Dorothy Sherman Severin, Ann L. Mackenzie. adv.; bk.rev.; bibl.; illus.; index; circ. 800. (back issues avail.; reprint service avail. from KTO) **Indexed:** Arts & Hum.Cit.Ind., Br.Hum.Ind., Curr.Cont., Ind.Bk.Rev.Hum., M.L.A.
—BLDSC shelfmark: 2855.910000.
Description: Devoted to the language, literature and civilization of Spain, Portugal and Latin America.

860 US ISSN 0007-5108
PQ6098.7
BULLETIN OF THE COMEDIANTES. 1949. s-a. $15 to individuals; institutions $30; students $10. University of California, Riverside, Department of Spanish & Portuguese, Riverside, CA 92521-0222. TEL 714-787-7334. FAX 714-787-3800. (Subscr. to: c/o Prof. Jose Antonio Madrigal, Dept. of Foreign Languages, Auburn University, Auburn, AL 36849) Ed. James Allan Parr. bk.rev.; circ. 550. (back issues avail.)
—BLDSC shelfmark: 2449.800000.
Description: Specializes in the drama of the Spanish Golden Age.

800 NE
BUMPER; literatuurmagazine voor het onderwijs. 1978. 4/yr. fl.31.75. Wolters-Noordhoff B.V., Damsport 157, 9728 PS Groningen, Netherlands. TEL 050-226922.

895 JA ISSN 0389-4029
BUNGAKU/LITERATURE. (Text in Japanese) 1933. q. 4800 Yen. Iwanami Shoten Publishers, 2-5-5 Hitotsubashi, Chiyoda-ku, Tokyo 101-02, Japan. FAX 03-3239-9618. (Dist. overseas by: Japan Publications Trading Co., Ltd., Box 5030, Tokyo International, Tokyo 100-31, Japan; Or: 1255 Howard St., San Francisco, CA 94103) **Indexed:** M.L.A.

890 JA
BUNGAKUKAI; a magazine on serious literature. (Text in Japanese) 1949. m. 9240 Yen. Bungei-Shunju Ltd., 3-23, kioi-cho, Chiyoda-ku, Tokyo, Japan. FAX 03-3265-4878. Ed. Yutaka Yukawa.

800 200 UK ISSN 0954-0970
BUNYAN STUDIES. 1988. s-a. £10 to individuals; institutions £20. Open University, Faculty of Arts, Walton Hall, Milton Keynes MK7 6AA, England. TEL 908-653674. FAX 908-653744. Ed. W.R. Owens. adv.; bk.rev.; circ. 250. (back issues avail.) **Indexed:** Hist.Abstr., Rel.Ind.One.
—BLDSC shelfmark: 2930.696100.
Description: Covers the life and works of John Bunyan and other related topics.

800 UK
BURNS CHRONICLE CLUB DIRECTORY. (Text in English and Scottish) 1892. a. £7.50 cloth bound; £4.50 paper bound. Burns Federation, Dick Institute, Elmbank Ave., Kilmarnock KAI 3BU, Scotland. Ed. James A. Mackay. adv.; bk.rev.; bibl.; charts; illus.; circ. 2,700.

813 US ISSN 0007-6333
BURROUGHS BULLETIN. 1947-1986; N.S. 1990. q. $28 (foreign $35) includes m. newsletter: Gridley Wave (effective Jan. 1990). Burroughs Bibliophiles, Edgar Rice Burroughs Collection, Ekstrom Library, University of Louisville, Louisville, KY 40292. TEL 502-588-6762. FAX 502-588-8753. Ed. George T. McWhorter. bk.rev.; film rev.; bibl.; illus.; circ. 800.
Description: Publishes scholarly articles on the literary works of Edgar Rice Burroughs, and news of the society's activities.

820 UK
BURROUGHSIANA. 1975. q. British E R B Society (Edgar Rice Burroughs), 45 Leith Towers, Brighton Rd., Sutton, Surrey SM2 5BY, England. Ed. Dick Ellingsworth.

BYDGOSKIE TOWARZYSTWO NAUKOWE. WYDZIAL NAUK HUMANISTYCZNYCH. PRACE. SERIA B (JEZYK I LITERATURA). see LINGUISTICS

809 US ISSN 0196-8998
BYRON SOCIETY NEWSLETTER. 1973. biennial. membership. Byron Society, American Committee, 259 New Jersey Ave., Collingswood, NJ 08108. Dir. Marsha M. Manns. circ. 2,000.

BYZANTINA AUSTRALIENSIA. see HISTORY — History Of Europe

BYZANTINE AND MODERN GREEK STUDIES. see LINGUISTICS

LITERATURE 2901

810 375.4 US ISSN 0007-8069
C E A CRITIC. (Includes: C E A Forum) 1939. 3/yr. $25 to individuals; libraries $30. College English Association, c/o Bege K. Bowers and Barbara Brothers, Eds., Dept. of English, Youngstown State University, Youngstown, OH 44555. TEL 216-742-3414. FAX 216-742-1998. adv.; index, cum.index; circ. 900. (also avail. in microform from UMI; reprint service avail. from UMI) **Indexed:** Abstr.Engl.Stud., Amer.Hum.Ind., Arts & Hum.Cit.Ind., Curr.Cont., M.L.A.
—BLDSC shelfmark: 3096.790000.
Description: Articles on current research and study on English literature and language, particularly as they apply to teaching in the college and university classroom.

C E C T A L CONFERENCE PAPERS SERIES. (Centre for English Cultural Tradition and Language) see LINGUISTICS

C L A JOURNAL. (College Language Association) see LINGUISTICS

800 US
C N L - WORLD REPORT. 1974. 6/yr. membership (includes Review of National Literatures). Council on National Literatures, Box 81, Whitestone, NY 11357. TEL 718-767-8380. Ed. Anne Paolucci. adv.; bk.rev.; circ. 1,200. (back issues avail.) **Indexed:** M.L.A.
Former titles (until 1985): C N L - Quarterly World Report (ISSN 0145-6873); (until Jan. 1978): Council on National Literatures Report.

C R: CENTENNIAL REVIEW. see HUMANITIES: COMPREHENSIVE WORKS

C R N L E REVIEWS JOURNAL. (Centre for Research in the New Literatures in English) see LITERARY AND POLITICAL REVIEWS

800 US ISSN 0883-9980
PR6023.E926
C S L BULLETIN. 1969. m. $10. New York C.S. Lewis Society, 419 Springfield Ave., Westfield, NJ 07090. Ed. Jerry L. Daniel. bk.rev.; circ. 550. **Indexed:** M.L.A.

810 US
C W M. 1989. a. $3. 112 South Market St., Johnstown, NY 12095. TEL 518-374-7143. Ed. David C. Kopaska-Merkel. circ. 100.
Description: Publishes portfolios of divergent works held together loosely by themes.

800 BL ISSN 0007-9316
CABORE.* 1968. 3/yr. Universidade Federal do Ceara, Faculdade de Letras, Av. da Universidade, Fortaleza, Ceara, Brazil. Ed. Linhares Filho. bk.rev.

CADMOS. see HISTORY — History Of Europe

810 US
CAESURA MAGAZINE. 1985. a. $5. Auburn University, Department of English, 9030 Haley Center, Auburn, AL 36849-5203. TEL 205-844-4620. Ed. Lex Williford. illus.; circ. 300. (back issues avail.)

810 US
CAFE REVIEW. 1989. m. $24. c/o Yes Books, 20 Danforth St., Portland, ME 04101. circ. 250.

840 FR ISSN 0007-9618
CAHIERS BOURBONNAIS; arts, lettres, regionalisme. 1957. 6/yr. Cour des Dames, 03140 Charroux, France. TEL 70-56-80-61. FAX 70-56-86-06. Dir. M. Jean Pierre Petit. adv.; bk.rev.; illus.; circ. 6,000. (also avail. in microfiche)

840 FR ISSN 0575-0415
CAHIERS CHARLES DU BOS. 1955. a. Societe des Amis de Charles Du Bos, 76 bis rue des Saints-Peres, 75007 Paris, France. circ. 400. (back issues avail.)

800 FR ISSN 0007-9650
CAHIERS D'ACTION LITTERAIRE. (Supplement avail.) 1955. 6/yr. 28 F. Jeunesses Litteraires de France, 117 bd. St.-Germain, 75006 Paris, France. adv.; bk.rev.; abstr.; illus.; stat.

CAHIERS DE CIVILISATION MEDIEVALE. see HISTORY

CAHIERS DE CIVILISATION MEDIEVALE. SUPPLEMENT. see HISTORY

LITERATURE

840   FR
CAHIERS DE JULES ROMAINS. 1976. a. price varies. (Societe des Amis de Jules Romains) Flammarion, 26 rue Racine, 75006 Paris, France.

800   FR
CAHIERS DE L'ENERGUMENE. 1982. 2/yr. $65. Editions Gerard-Julien Salvy, 14 rue du Mail, 75002 Paris, France. Eds. G. Grenier, G.S. Salvy. adv.; bk.rev.; circ. 1,800.
    Supersedes (1973-1979): Energumene.

840 320   FR
CAHIERS DE L'EST.* q. 80 F. Editions Albatros, 21 rue Cassette, 75006 Paris, France. Ed. Dumitru Tsepeneag. bk.rev.

830 430   FR   ISSN 0767-7529
CAHIERS DE L'INSTITUT D'ETUDES GERMANIQUES. a. Universite de Montpellier (Universite Paul Valery), Institut d'Etudes Germaniques, B.P. 5043, 34032 Montpellier Cedex 1, France. TEL 67-14-20-00.
    Description: Specializes in German literature, social studies and linguistics.

CAHIERS DE L'IROISE. see HISTORY — History Of Europe

840   LE   ISSN 0007-991X
CAHIERS DE L'ORONTE.* (Text in French) 1965. q. £22.($15) Immeuble Chidiac, Rue Said Akl, Beirut, Lebanon. Ed. Lody Aoueiss. adv.; bk.rev.; bibl.; charts; illus.; stat.

800 900   FR   ISSN 0769-0770
CAHIERS DE L'UNIVERSITE DE PERPIGNAN. 1986. s-a. price varies. Universite de Perpignan, 36, Chemin de la Passio Vella, 66025 Perpignan Cedex, France. TEL 68-66-20-00. FAX 68-66-20-19. TELEX 505 005 F UNIPERP. Ed. Jean Sagnes. adv.; bk.rev.; circ. 300 (controlled). (back issues avail.)

840   SZ   ISSN 0007-9847
CAHIERS DE LA RENAISSANCE VAUDOISE. (Text in French) 1926. irreg. (2-4/yr.) price varies. Place Saint-Francois 5, Case Postale 3414, CH-1002 Lausanne, Switzerland. Ed. Yves Gerhard. illus.; circ. 5,750.
    Description: Essays of political, historical, philosophical and religious essences.

800   FR   ISSN 0068-5089
CAHIERS DE SAINT-MICHEL DE CUXA. 1970. a. price varies. Association Culturelle de Cuxa, Centre Permanent de Recherches et d'Etudes Pre-Romanes et Romanes, Abbaye de Saint-Michel de Cuxa, Codalet, 66500 Prades, France. bk.rev. **Indexed:** Avery Ind.Archit.Per., RILA.

808   FR   ISSN 0766-4214
CAHIERS DE SEMIOTIQUE TEXTUELLE. 1984. q. (Centre de Semiotique Textuelle) Publidix, Universite de Paris X, 200 Av. de la Republique, 92001 Nanterre, France. FAX 47-21-67-44. Ed. Edmond Marc Lipiansky.

CAHIERS ELISABETHAINS; etudes sur la pre-renaissance et la renaissance anglaises. see HISTORY — History Of Europe

CAHIERS HAUT-MARNAIS; revue d'histoire, de lettres et d'art. see HISTORY

840   FR   ISSN 0753-4590
CAHIERS HENRI BOSCO. 1973. a. 100 F. Amitie Henri Bosco, Les Oliviers III, 76 av. des Baumettes, 06000 Nice, France. Ed. Claude Girault. bk.rev.; cum.index: 1973-1977, 1978-1982; circ. 1,500. (back issues avail.)
    Formerly: Amitie Henri Bosco. Cahiers (ISSN 0399-1121)

800   FR   ISSN 0008-0365
CAHIERS NATURALISTES. 1955. a. 160 F. (Societe Litteraire des Amis d'Emile Zola) Editions Grasset et Fasquelle, B.P. 12, 77580 Villers-Morin, France. Dir. Alain Pages. adv.; bk.rev.; bibl.; charts; cum.index; circ. 1,000. (back issues avail.) **Indexed:** M.L.A.

800   FR   ISSN 0084-8239
CAHIERS PAUL-LOUIS COURIER. 1968. s-a. 60 F. Societe des Amis de Paul-Louis Courier, Mairie de Veretz, 37270 Veretz, France. (Subscr. address: c/o M. Quilici, 18 d'Arsonval, 44600 Nazaire, France) Ed. Gabriel Spillebout. adv.; bibl.; illus.

840   FR   ISSN 0008-0454
CAHIERS RACINIENS. 1957. s-a. 60 F. Societe Racinienne, 52 rue Jacques- Dulud, 92200 Neuilly-sur-Seine, France. Ed. M. Jacques Masson-Forestier. bk.rev.; bibl.; illus.; play rev.; tr.lit.; index, cum.index covering 20 issues; circ. 1,000. (Table des Cahiers Raciniens avail.; reprint service avail. from SWZ)

800   RM
CAHIERS ROUMAINS D'ETUDES LITTERAIRES. (Text in English, French; occasionally German, Italian, Russian, Spanish) 1973. q. 60 lei($18) (Consiliul Culturii si Educatiei Socialiste) Editura Univers, Piata Scinteii 1, Bucharest, Rumania. TELEX 10376. (Subscr. to: ILEXIM, Str. 13 Decembrie Nr. 3, P.O. Box 136-137, Bucharest, Rumania) Ed. Romul Munteanu. adv.; bk.rev.; circ. 1,000. **Indexed:** Can.Rev.Comp.Lit, M.L.A.

840   FR
CAHIERS SAINT-EXUPERY. a. (Association des Amis d'Antoine de Saint-Exupery) Editions Gallimard, 5 rue Sebastien-Bottin, 75007 Paris, France. illus.

942   FR   ISSN 0220-5610
PR463
CAHIERS VICTORIENS ET EDOUARDIENS. (Text in English, French) 1973. s-a. 150 F. Universite de Montpellier (Universite Paul Valery), Centre d'Etudes et de Recherches Victoriennes et Edouardiennes, B.P. 5043, 34032 Montpellier Cedex 1, France. TEL 67-14-20-00. FAX 67-14-20-52. Ed. J.C. Amalric. adv.; bk.rev.; circ. 250. (also avail. in microform from UMI; back issues avail., reprint service avail. from UMI) **Indexed:** Arts & Hum.Cit.Ind., Curr.Cont., M.L.A.
    —BLDSC shelfmark: 2952.413000.
    Formerly (until 1977): Cahiers d'Etudes et de Recherche Victoriennes (ISSN 0339-2171)
    Description: Concerned not only with literature, but with every aspect of the "Victorian and Edwardian" cultural area.

850 851 398   IT
CALABRIA LETTERARIA.* 1954. m. L.24000($14) Rubbettino Editore, Viale dei Pini, 88049 Soveria Mannelli, Italy. Ed. Emilio Frangella. circ. 8,000. (back issues avail.)

CALABRIA NOBILISSIMA. see ART

810   US   ISSN 1040-8339
CALAPOOYA COLLAGE. 1970. a. $5. Calapooya Collage, Box 309, Monmouth, OR 97361. Ed. Thomas L. Ferte. adv.; bk.rev.; circ. 1,500. (tabloid format)

CALENDAR OF LITERARY FACTS. see LITERARY AND POLITICAL REVIEWS

820   FR   ISSN 0575-2124
PR1
CALIBAN; litteratures anglaises et nord-americaines. (Text in English or French; summaries in other languages) 1964. a. 80 F. (effective 1992). (Universite de Toulouse II (le Mirail)) Presses Universitaires du Mirail, 56 rue du Taur, 31069 Toulouse Cedex, France. TEL 61-22-58-31. FAX 61-21-84-20. Ed. Marcienne Rocard. (back issues avail.) **Indexed:** Abstr.Engl.Stud., M.L.A.
    —BLDSC shelfmark: 3010.725000.

800   US   ISSN 0890-7269
PN6101
CALIBAN. 1986. s-a. $10 to individuals; institutions $17. Lawrence R. Smith, Ed. & Pub., Box 4321, Ann Arbor, MI 48106. adv.; circ. 1,500. **Indexed:** Ind.Amer.Per.Verse.
    Description: International journal of literature, art, and music with a strong emphasis on the avant-garde.

810   US   ISSN 0045-3978
NX1
CALIFORNIA QUARTERLY; journal of fiction and poetry. 1971. irreg., (2-4/yr.). $14 for 4 issues. University of California, Davis, Department of English, 100 Sproul Hall, Davis, CA 95616. TEL 916-752-2729. Eds. Jack Hicks. adv.; illus.; circ. 500. (reprint service avail. from KTO) **Indexed:** Amer.Hum.Ind., Ind.Amer.Per.Verse.
    —BLDSC shelfmark: 3015.190000.

808 910.3   US   ISSN 0161-2492
NX506
CALLALOO; a journal of African-American and African arts and letters. (Text in English, French, Spanish) 1976. 4/yr. $21 to individuals (foreign $34.50); institutions $45 (foreign $57). Johns Hopkins University Press, Journals Publishing Division, 701 W. 40th St., Ste. 275, Baltimore, MD 21211. TEL 410-515-6987. FAX 410-516-6998. Ed. Charles H. Rowell. adv.; bk.rev.; film rev.; play rev.; bibl.; illus.; index; circ. 1,359. (back issues avail.) **Indexed:** A.I.P.P., Amer.Hum.Ind., Bk.Rev.Ind. (1987-), Child.Bk.Rev.Ind. (1987-), Ind.Amer.Per.Verse, M.L.A.
    —BLDSC shelfmark: 3015.428800.
    Description: Offers a rich mixture of fiction, poetry, plays, critical essays, cultural studies, interviews, and visual art.

CALLIOPE (BRISTOL). see LITERATURE — Poetry

CALLIOPE (PETERBOROUGH); world history for young people. see HISTORY

800   UK
CAMBRENSIS; short story quarterly magazine of Wales. 1987. q. £6. 41 Heol Fach, Cornelly, Bridgend, Mid-Glamorgan CF33 4LN, Wales. TEL 0656-741994. (Subscr. to: Blackwell's Periodicals Ltd., P.O. Box 40, Hythe Bridge St., Oxford, OX1 2EJ, England) Ed. Arthur Smith. adv.; illus.; circ. 500. (back issues avail.)

870 880   UK
CAMBRIDGE GREEK AND LATIN CLASSICS. irreg., latest 1985. price varies. Cambridge University Press, Edinburgh Bldg., Shaftesbury Rd., Cambridge CB2 2RU, England. TEL 0223-312393. FAX 0223-315052. TELEX 851817256. Eds. E.J. Kenney, P.E. Easterling.

CAMBRIDGE LATIN TEXTS. see LINGUISTICS

CAMBRIDGE MEDIEVAL CELTIC STUDIES. see HISTORY — History Of Europe

800   UK   ISSN 0008-199X
CAMBRIDGE QUARTERLY. 1964. 4/yr. £46($94) (Cambridge Quarterly Association) Oxford University Press, Oxford Journals, Pinkhill House, Southfield Road, Eynsham, Oxford OX8 1JJ, England. TEL 0865-882283. FAX 0865-882890. TELEX 837330 OXPRES G. Ed.Bd. adv.; bk.rev.; cum. index; circ. 900. **Indexed:** Abstr.Engl.Stud., Arts & Hum.Cit.Ind., Br.Hum.Ind., Curr.Cont., Hum.Ind., Ind.Bk.Rev.Hum., M.L.A., Mid.East: Abstr.& Ind.
    —BLDSC shelfmark: 3015.975000.
    Description: Principally literary criticism, includes articles on painting, sculpture, music and cinema.

CANADIAN AUTHOR & BOOKMAN. see PUBLISHING AND BOOK TRADE

800   CN
CANADIAN AUTHORS ASSOCIATION NEWSLINE. q. membership. Canadian Authors Association, 275 Slater St., 5th fl., Ottawa, Ont. K1P 5H9, Canada. TEL 613-233-2846. FAX 613-235-8237.

800   UK
CANADIAN C.S. LEWIS JOURNAL. 1979. q. $10. S. Schofield, Ed.& Pub., Dunsfold, Godalming, Surrey GU8 4PF, England. TEL 048-649-390. adv.; bk.rev.; circ. 203.

813   CN   ISSN 0045-477X
CANADIAN FICTION. (Text mainly in English; occasionally in French) 1971. q. Can.$30 (to institutions and foreign Can.$40). Geoffrey Hancock, Ed. & Pub., Box 946, Station F, Toronto, Ont. M4Y 2N9, Canada. FAX 519-273-4887. adv.; bk.rev.; illus.; circ. 2,000. (also avail. in microform from UMI; reprint service avail. from UMI; back issues avail.) **Indexed:** Abstr.Engl.Stud., Amer.Hum.Ind., Can.Lit.Ind., Can.Per.Ind., CMI, M.L.A.

CANADIAN JOURNAL OF IRISH STUDIES. see HUMANITIES: COMPREHENSIVE WORKS

LITERATURE

850 945 100　　　CN　ISSN 0705-3002
PQ4001
CANADIAN JOURNAL OF ITALIAN STUDIES. (Text in English, French and Italian) 1977. 4/yr. Can.$20($20) to individuals; institutions Can.$30 ($30). The Symposium Press, P.O. Box 5143, Station "E", Hamilton, Ont. L8S 1N8, Canada. TEL 416-525-9140. Ed. Stelio Cro. adv.; bk.rev.; circ. 300. **Indexed:** Amer.Hist.& Life, Arts & Hum.Cit.Ind., Can.Rev.Comp.Lit., Curr.Cont., Hist.Abstr., M.L.A.
—BLDSC shelfmark: 3031.780000.

820 700　　　CN　ISSN 0225-0500
CANADIAN JOURNAL OF NETHERLANDIC STUDIES/REVUE CANADIENNE D'ETUDES NEERLANDAISES. 1980. s-a. Can.$15 (membership). Canadian Association for the Advancement of Netherlandic Studies, Department of French, University of Windsor, Windsor, Ont. N9B 3P4, Canada. TEL 519-253-4232. FAX 519-973-7050. Ed. Basil D. Kingstone. adv.; bk.rev.; circ. 300. **Indexed:** M.L.A.
—BLDSC shelfmark: 3033.250000.

819　　　CN　ISSN 0008-4360
CANADIAN LITERATURE/LITTERATURE CANADIENNE; a quarterly of criticism and review. (Text in English, French) 1959. q. Can.$25 to individuals; institutions Can.$35. University of British Columbia, 223-2029 West Mall, Vancouver, B.C. V6T 1W5, Canada. TEL 604-822-3727. Ed. W.H. New. adv.; bk.rev.; bibl.; illus.; circ. 2,000. (also avail. in microform from UMI; reprint service avail. from CLA,UMI) **Indexed:** Abstr.Engl.Stud., Amer.Hum.Ind., Arts & Hum.Cit.Ind., Bk.Rev.Ind. (1990-), Can.Lit.Ind., Can.Per.Ind., Can.Wom.Per.Ind., Child.Bk.Rev.Ind. (1990-), CMI, Curr.Cont., Hum.Ind., Ind.Bk.Rev.Hum., LCR, M.L.A.
—BLDSC shelfmark: 3037.750000.
Description: Devoted to the study of all aspects of Canadian writing.

CANADIAN REVIEW OF AMERICAN STUDIES. see HISTORY — History Of North And South America

800 011　　　CN　ISSN 0319-051X
PN851
CANADIAN REVIEW OF COMPARATIVE LITERATURE/REVUE CANADIENNE DE LITTERATURE COMPAREE. (Text in English and French) 1974. q. Can.$37.50($40) institutions Can.$64.50($62). (Canadian Comparative Literature Association - Association Canadienne de Litterature Comparee) Academic Printing and Publishing, Box 4834, Edmonton, Alta. T6E 5G7, Canada. TEL 403-435-5898. FAX 403-435-5852. Ed. M.V. Dimic. bk.rev.; abstr.; bibl.; index; circ. 700. **Indexed:** Amer.Bibl.Slavic & E.Eur.Stud., Arts & Hum.Cit.Ind., Can.Rev.Comp.Lit., Curr.Cont., Ind.Bk.Rev.Hum., M.L.A., Mid.East: Abstr.& Ind.
—BLDSC shelfmark: 3044.640000.

820　　　CN
CANADIAN SHORT STORY LIBRARY. 1972. irreg. price varies. University of Ottawa Press, 603 Cumberland, Ottawa, Ont. K1N 6N5, Canada. TEL 613-564-2270.
Description: Focuses on the short story form.

800 700　　　US
CANVAS. 1987. a. $1. 6189 Helen C. White Hall, Madison, WI 53703. Eds. Mark V. Cushman, William Perry. circ. 500.

895.1　　　CC　ISSN 0496-3326
CAOYUAN/PRAIRIE; wenxue yuekan. (Text in Chinese) m. Y12($49.50) Caoyuan Wenxue Yuekan She, 15 Xilin Beilu, Huhhot, Inner Mongolia Autonomous Region 010020, People's Republic of China. (Dist. outside China by: China International Book Trading Corp., P.O. Box 399, Beijing, P.R.C.; Dist. in US by: China Books & Periodicals, Inc., 2929 24th St., San Francisco, CA 94110) Ed. Ding Mao.
Description: Contains short stories, northern Chinese poetry, prose, and essays.

811 700　　　CN　ISSN 0315-3754
PR9194.9
CAPILANO REVIEW. 1972. 3/yr. Can.$20 to individuals; Can. $25 to libraries. Capilano College, 2055 Purcell Way, N. Vancouver, B.C. V7J 3H5, Canada. TEL 604-984-1712. FAX 604-984-4985. Ed. Robert Sherrin. adv.; bk.rev.; illus.; circ. 1,000. (also avail. in microform from UMI; reprint service avail. from UMI) **Indexed:** Amer.Hum.Ind., Can.Lit.Ind., Can.Per.Ind.
Description: Journal of poetry, art work and short fiction.

800　　　JM　ISSN 1018-2926
▼**CARIBBEAN REVIEW OF BOOKS.** 1991. q. $10 (foreign $16). (University of the West Indies Publishers' Association) U W I Publishers Association, P.O. Box 139, Mona, Kingston 7, Jamaica, W.I. TEL 809-927-1201. FAX 809-927-2409. (Subscr. to: C R B, P.O. Box 42, Mona, Kingston 7, Jamaica, W.I.) adv.; bk.rev.; illus. (back issues avail.)

808　　　VI　ISSN 0893-1550
THE CARIBBEAN WRITER. 1987. a. $7. University of the Virgin Islands, Caribbean Research Institute, RR 2, Box 10,000, Kingshill, St. Croix, VI 00850. TEL 809-778-0246. FAX 809-778-6750. adv.; bk.rev.; circ. 1,000.
Description: Creative writing: poetry and fiction, with Caribbean as focus.

830.9　　　CN　ISSN 0317-7254
PT1
CARLETON GERMANIC PAPERS. 1973. a. Can.$3. Carleton University, Department of German, Ottawa, Ont. K1S 5B6, Canada. TEL 613-788-2116. FAX 613-788-3544. Ed.Bd. circ. 140. (back issues avail.) **Indexed:** Curr.Cont., M.L.A.
—BLDSC shelfmark: 3053.350000.

CARLYLE ANNUAL; essays on Thomas and Jane Carlyle and their circle. see BIOGRAPHY

CARNEGIE MAGAZINE; dedicated to art, science, literature and music. see ART

810　　　US　ISSN 1047-2789
CAROLINA LITERARY COMPANION. 1985. s-a. $8.50. Community Council of the Arts, Box 3554, Kinston, NC 28502-3554. TEL 919-527-2517. Ed. Nellvena Duncan Eutsler. circ. 225. (back issues avail.)
Description: Intended as a forum for Southern writers of general interest short stories and poetry.

808　　　US　ISSN 0008-6797
CAROLINA QUARTERLY. 1948. 3/yr. $10. University of North Carolina at Chapel Hill, Greenlaw Hall CB 3520, Chapel Hill, NC 27599-3520. TEL 919-962-0244. Ed. David Kellogg. adv.; illus.; circ. 800. (also avail. in microform from UMI; back issues avail.; reprint service avail. from UMI,ISI) **Indexed:** A.I.P.P., Amer.Hum.Ind., Arts & Hum.Cit.Ind., Bk.Rev.Ind. (1965-), Child.Bk.Rev.Ind. (1965-), Curr.Cont., Ind.Amer.Per.Verse, Ind.Bk.Rev.Hum.
Description: Contains fiction and poetry.

806　　　US
CAROUSEL; information for writers. 1977. bi-m. $30. Writer's Center, 7815 Old Georgetown Rd., Bethesda, MD 20814-2415. TEL 301-654-8664. Ed. Jane Fox. adv.; bk.rev.; circ. 6,000.

800 821　　　AT　ISSN 0815-452X
CARRIONFLOWER WRIT. 1985. irreg. Aus.$3. Nosukumo, G.P.O. Box 994-H, Melbourne, Vic. 3001, Australia. Ed. Javant Biarujia. circ. 500.
Description: Literary and art magazine in broadsheet format of eight folded pages.

800　　　IT
CARTE SCOPERTE. (Text in English and Italian) 1982. q. L.25000. Edizioni del Labirinto, Via Rosario 7, Casella Postale 178, 75100 Matera, Italy. Ed. Gianni Toti.

800 700　　　IT　ISSN 0008-7025
CARTE SEGRETE; rivista-libro di letteratura ed arte. 1967. q. L.8000($18) Edizioni Carte Segrete, Piazza d'Aracoeli 6, 00186 Rome, Italy. bk.rev.; abstr.; bibl.; charts; film rev.; illus.; pat.; play rev.; tr.lit.; circ. 8,000. **Indexed:** M.L.A.

CASOPIS PRO MODERNI FILOLOGII. see LINGUISTICS

800　　　UK　ISSN 0069-0961
CASSAL BEQUEST LECTURES. (Text in French) 1961. irreg. price varies. University of London, Senate House, London WC1E 7HU, England. TEL 071-636-8000.

800 780　　　FR
CASSETTE GAZETTE; audio magazine. (Text in English) 1971. q. 300 F.($40) Handshake Editions, 83 rue de la Tombe-Issoire, Atelier A2, 75014 Paris, France. Ed. Jim Haynes. circ. 1,000. (back issues avail.)

860　　　SP
CATALAN REVIEW. 1986. s-a. 4000 ptas.($30) to non-members; members 2000 ptas.($15). (North American Catalan Society) Publicacions de l' Abadia de Montserrat, Ausias March 92-98, Apdo. 244celona, Spain. Eds. Manuel Duran, Josep Roca-Pons.

849　　　SP　ISSN 0214-3089
CATALAN WRITING. (Text in English) 1988. s-a. Institucio de les Lletres Catalanes, Pg. de Gracia 41, 2n 1a, 08007 Barcelona, Spain. TEL 93-216-80-00. FAX 93-216-01-25. circ. 2,500.
Description: Provides information on Catalan literature. Promotes the diffusion of works by Catalan writers.

850 700 398　　　IT
CATALOGO DANTE. 1870. q. Libreria Gozzini, Via Ricasoli 49-103r, 50122 Florence, Italy. TEL 55-212433. FAX 55-211105. circ. 8,200.

810　　　US　ISSN 0896-7423
CATALYST (ATLANTA); a magazine for heart and mind. 1986. s-a. $10. Catalyst, Inc., 34 Peachtree St., Ste. 2330, Atlanta, GA 30303. TEL 404-730-5785. FAX 404-730-5798. Ed. Pearl Cleage. adv.; bk.rev.; illus.; circ. 5,000. (back issues avail.)

810　　　US　ISSN 0145-8310
CATHARTIC. 1974. 2/yr. $5. c/o Patrick M. Ellingham, Ed., Box 1391, Fort Lauderdale, FL 33302. TEL 305-967-9378. adv.; bk.rev.; index; circ. 200. (back issues avail.)
Description: Poetry magazine devoted to the unknown poet and works from the darker side of life.

800　　　US　ISSN 1045-9871
▼**CATHER STUDIES.** 1990. s-a. $25. University of Nebraska Press, 901 N. 17th St., Lincoln, NE 68588-0520. TEL 402-472-3581. FAX 402-472-6214. Ed. Susan J. Rosowski.
Description: Provides a forum for all aspects of Cather scholarship and criticism: biography, various critical approaches to the art of Willa Cather, her literary relationships and reputation, the artistic, historical, intellectual, religious, economic, political, and social background to her work.

800　　　US　ISSN 1048-8618
PS3505.A87
CATHER YEARBOOK. a. $19.95 to individuals; institutions $29.95. Edwin Mellen Press, 240 Portage Rd., Box 450, Lewiston, NY 14092. TEL 800-753-2788. FAX 716-754-4335. Ed.Bd.

808　　　US
CAUDA PAVONIS; studies in Hermeticism. 1974. 2/yr. $7.50 to individuals; libraries $10. Washington State University, Department of English, Pullman, WA 99164. TEL 509-335-3023. Ed. Stanton J. Linden. bk.rev.; abstr.; bibl.; circ. 450. (looseleaf format) **Indexed:** Ind.Bk.Rev.Hum., M.L.A.
Description: Publishes scholarly material on all aspects of alchemy and hermeticism and their influence on literature, philosophy, art, religion and the history of science and medicine.

CE MOIS-CI A L'ALLIANCE. see EDUCATION

800 300　　　PR
CEIBA. 1972. s-a. free. Universidad de Puerto Rico, Administracion de Colegios Regionales, Colegio Universitario Tecnologico de Ponce, Box 7186, Ponce, PR 00732. TEL 809-844-8181. Ed. Luz Ivette Martinez. bk.rev.; circ. 1,000. **Indexed:** Hort.Abstr.

LITERATURE

808 US ISSN 0741-0794
CEILIDH; an informal gathering for story and song. 1981. q. $15. Ceilidh, Inc., Box 6367, San Mateo, CA 94403. TEL 415-591-9902. Eds. Patrick S. Sullivan, Perry P. Oei. adv.; bk.rev.; circ. 500. (back issues avail.)

800 US ISSN 0147-3085
PQ6428
CELESTINESCA; boletin informativo internacional. (Text in English, French and Spanish) 1977. s-a. $8 (foreign $14). Michigan State University, Department of Romance Languages, E. Lansing, MI 48824. FAX 517-336-1858. Ed. Joseph T. Snow. bk.rev.; play rev.; illus.; circ. 360. (processed; back issues avail.) Indexed: M.L.A.
 Description: Specializes in the arts, particularly on Fernando de Roja's Spanish classic, "Celestina," including all other continuations, adaptations, translations, stagings and other tranformations of the work, from 1500 until now.

800 UK ISSN 0264-0856
CENCRASTUS; Scottish & international literature, arts & affairs. 1979. q. £9 to individuals; institutions £12. 1 Abbeymount Techbase, Edinburgh EH8 8EJ, Scotland. TEL 031-661-5687. Ed. Raymond J. Ross. adv.; bk.rev.; charts; illus.; circ. 3,000.
 —BLDSC shelfmark: 3102.403000.

CENTER FOR SOVIET AND EAST-EUROPEAN STUDIES IN THE PERFORMING ARTS. BULLETIN. see HUMANITIES: COMPREHENSIVE WORKS

820 UK ISSN 0069-164X
CENTRAL LITERARY MAGAZINE. 1873. a. 25p. 45 Sandhills Lane, Barnt Green, Nr. Birmingham, England. Ed. W.H.M. Sparks.

820 FR ISSN 0240-8864
CENTRE AIXOIS DE RECHERCHES ANGLAISES. ACTES DU COLLOQUE. (Text in French) irreg., no.11, 1990. price varies. Universite de Provence, Service des Publications, 29 av. Robert Schuman, 13621 Aix-en-Provence Cedex 1, France. TEL 42-20-09-16. (back issues avail.)

800 AE ISSN 0069-1720
CENTRE CULTUREL FRANCAIS, ALGER. RENCONTRES CULTURELLES.* 1970. irreg. price varies. Centre Culturel Francais, 7 rue Medecin-Capitaine Kassani Issad, Algiers, Algeria.

850 IT
CENTRO DI STUDI DI LETTERATURA ITALIANA IN PIEMONTE GUIDO GOZZANO. SAGGI E TESTI. 1965. irreg., no.10, 1985. price varies. Casa Editrice Leo S. Olschki, Casella Postale 66, 50100 Florence, Italy. TEL 055-6530684. FAX 055-6530214.

860 US ISSN 0277-6995
PQ6337
CERVANTES. (Text in English and Spanish) 1981. s-a. $17. Cervantes Society of America, Pomona College, Claremont, CA 91711. FAX 714-621-9609. (Subscr. to: Alison Weber, Department of Spanish, Italian and Portuguese, University of Virginia, Charlottesville, VA 22903) Ed. Michael McGaha. adv.; bk.rev.; circ. 350. (back issues avail.) Indexed: M.L.A.
 —BLDSC shelfmark: 3120.245500.

800 US ISSN 1054-1403
CERVANTES AND HIS TIMES. irreg. Peter Lang Publishing, Inc., 62 W. 45th St., 4th Fl., New York, NY 10036. TEL 212-302-6740. FAX 212-302-7574. Ed. Eduardo Urbina.
 Description: Publishes manuscripts that contribute to the understanding of Cervantes' work and his times.

891.86 NE ISSN 0009-0468
PG5000
CESKA LITERATURA/CZECH LITERATURE; casopis pro literarni vedu. (Text in Czech; summaries in English, German, Russian) 1953. bi-m. fl.228($125) (Czechoslovak Academy of Sciences, Institute for Czech and World Literature, CS) John Benjamins Publishing Co., Amsteldijk 44, P.O. Box 75577, 1070 AN Amsterdam, Netherlands. TEL 020-6738156. FAX 020-6739773. (In N. America: 821 Bethlehem Pike, Philadelphia, PA 19118. TEL 215-836-1200) Ed. Miroslav Cervenka. bk.rev.; bibl.; illus.; index; circ. 1,850. Indexed: Amer.Hist.& Life, Arts & Hum.Cit.Ind., Can.Rev.Comp.Lit., Curr.Cont., Hist.Abstr., M.L.A.
 Description: Studies the history and theory of literatures, especially Czech literature.

CESKY JAZYK A LITERATURA; casopis pro metodiku. see EDUCATION

800 US
CHAKRA. 1988. irreg. $2 per no. Freelance Press, Department ULR, Box 8551, F D R Sta., New York, NY 10022-9998. Ed. Liz Camps. adv.; illus.; circ. 1,000. (back issues avail.)
 Description: Journal of erotic, mystical, scififantastical, politcophilosophical, experimental and unusual writing and visual art.

810 US
CHALK CIRCLE. 1988. 4/yr. $15. Box 5038, Hoboken, NJ 07030. TEL 201-420-9235. circ. 500.

810 US
CHAMINADE LITERARY REVIEW. 1987. 2/yr? $10. 3140 Waialae Ave., Honolulu, HI 96816-1578. TEL 808-735-4723. circ. 350.

891.4 II ISSN 0009-1359
CHANDRABHAGA (WEST BENGAL). (Text in Bengali) 1967. w. Rs.7.50. Ed. Ramanath Sinha, P.O. Suri., Dist. Birbhum, West Bengal, India. circ. 834. Indexed: M.L.A.

800 US
CHANEY CHRONICAL. (Companion to: What's New About London, Jack) 1972. irreg. (1-2/yr). $0.50 per no. London Northwest, 929 South Bay Rd., Olympia, WA 98506. Ed. David H. Schlottman. bk.rev.; bibl. (processed)

895.1 CC
CHANG CHENG/GREAT WALL. (Text in Chinese) bi-m. Hebei Sheng Wenxue Yishu Jie Lianhehui, 2 Shizhuang Lu, Shigang Dajie, Shijiazhuang, Hebei 050000, People's Republic of China. TEL 745373. Ed. Ai Dong.

895.1 US
CHANGJIANG (DUOZHONG WENXUE) CONGKAN/YANGTZE LITERATURE. (Text in Chinese) bi-m. $45.50. China Books & Periodicals, Inc., 2929 24th St., San Francisco, CA 94110. TEL 415-282-2994. FAX 415-282-0994.

895.1 700 CC ISSN 0528-838X
CHANGJIANG WENYI/YANGTZ LITERATURE AND ART. (Text in Chinese) 1949. m. Y14.40($49.50) No. 1, Dong Ting 2 Lu, Wuchang, Wuhan, Hubei 430071, People's Republic of China. (Dist. outside China by: China International Book Trading Corp., P.O. Box 399, Beijing, P.R.C.; Dist. in US by: China Books & Periodicals, Inc., 2929 24th St., San Francisco, CA 94110. TEL 415-282-2994) Ed. Hong Yang. illus.

800 FR ISSN 0395-7845
CHANTS DES PEUPLES. vol.2, 1974. irreg. Editions Caracteres, 7 rue de l'Arbalete, 75005 Paris, France. TEL 43-37-96-98. Ed. Bruno Durocher. illus.

895.1 CC
CHAO SHENG. (Text in Chinese) bi-m. Shantou Shi Wenlian, No. 130, Xinxing Lu, Shantou, Guangdong 515031, People's Republic of China. TEL 254506. Ed. Wu Guoqu.
 Formerly: Shantou Wenyi.

052 800 UK ISSN 0308-2695
CHAPMAN; Scotland's quality literary magazine. (Text in English, Gaelic and Scots) 1970. 4/yr. £9.50($21) to individuals (foreign £11); institutions £11 ($24)(foreign £12.50). Chapman Magazine, 4 Broughton Place, Edinburgh EH1 3RX, Scotland. TEL 031-557-2207. Ed. Joy M. Hendry. adv.; bk.rev.; play rev.; circ. 2,000. (back issues avail.)
 Description: Publishes poetry, fiction, criticism, reviews, articles on theater, politics, language and the arts.

800 US
CHARACTERS IN 20TH-CENTURY LITERATURE. 1989. irreg. $49.95. Gale Research Inc., 835 Penobscot Bldg., Detroit, MI 48226. TEL 800-877-4253. FAX 313-961-6083. TELEX 810-221-7086. Ed. Laurie Lanzen Harris.

CHARIOTEER; an annual review of modern Greek culture. see GENERAL INTEREST PERIODICALS — Greece

810 US ISSN 0098-9452
PS501
CHARITON REVIEW. 1975. s-a. $7. Northeast Missouri State University, Kirksville, MO 63501. TEL 816-785-4499. Ed. Jim Barnes. adv.; bk.rev.; circ. 650. (back issues avail.) Indexed: A.I.P.P., Amer.Hum.Ind., Ind.Amer.Per.Verse.

820 UK ISSN 0308-0951
PR4863
CHARLES LAMB BULLETIN. N.S. 1973. q. $14 to individuals; $21 to institutions. Charles Lamb Society, c/o Willian Ruddick, Ed., 9 Dale View Gardens, Crawcrook, Ryton, Tyne and Wear NE40 4ED, England. bk.rev.; circ. 350. (back issues avail.) Indexed: Abstr.Engl.Stud., LCR, M.L.A.
 —BLDSC shelfmark: 3129.934000.
 Former titles: C.L.S. Bulletin & Charles Lamb Society. Journal.

460 860 US ISSN 0145-8973
PQ7081.A1
CHASQUI. 1972. 2/yr. $9 to indivisuals; libraries $12. College of William and Mary, Department of Modern Languages, Williamsburg, VA 23185. TEL 804-221-3691. Ed. Howard Fraser. adv.; bk.rev.; bibl.; circ. 300. (reprint service avail. from ISI) Indexed: Arts & Hum.Cit.Ind., Hisp.Amer.Per.Ind., M.L.A.
 —BLDSC shelfmark: 3132.028200.

800 US ISSN 0741-9155
CHATTAHOOCHEE REVIEW. 1980. q. $15. Dekalb College, 2101 Womack Rd., Dunwoody, GA 30338. TEL 404-551-3166. FAX 404-551-3201. Ed. Lamar York. adv.; bk.rev.; film rev.; play rev.; cum.index every 5 yrs.; circ. 1,000. (also avail. in microform from UMI; back issues avail.) Indexed: Amer.Hum.Ind.
 Description: Provides a forum for published but unacknowledged literary writers.

820 US
CHAUCER LIBRARY. 1978. irreg., no.4, 1989. price varies. University of Georgia Press, Athens, GA 30602. TEL 404-542-2830. FAX 404-542-0601.

820 US ISSN 0009-2002
PR1901
CHAUCER REVIEW; only quarterly journal in America focusing on medieval studies and literary criticism. Includes: Chaucer Research Report. 1966. q. $22.50 to individuals (foreign $30); institutions $35 (foreign $40). Pennsylvania State University Press, Barbara Bldg., Ste. C, 820 N. University Dr., University Park, PA 16802-1003. TEL 814-865-1327. FAX 814-863-1408. Ed. Robert Frank. adv.; bk.rev.; bibl.; circ. 1,300. (also avail. in microform from UMI; reprint service avail. from UMI) Indexed: Abstr.Engl.Stud., Curr.Cont., Hum.Ind., M.L.A.
 —BLDSC shelfmark: 3132.250000.

810 US ISSN 0009-2185
AP2
CHELSEA; a magazine for poetry, stories, essays, and translations. 1958. s-a. $14. Chelsea Associates, Inc., Box 5880, Grand Central Sta., New York, NY 10163. TEL 212-988-2276. Ed.Bd. adv.; cum.index; circ. 1,300. (also avail. in microform from UMI; back issues avail.; reprint service avail. from UMI, ISI) Indexed: Arts & Hum.Cit.Ind., Curr.Cont., Ind.Amer.Per.Verse.

LITERATURE

820   CN   ISSN 0317-0500
PR4453.C4
CHESTERTON REVIEW. 1974. q. Can.$30($30) G.K. Chesterton Society, St. Thomas More College, 1437 College Dr., Saskatoon, Sask. S7N 0W6, Canada. FAX 306-966-8904. Ed. J. Ian Boyd. adv.; bk.rev.; bibl.; index; circ. 1,500. **Indexed:** Amer.Hist.& Life, Amer.Hum.Ind., Hist.Abstr., M.L.A.
—BLDSC shelfmark: 3172.616000.

891.4   II   ISSN 0009-3432
CHHANDITA. (Text in Bengali) 1965. irreg. (10-12/yr.). Rs.10. B-59 Rabindra Nagar, Calcutta 700018, India. Ed. Gourgopal Das. adv.; bk.rev.; circ. 2,500. (also avail. in microform)

800 770   US
CHICAGO RENAISSANCE. 1976. a. $5.95. (Chicago Renaissance Workshop) Natural Resources Unlimited, 3531 Roesner Dr., Markham, IL 60426. Ed. Joe H. Mitchell. bk.rev.; circ. 3,000.

810   US   ISSN 0009-3696
AP2
CHICAGO REVIEW. 1946. q. $20 to individuals; institutions $35. Chicago Review, 5801 S. Kenwood, Chicago, IL 60637. TEL 312-702-0887. Ed. David Nicholls. adv.; bk.rev.; illus.; index; circ. 2,000. (also avail. in microfilm from UMI; back issues avail.; reprint service avail. from UMI) **Indexed:** A.I.P.P., Acad.Ind., Amer.Bibl.Slavic & E.Eur.Stud., Artbibl.Mod., Arts & Hum.Cit.Ind., Curr.Cont., Hum.Ind., Ind.Amer.Per.Verse, Ind.Bk.Rev.Hum., M.L.A.
—BLDSC shelfmark: 3172.720000.

800   CN   ISSN 0315-467X
CHIEN D'OR/GOLDEN DOG. (Text in English and French) 1972. irreg. c/o Editor, English Department, Carleton University, Ottawa, Ont. K1S 5B6, Canada. TEL 613-231-3847. Ed. Michael Gnarowski. illus.
Supersedes: Yes (ISSN 0044-0353)

CHILDREN'S ALBUM; children's crafts and creative writings. see *CHILDREN AND YOUTH — For*

CHILDREN'S BOOK REVIEW. see *CHILDREN AND YOUTH — For*

028.5   US   ISSN 0092-8208
PN1009.A1
CHILDREN'S LITERATURE (NEW HAVEN). 1972. a. price varies. (Children's Literature Foundation) Yale University Press, 302 Temple St., 92A Yale Sta., New Haven, CT 06520. TEL 203-432-0940. Ed. Francelia Butler. bk.rev.; illus.; cum.index: vols.1-5, 6-10, 11-15; circ. 2,700. **Indexed:** Bk.Rev.Ind. (1990-), Child.Bk.Rev.Ind. (1990-), Child.Lit.Abstr., M.L.A.
Description: Interdisciplinary journal featuring articles on various authors, illustrators, and periods of children's literature, as well as interpretative essays.

891.43   II
CHILDREN'S LITERATURE SERIES. (Text in Hindi) 1951. irreg., vol.29, 1963. price varies. Vishveshvaranand Vedic Research Institute, P.O. Sadhu Ashram, Hoshiarpur 146021, Punjab, India.

820   HK   ISSN 0069-3642
CHIMES.* 1961. irreg. free. University of Hong Kong, English Society, Hong Kong. **Indexed:** Ind.Chem.

810   US   ISSN 0009-4285
CHIMES (NOTRE DAME). a. free. Saint Mary's College, Notre Dame, IN 46556. TEL 219-284-4000. illus.; circ. 1,600.

800   CC
CHINESE FOLK CULTURE. (Text in Chinese) 1986. q. Y4.20. Zhongguo Minjian Wenyi Xiehui, Shanghai Fenhui - China Folk Literature and Arts Association, Shanghai Chapter, 675 Julu Road, Shanghai 200040, People's Republic of China. TEL 2475446. Ed. Jiang Bin. circ. 3,000.
Formerly (until 1990): Minjian Wenyi Jikan (ISSN 0540-1186)

895.1   CC   ISSN 0009-4617
DS777.55
CHINESE LITERATURE; fiction, poetry, art. French edition: Litterature Chinoise (ISSN 1000-9132) (Text in English) 1951. q. $16.50. (Wenhua Bu, Waiwen Ju - Ministry of Culture, Foreign Language Bureau) Zhongguo Wenxue Zazhishe - Chinese Literature Press, 24 Baiwanzhuang Lu, Beijing 100037, People's Republic of China.
TEL 832-3291. TELEX 222314-FLPDA-CN. (Dist. by: China International Book Trading Corp., P.O. Box 399, Beijing 100044, P.R.C.; Dist. in US by: China Books & Periodicals Inc., 2929 24th St., San Francisco, CA 94110. TEL 415-282-2994) Ed. He Jingzhi. bk.rev.; illus.; index; circ. 50,000. (also avail. in microform from UMI,MIM) **Indexed:** Arts & Hum.Cit.Ind.
Description: Contains new short stories by China's most popular contemporary authors and excerpts from best-selling novels. Includes selections from classical literature, poems, essays, biographical sketches, publishing news and color plates of classical and contemporary art.

890   US   ISSN 0161-9705
PL2250
CHINESE LITERATURE: ESSAYS, ARTICLES, REVIEWS. 1979. a. $25 to individuals; institutions $40 (foreign $65). Indiana University, Ballantine Hall 402, Bloomington, IN 47505. Eds. Eugene Eoyang, William H. Nienhauser. adv.; bk.rev.; circ. 350. **Indexed:** Arts & Hum.Cit.Ind., Curr.Cont., Ind.Bk.Rev.Hum.

800   CH
THE CHINESE PEN. 1972. q. NT.$400($18) International P.E.N. (Poets, Playwrights, Editors, Essayists, and Novelists), Taipei Chinese Center, 5th Fl., No. 33, Lane 180, Kwang Fu South Rd., Taipei 10553, Taiwan, Republic of China.
TEL 02-721-9101. Ed. Nancy Chang Ing. bk.rev.; illus.; cum.index; circ. 2,000.
Description: Translations of contemporary Chinese short stories, poetry and essays; includes listings of cultural activities in Taiwan. Includes an introduction to new artist with each issue. Contains traditional styles as well.

CHINOPERL PAPERS. see *ORIENTAL STUDIES*

808   US   ISSN 0277-7223
CB226
CHIRICU. (Text in English, Portuguese, Spanish) 1977. a. $5 to individuals; institutions $7. Indiana University, Chicano Riqueno Studies, 849 Ballantine Hall, Bloomington, IN 47405. TEL 812-855-5257. Ed. Edith Baez-Baez. adv.; bk.rev.; circ. 300. **Indexed:** Chic.Per.Ind., M.L.A.
Description: Includes scholarly essays, original poetry, fiction, theatre and art by Latinos and non-Latinos interested in Latino issues.

895.74   KN
CHOSON MUNHAK/KOREAN LITERATURE. (Text in Korean) m. Central Committee of the Korean Writers' Union, Pyongyang, N. Korea.

CHRISTIAN VISION. see *RELIGIONS AND THEOLOGY*

818   US
CHRISTMAS: THE ANNUAL OF CHRISTMAS LITERATURE AND ART. 1931. a. $10.95 paper. Augsburg Fortress, 426 S. Fifth St., Box 1209, Minneapolis, MN 55440. TEL 612-330-3300. Ed. Gloria E. Bengtson. circ. 67,000.
Formerly (until 1987): Christmas: An American Annual of Christmas Literature and Art (ISSN 0069-3928)

800   US   ISSN 0887-5731
E169.12
CHRONICLES; a magazine of American culture. 1977. m. $24. Rockford Institute, 934 N. Main St., Rockford, IL 61103. TEL 815-964-5813. FAX 815-965-1826. Ed. Thomas Fleming. adv.; bk.rev.; film rev.; play rev.; abstr.; illus.; index; circ. 13,500. (back issues avail.)
Formerly: Chronicles of Culture (ISSN 0163-1187)
Description: Reviews literature and the arts and examines social and political issues.

CHU FENG. see *FOLKLORE*

895.1   CC   ISSN 1003-2738
CHUANQI WENXUE XUANKAN/SELECTED LEGENDARY LITERATURE. (Text in Chinese) 1985. m. Y13.80. Henan Sheng Wenlian, No. 34, Jing 7 Lu, Zhengzhou, Henan 450003, People's Republic of China. TEL 334646. (Dist. overseas by: Jiangsu Publications Import & Export Corp., 56 Gao Yun Ling, Nanjing, Jiangsu, P.R.C.) Ed. Xing Guilun. adv.; bk.rev.; circ. 20,000.

895.1   CC   ISSN 1001-621X
CHUN FENG/SPRING BREEZE. (Text in Chinese) m. Changchun Shi Wenlian, 11, Jianhe Jie, Changchun, Jilin 130061, People's Republic of China. TEL 822690. Ed. Zhang Shaowu.

895.1   CH   ISSN 0303-0849
CHUNG-WAI LITERARY MONTHLY. (Text in Chinese) m. NT.$850 (Hong Kong HK.$46; elsewhere $53). c/o Department of Foreign Languages, National Taiwan University, Roosevelt Rd. Sec. 4, Taipei, Taiwan, Republic of China. TEL 02-3630231-2288. FAX 886-02-3639395. Ed. Kao Tien-En. adv.; bk.rev.
Description: Contains articles on literature, literary works, poetry, and translations of foreign literature.

870   IT   ISSN 0009-6687
CICERONIANA; rivista di studi Ciceroniani. 1959. irreg. L.20000. Centro di Studi Ciceroniani, Piazza dei Cavalieri di Malta 2, Rome, Italy. Dir. Scevola Mariotti.

810   US   ISSN 0009-6849
AS36
CIMARRON REVIEW. 1967. q. $12. Oklahoma State University, Department of English, 205 Morrill Hall, Stillwater, OK 74078-0135. TEL 405-744-9476. FAX 405-744-6326. Ed. Deborah Bransford. bk.rev.; cum.index every 2 yrs.; circ. 700. (also avail. in microfilm from UMI) **Indexed:** Amer.Hum.Ind., Ind.Amer.Per.Verse, M.L.A.
Description: Publishes fiction, poetry, essays and reviews, with regular features on international literatures.

890 701   II
CINMAY SMRTI PATHAGARA. (Text in Bengali) 1970. a. Rs.8. 26-8A Mahatma Gandhi Rd., Calcutta 9, India. adv.

700 100   FR   ISSN 0069-4177
CIRCE. 1969. irreg. 420 F. for 10 nos. Lettres Modernes, 73 rue du Cardinal Lemoine, 75005 Paris, France. TEL 1-43-54-46-09. Ed. Jean Burgos.

810   US
CITY RANT. 1989. irreg. $5.95. McOne Press, Box 50174, Austin, TX 78763. TEL 512-477-2269. Ed. John McElhenney. circ. 2,000.

860   CK   ISSN 0069-4444
CLASICOS COLOMBIANOS. 1954. irreg., no.8, 1980. price varies. Instituto Caro y Cuervo, Seccion de Publicaciones, Apdo. Aereo 51502, Bogota, Colombia.

CLASSIC; magazine of creative writing and art. see *LITERARY AND POLITICAL REVIEWS*

800   US   ISSN 0896-0011
PN681.5
CLASSICAL AND MEDIEVAL LITERATURE CRITICISM; excerpts from criticism of the works of world authors from classical antiquity through the fourteenth century, from the first appraisals to current evaluations. irreg. (1-2/yr.). $99. Gale Research Inc., 835 Penobscot Bldg., Detroit, MI 48226. TEL 313-961-2242. FAX 313-961-6083. TELEX 810-221-7086. Eds. Dennis Poupard, Jelena O. Krstovic.

800   US   ISSN 0197-2227
PN883
CLASSICAL AND MODERN LITERATURE: A QUARTERLY. 1980. q. $16 to individuals; institutions $19. C M L, Inc., Box 629, Terre Haute, IN 47808-0629. TEL 812-237-2362. Eds. James O. Loyd, Virginia Leon de Vivero. adv.; bk.rev.; index; circ. 400. **Indexed:** Bk.Rev.Ind. (1982-), Child.Bk.Rev.Ind. (1982-), Curr.Cont., M.L.A.
—BLDSC shelfmark: 3274.534000.
Description: Covers all aspects of classical and modern literatures. Uses the knowledge and depth of the scholar's own discipline to examine problems recurring in both classical and modern literature.

LITERATURE

870 930 UK ISSN 0069-4460
CLASSICAL ASSOCIATION. PROCEEDINGS. 1904. a. £3. Classical Association, St. John's College, Cambridge CB2 1TP, England. Ed. M. Schofield. adv.; circ. 4,000. (also avail. in microfilm)
Description: Text of presidental address, report of annual formal meeting, news from branches and a statement of accounts.

800 US
CLASSICAL DISCOURSE. irreg. Peter Lang Publishing, Inc., 62 W. 45th St., 4th Fl., New York, NY 10036. TEL 212-302-6740. FAX 212-302-7574. Ed. William Blake Tyrrell.
Description: Examines the narrative treatment of Greek and Roman antiquity. Provides a forum for new interpretative techniques.

CLASSICAL JOURNAL. see CLASSICAL STUDIES

850 IT
CLASSICI ITALIANI MINORI. irreg., latest no.18. price varies. Angelo Longo Editore, Via Paolo Costa 33, P.O. Box 431, 48100 Ravenna, Italy. TEL 0544-217026. Ed. Enzo Esposito. circ. 2,000.

800 410 US
CLASSICS AND TODAY'S WORLD. irreg. Peter Lang Publishing, Inc., 62 W. 45th St., 4th Fl., New York, NY 10036. TEL 212-302-6740. FAX 212-302-7574. Eds. Robert J. Ball, J.D. Ellsworth.
Description: Emphasizes the influence of ancient Greece and Rome on present-day languages, literature, and civilizations.

820 US ISSN 0069-4509
CLASSICS OF BRITISH HISTORICAL LITERATURE. 1970. irreg., no.14, 1984. price varies. University of Chicago Press, 5801 S. Ellis Ave., Chicago, IL 60637. TEL 312-702-7899. Ed. John L. Clive. (reprint service avail. from UMI,ISI)
Refereed Serial

841 FR ISSN 0755-1959
CLASSIQUES FRANCAIS DU MOYEN AGE. Variant title: C F M A. (Text in ancient French; summaries in French) 1910. q. free. Librairie Honore Champion, 7 quai Malaquais, 75006 Paris, France. TEL 46-34-07-29. FAX 46-34-64-06. Ed. Felix Lecoy. circ. 2,000. (back issues avail) Indexed: M.L.A.

808 US
CLEAR BEGINNINGS.* 1981. 3/yr. $3 per no. Clear Beginnings Women's Writers Workshops, c/o Pfender, 5533 38th Ave., N.E., Seattle, WA 98105-2203. Eds. Elizabeth Pfender, Marjorie Mitchell.

808 US
CLIFTON MAGAZINE. 1972. 3/yr. $15. University of Cincinnati, Communications Board, 201 TUC, Mail Location 65, Cincinnati, OH 45221. TEL 513-556-6379. Ed. Eden Casteel. adv.; bk.rev.; charts; illus.; play rev.; cum.index: 1972-1987; circ. 33,500.

800 US
CLINTON ST.. (Text in English; occasionally in Spanish) 1979. 3/yr. $12. Out of the Ashes Press, Box 3588, Portland, OR 97208. TEL 503-222-6039. Ed. David Milholland. adv.; bk.rev.; cum.index: 1979-1988; circ. 50,000. (tabloid format; back issues avail.)
Formerly: Clinton St. Quarterly.
Description: Forum of world affairs, literature, the environment and art.

CLIO (FORT WAYNE); a journal of literature, history, and the philosophy of history. see HISTORY

CLIPPER STUDIES IN THE THEATER. see THEATER

810 US
CLIPS FROM BEAR'S HOME MOVIES. 1985. irreg. $4. Dancing Bear Productions, Box 733, Concord, MA 01742. TEL 617-369-5592. Ed. Craig Ellis. circ. 500.

800 780 700 US ISSN 0740-9311
NX504
CLOCKWATCH REVIEW; a journal of the arts. 1983. 2/yr. $8. Clockwatch Review, Inc., c/o Department of English, Wesleyan University, Bloomington, IL 61702. TEL 309-556-3352. FAX 309-556-3411. Ed. James Plath. adv.; bk.rev.; illus.; index; circ. 1,500. Indexed: A.I.P.P., Amer.Hum.Ind., Ind.Amer.Per.Verse.
Description: Fiction, poetry, and interviews with contemporary artists and musicians.

808 US
CLUES (BOWLING GREEN); a journal of detection. 1980. s-a. $12.50. c/o Mrs. Pat Browne, Ed., Bowling Green State University, Bowling Green, OH 43403. TEL 419-372-7866. FAX 419-372-8095. adv.; bk.rev.; circ. 700. Indexed: Amer.Bibl.Slavic & E.Eur.Stud, M.L.A.

800 NE ISSN 0169-8672
CODICES MANUSCRIPTI BIBLIOTHECAE UNIVERSITATIS LEIDENSIS. 1910. irreg., vol.26, 1988. price varies. E.J. Brill, P.O. Box 9000, 2300 PA Leiden, Netherlands. TEL 071-312624. FAX 071-317532. TELEX 39296 BRILL NL. (N. America dist. addr.: E.J. Brill, 24 Hudson St., Kinderhook, NY 12106. TEL 800-962-4406) (Co-publisher: Leiden University Press)

800 US
COE REVIEW. 1972. a. $4. Student Senate of Coe College, 1220 First Ave., Cedar Rapids, IA 52402. TEL 319-399-8660. Ed. Becky L. Rieniets. circ. 500.
Formerly: Caravan.

800 US ISSN 1050-5873
Z881
COLBY QUARTERLY. 1943. q. $10. Colby College, Waterville, ME 04901. TEL 207-872-3000. Ed. Douglas Archibald. adv.; bibl.; illus.; index; circ. 800. (also avail. in microfilm) Indexed: Abstr.Engl.Stud., Amer.Hist.& Life, Arts & Hum.Cit.Ind., Curr.Cont., Hist.Abstr., M.L.A.
Formerly: Colby Library Quarterly (ISSN 0010-0552)

810 US ISSN 0084-8816
COLD-DRILL. 1970. a. $6. Boise State University, Department of English, 1910 University Dr., Boise, ID 83725. TEL 208-385-1999. Ed. Tom Trusky. charts; illus.

869 BL
COLECAO DOS AUTORES CELEBRES DA LITERATURA BRASILEIRA. 1988. irreg., latest 1989. Fundacao Casa de Rui Barbosa, Rua Sao Clemente, 134, Botafogo, 22260 Rio de Janeiro, RJ, Brazil. FAX 5371114.

869 BL
COLECAO ESCRITORES BRASILEIROS; antologia e estudos. 1982. irreg. Editora Atica, S.A., Rua Barao de Iguape, 110, Caixa Postal 8656, Sao Paulo, Brazil.

869 BL
COLECAO TIRANDO DE LETRA. 1984. irreg. EMW Editores Ltda., Caixa Postal 2025, CEP 01051 Sao Paulo, SP, Brazil. Ed. Alberto Avillas. circ. 3,000.

869 PO
COLECCAO ENSAIO. no.3, 1981. irreg. Edicoes Ro, Rua da Tojeirinha, 10, 2735 Cacem, Portugal.

869 PO
COLECCAO LITERATURA. irreg., no.12, 1982. (Instituto Nacional de Investigacao Cientifica, Centro de Linguistica) Universidade de Coimbra, Centro de Estudos Classico y Humanisticos, Faculdade de Letras, Coimbra, Portugal.

860 SP
COLECCION BIBLIOTECA DE CASTILLA Y LEON. SERIE LITERATURA. 1987. irreg., latest no.2. price varies. Universidad de Valladolid, Secretariado de Publicaciones, Avda. Ramon y Cajal, 7, 47005 Valladolid, Spain. TEL 983-423000. FAX 983-423003. TELEX 26357. (Co-sponsor: Junta de Casilla y Leon, Consejeria de Cultura y Bienestar Social)

800 AG
COLECCION ESTUDIOS LATINOAMERICANOS. 1972. irreg. Fernando Garcia Cambeiro (Dist.), Cochabamba 244, 1150 Buenos Aires, Argentina. Ed. Graciela Maturo. Indexed: P.A.I.S.For.Lang.Ind.

808 PY
COLECCION LITERATURA. irreg., no.3, 1983. El Lector, 25 de Mayo y Antequera, Asuncion, Paraguay.

COLECCION MIGUEL SALGUERO. see ETHNIC INTERESTS

860 SP
COLECCION POLIEDRO. irreg., no.10, 1981. Ediciones Rayuela, Claudio Coello, 19, Madrid-1, Spain.

860 NQ
COLECCION POPULAR DE LITERATURA NICARAGUENSE. DOCUMENTOS. 1982. irreg. Ministerio de Cultura, Apdo. 3514, Managua, Nicaragua. Ed. Ernesto Cardenal.

808 001.6 US
▼**COLIN'S MAGAZINE.** 1991. irreg. (approx. 2/yr.). $7 per no. Poets, Painters, Composers, 10524 35th Ave., S.W., Seattle, WA 98146. TEL 206-937-8155.
Description: Forum for literary discussion of contemporary culture and technology.

800 IT ISSN 0069-5165
COLLANA DI CULTURA. 1963. irreg., no.43, 1985. price varies. Edizioni dell' Ateneo S.p.A., P.O. Box 7216, 00100 Rome, Italy. circ. 1,000.

850 IT ISSN 0069-5203
COLLANA DI STUDI E SAGGI. 1959. irreg. price varies. Societa Accademica Romena, Foro Traiano 1a, 00187 Rome, Italy.

809 IT
COLLANA DI TESTI E DI CRITICA. 1964. irreg., no.31, 1990. price varies. Liguori Editore s.r.l., Via Mezzocannone 19, 80134 Naples, Italy. TEL 081-5527139. Ed. Giorgio Petrocchi.

800 920 NE
COLLECTION MONOGRAPHIQUE RODOPI EN LITTERATURE FRANCAISE CONTEMPORAINE. (Text in English, French) 1984. irreg. (approx. 2-5/yr.). price varies. Editions Rodopi B.V., Keizersgracht 302-304, 1016 EX Amsterdam, Netherlands. TEL 020-6227507. FAX 020-6380948. (US and Canada subscr. to: 233 Peachtree St., N.E., Ste. 404, Atlanta, GA 30303-1504, USA. TEL 800-225-3998; Subscr. in France to: Nordeal, B.P. 139, 30, rue de Verlinghem, F-59832 Lambersart, France) (Co-publisher: Nordeal)
Description: Presents various authors of contemporary French literature and poetry.

840 809 SZ
COLLECTION STENDHALIENNE. (Text in French) 1969. irreg., no.28, 1988. price varies. Librairie Droz S.A., 11 rue Massot, CH-1211 Geneva 12, Switzerland. TEL 022-466666. (Subscr. to: Base Postale 389, CH-1211 Geneva 12, Switzerland) Ed. V. Del Litto.

895 BE
COLLECTION VIETNAMIENNE. 1973. irreg., no.7, 1985. price varies. Librairie-Editions Thanh-Long, 34 rue Dekens, B-1040 Brussels, Belgium.

800 US ISSN 0093-3139
PR1 CODEN: COLTEY
COLLEGE LITERATURE. 1974. 3/yr. $23 to individuals (foreign $29); institutions $48 (foreign $53). West Chester University, 554 New Main, West Chester, PA 19383. TEL 215-436-2901. FAX 215-436-3150. Ed. Jerry McGuire. adv.; bk.rev.; index; circ. 900. (also avail. in microfilm from UMI; reprint service avail. from UMI) Indexed: Abstr.Engl.Stud., Amer.Bibl.Slavic & E.Eur.Stud., Amer.Hum.Ind., Arts & Hum.Cit.Ind., Bk.Rev.Ind. (1980-), Child.Bk.Rev.Ind. (1980-), Curr.Cont., LCR, M.L.A.
—BLDSC shelfmark: 3311.160000.
Description: Scholarly criticism dedicated to the needs of college and university teachers by providing them with access to innovative ways of studying and teaching new bodies of literature and experiencing old literatures in new ways.

COLLOQUI CREMONESE. see ART

COLLOQUIA GERMANICA; an international journal for Germanic philology and literary criticism. see *LINGUISTICS*

800   PO   ISSN 0010-1451
COLLOQUIO: LETRAS. 1971. q. $45 in Europe; elsewhere $55. Fundacao Calouste Gulbenkian, Av. de Berna 56-3o, 1093 Lisbon, Portugal. TEL 1-7935131. FAX 1-7935139. Dir. David Mourao Ferreira. circ. 4,000.
—BLDSC shelfmark: 3320.450000.

801   SZ   ISSN 0179-3780
COLLOQUIUM HELVETICUM; Schweizerhefte fuer allgemeine und vergleichende Literaturwissenschaft. (Text in English, French, German and Italian) 1985. s-a. 30 Fr.($24) Verlag Peter Lang AG, Jupiterstr. 15, CH-3000 Bern 15, Switzerland. TEL 031-321122. FAX 031-321131. TELEX 912651-PELA-CH.

810   US   ISSN 0194-0589
PS1
COLORADO NORTH REVIEW; a literary magazine for mental travellers. 1972. irreg. (2-3/yr.). $8 (effective thru 1992). University of Northern Colorado, Student Media Corporation, University Center, Greeley, CO 80639. TEL 303-351-1350. Ed. L. Christopher Baxter. adv.; illus.; circ. 2,500 (controlled). (back issues avail.)

810   US   ISSN 0161-486X
PN6010.5
COLUMBIA: A MAGAZINE OF POETRY AND PROSE. 1975. s-a. $15. Columbia University, School of the Arts, Writing Division, 404 Dodge Hall, Columbia University, New York, NY 10027. TEL 212-854-4391. (Dist. by: Fine Print, 6448 Hwy. 270 E., Ste. 13104, Austin, TX 78723. TEL 512-452-8709) Ed.Bd. adv.; circ. 1,250. (back issues avail.)
Description: Presents fiction, poetry and nonfiction by new and established writers.

800 378.1   US   ISSN 0010-1982
AP2
COLUMBIA REVIEW (NEW YORK). 1815. a. Columbia University, Columbia Review, 206 Ferris Booth Hall, New York, NY 10027. TEL 212-854-3611. circ. 500. (also avail. in microform from MIM) **Indexed:** C.L.I.

820   US   ISSN 0069-6412
PR251
COMITATUS; a journal of Medieval and Renaissance studies. 1970. a. $10 to individuals; institutions $15. University of California, Los Angeles, Center for Medieval and Renaissance Studies, 212 Royce Hall, 405 Hilgard Ave., Los Angeles, CA 90024-1485. TEL 310-825-1880. FAX 310-825-0655. Ed. Peter Moore. bk.rev.; circ. 500. (back issues avail.) **Indexed:** Arts & Hum.Cit.Ind., Curr.Cont., M.L.A.
—BLDSC shelfmark: 3330.930000.
Description: Interdisciplinary approach to Medieval and Renaissance studies. Articles provided by graduate students and new scholars.

840   FR   ISSN 0180-8214
AP20
COMMENTAIRE. 1978. q. 295 F.($60) (foreign 330 F.)(effective Jun. 1990). Commentaire, 116 rue du Bac, 75007 Paris, France. TEL 33-1-45-49-37-82. FAX 33-1-45-44-32-18. Ed. Jean-Claude Casanova. adv.; bk.rev.; circ. 5,500.
—BLDSC shelfmark: 3331.736000.

COMMON KNOWLEDGE. see *PHILOSOPHY*

808.8 950 001.3   US   ISSN 0732-6734
PR9080
COMMONWEALTH NOVEL IN ENGLISH. 1982. s-a. $14 to individuals; institutions $16. B S C Center for International Understanding, c/o Sudhakar R. Jamkhandi, Ed., Bluefield St. College, English Dept., Bluefield, WV 24701-2198. FAX 304-325-7747. adv.; bk.rev.; index; circ. 300. (back issues avail.) **Indexed:** Abstr.Engl.Stud., M.L.A.
—BLDSC shelfmark: 3340.947000.
Description: Examines the socio-political and economic landscapes in Commonwealth novels.

809   US   ISSN 0275-2069
COMMUNICATION AND THE HUMAN CONDITION. vol.2, 1973. irreg., latest vol.2. price varies. Gordon & Breach Science Publishers, 270 Eighth Ave., New York, NY 10011. TEL 212-206-8900. FAX 212-645-2459. TELEX 236735 GOPUB G. (Subscr. to: Box 786, Cooper Sta., New York, NY 10276. TEL 800-545-8398; UK subscr. to: P.O. Box 90, Reading, Berkshire RG1 8JL, England. TEL 0734-560-080) Ed. L. Thayer.
—BLDSC shelfmark: 3359.312000.
Refereed Serial

700   US   ISSN 0740-8943
PT2603.R397
COMMUNICATIONS FROM THE INTERNATIONAL BRECHT SOCIETY. 1970. s-a. $25. International Brecht Society, c/o W. Lewis, Dept. of Germanic and Slavic Language, University of Georgia, Athens, GA 30602. TEL 404-542-3663. Ed. Michael Gilbert. adv.; bk.rev.; play rev.; bibl.; circ. 400. (back issues avail.) **Indexed:** M.L.A.

800   US   ISSN 0195-7678
PN855
THE COMPARATIST. 1977. a. $15. Southern Comparative Literature Association, Comparatist, c/o Marcel Cornis-Pope, Ed., Department of English, Virginia Commonwealth Univ., Richmond, VA 23284-2005. TEL 804-367-1667. FAX 804-367-2171. bk.rev.; circ. 500. **Indexed:** Amer.Bibl.Slavic & E.Eur.Stud., Amer.Hum.Ind., Can.Rev.Comp.Lit, M.L.A.
—BLDSC shelfmark: 3363.741400.
Description: Journal of comparative literature published by the Southern Comparative Literature Association.

809   UK   ISSN 0144-7564
PN863   CODEN: CMCRE3
COMPARATIVE CRITICISM; a yearbook. 1979. a. $49 to individuals; institutions $79. (British Comparative Literature Association) Cambridge University Press, Edinburgh Bldg., Shaftesbury Rd., Cambridge CB2 2RU, England. TEL 0223-312393. FAX 0223-315052. TELEX 851817256. (North American orders to: Cambridge University Press, Journals Dept., 40 W. 20th St., New York, NY 10011, USA) Ed. Elinor Shaffer. (also avail. in microform from UMI) **Indexed:** M.L.A.
—BLDSC shelfmark: 3363.752750.
Description: Studies literary theory and criticism, comparative studies in terms of theme, genre, movement and influence.

809   US   ISSN 0010-4078
PN1601
COMPARATIVE DRAMA. 1967. q. $15 to individuals (foreign $18); institutions $25 (foreign $28). Western Michigan University, Department of English, Kalamazoo, MI 49008. TEL 616-387-2579. bk.rev.; bibl.; index; circ. 900. (also avail. in microform from UMI; back issues avail.; reprint service avail. from UMI) **Indexed:** Abstr.Engl.Stud., Amer.Bibl.Slavic & E.Eur.Stud., Arts & Hum.Cit.Ind., Bk.Rev.Ind. (1980-), Can.Rev.Comp.Lit., Child.Bk.Rev.Ind. (1980-), Curr.Cont., Hum.Ind., Ind.Bk.Rev.Hum., LCR, M.L.A., Mid.East: Abstr.& Ind.
—BLDSC shelfmark: 3363.755000.

800 778.534   US   ISSN 0899-9902
COMPARATIVE LITERARY AND FILM STUDIES: EUROPE, JAPAN, AND THE THIRD WORLD. irreg. Peter Lang Publishing, Inc., 62 W. 45th St., 4th Fl., New York, NY 10036. TEL 212-302-6740. FAX 212-302-7574. Ed. Douglas Radcliff-Umstead.
Description: Presents studies on major authors and film makers of the twentieth century who were involved in movements like Surrealism, Futurism, Structuralism, Hermeticism, the New Novel, Neorealism, New German Cinema, and Magic Realism.

809   US   ISSN 0010-4124
PN851
COMPARATIVE LITERATURE. (Text mainly in English; occasionally in French, German, Italian, Spanish) 1949. q. $12.50 to individuals; institutions $22.50. University of Oregon, Comparative Literature, 223 Friendly Hall, Eugene, OR 97403-1233. TEL 503-346-4022. FAX 503-346-4030. Ed. Steven Rendall. bk.rev.; index, cum.index: 1949-1963; circ. 3,000. (also avail. in microfiche from UMI; reprint service avail. from UMI) **Indexed:** Abstr.Engl.Stud., Amer.Bibl.Slavic & E.Eur.Stud., Arts & Hum.Cit.Ind., Bk.Rev.Ind. (1965-), Child.Bk.Rev.Ind. (1965-), Curr.Cont., Hum.Ind., Ind.Bk.Rev.Hum., LCR, M.L.A., Mid.East: Abstr.& Ind.
—BLDSC shelfmark: 3363.789000.

807   CN
COMPARATIVE LITERATURE IN CANADA/LITTERATURE COMPAREE AU CANADA. Variant title: C C L A Bulletin - A C L C Newsletter. s-a. $5. Canadian Comparative Literature Association - Association Canadienne de Litterature Comparee, c/o University of Alberta, Dept. of Comparative Literature, Edmonton, Alta. T6G 2E6, Canada. Ed. P.A. Robberecht.

809   US   ISSN 0010-4132
PN851
COMPARATIVE LITERATURE STUDIES. (Text in English, French, German, Italian, Spanish) 1963. q. $22.50 to individuals (foreign $30); institutions $35 (foreign $40). (Pennsylvania State University) Pennsylvania State University Press, Barbar Bldg., Ste. C, 820 N. University Dr., University Park, PA 16802-1003. TEL 814-865-1327. FAX 814-863-1408. adv.; bk.rev.; cum.index: vols.1-10; circ. 1,000. (also avail. in microform from UMI; reprint service avail. from UMI) **Indexed:** Abstr.Engl.Stud., Amer.Bibl.Slavic & E.Eur.Stud., Arts & Hum.Cit.Ind., Bk.Rev.Ind. (1976-), Can.Rev.Comp.Lit., Child.Bk.Rev.Ind. (1976-), Curr.Cont., Hum.Ind., Ind.Bk.Rev.Hum., M.L.A., Mid.East: Abstr.& Ind.
—BLDSC shelfmark: 3363.789500.

COMPUTATIONAL AND LINGUISTIC APPROACHES TO LITERATURE. see *LINGUISTICS — Computer Applications*

CONCEPTIONS SOUTHWEST; publicacion de literatura y arte de la Universidad de Nuevo Mexico. see *ART*

800 976   US
CONCHO RIVER REVIEW. 1987. s-a. $12. (Fort Concho Museum) Fort Concho Museum Press, 213 E. Ave. D, San Angelo, TX 76903-7099. TEL 915-657-4441.

800   US
CONCORD SAUNTERER. 1966-1992; suspended. a. membership. Thoreau Society, Inc., Thoreau Lyceum, 156 Belknap St., Concord, MA 01742. Ed. Thomas Blanding. circ. 2,000. (reprint service avail. from ISI) **Indexed:** Amer.Hum.Ind.

CONDITIONS; a feminist magazine of writing by women, with an emphasis on writing by lesbians. see *WOMEN'S INTERESTS*

800 940 700   US   ISSN 0891-1908
CONFERENCE ON EDITORIAL PROBLEMS: UNIVERSITY OF TORONTO. 1966. a. $29.50. (University of Toronto) A M S Press, Inc., 56 E. 13th St., New York, NY 10003. TEL 212-777-4700. FAX 212-995-5413. index. (back issues avail.)
Description: Bibliographical and textual articles taken from the conferences on editorial problems held annually at the University of Toronto.

810   US   ISSN 0010-5716
PS501
CONFRONTATION; a literary journal of Long Island University. 1968. s-a. $10. Long Island University, C.W. Post College, Dept. of English, Greenvale, NY 11548. TEL 516-299-2391. Ed. Martin Tucker. bk.rev.; illus.; circ. 2,000. (also avail. in microform from UMI; back issues avail.; reprint service avail. from UMI, ISI) **Indexed:** A.I.P.P., Arts & Hum.Cit.Ind., Curr.Cont., M.L.A.

808 US ISSN 0278-2324
PN6010.5
CONJUNCTIONS. 1981. s-a. $18 (foreign $25). P.O. Box 118, Bard College, Annandale-on-Hudson, NY 12504. TEL 212-477-1136. FAX 914-758-9654. Ed. Bradford Morrow. adv.; bk.rev.; circ. 7,500. **Indexed:** Ind.Bk.Rev.Hum.
Description: Anthology of contemporary, formally innovative poetry and fiction.

890 FR ISSN 0589-3496
CONNAISSANCE DE L'ORIENT. COLLECTION UNESCO D'OEUVRES REPRESENTATIVES. 1956. (Unesco, UN) Editions Gallimard, 5 rue Sebastien-Bottin, 75007 Paris, France. TEL 33-1-45-44-39-19.

CONNECTICUT ENGLISH JOURNAL. see EDUCATION

800 US
CONNECTICUT QUARTERLY. At head of title: C Q. 1979. q. $7.50. Asnuntuck Community College Press, Box 68, Enfield, CT 06082. TEL 203-745-1603. Ed. Carol Haber. bk.rev.; circ. 300.

800 US
CONNECTICUT WRITER. 1974. a. $7. Connecticut Writers League Inc., Box 10536, W. Hartford, CT 06110. Ed. Candice Hall. circ. 300. (back issues avail.)
Formerly (until 1981): Harvest (ISSN 0362-7888)

820 US ISSN 0010-6356
PR6005.O4
CONRADIANA; a journal of Joseph Conrad studies. 1968. 3/yr. $16 to individuals; institutions $28. Texas Tech University Press, Lubbock, TX 79409-1037. TEL 806-742-2982. Ed. David Leon Higdon. adv.; bk.rev.; abstr.; bibl.; illus.; index; circ. 646. (also avail. in microform from UMI) **Indexed:** Abstr.Engl.Stud., Amer.Hum.Ind., Curr.Cont., Ind.Bk.Rev.Hum., M.L.A.
—BLDSC shelfmark: 3417.860000.

800 700 FR ISSN 0760-629X
CONSEQUENCES. (Text and summaries in French) 1983. 2/yr. 230 F.($45) outside EEC 310 F. ($61)(effective Jan. 1991). (Centre National des Lettres) Impressions Nouvelles, 93, Quai de Valmy, 75010 Paris, France. Ed. Guy Lelong. adv.; bk.rev.; illus.; circ. 1,000. (back issues avail)

800 US
CONSERVATORY OF AMERICAN LETTERS NEWSLETTER. Short title: C A L Newsletter. 1986. q. $4. (Conservatory of American Letters) Dan River Press, Box 88, Thomaston, ME 04861. TEL 207-354-6550. Ed. Robert W. Olmsted. adv.; circ. 2,000.
Description: Advises members and other writers of things near and dear to the hearts of writers.

CONSTRUCTURA. see LINGUISTICS

CONTEMPORANEA; studi e testi. **see** HISTORY

839.82 500 NO
PT8890.A1
CONTEMPORARY APPROACHES TO IBSEN. (Text in English) 1951. s-a. price varies. Universitetsforlaget, Box 2959-Toeyen, N-0608 Oslo 6, Norway. (Dist. by: Oxford University Press, Distribution Services, Saxon Way West, Corby, Nothants NN 18 9ES, England; In U.S. dist. by: Oxford University Press, 200 Madison Ave., New York, NY 10016, USA) Eds. Bjoern Hemmer, Vigdis Ystad. bk.rev. (back issues avail.) **Indexed:** M.L.A.
Formerly: Ibsenaarboken (ISSN 0073-4365)

800 US ISSN 0069-9381
CONTEMPORARY DRAMA SERIES. 1971. irreg., no.4, 1979. $2.95. Proscenium Press, Box 361, Newark, DE 19711. TEL 302-764-8477. Ed. Robert Hogan. (reprint service avail. from UMI)

830 943 UK ISSN 0268-1331
CONTEMPORARY GERMAN STUDIES: OCCASIONAL PAPERS. (Text in English and German) 1985. irreg. (1-2/yr.). £2.50 per no. University of Strathclyde, Department of Modern Languages, 26 Richmond St., Glasgow G1 1XH, Scotland. TEL 041-552 4400. Eds. M. McGowan, M. Pender. circ. 420. (back issues avail.)
—BLDSC shelfmark: 3425.181875.
Description: Presents scholarly and academic research papers on the cultural, political, economic, sociological, literary, and educational issues affecting modern Germany.

809 US ISSN 0091-3421
PN771
CONTEMPORARY LITERARY CRITICISM SERIES; excerpts from criticism of the works of today's novelists, poets, playwrights, and other creative writers. 1973. irreg., vol.67, 1991. $108 per vol. Gale Research Inc., 835 Penobscot Bldg., Detroit, MI 48226. TEL 313-962-2242. FAX 313-961-6083. TELEX 810-221-7086. Ed. Roger Matuz. cum.index. **Indexed:** Child.Auth.& Illus., Perf.Arts Biog.Master Ind.
—BLDSC shelfmark: 3425.190600.
Description: Compendium of critical works on contemporary creative writers.

800 US ISSN 0010-7484
PN2
CONTEMPORARY LITERATURE. 1960. 4/yr. $23 to individuals; institutions $52. (University of Wisconsin-Madison, Department of English) University of Wisconsin Press, Journal Division, 114 N. Murray St., Madison, WI 53715. TEL 608-262-4952. FAX 608-262-7560. Ed. Thomas Schaub. adv.; bk.rev.; bibl.; cum.index every 2 yrs.; circ. 2,100. (also avail. in microform from UMI; back issues avail., reprint service avail from UMI) **Indexed:** Abstr.Engl.Stud., Amer.Bibl.Slavic & E.Eur.Stud., Amer.Hum.Ind., Arts & Hum.Cit.Ind., Curr.Cont., Hum.Ind., Ind.Bk.Rev.Hum., LCR, M.L.A., Mid.East: Abstr.& Ind.
—BLDSC shelfmark: 3425.191000.
Formerly: Wisconsin Studies in Contemporary Literature.

800 US
CONTEMPORARY WOMEN WRITERS OF SPAIN. irreg. Peter Lang Publishing, Inc., 62 W. 45th St., 4th Fl., New York, NY 10036. TEL 212-302-6740. FAX 212-302-7574. Ed. Alicia Ramos.

800 700 IT ISSN 0010-762X
CONTENUTI; bimestrale di lettere e arti. bi-m. L.40000. Editrice Pellegrini, Via Roma 74, Casella Postale 158, 87100 Cosenza, Italy. Ed. Luigi Pellegrini.

850 IT
CONTESTO; rivista di letteratura Italiana. 1977. 3/yr. L.16000($15) Argalia Editore, Via N. Sauro 1, 61029 Urbino, Italy. Dir. Claudio Varese. bibl.

800 SZ
CONTINENT CENDRARS. (Text in French) 1986. a. varies. (Universite de Berne, Centre D'Etudes Blaise Cendrars) Editions de la Baconniere S.A., P.O. Box 185, CH-2017 Boudry, Switzerland. TEL 038-421004. Ed. Jean-Carlo Flueckiger. bk.rev.

800 US ISSN 0899-4307
PQ226
CONTINUUM: PROBLEMS IN FRENCH LITERATURE FROM THE RENAISSANCE TO THE EARLY ENLIGHTENMENT. 1988. a. $57.50. (University of Virginia, Center for Advanced Studies) A M S Press, Inc., 56 E. 13th St., New York, NY 10003. TEL 212-777-4700. FAX 212-995-5413. Eds. David Lee Rubin, John D. Lion. bk.rev.; index.
—BLDSC shelfmark: 3425.720600.
Description: Essays and review articles on French literature from the Renaissance to the early Enlightenment.

CONTRIBUTIONS TO THE STUDY OF SCIENCE FICTION AND FANTASY. see LITERATURE — Science Fiction, Fantasy, Horror

808 US ISSN 0738-9345
CONTRIBUTIONS TO THE STUDY OF WORLD LITERATURE. 1983. irreg. price varies. Greenwood Press, Inc. (Subsidiary of: Greenwood Publishing Group Inc.), 88 Post Rd. W., Box 5007, Westport, CT 06881-5007. TEL 203-226-3571. FAX 203-222-1502. Ed. Leif Sjoberg. index.
—BLDSC shelfmark: 3461.461000.

869 BL
CONVERGENCIA. (Text in Portuguese, Spanish) 1976. s-a. Centro de Estudos do Real Gabinete Portugues de Leitura, Rua Luis de Comoes 30, 20000 Rio de Janeiro ZC21, Brazil. illus.

859 RM ISSN 0010-8243
CONVORBIRI LITERARE. 1867, N.S. 1972. m. 60 lei($10) Uniunea Scriitorilor din Republica Socialista Romania, Calea Victoriei 115, Bucharest, Rumania. (Subscr. to: ILEXIM, Str. 13 Decembrie Nr. 3, Box 136-137, 70116 Bucharest, Rumania) Ed. Corneliu Sturzu. bk.rev.; bibl.; circ. 3,000. **Indexed:** M.L.A.

800 910.09 US ISSN 1044-3495
COOL TRAVELER; literary publication about "place". 1988. q. $10. Rome Cappucino Review, Box 11975, Philadelphia, PA 19145. TEL 215-440-8257. Ed. Bob Moore. adv.; circ. 1,000. (back issues avail.)

808 US
COPULA. q. Copula Press, W. 1114 Indiana St., Spokane, WA 99205. Ed. James Bradford.

CORADDI. see ART

800 US ISSN 0010-8669
AP2
CORANTO. 1963. a. $10 per no. (University of Southern California, U S C Libraries) U S C Fine Arts Press, Research Annex, 3716 S. Hope St., Los Angeles, CA 90007. TEL 213-743-3939. Ed. Gerald Lange. bk.rev.; bibl.; circ. 2,000. **Indexed:** Abstr.Engl.Stud., M.L.A.
Description: Focuses on book-related topics. Includes information on the special collections holdings of the USC Libraries.

700 US ISSN 0363-4574
NX1
CORNFIELD REVIEW; an annual of the creative arts. 1976. 6. $4. Ohio State University, Marion Campus, 1465 Mt. Vernon Ave., Marion, OH 43302-5695. TEL 614-389-2361. Ed. Stuart Lishan. illus.; circ. 750.
Description: Presents poetry, short fiction and visual art, with an emphasis on Midwestern writers and artists.

801 100 US ISSN 0270-6687
PS536.2
CORONA. 1980. a. $7 to individuals; institutions $8.50. Montana State University, Department of History and Philosophy, Bozeman, MT 59717. TEL 406-994-5200. Eds. Lynda and Michael Sexson. adv.; bk.rev.; illus.; circ. 2,000. (back issues avail.) **Indexed:** Amer.Hum.Ind., M.L.A.

809 839.3 NE
CORPUS SACRAE SCRIPTURAE NEERLANDICAE MEDII AEVII. (Consists of: Catalogus, Miscellanea, Series Maior, Series Minor) 1970. irreg., latest 1984. E.J. Brill, P.O. Box 9000, 2300 PA Leiden, Netherlands. TEL 071-312624. FAX 071-317532. TELEX 39296 BRILL NL. (In N. America: E.J. Brill, 24 Hudson St., Kinderhook, NY 12106. TEL 800-962-4406) Ed. C.C. de Bruin.
Formerly: Verzameling van Middelnederlandse Bijbelteksten.

COSTERUS; essays in English and American language and literature. **see** LINGUISTICS

810 US
COTTONWOOD. 1965. 3/yr. $12 (foreign $15). Cottonwood Magazine and Press, Box J Kansas Union, University of Kansas, Lawrence, KS 66045. TEL 913-864-3777. Ed. George F. Wedge. bk.rev.; illus.; circ. 500. (back issues avail.) **Indexed:** Amer.Hum.Ind.
Former titles: Cottonwood Review (ISSN 0147-149X); Cottonwood (ISSN 0010-9843)
Description: Includes a wide variety of poetry and fiction, reviews and interviews.

840 FR ISSN 0998-6316
COURRIER-EXPRESSION. 1972. s-a. 5 F. Centre Culturel et Sportif de Vulaines, 5 rue Pasteur, Vulaines sur Seine 77870, France. (Affiliate: Federation des Oeuvres Complimentaires de l'Ecole Laigue) Ed. Leroux Henry Fonta. circ. 1,000. (tabloid format)

800 US ISSN 0738-7008
CRAB CREEK REVIEW. (In 3 vols.) 1983. 2/yr. $8 per vol. (foreign $13). Crab Creek Review Association, 4462 Whitman Ave., N., Seattle, WA 98103-7347. TEL 206-633-1090. Eds. Linda J. Clifton, Carol Orlock. adv.; circ. 500. (back issues avail.) **Indexed:** Ind.Amer.Per.Verse.
Description: Poetry, short fiction, and translations of poetry and short fiction from Greek, Latin, Chinese, Japanese, and modern work.

LITERATURE

800 US ISSN 0011-0841
PS580 CODEN: CCSCBX
CRAZYHORSE. 1960. s-a. $10. Crazyhorse Association, Department of English, University of Arkansas at Little Rock, 2801 S. University, Little Rock, AR 72204. TEL 501-569-3160. FAX 501-569-8323. Ed.Bd. adv.; bk.rev.; circ. 1,000. (back issues avail.) **Indexed:** M.L.A.
Description: Publishes poetry and short fiction.

808 US ISSN 0887-5308
CRAZYQUILT. 1986. q. $14.95. CrazyQuilt Press, Box 632729, San Diego, CA 92163-2729. TEL 619-688-1023. Ed. Jim Kitchen. adv.; bk.rev.; circ. 175. (back issues avail.)
Description: Fiction, nonfiction, black and white art and photos, poetry, and drama, as well as interviews with practicing writers.

895 JA
CREA; women's magazine for up-scale readers. 1989. 4800 Yen. Bungei Shunju Ltd., 3-23 Kioi-cho, Chiyoda-ku, Tokyo, Japan. Ed. Tadashi Saito.

800 US ISSN 0884-3457
PN6010.5
CREAM CITY REVIEW. 1975. s-a. $10 (effective Jan. 1990). University of Wisconsin-Milwaukee, English Department, Curtin Hall, Box 413, Milwaukee, WI 53201. TEL 414-229-4708. FAX 414-229-6329. Eds. Sandra Nelson, Kathleen Postma. adv.; bk.rev.; film rev.; play rev.; circ. 2,500. (back issues avail.) **Indexed:** A.I.P.P., Ind.Amer.Per.Verse.

820 II
CREATIVE FORUM. 1988. 2/yr. Rs.150($40) Bahri Publications, 997-A, Street No. 9, P.O. Box 4453, Gobindpuri, Kalkaji, New Delhi 110 019, India. TEL 6448606. FAX 92-11-64601796. Eds. U.S. Bahri, Ravinder K. Bahri.

CREATIVE WOMAN. see *WOMEN'S INTERESTS*

810 US ISSN 8756-0291
CREEPING BENT. 1984. s-a. $7. 433 West Market St., Bethlehem, PA 18018. TEL 215-866-5613. Ed. Joseph Lucia. bk.rev.; circ. 350. (back issues avail.)

800 US ISSN 0749-2871
CRESCENT REVIEW. 1983. s-a. $10. Crescent Review, Inc., 1445 Old Town Rd., Winston-Salem, NC 27106-3143. TEL 919-924-1851. Ed. Guy Nancekeville. adv.; circ. 300.
Description: Independent journal devoted only to short stories.

820 UK
CRIMSON CIRCLE MAGAZINE. 1969. q. £8 (effective Jan. 1991). Edgar Wallace Society, 7 Devonshire Close, Amersham, Bucks. HP6 5JG, England. TEL 0494-72-5398. Ed. John A. Hogan. bk.rev.; circ. 425.
Formerly (until 1985): Edgar Wallace Society Newsletter.

800 700 IT ISSN 0011-1406
CRISI E LETTERATURA; periodico di lettere filosofia arti. 1961. a. Gaetano Salveti, Ed.& Pub., Via Bu Meliana 12, 00195 Rome, Italy. (Subscr. to: Lago d'Iseo No.21, 00050 Santa Severa, Rome, Italy) bk.rev.; bibl.; illus.; circ. 3,000. (tabloid format)

860 US ISSN 0278-7261
PQ6001
CRITICA HISPANICA. (Text in English or Spanish) 1979. s-a. $27 (foreign $38). c/o Gregorio Martin, Ed., Department of Modern Language, Duquesne University, Pittsburgh, PA 15282. TEL 412-434-6415. FAX 412-434-5197. adv.; bk.rev.; circ. 500. **Indexed:** Arts & Hum.Cit.Ind., Chic.Per.Ind., Curr.Cont., Ind.Bk.Rev.Hum., M.L.A.
—BLDSC shelfmark: 3487.395500.

CRITICA LETTERARIA. see *LINGUISTICS*

840 US
CRITICAL BIBLIOGRAPHY OF FRENCH LITERATURE. 1951. irreg., vol.6, 1980. price varies. Syracuse University Press, 1600 Jamesville Ave., Syracuse, NY 13244. TEL 315-443-2597. Ed. Richard A. Brooks.

820 UK ISSN 0011-1562
AP4 CODEN: CRQUEF
CRITICAL QUARTERLY. 1959. q. £21.50($40) to individuals; institutions £36($65). Basil Blackwell Ltd., 108 Cowley Rd., Oxford OX4 1JF, England. TEL 0865-791100. (Subscr. addr.: c/o Marston Book Services, P.O. Box 87, Oxford OX2 ODT, England) Ed.Bd. adv.; bk.rev.; index; circ. 2,200. (back issues avail.) **Indexed:** Arts & Hum.Cit.Ind., Bk.Rev.Ind. (1988-), Br.Hum.Ind., Child.Bk.Rev.Ind. (1988-), Curr.Cont., Hum.Ind., Ind.Bk.Rev.Hum., M.L.A., Mid.East: Abstr.& Ind.
—BLDSC shelfmark: 3487.460000.
Description: Selections of new poetry, literary criticism, contemporary fiction and articles on modern writing.

899 900 100 AT
CRITICAL REVIEW. 1958. a. Aus.$10 (foreign AUS.$12). Australian National University, Research School of Social Sciences, Department of Philosophy, P.O. Box 4, Canberra, A.C.T. 2601, Australia. Ed. S.L. Goldberg. bk.rev.; circ. 1,100. (back issues avail.) **Indexed:** Abstr.Engl.Stud., Aus.P.A.I.S., Br.Hum.Ind., Hum.Ind., M.L.A., NRN.
Former titles: Critical Review Melbourne (ISSN 0070-1548); Critical Review. Melbourne-Sydney.

CRITICAL REVIEW; an interdisciplinary journal. see *LITERARY AND POLITICAL REVIEWS*

800 US
CRITICAL STUDIES; a journal of critical theory, literature, and culture. 1989. s-a. $12.50 to individuals; institutions $37.50. Editions Rodopi, 233 Peachtree St., N.E., Ste. 404, Atlanta, GA 30303-1504. Ed. Myriam Diaz-Diocaretz.

CRITICAL TEXTS: A REVIEW OF THEORY AND CRITICISM. see *LITERARY AND POLITICAL REVIEWS*

800 700 US ISSN 0011-1589
AS30.W3
CRITICISM; a quarterly for literature and the arts. 1959. q. $28 to individuals; institutions $45. Wayne State University Press, 5959 Woodward Ave., Detroit, MI 48202. TEL 313-577-6120. FAX 313-577-6131. Ed. Arthur Marotti. adv.; bk.rev.; illus.; index; circ. 1,175. (also avail. in microform from MIM,UMI; reprint service avail. from UMI,KTO; back issues avail.) **Indexed:** Abstr.Engl.Stud., Bk.Rev.Ind. (1965-), Child.Bk.Rev.Ind. (1965-), Curr.Cont., Film Lit.Ind. (1986-), Hum.Ind., Ind.Bk.Rev.Hum., M.L.A., Mid.East: Abstr.& Ind., RILA.
—BLDSC shelfmark: 3487.489000.
Description: Articles on artists, art, and literature from all periods, either individually or in their interrelationships, with an emphasis on post-structuralist critical approaches, feminist and new historicist interpretation.

CRITICON. see *LITERATURE — Poetry*

801 US ISSN 0011-1619
PN3503
CRITIQUE: STUDIES IN MODERN FICTION. 1956. q. $25 to individuals; institutions $45. (Helen Dwight Reid Educational Foundation) Heldref Publications, 1319 Eighteenth St., N.W., Washington, DC 20036-1802. TEL 202-296-6267. FAX 202-296-5149. Ed. Helen Strang. bk.rev.; index; circ. 1,500. (also avail. in microform; reprint service avail.) **Indexed:** Abstr.Engl.Stud., Arts & Hum.Cit.Ind., Curr.Cont., Hum.Ind., M.L.A.
—BLDSC shelfmark: 3487.489300.
Refereed Serial

800 FR ISSN 0070-1556
CRITIQUES DE NOTRE TEMPS ET....* 1970. irreg. 18.50 F. Editeur Garniere Freres, c/o Editions Pierre Bordas et Fils, 7 rue Princesse, 75006 Paris, France. circ. 10,000.

800 574 US ISSN 0890-8885
CROSS TIMBERS REVIEW. 1984. 2/yr. $6. Cisco Junior College, Cisco, TX 76437. TEL 817-442-2567. Ed. Monte Lewis. circ. 200.
Description: Poetry, short stories, reviews, and essays, focusing primarily on Southwestern U.S. culture and its environment. Features prominent authors and contributors from the area.

800 700 US ISSN 0739-2354
CROSSCURRENTS; a quarterly. 1980. q. $18. 2200 Glastonbury Rd., Westlake Village, CA 91361. TEL 818-991-1694. FAX 818-707-3401. Ed. Linda Brown Michelson. illus.; circ. 3,000. (back issues avail.) **Indexed:** Amer.Hum.Ind., Ind.Amer.Per.Verse, M.L.A.
Description: Focused innovative collections of contemporary literature.

820 SA
CRUX. (Text in English) 4/yr. R.11 (foreign R.14.40). Foundation for Education, Science and Technology, P.O. Box 1758, Pretoria 0001, South Africa. TEL 012-322-6404. FAX 012-320-7803. **Indexed:** Ind.S.A.Per., Lang.Teach.& Ling.Abstr.

CRYPT OF CTHULHU; pulp thriller and theological journal. see *LITERATURE — Science Fiction, Fantasy, Horror*

CTENAR; mesicnik pro praci s knihou. see *LIBRARY AND INFORMATION SCIENCES*

CUADERNO LITERARIO AZOR; literatura, poesia, arte, historia, etc., del ambito de la hispanidad. see *LITERARY AND POLITICAL REVIEWS*

CUADERNOS DE INVESTIGACION FILOLOGICA. see *LINGUISTICS*

807 860 AG
CUADERNOS PARA EL ESTUDIO DE LA ESTETICA Y LA LITERATURA. no.8, 1974. irreg. Universidad Nacional del Nordeste, Instituto de Letras, Resistencia, Chaco, Argentina.

700 NQ ISSN 0011-2569
CUADERNOS UNIVERSITARIOS. 1958. 4/yr. C.$12. (Universidad Nacional Autonoma de Nicaragua) Editorial Universitaria de la U N A N, Leon, Nicaragua. Ed. Alejandro Bravo. bk.rev.; circ. 1,000. **Indexed:** Amer.Hist.& Life, Hist.Abstr.

CUBA INTERNACIONAL. see *POLITICAL SCIENCE*

700 IT ISSN 0011-2798
CULTURA NEL MONDO. 1945. q. L.20000. La Cultura nel Mondo, Via Archimede 139, 00197 Rome, Italy. TEL 06-8072575. Ed. Leo Magnino. adv.; bk.rev.; circ. 5,000. (also avail. in microform)

809 870 IT
CULTURA NEOLATINA; revista di filologia romanza. 1941. q. L.70000 (foreign L.90000). (Istituto di Filologia Romanza) Mucchi Editore s.r.l., Via Emilia Est 1527, 41100 Modena, Italy. Ed. Aurelio Roncaglio. (back issues avail.) **Indexed:** M.L.A.

CULTURAL CORRESPONDENCE. see *LITERARY AND POLITICAL REVIEWS*

CULTURES DU CANADA FRANCAIS. see *HISTORY — History Of North And South America*

800 659.1 US
CUPID'S DESTINY. 1937. q. $36. Destiny Syndicate, Box 5637, Reno, NV 89513-5637. Ed. Kelly Williams. adv.; circ. 20,000. (back issues avail.)

800 410 US ISSN 0893-5963
CURRENTS IN COMPARATIVE ROMANCE LANGUAGES AND LITERATURES. (Text in English and other West European languages.) 1987. irreg., vol.2, 1988. Peter Lang Publishing, Inc., 62 W. 45th St., 4th Fl., New York, NY 10036. TEL 212-302-6740. FAX 212-302-7574. Eds. Tamara Alvarez-Detrell, Michael G. Paulson.
—BLDSC shelfmark: 3505.170000.
Description: Concentrates on literary and linguistic works with a comparative basis, usually drawing on two or more Romance language literatures.

800 UK
CURTAINS. 1971. s-a. price varies. Pressed Curtains, 4 Bower St., Maidstone, Kent ME16 8SD, England. Ed. Paul Buck. bk.rev.; circ. 400. (processed)

900 800 US ISSN 0737-139X
CUYAHOGA REVIEW. 1983. s-a. $10. Cuyahoga Community College (Western Campus), 11000 Pleasant Valley Rd., Parma, OH 44130. TEL 216-987-5000. Ed. Richard Charnigo. circ. 400. **Indexed:** M.L.A.
—BLDSC shelfmark: 3506.221500.

2910 LITERATURE

891.66 UK
CYFRES CLASURON YR ACADEMI. (Text in Welsh) 1980. irreg. price varies. (Welsh Academy) University of Wales Press, 6 Gwennyth St., Cathays, Cardiff CF2 4YD, Wales. TEL 0222-231919. FAX 0222-230908. Ed. P.J. Donovan.
Description: Covers the classics of Welsh literature previously only available in manuscript form.

820 II
CYGNUS; journal of research in English. (Text in English) 1979. s-a. Rs.30($15) Centre for Commonwealth Literature, Mohana, C-278 Niralanagar, Lucknow 226 007, India. Ed. A.K. Srivastava. circ. 1,000.

820 US ISSN 0011-4936
PR6023.A93
D H LAWRENCE REVIEW. 1968. 3/yr. $14 to individuals (foreign $15); institutions $20. University of Delaware, English Department, 204 Memorial Hall, Newark, DE 19716. TEL 302-454-1480. Ed. Dennis Jackson. adv.; bk.rev.; film rev.; play rev.; bibl.; index; circ. 750 (controlled). (also avail. in microform from UMI; back issues avail.) **Indexed:** Abstr.Engl.Stud., Amer.Hum.Ind., Arts & Hum.Cit.Ind., Curr.Cont., M.L.A.
—BLDSC shelfmark: 3579.501000.

800 US
D H LAWRENCE SOCIETY OF NORTH AMERICA. NEWSLETTER. 1981. s-a. membership. Ohio Northern University, Department of English, Ada, OH 45810. TEL 419-772-2101. (Subscr. to: Lydia Blanchard, Treas., 12503 Chateau Forest, San Antonio, TX 78230) Ed. Eleanor H. Green. film rev.; play rev.; bibl.; illus.; circ. 250. (looseleaf format; back issues avail.)
Description: Contains material of interest to Lawrence scholars and admirers.

800 NE
D Q R. (Dutch Quarterly Review); studies in literature. 1986. irreg., latest vol.8, 1990. price varies. Editions Rodopi B.V., Keizersgracht 302-304, 1016 EX Amsterdam, Netherlands. TEL 020-6227507. FAX 020-6380948. (US and Canada subscr. to: 233 Peachtree St., N.E., Ste. 404, Atlanta, GA 30303-1504, USA. TEL 800-225-3998) Ed.Bd. (reprint service avail. from SWZ)
Incorporates (1971-1991): Dutch Quarterly Review of Anglo American Letters (ISSN 0046-0842)

800 410 DK ISSN 0105-208X
D S L'S PRAESENTATIONSHAEFTE. 1975. a. DKK 12.20. Danske Sprog- og Litteraturselskab - Danish Society of Language and Literature, Frederiksholms Kanal 18A, DK-1220 Copenhagen K, Denmark. TEL 01-13-06-600. FAX 33-14-06-08. circ. 600.
Description: Deals with aspects or editions within the program of this editorial society.

DACOROMANIA; Jahrbuch fuer oestliche Latinitaet. see LINGUISTICS

800 700 US ISSN 0084-9537
NX600.D3
DADA - SURREALISM. 1970. a. $12 to individuals; institutions $15. Association for the Study of Dada and Surrealism, Univ. of Iowa, 425 EPB, Iowa City, IA 52242. adv.; bibl.; illus. (back issues avail.) **Indexed:** Amer.Hum.Ind., Artbibl.Mod., RILA.
—BLDSC shelfmark: 3509.642000.
Description: Critical essays, previously unpublished documents and extensive bibliographies on Dada and Surrealism.

DALHOUSIE REVIEW; a Canadian quarterly of literature and opinion. see LITERARY AND POLITICAL REVIEWS

891.7 BW
DALYAGLYADY LITARATURNY ZBORNIK. 1975. a. Vydavetstva Mastatskaya Litaratura, Prospekt Mashepava 11, 220600 Minsk, Byelarus. TEL 23-48-09. Ed.Bd.
Description: Contains translations of foreign literature and poetry into Belorussian.

810 US
DAMASCUS ROAD. 1959. irreg. (approx. a.), latest vol.10. $2.95 per no. c/o C.S. Hanna, Ed., 6271 Hill Dr., Allentown, PA 18104. TEL 215-395-6469. circ. 500. (also avail. in microform from UMI; reprint service avail. from UMI)

800 US
DAN RIVER ANTHOLOGY (YEAR). 1984. a. $9.95 paper; cloth $19.95. (Conservatory of American Letters) Dan River Press, Box 88, Thomaston, ME 04861. TEL 207-354-6550. (Subscr. to: Box 123, S. Thomaston, ME 04858) Ed. Richard S. Danbury III. circ. 1,000.
Description: Annual collection of fiction and poetry from all over the country.

DANDELION. see LITERATURE — Poetry

895.1 CC ISSN 0257-0165
DANGDAI/CONTEMPORARY ERA. (Text in Chinese; summaries in Chinese and English) 1979. bi-m. Y22.80($5) Renmin Wenxue Chubanshe - People's Literature Publishing House, 166 Chaonei Dajie, Beijing 100705, People's Republic of China. TEL 55-7553. (Dist. outside China by: China International Book Trading Corp., P.O. Box 399, Beijing, P.R.C.; Dist. in US by: China Books & Periodicals, Inc., 2929 24th St., San Francisco, CA 94110) Ed. Qin Zhaoyang. bk.rev.
Description: Publishes contemporary Chinese literature; novels, novelettes, short stories, poetry, prose, and reportage.

800 US ISSN 1001-1757
DANGDAI WAIGUO WENXUE/CONTEMPORARY FOREIGN LITERATURE. (Text in Chinese) q. $29.40. China Books & Periodicals, Inc., 2929 24th St., San Francisco, CA 94110. TEL 415-282-2994. FAX 415-282-0994.

895 CC
DANGDAI WENTAN/MODERN LITERARY WORLD. (Text in Chinese) bi-m. (Zhongguo Zuojia Xiehui, Sichuan Fenhui - Chinese Writers Association, Sichuan Chapter) Dangdai Wentan Bianjibu, No.85, Hongxing Zhonglu 2 Duan, Chengdu, Sichuan 610012. TEL 660070. Ed. Chen Zhaohong.

895.1 CC ISSN 1000-7946
DANGDAI XIAOSHUO/CONTEMPORARY NOVELS. (Text in Chinese) 1985. m. $40.40. Jinan Shi Wenlian, No. 104, Jing 10 Lu, Jinan, Shandong 250002, People's Republic of China. TEL 24544. (Dist. in US by: China Books & Periodicals, Inc., 2929 24th St., San Francisco, CA 94110. TEL 415-282-2994) Ed. Sun Guozhang.

895.1 CC
DANGDAI ZUOJIA/MODERN WRITERS. (Text in Chinese) bi-m. Changjiang Wenyi Chubanshe, No. 63, Xiyu Cun, Hankou, Wuhan, Hubei 430022, People's Republic of China. TEL 357031. Ed. Tian Zhongquan.

895.1 CC
DANGDAI ZUOJIA PINGLUN/CONTEMPORARY WRITERS REVIEW. (Text in Chinese; table of contents in English) bi-m. Y13.20. (Zhongguo Zuojia Xiehui, Liaoning Fenhui - China Writers' Association, Liaoning Chapter) Dangdai Zuojia Pinglun Zazhi She, 1 Wenxing Li, Shenyang Lu Erduan, Shenhe Qu, Shenyang, Liaoning 110011, People's Republic of China. (Dist. outside China by: China Publications Foreign Trade Corp., P.O. Box 782, Beijing, P.R.C.) Eds. Chen Yan, Zhang Songkui. adv.
Description: Contains literary criticism, reviews.

839.8 DK ISSN 0906-5369
▼**DANISH LITERARY MAGAZINE.** (Text in English) 1991. s-a. DKK 70($10) (Ministry of Foreign Affairs) Danish Literature Information Center, 38 Amaliegade, 1256 Copenhagen K, Denmark. TEL 45-33-32-07-25. FAX 45-33-91-15-45. (Co-sponsors: Ministry of Cultural Affairs, Ministry of Education) Ed. Thomas Thurah. adv.; bk.rev.; play rev.; bibl.; illus.; circ. 10,000.

850 US ISSN 0070-2862
PQ4331
DANTE STUDIES; with the Annual Report of the Dante Society. 1881. a. price varies. State University of New York Press, State University Plaza, Albany, NY 12246. TEL 518-472-5025. Ed. Anthony L. Pellegrini. adv.; circ. 350. (also avail. in microform from UMI; reprint service avail. from UMI,KTO)
Indexed: M.L.A.
Formerly (until 1980): Dante Society of America. Report with Accompanying Papers.

850 IT
▼**DANTOLOGIA.** 1990. irreg. price varies. (Centro Bibliografico Dantesco) Casa Editrice Leo S. Olschki, Casella Postale 66, 50100 Florence, Italy. TEL 055-6530684. FAX 055-6530214.

830 NE ISSN 0300-693X
PT177
DAPHNIS; Zeitschrift fuer Mittlere Deutsche Literatur. 1972. q. fl.190. Editions Rodopi B.V., Keizersgracht 302-304, 1016 EX Amsterdam, Netherlands. TEL 020-6227507. FAX 020-6380948. (In N. America: 233 Peachtree St. N.E., Ste. 404, Atlanta, GA 30303-1504. TEL 800-225-3998) Ed. Hans-Gert Roloff. adv.; bk.rev.; circ. 500. **Indexed:** Arts & Hum.Cit.Ind., Can.Rev.Comp.Lit, Curr.Cont., M.L.A.
—BLDSC shelfmark: 3533.200000.

890 IS ISSN 0334-0686
PJ5001
DAPPIM - RESEARCH IN LITERATURE. (Text in Hebrew; summaries in English) 1984. a. IS.28($25) Haifa University Press, Mount Carmel, Haifa 31999, Israel. TEL 04-247181. FAX 04-254184. Ed.Bd. circ. 500.

809.916 US
▼**THE DARK MAN: THE JOURNAL OF ROBERT E. HOWARD STUDIES.** 1990. irreg., vol.3, 1992. $5 per no. Necronomicon Press, 101 Lockwood St., W. Warwick, RI 02893. TEL 401-828-7161. FAX 401-738-6125. Ed. Rusty Burke. bk.rev. (back issues avail.)
Description: Covers the life and work of Robert E. Howard, fantasy and horror author, and creator of Conan.

810 US
DARK WINDS;* decadence fantasy magazine. 1982. a. $6. Gibbelin's Gazette Publications, c/o Veron Clark, Ed., 2810 Urbana Dr., Silver Spring, MD 20906-5033. adv.; bk.rev.; illus.; circ. 350.
Description: Features nonfiction and poetry.

891.7 LV
DAUGAVA. 1977. m. 14.40 Rub. (Soyuz Sovetskikh Pisatelei Latvii) Izdatel'stvo Daugava, Riga, Latvia. Ed. R. Trofimov. circ. 15,200. **Indexed:** M.L.A.

DAZHONG WENYI. see ART

895.1 CC
DAZHONG XIAOSHUO/POPULAR SHORT STORIES. (Text in Chinese) bi-m. Chunfeng Wenyi Chubanshe, 108 Beiyi Malu, Heping Qu, Shenyang, Liaoning 110001, People's Republic of China. TEL 363198. Ed. Li Qinxue.

DEATHREALM; the land where horror dwells. see LITERATURE — Science Fiction, Fantasy, Horror

810 705 US ISSN 0070-3141
PS501
DECEMBER; a magazine of the arts and opinion. 1958. irreg. $25 for 4 nos. December Press, Box 302, Highland Park, IL 60035. TEL 708-940-4122. Ed. Curt Johnson. adv.; bk.rev.; film rev.; illus.; circ. 1,200. (also avail. in microform from UMI; reprint service avail. from UMI,KTO; back issues avail.)
Description: Fiction and polemics.

890 US ISSN 0148-561X
PQ1
DEGRE SECOND: STUDIES IN FRENCH LITERATURE. 1976. a. $17. Virginia Polytechnic Institute and State University, Department of Foreign Languages, Blacksburg, VA 24061. TEL 703-231-5361. Ed. W. Pierre Jacoebee. adv.; bk.rev.; circ. 180. (back issues avail.) **Indexed:** M.L.A.
Formerly: Degre Second: Studies in French Literature from the Renaissance to the Present.

800 US ISSN 0011-7951
PN241.A1
DELOS. 1988. 4/yr. $20 to individuals; institutions $25; students $15. Center for World Literature, Inc., Box 2880, College Park, MD 20740. TEL 301-935-5263. adv.

808 960 SG
DEMB AK TEY/YESTERDAY AND TODAY; a journal of myths and legends. (Editions in English and French) q. $18. Centre d'Etude des Civilisations, Ministry of Culture, Dakar, Senegal. Ed.Bd. illus.

810   US   ISSN 0011-9210
DESCANT. 1955. 2/yr. $12 $18. Texas Christian University, Department of English, Fort Worth, TX 76129. TEL 817-921-7240. FAX 817-921-7333. Ed.Bd. circ. 450. **Indexed:** Abstr.Engl.Stud., Amer.Hum.Ind., Curr.Cont., M.L.A.
Incorporates (in 1979): Quartet (ISSN 0033-586X)

810   CN   ISSN 0382-909X
PR9194
DESCANT. 1970. 4/yr. Can.$22.47 to individuals; institutions Can.$31.03. Descant Arts and Letters Foundation, 245 Markham St., Toronto, Ont. M6J 2G7, Canada. TEL 416-603-0223. Ed. Karen Mulhallen. adv.; bk.rev.; circ. 1,000. **Indexed:** Amer.Hum.Ind., Arts & Hum.Cit.Ind., Can.Lit.Ind., Can.Per.Ind., CMI, Curr.Cont.
Description: Literary journal publishing poetry, fiction, essays and visuals.

895.9   II
DESH. (Text in Bengali) 1933. w. 6 Prafulla Sarkar St., Calcutta 700 001, India. TEL 33-274880. TELEX 215468. Ed. S. Ghosh. circ. 81,200.

DETSKAYA LITERATURA. see CHILDREN AND YOUTH — About

DEUTSCHE AKADEMIE FUER SPRACHE UND DICHTUNG. JAHRBUCH. see LINGUISTICS

830   GW
DEUTSCHE AKADEMIE FUER SPRACHE UND DICHTUNG. SCHRIFTENREIHE. 1954. irreg., no.60, 1986. price varies. Luchterhand Verlag, Heddesdorferstr. 31, Postfach 1780, 5450 Neuwied, Germany.

800   GW   ISSN 0420-0152
DEUTSCHE BIBLIOTHEK. 1968. irreg., vol.13, 1988. (Akademie der Wissenschaften der DDR) Akademie-Verlag Berlin, Leipziger Str. 3-4, 1086 Berlin, Germany. TELEX 114420-AVERL-DD.

830 500   GW   ISSN 0012-043X
DEUTSCHE LITERATURZEITUNG; fuer Kritik der internationalen Wissenschaft. 1880. m. DM.158.40. (Akademie der Wissenschaften der DDR) Akademie-Verlag Berlin, Leipziger Str. 3-4, 1086 Berlin, Germany. TELEX 114420-AVERL-DD. Ed. W. Hartke. adv.; bk.rev.; bibl.; stat.; index. **Indexed:** RILA.

DEUTSCHE OSTKUNDE; Vierteljahresschrift fuer Wissenschaft, Erziehung und Unterricht. see HISTORY — History Of Europe

830   GW   ISSN 0070-4318
PT105
DEUTSCHE SCHILLER-GESELLSCHAFT. JAHRBUCH. 1957. a. price varies. Alfred Kroener Verlag, Reinsburgstr. 56, 7000 Stuttgart 1, Germany. FAX 0711-6159946. Ed.Bd. circ. 3,000. **Indexed:** M.L.A.

820   GW   ISSN 0070-4326
DEUTSCHE SHAKESPEARE-GESELLSCHAFT WEST. JAHRBUCH. 1948. a. price varies, approx. DM.80. Verlag Ferdinand Kamp GmbH & Co. KG, Postfach 101309, 4630 Bochum, Germany. Ed. Werner Habicht. bk.rev.; circ. 2,000. **Indexed:** Abstr.Engl.Stud., Ind.Bk.Rev.Hum., M.L.A.
Description: Presents scholarly, critical and theater-oriented articles on Shakespeare and his work.

430 830   GW   ISSN 0070-4334
PT1375
DEUTSCHE TEXTE DES MITTELALTERS. vol.42, 1942. irreg., vol.75, 1989. price varies. Akademie-Verlag Berlin, Leipziger Str. 3-4, 1086 Berlin, Germany. TELEX 114420-AVERL-DD. (also avail. in microfiche from BHP) **Indexed:** M.L.A.

850   GW   ISSN 0070-444X
DEUTSCHES DANTE-JAHRBUCH. a. DM.68. (Dante Gesellschaft e.V.) Boehlau Verlag GmbH, Theodor-Heuss-Str. 76, 5000 Cologne 90, Germany. Ed. Marcella Roddewig. **Indexed:** M.L.A.

810   US
DEVIANCE. 1987. 3/yr. $13. Box 1706, Pawtucket, RI 02862. Ed. Lin Collette. circ. 500.
Description: Publishes poems, satire and translations.

DEVONSHIRE ASSOCIATION FOR THE ADVANCEMENT OF SCIENCE, LITERATURE AND ART. REPORT AND TRANSACTIONS. see ART

410 869   PO   ISSN 0870-8967
AP65
DIACRITICA. 1986. a. Esc.1700($12) Universidade do Minho, Centro de Estudos Portugueses, 4 719 Braga Codex, Portugal. TEL 053-676375. FAX 053-676387. bk.rev.; circ. 750.
Description: Covers university level interests such as theories of literature, philosophy and linguistics.

809   US   ISSN 0300-7162
PN80
DIACRITICS; a review journal of contemporary criticism. 1971. q. $19.90 to individuals (foreign $27.50); institutions $51 (foreign $56.60). (Cornell University) Johns Hopkins University Press, Journals Publishing Division, 701 W. 40th St., Ste. 275, Baltimore, MD 21211. TEL 410-516-6987. FAX 410-516-6998. Ed. Debra Castillo. adv.; bk.rev.; film rev.; bibl.; index, cum.index; circ. 1,290. (also avail. in microform from UMI; back issues avail.; reprint service avail. from SWZ,UMI) **Indexed:** Abstr.Engl.Stud., Amer.Hum.Ind., Arts & Hum.Cit.Ind., Curr.Cont., Film Lit.Ind. (1976-), Ind.Bk.Rev.Hum., Lang.& Lang.Behav.Abstr., LCR, M.L.A.
—BLDSC shelfmark: 3579.616000.
Description: Features articles in which contributors compare and analyze books on particular theoretical works and develop their own positions on the theses, methods, and theoretical implications of those works.

450   IT   ISSN 0012-2025
DIALETTI D'ITALIA.* (Text in Italian and Italian dialects) 1956; N.S. 1963. m. L.1000. Via Venti Settembre 26, 00187 Rome, Italy. Ed. Maria Teresa Martinozzi.

DIALOGOS HISPANICOS DE AMSTERDAM. see LINGUISTICS

800 300   FR
DIALOGUE. 1978. 2/yr. Universite de Montpellier (Universite Paul Valery), Centre d'Etudes et de Recherches Roumaines et des Traditions Orales Mediterraneennes, B.P. 5043, 34032 Montpellier Cedex 1, France. TEL 67-14-20-00. Ed. J. Lacroix.
Description: Specializes in Rumanian studies. Intended for specialists in the fields of literature, linguistics, cultural anthropology and for those interested in Rumanian and Mediterranean culture.

808   US
DIANA'S ALMANAC.* 1972. a. $4.50. Diana's Cards - Press, 10 Johnson Rd., Foster, RI 02825. Ed. Tom Ahern. circ. 1,000.

DIANSHI DIANYING WENXUE/TV AND FILM LITERATURE. see MOTION PICTURES

800   RU
DIAPASON; vestnik inostrannoi literatury. 1961. q. 9 Rub. Vsesoyuznaya Gosudarstvennaya Biblioteka Inostrannoi Literatury, Ul'anovskaya St., 1, VGBIL "Diapason", Moscow 109189, Russia. TEL 245-05-56. Ed. G. Zlobin. bk.rev.; circ. 9,000. (also avail. in microform)
Formerly (until 1991): Sovremennaya Khudozhestvennaya Literatura za Rubezhom (ISSN 0132-1390)

800   US
DIARIST'S JOURNAL. 1988. q. $12. Gazette Publications, Inc., 102 W. Water St., Lansford, PA 18232. TEL 717-645-4692. Ed. Edward Gildea. adv.; bk.rev.; circ. 500.
Description: Prints excerpts from diaries people are keeping today. Includes articles on diarists of today and yesterday.

820   US   ISSN 0742-5473
PR4579
DICKENS QUARTERLY. 1984. q. $15. University of Massachusetts, Department of English, Amherst, MA 01003. (Subscr. to: Dickens Society, President's Office, Grawemeyer Hall, Univ. of Louisville, Louisville, KY 40292) Ed. David Paroissien. adv.; bk.rev.; bibl.; circ. 500. **Indexed:** Abstr.Engl.Stud., Amer.Hum.Ind., Arts & Hum.Cit.Ind., Curr.Cont.; M.L.A.
—BLDSC shelfmark: 3580.239000.
Supersedes (1970-1984): Dickens Studies Newsletter (ISSN 0012-2432)
Description: Publishes articles, notes, reviews, and a checklist of Dickens studies.

820   US
DICKENS STUDIES ANNUAL: ESSAYS ON VICTORIAN FICTION. 1970. a. $45. (City University of New York, Victorian Committee) A M S Press, Inc., 56 E. 13th St., New York, NY 10003. TEL 212-777-4700. FAX 212-995-5413. Ed.Bd. index. (back issues avail.) **Indexed:** Amer.Hum.Ind., M.L.A.
Formerly: Dickens Studies Annual (ISSN 0084-9812)
Description: Scholarly articles on the life and work of Charles Dickens and other Victorian writers.

800   US
DICKEN'S UNIVERSE. irreg. Peter Lang Publishing, Inc., 62 W. 45th St., 4th Fl., New York, NY 10036. TEL 212-302-6740. FAX 212-302-7574. Ed. Charlotte Rotkin.
Description: Literary series on the life and letters of Charles Dickens.

820   UK   ISSN 0012-2440
PR4579
DICKENSIAN. 1905. 3/yr. £10 individuals; institutions £13. University of Kent at Canterbury, Eliot College, The University, Canterbury, Kent CT2 7NS, England. TEL 0227-764000. FAX 452196. TELEX 965449. Ed. Malcolm Andrews. adv.; bk.rev.; bibl.; illus.; index, cum.index; circ. 2,250. (also avail. in microform from HPL; reprint service avail. from KTO) **Indexed:** Abstr.Engl.Stud., Arts & Hum.Cit.Ind., Br.Hum.Ind., Curr.Cont., Ind.Bk.Rev.Hum., LCR, M.L.A.
—BLDSC shelfmark: 3580.242000.

400   US   ISSN 0360-215X
PN6081
DICTIONARY OF CONTEMPORARY QUOTATIONS. 1976. triennial. $55. John Gordon Burke Publisher, Inc., Box 1492, Evanston, IL 60204-1492. TEL 708-866-8625.
●Also available online.
Description: Records contemporary, historically, sociologically and politically significant quotes.

DICTIONARY OF LITERARY BIOGRAPHY. see BIOGRAPHY — Abstracting, Bibliographies, Statistics

800 920   US   ISSN 0731-7867
PS221
DICTIONARY OF LITERARY BIOGRAPHY YEARBOOK. 1981. a. $112. Gale Research Inc., 835 Penobscot Bldg., Detroit, MI 48226. TEL 313-961-2242. FAX 313-961-6083. TELEX 810-221-7086.
Description: Annual reference on works of literary biography.

860   US   ISSN 0163-0415
PQ6069
DIECIOCHO; Hispanic enlightenment, aesthetics and literary theory. (Text in English, Portuguese, Spanish) 1978. s-a. $12 to individuals; institutions $17 (effective Jan. 1992). c/o Dr. Eva M. Kahiluoto Rudat, Ed., 53 King Charles Ln., Newtown, PA 18940-2312. TEL 215-579-2995. bk.rev.; circ. 200. **Indexed:** Arts & Hum.Cit.Ind., Curr.Cont., M.L.A.
—BLDSC shelfmark: 3580.520000.

800   NE   ISSN 0166-5618
DIEPZEE; literaturmagazine voor het onderwijs. 1983. 6/yr. fl.30. Wolters-Noordhoff B.V., Damsport 157, 9728 PS Groningen, Netherlands. TEL (050)226922. (Subscr. to: Box 58, 9700 MB Groningen, Netherlands)
Formerly: Klapper.

LITERATURE

830   US   ISSN 0012-2882
AP2
DIMENSION (AUSTIN); contemporary German arts and letters. (Text in English, German) 1968. 3/yr. $16 to individuals; institutions $19. Box 26673, Austin, TX 78755. TEL 512-345-0622. Ed. A. Leslie Willson. index, cum.index: vols.1-10; circ. 800. (also avail. in microform from UMI; reprint service avail. from UMI) **Indexed:** Arts & Hum.Cit.Ind., CERDIC, M.L.A.
—BLDSC shelfmark: 3588.466000.

800   US
DIMENSIONS (WATERBURY). 1969. a. free. Mattatuck Community College, Student Legislative Congress, 750 Chase Pkwy., Waterbury, CT 06708. TEL 203-575-0328. Ed. Gloria D. Pond. circ. 1,000.
Description: Poetry, verse, drawings, and narrative sketches by students of Mattatuck Community College, Connecticut.

800   US   ISSN 1044-4149
DIONYSOS; the literature and intoxication triquarterly. 1989. 3/yr. $10 to individuals; institutions $15. University of Wisconsin at Superior, 1800 Grand Ave., Superior, WI 54880. FAX 715-394-8454. Ed. Roger Forseth. adv.; bk.rev.; circ. 150.
Description: Contains news notes and articles dealing with the cultural and aesthetic side of intoxication. Covers both the creative and destructive role of drinking and drug use in the lives and works of writers and artists.

DIRECTORY OF CARTOONISTS - GAGWRITERS - SHORT HUMOR MARKETS. see BUSINESS AND ECONOMICS — Trade And Industrial Directories

050 810 820   US   ISSN 0070-6094
Z2015.P4
DIRECTORY OF PERIODICALS PUBLISHING ARTICLES ON ENGLISH AND AMERICAN LITERATURE AND LANGUAGE.* 1959. irreg., 4th ed. 1975. $10 hardbound; paperback $3.50. Swallow Press, Inc., Box 2080, Chicago, IL 60690-2080. Eds. Donna Gerstenberger, George Hendrick.

800   PY
PQ7081.A1
DISCURSO; revista de temas hispanicos. (Former issuing body: University of Oklahoma, Department of Foreign Languages and Literatures) (Text in English, Portuguese and Spanish) 1983. s-a. $40 to individuals; institutions $50. (Centro de Estudios de Economia y Sociedad) Ediciones y Arte s.r.l., Estados Unidos 1461, Asuncion, Paraguay. TEL 59521-607-376. Ed. Javier Restrepo. adv.; bk.rev.; bibl.; circ. 1,000. (also avail. in microform from UMI; back issues avail.) **Indexed:** M.L.A.
Formerly: Discurso Literario (ISSN 0737-8742)

800   NE
DIVER; magazine for reading & literature. (Text in English) 1984. 3/yr. fl.27.50. Wolters-Noordhoff B.V., Damsport 157, 9728 PS Groningen, Netherlands. TEL (050)226922.

DIVREI HA-AKADEMIA HA-LEUMIT HA-YISRAELIT LEMADAIM. see HUMANITIES: COMPREHENSIVE WORKS

909.6   FR   ISSN 0012-4273
DIX-SEPTIEME SIECLE. 1948. q. 350 F. (effective 1991). Societe d'Etude du Dix-Septieme Siecle, Commission de Publication, c/o College de France, 11 Place Marcellin Berthelot, 75231 Paris Cedex 05, France. TEL 1-45-48-85-24. Dir. Georges Molinie. adv.; bk.rev.; cum.index: 1949-1959, 1960-1969, 1970-1979; circ. 1,500. **Indexed:** Amer.Hist.& Life, Arts & Hum.Cit.Ind., Bull.Signal., Curr.Cont., Hist.Abstr., M.L.A.
—BLDSC shelfmark: 9725.300000.
Description: Publishes news from books or colloquies about 17th century studies.

860   US
DOCUMENTACION CERVANTINA. 1978. irreg., no.11, 1991. price varies. Juan de la Cuesta - Hispanic Monographs, 270 Indian Rd., Newark, DE 19711. TEL 302-453-8695. FAX 302-453-8601. Ed. Thomas A. Lathrop. circ. 500. **Indexed:** M.L.A.

830 430   JA   ISSN 0387-2831
DOITSU BUNGAKU. s-a. free. Nippon Dokubungakkai, c/o Ikubundo, Hongo 5-30-21, Bunkyo-ku, Tokyo 113, Japan.

800   DK   ISSN 0106-4487
DOLPHIN. (Text in English) 1979. s-a. $38. Aarhus University Press, Aarhus University, Building 170, DK-8000 Aarhus C, Denmark. TEL 86-197033. FAX 86-198433. Ed.Bd. circ. 200.
—BLDSC shelfmark: 3616.620000.
Description: Studies in English and American literature and language; also media studies.

057.87 891.87   CS
DOMOVA POKLADNICA. a. 30 Kcs. Priroda, Krizkova 9, 815 34 Bratislava, Czechoslovakia.

DONG-A MUNHUA/EAST ASIA CULTURE. see ORIENTAL STUDIES

895.1   CC
DONG HAI/EAST CHINA SEA. (Text in Chinese) m. $36.80. Zhejiang Sheng Wenlian, 9, Jiande Lu, Hangzhou, Zhejiang 310006. TEL 778991. (Dist. in US by: China Books & Periodicals, Inc., 2929 24th St., San Francisco, CA 94110. TEL 415-282-2994)

895.1   CC
DONGJING WENXUE. (Text in Chinese) bi-m. Kaifeng Shi Wenlian, Shiwei Dayuan, Kaifeng, Henan 475000, People's Republic of China. TEL 31030. Ed. Xiao Yunxing.

800   US   ISSN 0882-486X
PR6023.E833
DORIS LESSING NEWSLETTER. 1976. s-a. $10 to individuals; libraries $12; foreign $14. Doris Lessing Newsletter, c/o K. Fishburn, English Department, Michigan State University, East Lansing, MI 48824-1036. Ed. Ruth Saxton. bk.rev.; circ. 200. (back issues avail.)
—BLDSC shelfmark: 3619.521000.

820 420   JA   ISSN 0046-063X
PE9
DOSHISHA LITERATURE; journal of English literature and philology. (Text in English) 1887. biennial. 1000 Yen($7) per no. Doshisha University, English Literary Society, Karasuma Imadegawa, Kamikyo-ku, Kyoto 602, Japan. Ed. Isamu Saito. bk.rev.; circ. 2,000. **Indexed:** Arts & Hum.Cit.Ind., Curr.Cont., Lang.& Lang.Behav.Abstr.
—BLDSC shelfmark: 3619.732000.
Formerly: Doshisha Bungaku.

800   JA   ISSN 0286-2832
DOSHISHA STUDIES IN FOREIGN LITERATURE. (Text in English, French, German, Japanese) 1971. irreg. 1000 Yen. Doshisha University, Gaikoku Bungakukai, Tanabe-cho, Kyoto 610-03, Japan. FAX 07746-5-7069. Ed. Osamu Kono. bk.rev.; circ. 2,000.
—BLDSC shelfmark: 3619.743000.

891.7   US
DOSTOEVSKY STUDIES. (Text in English, French, German and Russian) 1980. a. $10. International Dostoevsky Society, c/o Martin P. Rice, University of Tennessee, Department of Germanic and Slavic Languages, Knoxville, TN 37996. TEL 615-974-3421. Ed. Rudolf Neuhaeuser. bk.rev.; bibl.; circ. 300. (back issues avail.) **Indexed:** Amer.Bibl.Slavic & E.Eur.Stud., M.L.A.
Supersedes: International Dostoevsky Society Bulletin (ISSN 0047-0686)

378.1   UK   ISSN 0012-589X
DRAGON. (Editions in English and Welsh) 1966. a. University College of Wales, Students' Union, Aberystwyth, Dyfed, Wales. Eds. C. Larner, A. Thomas. adv.; bk.rev.; film rev.; illus.; record rev.; circ. 250.
Description: For students of Aberystwyth, using any literary material freely submitted by the students.

DRAMA CRITICISM. see THEATER

822   UK   ISSN 0070-7198
DRAMASCRIPTS SERIES. 1965. irreg., no.4, 1970. price varies. Oleander Press, 17 Stansgate Ave., Cambridge CB2 2QZ, England. (U.S. address: 80 Eighth Ave., Ste. 303, New York, NY 10011) Eds. Philip Ward, Wayne Schlepp.

800   CN   ISSN 0843-445X
DREAMS & VISIONS; new frontiers in Christian fiction. 1989. q. Can.$12($12) Skysong Press, R.R. 1, Washago, Ont. L0K 2B0, Canada. TEL 705-689-6226. Eds. Steve and Wendy Stanton. circ. 400. (back issues avail.)

830   SZ   ISSN 0012-6055
DREHPUNKT. (Text in German) 1969. 3/yr. 30 SFr. Lenos Verlag, Spalentorweg 12, CH-4051 Basel, Switzerland. (Subscr. to: Postfach 164, CH-4016 Basel, Switzerland) Ed.Bd. adv.; bk.rev.; illus.; circ. 1,500.

810   US   ISSN 0896-6362
PS3507.R55
DREISER STUDIES. 1970. s-a. $5 to individuals; institutions $7; outside N. America $14. Indiana State University, Department of English, Terre Haute, IN 47809. TEL 812-237-3164. FAX 812-237-2567. Ed. D. Vancil. bk.rev.; circ. 300. (back issues avail.) **Indexed:** Amer.Hum.Ind., Bibl.Engl.Lang.& Lit., Hum.Ind.
Formerly: Dreiser Newsletter (ISSN 0012-6098)
Description: Contains critical and textual essays, notes and reviews, and news on the literature of Theodore Dreiser and his peers.

DROOD REVIEW OF MYSTERY. see LITERATURE — Mystery And Detective

810 700 320   US   ISSN 0899-5443
DRUM; black literary experience. 1969. a. $3. 115 New Africa House, University of Massachusetts, Amherst, MA 01003. TEL 413-545-3185. Ed. Martha Grier-Deen. illus.; circ. 4,000. (back issues avail.)

DRYADE; revue artistique et litteraire. see ART

895.1   CC   ISSN 0257-0270
DU SHU/READING. (Text in Chinese) 1979. m. Y26.40($67.50) Shenghuo - Dushu - Xinzhi Sanlian Shudian, Life - Reading - Knowledge Joint Publishing Co., 166 Chaonei Dajie, Beijing 100706, People's Republic of China. TEL 4013360. (Dist. in US by: China Books & Periodicals, Inc., 2929 24th St., San Francisco, CA 94110. TEL 415-282-2994) Ed. Shen Changwen. bk.rev.; circ. 50,000.
Description: Primarily contains book reviews.

895.1   CC
DUANPIAN XIAOSHUO/SHORT STORIES. (Text in Chinese) m. Jilin Shi Wenlian, 7, Nanjing Jie, Jilin, Jilin 132001, People's Republic of China. TEL 452980. Ed. Ning Xuancheng.

DUE SOUTH; the biggest guide to what's on in the South. see ARTS AND HANDICRAFTS

895.1   CC
DUILIAN - MINJIAN DUILIAN GUSHI/ANTITHETICAL COUPLET - FOLK STORIES ABOUT ANTITHETICAL COUPLET. (Text in Chinese) bi-m. Shanxi Ribao She - Shanxi Daily Publishing Company, 24 Shuangtasi Jie, Taiyuan, Shanxi 030012, People's Republic of China. TEL 446561. Ed. Guo Huarong.

DUITSE KRONIEK; orgaan voor culturele betrekkingen met Duitsland. see POLITICAL SCIENCE — International Relations

DUPLEX PLANET. see FOLKLORE

DUQUESNE STUDIES. LANGUAGE AND LITERATURE SERIES. see LINGUISTICS

820 900   UK   ISSN 0012-7280
DURHAM UNIVERSITY JOURNAL. (Supplement avail.) 1876. 2/yr. £19 (foreign £22). University of Durham, School of English, Elvet Riverside, New Elvet, Dulham DH1 3JT, England. TEL 091-374-2744. Ed. P.E. Lewis. adv.; bk.rev.; index; circ. 500. (also avail. in microfilm from UMI; back issues avail.; reprint service avail. from UMI) **Indexed:** Abstr.Engl.Stud., Amer.Hist.& Life, Arts & Hum.Cit.Ind., Br.Archaeol.Abstr., Br.Hum.Ind., Curr.Cont., Hist.Abstr., Ind.Bk.Rev.Hum., M.L.A., Mid.East: Abstr.& Ind.
—BLDSC shelfmark: 3632.450000.
Description: Articles of academic interest on the arts, humanities, philosophy and Christian theology and church history.

DYSKUSJA. see ETHNIC INTERESTS

E A C R O T A N A L INFORMATION. (Eastern African Centre for Research on Oral Traditions and African National Languages) see LINGUISTICS

E A C R O T A N A L STUDIES & DOCUMENTS. (Eastern African Centre for Research on Oral Traditions and African National Languages) see LINGUISTICS

810 US ISSN 1054-3376
▼E L F. (Eclectic Literary Forum) 1991. 4/yr. $12 (foreign $20). E L F Associates, Inc., Box 392, Tonawanda, NY 14150. Ed. Cynthia K. Erbes. adv.; circ. 4,000. (back issues avail.)
Description: Publishes contemporary, well-crafted short fiction, poetry and essays on literary themes, including native American folklore and other special features.

820 US ISSN 0013-8304
PR1
E L H. (English Literary History) 1931. q. $19.50 to individuals (foreign $30.50); institutions $63 (foreign $72.50). Johns Hopkins University Press, Journals Publishing Division, 701 W. 40th St., Ste. 275, Baltimore, MD 21211. TEL 410-516-6987. FAX 410-516-6998. Ed. Ronald Paulson. adv.; circ. 755. (also avail. in microform from UMI; reprint service avail. from UMI,KTO) Indexed: Abstr.Engl.Stud., Acad.Ind., Amer.Hist.& Life, Arts & Hum.Cit.Ind., Curr.Cont., Hist.Abstr., Hum.Ind., LCR, Leg.Cont, M.L.A.
—BLDSC shelfmark: 3730.650000.
Description: Presents studies that interpret the historical conditions affecting major works in English and American literature--from the creation of those works to their subsequent life and present status.

810 US ISSN 0093-8297
PS1629
E S Q; a journal of the American Renaissance. 1955. q. $15 to individuals; institutions $20. Washington State University Press, Pullman, WA 99164-5910. TEL 509-335-3518. FAX 509-335-8568. Ed. Robert C. McLean. bk.rev.; bibl.; charts; illus.; circ. 625. Indexed: Abstr.Engl.Stud., Amer.Hum.Ind., Arts & Hum.Cit.Ind., Curr.Cont., Ind.Bk.Rev.Hum., M.L.A.
—BLDSC shelfmark: 3811.662000.
Formerly: Emerson Society Quarterly.

830 GW ISSN 0073-2885
E.T.A. HOFFMANN-GESELLSCHAFT. MITTEILUNGEN. 1938. a. DM.35. E.T.A. Hoffmann-Gesellschaft, Wetzelstr. 19, 8600 Bamberg, Germany. bk.rev.; circ. 850. (reprint service avail. from SWZ)

800 US
EADS BRIDGE; a literary review. 1972. a. $4. St. Louis University, English Department, St. Louis, MO 63108. TEL 314-658-3010. Ed. Avis Meyer. circ. 500.
Description: Contains prose, poetry, short stories, essays and graphics.

810 US ISSN 0012-8163
PS501
EARLY AMERICAN LITERATURE. 1966. 3/yr. $16.50 to individuals; institutions $22; foreign $26. (University of North Carolina at Chapel Hill, Department of English) University of North Carolina Press, Box 2288, Chapel Hill, NC 27515-2288. TEL 919-966-3561. FAX 919-966-3829. (Co-sponsor: Modern Language Association of America) Ed. Philip Gura. adv.; bk.rev.; bibl.; cum. index; circ. 800. Indexed: Abstr.Engl.Stud., Amer.Hist.& Life, Amer.Hum.Ind., Arts & Hum.Cit.Ind., Curr.Cont., Hist.Abstr., Hum.Ind., M.L.A., Rel.Ind.One.
—BLDSC shelfmark: 3642.930000.
Refereed Serial

EARLY DRAMA, ART, AND MUSIC REVIEW. see THEATER

EARTH'S DAUGHTERS; a feminist arts periodical. see WOMEN'S INTERESTS

800 US
ECLECTIC. a. free. West Georgia College, Carrollton, GA 30118. TEL 404-836-6512. circ. 1,000.

700 CK ISSN 0012-9410
AP63
ECO; revista de la cultura de occidente. 1961. m. $22. Libreria Buchholz, Av. Jimenez de Quesada 8-40, Bogota, Colombia. Ed. J.G. Cobo Borda. bk.rev.; circ. 4,500. Indexed: Hisp.Amer.Per.Ind., M.L.A.

ECOLE PRATIQUE DES HAUTES ETUDES. CENTRE DE RECHERCHES SUR LE PORTUGAL DE LA RENAISSANCE. SERIES TEXTES. see HISTORY — History Of Europe

840 CN ISSN 0013-0729
ECRITS DU CANADA FRANCAIS. 1954. 3/yr. Can.$24 for 4 nos. c/o Paul Beaulieu, 5754 Deom, Montreal, Que. H3S 2N4, Canada. Ed.Bd. adv.; bk.rev.; bibl.; circ. 2,500. Indexed: Pt.de Rep. 91982-).

839.5 NO ISSN 0013-0818
PN9
EDDA; Scandinavian journal for literary research. (Text in English and Norwegian) 1914. q. $51 to individuals; institutions $77. Universitetsforlaget, P.O. Box 2959-Toeyen, N-0608 Oslo 1, Norway, Norway. (U.S. addr.: Publications Expediting Inc., 200 Meacham Ave., Elmont, NY 11003) Eds. Steinar Gimnes, Jorunn Hareide. adv.; bk.rev.; index; circ. 950. Indexed: Can.Rev.Comp.Lit, Ind.Bk.Rev.Hum.

890 US ISSN 0364-6505
PJ2
EDEBIYAT; a journal of Middle Eastern and comparative literature. 1976-1980; N.S. 1989. s-a. $20 to individuals (foreign $25); students $10. University of Pennsylvania, Middle East Center, 838 Williams Hall-CU, Philadelphia, PA 19104-6305. TEL 215-898-6335. Ed. William L. Hanaway. adv.; bk.rev.; index; circ. 300. (back issues avail.; reprint service avail. from ISI) Indexed: Arts & Hum.Cit.Ind., Curr.Cont., Ind.Islam., M.L.A.
—BLDSC shelfmark: 3659.772000.

398 PE
EDICIONES DEL PUEBLO. no.38, 1983. irreg. Universidad Nacional "Daniel Aleides Carron", Av. Guzman Blanco 465, Of.204, Lima, Peru.

301.412 800 US
EDITH WHARTON REVIEW. 1984. s-a. $10 to individuals; institutions $20; foreign $15. Edith Wharton Society, Department of English, Long Island University, Brooklyn, NY 11201. TEL 718-403-1050. Ed. Annette Zilversmit. adv.; bk.rev.; bibl.; circ. 450.
Formerly (until 1990): Edith Wharton Newsletter.

809 028.1 GW ISSN 0931-3079
PN162
EDITIO; internationales Jahrbuch fuer Editionswissenschaft. (Text in English, French and German) 1987. a. DM.96. (Arbeitsgemeinschaft fuer Germanistische Edition) Max Niemeyer Verlag, Postfach 2140, 7400 Tuebingen 1, Germany. TEL 7071-81104. FAX 07071-87419. Ed. Winfried Woesler. adv.; bk.rev.
Description: Covers essays and reviews on scholarly editing of works in literature and philosophy.

839 439 DK ISSN 0070-9069
EDITIONES ARNAMAGNAEANAE. SERIES A. (Text in Danish, English, German, Icelandic, Norwegian, Swedish) 1958. irreg. price varies. Arnamagnaean Commission, Njalsgade 76, DK-2300 Copenhagen S, Denmark. TEL 31-542211. (Dist. by: C.A. Reitzels Boghandel A-S, Noerregade 20, DK-1165 Copenhagen K, Denmark)
Description: Presents critical edititions, primarily of Old Norse-Icelandic, mediaeval literature.

839 439 DK ISSN 0070-9077
EDITIONES ARNAMAGNAEANAE. SERIES B. (Text in Danish, English, German, Icelandic, Norwegian, Swedish) 1960. irreg. price varies. Arnamagnaean Commission, Njalsgade 76, DK-2300 Copenhagen S, Denmark. TEL 31-542211. (Dist. by: C.A. Reitzels Boghandel A-S, Noerregade 20, DK-1165, Copenhagen K, Denmark)
Description: Presents critical editions, primarily of Old Norse-Icelandic, mediaeval literature.

839 DK ISSN 0070-9085
EDITIONES ARNAMAGNAEANAE. SUPPLEMENTUM. 1963. irreg. Arnamagnaean Commission, Njalsgade 76, DK-2300 Copenhagen S, Denmark. TEL 31-542211. (Dist. by: C.A. Reitzels Boghandel A-S, Noerregade 20, DK-1165 Copenhagen K, Denmark)
Description: Critical editions of primarily Old Norse-Icelandic, mediaeval literature.

EDITOR & PUBLISHER SYNDICATE DIRECTORY; annual directory of syndicate services. see JOURNALISM

800 US ISSN 1060-2658
PN6014
EDITOR'S CHOICE; fiction, poetry and art from the U.S. small press. 1980. biennial. $12 paperback; hardcover $18. Spirit That Moves Us Press, Inc., Box 820, Jackson Heights, NY 11372-0820. TEL 718-426-8788. Ed. Morty Sklar. bibl.; illus.; circ. 4,200. Indexed: Amer.Hum.Ind., Ind.Amer.Per.Verse.
Description: Selections from small literary presses and magazines, from nominations made by their editors.

800 US ISSN 1048-8596
THE EDWARDEAN. a. $19.95 to individuals; institutions $29.95. Edwin Mellen Press, 240 Portage Rd., Box 450, Lewiston, NY 14092. TEL 800-753-2788. FAX 716-754-4335. Ed. Richard Hall.
Description: Covers the studies of Jonathan Edwards.

890 SP
EGAN; suplemento de literatura, del boletin de la real sociedad vascongada de los amigo del pais. (Text in Basque) 1948. s-a. 90 ptas. Real Sociedad Vascongada de los Amigos del Pais, Po. Ramon Ma. de Lili, 6-4o, Izqda., Apdo. 992, 20002 San Sebastian, Spain. TEL 285577.

810 UK
EIGHTEEN NINETIES SOCIETY. JOURNAL. 1963. a. membership. Eighteen Nineties Society, 17 Meton Hall Rd., Wimbledon, London SW19 3PP, England. Ed. G. Krishnamurti. adv.; bk.rev.; circ. 750. (processed) Indexed: Abstr.Engl.Stud.
Formerly: Francis Thompson Society. Journal (ISSN 0532-5781)

800 CN ISSN 0840-6286
PN3495
EIGHTEENTH-CENTURY FICTION. 1988. q. Can.$30 to individuals; institutions Can.$48; students Can.$22. University of Toronto Press, Journals Department, P.O. Box 1280, 1011 Sheppard Ave. W., Downsview, Ont. M3H 5H4, Canada. (U.S. Addr.: 340 Nagel Dr., Cheektowaga, NY 14225) Ed. David Blewett. adv.; illus.
—BLDSC shelfmark: 3665.227300.

EIGHTEENTH CENTURY LIFE. see HISTORY — History Of Europe

EIGHTEENTH-CENTURY STUDIES. see HISTORY

EIGHTEENTH CENTURY: THEORY AND INTERPRETATION. see HISTORY — History Of Europe

EIRE - IRELAND; a journal of Irish studies. see HUMANITIES: COMPREHENSIVE WORKS

800 FR ISSN 0013-4066
ELAN; poetique, litteraire et pacifiste. 1955. q. 50 F.($7) Louis Lippens, Ed. & Pub., 31 rue Foch, 59126 Linselles, France. bk.rev.; abstr.; bibl.; illus. (also avail. in microfilm from KTO) Indexed: Excerp.Med.

800 841 FR ISSN 0397-0051
ELAN POETIQUE LITTERAIRE ET PACIFISTE. 1955. q. 50 Fr.($7) Elan Poerique Litteraire et Pacifiste, 31 rue Foch, F-59126 Linselles, France. TEL 20-03.48.59. Ed. Louis Lippens.

800 US
ELDERLY IN THE LITERATURES OF THE GERMAN-SPEAKING COUNTRIES. irreg. Peter Lang Publishing, Inc., 62 W. 45th St., 4th Fl., New York, NY 10036. TEL 212-302-6740. FAX 212-302-7574. Ed. Gerd K. Schneider.

ELEMENTS. see ART

810 US
ELEPHANT-EAR. 1983. a. Irvine Valley College, School of Humanities, 5500 Irvine Center Dr., Irvine, CA 92720. TEL 714-559-9300. Ed. Linda Thomas. circ. 2,500.

808 CN
ELIXIR. a. Glendon College, Student Union, 2275 Bayview Ave., Toronto, Ont. M4N 3M6, Canada. TEL 416-487-6720. adv.; circ. 2,000.

LITERATURE

820   AU
ELIZABETHAN AND RENAISSANCE STUDIES. (Text in English) 1972. irreg., no.110, 1991. S.245. Universitaet Salzburg, Institut fuer Englische Sprache, Akademiestr. 24, A-5020 Salzburg, Austria. Ed. James Hogg. circ. 250. **Indexed:** M.L.A.

810   US   ISSN 0160-7545
PS3513.L34
ELLEN GLASGOW NEWSLETTER. 1974. s-a. membership. Ellen Glasgow Society, c/o Prof. Beverly Baker, 1004 Ridge Top Rd., Richmond, VA 23229. bk.rev.; bibl.; circ. 200. **Indexed:** M.L.A.

800   CN   ISSN 0046-1830
PR9194
ELLIPSE. (Text in English and French) 1969. 2/yr. Can.$10 to individuals; institutions Can.$12. Universite de Sherbrooke, Faculte des Lettres et Sciences Humaines, Box 10, Sherbrooke, Que. J1K 2R1, Canada. TEL 819-821-7277. Eds. Charly Bouchara, Patricia Godbout. adv.; bibl.; circ. 750. (also avail. in microform from MML,UMI; reprint service avail. from UMI) **Indexed:** Amer.Hum.Ind., Can.Lit.Ind., Pt.de Rep. (1982-).

800   US   ISSN 1040-1644
ELLIPSIS...; literature with a certain twist. 1988. s-a. $24 (foreign $32). Ellipsis Press, 105-A N. Santa Cruz Ave., Los Gatos, CA 95030. TEL 408-354-1481. FAX 408-354-1463. Ed. Joy Oestreicher. circ. 500. (back issues avail.)
Description: Devoted to literature reflecting the human condition, with a humorous twist.

800   US
EMPIRE!; the N Y State inmate literary arts journal. 1984. a. free. Department of Correctional Services, c/o Paul Gordon, Ed., Arthur Kill Correctional Facility, 2911 Arthur Kill Rd., Staten Island, NY 10309. TEL 718-356-7333. bk.rev.; circ. 5,000. (back issues avail.)

EMPORIA STATE RESEARCH STUDIES. see HISTORY — History Of North And South America

809.02   US   ISSN 0363-4841
PN661
ENCOMIA; bibliographical bulletin of the International Courtly Literature Society. 1975. a. $12. International Courtly Literature Society, c/o Dhira B. Mahoney, Sec.-Treas., Department of English, Arizona State University, Tempe, AZ 85287-0302. Ed. Maria Dobozy. adv.; bk.rev.; illus.; circ. 900. **Indexed:** M.L.A.
—BLDSC shelfmark: 3738.523000.

800   US   ISSN 0071-0164
ENCORE (BLACKSBURG). 1948. a. $2. National Association of Dramatic and Speech Arts, 255 Lane Hall, Virginia Tech University, Blacksburg, VA 24061. TEL 703-231-5812. Ed. H.D. Flowers, II. adv.; bk.rev.; circ. 2,000. (also avail. in microform from UMI; reprint service avail. from UMI) **Indexed:** Mag.Ind.
Description: Scholarly and creative writing about black theater and rhetoric.

051   CN   ISSN 1180-5331
▼**ENCYCLOPEDIA BANANICA.** 1990. 2/yr. $4 per no. Banana Productions, P.O. Box 3655, Vancouver, B.C. V6B 3Y8, Canada. TEL 604-876-6764.
Description: Publishes all types of material focusing on the banana, including news, poetry, satirical pieces, artwork, and language usage.

820   UK   ISSN 0013-8215
PR5
ENGLISH. 1935. 3/yr. £25($60) (foreign £33). English Association, The Vicarage, Priory Gardens, Bedford Park, London W4 1TT, England. Eds. Michael Baron, Peter Barry. adv.; bk.rev. (also avail. in microform from UMI; reprint service avail. from UMI) **Indexed:** Abstr.Engl.Stud., Arts & Hum.Cit.Ind., Br.Hum.Ind., Curr.Cont., Ind.Bk.Rev.Hum., Lang.& Lang.Behav.Abstr.
—BLDSC shelfmark: 3772.600000.
Description: Journal of literary criticism, publishing essays and reviews, aimed at readers in all forms of higher education, but in a style intelligible to all.

800 370   SA
ENGLISH ACADEMY REVIEW. (Text in English) a. R.18 (foreign R.28). English Academy of South Africa, P.O. Box 124, 2050 Wits, South Africa. TEL 011-716-3683. Ed. Ivan Rabinowitz. adv.; bk.rev.; play rev.; circ. 1,100. (back issues avail.)
Description: Contains South African literature, language and education, and creative writing.

807   UK
ENGLISH AND MEDIA MAGAZINE. 1979. s-a. £10.50 to individuals; institutions and foreign £21 (for 3 nos.). English Centre, Ebury Teachers Centre, Sutherland St., London SW1V 4LH, England. TEL 071-828-8560. FAX 071-821-6541. Ed. Michael Simons. adv.; bk.rev.; circ. 7,000. (back issues avail.)
Formerly: English Magazine (ISSN 0144-6487)

830   UK
ENGLISH GOETHE SOCIETY. PUBLICATIONS. 1886; N.S. 1972. a. $22. English Goethe Society, University College, Gower St., London W.C.1., England. Ed. Prof. F.M. Fowler. circ. 500.

810   US   ISSN 0013-8282
PE1
ENGLISH LANGUAGE NOTES. 1963. q. $20 to individuals; institutions $40; foreign $27. University of Colorado, English Language Notes, Box 226, Boulder, CO 80309. TEL 303-492-7176. Ed. J. Wallace Donald. adv.; bk.rev.; bibl.; index; circ. 1,222. (back issues avail; reprints avail.) **Indexed:** Abstr.Engl.Stud., Arts & Hum.Cit.Ind., Can.Rev.Comp.Lit, Curr.Cont., Hum.Ind., Ind.Bk.Rev.Hum., M.L.A., Ref.Sour.
—BLDSC shelfmark: 3775.040000.

820   US   ISSN 0013-8312
PR1
ENGLISH LITERARY RENAISSANCE. 1971. 3/yr. $20 to individuals; libraries $25. University of Massachusetts, Department of English, Amherst, MA 01003. TEL 413-545-0372. Ed. Arthur F. Kinney. adv.; bibl.; circ. 1,000. **Indexed:** Abstr.Engl.Stud., Amer.Hist.& Life, Amer.Hum.Ind., Arts & Hum.Cit.Ind., Curr.Cont., Hist.Abstr., M.L.A.
—BLDSC shelfmark: 3775.065000.
Description: Provides scholarly and critical essays, bibliographies and primary texts of English literary works written in England between 1485-1668. Including studies of the cultural and intellectual background of those texts.

820   US   ISSN 0364-3549
PR1
ENGLISH LITERATURE IN TRANSITION (1880-1920). 1957. q. $16. Robert Langenfeld, Ed. & Pub., Department of English, University of North Carolina, Greensboro, NC 27412-5001. TEL 919-334-5446. FAX 919-334-3281. Ed. Robert Langenfeld. adv.; bk.rev.; bibl.; cum.index: 1957-1972, 1973-1982; circ. 900. (also avail. in microform from JAI,MIM,UMI; reprint service avail. from UMI,KTO; back issues avail.) **Indexed:** Abstr.Engl.Stud., Arts & Hum.Cit.Ind., Bk.Rev.Ind. (1991-), Child.Bk.Rev.Ind. (1991-), Curr.Cont., Hum.Ind., Ind.Bk.Rev.Hum., M.L.A.
Formerly: English Fiction in Transition (ISSN 0013-8339)
Description: Contains essays and reviews fiction, poetry and culture in British literature.

080 800   UK   ISSN 0071-061X
ENGLISH LITTLE MAGAZINES. 1967. irreg., no.16, 1971. price varies. Frank Cass & Co. Ltd., Gainsborough House, 11 Gainsborough Rd., London E11 1RS, England. TEL 081-530-4226. FAX 081-530-7795. (Dist. in U.S. by: ISBS, 5602 N.E. Hassalo St., Portland, OR 97213-3640)

ENGLISH QUARTERLY. see EDUCATION — Teaching Methods And Curriculum

ENGLISH STUDIES; a journal of English language and literature. see LINGUISTICS

ENGLISH STUDIES IN AFRICA; a journal of the humanities. see HUMANITIES: COMPREHENSIVE WORKS

820   CN   ISSN 0317-0802
ENGLISH STUDIES IN CANADA. 1975. q. $45 to non-members. Association of Canadian University Teachers of English, Department of English, Carleton University, Ottawa, Ont. K1S 5B6, Canada. TEL 613-788-2317. FAX 613-788-2317. Ed. D.J. Wurtele. bk.rev.; circ. 1,000. **Indexed:** Arts & Hum.Cit.Ind., Can.Lit.Ind., Curr.Cont., Ind.Bk.Rev.Hum., M.L.A.
—BLDSC shelfmark: 3775.121000.

L'ENNEMI. see ART

860   UY   ISSN 0071-0679
ENSAYO Y TESTIMONIO.* irreg. Editorial Arca, Colonia 1263, Montevideo, Uruguay.

891 410   FR   ISSN 0300-2608
ENSEIGNEMENT DU RUSSE. 1968. s-a. price varies. Institut d'Etudes Slaves, 9 rue Michelet, F-75006 Paris, France. (Co-sponsor: Societe des Professeurs de Russe) Ed.Bd. bk.rev.; bibl.; circ. 700.

809 940   US   ISSN 0897-4888
ENVOI; a review journal of Medieval literature. 1988. s-a. $55. (Columbia University, Department of English and Comparative Literature) A M S Press, Inc., 56 E. 13th St., New York, NY 10003. TEL 212-777-4700. FAX 212-995-5143. Ed. Paul Spillenger.
Description: Essays and notices of scholarly books relating to medieval studies with emphasis on medieval literature.

800   US
EOTU. 1988. bi-m. $24 (foreign $25). 1810 W. State St., Ste. 115, Boise, ID 83702. FAX 208-342-4996. Ed. Larry D. Dennis. illus.; circ. 500.
Description: Features experimental fiction, art work and short stories.

700   PY   ISSN 0013-9726
EPOCA;* revista de cultura. vol.5, 1968. bi-m. 180 g.($5). Natalicio Talavera No. 336, Asuncion, Paraguay. Ed. Emilio Perez Chaves. bk.rev.; bibl. **Indexed:** Chic. Per.Ind.

810   US   ISSN 0145-1391
AP2
EPOCH (ITHACA); a magazine of contemporary literature. 1947. 3/yr. $11. Cornell University, 251 Goldwin Smith Hall, Ithaca, NY 14853. TEL 607-255-3385. Ed. Michael Koch. adv.; bk.rev.; cum.index every 2 yrs.; circ. 1,100. (also avail. in microform from UMI; reprint service avail. from UMI) **Indexed:** A.I.P.P., Arts & Hum.Cit.Ind., Ind.Amer.Per.Verse, Ind.Bk.Rev.Hum.

800 900   IT   ISSN 0394-5618
ERBA D'ARNO. 1980. q. L.30000 (foreign L.50000). Erba d'Arno, Via Castruccio 1, 50054 Fucecchio (Florence), Italy. TEL 0571-242093. Ed. Piero Malvolti. adv.; bk.rev.; cum.index; circ. 2,000. (back issues avail.)
Description: Covers historical research.

800 900   IT   ISSN 1120-4923
ERBA D'ARNO. QUADERNI; supplemento a Erba d'Arno. 1986. a. L.10000. Erba d'Arno, Via Castruccio 1, 50054 Fucecchio (Florence), Italy. TEL 0571-242093. Ed. Piero Malvolti. circ. 700.

800   IE
ERIU; journal devoted to Irish philology and literature. 1904. a. Royal Irish Academy, 19 Dawson St., Dublin 2, Ireland. TEL 01-762570. FAX 01-762346. Ed.Bd. **Indexed:** M.L.A.

800 700   AU   ISSN 0014-0252
EROEFFNUNGEN; Magazin fuer Literatur & bildende Kunst. (Text mainly in German; with English or Slovene) 1961. q. S.50. Hubert F. Kulterer, Ed. & Pub., Unter-Meidlinger Str. 16-18, A-1120 Vienna, Austria. adv.; illus.; play rev.; circ. 1,500.

808   US   ISSN 0887-5057
EROTIC FICTION QUARTERLY; a journal of erotic & other sexual fiction. 1985. irreg. $9.95 per no. E F Q Publications, Box 424958, San Francisco, CA 94142-4958. Ed. Richard Hiller. circ. 1,000.

ERTONG XIAOSHUO/SHORT STORIES FOR CHILDREN. see CHILDREN AND YOUTH — For

LITERATURE 2915

| 800 741.5 | UK | ISSN 0266-1667 |

ESCAPE. 1983. bi-m. £13.80($22) Escape Publishing, 156 Munster Rd., London SW6 5RA, England. Ed. Paul Gravett. film rev.; illus.; circ. 5,000. (back issues avail.)

| 860 100 | CK | ISSN 0120-1263 |

ESCRITOS. 1974. s-a. $1.50 per no. Universidad Pontificia Bolivariana, Escuela de Educacio y Humanidades, Biblioteca Central - Seccion Canje, Aptdo. 1178, Medellin, Colombia. TEL 2498957. FAX 2396683. TELEX 65047. Ed. Bernardo Lopera. adv.; bk.rev.; bibl.; circ. 1,000.

| 860 | VE | ISSN 1011-7989 |

ESCRITURA: TEORIA Y CRITICA LITERARIAS. 1976. s-a. $15 to individuals; institutions $35. Universidad Central de Venezuela, Consejo de Desarrollo Cientifico y Humanistico, Apdo. 65603, Caracas 1066-A, Venezuela. Ed. Rafael Di Prisco. adv.; bk.rev.; circ. 1,000.
 Description: Contains essays and study on theory and literary criticism with special emphasis on Latin American literature.

| 830 | AU | |

ESELSOHR.* 2/yr. G. Pilz, Stifterstrasse 4a, A-4320 Perg, Austria. illus.

| 840 | US | ISSN 0014-0767 |

ESPRIT CREATEUR; a critical quarterly of French literature. (Text in English and French) 1961. 4/yr. $17 to individuals; institutions $30. Esprit Createur, Inc., Box 25333, Baton Rouge, LA 70894. TEL 504-388-6713. Ed. John D. Erickson. adv.; bk.rev.; index; circ. 1,100. (also avail. in microfilm from UMI; reprint service avail. from UMI; back issues avail.) **Indexed:** Amer.Hum.Ind., Arts & Hum.Cit.Ind., Bk.Rev.Ind. (1980-), Child.Bk.Rev.Ind. (1980-), Curr.Cont., M.L.A.
 —BLDSC shelfmark: 3811.660200.

| 824 PR13 | US | ISSN 0071-1357 |

ESSAYS AND STUDIES. 1910. a. price varies. Humanities Press, 165 First Ave., Atlantic Highlands, NJ 07716-1289. TEL 908-872-1441. FAX 908-872-0717. **Indexed:** Abstr.Engl.Stud., Br.Hum.Ind., M.L.A.

| 808 PN22 | US | ISSN 0261-216X |

ESSAYS BY DIVERS HANDS. 1825. a. price varies. (Royal Society of Literature, UK) Boydell & Brewer, Box 41026, Rochester, NY 14604. TEL 716-275-0419. FAX 716-271-8778. **Indexed:** Abstr.Engl.Stud., M.L.A.

| 809 PR1 | UK | ISSN 0014-0856 |

ESSAYS IN CRITICISM; a quarterly journal of literary criticism. 1951. q. £68. Stephen Wall, Ed. & Pub., 6A Rawlinson Rd., Oxford OX2 6UE, England. adv.; bk.rev.; index, cum.index; circ. 2,250. (also avail. in microfilm from MIM,UMI; back issues avail.; reprint service avail. from SWZ,UMI) **Indexed:** Abstr.Engl.Stud., Acad.Ind., Arts & Hum.Cit.Ind., Br.Hum.Ind., Curr.Cont., Hum.Ind., Ind.Bk.Rev.Hum., M.L.A.
 —BLDSC shelfmark: 3811.690000.

| 800 PR6013.R44 | US | ISSN 0738-0763 |

ESSAYS IN GRAHAM GREENE; an annual review. 1987. a. $20. Penkevill Publishing Company, Box 212, Greenwood, FL 32443. TEL 904-569-2811. Ed. Peter Wolfe.

| 809 PN2 | US | ISSN 0094-5404 |

ESSAYS IN LITERATURE. 1974. s-a. $8 to individuals; institutions $10 (effective Jan. 1992). Western Illinois University, Department of English, Macomb, IL 61455. TEL 309-298-2212. Ed. Thomas P. Joswick. bibl.; rev. 600. **Indexed:** Abstr.Engl.Stud., Amer.Bibl.Slavic & E.Eur.Stud., Arts & Hum.Cit.Ind., Curr.Cont., LCR, M.L.A.
 —BLDSC shelfmark: 3811.699000.

| 800 PN2 | UK | ISSN 0308-888X |

ESSAYS IN POETICS. 1976. s-a. £13.50 to individuals (foreign £17.50); institutions £19.50 (£24). (British Neo-Formalist Circle) Drake Marketing Services Ltd., Market House, Market Place, Deddington, Oxford OX5 4SW, England. TEL 0869-38087. FAX 0869-37123. (Co-publisher: Oxon Publishers) Eds. J.M. Andrew, C.R. Pike. adv.; bk.rev.; circ. 300. **Indexed:** Arts & Hum.Cit.Ind., Curr.Cont., M.L.A.
 —BLDSC shelfmark: 3811.781000.

| 820 PR9180 | CN | ISSN 0316-0300 |

ESSAYS ON CANADIAN WRITING. (Text in English) 1974. 3/yr. Can.$20 to individuals; institutions Can.$40 (effective Jan. 1991). Canadian Literary Research Foundation, 307 Coxwell Ave., Toronto, Ont. M4L 3B5, Canada. TEL 416-694-3348. FAX 416-698-9906. Ed.Bd. adv.; bk.rev.; circ. 1,000. (also avail. in microfilm) **Indexed:** Abstr.Engl.Stud., Amer.Hum.Ind., Bk.Rev.Ind. (1980-), Can.Lit.Ind., Can.Per.Ind., Child.Bk.Rev.Ind. (1980-), CMI, Ind.Bk.Rev.Hum., M.L.A.
 —BLDSC shelfmark: 3811.678000.

ESSAYS ON FANTASTIC LITERATURE. see LITERATURE — Science Fiction, Fantasy, Horror

| 800 | US | ISSN 0071-1470 |

ESSENTIAL ARTICLES. 1961. irreg., no.11, 1985. price varies. Shoe String Press, Inc., 925 Sherman Ave., Hamden, CT 06514.
 Description: Anthologies of articles essential to the study of various periods and authors in the field of literature.

ESTRENO; journal on the contemporary Spanish theater. see THEATER

ESTUDIOS; revista trimestral publicada por los fraile de la orden de la merced. see RELIGIONS AND THEOLOGY

| 860 | MX | ISSN 0071-1691 |

ESTUDIOS DE LITERATURA. 1958. irreg., latest 1983. price varies. Universidad Nacional Autonoma de Mexico, Instituto de Investigaciones Esteticas, Circuito Mtro. Mario de la Cueva, Zona Cultural, Ciudad de la Investigacion en Humanidades, 04000 Mexico, D.F., Mexico.

| 860 | SP | ISSN 0071-1705 |

ESTUDIOS DE LITERATURA CONTEMPORANEA. 1968. irreg. price varies, $3-$5. Real Academia Espanola de la Lengua, Universidad de Santiago de Compostela, Coruna, Spain. circ. 2,000.

ESTUDIOS FILOLOGICOS. see LINGUISTICS

| 800 | BL | |

ESTUDOS BAIANOS. 1970. irreg. Cr.$290. Universidade Federal da Bahia, Centro Editorial e Didatico, Rua A. Viana s/n, Canela, Salvador, Bahia, Brazil. Ed.Bd. circ. 1,000.

| 830 PB5 | BL | ISSN 0101-837X |

ESTUDOS GERMANICOS. (Two annual issues: one on literature, and one on language) 1980. s-a. $1. Universidade Federal de Minas Gerais, Departamento de Letras Germanicas, Campus Pampulha, Av. Antonio Carlos, 6627, 30000 Belo Horizonte, Minas Gerais, Brazil. Ed. Julio Yeha. bk.rev.; circ. 1,000.
 —BLDSC shelfmark: 3813.064000.

ESTUDOS ITALIANOS EM PORTUGAL. see ART

ESTUDOS PORTUGUESES E AFRICANOS. see SOCIAL SCIENCES: COMPREHENSIVE WORKS

| 820 PR1 | FR | ISSN 0014-195X |

ETUDES ANGLAISES. (Text in English, French) 1937. q. $70. Didier Erudition, 6 rue de la Sorbonne, 75005 Paris, France. (Subscr. to: Didier Erudition, North American Fulfillment Office, P.O. Box 830350, Birmingham, AL 35283-0350, U.S.A.) Ed. S. Soupel. bk.rev.; bibl.; illus.; index; circ. 1,500. (processed; also avail. in microfilm from SWZ; reprint service avail. from SWZ) **Indexed:** Abstr.Engl.Stud., Arts & Hum.Cit.Ind., Curr.Cont., Ind.Bk.Rev.Hum., M.L.A.
 —BLDSC shelfmark: 3816.760000.

ETUDES BALKANIQUES. see HISTORY — History Of Europe

| 840 | SZ | ISSN 0531-9455 |

ETUDES BAUDELAIRIENNES. 1970. irreg., no.13, 1991. price varies. Editions de la Baconniere S.A., Box 185, CH-2017 Boudry, Switzerland. TEL 038-421004. Eds. Marc Eigeldinger, Claude Pichois. (reprint service avail. from UMI)

| 800 | SZ | ISSN 0014-2026 |

ETUDES DE LETTRES. 1926. 4/yr. 60 Fr. Universite de Lausanne, Faculte des Lettres, Batiment Central, CH-1015 Lausanne, Switzerland. Ed. Doris Jakubec. bk.rev.; bibl.; circ. 700. **Indexed:** Abstr.Engl.Stud., M.L.A.

| 400 900 | SZ | ISSN 0071-1934 |

ETUDES DE PHILOLOGIE ET D'HISTOIRE. (Text in English, French) 1967. irreg., no.45, 1991. price varies. Librairie Droz S.A., 11, rue Massot, CH-1211 Geneva 12, Switzerland. TEL 022-466666. FAX 022-472391.

ETUDES FINNO-OUGRIENNES. see LINGUISTICS

| 840 440 | CN | ISSN 0014-2085 |

ETUDES FRANCAISES. (Including section bibliographique) (Text in French) 1965. 3/yr. Can.$21 to individuals; institutions Can.$36. Presses de l'Universite de Montreal, C.P. 6128, Succ. A, Montreal, Que. H3C 3J7, Canada. TEL 514-343-6933. Ed. Robert Melancon. adv.; bk.rev.; bibl.; index; circ. 1,000. (also avail. in microform from MIM,UMI; reprint service avail. from UMI) **Indexed:** Amer.Hist.& Life, Arts & Hum.Cit.Ind., Can.Lit.Ind., Curr.Cont., Hist.Abstr., M.L.A., Pt.de Rep. (1979-).
 —BLDSC shelfmark: 3819.530000.

| 830 DD1 | FR | ISSN 0014-2115 |

ETUDES GERMANIQUES. 1946. q. $70. Didier Erudition, 6 rue de la Sorbonne, 75005 Paris, France. (Subscr. to: Didier Erudition, North American Fullfillment Office, P.O. Box 830350, Birmingham, AL 35283-0350, U.S.A.) Ed.Bd. adv.; bk.rev.; charts; index; circ. 2,000. (also avail. in microform from SWZ; reprint service avail. from SWZ) **Indexed:** Arts & Hum.Cit.Ind., Can.Rev.Comp.Lit, Curr.Cont., M.L.A.
 —BLDSC shelfmark: 3819.980000.

ETUDES IRLANDAISES; revue bilingue d'histoire, civilisation et litterature irlandaises. see HISTORY — History Of Europe

| 800 PQ2 | CN | ISSN 0014-214X |

ETUDES LITTERAIRES. 1968. 3/yr. Can.$22 to individuals (foreign Can.$26); institutions Can.$36. Presses de l'Universite Laval, Cite universitaire, Quebec, Que. G1K 7P4, Canada. TEL 418-656-3809. FAX 413-656-2600. Ed. Louise Francoeur. bk.rev. (also avail. in microfilm from UMI; reprint service avail. from UMI) **Indexed:** Arts & Hum.Cit.Ind., Can.Lit.Ind., Can.Rev.Comp.Lit, Curr.Cont., Ind.Bk.Rev.Hum., M.L.A., Pt.de Rep. (1979-).
 —BLDSC shelfmark: 3820.776000.
 Description: Each issue devoted to a writer, theme or genre and consists of studiesand unedited or little known documents.

| 840 | BE | |

ETUDES NERVALIENNES ET ROMANTIQUES. (Text in French) 1978. a. 350 BEF. Presses Universitaires de Namur, 8 Rempart de la Vierge, 5000 Namur, Belgium. FAX 32-19-23-03-91. TELEX 59222 FACNAM B. Ed. Pierre Rummens. bk.rev.; circ. 750. (back issues avail.)
 Description: Connected with the publication of the complete works of Gerard de Nerval.

| 840 | SZ | |

ETUDES RABELAISIENNES. (Text in English, French, German, Italian, Spanish) 1956. irreg., vol.24, 1991. price varies. Librairie Droz S.A., 11 rue Massot, CH-1211 Geneva 12, Switzerland. FAX 22-472391. circ. 800. **Indexed:** M.L.A.
 Description: Presents studies on the life and work of Francois Rabelais.

ETUDES ROMANES DE LUND. see LINGUISTICS

L

2916 LITERATURE

800   FR
ETUDES SUR LES MONDES HISPANOPHONES. no.5, 1965. biennial. price varies. Universite de Rennes II (Universite de Haute Bretagne), 6 Ave. Gaston Berger, 35043 Rennes, France. Ed.Bd. adv.; bk.rev.; circ. 500.
Former titles: Mondes Hispanophone et Lusophone (ISSN 0761-2397); Universite de Haute Bretagne. Centre d'Etudes Hispaniques, Hispano-Americaines et Luso-Bresiliennes. Travaux (ISSN 0080-0929)

800   US   ISSN 0146-7220
PS3545.E6
EUDORA WELTY NEWSLETTER. 1977. s-a. $2 (foreign $3). University of Toledo, Department of English, 2801 W. Bancroft, Toledo, OH 43606. TEL 419-537-2318. Ed. W.U. McDonald, Jr. bibl.; cum.index: 1977-1986; circ. 165. (back issues avail.) **Indexed:** Amer.Hum.Ind., LCR, M.L.A.
Description: Provides checklists of Eudora Welty's writing and of secondary materials, information about scholarly works in progress and forthcoming, and bibliographical notes on Welty texts, unrecorded appearances, and location of rare copies or editions.

810   US   ISSN 1040-9483
PS3529.N5
EUGENE O'NEILL REVIEW. 1977. 2/yr. $10 to individuals; institutions and foreign $15. Suffolk University, Department of English, c/o Frederick Wilkins, Ed., Boston, MA 02114. TEL 617-573-8272. adv.; bk.rev.; play rev.; abstr.; bibl.; index; circ. 550. (back issues avail.) **Indexed:** Abstr.Engl.Stud., LCR, M.L.A.
Formerly (until 1989): Eugene O'Neill Newsletter (ISSN 0733-0456)
Description: Essays on the life and works of Eugene O'Neill; reviews of his plays; news, letters and comments of interest to O'Neillians.

830 398   GW   ISSN 0531-2159
PT941.E9
EULENSPIEGEL-JAHRBUCH. 1960. a. DM.36. Verlag Peter Lang GmbH, Eschborner Landstr. 42-50, 6000 Frankfurt a.M. 90, Germany. TEL 069-7807050. FAX 069-785893. (Subscr. to: Dieter Scheller, Rathaus, 3307 Schoeppenstedt, Germany) Ed. Werner Wunderlich. adv.; bk.rev.; circ. 600. (back issues avail.)

809   GW   ISSN 0014-2328
PN4
EUPHORION; Zeitschrift fuer Literaturgeschichte. 1894. 4/yr. DM.135 (students DM.110). Carl Winter Universitaetsverlag GmbH, Lutherstr. 59, 6900 Heidelberg, Germany. Ed. Rainer Gruenter. adv.; bk.rev.; index; circ. 1,100. (reprint service avail. from KTO) **Indexed:** Arts & Hum.Cit.Ind., Can.Rev.Comp.Lit, Curr.Cont.
—BLDSC shelfmark: 3827.700000.

840   FR   ISSN 0046-2667
EUREKA.* 1971. m. c/o Jean LaPlace, Ed., 10 rue Kuss, 75013 Paris, France. bk.rev.

800 920   NE
EUROPEAN JOYCE STUDIES. 1989. a. price varies. Editions Rodopi B.V., Keizersgracht 302-304, 1016 EX Amsterdam, Netherlands. TEL 020-6227507. FAX 020-6380948. (US and Canada Subscr. to: 233 Peachtree St., N.E., Ste. 404, Atlanta, GA 30303-1504. TEL 800-225-3998) Eds. Christine van Boheemen, Fritz Senn.
Description: Offers "European" perspectives on James Joyce's works, their adaptations, annotations, and translations; studies in biography as well as current debates in criticism and Joyce's place in literary history.

800   US
▼**EUROPEAN ROMANTIC REVIEW.** 1990. s-a. $14 to individuals; institutions $22. Box 67885, Los Angeles, CA 90067. Ed. Frederick Burwick. bk.rev.

EUROPEAN STUDIES. see HISTORY — History Of Europe

800   US
PR6045.A97
EVELYN WAUGH NEWSLETTER AND STUDIES. 1967. 3/yr. $8. Evelyn Waugh Society, Nassau Community College, State University of New York, Department of English, Garden City, NY 11530. TEL 516-222-7187. Ed. Paul A. Doyle. adv.; bk.rev.; circ. 201. **Indexed:** Abstr.Engl.Stud., Amer.Hum.Ind., M.L.A.
Formerly (until Apr. 1990): Evelyn Waugh Newsletter (ISSN 0014-3693)
Description: Encourages research in the writings of Evelyn Waugh.

800   CN   ISSN 0315-3770
EVENT. 1971. 3/yr. Can.$13. Douglas College, P.O. Box 2503, New Westminster, B.C. V3L 5B2, Canada. TEL 604-527-5293. FAX 604-527-5095. Ed. Dale Zieroth. adv.; bk.rev.; circ. 1,000. (also avail. in microform from MML; back issues avail.; reprint service avail. from ISI) **Indexed:** Arts & Hum.Cit.Ind., Can.Lit.Ind.
Description: Presents reviews, fiction, poetry and visuals.

EVENTI E INTERVENTI. see ART

800   US   ISSN 1043-3333
EVERGREEN CHRONICLES; a journal of gay and lesbian literature. 1985. s-a. $15 to individuals; institutions $20. Box 8939, Minneapolis, MN 55408-0939. TEL 612-871-2547. Ed. James Berg. adv.; bk.rev.; circ. 400. (back issues avail.)
Description: Presents the works of lesbian and gay literary and visual artists.

801   PR
EXEGESIS. 1986. 3/yr. $12. Universidad de Puerto Rico, Colegio Universitario de Humacao, Humacao, PR 00791. TEL 809-850-0000. Ed. Marcos Reyes. bk.rev.; circ. 1,500.

809   US   ISSN 1041-2573
PN661
EXEMPLARIA; a journal of theory in Medieval and Renaissance studies. 1989. s-a. $20 to individuals; institutions $35. Medieval and Rennaissance Texts and Studies, LNG 99, State University of New York, Binghamton, NY 13902-6000. Ed. R.A. Shoaf. adv.; circ. 325.
—BLDSC shelfmark: 3836.227200.
Description: Concerns with both theoretical and experimental approaches to medieval and renaissance culture.
Refereed Serial

709   UK
EXETER STUDIES IN AMERICAN & COMMONWEALTH ARTS. 1970. irreg. (1-2/yr.). $10. University of Exeter, Centre for American & Commonwealth Arts, Queens Bldg., Exeter EX 4QH, England. FAX 0392-263108. Ed. R. Maltby. circ. 2,000.
Formerly: American Arts Pamphlet Series.

800   CN
EXILE. 1972. q. $25. Exile Editions Ltd., 69 Sullivan, Toronto, Ont., Canada. TEL 416-977-7937. Ed. Barry Callaghan. circ. 1,200. (also avail. in microfiche) **Indexed:** Arts & Hum.Cit.Ind., Curr.Cont.
Description: Publishes poetry, plays, novels, stories, drawings and paintings.

810   US   ISSN 0421-9090
EXILE; contemporary literature. 1953. biennial. Denison University, Granville, OH 43023. TEL 614-587-0810. illus. (also avail. in microfiche from BHP) **Indexed:** Arts & Hum.Cit.Ind., Curr.Cont.

800   US   ISSN 0195-3516
EXIT; a journal of the arts. 1976. irreg. $7 for 3 nos. Rochester Routes - Creative Arts Projects, 50 Inglewood Dr., Rochester, NY 14619. Eds. Frank Judge, Gregory FitzGerald. adv.; circ. 2,000.
Formerly: Entrance.

808.81   US   ISSN 1054-3937
EXIT 13 MAGAZINE. 1981. a. $5. Tom Plante Ed. & Pub., 22 Oakwood Ct., Fanwood, NJ 07023. TEL 908-889-5298. adv.; bk.rev.; circ. 500. (back issues avail.)
Formerly (until no.4, 1986): Berkeley Works.
Description: Poetic overview of contemporary life, with a strong focus on geography, travel, adventure and nature.

860   US   ISSN 0361-9621
PQ6001
EXPLICACION DE TEXTOS LITERARIOS. (Text in Spanish) 1972. s-a. $12 to individuals; libraries $20. California State University, Sacramento, Department of Foreign Languages, 6000 J St., Sacramento, CA 95819. TEL 916-454-6011. Ed. Jorge A. Santana. adv.; bk.rev.; cum.index; circ. 1,000. **Indexed:** Arts & Hum.Cit.Ind., Curr.Cont., Hisp.Amer.Per.Ind., M.L.A.

810   US   ISSN 0014-4940
PR1
EXPLICATOR. 1941. q. $25 to individuals; institutions $45. (Helen Dwight Reid Educational Foundation) Heldref Publications, 1319 Eighteenth St., N.W., Washington, DC 20036-1802. TEL 202-296-6267. FAX 202-296-5149. Ed. Nancy Geltman. adv.; index, cum.index: vols.1-20, 21-30; circ. 2,200. (also avail. in microform; reprint service avail. from KTO) **Indexed:** Abstr.Engl.Stud., Acad.Ind., Arts & Hum.Cit.Ind., Curr.Cont., Hum.Ind., M.L.A.
—BLDSC shelfmark: 3842.153000.
Refereed Serial

808 910.09   US
EXPLORATION; journal on the literature of exploration and travel. 1972. a. $3. Illinois State University, Department of English, Normal, IL 61761. Ed. Steven E. Kagle. bk.rev.; circ. 250. (back issues avail.) **Indexed:** Abstr.Engl.Stud.

EXPLORATIONS. see LINGUISTICS

810   US
EXPLORATIONS. 1980. a. $4. Alaska University, English Department, 11120 Glacier Highway, Juneau, AK 99801. Ed. Art Petersen. circ. 250.

EXPLORATIONS IN RENAISSANCE CULTURE. see HUMANITIES: COMPREHENSIVE WORKS

810   US   ISSN 0014-5017
EXPLORER (NOTRE DAME). 1960. s-a. $6. Explorer Publications Co., Box 210, Notre Dame, IN 46556. TEL 219-277-3465. Ed. Raymond John Flory. adv.; illus.; circ. 200. **Indexed:** Biol.Abstr.
Description: Magazine of verse, fiction, essays and photography.

820   AT   ISSN 0085-039X
EXPRESSION. 1964. a. Aus.$2. University of Wollongong, School of Education, P.O. Box 1144, Wollongong, N.S.W. 2500, Australia. Ed. R.W. Colvin. bk.rev.; circ. 400.

EXTRAPOLATION; journal of the scholarly study of science fiction and fantasy. see LITERATURE — Science Fiction, Fantasy, Horror

F A R C E. (Fine Arts Research and Communications Enterprises) see ART

820   AT   ISSN 0155-476X
F A W N S. 1977. a. Aus.$5. Fellowship of Australian Writers North Shore Regional, P.O. Box 15, Berowra 2081, Australia. TEL 02-4561142. Ed. Bettina Cummins. bk.rev.; circ. 150. (back issues avail.)
Description: Contains short stories, articles and poetry written by members.

830   GW   ISSN 0175-2200
FACHDIENST GERMANISTIK. 1983. m. DM.84. Iudicium Verlag, P.O. Box 701067, Waldfriedhofstr. 60, 8000 Munich 70, Germany. TEL 089-71847. Ed. Peter Kapitza.

FACTSHEET FIVE. see PUBLISHING AND BOOK TRADE

808   FR   ISSN 0182-1717
PQ1184
FAIRE PART. 1982. a. 180 F. Editions Faire Part, 17, Allee Jean Buclon, 26000 Valence, France. adv.
Description: Presents French prose and poetry works.

839.31   NE
FAMA. 1936. 8/yr. free. Stichting het Rijnlands Lyceum, Backershagenlaan 5, 2243 AB Wassenaar, Netherlands. Ed.Bd. adv.; bk.rev.; film rev.; play rev.; circ. 1,000.
Former titles: Krant; Scheepspraat (ISSN 0036-5971)

895.1 CC
FANG CAO. (Text in Chinese) m. Wuhan Shi Wenlian, No. 44, Jiefang Gongyuan Lu, Wuhan, Hubei 430010, People's Republic of China. TEL 24791. Ed. Guan Yonghe.

800 CC
FANG CAO DI. (Text in Chinese) bi-m. Y6. Fang Cao Di Bianjibu, 1-1 Huoyaoku, Huancheng Lu, Fuzhou, Fujian 350001, People's Republic of China. (Dist. overseas by: Jiangsu Publications Import & Export Corp., 56 Gao Yun Ling, Nanjing, Jiangsu, P.R.C.)
Description: Covers different styles of popular literature, music and critical approaches.

FANTASIA. see *LITERATURE — Science Fiction, Fantasy, Horror*

FANTASTIC WORLDS OF EDGAR RICE BURROUGHS. see *LITERATURE — Science Fiction, Fantasy, Horror*

891.439 PK
FANUS. (Text in Urdu) 1978. m. Rs.6. Rukhsanah Siham Mirza, Ludvika Mansion, 689 Central Commercial Area, PECHS, Karachi 29, Pakistan.

810 US
FARCE; Raleigh's review of alternative arts. 1988. 4/yr. $20 (students $12). Paper Plant, Box 543, Raleigh, NC 27602. TEL 919-834-9203. Ed. John Dancy-Jones. circ. 1,000.
Description: Publishes performative, dramatized works, urban lyrics, and the life of the mind.

808 US ISSN 0748-6022
FARMER'S MARKET. 1981. s-a. $8. Midwest Farmer's Market, Inc., Box 1272, Galesburg, IL 61402. Ed.Bd. circ. 500. **Indexed:** Amer.Hum.Ind., Ind.Amer.Per.Verse.
Description: Creative works of distinguished local, regional, and national writers, poets, and artists, in the Midwestern literary tradition.

891.4 II ISSN 0014-8571
FAROGH-I-URDU. (Text in Urdu) 1954. m. Rs.30. Idara-I-Farogh-I-Urdu, 37 Aminabad Park, Lucknow 1, India. Ed.Bd. adv.; bk.rev.; illus.; circ. 1,200.

FASETTE/FACETS/FACETTEN. see *EDUCATION*

808 US ISSN 0276-2072
FAT TUESDAY. (Each issue has distinctive title) 1981. a. $5. Fat Tuesday Publications, RD 2, Box 4220, Manada Gap Rd., Grantville, PA 17028. TEL 717-469-7159. Ed. F.M. Cotolo. adv.; illus.; circ. 200. (back issues avail.)
Description: Contains contemporary prose and poetry.

809 US ISSN 0884-2949
PS3511.A86
FAULKNER JOURNAL. 1985. s-a. $9 to individuals; institutions and foreign $15. c/o Dawn Trouard, University of Akron, Department of English, Akron, OH 44325-1906. TEL 216-972-7470. (Co-sponsors: University of Akron; Boston University) Ed. John T. Matthews. bibl.; illus.; circ. 400. (also avail. in microform from UMI; back issues avail.)
—BLDSC shelfmark: 3897.775000.

895.1 CC ISSN 1002-803X
FEI TIAN/FLYING APSARAS. (Text in Chinese) 1950. m. Y16.80($58.50) (Gansu Sheng Wenlian) Fei Tian Yuekanshe, 284, Donggang Xilu, Lanzhou, Gansu 730000, People's Republic of China. TEL 25803. (Dist. outside China by: Guoji Shudian - China International Book Trading Corp., P.O. Box 399, Beijing, P.R.C.; Dist. in US by: China Books & Periodicals, Inc., 2929 24th St., San Francisco, CA 94110. TEL 415-282-2994) Ed. Li Yunpeng. adv.; bk.rev.; circ. 11,000.
Formerly (until 1981): Gansu Wenxue.
Description: Publishes short stories, proses, poems and literary reviews.

800 US ISSN 1040-5607
FELL SWOOP; the all Bohemian review. 1983. s-a. $6. Acre Press, 1521 N. Lopez St., New Orleans, LA 70119. TEL 504-943-5198. Ed. X.J. Dailey. bk.rev.; circ. 500. (back issues avail.)
Description: Geared towards deflating the literature of our day which needs deflating.

FELLOWSHIP IN PRAYER. see *RELIGIONS AND THEOLOGY — Other Denominations And Sects*

FEMINARIA. see *WOMEN'S INTERESTS*

800 301.412 FR
FEMMES EN LITTERATURE. 1976. irreg. price varies. Editions Klincksieck, 11 rue de Lille, 75005 Paris, France. Dir. Patrice Laurent.

700 AU ISSN 0015-0029
DAS FENSTER; tiroler Kulturzeitschrift. 1968. s-a. S.160. Tiroler Landesregierung, Kulturreferat, Neues Landhaus, A-6010 Innsbruck, Austria. TEL 0512-576300. (Subscr. to: Haymon Verlag, Erzherzog Eugen-Str. 24, A-6020 Innsbruck, Austria) Ed. Wolfgang Pfaundler. adv.; bk.rev.; bibl.; illus.; circ. 3,600.
—BLDSC shelfmark: 3906.503000.

810 US ISSN 0046-3736
PN6010.5
FICTION. 1972. 2/yr. $10 per no.(foreign $15). c/o City College, Department of English, 138th St. and Convent Ave., New York, NY 10031. TEL 212-690-8170. Ed. Mark J. Mirsky. circ. 2,000. (also avail. in microform from UMI; reprint service avail. from UMI) **Indexed:** Amer.Hum.Ind.
Description: Published modern fiction that sets itself serious questions, sometimes in absurd and comic voices, interrogating the nature of the real and fantastic. Representing no particular school of fiction - naturalism, surrealism - except the innovative.

808.838 FR
FICTION. 1958? 4/yr. Societe Nouvelle des Edition Opta, 1 quai de Conti, 75006 Paris, France. (back issues avail.)

800 US ISSN 1046-1094
FICTION FORUM. 4/yr. $12. Chips Off the Writer's Block, Box 83371, Los Angeles, CA 90083. Ed. Wanda Windham. circ. 500.
Description: Forum for beginners to publish their work and have it critiqued by their peers.

800 US ISSN 0092-1912
PN3311
FICTION INTERNATIONAL. 1973. s-a. $14 to individuals; institutions $28. San Diego State University Press, San Diego, CA 92182. TEL 619-594-6220. adv.; bk.rev.; illus.; circ. 1,000. (also avail. in microform from UMI; reprint service avail. from UMI) **Indexed:** Abstr.Engl.Stud., Amer.Hum.Ind., Bk.Rev.Ind. (1980-), Child.Bk.Rev.Ind. (1980-).
—BLDSC shelfmark: 3918.715000.

890 II
FICTION REVIEW; a magazine of creative writing. 1982. m. Vikrant Press, 32 DSIDC Industrial Complex, Wazirpur Delhi 110 052, India. Ed. Jai Vrat. adv.

FILOLOGIA. see *LINGUISTICS*

FILOLOGIA MODERNA. see *LINGUISTICS*

FILOLOGIA POLSKA. see *LINGUISTICS*

FILOZOFSKI FAKULTET - ZADAR. RAZDIO FILOLOSKIH ZNANOSTI. RADOVI. see *LINGUISTICS*

800 IT
FINISTERE. s-a. Elitropia Edizioni, Casella Postale 421, 42100 Reggio Emilia, Italy.

FINNISCH-UGRISCHE MITTEILUNGEN. see *LINGUISTICS*

FIREWEED; a feminist quarterly. see *WOMEN'S INTERESTS*

FIRST LINE/YI XING. see *LITERATURE — Poetry*

810 US ISSN 1051-1695
FISH DRUM. 1988. irreg. (2-4/yr.). $10 for 4 nos. Fish Drum Magazine, 626 Kathryn Ave., Santa Fe, NM 87501. TEL 505-982-8340. Ed. Robert Winson. bk.rev.; circ. 500. (also avail. in magnetic tape)
Description: Emphasizes modern, lively poetry and prose, and includes visual art, scores, and interviews. Audio issues are all poetry, sometimes with music. Favors local poets.

800 301 US ISSN 0898-0233
FIVE FINGERS REVIEW. 1984. 2/yr. $15. Five Fingers Press, Box 15426, San Francisco, CA 94115-0426. TEL 415-431-8506. FAX 510-655-7904. Ed.Bd. adv.; circ. 1,500.
Description: Publishes poetry, fiction, nonfiction prose, essays and translations from diverse aesthetics and traditions.

821 UK
FIVE LEAVES LEFT. 1983. 3/yr. $10. 12 Colne Rd., Cowling, Keighley, West Yorkshire BD22 OBZ, England. circ. 500.

808 US
FLANNERY O'CONNOR AWARDS FOR SHORT FICTION. 1983. 2/yr. price varies. University of Georgia Press, Athens, GA 30602. TEL 404-542-2830. FAX 404-542-0601.

809 US ISSN 0091-4924
PS3565.C57
FLANNERY O'CONNOR BULLETIN. 1972. a. $5 to individuals; institutions $6. Georgia College, Department of English and Speech, Box 44, Milledgeville, GA 31061. TEL 912-453-4581. Ed.Bd. adv.; bk.rev.; circ. 1,000. (also avail. in microform from UMI; back issues avail.; reprint service avail. from UMI) **Indexed:** Abstr.Engl.Stud., Amer.Hum.Ind.

FLASH MARKET NEWS. see *PUBLISHING AND BOOK TRADE*

810 US ISSN 0147-1686
PS580
FLOATING ISLAND. 1976. irreg., no.4, 1989. $15. Floating Island Publications, Box 516, Point Reyes Sta., CA 94956. TEL 415-663-1181. Ed. Michael Sykes. illus.; circ. 2,000.
Description: Occasional anthology of poetry, fiction, photography, and graphic arts.

FLORILEGIUM; annual papers on late antiquity and the Middle Ages. see *CLASSICAL STUDIES*

810 US
▼**FLOWER.** 1991. 12/yr. 302 Laurie Court, Stillwater, MN 55082. Ed. Neil Cunningham. circ. 270.
Description: Publishes poetry, fiction, articles, art, criticism and letters.

830 GW ISSN 0724-1194
FLUGASCHE. (Text in English and German) 1981. q. DM.20($12) Flugasche Verlag, Lembergstr. 20, 7000 Stuttgart 1, Germany. TEL 0711-482446. Ed.Bd. adv.; bk.rev.; circ. 2,000. (back issues avail.)

FOCUS (KENT). see *LITERATURE — Science Fiction, Fantasy, Horror*

800 CN
FOCUS ON ROBERT GRAVES AND HIS CONTEMPORARIES. 1972. 2/yr. $5. University of Toronto, Department of English, 7 King's College Cir., Toronto, Ont. M5A 1A1, Canada. TEL 416-978-7223. (Co-publisher: University of Maryland, European Division) Ed. Patrick Quinn. bk.rev.; bibl.; circ. 600. (processed) **Indexed:** Amer.Hum.Ind., M.L.A.
Formerly (until no.7, May 1988): Focus on Robert Graves.
Description: Dedicated to the study of the literature of Robert Graves and of World War I era writer.

FOCUSES. see *EDUCATION — Teaching Methods And Curriculum*

FOLIO. see *PUBLISHING AND BOOK TRADE*

810 US ISSN 0015-5756
FOLIO (BIRMINGHAM). 1965. s-a. $3. A.H. Cather Publishing Co., 2501 Seventh Ave. S., Birmingham, AL 35222. TEL 205-252-6109. circ. 500. (processed; also avail. in microform from UMI) **Indexed:** Tr.& Indus.Ind.

FOLIO (BROCKPORT); essays on foreign languages and literature. see *HUMANITIES: COMPREHENSIVE WORKS*

LITERATURE

808 US
FOLIO (WASHINGTON); a literary journal. 1984. 2/yr. $10. American University, Department of Literature, 4400 Massachusetts Ave., N.W., Washington, DC 20016. TEL 202-885-2971. adv.; bk.rev.; circ. 400. (back issues avail.) Indexed: Graph.Arts Lit.Abstr.
Description: Prints quality fiction and poetry by established and new writers.

800 IT
FONDAMENTI. q. L.30000. Paideia Editrice, Via Corsica 130, 25125 Brescia, Italy. Ed. Giuseppe Scarpat.

800 808.81 BE
FONDATION MAURICE CAREME. (Text in French; special issues in English) 1978. a. free. Fondation Maurice Careme, Av. Nellie Melba, 14, B-1070 Brussels, Belgium. TEL 02-521-67-75. (Co-sponsor: Les Amis de Maurice Careme) circ. 12,500.
Description: Provides information on films, conferences, poetry readings and competitions in the honor of Maurice Careme, with emphasis on the French language.

830 GW ISSN 0015-6175
PT1863.Z7
FONTANE-BLAETTER. 1965. s-a. DM.8.50 per no. Deutsche Staatsbibliothek, Theodor Fontane Archiv, Dortustr. 30-34, Postfach 59, 1561 Potsdam, Germany. Ed. Manfred Horlitz. adv.; bk.rev. Indexed: M.L.A.

810 US
FOOTBALL: OUR WAY. 1984. 5/yr. $5. Our Way Publications, 5014 Starker Ave., Madison, WI 53716. TEL 608-241-0549. Ed. Dale Jellings. circ. 50.
Description: Publish literary works related to football.

810 US
FOOTHILL QUARTERLY. 1975. q. $4. Foothill Community College, 12345 El Monte Rd., Los Altos Hills, CA 94022. TEL 415-948-8590. Eds. Richard Maxwell, Neva V. Hacker. circ. 1,000.

FOOTWORK: THE PATERSON LITERARY REVIEW. see LITERATURE — Poetry

800 US ISSN 0749-9132
JF1525.I6
FOREIGN INTELLIGENCE LITERARY SCENE. 1982. 6/yr. $50. National Intelligence Study Center, 1800 K St., N.W., Ste. 1102, Washington, DC 20006. FAX 202-331-0109. Eds. Marjorie W. Cline, Dalton A. West. bk.rev.; circ. 1,000.

800 AA
FOREIGN LITERATURE. q. $30. Union des Ecrivains et Artistes d'Albanie, Tirana, Albania.

FORGOTTEN FANTASY LIBRARY. see LITERATURE — Science Fiction, Fantasy, Horror

800 US ISSN 0741-5702
PN6010.5
FORMATIONS. 1984. 3/yr. $16 to individuals (foreign $22); institutions $32 (foreign $38). Northwestern University Press, 625 Colfax St., Evanston, IL 60201-2807. TEL 708-491-5313. Eds. Jonathan Brent, Frances Padorr Brent. adv.; circ. 1,500. (also avail. in microform from UMI; back issues avail.; reprint service avail. from UMI) Indexed: M.L.A.
Description: Contains American fiction, important fiction in translation, essays on the arts, and photographs.

860 UY
FORO LITERATIO. 1977. s-a. $7.50. Editorial Geminis, El Uiejo Pancho 2585, Montevideo, Uruguay. (Editorial addr.: Casilla 12013, Montevideo, Uruguay) Ed. Julio Ricci. adv.; bk.rev.; circ. 1,000. Indexed: Hisp.Amer.Per.Ind.

830 NE ISSN 0168-9770
FORSCHUNGSBERICHTE ZUR D D R-LITERATUR. 1980. irreg. price varies. Editions Rodopi B.V., Keizersgracht 302-304, Amsterdam, Netherlands. TEL 020-6227507. FAX 020-6380948. (US and Canada subscr. to: 233 Peachtree St. N.E., Ste. 404, Atlanta GA 30303-1504, USA. TEL 800-225-3998) Ed. Gerd Labroisse.

891.8 CI ISSN 0015-8445
FORUM. (Text in Serbo-Croatian) 1962. 4/yr. 400 din. Jugoslavenska Akademija Znanosti i Umjetnosti, Razred za Suvremenu Knjizevnost, Zrinjski trg. 11, 41000 Zagreb, Croatia. TEL 041 433-849. Ed. Slavko Mihalic. index. Indexed: Abstr.Engl.Stud., Leg.Per., M.L.A.

800 NE ISSN 0015-8496
PN9
FORUM DER LETTEREN; tijdschrift voor taal- en letterkunde. 1960. q. fl.53.33 to individuals; institutions fl.62.86; students fl.47.62. (Nederlandse Organisatie voor Zuiver-Wetenschappelijk Onderzoek) Smits B.V., Westeinde 135, 2512 The Hague, Netherlands. Ed.Bd. adv.; bk.rev.; index; circ. 1,200. Indexed: Amer.Hist.& Life, Hist.Abstr., Ind.Bk.Rev.Hum., M.L.A.
Formerly: Museum.

FORUM FOR MODERN LANGUAGE STUDIES. see LINGUISTICS

890 US
FORUM INTERNATIONAL.* (Text in English, Russian) 1976. s-a. $12 for 3 yrs. c/o J. Glad, Ed., 3901 Connecticut Ave., N.W., Ste. 408, Washington, DC 20008. adv.; bibl.; circ. 500.
Formerly: Forum (College Park) (ISSN 0164-288X)

FORUM UNIVERSITAIRE. see SOCIAL SCIENCES: COMPREHENSIVE WORKS

895.1 CC
FOSHAN WENYI. (Text in Chinese) m. Foshan Shi Wenhua-ju, No. 36, Xinfeng Lu, Foshan, Guangdong 518000, People's Republic of China. TEL 248866. Ed. Liu Ning.

FOUNDATION; the review of science fiction. see LITERATURE — Science Fiction, Fantasy, Horror

FOURAH BAY STUDIES IN LANGUAGE AND LITERATURE. see LINGUISTICS

FRANCITE. see LINGUISTICS

FRANCOFONIA; studi e ricerche sulle letterature di lingua francese. see HISTORY — History Of Europe

FRANCOFONIA. QUADERNI. see HISTORY — History Of Europe

FRANKENLAND; Zeitschrift fuer Fraenkische Landeskunde und Kulturpflege. see HISTORY — History Of Europe

830 430 GW ISSN 0071-9226
FRANKFURTER BEITRAEGE ZUR GERMANISTIK. 1967. irreg., vol.15, 1977. price varies. Carl Winter Universitaetsverlag GmbH, Lutherstr. 59, 6900 Heidelberg, Germany. Indexed: M.L.A.

FRANKFURTER JUDAISTISCHE BEITRAEGE. see ETHNIC INTERESTS

FRAU OHNE HERZ; eine Zeitschrift fuer Frauen und andere Lesben. see WOMEN'S INTERESTS

800 US
FREE FOCUS. 1985. s-a. $5 (foreign $10). (Women's Literary Guild) Wagner Press, c/o Patricia D. Coscia, Ed., 224 82nd St., Brooklyn, NY 11209. TEL 718-680-3899. adv.; bk.rev.; illus.; circ. 200. (looseleaf format; back issues avail.)
Description: Features literature by women.

800 US ISSN 0016-0369
FREE LANCE; a magazine of poetry and prose. 1950. s-a. $2. Free Lance Poets and Prose Workshop, Inc., 6005 Grand Ave., Cleveland, OH 44104. Eds. Casper L. Jordan, Russell Atkins. bk.rev.; charts; play rev.; cum.index: vols.1-13; circ. 500. (also avail. in microfilm from KTO; back issues avail.)

800 CN
FREE SPEECH MONITOR. 6/yr. Can.$10. Canadian Association for Free Expression Inc., P.O. Box 332, Rexdale, Ont. M9W 5L3, Canada. TEL 416-236-1367. FAX 416-896-4037. Ed. James P. Rae.
Formerly: Free Speech.

820 CN ISSN 0705-1379
FREELANCE. 1970. m. (10/yr.). Can.$40 membership. Saskatchewan Writers Guild, P.O. Box 3986, Regina, Sask. S4P 3R9, Canada. Ed. April Davies. bk.rev.; circ. 700.
Description: Contains news and commentary on issues of interest to writers.

491 891 GW ISSN 0067-592X
FREIE UNIVERSITAET BERLIN. OSTEUROPA-INSTITUT. SLAVISTISCHE VEROEFFENTLICHUNGEN. (Title varies: Veroeffentlichungen der Abteilung fuer Slavische Sprachen und Literaturen) 1953. irreg., vol.74, 1991. price varies. (Freie Universitaet Berlin, Osteuropa Institut) Verlag Otto Harrassowitz, Taunusstr. 14, Postfach 2929, 6200 Wiesbaden 1, Germany. TEL 0611-530-0. FAX 0611-530570. TELEX 4186135. Ed.Bd. circ. 500.

800 GW ISSN 0071-9463
AS182
FREIES DEUTSCHES HOCHSTIFT, FRANKFURT AM MAIN. JAHRBUCH. (Text in English and German) 1962. a. varies. Max Niemeyer Verlag, Postfach 2140, 7400 Tuebingen 1, Germany. TEL 07071-81104. FAX 07071-87419. Ed.Bd. circ. 1,100. (back issues avail.) Indexed: M.L.A.
Description: Studies literature, mostly German, from 1750-1850.

FREMANTLE ARTS REVIEW. see ART

700 800 300 US ISSN 1052-3952
CR5061.U6
FRENCH AMERICAN REVIEW. 1930. 2/yr. $15 to non-members (foreign $18). American Society of the French Legion of Honor, 22 E. 60th St., New York, NY 10022. TEL 203-542-5539. FAX 203-542-5258. Ed. Sara Vagliano. bk.rev.; index; circ. 950. Indexed: M.L.A.
Former titles (until 1990, Winter): Laurels (ISSN 0270-3793); (until 1979): American Society Legion of Honor Magazine.

FRENCH - CANADIAN CIVILIZATION RESEARCH CENTER. CAHIERS/CENTRE DE RECHERCHE EN CIVILISATION CANADIENNE - FRANCAISE. CAHIERS. see HISTORY — History Of North And South America

840 944 UK ISSN 0016-1128
PQ1
FRENCH STUDIES; a quarterly review. (Supplement avail.: French Studies Bulletin (ISSN 0262-2750)) 1947. q. £35($70) Society for French Studies, c/o Dr. A.W. Raitt, Ed., Taylor Institution, St. Giles', Oxford OX1 3NA, England. bk.rev.; bibl.; tr.lit.; index; circ. 1,900. (back issues avail.; reprint service avail. from SCH) Indexed: Amer.Hist.& Life, Arts & Hum.Cit.Ind., Br.Hum.Ind., Curr.Cont., Hist.Abstr., Ind.Bk.Rev.Hum., Mid.East: Abstr.& Ind.
—BLDSC shelfmark: 4034.600000.
Description: Contains articles on French literature and French language with an occasional contribution on other aspects of French culture.

840 944 UK ISSN 0262-2750
FRENCH STUDIES BULLETIN. (Supplement to French Studies (ISSN 0016-1128)) (Text in English and French) 1981. q. free with subscr. to French Studies. Society for French Studies, c/o G. Chesters, Ed., Dept. of French, University of Hull, Hull HU6 8RX, England. circ. 1,900. (back issues avail.)
—BLDSC shelfmark: 4034.600500.
Description: Contains short notes, opinions and news items on all aspects of French culture and the teaching of French in institutions of higher education.

810 US
FRIENDS OF PEACE PILGRIM. 1987. 3/yr. free. 43480 Cedar Ave., Hemet, CA 92344. TEL 714-927-7678. circ. 10,500.

FROGPOND. see LITERATURE — Poetry

809 917.106 CN ISSN 0829-4976
FROM MY BOOKSHELF; books noted for you. 1972. m. free. George Bonavia International Productions, P.O. Box 826 Sta. B., Ottawa, Ont. K1P 5P9, Canada. Ed. George Bonavia. bk.rev.
Formerly: International Corner (ISSN 0316-6260)
Description: Reviews books on Canada and Canadian affairs as well as on subjects of interest to ethnocultural groups.

800 410 CH ISSN 1015-0021
P1
FU JEN STUDIES; literature & linguistics. (Text in English, German, and Spanish) 1968. a. $5 (effective 1990). Fu Jen University, College of Foreign Languages & Literatures - Fu Jen Ta Hsueh, 24205 Hsinchuang, Taipei, Taiwan, Republic of China. FAX 02-9014733. Ed. Heliena Krenn. circ. 300. (back issues avail.) **Indexed:** M.L.A.
—BLDSC shelfmark: 4047.745000.
  Description: Presents Chinese and Western literature and linguistics.

895.1 CC ISSN 0257-0297
FUJIAN WENXUE/FUJIAN LITERATURE. (Text in Chinese) 1951. m. Y18 (foreign 61.20). Fujian Sheng Wenlian, Fenghuang Chi, Xihong Lu, Fuzhou, Fujian 350002, People's Republic of China. TEL 711725. (Dist. in US by: China Books & Periodicals, Inc., 2929 24th St., San Francisco, CA 94110. TEL 415-282-2994) Ed. Cao Haibin.
  Description: Published literary works that depict the special economic zones in the province, rural towns, as well as relationships between people living on both sides of the Taiwan Straits.

895.65 301.412 JA
FUJINKORON. (Text in Japanese) 1916. m. Chuokoron-Sha Inc., 2-8-7, Kyobashi, Chuo-ku, Tokyo 104, Japan. TEL 03-3563-1261. Ed. Kazuo Matsumura. circ. 257,000.

895.1 CC
FURONG. (Text in Chinese) bi-m. Y18($58.80) Hunan Wenyi Chubanshe, 67, Yinpen Nanlu, Changsha, Hunan 410006, People's Republic of China. TEL 82988. (Dist. outside China by: China International Book Trading Corp., P.O. Box 399, Beijing, p.R.C.; Dist. in US by: China Books & Periodicals, Inc., 2929 24th St., San Francisco, CA 94110. TEL 415-282-2994) adv.

809 US
▼**FURTHER STATE(S) OF THE ART**; a critical catalogue of new American fiction. 1991. q. $2.50 per no. Marshall Communications, 100 Manhattan Ave., Ste. 1210, Union City, NJ 07087. TEL 201-601-0886. Ed. Phil Leggiere. bk.rev.
  Description: Reviews recent American fiction, with an eye for the unconventional and innovative.

G I P. (Germansk Instituts Publikationer) see LINGUISTICS

800 US
G W REVIEW. 1978. s-a. $6. George Washington University, Marvin Center, 800 21st St., N.W., Box 20, Washington, DC 20052. Eds. Roman S. Ponos, Joseph Dumas. bk.rev.; circ. 1,000.
  Description: Presents poetry, short fiction and interviews.

800 UK ISSN 0016-3929
AP75
GAIRM. (Text in Gaelic) 1952. q. £9 (typically set in Dec.). Gairm Publications, 29 Waterloo St., Glasgow G2, Scotland. FAX 041-221-1971. Ed. Derick S. Thomson. adv.; bk.rev.; illus.; index; circ. 2,000.
  Description: Covers Gaelic literary topics, plus fiction, poetry travel, history and current affairs.

GALACTIC CENTRAL BIBLIOGRAPHIES. see BIBLIOGRAPHIES

700 800 IT ISSN 0016-4097
GALLERIA. 1949. bi-m. L.20000. Casa Editrice Salvatore Sciascia, Corso Umberto 111, 93100 Caltanissetta, Italy. Ed. Leonardo Sciascia. adv.; bk.rev.

891.4 II ISSN 0016-4216
GALPAKABITA. (Text in Bengali) 1967. m. Rs.7($6.) Kamal Kumar Lahiri, 17-1-D Suriya Sen St., Calcutta 12, India. Ed. Krishna Gopal Mullick.

GAMUT. see LITERARY AND POLITICAL REVIEWS

807 860 PE ISSN 0254-797X
GARABATO; teoria, produccion y critica del texto narrativo. 1983. s-a. c/o Luis Fernando Vidal, Calle Uno 1242 Urbanizacion Corpac, Lima 27, Peru. Ed. Esteban Quiroz Cisneros.

860 700 US ISSN 8755-3651
EL GATO TUERTO/ONE-EYED CAT; gaceta de arte, literatura, etcetera, etcetera. (Text in English, Spanish) 1984. q. $8 to individuals; institutions $12. Ediciones el Gato Tuerto, Box 210277, San Francisco, CA 94121. TEL 504-866-8598. Ed. Carlota Caulfield. adv.; bk.rev.; circ. 1,000. (back issues avail.)
  Description: Looks at Hispanic literature.

800 GW ISSN 0720-2520
GAUKE'S JAHRBUCH. 1980. a. price varies. Gauke Verlag GmbH, Postfach 1320, 2322 Luetingen, Germany. Eds. Christoph and Gabriele Gauke.

GAUNTLET; exploring the limits of free expression. see LITERARY AND POLITICAL REVIEWS

869 US ISSN 0276-7910
PQ9470
GA'VEA - BROWN; revista bilingue de letras e estudos Luso-Americanos - a bilingual journal of Portuguese-American letters and studies. (Text in English, Portuguese) 1980. a. $10 to individuals; institutions $15. (Center for Portuguese & Brazilian Studies) Ga'vea - Brown Publications, Box O, Brown University, Providence, RI 02912.
TEL 401-863-3042. FAX 401-863-3700. TELEX 952095. Eds. One'simo T. Almeida, George Monteiro. bk.rev.; illus.; circ. 500. (back issues avail.)
  Description: Covers all things related to the Portuguese presence in North America. Includes studies and creative writing.

GAZZETTA DELLE ARTI. see ART

800 US
GEGENSCHEIN. 1971. irreg., approx. 4/yr. $5 per issue. Gegenschein Press, 421 Hudson St., Ste. 220, New York, NY 10014. TEL 212-989-7845. Ed. Phil Smith. circ. 750 (controlled).
  Formerly: Gegenschein Quarterly.

830 GW ISSN 0016-5883
GEHOERT GELESEN (MUNICH, 1954); Manuskriptauslese der interessantesten Sendungen des Bayerischen Rundfunks. 1954. m. DM.55. (Bayerischer Rundfunk) Ehrenwirth Verlag, Schwanthaler Str. 91, 8000 Munich 2, Germany. Ed. Reinhard Wittmann.

800 US ISSN 0016-6928
PN80
GENRE (NORMAN). 1968. q. $14 to individuals; institutions $27; foreign $30. University of Oklahoma, Department of English, 760 van Vleet Oval, Norman, OK 73019. TEL 405-325-4661. Ed. Ronald Schleifer. adv.; bk.rev.; circ. 700. (processed) **Indexed:** Abstr.Engl.Stud., Amer.Hum.Ind., Arts & Hum.Cit.Ind., Can.Rev.Comp.Lit, Curr.Cont., Ind.Bk.Rev.Hum., M.L.A., Mid.East: Abstr.& Ind.
—BLDSC shelfmark: 4116.340000.

800 GW
GEORG FORSTER: SAEMTLICHE SCHRIFTEN, TAGEBUECHER, BRIEFE. (Text in English and German) 1958. irreg., vol.17, 1989. (Akademie der Wissenschaften der DDR, Zentralinstitut fuer Literaturgeschichte) Akademie-Verlag Berlin, Leipziger Str. 3-4, 1086 Berlin, Germany. TELEX 114420-AVERL-DD.

800 UK
GEORGE ELIOT FELLOWSHIP REVIEW. 1970. a. £5.50. George Eliot Fellowship, 71 Stepping Stones Rd., Coventry, W. Midlands CV5 8JT, England. TEL 0203-592231. Eds. Beryl Gray, Graham Hanley. adv.; bk.rev.; circ. 400. **Indexed:** M.L.A.

800 054.1 US
GEORGE SAND STUDIES. Variant title: George Sand Newsletter. (Text in English and French) 1978. s-a. $12 to individuals; institutions $15; students $8. (Friends of George Sand) Hofstra University, Cultural Center, Hempstead, NY 11550.
TEL 516-560-5669. FAX 516-564-4297. Ed. Natalie Datlof. adv.; bk.rev.; bibl.; illus.; circ. 500. (back issues avail.)
  Formerly: Friends of George Sand Newsletter (ISSN 0161-6544)

810 US ISSN 0016-8386
AP2
THE GEORGIA REVIEW. 1947. q. $18 (foreign $23). University of Georgia, Georgia Review, Athens, GA 30602. TEL 706-542-3481. FAX 706-542-0047. Ed. Stanley W. Lindberg. adv.; bk.rev.; illus.; circ. 5,300. (also avail. in microform from UMI; talking book; Braille; back issues avail.; reprint service avail. from UMI) **Indexed:** A.I.P.P., Abstr.Engl.Stud., Amer.Hist.& Life, Bk.Rev.Ind. (1965-), Child.Bk.Rev.Ind. (1965-), Curr.Cont., Film Lit.Ind. (1976-), Hist.Abstr., Hum.Ind., Ind.Bk.Rev.Hum., Lang.& Lang.Behav.Abstr., M.L.A., Sociol.Abstr.
—BLDSC shelfmark: 4158.459000.
  Description: Contains fiction, essays, poetry; directed at interdisciplinary audience.

800 US ISSN 0884-8696
GEORGIA STATE LITERARY STUDIES. irreg., no.8, 1990. price varies. A M S Press, Inc., 56 E. 13th St., New York, NY 10003. TEL 212-777-4700. FAX 212-995-5413. Ed. Victor A. Kramer. index. (back issues avail.)

830 UK ISSN 0016-8777
AP4
GERMAN LIFE AND LETTERS. 1936. q. £38($79.50) to individuals; institutions £78.50($165). Basil Blackwell Ltd., 108 Cowley Rd., Oxford OX4 1JF, England. TEL 0865-791100. FAX 0865-791347. TELEX 837022-OXBOOK-G. Ed.Bd. adv.; bk.rev.; index; cum.index; circ. 800. (reprint service avail. from SCH,SWZ) **Indexed:** Arts & Hum.Cit.Ind., Br.Hum.Ind., Can.Rev.Comp.Lit, Curr.Cont., Ind.Bk.Rev.Hum., M.L.A.
—BLDSC shelfmark: 4162.124000.

GERMAN STUDIES REVIEW. see HISTORY — History Of Europe

GERMANIC REVIEW; devoted to studies dealing with the Germanic languages and literatures. see LINGUISTICS

830 FR
GERMANICA. 2/yr. 100 F. (effective 1992). Universite de Lille III, B.P. 149, F-59653 Villeneuve d'Ascq Cedex, France.

800 GW ISSN 0016-8904
PB3
GERMANISCH-ROMANISCHE MONATSSCHRIFT. 1909; N.S. 1950. 4/yr. DM.135 (students DM.110). Carl Winter Universitaetsverlag GmbH, Lutherstr. 59, 6900 Heidelberg, Germany. Ed. Conrad Wiedemann. adv.; bk.rev.; bibl.; index; circ. 1,100. **Indexed:** Arts & Hum.Cit.Ind., Curr.Cont., Ind.Bk.Rev.Hum., Lang.& Lang.Behav.Abstr., M.L.A., RILA.

430 CN ISSN 0317-4956
PT123.S58
GERMANO-SLAVICA. (Text in English, French, German) 1973. a. $12. University of Waterloo, Department of Germanic and Slavic Languages and Literature, Waterloo, Ont. N2L 3G1, Canada.
TEL 519-885-1211. FAX 519-885-1211. Ed. J. Whiton. adv.; bk.rev.; circ. 800. (back issues avail.) **Indexed:** Amer.Bibl.Slavic & E.Eur.Stud., Arts & Hum.Cit.Ind., Curr.Cont., M.L.A.
—BLDSC shelfmark: 4162.178000.

GESCHICHTE DES ARABISCHEN SCHRIFTTUMS. see HISTORY — History Of The Near East

800 US ISSN 0749-7644
PT2603.R397
GESTUS; a quarterly journal of Brechtian studies. 1985. 6/yr. $35 to individuals; institutions $80. Brecht Society of America, Inc., 59 S. New St., Dover, DE 19901. TEL 302-734-3740. FAX 302-734-9354. TELEX 984038 ESLUND. Ed. Dwight Steward. bk.rev.; circ. 250. (also avail. in microform; avail. on diskette)
●Also available online.

800 IS
GINAZIM. (Text in Hebrew) 1962. irreg. $7 per no. Association of Hebrew Writers in Israel, Rehov Kaplan 6, Tel Aviv 61070, Israel.

LITERATURE

850   IT   ISSN 0017-0496
PQ4001
GIORNALE STORICO DELLA LETTERATURA ITALIANA. 1883. q. (foreign L.122000)(effective 1992). Editore Loescher, Via Vittorio Amedeo II, 18, 10121 Turin, Italy. TEL 549-333. Ed.Bd. bk.rev.; bibl.; index. **Indexed:** Arts & Hum.Cit.Ind., Can.Rev.Comp.Lit., Curr.Cont., Ind.Bk.Rev.Hum., M.L.A.

820   UK   ISSN 0017-0615
PR4717
GISSING JOURNAL. 1965. q. £8 to individuals; institutions £12. Gissing Trust, 7 Town Ln., Idle, Bradford BD10 8PR, England. Ed. P. Coustillas. bk.rev.; bibl.; circ. 250. (processed) **Indexed:** Abstr.Engl.Stud., M.L.A.
    Formerly: Gissing Newsletter.
    Description: Concerns George Gissing (1857-1903).

820 284   UK   ISSN 0269-770X
GLASS (LEICESTER). 1986. irreg. £7. U C C F (Universities and Colleges Christian Fellowship), Literary Studies Group, 38 de Montfort St., Leicester LE1 7GP, England. TEL 0533-551700. FAX 0533-555672. Ed. John Gillespie. bk.rev.; circ. 150. (back issues avail.)
    Description: Aims to develop a Christian understanding of current issues in literary criticism.

808 701.18   US
GNOME BAKER. 1975. s-a. $15. Tongue Press, Box 23, Kew West, FL 33041. Eds. Madeleine Burnside, Andrew Kelly. adv.; circ. 825. (back issues avail.)

GOETEBORGER GERMANISTISCHE FORSCHUNGEN. see LINGUISTICS

830   GW   ISSN 0323-4207
PT2045
GOETHE-JAHRBUCH. 1880. a. DM.32. (Goethe-Gesellschaft, Weimar) Verlag Hermann Boehlaus Nachfolger, Meyerstr. 50a, 5300 Weimar, Germany. Ed. Werner Keller. bk.rev. **Indexed:** Arts & Hum.Cit.Ind., Curr.Cont., M.L.A.
    Formerly: Goethe-Gesellschaft. Jahrbuch (ISSN 0072-484X)

830   US
GOETHE NEWS AND NOTES. 1980. s-a. membership. Goethe Society of North America, Department of Germanic Languages, University of Michigan, Ann Arbor, MI 48109-1275. TEL 313-747-0242. Ed. Frederick Amrine. circ. 300. (looseleaf format)

830   GW
GOETHE WOERTERBUCH. 1966. a. W. Kohlhammer (Stuttgart), Hessbruehlstr. 69, Postfach 80 04 30, D-7000 Stuttgart 80, Germany.

830   US   ISSN 0734-3329
PT2046
GOETHE YEARBOOK. 1982. a. $48. (Goethe Society of North America) Camden House, Inc., Box 2025, Columbia, SC 29202. TEL 803-788-8689. FAX 803-736-9455. Ed. Thomas P. Saine. bk.rev.; bibl.; circ. 700. (back issues avail.) **Indexed:** M.L.A.
    Description: Includes essays on the German poet, novelist and dramatist Goethe. Includes bibliography of dissertations.

149.3   SZ
DAS GOETHEANUM. 1921. w. 90 Fr. (Allgemeine Anthroposophische Gesellschaft) Wochenschrift "Das Goetheanum", Postfach 134, CH-4143 Dornach, Switzerland. TEL 61-7017230. FAX 61-7017468. Eds. Martin Barkhoff, Manfred Krueger. adv.; bk.rev.; circ. 10,800.

810   US
GOING GAGA. 1988. 4/yr. $12. 2630 Robert Walker Place, Arlington, VA 22207. TEL 703-527-6032. Ed. Gareth Branwyn. circ. 300.

810   US
GOOD CLEAN FUN. 1988. 4/yr. $8. 1190 Maria Privada, Mountain View, CA 94040.

810   US   ISSN 0046-6158
GOOD OLD DAYS. vol.8, 1971. m. $12.97. House of White Birches Publishing, 306 E. Parr Rd., Berne, IN 46711. TEL 219-589-8471. Ed. Bettina Miller. adv.; charts; illus.; tr.lit.; circ. 106,561.
    Description: Contains photos, cartoons, features and poems from 1900-1949.

810   US   ISSN 1050-480X
GOOD OLD DAYS SPECIALS. 1973. bi-m. $14.95. House of White Birches Publishing, 306 E. Parr Rd., Berne, IN 46711. TEL 212-589-8471. Ed. Bettina Miller. adv.; charts; illus.; circ. 17,703.
    Former titles: Fireside Companion; Good Days Special Issues; Good Old Days Specials.
    Description: Contains features, photos, cartoons and poems from 1900-1949.

GOTHENBURG STUDIES IN ENGLISH. see LINGUISTICS

800   US
GRAB A NICKEL. 1975. irreg. (2-3/yr.). Barbour County Writers' Workshop, Box 2158, Alderson-Broaddus College, Philippi, WV 26416. TEL 304-457-1700. Ed. Barbara Smith. bk.rev.; circ. 1,000.

809   US   ISSN 0363-8057
PN80
GRADIVA; revista internazionale di lettura italiana - international journal of Italian literature. 1976. a. $25. c/o S. Morandina, Man. Ed., Department of French and Italian, State University of New York at Stony Brook, Stony Brook, NY 11794-3359. (Subscr. to: Box 831, Stony Brook, New York, NY 11790) Ed. Luigi Fontanella. adv.; bk.rev.; abstr.; illus.; circ. 300. **Indexed:** Arts & Hum.Cit.Ind., Curr.Cont., M.L.A.

800   US   ISSN 0145-7780
PS580
GRAHAM HOUSE REVIEW. 1976. a. $7.50. (Colgate University) Colgate University Press, Box 5000, Hamilton, NY 13346. TEL 315-824-1000. Eds. Peter Balakian, Bruce Smith. circ. 500. **Indexed:** Ind.Amer.Per.Verse.
    Description: Includes poetry, literary essays and interviews.

810   CN   ISSN 0315-7423
PR9194
GRAIN. 1973. 4/yr. Can.$15 to individuals; institutions Can.$20. Saskatchewan Writers Guild, P.O. Box 1154, Regina, Sask. S4P 3B4, Canada. TEL 306-757-6310. Ed. Geoffrey Ursell. circ. 1,200. **Indexed:** Amer.Hum.Ind., Can.Lit.Ind.
    Description: International literary and visual arts publication, presenting poetry short fiction and graphic arts.

810   US   ISSN 0734-5496
PN6010.5
GRAND STREET. 1981. q. $24 to individuals; institutions $28; foreign $34. Grand Street Publications, 131 Varick St., Rm. 906, New York, NY 10013. TEL 212-807-6548. FAX 212-807-6544. (Dist. by: W.W. Norton, 500 Fifth Ave., New York, NY 10110) Ed. Jean Stein. adv.; bk.rev.; circ. 4,000. (back issues avail.)
    —BLDSC shelfmark: 4210.060750.
    Description: Essays, stories, poems, art, photography and articles by noted authors, for a cosmopolitan audience.

860   UY   ISSN 0072-5439
GRANDES TODOS.* irreg. Editorial Arca, Colonia 1263, Montevideo, Uruguay.

057   GW   ISSN 0017-3185
AP50
GRANI; zhurnal literatury, iskusstva, nauki i obshchestvenno-politicheskoi mysli. (Text in Russian) 1946. q. DM.70. Possev-Verlag, Flursscheideweg 15, 6230 Frankfurt a.M. 80, Germany. TEL 069-341265. Ed. E.A. Breitbart-Samsonowa. adv.; bk.rev.; bibl.; circ. 2,000. (also avail. in microfilm from KTO; back issues avail.) **Indexed:** M.L.A.
    —BLDSC shelfmark: 0052.004000.

800   US   ISSN 0092-5268
PN171.P75
GRANTS AND AWARDS AVAILABLE TO AMERICAN WRITERS. 1969. biennial. $7.50 to individuals; institutions $12.50. P E N American Center, 568 Broadway, New York, NY 10012. TEL 212-334-1660. FAX 212-334-2181. Ed. John Morrone. circ. 4,500.
    Formerly: List of Grants and Awards Available to American Writers (ISSN 0075-983X)
    Description: Directory of prizes, awards, grants, residences and production opportunities for writers of all kinds.

800   US   ISSN 0743-7471
PS648.S5
GRAYWOLF ANNUAL. 1984. a. $8.95. Graywolf Press, 2402 University Ave., Ste. 203, St. Paul, MN 55114. TEL 612-222-8342. FAX 612-641-0036. Ed. Scott Walker. circ. 10,000. (back issues avail.)
    Description: Anthology of contemporary fiction or essays, often organized aroun a social theme or issue (ie. multi-cultural social change).

GREAT ISSUES OF THE DAY. see POLITICAL SCIENCE

800   AT
GREAT LAKES ADVOCATE. 1952. w. Aus.$30. Regional Publishers (N.S.W.) Pty. Ltd., 41 Helen St., Forster N.S.W. 2428, Australia. TEL 065-546688. FAX 065-556399. (Subscr. to: P.O. Box 138, Forster N.S.W. 2428, Australia) Ed. Susan Gogarty. adv.; bk.rev.; circ. 5,200.
    Description: Features local news, sports and letters.

810   US   ISSN 0160-2144
PS273
GREAT RIVER REVIEW. 1977. 2/yr. $9. Great River Review, Inc., 211 W. 7th St., Winona, MN 55987. TEL 507-454-6564. Ed. Orval Lund. adv.; bk.rev.; circ. 800. (back issues avail.)

GREEK INDEX PROJECT SERIES. see HISTORY — History Of Europe

800   US   ISSN 0895-9307
PS1
GREEN MOUNTAINS REVIEW. 1987. s-a. $8.50. Johnson State College, Box A58, Johnson, VT 05656. TEL 802-635-2356. Eds. Neil Shepard, Tony Whedon. adv.: B&W page $75; adv. contact: adv. contact: Kate Riley. bk.rev.; circ. 1,000. (back issues avail.)
    Description: Covers contemporary poetry and fiction. Includes literary essays and interviews.

810   US   ISSN 0017-4009
PS501
GREEN RIVER REVIEW. 1968. 3/yr. $6. Green River Press, Inc., SVSC Box 56, University Center, MI 48710. Ed. Raymond Tyner. bk.rev.; circ. 500. **Indexed:** M.L.A.

810   CN   ISSN 0824-2992
GREEN'S MAGAZINE; fiction for the family. 1972. q. $12. Green's Educational Publications, Inc., P.O. Box 3236, Regina, Sask. S4P 3H1, Canada. Ed. David Green. adv.; bk.rev.; illus.; index; circ. 400.

810   US   ISSN 0017-4084
GREENSBORO REVIEW. 1966. 2/yr. $8. University of North Carolina at Greensboro, English Department, Greensboro, NC 27412. TEL 919-334-5459. FAX 919-334-3281. Ed. Jim Clark. adv.; circ. 600. (also avail. in microfilm from UMI; reprint service avail. from UMI) **Indexed:** A.I.P.P., Amer.Hum.Ind.
    Description: Fiction and poetry.

700   SP   ISSN 0017-4181
GRIAL; revista gallega de cultura. (Text in Gallegan) 1963. q. 4000 ptas. Editorial Galaxia, S.A., Reconquista 1, Vigo, Spain. TEL 43-21-00. FAX 22-32-05. Ed. Carlos Casares. bk.rev.; circ. 2,000. **Indexed:** M.L.A.

GRIDLEY WAVE. see LITERATURE — Science Fiction, Fantasy, Horror

850   IT
GROTTA DELLA VIPERA; rivista trimestrale di cultura. 1975. q. L.20000. Via Istria 45, 09100 Cagliari, Italy. Ed. Antonio Cossu. adv.; bk.rev.; illus.; circ. 1,000.

820   FR
GROUPE DE RECHERCHE ET D'ETUDES NORD-AMERICAINES. ACTES DU COLLOQUE. (Text in English, French) irreg., no.12, 1990. price varies. Universite de Provence, Service des Publications, 29 av. Robert Schuman, 13621 Aix-en-Provence Cedex 1, France. TEL 42-20-09-16.

895   CC
GUANGXI WENXUE/GUANGXI LITERATURE. (Text in Chinese) m. Guangxi Wenlian, 28 Jianzhen Lu, Nanning, Guangxi 530023, People's Republic of China. TEL 22120.

LITERATURE

895.1   CC   ISSN 0257-022X
GUANGZHOU WENYI/GUANGZHOU LITERATURE. (Text in Chinese) 1976. m. $58.50. Guangzhou Shi Wenlian, CC , Wenhua Dalou, 4th Floor, No. 170, Wende Lu, Guangzhou, Guangdong 510030, People's Republic of China. (Dist. in US by: China Books & Periodicals, Inc., 2929 24th St., San Francisco, CA 94110. TEL 415-282-2994) Ed. Gao Naiyan.

895.4   BR
GUARDIAN MAGAZINE. (Text in English) 1953. m. 392-396 Merchant St., Botahtaung PO, P.O. Box 1522, Yangon, Union of Myanmar. TEL 01-70150. circ. 11,600.

895.1   CC
GUDIAN WENXUE ZHISHI. (Text in Chinese) bi-m. Y7.20. Jiangsu Guji Chubanshe, 165 Zhongyang Lu, Nanjing, Jiangsu 210009, People's Republic of China. Ed.Bd.
   Description: Encourages the reading and study of classical Chinese literature.

895.1   CC
GUDIAN WENXUE ZHISHI/CLASSIC LITERATURE KNOWLEDGE. (Text in Chinese) bi-m. Jiangsu Guji Chubanshe - Jiangsu Classic Literature Publishers, 165 Zhongyang Lu, Nanjing, Jiangsu 210009, People's Republic of China. TEL 631836. Ed. Gao Jiyan.

800   US   ISSN 0160-6565
PN452
GUEST AUTHOR; a directory of speakers. 1978. biennial. $9.95. Hermes Press, 51 Lenox St., Brockton, MA 02401. Eds. Jane Manthorne, Rose Moorachian. circ. 2,000.

GULLIVER; German-English Yearbook. see *LINGUISTICS*

890   JA
GUNZO. (Text in Japanese) 1946. m. Kodansha Ltd., International Division, 12-21 Otowa 2-chome, Bunkyo-Ku, Tokyo 112, Japan. TEL 03-3945-1111. FAX 03-3943-7814. TELEX J34509 KODANSHA. Ed. Katsuo Watanabe. circ. 30,000.

895.1   CC
GUSHI DAGUAN. (Text in Chinese) m. Shandong Wenyi Chubanshe, No. 8, Taibailou Donglu, Jining, Shandong 272117, People's Republic of China. TEL 213169. Ed. Shao Jianming.

800 028.5   CC
GUSHI DAWANG. (Text in Chinese) m. Shaonian Ertong Chubanshe - Children's Publishing Company, 1538 Yan'an Xilu, Shanghai 200052, People's Republic of China. TEL 2513025. Ed. Yu Hexian.

895.1   CC
GUSHI JIA/STORY TELLER. (Text in Chinese) bi-m. Henan Sheng Wenlian, No. 34, Jing 7 Lu, Zhengzhou, Henan 450003, People's Republic of China. TEL 334916. Ed. Du Daoheng.

800   CC   ISSN 1002-2554
GUSHI LIN. (Text in Chinese) 1984. bi-m. Y4.20($2.40) Fujian Sheng Wenlian, Fenghuang Chi, Xihong Lu, Fuzhou, Fujian 350002, People's Republic of China. TEL 32871. (Dist. overseas by: Jiangsu Publications Import & Export Corp., 56 Gao Yun Ling, Nanjing, Jiangsu, P.R.C.) (Co-sponsor: Zhongguo Minjian Yishujia Xiehui Fujian Fenhui) Ed. Wang Meitian. adv.
   Description: Publishes ancient and contemporary folk stories, legends and local customs.

895.1   CC
GUSHI SHIJIE. (Text in Chinese) m. Haiyan Chubanshe, No. 73, Nongye Lu, Zhengzhou, Henan 450002, People's Republic of China. TEL 551756. Ed. Gao Mingxing.

895.1   CC   ISSN 0257-0238
GUSHIHUI/STORYTELLER. (Text in Chinese) 1978. m. $58.50. Shanghai Wenyi Chubanshe - Shanghai Literature & Art Press, 74 Shaoxing Lu, Shanghai 200020, People's Republic of China. TEL 4372608. (Dist. in US by: China Books & Periodicals, Inc., 2929 24th St., San Francisco, CA 94110. TEL 415-282-2994)

830   GW
GUSTAV FREYTAG BLAETTER. 1954. a. DM.24 membership. Gustav Freytag Gesellschaft e.V., Bahnhofstr. 71, 4030 Ratingen 6, Germany. TEL 02102-67341. bk.rev.; bibl.; illus.; circ. 500.
   Description: Articles about Gustav Freytag and his times; information for members.

811   US
GUTS. irreg. Box 2730, Long Beach, CA 90801. Ed. Keith A. Dodson. (back issues avail.)

800   US   ISSN 0176-3148
GYPSY; literary magazine. 1984. s-a. $10. Vergin Press, c/o Belinda Subraman, 10708 Gay Brewer Drive, El Paso, TX 79935. Ed. Belinda Subraman. adv.; bk.rev.; circ. 1,000. (back issues avail.)
   Description: Features poetry, fiction, interviews and articles, as well as artwork by independent literary and visual artists.

GYPSY LORE SOCIETY. JOURNAL. see *ANTHROPOLOGY*

800   US   ISSN 1040-4015
PS3507.0726
H D NEWSLETTER. (Hilda Doolittle) 1987. s-a. $10. Dallas Institute of Humanities and Culture, 2719 Routh St., Dallas, TX 75201. TEL 214-871-2440. FAX 214-969-1884. Ed. Eileen Gregory. circ. 150. **Indexed:** M.L.A.
   Description: Provides a locus of literary interchange to those engaged in research and writing on HD. Includes essays, notes, queries, notices of work-in-progress and of recent events, and conferences.

820   UK   ISSN 0306-5480
H.G. WELLS SOCIETY NEWSLETTER. 1960. 2/yr. £12 to institutions. H.G. Wells Society, H.G. Wells Centre, Nene College, Eng. Dept., Moulton Park, Northampton NN2 7AL, England. Ed. Sylvia Hardy. bk.rev.; cum.index every five yrs.; circ. 300. (looseleaf format; reprint service avail.)

800   IS
H S L A. (Hebrew University Studies in Literature and the Arts) 1973. s-a. $12. (Hebrew University of Jerusalem, Institute of Languages, Literatures and Arts) Magnes Press, Hebrew University, Jerusalem 91 905, Israel. Ed.Bd. circ. 1,000. **Indexed:** Abstr.Engl.Stud., Arts & Hum.Cit.Ind., Curr.Cont., M.L.A., Mid.East: Abstr.& Ind.
   Formerly (until 1983): H S L (ISSN 0333-5690)

810 355.115   US
H V W P IN ACTION. s-a. $15 to individuals; institutions and veterans $8 (includes Veterans' Voice). Hospitalized Veterans Writing Project, Inc., 5920 Nall, Rm. 102, Mission, KS 66202. Ed. Ronnie Millard. circ. 1,585.

830   GW
HABELTS DISSERTATIONSDRUCKE. REIHE GERMANISTIK. 1973. irreg. price varies. Dr. Rudolf Habelt GmbH, Am Buchenhang 1, 5300 Bonn 1, Germany.

810   US
▼**HABERSHAM REVIEW.** 1991. 2/yr. $12. Box 10, Demorest, GA 30535. TEL 404-778-2215. Eds. David Greeve, Lisa H. Lumpkin.
   Description: Publishes poetry, fiction, interviews, satire, reviews with a regional (Southeastern U.S.) focus.

HACIA LA LUZ. see *HANDICAPPED — Visually Impaired*

895.1   CC
HAI OU/SEA GULL LITERATURE. (Text in Chinese) m. $54. Qingdao Shi Wenlian, No. 25, Xinhaoshan Lu, Qingdao, Shandong 266003, People's Republic of China. TEL 226996. (Dist. in US by: China Books & Periodicals, Inc., 2929 24th St., San Francisco, CA 94110. TEL 415-282-2994) Ed. Xu Banfu.

895.1   CC
HAI YAN. (Text in Chinese) m. Dalian Wenxue Yishujie Lianhehui - Dalian Literary and Art Circle Association, 6 Baiyunshan, Xigang-qu, Dalian, Liaoning 116012, People's Republic of China. TEL 336980. Ed. Bi Fuhua.

810   US
HAIGHT ASHBURY LITERARY JOURNAL. 1980. irreg. (1-2/yr.) $5 for 2 issues. c/o Alice Rogoff, 558 Joost Ave., San Francisco, CA 94127. Ed.Bd. adv.; bk.rev.; circ. 1,600. (back issues avail.)
   Description: Publishes poetry, stories, and interviews of writers.

800   CC
HAIXIA/STRAIT. (Text in Chinese) 1981. q. Y19.8($11.40) (effective 1992). Haixia Wenyi Chubanshe, 27 Degui Xiang, Fuzhou, Fujian 350001, People's Republic of China. TEL 522384. (Dist. overseas by: Jiangsu Publications Import & Export Corp., 56 Gao Yun Ling, Nanjing, Jiangsu, P.R.C.) Ed. Lin Zhengrang. bk.rev.
   Description: Features writers from both sides of the Taiwan Straits and from overseas Chinese communities.

808   US   ISSN 0733-6616
HAMBONE. 1974. a. $10 to individuals for two issues; institutions $14. Hambone, 134 Hunelt St., Santa Cruz, CA 95060. TEL 408-426-3072. Ed. Nathaniel Mackey. bk.rev.; circ. 700.

820   II   ISSN 0256-2480
PR2807
HAMLET STUDIES; an international journal of research on the tragedy of Hamlet Prince of Denmark. (Text in English) 1979. s-a. $18. R.W. Desai Publishing Company Ltd., Rangoon Villa, 1-10 W. Patel Nagar, New Delhi 110 008, India. Ed. R.W. Desai. adv.; bk.rev.; circ. 300. (also avail. in microform; back issues avail.; reprint service avail. from GMC)
   Indexed: Abstr.Engl.Stud., M.L.A.
   —BLDSC shelfmark: 4241.472000.

HANZI WENHUA/CHINESE CULTURE. see *HUMANITIES: COMPREHENSIVE WORKS*

808   US
HARBOUR REVIEW. 1982. s-a. $7 for 3 nos. University of Massachusetts, English Department, Boston, MA 02125. Ed. Stephen Strempek. bk.rev.; cum.index: 1982-1984; circ. 500. (back issues avail.)

810   US
HARD ROW TO HOE. 1982-1987; resumed 1988. 3/yr. $7. Hard Row to Hoe (Subsidiary of: Misty Hill Press), Box 541-I, Healdsburg, CA 95448. Ed. Joe E. Armstrong. bk.rev.; circ. 500.
   Description: Covers book reviews, short story and poetry of rural America.

810   US
HARP-STRINGS. 1989. 3/yr. $20. 310 S. Adams St., Beverly Hills, FL 32265. Ed. Madelyn Eastlund. circ. 200.

378.1   US   ISSN 0017-8004
HARVARD ADVOCATE. 1866. q. $15. Harvard Advocate Trustees, Inc., Advocate House, 21 South St., Cambridge, MA 02138. TEL 617-495-0737. adv.; bk.rev.; film rev.; play rev.; illus.; circ. 10,000. (also avail. in microform from UMI; back issues avail.; reprint service avail. from UMI)
   Description: Contains fiction, poetry, and art work by Harvard College students.

HARVARD CELTIC COLLOQUIUM. PROCEEDINGS. see *LINGUISTICS*

800 420   US   ISSN 0073-0513
HARVARD ENGLISH STUDIES. 1970. irreg., vol.17, 1991. Harvard University Press, 79 Garden St., Cambridge, MA 02138. TEL 617-495-2600. FAX 617-495-5898. **Indexed:** M.L.A., Rel.Ind.Two.
   —BLDSC shelfmark: 4265.940000.

800   US   ISSN 0073-0696
HARVARD STUDIES IN COMPARATIVE LITERATURE. 1910. irreg., no.41, 1991. price varies. Harvard University Press, 79 Garden St., Cambridge, MA 02138. TEL 617-495-2600. FAX 617-495-5898. **Indexed:** M.L.A.
   Refereed Serial

HARVARD - YENCHING INSTITUTE. MONOGRAPH SERIES. see *HISTORY — History Of Asia*

LITERATURE

807   BG
HARVEST: JAHANGIRNAGAR STUDIES IN LITERATURE.
(Text in English) vol.2, 1978. a. Tk.15($1)
Jahangirnagar University, Department of English,
Rm. 223, Savar, Dhaka, Bangladesh. Ed. Nurul
Islam. bk.rev.; circ. 300.
   Formerly (until vol.5, 1983): Jahangirnagar
University. Department of English. Bulletin.

800 700   US
HARVESTER. 1972. a. Lincoln Land Community
College, Humanities Division, Shephard Rd.,
Springfield, IL 62794-9256. TEL 217-786-2330.
Ed. Mary A. Fortner. circ. 1,000. (back issues avail.)

810   US   ISSN 0093-9625
PS571.H3
HAWAII REVIEW. 1972. 3/yr. $12. University of Hawaii,
Board of Publications, 2465 Campus Dr., Honolulu,
HI 96822. TEL 808-948-8548. (Subscr. to:
Department of English, 1733 Donaghho Rd.,
Honolulu, HI 96822) Ed. Jeanne Tsutsui. adv.;
bk.rev.; illus.; circ. 2,000. **Indexed:** A.I.P.P.,
Amer.Hum.Ind.
   Formerly: Hawaii Literary Review (ISSN 0090-8274)

808.8   US
▼**HEARTLANDS TODAY.** 1991. a. Firelands College,
Firelands Writing Center, Huron, OH 44839.

830   GW   ISSN 0073-1560
PT2296.A1
HEBBEL - JAHRBUECHER. a. price varies.
(Hebbel-Gesellschaft) Westholsteinische
Verlagsanstalt Boyens und Co., Am
Wulf-Isebrand-Platz, Postfach 1880, 2240 Heide,
Germany. TEL 0481-691-0. Ed.Bd.

830   AU
HEBBEL - MENSCH UND DICHTER IM WERK. irreg., no.3,
1990. price varies. Verband der Wissenschaftlichen
Gesellschaften Oesterreichs, Lindengasse 37,
A-1070 Vienna, Austria. TEL 932166.

895.1   CC   ISSN 1000-9663
HEBEI WENXUE/HEBEI LITERATURE. (Text in Chinese)
m. Hebei Sheng Wenxue Yishu Jie Lianhehui, 2
Shizhuang Lu, Shigang Dajie, Shijiazhuang, Hebei
050000, People's Republic of China. TEL 745831.

059.927 001.3   US
HEBREW ANNUAL REVIEW; a journal of biblical and
Hebraic studies. 1977. a. $30. Ohio State
University, Department of Judaic and Near Eastern
Languages and Literatures, 1841 Millikin Rd.,
Columbus, OH 43210. TEL 614-422-9255.
(Subscr. to: Student Book Exchange, 1086 N. High
St., Columbus, OH 43201) Ed. Reuben Ahroni. adv.;
circ. 750. **Indexed:** Lang.& Lang.Behav.Abstr., M.L.A.,
Rel.& Theol.Abstr. (1982-), Rel.Ind.One, Rel.Ind.One,
Sociol.Abstr.

HEBREW STUDIES; a journal devoted to Hebrew
language and literature of all periods. see
LINGUISTICS

800   II
HEENAYANA; literary and cultural quarterly. (Text in
Bengali and English) 1974. q. Rs.8($6) Subhas
Ghosal, Ed. & Pub., 33-D, Sreemohon Lane, Calcutta
700026, India. adv.; bk.rev.; circ. 1,000. (back
issues avail.)

830   GW   ISSN 0933-8721
HEFTE FUER OSTASIATISCHE LITERATUR. 1985. s-a.
DM.20. Iudicium Verlag, P.O. Box 701067,
Waldfriedhofstr. 60, 8000 Munich 70, Germany.
TEL 089-718747.

800   CC
HEHUA DIAN. (Text in Chinese) bi-m. Baoding Shi
Wenlian, 14 Yuhua Donglu, Baoding, Hebei 071000,
People's Republic of China. TEL 24139. Ed. Hao
Jianqi.

053.1   GW
HEIMATJAHRBUCH KREIS AHRWEILER. 1981. a.
DM.8.50. Kreisverwaltung Ahrweiler, Wilhelmstr.,
5483 Ahrweiler, Germany. TEL 02641-384206.
FAX 02641-384456. TELEX 2641915-KVAW. adv.;
bk.rev.

830 920   GW   ISSN 0073-1692
PT2328
HEINE-JAHRBUCH. 1962. a. DM.25.
(Heinrich-Heine-Institut, Duesseldorf) Hoffmann und
Campe Verlag, Harvestehuder Weg 45, 2000
Hamburg 13, Germany. Ed. Joseph A. Kruse. bk.rev.;
circ. 1,300. **Indexed:** M.L.A.

800   GW
HEINE SAEKULARAUSGABE:
WERKE-BRIEFWECHSEL-LEBENSZEUGNISSE. (Text in
French and German) 1970. irreg., vol.15, 1989.
Akademie-Verlag Berlin, Leipziger Str. 3-4, 1086
Berlin, Germany. TELEX 114420-AVERL-DD.
   Description: Compilation of Heine's work and
correspondence, in the original languages.

800   HU   ISSN 0017-999X
PN9
HELIKON; vilagirodalmi figyelo. (Text in Hungarian;
summaries in French and Russian) 1955. q.
$23.50. (Magyar Tudomanyos Akademia,
Irodalomtudomanyi Intezet) Akademiai Kiado,
Publishing House of the Hungarian Academy of
Sciences, P.O. Box 24, H-1363 Budapest, Hungary.
Eds. B. Kopeczi, L. Hopp. adv.; bk.rev.; index.
Indexed: Hist.Abstr., M.L.A.

840   US   ISSN 0160-0923
PA1
HELIOS (LUBBOCK). 1974. s-a. $15 to individuals;
institutions $27. (Classical Association of the
Southwestern United States) Texas Tech University
Press, Lubbock, TX 79409-1037.
TEL 806-742-2982. Ed. Steven M. Oberhelman.
adv.; bk.rev.; circ. 363. **Indexed:** Arts & Hum.Cit.Ind.
—BLDSC shelfmark: 4285.330000.

820 821   AT   ISSN 0155-9044
HELIX. 1978. 4/yr. Aus.$12. Victoria College, 119
Maltravers Rd., Ivanhoe 3079, Australia. Ed. David
Brooks. adv.; bk.rev.; film rev.; play rev.; illus.; circ.
2,000.

880 480   GW   ISSN 0018-0084
PA5201
HELLENIKA; Zeitschrift fuer deutsch-griechische
kulturelle und wirtschaftliche Zusammenarbeit.
1964. a. DM.20. (Ausgaben Neugriechische
Studien) Verlag Ferdinand Kamp, Am Dornbusch 28,
4630 Bochum, Germany. Ed. Isidora
Rosenthal-Kamarinea. adv.; bk.rev.; abstr.; bibl.; circ.
3,000. **Indexed:** Hist.Abstr., M.L.A.
—BLDSC shelfmark: 4285.465000.

806   US   ISSN 0739-7801
HEMINGWAY NEWSLETTER. 1981. s-a. membership.
Hemingway Society, c/o Charles M. Oliver, Ed., Ohio
Northern University, Department of English, Ada, OH
45810. TEL 419-772-2107. bibl.; illus.; stat.; circ.
700. (reprint service avail. from UMI)

809   US   ISSN 0276-3362
PS3515.E37
HEMINGWAY REVIEW. 1971. s-a. $9 to individuals;
institutions $15. Hemingway Society, c/o Charles M.
Oliver, Ed., Ohio Northern University, Department of
English, Ada, OH 45810. TEL 419-772-2107.
bk.rev.; bibl.; circ. 950. (also avail. in microform
from UMI; reprint service avail. from UMI) **Indexed:**
Abstr.Engl.Stud., Ind.Bk.Rev.Hum., M.L.A.
   Formerly (until 1981): Hemingway Notes (ISSN 0046-7243)

807   US   ISSN 0273-0340
PS2124
HENRY JAMES REVIEW. 1979. 3/yr. $21 to individuals
(foreign $23.25); institutions $35 (foreign $37.25).
(Henry James Society) Johns Hopkins University
Press, Journals Publishing Division, 701 W. 40th St.,
Ste. 275, Baltimore, MD 21211.
TEL 410-516-6987. FAX 410-516-6998. Ed.
Daniel Mark Fogel. adv.; bk.rev.; circ. 698. **Indexed:**
Abstr.Engl.Stud., Ind.Bk.Rev.Hum., LCR, M.L.A.
—BLDSC shelfmark: 4295.760000.
   Description: Critical essays and reviews by noted
critics of James, such as Leon Edel and Adeline
Tintner.

305.4 800   US   ISSN 0898-0241
HER OWN WORDS; women's history & literature media.
1987. q. $10. Her Own Words, Box 5264, Madison,
WI 53705. TEL 608-271-7083. Ed. Jocelyn Riley.
(back issues avail.)

820   UK   ISSN 0073-1927
HERBERT READ SERIES. 1961. irreg. £1.25($1.95)
Oleander Press, 17 Stansgate Ave., Cambridge CB2
2QZ, England. (U.S. address: 80 Eighth Ave., Ste.
303, New York, NY 10011) Ed. Philip Ward.

830   GW
HERMAEA; germanistische Forschungen N.F. irreg.,
no.65, 1992. Max Niemeyer Verlag, Postfach 2140,
7400 Tuebingen 1, Germany. TEL 07071-81104.
FAX 07071-87419. Eds. Hans Fromm,
Hans-Joachim Maehl. (back issues avail.) **Indexed:**
M.L.A.
   Description: Monographs on German language and
literature.

HERODOTE; revue de geographie et de geopolitique. see
GEOGRAPHY

809 400   JA   ISSN 0387-9348
HERON; essays on language & literature. (Text in
English and Japanese) 1966. a. Saitama Daigaku -
Saitama University, 255 Shimo-Okubo, Urawa-shi,
Saitama-ken 338, Japan. Ed.Bd. circ. 200.
   Description: Articles on American and English
literature, English linguistics and Japanology.

800   CS
HET. (Text in Hungarian) w. $65. (Cultural Union of
Hungarians in Czechoslovakia - CSEMADOK) Obzor,
Ceskoslovenskej Armady 35, 815 85 Bratislava,
Czechoslovakia.

810   US   ISSN 0888-4153
HIGH PLAINS LITERARY REVIEW. 1986. 3/yr. $20. High
Plains Literary Review, Inc., 180 Adams St., Ste.
250, Denver, CO 80206. TEL 303-320-6828. Ed.
Robert O. Greer, Jr. adv.; bk.rev.; circ. 1,100. (back
issues avail.)
   Description: Fiction, poetry, interviews, reviews, and
essays designed to bridge the gap between
academic and commercial literary quarterlies.

059.927   UA   ISSN 0378-4010
AL-HILAL. 1893. m. Dar al- Hilal, 16 Sharia
Muhammad Ezz el-Arab, Cairo, Egypt.
TEL 02-27954. TELEX 92703. Ed. Husain Mones.

810   US
HILL AND HOLLER; southern Appalachian mountains.
1983. a. $14. Seven Buffaloes Press, Box 249, Big
Timber, MT 59011. Ed. Art Cuelho. circ. 750.
   Description: Lifestyles and culture of Appalachian
mountain people.

890   II
HINDI KAHANI. (Text in Hindi) 1977. a. Rs.125($8)
Granthayan, 398 Sarvoday Nagar, Sasni Gate,
Aligarh 202001, India. Eds. Rakeshgupta, R.K.
Chaturvedi. circ. 1,100. (back issues avail.)

HINDUSTANI ZABAN. see LINGUISTICS

800   US   ISSN 1050-6802
HIPPO. 1988. s-a. $6. Chautauqua Press, 28834
Boniface Dr., Malibu, CA 90265.
TEL 213-457-7871. Ed. Karl Heiss. adv.; circ. 200.
(back issues avail.)

800   US   ISSN 0363-0471
PQ7081.A1   CODEN: HSPAEC
HISPAMERICA; revista de literatura. (Text in Spanish)
1972. 3/yr. $30. c/o Saul Sosnowski, Ed., 5 Pueblo
Court, Gaithersburg, MD 20878.
TEL 301-948-3494. adv.; bk.rev.; bibl.; circ. 1,000.
(back issues avail.) **Indexed:** Arts & Hum.Cit.Ind.,
Curr.Cont., Hisp.Amer.Per.Ind., M.L.A.
   Description: Devoted to Spanish-American
literature. Publishes essays, bibliographic notes, and
reviews, fiction, poetry, and interviews with leading
writers.

HISPANIC REVIEW; a quarterly journal devoted to
research in the Hispanic languages and literatures.
see LINGUISTICS

860 US ISSN 0018-2206
PQ6001
HISPANOFILA. (Text in English, Portuguese, Spanish) 1957. 3/yr. $18 to individuals; libraries $21. University of North Carolina at Chapel Hill, Department of Romance Languages, CB 3170, 238 Dey Hall, Chapel Hill, NC 27599-3170. TEL 919-962-1025. Ed. Fred M. Clark. bk.rev.; index, cum.index every 3 yrs.; circ. 500. (also avail. in microform from UMI; reprint service avail. from UMI) **Indexed:** Arts & Hum.Cit.Ind., Can.Rev.Comp.Lit., Curr.Cont., Ind.Bk.Rev.Hum., M.L.A.
—BLDSC shelfmark: 4315.785000.

860 407 056 370 GW ISSN 0720-1168
HISPANORAMA. (Text in German, Spanish) 1972. 3/yr. DM.40($12) Deutscher Spanischlehrerverband, Braillestr. 17, 8500 Nuernberg 90, Germany. TEL 0911-351561. Ed. Anton Bemmerlein. adv.; bk.rev.; bibl.; circ. 2,000.

100 800 SZ ISSN 0073-2397
HISTOIRE DES IDEES ET CRITIQUE LITTERAIRE. (Text in French; occasionally in English) 1954. irreg., no.297, 1991. price varies. Librairie Droz S.A., 11, rue Massot, CH-1211 Geneva 12, Switzerland. TEL 022-466666. FAX 022-472391. circ. 1,500.
—BLDSC shelfmark: 4316.009000.
Description: Examines the history of ideas and literary critique from an academic perspective.

810 793 US
HOB-NOB. 1969. s-a. $6 to individuals; libraries $5.50 (effective Jan. 1991). Mildred K. Henderson, Ed. & Pub., 994 Nissley Rd., Lancaster, PA 17601. TEL 717-898-7807. bk.rev.; circ. 450.
Former titles: Hob-Nob Annual; (until 1979): Hob-Nob Quarterly.
Description: Original prose, poetry, reviews, letters and cartoons.

800 AG
HOJAS LITERARIAS ILUSTRADAS. (Text in Spanish and Yiddish) vol.22, 1976. bi-m. free. Moises Knaphais, Ed. & Pub., Rem. Esc. de San Martin 2670-Dto. C., Buenos Aires, Argentina. adv.; bk.rev.; film rev.; play rev.; charts; illus.; circ. 3,000.

800 CN ISSN 1180-1670
▼**HOLE.** 1990. 2/yr. Can.$8. Hole Magazine, 147 Sweetland Ave., Ottawa, Ont. K1N 7V1, Canada. Eds. Louis Cabri, Robert Manery. bk.rev.; circ. 300.
Description: Magazine of critical writing, reading, poetry and prose.

808.8 700 CN
HOMINIDS, OH!. 1977. irreg. $3. Kiddelidivee Books, 1812-415 Willowdale Ave., Willowdale, Ont. M2N 5B4, Canada. Ed. Taral Wayne. circ. 800.
Former titles (until 1986): New Toy; March to the Beat of a Red Shift Drum.

808 FR
HOMMES ET LES LETTRES. irreg., vol.2, 1977. Editions l' Hermes, 31 rue Pasteur, 69007 Lyon, France. Ed. Jacques Goudet.

895.6 JA
HON. (Text in Japanese) 1977. m. Kodansha Ltd., International Division, 12-21 Otowa 2-chome, Bunkyo-ku, Tokyo 112, Japan. TEL 03-3945-1111. FAX 03-3943-7815. TELEX J34509 KODANSHA. Ed. Shunkichi Yabuki. circ. 50,000.
Description: Publishes short essays.

800 UK ISSN 0018-4543
AP4
HONEST ULSTERMAN. 1968. irreg. (3-4/yr.). £14 to individuals; institutions £17. Ulsterman Publications, 102 Elm Park Mansions, Park Walk, London SW10 0AP, England. Eds. Robert Johnstone, Ruth Hooley. adv.; bk.rev.; cum.index 1968-1985; circ. 1,000. (back issues avail.)

895 CC
HONG DOU. (Text in Chinese) m. Nanning Shi Wenlian, Minsheng Lu, Nanning, Guangxi 530012, People's Republic of China. TEL 26093. Ed. Wei Weizu.

895.1 CC
HONG YAN. (Text in Chinese) bi-m. Y21. (Chongqing Wenxue Yishu Jie Lianhehui) Hongyan Wenxue Zazhishe, 30, Chongqing Cun, Zhongshan 3rd Rd., Chongqing 630015, People's Republic of China. TEL 554065. illus.

801.953 CC
HONGLOUMENG XUEKAN/STUDIES ON A DREAM OF RED MANSIONS. (Text in Chinese; table of contents in English) q. Y12.80($34.70) (Zhongguo Yishu Yanjiuyuan - Chinese Art Academy) Wenhua Yishu Chubanshe, 17, Qianhai Xijie, Beijing 100009, People's Republic of China. TEL 651128. (Dist. outside China by: China International Book Trading Corp., P.O. Box 399, Beijing, P.R.C.; Dist. in US by: China Books & Periodicals, Inc., 2929 24th St., San Francisco, CA 94110. TEL 415-282-2994) Ed. Feng Qiyong. bk.rev.
Description: Presents literary and historical studies on all aspects of the eighteenth-century novel "Hong Lou Meng" (A Dream of Red Mansions).

801.953 CC ISSN 1001-277X
"HONGLOUMENG" YANJIU. (Subseries of: Fuyin Baokan Ziliao) (Text in Chinese) q. Y7. Zhongguo Renmin Daxue, Shubao Ziliao Zhongxin - China People's University, Book & Newspaper Information Center, P.O. Box 1122, Beijing 100007, People's Republic of China. TEL 441792. adv.
Description: Reprints articles and papers concerning the Qing dynasty novel "Hong Lou Meng" (A Dream of Red Mansions).

810 US
HOOSIER CHALLENGER.* 1956. q. $12. Claire Emerson, Ed. & Pub., 9423 Montgomery Rd., Cincinnati, OH 45242-7602. adv.; bk.rev.; illus.; tr.lit.

800 US
HOR-TASY. 1980. irreg. (approx a.). $2.95. Ansuda Publications, Box 158-B, Harris, IA 51345. Ed. Daniel R. Betz.
Description: Contains fiction only; uses psychological horror and pure fantasy - no science fiction.

800 GW ISSN 0018-4942
DIE HOREN; Zeitschrift fuer Literatur, Grafik und Kritik. 1955. q. DM.48. Wirtschaftsverlag NW, Verlag fuer neue Wissenschaft GmbH, Postfach 101110, 2850 Bremerhaven, Germany. TEL 0471-46093. Ed. Kurt Morawietz. adv.; bk.rev.; illus.; circ. 5,500. (reprint service avail. from KTO)

895.9 IO
HORISON. 1966. m. Jalan Gajah Mada 104-110A, Jakarta Barat, Indonesia. Eds. Mochtar Lubis, H.B. Jassin. circ. 4,000.

839.7 FI ISSN 0439-5530
HORISONT. (Text in Swedish) 1954. 6/yr. FIM 150 (SEK 220). Svenska Oesterbottens Litteraturfoerening, Kyrkoesplanaden 19 A 10, 65100 Vasa, Finland. TEL 961-128426. Ed. Maria Sandin. adv.; bk.rev.; play rev.; illus.; index; circ. 3,600.
—BLDSC shelfmark: 4326.792700.

810 US
HORIZONS BEYOND. 1983. 2/yr. $18. Baker Street Publications, Box 994, Metairie, LA 70004. TEL 504-734-8414. Ed. Sharida Rizzuto. circ. 9,000.

810 US
HORIZONS WEST. 1983. 2/yr. $18.60. Baker Street Publications, Box 994, Metairie, LA 70004. TEL 504-734-8414. Ed. Sharida Rizzuto. circ. 9,000.

860 861 US
HORIZONTES (PATERSON). 1983. a. $4. Passaic County Community College, Poetry Center, College Blvd., Paterson, NJ 07509. TEL 201-684-6555. Ed. Jose A. Villalongo, Sr. illus.; circ. 800.

HORROR FICTION NEWSLETTER. see LITERATURE — Science Fiction, Fantasy, Horror

891.439 PK
HOSHRUBA DA'IJIST. (Text in Urdu) 1978. m. Rs.65. Ali Aufyan Afagi, 20-B Model Town, Lahore, Pakistan.

810 US
HOT FLASHES. 1985. 10/yr. $15. 5926 Marquita Ave., Dallas, TX 75206-6116. circ. 200.

800 UK ISSN 0305-926X
PR4809.H15
HOUSMAN SOCIETY JOURNAL. 1974. a. £5.39. Housman Society, Mrs V. Richardson, 1 Warwick Hall Gardens, Bromsgrove B60 2AU, England. adv.; bk.rev.; bibl.; circ. 350. (back issues avail.) **Indexed:** M.L.A.
—BLDSC shelfmark: 4335.152500.

800 US ISSN 0888-3521
HOWLING DOG; a journal of letters, words and lines. 1985. s-a. $10. Parkville Publishing, 8419 Rhode Dr., Utica, MI 48087. TEL 313-254-5334. Ed. Mark Donovan. adv.; bk.rev.; illus.; circ. 500. (back issues avail.)
Description: Contains humor, fiction, poetry and art.

810 US
HOWLING MANSTRA. 1988. a. $5. Box 1821, La Crosse, WI 57602. TEL 608-785-0810. circ. 150.

894.2 US
HUA DE YUANYE/PRAIRIE OF FLOWERS. (Text in Mongolian) m. $54. China Books & Periodicals, Inc., 2929 24th St., San Francisco, CA 94110. TEL 415-282-2994. FAX 415-282-0994.

895.15 CC ISSN 1000-789X
HUACHENG. (Text in Chinese) 1979. bi-m. Y22.80($67.80) Huacheng Chubanshe, No. 11, Shuiyin Lu, Huanshi Donglu, Guangzhou, Guangdong 510075, People's Republic of China. TEL 768688. (Dist. outside China by: China International Book Trading Corp., P.O. Box 399, Beijing, P.R.C.; Dist. in US by: China Books & Periodicals, Inc., 2929 24th St., San Francisco, CA 94110. TEL 415-282-2994) Ed. Fan Hansheng. adv.

895.1 CC ISSN 1000-4823
HUANG HE/YELLOW RIVER. (Text in Chinese) 1985. bi-m. Y18. Zhongguo Zuojia Xiehui, Shanxi Fenhui - China Writer's Association, Shanxi Chapter, Dongsitiao Nanhuamen, Taiyuan, Shanxi 030001, People's Republic of China. TEL 382495. Ed. Shan Quan. circ. 10,000.

895.1 CC ISSN 1002-686X
HUAXI; qingnian wenxue yuekan. (Text in Chinese) 1978. m. Y14.40. 27, Shizi Lu, Guiyang, Guizhou 550001, People's Republic of China. Ed.Bd.
Description: Contains short stories, poetry, prose. Also includes translations.

800 700 PE
HUESO HUMERO. 1979. s-a. $9 per no. Mosca Azul Editores, Conquistadores 1130, Lima 27, Peru. Eds. Mirko Lauer, Abelardo Oquendo. bk.rev.; circ. 1,500. **Indexed:** Hisp.Amer.Per.Ind.

810 US
HUMERUS. 1988. 3/yr. $14. Box 222, Piermont, NY 10986. TEL 914-358-2371. circ. 1,500.

895.1 CC ISSN 0439-8106
HUNAN WENXUE/HUNAN LITERATURE. (Text in Chinese) m. $47.70. Hunan Sheng Wenlian, Building No. 17, Dongfeng 2 Cun, Changsha, Hunan 410003, People's Republic of China. TEL 24821. (Dist. in US by: China Books & Periodicals, Inc., 2929 24th St., San Francisco, CA 94110. TEL 415-282-2994) Ed. Wang Yiping.

894.51 HU ISSN 0439-9080
HUNGARIAN P.E.N./P.E.N. HONGROIS. (Text in English and French) 1961. a. free. Hungarian P.E.N. Club, Vorosmarty ter 1, 1051 Budapest, Hungary. Ed. Imre Szasz. adv.; bk.rev.; bibl.; circ. 1,000. **Indexed:** M.L.A.

HUNGARIAN STUDIES NEWSLETTER. see LINGUISTICS

HUNGRY MIND REVIEW; a Midwestern book review. see PUBLISHING AND BOOK TRADE

LITERATURE

810 US ISSN 0018-7895
Z733.S24
HUNTINGTON LIBRARY QUARTERLY; studies in English and American literature, history, and art. 1931. q. $46 (foreign $54). Huntington Library, Art Collections and Botanical Gardens, 1151 Oxford Rd., San Marino, CA 91108. TEL 818-405-2172. FAX 818-405-0225. Ed. Guilland Sutherland. bk.rev.; illus.; index; circ. 1,000. (also avail. in microfilm from UMI; reprint service avail. from UMI,KTO) Indexed: Abstr.Engl.Stud., Amer.Hist.& Life, Amer.Hum.Ind., Curr.Cont., Hist.Abstr., Hum.Ind., Ind.Bk.Rev.Hum., LCR, M.L.A.
—BLDSC shelfmark: 4337.460000.
Description: Publishes scholarly articles with special attention to the research fields of the Huntington Library collections, concentrating on the literature, history and art of the 16th to 18th centuries in Britain and America.

800 GW ISSN 0176-8123
HYDRONYMIA EUROPAEA. irreg., vol.6, 1990. price varies. (Akademie der Wissenschaften und der Literatur, Mainz, Klasse Literatur) Franz Steiner Verlag Wiesbaden GmbH, Birkenwaldstr. 44, Postfach 101526, 7000 Stuttgart 1, Germany. TEL 0711-2582-0. FAX 0711-2582290. Ed. Wolfgang P. Schmid.

890 KO
HYUNDAE MUNHAK. (Text in Korean) 1955. m. 17000 Won. Mokjung Bldg., 6th Floor, 1361-5 Seocho-dong, Seocho-ku, Seoul, S. Korea. Ed. Kim Kwang-Soo. circ. 200,000.

809 US ISSN 0161-9225
PN51
I & L. (Ideologies and Literature); a journal of Hispanic and Luso-Brazilian discourse analysis. (Text in English, French, Portuguese, Spanish) 1977. s-a. $18 to individuals; institutions $30. Prisma Institute, 4 Folwell Hall, 9 Pleasant St., S.E., University of Minnesota, Minneapolis, MN 55455. TEL 612-625-9028. Ed. James V. Romano. circ. 1,500. (back issues avail.) Indexed: Curr.Cont., Hisp.Amer.Per.Ind., M.L.A.

I B L A. (Institut des Belles Lettres Arabes) see ORIENTAL STUDIES

860 861 VE
I C A M; revista literaria. 1971. q. free. Alberto Jose Perez, Ed. & Pub., Urb. Manuel Palacios Fajardo, Bloque 4, Edif. 01, Apdo. 0302, Barinas, Venezuela. (Subscr. to: I C A M, Apartado de Correos 127, Barinas, Venezuela) bk.rev.; abstr.; bibl.; illus.; circ. 2,000. (back issues avail.)

800 US ISSN 0887-3615
I C L A BULLETIN. irreg. (approx. 3/yr.). $15 for 3 years. International Comparative Literature Association, c/o Steven P. Sondrup, Ed., Department of Comparative Literature, Brigham Young University, Provo, UT 84602. TEL 801-378-2579. circ. 4,000.

800 GW
I J B - REPORT. (Text mainly in German; occasionally in English, French; summaries in English) 1983. q. free. Internationale Jugendbibliothek - International Youth Library, Schloss Blutenburg, 8000 Munich 60, Germany. TEL 089-8112028. FAX 089-8117553. Ed. Andreas Bode. circ. 3,900.
Description: News about the children's literature scene and the activities of the library.

809 US ISSN 0271-9061
I.O. EVANS STUDIES IN THE PHILOSOPHY & CRITICISM OF LITERATURE. 1982. irreg., no.17, 1992 (approx. 4/yr.). price varies. Borgo Press, Box 2845, San Bernardino, CA 92406. TEL 714-884-5813. Ed. Boden Clarke.
—BLDSC shelfmark: 4563.747400.
Description: Includes monographs on general literary topics, histories and discussions of genre fiction, anthologies of essays on specific literary themes, philosophical discussions of literature, and books on related topics.

I U O M A MAGAZINE. (International Union of Mail Artists) see ART

I W I NEWSLETTER. (Illinois Writers, Inc.) see JOURNALISM

892.76 UA
IBDA/INNOVATION. (Text in Arabic) 1983. m. $12 to individuals; institutions $24. (Al-Hai'ah al-Misriyyah al-Aamah lil-Kuttab) Magallat Ibda', 27 Sharia Abd al-Khaliq Tharwat, P.O. Box 626, Cairo, Egypt. TEL 757691. Ed. Abd al-Qadir al-Qatt. adv.; bk.rev.; illus.
Description: Publishes short stories, poetry, plays and critical studies on the arts and literature in Egypt.

800 700 IE ISSN 0019-1027
ICARUS. 1950. irreg. (3-7/yr.). £15($20) to individuals; students £8($10). University of Dublin, Regents House, Trinity College, Dublin, Ireland. Ed.Bd. adv.; bk.rev.; film rev.; circ. 1,000.

810 US
ICARUS REVIEW. 1989. 2/yr. $6. McOne Press, Box 51074, Austin, TX 78763. TEL 512-477-2269. Ed. Mark Lawrence. circ. 400.

830 GW ISSN 0445-1821
ICH SCHREIBE; Zeitschrift fuer schreibende Arbeiter. vol.13, 1972. 4/yr. DM.11 per no. Zentralhaus-Publikationen, Dittrichring 4, 7010 Leipzig, Germany. Ed. Ursula Dauderstaedt. bk.rev.; bibl.; illus.

800 IS ISSN 0333-838X
PJ5001
IDENTITY. 1980. s-a. $25. Haberman Institute for Literary Research, P.O. Box 166, Lod 71101, Israel. TEL 08-244569. FAX 08-249466. Ed. Z. Malachi. adv.; bk.rev.; circ. 2,000. Indexed: Ind.Heb.Per.
Description: Studies in Jewish culture and literature.

860 AG ISSN 0019-1663
IGITUR REVISTA LITERARIA. no.4, 1967. q. Republica de Israel 115, Cordoba, Argentina. Ed. Carlos Cullere. adv.; bk.rev.; bibl.

890 IS
IGRA. a. P.O. Box 7145, Jerusalem 91 071, Israel. TEL 02-521201.

813 US
ILLINOIS SHORT FICTION. irreg. University of Illinois Press, 54 E. Gregory Dr., Champaign, IL 61820. TEL 217-333-0950.
Refereed Serial

ILOCOS REVIEW. see HISTORY — History Of Australasia And Other Areas

IMAGE. see ORIENTAL STUDIES

810 US ISSN 0748-1780
IMAGE MAGAZINE;* a magazine of the arts. (Text in English, German, Spanish) 1972. irreg. (approx. 3/yr.). $6. Cornerstone Press, Box 388, Arnold, MO 63010-0388. TEL 314-296-9662. Eds. Anthony J. Summers, James J. Finnegan. bk.rev.; illus.; circ. 750. (also avail. in microfiche)

IMAGERY TODAY. see PSYCHOLOGY

810 US
▼IMAGINATION MAGAZINE. 1990. 13/yr. $21. Box 781, Dolton, IL 60419. circ. 100.

800 IT
IMMAGINE RIFLESSA; rivista di sociologia della letteratura. 1977. s-a. L.19000($19) Tilgher-Genova s.a.s., Via Assarotti 52, 16122 Genoa, Italy. Ed. Nicolo Pasero. adv.; bk.rev.; index.

800 US ISSN 0741-6180
IN CONTEXT; a quarterly of humane sustainable culture. 1980. q. $18 (foreign $25). Context Institute, Box 11470, Bainbridge Island, WA 98110. TEL 206-842-0216. FAX 206-842-5208. Ed. Alan Atkinson. illus.; circ. 11,000.
Description: Information source about strategies for creating a more humane and sustainable culture.

895.6 JA
IN POCKET. (Text in Japanese) 1983. m. Kodansha Ltd., International Division, 12-21 Otowa 2-chome, Bunkyo-ku, Tokyo 112, Japan. TEL 03-3945-1111. FAX 03-3943-7815. TELEX J34509 KODANSHA. Ed. Yoshimi Sugiyama. circ. 80,000.
Description: Publishes essays and novels.

IN SEARCH OF A SONG. see CHILDREN AND YOUTH — For

808 910.03 US
IN TOUCH (CHICAGO). m. membership. International Black Writers Conference, Box 1030, Chicago, IL 60690. TEL 312-924-3818. bk.rev.
Description: Covers writing competitions, member activities and new books written by Afro-American writers.

INDAGINI E PROSPETTIVE. see POLITICAL SCIENCE

INDEPENDENT PUBLISHING REPORT. see JOURNALISM

820 US ISSN 0019-3763
PR5366
INDEPENDENT SHAVIAN. 1962. 3/yr. $15 to libraries and non-members (foreign $20). Bernard Shaw Society, Inc., Box 1373, Grand Central Sta., New York, NY 10163. Ed.Bd. adv.; bk.rev.; play rev.; index; circ. 300. (also avail. in microfilm from UMI; reprint service avail. from UMI) Indexed: Abstr.Engl.Stud., M.L.A.
—BLDSC shelfmark: 4375.920000.

820 II
INDIAN AUTHOR. (Text in English) 1976. q. Rs.20($4) Authors Guild of India, F-12 Jangpura Ext., New Delhi 110 014, India. TEL 11-615063. Ed.Bd. adv.; bk.rev.; circ. 2,000.

INDIAN HORIZONS. see HISTORY — History Of Asia

INDIAN JOURNAL OF AMERICAN STUDIES. see HISTORY — History Of North And South America

891.1 II ISSN 0019-5804
AP8
INDIAN LITERATURE. (Text in English) 1957. bi-m. Rs.20($12) National Academy of Letters - Sahitya Akademi, 35 Ferozeshah Rd., Rabindra Bhavan, New Delhi 110 001, India. TEL 38 20 50. Ed. D.S. Rao. adv.; bk.rev.; bibl.; illus.; index, cum.index; circ. 2,500. Indexed: Abstr.Engl.Stud., Arts & Hum.Cit.Ind., Curr.Cont., M.L.A.
Description: Devoted to the dissemination of Indian literature.

820 II ISSN 0019-6053
PK101
THE INDIAN P.E.N.. (Text in English) 1934. q. Rs.30($7.50) P.E.N. All-India Centre, Theosophy Hall, 40, New Marine Lines, Bombay 400 020, India. TEL 292175. Ed. Nissim Ezekiel. adv.; bk.rev.; circ. 750. Indexed: M.L.A.

801 808.1 II
INDIAN WRITER. (Text in English) 1986. q. Rs.20($15) to non-members. Writer's Club, C-23, Annanagar E., Madras 600 102, India. TEL 615370. TELEX 41-24064. Ed. P.K. Joy. bk.rev.; circ. 900.
Description: Covers literary news.

810 US
INDIANA ENGLISH. 1966. 3/yr. $10 to non-members. Indiana Council of Teachers of English, Inc., Department of English, Indiana State University, Terre Haute, IN 47809. TEL 812-237-3147. Ed. Robert Perrin. bk.rev.; circ. 800 (controlled). Indexed: Bibl.Engl.Lang.& Lit.
Former titles (until 1977): Indiana English Journal (ISSN 0019-6584); Indiana English Leaflet.

800 US ISSN 0738-386X
PS536.2
INDIANA REVIEW. 1975. 2/yr. $12 to individuals; institutions $15. 316 N. Jordan Ave., Indiana University, Bloomington, IN 47405. TEL 812-855-3439. Ed. Dorian Gossy. adv.; circ. 800. (back issues avail.) Indexed: A.I.P.P., Amer.Hum.Ind., Ind.Amer.Per.Verse.
Formerly: Indiana Writes (ISSN 0149-3361)
Description: Covers poetry, fiction, non-fiction prose, and personal essays, interviews and translations.

810 US
INDIGENOUS WORLD/MUNDO INDIGENA. (Text in English, Spanish) 1982. 2/yr. $20. 275 Grand View Ave., No. 103, San Francisco, CA 94114. TEL 415-647-1966. circ. 10,000.

800 320 II ISSN 0378-0856
INDO-IRANICA. (Text in English and Persian) 1946. q. $25. Iran Society, 12 Dr. M. Ishaque Rd., Calcutta 700 016, India. Ed. M.A. Majid. bk.rev.; illus.; circ. 750.

491.1 891.1 II
INDOLOGICAL STUDIES. Variant title: University of Delhi. Department of Sanskrit. Journal. (Text in English) 1972. s-a. University of Delhi, Department of Sanskrit, Delhi 110007, India.

860 MX ISSN 0186-7067
INFAME TURBA. 1986. m. Universidad Autonoma de Puebla, Coordinacion de Difusion Cultural, Reforma 913-altos, C.P. 72000, Puebla, Pue., Mexico. TEL 46 38 91. Ed. Alfonso Velez Pliego. adv.; bk.rev.; circ. 2,000.

810 US
INFINITE ONION. 1989. 5/yr. $5. Box 263, Colorado Springs, CO 80901. TEL 719-473-2647. circ. 1,000.

800 700 US ISSN 1050-7280
INFINITY LIMITED; a journal for the somewhat eccentric. (Text in English, French, Spanish) 1988. q. $12.95 to individuals; institutions $15. Ken and Genie Lester, 3243 Sydney Way, Box 2713, Castro Valley, CA 94546-0546. TEL 415-581-8172. Ed. Genie Lester. adv.; B&W page $100. bk.rev.; circ. 1,000. (back issues avail.)

840 FR ISSN 0020-0123
PN3
INFORMATION LITTERAIRE; revue illustree paraissant tous les deux mois pendant la periode scolaire. 1949. 5/yr. 235 F. Societe d'Edition les Belles Lettres, 95 bd. Raspail, 75006 Paris, France. Ed. M. Beaujeu. bk.rev.; bibl.; illus.; index; circ. 6,000. (reprint service avail. from KTO)
—BLDSC shelfmark: 4493.685000.

INFORMER; international poetry magazine. see LITERATURE — Poetry

810 US
INKBLOT. 1983. 4/yr. $12. Inkblot Publications, 439 49th St., Ste. 11, Oakland, CA 94609-2158. Ed. Theo Green. circ. 1,000.

808.1 US ISSN 0085-1884
INLET. 1972. a. free. Virginia Wesleyan College, Department of English, Norfolk, VA 23502. TEL 804-461-3232. Ed. Joseph Harkey. circ. 750.

820 CN
INNER SEARCH. 1990. 4/yr. $9. P.O. Box 3577, Station C, Ottawa, Ont. K1Y 4J7, Canada. circ. 180.

INNISFREE. see LITERATURE — Poetry

800 GW ISSN 0443-2460
INSEL-ALMANACH. 1905. a. price varies. Insel-Verlag, Lindenstr. 29, 6000 Frankfurt a.M. 1, Germany. (Dist. by: Suhrkamp Publishers New York Inc., 175 Fifth Ave., New York, NY 10010, USA) bk.rev.; circ. 5,000.
Description: Collection of essays on important writers from the history of world literature.

800 851 363.35 IT
INSIEME NELLA VALLE E ACCADEMIA INTERNATIONALE ARTE LETTERE SCIENZE DAFNI; ebdomadario artistico-poetico e di informazione del movimento i.n.v. 1973. m. L.25000. Movimento Independenti per la Pace, Via de Gasperi, I-92100 Agrigento, Italy. Ed. Giuseppe Amico. (tabloid format)
Formerly: Insieme nella Valle.

INSTITUT CATHOLIQUE DE PARIS. REVUE. see GENERAL INTEREST PERIODICALS — France

891.7 947 FR ISSN 0078-9976
INSTITUT D'ETUDES SLAVES, PARIS. BIBLIOTHEQUE RUSSE. (Text in French or Russian) 1912. irreg., vol.85, 1989. price varies. Institut d'Etudes Slaves, 9 rue Michelet, 75006 Paris, France. Indexed: M.L.A.

891.8 FR ISSN 0079-001X
PG13
INSTITUT D'ETUDES SLAVES, PARIS. TEXTES. 1926. irreg., vol.8, 1968. price varies. Institut d'Etudes Slaves, 9 rue Michelet, 75006 Paris, France.

891 943 FR ISSN 0079-0028
INSTITUT D'ETUDES SLAVES, PARIS. TRAVAUX. 1923. irreg., vol.33, 1990. price varies. Institut d'Etudes Slaves, 9 rue Michelet, 75006 Paris, France.

800 FR ISSN 0073-8212
INSTITUT DE RECHERCHE ET D'HISTOIRE DES TEXTES, PARIS. DOCUMENTS, ETUDES ET REPERTOIRES. 1958. a. price varies. Editions du C N R S, 1 Place Aristide Briand, 92195 Meudon Cedex, France. TEL 1-45-34-75-50. FAX 1-46-26-28-49. TELEX LABOBEL 204 135 F. (Subscr. to: Presses du C N R S, 20-22, rue Saint Amand, 75015 Paris, France. TEL 1-46-33-16-00) adv.; bk.rev.; index; circ. 1,500.

INSTITUT PROVINCIAL D'ETUDES ET RECHERCHES BIBLIOTHECONOMIQUES. MEMOIRES. see BIBLIOGRAPHIES

800 CK ISSN 0020-370X
INSTITUTO CARO Y CUERVO. NOTICIAS CULTURALES. 1961-1975; N.S. 1982. bi-m. Col.$180($6) Instituto Caro y Cuervo, Seccion de Publicaciones, Apdo. Aereo 51502, Bogota, Colombia. Ed.Bd. bk.rev.; bibl.; illus.; circ. 4,000.

860 CK
INSTITUTO CARO Y CUERVO. SERIE GRANADA ENTREABIERTA. 1973. irreg., no.53, 1990. price varies. Instituto Caro y Cuervo, Seccion de Publicaciones, Apdo. Aereo 51502, Bogota, Colombia.

860 400 CK ISSN 0073-9928
INSTITUTO CARO Y CUERVO. SERIE MINOR. 1950. irreg., no.31, 1988. price varies. Instituto Caro y Cuervo, Seccion de Publicaciones, Apdo. Aereo 51502, Bogota, Colombia. (back issues avail.)

800 RM
INSTITUTUL DE SUBINGINERI ORADEA. LUCRARI STIINTIFICE: SERIA LITERATURA. (Text in Rumanian, occasionally in English or French; summaries in English, French, German or Rumanian) irreg. Institutul de Subingineri Oradea, Calea Armatei Rosii Nr. 5, 3700 Oradea, Rumania.
Formerly: Institutul Pedagogic Oradea. Lucrari Stiintifice: Seria Literatura; which continues in part (in 1973): Institutul Pedagogic Oradea. Lucrari Stiintifice: Seria Filologie; which superseded in part (in 1971): Institutul Pedagogic Oradea. Lucrari Stiintifice: Seria A and Seria B; which was formerly (until 1969): Institutul Pedagogic Oradea. Lucrari Stiintifice.

INTERDISCIPLINARITE ETUDES PHILOSOPHIQUES ET LITTERAIRES. see PHILOSOPHY

840 FR ISSN 0154-5604
PN3
INTERFERENCE. s-a. 20 F. Universite de Rennes II (Universite de Haute Bretagne), Institut de Litterature, 6 av. Gaston-Berger, 35043 Rennes Cedex, France. Ed. Patrick Besnier.

840 700 FR ISSN 0074-1140
INTERFERENCES, ARTS, LETTRES. 1968. irreg. Lettres Modernes, 73 rue du Cardinal-Lemoine, 75005 Paris, France. TEL 1-43-54-46-09.

800 US ISSN 0888-2452
INTERIM (LAS VEGAS). 1944-1955; resumed 1986. 2/yr. $5 to individuals; institutions $8. c/o A. Wilber Stevens, Ed., Department of English, University of Nevada, Las Vegas, Las Vegas, NV 89154. TEL 702-739-3172. circ. 800. **Indexed:** Amer.Hum.Ind., Ind.Amer.Per.Verse.
Description: Publishes poetry and short fiction.

840 398 CN
INTERNATIONAL ARTHURIAN SOCIETY. NEWSLETTER. 1981. s-a. membership. Dalhousie University, Department of French, Halifax, N.S. B3H 3J5, Canada. TEL 902-494-2430. Ed. Hans R. Runte. circ. controlled.

840 FR ISSN 0571-5865
PC2012
INTERNATIONAL ASSOCIATION OF FRENCH STUDIES. CAHIERS. 1951. a. 150 Fr. International Association of French Studies, 11 place Marcelin-Berthelot, 75005 Paris, France. Ed. Robert Garapon. circ. 300.

INTERNATIONAL AUTHORS AND WRITERS WHO'S WHO. see BIOGRAPHY

LITERATURE 2925

800 CN ISSN 0315-4149
PN3311
INTERNATIONAL FICTION REVIEW. 1974. s-a. Can.$12 to individuals; institutions Can.$15. International Fiction Association, Department of German, Russian, University of New Brunswick, Fredericton, N.B., Canada. TEL 506-453-4636. FAX 506-453-4599. Ed. Saad Elkhadem. bk.rev.; index; circ. 600. (also avail. in microform from MML; back issues avail.; reprint service avail.) **Indexed:** Amer.Hum.Ind., Arts & Hum.Cit.Ind., Can.Rev.Comp.Lit., CMI, Curr.Cont., Hum.Ind., Ind.Bk.Rev.Hum., M.L.A., Mid.East: Abstr.& Ind.
—BLDSC shelfmark: 4540.187000.

800 860 US ISSN 0074-6495
INTERNATIONAL INSTITUTE OF IBERO-AMERICAN LITERATURE. CONGRESS PROCEEDINGS. MEMORIA. (Proceedings published by sponsoring university) 1939. irreg. International Institute of Ibero-American Literature - Institute Internacional de Literatura Iberoamericana, 1312 C.L., University of Pittsburgh, Pittsburgh, PA 15260. TEL 412-624-3359. FAX 412-624-8505. Ed. Alfredo A. Roggiano. adv.; bk.rev. (also avail. in microform from UMI; back issues avail.; reprint service avail. from UMI)

INTERNATIONAL JOURNAL OF SLAVIC LINGUISTICS AND POETICS. see LINGUISTICS

800 UK ISSN 0074-722X
INTERNATIONAL P.E.N. CONGRESS. REPORT. irreg. International P.E.N., 9-10 Charterhouse Bldgs., London EC1M 7AT, England.

INTERNATIONAL REVIEW OF AFRICAN AMERICAN ART; an international publication. see ART

830 GW ISSN 0340-4528
PT3
INTERNATIONALES ARCHIV FUER SOZIALGESCHICHTE DER DEUTSCHEN LITERATUR. (Text in English, French, German) 1976. s-a. DM.136. Max Niemeyer Verlag, Postfach 2140, 7400 Tuebingen 1, Germany. TEL 07071-81100. FAX 07071-87419. Ed.Bd. adv.; bk.rev.; bibl. (back issues avail.) **Indexed:** Arts & Hum.Cit.Ind., Can.Rev.Comp.Lit., Curr.Cont., M.L.A.
Description: Essays on social history of German literature, especially 18th through 20th centuries.

809 US
INTERPLAY; proceedings of symposia in comparative literature and the arts. 1982. irreg., latest no.6. price varies. (University of Southern California, Center for the Humanities, Comparative Literature Program) Undena Publications, Box 97, Malibu, CA 90265. TEL 805-746-5870. FAX 805-746-2728. (Dist. by: Crescent Academic Services, 29528 Madera Ave., Shafter, CA 93263) Ed. Moshe Lazar. (back issues avail.) **Indexed:** Amer.Hist.& Life, Hist.Abstr., M.L.A., PROMT.

850 IT
INTERPRETE. (Text in English or Italian) irreg., latest no.50. price varies. Angelo Longo Editore, Via Paolo Costa 33, P.O. Box 431, 48100 Ravenna, Italy. TEL 0544-217026. Ed. Aldo Scaglione.

800 US ISSN 0363-9991
INTERSTATE; a magazine of creative acts. 1974. irreg. $10 for 2 nos. Noumenon Foundation, Box 7068, University Sta., Austin, TX 78713. TEL 512-928-2911. Eds. Loris Essary, Mark Loeffler. bk.rev.; circ. 500. **Indexed:** Abstr.Mil.Bibl.

INTERVENTI CLASSENSI. see ART

INTERZONE. see LITERATURE — Science Fiction, Fantasy, Horror

860 US ISSN 0732-6750
PQ6001
INTI; revista de literatura hispanica. 1974. s-a. $25 to individuals; institutions $40. Providence College, Department of Modern Languages, Providence, RI 02918. FAX 401-865-2057. Ed. Roger B. Carmosino. adv.; bk.rev.; film rev.; bibl.; circ. 1,000. (back issues avail.) **Indexed:** Hisp.Amer.Per.Ind., M.L.A.

800 IT ISSN 0392-6095
INVENTARIO; rivista quadrimestrale di critica e letteratura. q. L.30000. Bi & Gi Editore, Casella Postale 2106, Verona, Italy. Ed. Pino Ruffo.

LITERATURE

IO. see ANTHROPOLOGY

820 UK
IOTA. 1988. 4/yr. $10. 67 Hady Crescent, Chesterfield, Derbyshire S41 0EB, England. TEL 0246-276532. Ed. David Holiday. circ. 300.

810 US ISSN 0021-065X
PS501
IOWA REVIEW. 1970. 3/yr. $15 to individuals; institutions $20. University of Iowa, Department of English, 308 EPB, Iowa City, IA 52242. TEL 319-335-0462. Ed. David Hamilton. adv.; bk.rev.; index; circ. 1,500. (also avail. in microform from UMI; back issues avail.; reprint service avail. from UMI,KTO) Indexed: A.I.P.P., Abstr.Engl.Stud., Access, Amer.Bibl.Slavic & E.Eur.Stud., Amer.Hum.Ind., Bibl.Engl.Lang.& Lit., Ind.Amer.Per.Verse, Ind.Bk.Rev.Hum., Leg.Per., M.L.A.
—BLDSC shelfmark: 4566.600000.
Description: Contains fiction, poetry and essays.

808 301.412 US ISSN 0271-8227
HQ1438.I7
IOWA WOMAN. 1980. q. $15 to individuals; institutions $15. Iowa Woman Endeavors, Inc., Box 680, Iowa City, IA 52244. Ed. Marianne Abel. adv.; bk.rev.; circ. 2,000. Indexed: Abstr.Pop.Cult., Hum.Ind.

800 US
IPSISSIMA VERBA; the very words. 1989. 2/yr. $2 per no. Haypenny Press, 211 New St., West Paterson, NJ 07424-3329. Ed. P.D. Jordan. adv.; illus. (back issues avail.)
Description: Writings in the first person.

860 FR ISSN 0291-2066
IRIS. 1980. a. 75 F. (foreign 100 F.). Universite de Montpellier (Universite Paul Valery), Centre de Recherches sur les Litteratures Iberiques et Iberoamericaines Modernes, B.P. 5043, 34032 Montpellier Cedex 1, France. TEL 67-14-20-00. Ed. P. Jourdan.
Description: Collection of unpublished poems and texts, studies in Spanish and Latin American poetry, novels, civilization and arts in the 19th and 20th centuries.

IRISH DRAMA SELECTIONS. see THEATER

800 UK ISSN 0140-895X
IRISH LITERARY STUDIES. 1977. irreg. Colin Smythe, Ltd., Box 6, Gerrards Cross, Buckinghamshire SL9 8XA, England. TEL 0753-886000. FAX 0753-886469. (Pub. in U.S. by: Barnes & Noble Books, 8705 Bollman Place, Savage, MD 20763) circ. 1,500. (reprint service avail. from ISI)
—BLDSC shelfmark: 4572.847000.
Description: Monographs and symposia on all aspects of Irish literature.

808 941.606 US ISSN 0733-3390
IRISH LITERARY SUPPLEMENT. 1982. s-a. $5 to individuals; libraries and foreign $6. Irish Studies, 114 Paula Blvd., Selden, NY 11784. TEL 516-698-8243. FAX 516-696-5008. Ed. Robert G. Lowery. adv.; bk.rev.; illus.; circ. 4,000. (also avail. in microfilm) Indexed: Amer.Hum.Ind., Bk.Rev.Ind. (1988-), Child.Bk.Rev.Ind. (1988-).
—BLDSC shelfmark: 4572.848000.

800 US ISSN 0075-0816
IRISH PLAY SERIES. 1968. irreg., no.18, 1981. price varies. Proscenium Press, Box 361, Newark, DE 19711. TEL 302-764-8477. Ed. Robert Hogan. (reprint service avail. from UMI)

IRISH SLAVONIC STUDIES. see HISTORY — History Of Europe

820 US
IRISH STUDIES SERIES. irreg. Syracuse University Press, 1600 Jamesville Ave., Syracuse, NY 13244. TEL 315-423-2597. Ed. Richard Fallis.

894 HU ISSN 0075-0824
IRODALOM - SZOCIALIZMUS. (Text in Hungarian; occasional summaries in German or Russian) 1959. irreg. price varies. (Magyar Tudomanyos Akademia) Akademiai Kiado, Publishing House of the Hungarian Academy of Sciences, Box 24, H-1363 Budapest, Hungary.

800 HU ISSN 0075-0832
IRODALOMELMELET KLASSZIKUSAI. 1963. irreg. price varies. (Magyar Tudomanyos Akademia) Akademiai Kiado, Publishing House of the Hungarian Academy of Sciences, Box 24, H-1363 Budapest, Hungary.

809 HU ISSN 0021-1478
IRODALOMTORTENET/LITERARY HISTORY. 1912; N.S. 1949. q. $20. (Magyar Irodalomtorteneti Tarsasag) Akademiai Kiado, Publishing House of the Hungarian Academy of Sciences, P.O. Box 24, H-1363 Budapest, Hungary. Ed. P. Nagy. bk.rev.; bibl. Indexed: Amer.Hist.& Life, Hist.Abstr., M.L.A.

809 HU ISSN 0075-0840
IRODALOMTORTENETI FUZETEK. 1950. irreg., vol.114, 1986. price varies. (Magyar Tudomanyos Akademia) Akademiai Kiado, Publishing House of the Hungarian Academy of Sciences, Box 24, H-1363 Budapest, Hungary. Indexed: M.L.A.

809 HU ISSN 0075-0859
IRODALOMTORTENETI KONYVTAR. (Text in Hungarian; occasional summaries in French or German) 1957. irreg., vol.38, 1983. price varies. (Magyar Tudomanyos Akademia) Akademiai Kiado, Publishing House of the Hungarian Academy of Sciences, Box 24, H-1363 Budapest, Hungary.

809 HU ISSN 0021-1486
IRODALOMTORTENETI KOZLEMENYEK/LITERARY HISTORY COMMUNICATIONS. (Text in Hungarian; summaries in English, French or Russian) 1891. bi-m. $23. (Magyar Tudomanyos Akademia, Irodalomtudomanyi Intezet) Akademiai Kiado, Publishing House of the Hungarian Academy of Sciences, P.O. Box 24, H-1363 Budapest, Hungary. Eds. F. Biro, T. Komlovszky. adv.; bk.rev.; illus.; index. Indexed: M.L.A.

800 800 UK ISSN 0140-7597
IRON. 1973. 3/yr. $25. Iron Press, 5 Marden Terrace, Cullercoats, North Shields, Tyne & Wear NE30 4PD, England. TEL 091-253 1901. Ed.Bd. adv.; bk.rev.; circ. 800. (back issues avail.)
Description: Magazine of contemporary writing and graphics.

810 US
IRON MOUNTAIN REVIEW. 1983. s-a. free. Emory & Henry College, Box 64, Emory, VA 24327. TEL 703-944-4121. Ed. John Lang. circ. 600. (back issues avail.)
Description: Contains essays and interviews with contemporary Southern Appalachian writers.

810 US
ISHMAEL. s-a. Brown University, Box 1947, Providence, RI 02912. TEL 401-863-1000. (Subscr. to: Box 1984, Providence, RI 02912) (Co-sponsor: Rhode Island School of Design) Eds. Bruce B. Redford, Jane Kallir. illus.

ISLAM AND THE MODERN AGE. see RELIGIONS AND THEOLOGY — Islamic

820 770 CN ISSN 0227-0773
ISLAND (LANTZVILLE). 3/yr. Can.$12 to individuals; institutions Can.$15. Box 256, Lantzville, B.C. V0R 2H0, Canada. Eds. John Marshall, Daphne Marlatt. Indexed: Can.Lit.Ind., So.Pac.Per.Ind.

800 AT ISSN 0156-8124
ISLAND MAGAZINE. 1979. q. Aus.$24 to individuals (foreign Aus.$35); institutions Aus.$34 (foreign Aus.$45). Island Magazine Inc., P.O. Box 207, Sandy Bay, Tas. 7005, Australia. FAX 002-202186. Ed. Cassandra Pybus. adv.; bk.rev.; circ. 1,000. (back issues avail.)

700 800 NZ ISSN 0110-0858
PZ1
ISLANDS; a New Zealand quarterly of arts and letters. 1972. q. NZ.$8. Robin Dudding, Ed. & Pub., 4 Sealy Rd., Torbay, Auckland 10, New Zealand. adv.; bk.rev.; film rev.; play rev.; illus.; index; circ. 2,000. Indexed: Abstr.Engl.Stud., So.Pac.Per.Ind.

ISSUE ONE. see LITERATURE — Poetry

800 400 IT
ISTITUTO UNIVERSITARIO ORIENTALE DI NAPOLI. ANNALI. SEZIONE ROMANZA. (Text in French, Italian, Portuguese and Spanish) 1959. 2/yr. L.60000($60) Herder Editrice e Libreria s.r.l., Piazza Montecitorio 117-120, 00186 Rome, Italy. TEL 67 94 628. FAX 678-47-51. TELEX 621427 NATEL. Ed. Raffaele Sirri.

ISTITUTO UNIVERSITARIO ORIENTALE DI NAPOLI. DIPARTIMENTO DI STUDI LETTERARI E LINGUISTICI DELL' OCCIDENTE. ANNALI: FILIOGIA GERMANICA. see LINGUISTICS

810 420 375.4 IT
ISTITUTO UNIVERSITARIO ORIENTALE DI NAPOLI. DIPARTIMENTO DI STUDI LETTERARI E LINGUISTICI DELL' OCCIDENTE. ANNUALI: STUDI DI ANGLISTICA. (Text in English, Italian) 1974. 3/yr. $60. (Istituto Universitario Orientale di Napoli, Dipartimento di Studi Letterari e Linguistici dell' Occidente) Herder Edtrice e Libreria s.r.l., Piazza Montecitorio 117-121, 00186 Rome, Italy. TEL 6794628. FAX 6784751.

830 430 375.4 IT
ISTITUTO UNIVERSITARIO ORIENTALE DI NAPOLI. DIPARTIMENTO DI STUDI LETTERARI E LINGUISTICI DELL' OCCIDENTE. ANNUALI: STUDI TEDESCHI. (Text in German, Italian) 1974. 3/yr. $60. (Istituto Universitario Orientale di Napoli, Dipartimento di Studi Letterari e Linguistici dell' Occidente) Herder Editrice e Libreria s.r.l., Piazza Montecitorio 117-121, 00186 Rome, Italy. TEL 6794628. FAX 6784751. (Dist. by: Herder Editrice e Libreria)

800 700 CI
ISTRA; kultura, knjizevnost drustvena pitjana. 1963. m. 100 din. Glas Istre, Obala Marsala Tita 10, Pula, Croatia. Ed. Mario Kalcic.

IT GOES ON THE SHELF. see LITERATURE — Science Fiction, Fantasy, Horror

850 808 US
ITALIAN QUARTERLY (NEW BRUNSWICK). (Text in English and Italian) vol.21, 1980. q. $15 to individuals; institutions $20. Rutgers University, Department of Italian, 18 Seminary Pl., New Brunswick, NJ 08903. TEL 908-932-7031. Ed.Bd. adv.; bk.rev.; circ. 1,050. (back issues avail.) Indexed: Amer.Hist.& Life, Hist.Abstr., M.L.A.

850 UK ISSN 0075-1634
PQ4001
ITALIAN STUDIES. 1937. a. £9.50. Society for Italian Studies, c/o Dr. C.S. Cairns, Department of Romance Studies, University College of Wales, Aberystwyth, Dyfed, Wales. Ed. Prof. B. Moloney. adv.; bk.rev.; bibl.; circ. 750. (back issues avail.) Indexed: Br.Hum.Ind., Ind.Bk.Rev.Hum., M.L.A.

ITALIANIST. see HISTORY — History Of Europe

850 IT
ITALIANISTICA. 1972. 3/yr. L.15000. Giardini Editori, Via Santa Bibbiana 28, 56100 Pisa, Italy. adv.; bk.rev.; circ. 2,000. Indexed: Can.Rev.Comp.Lit, M.L.A.

850 450 370 US ISSN 0021-3020
PC1068.U6
ITALICA (MADISON). (Text in English, Italian) 1924. q. $30 to individuals; institutions $40. American Association of Teachers of Italian, Department of French and Italian, University of Wisconsin, 618 Van Hise Hall, 1220 Linden Dr., Madison, WI 53706. TEL 608-262-3941. Ed. Robert Rodini. adv.; bk.rev.; bibl.; index; circ. 1,750. (tabloid format; also avail. in microform from UMI; reprint service avail. from UMI) Indexed: Arts & Hum.Cit.Ind., C.I.J.E., Curr.Cont., Ind.Bk.Rev.Hum., Lang.Teach.& Ling.Abstr., M.L.A.
—BLDSC shelfmark: 4588.380000.
Description: Represents all levels of the teaching of Italian literature, language and culture.

450 375.4 AU
ITALIENISCHE STUDIEN. 1978. a. DM.48. Italienisches Kulturinstitut Wien, AU , Ungargasse 43, A-1030 Vienna, Austria. bk.rev.; circ. 500.

IWATE UNIVERSITY. FACULTY OF EDUCATION. ANNUAL REPORT/IWATE DAIGAKU KYOIKUGAKUBU KENKYU NENPO. see SOCIAL SCIENCES: COMPREHENSIVE WORKS

891.7 BW
IZOBRAZITEL'NOE ISKUSSTVO BELORUSSII. 1977. q. 1.31 Rub. Izdatel'stvo Belarus', Leninskii Pr. 79, Minsk, Byelarus. circ. 6,000.

891.8 BN ISSN 0021-3381
PN9
IZRAZ; casopis za knjizevnu i umjetnicku kritiku. 1957. m. $15. (Republican Union of Culture) S O U R Svjetlost, P.O. Box 129, Petra Preradovica 3, 71000 Sarajevo, Bosnia Hercegovina. Ed. Dzevad Karahasan. bk.rev.; circ. 1,000. **Indexed:** M.L.A.

807 CN
J A S N A NEWS. 2/yr. membership. Jane Austen Society of North America, 4169 Lions Ave., North Vancouver, B.C. V7R 3S2, Canada. TEL 604-988-0479. (Subscr. to: JASNA, Membership Office, 1416 Rushden Dr., Sacremento, CA 95864) Ed. Paula Stephankowsky. bk.rev.; illus.; tr.lit.; circ. 3,500. (back issues avail.)
  Formerly: Jane Austen Society of North America News.
  Description: News and activities of the Jane Austen Society of North America.

J E G P: JOURNAL OF ENGLISH AND GERMANIC PHILOLOGY. see LINGUISTICS

820 UK ISSN 0305-8182
PR4612
JABBERWOCKY. 1969. irreg. (2-4/yr.) £8($15) to members; institutions £10($18). Lewis Carroll Society, 69 Ashby Rd., Woodville, Burton-on-Trent, Staffs., England. Ed. Selwyn H. Goodacre. adv.; bk.rev.; film rev.; play rev.; bibl.; illus.; circ. 400. (back issues avail) **Indexed:** Ind.Bk.Rev.Hum., M.L.A.
 —BLDSC shelfmark: 4616.320000.

800 II ISSN 0448-1143
PN851
JADAVPUR JOURNAL OF COMPARATIVE LITERATURE. (Text mainly in English, occasionally in Bengali; summaries in English) 1961. a. Rs.12.50($3) Jadavpur University, Department of Comparative Literature, Calcutta 32, India. Ed. Amiya Dev. index, cum.index vols.1-10; circ. 500. **Indexed:** Abstr.Engl.Stud., M.L.A.

830 407 GW ISSN 0173-6469
JAHRBUCH DER DEUTSCHDIDAKTIK. 1978. a. price varies. Gunter Narr Verlag, Dischingerweg 5, 7400 Tuebingen, Germany. TEL 07071-78091. FAX 07071-75288. Ed. H. Mueller-Michaels. circ. 750.

830 SZ
JAHRBUCH FUER INTERNATIONALE GERMANISTIK. 1969. s-a. $65.80. Verlag Peter Lang AG, Jupiterstr. 15, CH-3015 Bern, Switzerland. TEL 031-321122. FAX 031-321131. TELEX 912651-PELA-CH. Ed. Hans-Gert Roloff. bibl. **Indexed:** Can.Rev.Comp.Lit., Curr.Cont., M.L.A.

JAMAICA PICTORIAL. see MUSIC

809 920 US ISSN 0749-0291
PS3507.I267
JAMES DICKEY NEWSLETTER. 1984. s-a. $5 to individuals; institutions $10. Joyce M. Pair, Ed. & Pub., 2101 Womack Rd., Dunwoody, GA 30338. FAX 404-551-3201. bk.rev.; circ. 250. (back issues avail.) **Indexed:** Hum.Ind., M.L.A.
  Description: Covers the writings of James Dickey.

820 UK ISSN 0143-6333
JAMES JOYCE BROADSHEET. 1980. 3/yr. £5($12) University of Leeds, School of English, Leeds LS2 9JT, England. Ed.Bd. adv.; bk.rev.; film rev.; play rev.; illus.; circ. 1,000.
  Description: Literary reviews of studies on the author; including essays, review articles, retrospective reviews, verse, translations, news and artwork.

800 US ISSN 0899-3114
PR6019.09
JAMES JOYCE LITERARY SUPPLEMENT. 1987. s-a. $8. University of Miami, Department of English, Box 248145, Coral Gables, FL 33124. TEL 305-284-2182. FAX 305-284-6758. Ed. Bernard Benstock. adv.; bk.rev.; circ. 800.
  Description: Publishes reviews of books on James Joyce and occasionally, his contemporaries.

800 US
JAMES JOYCE NEWESTLATTER. 1969. 3/yr. $10. James Joyce Foundation, c/o English Dept., Ohio State University, 164 W. 17th Ave., Columbus, OH 43210. Ed. Morris Beja. bibl.; charts; illus.; stat.; circ. 500.
  Formerly: James Joyce Foundation Newsletter.

820 US ISSN 0021-4183
PR6019.09
JAMES JOYCE QUARTERLY. (Supplement avail.) 1963. q. $17 to individuals; institutions $18. (University of Tulsa) Academic Publications (Tulsa), 600 S. College Ave., Tulsa, OK 74104. TEL 918-631-2501. FAX 918-631-2033. Ed. Robert Spoo. adv.; bk.rev.; play rev.; bibl.; charts; illus.; cum.index: 1963-1983; circ. 1,400. (also avail. in microform from MIM,UMI; back issues avail.; reprint service avail. from SWZ,UMI) **Indexed:** Abstr.Engl.Stud., Amer.Hum.Ind., Arts & Hum.Cit.Ind., Curr.Cont., Hum.Ind., Ind.Bk.Rev.Hum., LCR, M.L.A.
 —BLDSC shelfmark: 4645.700000.

JAMES WHITE REVIEW; a gay men's literary quarterly. see HOMOSEXUALITY

892.7 UA
JAMI'AT TANTA. KULLIYYAT AL-ADAB. MAJALLAH/TANTA UNIVERSITY. FACULTY OF LITERATURE. JOURNAL. (Text in Arabic) irreg. Tanta University, Faculty of Literature, Tanta, Egypt.

894.8 II
JANASHAKTI NEWS WEEKLY. (Text in Malayalam) 1940. w. Rs.10. Cochin 682001, India. Ed. A.V. Vasavan. adv.; bk.rev.; illus.

895 JA
JAPANESE LITERATURE TODAY. (Text in English) 1959-1969; N.S. 1976. a. $18.50. Japan P.E.N. Club - Nihon P E N Kurabu, 265 Shuwa Residential Hotel, 9-1-7 Akasaka, Minato-ku, Tokyo, Japan. FAX 03-3402-5951. Ed. Masaaki Kanno. bk.rev.; circ. 2,500.
  Supersedes (in 1976): Japan P.E.N. News (ISSN 0075-3300)
  Description: Includes list of translations into foreign languages.

800 US
JAPANESE SCHOLARLY WORKS IN ENGLISH. irreg. Peter Lang Publishing, Inc., 62 W. 45th St., 4th Fl., New York, NY 10036. TEL 212-302-6740. FAX 212-302-7574. Ed. Kaoru Yamaguchi.

890 430 SZ ISSN 0721-3719
JAPANESE STUDIES IN GERMAN LANGUAGE AND LITERATURE/JAPANISCHE STUDIEN ZUR DEUTSCHEN SPRACHE UND LITERATUR. (Text in English, German) 1971. irreg. Verlag Peter Lang AG, Jupiterstr. 15, CH-3015 Bern, Switzerland. TEL 031-321122. FAX 031-321131. TELEX 912651-PELA-CH. Ed. Peter Lang. circ. 400. **Indexed:** M.L.A.

891 301 HU ISSN 0448-9144
JASZKUNSAG; social and artistic journal. 1954. 6/yr. $20.50. (Jasz - Nagykun - Szolnok Megyei Onkormanyzat) Verseghy Ferenc Megyei Konyvtar, Kossuth ter 4, Pf. 139, 5001 Szolnok, Hungary. TEL 06-56-41333. FAX 06-56-41806. Ed. Lajos Kormendi. bk.rev.; illus.; circ. 1,000.
  Description: Covers the life, traditions and social conflicts of the people of two historical regions of Eastern Hungary.

JAUNA GAITA. see ART

830 GW ISSN 0075-3580
PT2456
JEAN-PAUL-GESELLSCHAFT. JAHRBUCH. 1966. a. DM.55. C.H. Beck'sche Verlagsbuchhandlung, Wilhelmstr. 9, 8000 Munich 40, Germany. TEL 089-38189-338. FAX 089-38189-398. TELEX 5215085-BECK-D. Ed. Kurt Woelfel. bk.rev.; circ. 750. **Indexed:** M.L.A.

810 US ISSN 0889-759X
PR6035.H96
JEAN RHYS REVIEW. 1986. s-a. $14 to individuals (foreign $17); institutions $20 (foreign $23). Box 811, Planetarium Sta., New York, NY 10024-0539. TEL 212-884-5854. Ed. Nora Gaines. bk.rev.; bibl.; circ. 75. (back issues avail.) **Indexed:** M.L.A.
 —BLDSC shelfmark: 4663.465590.
  Description: Provides a forum for research in progress, bibliography, critical articles and reviews and announcements of forthcoming studies and conferences related to the work of Jean Rhys.

840 FR ISSN 0981-9185
J'ECRIS; journal d'information technique pour les ecrivains pratiquants. 1987. q. 235 F.($40) 85, rue des Tennerolles, Saint-Cloud 92210, France. Ed. Albert Sigusse. bk.rev.; circ. 1,000. (back issues avail.)

700 US ISSN 0021-5880
JEOPARDY. 1964. a. $4. College Hall 132, Western Washington University, Department of English, 516 High St., Bellingham, WA 98225. TEL 206-676-3118. bk.rev.; illus.; circ. 4,000. (back issues avail.) **Indexed:** A.I.P.P.

840 FR
JEUNESSES LITTERAIRES DE FRANCE. 1955. bi-m. 117 bd. Saint Germain, 75006 Paris, France. Ed. Jean Huguet.

JEZIK IN SLOVSTVO. see LINGUISTICS

895.1 CC ISSN 1001-6694
JIANGNAN; daxing wenxue. (Text in Chinese) bi-m. Zhongguo Zuojia Xiehui, Zhejiang Fenhui - China Writers' Association, Zhejiang Chapter, 9, Jiande Lu, Hangzhou, Zhejiang 310006, People's Republic of China.

JIDISCHE SCHTUDIES. see LINGUISTICS

895.1 355 CC
JIEFANGJUN WENYI/LITERATURE AND ART OF PEOPLE'S LIBERATION ARMY. (Text in Chinese) m. Y1.60($63) (Zhongguo Renmin Jiefangjun - Chinese People's Liberation Army) Jiefangjun Wenyi Chubanshe, A3, Xishiku Maowu Hutong, Beijing 100034, People's Republic of China. (Dist. outside China by: China International Book Trading Corp., P.O. Box 2820, Beijing, P.R.C.; Dist. in US by: China Books & Periodicals, Inc., 2929 24th St., San Francisco, CA 94110. TEL 415-282-2994) Ed. Ling Xingzheng. illus.

895.1 CC
JIN YAOSHI/GOLDEN KEY. (Text in Chinese) q. Nei Menggu Wenxue Yishujie Lianhehui - Inner Mongolian Literary and Art Circle Association, Huhhot, Nei Menggu 010020, People's Republic of China. TEL 663760. Ed. Ya Lin.

JINGU CHUANQI/MODERN AND ANCIENT LEGENDS. see FOLKLORE

895.1 CC
JINSHAN. (Text in Chinese) q. Zhenjiang Wenxue Yishu Jie Lianhehui - Zhenjiang Literary and Art Circle Association, 21 Jiefang Lu, Zhenjiang, Jiangsu 212001, People's Republic of China. TEL 221721. Ed. Chen Tupeng.

895.1 CC ISSN 0257-2915
JINYANG WENYI. (Text in Chinese) m. Y12($36.80) (Shanxi Sheng Qunzhong Yishuguan) Jinyang Wenyi Bianjibu, 1, Houjia Xiang, Taiyuan, Shanxi 030001, People's Republic of China. (Dist. outside China by: China International Book Trading Corp., P.O. Box 399, Beijing, P.R.C.; Dist. in US by: China Books & Periodicals, Inc., 2929 24th St., San Francisco, CA 94110. TEL 415-282-2994) adv.; illus.

899.2 II ISSN 0021-700X
JNANADHARA. (Text in Malayalam) 1969. m. Rs.3.60. P. Haridas, Ed. & Pub., Vakayar P.O., Kouni, Kerala, India. adv.; bk.rev.; film rev.; play rev.; abstr.; illus.; circ. 5,000.

LITERATURE

200   UK
JOHN CLARE SOCIETY JOURNAL. 1982. a. £7.50($20) John Clare Society, c/o Mrs. J. Mary Moyse, The Stables, 1A West Street, Helpston, Peterborough PE6 7DU, England. TEL 0733-252678. (Subscr. to: c/o Hon. Treasurer, 8 Priory Rd., Peterborough, PE3 6EB, England) Ed. John Goodridge. adv.; bk.rev.; circ. 500. (back issues avail.)
   Description: Examines the life and work of the poet John Clare.

806   US   ISSN 0738-9655
PR2248
JOHN DONNE JOURNAL: STUDIES IN THE AGE OF DONNE. 1982. 2/yr. $20 to individuals; libraries $30. North Carolina State University, Department of English, Box 8105, Raleigh, NC 27695-8105. TEL 919-737-3870. Eds. M. Thomas Hester, R.V. Young. adv.; bk.rev.; circ. 450. (back issues avail.) **Indexed:** M.L.A.

820   US   ISSN 0021-728X
PR1
JOHNSONIAN NEWS LETTER. 1940. q. $6 (foreign $6.50). University of Chicago, Department of English, 1050 E. 59th St., Chicago, IL 60637. TEL 312-702-7989. Ed. Stuart Sherman. bk.rev.; cum.index every 5 yrs.; circ. 1,800. (back issues avail.)
   Description: Provides news of interest to students, collectors, and scholars of 18th-century English literature, particularly of Samuel Johnson (1709-1784), English author and laxicographer, and his circle.

800   GW
JOSEF-ALBERS-SCHOOL. ALMANACH. 1978. s-a. DM.10($6) Zeppelinstr. 20, 4250 Bottrop, Germany. Ed. W. Boschmann. adv.; circ. 1,500.

810 770   US   ISSN 1045-084X
JOURNAL (COLUMBUS). 1972. 2/yr. $8. Ohio State University, Department of English, 421 W. Denney Hall, 164 W. 17th Ave., Columbus, OH 43210. TEL 614-292-4076. Ed. David Citino. adv.; bk.rev.; illus.; circ. 1,200. (back issues avail.) **Indexed:** A.I.P.P.
   Formerly (until 1987): Ohio Journal.
   Description: Includes contemporary fiction and poetry.

840   FR
JOURNAL DES LETTRES ET DE L'AUDIOVISUEL. vol.111, 1976. q. 100 F. Societe des Gens de Lettres de France, Hotel de Massa, 38 rue du Faubourg Saint-Jacques, 75014 Paris, France. bibl.; circ. 5,500.
   Formerly: Revue des Lettres (ISSN 0035-2128)

JOURNAL OF AMERICAN DRAMA AND THEATRE. see *THEATER*

800 950   NE   ISSN 0085-2376
PJ7501
JOURNAL OF ARABIC LITERATURE. (Supplement avail.: Studies in Arabic Literature (ISSN 0169-9903)) 1970. a. fl.120 (effective 1992). E.J. Brill, P.O. Box 9000, 2300 PA Leiden, Netherlands. TEL 071-312624. FAX 071-317532. TELEX 39296 BRILL NL. (In N. America: E.J. Brill, 24 Hudson St., Kinderhook, NY 12106. TEL 800-962-4406) Ed. M.M. Badawi. **Indexed:** Arts & Hum.Cit.Ind., Curr.Cont., Ind.Bk.Rev.Hum., M.L.A., Rel.Ind.One.
   —BLDSC shelfmark: 4947.170000.
   Description: Forum for discussion of Arabic literature, both classical and modern, by Arabs and non-Arabs.

800 792   UK   ISSN 0309-5207
PR6003.E282
JOURNAL OF BECKETT STUDIES. 1977. irreg. £14 for 2 nos. Calder Publications, 9-15 Neal St., London WC2H 9TU, England. TEL 071-497-1741. Ed. Stanley Gontarski. adv.; bk.rev.; illus. (back issues avail.) **Indexed:** Arts & Hum.Cit.Ind., Curr.Cont., Ind.Bk.Rev.Hum., M.L.A.
   —BLDSC shelfmark: 4951.240000.

819   CN   ISSN 0047-2255
PR9195.7
JOURNAL OF CANADIAN FICTION. (Text in English and French) 1972. q. Can.$18($20) J C F Press Association, 2050 Mackay St., Montreal, Que. H3G 2J1, Canada. Ed. Dr. John R. Sorfleet. adv.; bk.rev.; bibl.; circ. 1,500. **Indexed:** Abstr.Engl.Stud., Amer.Hum.Ind., Arts & Hum.Cit.Ind., Bibl.Engl.Lang.& Lit., Can.Lit.Ind., Can.Per.Ind., CMI, Curr.Cont., Hum.Ind., Ind.Bk.Rev.Hum., M.L.A.
   —BLDSC shelfmark: 4954.747000.

820   UK   ISSN 0021-9894
PR1
JOURNAL OF COMMONWEALTH LITERATURE. 1965. s-a. £25($85) to individuals; institutions £35. Bowker-Saur Ltd. (Subsidiary of: Reed International Books), 59-60 Grosvenor St., London W1X 9DA, England. TEL 071-493-5841. FAX 071-499-1590. (Subscr. to: Order Processing Dept., Butterworth Services, Borough Green, Sevenoaks, Kent TN15 8PH, England. TEL 0732-884567; N. America subscr. to: K.G. Saur, A Reed Reference Publishing Company, 121 Chanlon Rd., New Providence, NJ 07974. TEL 908-665-3576) Eds. Alastair Niven, Caroline Bundy. adv.; bibl.; circ. 1,200. (also avail. in microform from UMI; back issues avail.; reprint service avail. from UMI) **Indexed:** Abstr.Engl.Stud., Arts & Hum.Cit.Ind., Br.Hum.Ind., Can.Lit.Ind., Curr.Cont.Africa, Curr.Cont., Hum.Ind., M.L.A., So.Pac.Per.Ind.
   ●Also available on CD-ROM.
   —BLDSC shelfmark: 4961.300000.
   Description: Critical and bibliographical forum in the field of Commonwealth writing.

809   II   ISSN 0252-8169
PN851
JOURNAL OF COMPARATIVE LITERATURE AND AESTHETICS. (Text in English) 1978. s-a. Rs.60($9) Vishvanatha Kaviraja Institute of Comparative Literature and Aesthetics, B8 Sambalpur University, Jyotivihar 768 019, Orissa, India. TELEX 066382-314. Ed. Ananta Charan Sukla. adv.; bk.rev.; circ. 1,000. **Indexed:** M.L.A.

JOURNAL OF EVOLUTIONARY PSYCHOLOGY. see *PSYCHOLOGY*

400 860   US   ISSN 0147-5460
PC4001
JOURNAL OF HISPANIC PHILOLOGY. 1976. 3/yr. $30 to individuals (foreign $35); institutions $60 (foreign $74). Journal of Hispanic Philology Inc., Department of Modern Languages and Linguistics, Florida State University, Tallahassee, FL 32306. TEL 904-385-6130. FAX 904-385-5392. Ed. Daniel Eisenberg. adv.; bk.rev.; circ. 500. **Indexed:** Arts & Hum.Cit.Ind., Curr.Cont., Ind.Bk.Rev.Hum., Lang.& Lang Behav.Abstr., M.L.A.
   —BLDSC shelfmark: 4999.100000.

890   II   ISSN 0302-1319
PR9480
JOURNAL OF INDIAN WRITING IN ENGLISH. 1973. s-a. Rs.50($12) G.S. Balarama Gupta, Ed. & Pub., Department of English, Gulbarga University, Gulbarga 585 106, Karnataka, India. adv.; bk.rev.; circ. 1,500. (back issues avail.) **Indexed:** M.L.A.

820   US   ISSN 0047-2514
PR8830
JOURNAL OF IRISH LITERATURE. 1972. 3/yr. $12 to individuals; institutions $18. Proscenium Press, Box 361, Newark, DE 19711. TEL 302-764-8477. Ed.Bd. adv.; bk.rev.; bibl.; circ. 600. (also avail. in microform from UMI; reprint service avail. from UMI) **Indexed:** Amer.Hum.Ind., Arts & Hum.Cit.Ind., Curr.Cont., Ind.Bk.Rev.Hum., M.L.A.
   —BLDSC shelfmark: 5008.200000.

JOURNAL OF LATIN AMERICAN LORE. see *FOLKLORE*

JOURNAL OF LITERARY SEMANTICS. see *LINGUISTICS*

800   SA   ISSN 0256-4718
JOURNAL OF LITERARY STUDIES/TYDSKRIF VIR LITERATUURWETENSKAP. (Text in Afrikaans and English) 1985. q. R.20($14) to individuals; institutions R.28 ($20). (South African Society for General Literary Studies - Suid-Afrikaanse Vereniging vir Algemene Literatuurwetenskap) Bureau for Scientific Publications, P.O. Box 1758, Pretoria 0001, South Africa. TEL 012-429-6614. (Subscr. to: Dept. of Theory of Literature, UNISA, P.O. Box 392, Pretoria 0001, South Africa) (Co-sponsor: Haum Literary Group) Eds. Ina Graebe, Rory Ryan. bk.rev.; circ. 350. (back issues avail.)
   Description: Forum for discussion of literary theory, methodology, and research. Features articles and reviews aimed at students and lecturers.

JOURNAL OF MEDIEVAL AND RENAISSANCE STUDIES. see *HUMANITIES: COMPREHENSIVE WORKS*

800   II
JOURNAL OF MEDIEVAL INDIAN LITERATURE. 1977. s-a. Panjab University, Department of Medieval Indian Literature, Arts Block No. 3, Panjab University Campus, Chandigarh 160014, India.

JOURNAL OF MENTAL IMAGERY. see *PSYCHOLOGY*

800   US   ISSN 1053-6981
PN212   CODEN: JNLHEY
▼**JOURNAL OF NARRATIVE AND LIFE HISTORY.** 1991. q. $30 to individuals (foreign $55); institutions $80 (foreign $105). Lawrence Erlbaum Associates, Inc., 365 Broadway, Hillsdale, NJ 07642. TEL 201-444-4110. FAX 201-666-2394. Ed. Allyssa McCabe.
   —BLDSC shelfmark: 5021.178000.
   Description: Provides a forum for encountering diverse approaches to the genres known collectively as narratives and the content of many language games known as life histories.
   Refereed Serial

808   US   ISSN 0022-2925
PE1425
JOURNAL OF NARRATIVE TECHNIQUE. 1971. 3/yr. $20. Eastern Michigan University, Society for the Study of Narrative Literature, Ypsilanti, MI 48197. TEL 313-487-0150. Ed. George Perkins. bk.rev.; circ. 1,400. (also avail. in microfilm from UMI; back issues avail.; reprint service avail. from UMI) **Indexed:** Abstr.Engl.Stud., Amer.Hum.Ind., Arts & Hum.Cit.Ind., Curr.Cont., LCR, M.L.A.
   —BLDSC shelfmark: 5021.180000.

809 806   NZ   ISSN 0112-1227
JOURNAL OF NEW ZEALAND LITERATURE. 1983. s-a. NZ.$24. University of Otago, Department of English, P.O. Box 56, Dunedin, New Zealand. TEL 03-479-8636. FAX 64-3-479-2305. TELEX NZ 505601. Ed. L.O. Jones. circ. 300.
   —BLDSC shelfmark: 5022.815000.
   Description: Contains scholarly and critical essays and notes on New Zealand literature.

800 300   US   ISSN 0022-3840
AP2
JOURNAL OF POPULAR CULTURE. 1967. q. $25. (Modern Language Association of America, Popular Literature Section) Popular Press, Bowling Green State University, Bowling Green, OH 43403. TEL 419-372-7866. (Co-sponsors: Midwest Modern Language Association, Folklore Section; Popular Culture Association) Ed. Ray B. Browne. adv.; bk.rev.; charts; illus.; circ. 2,500. (also avail. in microform from MIM,UMI; microfiche from KTO; reprint service avail. from UMI) **Indexed:** Abstr.Engl.Stud., Acad.Ind., Amer.Hist.& Life, Artbibl.Mod., Arts & Hum.Cit.Ind., ASSIA, Bk.Rev.Ind. (1976-), CERDIC, Chic.Per.Ind., Child.Bk.Rev.Ind. (1976-), Commun.Abstr., Curr.Cont., Film Lit.Ind. (1973-), Hist.Abstr., Hum.Ind., LCR, M.L.A., Mid.East: Abstr.& Ind., Music Ind., RILA, SSCI.
   —BLDSC shelfmark: 5041.130000.

800   US
JOURNAL OF POPULAR LITERATURE. 1985. s-a. $12.50. Popular Press, Bowling Green State University, Bowling Green, OH 43403. Ed. Ray B. Browne. adv.; illus.

895 US ISSN 0091-5637
PK1501
JOURNAL OF SOUTH ASIAN LITERATURE. 1963. s-a. $21 to individuals (foreign $22); institutions $27 (foreign $28). Michigan State University, Asian Studies Center, 109 International Center, E. Lansing, MI 48824. TEL 517-353-1680. Eds. Carlo Coppola, Surjit Dulai. bk.rev.; bibl.; index; circ. 350. (also avail. in microform from UMI; reprint service avail. from UMI, ISI) **Indexed:** Arts & Hum.Cit.Ind., Curr.Cont., Ind.Bk.Rev.Hum., M.L.A.
—BLDSC shelfmark: 5066.003000.
Formerly: A Quarterly of South Asian Literature (ISSN 0025-0503)

800 FR ISSN 0294-0442
JOURNAL OF THE SHORT STORY IN ENGLISH. (Text in English) 1983. s-a. 140 Fr. (foreign 165 F.). (Centre d'Etudes et de Recherches sur la Nouvelle en Langue Anglaise) Presses de l'Universite d'Angers, Bibliotheque Universitaire, 5 Blvd. Lavoisier, 49045 Angers, France. TEL 41-35-21-00. (back issues avail.)
Description: Deals with the 19th and 20th century short stories in English from a historical and textual point-of-view. Includes translations of unpublished short stories and original interviews as well as studies related to the teaching of short stories.

890 300 CN ISSN 0228-1635
DK508.A2
JOURNAL OF UKRAINIAN STUDIES. (Text in English and Ukrainian) 1976. s-a. $15 to individuals; institutions $20. Canadian Institute of Ukrainian Studies, 352 Athabasca Hall, University of Alberta, Edmonton, Alta. T6G 2E8, Canada. TEL 403-492-2972. FAX 403-492-4967. Ed. David R. Marples. adv.; bk.rev.; bibl.; illus.; circ. 700. (back issues avail.; reprint service avail. from ISI, UMI) **Indexed:** Amer.Bibl.Slavic & E.Eur.Stud., Arts & Hum.Cit.Ind., Curr.Cont., M.L.A.
—BLDSC shelfmark: 5071.454000.
Formerly: Journal of Ukrainian Graduate Studies (ISSN 0701-1792)

800 BB ISSN 0258-8501
JOURNAL OF WEST INDIAN LITERATURE. 1986. s-a. $20. University of the West Indies, Department of English, P.O. Box 64, Bridgetown, Barbados, W.I. TEL 809-425-1310. FAX 809-425-1327. Ed. Mark A. McWatt. adv.; bk.rev.; bibl.; circ. 750. (back issues avail.)
Description: Publishes research in West Indian literature for students and scholars working in that field.

800 920 US ISSN 1049-0809
PR6019.09
▼**JOYCE STUDIES ANNUAL.** 1990. a. $25 to individuals; institutions $35. University of Texas Press, Box 7819, Austin, TX 78713-7819. TEL 512-471-4531. FAX 512-320-0668. TELEX 776453-UTEXPRES-AUS. Ed. Thomas Staley. adv.; circ. 400. (reprint service avail. from UMI)
Description: Publishes articles by leading Joyce scholars on Joyce and closely related topics.

JUGEND UND KULTUR. see *ART*

800 890 DK ISSN 0905-1678
JULEGAVEN. a. DKK 48. Lohses Forlag, Korskarvej 25, DK-7000 Fredericia, Denmark. Eds. Marie and Frank Laursen. circ. 300.
Formerly: Naar Lampen Taendes. Fortaellinger (ISSN 0107-8232)
Description: Contains fictional and non-fictional religious literature.

895.1 CC
JUN MA/STEED. (Text in Chinese) m. Hulun Bei'er Meng Wenxue Yishu Lianhehui - Hulun Bei'er League Literary and Art Circle Association, Shengli Dajie, Haila'er, Nei Menggu 021008, People's Republic of China. TEL 2145. Ed. Liu Qian.

JUNKANOO. see *THEATER*

JYVASKYLA STUDIES IN THE ARTS. see *ART*

800 GW
K L G: KRITISCHES LEXIKON ZUR DEUTSCHSPRACHIGEN GEGENWARTSLITERATUR. 1979. DM.285. Edition Text und Kritik GmbH, Levelingstr. 6a, 8000 Munich 80, Germany. TEL 089-432929. FAX 089-433997. Ed. Heinz Ludwig Arnold.

800 831 GW
K U L I M U. (Kunst, Literatur & Music) (Text in German, Serbo-Croatian, Slovene) 1974. 3/yr. DM.15($10) Verlag fuer Kunst, Literatur & Music, Marienstr. 6, 8400 Regensburg, Germany. TEL 0941-75805. Eds. U. Alberts, J. Hachmann. adv.; bk.rev.; circ. 1,000.

KABUL MOJALA. see *PHILOSOPHY*

800 US
KACH NAZAR; Armenian satirical & critical independent monthly. (Text in Armenian and English) 1970. m. $25 (effective Jan. 1991). Kach Nazar Publishing Co., 1036 N. Glendale Ave., Glendale, CA 91206. Ed. Ovanes Balayan. adv.; bk.rev.; bibl.; illus.; circ. 5,000. (tabloid format)

807 US ISSN 0894-6388
KAFKA SOCIETY OF AMERICA. JOURNAL. 1977. 2/yr. $15 to individuals; libraries $25; foreign $30. Temple University, Department of Germanic and Slavic Languages and Literatures, AB 335, Philadelphia, PA 19122. TEL 215-787-8282. Ed. Maria Luise Caputo-Mayr. bk.rev.; bibl.; circ. 400. (back issues avail.) **Indexed:** Amer.Bibl.Slavic & E.Eur.Stud., M.L.A.
—BLDSC shelfmark: 4810.170000.
Formerly (until 1983): Kafka Society of America. Newsletter (ISSN 0741-6202)
Description: Presents papers given at the meetings, other articles, essays, bibliographies, and materials of interest to Kafka scholars.

809 II
KAKATIYA JOURNAL OF ENGLISH STUDIES. Short title: K J E S. (Text in English) 1976. a. Rs.15($2) Kakatiya University, Department of English, Vidyaranyapuri, Warangal 506 009, India. Ed. A. Jaganmohana Chari. circ. 250.

895 II
KALAI MAGAL. (Text in Tamil) 1932. m. P.O. Box 604, Madras 600 004, India. TEL 44-76011. Ed. R. Narayanaswamy. circ. 22,700.

890 700 CE
KALAVA HA SAHITYAYA. (Text in Sinhalese) 1976. irreg. Rs.1. Nava Parapura, 26 Clifford Ave., Colombo 3, Sri Lanka.

808 700 US ISSN 0748-8742
PS153.P48
KALEIDOSCOPE (AKRON); international magazine of literature, fine arts and disability. 1979. s-a. $14 to individuals; institutions $12. (United Cerebral Palsy and Services for the Handicapped) Kaleidoscope Press (Akron), 326 Locust St., Akron, OH 44302. TEL 216-762-9755. FAX 216-762-0912. Ed. Darshan Perusek. adv.; bk.rev.; circ. 2,000. (also avail. in audio cassette; back issues avail.)
Description: Addresses the experience of disability through literature and the fine arts.

800 FI ISSN 0355-0311
PH325
KALEVALASEURAN VUOSIKIRJA. 1921. a. FIM 120. Suomalaisen Kirjallisuuden Seura, Hallituskatu 1, SF-00170 Helsinki, Finland. TEL 358-0-131237. cum.index 1921-70; circ. 2,000. **Indexed:** M.L.A.
Description: Contains articles on Finnish and Balto-Finnic folklife and cultural phenomena relating to an annually varying theme of research.

813 US ISSN 0022-7994
KALKI; studies in James Branch Cabell. 1965. irreg. $10 for 4 nos. James Branch Cabell Society, HC 63 Box 70A, E. Alstead, NH 03602-7705. Ed. Paul Spencer. bk.rev.; bibl.; illus.; index; circ. 200. (back issues avail.; also avail. on microfilm from JOH) **Indexed:** Amer.Hum.Ind., M.L.A.

895 II
KALKI. (Text in Tamil) 1941. w. 84-1C Race Course Rd., Guindy, Madras 600 032, India. TEL 48-431543. Ed. K. Rajendran. circ. 88,200.

808 301.412 US ISSN 0735-7885
NX504
KALLIOPE; a journal of women's art. 1979. 3/yr. $10.50. Florida Community College, Kalliope Writers' Collective, 3939 Roosevelt Blvd., Jacksonville, FL 32205. TEL 904-387-8211. Ed. Mary Sue Koeppel. bk.rev.; circ. 1,000. (also avail. in microform from UMI; back issues avail.)
Description: Provides a forum for the exchange and sharing of ideas for and by women. Publishes poetry, short fiction and b&w art work. Gives consideration to young and-or emerging artists and writers.

808 301.2 MW
KALULU; bulletin of Malawian oral literature and cultural studies. 1976. irreg. $5. Chancellor College, Writer's Group, Box 280, Zomba, Malawi.

800 340 JA ISSN 0453-1981
KANAZAWA UNIVERSITY. FACULTY OF LAW AND LITERATURE. STUDIES AND ESSAYS. (Text in English and Japanese) 1953. a. Kanazawa Daigaku, Hobungakubu - Kanazawa University, Faculty of Law and Literature, 1-1 Marunouchi, Kanazawa-shi, Ishikawa-ken 920, Japan. bibl.

800 700 CR ISSN 0378-0473
NX1.A1
KANINA; revista de artes y letras. 1976. s-a. $20. Editorial de la Universidad de Costa Rica, Apartado 75-2060, Ciudad Universitaria Rodrigo Facio, 2050 San Pedro, Montes de Oca, San Jose, Costa Rica. TEL 506-25-3133. FAX 506-24-9367. TELEX UNICORI 2544. Dir. Ivonne Robles Mohs. **Indexed:** Curr.Cont., M.L.A.

860 SP
KANTIL; revista mensual de literatura. (Text in Basque and Spanish) 1975. m. 750 ptas.($12) Apdo. 570 Marina, 4, San Sebastian, Spain. Ed. Raul Guerra Garrido. adv.; bk.rev.; film rev.; play rev.; illus.; circ. 3,000.

800 US ISSN 0022-8990
KARAMU. 1967. a. $4 to individuals; institutions $5. Karamu Association, English Department, Eastern Illinois University, Charleston, IL 61920. Ed. Peggy L. Brayfield. bk.rev.; illus.; circ. 400.
Description: Collection of fiction, poetry, art work, and artistic expression, selected from open submissions and published at Eastern Illinois University.

833 GW ISSN 0300-1989
PT2625.A848
KARL-MAY-GESELLSCHAFT. JAHRBUCH. 1970. a. price varies. Hansa Verlag, Nordbahnhofstr. 2, Postfach 1480, 2250 Husum, Germany. TEL 04841-6081. FAX 04841-61397. TELEX 28567. Ed.Bd. adv.; bk.rev. **Indexed:** M.L.A.

833 GW
KARL-MAY-GESELLSCHAFT. MITTEILUNGEN. 1969. q. membership. Karl-May-Gesellschaft e.V., Maximiliankorso 45, 1000 Berlin 28, Germany. TEL 030-4061033. Ed. Hansotto Hatzig. adv.; bk.rev.; circ. 1,450. (back issues avail.)
Description: Studies the work and life of German author Karl May (1842-1912).

830 831 GW
KARLSRUHER BOTE. 1946. s-a. $30. Kurt Ruediger, Ed. & Pub., Friedenstr. 16, 7500 Karlsruhe, Germany.

890 IS
AL-KARMIL. (Text in Arabic) a. Haifa University, Institute of Middle Eastern Studies, Ha-Carmel, Haifa 31 999, Israel.

891.4 II ISSN 0022-9318
KATHA-SAHITYA. (Text in Bengali) 1949. m. Rs.50. Mitra & Ghosh Publishers Pvt. Ltd., 10 Shyama Charan Dey St., Calcutta 700 073, India. Ed.Bd. adv.; bk.rev.; tr.lit.; circ. 32,135.

820 UK
KEATS - SHELLEY REVIEW.* 1910. a. £1.50. Keats - Shelley Memorial Association, c/o Wm. Dawson & Sons Ltd., Cannon House, Folkestone, Kent CT19 5EE, England. Ed. Dorothy Hewlett. adv.; cum.index: vols. 1-20; circ. 1,200. **Indexed:** Abstr.Engl.Stud., Arts & Hum.Cit.Ind., Curr.Cont., Ind.Bk.Rev.Hum., M.L.A.
Formerly (until 1986): Keats - Shelley Memorial Bulletin (ISSN 0453-4395)

LITERATURE

KEEL JA KIRJANDUS. see *LINGUISTICS*

800 US ISSN 0451-6338
KELSEY REVIEW. 1988. a. free. Mercer County Community College, Box B, Trenton, NJ 08690. TEL 609-586-4800. Ed. G. Robin Schore. bk.rev.; circ. 1,500. (back issues avail.)
Description: Presents fiction, poetry, essays (all subjects) written by people living and working in Mercer County, NJ.

895.1 CC
KEN CHUN NI. (Text in Chinese) m. Jiangsu Renmin Chubanshe, Qikan Bu, 165 Zhongyang Lu, Nanjing, Jiangsu 210009, People's Republic of China. TEL 639518. Ed. Wang Yuanhong.

800 810 US
KENNEBEC; a portfolio of Maine writing. 1975. a. free. University of Maine at Augusta, Augusta, ME 04330. TEL 207-621-3246. bk.rev.; circ. 5,000. (tabloid format)
Description: Examines and introduces literature by Maine writers.

810 US ISSN 0163-075X
AP2
KENYON REVIEW. 1939; N.S. 1979. 4/yr. $22 to individuals; institutions $24. Kenyon College, Box B, Gambier, OH 43022. TEL 614-427-3339. (Subscr. to: c/o Small Publishers Fulfillment Service, 202 Twin Oaks Drive, Syracuse, NY 13206) Ed. Marilyn Hacker. adv.; bk.rev.; index, cum.index (old series): 1939-1963; circ. 3,000. (also avail. in microfilm; reprint service avail. from UMI) Indexed: Abstr.Engl.Stud., Acad.Ind., Amer.Hum.Ind., Bk.Rev.Ind. (1965-), Child.Bk.Rev.Ind. (1965-), Hum.Ind., Ind.Bk.Rev.Hum., M.L.A.

820 UK
KEROUAC CONNECTION. 1984. 2/yr. £2($5) (Europe £3; Canada £4). 19 Worthing Rd., Patchway, Bristol BS12 5HY, England. Ed. Dave Moore. circ. 600.
Description: Devoted to the life and work of Jack Kerouac, with relevant articles and poems.

800 US
KESTREL CHAPBOOK SERIES. 1982. irreg. $4 per no. Holmgangers Press, 95 Carson Ct., Shelter Cove, CA 95489. TEL 707-986-7700. Ed. Gary Elder. circ. 250. (back issues avail.)

810 UK
KEYNOTES. q. membership. Eighteen Nineties Society, 17 Merton Hall Road, Wimbledon, London SW19 3PP, England.

KEYSTROKES. see *PUBLISHING AND BOOK TRADE*

KHOJ DARPAN. see *FOLKLORE*

891.553 IR ISSN 1017-415X
▼**KILK - MAHNAMAH-I ADABI VA HUNARI/KELK - REVIEW OF ART AND LITERATURE.** (Text in Farsi) 1990. m. $38 in Asia, Europe; $56 in N. America. K.S. Jawadi, Ed.& Pub., P.O. Box 13145-916, Teheran, Iran. bk.rev.

KING SAUD UNIVERSITY. JOURNAL. ARTS. see *ART*

813 US
KINGFISHER. 1987. 2/yr. $10. Box 9783, N. Berkeley, CA 94709. TEL 415-893-4852. Ed. Barbara Schultz. adv.; bk.rev.; circ. 1,500. (back issues avail.)

813 UK ISSN 0023-1738
PR4856
KIPLING JOURNAL. 1927. q. membership. Kipling Society, Schomberg House, 2nd floor, 80-82 Pall Mall, London SW1Y 5HF, England. Ed. G.H. Webb. adv.; bk.rev.; bibl.; illus.; circ. 1,000. Indexed: Abstr.Engl.Stud., Br.Hum.Ind., Hum.Ind, M.L.A.
—BLDSC shelfmark: 5097.330000.
Description: Literary and historical review focused on the prose and verse, and life and times, of Rudyard Kipling.

891.92 US ISSN 0017-6613
KIR - OU - KIRK. (Text in Armenian & English) 1956. a. free. Armenian Literary Society - New York, Inc., 77 Everett Rd., Demarest, NJ 07627. TEL 201-767-1494. Ed. Arthur Hamparian. bk.rev.; play rev.; circ. 900 (controlled).
Formerly: Haghordagroutiun.

890 PK
KIRAN.* (Text in Urdu) 1978. m. Rs.60. 37 Urdu Bazar, Karachi, Pakistan.

KISWAHILI. see *LINGUISTICS*

820 SA
KLASGIDS. (Text in Afrikaans) 4/yr. R.11 (foreign R.14.40). Foundation for Education, Science and Technology, P.O. Box 1758, Pretoria 0001, South Africa. TEL 012-322-6404. FAX 012-320-7803. Indexed: Ind.S.A.Per., M.L.A.

KLAUS GROTH GESELLSCHAFT. JAHRESGABEN. see *LINGUISTICS*

830 GW ISSN 0075-6318
KLEINE DEUTSCHE PROSADENKMAELER DES MITTELALTERS; Erst und Neuausgaben der Forschungstelle fuer deutsche prosa des Mittelalters. 1965. irreg. price varies. (Seminar fuer Deutsche Philologie) Wilhelm Fink Verlag, Ohmstr. 5, 8000 Munich 40, Germany. Ed. Georg Steer.

800 GW ISSN 0722-8899
KLEIST-JAHRBUCH. 1980. a. price varies. Erich Schmidt Verlag GmbH & Co. (Bielefeld), Viktoriastr. 44a, Postfach 7330, 4800 Bielefeld 1, Germany. TEL 0521-583080. Ed. Hans Joachim Kreutzer. bk.rev. (back issues avail.)
—BLDSC shelfmark: 5099.151000.

859 RM
KNJIEVNI JIVOT. (Text in Serbian) 1957. s-a. 48 lei. Uniunea Scriitorilor din Republica Socialista Romania, Calea Victoriei 115, Bucharest, Rumania. (Subscr. to: ILEXIM, Str. 13 Decembrie Nr. 3, Box 136-137, 70116 Bucharest, Rumania) Ed. Slavomir Gvozdenovici. bk.rev.; abstr.; illus.

900 100 YU
KNJIZEVNA KRITIKA; casopisu za umetnicku, istorijsku i filosofsku kritiku. 1970. bi-m. 60000 din.($15) Izdavacko Preduzece Rad, Moshe Pijade 12, Belgrade, Yugoslavia. Ed. Milivoj Srebro. adv.; bk.rev.; circ. 1,200. Indexed: M.L.A.
Description: Covers criticism and aesthetics in literature.

809 CI ISSN 0455-0463
PN9
KNJIZEVNA SMOTRA; casopis za svjetsku knjizevnost. (Text in Croatian) 1969. q. 120 din.($6.50) Hrvatsko Filolosko Drustvo, Djure Salaja 3, 41000 Zagreb, Croatia. Ed. Zdravko Malic. bk.rev.; illus.; circ. 1,500.

057.8 YU ISSN 0023-2408
KNJIZEVNOST. (Text in Serbo-Croatian) 1946. m. $50. Udruzenje za Ekonomiju Samoupravljanja, Zmaj Jovina 12, P.O. Box 611, 11000 Belgrade, Yugoslavia. (Subscr. to: Prosveta, Terazije 16, Belgrade, Yugoslavia) Ed. Vuk Krnjevic. circ. 2,000.

KNJIZEVNOST I JEZIK. see *LINGUISTICS*

808.068 US ISSN 0271-1990
THE KORBIN LETTER; concerning children's books about real people, places and things. 1980. 7/yr. $12. 732 Greer Rd., Palo Alto, CA 94303. TEL 415-856-6658. Ed. Dr. Beverly Korbin. bk.rev. (back issues avail.)

810 US
▼**KOKOPELLI NOTES.** 1990. 4/yr. $12. Box 8186, Asheville, NC 28814. Ed. Patrick Clark. circ. 800.
Description: General literary journal.

910.03 323.4 CN ISSN 0835-2445
KOLA. 1987. 3/yr. $12 to individuals; institutions $18. C.P. 1602, Place Bonaventure, Montreal, Que. H5A 1H6, Canada. Ed. Horace I. Goddard. adv.; bk.rev.; circ. 300. (back issues avail.)
Description: Provides a forum for creative artists who have an interest in publicizing works that reflect the black experience around the world.

KONINKLIJKE ACADEMIE VOOR NEDERLANDSE TAAL- EN LETTERKUNDE. JAARBOEK. see *LINGUISTICS*

400 800 BE ISSN 0770-786X
KONINKLIJKE ACADEMIE VOOR NEDERLANDSE TAAL- EN LETTERKUNDE. VERSLAGEN EN MEDEDELINGEN. 1887; N.S. 1958. irreg. price varies. Koninklijke Academie voor Nederlandse Taal- en Letterkunde, Koningstraat 18, B-9000 Ghent, Belgium. FAX 091-23-27-18. bibl.; illus.; index. Indexed: Nutr.Abstr.

890 RU
KONTEKST. a. $3. (Akademiya Nauk S.S.S.R., Institut Mirovoi Literatury) Izdatel'stvo Nauka, 90 Profsoyuznaya ul., 117864 Moscow, Russia. TEL 234-05-84. (Dist. by: Mezhdunarodnaya Kniga, ul. Dimitrova D.39, 113095 Moscow, Russia) Ed.Bd. circ. 7,700.

KOSMOSKYNA. see *LITERATURE — Science Fiction, Fantasy, Horror*

KRATYLOS; kritisches Berichts- und Rezensionsorgan fuer indogermanische und allgemeine Sprachwissenschaft. see *LINGUISTICS*

800 GW ISSN 0342-4626
KRAUS-HEFTE. 1977. 4/yr. DM.44. Edition Text und Kritik GmbH, Levelingstr. 6a, 8000 Munich 80, Germany. TEL 089-432929. FAX 089-433997. Eds. Christian Wagenknecht, Sigurd Scheichl.

KRCKI ZBORNIK. see *HISTORY — History Of Europe*

800 PL ISSN 0867-1125
▼**KRESY.** 1990. q. 48000 Zl.($40) (effective 1992). Stowarzyszenie Literackie Kresy, Ul. Irydiona 4 m.11, 20-624 Lublin, Poland. Ed. Grzegorz Filip. adv.; bk.rev.

891.4 II ISSN 0023-4737
KRISHANU. (Text and summaries in Bengali) 1968. q. Rs.5($4) Malim Dulta, 18 Surja Sen St., Calcutta, West Bengal, India. Ed. Dinesh Chandra Sinha. adv.; bk.rev.; film rev.; play rev.; circ. 1,000.

891.4 II ISSN 0023-4745
KRISHNACHURA. (Text in Bengali) 1970. s-a. Rs.2($0.28) Prodyut Kumar Som, 19 Nagar Bagan, Haltu, Parganas 24, West Bengal, India. Ed. Sumanta Som.

809 HU ISSN 0023-4818
PH3001
KRITIKA. (Summaries in French, German and Russian) 1963. m. $25. (Magyar Tudomanyos Akademia, Irodalomtudomanyi Intezet) Lapkiado Vallalat, Lenin korut 9-11, 1073 Budapest 7, Hungary. TEL 222-408. (Subscr. to: Kultura, Box 149, H-1389 Budapest, Hungary). Indexed: Curr.Cont.

KRITIKON LITTERARUM; international book review for American, English, Romance and Slavic studies and for linguistics. see *LINGUISTICS*

809 BE
KTEMATA. (Text in French) 1974. irreg., latest no.10, 1989. 1200 Fr. Editions Peeters s.p.r.l., Bondgenotenlaan 153, B-3000 Leuven, Belgium. TEL 016-235170. FAX 016-228500. TELEX 65981 PULB.

800 KR ISSN 0201-419X
KULTURA SLOVA; respublikanskii mezhvidomchyi zbirnyk naukovykh prac. (Text in Ukrainian; summaries in Russian) 1967. s-a. (Akademiya Nauk Ukrainskoi S.S.R., Institut Movoznavstva im. O.O. Potebni) Izdatel'stvo Naukova Dumka, c/o Yu.A. Khramov, Dir, Ul. Repina, 3, Kiev 252 601, Ukraine. TEL 229-02-92. (Subscr. to: Mezhdunarodnaya Kniga, Moscow, G-200, Russia) Ed. S.Y. Ermolenko.
—BLDSC shelfmark: 0094.740000.

KUMAR. see *ART*

895.1 355 CC
KUN LUN/ARMY LITERATURE. (Text in Chinese) bi-m. Y22.80($67.80) Jiefangjun Wenyi Chubanshe, A3, Xishiku Maowu Hutong, Beijing 100034, People's Republic of China. (Dist. overseas by: China International Book Trading Corp., P.O. Box 399, Beijing, P.R.C.; Dist. in US by: China Books & Periodicals, Inc., 2929 24th St., San Francisco, CA 94110. TEL 415-282-2994).
Description: Contains short stories, poetry, and prose, emphasizing military themes.

800   II
KUNAPIPI. Association for Commonwealth Literature and Language Studies, Indian Branch, Department of English, University of Mysore, Manasagangotri, Mysore 570006, India. **Indexed:** Curr.Cont.Africa, M.L.A., So.Pac.Per.Ind.
    Formerly (until 1979): Commonwealth Newsletter.

800   II
KURINJI QUARTERLY.* (Text in English) 1973. q. Rs.12. 536 Raja Basantha Roy Rd., Calcutta, India. Ed. M. Srinivasan. adv.; bibl.
    Description: Indian vernacular literature in translation.

KWARTALNIK NEOFILOLOGICZNY. see *LINGUISTICS*

810   JA   ISSN 0454-8132
KYUSHU AMERICAN LITERATURE. (Text in English) 1960. a. (Kyushu American Literature Society - Kyushu Amerika Bungaku-Kai) Kyushu University, College of General Education, 4-2-1 Ropponmatsu, Chuo-Ku, Fukuoka 810, Japan. TEL 092-731-8745. FAX 011-81-092-771-4161. adv.; bk.rev.; bibl.; circ. 450. **Indexed:** Curr.Cont., M.L.A.
    —BLDSC shelfmark: 5135.030000.

890   DK   ISSN 0109-5390
L AE S. (Litteratur, Aestetik, Sprog) 1983. s-a. free. Aarhus Universitet, Institut for Nordisk Sprog og Litteratur, Niels Juelsgade 84, 8200 Aarhus N, Denmark. TEL 06-136711. Ed.Bd. illus.

L B I NEWS. (Leo Baeck Institute) see *HISTORY*

810 301.415   US
L G L C NEWSLETTER. 1983. 6/yr. $15. Libertarians for Gay and Lesbian Concerns, Box 447, Chelsea, MI 48118. TEL 313-475-9792. circ. 300.

L G S N: LESBIAN AND GAY STUDIES NEWSLETTER. see *HOMOSEXUALITY*

L I A S: SOURCES AND DOCUMENTS RELATING TO THE EARLY MODERN HISTORY OF IDEAS.. see *HISTORY*

800   US   ISSN 1043-6928
       CODEN: LINTEX
▼**L I T: LITERATURE INTERPRETATION THEORY.** 1991. 4/yr. $53. Gordon and Breach Science Publishers, 270 Eighth Ave., New York, NY 10011. TEL 212-206-8900. FAX 212-645-2459. TELEX 236735 GOPUB UR. (Subscr. to: Box 786, Cooper Sta., New York, NY 10276. TEL 800-545-8398; UK subscr. to: P.O. Box 90, Reading, Berkshire RG1 8JL, England. TEL 0734-560-080) Ed. Lee Jacobus. (also avail. in microform)
    —BLDSC shelfmark: 5276.270000.
    Refereed Serial

LABYRINTHOS. see *ART*

800   AG   ISSN 0023-7280
LAGRIMAL TRIFURCA. 1968. q. Arg.$2000($20) Ocampo 1812, Rosario, Argentina. Ed. Francisco E. Gandolfo. adv.; bk.rev.; bibl.; circ. 1,000. (looseleaf format)

LAMAR LECTURE SERIES. see *HISTORY*

839   NE
LAMPAS; tijdschrift voor Nederlandse classici. 5/yr. fl.62.50. Dick Coutinho B.V., P.O. Box 10, 1399 ZG Muiderberg, Netherlands. TEL 02942-1886. Ed.Bd.
    Description: For Dutch classicists.

809   US   ISSN 0737-0555
PS3515.U274
LANGSTON HUGHES REVIEW. 1982. 2/yr. $10. (Langston Hughes Society) Brown University, Afro-American Studies Program, Box 1904, Providence, RI 02912. TEL 401-863-3898. Ed. George Houston Bass. adv.; bk.rev.; index; circ. 300. (back issues avail.) **Indexed:** M.L.A.
    Description: Concerned with the life and writings of Langston Hughes. Articles on information relevant to a critical study of the Hughesian tradition.

LANGUAGE AND CULTURE. see *LINGUISTICS*

LANGUAGE AND LITERATURE. see *LINGUISTICS*

LANGUAGE FORUM. see *LINGUISTICS*

LANGUAGE FORUM MONOGRAPH SERIES. see *LINGUISTICS*

LANGUAGE QUARTERLY. see *LINGUISTICS*

LANGUAGES OF DESIGN; formalisms for word, images and sound. see *LINGUISTICS — Computer Applications*

800 400   FR   ISSN 0457-1320
LANGUES ET STYLES. 1959. irreg., latest no.9, 1983. Lettres Modernes, 73, rue du Cardinal Lemoine, 75005 Paris, France. TEL 022-466666. FAX 022-472391. (Dist. outside France by: Librairie Droz S.A., 11, rue Massot, CH-1211 Geneva 12, Switzerland.)
    Description: Part of "Editions 'Lettres Modernes'."

LANGUES MODERNES. see *LINGUISTICS*

800   CN   ISSN 0382-8824
LAOMEDON REVIEW. vol.2, 1976. irreg. (1-2/yr.) Can.$5. c/o Erindale College, University of Toronto, Mississauga, Ont. L5L 1C6, Canada. TEL 416-978-2011. Ed. Linda J. Kuschnir. illus.

860   US   ISSN 0888-5613
LATIN AMERICAN INDIAN LITERATURES JOURNAL; a review of American Indian texts and studies. 1977. s-a. $25 to individuals (foreign $28); institutions $35 (foreign $41). Penn State University, McKeesport, University Dr., McKeesport, PA 15132. TEL 412-675-9466. Ed. Mary H. Preuss. adv.; bk.rev.; bibl.; circ. 500. (back issues avail.) **Indexed:** Arts & Hum.Cit.Ind., Curr.Cont., Hisp.Amer.Per.Ind., M.L.A., Rel.Ind.One.
    —BLDSC shelfmark: 5160.064500.
    Supersedes (in 1985): Latin American Indian Literatures (ISSN 0160-8045)

860   US   ISSN 0047-4134
PQ7081.A1
LATIN AMERICAN LITERARY REVIEW. 1972. s-a. $33. (University of Pittsburgh, Department of Hispanic Languages and Literatures) Latin American Literary Review, Cathedral of Learning, 1309, Pittsburgh, PA 15260. TEL 412-351-1477. FAX 412-351-6831. Ed.Bd. adv.; bk.rev.; index; circ. 1,250. (also avail. in microform from UMI) **Indexed:** Arts & Hum.Cit.Ind., Curr.Cont., Hisp.Amer.Per.Ind, M.L.A.
    Description: Essays on and reviews of literature by Latin American writers, as well as English translations of poems, plays, stories, and novel excerpts.

LATIN AMERICAN THEATRE REVIEW; a journal devoted to the theatre and drama of Spanish & Portuguese America. see *THEATER*

859   RM
LATO. (Text in Hungarian) 1953. m. 144 lei. Uniunea Scriitorilor din Republica Socialista Romania, Calea Victoriei 115, Bucharest, Rumania. (Subscr. to: ILEXIM, Str. 13 Decembrie Nr. 3, Box 136-137, 70116 Bucharest, Rumania) Ed. Bela Marko. bk.rev.; film rev.; abstr.; charts; illus.; circ. 5,000.
    Formerly: Igaz Szo.

808   US   ISSN 0023-9003
PS221
LAUREL REVIEW (MARYVILLE). 1960. s-a. $8 (effective 1987). GreenTower Press, c/o Loren C. Gruber, Business Mgr., Dept. of English, Northwest Missouri State University, Maryville, MO 64468. TEL 816-562-1265. Ed.Bd. adv.; circ. 750. (also avail. in microfilm; back issues avail.) **Indexed:** A.I.P.P., Ind.Amer.Per.Verse.

LEA. see *BIBLIOGRAPHIES*

810 820   US   ISSN 0075-8396
LEBARON RUSSELL BRIGGS PRIZE HONORS ESSAYS IN ENGLISH. 1965. irreg. $5.95. Harvard University, Department of English, Cambridge, MA 02138. (Dist. by: Harvard University Press, 79 Garden St., Cambridge, MA 02138)

LECTOR. see *PUBLISHING AND BOOK TRADE*

200 800   FR   ISSN 0024-0125
LECTURE ET TRADITION; bulletin litteraire, contrerevolutionnaire. 1966. m. 90 F. (foreign 110 F.). Diffusion de la Pensee Francaise, Chire-en-Montreuil, 86190 Vouille, France. TEL 49-51-83-04. Ed. Jean Auguy. adv.; bk.rev.; bibl.; circ. 4,000.

801 944   IT
LECTURES. (Text in French, Italian) 1979. s-a. L.22000. Edizioni dal Sud, Via Gen. Bellomo 71, Bari 70100, Italy. Ed. Vito Carofiglio. bk.rev.; circ. 1,000.
    Formerly: Lectures da Roland Barthes.

808.81   US
LEDGE POETRY & FICTION MAGAZINE. 1988. s-a. $9. 64-65 Cooper Ave., Glendale, NY 11385. Ed. Timothy Monaghan. adv.; circ. 500.
    Formerly (until 1991): Ledge Poetry and Prose Magazine (ISSN 1046-2724)

900 800   UK   ISSN 0024-0281
AS12
LEEDS PHILOSOPHICAL AND LITERARY SOCIETY. PROCEEDINGS. LITERARY AND HISTORICAL SECTION. 1925. irreg. (3-4/yr.). price varies. Leeds Philosophical and Literary Society, Central Museum, Calverley St., Leeds 2, England. Ed. I.S. Moxon. charts; illus.; index; circ. 650. **Indexed:** Br.Hum.Ind., Hist.Abstr., Sci.Abstr.
    —BLDSC shelfmark: 6746.900000.
    Description: Explores areas of scholarly, literary or historical study.

820   UK   ISSN 0075-8566
PE10
LEEDS STUDIES IN ENGLISH. N.S. 1967. a. price varies. Leeds Studies in English, University of Leeds, School of English, Leeds LS2 9JT, England. Ed. A. Wawn. (reprint service avail. from KTO) **Indexed:** Br.Archaeol.Abstr., M.L.A.
    Supersedes: Leeds Studies in English and Kindred Languages.

375.4 420   UK   ISSN 0075-8574
LEEDS TEXTS AND MONOGRAPHS. NEW SERIES. 1966; N.S. 19?? irreg. price varies. Leeds Studies in English, University of Leeds, School of English, Leeds LS2 9JT, England. TEL 0532-334738. FAX 0532-334774. Ed. P. Meredith. **Indexed:** M.L.A.

800 305.4   US   ISSN 0748-4321
PS149
LEGACY (UNIVERSITY PARK); a journal of nineteenth-century American women writers. 1984. s-a. $17.50 to individuals (foreign $20); institutions $20 (foreign $23). Penn State University Press, Barbara Bldg., Ste. C, 820 N. University Dr., University Park, PA 16802-1003. TEL 814-865-1327. FAX 814-863-1408. Ed.Bd. adv.; bk.rev.; circ. 450. (reprint service avail. from UMI) **Indexed:** Bk.Rev.Ind., Child.Bk.Rev.Ind., M.L.A., Wom.Stud.Abstr. (1984-).
    —BLDSC shelfmark: 5181.309500.

052   UK   ISSN 0141-3511
       CODEN: TLLPAE
LEICESTER LITERARY & PHILOSOPHICAL SOCIETY. TRANSACTIONS. 1879. a. £3($5) Leicester Literary & Philosophical Society, c/o Leicestershire Museums, 96 New Walk, Leicester, England. TEL 0533-715265. Ed. T.D. Ford. bk.rev.; circ. 300. (back issues avail.)
    —BLDSC shelfmark: 8978.300000.

830   NE   ISSN 0169-8559
LEIDSE GERMANISTISCHE EN ANGLISTISCHE REEKS. 1962. irreg., vol.21, 1983. price varies. E.J. Brill, P.O. Box 9000, 2300 PA Leiden, Netherlands. TEL 071-312624. FAX 071-317532. TELEX 39296 BRILL NL. (N. America dist. addr.: E.J. Brill, 24 Hudso St., Kinderhook, NY 12106. TEL 800-962-4406) (Co-publisher: Leiden University Press)
    Description: German and English studies of the University of Leiden.

LEIDSE ROMANISTISCHE REEKS. see *LINGUISTICS*

892   IS
LEKET.* (Editions in English and Hebrew) irreg. World Zionist Organization, P.O. Box 92, Jerusalem 91920, Israel. Ed. David Hardan. illus.

830   US   ISSN 0075-8833
PT2405.5
LESSING YEARBOOK. (Text in English or German) 1969. a. price varies. (Lessing Society) Wayne State University Press, 5959 Woodward Ave., Detroit, MI 48202. TEL 089-432929. Ed. G. Hillen. bk.rev. **Indexed:** M.L.A.

LITERATURE

891.8   YU   ISSN 0025-5939
LETOPIS MATICE SRPSKE. 1825. m. 200 din. Matica Srpska, Matice Srpske 1, Novi Sad, Vojvodina, Yugoslavia. Ed. Dimitrije Vucenov. adv.; bk.rev.; bibl.; index.
—BLDSC shelfmark: 0097.375000.

LETRA GRANDE, ARTE Y LITERATURA. see *ART*

800 861   AG   ISSN 0326-2928
PQ7600
LETRAS DE BUENOS AIRES. 1980. q. $20 for 3 nos. Tagle 2572, 6 Piso D, 1425 Buenos Aires, Argentina. TEL 1-802-1510. Ed. Victoria Pueyrredon. adv.; bk.rev.; circ. 6,000.

800 700   EC
LETRAS DEL ECUADOR. 1944. m. Casa de la Cultura Ecuatoriana, Avda. 6 de Diciembre, Casilla 67, Quito, Ecuador. Dir. Teodoro Vanegas Andrade.

860 376   US   ISSN 0277-4356
PQ6055
LETRAS FEMENINAS. (Text in English, Portuguese, Spanish) 1974. 2/yr. $20 to individuals; libraries $25. Asociacion de Literatura Femenina Hispanica, Department of Modern Languages, University of Nebraska, Lincoln, NE 68588-0315. TEL 402-472-3710. Ed. Adelaida L. Martinez. adv.; bk.rev.; circ. 400. (back issues avail.) **Indexed:** Ind.Amer.Per.Verse, M.L.A.

700   MX   ISSN 0024-1245
LETRAS POTOSINAS; vocero de cultura. vol.27, 1969. q. Mex.$40. Luis Chessal Iturbide 505, San Luis Potosi, Mexico. Ed. Jesus C. Perez. adv.; bk.rev.; bibl.

806 383   US   ISSN 0882-3804
LETTER EXCHANGE; a magazine for letter writers. 1982. 3/yr. $18. Readers' League, Box 6218, Albany, CA 94706. TEL 510-526-7412. Ed. Stephen Sikora. adv.; bk.rev.; circ. 3,000.
    Formerly (until 1983): Readers' League Catalogue of Correspondence.

850   IT
LETTERATURE. 1983. irreg., no.24, 1991. price varies. Liguori Editore s.r.l., Via Mezzocannone, 19, 80134 Naples, Italy. TEL 081-5227139. Ed. GianCarlo Mazzacurati.

809   IT
LETTERATURE D'AMERICA. 1980. q. L.40000. (Universita degli Studi di Roma "La Sapienza") Bulzoni Editore, Via dei Liburni 14, 00185 Rome, Italy. Ed. Dario Puccini. **Indexed:** M.L.A.

850   IT   ISSN 0024-1334
PQ4001
LETTERE ITALIANE. 1949. q. L.68000 (foreign L.85000). Universita di Padova e di Torino, Istituti di Letteratura Italiana, Casella Postale 66, 50100 Florence, Italy. TEL 055-6530684. FAX 055-6530214. Eds. Vittore Branca, Carlo Ossola. adv.; bk.rev.; cum.index 1949-1979; circ. 1,200. **Indexed:** Can.Rev.Comp.Lit., Curr.Cont.
—BLDSC shelfmark: 5185.175000.

850   IT   ISSN 0075-8892
LETTERE ITALIANE. BIBLIOTECA; studi e testi. 1961. irreg., vol.39, 1991. price varies. Casa Editrice Leo S. Olschki, Casella Postale 66, 50100 Florence, Italy. TEL 055-6530684. FAX 055-6530214. Eds. Vittore Branca, Carlo Ossola. circ. 1,000.

850   IT
LETTERE ITALIANE. SAGGI. 1959. irreg., no.42, 1991. price varies. Casa Editrice Leo S. Olschki, Casella Postale 66, 50100 Florence, Italy. TEL 055-6530684. FAX 55-6530214. circ. 1,200.

850   IT   ISSN 0024-1350
LETTORE DI PROVINCIA; testi - ricerche - critica. 1970. q. L.30000 (foreign L.50000). Angelo Longo Editore, Via Paolo Costa 33, P.O. Box 431, 48100 Ravenna, Italy. TEL 0544-217026. Ed. Tino Dalla Valle. adv.; bk.rev.; bibl.; circ. 3,000.

800   GW
LETTRE INTERNATIONAL. (Text and summaries in German) 1988. q. DM.48 (foreign DM.64). Dominicusstr. 3, 1000 Berlin 62, Germany. TEL 030-788-1682. Eds. Frank Berberich, Antonin Liehm. circ. 30,000. (tabloid format; back issues avail.)

800 700 100   FR   ISSN 0024-1369
LETTRES; poesie, philosophie, litterature, arts, critique. 1945. q. 200 F. Editions Andre Silvaire, 20 rue Domat, 75005 Paris, France. illus.

800   AA
LES LETTRES ALBANAISES. (Text in French) q. $12. Lidhja e Shkrimatareve dhe e Artisteve te Shqiperise - Union des Ecrivains et Artistes d'Albanie, Baboci 37z, Tirana, Albania. TEL 42-27989. (Editorial office addr.: Rruga Konferenca e Pezes, Tirana, Albania. TEL 42-22691) Diana Culi.

301.415   GR
LETTRES EOLIENNES/EOLIKA GRAMMATA; revue bimensuelle d'art de Lesbos. 1971. bi-m. Dr.40. Nireos 41, P. Faliron, Athens, Greece. Ed. K. Valetas. bk.rev.; bibl.

800 900   FR
LETTRES ET CULTURES DE LANGUES FRANCAISES. 1984. 2/yr. 220 F. Association des Ecrivains de Langue Francaise (ADELF), 14 rue Broussais, 75014 Paris, France. TEL 43-21-95-99. Ed. Charles Saint-Prot. adv.; bk.rev.; circ. 3,200.

800   FR
LETTRES MEDIEVALES. 1984. irreg. Librairie A.G. Nizet, 3 bis place de la Sorbonne, 75005 Paris, France. TEL 43-54-79-76. Ed. Jacques De Caluwe. circ. 500.

840   CN   ISSN 0382-084X
LETTRES QUEBECOISES; revue de l'actualite litteraire. (Text in French) 1976. q. Can.$18. Editions Jumonville, Box 1840, Succursale B, Montreal, Que. H3B 3L4, Canada. Ed. Andre Vanesse. adv.; bk.rev.; play rev.; illus.; circ. 5,500. (back issues avail.) **Indexed:** C.L.I., Can.Lit.Ind., Can.Per.Ind., M.L.A., Pt.de Rep. (1979-), RADAR.

870   BE   ISSN 0024-1415
LES LETTRES ROMANES. (Supplement avail.) 1947. q. 850 Fr. (foreign 950 Fr.). Faculte de Philosophie et Lettres, Place Blaise Pascal 1, B-1348 Louvain-la-Neuve, Belgium. Ed. G. Jacques. bk.rev.; bibl.; index; circ. 600. (back issues avail.) reprint service avail. from ISI) **Indexed:** Arts & Hum.Cit.Ind., Can.Rev.Comp.Lit., Curr.Cont., Ind.Bk.Rev.Hum.
    Description: Publishes original articles on the scientific study of romance language literatures and their history.

800   FR   ISSN 0024-1423
LETTRISME. 1957. m. 1000 F. (Centre de Creativite) Librairie-Edition la Guilde, 18 rue de Turbigo, 75002 Paris, France. TEL 42-33-39-09. Ed. Maurice Lemaitre. bk.rev.; bibl.; illus.; circ. 200.
—BLDSC shelfmark: 5185.227000.

850   IT   ISSN 0459-1623
PQ4331
LETTURE CLASSENSI; letture dantesche. (Text in Italian) 1966. a. L.40000. Angelo Longo Editore, Via Paolo Costa 33, P.O. Box 431, 48100 Ravenna, Italy. TEL 0544-217026. adv.; cum.index; circ. 2,000.

840   IS   ISSN 0992-0757
LEVANT. (Text in French) 1984. a. $30. Haifa University, Faculty of Humanities, Ha-Carmel, Haifa 31 999, Israel. FAX 052-584192. circ. 1,000.
    Formerly: Approches.

840   FR
LEVANT - CAHIERS DE L'ESPACE MEDITERRANEEN. 1987. a. 95 F. Editions de l'Eclat, Combas, 30250 Sommieres, France. TEL 66-77-87-63. Ed. Michel Elial.

LEXIS; revista de linguistica y literatura. see *LINGUISTICS*

895   CC
LI JIANG/LI RIVER. (Text in Chinese) q. Li Jiang Chubanshe, 159 Nanhuan Lu, Nanning, Guangxi 541002, People's Republic of China. TEL 223929. Ed. Nie Zhenning.

LIAISON. see *HANDICAPPED — Visually Impaired*

891.6   FR   ISSN 0024-1733
AL LIAMM. (Text in Breton) 1946. bi-m. 150 F. (Association al Liamm) P. Le Bihan, 16 rue des Fours a Chaux, 35400 Saint-Malo, Brittany, France. Ed. R. Huon. adv.; bk.rev.; bibl.; charts; illus.; circ. 730.

LIANHUANHUA YISHU/ART OF PICTORIAL STORIES. see *ART*

810   US
LIBIDO; the journal of sex and sensibility. 1988. 4/yr. $26. Box 146721, Chicago, IL 60614. TEL 312-281-0805. circ. 7,000.

LIBROS DE MEXICO. see *PUBLISHING AND BOOK TRADE*

028.1 860   PY   ISSN 0257-3555
LIBROS PARAGUAYOS. 1972. a. $8. Distribuidor Internacional Publicaciones Paraguayas, P.O. Box 2507, Torreani Viera, 551, Villa Mora, Asuncion, Paraguay. TEL 595-21-660991. FAX 595-21-94271. TELEX DIPP 660991. Eds. Margarita Kallsen, Sofia Marecky. bk.rev.; circ. 1,000. (also avail. in microfiche)

LICHTENBERG-JAHRBUCH. see *BIOGRAPHY*

LIFTOUTS; a review of books and language work. see *PUBLISHING AND BOOK TRADE*

800   US   ISSN 0743-913X
PS595.H8
LIGHT YEAR; the biennial of light verse & funny poems. 1983. biennial. $15.95. Bits Press, English Department, Case Western Reserve University, Cleveland, OH 44106. TEL 216-795-2810. Ed. Robert Wallace. circ. 3,600. (back issues avail.)

808.838   US   ISSN 0887-4328
LIGHTHOUSE (AUBURN). 1986. bi-m. $7.95. Lighthouse Publications, Box 1377, Auburn, WA 98071-1377. Ed. Tim Clinton. circ. 300.
    Formerly: Lighthouse Magazine.
    Description: Fiction and poetry for family reading.

850   IT
LIGUORI EDITORE. MONOGRAFIE. 1984. irreg., no.3, 1988. price varies. Liguori Editore s.r.l., Via Mezzocannone, 19, 80134 Naples, Italy. TEL 081-5227139. Eds. G. Mazzacurati, V. Russo.

800   PH   ISSN 0115-6144
LIKHA; D L S U literary journal. (Text in English and Filipino) 1979. s-a. P.85($10.50) (De La Salle University, Literature Department) De La Salle University Press, 2401 Taft Ave., Manila, Philippines. TEL 2-595177. Ed. Ma. Lourdes S. Bautista. adv.; bk.rev.; circ. 300.
    Description: Publishes literary works of university faculty and writers.

LILI. (Zeitschrift fuer Literaturwissenschaft und Linguistik) see *LINGUISTICS*

LILI. BEIHEFTE. (Zeitschrift fuer Literaturwissenschaft und Linguistik) see *LINGUISTICS*

810   US
LILIPUT REVIEW. 1989. irreg. $12. 207 S. Milvale Ave., Ste. 3, Pittsburgh, PA 15224. Ed. Don Wentworth. circ. 150.

808 808.81   US   ISSN 0899-5966
LIMESTONE; a literary journal. 1979. a. $3. University of Kentucky, Department of English, 1215 Patterson Office Tower, Lexington, KY 40506. TEL 606-257-7008. Ed. Matthew J. Bond. adv.; bk.rev.; circ. 1,000. (back issues avail.)
    Formerly: Fabbro (ISSN 0748-2418)

800   IT
LINEA D'OMBRA; mensile di storie, immagini, discussioni. 1983. m. (foreign L.85000). MassMedia Edizioni s.r.l., Via Gaffurio 4, 20124 Milan, Italy. adv.; bk.rev.; index.

895   CC
LING SHUI. (Text in Chinese) q. Nannong Diqu Wenlian, You'ai Lu, Nanning, Guangxi 530001, People's Republic of China. TEL 34608. Ed. Huang Quan'an.

800   GW
LINGUA.* (Text in English and German) q. DM.180 to individuals; institutions DM.240. Cobra Verlag, Schlossgang 15, Postfach 1166, 2250 Husum, Germany. Ed. Wendelin Rader. bk.rev.; index.

LINGUA E CULTURA. see *LINGUISTICS*

800 850 IT
LINGUA E LETTERATURA. 1983. s-a. Istituto Universitario di Lingue Moderne, Piazza Volontari 3, 20145 Milan, Italy. Dir. Carlo Bo. Indexed: M.L.A.

LINGUA E LITERATURA. see *LINGUISTICS*

LINGUA E STILE. see *LINGUISTICS*

LINGUISTIC & LITERARY STUDIES IN EASTERN EUROPE. see *LINGUISTICS*

LINGUISTICA E LETTERATURA. see *LINGUISTICS*

LINGUISTICA PRAGENSIA. see *LINGUISTICS*

LINGUISTICA Y LITERATURA. see *LINGUISTICS*

800 US ISSN 8756-5609
PS3562.I515
LININGTON LINEUP. 1984. bi-m. $12 (foreign $15). (Elizabeth Linington Society) Gloucester Researchers, 1223 Glen Terrace, Glassboro, NJ 08028-1315. TEL 609-589-1571. Ed. Rinehart S. Potts. adv.; bk.rev.; film rev.; abstr.; bibl.; illus.; circ. 400. (back issues avail.)
Description: Covers the life and writings of Elizabeth Linington a.k.a. Anne Blaisdell, Lesley Egan, Egan O'Neill, and Dell Shannon.

820 AT ISSN 0817-458X
LINQ. 1971. 3/yr. Aus.$20 to individuals; institutions Aus.$25. (English Language & Literature Association) James Cook University of North Queensland, Department of English, Townsville, Qld. 4811, Australia. Ed.Bd. bk.rev.; circ. 400. Indexed: M.L.A.

840 FR
LIRE.* 1975. m. 170 F. Groupe Expansion, 38 ave Hoche, 75008 Paris, France. TEL 1-42-89-05-98. FAX 1-45-63-48-14. Ed. Jean-Maurice de Montremy. abstr.; circ. 125,070.

830 GW ISSN 0340-7888
LITERARISCHER VEREIN IN STUTTGART. BIBLIOTHEK. Abbreviated title: B L V S. 1842. irreg., vol.316, 1992. price varies. Anton Hiersemann Verlag, Rosenbergstr. 113, Postfach 140155, 7000 Stuttgart 1, Germany. TEL 0711-638265. FAX 0711-6369010.

891.86 CS ISSN 0300-2446
PG5000
LITERARNI MESICNIK. 1972. 10/yr. 60 Kcs.($26.40) Svaz Ceskoslovenskych Spisovatelu, Narodni tr. 11, 111 47 Prague 1, Czechoslovakia. (Subscr. to: Artia, Ve Smeckach 30, 111 27 Prague 1, Czechoslovakia) (Co-sponsor: Czechoslovakia. Ministerstvo Kultury Ceske Socialisticke Republiky) Ed. Oldrich Rafaj. bk.rev.; illus.; index; circ. 15,000. Indexed: M.L.A.

891.87 780 CS
LITERARNO - MUZEJNY LETOPIS. (Text in Slovak; summaries in German and Russian) 1967. a. price varies. Matica Slovenska, Literarne Muzeum, Ul. Mudronova 26, 036 52 Martin, Czechoslovakia. TEL 0842-313-71. FAX 0842-324-54. TELEX 075 331. Ed. Imrich Sedlak. bk.rev.
Formerly: Letopis Pamatnika Slovenskej Literatury (ISSN 0075-8841)

891.87 CS ISSN 0075-9872
PG5400
LITERARNY ARCHIV. (Text in Slovak) 1964. irreg. (approx. a.). price varies. Matica Slovenska, Archiv Literatury a Umenia, Ul. L. Novomeskeho 32, 036 52 Martin, Czechoslovakia. TEL 0842-313-71. FAX 0842-324-54. TELEX 075 331. Ed. Michal Kocak. bk.rev.

806 070.5 070 US
LITERARY AGENTS OF NORTH AMERICA. 1983. biennial. $29.95. Research Associates International, 340 E. 52 St., New York, NY 10022. TEL 212-980-9179. Eds. Arthur Orrmont, Leonie Rosenstiel. adv.
Formerly: Literary Agents of North America Marketplace.

LITERARY CAVALCADE. see *CHILDREN AND YOUTH — For*

820 II ISSN 0255-2779
LITERARY ENDEAVOUR; a quarterly journal devoted to English studies. (Text in English) 1979. q. Rs.30($10) (New Accents) Dr. L. Adinarayana, Pub., F-3, Block 6, HIG, Opp. Water Tank, Bagh Lingampalli, Hyderanad 500 044, India. Ed. C.R. Nagendran. adv.; bk.rev.; circ. 600. Indexed: M.L.A.
—BLDSC shelfmark: 5276.636050.
Description: Highlights regional literature. Aims to promote an awareness of modern trends and critical approaches to literature. Includes research and reports of conferences and seminars.

800 II ISSN 0024-4554
AP8
LITERARY HALF-YEARLY. (Text in English) 1960. s-a. Rs.60($20) (Institute of Commonwealth and American Studies and English Language) Literary Press, Anjali 96, 7th Main, Jayalakshmipuram, Mysore 570 012, India. (Co-sponsor: Centre for Commonwealth Literature and Research) Ed. H.H. Anniah Gowda. adv.; bk.rev.; bibl.; illus.; index; circ. 1,000. (reprint service avail.) Indexed: Abstr.Engl.Stud., M.L.A.

800 070 US ISSN 0732-6637
PN4878.3
LITERARY MAGAZINE REVIEW. 1981. q. $12.50. Kansas State University, English Department, Manhattan, KS 66506. TEL 316-532-6716. Ed. G.W. Clift. bk.rev.; index; circ. 500. (back issues avail.) Indexed: Amer.Hum.Ind., Bk.Rev.Ind. (1986-), Child.Bk.Rev.Ind. (1986-).
—BLDSC shelfmark: 5276.644500.
Description: Devoted to reviews of the specific contents of magazines publishing fiction or poetry.

820 810 US ISSN 0075-9902
PR13
LITERARY MONOGRAPHS. 1967. irreg. University of Wisconsin Press, 114 N. Murray St., Madison, WI 53715. (reprint service avail. from UMI)

801 US ISSN 0160-8703
PN56.N16
LITERARY ONOMASTICS STUDIES. 1974. a. $12. University of Georgia, Department of English, Athens, GA 30602. (Co-sponsor: American Name Society) Ed. Grace Alvarez-Altman. adv.; circ. controlled. Indexed: Chic.Per.Ind., M.L.A.

800 028 PK ISSN 0075-9929
LITERARY PRIZES IN PAKISTAN. (Text in English) 1964. a. Rs.4.($1.) National Book Council of Pakistan, Theosophical Hall, M.A. Jinnah Rd., Karachi, Pakistan.
Formerly: Incentives for Better Books in Pakistan.

809 US ISSN 0891-6365
PN73
LITERARY RESEARCH: A JOURNAL OF SCHOLARLY METHOD AND TECHNIQUE. 1976. q. $15 (foreign $20). Literary Research Association, Department of English, University of Maryland, College Park, MD 20742. TEL 301-405-3758. FAX 301-314-9320. Ed. Michael J. Marcuse. adv.; bk.rev.; cum.index; circ. 300. (back issues avail.) Indexed: Amer.Hum.Ind., Arts & Hum.Cit.Ind., Curr.Cont., Ind.Bk.Rev.Hum., M.L.A.
—BLDSC shelfmark: 5276.653960.
Formerly (until vol.11, no.1, 1986): Literary Research Newsletter (ISSN 0362-1294)
Description: Covers all aspects of literary research including enumerative and descriptive bibliography, textual criticism and pedagogy.

800 US ISSN 0024-4589
AP2
LITERARY REVIEW; an international journal of contemporary writing. 1957. q. $18. Fairleigh Dickinson University, Literary Review, 285 Madison Ave., Madison, NJ 07940. TEL 201-593-8564. Ed. Walter Cummins. adv.; bk.rev.; index; circ. 2,000. (also avail. in microform from MIM,UMI; reprint service avail. from UMI) Indexed: A.I.P.P., Amer.Bibl.Slavic & E.Eur.Stud., Arts & Hum.Cit.Ind., Curr.Cont., Hum.Ind., Ind.Amer.Per.Verse, Ind.Bk.Rev.Hum., M.L.A., Mid.East: Abstr.& Ind.
—BLDSC shelfmark: 5276.655000.

800 070.5 US ISSN 0024-4597
LITERARY SKETCHES; a magazine of interviews, reviews and memorabilia. 1961. m. $7. Olivia Murray Nichols, Ed. & Pub., Box 810571, Dallas, TX 75381-0571. TEL 214-243-8776. adv.; bk.rev.; charts; cum.index 1962-1986, 1987-1991; circ. 500. Indexed: Abstr.Engl.Stud.
Description: Non-scholarly articles on books and authors of all periods, reviews, trivia, and literary quizzes.

891.4 II ISSN 0024-4600
LITERARY STUDIES; a quarterly review of literature and criticism from the Panjab. (Text in English) 1970. q. Rs.20($10.) Razdan House, Sirhindi Darwaza, Patiala, Panjab, India. Ed. Brij M. Razdan. adv.; bk.rev.

807 PL
LITERARY STUDIES IN POLAND. (Text in English, French, German) irreg., latest vol.20, 1988. price varies. (Polish Academy of Sciences, Institute of Literary Research) Ossolineum, Publishing House of the Polish Academy of Sciences, Rynek 9, 50-106 Wroclaw, Poland. TEL 386-25. (Dist. by: Ars Polona, Krakowskie Przedmiescie 7, 00-068 Warsaw, Poland) Ed. Hanna Dziechcinska.

895.1 CH
LITERARY TAIWAN/WEN HSUEH CHIEH. (Text in Chinese) 1982. q. NT.$400 in ROC; Europe & USA $18; Asia $20. No. 8, Lane 3, Cheng Yi Rd., Ling Ya District, Kaohsiung, Taiwan, Republic of China. TEL 07-771-2027. (Subscr. in US to: Mr. Wen-Hsiung Hsu, 210 Oakmont Dr., Deerfield, IL 60015)

800 700 GW ISSN 0024-4627
DER LITERAT; Fachzeitschrift fuer Literatur und Kunst. 1958. m. DM.65. Verlag der Literat, Hohlweg 27, Postfach 2129, 6232 Bad Soden, Germany. TEL 06174-1764. FAX 06174-24626. Ed. Inka Bohl. adv.; bk.rev.; film rev.; play rev.; circ. 3,000.

LITERATOR; journal of literary criticism and linguistics. see *LINGUISTICS*

830 GW
LITERATUR. 1983. a. DM.9.50. Lamuv Verlag GmbH, Duestere Str. 3, D-3400 Goettingen, Germany. Eds. Christoph Heubner, Alwin Meyer. circ. 15,000. (back issues avail.)

800 831 AU ISSN 0024-466X
PN4
LITERATUR & KRITIK; oesterreichische Monatsschrift. 1966. 5/yr. S.380. Otto Mueller Verlag, Postfach 167, A-5021 Salzburg, Austria. TEL 0662-881974. Ed. Karl-Markus Gauss. bk.rev.; index; circ. 2,500. (back issues avail.)

830 AU
LITERATUR AUS OESTERREICH; Texte zeitgenoessischer Autoren. 1955. bi-m. S.250. (Arbeitsgemeinschaft Literatur) Malek Verlag GmbH, Wienerstr. 127, A-3500 Krems, Austria. FAX 02732-74939. Ed. Johannes Twaroch. adv.; bk.rev.; bibl.; circ. 4,000.
Formerly (until 1986): Heimatland (ISSN 0017-9779)

830 GW ISSN 0930-4010
PT3803.H4
DER LITERATUR BOTE. q. DM.20. (Hessisches Literaturbuero) Dipa-Verlag, Nassauer Str. 1-3, 6000 Frankfurt a.M. 50, Germany. TEL 069-586910. FAX 069-576128.

830 GW ISSN 0343-1657
PT3
LITERATUR FUER LESER; Zeitschrift fuer Interpretationspraxis und geschichtliche Texterkenntnis. 1968. q. DM.56.80. Verlag Peter Lang, Eschborner Landstr. 42-50, 6000 Frankfurt a.M. 90, Germany. Eds. Rolf Geissler, Herbert Kaiser. adv. (back issues avail.)
Description: Collection of critical essays and interpretations of important literary works.

800 GW ISSN 0178-6857
LITERATUR IN BAYERN. 1985. q. DM.24. F.A. Herbig Verlagsbuchhandlung GmbH, Thomas-Wimmer-Ring 11, 8000 Munich 22, Germany. FAX 089-235008-44. TELEX 5215045-LAHE-D. Ed. Prof. Dietz-Ruediger Moser. adv.; bk.rev.; circ. 3,000.

LITERATURE

830 GW
LITERATUR UND GESCHICHTE. EINE SCHRIFTENREIHE. 1970. irreg. price varies. Lothar Stiehm Verlag, Hausackerweg 16, 6900 Heidelberg, Germany. **Indexed:** M.L.A.

800 GW ISSN 0232-315X
LITERATUR UND GESELLSCHAFT. 1972. irreg., vol.99, 1989. (Akademie der Wissenschaften der DDR) Akademie-Verlag Berlin, Leipziger Str. 3-4, 1086 Berlin, Germany. TELEX 114420-AVERL-DD.

800 GW ISSN 0075-9937
LITERATUR UND WIRKLICHKEIT. 1967. irreg., latest vol.24. price varies. Bouvier Verlag Herbert Grundmann, Am Hof 32, Postfach 1268, 5300 Bonn 1, Germany. Ed. Karl Otto Conrady.

830 GW ISSN 0938-1767
LITERATUR ZUM ANGEWOEHNEN. 1983. irreg., no.53, 1992. DM.10. M. und N. Boesche, Laurinsteig 14a, 1000 Berlin 28, Germany. TEL 030-4019009.

891.8 PL
LITERATURA. 1972. m. $23. Ul. Koszykowa 6A, 00-562 Warsaw, Poland. (Dist. by: Ars Polona-Ruch, Krakowskie Przedmiescie 7, Warsaw, Poland) Ed. Jacek Syski. bk.rev.; illus.; circ. 64,800.
Supersedes: Wspolczesnosc (ISSN 0510-9744)

800 HU ISSN 0133-2368
PH3001
LITERATURA. (Text in Hungarian; summaries in English and Russian) 1974. q. $19.50. (Magyar Tudomanyos Akademia, Irodalomtudomanyi Intezet) Akademiai Kiado, Publishing House of the Hungarian Academy of Sciences, P.O. Box 24, H-1363 Budapest, Hungary. Ed. Gy. Bodnar. adv.; bk.rev. **Indexed:** M.L.A.

800 LI ISSN 0202-3296
LITERATURA. (Text and summaries in English, German, Lithuanian, Polish, Russian) 1958. 3/yr. price varies. (Vilniaus Universitetas - Vilnius University) Leidykla Mokslas, Zvaigzdziu g-ve, 23, 232050 Vilnius, Lithuania. TEL 45-85-26. TELEX 261107 LMOK SU. (Co-sponsor: Lithuanian Ministry of Culture and Education) Ed. V. Areska. circ. 500. (also avail. in microfilm from KTO)
—BLDSC shelfmark: 5276.678000.
Description: Focuses on problems of Lithuanian, Russian, Germanic-Romance and antique literature.

860 US ISSN 0730-0220
PQ7900
LITERATURA CHILENA; creacion y critica. 1977. irreg. $16 to individuals; institutions $22. Ediciones de la Frontera, Box 3013, Hollywood, CA 90078. Ed. David Valjalo. bk.rev.; circ. 3,000.
Formerly (until 1981): Literatura Chilena en el Exilio (ISSN 0278-7288)

891.7 RU
LITERATURA DREVNEI RUSI. 1975. irreg. 1 Rub. Moskovskii Gosudarstvennyi Pedagogicheskii Institut, Kafedra Russkoi Literatury, Moscow, Russia. circ. 1,000.

891.7 BW ISSN 0024-4686
LITERATURA I MASTATSTVA. vol.43, 1976. s-w. $8.40. Ministerstvo Kul'tury, Minsk, Byelarus. Ed. L.Y. Pzoksha. bk.rev.; illus.; index. (also avail. in microform from MIM)

499.992 BL ISSN 0024-4694
LITERATURA KAJERO;* monata kultura kajero en esperanto. (Text in Esperanto) 1968. m. Cr.$10.($3.) Henerik Kocher, Ed. & Pub., Rua Baltasar Lisboa 34, ZC-11 Rio de Janeiro GB, Brazil.

800 PL
LITERATURA NA SWIECIE. m. $19.80. Wydawnictwo Wspolczesne R S W "Prasa-Ksiazka-Ruch", Ul. Wiejska 12, 00-420 Warsaw, Poland. TEL 48-22-285330. (Subscr. to: RSW "Prasa-Ksiazka-Ruch" Centrala Kolportazu i Wydawnictw, ul. Towarowa 28, 00-958 Warsaw, Poland; Editorial addr.: ul. Sienkiewicza 12, IV p., pok, 423, 00-010 Warsaw, Poland. TEL 48-22-274791) Ed. Waclaw Sadkowski. bk.rev.

891.7 RU
LITERATURA OB ARKHANGEL'SKOI OBLASTI. 1973. a. (Arkhangel'skaya Oblastnaya Biblioteka, Bibliograficheskii Otdel) Severo-Zapadnoe Knizhnoe Izdatel'stvo, Arkhangel'sk, Russia.

869 BL
LITERATURA POPULAR EM VERSO. 1983. irreg. Fundacao Casa de Rui Barbosa, Rua Sao Clemente 134, Botafogo 22260, Rio de Janeiro RJ, Brazil. FAX 5371114.

371.3 RU ISSN 0130-3414
LITERATURA V SHKOLE. 1914. bi-m. 2.70 Rub. (Ministerstvo Prosveshcheniya) Izdatel'stvo Prosveshchenie, 3-i Proezd Mar'inoi Roshchi, 41, Moscow, Russia. TEL 289-44-34. TELEX 111999 PARK. (Co-sponsor: Ministerstvo Narodnogo Obrazovaniya R.S.F.S.R.) Ed. N.L. Krupina. bk.rev.; bibl.; illus.; circ. 286,986.
Description: Aimed at literature teachers in grades 4-10. Presents materials on classical Russian and modern Soviet literature. Also contains articles on methodology of teaching literature in school.

860 PE
LITERATURAS ANDINAS. 1988. s-a. $12. Instituto de Estudios.Cultura y Sociedad en los Andes, San Martin 771, Juaja, Peru.

LITERATURE AND BELIEF. see *RELIGIONS AND THEOLOGY*

052 US ISSN 0306-1973
AS122.T45
LITERATURE & HISTORY. 1975-1988; N.S. 1990. s-a. $29. Ohio State University, Department of English, 421 W. Denney Hall, 164 W. 17th Ave., OH 43210. TEL 614-292-4076. Ed. John N. King. adv.; bk.rev.; circ. 600. **Indexed:** Abstr.Pop.Cult., Amer.Hist.& Life, Arts & Hum.Cit.Ind., Bk.Rev.Ind. (1984-1990), Child.Bk.Rev.Ind. (1984-1990), Curr.Cont., Hist.Abstr., Ind.Bk.Rev.Hum., LCR, M.L.A.
—BLDSC shelfmark: 5276.713000.
Description: Explores the relations among writing, history, and ideology.

808 610 US ISSN 0278-9671
PN56.M38
LITERATURE & MEDICINE. 1982. s-a. $18 to individuals (foreign $18.30); institutions $32. (University of Texas Medical Branch at Galveston, Institute for the Medical Humanities) Johns Hopkins University Press, Journals Publishing Division, 701 W. 40th St., Ste. 275, Baltimore, MD 21211. TEL 410-565-6987. FAX 410-565-6998. Ed. Anne Hudson Jones. adv.; circ. 592. (back issues avail.) **Indexed:** Arts & Hum.Cit.Ind., Curr.Cont., M.L.A.
—BLDSC shelfmark: 5276.714500.
Description: Covers an emerging new specialty in the medical humanities.

809 150 US ISSN 0024-4759
PN49 CODEN: LIPSA
LITERATURE AND PSYCHOLOGY; a quarterly journal of literary criticism as informed by depth psychology. 1951-1981; resumed 1984. q. $12 to individuals; institutions $20. c/o Morton Kaplan and Richard Feldstein, Eds., Department of English, Rhode Island College, Providence, RI 02908. bk.rev.; bibl.; circ. 1,000. (also avail. in microform from UMI; reprint service avail. from SWZ,UMI) **Indexed:** Abstr.Engl.Stud., Amer.Bibl.Slavic & E.Eur.Stud., Curr.Cont., Film Lit.Ind. (1990-), Hum.Ind., Ind.Bk.Rev.Hum., M.L.A., Mid.East: Abstr.& Ind., Psychol.Abstr.

839 NE
LITERATURE AND SOCIETY IN THE SEVENTEENTH CENTURY. 1983. irreg. price varies. Dick Coutinho B.V., P.O. Box 10, 1399 ZG Muiderberg, Netherlands. TEL 02942-1888.

800 100 US ISSN 1040-7928
LITERATURE AND THE SCIENCES OF MAN. irreg. Peter Lang Publishing, Inc., 62 W. 45th St., 4th Fl., New York, NY 10036. TEL 212-302-6740. FAX 212-302-7574. Ed. Peter Heller.

800 700 US ISSN 0888-3890
LITERATURE AND THE VISUAL ARTS: NEW FOUNDATIONS. irreg. Peter Lang Publishing, Inc., 62 W. 45th St., 4th Fl., New York, NY 10036. TEL 212-302-6740. FAX 212-302-7574. Ed. Ernest B. Gilman.
—BLDSC shelfmark: 5276.717000.
Description: Explores the interrelationships of literature and the visual arts, including film.

800 UK ISSN 0269-1205
PN49
LITERATURE AND THEOLOGY. 1987. 4/yr. £48($93) Oxford University Press, Oxford Journals, Pinkhill House, Southfield Road, Eynsham, Oxford OX8 1JJ, England. TEL 0865-882283. FAX 0865-882890. TELEX 837330 OXPRES G. Ed. Rev. David Jasper. adv.; bk.rev.; circ. 750. **Indexed:** Rel.& Theol.Abstr. (1989-).
—BLDSC shelfmark: 5276.716000.
Description: Interdisciplinary study of serious interest to both theologians and to students of literature.

THE LITERATURE BASE. see *CHILDREN AND YOUTH — For*

800 US ISSN 0024-4767
PN2
LITERATURE EAST AND WEST. Short title: L E & W. 1954. q. $10. c/o Department of Oriental and African Languages and Literatures, University of Texas, Austin, 2601 University Ave., Austin, TX 78712. Ed. Michael Hillman. adv.; bk.rev.; index; circ. 500. (also avail. in microform from MIM,UMI; reprint service avail. from UMI,ISI) **Indexed:** Abstr.Engl.Stud., Curr.Cont., M.L.A., Mid.East: Abstr.& Ind.

LITERATURE - FILM QUARTERLY. see *MOTION PICTURES*

800 US
LITERATURE OF EXCLUSION IN SPAIN. irreg. Peter Lang Publishing, Inc., 62 W. 45th St., 4th Fl., New York, NY 10036. TEL 212-302-6740. FAX 212-302-7574. Ed. Benito Brancaforte.
Description: Explores problems of exclusion from the perspective of the dominant groups and that of the excluded.

891.8 XN ISSN 0024-4791
PG1161
LITERATUREN ZBOR; jezik, literatura, nastavi, prikazi. (Text in Macedonian) 1954. s-a. 15 din.($4.20) Drustvoto za Makedonski Jazik i Literatura, Grigor Prlicev 5, 91000 Skopje, Macedonia. (Co-sponsor: Institut za Makedonski Jazik, Skopje) Ed. Blagoja Karilin. **Indexed:** M.L.A.

891.8 BU ISSN 0324-0495
LITERATURNA MISAL. (Contents page in English and French) 1957. 10/yr. 1.30 lv. per no. (Bulgarska Akademiia na Naukite, Institut za Literatura) Publishing House of the Bulgarian Academy of Sciences, Acad. G. Bonchev St., Bldg. 6, 1113 Sofia, Bulgaria. (Dist. by: Hemus, 6, Rouski Blvd., 1000 Sofia, Bulgaria) Ed. Pantelei Zarev. bk.rev.; index; circ. 1,660. **Indexed:** Can.Rev.Comp.Lit., M.L.A.

LITERATURNAYA ROSSIYA. see *LITERARY AND POLITICAL REVIEWS*

890 GS
LITERATURNYE VZAIMOSVYAZI. (Text in Georgian and Russian) vol.6, 1976. price varies. (Akademiya Nauk Gruzinskoi S.S.R., Institut Istorii Gruzinskoi Literatury) Izdatel'stvo Metsniereba, Ul. Kutuzova 19, Tbilisi, Georgia. Ed.Bd. bibl.; circ. 900.

891.7 AJ ISSN 0024-4864
LITERATURNYI AZERBAIDZHAN. 1942. m. 16.20 Rub. Soyuz Pisatelei Azerbaidzhanskoi S.S.R., Ul. Khagani 25, Baku, Azerbaijan. bk.rev.; bibl.; charts; illus.; circ. 3,460.

830 GW ISSN 0075-997X
PT13
LITERATURWISSENSCHAFTLICHES JAHRBUCH. NEUE FOLGE. 1960. a. price varies. (Goerres-Gesellschaft) Duncker und Humblot GmbH, Postfach 410329, 1000 Berlin 41, Germany. TEL 030-7900060. FAX 030-79000631. Ed.Bd. bk.rev. **Indexed:** Can.Rev.Comp.Lit, M.L.A.
—BLDSC shelfmark: 5276.739500.

810 IT
LITERRATURE D'AMERICA. 1979. q. L.40000. (Universita degli Studi di Roma, Dipartamento di Studi Americani) Bulzoni Editore, Via dei Liburni 14, 00185 Rome, Italy. TEL 06-4455207. FAX 06-4450355. Ed. Dario Puccini.

800 GW
LITFASS; Zeitschrift fuer Literatur. 1976. q. DM.35.20. Piner Verlag, Georgenstr. 4, D-8000 Munich, Germany. Ed. Uwe Heldt. adv.; bk.rev.; bibl.; illus.; stat.; tr.lit.; index; circ. 4,000.

LITERATURE

800   NE   ISSN 0169-8702
LITTERAE TEXTUALES; a series on manuscripts and their texts. 1972. irreg. price varies. E.J. Brill, P.O. Box 9000, 2300 PA Leiden, Netherlands. TEL 071-312624. FAX 071-317532. TELEX 39296 BRILL NL. (In N. America: E.J. Brill, 24 Hudson St., Kinderhook, NY 12106. TEL 800-962-4406) Eds. A. Gruys, J.P. Gumbert.

800   PL   ISSN 0084-3008
LITTERARIA; teoria literatury-metodologia-kultura-humanistyka. 1969. irreg., vol.18, 1987. price varies. (Wroclawskie Towarzystwo Naukowe) Ossolineum, Publishing House of the Polish Academy of Sciences, Rynek 9, Wroclaw, Poland. TELEX 0712771 OSS PL. (Dist. by: Ars Polona-Ruch, Krakowskie Przedmiescie 7, Warsaw, Poland) (Co-sponsor: Polska Akademia Nauk) Ed. Jan Trzynadlowski. bk.rev.; circ. 700. (also avail. in microfilm)
Description: Devoted to Polish literature of the past and present, comparative literature, sociology of literature, and literary criticism.

891.87   CS
LITTERARIA. irreg. price varies. (Slovenska Akademia Vied, Literarnovedny Ustav) Veda, Publishing House of the Slovak Academy of Sciences, Klemensova 19, 814 30 Bratislava, Czechoslovakia. (Dist. by: Slovart, Nam. Slobody 6, 817 64 Bratislava, Czechoslovakia)

800 400   NE
▼**LITTERARIA PRAGENSIA**. 1991. 2/yr. fl.96($49) (Czechoslovak Academy of Sciences, Institute for Czech and World Literature, CS) John Benjamins Publishing Co., Amsteldijk 44, P.O. Box 75577, 1070 AN Amsterdam, Netherlands. TEL 020-6738156. FAX 020-6739773. (In N. America: 821 Bethlehem Pike, Philadelphia, PA 19118. TEL 215-836-1200) (back issues avail.)
Supersedes in part (1958-1991): Philologica Pragensia (ISSN 0048-3885)
Description: Contemporary literary and cultural studies, with an emphasis on literary discourse.

800   FR   ISSN 0047-4800
LITTERATURE. 1971. q. 270 F. Larousse, 17 rue du Montparnasse, 75280 Paris Cedex 06, France. (Dist. by: Gauthier-Villars, Centrale des Revues, 11 rue Gossin, 92543 Montrouge Cedex, France. TEL 1-46-56-52-66) Ed.Bd. bk.rev.; bibl. **Indexed:** Arts & Hum.Cit.Ind., Curr.Cont., M.L.A.
—BLDSC shelfmark: 5277.495000.

800   CC   ISSN 1000-9132
LITTERATURE CHINOISE. English edition: Chinese Literature (ISSN 0009-4617) (Text in French) q. (Wenhua Bu, Waiwen Ju - Ministry of Culture, Foreign Language Bureau) Zhongguo Wenxue Zazhishe - Chinese Literature Press, 24 Baiwanzhuang Lu, Beijing 100037, People's Republic of China. TEL 8323291. (Dist. outside China by: China International Book Trading Corp., P.O. Box 399, Beijing, P.R.C.) Ed. Yin Shuxun.

840   FR   ISSN 0563-9751
PN3
LITTERATURES. 1951. s-a. 150 F. to individuals; students 120 F. (effective 1992). (Universite de Toulouse II (le Mirail)) Presses Universitaires du Mirail, 56 rue du Taur, 31000 Toulouse, France. TEL 61-22-58-31. FAX 61-21-84-20. Ed. Claude Sicard. (back issues avail.) **Indexed:** M.L.A.
—BLDSC shelfmark: 5277.750000.
Description: Covers French, German, Italian and slavic-language literature; comparative literature; theatrical, musical and cinematographic studies.

LITTLE BALKANS REVIEW; Southeast Kansas literary and graphics quarterly. see ART

810   US   ISSN 0024-5054
LITTLE REVIEW. 1969. irreg. $6. Little Review Press, Marshall University, Huntington, WV 25701. TEL 304-696-6499. Ed. John McKernan. bk.rev.; circ. 1,000. (also avail. in microfilm from UMI) **Indexed:** Ind.Amer.Per.Verse.
Description: Focuses on literature; contemporary poetry and poetic theory.

800   US
LIVE LETTERS. 1974. s-a. $20. Center for Live Letters, 156 Hunter St., Kingston, NY 12401. FAX 914-338-5986. bk.rev.; illus.; circ. 500. (back issues avail.)
Formerly: Letters.

860   UK   ISSN 0261-1538
LIVERPOOL MONOGRAPHS IN HISPANIC STUDIES. 1982. irreg. (1-3/yr.) price varies. Francis Cairns (Publications), c/o the University, Leeds LS2 9JT, England. Ed. James Higgins. **Indexed:** M.L.A.

808 200   US
LIVING STREAMS; the Christian writers journal. 1988. q. $18. P.O. Box 1321, Vincennes, IN 47591. Ed. Kevin Hrebik.
Description: Collection of contemporary Christian prose and poetry.

800   UK   ISSN 0076-0188
LLEN CYMRU. (Text in Welsh) 1950. irreg. £5. (Board of Celtic Studies) University of Wales Press, 6 Gwennyth St., Cathays, Cardiff CF2 4YD, Wales. TEL 0222-231919. FAX 0222-230908. Ed. C.W. Lewis. adv.; bk.rev.; circ. 250. (also avail. in microfilm from UMI; reprint service avail. from UMI) **Indexed:** M.L.A.
Description: Research in Welsh language and Welsh literary history.

LO GAI SABER. see LINGUISTICS

800   PL   ISSN 0076-0404
LODZKIE TOWARZYSTWO NAUKOWE. PRACE WYDZIALU JEZYKOZNAWSTWA, NAUKI O LITERATURZE I FILOZOFII. (Text in Polish; summaries in English, French, Russian) 1947. irreg., no.87, 1986. price varies. Ossolineum, Publishing House of the Polish Academy of Sciences, Rynek 9, 50-106 Wroclaw, Poland. TELEX 0712771 OSS PL. (Dist. by: Ars Polona-Ruch, Krakowskie Przedmiescie 7, 00-068 Warsaw, Poland) (Co-sponsor: Polska Akademia Nauk)

800   US
LOEB CLASSICAL LIBRARY. irreg., no.475, 1990. $15.50. Harvard University Press, 79 Garden St., Cambridge, MA 02138. TEL 617-495-2600. FAX 617-495-5898.
Refereed Serial

810   US   ISSN 0047-5033
LONDON COLLECTOR. 1970. s-a. $1. Wolf House Books, Box 6657, Grand Rapids, MI 49506-0657. Ed. Richard Weiderman. adv.; bk.rev.; circ. 150. (processed)
Description: Covers the life and work of Jack London.

830   UK
PT1
LONDON GERMAN STUDIES. 1980. irreg., latest 1992. price varies. University of London, Institute of Germanic Studies, 29 Russell Square, London WC1B 5DP, England. TEL 071-580-2711. FAX 071-436-3497. circ. 500.
Description: Selection of essays previously given as lectures at the institute.

820   UK   ISSN 0024-614X
LONDON REVIEW.* 1967. s-a. 40p.($0.96) 45 Manor Rd., Ashford, Middx., England. Ed. T.F. Evans. adv.; circ. 500.

800   US   ISSN 8756-5099
PS536.2
LONG POND REVIEW. 1975. a. $3 per no. to individuals; institutions $5. Long Pond Review Press, Suffolk County Community College, English Dept., Selden, NY 11784. TEL 516-451-4153. Ed. Russell Steinke. adv.; bk.rev.; circ. 500.

800   US   ISSN 0895-9773
LONG SHOT. 1982. 2/yr. $10. Long Shot Productions, Box 6231, Hoboken, NJ 07030. Ed.Bd. adv.; circ. 1,000. (back issues avail.)

800   US   ISSN 0741-4242
LONG STORY. 1983. a. $5. 11 Kingston St., North Andover, MA 01845. TEL 508-686-7638. Ed. R.P. Burnham. circ. 500. (back issues avail.) **Indexed:** A.I.P.P., Amer.Hum.Ind.

890   II   ISSN 0377-1083
LORE; magazine of new writing. (Text in English) 1974. m. Rs.10. (Delhi Writers Club) Rami Press, 48 Mandirwali Gali, Yusof Sarai, New Delhi, India. Ed. M. C. Bose. adv.; bk.rev.; bibl.

800 900   US   ISSN 0091-2948
NX504
LOST GENERATION JOURNAL. 1973. a. $10. Deloris & Tom Wood, Eds. & Pubs., Route 5, Box 134, Salem, MO 65560. TEL 314-364-5900. adv.; bk.rev.; circ. 500. (back issues avail.) **Indexed:** Abstr.Engl.Stud., Abstr.Pop.Cult., Amer.Hum.Ind., M.L.A.
Description: Covers American writers, performers and artists in Europe (mainly Paris) from 1919 to 1939.

896 892 895   UA   ISSN 0002-0664
PN2
LOTUS; Afro-Asian writings. 1968. q. Permanent Bureau of Afro-Asian Writers, 104 Sharia Kasr El-Aini, Cairo, Egypt. Ed. Youssef El Sebai. bk.rev.; bibl.; illus.
Formerly: Afro-Asian Writings.

800   US   ISSN 0890-0477
LOUISIANA LITERATURE. 1984. s-a. $10 to individuals; institutions $12.50. Southeastern Louisiana University, English Department, Box 792, Hammond, LA 70402. Ed. Tim Gautreaux. adv.; bk.rev.; circ. 650.
Formerly: L A Lit - Lousiana Literature.
Description: Essays relevant to Louisiana's literature, history and art. Includes poetry and fiction.

800   US   ISSN 0148-3250
PS501
LOUISVILLE REVIEW. 1976. s-a. $7 (typically set in May). (University of Louisville) Louisville Review Corporation, Louisville, KY 40292. TEL 502-588-6801. Ed. Sena Naslund. circ. 500.
Description: Contains poetry and fiction, plus children's (K-12) work in the spring.

LOVECRAFT STUDIES. see LITERATURE — Science Fiction, Fantasy, Horror

LOVING BROTHERHOOD NEWSLETTER; a journal for personal and planetary transformation. see HOMOSEXUALITY

810   US
LOWLANDS REVIEW. 1975. s-a. $3 per no. 6048 Perrier, New Orleans, LA 70118. Ed. Tom Whalen. bk.rev.; circ. 400.

895.1   CC
LU MING. (Text in Chinese) bi-m. Baotou Shi Wenlian - Baotou Municipal Literary and Art Circle Association, Jinrong Dalou (Financial Building), Kundulun-qu, Baotou, Nei Menggu 014010, People's Republic of China. TEL 62935. Ed. Ge Fei.

LU XUN YANJIU YUEKAN/LU XUN STUDIES MONTHLY. see BIOGRAPHY

859   RM
LUCEAFARUL. 1958. w. 208 lei. Uniunea Scriitorilor din Republica Socialista Romania, Calea Victoriei 115, Bucharest, Rumania. (Subscr. to: ILEXIM, Str. 13 Decembrie Nr. 3, Box 136-137, 70116 Bucharest, Rumania) Ed. Nicolae Dan Runtelata. bk.rev.; film rev.; play rev.; charts; illus.; circ. 7,000. **Indexed:** M.L.A.

860   CK
LUCIERNAGA. 1981. bi-m. Apartado Aereo 8663, Cali, Colombia.

800   BE
LUCRE-HATIF. 1962. m. 300 Fr. Institut Catholique des Hautes Etudes Commerciales, Cercle des Etudiants, 2 Bd. Brand Whitlock, B-1040 Brussels, Belgium. TEL 02-732-01-50. Ed. Marc Jossart. adv.; bk.rev.; film rev.; illus.; circ. 800. (processed)
Formerly: Confins (ISSN 0010-5694)
Description: Informs students, teachers, and members of events in the ICHEC. Contains interesting surveys about the students.

700 800   YU
LUMINA. (Text in Rumanian) 1946. $5.70. Libertatea, Zarka Zrenjanina 7, Pancevo, Serbia, Yugoslavia. Ed. Ion Balan. bibl.

850   IT
LUNARIONUOVO. bi-m. L.15000. Mario Grasso, Ed. & Pub., Via Duca d'Aosta 90, 95037 San Giovanni La Punta, Italy.

LITERATURE

850 IT
▼LUOGHI DELL'ANIMA. 1990. irreg. price varies. Ligouri Editrice s.r.l., Via Mezzocannone 19, 80134 Naples, Italy. TEL 081-5227139. Ed. Elena Vitas.

808.81 FR ISSN 0754-927X
LUVAH. 1982. q. 100 F.($15) (effective 1991). Association Luvah, 25220 Amagney, France. Ed. Louis Ucciani. circ. 300. (back issues avail.)

810 US ISSN 0163-755X
PN843
M E L U S. 1974. 4/yr. (in 1 vol.). $40 (foreign $48). Society for the Study of the Multi-Ethnic Literature of the United States, 272 Bartlett Hall, Dept. of English, Univ. of Mass., Amherst, MA 01003. TEL 413-545-3166. FAX 413-545-3880. Ed. Joseph T. Skerrett, Jr. adv.; bk.rev.; circ. 900. (also avail. in microform from UMI) Indexed: Abstr.Anthropol., Abstr.Engl.Stud., Amer.Bibl.Slavic & E.Eur.Stud., Amer.Hum.Ind., Arts & Hum.Cit.Ind., Curr.Cont., Hum.Ind. Key Title: Melus.
   Description: Presents research, scholarly essays, and interviews of interest to those concerned with the multi-ethnic scope of America's literature, including Asian-American, African-American, Hispanic-American, Native-American and immigrant European literature.

M L A INTERNATIONAL BIBLIOGRAPHY OF BOOKS AND ARTICLES ON THE MODERN LANGUAGES AND LITERATURES. (Modern Language Association of America) see BIBLIOGRAPHIES

M L A NEWSLETTER (NEW YORK). (Modern Language Association of America) see LINGUISTICS

808 US ISSN 0738-9469
PS501
M S S MAGAZINE. 1961. irreg. (2-3/yr.). $10 to individuals; institutions $15. State University of New York at Binghamton, Binghamton, NY 13901. Ed. L.M. Rosenberg. adv.; bk.rev.; illus.; circ. 1,000. (back issues avail.)

M 5 V MAGAZINE. see ART

800 028.5 IS ISSN 0334-2867
MA'AGALAI KERI'A. (Text in Arabic, Hebrew) 1977. s-a. IS.27($25) (Haifa University, Center for Children's Literature) Haifa University Press, Mount Carmel, Haifa 31999, Israel. TEL 04-247181. FAX 04-254184. Ed. Adir Cohen. circ. 400.

MAARAV; a journal for the study of the northwest semitic languages and literatures. see LINGUISTICS

890 920 011 IS
MABUA/FOUNTAIN; religious creation in literature, society and thought. (Text and summaries in Hebrew) 1965. a. $20. Association of Religious Writers, 58 King George St., Jerusalem 91073, Israel. Ed. Ya'akov Edelstein. adv.; bk.rev.; circ. 2,000. (back issues avail.) Indexed: Ind.Heb.Per.

800 700 XN ISSN 0350-3089
MACEDONIAN REVIEW; history, culture, literature, arts. (Text in English) 1971. 3/yr. $20 (effective Jan. 1991). Kulturen Zivot - Cultural Life, Ruzveltova, 6, P.O. Box 85, 91001 Skopje, Macedonia. Ed. Boris Vishinski. bk.rev.; illus. (reprint service avail. from UMI) Indexed: Amer.Hist.& Life, Hist.Abstr., M.L.A.

800 976 US ISSN 0885-467X
AS36
MCNEESE REVIEW. 1948. a. $3 (foreign $4.25). McNeese State University, Box 92940, Lake Charles, LA 70609. TEL 318-475-5127. Ed. Benjamin C. Harlow. circ. 200. (back issues avail.) Indexed: Abstr.Engl.Stud.
   Description: Presents original, previously unpublished manuscripts and documented research of a scholarly nature.

800 US
MCWINNERS MAGAZINE.* 1975. irreg. $12 to individuals; institutions $15. Alex N. Scandalios, Ed. & Pub., Box 8611, Santa Fe, CA 92067-8611. adv.; bk.rev.; circ. 30,000.
   Former titles: Winners Magazine & Willmore City.

800 US ISSN 1054-2655
▼MAD RIVER; a journal of essays. 1991. 3/yr. $18. Wright State University, 006 U.C., Dayton, OH 45435. TEL 513-873-2031. Ed. Charles S. Taylor. bk.rev.
   Description: Multidisciplinary journal of essays, original works of art, and reviews of classical and jazz CDs.

895.49 NP
MADHUPARKA. (Text in Nepali) 1986. m. Dharma Path, P.O. Box 23, Kathmandu, Nepal. TEL 222278. Ed. Krishna Bhakta Shrestha. circ. 20,000.

MAGAZIN POLOVNIKA. see SPORTS AND GAMES — Outdoor Life

800 FR ISSN 0024-9807
PN3
MAGAZINE LITTERAIRE. 1966. m. 335 F. (foreign 450 F.)(effective Mar.1992). Magazine-Expansion, 40, rue des Saints-Peres, 75007 Paris, France. TEL 45-44-14-51. FAX 45-48-86-36. Ed. Jean-Jacques Brochier. adv.; bk.rev.; circ. 95,000. Indexed: Pt.de Rep. (1979-).
—BLDSC shelfmark: 5333.470000.

100 700 US ISSN 0196-8432
MAGIC CHANGES; the annual for independent artists. 1979. a. $5. (Order of the Celestial Otter) Celestial Otter Press, c/o John Sennett, Ed., Box 658, Warrenville, IL 60555-9269. TEL 708-416-3111. adv.; bk.rev.; circ. 500. (back issues avail.)

MAGICAL BLEND; a transformative journey. see NEW AGE PUBLICATIONS

028.1 US ISSN 0163-3058
Z1219
MAGILL'S LITERARY ANNUAL. a. $70. Salem Press, Box 1097, Englewood Cliffs, NJ 07632. TEL 201-871-3700. FAX 201-871-8668. Ed. F.N. Magill. Indexed: Amer.Bibl.Slavic & E.Eur.Stud.
   Formerly: Masterplots Annual.

MAGPIES; talking about books for children. see CHILDREN AND YOUTH — About

894.51 HU ISSN 0076-2385
MAGYAR IRODALOMTORTENETIRAS FORRASAI; fontes ad historiam litterariam Hungariae spectantes. 1960. irreg. price varies. (Magyar Tudomanyos Akademia) Akademiai Kiado, Publishing House of the Hungarian Academy of Sciences, Box 24, H-1363 Budapest, Hungary.

891.4 II ISSN 0025-049X
MAHENJODARO. (Text in Bengali) 1959. q. Rs.3. 5514 Natabar Pal Rd., Howrah, West Bengal, India. Ed. Samir Ray. bk.rev.; film rev.; play rev.; abstr.; illus.; circ. 2,300.

MAIA; rivista di letterature classiche. see CLASSICAL STUDIES

800 US
MAINE SCHOLAR. 1988. a. $15. University of Maine, Honors Program, 96 Falmouth St., Portland, ME 04103. Ed. Jeremiah P. Conway.

820 UK ISSN 0025-0848
MAINLY.* 1965. irreg. (2-4/yr.). 2s. 6d. per no.($.75). Carregraff, Graig Las, Talybont, Brecon, Wales. Eds. Lyndon Puw, Chrissie Smith. bk.rev.; illus.; circ. 1,000.

830 GW ISSN 0076-2784
MAINZER REIHE. 1960. irreg. price varies. (Akademie der Wissenschaften und der Literatur, Mainz) Hase und Koehler Verlag KG, Bahnhofstr. 6, 6500 Mainz 1, Germany. FAX 06131-227952. TELEX 4187850. adv.; bk.rev. Indexed: Math.R.

810 418.02 GW ISSN 0170-9135
MAINZER STUDIEN ZUR AMERIKANISTIK. (Text in English, German) 1972. irreg., no.24, 1991. Verlag Peter Lang GmbH, Eschborner Landstr. 42-50, 6000 Frankfurt a.M. 90, Germany. TEL 069-7807050. FAX 069-785893. Ed. Hans Galinsky. circ. 225. (back issues avail.)

892.7 SY ISSN 0002-4031
PJ6001
MAJMA' AL-LUGHAH AL-ARABIYYAH. MAJALLAH/ARAB LANGUAGE ACADEMY. JOURNAL. 1921. q. $9. Majma' al-Lughah al-Arabiyyah - Arab Language Academy, P.O. Box 327, Damascus, Syria. Ed. Dr. Shakir al-Faham. bk.rev.; index, cum.index; circ. 2,000.
   Description: Covers Arabic culture and traditions in language, history and literature.

800 UK
MAJOR EUROPEAN AUTHOR SERIES. irreg. price varies. Cambridge University Press, Edinburgh Bldg., Shaftesbury Rd., Cambridge CB2 2RU, England. TEL 0223-312393. FAX 0223-315052. TELEX 851817256.

MAKEDONSKA AKADEMIJA NA NAUKITE I UMETNOSTITE. ODDELENIE ZA LINGVISTIKA I LITERATURNA NAUKA. PRILOZI/MACEDONIAN ACADEMY OF SCIENCES AND ARTS. SECTION OF LINGUISTICS AND LITERARY SCIENCES. CONTRIBUTIONS. see LINGUISTICS

899 MY ISSN 0128-1186
MALAY LITERATURE. (Text in English and Malay) 1967. s-a. M.$20 to individuals (institutions M.$24); foreign individuals $5 (institutions $7). National Language and Literary Agency of Malaysia - Dewan Bahasa dan Pustaka Malaysia, Box 10803, 50926 Kuala Lumpur, Malaysia. FAX 03-2482726. TELEX MA 32683. Ed. S. Jaafar Husin. adv.; bk.rev.; circ. 3,000. Indexed: M.L.A.
   Formerly (until 1989): Tenggara.
   Description: Introduces to the world the literature of the Malay region of Indonesia, Malaysia, Brunei Darussalam and Singapore.

700 UK ISSN 0308-6674
MALLORN. 1970. a. £15. Tolkien Society, 357 High St., Flat 5, Cheltenham, Glos. GL50 3HT, England. TEL 0242-577232. bk.rev.; bibl.; circ. 900. Indexed: Child.Lit.Abstr., M.L.A.
   Description: Essays on elvish language and writings, poetry and art work from members of the Society.

MAN AND NATURE/HOMME ET LA NATURE. see HISTORY

990 FJ ISSN 0379-5268
MANA; South Pacific journal of language and literature. (Text in English) 1973. 2/yr. F.$4. South Pacific Creative Arts Society, c/o IPS, Box 1168, Suva, Fiji. FAX 679-301594. adv.; bk.rev.; illus.; circ. 1,500. Indexed: M.L.A., So.Pac.Per.Ind.
   Formerly: Mana Annual of Creative Writing.

MANG YUAN. see ART

895.1 CC
MANG ZHONG. (Text in Chinese) m. $63. Mang Zhong Zazhishe, 29 Shiwei Lu, Heping-qu, Shengyang, Liaoning 110003, People's Republic of China. (Dist. in US by: China Books & Periodicals, Inc., 2929 24th St., San Francisco, CA 94110. TEL 415-282-2994) Ed. Liu Wenyu.

820 700 PH
MANILA REVIEW; Philippines journal of literature and the arts. (Text in English) 1975. q. P.25($5) Department of Public Information, c/o Bureau of National and Foreign Information, U P L Building, Box 3396, Intramuros, Manila, Philippines. Ed. Gregorio C. Brillantes. bk.rev.; film rev.; charts; illus.

820 II
MANIPUR STATE KALA AKADEMI. QUARTERLY JOURNAL. (Text in English) vol.2, 1977. q. Rs.8. Manipur State Kala Akademi, Jawaharlal Nehru Manipur, Dance Academy, Imphal, India. Ed.Bd. bk.rev.

800 808.81 US ISSN 1045-7909
PN771 CODEN: MANOE7
MANOA; a Pacific journal of international writing. 1989. s-a. $15 to individuals (foreign $18); institutions $18 (foreign $22). University of Hawaii Press, Journals Department, 2840 Kolowalu St., Honolulu, HI 96822. TEL 808-948-8833. FAX 808-988-6052. Ed. Robert Shapard. adv.; bk.rev.; illus.; circ. 726. (back issues avail.; reprint service avail. from UMI)
   Description: International literary review presents fiction, poetry, artwork and articles of current cultural and literary interest.
   Refereed Serial

091 900   US   ISSN 0025-2603
Z6602
MANUSCRIPTA; a journal devoted to manuscript studies. (Text mainly in English; occasionally in other languages) 1957. 3/yr. $18. St. Louis University, Pius XII Memorial Library, 3650 Lindell Blvd., St. Louis, MO 63108. TEL 314-658-3090. Ed. Charles Ermatinger. adv.; bk.rev.; bibl.; illus.; cum.index; circ. 1,000. (also avail. in microfilm) **Indexed:** Amer.Bibl.Slavic & E.Eur.Stud., Amer.Hist.& Life, Amer.Hum.Ind., Arts & Hum.Cit.Ind., Cath.Ind., CERDIC, Curr.Cont., Hist.Abstr., Ind.Bk.Rev.Hum., M.L.A., Old Test.Abstr., RILA.

800   RM
MANUSCRIPTUM. (Text in Romanian; summaries in English, French, German, Russian) 1970. q. 40 lei($16) Muzeul Literaturii Romane, Str. Fundatiei Nr. 4, Bucharest, Rumania. TEL 502096. (Subscr. to: ILEXIM, Str. 13 Decembrie Nr. 3, P.O. Box 136-137, Bucharest, Rumania) adv.; bk.rev.; circ. 3,000. **Indexed:** M.L.A.

830 700   AU   ISSN 0025-2638
PT1141.A2
MANUSKRIPTE; Zeitschrift fuer Literatur, Kunst, Kritik. 1960. 4/yr. S.300. Forum Stadtpark, Stadtpark 1, A-8010 Graz, Austria. Eds. Guenther Waldorf, Alfred Kolleritsch. adv.; bk.rev.; circ. 4,000.

895.1   CC
MANZU WENXUE/MANCHU LITERATURE. (Text in Chinese) bi-m. $20.70. Manzu Wenxue Zazhishe, 107 Qijing Jie, Dandong, Liaoning 118000, People's Republic of China. TEL 27950. (Dist. in US by: China Books & Periodicals, Inc., 2929 24th St., San Francisco, CA 94110. TEL 415-282-2994)

808   BS
MARANG. 1977. s-a. 75 Thebe per no. University of Botswana, Department of English, c/o Library, Private Bag 0022, Gaborone, Botswana. Ed. B.L. Leshoai.
Description: Includes creative writing.

830   GW
MARBACHER MAGAZIN. 1976. q. DM.37. Deutsche Schillergesellschaft e.V., Schillerhoehe 8-10, 7142 Marbach a.N., Germany. TEL 07144-6061. FAX 07144-15976.

MARCHE ROMANE. see *LINGUISTICS*

800   BE   ISSN 0025-293X
AP22
MARGINALES; revue des idees et des lettres. 1945. m. $12. Reui Fayt, Bd. General Jacques 159, B-1050 Brussels, Belgium. Ed. Reui Fayt. bk.rev.; play rev.; illus.; circ. 1,000.

810   US
MARI SANDOZ HERITAGE. 1971. s-a. $4. Mari Sandoz Heritage Society, c/o Chadron State College, Chadron, NE 69337. TEL 308-432-4451. Ed. Wayne Britt. adv.; illus.; circ. 200.

810   US   ISSN 0025-3499
PS1329
MARK TWAIN JOURNAL. 1936. s-a. $15 (foreign $16). c/o Department of English, College of Charleston, Charleston, SC 29424. TEL 803-792-5664. Ed. Thomas A. Tenney. illus.; cum.index; circ. 800. (also avail. in microform from UMI; reprint service avail. from ISI,KTO) **Indexed:** Abstr.Engl.Stud., Amer.Hum.Ind., Arts & Hum.Cit.Ind., Bibl.Engl.Lang.& Lit., Curr.Cont., LCR, M.L.A., RILA.
—BLDSC shelfmark: 5381.385000.

810   US   ISSN 0272-6378
PS1329
MARK TWAIN SOCIETY BULLETIN. 1978. s-a. $5 (foreign $6). Mark Twain Society, Inc., Box 3225, Elmira, NY 14905. Eds. Robert Jerome, Herbert Wisbey. bk.rev.; illus.; circ. 500.

806   US
MARLOWE SOCIETY OF AMERICA NEWSLETTER. 1980. 2/yr. $15 (foreign $20). Marlowe Society of America, c/o English Department, Box 2275-A, South Dakota State University, Brookings, SD 57007. Ed. Bruce Brandt. circ. 200.

810   US   ISSN 0025-3979
MARQUETTE JOURNAL. 1903. irreg. (4-6/yr.). $12. Marquette University, 1131 W. Wisconsin Ave., Milwaukee, WI 53233. TEL 414-288-7057. Ed. Lisa Sink. adv.; circ. 5,000.
Description: Student publication.

MARYLAND ENGLISH JOURNAL. see *EDUCATION — Teaching Methods And Curriculum*

809 491.8   CS
MASARYKOVA UNIVERZITA. FILOZOFICKA FAKULTA. SBORNIK PRACI. D: RADA LITERARNEVEDNA. 1955. irreg. (approx. a.). price varies. Masarykova Univerzita, Filozoficka Fakulta, A. Novaka 1, 660 88 Brno, Czechoslovakia.
Formerly: Univerzita J.E. Purkyne. Filozoficka Fakulta. Sbornik Praci. D: Rada Literarnevedna (ISSN 0231-7818)
Description: Covers the theory and history of Czech, Soviet, Russian (pre-revolutionary), and other Slavonic literatures.

MASARYKOVA UNIVERZITA. FILOZOFICKA FAKULTA. SBORNIK PRACI. K: RADA GERMANISTICKO - ANGLISTICKA. see *LINGUISTICS*

MASARYKOVA UNIVERZITA. FILOZOFICKA FAKULTA. SBORNIK PRACI. L: RADA ROMANISTICKA. see *LINGUISTICS*

805   IR
MASHHAD UNIVERSITY. FACULTY OF LETTERS AND HUMANITIES. JOURNAL. (Text in Persian) 1965. q. Rs.150($5) Mashhad University, Faculty of Letters and Humanities, Mashhad, Iran. Ed. M.J. Yahaghi. bk.rev.; circ. 1,000.
Formerly: University of Ferdowsi. Faculty of Letters and Humanities. Journal.

810   US   ISSN 0047-6161
PR1
MASSACHUSETTS STUDIES IN ENGLISH. 1967. s-a. $10 to individuals; institutions $14. Bartlett Hall, University of Massachusetts, Amherst, MA 01003. TEL 413-545-2332. Ed. Marcy Tanter. adv.; index; circ. 275. (also avail. in microfilm; back issues avail.) **Indexed:** M.L.A. (until 1986).
—BLDSC shelfmark: 5980.863000.
Description: Publishes essays which discuss a wide array of critical and scholarly approaches to literature.

890   NE   ISSN 0932-9714
CODEN: MAATEP
MATATU; journal for African culture. (Text in English, French, German) 1987. s-a. fl.45($22.50) to individuals; institutions fl.80($40). Editions Rodopi B.V., Keizersgracht 302-304, 1016 EX Amsterdam, Netherlands. TEL 020-6227507. FAX 020-6380948. Ed. Holger G. Ehling. adv.; bk.rev.; circ. 500.
Description: Concerned with all aspects of Black and African studies.

MATILDA MAGAZINE: LITERARY AND ART MAGAZINE. see *LITERATURE — Poetry*

800   CN   ISSN 0318-3610
MATRIX; writing worth reading. 1975. 3/yr. Can.$15 to individuals; institutions Can.$22. Linda Leith, Ed. & Pub., P.O. Box 100, Ste.Anne de Bellevue, Que. H9X 3L4, Canada. TEL 514-457-3880. adv.; bk.rev.; circ. 2,000. **Indexed:** Can.Lit.Ind.

MATRIX; the newsletter of the British Science Fiction Association. see *LITERATURE — Science Fiction, Fantasy, Horror*

800   AT
MATTOID. 1979. 3/yr. Aus.$25. Deakin University, Deakin Literary Society, Vic. 3217, Australia. FAX 052-272018. TELEX DUNIV AA35625. Ed. Brian Edwards. adv.; bk.rev.; circ. 650. (back issues avail.)
Description: Literary journal that publishes poetry, fiction, interviews, reviews and graphics.

892   SY
MAWQIF AL-ADABI. (Some numbers issued in combined form) 1971. m. £S1($28) Ittihad al-Kuttab al-Arab - Arab Writers Union, Mezzeh, P.O. Box 3230, Damascus, Syria. Ed. A. Abu-Haif. adv.; bk.rev.; illus.; circ. 4,000.

MEANJIN; a magazine of literature, art and discussion. see *LITERARY AND POLITICAL REVIEWS*

808   US
MECHANICS, A WRITER'S QUARTERLY.* q. 71 Camelot Rd., Poughkeepsie, NY 12601-5914. Ed. Ginger Bisanz.

890   IE   ISSN 0332-4265
MEDIAEVAL AND MODERN IRISH SERIES. 1931. irreg., vol.25, 1978. Dublin Institute for Advanced Studies, 10 Burlington Rd., Dublin 4, Ireland. TEL 680748. FAX 680561.

890   IE   ISSN 0332-4230
MEDIAEVAL AND MODERN WELSH SERIES. 1957. irreg., vol.9, 1988. Dublin Institute for Advanced Studies, 10 Burlington Rd., Dublin 4, Ireland. TEL 680748. FAX 680561.

800 940   CN   ISSN 0316-0874
MEDIAEVAL SOURCES IN TRANSLATION. 1949. irreg. price varies. Pontifical Institute of Mediaeval Studies, 59 Queen's Park Crescent E., Toronto, Ont. M5S 2C4, Canada. TEL 416-926-7144. FAX 416-926-7276. circ. 1,000.
—BLDSC shelfmark: 5525.279000.

MEDIAEVALIA. see *HISTORY — History Of Europe*

MEDIEVAL ACADEMY BOOKS. see *HISTORY — History Of Europe*

MEDIEVAL ACADEMY REPRINTS FOR TEACHING. see *HISTORY — History Of Europe*

800   NE   ISSN 0169-9059
MEDIEVAL AND RENAISSANCE AUTHORS. 1976. irreg., vol.10, 1988. price varies. E.J. Brill, P.O. Box 9000, 2300 PA Leiden, Netherlands. TEL 071-312624. FAX 071-317532. TELEX 39296 BRILL NL. (In N. America: E.J. Brill, 24 Hudson St., Kinderhook, NY 12106. TEL 800-962-4406) Eds. John Norton-Smith, Douglas Gray.

MEDIEVAL AND RENAISSANCE DRAMA IN ENGLAND; an annual gathering of research, criticism, and reviews. see *THEATER*

800   US   ISSN 1048-8588
MEDIEVAL AND RENAISSANCE YEARBOOK. a. $19.95 to individuals; institutions $29.95. Edwin Mellen Press, 240 Portage Rd., Box 450, Lewiston, NY 14092. TEL 800-753-2788. FAX 716-754-4335. Ed. Guy R. Mermier. bk.rev.

MEDIEVALIA ET HUMANISTICA; studies in medieval and renaissance culture. see *HISTORY — History Of Europe*

879 410   UK   ISSN 0025-8385
PB1
MEDIUM AEVUM. 1932. s-a. £24($54) (effective Jan. 1992). Society for the Study of Mediaeval Languages and Literature, c/o Dr. D.G. Pattison, Hon. Treas., Magdalen College, Oxford OX1 4AU, England. Ed.Bd. adv.; bk.rev.; index. cum.index: 1932-1957; 1957-1981; circ. 1,100. (also avail. in microfilm; back issues avail.) **Indexed:** Abstr.Engl.Stud., Arts & Hum.Cit.Ind., Br.Hum.Ind., Can.Rev.Comp.Lit., Hum.Ind., Ind.Bk.Rev.Hum., M.L.A., Mid.East: Abstr.& Ind.
—BLDSC shelfmark: 5534.790000.
Description: Articles, notes and reviews on medieval European languages and literature.

056.1   PE
MELIBEA. 1975. irreg. Casimiro Ulloa, 125, Lima, Peru. illus.

810   US   ISSN 0193-8991
MELVILLE SOCIETY EXTRACTS. 1969. 4/yr. $7 to individuals (foreign $8); libraries $10. c/o John Wenke, Treas., Department of English, Salisbury State University, Salisbury, MD 21801-6837. Ed. John Bryant. adv.; bk.rev.; illus.; circ. 750. (back issues avail.) **Indexed:** Abstr.Engl.Stud., Amer.Hum.Ind., LCR, M.L.A.
Former titles: Extracts (ISSN 0193-7626); Melville Society Newsletter (ISSN 0076-633X); **Incorporates:** Melville Society. Special Publication (ISSN 0076-6348)

800   US   ISSN 0732-2968
PS536.2
MEMPHIS STATE REVIEW. 1980. s-a. $3 to individuals; institutions $5.56. Memphis State University, Department of English, Memphis, TN 38152. TEL 901-454-4438. Ed. Sharon Bryan. adv.; bk.rev.; circ. 1,000.

LITERATURE

810   US   ISSN 0025-9233
PS3525.E43
MENCKENIANA. 1962. q. $12 (foreign US $15). Enoch Pratt Free Library, 400 Cathedral St., Baltimore, MD 21201-4484. TEL 301-396-5494. FAX 301-396-5856. Ed. Charles Fecher. bk.rev.; bibl.; circ. 700. (also avail. in microform from UMI)
Indexed: Abstr.Engl.Stud., Amer.Hum.Ind., Curr.Cont., M.L.A.

895.1   CC   ISSN 0539-323X
MENG YA. (Text in Chinese) m. $63.90. (Zhongguo Zuojia Xiehui, Shanghai Fenhui - China Writers' Association, Shanghai Chapter) Meng Ya Bianjibu, 200 Yan'an Xilu, Shanghai 200040, People's Republic of China. TEL 2581613. (Dist. in US by: China Books & Periodicals, Inc., 2929 24th St., San Francisco, CA 94110. TEL 415-282-2994)

289.7 800   CN   ISSN 0315-8101
MENNONITE MIRROR. (Text in English and German) 1971. 10/yr. Can.$20. Mennonite Literary Society, 207-1317A Portage Ave., Winnipeg, Man. R3G 0V3, Canada. TEL 204-786-2289. FAX 204-783-0898. Ed. Ruth Vogt. adv.; bk.rev.; illus.; circ. 7,000. (also avail. in microfilm)

MENSUEL 25. see ART

810   US
▼**MERCURY RISING.** 1991. m. $10. 564 Mission St., Ste. 152, San Francisco, CA 94105. circ. 750.
Description: General literary journal.

820   AT   ISSN 0728-5914
PN2
MERIDIAN; La Trobe University English review. 1982. s-a. Aus.$28 to individuals; institutions Aus.$36.50 (foreign Aus.$39.50). (La Trobe University, Department of English) La Trobe University Press, Bundoora, Vic. 3083, Australia. FAX 03-470-2011. TELEX AA 33143. Ed. John Barnes. adv.; bk.rev.; circ. 600.

800 200   US   ISSN 0894-4857
BX4705.M542
MERTON ANNUAL: STUDIES IN THOMAS MERTON, RELIGION, CULTURE, LITERATURE, AND SOCIAL CONCERNS. 1988. a. $42.50. A M S Press, Inc., 56 E. 13th St., New York, NY 10003. TEL 212-777-4700. FAX 212-995-5413. Ed.Bd. bk.rev.; index.
Description: Publishes articles about Thomas Merton and matters of major concern in his life and work as a writer, monk, and spiritual leader.

THE MERTON SEASONAL: A QUARTERLY REVIEW. see RELIGIONS AND THEOLOGY

MERVYN PEAKE REVIEW. see LITERATURE — Science Fiction, Fantasy, Horror

891   LI
▼**METAI.** 1991. m. Gedimino pr.37, Vilnius 232600, Lithuania. TEL (0122) 617-344. Ed. Juozas Aputis.

METAPHOR AND SYMBOLIC ACTIVITY. see LINGUISTICS

METHODIST HISTORY. see RELIGIONS AND THEOLOGY — Protestant

800   US   ISSN 0543-615X
AP95.L5
METMENYS; kuryba ir analize. (Text in Lithuanian) 1959. s-a. $15. (Metmenys Corp.) A M & M Publications, 7338 S. Sacramento, Chicago, IL 60629. TEL 312-436-5369. Ed. Vytautas Kavolis. bk.rev.; cum.index 1959-1973; 1973-1985; circ. 1,000. **Indexed:** Amer.Bibl.Slavic & E.Eur.Stud.

800 700   AT
MEUSE. 1977. biennial (plus special nos.). Aus.$15 to individuals; institutions Aus.$18. Meuse Press, Box 61, Wentworth Bldg., Sydney University, Sydney, N.S.W. 2006, Australia. Eds. Les Wicks, Bill Farrow. bk.rev.; circ. 1,000. (back issues avail.)
Incorporates: Rochford St. Press.

830   GW
MEZZOTINTO; Zeitschrift fuer Literatur. 1981. a. DM.5. Stiefmuetterchenweg 18, 2000 Hamburg 52, Germany. TEL 040-806657. Ed. Harry Springer.

MICHIGAN GERMANIC STUDIES. see LINGUISTICS

801   US   ISSN 0076-8103
MICHIGAN SLAVIC CONTRIBUTIONS. (Text in English, Russian and Slavic languages) 1968. irreg., latest 1984. price varies. University of Michigan, Department of Slavic Languages and Literatures, 3040 Modern Language Bldg., Ann Arbor, MI 48109. TEL 313-763-4496. FAX 313-764-3521. Ed. Ladislav Matejka. **Indexed:** M.L.A.

890 491.8 375.4   US   ISSN 0543-9930
PG13
MICHIGAN SLAVIC MATERIALS. 1961. a. University of Michigan, Department of Slavic Languages and Literatures, 3040 Modern Language Bldg., Ann Arbor, MI 48109. TEL 313-763-4496. FAX 313-764-3521. Ed. Ladislav Matejka.

891.7   US
MICHIGAN SLAVIC TRANSLATIONS. 1972. irreg., no.6, 1983. University of Michigan, Department of Slavic Languages and Literatures, 3040 Modern Language Bldg., Ann Arbor, MI 48104. TEL 313-763-4496. FAX 313-764-3521. Ed. Ladislav Matejka.

890   US
MICHIGAN STUDIES IN THE HUMANITIES. 1980. irreg., vol.7, 1988. University of Michigan, Department of Slavic Languages and Literatures, 3040 Modern Language Bldg., Ann Arbor, MI 48109. TEL 313-763-4496. FAX 313-764-3521. Ed. Ladislav Matejka. **Indexed:** M.L.A.

800   US   ISSN 0190-2911
MIDAMERICA. 1973. a. $7.50 per no. Society for the Study of Midwestern Literature, Ernst Bessey Hall, Michigan State University, East Lansing, MI 48824. TEL 517-355-1855. Ed. David D. Anderson. bk.rev.; circ. 1,000. (back issues avail.) **Indexed:** Abstr.Engl.Stud., M.L.A.
Formerly: Midwestern Annual.

800 808.81 700   US   ISSN 0892-970X
MIDCOASTER. 1986. a. $4.50. Peter Blewett, Ed. & Pub., 2750 N. 45th. St., Milwaukee, WI 53210. TEL 414-442-2807. circ. 500. (back issues avail.)
Description: Covers short fiction, poetry and art.

MIDDLEBURY STUDIES IN RUSSIAN LANGUAGE AND LITERATURE. see LINGUISTICS

800 770   US   ISSN 0886-7976
MIDLAND REVIEW. 1985. a. $6.90. Oklahoma State University, English Department, Morrill Hall, Stillwater, OK 74078. TEL 405-744-9474. adv.; bk.rev.; circ. 500.
Description: Covers contemporary literature, literary criticism and art.

800   US   ISSN 0742-5562
P1.A1
MIDWEST MODERN LANGUAGE ASSOCIATION. JOURNAL. 1968. s-a. $15. Midwest Modern Language Association, 302 English-Philosophy Bldg., University of Iowa, Iowa City, IA 52242. TEL 319-335-0331. Ed. Rudolf Kueneli. adv.; bk.rev.; bibl.; circ. 2,000. (back issues avail.) **Indexed:** Amer.Hum.Ind., Arts & Hum.Cit.Ind., Curr.Cont.
—BLDSC shelfmark: 4825.950000.
Formerly (until 1984): Midwest Modern Language Association. Bulletin (ISSN 0026-3419)

810   US
MIDWESTERN MISCELLANY. irreg. membership. Society for the Study of Midwestern Literature, 240 Ernst Bassey Hall, Michigan State University, East Lansing, MI 48824. TEL 517-355-1855. **Indexed:** Mich.Mag.Ind.

891.8   PL   ISSN 0026-3567
MIESIECZNIK LITERACKI. 1966. m. $9.90. Wydawnictwo Wspolczesne R S W "Prasa-Ksiazka-Ruch", Ul. Wiejska 12, 00-420 Warsaw, Poland. TEL 48-22-285330. (Dist. by: Ars Polona-Ruch, Krakowskie Przedmiescie 7, Warsaw, Poland) Ed. Wlodzimierz Sokorski. circ. 12,000. **Indexed:** M.L.A.

800   IS
MIFGASH. 1984. a. Jewish-Arab Institute, Beit Berl, Doar Kfar Saba 44 905, Israel.

800   US   ISSN 0163-2469
MILFORD SERIES; popular writers of today. 1976. irreg., no.72, 1989 (6-10/yr.). price varies. Borgo Press, Box 2845, San Bernardino, CA 92406. TEL 714-884-5813. Ed. Dale Salwak. circ. 2,000.
—BLDSC shelfmark: 6551.700000.
Incorporates (1988-1991): Starmont Contemporary Writers Series (ISSN 0738-0119)
Description: Series of critical monographs on and interviews with genre and mainstream writers of the twentieth century.

810   US
▼**MILIM.** 1990. 3/yr. $8. 324 Ave. F, Brooklyn, NY 11218. Ed. Y. David Shulman. circ. 800.
Description: Literary magazine that provides a forum for people involved with Torah.

820   US   ISSN 0026-4326
PR3579
MILTON QUARTERLY. 1967. q. $15 to individuals; libraries $24. Ohio University English Department, Ellis Hall, Ohio University, Athens, OH 45701. TEL 614-593-2829. (Co-sponsors: Medieval & Renaissance Texts & Studies, S U N Y Binghamton) Ed. Roy C. Flannagan. adv.; bk.rev.; abstr.; illus.; index; circ. 1,100. (also avail. in microform from MIM,UMI; back issues avail.; reprint service avail. from UMI, ISI) **Indexed:** Abstr.Engl.Stud., Amer.Hum.Ind., Arts & Hum.Cit.Ind., Curr.Cont., Hum.Ind., Ind.Bk.Rev.Hum., M.L.A.
—BLDSC shelfmark: 5774.550000.
Formerly (until 1969): Milton Newsletter (ISSN 0146-4922)
Description: Focuses on scholarly articles and texts dealing with John Milton and his milieu.

821.4   US   ISSN 0076-8820
PR3579
MILTON STUDIES. 1969. a. $34.95. University of Pittsburgh Press, 127 N. Bellefield Ave., Pittsburgh, PA 15260. TEL 412-624-4111. FAX 412-624-0777. Ed. James Simmonds. **Indexed:** Abstr.Engl.Stud., M.L.A.
—BLDSC shelfmark: 5774.570000.

810   US
MILWAUKEE UNDERGRADUATE REVIEW. 1989. 2/yr. $5. Box 71079, Milwaukee, WI 53211. circ. 600.
Description: Publishes literary works by undergraduates across the country.

869   BL
MINAS GERAIS SUPLEMENTO LITERARIO. 1966. w. Cr.$5200 for 6 mos. ($200). Imprensa Oficial do Estado, Av. Augusto de Lima, 270, Ramal 197, 30190 Belo Horizonte, Brazil. TEL 031-273-2088. FAX 031-273-3700. TELEX 318227. Ed. Jose Maria Caetano de Freitas de Mata Mourao. bk.rev.; circ. 5,000. **Indexed:** M.L.A.

800   US
MINAS TIRITH EVENING STAR. 1967. q. $5. (American Tolkien Society) W.W. Publications, Box 373, Highland, MI 48357-0373. TEL 813-585-0985. Ed. Philip Helms. adv.; bk.rev.; circ. 300. (back issues avail.)
Description: Publishes articles on and stories in the manner of J.R.R. Tolkien and his son Christopher J.R. Tolkien.

800   CC
MINGZUO XINSHANG/BEST WORKS OF LITERATURE. (Text in Chinese) bi-m. $31.50. Beiyue Wenyi Chubanshe, 46 Jiefang Lu, Taiyuan, Shanxi 030002, People's Republic of China. TEL 227068. (Dist. in US by: China Books & Periodicals, Inc., 2929 24th St., San Francisco, CA 94110. TEL 415-282-2994)

MINJIAN WENXUE. see FOLKLORE

MINJIAN WENXUE LUNTAN/TRIBUNE OF FOLK LITERATURE. see FOLKLORE

800   US   ISSN 0890-0566
MINNESOTA LITERATURE; a newsletter by and for Minnesota writers and supporters of literature. 1973. m. (Sep.-Jun.). $10. 1 Nord Circle, St. Paul, MN 55127. Ed. Mary Bround Smith. adv.; circ. 750.
Description: Announcements, opportunities, and publication news affecting writers and supporters of literature in the state. Also includes opinion essays.

810   US   ISSN 0026-5667
AP2
MINNESOTA REVIEW; a journal of committed writing; fiction, poetry, essays, reviews. 1960. s-a. $8 to individuals; institutions $16. Minnesota Review Press, English Dept., East Carolina Univ., Greenville, NC 27858-5350. TEL 516-246-5080. Ed.Bd. adv.; bk.rev.; illus.; circ. 1,000. (also avail. in microfilm from UMI; reprint service avail.) **Indexed:** Abstr.Engl.Stud., Arts & Hum.Cit.Ind., Bk.Rev.Ind. (1989-), Chic.Per.Ind., Child.Bk.Rev.Ind. (1989-), Curr.Cont., Film Lit.Ind. (1976-), M.L.A.
—BLDSC shelfmark: 5810.463400.
Description: Distinguished fiction, poetry, essays, and reviews on a diverse range of subjects and content.

895.1   CC   ISSN 0257-2850
MINZU WENXUE/JOURNAL OF MINORITY LITERATURE. (Text in Chinese) 1981. m. Y10.80($47.70) Zhongguo Zuojia Xiehui - China Writers' Association, 27, Balizhuang Nanli, Beijing 100025, People's Republic of China. TEL 5005971. (Dist. outside China by: China International Book Trading Corporation, P.O. Box 399, Beijing, P.R.C.; Dist. in US by: China Books & Periodicals, Inc., 2929 24th St., San Francisco, CA 94110. TEL 415-282-2994) Ed. Jin Zhe.

895.1   CC
MINZU WENXUE YANJIU/RESEARCH IN NATIONAL MINORITY LITERATURE. (Text in Chinese) 1983. q. $16.50. Zhongguo Shehui Kexueyuan, Minzu Wenxue Yanjiusuo - Chinese Academy of Social Sciences, Institute for National Minority Literature, 5, Jiannei Dajie, Beijing 100732, People's Republic of China. TEL 5137744. (Dist. in US by: China Books & Periodicals, Inc., 2929 24th St., San Francisco, CA 94110. TEL 415-282-2994) Ed. Liu Kuizhi.
Description: Publishes research articles on folk literature and literature by historical and contemporary writers of China's national minority groups. Also includes important investigative reports on minority literature.

895.1   CC
MINZU ZUOJIA. (Text in Chinese) bi-m. Y9.60. Minzu Zuojia Zazhi She, Urumqi, Xinjiang Weiwuer Zizhiqu, People's Republic of China. (Dist. outside China by: China Publications Foreign Trade Corp., P.O. Box 782, Beijing, P.R.C.) Ed. Zhang Shirong. illus.
Description: Publishes literature by writers of minority nationalities, especially those in Xinjiang.

MIORITA; a journal of Roumanian studies. see *ETHNIC INTERESTS*

MIRAS-I FIRHANGI. see *ARCHAEOLOGY*

MISCELLANEA BYZANTINA MONACENSIA. see *HISTORY — History Of Europe*

820   II   ISSN 0026-5896
MISCELLANY. (Text in English) 1960. bi-m. $18. Writers Workshop, 162-92 Lake Gardens, Calcutta 700045, India. Ed. P. Lal. bk.rev.; circ. 1,000.
Formerly: Writers Workshop Miscellany.

810   US   ISSN 0026-590X
MISCELLANY;* a Davidson review. 1965. s-a. $2. Davidson College, Box 218, Davidson, NC 28036. TEL 704-892-2000. Ed. William Barnes. circ. 1,500. (tabloid format)

MISSISSIPPI HISTORY NEWSLETTER. see *HISTORY — History Of North And South America*

810   US
MISSISSIPPI MUD. 1973. irreg. $19 for 4 nos. 1336 S.E. Marion St., Portland, OR 97202. TEL 503-236-9962. Ed. Joel Weinstein. adv.; bk.rev.; circ. 1,500. (reprint service avail. from UMI,ISI)

810   US   ISSN 0047-7559
PS501
MISSISSIPPI REVIEW. 1972. s-a. $15. University of Southern Mississippi, Center for Writers, Box 5144, Southern Station, Hattiesburg, MS 39406. TEL 601-266-4321. Ed. Frederick Barthelms. adv.; bk.rev.; index; circ. 1,500. (also avail. in microform from UMI) **Indexed:** A.I.P.P., Amer.Hum.Ind.

810   US   ISSN 0270-3521
MISSISSIPPI VALLEY REVIEW. 1971. 2/yr. $6. Western Illinois University, Department of English, Macomb, IL 61455. TEL 309-298-1514. Ed. Forrest Robinson. circ. 450.

800   US   ISSN 0191-1961
PS1
MISSOURI REVIEW. 1977. 3/yr. $15 (effective Jan. 1992). University of Missouri, Columbia, Department of English, 1507 Hillcrest Hall, Columbia, MO 65211. TEL 314-882-4474. Eds. Speer Morgan, Greg Michalson. adv.; bk.rev.; circ. 4,000. **Indexed:** Amer.Hum.Ind., M.L.A.

800   IT   ISSN 0392-6397
MISURE CRITICHE; rivista trimestrale di litteratura e cultura varia. (Text in English, French, Italian) 1970. q. L.48000 (foreign L.80000). Fratelli Conte Editori, Via Andrea d'Isernia, 59, 80122 Naples, Italy. TEL 683667. (Subscr. to: Corso V. Emanuele, 14, 41000 Salerno, Italy) Ed. Gioacchino Paparelli. adv.; bibl.; circ. 1,000. (back issues avail.)
Description: Reviews Italian and comparative literature.

830   US   ISSN 0026-7503
PT3810
MODERN AUSTRIAN LITERATURE. (Text and summaries in English and German) 1961. q. $20 to individuals (foreign $25); libraries $30 (foreign $35). International Arthur Schnitzler Research Association, c/o Donald G. Daviau, Ed., Department of Literatures and Languages, University of California, Riverside, CA 92521. TEL 714-787-5603. FAX 714-787-3800. adv.; bk.rev.; play rev.; abstr.; bibl.; circ. 700. (processed; also avail. in microfiche; cards; record; reprint service avail. from UMI) **Indexed:** Amer.Bibl.Slavic & E.Eur.Stud., Arts & Hum.Cit.Ind., Curr.Cont., M.L.A.
—BLDSC shelfmark: 5883.695000.
Description: Devoted to 19th and 20th century Austrian literature and culture.

895.1   US   ISSN 0190-2369
PL2303
MODERN CHINESE LITERATURE. 1984. s-a. $15 to individuals; institutions $25; students $10. University of Colorado, Department of Oriental Languages, Campus Box 279, Boulder, CO 80309-0279. TEL 303-492-3486. FAX 303-492-7272. Ed. Howard Goldblatt. adv.; bk.rev.; circ. 300. **Indexed:** M.L.A.

822   CN   ISSN 0026-7694
MODERN DRAMA. 1958. q. Can.$22.50 to individuals; institutions Can.$40; students Can.$15. (University of Toronto, Graduate Centre for Study of Drama) University of Toronto Press, Journals Department, P.O. Box 1280, 1011 Sheppard Ave. W., Downsview, Ont. M3H 5V4, Canada. TEL 416-667-7781. FAX 416-667-7832. (U.S. Addr.: 340 Nagel Dr., Cheektowaga, NY 14225) Ed. J. Astington. adv.; bk.rev.; bibl.; index; circ. 2,260. (back issues avail.) **Indexed:** Acad.Ind., Amer.Bibl.Slavic & E.Eur.Stud., Can.Per.Ind., Curr.Cont., Film Lit.Ind. (1973-), Hum.Ind., Ind.Bk.Rev.Hum., M.L.A., Mid.East: Abstr.& Ind., Ref.Sour.
—BLDSC shelfmark: 5886.190000.

813   US   ISSN 0026-7724
PS379
MODERN FICTION STUDIES; a critical quarterly devoted to criticism, scholarship and bibliography of American, English and European fiction since about 1880. 1955. 4/yr. $15 to individuals; institutions $18; foreign $20. Purdue University, Department of English, West Lafayette, IN 47907. TEL 317-494-3758. Ed. William T. Stafford. bk.rev.; bibl.; circ. 4,000. (also avail. in microform from UMI; reprint service avail. from UMI,KTO) **Indexed:** Abstr.Engl.Stud., Acad.Ind., Amer.Bibl.Slavic & E.Eur.Stud., Arts & Hum.Cit.Ind., Bk.Rev.Ind. (1977-), Chic.Per.Ind., Child.Bk.Rev.Ind. (1977-), Curr.Cont., Hum.Ind., Ind.Bk.Rev.Hum., M.L.A., Mid.East: Abstr.& Ind.
—BLDSC shelfmark: 5886.550000.

070.5 899   IS   ISSN 0334-4266
PJ5001
MODERN HEBREW LITERATURE. 1975. s-a. $9. Institute for the Translation of Hebrew Literature, P.O. Box 10051, Ramat Gan 52001, Israel. TEL 03-5796830. Ed. Gershon Shaked. bk.rev.; index; circ. 2,000. (also avail. in microform from UMI; reprint service avail. from UMI) **Indexed:** Arts & Hum.Cit.Ind., Curr.Cont., M.L.A., Mid.East: Abstr.& Ind.
—BLDSC shelfmark: 5886.810000.
Incorporates: Hebrew Book Review.

810.9 296   US   ISSN 0270-9406
PS153.J4
MODERN JEWISH STUDIES ANNUAL. a. Queens College Press, c/o Joseph Landis, NSF 35U, Kiely 1309, Flushing, NY 11367. TEL 718-520-7067.
Formerly: Conference on Modern Jewish Studies Annual (ISSN 0270-9392).

400   US   ISSN 0026-7929
PB1
MODERN LANGUAGE QUARTERLY. 1940. q. $20 to individuals; institutions $26. University of Washington, Department of English GN-30, Seattle, WA 98195. TEL 206-543-6827. FAX 206-685-2673. Eds. John C. Coldewey, Marshall Brown. bk.rev.; index; circ. 1,600. (also avail. in microform from MIM,UMI) **Indexed:** Abstr.Engl.Stud., Acad.Ind., Amer.Bibl.Slavic & E.Eur.Stud., Arts & Hum.Cit.Ind., Curr.Cont., Hum.Ind., Ind.Bk.Rev.Hum., M.L.A., Mid.East: Abstr.& Ind.
—BLDSC shelfmark: 5887.550000.
Description: Focuses on literary scholarship and criticism, medieval to modern.

400   UK   ISSN 0026-7937
PB1
MODERN LANGUAGE REVIEW. 1905. q. $112. Modern Humanities Research Association, King's College, London WC2 R 2LS, England. (Vols. 1-69 avail. from Wm. Dawson & Sons Ltd., Cannon House, Folkstone, Kent, England) Ed.Bd. bk.rev.; circ. 1,800. (also avail. in microfilm from BHP) **Indexed:** Abstr.Engl.Stud., Arts & Hum.Cit.Ind., Bk.Rev.Ind. (1965-), Br.Hum.Ind., Can.Rev.Comp.Lit., Chic.Per.Ind., Child.Bk.Rev.Ind. (1965-), Curr.Cont., Hum.Ind., Ind.Bk.Rev.Hum., M.L.A., Mid.East: Abstr.& Ind., Ref.Sour., Soc.Sci.Ind.
—BLDSC shelfmark: 5887.600000.

400   US   ISSN 0047-7729
PB1
MODERN LANGUAGE STUDIES. 1971. 4/yr. $25. Northeast Modern Language Association, English Department, Brown University, Box 1852, Providence, RI 02912. TEL 401-863-3756. Ed. David H. Hirsch. adv.; bk.rev.; bibl.; circ. 2,300. (also avail. in microform from UMI) **Indexed:** Abstr.Engl.Stud., Amer.Bibl.Slavic & E.Eur.Stud., Arts & Hum.Cit.Ind., Curr.Cont., Ind.Bk.Rev.Hum., M.L.A., Mid.East: Abstr.& Ind.
—BLDSC shelfmark: 5887.650000.
Formerly: North East Modern Language Association. Newsletter.

MODERN PHILOLOGY; a journal devoted to research in medieval and modern literature. see *LINGUISTICS*

MODERNA SPRAAK. see *LINGUISTICS*

840   CN   ISSN 0225-1582
MOEBIUS; Ecritures et Litterature. 1976. q. Can.$30 (foreign Can.$40) to individuals; Can.$45 (foreign Can.$55) to institutions. Editions Triptyque, C.P. 5670, succ. C, Montreal (QC) H2X 3N4, Canada. TEL 514-524-5900. bk.rev.; circ. 800. (back issues avail.)

800   II
MOKO. Association for Commonwealth Literature and Language Studies, Indian Branch, Department of English, University of Mysore, Manasagangotri, Mysore 570006, India.

808   UK
MOMENTUM. 1985. 3/yr. £3.40 (foreign £4.40). Wrexham Writers' Workshop, Almere Farm, Rossett, Wrexham, Clwyd LL12 0BY, Wales. Ed. Pamela Goodwin. (back issues avail.)
Description: Short stories, poems, articles of literary interest.

MONAD; essays on science fiction. see *LITERATURE — Science Fiction, Fantasy, Horror*

2940 LITERATURE

MONATSHEFTE. see *LINGUISTICS*

895   MP
MONGOL ROMAN/MONGOLIAN NOVEL. (Text in Mongolian) q. Union of Writers, Ulan Bator, Mongolia. TEL 20812. Ed. Ts. Shuger.

800 770 700   US
THE MONOCACY VALLEY REVIEW. 1985. s-a. $8. Mount Saint Mary's College, Emmitsburg, MD 21727. TEL 301-447-6122. Ed. William Heath. bk.rev.; illus.; circ. 500 (controlled).
    Description: Includes poetry, short fiction, non-fiction prose, reviews, photography and line drawings.

891.8 940   PL   ISSN 0077-0531
MONOGRAFIE SLAWISTYCZNE. 1959. irreg., vol.53, 1986. price varies. (Polska Akademia Nauk, Komitet Slowianoznawstwa) Ossolineum, Publishing House of the Polish Academy of Sciences, Rynek 9, 50-106 Wroclaw, Poland. TELEX 0712771 OSS PL. (Dist. by: Ars Polona-Ruch, Krakowskie Przedmiescie 7, Warsaw, Poland)

MONOGRAPHS IN MODERN DUTCH STUDIES. see *HISTORY — History Of Europe*

MONOGRAPHS IN MODERN LANGUAGES. see *LINGUISTICS*

810   US
MONTANA REVIEW. 1979. biennial. $9. (Owl Creek Foundation) Owl Creek Press, 1620 N. 45th St. Rm. 205, Seattle, WA 98103. TEL 206-633-5929. Ed. Rich Ives. adv.; bk.rev.; illus.; circ. 1,000.

800   US   ISSN 0196-2604
PS3521.E735
MOODY STREET IRREGULARS; a Jack Kerouac newsletter. (Text in English, French) 1978. s-a. $10 to individuals; institutions $15. Moody Street Irregulars, Inc., Box 157, Clarence Center, NY 14032. Ed. Joy Walsh. adv.; bk.rev.; film rev.; play rev.; bibl.; charts; illus.; stat.; tr.lit.; circ. 1,000. (back issues avail.) **Indexed:** M.L.A.
    —BLDSC shelfmark: 5966.397000.

809   CN   ISSN 0027-1276
PN2
MOSAIC (WINNIPEG, 1967); a journal for the interdisciplinary study of literature. (Text in English, French) 1967. q. Can.$20 to individuals; institutions Can.$32. University of Manitoba, 208 Tier Bldg., Winnipeg, Man. R3T 2N2, Canada. TEL 204-474-9763. FAX 204-261-9086. (Co-sponsor: Social Sciences and Humanities Research Council of Canada) Ed. Dr. Evelyn J. Hinz. adv.: adv.: B&W page Can.$100. illus.; index; circ. 1,300. (also avail. in microform from UMI; back issues avail.) **Indexed:** Abstr.Engl.Stud.; Amer.Hum.Ind.; Arts & Hum.Cit.Ind.; Can.Lit.Ind.; Can.Per.Ind., CMI, Hum.Ind., Ind.Bk.Rev.Hum.; LCR, M.L.A., RILA, RILM.
    —BLDSC shelfmark: 5967.483500.
    Formerly (until 1978): Journal for the Comparative Study of Literature and Ideas.
    Description: Theoretical and practical essays explore literary works or issues from an interdisciplinary perspective.

891.7   RU   ISSN 0131-2332
AP50
MOSKVA; literary magazine. 1957. m. 24 Rub. Soyuz Pisatelei Rossiiskoi S.F.S.R., Moskovskoe Otdelenie, Arbat 20, 121918 Moscow, Russia. TEL (095) 291-71-10. Ed. M.N. Alekseev. bk.rev.; illus.; tr.bibl.; index; circ. 160,000. **Indexed:** Curr.Dig.Sov.Press.
    —BLDSC shelfmark: 0118.550000.

800   CI   ISSN 0006-9833
PG560
MOST/BRIDGE/PONT/PUENTE; jugoslavia revuo pri kroata literaturo. (Text in various languages) N.S. 1981. 4/yr. $12. Drustvo Knjizevnika Hrvatske, Trg Republike 7-I, 41000 Zagreb, Croatia. TEL 041-274-211. Ed. Milivoj Solar. **Indexed:** Amer.Bibl.Slavic & E.Eur.Stud.
    Description: Review of Croatian literature.

MOSTOVI. see *LINGUISTICS*

MOVEMENTS IN THE ARTS. see *ART*

895.1   CC
MUDAN/PEONY. (Text in Chinese) bi-m. Luoyang Shi Wenlian, No. 135, Zhongzhou Zhonglu, Luoyang, Henan 471000, People's Republic of China. TEL 37165. Ed. Han Li.

820   NE
MUENCHENER STUDIEN ZUR NEUEREN ENGLISCHEN LITERATUR/MUNICH STUDIES IN ENGLISH LITERATURE. 1986. irreg., latest vol.4, 1987. price varies. John Benjamins Publishing Co., Amsteldijk 44, P.O. Box 75577, 1070 AN Amsterdam, Netherlands. TEL 020-6738156. FAX 020-6739773. (In N. America: 821 Bethlehem Pike, Philadelphia, PA 19118. TEL 215-836-1200) Ed. Ulrich Broich.

430 830   GW   ISSN 0077-1872
MUENCHNER GERMANISTISCHE BEITRAEGE. 1968. irreg. price varies. Wilhelm Fink Verlag, Ohmstr. 5, 8000 Munich 40, Germany. Ed.Bd.

MULIKA. see *LINGUISTICS*

MUNDUS. see *PUBLISHING AND BOOK TRADE*

892   US
MUNDUS ARABICUS. 1981. a. $30. Dar Mahjar Inc., Box 56, Cambridge, MA 02238. Ed.Bd. circ. 350. **Indexed:** Ind.Islam.

892.7   TS
AL-MUNTADA. 1983. m. Dubai Literary Club - Nadi Dubai al-Adabi, P.O. Box 9339, Dubai, United Arab Emirates. TEL 377464. Ed. Ahmed bin Said al-Maktum. circ. 2,000.
    Description: Publishes stories, poetry and articles on Arabic literature.

800   NR   ISSN 0331-3468
PR9387.5
MUSE; journal of creative and critical writing from Nsukka. 1963. a. £N2. University of Nigeria, Department of English, Nsukka, Nigeria. Ed. Onyedika L. Okwuonu. adv.; bk.rev.; circ. 1,500.

809   IT
MUSEUM CRITICUM. vol.10, 1975. irreg. price varies. Giardini Editori e Stampatori, Via Santa Bibbiana 28, 56100 Pisa, Italy. TEL 050 502531. Ed. Benedetto Marzullo.

830   GW
MUSIL - FORUM. (Text in English, French, German) 1974. a. DM.45. Internationale Robert-Musil-Gesellschaft, Universitaet, Gebaeude 35, 6600 Saarbruecken 11, Germany. TEL 0681-3023334. bk.rev.; index; circ. 500.

890 069.9   PL   ISSN 0324-8925
PG7001
MUZEUM LITERATURY IM. ADAMA MICKIEWICZA. BLOK-NOTES. 1959. irreg. price varies. Muzeum Literatury im. Adama Mickiewicza, Rynek Starego Miasta 20, 00-272 Warsaw, Poland. TEL 31-40-61. Ed. Malgorzata Kucza-Kuczynska. illus.; circ. 600. (back issues avail.)

810 910.03   US
MWENDO. 1973. s-a. $1 per copy. Coe College, Black Student Educational Organization, Box 577, Cedar Rapids, IA 52402. TEL 319-399-8660. Ed. Latonia Williams. bk.rev.; bibl.; circ. 350.

895.4   BR
MYAWADDY MAGAZINE. (Text in Burmese, English) 1952. m. Myawaddy Press, 181-3 Sule Pagoda Rd., Yangon, Union of Myanmar. circ. 4,200.

800 371.3   US
N A Y W NEWS.* 1986. 4/yr. $15. National Association for Young Writers, Inc., Box 228, Sandusky, MI 48471. TEL 505-982-8596. (Subscr. to: NAYW, Box 3000, Dept YW, Denville, NJ 07834) Ed. Sheila Cowing. circ. 500. (tabloid format; back issues avail.)
    Description: Features professionally written articles on all aspects of teaching writing. Includes market information for young writers. Designed to stimulate those who teach writing to children.

800 700   US
N E A GRANTMAKING PROGRAMS: CHALLENGE AND ADVANCEMENT. a. National Endowment for the Arts, Public Information Office, 1100 Pennsylvania Ave., N.W., Washington, DC 20506. TEL 202-682-5400.
    Supersedes in part: Advancement 2: Literature, Media Arts, Opera, Musical Theater, Visual Arts.
    Description: Grant application guidelines.

800   US
N E A GRANTMAKING PROGRAMS: LITERATURE. a. free. National Endowment for the Arts, Public Information Office, 1100 Pennsylvania Ave., N.W., Washington, DC 20506. TEL 202-682-5400.
    Description: Grant application guidelines.

850 808   US
N E M L A ITALIAN STUDIES; selected proceedings of the Italian section. (Text in English, Italian) 1977. a. $6. Northeast Modern Language Association Conference, Italian Section, Rutgers University, Department of Italian, 18 Seminary Pl., New Brunswick, NJ 08903. TEL 908-932-7536. Ed. Umberto C. Mariani. adv.; bk.rev. (back issues avail.)

810   US   ISSN 0163-8246
PS221
N M A L: NOTES ON MODERN AMERICAN LITERATURE. 1976. 3/yr. $5. A B C Publishing Co., c/o St. John's University, Department of English, Jamaica, NY 11439. TEL 718-990-6161. Eds. Edward Guereschi, Lee Richmond. circ. 500. **Indexed:** M.L.A.
    Formerly: Notes on Modern American Literature (ISSN 0164-1360)

830 053.1   AU
N O I INTERNATIONAL; Mensch, Gesellschaft, Kultur, Umwelt. vol.11, 1972. q. S.280. N O I-Verlag, Morrestrasse 13, A-9020 Klagenfurt, Austria. Ed. Dr. Dietfried Schoenemann. bk.rev.; bibl.

N W C NEWSLETTER. see *JOURNALISM*

891.7   US
NABOKOVIAN. (Text mainly in English; occasionally in Russian) 1978. s-a. $9 to individuals; institutions $11. Vladimir Nabokov Society, c/o Stephen Jan Parker, Ed., Slavic Languages & Literatures, University of Kansas, Lawrence, KS 66045. TEL 913-864-3313. bk.rev.; bibl.; circ. 285. **Indexed:** Amer.Bibl.Slavic & E.Eur.Stud.; M.L.A.
    Formerly (until 1984): Vladimir Nabokov Research Newsletter.

NACHBARSPRACHE NIEDERLAENDISCH. see *LINGUISTICS*

800   HU
NAGYVILAG. 1956. m. $28.50. Szechenyi u. 1, 1054 Budapest, Hungary. TEL 132-1160. Ed. Laszlo Kery. circ. 12,000.
    Description: Reviews world literature.

860 028.1   PY   ISSN 1012-5507
NANDE REKO; cuaderno de literatura popular. 1980. s-a. $14. Distribuidor Internacional Publicaciones Paraguayas, P.O. Box 2507, Torreani Viera, 551, Villa Mora, Asuncion, Paraguay. TEL 595-21-660991. FAX 595-21-94271. TELEX DIPP 660991. Ed. Rudi Torga. bk.rev.; circ. 1,000.

895   CC
NANFANG WENTAN. (Text in Chinese) bi-m. Guangxi Wenlian, 28 Jianzheng Lu, Nanning, Guangxi 530023, People's Republic of China. TEL 23613. Ed. Li Chaohong.

895   CC
NANFANG WENXUE/SOUTHERN LITERATURE. (Text in Chinese) bi-m. Guilin Shi Wenlian, Rongcheng Lu, Guilin, Guangxi 541001, People's Republic of China. TEL 224578. Ed. Zeng Xianrui.

895.1   CC   ISSN 0257-2885
NANFENG/SOUTH WIND; folk literature of Guizhou. (Text in Chinese) 1983. bi-m. $16.20. Guizhou Sheng Wenlian, 66, Kexue Lu, Guiyang, Guizhou 550002, People's Republic of China. TEL 25616. (Dist. in US by: China Books & Periodicals, Inc., 2929 24th St., San Francisco, CA 94110. TEL 415-282-2994) Ed. Tian Bing.

059.94   HU   ISSN 0547-2075
NAPJAINK. m. $23. Borsod Megyei Lapkiado Vallalat, Bajcsy-Zsilinszky u. 15, 3527 Miskolc, Hungary. (Subscr. to: Kultura, Box 149, H-1389 Budapest, Hungary.)

800 700 720　　　BU　ISSN 0205-1109
NARODNA KULTURA. 1957. w. 6.50 lv. (Komitet za Kultura - Committee for Culture) Foreign Trade Co. "Hemus", 7 Levsky St., 1000 Sofia, Bulgaria. Ed. Koprinka Chervenkova. adv.; bk.rev.; circ. 50,000. (also avail. in microfilm from NRP)

860　　　UY　ISSN 0077-2801
NARRADORES DE ARCA.* irreg. Editorial Arca, Colonia 1263, Montevideo, Uruguay.

NARRATIVA LATINOAMERICANA. see *HISTORY — History Of North And South America*

810　　　US　ISSN 0077-2879
NASSAU REVIEW. 1964. a. free. Nassau Community College, SUNY, Department of English, Garden City, NY 11530. TEL 516-222-7187. Ed. Paul A. Doyle. circ. 1,200. **Indexed:** M.L.A.

810　　　US　ISSN 0073-1382
NATHANIEL HAWTHORNE JOURNAL. (1979 and 1980 were cancelled) 1971. irreg. $70. Gale Research Inc., 835 Penobscot Bldg., Detroit, MI 48226. TEL 313-961-2242. FAX 313-961-6083. TELEX 810-221-7086. Ed. C.E. Frazer Clark, Jr. **Indexed:** M.L.A.
   Description: Articles on the works of Nathaniel Hawthorne.

806　　　US　ISSN 0890-4197
PS1879
NATHANIEL HAWTHORNE REVIEW. 1975. s-a. $10. (Nathaniel Hawthorne Society) Bowdoin College, Hawthorne-Longfellow Library, Brunswick, ME 04011. TEL 207-725-3281. Ed. John Idol, Jr. bk.rev.; bibl.; circ. 440. **Indexed:** Amer.Hum.Ind., M.L.A.
   Formerly: Nathaniel Hawthorne Society. Newsletter (ISSN 0162-9824)

808　　　US
NATIONAL DIRECTORY OF STORYTELLING. a. $40 membership (foreign $50) includes Yarnspinner and Storytelling Magazine. National Association for the Preservation and Perpetuation of Storytelling, Box 309, Jonesborough, TN 37659.
TEL 615-753-2171. FAX 615-753-9331.
   Description: Guide to professional storytellers, storytelling publications, events and organizations throughout the U.S.

NATIONAL FOUNDATION FOR ADVANCEMENT IN THE ARTS. ANNUAL REPORT. see *ART*

890　　　JA　ISSN 0387-3447
NATIONAL INSTITUTE OF JAPANESE LITERATURE. BULLETIN/KOKUBUNGAKU KENKYU SHIRYOKAN KIYO. (Text in Japanese) 1975. free. National Institute of Japanese Literature - Kokubungaku Kenkyu Shiryokan, 1-16-10 Yutokacho, Shinagawa-ku, Tokyo 142, Japan.
FAX 03-785-7051.

800　　　US
NATIONAL POETRY MAGAZINE OF THE LOWER EAST SIDE. vol.3,no.1, 1988. q. Box 1351, Cooper Station, New York, NY 10276. Eds. Stephen Paul Miller, Jim Feast.

890　　　US
NAUKOVE TOVARYSTVO IMENI SHEVCHENKA. UKRAINSKA LITERATURNA BIBLIOTEKA/UKRAINIAN LITERARY LIBRARY. (Text in Ukrainian; summaries in English) 1881. irreg. price varies. Shevchenko Scientific Society, 63 Fourth Ave., New York, NY 10003.

895　　　CE
NAVA YUGAYA. (Text in Sinhala) 1956. fortn. Lake House, D.R. Wijewardene Mawatha 1, Colombo 10, Sri Lanka. TEL 1-21181. Ed. S.N. Senanayake. circ. 57,000.

880　　　GR　ISSN 0028-1735
AP85
NEA HESTIA. 1927. bi-m. $324. G.C. Eleftheroudakis S.A., 4 Nikis St., 10563 Athens, Greece.
TEL 01-3222255. FAX 01-3239821. Ed. P. Charis. adv.; bk.rev.; bibl.; illus.; index.

880　　　GR
NEA POREIA; magazine on literature. (Text and summaries in Greek) 1955. q. Dr.1,600($30) Nea Poreia, Venizelou 14, 54624 Thessaloniki, Greece. TEL 31-273450. Ed. Tilemachos Alaveras. bk.rev.; bibl.; cum.index; circ. 1,300. (back issues avail.)

808　　　US　ISSN 0741-1316
NEBO; a literary journal. 1983. s-a. $6. Arkansas Tech University, Department of English, Russellville, AR 72801. TEL 501-968-0256. Eds. B.C. Hall, Michael Karl Ritdie. bk.rev.; circ. 500. (back issues avail.)

800　　　US　ISSN 8755-514X
NEBRASKA REVIEW. 1971. s-a. $6. University of Nebraska, Omaha, Writer's Workshop, Arts & Sciences Hall 212, Omaha, NE 68182-0324.
TEL 402-554-2771. Eds. Art Homer, Richard Duggin. adv.; circ. 750. **Indexed:** A.I.P.P.
   Formerly (until 1984): Smackwarm.
   Description: Literary magazine that publishes fiction and poetry.

810　　　US　ISSN 0162-3818
PS648.S3
NEBULA WINNERS.* 1965. a. price varies. Arbor House Publishing Co. (Subsidiary of: William Morrow), 105 Madison Ave., 17th Fl., New York, NY 10016.
TEL 212-889-3050. Ed. Marta Randall.
   Formerly: Nebula Award Stories (ISSN 0077-6408)

HET NEDERLANDSE BOEK. see *LITERARY AND POLITICAL REVIEWS*

NEEUROPA. see *ART*

891.553　　　IR
NEGIN. m. M. Enayat, Ed. & Pub., Vali Asar Ave., Adl St. 52, Teheran, Iran.

800　　　NE　ISSN 0324-4652
PN851
NEOHELICON; acta comparationis litterarum universarum. (Text in English, French, German, Russian) 1973. s-a. fl.252($138) (effective 1992). (International Comparative Literature Association, HU) John Benjamins Publishing Co., Amsteldijk 44, P.O. Box 75577, 1070 AN Amsterdam, Netherlands. TEL 020-6738156.
FAX 020-6739773. (In N. America: 821 Bethlehem Pike, Philadelphia, PA 19118. TEL 215-836-1200) Eds. M. Szabolcsi, G.M. Vajda. bk.rev.; bibl. **Indexed:** Arts & Hum.Cit.Ind., Can.Rev.Comp.Lit, Curr.Cont.
   —BLDSC shelfmark: 6075.606500.
   Description: Studies in comparative and world literature.

NEOPHILOLOGUS; an international journal, devoted to the study of modern and mediaeval literature, including general linguistics, literary theory and comparative literature. see *LINGUISTICS*

830　　　GW　ISSN 0077-7668
NEUDRUCKE DEUTSCHER LITERATURWERKE. N.S. 1961. irreg., no.45, 1991. price varies. Max Niemeyer Verlag, Postfach 2140, 7400 Tuebingen 1, Germany. TEL 07071-81104.
FAX 07071-87419. (back issues avail.) **Indexed:** M.L.A.
   Continues: Neudrucke Deutscher Literaturwerke des XVI und XVII Jahrhunderts & Neudrucke Deutscher Literaturwerke des XVIII und XIX Jahrhunderts.
   Description: Editions of German literature in the 16th and 17th centuries, in part also the 18th and 19th centuries.

830　　　GW　ISSN 0077-7676
NEUDRUCKE DEUTSCHER LITERATURWERKE. SONDERREIHE. 1964. irreg. price varies. Max Niemeyer Verlag, Postfach 2140, 7400 Tuebingen 1, Germany. TEL 07071-81104.
FAX 07071-87419. (back issues avail.)
   Description: Editions of German literature in the 16th and 17th centuries, in part also the 18th and 19th centuries.

830　　　GW　ISSN 0028-3150
PT3
NEUE DEUTSCHE LITERATUR. Short title: N D L. 1953. m. DM.120. Aufbau-Verlag Berlin und Weimar, Franzoesische Str. 32, 1086 Berlin, Germany. TEL 030-2202421. FAX 030-2298637. Ed. Werner Liersch. adv.; bk.rev.; film rev.; play rev.; index.
   —BLDSC shelfmark: 6077.330000.

859　　　RM
NEUE LITERATUR. (Text in German) 1953. m. 144 lei. Uniunea Scriitorilor din Republica Socialista Romania, Calea Victoriei 115, Bucharest, Rumania. (Subscr. to: ILEXIM, Str. 13 Decembrie Nr. 3, Box 136-137, 70116 Bucharest, Rumania) Ed. Arnold Hauser. bk.rev.; play rev.; abstr.; illus.

808.068 371.3
028.5　　　US　ISSN 0895-1381
THE NEW ADVOCATE. 1981-1986 (vol.5); N.S. 1987. 4/yr. $45 (Canada $55; elsewhere $65). (University of Georgia, College of Education) Christopher - Gordon Publishers, Inc., 480 Washington St., Norwood, MA 02062.
TEL 617-762-5577. Ed. Joel Taxel. adv.; bk.rev.; charts; illus.; stat.; index; circ. 7,500. (back issues avail.) **Indexed:** Bk.Rev.Ind. (1990-), Child.Bk.Rev.Ind. (1990-), Child.Lit.Abstr.
   —BLDSC shelfmark: 6081.725000.
   Formerly (until 1987): Advocate (Athens) (ISSN 0730-3114)
   Description: Features articles on using children's literature in the classroom, across the curriculum.

800 100 200　　　US　ISSN 1048-8545
B3090
NEW ATHENAEUM/NEUES ATHENAEUM. (Text in English, German) a. $19.95 to individuals; institutions $29.95. Edwin Mellen Press, 240 Portage Rd., Box 450, Lewiston, NY 14092.
TEL 800-753-2788. FAX 716-754-4335. Ed. Ruth Richardson.
   Description: Scholarly journal specializing in Schleiermacher and Schlegel Research and other Nineteenth-Century studies.

820　　　CN　ISSN 0832-932X
PR9194
NEW CANADIAN REVIEW. 1987. 3/yr. Can.$21 (foreign $25). P.O. Box 717, Pointe-Claire-Dorval, Que. H9R 4S8, Canada. TEL 514-636-9845. Ed. Lino Leitao. adv.; bk.rev.; circ. 500. (microform from MML; back issues avail.)
   Description: Multi-cultural literary journal.

807　　　US
NEW CANTERBURY LITERARY SOCIETY NEWSLETTER. 1973. q. free. (New Canterbury Literary Society) Norman T. Gates, Ed. & Pub., 520 Woodland Ave., Haddonfield, NJ 08033. bk.rev.; circ. 100 (controlled).
   Description: Covers the author Richard Aldington (1892-1962).

800 410　　　AT
NEW CEYLON WRITING; creative and critical writing of Sri Lanka. 1970. irreg. Aus.$20. Post-Colonial Literatures & Language Research Centre, School of English & Linguistics, Nacquarie University, North Ryde, N.S.W. 2109, Australia. TEL 02-805-8776. FAX 02-805-7849. Ed. Yasmine Gooneratne. adv.; bk.rev.; play rev.; abstr.; bibl.; circ. 250.

810　　　US　ISSN 0028-4467
NEW COLLAGE MAGAZINE. 1970. 3/yr. $6. (New Collage Foundation) New Collage Press, 5700 N. Tamiami Trail, Sarasota, FL 34243-2197.
TEL 813-359-4248. Ed. A. McA. Miller. bk.rev.; circ. 700. (back issues avail.) **Indexed:** A.I.P.P., Ind.Amer.Per.Verse.

800　　　UK　ISSN 0950-5814
PN851
NEW COMPARISON; a journal of comparative and general literary studies. 1975. 2/yr. £12 to individuals; institutions £24. Berg Publishers Ltd., 150 Cowley Rd., Oxford OX4 1JJ, England. Ed. Susan Bassnet. bk.rev.; circ. 250.
   —BLDSC shelfmark: 6082.883000.
   Formerly (until 1984): Comparison (ISSN 0307-8000)

800　　　US　ISSN 0891-0073
NEW CONNECTIONS: STUDIES IN INTERDISCIPLINARITY. irreg. Peter Lang Publishing, Inc., 62 W. 45th St., 4th Fl., New York, NY 10036. TEL 212-302-6740. FAX 212-302-7574. Ed. Shirley Paolini.
   —BLDSC shelfmark: 6082.894240.
   Description: Focuses on the interrelationships between literature and other arts, science, philosophy, law, psychology, anthropology, and religion.

LITERATURE

800   SA
AP9
NEW CONTRAST; South African literary journal. (Text in Afrikaans, English, Xhosa) 1960. q. R.20($20) South African Literary Journal Ltd., Box 3841, Cape Town 8000, South Africa. TEL 021-477280. Ed. Douglas Reid Skinner. adv.; bk.rev.; illus.; index every 5 yrs.; circ. 1,000. (back issues avail.) Indexed: Ind.S.A.Per., M.L.A.
    Formerly: Contrast (ISSN 0589-574X); Incorporates (1983-1990): Upstream (ISSN 0258-7416)

800 700   UK
NEW DEPARTURES; international review of literature & the lively arts. 1959. a. $10. c/o Michael Horovitz, Ed., Mullions, Piedmont, Bisley, Stroud, Glos. GL6 7BU, England. adv.; bk.rev.; circ. 10,000.

808   US
NEW DIRECTIONS (NEW YORK, 1936). 1936. irreg., no.55, 1991. price varies. New Directions Books, 80 Eighth Ave., New York, NY 10011. TEL 212-255-0230. FAX 212-255-0231. Ed. James Laughlin. bk.rev. (reprint service avail. from KTO)
    Description: Showcase for writers extending the frontiers of literature.

810 974   US   ISSN 0028-4866
F1
NEW ENGLAND QUARTERLY; a historical review of New England life and letters. 1928. q. $20 to individuals; institutions $25. New England Quarterly, Inc., Meserve Hall, 2nd Fl., Boston, MA 02115. TEL 617-437-2734. FAX 617-437-2661. Ed. William M. Fowler. adv.; bk.rev.; index; circ. 2,400. (also avail. in microform from UMI; reprint service avail. from UMI) Indexed: Abstr.Engl.Stud., Acad.Ind., Amer.Hist.& Life, Arts & Hum.Cit.Ind., Bk.Rev.Ind. (1965-), CERDIC, Child.Bk.Rev.Ind. (1965-), Curr.Cont., Hist.Abstr., Hum.Ind., Ind.Bk.Rev.Hum., M.L.A., Rel.& Theol.Abstr. (1990-).
—BLDSC shelfmark: 6084.027000.

810   US   ISSN 1053-1297
PN2
NEW ENGLAND REVIEW. 1978. q. $15 to individuals; institutions $40. (Middlebury College) Middlebury College Publications, Middlebury College, Middlebury, VT 05753. TEL 802-388-3711. Eds. T.R. Hummer, Devon Jerrild. adv.; bk.rev.; circ. 3,000. (also avail. in microform from UMI; back issues avail.; reprint service avail. from UMI) Indexed: A.I.P.P., Amer.Bibl.Slavic & E.Eur.Stud., Arts & Hum.Cit.Ind., Bk.Rev.Ind. (1980-), Child.Bk.Rev.Ind. (1980-), Curr.Cont., Ind.Amer.Per.Verse, Ind.Bk.Rev.Hum., M.L.A.
—BLDSC shelfmark: 6084.028400.
    Former titles (until 1990): New England Review and Bread Loaf Quarterly (ISSN 0736-2579); (until 1982): New England Review (ISSN 0164-3177)
    Description: Contemporary poetry, essays, fiction, reviews, interviews and translations.

830 410   US   ISSN 0889-0145
NEW GERMAN REVIEW; a journal of Germanic studies. (Text in English, German) 1985. a. $5 to individuals; institutions $8. University of California, Los Angeles, Department of Germanic Languages, 302 Royce Hall, Los Angeles, CA 90034. TEL 213-825-3955. Ed. Harald Weilnboeck. bk.rev. (back issues avail.)
    Description: Publishes articles on German literature, language, culture and literary theory.

830   UK   ISSN 0307-2770
PF3001
NEW GERMAN STUDIES. 1973. 3/yr. £5 to individuals; institutions £7(effective 1992). University of Hull, Department of German, Hull HU6 7RX, England. FAX 0482-465991. Eds. A.D. Best, A.R. Deighton. adv.; bk.rev.; index; circ. 250. Indexed: M.L.A.
—BLDSC shelfmark: 6084.217000.

820   UK
NEW HOPE INTERNATIONAL ZINE. 1970. 6/yr. $20. New Hope International, 20 Werneth Ave., Gee Cross, Hyde, Cheshire SK14 5NL, England. TEL 061-351-1878. circ. 800.

810   US
NEW KENT QUARTERLY. 1956. a. $1.25 per no. Kent State University, Department of English, Satterfield Hall, Kent, OH 44242. TEL 216-672-2121. Ed. Kimberly Littlepage. adv.; illus.; circ. 1,500. (processed) Indexed: A.I.P.P.
    Former titles: Human Issue (ISSN 0018-7232); Kent Quarterly.

800   US   ISSN 0145-8388
NEW LAUREL REVIEW. 1971. a. $8 to individuals; libraries $10. (New Orleans Poetry Forum) Smoke Bend Publishing, 828 Lesseps St., New Orleans, LA 70117. TEL 504-947-6001. Ed. Lee Meitzen Grue. adv.; bk.rev.; circ. 500. Indexed: M.L.A.
—BLDSC shelfmark: 6084.344000.

378.1   US   ISSN 0146-4930
PS501
NEW LETTERS; a magazine of fine writing. 1934. q. $17 to individuals; institutions $20. University of Missouri, Kansas City, 5100 Rockhill Rd., Kansas City, MO 64110. TEL 816-235-1168. FAX 816-235-5191. Ed. James McKinley. adv.; bk.rev.; index; circ. 1,500. Indexed: A.I.P.P., Abstr.Engl.Stud., Amer.Hum.Ind., Arts & Hum.Cit.Ind., Curr.Cont., Ind.Amer.Per.Verse, Ind.Bk.Rev.Hum., M.L.A.
    Former titles (until vol.37, 1971): University Review (ISSN 0042-0379); (until vol.30, 1964): University of Kansas City Review; (until vol.8, 1942): University Review.

809   US   ISSN 0028-6087
PR1
NEW LITERARY HISTORY; a journal of theory and interpretation. 1969. 4/yr. $22 to individuals (foreign $32); institutions $69 (foreign $78.10). (University of Virginia) Johns Hopkins University Press, Journals Publishing Division, 701 W. 40th St., Ste. 275, Baltimore, MD 21211. TEL 410-516-6987. FAX 410-516-6998. Ed. Ralph Cohen. adv.; index. cum.index: vols.1-10; circ. 2,192. (also avail. in microform from UMI; back issues avail.; reprint service avail. from UMI) Indexed: Abstr.Engl.Stud., Amer.Hist.& Life (until 1990), Arts & Hum.Cit.Ind., Bibl.Engl.Lang.& Lit., Can.Rev.Comp.Lit., Curr.Cont., Film Lit.Ind. (1990-), Hist.Abstr. (until 1990), Hum.Ind., Lang.& Lang.Behav.Abstr., LCR, M.L.A., Sociol.Abstr.
—BLDSC shelfmark: 6084.457000.
    Description: Focuses on theory and interpretation--the reasons for literary change, the definitions of periods, and the evolution of styles, conventions, and genres.

800   AT   ISSN 0314-7495
PR9080
NEW LITERATURES REVIEW. 1975. s-a. Aus.$10. University of Wollongong, Department of English, P.O. Box 1144, Wollongong, N.S.W. 2500, Australia. TEL 042-213-555. FAX 042-213-477. Co-sponsor: New Literatures Research Centre) Ed.Bd. adv.; bk.rev.; circ. 250. (back issues avail.) Indexed: Aus.P.A.I.S., M.L.A., So.Pac.Per.Ind.

808   US   ISSN 0193-5356
NEW MEXICO INDEPENDENT. 1895. fortn. $20. Independent Publishing Company, Inc., c/o Mark D. Acuff, Ed., Box 1706, Casa Grande, AZ 85222. adv.; bk.rev.; film rev.; play rev.; circ. 8,000. (tabloid format; back issues avail.)

800 700   IT   ISSN 0028-6354
NEW MORALITY;* concerned with new literature, art and criticism. (Text in English, French, Italian, Spanish) 1961. q. L.5000.($10) Via della Penna 51, Rome, Italy. Dir. Francine Virduzzo.

810 770   US   ISSN 0028-6400
AP2
NEW ORLEANS REVIEW. 1968. 4/yr. $30. Loyola University, Box 195, New Orleans, LA 70118. TEL 504-865-2294. Ed. John Mosier. adv.; film rev.; illus.; circ. 600. (also avail. in microform from UMI; reprint service avail. from UMI) Indexed: A.I.P.P., Abstr.Engl.Stud., Amer.Bibl.Slavic & E.Eur.Stud., Amer.Hum.Ind., Arts & Hum.Cit.Ind., Curr.Cont., Film Lit.Ind. (1980-), Ind.Amer.Per.Verse, Ind.Bk.Rev.Hum., M.L.A.
—BLDSC shelfmark: 6084.843000.
    Description: Literary journal specializing in poetry, fiction, photography, and film and literary criticism.

808   US
NEW RAIN. (Text in English, French, Spanish) 1981. a. price varies. Blind Beggar Press, Box 437, Williamsbridge Station, Bronx, NY 10467. TEL 914-683-6792. Ed. Gary Johnston. adv.; illus.; circ. 1,000. (back issues avail.)

820   UK   ISSN 0028-6540
PR3532
NEW RAMBLER. 1941. a. $7. Johnson Society of London, 10 Beaumont Buildings, Oxford OX1 2LL, England. Ed. David Parker. adv.; bk.rev.; circ. 300. (back issues avail.) Indexed: Abstr.Engl.Stud.

800 700   US   ISSN 0028-6575
NX1
THE NEW RENAISSANCE; an international magazine of ideas and opinions, emphasizing literature & the arts. 1968. s-a. $14.50 (Canada $15.50; Mexico and Europe $16.50; elsewhere $17.50) for 3 nos. Friends of the New Renaissance, Inc., 9 Heath Rd., Arlington, MA 02174. Ed. Louise T. Reynolds. bk.rev.; film rev.; play rev.; illus.; index; circ. 1,700. (back issues avail.) Indexed: A.I.P.P., Abstr.Engl.Stud., Alt.Press Ind., Amer.Hum.Ind., Ind.Amer.Per.Verse.

808   UK   ISSN 0260-3268
NEW TOLKIEN NEWSLETTER; a review of the works of J.R.R. Tolkien. 1980. 3/yr. £1.85. Widcombe Press, 16 Prior Park Bldgs., Bath, Avon BA2 4NP, England. Ed. Elizabeth Holland. adv.; bk.rev.; illus.; circ. 1,000.

800 770   US
NEW VIRGINIA REVIEW. 1978. a. $13.50. New Virginia Review, Inc., 1306 E, Cary St., Ste. 2A, Richmond, VA 23219. TEL 804-782-1043. circ. 2,000.

820   TR   ISSN 0254-9549
THE NEW VOICES. (Text in English) 1973. s-a. $10. P.O. Box 3254, Diego Martin, Trinidad & Tobago, W.I. TEL 809-637-4516. Ed. Anson Gonzalez. adv.; bk.rev.; illus.; circ. 300.

810   US
NEW VOICES (CLINTONDALE).* 1972. a. $3. Box 308, Clintondale, NY 12515. circ. 500.

800   US   ISSN 0895-6510
NEW WRITER'S MAGAZINE. 1986. bi-m. $12. Sarasota Bay Publishing, Box 5976, Sarasota, FL 34277. TEL 813-953-7903. Ed. George J. Haborak. adv.; bk.rev.; circ. 5,000. (back issues avail.)
    Description: Features articles for new, aspiring writers with information on how to break into the freelance market.

NEW YORK TIMES BOOK REVIEW. see *PUBLISHING AND BOOK TRADE*

NEW YORK TIMES BOOK REVIEW (MICROFORM EDITIONS). see *PUBLISHING AND BOOK TRADE*

NEW YORK UNIVERSITY STUDIES IN FRENCH CULTURE AND CIVILIZATION. see *HISTORY. — History Of Europe*

840 440   NZ   ISSN 0110-7380
PQ9
NEW ZEALAND JOURNAL OF FRENCH STUDIES. 1980. s-a. NZ.$20. Massey University, Department of Modern Languages, Palmerston North, New Zealand. TEL 06-3- 505633. Ed. Emeritus J. Dunmore. bk.rev.; circ. 200. (back issues avail.)
—BLDSC shelfmark: 6094.150000.
    Description: Scholarly articles on all aspects of French language, literature and culture.

NEWORLD; the multicultural magazine of the arts. see *ART*

810   US   ISSN 0276-5241
AP2
NEWPORT REVIEW.* 1979. a. $5. Newport Art Museum, c/o Stuart Blazer, Ed., Box 175, Adamsville, RI 02801-0175. TEL 401-848-2100. adv.; circ. 1,000.

800   US   ISSN 0737-4011
NEWSBANK REVIEW OF THE ARTS: LITERATURE. 1972. m. (q. and a. cumulations). price varies. NewsBank, Inc., 58 Pine St., New Canaan, CT 06840-5426. TEL 203-966-1100. FAX 203-966-6254. Ed. C. Dyer. bk.rev. (also avail. in microfiche; reprint service avail.)

810 US ISSN 0194-4118
NEWSCRIBES; a literary magazine. 1976. s-a. $5. Newscribes Group, 1223 Newkirk Ave., Brooklyn, NY 11230. Ed. Vincent Campo. adv.; circ. 800.

808.87 CN ISSN 0384-1642
NEWSPACKET. 1970. 3/yr. Can.$10. Stephen Leacock Associates, P. O. Box 854, Orillia, Ont. L3V 6K8, Canada. Ed. Jim Harris. adv.; bk.rev.; illus.; circ. 3,500.
  Description: Newsletter on humor, with emphasis on humor in Canada. Includes news of the Leacock Associates and topical columns.

800 US
NEXUS (DAYTON). 1965. 3/yr. $15. Wright State University, 006 U.C., Dayton, OH 45435. TEL 513-873-2031. Ed. Ted Cains. adv.; bk.rev.; circ. 2,000. (back issues avail.) Indexed: Rel.Ind.One.

NIEUWE TAALGIDS; tijdschrift voor neerlandici. see *LINGUISTICS*

800 100 US ISSN 0278-6079
NIGHTSUN; a journal of poetry, fiction, and interviews. 1981. a. $6.50. Frostburg State University, Department of English, Frostburg, MD 21532. Eds. Douglas DeMars, Barbara Wilson. adv.; bk.rev.; circ. 500. (back issues avail.)

810 US ISSN 1055-842X
▼**NIHILISTIC REVIEW**; the magazine for those without convention. 1990. q. $18. Pessimism Press, Inc., Box 1074, S. Sioux City, NE 68776. TEL 402-494-3110. Eds. Maxwell Gaddis, Camilla Danielson-Oregon. adv.; bk.rev.; film rev.; illus.; circ. 850. (back issues avail.)
  Description: Publishes iconoclastic poetry and short fiction in the tradition of Charles Bukowski and Jack Kerouac.

890 JA ISSN 0386-9903
NIHON BUNGAKU/JAPANESE LITERATURE. (Text in Japanese) 1952. m. 930 Yen per no. Nihon Bungaku Kyokai - Japanese Literature Association, 2-17-10 Minami-otsuka, Toshima-ku, Tokyo, Japan. FAX 03-3941-2740. Ed. Hiromi Hyodo. adv.; bk.rev.

808 US ISSN 0029-053X
SK223.H9
NIMROD; international journal of fiction and poetry. 1956. s-a. $11.50 (foreign $16). Arts and Humanities Council of Tulsa, 2210 S. Main, Tulsa, OK 74114. TEL 918-584-3333. (Dist. by: Council Oak Distributing, 1428 S. St. Louis, Tulsa, OK 74120. TEL 800-247-8850) Ed. Francine Ringold. adv.; circ. 3,200. (back issues avail.) Indexed: Amer.Hum.Ind., Ind.Amer.Per.Verse.

840 US ISSN 0146-7891
PQ1
NINETEENTH CENTURY FRENCH STUDIES. (Text in English and French) 1972. q. $28 to individuals; institutions $32. State University of New York, College at Fredonia, Department of Foreign Languages, Fredonia, NY 14063. TEL 716-673-3387. Ed. T. H. Goetz. adv.; bk.rev.; bibl.; index; circ. 800. (also avail. in microfilm from UMI; reprint service avail. from UMI) Indexed: Arts & Hum.Cit.Ind., Curr.Cont., Ind.Bk.Rev.Hum., M.L.A.
  —BLDSC shelfmark: 6113.230200.

800 US ISSN 0732-1864
PN761
NINETEENTH-CENTURY LITERARY CRITICISM. 1981. 3/yr. $108 per vol. (effective Nov. 1991). Gale Research Inc., 835 Penobscot Bldg., Detroit, MI 48226. TEL 313-961-2242. FAX 313-961-6083. TELEX 810-221-7086. Ed. Paula Kepos.

813 US ISSN 0891-9356
PR451
NINETEENTH-CENTURY LITERATURE (BERKELEY). 1945. q. $21 to individuals (foreign $26); institutions $36 (foreign $41); students $15 (foreign $20). University of California Press, Journals Division, 2120 Berkeley Way, Berkeley, CA 94720. TEL 510-642-4191. FAX 510-643-7127. Eds. G.B. Tennyson, Thomas Wortham. adv.; bk.rev.; index. cum.index; circ. 2,400. (also avail. in microfilm from UMI; back issues avail.; reprint service avail. from UMI) Indexed: Abstr.Engl.Stud., Acad.Ind., Arts & Hum.Cit.Ind., Bk.Rev.Ind. (1986-), Child.Bk.Rev.Ind. (1986-), Curr.Cont., Hist.Abstr., Hum.Ind., Ind.Bk.Rev.Hum., M.L.A., Ref.Sour.
  Formerly: Nineteenth-Century Fiction (ISSN 0029-0564)
  Description: Provides new research in scholarship, criticism, comparative studies and new editions of 19th century English and American literature.
  Refereed Serial

800 US
NINETEENTH-CENTURY LITERATURE (ROCHESTER). irreg. University of Rochester Press, c/o Robert Easton, Man. Ed., Box 41026, Rochester, NY 14604. TEL 716-275-4019. Indexed: Acad.Ind.

824 US
PR4023
NINETEENTH-CENTURY PROSE. 1974. 2/yr. $20. Department of Languages & Literature, Mesa State College, Box 2647, Grand Junction, CO 81502. TEL 303-248-1385. Ed. Barry Tharaud. adv.; bk.rev.; bibl.; circ. 400. (back issues avail.) Indexed: Abstr.Engl.Stud., Amer.Hum.Ind., Arts & Hum.Cit.Ind., Curr.Cont., LCR, M.L.A.
  Former titles (until 1989): Arnoldian (ISSN 0160-4848); Arnold Newsletter (ISSN 0094-5897)

800 US ISSN 0893-7931
CB415
NINETEENTH-CENTURY STUDIES. 1987. a. $25. (Southeastern Nineteenth-Century Studies Association) The Citadel - The Military College of South Carolina, Department of English, Charleston, SC 29409. Ed. Suzanne O. Edwards. bk.rev.; circ. 200. Indexed: M.L.A.
  —BLDSC shelfmark: 6113.231630.
  Description: Interdisciplinary journal focusing on Nineteenth-Century art, culture, and science.
  Refereed Serial

810 US ISSN 0199-3941
NIT & WIT; Chicago's arts magazine. 1977-1985; resumed 1986. bi-m. $12. Nit & Wit Publishing, Box 627, Geneva, IL 60134-0627. TEL 708-232-9496. Eds. Marie Aguirre, Harrison McCormick. adv.; bk.rev.; illus.; circ. 6,000. Indexed: A.I.P.P.

NNIDNID: SURREALITY. see *ART*

810 US
NOCTURNAL NEWS. 1983. 3/yr. $11. Baker Street Publications, Box 994, Metairie, LA 70004. TEL 504-734-8414. Ed. Sharida Rizzuto. circ. 9,000.

NONGCUN QINGNIAN/COUNTRY YOUTH. see *CHILDREN AND YOUTH — For*

NORDEUROPA STUDIEN. see *SOCIAL SCIENCES: COMPREHENSIVE WORKS*

NORDISTICA GOTHOBURGENSIA. see *LINGUISTICS*

839.82 NO ISSN 0078-1266
PT8301
NORSK LITTERAER AARBOK. (Text mainly in Norwegian; partly Danish and Swedish) 1966. a. NOK 234. Norske Samlaget, Boks 4672 Sofienberg, 0506 Oslo 5, Norway. TEL 02-687600. FAX 02-687502. Eds. H. Skei, E. Vannebo. circ. 1,500. Indexed: M.L.A.
  Description: Essays on Scandinavian, mainly Norwegian, 20th century literature, and an annotated bibliography of Norwegian research in literature.

800 327 MX
NORTE; revista hispanoamericano. 1929. bi-m. $7 per no. Frente de Afirmacion Hispanista A.C., Lago Ginebra No. 47 C, Mexico 17 D.F., Mexico. Dir. Fredo Arias de la Canal. adv.; illus.; circ. 2,000. Indexed: Amer.Hist.& Life, Hist.Abstr.

800 US ISSN 0891-4109
NORTH AMERICAN STUDIES IN NINETEETH-CENTURY GERMAN LITERATURE. (Text in English and other West European languages) 1988. irreg. Peter Lang Publishing, Inc., 62 W. 45th St., 4th Fl., New York, NY 10036. TEL 212-302-6740. Ed. Jeffrey Sammons.
  —BLDSC shelfmark: 6148.257000.

840 US
NORTH CAROLINA STUDIES IN THE ROMANCE LANGUAGES AND LITERATURES.. (Text in English, French, Italian, Latin, Portuguese, Spanish) 1940. irreg., no.231, 1988. price varies. University of North Carolina at Chapel Hill, Department of Romance Languages, CB 3170, 238 Dey Hall, Chapel Hill, NC 27599-3170. TEL 919-962-1025. Ed. Maria A. Salgado. Indexed: M.L.A.
  Formerly: Studies in the Romance Languages and Literatures (ISSN 0081-8666)

800 US
NORTH STONE REVIEW. 1971-19??; resumed no.9, 1990. irreg. (1-2/yr). $15. D Station, Box 14098, Minneapolis, MN 55414. Ed. James Naiden. adv.; bk.rev.; illus.; circ. 1,500. (also avail. in microform from UMI; reprint service avail. from UMI)

810 US
NORTHEAST (LA CROSSE). 1962. s-a. $33 to individuals; institutions $38. Juniper Press, 1310 Shorewood Dr., La Crosse, WI 54601. TEL 608-788-0096. Eds. John Judson, Joanne Judson. bk.rev.; cum.index every 5 yrs.; circ. 400. Indexed: A.I.P.P., Ind.Little Mag.
  Description: Contains contemporary poetry, short stories, and graphics.

800 US
NORTHEAST JOURNAL. 1978. a. $5. Northeast Journal, Box 2321, Providence, RI 02906-0321. TEL 401-785-0553. Eds. Dawne Anderson, Dennis Holt. bk.rev.; circ. 500.
  Description: Contains nationwide poetry and short prose, with emphasis on Rhode Island and the Northeast.

NORTHERN LIGHTS STUDIES IN CREATIVITY. see *ART*

800 US ISSN 0190-3012
NORTHERN NEW ENGLAND REVIEW. 1973. a. $5. Franklin Pierce College, Box 825, Rindge, NH 03461. TEL 603-899-5111. Ed. Alexandra Fox. adv.; bk.rev.; circ. 600 (controlled). (back issues avail.) Indexed: A.I.P.P., M.L.A.

800 550 UK ISSN 0308-4809
NORTHUMBRIANA; True Northumberland's own magazine. (Text in English and Northumbrian) 1975. irreg. (approx. 3/yr.). Morpeth Northumbrian Gathering Committee, Westgate House, Dogger Bank, Morpeth, Northumberland NE61 1RF, England. TEL 0670 513308. Ed. Roland Bibby. adv.; bk.rev.; circ. 750.
  Description: Discusses dialect and writings, history, lore and legend, landscape, architecture, balladry, song, music, dance & crafts.

820 821 CN ISSN 0706-0955
NORTHWARD JOURNAL; a quarterly of northern arts. 1974. q. Can.$20. 439 Wellington St. W., 3rd fl., Toronto, Ont. M5V 1E7, Canada. TEL 416-593-2730. Ed. Robert Stacey. adv.; bk.rev.; circ. 700. (also avail. in microfilm from MML) Indexed: Can.Lit.Ind.
  Description: Poetry, fiction, prose, art and reviews with a northern perspective.

810 US ISSN 0029-3423
AP2
NORTHWEST REVIEW. 1957. 3/yr. $14. University of Oregon, Northwest Review, 369 Prince Lucien Campbell Hall, Eugene, OR 97403. TEL 503-346-3957. Ed. John Witte. adv.; bk.rev.; film rev.; play rev.; circ. 1,000. (also avail. in microform from UMI; back issues avail.; reprint service avail. from UMI) Indexed: A.I.P.P., Amer.Hum.Ind., Ind.Amer.Per.Verse, Ind.Bk.Rev.Hum., M.L.A.
  —BLDSC shelfmark: 6151.950000.
  Description: Contains original and vital literary and critical works.

LITERATURE

810 US
NORWOTTUCK. 1972. s-a. $3. Hampshire College, Amherst, MA 01002. TEL 413-549-4600. Ed. Richard Waks. bk.rev.; circ. 2,000. **Indexed:** Ind.Amer.Per.Verse.
  Formerly (until vol.7, 1978): Boxspring.

070 840 BE
NOS LETTRES. 1968. m. 400 BEF (foreign 520 BEF). Association des Ecrivains Belges de Langue Francaise, Maison des Ecrivains, Chaussee de Wavre 150, B-1050 Brussels, Belgium. TEL 02-512-29-68. Ed. Roger Foulon. adv.; bk.rev.; play rev.; illus.; circ. 600.
  Formerly (until 1991): Nos Lettres. Informations (ISSN 0029-3717)

800 US ISSN 0892-2616
NOSTALGIA (ORANGEBURG); a sentimental state of mind. 1986. s-a. $5. Nostalgia Publications, Box 2224, Orangeburg, SC 29116. TEL 803-534-9844. Ed. Connie Lakey Martin. adv.; bk.rev.; illus.; circ. 1,000. (back issues avail.)
  Description: Features short stories and poems of a nostalgic content.

NOSTRO TEMPO; settimanale cattolico. see ART

800 180 900 US ISSN 0883-6337
NOTEBOOK (BARSTOW)/CUADERNO; a literary journal. (Text in English, some Spanish) 1985. a. $8 to individuals; institutions $10. Esoterica Press, P.O. Box 15607, Albuquerque, NM 87174-0607. Ed. Yoly Zentella. adv.; bk.rev.; circ. 200. (back issues avail.) **Indexed:** Amer.Hum.Ind., Chic.Per.Ind.
  Description: Humanistic literature emphasizing Latino literature.

820 AT ISSN 0156-806X
NOTES & FURPHIES. 1978. s-a. Aus.$12. Association for the Study of Australian Literature, c/o University of New England, Department of English, Armidale, NSW 2351, Australia. TEL (067)73-2604. Eds. Julian Croft, Ken Stewart. circ. 700. (back issues avail.)
  Description: Newsletter for undergraduate and post-graduate researchers in Australian literature.

820 UK ISSN 0029-3970
AG305
NOTES AND QUERIES; for readers and writers, collectors and librarians. 1849. 4/yr. £47($96) Oxford University Press, Oxford Journals, Pinkhill House, Southfield Road, Eynsham, Oxford OX8 1JJ, England. TEL 0865-882283. FAX 0865-882890. TELEX 837330 OXPRES G. Ed.Bd. adv.; bk.rev.; index. cum.index published irregularly; circ. 1,700. (also avail. in microform from UMI) **Indexed:** Abstr.Engl.Stud., Arts & Hum.Cit.Ind., Br.Archaeol.Abstr., Br.Hum.Ind., Curr.Cont., Hist.Abstr., Hum.Ind., Ind.Bk.Rev.Hum., M.L.A., RILA.
  —BLDSC shelfmark: 6165.040000.
  Description: Covers the English language and literature, lexicography, history and scholarly antiquarianism.

800 US ISSN 0029-4047
NOTES ON CONTEMPORARY LITERATURE. 1971. q. $5 to individuals; libraries $10; foreign $20. c/o English Department, West Georgia College, Carollton, GA 30118. TEL 404-834-3282. Ed.Bd. adv.; bk.rev.; index; circ. 250. **Indexed:** Abstr.Engl.Stud., LCR, M.L.A.
  —BLDSC shelfmark: 6166.650000.

810 US ISSN 0029-4071
PS266.M7
NOTES ON MISSISSIPPI WRITERS. 1968. s-a. $4. University of Southern Mississippi, Department of English, Hattiesburg, MS 39401. TEL 601-266-4319. Ed. Hilton Anderson. bk.rev.; bibl.; index; circ. 250. (back issues avail.) **Indexed:** Abstr.Engl.Stud., M.L.A.

840 UK ISSN 0029-4586
PQ1
NOTTINGHAM FRENCH STUDIES. (Text in English and French) 1962. s-a. £10($24) (University of Nottingham, Department of French) Nottingham University Press, Nottingham, England. TEL 0602-484848. FAX 0602-420825. TELEX 37346-UNINOT-G. Ed.Bd. circ. 500. **Indexed:** Arts & Hum.Cit.Ind., Br.Hum.Ind., Curr.Cont., M.L.A.

800 FR ISSN 0550-1326
NOUVEAU COMMERCE. (Supplement avail.: Nouveau Commerce de la Lecture (ISSN0223-3533)) 1963. 2/yr. 310 F. includes supplement. A C N C Nouveau Commerce, Librarie Anima, 3 rue Ravignan, 75018 Paris, France. TEL 1-42-64-05-25. bk.rev.; abstr.; bibl.; cum.index; circ. 1,000 (controlled). (tabloid format)
  —BLDSC shelfmark: 6176.319000.

840 FR ISSN 0223-3533
NOUVEAU COMMERCE DE LA LECTURE. (Supplement to: Nouveau Commerce (ISSN 0550-1326)) 1972. irreg. included in subscr. to Nouveau Commerce. A C N C Nouveau Commerce, 80, rue des Archives, 75003 Paris, France. TEL 42-72-99-03. bk.rev.; abstr.; bibl.; circ. 1,000.

840 920 FR ISSN 0078-2165
NOUVELLE BIBLIOTHEQUE NERVALIENNE. (Consists of two subdivisions: Textes and Etudes et Documents; subdivisions are numbered consecutively within the main series) 1959. irreg. Lettres Modernes, 73 rue du Cardinal Lemoine, 75005 Paris, France. TEL 1-43-54-46-09.

NOVA TELLUS; anuario del centro de estudios clasicos. see HUMANITIES: COMPREHENSIVE WORKS

813 US ISSN 0029-5132
PN3311
NOVEL: A FORUM ON FICTION. 1967. 3/yr. $13.20 to individuals; institutions $12. Brown University, Box 1984, Providence, RI 02912. TEL 414-863-2154. Ed.Bd. bk.rev.; index; circ. 1,500. (also avail. in microform from UMI; reprint service avail. from UMI) **Indexed:** Abstr.Engl.Stud., Acad.Ind., Amer.Bibl.Slavic & E.Eur.Stud., Arts & Hum.Cit.Ind., Can.Rev.Comp.Lit., Curr.Cont., Hum.Ind., Ind.Bk.Rev.Hum., M.L.A.
  —BLDSC shelfmark: 6180.235000.

808 US ISSN 0897-9812
PN3355
NOVEL & SHORT STORY WRITER'S MARKET. a. $19.95. F & W Publications, Inc., 1507 Dana Ave., Cincinnati, OH 45207. TEL 513-531-2222. Ed. Robin Gee. circ. 20,000.
  Formerly (until 1988): Fiction Writer's Market (ISSN 0275-2123)
  Description: Provides 1,900 listings of fiction publishers, plus 20 articles on fiction writing and marketing techniques.

895.1 CH
NOVELISTIC WORKS/HSIAO SHUO CH'UANG TSO. (Text in Chinese) 1962. m. NT.$1500 in ROC; Hong Kong HK.$430; elsewhere NT.$1700 ($61). P.O. Box 3914, Taipei, Taiwan, Republic of China. TEL 02-931-9087. FAX 02-934-3887. (Or: No. 11, Lane 102, Hsinglung Rd. Sec. 1, Taipei, Taiwan, R.O.C.) Ed. Hsieh Hsueh-chun. adv.

808 333.7 US ISSN 0896-2693
F217.A65
NOW AND THEN. 1984. 3/yr. $10 to individuals; institutions $12. East Tennessee State University, Center for Appalachian Studies and Services, Box 70556, Johnson City, TN 37614-0556. TEL 615-929-5348. FAX 615-929-5770. Ed. Pat Arnow. bk.rev.; circ. 1,600.
  ●Also available online.
  Former Titles: Second Growth; Appalachian Nature and Culture.
  Description: Contains poetry, fiction, essays, interviews, photos and graphics focusing on life in the Appalachian mountains.

896 NR
NSUKKA STUDIES IN AFRICAN LITERATURE. 1977. s-a. University of Nigeria, Department of English, Nsukka, Nigeria. (Co-sponsor: Department of Languages) bk.rev. **Indexed:** Arts & Hum.Cit.Ind., Curr.Cont.

800 US
NUESTRA VOZ. irreg. Peter Lang Publishing, Inc., 62 W. 45th St., 4th Fl., New York, NY 10036. TEL 212-302-6740. FAX 212-302-7574. Ed. Amy Williamsen.
  Description: Covers women writers in Spain and Latin America and introduces them to new audiences.

056.1 CU
NUEVA GACETA DE CUBA. m. $20 in N. America; S. America $26; Europe $29; elsewhere $41. (Union de Escritores y Artistas de Cuba) Ediciones Cubanas, Obispo No. 527, Aptdo. 605, Havana, Cuba. illus.; circ. 10,000.
  Former titles: Nueva Gaceta; Gaceta de Cuba.

NUEVA REVISTA DE FILOLOGIA HISPANICA. see LINGUISTICS

NUEVA REVISTA DEL PACIFICO. see LINGUISTICS

820 CN ISSN 0823-2490
NUIT BLANCHE; l'actualite du livre. 4/yr. Can.$15 (foreign Can.$25). 1026 rue Saint-Jean, No. 403, Quebec, Que. G1R 1R7, Canada. TEL 418-692-1354. FAX 418-692-1355. Ed. A.M. Guerineau. **Indexed:** Pt.de Rep. (1989-).

NUMBER ONE. see LITERATURE — Poetry

800 IT ISSN 0029-6155
NUOVA CORRENTE; rivista di letteratura e filosofia. (Text in Italian; occasionally in English, French, German) 1954. s-a. L.25000($25) Tilgher-Genova s.a.s., Via Assarotti 52, 16122 Milan, Italy. Eds. Mario Boselli, Giuseppe Sertoli. adv.; bk.rev.; index. **Indexed:** Abstr.Engl.Stud.
  —BLDSC shelfmark: 6184.908500.

850 IT ISSN 0391-8548
NUOVA UNIVERSALE STUDIUM. 1974. irreg., latest no.60. price varies. Edizioni Studium, Via Cassiodoro 14, 00193 Rome, Italy.

800 CC
NUZI WENXUE/WOMEN'S LITERATURE. (Text in Chinese) m. Shijiazhuang Wenxue Yishu Jie Lianhehui, 19 Tannan Lu, Shijiazhuang, Hebei 050011, People's Republic of China. TEL 45845. Ed. Zhang Guangmin.

NYELV- ES IRODALOMTUDOMANYI KOZLEMENYEK. see LINGUISTICS

891.7 RU
O LITERATURE DLYA DETEI. vol.20, 1976. irreg. 0.36 Rub. per no. Izdatel'stvo Detskaya Literatura, Nab. Kutuzova 6, 192187 St. Petersburg, Russia. circ. 10,000.

840 FR ISSN 0294-4480
O R A C L. 1982. q. 220 F. Office Regional d'Action Culturelle, Musee Sainte-Croix, 86000 Poitiers, France. TEL 49415900. (Subscr. to: Georges Bonnet, 4 rue de la Trinite, 86000 Poitiers, France) bk.rev.; circ. 1,000. (back issues avail.)

820 UK
OASIS (LONDON). 1969. 6/yr. $15. Oasis Books, 12 Stevenage Rd., London SW6 6ES, England. TEL 071-726-5059. Ed. Ian Robinson. adv.; bk.rev.; index every 3 yrs.; circ. 500. (back issues avail.)
  Incorporating: Expression (ISSN 0029-7410)

891.85 PL ISSN 0078-2963
OBRAZ LITERATURY POLSKIEJ. 1965. irreg. price varies. Panstwowe Wydawnictwo Naukowe, Ul. Miodowa 10, 00-950 Warsaw, Poland.

800 910.03 US ISSN 0888-4412
PR1110.B5
OBSIDIAN II: BLACK LITERATURE IN REVIEW. 1975. 3/yr. $12. North Carolina State University, Box 8105, Raleigh, NC 27695-8105. TEL 919-515-3870. Ed. Gerald Barrax. adv.; bk.rev.; index; circ. 500. (also avail. in microform from UMI; reprint service avail. from UMI) **Indexed:** Amer.Hum.Ind., Arts & Hum.Cit.Ind., Curr.Cont., Ind.Amer.Per.Verse, Ind.Bk.Rev.Hum., M.L.A.
  Formerly: Obsidian: Black Literature in Review (ISSN 0360-6724)
  Description: Review for the study and cultivation of creative works in English by black writers worldwide, with scholarly critical studies by all writers on black literature in English.

891.81 BU ISSN 0029-7852
AP4
OBZOR; Bulgarian quarterly review of literature & the arts. (Editions in English, French and Spanish) 1967. q. 4 lv.($5) (Komitet za Izkustvo i Kultura) Foreign Trade Co. "Hemus", 7 Levsky St., 1000 Sofia, Bulgaria. (Co-sponsor: Suiuz na Bulgarski Pisateli) Ed. Liliana Stefanova. bk.rev.; bibl.; illus.; index; circ. 3,000 (English ed.). (also avail. in microform from UMI; reprint service avail. from UMI) **Indexed:** Arts & Hum.Cit.Ind., Curr.Cont.

430 400 940 UK ISSN 0307-7497
OCCASIONAL PAPERS IN GERMAN STUDIES. (Text in English with German quotations) 1972. irreg. 75p. per no. University of Warwick, Department of German Studies, Coventry CV4 4AL, England. (Co-sponsor: Volkswagen Foundation) Ed. Tony Phelan. circ. 200.

807 407 US ISSN 0739-8972
PG1
OCCASIONAL PAPERS IN SLAVIC LANGUAGES AND LITERATURE. 1982. irreg. University of Washington, Department of Slavic Languages and Literature, DP-32, Seattle, WA 98195. FAX 206-543-9285.
  Description: Presents research papers and covers literature and linguisitcs

OCTOBER. see *ART*

809 DK ISSN 0106-2212
ODENSE UNIVERSITET. LABORATORIUM FOR FOLKESPROGLIG MIDDELALDERLITTERATUR. MINDRE SKRIFTER. 1977. irreg. price varies. Odense Universitet, Laboratorium for Folkesproglig Middelalterlitteratur, Odense, Denmark. circ. 100.

800 DK ISSN 0078-3323
ODENSE UNIVERSITY STUDIES IN LITERATURE. (Text in Danish; summaries in English) 1969. irreg., vol.28, 1991. price varies. Odense University Press, Campusvej 55, DK-5230 Odense M, Denmark. TEL 66-157999. (back issues avail.)

ODENSE UNIVERSITY STUDIES IN SCANDINAVIAN LANGUAGES AND LITERATURES. see *LINGUISTICS*

820 MW
ODI; the muse. (Text in English) 1974. q. $6. Chancellor College, Writers' Group, P.O. Box 280, Zomba, Malawi. Ed. A.J. Nazombe. **Indexed:** M.L.A.

800 700 PL ISSN 0472-5182
AP54
ODRA. 1961. m. $55. (Ministry of Culture) Agencja Autorska, Hipoteczna 2, P.O. Box 133, 00-950 Warsaw, Poland. TEL 48-22-27-6061. FAX 48-22-27-5882. TELEX ZAIKS PL 812472. (Editorial addr.: Redakcja Odry, ul. Podwale 64, Wroslaw, Poland. TEL 255-16) bk.rev.; circ. 8,500.
  Description: Cultural-social review, includes poetry, prose, essays, art, politics.

ODU; a journal of West African studies. see *HISTORY — History Of Africa*

838 AU
OESTERREICHISCHE AKADEMIE DER WISSENSCHAFTEN. KOMMISSION FUER LITERATURWISSENSCHAFT. VEROEFFENTLICHUNGEN. (Subseries of: Oesterreichische Akademie der Wissenschaften. Philosophisch-Historische Klasse. Sitzungsberichte) 1973. irreg. Verlag der Oesterreichischen Akademie der Wissenschaften, Dr. Ignaz-Seipel-Platz, A-1010 Vienna, Austria. FAX 0222-5139541.

OESTERREICHISCHE AKADEMIE DER WISSENSCHAFTEN. PHILOSOPHISCH-HISTORISCHE KLASSE. SITZUNGSBERICHTE. see *HISTORY — History Of Europe*

OESTERREICHISCHE AUTORENZEITUNG. see *PATENTS, TRADEMARKS AND COPYRIGHTS*

809 840 GW ISSN 0338-1900
PQ2
OEUVRES ET CRITIQUES; revue international d'etude de la reception critique des oeuvres litteraires de langue Francaise. (Text in English, French and German) 1976. 2/yr. DM.68. Gunter Narr Verlag, Dischingerweg 5, 7400 Tubingen 5, Germany. TEL 07071-78091. FAX 07071-75288. Ed. Wolfgang Leiner. adv.; bk.rev.; bibl.; tr.lit.; circ. 3,000. (back issues avail.) **Indexed:** Arts & Hum.Cit.Ind., Curr.Cont., M.L.A.

810 US
OFF MAIN STREET. 1986. a. $3.50. Ferris State College, Languages and Literature Department, Big Rapids, MI 49307. TEL 616-796-8762. Eds. David Vinopal, John Caserta.

OHIO REVIEW. see *LITERATURE — Poetry*

810 US ISSN 0030-1248
OHIOANA QUARTERLY. 1957. q. $20. Ohioana Library Association, 1105 Ohio Departments Bldg., 65 S. Front St., Columbus, OH 43215. TEL 614-466-3831. Ed. Barbara S. Maslekoff. bk.rev.; bibl.; illus.; circ. 2,500. **Indexed:** Abstr.Engl.Stud., Amer.Hum.Ind.
  Formerly: Ohioana.

810 960 NR ISSN 0331-0566
PR9898.N5
OKIKE; an African journal of new writing. 1971. 3/yr. $12. Okike Arts Centre, Box 53, Nsukka, Nigeria. Ed. Chinua Achebe. adv.; bk.rev.; illus.; index; cum.index; circ. 5,500. **Indexed:** Arts & Hum.Cit.Ind., Curr.Cont., Curr.Cont.Africa, M.L.A.
—BLDSC shelfmark: 6252.860000.

891.8 YU ISSN 0030-1949
OKTOBAR; list za knjizevnost, umetnost i kulturu. 1966. d. 18 din.($3.) Kulturno Prosvetna Zajednica Opstine Kraljevo, Cara Dusana 32, Kraljevo, Yugoslavia. Ed. Jovan Markovic.

800 429 US ISSN 0030-1973
PE101
OLD ENGLISH NEWSLETTER. 1967. s-a. $5 to individuals; institutions $10. (Modern Language Association of America, Old English Group) State University of New York at Binghamton, Center for Medieval and Early Renaissance Studies, Binghamton, NY 13901. TEL 607-777-2130. Ed. Paul E. Szarmach. bibl.; circ. 975. (back issues avail.; reprint service avail. from ISI) **Indexed:** LCR, M.L.A.

OLD LADY OF THREADNEEDLE STREET. see *GENERAL INTEREST PERIODICALS — Great Britain*

810 US
OLD RED KIMONO. 1972. a. Floyd College, Humanities Division, Box 1864, Rome, GA 30163. TEL 404-295-6312. Eds. Jon Hershey, Ken Anderson. index; circ. 1,200. (processed)
  Description: Contains poetry and very short stories that are concise and imagistic, not sentimental or didactic.

700 US ISSN 0316-4055
NX1
ONTARIO REVIEW. 1974. s-a. $10 (foreign $12). O. R. Press, Inc., 9 Honey Brook Dr., Princeton, NJ 08540. TEL 609-737-7497. Ed. Raymond J. Smith. adv.; cum.index: 1974-1987; circ. 1,100. (also avail. in microfilm; back issues avail.) **Indexed:** A.I.P.P., Amer.Hum.Ind., Ind.Amer.Per.Verse, LCR, M.L.A.
  Description: Publishes poetry, fiction, essays and graphics by both newer and more established writers and artists. Contains interviews with distinguished authors.

ONTHEBUS. see *LITERATURE — Poetry*

800 JA
OORU YOMIMONO/ALL READING MATTERS. 1930. m. 9120 Yen. Bungei Shunju Ltd., 3-23,Kioi-cho, Chiyoda-ku, Tokyo, Japan. FAX 03-3265-4878. Ed. Masaru Nakai. circ. 121,940.

OPEN DEUR. see *ART*

OPERA SLAVICA. NEUE FOLGE. see *LINGUISTICS*

ORAL TRADITION. see *FOLKLORE*

ORBIS; an international journal of poetry and prose. see *LITERATURE — Poetry*

LITERATURE 2945

807 DK ISSN 0105-7510
PN1
ORBIS LITTERARUM; international review of literary studies. (Text in English, French, or German) 1946-1950; resumed 1954. 6/yr. DKK 1035. Munksgaard International Publishers Ltd., 35 Noerre Soegade, P.O. Box 2148, DK-1016 Copenhagen K, Denmark. TEL 33-127030. FAX 33-129387. TELEX 19431-MUNKS-DK. Ed. Morten Noejgaard. adv.; bk.rev.; index,cum.index: vols.1-8, 1943-1950 in vol. 8; circ. 600. (also avail. in microform from SWZ; reprint service avail. from ISI,SWZ) **Indexed:** Arts & Hum.Cit.Ind., Can.Rev.Comp.Lit., Curr.Cont., Ind.Bk.Rev.Hum., M.L.A., Mid.East: Abstr.& Ind.

ORDEN POUR LE MERITE FUER WISSENSCHAFTEN UND KUENSTE. REDEN UND GEDENKWORTE. see *HUMANITIES: COMPREHENSIVE WORKS*

800 UK
ORDINARY LIVES. 1976. irreg. £6.95. Dennis Dobson Books Ltd., 80 Kensington Church St., London W8 4BZ, England.

800 100 US ISSN 0897-2648
ORGANICA; a magazine of arts & activism. 1982. q. free. (Aubrey Organics) Organica Press, 4419 N. Manhattan Ave., Tampa, FL 33614. FAX 813-876-8166. Ed. Susan Hussey. bk.rev.; circ. 300,000.

890 PK
ORIENTAL COLLEGE. MAGAZIN. (Text in Urdu) vol.40, 1964. q. Rs.15 per no. University of the Punjab, Oriental College, Lahore, Pakistan.

ORIENTALISTISCHE LITERATURZEITUNG; Zeitschrift fuer die Wissenschaft vom ganzen Orient und seinen Beziehungen zu den angrenzenden Kulturkreisen. see *ORIENTAL STUDIES*

800 RM ISSN 0030-560X
PC601
ORIZONT. 1949. w. 1 lei per no. Uniunea Scriitorilor din Republica Socialista Romania (Timisoara), Str. Rodnei Nr. 1, Timisoara, Rumania. Ed. Ion Ariesanu. bk.rev.; play rev.; bibl.; illus.; circ. 5,000.

800 020 US ISSN 0730-3475
ORO MADRE.* (Text in English, Spanish) 1980. q. $14. Ruddy Duck Press, 55 Vernon Pl., Buffalo, NY 14214-2013. Ed. L. Glazier. adv.; bk.rev.; cum.index: 1980-1985; circ. 1,000. (back issue avail.) **Indexed:** Ind.Amer.Per.Verse.

800 930 IT ISSN 0030-5790
ORPHEUS; rivista di umanita classica e cristiana. 1954. s-a. L.40000 (foreign L.70000)(effective 1993). Centro Studi Antico Cristianesimo, Universita di Catania, Facolta di Lettere, 95131 Catania, Sicily, Italy. Ed. Carmelo Curti. bk.rev.; index; circ. 1,200.
—BLDSC shelfmark: 6293.545000.

053.5 SZ
ORTE; Schweizer Literaturzeitschrift. 1974. 5/yr. 10 Fr. Orte Verlag, Wirtschaft "Kreuz", CH-9429 Zelg-Wolfhalden, Switzerland. Ed. Werner Bucher. adv.

700 US ISSN 0095-019X
OSIRIS (DEERFIELD); an multilingual poetry journal. (Text in English, French, German, Italian, Polish, Spanish) 1972. s-a. $10. Box 297, Deerfield, MA 01342. TEL 413-774-4027. Ed. Andrea Moorhead. illus.; circ. 1,000. **Indexed:** A.I.P.P., Amer.Hum.Ind., Ind.Amer.Per.Verse.
  Description: Publishes poetry in different languages, most with English translation.

OSNOVAC. see *ART*

890 XN ISSN 0352-1362
OSOGOVSKI GLAS. (Text in Macedonian) a. Literaturen Klug "Nadezi", 91320 Kratovo, Macedonia. TEL 0901 81-193.

808 US ISSN 8756-4696
PS642
OTHER VOICES. 1985. s-a. $16 for 4 nos. to individuals (foreign $28); institutions $18. Other Voices, Inc., University of Illinois at Chicago, Department of English MC 162, Box 4348, Chicago, IL 60680. TEL 312-413-2209. Eds. Sharon Fiffer, Lois Hauselman. adv.; circ. 1,500. **Indexed:** Can.Wom.Per.Ind.
  Description: Dedicated to original and diverse stories and novel-excerpts.

LITERATURE

809   IT   ISSN 0391-2639
OTTO-NOVECENTO; rivista bimestrale di critica letteraria. 1977. bi-m. L.78000. Edizioni Otto-Novecento, Piazza Giovanni XXIII, no. 2, 21022 Azzate (Va), Italy. FAX 0332-458395. Ed. Umberto Colombo. adv.; bk.rev.

850   IT
OTTO - NOVECENTO RITROVATO. 1985. irreg., no.6, 1990. price varies. Liguori Editore s.r.l., Via Mezzocannone, 19, 80134 Naples, Italy. TEL 081-5227139. Eds. F. Bruni, A. Palermo.

800   US
OUROBOROS. 1985. irreg. (2-3/yr.). $4.50 per no. 3912 24th St., Rock Island, IL 61201. Ed. Erskine Carter. circ. 300. (back issues avail.)
   Description: Fiction, poetry and art.

800   US   ISSN 0739-4969
OUTERBRIDGE. 1975. a. $5. City University of New York, College of Staten Island, Department of English A324, 715 Ocean Terrace, Staten Island, NY 10301. TEL 718-390-7654. Ed. Charlotte Alexander. bk.rev.; cum.index in no. 8-9 and no. 18-19; circ. 500. (back issues avail.) **Indexed:** Hum.Ind., Ind.Amer.Per.Verse.
   Description: Seeks professionalism in literature. Regulates theme issues (rural, urban, Southern, war, childhood, interdisciplinary, immigrant-migrant). Slight bias toward new, less published voices.

821   AT   ISSN 0813-5886
OUTRIDER. 1984. s-a. Aus.$15. (Australia Council Literature Board) Phoenix Publications Brisbane, c/o Prof. M. Jurgensen, P.O. Box 210, Indooroopilly, Qld. 4068, Australia. TEL 371-6166. Ed. Manfred Jurgensen. adv.; bk.rev.; circ. 2,000.
   Description: Publishes literary prose, poetry and articles dealing with literature in Australia.

807   US
OWEN WISTER REVIEW. 1978. 2/yr. $6 (typically set in Sept). University of Wyoming, Student Publications, Box 4238, University Station, Laramie, WY 82071. Ed. Spence Keralis. bk.rev.; circ. 500.

810   US
OXALIS. 1988. 4/yr. $18. Box 3993, Kingston, NY 12401. TEL 914-687-7942. Ed. Shirley Powell. circ. 300.

820   US
OXFORD ENGLISH MONOGRAPHS. irreg. price varies. Oxford University Press, 200 Madison Ave., New York, NY 10016. TEL 212-679-7300. Ed.Bd. **Indexed:** M.L.A.

830 410   UK   ISSN 0078-7191
PT1
OXFORD GERMAN STUDIES. (Text and summaries in English and German) 1966. a. $35. (Fiedler Foundation) Willem A. Meeuws, Pub., 11 Broad St., Oxford OX1 3AR, England. TEL 0865-242939. Eds. N. Palmer, T.J. Reed. adv.; bk.rev.; circ. 500. (back issues avail.) **Indexed:** Curr.Cont., M.L.A.
—BLDSC shelfmark: 6321.005000.

800 100   UK
OXFORD LITERARY REVIEW; critical analyses of literary, philosophical, political and psycho-analytic theory. 1974. a. £8($13.75) to individuals; institutions £18($35). Wadham College, Oxford OX1 3PN, England. Ed.Bd. adv.; bk.rev.; circ. 1,000. **Indexed:** Arts & Hum.Cit.Ind., Curr.Cont., M.L.A.
   Former titles: Oxford Literary Review: A Post-Structuralist Journal; Oxford Literary Review (ISSN 0305-1498)

811.051   US
OXFORD MAGAZINE. 1985. s-a. $7. Miami University, Department of English, Oxford, OH 45056. Ed. Kathryn Lacey. adv.; circ. 250. (back issues avail.)
   Description: National journal publishing new poetry, fiction, and essays.

800   US
OXFORD MODERN LANGUAGE AND LITERATURE MONOGRAPHS. irreg. price varies. Oxford University Press, 200 Madison Ave., New York, NY 10016. TEL 212-679-7300. Ed.Bd. **Indexed:** M.L.A.

OXFORD SLAVONIC PAPERS. see HISTORY — History Of Europe

OXFORD THEATRE TEXTS. see THEATER

810   US
OYEZ REVIEW. 1966. a. $7.50 for 2 issues. Roosevelt University, 430 S. Michigan Ave., Chicago, IL 60605. TEL 312-341-2017. FAX 312-341-2017. Ed. Angela Lewis. adv.; bk.rev.; illus.; circ. 750. (back issues avail.)

OZ TRADING POST. see HOBBIES

OZIANA. see CLUBS

800 808.81   IT
L'OZIO; almanacco di letteratura. 1980. s-a. L.35000($37) Edizioni Amadeus, Corso Mazzini 10/39, 31044 Montebelluna, Italy. TEL 0423-85617. FAX 0423-601085. Ed. Antonio Facchin. (back issues avail.; reprint service avail.)

800   US
P E NEWSLETTER. 1971. q. $8. P E N American Center, 568 Broadway, New York, NY 10012. TEL 212-334-1660. FAX 212-334-2181. Ed. Naomi Bliven. circ. 3,000.
   Description: Reports on PEN programs in the US and abroad.

P - FORM; performance art magazine. see ART

800 406   US   ISSN 0030-8129
PB6
P M L A. (Supplements avail.) 1884. 6/yr. membership; libraries $100 (effective 1993). Modern Language Association of America, 10 Astor Pl., New York, NY 10003. TEL 212-475-9500. FAX 212-477-9863. Ed. Domna Stanton. adv.; index; circ. 35,500. (also avail. in microfilm from UMI; reprint service avail. from ISI,KTO,UMI) **Indexed:** Abstr.Engl.Stud., Arts & Hum.Cit.Ind., Curr.Cont., Hum.Ind., Lang.& Lang.Behav.Abstr., M.L.A., Mid.East: Abstr.& Ind.
—BLDSC shelfmark: 6541.092000.
   Description: Publishes scholarly and critical articles, professional notes, letters. Lists fellowships, forthcoming meetings.

850   US   ISSN 1042-4822
PQ4835.I7
P S A. 1970. a. $15 to individuals; institutions $30. Pirandello Society of America, Box 81, Whitestone, NY 11357. TEL 718-767-8380. Ed. A. Paolucci. adv.; circ. 600. (back issues avail.)
   Formerly: Pirandello Society Newsletter.
   Description: Articles on Pirandello's work and his influence on contemporary theater. Includes fiction.

800 500   US   ISSN 0886-1102
P S L S. (Publication of the Society for Literature and Science) 1985. q. $25. Society for Literature and Science, c/o Prof. Kenneth J. Knoespel, Department of Literature, Communication, and Culture, Georgia Institute of Technology, Atlanta, GA 30332-0165. TEL 617-437-2512. adv.; bk.rev.; circ. 560. (tabloid format; back issues avail.)
   Description: Surveys the relationship between literature and science and the historical, philosophical, and broader cultural implications of that relationship.

800 400   US   ISSN 0078-7469
P1.A1
PACIFIC COAST PHILOLOGY. (Text mainly in English; occasionally in French and German) 1966. a. $6. Philological Association of the Pacific Coast, c/o Cyndia Clegg, Dept. of Humanities, Pepperdine University, Malibu, CA 90263-4275. circ. 1,300.
—BLDSC shelfmark: 6329.010000.

800   II
PAHAL. (Text in Hindi) 1973. q. Rs.10($5) 763 Agrawal Colony, Jabalpur, India.
   Description: Includes poems, essays and short stories.

810   US   ISSN 0090-5674
PS3531.082
PAIDEUMA; a journal devoted to Ezra Pound scholarship. 1972. 3/yr. $18 to individuals; institutions $35. National Poetry Foundation, 302 Neville Hall, University of Maine, Orono, ME 04469. TEL 207-581-3814. Ed. C.F. Terrell. adv.; bk.rev.; bibl.; circ. 1,000. **Indexed:** Abstr.Engl.Stud., Amer.Hum.Ind., Arts & Hum.Cit.Ind., Curr.Cont., Ind.Bk.Rev.Hum., M.L.A.
—BLDSC shelfmark: 6333.781000.

800   US   ISSN 0094-1964
PN6099.6
PAINTBRUSH; a journal of poetry, translations and letters. 1974. s-a. $9 to individuals; institutions $12. Northeast Missouri State University, Language and Literature Division, Kirksville, MO 63501. TEL 816-785-4185. FAX 816-785-4181. Ed. Benjamin Bennani. adv.; bk.rev.; circ. 500. (back issues avail.; reprint service avail. from ISI) **Indexed:** Arts & Hum.Cit.Ind., Ind.Amer.Per.Verse, M.L.A.

PAINTED BRIDE QUARTERLY. see LITERATURE — Poetry

891.92   LE   ISSN 0030-9613
PAKIN.* (Text in Armenian) 1962. m. Dr. Artin Kazandjian, Pub., Spears St., Box 4176, Beirut, Lebanon. Ed. Gard Sassouny. bk.rev.; illus.; index; circ. 2,000.

860 972   US   ISSN 0277-1535
PQ7070
LA PALABRA. 1979. a. $20. La Palabra, 1616 E. Westchester Dr., Tempe, AZ 85283. Ed. Justo S. Alarcon. **Indexed:** M.L.A.

700   IT   ISSN 0031-0255
PALAESTRA. (Text in Italian and Latin) 1962. bi-m. Via Tiglio S. Biagio, Maddaloni 81024, Italy. Ed. Gaspare Caliendo. bk.rev.; film rev.; play rev.; bibl.; illus.; index, cum.index; circ. 1,000 (controlled). (tabloid format; also avail. in cards)

800   UK
PALATINATE. 1948. 23/yr. £5.75. University of Durham, Students Union, Dunham Hse., New Ehet, Durham DH1 3AN, England. TEL 091-3743318. FAX 091-3743740. adv.; bk.rev.; circ. 4,500. (also avail. in microform from UMI; reprint service avail. from UMI)
   Formerly: Phalanx.

891.85   PL   ISSN 0031-0514
PG7001
PAMIETNIK LITERACKI. (Contents page in English, Polish and Russian) 1902. q. $80. (Polska Akademia Nauk, Instytut Badan Literackich) Ossolineum, Publishing House of the Polish Academy of Sciences, Rynek 9, Wroclaw, Poland. TELEX 0712771 OSS PL. (Dist. by: Ars Polona-Ruch, Krakowskie Przedmiescie 7, Warsaw, Poland) Ed. B. Zakrzewski. bk.rev.; bibl.; index; circ. 1,250. **Indexed:** Arts & Hum.Cit.Ind., Curr.Cont., M.L.A.
   Description: Devoted to the history and criticism of Polish literature.

810   US   ISSN 0031-059X
PAN AMERICAN REVIEW.* (Text mainly in English, occasionally in Spanish) 1970. irreg. $6. Wade Press, Box 3427, Edinburg, TX 78540-3427. Ed. Seth Wade.

PAN-EROTIC REVIEW. see ART

810   US   ISSN 0738-8705
PANHANDLER. 1976. s-a. $8 includes Chapbook. University of West Florida, English Department, Pensacola, FL 32514. TEL 904-474-2923. Ed. Michael Yots. adv.; bk.rev.; circ. 900. **Indexed:** Amer.Hum.Ind.
   Description: Presents poetry and fiction nationally.

800 808.81   CS
PANORAMA OF CZECH LITERATURE. German edition: Panorama der Tschechischen Literatur. Spanish edition: Panorama de la Literatura Checa. French edition: Panorama de la Litterature Tcheque. Russian edition: Panorama Cheshskoi Literatury. (Editions in French, German, Russian and Spanish) 1980. biennial. free. (Union of Czech Writers) Panorama, Halkova 1, 120 72 Prague 2, Czechoslovakia. (Co-sponsors: Czech Literary Fund, DILIA Theatrical and Literary Agency) Ed. Ivo Kral. circ. 3,000.

808   UK   ISSN 0951-4546
PANURGE. 1984. s-a. $22. 15 Westwood Ave., Heaton, Newcastle Upon Tyne NE6 5QT, England. TEL 091-232 7669. Ed. David Almond. adv.; bk.rev.; illus.; circ. 1,000. (back issues avail.)
   Description: Short fiction by new and up-and-coming writers.

860   CR   ISSN 0048-2854
PAPEL IMPRESO. 1971. m. free. Ministerio de Cultura, Juventud y Deportes, Departamento de Publicaciones, Apdo. 10227, San Jose, Costa Rica. Ed. Victor Julio Peralta. bibl.; illus.

LITERATURE 2947

800 US
PAPER BAG. 1988. q. $10 (foreign $15). Paper Bag Press, Box 268805, Chicago, IL 60626-8805. TEL 312-285-7972. Ed. Michael H. Brownstein. circ. 500. (back issues avail.)
Description: Publishes poetry and short short stories.

PAPERBACK INFERNO. see *LITERATURE — Science Fiction, Fantasy, Horror*

808.838 US
PAPERBACK PREVIEWS. 1966. m. $15 (foreign $30). Box 6781, Albuquerque, NM 87197. TEL 505-345-5925. Ed. Gypsy Kemp. bk.rev. (tabloid format)

809 028.5 AT ISSN 1034-9243
PAPERS: EXPLORATIONS INTO CHILDREN'S LITERATURE. 3/yr. Aus.$35 (New Zealand Aus.$41.50; elsewhere Aus.$48.50). Magpies Magazine, 10 Armagh St., Victoria Park, W.A. 6100, Australia. TEL 09-361-8288. FAX 09-361-8295.
Description: Contains critical essays - comparative, evaluative and historical - on children's literature.

808 US ISSN 0736-9123
AS30
PAPERS IN COMPARATIVE STUDIES. 1981. irreg. $10. Ohio State University, Division of Comparative Studies in the Humanities, 306 Dulles Hall, 230 W. 17th Ave., Columbus, OH 43210-1311. TEL 614-292-2559. Eds. Richard Bjornson, Marilyn R. Waldman. circ. 200. (back issues avail.)

400 800 US ISSN 0031-1294
PR1
PAPERS ON LANGUAGE AND LITERATURE; a quarterly journal. 1965. q. $12 to individuals; institutions $24 (foreign $26). Southern Illinois University, Edwardsville, Edwardsville, IL 62026-1434. TEL 618-692-2119. FAX 618-692-3509. Ed. Dickie Spurgeon. adv.; bk.rev.; abstr.; index. cum.index; circ. 850. (also avail. in microform from UMI; reprint service avail. from UMI) **Indexed:** Abstr.Engl.Stud., Amer.Bibl.Slavic & E.Eur.Stud., Arts & Hum.Cit.Ind., Curr.Cont., Hum.Ind., Ind.Bk.Rev.Hum., Lang.& Lang.Behav.Abstr., M.L.A., Mid.East: Abstr.& Ind.
—BLDSC shelfmark: 6396.950000.
Description: Papers on literary history, analysis, stylistics and evaluation.

800 NE ISSN 0169-9652
PAPYROLOGICA LUGDUNO-BATAVA. 1941. irreg., vol.25, 1991. price varies. E.J. Brill, P.O. Box 9000, 2300 PA Leiden, Netherlands. TEL 071-312624. FAX 071-317532. TELEX 39296 BRILL NL. (In N. America: E.J. Brill, 24 Hudson St., Kinderhook, NY 12106. TEL 800-962-4406) Ed.Bd.
Description: Explores international papyrus studies.

808 US ISSN 1055-761X
▼**THE PARADOXIST MOVEMENT.** (Text and summaries in English, French, Rumanian) 1991. a. $6.99 (typically set in Sep.). (Paradoxist Association) Xiquan Publishing House, Box 42561, Phoenix, AZ 85080. Ed. Florentin Smarandache. adv.
Description: Covers avant-garde literature and promotes the Paradoxist literary movement originating in Rumania in 1980.

800 700 IT ISSN 0031-1650
PN5
PARAGONE; rivista mensile di arte figurativa e letteratura. 1950. m. L.300000. Casa Editrice G. C. Sansoni Editore Nuova S.p.A., Via Benedetto Varchi 47, 50132 Florence, Italy. Eds. Cesare Garboli, Mina Gregori. illus.; index. **Indexed:** Artbibl., Arts & Hum.Cit.Ind., Avery Ind.Archit.Per., Can.Rev.Comp.Lit., Curr.Cont., M.L.A., RILA.

800 CN
PARAGRAPH. 1979. q. Can.$14 to individuals; institutions Can.$20 (typically set in Jan.). The Mercury Press, 137 Birmingham St., Stratford, Ont. N5A 2T1, Canada. Ed. Beverly Daurio. adv.; bk.rev.; index; circ. 2,000. (also avail. in microform from MML; back issues avail.) **Indexed:** Can.Lit.Ind., Can.Per.Ind., CMI, Ind.Amer.Per.Verse.
Former titles: Cross-Canada Writers' Magazine & Cross-Canada Writers' Quarterly (ISSN 0227-2652); New Writers' News.

800 UK ISSN 0264-8334
PN80
PARAGRAPH. 1983. 3/yr. £34($66) (Modern Critical Theory Group) Oxford University Press, Oxford Journals, Pinkhill House, Southfield Road, Eynsham, Oxford OX8 1JJ, England. TEL 0865-882283. FAX 0865-882890. TELEX 837330 OXPRESS G. (U.S. subscr. to: 200 Madison Ave., New York, NY 10016) Ed.Bd. adv.; bk.rev.; circ. 500.
—BLDSC shelfmark: 6404.820000.
Description: Explores critical theory and its application to literature and the arts.

810 US ISSN 0891-7248
PARAGRAPH. 1985. 3/yr. $8. Oat City Press, Box 326, Tuscaloosa, AL 35401. TEL 205-759-2994. Eds. Walker Rumble, Karen Donovan. adv.; circ. 500.
Description: Publishes paragraphs of 200 words or less on a variety of topics, and favors both innovation and brief bursts of "ordered sensibility."

800 FR ISSN 0078-9429
PARALOGUE. 1965. irreg., no.5, 1972. Lettres Modernes, 73, rue de Cardinal Lemoine, 75005 Paris, France. TEL 022-466666. FAX 022-472391. (Dist. outside France by: Librairie Droz S.A., 11, rue Massot, CH-1211 Geneva 12, Switzerland)
Description: Covers classical literature of France. From the "Editions 'Lettres Modernes'".

300 AT ISSN 0313-6221
CB351
PARERGON. 1971. biennial. Aus.$25. Australian and New Zealand Association for Medieval and Renaissance Studies, University of Sydney, Department of English, Sydney, N.S.W. 2006, Australia. FAX 02-692-2434. TELEX AA26169 UNISYD. Ed. D. Speed. bk.rev.; circ. 300. **Indexed:** Arts & Hum.Cit.Ind., Aus.P.A.I.S., Curr.Cont., M.L.A.
—BLDSC shelfmark: 6406.298000.
Description: Presents scholarly papers on all aspects of Medieval and Renaissance culture.
Refereed Serial

800 US ISSN 0031-2037
AP4
PARIS REVIEW. 1953. q. $25. Paris Review, Inc., 541 E. 72nd St., New York, NY 10021. TEL 212-861-0016. FAX 212-861-0282. (Subscr. to: 45-39 171st Pl., Flushing, NY 11358) Ed. George A. Plimpton. adv.; illus.; cum.index; circ. 8,000. (also avail. in microform from MIM,UMI; back issues avail.; reprint service avail. from UMI,ISI) **Indexed:** A.I.P.P., Abstr.Engl.Stud., Acad.Ind., Arts & Hum.Cit.Ind., Curr.Cont., Hum.Ind., Ind.Amer.Per.Verse, Mag.Ind., Soc.Sci.Ind.
—BLDSC shelfmark: 6406.605700.

840 FR ISSN 0181-5210
PARIS VOICES. 1978. q. 36 F.($9) c/o Shakespeare & Co., 37 rue de la Bucherie, 75005 Paris, France. Ed. Ken Timmerman.

820 UK ISSN 0031-210X
PARK.* 1968. q. 25s.($5) Ferry Press, 177 Green Lane, London S.E.9, England. Ed. Andrew Crozier.

PARKH. see *LINGUISTICS*

800 440 375.4 FR ISSN 1151-941X
PARLANGHE. s-a. 350 F. Geste Editions, Maison des Ruralies, B.P. 1, 79230 Vouille, France. TEL 49-75-67-71. Ed. Michel Gautier.
Description: Studies dialects of the Poitou area.

800 FI ISSN 0031-2320
PN9
PARNASSO. 1951. 8/yr. Fmk.249. (Finnish Cultural Foundation) Yhtyneet Kuvalehdet Oy, Maistraatinportti 1, 00240 Helsinki, Finland. TEL 0-15661. FAX 0-1566505. TELEX 121364. Ed. Jarkko Laine. adv.; bk.rev.; film rev.; play rev.; charts; index; circ. 5,289. **Indexed:** M.L.A.

801 AF
PASHTO ACADEMY. MONTHLY JOURNAL. (Text in Pashto) no.9, 1976. m. Pashto Academy, 26th Saratan Wat, Kabul, Afghanistan.

PASHTU QUARTERLY. see *LINGUISTICS*

809 DK ISSN 0901-8883
PASSAGE. 1980. 2/yr. DKK 210. Aarhus Universitet, Institut for Litteraturhistorie, B 328, 8000 Aarhus C, Denmark. bk.rev.; illus.
Formerly: Aarhus Universitet. Institut for Litteraturhistorie. Skrifter (ISSN 0107-8631)

830 701.18 GW ISSN 0933-7253
NX550.M36
PASSAGEN; Mannheimer Zeitschrift fuer Literatur und Kunst. 1988. q. DM.32($17) Edition Passagen, Leutweinstr. 23, Postfach, 6800 Mannheim 81, Germany. TEL 0621-892928. Ed. Helmut Riemenschneider. bk.rev.; circ. 4,000. (back issues avail)

808 US ISSN 0278-0828
PASSAGES NORTH. 1979. s-a. $5 (foreign $8). Bay Arts Writers Guild, c/o Kalamazoo College, 1200 Academy St., Kalamazoo, MI 49007-3291. TEL 616-383-5700. FAX 616-383-5688. Ed. Ben Mitchell. adv.; circ. 2,600. (tabloid format; back issues avail.) **Indexed:** Amer.Hum.Ind., Ind.Amer.Per.Verse.
Description: Contains poetry, short fiction, work in translation, essays, criticism, reviews, photography and graphic art from established and emerging writers and artists.

830 GW ISSN 0724-0708
PASSAUER PEGASUS; Zeitschrift fuer Literatur. 1983. s-a. DM.20. c/o Karl Krieg, Ed., Woerthstr. 8, 8390 Passau, Germany. TEL 0851-56189. adv.; bk.rev.; circ. 600.
Description: New literature in German: poems, short stories, essays.

809 UK ISSN 0264-8342
PR5136
PATER NEWSLETTER. 1977. s-a. £3($6) Centre for Extra-Mural Studies, Birkbeck College, 26 Russell Square, London WC1B 5DQ, England. (U.S. addr.: University of West Virginia, Morgantown, WV) Eds. Hayden Ward, Laurel Brake. bk.rev.; circ. 100.
Description: Contains news, work in progress, articles, reviews, dissertations, and current annotated book and periodical bibliographies on Pater and related topics.

891.4 II ISSN 0031-3122
PATRANU; world's first mini magazine. (Text in Bengali) 1970. m. Rs.3.40($0.50) K. Chatterjee, Pub., 122-A Ballygunge Gardens, Calcutta 19, India. Ed. A. Chatterji. adv.; bk.rev.; film rev.; play rev.; illus.; circ. 5,000. (tabloid format)

810 US
PAX; a journal for peace through culture. 1983. 2/yr. $4 per no. 217 Pershing, San Antonio, TX 78209. Ed. Bryce Milligan. adv.; circ. 600.

808 US
PELLENNORATH. 1980. irreg., no.5, 1982. $4 for five issues. Pandemonium Press, 1273 Crest Dr., Encinitas, CA 92024. Ed. R.C. Walker. (back issues avail.)

808 US ISSN 0031-4242
THE PEN WOMAN. 1922. 6/yr. $7. National League of American Pen Women, Inc., Pen Arts Bldg., 1300 17th St., N.W., Washington, DC 20036. TEL 202-785-1997. adv.; bk.rev.; illus.; circ. 5,000. (back issues avail.)
Description: Presents news about members, and articles relating to art, letters, and music. Includes members' poetry, music composition, and artwork, as well as personality profiles.

800 US
PENDRAGON; a literary review. 2/yr. Valdosta State College, English Department, Valdosta, GA 31698. TEL 912-333-5946. Ed. Hetaher Tapley. circ. 450.

PENNSYLVANIA PORTFOLIO; a literary review about Pennsylvania authors, books & libraries. see *BIOGRAPHY*

800 US ISSN 8756-5668
PENNSYLVANIA REVIEW. 1985. s-a. $10. University of Pittsburgh, Department of English, 526 C.L., Pittsburgh, PA 15260. TEL 412-624-0026. Ed. Lori Jakiela. adv.; bk.rev.; circ. 750. (back issues avail.)
Description: Presents contemporary prose and poetry.

PENSIERO ED ARTE. see *LITERARY AND POLITICAL REVIEWS*

800 UK
PEOPLE LIKE THAT. 1970. irreg. Central London Adult Education Institute, 6 Bolt Court, Fleet St., London E.C.4, England. Ed. Bernard Miller. illus.

LITERATURE

800 US ISSN 0149-0516
PN6010.5
PEQUOD; a journal of contemporary literature and literary criticism. 1966-1984; resumed 1985. 2/yr. $13.50 to individuals; institutions $21.00. 817 West End Ave., New York, NY 10025. TEL 212-998-8828. Ed. Mark Rudman. adv.; circ. 550. Indexed: A.I.P.P., Amer.Bibl.Slavic & E.Eur.Stud., M.L.A.

800 US ISSN 0740-7890
PERMAFROST; a literary journal. 1977. 2/yr. $7. University of Alaska, Fairbanks, English Department, Fairbanks, AK 99775-0640. TEL 907-474-7193. circ. 500. Indexed: A.I.P.P.

PERPJEKJA E JONE/OUR EFFORT. see *ART*

800 PK
PERSPECTIVE. (Text in English) vol.6, 1972. m. Rs.18($6) Pakistan Publications, Box 183, Shahrah Iraq, Karachi 1, Pakistan. Ed. M. R. Siddiqui. adv.; bk.rev.

809 CN ISSN 0821-0314
PR4036
PERSUASIONS. 1979. a. membership. Jane Austen Society of North America, 4169 Lions Ave. N., Vancouver, B.C. V7R 3S2, Canada. TEL 604-988-0479. (Subscr. to: 221 Nevin St., Lancaster, PA 17603) Ed. Gene Koppel. circ. 2,500. (back issues avail.)
Description: Focuses on Jane Austen, her family, her art and her times.

800 CN ISSN 0835-9628
PERSUASIONS, OCCASIONAL PAPERS. 1979. a. $5 per no. Jane Austen Society of North America, 4169 Lions Ave., North Vancouver, B.C. V7R 3S2, Canada. TEL 604-988-0479. (Subscr. to: 221 Nevin St., Lancaster, PA 17603) Ed. Gene Koppel. illus.; circ. 150.

890 IS
PESEFAS. 1988. q. Eked, P.O. Box 11138, Tel Aviv, Israel. TEL 03-283648. circ. 2,000.

800 HU ISSN 0524-8906
PH3002
PETOFI IRODALMI MUZEUM EVKONYVE/YEARBOOK OF THE LITERARY MUSEUM. 1958. biennial. Muzsak, Kartacs u. 24-26, 1139 Budapest 13, Hungary. Ed. Ferenc Botka.

800 NQ ISSN 0031-6652
NX7
EL PEZ Y LA SERPIENTE; revista de cultura. 1961. s-a. C.$41($6) Pablo A. Cuadra, Ed. & Pub., Apdo Postal 192, Managua, Nicaragua. FAX 5052-43569. TELEX 375-2051. bk.rev.; illus.; circ. 1,000.
Description: Includes poetry, literary criticism, history, anthropology, and art from the most prominent intellectuals in Central America.

PHI SIGMA IOTA FORUM. see *LINGUISTICS*

800 GW
PHILOLOGISCHE STUDIEN UND QUELLEN. 1960. irreg. Erich Schmidt Verlag GmbH & Co. (Berlin), Genthiner Str. 30 G, 1000 Berlin 30, Germany. (Subscr. addr.: Zweigniederlassung Bielefeld, Viktoriastr. 44a, 4800 Bielefeld 1, Germany) Eds. Hugo Steger, Hartmut Steinecke.

800 NE ISSN 0166-5030
PHILOSOPHIA PATRUM; interpretations of patristic texts. 1971. irreg., vol.8, 1986. price varies. E.J. Brill, P.O. Box 9000, 2300 PA Leiden, Netherlands. TEL 071-312624. FAX 071-317532. TELEX 39296 BRILL NL. (In N. America: E.J. Brill, 24 Hudson St., Kinderhook, NY 12106. TEL 800-962-4406) Eds. J.H. Waszink, J.C.M. van Winden.

PHILOSOPHY AND LITERATURE. see *PHILOSOPHY*

800 US ISSN 0270-868X
PHOEBE. 1972. s-a. $8. George Mason University, 4400 University Drive, Fairfax, VA 22030. TEL 703-993-2915. Ed. Rex Batson. adv.; bk.rev.; illus.; circ. 2,500.
Description: Features fiction, poetry, and photographs.

820 UK
PHOENIX BROADSHEET. 1972. irreg. free. 78 Cambridge St., Leicester LE3 0JP, England. TEL 547419. Ed. Toni Savage.

800 US
PHOENIX LITERATURE. 1929. irreg., latest 1985. price varies. University of Chicago Press, 5801 S. Ellis Ave., Chicago, IL 60637. TEL 312-702-7899. (Subscr. to: 11030 Langley Ave., Chicago, IL 60628)
Refereed Serial

PICK OF THE YEAR; a selection of 50 recommended books, chosen for families, tried and tested by children, and voted the best of (year). see *CHILDREN AND YOUTH — For*

PIE/PIADA; rassegna d'illustrazione Romangnola. see *FOLKLORE*

808 AG
PIE DE PAGINA. 1982. q. Av. Belgrano 2358, 1069 Buenos Aires, Argentina. Eds. Alberto Castro, Gabriela Borgna.

PIEDMONT LITERARY REVIEW. see *LITERATURE — Poetry*

800 US
PIEGAN STORYTELLER. 1976. q. $10 in N.Amer.; elsewhere $15. James Willard Schultz Society, 135 Wildwood Dr., New Bern, NC 28562-9530. Ed. David C. Andrews. adv.; bk.rev.; bibl.; illus.; circ. 300.

800 US ISSN 0362-5214
PS615
PIG IRON; the annual thematic anthology of contemporary literature. 1975. a. $9 to individuals; institutions $10. Pig Iron Press, Box 237, Youngstown, OH 44501. TEL 216-783-1269. Ed. Jim Villani. bibl.; illus.; circ. 1,000. (also avail. in microfilm from UMI; back issues avail.) **Indexed:** Ind.Amer.Per.Verse.
Description: Concentrates on specific themes selected for their literary and popular culture appeal.

800 US ISSN 0192-8716
PIKESTAFF FORUM. 1978. a. $10 for 6 nos. Pikestaff Publications, Inc., Box 127, Normal, IL 61761. TEL 309-452-4831. Eds. Robert D. Sutherland, James R Scrimgeour. bk.rev.; index; circ. 1,000. (tabloid format; back issues avail.) **Indexed:** Ind.Amer.Per.Verse.
Description: Presents poetry, fiction, commentary and profiles of other editors and magazines. Includes a young writers feature for authors aged 7-17.

PINTER REVIEW: ANNUAL ESSAYS. see *THEATER*

891.85 PL ISSN 0079-211X
PISARZE SLASCY 19 I 20 WIEKU. 1965. irreg. price varies. Slaski Instytut Naukowy, Ul. Graniczna 32, 40-956 Katowice, Poland. (Dist. by: Ars Polona-Ruch, Krakowskie Przedmiescie 7, Warsaw, Poland)

800 700 778.5 CI
PITANJA; mjesecnik: drustvo, znanost, kultura. 1969. m. 200 din.($12.50) Savez Socijalisticke Omladine Hrvatske, Zagreb, Centar Drustvenih Djelatnosti, Opaticka 10, 41001 Zagreb, Croatia. Ed. Neven Mates. bk.rev.; film rev.; bibl.; illus.

808.8 US
▼**PITTSBURGH QUARTERLY**. 1991. q. $12. 36 Haberman Ave., Pittsburgh, PA 15211-2144. Ed. Frank Correnti. adv.

806 AT ISSN 0311-0753
PLAIN TURKEY. 1973. irreg. Aus.$6. Mt. Isa Writers Workshop, 97 Trainor St., Mt. Isa, Qld. 4825, Australia. Ed. R. Algie.

890 FR ISSN 0750-9189
PLANEDENN. 1979. q. 150 F.($24) Editions Skol Vreizh, 20 rue de Kerscoff, 29600 Morlaix, France. TEL 98-62-17-20.
Description: Contains studies, reviews of theater pieces, news and interviews.

820 UK ISSN 0048-4288
PLANET; the Welsh internationalist. 1970. bi-m. £11($30) (foreign £12). P.O. Box 44, Aberystwyth, Dyfed, Wales. TEL 0970-611255. FAX 0970-623311. Eds. John Barnie, Gwen Davies. bk.rev.; illus.; index; circ. 1,400. **Indexed:** Abstr.Engl.Stud.

800 US
PLANET DRUM BUNDLES. 1973. irreg. $15. Planet Drum Foundation, Box 31251, San Francisco, CA 94131. TEL 415-285-6556. circ. 3,000.
Formerly: Planet Drum.

808 200 US
PLANET WALK. 1982. q. $20. Box 701, Inverness, CA 94937. Ed. John Francis. bk.rev.; circ. 300.
Formerly: Planet Walker.
Description: Journal of pilgrimage along with news of other pilgrims.

820 920 UK
PLANTAGENET PRODUCTIONS; libraries of spoken word recordings, of stagescripts, and of family papers. 1974. irreg. Westridge (Open Centre), Highclere, Nr. Newbury, Royal Berkshire RG15 9PJ, England. TEL 0635-253322. Ed. Dorothy Rose Gribble.
Former titles: Milton Traditions & Gribble Annals.
Description: Recordings of poetry, philosophy, narrative (existing titles); stagescripts of short plays, stories suitable for recital; family papers and history.

830 GW ISSN 0931-3931
PLATTDUETSCH LAND UN WATERKANT. (Text in Low-German (Plattdeutsch)) 1916. s-a. DM.10 (free to members). Quickborn Vereinigung fuer Niederdeutsche Sprache und Literatur e.V., Alexanderstr. 16, 2000 Hamburg 1, Germany. TEL 040-240809. Ed. Gerd Spiekermann. adv.; bk.rev.; circ. 1,000. (back issues avail.)
Description: Short stories, poems, plays and essays in Low-German dialect.

PLAYS & PLAYWRIGHTS. see *THEATER*

860 US
PLAZA. (Text in Spanish) 1977. s-a. $4 to individuals; institutions $8. Plaza Editores, Harvard University, 201 Boylston Hall, Cambridge, MA 02138. Ed.Bd. circ. 350. (back issues avail.) **Indexed:** M.L.A.

890 JA
PLEIADES/SUBARU. (Text in Japanese) 1970. bi-m. 630 Yen. Shueisha Inc., 5-10, 2-chome, Hitotsubashi, Chiyoda-ku, Tokyo 101-50, Japan. TEL 03-3230-6104. Ed. Nobuhiro Kano. circ. 10,000.

800 IT
PLEIADI. irreg.. latest no.45. price varies. Angelo Longo Editore, Via Paolo Costa 33, P.O. Box 431, 48100 Ravenna, Italy. TEL 0544-217026. Ed. Franco Mollia. circ. 2,500.

840 FR
PLEIN CHANT; cahiers trimestriels de litterature. 1971. q. 180 F. Editions Plein Chant, Bassac, 16120 Chateauneuf-sur-Charente, France. Ed. Edmond Thomas. adv.; bk.rev.; bibl.; illus.; index; circ. 1,000 (controlled). (back issues avail.)

840 700 BE ISSN 0295-1630
PLEINE MARGE; cahiers de litterature, d'arts plastiques et de critique. (Text in French) vol.10, 1989. 2/yr. 1200 Fr. Editions Peeters s.p.r.l., Bondgenotenlaan 153, B-3000 Leuven, Belgium. TEL 016-235170. FAX 016-228500. Ed. J. Chenieux. adv. (back issues avail.)

810 US ISSN 0048-4474
NX1
PLOUGHSHARES; a journal of new writing. 1971. 3/yr. $19 to individuals; institutions $22 (foreign $27). Ploughshares, Inc., Emerson College, 100 Beacon St., Boston, MA 02116. TEL 617-578-8753. (Co-sponsors: Massachusetts Council on the Arts; National Endowment for the Arts; Emerson College) Ed.Bd. adv.; bk.rev.; illus.; index, cum.index: vols.1-6; circ. 3,800. (also avail. in microfilm from UMI; back issues avail.; reprint service avail. from UMI) **Indexed:** Amer.Hum.Ind., Arts & Hum.Cit.Ind., Bk.Rev.Ind., Curr.Cont., GeoRef., Ind.Amer.Per.Verse, M.L.A.
Description: Introduces new American writing, guest-edited by major writers.

PLUG; maandelijks informatieblad van het Cultureel Jongeren Paspoort. see *THEATER*

860   MX   ISSN 0185-4925
NX7
PLURAL; critica-arte-literatura. (Text in Spanish) 1971. m. Mex.$30($1.80) Compania Editorial Excelsior S. C. L., Reforma 18, 1er piso, Delegacion Cuauhtemoc, 06600 Mexico 1, DF, Mexico. Dir. Jaime Labastida. adv.; bk.rev.; illus.; circ. 16,000. (tabloid format) Indexed: Hisp.Amer.Per.Ind., M.L.A.
—BLDSC shelfmark: 6541.012000.

800   FR   ISSN 0765-1112
PC2002
PLURIAL; revue de litterature francophone, la femme et la famille traditionnelle. 1988. a. 80 F. Presses Universitaires de Rennes II, 6, Av. Gaston-Berger, 35043 Rennes Cedex, France. TEL 99-33-52-52.

THE POE MESSENGER. see LITERATURE — Poetry

POESIE UND WISSENSCHAFT. SAMMLUNG. see LITERATURE — Poetry

POETES ET PROSATEURS DU PORTUGAL. see LITERATURE — Poetry

POETI E PROSATORI TEDESCHI. see LITERATURE — Poetry

POETIC DRAMA AND POETIC THEORY. see LITERATURE — Poetry

800 410   GW   ISSN 0303-4178
P3
POETICA; Zeitschrift fuer Sprach- und Literaturwissenschaft. 1967. q. fl.160. Wilhelm Fink Verlag, Ohmstr. 5, 8000 Munich 40, Germany. TEL 089-348017. FAX 089-341378. Ed.Bd. adv.; bk.rev.; bibl.; index; circ. 1,000. (back issues avail.) Indexed: Can.Rev.Comp.Lit, Curr.Cont., Ind.Bk.Rev.Hum., M.L.A.
—BLDSC shelfmark: 6541.740000.
Description: Contains essays and discussions on literary theory and history, classical and modern philology. Includes book reviews and bibliography.

800   NE   ISSN 0304-422X
PN45
POETICS; journal for empirical research on literature, the media and the arts. (Text in Dutch, English and French) 1972. 6/yr. fl.386 (effective 1992). North-Holland (Subsidiary of: Elsevier Science Publishers B.V.), P.O. Box 211, 1000 AE Amsterdam, Netherlands. TEL 020-5803911. FAX 020-5803598. TELEX 18582 ESPA NL. (Subscr. in U.S. and Canada to: Elsevier Science Publishing Co., Inc., Box 882, Madison Sq. Sta., New York, NY 10159. TEL 212-989-5800) Ed. C.J. van Rees. bk.rev. (also avail. in microform from RPI; back issues avail.; reprint service avail. from SWZ) Indexed: Abstr.Engl.Stud., Arts & Hum.Cit.Ind., Curr.Cont., Ind.Bk.Rev.Hum.
—BLDSC shelfmark: 6541.744000.
Description: Interdisciplinary journal covering theoretical and empirical research in literature, the media and the arts.
Refereed Serial

POETICS JOURNAL. see LITERARY AND POLITICAL REVIEWS

POETRY IRELAND REVIEW. see LITERATURE — Poetry

POETS & WRITERS MAGAZINE. see LITERATURE — Poetry

800 700   US
POETS, PAINTERS, COMPOSERS. 1984. a. $50. Poets, Painters, Composers, 10254 35th Ave., S.W., Seattle, WA 98146. TEL 206-937-8155. Ed. Joseph Keppler. bk.rev.; illus.; circ. 300. (back issues avail.)
Description: Multi-media art and literary publication.

810   US
POISON PEN WRITERS NEWS. 1983. 3/yr. $12. Baker Street Publications, Box 994, Metairie, LA 70004. TEL 504-734-8414. Ed. Sharida Rizzuto. circ. 9,000.
Description: Covers the writers market and writing.

POLICORDO; revista quadrimestale di cultura, letteratura, arte. see HUMANITIES: COMPREHENSIVE WORKS

810 320   US
POLIT; a journal of literature and politics. 1977. s-a. $6. Southeastern Massachusetts University, Department of English, North Dartmouth, MA 02747. TEL 617-999-8274. (Co-sponsor: Department of English, University of Alabama, Birmingham) Eds. Robert Waxler, Carl Schinasi.

891   PL   ISSN 0551-3707
POLONISTYKA. 1948. 10/yr. $17.50. (Ministerstwo Edukacji Narodowej) Wydawnictwa Szkolne i Pedagogiczne, Pl. Dabrowskiego 8, 00-950 Warsaw, Poland. TEL 48 22 26-89-71. (Dist. by: Ars Polona-Ruch, Krakowskie Przedmiescie 7, Warsaw, Poland) circ. 15,830.
Description: Presents contemporary literary and linguistic research, with articles on literary studies and on culture, the methodology of teaching Polish, and research on Polish writers' works and different literary epochs.

POLSKA AKADEMIA NAUK. INSTYTUT SLAWISTIKI. PRACE SLAWISTYCZNE. see LINGUISTICS

809   PL   ISSN 0554-579X
POLSKA AKADEMIA NAUK. ODDZIAL W KRAKOWIE. KOMISJA HISTORYCZNOLITERACKA. PRACE. (Text in English, French and Polish) 1961. irreg., no.46, 1987. price varies. Ossolineum, Publishing House of the Polish Academy of Sciences, Rynek 9, Wroclaw, Poland. TELEX 0712771 OSS PL. (Dist. by: Ars Polona-Ruch, Krakowskie Przedmiescie 7, Warsaw, Poland) Ed. Jan Nowakowski.
Description: Presents the history of Polish and other European literature.

POLSKA AKADEMIA NAUK. ODDZIAL W KRAKOWIE. KOMISJA HISTORYCZNOLITERACKA. ROCZNIK. see HISTORY

891.8   PL   ISSN 0079-3434
POLSKA AKADEMIA NAUK. ODDZIAL W KRAKOWIE. KOMISJA SLOWIANOZNAWSTWA. PRACE. (Text in Polish; summaries in English and Russian) 1962. irreg., no.46, 1987. price varies. Ossolineum, Publishing House of the Polish Academy of Sciences, Rynek 9, 50-106 Wroclaw, Poland. TELEX 0712771 OSS PL. (Dist. by: Ars Polona-Ruch, Krakowskie Przedmiescie 7, Warsaw, Poland) Ed. Ryszard Luzny.
Description: Covers works on Slavonic linguistics and literature.

POLYLINGUA; a college journal of foreign languages. see LINGUISTICS

891.7   BW   ISSN 0130-8068
POLYMYA. (Text in Byelorussian) 1922. m. 12 Rub. (Sayuz Pismennikow Belarusskai S.S.R. - Soyuz Pisatelei Belorusskoi S.S.R.) Izdatel'stvo Polymya, Ul. Zakharova 19, Minsk, Byelarus. Ed. S.I. Zakonnikov. bk.rev.; play rev.; bibl.; index; circ. 9,500.

POMPEBLEDEN; tydskrift foar Fryske Studzje. see LINGUISTICS

839   NE
POPULAIRE LITERATUUR; een reeks teksten uit de late Middeleeuwen. 1979. irreg. price varies. Dick Coutinho B.V., P.O. Box 10, 1399 ZG Muiderberg, Netherlands. TEL 02942-1888.

839   NE
POPULAR ESSAYS FROM THE LATE REPUBLIC. 1983. irreg. price varies. Dick Coutinho B.V., P.O. Box 10, 1399 ZG Muiderberg, Netherlands. TEL 02942-1888.

808   US   ISSN 8756-5978
PORTABLE LOWER EAST SIDE. 1984. 2/yr. $12 to individuals; institutions $20. P L E S, Box 30323, New York, NY 10011-0103. Ed. Arthur Nersesian. adv.; bk.rev.; circ. 2,000. (back issues avail.)
—BLDSC shelfmark: 6539.445000.
Description: Fiction, poetry, photography and non-fiction with a realistic and documentary approach. Each issue focuses on a specific ethnicity or aspect of life in New York City.

800 850   IT
PORTICO. (In 2 parts: Letteratura Italiana; Letteratura Straniera) irreg., latest LI no.59, LS no.134. price varies. Angelo Longo Editore, Via Paolo Costa 33, P.O. Box 431, 48100 Ravenna, Italy. TEL 0544-217026. Ed. Antonio Piromalli. circ. 3,000.

LITERATURE 2949

800   US
PORTLAND REVIEW MAGAZINE. 1955. 2/yr. $10. Portland State University, Box 751, Portland, OR 97207. TEL 503-725-4533. FAX 503-725-4882. Ed. J.E. Sellon. adv.; bk.rev.; circ. 2,000. Indexed: Ind.Amer.Per.Verse.
Former titles: International Portland Review; Portland Review (ISSN 0360-3091)
Description: Features poetry, fiction, experimental writing, artwork and photography.

869   UK   ISSN 0267-5315
DP532
PORTUGUESE STUDIES. (Text mainly in English, occasionally in Portuguese) 1985. a. $52. Modern Humanities Research Association, Kings College, Strand, London WC2R 2LS, England.
—BLDSC shelfmark: 6557.300000.
Description: Devoted to the literature, culture, and history of Portugal, Brazil and the Portuguese-speaking countries in Africa. Includes articles, reviews, literary translation and a survey of research recently completed at universities in the U.K.

POSTCARD ART - POSTCARD FICTION. see ART

800   US
▼POSTMODERN CULTURE; an electronic journal of interdisciplinary criticism. (Not avail. in print) 1990. 3/yr. $15 to individuals on disk or fiche; institutions $30 (free electronically). Box 8105, Raleigh, NC 27695. TEL 919-832-7808. Eds. Eyal Amiran, John Unsworth. (also avail. in microfiche)
●Also available on CD-ROM.
Description: Literary review.

806   US
POSTSCRIPT. 1981. q. membership. Washington Irving Society, 150 White Plains Rd., Tarrytown, NY 10591. circ. 150.

808.838   CN   ISSN 0226-0840
THE POTTERSFIELD PORTFOLIO; new fiction, essays, poetry, plays and artwork in English and French. 1979. s-a. Can.$12 (foreign $15). Wild East Publishing Co-operative Ltd., P.O. Box 1135, Sta. A, Fredericton, N.B. E3B 5C2, Canada. TEL 506-454-5127. Ed.Bd. adv.; bk.rev.; circ. 1,000. (also avail. in microform from MML) Indexed: Amer.Hum.Ind., Amer.Hum.Ind., Can.Lit.Ind., CMI, Ind.Amer.Per.Verse.

800   US   ISSN 1058-7691
POWYS NOTES. 1985. s-a. $12 membership; institutions $15. Powys Society of North America, Dept. of English, Valparaiso University, Valparaiso, IN 46383. (Subscr. to: Constance Harsh, Dept. of English, Colgate University, Hamilton, NY 13346-1398. TEL 315-824-7294) Ed. Richard Maxwell. bk.rev.; circ. 150.
Description: Publishes history and criticism relating to literary members of the Powys family.

820   UK   ISSN 0309-1619
PR6031.O867
POWYS REVIEW. 1977. a. £5. c/o Belinda Humfrey, Ed., Department of English, Saint David's University College, Lampeter, Dyfed SA48 7ED, Wales. TEL 0570-422351. FAX 0570-423423. adv.; bk.rev.; play rev.; bibl.; circ. 1,000. Indexed: Arts & Hum.Cit.Ind., Curr.Cont., M.L.A.
—BLDSC shelfmark: 6579.030000.

891.85   PL   ISSN 0079-4791
PG7001
PRACE POLONISTYCZNE. 1951. a. price varies. (Lodzkie Towarzystwo Naukowe) Ossolineum, Publishing House of the Polish Academy of Sciences, Rynek 9, 50-106 Wroclaw, Poland. TELEX 0712771 OSS PL. (Dist. by: Ars Polona-Ruch, Krakowskie Przedmiescie 7, 00-068 Warsaw, Poland) (Co-sponsor: Polska Akademia Nauk) Ed. Z. Skwarczynski. bk.rev.; circ. 800. (also avail. in microfilm)
—BLDSC shelfmark: 6591.500000.
Description: Polonistic works on prose and poetry of Polish writiers.

891.4   II   ISSN 0032-6550
PRAGATI. (Text in Bengali) 1966. m. Rs.10. Nava Niketan, 39B Dent Mission Rd., Calcutta 700 023, India. Ed. Mrinal Chatterjee. adv.; bk.rev.; film rev.; play rev.; circ. 1,500.

LITERATURE

810   CN   ISSN 0821-1124
PRAIRIE FIRE; a Canadian magazine of new writing. 1978. 4/yr. Can.$24 to individuals; institutions Can.$32. Prairie Fire Press, Inc., 423-100 Arthur St., Winnipeg, Man. R3B 1H3, Canada. TEL 204-943-9066. FAX 204-942-1555. Ed. Andris Taskans. adv.; bk.rev.; circ. 1,200. **Indexed:** Can.Lit.Ind., Can.Lit.Ind., Ind.Amer.Per.Verse, Ind.Amer.Per.Verse.
Incorporates: Writers News Manitoba.
Description: Literary writing and criticism from Canada's prairie provinces.

820   CN   ISSN 0827-2921
PRAIRIE JOURNAL. 1983. s-a. Can.$6 to individuals; institutions Can.$12. Prairie Journal Press, P.O. Box G997, Sta. G, Calgary, Alta. T3A 3G2, Canada. Ed. A. Burke. adv.; bk.rev.; circ. 500. (also avail. in microform from MML) **Indexed:** Can.Lit.Ind.
Description: Contains a mix of poetry, fiction, articles, reviews, drama and essays.

810   US   ISSN 0032-6682
AP2
PRAIRIE SCHOONER. 1927. q. $17 to individuals; institutions $19. University of Nebraska, Lincoln, 201 Andrews Hall, Lincoln, NE 68588-0334. TEL 402-472-3191. FAX 402-472-4636. TELEX 484-240 U NEBR. (Dist. by: Ingram Periodicals, Box 7000, La Vergne, TN 37086-7000) Ed. Hilda Raz. adv.; bk.rev.; circ. 2,700. (also avail. in microfilm from UMI; back issues avail.; reprint service avail. from UMI,KTO) **Indexed:** A.I.P.P., Arts & Hum.Cit.Ind., Bk.Rev.Ind. (1965-), Child.Bk.Rev.Ind. (1965-), Curr.Cont., Hum.Ind., Ind.Bk.Rev.Hum., M.L.A.
—BLDSC shelfmark: 6598.554000.
Description: Contains stories, poems, interviews, imaginative essays, translations, plus reviews of current books of poetry and fiction.

800   II
PRAKALPANA SAHITYA/PRAKALPANA LITERATURE. (Text in Bengali and English) 1977. a. Rs.6. c/o Vattacharja Chandan, Ed., P-40 Nandana Park, Calcutta 700 034, India. TEL 77327. (Dist. in West by: Flatland, Box 2420, Fort Bragg, CA 95437-2420, USA) bk.rev.; circ. 1,000.
Description: Promotes alternative and experimental Sarbangin poetry and literature.

491 891   II
PRAKRIT TEXT SOCIETY. PUBLICATIONS. irreg. price varies. Prakrit Text Society, c/o Lalbhai Dalpatbhai Institute of Indology, Near Gujarat University, P.O. Navarangpura, Ahmedabad 380 009, India.

PRAMPRA. see FOLKLORE

801 700   II   ISSN 0970-2849
PRATIBHA INDIA; journal of Indian art, culture and literature. (Text in English) 1981. q. Rs.65 (foreign $15 or £8). Sneh Bharti - Charitable Trust, B-2, I.P. Staff Flats, Shamnath Marg, Delhi 110 054, India. TEL 292-7815. Eds. Aruna Sitesh, Sitesh Aloke. adv.; bk.rev.; illus.; circ. 1,400.
Description: Promotes the study and creation of modern Indian literature and poetry. Includes translations of stories from various languages (Bengali, Urdu, Tamil, Marathi, as well as others). Features articles on the lives and works of authors and artists.

850   IT
PRATO PAGANO; giornale di nuova letteratura. 3/yr. L.20000. Il Melograno - Edizione ABETE, Via Torburtina, 655, Rome, Italy.

891.1   II   ISSN 0303-2906
PRAYAASA. (Text in English, Hindi) 1975? irreg., latest Mar. 1989. Jawaharlal Nehru University, Literary Club, Cultural Committee, Dean of Students' Office, New Dehli 110 067, India. Eds. Siyaram Sharma (Hindi), Prashant Kumar Misra (English). bibl.; illus.
Description: Provides a forum for students' essays, analyses, translations and poems. Each issue has separate autonomous English and Hindi sections.

809   US   ISSN 0163-4631
PN2
PRECISELY; a critical journal. 1977. 2/yr. $8 for 4 nos. R K Editions, Box 73, Canal St., NY 10013. Eds. Richard Kostelanetz, Stephen Scobie. bk.rev.; circ. 300. (back issues avail.) **Indexed:** M.L.A.
Description: Devoted to extended critical essays on innovative literature of the past three decades.

PREPUBLICATIONS. see LINGUISTICS

800 700   FR   ISSN 0336-321X
PRESENCE DES LETTRES ET DES ARTS.* 1964. q. 120 F. Cercle International de la Pensee et des Arts Francais, Arquian, 58310 Saint Armand en Puisage, France. Ed. A. Pourtier. adv.; bk.rev.; illus.; circ. 3,000.
Formerly: Presence des Lettres des Arts (ISSN 0032-7654)

840   CN   ISSN 0048-5195
PRESENCE FRANCOPHONE. 1970. s-a. $8. (Universite de Sherbrooke, Centre d'Etude des Litteratures d'Expression Francaise) Editions Paulines, 250 Nord Bd. St. Francois, Sherbrooke, Que., Canada. TEL 819-821-7000. Ed. Rodolphe Lacasse. adv.; bk.rev.; illus.; circ. 2,000. **Indexed:** M.L.A., Pt.de Rep. (1985-).

PREVIEW (ANN ARBOR); professional and reference literature review. see LIBRARY AND INFORMATION SCIENCES

891   RU
PRIAMUR'E MOE; literaturno-khudozhestvennyi sbornik. irreg. 1.05 Rub. Khabarovskoe Knizhnoe Izdatel'stvo, Ul. Lenina, 181, Blagoveshchensk, Russia. illus.

PRILOZI ZA KNJIZEVNOST, JEZIK, ISTORIJU I FOLKLOR. see LINGUISTICS

PRIMAVERA (CHICAGO). see WOMEN'S INTERESTS

800   XV   ISSN 0351-1189
PG1900.A1
PRIMERJALNA KNJIZEVNOST. (Text in Slovenian; summaries in English, French, German) 1978. s-a. 300 SLT($20) Slovensko Drustvo za Primerjalno Knjizevnost, Askerceva 12, 61000 Ljubljana, Slovenia. TEL 061-156-068. FAX 061-155-253. Ed. Darko Dolinar. bk.rev.; bibl.; circ. 500. (back issues avail.) **Indexed:** M.L.A.
Description: Covers all aspects of comparative literature for literary scholars and students.

800   UK   ISSN 0269-2619
PRINCESS GRACE IRISH LIBRARY. 1986. irreg. price varies. Colin Smythe Ltd., P.O. Box 6, Gerrards Cross, Buckinghamshire SL9 8XA, England. TEL 0753-886600. FAX 0753-886469. (Distr. in U.S. by: Barnes & Noble Books, 8705 Bollman Place, Savage, MD 20763) circ. 1,500. (reprint service avail. from ISI)
—BLDSC shelfmark: 6612.932300.
Description: Collections of papers given at the Princess Grace Irish Library conferences, or collections of essays commissioned by the Library.

800   UK   ISSN 0950-5121
PRINCESS GRACE IRISH LIBRARY LECTURES. 1986. irreg. Colin Smythe Ltd., P.O. Box 6, Gerrards Cross, Buckinghamshire SL9 8XA, England. TEL 0753-886600. FAX 0753-886469. (Distr. in U.S. by: Dufour Editions, Box 449, Chester Springs, PA 19425) circ. 750. (reprint service avail. from ISI)
—BLDSC shelfmark: 6612.932400.
Description: Texts of individual lectures given at the Princess Grace Irish Library.

800   US   ISSN 0079-5186
PRINCETON ESSAYS IN LITERATURE.. 1964. irreg. price varies. Princeton University Press, 3175 Princeton Pike, Lawrenceville, NJ 08648. TEL 609-896-1344. FAX 609-895-1081. (reprint service avail. from UMI)

PRINCETON LIBRARY OF ASIAN TRANSLATIONS. see ORIENTAL STUDIES

819   CN   ISSN 0032-8790
AP5
PRISM INTERNATIONAL; a journal of contemporary writing. (Text in English) 1959. 4/yr. Can.$16 to individuals; institutions Can.$22. University of British Columbia, Creative Writing Department, E462-1866 Main Mall, Vancouver, B.C. V6T 1Z1, Canada. TEL 604-822-2514. Ed. Roger Cove. bk.rev.; cum.index; circ. 1,100. (also avail. in microform from UMI; reprint service avail. from UMI,KTO; back issues avail.) **Indexed:** Amer.Bibl.Slavic & E.Eur.Stud., Amer.Hum.Ind., Arts & Hum.Cit.Ind., Can.Lit.Ind., Curr.Cont.

820   II
PROBITAS; devoted to literature and culture. (Text in English) Rs.3($2) per no. Aruna Printing Works, Berhampur 760002, India.

PROFESSION. see LINGUISTICS

840   FR   ISSN 0181-0146
PROMETHEE; magazine bimestriel de creation et de recherches de la pensee. 1972. bi-m. 200 F. Promethee, c/o Octave Prour, Ed., B.P. 166-10, 75463 Paris Cedex 10, France. adv.; bk.rev.; circ. 4,000.

PROMISE. see LITERATURE — Poetry

PROOFTEXTS; a journal of Jewish literary history. see RELIGIONS AND THEOLOGY — Judaic

800 100   US   ISSN 0734-3027
PROPHETIC VOICES; an international literary journal. 1983. s-a. $14 to individuals; institutions and foreign $16. Heritage Trails Press, 94 Santa Maria Dr., Novato, CA 94947. FAX 415-897-5679. Ed.Bd. circ. 400. (back issues avail.)
Description: Views the poet as prophet. Concerned with world issues such as the preservation of animals and the environment.

800   UK   ISSN 0144-0357
PR750
PROSE STUDIES; history, theory, criticism. 1978. 3/yr. £24($35) to individuals; institutions £52($80). Frank Cass & Co. Ltd., Gainsborough House, 11 Gainsborough Rd., London E11 1RS, England. TEL 081-530-4226. FAX 081-530-7795. Eds. Ronald J. Corthell, T.H. Corns. adv.; bk.rev. **Indexed:** Ind.Bk.Rev.Hum., M.L.A.
—BLDSC shelfmark: 6927.440000.
Description: Covers the academic study of non-fictional prose.

850   IT
PROSPETTIVE CULTURALI. 1975. bi-m. L.20000. (Associazione Culturale dei Medici Artisti Italiani) Societa Editrice Napoletana s.r.l., Corso Umberto I, 34, 80138 Naples, Italy. Ed. A. Spagnuolo. adv.; bk.rev.; circ. 500.
Formerly: Nuove Prospettive Letterarie.

800 700 780   AU   ISSN 0555-5027
NX548.A1
PROTOKOLLE; Wiener Halbjahresschrift fuer Literatur, Bildende Kunst und Musik. s-a. S.175. Jugend und Volk Verlagsgesellschaft, Anschuetzg. 1, A-1153 Vienna, Austria. TEL 0222-8120517. FAX 0222-8120517-27. Ed. Otto Breicha. illus. **Indexed:** Artbibl.Mod.
Description: Journal of literature and the arts.

840   US   ISSN 0048-5659
PQ2631.R63
PROUST RESEARCH ASSOCIATION NEWSLETTER. (Text in English and French) 1969. s-a. free. Proust Research Association, c/o J. Theodore Johnson, Ed., Department of French and Italian, University of Kansas, Lawrence, KS 66045. TEL 913-864-3388. Ed.Bd. bk.rev.; abstr.; bibl.; circ. 250. **Indexed:** M.L.A.
Description: Forum for the discussion of problems relating to current research on Marcel Proust.

PROVINCETOWN ARTS. see ART

800 700   IS   ISSN 0334-4975
PROZA; literary and art magazine. 1976. m. P.O. Box 969, Ramat Gan 52 109, Israel. Ed. Yossi Creme.

PRUDENTIA. see HISTORY

800   US
PUB. 1979. biennial. $7.95 for 3 nos. Ansuda Publications, Box 158-B, Harris, IA 51345. Ed. Daniel Betz. adv.; circ. 350.
Description: Contains socially-oriented poetry and fiction.

840 440   SZ   ISSN 0079-7812
PUBLICATIONS ROMANES ET FRANCAISES. no.9, 1933. irreg, no.198, 1991. price varies. Librairie Droz S.A., 11, rue Massot, CH-1211 Geneva 12, Switzerland. TEL 022-466666. FAX 022-472391. circ. 800. **Indexed:** M.L.A.
Description: Brings out linguistic, psychological and historical analyses of classical and modern literature.

| 810 | US | ISSN 0890-3433 |

PUCKERBRUSH REVIEW. 1978. 2/yr. $8. Puckerbrush Press, 76 Main St., Orono, ME 04473. TEL 207-581-3832. Ed. Constance Hunting. adv.; bk.rev.; illus.; circ. 250.
   Description: Interviews Maine writers, features, poetry, fiction and essays with a Maine focus.

| 800 | US | ISSN 0738-517X |
| PS580 | | |

PUERTO DEL SOL. 1961-1976; resumed 1980. s-a. $7.75. New Mexico State University, Department of English, Box 3E, Las Cruces, NM 88003. TEL 505-646-2345. Ed. Kevin McIlvoy. adv.; bk.rev.; bibl.; illus.; circ. 750. **Indexed:** A.I.P.P., Amer.Hum.Ind., Chic.Per.Ind., Ind.Amer.Per.Verse.

PULPHOUSE - A FICTION MAGAZINE. see LITERATURE — Science Fiction, Fantasy, Horror

PULPHOUSE FICTION SPOTLIGHT. see LITERATURE — Science Fiction, Fantasy, Horror

| 800 | US | ISSN 1055-1492 |

PUN AMERICAN NEWSLETTER; jest for fun. 1989. q. $9.95 for 6 nos. Pun American Newsletter, 1165 Elmwood Place, Deerfield, IL 60015. TEL 708-945-1790. Ed. Robert S. Aitchison. bk.rev.; circ. 600.
   Description: Covers puns, pictures, cartoons and photographs mainly contributed by subscribers nation wide.

| 808.87 | CN | ISSN 0712-1318 |

PUNDIT. 1981. m. $20. International Save the Pun Foundation, Box 5040, Sta. A, Toronto, Ont. M5W 1N4, Canada. TEL 416-922-1100. FAX 416-922-1100. Ed. John S. Crosbie. bk.rev. (looseleaf format)
   Description: Seeks to encourage literacy by supplying word-play to members worldwide. Conducts contests involving word games.

| 800 792 | PL | ISSN 0208-8363 |

PUNKT; kwartalnik gdanskich srodowisk tworczych. 1979. q. Wydawnictwo Morskie, Ul. Szeroka 38-40, 80-835 Gdansk, Poland. TEL 31-10-31. Ed. Edward Mazurkiewicz. bk.rev.; play rev.; illus.
   Description: Literary magazine.

| 378.1 | MX | ISSN 0033-4367 |

PUNTO DE PARTIDA. 1967. bi-m. Mex.$15($2.50) Universidad Nacional Autonoma de Mexico, Direccion General de Difusion Cultural, Ciudad Universitaria, Villa Obregon, Mexico 20 D.F., Mexico. Ed. Dir. Eugenia Revueltas. bibl.; illus.

PURDUE UNIVERSITY MONOGRAPHS IN ROMANCE LANGUAGE. see LINGUISTICS

| 890 | BG | |

PURNASA. (Text in Bengali) 1976. m. Tk.2. Bijan Bihari Goldar, Ed. & Pub., 143 Shahid Samsuzzoha Hall, Rajshahi University, Rajshahi, Bangladesh.

| 810 | US | ISSN 0149-7863 |
| PS501 | | |

PUSHCART PRIZE: BEST OF THE SMALL PRESSES. 1976. a. $28.50. Pushcart Press, Box 380, Wainscott, NY 11975. TEL 516-324-8335. Ed. Bill Henderson. index; circ. 10,000. (back issues avail.)
   Description: Covers selections from small, independent book presses and literary magazines.

PUSHTO. see LINGUISTICS

| 810 | US | ISSN 0278-1891 |
| PS3566.Y55 | | |

PYNCHON NOTES. 1979. 2/yr. $9 (foreign $12). c/o Bernard Duyfhuizen, Man. Ed., English Dept., Univ. of Wisconsin, Eau Claire, WI 54702-4004. TEL 715-836-3165. FAX 715-836-2380. Eds. John M. Krafft, Khachig Tololyan. adv.; bk.rev.; bibl.; circ. 250. **Indexed:** Abstr.Engl.Stud., LCR, M.L.A.
—BLDSC shelfmark: 7161.765000.
   Description: Notes and essays of any length considering the writings of Thomas Pynchon from any critical angle and in any literary, historical or cultural context.

| 800 | CS | |

PYRAMIDA. m. $94. (Socialist Academy of Slovakia) Obzor, Ceskoslovenskej Armady 35, 815 85 Bratislava, Czechoslovakia.

| 895.1 | CC | |

QING MING; wenxue shuang yuekan. (Text in Chinese) 1979. bi-m. Y22.80($69.10) 9, Suzhou Lu, Hefei, Anhui 230001, People's Republic of China. (Dist. outside China by: Guoji Shudian - China International Book Trading Corp., P.O. Box 399, Beijing, P.R.C.; Dist. in US by: China Books & Periodicals, Inc., 2929 24th St., San Francisco, CA 94110. TEL 415-282-2994) adv.; circ. 160,000.
   Description: Literary magazine that covers stories, proses and reviews.

| 895.1 | CC | |

QINGCHUN/YOUTH. (Text in Chinese) m. Nanjing Shi Wenlian, 19 Lanyuan, Nanjing, Jiangsu 210018, People's Republic of China. TEL 631931. Ed. Chen Jian.

| 895.1 | CC | ISSN 0257-5795 |

QINGHAI HU/QINGHAI LAKE. (Text in Chinese) 1970. m. $45. Qinghai Sheng Wenlian, No. 12, Huanghe Lu, Xining, Qinghai 810001, People's Republic of China. TEL 45083. (Dist. in US by: China Books & Periodicals, Inc., 2929 24th St., San Francisco, CA 94110. TEL 415-282-2994) Ed. Li Shijing.

| 895.1 | CC | |

QINGNIAN WENXUE/YOUTH LITERATURE. (Text in Chinese) m. Y1.80($57.60) Zhongguo Qingnian Chubanshe, Qikan Bu, 21, Dongsi 12 Tiao, Beijing 100708, People's Republic of China. TEL 442125. (Dist. outside China by: China International Book Trading Corp., P.O. Box 399, Beijing, P.R.C.; Dist. in US by: China Books & Periodicals, Inc., 2929 24th St., San Francisco, CA 94110. TEL 415-282-2994) Ed. Chen Haozeng.

| 895.1 | CC | |

QINGNIAN WENXUEJIA/YOUNG WRITERS. (Text in Chinese) m. Qiqiha'er Shi Wenlian, Tiyuchang Nan 2 Men, Hecheng, Qiqiha'er, Heilongjiang 142, People's Republic of China. TEL 72248. Ed. Guo Dabin.

| 895.1 | CC | ISSN 1003-1669 |

QINGNIAN ZUOJIA/YOUNG WRITERS; wenxue shuang yuekan. (Text in Chinese) 1981. bi-m. Y15. (Chengdu Shi Xinwen Chubanju - Chengdu News Publishing Bureau) Qingnian Zuojia Zazhishe, 44, Beixin Jie, Chengdu, Sichuan 610016, People's Republic of China. TEL 28719. Ed. Yang Zhengtai. adv.
   Description: Publishes prose, poetry, short stories, novelettes, and satirical and humorous stories.

| 895.1 | CC | |

QIYE WENHUA/ENTERPRISE CULTURE. (Text in Chinese) bi-m. Heilongjiang Zuojia Qiyejia Lianyihui, 16, Yaojing Jie, Nangang-qu, Harbin, Heilongjiang 150006, People's Republic of China. TEL 30993. Ed. Li Chunren.

| 850 | CN | ISSN 0226-8043 |

QUADERNI D'ITALIANISTICA. 1980. s-a. Can.$20($20) (effective 1991). Canadian Society for Italian Studies, University of Toronto, Dept. of Italian, Toronto, Ont. M5S 1A1, Canada. FAX 416-978-5593. Ed. Massimo Ciavolella. adv.; bk.rev.; circ. 450. (reprint service avail. from ISI) **Indexed:** Arts & Hum.Cit.Ind., Curr.Cont., M.L.A.
—BLDSC shelfmark: 7166.363000.

| 850 410 851 | IT | ISSN 1120-9178 |

QUADERNI DI LINGUE E LETTERATURE. (Text in English, French, German, Modern Greek, Italian, Russian, Spanish) 1976. a. exchange basis. Universita degli Studi di Verona, Facolta di Lingue e Letterature Straniere, 37129 Verona, Italy. FAX 045-38792. Ed. Anna Maria Babbi. bk.rev.; circ. 500.

QUADERNI IBERO-AMERICANI; attualita culturale Penisola Iberica America-Latina. see LINGUISTICS

| 850 | | ISSN 0394-2694 |

QUADERNI VENETI. 1985. s-a. L.45000 (foreign L.63000). (Centro Interuniversitario di Studi Veneti) Angelo Longo Editore, Via Paolo Costa 33, P.O. Box 431, 48100 Ravenna, Italy. TEL 0544-217026. Ed. Giorgio Padoan. adv.; index. (back issues avail.)

| 800 410 | FR | |

QUADRANT. (Text in French, Portuguese, Spanish) 1984. a. 50 F. Universite de Montpellier (Universite Paul Valery), B.P. 5043, 34032 Montpellier Cedex 1, France. TEL 67-14-20-00. circ. 500. (back issues avail.)
   Description: Covers Portuguese and Brazilian literature and linguistics.

| 895.1 | CC | |

QUANZHOU WENXUE/QUANZHOU LITERATURE. (Text in Chinese) bi-m. Y4.50. Quanzhou Shi Wenlian, 412 Zhongshan Zhonglu, 2nd Floor, Quanzhou, Fujian 362000, People's Republic of China. TEL 222364. (Dist. overseas by: Jiangsu Publications Import & Export Corp., 56 Gao Yun Ling, Nanjing, Jiangsu, P.R.C.) Ed. Chen Zhize.

| 819 | CN | ISSN 0033-5266 |
| PS501 | | |

QUARRY. 1952. q. Can.$24 to individuals; institutions $32. Quarry Press, Inc., Box 1061, Kingston, Ont. K7L 4Y5, Canada. TEL 613-548-8429. Ed. Bob Hilderley. adv.; bk.rev.; circ. 1,000. (also avail. in microfilm from MML; microfiche from UMI) **Indexed:** Amer.Hum.Ind., C.P.I., Can.Lit.Ind., Can.Per.Ind., CMI, Ind.Amer.Per.Verse.

| 800 | US | ISSN 1055-1492 |

QUARRY FARM PAPERS. 1989. irreg. $5 (members $4). Elmira College, Center for Mark Twain Studies, Box EC 7035, Elmira, NY 14901. TEL 607-732-0993. Ed. Darryl Baskin. circ. 1,000.

| 810 | US | ISSN 0893-3103 |
| PS501 | | |

THE QUARTERLY (NEW YORK); the magazine of new writing. 1987. q. $48 (Canada $40); elsewhere $46). Vintage: Random House, 201 E. 50th St., New York, NY 10022. TEL 212-572-2128. FAX 212-572-2593. TELEX 960550. Ed. Gordon Lish. adv.; circ. 15,000.
   Description: Aims to deliver to an international readership the strongest samples of contemporary prose fiction and poetry available in the marketplace.

| 810 | US | ISSN 0194-4231 |

QUARTERLY WEST. 1976. s-a. $9. University of Utah, Quarterly West, 317 Olpin Union, Salt Lake City, UT 84112. TEL 801-581-3938. Eds. Tom Hazuka, Bernie Wood. adv.; bk.rev.; circ. 1,000. (back issues avail.) **Indexed:** A.I.P.P., Amer.Hum.Ind., Ind.Amer.Per.Verse.

| 800 | US | ISSN 0737-3759 |
| F1051 | | |

QUEBEC STUDIES. 1983. s-a. $30 to individuals; institutions $40. American Council for Quebec Studies, c/o Karen Gould, Ed., Department of Romance Languages, Bowling Green State University, Bowling Green, OH 43403-0189. TEL 419-372-2667. FAX 419-372-7332. adv.; bk.rev.; circ. 800.
   Description: Provides essays on Quebec society and French-Canadian culture.

QUESTION DE. see PARAPSYCHOLOGY AND OCCULTISM

| 800 700 | US | ISSN 1041-8385 |
| PN1 | | |

QUI PARLE; a journal of literary studies. 1986. s-a. $10 to individuals; institutions $20. University of California, Berkeley, Doreen B. Townsend Center for the Humanities, 460 Stephens Hall, Berkeley, CA 94720. TEL 510-643-9670. FAX 510-643-8245. adv.; bk.rev.; circ. 1,000. (back issues avail.)
   Description: Interdisciplinary journal of contemporary literary theory and criticism.

QUICKBORN; Zeitschrift fuer plattdeutsche Sprache und Dichtung. see LINGUISTICS

| 830 | GW | |

QUICKBORN BUECHER. (Text in German and Low-German (Plattdeutsch)) 1913. a. free to members. Quickborn Vereinigung fuer Niederdeutsche Sprache und Literatur e.V., Alexanderstr. 16, 2000 Hamburg 1, Germany. TEL 040-240809. adv.; bk.rev.; circ. 3,000.

| 860 | SP | ISSN 0211-3325 |
| PN778 | | |

QUIMERA. 1980. m. $63. Montesinos Editor, S.A., Maignon, 26, 3, 08024 Barcelona, Spain. TEL 210-69-06. Ed. Miguel Riera. adv.; bk.rev.; circ. 21,500. (controlled).
   Description: Contains interviews with writers and general articles about literary books.

QUINQUEREME; new studies in modern languages. see LINGUISTICS

2952 LITERATURE

840   FR   ISSN 0048-6493
AP20
QUINZAINE LITTERAIRE. 1966. fortn. 395 F. (foreign 520 F.). S E L I S la Quinzaine Litteraire, 43, rue du Temple, 75004 Paris 4, France. TEL 48-87-48-58. FAX 48-87-13-01. Ed. Maurice Nadeau. circ. 40,000. (also avail. in microform from UMI; reprint service avail. from UMI) **Indexed:** Arts & Hum.Cit.Ind., Curr.Cont., M.L.A.
—BLDSC shelfmark: 7218.180000.

808 891.82   CI   ISSN 0352-7654
QUORUM; literary journal. (Text in Croatian, English, Serbian) 1986. bi-m. $40. Savez Omladine Hrvatske, Republicki Savjet, Franza Mehringa 14, 41000 Zagreb, Croatia. TEL 041-51-46-79. Ed. Miroslav Micanovic. adv.; bk.rev.; art rev.; film rev.; circ. 2,000.

800   GW   ISSN 0723-0338
PR13
R E A L YEARBOOK. (Research in English and American Literature) (Text in English) 1982. a. DM.168. Gunter Narr Verlag, Dischingerweg 5, 7400 Tuebingen 5, Germany. TEL 07071-78091. FAX 07071-75288. Ed.Bd. adv.; bibl.; circ. 800. (back issues avail.)
—BLDSC shelfmark: 9416.150000.

R I F NEWSLETTER. (Reading Is Fundamental, Inc.) see *EDUCATION*

R I S D VOICE. (Rhode Island School of Design) see *ART*

830 920   GW   ISSN 0075-2371
PT2451.Z5
RAABE-GESELLSCHAFT. JAHRBUCH. 1960. a. DM.78. (Raabe-Gesellschaft) Max Niemeyer Verlag, Postfach 2140, 7400 Tuebingen 1, Germany. TEL 0531-75225. FAX 07071-87419. Eds. Josef Daum, Hans-Juergen Schrader. bk.rev.; circ. 1,000. (reprint service avail. from SWZ)

800   US   ISSN 0731-4817
PN2
RACKHAM JOURNAL OF THE ARTS AND HUMANITIES. (Text in English, French, German) 1971. a. $4 to individuals; institutions $5. University of Michigan, 411 Mason Hall, Ann Arbor, MI 48109. TEL 313-763-2351. Ed. Thomas Mussio, Mary Lacey. adv.; circ. 300. **Indexed:** Abstr.Engl.Stud., Amer.Hum.Ind., M.L.A.
Formerly: Rackham Literary Studies (ISSN 0360-7887)

RADAR; international magazine for creativity. see *ART*

RADAR - SEI; rivista mensile di attualita-arte-cultura. see *ART*

810   CN   ISSN 0826-5909
PN771 db .R33
RADDLE MOON. 1978. 2/yr. Can.$12($12) to individuals; institutions Can.$18 (foreign US$$18). Raddle Moon Press, 9060 Ardmore Dr., Sidney, B.C. V8L 3S1, Canada. TEL 604-736-9769. FAX 604-732-7367. Ed. Susan Clark. adv.; bk.rev.; illus.; circ. 700.
Supersedes (in 1984): From an Island (ISSN 0706-8093); **Formerly:** Introductions from an Island (ISSN 0318-3270)
Description: Publishes post-language-centered and new lyric poetry, open texts and poetics; essays (personal, literary and critical); forums on various topics of current concern, photographs and image - text works.

891.7   KR   ISSN 0131-8136
RADUGA. 1927. m. 20.40 Rub. (Spilka Pys'mennykiv Ukrainy) Vydavnytstvo Radyanskii Pismennik, Chkalova, 52, Kiev, Ukraine. Ed. A.P. Rogatchenko. bk.rev.; film rev.; play rev.; bibl.; illus.; circ. 30,000. **Indexed:** M.L.A.

891.7   KR   ISSN 0131-0194
PG3900
RADYANS'KE LITERATUROZNAVSTVO. 1957. m. 6.60 Rub.($17.40) (Akademiya Nauk Ukrainskoi S.S.R., Institut Literatury im. T.G. Shevchenko) Izdatel'stvo Naukova Dumka, c/o Yu.A. Khramov, Dir, Ul. Repina, 3, Kiev 252 601, Ukraine. TEL 229-24-56. (Co-sponsor: Soyuz Pisatelei Ukrainy) Ed. V.G. Belyaev. bk.rev.; bibl.; illus.; index; circ. 2,895.

RAGIONI CRITICHE; rivista di studi lingustici e letterari. see *LINGUISTICS*

890   US
DS251
RAHAVARD PERSIAN JOURNAL. 1982. q. $28 (foreign $36). Hassan Shahbaz, Ed. & Pub., Box 24640, Los Angeles, CA 90024. adv.; bk.rev.; circ. 3,000.
Formerly: Rahavard (ISSN 0742-8014)
Description: For the preservation of the Persian culture among Iranian immigrants.

820 420   II   ISSN 0448-1690
PR1
RAJASTHAN UNIVERSITY STUDIES IN ENGLISH. (Text in English) 1963. a. $6. University of Rajasthan, Department of English, Gandhi Nagar, Jaipur 302004, India. Ed. Jasbir Jain. bk.rev.; circ. 250.
Indexed: M.L.A.

800   US
RAMBUNCTIOUS REVIEW. 1984. a. $10 for 3 nos. Rambunctious Press, Inc., 1221 W. Pratt Blvd., Chicago, IL 60626. Ed.Bd. circ. 300. (back issues avail.)

830   AU
DIE RAMPE (LINZ). 1975. s-a. S.80. Amt der Oberoesterreich Landesregierung, Kulturabteilung, Spittelwiese 4, A-4010 Linz, Austria. Ed.Bd. adv.; bk.rev.; circ. 2,000.

RAMPIKE MAGAZINE. see *ART*

890   BG
RAMPURA SAHITYA PARISHADA PATRIKA. (Text in Bengali) s-a. Tk.6. Rangpur Sahitya Parishad, Rangpur, Bangladesh.

RAM'S HORN. see *LINGUISTICS*

800   US   ISSN 0275-1607
AS30
RARITAN; a quarterly review. 1981. q. $16 to individuals; institutions $20. Rutgers University, 31 Mine St., New Brunswick, NJ 08903. TEL 908-932-7887. FAX 908-932-7855. Ed. Richard Poirier. adv.; bk.rev.; circ. 3,500. **Indexed:** Abstr.Engl.Stud., Amer.Hum.Ind., Arts & Hum.Cit.Ind., Film Lit.Ind. (1989-), Hum.Ind., M.L.A.
—BLDSC shelfmark: 7291.875000.
Description: Interdisciplinary journal publishing critical writing on literature, film, art, philosophy and anthropology.

850   IT   ISSN 0033-9423
RASSEGNA DELLA LETTERATURA ITALIANA. 1893. q. L.160000. Casa Editrice G. C. Sansoni Editore Nuova S.p.A., Via Benedetto Varchi 47, 50132 Florence, Italy. Ed. Walter Binni. adv.; bk.rev.; abstr.; bibl.; index; circ. 1,000. **Indexed:** Arts & Hum.Cit.Ind., Can.Rev.Comp.Lit, Curr.Cont., M.L.A.

RASSEGNA MENSILE DI ISRAEL. see *RELIGIONS AND THEOLOGY — Judaic*

RASSEGNA SOVIETICA; rivista bimestrale di cultura. see *ART*

800   RU   ISSN 0235-4241
RASSKAZ. 1978. a. Izdatel'stvo Sovremennik, Horoshevskaya, 62, Moscow 123007, Russia. TEL 941-40-08.
Description: Presents a collection of the best stories published in the Soviet literary magazines during previous year.

800   NE
RASTER. 1977. q. fl.95. Uitgeverij De Bezige Bij, Van Miereveldstraat 1, 1071 DW Amsterdam, Netherlands. TEL 020-73-67-31. FAX 020-76-19-48. Ed.Bd. circ. 900.

890   PK
RAVI. (Issued in 3 parts) (Text in English, Panjabi or Urdu) 1906. a. price varies. Government College, Lahore, Pakistan.

891.4   XN   ISSN 0034-0227
RAZGLEDI; spisanije za literatura, umetnost i kultura. (Text in Macedonian) 1958. m. 300 din. Ul. Ivo Ribar-Lola 66, Box 345, 91000 Skopje, Macedonia. Ed. Danilo Kocevski. circ. 1,000. **Indexed:** M.L.A.
—BLDSC shelfmark: 0140.216000.

800 001.3 700   XN   ISSN 0351-3769
RAZVITOK. (Text in Macedonian) 1963. m. 1600 din.($4) R.O. B.I.D. "Mistirkov", Koment Ohridski bb, Bitola, Macedonia. TEL 22-951-097.

800   US
THE READER'S ADVISER; a layman's guide to literature. (In 6 vols.; Vol. 1: The Best in American and British Fiction, Poetry, Essays, Literary Biography, Bibliography, and Reference; Vol. 2: The Best in American and British Drama and World Literature in English Translation; Vol. 3: The Best in General Reference Literature, the Social Sciences, History, and the Arts; Vol. 4: The Best in the Literature of Philosophy and World Religions; Vol. 5: The Best in the Literature of Science, Technology, and Medicine; Vol. 6: Indexes) 1927. irreg., 13th ed., 1988. $411. R.R. Bowker, A Reed Reference Publishing Company, Division of Reed Publishing (USA) Inc., 121 Chanlon Rd., New Providence, NJ 07974. TEL 800-521-8110. FAX 908-555-6688. TELEX 138 755. (Subscr. to: Order Dept., Box 31, New Providence, NJ 07974)
Description: Profiles authors, annotated bibliographies (with prices) of selected in-print works by and about them.

809   AT   ISSN 0155-218X
READING TIME. 1957. q. Aus.$25. Children's Book Council of Australia, P.O. Box 62, Turvey Park, Wagga Wagga, N.S.W. 2650, Australia. FAX 069-25-4907. Ed. John Cohen. adv.; bk.rev.; index; circ. 2,200. **Indexed:** Aus.P.A.I.S., Child.Lit.Abstr., Gdlns.
—BLDSC shelfmark: 7301.430000.

500 700 800   SP   ISSN 0034-060X
AS302
REAL ACADEMIA DE CORDOBA DE CIENCIAS, BELLAS LETRAS Y NOBLES ARTES. BOLETIN. 1922. a. 200 ptas. Real Academia de Cordoba de Ciencias, Bellas Letras y Nobles Artes, Ambrosia de Morales 9, Cordoba, Spain. bk.rev.; abstr.; charts; illus.; upd. 3 91130; circ. 500. **Indexed:** Amer.Hist.& Life, Hist.Abstr.

800   SP
REAL ACADEMIA SEVILLANA DE BUENAS LETRAS. BOLETIN. irreg., latest no.17. price varies. (Real Academia Sevillana de Buenas Letras) Universidad de Sevilla, Servicio de Publicaciones, San Fernando, 4, 41004 Seville, Spain. TEL 954-22-8071. FAX 954-22-1315.

800   US
REAL FICTION. 1982. 2/yr. $15 to individuals; institutions $25. 298 9th Ave., San Francisco, CA 94118. Ed. Genevieve Belfiglio. adv.; circ. 200.

REAL LIFE MAGAZINE. see *ART*

820   CN
REAPPRAISALS; Canadian writers. 1974. irreg. University of Ottawa Press, 603 Cumberland, Ottawa, Ont. K1N 6N5, Canada. TEL 613-564-2270. Ed. Lorraine McMullen.
Description: Articles on Canadian authors or on related topics in English-Canadian literature.

830 430   FR   ISSN 0399-1989
DD61
RECHERCHES GERMANIQUES. (Text in French, German) 1971. a. price varies. Universite de Strasbourg II, 22 rue Descartes, 67084 Strasbourg, France. Ed. G.L. Fink. bibl.; circ. 800. (back issues avail.) **Indexed:** M.L.A.
Description: Covers research in German culture and literature.

860 869 791.43   FR
RECHERCHES IBERIQUES ET CINEMATOGRAPHIQUES. 1960. 2/yr. 119 F. (foreign 139 F.). Universite de Strasbourg II, Institut d'Etudes Iberiques, 25 rue du Marechal Juin, 67084 Strasbourg Cedex, France. TEL 88-36-51-47. Eds. Duarte Mimoso-Ruiz, Jean-Pierre Prevost.
Former titles: Recherches Iberiques Strasbourg II (ISSN 0755-2807) & Universite de Strasbourg. Institut d'Etudes Latino-Americaines. Travaux.

800   FR   ISSN 0769-0886
PQ1979
RECHERCHES SUR DIDEROT ET SUR L'ENCYCLOPEDIE. 1986. s-a. 180 F. to members (foreign 220 F.); institutions 250 F. Societe Diderot, 7, Route de la Reine, 92100 Boulogne, France. (Subscr. to: Klincksieck, 11 rue de Lille, 75007 Paris, France) Ed. Anne-Marie Chouillet. adv.; bk.rev.; illus.

RECORDER (SEARCY). see *EDUCATION — Higher Education*

LITERATURE

RECORDS OF EARLY ENGLISH DRAMA NEWSLETTER. see *THEATER*

800 US ISSN 0300-6425
RECOVERING LITERATURE; a journal of contextualist criticism. 1972. irreg. (1-3/yr.) $6. Box 805, Alpine, CA 91903. Ed. Gerald J. Butler. adv.; bk.rev.; circ. 250. (back issues avail.) **Indexed:** Abstr.Engl.Stud.

RED BASS. see *LITERARY AND POLITICAL REVIEWS*

810 US ISSN 0034-1967
PS501
RED CEDAR REVIEW. 1962. s-a. $10. Red Cedar Press, 325 Morrill Hall, Michigan State University, E. Lansing, MI 48824. TEL 517-355-9656. FAX 517-355-7570. Ed. Anne Marie Carey. bk.rev.; circ. 500.

810 US
RED WEATHER;* poems, translations, essays, reviews. irreg. (approx. 4/yr.) $2.50 per no. c/o Bruce Taylor, 448 W. Grand Ave., Eau Claire, WI 54703-5330. bk.rev.; circ. 400.

810 US ISSN 0887-5715
REDNECK REVIEW. Variant title: Redneck Review of Literature. 1975. 2/yr. $15 (typically set in Spring). 2919 N. Downer Ave., Milwaukee, WI 53211-3335. TEL 414-332-6881. Ed. Penelope Reedy. adv.; bk.rev.; circ. 500. **Indexed:** Amer.Hum.Ind.
Description: Presents and explores the contemporary literature of the American West. Includes essays, poetry, fiction.

830 GW ISSN 0138-340X
PN4
REFERATEDIENST ZUR LITERATURWISSENSCHAFT. 1969. q. DM.36.20. Akademie der Wissenschaften, Zentralinstitut fuer Literaturgeschichte, Prenzlauer Promenade 149-152, 1100 Berlin, Germany. Ed.Bd.

860 AG
REFERENTE; el ojo que mira. 1981. q. Ediciones La Tabla de Esmeralda, Pena 2141, Buenos Aires, Argentina. Ed.Bd.

800 745.1 US
REFLECT. 1979-1987; resumed 1988. q. $8. 3306 Argonne Ave., Norfolk, VA 23509. TEL 804-857-1097. Ed. William S. Kennedy. adv.; bk.rev.; circ. 100.
Description: Specializes in spiral mode poetry, featuring euphony mysticism and succinct impersonal writing.

811 US ISSN 0484-2650
REFLECTION (SPOKANE); Gonzaga's literary magazine. 1960. a. free. Gonzaga University, Spokane, WA 99258. TEL 509-328-4220. FAX 509-484-2818. circ. 800.
Description: Contains literary pieces (prose and poetry) contributed by both faculty and students.

830 430 375.4 GW
REGENSBURGER BEITRAEGE ZUR DEUTSCHEN SPRACH- UND LITERATURWISSENSCHAFT. REIHE A: QUELLEN. irreg. Verlag Peter Lang GmbH, Eschborner Landstr. 42-50, 6000 Frankfurt a.M. 90, Germany. TEL 069-7807050. FAX 069-785893. Ed. Bernhard Gajek.

830 430 GW
REGENSBURGER BEITRAEGE ZUR DEUTSCHEN SPRACH- UND LITERATURWISSENSCAHFT. REIHE B: UNTERSUCHUNGEN. irreg., no.50, 1991. Verlag Peter Lang GmbH, Eschborner Landstr. 42-50, 6000 Frankfurt a.M. 90, Germany. TEL 069-7807050. FAX 069-785893. Ed. Bernhard Gajek.

DER REGGEBOGE/RAINBOW. see *ETHNIC INTERESTS*

894 HU ISSN 0080-0570
REGI MAGYAR PROZAI EMLEKEK. (Text in Hungarian; occasional summaries in German) 1968. irreg. price varies. (Magyar Tudomanyos Akademia) Akademiai Kiado, Publishing House of the Hungarian Academy of Sciences, Box 24, H-1363 Budapest, Hungary.

800 UK ISSN 0757-8237
REIMPRESSION. 1984. irreg., latest vol.9. Gordon & Breach Science Publishers, P.O. Box 90, Reading, Berkshire RG1 8JL, England. TEL 0734-560-080. FAX 0734-568-211. TELEX 849870 SCIPUB G. (US addr.: Box 786, Cooper Sta., New York, NY 10276. TEL 800-545-8398) Ed.Bd.
Refereed Serial

809.915 NE ISSN 0925-4757
PN690.A6
REINARDUS. 1988. a. fl.100($52) (International Reynard Society) John Benjamins Publishing Co., Amsteldijk 44, P.O. Box 75577, 1070 AN Amsterdam, Netherlands. TEL 020-6738156. FAX 020-6739773. (In N. America: 821 Bethlehem Pike, Philadelphia, PA 19118. TEL 215-836-1200) Eds. Brian Levy, Paul Wackers. (back issues avail.)
Description: Promotes comparative research in the fields of mediaeval comic, satirical, didatic, and allegorical literature, with emphasis on the beast epic, fable and fabliau, including later developments into the modern era.

810 US
RELIGION AND LITERATURE. 1957; N.S. vol.8, 1972. 3/yr. $15 to individuals; libraries $18. University of Notre Dame, Department of English, Notre Dame, IN 46556. TEL 219-239-5725. Eds. James Dougherty, Thomas Werge. adv.; bk.rev.; bibl.; circ. 500. (processed; also avail. in microform from UMI; back issues avail.) **Indexed:** Abstr.Engl.Stud., Amer.Hum.Ind., Arts & Hum.Cit.Ind., Cath.Ind., CERDIC, Curr.Cont., M.L.A., Rel.& Theol.Abstr. (1983-), Rel.Ind.One.
Formerly: Notre Dame English Journal (ISSN 0029-4500)

800 808.8 US ISSN 1053-7201
▼**REMARK (NEW YORK);** a journal of essays and reviews. 1990. q. $9 to individuals; institutions $11; foreign $27. Again & Again Press, Box 20041, Cherokee Sta., New York, NY 10028. TEL 212-734-2149. Ed. Laurel Speer.

800 909 CN ISSN 0034-429X
CB359
RENAISSANCE AND REFORMATION/RENAISSANCE ET REFORME. (Text in English, French) 1964. q. Can.$20 to individuals; institutions Can.$35. (Canadian Society for Renaissance Studies) University of Guelph, Guelph, Ont. N1G 2W1, Canada. Ed. Francois Pare. bk.rev.; index; circ. 700. (processed; reprint service avail. from ISI) **Indexed:** Arts & Hum.Cit.Ind, Bk.Rev.Ind. (1980-), Can.Rev.Comp.Lit, Child.Bk.Rev.Ind. (1980-), Curr.Cont., Hist.Abstr., Ind.Bk.Rev.Hum., M.L.A.
—BLDSC shelfmark: 7356.865100.

RENAISSANCE DRAMA. see *THEATER*

800 US
RENAISSANCE PAPERS. 1955. a. $20. Southeastern Renaissance Conference, Box 8105, English Dept., NCSU, Raleigh, NC 27695-8105. TEL 919-737-3866. Eds. Barbara J. Baines, George W. Williams. circ. 500.

800 US ISSN 0034-4338
CB361
RENAISSANCE QUARTERLY. 1954. q. $60 to individuals; institutions $55. Renaissance Society of America, 1161 Amsterdam Ave., New York, NY 10027. TEL 212-280-2318. FAX 212-749-3163. Ed.Bd. adv.; bk.rev.; bibl.; illus.; index; circ. 3,000. (also avail. in microform from UMI,KTO; back issues avail. from KTO; reprint service avail. from KTO) **Indexed:** Abstr.Engl.Stud., Arts & Hum.Cit.Ind., Bk.Rev.Ind., Child.Bk.Rev.Ind. (1980-), Curr.Cont., Hist.Abstr., Hum.Ind., Ind.Bk.Rev.Hum., M.L.A., RILA.
—BLDSC shelfmark: 7356.866000.
Incorporates: Studies in the Renaissance (ISSN 0081-8658); **Formerly:** Renaissance News.

809 US ISSN 0034-4346
PN2
RENASCENCE; essays on values in literature. 1948. q. $20 (foreign $23). Marquette University Press, 1324 W. Wisconsin Ave., Milwaukee, WI 53233. TEL 414-224-1564. Ed. Dr. Joseph Schwartz. adv.; bk.rev.; index; circ. 825. (also avail. in microform from UMI; back issues avail.; reprint service avail. from UMI) **Indexed:** Abstr.Engl.Stud., Cath.Ind., Curr.Cont., Hum.Ind., LCR, M.L.A.
—BLDSC shelfmark: 7356.883000.
Description: Concerned with the study of values in literature.

895.1 CC ISSN 0258-8218
RENMIN WENXUE/PEOPLE'S LITERATURE. (Text in Chinese) 1950. m. Y23.40($71.10) Zuojia Chubanshe, 10, Nongzhanguan Nanli, Beijing 100026, People's Republic of China. TEL 500-3120. (Dist. outside China by: China International Book Trading Corp., P.O. Box 399, Beijing, P.R.C.; Dist. in US by: China Books & Periodicals, Inc., 2929 24th St., San Francisco, CA 94110. TEL 415-282-2994) Ed. Liu Xinwu.
Description: Contains short stories, essays, poetry. Includes children's literature.

830 GW
REPERTORIA HEIDELBERGENSIA. 1976. irreg. price varies. Verlag Lambert Schneider, Hausackerweg 16, 6900 Heidelberg, Germany.

860 CR ISSN 0252-8479
REPERTORIO AMERICANO. 1974. q. Col.30($8) Universidad Nacional, Instituto de Estudios Latinoamericanos, Apdo. 86, Heredia, Costa Rica. Eds. Maria R. de Bonilla, Isaac F. Azofeifa. adv.; bk.rev.; bibl.; illus.; cum.index: vols. 1-5; circ. 1,000. (tabloid format) **Indexed:** Hisp.Amer.Per.Ind.

THE REPORT (EUGENE). see *LITERATURE — Science Fiction, Fantasy, Horror*

859 RM
REPUBLICII SOCIALISTE ROMANIA. BIBLIOGRAFIA; carti-albume-harti. a. (Biblioteca Centrala de Stat a Republicii Socialiste Romania) Rompres - Filatelia, P.O. Box 12-201, 78104 Bucharest, Rumania. TELEX 10376 PRSFIR.

896 US ISSN 0034-5210
PL8010
RESEARCH IN AFRICAN LITERATURES. 1970. q. $30 to individuals; institutions $55. Indiana University Press, 601 N. Morton St., Bloomington, IN 47404. TEL 812-855-9449. Ed. Richad Bjornson. adv.; bk.rev.; bibl.; charts; illus.; stat.; index; circ. 670. (also avail. in microform from KTO,MIM,UMI; reprint service avail. from UMI) **Indexed:** Abstr.Engl.Stud., Arts & Hum.Cit.Ind., Curr.Cont., Curr.Cont.Africa, Hum.Ind., Ind.Bk.Rev.Hum., Lang.& Lang.Behav.Abstr., M.L.A., Sociol.Abstr.
—BLDSC shelfmark: 7714.380000.
Description: Features historical, biographical, and theoretical studies of the written and oral literatures of Africa.

RESENA DE LITERATURA, ARTE Y ESPECTACULOS. see *ART*

830 GW
RESONANZ; Kunst, Poesie und Literatur der Gegenwart. m. DM.48. Verlag Michael Bonitz, Herforderstr. 1, 4925 Kalletal, Germany. Ed. Raphael Bonitz.

801 055 IT
RESPONSABILITA DEL SAPERE. 1947. s-a. $16. Via G. Carini, 24-28, Rome, Italy. Ed. G. Arcidiacono. bk.rev.

RESPONSE (NEW YORK, 1967); a contemporary Jewish review. see *ETHNIC INTERESTS*

820 US ISSN 0162-9905
PR437
RESTORATION: STUDIES IN ENGLISH LITERARY CULTURE, 1660-1700. 1977. s-a. $8 for 6 issues (foreign $18). James Madison University, College of Letters and Sciences, Harrisonburg, VA 22807. Ed. J.M. Armistead. bibl.; circ. 500. (back issues avail.) **Indexed:** M.L.A.
—BLDSC shelfmark: 7777.815000.
Description: Scholarly articles on literature and contexts, annotated bibliography, and announcements.

LITERATURE

809 420 375.4 US ISSN 0190-3233
PR1
REVIEW (CHARLOTTESVILLE). 1979. a. $30. (Virginia Polytechnic Institute and State University) University Press of Virginia, Box 3608 University Sta., Charlottesville, VA 22903. TEL 804-924-3468. (Co-sponsor: Pennsylvania State University) Eds. James O. Hoge, James L.W. West III. circ. 1,500.
  Description: Reviews and essays of greater length than in most scholarly journals.

809 US ISSN 0890-5762
F1401
REVIEW: LATIN AMERICAN LITERATURE AND ARTS. 1968-1982; resumed 1984. 2/yr. $14 to individuals; institutions $22 (foreign $26). Americas Society, 680 Park Ave., New York, NY 10021. TEL 212-249-8950. Ed. Alfred J. MacAdam. adv.; bk.rev.; film rev.; play rev.; illus.; circ. 5,000. (also avail. in microfiche from UMI; back issues avail.)
  Indexed: M.L.A.
  Description: Work in English translation by and about leading Latin American writers as well as articles on Latin American visual and performing arts.

800 US ISSN 0276-0045
PN3503
REVIEW OF CONTEMPORARY FICTION. 1981. 3/yr. $17 to individuals; institutions $24. Review of Contemporary Fiction, Inc., 1817 North 79th St., Elmwood Park, IL 60635. TEL 708-355-4300. FAX 708-355-5187. (Subscr. to: Dalkey Archive Press, 1817 N. 79th Ave., Elmwood Park, IL 60635) Ed. John O'Brien. adv.; bk.rev.; index; circ. 2,780. (also avail. in microform from UMI; back issues avail.) **Indexed:** Amer.Hum.Ind., Bk.Rev.Ind. (1986-), Child.Bk.Rev.Ind. (1986-), LCR, M.L.A.
  —BLDSC shelfmark: 7789.080000.
  Description: Each issue devoted to one or two significant (but often neglected) contemporary novelists.

820 UK ISSN 0034-6551
PR1
REVIEW OF ENGLISH STUDIES; a quarterly journal of English literature and the English language. 1925; N.S. 1950. q. £56($106) Oxford University Press, Oxford Journals, Pinkhill House, Southfield Road, Eynsham, Oxford OX8 1JJ, England. TEL 0865-882283. FAX 0865-882890. TELEX 8373300 OXPRES G. Ed. R.E. Alton. adv.; bk.rev.; bibl.; index; circ. 2,200. (also avail. in microform from UMI) **Indexed:** Abstr.Engl.Stud., Acad.Ind., Arts & Hum.Cit.Ind., Bk.Rev.Ind. (1965-), Br.Hum.Ind., Child.Bk.Rev.Ind. (1965-), Curr.Cont., Hum.Ind., Ind.Bk.Rev.Hum., Lang.& Lang.Behav.Abstr.
  —BLDSC shelfmark: 7790.520000.
  Description: Presents English literature and the English language from the earliest period up to the present day.

REVIEW OF LATIN AMERICAN STUDIES. see *HISTORY — History Of North And South America*

800 US ISSN 0034-6640
PN2
REVIEW OF NATIONAL LITERATURES. 1970. a. membership (includes C N L - World Report). Council on National Literatures, Box 81, Whitestone, NY 11357. TEL 718-767-8380. Ed. Anne Paolucci. adv.; bk.rev.; abstr.; bibl.; circ. 1,200. (back issues avail.) **Indexed:** Abstr.Engl.Stud., Arts & Hum.Cit.Ind., Curr.Cont., M.L.A., Mid.East: Abstr.& Ind.
  —BLDSC shelfmark: 7793.520000.

REVISTA AMERICANA DE ESTUDIOS SEMIOTICOS Y CULTURALES/AMERICAN JOURNAL OF SEMIOTIC AND CULTURAL STUDIES. see *LINGUISTICS*

REVISTA AWRAQ. see *HISTORY — History Of Europe*

869 BL ISSN 0486-6460
PQ9212
REVISTA CAMONIANA. 1964-1971; N.S. 1978. biennial. $10. Universidade de Sao Paulo "Armando de Salles Oliveira", Centro de Estudos Portugueses, Cidade Universitaria, C.P. 8105, 05508 Cidade Universitaria, Sao Paulo, Brazil. Ed. Maria H. Ribeiro da Cunha. bk.rev.; bibl.; illus.; circ. 2,000.

700 BL ISSN 0034-7353
REVISTA CAMPINENSE DE CULTURA.* vol.3, 1966. q. Comissao Cultural do Municipio Prefeitura, Municipal de Campina Grande, Paraiba, Brazil. Ed. Elpidio De Almeida. bk.rev.

REVISTA CANARIA DE ESTUDIOS INGLESES. see *LINGUISTICS*

860 SP ISSN 0378-200X
REVISTA CASTILLA. 1980. irreg., vol.15, 1990. 1200 ptas. Universidad de Valladolid, Secretariado de Publicaciones, Departamento de Literatura Espanola, Avda. de Ramon y Cajal, 7, 47005 Valladolid, Spain. TEL 983-423000. FAX 983-423003. TELEX 26357.

800 CL ISSN 0048-7651
PQ7900
REVISTA CHILENA DE LITERATURA. 1970. 2/yr. $30. Universidad de Chile, Departamento de Literatura, Casilla 10136, Santiago, Chile. TEL 2725978. FAX 2725977. Ed. Hugo Montes. bk.rev.; bibl.; circ. 1,000. Indexed: Arts & Hum.Cit.Ind., Curr.Cont., Hisp.Amer.Per.Ind., M.L.A.
  Formerly: Facultad de Filosofia y Humanidades. Boletin.

700 RM ISSN 0034-754X
REVISTA CULTULUI MOZAIC/REVIEW OF THE MOSAIC CREED. (Text in English, Hebrew, Rumanian and Yiddish) 1956. bi-m. Federatia Comunitatilor Evreiesti din Republica Socialista Romania, Str. Lapusna nr.9, 70478 Bucharest, Rumania. TEL 132583. FAX 162780. adv.; bk.rev.; illus.; circ. 9,800.

860 US ISSN 0252-8843
PQ7081.A1
REVISTA DE CRITICA LITERARIA LATINOAMERICANA. (Text in Spanish) 1975. s-a. $35. Latinoamericana Editores, 1309 C.L., University of Pittsburgh, Pittsburgh, PA 15260. TEL 412-624-5225. Dir. Antonio Cornejo Polar. adv.; bk.rev.; bibl.; circ. 1,225. (back issues avail.) **Indexed:** Arts & Hum.Cit.Ind., Chic.Per.Ind., Curr.Cont., Hisp.Amer.Per.Ind., M.L.A.

REVISTA DE ESTUDIOS COLOMBIANOS. see *HISTORY — History Of North And South America*

860 460 US ISSN 0034-818X
REVISTA DE ESTUDIOS HISPANICOS. (Text in English, Spanish) 1967. 3/yr. $21 to individuals; institutions $28.50 (foreign $30); students $17; (typically set in Aug.) Washington University, One Brookings Dr., St. Luois, MO 63130-4899. TEL 314-935-5175. FAX 314-726-3494. Ed. Michale Mudrovic. adv.; bk.rev.; bibl.; circ. 600. (also avail. in microform from UMI; back issues avail.; reprint service avail. from UMI) **Indexed:** Arts & Hum.Cit.Ind., Curr.Cont., Ind.Bk.Rev.Hum., M.L.A.
  —BLDSC shelfmark: 7854.507000.
  Description: Articles and reviews of books dealing with the literature of Spain and Latin America.

REVISTA DE FILOLOGIA. see *LINGUISTICS*

869 BL ISSN 0101-3505
P1.A1 CODEN: RLETD 6
REVISTA DE LETRAS. (Text in Portuguese; summaries in English and Portuguese) 1959-1977; resumed 1980. a. $30 or exchange basis. Universidade Estadual Paulista, Av. Vicente Ferreira 1278, Caixa Posta 603, 17.500 Marilia SP, Brazil. TEL 0144-33-1844. FAX 0144-22-2504. TELEX 111 9016 UJME BR. bk.rev.; bibl.; circ. 1,000. **Indexed:** Hisp.Amer.Per.Ind., Lang.& Lang.Behav.Abstr., M.L.A., Sociol.Abstr.
  —BLDSC shelfmark: 7863.605000.
  Description: Studies in Brazilian literature.

860 100 SP
REVISTA DE LITERATURA. s-a. 3300 ptas. (foreign 4950 ptas.). Consejo Superior de Investigaciones Cientificas (C.S.I.C.), Instituto de Filologia, Duque de Medinaceli, 6, 28014 Madrid, Spain. Dir. Miguel Angel Garrido.

860 CU ISSN 0138-6948
REVISTA DE LITERATURA CUBANA. 1982. s-a. $12. (Union de Escritores y Artistas de Cuba (UNEAC)) Empresa Ediciones Cubanas, Vicedireccion de Exportacion, O'Reilly No. 407, Havana, Cuba. (Dist. by: Ediciones Cubanas, Obispo No. 527, Apdo 605, Havana, Cuba) Ed.Bd. bk.rev.; circ. 10,000.
  Description: Presents research and critical studies on authors, works, topics, personages, trends, stages and characteristics of Cuban literature, including bibliographic summaries of literary criticism.

860 VE
REVISTA DE LITERATURA HISPANOAMERICANA. 1970. s-a. $7. Universidad de Zulia, Centro de Estudios Literarios, Apartado 1490, Maracaibo, Venezuela. Ed. J.A. Castro. bk.rev.; circ. 1,000.

860 US ISSN 0034-9593
PQ6001
REVISTA HISPANICA MODERNA; devoted to the study of the literature of Latin America, Portugal and Spain. (Text in Portuguese or Spanish) 1934. s-a. $20 to individuals (foreign $25); institutions $30 (foreign $35). Columbia University, Hispanic Institute of the United States, 612 W. 116th St., New York, NY 10027. TEL 212-854-4187. FAX 212-854-8787. Eds. G. Sobejano, J.Alazraki. adv.; bk.rev.; bibl.; charts; illus.; index; circ. 1,200. (also avail. in microform from BHP) **Indexed:** Arts & Hum.Cit.Ind., Curr.Cont., M.L.A.
  —BLDSC shelfmark: 7858.370000.

860 US ISSN 0034-9631
PQ7081.A1
REVISTA IBEROAMERICANA. (Text in Portuguese, Spanish) 1938. 4/yr. $40 to individuals (Latin America $25); institutions $60 (Latin America $30). International Institute of Ibero-American Literature - Instituto Internacional de Literature Iberoamericana, 1312 C.L., University of Pittsburgh, Pittsburgh, PA 15260. TEL 412-624-3359. FAX 412-624-8505. Ed. Dr. Alfredo A. Roggiano. adv.; bk.rev.; circ. 1,800. (also avail. in microform from UMI; back issues avail.; reprint service avail. from UMI,KTO) **Indexed:** Arts & Hum.Cit.Ind., Curr.Cont., Hisp.Amer.Per.Ind., M.L.A.
  —BLDSC shelfmark: 7858.810000.

869 BL ISSN 0100-0888
PB5
REVISTA LETRAS. 1953. a. exchange only. Universidade Federal do Parana, Setor de Ciencias Humanas, Letras e Artes, Caixa Postal 441, 80001 Curitaba PR, Brazil. FAX 041-2642243. TELEX 415100. Ed. Joao Alfredo dal Bello. bk.rev.; circ. 800. **Indexed:** M.L.A.

850 IT ISSN 0080-2441
REVISTA SCRIITORILOR ROMANI. (Text in Rumanian) 1962. a. price varies. Societa Accademica Romena, Foro Traiano 1a, 00187 Rome, Italy.

400 800 CL ISSN 0035-0451
P9
REVISTA SIGNOS DE VALPARAISO; estudios de lengua y literatura. Variant title: Revista Signos. (Text in Spanish; summaries in English, French and Spanish) 1967. a. $33. (Universidad Catolica de Valparaiso, Instituto de Literatura y Ciencias del Languaje) Ediciones Universitarias de Valparaiso, Casilla 1415, Valparaiso, Chile. TEL 252900. FAX 032-272746. TELEX 230389 UCVAL CL. Dir. Eduardo Godoy G. bk.rev.; circ. 300. **Indexed:** M.L.A.

800 CU ISSN 0864-1315
REVOLUCION Y CULTURA. 1976. bi-m. $30 in America; elsewhere $36. Ministerio de Cultura, Comite Estatal de Colaboracion Economica, Calle 1 No. 201 esq. B Vedado, Havana, Cuba. (Dist. by: Ediciones Cubanas, Obispo No. 527, Apdo. 605, Havana, Cuba) Dir. Romualdo Santos. bk.rev.; circ. 20,000. (also avail. in microfilm)

840 CN ISSN 0839-458X
PQ2625.A716
REVUE ANDRE MALRAUX REVIEW. (Text in English, French) 1969. s-a. Can.$24($24) to individuals; institutions Can.$30($30). Malraux Society, c/o Dr. Robert S. Thornberry, Univ. of Alberta, Dept. of Romance Languages, Edmonton, Alta. T6G 2E6, Canada. TEL 403-492-2003. FAX 403-474-8149. (Subscr. to: c/o Prof. Susan McLean McGrath, 615 W. May St., Mount Pleasant, MI 48858) Ed.Bd. bk.rev.; bibl.; cum.index every 3 yrs.; circ. 350. **Indexed:** M.L.A.
  Formerly: Melanges Malraux Miscellany (ISSN 0025-892X)
  Description: Devoted to all aspects of the life, works and influence of Andre Malraux (1901-1976).

LITERATURE 2955

800 961   US   ISSN 0890-6998
REVUE C E L F A N - C E L F A N REVIEW. (Text in English, French) 1981. 3/yr. $7.50 (foreign $10). Center for the Study of the Francophone Literature of North Africa, Department of French and Italian (022-37), Temple University, Philadelphia, PA 19122. TEL 215-787-8529. Ed. Eric Sellin. bk.rev.; bibl.; illus.; circ. 200. (back issues avail.)
Description: Scholarly criticism and creative works of French-language literature of North Africa.

860   FR   ISSN 0249-6356
REVUE CO-TEXTES. 2/yr. Universite de Montpellier (Universite Paul Valery), B.P. 5043, 34032 Montpellier Cedex 1, France. TEL 67-14-20-00.

800 944   FR
REVUE D'HISTOIRE DES TEXTES. a. price varies. (Centre National de la Recherche Scientifique) Editions du C N R S, 1 Place Aristide Briand, 92195 Meudon Cedex, France. TEL 1-45-34-75-50. FAX 1-46-26-28-49. TELEX LABOBEL 204 135 F. (Subscr. to: Presses du C N R S, 20-22, rue Saint Amand, 75015 Paris, France. TEL 1-45-33-16-00) adv.; bk.rev.; index; circ. 1,250 (controlled).

809   FR   ISSN 0035-2411
PQ2
REVUE D'HISTOIRE LITTERAIRE DE LA FRANCE. 1894. bi-m. 70 ECU($86) (Societe d'Histoire Litteraire de la France) Armand Colin (Subsidiary of: Masson), 103 bd. Saint-Michel, 75005 Paris, France. TEL 1-46-34-19-12. FAX 1-43-26-96-38. TELEX 201 269 F. Ed. Rene Pomeau. adv.; bk.rev.; bibl.; circ. 2,700. (also avail. in microfiche from BHP)
Indexed: Can.Rev.Comp.Lit., Curr.Cont., Hist.Abstr., Ind.Bk.Rev.Hum., M.L.A., RILA.

801 400   FR   ISSN 0982-6548
REVUE DE BIBLIOLOGIE. 2/yr. 75 F. Societe de Bibliologie et de Schematisation (S B S), 36 av. d'Italie, Tour Rubis, 75013 Paris, France.
Formed by the merger of: Schema et Schematisation (ISSN 0586-7606); Bulletin d'Informations Internationales de Bibliologie.

809   FR   ISSN 0035-1466
PN851
REVUE DE LITTERATURE COMPAREE. (Text in English, French, German, Italian, Spanish) 1921. q. $74. Didier Erudition, 6 rue de la Sorbonne, 75005 Paris, France. (Subscr. to: Didier Erudition, North American Fullfillment Office, P.O. Box 830350, Birmingham, AL-35283-0350) Ed. J. Voisine. adv.; bk.rev.; bibl.; charts; cum.index every 10 yrs.; circ. 2,000. (also avail. in microform from BHP; reprint service avail. from SCH) **Indexed:** Can.Rev.Comp.Lit., Curr.Cont., Ind.Bk.Rev.Hum., M.L.A.
Formerly: Etudes de Litterature Etrangere et Comparee (ISSN 0071-1918)

REVUE DES ETUDES AUGUSTINIENNES. see RELIGIONS AND THEOLOGY

891 943   FR   ISSN 0080-2557
PG1
REVUE DES ETUDES SLAVES. 1921. q. 400 F. Institut d'Etudes Slaves, 9 rue Michelet, 75006 Paris, France. bk.rev.; circ. 600. **Indexed:** Can.Rev.Comp.Lit, Hist.Abstr.

809   FR   ISSN 0035-2136
PN3
REVUE DES LETTRES MODERNES; histoire des idees et des litteratures. 1954. irreg. (6-10/yr.). 940 F. for 50 nos. Lettres Modernes, 73 rue du Cardinal Lemoine, 75005 Paris, France. Ed. M.J. Minard. bk.rev.; bibl. **Indexed:** M.L.A.

840   FR   ISSN 0425-4791
REVUE DES LETTRES MODERNES. ETUDES BERNANOSIENNES. 1960. a. 940 F. Lettres Modernes, 73 rue du Cardinal Lemoine, 75005 Paris, France. Ed. Michel Esteve. bk.rev. (back issues avail.)

LA REVUE DES REVUES. see BIBLIOGRAPHIES

REVUE ROMANE. see LINGUISTICS

808   US   ISSN 1047-2207
RHODODENDRON. (Text in English, French, German, Spanish) 1984. q. $15. Guerilla Poetics, Inc., 879 Bell St., E. Palo Alto, CA 94303. TEL 415-324-0206. Ed. Steven Jacobsen. adv.; bk.rev.; circ. 250. (back issues avail.)

869   BL
RHYTHMUS. 1981. q. Univerdidade Estadual Paulista Julio De Mesquita Filho, Instituto de Biociencias, Letras e Ciencias Exatas, 15100 Campus de Sao Jose do Rio Preto SP, Brazil.

RICHMOND QUARTERLY. see HISTORY — History Of North And South America

439.31 417   NE   ISSN 0012-6209
RIJKSUNIVERSITEIT TE GRONINGEN. NEDERSAKSISCH INSTITUUT. DRIEMAANDELIJKSE BLADEN; taal en volksleven in het oosten van Nederland. (Text in Dutch, German) 1902; N.S. 1949. q. fl.15. Stichting Sasland, Postbus 1127, 9701 BC Groningen, Netherlands. Ed. J. van der Kooi. bk.rev.; illus.; maps; circ. 400.

810   US
RIPPLES;* the poetry and fiction magazine. 1973. 4/yr. $18.50. Shining Waters Press, 2840 Canterbury Rd., Ann Arbor, MI 48104-5021. TEL 313-662-8446. Eds. Jim & Karen Schaefer. adv.; bk.rev.; circ. 1,000.

800   IT
RIVISTA DI LETTERATURE MODERNE E COMPARATE. (Text in English, French and Italian) 1946. q. L.60000 (foreign L.90000)(effective 1992). Pacini Editore s.r.l., Via Gherardesca 1, 56014 Ospedaletto (Pisa), Italy. TEL 050-982439. FAX 050-983906. Eds. G. Pellegrini, A. Pizzorusso. adv.; bk.rev.; circ. 520. **Indexed:** Arts & Hum.Cit.Ind., Can.Rev.Comp.Lit., Curr.Cont., M.L.A.

800 851   IT
RIVISTA LETTERARIA; quadrimestrale di critica letteraria e cultura varia. 1978. 3/yr. L.5000($5) Giuseppe Amalfitano Editore, Corso Garibaldi, 15, I-80074 Casamicciola Terme (Naples), Italy. adv.; bk.rev. (back issues avail.)

RIVISTA ROSMINIANA DI FILOSOFIA E DI CULTURA. see PHILOSOPHY

810   US   ISSN 0035-7367
PS50
ROANOKE REVIEW. 1967-1982; resumed 1985. s-a. $5.50. Roanoke College, Department of English, Salem, VA 24505. TEL 703-375-2367. Ed. Robert R. Walter. circ. 300. (processed)

820   UK   ISSN 0307-8957
PR4329
ROBERT BURNS CHRONICLE. 1892. a. £7.50 cloth bound; £4.50 paper bound. Burns Federation, Dick Institute, Elmbank Avenue, Kilmarnock KAI 3BU, Scotland. Ed. James A. Mackay. adv.; bk.rev.; bibl.; illus.; cum.index; circ. 3,000.

ROBERT E. HOWARD'S FIGHT MAGAZINE. see LITERATURE — Adventure And Romance

ROC SCIENCE FICTION ADVANCE. see LITERATURE — Science Fiction, Fantasy, Horror

800 700 770   US   ISSN 1046-0985
ROCKFORD REVIEW. 1971. a. $6. Rockford Writers' Guild, Box 858, Rockford, IL 61105. Ed. David Ross. circ. 500. (back issues avail.)
Description: Poetry, short fiction, one-act plays, essays, and black and white art work.

ROCKY MOUNTAIN MEDIEVAL AND RENAISSANCE ASSOCIATION. JOURNAL. see HISTORY — History Of Europe

800   US   ISSN 0361-1299
PB1
ROCKY MOUNTAIN REVIEW OF LANGUAGE AND LITERATURE. 1946. 4/yr. $20 to individuals; institutions $25. Rocky Mountain Modern Language Association, Department of English, Boise State University, Boise, ID 83725. TEL 208-385-3426. FAX 208-385-3401. Ed. Carol A. Martin. adv.; bk.rev.; charts; illus.; circ. 1,500. **Indexed:** Abstr.Engl.Stud., Amer.Hum.Ind., Arts & Hum.Cit.Ind., Bibl.Engl.Lang.& Lit., Bk.Rev.Ind. (1981-), Chic.Per.Ind., Child.Bk.Rev.Ind. (1981-), Curr.Cont., Lang.& Lang.Behav.Abstr., M.L.A.
Formerly: Rocky Mountain Modern Language Association. Bulletin (ISSN 0035-7626)

800   NE
RODOPI PERSPECTIVES ON MODERN LITERATURE. (Text in English) 1988. irreg. price varies. Editions Rodopi B.V., Keizersgracht 302-304, 1016 EX Amsterdam, Netherlands. TEL 020-6227507. FAX 020-6380948. (US and Canada subscr. to: 233 Peachtree St., N.E., Ste. 404, Atlanta, GA 30303-1504. TEL 800-225-3998) Ed. David Bevan.

890   II
ROHINI. (Text in Marathi) m. V.S. Kane, Ed. & Pub., White House, Tilak Rd., Pune 411 030, India. circ. 3,000.

813   US   ISSN 0145-5753
PS3545.A653
ROHMER REVIEW. 1968. irreg. $3 per no. 4 Forest Ave., Salem, MA 01970-4517. TEL 508-744-0885. Ed. Robert E. Briney. bk.rev.; illus.; circ. 400. **Indexed:** Abstr.Pop.Cult.
Description: Covers all aspects of the life and work of British thriller writer Sax Rohmer, creator of Dr. Fu Manchu.

810   US   ISSN 0892-6956
ROHWEDDER; international journal of literature and art. 1986. s-a. $12 to individuals; institutions $18. Rough Weather Press, Box 29490, Los Angeles, CA 90029. TEL 213-256-5083. Eds. Hans-Jurgen Schacht, Robert Dassanowsky-Harris. adv.; circ. 1,500 (controlled).

407   US   ISSN 0035-7995
PC1
ROMANCE NOTES. (Text in English, French, Italian, Portuguese, Spanish) 1959. 3/yr. $18. University of North Carolina at Chapel Hill, Department of Romance Languages, CB 3170, 238 Dey Hall, Chapel Hill, NC 27599-3170. TEL 919-962-1025. Ed. Ed. Montgomery. cum.index; circ. 650. (also avail. in microform from MIM; back issues avail.) **Indexed:** Arts & Hum.Cit.Ind., Curr.Cont., M.L.A.
—BLDSC shelfmark: 8019.460000.

ROMANCE OF LIFE. see ART

ROMANCE PHILOLOGY. see LINGUISTICS

809   UK   ISSN 0263-9904
ROMANCE STUDIES. 1982. s-a. £10 to individuals (foreign £12); institutions £15 (foreign £17). University College of Swansea, School of European Languages, c/o George Evans, Bus. Mgr., School of European Languages, Singleton Park, Swansea, W. Glamorgan SA2 8PP, England. FAX 295710. Ed. Valerie Minogue. adv.; circ. 200.
—BLDSC shelfmark: 8019.480000.
Description: Each issue is devoted to a specific theme or writer.

800   GW   ISSN 0557-2614
ROMANFUEHRER; der Inhalt der Romane und Novellen der Weltliteratur. 1952. irreg., vol.26, 1992. DM.178 per no. Anton Hiersemann Verlag, Rosenbergstr. 113, Postfach 140155, 7000 Stuttgart 1, Germany. TEL 0711-638265. FAX 0711-6369010. Ed. Bernd Graef.

859   RM   ISSN 0048-8550
AP86
ROMANIA LITERARA. 1954. w. 260 lei($15) Uniunea Scriitorilor din Republica Socialista Romania, Calea Victoriei 115, Bucharest, Rumania. (Subscr. to: ILEXIM, Str. 13 Decembrie Nr. 3, Box 136-137, 70116 Bucharest, Rumania) Dir. Nicolae Manolescu. bk.rev.; film rev.; play rev.; charts; illus.; circ. 25,000. (also avail. in microfilm from NRP) **Indexed:** M.L.A.
Supersedes (in 1968): Gazeta Literara.

ROMANIC REVIEW. see LITERATURE — Adventure And Romance

ROMANICA GOTHOBURGENSIA. see LINGUISTICS

ROMANICA HELVETICA. see LINGUISTICS

LITERATURE

870 GW ISSN 0035-8126
PC3
ROMANISCHE FORSCHUNGEN. (Text in English, French, German, Italian and Spanish) 1883. 4/yr. DM.228. Vittorio Klostermann, Frauenlobstr. 22, 6000 Frankfurt a.M. 90, Germany. TEL 069-774011. FAX 069-708038. Ed. Wido Hempel. adv.; bk.rev.; bibl.; index; circ. 800. (reprint service avail. from SCH,KTO) **Indexed:** Arts & Hum.Cit.Ind., Curr.Cont., Ind.Bk.Rev.Hum., M.L.A.

890 920 DK ISSN 0106-8253
ROMANSERIER OG SELVBIOGRAFISKE SERIER. a. DKK 92.60. Bibliotekscentralen, Tempovej 7-11, DK-2750 Ballerup, Denmark. TEL 2-974000. FAX 2-655310.

800 FR ISSN 0048-8593
ROMANTISME; revue du dix-neuvieme siecle. 1971. 4/yr. 330 F.($84.31) (Societe des Etudes Romantiques) Editions Centre de Documentation Universitaire et de la Societe d'Edition d'Enseignement Superieur Reunies (CDU & SEDES), 88 bd. Saint Germain, 75005 Paris, France. TEL 325-23-23. FAX 46-33-57-15. TELEX EDSEDES 206701F. adv.; bk.rev. **Indexed:** Can.Rev.Comp.Lit, Curr.Cont., M.L.A.
—BLDSC shelfmark: 8019.950000.

800 RU
ROMANTIZM V RUSSKOI I SOVETSKOI LITERATURE. 1973. irreg. 68 Rub. Kazanskii Universitet, Ul. Lenina, 4-5, Kazan, Russia.

800 305.412 CN ISSN 0316-1609
ROOM OF ONE'S OWN; a feminist journal of literature and criticism. 1975. q. Can.$15 to individuals (foreign Can.$20); institutions Can.$20 (foreign Can.$25). Growing Room Collective, Box 46160, Station G, Vancouver, B.C. V6R 4G5, Canada. Ed.Bd. adv.; bk.rev.; circ. 1,200. (also avail. in microform from UMI; back issues avail.; reprint service avail. from UMI) **Indexed:** Amer.Hum.Ind., Can.Lit.Ind., Can.Wom.Per.Ind., M.L.A., Stud.Wom.Abstr.

890 II
ROOPVATI. (Text in English, Punjabi) 1970. Rs.7. Pritam Singh, Pleasure Garden Market, Chadni Chowk, Delhi 6, India. Ed. Mrs. Kailash Puri. adv.; bibl.; illus.

ROSSICA OLOMUCENSIA. see *LINGUISTICS*

ROUND TABLE (ROCHESTER); a journal of poetry and fiction. see *LITERATURE* — *Poetry*

800 US
ROUND TABLE: A JOURNAL OF POETRY & FICTION. 1984. a. $12.50. Box 18763, Rochester, NY 14618. TEL 716-244-0623. Eds. Alan Lupack, Barbara Tepa Lupack. circ. 125. (back issues avail.)

ROYAL IRISH ACADEMY. PROCEEDINGS. SECTION C: ARCHAEOLOGY, CELTIC STUDIES, HISTORY, LINGUISTICS AND LITERATURE. see *ARCHAEOLOGY*

820 UK
ROYAL SHAKESPEARE COMPANY. PUBLICATION. 1978. a. £3.75. R S C Publications, Barbican Theatre, London EC2Y 8BQ, England. Ed. Simon Trussler.

891.85 PL ISSN 0035-9602
PG7001
RUCH LITERACKI. 1960. bi-m. $28.80. (Polska Akademia Nauk, Oddzial w Krakowie, Komisja Historycznoliteracka) Ossolineum, Publishing House of the Polish Academy of Sciences, Rynek 9, Wroclaw, Poland. TELEX 0712771 OSS PL. (Dist. by: Ars Polona-Ruch, Krakowskie Przedmiescie 7, Warsaw, Poland) (Co-sponsor: Towarzystwo Literackie Im. A. Mickiewicza) Ed. S. Jaworski. bk.rev.; bibl.; circ. 1,700. **Indexed:** M.L.A.
Description: History of Polish literature in international relations, literary theory, Slavonic literature.

800 GW ISSN 0557-4404
RUECKERT STUDIEN. irreg., vol.5, 1990. (Rueckert Gesellschaft e.V.) Verlag Otto Harrassowitz, Taunusstr. 14, Postfach 2929, 6200 Wiesbaden 1, Germany. TEL 0611-530-0. FAX 0611-530-570. TELEX 4186135. Ed.Bd.

800 GW ISSN 0933-9094
RUECKERT ZU EHREN; eine Schriftenreihe der Rueckert Gesellschaft. 1988. irreg., vol.3, 1990. (Rueckert Gesellschaft) Verlag Otto Harrassowitz, Taunusstr. 14, Postfach 2929, 6200 Wiesbaden 1, Germany. TEL 0611-530-0. FAX 0611-530-570. TELEX 4186135.

891.4 II ISSN 0035-9963
RUPAMBARA. (Text in English) q. $8. 22B Pratapaditya Rd., Calcutta 26, India. Ed. Swadesh Bharati.

RUSISTIKA. see *LINGUISTICS*

RUSKY JAZYK VE SKOLE; casopis pro vyucovani rustine na ceskoslovenskych skolach. see *EDUCATION*

890 NE ISSN 0304-3479
RUSSIAN LITERATURE; Croatian and Serbian, Czech and Slovak, Polish. 1972. 8/yr.(in 2 vols.; 4 nos./vol.) fl.730 (effective 1992). North-Holland (Subsidiary of: Elsevier Science Publishers B.V.), P.O. Box 211, 1000 AE Amsterdam, Netherlands. TEL 020-5803911. FAX 020-5803598. TELEX 18582 ESPA NL. (Subscr. in U.S. and Canada to: Elsevier Science Publishing Co., Inc., Box 882, Madison Sq. Sta., New York, NY 10159. TEL 212-989-5800) Eds. N.A. Nilsson, J. van der Eng. (also avail. in microform from RPI; back issues avail.; reprint service avail. from ISI,SWZ) **Indexed:** Curr.Cont.
—BLDSC shelfmark: 8052.739000.
Description: Devoted to special topics of Russian literature with contributions on related subjects in Croatian, Serbian, Czech, Slovak and Polish literatures.
Refereed Serial

891.7 491.7 700 UK
RUSSIAN POETICS IN TRANSLATION. 1973. irreg. price varies. (University of Essex, Department of Literature) R P T Publications, c/o N. Drake, Marketing Services, Deddington, Oxford OX5 4SW, England. FAX 0869-37123. bibl.; circ. 800. **Indexed:** M.L.A.

891.7 US
PN2
RUSSIAN STUDIES IN LITERATURE; a journal of translations. 1964. q. $286 to institutions. M.E. Sharpe, Inc., 80 Business Park Dr., Armonk, NY 10504. FAX 914-273-2106. Ed. Deming Brown. adv.; index. **Indexed:** Arts & Hum.Cit.Ind., Curr.Cont., M.L.A.
Formerly: Soviet Studies in Literature (ISSN 0038-5875)
Refereed Serial

809 US
RUTGERS AMERICAN WOMEN WRITERS SERIES. 1986. irreg., latest 1991. price varies. Rutgers University Press, 109 Church St., New Brunswick, NJ 08901. TEL 908-932-7762. FAX 908-932-7039. (Dist. by: Rutgers University Press Distribution Center, Box 4869, Hampden Sta., Baltimore, MD 21211. TEL 410-516-6947)

800 US
S C L A NEWSLETTER. 1975. biennial. $15 includes membership. Southern Comparative Literature Association, S C L A Newsletter, c/o David Parsell, Dept. of Classical & Modern Languages, Furman University, Greenville, SC 29613. (Subscr. to: c/o Dr. Carolyn Hodges, Department of German, University of Tennessee, Knoxville, TN 37996-0470) bk.rev.; bibl.; circ. 500.
Description: Provides news of the association.

S F W A BULLETIN. (Science Fiction Writers of America) see *LITERATURE* — *Science Fiction, Fantasy, Horror*

S K M. (Schweizer Kontakt) see *SOCIOLOGY*

808.838 US
S P W A O SHOWCASE. 1980. a. $5. (Small Press Writers and Artists Organization) Regions Press, c/o Sec./Treas., 13 Southwood Dr., Woodland, CA 95695. TEL 916-661-9231. Ed. Joe Morey. circ. 300.

800 SP ISSN 0213-6449
SABER LEER; revista critica de libros. 1987. m. Fundacion Juan March, Servicio de Informacion y Prensa, Castello, 77, 28006 Madrid, Spain. TEL 435 42 40. circ. 20,000.

810 640 US
SADIE'S CHATTER. 1972. m. $6. Box 2061, Tulsa, OK 74101. Ed. Doris Gist. adv.; bk.rev.; illus.; circ. 1,000.

839.6 949.12 IC ISSN 0558-1257
SAFN TIL SOEGU ISLANDS OG ISLENZKRA BOKMENNTA. 1856. irreg. Hid Islenzka Bokmenntafelag, Sidumula 21, P.O. Box 8935, 128 Reykjavik, Iceland. circ. 700.

800 US ISSN 1056-2591
▼**THE SAGARIN REVIEW.** 1991. a. $4. c/o The Saul Brodsky Jewish Community Library, 12 Millstone Campus Dr., St. Louis, MO 63146-5776. TEL 314-432-0200. Ed. Howard Schwartz.

890 II
SAHITYA CHINTA. (Text in Bengali) 1971. s-a. Rs.5 per no. Sahita Chinta Prokashani, 311 Ganguli Bagan Lane, Calcutta 47, India. Ed. Kiranshanker Sengupta. adv.; bk.rev.; circ. 1,250.
Description: Articles on traditions and trends of literary activities in India and abroad, includes short stories, poems and reviews.

378.1 US ISSN 0036-2751
PS1
ST. ANDREWS REVIEW. 1970. s-a. $14. (St. Andrews Presbyterian College) St. Andrews Press, Laurinburg, NC 28352. TEL 919-276-3652. Ed. Ronald H. Bayes. adv.; bk.rev.; play rev.; illus.; circ. 500. (also avail. in microform from UMI; reprint service avail. from UMI) **Indexed:** A.I.P.P.

916.606 NR ISSN 0795-2864
SAIWA; a journal of communication. (Text in English) 1981. a. £N15($8) Ahmadu Bello University, Department of English, Zaria, Kaduna State, Nigeria. Ed. O.S. Ogede. circ. 500.
Description: Attempts to break new ground in the praxis and study of African writing.

820 IE
SALMON INTERNATIONAL LITERARY JOURNAL. (Text in English, Gaelic) 1981. 3/yr. £6($22) (Arts Council) Salmon Publishing, The Bridge Mills, Galway, Ireland. TEL 091-62587. Ed. Jessie Lendennie. circ. 1,000.

801 II
SAMBALPUR UNIVERSITY. POST-GRADUATE DEPARTMENT OF ORIYA. JOURNAL. (Text in Oriya) no.2, 1976. a. Sambalpur University, Post Graduate Department of Oriya, Jotibihara, Sambalpur, India.

891.43 II
SAMBODHANA. (Text in Hindi) 1966. q. Rs.1000. Gulfam Khan, Chand Pole, Kankroli 313324, Rajasthan, India. Ed. Omar Mewari. adv.; bk.rev.; circ. 1,100.

SAMBRE ET HEURE. see *HISTORY*

895.1 CC
SAN YUE SAN. Zhuang edition: Sam Nyied Sam. (Editions in Chinese and Zhuang) 1983. bi-m. Y7.50($18.50) Guangxi Minzu Chubanshe, No. 8, Xinghu Lu Bei 2 Li, Nanning, Guangxi 530022, People's Republic of China. TEL 42719. (US subscr. to: China Books & Periodicals, Inc., 2929 24th St., San Francisco, CA 94110) Ed. Wei Wenjun. bk.rev.; circ. 20,000.
Description: Presents folk and contemporary literature by and about minority nationalities in southern China, primarily those in Guangxi. Also publishes research on the history, culture, languages, and customs of various minorities. Columns introduce famous places, persons, drama works, and history pertaining to minority ethnic groups.

810 US
SANDSCRIPT. 1977. 2/yr. $5. Cape Cod Writers, Inc., 1480 Masters Cir., Ste. 171, Delray Beach, FL 33445. TEL 617-362-6078. Eds. Barbara Oeffner, Jean Lunn. adv.; bk.rev.; illus.; circ. 300.

895.1 CC
SANJIAO ZHOU. (Text in Chinese) bi-m. Nantong Wenxue Yishu Jie Lianhehui - Nantong Literary and Art Circle Association, 2 Wenfeng Lu, Nantong, Jiangsu 226001, People's Republic of China. TEL 513929. Ed. Zhang Songlin.

810   US   ISSN 0899-9848
PS659
SANTA MONICA REVIEW. 1988. s-a. $12. Santa Monica College, 1900 Pico Blvd., Santa Monica, CA 90405. TEL 213-450-5150. Ed. James Krusoe. adv.; circ. 1,200.
  Description: Presents fiction, poetry and essays by contemporary writers.

895.1   CC   ISSN 0257-5809
SANWEN/PROSE MONTHLY. (Text in Chinese) 1980. m. $35. Baihua Wenyi Chubanshe, Chifeng Dao 130, Heping Qu, Tianjin 300041, People's Republic of China. TEL 706986. (Dist. in US by: China Books & Periodicals, Inc., 2929 24th St., San Francisco, CA 94110. TEL 415-282-2994)

800   CC
SANWEN BAIJIA. (Text in Chinese) bi-m. Xingtai Diqu Wenlian, 76 Xinxi Jie, Xingtai, Hebei 054001, People's Republic of China. TEL 4084. Ed. Xiao Shanbi.

895.1   CC
SANWEN XUANKAN. (Text in Chinese) m. Y0.98 per no. Henan Sheng Wenlian, No. 34, Jing 7 Lu, Zhengzhou, Henan 450003, People's Republic of China. TEL 334625. Ed. Bian Ka.
  Description: Publishes selected prose.

SANYUEFENG/SPRING BREEZES. see HANDICAPPED

SAPPHIC TOUCH; a journal of lesbian erotica. see WOMEN'S INTERESTS

SARI. see LINGUISTICS

891.4   II   ISSN 0036-4797
SARIKA. (Text in Hindi) fortn. $37. Bennett, Coleman & Co., Ltd. (New Delhi), Times House, 7 Bahadur Shah Zafar Marg, New Delhi 110002, India. (U.S. subscr. address: Kalpana, 42-75 Main St., Flushing, NY 11355) Ed. A.N. Mudgil. circ. 40,000.

891.4   II
SARITA. (Text in Hindi) 1945. fortn. Rs.300. Delhi Press Patra Prakashan Ltd., Delhi Press Bldg., E-3 Jhandewala Estate, New Delhi 110 055, India. Ed. Vishwa Nath. adv.; illus.; circ. 275,000.

890   II   ISSN 0303-3074
SARVOTKRUSHTA MARATHI KATHA. (Text in Marathi) vol.9, 1974. a. Rs.16($2) c/o Mrs. Chhaya Kolarkar, Ed., 43-348 Sant Tukaram Nagar, Pimpri, Poona 411018, India. circ. 1,500. (back issues avail.)

890   II   ISSN 0581-8532
SATAPITAKA. INDO-ASIAN LITERATURES. 1957. irreg. price varies. (International Academy of Indian Culture) Aditya Prakasham, F-14-65, Model Town II, New Delhi 110 009, India. TEL 7125436. FAX 91-11-3282047. Ed. Lokesh Chandra. circ. 100.

808   US
SATCHELL'S WRITER'S CLUB NEWSLETTER. 1985. q. $2.50 per no. Satchell's Publishing, 3124 Fifth Ave., Richmond, VA 23222. TEL 804-329-2130. Ed. Roswitha Petretschek. illus.

890   II
SATTAR DASHAK. (Text in Bengali) 1971. q. Rs.30. Gita Ganguli, 92-1 Charu Chandra Place, East Calcutta 700 033, India. TEL 423768. Ed. Jitesh Gangopadhaya. adv.; bk.rev.; circ. 15,000.
  Description: Provides articles on literature, economy and culture.

SATURDAY EVENING POST. see GENERAL INTEREST PERIODICALS — United States

806   US   ISSN 0735-1550
PS3503.E4488
SAUL BELLOW JOURNAL. 1982. 2/yr. $20 to individuals; institutions $15. 6533 Post Oak Dr., West Bloomfield, MI 48322. Ed. Liela Goldman. bk.rev.; circ. 300. **Indexed:** Abstr.Engl.Stud., M.L.A.
  —BLDSC shelfmark: 8077.204000.
  Supersedes: Saul Bellow Newsletter.
  Description: Critical essays, biographical articles, and annotated bibliography on Saul Bellow and his works.

808   US
SAUL BELLOW SOCIETY NEWSLETTER. vol.4, 1989. q. Brigham Young University, English Department, 3146 Jesse Knight Humanities Bldg., Provo, UT 84602. TEL 801-378-2948.

SAVACOU; a journal of the Caribbean artists movement. see ART

891.8   YU   ISSN 0036-519X
SAVREMENIK; mesecni knjizevni casopis. (Text in Serbo-Croatian) 1955. m. $0.05. Knjizevne Novine, Francuska 7, 11000 Belgrade, Yugoslavia. Ed. Pavle Zoric. bk.rev.; circ. 1,500. **Indexed:** M.L.A.

SCANDINAVIAN STUDIES (EUGENE). see LINGUISTICS

800 890   UK   ISSN 0036-5653
PT7001
SCANDINAVICA. (Text in English, French, German) 1962. s-a. $45. (School of Modern Languages and European History) Norvik Press, University of East Anglia, Norwich NR4 7TJ, England. TEL 0603-56161. FAX 0603-250599. Ed. Janet Garton. adv.; bk.rev.; bibl.; cum.index every 10 yrs.; circ. 500. (back issues avail.) **Indexed:** Hist.Abstr.

SCANDO-SLAVICA. see LINGUISTICS

800   CN
SCAT!. 1983. a. University of Toronto, Innis College, 2 Sussex Ave., Toronto, Ont. M5S 1A1, Canada. Ed. Yukio Koglin. bk.rev.; circ. 500.

SCAVENGER'S NEWSLETTER. see JOURNALISM

830   GW   ISSN 0937-2644
SCHLESWIG-HOLSTEIN. JAHRBUCH - HEIMATKALENDER. 1938. a. DM.11.90. (Schleswig-Holsteinischer Heimatbund) Heinrich Moeller Soehne GmbH, Bahnhofstr. 12-16, 2370 Rendsburg, Germany. TEL 04331-591101. FAX 04331-591100. adv.; bk.rev.; illus.; circ. 10,000.
  Formerly: Schleswig-Holsteinischer Heimatkalender.

SCHOOL MAGAZINE. see CHILDREN AND YOUTH — For

830 831   GW   ISSN 0174-2132
SCHREIBHEFT; Zeitschrift fuer Literatur. 1977. s-a. DM.52. Rigodon-Verlag, Nieberdingstr. 18, 4300 Essen 1, Germany. TEL 0201-778111. FAX 0221-715174. Ed. Norbert Wehr.

809   GW   ISSN 0430-5809
SCHRIFTEN AUS DEM FINNLAND-INSTITUT KOELN. 1961. irreg., no.15, 1987. price varies. Helmut Buske Verlag Hamburg, Friedrichsgaber Weg 138, Postfach 1249, 2000 Norderstedt, Germany. Ed. Fritz Keese.

SCHWARZER FADEN; Vierteljahresschrift fuer Lust und Freiheit. see POLITICAL SCIENCE

800   PP
SCOPE. irreg. price varies. National Research Institute, Cultural Studies Division, P.O. Box 5854, Boroko, NCD, Papua New Guinea. TEL 675-26-0300. FAX 675-26-0312.

820   UK
SCOTLIT. 1989. s-a. £24 (typically set in May). Association for Scottish Literary Studies (Dundee), c/o Univeristy of Aberdeen, Dept of English, Aberdeen AB9 2UB, Scotland. adv.; circ. 3,000.
  Supersedes (1974-1987): A S L S Newsletter.
  Description: Information about Scottish literature, publications and conferences.

820   UK   ISSN 0305-0785
PR8514
SCOTTISH LITERARY JOURNAL. 1974. s-a. £24 to individuals; institutions £40 (typically set in May). Association for Scottish Literary Studies, Dept. of English, University of Aberdeen, Old Aberdeen AB9 2UB, Scotland. TEL 0224-272634. Ed. J.H. Alexander. adv.; bk.rev.; cum.index; circ. 820 (controlled). **Indexed:** Abstr.Engl.Stud., Arts & Hum.Cit.Ind., Curr.Cont., Ind.Bk.Rev.Hum., M.L.A.
  —BLDSC shelfmark: 8210.693000.
  Supersedes: Scottish Literary News (ISSN 0048-9794)
  Description: Academic journal about Scottish literature of all periods.

800 940   UK   ISSN 0265-3273
PG1
SCOTTISH SLAVONIC REVIEW. 1983. 2/yr. £10($20) to individuals; institutions £15($30). University of Glasgow, Department of Slavonic Languages & Literature, Hetherington Building, Glasgow G12 8QQ, Scotland. TEL 041-339-8855. FAX 041-339-1110. TELEX 777070-UNIGLA. Ed. Peter Henry. adv.; bk.rev.; circ. 400.
  —BLDSC shelfmark: 8211.240000.
  Description: Covers the languages, literature, history, cultures and the arts of East Europe. Explores historical and cultural links between Eastern Europe and Scotland.

808 700   US   ISSN 0890-4596
SCREAM MAGAZINE. 1985. s-a. $10. Alternative Crimes Publishing, Box 10363, Raleigh, NC 27605. TEL 919-834-7542. Ed. Russell Judd Boone. adv.; bk.rev.; illus.; index, cum.index; circ. 2,000. (back issues avail.)
  Description: Promotes comics as an art form equal to literature, fine art and poetry.

800   US
SCRIBBLER. 1988. bi-m. Box 671, Madison, AL 35758. TEL 205-837-6434.

890   IE   ISSN 0332-4249
SCRIBHINNI GAEILGENA NA BRATHAR MIONUR. (Text in Gaelic) 1952. irreg., vol.11, 1976. Dublin Institute for Advanced Studies, 10 Burlington Rd., Dublin 4, Ireland. TEL 680748. FAX 680561.

820   US   ISSN 0190-731X
SCRIBLERIAN AND THE KIT-CATS; a newsjournal devoted to Pope, Swift, and their circle, the Kit-Cats and Dryden. 1968. s-a. $9 to individuals; institutions $12. Temple University, Department of English, Anderson Hall, Rm. 1038, Philadelphia, PA 19122. TEL 215-787-4717. (Co-sponsors: Northeastern University, Goldsmith's College, University of London, Queen's University) Ed. Bill Hatter. adv.; bk.rev.; bibl.; illus.; circ. 1,200. (back issues avail.) **Indexed:** Amer.Hum.Ind., Curr.Cont., Ind.Bk.Rev.Hum., M.L.A.
  Formerly: Scriblerian (ISSN 0036-9640) Formerly: Scriblerian (ISSN 0036-9640)

800   AT   ISSN 0725-0096
PN2
SCRIPSI. 1981. q. Aus.$30($40) Oxford University Press Australia, c/o Ormond College, Parkville, Vic. 3052, Australia. FAX 03-347-8084. (Subscr. to: Oxford University Press Australia, 253 Normandy Rd., S. Melbourne, Vic. 3205, Australia) Eds. Michael Heyward, Peter Craven. adv.; bk.rev.; circ. 2,000. (back issues avail.)
  —BLDSC shelfmark: 8211.859575.

SCRIPTA ISLANDICA. see LINGUISTICS

870   IE   ISSN 0332-4214
SCRIPTORES LATINI HIBERNIAE. (Text in Latin) 1955. irreg., vol.11, 1981. Dublin Institute for Advanced Studies, 10 Burlington Rd., Dublin 4, Ireland. TEL 680748. FAX 680561.
  Description: Works in Latin by medieval Irish writers.

860   DR
SCRIPTURA. irreg. Universidad Autonoma de Santo Domingo, Depto. de Letras, Apdo. 1355, Santo Domingo, Dominican Republic. **Indexed:** New Test.Abstr., Rel.Ind.One.

808 384 791.43   US   ISSN 0734-8592
PN1993.5.U718
SCRIPTWRITERS MARKET. 1979. a. $28.95. Scriptwriters - Filmmakers Publishing Co., 8033 Sunset Blvd., No. 306, Hollywood, CA 90046. TEL 818-762-3726. Eds. Leslie Gates, David Buffum. adv.; circ. 10,000.

800   IT
SCRITTURA SCENICA. 1971. q. L.27000. Bulzoni Editore, Via dei Liburni 14, 00185 Rome, Italy. Dir. Giuseppe Bartolucci. bk.rev.; bibl.

800   CN   ISSN 0227-5090
SCRIVENER. 1980. a. Can.$5($5) Scrivener Press, 853 Sherbrooke St. W., Montreal, Que. H3A 2T6, Canada. TEL 514-398-6588. Ed.Bd. adv.; bk.rev.; circ. 800.
  Description: New Canadian and American poetry, short fiction, essays and art.

2958 LITERATURE

800 PO ISSN 0037-0177
AP65
SEARA NOVA (LISBON, 1921).* 1921. m. Esc.300($9) Empresa de Publicidade Seara Nova, S.A.R.L., Av. Santos Dumont, 57-2, 1000 Lisbon, Portugal. TEL 01-761131. Ed. Jose Garibaldi. adv.; bk.rev.; film rev.; play rev.; record rev.; chart.; illus.; circ. 15,000. **Indexed:** M.L.A.

810 US ISSN 0147-6629
PS536.2
SEATTLE REVIEW. 1978. s-a. $10. University of Washington, Department of English, Padelford Hall, GN-30, Seattle, WA 98195. TEL 206-543-9865. Ed. Donna Gerstenberger. adv.; circ. 300. (back issues avail.) **Indexed:** A.I.P.P.
Supersedes: Assay (ISSN 0004-5004)

800 RM ISSN 0037-0517
PN6065.R8
SECOLUL 20; revista de literatura universala. 1961. m. 204 lei($15) Uniunea Scriitorilor Din Republica Socialista Romania, Calea Victoriei 115, Bucharest, Rumania. (Subscr. to: ILEXIM, Str. 13 Decembrie Nr. 3, Box 136-137, 70116 Bucharest, Rumania) Ed. Dan Haulica. bk.rev.; illus.; cum.index; circ. 8,000.

810 811 US ISSN 0095-1730
PS501
SEEMS. 1971. irreg. $16. c/o Karl Elder, Ed., Lakeland College, Box 359, Sheboygan, WI 53081. TEL 414-565-3871. circ. 250. **Indexed:** Access.

895 MY
SEJAHTERA. (Text in English or Malay) a. University of Malaya, Islamic Students' Union - Persatuan Mahasiswa Islam Universiti Malaya, 59100 Kuala Lumpur, Malaysia.

SELECTA (CORVALLIS). see LINGUISTICS

SELECTED WORKS OF JUAN LUIS VIVES. see HISTORY — History Of Europe

SELSKAB FOR NORDISK FILOLOGI. AARSBERETNING. see LINGUISTICS

430 CN ISSN 0037-1939
PF3001
SEMINAR; a journal of Germanic studies. (Text in English, French and German) 1965. q. Can.$35. (Canadian Association of University Teachers of German) University of Toronto Press, Journals Department, P.O. Box 1280, 1011 Sheppard Ave. W., Downsview, Ont. M3H 5V4, Canada. TEL 416-667-7781. FAX 416-667-7832. (U.S. Address: 340 Nagel Dr., Cheektowaga, NY 14225) Ed. R. Symington. adv.; bk.rev.; charts; index; circ. 776. **Indexed:** Amer.Bibl.Slavic & E.Eur.Stud., Curr.Cont., Ind.Bk.Rev.Hum., M.L.A.
—BLDSC shelfmark: 8239.352000.

800 051 US ISSN 1053-9115
SENSATIONS. 1987. s-a. $30 for 5 nos. David Messineo, Ed. & Pub., c/o 2 Radio Ave., A5, Secaucus, NJ 07094. Ed.Bd. adv.; illus.; circ. 120. (back issues avail.)
Description: Literary magazine covering American poetry from 1565 to 1625. Also includes contemporary poetry and fiction.

860 CR
SERIE ESTUDIOS LITERARIOS. 1975. irreg. free (not for international distribution). Ministerio de Cultura, Juventud y Deportes, Dept. de Publicaciones, Apdo. 10227, San Jose, Costa Rica.

800 410 II ISSN 0254-0193
SERIES IN ENGLISH LANGUAGE AND LITERATURE. (Text in English) 1978. irreg. price varies. Bahri Publications, 997-A, Street No. 9, Gobindpuri, Kalkaji, New Delhi 110 019, India. TEL 644-5710. Ed. Ujjal Singh Bahri.
Description: Academic series on English language and literature.

SERIES IN SIKH HISTORY AND CULTURE. see HISTORY — History Of Asia

850 IT ISSN 0037-2498
SERPE; rivista letteraria. 1952. q. $20. (Associazione dei Medici Scrittori Italiani) Edizioni Clinica Europea, Via Concordia 20, 00183 Rome, Italy. TEL 7576475. Ed. Fausto Federici. adv.; bk.rev.; record rev.; index; circ. 12,000.

840 FR ISSN 0992-2660
SERPENT A PLUMES. q. 225 F. (foreign 275 F.). Association pour le Promotion de la Nouvelle, 78 rue du Bac, 75007 Paris, France. TEL 45-48-58-89. Ed. Pierre Astier.

800 IS
SEVEN GATES. (Text in English) 1985. 3/yr. Youval Tal Ltd., P.O. Box 2160, Jerusalem 91 021, Israel.

800 UK ISSN 0268-117X
THE SEVENTEENTH CENTURY. 1986. s-a. £10 to individuals; institutions £15. University of Durham, Centre for 17th Century Studies, Palace Green, Durham DH1 3RN, England. Ed. R.G. Maber. adv.
—BLDSC shelfmark: 8253.947900.
Description: Interdisciplinary journal concerned with all aspects of the seventeenth century, including literature, theology, philosophy, natural science, music and visual arts.

840 844 UK ISSN 0265-1068
DC33.4
SEVENTEENTH CENTURY FRENCH STUDIES. (Text in English and French) 1979. a. £6 to individuals; institutions £8. Society for Seventeenth Century French Studies, School of Modern Languages and European History, University of East Anglia, Norwich NR4 7TJ, England. TEL 0603-56161. FAX 0603-58553. TELEX 975197. Ed. C.N. Smith. adv.; bk.rev.; circ. 300. **Indexed:** M.L.A.
Formerly (until 1984): Society for Seventeenth Century French Studies. Newsletter (ISSN 0142-5080)
Description: All aspects of French seventeenth-century culture, literature and history.

800 US ISSN 0037-3028
PR1
SEVENTEENTH - CENTURY NEWS. (Including: Neo-Latin News) 1942. q. $6. (Milton Society of America) Texas A & M University, Department of English, College Station, TX 77843. TEL 409-845-3400. Eds. J. Max Patrick, Harrison T. Meserole. adv.; bk.rev.; abstr.; circ. 1,200. (also avail. in microform from UMI; reprint service avail. from UMI) **Indexed:** Abstr.Engl.Stud., Arts & Hum.Cit.Ind., Bk.Rev.Ind. (1981-), Child.Bk.Rev.Ind. (1981-), Curr.Cont., Ind.Bk.Rev.Hum., M.L.A.
—BLDSC shelfmark: 8253.950000.

800 US ISSN 0893-6900
SEVENTEENTH - CENTURY TEXTS AND STUDIES. (Text in English and other West European languages) 1987. irreg. Peter Lang Publishing, Inc., 62 W. 45th St., 4th Fl., New York, NY 10036. TEL 212-302-6740. Ed. Anthony Low.
—BLDSC shelfmark: 8253.953000.
Description: Concerned with English non-dramatic poetry and prose from about the time of Donne and Jonson to the death of Milton.

810 US ISSN 0037-3052
AP2
SEWANEE REVIEW. 1892. q. $15 to individuals; institution $20. University of the South, Sewanee Review, Sewanee, TN 37375-4000. TEL 615-598-1246. Ed. George Core. adv.; bk.rev.; circ. 3,400. (also avail. in microform from KTO,BHP; back issues avail.; reprint service avail. from UMI,KTO) **Indexed:** A.I.P.P., Abstr.Engl.Stud., Acad.Ind., Arts & Hum.Cit.Ind., Bibl.Engl.Lang.& Lit., Bk.Rev.Ind. (1965-), Child.Bk.Rev.Ind. (1965-), Hum.Ind., Ind.Amer.Per.Verse, Ind.Bk.Rev.Hum., LCR, M.L.A., Mag.Ind.
—BLDSC shelfmark: 8254.250000.

800 US ISSN 0893-6889
SEXUALITY AND LITERATURE. (Text in English and other West European languages) 1988. irreg. Peter Lang Publishing, Inc., 62 W. 45th St., 4th Fl., New York, NY 10036. TEL 212-302-6740. FAX 212-302-7574. Ed. John Maynard.

SEZ; a multi-racial journal of poetry & people's culture. see ETHNIC INTERESTS

800 GW ISSN 0080-9128
PR2889
SHAKESPEARE - JAHRBUCH. 1864. a. DM.32. (Deutsche Shakespeare Gesellschaft) Verlag Hermann Boehlaus Nachfolger, Meyerstr. 50a, 5300 Weimar, Germany. Ed. Guenther Klotz. bk.rev. (reprint service avail. from KTO) **Indexed:** M.L.A.

820 US ISSN 0037-3214
PR2885
SHAKESPEARE NEWSLETTER. 1951. 4/yr. (Sept.-May). $12 (foreign $14). Louis Marder, Ed. & Pub., 1217 Ashland Ave., Evanston, IL 60202. TEL 708-475-7550. FAX 708-475-2415. adv.; bk.rev.; abstr.; bibl.; film rev.; play rev.; stat.; tr.lit.; index; circ. 2,000. (back issues avail.) **Indexed:** Abstr.Engl.Stud., LCR, M.L.A.
Description: Shakespeare news, digests of scholarly articles, lectures, dissertations, new books, original articles, authorship question, computer scholarship, latest critical and historical discoveries, Shakespeare festivals and programs.

800 US
SHAKESPEARE OXFORD SOCIETY. NEWSLETTER. 1957. q. $25. Shakespeare Oxford Society, c/o Victor Crichton, Membership Chairman, 207 W. 106th St., Apt. 10B, New York, NY 10025. Ed. Morse Johnson. bk.rev.; circ. 500.

820 US ISSN 0037-3222
PR2885
SHAKESPEARE QUARTERLY. 1950. 5/yr. $35 to individuals; institutions $45. Folger Shakespeare Library, 201·E. Capitol St., S.E., Washington, DC 20003-1094. TEL 202-544-4600. FAX 202-544-4623. Ed. Barbara A. Mowat. adv.; bk.rev.; bibl.; illus.; circ. 4,000. (also avail. in microform from UMI; microfiche; reprint service avail. from UMI) **Indexed:** Abstr.Engl.Stud., Acad.Ind., Arts & Hum.Cit.Ind., Bk.Rev.Ind. (1986-), Child.Bk.Rev.Ind. (1986-), Curr.Cont., Film Lit.Ind. (1974-), Hum.Ind., Ind.Bk.Rev.Hum., M.L.A.
—BLDSC shelfmark: 8254.586000.

820 JA ISSN 0582-9402
SHAKESPEARE STUDIES. (Text in English) 1962. a. 6000 Yen($5) Shakespeare Society of Japan, 501 Kenkyusha Bldg. 9, 2-chome Kanda-Surugadai, Chiyoda-ku, Tokyo 101, Japan. FAX 03-3233-3398. Ed. Yasunari Takahashi. circ. 1,200. **Indexed:** Hum.Ind., M.L.A.

809 US ISSN 0582-9399
PR2885
SHAKESPEARE STUDIES; an annual gathering of research, criticism & review. 1965. a. $25. Burt Franklin & Co., Inc., Box 856, New York, NY 10014. TEL 212-627-0027. **Indexed:** Hum.Ind., Ind.Bk.Rev.Hum., M.L.A.
—BLDSC shelfmark: 8254.586500.

822 UK ISSN 0080-9152
PR2888
SHAKESPEARE SURVEY. 1948. a. price varies. Cambridge University Press, Edinburgh Bldg., Shaftesbury Rd., Cambridge CB2 2RU, England. TEL 0223-312393. FAX 0223-315052. TELEX 851817256. Ed. Stanley Wells. index, cum.index: vols. 1-10, 11-10, 21-30. **Indexed:** Abstr.Engl.Stud., Acad.Ind., Arts & Hum.Cit.Ind., Curr.Cont., Hum.Ind., M.L.A.
—BLDSC shelfmark: 8254.586800.

800 US
SHAKESPEARE WORLDWIDE. 1974. a. $45. A M S Press, Inc., 56 E. 13th St., New York, NY 10003. TEL 212-777-4700. FAX 212-995-5413. (back issues avail.)
Formerly: Shakespeare Translation.
Description: Collection of reviews of performances of Shakespeare in non-English speaking countries.

800 US ISSN 1045-9456
PR2885
SHAKESPEARE YEARBOOK. a. $29.95. Edwin Mellen Press, 240 Portage Rd., Box 450, Lewiston, NY 14092. TEL 800-753-2788. FAX 716-754-4335. Ed. Linda Kay Hoff.
Description: Focuses on cultural continuity.

807 US ISSN 0883-9123
PR2965
SHAKESPEAREAN CRITICISM. 1984. irreg., vol.16, 1991. $114. Gale Research Inc., 835 Penobscot Bldg., Detroit, MI 48226. TEL 800-877-4253. FAX 313-961-6083. TELEX 810-221-7086. Ed. Sandra Williamson. abstr.; bibl.; illus.
—BLDSC shelfmark: 8254.586950.
Description: Guide to contemporary forms of Shakespearean criticism.

895.1   CC
SHAN CHA/CAMELLIA; minzu minjian wenxue shuangyuekan. (Text in Chinese) bi-m. $22.50. Yunnan Shehui Kexueyuan, Minzu Wenxue Yanjiusuo - Yunnan Academy of Social Sciences, Institute of Minority Nationalities Literature, 45, Qixiang Lu, Kunming, Yunnan 650032, People's Republic of China. TEL 42039. (Dist. outside China by: China International Book Trading Corp., P.O. Box 399, Beijing, P.R.C.; Dist. in US by: China Books & Periodicals, Inc., 2929 24th St., San Francisco, CA 94110. TEL 415-282-2994) Ed. Li Zuanxu.
  Description: Contains folk literature and literature of minority nationalities.

895.1   CC   ISSN 0257-5817
SHANDONG WENXUE/SHANDONG LITERATURE. (Text in Chinese) 1980. m. Y15.60($56.70) (Zhongguo Zuojia Xiehui, Shandong Fenhui - China Writers' Association, Shandong Chapter) Shandong Wenxue She, No.10, Honglou Nanlu, Jinan, Shandong 250100, People's Republic of China. TEL 46573. (Dist. overseas by: China International Book Trading Corp., P.O. Box 399, Beijing, P.R.C.; Dist. in US by: China Books & Periodicals, Inc., 2929 24th St., San Francisco, CA 94110) Ed. Qiu Xun. bk.rev.

800   CC   ISSN 1000-4831
SHANGHAI GUSHI/SHANGHAI STORIES. (Text in Chinese) m. Shanghai Qunzhong Yishu-guan - Shanghai Municipal Mass Art Gallery, 226 Huangling Beilu, Shanghai 200003, People's Republic of China. TEL 3278219. Ed. Xu Weixin.

895.1   CC   ISSN 0582-9542
SHANGHAI WENXUE/SHANGHAI LITERATURE. dangdai xintansuo, xinwenxue. (Text in Chinese; table of contents in English) 1959-1963; N.S. 1977. m. Y20.40($72) (Shanghai Wenxue Bianjibu) Shanghai Wenyi Chubanshe - Shanghai Arts Press, 675 Julu Road, Shanghai 200040, People's Republic of China. (Dist. outside China by: China International Book Trading Corp., P.O. Box 399, Beijing, P.R.C.; Dist. in US by: China Books & Periodicals, Inc., 2929 24th St., San Francisco, CA 94110. TEL 415-282-2994) Ed. Ba Jin. adv.
  Formerly: Wenyi Yuebao.

895.1   CC   ISSN 0559-7218
SHANHUA/MOUNTAIN BLOSSOMS (GUIZHOU). (Text in Chinese) m. $49.50. Guizhou Sheng Wenlian, No. 66, Kexue Lu, Guiyang, Guizhou 550002, People's Republic of China. TEL 23844. (Dist. in US by: China Books & Periodicals, Inc., 2929 24th St., San Francisco, CA 94110. TEL 415-282-2994) Ed. Wen Zhiqiang.

810 700   US
SHANKPAINTER. 1970. a. free. Fine Arts Work Center in Provincetown, Inc., Box 565, 24 Pearl St., Provincetown, MA 02657. TEL 508-487-9960. illus.; circ. 700.
  Description: Publishes the works by the Center's writing and visual fellows.

800   CC
SHANXI MINJIAN WENXUE/SHANXI FOLK LITERATURE. (Text in Chinese) bi-m. Zhongguo Minjian Wenyijia Xiehui, Shanxi Fenhui - China Folk Artists Assocition, Shanxi Chapter, 62 Yingze Dajie, Taiyuan, Shanxi 030001, People's Republic of China. TEL 446952. Ed. Liu Qi.

895.1   CC   ISSN 0257-5906
SHANXI WENXUE/SHANXI LITERATURE. (Text in Chinese) 1982. m. $47.70. Shanxi Wenxue Yuekan She, Taiyuan, Shanxi, People's Republic of China. (Dist. by: China Books & Periodicals, Inc., 2929 24th San Francisco, CA 94110. TEL 415-282-2994)
  Formerly: Fen Shui.

895.1   CC
SHAONAN SHAONU/BOYS AND GIRLS. (Text in Chinese) bi-m. Y10.80. Zhongguo Zuojia Xiehui, Guangdong Fenhui - China Writers' Association, Guangdong Chapter, No. 75, Wende Lu, Guangzhou, Guangdong 510030, People's Republic of China. TEL 330050. Ed. Guan Xizhi.

SHAONIAN WENYI/LITERATURE & ART FOR JUVENILES. see CHILDREN AND YOUTH — For

890   IS
AL-SHARQ; literary quarterly. (Text in Arabic) 1970. q. $40. Al-Mashreq Ltd., P.O. Box 69, Shfaram, Israel. TEL 04-966079. FAX 04-866129. Ed. Dr. Mahmoud Abassi.

820   UK   ISSN 0037-3346
SHAVIAN. 1946. a. £5($12) Shaw Society, 6 Stanstead Grove, London SE6 4UD, England. (Subscr. to: Mr. D. Sutherland, 155a N. View Rd., London N8 7ND, England) adv.; bk.rev.; cum.index: vol.1, 1953-1959; vol.2, 1960-1963; circ. 550. (also avail. in microform from UMI; reprint service avail. from UMI) Indexed: Abstr.Engl.Stud, M.L.A.

820   US   ISSN 0741-5842
PR5366
SHAW ANNUAL. Variant title: Shaw: the annual of Bernard Shaw Studies. 1951. a. price varies. Pennsylvania State University Press, Barbara Bldg., Ste. C, 820 N. University Dr., University Park, PA 16802-1003. TEL 814-865-1327. FAX 814-863-1408. Ed. Fred D. Crawford. bk.rev.; bibl.; illus.; index, cum.index: 1950-1975; circ. 750. (also avail. in microform from UMI; reprint service avail. from UMI,KTO) Indexed: Abstr.Engl.Stud., Amer.Hum.Ind., Curr.Cont., Ind.Bk.Rev.Hum., M.L.A.
  Formerly: Shaw Review (ISSN 0037-3354)

800   UK
SHAW SOCIETY NEWSLETTER. 1976. q. £5($12) membership. Shaw Society, 6 Stanstead Grove, London SE6 4UD, England. (Subscr. to: Mr. D.A. Sutherland, 155a North View Rd., London N8 7ND, England) Ed. T.E. Evans. adv.; bk.rev.; circ. 500. (looseleaf format)
  Formerly: Shaw Newsletter (ISSN 0309-0396)

800   CC
SHENZHOU CHUANQI. (Text in Chinese) bi-m. Huashan Wenyi Chubanshe, 45 Beima Lu, Shijiazhuang, Hebei 050071, People's Republic of China. TEL 742501. Ed. Ning Xuancheng.

890   UK
SHETU-BONDHA; the Bengali literary bi-monthly magazine. 1976. bi-m. £2($10) Shetu-Bondha Publications, 113 Harold Rd., London E13 0SG, England. Ed. Khalilur Rahamn. bk.rev.; circ. 6,000. (back issues avail.)

895.1   CC   ISSN 0257-5841
PL2653
SHI YUE/OCTOBER; wenxue shuang yuekan. (Text in Chinese) 1978. bi-m. Y22.80($68.20) Beijing Chubanshe, 6, Beisanhuan Zhonglu, Beijing 100011, People's Republic of China. TEL 201-2336. FAX 201-2339. (Dist. overseas by: Guoji Shudian - China International Book Trading Corp., P.O. Box 399, Beijing, P.R.C.; Dist. in US by: China Books & Periodicals, Inc., 2929 24th St., San Francisco, CA 94110. TEL 415-282-2994) Ed. Xie Dajun. circ. 123,000.
  Description: Literary magazine of Beijing.

895.1   CC
SHIDAI WENXUE. (Text in Chinese) bi-m. Zhongguo Zuojia Xiehui, Shandong Fenhui - China Writers' Association, Shandong Chapter, No. 10, Hongjialou Nanlu, Jinan, Shandong 250100, People's Republic of China. TEL 48869. Ed. Feng Deying.

800   CC   ISSN 0583-0206
SHIJIE WENXUE/WORLD LITERATURE. (Text in Chinese; table of contents in English) 1959. bi-m. $47.30. Shehui Kexue Zazhishe, A-158 Gulou Xidajie, Beijing 100720, People's Republic of China. (Dist. in US by: China Books & Periodicals, Inc., 2929 24th St., San Francisco, CA 94110. TEL 415-282-2994)
  Formerly: Yi Wen.
  Description: Introduces modern writers and their works. Also presents important literary trends, critical essays, cultural exchanges, and the latest developments in literature.

891.4   II
SHIRAZA. (Editions in Dogri, Gojri, Hindi, Kahmiri, Pahari, Punjabi and Urdu) 1969. bi-m. Rs.10. Jammu and Kashmir Academy of Art, Culture and Languages, Canal Road, Jammu 180001, India. Ed. Amrik Singh. bk.rev.; bibl.; circ. 500.

SHOE TREE; the literary magazine by and for young writers 6-14. see CHILDREN AND YOUTH — For

SHOOTING STAR REVIEW. see ETHNIC INTERESTS

808   US
▼**SHORT FICTION BY WOMEN**. 1991. 3/yr. $18. Box 1276, Stuyvesant Sta., New York, NY 10009. TEL 212-255-0276. Ed. Rachel Whalen.
  Description: Short stories and novel excerpts from new and established writers.

800   US   ISSN 0080-9403
SHORT PLAY SERIES. 1966. irreg., no.8, 1982. price varies. Proscenium Press, Box 361, Newark, DE 19711. TEL 302-764-8477. Ed. Robert Hogan. (reprint service avail. from UMI)

800   US
SHORT STORY CRITICISM. irreg., vol.7, 1991. $79. Gale Research Inc., 835 Penobscot Bldg., Detroit, MI 48226-4094. TEL 313-961-2242. FAX 313-961-6083. TELEX 810-221-7086.
  Description: Excerpts significant passages from criticism on the works of the great short story writers of the world throughout history.

810   US   ISSN 0147-7706
PZ1.A1
SHORT STORY INTERNATIONAL. Short title: S S I. 1977. bi-m. $24. International Cultural Exchange, 6 Sheffield Rd., Great Neck, NY 11021. TEL 516-466-4166. (Subscr. to: Box 405, Great Neck, NY 11022) Ed. Sylvia Tankel. circ. 75,000.

890   JA
SHOSETSU GENDAI. (Text in Japanese) 1963. m. Kodansha Ltd., International Division, 12-21 Otowa 2-chome, Bunkyo-Ku, Tokyo 112, Japan. TEL 03-3945-1111. FAX 03-3943-7815. TELEX J34509 KODANSHA. Ed. Shinichi Hirota. circ. 150,000.
  Description: Publishes serialised novels and short stories for adults.

895.65   JA
SHOSETSU SHINCHO. (Text in Japanese) 1947. m. Shincho-Sha, 71, Yarai-cho, Shinjuku-ku, Tokyo 162, Japan. TEL 03-3266-5235. Ed. Masaji Yokoyama. circ. 360,000.

895.1   CC   ISSN 0583-1288
SHOU HUO/HARVEST: A LITERARY MAGAZINE; a widely circulated national magazine devoted to pure literature. (Text in Chinese) bi-m. Y24($70) Shouhuo Wenxue Zazhishe, 675 Julu Lu, Shanghai 200040, People's Republic of China. TEL 4335176. (Dist. outside China by: China International Book Trading Corp., P.O. Box 399, Beijing, P.R.C.; Dist. in US by: China Books & Periodicals, Inc., 2929 24th St., San Francisco, CA 94110. TEL 415-282-2994) Ed. Ba Jin.
  Description: Contains short stories, prose, movie scripts, and other literary works.

SHU LIN/BOOK FOREST. see PUBLISHING AND BOOK TRADE

895.4   BR
SHU MA WA MAGAZINE. (Text in Burmese) m. 146 Western Wing, Bogyoke Market, Yangon, Union of Myanmar.

808.87   II
SHUGOOFA; humorous Urdu monthly. (Text in Urdu) 1969. m. Rs.50. 31 Bachelor's Quarters, Moazamjahi Market, Hyderabad 500001, India. TEL 557716. Ed. Dr. S. Mustafa Kamal. adv.; bk.rev.; illus.; circ. 2,700.

895.1   US   ISSN 0257-585X
SHUOFANG/SHUOFANG LITERATURE (Text in Chinese) 1973. m. $44. China Books & Periodicals, Inc., 2929 24th St., San Francisco, CA 94110. TEL 415-282-2994. FAX 415-282-0994.

892.7   TS
SHU'UN ADABIYYAH/LITERARY AFFAIRS. (Text in Arabic) 1987. q. Ittihad Kuttab wa Udaba' al-Imarat - Emirates Writers Union, P.O. Box 4321, Sharjah, United Arab Emirates. TEL 350769. Ed. Muhammad Abdullah al-Muttawi. circ. 2,000.
  Description: Covers contemporary literary issues in the Arab world, with a focus on the U.A.E.

LITERATURE

895.1   CC
SICHUAN WENXUE/SICHUAN LITERATURE. (Text in Chinese) 1953. m. Y18. Zhongguo Zuojia Xiehui, Sichuan Fenhui - China Writers' Association, Sichuan Chapter, 85, Sec.2, Hongxing Lu, Chengdu, Sichuan 610012, People's Republic of China. TEL 665271. (Dist. outside China by: China International Book Trading Corp., P.O. Box 399, Beijing, P.R.C.; Dist. in US by: China Books & Periodicals, Inc., 2929 24th St., San Francisco, CA 94110. TEL 415-282-2994) Ed. Deng Yizhong. bk.rev.; illus.
    Formerly (until 1991): Xiandai Zuojia (ISSN 0258-0004)
    Description: Publishes novels, essays, and poetry.

840   FR
SIECLE ECLATE: DADA, SURREALISME ET LES AVANT-GARDES. 1974. irreg. Lettres Modernes, 73 rue du Cardinal Lemoine, 75005 Paris, France. circ. 2,500.

892.4   IS   ISSN 0037-4792
SIFRIYA LAAM. 1958. m. $70. Am Oved Ltd. Publishers, Box 470, Tel Aviv, Israel. circ. 20,000.

892.4   IS   ISSN 0017-8284
PJ5001
HA-SIFRUT/LITERATURE; journal for the study of literary theory, Hebrew and comparative. (Text in Hebrew; summaries in English) 1968. q. $36. Tel Aviv University, Porter Institute, Ramat Aviv, Tel Aviv, Israel. Ed. Itamar Even-Zohar. bk.rev.; circ. 1,100. (back issues avail.) **Indexed:** Ind.Heb.Per., Lang.& Lang.Behav.Abstr., M.L.A.

860   US   ISSN 0740-946X
PQ6072
SIGLO XX/20TH CENTURY. (Text and summaries in English and Spanish) 1983. s-a. $25. (Twentieth Century Spanish Association of America) Society of Spanish and Spanish-American Studies, Department of Spanish and Portuguese, University of Colorado, Campus Box 278, Boulder, CO 80309-0278. TEL 303-492-7308. FAX 303-492-3699. Ed. Luis T. Gonzalez. index; circ. 700. (back issues avail.) **Indexed:** M.L.A.
    Description: Attempts to foster dialogue on twentieth century Spanish and Spanish-American literatures and to facilitate the development of the many critical avenues available to the specialist.

SIGNAL; approaches to children's books. see CHILDREN AND YOUTH — About

800   CC   ISSN 1001-0165
SIHAI; dangtai haiwai huaren wenxue. (Text in Chinese) bi-m. Zhongguo Wenlian Chuban Gongsi, 10 Nongzhanguan Nanli, Beijing 100026, People's Republic of China. TEL 5005588. Ed. Qin Mu.
    Description: Presents literary works by Chinese writers living abroad.

830   GW   ISSN 0173-6310
SILHOUETTE; Literatur-International. (Text mainly in German; occasionally in English, Hebrew) 1980. a. DM.10. M. und N. Boesche, Laurinsteig 14a, 1000 Berlin 28, Germany. TEL 030-4019009. Ed. Tilly Boesche-Zacharow. bk.rev.

SILLAGES. see LINGUISTICS

895.1   US   ISSN 1000-7792
SILU/SILK ROAD. (Text in Chinese) 1978. bi-m. $13.10. (Kashi Wen-Lian, CC) China Books & Periodicals, Inc., 2929 24th St., San Francisco, CA 94110. TEL 415-282-2994. FAX 415-282-0994.

810   US   ISSN 0164-1085
PS536.2
SILVERFISH REVIEW. 1979. irreg. (approx. 3/yr.). $12 to individuals; institutions $15. Box 3541, Eugene, OR 97403. TEL 503-344-5060. Ed. Rodger Moody. adv.; bk.rev.; circ. 750. (back issues avail.) **Indexed:** Amer.Hum.Ind., Ind.Amer.Per.Verse.
    Description: Prints poetry, fiction, essays, translations, interviews and poetry chapbooks.

830   SZ   ISSN 0259-6415
PT1732
SIMPLICIANA; Schriften der Grimmelshausen Gesellschaft. (Text in German) 1979. a. Verlag Peter Lang AG, Jupiterstr. 15, CH-3000 Bern 15, Switzerland. TEL 031-321122. FAX 031-321131. TELEX 912651-PELA-CH.

890   KO
SIMUNHAK. m. 3000 Won. Simunhak Sa, 34 Hap-dong, Sodaemun-ku, Seoul, S. Korea. Ed. Dok-su Moon. adv.; bk.rev.

810   US   ISSN 0198-9855
PS508.W7
SING HEAVENLY MUSE!; women's poetry and prose. 1978. s-a. $19 to individuals; institutions $21. Box 132320, Minneapolis, MN 55414. Ed. Sue Ann Martinson. circ. 500. (back issues avail.)

890   SI   ISSN 0129-3117
SINGAPORE LITERATURE.* (Text in Chinese) 1976. q. S.$19.50 for 10 nos. Singapore Literature Society, 122B Slims Ave., Singapore 1438, Singapore. Ed. Luo-Ming. circ. 8,000.

810   US
SINGLE TODAY. 1987. 12/yr. $25. 2500 Mt. Moriah, Ste. 185, Memphis, TN 38115. TEL 901-365-3988. Ed. Paula M. Pederson. circ. 15,000.

SINISTER WISDOM; a journal for the lesbian imagination in the arts and politics. see WOMEN'S INTERESTS

800   GW   ISSN 0037-5756
AP30
SINN UND FORM; Beitraege zur Literatur. 1949. bi-m. DM.57 (foreign DM.57). Verlag Ruetten und Loenig, Franzoesische Str. 32, 1080 Berlin, Germany. TEL 2202421. Ed. Sebastian Kleinschmidt. bk.rev.; film rev.; play rev.; circ. 4,000. **Indexed:** Arts & Hum.Cit.Ind., Ind.Bk.Rev.Hum., M.L.A.
—BLDSC shelfmark: 8285.580000.

SINO-PLATONIC PAPERS. see HISTORY — History Of Asia

800   NE
SIRENE. (Text in German) 1985. 3/yr. fl.26. Wolters-Noordhoff B.V., Damsport 157, 9728 PS Groningen, Netherlands. TEL 050-226922.

808.8 305.4   US
▼**SISTERSONG;** women across cultures. 1992. 3/yr. Sistersong, Box 7045, Pittsburgh, PA 15213. bk.rev.
    Description: Poetry, fiction, essays, journal entries and artwork by women artists.

SITES. see ARCHITECTURE

890   GW
SKANDINAVISTIK; Zeitschrift fuer Sprache, Literatur und Kultur der nordischen Laender. 1970. s-a. DM.46. Verlag J.J. Augustin GmbH, Am Fleth 36-37, 2208 Glueckstadt, Germany. Ed. Otto Oberholzer. **Indexed:** Arts & Hum.Cit.Ind.

839.6 949.12   IC   ISSN 0256-8446
SKIRNIR. 1827. s-a. ISK 2200. Hid Islenzka Bokmenntafelag, Sidumula 21, P.O. Box 8935, 128 Reykjavik, Iceland. adv.; bk.rev.; cum.index; circ. 2,000. **Indexed:** M.L.A.
    Formerly: Islenzk Sagnabloed.

800 378.198   US
SKYLARK. 1972. a. $5.00. Purdue University Calumet, 2200 169th St., Hammond, IN 46323. TEL 219-989-2262. Ed. Pamela Hunter. adv.; circ. 800. (back issues avail.)

800   CN
SKYLARK (BEAUPORT). s-a. £5($8) Suzanne Fortin, Ed. & Pub., 2110 Charleroi, No. 8, Beauport, Quebec G1E 3S1, Canada.

808   US
SLAVIC AND EAST EUROPEAN ARTS. 1982. 2/yr. $15. (State University of New York, Stonybrook, Department of Germanic and Slavic Languages, Slavic and East European Arts) Slavic Cultural Center Press, Stonybrook, NY 11794. Ed. E.J. Czerwinski. adv.; circ. 1,500.

808   US   ISSN 0737-7002
NX542
SLAVIC AND EUROPEAN ARTS. 1982. s-a. $15. (State University of New York, Stony Brook, Department of Germanic and Slavic Literatrs) Slavic Cultural Center Press, Stony Brook, NY 11794. Ed. E.J. Czerwinski. adv.; circ. 800.

SLAVIC REVIEW; American quarterly of Soviet and East European studies. see SOCIAL SCIENCES: COMPREHENSIVE WORKS

800   US
SLAVIC WESTERN LITERARY RELATIONS. irreg. Peter Lang Publishing, Inc., 62 W. 45th St., 4th Fl., New York, NY 10036. TEL 212-302-6740. FAX 212-302-7574. Ed. Albert Kipa.
    Description: Covers comparative studies in the fields of the various Western and Eastern European literatures, languages, and cultures.

SLAVICA LUNDENSIA. see LINGUISTICS

SLAVICA SLOVACA. see LINGUISTICS

SLAVISTICNA REVIJA; journal for linguistics and literary sciences. see LINGUISTICS

830 430   GW   ISSN 0583-5429
SLAVISTISCHE BEITRAEGE. (Text in English and German) 1960. irreg. price varies. Verlag Otto Sagner, Postfach 340108, 8000 Munich 34, Germany. TEL 089-522027. TELEX 5216711-KUSAD. Ed.Bd. circ. 300. (back issues avail.)

491 940   UK   ISSN 0037-6795
D377.A1
SLAVONIC AND EAST EUROPEAN REVIEW. 1922. q. $130. Modern Humanities Research Association, Kings College, Strand, London WC2R 2LS, England. Ed.Bd. adv.; bk.rev.; illus.; index, cum.index; circ. 1,000. (reprint service avail. from SCH) **Indexed:** Acad.Ind., Arts & Hum.Cit.Ind., Br.Hum.Ind., Hist.Abstr., Hum.Ind., Ind.Bk.Rev.Hum., Lang.& Lang.Behav.Abstr., M.L.A., RILA, SSCI.
—BLDSC shelfmark: 8309.390000.

810   US
SLEUTH JOURNAL. 1983. irreg. (2-4/yr.). $28 for 4 issues. Baker Street Publications, Box 994, Metairie, LA 70004. TEL 504-734-8414. Ed. Sharida Rizzuto. circ. 10,000.

891.87   CS   ISSN 0037-6973
PG5400
SLOVENSKA LITERATURA/SLOVAK LITERATURE; revue pre literarnu vedu a kritiku. (Text in Slovak; contents page and summaries also in German and Russian) 1954. bi-m. 84 Kcs.($21) (Slovenska Akademia Vied, Literarnovedny Ustav) Veda, Publishing House of the Slovak Academy of Sciences, Klemensova 19, 814 30 Bratislava, Czechoslovakia. (Dist. in Western countries by: John Benjamins B.V., Amsteldijk 44, Amsterdam (Z.), Netherlands) Ed. Dalimir Hajko. adv.; bk.rev.; abstr.; bibl.; cum.index.
    Description: Evaluates the heritage of Slovak classical literature, and analyzes works and problems of socialist literature.

SLOVENSKA REC/SLOVAK LANGUAGE; casopis pre vyskum a kulturu slovenskeho jazyka. see LINGUISTICS

891.87 700   CS   ISSN 0037-7007
SLOVENSKE POHLADY NA LITERATURU A UMENIE. 1846. m. 120 Kcs.($108) (Asociacia Slovenskych Sposovatelov - Association of Slovak Writers) Vydavatel'stvo Slovensky Spisovatel', Laurinska 2, 813 67 Bratislava, Czechoslovakia. (Subscr. to: Slovart, Gottwaldovo nam. 47, 805-32 Bratislava, Czechoslovakia) Ed. Jan Strasser. bk.rev.; circ. 6,000.
    Description: For literary scientists, critics, teachers of Slovak in all schools, students, cultural and eductional workers, editors and all those interested in Slovak literature. Contains studies and articles from the history and theory of literature.

SLOW DANCER. see LITERATURE — Poetry

810   US   ISSN 0037-721X
SMALL POND MAGAZINE OF LITERATURE; journal of poetry, short fiction and opinion. Variant title: Small Pond. 1964. 3/yr. $8. Napoleon St. Cyr, Ed. & Pub., Box 664, Stratford, CT 06497. TEL 203-378-4066. adv.; bk.rev.; cum.index: 1964-69, 1970-74, 1975-78, 1978-81, 1982-84, 1985-88; circ. 300. (also avail. in microform from UMI; reprint service avail. from UMI) **Indexed:** A.I.P.P., Ind.Amer.Per.Verse.

810 US
SNOWY EGRET. 1922. s-a. $12. Karl Barnebey, Ed. & Pub., Box 9, Bowling Green, IN 47833. bk.rev.; illus.; index, cum.index every 10 yrs.; circ. 400. **Indexed:** A.I.P.P.
   Description: Literary, artistic, philosophic and historical responses to nature. Presents artwork, poetry, fiction and non-fiction.

806 AG
SOCIEDAD ARGENTINA DE ESCRITORES. BOLETIN. 1975. Sociedad Argentina de Escritores, Uruguay 1371, Buenos Aires 1016, Argentina. Ed. Horacio Esteban Ratti.

800 410 SP ISSN 0212-3223
PH5001
SOCIEDAD DE ESTUDIOS VASCOS. CUADERNOS DE SECCION. LENGUA Y LITERATURA. 1982. irreg. Eusko Ikaskuntza, S.A., Legazpi, 10-1, 20004 Donostia-San Sebastian, Spain. TEL 425 111.

840 FR
SOCIETE ACADEMIQUE DES ARTS LIBERAUX DE PARIS. COLLECTION. 1963. 4/yr. free. Societe Academique des Arts Liberaux de Paris, 3 av. de Chanzy, B.P. 49, 94210 la Varenne-St. Hilaire, France. TEL 42-83-36-03. Ed. Claude Cotti. circ. 1,500.
   Formerly: Societe Academique des Arts Liberaux de Paris. Anthologie des Societaires (ISSN 0081-072X)

840 FR ISSN 0081-0754
SOCIETE CHATEAUBRIAND. BULLETIN. NOUVELLE SERIE. 1930; N.S. 1957. a. 200 F. Societe Chateaubriand, Secretariat General, 122 bd. de Courcelles, 75017 Paris, France. TEL 42-27-34-41. Ed.Bd. bk.rev.; circ. 600.

801 400 FR ISSN 0982-6548
SOCIETE DE BIBLIOLOGIE ET DE SCHEMATISATION. ALMANACH. 2/yr. 22 F. per no. Societe de Bibliologie et de Schematisation (S B S), 36 av. d'Italie, Tour Rubis, 75013 Paris, France.

800 FR ISSN 0583-8452
PQ2631.R63
SOCIETE DES AMIS DE MARCEL PROUST ET DES AMIS DE COMBRAY. BULLETIN. 1950. a. 160 F.($35) Societe des Amis de Marcel Proust, 11, rue Martel, 75010 Paris, France. TEL 42-46-89-64. Eds. Elyane Dezon-Jones, Anne Borrel. adv.; bk.rev.; circ. 2,500. (back issues avail) **Indexed:** M.L.A.
   Description: Covers unpublished Proust documents and original studies.

SOCIETE DES SCIENCES ET DES LETTRES DE LODZ. BULLETIN. see SCIENCES: COMPREHENSIVE WORKS

800 700 FR
SOCIETE DES SCIENCES, LETTRES ET ARTS DE BAYONNE. BULLETIN. a. Societe des Sciences, Lettres et Arts de Bayonne, Musee Basque, 1 rue Marengo, 64100 Bayonne, France. (back issue avail.)

820 FR
SOCIETE FRANCAISE SHAKESPEARE. ACTES DU CONGRES. (Text in French) 1981. a. price varies. (Societe Francaise Shakespeare) Librarie Touzot, 38 rue Saint Sulpice, 75278 Paris Cedex 06, France.

800 SW
SOCIETE ROYALE DE LETTRES DE LUND. BULLETIN/KUNGLIGA HUMANISTISKA VETENSKAPSSAMFUNDET I LUND. AARSBERATTELSE. (Text in French) a. Almqvist & Wiksell International, Box 638, S-101 28 Stockholm, Sweden. **Indexed:** Amer.Hist.& Life.

800 FR ISSN 0221-7945
SOCIETE THEOPHILE GAUTIER. BULLETIN. 1977. a. 110 Fr. Universite de Montpellier (University Paul Valery), B.P. 5043, 34032 Montpellier Cedex 1, France. TEL 67-14-20-00. Ed. Claudine Lacoste.

SOCIETY FOR ARMENIAN STUDIES. JOURNAL. see ETHNIC INTERESTS

800 US ISSN 0741-5753
E184.G3
SOCIETY FOR GERMAN - AMERICAN STUDIES. NEWSLETTER. 1979. 4/yr. $20. Society for German - American Studies, c/o William Roba, Treas., 500 Belmont Rd., Bettendorf, IA 52722. TEL 319-359-7531. Ed. La Vern J. Rippley. bk.rev.; circ. 1,000.
   Description: Articles concerning the society, as well as information about the activities of other organizations with similar purposes. Includes short articles on German-Americana.

850 UK
PQ4835.I7
SOCIETY FOR PIRANDELLO STUDIES. YEARBOOK. 1981. a. £7.95. Society for Pirandello Studies, c/o E. Schachter, Ed., Keynes College, University of Kent, Canterbury CT2 7NP, England. FAX 0227-475472. bk.rev.; illus.; circ. 300.
   Formerly: British Pirandello Society. Yearbook (ISSN 0260-9215)

800 940 700 UK ISSN 0264-8571
SOCIETY FOR RENAISSANCE STUDIES. BULLETIN. 1983. 2/yr. $20 to non-members. Society for Renaissance Studies, c/o Richard Simpson, Hon. Treasurer, 12A Manley St., London NW1 8LT, England. Ed. Constance Blackwell. bk.rev.; tr.lit.; circ. 640. (back issues avail.)

800 700 100 UK
SOCIETY FOR RENAISSANCE STUDIES. OCCASIONAL PAPERS. 1973. irreg. $20. Society for Renaissance Studies, c/o Richard Simpson, Hon. Treasurer, 12A Manley St., London NW1 8LT, England. Ed. Peter Denley. circ. 640. (back issues avail.)

810 US ISSN 0085-6304
PS501
SOCIETY FOR THE STUDY OF MIDWESTERN LITERATURE. NEWSLETTER. 1971. 3/yr. $5 (includes Midwestern Miscellany). Society for the Study of Midwestern Literature, 240 Ernst Bessey Hall, Michigan State University, East Lansing, MI 48824. TEL 517-355-1855. Ed. David D. Anderson. adv.; bibl.; circ. 400. (processed) **Indexed:** Abstr.Engl.Stud., M.L.A., Mich.Mag.Ind.

810 US ISSN 0197-8071
PS261
SOCIETY FOR THE STUDY OF SOUTHERN LITERATURE. NEWSLETTER. Short title: S S S L. 1968. 2/yr. $4.50 (foreign $5). Society for the Study of Southern Literature, Department of English, Loyola University, New Orleans, LA 70118. TEL 504-865-2476. (Alt. addr.: University of Southern Mississippi, Southern Sta., Box 5078, Hattiesburg, MS 39406-5078) Ed. Stephen Young. circ. 400.

800 CN ISSN 0701-9890
SOCIETY OF THE SEVEN SAGES NEWSLETTER. 1976. a. Dalhousie University, Department of French, Halifax, N.S. B3H 3J5, Canada. TEL 902-494-2430. Ed. Hans R. Runte. adv.; bk.rev.; circ. 120. (back issues avail.)
   Description: Literary research on the Book of Sinbad and the Seven Sages of Rome.

800 FR ISSN 0985-5939
SOCIOCRITICISM. (Editions in English, French, Spanish) 2/yr. Universite de Montpellier (Universite Paul Valery), B.P. 5043, 34032 Montpellier Cedex 1, France. TEL 67-14-20-00. Ed. Edmond Cros.
   —BLDSC shelfmark: 8319.565000.
   Description: Dedicated to promoting a new conception of the sociohistorical study of literature and culture.

800 301 US ISSN 1043-5727
SOCIOCRITICISM: LITERATURE, SOCIETY, AND HISTORY. irreg. Peter Lang Publishing, Inc., 62 W. 45th St., 4th Fl., New York, NY 10036. TEL 212-302-6740. FAX 212-302-7574. Ed. James F. Gaines.
   Description: Focuses on the early modern period in the Western European literatures (approximately 1550-1850). Examines the relationship between literary art forms and socio-historical structures, tensions, or mentalities.

800 US
SOME. 1972. s-a. $5 for 3 nos.; institutions $9. 309 W. 104 St., Apt. 9d, New York, NY 10025. Ed.Bd. bk.rev.; circ. 1,000.

810 US
SOME FRIENDS. 1972. irreg. (approx. 1/yr.). $1.50. c/o Terry J. Cooper, Ed., Box 6395, Tyler, TX 76701. TEL 214-597-1258. circ. 500.

810 US
SOME OTHER MAGAZINE. 1978. s-a. $6. Some Other Magazine, 47 Hazen Ct., Wayne, NJ 07470. TEL 201-696-9230. Ed. Robert Richman. adv.; bk.rev.; circ. 250. (back issues avail.)

SOMETHING ABOUT THE AUTHOR. see CHILDREN AND YOUTH — For

895.7 CC
SONGHUA JIANG/SONGHUA RIVER. (Text in Korean) bi-m. Harbin Shi Chaoxianzu Yishuguan - Harbin Korean Art Center, 43, Zhongyang Dajie, Daoli-qu, Harbin, Heilongjiang 150010, People's Republic of China. TEL 415131. Ed. Li Qingzhao.

800 US
SONOMA MANDALA. 1974. a. $8. Sonoma State University, English Department, Rohnert Park, CA 94928. TEL 717-664-2140. FAX 707-664-3902. Ed. Elizabeth Herron. circ. 500. (back issues avail.)
   Description: International literary magazine focusing on fiction and poetry.

810.8 US ISSN 0275-5203
PS1
SONORA REVIEW. 1980. s-a. $10. University of Arizona, Department of English, Tucson, AZ 85721. TEL 602-621-1836. Ed. Tony Brown. bk.rev.; circ. 600. (back issues avail.)
   Supersedes: University of Arizona. Department of English. Graduate English Papers (ISSN 0066-7536)
   Description: Presents contemporary fiction, non-fiction and poetry.

SOOCHOW JOURNAL OF FOREIGN LANGUAGES AND LITERATURES. see LINGUISTICS

SOUNDINGS (SANTA BARBARA); collections of the University Library. see LIBRARY AND INFORMATION SCIENCES

800 US
SOUNDINGS EAST. 1978. s-a. $6. Salem State College, 352 Lafayette St., Dept. of English, Salem, MA 01970-4589. TEL 508-741-6000. Ed. Jasper A. Swininch. illus.; circ. 2,500. **Indexed:** A.I.P.P.
   Formerly: Soundings (Salem); **Supersedes** (1973-1978): Gone Soft (ISSN 0362-1219)
   Description: Contains original poetry, fiction and artwork.

SOUTH AFRICAN JOURNAL OF AFRICAN LANGUAGES. see LINGUISTICS

492 US ISSN 0275-9527
PK180
SOUTH ASIAN REVIEW.* 1977. s-a. $10. South Asian Literary Association, c/o Univ. of North Florida, Jacksonville, FL 32216. Ed. Satya S. Pachori. circ. 100. **Indexed:** M.L.A.

806 US
SOUTH ATLANTIC MODERN LANGUAGE ASSOCIATION AWARDS. 1977. a. price varies. University of Georgia Press, Athens, GA 30602. TEL 404-542-2830. FAX 404-542-0601.

SOUTH ATLANTIC REVIEW. see LINGUISTICS

810 US ISSN 0038-3163
PS558.S6
SOUTH CAROLINA REVIEW. 1968. 2/yr. $7 to individuals; institutions $8; foreign $7.50. Clemson University, Department of English, Clemson, SC 29634-1503. TEL 803-656-3151. Ed. R.J. Calhoun. adv.; bk.rev.; circ. 600. (back issues avail.) **Indexed:** A.I.P.P., Abstr.Engl.Stud., Amer.Hum.Ind., Bk.Rev.Ind. (1980-), Child.Bk.Rev.Ind. (1980-), Ind.Amer.Per.Verse, Ind.Bk.Rev.Hum., M.L.A.
   —BLDSC shelfmark: 8350.200000.

LITERATURE

810 US ISSN 0038-3368
AP2
SOUTH DAKOTA REVIEW. 1963. 4/yr. $15 (foreign $16). University of South Dakota, Department of English, Vermillion, SD 57069. TEL 605-677-5229. Ed. John R. Milton. bibl.; illus.; index; circ. 600. (also avail. in microform from UMI; back issues avail.; reprint service avail. from UMI) **Indexed:** A.I.P.P., Abstr.Engl.Stud., Amer.Hum.Ind., Arts & Hum.Cit.Ind., Curr.Cont., Ind.Amer.Per.Verse, M.L.A. —BLDSC shelfmark: 8351.350000.
  Description: Includes fiction, poetry, articles and essays, frequently with an eclectic emphasis on the American West.

SOUTHEASTERN FRONT. see ART

SOUTHEASTERN WRITING CENTER ASSOCIATION. SELECTED PAPERS. see EDUCATION — Teaching Methods And Curriculum

820 AT ISSN 0038-3732
AP7
SOUTHERLY; a review of Australian literature. 1939. q. Aus.$35 (foreign Aus.$45). English Association, Sydney Branch, 2 Belgrave St., Cremorne, N.S.W. 2090, Australia. TEL 02-692-2589. FAX 02-692-4203. (Subscr. to: P.O. Box 187, Rozelle, N.S.W. 2039) Ed. Elizabeth Webby. adv.; bk.rev.; index; circ. 1,200. (also avail. in microform from UMI; reprint service avail. from UMI) **Indexed:** Abstr.Engl.Stud., Arts & Hum.Cit.Ind., Aus.P.A.I.S., Curr.Cont., Gdlns.
  Description: Contains literary criticism, interviews with writers, contemporary stories and poetry.

800 US
SOUTHERN CALIFORNIA ANTHOLOGY. 1983. a. $7.95. University of Southern California, Master of Professional Writing Program, WPH 404, Los Angeles, CA 90089-4034. TEL 213-740-3252. Eds. James Reagan, Richard Paul Aloia, Jr. circ. 1,000. (back issues avail.)
  Description: Presents poetry, short stories, novel excerpts and interviews with writers.

810 US ISSN 0038-4291
PS261
SOUTHERN LITERARY JOURNAL. 1968. s-a. $15 (foreign $18). (University of North Carolina at Chapel Hill, Department of English) University of North Carolina Press, Box 2288, Chapel Hill, NC 27515-2288. TEL 919-966-3561. FAX 919-966-3829. Eds. Fred Hobson, Kimbal King. adv.; bk.rev.; a. index; circ. 700. (also avail. in microform from UMI; reprint service avail. from UMI) **Indexed:** Abstr.Engl.Stud., Arts & Hum.Cit.Ind., Curr.Cont., Hist.Abstr., Hum.Ind., Ind.Bk.Rev.Hum., M.L.A.
  —BLDSC shelfmark: 8354.290000.
  Refereed Serial

800 US ISSN 1042-6604
F209
SOUTHERN READER. 1989. q. $2.50. Southern Reader Corporation, 114 S.Lamar, Box 1827, Oxford, MS 38655. TEL 601-234-2596. FAX 601-234-2572. Ed. R.J. Bedwell. adv.; bk.rev.; circ. 7,000.
  Description: Contemporary journalism and fiction on the South.

820 AT ISSN 0038-4526
PR1
SOUTHERN REVIEW; literary and interdisciplinary essays. 1963. 3/yr. Aus.$25 to individuals; institutions Aus.$40; students and unemployed Aus.$15. University of Adelaide, Department of English, Adelaide 5000, Australia. FAX 08-232-3375. Ed.Bd. adv.; bk.rev.; index; circ. 500. (back issues avail.) **Indexed:** Abstr.Engl.Stud., Arts & Hum.Cit.Ind., Aus.P.A.I.S., Curr.Cont., M.L.A.
  —BLDSC shelfmark: 8354.920000.

810 US ISSN 0038-4534
AP2
SOUTHERN REVIEW; a literary and critical quarterly magazine. 1935-1942; resumed 1965. q. $15 to individuals; institutions $30. Louisiana State University, 43 Allen Hall, Baton Rouge, LA 70803. TEL 504-388-5108. FAX 504-388-5098. Eds. James Olney, Dave Smith. adv.; bk.rev.; index; circ. 3,000. (also avail. in microform from UMI; microfiche from KTO; reprint service avail. from UMI,KTO) **Indexed:** A.I.P.P., Abstr.Engl.Stud., Amer.Hum.Ind., Arts & Hum.Cit.Ind., Bk.Rev.Ind. (1976-), Child.Bk.Rev.Ind. (1976-), Curr.Cont., Hist.Abstr., Hum.Ind., Ind.Amer.Per.Verse, Ind.Bk.Rev.Hum.

SOUTHWESTERN (GEORGETOWN). see COLLEGE AND ALUMNI

808 US ISSN 0276-7155
PS501
SOUTHWESTERN REVIEW. s-a. $2. University of Southwestern Louisiana, Department of English, Box 44691, Lafayette, LA 70504. TEL 318-231-6908. Ed. Laura Ellen Brown. circ. 1,000.
  Description: Presents poetry, fiction, black and white photography, and black and white artwork.

810 US ISSN 0098-499X
SOU'WESTER (EDWARDSVILLE); literary magazine. 1960. 3/yr. $10. Southern Illinois University, Edwardsville, Edwardsville, IL 62026-1438. TEL 618-692-3190. Ed. Fred W. Robbins. circ. 300 (controlled). (back issues avail)
  Description: Contains poetry and short fiction.

891.92 AI ISSN 0038-5018
SOVETAKAN GRAKANUTIUN. 1934. m. 18 Rub. Soyuz Pisatelei Armyanskoi S.S.R., Erevan, Armenia. Ed.Bd. bk.rev.; bibl.; illus.; play rev.; stat.; circ. 8,000.

891.7 RU
SOVETSKAYA LITERATURA, TRADITSII I NOVATORSTVO. 1976. irreg. 0.68 Rub. per issue. Leningradskii Universitet, Universitetskaya Nab. 7-9, St. Petersburg B-164, Russia. Ed. L. Gladkovskaya. circ. 6,550.

891 FR ISSN 0303-111X
SOVETSKIE LJUDI SEGODNJA/VIE QUOTIDIENNE EN U.R.S.S. PRISE SUR LE VIF. (In two series Textes Litteraires and Dossiers) (Text in Russian; notes and comments in French or Russian) 1969. irreg. price varies. Institut d'Etudes Slaves, 9 rue Michelet, 75006 Paris, France.

891.7 RU ISSN 0202-1870
SOVIET LITERATURE. Short title: S L. Russian edition: Sovetskaya Literatura (ISSN 0038-5557) (Editions in Chech, English, French, German, Hungarian, Polish, Russian, Slovak, Spanish) 1948. m. $25.50. Soyuz Pisatelei S.S.S.R., 1-7 Kutuzovskii Prospekt, 121248 Moscow, Russia. (U.S. subscr. to: Creative Subscription Service, 1671 E. 16th St., Ste. 189, Brooklyn, NY 11229-2901) Ed. Savva Dangulov. illus.; index. (also avail. in microform from MIM) **Indexed:** Arts & Hum.Cit.Ind., Curr.Cont., Hum.Ind., M.L.A.
  —BLDSC shelfmark: 8359.435000.
  Description: Includes new works by established writers and poets; a section devoted to new talents; previously unknown pages from works of outstanding philosophers and writers of the past as well as comment by leading critics of literature in the USSR on new books as they are released for publication.

SOW'S EAR. see LITERARY AND POLITICAL REVIEWS

820 AT ISSN 0313-1459
SPAN. 1975. 2/yr. Aus.$20 to individuals; institutions $30. Murdoch University, English & Comparative Literature, Murdoch, W.A. 6150, Australia. TEL 09-332-3504. FAX 09-332-2507. (Co-sponsor: South Pacific Association for Commonwealth Literature and Language Studies) Ed. Kateryna Arthur. bk.rev.; bibl.; cum.index; circ. 250. (back issues avail.)

860 460 UK
SPANISH STUDIES; modern literature, history and politics. 1979. a. £8.90 for 4 years. c/o Mrs. Olga Kenyon, Ed. & Pub., 29 Woodsyre, Sydenham hill, London SE26 6SS, England. adv.; bk.rev.; play rev.; circ. 300. (back issues avail.)

SPANISH TODAY. see LINGUISTICS

810 US
SPARROW (SANTA ROSA).* 1972. m. $0.75 per no. Black Sparrow Press, 24 10th St., Santa Rosa, CA 94501-4714. Ed. John Martin. circ. 1,500. **Indexed:** Abstr.Engl.Stud.

890 970.1 US
SPAWNING THE MEDICINE RIVER. 3/yr. $6. Institute of American Indian Arts Press, St. Michael Dr., Santa Fe, NM 87501. Ed. Philip Foss.

800 US ISSN 0894-8852
SPEAR SHAKER REVIEW. 1987-1988; resumed 1991. q. $24. Spear Shaker Press, Box 308, Napanoch, NY 12458. Ed. Stephanie Caruana. adv.; bk.rev.; illus.; circ. 1,000.
  Description: Current research and opinion regarding the authorship of the "Shake-speare" plays and poetry, from the point of view that the most likely candidate is Edward de Vere, the 17th Earl of Oxford.

SPECIMINA PHILOLOGIAE SLAVICAE. see LINGUISTICS

SPECTRUM (AMHERST). see ART

800 378 US ISSN 0895-8270
SPECTRUM (PAXTON). 1985. s-a. $7. Anna Maria College, Sunset Lane, Box 72-F, Paxton, MA 01612. TEL 508-757-4586. Ed. Robert Goepfert. bk.rev.; circ. 1,000.
  Description: Multidisciplinary presentation of scholarly articles, fiction, poetry, art, and photography.

SPECULUM; a journal of Medieval studies. see HISTORY — History Of Europe

SPECULUM ANNIVERSARY MONOGRAPHS. see HISTORY — History Of Europe

800 IT
SPECULUM ARTIUM. (Text in English, French and Italian) irreg., latest no.18. price varies. Angelo Longo Editore, Via Paolo Costa 33, P.O. Box 431, 48100 Ravenna, Italy. TEL 0544-217026. Ed. Aldo Scaglione. circ. 2,500. **Indexed:** M.L.A.

830 301 NE ISSN 0165-084X
SPEKTATOR; tijdschrift voor neerlandistiek. 1970. 6/yr. fl.80 to individuals; institutions fl.130. (Stichting Heliogabalos) I C G Publications, P.O. Box 509, 3300 AM Dordrecht, Netherlands. TEL 078-510454. FAX 078-510972. Ed.Bd. adv.; bk.rev.; bibl.; circ. 300. **Indexed:** M.L.A., Sociol.Abstr.

SPEKTRUM; Vierteljahresschrift fuer Dichtung und Originalgrafik. see ART

830 GW ISSN 0177-6185
SPEKTRUM DES GEISTES; Literaturkalender. 1951. a. DM.14.80. Husum Druck- und Verlagsgesellschaft mbH, Nordbahnhofstr. 2, Postfach 1480, 2250 Husum, Germany. TEL 04841-6081. FAX 04841-61397. TELEX 28567. Eds. Alix and Ingwert Paulsen. adv.; bk.rev.; circ. 10,000.

820 US ISSN 0038-7347
SPENSER NEWSLETTER. 1970. 3/yr. $6.50 (foreign $11). Darryl J. Gless, Ed.& Pub., CB No. 3520, English Department, Greenlaw Hall, University of North Carolina, Chapel Hill, NC 27599. TEL 919-966-5110. adv.; bk.rev.; index; circ. 700. (also avail. in microform from UMI; reprint service avail. from UMI) **Indexed:** Ind.Bk.Rev.Hum.

809 CN ISSN 0319-0188
SPHINX; a magazine of literature and society. 1974. s-a. Can.$3.50 to individuals; Can. $7.50 to institutions. University of Regina, Department of English, Regina, Sask. S4S 0A2, Canada. Ed.Bd. bk.rev.; illus.; circ. 250. (also avail. in microform from MML) **Indexed:** M.L.A.
  —BLDSC shelfmark: 8413.615000.

SPHINX WOMEN'S INTERNATIONAL LITERARY ART REVIEW. see ART

808 US
SPIDERWEB. 1982. q. $10. Corsair Press, Drawer F, M I T Branch Station, Cambridge, MA 02139. adv.

839.31   BE   ISSN 0038-7479
SPIEGEL DER LETTEREN; tijdschrift voor Nederlandse literatuurgeschiedenis en voor literatuurwetenschap. (Text in Dutch) 1956. 4/yr. 1280. Editions Peeters s.p.r.l., Bondgenotenlaan 153, B-3000 Leuven, Belgium. TEL 016-235170. FAX 016-228500. Ed.Bd. bk.rev.; index. (back issues avail.) **Indexed:** Arts & Hum.Cit.Ind., M.L.A.
—BLDSC shelfmark: 8413.795000.

830   GW   ISSN 0722-7833
PN4
SPIEL; Siegener Periodicum zur int. empirischen Literaturwissenschaft. 1982. s-a. Verlag Peter Lang GmbH, Eschborner Landstr. 42-50, 6000 Frankfurt a.M. 90, Germany. TEL 069-7807050. FAX 069-785893. Ed.Bd. circ. 500.
—BLDSC shelfmark: 8413.799100.

SPIRAL. see *WOMEN'S INTERESTS*

800   US   ISSN 0364-4014
PS580
THE SPIRIT THAT MOVES US. 1975. irreg. price varies. Spirit That Moves Us Press, Inc., Box 820, Jackson Heights, NY 11372-0820. TEL 718-426-8788. Ed. Morty Sklar. adv.; index; circ. 2,500. (back issues avail.) **Indexed:** Amer.Hum.Ind., Ind.Amer.Per.Verse.
Description: Presents fiction, poetry and art. Special issues include one of a collection of poetry by Jaroslav Seifert, published before he won the Nobel Prize for literature.

808 796.357   US   ISSN 8755-741X
SPITBALL; the literary baseball magazines. 1981. q. $12. c/o Mike Shannon, Ed., 6224 Collegevue, Cincinnatti, OH 45224-1922. adv.; bk.rev.; film rev.; play rev.; illus.; circ. 10,000. (back issues avail.)
Description: Completely devoted to baseball poetry and fiction.

810   US
▼**SPONTANEOUS COMBUSTION**. 1991. irreg. (1-2/yr.). $3.50 for 2 issues. 3320 Vista Rocosa, Escondido, CA 92029. Ed. James C. Kaufman.
Description: Publishes poetry, fiction, art and cartoons.

800   GW   ISSN 0038-8475
P3
SPRACHE IM TECHNISCHEN ZEITALTER; Literatur im technischen Zeitalter. 1961. q. DM.44. Literarisches Colloquium Berlin, Am Sandwerder 5, 1000 Berlin 39, Germany. TEL 030-8169960. FAX 030-81699619. Eds. Walter Hollerer, Norbert Miller. adv.; bk.rev.; charts; index; circ. 1,800. **Indexed:** Phil.Ind.
Description: Forum for discussing and presenting contemporary and modern literature.

SPRACHE UND LITERATUR IN WISSENSCHAFT UND UNTERRICHT. see *LINGUISTICS*

800   AU   ISSN 0038-8483
P3   CODEN: SPRAEK
SPRACHKUNST; Beitraege zur Literaturwissenschaft. (Text in English, French, German and Russian) 1970. s-a. DM.60. Verlag der Oesterreichischen Akademie der Wissenschaften, Dr. Ignaz-Seipel-Platz 2, A-1010 Vienna, Austria. FAX 0222-5139541. Ed.Bd. bk.rev.; index. **Indexed:** Arts & Hum.Cit.Ind., Can.Rev.Comp.Lit, Ind.Bk.Rev.Hum., M.L.A.
—BLDSC shelfmark: 8419.873000.

SPRACHPRAXIS; Arbeitsmaterial fuer Deutsch lernende Auslaender. see *EDUCATION — Adult Education*

800   US   ISSN 0884-1934
SQUARE ONE; a magazine of fiction. 1984. a. $14 for 2 nos. Tarkus Press, Box 11921, Milwaukee, WI 53211. TEL 414-964-1994. Ed. William D. Gagliani. adv.; circ. 250. (back issues avail.)
Description: Varied general fiction for well-educated readers interested in the human and inhuman experience.

891.92 491.92   YU   ISSN 0081-3990
SRPSKA AKADEMIJA NAUKA I UMETNOSTI. ODELJENJE JEZIKA I KNJIZEVNOSTI. POSEBNA IZDANJA. (Text in Serbo-Croatian; summaries in English, French, German or Russian) 1950. irreg. price varies. Srpska Akademija Nauka i Umetnosti, Knez Mihailova 35, 11001 Belgrade, Serbia, Yugoslavia. FAX 38-11-182-825. TELEX 72593 SANU YU. (Dist. by: Prosveta, Terazije 16, Belgrade, Serbia, Yugoslavia) circ. 1,000.

820   UK   ISSN 0038-9366
AP4
STAND MAGAZINE. 1952. q. £11($22) Stand Magazine, 179 Wingrove Rd., Newcastle Upon Tyne NE4 9DA, England. TEL 091-273-328. Ed.Bd. adv.; bk.rev.; cum.index; circ. 4,500. **Indexed:** Abstr.Engl.Stud., Bk.Rev.Ind. (1988-), Child.Bk.Rev.Ind. (1988-), Curr.Cont., Ind.Amer.Per.Verse, Ind.Bk.Rev.Hum.
●Also available online.
—BLDSC shelfmark: 8430.241500.
Description: Short stories, poetry and reviews.

840 850   US
STANFORD FRENCH & ITALIAN STUDIES. 1975. irreg. (approx. 4 vols./yr.). price varies. (Stanford University, Department of French and Italian) Anma Libri, Box 876, Saratoga, CA 95071. TEL 408-741-1522. Ed. Marc Bertrand. **Indexed:** M.L.A.
Description: Monographs on French and Italian language literature, culture and history.

840 944   US   ISSN 0163-657X
PQ1
STANFORD FRENCH REVIEW. (Text in English and French) 1977. 3/yr. $74.50. (Stanford University, Department of French & Italian) Anma Libri, Box 876, Saratoga, CA 95071. TEL 408-741-1522. Ed. Jean-Marie Apostolides. (back issues avail.; reprint service avail. from ISI) **Indexed:** Arts & Hum.Cit.Ind., Curr.Cont., M.L.A.
—BLDSC shelfmark: 8431.370000.
Description: Scholarly articles on French literature, language and culture.

840   US   ISSN 0730-6857
PQ4001
STANFORD ITALIAN REVIEW. (Text in English and Italian) 1979. irreg. $64.50. (Stanford University, Department of French and Italian) Anma Libri, Box 876, Saratoga, CA 95071. TEL 408-741-1522. Ed. John Freccero. **Indexed:** Arts & Hum.Cit.Ind., M.L.A.
—BLDSC shelfmark: 8432.060000.
Description: Scholarly articles on Italian literature, language and culture.

808   US   ISSN 0886-666X
STANFORD LITERATURE REVIEW. 1984. s-a. $64.50. (Stanford University, Department of French and Italian) Anma Libri, Box 876, Saratoga, CA 95071. TEL 408-741-1522. Ed. Hans Ulrich Gumbrecht. **Indexed:** M.L.A.
Description: Scholarly articles on comparative literature.

808   US
STANFORD LITERATURE STUDIES. 1984. 2/yr. $37.50 per vol. (Stanford University, Department of French and Italian) Anma Libri, Box 876, Saratoga, CA 95071. TEL 408-741-1522.
Description: Monographs on French, Italian and comparative literature.

800   US   ISSN 0890-6270
STARMONT POPULAR CULTURE STUDIES. 1988. irreg., no.16, 1990. price varies. Borgo Press, Box 2845, San Bernardino, CA 92406. TEL 714-884-5813.
Description: Monographs on popular culture, including collections of stories from pulp sources, critical works on genre writers, and facsimile anthologies.

800   US   ISSN 0885-0658
STARMONT PULP & PAPER DIME NOVEL STUDIES. 1988. irreg., no.4, 1989. price varies. Borgo Press, Box 2845, San Bernardino, CA 92406. TEL 714-884-5813.
Description: Critical monographs on pulp magazine and dime novel authors and themes.

809   US   ISSN 0737-1306
STARMONT STUDIES IN LITERARY CRITICISM. irreg., no.44, 1992. Borgo Press, Box 2845, San Bernardino, CA 92406. TEL 714-884-5813.
—BLDSC shelfmark: 8436.060000.
Description: Monographs and essays on genre literature, complete with bibliographies and indexes.

800 821   UK
START MAGAZINE OF LITERATURE AND THE ARTS. 1978. 4/yr. $24. Start, 31 The Wells Rd., St. Ann's, Nottingham NG3 3AP, England. TEL 602 50 54 99. Ed. Charles Mansfield. adv.; bk.rev.; rec.; illus.; circ. 1,800. (processed; back issues avail.)
Formerly (until 1984): Start (ISSN 0267-2502)

LITERATURE   2963

810   US
STARTING FROM PAUMANOK. 1985. 3/yr. membership. Walt Whitman Birthplace Association, 246 Old Walt Whitman Rd., Huntington Station, NY 11746. TEL 516-427-5340. Ed. Barbara Bart. circ. 300. (back issues avail.)

800 700   RM   ISSN 0039-0852
STEAUA. 1953. m. 144 lei($10) Uniunea Scriitorilor din Republica Socialista Romania, Calea Victoriei 115, Bucharest, Rumania. (Subscr. to: ILEXIM, Str. 13 Decembrie Nr. 3, Box 136-137, 70116 Bucharest, Rumania) Ed. Aurel Rau. bk.rev.; illus.; index; circ. 3,500. **Indexed:** M.L.A.

810   US
STEINBECK BIBLIOGRAPHY SERIES. 1986. irreg. price varies. Steinbeck Research Institute, c/o English Dept., Ball State Univ., Muncie, IN 47306. Ed. Tetsumaro Hayashi.

810 016   US
STEINBECK ESSAY SERIES. 1986. irreg. price varies. Steinbeck Research Institute, c/o English Dept., Ball State Univ., Muncie, IN 47306. Ed. Tetsumaro Hayashi.

810   US   ISSN 0085-6746
PS3537.T3234
STEINBECK MONOGRAPH SERIES. 1971. irreg., no.13, 1988. price varies. Steinbeck Research Institute, c/o English Dept., Ball State University, Muncie, IN 47306. TEL 317-285-8389. Ed. Tetsumaro Hayashi. adv.; bk.rev.; circ. 600. (also avail. in microfilm from UMI; reprint service avail. from UMI,KTO) **Indexed:** Abstr.Engl.Stud., Arts & Hum.Cit.Ind., Curr.Cont., M.L.A.

810   US   ISSN 0039-100X
PS3537.T3234
STEINBECK QUARTERLY. 1968. 2/yr. $25 (foreign $30). Steinbeck Research Institute, c/o English Dept., Ball State University, Muncie, IN 47306. TEL 317-285-5688. Ed. Tetsumaro Hayashi. adv.; bk.rev.; abstr.; bibl.; index; circ. 650. (also avail. in microform from UMI; reprint service avail. from UMI,KTO) **Indexed:** Abstr.Engl.Stud., Amer.Hum.Ind., Arts & Hum.Cit.Ind., Curr.Cont., M.L.A.
—BLDSC shelfmark: 8464.109800.
Formerly (until 1969): Steinbeck Newsletter.

830   AU
STERZ; Zeitschrift fuer Literatur, Kunst und Kulturpolitik. 1977. q. S.180($25) Mandellstr. 10, A-8010 Graz, Austria. TEL 0316-824146. Ed.Bd. adv.; circ. 8,000.

STILETTO. see *LITERATURE — Poetry*

809   SW   ISSN 0491-0869
STOCKHOLM STUDIES IN HISTORY OF LITERATURE. (Subseries of Acta Universitatis Stockholmiensis) (Text in English and Spanish) 1956. irreg., no.31, 1987. price varies. (Stockholms University) Almqvist & Wiksell International, Box 638, S-101 28 Stockholm, Sweden. Eds. O. Lindberger, I. Jonsson. (back issues avail.)

890   SW
STOCKHOLM STUDIES IN RUSSIAN LITERATURE. (Subseries of Acta Universitatis Stockholmiensis) (Text in Russian; summaries in English) irreg., latest no.24, 1988. price varies. (Stockholms Universitet) Almqvist & Wiksell International, Box 638, S-101 28 Stockholm, Sweden. Ed. Nils Ake Nilsson. **Indexed:** M.L.A.

STONY THURSDAY BOOK. see *LITERATURE — Poetry*

820   UK
STORIA. s-a. Pandora Press, 15-17 Broadwick St., London W1V 1FP, England.

808   US   ISSN 0742-2113
PN6010.5
STORIES. 1982. q. $18. Stories and Stories for Children, Inc., Box 1467, Arlington, MA 02174-0022. Ed. Amy R. Kaufman. adv.; circ. 5,000.

820   US   ISSN 0081-5861
STORIES FROM THE HILLS. 1970. a. $4. Morris Harvey College Publications, Charleston, WV 25304. TEL 304-346-9471. Ed. William Plumley. circ. 2,000.

LITERATURE

800 US ISSN 1045-0831
PZ1.A1
STORY. 1931. q. $17. F & W Publications, Inc., 1507 Dana Ave., Cincinnati, OH 45207. TEL 513-531-2222. FAX 513-531-4744. (Subscr. to: Box 396, Mt. Morris, IL 61054) Ed. Lois Rosenthal. adv.; circ. 25,000. (reprint service avail. from KTO) **Indexed:** Access (1990-).
Description: Features general interest stories of literary merit.

800 US ISSN 0039-1999
STORY ART; a magazine for storytellers. 1934. q. $6. National Story League, c/o Gertrude Stirnaman, 3516 Russell, Ste. 6, St. Louis, MO 63104. (Subscr. to: Mrs. Thomas G. Reighart, Ed., 872 High St., No. 5710, Canal Fulton, OH 44614) bk.rev.; circ. 3,100.

800 US
▼**STORY RHYME GREETING LETTERS UPDATE.** 1992. a. $5 (Canada $7; elsewhere $8). Story Rhyme Greeting, c/o Prosperity & Profits Unlimited, Box 570213, Houston, TX 77257. TEL 713-867-3438. Ed.Bd.

800 US
STORYETTE. q. $12. Lott Publishing Co., Box 1107, Santa Monica, CA 90406. TEL 213-397-4217. Ed. Davis Lott. circ. 10,000. (tabloid format)
Description: Offers short stories only.

800 US
STORYQUARTERLY. 1975. 2/yr. $12 for 4 nos. to individuals; institutions $14. StoryQuarterly, Inc., Box 1416, Northbrook, IL 60065. TEL 708-564-8891. (Dist. by: B. DeBeor, 113 Centre St., Nutley, NJ 07110) Eds. Anne Brashler, Diane Williams. adv.; bk.rev.; illus.; circ. 1,500. **Indexed:** Amer.Hum.Ind.

808 US ISSN 1048-1354
STORYTELLING MAGAZINE. 1984. q. $40 membership (foreign $50) includes Yarnspinner and National Directory of Storytelling. National Association for the Preservation and Perpetuation of Storytelling, Box 309, Jonesborough, TN 37659. TEL 615-753-2171. FAX 615-753-9331. Ed. Mary C. Weaver. adv.; bk.rev.; illus.; circ. 3,300.
Formerly (until 1989): National Storytelling Journal (ISSN 0743-1104)
Description: Showcases contemporary storytelling and the oral tradition and informs readers of developments in the art and its applications, particularly in education and the helping professions.

891.86 CS ISSN 0081-5896
Z674
STRAHOVSKA KNIHOVNA. (Text in Czech; summaries in French and German) 1966. a. price varies. Pamatnik Narodniho Pisemnictvi, Strahovske nadv. 132, Prague 1, Czechoslovakia. Ed. Pravoslav Kneidl. **Indexed:** Hist.Abstr.

808 US
STRAITS. 1982. m. $5. Detroit River Press, c/o Glen Mannisto, 39 Moss, Highland Park, MI 48203.

STRATHCLYDE MODERN LANGUAGE STUDIES. see LINGUISTICS

STRINDBERGIANA. see THEATER

STRUGGLE; a magazine of proletarian revolutionary literature. see POLITICAL SCIENCE

809 IT ISSN 0039-2618
STRUMENTI CRITICI. 1966. 3/yr. L.110000. Societa Editrice Il Mulino, Strada Maggiore, 37, 40125 Bologna, Italy. TEL 051-256011. FAX 051-256034. Ed.Bd. adv.; bk.rev.; bibl.; index; circ. 1,000. (back issues avail.) **Indexed:** Arts & Hum.Cit.Ind., Can.Rev.Comp.Lit, Curr.Cont., M.L.A.

STUDI ALBANESI. STUDI E TESTI. see LINGUISTICS

850 IT
STUDI DANTESCHI (FLORENCE). 1920. a. L.70000($45) (Societa Dantesca Italiana) Casa Editrice G. C. Sansoni Editore Nuova S.p.A., Via Banedetto Varchi 47, 50132 Florence, Italy. TEL 055 294580. circ. 1,000.

840 IT ISSN 0585-4768
PQ5
STUDI DI LETTERATURA FRANCESE. (Text in language of authors) 1967. a. price varies. (Universita degli Studi di Milano, Seminario di Lingue e Letterature Neolatine) Casa Editrice Leo S. Olschki, Casella Postale 66, 50100 Florence, Italy. TEL 055-6530684. FAX 055-6530214. Ed. Enea Balmas. circ. 1,000. **Indexed:** M.L.A.

STUDI E PROBLEMI DI CRITICA TESTUALE. see LINGUISTICS

809 IT
STUDI E TESTI DELL'ANTICHITA. 1975. irreg., no.18, 1984. price varies. Societa Editrice Napoletana s.r.l., Corso Umberto I 34, 80138 Naples, Italy. Ed. Fabio Cupaiuolo.

809 850 IT
STUDI E TESTI DI LETTERATURA ITALIANA. 1974. irreg., no.21, 1984. price varies. Societa Editrice Napoletana s.r.l., Corso Umberto I 34, 80138 Naples, Italy.

STUDI FRANCESI; cultura e civilta letteraria della Francia. see LINGUISTICS

830 IT ISSN 0039-2952
PT5
STUDI GERMANICI. 1935-19??; resumed 1963. 1/yr. L.50000. (Istituto Italiano di Studi Germanici) Herder Editrice e Libreria s.r.l., Piazza Montecitorio, 120, 00186 Rome, Italy. TEL 67-94-628. FAX 678-47-51. Ed. Paolo Chiarini. adv.; bk.rev.; bibl.; circ. 1,000.
Description: Contains articles and essays on Germanic languages and literatures written by Italian and foreign scholars.

800 IT ISSN 0585-492X
STUDI ISPANICI. 1962. a. L.185000. Giardini Editori e Stampatori, Via Santa Bibbiana 28, 56100 Pisa, Italy. TEL 050 502531. Ed.Bd. **Indexed:** M.L.A.

850 IT
STUDI NOVECENTESCHI. 3/yr. L.70000. Giardini Editori e Stampatori, Via Santa Bibbiana 28, 56100 Pisa, Italy. TEL 050 502531. Ed.Bd. **Indexed:** M.L.A.

800 851 IT
STUDI PIEMONTESI. 1972. s-a. L.72000. Centro Studi Piemontesi, Via O. Revel 15, 10121 Turin, Italy. TEL 537-486. adv.; bk.rev.; circ. 1,200. (back issues avail.)

850 IT ISSN 0081-6248
STUDI SECENTESCHI. 1961. a. price varies. Casa Editrice Leo S. Olschki, Casella Postale 66, 50100 Florence, Italy. TEL 055-6530684. FAX 055-6530214. Ed. Martino Capucci. bk.rev.; index; circ. 1,000. **Indexed:** Hist.Abstr., M.L.A., RILA.

850 IT ISSN 0081-6256
PQ4646
STUDI TASSIANI. 1951. a. L.50000. Centro di Studi Tassiani, Comune di Bergamo - Biblioteca, Piazza Vecchia 15, 24100 Bergamo, Italy. FAX 035-240655. cum.index vols.1-10, vols.11-20.

800 900 100 IT
AS221
STUDI URBINATI. SERIE B: SCIENZE UMANE E SOCIALI. N.S. 1950. a. L.95000. (Universita degli Studi di Urbino) Edizioni Quattroventi, Casella Postale 156, 61029 Urbino, Italy. Ed. Carlo Bo. bk.rev.; charts; illus.; index. **Indexed:** Arts & Hum.Cit.Ind., Curr.Cont.
Former titles (until 1988): Studi Urbinati. Serie B: Letteratura, Storia, Filsofia (ISSN 0039-3088); Studi Urbinati. Serie B: Letteratura.

STUDIA ANGLICA POSNANIENSIA; international review of English Studies. see LINGUISTICS

880 US ISSN 0899-9929
STUDIA CLASSICA. irreg. Peter Lang Publishing, Inc., 62 W. 45th St., 4th Fl., New York, NY 10036. TEL 212-302-6740. FAX 212-302-7574. Eds. Anthony J. Podlecki, John C. Overbeck.
—BLDSC shelfmark: 8482.376800.
Description: Examines various aspects of the Graeco-Roman world syntopically.

830 PL ISSN 0137-2467
PF3003
STUDIA GERMANICA POSNANIENSIA. (Text in German) 1971. irreg., no.16, 1989. price varies. Adam Mickiewicz University Press, Nowowiejskiego 55, 61-734 Poznan, Poland. TEL 527-380. FAX 61-526425. TELEX 413260 UAMPL. Eds. Stefan H. Kaszynski, A. Bzdega. bk.rev.; bibl. **Indexed:** Lang.& Lang.Behav.Abstr.
—BLDSC shelfmark: 8482.831000.
Description: An international review of German studies. Contains articles and papers in German linguistics and literature.

891 941.5 IE ISSN 0081-6477
PB1201
STUDIA HIBERNICA. 1961. a. £3. St. Patrick's College, Editorial Committee, Dublin 9, Ireland. Ed. D.F. Cregan. bk.rev.; circ. 1,000. **Indexed:** Br.Archaeol.Abstr., Hist.Abstr., M.L.A.

801 830 HU ISSN 0209-9403
STUDIA POETICA. (Text in English, German) 1980. irreg. exchange basis. Attila Jozsef University, c/o E. Szabo, Exchange Librarian, Dugonics ter 13, P.O.B. 393, Szeged H-6701, Hungary. (Dist. in Western countries by: Harry Munchberg, Hahnenkleerstr. 14, D-3394, Langelsheim) Eds. Arpad Bernath, Karoly Csuri. circ. 500.
Description: Examines literary theory and analysis and attempts to apply the methods of semiotics, linguistics and logical semantics to works of literature.

809 PL ISSN 0137-4389
STUDIA POLONO-SLAVICA ORIENTALIA. ACTA LITTERARIA. a. price varies. (Polska Akademia Nauk, Instytut Slowianoznawstwa, Pracownia Literatur Wschodnioslowianskich) Ossolineum, Publishing House of the Polish Academy of Sciences, Rynek 9, Wroclaw, Poland. TELEX 0712771 OSS PL. (Dist. by: Ars Polona-Ruch, Krakowskie Przedmiescie 7, Warsaw, Poland) Ed. Bazyli Bialokozowicz.

STUDIA ROMANICA ET ANGLICA ZAGRABIENSIA. see LINGUISTICS

STUDIA ROSENTHALIANA; tijdschrift voor Joodse wetenschap en geschiedenis in Nederland/journal for Jewish literature and history in the Netherlands. see ETHNIC INTERESTS

800 PL ISSN 0081-6884
PG2025
STUDIA ROSSICA POSNANIENSIA. (Text in Polish and Russian; summaries in English and Russian) 1970. irreg., vol.20, 1988. price varies. Adam Mickiewicz University Press, Nowowiejskiego 55, 61-734 Poznan, Poland. TEL 527-380. FAX 61-526425. TELEX 413260 UAMPL. Eds. Zbigniew Baranski, Leszek Ossowski. bk.rev.; circ. 700. **Indexed:** Lang.& Lang.Behav.Abstr.
Description: Papers in Russian and Polish divided into areas of literature, linguistics and methods of teaching.

800 PL ISSN 0081-6949
STUDIA STAROPOLSKIE. 1953. irreg., vol.53, 1987. price varies. (Polska Akademia Nauk, Instytut Badan Literackich) Ossolineum, Publishing House of the Polish Academy of Sciences, Rynek 9, Wroclaw, Poland. TELEX 0712771 OSS PL. (Dist. by: Ars Polona-Ruch, Krakowskie Przedmiescie 7, Warsaw, Poland)

STUDIA UNIVERSITATIS "BABES-BOLYAI". PHILOLOGIA. see LINGUISTICS

STUDIA URALO-ALTAICA. see LINGUISTICS

800 PL ISSN 0081-7112
STUDIA Z OKRESU OSWIECENIA. (Text in Polish; summaries in English and French) 1964. irreg., vol.20, 1986. price varies. (Polska Akademia Nauk, Instytut Badan Literackich) Ossolineum, Publishing House of the Polish Academy of Sciences, Rynek 9, Wroclaw, Poland. TELEX 0712771 OSS PL. (Dist. by: Ars Polona-Ruch, Krakowskie Przedmiescie 7, Warsaw, Poland) Ed.Bd. bibl.; circ. 1,000.

830 GW ISSN 0081-7236
STUDIEN ZUR DEUTSCHEN LITERATUR. 1966. irreg., no.118, 1991. price varies. Max Niemeyer Verlag, Postfach 2140, 7400 Tuebingen 1, Germany. TEL 07071-81104. FAX 07071-87419. Ed.Bd. (back issues avail.) **Indexed:** M.L.A.
Description: Monographs on German literature, especially since the 17th century.

STUDIEN ZUR ENGLISCHEN PHILOLOGIE, NEUE FOLGE. see *LINGUISTICS*

830 GW ISSN 0340-594X
STUDIEN ZUR GERMANISTIK, ANGLISTIK UND KOMPARATISTIK. 1970. irreg., vol.116, 1985. price varies. Bouvier Verlag Herbert Grundmann, Am Hof 32, Postfach 1268, 5300 Bonn 1, Germany. Eds. A. Arnold, A. Hass. **Indexed:** M.L.A.

800 GW ISSN 0340-9023
STUDIEN ZUR LITERATUR DER MODERNE. 1976. irreg., vol.13, 1985. price varies. Bouvier Verlag Herbert Grundmann, Am Hof 32, Postfach 1268, 5300 Bonn 1, Germany. Ed. Helmut Koopmann.

860 301 GW ISSN 0340-5990
STUDIEN ZUR LITERATUR- UND SOZIALGESCHICHTE SPANIENS UND LATEINAMERIKAS. 1975. irreg., no. 7, 1984. price varies. Bouvier Verlag Herbert Grundmann, Am Hof 32, Postfach 1268, 5300 Bonn 1, Germany. Ed. Martin Franzbach.

STUDIES IN AFRICAN AND AFRO-AMERICAN CULTURE. see *HISTORY — History of Africa*

896 US
STUDIES IN AFRICAN LITERATURE. irreg., latest no.5. $39.95 per no. Edwin Mellen Press, 240 Portage Rd., Box 450, Lewiston, NY 14092. TEL 716-754-8566. FAX 716-754-4335.

810 US ISSN 0091-8083
PS370
STUDIES IN AMERICAN FICTION. 1973. 2/yr. $6 to individuals (foreign $9); institutions $10 (foreign $12). Northeastern University, Department of English, Boston, MA 02115. TEL 617-437-3687. Ed. James Nagel. adv.; bk.rev.; circ. 1,300. **Indexed:** Abstr.Engl.Stud., Amer.Hum.Ind., Arts & Hum.Cit.Ind., Curr.Cont., Ind.Bk.Rev.Hum., M.L.A.
—BLDSC shelfmark: 8489.059000.

808 970.1 US ISSN 0730-3238
STUDIES IN AMERICAN INDIAN LITERATURES. 1977. q. $6. Columbia University, 603 Lewisohn Hall, New York, NY 10027. TEL 212-280-8253. Ed. Karl Kroeber. bk.rev.; bibl.; circ. 250. (back issues avail.)

STUDIES IN AMERICAN JEWISH LITERATURE. see *ETHNIC INTERESTS*

810 US
STUDIES IN AMERICAN LITERATURE. irreg., latest no.16. $39.95 per no. Edwin Mellen Press, 240 Portage Rd., Box 450, Lewiston, NY 14092. TEL 716-754-8566. FAX 716-754-4335.

892.7 NE ISSN 0169-9903
STUDIES IN ARABIC LITERATURE. (Supplement to: Journal of Arabic Literature (ISSN 0085-2376)) 1971. irreg., no.15, 1992. price varies. E.J. Brill, P.O. Box 9000, 2300 PA Leiden, Netherlands. TEL 071-312624. FAX 071-317532. TELEX 39296 BRILL NL. (In N. America: E.J. Brill, 24 Hudson St., Kinderhook, NY 12106. TEL 800-962-4406)

808 910.03 US ISSN 0738-0755
PS153.N5
STUDIES IN BLACK AMERICAN LITERATURE. 1984. a. price varies. Penkevill Publishing Company, Box 212, Greenwood, FL 32443. Eds. Joe Weixlmann, Houston A. Baker, Jr. adv.; circ. 500.
—BLDSC shelfmark: 8489.699500.

809 JA
STUDIES IN BRITISH & AMERICAN LITERATURE/EI-BEIBUNGAKU. (Text in English or Japanese) a. Komazawa University, 1-23-1 Komazawa, Setagaya-ku, Tokyo 154, Japan.
Formerly: Gaikoku Bungaku Kenkyu.

890 US
STUDIES IN BRITISH LATERATURE. irreg., latest no.16. $39.95 per no. Edwin Mellen Press, 240 Portage Rd., Box 450, Lewiston, NY 14092. TEL 716-754-8566. FAX 716-754-4335.

820 US ISSN 0095-4489
PR4229
STUDIES IN BROWNING AND HIS CIRCLE; a journal of criticism, history and bibliography. 1968. a. $17.50. Baylor University, Armstrong Browning Library, B U Box 7152, B U Box 7152, TX 76798-7152. TEL 817-755-3566. Ed. Roger L. Brooks. bk.rev.; cum.index; circ. 650. **Indexed:** Abstr.Engl.Stud., Amer.Hum.Ind., Arts & Hum.Cit.Ind., Curr.Cont., Ind.Bk.Rev.Hum., M.L.A.
—BLDSC shelfmark: 8489.730000.
Formerly: Browning Newsletter (ISSN 0007-2532)

800 CN ISSN 0380-6995
PR9180
STUDIES IN CANADIAN LITERATURE. 1976. s-a. Can.$14($18) to individuals; institutions Can.$20 ($24). University of New Brunswick, Department of English, Fredericton, N.B. E3B 5A3, Canada. TEL 506-453-4598. FAX 506-453-4599. Ed.Bd. adv.; circ. 700. **Indexed:** Abstr.Engl.Stud., Amer.Hum.Ind., Arts & Hum.Cit.Ind., Can.Lit.Ind., Can.Per.Ind., CMI, Curr.Cont., M.L.A.
—BLDSC shelfmark: 8489.815000.

880 US
STUDIES IN CLASSICS. irreg. $39.95. Edwin Mellen Press, 240 Portage Rd., Box 450, Lewiston, NY 14092. TEL 716-754-8566. FAX 716-754-4335.

809 US ISSN 0081-7775
STUDIES IN COMPARATIVE LITERATURE (CHAPEL HILL). (Text in English, French, German, Italian, Latin, and Spanish) 1950. irreg., no.63, 1988. price varies. (University of North Carolina at Chapel Hill, Department of English) University of North Carolina Press, Box 2288, Chapel Hill, NC 27515-2288. TEL 919-966-3561. FAX 919-966-3829. (reprint service avail. from UMI)
—BLDSC shelfmark: 9116.210000.
Refereed Serial

800 US
STUDIES IN COMPARATIVE LITERATURE (LEWISTON). irreg., latest vol.18. $39.95 per no. Edwin Mellen Press, 240 Portage Rd., Box 450, Lewiston, NY 14092. TEL 716-754-8566. FAX 716-754-4335.

820.9 410 JA ISSN 0039-3649
PR1
STUDIES IN ENGLISH LITERATURE/EIBUNGAKU KENKYU. (Text in English and Japanese) 1919. 3/yr. 6000 Yen. English Literary Society of Japan – Nihon Eibungakkai, 501 Kenkyusha Bldg., 9 Surugadai 2-chome, Kanda, Chiyoda-ku, Tokyo 101, Japan. FAX 03-3233-3398. Ed. Hiroyuki Ide. adv.; bk.rev.; cum.index; circ. 3,800. **Indexed:** Curr.Cont.

820 US ISSN 0039-3657
PR1
STUDIES IN ENGLISH LITERATURE 1500-1900. 1961. q. $25 to individuals; institutions $30 (foreign $35). Rice University, Box 1892, Houston, TX 77251. TEL 713-527-8101. FAX 713-285-5207. Ed. Robert L. Patten. circ. 2,000. (also avail. in microform from UMI; back issues avail.; reprint service avail. from SCH,UMI) **Indexed:** Abstr.Engl.Stud., Acad.Ind., Arts & Hum.Cit.Ind., Biog.Ind., Curr.Cont., Hum.Ind., M.L.A.
—BLDSC shelfmark: 8490.521000.
Description: Each issue covers a different period of literature from the Renaissance to 19th century, with a review of current scholarship in that period.

800 US
STUDIES IN EXPERIMENTAL LITERATURE. irreg. Edwin Mellen Press, 240 Portage Rd., Box 450, Lewiston, NY 14092. TEL 716-754-8566. FAX 716-754-4335.

890 US
STUDIES IN FRENCH LITERATURE. irreg., latest no.13. $39.95 per no. Edwin Mellen Press, 240 Portage Rd., Box 450, Lewiston, NY 14092. TEL 800-753-2788. FAX 716-754-4335.

840 US
STUDIES IN GERMAN LANGUAGE AND LITERATURE. irreg., latest vol.8. $39.95 per no. Edwin Mellen Press, 240 Portage Rd., Box 450, Lewiston, NY 14092. TEL 716-754-8566. FAX 716-754-4335.

830 US
STUDIES IN GERMAN LITERATURE OF THE 18TH AND 19TH CENTURIES. irreg. Peter Lang Publishing, Inc., 62 W. 45th St., 4th Fl., New York, NY 10036. TEL 212-302-6740. FAX 212-302-7574. Ed. Christopher Herin.
Description: Devoted to German literature from the Enlightenment to Post-Romanticism (1750-1830) within a European context.

800 UK ISSN 0960-6025
STUDIES IN HOGG AND HIS WORLD. 1982. a. £12.50. James Hogg Society, Department of English Studies, University of Stirling, Stirling FK9 4LA, Scotland. Ed. G.H. Hughes. adv.; bk.rev.; circ. 100.
Formerly (until 1989): James Hogg Society. Newsletter (ISSN 0263-7022)
Description: Contains essays and texts of interest to students of the Scottish writer James Hogg (1770-1835).

STUDIES IN ISLAM. see *RELIGIONS AND THEOLOGY — Islamic*

800 US ISSN 1043-5794
STUDIES IN ITALIAN CULTURE: LITERATURE IN HISTORY. irreg. Peter Lang Publishing, Inc., 62 W. 45th St., 4th Fl., New York, NY 10036. TEL 212-302-6740. FAX 212-302-7574. Ed. Aldo Scaglione.

850 US
STUDIES IN ITALIAN LITERATURE. irreg. $39.95 per no. Edwin Mellen Press, 240 Portage Rd., Box 450, Lewiston, NY 14092. TEL 800-753-2788. FAX 716-754-4335.

STUDIES IN LANGUAGE COMPANION SERIES. see *LINGUISTICS*

800 US
STUDIES IN LITERATURE AND CRITICISM. irreg. price varies. Burt Franklin & Co., Inc., Box 856, New York, NY 10014. TEL 212-627-0027.

800 US
STUDIES IN MEDIAEVAL LITERATURE. irreg., latest no.12. $39.95 per no. Edwin Mellen Press, 240 Portage Rd., Box 450, Lewiston, NY 14092. TEL 800-753-2788. FAX 716-754-4335.

807 US
STUDIES IN MEDIEVAL AND RENAISSANCE TEACHING. 1973. a. $10. c/o J. Hample, Ed., College of Arts and Sciences, Indiana State University, Terre Haute, IN 47809. TEL 812-237-2788. adv.; bk.rev.; film rev.; play rev.; circ. 500.
Formerly (until 1982): Ralph.

STUDIES IN MEDIEVAL CULTURE. see *HISTORY*

890 US
STUDIES IN MIDDLE EASTERN LITERATURES. 1972. irreg., no.11, 1984. price varies. Bibliotheca Islamica, Inc., Box 14474, University Sta., Minneapolis, MN 55414.

830 US ISSN 0888-3904
STUDIES IN MODERN GERMAN LITERATURE. 1987. irreg. Peter Lang Publishing, Inc., 62 W. 45th St., 4th Fl., New York, NY 10036. TEL 212-302-6740. Ed. Peter D.G. Brown.

STUDIES IN NEW ENGLAND THOUGHT AND LITERATURE. see *PHILOSOPHY*

STUDIES IN OLD GERMANIC LANGUAGES AND LITERATURES. see *LINGUISTICS*

809 US
STUDIES IN RENAISSANCE LITERATURE. irreg., latest no.12. $39.95 per no. Edwin Mellen Press, 240 Portage Rd., Box 450, Lewiston, NY 14092. TEL 716-754-8566. FAX 716-754-4335.

479 US
STUDIES IN ROMANCE LANGUAGES & LITERATURES. 1970. irreg., latest 1988. price varies. University Press of Kentucky, 663 S. Limestone St., Lexington, KY 40508-4008. TEL 606-257-2951. FAX 606-257-2984. Ed. John E. Keller. (reprint service avail. from UMI) **Indexed:** M.L.A.
Formerly: Studies in Romance Languages (ISSN 0085-6894)

2966 LITERATURE

800 US ISSN 0039-3762
PN751
STUDIES IN ROMANTICISM. 1961. q. $20 to individuals (foreign $22); institutions, $49.50 (foreign $51.50). Boston University, Graduate School, 236 Bay State Rd., Boston, MA 02215. TEL 617-353-2505. (Subscr. to: Boston University Scholarly Publications, 985 Commonwealth Ave., Boston, MA 02215. TEL 617-353-4106) Ed. David Wagenknecht. adv.; bk.rev.; index, cum.index: vols.1-10; circ. 1,800. (also avail. in microform from UMI; reprint service avail. from UMI) **Indexed:** Abstr.Engl.Stud., Artbibl.Mod., Can.Rev.Comp.Lit., Curr.Cont., Hist.Abstr., Hum.Ind., Ind.Bk.Rev.Hum., M.L.A., RILA.
—BLDSC shelfmark: 8491.450000.
Description: Covers the literature, music and art of the Romantic period in England, Europe, and America. Examines Third World parallels.

STUDIES IN SEMIOTICS AND LITERATURE. see LINGUISTICS

813 US ISSN 0039-3789
PN3311
STUDIES IN SHORT FICTION. 1963. q. $18 to individuals; libraries $21. Newberry College, 2100 College St., Newberry, SC 29108. TEL 803-276-5195. FAX 803-321-5232. Ed. Michael J. O'Shea. bk.rev.; bibl.; index; circ. 1,775. (also avail. in microform from UMI; reprint service avail. from UMI) **Indexed:** Abstr.Engl.Stud., Abstr.Pop.Cult., Amer.Bibl.Slavic & E.Eur.Stud., Arts & Hum.Cit.Ind., Bk.Rev.Ind. (1986-), Child.Bk.Rev.Ind. (1986-), Curr.Cont., Hisp.Amer.Per.Ind., Hum.Ind., Ind.Bk.Rev.Hum., M.L.A., Mid.East: Abstr.& Ind.
—BLDSC shelfmark: 8491.580000.

890 US
STUDIES IN SLAVIC LANGUAGE AND LITERATURE. irreg., latest no.7. Edwin Mellen Press, 240 Portage Rd., Box 450, Lewiston, NY 14092. TEL 716-754-8566. FAX 716-754-4335.

899 NE ISSN 0169-0175
STUDIES IN SLAVIC LITERATURE AND POETICS. Short title: S S P. 1981. irreg. price varies. Editions Rodopi B.V., Keizersgracht 302-304, 1016 EX Amsterdam, Netherlands. TEL 020-6227507. FAX 020-6380948. (US and Canada subscr. to: 233 Peachtree St. N.E., Ste. 404, Atlanta, GA 30303-1504. TEL 800-225-3998) Ed.Bd. **Indexed:** M.L.A.

807 US ISSN 0190-2407
PR1901
STUDIES IN THE AGE OF CHAUCER. 1979. a. $30. Ohio State University, Department of English, 421 W. Denney Hall, 164 W. 17th Ave., Columbus, OH 43210. (Subscr. to: Christian Zacher, Center for Medieval & Renaissance Studies, Ohio State Univ., 322 Dulles Hall, 230 W. 17th Ave., Columbus, OH 43210-1311) Ed. Lisa J. Kiser. bk.rev.; bibl.; index; circ. 700. (back issues avail.)
—BLDSC shelfmark: 8488.952000.

800 US ISSN 0149-015X
PS201
STUDIES IN THE AMERICAN RENAISSANCE. 1977. a. $35. (University of South Carolina) University Press of Virginia, Box 3608, Charlottesville, VA 22903. TEL 804-924-3468. FAX 804-982-2655. Ed. Joel Myerson. bk.rev.; bibl.; illus.; circ. 750. **Indexed:** Amer.Hist.& Life, Amer.Hum.Ind., Hist.Abstr., M.L.A., Rel.Ind.One.
—BLDSC shelfmark: 8489.090000.
Description: Articles on the literature of the American Renaissance.

830 US ISSN 0081-8593
PD25
STUDIES IN THE GERMANIC LANGUAGES AND LITERATURES. 1949. irreg., no.114, 1992. price varies. (University of North Carolina at Chapel Hill, Department of English) University of North Carolina Press, Box 2288, Chapel Hill, NC 27515-2288. TEL 919-966-3561. FAX 919-966-3829. (reprint service avail. from UMI)
Refereed Serial

800 US
STUDIES IN THE HISTORICAL NOVEL. irreg., latest no.2. $39.95 per no. Edwin Mellen Press, 240 Portage Rd., Box 450, Lewiston, NY 14092. TEL 716-754-8566. FAX 716-754-4335.

800 US ISSN 0039-3819
PR1
STUDIES IN THE LITERARY IMAGINATION. 1968. s-a. $5. Georgia State University, Department of English, Graduate Faculty, 31 Gilmer St., Atlanta, GA 30303. TEL 404-658-2900. Ed. Dr. R. Barton Palmer. circ. 4,000 (controlled). (also avail. in microform from UMI; back issues avail.; reprint service avail. from UMI) **Indexed:** Abstr.Engl.Stud., Amer.Bibl.Slavic & E.Eur.Stud., Amer.Hum.Ind., Arts & Hum.Cit.Ind., Film Lit.Ind. (1983-), Hum.Ind., M.L.A.
—BLDSC shelfmark: 8491.037000.

813 US ISSN 0039-3827
PN3311
STUDIES IN THE NOVEL. 1969. q. $15 to individuals; libraries $25; (foreign $35). University of North Texas, English Department, Denton, TX 76203. TEL 817-565-2025. (Subscr. addr.: Box 13706, North Texas Sta., Denton, TX 76203) Ed. Gerald A. Kirk. adv.; bk.rev.; bibl.; index; circ. 1,800. (also avail. in microform from UMI; reprint service avail. from UMI) **Indexed:** Abstr.Engl.Stud., Amer.Bibl.Slavic & E.Eur.Stud., Arts & Hum.Cit.Ind., Curr.Cont., Hum.Ind., Ind.Bk.Rev.Hum., LCR, M.L.A., Mid.East: Abstr.& Ind.
—BLDSC shelfmark: 8491.157000.

800 US
STUDIES IN THE ROMANTIC AGE. (Text in English and other West European language.) 1988. irreg. Peter Lang Publishing, Inc., 62 W. 45th St., 4th Fl., New York, NY 10036. TEL 212-302-6740. Ed. Charles I. Patterson.

800 US ISSN 0145-7888
PN771
STUDIES IN TWENTIETH CENTURY LITERATURE. 1976. s-a. $15 to individuals; institutions $20. Kansas State University, Department of Modern Languages, Eisenhower 104, Manhattan, KS 66506-1003. TEL 913-532-6760. FAX 913-532-7114. (Co-sponsor: University of Nebraska-Lincoln) Ed.Bd. adv.; bk.rev.; cum.index; circ. 450. **Indexed:** Amer.Bibl.Slavic & E.Eur.Stud., Amer.Hum.Ind., Arts & Hum.Cit.Ind., Curr.Cont., M.L.A., Mid.East: Abstr.& Ind.
—BLDSC shelfmark: 8491.832000.
Description: Devoted to literary theory and practical criticism of 20th century literature written in French, German, Russian, and Spanish. Focuses on poetry, prose, drama, and literary theory.

800 420 US ISSN 1043-8580
STUDIES OF WORLD LITERATURE IN ENGLISH. irreg. Peter Lang Publishing, Inc., 62 W. 45th St., 4th Fl., New York, NY 10036. TEL 212-302-6740. FAX 212-302-7574. Ed. Norman R. Cary.
Description: Encompasses criticism of modern English-language literature from outside the United States, Great Britain, and Ireland; literature by writers from Canada, Africa, Asia, the Pacific, and the Caribbean.

800 US
STUDIES ON THEMES AND MOTIFS IN LITERATURE. irreg. Peter Lang Publishing, Inc., 62 W. 45th St., 4th Fl., New York, NY 10036. TEL 212-302-6740. FAX 212-302-7574. Ed. Horst Daemmrich.
Description: Covers cross-cultural patterns as well as the entire range of national literatures.

840 940 UK ISSN 0435-2866
PQ2105.A2
STUDIES ON VOLTAIRE AND THE EIGHTEENTH CENTURY. (Text in English and French) 1955. irreg. (approx. 12/yr.). price varies. Voltaire Foundation, Taylor Institution, St. Giles, Oxford OX1 3NA, England. TEL 0865-270250. FAX 0865-270740. Ed. H.T. Mason. cum.index: 1955-64, 1965-70. (also avail. in microfiche from VFN; back issues avail.) **Indexed:** M.L.A.

800 300 AT
STUDIO; a journal of Christians writing. 1980. q. Aus. $40. Studio, 727 Peel St., Albury, N.S.W. 2640, Australia. TEL 060-21-1135. Ed. Paul Grover. bk.rev.; circ. 300. (back issues avail.)
Formerly: Christians Writing (ISSN 0729-4042)
Description: Presents work of literary merit, offers a venue for new and aspiring writers, and seeks to create a sense of community among Christian writers.

STUDY GROUP ON EIGHTEENTH-CENTURY RUSSIA. NEWSLETTER. see HISTORY — History Of Europe

800 GW
STUTTGARTER ARBEITEN ZUR GERMANISTIK. (Text and summaries in English, German) 1975. irreg. price varies. Verlag Hans-Dieter Heinz, Steiermaerkerstrasse 132, 7000 Stuttgart 30, Germany. Ed.Bd. circ. 400. (back issues avail.) **Indexed:** M.L.A.

801 US ISSN 0039-4238
PE1
STYLE (DEKALB). 1966. q. $24 to individuals; institutions $36. Northern Illinois University, Department of English, DeKalb, IL 60115. TEL 815-753-0611. FAX 815-753-1824. Ed. Harold F. Mosher, Jr. adv.; bk.rev.; bibl.; circ. 600. (also avail. in microfilm from UMI; talking book; Braille; back issues avail.; reprint service avail. from UMI) **Indexed:** Abstr.Engl.Stud., Arts & Hum.Cit.Ind., Lang.& Lang.Behav.Abstr., M.L.A.
—BLDSC shelfmark: 8501.803000.
Description: Articles analyze stylistic features of literature, ranging from traditional subjects such as diction, grammar and metrics, to the theory of literature, the process of reading, and problems of narratology.

869 BL
STYLOS. 1980. irreg., no.43, 1981. Universidade Estadual Paulista Julio de Mesquita Filho, Instituto de Biociencias, Letras e Ciencias Exatas, Rua Cristovao Colombo 2265-J. Nazareth, 15100 Campus de Sao Jose do Rio Preto SP, Brazil.

879.9 US ISSN 0049-2426
PN2
SUB-STANCE. (Text in English and French) 1971. 3/yr. $19 to individuals; institutions $65. University of Wisconsin Press, 114 N. Murray St., Madison, WI 53715. TEL 608-262-4952. FAX 608-262-7560. Eds. Sydney Levy, Michel Pierssens. adv.; bk.rev.; cum.index: 1971-1978; circ. 750. (processed; also avail. in microform from UMI; reprint service avail. from UMI) **Indexed:** Amer.Hum.Ind., Arts & Hum.Cit.Ind., Curr.Cont., M.L.A., Sociol.Abstr.
—BLDSC shelfmark: 8503.480000.

810 CN
SUB-TERRAIN. 1988. 4/yr. $8. P.O. Box 1575, Sta. A, Vancouver, B.C. V6C 2P7, Canada. TEL 604-876-8710. circ. 500.

892 II
SUBH-I-ADAB. (Text in Urdu) 1974. m. Rs.20. Nazir Ahmad Nuri, Mahmood Manzil Gwynne Rd., Lakhnau, India. illus.

808 US
SUBTLE JOURNAL OF RAW COINAGE. 1987. m. $10. D B Q P, 317 Princetown Rd., Schenectady, NY 12306. Ed. Geof Huth.
Description: Publishes undefined invented words and short pieces of experimental writing comprised exclusively of invented words, as a means of exploring the creation of language and the invention of meaning.

SUEDOSTDEUTSCHES KULTURWERK. VEROEFFENTLICHUNGEN. REIHE A: KULTUR UND DICHTUNG. see HISTORY — History Of Europe

SUEDOSTDEUTSCHES KULTURWERK. VEROEFFENTLICHUNGEN. REIHE B: WISSENSCHAFTLICHE ARBEITEN. see HISTORY — History Of Europe

SUEDOSTDEUTSCHES KULTURWERK. VEROEFFENTLICHUNGEN. REIHE C: ERINNERUNGEN UND QUELLEN. see HISTORY — History Of Europe

SUEDOSTDEUTSCHES KULTURWERK. VEROEFFENTLICHUNGEN. REIHE D: KLEINE SUEDOSTREIHE. see HISTORY — History Of Europe

830 GW
SUEVICA - BEITRAEGE ZUR SCHWABISCHEN LITERATUR- UND GEISTESGESCHICHTE. 1981. biennial. price varies. (Justinus-Kerner-Verein) Verlag Hans-Dieter Heinz, Steiermaerker Str. 132, 7000 Stuttgart 30, Germany. Ed. Hartmut Froeschle.
Formerly: Beitraege zur Schwabischen Literatur- und Geistesgeschichte und Mitteilungen des Justinius Kerner-Vereins und Fraunenvereins.

| 895.15 | CC | ISSN 1000-7903 |

SUIBI/RANDOM NOTES. (Text in Chinese) 1979. bi-m. $38.30. Huacheng Chubanshe, No. 11, Shuiyin Lu, Huanshi Donglu, Guangzhou, Guangdong 510075, People's Republic of China. TEL 768688. (Dist. in US by: China Books & Periodicals, Inc., 2929 24th St., San Francisco, CA 94110. TEL 415-282-2994) Ed. Huang Weijing.

SUID-AFRIKAANSE AKADEMIE VIR WETENSKAP EN KUNS. NUUSBRIEF. see *SCIENCES: COMPREHENSIVE WORKS*

| 800 | | BG |

SUJANESHU. (Text in Bengali) m. 15-16 Goalnagar Lane, Dhaka 1, Bangladesh. Eds. Ahmad Rafiq, Kazi Abdul Halim.

| 800 051 | US | ISSN 0730-305X |
| PS501 | | |

SULFUR; a literary bi-annual of the whole art. 1980. 2/yr. $13 to individuals (foreign $17); institutions $19 (foreign $23)(effective Jan. 1, 1991). Clayton Eshleman, Ed. & Pub., 210 Washtenaw, Ypsilanti, MI 48197-2526. TEL 313-483-9787. (Alt. addr.: c/o English Department, Eastern Michigan University, Ypsilanti, MI 48197) adv.; bk.rev.; bibl.; illus.; circ. 2,000. (back issues avail.). **Indexed:** Bk.Rev.Ind. (1986-), Child.Bk.Rev.Ind. (1986-), PROMT.
Supersedes (1967-1972): Caterpillar (ISSN 0008-784X)

| 800 | | CC |

SULIAN WENXUE (LIANKAN)/RUSSIAN LITERATURE. (Text in Chinese) bi-m. $27.50. (Beijing Shifan Daxue - Beijing Normal University) Beijing Shifan Daxue Chubanshe - Beijing Normal University Press, Beijing 100088, People's Republic of China. (Dist. overseas by: China International Book Trading Corp., P.O. Box 399, Beijing, P.R.C.; Dist. in US by: China Books & Periodicals, Inc., 2929 24th St., San Francisco, CA 94110. TEL 415-282-2994) (Co-sponsors: Beijing Waiyu Xueyuan - Beijing Institute of Foreign Languages; Wuhan Daxue - Wuhan University) bk.rev.
Formed by the 1990 merger of: Sulian Wenxue & Dangdai Sulian Wenxue & Esu Wenxue.
Description: Publishes works of Soviet Russian literature, as well as reviews, columns, and literary and publishing news.

| 808 | US | ISSN 0741-0271 |

SUNRUST. 1983. s-a. $8. Dawn Valley Press, Box 58, New Wilmington, PA 16142. TEL 412-946-2948. Eds. Nancy Esther James, James A. Perkins. bk.rev.; circ. 300. (back issues avail.)
Description: Poetry, prose, art and photography emphasizing the moods, places and people of rural America.

SUPLEMENTO LITERARIO DE REVOLUCION Y CULTURA. see *LITERARY AND POLITICAL REVIEWS*

| 891.553 | | IR |

SURAH. 1989. m. Rs.250 per no. Hawzah-i Hunari Sazman-i Tablighat-i Islami, 213 Summaiyah St., P.O. Box 1677-15815, Teheran, Iran. illus.

| 891.439 | | PK |

SURAT. (Text in Urdu) 1979. m. Rs.6. Meyar Publications, Box 3195, Karachi 29, Pakistan. Ed. Sayyid Wajahat Ali.

| 820 | NE | ISSN 0921-2981 |

SURPLUS; tijdschrift over literatuur van vrouwen (women's review of books). 1987. bi-m. fl.27.50. Surplus Foundation, Postbus 16572, 1001 RB Amsterdam, Netherlands. TEL 020-6207767. adv.; bk.rev.; circ. 1,000. (back issues avail.)

| 891.4 | II | ISSN 0039-6370 |

SUSHAMA. (Text in Hindi) 1959. m. Rs.100 (foreign Rs.650). Shama Magazine, 13-14 Asaf Ali Rd., New Delhi 110002, India. TEL 91-11-732666. FAX 91-11-736539. TELEX 3161601 SHAMA-IN. Ed.Bd. adv. 80,333.

| 895 791.43 | | II |

SUSHMITA. (Text in Hindi) 1989. w. 13-14 Asaf Ali Rd., New Delhi 110 002, India. TEL 11-732666. FAX 11-736539. TELEX 3161601. Ed. M. Yunus Dehlvi. circ. 50,000.
Description: Covers literature, films and television.

| 806 | | SW |

SVERIGES FOERFATTARFOERBUND. MEDLEMSFOERTECKNING/SWEDISH WRITERS ASSOCIATION. MEMBERSHIP ROLL. a. membership. Sveriges Foerfattarfoerbund, Drottninggatan 88 B, 111 36 Stockholm, Sweden. TEL 08-791-22-80. FAX 08-791-22-85. Ed. Inger Aerlemalm.

| 891.7 491.7 | | NE |

▼**SVET LITERATURY/WORLD OF LITERATURE.** (Text in Czech) 1991. 2/yr. fl.93($48) (effective 1992). (Czechoslovak Academy of Sciences, Institute for Czech and World Literature, CS) John Benjamins Publishing Co., Amsteldijk 44, P.O. Box 75577, 1070 AN Amsterdam, Netherlands. TEL 020-6738156. FAX 020-6739773. (In N. America: 821 Bethlehem Pike, Philadelphia, PA 19118. TEL 215-836-1200) bk.rev. (back issues avail.)
Supersedes in part (1956-1991): Ceskoslovenska Rusistika (ISSN 0009-0638)
Description: Covers European and American literatures with a comparative and interdisciplinary focus, including examinations of interpretative methods.

| 891.86 | CS | ISSN 0039-7075 |

SVETOVA LITERATURA; revue zahranicnich literatur. 1956. bi-m. 210 Kcs.($51.40) (typically set in Dec.). Odeon, Nakladatelstvi Krasne Literatury a Umeni, Narodni tr. 36, 115 86 Prague 1, Czechoslovakia. (Subscr. to: Svetova Literatura, Na Florenci 3, 115 86 Prague 1, Czechoslovakia) Ed. Anna Kareninova-Furekova. adv.; bk.rev.; illus.; circ. 9,000.
Description: Literary review of literature outside Czechoslovakia.

| 800 | | |

SVOBODNA SKOLA/FREE THINKING SCHOOL. 1896. m. $5 (foreign $6). (Bohemian Freethinkers Association) Free Thinking Schools, 5701 W. 22nd Pl., Cicero, IL 60650. TEL 708-656-9810. Ed. Savo Roknic. adv.; illus.; circ. 600.
Description: Features stories, history and customs of their forefathers.

| 800 | US | ISSN 1045-7682 |

SWAMP ROOT.* 1988. 3/yr. $12 to individuals; institutions $15. Box 31, Hot Springs, SD 57747-0031. TEL 615-562-7082. Ed. Al Masarik. bk.rev. (back issues avail.) **Indexed:** Amer.Hum.Ind., Ind.Amer.Per.Verse.
Description: Publishes poetry, essays, reviews, and interviews.

| 820 | | UK |

SWANSEA REVIEW. 1975. 3/yr. £1.50. University College of Swansea, Department of English, Mandela House, Singleton Park, Swansea SA2 8PP, Wales. Ed.Bd. adv.; bk.rev.
Formerly (until 1986): Prospect (ISSN 0306-5529)

| 808 | US | ISSN 0277-447X |

SWIFT KICK. 1980. irreg., no.8, 1988. $20 for 4 nos. to individuals; institutions $40. 1711 Amherst St., Buffalo, NY 14214. TEL 716-837-7778. Ed. Robin Kay Willoughby. circ. 150.

| 810 | US | ISSN 1043-1497 |
| PS501 | | |

SYCAMORE REVIEW. 1989. s-a. $9. Purdue University, Department of English, W. Lafayette, IN 47907. TEL 317-494-3783. Ed. Henry Hughes. adv.; circ. 1,000. (back issues avail.)
Description: Includes fiction, poetry, personal essays, and translations.

| 820 375.4 | | AT |

SYDNEY STUDIES IN ENGLISH. 1975. a. $8.50. University of Sydney, Department of English, Sydney, N.S.W. 2006, Australia. Eds. G.A. Wilkes, A.P. Riemer. bk.rev.; circ. 1,000. (back issues avail.)
Description: Devoted to criticism and scholarship in English literature and drama.

| 870 | | BE |

SYMBOLAE. SERIES D. LITERARIA. (Text in Dutch, English) 1987. irreg., vol.5, 1990. price varies. Leuven University Press, Krakenstraat 3, B-3000 Leuven, Belgium. TEL 016-284175. FAX 016-284176. Ed.Bd.

| 800 | US | ISSN 0039-7709 |
| PB1 | | CODEN: SYMPEZ |

SYMPOSIUM; a quarterly journal in modern foreign literatures. (Text mainly in English; occasionally in French, German, Italian, Portuguese and Spanish) 1946. q. $30 to individuals; institutions $56. (Syracuse University, Department of Romance Languages) Heldref Publications, 1319 Eighteenth St., N.W., Washington, DC 20036-1802. TEL 202-296-6267. FAX 202-296-5149. (Co-sponsor: Helen Dwight Reid Educational Foundation) Ed. Jeanne Bebo. adv.; bk.rev.; circ. 700. (also avail. in microform; reprint service avail. from KTO) **Indexed:** Hum.Ind., Ind.Bk.Rev.Hum.
—BLDSC shelfmark: 8582.880000.
Refereed Serial

| 800 | US | ISSN 1048-8561 |
| CB351 | | |

SYNOPSIS (LEWISTON); a yearly volume of book reviews. a. $19.95 to individuals; institutions $29.95. Edwin Mellen Press, 240 Portage Rd., Box 450, Lewiston, NY 14092. TEL 800-753-2788. FAX 716-754-4335. Eds. Guy R. Mermier, Mercedes Vaquero.

| 850 | | RM |

SYNTHESIS; Bulletin du Comite National Roumain de Litterature Comparee. (Text in English, French, German, Italian, Spanish) 1972. a. 30 lei($42) Editura Academiei Romane, Calea Victoriei 125, 79717 Bucharest, Rumania. (Dist. by: Rompresfilatelia, Calea Grivitei 64-66, P.O. Box 12-201, 78104 Bucharest, Rumania) Ed. Zoe Dumitrescu Busulenga. bk.rev. **Indexed:** Chem.Infd., Hist.Abstr.

| 810 | | US |

T A W T E.* (Texas Artists, Writers and Thinkers in Exile); a journal of Texas culture. (Text in English, some Spanish) 1974. s-a. $6 for 2 yrs. or $1.50 per no. Thorp Springs Press, 1002 Lorrain St., Austin, TX 78703-4829. Eds. Paul Foreman, Bob Burleson. bk.rev.; film rev.; circ. 2,000.

| 860 | US | ISSN 1045-8875 |
| E184.M5 | | |

T Q S NEWS. (Tonatiuh-Quinto Sol); a contemporary newsletter of eclectic Chicano thought. (Text in English and Spanish) 1976-1982; resumed 1984. q. $14. T Q S Publications (Subsidiary of: Tonatiuh-Quinto Sol International), Box 9275, Berkeley, CA 94709. TEL 510-655-8036. FAX 510-601-6938. Ed. Octavio I. Romano. bk.rev.; circ. 1,000. (back issues avail.) **Indexed:** Hisp.Amer.Per.Ind.
Formerly (until Jan. 1989): Grito del Sol Collection; **Supersedes:** Grito del Sol (ISSN 0742-1877)
Description: News about education, health, literature, research, consumer issues and student scholarships.

| 800 | | II |

TAGORE INTERNATIONAL. (Text in English) 1985. s-a. Rs.50($10) Tagore Research Institute, Rabindra Charcha Bhavan, 97C S.P. Mukherjee Rd., Calcutta 700 026, India. TEL 42-4386. Ed. Manjula Bose. bk.rev.; circ. 500.
Description: Academic journal and news bulletin on the Bengali poet and writer Rabindranath Tagore.

| 895.1 | | CC |

TAIGANG WENXUE XUANKAN/SELECTED TAIWAN AND HONG KONG LITERARY WORKS. (Text in Chinese) m. Y26.40. Fujian Sheng Wenlian, Fenghuang Chi, People's Republic of China, Fuzhou, Fujian 350002. TEL 711725. (Dist. overseas by: Jiangsu Publications Import & Export Corp., 56 Gao Yun Ling, Nanjing, Jiangsu, P.R.C.) Ed. Ji Zhong.
Description: Introduces literary works by overseas Chinese writers in Taiwan, Hong Kong, Macao and other areas.

| 895.1 | | CH |

TAIWAN LITERATURE/T'AI-WAN WEN I. (Text in Chinese) 1964. bi-m. NT.$500 in ROC; Asia $31; elsewhere $35. 6F, No. 1-1, Lane 52, Roosevelt Rd. Sec. 4, Taipei, Taiwan, Republic of China. (Orders to: 3F, No. 65 An-ho Rd., Taipei, Taiwan, R.O.C.) Ed. Wang Ming-Huang. adv.

LITERATURE

700 800 NZ ISSN 0114-4138
TAKAHE. 1989. q. NZ.$24. Takahe Publishing Collective, P.O. Box 13-335, Christchurch 1, New Zealand. TEL 03-3558-337. Ed.Bd. adv.; circ. 225.
Description: Publishes short fiction and poetry (including translations) from emergent and established writers.

810 US
TALKING STICK. 1988. 4/yr. donation. 8002B Dollyhyde Rd., Mt. Airy, MD 21771. TEL 301-829-2460. Ed. Bruce W. Barth. circ. 5,000.
Description: Publishes poetry, fiction, articles, art, photos, cartoons, interview, reviews, non-fiction, and news items.

800 NQ ISSN 0039-9221
TALLER. 1968; N.S. no.10, 1975. 3/yr. Can.$5. (Universidad Nacional Autonoma de Nicaragua) Editorial Universitaria de la U N A N, Leon, Nicaragua. Ed. Jaime Buitrago. (processed)

860 CL ISSN 0716-0798
TALLER DE LETRAS. (Some vols. accompanied by supplements) 1971. a. $25. Pontificia Universidad Catolica de Chile, Instituto de Letras, Pte. Batlle y Ordonez, 3300, Campus Oriente U.C., Casilla 6277, Correo 22, Santiago, Chile. FAX 562-2225515. TELEX 240395 PUC VA-CL. Ed. Ileana Cabrera de Hagel. bk.rev.; bibl.; illus.; index; circ. 1,000.

809 895.1 CH ISSN 0049-2949
PL2250
TAMKANG REVIEW; a journal mainly devoted to comparative studies between Chinese and foreign literatures. (Text in English) 1970. q. NT.$1200($40) Tamkang University, Graduate Institute of Western Languages and Literature, Tamsui, Taipei Hsien, Taiwan 25137, Republic of China. Ed. Chang-fang Chen. adv.; bk.rev.; circ. 1,000. (back issues avail.) **Indexed:** Arts & Hum.Cit.Ind., Curr.Cont., M.L.A.
—BLDSC shelfmark: 8601.620000.

895 VN
TAP CHI TAC PHAM VAN HOC. 1987. m. Viet-Nam Writers' Association, 65 Nguyen Du St., Hanoi, Socialist Republic of Vietnam. TEL 52442. Ed. Nguyen Dinh Thi. circ. 15,000.

895 VN
TAP CHI VAN HOC/LITERATURE MAGAZINE. m. Institute of Literature, 20 Ly Thai To St., Hanoi, Socialist Republic of Vietnam. TEL 52895. Ed. Phong Le.

800 792 US ISSN 0887-9257
TAPROOT. 1984. q. $10. Burning Press, Box 18817, Cleveland Heights, OH 44118. Ed. Robert Drake. bk.rev.; circ. 250.
Description: Journal of avant-garde and experimental language, graphic, and audio arts.

810 US
TAPROOT LITERARY REVIEW. 1987. irreg. (1-2/yr.). $5.50. 302 Park Rd., Ambridge, PA 15003. TEL 412-266-8476. circ. 500.

TEACHERS & WRITERS MAGAZINE. see EDUCATION — Teaching Methods And Curriculum

890 PL ISSN 0867-0633
PN9
TEKSTY DRUGIE. 1972-1981 (no.6-60); resumed 1990 (Apr.). bi-m. $36. Polska Akademia Nauk, Instytut Badan Literackich, Nowy Swiat 72, Palac Staszica, pok. 128, 00-330 Warsaw, Poland. (Co-sponsor: Komitet Nauk o Literaturze Polskiej) Ed. R. Nycz. adv.; bk.rev.; circ. 1,500. **Indexed:** M.L.A.
Formerly (until 1981): Teksty (ISSN 0324-8208)
Description: Focuses on theory and practice of new approaches to literature, especially to Polish literature.

800 IS ISSN 0792-1683
TEL AVIV REVIEW. 1988. a. $12 to individuals (foreign $18); institutions $24 (foreign $30). Ah'shav Publishers, 3 Smolenskin St., P.O. Box 3421, Tel Aviv 63415, Israel. TEL 03-5245120. (Dist. worldwide, except in Israel and UK by: Duke University Press, 6697 College Sta., Durham, NC 27708) Ed. Gabriel Moked. adv.; circ. 3,700.
Description: Dedicated to translations from ancient and modern Hebrew literature and to the poetry, fiction, drama and essays of non-Israeli writers.

808 301.4157 US
TELEWOMAN. 1979. m. $20. Telewoman, Inc., Box 2306, Pleasant Hill, CA 94523. Ed. Anne D'Arcy. adv.; bk.rev.; illus.; circ. 500.

TELICOM. see PHILOSOPHY

895.6 JA
TELS PRESS. (Text in English) 1977. a. 1000 Yen($7.50) Tel Press, c/o 2nd Fl., Nakijima Bldg., 1-26-7 Umegaoka, Setagaya-ku, Tokyo 154, Japan. TEL 03-3706-5055. Ed. John Evans.

800 IT
TEMPO. 1981. m. L.60000. Edizioni Scientifiche Italiane S.p.A., Via Chiatamone, 7, I-80121 Naples, Italy. Ed. Angelo G. Sabatini. adv.; circ. 2,000.

TEMPORARY CULTURE. see LITERARY AND POLITICAL REVIEWS

800 US ISSN 0497-2384
PS1
TENNESSEE STUDIES IN LITERATURE. 1956. a. price varies. (University of Tennessee, Department of English) University of Tennessee Press, Knoxville, TN 37996-0325. TEL 615-974-3321. bibl.; cum.index. (also avail. in microform from UMI; back issues avail.; reprint service avail. from UMI) **Indexed:** Amer.Hum.Ind., M.L.A.
—BLDSC shelfmark: 8790.740000.

800 US
TENNESSEE WILLIAMS LITERARY JOURNAL. 1989. s-a. $40. c/o Clare Beth Pierson, Mgr. Ed., 4517 Cleary Ave., Metairie, LA 70000. Ed. W. Kenneth Holditch.
Description: Devoted to the study of the life and works of America's premier playwright. Contains critical articles on Tennessee Williams and/or his work, calendar of current production of his plays, news concerning recent publications, and updated bibliographies.

820 UK ISSN 0082-2841
PR5579
TENNYSON RESEARCH BULLETIN. 1967. a. membership. Tennyson Society, Tennyson Research Centre, Central Library, Free School Lane, Lincoln LN2 1EZ, England. TEL 552866-0522. Ed.Bd. bk.rev.; index, cum.index every 5 yrs.; circ. 500. **Indexed:** M.L.A.
—BLDSC shelfmark: 8790.768000.

820 UK ISSN 0082-285X
PR5579
TENNYSON SOCIETY, LINCOLN, ENGLAND. MONOGRAPHS. 1969. irreg., no.11, 1987. membership. Tennyson Society, Tennyson Research Centre, Central Library, Free School Lane, Lincoln LN2 1EZ, England. TEL 552866-0522. Ed.Bd. circ. 500.
—BLDSC shelfmark: 8790.770000.

820 UK ISSN 0307-3572
TENNYSON SOCIETY, LINCOLN, ENGLAND. OCCASIONAL PAPERS. 1974. irreg., no.8, 1990. membership. Tennyson Society, Tennyson Research Centre, Central Library, Free School Lane, Lincoln LN2 1EZ, England. TEL 552866-0522.
—BLDSC shelfmark: 8790.775000.

820 UK ISSN 0082-2868
TENNYSON SOCIETY, LINCOLN, ENGLAND. REPORT. 1961. a. free. Tennyson Society, Tennyson Research Centre, Central Library, Free School Lane, Lincoln LN2 1EZ, England. TEL 552866-0522. circ. 500.

800 II
TENOR. (Text in English) 1978. s-a. Rs.50 foreign $10 (effective Sep. 1991). M. Sivaramkrishna, 3-6-226-1, Himayatnagar, Hyderabad 500 029, India. Ed.Bd. adv.; bk.rev.; circ. 200.
Description: Promotes culture, literature and translation.

895 MY
TENQQARA; journal of Southeast Asian literature. (Text in English, Indonesian, Malay) 1967. s-a. $7. Dewan Behasa dan Pustaka, P.O. Box 10803, Kuala Lumpur, Malaysia. adv.; illus.
Description: Presents literary works and critical essays on and from Malaysia, Philippines, Singapore, and Thailand.

TEORIA LITERARIA: TEXTO Y TEORIA. see LITERARY AND POLITICAL REVIEWS

895.1 CC
TEQU WENXUE. (Text in Chinese) m. Y2.80 per no. Shenzhen Wenlian, 13, Guiyuan Lu, 4th Floor, Shenzhen, Guangdong 518001, People's Republic of China. TEL 226304. Ed. Dai Musheng. adv.; illus.

808 US
TERMINO. q. Box 8905, Cincinnati, OH 45208. TEL 513-232-1548. Eds. Roberto Madrigal Ecay, Manuel F. Ballagas.

840 FR
TERRE LORRAINE.* 1970. 4/yr. 50 F. Association pour le Rayonnement des Lettres, des Arts et des Sciences, c/o Andre Leclere, 80 rue de Miromesnil, 75008 Paris, France. (Subscr. address: c/o J. de Ravinel, 32 rue de Viller, 54300 Luneville, France) adv.; bk.rev.; bibl.; illus.; circ. 1,000.

144 IT
TESTI E STUDI UMANISTICI. irreg., latest no.3. L.30000. Angelo Longo Editore, Via Paolo Costa 33, P.O. Box 431, 48100 Ravenna, Italy. TEL 0544-217026. Eds. Giorgio Padoan, Manlio Pastore Stocchi. circ. 1,500.

810 US ISSN 0885-2685
TEXAS REVIEW. 1976. s-a. $10. Sam Houston State University, English Department, Huntsville, TX 77340. TEL 409-294-1429. Ed. Paul Ruffin. adv.; bk.rev.; circ. 750. **Indexed:** A.I.P.P., M.L.A.
Formerly (until 1979): Sam Houston Literary Review.

810 US ISSN 0040-4691
AS30
TEXAS STUDIES IN LITERATURE AND LANGUAGE; a journal of the humanities. 1959. q. $23 to individuals; institutions $37. University of Texas Press, Box 7819, Austin, TX 78713. TEL 512-471-4531. Eds. Jerome Bump, William J. Scheick. adv.; index; circ. 1,000. (also avail. in microform from KTO,MIM,UMI; reprint service avail. from UMI) **Indexed:** Abstr.Engl.Stud., Amer.Bibl.Slavic & E.Eur.Stud., Arts & Hum.Cit.Ind., Curr.Cont., Hum.Ind., Lang.& Lang.Behav.Abstr., M.L.A., Sociol.Abstr.
—BLDSC shelfmark: 8800.180000.
Description: Publishes essays reflecting a variety of critical approaches and covers all periods of literary history.

808.8 US ISSN 0899-2193
TEXAS TECH UNIVERSITY. INTERDEPARTMENTAL COMMITTEE ON COMPARATIVE LITERATURE. STUDIES IN COMPARATIVE LITERATURE. 1968. a. price varies. Texas Tech University Press, Lubbock, TX 79409-1037. TEL 806-742-2982. Ed. Wendell M. Aycock. illus. **Indexed:** Abstr.Engl.Stud., M.L.A.
—BLDSC shelfmark: 8490.254300.
Formerly (until vol.17): Texas Tech University. Interdepartmental Committee on Comparative Literature. Proceedings of the Comparative Literature Symposium (ISSN 0084-9103)

810 US
TEXAS TRAVELER. 1970. s-a. $3. Josephine Payne, Ed. & Pub., 2205AA Echols St., Bryan, TX 77801. TEL 409-823-7723. adv.; bk.rev.; circ. 200. (processed)

TEXT; an interdisciplinary journal for the study of discourse. see HUMANITIES: COMPREHENSIVE WORKS

800 US ISSN 0736-3974
P47
TEXT (NEW YORK); transactions. 1984. a. $45. (Society for Textual Scholarship) A M S Press, Inc., 56 E. 13th St., New York, NY 10003. TEL 212-777-4700. FAX 212-995-5413. Eds. D.C. Greetham, W. Speed Hill. (back issues avail.)
—BLDSC shelfmark: 8800.612500.
Description: Annual collection of articles on textual scholarship originating from bi-annual conferences held by the Society for Textual Scholarship.

800 GW ISSN 0933-4769
TEXT UND KONTEXT; Romanische Literaturen und allgemeine Literaturwissenschaft. irreg., vol.8, 1992. price varies. Franz Steiner Verlag Wiesbaden GmbH, Birkenwaldstr. 44, Postfach 101526, 7000 Stuttgart 1, Germany. TEL 0711-2582-0. FAX 0711-2582290. TELEX 723636-DAZD. Ed. Klaus W. Hempfer.

LITERATURE

800   GW   ISSN 0040-5329
PN4
TEXT UND KRITIK; Zeitschrift fuer Literatur. 1962. q. DM.58. Edition Text und Kritik GmbH, Levelingstr. 6a, 8000 Munich 80, Germany. TEL 089-432929. FAX 089-433997. Ed. Heinz Ludwig Arnold. adv. **Indexed:** Curr.Cont., M.L.A.
—BLDSC shelfmark: 8800.630000.

800 320   GW   ISSN 0081-3257
TEXTAUSGABEN ZUR FRUEHEN SOZIALISTISCHEN LITERATUR IN DEUTSCHLAND. 1963. irreg., vol.26, 1988. price varies. (Akademie der Wissenschaften der DDR, Zentralinstitut fuer Literaturgeschichte) Akademie-Verlag Berlin, Leipziger Str. 3-4, 1086 Berlin, Germany. TELEX 114420-AVERL-DD. Ed. Ursula Muenchow.

800   CN   ISSN 0715-8920
TEXTE; revue de critique et de theorie litteraire. (Text in French) 1981. a. Can.$36. Trinity College, Toronto, Ont. M5S 1H8, Canada. (Subscr. to: 5201 Dufferin St., Downsview, Ont. M3H 5T8 Canada) Ed. A. Oliver. bk.rev.; circ. 280. (back issues avail.)
—BLDSC shelfmark: 8800.635200.
Description: Seeks to provide a forum for dialogue between the different approaches to the study of the literary text by bringing together work on a given topic with its critical debates, its analytical bibliographies and indexes.

800   GW
TEXTE DES SPAETEN MITTELALTERS UND DER FRUEHEN NEUZEIT. 1956. irreg. Erich Schmidt Verlag GmbH & Co. (Berlin), Genthiner Str. 30 G, 1000 Berlin 30, Germany. TEL 030-2500850. (Subscr. addr.: Zweigniederlassung Bielefeld, Viktoriastr. 44a, 4800 Bielefeld 1, Germany) Eds. Karl Stackmann, Stanley N. Werbow.

830 430   FR   ISSN 0981-1907
TEXTE ET L'IDEE. 1986. a. 70 Fr. (Universite de Nancy II, Centre de Recherches Germaniques) Association le Texte et l'Idee, 23 Blvd. Albert 1er, 54015 Nancy Cedex, France. TEL 80-61-41-22. Ed. Jean-Marie Paul.
Description: Covers German literature and history of ideas.

808   GW
TEXTEN UND SCHREIBEN. bi-m. DM.61.60. Hans Holzmann Verlag KG, Gewerbestr. 2, Postfach 1342, 8939 Bad Woerishofen, Germany.

840   SZ
TEXTES LITTERAIRES FRANCAIS. (Text in French) 1895. irreg., no.406, 1991. price varies. Librairie Droz S.A., 11 rue Massot, CH-1211 Geneva 12, Switzerland. TEL 022-466666. FAX 022-472391.
Description: Features letters and poetry.

820   UK   ISSN 0950-236X
TEXTUAL PRACTICE. 1987. 3/yr. £24($48) to individuals; institutions £38.50($72). Routledge, 11 New Fetter Lane, London EC4P 4EE, England. Ed. Terence Hawkes. adv.; bk.rev.; circ. 400.
—BLDSC shelfmark: 8813.780460.
Description: Develops the concept of "textuality". Centers on the study of literature, philosophy, law, history of science, sociology, feminism and cultural and media studies.

800   US
THACKERAY NEWSLETTER. 1975. s-a. $2.50. Mississippi State University, English Department, Drawer E, Mississippi State, MS 39762. TEL 601-325-3644. Ed. P.L. Shillingsburg. bk.rev.; circ. 70. (back issues avail.) **Indexed:** Amer.Hum.Ind., M.L.A.
Description: News notes, recent studies, and scholarly notes relating to William Makepeace Thackeray.

820   CN   ISSN 0706-5604
PN6147
THALIA; a journal of studies in literary humor. (Text in English; occasionally in French) 1978. s-a. Can.$15($15) to individuals; libraries Can.$18($18). Association for the Study of Humor, c/o Jacqueline Tavernier-Courbin, Ed., Dept. of English, University of Ottawa, Ottawa, Ont. K1N 6N5, Canada. TEL 613-564-2311. FAX 613-564-9175. adv.; bk.rev.; illus.; index; circ. 500. (back issues avail.; reprint service avail. from ISI) **Indexed:** Abstr.Engl.Stud., Arts & Hum.Cit.Ind., Curr.Cont., M.L.A.
—BLDSC shelfmark: 8814.185000.

830 920   GW   ISSN 0082-3880
THEODOR-STORM-GESELLSCHAFT. SCHRIFTEN. 1952. a. price varies. Westholsteinische Verlagsanstalt Boyens und Co., Am Wulf-Isebrand-Platz, Postfach 1880, 2240 Heide, Germany. TEL 0481-691-0. Eds. Karl E. Laage, Friedrich Heitmann.

THIRD DEGREE (NEW YORK). see LITERATURE — Mystery And Detective

820   UK
THIRD HALF. 1987. q. £6.25. K.T. Publications, 16 Fane Close, Stamford, Lincs. PE9 1HG, England. TEL 0780-54193. Ed. Kevin Troop. (back issues avail.)

800   UK   ISSN 0268-5418
THOMAS HARDY JOURNAL. 1975. 3/yr. $30. Thomas Hardy Society Ltd., c/o Prof. Norman Page, Ed., 23 Braunston Road, Oakham, Rutland LE15 6LD, England. TEL 0572-756358. (Subscr. to: John Maybery, 59 Yonder Street, Ottery St. Mary, Devon EX11 1HF, England) adv.; bk.rev.; circ. 1,500.
—BLDSC shelfmark: 8820.230670.
Formerly (until 1985): Thomas Hardy Society. Review (ISSN 0307-1642)
Description: Provides information about the Society's activities. Includes letters, reviews and articles about Hardy's writings, his life and his background.

820   UI   ISSN 0082-416X
PR4752
THOMAS HARDY YEAR BOOK. 1970. a. 4p. Toucan Press, Saravia, Rue des Monts, Delancey Park, St. Sampson, Guernsey, Channel Islands. Eds. J. Stevens Cox, G. Stevens Cox. adv.; bk.rev.; circ. 2,000. **Indexed:** Br.Hum.Ind., M.L.A.
Description: Prints scholarly articles on Thomas Hardy and other Victorian authors.

800   SZ   ISSN 0082-4186
PT2625.A44
THOMAS MANN GESELLSCHAFT. BLAETTER. 1958. a. price varies. Thomas Mann Gesellschaft, Raemistr. 5, CH-8001 Zurich, Switzerland. bk.rev.; circ. 1,000.

810   US   ISSN 0276-5683
PS3545.O337
THOMAS WOLFE REVIEW. 1977. s-a. $10. Thomas Wolfe Society, c/o John S. Phillipson, Ed., Dept. of English, University of Akron, Akron, OH 44325. TEL 216-972-7470. abstr.; illus.; circ. 600. (reprint service avail. from ISI) **Indexed:** Abstr.Engl.Stud., Amer.Hum.Ind., Arts & Hum.Cit.Ind., M.L.A.
Formerly: Thomas Wolfe Newsletter (ISSN 0148-1789)

810   US
THOMAS WOLFE SOCIETY. PROCEEDINGS. 1981. a. membership. Thomas Wolfe Society, c/o Dr. John S. Phillipson, Dept. of English, University of Akron, Akron, OH 44325. TEL 216-972-7470. circ. 600.
Formerly (until 1989): Thomas Wolfe Society. Summer Report and Membership List.

810   US   ISSN 0040-6406
PS3053
THOREAU SOCIETY BULLETIN; devoted to the life and writings of Henry David Thoreau. 1941. q. $20. Thoreau Society, Inc., Rt. 2, Box 36, Ayden, NC 28513. TEL 919-355-0620. FAX 919-355-5280. Ed. Bradley P. Dean. bk.rev.; bibl.; charts; illus.; circ. 2,000. (processed; also avail. in microform from UMI; reprint service avail. from UMI) **Indexed:** Amer.Hum.Ind., LCR, M.L.A.

THORNDYKE FILE. see LITERATURE — Adventure And Romance

808.882 100   US   ISSN 0886-6481
THOUGHTS FOR ALL SEASONS; the magazine of epigrams. 1976. irreg., vol.4, 1992. $4.75. Valley Press, 11530 S.W. 99th St., Miami, FL 33176-2516. TEL 305-598-8599. Ed. Michel P. Richard. adv.; circ. 1,000. (back issues avail.)
Description: Presents original epigrams and black and white illustrations and essays about the epigram as a literary form.

810   US   ISSN 0275-1410
THREEPENNY REVIEW. 1980. q. $12. Box 9131, Berkeley, CA 94709. TEL 510-849-4545. FAX 510-849-4551. Ed. Wendy Lesser. adv.; bk.rev.; circ. 8,000. (tabloid format; also avail. in microfilm from UMI; reprint service avail. from UMI) **Indexed:** Alt.Press Ind., Bk.Rev.Ind. (1981-), Child.Bk.Rev.Ind. (1981-), Ind.Amer.Per.Verse.
—BLDSC shelfmark: 8820.341600.

820   UK   ISSN 0040-6562
AP4
THRESHOLD. 1957. irreg., no. 31, 1980. price varies. Lyric Players Theatre, 55 Ridgeway St., Belfast 9, N. Ireland. Ed. John Boyd. bk.rev.; circ. 1,000.
—BLDSC shelfmark: 8820.341800.

059.958   BR
THWE - THAUK MAGAZINE. 1946. m. 185 48th St., Yangon, Union of Myanmar.

895.1   CC
TIAN NAN. (Text in Chinese) bi-m. Zhongguo Minjian Wenyijia Xiehui, Guangdong Fenhui - China Folk Artists' Association, Guangdong Chapter, No. 170, Wende Beilu, Guangzhou, Guangdong 510030, People's Republic of China. TEL 346887. Ed. Lin Zesheng.

895.1   CC
TIANCHI. (Text in Chinese) m. Zhongguo Zuojia Xiehui, Yanbian Fenhui, 22, Henan Jie, Yanji, Jilin 133001, People's Republic of China. TEL 512901. Ed. Liu Dechang.

800   BE   ISSN 0774-1847
TIJDSCHRIFT VOOR DE STUDIE VAN DE VERLICHTING EN VAN HET VRIJE DENKEN/REVIEW FOR THE STUDY OF ENLIGHTENMENT AND FREE-THINKING. (Text in Dutch, English, French, German) 1973. 4/yr. 800 Fr. Vrije Universiteit Brussel, Centrum voor Studie van de Verlichting en van het Vrije Denken, Pleinlaan 2, B. 416, B-1050 Brussels, Belgium. Ed. E. Walravens. bk.rev.; circ. 500.
Formerly (until 1980): Tijdschrift voor de Studie van de Verlichting.

830 439.3   NE   ISSN 0040-7550
PF4
TIJDSCHRIFT VOOR NEDERLANDSE TAAL- EN LETTERKUNDE. 1881. 4/yr. fl.98 to individuals; institutions fl.148(effective 1992). (Maatschappij der Nederlandse Letterkunde) E.J. Brill, P.O. Box 9000, 2300 PA Leiden, Netherlands. TEL 071-312624. FAX 071-317532. TELEX 39296 BRILL NL. (In N. America: E.J. Brill, 24 Hudson St., Kinderhook, NY 12106. TEL 800-962-4406) Ed. G.C. Zieleman. bk.rev.; cum.index. **Indexed:** Curr.Cont., M.L.A.

800 700   UK   ISSN 0040-7895
AP4
TIMES LITERARY SUPPLEMENT. 1902. w. $110. Times Supplements Ltd., Priory House, St. John's Lane, London EC1M 4BX, England. TEL 071-253-3000. FAX 071-251-4698. TELEX 264971. Ed. Ferdinand Mount. adv.; bk.rev.; illus.; mkt.; index; circ. 27,338. (tabloid format; also avail. in microform from RPI) **Indexed:** Acad.Ind., Bk.Rev.Dig., Bk.Rev.Ind. (1965-), Br.Hum.Ind., Chic.Per.Ind., Child.Bk.Rev.Ind. (1965-), Gdlns., Hum.Ind., Mid.East: Abstr.& Ind., Ref.Sour., RILA, RILM.
—BLDSC shelfmark: 8853.810000.

TIMP LIBER. see ART

895.1   SW
TODAY LITERARY MAGAZINE/JINTIAN. (Text in Chinese) 1978-1980; resumed 1990. q. $24 to individuals; institutions $32. Today Literary Foundation, P.O. Box 50025, S-104 05 Stockholm, Sweden. TEL 46-8-161315. FAX 46-8-155464. Eds. Bei Dao, Chen Maiping.
Description: Contains literature by Chinese writers living in exile, or works by writers still inside the mainland whose works cannot be published in China for political reasons.

820 810 410   JA   ISSN 0385-406X
TOHOKU GAKUIN UNIVERSITY REVIEW; essays and studies in English language and literature. (Text in English and Japanese) 1958. a. 2000 Yen($12) Literary, Economic and Juristic Association, Tohoku Gakuin University, 3-1 Tsuchitoi 1-Chome, Sendai 980, Japan. Ed. Yukio Igarashi. bk.rev.; circ. 2,000. **Indexed:** MLA.

LITERATURE

800   JA   ISSN 0563-6760
TOKAI DAIGAKU KIYO. BUNGAKUBU/TOKAI UNIVERSITY. FACULTY OF LETTERS. BULLETIN. (Text mainly in Japanese; contents page in European languages) no.25, 1976. s-a. exchange basis. (Tokai Daigaku, Bungakubu - Tokai University, Faculty of Literature) Tokai Daigaku Shuppankai - Tokai University Press, Shinjuko Tokai Bldg., 27-4 Shinjuku 3-chome, Shinjuku-ku, Tokyo 160, Japan. TEL 03-356-1541. Ed. Keitaro Syoju. illus.; cum.index: vols.1-25.
   Formerly: Tokai University. Faculty of Literature. Bulletin.

TOME; the dark works of great minds, and the great works of dark minds. see LITERATURE — *Science Fiction, Fantasy, Horror*

TOOK. see *LITERARY AND POLITICAL REVIEWS*

810   US
TOP STORIES. 1979. irreg. (approx. 3/yr.). $14.50 to individuals; institutions $16.50. 228 Seventh Ave., New York, NY 10011. TEL 212-989-3869. Ed. Anne Turyn. circ. 2,000. (back issues avail.)

IL TORCHIO ARTISTICO E LETTERARIO; organo ufficiale di stampa dell'Accademia Culturale d'Europa. see *ART*

839.74   DK   ISSN 0904-8987
TORDENSKJOLD; a newsletter about Danish literature today. (Text in English) q. DKK 25 per no. Danish Writers Association, Tordenskjolds Gaard, Strandgade 6, st., DK-1041 Copenhagen K, Denmark. TEL 45-31-95-51-00. Ed.Bd. bk.rev.

940   CN   ISSN 0082-5050
TORONTO MEDIAEVAL LATIN TEXTS. 1972. irreg. $6.75. Pontifical Institute of Mediaeval Studies, 59 Queen's Park Crescent. E., Toronto, Ont. M5S 2C4, Canada. TEL 416-926-7144. FAX 416-926-7276. Ed.Bd.
—BLDSC shelfmark: 8868.770000.

809 820   CN
TORONTO OLD ENGLISH SERIES. 1970. irreg. price varies. (University of Toronto, Centre for Medieval Studies) University of Toronto Press, 5201 Dufferin St., Downsview, Ont. M3H 5T8, Canada. TEL 416-667-7791. FAX 416-667-7832. (U.S. address: 340 Nagel Drive, Cheektowaga, NY 14225) Ed. Roberta Frank.

TORONTO SOUTH ASIAN REVIEW. see *LITERARY AND POLITICAL REVIEWS*

LA TORRE. see *LINGUISTICS*

860   AG
TORRE DE PAPEL. bi-m. Av. del Liberatador 930, 2 Piso, Buenos Aires, Argentina. bk.rev.

891.85   PL   ISSN 0067-7787
TOWARZYSTWO LITERACKIE IM. A. MICKIEWICZA. BIBLIOTEKA. 1960. irreg., vol.17, 1984. price varies. Ossolineum, Publishing House of the Polish Academy of Sciences, Rynek 9, 50-106 Wroclaw, Poland. TELEX 0712771 OSS PL.

800   JA   ISSN 0285-9033
TOYOTA FOUNDATION OCCASIONAL REPORT. (Text in English) 1981. s-a. free. Toyota Foundation, Shinjuku-Mitsui Bldg., 37F, 2-1-1 Nishi-Shinjuku, Shinjuku-ku, Tokyo 163, Japan. TEL 03-3344-1701. FAX 03-3342-6911. Eds. Shukuko Matsumoto, Becky M. Davis. bk.rev.; circ. 4,000.
   Description: Introduces policies, activities, projects, and grantees of the foundation.

820   UK
TRAETHODYDD; cylchgrawn chwarterol at wasanaeth crefydd, diwinyddiaeth, athroniaeth a llenyddiaeth. (Text in Welsh) 1845. q. £1.25. Llyfrfa'r Methodistiaid Calfinaidd, Caernarfon, North Wales. Ed. J.E. Caerwyn Williams. bk.rev.; circ. 450.
   Indexed: Abstr.Engl.Stud.

860   HO
TRAGALUZ. 1986. bi-m. $30. Editorial Guaymuras, S.A., Apdo. Postal 1843, Tegucigalpa, D.C., Honduras. TEL 37-54-33. Ed. Helen Umana.

800   US
TRANSIENT. 1973. irreg., no. 6, 1977. $5. Transient Press, Box 4662, Albuquerque, NM 87106. TEL 505-242-6600. Ed. Ken Saville. circ. 250.
   Formerly: Is.

800   US   ISSN 0093-9307
PN241
TRANSLATION (NEW YORK, 1972). 1972. s-a. $18. Translation Center, 412 Dodge Hall, Columbia University, New York, NY 10027. TEL 212-854-2305. FAX 212-749-0397. Ed. Frank MacShane. adv.; bk.rev.; circ. 2,000.
   Description: Dedicated to finding and publishing the best translations of foreign, contemporary literature.

TRAVAUX DE LINGUISTIQUE ET DE LITTERATURE. see *LINGUISTICS*

891.1   II
TREND. (Text in English) q. Rs.4. Pathikrit Association, 88-B Bipin Behari Ganguli St., Calcutta 12, India.
   Description: A literary and cultural journal.

800   US
TRIBUTARY. q. $2.50 per no. Rockford Writers' Guild, Box 858, Rockford, IL 61105. Ed. David Ross.
   Description: Publishes very short poetry and prose pieces.

TRICYCLE; the Buddhist review. see *RELIGIONS AND THEOLOGY — Buddhist*

800 398   US   ISSN 0360-3385
PN57.T8
TRISTANIA; a journal devoted to Tristan studies. 1975. a. $9.95 to individuals; institutions $19.95. (Tristan Society) Edwin Mellen Press, 240 Portage Rd., Box 450, Lewiston, NY 14092. TEL 800-753-2788. FAX 716-754-4335. Ed. Lewis A.M. Sumberg. bk.rev.; bibl. (back issues avail.) **Indexed:** M.L.A.
—BLDSC shelfmark: 9050.694500.

891.4   II   ISSN 0041-3135
AP8
TRIVENI; a literary and cultural quarterly. (Text in English) 1928. q. Rs.50. Ravi Academic Society, 3-7 Brodipet, Guntur 522 002, India. Ed. C.N.V. Dhan. adv.; bk.rev.; circ. 2,000. **Indexed:** M.L.A.

800 700   UK
TRIVIUM. 1966. a. £7.50. Saint David's University College, Lampeter, Dyfed SA48 7ED, Wales. FAX 0570-423423. Ed. C.C. Eldridge. adv.; bk.rev.; circ. 300. **Indexed:** Abstr.Engl.Stud., Arts & Hum.Cit.Ind., M.L.A.
   Description: Devoted to the arts and related subjects.

839.2   NE   ISSN 0041-3348
TROTWAER; literer tydskrift. (Text in Frisian) 1969. bi-m. fl.47.50 to individuals (foreign fl.60); students fl.37.50. Koperative Utjowerij, Postbus 156, 8700 AD Boalsert-Bolsward, Netherlands. TEL 05157-5055. Ed. Koby van der Zwaag-Kampman. adv.; bk.rev.; bibl.; illus.; circ. 350.

TRUE POLICE CASES. see *CRIMINOLOGY AND LAW ENFORCEMENT*

800   US
TRULY FINE. 1974. irreg. $1.50. Truly Fine Press, Box 891, Bemidji, MN 56601. Ed. Jerry Madson. bk.rev.; circ. 500. (back issues avail.)
   Formerly: Truly Fine Press.

895   MP
TSOG/SPARK. 1944. bi-m. Union of Writers, Ulan Bator, Mongolia. Ed. Ts. Natsagdorj.

420.5 809   JA   ISSN 0496-3547
TSUDA REVIEW. (Text in English) 1956. a. exchange basis. Tsuda College - Tsuda Juku Daigaku, 2-1-1 Tsuda-machi, Kodaira-shi, Tokyo 187, Japan. FAX 0423-41-2444. circ. 1,000. **Indexed:** Abstr.Engl.Stud.
   Description: Covers English literature and linguistics.

810   US
TUCUMCARI LITERARY REVIEW. (Text mainly in English; occasionally in Spanish) 1988. bi-m. $12 (foreign $20). 3108 W. Bellevue Ave., Los Angeles, CA 90026. TEL 213-413-0789. Ed. Troxey Kemper. circ. 150.
   Description: Covers poetry, fiction, essays; includes non-fiction articles and nostalgia.

808 305.4   US   ISSN 0732-7730
PN471
TULSA STUDIES IN WOMEN'S LITERATURE. 1982. s-a. $12 to individuals; institutions $14; students $10. University of Tulsa, Tulsa Studies in Women's Literature, 600 S. College Ave., Tulsa, OK 74104. TEL 918-631-2503. Ed. Holly Laird. adv.; bk.rev.; circ. 500. (also avail. in microfilm from UMI; back issues avail.) **Indexed:** Arts & Hum.Cit.Ind., Bk.Rev.Ind. (1989-), Child.Bk.Rev.Ind. (1989-), M.L.A., Stud.Wom.Abstr., Wom.Stud.Abstr. (1982-).
—BLDSC shelfmark: 9070.480000.
   Description: Scholarly articles, notes and queries on literature from all time periods and places, including foreign-language literature, and from every genre: poetry, prose, drama, essays, diaries, memoirs, journalism and criticism. Focuses on women and writing, feminist critical and literary theory.

895.1   US
TUO LING/CAMEL BELLS. (Text in Chinese) bi-m. $35.60. China Books & Periodicals, Inc., 2929 24th St., San Francisco, CA 94110. TEL 415-282-2994. FAX 415-282-0994.

494.35   TU   ISSN 0041-4220
TURK DILI. 1951. m. $40. Turkish Language Institute - Turk Dil Kurumu, 217 Ataturk Bulvari, Ankara, Turkey. TEL 4-1268124. FAX 4-1285288. Ed. Hasan Eren. adv.; bk.rev.; bibl.; charts; stat.; index; circ. 11,650.
—BLDSC shelfmark: 9071.940000.

830   GW   ISSN 0723-8177
TURMSCHREIBER KALENDER; ein Bayerisches Hausbuch auf das Jahr. 1982. a. DM.19.80. W. Ludwig Verlag, Goethestr. 43, 8000 Munich 2, Germany. TEL 089-5148-0. FAX 089-5148-229. circ. 11,000. (back issues avail.)

TURN-OF-THE-CENTURY WOMEN. see *WOMEN'S INTERESTS*

800 811   US   ISSN 0896-5951
TURNSTILE. 1988. a. $6.50. Turnstile Press, 175 Fifth Ave., Ste. 2348, New York, NY 10010. Ed. Mitchell Nauffets. adv.; circ. 1,500. (back issues avail.)
   Description: Introduces non-commercial works of poetry, fiction, essays, interviews.

810   US   ISSN 0041-4573
PS1329
TWAINIAN. 1939. bi-m. membership. Mark Twain Research Foundation, Inc., Perry, MO 63462. TEL 314-565-3570. Ed. Mrs. Chester L. Davis. bk.rev.; circ. 400. **Indexed:** Abstr.Engl.Stud., Hist.Abstr.
   Description: Articles and essays on the wisdom of Mark Twain as taught by his life and his writings.

821   AT
TWEED. 1972. q. Aus.$4($5) c/o Janice M. Bostok, Ed., Box 304, Murwillumbah, N.S.W. 2484, Australia. bk.rev.; illus.; circ. 200. (back issues avail.)

800   NE   ISSN 0166-1868
TWEEDE RONDE; tijdschrift voor literatuur. 1980. q. fl.44. Bert Bakker, Herengracht 406, 1017 BX Amsterdam, Netherlands. TEL 020-6263588. Ed.Bd. circ. 2,000.
   Description: Publishes poems, essays and short stories.

800   US   ISSN 0897-7844
TWENTIETH - CENTURY AMERICAN JEWISH WRITERS. irreg. Peter Lang Publishing, Inc., 62 W. 45th St., 4th Fl., New York, NY 10036. TEL 212-302-6740. FAX 212-302-7574. Ed. Daniel Walden.
   Description: Covers the Jewish writer in 20th Century America.

LITERATURE

809 US ISSN 0276-8178
PN771
TWENTIETH - CENTURY LITERARY CRITICISM; excerpts from criticism of the works of novelists, poets, playwrights, and other creative writers of the era 1900-1960. 1978. irreg., vol.43, 1992. $108. Gale Research Inc., 835 Penobscot Bldg., Detroit, MI 48277-0748. TEL 313-961-2242. FAX 313-961-6083. TELEX 810-221-7086. Ed. Paula Kepos. bibl.; index. (back issues avail.) **Indexed:** Child.Auth.& Illus.
  Description: Covers twentieth century creative writing to 1960.

800 US ISSN 0041-462X
PN2
TWENTIETH CENTURY LITERATURE; a scholarly and critical journal. 1955. q. $25 to individuals (foreign $30); institutions $30 (foreign $34). Hofstra University, 203 Student Center, Hemstead, NY 11550. TEL 516-463-5460. Ed. William McBrien. adv.; abstr.; bibl.x.; index; circ. 3,000. (also avail. in microform from ISI,KTO,UMI) **Indexed:** Abstr.Engl.Stud., Acad.Ind., Arts & Hum.Cit.Ind., Bibl.Engl.Lang.& Lit., Bibl.Ind., Curr.Cont., Hum.Ind., LCR, M.L.A., Mid.East: Abstr.& Ind.
  —BLDSC shelfmark: 9076.850000.

051 700 US
▼**XXIST CENTURY;** a new quarterly of art, politics, literature and ideas. 1991. 3/yr. $7.50 per no. Rizzoli International Publishers, Inc., 300 Park Ave. S., New York, NY 10010. TEL 212-387-3400. FAX 212-387-3535. Ed. Gini Alhadeff. illus.

TWISTED. see *LITERATURE — Science Fiction, Fantasy, Horror*

820 UK ISSN 0041-4670
TWO RIVERS.* 1969. q. 32s.($4) 28 Tottenham St., London W.1, England. Eds. Martin Green, Paul Durcan. circ. 1,010.

810.8 CN ISSN 0226-3440
U.C. REVIEW. Variant title: University College Literary Review. a. University of Toronto, University College, Toronto, Ont. M5S 1A1, Canada. TEL 613-978-2011. illus.

820 SA ISSN 0041-5359
PR1
U N I S A ENGLISH STUDIES. 1963. s-a. R.11($7.50) University of South Africa, Department of English, P.O. Box 392, Pretoria 0001, South Africa. FAX 012-429-3221. TELEX 350068. Ed. S.G. Kossick. adv.; bk.rev.; abstr.; bibl.; illus.; circ. 2,858. **Indexed:** M.L.A.
  —BLDSC shelfmark: 9090.782000.

808.81 808.81 US ISSN 0362-7012
PS501
U S 1 WORKSHEETS. 1973. a. $8. U S 1 Poets' Cooperative, Box 57, Roosevelt, NJ 08551-0057. (Subscr. to: Postings, Box 1, Ringoes, NJ 08551. TEL 908-782-6492) circ. 500. (back issues avail.) **Indexed:** Ind.Amer.Per.Verse.

800 HU ISSN 0041-5952
AP82
UJ IRAS. 1961. m. $27. (Magyar Irok Szovetsege) Lapkiado Vallalat, Lenin korut 9-11, 1073 Budapest 7, Hungary. TEL 222-408. (Subscr. to: Kultura, Box 149, H-1389 Budapest, Hungary) Ed. Ferenc Juhasz. bk.rev.; circ. 20,000. **Indexed:** M.L.A.

890 KR
UKRAINS'KE LITERATUROZNAVSTVO. vol.28, 1977. 1.00 Rub. per no. (L'vovskii Gosudarstvennyi Universitet) Izdatel'stvo Vysshaya Shkola, L'vovskoe Otdelenie, Ul. Universitetskaya, 1, Lvov, Ukraine. Ed. I. Doroshenko. bibl.; circ. 1,000.

914.1 941 UK ISSN 0954-3392
ULSTER EDITIONS AND MONOGRAPHS. 1988. irreg. Colin Smythe Ltd., P.O. Box 6, Gerrards Cross, Buckinghamshire SL9 8XA, England. TEL 0753-886000. FAX 0753-886469. circ. 1,200.
  —BLDSC shelfmark: 9082.741800.
  Description: Collections of essays on Northern Irish literary and historical matters.

ULYSSES INTERNATIONAL; magazine du sud en France. see *ETHNIC INTERESTS*

UMBRUCH; Zeitschrift fuer Kultur. see *ART*

890 JA
UMI/SEA. (Text in Japanese) 1969. m. 9450 Yen. Chuokoron-Sha, Inc., 2-8-7 Kyobashi, Chuo-ku, Tokyo 104, Japan. Ed. Marie Miyata. **Indexed:** Chem.Abstr.

801 CI
UMJETNOST RIJECI/WORD ART; casopis za znanost o knjizevnosti. vol.24, 1980. q. 180 din.($20) Sveuciliste u Zagrebu, Filozofski Fakultet, Dure Salaja 3, 41000 Zagreb, Croatia. (Dist by: IKP "Mladost" Export-Import, Ilica 30, 41000 Zagreb, Croatia) **Indexed:** Can.Rev.Comp.Lit.

800 TZ ISSN 0011-6696
UMMA; a magazine of original writing. (Text in English and Kiswahili) 1966. 2/yr. EAs.15($3) University of Dar es Salaam, Department of Literature, Box 35041, Dar es Salaam, Tanzania. TELEX 41327 UNISCIE TANZANIA. Ed. Clement L. Ndulute. bk.rev.; circ. 600. (also avail. in microfilm from UMI; reprint service avail. from KTO,UMI) **Indexed:** Curr.Cont.Africa, M.L.A.
  Formerly: Darlite.

890 SW
UNGA DIKTARA. a. Bokfoerlaget Inferi, Box 167, 821 01 Bollnaes 1, Sweden.

808.83 II ISSN 0041-6762
PN2
UNILIT. (Text in English) 1961. m. Rs.20($6) Viswa Sahiti, 6-3-195 New Bhoiguda, Secunderabad 500003, India. Ed. Pothukuchi Sambasivarao. adv.; bk.rev.; circ. 2,000. **Indexed:** M.L.A.
  Description: Special focus on world problems and scientific material.

860 CU ISSN 0041-6770
NX7
UNION. 1962. q. $10 in N. America; S. America $12; Europe $17. (Union de Escritores y Artistas de Cuba (UNEAC)) Ediciones Cubanas, Obispo No. 527, Aptdo. 605, Havana, Cuba. Ed. Otto Fernandez. bk.rev.; illus.; circ. 5,000.

700 SG ISSN 0253-584X
UNIR: ECHO DE SAINT LOUIS. (Includes supplement) 1956. q. 500 Fr.CFA. (Centre Catholique d'Information) Jean Vast Ed. & Pub., B.P. 160, 1 rue Neuville, Saint Louis, Senegal. adv.; illus.
  Supersedes (1906-1918): Echo de Saint.

800 US
▼**UNIROD.** 1991. irreg. $10 for 2 issues. Firsten Tightbell Publishing, c/o Kenward G. Bradley, Ed., 4214-B Filbert Ave., Atlantic City, NJ 08401-1070. **Description:** Includes fiction and art, especially experimental and unusual works.

UNIVERSAL BLACK WRITER. see *ETHNIC INTERESTS*

860 100 SP
UNIVERSIDAD COMPLUTENSE DE MADRID. REVISTA. 1940. bi-m. Universidad Complutense de Madrid, Facultad de Filosofia y Letras, Ciudad Universitaria, Madrid 3, Spain. bk.rev.; bibl. **Indexed:** Hist.Abstr.
  Formerly (until 1972): Universidad de Madrid. Revista (ISSN 0541-8607)

860 UY ISSN 0250-6556
PB5
UNIVERSIDAD DE LA REPUBLICA. FACULTAD DE HUMANIDADES Y CIENCIAS. REVISTA. SERIE LETRAS. N.S. 1979. irreg. exchange basis. Universidad de la Republica, Facultad de Humanidades y Ciencias, Seccion Revista, Tristan Narvaja 1674, Montevideo, Uruguay. Dir. Beatriz Martinez Osorio.
  Supersedes in part: Universidad de la Republica. Facultad de Humanidades y Ciencias. Revista.

860 VE
UNIVERSIDAD DE LOS ANDES. ESCUELA DE LETRAS. ANUARIO.* 1975. a. exchange basis. Universidad de los Andes, Escuela de Letras, Via los Chorras de Milla, C.P. 5101, Merida, Venezuela. Ed.Bd

UNIVERSIDAD DE MURCIA. ESTUDIOS ROMANICOS. see *LINGUISTICS*

860 SP
UNIVERSIDAD DE NAVARRA. DEPARTAMENTO DE LITERATURA ESPANOLA. COLECCION PUBLICACIONES. 1974. irreg., no.9, 1986. price varies. Ediciones Universidad de Navarra, S.A., Apdo. 396, 31080 Pamplona, Spain. TEL 94 825 6850.

UNIVERSIDAD DE SAN CARLOS. REVISTA; artes - literatura - ciencias humanas. see *ART*

800 SP
UNIVERSIDAD DE SEVILLA. COLECCION DE BOLSILLO. irreg., latest no.109. Universidad de Sevilla, Servicio de Publicaciones, San Fernando, 4, 41004 Seville, Spain. TEL 954-22-8071. FAX 954-22-1315.

860 UY ISSN 0077-1252
UNIVERSIDAD DE URUGUAY. DEPARTAMENTO DE LITERATURA IBEROAMERICANA PUBLICACIONES.* irreg. Universidad de Uruguay, Departamento de Literatura Iberoamericana, Montevideo, Uruguay.

UNIVERSIDAD VERACRUZANA. CENTRO DE INVESTIGACIONES LINGUISTICO-LITERARIAS. TEXTO-CRITICO. see *LINGUISTICS*

800 PO
UNIVERSIDADE DE LISBOA. FACULDADE DE LETRAS. REVISTA. 1933. 2/yr. Esc.800($6) Universidade de Lisboa, Faculdade de Letras, Cidade Universitaria, 1699 Lisbon Codex, Portugal. FAX 760063. Ed.Bd. bk.rev.; bibl.; circ. 1,500.

869 BL ISSN 0079-9327
PQ9644
UNIVERSIDADE FEDERAL DE MINAS GERAIS. CORPO DISCENTE. REVISTA LITERARIA.. Cover title: R L; Revista Literaria. 1966. a. free. Universidade Federal de Minas Gerais, Centro de Extensao da Faculdade de Letras, Av. Antonio Carlos, 6.627-4 Andar-Sala 451, Caixa Postal 905, Belo Horizonte-MG, Brazil. Ed.Bd. bk.rev.; illus.; circ. 2,000.
  Description: Presents Brazilian poetry, short stories, essays and art.

850 100 IT ISSN 0078-7728
UNIVERSITA DEGLI STUDI DI PADOVA. FACOLTA DI LETTERE E FILOSOFIA. OPUSCOLI ACCADEMICI. 1937. irreg., vol.18, 1989. price varies. Casa Editrice Leo S. Olschki, Casella Postale 66, 50100 Florence, Italy. TEL 055-6530684. FAX 055-6530214. circ. 1,000.

850 100 IT ISSN 0078-7736
UNIVERSITA DEGLI STUDI DI PADOVA. FACOLTA DI LETTERE E FILOSOFIA. PUBBLICAZIONI. 1932. irreg., vol.62, 1988. price varies. Casa Editrice Leo S. Olschki, Casella Postale 66, 50100 Florence, Italy. TEL 055-6830684. FAX 055-6530214. circ. 1,000.

850 100 IT
UNIVERSITA DEGLI STUDI DI SIENA. FACOLTA DI LETTERE E FILOSOFIA. ANNALI. 1980. a. price varies. (Universita degli Studi di Siena, Facolta di Lettere e Filosofia) Casa Editrice Leo S. Olschki, Casella Postale 66, 50126 Florence, Italy. TEL 055-6530684. FAX 055-6530214. Ed. M. Bettini.

UNIVERSITA DI NAPOLI. FACOLTA DI LETTERE E FILOSOFIA. ANNALI. see *HISTORY*

491 CS
UNIVERSITA PALACKEHO. FILOSOFICKA FAKULTA. SLAVICA. (Subseries of its Philologica) (Text in Czech; summaries in French or German) 1971. irreg. 8.50 Kcs. Statni Pedagogicke Nakladatelstvi, Ostrovni 30, 113 01 Prague 1, Czechoslovakia. bibl.; illus.
  Supersedes: Series Slavica.

UNIVERSITA PALACKEHO. PEDAGOGICKA FAKULTA. SBORNIK PRACI: RUSKY JAZYK A LITERATURA. see *LINGUISTICS*

700 500 800 GW ISSN 0341-0129
AP4
UNIVERSITAS (ENGLISH EDITION); quarterly German review of the arts and sciences. 1956. q. DM.62 (students DM.46). Wissenschaftliche Verlagsgesellschaft mbH, Postfach 105339, 7000 Stuttgart 10, Germany. TEL 0711-2582-0. FAX 0711-2582-290. TELEX 723636-DAZ-D. Ed. H.W. Baehr. circ. 5,100.
  —BLDSC shelfmark: 9101.344000.

LITERATURE

700 500 800   GW   ISSN 0041-9079
AP30   CODEN: UNIVA8
UNIVERSITAS (GERMAN EDITION); Zeitschrift fuer interdisziplinaere Wissenschaft. English edition (ISSN 0341-0129); Spanish edition (ISSN 0341-0102) 1946. m. (German ed.); q. (English and Spanish eds.). DM.89.40 (students DM.67.40). (Institute for Scientific Cooperation) Wissenschaftliche Verlagsgesellschaft mbH, Postfach 105339, 7000 Stuttgart 10, Germany. TEL 0711-2582-0. FAX 0711-2582-290. TELEX 723636-DAZ-D. Ed. Ch. Rotta. adv.; bk.rev.; film rev.; play rev.; abstr.; bibl.; index; circ. 7,600 (German ed.). **Indexed:** Chem.Abstr., Curr.Cont., Phil.Ind.

700 500   GW   ISSN 0341-0102
UNIVERSITAS (SPANISH EDITION); revista trimestral alemana de letras, ciencias y arte. 1962. q. DM.62 (students DM.46). Wissenschaftliche Verlagsgesellschaft mbH, Postfach 105339, 7000 Stuttgart 10, Germany. TEL 0711-2582-0. FAX 0711-2582-290. TELEX 723636-DAZ-D. Ed. H.W. Baehr. circ. 4,700.

850   RM   ISSN 0379-7899
UNIVERSITATEA "AL. I. CUZA" DIN IASI. ANALELE STIINTIFICE. SECTIUNEA 3F: LITERATURA. (Text in English, French, German, Rumanian, Russian) 1955. a. 35 lei. Universitatea "Al. I. Cuza" din Iasi, Calea M. Eminescu 11, Jassy, Rumania. (Subscr. to: ILEXIM, Str. 13 Decembrie Nr. 3, P.O. Box 136-137, Bucharest, Rumania) Ed. Ion Apetroaie. bk.rev.; abstr.; charts; illus.; circ. 300.
—BLDSC shelfmark: 0869.650000.
Description: Covers the history of Rumanian literature, its theories of aesthetics, as well as comparative and universal literature.

UNIVERSITE CATHOLIQUE DE LOUVAIN. FACULTE DE PHILOSOPHIE ET LETTRES. TRAVAUX. see *HUMANITIES: COMPREHENSIVE WORKS*

880   FR   ISSN 0065-4981
UNIVERSITE D'AIX-MARSEILLE I. CENTRE D'ETUDES ET DE RECHERCHES HELLENIQUES. PUBLICATIONS. 1958. irreg. Universite d'Aix-Marseille I (Universite de Provence), Centre d'Etudes et de Recherches Helleniques, Service des Publications, 13621 Aix en Provence, France.

UNIVERSITE D'ODENSE. ETUDES ROMANES. see *LINGUISTICS*

800   FR   ISSN 0399-0443
F1022
UNIVERSITE DE BORDEAUX III. CENTRE DE RECHERCHES SUR L'AMERIQUE ANGLOPHONE. ANNALES. N.S. 1976. a. 120 F.($20) (typically set in July). Maison des Sciences de l'Homme d'Aquitaine, Esplanade des Antilles, Domaine Universitaire, 33405 Talence Cedex, France. TEL 56-84-68-00.
FAX 56-84-68-10. (Dist. by: Presses Universitaires de Bordeaux, Domaine Universitaire, 33405 Talence Cedex, France. TEL 56-84-50-20) Ed. J.F. Beranger. adv.; circ. 200.
●Also available online.
Description: Covers minority literature in the U.S.: Hispanic, Jewish, Indian, Italian and Greek.

001.3   FR
UNIVERSITE DE DAKAR. FACULTE DES LETTRES ET SCIENCES HUMAINES. ANNALES. 1971? a. Presses Universitaires de France, Departement des Revues, 14 Avenue du Bois-de-l'Epine, B.P.90, 91003 Evry Cedex, France. TEL 1-60-77-82-05.
FAX 1-60-79-20-45. TELEX PUF 600 474 F. Ed. Jacques Gengoux. bibl.; charts; illus. (reprint service avail. from KTO) **Indexed:** Deep Sea Res.& Oceanogr.Abstr.

800 700   SZ   ISSN 0041-915X
UNIVERSITE DE LAUSANNE. FACULTE DES LETTRES. PUBLICATIONS. (Text in French; occasionally in English) 1930. irreg., no.32,1989. price varies. Librairie Droz S.A., 11, rue Massot, CH-1211 Geneva 12, Switzerland. TEL 022-466666. FAX 022-472391.
Description: Explores literary, religious and political perspectives of historical studies.

800   SZ   ISSN 0077-7633
UNIVERSITE DE NEUCHATEL. FACULTE DES LETTRES. RECUEIL DE TRAVAUX. 1905. irreg., no.41, 1989. price varies. Librairie Droz S.A., 11, rue Massot, CH-1211 Geneva 12, Switzerland.
TEL 022-466666. FAX 022-472391. circ. 500.
—BLDSC shelfmark: 7329.698000.
Description: Covers art, literature, linguistics, banking and architecture of historic and modern Europe.

UNIVERSITE DE POITIERS. CENTRE D'ETUDES SUPERIEURES DE CIVILISATION MEDIEVALE. PUBLICATIONS. see *HISTORY*

UNIVERSITE DE STRASBOURG II. CENTRE DE PHILOLOGIE ET LITTERATURES ROMANES. ACTES ET COLLOQUES. see *LINGUISTICS*

UNIVERSITE DE STRASBOURG II. INSTITUT DE PHONETIQUE. TRAVAUX. see *LINGUISTICS*

890 410   TI
UNIVERSITE DE TUNIS. ECOLE NORMALE SUPERIEURE. SECTION A: LETTRES ET SCIENCES HUMAINES. SERIE 1: LANGUE ET LITTERATURE. 1977. irreg. Universite de Tunis, Ecole Normale Superieure, Tunis, Tunisia.

UNIVERSITETET I OSLO. SLAVISK-BALTISK AVDELING. MEDDELELSER. see *LINGUISTICS*

820   II
UNIVERSITY OF CALCUTTA. DEPARTMENT OF ENGLISH. JOURNAL. (Text in English) vol.4, 1969. s-a. Rs.15. University of Calcutta, Department of English, Asutosh Bldg., Calcutta 700073, India. Ed. A.K. Dasgupta. bk.rev.; bibl.; circ. 1,000.
Formerly: University of Calcutta. Department of English. Bulletin (ISSN 0008-0691)

UNIVERSITY OF CINCINNATI STUDIES IN HISTORICAL AND CONTEMPORARY EUROPE. see *HISTORY — History Of Europe*

809   US   ISSN 0196-2280
PN2
UNIVERSITY OF HARTFORD STUDIES IN LITERATURE; a journal of interdisciplinary criticism. 1969. 3/yr. $7.50 to individuals; libraries $9. University of Hartford, English Department, 200 Bloomfield Ave., W. Hartford, CT 06117. TEL 203-243-4574. Ed. Michael Walsh. adv.; bk.rev.; cum.index; circ. 500 (controlled). (also avail. in microform from UMI; reprint service avail. from UMI) **Indexed:** Abstr.Engl.Stud., Amer.Bibl.Slavic & E.Eur.Stud., Amer.Hum.Ind., Arts & Hum.Cit.Ind., Can.Rev.Comp.Lit., Curr.Cont., LCR, M.L.A.
Formerly (until vol.9, no.2, 1977): Hartford Studies in Literature (ISSN 0017-7989)

UNIVERSITY OF KERALA. DEPARTMENT OF TAMIL. RESEARCH PAPERS. see *LINGUISTICS*

830   UK   ISSN 0144-9850
UNIVERSITY OF LONDON. INSTITUTE OF GERMANIC STUDIES. BITHELL MEMORIAL LECTURES. 1975. biennial. £2. University of London, Institute of Germanic Studies, 29 Russell Square, London WC1B 5DP, England. TEL 071-580-2711.
FAX 071-436-3497. Ed.Bd. circ. 1,000.
Description: Published version of the Institute of Germanic Studies endowed lecture.

830   UK   ISSN 0266-7932
UNIVERSITY OF LONDON. INSTITUTE OF GERMANIC STUDIES. BITHELL SERIES OF DISSERTATIONS. 1979. irreg. University of London, Institute of Germanic Studies, 29 Russell Square, London WC1B 5DP, England. TEL 071-580-2711. FAX 071-436-3497. (Co-sponsor: Modern Humanities Research Association) Ed.Bd. circ. 500.
Description: Theses in German studies previously accepted for a higher degree in a university in the British Isles.

830   UK   ISSN 0076-0803
UNIVERSITY OF LONDON. INSTITUTE OF GERMANIC STUDIES. LIBRARY PUBLICATIONS. 1961. irreg. price varies. University of London, Institute of Germanic Studies, 29 Russell Sq., London WC1B 5DP, England. TEL 071-580-2711. FAX 071-436-3497. circ. 500.
Description: Special catalogues and guides relating to the collections of the library of the Institute of Germanic Studies.

830   UK   ISSN 0076-0811
UNIVERSITY OF LONDON. INSTITUTE OF GERMANIC STUDIES. PUBLICATIONS. 1956. irreg. price varies. University of London, Institute of Germanic Studies, 29 Russell Sq., London WC1B 5DP, England. TEL 071-580-2711. FAX 071-436-3497. circ. 400.
—BLDSC shelfmark: 7081.855000.
Description: Monographs and volumes of essays on topics in German language and literature.

820   US   ISSN 0278-310X
PR5.M5
UNIVERSITY OF MISSISSIPPI STUDIES IN ENGLISH. 1960. a. $20. University of Mississippi, Department of English, University, Lafayette Co., MS 38677. TEL 601-232-7439. Ed. Benjamin F. Fisher IV. adv.; bk.rev.; circ. 450. (also avail. in microform from UMI) **Indexed:** Abstr.Engl.Stud., M.L.A.
Formerly: University of Mississippi. Studies in English. New Series.

491.1 891.1   II   ISSN 0448-1712
UNIVERSITY OF RAJASTHAN. STUDIES IN SANSKRIT AND HINDI. 1965. irreg. University of Rajasthan, Departments of Sanskrit and Hindi, Gandhi Nagar, Jaipur 302004, India.

800   US
UNIVERSITY OF TEXAS STUDIES IN CONTEMPORARY SPANISH-AMERICAN FICTION. irreg. Peter Lang Publishing, Inc., 62 W. 45th St., 4th Fl., New York, NY 10036. TEL 212-302-6740.
FAX 212-302-7574. Ed. Robert Brody.

UNIVERSITY OF THE NORTH. COMMUNIQUE. see *EDUCATION*

820   CN   ISSN 0082-5336
UNIVERSITY OF TORONTO ROMANCE SERIES. (Text in English; occasionally in French) 1949. irreg. price varies. (Department of Romance Languages) University of Toronto Press, 5201 Dufferin St., Downsview, Ont. M3H 5T8, Canada.
TEL 416-667-7761. FAX 416-667-7832. (U.S. address: 340 Nagel Drive, Cheektowaga, NY 14225) **Indexed:** M.L.A.

820
UNIVERSITY OF TULSA. MONOGRAPH SERIES. 1966. irreg., nos.22-23, 1989. price varies. University of Tulsa, 600 S. College Ave., Tulsa, OK 74104. circ. 300. (also avail. in microfilm from UMI; back issues avail.) **Indexed:** M.L.A.
Formerly: University of Tulsa. Department of English. Monograph Series (ISSN 0082-6812)

UNIVERSITY STUDIES IN MEDIEVAL AND RENAISSANCE LITERATURE. see *HISTORY*

UNIVERZITA KOMENSKEHO. FILOZOFICKA FAKULTA. ZBORNIK: PHILOLOGICA. see *LINGUISTICS*

UNIVERZITA PALACKEHO. PEDAGOGICKA FAKULTA. SBORNIK PRACI: CESKY JAZYK A LITERATURA. see *LINGUISTICS*

891.85 943   PL   ISSN 0072-0488
UNIWERSYTET GDANSKI. WYDZIAL HUMANISTYCZNY. ZESZYTY NAUKOWE. PRACE HISTORYCZNO-LITERACKIE. (Text in Polish; summaries in English and Russian) 1972. irreg. price varies. Uniwersytet Gdanski, Wydzial Humanistyczny, c/o Biblioteka Glowna, Ul. Armii Krajowej 110, 81-824 Sopot, Poland. TEL 51-0061. TELEX 051-2247 BMOR PL. (Dist. by: Ars Polona-Ruch, Krakowskie Przedmiescie 7, 00-680 Warsaw, Poland) circ. 250.
Description: Contains articles and book reviews on the theory and history of literature, particularly Polish literature.

891.85   PL   ISSN 0083-436X
PG7003
UNIWERSYTET JAGIELLONSKI. ZESZYTY NAUKOWE. PRACE HISTORYCZNOLITERACKIE. (Vol. 3- called also vol. 5-, continuing the volume numbering of Seria Nauk Spolecznych. Filologia, which it supersedes) (Text mainly in Polish; occasionally in English, French or Russian; summaries in English, French, German, Russian) 1955. irreg. price varies. Panstwowe Wydawnictwo Naukowe, Miodowa 10, 00-251 Warsaw, Poland. (Dist. by: Ars Polona, Krakowskie Przedmiescie 7, 00-068 Warsaw, Poland) Ed. St. Jaworski. circ. 600.

809 PL ISSN 0208-5453
UNIWERSYTET SLASKI W KATOWICACH. PRACE NAUKOWE. PRACE HISTORYCZNOLITERACKIE. (Text in French and Polish; summaries in English, French, Polish, Russian) 1959. irreg. price varies. Wydawnictwo Uniwersytetu Slaskiego, Ul. Bankowa 14, 40-007 Katowice, Poland. TEL 48-32-596-915. FAX 48-32-599-605. TELEX 0315584 USKPL. (Dist. by: CHZ Ars Polona, P.O. Box 1001, 00-950 Warsaw, Poland)
Description: Covers Polish and French literature.

800 PL ISSN 0208-5038
UNIWERSYTET SLASKI W KATOWICACH. PRACE NAUKOWE. RUSYCYSTYCZNE STUDIA LITERATUROZNAWCZE. (Text in Polish and Russian; summaries in English, Polish or Russian) 1977. irreg. price varies. Wydawnictwo Uniwersytetu Slaskiego, Ul. Bankowa 14, 40-007 Katowice, Poland. TEL 48-32-596-915. FAX 48-32-599-605. TELEX 0315584 USKPL. (Dist. by: CHZ Ars Polona, P.O. Box 1001, 00-950 Warsaw, Poland)
Description: Covers history and the present image of Russian and Soviet literature: studies of works, groups of works and trends in literary theory.

830 GW ISSN 0083-4564
UNTERSUCHUNGEN ZUR DEUTSCHEN LITERATURGESCHICHTE. 1962. irreg., no.61, 1991. price varies. Max Niemeyer Verlag, Postfach 2140, 7400 Tuebingen 1, Germany. TEL 07071-81104. FAX 07071-87419. (back issues avail.) Indexed: M.L.A.
Description: Monographs on German literature.

800 IT ISSN 0042-0646
UOMINI E IDEE; rivista di letteratura, sociologia e arte. 1958. bi-m. Via Poggio de Mari 16, 80129 Naples, Italy. Ed. Corrado Piancastelli. adv.; bk.rev.; illus.; circ. 5,000.

810 700 US
URBANUS - RAIZIRR. 1988. s-a. $10. Box 192561, San Francisco, CA 94119-2561. Eds. Peter Drizhal, Cameron Bamberger. circ. 300.
Formerly: Urbanus.
Description: Aims for "dangerous" material, experimental or mainstream; includes poetry, fiction, art, and other writings; socially oriented - non-sexist.

US WURK; tydskrift foar Frisistyk. see LINGUISTICS

890 300 TZ
UTAFITI; journal of the faculty of arts and social science. 1976. s-a. $25. University of Dar es Salaam, Faculty of Arts and Social Science, TZ , P.O. Box 35051, Dar es Salaam, Tanzania. FAX 48274. Ed. Joseph L. Mbele. bk.rev.; circ. 600. Indexed: Curr.Cont.Africa.

800 410 US ISSN 0171-726X
UTAH STUDIES IN LITERATURE AND LINGUISTICS. irreg. Peter Lang Publishing, Inc., 62 W. 45th St., 4th Fl., New York, NY 10036. TEL 212-302-6740. FAX 212-302-7574. Ed. Wolff A. von Schmidt.

891.4 II ISSN 0042-157X
UTHON/PLATFORM.* (Text and summaries in Bengali) 1968. 6/yr. Rs.4($1) (Chandita Prakasani) Raja Rammohan Sarani, Dipok Dey, 107-2 Amherst St., Calcutta 9, India. Ed. Samir Kumar Dey. bk.rev.; illus.; circ. 1,500.
Formerly: Natunkatha.

859 RM
UTUNK. (Text in Hungarian) 1946. w. 156 lei. Uniunea Scriitorilor din Republica Socialista Romania, Calea Victoriei 115, Bucharest, Rumania. (Subscr. to: ILEXIM, Str. 13 Decembrie Nr. 3, Box 136-137, 70116 Bucharest, Rumania) Ed. Letay Lajos. bk.rev.; film rev.; play rev.; charts; illus.

890 UZ
UZBEK TILI VA ADABIETI. bi-m. 7.80 Rub. Izdatel'stvo Fan, Pr. M. Gor'kogo 79, Tashkent, Uzbekistan. circ. 19,820.

808 US ISSN 0887-8633
V L S. (Voice Literary Supplement) (Supplement to: Village Voice) 1981. m. (10/yr.). $17 (foreign $33). V V Publishing Corporation, 36 Cooper Sq., New York, NY 10003. (Subscr. to: Department VLS, Box 3000, Denville, NJ 07834. TEL 800-562-1973) Ed. M. Mark. adv.; bk.rev.; illus. (tabloid format) Indexed: Bk.Rev.Ind. (1982-), Child.Bk.Rev.Ind. (1982-).
Description: Features book reviews, fiction and critical essays.

800 808.81 SZ ISSN 0259-6512
V W A; revue litteraire. (Text in French) 1983. 2/yr. 62 Fr. V W A, Case Postale 172, 2301 La-Chaux-de-Fonds, Switzerland. TEL 39-282418. FAX 39-281332. Ed.Bd. illus.; circ. 1,000. (back issues avail.)

891.553 IR
VAHID. w. S. Vahidnia, Ed. & Pub., 55 Jomhoori Islami Ave., Jam St., Teheran, Iran.

840 FR ISSN 0760-5641
VALENCIENNES. 1976. a. 100 F. Presses Universitaires de Valenciennes, Le Mont Houy, 59326 Valenciennes Cedex, France. Ed. J.P. Giusto. adv.; circ. 500. (back issues avail.)
Formerly (until 1981): Cahiers de l'U E R Froissart.

VAMPIRE JOURNAL. see LITERATURE — Science Fiction, Fantasy, Horror

895 VN
VAN NGHE/ARTS AND LETTERS. 1949. w. Vietnamese Writers' Union, 17 Tran Quoc Toan, Hanoi, Socialist Republic of Vietnam. TEL 64430. Ed. Huu Thinh. circ. 40,000.

895 VN
VAN NGHE QUAN DOI/ARMY LITERATURE AND ARTS. 1957. m. 4 Ly Nam De St., Hanoi, Socialist Republic of Vietnam. TEL 54378. Ed. Dung Ha. circ. 50,000.

810 US
▼VANDELOECHT'S FICTION MAGAZINE. 1991. 4/yr. $8. Box 515, Montross, VA 22520.

800 TU ISSN 0042-2762
VARLIK. 1933. m. $30. Varlik Yayinlari A.S., Cagaloglu Yokusu 40, Istanbul, Turkey. FAX 1-5129528. Ed. Filiz Nayir Deniztekin. adv.; bk.rev.; circ. 6,000.

VECTOR. see LITERATURE — Science Fiction, Fantasy, Horror

860 AG
VENGA QUE LE CUENTO; publicacion periodica aleatoria de narradores Argentinos. no. 1974. irreg. Prudan 1330, Buenos Aires, Argentina. adv.; illus.

VENT - ART. see ART

VENTURE; bi-annual review of English language and literature. see LINGUISTICS

800 SZ
VERSANTS; revue suisse des litteratures romanes. (Text in French, Italian and Spanish) 1981. 2/yr. 42 SFr. (Collegium Romanicum, Association des Romanistes Suisses) Editions de la Baconniere S.A., P.O. Box 185, CH-2017 Boudry, Switzerland. TEL 038-421004.

800 GW ISSN 0170-3633
VERSCHOLLENE UND VERGESSENE. irreg. price varies. (Akademie der Wissenschaften und der Literatur, Mainz, Klasse der Literatur) Franz Steiner Verlag Wiesbaden GmbH, Birkenwaldstr. 44, Postfach 101526, 7000 Stuttgart 1, Germany. TEL 0711-2582-0. FAX 0711-2582290. TELEX 723636-DAZD.

800 808.81 US ISSN 0268-3830
VERSE. 1984. 3/yr. $12. College of William and Mary, English Department, Williamsberg, VA 23186. TEL 804-221-3922. Ed. Henry Hart. adv.; bk.rev.; circ. 800. (back issues avail.)
Description: International literary publication featuring poems, reviews and essays.

891.8 YU ISSN 0042-4536
VESELI SVET;* humoristicki magazin. (Text in Serbo-Croatian) vol.10, 1970. m. 3 din. Dnevnik, Bulevar 23, Oktobra 31, Novi Sad, Yugoslavia. Ed. Mitar Milosevic.

LITERATURE 2973

830 NE
VESTDIJKKRONIEK. 1973. q. fl.45. Vestdijkkring, Het Erf 19, 8102 KE Raalte, Netherlands. TEL 05720-54291. Ed.Bd. adv.; bk.rev.; circ. 800.

IL VESUVIO; fiaccola ercolanese. see ART

890 RU
VETER STRANSTVII. 1965. irreg. 1.30 Rub. per no. Izdatel'stvo Fizkul'tura i Sport, Kalyaevskaya Ul., 27, Moscow K-6, Russia. Ed.Bd. illus.; circ. 150,000.

810 US ISSN 0504-0779
PS508.V45
VETERANS' VOICES. 1952. 3/yr. $15 (includes HVWP in Action). Hospitalized Veterans Writing Project, Inc., 5920 Nall, Rm. 102, Mission, KS 66202. TEL 913-432-1214. Ed. Margaret Cathcart Clark. circ. 1,500.

VIATA CAPITALEI. see ART

859 RM ISSN 0042-5052
VIATA ROMINEASCA. 1906. m. 144 lei($10) Uniunea Scriitorilor din Republica Socialista Romania, Calea Victoriei 115, Bucharest, Rumania. (Subscr. to: ILEXIM, Export-Import Presa, Str. 13 Decembrie Nr. 3, Box 136-137, 70116 Bucharest, Rumania) Ed. Ioanichie Olteanu. bk.rev.; abstr.; circ. 2,900. Indexed: M.L.A.

800 700 780 CN ISSN 0821-6827
VICE VERSA MAGAZINE. 1983. bi-m. Can.$18 to individuals; institutions Can.$25. Editions Vice Versa Inc., C.P. 991, Succ. A, Montreal, Que. H3C 2W9, Canada. TEL 514-393-1853. FAX 514-843-5681. Ed. Lamberto Tassinari. adv.; bk.rev.; circ. 10,000. (tabloid format) Indexed: Pt.de Rep. (1989-).
Formerly: Guernica Review.

800 US ISSN 0042-5192
PR1
VICTORIAN NEWSLETTER. 1952. s-a. $5 (foreign $6). Western Kentucky University, College of Arts and Humanities, FAC 200, Bowling Green, KY 42101. TEL 502-745-2345. (Co-sponsor: Modern Language Association) Ed. Ward Hellstrom. circ. 900. (also avail. in microfilm; reprint service avail. from UMI) Indexed: Abstr.Engl.Stud., Avery Ind.Archit.Per.
—BLDSC shelfmark: 9232.655000.

VICTORIAN PERIODICALS REVIEW. see JOURNALISM

820.9 CN ISSN 0848-1512
VICTORIAN REVIEW. 1972. s-a. Can.$25 membership to individuals; institutions Can.$30. Victorian Studies Association of Western Canada, c/o Prof. G. Stephenson, Ed., Dept. of English, University of Alberta, Edmonton, Alta. T6G 2E5, Canada. TEL 403-492-7821. FAX 403-492-8142. adv.; bk.rev.; circ. 200. Indexed: Abstr.Engl.Stud.
—BLDSC shelfmark: 9232.690000.
Formerly: Victorian Studies Association of Western Canada. Newsletter (ISSN 0703-5500)

800 US ISSN 0169-1724
VIENNESE HERITAGE/WIENER ERBE. 1984. irreg., no.3, 1990. price varies. John Benjamins Publishing Co., 821 Bethlehem Pike, Philadelphia, PA 19118. TEL 215-836-1200. FAX 215-836-1204. (And: Amsteldijk 44, P.O. Box 75577, 1070 AN Amsterdam, Netherlands. TEL 020-6762325) Eds. Achim Eschbach, Walter H. Schmitz.

VIGILIA. see RELIGIONS AND THEOLOGY — Roman Catholic

800 US
VILLAGE IDIOT. (Text mainly in English) 1970. 3/yr. $7. Mother of Ashes Press, Box 66, Harrison, ID 83833-0066. TEL 208-689-3738. circ. 200.
Description: Original poems, pictures, and stories by contemporary authors.

373.4 UK ISSN 0264-5564
VINAVER STUDIES IN FRENCH. 1984. irreg. price varies. Francis Cairns (Publications), c/o The University, Leeds LS2 9JT, England. Eds. Jane H.M. Taylor, A.R.W. James.
—BLDSC shelfmark: 9236.850900.

LITERATURE

800 NO ISSN 0042-6288
PN9
VINDUET; Gyldendal's literary magazine. 1947. q. NOK 260 to individuals; institutions NOK 325; students NOK 190. Gyldendal Norsk Forlag, Sehesteds gt. 4, 0164 Oslo 1, Norway. FAX 02-425953. TELEX 72880 GYLDN N. (Subscr. to: Forlagsentralen, Tidsskriftavd., P.O. Box 150 Furuset, 1001 Oslo 1, Norway) Ed. H.W. Freihow. adv.; bk.rev.; circ. 3,800. **Indexed:** M.L.A.
—BLDSC shelfmark: 9236.854000.

810 US
VINTAGE NORTHWEST. 1980. 2/yr. $2.25 per no.(typically set in Jan.). Box 193, Bothell, WA 98041. TEL 206-487-1201. Ed. Lawrence T. Campbell. adv.; circ. 500.
Description: Seasonal literary magazine featuring creative writing only from persons age 50 and older.

809 US
VIRGINIA WOOLF MISCELLANY. 1973. s-a. membership. (Virginia Woolf Society) Sonoma State University, Department of English, Rohnert Park, CA 94928. TEL 707-664-2140. Ed.Bd. bk.rev.; bibl.; circ. 1,300. **Indexed:** Abstr.Engl.Stud., Amer.Hum.Ind.
Description: Forum to exchange information about Virginia Woolf.

VIRITTAAJAA. see *LINGUISTICS*

891.2 II
VISHVA SAMSKRTAM. (Text in Sanskrit) q. Rs.15. Vishveshvaranand Vedic Research Institute, P.O. Sadhu Ashram, Hoshiarpur 146021, Punjab, India. Ed. Veda Prakasha.
Description: Presents articles on Sanskrit language, literature and culture.

VISIONARY COMPANY: A MAGAZINE OF THE TWENTIES. see *ART*

891.4 II ISSN 0042-7179
VISVA - BHARATI PATRIKA. (Text in Bengali) 1942. q. Rs.23.60. Visva - Bharati University, Publishing Department, 6 Acharya Jagadish Bosh Rd., Calcutta 700017, India. Ed. Surajit Chandra Sinha. adv.; bk.rev.; illus.; index; circ. 2,700.

891.4 II ISSN 0042-7209
VISWA RACHANA. (Text in Telugu) 1960. fortn. Rs.50. Viswa Sahiti, 6-3-195 New Bhoiguda, Secunderabad 500003, India. Ed. Pothukuchi Sambasivarao. adv.; bk.rev.; film rev.; play rev.; circ. 3,000.
Formerly: Viswa Sahiti.
Description: Special focus on the exchange of world literature.

VLAANDEREN; tijdschrift voor kunst en letteren. see *ART*

VOCE DI FIUME. see *HISTORY*

800 700 IT
VOCI DEL NOSTRO TEMPO. 1972. bi-m. Via S. Anna 223, 97100 Ragusa, Italy. Ed. Gerlando Bordore. bibl.; illus.

840 CN ISSN 0318-9201
PQ3900
VOIX ET IMAGES. 1976. q. Can.$23 (foreign Can.$25). Universite du Quebec a Montreal, Service des Publications, C.P. 8888, Succ. "A", Montreal, Que. H3C 3P8, Canada. TEL 514-987-7747. Ed. Lucie Robert. **Indexed:** Can.Lit.Ind., M.L.A., Pt.de Rep. (1981-).
—BLDSC shelfmark: 9251.535000.

808 US
VOLCANO REVIEW. 1979. s-a. $15. Peninhand Press, Box 82699, Portland, OR 97282. Ed. Tom Janisse.

830 NE
VOORZETTEN. 1985. irreg. price varies. (Nederlandse Taalunie) Stichting Bibliographia Neerlandica, P.O. Box 90751, 2509 LT The Hague, Netherlands. TEL (070)31 02 85. Ed. Oscar de Wandel.
Description: Publication devoted to the integration of the Netherlands and the Dutch speaking community in Belgium, concerning the Dutch language. Each volume covers a single topic.

891.7 RU ISSN 0042-8795
PN9
VOPROSY LITERATURY. 1957. m. 29.40 Rub. (Soyuz Pisatelei S.S.S.R.) Izdatel'stvo Izvestiya, Pl. Pushkina, 5, 103798 Moscow, Russia. (Co-sponsor: Akademiya Nauk S.S.S.R. Institut Mirovoi Literatury im. A.M. Gor'kogo) Ed. V. Ozerov. adv.; bk.rev.; index; circ. 25,000. (also avail. in microfiche from NRP) **Indexed:** Can.Rev.Comp.Lit., Curr.Dig.Sov.Press, M.L.A.
Description: Literary criticism and scholarship.

800 374 GW ISSN 0172-5300
VOX LATINA. 1965. q. DM.28. Societas Latina, Fachbereich 6.3, Universitaet, 6600 Saarbruecken, Germany. Ed. Caelestis Eichenseer. adv.; bk.rev.; index; circ. 1,500. (back issues avail.)

VOX ROMANICA; annales helvetici explorandis linguis romanicis destinati. see *LINGUISTICS*

VRISHCHIK. see *ART*

860 MX
VUELTA.* 1976. m. $30. Amigos del Arte A.C., Ave. Contreras 516, piso 3, Col. San Jeronimo Lidice, 10200 Mexico D.F., Mexico. (U.S. subscr. to: Overseas Book Mart, 313 Third St., Bloomington, IN 47401) Ed.Bd. adv.; bk.rev.; illus.; index; circ. 12,000. **Indexed:** Hisp.Amer.Per.Ind., M.L.A.

800 US
WAIGUO WENXUE/FOREIGN LITERATURE. (Text in Chinese) m. $36. China Books & Periodicals, Inc., 2929 24th St., San Francisco, CA 94110. TEL 415-282-2994. FAX 415-282-0994.

800.953 CC ISSN 1001-2885
WAIGUO WENXUE YANJIU/FOREIGN LITERATURE STUDIES. (Subseries of: Fuyin Baokan Ziliao) (Text in Chinese) 1978. q. Y42($30) Zhongguo Renmin Daxue, Shubao Ziliao Zhongxin - China People's University, Book & Newspaper Information Center, P.O. Box 1122, Beijing 100007, People's Republic of China. TEL 441792. (Dist. in US by: China Books & Periodicals, Inc., 2929 24th St., San Francisco, CA 94110. TEL 415-282-2994)
Description: Reprints papers and articles on foreign literature.

810 US ISSN 0737-0679
PS3229
WALT WHITMAN QUARTERLY REVIEW. 1955. q. $12 to individuals; institutions $15. University of Iowa, Department of English, 308 E P B Bldg., Iowa City, IA 52242. (Co-sponsor: Graduate College) Ed. Edwin Folsom. adv.; bk.rev.; bibl.; illus.; cum.index every 5 yrs.; circ. 468. (also avail. in microform from MIM,UMI; back issues avail.) **Indexed:** Abstr.Engl.Stud., Amer.Hum.Ind., Arts & Hum.Cit.Ind., Curr.Cont., Ind.Bk.Rev.Hum., M.L.A.
Former titles (until 1982): Walt Whitman Review (ISSN 0043-017X); Walt Whitman Newsletter.
Description: Provides scholarly articles and literary criticism about Walt Whitman.

830 GW ISSN 0930-0279
WALTHARI; Zeitschrift fuer Literatur. 1984. s-a. DM.27. Walthari Verlag, Postfach 440, 6785 Muenchweiler-Rod., Germany. Ed. Erich Dauenhauer. bk.rev. (back issues avail.)

WANBLI HO/EAGLE'S VOICE. see *ETHNIC INTERESTS*

800 US ISSN 1046-6967
PN56.W3
WAR, LITERATURE, AND THE ARTS. 1989. s-a. $10 to individuals; institutions $20. United States Air Force Academy, Department of English, Colorado Springs, CO 80840. TEL 719-472-3930. FAX 719-472-3135. Ed. Lt. Col. Donald Anderson. bk.rev.
—BLDSC shelfmark: 9261.811450.

809 US ISSN 0083-7210
WARD - PHILLIPS LECTURES IN ENGLISH LANGUAGE AND LITERATURE. 1967. irreg., no.12, 1987. price varies. (University of Notre Dame, Department of English) University of Notre Dame Press, Notre Dame, IN 46556. TEL 219-239-6346. **Indexed:** Cath.Ind.

819 CN ISSN 0043-0412
WASCANA REVIEW. 1966. s-a. Can.$7. University of Regina, Regina, Sask. S4S 0A2, Canada. TEL 306-584-4316. Ed. Joan Givner. bk.rev.; circ. 500. (tabloid format) **Indexed:** Abstr.Engl.Stud., Amer.Hum.Ind., Can.Lit.Ind., M.L.A.
—BLDSC shelfmark: 9261.972000.

808 JA
WASEDA BUNGAKU. m. Kodansha Ltd., P.R. Division, 12-21, Otowa, 2-chome, Bunkyo-ku, Tokyo 112, Japan. Ed. Waseda Bungaku-kai. circ. 3,000.

800 US ISSN 1041-5874
WATER ROW REVIEW. 1987. q. $20. Water Row Books Inc., Box 438, Sudbury, MA 01776. TEL 508-443-8910. Ed. Cisco Harland. adv.; bk.rev.; bibl.; circ. 3,500. (back issues avail.)
Description: Dedicated to "Beat" generation authors and their work.

800 US ISSN 0363-1230
PN6010.5
WEBSTER REVIEW. 1974. a. $5. (Webster University) Webster Review, Inc., 470 E. Lockwood, Webster Groves, MO 63119. TEL 314-432-2657. Ed. Nancy Schapiro. circ. 600. (back issues avail.) **Indexed:** A.I.P.P., Ind.Amer.Per.Verse, M.L.A.
Description: Contains works by little-known American authors and translations of major foreign authors.

800 AU ISSN 0043-2199
WEIMARER BEITRAEGE; Zeitschrift fuer Literaturwissenschaft, Aesthetik und Kultur. 1955. m. DM.144. Passagen Verlag, Walfischgasse 15-14, A-1010 Vienna, Austria. FAX 0222-5126327. Ed. Peter Engelmann. adv.; bk.rev.; index; circ. 1,200. **Indexed:** Arts & Hum.Cit.Ind., Can.Rev.Comp.Lit., Ind.Bk.Rev.Hum., M.L.A.

830 GW
WEISS - BLAETTER. 1983. s-a. DM.16($6) Rigodon-Verlag, Nieberdingstr. 18, 4300 Essen 1, Germany. TEL 0201-778111. FAX 0201-775114. (Subscr. to: Sven Spieker, Ed., Glockenstr. 18, 5300 Bonn 1, Germany) bibl. (back issues avail.)

WEISSES MINARETT. see *RELIGIONS AND THEOLOGY — Islamic*

895.1 CC
WEIXING XIAOSHUO XUANKAN. (Text in Chinese) bi-m. Weixing Xiaoshuo Xuankan Zazhishe, No.5, Xinwei Lu, Nanchang, Jiangxi 330002, People's Republic of China. TEL 331727. Ed. Lu Yun.

820 UK ISSN 0263-1776
WELLSIAN. 1960. s-a. £10 to institutions. H.G. Wells Society, H.G. Wells Centre, Nene College, Eng. Dept., Moulton Park, Northampton NN2 7AL, England. Ed. Michael Draper. bk.rev.; bibl.; cum.index every 5 yrs.; circ. 300. (also avail. in microform from UMI)

800 GW ISSN 0043-2520
PG1
DIE WELT DER SLAVEN. (Text in English, French, German and Russian) 2/yr. DM.120. Verlag Otto Sagner, Postfach 340108, 8000 Munich 34, Germany. TEL 089-522027. TELEX 5216711-KUSAD. Ed. Peter Rehder. circ. 450. (back issues avail.) **Indexed:** Arts & Hum.Cit.Ind.
—BLDSC shelfmark: 9294.730000.

800 CC ISSN 1000-6222
WENHUA YICONG. (Text in Chinese) 1980. q. Y4.40. Tianjin Waiyu Xueyuan - Tianjin Foreign Language Institute, 117 Machang Dao, Hexi Qu, Tianjin 300204, People's Republic of China. TEL 390181. Ed. Lu Jiaqi. circ. 2,000.
Description: Publishes translated articles on world literature, art, history, geography, archaeology, tourism and popular science.

WENHUA YULE/CULTURE & RECREATION. see *LEISURE AND RECREATION*

WENSHI ZHISHI/KNOWLEDGE OF LITERATURE AND HISTORY. see *SOCIAL SCIENCES: COMPREHENSIVE WORKS*

895.1 CC
WENXUE BAO/LITERATURE PRESS. (Text in Chinese) w. $55.50. No. 14, Alley 606, Huaihai Zhonglu, Shanghai 200020, People's Republic of China. (Dist. in US by: China Books & Periodicals, Inc., 2929 24th St., San Francisco, CA 94110) (newspaper)

895.1 CC
WENXUE DAGUAN. (Text in Chinese) m. Zhongguo Zuojia Xiehui, Liaoning Fenhui - China Writers' Association, Liaoning Chapter, 7 Shaoshuaifu Houxiang, Chaoyang Jie, Shenhe Qu, Shenyang, Liaoning 110011, People's Republic of China. TEL 443806. Ed. Chi Songnian.

895.1 CC
WENXUE GANG. (Text in Chinese) Ningbo Shi Wenlian, 220, Yaoxing Jie, Ningbo, Zhejiang 315000, People's Republic of China. (Dist. outside China by: China Publications Foreign Trade Corp., P.O. Box 782, Beijing, P.R.C.) Ed. Li Jianshu.

800.953 CC ISSN 0511-4683
WENXUE PINGLUN/LITERARY REVIEW. (Text in Chinese; table of contents in English) 1959. bi-m. Y19.80($50.90) (Zhongguo Shehui Kexueyuan, Wenxue Yanjiusuo - Chinese Academy of Social Sciences, Institute of Literature) Shehui Kexue Zazhishe, 158 A Gulou Xidajie, Beijing 100720, People's Republic of China. (Dist. outside China by: China International Book Trading Corp., P.O. Box 399, Beijing, P.R.C.; Dist. in US by: China Books & Periodicals, Inc., 2929 24th St., San Francisco, CA 94110. TEL 415-282-2994) bk.rev.
—BLDSC shelfmark: 5276.654540.

895.1 CC
WENXUE PINGLUNJIA/LITERARY CRITICS. (Text in Chinese) bi-m. Y7.80. Zhongguo Zuojia Xiehui, Shandong Fenhui - China Writers' Association, Shandong Chapter, 10, Honglou Nanlu, Jinan, Shandong 250100, People's Republic of China. Eds. Wang Guangdong, Li Jizhao. adv.
Description: Publishes literary criticism.

895.15 CC
WENXUE QINGNIAN/YOUTH LITERATURE JOURNAL. (Text in Chinese) 1981. m. Wenxue Qingnian Bianjibu, Mu Tse Fang 27, Wenzhou, Zhejiang, People's Republic of China. TEL 3578. Ed. Chen Yushen. circ. 80,000.

895.1 CC
WENXUE SHAONIAN/ADOLESCENT LITERATURE. (Text in Chinese) bi-m. Liaoning Shaonian Ertong Chubanshe, 2, Nanjing Jie 6 Duan 1 Li, Shenyang, Liaoning 110011, People's Republic of China. TEL 365076. Ed. Wu Qingxian.

895.1 CC ISSN 0257-5914
WENXUE YICHAN/LITERARY HERITAGE. (Text in Chinese; table of contents in English) q. Y12($31.50) (Zhongguo Shehui Kexueyuan, Wenxue Yanjiusuo - Chinese Academy of Social Sciences, Institute of Literature) Shehui Kexue Zazhishe, 158 A Gulou Xidajie, Beijing 100720, People's Republic of China. (Dist. outside China by: China International Book Trading Corp., P.O. Box 399, Beijing, P.R.C.; Dist. in US by: China Books & Periodicals, Inc., 2929 24th St., San Francisco, CA 94110) Eds. Xu Gongchi, Lu Huifen.

895.1 CC ISSN 0258-8226
WENYI BAO/LITERATURE & ART GAZETTE. (Text in Chinese) 1949. d. Y182.50. (Zhongguo Zuojia Xiehui - China Writers' Association) Wenyi Bao She, 6th Fl., No. 10, Nongzhanguan Nanli, Beijing 100026, People's Republic of China. TEL 500-5588. (Dist. in US by: China Books & Periodicals, Inc., 2929 24th St., San Francisco, CA 94110. TEL 415-282-2994) Ed. Zheng Bonong. (newspaper)

801 CC ISSN 0257-0254
WENYI LILUN YANJIU/THEORETICAL STUDIES IN LITERATURE AND ART. (Text in Chinese; table of contents in English) 1980. bi-m. Y11.88($36) Huadong Shifan Daxue, Zhongwen Xi - East China Normal University, Department of Chinese, 3663 Zhongshan Beilu, Shanghai 200062, People's Republic of China. (Dist. overseas by: China International Book Trading Corp., P.O. Box 399, Beijing, P.R.C.; Dist. in US by: China Books & Periodicals, Inc., 2929 24th St., San Francisco, CA 94110) (Co-sponsor: Zhongguo Wenyi Lilun Xuehui - Chinese Society of Literature and Art Theory) Eds. Xu Zhongyu, Qian Gurong.

895.1 700 CC ISSN 0257-5876
WENYI YANJIU/LITERATURE AND ART STUDIES. (Text in Chinese; table of contents in English) 1979. bi-m. Y16.80($36) (Zhongguo Yishu Yanjiuyuan - China Art Institute) Wenhua Yishu Chubanshe, 17, Qianhai Xijie, Xi Cheng Qu, Beijing 100009, People's Republic of China. TEL 651128. (Dist. outside China by: China International Book Trading Corp., P.O. Box 399, Beijing, P.R.C.; Dist. in US by: China Books & Periodicals, Inc., 2929 24th St., San Francisco, CA 94110. TEL 415-282-2994) Ed. Yang Liu.

700 CN
AP2
WEST COAST LINE; a journal of contemporary writing and criticism. 1966. 3/yr. Can.$15 to individuals; institutions $18. Simon Fraser University, West Coast Review Publishing Society, Burnaby, B.C. V5A 1S6, Canada. TEL 604-291-4287. Ed. Roy Miki. adv.; bk.rev.; bibl.; illus.; circ. 750. (also avail. in microform from UMI; reprint service avail. from UMI) **Indexed:** Abstr.Engl.Stud., Amer.Hum.Ind., Can.Lit.Ind., Can.Per.Ind., CMI, Ind.Amer.Per.Verse, Ind.Bk.Rev.Hum., M.L.A.
Formerly: West Coast Review (ISSN 0043-311X)
Description: Contains contemporary poetry, fiction, essays, reviews of modern art, literature. International in scope, but emphasis is on Canadian writing.

800 US
WEST VIRGINIA ASSOCIATION OF COLLEGE ENGLISH TEACHERS. BULLETIN. 1955. a. $2. West Virginia Association of College English Teachers, Department of English, Marshall University, Huntington, WV 25701. TEL 304-696-6600. Ed. Joan F. Gilliland. bk.rev.; circ. 200. (back issues avail.) **Indexed:** M.L.A.

820 AT ISSN 0043-342X
AP7
WESTERLY. 1956. q. Aus.$20. University of Western Australia, Centre for Studies in Australian Literature, Nedlands, W.A. 6009, Australia. (Co-sponsors: Australia Council, W.A. Department for the Arts) Ed.Bd. adv.; bk.rev.; illus.; circ. 900. **Indexed:** Abstr.Engl.Stud., Arts & Hum.Cit.Ind., Aus.P.A.I.S., Curr.Cont., Gdlns.
—BLDSC shelfmark: 9300.171500.

810 US ISSN 0043-3462
PS271
WESTERN AMERICAN LITERATURE. 1966. q. $12 to individuals; institutions $30. Western Literature Association, Utah State University, English Dept., Logan, UT 84322-3200. TEL 801-750-1603. Ed. Thomas J. Lyon. adv.; bk.rev.; bibl.; index; circ. 900. (also avail. in microform from UMI; back issues avail.; reprint service avail. from ISI,UMI) **Indexed:** Abstr.Engl.Stud., Arts & Hum.Cit.Ind., Amer.Hum.Ind., Arts & Hum.Cit.Ind., Bk.Rev.Ind. (1981-), Chic.Per.Ind., Child.Bk.Rev.Ind. (1981-), Curr.Cont., Film Lit.Ind. (1990-), Hist.Abstr., Ind.Bk.Rev.Hum., LCR, M.L.A., Ref.Sour.
—BLDSC shelfmark: 9300.183000.

700 800 US ISSN 0043-3845
AP2
WESTERN HUMANITIES REVIEW. 1947. q. $18 to individuals; institutions $24. University of Utah, Department of English, Salt Lake City, UT 84112. TEL 801-581-6168. Ed. Barry Weller. index; circ. 1,000. (also avail. in microform from MIM,UMI; back issues avail.; reprint service avail. from SCH,UMI) **Indexed:** A.I.P.P., Abstr.Engl.Stud., Amer.Bibl.Slavic & E.Eur.Stud., Amer.Hist.& Life, Amer.Hum.Ind., Arts & Hum.Cit.Ind., Bk.Rev.Ind. (1965-), Child.Bk.Rev.Ind. (1965-), Curr.Bk.Rev.Cit., Curr.Cont., Film Lit.Ind. (1990-), Ind.Bk.Rev.Hum., LCR, M.L.A., Media Rev.Dig., Mid.East. Abstr.& Ind.
—BLDSC shelfmark: 9300.820000.

WESTERN ILLINOIS REGIONAL STUDIES. see
HISTORY — History Of North And South America

WESTWIND (LOS ANGELES); U C L A's journal of the arts. see *ART*

800 070.5 US ISSN 0896-6354
WHAT IS TO BE READ. 1984. bi-m. $25. Cooperative Economics News Service, 1736 Columbia Rd., N.W., Ste. 202, Washington, DC 20009. TEL 202-387-1753. Ed. Henry Leland. circ. 2,500. (looseleaf format; also avail. on diskette; back issues avail.)
Description: Read primarily by academic social scientists. Publishes book reviews of current academic, scholarly, and college textbooks in economics, sociology, labor studies, women's studies, urban affairs, and educational software.

810 US ISSN 0278-4947
WHAT'S COOKING IN CONGRESS?. 1979. biennial. $9.95. (Harian Creative Associates) Harian Creative Press-Books, 47 Hyde Blvd., Ballston Spa, NY 12020. TEL 518-885-7397. Eds. Harry Barba, Marian Barba. circ. 5,000.
Former titles: Harian Creative Press; Harian Press (ISSN 0017-7776)

800 US
WHAT'S NEW ABOUT LONDON, JACK?. (Companion to Chaney Chronical) 1971. 4/yr. $10. London Northwest, 929 South Bay Rd., Olympia, WA 98506. Ed. David H. Schlottman. adv.; bk.rev.; film rev.; play rev.; bibl.; circ. 70. (processed)
Description: Covers the life and works of the author Jack London.

800 700 US ISSN 1055-8659
WHETSTONE (BARRINGTON). 1983. a. $6.25. Barrington Area Arts Council, Box 1266, Barrington, IL 60011. TEL 708-382-5626. Ed.Bd. circ. 500. (back issues avail.)
Description: Presents poetry, short stories, novel excerpts, critical essays and interviews.

808 US
WHICH WAY.* irreg., no. 4, 1982. c/o Don Byrd, 51 Marlboro Rd., Delmar, NY 12054-2924. Eds. Jed Rasula, Don Byrd.

808 US
WHISKEY ISLAND MAGAZINE. 1978. 2/yr. $8. Cleveland State University, University Center, Cleveland, OH 44115. TEL 216-687-2056. Ed. Cynthia Meyer Sabik. circ. 2,000.

800 US
WHITE ARMS MAGAZINE.* 1974. q. $5. c/o Dana Wichern, 10215 Hickory Valley Dr., Fort Wayne, IN 46815. illus.; circ. 500. (also avail. in microform from UMI)

800 US ISSN 0882-066X
PS536.2
WIDENER REVIEW; poetry, fiction, essays, reviews. 1984. a. $4. Widener University, Humanities Division, Chester, PA 19013. TEL 215-499-4341. Ed. Michael Clark. bk.rev.; circ. 250. (back issues avail.)

800 GW
WIELANDS BRIEFWECHSEL. 1963. irreg., vol.5, 1983. (Akademie der Wissenschaften der DDR) Akademie-Verlag Berlin, Leipziger Str. 3-4, 1086 Berlin, Germany. TELEX 114420-AVERL-DD.

830 AU ISSN 0083-9906
WIENER ARBEITEN ZUR DEUTSCHEN LITERATUR. 1970. a. price varies. Wilhelm Braumueller, Universitaets-Verlagsbuchhandlung GmbH, Servitengasse 5, A-1092 Vienna, Austria. TEL 0222-348124. FAX 0222-310-2805. Eds. Wendelin Schmidt-Dengler, Werner Welzig. index; circ. 1,000. **Indexed:** M.L.A.

WIENER BEITRAEGE ZUR ENGLISCHEN PHILOLOGIE. see
LINGUISTICS

830 831 AU ISSN 0250-443X
WIENER - GOETHE - VEREIN. JAHRBUCH. 1878. a. S.250. Verlag Fassbaender, Lichtgasse 10, A-1150 Vienna, Austria. Ed. Herbert Zeman. adv.; bk.rev.; circ. 700. (reprint service avail. from KTO)
Description: Covers the development of Austrian literature from the 18th to the 20th century.

WIENER JOURNAL; gegruendet von Jorg Mauthe. see
GENERAL INTEREST PERIODICALS — Austria

WIENER ROMANISTISCHE ARBEITEN. see *LINGUISTICS*

WIENER SLAWISTISCHER ALMANACH. see *LINGUISTICS*

2976 LITERATURE

800 US
WILD ABOUT WILDE NEWSLETTER. 1986. s-a. $5. McCaffrey Publishing, 2542 Vance Dr., Mt. Airy, MD 21771. TEL 410-875-0699. Ed. Carmel McCaffrey. bk.rev.; play rev.; circ. 350. (back issues avail.)
Description: Concerns the work of Oscar Wilde - both his work and any new publications about his work.

800 US
WILLA CATHER PIONEER MEMORIAL & EDUCATIONAL FOUNDATION NEWSLETTER. 1957. q. $15. Willa Cather Pioneer Memorial & Educational Foundation, 326 N. Webster, Red Cloud, NE 68970. TEL 402-746-2653. Ed. John Murphy. bk.rev.; illus.; circ. 2,000. (looseleaf format)

378.1 US ISSN 0043-5600
LH1.W64
WILLIAM AND MARY REVIEW. 1962. s-a. $10. College of William and Mary, Williamsburg, VA 23185. TEL 804-253-4895. Ed. William Clark. illus.; circ. 3,000.
Description: Publishes fiction, non-fiction, poetry, and visual art in a four-color format.

808 US ISSN 0196-6286
PS3545.I544
WILLIAM CARLOS WILLIAMS REVIEW. 1975. s-a. $8 to individuals; institutions $10. Swarthmore College, Department of English, Swarthmore, PA 19081-1397. TEL 215-774-7152. FAX 215-328-8673. Ed. Peter Schmidt. adv.; bk.rev.; circ. 375. (back issues avail.) **Indexed:** Abstr.Engl.Stud., Amer.Hum.Ind., Arts & Hum.Cit.Ind., M.L.A.
—BLDSC shelfmark: 9318.912100.
Description: Covers the life and art of the American poet William Carlos Williams, 1883-1963. Includes previously unpublished Williams documents, scholarly articles and notes, announcements and current bibliographic listings.

808 US ISSN 0739-1277
PS571.W2
WILLOW SPRINGS; poetry, translations, fiction, essays, artwork. 1977. s-a. $8. Eastern Washington University, P.U.B. Box 1063, MS-1, Cheney, WA 99004. TEL 509-458-6429. Ed. Nance Van Winckel. adv.; bk.rev.; circ. 1,000. (back issues avail.) **Indexed:** Amer.Hum.Ind.
Description: Poetry, fiction, non-fiction and artwork.

800 US ISSN 0361-2481
PS501
WIND. 1971. irreg. $7 for 2 nos. to individuals; institutions $8 (foreign $12). Wind Press, Box 809K, R.F.D. Route No. 1, Pikeville, KY 41501. TEL 606-631-1129. Ed. Quentin R. Howard. bk.rev.; circ. 500. (back issues avail.) **Indexed:** Ind.Amer.Per.Verse.

800 700 US ISSN 0888-0832
WINDHAM PHOENIX. 1985. m. $12. Phoenix Publishing Co., Box 752, Willimantic, CT 06226. Eds. Michael J. Westerfield, Mark Svetz. illus.; circ. 1,000. (back issues avail.)

808 700 CN ISSN 0822-2363
WINDSCRIPT. 1983. s-a. Can.$6. Saskatchewan Writers Guild, 2049 Lorne St., Regina, Sask. S4P 2M4, Canada. Ed. Cathy Wall. adv.; circ. 3,500. (back issues avail.)
Description: Journal of black and white artwork, poetry and prose by Saskatchewan high school students.

810 US ISSN 0147-3166
PS3501.N4
WINESBURG EAGLE. 1975. s-a. $8. Dept. of English, Virginia Tech, Blacksburg, VA 24061. Eds. Charles E. Modlin, Hilbert H. Campbell. adv.; bk.rev.; cum.index every 2 yrs.; circ. 150. (back issues avail.) **Indexed:** M.L.A.
Description: Provides critical, biographical and bibliographical articles about Sherwood Anderson.

WISCONSIN ACADEMY REVIEW. see ART

WISCONSIN ENGLISH JOURNAL. see EDUCATION — Teaching Methods And Curriculum

800 US ISSN 1050-7035
AS30
▼**WITTENBERG REVIEW;** undergraduate journal of the liberal arts. 1990. s-a. free. Wittenberg University, Box 720, Springfield, OH 45501. TEL 513-327-6231. Ed. Richard P. Veler.

800 700 US
WITTENBERG REVIEW OF LITERATURE AND ART. 1977. a. Wittenberg University, Box 720, Springfield, OH 45501. TEL 513-327-6231. Ed. Pete Staubitz. illus.; circ. 900.

WOLFENBUETTELER BIBLIOTHEKS - INFORMATIONEN. see HISTORY

WOLFENBUETTELER RENAISSANCE MITTEILUNGEN. see HISTORY — History Of Europe

WOLFENBUETTELER STUDIEN ZUR AUFKLAERUNG. SCHRIFTENREIHE. see HISTORY

810 US ISSN 1042-1491
WOMAN OF MYSTERY. 1986. m. $30. Wom'n, Box 1616, Canal St. Sta., New York, NY 10013. Ed. Amy Lubelski. circ. 600.

WOMAN OF POWER; a magazine of feminism, spirituality, and politics. see WOMEN'S INTERESTS

800 305.4 US ISSN 0147-1759
PN481
WOMEN & LITERATURE; a journal of women writers and the literary treatment of women. 1974; N.S. 1981. irreg. price varies. Holmes & Meier Publishers, Inc., 30 Irving Pl., New York, NY 10003. TEL 212-245-4100. FAX 212-254-4104. (U.K. addr.: Book Representation & Distribution, Ltd., P.O. Box 17, Canvey Island, Essex SS8 8HZ, England. TEL 0268-696280) Ed. Janet M. Todd. adv.; bk.rev.; bibl. (also avail. in microform from MIM,UMI; back issues avail.) **Indexed:** Abstr.Engl.Stud., Amer.Hum.Ind., Arts & Hum.Cit.Ind., Curr.Cont., Hum.Ind., M.L.A., Stud.Wom.Abstr.
Formerly: Mary Wollstonecraft Journal (ISSN 0193-7103)
Description: Each volume focuses on a specific theme in literary or artistic criticism.

800 301.42 US ISSN 1056-4535
WOMEN WRITERS OF ITALY. irreg. price varies. Peter Lang Publishing, Inc., 62 W. 45th St., 4th Fl., New York, NY 10036. TEL 212-302-6740. Ed. Susan Briziarelli.
Description: Focuses on Italian women writers, mostly from the nineteenth and twentieth centuries. Includes translations, essays and Italian feminist criticism.

800 US
WOMEN WRITING NEWSLETTER.* 1975. bi-m. $6. c/o Women Writing Press, 151 Oakwook Ln., Ithaca, NY 14850.

WOOLNER INDOLOGICAL SERIES. see PHILOSOPHY

810 US
WOOSTER REVIEW. 1984. 2/yr. $5. College of Wooster, Wooster, OH 44691. Eds. Stuart Safford, Carrie Allison.

WORD WRAP. see PUBLISHING AND BOOK TRADE

820 US ISSN 0043-8006
PR1
WORDSWORTH CIRCLE. 1970. q. $15. c/o Marilyn Gaull, Ed., Dept. of English, New York University, NY 10003. (Subscr. to: Dept. of English, Temple Univ., Philadelphia, PA 19122) adv.; bk.rev.; bibl.; index; circ. 1,000. (also avail. in microform from UMI; back issues avail.) **Indexed:** Abstr.Engl.Stud., Amer.Hum.Ind., Arts & Hum.Cit.Ind., Ind.Bk.Rev.Hum., M.L.A.
Description: Covers the writers and artists who lived during the Romantic Era (1760-1850).

820 CN
WORKING TITLE. 1972. q. free. Alberta Culture, Film & Literary Arts, 12th Fl., CN Tower, 10004 104th Ave., Edmonton, Alta. T5J 0K5, Canada. TEL 403-427-2554. FAX 403-427-5362. Ed. Scot Morison. adv.; bk.rev.; circ. 6,000.
Former titles: Alberta Film and Literary Arts Bulletin (ISSN 0835-4685); (until 1987): Alberta Authors Bulletin (ISSN 0707-994X)

800 001.3 US ISSN 0886-2060
WORKS AND DAYS; essays in the socio-historical dimensions of literature and the arts. 1979. s-a. $7 to individuals (foreign $10); institutions $12 (foreign $15). Indiana University of Pennsylvania, English Department, 110 Leonard Hall, Indiana, PA 15705. TEL 412-357-6486. FAX 412-357-6213. Ed. David B. Downing. index; circ. 300. (back issues avail.) **Indexed:** Hum.Ind.
Description: Multidisciplinary essays on the relations between literature and arts and their socio-historical and socio-cultural contents.

028 US ISSN 0196-3570
Z1007
WORLD LITERATURE TODAY; a literary quarterly of the University of Oklahoma. 1927. q. $24 to individuals; institutions $36. 110 Monnet Hall, University of Oklahoma, Norman, OK 73019-0375. TEL 405-325-4531. FAX 405-325-7495. Ed. Djelal Kadir. adv.; bk.rev.; bibl.; index; circ. 2,200. (also avail. in microform from UMI; reprint service avail. from KTO,UMI) **Indexed:** Amer.Bibl.Slavic & E.Eur.Stud., Arts & Hum.Cit.Ind., Bk.Rev.Dig., Bk.Rev.Ind. (1977-), Chic.Per.Ind., Child.Bk.Rev.Ind. (1977-), Curr.Cont.Africa, Curr.Cont., Hisp.Amer.Per.Ind., Hum.Ind., Lang.& Lang.Behav.Abstr., M.L.A., Mid.East: Abstr.& Ind.
—BLDSC shelfmark: 9356.558600.
Formerly: Books Abroad (ISSN 0006-7431)
Description: Presents literary essays and book reviews from all over the world.

820 CN
WORLD LITERATURE WRITTEN IN ENGLISH. 2/yr. Can.$20 to individuals; institutions Can.$30. University of Toronto Press, Journals Department, P.O. Box 1280, 1011 Sheppard Ave. W., Downsview, Ont. M3H 5V4, Canada. TEL 416-667-7781. Ed. D. Brydon.

WORLD PRESS REVIEW; news and views from around the world. see LITERARY AND POLITICAL REVIEWS

800 CN ISSN 0316-3768
WRIT. 1970. a. Can.$18($18) for 2 yrs. c/o Innis College, 2 Sussex Ave., Toronto, Ont. M5S 1J5, Canada. TEL 416-978-4871. FAX 416-978-5503. Eds. Roger Greenwald, Richard Lush. adv.; index; circ. 700. (back issues avail.)
Description: Presents poetry, fiction, and translations of 20th century authors.

808 UK ISSN 0260-2776
WRITER (PENZANCE). 1963. a. £9. United Writers Publications Ltd., Ailsa, Castle Gate, Penzance TR20 8BG, Cornwall, England. Ed. Sydney Sheppard. adv.; bk.rev.; illus.; mkt.; tr.lit.; circ. 4,000.
Incorporates: Writer's Review (ISSN 0043-9568)
Description: Publication for writers and poets.

808 UK
WRITERS' AND POETS' YEARBOOK. a. United Writers Publications Ltd., Ailsa, Castle Gate, Penzance TR20 8BG, England.

810 US ISSN 0960-2992
TP1
WRITERS FORUM. 1974. a. $10. University of Colorado at Colorado Springs, Colorado Springs, CO 80933-7150. TEL 719-599-4023. (Subscr. to: University Press of Colorado, Box 849, Niwot, CO 80554. TEL 303-530-5337) Ed. Alex Blackburn. adv.; circ. 1,000. (also avail. in microfiche; back issues avail.)
Description: Fiction, poetry, and essays on western American literature.

800 US
WRITERS GAZETTE. 1984. m. $19. Trouvere Company, Rt. 2, Box 290, Eclectic, AL 36024. Ed. Brenda Williamson. adv.; bk.rev.; circ. 1,200.
Formerly: Writer's Gazette Newsletter.

806 US
WRITERS GUILD OF AMERICA, EAST. NEWSLETTER. 1972. m. membership. Writers Guild of America, East, Inc., 555 W. 57th St., New York, NY 10019. TEL 212-767-7800. Ed. Martin G. Waldman. adv.; bk.rev.; circ. 3,500 (controlled).

LITERATURE   2977

800   US   ISSN 1055-1948
WRITERS GUILD OF AMERICA, WEST. JOURNAL. 1963. 11/yr. $40. Writers Guild of America, West, 8955 Beverly Blvd., West Hollywood, Los Angeles, CA 90048. TEL 310-550-1000. Ed. William Meis. adv.; illus.; circ. 10,000.
   Formerly (until Nov. 1988): Writers Guild of America, West. Newsletter (ISSN 0043-9533)
   Description: Looks at TV and screen writing for union members.

810   US
THE WRITER'S HAVEN LITMAG. bi-m. Box 413, Joaquin, TX 75954. Ed. Marcella Owens.

WRITERS INK. see *PUBLISHING AND BOOK TRADE*

808 070   US   ISSN 0891-8759
WRITERS' JOURNAL (N. ST. PAUL). 1980. bi-m. $18 (foreign $29). Minnesota Ink, Inc., 27 Empire Dr., St. Paul, MN 55103-1861. TEL 612-433-3626. Ed. Valerie Hockert. adv.; bk.rev.; index; circ. 35,000. (back issues avail.; reprint service avail.)
   Incorporates (in1990): Minnesota Ink; Former titles: Inkling Literary Journal & Inkling (ISSN 0734-7138)
   Description: Information, news, and practical advice for freelance writers, communicators, and consultants.

820   UK   ISSN 0957-3577
WRITERS NEWS. 1959. m. £44.90. Writers News Ltd., P.O. Box 4, Nairn IV12 4HU, Scotland. TEL 0667-54441. (Subscr. to: Stonehart Subscription Services, Writers News, Hainault Road, Little Heath, Romford, RM6 5NP, England) Ed. Richard Bell. adv.; bk.rev.; circ. 400.
   Incorporates: Writing Magazine (ISSN 0308-2024); Writing Published (ISSN 0049-8211)
   Description: Publishes articles, short stories, poetry, information for writers and poets.

800   UK   ISSN 0141-5050
WRITERS OF WALES. 1970. irreg. price varies. (Welsh Arts Council) University of Wales Press, 6 Gwennyth St., Cathays, Cardiff CF2 4YD, Wales. TEL 0222-231919. FAX 0222-230908. Eds. Meic Stephens, R. Brinley Jones.
   Description: Promotes interest in Welsh authors for an English-speaking audience.

800 821   UK   ISSN 0267-1360
WRITERS' OWN MAGAZINE. 1982. q. £6 (foreign £8)(effective Mar. 1992). 121 Highbury Grove, Clapham, Bedford MK41 6DU, England. TEL 0234-365982. (Subscr. to: Basil Blackwell Ltd., P.O. Box 40, Hythe Bridge Street, Oxford ON 2EU, England) Ed. Eileen M. Pickering. adv.; bk.rev.; circ. 150.

828   II
WRITERS WORKSHOP LITERARY READER. (Text in English) 1972. irreg. Rs.60 cloth; paperback Rs.15. Writers Workshop, 162-92 Lake Gardens, Calcutta 700045, India. Ed. P. Lal. circ. 1,000.

WRITERS' WORLD. see *JOURNALISM*

820   CN   ISSN 0706-1889
WRITING. 1980. 3/yr. Can.$15($18) (outside Canada and US Can.$20). Box 69609, Station "K", Vancouver, B.C. V5K 4W7, Canada. TEL 604-688-6001. Ed. Jeff Derksen. bk.rev.; illus.; circ. 750. (back issues avail.) **Indexed:** Can.Lit.Ind.
   Description: A journal of socially committed and experimental poetry and fiction from Canada, the United States and Great Britain.

808 370   US   ISSN 0194-5475
WRITING (NORTHBROOK); the continuing guide to written communication. 1981. m. (Sep.-May). $5.25. General Learning Corporation, Curriculum Innovations Group, 60 Revere Dr., Northbrook, IL 60062-1563. TEL 708-564-4070. (Subscr. to: Box 3060, Northbrook, IL 60065-3060) Ed. Alan Lenhoff. (also avail. in microfiche from UMI; reprint service avail. from UMI)
   Formerly: Current Media.
   Description: Articles, essays, interviews, technical advice, and word challenges pertaining to the craft of writing, for college-bound students.

810   US   ISSN 0084-2745
WRITING (SAN FRANCISCO). 1964. irreg., no.43, 1983. price varies. Four Seasons Foundation, Box 31190, San Francisco, CA 94131. (Subscr. to: Subco, Box 168, Monroe, OR 97456) Ed. Donald Allen. circ. 3,000. (also avail. in microfiche from UMI)

800   US   ISSN 1053-7937
WRITING ABOUT WOMEN: FEMINIST LITERARY STUDIES. irreg. Peter Lang Publishing, Inc., 62 W. 45th St., 4th Fl., New York, NY 10036. TEL 212-302-6740. FAX 212-302-7574. Ed. Esther K. Labovitz.
   Description: Devoted to feminist studies on past and contemporary women authors, exploring social, psychological, political, economic, and historical insights using an interdisciplinary approach.

808   US   ISSN 0277-7789
PE1001
WRITING INSTRUCTOR. 1981. q. $16 to individuals; institutions $20. T W I (The Writing Instructor), University of Southern California, 817 W. 34th St., Los Angeles, CA 90089. Ed. David Blakesley. adv.; bk.rev.; cum.index; circ. 1,000. (back issues avail.)
   —BLDSC shelfmark: 9364.758500.

808   US
WRITING RESEARCH. 1984. irreg. price varies. Ablex Publishing Corporation, 355 Chestnut St., Norwood, NJ 07648. TEL 201-767-8450. FAX 201-767-6717. TELEX 135-393. Ed. Marcia Farr.

808 372   US   ISSN 0894-5837
LB1576
WRITING TEACHER (SAN ANTONIO). 1987. 5/yr. (during school yr.). $25 (foreign $31). E C S Learning Systems, Inc., Box 791437, San Antonio, TX 78279-1437. TEL 512-438-4262. FAX 512-438-4263. Ed. Lori Mammen. adv.; bk.rev.
   Description: For teachers K-8. Provides practical ideas for classroom activities.

WRITTEN COMMUNICATION; a quarterly journal of research, theory, and application. see *COMMUNICATIONS*

800   GW   ISSN 0341-2172
WUPPERTALER SCHRIFTENREIHE LITERATUR. 1976. irreg., vol.22, 1982. price varies. Bouvier Verlag Herbert Grundmann, Am Hof 32, Postfach 1268, 5300 Bonn 1, Germany. (Subscr. to: VVA Guetersloh, Postfach 7777, D-4830 Guetersloh 1, Germany) Ed.Bd.
   Formerly: Gesamthochschule Wuppertalerschriftenreihe Literaturwissenschaft.

800   US   ISSN 0884-2930
WYOMING; the hub of the wheel...a journey for universal spokesmen. 1985. a. $10. Willow Bee Publishing House, Box 9, Saratoga, WY 82331. TEL 307-326-5214. Eds. Lenore A. Senior, Dawn Senior. circ. 500. (back issues avail.) **Indexed:** Amer.Hum.Ind.
   Description: Themes include peace (from international peace to personal peace), the human race, positive relationships, the human spirit and possibilities.

809   PL
WYZSZA SZKOLA PEDAGOGICZNA IM. KOMISJI EDUKACJI NARODOWEJ W KRAKOWIE. ROCZNIK NAUKOWO-DYDAKTYCZNY. PRACE HISTORYCZNOLITERACKIE. 1961. irreg., no.10, 1986. price varies. Wydawnictwo Naukowe W S P, Ul. Karmelicka 41, 31-128 Krakow, Poland. TEL 33-78-20. (Co-sponsor: Ministerstwo Edukacji Narodowej)

WYZSZA SZKOLA PEDAGOGICZNA IM. KOMISJI EDUKACJI NARODOWEJ W KRAKOWIE. ROCZNIK NAUKOWO-DYDAKTYCZNY. PRACE ROMANISTYCZNE. see *LINGUISTICS*

891.7   PL   ISSN 0239-7986
WYZSZA SZKOLA PEDAGOGICZNA IM. KOMISJI EDUKACJI NARODOWEJ W KRAKOWIE. ROCZNIK NAUKOWO-DYDAKTYCZNY. PRACE RUSYCYSTYCZNE. 1964. irreg., no.5, 1987. price varies. Wydawnictwo Naukowe W S P, Ul. Karmelicak 41, 31-128 Krakow, Poland. TEL 33-79-20. (Co-sponsor: Ministerstwo Edukacji Narodowej)

WYZSZA SZKOLA PEDAGOGICZNA IM. KOMISJI EDUKACJI NARODOWEJ W KRAKOWIE. ROCZNIK NAUKOWO-DYDAKTYCZNY. PRACE Z DYDAKTYKI LITERATURY I JEZYKA POLSKIEGO. see *LINGUISTICS*

890   PL   ISSN 0324-9050
WYZSZA SZKOLA PEDAGOGICZNA, OPOLE. ZESZYTY NAUKOWE. SERIA A. FILOLOGIA POLSKA. 1975. irreg., vol.29, 1990. price varies or exchange basis. Wyzsza Szkola Pedagogiczna, Opole, Oleska 48, 45-951 Opole, Poland. TEL 48 77 383-87. (Dist. by: Ars Polona-Ruch, Krakowskie Przedmiescie 7, Warsaw, Poland)
   —BLDSC shelfmark: 9512.478964.
   Incorporates: Wyzsza Szkola Pedagogiczna, Opole. Zeszyty Naukowe. Seria A. Historia Literatury (ISSN 0078-5407)

890   PL   ISSN 0474-2974
HC10
WYZSZA SZKOLA PEDAGOGICZNA, OPOLE. ZESZYTY NAUKOWE. SERIA A. FILOLOGIA ROSYJSKA. (Text in Polish and Russian; summaries in Russian) 1962. irreg., vol.27, 1988. price varies or exchange basis. Wyzsza Szkola Pedagogiczna, Opole, Oleska 48, 45-951 Opole, Poland. TEL 48 77 383-87. (Dist. by: Ars Polona-Ruch, Krakowskie Przedmiescie 7, Warsaw, Poland)
   —BLDSC shelfmark: 9512.478968.

810   US
X I B. 1991. irreg. (3-4/yr.) $8. X I B Publications, Box 262112, San Diego, CA 92126. circ. 500.
   Description: Publishes poetry, fiction, art, photos, cartoons, satire, and collages.

700 800   US
XALMAN. (Text in English and Spanish) 1974. s-a. $4 to individuals; institutions $10. Casa de la Raza, Inc., 601 E. Montecito St., Santa Barbara, CA 93103. Eds. Armando Vellejo, Manuel Unzueta. film rev.; play rev.; illus.; circ. 1,000.

300 001.3   US   ISSN 0887-6681
XAVIER REVIEW. 1980. s-a. $10 to individuals; institutions $15. Xavier University of Louisiana, Box 110C, New Orleans, LA 70125. TEL 504-486-7411. FAX 504-488-3320. Eds. Thomas Bonner Jr., Robert E. Skinner. bk.rev.; circ. 500. (back issues avail.) **Indexed:** M.L.A.
   Description: Publishes short fiction, novels in progress, poetry, drama, criticism, literary history and essays.

895.1   CC
XIAMEN WENXUE/XIAMEN LITERATURE. (Text in Chinese) m. Y7.60 (foreign $4.30). Xiamen Shi Wenlian, 2 Gongyuan Nanlu, Xiamen, Fujian 361003, People's Republic of China. TEL 25376. (Dist. overseas by: Jiangsu Publications Import & Export Corp., 56 Gao Yun Ling, Nanjing, Jiangsu, P.R.C.) Ed. Chen Yuanlin.
   Description: Comprehensive treatment of literary activities in the Xiamen Special Economic Zone.

895.1   CC
XIAO XIAOSHUO XUANKAN. (Text in Chinese) m. Zhengzhou Shi Wenlian, No. 12, Yihe Lu, Zhengzhou, Henan 450007, People's Republic of China. TEL 449795. Ed. Wang Baomin.
   Description: Publishes fictional vignettes.

800   CC
XIAOSHUO/SHORT STORIES. (Text in Chinese) q. Zhongguo Qingnian Chubanshe, Qikan Bu, 21, Dongsi 12 Tiao, Beijing 100708, People's Republic of China. TEL 442125. Ed. Xu Dai.

800   CC
XIAOSHUO JIA/NOVELISTS. (Text in Chinese) bi-m. Baihua Wenyi Chubanshe, 130 Chifeng Dao, Tianjin 300041, People's Republic of China. TEL 704723. Ed. Zheng Faqing.

895.1   CC
XIAOSHUO JIE/WORLD OF NOVELS. (Text in Chinese) 1980. s-m. Y12($67.30) (Nanchang Wenyi Lianhehui - Nanchang Association of Literature and Art) Shanghai Wenyi Chubanshe - Shanghai Literature and Art Press, 74 Shaoxing Lu, Shanghai 200020, People's Republic of China. TEL 4372608. (Dist. in US by: China Books & Periodicals, Inc., 2929 24th St., San Francisco, CA 94110. TEL 415-282-2994) Ed. Feng Zhaopin. adv.; bk.rev.; circ. 62,000. (back issues avail.)
   Formerly: Nanyuan Xiaoshuo - Novels of Nanyuan.
   Description: Aims to foster young writers.

L

LITERATURE

895.1   CC
XIAOSHUO LIN. (Text in Chinese) bi-m. (Harbin Shi Wenlian) Xiaoshuo Lin Zazhishe, 91, Tiandi Jie, Daoli-qu, Harbin, Heilongjiang 150010, People's Republic of China. TEL 414197. Ed. Jiang Wei.

895.1   CC   ISSN 1004-2164
XIAOSHUO PINGLUN/SHORT STORY REVIEWS. (Text in Chinese) 1985. bi-m. Y12. (Zhongguo Zuojia Xiehui, Shaanxi Fenhui - China Writers' Association, Shaanxi Chapter) Xiaoshuo Pinglun She, 71, Jianguo Lu, Xi'an, Shaanxi 710001, People's Republic of China. TEL 718615. (Co-sponsor: Zhongguo Xiaoshuo Xuehui) bk.rev.; circ. 3,000.
  Description: Publishes literary criticism and comments.

895.1   CC
XIAOSHUO TIANDI. (Text in Chinese) m. Jiangxi Sheng Wenlian, No.104, Bayi Dadao, Nanchang, Jiangxi 330006, People's Republic of China. TEL 65070. Ed. Feng Zhaoping.

895.1   CC   ISSN 0257-5604
XIAOSHUO XUANKAN/SELECTED SHORT STORIES. (Text in Chinese) 1980. m. $71.10. Zuojia Chubanshe, Shatan Beijie 2, Beijing, People's Republic of China. (Dist. in US by: China Books & Periodicals, Inc., 2929 24th St., San Francisco, CA 94110. TEL 415-282-2994)

895.1   CC   ISSN 0257-9413
XIAOSHUO YUEBAO/SHORT STORIES MONTHLY. (Text in Chinese) 1980. m. Y18($61.20) Baihua Wenyi Chubanshe, Chifeng Dao 130, Heping Qu, Tianjin 300041, People's Republic of China. (Dist. outside China by: China International Book Trading Corp., P.O. Box 399, Beijing, P.R.C.; Dist. in US by: China Books & Periodicals, Inc., 2929 24th St., San Francisco, CA 94110. TEL 415-282-2994) Eds. Zheng Faqing, Li Zigan. adv.
  Description: Contains short stories.

XIE ZUO/WRITING. see *JOURNALISM*

895   CC
XIJIANG YUE. (Text in Chinese) bi-m. Wuzhou Shi Wenhua Ju, 102 Dazhongshang Lu, Wuzhou, Guangxi 543000, People's Republic of China. TEL 22347. (Co-sponsor: Wuzhou Shi Wenlian) Ed. Luo Geding.

895.1   CC
XIJU WENXUE/DRAMA LITERATURE. (Text in Chinese) m. Jilin Sheng Xiju Chuangzuo Pinglun Shi, Jianshe Guangchang, Changchun, Jilin 130021, People's Republic of China. TEL 52994. Ed. Li Wenhua.

895.1   CC
XIN LIAOZHAI. (Text in Chinese) bi-m. Shandong Sheng Wenlian, No. 117, Jing 6 Lu, Jinan, Shandong 250001, People's Republic of China. TEL 21475. Ed. Li Chuanrui.

895.1   CC   ISSN 0257-5647
XIN WENXUE SHILIAO/HISTORICAL MATERIALS OF NEW LITERATURE. (Text in Chinese) 1978. q. Y14($43.10) Renmin Wenxue Chubanshe - People's Literature Publishing House, 166 Chaonei Dajie, Beijing 100705, People's Republic of China. (Dist. outside China by: China International Book Trading Corp., P.O. Box 399, Beijing, P.R.C.; Dist. in US by: China Books & Periodicals, Inc., 2929 24th St., San Francisco, CA 94110. TEL 415-282-2994) Eds. Niu Han, Chen Zaochun. (back issues avail.)
  Description: Contains articles and investigations in the history of literature.

895.1   CC
XING HUO/SPARK. (Text in Chinese) m. Jiangxi Sheng Wenlian, No. 147, Bayi Dadao, Nanchang, Jiangxi 330006, People's Republic of China. TEL 63230. Ed. Shu Xinbo.

895.1   CC
XINYUAN. (Text in Chinese) bi-m. Shidai Wenyi Chubanshe, Fu 136, Stalin Street, Changchun, Jilin 130022, People's Republic of China. TEL 884440. Ed. Jin Zhongming.

808   CC   ISSN 1000-3584
XIUCI XUEXI/RHETORIC STUDY. (Text in Chinese) 1982. q. $13.80. (Fudan University, Chinese Language and Literature Institute) Fudan University Press, 220 Handan Lu, Shanghai 200433, People's Republic of China. TEL 5480906. (Dist. in US by: China Books & Periodicals, Inc., 2929 24th St., San Francisco, CA 94110. TEL 415-282-2994)

895.4   CC
XIZANG WENXUE/TIBETAN LITERATURE. (Editions in Chinese, Tibetan) bi-m. Y7.20($20.70) (Xizang Wenlian - Tibetan Artists Association) Xizang Wenxue Bianjibu, Lhasa, Xizang (Tibet) 850001, People's Republic of China. TEL 22382. (Dist. in US by: China Books & Periodicals, Inc., 2929 24th St., San Francisco, CA 94110. TEL 415-282-2994)

800   US
XTRAS.* 1975. irreg., no.19, 1988. price varies. From Here Press, Box 2740, Santa Fe, NM 87504-2704. Eds. William J. Higginson, Penny Harter. circ. 750. (back issues avail.)

820   CN   ISSN 0704-5697
Y E R MONOGRAPH SERIES. (Yeats Eliot Review) 1978. irreg. Can.$8. University of Victoria, Department of English, Victoria, B.C. V8W 2Y2, Canada. TEL 604-721-7211. **Indexed:** M.L.A.

891.553   IR
YAGHMA. 1948. m. Habib Yaghmaie, Ed. & Pub., 15 Khaneqah Ave., Teheran, Iran. TEL 021-305344.

840   US   ISSN 0044-0078
DC1
YALE FRENCH STUDIES. 1948. s-a. price varies. Yale University Press, 92A Yale Sta., New Haven, CT 06520. TEL 203-432-0940. Ed. Liliane Greene. adv.; circ. 2,500. (also avail. in microform from UMI; reprint service avail. from KTO) **Indexed:** Acad.Ind., Arts & Hum.Cit.Ind., Can.Lit.Ind., Curr.Cont., Hum.Ind., M.L.A.
  —BLDSC shelfmark: 9369.970000.

800   UK   ISSN 0893-5378
PN2
YALE JOURNAL OF CRITICISM; interpretation in the humanities. 1987. s-a. £30($27.50) to individuals; institutions £75($75). Basil Blackwell Ltd., 108 Cowley Rd., Oxford OX4 1JF, England. TEL 0865-791100. FAX 0865-791347. TELEX 837022-OXBOOK-G. Ed.Bd. adv. (back issues avail.) **Indexed:** Acad.Ind.
  —BLDSC shelfmark: 9370.005000.
  Description: Essays of an interpretive or theoretical nature in all fields of the humanities.

YALE JOURNAL OF LAW & THE HUMANITIES. see *HUMANITIES: COMPREHENSIVE WORKS*

810   US   ISSN 0148-4605
PS501
YALE LITERARY MAGAZINE. 1831. s-a. $35. Box 243A, Yale Sta., New Haven, CT 06520. TEL 203-497-8213. Ed. Kathryn Haines. adv.; bk.rev.; play rev.; circ. 5,000. (also avail. in microform from UMI; reprint service avail. from UMI) **Indexed:** A.I.P.P., Amer.Bibl.Slavic & E.Eur.Stud., Hum.Ind., Soc.Sci.Ind.
  Former titles (until 1976): Yale Lit (ISSN 0148-4532); Yale Literary Magazine (ISSN 0044-0108)

820 810   US   ISSN 0084-3482
YALE STUDIES IN ENGLISH. 1898. irreg., no.196, 1987. price varies. Yale University Press, 92A Yale Sta., New Haven, CT 06520. TEL 203-432-0940. **Indexed:** M.L.A.
  —BLDSC shelfmark: 9370.750000.

895.1   CC   ISSN 1003-4099
YALUJIANG/YALU RIVER. (Text in Chinese) 1946. m. Y20.40($61.20) (Liaoningsheng Zuojia Xiehui - Liaoning Writers' Association) Yalujiang Wenxue Yuekan She - Yalu River Literature Magazine House, No.7, Shaoshuaifu Hou Xiang, Chaoyang Jie, Shenhe Qu, Shenyang, Liaoning 110011, People's Republic of China. TEL 024-443514. (Dist. overseas by: China International Book Trading Corp., P.O. Box 399, Beijing, P.R.C.; Dist. in US by: China Books & Periodicals, Inc., 2929 24th St., San Francisco, CA 94110) Ed. Chi Songnian. bk.rev.; circ. 10,000.

895.1   CC   ISSN 1001-6104
YAN HE/YAN RIVER. (Text in Chinese) 1956. m. Y1.50($61.20) (Zhongguo Zuojia Xiehui, Shaanxi Fenhui - China Writers Association, Shaanxi Chapter) Yan He Wenxue Yuekanshe, 71, Jianguo Lu, Xi'an, Shaanxi 710001, People's Republic of China. (Dist. outside China by: China International Book Trading Corp., P.O. Box 399, Beijing, P.R.C.; Dist. in US by: China Books & Periodicals, Inc., 2929 24th St., San Francisco, CA 94110) Ed. Bai Miao. illus.

810.8   US
YARDBIRD READER. Variant title: Y'bird. 1971. s-a. $7.50. Yardbird Publishing Co., Box 2370, Station A, Berkeley, CA 94702. Ed. Glenn Myles. adv.; bk.rev.; illus.; circ. 3,000.

808   US
YARNSPINNER. 8/yr. $40 membership (foreign $50)(includes Storytelling Magazine and National Directory of Storytelling). National Association for the Preservation and Perpetuation of Storytelling, Box 309, Jonesborough, TN 37659. TEL 615-753-2171. FAX 615-753-9331.

059.94   GW
YAZIN. (Text in Turkish) 1982. 6/yr. DM.30. Yazin Verlag, Kasselerstr. 1a, 6000 Frankfurt a.M. 90, Germany. FAX 069-7074628. Ed. Engin Erkiner. adv.; bk.rev.; illus.; circ. 1,000. (back issues avail.)

800   US   ISSN 0084-3695
PN851
YEARBOOK OF COMPARATIVE AND GENERAL LITERATURE. (Issued 1952-60 as subseries of University of North Carolina, Studies in Comparative Literature) 1952. a. $12.50 to individuals; libraries $17.50 per vol. Indiana University, Comparative Literature Program, Ballantine Hall 402, Bloomington, IN 47405. TEL 812-855-2140. (Vols.1-11 (1952-62) avail. from Scribner Distribution Center, Inc.: 12 Vreeland Ave., Totowa, NJ 07512) Ed. Gilbert Chaitin. bk.rev.; circ. 1,375. (also avail. in microform from UMI; reprint service avail. from UMI) **Indexed:** Abstr.Engl.Stud., Amer.Bibl.Slavic & E.Eur.Stud., Amer.Hum.Ind., Can.Rev.Comp.Lit., Ind.Bk.Rev.Hum., LCR, M.L.A.
  —BLDSC shelfmark: 9411.623300.

YEARBOOK OF ENGLISH STUDIES. see *HUMANITIES: COMPREHENSIVE WORKS*

YEARBOOK OF EUROPEAN STUDIES/ANNUAIRE D'ETUDES EUROPEENNES. see *POLITICAL SCIENCE — International Relations*

800   US
YEARBOOK OF GERMAN - AMERICAN STUDIES. (Text and summaries in English and German) 1969. a. $20 (foreign $25). Society for German - American Studies, c/o Willailm Roba, Treas., 500 Belmont Rd., Bettendorf, IA 52722. Eds. Helmut Huelsbergen, William Keel. adv.; bk.rev.; bibl.; circ. 400. (back issues avail.) **Indexed:** M.L.A.
  Supersedes (after vol.15): Journal of German - American Studies; **Formerly** (until vol.11, 1976): German - American Studies (ISSN 0046-5836)
  Description: Articles on German-American history, literature and culture.

YEARBOOK OF INTERDISCIPLINARY STUDIES IN THE FINE ARTS. see *ART*

840 947   US   ISSN 0149-7219
DR201
YEARBOOK OF ROMANIAN STUDIES. 1976. a. $5. Romanian Studies Association of America, c/o Paul G. Teodorescu, Ed., 7 John Circle, No. 4, Salinas, CA 93905. adv.; bk.rev.; circ. 250. **Indexed:** Amer.Bibl.Slavic & E.Eur.Stud., M.L.A.

820.6   US   ISSN 0084-4144
PE58
YEAR'S WORK IN ENGLISH STUDIES. 1919. a. price varies. Humanities Press, 165 First Ave., Atlantic Highlands, NJ 07716-1289. TEL 908-872-1441. FAX 908-872-0717. bk.rev.; index. **Indexed:** Br.Hum.Ind., Hum.Ind., M.L.A.
  Description: Summarizes and evaluates all books and articles relating to the study of English language and literature.

809 US ISSN 0742-6224
PR5906
YEATS; an annual of critical and textual studies. 1983. a. University of Michigan Press, Box 1104, Ann Arbor, MI 48106. TEL 313-764-4392. FAX 313-936-0456. TELEX 4320815. Ed. Richard J. Finneran. bk.rev.
Description: Presents current scholarship on W.B. Yeats: articles, annual bibliographies and dissertation abstracts.

YEATS ELIOT REVIEW. see LITERATURE — Poetry

808 808.81 US ISSN 0736-9212
PS509.E7
YELLOW SILK; journal of erotic arts. 1981. q. $38 to institutions. Verygraphics, Box 6374, Albany, CA 94706. TEL 510-644-4188. Eds. Lily Pond, Marnie Purple. adv.; bk.rev.; illus.; circ. 16,000. (back issues avail.) **Indexed:** Alt.Press Ind., Ind.Amer.Per.Verse.
Description: Presents articles on literature and art, short stories and poetry, and illustrations of paintings and photographs.

296 830 IS ISSN 0334-9594
YERUSHOLAIMER ALMANAKH. (Text in Yiddish) 1973. a. $15. Yidishe Shrayber Grupe in Yerusholaim - Yiddish Writers Group in Jerusalem, Shederot Eshkol 12-6, Jerusalem, Israel. Ed. Yoysef Kerler. bk.rev.; illus.; circ. 700. **Indexed:** M.L.A.

810 US
YESTERDAY'S MAGAZETTE. 1973. 6/yr. $10. Independent Publishing Co., Box 15126, Sarasota, FL 34277. TEL 813-922-7080. Ed. E.P. Burke. circ. 6,500.
Description: Publishes literary works including poetry with a nostalgic theme.

800 US
YIDDISH. 1973. q. $15. Queens College Press, c/o Joe Landis, NSF 350, Kiely 1309, Flushing, NY 11367. TEL 718-520-7067. Ed. Joseph C. Landis. adv.; bk.rev.; circ. 800. (back issues avail.) **Indexed:** Arts & Hum.Cit.Ind., Curr.Cont., M.L.A.

800 CC ISSN 1001-1897
YILIN/TRANSLATIONS: A QUARTERLY OF FOREIGN LITERATURE; waiguo wenxue jikan. (Text in Chinese) 1979. q. $43.10. Yilin Chubanshe, 165 Zhongyang Lu, Nanjing, Jiangsu 210009, People's Republic of China. TEL 631317. (Dist. in US by: China Books & Periodicals, Inc., 2929 24th St., San Francisco, CA 94110. TEL 415-282-2994) Ed. Li Jingduan.

895.1 791.43 CC
YINGJU XINZUO/NEW FILM AND PLAY SCRIPTS. (Text in Chinese) bi-m. Jiangxi Sheng Wenxue Yishu Yanjiusuo - Jiangxi Institute of Literature and Art, No.89, Beijing Xilu, Nanchang, Jiangxi 330046, People's Republic of China. TEL 332920. Ed. Tao Xuehui.

895.1 791.43 CC
YINGSHI WENXUE/FILM AND TELEVISION LITERATURE. (Text in Chinese) bi-m. Shandong Sheng Yingshi Zhizuo Zhongxin, No. 55, Wenhua Donglu, Jinan, Shandong 250014, People's Republic of China. TEL 44921. Ed. Teng Jingde.

YISHUJIA/ARTIST. see ART

YORUBA. see LINGUISTICS

895.1 CH
YU SHIH WEN I. (Text in Chinese) m. NT.$700 in ROC; Asia $51; elsewhere $56. 3F, No. 66-1, Chungking S. Rd. Sec. 1, Taipei, Taiwan, Republic of China. TEL 02-311-2832. FAX 02-311-3309. Ed. Tuan Tsai-Hua.

895 CC
YUEDU YU XIEZUO/READING AND WRITING. (Text in Chinese) m. Guangxi Daxue, Zhongwen Xi - Guangxi University, Chinese Department, Nanning, Guangxi 530004, People's Republic of China. TEL 33442. Ed. Liao Chaoran.

YUGNTRUF; Yiddish student quarterly. see ETHNIC INTERESTS

895.1 CC ISSN 0512-9664
YUHUA/RAIN FLOWER. (Text in Chinese) m. (Jiangsu Zuojia Xiehui - Jiangsu Writers Association) Yuhua Bianjibu, 10 Hunan Lu, Nanjing, Jiangsu 210009, People's Republic of China. TEL 638636. Ed. Ye Zhicheng.

YUVA BHARATI; voice of youth. see CHILDREN AND YOUTH — For

891.85 PL ISSN 0084-4411
PG7001
Z DZIEJOW FORM ARTYSTYCZNYCH W LITERATURZE POLSKIEJ. (Text in Polish) 1963. irreg., vol.69, 1986. price varies. (Polska Akademia Nauk, Instytut Badan Literackich) Ossolineum, Publishing House of the Polish Academy of Sciences, Rynek 9, 50-106 Wroclaw, Poland. TELEX 0712771 OSS PL. (Dist. by: Ars Polona-Ruch, Krakowskie Przedmiescie 7, Warsaw, Poland)
Description: Series of monographs on artistic forms in Polish literature.

ZA CASOPIS: KOVCEZIC. see LINGUISTICS

809 PL ISSN 0084-4446
PN1
ZAGADNIENIA RODZAJOW LITERACKICH/PROBLEMES DES GENRES LiTTERAIRES. (Text in English, French, German, Italian, Polish and Russian) 1958. s-a. $28. (Lodzkie Towarzystwo Naukowe) Ossolineum, Publishing House of the Polish Academy of Sciences, Rynek 9, Wroclaw, Poland. TELEX 0712771 OSS PL. (Dist. by: Ars Polona - Ruch, Krakowskie Przedmiescie 7, Warsaw, Poland) (Co-sponsor: Polska Akademia Nauk) Ed. Jan Trzynadlowski. bk.rev.; circ. 800. **Indexed:** Abstr.Engl.Stud., Can.Rev.Comp.Lit., M.L.A.
Description: An international periodical devoted to the theory of literature. Authors from various countries.

ZAYRAY. see LINGUISTICS

891.82 YU ISSN 0084-5183
PG1400
ZBORNIK ISTORIJE KNJIZEVNOSTI/RECUEIL DES TRAVAUX DE L'HISTOIRE DE LA LITTERATURE. (Text in Serbo-Croatian; summaries in English, French, German or Russian) 1960. irreg. price varies. Srpska Akademija Nauka i Umetnosti, Odeljenje Jezika i Knjizevnosti, Knez Mihailova 35, 11001 Belgrade, Serbia, Yugoslavia. FAX 38-11-182-825. TELEX 72593 SANU YU. (Dist. by: Prosveta, Terazije 16, Belgrade, Serbia, Yugoslavia) circ. 1,000. **Indexed:** M.L.A.

891.82 YU ISSN 0084-5205
ZBORNIK ZA ISTORIJU, JEZIK I KNJIZEVNOST SRPSKOG NARODA. SPOMENICI NA SRPSKOM JEZIKU. (Text in Serbo-Croatian; summaries in English, French, German or Russian) 1902. irreg. price varies. Srpska Akademija Nauka i Umetnosti, Knez Mihailova 35, 11001 Belgrade, Serbia, Yugoslavia. FAX 38-11-182-825. TELEX 72593 SANU YU. (Dist. by Prosveta, Terazije 16, Belgrade, Serbia, Yugoslavia) circ. 1,000.

820 810 GW ISSN 0044-2305
PR1
ZEITSCHRIFT FUER ANGLISTIK UND AMERIKANISTIK. (Text in English, German) 1953. 4/yr. DM.72. Verlag Langenscheidt KG, Crellestr. 28-30, 1000 Berlin 62, Germany. FAX 030-780002-15. TELEX 183175 EKGBL. Ed. Helmut Heuermann. adv.; bk.rev.; bibl.; index; circ. 1,500. **Indexed:** Arts & Hum.Cit.Ind., Can.Rev.Comp.Lit., M.L.A.
Description: Covers literature, literary history, language, linguistics, and semantics. Includes reports of events, and book discussions.

ZEITSCHRIFT FUER ARABISCHE LINGUISTIK/JOURNAL OF ARABIC LINGUISTICS/JOURNAL DE LINGUISTIQUE ARABE. see LINGUISTICS

ZEITSCHRIFT FUER CELTISCHE PHILOLOGIE. see LINGUISTICS

830 GW ISSN 0323-7982
PF3003
ZEITSCHRIFT FUER GERMANISTIK. q. DM.120. Europaeischer Verlag der Wissenschaften, Kurzestr. 11, 1254 Schoeneiche, Germany.
Description: Covers literary history, language, linguistics, semantics, and philosophy. Includes announcements of events, and book discussions.

ZEITSCHRIFT FUER ROMANISCHE PHILOLOGIE. see LINGUISTICS

ZEITSCHRIFT FUER ROMANISCHE PHILOLOGIE. BEIHEFTE. see LINGUISTICS

ZENTRALINSTITUTS FUER ALTE GESCHICHTE UND ARCHAEOLOGIE. VEROEFFENTLICHUNGEN. see HISTORY

800 FR ISSN 0751-0357
ZESZYTY LITERACKIE. (Text in Polish) 1983. q. 200 F.($40) Association Cahiers Litteraires, B.P. No 234, 75464 Paris Cedex 10, France. FAX 42-46-13-71. Ed. Barbara Torunczyk.

895.1 CC
ZHANGHUI XIAOSHUO. (Text in Chinese) bi-m. Heilongjiang Sheng Wenlian, 16, Yaojing Jie, Nangang-qu, Harbin, Heilongjiang 150006, People's Republic of China. TEL 30826. Ed. Xiao Yingjun.
Description: Publishes a type of traditional Chinese novel with each chapter headed by a couplet giving the gist of its content.

895.1 CC
ZHANJIANG WENXUE/ZHANJIANG LITERATURE. (Text in Chinese) bi-m. Zhanjiang Shi Wenlian, Renmin Dadao Nan, Xiashan, Zhanjiang, Guangdong 224155, People's Republic of China. TEL 224155. Ed. Ou-yang Qi.

800 CC
ZHISHAN. (Text in Chinese) 1979. q. Zhangzhou Shi Wenlian, Shengli Lu, Zhangzhou, Fujian 363000, People's Republic of China. TEL 27182. (Dist. overseas by: Jiangsu Publications Import & Export Corp., 56 Gao Yun Ling, Nanjing, Jiangsu, P.R.C.) Ed. Chen Wenhe.

800 CC
ZHONG WAI SHUZHAI. (Text in Chinese) bi-m. Shanghai Renmen Chubanshe, Qikan Bu, 54 Shaoxing Lu, Shanghai 200020, People's Republic of China. TEL 4335250. Ed. Wu Shiyu.

895.15 CC ISSN 1002-7564
ZHONGGUO GUSHI/CHINESE STORIES. (Text in Chinese) 1985. bi-m. Y23. Zhongguo Gushi Zazhishe, 94 Dingziqiao Lu, Wuchang Qu, Wuhan, Hubei 430064, People's Republic of China. TEL 027-712847. (Dist. outside China by: Guoji Shudian - China International Book Trading Corp., P.O. Box 399, Beijing, P.R.C.) adv.; bk.rev.; circ. 1,000,000.
Description: Publishes legendary novels, historical stories and biographies.

ZHONGGUO QINGNIAN/CHINESE YOUTH. see CHILDREN AND YOUTH — For

ZHONGGUO QINGNIAN BAO/CHINESE YOUTH DAILY. see CHILDREN AND YOUTH — For

ZHONGGUO TUSHU PINGLUN/CHINESE BOOK REVIEWS. see PUBLISHING AND BOOK TRADE

895.1 CC ISSN 1001-2907
ZHONGGUO XIANDAI, DANGDAI WENXUE YANJIU. (Subseries of: Fuyin Baokan Ziliao) (Text in Chinese) m. Y67.20. Zhongguo Renmin Daxue, Shubao Ziliao Zhongxin - China People's University, Book & Newspaper Information Center, P.O. Box 1122, Beijing 100007, People's Republic of China.
Description: Contains reprinted papers and articles on modern and contemporary Chinese literature.

895.1 CC ISSN 1000-8896
ZHONGGUO XIBU WENXUE. (Text in Chinese) m. Y19.2. Xinjiang Renmin Chubanshe, Qikan Bu, 306, Jiefang Lu, Urumqi, Xinjiang 830001, People's Republic of China. TEL 25358. (Dist. outside China by: China Publications Foreign Trade Corp., P.O. Box 782, Beijing, P.R.C.) Ed. Chen Bozhong. adv.; illus
Description: Publishes short stories, prose, and poetry from the Xinjiang Uighur Autonomous Region and other areas of western China.

2980 LITERATURE — ABSTRACTING, BIBLIOGRAPHIES, STATISTICS

895.1   CC
ZHONGGUO ZUOJIA; daxing wenxue shuangyuekan. (Text in Chinese) bi-m. Y22.80($67.80) 2, Shatan Beijie, Beijing 100720, People's Republic of China. (Dist. outside China by: China International Book Trading Corp., P.O. Box 399, Beijing, P.R.C.; Dist. in US by: China Books & Periodicals, Inc., 2929 24th St., San Francisco, CA 94110. TEL 415-282-2994) Ed. Feng Mu. adv.
    Description: Contains short stories and essays, as well as interviews with and articles about Chinese writers.

895.1   CC
ZHONGPIAN XIAOSHUO/NOVELETTE. (Text in Chinese) m. Y38.40. Zhongpian Xiaoshuo Bianjibu, 27 Degui Xiang, Fuzhou, Fujian 350001, People's Republic of China. (Dist. overseas by: Jiangsu Publications Import & Export Corp., 56 Gao Yun Ling, Nanjing, Jiangsu, P.R.C.)
    Description: Covers critically acclaimed novelettes selected from all the literary magazines and journals in the country as well as novelettes by overseas Chinese writers. Serves as a reference for writers, critics, and libraries.

895.1   CC
ZHONGPIAN XIAOSHUO XUANKAN/SELECTED NOVELLE. (Text in Chinese) bi-m. Haixia Wenyi Chubanshe, 27 Degui Xiang, Fuzhou, Fujian 350001, People's Republic of China. TEL 533457. Ed. Zhang Jiexing.

895.1   CC
ZHONGSHAN; a literary bi-monthly. (Text in Chinese) bi-m. Y$62.40. (Jiangsu Zuojia Xiehui - Jiangsu Writers Association) Zhongshan Bianjibu, 10 Hunan Lu, Nanjing, Jiangsu 210009, People's Republic of China. TEL 638819. (Dist. in US by: China Books & Periodicals, Inc., 2929 24th St., San Francisco, CA 94110. TEL 415-282-2994)

895.1   CC
ZHONGWAI GUSHI/CHINESE AND FOREIGN STORIES. (Text in Chinese) bi-m. Zhongguo Minjian Wenyijia Xiehui, Shanxi Fenhui - China Folk Artists' Association, Shanxi Chapter, 62 Yingze Dajie, Taiyuan, Shanxi 030001, People's Republic of China. TEL 446952. Ed. Liu Qi.

ZHONGWAI GUSHI CHUANQI. see LITERATURE — Adventure And Romance

895.1   CC
ZHONGWAI WENXUE/CHINESE AND FOREIGN LITERATURE. (Text in Chinese) bi-m. Chunfeng Wenyi Chubanshe, 108 Beiyi Malu, Shenyang, Liaoning 110061, People's Republic of China. TEL 363198. Ed. Liu Lieheng.

800   CC
ZHUANJI WENXUE/BIOGRAPHICAL LITERATURE. (Text in Chinese) 1984. bi-m. $3. Wenhua Yishu Chubanshe - Culture and Art Publishers, 17 Qianhai Xijie, Beijing 100009, People's Republic of China. TEL 655992. Ed. Liu Jingzi. circ. 50,000.

895.1   CC
ZHUOMUNIAO/WOODPECKER. (Text in Chinese) bi-m. $49.50. Qunzhong Chubanshe, 14, Dongchang'anjie, Beijing 100741, People's Republic of China. TEL 545108. (Dist. in US by: China Books & Periodicals, Inc., 2929 24th St., San Francisco, CA 94110. TEL 415-282-2994) Ed. Sun Zhongyi.

ZLATY MAJ; casopis o detske literature. see CHILDREN AND YOUTH — For

800   VE
ZONA FRANCA. m. Conda esq. Carmelitas, Caracas, Venezuela.

800 700   US   ISSN 0887-0411
HT101
ZONE (NEW YORK). 1986. irreg., no.6, 1992. price varies. Zone Books, 611 Broadway, Ste. 608, New York, NY 10012. TEL 212-529-5674. (Dist. by: M I T Press, 55 Hayward St., Cambridge, MA 02142. TEL 800-356-0343) Ed.Bd. illus. (back issues avail.)
    Description: Publishes essays, cultural criticism, and artist projects.

806   US
ZORA NEALE HURSTON FORUM. 1986. 2/yr. $15 to individuals; institutions $21. Zora Neale Hurston Society, Box 550, Morgan State University, Baltimore, MD 21239. Ed. Ruthe T. Sheffey. bk.rev.; circ. 200.

895.1   CC
ZUOJIA; wenxue yuekan. (Text in Chinese) m. Y18($61.20) 111 Sidalin Dajie, Changchun, Jilin 130021, People's Republic of China. TEL 883677. (Dist. outside China by: China International Book Trading Corp., P.O. Box 399, Beijing, P.R.C.; Dist. in US by: China Books & Periodicals, Inc., 2929 24th St., San Francisco, CA 94110) adv.; bk.rev.

895.1   CC   ISSN 0494-1101
ZUOPIN. (Text in Chinese) m. $115.50. Zhongguo Zuojia Xiehui, Guangdong Fenhui - China Writers Association, Guangdong Chapter, No. 75, Wende Lu, Guangzhou, Guangdong 510030, People's Republic of China. TEL 334179. (Dist. in US by: China Books & Periodicals, Inc., 2929 24th St., San Francisco, CA 94110. TEL 415-282-2994) Ed. Huang Peiliang.

895.1   CC
ZUOPIN YU ZHENGMING. (Text in Chinese) m. Y1.60 per no. Wenhua Yishu Chubanshe, 17, Qianhai Xijie, Xi Cheng Qu, Beijing 100009, People's Republic of China. (Editorial addr.: P.O. Box 2913, Beijing, P.R.C.) bk.rev.
    Description: Contains controversial stories and drama, followed by literary criticism.

ZUOWEN CHENGGONG ZHI LU/WAYS TO A SUCCESSFUL COMPOSITION. see EDUCATION

800   US
▼**ZUZU PETAL QUARTERLY**; journal of the written arts. 1992. q. $5. Somerset Creamtree Press, Box 4476, Allentown, PA 18105. TEL 215-821-1324. Ed. T. Dunn.

ZVEZDA; literaturno-khudozhestvennyi i obshchestvenno-politicheskii zhurnal. see LITERARY AND POLITICAL REVIEWS

800   GW   ISSN 0934-6155
ZWISCHEN ORIENT UND OKZIDENT. 1988. irreg., vol.2, 1991. (Rueckert Gesellschaft e.V.) Verlag Otto Harrassowitz, Taunusstr. 14, Postfach 2929, 6200 Wiesbaden 1, Germany. TEL 0611-530-0. FAX 0611-530-570. TELEX 4186135.

800 700   US   ISSN 8756-5633
PS561
ZYZZYVA. 1985. q. $20. Zyzzyva, Inc., 41 Sutter St., Ste. 1400, San Francisco, CA 94104. TEL 415-255-1282. Ed. Howard Junker. adv.; bk.rev.; circ. 3,500. (back issues avail.) **Indexed:** Amer.Hum.Ind., Ind.Amer.Per.Verse.

810 301.412   US   ISSN 0094-3320
PS508.W7
13TH MOON; a feminist literary magazine. 1973. irreg. $8 per vol. to individuals; institutions $16. 13th Moon, Inc., Dept. of English, SUNY at Albany, 1400 Washington Ave., Albany, NY 12222. Ed. Judith E. Johnson. adv.; bk.rev.; illus.; circ. 2,000. (back issues avail.) **Indexed:** A.I.P.P., Abstr.Pop.Cult., Amer.Hum.Ind., Ind.Amer.Per.Verse.
    Description: Presents poetry, fiction and critical articles with a feminist perspective, includes special focus on translations.

809   FR
27 RUE JACOB. m. Editions du Seuil, 27 rue Jacob, 75261 Paris Cedex 06, France. bk.rev.; abstr.; illus.

LITERATURE — Abstracting, Bibliographies, Statistics

820 016   AT
A.A.T.E. GUIDE TO ENGLISH BOOKS AND RESOURCES. 1970. a. Aus.$4 (Aus.$15 for combined subscr. with English in Australia). Australian Association for the Teaching of English, P.O. Box 203, Norwood, S.A. 5067, Australia. Ed. R. Leonarder. adv.; bk.rev.; index; circ. 5,000.
    Formerly: A.A.T.E. Guide to English Books (ISSN 0084-7216)
    Description: Contains reviews of new text-books and fiction relevant to teachers and librarians.

A M S STUDIES IN MODERN LITERATURE. see LITERATURE

A M S STUDIES IN THE EIGHTEENTH CENTURY. see LITERATURE

A M S STUDIES IN THE NINETEENTH CENTURY. see LITERATURE

A M S STUDIES IN THE RENAISSANCE. see LITERATURE

A M S STUDIES IN THE SEVENTEENTH CENTURY. see LITERATURE

ABSTRACTS OF BULGARIAN SCIENTIFIC LITERATURE. LINGUISTICS AND LITERATURE. see LINGUISTICS — Abstracting, Bibliographies, Statistics

810 016   UK   ISSN 0001-3560
PE25
ABSTRACTS OF ENGLISH STUDIES. 1958. 4/yr. £24($35) to individuals; institutions £45($69.50). (University of Calgary, Department of English, CN) Basil Blackwell Ltd., 108 Cowley Road, Oxford OX4 1JF, England. TEL 0865-791100. FAX 0865-791347. TELEX 837022-OXBOOK-G. Eds. Jerve Paquette, W. Monday. abstr.; index; circ. 1,300. (also avail. in microform from UMI)
—BLDSC shelfmark: 0564.220000.
    Description: Abstracts from hundreds of journals on American and English literature, world literature and related languages.

AMERICAN HUMANITIES INDEX. see HUMANITIES: COMPREHENSIVE WORKS — Abstracting, Bibliographies, Statistics

810 016   US   ISSN 0002-9823
AMERICAN LITERARY REALISM. 1967. 3/yr. $25 (foreign $31). (University of New Mexico, Department of English) McFarland & Company, Inc., Box 611, Jefferson, NC 28640. TEL 919-246-4460. Eds. James Barbour, Robert E. Fleming. adv.; bk.rev.; illus.; index; circ. 600. (reprint service avail. from KTO) **Indexed:** Abstr.Engl.Stud., Amer.Hist.& Life, Amer.Hum.Ind., Arts & Hum.Cit.Ind., Curr.Cont., Hist.Abstr., Ind.Bk.Rev.Hum., M.L.A., Ref.Sour.
—BLDSC shelfmark: 0840.760000.

808.838   US
ANATOMY OF WONDER; a critical guide to science fiction. 1975. irreg., 3rd ed., 1987. $44.95 hardcover. R.R. Bowker, A Reed Reference Publishing Company, Division of Reed Publishing (USA) Inc., 121 Chanlon Rd., New Providence, NJ 07974. TEL 800-521-8110. FAX 908-665-6688. TELEX 138 755. (Subscr. to: Order Dept., Box 31, New Providence, NJ 07974) Ed. Neil Barron.

420 016   UK   ISSN 0066-3786
Z2011
ANNUAL BIBLIOGRAPHY OF ENGLISH LANGUAGE AND LITERATURE. 1920. a. $204. Modern Humanities Research Association, Kings College, London WC2R 2LS, England. (Vols. 1-39 avail. from: Wm. Dawson & Sons Ltd., Cannon House, Folkstone, Kent, England) Eds. E. Erskine, M.J. De Marr. (also avail. in microform from BHP)

016 820   UK   ISSN 0307-9864
Z2057
ANNUAL BIBLIOGRAPHY OF SCOTTISH LITERATURE. 1969. a. £9($19) to personal subscriber £11 (24) to institutions. Library Association, Scottish Group, Edinburgh University Library, Edinburgh EH8 9LJ, Scotland. Eds. J. Kidd, R.H. Carnie. adv.; bk.rev.; circ. 400. **Indexed:** Abstr.Engl.Stud., LISA.

800 016   CN   ISSN 0227-1400
Z2019
ANNUAL BIBLIOGRAPHY OF VICTORIAN STUDIES. 1977. a. LITIR Database, c/o Department of English, University of Alberta, Edmonton, Alta. T6G 2E5, Canada. TEL 403-432-3258. Eds. Brahma Chaudhuri, Fred Radford. cum.index every 5 yrs.

APPLAUSE THEATRE BOOK REVIEW & CATALOG. see LITERATURE

LITERATURE — ABSTRACTING, BIBLIOGRAPHIES, STATISTICS

800   FR
Z1000
ARGUS DU LIVRE DE COLLECTION. (Text in English, French) 1981. a. 980 F. Editions du Cercle de la Librairie, 35 rue Gregoire-de-Tours, 75006 Paris, France.
Former titles: Argus du Livre de Collection et de l'Autographe (ISSN 0764-8111); Argus du Livre Ancien et Moderne (ISSN 0242-5823)

AUSTRALIAN BOOK COLLECTOR. see *LITERATURE*

860 016   SP
BIBLIOGRAFIA DE LA LITERATURA HISPANICA. 1960. irreg. Consejo Superior de Investigaciones Cientificas (C.S.I.C.), Instituto de Filologia, Vitruvio, 8, 28006 Madrid, Spain. Ed. Jose Simon Diaz.

809 016   IT
BIBLIOGRAFIA E STORIA DELLA CRITICA. irreg., latest no.7. price varies. Angelo Longo Editore, Via Paolo Costa 33, P.O. Box 431, 48100 Ravenna, Italy. TEL 0544-217026. Ed. Enzo Esposito. circ. 2,000.

800 011   YU   ISSN 0350-1450
BIBLIOGRAFIJA DOMACIH I STRANIH KNJIGA. (Text in Serbo-Croatian) 1952. 6/yr. Centar za Vojnonaucnu Dokumentaciju i Informacije, Balkanska 53, Belgrade, Yugoslavia. Ed. Aleksander Nikovic.
Description: Covers contemporary domestic and foreign literature.

059   YU   ISSN 0351-1537
BIBLIOGRAFIJA ROTO STAMPE I STRIPOVA. 1974. a. $105. Jugoslovenski Bibliografsko-Informacijski Institut (YUBIN) - Yugoslav Institute for Bibliography and Information, Terazije 26, Belgrade, Serbia, Yugoslavia. FAX 11-687-760. Ed. Radomir Glavicki.

016 830   GW   ISSN 0341-9363
BIBLIOGRAPHIE DER DEUTSCHEN SPRACH- UND LITERATURWISSENSCHAFT. 1957. a. DM.200. Vittorio Klostermann, Frauenlobstr. 22, Postfach 900601, 6000 Frankfurt a.M. 90, Germany. TEL 069-774011. FAX 069-708038. Ed. Bernhard Kossmann. circ. 2,000.
Formerly: Bibliographie der Deutschen Literaturwissenschaft.

016 840   GW   ISSN 0523-2465
Z2171
BIBLIOGRAPHIE DER FRANZOESISCHEN LITERATURWISSENSCHAFT. 1960. a. DM.290. Vittorio Klostermann, Frauenlobstr. 22, 6000 Frankfurt a.M. 90, Germany. TEL 069-774011. FAX 069-708038. Ed. Astrid Klapp-Lehrmann. circ. 1,500.

830 430 016   GW   ISSN 0172-3960
BIBLIOGRAPHIE LINGUISTISCHER LITERATUR; bibliography of general linguistics and of English, German and Romance linguistics. (Text in English) 1978. a. DM.496. Vittorio Klostermann, Frauenlobstr. 22, Postfach 900601, 6000 Frankfurt a.M. 90, Germany. TEL 069-774011. FAX 069-708038. Ed. Klaus Dieter Lehmann.
Formerly (1976-1978): Bibliographie Unselbstaendiger Literatur-Linguistik.

800   SZ
BIBLIOGRAPHIE ZUR DEUTSCHSPRACHIGEN SCHWEIZERLITERATUR. 1976. a. 30 Fr. Bibliotheque Nationale Suisse, Hallwylstr. 15, CH-3003 Berne, Switzerland. Ed. Gaby Rauch. bk.rev.; circ. 75.

830   GW   ISSN 0523-2767
BIBLIOGRAPHIEN ZUR DEUTSCHEN LITERATUR DES MITTELALTERS. 1966. irreg., vol.10, 1989. price varies. Erich Schmidt Verlag GmbH & Co. (Bielefeld), Viktoriastr. 44a, Postfach 7330, 4800 Bielefeld 1, Germany. TEL 0521-583080. Eds. Ulrich Pretzel, Wolfgang Bachofer. (back issues avail.) **Indexed:** M.L.A.

840   GW   ISSN 0171-0125
BIBLIOGRAPHIEN ZUR ROMANISTIK. (Text in French) 1981. irreg. price varies. Edition Gemini, Juelichstr. 7, 5030 Huerth-Efferen, Germany. TEL 02233-63550. Ed. Gernot U. Gabel. circ. 200. (back issues avail.)

810   US   ISSN 0742-6860
BIBLIOGRAPHIES AND INDEXES IN AMERICAN LITERATURE. 1984. irreg. price varies. Greenwood Press, Inc. (Subsidiary of: Greenwood Publishing Group Inc.), 88 Post Rd. W., Box 5007, Westport, CT 06881-5007. TEL 203-226-3571. FAX 203-222-1502.
—BLDSC shelfmark: 1993.097100.

808.338   US   ISSN 1053-4636
BIBLIOGRAPHIES AND INDEXES IN SCIENCE FICTION, FANTASY, AND HORROR. 1987. irreg. price varies. Greenwood Press, Inc. (Subsidiary of: Greenwood Publishing Group Inc.), 88 Post Rd. W., Box 5007, Westport, CT 06881-5007. TEL 203-226-3571. FAX 203-222-1502.

808   US   ISSN 0742-6801
BIBLIOGRAPHIES AND INDEXES IN WORLD LITERATURE. 1984. irreg. price varies. Greenwood Press, Inc. (Subsidiary of: Greenwood Publishing Group Inc.), 88 Post Rd. W., Box 5007, Westport, CT 06881-5007. TEL 203-226-3571. FAX 203-222-1502.
—BLDSC shelfmark: 1993.097600.

BIBLIOGRAPHIES OF MODERN AUTHORS. see *BIBLIOGRAPHIES*

808   II
BIBLIOGRAPHY OF INDIAN WRITING IN ENGLISH SERIES. (Text in English) 1983. irreg. (approx. biennial). Rs.25($5) Concept Publishing Company, A 15-16, Commercial Block, Mohan Garden, New Delhi 110 059, India. TEL 011-5554-042. Ed. Hilda Ponter. bibl.
Description: Includes biographical factors and critical opinions.

011 899   IS   ISSN 0334-309X
Z7070
BIBLIOGRAPHY OF MODERN HEBREW LITERATURE IN TRANSLATION. 1979. a. $20. Institute for the Translation of Hebrew Literature, P.O. Box 10051, Ramat Gan 52001, Israel. TEL 03-5796830. Ed. Nilli Raz. bk.rev.; index; circ. 200. (reprint service avail. from UMI)

860   CU
BIBLIOTECA NACIONAL JOSE MARTI. BOLETIN BIBLIOGRAFICO. LITERATURA. 1986. m. Biblioteca Nacional Jose Marti, Plaza de la Revolucion, Obispo 527, Apdo. 605, Havana, Cuba.

810   US   ISSN 0742-695X
BIO-BIBLIOGRAPHIES IN AMERICAN LITERATURE. 1984. irreg. price varies. Greenwood Press, Inc., 88 Post Rd. W., Box 5007, Westport, CT 06881-9990. TEL 203-226-3571.

808   US   ISSN 0894-2323
BIO-BIBLIOGRAPHIES IN WORLD LITERATURE. irreg. price varies. Greenwood Press, Inc. (Subsidiary of: Greenwood Publishing Group Inc.), 88 Post Rd. W., Box 5007, Westport, CT 06881-5007. TEL 203-226-3571. FAX 203-222-1502.

BOOK REVIEW INDEX; indexes all reviews in 460 periodicals. see *PUBLISHING AND BOOK TRADE — Abstracting, Bibliographies, Statistics*

BOOK REVIEW INDEX: ANNUAL CLOTHBOUND CUMULATIONS. see *PUBLISHING AND BOOK TRADE — Abstracting, Bibliographies, Statistics*

BOOKS AND ARTICLES ON ORIENTAL SUBJECTS PUBLISHED IN JAPAN. see *ORIENTAL STUDIES — Abstracting, Bibliographies, Statistics*

BORGO LITERARY GUIDES. see *LITERATURE*

800 016   FR   ISSN 0007-5582
Z6513
BULLETIN SIGNALETIQUE. PART 523: HISTOIRE ET SCIENCES DE LA LITTERATURE. 1947. q. 470 F. Centre National de la Recherche Scientifique, Institut de l'Information Scientifique et Technique, 54 bd. Raspail, 75270 Paris Cedex 06, France. FAX 45487015. TELEX MSH 203104 F. cum.index.
●Also available online. Vendor(s): Telesystemes - Questel.

820 011   CN
CANADIAN LITERATURE INDEX. 1985. a. $195. E C W Press, 307 Coxwell Ave., Toronto, Ont. M4L 3B5, Canada. Ed. Janet Fraser. circ. 250.
Description: Comprehensive reference guide to more than 100 English and French-Canadian literary periodicals and newspapers.

016 880   US   ISSN 0528-2594
CATALOGUS TRANSLATIONEM ET COMMENTATORIUM; Medieval and Renaissance Latin translations. 1960. irreg., latest vol.6. price varies. Catholic University of America Press, 620 Michigan Ave., N.E., Washington, DC 20064. TEL 202-319-5052. (reprint service avail. from UMI)

800   FR
DP501
CENTRE CULTUREL PORTUGAIS. ARCHIVES. 1969. a. 350 F. Centre Culturel Portugais, Fondation Calouste Gulbenkian, 51 Ave. d'Iena, 75116 Paris, France. TEL 47-20-86-84. FAX 40-70-98-79. TELEX GULBENF 620176F. (Subscr. to: Jean Touzot, Editeur Libraire, 38 rue Saint-Sulpice, 75006 Paris, France. TEL 43-26-03-88) Ed. Maria De Lourdes Belchior. bk.rev.; circ. 1,000.
Formerly: Centro Cultural Portugues. Arquivos (ISSN 0590-966X)

CHILDREN'S AUTHORS AND ILLUSTRATORS; an index to biographical dictionaries. see *BIOGRAPHY — Abstracting, Bibliographies, Statistics*

CHILDREN'S BOOKS IN PRINT. see *BIBLIOGRAPHIES*

860   NQ
CUADERNOS DE BIBLIOGRAFIA NICARAGUENSE. s-a. Biblioteca Nacional Ruber Dario, Managua, Nicaragua.

CURRENT RESEARCH IN FRENCH STUDIES AT UNIVERSITIES AND POLYTECHNICS IN THE UNITED KINGDOM AND IRELAND. see *LINGUISTICS — Abstracting, Bibliographies, Statistics*

015   DK   ISSN 0070-2714
DANIA POLYGLOTTA; literature on Denmark in languages other than Danish and books of Danish interest published abroad. 1947; N.S. 1969. a. price varies. Kongelige Bibliotek, Danish Department, Christians Brygge 8, 1219 Copenhagen K, Denmark. (Avail. on exchange basis from: I.D.E., Denmarks Institut for International Udveksling, Amaliegade 38, DK-1256 Copenhagen K, Denmark) Eds. Sven C. Jacobsen, Jan William Rasmussen.

016   NE   ISSN 0167-2185
DEUTSCHE BUECHER. (Text in German) 1971. q. fl.165. Editions Rodopi B.V., Keizersgracht 302-304, 1016 EX Amsterdam, Netherlands. TEL 020-6227507. FAX 020-6380948. (US and Canada subscr. to: 233 Peachtree St. N.E., Ste. 404, Atlanta GA 30303-1504. TEL 800-225-3998) Ed.Bd. circ. 1,000.
Formerly: Duitse Boek (ISSN 0046-080X)

DOCUMENTATIEBLAD: THE ABSTRACTS JOURNAL OF THE AFRICAN STUDIES CENTRE LEIDEN. see *SOCIAL SCIENCES: COMPREHENSIVE WORKS — Abstracting, Bibliographies, Statistics*

E I. (Excerpta Indonesica) see *ANTHROPOLOGY — Abstracting, Bibliographies, Statistics*

800 011   US   ISSN 0014-083X
AI3
ESSAY AND GENERAL LITERATURE INDEX. 1900. s-a. (a. and 5 year cumulations). $100. H.W. Wilson Co., 950 University Ave., Bronx, NY 10452. TEL 800-367-6770. FAX 212-538-2716. TELEX 4990003HWILSON. Ed. John Greenfieldt. cum. index: 1900-1969. (also avail. in magnetic tape)
●Also available online. Vendor(s): Wilsonline (File EGL).
Also available on CD-ROM. Producer(s): H.W. Wilson (WILSONDISC).
—BLDSC shelfmark: 3811.671400.
Description: Index to collections of essays and works of a composite nature that have reference value.

LITERATURE — ABSTRACTING, BIBLIOGRAPHIES, STATISTICS

800 011 US ISSN 0160-4880
Z5916
FICTION CATALOG. quinquennial, plus a. supplement. $80. H.W. Wilson Co., 950 University Ave., Bronx, NY 10452. TEL 800-367-6770. FAX 212-538-2716. TELEX 4990003HWILSON. Ed. Juliette Yaakov.
  Description: An annotated list of the best new and established English-language fiction, with title and subject index.

800 US ISSN 0271-6607
FRENCH LITERATURE SERIES. 1974. a. $15 to individuals; institutions & libraries $25. University of South Carolina, Department of Foreign Languages, Columbia, SC 29208. TEL 803-777-4881. Ed. Freeman G. Henry. bibl.; circ. 300. (back issues avail.) **Indexed:** M.L.A.
  —BLDSC shelfmark: 4034.350000.

800 GW
FRITZ-HUESER-INSTITUT FUER DEUTSCHE UND AUSLAENDISCHE ARBEITERLITERATUR. INFORMATIONEN. 1967. irreg. Fritz-Hueser-Institut fuer Deutsche und Auslaendische Arbeiterliteratur, Ostenhellweg 56-58, 4600 Dortmund 1, Germany. TEL 0231-542-23227. circ. 600.
  Description: News about books and documents in the institute's archives.

430 830 016 GW ISSN 0016-8912
Z2235.A2
GERMANISTIK; internationales Referatenorgan mit bibliographischen Hinweisen. 1960. q. DM.126. Max Niemeyer Verlag, Postfach 2140, 7400 Tuebingen 1, Germany. TEL 07071-81104. FAX 07071-87419. Ed. Matthias Reifegerste. adv.; bk.rev.; bibl.; index; circ. 1,900. (back issues avail.) **Indexed:** M.L.A.
  Description: Bibliography listing new works and essays on German language and literature.

GREECE. NATIONAL STATISTICAL SERVICE. CULTURAL STATISTICS. see ART — Abstracting, Bibliographies, Statistics

016 US ISSN 0090-9130
Z1231.P7
INDEX OF AMERICAN PERIODICAL VERSE. 1971. a. Scarecrow Press, Inc., 52 Liberty St., Box 4167, Metuchen, NJ 08840. TEL 800-537-7107. Eds. Rafael Catata, James D. Anderson. circ. 3,000.
  Description: Indexes poems published by periodicals from Canada, the U.S. and Puerto Rico. Includes "little magazines" with limited distribution.

800 016 UK
INDEX OF ENGLISH LITERARY MANUSCRIPTS. 1980. irreg. price varies. Mansell Publishing Ltd., Villiers House, 41-47 Strand, London WC2N 5JE, England. TEL 071-839-4900. FAX 071-839-1804. (Dist. in U.S. by: Publishers Distribution Center, P.O. Box C831, Rutherford, NJ 07070)
  Description: Lists, describes and locates texts by some 270 major British and Irish authors from 1450 to 1900.

INDICE ESPANOL DE HUMANIDADES. SERIES C: LINGUISTICS AND LITERATURE. see LINGUISTICS — Abstracting, Bibliographies, Statistics

810 US
▼**INTERACTIONS OF MAN & ANIMALS;** a quarterly bibliography. 1990. 4/yr. $50. 8732 Rock Springs Rd., Penryn, CA 95663. Ed. David C. Anderson. bk.rev.; circ. 60.
  Description: Cites journal articles, books and book reviews on the human-animal relationship, often quoting the journal abstract or conclusions. Also publishes short articles and news to promote bibliographic access to this multidisciplinary literature.

INTER-AMERICAN REVIEW OF BIBLIOGRAPHY/REVISTA INTERAMERICANA DE BIBLIOGRAFIA. see HUMANITIES: COMPREHENSIVE WORKS — Abstracting, Bibliographies, Statistics

820 398 CN ISSN 0074-1388
Z8045
INTERNATIONAL ARTHURIAN SOCIETY. BIBLIOGRAPHICAL BULLETIN/SOCIETE INTERNATIONALE ARTHURIENNE. BULLETIN BIBLIOGRAPHIQUE. (Text in English and French) 1949. a. $18 to non-members; members $15. International Arthurian Society, c/o Hans R. Runte, Sec.-Treas., Dalhousie University, Department of French, Halifax, N.S. B3H 3J5, Canada. TEL 902-494-2430. Ed. Douglas Kelly. bk.rev.; bibl.; circ. 1,000. (also avail. in microform from SWZ; back issues avail.; reprint service avail. from SWZ) **Indexed:** MLA.
  Supersedes: International Arthurian Society. Report on Congress (ISSN 0074-1396)

INTERNATIONAL RARE BOOK PRICES - LITERATURE. see PUBLISHING AND BOOK TRADE — Abstracting, Bibliographies, Statistics

INTERNATIONAL RARE BOOK PRICES - MODERN FIRST EDITION. see PUBLISHING AND BOOK TRADE — Abstracting, Bibliographies, Statistics

011 SW ISSN 0349-5426
KOMMUNAL LITTERATUR. 1952. bi-m. SEK 245. Bibliotekstjaenst AB, Box 200, 221 00 Lund, Sweden. TEL 46-180-000. circ. 1,600.
  Formerly: Kommunal Litteraturtjaenst (ISSN 0023-3056)

800 011 MX ISSN 0024-1210
LETRAS;* publicacion literaria y bibliografica. vol.36,1970. bi-m. Libreria y Ediciones Botas S. A., Justo Sierra no. 52, Mexico 1, D.F., Mexico. Ed. Gilberto Basa. bk.rev.; bibl.

016 US
LEWIS CARROLL SOCIETY OF NORTH AMERICA. CHAPBOOK. Variant title: Carroll Studies. 1975. a. $20. Lewis Carroll Society of North America, 617 Rockford Rd., Silver Spring, MD 20902. Ed. Charles Lovett. circ. 350.

LIBROS PARAGUAYOS. see LITERATURE

LIGHT'S LIST OF LITERARY MAGAZINES (YEAR). see LITERARY AND POLITICAL REVIEWS — Abstracting, Bibliographies, Statistics

890 NE
LITERAIRE TIJDSCHRIFTEN IN NEDERLAND; bibliografische beschrijvingen, analytische inhoudsopgaven en indices. 1975-1986 (no.6). irreg. price varies. De Graaf Publishers, P.O. Box 6, 2420 AA Nieuwkoop, Netherlands. TEL 01725-71461.

809 011 US ISSN 0733-2165
Z2011
LITERARY CRITICISM REGISTER; a monthly listing of studies in English and American literature. 1983. m. $34 to individuals; institutions $59. Literary Criticism Register, Box 2086, DeLand, FL 32721. TEL 904-736-6029. Ed. Sims D. Kline. adv.; cum.index; circ. 600.
  Description: Listing of bibliographic information for recent articles, books, and dissertations in the field.

800 016 PL ISSN 0075-9945
LITERATURA PIEKNA. ADNOTOWANY ROCZNIK BIBLIOGRAFICZNY. 1954. a. 8000 Zl.($28) (Biblioteka Narodowa, Instytut Bibliograficzny) Stowarzyszenie Bibliotekarzy Polskich, Konopczynskiego 5-7, 00-953 Warsaw, Poland. TEL 275296. (Dist. by: Ars Polona-Ruch, Krakowskie Przedmiescie 7, 00-068 Warsaw, Poland) circ. 5,500.

890 DK ISSN 0108-7215
LITTERATUR PAA INDVANDRERSPROG I DANSKE FOLKEBIBLIOTEKER. 1983. a. DKK 819.67. Bibliotekscentralen, Tempovej 7-11, 2750 Ballerup, Denmark. TEL 2-974000. FAX 2-655310.
  ●Also available online.

800 400 016 US ISSN 0197-0380
P1.A1
M L A DIRECTORY OF PERIODICALS; a guide to journals and series in languages and literatures. 1979. triennial. $115. Modern Language Association of America, 10 Astor Pl., New York, NY 10003. TEL 212-475-9500. FAX 212-477-9863. circ. 1,500.
  Description: Provides detailed information of periodicals on language, literature, linguistics and folklore.

808.838 US
Z5917.S36
N E S F A INDEX TO SHORT SCIENCE FICTION. 1966. a. price varies. New England Science Fiction Association Inc., Box G., MIT Branch, Cambridge, MA 02139. Ed. Anthony Lewis. circ. 1,000.
  Former titles: N.E.S.F.A. Index: Science Fiction Magazines and Anthologies (ISSN 0361-3038); (until 1970): Index to the Science Fiction Magazines (ISSN 0579-6059)

809 011 RU ISSN 0134-2797
NOVAYA INOSTRANNAYA LITERATURA PO OBSHCHESTVENNYM NAUKAM. LITERATUROVEDENIE; bibliograficheskii ukazatel' 1954. m. 8.40 Rub. Akademiya Nauk S.S.S.R., Institut Nauchnoi Informatsii po Obshchestvennym Naukam, Ul. Krasikova 28-21, 117418 Moscow V-418, Russia. Ed. M. Ya. Kurashova.

809 011 RU ISSN 0134-2770
NOVAYA SOVETSKAYA LITERATURA PO OBSHCHESTVENNYM NAUKAM. LITERATUROVEDENIE; bibliograficheskii ukazatel' 1953. m. 9.60 Rub. Akademiya Nauk S.S.S.R., Institut Nauchnoi Informatsii po Obshchestvennym Naukam, Ul. Krasikova 28-21, 117418 Moscow V-418, Russia. Ed. Yu.D. Ruskin.

809 RU ISSN 0202-2095
PN9
OBSHCHESTVENNYE NAUKI V S.S.S.R. LITERATUROVEDENIE; referativnyi zhurnal. 1973. bi-m. 4.20 Rub. Akademiya Nauk S.S.S.R., Institut Nauchnoi Informatsii po Obshchestvennym Naukam, Ul. Krasikova 28-21, 117418 Moscow V-418, Russia. Ed. Ch.G. Buseinov.

809 RU ISSN 0202-2117
OBSHCHESTVENNYE NAUKI ZA RUBEZHOM. LITERATUROVEDENIE; referativnyi zhurnal. 1973. bi-m. 4.20 Rub. Akademiya Nauk S.S.S.R., Institut Nauchnoi Informatsii po Obshchestvennym Naukam, Ul. Krasikova 28-21, 117418 Moscow V-418, Russia. Ed. L.G. Andreev.

810 US
OTISIAN DIRECTORY. 1988. 4/yr. $8. Box 235, Williamstown, MA 01267-0235. circ. 500.

011 UK
P E N INTERNATIONAL. (Issued with the assistance of UNESCO) (Text and titles in English and French) 1950. s-a. £6($8) International P.E.N., 9-10 Charterhouse Bldgs., London EC1M 7AT, England. (U.S. address: F.W. Faxon Co., Inc., 15 Southwest Park, Westwood, MA 02090) Ed. Peter Day. adv.; bk.rev.; index; circ. 1,400. **Indexed:** Mid.East: Abstr.& Ind.
  Formerly: International P.E.N. Bulletin of Selected Books (ISSN 0020-823X)

808 US
PITTSBURGH SERIES IN BIBLIOGRAPHY. 1972. a. price varies. University of Pittsburgh Press, 127 North Bellefield Ave., Pittsburgh, PA 15260. TEL 412-624-4110. FAX 412-624-7380. Ed. Matthew J. Bruccoli.

PLATTDEUTSCHE BIBLIOGRAPHIE; laufendes Verzeichnis der Neuerscheinungen und Neuauflagen auf dem Gebiet der Plattdeutschen Sprache und Literatur. see LINGUISTICS — Abstracting, Bibliographies, Statistics

800 016 US ISSN 0554-3037
Z5781
PLAY INDEX. 1949. quinquennial. price varies. H.W. Wilson Co., 950 University Ave., Bronx, NY 10452. TEL 800-367-6770. FAX 212-538-2716. TELEX 4990003 HWILSON. Ed. Juliette Yaakov.
  Description: Author, title, and subject index to individual plays and plays in collections, with separate cast analysis.

LITERATURE — ADVENTURE AND ROMANCE

808.81   US   ISSN 0736-3966
PN1022
POETRY INDEX ANNUAL. 1982. a. $54.99. Roth Publishing, Inc., 185 Great Neck Rd., Great Neck, NY 11021. TEL 516-466-3676. FAX 516-829-7746. (back issues avail.)

891.85 016   PL   ISSN 0079-3590
POLSKA BIBLIOGRAFIA LITERACKA. 1944. irreg. price varies. (Polska Akademia Nauk, Instytut Badan Literackich) Panstwowe Wydawnictwo Naukowe, Ul. Miodowa 10, 00-251 Warsaw, Poland. (Dist. by: Ars Polona, Krakowskie Przedmiescie 7, 00-068 Warsaw, Poland) Ed. J. Czachowska. circ. 700.

811   US   ISSN 1040-5461
PS580
ROTH'S AMERICAN POETRY ANNUAL; a reference guide to poetry published in the United States during (year). 1988. a. $60. Roth Publishing, Inc., 185 Great Neck Rd., Great Neck, NY 11021. TEL 516-466-3676. FAX 516-829-7746. (back issues avail.)
    Incorporates (1985-1986): Annual Survey of American Poetry; (1983-1986): American Poetry Index (ISSN 0741-3165); (1984-1986): Annual Index to Poetry in Periodicals (ISSN 0882-195X)

890   SW   ISSN 0348-6133
PT9201
SAMLAREN; tidskrift for Svensk litteraturvetenskaplig forskning. (Text and summaries in English, German and Swedish) 1880. a. SEK 85. (Litteraturvetenskapliga Institutionen) Almqvist & Wiksell International, Box 638, S-101 28 Uppsala, Sweden. Ed. Ulf Wittrock. bk.rev.; circ. 1,000. (back issues avail.)

808.838   US
SCIENCE FICTION AND FANTASY RESEARCH INDEX. 1981. irreg., approx. a., latest 1988-89. price varies. S F B R I, 3608 Meadow Oaks Ln., Bryan, TX 77802. TEL 409-845-2316. Ed. H.W. Hall. circ. 500.
    Formerly: Science Fiction Research Index.

808 011   US
SCIENCE FICTION, FANTASY, & HORROR; comprehensive bibliography of books and short fiction published in the English language. 1984. a. price varies. Locus Publications, Box 13305, Oakland, CA 94661. TEL 510-339-9198. FAX 510-399-8144. Eds. Charles N. Brown, William G. Contento. circ. 500.
    Former titles (until 1986): Science Fiction in Print; (until 1985): Science Fiction, Fantasy, and Horror.
    Description: Provides a comprehensive listing of the output in books and magazines for each year by author, title, and subject category.

SENALES; revista bibliografica. see PUBLISHING AND BOOK TRADE — Abstracting, Bibliographies, Statistics

800 016   US   ISSN 0360-9774
Z5917.S5
SHORT STORY INDEX; an index to stories in collections and periodicals. 1900. a. (plus 5 yr. cumulation). $125. H.W. Wilson Co., 950 University Ave., Bronx, NY 10452. TEL 800-267-6770. FAX 212-538-2716. TELEX 4990003HWILSON. Ed. Juliette Yaakov.
● Also available online. Vendor(s): Wilsonline.

T A P; newsletter for the communications revolution. (Technological Assistance Program) see LITERATURE — Science Fiction, Fantasy, Horror

800   DK
UDENLANDSK LITTERATUR I DANSKE FOLKEBIBLIOTEKER. 1972. a. DKK 141($35.25) Bibliotekscentralen, Tempovej 7-11, DK-2750 Ballerup, Denmark. TEL 2-974000. FAX 2-655310.
● Also available online.
    Formerly: Udenlandsk Litteratur i Danske Folkebiblioteker. Skoenlitteratur (ISSN 0106-6641)

016 800   AT   ISSN 0158-3921
VICTORIAN FICTION RESEARCH GUIDES. 1979. irreg. (3-4/yr.). Aus.$34. University of Queensland, Department of English, St. Lucia, Qld. 4072, Australia. Ed. P.D. Edwards. circ. 300. (back issues avail.) **Indexed:** M.L.A.

810 808.02   US   ISSN 1049-8621
PS129
WHO'S WHO IN WRITERS, EDITORS & POETS IN THE UNITED STATES & CANADA; a biographical directory. biennial, 3rd ed., 1990. $97. December Press, Box 302, Highland Park, IL 60035. TEL 708-940-4122. Ed. Curt Johnson.
    Formerly: Who's Who in U S Writers, Editors and Poets (ISSN 0885-4521)
    Description: Gives vital statistics and bibliographies of 10,000 U.S. and Canadian writers, editors and poets.

YEAR'S WORK IN MODERN LANGUAGE STUDIES. see LINGUISTICS — Abstracting, Bibliographies, Statistics

ZA CASOPIS: KOVCEZIC. see LINGUISTICS

LITERATURE — Adventure And Romance

808.838   US   ISSN 0739-3881
AFFAIRE DE COEUR; West Coast leading romance publication. 1979. m. $28. Keenan - Snead, Inc., 1555 Washington Ave., San Leandro, CA 94577. TEL 510-357-5665. FAX 510-357-3117. Ed. Louise Snead. adv.; bk.rev.; bibl.; circ. 115,000.
    Description: Features articles on romance and mystery, including fiction and some non-fiction.

808.838   IT
ALTER-ALTER. 1974. m. L.42000. Rizzoli Editore-Corriere della Sera, Via A. Rizzoli 2, 20132 Milan, Italy. Ed. F. Serra.

056.9   BL   ISSN 0008-5944
CAPRICHO. 1952. m. $90. Editora Abril, S.A., Av. Otaviano Alves de Lima 4,400, 04575 Sao Paulo, Brazil. TEL 011-877-1315. FAX 011-8643796. TELEX 011-80260 EDAB BR. (Subscr. to: Rua do Curtume, 769 CEP 05065 Lapa, Sao Paulo, Brazil.) Ed. Roberto Civita. adv.; film rev., illus.; circ. 190,888.
    Description: For the young woman, covers beauty and makeup, health, sex. love, relationships, people and leisure.

056.1   MX
CAPRICHO. 1967. w. Mex.$120($12) Publicaciones Herrerias, S.A., Morelos 16, planta baja, 06040 Mexico D. F., Mexico. TEL 5-512-4903. Ed. Maria Espinosa. adv.; circ. 320,000.

056.9   BL
CARICIA. 1975. m. Av. Marquez de Sao Vicente 1771, 01139 Rio de Janeiro RJ, Brazil. TEL 11-826-6777. TELEX 11-26070. Dir. Angel Rossi. adv.; illus.; circ. 210,000.

808.838   IT
CHARME. m. Edizioni Lancio, Via Tiburtina km 11.550, Rome, Italy. adv.

055.1   IT   ISSN 0009-8426
CLASSICI DEL GIALLO. no.87, 1970. fortn. L.156000 (foreign L.150800). Arnoldo Mondadori Editore S.p.A., Casella Postale 1833, 20101 Milan, Italy. TEL 3199345. Ed. Laura Grimaldi. circ. 29,715.

808   IT
CLASSICI URANIA. 1977. m. L.72000 (foreign L.69600). Arnoldo Mondadori Editore S.p.A., Casella Postale 1833, 20101 Milan, Italy. TEL 3199345. Ed. Laura Grimaldi. circ. 12,624.

808   AG
CLEPSIDRA. 1984. 4/yr. (Ediciones Filofalsi) Fernando Garcia Cambeiro (Dist.), Cochabamba 244, 1150 Buenos Aires, Argentina.

COMICS INTERVIEW. see ART

808   US
DARING.* 1967. bi-m. Candar Publishing Co., 15-05 Jorden Ct., 102-B Upper, Bayside, NY 11360-1148. Ed. Dan Sontup.

THE DARK MAN: THE JOURNAL OF ROBERT E. HOWARD STUDIES. see LITERATURE

808   IT
DARLING; mensile de fotoromanzi - attualita. vol.8, 1974. m. L.350 per no. Edizioni Lancio, Via Tiburtina KM 11550, 00131 Rome, Italy. FAX 06-4110948. TELEX 622141 LANCIO I. adv.; illus.; circ. 235,000.

808   HU   ISSN 0864-9227
▼**DENISE.** 1990. m. $34 (effective 1992). Harlequin Magyarorszag Kft., Bartok Bela ut. 104, 1113 Budapest 11, Hungary. (Subscr. to: P.O.B. 149, 1389 Budapest 62, Hungary) Ed. Teglasy Imre.

808.838 790.1   US
DIFFERENT WORLDS; the magazine for adventurers. 1979. bi-m. $15. Sleuth Publications, Ltd., 2814 19th St., San Francisco, CA 94110. Ed. Tadashi Ehara. adv.; bk.rev.; circ. 5,000. (back issues avail.)

808.83   GW
EDELWEISS BERG-ROMAN. 1971. w. Zauberkreis Verlag, Karlsruher Str. 22, Postfach 2300, 7550 Rastatt, Germany. Ed. R. Greiser.

056.1 808.838   MX
ESCANDALO.* 1978. fortn. $47. Corporacion Editorial S.A., Lucio Blanco 435, Col. San Juan Tlihuaca, 02400 Mexico D.F., Mexico. Ed. Javier Ortiz Camorlinga. adv.; film rev, illus.; circ. 100,000.

808   GW
FRAGILE; comics handle with care. 1985. q. DM.2. Fragile Comic Group, c/o Michael Hackl, Ed., Ziegelstr. 6, 7326 Heiningen, Germany. TEL 07161-43576. circ. 200. (back issues avail.)

808.838   FR
GALAXIE - BIS. 1962? 24/yr. Societe Nouvelle des Edition Opta, 1 quai de Conti, 75006 Paris, France.

055.1   IT
GRAFFITI.* 1979. m. L.50000($55) Citta Armoniosa, Via Spallanzani 3, 42100 Reggio Emilia, Italy.

055.1   IT
GRAND HOTEL. 1946. w. L.91500. Casa Editrice Universo S.p.A., Via M. de Vizzi 35, 20092 Cinisello Balsamo (MI), Italy. Ed. Alberto Tagliati. adv.; circ. 450,000.

056.9   BL   ISSN 0017-3142
GRANDE HOTEL. 1947. fortn. $85. Editora Vecchi, S.A., Rua do Resende 144, Rio de Janeiro, Brazil. Ed. Amalia Vecchi. illus.

HEARTLAND CRITIQUES. see LITERARY AND POLITICAL REVIEWS

808.838   IT
IDILLIO. m. Edizioni Lancio, Via Tiburtina km 11.550, Rome, Italy. adv.

051   US   ISSN 0020-9813
INTIMATE STORY.* 1948-1982; resumed 1983. m. Charlton Publishers, c/o Miracle Publishing Company, 1275 E. 51 St., Ste. 6H, Brooklyn, NY 11234-2234. TEL 212-868-1210. Ed. Sheila Steinbach. adv.; circ. 215,000.

055.1   IT
INVENZIONE.* 1978. m. L.50000($55) Citta Armoniosa, Via Spallanzani 3, 42100 Reggio Emilia, Italy.

ISKATEL. see CHILDREN AND YOUTH — For

808.838   IT
KISS. m. $15 ($22 to Canada; elsewhere $30). Edizioni Lancio, Via Tiburtina km 11.550, Rome, Italy. (Subscr. in N. America to: Lancio U S A, 630 Third Ave., New York, NY 10017. TEL 212-986-9023) adv.

808.838   IT
KOLOSSAL. m. Edizioni Lancio, Via Tiburtina km 11.500, Rome, Italy. adv.

808.838   IT
LETIZIA. fortn. Edizioni Lancio, Via Tiburtina km 11.550, Rome, Italy. adv.

LITERATURE — ADVENTURE AND ROMANCE

808.828 UK
LOVING. m. £10.80 (foreign £17.70). I P C Magazines Ltd., Holborn Group (Subsidiary of: Reed Business Publishing Ltd.), Kings Reach Tower, Stamford St., London SE1 9LS, England. TEL 071-261-5000. Ed. Lorna Read. adv.; circ. 50,627.
  Incorporates: True Monthly.
  Description: Publishes romance fiction and articles on health and beauty topics for a young adult audience.

808.838 IT
LUCKY. m. Edizioni Lancio, Via Tiburtina km 11.550, Rome, Italy. adv.

MANSCAPE. see *HOMOSEXUALITY*.

808.838 IT
MARINA. m. Edizioni Lancio, Via Tiburtina km 11.550, Rome, Italy. adv.

MERVEILLES & CONTES/MARVELS & TALES/WUNDER & MAERCHEN/MARAVILLAS & CUENTOS/MERAVIGLIE & RACCONTI. see *FOLKLORE*.

808.838 UK ISSN 0960-832X
▼**MILLION;** the magazine of popular fiction. 1991. bi-m. £12($24) Popular Fictions, 217 Preston Drove, Brighton BN1 6FL, England. TEL 0273-504710. Ed. David Pringle. adv.; bk.rev.; film rev.; bibl.; illus. (back issues avail.)
  Description: Publishes author profiles, interviews, and articles about popular fiction past and present, including mystery, adventure, pulp magazine, western, and romance.

808 US ISSN 0747-1637
MILTON CANIFF'S STEVE CANYON MAGAZINE.* Short title: Steve Canyon Magazine. 1982. q. $40. Kitchen Sink Press, Inc., Rt. 1, Box 329, Princeton, WI 54968. TEL 414-295-6922. FAX 414-295-6878. Ed. Peter Poplaski. adv.; bk.rev.; bibl.; charts; illus.; circ. 5,000.
  Description: Covers the career of the eighty-year-old active cartoonist. Includes autobiographical material, comic strip reprints & letters.

808.838 DK
MIT LIVS NOVELLE. 1964. 12/yr. DKK 98 for 6 mos. Interpresse A-S, Noerregade 7A, DK-1165 Copenhagen K, Denmark. TEL 33-33-75-35. FAX 33-33-75-05. Ed. Hanne Williams. adv.; circ. 35,493.

058 SW
MITT LIVS NOVELL. 1964. w. SEK 548. Ungdomsfoerlaget, Baellstavaegen 6, Box 74, 172 22 Sundbyberg, Sweden. Ed. Karin Krausz. circ. 46,200.

051 US ISSN 0026-8399
MODERN ROMANCES. 1930. m. $14.95. Macfadden Women's Media, Inc., 233 Park Ave. S., New York, NY 10003. TEL 212-979-4800. Ed. Cheryl Clark-King. adv.; illus. (also avail. in microform from MCA)

MUJERES Y MUCHACHA. see *MEN'S INTERESTS*.

808.838 US
MYSTERY & ADVENTURE SERIES REVIEW. 1980. s-a. $10 for 4 nos. Fred Woodworth, Ed. & Pub., Box 3488, Tucson, AZ 85722. circ. 700. (back issues avail.)
  Description: Examination, preservation and collecting of old juvenile adventure books.

808.838 IT
NOI DUE. m. Edizioni Lancio, Via Tiburtina km 11.550, Rome, Italy. adv.

NOUS DEUX PRESENTE. see *GENERAL INTEREST PERIODICALS — France*.

056.1 MX
NOVELA MUSICAL. 1968. w. Mex.$150($15) Publicaciones Herrerias, S.A., Morelos 16, planta baja, 06040 Mexico D.F., Mexico. 5-518-5481. Ed. Maria Espinosa. adv.; circ. 300,000.

056.1 MX
NOVELAS DE AMOR. 1960. w. Mex.$3 per no. Publicaciones Herrerias S.A., Morelos 16, planta baja, 06040 Mexico D.F., Mexico. 5-518-5481. Ed. Alicia Ibanez Parkman. adv.; circ. 360,000.

808 UK
OH BOY MONTHLY. 1985. m. I P C Magazines Ltd., Holborn Group (Subsidiary of: Reed Business Publishing Ltd.), King's Reach Tower, Stamford St., London SE1 9LS, England. TEL 071-261 5000. Ed. June Smith. circ. 29,996.
  Incorporates: Photo Love Monthly.

808 US
OMAHA (PRINCETON);* the cat dancer. 1981. bi-m. $15. Kitchen Sink Press, Inc., Rt. 1, Box 329, Princeton, WI 54968. TEL 414-295-6922. FAX 414-295-6878. Eds. Reed Waller, Kate Worley. illus.; circ. 12,000. (back issues avail; reprint service avail.)

808.838 US
ORACLE SCIENCE FICTION AND FANTASY MAGAZINE. 1982. q. $7.20. Science Fiction and Fantasy Productions, Inc., 21111 Mapleridge, Southfield, MI 48075. TEL 313-355-9827. Ed. Dave Lillard. circ. 5,000. (back issues avail.)
  Formerly: Oracle Science Fiction and Fantasy Anthology Magazine (ISSN 0736-2862)

051 US ISSN 0031-5613
PERSONAL ROMANCES.* 1937-1982; resumed 1983. m. $9. Charlton Publishers, c/o Miracle Publishing Company, 1275 E. 51st St., Ste. 6H, Brooklyn, NY 11234-2234. TEL 212-868-1210. Ed. Sheila Steinbach. adv.; circ. 330,000.

808 US
PHOTOROMANCE DARLING. m. $1.50 per no. Lancio U S A, 630 Third Ave., New York, NY 10017. TEL 212-986-9023. FAX 212-972-9769.

808 US
PORTENTS.* 1986. 3/yr. $10. 2239 Wilderness, Germantown, TN 38139-5324. Ed. Deb Rasmussen. circ. 350.
  Description: Offers entertaining short stories.

053.1 AU ISSN 0033-7218
R Z - ILLUSTRIERTE ROMANZEITUNG. 1935. w. S.397. Verlag A. Kirsch, Kaiserstr. 8-10, A-1072 Vienna, Austria. Ed. H. Adfassnig. bk.rev.; film rev.; illus.; circ. 59,000.

808.838 IT
RAGAZZA IN. 1979. w. L.700 per no. Lady M, Via Nicotera 24, 00195 Rome, Italy. Ed. Nicola De Feo. adv.; circ. 300,000.

808 UK
RED LETTER. w. D.C. Thomson & Co. Ltd., Albert Square, Dundee DD1 9QJ, Scotland. **Indexed:** Alt.Press Ind., M.L.A.

052 UK ISSN 0034-2068
RED STAR WEEKLY. 1929. w. D.C. Thomson & Co. Ltd., Albert Square, Dundee DD1 9QJ, Scotland. adv.

808.838 US
ROBERT E. HOWARD'S FIGHT MAGAZINE. irreg., no.3, 1992. $4.50 per no. Necronomicon Press, 101 Lockwood St., W. Warwick, RI 02893. TEL 401-828-7161. FAX 401-738-6125.
  Description: Publishes pulp fiction stories.

808.03 US ISSN 0883-1157
P1
ROMANCE QUARTERLY. (Text in English or any Romance language) 1954. q. $18 to individuals; institutions $28. University Press of Kentucky, 663 S. Limestone St., Lexington, KY 40508-4008. TEL 606-257-2951. FAX 606-257-2984. Ed. Brian J. Dendle. adv.; bk.rev.; index, cum.index; circ. 500. (also avail. in microfilm from UMI; reprint service avail. from UMI) **Indexed:** Arts & Hum.Cit.Ind., Chic.Per.Ind., Curr.Cont., Ind.Bk.Rev.Hum., Lang.& Lang.Behav.Abstr., M.L.A., RILA.
  —BLDSC shelfmark: 8019.474000.
  Former titles (until 1986): Kentucky Romance Quarterly (ISSN 0364-8664); Kentucky Foreign Language Quarterly (ISSN 0023-0332)
  Description: Scholarly articles relating to Romance literature and liguistic topics.

808.03 US ISSN 0035-8118
PC1
ROMANIC REVIEW. (Text in several languages) 1910. q. $25. Columbia University, c/o Prof. Michael Riffaterre, Ed., 518 Philosophy Hall, Columbia University, New York, NY 10027. TEL 212-854-2500. adv.; bk.rev.; index; circ. 1,500. (also avail. in microform from UMI; reprint service avail. from KTO) **Indexed:** Arts & Hum.Cit.Ind., Hum.Ind., Ind.Bk.Rev.Hum., M.L.A.
  —BLDSC shelfmark: 8019.770000.

808.838 US
ROMANTIC TIMES; for readers of romantic and contemporary fiction. 1981. m. $36. Romantic Times Publishing Group, 55 Bergen St., Brooklyn, NY 11201. TEL 718-237-1097. FAX 718-624-4231. Ed. Kathryn Falk. adv.; bk.rev.; circ. 135,000.
  Incorporates (1986-1991): Rave Reviews.

058.82 NO ISSN 0035-8142
ROMANTIKK. 1937. w. NOK 624($93) Bladkompaniet A-S, Postbox 148, Kalbakken, 0902 Oslo 9, Norway. TEL 02-257190. FAX 02-165059. Ed. Gustav M. Galaasen. adv.; illus.; circ. 55,500.

808.03 808.83 011 US ISSN 0161-682X
PS1462
THE ROMANTIST. 1977. a. $10. F. Marion Crawford Memorial Society, Saracinesca House, 3610 Meadowbrook Ave., Nashville, TN 37205. TEL 615-292-9695. Ed.Bd. adv.; bk.rev.; circ. 300 (controlled). (back issues avail.) **Indexed:** M.L.A.
  Description: Devoted to the study of modern manifestations of the Romantic tradition with emphasis on fantastic and imaginative literature. Contains a special section on Francis Marion Crawford.

056.1 MX ISSN 0036-0430
RUTAS DE PASION; photo novels. 1965. w. Editorial Mex-Ameris, S.A., Av. Morelos 16, 4o piso, 06040 Mexico, D.F. TEL 5-521-4690. Ed. Dea Maria Revilla. adv.; illus.; circ. 115,000.

051 US ISSN 0037-0649
AP2
SECRETS. 1936. q. Macfadden Women's Media, Inc., 233 Park Ave. S., New York, NY 10003. TEL 212-979-4800. Ed. Patricia Byrdsong. adv.

808 UK
SECRETS. 1932. w. D.C. Thomson & Co. Ltd., Albert Square, Dundee DD1 9QJ, Scotland.

808.838 IT
SEGRETISSIMO. 1960. fortn. L.156000 (foreign L.150800). Arnoldo Mondadori Editore S.p.A., Casella Postale 1833, 20101 Milan, Italy. TEL 3199345. Ed. Laura Grimaldi. circ. 21,388.

056.9 BL ISSN 0037-2862
SETIMO CEU. 1958. m. $21. Bloch Editores S.A., Rua Frei Caneca 511, Rio de Janeiro GB, Brazil. Ed. Tarlis Batista. adv.; circ. 250,000.

808.838 US
SHAVERTON. 4/yr. $8. 309 Coghlan St., Vallejo, CA 94590. Ed. Richard Toronto. illus.

808.838 IT
SOGNO. fortn. Edizioni Lancio, Via Triburtina km 11.550, Rome, Italy. adv.

STAR WAR COLLECTION TRADING POST. see *HOBBIES*.

808.03 US
STUDIES IN EPIC AND ROMANCE LITERATURE. irreg., latest no.3. $39.95 per no. Edwin Mellen Press, 240 Portage Rd., Box 450, Lewiston, NY 14092. TEL 716-754-8566. FAX 716-754-4335.

808.838 US ISSN 0145-5575
PR6011.R43
THORNDYKE FILE. 1976. s-a. $5. c/o Philip T. Asdell, Ed., R.R. 5, Box 355, Frederick, MD 21701. circ. 100.

051 US ISSN 0041-3550
TRUE LOVE. 1931. m. $14.95. Macfadden Women's Media, Inc., 233 Park Ave. S., New York, NY 10003. TEL 212-979-4800. Ed. Marcia Pomerantz. (also avail. in microform from MCA)

808	KE

TRUE LOVE. w. Drum Publications (EA Ltd.), Mutual Bldg., P.O. Box 43372, Kimathi St., Nairobi, Kenya. TEL 23684. Ed. B.B. Garth. circ. 35,000.

808.838	US	ISSN 0199-0020

TRUE ROMANCE. m. $14.95. Macfadden Women's Media, Inc., 233 Park Ave. S., New York, NY 10003. TEL 212-979-4800. Ed. Jean Sharbel.

052	UK

TRUE ROMANCES. 1934. m. £11.40 (foreign £26). Argus Consumer Publications Ltd., 2-4 Leigham Ct. Rd., London SW16 2PD, England. FAX 081-769-6052. Ed. Ann Jaloba. adv.; illus.

052	UK

TRUE STORY. 1922. m. £11.40 (foreign £26). Argus Consumer Publications Ltd., 2-4 Leigham Ct. Rd., London SW16 2PD, England. FAX 081-769-6052. Ed. Veronica Dunn. adv.; illus.

808.838	US	ISSN 0195-3117

TRUE STORY. 1919. m. $17.97 (foreign $23.97). Macfadden Women's Media, Inc., 233 Park Ave. S., New York, NY 10003. TEL 212-979-4800. Ed. Susan Weiner. circ. 1,349,213.
  Description: Short-story romances.

808.838	IT

URANIA. 1952. fortn. L.117000 (foreign L.119600). Arnoldo Mondadori Editore S.p.A., Casella Postale 1833, 20101 Milan, Italy. TEL 3199345. Ed. Laura Grimaldi. circ. 27,126.

808.83	GW

WAHRE GESCHICHTEN. 1973. s-m. Erich Pabel KG, Karlsruher Str. 31, Postfach 1780, 7550 Rastatt, Germany. Ed. Ingeborg Kunze-Gluck. circ. 315,000.

808	JA

WEEKLY NOVELS/SHUKAN SHOSETSU. (Text in Japanese) 1972. fortn. 7200 Yen. Jitsugyo no Nihon Sha, Ltd., 3-9 Ginza, 1-chome, Chuo-ku, Tokyo, Japan. Ed. Nobuyoshi Yoshida.

808	US

WILDCAT SPECIAL.* 1970. q. $1.50. Candar Publishing Co., 15-05 Jorden Ct., 102-B Upper, Bayside, NY 11360-1148. Ed. Dan Sontup. adv.; illus.

808.8	US

▼**XENOPHILIA.** 1991. s-a. $3 per no. (£2.50 in UK). 904 Old Town Ct., Cupertino, CA 95014. (Subscr. in UK to: Chris Reed, NSFA, P.O. Box 625, Sheffield S1 3GY, England) Ed. Joy Ostreicher.
  Description: Fantastic and unusual poetry.

808.838	US

XENOZOIC TALES.* 1987. s-a. $15 for 6 nos. Kitchen Sink Press, Inc., Rte.1, Box 329, Princeton, WI 54968. TEL 414-295-6922. FAX 414-295-6878. Ed. Dave Schreiner. circ. 10,000. (back issues avail.)

808	KO

YADAM & SILHWA. (Text in Korean) 1960. m. 56400 Won. Bupjisa, 30-21 Mukjungdong, Jungku, Seoul, S. Korea. (Subscr to: Seoul & Records, 3345 N. Clark St., Chicago, IL 60657, U.S.A.) Ed. Kim Jee Wun. illus.; circ. 7,000. (also avail. in talking book)

808.03 895.1	CC

ZHONGWAI GUSHI CHUANQI. (Text in Chinese) bi-m. Jiangxi Renmin Chubanshe, Qikan Bu, No.5, Xinwei Lu, Nanchang, Jiangxi 330002, People's Republic of China. TEL 333180. Ed. Zhou Rongfang.

808.838	US	ISSN 0886-8743

2 A M MAGAZINE; horror, fantasy and science fiction. 1986. q. $19 (foreign $23). Two A M Publications, Box 6754, Rockford, IL 61126-1754. TEL 815-397-5901. Ed. Gretta McCombs Anderson. adv.; bk.rev.; film rev.; circ. 1,000. (back issues avail.)
  Description: Stories, poetry, articles and art for adult readers of fantasy, science fiction and horror literature.

LITERATURE — Mystery And Detective

813	US	ISSN 0002-5224

ALFRED HITCHCOCK'S MYSTERY MAGAZINE. 1956. 15/yr. $31.97. Dell Magazines, 380 Lexington Ave., New York, NY 10168-0035. TEL 212-557-9100. (Subscr. to: Box 7054, Red Oak, IA 51591. TEL 800-333-3311) Ed. Cathleen Jordan. adv.; bk.rev.; film rev.; illus.; circ. 245,000. (also avail. in microfilm from UMI) **Indexed:** Amer.Hum.Ind.

813	US	ISSN 0004-217X
PS374.D4		

ARMCHAIR DETECTIVE; a quarterly journal of fiction and criticism devoted to the appreciation of mystery, detective and suspense fiction. 1967. q. $26. Mysterious Press, 129 W. 56th St., New York, NY 10019. TEL 212-765-0902. FAX 212-265-5478. Ed. Kathy Daniel. adv.; bk.rev.; film rev.; bibl.; cum.index: vols.1-10; circ. 3,500. (back issues avail.) **Indexed:** Bk.Rev.Ind. (1986-), Child.Bk.Rev.Ind. (1986-), Film Lit.Ind. (1977-), M.L.A.

AUGUST DERLETH SOCIETY. NEWSLETTER. see *LITERATURE*

813	US	ISSN 0005-4070
PR4623		

BAKER STREET JOURNAL; an irregular quarterly of Sherlockiana. 1946. q. $17.50. Fordham University Press, University Box L, Bronx, NY 10458-5172. TEL 212-579-2321. Ed. Philip A. Shreffler. adv.; bk.rev.; bibl.; illus.; index; circ. 1,600. (also avail. in microform from UMI; back issues avail.; reprint service avail. from UMI) **Indexed:** Abstr.Engl.Stud., Amer.Hum.Ind., M.L.A.
—BLDSC shelfmark: 1859.980000.

808	US

BEST DETECTIVE CASES. bi-m. $1.50 per no. Globe Communications Corp. (New York), 441 Lexington Ave., New York, NY 10017. TEL 800-472-7744.

BOOKS ARE EVERYTHING. see *LITERATURE*

808.838 800	US

BROWNSTONE MYSTERY GUIDES. 1985. irreg., no.17, 1992. price varies. Borgo Press, Box 2845, San Bernardino, CA 92406. TEL 714-884-5813. Eds. Dale Salwak, Guy M. Townsend.
  Formerly: Brownstone Chapbook Series.
  Description: Essays and bibliographies on the mystery writers of our times.

808	US

CRYPTOGRAM DETECTIVE. 1988. bi-m. $16. Barton Company, 8137 Seash, Portland, OR 97215. TEL 503-256-2393. Ed. Orajoan Barton.
  Description: Contains detective McCann stories, humor, and oddities.

808	US

DETECTIVE CASES. bi-m. Globe Communications Corp. (New York), 441 Lexington Ave., New York, NY 10017. TEL 212-472-4040. Ed. Dominick A. Merle.

808	US

DETECTIVE DRAGNET. bi-m. Globe Communications Corp. (New York), 441 Lexington Ave., New York, NY 10017. TEL 212-472-4040. Ed. Dominick A. Merle.

808	US

DETECTIVE FILES. bi-m. Globe Communications Corp. (New York), 441 Lexington Ave., New York, NY 10017. TEL 800-472-7744. Ed. Dominick A. Merle.

809.916	US	ISSN 0893-0252
PN3448.D4		

DROOD REVIEW OF MYSTERY. 1982. m. $20. Jim Huang, Ed. & Pub., 5047 W. Main St., No. 110, Kalamazoo, MI 49009. TEL 617-499-9578. adv.; bk.rev.; index; cum.index; circ. 1,700. (back issues avail.)
  Description: News and opinion on the latest in mystery, suspense and detective fiction.

808.838	JA

E Q. (Text in Japanese) 1977. bi-m. 3000 Yen. Kobunsha Publishers Co. Ltd., 12-13, 2-chome, Otowa, Bunkyo-ku, Tokyo, Japan. Ed. Hisanori Taniguchi.
  Description: Contains mystery stories.

813	US	ISSN 0013-6328

ELLERY QUEEN'S MYSTERY MAGAZINE. 1941. 15/yr. $31.97. Dell Magazines, 380 Lexington Ave., New York, NY 10168-0035. (Subscr. to: Box 7051, Red Oak, IA 51591. TEL 800-333-3053) Ed. Janet Hutchings. adv.; bk.rev.; film rev.; play rev.; circ. 230,000. (also avail. in microform from UMI) **Indexed:** Amer.Hum.Ind.

813	US	ISSN 0016-2043

FRONT PAGE DETECTIVE. m. (9/yr.). $13. R G H Publishing Corp., 460 W. 34th St., New York, NY 10001. Ed. Rose Mandelsberg. adv.; illus.

808.838	US	ISSN 0193-533X
PS3537.T733		

GAZETTE (NEW YORK). 1979. q. membership. Wolfe Pack, Box 822, Ansonia Sta., New York, NY 10023. Ed. Joel Levy. circ. 500. **Indexed:** Mid.East: Abstr.& Ind.
  Description: Contains material about Nero Wolfe and his creator, Rex Stout.

808.838	IT

GIALLO MONDADORI. 1928. w. L.234000 (foreign L.239200). Arnoldo Mondadori Editore S.p.A., Casella Postale 1833, 20101 Milan, Italy. TEL 3199345. Ed. Laura Grimaldi. circ. 24,310.
  Description: Contains mystery stories.

808.838	US

HARDBOILED DETECTIVE. q. $20 for 6 issues (foreign $26). Gryphon Publications, Box 209, Brooklyn, NY 11228-0209.
  Formed by the merger of: Detective Story Magazine & Hardboiled.
  Description: Publishes original fiction by new and professional talent.

808	US

HEADQUARTERS DETECTIVE. bi-m. Globe Communications Corp. (New York), 441 Lexington Ave., New York, NY 10017. TEL 800-472-7744. Ed. Dominick A. Merle.

813	US	ISSN 0020-1847

INSIDE DETECTIVE. m. (9/yr.). $13. R G H Publishing Corp., 460 W. 34th St., New York, NY 10001. Ed. Rose Mandelsberg. adv.; illus.

808.838 057	RU

▼**INTERPOL - MOSKVA.** 1991. 12/yr. 10 Rub. P. Severnyi, 1-ya Liniya, d.1, 127204 Moscow, Russia. Ed. Valerii Volodchenko. circ. 250,000.

895.15	CC	ISSN 1001-0459

JINGTAN FENGYUN. (Text in Chinese) m. Y14.40. Fujian Sheng Gong'an Ting - Fujian Provincial Bureau of Public Security, No. 147, Beida Lu, Fuzhou, Fujian 350003, People's Republic of China. TEL 536739. (Dist. overseas by: Jiangsu Publications Import & Export Corp., 56 Gao Yun Ling, Nanjing, Jiangsu, P.R.C.) Ed. Lin Zhangfu.
  Description: Features police stories and foreign detective stories.

058	NO	ISSN 0800-0484

KRIMINAL JOURNALEN. (Editions in Norwegian and Swedish) 1953. fortn. NOK 400($72) Ernst Poleszynski & Co., Fridtjof Nansens Plass 6, Oslo 1, Norway. (Subscr. to: Postboks 1594 Vika, Oslo 1, Norway) Ed. Dag Loensjoe. adv.; illus.; circ. 70,000. (back issues avail.)

808.838	US

M W A ANNUAL. 1949. a. membership. Mystery Writers of America, Inc., 17 E. 47th St., 6th fl., New York, NY 10017-1420. TEL 212-888-8171. adv.; circ. 3,000.
  Description: Articles and thoughts of various mystery writers in celebration of the Edgar Allan Poe Awards.

808.838	IT

MARTIN MYSTERE. 1982. m. $15. Daim Press, Via Buonarroti 38, 20145 Milan, Italy. TEL 02 46 94 778. Eds. Sergio Bonelli, Alfredo Castelli. circ. 50,000. (back issues avail.)

364.12	US	ISSN 0025-5017
AP2		

MASTER DETECTIVE. 1929. m. (9/yr.). $13. R G H Publishing Corp., 460 W. 34th St., New York, NY 10001. Ed. Art Crockett. adv.; bk.rev.; charts; illus.; stat.; circ. 175,000.

LITERATURE — POETRY

808.83   AT   ISSN 1035-9761
▼**MEAN STREETS.** 1990. q. Aus.$25($28) What Goes On Pty. Ltd., 214 Hat Hill Rd., Blackheath, N.S.W. 2785, Australia. TEL 61-47-876049. FAX 61-47-876050. Ed. Stuart Coupe. adv.; bk.rev.; bibl.; circ. 6,000. (back issues avail.)
Description: Covers all areas of crime, mystery and detective fiction, both Australian and international.

MILLION; the magazine of popular fiction. see *LITERATURE — Adventure And Romance*

808.838   JA
MU. 1979. m. 5880 Yen. Gakken Co. Ltd., 40-5, 4-chome, Kamiikedai, Ohta-ku, Tokyo 145, Japan. Ed. Masao Ota.
Description: Contains mystery stories.

808.838   II
MUJRIM. (Text in Urdu) 1959. m. 13-14 Asaf Ali Rd., New Delhi 110 002, India. TEL 11-732666. TELEX 3161601. Ed. M. Yunus Dehlvi. circ. 35,000.
Description: Publishes detective fiction.

MYSTERY & ADVENTURE SERIES REVIEW. see *LITERATURE — Adventure And Romance*

808.83   US   ISSN 0000-0302
PN3448.D4
MYSTERY & DETECTION ANNUAL.* 1972. a. 152 S. Clark Dr., Beverly Hills, CA 90211. bk.rev.; circ. 1,200. **Indexed:** M.L.A.

808.83   US
MYSTERY NOTEBOOK. 1984. irreg. $7.50 per no. Stephen Wright, Ed. & Pub., Box 1341, F.D.R. Sta., New York, NY 10150-1341. bk.rev.; circ. 1,000. (back issues avail.)
Formerly: Stephen Wright's Mystery Notebook (ISSN 0740-8870)
Description: Essays on specific mysteries and their writers.

808.838   US   ISSN 1043-3473
MYSTERY READERS JOURNAL. 1985. q. $22.50 to individuals; $35 (foreign $35); libraries $35 (typically set in Jan.). Mystery Readers International, Box 8116, Berkeley, CA 94707-8116. TEL 510-339-2800. Ed. Janet A. Rudolph. bk.rev.; circ. 1,500. (back issues avail.)
Formerly: Mystery Readers of America Journal.
Description: Thematic mystery review. Each issue contains articles, interviews, and reviews on a specific theme, as well as special columns, a calendar of events, and other mystery-related material.

808.83   US
MYSTERY SCENE. 1985. 6/yr. $35 for 7 nos. (foreign $63.50)(effective 1992). Fedora, Inc., Box 669, Cedar Rapids, IA 52406-0669. TEL 319-363-9868. Ed. Ed Gorman. adv.; B&W page $450; trim 7 1/2 x 9 1/2; adv. contact: Ed Gorman. bk.rev.; bibl.; illus.; circ. 8,000. (back issues avail.)
Description: Professional journal for mystery and genre fiction writers, editors and publishers. Includes author interviews, industry news and trends, coverage of recent events and upcoming meetings and conventions.

808.838   US
▼**MYSTERY SCENE AUTHOR'S CHOICE MONTHLY.** 1991. m. $50. Pulphouse Publishing, Inc., Box 1227, Eugene, OR 97440. TEL 503-344-6742. FAX 503-683-3412. Eds. Martin Greenberg, Ed Gorman.
Description: Short mystery story collections featuring individual authors.

808.838   JA
MYSTERY STORIES/SHOSETSU SUIRI. (Text in Japanese) 1961. m. 7440 Yen. Futabasha Publishers, 3-28, Higashi-Gokencho, Shinjuku-ku, Tokyo, Japan. Ed. Masaharu Takano.

808.83   US   ISSN 0737-5840
BV5077.G7
MYSTICS QUARTERLY. 1975. q. $12 to individuals; institutions $15. University of Cincinnati, Department of English, Cincinnati, OH 45221. TEL 319-335-4645. Ed. Elizabeth Armstrong. bk.rev.; bibl.; circ. 450. (also avail. in microform; back issues avail.; reprint service avail. from UMI) **Indexed:** M.L.A.
Formerly (until 1984): Fourteenth Century English Mystics Newsletter.

808.838   US
NEBULOUSFAN.* 1977. irreg., no.10, 1988. (Wing Nuts Wing Club) David Thayer, Ed. & Pub., Box 905, Euless, TX 76039-0905. TEL 817-485-0683. bk.rev.; illus.; circ. 200.
Description: Amateur science fiction humor magazine. Includes fiction, correspondence, humor, criticism, fanzines, cartoons, conventions, art and fun.

813   US   ISSN 0030-0306
OFFICIAL DETECTIVE STORIES. 1930. m. $17. R G H Publishing Corp., 460 W. 34th St., New York, NY 10001. Ed. Art Crockett. adv.; bk.rev.; charts; illus.; stat.; circ. 265,000.
Incorporates: Actual Detective.

808   US
P I MAGAZINE. (Private Investigator); facts and fiction about the world of private investigators. 1988. q. $16. 755 Bronx, Toledo, OH 43609. TEL 419-382-0967. Ed. Bob Mackowiak. adv.; bk.rev.; film rev.; illus.; circ. 600. (back issues avail.)
Description: Contains stories of real investigators' unsolved missing persons cases.

PAPERBACK PARADE. see *PUBLISHING AND BOOK TRADE*

808.838   US
SERPENTINE MUSE. 1975. q. $10. Adventuresses of Sherlock Holmes, c/o Evelyn Herzog, 360 W. 21st St., New York, NY 10011. TEL 212-527-7789. Ed. Patricia E. Moran. adv.; bk.rev.; film rev.; play rev.; bibl.; charts; illus.; circ. controlled. (back issues avail.)
Formerly: Adventuresses of Sherlock Holmes Newsletter.
Description: Sherlockiana: scion society of the Baker Street Irregulars.

808.83   UK   ISSN 0037-3621
PR4623
SHERLOCK HOLMES JOURNAL. 1952. s-a. $15. Sherlock Holmes Society of London, c/o Cdr. G.S. Stavert, 3 Outram Road, Southsea, Hants. PO5 1QP, England. TEL 0705-812104. Ed. N. Utechin. bk.rev.; illus.; cum.index every 2 yrs.; circ. 1,600.

808.838   US   ISSN 1040-4937
SHERLOCKIAN TIDBITS. 1987. q. $4. 42 Melrose Pl., Montclair, NJ 07042. Ed. Arnold Korotkin. bk.rev.; circ. 221. (back issues avail.)
Description: Covers items of interest pertaining to the adventures, life and times of Sherlock Holmes.

808.838   US
SOUTH OF THE MOON. 1968. a. $5 (effective Jan. 1991). American Private Press Association, 562 N. First Ave., Stayton, OR 97383. TEL 503-769-6122. FAX 503-769-4520. Ed. M. Horvat. bk.rev.; film rev.; circ. 750.
Description: Contains a listing of press associations which concentrate on different genres including mystery and detective, science fiction, fantasy, and horror.

813   US   ISSN 0038-996X
STARTLING DETECTIVE. 1929. bi-m. $7.20 for 12 nos. Globe Communications Corp. (New York), 441 Lexington Ave., New York, NY 10017. TEL 800-472-7744. Ed. Dominick A. Merle. adv.; illus.

808.83   US   ISSN 0161-7222
BL625
STUDIA MYSTICA. 1978. q. $14 to individuals; institutions $20. Texas A & M University, Department of English, College Sta., TX 77843-4227. TEL 409-845-8318. Ed. Robert Boenig. adv.; bk.rev.; film rev.; illus.; play rev.; circ. 500. (back issues avail.; reprint service avail. from ISI) **Indexed:** Arts & Hum.Cit.Ind., Curr.Cont., M.L.A., Rel.& Theol.Abstr. (1990-), Rel.Ind.One.
—BLDSC shelfmark: 8483.075000.
Description: Scholarly articles, poetry, prose fiction, essays, reviews, and other art forms pertaining to mystical experience.

813   US   ISSN 0040-6139
THIRD DEGREE (NEW YORK). 1946. m. membership. Mystery Writers of America, Inc., 17 E. 47th St., 6th fl., New York, NY 10017-1420. TEL 212-888-8171. circ. 2,500.

808.838   US   ISSN 0041-3488
TRUE CONFESSIONS. 1922. m. $14.95. Macfadden Women's Media, Inc., 233 Park Ave. S., New York, NY 10003. TEL 212-979-4800. Ed. H. Marie Atkocius. adv.; illus. (also avail. in microform from MCA)

808.838   US   ISSN 0041-350X
TRUE DETECTIVE. 1924. m. $17. R G H Publishing Corp., 460 W. 34th St., New York, NY 10001. Ed. Art Crockett. adv.; bk.rev.; charts; illus.; stat.; circ. 250,000.

808.838   US   ISSN 0199-0012
TRUE EXPERIENCE. 1925. m. $14.95. Macfadden Women's Media, Inc., 233 Park Ave. S., New York, NY 10003. TEL 212-979-4800. (Subscr. to: Box 10015, Des Moines, IA 50340) Ed. Jean Silberg.

813   US   ISSN 0042-4129
VERMISSA HERALD;* a journal of Sherlockian affairs. 1967. q. $2. Scowrers & Molly Maguires of San Francisco, 4712 17th St., San Francisco, CA 94117. Ed. William A. Berner. adv.; bk.rev.; bibl.; circ. 200.

808.838 820   UK
WINTER'S CRIMES. a. MacMillan Press Ltd, Houndmills, Basingstoke, Hampshire RG2 2XS, England.

LITERATURE — Poetry

821   UK
A. 1969. irreg. £75. Alphabox Press, Flat 1, 41 Mapesbury Rd., London NW2 4HJ, England. circ. 300.
Description: Publishes poems.

700   AG   ISSN 0002-4090
A L A; organo de fomento cultural y de circulacion internacional. vol.11, 1975. q. $10. Conesa 1330, Buenos Aires, Argentina. Dir. Mercedes Fernandez Zalazar. illus. **Indexed:** E.I.

808.81   US   ISSN 0734-7618
A M S ARS POETICA. 1983. irreg., no.5, 1989. price varies. (Abrahams Magazine Service) A M S Press, Inc., 56 E. 13th St., New York, NY 10003. TEL 212-777-4700. FAX 212-995-5413. (back issues avail.)
—BLDSC shelfmark: 0859.497000.
Description: Series of monographs, bibliographies and reference works devoted to particular topics in literature and poetry.

841 800   FR
A R P A CAHIERS DE RECHERCHE POETIQUE. 1977. q. 170 Fr.($20) Association de Recherche Poetique en Auvergne, 11 rue Sarrail, 63000 Clermont-Ferrand, France. circ. 500. (back issues avail.)

811   US
A VOICE WITHOUT SIDES. 1987. irreg. (approx. 2/yr.). 317 Princetown Rd., Schenectady, NY 12306-2022. circ. 30.
Description: Publishes short avant-garde poetry and visual arts in strange formats.

808.81   US   ISSN 0886-4047
ABACUS (ELMWOOD). 1984. every 6 weeks. $21. Potes & Poets Press, Inc., 181 Edgemont Ave., Elmwood, CT 06110. TEL 203-233-2023. Ed. Peter Ganick. circ. 150. (back issues avail.) **Indexed:** Avery Ind.Archit.Per.
Description: Experimental and language-centered poetry.

811   US
ABBEY; the journal of literary brouhaha. 1970. q. $2. (South Canada Broccoli Federation) White Urp Press, 5360 Fallriver Row Ct., Columbia, MD 21044. Ed. David Greisman. adv.; bk.rev.; play rev.; bibl.; illus.; circ. 200 (controlled).

811   US   ISSN 0361-1663
PS325
ABRAXAS. 1968. irreg. $12. Abraxas Press, Inc., 2518 Gregory St., Madison, WI 53711. TEL 608-238-0175. Ed. Ingrid Swanberg. adv.; bk.rev.; cum.index: 1968-1982; circ. 600. (back issues avail.) **Indexed:** Amer.Hum.Ind.
Description: Independent, contemporary, small press journal publishing poetry and poetry in translation.

808.81 UK ISSN 0143-7488
ACADEMUS POETRY MAGAZINE. 1979. s-a. 38 Courtenay St., Cheltenham, Glos. GL5 4LR, England.

810 US
ACADEMY OF AMERICAN POETS. LAMONT POETRY SELECTION AND WALT WHITMAN SELECTION. 1954. a. $45. Academy of American Poets, 177 E. 87th St., New York, NY 10128.
Formerly: Academy of American Poets. Lamont Poetry Selections (ISSN 0515-2003)
Description: Introduces the winner of the Walt Whitman award, which is an annual first book selection of a previously unpublished poet. The Lamont poetry selection is an annual second book award.

L'ACERBA; periodico di tecnica (artistica, letteraria, libraria) culturale. see *LITERATURE*

861 MX ISSN 0185-3082
ACTA POETICA. 1979. a. price varies. Universidad Nacional Autonoma de Mexico, Instituto de Investigaciones Filologicas, Ciudad Universitaria, C.P. 04510, Mexico 21 D.F., Mexico.

841 FR ISSN 0001-7477
ACTION POETIQUE. 1950. q. 300 F. Editions Action Poetique, La Fontaine au Bois Pav. 2, 25 rue J. Mermoz, 77210 Avon, France. Ed. Henri Deluy. adv.; bk.rev.; illus.; circ. 2,000.

811 US ISSN 0749-3908
PN2
ACTS (SAN FRANCISCO); a journal of new writing. 1982. s-a. $12 to individuals; institutions $16. 514 Guerrero St., San Francisco, CA 94110-1017. TEL 415-431-8297. Ed. David Levi Strauss. adv.; bk.rev.; circ. 1,500. Indexed: A.I.P.P., Amer.Hum.Ind.
Description: Contemporary radical poetry, "analytic lyric," word-image work and photography. Special book issues on selected subjects.

821 UK ISSN 0964-0304
ACUMEN MAGAZINE. 1985. s-a. £6($25) 6 The Mount, Higher Furzeham, Brixham, S. Devon TQ5 8QY, England. TEL 0803-851098. Ed. Patricia Oxley. adv.; bk.rev.; circ. 600. (back issues avail)
Description: Contains poetry, articles about poetry, and interviews with poets.

811 US
ADROIT EXPRESSION. 1986. 2/yr. $5. Box 73, Courtney, PA 15029. Ed. Xavier F. Aguilar. circ. 50.

ADVOCATE (PRATTSVILLE). see *LITERATURE*

808.81 700 US ISSN 0894-2633
AERIAL. 1985. a. $20 for 3 nos. Edge Books, Box 25642, Washington, DC 20007. TEL 202-333-1544. Ed. Rod Smith. adv.; bk.rev.; bibl.; circ. 1,000. (back issues avail.)
Formerly: Ariel.

811 US
AERIE. vol.4, 1974. a. $2. University of Southern Indiana, Publication Dept., 8600 University Blvd., Evansville, IN 47712. TEL 812-464-1954. FAX 812-464-1960. illus.
Formerly (until 1979): Moving Finger.

811 US
AERO SUN-TIMES. 1974. 4/yr. 44 N. Last Chance Gulch No. 9, Helena, MT 59601. TEL 406-443-7272. Ed. Wilbur Wood.
Description: Publishes mainly short poems on the themes of energy or environment.

821 UK ISSN 0002-0796
AGENDA. 1959. q. £15($30) to individuals; libraries £20($40). Agenda & Editions Charitable Trust, 5 Cranbourne Court, Albert Bridge Rd., London SW11 4PE, England. TEL 01-228 0700. Ed. William Cookson. adv.; bk.rev.; circ. 2,000. (also avail. in microfilm from UMI) Indexed: Abstr.Engl.Stud., Br.Hum.Ind., Geo.Abstr., M.L.A., So.Pac.Per.Ind.
—BLDSC shelfmark: 0736.242500.

811 US
▼**AGOG.** 1990. 4/yr. 340 22nd St., Brooklyn, NY 11215. TEL 718-965-3871. circ. 100.

811 US
AHSAHTA. 1975. 3/yr. $4.95 per no. Boise State University, Department of English, 1910 University Dr., Boise, ID 83725. TEL 208-385-1246. Ed. Tom Trusky. circ. 500.

800 700 770 US
AILERON; a literary journal. 1980. a. $12 for 4 nos. Aileron Press, Box 891, Austin, TX 78767-0891. Ed. Ric Williams. circ. 200.
Description: Poetry with occasional short fiction.

AIREINGS. see *LITERATURE*

891.43 II ISSN 0970-096X
AKAVITA. (Text in Hindi) q. Rs.40($12) Samkaleen Prakashan, 2762 Rajguru Marg, New Delhi 110 055, India.

831 GW ISSN 0002-3957
PT1141.A2
AKZENTE; Zeitschrift fuer Literatur. 1954. bi-m. DM.55.80. Carl Hanser Verlag, Kolbergerstr. 22, Postfach 860420, 8000 Munich 80, Germany. TEL 089-926940. Ed. Michael Krueger. adv.; bk.rev.; index; circ. 4,500. Indexed: Arts & Hum.Cit.Ind., Curr.Cont., M.L.A.

811 US
ALABAMA DOGSHOE MOUSTACHE. 1987. q. $5. D B Q P, 317 Princetown Rd., Schenectady, NY 12306-2022. circ. 100.
Description: Publishes linguistically daring poetry.

841 FR
ALBATROS. q. 180 F. (foreign 190 F.)(effective 1991). Academie des Poetes Classiques de France, 40 rue de Bretagne, 75003 Paris, France. Ed. Jean de Lost-Pic. bk.rev.
Description: French poetry in the classical form.

811 US
ALBATROSS. 1986. 2/yr. $5. Anabiosis Press, 125 Horton Ave., Englewood, FL 33981. Eds. Richard Smyth, Richard Brobst. circ. 500.
Description: Publishes free-style, narrative poetry on environment and nature.

ALCHEMIST. see *LITERATURE*

811 US
ALDEBARAN. 1971. s-a. $10. c/o Roger Williams College, Old Ferry Rd., Bristol, RI 02809. TEL 401-253-1040. Ed. Debra L. Malewicki. illus.; circ. 200. (back issues avail.)

811 US ISSN 0002-5089
PS615
ALDEBARAN REVIEW. 1968. 3/yr. $8. 2209 California, Berkeley, CA 94703. Ed. John Oliver Simon. circ. 1,000. Indexed: ACCESS.

821 UK ISSN 0140-5136
ALEMBIC. 1973. irreg. $20 for 2 nos. 88 Ashburnham Rd., London NW10 5SE, England. Ed. Robert Hampson. adv.; bk.rev.; bibl.; circ. 200. (back issues avail.)

808.81 UA
ALIF; journal of comparative poetics. (Text in Arabic, English; occasionally in French) 1981. a. $15 to individuals; institutions $30. American University in Cairo, Department of English and Comparative Literature, P.O. Box 2511, Cairo, Egypt. FAX 355-7565. TELEX 92224 AUCAI UN. Ed. Ferial Ghazoul. adv.; circ. 500. (back issues avail.) Indexed: Mid.East: Abstr.& Ind.
Description: Each issue focuses on a specific theme; responses are articulated by writers in different disciplines and cultures.

851 IT
ALIGHIERI. s-a. Piazza Sonnino, 5, Rome, Italy. Ed. A. Vallone. Indexed: M.L.A.

ALL AREA. see *ART*

811 US
ALL AVAILABLE LIGHT. 1989. 2/yr. $6. McOne Press, Box 50174, Austin, TX 78763. Ed. Jason Freeman. circ. 200.
Description: Publishes poems that don't shout their spiritual content, but whisper through language, sound and rhythm.

821 UK
ALL IN; wallstickers. (Poster format) 1968. s-a. £1. c/o Nina Steane, Ed., 31 Headlands, Kettering, Northants., England. circ. 50.

831 053 GW ISSN 0720-3098
PT1141.A2
ALLMENDE. 1981. q. DM.53. Elster Verlag, Schillerstr. 7, 7570 Baden-Baden, Germany. TEL 07221-29590. FAX 07221-25973. Ed.Bd. adv.; index; circ. 3,000. (back issues avail.)

ALPHA BEAT SOUP. see *LITERATURE*

811 US
THE ALTERED MIND. 1989. 6/yr. $8. Box 1083, Claremont, CA 91711. TEL 714-949-9531. circ. 800.

811 700 US
ALTERNATIVE PRESS.* 1969. 3/yr. $15. 1207 Henry St., Ann Arbor, MI 48104-4340. Eds. Ann Mikolowski, Ken Mikolowski.

811 US
AMANITA BRANDY. 1980. 4/yr. $6. W. Paul Ganley, Ed. & Pub., Box 149, Amherst Branch, Buffalo, NY 14226-0149. TEL 716-839-2415. circ. 150.

811 US ISSN 1043-8947
AMARANTH REVIEW. 1989. s-a. $10. Window Publications, Box 56325, Phoenix, AZ 85079. TEL 602-527-8085. Ed. Dana L. Yost. adv.; bk.rev.; circ. 1,500. (back issues avail.)

811 US
AMERICAN COLLEGIATE POETS. 1975. 2/yr. $12.50. International Publications, Box 44044-L, Los Angeles, CA 90044. TEL 213-755-1814. circ. 500.

808 US ISSN 1051-5062
▼**AMERICAN LITERARY REVIEW.** 1990. s-a. $10. University of North Texas, Box 13615, Denton, TX 76203. Ed. J.F. Kobler.
Description: Publishes previously unpublished poems and short stories in English, representative of all states and both American continents.

AMERICAN OXONIAN. see *LITERARY AND POLITICAL REVIEWS*

811 US ISSN 0095-1684
PS301
AMERICAN POETRY AND POETICS. 1974. q. $9. Box 348, 218 S. Egan Ave., Madison, SD 57042. Eds. L. Eric Johnson, Oliver H. Evans. bk.rev.

811 US
AMERICAN POETRY ANTHOLOGY.* 1981. irreg. (3-4/yr.). $40. American Poetry Association, Box 51007, Seattle, WA 98115-1007. Ed. John Frost. circ. 10,000.

800 US ISSN 0360-3709
PS580
AMERICAN POETRY REVIEW (PHILADELPHIA). 1972. bi-m. $14. World Poetry, Inc., 1721 Walnut St., Philadelphia, PA 19103. TEL 215-496-0439. Ed. David Bonanno. adv.; bk.rev.; play rev.; illus.; circ. 24,000. (tabloid format; also avail. in microfilm from UMI; reprint service avail. from UMI) Indexed: A.I.P.P., Amer.Hum.Ind., Arts & Hum.Cit.Ind., Bk.Rev.Ind. (1976-), Child.Bk.Rev.Ind. (1976-), Curr.Cont., Ind.Bk.Rev.Hum., M.L.A., New Per.Ind.

811 US
AMERICAN POETRY SERIES. 1973. irreg. price varies. Ecco Press Ltd., 100 W. Broad St., Hopewell, NJ 08525. TEL 509-466-4748. FAX 609-466-4706.

811 US
AMERICAS REVIEW. 1985. a. $4 to individuals; institutions $6. Box 7681, Berkeley, CA 94707. TEL 415-845-2089. Ed. Gerald Gray. circ. 1,000.
Description: Publishes poems of a political nature. Also sponsors a contest.

821 UK ISSN 0951-2500
AMMONITE. 1986. irreg. £3. Ammonite Publications, 12 Priory Mead, Bruton, Somerset BA10 0DZ, England. TEL 813349. Ed. John Howard Greaves. adv.; bk.rev.; circ. 100. (back issues avail.)
Description: Poetry, prose and artwork toward the second millenium.

808.81 US
THE AND REVIEW. 1989. 2/yr. $5. 10485 Iams Rd., Plain City, OH 43064. bk.rev.

LITERATURE — POETRY

808.81 US
ANDROGYNE; a rebus of poetry, fiction & graphic art. 1971. a. $4. Androgyne Books, 930 Shields St., San Francisco, CA 94132. Ed. Ken Weichel. adv.; bk.rev.; circ. 500. (back issues avail.)

811 US
ANIMAL TALES. 1989. 6/yr. $19.95. Box 2220, Payson, AZ 85547-2220. Ed. Berta I. Cellers.

811 US
▼**ANT FARM.** 1990. 2/yr. $8. Box 15513, Santa Fe, NM 87506. TEL 506-473-0290. Ed. Kate Bremer. circ. 250.
   Description: Publishes poems of four lines or less.

811 US
ANT SPOIM - SMASH APATHY. 1981. 2/yr. free. Box 1216, Fairlawn, NJ 07410. circ. 300.

811 US
ANTI-ISOLATION; new arts in Wisconsin. 1984. irreg. 1341 Williamson, Madison, WI 53703. Eds. Miekal and Elizabeth Was. circ. 1,000.
   Description: Seeks innovative poetry, audio and visual arts.

ANTIETAM REVIEW. see LITERATURE

861 AG
ANTOLOGIA POETICA DEL PARTIDO DE ESTEBAN ECHEVERRIA. 1979. a. Arg.$10000. (Asociacion de Artes y Letras de Esteban Echeverria) Ediciones Agon, Charcas 3918, 1425 Buenos Aires, Argentina. Dir. Maria E. Dubecq.

849.9 SP
ANUARI VERDAGUER; estudis textos ressenyes bibliografia cronica. (Text in Catalan) 1987. a. 2500 ptas. (typically set in Jan.). (Escola Universitaria de Mestres d'Osona) E U M O Editorial, S.A., C. de Miramarges s-n, 08500 Vic, Spain. TEL 93-8860794. FAX 3-8891063. Ed.Bd. bk.rev.

861 CK
AQUARIMANTIMA. 1973. irreg. Apdo. Aereo 3845, Medellin, Colombia.

861 AG
AQUARIO; revista internacional de poesia. 1977. irreg. $2.50. Aquario, Paraguay 647, Buenos Aires, Argentina. Eds. Sergio Chaves, Sigfrido Radaelli.

821 UK ISSN 0003-7303
PR1170
AQUARIUS; poetry magazine. 1968. q. £3($40) c/o Eddie S. Linden, Ed., 116 Sutherland Ave., Flat 10 - Rm. A, London W.9., England. TEL 071-289-4338. adv.; bk.rev.; circ. 3,000.
   Description: Each issue focuses on one of England's great poets.

811 US
AQUATERRA, WATER CONCEPTS FOR THE ECOLOGICAL SOCIETY. 1986. 2/yr. $10. Route 3, Box 720, Eureka Springs, AR 72632. Ed. Jacqui Froelich. circ. 3,000.
   Description: Publishes poems on the theme of water and water related subjects.

811 US
ARACHNE. 1979. q. $18 to individuals; institutions $20. Arachne, Inc., 162 Sturges St., Jamestown, NY 14701. TEL 716-488-0417. Ed. Susan L. Leach. bk.rev.; circ. 500. (back issues avail.)

ARC. see LITERATURE

808.81 US
ARCHIVE FOR NEW POETRY NEWSLETTER. 1978. 3/yr. free. (Archive for New Poetry) University of California, San Diego, Central University Library, La Jolla, CA 92093-0175. TEL 619-534-2533. Ed. Bett Miller. bk.rev.; circ. 400.
   Description: Reports on the archive's acquisitions. Includes poetry.

808.8 US ISSN 0883-9824
ARGONAUT. 1972. a. $5 (Canada $6; elsewhere $7.50)(effective Jan. 1991). Argo Press, Box 4201, Austin, TX 78765-4201. Ed. Michael E. Ambrose. adv.; illus.; circ. 500.
   Description: Presents anthology of weird fantasy and science fiction.

808.1 FR ISSN 0066-734X
ARGUS DE LA POESIE FRANCAISE.* 1971. irreg. 30 F. Association Poesie Vivante France, B.P.8, 01210 Ferney-Voltaire, France.

811 CN
ARIEL; a review of international English literature. 1970. 4/yr. Can.$14 to individuals; institutions Can.$22. University of Calgary Press, Calgary, Alta. T2N 1N4, Canada. TEL 403-220-4657. Ed. V.J. Ramraj. circ. 925.
   Description: Publishes new poems.

811 US
THE ARK (CAMBRIDGE). 1970. a. $5. Ark, 35 Highland Ave., Cambridge, MA 02139-1015. TEL 617-547-0852. Ed. Geoffrey Gardner. circ. 1,500.
   Description: Publishes poems including translations.

ARSENAL; surrealist subversion. see ART

ARSENALE; trimestrale di letteratura. see LITERATURE

ART AND POETRY TODAY. see ART

ART ET POESIE. see ART

808.81 700 US
ARTEMIS - ARTISTS AND WRITERS; artists and writers from the Blue Ridge Mountains. 1977. a. $8. Artemis - Artists and Writers, Inc., Box 8147, Roanoke, VA 24014. TEL 703-774-8440. FAX 703-344-7485. Ed.Bd. circ. 1,200.
   Formerly: Artemis.

811 US
ASH. 1989. 4/yr. $4. 121 Gregory Ave., No. B-7, Passaic, NJ 07055. TEL 201-471-8378. circ. 125.

861 US
ASOCIACION DE HISPANISTAS DE LAS AMERICAS. COLECCION MONOGRAFIAS. 1981. irreg., no.3, 1987. $3. Asociacion de Hispanistas de las Americas, 3600 S.W. 9th Terrace, Apt. 4, Miami, FL 33135. Ed. Gladys Zaldivar. circ. 500.
   Formerly: Coleccion Vortex (ISSN 0277-6782)

808.81 US ISSN 0896-1344
ASYLUM. 1985. s-a. $10 to individuals (foreign $12); institutions $15 (foreign $17). Asylum Arts Publishing, Box 6203, Santa Maria, CA 93456. TEL 805-928-8774. Ed. Greg Boyd. adv.; bk.rev.; circ. 700.
   Description: Publishes original short stories and poetry, with an emphasis on dream and fantasy.

808.81 700 US
ATTICUS REVIEW; a journal of experimental poetry, fiction, graphics and criticism. 1983. s-a. $8. Atticus Press, Box 927428, San Diego, CA 92192. TEL 691-357-5512. Ed. Harry Polkinhorn. circ. 125.

811 US
AVALON DISPATCH. irreg. (3-4/yr.). membership. (Avalon Poets) Vernon Payne, Ed. & Pub., 212 W. First St., San Angelo, TX 76901. circ. 500.

861 VE ISSN 0005-2426
AXIAL;* revista de poesia. 1966. q. Bs.1($1) (Grupo Literario Axial) Editorial Axial, Apartado Postal 62, Merida, Venezuela. Ed. Lubio Cardozo. bk.rev.; bibl.; illus.; circ. 1,000(controlled).

B-CITY. see LITERATURE

811 US
BABY SUE. 1985. 2/yr. $8. Box 1111, Decatur, GA 30031. TEL 404-875-8951. Ed. Don W. Seven. circ. 5,000.

808.81 US
BACKBOARD. 1976. irreg. free. Backspace Ink, 1131 Galvez Dr., Pacifica, CA 94044. TEL 415-355-4640. Ed. Joanne Shwed. circ. 200. (back issues avail.)

BAD HAIRCUT. see POLITICAL SCIENCE

811 US
BAD HENRY REVIEW. 1981. s-a. $12. 44 Press, Box 150045, Van Brunt Sta., Brooklyn, NY 11215-0001. Ed.Bd. adv.; bk.rev.; circ. 750.

811 SP
BAHIA; pliegos poeticos del campo de Gibraltar. 1967. 8/yr. 375 ptas. Ediciones Bahia, Fray Bartolome Bloque 1, 6-A, Algeciras, Cadiz, Spain. Dir. Manuel Fernandez Mota. bibl.; circ. 500.

800 700 US ISSN 1052-3154
▼**BAKUNIN.** 1990. s-a. $12 to individuals; institutions $16. Box 1853, Simi Valley, CA 93062. TEL 818-991-2900. Ed. Jordan Jones. adv.; bk.rev.; illus.
   Description: For the dead Russian anarchist in all of us. Includes poetry, fiction, art, essays, plays, and reviews.

811 CN ISSN 0005-4399
BALLSOUT.* 1969. $3. Pendejo Press, 3358 W. First Ave., Vancouver, B.C., Canada. Ed. Bertram Maird. illus.

811 CN
BARBIZON MAGAZINE. 1983. 8/yr. $15. Barbizon House, R.R. 1, Lumby, B.C. V0E 2G0, Canada. TEL 604-547-6621. circ. 2,500.

BARE NIBS. see THEATER

811 US
BASEBALL: OUR WAY. 1984. 10/yr. $9. Our Way Publications, 5014 Starker Ave., Madison, WI 53716. TEL 608-241-0549. Ed. Dale Jellings. circ. 50.

808.81 US
▼**BE SOMEBODY, BE YOURSELF LETTER**; greetings update. 1992. a. $5 (Canada $7; elsewhere $8). Continnuus, c/o Prosperity & Profits Unlimited, Box 570213, Houston, TX 77257. TEL 713-867-3438. Ed.Bd.

821 UK
BEAT SCENE. 1988. 7/yr. $24 for 4 issues. Beat Scene Press, 27 Court Leet, Binley Woods, Coventry, Warwickshire CV3 2JO, England. TEL 0202-543604. circ. 200.

811 US ISSN 0005-8661
PS301
BELOIT POETRY JOURNAL. (Supplement avail.: Beloit Poetry Journal. Chapbook) 1950. q. $8 to individuals; institutions $12. Beloit Poetry Journal Foundation, Inc., Box 154, R.F.D. 2, Ellsworth, ME 04605. TEL 207-667-5598. Ed. Marion K. Stocking. bk.rev.; cum.index: 1950-1975; circ. 1,200. (back issues avail.) Indexed: Amer.Hum.Ind., Arts & Hum.Cit.Ind., Curr.Cont., Ind.Amer.Per.Verse, Ind.Little Mag.
   Description: Introduces strong new writers. Includes occasional chapbooks.

811 US ISSN 0067-5695
BELOIT POETRY JOURNAL. CHAPBOOK. (Included in Beloit Poetry Journal) 1951. irreg., vol.40, 1990 (approx. biennial). $5. Beloit Poetry Journal Foundation, Inc., Box 154, R.F.D. 2, Ellsworth, ME 04605. TEL 207-667-5598. Ed. Marion K. Stocking. bk.rev.; circ. 1,200. Indexed: Amer.Hum.Ind., Ind.Amer.Per.Verse.

808.81 II
BENGALI INTERNATIONAL.* (Text in English) 1972. bi-m. 107-2 Raja Rammohan Sarani, Calcutta 9, India. Ed. Samir De. adv.

808.81 US
BERKELEY POETRY REVIEW. 1973. s-a. $10. University of California, Berkeley, 700 Eshleman Hall, Berkeley, CA 94720. Ed. Cynthia Pierce. adv.; bk.rev.; circ. 750.
   Description: Publishes student work of national interest; regularly features Thom Gunn, Ishmael Reed, Robert Pinsky and August Kleinzahler.

861 BL
BIBLIOTECA ALFA-OMEGA DE POESIA BRASILEIRA: SERIE 1. 1983. irreg. Editora Alfa-Omega, Rua Lisboa, 489, 05413 Sao Paulo, Brazil. TEL (011) 852-6400. TELEX 22888XPSP BR.

811 US
BIG CIGARS. 1986. 2/yr. P.O.N. Press, 1625 Hobart St., N.W., Washington, DC 20009. Ed. Jose Padua. circ. 300.

LITERATURE — POETRY

811 US
BIG HAMMER. 1988. biennial. $6. Box 1698, New Brunswick, NJ 08901. TEL 908-249-2645. Ed. David Roskos. circ. 800.

BIM. see *LITERATURE*

808.81 US ISSN 1047-2258
BIRMINGHAM POETRY REVIEW. 1988. 2/yr. $3. English Department, University of Alabama, Birmingham, AL 35294. TEL 205-934-8573. Ed. Robert Collins. circ. 600. (back issues avail.)

808.81 700 US ISSN 8756-0666
BLACK BEAR REVIEW. 1985. s-a. $10. Black Bear Publications, 1916 Lincoln St., Croydon, PA 19021-8026. TEL 215-788-3543. Eds. Ave Jeanne, Ron Zettlemoyer. adv.; bk.rev.; bibl.; illus.; circ. 550.

811 US
BLACK BUZZARD REVIEW. 1988. a. $16. Black Buzzard Press, 1110 Seaton La., Falls Church, VA 22046. Ed. Bradley R. Strahan. circ. 300.
   Description: Publishes all types of poetry except typographical poems.

811 US
BLACK JACK & VALLEY GRAPEVINE. 1973. a. $4.75. Seven Buffaloes Press, Box 249, Big Timber, MT 59011. Ed. Art Cuelho. circ. 750.
   Description: Publishes rural poetry, farm and ranch, especially material from the Southern Appalachian region.

811 US
BLACK MULLET REVIEW. 1986. 2/yr. $3 per no. Jubilee Press, Box 22814, Tampa, FL 33622. circ. 250.

811 US
BLACK RIVER REVIEW. 1985. a. $3.50. 855 Mildred, Lorain, OH 44052-1213. TEL 216-244-9654. Eds. Kaye Coller, Deborah S. Glaefke. adv.; bk.rev.; circ. 400.

819 CN ISSN 0045-2270
BLACKFISH.* 1971. 3/yr. $2. 1851 Moore St., Burnaby 2, B.C., Canada. Eds. B.T. Brett, Allan Safarik. illus.

811 US
BLACKLIST. 1989. 6/yr. $3. Box 1417, Salt Lake City, UT 84110. TEL 801-972-6739. circ. 500.

808.81 700 US ISSN 0888-529X
BLADES;* a tiny magazine. (Text in English, Portuguese, Spanish) 1977. 3/yr. $2. Poporo Press, 182 Orchard Rd., Newark, DE 19711-5208. Eds. JoAnn Balingit, Francis Poole. circ. 175. (back issues avail.)
   Description: Presents poetry written in the language submitted.

811 US
▼**BLANK GUN SILENCE.** 1991. 3/yr. $6. 1240 William St., Racine, WI 53402. TEL 414-639-2406. Ed. Dan Nielsen. circ. 200.
   Description: Publishes concise, tight and startling poems.

808.81 US ISSN 0737-9269
PS615
BLIND ALLEYS; a journal of contemporary poetry. 1982. s-a. $11 to individuals; institutions $13. 7th Son Press, Rutgers University, Box 29, Camden, NJ 08102. TEL 609-757-6117. Ed. Michael S. Weaver. adv.; bk.rev.; circ. 300.

800 US
BLUE BUILDINGS. 1979. irreg. (1-2/yr.). $8 per no. 1215 25th St., Apt. F, Des Moines, IA 50311-3005. TEL 515-277-4298. Ed.Bd. circ. 500.

811 US
BLUE GUITAR. 1989. 4/yr. $12. 3022 North 5th St., Harrisburg, PA 17110. circ. 300.

811 US
BLUE PIG.* 1968. irreg. $5. 23 Cedar St., Northampton, MA 01060. circ. 250.

811 770 US ISSN 0886-4187
BLUE PITCHER;* a biannual magazine of poetry and photography. 1986. s-a. $7.50 for 2 yrs. Unicorn Press, Inc., 200 E. Bessemer Ave, Greensboro, NC 27401-1416. TEL 919-852-0281. Ed. Sarah Lindsay. adv.; circ. 1,000(controlled).

811 US ISSN 0197-7016
PS580
BLUE UNICORN; a tri-quarterly of poetry. 1977. 3/yr. $14 (foreign $18). Blue Unicorn, Inc., 22 Avon Rd., Kensington, CA 94707. TEL 510-526-8439. Ed.Bd. circ. 500. **Indexed:** A.I.P.P.

810 820 US ISSN 0882-648X
BOGG; a journal of North American and British poetry, prose poems, reviews, and essays on small press publishing. 1968. irreg. (2-3/yr.). $12 for 3 nos. Bogg Publications, 422 N. Cleveland St., Arlington, VA 22201. TEL 703-243-6019. (U.K. subscr. to: 31, Belle Vue St., Filey, North Yorkshire YO14 9HU) Eds. John Elsberg, George Cairncross. bk.rev.; circ. 750 (controlled). (back issues avail.) **Indexed:** Ind.Amer.Per.Verse.

811 US
BOLD PRINT. 1982. a. $3. 2211 Stuart Ave., 1st Fl., Richmond, VA 23220. Ed. Kyle Hogg.

808.81 US
BONE & FLESH. 1988. a. $7. Bone & Flesh Publications, Box 349, Concord, NH 03302. Ed. Lester Hirsh. circ. 199. (back issues avail.)

BOOKENDS. see *LIBRARY AND INFORMATION SCIENCES*

808.8 US
▼**BORDERLANDS.** 1992. 2/yr. Borderlands, Box 49818, Austin, TX 78765. Ed.Bd. bk.rev.
   Description: Poetry and essays acknowledging historical, political, social and spiritual connection.

821 CN
BOREAL INTERNATIONAL; poesia Espanola en el Canada. (Text in Spanish) 1976. 2/yr. Can.$2. Box 262, Victoria Station, Montreal, Que., Canada. Ed. Manuel Betanzos-Santos. bibl.; illus.
   Supersedes: Boreal (ISSN 0006-7717)

BOTTOM LINE PUBLICATIONS. see *LITERARY AND POLITICAL REVIEWS — Abstracting, Bibliographies, Statistics*

BOUNDARY 2; an international journal of literature and culture. see *LITERATURE*

899 KR
BOYAN. (Text in Ukrainian) 1968. s-a. 0.50 Rub. per no. Vydavnytstvo Radyanskii Pismennik, Chkalova, 52, Kiev, Ukraine. TEL 216-62-72. Ed. L. Golota. circ. 8,000.
   Formerly (until 1992): Poeziya (Kiev) (ISSN 0554-4084)

808.81 UK
BRADFORD POETRY. 1982. s-a. £3. Prontaprint, 9 Woodvale Way, Bradford, West Yorkshire BD7 2SJ, England. TEL 0274-575993. Ed. Clare Chapman. circ. 200. (back issues avail.)
   Formerly: Bradford Poetry Quarterly.
   Description: Covers all types of poetry.

811 US
BRANCH REDD REVIEW. 1976. irreg. $10 per no. Branch Redd, 4805 B St., Philadelphia, PA 19120. TEL 215-324-1462. Ed. William David Sherman. circ. 400.
   Description: Publishes post-modern poetry.

BRAVE NEW WORD; contemporary Australian short stories and poetry. see *LITERATURE*

808.81 US ISSN 0275-6080
BRAVO; the poet's magazine. 1980. a. $5. Bravo Editions, c/o John Edwin Cowen, Ltd., 1081 Trafalgar St., Teaneck, NJ 07666. Ed. Jose Garcia Villa. circ. 1,000. (back issues avail.)

808.81 US
▼**THE BRIDGE (OAK PARK);** a journal of fiction and poetry. 1991. s-a. $8. 14050 Vernon St., Oak Park, MI 48237. Ed. Jack Zucker. adv.

821 CN ISSN 0382-5272
BRITISH COLUMBIA MONTHLY. 1972. irreg. (6-10/yr.). Can.$20 to individuals; institutions Can.$35. B.C. Monthly Press, Box 48884, Vancouver, B.C. V7X 1A8, Canada. Ed. Gerry Gilbert. adv.; bk.rev.; index; circ. 350.

811 US
BROKEN STREETS. 1979. q. $12. Broken Streets, 57 Morningside Dr., E., Bristol, CT 06010. Ed. Ron Grossman. adv.; circ. 100. (back issues avail.)

890 AT ISSN 0310-2467
BRONZE SWAGMAN BOOK OF BUSH VERSE. 1972. a. Aus.$8. Winton Tourist Promotion Association, Box 44, Winton, Qld. 4735, Australia. FAX 076-571502. circ. 1,500.

808 US
BROOKLYN REVIEW. 1984. a. $5. City University of New York, Brooklyn College, Department of English, Brooklyn, NY 11210.
   Formerly (until 1983): Junction Magazine.
   Description: Publishes poetry and fiction.

821 UK
BROWNING SOCIETY NOTES. 1970. 2/yr. £12.50($35) to individuals; institutions £15($40). Browning Society, c/o Michael Meredith, Ed., The Timbralls, Eton College, Windsor, Berks. SL4 6HB, England. adv.; bk.rev.; index; circ. 225. (processed; back issues avail.) **Indexed:** M.L.A.
   Description: Essays and book reviews on the lives and works of Robert Browning and Elizabeth Barrett Browning.

808.81 US ISSN 0897-7356
BRUSSELS SPROUT. 1980. 3/yr. $15 (foreign $20). Box 1551, Mercer Island, WA 98040. TEL 206-232-3239. Ed. Francine Porad. bk.rev.; circ. 300.
   Description: Journal of contemporary Haiku and art.

810 US
BURNT SIENNA. 1979. a. $2.50. Box 7495, Berkeley, CA 94707. Ed. Charles Heimler. circ. 1,000.

821 UK ISSN 0301-7257
PR4379
BYRON JOURNAL. 1973. a. £3. Byron Society Journal Ltd., 6 Gertrude St., London SW10 OJN, England. TEL 01-352 5112. Ed.Bd. adv.; bk.rev.; circ. 2,000. (back issues avail.) **Indexed:** Arts & Hum.Cit.Ind., Curr.Cont., M.L.A.
   —BLDSC shelfmark: 2941.550000.

808.81 US
C A L ANTHOLOGY. 1987. a. $12.45. (Conservatory of American Letters) Norwoods Press, Box 88, Thomaston, ME 04861. TEL 207-354-6550. Ed. Robert Olmsted. circ. 1,000.

811 CN ISSN 0702-7958
C.S.P. WORLD NEWS. 1962. m. Can.$15. Guy Claude Hamel Foundation, 1307 Bethamy Lane, Gloucester, Ont. K1J 8P3, Canada. TEL 613-741-8675. Ed. Guy F. Claude Hamel. adv.; bk.rev.; film rev. (looseleaf format)

811 US
CACANADADADA REVIEW. 1989. 2/yr. $6. Box 1283, Port Angeles, WA 98362. TEL 206-325-5541. Ed. Jack Estes. circ. 300.
   Description: Publishes experimental poetry and satire.

CAESURA MAGAZINE. see *LITERATURE*

811 US ISSN 0007-9537
CAFE SOLO. (Text mainly in English; occasionally in other languages) 1969. q. $30. (India Inc.) Solo Press, c/o Luschei, Box 2814, Atascadero, CA 93422. TEL 805-543-1058. Ed. Glenna Luschei. bk.rev.; illus.; circ. 500.

811 US
CAFETERIA. 1971. irreg. $3. Cafeteria Press, 1724 Woodland Ave., Modesto, CA 95351. TEL 209-523-8916. Eds. Gordon Preston, Rick Robbins. bk.rev.; circ. 300.

CAHIERS DE L'IROISE. see *HISTORY — History Of Europe*

CAHIERS DE POETIQUE COMPAREE. see *ORIENTAL STUDIES*

LITERATURE — POETRY

841 BE
CAHIERS NIVELLOIS. 1978. irreg. 250 Fr. Association Culturelle et Dialectale de la Region Nivelloise, Allee des Couterelles 4, 1400 Nivelles, Belgium.

841 FR
CAHIERS TRISTAN L'HERMIT. 1979. a. price varies. Rougerie Editeur, Mortemart, 87330 Mezieres-sur-Issoire, France. Ed. M. Carriat. **Indexed:** Can.Rev.Comp.Lit.

CALABRIA LETTERARIA. see *LITERATURE*

811 US ISSN 0896-6338
CALIFORNIA STATE POETRY QUARTERLY. 1973. 3/yr. membership. 1200 E. Ocean Blvd., Ste. 64, Long Beach, CA 90802. TEL 714-495-0925. Ed. John Brander. circ. 500.

800 US
CALLIOPE (BRISTOL). 1977. s-a. $5. Roger Williams College, Creative Writing Program, Bristol, RI 02809. TEL 401-254-3217. Ed. Martha Christina. circ. 300. (back issues avail.)

808.81 US ISSN 1051-1857
PN6010.5
CALYPSO;* journal of narrative poetry and poetic fiction. 1989. a. $6. c/o Susan Richardson, Ed., 1829 Arnold Way, Ste. 503, Alpine, CA 91901-3708. bk.rev.; circ. 200. (back issues avail.)
Description: Shows how characteristics of fiction stregthen poetry and vice versa.

CALYX; a journal of art & literature by women. see *ART*

821 CN ISSN 0704-5646
PR9190.2
CANADIAN POETRY (LONDON, ONT.); studies, documents, reviews. 1977. s-a. Can.$15 to individuals; institutions Can.$18. c/o Department of English, University of Western Ontario, London, Ont. N6A 3K7, Canada. TEL 519-661-3374. Ed. D.M.R. Bentley. bk.rev.; circ. 400. **Indexed:** Amer.Hum.Ind., Hum.Ind., M.L.A.
—BLDSC shelfmark: 3044.026900.
Description: Devoted to the study of Canadian poetry from all periods and regions.

821 UK
CANDELABRUM POETRY MAGAZINE. 1970. a. £12. Red Candle Press, 9 Milner Rd., Wisbech PE13 2LR, England. TEL 0945-581067. Ed. M.L. McCarthy. adv.; bk.rev.; cum.index; circ. 1,000.

811 770 US ISSN 0146-2199
CAPE ROCK; a journal of poetry. 1964. s-a. $5. Southeast Missouri State University, Department of English, Cape Girardeau, MO 63701. TEL 314-651-2500. Ed. Harvey Hecht. index; circ. 700. (back issues avail.) **Indexed:** A.I.P.P., Ind.Amer.Per.Verse.
Former titles (until 1975): Cape Rock Journal (ISSN 0008-5812); Cape Rock Quarterly.

861 AG
CAPITAL DE LA POESIA. vol.5, 1973. bi-m. Calle Libertad, Casa 16, Barrio los Olivos, Villa Dolores (CBA), Argentina. Ed.Bd.

808.81 FR ISSN 0008-6134
CARACTERES; revue internationale de poesie. (Text mainly in French; occasionally in English) 1950. irreg. 150 F. Editions Caracteres, 7 rue de l'Arbalete, 75005 Paris, France. TEL 43-37-96-98. Ed. Bruno Durocher.

CARRIONFLOWER WRIT. see *LITERATURE*

811 US
CAT FEET. 1977. s-a. $2.50. College of Notre Dame, Department of English, 1500 Ralston Ave., Belmont, CA 94002. Ed. Sylvia Rogers, M.D. bk.rev.; circ. 300. (back issues avail.)

CATALYST (SEATTLE). see *ART*

808.81 US ISSN 1058-6326
CATHARSIS. 2/yr. $10. Chips Off the Writer's Block, Box 83371, Los Angeles, CA 90083. Ed. Wanda Windham. circ. 200.
Description: Journal of poetry by beginning poets.

811 US ISSN 0883-9174
CELEBRATION. 1975. irreg., no.5, 1985. $8 for 4 nos. Prospect Press, 2707 Lawina Rd., Baltimore, MD 21216-1608. Ed. William J. Sullivan. circ. 300.

808.81 US
CENTER STAGE (MAITLAND).* m. 540 S. Maitland Ave., Maitland, FL 32751.

811 US
CENTERING. 1973. irreg. $5 per no. Years Press, ATL EBH, Michigan State University, East Lansing, MI 48824-1033. TEL 517-355-3506. Ed. F. Richard Thomas. circ. 300.
Description: Each issue focuses on either poetry, or short fiction from one author; past authors included Roger Pfingston, Stephen Dunning, Lee Upton, Dan Seiters, Leonora Smith, Alice Friman.

808.81 BE ISSN 0771-6443
CENTRE INTERNATIONAL D'ETUDES POETIQUES. COURRIER. 1954. 4/yr. 800 Fr. (effective 1992). Archives et Musee de la Litterature, Bibliotheque Royale, 4 bd. de l'Empereur, B-1000 Brussels, Belgium. TEL 519-55-80. Eds. Fernand Verhesen, Frans de Haes. adv.; bibl.; circ. 1,000.

851 IT
CERVO VOLANTE. 10/yr. L.65000. Etrusculudens, Via Bargo 39, 00166 Rome, Italy.

811 US ISSN 1046-8897
PS501
CHIRON REVIEW; a poetry journal. 1982-1988; resumed 1989. q. $8 to individuals (foreign $16); institutions $20. Chiron Review Press, 1514 Stone, Great Bend, KS 67503-4027. TEL 316-792-5025. Ed. Michael Hathaway. adv.; bk.rev.; circ. 2,000. (tabloid format; also avail. in microform from UMI; back issues avail.) **Indexed:** Amer.Hum.Ind.
Formerly (until Mar. 1989): Kindred Spirit (ISSN 0898-5502)

811 760 US
CHOICE (BINGHAMTON); a magazine of poetry and graphics. 1961. a. $5. State University of New York at Binghamton, Box Z, Binghamton, NY 13901. TEL 607-798-2000. Eds. Milton Kessler, John Logan. circ. 1,000.

811 US
▼**CHRISTIAN POET.** 1992. irreg. 2745 Monterey Hwy., No. 76, San Jose, CA 95111-3129. Ed. Richard Soos.
Description: Publishes single author collections of Christian poetry.

CHUNG-WAI LITERARY MONTHLY. see *LITERATURE*

CI KAN/VERSES. see *MUSIC*

808.81 US ISSN 0891-2386
CICADA. 1985. q. $14 (foreign $19). Amelia, 329 "E" St., Bakersfield, CA 93304. TEL 805-323-4064. Ed. Frederick A. Raborg. illus.; circ. 600.

811 US
CINCINNATI POETRY REVIEW. 1975. s-a. $3 per no. English Department, 069, University of Cincinnati, Cincinnati, OH 45221. TEL 513-556-3922. Ed. Dallas Wiebe. adv.; bibl.; circ. 1,000. (back issues avail.)
Description: Publishes original and unpublished poetry of all kinds.

811 US
CIRCLE (PORTLAND); a periodical of reversible poetry. 1975. biennial. $2 per no. Circle Forum, Box 176, Portland, OR 97207. Ed. J.M. Gates. bk.rev.; circ. controlled. **Indexed:** CERDIC.

811 UK
CIRCLE IN THE SQUARE BROADSHEET. 1966. 2/yr. 30p.($1) Bristol Arts Centre, 415 King Square, Bristol 2, England. Ed. Bill Pickard. circ. 500.
Formerly: Poetry of the Circle in the Square.

811 US
CIRCLETS; an occasional newsletter of reversible poetry. no. 4, 1977. irreg. Circle Forum, Box 176, Portland, OR 97207.

861 SP
CIRCULO POETICO; cuadernos de poesia. (Text in English, Spanish) 1970. a. $10 to individuals; institutions $25. Circulo de Cultura Panamericano, 16 Malvern Pl., Verona, NJ 07044. TEL 201-239-3125. Ed. Ana H. Raggi. illus.; circ. 800.

808.81 US
CITY LIGHTS REVIEW. 1987. a. City Lights Books, 261 Columbus Ave., San Francisco, CA 94133. TEL 415-362-1901. Eds. Lawrence Ferlinghetti, Nancy J. Peters. circ. 5,000.

841 FR
CLIVAGES. 1974. irreg., no.8, 1991. price varies. Editions Clivages, 5 rue Sainte-Anastase, 75003 Paris, France. TEL 42-72-40-02. Ed. Jean P. Leger. adv.; illus.

808.81 US
CLOUDLINE. biennial. Wind Vein Press, Box 462, Ketchum, ID 83340.

811 US
▼**COFFEEHOUSE POETS' QUARTERLY.** 1990. 4/yr. $8. Box 15123, San Luis Obispo, CA 93406. TEL 805-541-4553. Ed. Ray Foreman. circ. 300.
Description: Publishes poems of everyday experience and psychological penetration and insight.

811 US
▼**COKEFISH.** 1990. m. $17. Ana Pine, Ed. & Pub., Box 683, Long Valley, NJ 07853. TEL 908-876-3824. circ. 150.

861 PO
COLECCAO FORMA. irreg., no.16, 1983. Editorial Presenca, Lda., Rua Augusto Gil, 35-A, 1000 Lisbon, Portugal.

869 PO
COLECCAO: POESIA (LISBON). 1982. irreg. Edicoes CASO, R. Cons. A. Pedroso, 59-2 E, Lisbon, Portugal.

869 PO
COLECCAO POESIA (PORTO). 1979. irreg., no.18, 1991. price varies. Edicoes Afrontamento, Lda., Rua de Costa Cabral, 859, Apdo. 2009, 4201 Porto Codex, Portugal. TEL 489271. FAX 491777.

861 SP
COLECCION "BAHIA". irreg., no.10, 1979. Ediciones Bahia, Fray Bartolome Bloque 1, Algeciras, Spain. Ed. Manual Fernandez Mota. circ. 700.

861 SP
COLECCION PENTESILEA. 1978. irreg. Ediciones Caballo Griego para la Poesia, Bolonia 3, Madrid 28, Spain. Ed. Maya Smerdou Altolaguirre.

861 AG
COLECCION POESIA DEL NUEVO TIEMPO. no.3, 1976. irreg. Ediciones Tres Tiempos, Av. Belgrano 225, Buenos Aires, Argentina. Ed. Sigfrido Radaelli. illus.

861 MX
COLECCION SIGNO Y SOCIEDAD. irreg., no.4, 1980. Universidad Autonoma de Puebla, 4 Sur 104, Puebla, Mexico.

851 IT
COLLANA DI POESIA. 1974; N.S. 1977. irreg., no.26, 1981. price varies. Societa Editrice Napoletana s.r.l., Corso Umberto I 34, 80138 Naples, Italy. Ed. Domenico Rea.

810 US
▼**COLOR WHEEL.** 1990. 2/yr. $8. 700 Elves Press, 4 Washington Court, Concord, NH 03301. Eds. William Szostak, Frederick Moe. circ. 300.
Description: Publishes mildly experimental poems and long poems.

COLUMBIA: A MAGAZINE OF POETRY AND PROSE. see *LITERATURE*

811 US ISSN 0887-1612
CONDITIONED RESPONSE. 1982. s-a. $6 for 3 nos. Conditioned Response Press, Box 3816, Ventura, CA 93006. Ed. John McKinley. bk.rev.; circ. 200. (back issues avail.)

CONFRONTATION; a literary journal of Long Island University. see *LITERATURE*

808.81 792   US   ISSN 0277-7770
CONNECTICUT POETRY REVIEW. 1981. a. $3. Box 3783, New Haven, CT 06525. Eds. J. Claire White, James Wm. Chichetto. bk.rev.; circ. 500. (back issues avail.) **Indexed:** Amer.Hum.Ind., Ind.Amer.Per.Verse.
   Description: Works by noted poets, with each issue focusing on a review of or interview with a noted author.

811   US   ISSN 0897-0998
CONNECTICUT RIVER REVIEW; a national journal of poetry. 1978. s-a. $10. Connecticut Poetry Society, Inc., Box 2171, Bridgeport, CT 06608. TEL 203-753-7815. Ed. Robert M. Isaacs. circ. 600. (back issues avail.) **Indexed:** Amer.Hum.Ind.

808.81   CN
CONSPIRACY OF SILENCE.* 2/yr. 30 Charles St. W., Ste. 1420, Toronto, Ont. M4Y 1R5, Canada.

811   US   ISSN 0197-6796
PS615
CONTACT 2; a poetry review. 1976. s-a. $10 to individuals; institutions $16. Contact II Publications, Box 451, Bowling Green Sta., New York, NY 10004. TEL 212-674-0911. Eds. Maurice Kenny, J.G. Gosciak. adv.; bk.rev.; bibl.; illus.; circ. 2,000. (back issues avail.) **Indexed:** A.I.P.P., Access, Amer.Hum.Ind., Ind.Amer.Per.Verse.
   Formerly: Contact; **Supersedes:** Dodeca.

811   US
CONTEMPORARY POETRY SERIES. 1969. 4/yr. price varies. University of Georgia Press, Athens, GA 30602. TEL 404-542-2830. FAX 404-542-0601.

811   CN   ISSN 0831-9502
PR9195.1
CONTEMPORARY VERSE TWO; a magazine of Canadian poetry and criticism. 1975. q. Can.$18 to individuals; institutions Can.$24. P.O. Box 3062, Winnipeg, Man. R3C 4E5, Canada. TEL 204-949-0511. Ed.Bd. adv.; bk.rev.; circ. 700. **Indexed:** Ind.Bk.Rev.Hum.
   Formerly (until 1985): C V 2 (ISSN 0319-6879)
   Description: Feminist poetry journal that intends to promote, strengthen and unify women.

808.81   US   ISSN 1045-2265
CONTEXT SOUTH. 1961. s-a. $10. Context South Foundation, c/o David Breeden, Ed., Box 4504, 2100 Memorial Blvd., Kerrville, TX 78028-5611. TEL 501-972-6095. adv.; bk.rev.; film rev.; circ. 500. (back issues avail.)
   Former titles (until 1989): Dasein (ISSN 0011-6807); (until 1987): Nycticorax.

851   IT
COOPERATIVA ANTIGRUPPO SICILIANO. 1968. 3/yr. $15. Cooperativa Editrice Antigruppo Siciliano, Villa Schammachanat, Via Argentaria Km 4, Trapani, Sicily, Italy. TEL 0923-38681. (Co-publisher: Cross-Cultural Communications) Ed. Ignazio Navarra. circ. 1,000.

861   AG   ISSN 0010-8766
CORMORAN Y DELFIN; revista planetaria de poesia. 1963. q. $4. F.F. Amador, 1805, Olivos, Buenos Aires, Argentina. Ed. Ariel Canzani. cum.index.

808.81   US
CORRIDORS.* 1979. Detroit Writer's Guild, c/o Anthony Ambrogio, 820 Notre Dame St., Grosse Pointe, MI 48230-1242. Ed. Jane Dobija. (back issues avail.)
   Description: Contains contemporary poetry and fiction by Detroit area writers.

811   US
CORVALLIS STREETS POETRY MAGAZINE. 1989. q? $24. Box 2291, Corvallis, OR 97339. TEL 503-758-8244. circ. 3,000.

811   US
COYDOG REVIEW. 1984. a. $5. Box 2608, Aptos, CA 95001. TEL 408-761-1824. Ed. Candida Lawrence. circ. 300.
   Description: Publishes poems.

811   US
CRAMPED AND WET. 1988. 4/yr. $1.50 per no. 1012 29th, Sioux City, IA 51104. circ. 150.

808.81   US
CRAWLSPACE.* 1980. s-a. $3. Crawlspace Press, c/o Dennis Gulling, Ed., 826 N. 1st St., Rockford, IL 61107. circ. 150. (back issues avail.)

811   US
CREATIVE MOMENT WORLD POETRY AND CRITICISM;* a semi-annual of creative writing and criticism. 1972. s-a. $4. Poetry Eastwest Publications, 790 Mckay St., Sumter, SC 29150-3217. Ed. Syed Amanuddin. adv.; bk.rev.; circ. 300. (also avail. in microfilm from UMI; back issues avail.; reprint service avail. from UMI) **Indexed:** Abstr.Engl.Stud., M.L.A.
   Former titles (until 1976): Creative Moment and Poetry Eastwest; (until 1975): Creative Moment (ISSN 0045-897X)

811   US   ISSN 0011-0930
Discard
CREATIVE WRITING. vol.30, 1979. bi-m. $7. National Poetry Press, Box 218, Agoura, CA 91301. TEL 818-889-7477. Ed. R. Lott. bk.rev.; circ. 500.

CRISI E LETTERATURA; periodico di lettere filosofia arti. see LITERATURE

861 860   FR   ISSN 0247-381X
CRITICON. (Text in Spanish) 1978. 3/yr. 180 F. (effective 1992). (Universite de Toulouse-Le Mirail, France-Iberie Recherche) Presses Universitaires du Mirail, 56 rue du Taur, 31000 Toulouse, France. TEL 61-22-58-31. FAX 61-21-84-20. Ed. Robert Jammes. adv.; bk.rev.; circ. 500. **Indexed:** M.L.A. —BLDSC shelfmark: 3487.489100.

811   US
CROOKED ROADS. 1989. 3/yr. $5. Wheel of Fire Press, Box 32631, Kansas City, MO 64111. circ. 180.

808.81   US   ISSN 0896-4610
CROSS-BIAS; the newsletter of the friends of Bemerton honoring George Herbert 1593-1633. 1975. a. $5. Friends of Bemerton, English Department, c/o Edmund Miller, Ed., English Dept., C.W. Post Campus, Long Island University, Greenvale, NY 11548-0570. TEL 516-299-2391. bibl.; charts; circ. 450. (back issues avail.)
   Description: For scholars interested in George Herbert and seventeeth-century English literature.

811   US   ISSN 0318-6075
CROSS COUNTRY;* magazine of Canadian-U.S. poetry. 1974. 3/yr. $7.50. Cross Country Press, 32 Haviland Rd., Ridgefield, CT 06877. (Can. address: 27 Tunstall, Senneville, Que. H9X 1T3) Ed.Bd. adv.; bk.rev.; illus. circ. 500. **Indexed:** Amer.Hum.Ind.

▼**CROTON BUG.** 1991. 4/yr. Box 11166, Milwaukee, WI 53211. TEL 414-374-0625. Ed. R.A. Melendez. illus.

808.81   DR   ISSN 0257-6457
CUADERNOS DE POETICA. 1983. 3/yr. RD.$45($25) to individuals; institutions RD.$75($30). Editora Alfa y Omega, Apartado Postal 1736, Santo Domingo, Dominican Republic. Ed. Diogenes Cespedes. adv.; bk.rev.; circ. 1,000.
   Description: Dedicated to poetical theory, literary criticism, linguistics and literary creation.

861   PE   ISSN 0011-2550
PQ8450
CUADERNOS TRIMESTRALES DE POESIA. 1951. q. Grupo Poesia, Casilla 151, Trujillo, Peru. circ. 1,000.

▼**CULTURE CONCRETE.** 1990. 4/yr. $16. 2141-C Mission St., Ste. 305, San Francisco, CA 94110-9839. TEL 415-285-4286. Ed. Dave Hayman. circ. 14,000.

808.81   US   ISSN 0731-7980
PS580
CUMBERLAND POETRY REVIEW. 1981. s-a. $14 to individuals; institutions $17 (foreign $23). Poetics, Inc., Box 120128, Acklen Sta., Nashville, TN 37212. Ed.Bd. circ. 500. (back issues avail.) **Indexed:** A.I.P.P., Ind.Amer.Per.Verse. —BLDSC shelfmark: 3491.812000.
   Description: Devoted to poetry and poetry criticism. Presents poets of diverse origins for a varied audience.

811   US
▼**CURLEY.** 1990. 4/yr. $8. Box 23521, Providence, RI 02903.

811   US   ISSN 0734-9963
PS501
CUTBANK. 1973. 2/yr. $12. University of Montana, Associated Students, Department of English, Missoula, MT 59812. TEL 406-243-0211. Ed. Dennis Held. adv.; bk.rev.; circ. 400. (back issues avail.) **Indexed:** A.I.P.P., ACCESS, Ind.Amer.Per.Verse, Ind.Little Mag.
   Description: National literary magazine with a Montana focus that inlcudes poetry, ficition, plus black-and-white art.

821   UK
CYFRES BARDDONIAETH PWYLLGOR CYFIEITHIADAU YR ACADEMI. (Text in Welsh) 1980. irreg. price varies. (Welsh Academy) University of Wales Press, 6 Gwennyth St., Cathays, Cardiff CF2 4YD, Wales. TEL 0222-231919. FAX 0222-230908.
   Description: Translations of poetry from many languages (Polish, Irish, Chinese and French) into Welsh.

821   CN
DANDELION. 1975. s-a. $10. Alexandra Centre, 922 9th Ave. S.E., Calgary, Alta. T2G 0S4, Canada. Ed. Chris Horgan. adv.; bk.rev.; circ. 800.

839   DK   ISSN 0107-4431
DANSK DIGTREGISTER. 1981. a. DKK 1784. Bibliotekscentralen, Tempovej 7-11, DK-2750 Ballerup, Denmark. TEL 2-974000. FAX 2-655310.
   Formerly: Dansk Digtkatalog.

DARK WINDS; decadence fantasy magazine. see LITERATURE

811   US
▼**DEAD BEAT POET PRODUCTION.** 1990. 6/yr. 500 North River Oaks, Indialantic, FL 32903. TEL 407-952-0563. circ. 100.

811   US
DEANOTATIONS. 1984. 6/yr. $10. 11919 Moss Point Lane, Reston, VA 22094. Ed. Dean Blehert. circ. 2,800.
   Description: Contains original short, humorous poems.

811   US
DESDE ESTE LADO/FROM THIS SIDE. 1987. a. $10. Box 18458, Philadelphia, PA 19120. circ. 700.

DEUTSCHE BIBLIOTHEK. see LITERATURE

811   US
DEVIL'S MILLHOPPER. 1976. s-a. $5. Devil's Millhopper Press, College of Humanities, University of South Carolina at Aiken, 171 University Parkway, Aiken, SC 29801. TEL 803-648-6851. Ed. Stephen Gardner. adv.; circ. 500. (back issues avail.)

811   US
DIAL-A-POEM POETS. 1971. 4/yr. $8.98. Giorno Poetry Systems Institute, Inc., 222 Bowery, New York, NY 10012. TEL 212-925-6372. FAX 212-966-7574. Ed. John Giorno. circ. 10,000. (record; also avail. in audio cassette; video cassette; also avail. on compact disc)

821   II
DIALOGUE INDIA;* Indian poetry review. (Text in English) 6/yr. Rs.50. Dialogue Publications, 5 Pearl Rd., Calcutta 17, India. Ed. Pritish Nandy. bk.rev.; illus. (back issues avail.)
   Formerly: Dialogue Calcutta (ISSN 0012-2270)

811   US
DIAMOND HITCHHIKER COBWEBS. 1986. 6/yr. Nuclear Trenchcoated Subway Prophets Publications, 118 E. Goodheart Ave., Lake Mary, FL 32746. circ. 500.

811   US   ISSN 0046-0222
PS501
DIANA'S BIMONTHLY.* Variant title: Diana's Bimonthly Almanac. 1972. s-a. $6. Diana's Cards - Press, 10 Johnson Rd., Foster, RI 02825. Ed. Tom Ahern. circ. 2,000.

DICHTER UND ZEICHNER. see ART

LITERATURE — POETRY

811 US ISSN 0164-1492
Z8230.5
DICKINSON STUDIES. 1968. s-a. $100 for 3 yrs. (Dickinson-Higginson Society) Dickinson-Higginson Press, 1330 Massachusetts Ave. NW, No. 503, Washington, DC 20005-4150. Ed. Frederick L. Morey. adv.; bk.rev.; bibl.; illus.; cum.index; circ. 250. (reprint service avail. from UMI,ISI) **Indexed:** Arts & Hum.Cit.Ind., Curr.Cont., M.L.A.
Formerly: Emily Dickinson Bulletin (ISSN 0046-1881)

808.81 II
DIPAVALI. (Text in Marathi) vol.33, 1977. a. Rs.25. Ravindra Kesava Kothavale, 316 Prasad Chambers, Bombay 400 004, India. TEL 8112044. Ed. Ashok Kothavale. adv.; circ. 10,000.

811 US ISSN 0734-0605
PS129
DIRECTORY OF AMERICAN POETS AND FICTION WRITERS. 1973. biennial. $23.95 to individuals; institutions $25.95. Poets & Writers, Inc., 72 Spring St., New York, NY 10012. TEL 212-226-3586. FAX 212-226-3963. **Indexed:** Child.Auth.& Illus.
Formed by the merger of: Directory of American Poets; Directory of American Fiction Writers.
Description: Reference for publishers, administrators, agents and others who need access to writers. Lists names and addresses of over 6,800 poets and fiction writers who publish their work in the U.S., with information on each author's publications.

808.81 US
DIRECTORY OF LITERARY MAGAZINES. 1981. a. $12.95. Council of Literary Magazines and Presses, 154 Christopher St., Ste. 3C, New York, NY 10014-2839. TEL 212-741-9043. index; circ. 3,500.

808.81 070.5 US
DIRECTORY OF POETRY PUBLISHERS. a. $15.95. Dustbooks, Box 100, Paradise, CA 95967. TEL 916-877-6110. circ. 2,000.
Description: Lists poetry publishers worldwide including full data concerning each one.

DISCRETE EPHEMERA. see ART

811 US ISSN 0749-260X
DOG RIVER REVIEW. 1982. s-a. $7. Trout Creek Press, 5976 Billings Rd., Parkdale, OR 97041. TEL 503-352-6494. Ed. Laurence F. Hawkins, Jr. bk.rev.; circ. 300.

811 US
DOLPHIN-MOON PRESS "SIGNATURES" SERIES. 1985. s-a. $10. Dolphin-Moon Press, Box 22262, Baltimore, MD 21203. circ. 1,000.
Supersedes (1973-1985): Atlantic Triannual; Caim.
Description: Poetry sampling of established and new writers.

811 US
▼**DRAGONFANG.** 1990. 2/yr. $8 for 3 issues. 9047 South River Rd., Waterville, OH 43566. TEL 419-878-7246. circ. 150.

811 US ISSN 0364-359X
PS593.H3
DRAGONFLY; east-west haiku quarterly. 1965. q. $12. Middlewood Press, Box 11236, Salt Lake City, UT 84147-0236. Ed. Richard E. Tice. bk.rev.; circ. 400. (processed)
Formerly: Haiku Highlights (ISSN 0017-6664)
Description: Presents English haiku, translations of Japanese haiku, and articles about haiku.

DREAM JOURNAL.* q. $9. 1508 Taylor St. No. 4, San Francisco, CA 94133.

811 US ISSN 0897-0238
DREAMS AND NIGHTMARES. 1986. irreg. (approx. q.). $5 for 4 nos. David C. Kopaska-Merkel, Ed. & Pub., 1300 Kicker Rd., Tuscaloosa, AL 35404-3954. TEL 205-553-2284. adv.; illus.; circ. 200. (back issues avail.)
Description: Literary journal of speculative poetry. Introduces new writers.

811 US
▼**DRY CRIK REVIEW.** 1990. 4/yr. $20. Box 51, Lemon Cove, CA 93244. TEL 209-597-2512. Ed. John C. Dofflemyer. circ. 250.

DUFU YANJIU XUEKAN/JOURNAL OF DUFU STUDIES. see LITERARY AND POLITICAL REVIEWS

811 US
DUMARS REVIEWS. 1987. 4/yr. $7.50. Box 810, Hawthorne, CA 90251. circ. 100.

811 US
▼**DUSTY DOG.** 1990. 3/yr. $7. John Pierce, Ed. & Pub., Box 1103, Zuni, NM 87327. TEL 505-782-4958. circ. 300.
Description: Publishes high caliber, well-crafted long poems.

808.81 700 US ISSN 0190-1761
EARTHWISE LITERARY CALENDAR. a. $9.95 to non-members. (Florida State Poets Association, Inc. (FSPA), Miami Earth Chapter) Earthwise Publications, Box 680536, Miami, FL 33168. TEL 305-653-2875.
Description: For poets concerned with environment and peace.

808.81 333.7 US
EARTHWISE REVIEW; a journal of poetry. 1978. q. $25. Earthwise Publications, Box 680536, Miami, FL 33168. TEL 305-653-2875. Ed. Barbara Holley. adv.; bk.rev.; illus.; circ. 1,000.
Former titles (until 1989): Earthwise; Earthwise Newsletter; Earthwise News (ISSN 0190-1761)
Description: Contains environmentally concerned literature, mainly poetry.

811 CN
ECLECTIC MUSE. 1989. 3/yr. $20. 340 West 3rd St., Ste. 107, North Vancouver, B.C. V7M 1G4, Canada. TEL 604-984-7834. circ. 200.
Description: Publishes poems, especially from women poets.

811 US
ECOS; a journal of Latino people's culture. 1980. a. $3. Abrazo Press, Box 2890, Chicago, IL 60690-2890. TEL 312-935-6188. circ. 800.

861 UK ISSN 0260-2113
ECUATORIAL; poetry. (Text in English, Portuguese and Spanish) 1978. irreg. King's College, Department of Spanish, c/o Dr. William Rowe, Strand, London WC2R, England.

808.81 US
EDITOR'S DESK. 1981. m. $16. 709 S.E. 52nd Ave., Ocala, FL 32671. TEL 904-694-2303. Eds. Florence F. Bradley, Susie Pettrey. adv.; bk.rev.; circ. 500.
Formerly: All Around the Editor's Desk.

821 CN
EGORAG. m. Can.$35. 4836 Ross St., Red Deer, Alta. T4N 5E8, Canada.

EIGHTIES; a magazine of poetry and opinion. see LITERARY AND POLITICAL REVIEWS

808 IS
EITIONE 77 LESIFRUT VELETARBUT. (Text in Hebrew) 1977. m. $35. Writers and Artists Association for Literature and Culture in Israel, Box 16452, Tel Aviv, Israel. Ed. Jakob Besser. adv.; bk.rev.

890 II
EK BACHARER SRESTHA KABITA. (Text in Bengali) 1973. a. Rs.4($1) c/o Mrs. Bhaswati Sinha, 36 Ballygunge Place, Calcutta 19, India. Eds. M. Manindra Gupta, Ranjit Sinha. adv.; illus.; stat.; circ. 1,000.

841 FR
ELAN POETIQUE ET LITTERAIRE. 1955. q. 31 rue Foch, 59000 Linselles, France. Ed. Louis Lippens.

ELAN POETIQUE LITTERAIRE ET PACIFISTE. see LITERATURE

808.81 US
ELEVENTH MUSE. 1983. s-a. $8. Poetry West, Box 2413, Colorado Springs, CO 80901. TEL 719-591-8210. Ed.Bd. adv.; bk.rev.; circ. 300. (back issues avail.)

808.81 US ISSN 0731-0382
EMBERS. 1979. s-a. $11. Embers Horizons, Inc., Box 404, Guilford, CT 06437. TEL 203-453-2328. Ed. Katrina Van Tassel. circ. 500. (back issues avail.)

EMERALD CITY COMIX & STORIES; fiction, poetry, news, reviews, humor. see LITERARY AND POLITICAL REVIEWS

811 US ISSN 0271-5023
PS580
EN PASSANT POETRY. 1975. irreg. $6. (En Passant Literary Association) En Passant Press, 4612 Sylvanus Dr., Wilmington, DE 19803. Ed. James A. Costello. bk.rev.; illus.; circ. 500. **Indexed:** Ind.Amer.Per.Verse.
Formerly: En Passant Poetry Quarterly (ISSN 0363-3780)

841 FR ISSN 0013-7103
ENCRES VIVES. 1960. q. 80 F. c/o Michel Cosem, Ed., Engomer, 09800-Castillon, France. adv.; bk.rev.; film rev.; circ. 1,000.

ENGLISH. see LITERATURE

ENGLISH GOETHE SOCIETY. PUBLICATIONS. see LITERATURE

800 808.81 SA ISSN 0257-2036
ENSOVOORT; a poetry magazine. (Text in Afrikaans and English) 1981. s-a. R.10 to individuals; institutions R.15. Ensovoort, P.O. Box 30314, Les Marais, Pretoria 0038, South Africa. Ed. Johann Lodewik Marais. adv.; bk.rev.; circ. 1,000. (back issues avail.) **Indexed:** Ind.S.A.Per.

821 UK ISSN 0013-9394
PR1225
ENVOI; a poetry magazine. 1957. 3/yr. £6 (foreign £7). c/o Anne Lewis-Smith, Ed., Pen Ffordd, Newport, Dyfed SA42 0QT, Wales. TEL 0239-820285. adv.; bk.rev.; circ. 800.

811 US
ENVOY (NEW YORK). 1964. a. membership. Academy of American Poets, 177 E. 87th St., New York, NY 10128. Ed. Jennifer O'Grady. circ. 3,000. **Indexed:** Cath.Ind., CERDIC.
Formerly (until 1976): Detonator (ISSN 0011-9598)

EPOCH (ITHACA); a magazine of contemporary literature. see LITERATURE

808.81 SP ISSN 0211-8181
EQUIVALENCIAS/EQUIVALENCES. 1982. 3/yr. $29. Fundacion Fernando Rielo, Jorge Juan 102, 2nd B, 28009 Madrid, Spain. TEL 34-1 275 4091. (U S addr.: 143-8 84th Dr., Briarwood, NY 11435) Ed. Justo Jorge Padron. bk.rev.; circ. 2,000.

821 UK
EQUOFINALITY. 1982. biennial. 147 Selly Oak Rd., Birmingham B30 1HN, England. Eds. Rod Mengham, John Wilkinson. circ. 300.
Description: Publishes experimental poetry, long poems and serial poems.

811 US
EREHWON; journal of lucid poetry. 1966. s-a. $6. Pandemonium Press, 1273 Crest Dr., Encinitas, CA 92024. Ed. R.C. Walker. circ. 200. (back issues avail.)

811 US
ESCHEW OBFUSCATION REVIEW. bi-m? Pen-Dec Press, 3922 Monte Carlo, Kentwood, MI 49512. TEL 616-942-0056.

861 CK ISSN 0014-0562
ESPARAVEL; gaceta de poesia. 1967. 10/yr. Col.50. Apartado Aereo 2670, Cali, Colombia. Ed. Helcias Martan Gongora. adv.; illus.

ETUDES BAUDELAIRIENNES. see LITERATURE

EXACT CHANGE; a journal of the American landscape. see ARCHITECTURE

811 US ISSN 0014-4770
EXPERIMENT; a magazine of new poetry. 1944. irreg. $5.20. Experiment Press, 6565 N.E. Windermere Rd., Seattle, WA 98105-2057. TEL 206-527-4172. Ed. Carol Ely Harper. adv.; bk.rev.; illus.; index; circ. 400.

811 US
▼**EXPERIMENT IN WORDS.** 1990. a. $5. Box 470186, Fort Worth, TX 76147. TEL 817-763-0158. circ. 200.

LITERATURE — POETRY

811 US
▼**EXPERIMENTAL BASEMENT**. 1991. 3/yr. $8. Experimental Press, 3740 N. Romero Rd., Ste. A-191, Tucson, AZ 85705. TEL 602-293-3287. circ. 150.

821 UK ISSN 0014-536X
EXPRESSION ONE. 1962. q. £0.75($1.25) c/o Leslie Surridge, Ed., 5 Avon Rd., Waltham Forest, London E17 3RB, England. index; circ. 300.
Formerly: Expression.

811 US
EXPRESSIONS: FIRST STATE JOURNAL. 1986. 2/yr. $8. Box 4064, Greenville, DE 19807. Ed. Joanne Petrizzi. circ. 350.

F A R C E. (Fine Arts Research and Communications Enterprises) see ART

F A W N S. (Fellowship of Australian Writers North Shore Regional) see LITERATURE

FANTASY COMMENTATOR. see LITERATURE — Science Fiction, Fantasy, Horror

811 US ISSN 1041-4886
FEDERAL POET. 1943. s-a. $10 (effective 1990). Federal Poets of Washington D.C., Box 65400, Washington, DC 20035. TEL 301-572-6803. Ed. Ingeborg Carsten Miller. adv.; bibl.; circ. 200.

808.81 US
FEH!; a journal of odious poetry. (Text in English, French) 1986. 3/yr. $5. Feh! Press, 2226 Hennepin Ave., Box 20, Minneapolis, MN 55405. Ed. Simeon Stylites. adv.; circ. 200.
Description: Poetry and some prose in the following areas: humor, satire, nonsense, eccentricity, madness and social criticism.

811 US
FELICITY. 1988. m. $15. Star Route, Box 21AA, Artemas, PA 17211. TEL 814-458-3102. Ed. Kay Weems. circ. 200.

811 CN ISSN 0015-0630
PR9291.N4
FIDDLEHEAD. 1945. q. $18 to individuals; institutions $28. University of New Brunswick, Campus House, P.O. Box 4400, Fredericton, N.B. E3B 5A3, Canada. TEL 506-453-3501. FAX 506-453-4599. (Co-sponsors: Canada Council; Provincial Government; Saint Thomas University) Ed. Don McKay. adv.; bk.rev.; circ. 1,050. (also avail. in microfilm from MML,UMI; back issues avail.; reprint service avail. from KTO) **Indexed**: Amer.Hum.Ind., Arts & Hum.Cit.Ind., Can.Lit.Ind., Can.Per.Ind., CMI, Curr.Cont., Ind.Bk.Rev.Hum.

811 US ISSN 0015-0657
PN6099.6
FIELD; contemporary poetry and poetics. 1969. s-a. $12. Oberlin College, Rice Hall, Oberlin, OH 44074. TEL 216-775-8121. Eds. David P. Young, Stuart Friebert. bk.rev.; circ. 2,500. (also avail. in microfilm from UMI; back issues avail.) **Indexed**: A.I.P.P., Amer.Bibl.Slavic & E.Eur.Stud., Ind.Bk.Rev.Hum.

811 US
FIFTY CELL.* 1975. q. free. Connecticut Correctional Institution, 900 Milldale Rd., Cheshire, CT 06410. TEL 203-272-5391. Ed. D.W. Donzella. illus.; circ. 500.

808.81 US ISSN 0737-4704
PS615
FINE MADNESS. 1982. s-a. $9. Box 31138, Seattle, WA 98103-1138. Ed.Bd. bk.rev.; circ. 800.

895.1 US
FIRST LINE/YI XING. (Text mainly in Chinese; occasionally in English) 1987. q. $10 (foreign $16). c/o Kuan-Fong Institute of East Asian Studies, Pace University, Pace Plaza, NY 10038-1502. (Subscr. to: Box 418, New York, NY 10013-0418) Ed. Yan Li. adv.; illus.
Description: Contains mainly original poetry by writers from around the world. Accepts contributions from readers. Also includes poetry translations and short prose works.

FLAMMES VIVES. see LITERARY AND POLITICAL REVIEWS

811 US
FLORIDA STATE POETRY SOCIETY. SELECTED POEMS. 1966. a. membership. Florida State Poetry Society, Inc., 1110 N. Venetian Dr., Miami Beach, FL 33139. Ed. Frances Clark Handler. circ. 17,500.

FOLIO (WASHINGTON); a literary journal. see LITERATURE

FONDATION MAURICE CAREME. see LITERATURE

FOOLSCAP. see LITERARY AND POLITICAL REVIEWS

808.8 US
FOOTWORK: THE PATERSON LITERARY REVIEW. 1979. s-a. $5. Passaic County Community College, Poetry Center, College Blvd., Paterson, NJ 07509. TEL 201-684-6555. Ed. Maria Gillan. adv.; bk.rev.; circ. 1,000.
Formerly: Footwork Magazine.

811 US ISSN 0887-0896
FOR POETS ONLY. 1985. 4/yr. $3 per no. Box 4855, Schenectady, NY 12304. Ed. L.M. Walsh. circ. 150. **Indexed**: Amer.Hum.Ind.
Description: Collection of poetry and poets' comments.

808.81 US ISSN 0894-4008
NX504
FOREHEAD; a journal of writing and art. 1987. irreg. Beyond Baroque Foundation, Box 2727, Venice, CA 90291. TEL 213-822-3006. FAX 310-827-7432. Ed. Erica Bornstein. bk.rev.; circ. 2,000.

808.81 US ISSN 1046-7874
PS615
▼**THE FORMALIST**; a journal of metrical poetry. 1990. s-a. $12 to individuals (foreign $15); libraries $14 (foreign $115. 320 Hunter Dr., Evansville, IN 47711. TEL 812-479-9624. Ed. William Baer. bk.rev. (back issues avail.)
Description: Devoted entirely to formal, metrical verse and publishing contemporary poetry and translations that participate in the great tradition of metrical poetry from Chaucer to Frost.

821 UK ISSN 0015-7740
FORMAT. 1966. irreg. £0.50. Stilt Press, c/o Alan & Joan Tucker, The Bookshop, Stroud, Gloucestershire, England. FAX 0453-766899. Ed. Alan Tucker. circ. 150 (controlled). (processed)

FRAENKISCHER HAUSKALENDER UND CARITASKALENDER. see BIOGRAPHY

FREE LANCE; a magazine of poetry and prose. see LITERATURE

808.81 US ISSN 1041-0945
FREE LUNCH. 1989. 3/yr. $10 (foreign $13)(free to qualified poets). Free Lunch Arts Alliance, 27301 Ventosa, Mission Viejo, CA 92691. (Subscr. to: Box 7647, Laguna Niguel, CA 92607-7647) Ed. Ron Offen. adv.; circ. 1,000. (back issues avail.) **Indexed**: Ind.Amer.Per.Verse.
Description: Covers poetry and news about poetry contests, new markets, grants, and deadlines for grants.

811 US
FROG GONE REVIEW. 1989. a. $4. Box 46308, Mt. Clemens, MI 48046. TEL 313-263-3399. Ed. Greg Shindler. circ. 500.
Description: Publishes witty, clever poems.

808.81 US
FROGPOND. 1978. q. $20 (foreign $28). Haiku Society of America, Inc., 87 Bayard Ave., N. Haven, CT 06473. TEL 203-281-9653. Ed. Sylvia Forges-Ryan. bk.rev.; circ. 600. (back issues avail.)
Description: Publishes contemporary English-language haiku, with occasional essays, renga and tanka, news briefs, listings of new books of haiku and translations from Japanese and other languages.

811 CN ISSN 0046-5267
FULL TIDE.* 1936. s-a. membership. Vancouver Poetry Society, c/o 4602 Prospect Rd., North Vancouver, B.C., Canada. Ed. Borghild Valeria.

821 UK ISSN 0306-1256
GALLERY. 1975. a. £2.50. Gallery Publications, c/o Valerie Sinason, Ed., 3 Honeybourne Rd., London NW6 1HH, England. adv.; bk.rev.; illus.; circ. 1,000.

808.81 US ISSN 0016-4100
GALLEY SAIL REVIEW; a journal of poetry. 1958. 3/yr. $8. 1630 University Ave., Ste. 42, Berkeley, CA 94703. TEL 415-486-0187. Ed. Stanley McNail. bk.rev.; circ. 500. **Indexed**: A.I.P.P., Amer.Hum.Ind.
Description: Seeks to encourage public appreciation of contemporary poetry.

811 US
GANDHABBA. 1984. a. $3.50 to individuals; institutions $4.50; lifetime $50. 622 E. 11th St., New York, NY 10007. TEL 212-533-3893. Ed. Tom Savage. circ. 300.
Description: Thematical-oriented contemporary poetry.

821 UK
GENERA. 1971. irreg. £14($30) for 4 nos. c/o Colin Simms, Ed., Low Woodhead North, Bellingham, Northumberland NE48 2HX, England. illus.; circ. 1,000. (back issues avail.)
Formerly: North York Poetry.

808.81 700 US ISSN 0896-7431
GENERATOR. 1987. a. $5. Generator Press, 8139 Midland Rd., Mentor, OH 44060. TEL 216-951-3209. Ed. John Byrum. circ. 125. (back issues avail.)
Description: Provides a forum for the intersection and cross-fertilization of language and visual poetries.

GEORG FORSTER: SAEMTLICHE SCHRIFTEN, TAGEBUECHER, BRIEFE. see LITERATURE

811 US ISSN 0161-7435
PR3508
GEORGE HERBERT JOURNAL. 1977. s-a. $7 to individuals (foreign $10); institutions $15. c/o Sidney Gottlieb, Ed., English Department, Sacred Heart University, 5151 Park Ave., Fairfield, CT 06432. TEL 203-371-7816. adv.; bk.rev.; circ. 450. **Indexed**: Abstr.Engl.Stud., Amer.Hum.Ind., M.L.A.
—BLDSC shelfmark: 4158.207800.
Description: Articles, essays, notes, and reviews on the life and scholarly studies of this English clergyman and poet. Discusses the theologic, social, and literary climate of his period.

821 CN ISSN 0704-6286
GERMINATION. 1976. s-a. Can.$7($9) Owl's Head Press, 428 Yale Ave., Riverview, N.B. E1B 2B5, Canada. Ed. Allan Cooper. adv.; bk.rev.; circ. 500. (back issues avail.) **Indexed**: Can.Lit.Ind., Ind.Amer.Per.Verse.

808.8 US ISSN 0898-4557
AS30
GETTYSBURG REVIEW. 1988. q. $15 (effective Jan. 1991). Gettysburg College, Gettysburg, PA 17325-1491. TEL 717-337-6770. FAX 717-337-6775. Ed. Peter Stitt. adv.; bk.rev.; illus.; index; circ. 2,500.
Description: Interdisciplinary magazine of arts and ideas. Features poetry, fiction, essays, and essay-reviews by both beginning and established writers and artists.

811 US ISSN 0016-9633
PS501
GHOST DANCE; the international quarterly of experimental poetry. 1968. irreg. (1-2/yr.). $6. Ghost Dance Press, Dept. of American Thought and Language (EBH), Michigan State University, E. Lansing, MI 48823. Ed. Hugh B. Fox. circ. 300. (also avail. in microfilm from UMI; reprint service avail. from UMI)

808.81 884.55 US
GIORNO POETRY SYSTEMS L P'S, C D'S, CASSETTES & GIORNO VIDEO PAK SERIES. 1967. s-a. Giorno Poetry Systems Institute, Inc., 222 Bowery, New York, NY 10012. TEL 212-925-6372. FAX 212-966-7574. Ed. John Giorno. circ. 17,500.
Description: Poets working with performance, music and video.

811 US
GLASS WILL. 1986. irreg., latest 1986. $5.95 per no. (Toledo Poets Center) Toledo Poets Center Press, 32 Scott House, University of Toledo, Toledo, OH 43606. TEL 419-537-2983. Ed. Joel Lipman. circ. 750. (back issues avail.)
Description: Presents ecclectic regional poetry in a book format.

LITERATURE — POETRY

821 UK ISSN 0141-1241
GLOBAL TAPESTRY JOURNAL; mind-opening & post-underground creativity. 1964. irreg. £7($21) B.B. Bks, Spring Bank, Longsight Rd., Copster Green, Blackburn, Lancs. BB1 9EU, England. TEL 0254-249128. Ed. David Cunliffe. adv.; bk.rev.; illus.; circ. 1,050. (processed; also avail. in microform)
Incorporates: P M Newsletter (Blackburn) (ISSN 0030-8145)

811 US
▼**GLOBE LITERARY**. 1990. a. 3625 Greenwood North, Seattle, WA 98103. Eds. P. Scheldt, D. Sprague.

811 US
GO MAGAZINE. 1988. 26/yr. free. 1139 N. Laura St., Jacksonville, FL 32206. TEL 904-354-4382. circ. 10,000.

811 US
GOLDEN ISIS. 1980. q. $10. 23233 Saticoy St., Bldg. 105, Ste. 137, W. Hills, CA 91304-5300. Ed. Gerina Dunwich. adv.; bk.rev.; circ. 3,600.
Description: Contains pagan art, Wiccan news, reviews, white magick and goddess-inspired poetry.

331.88 ISSN 0017-1638
DI GOLDENE KEYT. (Text in Yiddish) 1949. q. $30. Histadrut, Beit Hamlin, 30 Weizmann St., Tel Aviv, Israel. TEL 03-216059. Ed. A. Sutzkever. Indexed: M.L.A.

811 US
▼**GOPHERWOOD REVIEW**. 1990. 2/yr. $7. Box 58784, Houston, TX 77258. TEL 713-532-1622. Eds. S. Reiff, S. Crowson. circ. 200.
Description: Biased toward experimental and surreal poetry.

811 US
GRASSLANDS REVIEW. 1989. 2/yr. $4. Box 13706, Denton, TX 76203. TEL 817-565-2025. circ. 300.

811 US ISSN 0191-0760
GRAVIDA;* a quarterly journal of poetry. Variant title: Gravida-Bridging. 1972. q. $4. (Women's Poetry Collective) Gravida, Ltd., Box 616, Bethpage, NY 11714-0616. Ed.Bd. bk.rev.; circ. 600.

GREAT TAO. see RELIGIONS AND THEOLOGY — Buddhist

821 UK ISSN 0017-3967
GREEN ISLAND. 1967. s-a. $75. c/o David A. Kilburn, Ed., Flat 2, 126 Long Acre, London WC2E 9PE, England. illus.; cum.index; circ. 400. Indexed: HR Rep.

GREEN MOUNTAINS REVIEW. see LITERATURE

GREEN RIVER REVIEW. see LITERATURE

810 US
GREEN ZERO. 1990. 4/yr. $2. Box 3104, Shiremanstown, PA 17011. TEL 717-732-7191. circ. 150.

811 US
GROUND WATER REVIEW. 1984. irreg. $4.50. Talking Leaves Press, 730 East Smith St., Warsaw, IN 46580. TEL 219-269-7680. Ed. George Kalamaras. circ. 200.
Description: Publishes experimental and long poems.

861 PR ISSN 0017-498X
GUAJANA.* 1962. 3/yr. $2.00. Las Palmas 1059, Santurce, PR 00907. Ed. Vicente Rodriguez Nietzsche.

821 UK
GUILDHALL POETS. a. £0.35. 19 Rugwood Rd., Flackwell Heath, High Wycombe HP10 9HA, England.

890 IS ISSN 0333-7588
PJ5041
HADARIM; poetry review. (Text in Hebrew) 1981. s-a. Gordon Gallery Ltd., 95 Ben Yehuda Street, Tel Aviv 63401, Israel. FAX 03-240935. Ed. Helit Yeshurun. adv.; bk.rev.; circ. 1,500. (back issues avail.) Indexed: Ind.Heb.Per.

811 US
HAIKU HEADLINES; a monthly newsletter of haiku and senryu. 1988. m. $18 (Canada $19.20; elsewhere $23). 1347 W. 71st St., Los Angeles, CA 90044. TEL 213-778-5337. David Priebe (Renge). circ. 155.

808.81
HAIKU ZASSHI ZO.* (Text in English, French, Hungarian, Japanese, Russian, Sanskrit, Spanish) 1983. s-a. $6. Haiku Zasshi Zo Publishing Co., 325 N. 125th St., Seattle, WA 98133-8123. TEL 206-524-9692. Ed. George Klacsauzky. circ. 800. (back issues avail.)
Description: Covers haiku poetry and Japanese arts that influence writing haiku.

808.81
HALF TONES TO JUBILEE. 1986. a. $4. Pensacola Junior College, 1000 College Blvd., Pensacola, FL 32504. TEL 904-484-1418. FAX 904-484-1826. Eds. Walter F. Spara, Allan Peterson. bk.rev.; circ. 500. (back issues avail.)

811 US
▼**HAMMERS**. 1990. irreg. $10. 1718 Sherman, Ste. 205, Evanston, IL 60201. Ed. Nat David. circ. 500.

811 US
HAMPDEN-SYDNEY POETRY REVIEW. 1975. s-a. $12. Hampden-Sydney College, Box 126, Hampden-Sydney, VA 23943. TEL 804-223-8209. Ed. Tom O'Grady. bk.rev.; circ. 750. (back issues avail.) Indexed: A.I.P.P.

808.81 NE ISSN 0017-7148
HAND VOL PLUIS.* (Text in Dutch, English and French) 1967. fl.2.50($0.75) Morsestraat 24, The Hague, Netherlands. Ed.Bd.

811 US ISSN 0440-2316
PS580
HANGING LOOSE. 1966. 3/yr. $12.50 to individuals, institutions $15. Hanging Loose Press, 231 Wyckoff St., Brooklyn, NY 11217. TEL 718-643-9559. Ed.Bd. cum.index every 12 nos.; circ. 1,500. (also avail. in microform from UMI; back issues avail.; reprint service avail. from UMI) Indexed: Ind.Amer.Per.Verse.
Formerly: Things (ISSN 0563-4660)
Description: Includes fiction, poetry, and art, with emphasis on new writers.

811 US ISSN 0046-6832
PS615
HAPPINESS HOLDING TANK.* 1970. irreg. $4. Stone Press, 9727 S.E. Reedway St., Portland, OR 97266-3738. TEL 517-349-0552. Ed. Albert Drake. bk.rev.; illus.; circ. 300. (processed; back issues avail.) Indexed: Bk.Rev.Ind.

811 US
HARBOR REVIEW. 1982. 3/yr. $7 to individuals; institutions $10. University of Massachusetts, English Department, Boston, MA 02125. TEL 617-929-8300. Eds. Charles Grace Anastas, Stephen Strempek. circ. 250.

808.81
HARVEST (SALEM). bi-m. 23222 Latona Dr., N.E., Salem, OR 97303.

811 US
HAUNTED JOURNAL. 1983. irreg. (2-4/yr.). $28 for 4 issues. Baker Street Publications, Box 994, Metairie, LA 70004. TEL 504-734-8414. Ed. Sharida Rizzuto. circ. 9,000.

808.81 US ISSN 0887-5170
HAYDEN'S FERRY REVIEW. 1986. s-a. $10. Arizona State University, Student Publications, Matthews Center, Tempe, AZ 85287-1502. TEL 602-965-1243. FAX 602-965-8484. Ed. Salima Keegan. adv.; circ. 1,000. (back issues avail.)

811 US
HEADWATERS REVIEW. 2/yr. $15 for 3 issues. Box 13682, Dinkytown Station, Minneapolis, MN 55414.

811 US
▼**HEART & SOUL**. 1991. 4/yr. $5. Box 1144, League City, TX 77574. TEL 713-332-5048. Ed. Rhonda Cook.
Description: Publishes poems and short stories.

811 US
HEATHENZINE. 1989. 6/yr. $12. 511 West Sullivan St., Olean, NY 14760. Ed. Ken Wagner. circ. 150.
Description: Publishes modernist and experimental poems.

808.81 US ISSN 1042-5381
HEAVEN BONE. 1986. s-a. $14.95. Heaven Bone Press, Box 486, Chester, NY 10918. TEL 914-469-9018. Eds. Kirpal Gordon, Steven Hirsch. adv.; bk.rev.; circ. 800. (back issues avail.)
Formerly: New Age Literary Arts.
Description: Includes esoteric and spiritual poetry, stories and reviews. Focus is on spiritual, metaphysical and experimental literary concerns.

HEINE SAEKULARAUSGABE: WERKE-BRIEFWECHSEL-LEBENSZEUGNISSE. see LITERATURE

800 II
HELICON.* (Text in English) 1971. m. Rs.10. 10-3C Nepal Bhattacharya St., Calcutta 26, India. Eds. Jyotirmoy Chatterjee, Suddha Sattwa Bovt. adv.

HELIX. see LITERATURE

808.81 US ISSN 1044-5331
PS615
▼**HELLAS**; a journal of poetry and the humanities. 1990. s-a. $12. 304 S. Tyson Ave., Glenside, PA 19038. TEL 215-884-1086. Ed. Gerald Harnett. adv.; bk.rev.; circ. 750. (back issues avail.)
Description: Includes modern poetry with criticism of modern poetry. Provides scholarly articles on Greek, Latin, and Renaissance English, as well as European literature.

811 US
HELTER SKELTER. 1987. a. $10 for 4 yrs. 979 Golf Course Dr., Ste. 223, Rohnert Park, CA 94928. TEL 408-624-7066. Ed. Anthony Boyd.

811 808.8 US
HENDERSON COMMUNITY COLLEGE LITERARY MAGAZINE. 1988. Henderson Community College, 2660 S. Green St., Henderson, KY 42420. TEL 502-827-1867. Ed. Noelle R. Wallace. illus. (back issues avail.)
Description: Presents poetry, short stories, and nonfiction prose.

821 II
HESPERUS REVIEW. 1988. q. $10 (effective 1991). Gautam Chandra Chunder, Ed. & Pub., 23 Nirmal Chunder St., Calcutta 700 012, India. TEL 26-8248. adv.; circ. 500.

811 US ISSN 0018-1188
HEY LADY. (Supplements avail.) 1969. 10/yr. free. Morgan Press, 1819 N. Oakland Ave., Milwaukee, WI 53202. TEL 414-272-3256. Ed. Edwin H. Burton. illus.; circ. 500.

811 US
HIDDEN SPRINGS REVIEW. 1985. 4/yr. $10. Box 29613, Los Angeles, CA 90029. TEL 213-664-0007. Ed. Moneim A. Fadali. circ. 1,000.

821 US ISSN 0164-145X
PS580
HIGGINSON JOURNAL. 1971. s-a. free (with subscr. to Dickinson Studies). Dickinson-Higginson Press, 1330 Massachusetts Ave. NW, No. 503, Washington, DC 20005-4150. Ed. F.L. Morey. adv.; bk.rev.; bibl.; charts; illus.; circ. 250. (reprint service avail. from UMI,ISI) Indexed: A.I.P.P., Curr.Cont., M.L.A.
Formerly: Higginson Journal of American Poetry.

811 US ISSN 0018-179X
HIKA. 1936. 2/yr. $12. Kenyon College, Box B, Gambier, OH 43022. TEL 614-427-2244. Eds. Bret Benjamin, Julie Emig. adv.; circ. 2,000. (processed)

811 US ISSN 0018-2036
PS580
HIRAM POETRY REVIEW. 1966. s-a. $4. Hiram College, English Department, Box 162, Hiram, OH 44234. TEL 216-569-3211. Eds. Hale Chatfield, Carol Donley. bk.rev.; circ. 500. (also avail. in microform from UMI; back issues avail.; reprint service avail. from UMI) Indexed: A.I.P.P., Ind.Amer.Per.Verse, Ind.Bk.Rev.Hum., Ind.Little Mag.

LITERATURE — POETRY

811 US
HOBO STEW REVIEW. 1984. 4/yr. $5. Hobo Stew, 2 Eliot St., Ste. 1, Somerville, MA 02143. circ. 45.

861 AG
HOJAS DE POESIA. irreg. $2.50. Aquario, Paraguay 647, Buenos Aires, Argentina. Eds. Sergio Chaves, Sigfrido Radaelli. (poster format)

811 US ISSN 0147-2631
HOLLOW SPRING REVIEW OF POETRY. 1975. s-a. $6. Hollow Spring Press, R.D. 1, Chester, MA 01011. Ed. Alexander Harvey. adv.; bk.rev.; circ. 1,200.

800 US
HOME PLANET NEWS. 1979. q. $8. Home Planet Publications, Box 415, Stuyvesant Sta., New York, NY 10009. TEL 718-769-2854. Eds. Donald Lev, Enid Dame. adv.; bk.rev.; play rev.; circ. 1,000. (tabloid format)
  Description: Literary - arts journal emphasizing poetry.

HONEST ULSTERMAN. see *LITERATURE*

HOOFSTRIKES NEWSLETTER. see *ANIMAL WELFARE*

821 CN ISSN 0094-9086
PR4803.H44
HOPKINS QUARTERLY. 1974. q. Can.$8($8) Language Studies Dept., Mohawk College, P.O. Box 2034, Hamilton, Ont. L8N 3T2, Canada. TEL 416-575-1212. Ed. Richard F. Giles. adv.; bk.rev.; index; circ. 375. (back issues avail.) **Indexed:** Abstr.Engl.Stud., Amer.Hum.Ind., Arts & Hum.Cit.Ind., Curr.Cont., M.L.A.
  —BLDSC shelfmark: 4326.755000.

861 SP ISSN 0212-9442
HORA DE POESIA. (Text mainly in Spanish; occasionally in other European languages.) 1979. bi-m. $43. Lentini Editor, Hipolito Lazaro 19-23, Esc. Dcha., Entlo 3a, 08025 Barcelona, Spain. TEL 93-213-30-40. Ed. Javier Lentini. adv.; bk.rev.; index; circ. 1,300. (back issues avail.)

HORNS OF PLENTY; Malcolm Cowley and his generation. see *LITERARY AND POLITICAL REVIEWS*

800 US ISSN 0278-4173
HOT WATER REVIEW.* 1976. a. $6. Hot Water Review, Inc., 9 Stuyvesant Oval, No. 5F, New York, NY 10009-1917. Ed. Peter Bushyeager. adv.; circ. 1,000.

808.81 301.412 US ISSN 1056-0815
HOUSEWIFE - WRITER'S FORUM. 1988. bi-m. $15. Deneb Publishing, Box 780, Lyman, WY 82937. TEL 307-786-4513. Ed. Diane Wolverton. adv.; bk.rev.; circ. 1,000. (back issues avail.)
  Description: For the woman writer who juggles husband, kids and housework with the pursuit of being published.

HUACHENG. see *LITERATURE*

HUAXI; qingnian wenxue yuekan. see *LITERATURE*

808.81 US ISSN 1047-0158
HUBBUB. 1983. 2/yr. $5. 5344 S.E. 38th, Portland, OR 97202. TEL 503-775-0370. Ed. Lisa Steinman. adv.; bk.rev.; circ. 300. (back issues avail.)
  Description: Presents contemporary poetry.

811 US
▼**HWUP!;** a forum for poets. 1991. 11/yr. $15 (foreign $18). Box 13743, Tallahassee, FL 32317. TEL 904-893-3878. Ed. Larry Gross. circ. 200.
  Description: Discusses pleasures and pitfalls of poetry and promotes a larger market for chapbooks.

811 US ISSN 0018-8328
HYPERION (AUSTIN);* a poetry journal. 1969. q. $4. Thorp Springs Press, 1002 Lorrain St., Austin, TX 78703-4827. (Subscr. to: c/o Judy Hogan, 300 Barlay, Chapel Hill, NC 27514) Ed.Bd. bk.rev.; circ. 2,000. (processed)

I C A M; revista literaria. see *LITERATURE*

IBDA/INNOVATION. see *LITERATURE*

813 500 GW ISSN 0720-8782
AS181
IBYKUS; Zeitschrift fuer Poesie, Wissenschaft und Staatskunst. 1981. q. DM.35. Dr. Boettiger Verlags GmbH, Dotzheimer Str. 166, 6200 Wiesbaden, Germany. TEL 06121-806955. FAX 06121-884101. adv.; bk.rev.; circ. 14,500. (back issues avail.)

811 US ISSN 0019-137X
IDEALS. 1944. 8/yr. $19.95. Ideals Publishing Corp. (Nashville) (Subsidiary of: Gutenberghus Company), 565 Marriott Dr., Box 148000, Nashville, TN 37210. TEL 615-885-8270. FAX 615-885-9578. Ed. Patricia Dingry. illus.; circ. 274,000. (also avail. in microform from UMI) **Indexed:** Jun.High.Mag.Abstr.

811 US
IDEOLOGY OF MADNESS. 1985. 4/yr. $5. Box 1742, Arlington, TX 76012. circ. 300.

821 AT
IDIOM 23. 1988. 2/yr. Aus.$10. University of Central Queensland, Rockhampton, Qld. 4702, Australia. TEL 0011-079-360655. circ. 350.

811 US
IKON. 1982. 2/yr. $9.50. Box 1355, Stuyvesant Sta., New York, NY 10009. Ed. Susan Sherman. circ. 1,750.

821 UK ISSN 0736-4725
ILLUMINATIONS. 1983. a. £10($20) Rathasker Press, Ryde School, Queens Rd., Ryde, Isle of Wight, PO33 3BE, England. Ed. Simon Lewis. circ. 500. (back issues avail.)
  Description: Features international poetry and short fiction from new and established writers.

821 AT
IMAGO. 1988. 2/yr. Aus.$12.50. Queensland University of Technology, School of Communication, P.O. Box 2434, Brisbane, Qld. 4001, Australia. TEL 07-223-2111. circ. 500.

IMPETUS. see *ART*

811 PE ISSN 0300-4031
IN TERRIS; revista de poesia. 1967. irreg. Livio Gomez Flores, Ed. & Pub., Francisco Cornejo 847, Tacna, Peru. adv.; bk.rev.; illus.; circ. 1,000. (also avail. in microform; back issues avail.)

821 UK
INCEPT.* s-a. £1. c/o Eric Harrison, Ed., 3 Grantley Close, Shalford, Surrey, England.

851 IT
INCOGNITA. 1982. q. L.30000. Societa Editrice Napoletana s.r.l., Corso Umberto 1, 34, 80138 Napoli, Italy. Ed. Giancarlo Majorino.

821 II
INDIAN VERSE; voice of the Indian poets. 1973. q. Rs.10($4) 9-3 Tamer Lane, Calcutta 9, India. Ed.Bd.

INDIAN WRITER. see *LITERATURE*

808.8 UK ISSN 0020-0840
INFORMER; international poetry magazine. 1966. q. 12s.($1.50) Circle Books, 15 Linkside Ave., Five Mile Drive, Oxford, England. Ed. Keith Armstrong. adv.; bk.rev.; bibl.; illus.; circ. 400. (processed)

808.81 UK ISSN 0951-0427
INKSHED - POETRY AND FICTION. 1986. 3/yr. £6($10) 387 Beverley Rd., Hull HU5 1LS, England. TEL 0482-440694. Ed.Bd. adv.; bk.rev.; circ. 400.

808.81 950 CN ISSN 0714-2870
INKSTONE; a magazine of haiku. 1983. irreg. Can.$15($15) P.O. Box 67, Station "H", Toronto, Ont. M4C 5H7, Canada. TEL 416-531-5688. Ed.Bd. bk.rev.; circ. 100. (back issues avail.)
  Description: Traditional and experimental Haiku poetry.

811 810 US
INNISFREE. 1981. 6/yr. $22. Appleseed, Box 277, Manhattan Beach, CA 90266. TEL 310-545-2607. FAX 310-546-5862. Ed. Rex Winn. bk.rev.; circ. 300.

810.8 US ISSN 0094-2715
PS508.C6
INSCAPE (PASADENA). vol.33, 1977. a. $1. Pasadena City College, 1570 E. Colorado Blvd., Pasadena, CA 91106. TEL 818-578-7123. illus.
  —BLDSC shelfmark: 4516.776000.
  Supersedes (since vol.30): Pipes of Pan.

811 US
INSECTS ARE PEOPLE TOO. 1989. a. $3. Box 146486, Chicago, IL 60614. TEL 312-777-8686. circ. 1,000.

INSIEME NELLA VALLE E ACCADEMIA INTERNATIONALE ARTE LETTERE SCIENZE DAFNI; ebdomadario artistico-poetico e di informazione del movimento i.n.v. see *LITERATURE*

861 US
INTERNATIONAL POETRY. (Text in English, French, German, Italian, Portuguese, Spanish) 1973. a. $22. International Writers and Artists Association, Bluffton College, Bluffton, OH 45817. TEL 419-358-3418. Ed. Teresinka Pereira. bk.rev.; circ. 500.
  Formerly: Poema Convidado.

808.81 US ISSN 0748-9676
INTERNATIONAL UNIVERSITY POETRY QUARTERLY. 1974. q. $200. (International University Foundation) International University Press, 1301 S. Noland Rd., Independence, MO 64055. TEL 816-461-3633. Ed. John Wayne Johnston. adv.; bk.rev.; circ. 425. (looseleaf format; back issues avail.)

051 US ISSN 0147-4936
PN6099.6
INVISIBLE CITY. 1971. irreg. (approx. 1/yr.). $3 to individuals; libraries $5. Red Hill Press, Box 2853, San Francisco, CA 94126. TEL 415-527-1018. Eds. John McBride, Paul Vangelisti. bk.rev.; circ. 1,000. (tabloid format; also avail. in microform) **Indexed:** Access.
  Formerly: Red Hill Press (ISSN 0034-2009)

IPSISSIMA VERBA; the very words. see *LITERATURE*

821 UK ISSN 0266-111X
ISSUE ONE. 1984. q. £1($6) Eon Publications, 2 Tewkesbury Dr., Grimsby, South Humberside DN34 4TL, England. Ed. Ian Brocklebank. adv.; circ. 200.
  Description: Publishes works of new and established writers.

811 301.412 US
ITHACA WOMEN'S ANTHOLOGY. 1976. a. $3.80. Box 582, Ithaca, NY 14850. Ed.Bd. circ. 350.

811 US
JABBERWOCKY. 1989. 2/yr. $10. Chimera Connections, Inc., 502 N.W. 75th St., Ste. 197, Gainesville, FL 32607-1608. TEL 908-332-6586. Ed. Duane Bray. circ. 1,000.

811 US ISSN 1042-7082
PS325
JACARANDA REVIEW. 1985. s-a. $10. University of California, Los Angeles, Department of English, 405 Hilgard Ave., Los Angeles, CA 90024. TEL 213-825-7411. Ed. Katherine Swiggart. adv.; bk.rev.; circ. 2,000. **Indexed:** Ind.Amer.Per.Verse.

830 GW
JAHRBUCH DEUTSCHER DICHTUNG. 1965. a. Kurt Ruediger, Ed. & Pub., Friedenstr. 16, 7500 Karlsruhe, Germany.

808.81 FR ISSN 0184-8100
JALONS. 1977. 3/yr. 80 F.($17) for 4 nos. Chris and Jean-Paul Mestas, Eds. & Publs., 7 rue Georges Courteline, 37310 Chambourg sur Indre, France. TEL 47-92-56-03. circ. 400.

808.81 II
JAMINRAITU. (Text in Telugu) a. Zamin Ryot Press, 170 Thippajuvari St, Nellore 524001, India.

JAUNA GAITA. see *ART*

JEOPARDY. see *LITERATURE*

JOHN CLARE SOCIETY JOURNAL. see *LITERATURE*

LITERATURE — POETRY

841 BE
JOURNAL DES POETES. 1931. 8/yr. 600 Fr.($16) Maison Internationale de la Poesie, Chaussee de Wavre 150, B-1050 Brussels, Belgium. FAX 5119122. Eds. A. Haulot, P. Jones. adv.; bk.rev.

808.81 CN ISSN 0705-1328
PR9190.25
JOURNAL OF CANADIAN POETRY. (Text in English, French) 1978-1982; resumed 1986. a. Can.$12.95. Borealis Press Limited, 9 Ashburn Dr., Nepean, Ont. K2E 6N4, Canada. TEL 613-224-6837. Ed. David Staines. adv.; bk.rev.; circ. 300. (back issues avail.) Indexed: CMI.
—BLDSC shelfmark: 4954.753000.

811 US ISSN 0363-4205
PS549.N5
JOURNAL OF NEW JERSEY POETS. 1976. s-a. $7. County College of Morris, 214 Center Grove Rd., Randolph, NJ 07869. TEL 201-328-5471. Ed.Bd. adv.; bk.rev.; circ. 500. Indexed: Ind.Amer.Per.Verse.
Description: Publishes poems written by poets who live or who have lived or worked in New Jersey.

808.81 616.89 US ISSN 0889-3675
CODEN: JPTHEK
JOURNAL OF POETRY THERAPY; the interdisciplinary journal of practice, theory, research, and education. 1987. q. $125 (foreign $145). (National Association for Poetry Therapy) Human Sciences Press, Inc. (Subsidiary of: Plenum Publishing Corp.), 233 Spring St., New York, NY 10013-1578. TEL 212-620-8000. FAX 212-463-0742. Ed. Nicholas Mazza. adv. (reprint service avail. from UMI) Indexed: Soc.Work Res.& Abstr.
—BLDSC shelfmark: 5040.820000.
Description: Addresses the use of poetics in health, mental health, education, and other human service settings, focusing on the use of language in therapy.
Refereed Serial

811 US
JUNCTION. 1973. a. $1.50. City University of New York, Brooklyn College, Graduate Student Organization, La Guardia Hall, Rm. 237C, Brooklyn, NY 11210. TEL 718-780-5485. Ed. Marshall Scott Grossman. bk.rev.; bibl.; circ. 600.

808.81 US
JUNIOR EDITOR. 1985. bi-m. $20 to individuals; teachers $10. Editor's Desk, 709 S.E. 52nd Ave., Ocala, FL 32671. TEL 904-694-2303. Eds. Florence F. Bradley, Susie Pettrey. illus.; circ. 275.
Description: For students of all ages.

861 VE ISSN 0047-3030
K: REVISTA DE POESIA.* 1971. 6/yr. Bs.20($4.) Lubio Cardozo y Juan Pinto, Eds. & Pubs., Apartado 410, Herida, Venezuela. bk.rev.; bibl.; tr.lit.; circ. controlled. (processed)

K U L I M U. (Kunst, Literatur & Music) see LITERATURE

808 II
KALAMI RISHATE. (Text in Punjabi) m. Rs.10. Krishan Lal Parwana, 9 Connaugh Circus, Jullundur 144001, India. bk.rev.

811 700 US
KALDRON. 1976. irreg. (1-2/yr.). $5 price varies. Box 7164, Halcyon, CA 93420-7164. Ed. Karl Kempton. bk.rev.; circ. 1,000.
Description: Covers visual poetry from around the world.

KARLSRUHER BOTE. see LITERATURE

891.41 II ISSN 0022-9547
KAVITA. (Text in Gujarati) 1967. bi-m. Rs.10 (foreign Rs.160)(effective 1989). Saurashtra Trust, Janmabhoomi Bhavan, Janmabhoomi Marg, Fort, Bombay 400 001, India. TEL 2870831. Ed. Suresh Dalal. adv.; bk.rev.; circ. 2,200.
Description: Presents literature, emphasizes poetry.

811 US
KAVITHA. 1982. s-a. $6. 4408 Wickford Rd., Baltimore, MD 21210. TEL 301-467-4316. Eds. Thomas Dorsett, Kammana Nirmala. circ. 500.

894.811 II
KAVITHAMANDALAM. (Text in Tamil) 1973. m. Rs.5. Vanambadi, 5 East Maada St., Mylapore, Madras 600004, India.
Description: Contains Tamil poetry.

808.81 II
KAVYA BHARATI. (Text in English) 2/yr. Rs.20($2.50) United States Department of English, American College, Madurai 625002, Tamil Dadu, India.

821 US ISSN 0453-4387
PR4836
KEATS - SHELLEY JOURNAL; Keats, Shelley, Byron, Hunt, and their circles. 1952. a. $20 to individuals; institutions $28. Keats - Shelley Association of America, Inc., c/o Stuart Curran, Ed., Dept. of English, University of Pennsylvania, Philadelphia, PA 19104-6273. bk.rev.; bibl.; circ. 1,000. (also avail. in microfilm; reprint service avail. from KTO) Indexed: Abstr.Engl.Stud., Arts & Hum.Cit.Ind., Curr.Cont., Hum.Ind., Ind.Bk.Rev.Hum., M.L.A., RILA.

KENNEBEC; a portfolio of Maine writing. see LITERATURE

821 AT
KHASMIK POETRY QUARTERLY.* 1974. q. Aus.$6. 26 Breillat St., Sydney 2038, Australia. illus.

811 US
KIOSK. 1987. 3/yr. $6. 317 West 106th St., Ste. 2-C, New York, NY 10025-3648. Eds. Charles Ward, Adam Ward. circ. 500.
Description: Publishes poems and fiction.

891 II
KOBISENA. (Text in Bengali and English) 1972. s-a. Rs.4. c/o Vattacharja Chandan, Ed., P-40 Nandana Park, Calcutta 700 034, India. TEL 777327. circ. 1,000.
Description: Promotes experimental and avant-garde Sarbangin poetry.

811 US
▼**KUMQUAT MERINGUE.** 1990. irreg. (2-3/yr.). $5. Box 5144, Rockford, IL 61125. TEL 815-968-0713.

KUUMBA. see HOMOSEXUALITY

800 US ISSN 0896-8705
LACTUCA. 1986. 3/yr. $10. Lactuca Publications, Box 621, Suffern, NY 10901. TEL 914-356-9236. Ed. Mike Selender. bk.rev.; circ. 700. Indexed: A.I.P.P., Amer.Hum.Ind., Ind.Amer.Per.Verse.

LAGRIMAL TRIFURCA. see LITERATURE

808 UK
THE LAST EVER MELODIC SCRIBBLE. 1984. 3/yr. $10. Pretty Publications, 81 Castlerigg Dr., Burnley, Lancashire BB12 8AT, England. Ed. Andrew Savage. adv.; bk.rev.; illus.; circ. 300. (back issues avail.)
Formerly: International Melodic Scribble.
Description: Presents rhymed and free verse, both humorous and sad.

811 US
LEGACIES IN TIME. 1989. 4/yr. $18. Proving Grounds International, Inc., Box 1074, Jackson, MI 49204. TEL 517-782-1075. circ. 600.

811 700 US
LEGACY (NASHVILLE). 1984. s-a. free. Trevecca Nazarene College, 333 Murfreesboro Rd., Nashville, TN 37203. TEL 615-248-1200. Ed. Scott A. Stargel. illus.; circ. 750. (back issues avail.)

LETRAS DE BUENOS AIRES. see LITERATURE

861 NQ
LETRAS DE NICARAGUA. irreg., no.3, 1982. Editorial Nueva Nicaragua, Paseo Salvador Allende, Km. 3, 1-2 Carretera Sur, Apdo. Postal RP-073, Managua, Nicaragua.

811 US
LETTERS FROM LIMERICK. 1980. q. $20. Limerick League, Inc., 1212 Elsworth St., Philadelphia, PA 19147. Ed. J. Beauregard Pepys. adv.; bk.rev.; circ. 1,500.

808.81 US
LEWISTON POETRY. irreg., latest no.20. $14.95 per no. Edwin Mellen Press, 240 Portage Rd., Box 450, Lewiston, NY 14092. TEL 800-753-2788. FAX 716-754-4335.

AL LIAMM. see LITERATURE

054.1 CN ISSN 0024-2020
AP21
LIBERTE. 1959. bi-m. Can.$30 (foreign $35). Collectif Liberte Inc., C.P. 399, Succ. Outremont, Montreal, Que. H2V 4N3, Canada. FAX 514-274-0201. Ed. Francois Hebert. adv.; bk.rev.; tr.lit.; circ. 3,000. (also avail. in microform from UMI; reprint service avail. from UMI, ISI) Indexed: Arts & Hum.Cit.Ind., Can.Lit.Ind., Can.Per.Ind., Curr.Cont., Pt.de Rep. (1983-), RADAR.
—BLDSC shelfmark: 5186.763000.

LIFTOUTS; a review of books and language work. see PUBLISHING AND BOOK TRADE

811 US
LIGHTNING SWORD. 1986. irreg. $1 per no. A P K L Publications, Box 371, Woodstock, NY 12498. Ed. Stephen Mark Rafalsky. circ. 1,000.

811 US ISSN 0743-2909
LIMBERLOST REVIEW. 1976. irreg. (2-3/yr.) $9.95 per no. HC 33, Box 1113, Boise, ID 83706-9702. Ed. Richard Ardinger. circ. 1,000.
Description: Often devoted to the works of poets in the form of chapbooks.

811 US
LIME GREEN BULLDOZERS (AND OTHER RELATED SPECIES). 1986. 2/yr. $3 per no. 1003 Ave. X, Apt. A, Lubbock, TX 79401. TEL 806-744-7412. circ. 300.

LIMESTONE; a literary journal. see LITERATURE

821 UK ISSN 0459-4541
LINES REVIEW. 1952. q. £8.50($17) (Scottish Arts Council) Macdonald Publishers, Edgefield Rd., Loanhead, Midlothian, Scotland. TEL 031-440 0246. FAX 031-440-0315. Ed. Tessa Ransford. adv.; bk.rev.; circ. 1,000.
Description: Publishes poetry in English, Scots and Gaelic. Includes Erropean languages in translation.

811 US ISSN 0893-620X
LIP SERVICE. 1986. a. $4. Lip Service, Inc., Box 23231, Washington, DC 20026-3231. TEL 703-549-1747. Ed. Robert Haynes. circ. 250.

811 US ISSN 0278-0933
LIPS (MONTCLAIR). 1981. 3/yr. $9 to individuals; institutions $12. Lips Press, Box 1345, Montclair, NJ 07042. TEL 201-662-1303. Ed. Laura Boss. adv.; circ. 1,000. Indexed: A.I.P.P., Ind. Amer. Per. Verse.

808.81 US ISSN 1049-9598
▼**LITERARY CREATIONS.*** 1990. m. $8. Imagery Publications, Box 1339, Albany, OR 97321-0440. Ed. Margaret L. Ingram. adv.; bk.rev.; circ. 300. (tabloid format; back issues avail.)

LITERARY TAIWAN/WEN HSUEH CHIEH. see LITERATURE

LITERATUR & KRITIK; oesterreichische Monatsschrift. see LITERATURE

831 GW ISSN 0932-4623
LITERATUR UM 11. 1987. s-a. DM.15. (Europae Literae) Diagonal Verlag, Postfach 1248, 3550 Marburg, Germany. TEL 06421-681936. FAX 06421-681733. Eds. Ludwig Legge, Anne Neuschaefer. (back issues avail.)

LITERATUR UND GESELLSCHAFT. see LITERATURE

800 DK ISSN 0107-0916
LITTERATURTOLKNINGER. 1980. triennial. DKK 617.20. Bibliotekscentralen, Tempovej 7-11, 2750 Ballerup, Denmark. TEL 2-974000. FAX 2-655310.

LITTLE REVIEW. see LITERATURE

LOBBY PRESS NEWSLETTER. see LITERARY AND POLITICAL REVIEWS

808.81 US
LOCKERT LIBRARY OF POETRY IN TRANSLATION. 1967. irreg., latest 1991. price varies. Princeton University Press, 3175 Princeton Pike, Lawrenceville, NJ 08648. TEL 609-896-1344. FAX 609-895-1081. (reprint service avail. from UMI)

841 FR
LOLA-FISH. (Text in English) 1989. 6/yr. $6. 36, Residence Jean Mace, 28300 Mainvilliers, France.

800 US
LONG ISLAND POETRY COLLECTIVE. NEWSLETTER. 1974. 6/yr. membership. Long Island Poetry Collective, Inc., Box 773, Huntington, NY 11743. Ed. Sue Kain. circ. 100.

811 US
LONGHOUSE. 1973. a. $10. Bob Arnold, Ed. & Pub., Jacksonville Stage, Brattleboro, VT 05301. TEL 802-254-4242. bk.rev.; circ. 200.
 Description: Contains works by unknowns and outsiders.

811 US
▼**THE LOOGIE.** 1990. 6/yr. $6. 435 Probasco, Ste. 3, Cincinnati, OH 45220. TEL 513-281-1353. circ. 50.

811 US
LOOK QUICK. 1975. irreg. (approx. 2/yr.). $2 per no. Quick Books, Box 222, Pueblo, CO 81002. Eds. Joel Scherzer, Robbie Rubinstein. bk.rev.; circ. 200. (also avail. in microfilm; back issues avail.)

811 US ISSN 0734-0699
LOONFEATHER; a magazine of poetry, short prose and graphics. 1979. 2/yr. $7.50. Loonfeather Press, 426 Bemidji Ave., Bemidji, MN 56601. TEL 218-751-4869. Eds. Betty Rossi, Marsh Muirhead. adv.; circ. 300. (back issues avail.)

811 US
LOUDER THAN BOMBS. 1990. 6/yr. $10. Seminal Life Press, 2313 Santa Anita Ave., S. El Monte, CA 91733. TEL 818-575-1887. Ed. Bryan Ha. circ. 200.

811 US ISSN 0897-6481
LUCIDITY; quarterly journal of verse. 1985. q. $8. Bear House Publishing, RR 02, Box 94, Eureka Springs, AR 72632-9505. TEL 501-253-9351. Ed. Ted. O Badger. bk.rev.; circ. 260. (back issues avail.)
 Description: Features life-related poetry.

LUCRE-HATIF. see LITERATURE

808.81 US ISSN 1051-5968
▼**LULLWATER REVIEW.** 1990. 3/yr. $12 to individuals (foreign $15); institutions $15 (foreign $18). Emory University, Box 22036, Atlanta, GA 30322. TEL 404-727-6181. circ. 1,000. (back issues avail.) **Indexed:** Amer.Hum.Ind., Ind.Amer.Per.Verse.

LUVAH. see LITERATURE

LYNX; a quarterly journal of renga. see ORIENTAL STUDIES

LYRA. see LITERARY AND POLITICAL REVIEWS

811 US ISSN 0024-7820
PS301
LYRIC. 1921. q. $10 (foreign $12). Leslie Mellichamp, Ed. & Pub., 307 Dunton Dr. S.W., Blacksburg, VA 24060. TEL 703-552-3475. index; circ. 900.
 Description: Publishes only original, unpublished poetry.

811 US ISSN 0076-1699
LYRICAL IOWA; poetry by Iowa authors. 1946. a. $6. Iowa Poetry Association, 2325 61st St., Des Moines, IA 50322. TEL 515-279-1106. Ed. Lucille Morgan Wilson. circ. 800.

MABUA/FOUNTAIN; religious creation in literature, society and thought. see LITERATURE

811 US
MAC GUFFIN. 1983. 3/yr. $10. Schoolcraft College, 18600 Haggerty Rd., Livonia, MI 48152. TEL 313-462-4400. Ed. Arthur J. Lindenberg. circ. 500.

811 US
MACGUFFIN. 1984. 3/yr. $10. Schoolcraft College, English Department, 18600 Haggerty Rd., Livonia, MI 48152. TEL 313-462-4400. Ed. Arthur J. Lindenberg. circ. 500. (back issues avail.)

811 US
▼**MAD POETS REVIEW.** 1990. 2/yr. $6. 1074 Hopkins Ave., Glenolden, PA 19036.
 Description: Publishes poems of various forms and styles.

811 US
MADISON REVIEW. 1979. s-a. $4 per no. University of Wisconsin, Department of English, Helen C. White Hall, 600 N. Park St., Madison, WI 53706. TEL 608-263-3800. Ed.Bd. adv.; illus.; circ. 500.
 Supersedes (1968-1979): Bloodroot (Madison); Modine Gunch (ISSN 0026-8763)

818 US ISSN 8755-8785
MAGAZINE OF SPECULATIVE POETRY. 1984. q. $11. Magazine of Speculative Poetry, Box 564, Beloit, WI 53512. Eds. Roger Dutcher, Mark Rich. adv.; bk.rev.; circ. 200. (back issues avail.)
 Description: Presents poetry, reviews and articles on speculative poetry, the equivalent of speculative fiction.

MAGE; a magazine of fantasy & science fiction. see LITERATURE — Science Fiction, Fantasy, Horror

MAGIRA. see LITERATURE — Science Fiction, Fantasy, Horror

808.81 PR
MAIRENA. 1979. s-a. $6 to individuals; institutions $15(effective Jan. 1991). Manuel de la Puebla, Ed. & Pub., 1656 C. Penasco - Paradise, San Juan, PR 00926-3127. TEL 809-250-8197. adv.; bk.rev.; circ. 1,000.

811 CN ISSN 0025-1216
MALAHAT REVIEW. 1967. 4/yr. Can.$15 to individuals; institutions Can.$25. University of Victoria, Box 3045, Victoria, B.C. V8W 3P4, Canada. TEL 604-721-8524. FAX 604-721-8653. Ed. Constance Rooke. adv.; illus.; cum.index: 1967-1977; circ. 1,800. **Indexed:** Abstr.Engl.Stud., Amer.Bibl.Slavic & E.Eur.Stud., Amer.Hum.Ind., Arts & Hum.Cit.Ind., Can.Lit.Ind., Can.Per.Ind., Curr.Cont., Hum.Ind, Ind.Amer.Per.Verse, M.L.A.

840 SZ ISSN 0076-3748
LA MANDRAGORE QUI CHANTE. 1961. irreg., latest vol.44, 1991. price varies. Editions de la Baconniere S.A., Box 185, CH-2017 Boudry, Switzerland. TEL 038-421004. Ed. Marc Eigeldinger. (reprint service avail. from UMI)

808 US ISSN 0885-9205
MANHATTAN POETRY REVIEW; a magazine of contemporary American poetry. 1982. s-a. $12 (foreign $25). Box 8207, New York, NY 10150. TEL 212-355-6634. Ed. Elaine Reiman-Fenton. circ. 500.

808.81 US ISSN 0275-6889
PN1010
MANHATTAN REVIEW. 1980. a. $10 to individuals; institutions $14. Manhattan Review Press, c/o Philip Fried, Ed., 440 Riverside Dr., Apt. 45, New York, NY 10027. TEL 212-932-1854. adv.; bk.rev.; circ. 500. (back issues avail.) **Indexed:** A.I.P.P., Amer.Hum.Ind., Ind.Amer.Per.Verse.

821 US ISSN 0025-2166
MANIFOLD;* review of poetry and the arts. 1962. q. 12s.($2.) 99 Vera Ave., London N.21, England. bk.rev.

MANIPUR STATE KALA AKADEMI. QUARTERLY JOURNAL. see LITERATURE

808.81 US ISSN 0894-2242
MANKATO POETRY REVIEW. 1984. s-a. $4. Mankato State University, English Department, Box 53, Mankato, MN 56001. TEL 507-389-5511. Ed. Roger Sheffer. bk.rev.; circ. 200. (back issues avail.)

808.81 US ISSN 0886-5957
MANNA. 1978. s-a. $6 (Canada and Mexico $7; elsewhere $12)(effective Sep.1991). FishDown Press, 2966 W. Westcove Dr., W. Valley City, UT 84119-5940. Ed.Bd. circ. 200.
 Description: Collection of serious, humorous and inspirational poetry with strong imagery.

MANOA; a Pacific journal of international writing. see LITERATURE

821 UK
MAR. 1989. 2/yr. £3. New River Project, 89A Petherton Rd., London N5 2QT, England.

MARBACHER MAGAZIN. see LITERATURE

811 US
MARTHA'S VINEYARD MAGAZINE. 1985. 4/yr. $15. Box 66, Edgartown, MA 02539. TEL 508-627-4311. Ed. Julia Wells. circ. 13,000.

808.81 US
MARYLAND POETRY REVIEW. 1986. s-a. $15. Maryland State Poetry and Literary Society, Drawer H, Catonsville, MD 21228. TEL 301-385-0541. Ed. R. Klein. bk.rev.; circ. 1,000. (back issues avail.)
 Description: Promotes national and international literary artists.

811 US
MATI. 1975. q. $5.50. Ommation Press, 5548 N. Sawyer Ave., Chicago, IL 60625. Ed. Effie Mihopoulos. adv.; circ. 1,000.
 Description: Features both academic and experimental poetry.

808.81 800 AT
MATILDA MAGAZINE: LITERARY AND ART MAGAZINE. 1980. q. Aus.$5. (Brunswick Poetry Workshop) Matilda Publications, 7 Mountfield St., Brunswick, Vic. 3056, Australia. Eds. Albert Hayes, Fonda Zenofon. adv.; bk.rev.; circ. 1,000.
 Former titles: Matilda Literary and Art Magazine (ISSN 0810-2740); Matilda Literary Magazine (ISSN 0159-7841)

808.81 890 US ISSN 8755-7266
MATRIX (URBANA). 1976. a. $8 (effective Sep. 1991). (Channing-Murray Foundation) Red Herring Press, c/o Channing-Murray Foundation, 1209 W. Oregon St., Urbana, IL 61801. TEL 217-344-1176. Eds. Carmen M. Pursifull, Ruth S. Walker. circ. 300. (back issues avail.)
 Description: Features poetry on all subjects, diverse styles. Contains selected work by members of Red Herring poetry workshop.

808.81 US
MAYFLY; a magazine of Haiku. 1986. 3/yr. $10. High-Coo Press, 4634 Hale Dr., Decatur, IL 62526-1117. TEL 217-877-2966. Ed. Randy Brooks. circ. 200.
 Description: Features Haiku in English.

ME. see ART

811 US
ME MAGAZINE. 1980. irreg. $20. Pittore Euforico, Box 1132, Peter Stuyvesant Station, New York, NY 10009. TEL 212-673-2705. Ed. Carlo Pittore. circ. 2,000.
 Description: Publishes poems about the "me", the subjective.

808.21 US
ME TOO.* 1974. a. $1.50. Me Too, Inc., 112 W. 34th St., New York, NY 10001. TEL 212-594-9224.

811 US
MEASURE.* 1971. s-a. $6. Tribal Press, c/o Howard McCord, Ed., 15431 San Ridge Rd., Bowling Green, OH 43402. bk.rev.; circ. 200-500. (reprint service avail. from KTO)

808.81 BG
MEIRA. (Text in Manipuri) bi-m. Tk.5. Bangladesh Manipuri Sahitya Sangsad, Taponan, Lamabazar, Sylhet - 3100, Bangladesh. Ed. A.K. Sheram.
 Formerly (until 1989): Dipanvita

808.81 US ISSN 0025-8954
MELE; international poetry letter. (Text in various languages) 1965. a. $4. University of Hawaii, Department of European Languages and Literature, Honolulu, HI 96822. TEL 808-948-8520. Ed. Stefan Baciu. (processed)

811 US
MELLEN POETRY SERIES. irreg., latest no.19. $14.95 per no. Edwin Mellen Press, 240 Portage Rd., Box 450, Lewiston, NY 14092. TEL 716-754-8566. FAX 716-754-4335.

LITERATURE — POETRY

821 UK
MEMES. 1989. irreg. (2-3/yr.). $10. c/o 38 Molesworth Rd., Plymouth, Devonshire PL7 4NT, England. circ. 250.

MENSUEL 25. see *ART*

811 US
METAPHOR. 1985. 4/yr. $7. 109 Minna St., Ste. 153, San Francisco, CA 94105. TEL 415-641-7231. circ. 250.

811 US
MID COASTER. 1986. a. $4. 2750 North 45th St., Milwaukee, WI 53210-2429. Ed. Peter Blewett. circ. 500.

MIDCOASTER. see *LITERATURE*

811 US ISSN 0026-3346
MIDWEST CHAPARRAL.* 1942. 2/yr. $3 (non-members $4). Midwest Federation of Chaparral Poets, c/o Margaret Wolff Garland, Ed., 225 3rd St. S.E., Waverly, IA 50677-3509. TEL 319-352-1716. bk.rev.; circ. 150.
  Description: Introduces poetry by members and subscribers. Includes some humorous verse.

811 US ISSN 0745-8738
MIDWEST POETRY REVIEW; a family of poets. 1980. q. $20 (Canada $25; elsewhere $30). River City Publishers, Box 4776, Rock Island, IL 61201. Ed. Tom Tilford. adv.; bk.rev.; circ. 10,000.
  Description: Literary magazine by and for poets, devoted only to poetry.

821 US ISSN 0540-0961
MILTON SOCIETY OF AMERICA. PROCEEDINGS. 1953. a. $5. Milton Society of America, c/o Albert C. Labriola, Ed., Department of English, Duquesne University, 600 Forbes Ave., Pittsburgh, PA 15282. TEL 412-434-6420. circ. 450.

808.5 US ISSN 8756-1549
MIND IN MOTION; a magazine of poetry and short prose. 1985. q. $14 (foreign $18). Mind in Motion Publications, Box 1118, Apple Valley, CA 92307. TEL 619-248-6512. Ed. Celeste Goyer. circ. 250. (back issues avail.)
  Description: General literary quarterly on poetry and short fiction.

808.8 US
MINETTA REVIEW; all-university literary journal. 1974. 2/yr. membership only. New York University, Student Activities, 21 Washington Pl., Box 168, New York, NY 10003. TEL 212-998-4700. Ed. Eddie Pereira. circ. 7,000.

MINJIAN GUSHI/FOLK TALES. see *FOLKLORE*

800 US
MINOTAUR. 1975. q. $12. Minotaur Press, Box 4039, Felton, CA 95018. Ed. Jim Gove. bk.rev.; circ. 150 (paid); 150 (controlled). (back issues avail.)
  Description: Publishes contemporary poetry.

MIRAGE; the magazine of the arts. see *ART*

811 US
MIRRORS; in the spirit of Haiku. 1988. q. $20 (foreign $25). Box 1250, Gualala, CA 95445. TEL 707-882-2226. FAX 707-884-1232. Ed. Jane Reichhold. adv.; bk.rev.; circ. 130.
  Description: Subscriber-produced haiku poetry magazine. Contents of each page is totally in the control of the person submitting that page. Includes haiku, senryu, renga, tanka, and haibun.

811 US ISSN 0026-7244
MOCCASIN. 1937. s-a. $12. League of Minnesota Poets, 732 Garfield Ave., North Mankato, MN 56001. Ed. Patricia M. Johnson. circ. 179.

811 US ISSN 0026-7821
PS593.H3
MODERN HAIKU. 1969. 3/yr. $13. Robert Spiess, Ed. & Pub., Box 1752, Madison, WI 53701. TEL 608-233-2738. bk.rev.; circ. 650. (back issues avail.) **Indexed:** Ind.Bk.Rev.Hum.
  Description: Presents haiku and senryu poetry.

811 US ISSN 0026-7848
MODERN IMAGES.* 1968. q. $12.95. Modern Images Poets Committee, c/o Morgan-Mod-Images, 1217 Champaign Ave., Mattoon, IL 61938-3167. Ed. Sue A. Morgan. bk.rev.; circ. 100.

811 US
MOONSTONE BLUE, NIGHT ROSES. 1986. irreg. $3 per no. Box 393, Prospect Heights, IL 60070. TEL 708-392-2435. Ed. Allen T. Billy. circ. 250.

808.81 CN ISSN 0228-7404
MOOSEHEAD REVIEW. 1978. a. Can.$5.50. Moosehead Press, Box 169, Ayer's Cliff, Que. JOB 1C0, Canada. Ed. Robert Allen. bk.rev.; circ. 350.

081 US ISSN 0740-1205
PS615
MR. COGITO. 1973. irreg. $9 for 3 nos. Mr. Cogito Press, Humanities Division, Pacific University, Forest Grove, OR 97116. TEL 503-226-4135. Eds. Robert A. Davies, John M. Gogol. circ. 500.
  Description: Publishes poetry, some emphasis on translations. Also graphics; contests.

808.81 700 US
MUDFISH; art and poetry. 1983. a. $8. Box Turtle Press, 184 Franklin St., New York, NY 10013. TEL 212-219-9278. Ed. Jill Hoffman. adv.; circ. 1,500. (back issues avail.)
  Description: Contemporary poems interspersed with contemporary art.

808.81 US
MUSE - PIE. 1980. s-a. $5. 73 Pennington Ave., Passaic, NJ 07055. TEL 201-777-3588. Ed. R.W. Grandinetti Rader. circ. 300.

821 CN
MUSELETTER. no.13, 1974. s-a. Can.$25 (typically set in Apr.). League of Canadian Poets, 24 Ryerson Avenue, Toronto, Ont. M5T 2P3, Canada. TEL 416-363-5047. FAX 416-860-0826. Ed. Richard Lush. adv.; circ. 400. (back issues avail.)
  Formerly: League of Canadian Poets. Newsletter (ISSN 0319-6658)
  Description: Information about and for members, poetry, essays, market and contest news.

811 US
▼**MY LEGACY.** 1990. 4/yr. $12. Star Rte., Box 21AA, Artemas, PA 17211. TEL 814-458-3102. Ed. Kay Weems. circ. 150.
  Description: Publishes only English poems, no translations.

N E A GRANTMAKING PROGRAMS: LITERATURE. (National Endowment for the Arts) see *LITERATURE*

808.81 US
N.P.D.C. NEWSLETTER. 1965. bi-m. membership. Florida State Poetry Society, Inc., National Poetry Day Committee, 1110 N. Venetion Dr., Miami Beach, FL 33139. Ed. Frances Clark Handler. bk.rev.; play rev.; stat.; circ. 17,000. (tabloid format)

811 US
N R G. 1976. 2/yr. $4. 6735 S.E. 78th St., Portland, OR 97206. Ed. Dan Raphael. bk.rev.; charts; illus.; stat.; circ. 1,000. (tabloid format; back issues avail.)
  Description: Avant-garde poetry

839.311 NE ISSN 0027-7355
NAAR MORGEN. 1970. q. fl.25. Opwenteling, Cooperatieve Vereniging voor Presentatie van Literatuur U.A., Postbus 6254, 5600 HG Eindhoven, Netherlands. TEL 040-455442. Ed.Bd. circ. 500.

821 IE
NEPTUNE'S KINGDOM; poetry review. (Text in English) 1972. irreg. 10p.($1) per issue. c/o Martin Gleeson, Ed., 5 Victoria Terrace, Kilkee, Co. Clare, Ireland. bk.rev.; illus.; circ. 500.

831 GW ISSN 0342-9547
NEUE BEITRAEGE ZUR GEORGE-FORSCHUNG. 1976. a. DM.16.80. Gesellschaft zur Foerderung der Stefan-George-Gedenkstaette Bingen e.V., Nostadtstr. 119, 6530 Bingen a.R., Germany. TEL 06721-44126. (Subscr. to: Verlag Brigitte Guderjahn, Im Anger 5, 6900 Heidelberg, Germany) circ. 400.

808.81 US ISSN 0893-7842
NEW AMERICAN WRITING. 1971. s-a. $6 to individuals; institutions $8; foreign $10. Oink! Press, Inc., 2920 W. Pratt Blvd., Chicago, IL 60645. FAX 312-262-9605. Eds. Maxine Chernoff, Paul Hoover. adv.; bk.rev.; circ. 2,000. **Indexed:** Amer.Hum.Ind., Ind.Amer.Per.Verse.
  Formerly (until 1986): Oink! (ISSN 0883-8518)
  Description: Contains avant-garde poetry, short fiction, and essays on poetics.

821 UK ISSN 0262-558X
N6768
NEW ARCADIAN JOURNAL. (Each issue has distinctive title) 1981. s-a. £25 (foreign £35). New Arcadian Press, 13 Graham Grove, Burley, Leeds LS4 2NF, England. TEL 0532-304608. Ed. Patrick Eyres. illus. (back issues avail.)
  —BLDSC shelfmark: 6082.082000.

NEW CANADIAN REVIEW. see *LITERATURE*

952 JA ISSN 0911-6567
NEW CICADA; haiku poetry magazine. (Text in English) 1984. s-a. 1000 Yen($6) Tadao Okazaki, Ed. & Pub., 40-11 Kubo, Hobara, Fukushima 960-06, Japan. (back issues avail.)
  Description: Devoted to the definition of traditional haiku as a ballad, and to free-verse haiku.

821 SA
NEW COIN POETRY. 1965. s-a. R.1150($14) £7.50(typically set in Jan.). Rhodes University, Institute for the Study of English in Africa, P.O. Box 94, Grahamstown 6140, South Africa. Ed. Robert Berold. circ. 450. **Indexed:** Ind.S.A.Per.
  Formerly: New Coin (ISSN 0028-4459)

811 US
NEW DAY PUBLICATIONS. 1987. 4/yr. $10. Rte. 4, Box 10, Eupora, MS 39744. TEL 801-258-2935. Ed. Brenda Davis.

NEW DIRECTIONS (NEW YORK, 1936). see *LITERATURE*

NEW DOG. see *LITERARY AND POLITICAL REVIEWS*

831 LU
NEW EUROPE. 1972. 4/yr. Europeditor, P.O. Box 212, Luxemburg, Luxembourg.

821 UK
NEW HOPE INTERNATIONAL REVIEW. 1980. s-a. £10($25) New Hope International, 20 Werneth Ave., Gee Cross, Hyde, Cheshire SK14 5NL, England. TEL 061-351-1878. Ed. Gerald England. adv.; bk.rev.; illus.; cum.index; circ. 1,000. (back issues avail.)
  Formerly: New Hope International Review Supplement.
  Description: Review of books, magazines, cassettes, CDs and PC software. Covers literature, music, art, socio-politics, religion and small press.

821 UK
NEW HOPE INTERNATIONAL WRITING. (Text mainly in English; occasionally in other languages) 1980. 6/yr. £10($25) including New Hope International Review. New Hope International, 20 Werneth Avenue, Gee Cross, Hyde SK14 5NL, England. TEL 061-351-1878. Ed. Gerald England. adv.; bk.rev.; cum.index: 1980-1989; circ. 1,000. (back issues avail.)
  Formerly: New Hope International (ISSN 0260-7948); Supersedes: Osgoldcross Review.
  Description: Poetry, prose and original artwork from around the world.

NEW LITERATURE AND IDEOLOGY. see *LITERARY AND POLITICAL REVIEWS*

808.81 US ISSN 0253-293X
NEW MUSES. 1976. q. price varies. Federation of International Poetry Associations, Drawer 579, Santa Claus, IN 47579. Ed. Carol L. Abell. bk.rev.; circ. 2,000.
  Description: Serves the presidents, directors, and members of organizations, societies and groups affiliated with the federation.

NEW ORLEANS REVIEW. see *LITERATURE*

811 US
NEW POETS SERIES - CHESTNUT HILLS PRESS. 1971. 4/yr. price varies. New Poets Series, Inc., 541 Piccadilly Rd., Baltimore, MD 21204. Ed. Clarinda Harriss. circ. 1,000.

811 US ISSN 0894-6078
NEW PRESS; a literary quarterly. 1984. q. $12. 53-35 Hollis Ct. Blvd., Flushing, NY 11365. TEL 718-217-7464. Ed. Robert Dunn. adv.; circ. 1,000. (back issues avail.)
  Description: Features short stories, poetry, commentary, and personal journalism with illustrations.

LITERATURE — POETRY

811 US
NEW SINS. 1989. 2/yr. $3. Rane Arroyo, Ed. & Pub., Box 7157, Pittsburgh, PA 15213. TEL 412-621-5611. circ. 200.

821 UK
NEW SPOKES. 1985. 2/yr. £7.50 (foreign £9). c/o The Orchard House, 45 Clophill Rd., Upper Gravenhurst, Bedford MK45 4JH, England. TEL 0462-711195. Eds. Donald Atkinson. bk.rev.; illus.; circ. 300.
  Formerly (until 1991): Spokes (ISSN 0268-294X)

808 US
NEW VOICES (METHUEN). 1979. a. $4. 24 Edgewood Terrace, Methuen, MA 01844. TEL 617-685-3087. Ed. Lorraine Moreau-Laverriere. circ. 300. (back issues avail.)

NEW WRITER'S MAGAZINE. see LITERATURE

811 US ISSN 0028-7482
PS580
NEW YORK QUARTERLY. Short title: N Y Q. 1970-1979; resumed 1985. 3/yr. $15 to individuals; institutions $25. National Poetry Foundation, 302 Neville Hall, University of Maine, Orono, ME 04469. Ed. William Packard. adv.; bibl.; cum.index every 10 nos.; circ. 3,500. (back issues avail.) **Indexed:** Curr.Cont.

NEW ZEALAND JOURNAL OF FRENCH STUDIES. see LITERATURE

808.81 US ISSN 0743-6882
NEWSLETTER INAGO. 1979. m. $17 (foreign $19)(effective 1992). Box 26244, Tucson, AZ 85726-6244. TEL 602-294-7031. Ed. Del Reitz. circ. 100.

821 CN ISSN 0828-8496
NEXT EXIT. 1980. s-a. Can.$6($6) 92 Helen St., Kingston, Ont. K7L 4P3, Canada. TEL 613-549-6790. Ed. Eric Folsom. bk.rev.; circ. 150.
  Description: Contemporary poems from around the world.

NEXUS (DAYTON). see LITERATURE

811 US
NIAGARA MAGAZINE.* 1974. 3/yr. $7 for 4 issues. 17 Burnside St., Upper Montclair, NJ 07043-1324. Ed. Neil Baldwin. circ. 500. (back issues avail)

NIHILISTIC REVIEW; the magazine for those without convention. see LITERATURE

NIMROD; international journal of fiction and poetry. see LITERATURE

811 US
NOCTURNAL LYRIC. 1987. 6/yr. $10. Box 2602, Pasadena, CA 91101. circ. 200.

811 US
NOOSPAPERS. 1986. 3/yr. $8. Open Dialogue, Inc., 215 N. Ave. West, Ste. 21, Westfield, NJ 07090. TEL 201-249-0280. circ. 200.

808.81 IT
NORDSEE; poesia in forma di manifesto. (Summaries in English) 1977. q. L.10000. Maurizio Maldini, Ed. & Pub., Via A. Romagnoli, 39, 40137 Bologna, Italy.
  Formerly: Nordsee - Cerchio.

811 US
▼**NORTHEASTARTS MAGAZINE.** 1990. 4/yr. $8. J.F.K. Station, Box 6061, Boston, MA 02114. circ. 600.

820 UK ISSN 0078-1738
NORTHERN HOUSE PAMPHLET POETS. 1964. irreg. price varies. Northern House, 19 Haldane Terrace, Newcastle-upon-Tyne NE2 3AN, England. Ed.Bd. adv.; bk.rev.; circ. 1,000. (back issues avail.)
  ●Also available online.

NORTHLAND QUARTERLY. see LITERARY AND POLITICAL REVIEWS

NORTHWARD JOURNAL; a quarterly of northern arts. see LITERATURE

811 US
NOSTOC. 1973. s-a. $10. Arts End Books, Box 162, Newton, MA 02168. Ed. Marshall Brooks. adv.; bk.rev.; circ. 500. (back issues avail.)

NOUVEAU COMMERCE. see LITERATURE

808.81 FR ISSN 0294-4030
PQ1184
NOUVELLE TOUR DE FEU; revue de creation poetique. 1946. bi-m. 200 F. Editions du Soleil Natal, 8 bis rue Lormier, 91580 Etrechy, France. Ed. Michel Heroult. bk.rev.; illus.; circ. 3,000.
  Formerly (until 1982): Tour de Feu (ISSN 0040-9731)

861 BL
NOVA POESIA BRASILEIRA. 1983. 10/yr. $10. Shogun Editora e Arte Ltda., Caixa Postal 43.021, CEP 22052, Rio de Janeiro, Brazil. TEL 021-2559494. circ. 12,000.

861 CL
NUEVA LINEA;* revista de literatura y arte. 1976. q. Esc.45($5) or exchange. Editorial Nueva Linea, Apdo. Postal 14.978, Stgo. 21, Santiago, Chile. Ed. Bd. bk.rev.; circ. 1,500.

871 SP
NUEVA POETICA ANDALUZA.* 1981. irreg. Editorial Cajal, Paseo de Almeria 1810, Apdo. 456, 04080 Almeria, Spain.

808.81 700 US ISSN 0898-1140
PQ7074.5
LA NUEZ; literary magazine. (Text in Spanish) 1988. q. $12 to individuals; institutions $15; foreign $18. Box 1655, New York, NY 10276. TEL 212-260-3130. Ed. Rafael Bordao. adv.; bk.rev.; circ. 1,000.
  Description: Contains poetry, essays, short fiction, criticism, interviews, reviews and original artwork and photography.

808.81 800 US
NUMBER ONE. 1973. a. free. Volunteer State Community College, Humanities Division, Nashville Pike, Gallatin, TN 37066. TEL 615-452-8600. Ed. Jeanne Irelan. circ. 1,000 (controlled).
  Description: Features poetry and short fiction from established writers, faculty and students.

821 UK ISSN 0950-2858
NUMBERS. 1986. s-a. £4.50($11.50) Numbers Publishing Ltd., 6 Kingston St., Cambridge, Cambs. CB1 2NU, England. TEL 0223-353425. Ed.Bd. adv.; circ. 1,000. (back issues avail.)

851 IT
NUOVA RASSEGNA: RIVISTA TRIMESTRALE. q. L.40000. Editrice Pellegrini, Via Roma 74, Casella Postale 158, 87100 Cosenza, Italy. Ed. Luigi Pellegrini-Cosenza. illus.
  Formerly: Poeti della Nuova Italia (ISSN 0032-1982)

821 US
NUTSHELL. 1988. 4/yr. £6. 8 George Marston Rd., Ernsford Grange, Coventry CV3 2HH, England. Ed. Chris Nankivell. circ. 200.

811 US
NYCTICORAX (CITRUS HEIGHTS). 1985. 3/yr. $10. 8420 Olivine Ave., Citrus Heights, CA 95610-2721. Ed. John A. Youril. circ. 650.
  Description: Publishes poetry, including translated poems.

808.81 US
O. ARS. 1981. s-a. $10. O. Ars, Inc., 21 Rockland Rd., Weare, NH 03281. TEL 603-529-1060. Ed. Don Wellman. adv.; bk.rev.; illus.; circ. 1,000. (back issues avail.) **Indexed:** M.L.A.
  Description: Covers poetry, visual language and theory.

808.81 US ISSN 0896-3053
O-BLEK; a journal of language arts. 1987. 2/yr. $15 (effective Jan. 1990). Garlic Press Foundation, Inc., Box 1242, Stockbridge, MA 01262. TEL 413-528-0462. Eds. J. Connell McGrath, Peter Gizzi. circ. 300. (back issues avail.)
  Description: Includes prose and poetry with emphasis on experimental and lyric creative writing.

808.81 II
OCARINA; Journal of poetry and aesthetics. (Text in English) 1968. bi-m. price varies. Tagore Institute of Creative Writing, International, Diparun, T-29B, Seventh Ave., Madras 600 090, India. Ed. Amal Ghose. adv.; circ. 5,000.

811 US
ODESSA POETRY REVIEW. 1984. 4/yr. $16. RR 1, Box 39, Odessa, MO 64076. Ed. Jim Wyzard. circ. 600.

811 US
OFFICE NUMBER ONE. 1989. 6/yr. $8.84 for 8 issues. 1709 San Antonio St., Austin, TX 78701. TEL 512-320-8243. circ. 2,000.

811 810 US ISSN 0360-1013
AS30
OHIO REVIEW. 1959. 3/yr. $12. Ohio University, Ellis Hall, Athens, OH 45701-2979. TEL 614-593-1900. Ed. Wayne Dodd. adv.; bk.rev.; illus.; index; circ. 2,000. (also avail. in Braille; back issues avail.) **Indexed:** A.I.P.P., Abstr.Pop.Cult., Amer.Hum.Ind., Arts & Hum.Cit.Ind., Curr.Cont., Ind.Amer.Per.Verse, Ind.Bk.Rev.Hum., LCR, M.L.A. —BLDSC shelfmark: 6247.236000.
  Description: Devoted to contemporary American poetry, fiction, and essays.

811 US
OIKOS; a journal of ecology and community. 1980. a. $11.50 for 4 issues. 55 Magnolia Ave., Denville, NJ 07834. circ. 1,200.

808.81 US
OLD HICKORY REVIEW. 1969. s-a. $12. Jackson Writers Group, Box 1178, Jackson, TN 38302. TEL 901-424-3277. (Co-sponsor: Jackson Arts Council) Ed.Bd. circ. 300. (back issues avail.)
  Description: Focuses on promoting the literary craft and encouraging writers.

840 US ISSN 0381-9132
PN689
OLIFANT. (Text in English, French, German or Spanish) 1973; N.S. 1986. 2/yr. $12 to individuals (foreign $15); institutions $18 (foreign $24). University of Virginia, Dept. of French, Charlottesville, VA 22903. TEL 804-924-4627. Ed. Robert F. Cook. bk.rev.; abstr.; bibl.; index; circ. 450. (back issues avail.) **Indexed:** Amer.Hum.Ind., Can.Rev.Comp.lit, Curr.Cont, M.L.A. —BLDSC shelfmark: 6255.450000.
  Description: Examines all studies and reviews on the Medieval Romance epic.
  Refereed Serial

821 NR
OMABE; poetry from Nsukka. (Text in English) 1972. irreg. (approx. 3/yr.). £N3($4.50) University of Nigeria, Department of English, Nsukka, Nigeria. Ed. Ossie Onuora Enekwe. illus.; circ. 1,000. (back issues avail.)
  Formerly: Omaba.

808.81 UK ISSN 0308-4752
OMENS; poetry magazine. 1971. q. £1.50($5) 130 Letchworth Rd., Leicester LE3 6HF, England. Eds. John Martin, Sam Brown. adv.; illus.; circ. 500. (back issues avail.)

811 US
OMNIFIC. 1989. 4/yr. $12. Star Route, Box 21AA, Artemas, PA 17211. TEL 814-458-3102. Ed. Kay Weems. circ. 200.

811 US
ON GOGOL BOULEVARD; networking bulletin for dissidents from East and West. 1987. irreg. (3-4/yr.). $5 (foreign $10). 151 1st Ave., Ste. 62, New York, NY 10003. TEL 212-206-8463. circ. 2,000.

811 US ISSN 1043-884X
ONTHEBUS. 1989. 2/yr. $24 to individuals; institutions $30 for 3 nos. Bombshelter Press, 6421 1-2 Orange St., Los Angeles, CA 90048. TEL 213-651-5488. Ed. Jack Grapes. adv.; bk.rev.; illus.; circ. 3,000. (back issues avail.)
  Description: Contains poetry, stories, interviews, translations, and photographs.

052 UK ISSN 0030-4425
ORBIS; an international journal of poetry and prose. 1968. q. £14($30) 199 The Long Shoot, Nuneaton, Warwickshire CV11 6JQ, England. TEL 203-327440. FAX 203-364402. Ed. Mike Shields. adv.; bk.rev.; index; circ. 1,000.
  Incorporates: Scrip.

L

3000 LITERATURE — POETRY

821   UK   ISSN 0030-459X
ORE. 1954. irreg. (1-2/yr.). £1.85 per no. c/o Eric Ratcliffe, Ed., 7 the Towers, Stevenage, Herts., SG1 1HE, England. adv.; bk.rev.
 Description: Poetry reflecting myth, legend and spiritual consciousness.

808.81   US
OREAD. q. Box 12628, San Luis Obispo, CA 93406.

800   US   ISSN 0162-296X
ORPHEUS; the magazine of poems. 1980. 3/yr. $12.50. Illuminati, Box 67E07, Los Angeles, CA 90067-1407. Ed. P. Schneidre. circ. 1,100.

811   US   ISSN 0030-5804
ORPHIC LUTE. 1952. q. $10. Paradox Press, c/o Patricia Doherty Hinnebusch, Ed., 526 Paul Pl., Los Alamos, NM 87544. TEL 505-672-3116. bk.rev.; circ. 250. (processed)
 Description: Publishes lyric poems and short verse forms, especially traditional haiku.

821   UK   ISSN 0307-0786
OSTRICH. 1971. q. 60p.($3) Erdesdun Pomes, 10 Greenhaugh Rd., South Wellfield, Whitley Bay, Tyne and Wear NE25 9HF, England. Ed. Keith Armstrong. bk.rev.; illus.; circ. 500. (also avail. in microfilm from HPL)

821   UK
OTTER. 1988. 3/yr. £5. Parford Cottage, Chagford, Newton Abbot TL13 8JR, England. Ed. C. Southgate. circ. 400.

OUROBOROS. see *LITERATURE*

821   UK   ISSN 0950-7264
OUTPOSTS POETRY QUARTERLY. 1943. q. £10($24) Hippopotamus Press, 22 Whitewell Road, Frome, Somerset BA11 4EL, England. TEL 0373-66653. Ed. Roland John. adv.; bk.rev.; circ. 2,300. (back issues avail.)
 Formerly: Outposts (ISSN 0030-7297)

811   US
OUTRE. 1986. 2/yr. $1.50 per no. 2251 Helton Dr., Ste. N7, Florence, AL 35630. TEL 205-767-3324. Ed. Jake Berry. circ. 150.

OUTRIDER. see *LITERATURE*

821   UK
OVERSPILL;* for the longer poem. 1972. 5/yr. £1($3.50) c/o Eric Harrison, Ed., Grantley Close, Shalford, Nr. Guildford, Surrey, England. circ. 100. (processed)

811   US
▼**OVERVIEW (WOODRIDGE).** 1991. 2/yr. $8. Overview Ltd., Box 211, Woodridge, NJ 07075. TEL 201-438-9069. Ed. Joseph Lanciotti. circ. 450.

800   UK
OXFORD POETRY. 1983. 3/yr. £6 (foreign £7.50). (Magdalen Coll.) Oxford Poetry, Oxford OX1 4AU, England. Ed. Mark Wormald. adv.; bk.rev.; circ. 650. (back issues avail.)
 Description: Publishes a combination of new poetry, interviews and reviews of new and established poets.

L'OZIO; almanacco di letteratura. see *LITERATURE*

P - FORM; performance art magazine. see *ART*

811   US
P L G C NEWSLETTER. 1975. q. $20 membership. Poets' League of Greater Cleveland, Box 91801, Cleveland, OH 44101. TEL 216-932-8444. Ed. John Byrum. bk.rev.; bibl.; circ. 800.
 Description: Attempts to establish, maintain and improve a regional, cultural, educational, intellectual and social climate in which the practice of art and poetry may prosper.

821   UK   ISSN 0144-7076
PN1010
P N REVIEW. 1971. bi-m. £21.50($39) to individuals; institutions £28($50). Carcanet Press Ltd., 208 Corn Exchange, Manchester M4 3BQ, England. FAX 061-832-0084. Ed. Michael Schmidt. adv.; bk.rev.; cum.index; circ. 2,000. Indexed: M.L.A.
 —BLDSC shelfmark: 6541.101000.
 Supersedes (in 1976): Poetry Nation (ISSN 0308-2636); Carcanet (ISSN 0008-624X)
 Description: For poets and poetry readers of all ages. Contains poetry, fiction, interviews and major essays.

811   US
P R C NEWSLETTER AND CALENDAR. 1979. m. membership. Poetry Resource Center of Michigan, 111 E. Kirby, Detroit, MI 48202. Ed. Lee Schreiner. circ. 4,000.
 Description: News of poetry in or about Michigan.

PACIFIC REVIEW; a magazine for poetry and prose. see *LITERARY AND POLITICAL REVIEWS*

811   US   ISSN 0362-7969
PS580
PAINTED BRIDE QUARTERLY. 1973. q. $16 to individuals; institutions $20. Painted Bride Quarterly, Inc., 230 Vine St., Philadelphia, PA 19106. TEL 215-925-9914. Ed.Bd. adv.; bk.rev.; circ. 1,000. Indexed: Amer.Hum.Ind., Ind.Amer.Per.Verse.
 Description: Presents poetry, fiction and essays by Pennsylvania writers and their peers nationwide.

811   US
▼**PAINTED HILLS REVIEW.** 1990. 4/yr. $10 to individuals; institutions $12. Box 494, Davis, CA 95617-0494. TEL 916-756-5987. Ed. Michael Ishii. circ. 250.

811   GW   ISSN 0179-9711
PALETTE; Zeitschrift fuer Literatur von Randgruppen. 1985. 2/yr. DM.35. Verein zur Foerderung von Randgruppenkultur, Kantstrasse 33, 8600 Bamberg, Germany. TEL 0951-47087. Ed. Arno Jesse. adv.; bk.rev.; circ. 500. (back issues avail.)

808.81   US   ISSN 0092-5535
PN6099.6
PANJANDRUM POETRY JOURNAL. 1972. irreg. $16 per 3 nos. Panjandrum Press, Inc., 5428 Hermitage Ave., North Hollywood, CA 91607. TEL 818-985-7259. Ed. Dennis Koran. circ. 1,250.

PANORAMA OF CZECH LITERATURE. see *LITERATURE*

811   US
PAPER RADIO. 1986. 2/yr. $10. Box 85302, Seattle, WA 98145-1302. Ed. N.S. Kvern. circ. 500.
 Description: Publishes experimental poetry, humor, weirdness, and surrealism.

811   US
PAPER TOADSTOOL. 1989. irreg. (2-3/yr.). 4946 West Point Way, West Valley, UT 84120. TEL 801-972-8236. circ. 500.

PARLANGHE. see *LITERATURE*

811   US   ISSN 0748-8785
PARNASSUS LITERARY JOURNAL. 1975. 3/yr. $12. Kudzu Press, Box 1384, Forest Park, GA 30051. TEL 404-366-3177. Ed. Denver Stull. bk.rev.; circ. 200. (back issues avail.)
 Description: Collection of poetry and essays pertaining to poetry by unsolicited contributors, emphasizing poetic structure and forms with a neo-romantic content.

811   US   ISSN 0048-3028
PN6099.6
PARNASSUS: POETRY IN REVIEW. 1972. s-a. $18 to individuals; institutions $36. Poetry in Review Foundation, 41 Union Sq. W., Rm. 804, New York, NY 10003. TEL 212-463-0889. Ed. Herbert Leibowitz. adv.; bk.rev.; index; circ. 2,500. (also avail. in microfilm) Indexed: Abstr.Engl.Stud., Amer.Bibl.Slavic & E.Eur.Stud., Amer.Hum.Ind., Arts & Hum.Cit.Ind., Bk.Rev.Ind. (1980-), Child.Bk.Rev.Ind. (1980-), Curr.Cont., Ind.Bk.Rev.Hum., LCR, M.L.A.
 —BLDSC shelfmark: 6406.875000.

800   US   ISSN 1043-3325
PARTING GIFTS. 1988. s-a. $8. March Street Press, 3006 Stonecutter Terrace, Greensboro, NC 27405. Ed. Robert Bixby. circ. 100. Indexed: Ind.Amer.Per.Verse.
 Description: Experimental poetry and prose.

811   US   ISSN 0031-2649
PS571.S8
PASQUE PETALS. 1926. 10/yr. $15. South Dakota State Poetry Society, 909 E. 34 St., Sioux Falls, SD 57105-0326. TEL 605-338-9156. Ed. Barbara Stevens. bk.rev.; circ. 200.

811   US   ISSN 0749-6761
PATRIOT. 1984. a. $10. Runaway Publications, Box 1172, Ashland, OR 97520-0040. TEL 503-482-2578. Ed. James L. Berkman. circ. 100 (controlled). (back issues avail.)
 Description: Looks at the cutting edge of American poetry from a hard line perspective.

821   UK
PAUSE. 1969. 2/yr. $10. National Poetry Foundation, 27 Mill Rd., Fareham, Hampshire, England. Eds. Jonathon Clifford, Helen Robinson. circ. 600.

811   US
PEARL. 1987. 2/yr. $10. 3030 E. Second St., Long Beach, CA 90803. TEL 213-434-4523. Ed. Joan Jobe Smith. circ. 500.

811   US   ISSN 0031-3696
PS580
PEBBLE; a magazine of poetry. 1968. 2/yr. Best Cellar Press, Department of English, University of Nebraska, NE 68588. Ed. Greg Kuzma. bk.rev.

811   CN
PECKERWOOD. 1987. 3/yr. $2. 1503-1465 Lawrence Ave. West, Toronto, Ont. M6L 1B2, Canada. TEL 416-248-2675. Ed. Emie Ourique. circ. 200.

868   US   ISSN 0888-322X
PEGASUS (NEVADA). 1986. q. $12.50. Pegasus Publishing, 525 Ave. B, Boulder City, NV 89005. TEL 702-294-1522. Ed. M.E. Hildebrand. circ. 200. (back issues avail.)

808.81   US
THE PEGASUS REVIEW. 1980. bi-m. $7. Pegasus Review, Box 134, Flanders, NJ 07836. TEL 201-927-0749. Ed. Arthur L. Bounds. circ. 160. (back issues avail.)

821   UK
PEN: UMBRA. 1989. irreg. (1-2/yr.). $5 per no. 1 Beeches Close, Saffron Walden, Essex CB11 4BU, England.

811   US
▼**PENINHAND.** 1990. 2/yr. $2. Peninhand Press, Box 82699, Portland, OR 97282. Ed. Tom Janisse. circ. 500.

811   US   ISSN 0031-4307
PENINSULA POETS. 1947. s-a. $12. Poetry Society of Michigan, 3781 Lodge Ln., Trenton, MI 48183. Ed. Gwendolen Funston. bk.rev.; circ. 300.
 Description: Anthology of poetry by members of the society.

821   UK   ISSN 0306-140X
PENNINE PLATFORM; poetry magazine. 1973. 3/yr. £7 (foreign £15). Brian Merrikin Hill, Ed. & Pub., Ingmanthorpe Hall Farm Cottage, Wetherby, W. Yorks. LS22 5EQ, England. TEL 0937-584674. adv.; bk.rev.; circ. 350.
 Formerly (until 1975): Platform (Luddendenfoot) (ISSN 0032-1389)

808.81   US
PENTATETTE. 1981. m. $20 includes membership. Limerick Special Interest Group, Box 365, Moffet, CA 94035. bk.rev.

811   US
PERCEPTIONS (MISSOULA). 1982. 3/yr. $10. 1317 S. Johnson St., Missoula, MT 59801-4805. TEL 406-543-5875. circ. 100.

808.81   US   ISSN 0890-622X
PEREGRINE; the journal of Amherst writers & artists. 1983. a. $5 per no. Amherst Writers & Artists Press, Inc., Box 1076, Amherst, MA 01004. TEL 413-253-3307. Ed.Bd. adv.; circ. 500. (back issues avail.)

LITERATURE — POETRY

808.81   US
PHASE AND CYCLE. 1988. s-a. $5. Phase and Cycle Press, 3537 E. Prospect, Ft. Collins, CO 80525. TEL 303-482-7573. Ed. Loy Banks. circ. 200. (back issues avail.)
   Description: Publishes poetry for the university community.

811   US
PHOENIX POETS. 1960. irreg., latest 1986. price varies. University of Chicago Press, 5801 S. Ellis Ave., Chicago, IL 60637. TEL 708-702-7899. (Subscr. to: 11030 Langley Ave., Chicago, IL 60628) Ed. Robert von Hallberg.
   Refereed Serial

808   US
PIDDIDDLE.* 1985. 3/yr. $4. 1521 Foxfire Dr., College Station, TX 77840-5619. Ed. Janet McCann. circ. 500. (back issues avail.)

800   US   ISSN 0275-357X
PIEDMONT LITERARY REVIEW. 1976. q. $12. Piedmont Literary Society, 1017 Spanish Moss Ln., Breaux Bridge, LA 70517. TEL 804-793-0956. Ed. Gail White. bk.rev.; circ. 400. (back issues avail.)
   Description: Focuses on poetry, particularly rhymed poetry.

808.81   US
PIG IN A PAMPHLET.* 8/yr. $1 for 3 nos. 331 Ridge Point Cir., No. 15, Bridgeville, PA 15017-1530. Ed. Harry Calhoun.

811   US
PIKEVILLE REVIEW. 1987. a. $4. Humanities Dept., Pikeville College, Pikeville, KY 41501. TEL 606-437-4046. Ed. James Alan Riley. circ. 500.

808.81   US
PITT POETRY SERIES. 1968. 7/yr. price varies. University of Pittsburgh Press, 127 North Bellefield Ave., Pittsburgh, PA 15260. TEL 412-624-4111. FAX 412-624-7380. Ed. Ed Ochester.

PITTSBURGH QUARTERLY. see *LITERATURE*

808.81   US
PIVOT (NEW YORK). 1951. a. $5. Pivot Associates, 221 S. Barnard, State College, PA 16801. Ed. Martin Mitchell. adv.; circ. 2,225.

808.8   US   ISSN 0730-6172
PLAINS POETRY JOURNAL. 1982. 2/yr. $18. Stronghold Press, Box 2337, Bismarck, ND 58502. Ed. Jane Greer. circ. 550. (back issues avail.)
   Description: Presents American poetry.

808.81   US
PLAINSONG. 1979. irreg. $7 for 2 nos. Plainsong, Inc., Box 8245, Western Kentucky University, Bowling Green, KY 42101. TEL 502-745-5708. Ed.Bd. adv.; bk.rev.; circ. 500.

811   US
PLASTIC TOWER. 1989. 4/yr. $8. Box 702, Bowie, MD 20718. Eds. Carol Brown, Roger Kyle-Keith. circ. 200.

821   CN   ISSN 0840-707X
PLOWMAN. 1988. 4/yr. Can.$5. Box 414, Whitby, Ont. L1N 5S4, Canada. Ed. T. Scavetta. circ. 10,000.
   Description: Magazine of original poetry.

811   US
▼**PLUM REVIEW.** 1990. 2/yr. $10. Box 3557, Washington, DC 20007. Ed. Christina Daub. bk.rev.
   Description: Carries poems, translations, reviews, and interviews with prominent authors.

841   FR   ISSN 0152-0032
PN1010
PO & SIE. 1977. q. 215 F. (foreign 235 F.). Editions Belin, 8 rue Ferou, 75278 Paris Cedex 06, France. TEL 46-34-21-42. FAX 43-25-18-29. TELEX 202970F LIBELIN. Ed. Michel Deguy. adv.; bk.rev.; circ. 500. **Indexed:** M.L.A.

811   US   ISSN 0079-2438
POCKET POETS SERIES. 1955. irreg., no.46, 1989. price varies. City Lights Books, 261 Columbus Ave., San Francisco, CA 94133. TEL 415-362-1901.

809   US   ISSN 0276-3737
PS2631
THE POE MESSENGER. 1969. a. $2. Poe Foundation, Inc., 1914-16 E. Main St., Richmond, VA 23223. Ed. Agnes Bondurant Marcuson. bk.rev.; play rev.; bibl.; illus.; circ. 550. (back issues avail.) **Indexed:** Amer.Hum.Ind.
   Description: Presents poetry, critical and historical information on the life of Edgar Allan Poe, includes list of Foundation activities and events.

811   US   ISSN 0032-1885
PS580
POEM. 1967. 2/yr. $10. Huntsville Literary Association, Box 919, Huntsville, AL 35804. TEL 205-536-9038. Ed. N.F. Dillard. index every 6 nos; circ. 600. (back issues avail.) **Indexed:** A.I.P.P.

861   UY   ISSN 0079-2462
POESIA.* irreg. Editorial Arca, Colonia 1263, Montevideo, Uruguay.

861   VE   ISSN 0032-1893
PQ8544
POESIA DE VENEZUELA. 1963. bi-m. Bs.12($3) or exchange basis. Apdo. Postal 1114, Caracas 1010A, Venezuela. TEL 74-43-61. Ed. Pascual Venegas Filardo. adv.; bk.rev.
   Description: Presents poetry from Venezuela, with emphasis on contemporary poets.

861   AG   ISSN 0032-1907
POESIA EN LA CALLE.* 1966. m. Habitante, Chacabuco 1380, Catamarca, Argentina. Ed. Luis Arganaraz.

861   PN
POESIA PANAMENA ACTUAL. 1979. a. price varies. (Direccion Nacional de Extension Cultural, Departamento de Letras) Editorial Mariano Arosemena (INAC), Apdo. 662, Panama 1, Panama. TEL 62-2811.

841   FR
POESIE (YEAR). 1984. 5/yr. 275 F. (foreign 300 F.). (Maison de la Poesie de Paris) Pierre Seghers, 228 bd. Raspail, 75014 Paris, France. adv.; bk.rev.
   Description: Forum for young unknown poets in France as well as the rest of the world.

841   FR   ISSN 0048-4563
PQ1160
POESIE PRESENTE. 1971. q. 290 F. Rougerie Editeur, Mortemart, 87330 Mezieres-sur-Issoire, France.
   Description: Publishes current French poetry.

811   US   ISSN 0364-4022
POESIE - U.S.A.. (Text in French) 1977. q. $10. Pierre E. Chanover, Ed. & Pub., Box 1516, Melville, NY 11747. adv.; circ. 500. (back issues avail.)

830   GW
POESIE UND WISSENSCHAFT. SAMMLUNG. 1967. irreg. price varies. Lothar Stiehm Verlag, Hausackerweg 16, 6900 Heidelberg, Germany. **Indexed:** M.L.A.

841   FR
POESIE 1. 1969. q. 165 F.($29) Le Cherche Midi Editeur, 87 rue de Sevres, 75006 Paris, France. Ed. Jean Orizet. adv.; bk.rev.

821   II   ISSN 0032-194X
POET. (Six international and six pan-continental issues) (Text in English) 1960. m. Rs.20. World Poetry Society Intercontinental, c/o Dr. Krishna Srinivas, Ed., 118 Raja St., Madras 600042, India. TEL 2350186. bk.rev.; circ. 1,000. (also avail. in microfilm from UMI; reprint service avail. from UMI)

811   US
POET; peu a peu. 1973. a. $11.50. Fine Arts Society, 2314 W. Sixth St., Mishawaka, IN 46544. Ed. Doris Nemeth. adv.; illus.; circ. 1,000. (controlled). (reprint service avail. from UMI)

811   US   ISSN 0032-1958
PS501
POET AND CRITIC. 1965. 3/yr. $18 (foreign $21). Iowa State University, Department of English, 203 Ross Hall, Ames, IA 50011. TEL 515-294-2180. Ed. Neal Bowers. adv.; bk.rev.; illus.; circ. 400. (also avail. in microform from UMI; reprint service avail. from UMI) **Indexed:** A.I.P.P., Abstr.Engl.Stud., Arts & Hum.Cit.Ind., Curr.Cont., Ind.Amer.Per.Verse.
   —BLDSC shelfmark: 6541.734000.

808.81   US   ISSN 0032-1966
PN2
POET LORE; a quarterly of world literature. 1889. q. $15 to individuals; institutions $24. Writer's Center, 7815 Old Georgetown Rd., Bethesda, MD 20814-2415. TEL 301-654-8664. Ed. Philip Jason. adv.; bk.rev.; index; circ. 700. (also avail. in microform; back issues avail.; reprint service avail.) **Indexed:** A.I.P.P., Amer.Bibl.Slavic & E.Eur.Stud, Arts & Hum.Cit.Ind., Curr.Cont., Ind.Amer.Per.Verse, Ind.Bk.Rev.Hum.

811   US
POET NEWS.* 1979. m. $18. Sacramento Poetry Center, 4750 Monterey Way, Sacramento, CA 95822-1258. Ed.Bd. adv.; bk.rev.; circ. 1,200.
   Description: Publishes poetry, essays and articles related to the craft, translations of non-English works and short fiction.

861   PY
POETAS.* 1977. irreg. (Paraguay PEN Centre) Fondo Editor Paraguayo, San Rafael 658, Asuncion, Paraguay.

811 869   BL
POETAS BRASILEIROS DE HOJE (YEAR). a. Shogun Editora e Arte Ltda., Caixa Postal 43.021, CEP 22052 Rio de Janeiro, Brazil. TEL 021-2559494.

811   FR   ISSN 0079-2470
POETES ET PROSATEURS DU PORTUGAL. 1970. irreg., latest 1981. price varies. Centre Culturel Portugais, Fondation Calouste Gulbenkian, Centre Culturel Portugais, 51, ave. d'Iena, 75116 Paris, France. TEL 1-47-20-86-84. FAX 1-40-70-98-79. (Subscr. to: Jean Touzot, 38 rue Saint-Suplice, 75006 Paris, France) (reprint service avail. from KTO)

830   IT   ISSN 0079-2500
POETI E PROSATORI TEDESCHI. 1962. irreg., no.7, 1982. price varies. Edizioni dell' Ateneo S.p.A., Box 7216, 00100 Rome, Italy. Ed. Paolo Chiarini. circ. 1,000.

820   AU
POETIC DRAMA AND POETIC THEORY. (Text in English) 1972. irreg., no. 77, 1991. S.245. Universitaet Salzburg, Institut fuer Englische Sprache, Akademiestr. 24, A-5020 Salzburg, Austria. Ed. James Hogg. circ. 200.

811   US
POETIC JUSTICE. 1982. irreg. (approx. a.). $10 for 4 issues. 8220 Rayford Dr., Los Angeles, CA 90045. Ed. Alan C. Engebretsen. circ. 200.

811   US
POETIC PAGE. 1989. 6/yr. $10. Poetic Page, Box 71192, Madison Heights, MI 48071-0192. TEL 313-548-0865. Ed. Denise Martinson. circ. 250.

811   US
POETIC SPACE. 1983. 2/yr. $10. Box 11157, Eugene, OR 97440. Eds. Don Hildenbrand, Thomas Strand. adv.; bk.rev.; circ. 800. (back issues avail.)
   Description: Features poetry, short fiction, art and black and white sketches.

POETICA; an international journal of linguistic-literary studies. see *LINGUISTICS*

851   IT
POETICA; mensile di poesia e critica diretto da Dante Maffia e Luigi Reina. m. L.25000. EdiSud, Via Leopoldo Cassese, 26, 84100 Salerno (NA), Italy.

808.81   US   ISSN 1043-0814
POETICS. 1987. 3/yr. $6. Great Lakes Poetry Press, Box 56703, Harwood Heights, IL 60656. TEL 312-478-1761. Ed. Chuck Kramer. adv.; circ. 10,000. (tabloid format)
   Description: Informs readers of news events in American poetry and profiles American poets.

811   US
POETIDINGS. 1973. m. membership. New Jersey Poetry Society, P.O. Box 217, Wharton, NJ 07885. Ed.Bd. adv.; bk.rev.; circ. 200. (processed)

811   US
POETPOURRI. 1986. s-a. $8. (Comstock Writers' Group, Inc.) Saltfire Press, 907 Comstock Ave., Syracuse, NY 13210. TEL 315-475-0339. Ed.Bd. circ. 500. (back issues avail.)

L

LITERATURE — POETRY

808.81 II ISSN 0970-7182
POETRY. (Text in English) 1975. s-a. Rs.40 (effective 1992). (Berhampur University, Department of English) Poetry Publications, 51L Ranguni Bandha St., Berhampur 760 009, India. Ed. N. Mohanty. adv.; bk.rev.

811 US ISSN 0032-2032
PS301
POETRY (CHICAGO). 1912. m. $25. Modern Poetry Association, 60 W. Walton St., Chicago, IL 60610. TEL 312-280-4870. Ed. Joseph Parisi. adv.; bk.rev.; index; circ. 7,000. (also avail. in microform from UMI; Braille; reprint service avail. from UMI; back issues avail.) Indexed: A.I.P.P., Acad.Ind., Access (1980-), Biog.Ind., Bk.Rev.Dig., Bk.Rev.Ind. (1965-), Child.Bk.Rev.Ind. (1965-), Curr.Cont., Ind.Amer.Per.Verse, Ind.Bk.Rev.Hum., Mag.Ind., Pop.Per.Ind.
—BLDSC shelfmark: 6541.753000.
Description: Devoted entirely to verse, from Auden to Ashbery, Pound to Pinsky, Stevens to Soto--voices both famous and new. Includes news notes and books received.

821 UK ISSN 0260-9339
POETRY AND LITTLE PRESS INFORMATION. 1970. 3/yr. £4.50. Association of Little Presses, 89A Petherton Rd., London N5 2QT, England. Eds. Bill Griffiths, Bob Cobbing. circ. 500.
—BLDSC shelfmark: 6541.755000.
Formerly (unitl 1980): Poetry Information (ISSN 0048-4598)

821 UK
POETRY ANTHOLOGY. a. £19.50. Poetry Book Society Ltd., 21 Earls Court Sq., London SW5 9DE, England.
Formerly: Poetry Supplement.
Description: New, previously unpublished poems from well known British poets.

821 AT ISSN 0032-2059
PR9548
POETRY AUSTRALIA. 1964. a. $20 (effective 1992). South Head Press, Market Place, Berrima, N.S.W. 2577, Australia. TEL 048-771421. Ed. John Millet. adv.; bk.rev.; index; circ. 2,250. Indexed: Abstr.Engl.Stud, Arts & Hum.Cit.Ind., Br.Hum.Ind., Curr.Cont., M.L.A.
—BLDSC shelfmark: 6541.758000.

821 UK
POETRY BOOK SOCIETY BULLETIN. 1952. q. £24. Poetry Book Society Ltd., 21 Earls Court Sq., London SW5 9DE, England. Ed. M Smart. adv.; bk.rev.; circ. 2,000.
Formerly: New Poems.
Description: Articles and news about contemporary British poetry.

821 CN
POETRY CANADA. 1979. q. Can.$16 to individuals; institutions Can. $32. Quarry Press, Inc., Box 1061, Kingston, Ont. K7L 4Y5, Canada. TEL 613-548-8429. Eds. Barry Dempster, Bob Hilderly. adv.; bk.rev.; circ. 1,800. (also avail. in microfilm) Indexed: Can.Lit.Ind., CMI, Ind.Amer.Per.Verse.
Formerly: Poetry Canada Review (ISSN 0709-3373)
Description: Features essays on poetry, in-depth interviews, coast-to-coast poetry news articles, and notices of new poetry releases.

808.81 US
POETRY COMICS.* q? $7 for 4 nos. c/o Dave Morice, Ed., 618 Eighth Ave., Coralville, IA 52241-1905.

808.81 US
THE POETRY CONNECTION. 1988. bi-m. $25. Sylvia Shichman, Ed. & Pub., 301 E. 64th St., No. 6K, New York, NY 10021. TEL 212-249-5494. circ. 200. (back issues avail.)
Description: Includes a listing of poetry contests, information on poetry activities and poetry information books.

800
▼**POETRY CRITICISM.** 1990. biennial. $75. Gale Research Inc., 835 Penobscot Bldg., Detroit, MI 48226-4094. TEL 313-961-2242. FAX 313-961-6083. TELEX 810-221-7086. Ed. Robyn V. Young.
Description: Presents overviews of 12-15 major poets from all time periods and from around the world in each volume.

821 UK
POETRY DURHAM. 1982. 3/yr. £4.50. University of Durham, School of English, Elvet Riverside, New Elvet, Durham DH1 3JT, England. TEL 091-374-2730. Ed.Bd. adv.; circ. 600.

811 US ISSN 0197-4009
PN1271
POETRY EAST. 1980. 2/yr. $12. Department of English, De Paul University, 802 W. Belden Ave., Chicago, IL 60614-3214. TEL 312-362-5114. FAX 312-362-5684. Ed. Richard Jones. adv.; bk.rev.; index; circ. 1,500. (back issues avail.) Indexed: Ind.Amer.Per.Verse.

811 US ISSN 0737-4747
POETRY FLASH; a poetry review and literary calendar for the West. 1972. m. $12 (foreign $22). Joyce Jenkins, Ed. & Pub., Box 4172, Berkeley, CA 94704. TEL 510-525-5476. Ed. Joyce Jenkins. adv.; bk.rev.; illus.; circ. 18,000.

821 CN ISSN 0838-200X
POETRY HALIFAX DARTMOUTH. (Text in English, French) 1986. bi-m. Can.$15($20) Firefly Poetry Group, 5280 Green St., No. 27008, Halifax, N.S. B3H 1N0, Canada. Ed. Mark Hamilton. bk.rev.; circ. 250.
Formerly (until no.17): B S P S Journal.

821 IE
POETRY IRELAND REVIEW. 1981. q. I£12($32) 44 Upper Mount St., Dublin 2, Ireland. TEL 01-610320. Ed. Peter Denman. adv.; bk.rev.; circ. 1,000. (back issues avail.)

808.81 JA
POETRY KANTO. (Text in English, Japanese) 1984. a. Kanto Poetry Center, Kanto Gakuin University, 1641 Kamariya, Kanazawa-ku, Yokohama 236, Japan. TEL 045-781-2001. Ed. William I. Elliott. circ. 800. (back issues avail.)
Description: Contains quality contemporary poetry by new and established poets from around the world.

811 US ISSN 0275-1739
PS1
POETRY - L A. 1980. s-a. $8. Peggor Press, Box 84271, Los Angeles, CA 90073. TEL 213-472-6171. Ed. Helen Friedland. circ. 500. (back issues avail.)
Description: An anthology of original poetry by both established and previously unpublished Los Angeles area writers.

811 US ISSN 0048-4601
POETRY MISCELLANY. 1971. 2/yr. $3. University of Tennessee at Chattanooga, Department of English, Chattanooga, TN 37402. TEL 615-755-4269. Ed. Richard Jackson. adv.; bk.rev.; circ. 600.

808.81 US
POETRY NEW YORK; a journal of poetry and translation. 1985. a. $5. City University of New York, English Department - Poetry New York, Graduate Center, 33 W. 42nd St., New York, NY 10036. (Dist. by: Berhard De Boer, Inc., 113 E. Center St., Nutley, NJ 07110) Eds. Cheryl Fish, Burt Kimmelman. circ. 500.

895.61 JA ISSN 0032-2105
POETRY NIPPON. (Text in English) 1967. q. 3500 Yen($29) (Poetry Society of Japan) Poetry Nippon Press, 5-11-2 Nagaike-cho, Showa-ku, Nagoya 466, Japan. Ed. Atsuo Nakagawa. adv.; bk.rev.; illus.; index; circ. 500. (processed; also avail. in microfiche)

811 US ISSN 0032-2113
AP2
POETRY NORTHWEST. 1959. q. $10. University of Washington, 4045 Brooklyn Ave. N.E., Seattle, WA 98105. TEL 206-685-4750. (Subscr. to: Edith Bowmar, Graduate School , University of Washington, AG-10, Seattle, WA 98195. TEL 206-543-5900) Ed. David Wagoner. circ. 1,500. Indexed: A.I.P.P., Amer.Hum.Ind.
Description: Poetry by young American poets.

821 UK ISSN 0143-3199
POETRY NOTTINGHAM; today's magazine for international poetry. 1941. q. £7 (foreign £12). Nottingham Poetry Society, Summer Cottage, West St., Shelford, Notts. NG12 1EJ, England. TEL 0602-334540. Ed.Bd. adv.; bk.rev.; circ. 300. (back issues avail.)

821 UK
POETRY NOW. 1983. q. £8($25) 33 Belgrade Rd., Stoke Newington, London N16, England. Eds. Ravi Mirchandani, Rian Cooney.
Incorporates (in Oct., 1984): Cambridge Poetry Magazine.

811 US
POETRY OF THE PEOPLE. 1986. m. $8. Box 13077, Gainesville, FL 32604. TEL 904-375-3324. Ed. Paul Cohen. circ. 1,000.
Description: Publishes satire.

811 US
POETRY PEDDLER. 1988. bi-m. $10 (foreign $12). Snowbound Press, Box 250, W. Monroe, NY 13167. TEL 315-676-2050. Eds. J.J. Snow, A.M. Ryant. circ. 150. (back issues avail.)

811 US ISSN 0554-3983
PS301
POETRY PILOT. 1937. m. $25. Academy of American Poets, 177 E. 87th St., New York, NY 10128.
Formerly (until 1943): Doggerel.

821 UK ISSN 0306-0195
POETRY POST. 1973. 2/yr. £0.75. Ver Poets, 61 & 63 Chiswell Green Lane, St. Albans, Herts AL2 3AL, England. TEL 0727-867005. Ed. May Badman.

808.81 US
POETRY PROJECT NEWSLETTER. 1967. 4/yr. (bi-m. Oct. to May). $20. Poetry Project Ltd., St. Mark's Church in-the-Bowery, Second Ave. & 10th St., New York, NY 10003. TEL 212-674-0910. Ed. Lynn Crawford. adv.; bk.rev.; circ. 3,500.
Description: Contains poetry, articles, transcripts of symposia presentations, and annotated calendars of readings and events at the Poetry Project.

821 UK
POETRY QUARTERLY. 1975. irreg. £5.75($15) Curlew Press, Hare Cottage, Kettlesing, Harrogate, Yorkshire, England. TEL 770686. Ed. P.J. Precious.

821 UK ISSN 0032-2156
PN1010
POETRY REVIEW. 1909. q. £21($38) to individuals; institutions and libraries £26($45). Poetry Society Inc., 21 Earls Court Sq., London SW5 9DE, England. TEL 071-373-7861. FAX 071-244-7388. Ed. Peter Forbes. adv.; bk.rev.; circ. 5,000. (reprint service avail. from ISI) Indexed: A.I.P.P., Arts & Hum.Cit.Ind., Curr.Cont., Ind.Bk.Rev.Hum., M.L.A.
—BLDSC shelfmark: 6541.777000.
Description: New poetry, reviews and features on poetry worldwide.

808.81 US
POETRY SOCIETY OF AMERICA NEWSLETTER. 3/yr. $35. Poetry Society of America, 15 Gramercy Park, New York, NY 10003. TEL 212-254-9628. Ed. Jonathan Shapiro. adv.; bk.rev.; tr.lit.; circ. 2,700. (back issues avail.)
Description: Interviews, articles and other information of interest to poets.

808.81 II
POETRY TIME; a quarterly of creative literature. (Supplement avail.) (Text in English) q. Rs.40 (foreign $20). Poetry Time Publication, Giri Road, Berhampur 760 005, India. Ed. Laxmi Narayan Mahapatra. adv.; bk.rev.; circ. 2,000.
Description: Includes poems from India and abroad.

811 US
POETRY: U S A QUARTERLY. 1985. q. $10. (National Poetry Association, Inc.) Poetry: U S A Publishers, 2569 Maxwell Ave., Oakland, CA 94601. TEL 510-532-3737. Ed. Jack Foley. adv.; index; circ. 10,000. (tabloid format; back issues avail.)
Formerly (until 1989): Poetry: San Francisco Quarterly.
Description: Includes eclectic articles and poetry, including homeless, prisoner and children's poetry as well an international section.

821   UK   ISSN 0032-2202
PR8954.5
POETRY WALES; Cylchgrawn Cenedlaethol o Farddoniaeth Newydd. (Text mainly in English; occasionally in Welsh) 1965. 4/yr. £8 (outside UK £15). (Welsh Arts Council) Poetry Wales Press, Andmar House, Trewsfield Industrial Estate, Tondu Rd., Bridgend, Mid-Glam. CF31 4LJ, Wales. TEL 0656-767834. Ed. Mike Jenkins. adv.; bk.rev.; circ. 1,000. (reprint service avail. from ISI) **Indexed:** Curr.Cont.
—BLDSC shelfmark: 6541.785000.
    Description: Covers poetry, critical essays and reviews, often with a Welsh connection.

811 810   US   ISSN 0891-6136
PS129
POETS & WRITERS MAGAZINE. 1972. 6/yr. $18 to individuals; institutions $25. Poets & Writers, Inc., 72 Spring St., New York, NY 10012. TEL 212-226-3586. FAX 212-226-3963. Ed. Darlyn Brewer. adv.; circ. 36,000. (also avail. in microform from UMI; reprint service avail. from UMI)
    Formerly (until 1987): Coda: Poets and Writers Newsletter (ISSN 0091-5645)
    Description: Provides essays, interviews with writers, news and commentary on publishing, political issues and practical topics of interest to writers. Includes coverage of grants and awards, deadlines for applications and calls for manuscript submissions.

808.81   US
POETS AT WORK. 1985. bi-m. $16. Jessee Poet Publications, Box 113, VAMC 325 New Castle Road, Butler, PA 16001. Ed. Jessee Poet. adv.; circ. 350. (back issues avail.)
    Description: Publishes contributions of subscribers.

POET'S HANDBOOK; 2,300 poetry publishers. see *BIBLIOGRAPHIES*

808.81   II
POETS INTERNATIONAL. 1983. q. Rs.50($16) 361, 11th Cross, 2nd Block, Jayanagar, Bangalore 560 011, India. TEL 607 818. Eds. Mohamed Fakruddin, D. Litt. adv.; bk.rev.; circ. 1,000.

811   US   ISSN 0883-5470
PN1059.M3
POET'S MARKET; where and how to publish your poetry. 1986. a. $19.95. F & W Publications, Inc., 1507 Dana Ave., Cincinnati, OH 45207. TEL 513-531-2222. FAX 513-531-4744. Ed. Michael Bugeja. index; circ. 25,000.
    Description: Provides 1,700 listings of magazines, chapbook publishers, greeting card companies and other companies and other markets interested in poetry submissions.

811   US
POET'S NEWSLETTER. 1989. 2/yr. $2.50 per no. 609C Idlewild Cir., Birmingham, AL 35205. TEL 205-323-5690. Ed. Bettye K. Wraye. bk.rev.; circ. 200.
    Description: Poetry, fiction, essays and interviews.

808.81   US   ISSN 0146-3136
POETS ON:. 1976. s-a. $8. Poets On:, 29 Loring Ave., Mill Valley, CA 94941. TEL 415-381-2824. Ed. Ruth Daigon. bk.rev.; circ. 450. **Indexed:** A.I.P.P.
    Description: Explores basic human concerns through poetry, each issue focusing on a specific topic.

811   US
POETS' ROUNDTABLE. 1939. 6/yr. $6 (membership). 826 South Center St., Terre Haute, IN 47807. TEL 812-234-0819. Ed. Esther Alman. circ. 2,000 (controlled).

811   PL   ISSN 0079-2527
POETYKA. ZARYS ENCYKLOPEDYCZNY. 1956. irreg., latest 1984. price varies. (Polska Akademia Nauk, Instytut Badan Literackich) Ossolineum, Publishing House of the Polish Academy of Sciences, Rynek 9, 50-106 Wroclaw, Poland. TELEX 0712771 OSS PL. (Dist. by: Ars Polona-Ruch, Krakowskie Przedmiescie 7, Warsaw, Poland) Ed. Lucylla Pszczolowska.
    Description: An Encyclopedic outline on problems of language, prosody, styles and figures in poetry.

899   RU
POEZIYA (MOSCOW). vol.20, 1977. irreg. 0.99 Rub. per issue. Izdatel'stvo Molodaya Gvardiya, Novodmitrovskaya ul. 5A, 125015 Moscow, Russia. Ed. N. Starshinov. illus.; circ. 65,000.

891.85   PL   ISSN 0032-2237
PN1010
POEZJA.* 1965. m. $9.90. Ul. Nowy Swiat 58, 00-950 Warsaw, Poland. TEL 48-22-261096. (Dist. by: Ars Polona-Ruch, Krakowskie Przedmiescie 7, Warsaw, Poland) Ed. Marek Wawrzkiewicz. circ. 7,500. **Indexed:** M.L.A.

841   FR   ISSN 0032-2369
POINTS ET CONTREPOINTS. 1935. q. 80 F. 19 rue Gerando, 75009 Paris, France. Ed. Jean Loisy. adv.; bk.rev.

808.81   FR   ISSN 0766-1924
POLYPHONIES. 1985. 2/yr. 140 F. B.P. 189, 75665 Paris Cedex 14, France. TEL 45-43-68-89. Ed. Pascal Culerrier. bk.rev.
    Description: Opens French literature to major productions of lyric poetry.

811   US
PORTRAITS POETRY MAGAZINE. 1989. 3/yr. $10. 8312 123rd St. E., Puyallup, WA 98373. TEL 206-848-5827. Ed. Jay L. Chambers. circ. 200.

808.81   US   ISSN 1041-9926
POTATO EYES; Appalachian voices. 1989. s-a. $11. Nightshade Press, Box 76, Ward Hill, Troy, ME 04987. TEL 207-948-3427. Eds. Carolyn Page, Roy Zarucchi. bk.rev.; circ. 800. (back issues avail.)
    Description: Presents poetry, short stories, literary reviews, and art by authors and artists from the United States and Canada.

THE POTTERSFIELD PORTFOLIO; new fiction, essays, poetry, plays and artwork in English and French. see *LITERATURE*

851   IT   ISSN 0032-5686
POTY CUNTU;* e chiddus cun ti piaci ti lu canci. vol.42, 1967. s-m. L.1200.($3) Accademia Dialettale Siciliana Giovanni Meli, Viale delle Sirene 15, 90149 Palermo, Sicily, Italy. Ed. Dir. Peppino Denaro. (newspaper)

PRAIRIE JOURNAL. see *LITERATURE*

811   US
PRINCETON SERIES OF CONTEMPORARY POETS. 1975. irreg. price varies. Princeton University Press, 3175 Princeton Pike, Lawrenceville, NJ 08648. TEL 609-896-1344. FAX 609-895-1081. (reprint service avail. from UMI)

895.65   JA
PRINTED MATTER. (Text in English) 1970. bi-m. (plus 2 special issues). 3000 Yen. Tels Press, 3-31-14-207 Ikebukuro Honcho, Toshima-ku, Tokyo 170, Japan. Ed. John Evans. circ. 200.

821   AT   ISSN 0816-3065
PRINTS. 1985. q. Aus.$10. Possum Paw Press, P.O. Box 137, Monbulk, Vic. 3793, Australia. Ed. Louise Rockne. circ. 100. (back issues avail.)
    Description: Publishes poetry, short fiction and photography, black and white graphics, bi-lingual poems.

821   UK
PROEM PAMPHLETS. 1976. irreg. price varies. Festival Office, Ilkley, West Yorkshire LS29 8DG, England. Ed. Michael Dawson. circ. 875.

808   US
PROMISE. 1989. q. $6. Bob Murphy, Ed. & Pub., Box 24, Bronston, KY 42518. TEL 606-561-4602. adv.; circ. 1,000.
    Description: Encourages aspiring writers to submit quality modern poetry and fiction.

811   US
PROSPECT REVIEW. 1989. a. $12. 557 Tenth St., Brooklyn, NY 11215.

851 055   IT
PROSPETTIVE CULTURALI CALABRESI. q. Corso Telesio, 34-36, Cosenza, Italy. Ed. M. Zuccaro.

861   SP
PROVINCIA; coleccion de poesia. 1970. irreg. 2500 ptas.($20) for 6 nos. Institucion "Fray Bernardino de Sahagun", Edificio Fierro, Puerta de la Reina, 1, Leon, Spain. circ. 1,000.

861   AG
PROVINCIA. 1967. s-m. $2. Rafael M. Altamirano, Ed. & Pub., Calle Libertad, Casa 16 B, Barrio los Olivos 5870, Villa Dolores, Argentina. bk.rev.
    Description: Covers poetry and other literary works.

821   UK
PSYCHOPOETICA; a magazine of psychologically-based poetry. 1978. s-a. £2.80($6) Psychopoetica Publications, University of Hull, Dept. of Psychology, Hull HU6 7RX, England. TEL 0482-465581. Ed. Geoff Lowe. bk.rev.; circ. 300. (back issues avail.)

811   US
PTOLEMY. 1979. a. $2. David Vajda, Ed. & Pub., Box 908, Browns Mills, NJ 08015. TEL 609-893-0896. circ. 250.

811   US   ISSN 0196-5913
PUDDING MAGAZINE; international journal of applied poetry. 1980. irreg. $12.75 for 3 nos. Pudding House Publications, c/o Pudding House Bed & Breakfast for Writers, 60 N. Main St., Johnstown, OH 43031. Ed. Jennifer Welch Bosveld. adv.; bk.rev.; circ. 1,400. **Indexed:** A.I.P.P.

861   AG   ISSN 0033-4391
PUNTO OMEGA.* 1968. bi-m. Arg.$1000. Envios, Gualeguaychu 882, Buenos Aires, Argentina. Ed. Edmundo J. Knlino. adv.; bk.rev.; bibl.

811   UK
PURPLE HEATHER PUBLICATIONS. 1981. bi-m. £9($24) Yorkshire Arts Association, 12 Granby Terrace, Headingley, Leeds, West Yorkshire LS6 3BB, England. TEL 0532-785878. Ed. Richard Mason. circ. 500. (also avail. in audio cassette; back issues avail.)

821   UK
PURPLE PATCH. 1976. 6/yr. £5. 8 Beaconview House, Charlemont Farm, West Bromwich, West Midlands, England. Ed. Geoff Stevens.

QINGNIAN WENXUE/YOUTH LITERATURE. see *LITERATURE*

QINGNIAN ZUOJIA/YOUNG WRITERS; wenxue shuang yuekan. see *LITERATURE*

QUADERNI DI LINGUE E LETTERATURE. see *LITERATURE*

808   IT   ISSN 0079-8274
QUADERNI DI POESIA NEOGRECA. 1967. irreg., no. 7, 1987. price varies. Istituto Siciliano di Studi Bizantini e Neoellenici, Via Noto, 34, 90141 Palermo, Italy. TEL 091-625-9541.

800   US   ISSN 0748-0873
AP2
QUARTERLY REVIEW OF LITERATURE POETRY SERIES. Variant title: Q R L Poetry Series. 1943. a. $20 paperback (2 vols.); $20 hardback (1 vol.). 26 Haslet Ave., Princeton, NJ 08540. TEL 609-921-6976. Eds. Theodore & Renee Weiss. adv.; circ. 3,000. (back issues avail.) **Indexed:** A.I.P.P., Acad.Ind., Arts & Hum.Cit.Ind., Curr.Cont., Ind.Little Mag., R.G.
    Former titles: Quarterly Review of Literature Contemporary Poetry Series; Quarterly Review of Literature (ISSN 0033-5819)
    Description: Publishes books of poetry, long poems, poetic plays and books of translations chosen in open competition. Includes photographs, biographies and statements about writing by the authors.

851   IT   ISSN 0048-6213
QUASI;* testi poetici e altre approssimazioni. 1971. 2/yr. L.22999. L. Manzuoli, Via Cairoli 86, 50131 Florence, Italy. Eds. Giuseppe Favati, G. Zagarrio. bk.rev.; illus.; circ. 1,000. (back issues avail.)

811   US
QUICKENINGS IN TRILLUM LAND. 1974. 2/yr. $4.75. 4344 S.W. Concord, West Seattle, WA 98136. Ed. Jessie T. Haraska. illus.

851   IT
QUINTA GENERAZIONE: RIVISTA DE POESIA. 1973. m. L.6500. Editrice Forum, Via Pedrali 27, 47100 Forli, Italy. Ed. Domenico Cara. bk.rev.; bibl.

3004 LITERATURE — POETRY

808.81   II
RABINDRA BHARATI JOURNAL. (Text in English) 1968. irreg., latest issue, 1973. Rs.2. Rabindra Bharati University, 6-4 Dwarkanath Tagore Ln., Calcutta 700007, India. Ed. Ramendranath Mullick. circ. 500.
   Description: Contains essays and poems.

811   US   ISSN 0148-0162
PS615
RACCOON. 1977. irreg. (2-3/yr.). $15. Ion Books, Inc., Box 111327, Memphis, TN 38111-1327. TEL 901-323-8858. Ed. David Spicer. bk.rev.; index; circ. 500. (back issues avail.) **Indexed:** Amer.Hum.Ind., Ind.Amer.Per.Verse.

RADAR - SEI; rivista mensile di attualita-arte-cultura. see ART

811   US
RAFALE. (Text in English, French) 1977. 4/yr. $10. 126 College Ave., Orono, ME 04469. TEL 207-581-3764. Ed. Richard L. Belair. circ. 4,500.
   Description: Encourages the Franco-American artistic expression.

917.306   US   ISSN 0891-0545
RAFT; a journal of Armenian poetry and criticism. 1987. a. $17.50 to individuals; institutions $30 (for 2 yrs.). c/o John A.C. Greppin, Ed., Cleveland State University, Cleveland, OH 44115. TEL 216-687-3967. FAX 216-687-9366. TELEX 810-421-8252. adv.; bk.rev.; bibl.; circ. 225.
   ●Also available online.
   Description: Intends to serve the needs of those interested in Armenian poetry and criticism who would read it in translation.

808.81   US
RAM - THE LETTER BOX. 1974. q. $25. Fordham University, Box B, Bronx, NY 10458. Ed.Bd. adv.; bk.rev.; circ. 6,000.

811   US
RAT RACE RECORD. 1988. 4/yr. $4. Box 1611, Union, NJ 07083. circ. 250.

811   US
▼**RAYSTOWN REVIEW.** 1990. a. $3. RD 1, Box 205, Schellsburg, PA 15559. circ. 500.

808.81   US
REALITIES. 1975. m. $5. Realities Library, 2745 Monterey Hwy. No. 76, San Jose, CA 95111. Ed. Richard A. Soos, Jr. bk.rev.; circ. 500.
   Former titles: Poet; Monthly Poetry Anthology (ISSN 0146-695X); Seven Stars Poetry.

808.81 301.412
REBIRTH OF ARTEMIS. 1982. s-a. $9. Astra Publications, 24 Edgewood Terr., Methuen, MA 01844. TEL 617-685-3087. Ed. Lorraine Moreau-Laverriere. circ. 500. (back issues avail.)

811   US   ISSN 0147-0396
REBIS CHAPBOOK SERIES. 1977. irreg., unnumbered. Allegany Mountain Press, 111 N. 10th St., Olean, NY 14760. Ed. H. Ruggieri. circ. 300.

811   US
RECORD SUN. 1969. 4/yr. $8. Poet Papers, Box 528, Topanga, CA 90290. circ. 8,000.

RED CEDAR REVIEW. see LITERATURE

811   US
▼**RED DANCEFLOOR.** 1990. 4/yr. $3.50 per no. Box 3051, Canoga Park, CA 91306. TEL 818-785-7650. Ed. David Goldschlag. circ. 450.

811   US
▼**RED DIRT.** 1991. 2/yr. $10 to individuals; institutions and foreign $20. 1630 30th St., Ste. A-307, Boulder, CO 80301. circ. 1,500.

811   US
RED PAGODA; a journal of haiku. 1983. q. $16 (foreign $24). Lewis Sanders, Ed. & Pub., 125 Taylor St., Jackson, TN 38301. TEL 901-427-7714. bk.rev.; circ. 130.

811 028.5   US
REFLECTIONS (DUNCAN FALLS); the national student poetry magazine for grades K-12. 1980. s-a. $5. Duncan Falls Junior High Journalism Group, Box 368, Duncan Falls, OH 43734. TEL 614-674-5209. Ed. Dean Harper. adv.; circ. 1,000. (also avail. in Braille; record; video cassette; back issues avail.) **Indexed:** Avery Ind.Archit.Per., ERIC.

808.81   US
RENEGADE (BLOOMFIELD HILLS). 1988. s-a. $5.90. Box 314, Bloomfield Hills, MI 48303. Ed. Michael E. Nowicki. adv.; circ. 100.

RENMIN WENXUE/PEOPLE'S LITERATURE. see LITERATURE

RESONANCE (NEW YORK); new voices for a new age. see NEW AGE PUBLICATIONS

811   US
THE REVIEW (PORTLAND); words and images. 1974. a. $5.50. University of Southern Maine, 96 Falmouth St., Portland, ME 04103. TEL 207-780-4186. Ed. John Bowman. adv.: B&W page $135; trim 9 3/4 x 6 1/2; adv. contact: Laura Lee Fitzgerald. bk.rev.; circ. 400.
   Former titles: Portland Review of the Arts; Presumpscot Review.

811   US
REVIEW LA BOOCHE. 1976. 2/yr. $6. 110 South Ninth, Columbia, MO 65201. circ. 500.

861   AG
REVISTA ACENTO. 1981. bi-m. $10. Fundacion Shaw, Cerrito 1154, Buenos Aires, Argentina. Eds. Juan Forn, Enrique Valiente Noailles. circ. 1,200.

861   CR
REVISTA DE POESIA CENTROAMERICANA.* Title varies: Revista Centroamericana de Poesia. 1974. q. Universidad de Costa Rica, Instituto de Estudios Centroamericanos, C.U. Rodrigo Facio, San Pedro de Montes de Oca, San Jose, Costa Rica. Ed. Manlio Argueta. illus.

808.81   US
RHINO. 1976. a. $5. Poetry Forum, 8403 W. Normal Ave., Niles, IL 60648. Eds. Kay Meier, Martha Vertreace. index; circ. 500. (back issues avail.)
   Description: Publishes free verse poetry.

821   UK   ISSN 0268-5981
RIALTO. 1984. 3/yr. £8 (Europe £11; U.S. £15; elsewhere £15.50)(effective Jan. 1992). 32 Grosvenor Rd., Norwich, NR2 2PZ, England. Eds. Michael Mackmin, John Wakeman. illus.; circ. 1,000. (back issues avail.)
   Description: A magazine of and about new poetry.

831   GW   ISSN 0720-0463
RIND UND SCHLEGEL; Zeitschrift fuer Poesie. 1977. q. DM.26. Klaus Friedrich, Ed. & Pub., Ursulastr. 10, D-8000 Munich 40, Germany. TEL 089-342550. adv.; bk.rev.; circ. 1,500.
   Description: Includes a collection of contemporary poetry.

821   US   ISSN 0893-9721
RIVER RAT REVIEW. 1987-1989; resumed no.6, 1992. a. $4. Box 24198, Lexington, KY 40524. TEL 606-277-8601. Ed. Daryl Rogers. bk.rev.; circ. 200. (back issues avail.)

811   US
RIVERRUN. a. $4. Brooklyn College, English Department, Bedford Ave. and Avenue H, Brooklyn, NY 11210. TEL 718-780-5195. Ed. Carlos Serrano.

811   US
RIVERWIND. 1977. a. $2.50. (Hocking College) Riverwind Press, General Studies, Hocking College, Nelsonville, OH 45764. TEL 614-753-3591. Ed.Bd. bk.rev.; circ. 400.
   Description: Presents literature from many genres.

RIVISTA LETTERARIA; quadrimestrale di critica letteraria e cultura varia. see LITERATURE

811   US   ISSN 0148-3730
PS580
ROAD-HOUSE. 1975. irreg. (5-6/yr.) $1.50. Todd Moore, Ed. & Pub., 900 W. 9th St., Belvidere, IL 61008. TEL 815-544-9581. bk.rev.; circ. 100. (back issues avail.)

ROANOKE REVIEW. see LITERATURE

890   BG
ROBABARA. (Text in Bengali) 1978. w. Tk.4. New Nation Printing Press, 1, Ramkrishna Mission Rd., Dhaka 3, Bangladesh.

808.81   US
ROBERT FROST NEWSLETTER. q. $5. St. Michael's Academy, Robert Frost Society, Box 9102, College Station, TX 77840. (Subscr. to: Ronald Bieganowski, Marquette University, Dept. of English, Milwaukee, WI 53233)

811   US   ISSN 0300-7936
PS3519.E27
ROBINSON JEFFERS NEWSLETTER. 1962. q. $10. California State University, Department of English, 1250 Bellflower Blvd., Long Beach, CA 90840. FAX 310-985-2369. (Co-sponsors: California State University, Long Beach; Occidental College) Ed. Robert Brophy. bk.rev.; abstr.; circ. 200. (processed; also avail. in microfilm) **Indexed:** Abstr.Engl.Stud., LCR, M.L.A.

821   UK   ISSN 0144-7262
ROCK DRILL. 1980. irreg. £1.20($4.80) Supranormal Cassettes, 15 Oakapple Rd., Southwick, Sussex BN4 4YL, England. Eds. Robert Sheppard, Penelope Bailey. adv.; bk.rev.; circ. 200. (back issues avail.)

800   US
ROUND TABLE (ROCHESTER); a journal of poetry and fiction. 1984. a. $12.50. Round Table Publications, Box 18673, Rochester, NY 14618. TEL 716-244-0623. Eds. Alan Lupack, Barbara Tepa Lupack. circ. 150. (back issues avail.)
   Description: Original poetry and fiction. Alternate issues include poetry and fiction on the Arthurian legends.

811   US
▼**ROWBOAT.** 1990. irreg. (6-8/yr). $5. c/o MFA Creative Writing Program, 452 Bartlett Hall, Massachusetts University, Amherst, MA 01003. Ed. Greg Bachar. circ. 500.

811   US   ISSN 0882-018X
RUNDY'S JOURNAL AND CONFEDERATION COURIER. 1976. s-a. $8 for 4 issues. Rundy's Journal, 217 Elizabeth St., 7, New York, NY 10012. TEL 212-966-1233. Ed. John A. Craig. circ. 350. (back issues avail.)

811   US
▼**RYAN'S REVIEW.** 1990. 4/yr. $4. Telstar Publishing, 7810 Bertha Ave., Parma, OH 44129-3110. circ. 125.
   Description: Publishes poetry by children under the age of 16.

808.81   US   ISSN 0891-2378
S P S M & H. (Shakespeare, Petrarch, Sidney, Milton & Hopkins) 1986. q. $14. Amelia, 329 "E" St., Bakersfield, CA 93304. TEL 805-323-4064. Ed. Frederick A. Raborg, Jr. bk.rev.; illus.; circ. 600. (back issues avail.)
   Description: Presents sonnets, artricles, fiction about or including sonnets; original illustrations and appropriate sophisticated cartoons.

811   CN
▼**SACRED FIRE.** 1990. 4/yr. $20. P.O. Box 91980, West Vancouver, B.C. V7V 4S4, Canada. TEL 604-922-8745. Ed. Robert Augustus Masters. circ. 20,000.

808.81   US   ISSN 0735-4665
PS301
SAGETRIEB. 1982. 3/yr. $18 to individuals; institutions $35. National Poetry Foundation, 302 Neville Hall, University of Maine, Orono, ME 04469. TEL 207-581-3814. Ed. Carroll F. Terrell. adv.; bk.rev.; circ. 300. **Indexed:** Abstr.Engl.Stud., Amer.Hum.Ind., M.L.A.
   —BLDSC shelfmark: 8069.272270.

808.81   US   ISSN 0885-5013
PS508.M4
SAGUARO. (Text in English, Spanish) 1984. a. $9 to individuals; institutions $15. University of Arizona, Mexican American Studies and Research Center, Douglas Bldg., Rm. 315, Tucson, AZ 85721. TEL 602-621-7551. FAX 602-621-7966. Ed. Charles Tatum. adv. (back issues avail.)

ST. ANDREWS REVIEW. see *LITERATURE*

811 US
ST. MAWR. (Text in English, French, Spanish) 1975. s-a. $16.50 (effective Aug. 1991). 496a Hudson St., Ste. K118, New York, NY 10014. FAX 212-787-9653. Ed. J.H. Kennedy. adv.; charts; illus.; circ. 1,000. (avail. on diskette, audio tape)
Formerly (until vol.3, 1977): Veins, Journal of Jazz Poetry.

811 US
▼**SALAD.** 1990. 2/yr. $12. Box 64980-306, Dallas, TX 75206. circ. 1,000.

821 IE ISSN 0790-1631
PR8848
SALMON. (Text in English, Gaelic) 1981. 3/yr. £6($22) Salmon Publishing, The Bridge Mills, Galway, Ireland. TEL 091-62587. Ed. Jessie Lendennie. adv.; circ. 1,000. (back issues avail.)
Description: Contemporary poetry and short stories primarily by Irish writers, as well as international writers.

831 AU
SALZ; Salzburger Literaturzeitung. 1975. q. S.40. Salzburger Literaturforum Leselampe, Kaigasse 27-I, A-5020 Salzburg, Austria. TEL 41327. bk.rev.; circ. 6,200. (back issues avail.)

821 UK ISSN 0954-6499
SAMIZDAT. 1970. bi-m. £20 (foreign £24). Pluto Publishing Ltd., 345 Archway Rd., London N6 5AA, England. FAX 081-348-9133. TELEX 262433. Ed. Martin Linton. adv.; bk.rev.; circ. 2,000. (back issues avail.)
—BLDSC shelfmark: 8071.990400.
Incorporates: Total Creative Plunge.
Description: Analysis of current British political life, written by journalists, academics, and politicians.

895 II ISSN 0970-0986
SAMKALEEN KALA AUR KAVITA. (Text in Hindi) 1982. q. Rs.80($24) Samkaleen Prakashan, 2762 Rajguru Marg, New Delhi 110 055, India. Ed. Krishan Khullar. adv.; bk.rev.; illus.; circ. 1,050.

811 US ISSN 0196-2884
SAN FERNANDO POETRY JOURNAL. 1978. q. $10. Kent Publications, Inc., 18301 Halsted St., Northridge, CA 91325. TEL 213-349-2080. Ed. Richard Cloke. adv.; bk.rev.; circ. 1,000. (back issues avail.)
Indexed: Ind.Amer.Per.Verse.
Description: Collection of contemporary, liberal poetry focusing on social, political, and environmental issues.

811 US
▼**SAN MIGUEL QUARTERLY.** 1990. biennial. 1200 E. Ocean Blvd., No.64, Long Beach, CA 90802. Ed. John Brander. circ. 400.

811 US
SAN MIGUEL REVIEW. 1973. a. 1200 E. Ocean Boulevard, No.64, Long Beach, CA 90802. TEL 213-495-0925. circ. 800.

SARGASSO; theater, film, poetry, performance, criticism. see *LITERARY AND POLITICAL REVIEWS*

808.1 CN ISSN 0080-6560
SASKATCHEWAN POETRY BOOK. 1936. biennial. Can.$4. Saskatchewan Poetry Society, 3104 College Avenue, Regina, Sask. S4T 1V7, Canada. Ed.Bd. circ. 600. (back issues avail.)

821 AT
SCARP. 1982. 2/yr. $12. Five Islands Press Cooperative Ltd., P.O. Box 1144, Wollongong, N.S.W. 2500, Australia. TEL 042-270985. circ. 1,000.

808.81 US
SCHLEGEL TRANSLATIONS. irreg., latest no.3. $39.95 per no. Edwin Mellen Press, 240 Portage Rd., Box 450, Lewiston, NY 14902. TEL 716-754-8566. FAX 716-754-4335.

SCHREIBHEFT; Zeitschrift fuer Literatur. see *LITERATURE*

808.81 US
SCORE (OAKLAND); a magazine of visual poetry. 1983. a. $12 for 2 issues. Score Publications, 491 Mandana Blvd., No. 3, Oakland, CA 94610. TEL 415-268-9284. Ed.Bd. bk.rev.; circ. 250. (back issues avail.)

821 UK
SCRATCH. no.5, 1991. 3/yr. £4. Mark Robinson, Ed. & Pub., 24 Nelson St., The Groves, York YO3 7NJ, England.
Description: Small press poetry magazine.

811 US
SCREAM OF THE BUDDHA. 1989. 4/yr. $35. Buddha Rose Publications, Box 902, Hermosa, CA 90254. TEL 213-318-6743. Ed. Scott Shaw. circ. 1,108.

SCREE. see *LITERARY AND POLITICAL REVIEWS*

808.81 070 US
SE LA VIE WRITER'S JOURNAL. 1987. q. $14 in US; Canada $16; elsewhere $18. Rio Grande Press, Box 371371, El Paso, TX 79937. TEL 915-595-2625. Ed. Rosalie Avara. adv.; bk.rev.; circ. 300.
Formerly (until **1989):** Se la Vie Poetry Newsletter.
Description: Dedicated to encouraging novice writers, poets and artists by giving them a chance at getting published.

SEEMS. see *LITERATURE*

811 US ISSN 0037-2145
PN6010.5
SENECA REVIEW. 1970. s-a. $8. Hobart & William Smith Colleges, Geneva, NY 14456. TEL 315-789-5500. Ed. Deborah Tall. adv.; bk.rev.; illus.; circ. 600. (back issues avail.) **Indexed:** A.I.P.P., Amer.Hum.Ind., Ind.Amer.Per.Verse.
Description: Contemporary poetry, translations and essays on contemporary poetry.

821 UK ISSN 0140-1165
SEPIA. 1977. 3/yr. $3. Kawabata Press, Knill Cross House, Hr. Anderton Rd., Millbrook, Torpoint, Cornwall, England. Ed. Colin David Webb. bk.rev.; circ. 100.
Description: Poetry and prose.

811 UK
SERIE D'ECRITURE. 1980. a. $9.50. Spectacular Diseases, 83-b London Rd., Peterborough, Cambs. PE2 9BS, England. circ. 500.

811 US
SHARING.* 1982. q. $12. (Western Sun Associates, Inc.) Western Sun Publications, 201 S. 1st Ave., Yuma, AZ 85364. Eds. Carson E. Bench, Alex Starch. circ. 200. **Indexed:** Rehabil.Lit.

811 US
SHATTERED WIG REVIEW. 1988. 2/yr. $6. 523 East 38th St., Baltimore, MD 21218. TEL 301-243-6888. circ. 500.
Description: Publishes prose poetry and concrete poetry.

895.1 CC
SHI SHEN/POEMS DEITY. (Text in Chinese) m. Hebei Sheng Wenxue Yishu Lianhehui, 2 Shizhuang Lu, Shigang Dajie, Shijiazhuang, Hebei 050000, People's Republic of China. TEL 741808.

895.1 CC ISSN 0583-0230
PL2543
SHIKAN/POETRY. (Text in Chinese) 1957. m. Y15.60($44) (Zhongguo Zuojia Xiehui - China Writers' Association) Shikan She, 10, Nongzhanguan Nanli, Beijing 100026, People's Republic of China. (Dist. overseas by: China International Book Trading Corporation, P.O. Box 2820, Beijing, P.R.C.; Dist. in US by: China Books & Periodicals, Inc., 2929 24th St., San Francisco, CA 94110. TEL 415-282-2994)

895.1 CC
SHILIN. (Text in Chinese) q. Harbin Wenlian, Shilin Bianjibu, 12, Gongchang Jie, Daoli-qu, Harbin, Heilongjiang 150010, People's Republic of China. TEL 410478. Ed. Jiang Wei.

895.1 CC
SHIREN/POET. (Text in Chinese) bi-m. Zhongguo Zuojia Xiehui, Jilin Fenhui - Chinese Writers Association, Jilin Chapter, Fu 111, Stalin Street, Changchun, Jilin 130022, People's Republic of China. TEL 884790. Ed. Lu Ping.

811 US
SHIRIM; a Jewish poetry journal. 1982. s-a. $7. c/o Hillel Macor, 2405 Hollister Terrace, Glendale, CA 91206. Ed. Marc Steven Dworkin. circ. 700.

811 US
SHOTS. 1986. 6/yr. $15. Box 109, Joseph, OR 97846. circ. 1,600.

SICHUAN WENXUE/SICHUAN LITERATURE. see *LITERATURE*

808.81 284 US ISSN 0889-9118
SILVER WINGS; poems. 1983. q. $7. Poetry on Wings, Inc., Box 1000, Pearblossom, CA 93553-1000. TEL 805-264-3726. Ed. Jackson Wilcox. bk.rev.; circ. 450. (back issues avail.)
Description: Ecumenical poetry of inspiration.

808.81 US
THE SINGLE HOUND; the poetry and image of Emily Dickinson. 1989. s-a. $12 to individuals (foreign $15); institutions $20 (foreign $23). Box 598, Newmarket, NH 03857. TEL 603-659-2685. Ed. Andrew Leibs. bk.rev.; circ. 300. (avail. on 3.5 inch floppy disk)
Description: Explores the poetry and life of Emily Dickinson.

THE SINGLE SCENE (GAHANNA). see *SINGLES' INTERESTS AND LIFESTYLES*

811 US
▼**SISYPHUS.** 1990. 6/yr. $12. 8 Asticou Rd., Boston, MA 02130. Ed. Christopher Corbett-Fiacco.

808.81 US ISSN 0893-7095
SLANT: A JOURNAL OF POETRY. 1987. a. $10. University of Central Arkansas, Conway, AR 72035. TEL 500-450-5107. (Subscr. to: UCA, Box 5063, Conway, AR 72032) Ed. Richard Hudson. circ. 300. (back issues avail.)
Description: Presents traditional and modern poetry from all regions.

SLATE & STYLE. see *HANDICAPPED — Visually Impaired*

811 US
SLEEPWALKER'S JOURNAL. 1989. 2/yr. free. 820 North Park St., Columbus, OH 43215. TEL 614-294-2922.

811 700 770 US ISSN 0749-0771
SLIPSTREAM (NIAGARA FALLS). 1981. s-a. $8.50. Slipstream Publications, Box 2071, New Market Sta., Niagara Falls, NY 14301. TEL 716-282-2616. Ed.Bd. circ. 300. **Indexed:** Ind.Amer.Per.Verse.

800 UK ISSN 0143-1412
PR1170
SLOW DANCER. 1977. s-a. £6($20) for 2 yrs. Slow Dancer Press, 58 Rutland Rd., West Bridgford, Nottingham NG2 5DG, England. TEL 0602-821518. (U.S. subscr. to: Alan Brooks, R.F.D. 1, Box 3010, Lubec, ME 04652) Ed. John Harvey. bk.rev.; illus.; circ. 500. (back issues avail.)
Description: A magazine of British and American writing; mainly, but not exclusively, poetry.

811 US
SLOW MOTION MAGAZINE.* 1985. s-a. $6. c/o Ona Gritz, 160 W. 84th ST., A No. 11, New York, NY 10024-4666. Ed.Bd. circ. 250. (back issues avail.)

SMALL POND MAGAZINE OF LITERATURE; journal of poetry, short fiction and opinion. see *LITERATURE*

821 UK ISSN 0262-852X
SMOKE. 1974. s-a. $5 for 3 nos. Windows Project, 22 Roseheath Dr., Halewood, Liverpool L26 9UH, England. Ed. Dave Ward. circ. 1,000. (also avail. in microfiche from BHP; back issues avail.)
Description: Features poetry, short prose, and art work.

811 US
▼**SNAIL'S PACE REVIEW.** 1991. 2/yr. $8. R.R. 2, Box 363, Brownell Rd., Cambridge, NY 12816. TEL 518-692-9953. Ed. Darby Penney. circ. 250.

811 US
SNAKE NATION REVIEW. 1989. 2/yr. $15. 2920 North Oak, Valdosta, GA 31602. TEL 912-242-1503. circ. 200.

LITERATURE — POETRY

811   US
SNUG. 1988. 2/yr. $2 per no. 1327 High Rd., Ste. Y-6, Tallahassee, FL 32304. TEL 904-224-9196. circ. 100.

841   FR   ISSN 0081-0908
SOCIETE DES POETES FRANCAIS. ANNUAIRE. 1902. a. Societe des Poetes Francais, Hotel de Massa, 38 rue du Faubourg Saint-Jacques, 75014 Paris, France.
   Description: Four-year bulletin report of conferences and news of the society, recent awards and prizes given.

841   FR   ISSN 0296-6867
SOCIETE DES POETES FRANCAIS. BULLETIN TRIMESTRIEL. no. 173, 1976. 4/yr. membership. Societe des Poetes Francais, 38 rue du Faubourg Saint-Jacques, 75014 Paris, France.

808.8   US
SOLO FLYER. 1987. 3/yr. Spare Change Poetry, 2115 Clearview N.E., Massillon, OH 44646. Ed. David B. McCoy. circ. 50.
   Formerly: Quatra.
   Description: Each issue presents poetry by an individual author.

810   US
SOUNDS OF POETRY. (Text in English, Spanish) 1983. q. $5. (Latino Poets Association) Jacqueline Sanchez, Pub., 8761 Avis, Detroit, MI 48209. TEL 313-843-8478. Ed. Jousseline Sanchez. bk.rev.; circ. 250.

811   US   ISSN 0887-2074
SOUTH COAST POETRY JOURNAL. 1986. s-a. $9 to individuals; institutions $10. California State University, Fullerton, Department of English, Fullerton, CA 92634. TEL 714-773-3163. Ed. John J. Brugaletta. adv.; bk.rev.; index; circ. 700. (back issues avail.)

811   US
SOUTH FLORIDA POETRY INSTITUTE PRESENTS THE REVIEW. 1983. s-a. $10 to individuals; institutions $11. South Florida Poetry Institute, Box 6124, Fort Lauderdale, FL 33310-6124. TEL 305-421-0980. Eds. M. Carlton, D. Simon. adv.; bk.rev.; circ. 500. (back issues avail.)
   Formerly: South Florida Poetry Review (ISSN 0885-0720)
   Description: Provides a forum for the works of well-known and new poets.

811   US   ISSN 0038-447X
PS580
SOUTHERN POETRY REVIEW. 1958. s-a. $8 (foreign $10). Dept. of English, Univ. of North Carolina, Charlotte, NC 28223. TEL 704-547-4309. Eds. Lucinda Grey, Ken McLaurin. bk.rev.; circ. 1,100. (also avail. in microform from UMI; reprint service avail. from UMI) **Indexed:** Ind.Amer.Per.Verse.

811   US
SOUTHWESTERN DISCOVERIES. 1986. 3/yr. $8.10. 15 Calle Bienvenida, Tijeras, NM 87059. TEL 505-247-8736. Ed. Holly Wilson. circ. 500.

SOU'WESTER (EDWARDSVILLE); literary magazine. see *LITERATURE*

SOW'S EAR. see *LITERARY AND POLITICAL REVIEWS*

811   US
SOW'S EAR POETRY JOURNAL. 1988. 4/yr. $10. 245 McDowell St., Bristol, TN 37620. TEL 615-764-1625. Eds. Errol Hess, Larry Richman. circ. 750.

861 811   US
SPANISH AND SPANISH-AMERICAN POETRY. irreg. Peter Lang Publishing, Inc., 62 W. 45th St., 4th Fl., New York, NY 10036. TEL 212-302-6740. FAX 212-302-7574. Ed. Manuel Mantero.

821   II
SPARK; an anthology of Indian poetry. (Text in English) 1975. s-a. Rs.6($2) per no. Spark Publications, 81 Raja Basanta Roy Rd., Calcutta 700 029, India. Ed. Santosh Kuman Adhikari. adv.; bk.rev.; circ. 500.
   Description: Includes poetry, short profiles of poets, views and reviews.

811   US
SPARROW (WEST LAFAYETTE); the politically incorrect verse magazine. 1954. a. $7. Sparrow Press, 103 Waldron St., W. Lafayette, IN 47906. TEL 317-743-1991. Eds. Felix Stefanile, Selma Stefanile. illus.; circ. 900. (also avail. in microform from UMI; reprint service avail. from UMI) **Indexed:** Ind.Amer.Per.Verse.
   Former titles (until 1991, no.58): Sparrow Poverty Pamphlets (ISSN 0885-9477); (until no.34): Sparrow (ISSN 0038-6588)
   Description: Publishes contemporary sonnets.

SPEKTRUM; Vierteljahresschrift fuer Dichtung und Originalgrafik. see *ART*

808.81   US   ISSN 0195-9468
PR2362
SPENSER STUDIES; a Renaissance poetry annual. 1980. a. $45. A M S Press, Inc., 56 E. 13 St., New York, NY 10003. TEL 212-777-4700. FAX 212-995-5413. Eds. Patrick Cullen, Thomas P. Roche, Jr. (back issues avail.) **Indexed:** M.L.A. —BLDSC shelfmark: 8411.772000.
   Description: Articles on the works of Edmund Spenser and other Renaissance poets.

SPIRAL. see *WOMEN'S INTERESTS*

811   US   ISSN 0038-7584
PS301
SPIRIT (SOUTH ORANGE); a magazine of poetry. 1934. s-a. $4. Seton Hall University, Department of English, South Orange, NJ 07079. TEL 201-761-9000. FAX 201-761-9596. Ed. David Rogers. adv.; bk.rev.; index; circ. 650. (also avail. in microform from UMI; reprint service avail. from UMI) **Indexed:** A.I.P.P., Cath.Ind., M.L.A.

811   US
▼**SPIT.** 1990. 2/yr. $6. 529 2nd St., Brooklyn, NY 11215. TEL 718-499-7343. circ. 400.

SPONTANEOUS COMBUSTION. see *LITERATURE*

811   US   ISSN 0738-8993
SPOON RIVER QUARTERLY. 1976. s-a. $12 to individuals; institutions $15. (Illinois State University, English Department) Illinois State University Publications Center, Normal, IL 61761. TEL 309-438-7906. Ed. Lucia C. Getsi. adv.; illus.; circ. 400. **Indexed:** A.I.P.P.

811   US
SPRING RAIN. 1971. irreg. (2-4/yr.). $10. Spring Rain Press, Box 277, Port Townsend, WA 98368. Ed. Karen Gates. circ. 500.

821   SA   ISSN 0258-7211
STAFFRIDER. 1978. q. R.12. Ravan Press (Pty.) Ltd., Box 31134, Braamfontein 2017, Transvaal, South Africa. Ed.Bd. adv.; bk.rev.; play rev.; circ. 7,000. **Indexed:** Ind.S.A.Per.

821   US
STAPLE. 1983. 3/yr. £7. Derbyshire College of H E, Mickleover, Derby, Derbyshire DE3 5GX, England. Eds. Donald Measham, Bob Windsor. circ. 600.

811   US
STAR ROUTE JOURNAL. 1978. 10/yr. $12. Box 1451, Redway, CA 95560. TEL 707-923-3351. Ed. Mary Siler Anderson. circ. 800.

STARLIGHT. see *RELIGIONS AND THEOLOGY — Protestant*

START MAGAZINE OF LITERATURE AND THE ARTS. see *LITERATURE*

821   UK   ISSN 0039-1212
STEREO HEADPHONES; an occasional magazine of the new experimental poetries. (Text in English, French, German and Italian) 1969. irreg. (2-3/yr.). £4($7.50) per no. Church Steps, Kersey, Near Ipswich, Suffolk, England. (Also avail from: Nicholas Zurbrugg, Ed., School of Humanities, Griffith University, Nathan, Brisbane, Qld. 4111, Australia) adv.; bk.rev.; bibl.; illus.; circ. 1,000. (tabloid format; also avail. in cards)

851   IT   ISSN 0393-9480
STEVE; rivista di poesia. 1981. a. L.40000 includes suppl. Edizioni del Laboratorio di Poesia, Via Monte Sabotino 69, 41100 Modena, Italy. TEL 361 560. FAX 059-217497. Ed. Carlo Alberto Sitta. adv.; bk.rev.; circ. 500.

891   RU
STIKHI. (Subseries of: Repertuar Khudozhestvennoi Samodeyatel'nosti. Seriya-Repertuarnye Sborniki) 1967. irreg. Izdatel'stvo Iskusstvo, Vorotnikovskii pereulok 11, Moscow, Russia.

811   US
STILE.* 1974. s-a. $2.50 for 3 nos. Stile Press, c/o Dennis Ray, Ed., Rt.1 Box 114, Ashland, MO 65010-9735. bk.rev.; circ. 100. (also avail. in microform)

808.8   US   ISSN 1043-9501
PS536.2
STILETTO. 1989. irreg. Howling Dog Press, Box 5987, Westport Sta., Kansas City, MO 64111. Ed. Michael Annis. illus.

821 820   IE
STONY THURSDAY BOOK. (Text in English and Gaelic) 1975. irreg., no. 8, 1982-83. £2($4.50) John Liddy, Ed. & Pub., 128 Sycamore Ave., Rath Bhan, Limerick, Ireland. bk.rev.; play rev.; bibl.; illus.; circ. 1,000. (back issues avail.)

811   US
STROKER;* a poem-prose-art review. 1974. 3/yr. $9. Stroker Press, c/o Irving Stettner, Ed., 124 N. Main St., No.1, Shavertown, PA 18708-1416. adv.; bk.rev.; circ. 500.

811   US
STROPHES. 1964. q. $3. National Federation of State Poetry Societies Inc., RR 3, Box 348, Alexandria, IN 46001. TEL 317-754-7082. Ed. Kay Kinnaman. circ. 8,500.
   Description: Informs poets of contest news, convention news, poetry news, for members only.

851   IT
STRUMENTI DI LESSICOGRAFIA LETTERARIA ITALIANA. 1987. irreg., no.8, 1990. price varies. Casa Editrice Leo S. Olschki, Casella Postale 66, 50100 Florence, Italy. TEL 055-6530684. FAX 055-6530214.

STUDI PIEMONTESI. see *LITERATURE*

STUDIA POETICA. see *LITERATURE*

821   US   ISSN 1043-5751
▼**STUDIES IN GERARD MANLEY HOPKINS.** 1990. irreg. Peter Lang Publishing, Inc., 62 W. 45th St., 4th Fl., New York, NY 10036. TEL 212-302-6740. FAX 212-302-7574. Ed. Todd K. Bender.

811   US
STUDIO ONE. 1976. a. free. College of St. Benedict, St. Joseph, MN 56374. circ. 900.

811 323.4   US   ISSN 1040-614X
SUBVERSIVE AGENT. 1988. a. $3. Arcady Publishing, Inc., 4622 Oliver Ave., N., Minneapolis, MN 55412. TEL 612-521-2205. Ed. Paul Jentz. adv.; bk.rev.; illus.; circ. 2,000. (tabloid format; back issues avail.)
   Description: Publishes political and surreal poetry with an avant-garde sense of language. Looks for "writers who take chances."

841   FR   ISSN 0049-2450
SUD; revue litteraire. (Supplement avail.) 1970. 6/yr. 545 F. 62, rue Sainte, 13001 Marseille, France. TEL 91-33-60-68. Ed. Yves Broussard. adv.; bk.rev.; circ. 2,000.

811   US   ISSN 0735-7133
PS501
SUN DOG: THE SOUTHEAST REVIEW. 1979. s-a. $8 to individuals; institutions $10. Florida State Student Writing Association, c/o English Dept., Florida State Univ., 406 Williams Bldg., Tallahassee, FL 32306. TEL 904-644-4230. Ed.Bd. adv.; bk.rev.; circ. 1,250.
   Formerly: Sun Dog.

811   US
SUNDOG. 1979. a. $2. Rte. 1, Box 56, Chokio, MN 56221. TEL 612-324-7456. circ. 125.

SWEDISH BOOK REVIEW. see *PUBLISHING AND BOOK TRADE*

SYCAMORE REVIEW. see *LITERATURE*

808.81   HU   ISSN 0586-3783
SZEP VERSEK. 1964. a. 88 Ft. Magveto Kiado, Vorosmarty ter 1, Budapest V, Hungary. TELEX 223502-MAGVE-H. Ed. Miklos Jovanovics.

861   AG
TABLA REDONDA. 1983. 4/yr. Rincon 110, Buenos Aires, Argentina. Ed. Adela Martinez del Castillo.

TAKAHE. see *LITERATURE*

808.81   US   ISSN 0898-8684
PS325
TALISMAN; a journal of contemporary poetry and poetics. 1988. s-a. $9 to individuals; institutions $13. Box 1117, Hoboken, NJ 07030. Ed. Edward Foster. adv.; bk.rev.; circ. 650.
  Description: Presents poetry, prose and interviews of contemporary artists worldwide.

TALKING STICK. see *LITERATURE*

851   IT
TAM TAM. 1972. q. L.35000($40) Via Val d'Enza 228, 42049 S. Ilario D' Enza (Reggio Emilia), Italy. TEL 0522-674756. Ed. Bianca Maria Bonazzi. adv.; bk.rev.; circ. 1,500.

811   US   ISSN 0162-1017
PS615
TAMARISK.* 1975. s-a. $10. 1200 Farrell Terr., Rahway, NJ 07065-2729. Eds. Dennis Barone, Deborah Ducoff-Barone. adv.; bk.rev.; circ. 300. **Indexed:** A.I.P.P.

811   US   ISSN 0896-064X
PS501
TAMPA REVIEW. 1988. s-a. $10. University of Tampa, Humanities Division, Box 19F, Tampa, FL 33606-1490. TEL 813-253-3333. FAX 813-251-0016. Ed. Richard Mathews. circ. 450. **Indexed:** Ind.Amer.Per.Verse.
  Supersedes (1972-1987): Abatis; **Formerly:** U T Review.
  Description: Features poetry, fiction, articles, interviews, translations and art.

811   US
TAPAS. 1989. 3/yr. $10. 4017A Shenandoah, St. Louis, MO 63110. TEL 314-772-8237. circ. 350.

808.81   US
TAPJOE;* an Anaprocrustean poetry journal of Enumclaw. 1987. s-a. $6.50 for 4 nos. Red Ink - Black Hole Productions, Box 632, Leavenworth, WA 98826-0632. circ. 200.
  Description: Emphasizes poetry with a slant towards environmental or social issues.

811   US   ISSN 0039-9639
TAR RIVER POETRY. 1978. 2/yr. $8. East Carolina University, Department of English, Greenville, NC 27834-4353. TEL 919-757-6041. Ed. Peter Makuck. adv.; bk.rev.; illus.; circ. 1,000. (tabloid format) **Indexed:** Amer.Hum.Ind., Ind.Amer.Per.Verse.

808.81   IT   ISSN 0394-3518
PN1059.E94
TAVERNA DI AUERBACH; rivista internazionale di Poetiche Intermediali. (Text in Italian; summaries in English) 1987. 3/yr. L.35000($30) Hetea Editrice di Enzo Tofani & Co., Via Colleprata, 374, 03011 Alatri (FR), Italy. TEL (0775) 434026. FAX 0775-450096. (Subscr. to: Hetea Editrice di Enzo Tofani & Co., San Quiziano, 03011 Alatri (FR), Italy) Ed. Giovanni Fontana. adv.; bk.rev.; bibl.; illus.; circ. 1,000. (back issues avail.)
  Description: Forum dealing with the structure of text, the matter of language and experimentation of all possible textual consistencies.

851   IT
TECHNE; rivista di poesia e non. 1986. a. L.24000($26) Campanotto Editore, Via Michelini 1, 33100 Udine, Italy. TEL 055 217882. (Subscr. to: Via del Moro 11, 50123 Florence, Italy) Ed.Bd. (back issues avail.)

811   US   ISSN 0883-1599
PN6099.6
TEMBLOR; contemporary poets. 1985. s-a. $16 to individuals; institutions $20. 4624 Cahuenga Blvd., Ste. 307, North Hollywood, CA 91602. TEL 818-449-1276. Ed. Leland Hickman. adv.; bk.rev.; circ. 1,000. (back issues avail.) **Indexed:** Amer.Hum.Ind., Ind.Amer.Per.Verse.

811   US
TEMM POETRY MAGAZINE. 1989. m. $12. Split Personality Press, 511 West Sullivan St., Olean, NY 14760. Ed. Ken Wagner. circ. 200.

808.81   US
TEMPEST ANTHOLOGY. irreg. $10. Earthwise Publications, Box 680-536, Miami, FL 33168. TEL 305-653-2875. Ed. Barbara Holley. illus.; circ. 250.
  Formerly: Tempest Poetry Journal.

TEMPORARY CULTURE. see *LITERARY AND POLITICAL REVIEWS*

811   US   ISSN 0197-890X
PS615
TENDRIL;* a poetry magazine. 1977. 3/yr. $12 to individuals; institutions $14. Tendril, Inc., Box 2626, Key West, FL 33045-2626. adv.; bibl.; illus.; cum.index: 1977-1980; circ. 1,800. **Indexed:** A.I.P.P., Ind.Amer.Per.Verse.

808 418   US
TERRA POETICA; a multilingual magazine of poetry. 1979. irreg., vol.2, no.2, 1983. $5. State University of New York at Buffalo, Department of Modern Languages, 910 Clemens Hall, Buffalo, NY 14260. TEL 716-636-2191. Ed. Jorge Guitar. circ. 500. (back issues avail.)

811   US
▼**THEATER OF BLOOD.** 1990. every 9 months. $7. Box 620, Orem, UT 84059-0620. circ. 150.

808.81   US   ISSN 1041-4851
THEMA. 1988. q. $16 (foreign $21). Thema Literary Society, 4312 Napoli Dr., Metairie, LA 70002. TEL 504-887-1263. (Subscr. to: Box 74109, Metairie, LA 70033-4109) Ed. Virginia Howard. circ. 300. (back issues avail.)
  Description: Contains thematically arranged poetry and fiction.

811   US
THEMATIC POETRY QUARTERLY. 1971. q. $12. Audio-Visual Poetry Foundation, 400 Fish Hatchery Rd., Marianna, FL 32446. TEL 904-482-3890. Ed. W.I. Throssell. circ. 100.

811   US
THIRD EYE. 1976. s-a. $2.50. Third Eye Publications, 189 Kelvin Dr., Buffalo, NY 14223. Ed. Patrick Lally. bk.rev.; circ. 500. (back issues avail.) **Indexed:** A.I.P.P.

811   US
THIRD LUNG REVIEW. 1985. a. $3. Third Lung Press, Box 361, Conover, NC 28613. TEL 704-465-1254. circ. 150.

811   US   ISSN 0747-9727
THIRTEEN (PORTLANDVILLE). 1982. q. $5. M A F Press, Thirteen Poetry Magazine, Box 392, Portlandville, NY 13834. TEL 607-286-7500. Ed. Ken Stone. bk.rev.; circ. 350. **Indexed:** Hum.Ind.

THIS AND THAT. see *CHILDREN AND YOUTH — For*

811   US   ISSN 0362-4846
PS580
THREE RIVERS POETRY JOURNAL. 1973. s-a. $10 for 2 years. Three Rivers Press, P.O. Box 21, Carnegie-Mellon University, Pittsburgh, PA 15213. TEL 412-268-2861. Ed. Gerald Costanzo. adv.; bk.rev.; circ. 1,000. (processed; also avail. in microform from UMI) **Indexed:** A.I.P.P.

800   CN   ISSN 0824-7579
TIDEPOOL; anthology of haiku and short poetry. 1984. a. Can.$5($5) Hamilton Haiku Press, 4 E. 23rd St., Hamilton, Ont. L8V 2W6, Canada. TEL 416-383-2857. Ed. Herb Barrett. circ. 300. (also avail. in microfilm; back issues avail.)

821   CN
TIGER LILY MAGAZINE; the magazine by women of colour. 1986. 5/yr. $14.95. P.O. Box 756, Stratford, Ont., Canada. TEL 519-271-7045. circ. 15,000.

TIME OF SINGING; a magazine of Christian poetry. see *RELIGIONS AND THEOLOGY*

821   AT
TIMESTREAM. 1971. bi-m. Aus.$1. c/o Richard Coady, Ed., Box a360, Sydney South 2000, New South Wales, Australia. circ. controlled.

811   US
TIN WREATH. 1985. q. free. Box 13401, Albany, NY 12212-3401. Ed. David Gonsalves. circ. 250.

811   US
TOAD HIWAY. 1988. irreg. $4 for 3 no. Toad Hiway Press, Box 44, Universal, IN 47884. TEL 317-832-8918. Ed. Doug Martin. circ. 200.

821   UK
TOLL GATE JOURNAL. 1983. 2/yr. $10. 12 Colne Rd., Cowling, Keighley, West Yorkshire BD22 OBZ, England. circ. 500.

861   UY
TORRE DE LOS PANORAMAS. 1972. q. Centro de Investigacion, Informacion y Difusion de la Joven Poesia Uruguaya, Avda. Centenario 3923 Ap. 008 Blok.H., Montevideo, Uruguay. Ed.Bd. adv.; bk.rev.; illus.; circ. 1,500.

808.8   US
TOUCHSTONE (HOUSTON); literary journal. 1976. $5. Touchstone Press, Box 8308, The Woodlands, TX 77387-8308. Ed. William Laufer. adv.; bk.rev.; illus.; circ. 1,000. (back issues avail.) **Indexed:** Amer.Hum.Ind.

821   CN   ISSN 0495-9701
TOWER. 1951. s-a. Can.$6. Tower Poetry Society, c/o Dundas Public Library, 18 Oglivie St., Dundas, Ont., Canada L9H 2S2. Ed. Joanna Lawson. circ. 300. (back issues avail.)

841   FR   ISSN 0041-0276
TRACES; cahiers trimestriels de lettres et d'arts. 1963. q. 88 F. Editions Traces, 44330 Le Pallet, France. Ed. Michel-Francois Lavaur. bk.rev.; illus.; circ. 700. (also avail. in microform from UMI)

811   US
▼**TRANS-MISSOURI ART VIEW.** 1990. m. 1506 Harney St., Omaha, NE 68102. Ed. Marilyn Coffey. circ. 2,300.

811   US
TRAY FULL OF LAB MICE PUBLICATIONS. 1989. 2/yr. $6. Box 303, Durham, NH 03824. Eds. Melissa Jasper, Matt Jasper. circ. 2,500.

808.1   US   ISSN 0085-7378
TREEWELL.* 1968. a. $1. Johnson C. Smith University, 100 Beatties Ford Rd., Charlotte, NC 28216. TEL 704-378-1000. Ed. Carolyn McClair. bk.rev.; illus.; circ. 500.

051   US
TRIBE; an American gay journal. 1989. q. $22. Columbia Publishing Co., 234 E. 25th St., Baltimore, MD 21218. Ed.Bd. illus.
  Description: Gay literary journal offering about 100 edited and printed essays, poems and stories.

TURNSTILE. see *LITERATURE*

TWEED. see *LITERATURE*

U.C. REVIEW. see *LITERATURE*

U S 1 WORKSHEETS. see *LITERATURE*

811   HU   ISSN 0082-7312
UJ MAGYAR NEPKOLTESI GYUJTEMENY. 1955. irreg. price varies. (Magyar Tudomanyos Akademia) Akademiai Kiado, Publishing House of the Hungarian Academy of Sciences, P.O. Box 24, H-1363 Budapest, Hungary.

861   AG   ISSN 0326-9779
PQ7748
ULTIMO REINO; revista de poesia. 1979. q. Arg.$2000($20) Ediciones Ultimo Reino, Av. Juan B. Justo 3167, 1414 Buenos Aires, Argentina. TEL 8555-3472. Ed. Gustavo Mario Margulies. adv.; bk.rev.; illus.; circ. 1,800.

811   US
▼**UNBRIDLED LUST!.** 1990. bi-m. $15. Unbridled Lust! Publishing, 8 Elm St., Ste. 2, Orono, ME 04473. TEL 207-866-3535. Eds. Brad Finch, Matt LeClair. circ. 500.

821   CN   ISSN 0838-6749
UNDERPASS. 1987. a. Can.$6.95($6.95) Underpass Press, 574-21, 10405 Jasper Ave., Edmonton, Alta., Canada. Ed. Barry Hammond. circ. 200 (controlled). (back issues avail.)
  Description: Avant-garde, concrete, urban, discursive prose and poetry.

LITERATURE — POETRY

943.1 US
UNICORN GERMAN SERIES.* (Text in English and German) 1968. irreg. $5 paper; $15 cloth. Unicorn Press, Inc., Box 3307, Greensboro, NC 27402. Ed. Teo Savory. adv.; bk.rev.; circ. 2,000. (back issues avail.)

821 CN
▼**UNION SHOP BLUFF.** 1990. bi-m. $6. 205A Liverpool St., Cuelph, Ont. N1H 2L6, Canada. TEL 519-767-1998. circ. 120.

811 US
▼**UNIROD MAGAZINE.** 1990. bi-m. $12. 4214-B Filbert Ave., Atlantic City, NJ 08401. circ. 100.

861 CK ISSN 0120-0992
UNIVERSIDAD DE LOS ANDES. CUADERNOS DE FILOSOFIA Y LETRAS. 1973. irreg. Universidad de los Andes, Facultad de Humanidades y Ciencias Sociales, Comite de Publicaciones, Bogota, Colombia. bibl.; circ. 1,000.
Formerly: Universidad de los Andes. Cuadernos de Letras.

811 US ISSN 0049-5557
PS580
UNMUZZLED OX. 1971. irreg. $20. (Soho Baroque Opera Company, Inc.) Unmuzzled Ox Foundation, Ltd., 105 Hudson St., New York, NY 10013. TEL 212-226-7170. Ed. Michael Andre. adv.; bk.rev.; bibl.; illus.; circ. 20,000 (controlled). **Indexed:** Amer.Hum.Ind., Ind.Amer.Per.Verse.
Description: Publishes fiction and original writing.

808.81 US
UPSTREAM; the Literary Center quarterly. 1984. q. $15. Literary Center, Box 85116, Seattle, WA 98105. Ed. Sarah Sarai. adv.; bk.rev.; circ. 1,700.
Formerly: Literary Center Quarterly.
Description: Provides a forum for writers and small presses in the Pacific North West.

821 UK ISSN 0142-128X
URBANE GORILLA. 1970. s-a. £1.50. Raven Publications, 29 Parker's Rd., Sheffield S10 1BN, England. Ed. Ed Tork. adv.; bk.rev.; circ. 1,000.

URBANUS - RAIZIRR. see LITERATURE

811 US ISSN 0146-8510
UROBOROS. 1975. 2/yr. $5. Allegany Mountain Press, 111 North Tenth Street, Olean, NY 14760. Eds. Ford & Helen Ruggieri. bk.rev.; bibl.; illus.; circ. 500. (also avail. in microfilm) **Indexed:** Access.
Formerly (until vol. 2, 1976): Allegany Poetry.

890 BG
UTSABA. (Text in Bengali) a. Tk.5. 113 Jagannath Saha Rd., Dhaka 1, Bangladesh. Ed. Syed Zafar Ali.

V L S. (Voice Literary Supplement) see LITERATURE

V W A; revue litteraire. see LITERATURE

811 US
VAGABOND CHAPBOOK.* vol. 6, 1976. irreg. $1 per no. Vagabond Press, 605 E. 5th Ave., Ellensburg, WA 98926-3201.

841 FR ISSN 0153-9620
PQ1160
VAGABONDAGES. 1978. 4/yr. 160 F. (foreign 220 F.). Association Paris-Poete, 3 rue Seguier, 75006 Paris, France. adv.; bk.rev.

VARLIK. see LITERATURE

821 UK
VER POETS VOICES. 1968. 2/yr. £1.50. Ver Poets, 61 & 63 Chiswell Green Lane, St. Albans, Herts. AL2 3AL, England. TEL 0727-867005. Ed. May Badman.
Formerly: Ver Poets Broadsheets.

861 SP
VERDE YERBA;* antologia hispanoamericana de poesia. no.10, 1972. irreg. Carabela, Pi i Margall 53, 08024 Barcelona, Spain.

VERSE. see LITERATURE

811 US
VERVE. 1989. 4/yr. $12 (foreign $18)(effective 1992). Box 3025, Simi Valley, CA 93093. Ed. Ron Reichick. circ. 250.

811 US ISSN 0042-5206
PR500
VICTORIAN POETRY. 1963. q. $15 to individuals; institutions $25. West Virginia University, Victorian Poetry Office, Dept. of English, Morgantown, WV 26506. TEL 304-293-3107. FAX 304-293-7417. Ed. Hayden Ward. adv.; bk.rev.; index, cum.index; circ. 1,200. (also avail. in microfilm from UMI; reprint service avail. from KTO) **Indexed:** Abstr.Engl.Stud., Arts & Hum.Cit.Ind., Curr.Cont., Hum.Ind., Ind.Bk.Rev.Hum., LCR, M.L.A.
—BLDSC shelfmark: 9232.665000.
Description: Examines Victorian poetry, 1830-1914.

811 US
VIRGIN MEAT. 1986. 4/yr. $7. 2325 West Ave., K-15, Lancaster, CA 93536. TEL 805-722-1758. Ed. Steve Blum. circ. 300.

821 UK
VISION ON. a. £1.50. Ver Poets, 61 & 63 Chiswell Green Lane, St. Albans, Herts AL2 3AL, England. TEL 0727-867005. Ed. May Badman.

800 US
VISIONS INTERNATIONAL; the world journal of illustrated poetry. 1979. 3/yr. $14. (Visions International Arts Synergy, Inc.) Black Buzzard Press, 1110 Seaton Lane, Falls Church, VA 22046-3920. TEL 703-241-8626. Ed. Bradley R. Strahan. bk.rev.; illus.; circ. 750. (back issues avail.) **Indexed:** Amer.Hum.Ind., Ind.Amer.Per.Verse.
Formerly: Visions (ISSN 0194-1690)
Description: Contains poetry and translation of poetry with original artwork done specifically for the poems.

811 US ISSN 0042-8280
VOICES INTERNATIONAL. 1966. q. $10. Voices International, Co., 1115 Gillette Drive, Little Rock, AR 72207. TEL 501-225-0166. Ed. Clovita Rice. adv.; bk.rev.; circ. 500.

821 IS ISSN 0333-676X
VOICES - ISRAEL; magazine of English language poetry in Israel. (Text in English) 1972. a. price varies. Voices Group of Israeli Poets in English, c/o Mark Levinson, Ed., P.O. Box 5780, Herzliya 46157, Israel. adv.; circ. 350. (also avail. on diskette)
Description: Anthology of English language poetry written by poets in Israel and abroad; includes translations.

808.81 US
VOL. NO. MAGAZINE. (Volume Number); from California - a literary/visual experience. (Text in English; occasionally in Spanish) 1956. s-a. $5. (Santa Clarita Valley Poets) Los Angeles Poetry Press, 24721 Newhall Ave., Newhall, CA 91321. TEL 805-254-0851. Eds. Richard J. Weekley, Donald McLeod. adv.; bk.rev.; circ. 300. (back issues avail.)

VOX MAGAZINE. see LITERARY AND POLITICAL REVIEWS

810 US ISSN 0095-5388
PS301
VOYAGES TO THE INLAND SEA. (Former issuing body: University of Wisconsin-La Crosse) 1971-1979; N.S. 1981. irreg. $33 includes Northeast (La Crosse). Juniper Press, 1310 Shorewood Dr., La Crosse, WI 54601. TEL 608-788-0096. circ. 500.

890 US ISSN 0888-5257
PG3542
VSTRECHI; almanac. (Text in Russian) 1977. a. $10. Encounters, 7738 Woodbine Ave., Philadelphia, PA 19151. Ed. Valentina Sinkevich. bk.rev.; circ. 500.
Formerly: Perekrestki (ISSN 0160-5534)

811 US
WALKING AND SINNING. 1989. a. Accelerator Press, 1708 Martin Luther King Jr. Way, No. 4, Berkeley, CA 94709. TEL 415-549-2815. Ed. J.D. Buhl. circ. 250.

811 US ISSN 0148-7132
WALLACE STEVENS JOURNAL. 1977. biennial. $20 to individuals; institutions $25 (foreign $30). Wallace Stevens Society, Inc., c/o Clarkson University, Potsdam, NY 13699-5750. TEL 315-268-3987. FAX 315-268-4475. Ed. John N. Serio. adv.; bk.rev.; bibl.; circ. 600. **Indexed:** Abstr.Engl.Stud., Arts & Hum.Cit.Ind., Curr.Cont., M.L.A., Tr.& Indus.Ind.
—BLDSC shelfmark: 9261.497500.

811 US
WASHOUT REVIEW.* 1975. irreg. $6. Mildred Publishing, 961 Birchwood Ln., Schenectady, NY 12309-3118. Eds. Ellen Biss, Kathryn Poppino. illus.; circ. 500. (back issues avail.)

WATER ROW REVIEW. see LITERATURE

811 US ISSN 0197-4777
WATERWAYS; poetry in the mainstream. 1978. 11/yr. $20. (Waterways Project) Ten Penny Players, Inc., 393 St. Pauls Ave., Staten Island, NY 10304-2127. TEL 718-442-7429. FAX 718-442-4978. Eds. Barbara Fisher, Richard Alan Spiegel. circ. 200. (back issues avail.)
Formerly: N Y S Waterways Project Magazine.
Description: Publishes poetry primarily by contemporary Americans (professional and child poets).

811 US
WE ARE THE WEIRD. 1985. 52/yr. $35. Box 2002, Dallas, TX 75221. TEL 214-692-8601. circ. 2,700.

811 US
WE MAGAZINE (SANTA CRUZ). 1986. 4/yr. $15. We Press, Box 1503, Santa Cruz, CA 95061. TEL 408-427-9711. circ. 800.

821 AT
WEBBER'S. 1989. 2/yr. $15. 15 McKillop St., Melbourne, Vic. 3000, Australia. Ed. Peter Gebhardt. circ. 1,000.

811 US ISSN 0511-4934
WESLEYAN POETRY PROGRAM. 1959. s-a. Wesleyan University Press, 110 Mt. Vernon St., Middletown, CT 06457. TEL 203-344-7918. FAX 203-344-7977. (Co-publisher: University Press of New England)

808.7 US ISSN 0149-6441
PN6010.5
WEST BRANCH. 1977. 2/yr. $7 (effective Sept. 1990). Bucknell University, Bucknell Hall, Lewisburg, PA 17837. TEL 717-524-1853. Eds. Karl Patten, Robert Taylor. bk.rev.; illus.; circ. 500. **Indexed:** A.I.P.P., Ind.Amer.Per.Verse.
Description: Features poetry and fiction.

810 US ISSN 0049-7223
WEST END;* a magazine of poetry and politics. 1971. s-a. $5. c/o G.D. Kaliss, Ed., 1777 East-West Rd., Ste. 1435, Honolulu, HI 96848-0001. bk.rev.; charts; illus.; circ. 1,000.

811 US ISSN 0890-9024
PS3229
WEST HILLS REVIEW; a Walt Whitman Journal. 1979. a. $6. Walt Whitman Birthplace Association, 246 Old Walt Whitman Rd., Huntington Sta., NY 11746. TEL 516-427-5240. Ed. William A. Fahey. bk.rev.; circ. 1,200.

811 US
WESTERFIELD'S REVIEW.* 1976. s-a. $5. Ashford Press, Box 513, Willimantic, CT 06226-0513. Ed. M.J. Westerfield. bk.rev.; illus.; circ. 750. (back issues avail.)
Formerly (until 1981): Sarcophagus.

WESTWORDS. see ART

821 UK ISSN 0307-7276
WEYFARERS. 1972. 3/yr. $14. Guildford Poets Press, 9 White Rose Lane, Woking Surrey GU22 7JA, England. Ed.Bd. bk.rev.; circ. 300.
Description: International poetry magazine for all kinds of poetry, especially mainstream poetry of 40 lines or less.

808 CN ISSN 0827-1828
WHAT; poetry, fiction, drama, criticism. 1985. bi-m. Can.$12($12) to individuals; institutions Can.$24($24). Box 338, Sta. "J", Toronto, Ont. M4J 4Y8, Canada. TEL 416-588-5268. Ed.Bd. adv.; bk.rev.; bibl.; play rev.; circ. 10,000. (tabloid format; back issues avail.)

811 US
WHETSTONE (SIERRA VISTA);* a Southwest poetry magazine. 1978. 3/yr. $5. San Pedro Press, c/o Michael Bowden, Ed., 514 W. Mallard Ctr., Sierra Vista, AZ 85635-3534.

LITERATURE — POETRY

811 US
▼WHISPERING PALM. 1991. m. Box 6523, Lake Worth, FL 33466. circ. 1,500.

811 US
WHITE CLOUDS REVUE. 1987. irreg. (2-3/yr.). $12 for 4 issues. Box 462, Ketchum, ID 83340. circ. 250.

811 US ISSN 0511-8832
PS3279
WHITTIER NEWSLETTER. 1966. a. free. Whittier Clubs of Haverhill and Amesbury, c/o Howard W. Curtis, Ed., Haverhill Public Library, Haverhill, MA 01830. bk.rev.; bibl.; circ. 600. (looseleaf format; back issues avail.)

811 US
WHOLE NOTES. 1984. 2/yr. $6. Daedalus Press, Box 1374, Las Cruces, NM 88004. TEL 505-382-7446. Ed. Nancy Peters Hastings. circ. 400.

811 US
▼WICKED MYSTIC. 1990. m. $39.95. Box 3087, Dept. 222, Astoria, NY 11103. TEL 718-545-6713. circ. 500.

WIELANDS BRIEFWECHSEL. see *LITERATURE*

WIENER - GOETHE - VEREIN. JAHRBUCH. see *LITERATURE*

811 US
WILDFLOWER. 1981. irreg. (6-8/yr.). $5. Wildflower Press, Box 4757, Albuquerque, NM 87196-4757. Ed. Jeanne Shannon. circ. 75.
  Description: Publishes experimental, imagistic poetry that draws upon the haiku tradition.

811 US ISSN 0893-3375
WINDFALL. 1979. irreg. (approx a.). $5. Windfall Prophets Press, Department of English, University of Wisconsin, Whitewater, WI 53190. TEL 414-472-1036. Ed. Ron Ellis. bk.rev.; circ. 300.

808.81 CN ISSN 0847-1762
WINDHORSE REVIEW. 1982. s-a. Can.$9 to individuals; institutions Can.$12 (effective June 1991). Samurai Press, RR 3, Box 3140, Yarmouth, N.S. B5A 4A7, Canada. Ed. John Castleburg. circ. 500.
  Description: Contempletive poetics and art.

811 US ISSN 0043-5716
PS580
WINDLESS ORCHARD; a quarterly magazine of photography and contemporary poetry. 1970. irreg., no.55, 1990. $10 for 3 nos. Robert Novak, Ed. & Pub., c/o English Dept., Indiana University, Fort Wayne, IN 46805. TEL 219-481-6841. bk.rev.; illus.; circ. 300. (also avail. in microfilm from UMI; reprint service avail. from UMI) Indexed: Ind.Amer.Per.Verse.

811 US ISSN 0043-6631
AP2
WISCONSIN REVIEW. 1966. 3/yr. $6. University of Wisconsin - Oshkosh, Box 158, Radford Hall, Oshkosh, WI 54901. TEL 414-424-2267. Ed. Mike Beirne. bk.rev.; play rev.; illus.; circ. 400. (back issues avail.)
  —BLDSC shelfmark: 9325.895000.
  Description: Contains new poetry, fiction, reviews, essays, interviews, and artwork.

811 US ISSN 1052-3162
WITHOUT HALOS. 1983. a. $5. (Ocean County Poets Collective) Without Halos Press, Box 1342, Pt. Pleasant Beach, NJ 08742. Ed. Frank Finale. circ. 1,000. (back issues avail.)

808.81 US ISSN 0891-1371
AP2
WITNESS (FARMINGTON HILLS). 1987. s-a. $12 to individuals; institutions $18. Oakland Community College, 27055 Orchard Lake Rd., Farmington Hills, MI 48334. TEL 313-471-7740. Ed. Peter Stine. adv.; bk.rev.; circ. 2,500 (controlled). (back issues avail.)
  Description: Literature illuminating political and social issues around globe. Presents writer as witness.

821 UK ISSN 0043-7107
IVENHOE PARK REVIEW.* 1966. 4/yr. 25s.($5) Ferry Press, 177 Green Lane, London SE9, England. Ed. A. Crozier. bk.rev.; circ. 500.

811 US ISSN 0195-6183
WOMAN POET. 1980. irreg., no.4, 1992. $19.95 hardcover; paperback $12.95. Women-in-Literature, Inc., Box 60550, Reno, NV 89506. TEL 702-972-1671. Ed. Elaine Dallman. bk.rev.; circ. 3,000. (back issues avail.)

811 US ISSN 8756-5277
WORCESTER REVIEW. 1973. a. $15. Worcester County Poetry Association, 6 Chatham St., Worcester, MA 01609. TEL 508-797-4770. Ed. Rodger Martin. adv.; bk.rev.; circ. 1,000. (back issues avail.)
  Description: Contains poetry, articles about poetry, fiction, critical articles with a New England connection, and graphics.

811 US ISSN 0043-8154
THE WORLD (NEW YORK). 1966-1984; resumed no.42, 1992. 4/yr. $20. Poetry Project Ltd., St. Marks Church in-the-Bowery, Second Ave. & 10th St., New York, NY 10003. TEL 212-674-0910. Ed. Lewis Warsh. Indexed: Abstr.Mil.Bibl.

811 US
▼WORLD LETTER. 1991. irreg. $4 per no. 2726 E. Court St., Iowa City, IA 52245. TEL 319-337-6022. Ed. Jon Cone. illus.

811 US
WORLD OF POETRY.* 1975. q. $10. 701 Dix Oeanne Ave., Sacramento, CA 95815-3121. Ed.Bd. circ. 250,000.

811 US ISSN 0043-9401
PS580
WORMWOOD REVIEW. 1959. q. $10. Wormwood Books and Magazines, Box 4698, Stockton, CA 95204-0698. TEL 209-466-8231. Ed. M. H. Malone. bk.rev.; bibl.; illus.; cum.index; circ. 700. (also avail. in microform from UMI) Indexed: A.I.P.P., Amer.Hum.Ind.
  Description: Prose poems and poems of all styles communicating the temper of current times.

811 US
▼WRITE NOW!. 1990. 6/yr. $12. Right Here Publications, Box 1014, Huntington, IN 46750. circ. 250.

WRITERS' AND POETS' YEARBOOK. see *LITERATURE*

811 US
WRITERS' BLOC. 1985. 4/yr. $10. Box 212, Marysville, OH 43040. TEL 513-642-8019. circ. 300.

WRITERS' OWN MAGAZINE. see *LITERATURE*

808.81 US
WRITER'S VOICE. 1988. q. $13. 1630 Lake Dr., Haslett, MI 48840. TEL 517-339-8754. Ed. Lisa Roose-Church. adv.; bk.rev.
  Formerly (until 1990): Poetry Magic.

WRITING. see *LITERATURE*

821 UK
X-CALIBRE. 1986. a. £3. Nemeton Publishing, P.O. Box 780, Bristol BS99 5BB, England. TEL 44-272-715144. Eds. Ken Taylor, Juli Taylor. circ. 500.

811 US ISSN 0146-0463
XANADU; a literary journal. 1975. a. $5. Long Island Poetry Collective, Inc., Box 773, Huntington, NY 11743. Ed.Bd. circ. 300. (back issues avail.)

XENOPHILIA. see *LITERATURE — Adventure And Romance*

811 US
XEROLAGE. 1985. 4/yr. $10. 1341 Williamson, Madison, WI 53703. TEL 608-258-1305. Eds. Miekal & Elizabeth Was. circ. 500.
  Description: Features visual poetry, copy art and collage graphics.

070.5 808.81 US
XEROTIC EPHEMERA. 1984. irreg., no.8, 1991. $4 per no. Permeable Press, 900 Tennessee, Studio 15, San Francisco, CA 94107. TEL 415-648-2175. FAX 415-648-2180. Ed. Brian C. Clark. bk.rev.; circ. 300.
  Former titles: Naked Review; (Until 1988): Comet Halley.
  Description: Literary journal dedicated to exposing assumptions. Provides a "radical reinterpretation" of fiction and poetry. Includes essays.

895.1 CC
XINGXING SHIKAN/STAR POETRY JOURNAL. (Text in Chinese) m. Zhongguo Zuojia Xiehui, Sichuan Fenhui - China Writers Association, Sichuan Chapter, 85, Hongxing Lu 2 Duan, Chengdu, Sichuan 610012, People's Republic of China. TEL 660846. Ed. Ye Yanbin.

811 US ISSN 0084-3458
YALE SERIES OF YOUNGER POETS. 1919. a. price varies. Yale University Press, 92A Yale Sta., New Haven, CT 06520. TEL 203-432-0940. Ed. James Dickey.

811 US
YARROW; a journal of poetry. 1981. s-a. $1.50 per no. Kutztown State College, English Department, Kutztown, PA 19530. TEL 215-683-4353. Ed. Harry Humes. circ. 350.

808.81 US
(YEAR) PEACE CALENDAR. a. War Resisters League, 339 Lafayette St., New York, NY 10012. TEL 212-228-0450. FAX 212-228-6193.
  Description: Includes one page of poetry or prose with illustrations for each week of the year.

820 CN ISSN 0704-5700
PS3509.L43
YEATS ELIOT REVIEW. 1974. a. Can.$12 for 2 years to institutions. University of Victoria, Department of English, Victoria, B.C. V8W 2Y2. TEL 604-721-7211. Ed. Shyamal Bagchee. bk.rev.; bibl. Indexed: Abstr.Engl.Stud., Amer.Hum.Ind., Arts & Hum.Cit.Ind., Curr.Cont., Ind.Bk.Rev.Hum., M.L.A.
  —BLDSC shelfmark: 9418.040000.
  Incorporates: T.S. Eliot Review (ISSN 0318-6342); T.S. Eliot Newsletter (ISSN 0315-1174)

811 US
▼YELLOW PAGES. 1990. 4/yr. $12. Telstar Publishing, 7810 Bertha Ave., Parma, OH 44129-3110. circ. 125.

YELLOW SILK; journal of erotic arts. see *LITERATURE*

YET ANOTHER SMALL MAGAZINE. see *LITERARY AND POLITICAL REVIEWS*

891.43 II ISSN 0970-0978
YUVA KAVI. (Text in Hindi) q. 40($12) Samkaleen Prakashan, 2762 Rajguru Marg, New Delhi 110 055, India.

811 US ISSN 0049-8505
ZAHIR. 1970. s-a. $4 to individuals; institutions $6. Diane Kruchkow, Ed. & Pub., Weeks Mills, New Sharon, ME 04955. TEL 207-778-3436. adv.; bk.rev.; circ. 1,000. Indexed: Access, Ind.Amer.Per.Verse.

821 UK
ZENOS. 1982. 3/yr. £3. 59 B Ilkeston Rd., Nottingham NG7 3GR, England. circ. 1,000.

ZHONGGUO XIBU WENXUE. see *LITERATURE*

821 UK ISSN 0260-7654
ZIP; poetry magazine. 1980. irreg. $4. Iris Services Co-operative, 1A Oldham St., Hyde, Cheshire SK14 1LJ, England. Ed. Sandy Gort. adv.; illus.; circ. 1,000. Indexed: Graph.Arts Lit.Abstr.

811 US ISSN 0888-000X
PS580
ZONE 3. 1986. 3/yr. $8 to individuals; institutions $10 (foreign $11). Austin Peay State University, Center for the Creative Arts, Box 4565, Clarksville, TN 37044. TEL 615-648-7031. Eds. Malcolm Glass, David Till. circ. 500.
  Description: Publishes work from the U.S. and abroad.

ZVEZDA; literaturno-khudozhestvennyi i obshchestvenno-politicheskii zhurnal. see *LITERARY AND POLITICAL REVIEWS*

811 US
2AM MAGAZINE. 1986. 4/yr. $19. 2AM Publications, Box 6754, Rockford, IL 61125-1754. TEL 815-397-5901. Ed. Gretta McCombs Anderson. circ. 1,000.

LITERATURE — SCIENCE FICTION, FANTASY, HORROR

811 US
5 AM. 1987. 2/yr. $6. 1109 Milton Ave., Pittsburgh, PA 15218. circ. 750.
Description: Publishes mostly poems ignored by other magazines.

811 US
11 X 13 - BROADSIDE. 4/yr. $5. Toledo Poets Center Press, 32 Scott House, University of Toledo, Toledo, OH 53606. Ed. Joel Lipman. circ. 1,000.

LITERATURE — Science Fiction, Fantasy, Horror

808.81 US
ABORIGINAL SCIENCE FICTION. 1986. q. $14. Absolute Entertainment Inc., Box 2449, Woburn, MA 01888-0849. Ed. Charles C. Ryan. adv.; bk.rev.; film rev.; illus.; circ. 31,000. (back issues avail.)
Formerly: Aboriginal S F (ISSN 0888-3475)

808.838 US
AFTER HOURS. no.12, 1991. 4/yr. $4 per no. Box 538, Sunset Beach, CA 90742. TEL 714-840-0606.
Description: Small press horror fiction, with author interviews.

808.8 RU
▼**ALIENS.** (Text in English) 1992. q. £1.95($2.95) per no. c/o Yevgeny Maidannikoff, 144 Kashirskoye Hig., Bldg. 2, 115561 Moscow, Russia. (Or: c/o Alexander Vasilkovsky, 36 Pyatidesyatileta Oktyabra av., Apt. 51, 252148, Kiev, Ukraine) Eds. Yevgeny Maidannikoff, Alexander Vasilkovsky.
Description: Showcases post-Soviet science fiction writing and art for Western audiences, with news of literary and fan activities in the former Soviet Union.

808.838 US ISSN 1058-0751
AMAZING STORIES. 1926. m. $30 (foreign $50). T S R Inc., Box 111, Lake Geneva, WI 53147. TEL 414-248-3625. FAX 414-248-0389. (Subscr. to: T S R Inc., Box 5695, Boston, MA 02206. TEL 800-372-4667) Ed. Kim Mohan. adv.; bk.rev.; circ. 10,000. (also avail. in microfilm from KTO)
Formerly: Amazing Science Fiction Stories (ISSN 0279-1706)
Description: Publishes science fiction, fantasy and horror short stories plus science fact articles, and opinion essays.

813 808.838 US ISSN 0161-2328
PZ1.A1
ANALOG SCIENCE FICTION & FACT. 1930. 15/yr. $34.95. Dell Magazines, 380 Lexington Ave., New York, NY 10168-0035. TEL 212-557-9100. (Subscr. to: Box 7060, Red Oak, IA 51591. TEL 800-333-4561) Ed. Stanley Schmidt. adv.; bk.rev.; charts; illus.; index; circ. 90,000. (also avail. in microform from UMI; reprint service avail. from UMI)
Indexed: Acad.Ind., Access (1975-), Bk.Rev.Ind. (1977-), Child.Bk.Rev.Ind. (1977-), Mag.Ind.
Formerly: Analog Science Fact - Science Fiction (ISSN 0003-2603)

ANATOMY OF WONDER; a critical guide to science fiction. see *LITERATURE — Abstracting, Bibliographies, Statistics*

808.8 UK
▼**ARCANUM.** 1991. irreg. £3.50 per no. 15 Oxford St., Mexborough, S. Yorks. S64 9RL, England. Ed. Stephen Sennitt.

808.838 AG ISSN 0004-1084
ARGENTINE SCIENCE FICTION REVIEW. (Text in English) 1969. 2/yr. $2 per no. Argentine Science Fiction Review Publications, Casilla 3869, Correo Central, Buenos Aires, Argentina. Ed. Hector R. Pessina. adv.; bk.rev.; film rev.; bibl.; illus.; circ. 500.

808.838 US
ARKHAM SAMPLER; a complement to Etchings & Odyssey. 1983. q. $7. Strange Company, Box 864, Madison, WI 53701. Ed.Bd. circ. 500.

808.838 US
▼**ATOPOS.** 1990. every 9 mos. $14 for 3 nos. 233 Lazy Acre Rd., Wausau, WI 54401. TEL 715-845-1421. Ed. Hal H. Hintze. adv.; illus.; circ. 500. (back issues avail.)
Description: Publishes speculative fiction, science fiction, horror and fantasy stories and related articles.

808.8 UK
AUGURIES. no.14, 1991. 4/yr. £7($18) 48 Anglesey Rd., Alverstoke, Gosport, Hants. PO12 2EQ, England. (Subscr. in U.S. to: Anne Marsden, 1052 Calle del Cerro, No. 708, San Clemente, CA 92672. TEL 714-361-3791) Ed. Nik Morton. bk.rev.; illus.
Description: Publishes traditional science fiction stories.

AUGUST DERLETH SOCIETY. NEWSLETTER. see *LITERATURE*

808.8 AT
AUREALIS. no.3, 1991. 4/yr. Aus.$24 (foreign Aus.$39; in UK £10). Chimaera Publications, P.O. Box 538, Mount Waverly, Vic. 3149, Australia. (Subscr. in UK to: Chris Reed, NSFA, P.O. Box 625, Sheffield S1 3GY, England)
Description: Australian science fiction for readers with traditional preferences.

808.838 US ISSN 0275-3715
AURORA (MADISON); S F science fiction-speculative feminism. Variant title: Aurora S F. 1975. irreg. (approx. 2/yr.). $10 for 3 nos. Society for the Furtherance and Study of Fantasy and Science Fiction, Inc. (SF3), Box 1624, Madison, WI 53701-1624. Ed. Diane Martin. adv.; bk.rev.; film rev.; circ. 500. (back issues avail.) *Indexed:* Stud.Wom.Abstr.
Formerly: Janus.

808.838 AT ISSN 0155-8870
AUSTRALIAN S F NEWS. (Science Fiction) 1978. q. Mervyn R. Binns, Ed. & Pub., 1 Glen Eira Rd., Ripponlea, Vic. 3182, Australia. TEL 03 531 5879. (Subscr. to: P.O. Box 5879, Elsternwick, Vic. 3185, Australia) bk.rev.; circ. 300. (back issues avail.)
Description: News about authors, books being published, reviews, and fan club activities.

808.838 US
AUTHOR'S CHOICE; a monthly magazine of author collections. 1989. m. $39. Pulphouse Publishing, Inc., Box 1227, Eugene, OR 97440. TEL 503-344-6742. FAX 503-683-3412. Ed. Kristine Kathryn Rusch. circ. 2,500. (back issues avail.)
Formerly (until no.28, 1992): Author's Choice Monthly.
Description: Publishes collections of short science fiction, horror, and fantasy, featuring the work of a single author.

B C S F A-ZINE. (British Columbia Science Fiction Association) see *CLUBS*

808.81 UK ISSN 0269-9990
BACK BRAIN RECLUSE; new speculative fiction. Cover title: B B R. irreg., approx. 3/yr., no.20, 1992. £11($36) for 4 nos. (effective 1992). P.O. Box 625, Sheffield S1 3GY, England. (U.S. addr.: c/o Anne Marsden, 1052 Calle del Cerro, No. 708, San Clemente, CA 92672. TEL 714-361-3791) Ed. Chris Reed. adv.; bk.rev.; bibl.; illus.
Description: Publishes a variety of innovative short fiction, with essays and non-fiction covering the science fiction scene around the world.

813 US ISSN 0095-7119
PZ1.A1
BEST SCIENCE FICTION OF THE YEAR. 1972. a. $2.50. Ballantine Books, 201 E. 50th St., New York, NY 10022. TEL 212-751-2600.

808.838 US
BEYOND SCIENCE FICTION. 1971. a. $5. c/o Rey King, Ed., 414 S. 41st St., Richmond, CA 94804. TEL 415-658-0233. circ. 2,000.
Formerly: Cosmic Circus.

BIBLIOGRAPHIES AND INDEXES IN SCIENCE FICTION, FANTASY, AND HORROR. see *LITERATURE — Abstracting, Bibliographies, Statistics*

BLACK COUNTRY GHOSTS AND MYSTERIES. see *FOLKLORE*

BOOKS ARE EVERYTHING. see *LITERATURE*

791.43 US
CASTLE DRACULA; dedicated to the appreciation, promotion, & preservation of supernatural fiction in literature, films, theater, TV & all media. 1967. q. $7. Gothick Gateway, c/o Gordon R. Guy, Ed., Box 423, Glastonbury, E. Hartford, CT 06033. adv.; bk.rev.; film rev.; illus.; circ. controlled. (processed)
Formerly: Count Dracula Society Quarterly (ISSN 0011-0051)

808.838 US
CEMETERY DANCE. q. $15. Cemetery Dance Publications, Box 18433, Baltimore, MD 21237. bk.rev.; film rev.; illus. (back issues avail.)
Description: Publishes horror and fantasy short stories, interviews and author profiles.

CINEFANTASTIQUE. see *MOTION PICTURES*

808.838 PL
COLLAPS. irreg. membership. Gdanski Klub Fantastyki, P.O. Box 76, 80-325 Gdansk 37, Poland. Dir. Krzysztof Papierkowski. illus.
Description: Science fiction fanzine.

808.838 US
COMPANION IN ZEOR. 1978. irreg. price varies. Karen Litman, Ed. & Pub., 307 Ashland Ave., McKee City, NJ 08232. TEL 609-645-6938. adv.; bk.rev.; film rev.; play rev.; circ. 300. (also avail. in audio cassette; back issues avail.)
Description: Presents work of amateur writers who set their stories in any of the Lichtenberg "universes."

800 US ISSN 0193-6875
CONTRIBUTIONS TO THE STUDY OF SCIENCE FICTION AND FANTASY. 1982. irreg., no.54, 1992. price varies. Greenwood Press, Inc. (Subsidiary of: Greenwood Publishing Group Inc.), 88 Post Rd. W., Box 5007, Westport, CT 06881-5007. TEL 203-226-3571. FAX 203-222-1502. Ed. Marshall Tymn.
—BLDSC shelfmark: 3461.456000.

813 808.838 UK ISSN 0010-9576
COSMOS.* 1969. m. $4.50. c/o Walter Gillings, Ed., 115 Wanstead Park Rd., Ilford, Essex, England. adv.; bk.rev.
Description: Contains science fiction stories.

808.838 UK
CRITICAL WAVE. no.18, 1990. bi-m. £5 (£7 outside UK). Critical Wave Publications, 33 Scott Rd., Olton, Solihull, W. Midlands B92 7LQ, England. Eds. Steve Green, Martin Tudor.
Description: Science fiction news magazine, with author interviews.

809.916 US
CRYPT OF CTHULHU; pulp thriller and theological journal. 1981. irreg. (1-2/yr.), no.80, 1991. $5 per no. Necronomicon Press, 101 Lockwood Ave., W. Warwick, RI 02893. TEL 401-828-7161. FAX 401-738-6125. Ed. Robert M. Price. adv.; bk.rev.; film rev.; circ. 650. (back issues avail.)
Description: Publishes general critical articles examining the literary, biographical and mythological sources of the supernatural fiction of H.P. Lovecraft, creator of the Cthulhu Mythos, and of works by his literary disciples. Occasionally includes fiction by fans and major writers in the field.

808.838 367 US
CUBE. 1983. bi-m. membership. Society for the Furtherance and Study of Fantasy and Science Fiction, Inc. (SF3), Box 1624, Madison, WI 53701-1624. TEL 608-251-6226. Ed. Spike Parsons. bk.rev.; circ. 100. (looseleaf format; back issues avail.)

808.838 UK
CYPHER.* irreg. (approx. s-a.). £1.50 for 5 nos.; in U.S. $3 for 4 nos. 17829 Peters, Roseville, MI 48066. Ed. Cy Gianvin. adv.; bk.rev.; film rev.; illus.; circ. 500.
Description: Contains science fiction reviews.

808.838 PL
▼**CZERWONY KARZEL/RED DWARF.** (Text in Polish) 1991. irreg. membership. Gdanski Klub Fantastyki, P.O. Box 76, 80-325 Gdansk 37, Poland. Dir. Krzysztof Papierkowski. illus.
Description: Science fiction stories by Polish writers, translations of Western authors, critical articles, and news of science fiction activities in Poland.

LITERATURE — SCIENCE FICTION, FANTASY, HORROR

808.838   UK
DARK HORIZONS. no.31, 1990. irreg. £10($24) membership. British Fantasy Society, c/o Di Wathen, 15 Stanley Rd., Morden, Surrey SM4 5DE, England. Ed. Phil Williams.

THE DARK MAN: THE JOURNAL OF ROBERT E. HOWARD STUDIES. see *LITERATURE*

808.838   US   ISSN 1049-0892
DEAD OF NIGHT.* 1989. q. $15. Dead of Night Publications, 916 Shaker Rd., Ste. 143, Longmeadow, MA 01106-2416. Ed. L. Lin Stein. adv.; bk.rev.; film rev.; illus.; circ. 400. (back issues avail.)
Description: Contains horror fiction, particularly concerning vampires.

808   US
DEATHREALM; the land where horror dwells. 4/yr. $15. Mark Rainey, Ed. & Pub., 3223-F Regents Park Ln., Greensboro, NC 27405. illus.
Description: Publishes horror fiction and dark fantasy.

808.8   UK
DEMENTIA 13. no.5, 1991. irreg. £2.50 per no. 17 Pinewood Ave., Sidcup, Kent DA15 8BB, England. Ed. Pam Creais. illus.
Description: Macabre, strange and weirdly erotic fiction.

398 808.81   US
DRACULA NEWS JOURNAL. 1980. q. membership. (Dracula Unlimited) Dracula Press, Penthouse N., 29 Washington Sq. W., New York, NY 10011. TEL 212-533-5018. Ed. James Martin. adv.; bk.rev.; circ. 2,950.
Description: Concerning vampirism in all its forms and guises.

808.8   UK
▼DREAM CELL. 1991. irreg. £1 per no. c/o 7 Walmersley Rd., New Moston, Manchester M10 0RS, England. Ed. Shan Schofield.

DREAMS AND NIGHTMARES. see *LITERATURE — Poetry*

808.8   CN
▼EDGE DETECTOR. 1991. 4/yr. $15 (£9 in UK). 1850 Lincoln Ave., No. 803, Montreal, Que. H3H 1H4, Canada. (Subscr. in UK to: Chris Reed, NSFA, P.O. Box 625, Sheffield S1 3GY, England) Ed. Glenn Grant.
Description: Publishes speculative and experimental fiction, critical essays and original artwork.

808.838   US
ELDRITCH SCIENCE. 1987. s-a. $12. Greater Medford Science Fiction Society, 87-6 Park, Worchester, MA 01605. Ed. George Phillies. bk.rev.; circ. 250. (back issues avail.)
Description: Publishes science fiction and fantasy short stories, poetry and art.

808.838   US   ISSN 0891-9593
ESSAYS ON FANTASTIC LITERATURE. 1986. irreg., no.12, 1992. price varies. Borgo Press, Box 2845, San Bernardino, CA 92406. TEL 714-884-5813. Ed. Robert Reginald.
Description: Short essays on science fiction and fantasy by critics and professionals in the genre.

808.838   US
ETCHINGS & ODYSSEYS; a special tribute to Weird Tales. 1973. s-a. price varies. Strange Company, Box 864, Madison, WI 53701. Ed.Bd. circ. 750.

809.9   US   ISSN 0014-5483
PN3448.S45
EXTRAPOLATION; journal of the scholarly study of science fiction and fantasy. 1959. q. $15 to individuals; institutions $25. Kent State University Press, Kent, OH 44242. TEL 216-672-7913. Ed. Donald M. Hassler. adv.; bk.rev.; bibl.; cum.index; vols. 1-14; circ. 1,000. (also avail. in microfrom from UMI; reprint service avail. from UMI) **Indexed:** Abstr.Engl.Stud., Acad.Ind., Amer.Bibl.Slavic & E.Eur.Stud., Arts & Hum.Cit.Ind., Bk.Rev.Ind. (1988-), Child.Bk.Rev.Ind. (1988-), Curr.Cont., Hum.Ind., M.L.A.
—BLDSC shelfmark: 3854.460000.

808.838   UK   ISSN 0959-4558
▼EXUBERANCE. 1990. q. £6.50($15) 34 Croft Close, Chipperfield, Herts. WD4 9PA, England. Ed. Jason R. Smith.
Description: Publishes science fiction.

808.838   IE
F T L (Faster than Light) q. $18. Irish Science Fiction Association, c/o Brendan Ryder, 30 Beverly Downs, Knocklyon Rd., Templeogue, Dublin 16, Ireland. (Subscr. in U.S. to: Anne Marsden, 1052 Calle del Cerro, No. 708, San Clemente, CA 92672-6068. TEL 714-361-3791)

808.8   GW
FANDOM NEWSLETTER. no.38, 1991. m. Science Fiction Club Deutschland, c/o Matthias Hofmann, Kirchbergstr. 14, 78000 Freiburg im Breisgau, Germany. bk.rev.; film rev.; illus.
Description: Author interviews, convention and publishing news for the science fiction community.

700 800 831   GW
FANTASIA. 1978. q. DM.40($24) Erster Deutscher Fantasy Club e.V., Postfach 1371, 8390 Passau, Germany. Ed. Franz Schroepf. adv.; bk.rev.; film rev.; illus.; circ. 800. (back issues avail.)

808.838   US   ISSN 0094-2375
FANTASIAE (LOS ANGELES). 1973. m. membership. Fantasy Association, Box 24560, Los Angeles, CA 90024. Ed. Ian M. Slater. bk.rev.; cum.index; circ. 500.

809.916 813   UK
FANTASTIC WORLDS OF EDGAR RICE BURROUGHS.* 1976. q. £2.50. British E.R.B. Society (Edgar Rice Burroughs), 56 Leith Towers, Brighton Rd., Sutton, Surrey SM2 5BY, England.

808.383   PL
FANTASTYKA. 1982. m. (plus q. ed. for children and q. comic ed.) Ul. Mokotowska 5-6, 00-640 Warsaw, Poland. TEL 48-22-253475. Ed. Adam Hollanek. circ. 149,300.

808.81   US   ISSN 1051-5011
FANTASY COMMENTATOR. 1943. s-a. $10. A. Langley Searles, Ed. & Pub., 48 Highland Cir., Bronxville, NY 10708-5909. TEL 914-961-6799. bk.rev.; bibl.; index; circ. 500. (back issues avail.)
Description: Devoted to articles, reviews and verse in the area of science-fiction and fantasy.

808.838   UK
FANTASY TALES; a paperback magazine of fantasy and terror. 1977. s-a. £2.95($3.95) per no. Robinson Publishing, 194 Station Rd., Kings Heath, Birmingham B14 7TE, England. TEL 01-493-1064. TELEX 28905 MON REFG REF 778. (Subscr. addr.: 11 Shepherd House, Shepherd St., London W1Y 7LD, England) Eds. Stephen Jones, David Sutton. adv.; bk.rev.; illus.; circ. 20,000.

FANTASYWELT; das Fachmagazin fur Rollenspieler. see *SPORTS AND GAMES*

808.838   UK   ISSN 0964-1890
▼FAR POINT. 1991. 6/yr. £11 (foreign £17). Victoria Publications, P.O. Box 47, Grantham, Lincs. NG31 8RJ, England. bk.rev.; illus. (back issues avail.)
Description: Science fiction and fantasy stories, criticism, and convention news.

808.838   UK
▼FAX 21. 1991. 4/yr. £9.50($20) Tony Lee, Ed. & Pub, 13 Hazely Combe, Arreton, Isle of Wight PO30 3AJ, England. (Subscr. in U.S. to: Anne Marsden, 1052 Calle del Cerro, No. 708, San Clemente, CA 92672-6068. TEL 714-361-3791)
Description: Science fiction stories in the guise of provocative news reports from 50 years in the future.

808.838   US
FILE 770. 1978. bi-m. $8. File 770, 5828 Woodman Ave., No. 2, Van Nuys, CA 91401. Ed. Michael Glyer. bk.rev.; illus.; stat.; circ. 450.
Description: Contains science fiction stories.

808.838   US
FIRST FANDOM MAGAZINE. 1959. 2/yr. membership. Pulp Era Press, 413 Ottokee St., Wauseon, OH 43567-1133. Ed. Lynn A. Hickman. bk.rev.; bibl.; illus.; stat.; circ. 350. (processed)
Description: Covers science fiction, with articles on magazines, authors, and artists.

FLICKERS 'N' FRAMES. see *MOTION PICTURES*

808.838   UK
FOCUS (KENT). 3/yr. £12 includes Matrix, Paperback Inferno and Vector. British Science Fiction Association Ltd., 49 Station Rd., Haxby, York YO3 8LU, England. (Subscr. to: 29 Thornville Rd., Hartlepool, Cleveland TS26 8EW, England) Ed. Cecil Nurse. (back issues avail.)
Description: Magazine for those interested in writing science fiction.

808.838   US   ISSN 0163-6251
FORGOTTEN FANTASY LIBRARY. 1980. irreg., no.25, 1992. price varies. Borgo Press, Box 2845, San Bernardino, CA 92406. TEL 714-884-5813. Eds. Douglas Menville, Robert Reginald.
Description: Classics of imaginative literature.

058   DK   ISSN 0108-6715
FORUM FABULATORUM; magasin for fantastisk litteratur. (Text in Danish) 1982. s-a. DKK 50 (foreign DKK 66). Morten R. Soerensen Ed. & Pub., Cort Adelersgade 5, 2 tv., 1053 Copenhagen K, Denmark. bk.rev.; illus.; circ. 250.
Description: Contains mainly fiction, native and in translation, both well known and new writers, and original artwork.

808.838   UK   ISSN 0306-4964
PS374.S35
FOUNDATION; the review of science fiction. 1972. 3/yr. £10($20) Science Fiction Foundation, Polytechnic of East London, Longbridge Rd., Dagenham, Essex RM8 2AS, England. TEL 081-590-7722. FAX 081-590-7799. Ed. E. James. adv.; bk.rev.; film rev.; bibl.; cum.index; circ. 1,000. (back issues avail.) **Indexed:** M.L.A.
—BLDSC shelfmark: 4024.855000.
Description: Articles on science fiction, by critics and science fiction writers.
Refereed Serial

808.838   PL
GALACTICA. irreg. membership. Gdanski Klub Fantastyki, P.O. Box 76, 80-325 Gdansk 37, Poland. Dir. Krzysztof Papierkowski.
Description: Science fiction fanzine.

808.838 *   UK   ISSN 0955-0933
THE GATE; science fiction and fantasy. 1989. irreg., no.3, 1991. £6 for 4 nos. W Publishing, 28 Saville Rd., Westwood, Peterborough PE3 7PR, England. FAX 0733331511. Ed. Richard Newcombe. bk.rev.; illus.; circ. 2,000.

GAUNTLET; exploring the limits of free expression. see *LITERARY AND POLITICAL REVIEWS*

808.838 813   US   ISSN 0017-419X
GRIDLEY WAVE. 1958; N.S. 1990. m. $28 membership (foreign $35) includes q. Burroughs Bulletin. Burroughs Bibliophiles, Edgar Rice Burroughs Collection, Ekstrom Library, University of Louisville, Louisville, KY 40292. TEL 502-588-6762. FAX 502-588-8753. Ed. George T. McWhorter. bk.rev.; film rev.; bibl.; illus.; circ. 800.
Description: Concerns the writings of Edgar Rice Burroughs, and includes news of society activities.

800   US   ISSN 0897-9707
GRUE MAGAZINE. 1985. 3/yr. $13. Hell's Kitchen Productions, Inc., Box 370, Times Sq. Sta., New York, NY 10108-0370. TEL 212-245-2329. Ed. Peggy Nadramia. adv.; illus.; circ. 1,300. (back issues avail.)
Description: Contains horror and dark fantasy fiction and poetry.

808.838   CN
GUARD THE NORTH. 1970. q. Can.$5. Box 65583, Vancouver, B.C. V5N 5K5, Canada. Ed. D. Say. adv.; bk.rev.; film rev.; circ. 300.
Description: Contains science fiction stories.

800   US
▼HAUNT OF FEAR. 1991. bi-m. $12 (foreign $17). Russ Cochran Publisher, Ltd., Box 469, W. Plain, MO 65775-0469. TEL 417-256-2224.

LITERATURE — SCIENCE FICTION, FANTASY, HORROR

808.8 US ISSN 1043-3503
PS648.H6
HAUNTS; tales of unexpected horror and the supernatural. 1984. q. $13. Nightshade Publications, Box 3342, Providence, RI 02906-0742. TEL 401-781-9438. Ed. Joseph K. Cherkes. adv.; bk.rev.; circ. 1,000.

817 US
HEAVY METAL; the adult illustrated fantasy magazine. Short title: H M. 1977. bi-m. $11.95. Metal Mammoth, 584 Broadway, Ste. 608, New York, NY 10012. TEL 212-274-8462. Ed. Julie Simmons-Lynch. adv. contact: Howard Jurofsky. illus.; circ. 140,000. (back issues avail.)

808.8 US ISSN 1049-0310
HORROR FICTION NEWSLETTER. 1989. m. $10. Gothic Press, 4998 Perkins Rd., Baton Rouge, LA 70808-3043. TEL 504-766-2906. Ed. Gary William Crawford. bk.rev.; film rev.; tr.lit. (back issues avail.)
Description: Contains news and reviews of current horror literature.

808 US ISSN 0748-2914
HORROR SHOW; an adventure in terror. 1982. q. $14. Phantasm Press, 14848 Misty Springs Ln., Oak Run, CA 96069. TEL 916-472-3540. Ed. David B. Silva. adv.; bk.rev.; film rev.; circ. 54,000.
Description: Presents contemporary tales of the macabre, illustrations, and inside tips on the horror field.

808 US
HORROR: THE ILLUSTRATED BOOK OF FEARS.* q. 402 Stanton Ln., Crete, IL 60417-4332. Ed. Mort Castle.
Description: Features fiction, poetry, spot illustrations, and comics.

808.838 CS
IKARIE. no.8, 1991. irreg. Na Cihadle 55, 16000 Prague 6, Czechoslovakia. Ed. Eva Hauser. illus.
Description: Czechoslovakian science fiction magazine, with fiction, including foreign writers in translation, interviews, and news of the science fiction world.

808.83 CN ISSN 0709-8855
IMAGINE; science-fiction et litteratures de l'imaginaire. (Text in French) 1979. q. Can.$20 (effective Jan. 1991). Publications les Imaginoides, 3418 rue de la Paix, Sainte-Foy, Que. G1X 3W6, Canada. TEL 418-658-9966. FAX 418-658-6100. Ed. Marc Lemaire. adv.; bk.rev.; film rev.; play rev.; illus.; index; circ. 600. (back issues avail.)
Description: Covers fiction and studies in the field of science fiction.

808.8 LI
INFOSFERA. (Text in English) irreg. Antakalnio 65-33, Vilnius 232040, Lithuania. Ed. Gediminas Beresnevicius.
Description: News on science fiction activities in Lithuania.

808.838 UK ISSN 0264-3596
INTERZONE. 1982. m. £26($52) (effective Nov. 1991). 217 Preston Drove, Brighton BN1 6FL, England. TEL 0273-504710. (N. America dist.: Worldswide Magazine Distributors Ltd., 225 Bysham Park Dr., Unit 14, Woodstock, Ontario, N4T 1P1, Canada. TEL 519-539-0200) Ed. David Pringle. adv.; bk.rev.; film rev.; illus.; cum.index: 1982-1991 in no.50; circ. 10,000. (back issues avail.)
Description: Specializing in new science fiction and fantasy stories.

808.838 US ISSN 0162-2188
PN6120.95
ISAAC ASIMOV'S SCIENCE FICTION MAGAZINE. 1976. 15/yr. $34.95. Dell Magazines, 380 Lexington Ave., New York, NY 10168-0035. TEL 212-557-9100. (Susbcr. to: Box 7057, Red Oak, IA 51591. TEL 800-333-4108) Ed. Gardner Dozois. adv.; bk.rev.; circ. 90,000. (also avail. in microform from UMI; reprint service avail. from UMI) **Indexed:** Amer.Hum.Ind.

808.838 US
IT GOES ON THE SHELF. 1979. irreg., no.8, 1991. free or exchange basis. Purple Mouth Press, 713 Paul St., Newport News, VA 23605. TEL 804-380-6595. Ed. Ned Brooks. adv.; bk.rev.; circ. 350.
Former titles: Skiffy Thyme; Skiffy Bag.
Description: Reviews books and related materials of interest to science fiction and fantasy readers and collectors.

808.8 LI
KAUKAS. irreg. (2-3/yr.). Radvilenu 56a-35, Kaunas 28, Lithuania. Ed. Gintaras Aleksonis. bk.rev.; film rev.
Description: Publishes science fiction and fantasy from Lithuanian authors and around the world.

808.838 FI ISSN 0785-2517
KOSMOSKYNA. (Text in English) no.2, 1990. 3/yr. Finnish Science Fiction Writers Association, Servin-Maijan tie 6F 94, SF-02150 Espoo, Finland. Ed. Jyrki J.J. Kasvi.

808.83 US ISSN 0047-4959
LOCUS (OAKLAND); the newspaper of the science fiction field. 1968. m. $35 to individuals; institutions $38. Locus Publications, Box 13305, Oakland, CA 94661. TEL 510-339-9198. FAX 510-339-8144. Ed. Charles N. Brown. adv.; bk.rev.; index; circ. 9,000. (back issues avail.) **Indexed:** Bk.Rev.Ind. (1989-).
Description: Trade journal aimed at publishers, authors and interested readers of science fiction.

809.916 US
LOVECRAFT STUDIES. 1979. 2/yr. $10. Necronomicon Press, 101 Lockwood St., W. Warwick, RI 02893. TEL 401-828-7161. FAX 401-738-6125. Ed. S.T. Joshi. bk.rev. (back issues avail.)
Description: Studies the life and writings of H.P. Lovecraft, horror and supernatural fiction author, and creator of the Cthulhu Mythos.

808.8 US
▼**THE LYRE.** 1991. irreg. £2.20($5) per no. Nicholas Mahoney, Ed. & Pub., 275 Lonsdale Ave., Intake, Doncaster DN2 6HJ, England. (Subscr. in U.S. to: Anne Marsden, 1052 Calle del Cerro, No. 708, San Clemente, CA 92672. TEL 714-361-3791)
Description: Original science fiction stories and author interviews.

813 US ISSN 0024-984X
AP2
MAGAZINE OF FANTASY AND SCIENCE FICTION. 1949. m. (combined Oct.-Nov.). $26. Mercury Press, Inc., Jewell St., Box 56, Cornwall, CT 06753. TEL 203-672-6376. FAX 203-672-2643. Ed. Kristine Rusch. adv.; bk.rev.; film rev.; charts; illus.; circ. 61,500. (also avail. in microfilm from UMI) **Indexed:** Amer.Hum.Ind., Bk.Rev.Ind. (1969-), Child.Bk.Rev.Ind. (1969-), Mag.Ind.
Incorporates: Venture Science Fiction.
Description: Contains short stories, novellas, novelettes, and a science column.

808.838 700 US
MAGE; a magazine of fantasy & science fiction. 1984. s-a. $6. Colgate University, Student Activities Office, Hamilton, NY 13346. TEL 315-824-1000. Ed. Sonya Gulatt. adv.; bk.rev.; illus.; circ. 750. (back issues avail.)
Description: Short stories, poetry, commentary, reviews, articles and illustrations in the genres of fantasy and science fiction.

830 831 700 GW
MAGIRA. 1967. a. $4 per no. Erster Deutscher Fantasy Club e.V., Postfach 1371, 8390 Passau, Germany. Ed. Hubert Strassl. adv.; bk.rev.; bibl.; illus.; circ. 1,300.

808.838 US ISSN 0897-9286
PS648.F3
MARION ZIMMER BRADLEY'S FANTASY MAGAZINE. 1988. q. $16 in U.S.; Canada $24; elsewhere $38. Marion Zimmer Bradley Ltd., Box 249, Berkeley, CA 94701. TEL 510-601-9000. Eds. Marion Zimmer Bradley, Jan Burke. (back issues avail.)
Description: Contains fantasy short stories and articles on fiction writing.

810 US
MASIFORM D. 1971. a. $7.50 per no. Poison Pen Press, 627 E. Eighth St., Brooklyn, NY 11218. TEL 718-853-8121. Ed. Devra Michele Langsam. illus.; circ. 500. (reprint service avail.)
Description: Publishes original fiction based on the Star Trek television shows and movies.

808.838 UK ISSN 0307-3335
MATRIX; the newsletter of the British Science Fiction Association. 1979. bi-m. £12 includes Focus, Paperback Inferno, and Vector. British Science Fiction Association Ltd., 16 Aviary Pl., Leeds, LS12 2NP, England. (Subscr. to: Membership Secretary, 33 Thornville Rd., Hartlepool, Cleveland TS26 8EW, England) Ed. Jenny Glover. adv.
Formerly: Science Fiction Media News (ISSN 0143-3725)
Description: News and articles on all aspects of science fiction.

800 700 UK ISSN 0309-1309
PR6031.E183
MERVYN PEAKE REVIEW. 1975. s-a. £14. Mervyn Peake Society, 2 Mount Park Rd., Ealing W5 2RP, England. TEL 081-566-9307. FAX 081-991-0559. adv.; bk.rev.; play rev.; abstr.; illus.; circ. 300. (back issues avail.) **Indexed:** Abstr.Engl.Stud., M.L.A.
Formerly: Mervyn Peake Society Newsletter.

808 US
▼**MIDNIGHT EXPRESS.*** 1991. m. $15. Shannon Riley, Ed. & Pub., Box 36, Ripley, MS 38663. adv.; bk.rev.; illus.; circ. 250.
Description: Market news and information source covering the horror and dark fantasy genres.

808.838 US
MIDNIGHT GRAFFITI. 4/yr. $4.95 per no. 13101 Sudan Rd., Poway, CA 92064. Ed. James van Mise.
Description: Small press horror fiction magazine.

MILLION; the magazine of popular fiction. see LITERATURE — Adventure And Romance

808.838 US
▼**MONAD;** essays on science fiction. 1990. irreg. $18 for 4 nos. (Writer's Notebook Press) Pulphouse Publishing, Inc., Box 1227, Eugene, OR 97440. TEL 503-344-6742. FAX 503-683-3412. Ed. Damon Knight. bk.rev.; index; circ. 500. (back issues avail.)

808.83 US
MYTHIC CIRCLE. 1981. 3/yr. $18 to non-members; members $13. Mythopoeic Society, Box 6707, Altadena, CA 91003-6707. Ed.Bd. circ. 200.
Formerly (until Feb. 1987): Mythellany.
Description: A fantasy writer's workshop in print, includes fiction, poetry and art. Extensive reader feedback is a special feature.

808.83 US ISSN 0146-9339
PR478.F35
MYTHLORE; a journal of J.R.R. Tolkien, C.S. Lewis, Charles Williams, and the genres of myths and fantasy studies. 1969. q. $13 to individuals; institutions $16. Mythopoeic Society (Los Angeles), 742 S. Garfield Ave., Monterey Park, CA 91754-3951. TEL 213-384-9420. (Subscr. to: P.O. Box 6707, Altadena, CA 91001) Ed. Glen M. Goodknight. adv.; bk.rev.; illus.; circ. 1,000. (also avail. in microform from UMI; reprint service avail. from UMI) **Indexed:** Abstr.Engl.Stud., Amer.Hum.Ind., Arts & Hum.Cit.Ind., Curr.Cont., M.L.A.
—BLDSC shelfmark: 6001.050000.
Supersedes (1964-1972): Tolkien Journal (ISSN 0040-909X)

808.83 US ISSN 0146-9347
MYTHPRINT. 1970. m. $12.50. Mythopoeic Society, Box 6707, Altadena, CA 91003-6707. Ed. David Bratman. adv.; bk.rev.; film rev.; index; circ. 300.
Formerly (until 1969): Mythopoeic Society. Bulletin.
Description: Provides information on meetings and conventions.

N E S F A INDEX TO SHORT SCIENCE FICTION. (New England Science Fiction Association Inc.) see LITERATURE — Abstracting, Bibliographies, Statistics

LITERATURE — SCIENCE FICTION, FANTASY, HORROR

808.83 US
▼NECROFILE; the review of horror fiction. 1991. 4/yr. $10. Necronomicon Press, 101 Lockwood St., W. Warwick, RI 02893. TEL 401-828-7161. FAX 401-738-6125. Eds. Stefan Dziemianowicz, S.T. Joshi. bk.rev.; bibl. (back issues avail.)
Description: Features extended critical reviews of contemporary horror titles, capsule reviews of recent and forthcoming works, and a complete listing of all American and British horror titles published during the preceding three months.

808.838 CN ISSN 0229-1932
NEW CANADIAN FANDOM. (Text in English, French) 1981. irreg. Can.$2 per no. Negative Entropy Press, Box 4655, P.S.S.E., Edmonton, Alta. T6E 5G5, Canada. Ed. Robert Runte. adv.; bk.rev.; film rev.; circ. 500.
Description: Commentary on Canadian speculative fiction, personal essays, and letters.

808.8 UK
NEW DAWN FADES. no.9, 1991. irreg. £1.50 per no. 2 Woodfield Ave., Colinston, Edinburgh EH13 0HX, Scotland. Ed. Gavin Boynter.

808.838 UK ISSN 0963-0805
NEW MOON; science fiction. 1985. q. £8 (foreign £10). Trevor Jones, Ed. & Pub., 1 Ravenshoe, Godmanchester, Huntingdon, Cambs. PE18 8DE, England. TEL 0480-451600. Ed. George Townsend. bk.rev.; circ. 1,000.
Formerly (until July 1991): Dream Science Fiction.

808 US ISSN 0886-2451
NEW PATHWAYS.* 1986. bi-m. $25 (foreign $36). M G A Services, 725 E. Interstate 30, Ste. 304, Garland, TX 75043-4043. (Subscr. to: Box 863994, Plano, TX 75086-3994) Ed. Michael G. Adkisson. bk.rev.; illus.; circ. 1,500.

808.838 CN
NEW VENTURE.* 1975. q. $4. c/o Stephen Fahnestalk, Ed., 7616 86th Ave., Edmonton, Alta. T6C 1H7, Canada. bk.rev.; film rev.; illus.; circ. 300.
Description: Contains science fiction stories.

808.838 US ISSN 1052-9438
PN3433
NEW YORK REVIEW OF SCIENCE FICTION. 1988. m. $25 to individuals; institutions $29; foreign $37. Dragon Press, Box 78, Pleasantville, NY 10570. TEL 914-769-5545. adv.; bk.rev.; bibl.; circ. 1,000. (back issues avail.)
Description: Publishes essays and reviews on horror, fantasy and science fiction.

808.838 PL
▼NIE Z TEJ ZIEMI/NOT FROM THAT WORLD. 1990. m. Ul. Kopernika 8-18, 00-367 Warsaw, Poland. TEL 48-22-264378. FAX 48-22-279620. Ed. Adam Hollanek. circ. 20,000.
Description: Covers para-science, ghost stories, and more.

808.838 US
NIEKAS. 1962-1969; resumed 1977. s-a. $15 for 4 nos. Niekas Publications, 380 Morrill St., Gilford, NH 03246. Ed.Bd. adv.; bk.rev.; film rev.; illus.; circ. 1,000.
Description: Covers science fiction and fantasy literature genres.

808.838 UK
NIGHTFALL. no.2, 1990. irreg. £5($10) for 3 nos. 18 Lansdowne Rd., Sydney, Crewe, Cheshire CW1 1JY, England. Ed. Noel K. Hannan. illus.
Description: Science fiction magazine.

808.838 US
NOVA EXPRESS; where the absurd meets the sublime. 1987. q. $10 (typically set in Jan.). White Car Publications, Nova Express, P.O. Box 27231, Austin, TX 78755. TEL 512-345-5629. Ed. Michael Sumbera. adv.; bk.rev.; bibl.; index; circ. 700. (back issues avail.)
Description: Small press review of science fiction, fantasy and horror, plus interviews.

808.838 UK
▼ORION. 1991. 3/yr. £4.50. Orion, 3 Bower St., Reddish, Stockport, Ches. SK5 6NW, England. Ed. Alan Garside. illus.
Description: Publishes speculative fiction.

808.838 US
OTHER WORLDS. 1988. a. $4. Gryphon Publications, Box 209, Brooklyn, NY 11228-0209. Ed. Gary Lovisi. adv.; bk.rev. (back issues avail.)

808.838 US
OWLFLIGHT; alternative science fiction and fantasy. 1981. irreg. $10 for 3 nos. Unique Graphics, 1025 55th St., Oakland, CA 94608. TEL 415-655-3024. Ed. Millea Kenin. adv.; bk.rev.; circ. 1,000. (back issues avail.)

500 808.838 US
PABLO LENNIS; science fiction, fantasy, science. 1976. m. $12. (Fandom House) Deneb Press, 30 N. 19th St., Lafayette, IN 47904. Ed. John Thiel. adv.; bk.rev.; film rev.; play rev.; charts; illus.; circ. 100.

808.838 US ISSN 0275-519X
PANDORA. 1978. 2/yr. $10. 2844 Grayson, Ferndale, MI 48220. Ed. Meg MacDonald. adv.; bk.rev.; illus.; circ. 700. (back issues avail.)
Formerly: Pandora, a Femzine.
Description: Focuses on character-intensive science fiction and fantasy stories and poetry.

028.1 UK ISSN 0260-0595
PAPERBACK INFERNO. 1977. 6/yr. £12 includes Focus, Matrix and Vector. British Science Fiction Association Ltd., The Flaxyard, Woodfield Ln., Little Neston, Wirral, Cheshire L62 4BT, England. (Subscr. to: 29 Thornville Rd., Hartlepool, Cleveland TS26 8EW, England) Ed. Andy Sawyer.
Formerly (until vol.3, 1979): Paperback Parlour.
Description: Reviews of science fiction paperback books.

PAPERBACK PARADE. see PUBLISHING AND BOOK TRADE

PAPERBACK PREVIEWS. see LITERATURE

808.8 US
PEEPING TOM. no.4, 1991. 4/yr. £5.50($16) David Bell, Ed. & Pub., 15 Nottingham Rd., Ashby-de-la-Zouche, Leicestershire LE6 5DJ, England. (Subscr. in U.S. to: Anne Marsden, 1052 Calle del Cerro, No. 708, San Clemente, CA 92672. TEL 714-361-3791)
Description: Menacing and bizarre tales of horror and the macabre.

808.838 UK
PERCHANCE. no.6, 1991. irreg. £1 per no. Jim Johnston, Ed. & Pub., 44 Hillcrest Dr., Doagh Rd., Newtownabbey, Co. Antrim BT36 6EQ, N. Ireland.
Description: Unusual new stories and scenarios for role-playing game enthusiasts.

808.838 GW
PHANTASTISCHE ZEITEN. 1987. bi-m. DM.30. Trivial Verlag, Marienstr. 3, 3000 Hannover 1, Germany. TEL 0511-329097. Eds. Kurt Werth, Michael Uffelmann. film rev.; illus.; circ. 10,000. (back issues avail.)

808.83 US
POE STUDIES ASSOCIATION NEWSLETTER. 1973. 2/yr. $8. (Poe Studies Association) Pennsylvania State University, DuBois Campus, Dubois, PA 15801. TEL 814-375-1218. (Subscr. to: Dennis Eddings, Humanities, Western Oregon State College, Monmouth, OR 97361) Ed. Richard Kopley. bk.rev.; circ. 250.
Description: Review of works on Poe and Poe-related activities.

808.83 US ISSN 0090-5224
PS2631
POE STUDIES - DARK ROMANTICISM. 1968. 2/yr. $8 to individuals; institutions $12. Washington State University Press, Pullman, WA 99164-5910. TEL 509-335-3518. Ed. Alexander Hammond. bk.rev.; bibl.; circ. 550. (reprint service avail. from UMI) Indexed: Abstr.Engl.Stud., Amer.Hum.Ind., Arts & Hum.Cit.Ind., Curr.Cont., Ind.Bk.Rev.Hum., M.L.A.
Formerly: Poe Newsletter (ISSN 0032-1877)

808.838 SA
PROBE. no.80, 1990. q. R.25 (foreign R.30). Science Fiction South Africa, P.O. Box 2538, Primrose 1416, South Africa. Ed. Cornelius van Niekerk. adv.; bk.rev.; video rev.; circ. 200.
Description: Publishes short science fiction stories, critical articles on science fiction topics, and members' letters and comments.

PSYCHOTRONIC VIDEO. see COMMUNICATIONS — Video

808.838 US
PULP VAULT. no.9, 1991. irreg. $6 per no. 6942 N. Oleander, Chicago, IL 60631. TEL 312-763-8763. Ed. Doug Ellis. bibl.
Description: For pulp-fiction enthusiasts.

808.838 US
▼PULPHOUSE - A FICTION MAGAZINE. 1991. m. $39 for 13 nos. (includes Pulphouse Fiction Spotlight)(effective 1992). Pulphouse Publishing, Inc., Box 1227, Eugene, OR 97440. TEL 503-344-6742. FAX 503-683-3412. Ed. Dean Wesley Smith. adv.; bk.rev.; film rev.; video rev.; illus.; tr.lit.; circ. 10,000. (back issues avail.)
Formerly (until no.4, 1991): Pulphouse - A Weekly Fiction Magazine.
Description: Publishes original science fiction, fantasy, and horror, with nonfiction and critical articles.

808.838 US
▼PULPHOUSE FICTION SPOTLIGHT. 1992. fortn. $26 (free to Pulphouse subscribers). Pulphouse Publishing, Inc., Box 1227, Eugene, OR 97440. TEL 503-344-6742. FAX 503-683-3412. Ed. Dean Wesley Smith. adv.; illus.
Description: Short horror and fantasy stories, with news of recent Pulphouse releases.

808.838 US
QUANTUM (GAITHERSBURG); science fiction and fantasy review. 1973. 3/yr. $7 (foreign $10). Thrust Publications, 8217 Langport Terr., Gaithersburg, MD 20877-1134. TEL 301-948-2514. Ed. D. Douglas Fratz. adv.; bk.rev.; film rev.; illus.; circ. 1,700. (back issues avail.) Indexed: Amer.Hum.Ind., Tr.& Indus.Ind.
Formerly (until 1990): Thrust (Gaithersburg) (ISSN 0198-6686)

808.8 UK
▼R E M. 1991. 4/yr. £7. R E M Publications, 19 Sandringham Rd., London NW2 5EP, England. Ed. Arthur Straker. adv.; bk.rev.; illus.
Description: Alternative science fiction.

808.838 US
THE REPORT (EUGENE). 1984. q. $30. (Writer's Notebook Press) Pulphouse Publishing, Inc., Box 1227, Eugene, OR 97440. TEL 503-344-6742. FAX 503-683-3412. Eds. Christina York, Steve York. adv.; circ. 500. (back issues avail.)

051 US ISSN 0035-5518
RIPLEY'S BELIEVE IT OR NOT; true ghost stories. 1964. 7/yr. Western Publishing Co., Inc., 1220 Mound Ave., Racine, WI 53404. TEL 414-633-2431. Ed. Wallace I. Green.

808.838 US
RISING STAR. 1983. bi-m. $7.50. Star - Sword Publications, 47 Byledge Rd., Manchester, NH 03104. Ed. Scott E. Green. adv.; bk.rev.; circ. 120.
Description: Publishes market information for writers and artists in the sci-fi, fantasy and horror genres.

808.83 US ISSN 0889-2326
RIVERSIDE QUARTERLY. 1964. irreg., vol.8, no.4, 1991. $8 for 4 nos. 807 Walters St., No. 107, Lake Charles, LA 70605-4665. TEL 318-477-7943. Ed. Lee Sapiro. adv.; bk.rev.; film rev.; illus.; circ. 1,100. (processed; also avail. in microform from MML;UMI; reprint service avail. from UMI) Indexed: Abstr.Engl.Stud., M.L.A.
Description: Literary magazine for science-fiction and fantasy. Includes criticism, letters and poetry.

808.838 US
ROC SCIENCE FICTION ADVANCE. 1989. bi-m. free. Penguin Books U S A, Inc., Roc Science Fiction Department, 375 Hudson St., New York, NY 10014. TEL 212-366-2000. Eds. John Silbersack, Christopher Schelling. bk.rev.; illus. (tabloid format)
Formerly: Signet S F Advance.
Description: Features author interviews and news of upcoming book releases.

THE ROMANTIST. see LITERATURE — Adventure And Romance

L

LITERATURE — SCIENCE FICTION, FANTASY, HORROR

808.838   AT
S F COMMENTARY. (Science Fiction) 1969. q. Aus.$35($25) Bruce Gillespie, Ed. & Pub., P.O. Box 5195AA, Melbourne, Vic. 3001, Australia. adv.; bk.rev.; circ. 500.
    Description: Contains short reviews of science fiction and fantasy.

813   US   ISSN 0036-1364
PS374.S35
S F W A BULLETIN. 1965. q. $14. (Science Fiction Writers of America) Pulphouse Publishing, Inc., Box 1227, Eugene, OR 97440. TEL 503-344-6742. FAX 503-683-3412. Ed. Dan Hatch. adv.; bk.rev.; illus.; circ. 1,500. (processed; also avail. in microform from UMI; reprint service avail. from UMI)

808.838   UK
▼**SCHEHERAZADE.** 1991. irreg. £6 for 4 nos. Liz Counihan, Ed. & Pub., St. Ives., Maypole Rd., E. Grinstead, W. Sussex RH19 1HL, England. illus.
    Description: Publishes short fantastic fiction with a non-technologcial slant, and author interviews.

808.838   US
SCIENCE - FANTASY CORRESPONDENT. 1977. 3/yr. $25. c/o Carrollton Clark, 9122 Rosslyn, Arlington, VA 22209. Ed. Willis Conover. illus.

808.83   AT   ISSN 0314-6677
SCIENCE FICTION; a review of speculative literature. 1977. 4/yr. Aus.$24($39) (typically set in Nov.). University of Western Australia, Department of English, c/o Dr. Van Ikin, Ed., Nedlands, W.A. 6009, Australia. FAX 61-9-380-1030. adv.; bk.rev.; circ. 1,000. (back issues avail.)
    Description: Essays, articles and interviews in the field of science fiction.

808.838   US
SCIENCE FICTION AND FANTASY BOOK REVIEW ANNUAL; a magazine of book news, reviews and commentary. 1978. a. $65. Greenwood Press, Inc. (Subsidiary of: Greenwood Publishing Group Inc.), 88 Post Rd. W., Box 5007, Westport, CT 06881-5007. TEL 203-226-3571. FAX 203-222-1502. Ed. Robert A. Collins. adv.; film rev.; abstr.; illus.; tr.lit.; index; circ. 3,000. (back issues avail.) **Indexed:** Bk.Rev.Ind. (1982-1987), Child.Bk.Rev.Ind. (1982-1987).
    Former titles (until 1990): Fantasy Review (ISSN 0747-234X); S F and Fantasy Review; Fantasy Newsletter (ISSN 0199-3151); Incorporates (in 1983): Science Fiction and Fantasy Book Review (ISSN 0163-4348)

SCIENCE FICTION AND FANTASY RESEARCH INDEX. see LITERATURE — Abstracting, Bibliographies, Statistics

808.838   US
SCIENCE FICTION AND FANTASY WORKSHOP. 1980. m. $10. 1193 S. 1900 E., Salt Lake City, UT 84108. TEL 801-582-2090. Ed. Kathleen D. Woodbury. circ. 450. (back issues avail.)
    Description: Covers writing and marketing of science fiction, fantasy and horror stories of all lengths.

070.5 808   US   ISSN 0195-5365
SCIENCE FICTION CHRONICLE; the monthly science fiction and fantasy newsmagazine. 1979. m. $33 in Canada $36; elsewhere $41. S F Chronicle, Box 2730, Brooklyn, NY 11202-0056. TEL 718-643-9011. FAX 718-643-9011. Ed. Andrew Porter. adv.; bk.rev.; illus.; circ. 6,000. (also avail. in microform from UMI; reprint service avail. from UMI) **Indexed:** Amer.Hum.Ind., Bk.Rev.Ind. (1981-1983, 1985-), Child.Bk.Rev.Ind. (1981-1983, 1985-), M.L.A.
    Incorporating (as of 1984): Starship (ISSN 0195-9379); Which was formerly: Algol (ISSN 0002-5364)
    Description: Newsmagazine for professionals and readers with news stories, pre-publication buyer's guide, 400 or more reviews yearly, market news, columns, overseas news, author signings.

SCIENCE FICTION CONVENTION REGISTER. see MEETINGS AND CONGRESSES

808.8   US
▼**SCIENCE FICTION EYE.** Short title: S F Eye. 1990. 6/yr. $18 (£11 for 4 nos. in UK). S F Eye, Box 18539, Asheville, NC 28814. (Subscr. in UK to: Chris Reed, NSFA, P.O. Box 625, Sheffield S1 3GY, England) bk.rev.
    Description: Critical articles and interviews in the science fiction field.

SCIENCE FICTION, FANTASY, & HORROR; comprehensive bibliography of books and short fiction published in the English language. see LITERATURE — Abstracting, Bibliographies, Statistics

808.838   GW   ISSN 0930-2492
SCIENCE FICTION MEDIA; Informationsdienst fuer science fiction und fantasy. 1984. m. DM.36($35) Pegasus S.F., Bietigheimerstr. 15, D-7149 Frieberg, Germany. TEL 07141-71417. bk.rev.; film rev.; bibl.; circ. 700. (back issues avail.)

813   US   ISSN 0048-9646
SCIENCE FICTION RESEARCH ASSOCIATION NEWSLETTER. 1971. m. membership. Science Fiction Research Association, c/o Ronald Tweet, Ed., 3900 Eighth Ave., Rock Island, IL 61201. bk.rev.; bibl.; circ. 500.

808.83   US   ISSN 0091-7729
PN3448.S45
SCIENCE-FICTION STUDIES. 1973. 3/yr. $14 to individuals; institutions $21. (DePauw University) S F - T H, Inc., c/o Prof. Arthur B. Evans, DePauw University, Greencastle, IN 46135. TEL 317-658-4758. FAX 317-658-4177. adv.; bk.rev.; index; circ. 1,200. (also avail. in microform from SWZ; reprint service avail. from SWZ) **Indexed:** Abstr.Engl.Stud., Amer.Hum.Ind., Arts & Hum.Cit.Ind., Bk.Rev.Ind. (1988-), Child.Bk.Rev.Ind. (1988-), Curr.Cont., Hum.Ind., Ind.Bk.Rev.Hum., M.L.A.
    —BLDSC shelfmark: 8145.182000.

808.838   GW   ISSN 0048-9654
SCIENCE FICTION TIMES. 1959. m. DM.54. Corian Verlag Heinrich Wimmer, Bernhard-Monath-Str. 24a, D-8901 Meitingen, Germany. Eds. Uwe Anton, Ronald M. Hahn. adv.; bk.rev.; film rev.; bibl.; circ. 1,000.

808.838   US   ISSN 0164-1093
PS374.S35
SCIENCE FICTION VOICES. 1979. irreg. (approx. a.). price varies. Borgo Press, Box 2845, San Bernardino, CA 92406. TEL 714-884-5813. Ed. Robert Reginald.

808.838   US   ISSN 0882-1348
SCIFANT. 1986. m. $24. Luna Ventures, Box 398, Suisun, CA 94585. Ed. Paul Doerr. adv.; bk.rev. (microfiche; back issues avail.)
    Description: Covers science fiction, fantasy, horror, space, and other similar fiction and nonfiction subjects, especially for new writers and artists.

808.838   US
SCREAM FACTORY. no.7, 1991. irreg. 4884 Pepper Wood Way, San Jose, CA 95124. Ed. Peter Enfantino.

808.838   NE
SHARDS OF BABEL. (Text in English) bi-m. fl.25($15) for 8 nos. Roelof Goudriaan, Ed. & Pub., Caan van Necklaan 63, 2281 BB Rijswijk, Netherlands. bibl.
    Description: Comprehensive coverage of European science fiction literary activity, including conventions, new magazines, fan news, and schedules of upcoming events.

808.838   UK   ISSN 0959-8006
▼**SKELETON CREW.** 1990. m. £23.40($56) Argus House, Boundary Way, Hempstead HP2 7ST, England. Ed. Dave Reeder. illus.
    Description: Contains horror fiction.

SOUTH OF THE MOON. see LITERATURE — Mystery And Detective

808.838   US   ISSN 0271-2512
SPACE AND TIME. 1966. s-a. $9.50. c/o Gordon Linzner, Ed., 138 W. 70 St., 4-B, New York, NY 10023-4432. adv.; illus.; circ. 400.
    Description: Presents a collection of fantasy and science fiction.

808.838 790.13   UK
SPACE VOYAGER. 1982. q. £7.50($15) Model & Allied Publications Ltd., Wolsey House, Wolsey Rd., Hemel Hempstead, Herts HP2 4SS, England. adv.; illus.; circ. 30,000.
    Formerly: New Voyager.

STAR TREK: THE OFFICIAL FAN CLUB MAGAZINE. see COMMUNICATIONS — Television And Cable

808.838   UK   ISSN 0955-114X
STARBURST. no.145, 1990. m. £22($40) Visual Imagination Ltd., P.O. Box 371, London SW14 8JL, England. TEL 081-878-5486. Ed. Stephen Payne. adv.: B&W page #500, color page #750; trim 184 x 268. film rev.; illus.; circ. 40,000.
    Description: Covers science fiction, horror, and fantasy media events and developments, with interviews and feature articles.

STARLOG; magazine of the future. see COMMUNICATIONS — Television And Cable

808.83   US   ISSN 0272-7730
STARMONT READER'S GUIDES. irreg., no.62, 1992. Borgo Press, Box 2845, San Bernardino, CA 92406. TEL 714-884-5813. Ed. Roger C. Schlobin. index. —BLDSC shelfmark: 8436.050000.
    Description: Critical monographs on science fiction and fantasy authors, complete with chronologies, bibliographies, and notes.

808.83   US   ISSN 0738-0127
STARMONT REFERENCE GUIDES. 1983. irreg., no.18, 1991. price varies. Borgo Press, Box 2845, San Bernardino, CA 92406. TEL 714-884-5813. Ed. T.E. Dikty. circ. 300.
    Description: Monograph series of reference books on science fiction and fantasy.

808.838   UK
▼**STRANGE ATTRACTOR.** 1992. irreg. Rick Cadger, Ed. & Pub., 111 Sundon Rd., Houghton Regis, Dunstable, Beds LU5 5NL, England.
    Description: Strange science fiction, fantasy and horror stories.

808.838   US
STRANGE PLASMA. no.4, 1991. q. $16 (foreign $23). Edgewood Press, Box 264, Cambridge, MA 02238. Ed. Steve Pasechnick.
    Description: Speculative fiction magazine with interviews and critical articles.

808.838   US
STUDIES IN WEIRD FICTION. 1987. 2/yr. $10. Necronomicon Press, 101 Lockwood St., W. Warwick, RI 02893. TEL 401-828-7161. FAX 401-738-6125. Ed. S.T. Joshi. (back issues avail.)
    Description: Publishes critical articles and reviews in the field of fantasy, horror and supernatural fiction subsequent to Edgar Allan Poe.

808.838 800 001.6   US
T A P; newsletter for the communications revolution. 1971-1984; resumed 1989. m. $10. Technological Assistance Program, P.O. Box 20264, Louisville, KY 40250. Ed. Ed White. adv.; bk.rev.; film rev.; charts; illus.; pat.; tr.lit.; index; circ. 1,000. (back issues avail.)
    Formerly (until 1974): Y I P L
    Description: "Cyberpunk" magazine: some fiction, some technical articles on computers and telecommunications.

T V ZONE. see COMMUNICATIONS — Television And Cable

808.838   US
▼**TALES FROM THE CRYPT.** 1991. bi-m. $12 (foreign $17). Russ Cochran Publisher Ltd., Box 469, W. Plains, MO 65775-0469. TEL 417-256-2224.

808.838   US
▼**TEKELI - LI! JOURNAL OF TERROR.** 1991. q. $20 (foreign $30). Montilla Publications, 106 Hanover Ave., Pawtucket, RI 02861. bk.rev.; film rev.; illus.
    Description: Devoted to the appreciation of horror fiction from Poe and Lovecraft to other contemporary authors of the same genre.

TEMPORARY CULTURE. see LITERARY AND POLITICAL REVIEWS

808.838 UK
▼**TERRITORIES**. 1992. irreg. £1.80 per no. c/o McNair, 65 Niddrie Rd., Strathbungo, Glasgow G42 8PT, Scotland. Ed. Erich Zann. bk.rev.
  Description: Publishes unconventional fiction and critical articles for science fiction enthusiasts.

808.83 AT ISSN 1031-3001
TERROR AUSTRALIS: THE AUSTRALIAN HORROR & FANTASY MAGAZINE. 1988. q. Aus.$25($31) R'lyeh Texts, P.O. Box A281, Sydney South, N.S.W. 2000, Australia. TEL 02-560-9054. FAX 02-818-5602. Ed. Leigh D. Blackmore. adv.; bk.rev.; film rev.; play rev.; bibl.; illus.; circ. 500. (back issues avail.)
  Description: Covers horror fiction, poetry and art by Australian writers and artists; scholarly and popular level; includes reviews and news.

808.838 US
THINGS TO COME. 1953. 14/yr. membership. Science Fiction Book Club, 245 Park Ave., New York, NY 10167. Ed. Ellen Asher.

810 US ISSN 1050-0421
TOME; the dark works of great minds, and the great works of dark minds. 1989. q. $12. Grub St. Publications, 454 Munden Ave., Norfolk, VA 23505. TEL 804-588-0583. Ed. Daivd N. Wilson. adv.; bk.rev.; circ. 1,000. (back issues avail.)
  Description: Contains horror, science fiction, fantasy, poetry, artwork, and surrealistic fiction.

808.83 US
TWISTED. 1985. irreg. $6 per no. Christine Hoard, Ed. & Pub., Box 1249, Palmetto, GA 30268-1249. bk.rev.; film rev.; illus.; circ. 300. (back issues avail.)
  Description: Covers horror and fantasy fiction, poetry, art, and reviews.

UNILIT. see *LITERATURE*

810 US
VAMPIRE JOURNAL. 1983. irreg. (2-4/yr.). $28. Baker Street Publications, Box 994, Metairie, LA 70004. TEL 504-734-8414. Ed. Sharida Rizzuto. circ. 9,000.
  Description: Devoted to vampirism in literature, legend and film.

808.83 US
▼**VAULT OF HORROR**. 1991. bi-m. $12 (foreign $17). Russ Cochran Publisher, Ltd., Box 469, W. Plains, MO 65775-0469. TEL 417-256-2224.

808.838 UK ISSN 0505-0448
VECTOR. 1958. bi-m. £12 includes Focus, Matrix and Paperback Inferno. British Science Fiction Association Ltd., 37 Firs Rd., Milnethorpe, Cumbria LA7 7QF, England. (Subscr. to: 29 Thornville Rd., Hartlepool, Cleveland TS26 8EW, England) Eds. B. Parkinson, K. McVeigh. adv.; bk.rev.; illus.; index; circ. 1,000. (back issues avail.)
  Description: Devoted to all aspects of science fiction. Includes author interviews, critical articles.

808.838 PL
WAMPIURS WARS. irreg. membership. Gdanski Klub Fantastyki, P.O. Box 76, 80-325 Gdansk 37, Poland. Dir. Krzysztof Papierkowski.
  Description: Science fiction "fanzine".

808.838 US
WARP FOUR; the magazine of science fiction, fantasy and horror. 1970. q. $4. c/o John R. Racano, Ed., 113 Cleveland Ave., Colonia, NJ 07067. TEL 201-679-7756. adv.; bk.rev.; illus.

808.838 US ISSN 0898-5073
PS509.F3
WEIRD TALES. 1923. q. $24 for 6 nos. Terminus Publishing Co., Inc., Box 13418, Philadelphia, PA 19101-3418. TEL 215-382-5415. Ed. Darrell Schweitzer. adv.; bk.rev.; circ. 8,000. (back issues avail.)
  Description: Fantastic fiction in the tradition of H.P. Lovecraft and Ray Bradbury.

808.838 US ISSN 8755-7452
WEIRDBOOK. 1968. s-a. $25 for 7 nos. Weirdbook Press, Box 149, Amherst Br., Buffalo, NY 14226. TEL 716-839-2415. Ed. W. Paul Ganley. illus.; circ. 900. (back issues avail.)
  Description: Focuses on fantasy - supernatural fiction, poetry and art.

WESTWIND (SEATTLE). see *CLUBS*

808.838 US
WHISPERS. 1973. irreg., latest 1992. $15.95. Whispers Press, 70 Highland Ave., Binghamton, NY 13905. TEL 607-729-6920. Ed. Stuart David Schiff. adv.; bk.rev.; illus.; circ. 3,000.
  Description: Publishes original science fiction and fantasy stories and novellas by eminent writers including Ray Bradbury, Avram Davidson, Lucius Shepard, and others.

808.838 US
WONDER; the international magazine of fantasy, science-fiction and horror. 1982. q. $26. Wonder Press, Box 58367, Louisville, KY 40268-0367. Ed. Walter Gammons. adv.; bk.rev.; film rev.; illus.; index; circ. 2,000.
  Formerly: Spectrum Stories.

808.83 UK ISSN 0954-3902
WORKS; magazine of speculative and imaginative fiction. 1989. s-a. £5.50. Works Publishing, 12 Blakestones Rd., Slaithwaite, Huddersfield, Yorks HO7 5JQ, England. Ed. Dave Hughes. bk.rev.; circ. 2,000.

808.838 US ISSN 0735-3995
WORLD S F NEWSLETTER. 1980. q. $15. World S F, International Science Fiction Association of Professionals, 855 S. Harvard Dr., Palatine, IL 60067-7026. Ed. Jim Goddard. circ. 600. (back issues avail.)

808.838 UK
▼**XENOS**; science fiction - fantasy magazine. 1990. bi-m. £11. S.V. Copestake, 29 Prebend St., Bedford MK40 1QN, England. TEL 0234-49067.
  Description: Publishes new science fiction and fantasy from new writers.

808.838 US
YEAR'S BEST HORROR STORIES. 1972. a. $3.95. DAW Books, Inc., 375 Hudson St., New York, NY 10014-3658. TEL 212-366-2096. FAX 212-366-2090. Ed. Karl Edward Wagner.
  Description: Collection of best horror stories published during the preceding year.

808.838 US
YEAR'S BEST SCIENCE FICTION; annual collection. 1984. a. $15.95 paperback; hardcover $27.95. St. Martin's Press, 175 Fifth Ave., New York, NY 10010. TEL 212-674-5151. Ed. Gardner Dozois. bibl.; circ. 15,000. (back issues avail.)

808.838 GW ISSN 0930-0007
ZAUBERZEIT. 1986. bi-m. DM.40 (foreign DM.60). Laurin Verlag, Luruper Chaussee 125, 2000 Hamburg 50, Germany. TEL 040-816565. Ed. Juergen Pirner. adv.; bk.rev.; index.

808.838 UK
▼**ZERO HOUR**. 1991. irreg. £7 for 4 nos. 20 Thorpe Green Dr., Leymour, Golcar, Huddersfield HD7 4QU, England. (U.S. subscr. to: Anne Marsden, 1052 Calle del Cerro, No. 708, San Clemente, CA 92672. TEL 714-361-3791).
  Description: Strange art and fiction.

MACHINERY 3015

LUMBER AND WOOD

see *Forests and Forestry–Lumber and Wood*

MACHINE THEORY

see *Computers–Machine Theory*

MACHINERY

see also *Agriculture–Agricultural Equipment*

621.8 GW ISSN 0340-5745
A.G.T. DOKUMENTATION. 1972. 4/yr. DM.47.40. A.G.T. Verlag Thum GmbH, Teinacher Str. 34, Postfach 109, 7140 Ludwigsburg, Germany. TEL 07141-33046. FAX 07141-33828. TELEX 7264853. Ed. K-P. Koerber. circ. 10,000.
  Description: All fields of drive and gear engineering, electrical engineering and electronics, CAD-CAM systems, practical hydraulics and pneumatics.

621.9 IT ISSN 0393-0483
A M U (Annuario Italiano Macchine Utensili e Complementari) 1966. a. L.50000 (foreign L.90000). Tecniche Nuove s.p.a., Via C. Menotti, 14, 20129 Milan, Italy. TEL 02-75701. FAX 02-7570205. circ. 5,000.
  Description: Names and addresses of 1800 Italian producers together with a description of their products.

676 621.9 US
A P M A NEWSLETTER. 1979. m. American Paper Machinery Association, 7297 Lee Hwy., Unit N, Falls Church, VA 22042. Ed. Frank McManus. circ. 100. (back issues avail.)
  Formerly: P P M M A Newsletter.

A T M DIRECTORY. (Automated Teller Machines) see *BUSINESS AND ECONOMICS — Trade And Industrial Directories*

621.92 US ISSN 0195-0932
ABRASIVE ENGINEERING SOCIETY MAGAZINE. 1963. q. $30 (foreign $65). Abrasive Engineering Society, Meadowlark Technical Services, 108 Elliot Dr., Butler, PA 16001. TEL 412-282-6210. FAX 412-282-6210. Ed. Theodore L. Giese. adv.; bk.rev.; charts; illus.; tr.lit.; circ. 2,500. (back issues avail.) Indexed: Met.Abstr., World Alum.Abstr.—BLDSC shelfmark: 0549.790000.
  Former titles: Abrasive Technology; Abrasive Methods (ISSN 0001-3285)

ADVANCED MANUFACTURING TECHNOLOGY; monthly report on the use of robots in manufacturing. see *COMPUTERS — Automation*

AGRARGEWERBLICHE WIRTSCHAFT. see *AGRICULTURE — Agricultural Equipment*

ALAMBRE; revista tecnica para la produccion y manufacturacion de alambres, barras y derivados y todos los sectores marginales. see *ENGINEERING — Electrical Engineering*

AMERICAN MACHINIST (1988). see *BUSINESS AND ECONOMICS — Production Of Goods And Services*

621.9 IT
AMMONITORE. 1954. w. L.20500. Editrice Giornale L'Ammonitore s.n.c., Via Desenzano 8, Milan, Italy. Ed. Mino Tenaglia. adv.; circ. 32,140.

621.9 FR
ANNUAIRE NATIONAL DES MATIERES PREMIERES DE RECUPERATION ET DU MATERIEL D'OCCASION. 1953. a. 60 F. S E P Edition, 194-196 rue Marcadet, 75018 Paris, France. adv.

ANNUARIO A N D I L (YEAR). (Associazione Nazionale degli Industriali dei Laterizi) see *CERAMICS, GLASS AND POTTERY*

MACHINERY

621.9 — SI — ISSN 0129-5519
ASIA PACIFIC METALWORKING EQUIPMENT NEWS. (Text in English) 1987. m. S.$98($90) (effective 1991). Asia Pacific Technology Publications Pte. Ltd., 24 Peck Seah St., 03-00 Nehsons Bldg., Singapore 0207, Singapore. TEL 222-3422. FAX 222-5587. TELEX RS 28366 SAFAN. Ed. C.S. Sharma. circ. 9,700. (back issues avail.)

621.9 — HK — ISSN 1015-5023
ASIAMAC JOURNAL; the machine-building and metal-working journal for the Asia Pacific Region. (Text in English) 1989. 4/yr. HK.$140($30) for Asia; elsewhere $34 (typically set in July). Adsale Publishing Company, Tung Wai Commercial Bldg., 21st Fl., 109-111 Gloucester Rd., Wanchai, Hong Kong. TEL 892-0511. FAX 838-4119. TELEX 63109-ADSAP-HX. (Subscr. to: P.O. Box 20032, Hennessy Rd., Hong Kong) Ed. Joyce Li. adv. (back issues avail.)
Description: Focuses on technology and market trends for machine builders and management in the Asia Pacific area.

621.8 — FR
ASSEMBLAGES ADHESIFS; soudage, colles et adhesifs, fixations mecaniques. no.32, 1976. bi-m. (7/yr.). 280 F. (foreign 360 F.). S O P R O G E, S.A., 7 ter, Cour des Petites-Ecuries, 75010 Paris, France. Ed. H. Thiron. adv.; circ. 5,000.
Incorporates: Adhesifs (ISSN 0044-6254)

ASSOCIATED EQUIPMENT DISTRIBUTORS. RENTAL RATES COMPILATION; nationally averaged rental rates for construction equipment including complete model specifications. see *BUILDING AND CONSTRUCTION*

621.9 — US
ASSOCIATION FOR COMPUTING MACHINERY. COMPUTER SERVICE. q. Association for Computing Machinery, 1515 Broadway, 17th Fl., New York, NY 10036. TEL 212-869-7440.

621.9 — US
ASSOCIATION FOR COMPUTING MACHINERY. CONFERENCE PROCEEDINGS. a. Association for Computing Machinery, 1515 Broadway, 17th Fl., New York, NY 10036. TEL 212-869-7440.

ASU HYVIN. see *BUILDING AND CONSTRUCTION — Hardware*

621.75 — US — ISSN 0005-1071
TJ1180.A1 — CODEN: AUMAAW
AUTOMATIC MACHINING. 1939. m. free to qualified personnel. Screw Machine Publishing Co., Inc., 100 Seneca Ave., Rochester, NY 14621. TEL 716-338-1522. Ed. Donald E. Wood. adv.; bk.rev.; charts; illus.; circ. 16,000. **Indexed:** Sci.Abstr.
—BLDSC shelfmark: 1829.200000.
Description: For engineers and managers of metalworking plants. Contains articles on plant modernization, management techniques, automation applications and computer-aided design.

AUTOMOBILE & TRACTOR; ancillary & agri equipment. see *AGRICULTURE — Agricultural Equipment*

BAENDER, BLECHE, ROHRE; Fachzeitschrift fuer Walzwerkstechnik, Blechbearbeitung, gezogene und geschweisste Rohre. see *METALLURGY*

BAUSTOFF, RECYCLING UND DEPONIETECHNIK. see *ENGINEERING — Engineering Mechanics And Materials*

BETRIEBSTECHNIK; Monatsmagazin fuer Betriebsleiter. see *ENGINEERING*

621.9 — US
BLACK BOOK AUCTION REPORT. m. and a. eds. $195 for monthly ed.; annual ed. $180. Black Book, Box 758, Gainesville, GA 30503. TEL 404-532-4111. FAX 404-287-0585. Ed. Michael Clark.
Formerly: I M N Auction Report.
Description: Pricing service for metalworking, plastic, and woodworking machinery.

BLECH-ROHRE-PROFILE; Fachzeitschrift fuer die Herstellung, Verarbeitung und Veredelung von Band, Blech, Rohren und Profilen einschliesslich aller Randgebiete. see *METALLURGY*

621.9 — US — ISSN 0006-5498
BODINE MOTORGRAM. 1916. bi-m. free. Bodine Electric Company, 2500 W. Bradley Place, Chicago, IL 60618. TEL 312-478-3515. Ed. J.J. Kester. adv.; charts; illus.; circ. 10,000.

BOVAGBLAD. see *TRANSPORTATION — Automobiles*

621 — FR — ISSN 1148-7305
TJ212 — CODEN: BEAUE3
BUREAUX D'ETUDES. 9/yr. 395 F. (foreign 459 F.). C E P Information Technologie, Immeuble Europais, 26 rue d'Oradour sur Glane, 75504 Paris Cedex 15, France. TEL 1-44-25-31-31. FAX 1-45-57-35-06. TELEX 270 589 F. Ed. Jean-Francois Desclaux. adv.; circ. 8,000.
Formerly: Bureaux d'Etudes Automatise (ISSN 0296-8517); Which was formed by the merger of: Nouvel Automatisme (ISSN 0220-8482); Bureaux d'Etudes (ISSN 0245-9981); Which was formerly (until 1983): Composants Mecaniques, Electriques et Electroniques (ISSN 0339-1558)
Description: Covers industrial design and CAD.

621.9 — US
C E M A BULLETIN. q. Conveyor Equipment Manufacturers Association, 932 Hungerford Dr., Ste. 36, Rockville, MD 20850. TEL 301-738-2448. FAX 301-738-0076. Ed. R.J. Lloyd.

658.7 — CN — ISSN 0008-3836
CANADIAN INDUSTRIAL EQUIPMENT NEWS; reader service on new, improved and redesigned industrial equipment & supplies. 1940. m. Can.$50.29($49) (foreign $50). Southam Business Communications Inc. (Subsidiary of: Southam Inc.), 1450 Don Mills Rd., Don Mills, Ont. M3B 2X7, Canada. TEL 416-445-6641. FAX 416-442-2261. Ed. Olga Markovich. adv.; illus.; tr.lit.; circ. 34,211.

621.9 669 — CN — ISSN 0008-4379
TJ1 — CODEN: CMCHA3
CANADIAN MACHINERY & METALWORKING. 1905. m. Can.$32. Maclean Hunter Ltd., Business Publication Division, Maclean-Hunter Bldg., 777 Bay St., Toronto, Ont. M5W 1A7, Canada. TEL 416-596-5720. Ed. Jim Barnes. adv.; bk.rev.; stat.; tr.lit.; circ. 16,158. (also avail. in microfilm; back issues avail.)
Formerly: Canadian Machinery and Metallurgy.

CANTERAS Y EXPLOTACIONES; revista tecnica de maquinaria para canteras, minas, cementos y obras hidraulicas. see *MINES AND MINING INDUSTRY*

621.9 — SA
CAPE BUSINESS ENQUIRER. bi-m. Communications Group, Group Marketing Division, P.O. Box 2735, Johannesburg 2000, South Africa. Ed. Penny Moore. circ. 3,600. (tabloid format)

CATALOG OF U.S. VALVES. see *BUSINESS AND ECONOMICS — Trade And Industrial Directories*

621.9 — CC — ISSN 1001-2281
CHILUN/GEAR. (Text in Chinese) q. Jidian Bu, Zhengzhou Jixie Yanjiusuo, Zhongyuan Lu, Zhengzhou, Henan 450052, People's Republic of China. TEL 447102. Ed. Xu Hongji.

CHINA, REPUBLIC. MACHINERY AND ELECTRICAL APPARATUS INDUSTRY YEARBOOK/CHUNG HUA MIN KUO CHI CH'I YU TIEN KUNG CH'I TS'AI NIEN CHIEN. see *ELECTRONICS*

621.9 — HK
CHINAMAC JOURNAL/JIXIE ZHIZAO; a machine building & metal working journal for P.R. China. (Text in Chinese; table of contents in Chinese, English) 1987. 3/yr. HK.$117($30) for Asia; elsewhere $33 (typically set in July). (Ministry of Machinery and Electronics Industry, Beijing Machine Tool Research Institute, CC) Adsale Publishing Company, Tung Wai Commercial Bldg., 21st Fl., 109-111 Gloucester Rd., Wanchai, Hong Kong. TEL 892-0511. FAX 838-4119. TELEX 63109 ADSAP HX. (Subscr. to: P.O. Box 20032, Hennessy Rd., Hong Kong) Ed. Josephine Cheng. adv.; circ. 20,000. (back issues avail.)
Description: Introduces to China advanced foreign technology, market trends and products in the machine building and metal-working industries.

681.7 — UK — ISSN 0305-7046
CLOTHING MACHINERY TIMES. 1960. 5/yr. £11. Sewing Machine Times Ltd., 24 Osborn St., London E1 6TJ, England. TEL 01-247 3050. FAX 01-247-0599. Ed. Wilfred Rodwell. adv.; bk.rev.; illus.; circ. 3,000. **Indexed:** Text.Tech.Dig., World Text.Abstr.
Incorporates: Clothing Machinery, Plant & Equipment Review; **Formerly:** Industrial Sewing Machine Times (ISSN 0046-9254)
Description: Addresses the state of sewing machinery and allied productive equipment in the garment industry.

621.9 608.7 — US
COMPRESSOR NEWS AND PATENTS. 1975. m. (10/yr.). $60. Impact Publications, Box 3113, Ketchum, ID 83340-3113. TEL 208-726-2133. pat.
Formerly: Compressor News (ISSN 0884-2264)
Description: Contains new product information, current technical article titles, new books, future seminars and new patent gazette summaries concerning compressors.

621.9 — US
COMPUTER LISTING SERVICE'S MACHINERY & EQUIPMENT GUIDE. 1969. m. Wineberg Publications, 7842 N. Lincoln Ave., Skokie, IL 60077. TEL 708-676-1900. Ed. Joel Wineberg.
Formerly: Computer Listing Service's Machinery, Electrical, Industrial and Plant Equipment.

621.9 — UK — ISSN 0950-9178
CONDITION MONITORING JOURNAL. 1987. q. $215 (foreign £120). S T I Ltd., 4 Kings Meadow, Ferry Hinksey Rd., Oxford OX2 0DU, England. TEL 0865-798898. FAX 0865-798788. (Dist. in U.S. by: Air Science Co., P.O. Box 143, Corning, NY 14830. TEL 607-962-5591) Ed. Clare Farley. circ. 150. (back issues avail.)

621.9 — UK — ISSN 0307-0018
CRANES TODAY. 1972. m. £32($100) United Trade Press Ltd., U.T.P. House, 33-35 Bowling Green Ln., London EC1R 0DA, England. TEL 01-837 1212. Ed. Graham Brent. adv.; bk.rev.; circ. 9,049. **Indexed:** Br.Tech.Ind.
—BLDSC shelfmark: 3487.018300.

621.9 — US — ISSN 0011-4189
CODEN: CTEGAP
CUTTING TOOL ENGINEERING. 1955. 9/yr. $30. C T E Publications Inc., 464 Central Ave., Northfield, IL 60093. TEL 708-441-7520. FAX 708-441-8740. Ed. Don Nelson. adv.; bk.rev.; charts; illus.; tr.lit.; index; circ. 38,750. (also avail. in microform from UMI; reprint service avail. from UMI) **Indexed:** Ind.Med., ISMEC, Met.Abstr., World Alum.Abstr.
—BLDSC shelfmark: 3506.200000.

621.9 — US
CUTTING TOOL - MACHINING DIGEST. 1984. m. $145 non-members (foreign $155); members $120 (foreign $130). A S M International, Materials Information, Materials Park, OH 44073. TEL 216-338-5151. FAX 216-338-4634. TELEX 980-619. (UK addr.: Institute of Metals, Materials Information, 1 Carlton House Terr., London SW1Y 5DB, England. TEL 071-839-4071) Ed. H. David Chafe.
Formerly: Cutting Tool Technology Digest.

621.86 — GW — ISSN 0723-7901
D H F - DEUTSCHE HEBE- UND FOERDERTECHNIK; German material handling magazine. 1955. m. DM.103.80. A.G.T. Verlag Thum GmbH, Teinacher Str. 34, Postfach 109, 7140 Ludwigsburg, Germany. TEL 07141-33046. FAX 07141-33828. TELEX 7264853. Ed. Hans Strothteicher. circ. 11,843. **Indexed:** C.I.S. Abstr., Excerp.Med., Fluidex, INIS Atomind.
Description: Presents information concerning lifting and materials-handling technology, transport rationalization, storage and transshipment technology.

621.9 — GW — ISSN 0011-507X
D N Z INTERNATIONAL. (Die Naehmaschinen-Zeitung) 1879. m. DM.102. Bielefelder Verlagsanstalt GmbH & Co. KG, Niederwall 53, Postfach 1140, 4800 Bielefeld, Germany. TEL 0521-595-520. adv.; bk.rev.; charts; illus.; mkt.; pat.; tr.lit.; index; circ. 5,000. **Indexed:** World Text.Abstr.
Formerly: D N Z. Deutsche Naehmaschinen-Zeitung.

DESIGN NEWS; news for OEM design engineers. see *TECHNOLOGY: COMPREHENSIVE WORKS*

621.9 US
DESIGN NEWS O E M - SUPPLIERS SPECIAL ISSUE. 1970. a. $50. Cahners Publishing Company (Newton) (Subsidiary of: Reed International PLC), Division of Reed Publishing (USA) Inc., 275 Washington St., Newton, MA 02158-1630. TEL 617-964-3030. FAX 617-558-4470. (Subscr. to: 44 Cook St., Denver, CO 80206. TEL 800-662-7776) Ed. Robert Sant Fournier. circ. controlled. (reprint service avail. from UMI)
Former titles: Design News Electrical - Electronic Directory; Design News Electrical - Electronic Reference Edition. Incorporates: Design News Fastening Directory (ISSN 0190-2288); Which was formerly: Design News Fastening Reference Edition; Design News. Fastening (ISSN 0190-2296); Incorporates: Design News Fluid Power Directory; Which was formerly: Design News Fluid Power Reference Edition; Design News. Fluid Power (ISSN 0164-2871); Design News Annual. Fluid Power Edition; Incorporates: Design News Materials Directory; Which was formerly: Design News Materials Reference Edition; Design News. Materials (ISSN 0164-2839); Design News Annual. Materials Edition; Incorporates: Design News Power Transmission Directory; Which was formerly: Design News Power Transmission Reference Edition.

621.9 SI ISSN 0218-2610
▼**DIE & MOULD TECHNOLOGY INTERNATIONAL.** (Text in English) 1991. q. S.$62($45) Asia Pacific Technology Publications Pte. Ltd., 24 Peck Seah St., 03-00 Nehsons Bldg., Singapore 0207, Singapore. TEL 222-3422. FAX 222-5587. TELEX RS 28366 SAFAN. Ed. C.S. Sharma. circ. 4,000. (back issues avail.)

621 669 US ISSN 1056-6090
TS229
▼**DIE CASTING BUYERS GUIDE.** 1990. a. $44.95. Die Casting Industry Publishing, 403-A N. Salem Ave., Arlington Heights, IL 60005. TEL 708-577-5772. FAX 708-577-5282. adv.; circ. 6,000.
Formerly (until 1991): Die Casting Industry Blue Book.
Description: Contains alphabetical listing of machinery, equipment, products, materials, services and supplies used by die casters.

621.9 US
DIEMAKING, STAMPING & EDMING. 1974. bi-m. Eagle Publications, Inc., 42400 Nine Mile Rd., Ste. B, Novi, MI 48050. TEL 800-783-3491. FAX 313-347-3492. Ed. Ed Gillis. adv.; bk.rev.; circ. 27,000.
Formed by the 1991 merger of: American Tool, Die and Stamping News (ISSN 0192-5709) & E D M Digest (ISSN 0199-3550)

621.9 US
▼**DOWNTIME.** 1991. bi-m. 765 Churchville Rd., Southampton, PA 18966. TEL 215-355-1034. FAX 215-355-3931. Ed. John Stevens. adv.; circ. 65,000.
Description: Covers new technology and information for maintenance and repair decision makers.

DRAHT; Fachzeitschrift fuer alle Bereiche der Herstellung und Verarbeitung von Draehten und Stangen einschliesslich aller Randgebiete. see *METALLURGY*

DRVNA INDUSTRIJA. see *FORESTS AND FORESTRY — Lumber And Wood*

621.9 US
E D M TODAY. bi-m. E D M Publications Inc., 1212 Rte. 23 North, Butler, NJ 07405. TEL 201-838-3130. FAX 201-838-3380. Ed. Jack Sebzda Sr.

E P E. (European Production Engineer) see *ENGINEERING — Mechanical Engineering*

338.4 621.9 US ISSN 0070-8550
HD9703.U48
ECONOMIC HANDBOOK OF THE MACHINE TOOL INDUSTRY. 1967. a. $55. N M T B A - Association for Manufacturing Technology, 7901 Westpark Dr., McLean, VA 22102. TEL 703-893-2900. FAX 703-827-5263. circ. 2,000. **Indexed:** SRI.
Description: Information on the U.S. and international machine tool industries, including orders, production, consumption and trade.

ELECTRIC MACHINES AND POWER SYSTEMS. see *ENGINEERING — Electrical Engineering*

EMBALLERING. see *PACKAGING*

621.9 FR
ENERGIE FLUIDE - L'AIR INDUSTRIEL; la pneumatique industrielle: production, traitements et applications de l'air comprime. 1972. 9/yr. 350 F. (foreign 480 F.). Editions U. Boucoiran, 7 ter, Cour des Petites-Ecuries, 75010 Paris, France. Ed. H. Thiron. abstr.; bibl.; tr.lit.; circ. 5,000. (back issues avail.)
Formerly: Air Industriel.

ENGENHARIA AGRICOLA. see *AGRICULTURE*

ENGINEERED SYSTEMS; serving the heating, ventilating, air conditioning and refrigerating engineering community. see *HEATING, PLUMBING AND REFRIGERATION*

621.8 US ISSN 0733-3056
TA725
EQUIPMENT MANAGEMENT. 1972. 12/yr. $30. Randall Publishing Co., Box 2029, Tuscaloosa, AL 35403. TEL 205-349-2990. Ed. Larry Green. adv.; illus.; circ. 76,097. **Indexed:** ABI Inform.
Formerly (until 1982?): Heavy Duty Equipment Maintenance-Management (ISSN 0090-5178)

EQUIPMENT MANUFACTURERS INSTITUTE. FIRST OF THE WEEK NEWSLETTER. see *AGRICULTURE — Agricultural Equipment*

EQUIPMENT MANUFACTURERS INSTITUTE. RETAIL SALES REPORTS. see *AGRICULTURE — Agricultural Equipment*

EQUIPMENT MANUFACTURERS INSTITUTE. STATE OF THE INDUSTRY. see *AGRICULTURE — Agricultural Equipment*

621.9 658.7 US ISSN 1057-7262
EQUIPMENT WORLD. 1979. bi-m. $58. Randall Publishing Co., Box 2029, Tuscaloosa, AL 35401. TEL 800-633-5953. adv.; circ. 87,918.
Description: Provides information and insight needed to make business decisions when buying, renting, leasing, selling or using equipment from earthmovers to pickups.

F B M - FERTIGUNGSTECHNOLOGIE. see *METALLURGY*

658.7 SA
FACTORY EQUIPMENT & MATERIALS. Abbreviated title: F E M. (Text in English) 1968. m. R.42. National Publishing (Pty) Ltd., P.O. Box 2735, Johannesburg 2000, South Africa. TEL 011-835-2221. FAX 011-835-1943. TELEX 82735-SA. Ed. Charleen Clark. adv.; illus.; circ. 11,439. (tabloid format) **Indexed:** INIS Atomind.
Formerly: Factory Equipment and Materials for Southern Africa (ISSN 0014-6552)

FACULTAD NACIONAL DE AGRONOMIA MEDELLIN. REVISTA. see *AGRICULTURE*

621.9 GW
FERTIGUNG; Fachmagazin fuer Bearbeitung, Montage, Kontrolle. 1973. m. DM.158. Verlag Moderne Industrie, Justus-von-Liebig-Str. 1, 8910 Landsberg, Germany. TEL 08191-125-0. FAX 08191-125-483. TELEX 527208. Ed. Hubert Winkler. adv.; bk.rev.; illus.; index; circ. 13,000.
Formerly: Moderne Fertigung (ISSN 0344-7596)

IL FILO METALLICO; rivista tecnica per la produzione e lavorazione di fili, barre e derivati vergella e settori annessi. see *ENGINEERING — Electrical Engineering*

621.9 US
▼**FLUID POWER SERVICE CENTER.** 1991. q. Penton Publishing Co., 1100 Superior Ave., Cleveland, OH 44114. TEL 216-696-7000. FAX 216-696-7648. Ed. Tobi Goldoftas. adv.; circ. 8,010.
Description: Covers the maintenance, repair and overhaul of fluid power systems and components used on mobile and industrial machinery.

621.86 GW ISSN 0015-5233
FOERDERMITTEL-JOURNAL; Materialfluss, Lager, Transport und Verpackung. 1969. m. free. Europa-Fachpresse-Verlag GmbH (Subsidiary of: Sueddeutscher Verlag), Thomas-Dehler-Str. 27, 8000 Munich 83, Germany. TEL 089-67804-0. Ed. Peter Scherr. adv.; charts; illus.; circ. 17,000. **Indexed:** Sci.Abstr.

MACHINERY 3017

621.9 SZ
FOERDERMITTELKATALOG; Logistik - Foerdern - Lagern - Verteilen. 1969. a. 25 Fr. Verlag Binkert AG, CH-4335 Laufenburg, Switzerland. TEL 064-697272. FAX 064-697333. Ed. Walter Meier-Schmid. adv.; circ. 4,150.

621.86 GW ISSN 0015-5241
FOERDERN UND HEBEN; independent periodical for rationalisation and automation in mechanical handling and storing. (Includes special issues) (Text in German; contents page in English and German) 1951. m. DM.236 (foreign DM.274). Vereinigte Fachverlage GmbH, Lise-Meitner-Str. 2, Postfach 2760, 6500 Mainz, Germany. TEL 06131-992-01. FAX 06131-992-100. TELEX 04-187752. Ed. Reiner Wesselowski. adv.; bk.rev.; abstr.; charts; illus.; index; circ. 12,000. **Indexed:** C.I.S. Abstr., INIS Atomind., ISMEC, Met.Abstr., World Alum.Abstr.

FOOD MANUFACTURE INGREDIENT AND MACHINERY SURVEY. see *FOOD AND FOOD INDUSTRIES*

621.9 HU ISSN 0016-8572
GEP. (Text in Hungarian; summaries and contents page in English, German, and Russian) 1949. m. $38.50. (Gepipari Tudomanyos Egyesulet - Scientific Society of Mechanical Engineering) Lapkiado Vallalat, Lenin korut 9-11, 1073 Budapest 7, Hungary. TEL 222-408. (Subscr. to: Kultura, Box 149, H-1389 Budapest, Hungary) Ed. Kornel Lehofer. adv.; bk.rev.; charts; illus.; circ. 3,600. **Indexed:** Appl.Mech.Rev., Chem.Abstr., Hung.Build.Bull., INIS Atomind.

621.9 HU ISSN 0016-8580
CODEN: GEPGAJ
GEPGYARTASTECHNOLOGIA. (Text in Hungarian; summaries in English, German and Russian) 1961. m. $41.50. (Gepipari Tudomanyos Egyesulet) Lapkiado Vallalat, Lenin korut 9-11, 1073 Budapest 7, Hungary. TEL 222-408. (Subscr. to: Kultura, Box 149, H-1389 Budapest, Hungary) Ed. Geza Lang. charts; illus. **Indexed:** Appl.Mech.Rev., C.I.S. Abstr., Chem.Abstr., Fluidex, Met.Abstr., World Alum.Abstr. —BLDSC shelfmark: 4161.400000.

665.5 CI ISSN 0350-350X
CODEN: GOMABN
GORIVA I MAZIVA/FUELS AND LUBRICANTS. (Text in Serbocroatian; summaries in English) 1962. bi-m. 1,500 din.($40) Savez Drustava za Primenu Goriva i Maziva Jugoslavije - Union of Societies for Application of Fuels and Lubricants of Yugoslavia, Berislaviceva 6, 41000 Zagreb, Croatia. TEL 041-442-948. Ed. Valdimir Savic. adv.; bk.rev.; circ. 1,100. **Indexed:** Chem.Abstr.
Formerly (until 1972): Tehnika Podmazivanja i Primjena Goriva (ISSN 0497-1035)

GOVERNMENT EQUIPMENT NEWS. see *BUSINESS AND ECONOMICS — Trade And Industrial Directories*

621.9 NE
GRASSO CONTACT. 1943. bi-m. free. Grasso's Koninklijke Machinefabrieken N.V., Parallelweg 27, S-Hertogenbosch, Netherlands. TEL 073-283111. FAX 073-210310. Ed.Bd. bk.rev.; play rev.; charts; illus.; index; circ. 1,600. (controlled).
Former titles (until 1989): Grassortiment; (until 1974): Grasso Mededelingen (ISSN 0017-3525)
Description: For employees and others interested in the company.

621.9 MX
GUIA DE LA INDUSTRIA: EQUIPO Y APARATOS; para laboratorios y plantas. 1962. a. Mex.$100000($50) Informatica Cosmos, S.A. de C.V., Fernandex Arrieta 5-101, Col. Los Cipreses, 04830 Mexico D.F., Mexico. TEL 677-48-68. FAX 679-35-75. Ed. Cesar Macazaga. adv.
Formerly: Equipo.

621.9 MX
GUIA DE LA INDUSTRIA: EQUIPO Y MATERIALES. 1968. a. Mex.$100000($50) Informatica Cosmos, S.A de C.V., Fernando Arrieta 5-101, Col. Los Cipreses, 04830 Mexico D.F., Mexico. TEL 677-48-68. FAX 679-35-75. Ed. Catalina Ramirez de Arellano. circ. 5,000.

MACHINERY

621.8 658.7   UK
HANDLING EQUIPMENT DIRECTORY (YEAR); unit loads, fluids, loose materials. 1989. a. £22($44) Lincoln Publications, 28 Centre Point House, St. Giles High St., London WC2 8LW, England. TEL 071-240-5562. FAX 071-497-2811. Eds. R. Feather, J. Hardwick. (back issues avail.)
   Description: Lists manufacturers and suppliers of handling equipment for unit loads, fluids, and loose materials, including powders.

HARD HAT NEWS. see *BUILDING AND CONSTRUCTION*

HERION - INFORMATIONEN. see *ENGINEERING — Hydraulic Engineering*

HIGH GEAR. see *AERONAUTICS AND SPACE FLIGHT*

HOLZ - KURIER; forst- und holzwirtschaftlicher Wochendienst. see *FORESTS AND FORESTRY — Lumber And Wood*

621.9   US   ISSN 0744-6640
TT205.A1
HOME SHOP MACHINIST; dedicated to precision metalworking. 1982. bi-m. $22.50. Village Press, Inc., Box 1810, Traverse City, MI 49685-1810. TEL 616-941-7160. Ed. Joe D. Rice. adv.; bk.rev.; illus.; stat.; index; circ. 23,013. (also avail. in microform from UMI; reprint service avail. from UMI)
   Description: Features articles on metalworking projects; focuses on lathe work, drilling, milling, grinding, foundry and micro-machines. Includes detailed drawings and photography.

HUAGONG JIXIE/CHEMICAL ENGINEERING AND MACHINERY. see *ENGINEERING — Chemical Engineering*

I E N: INDUSTRIAL EQUIPMENT NEWS; what's new in equipment, parts, materials. see *BUSINESS AND ECONOMICS — Marketing And Purchasing*

621.9   SP   ISSN 0210-1777
I M H E. (Informacion de Maquinas - Herramienta Equipos y Accesorios) (Text in Spanish; summaries in English) 1974. m. (10/yr.). $170. Ediciones Tecnicas Izaro S.A., Mazustegui 2 - 4, planta, E-48006 Bilbao, Spain. FAX 394-4162743. Ed. D. Ramon Urizar. adv.; bk.rev.; bibl.; illus.; index; circ. 5,050. **Indexed**: Ind.SST.

621.9 540   GW   ISSN 0342-6319
I W - REPORT; Informationen fuer die technisch-industrielle Werbung und Verkaufsfoerderung. 1971. m. DM.93. Text Verlag GmbH, Postfach 106124, 2000 Hamburg, Germany. Ed. Ralph Schneider. adv.; bk.rev.; circ. 3,000. (back issues avail.)

621.9 608.7   US   ISSN 1056-1536
IMPACT PUMP NEWS PATENTS. 1971. m. (10/yr.). $100. Impact Publications, Box 3113, Ketchum, ID 83340-3113. TEL 208-726-2133. pat.
   Former titles: Impact Pump Patents & Impact Pumps, Pumps-Compressors (ISSN 0883-7627)
   Description: Contains recent patent gazette summaries, new product information, current technical articles, new books and future seminars.

697 621.9   IT   ISSN 0394-1582
IMPIANTISTICA ITALIANA. 1988. m. $137. (Associazione Nazionale Impiantistica Industriale) Editoriale P E G SpA, Via Fratelli Bressan 2, 20126 Milan, Italy. TEL 02-25-79-841. FAX 02-25-52-779. TELEX 323088 PEGMOS I. Ed. Arrigo Pareschi. adv.; charts; illus.; stat.; circ. 6,500. (back issues avail.)
   Description: Concerned with industrial plant installation and various aspects related to industrial engineering as well as, advanced production technologies.

IMPLEMENT & TRACTOR; the business magazine of the farm and industrial equipment industry. see *AGRICULTURE — Agricultural Equipment*

IN-PAK; packaging and handling: from process to shelf. see *PACKAGING*

INDUSTRIA MERCATO; rivista dell'industria meccanica. see *ENGINEERING — Mechanical Engineering*

INDUSTRIAL EQUIPMENT NEWS. see *BUSINESS AND ECONOMICS — Marketing And Purchasing*

658.7   KO
INDUSTRIAL EQUIPMENT NEWS KOREA. 1986. m. Monthly Korea Co., Ltd., 113-6, Rm. 302, Dongjak-ku Sando 1 Dong, Seoul, Korea. TEL 787-22592. (U.S. addr.: Thomas International Publishing Co., One Penn Plaza, New York, NY 10119) circ. 5,446.

621.9 659.1
INDUSTRIAL EXCHANGE & MART. 1976. w. £120. Link House Advertising Periodicals Ltd., 25 West St., Poole, Dorset BH15 1LL, England. TEL 0202-671171. FAX 0202-671171. TELEX 417109. circ. 34,225.
   Description: Marketplace guide to industrial and commercial plants, equipment, buildings, transport, services, and products, with a full index of classifications and announcements of auctions and sales.

621.8 380.52   UK
INDUSTRIAL HANDLING & STORAGE. 1979. 6/yr. £40 (foreign £50). Trinity Publishing Ltd., Times House, Station Approach, Ruislip, Middx. HA4 8NB, England. TEL 0895-677677. FAX 0895-676027. Ed. Geoff Bone. adv.; circ. 20,000. **Indexed**: Account.& Data Proc.Abstr.

658   US   ISSN 1047-4374
INDUSTRIAL MACHINE TRADER. w. $79. Heartland Communications, Inc., 1003 Central Ave., Fort Dodge, IA 50501. TEL 515-955-1600.
   Description: Keeps potential buyers and sellers current on supply and demand of machinery in the machine tool industry.

621.9   US
INDUSTRIAL MACHINERY: LATIN AMERICAN INDUSTRIAL REPORT. (Avail. for each of 22 Latin American countries) 1985. a. $435 per country report. Aquino Productions, Box 15760, Stamford, CT 06901. TEL 203-325-3138.

621.9   US   ISSN 0019-8455
INDUSTRIAL MACHINERY NEWS.* 1953. 12/yr. $40. Hearst Business Media Corporation, I M N Division, 645 Stewart Ave., Garden City, NY 11530-4709. TEL 313-828-7000. FAX 313-828-7008. Ed. Gregory A. Jones. adv.; bk.rev.; charts; stat.; tr.lit.; circ. 70,000. (tabloid format; back issues avail.)

621.9   US
INDUSTRIAL MARKET PLACE. 1951. fortn. $125. Wineberg Publications, 7842 N. Lincoln Ave., Skokie, IL 60077. TEL 708-676-1900. FAX 708-676-0063. TELEX 327489. Ed. Joel Wineberg. adv.; circ. 21,000. (tabloid format; back issues avail.)
   Description: Contains advertising on machinery and equipment from plants and factories nationwide.

INDUSTRIAL PRODUCTS FINDER. see *BUSINESS AND ECONOMICS — Trade And Industrial Directories*

621.9   US
INDUSTRIAL PUMP & VALVE.* 1984. bi-m. Industrial Pump Company, 20509 W. 7 Mile Rd., Detroit, MI 48219. TEL 313-531-4771. Ed. Linda Brown. adv.; circ. 21,029.

621.9   GW   ISSN 0174-7215
INDUSTRIE-AUSRUESTUNGS-MAGAZIN. 1979. 6/yr. free. Konradin-Verlag Robert Kohlhammer GmbH, Ernst-Mey-Str. 8, Postfach 100252, 7022 Leinfelden-Echterdingen 1, Germany. TEL 0711-7594-0. Ed. Peter Schaeuble. adv.; bk.rev.; charts; circ. 25,226 (controlled).
   Description: Product-orientated details for all fields of industrial equipment.

621.9   GW   ISSN 0172-7117
INDUSTRIEBEDARF. 1976. m. DM.60. Verlag W. Sachon, Schloss Mindelburg, Postfach 1463, 8948 Mindelheim, Germany. TEL 08261-999-0. FAX 08261-999-132. TELEX 539624. Ed. Peter Schmid. circ. 6,665.

INDUSTRIES MECANIQUES. see *ENGINEERING — Mechanical Engineering*

621.8   GW   ISSN 0170-6993
INSTANDHALTUNG; Zeitschrift fuer Wartung, Inspektion, Instandsetzung. 1972. bi-m. DM.84. Verlag Moderne Industrie, Justus-von-Liebig-Str., 8910 Landsberg, Germany. TEL 08191-125-0. FAX 08191-125-483. TELEX 527208. Ed. Klaus Hader. bk.rev.; illus.; circ. 12,000.

INSTYTUT OBROBKI SKRAWANIEM. ZESZYTY NAUKOWE. see *ENGINEERING — Engineering Mechanics And Materials*

629.1   US
INTERNATIONAL GAS TURBINE AND AEROENGINE TECHNOLOGY REPORT. a. free. International Gas Turbine Institute, 6085 Barfield Rd., Ste. 207, Atlanta, GA 30338. TEL 404-847-0072. FAX 404-847-0151. adv.; circ. 20,000.

INTERNATIONAL JOURNAL OF ADVANCED MANUFACTURING TECHNOLOGY. see *ENGINEERING — Mechanical Engineering*

INTERNATIONAL JOURNAL OF APPLIED PNEUMATICS. see *ENGINEERING — Mechanical Engineering*

621.9   US   ISSN 0890-6955
TJ1180.A1   CODEN: IMTME3
INTERNATIONAL JOURNAL OF MACHINE TOOLS & MANUFACTURE; design, research & application. 1961. 6/yr. £285 (effective 1992). Pergamon Press, Inc., Journals Division, 660 White Plains Rd., Tarrytown, NY 10591-5153. TEL 914-524-9200. FAX 914-333-2444. (And: Headington Hill Hall, Oxford OX3 0BW, England. TEL 0865-794141) Ed. R. Davies, T.A. Dean. adv.; bk.rev.; charts; illus.; index; circ. 1,000. (also avail. in microform from MIM,UMI; reprint service avail. from UMI) **Indexed**: Appl.Mech.Rev., Br.Tech.ind., Curr.Cont., Eng.Ind., ISMEC, Sh.& Vib.Dig.
   —BLDSC shelfmark: 4542.323000.
   Formerly: International Journal of Machine Tool Design and Research (ISSN 0020-7357); Which supersedes: Advances in Machine Tool Design and Research (ISSN 0065-2857)
   Refereed Serial

621.9   II   ISSN 0047-0996
INTERNATIONAL PRESS CUTTING SERVICE: MACHINE TOOL AND IRON STEEL INDUSTRY. 1967. w. $65. International Press Cutting Service, Box 63, Allahabad 211001, India. Ed. N. Khanna. bk.rev.; index; circ. 1,200. (processed)

INTERNATIONAL TRENDS IN MANUFACTURING TECHNOLOGY. see *TECHNOLOGY: COMPREHENSIVE WORKS*

658.5   IE   ISSN 0047-1453
IRISH EQUIPMENT NEWS. 1969. m. free. Maxwell Publications, Kaima House, 49 Wainsfort Park, Terenure, Dublin 6, Ireland. Ed. Eugene McGee. adv. (tabloid format)

669 621.9 620   GW   ISSN 0940-8789
J O T. (Journal fuer Oberflaechentechnik) 1961. m. DM.178 (foreign DM.184). Heinrich Vogel Fachzeitschriften GmbH, Neumarkter Str. 18, Postfach 802020, 8000 Munich 80, Germany. TEL 089-43180-0. Ed. Jochen Korch. adv.; bk.rev.; bibl.; charts; illus.; mkt.; pat.; tr.lit.; index; circ. 10,200. **Indexed**: Chem.Abstr., Dok.Arbeitsmed., Excerp.Med., Met.Abstr., World Alum.Abstr., World Surf.Coat.
   Formerly: Oberflaeche und J O T (ISSN 0170-4044); Formed by the merger of: Oberflaeche (ISSN 0029-7488); J O T (Journal fuer Oberflaechentechnik) (ISSN 0021-3756); Supersedes: Journal fuer die Gesamte Oberflaechentechnik.

JAPANESE JOURNAL OF TRIBOLOGY. see *ENGINEERING — Mechanical Engineering*

JERN- OG MASKININDUSTRIEN. see *ENGINEERING*

621.9 720   CC   ISSN 1001-554X
JIANZHU JIXIE/ARCHITECTURAL MACHINERY. (Text in Chinese) m. (Beijing Jianzhu Jixie Zonghe Yanjiusuo - Beijing Architectual Machinery Comprehensive Research Institute) Jianzhu Jixie Bianjibu, 21 Wanjia Hutong, Andingmennei, Beijing 100007, People's Republic of China. TEL 485223. Ed. Zhang Shiying.

621.9   CC   ISSN 1000-3738
TA401
JIXIE GONGCHENG CAILIAO. (Text in Chinese) bi-m. Shanghai Cailiao Yanjiusuo - Shanghai Material Research Institute, 99 Handan Lu, Shanghai 200433, People's Republic of China. TEL 5420775. Ed. Feng Guoguang.
   —BLDSC shelfmark: 5396.012000.

621.9   CC   ISSN 1001-0513
JIXIE KEXUE YU JISHU. (Text in Chinese) bi-m. Jiangsu Sheng Jixie Yanjiu Shejiyuan, 445 Changhong Lu, Nanjing, Jiangsu 210012, People's Republic of China. TEL 201741. Ed. Cao Zhichao.

621.9   CC
JIXIE SHEJI YU YANJIU. (Text in Chinese) q. Shanghai Jixie Gongcheng Xuehui - Shanghai Mechanical Engineering Society, Shanghai Jiaotong Daxue, 1954 Huanshan Lu, Shanghai 200030, People's Republic of China. TEL 4310310. Ed. Huang Buyu.

612.9   CC   ISSN 1000-4998
JIXIE ZHIZAO. (Text in Chinese) m. Shanghai Jidian Gongye Guanliju, 27 Huqiu Lu, Shanghai 200002, People's Republic of China. TEL 3217280. Ed. Zhu Run.

JOURNAL OF MATERIALS PROCESSING TECHNOLOGY. see *ENGINEERING — Mechanical Engineering*

621.9   II   ISSN 0449-5721
TS191
JOURNAL OF PLANT AND MACHINERY. (Text in English) s-a. T.S.K. Rao, Ed. & Pub., 2235 Bhutgoswami Vattaram, Manojiappa St., Thanjavur 613001, India. charts; illus.

621.9   US   ISSN 0022-4898
TE208.5   CODEN: JTRMAF
JOURNAL OF TERRAMECHANICS. 1964. 6/yr. £215 (effective 1992). (International Society for Terrain Vehicle Systems) Pergamon Press, Inc., Journals Division, 660 White Plains Rd., Tarrytown, NY 10591-5153. TEL 914-524-9200. FAX 914-333-2444. (And: Headington Hill Hall, Oxford OX3 0BW, England. TEL 0865-794141) Ed. John R. Radforth. adv.; bk.rev.; abstr.; charts; illus.; pat.; tr.lit.; cum.index; circ. 1,100. (also avail. in microform from MIM,UMI; back issues avail.) **Indexed:** Agri.Eng.Abstr., Appl.Mech.Rev., Curr.Cont., Excerp.Med., GeoRef, Geotech.Abstr.
—BLDSC shelfmark: 5069.030000.
Description: Covers recent research and developments in off-road locomotion, soil excavation, and related engineering aspects, including vehicle design, construction, maintenance and operation.
Refereed Serial

KHIMICHESKOE I NEFTYANOE MASHINOSTROENIE/CHEMICAL AND OIL INDUSTRY. see *ENGINEERING — Chemical Engineering*

681.7   UK
KNITTING AND SEWING MACHINE TIMES. 1939. 5/yr. £9.50. Sewing Machine Times Ltd., 24 Osborn St., London E1 6TJ, England. TEL 01-247 3050. FAX 01-247-0599. Ed. Shirley Barnett. adv.; circ. 2,000. **Indexed:** World Text.Abstr.
Formerly: Sewing Machine Times (ISSN 0049-030X)
Description: Deals with home sewing and knitting products; extends to allied fields of haberdashery, crafts, and sewing patterns.

621.9   FI   ISSN 0355-0729
KONEVIESTI. (Text in Finnish) 1952. fortn. FIM 235. Viestilehdet Oy, Revontulentie 8b, 02100 Espoo 10, Finland. TEL 90-131151. FAX 0-131-15209. Ed. Tarmo Luoma. adv.; circ. 53,500 (controlled). (tabloid format)
Description: Covers farm and forest mechanization, contractor and entrepreneur machinery, cattle and pig mechanization, and farm buildings.

621.9   GW   ISSN 0720-5953
                         CODEN: KMAGAA
KONSTRUKTION; Zeitschrift fuer Konstruktion und Entwicklung im Maschinen, Apparate- und Geraeetbau. (Text in German) 1949. m. DM.312($175) (Verein Deutscher Ingenieure, Gesellschaft Entwicklung Konstruktion Vertrieb) Springer-Verlag, Heidelberger Platz 3, D-1000 Berlin 33, Germany. TEL 030-8207-1. (Also Heidelberg, Tokyo, Vienna, and New York) Ed. W. Beitz. adv.; bk.rev.; abstr.; bibl.; charts; illus.; pat.; index; circ. 6,000. (also avail. in microform from MIM; back issues avail.; reprint service avail. from ISI) **Indexed:** Eng.Ind, Excerp.Med., Fluidex, INIS Atomind., Sh.& Vib.Dig.
—BLDSC shelfmark: 5112.000000.
Formerly (until 1981): Konstruktion im Maschinen-, Apparate- und Geraeetbau (ISSN 0023-3625)

621.9 918   US
LATIN AMERICAN METAL MECHANIC & ELECTRONIC INDUSTRY DIRECTORY. a. Aquino Productions, Box 15760, Stamford, CT 06901. TEL 203-325-3138. Ed. Andres C. Aquino. adv.

621.8   US
LIFT EQUIPMENT. 1988. bi-m. $24 (foreign $60). Group III Communications, 10229 E. Independence Ave., Independence, MO 64053. TEL 816-254-8735. FAX 816-254-2128. adv.; bk.rev.; circ. 16,089.
Description: Reports on information about lifting personnel and materials aloft. Covers safety products and regulations, new equipment, and maintenance.

LINYE JIXIE/FORESTRY MACHINERY. see *FORESTS AND FORESTRY*

621.9   US
LOCATOR OF USED MACHINERY, EQUIPMENT & PLANT SERVICES. 1969. m. $38. Machinery Information Systems, Inc., 1110 Spring St., Silver Spring, MD 20910. TEL 301-585-9498. FAX 301-585-9460. TELEX 898-400. adv.; circ. 143,000.
Formerly: Locator (Silver Spring) (ISSN 0460-1327)
Description: Directory of used metalworking machinery and manufacturing plant supplies.

621.9   US   ISSN 0741-8760
TJ1   CODEN: LCOVAW
LOCOMOTIVE. 1867. q. free. Hartford Steam Boiler Inspection and Insurance Co., One State St., Hartford, CT 06102. TEL 203-722-1866. Ed. Nancy E. Bergeron. illus.; cum.index every 2 yrs.; circ. 50,000. (also avail. in microfiche)

LOLA SAOPSTENJA/LOLA PROCEEDINGS. see *ENGINEERING — Mechanical Engineering*

621.9   GW
M A N ROLAND REVUE; pictures and reports from the world of sheet-fed offset. (Text in Dutch, English, Finnish, French, German, Italian, Japanese, Spanish, Swedish) 1970. s-a. free. M A N - Roland Druckmaschinen Aktiengesellschaft, Christian-Pless-Str. 6-30, Postfach 101264, 6050 Offenbach a.M., Germany. FAX 069-83051030. circ. 130,000. (back issues avail.) **Indexed:** Print.Abstr.
Former titles: M A N Roland News Extra; M A N - Roland Revue; **Supersedes:** M A N Roland Nachrichten.

621.8   US
M H I NEWS. 1945. q. free to members. Material Handling Institute, 8720 Red Oak Blvd., Ste. 201, Charlotte, NC 28217-3992. TEL 704-522-8644. FAX 704-522-7826. Ed. Lisa Woodieenreich. bk.rev.; circ. 1,000.
Incorporates (in 1987): Material Handling Education News.
Description: Deals with the storage, movement, control or protection of materials like cranes, storage containers, and guided vehicle systems.

621.9   US
▼**M S C BUYER'S REFERENCE.** 1990. a. M S C Industrial Supply Co., 151 Sunnyside Blvd., Plainview, NY 11803. TEL 516-349-7100. adv.: B&W page $5400, color page $6500; trim 8 1/4 x 10. circ. 179,000.
Description: Contains product information for OEM-MRO industrial buyers.

MAARAKENNUS JA KULJETUS/EARTH CONSTRUCTION AND TRANSPORT. see *TRANSPORTATION — Trucks And Trucking*

621.9   IT   ISSN 0024-8959
MACCHINE; rassegna tecnica dell'industria meccanica. 1948. 11/yr. L.110000. (Editoriale Tecnica Macchine) E T M, S.r.l., Via Roncaglia 14, 20146 Milan, Italy. TEL 02-48010095. FAX 02-48010011. adv.; bk.rev.; abstr.; bibl.; charts; illus.; index; circ. 11,000.
Description: Technical review of the mechanical engineering industry. Workshop and engineering technique, metrology, tooling, production and organization.

621.9   II   ISSN 0024-9092
MACHINE AND MACHINERY. (Text in English) 1968. m. Rs.40. L.K. Pandeya, Ed. & Pub., Block F, 105C New Alipore, Calcutta 700053, India.

621.9   II   ISSN 0541-6388
TJ1   CODEN: MBUIAR
MACHINE BUILDING INDUSTRY. (Text in English) 1962. m. Rs.30. (Indian Machine Tool Manufacturers' Association) Chary Publications, 14 Sidh Prasad, Ghatkopar Mahul Rd., Tilak Nagar, Bombay 400089, India. Ed. S.T. Chary. adv.; charts; illus.; circ. 5,000.

621.9   FR   ISSN 0758-1874
MACHINE - OUTIL PRODUIRE. 1983. m. 630 F. Societe Francaise d'Editions Techniques (SOFETEC), 20 rue de la Saussiere, 92100 Boulogne, France. TELEX 206 848 F. Ed. Eleonore Robert. adv.; bk.rev.; charts; illus.; circ. 12,000. **Indexed:** Met.Abstr., World Alum.Abstr.

621.9   UK
MACHINE TOOL SELECTOR. 1978. 3/yr. A.G.B. Hulton Ltd., Warwick House, Azalea Dr., Swanley, Kent BR8 8JE, England. adv.; circ. 18,634.

621   CN   ISSN 0831-8603
MACHINERY & EQUIPMENT M R O. (Machinery and Equipment Maintenance Repair Overhaul) 1985. bi-m. Can.$42($68) (effective Feb. 1990). Southam Business Communications Inc., 1450 Don Mills Rd., Don Mills, Ont. M3B 2X7, Canada. TEL 416-445-6641. FAX 416-442-2077. Ed. William Roebuck. adv.; bk.rev.; circ. 25,000 (controlled). (tabloid format; back issues avail.)
Description: Directed to people responsible for mechanical and electrical maintenance, and maintenance shop operations. Focuses on mechanical power transmission, fluid power (hydraulics and pneumatics), health and safety, shop tools, electrical and electronic components.

621.9   II   ISSN 0047-5351
MACHINERY & MACHINE TOOL JOURNAL. (Text in English) 1958. m. Rs.18($3) 5-A Daryaganj, Ansari Rd., New Delhi 110002, India. Ed. R.C. Hersolay. adv.; bk.rev.; illus.; stat.; index; circ. 7,000. (tabloid format)

621.9 658.5   UK   ISSN 0024-919X
TJ1   CODEN: MPREAU
MACHINERY AND PRODUCTION ENGINEERING; a journal of production engineering and machine tools. 1912. s-m. free in U.K. Findlay Publications Ltd., Franks Hall, Franks Lane, Horton Kirby, Kent DA4 9LL, England. TEL 0322-22222. Ed. Chris Powley. adv.; bk.rev.; charts; illus.; mkt.; s-a index; circ. 15,500. (also avail. in microform from UMI) **Indexed:** B.C.I.R.A., BMT, Br.Tech.Ind., C.I.S. Abstr., Cadscan, Eng.Ind., Fluidex, ISMEC, Lead Abstr., Met.Abstr., Robomat, Sci.Abstr., World Alum.Abstr., World Text.Abstr., Zincscan.
—BLDSC shelfmark: 5328.200000.
Formerly: Machinery.

620.16   AU
MACHINERY AND STEEL. English edition of: Maschinen & Stahlbau. (Text in English) vol.14, 1972. 5/yr. S.330. Fachverband der Maschinen und Stahlbauindustrie Oesterreichs, Wiedner Hauptstrasse 63, 1045 Vienna 63, Austria. Ed.Bd. adv.; charts; illus.; tr.lit. **Indexed:** Met.Abstr., Sh.& Vib.Dig., World Alum.Abstr.
Description: Trade publication for the machinery and steel construction industry, featuring technical research and new developments. Includes industry news, and new product information.

621.9   UK   ISSN 0305-3121
MACHINERY BUYERS' GUIDE. 1926. a. free in U.K. Findlay Publications Ltd., Franks hall, Franks Lane, Horton Kirby, Kent DA4 9LL, England. Ed. F.A.J. Browne. adv.; circ. 8,000. **Indexed:** Copper Abstr.
Formerly: Machinery's Annual Buyer's Guide (ISSN 0076-2040)

621   US
MACHINERY: LATIN AMERICAN INDUSTRIAL REPORT. 1985. a. $235 per country report. Aquino Productions, Box 15760, Stamford, CT 06901. TEL 203-325-3138. Ed. Andres C. Aquino.

MACHINERY

621.9   UK
MACHINERY MARKET; the commercial engineering journal. 1879. w. £56($104) (effective Sept. 1990). Machinery Market Ltd., 6 Blyth Rd., Bromley, Kent BR1 3RX, England. TEL 081-460 4224. FAX 081-290-1668. Ed. A.J. Barker. adv.; bk.rev.; abstr.; charts; illus.; mkt.; pat.; stat.; tr.mk.; circ. 9,400. **Indexed:** Eng.Ind.
    Formerly: Machinery Market and the Machinery and Engineering Materials Gazette (ISSN 0024-9211)
    Description: Lists thousands of machine tools for sale with editorial features and comment.

621.9   US   ISSN 8756-923X
MACHINERY OUTLOOK; heard in the dirt. 1984. m. $295 (foreign $345). Manfredi & Associates, 1110 Lake Cook Rd., Ste. 145, Buffalo Grove, IL 60089. TEL 708-215-2999. FAX 708-215-0455. Ed. Frank Manfredi. bk.rev. (looseleaf format; back issues avail.)
    Description: Covers construction and mining machinery markets and trends.

621.9   US
MACHINERY TRADER. 1978. w. Peed Corporation, Box 85670, Lincoln, NE 68501. TEL 402-477-8900. circ. 212,000. (tabloid format)

621.9   UK
MACHINERY WORLD. 1983. m. £30($60) Sheen Publishing Ltd., 50 Queens Rd., Buckhurst Hill, Essex IG9 5DD, England. TEL 081-504-1661. FAX 081-505-4336. TELEX 296620-SHEEN-G. Ed. Peter Ashmore. circ. 10,000.
    Formerly: World Machinery.

621.9   FR   ISSN 0047-536X
MACHINES PRODUCTION. 1971. w. 885 F.($83) Societe Francaise d'Editions Techniques (SOFETEC), 20 rue de la Saussiere, 92100 Boulogne, France. TELEX 206 848. Ed. Jean Daniel Cyssau. adv.; bk.rev.; illus.; index; circ. 20,000. **Indexed:** World Alum.Abstr.

621.9   US
MACHINING TECHNOLOGY. q. $45 to individuals; institutions $60. Society of Manufacturing Engineers, One SME Dr., Box 930, Dearborn, MI 48121-0930. TEL 313-271-1500. FAX 313-271-2861. TELEX 297742 SME UR (VIA RCA).

MACHINIST. see *LABOR UNIONS*

MACHINIST. see *ENGINEERING — Mechanical Engineering*

MANUFACTURING ENGINEERING. see *ENGINEERING*

621.86   SP   ISSN 0025-2646
MANUTENCION Y ALMACENAJE. 1965. 11/yr. 13566 ptas. (foreign 15796 ptas.). (Federation Europeenne de la Manutention, Comite Nacional Espanol) Compania Espanola de Editoriales Tecnologicas Internacionales, S.A., Concepcion Arenal, 5, 08027 Barcelona, Spain. Ed. Ferran Puig. adv.; bk.rev.; illus.; tr.lit.
    —BLDSC shelfmark: 5368.490000.

621.9 669   BL   ISSN 0025-2700
TJ4
MAQUINAS & METAIS. 1964. m. $80. Aranda Editora Ltda., Rua D. Elisa no. 167, Perdizes, 01155 Sao Paulo, SP, Brazil. TEL 011-826-4511. FAX 011-669585. Ed. Jose Roberto Gonzalves. adv.; bk.rev.; circ. 19,000 (controlled). **Indexed:** PROMT.

621.9   SZ   ISSN 0025-2840
MARCHE SUISSE DES MACHINES. German edition: Schweizer Maschinenmarkt (ISSN 0036-7397) (Text in French) 1933. fortn. 78 SFr. (foreign 125 SFr.). Fachpresse Goldach, CH-9403 Goldach, Switzerland. TEL 071-416781. FAX 071-413881. Ed. Joerg Naumann. adv.; abstr.; illus.; stat.; index; circ. 8,000.

621.9   GW   ISSN 0340-5737
TJ3
DIE MASCHINE. Short title: D I M A. 1946. 10/yr. DM.94.50. A.G.T. Verlag Thum GmbH, Teinacher Str. 34, Postfach 109, 7140 Ludwigsburg, Germany. TEL 07141-33046. FAX 07141-33828. TELEX 7264853. Ed. L. Friedrich. circ. 10,057. **Indexed:** INIS Atomind.
    Description: Construction and operation of machine tools for cutting, non-cutting, metal-removing and forming production methods.

621.9   GW   ISSN 0025-4452
MASCHINE UND WERKZEUG; Fachblatt fuer Neukonstruktionen Betriebstechnik, Fabrik- u. Werkstatt-Bedarf. (Issued in three sections: Betriebsbedarf Lagern und Verteilen; Fertigungstechnik; Konstruktion und Entwicklung; Includes two supplements: "Chefbuero" and "Betriebsfuhrpark".) 1899. fortn. DM.100 for all three sections. Media Mail Verlagsgesellschaft, Postfach 2453, 8630 Coburg, Germany. TEL 09561-6491-0. FAX 09561-6180. TELEX 663241. adv.; bk.rev.; illus.; tr.lit.; cum.index covering 70 yrs.; circ. 25,000.
    Description: Comprehensive coverage of manufacturing technology.

621.9   AU
MASCHINEN REPORT INTERNATIONAL. 1974. q. S.80. Technopress Fachzeitschriften Verlagsgesellschaft mbH, Postfach 176, A-1191 Vienna-19, Austria. Ed. Helmut Tober. adv.; bk.rev.; charts; illus.; tr.lit.; circ. 10,000.

621.9 693.7   AU
MASCHINEN UND STAHLBAU. English edition: Machinery and Steel. 1959. 5/yr. S.330. Fachverband der Maschinen und Stahlbauindustrie Oesterreichs, Wiedner Hauptstr. 63, 1045 Vienna 63, Austria. adv.; charts; circ. 5,000.
    Formerly: Maschinen- und Stahlbauindustrie in Oesterreich (ISSN 0025-4460)

621.9   SZ
MASCHINENBAU. 1972. m. 58 Fr.($39) Olympia Verlag AG, Postfach, CH-8021 Zurich, Switzerland. TEL 01-242 95 45. Ed. C. Schlumpf. circ. 12,000.

621.9   GW   ISSN 0025-4487
MASCHINENBAU UND FERTIGUNGSTECHNIK DER U D S S R. 1959. m. DM.375. Institut fuer Wissenschaftliche Information aus der Sowjetunion, Postfach 721, 5100 Aachen, Germany. Ed. J. Peklenik. charts; illus.; tr.lit.; index; circ. 2,000.

621.9   GW   ISSN 0341-5775
MASCHINENMARKT. 1895. w. DM.265. Vogel-Verlag und Druck KG, Max-Planck-Str. 7-9, Postfach 6740, 8700 Wuerzburg 1, Germany. TEL 0931-418-0. Ed. Hasso Reschenberg. adv.; bk.rev.; charts; illus.; mkt.; tr.lit.; index; circ. 45,000. **Indexed:** C.I.S. Abstr., Chem.Abstr., Excerp.Med., Fluidex, INIS Atomind., Key to Econ.Sci., Met.Abstr., Packag.Sci.Tech., Sci.Abstr., Sh.& Vib.Dig., World Alum.Abstr.
    —BLDSC shelfmark: 5384.950000.

621.9   GW   ISSN 0025-4517
TJ3   CODEN: MSCNA3
MASCHINENSCHADEN; Zeitschrift fuer Risikotechnologie. (Text in German; summaries in Dutch, English, French, Italian) 1924. bi-m. DM.130. Allianz Versicherungs-AG, Koeniginstr. 28, Postfach 440124, 8000 Munich 44, Germany. Eds. E. Siepe, J.M. Zimmer. bk.rev.; illus.; circ. 8,400. **Indexed:** C.I.S. Abstr., Cadscan, Chem.Abstr, Eng.Ind., Excerp.Med., Fuel & Energy Abstr., INIS Atomind., Lead Abstr., Met.Abstr., Sci.Abstr., Sh.& Vib.Dig., World Alum.Abstr., Zincscan.
    —BLDSC shelfmark: 5385.050000.

621.9 621.3   AU   ISSN 0025-4533
MASCHINENWELT - ELEKTROTECHNIK. 1946. 10/yr. S.600. Reinhold Schmidt Verlag, Kastanienweg 9, A-2362 Biedermannsdorf, Austria. TEL 02236-72469. FAX 02236-72469. Ed. Ch. Schwestka. adv.; bk.rev.; illus.; pat.; index; circ. 7,300. **Indexed:** Excerp.Med.
    Formerly: Maschinenwelt und Elektrotechnik.

621.9   RU   ISSN 0025-4568
       CODEN: MASHA7
MASHINOSTROITEL'. 1931. m. $15. Izdatel'stvo Mashinostroenie, 4, Stromynsky Lane, Moscow, 107076, Russia. Ed. E.M. Korolenko. bk.rev.; bibl.; charts; illus.; index. (tabloid format) **Indexed:** C.I.S. Abstr., Chem.Abstr, INIS Atomind.
    —BLDSC shelfmark: 0103.200000.

621.9   RU   ISSN 0025-4576
TJ4   CODEN: MSNVAE
MASHINOVEDENIE. English translation: Soviet Machine Science (US ISSN 0739-8999) 1965. bi-m. $19.20. (Akademiya Nauk S.S.S.R.) Izdatel'stvo Nauka, Fizmatlit, Leninskii prospekt, 15, 117071 Moscow, V-71, Russia. charts; illus.; index. **Indexed:** Appl.Mech.Rev., Chem.Abstr, INIS Atomind., Met.Abstr., World Alum.Abstr.

621.8   YU   ISSN 0461-2531
MASINSTVO. (Issued also as part of Tehnika) (Text in Serbocroatian; summaries in English, Russian) vol. 24, 1975. m. $50. Savez Inzenjera i Tehnicara Jugoslavije, Kneza Milosa 9, Box 187, 11000 Belgrade, Yugoslavia. Ed. Mirko Josifovic.

621.9 388.12   SW   ISSN 0345-7788
MASKINKONTAKT. 1966. m. SEK 598 in Sweden; other Nordic countries SEK 2400; elsewhere SEK 2800. V MaskinKontakt AB, Datavaagen 10, S-436 32 Askim, Sweden. TEL 031-680005. FAX 46-31-68-00-09. TELEX 21131. Ed. Bjoern Johansson. adv.; circ. 14,000.
    Description: Lists suppliers of primarily second-hand H6Vs, construction machinery, gravel machinery, forestry and lumbering machinery, cranes and lifting appliances.

621.9   DK   ISSN 0047-6102
MASKINMESTEREN. 1890. m. DKK 96. Maskinmestrenes Forening - Marine Engineer Officers' Association, Sankt Annae Plads 16, DK-1250 Copenhagen K, Denmark. adv.; circ. 10,500.

621.86   US   ISSN 0025-5262
       CODEN: MHENA4
MATERIAL HANDLING ENGINEERING; technical magazine for material handling, packaging and shipping specialists. 1945. m. $45 (free to qualified personnel). Penton Publishing (Subsidiary of: Pittway Company), 1100 Superior Ave., Cleveland, OH 44114-2543. TEL 216-696-7000. FAX 216-696-8765. (Subscr. to: Box 95759, Cleveland, OH 44101) Ed. Bernard Knill. adv.; charts; illus.; stat.; tr.lit.; circ. 105,600 (controlled). (also avail. in microform from UMI; reprint service avail. from UMI) **Indexed:** A.S.& T.Ind., ABI Inform, B.P.I., CAD CAM Abstr., Eng.Ind, Ind.Sci.Rev., Int.Packag.Abstr., Robomat., Sci.Abstr.
    —BLDSC shelfmark: 5393.280000.
    Description: Offers comprehensive information on the technology and processes used in industrial material handling. Articles cover systems presently in use, new product developments, management techniques and the operations of individual companies.

621.86   US
MATERIAL HANDLING ENGINEERING HANDBOOK AND DIRECTORY. biennial. $35 (free to qualified personnel). Penton Publishing (Subsidiary of: Pittway Company), 1100 Superior Ave., Cleveland, OH 44114-2543. TEL 216-696-7000. FAX 216-696-8765. (Subscr. to: Box 95759, Cleveland, OH 44101) Ed. Bernard Knill. circ. 113,000 (controlled). (reprint service avail. from UMI)

MACHINERY 3021

621.86 UK ISSN 0025-5351
MATERIALS HANDLING NEWS. 1955. m. £160($227.50) Reed Business Publishing Group, Enterprise Division, Quadrant House, The Quadrant, Sutton, Surrey SM2 5AS, England. TEL 081-652-3227. FAX 081-652-8991. (Subscr. to: Oakfield House, Perrymount Rd., Haywards Heath, W. Sussex RH16 3DH, England. TEL 444-445566) Ed. Roderick Robinson. adv.; bk.rev.; index; circ. 36,724 (controlled). (also avail. in microform from UMI; back issues avail.) Indexed: Account.& Data Proc.Abstr., BMT, Br.Ceram.Abstr., Br.Tech.Ind., C.I.S. Abstr., CAD CAM Abstr., Environ.Abstr., Ergon.Abstr., Int.Packag.Abstr., ISMEC, Key to Econ.Sci., Mgmt.& Market.Abstr., Robomat., World Text.Abstr.
—BLDSC shelfmark: 5395.025000.
Incorporates: Mechanical Handling International; Which was formerly: Mechanical Handling (ISSN 0025-6528)
Description: Contains information on all aspects of materials handling and storage systems in manufacturing, distribution and storage industries.

MECHANICS OF STRUCTURES AND MACHINES; an international journal. see ENGINEERING — Mechanical Engineering

MECHANIK; miesiecznik naukowo-techniczny. see ENGINEERING — Mechanical Engineering

MEKHANIZATSIYA STROITEL'STVA. see ENGINEERING — Civil Engineering

MESTNYI PROIZVODSTVENNYI OPYT V PROMYSHLENNOSTI/LOCAL LEVEL EXPERIENCE IN THE MANUFACTURING INDUSTRY; nauchno-tekhnicheskii referativnyi sbornik. see ENGINEERING — Mechanical Engineering

671 NE ISSN 0026-0460
METAAL & KUNSTSTOF. 1963. fortn. fl.215. Uitgeversmaatschappij C. Misset B.V., Hanzestr. 1, 7006 RH Doetinchem, Netherlands. TEL 08340-49911. FAX 08340-43839. TELEX 45481. (Subscr. to: Postbus 4, 7000 BA Doetinchem, Netherlands) Ed. Th. Evers. adv.: B&W page fl.2395; trim 215 x 285; adv. contact: Cor van Nek. bk.rev.; charts; illus.; mkt.; pat.; stat.; circ. 8,090. Indexed: Excerp.Med., Key to Econ.Sci.
Description: Technical magazine for the engineering and machinery industry.

671 621.3 NE
METALEKTRO PROFIEL;* informatie over de metaal- en elektrotechnische industrie. 1961. m. fl.50($10) (Vereniging F M E) Haagse Drukkerij en Uitgeversmaatschapij B.V., P.B. 30111, 2500 GC The Hague, Netherlands. TELEX 32157-FME-NL. Ed. Jos de Gruiter. adv.; charts; illus.; stat.; circ. 4,900. Indexed: Key to Econ.Sci.
Formerly: Metalektro Visie (ISSN 0026-0738)

METALES Y METALURGIA. see METALLURGY

METALWORKING PRODUCTION & PURCHASING; Canadian publication for production, purchasing & management in metalworking. see METALLURGY

METLFAX. see METALLURGY

MINING AND ALLIED MACHINERY CORPORATION. ANNUAL REPORT. see MINES AND MINING INDUSTRY

621.75 US ISSN 0026-8003
TJ1 CODEN: MMASAY
MODERN MACHINE SHOP. 1928. m. $30 (foreign $60). Gardner Publications, Inc., 6600 Clough Pike, Cincinnati, OH 45244-4090. TEL 513-231-8020. FAX 513-231-2818. Ed. Kenneth M. Gettelman. adv.; charts; illus.; tr.lit.; circ. 106,000. (also avail. in microform from UMI; reprint service avail.) Indexed: A.S.& T.Ind., Bus.Ind., Chem.Abstr., Ind.Sci.Rev., ISMEC, Met.Abstr., Sci.Abstr., Tr.& Indus.Ind., World Alum.Abstr.
Description: Offers comprehensive information on all aspects of the manufacturing and machining industry. Provides coverage of engineering, industrial robots, research and developments, programming, safety requirements and equipment.

621.86 US ISSN 0026-8038
TS149 CODEN: MMHHA2
MODERN MATERIALS HANDLING. 1946. 14/yr. (includes a Casebook Directory, a. Planning Guidebook). $74.95 (Canada $106.95; Mexico $99.95; elsewhere $114.95). Cahners Publishing Company (Newton) (Subsidiary of: Reed International PLC), Division of Reed Publishing (USA) Inc., 275 Washington St., Newton, MA 02158-1630. TEL 617-964-3030. FAX 617-558-4402. (Subscr. to: 44 Cook St., Denver, CO 80206. TEL 800-662-7776) Ed. Raymond Kulwiec. adv.; bk.rev.; charts; illus.; tr.lit.; index; circ. 105,835. (also avail. in microform from RPI) Indexed: A.I.Abstr., A.S.& T.Ind., ABI Inform, BPIA, Bus.Ind., CAD CAM Abstr., Comput.Lit.Ind., Eng.Ind., Ind.Sci.Rev., Int.Packag.Abstr., Packag.Sci.Tech., PROMT, Robomat., Sci.Abstr., Tr.& Indus.Ind.
—BLDSC shelfmark: 5889.500000.
Description: For managers and engineers who buy or specify equipment used to move, store, control and protect products throughout the manufacturing and warehousing cycles. Covers trucks, conveyors, storage systems, overhead handling, computers, automatic identification, yard and plant services equipment, and packaging materials and machinery.

621.86 US
MODERN MATERIALS HANDLING CASEBOOK DIRECTORY. (Suppl. to: Modern Materials Handling) a. Cahners Publishing Company (Newton) (Subsidiary of: Reed International PLC), Division of Reed Publishing (USA) Inc., 275 Washington St., Newton, MA 02158-1630. TEL 617-964-3030. FAX 617-558-4402. (Subscr. to: 44 Cook St., Denver, CO 80206. TEL 800-662-7776)
Description: Where-to source for equipment purchases.

621.86 US
MODERN MATERIALS HANDLING PLANNING GUIDEBOOK. (Suppl. to: Modern Materials Handling) a. Cahners Publishing Company (Newton) (Subsidiary of: Reed International PLC), Division of Reed Publishing (USA) Inc., 275 Washington St., Newton, MA 02158-1630. TEL 617-964-3030. FAX 617-558-4402. (Subscr. to: 44 Cook St., Denver, CO 80206. TEL 800-662-7776)
Description: How-to guide for determining plant needs for finding new ways to increase productivity.

621.9 US
MODERN WOODWORKING. 1988. bi-m. $15. Target Marketing Magazine Group (Subsidiary of: Associations Publications, Inc.), 167 Hwy. 72 E., Box 640, Collierville, TN 38017. TEL 901-853-6437. FAX 901-853-6437. Ed. Owen Proctor. adv.; circ. 9,905.
Formerly: Cutting Tool Business.
Description: Features new technology in cutting tool design and application.

LE MONITEUR - MATERIELS ET CHANTIERS. see BUILDING AND CONSTRUCTION

621.9 FR ISSN 0297-8717
MOULES, MODELES ET MAQUETTES. 1964. q. 200 F. Centre d'Etudes de la Productivite dans les Industries du Moule, Modele et Maquette, 39141 rue Louis Blanc, 92400 Courbevoie Cedex 72, France. TEL 33-1-47-17-63-57. FAX 33-1-47-17-63-60. Ed. Bertrand Kahn. adv.; bk.rev.
Formerly: Moules et Modeles (ISSN 0153-9604)

621.9 SW
MOVING;* kundtidning med aktuelle information. 1974. q. Gillelije Sten och Grus, Havnen, 3250, Gilleleje, Sweden. charts; illus.

621.9 658 US
MY LITTLE SALESMAN HEAVY EQUIPMENT CATALOG. 1958. m. $12. Industrial Publishing Co., Box 70208, Eugene, OR 97401. TEL 503-342-1201. FAX 503-342-3307. adv.; B&W page $810; adv. contact: John Hallberg. circ. 26,000.
Description: Provides information to those buying or selling heavy equipment.

N C S INTEGRATED MANUFACTURING. (Numerical Control Society - AIMTECH) see ENGINEERING — Mechanical Engineering

621.8 BL
N E I BRAZIL: NOTICIARIO DE EQUIPAMENTOS INDUSTRIAIS. 1974. m. $125. T L Publicacoes Industriais Ltda., R. Brig. Tobias, 356, 4 andar, 01032 Sao Paulo, SP, Brazil. TEL 011-2271022. FAX 011-2289373. TELEX 011-30562 TLPB. Ed. Raul Gonzalez Simon. circ. 30,000. (tabloid format; back issues avail.)
Description: Provides information about new industrial products in all industries.

621.8 BL
N E I SPANISH AMERICA: NOTICIARIO DE EQUIPOS INDUSTRIALES. 1977. 6/yr. $35. T L Publicacoes Industriais Ltda., Caixa Postal 3349, 01060 Sao Paulo, SP, Brazil. TEL 001-227-1022. FAX 011-2289373. TELEX 011-30562 TLPB. Ed. Raul Gonzalez Simon. circ. 32,000.
Formerly: N E I - L A.

621.9 330 US
N E S D A QUARTERLY NEWSLETTER. 1982. q. $35 to non-members. National Equipment Servicing Dealers Association, Box 2116, Peoria, AZ 85380-2116. TEL 602-566-0997. Ed. Norman Beck. adv.; circ. 2,500. (back issues avail.)
Description: Provides information about the business practices and customer relations in the lawn and garden outdoor power equipment servicing industry.

621.9 NE ISSN 0027-7339
NAAIMACHINE - NIEUWS. 1944. m. fl.135. (Algemene Vereniging van Naaimachinehandelaren) Naaimachine Nieuws, Postbus 57, 2390 AB Hazerswoude, Netherlands. TEL 01728-7167. FAX 01728-7542. Ed. G.K.P. Rozendal. adv.; bk.rev.; abstr.; illus.; pat.; tr.lit.; tr.mk.; circ. 1,000.
Description: Trade journal for the sewing machine industry.

621.9 US
NATIONAL TOOLING AND MACHINING ASSOCIATION. BUYERS GUIDE. 1968. a. $90. National Tooling and Machining Association, 9300 Livingston Rd., Ft. Washington, MD 20744. TEL 301-248-6200. FAX 301-248-7104. Ed. Mark Jeschke. adv.; circ. 25,000.
Formerly: National Tool, Die and Precision Machining Association. Buyers Guide.
Description: Complete listings of tooling and machining capabilities of the members of the National Tooling and Machining Association, with cross-references for 95 major machining capabilities.

NEIRANJI GONGCHENG/CHINESE INTERNAL COMBUSTION ENGINE ENGINEERING. see ENGINEERING — Engineering Mechanics And Materials

621.9 530 JA ISSN 0385-6542
T1
NEW TECHNOLOGY JAPAN. (Text in English) 1972. m. 16800 Yen($140) Japan External Trade Organization, Machinery and Technology Department, 2-5 Toranomon 2-chome, Minato-ku, Tokyo 105, Japan. TEL 03-582-5184. FAX 03-587-2485. TELEX J24873. Ed. Takehisa Okabe. circ. 2,000. (back issues avail.)
—BLDSC shelfmark: 6088.840400.
Formerly: Japan Industrial and Technology Bulletin.
Description: Presents new technology and developments in high-tech research.

621.9 NZ ISSN 0028-8756
NEW ZEALAND TENDERS GAZETTE. vol.7, 1970. w. Mercantile Gazette Marketing, 8 Sheffield Crescent, P.O. Box 20034, Bishopdale, Christchurch, New Zealand. FAX 03-584-490. adv.; illus.; circ. 3,000.

621.9 US ISSN 0028-9159
NEWS FROM THE GUTTER. 1961. irreg. (2-4/yr.) free. Power Curbers Inc., Box 1639, Salisbury, NC 28144. TEL 704-636-5871. Ed. Richard Messinger. charts; illus.; stat.; circ. 17,500.

621.9 JA
NIPPON THOMPSON COMPANY. ANNUAL REPORT. a. Nippon Thompson Co. Ltd., 2-19-19 Takanawa, Minato-ku, Tokyo 108, Japan. TEL 03-448-5850. FAX 03-447-7637.

NORTH CAROLINA METALWORKING DIRECTORY. see BUSINESS AND ECONOMICS — Trade And Industrial Directories

M

MACHINERY

NOTICIARIO DE TESTES E LABORATORIOS. see *INSTRUMENTS*

621.9   IT   ISSN 0029-4438
NOTIZIE OLIVETTI. 1952. m. free. C. Olivetti & Co., S.p.A., Via G. Jervis, 77, 10015 Ivrea (Turin), Italy. TEL 125-522639. FAX 125-523884. TELEX 210030. Ed. Rolando Argentero. circ. 39,000.
Indexed: C.I.S. Abstr.
Formerly: Notizie di Fabbrica.
Description: Provides a view of Olivetti's corporate activities, also looks at technology and marketing.

621.8   SP   ISSN 0210-0118
NOVAMAQUINA 2000; maquina-nerramienta y produccion automatizada mecanica. 1975. m. 8500 ptas.($134) Pulsar, S.A., Gran Via Corts Catalanes, 322-324, 08004 Barcelona, Spain. TEL 3-425-45-44. FAX 3-425-03-68. Ed. Daniel Crespo. adv.; bk.rev.; bibl.; charts; illus.; circ. 5,000.
Indexed: Ind.SST.

OELHYDRAULIK UND PNEUMATIK; Zeitschrift fuer Fluidtechnik. see *ENGINEERING — Mechanical Engineering*

621.9   AU
OESTERREICHISCHE NAEHMASCHINEN- UND ZWEIRAD-ZEITUNG. 1964. 16/yr. S.200. (Verband des Naehmaschinen- und Fahrradhandels und Gewerbes Oesterreichs) Verlag Michael Fischer, Neulerchenfelderstr. 8, A-1160 Vienna, Austria. Ed. Michael Fischer. adv.; abstr.; bibl.; charts; illus.; stat.; tr.lit.; circ. 4,000.
Formerly: Oesterreichische Naehmaschinen- und Fahrrad-Zeitung (ISSN 0029-9324)

OFF ROAD AND 4 WHEEL DRIVE. see *TRANSPORTATION — Automobiles*

OFFICIAL GUIDE: TRACTORS AND FARM EQUIPMENT. see *AGRICULTURE — Agricultural Equipment*

OFFICIAL INDUSTRIAL EQUIPMENT GUIDE. see *AGRICULTURE — Agricultural Equipment*

621.9   IT
OLIVETTI NEWS. (Text in English) 1985? m? C. Olivetti & Co., S.p.A., Via G. Jervis, 77, 10015 Ivrea (Turin), Italy. TEL 125-522639. FAX 125-523884. TELEX 210030. circ. 13,000.
Description: Covers general Olivetti corporate activities and marketing technology.

OUTDOOR POWER EQUIPMENT OFFICIAL GUIDE. see *AGRICULTURE — Agricultural Equipment*

621.9 621   JA   ISSN 0474-9847
OYO KIKAI KOGAKU/MECHANICAL ENGINEERING APPLICATIONS. (Text in Japanese) 1960. m. 12000 Yen (foreign 26000 Yen.) effective Apr. 1989. Taiga Shuppan Publications Co., 1-13, Kanda, Awaji-Cho, chiyoda-Ku, Tokyo 101, Japan. FAX 8132536448. adv.; circ. 18,000. (back issues avail.) **Indexed:** JCT, JTA.

PACKAGE PRINTING & CONVERTING; diemaking and diecutting, flexography, gravure and offset. see *PRINTING*

PLANT SERVICES. see *ENGINEERING — Mechanical Engineering*

PLASTICS MACHINERY AND EQUIPMENT; for those who select and buy plastics processing machinery and equipment. see *PLASTICS*

621.9   GW
POLAR INFORMATION. 1966. irreg., (approx. 2/yr.). free. Polar Mohr, P.O. Box 1220, Hattersheimer Str. 16-34, 6238 Hofheim, Germany. TEL 06192-2040. FAX 06192-22193. circ. 125,000. (back issues avail.)

621.9   PL   ISSN 0324-9646
POLITECHNIKA WROCLAWSKA. INSTYTUT KONSTRUKCJI I EKSPLOATACJI MASZYN. PRACE NAUKOWE. KONFERENCJE. 1973. irreg., no.19, 1991. price varies. Politechnika Wroclawska, Wybrzeze Wyspianskiego 27, 50-370 Wroclaw, Poland. FAX 22-36-64. TELEX 712559 PWRPL. (Dist. by: Ars Polona-Ruch, Krakowskie Przedmiescie 7, Warsaw, Poland) illus.

620   PL   ISSN 0324-962X
POLITECHNIKA WROCLAWSKA. INSTYTUT KONSTRUKCJI I EKSPLOATACJI MASZYN. PRACE NAUKOWE. MONOGRAFIE. (Text in Polish; summaries in English and Russian) 1969. irreg., no.15, 1991. price varies. Politechnika Wroclawska, Wybrzeze Wyspianskiego 27, 50-370 Wroclaw, Poland. FAX 22-36-64. TELEX 712559 PWRPL. (Dist. by: Ars Polona-Ruch, Krakowskie Przedmiescie 7, Warsaw, Poland)

620   PL   ISSN 0324-9638
POLITECHNIKA WROCLAWSKA. INSTYTUT KONSTRUKCJI I EKSPLOATACJI MASZYN. PRACE NAUKOWE. STUDIA I MATERIALY. (Text in Polish: summaries in English and Russian) 1970. irreg., no.25, 1989. price varies. Politechnika Wroclawska, Wybrzeze Wyspianskiego 27, 50-370 Wroclaw, Poland. FAX 22-36-64. TELEX 712559 PWRPL. (Dist. by: Ars Polona-Ruch, Krakowskie Przedmiescie 7, Warsaw, Poland)

621.9   PL   ISSN 0239-3182
POLITECHNIKA WROCLAWSKA. INSTYTUT KONSTRUKCJI I EKSPLOATACJI MASZYN. PRACE NAUKOWE. WSPOLPRACA. (Text in Polish; summaries in English, Russian) 1979. irreg., no.4, 1991. price varies. Politechnika Wroclawska, Wybrzeze Wyspianskiego 27, 50-370 Wroclaw, Poland. FAX 22-36-64. TELEX 712559 PWRPL. (Dist. by: Ars Polona-Ruch, Krakowskie Przedmiescie 7, Warsaw, Poland)

621.9   KR   ISSN 0372-6053
TJ241   CODEN: VKPIAS
POLITEKHNICHNYI INSTYTUT KIEV. VESTNIK. SERIYA MASHINOSTROENIYA. (Text in Russian; summaries in English) irreg. 1.21 Rub. Politekhnichnyi Instytut, Brest-Litovskii pr., 39, Kiev, Ukraine. illus.
—BLDSC shelfmark: 0028.438000.

POWDER HANDLING & PROCESSING. see *TECHNOLOGY: COMPREHENSIVE WORKS*

621.9   JA   ISSN 0387-3544
PRESS WORKING/PURESU GIJUTSU. (Text in Japanese) 1963. m. 1000 Yen per no. Industrial Daily News Ltd. - Nikkan Kogyo Shinbun Ltd., 1-8-10 Kudan Kita, Chiyoda-ku, Tokyo 102, Japan. circ. 30,000.
Description: Specializes in the technologies for metal mold designing, manufacturing and machining in all fields of industries centering around plastic processing.

PREVISIONS GLISSANTES DETAILLEES EN PERSPECTIVES SECTORIELLES (VOL.5): CONSTRUCTION DE MACHINES. see *BUSINESS AND ECONOMICS — Economic Situation And Conditions*

PREVISIONS GLISSANTES DETAILLEES EN PERSPECTIVES SECTORIELLES (VOL.6): EQUIPEMENT INDUSTRIEL. see *BUSINESS AND ECONOMICS — Economic Situation And Conditions*

PREVISIONS GLISSANTES DETAILLEES EN PERSPECTIVES SECTORIELLES (VOL.7): MECANIQUE DE PRECISION. see *BUSINESS AND ECONOMICS — Economic Situation And Conditions*

621   KR   ISSN 0131-2928
TJ241   CODEN: PRMSDT
PROBLEMY MASHINOSTROENIYA; respublikanskii mezhvedomstvennyi sbornik nauchnykh trudov. 1975. 2/yr. 0.82 Rub. per no. (Akademiya Nauk Ukrainskoi S.S.R., Institut Problem Mashinostroeniya) Izdatel'stvo Naukova Dumka, c/o Yu.A. Khramov, Dir, Ul. Repina, 3, Kiev 252 601, Ukraine. (Subscr. to: Mezhdunarodnaya Kniga, Moscow, G-200, Russia) Ed. A.N. Podgornyi. illus. **Indexed:** Chem.Abstr.
—BLDSC shelfmark: 0133.407000.

621.9   AT
PRODUCTION MACHINERY. 1948. m. Aus.$30. Business Press International Pty. Ltd., 162 Goulburn St., Darlinghurst, N.S.W. 2010, Australia. TEL 266-9711. FAX 267-1223. Ed. Peter Tyldsley. adv.; circ. 5,000. **Indexed:** Chem.Abstr., Eng.Ind.
Formerly: Australian Machinery and Production Engineering (ISSN 0004-9719)

621.75   DK   ISSN 0106-0104
PRODUKTIONS NYT. 1963. 16/yr. free. Christtreu, Strandlodsvei 48, DK-2300 Copenhagen S, Denmark. TEL 32-844848. FAX 31-582055. Ed. B. Remby. adv.; bk.rev.; charts; illus.; circ. 12,816 (controlled).
Formerly: Vaerksteds Nyt (ISSN 0042-2126)

621.9 669   DK
PRODUKTIONS NYTS LEVERANDOERREGISTER. 1963. a. Christtreu, Strandlodsvei 48, DK-2300 Copenhagen S, Denmark. TEL 32-844848. FAX 31-582055. adv.; circ. 12,816.

621.9   IT
PROGETTARE. 1979. m. L.103000 (foreign L.158000). (Associazione Italiana Progettisti Industriali) Etas s.r.l., Via Mecenate, 91, 20138 Milan, Italy. TEL 02-580841. FAX 02-5064867. Ed. Carlo Prono. adv.; circ. 6,436.
Description: Design of machines, equipment, devices and systems; dimensioning and application criteria for components.

621.9   IT   ISSN 0392-4823
PROGETTISTA INDUSTRIALE. 1981. 9/yr. L.70000 (foreign L.180000)(effective 1992). (P R O M A C) Tecniche Nuove s.p.a., Via Menotti 14, 20129 Milan, Italy. TEL 02-75701. FAX 02-7570205. Ed. G. Nardella. circ. 5,500.
Description: Covers exhibition and congress of components, equipment and systems for the design of machines and commercial plants.

621.9
PROGETTO: RIVISTA DI PROGETTAZIONE DI MACCHINE. 1979. m. (10/yr.). L.25000. ERIS S.p.A., Via E. Tellini, 14, 20155 Milan, Italy. TEL 02-33103305. FAX 02-33104245. TELEX 323314 ERIS I. adv.; circ. 6,500.

621.9   US
PROGRESS IN MATERIALS HANDLING AND LOGISTICS. 1989. a. $79.50. Springer-Verlag, 175 Fifth Ave., New York, NY 10010. TEL 212-460-1500. (Subscr. to: 44 Hart Way, Secaucus, NJ 07094) Eds. Ira W. Pence, John A. White.
Description: Provides an overview of current knowledge in the field of material handling and logistics.

690   SA
PROMAT NEWS; what's new in plant methods and industrial automation. 1951. m. R.64 (foreign R.89)(effective 1992). (South African Institute of Materials Handling) Thomson Publications (Subsidiary of: Times Media Ltd.), P.O. Box 56182, Pinegowrie 2123, South Africa. TEL 011-789-2144. FAX 011-789-3196. Ed. Erich Viedge. adv.; bk.rev.; illus.; circ. 9,894. **Indexed:** Ind.S.A.Per.
Formerly: South African Materials Handling News (ISSN 0025-6579); Supersedes (1946-1951): S.A. Mechanised Handling Equipment (ISSN 0038-2450)

621.9 696   US   ISSN 0887-5081
PUMP NEWS. 1974. m. (10/yr.). $30. Impact Publications, Box 3113, Ketchum, ID 83340-3113. TEL 208-726-2133.
Description: Contains new product, book and software information; current technical article titles and future seminars.

621.9   US
▼**QUALITY IN MANUFACTURING.** 1991. bi-m. $75 (Canada $95; elsewhere $125). Huebcore Communications, Inc., 29100 Aurora Rd., Solon, OH 44139. TEL 216-248-1125. FAX 216-248-0187. (Subscr. to: Box 21640, Eagan, MN 55121-0640. TEL 612-686-0303) Ed. Joseph C. Quinlan. adv.; circ. 61,200.
Description: Features how-to, problem solving articles focusing on practical applications of quality technologies and processes.

RASSEGNA DI MECCANICA; mensile di tecnica e organizzazione. see *TECHNOLOGY: COMPREHENSIVE WORKS*

REMINDER PLUS. see *ADVERTISING AND PUBLIC RELATIONS*

658.2 658.5   US   ISSN 0034-4818
REPORTERO INDUSTRIAL; new equipment, machinery and techniques for industry. (Text in Spanish) 1943. 9/yr. Keller International Publishing Corporation, 150 Great Neck Rd., Great Neck, NY 11021. TEL 516-829-9210. FAX 516-829-5414. TELEX 221-574 KELLE. Ed. Felicia M. Morales. adv.; charts; illus.; tr.lit.; circ. 40,302 (controlled). (tabloid format)

REPRESENTATIVE. see *AGRICULTURE — Agricultural Equipment*

MACHINERY

621.9   CU
REVISTA DE CONSTRUCCION DE MAQUINARIAS. q. $25 in N. America; S. America $26; Europe $28. (Ministerio de Educacion Superior, Departamento de Seleccion y Adquisicion) Ediciones Cubanas, Obispo No. 527, Apdo. 605, Havana, Cuba.

621.9   BL
REVISTA DE PRECOS PARA INSTALACOES ELETRICAS E HIDRAULICAS. 1968. m. $300. Editora Revista de Precos Ltda., Av. N. Sa de Copacabana, 749 gr. 801, Rio de Janeiro, RJ, Brazil. Ed. Tatiana Salme Lowjagin. adv.; circ. 16,000.

REVUE POLYTECHNIQUE. see *TECHNOLOGY: COMPREHENSIVE WORKS*

621.9   IT   ISSN 0035-6301
     CODEN: RVMCAS
RIVISTA DI MECCANICA. (Text in Italian; summaries in English) 1950. fortn. L.110000 (foreign L.230000). Gruppo Editoriale Fabbri S.p.A., Divisione Periodici, Via Mecenate, 91, 20138 Milan, Italy. TEL 02 50951. FAX 02-55400388. Ed. Sergio Oltolini. circ. 9,251. **Indexed:** C.I.S. Abstr., Chem.Abstr, Fluidex.
—BLDSC shelfmark: 7989.800000.

ROBOTICS TODAY. see *COMPUTERS — Automation*

SCHIFFSBETRIEBSTECHNIK FLENSBURG. see *TRANSPORTATION — Ships And Shipping*

621.9   SZ   ISSN 0036-7397
SCHWEIZER MASCHINENMARKT; die praxisnahe technische Fachzeitschrift. French edition: Marche Suisse des Machines (ISSN 0025-2840) 1900. w. 135 SFr. (includes annual buying guide: Revue)(foreign 260 SFr.). Fachpresse Goldach, CH-9403 Goldach, Switzerland. TEL 071-416611. FAX 071-413881. Ed. Joerg Naumann. adv.; bk.rev.; illus.; circ. 15,000. (also avail. in microform from UMI; reprint service avail. from UMI) **Indexed:** C.I.S. Abstr., Excerp.Med., Met.Abstr., World Alum.Abstr.
—BLDSC shelfmark: 8112.320000.

SCOTTISH INDUSTRIAL HISTORY. see *TECHNOLOGY: COMPREHENSIVE WORKS*

621.9   GW   ISSN 0176-2656
SEKUNDAER-ROHSTOFFE; Fachzeitschrift fuer Rohstoffhandel, Wiederverwertung und Recycling-Technik. 1984. m. DM.80 (foreign DM.98). Peter Polz Verlag, Grubmuehlerfeldstr. 54, Postfach 1324, 8035 Gauting, Germany. TEL 089-8507727. adv.; bk.rev.; charts; illus.; circ. 3,800. (back issues avail.)
Description: International trade with secondary materials, recycling, recycling plants and developments in machinery.

SEL'SKII MEKHANIZATOR. see *AGRICULTURE — Agricultural Equipment*

SEN'I KIKAI GAKKAISHI. see *TEXTILE INDUSTRIES AND FABRICS*

621.8 001.6   UK   ISSN 0260-2288
TA165   CODEN: SNRVDY
SENSOR REVIEW. q. $399.95. M C B University Press Ltd., 62 Toller Ln., Bradford, W. York BD8 9BY, England. TEL 0274-499821. FAX 0274-547143. TELEX 51317-MCBUNI-G. Ed. Clive Loughlin. **Indexed:** A.I.Abstr., B.C.I.R.A., CAD CAM Abstr., Robomat., Sci.Abstr.
●Also available online. Vendor(s): Data-Star, DIALOG.
—BLDSC shelfmark: 8241.782000.
Description: Offers international coverage of sensor technology in advanced manufacturing processes to engineers, researchers, and managers.

621.9 631.3   US
SERVICING DEALER; for the competitive edge. 1987. 10/yr. $30. Communications Group, Inc., 3703 N. Main St., Ste. 108, Rockford, IL 61103-1677. TEL 815-633-2680. FAX 815-633-6880. Ed. Craig Wyatt. adv.; circ. 23,000 (controlled).
Description: Business magazine for outdoor power equipment servicing dealers. Includes articles on technical, management, and industry news topics.

621.9   CC
SHANGHAI JICHUANG/SHANGHAI MACHINE TOOL. (Text in Chinese) q. Shanghai Jichuang Yanjiusuo - Shanghai Machine Tool Research Institute, 681 Huai'an Lu, Shanghai 200041, People's Republic of China. TEL 2565880. Ed. Dong Shankang.

621.9   CN
SHOP; national newspaper of used & new equipment. 1942. m. Can.$35($45) Southam Business Communications Inc. (Subsidiary of: Southam Inc.), 1450 Don Mills Rd., Don Mills, Ont. M3B 2X7, Canada. TEL 416-445-6641. FAX 416-442-2077. Ed. Dick Stubbs. adv.; bk.rev.; circ. 11,671 (controlled). (tabloid format)

621.9   UK   ISSN 0143-8557
SOLIDS HANDLING; the journal of bulk materials management. 1979. bi-m. £40 (foreign £50). Trinity Publishing Ltd., Times House, Station Approach, Ruislip, Middx. HA4 8NB, England. TEL 0895-677677. FAX 0895-676027. Ed. Lena Mithani. adv.; circ. 7,000. **Indexed:** Br.Ceram.Abstr., Fluidex, World Surf.Coat.
—BLDSC shelfmark: 8327.560000.

621.9   SA   ISSN 0036-0848
SOUTH AFRICAN MACHINE TOOL REVIEW. (Text in English) 1968. m. R.104. George Warman Publications (Pty.) Ltd., P.O. Box 3847, Cape Town 8000, South Africa. TEL 021-12-5320. FAX 021-26-1332. TELEX 5-21849 SA. Ed. Paddy Attwell. adv.; bk.rev.; illus.; circ. 3,800. **Indexed:** Met.Abstr., World Alum.Abstr.
Description: Focuses on machine tools, accessories and modern tool practice.

621.9   SA
SOUTH AFRICAN MECHANICS HANDBOOK. (Text in Afrikaans and English) a. R.1.25. Union Trades Directories (Pty) Ltd., 22-24 North Block, Mutual Sq., Davenport Rd., Box 687, Durban 4000, South Africa. adv.

SOUTHERN FARM EQUIPMENT MANUFACTURERS. NEWSLETTER. see *AGRICULTURE — Agricultural Equipment*

621.9   US   ISSN 0144-6622
TJ1   CODEN: SORSDW
SOVIET ENGINEERING RESEARCH. English translation of: Stanki i Instrumenty; Vestnik Mashinostroeniya (UR ISSN 0038-9811) 1959. m. $750 uS and Canada; UK $445; elsewhere $825. (British Library, Lending Division) Allerton Press, Inc., 150 Fifth Ave., New York, NY 10011. TEL 212-924-3950. Ed. T.B. Snape. abstr.; bibl.; charts; illus.; index; circ. 350. (back issues avail.) **Indexed:** ASCA, Chem.Abstr., Curr.Cont., Eng.Ind., Excerp.Med., Fluidex, ISMEC, Met.Abstr., RAPRA, Risk Abstr., Robomat, Sci.Abstr.
—BLDSC shelfmark: 0421.760000.
Formed by the merger of: Machines and Tooling (ISSN 0024-922X) & Russian Engineering Journal (ISSN 0036-0228)

SOVIET SURFACE ENGINEERING AND APPLIED ELECTROCHEMISTRY. see *ENGINEERING — Mechanical Engineering*

621.9   UK   ISSN 0263-5038
SPON'S PLANT AND EQUIPMENT PRICE GUIDE. 1982. a. £190($295) E. & F.N. Spon Ltd., 7 St. Peter's Pl., Brighton BN1 6TB, England. TEL 0273-6800416. FAX 0273-606588.
Formerly: Plant and Equipment Guide.

STEAMBOATING. see *SPORTS AND GAMES — Boats And Boating*

621.9   RU   ISSN 0039-2391
STROITEL'NYE I DOROZHNYE MASHINY. 1956. m. $21. Izdatel'stvo Mashinostroenie, 4, Stromynsky Lane, Moscow, 107076, Russia. (Co-sponsor: Ministerstvo Stroitel'nogo, Dorozhnogo i Kommunal'nogo Mashinostroeniya) bk.rev.; charts; illus.; tr.lit.; index; circ. 14,000. **Indexed:** Chem.Abstr.
—BLDSC shelfmark: 0172.500000.

621.9   CS   ISSN 0039-2456
STROJIRENSKA VYROBA/ENGINEERING PRODUCTION. (Text in Czech; summaries in English, German, Polish, Russian) 1953. m. $58.30. Nakladatelstvi Technicke Literatury, Spalena 51, 113 02 Prague 1, Czechoslovakia. (Dist. by: Artia, Ve Smeckach 30, 111 27 Prague 1, Czechoslovakia) Ed. Eva Kissova. adv.; bk.rev.; abstr.; charts; illus.; tr.lit.; index; circ. 14,000. **Indexed:** Appl.Mech.Rev., C.I.S. Abstr., Met.Abstr., World Alum.Abstr.

621.9   CS   ISSN 0039-2464
     CODEN: STRJA3
STROJIRENSTVI. (Text in Czech; summaries in English, German, Russian) 1950. m. $64.10. (Federalni Ministerstvo Hutnictvi, Strojirenstvi a Eletrotechniky) Nakladatelstvi Technicke Literatury, Spalena 51, 113 02 Prague 1, Czechoslovakia. (Dist. by: Artia, Ve Smeckach 30, 111 27 Prague 1, Czechoslovakia) adv.; bk.rev.; abstr.; charts; illus.; pat.; index; circ. 6,500. **Indexed:** Appl.Mech.Rev., C.I.S. Abstr., Chem.Abstr., Met.Abstr., World Alum.Abstr.

STROJNICKY CASOPIS/MECHANICAL ENGINEERING MAGAZINE. see *ENGINEERING — Mechanical Engineering*

SUCCESSFUL DEALER. see *TRANSPORTATION — Trucks And Trucking*

SULZER TECHNICAL REVIEW. see *ENGINEERING*

621.46   US   ISSN 0092-1661
TK4058
SYMPOSIUM ON INCREMENTAL MOTION CONTROL SYSTEMS AND DEVICES. PROCEEDINGS. 1972. a. $80. Incremental Motion Control Systems Society, Box 2772, Station A, Champaign, IL 61825. TEL 217-356-1523. FAX 217-356-2356. Ed. B.C. Kuo. illus.; circ. 500. **Indexed:** Comput.Cont. Key Title: Proceedings. Annual Symposium. Incremental Motion Control Systems and Devices.
Description: Provides an up-to-date review of existing technology and recent advances in systems research. Also contains exhibits with technical displays.

TAASIOT. see *BUSINESS AND ECONOMICS — Labor And Industrial Relations*

621.9   CH
TAIWAN MACHINERY. (Text in English) 1980. 2/yr. NT.$1400($60) in Asia, Middle East, Oceania; elsewhere $70. China Economic News Service, 561 Chung Hsiao E. Rd. Sec. 4, Taipei, Taiwan 10516, Republic of China. TEL 2-642-2629. FAX 2-642-7422. TELEX 27710-CENSPC. (Subscr. to: P.O. Box 43-60, Taipei, Taiwan, R.O.C.)

621.9   CH
TARGET MACHINERY & HARDWARE. Cover title: T M H. m. $60 (foreign $70). United Pacific International Inc., P.O. Box 81-417, Taipei, Taiwan, Republic of China. TEL 02-7150751. FAX 02-7169493. TELEX 28784-UNIPAINC. adv.
Description: Information on hardware and auto supplies, including building supplies and machinery.

621.9   SZ   ISSN 0040-0866
T4   CODEN: TCHNAR
TECHNICA; international technical review. (Text in German) 1951. 26/yr. 95 Fr. Industrie-Verlag AG, Postfach, CH-8032 Zurich, Switzerland. Ed. M Gysi. adv.; bk.rev.; illus.; index; circ. 22,800. **Indexed:** BMT, C.I.S. Abstr., Chem.Abstr., Excerp.Med., Met.Abstr., Sci.Abstr.
—BLDSC shelfmark: 8614.850000.
Description: Devoted to research in all fields of technology in the machine industry. Covers mechanization, automation, controls, manufacturing, instruments and materials. Includes reports of events, new products, industry news, and positions available.

TECHNISCHE REVUE. see *TECHNOLOGY: COMPREHENSIVE WORKS*

TECNICA E INDUSTRIA. see *TECHNOLOGY: COMPREHENSIVE WORKS*

TECNO 2000; revista per a la innovacio tecnologica a l'empresa. see *TECHNOLOGY: COMPREHENSIVE WORKS*

MACHINERY

671.3 621   IT
TECNOLOGIA DELLA DEFORMAZIONE. 1962. bi-m. L.50000 (foreign L.75000). (Editoriale Tecnica Macchine) E T M S.r.l., Via Roncaglia 14, 20146 Milan, Italy. TEL 02-48010095. FAX 02-48010011. adv.; bk.rev.; charts; illus.; tr.lit.; index; circ. 5,500. **Indexed:** Met.Abstr., World Alum.Abstr.
Formerly (until 1987): Tranciatura Stampaggio (ISSN 0041-1027)
Description: Technical review of metal deformation.

TEKHNIKA V SEL'SKOM KHOZYAISTVE. see *AGRICULTURE — Agricultural Equipment*

TEXTILE MACHINERY SOCIETY OF JAPAN. JOURNAL. see *TEXTILE INDUSTRIES AND FABRICS*

TIMBER TRADES JOURNAL AND WOOD PROCESSING. see *FORESTS AND FORESTRY — Lumber And Wood*

621.9   US
TIMKEN MAGAZINE. (Text in English, French) 1945. 4/yr. free. Timken Co., 1835 Dueber Ave. S.W., Canton, OH 44706. TEL 216-438-3825. FAX 216-438-4118. Ed. Keith Price. illus.; circ. 31,000.

671   NE
TOELEVEREN EN UITBESTEDEN. (Supplement to: Metaal en Kunststof) bi-m. fl.185 (includes Metaal en Kunststof). Uitgeversmaatschappij C. Misset B.V., Hanzestr. 1, 7006 RH Doetinchem, Netherlands. TEL 08340-49911. FAX 08340-43839. TELEX 45481. (Subscr. to: Postbus 4, 7000 BA Doetinchem, Netherlands) Ed. Th. Evers. adv.: B&W page fl.2265; unit 187 x 257; adv. contact: Cor van Nek. circ. 6,000 (controlled).
Description: Information about all aspects of supply and subcontracting in the metal and plastics industries.

621.9   US   ISSN 0040-9243
                                          CODEN: TOPRAR
TOOLING & PRODUCTION; the magazine of metalworking manufacturing. 1934. m. $90 (Canada $125; elsewhere $195). Huebcore Communications, Inc., 29100 Aurora Rd., Ste. 200, Solon, OH 44139. TEL 216-248-1125. FAX 612-686-0214. (Subscr. to: Box 21640, Eagan, MN 55121-0640. TEL 612-686-0303) Ed. Stan Modic. adv.; bk.rev.; charts; illus.; stat.; tr.lit.; index, cum.index; circ. 80,000. (also avail. in microform from UMI) **Indexed:** A.S.& T.Ind., ASCA, Bus.Ind., Eng.Ind, ISMEC, Met.Abstr., PROMT, Sci.Abstr., Tr.& Indus.Ind., World Alum.Abstr.
●Also available online. Vendor(s): DIALOG.
—BLDSC shelfmark: 8867.000000.
Description: Emphasis on manufacturing technology for improved productivity.

621.8   JA
TOYODA MACHINE WORKS TECHNICAL REVIEW/TOYODA KOKI GIHO. (Text in Japanese) 1960. q. Toyoda Machine Works Ltd. - Toyoda Koki K. K., 1-1 Asahi-cho, Kariya, Aichi 448, Japan. Ed. Hiroaki Asano. bibl.; charts; illus.; pat.; cum.index; circ. 1,400(controlled).
Formerly: Toyoda Technical Review (ISSN 0041-0152)

621.9   JA   ISSN 0493-6779
TRADE TIMES. (Text in English) 1956. m. 7200 Yen($35) (Japan Machinery Exporters' Association) Trade Times, Ltd., 5-16, Nishi-Shinbashi 1-chome, Minato-ku, Tokyo, Japan. Ed. Fumihiro Yoshimura. adv.; illus.; pat.; circ. 35,000. (also avail. in microform) **Indexed:** Met.Abstr., World Alum.Abstr.

TRAKTOR- OG LANDBRUGSBLADET. see *AGRICULTURE — Agricultural Equipment*

LE TREFILE; revue technique consacree a tous les domaines de la production et transformation de fils metalliques et barres, y compris tous les domaines annexes. see *ENGINEERING — Electrical Engineering*

TRIBOLOGIST. see *ENGINEERING — Mechanical Engineering*

621.9   US
TURBOMACHINERY MAINTENANCE NEWSLETTER. m. Turbomachinery Maintenance Institute, Inc., Box 5550, Norwalk, CT 06856-5550. TEL 203-853-6015. FAX 203-852-8175. Ed. Rena Hines.

621.9   US
TURBOMACHINERY SYMPOSIUM. PROCEEDINGS. 1972. a. $50. Texas A & M University, Department of Mechanical Engineering, Turbomachinery Laboratory, College Station, TX 77843. TEL 409-845-8943. FAX 409-845-1835. Ed. Jean C. Bailey. circ. 1,500. **Indexed:** Sh.& Vib.Dig.

621.9 669   US
U S S R REPORT: MACHINE TOOLS AND METAL - WORKING EQUIPMENT. irreg. (approx. 10/yr.). $5 per no. U.S. Joint Publications Research Service, Box 12507, Arlington, VA 22209. TEL 703-487-4630. (Orders to: NTIS, Springfield, VA 22161)

UMFORMTECHNIK. see *METALLURGY*

621.9   US   ISSN 0085-6916
UNIVERSITAET STUTTGART. INSTITUT FUER STEUERUNGSTECHNIK DER WERKZEUGMASCHINEN UND FERTIGUNGSEINRICHTUNGEN. I S W BERICHTE. 1972. irreg. price varies. (Universitaet Stuttgart, GW) Springer-Verlag, 175 Fifth Ave., New York, NY 10010. TEL 212-460-1500. (Also: Berlin, Heidelberg, Tokyo and Vienna) (reprint service avail. from ISI)

621.9   US   ISSN 1045-3954
USED EQUIPMENT DIRECTORY. 1949. m. $30 (foreign $100). Penton Publishing (Hasbrouck Heights) (Subsidiary of: Pittway Company), 611 Rte. 46 W., Hasbrouck Heights, NJ 07604-3120. TEL 800-526-6052. FAX 201-393-9553. Ed. James J. Mack. adv.; circ. 75,000 (controlled). (also avail. in microform; reprint service avail. from UMI)
●Also available online.
Description: Lists over 34,000 available used machines and equipment from more than 800 dealers, with a rotational circulation list of over 150,000 plants and a monthly distribution of 75,000 users of mechanical tools, metalworking, chemical, plastic, power, electrical, and other industrial equipment.

USINE NOUVELLE; technology and economics. see *TECHNOLOGY: COMPREHENSIVE WORKS*

621.9   IT   ISSN 0392-6567
                                    CODEN: UTEND9
UTENSIL. 1978. 9/yr. L.75000 (foreign L.100000). E T M, S.r.l., Via Roncaglia 14, 20146 Milan, Italy. TEL 02-48010095. FAX 02-48010011. adv.; bk.rev.; charts; illus.; tr.lit.; index; circ. 12,000. **Indexed:** Chem.Abstr., Met.Abstr., World Alum.Abstr.
Description: Review of technology and marketing for the industry. Deals in the field of the tools trade, mechanical and manual operated tools, accessories, abrasives, equipment gauges and products for mechanical works.

V D I INFORMATIONSDIENST. DRAHTHERSTELLUNG U. DRAHTERZEUGNISSE. (Verein Deutscher Ingenieure) see *ENGINEERING — Abstracting, Bibliographies, Statistics*

621.9 330   US
VALVE MAGAZINE. 1982. q. $28 (foreign $40). Valve Manufacturers Association of America, 1050 17th St., N.W., Ste. 701, Washington, DC 20036. TEL 202-331-8105. (Subscr. to: 901 S. Highland St., Ste. 105, Arlington, VA 22204) Ed. Elizabeth Tober-Lyon. adv.; stat.; tr.lit.; circ. 23,000.
Description: Covers issues and applications surrounding the U.S. valve industry. Includes information on the activities of the Association.

VALVE NEWS. see *HEATING, PLUMBING AND REFRIGERATION*

621.9   DK
VEJVISER FOR MASKININDUSTRIEN. 1950. a. Industriens Forlag, Gl. Koege Landevej 41, 2500 Valby, Denmark. TEL 31 46 78 22. Ed. G.F. Kentorp. adv.; circ. 4,000.

VEREIN DEUTSCHER INGENIEURE. INFORMATIONSDIENST. INSTANDHALTUNG. see *ENGINEERING — Abstracting, Bibliographies, Statistics*

621.75   SW   ISSN 0042-4056
TJ4   CODEN: VSTDAL
VERKSTAEDERNA. 1905. 12/yr. SEK 350. Sveriges Verkstadsfoerening, P.O. Box 5510, S-114 85 Stockholm, Sweden. TEL 46-8-782-0800. FAX 46-8-782-0994. Ed. Stefan Hallberg. adv.; bk.rev.; charts; illus.; tr.lit.; index; circ. 16,732. (also avail. in microfilm) **Indexed:** C.I.S. Abstr.
Description: Covers methods and equipment for productive mechanical and electrotechnical workshops. Includes education, planning and logistics.

W T - WERKSTATTSTECHNIK; Zeitschrift fuer industrielle Fertigung. see *TECHNOLOGY: COMPREHENSIVE WORKS*

621.9 620 621 600   GW   ISSN 0043-2792
                                      CODEN: WKUBA9
WERKSTATT UND BETRIEB; Zeitschrift fuer Maschinenbau, Konstruktion und Fertigung. 1867. m. DM.146.40. Carl Hanser Verlag, Kolbergerstr. 22, Postfach 860420, 8000 Munich 80, Germany. TEL 089-926940. Ed. Herbert Schulz. adv.; bk.rev.; charts; illus.; mkt.; pat.; tr.lit.; index, cum.index; circ. 11,500. **Indexed:** C.I.S. Abstr., Chem.Abstr., Eng.Ind., Excerp.Med., Int.Aerosp.Abstr., Met.Abstr., Sci.Abstr., World Alum.Abstr.
—BLDSC shelfmark: 9296.000000.

621.8   GW
▼**WERKZEUG & FORMENBAU.** 1991. q. DM.84 (foreign DM.90). Verlag Moderne Industrie, Justus-von-Liebig-Str. 1, Postfach 1751, 8910 Landsberg, Germany. TEL 08191-125-0. FAX 08191-125-483. Eds. Hubert Winkler, Wolfgang Klingauf. adv.: B&W page DM.5260; trim 257 x 178; adv. contact: Franz Krauss. circ. 10,500.

621.9   GW   ISSN 0936-8760
WERKZEUGE. s-a. DM.50. Verlag Moderne Industrie, Justus-von-Liebig-Str. 1, Postfach 1751, 8910 Landsberg, Germany. TEL 08191-125-0. FAX 08191-125-483. Ed. Wolfgang Klingauf. adv.; illus.

621.9   US
WESTERN METALWORKING DIRECTORY;* complete buying guide for all machine shop requirements. 1988. a. $55. De Roche Publications, 12 Del Italia, Irvine, CA 92714-5355. Ed. David J. De Roche. adv.; circ. 22,000. (tabloid format; back issues avail.)
Description: Concerned with the metal working industry.

621.9   PL   ISSN 0043-521X
WIADOMOSCI WARSZTATOWE. 1968. fortn. $18. (Stowarzyszenie Inzynierow i Technikow Mechanikow Polskich) Oficyna Wydawnicza SIMP Press, Ltd., Ul. Zurawia 22, 00-515 Warsaw, Poland. (Dist. by: Ars Polona-Ruch, Krakowskie Przedmiescie 7, Warsaw, Poland) adv.; bk.rev.; film rev.; bibl.; illus.; pat.; circ. 34,000. (tabloid format)

WOOD BASED PANELS INTERNATIONAL. see *FORESTS AND FORESTRY — Lumber And Wood*

WOOD MACHINERY MANUFACTURERS OF AMERICA. BUYER'S GUIDE AND DIRECTORY. see *FORESTS AND FORESTRY — Lumber And Wood*

338   US   ISSN 0043-8561
WORLD INDUSTRIAL REPORTER; new equipment, machinery and techniques for industry. Spanish edition: Reportero Industrial. (Supplements avail.: Infochem, Infomet) 1943. 9/yr. free to qualified personnel. Keller International Publishing Corporation, 150 Great Neck Rd., Great Neck, NY 11021. TEL 516-829-9210. FAX 516-829-5414. TELEX 221574 KELLE. Felicia M. Morales. adv.; abstr.; charts; illus.; tr.lit.; circ. 42,119. (tabloid format)

621.9 639.2   CC   ISSN 1001-2451
YUYE JIXIE YIQI. (Text in Chinese) bi-m. Zhongguo Shuichan Kexue Yanjiuyuan - China Aquatic Science Research Institute, 63 Chifeng Lu, Shanghai 200092, People's Republic of China. TEL 5417260. Ed. Chen Sheng.

621.9 620 621 600 GW ISSN 0044-3743
CODEN: ZTWFAP
Z W F - C I M. (Zeitschrift fuer Wirtschaftliche Fertigung und Automatisierung) 1879. m. DM.154.80. Carl Hanser Verlag GmbH, Pascalstr. 8-9, 1000 Berlin 10, Germany. TEL 030-39006226. FAX 030-3911037. Ed. Guenter Spur. adv.; bibl.; charts; illus.; index; circ. 5,020. **Indexed:** Chem.Abstr., Sci.Abstr.
—BLDSC shelfmark: 9492.210000.

9N - 2N - 8N NEWSLETTER. see AGRICULTURE — Agricultural Equipment

MACHINERY — Abstracting, Bibliographies, Statistics

621.9 016 RU ISSN 0131-7970
EKSPRESS-INFORMATSIYA. DETALI MASHIN. 1959. 48/yr. 38.20 Rub. Vsesoyuznyi Institut Nauchno-Tekhnicheskoi Informatsii (VINITI), Baltiiskaya ul., 14, Moscow A-219, Russia. (Subscr. to: Mezhdunarodnaya Kniga, Dimitrova ul. 39, 113095 Moscow, Russia)

621.8 016 RU
EKSPRESS-INFORMATSIYA. PODVODNO-TEKHNICHESKIE, VODOLAZNYE I SUDOPOD'EMNYE RABOTY. GIDROTEKHNICHESKIE SOORUZHENIYA. 1970. 48/yr. 37.40 Rub. Vsesoyuznyi Institut Nauchno-Tekhnicheskoi Informatsii (VINITI), Baltiiskaya ul., 14, Moscow A-219, Russia. (Subscr. to: Mezhdunarodnaya Kniga, Dimitrova ul. 39, 113095 Moscow, Russia)
Formerly: Ekspress-Informatsiya. Podvodno-Tekhnicheskie, Vodolaznye i Sudopod'emnye Raboty. (ISSN 0131-0321)

621.9 GW ISSN 0343-6411
FACHBUCHVERZEICHNIS MASCHINENBAU (YEAR). 1900. a. DM.3.10. Fr. Weidemanns Buchhandlung (H.Witt), Georgstr. 11, Postfach 6406, 3000 Hannover 1, Germany. TEL 0511-14014. FAX 0511-325971. Ed. Kaethe Deichmann. circ. 20,000.

GEPESZETI SZAKIRODALMI TAJEKOZTATO/MACHINERY ABSTRACTS. see ENGINEERING — Abstracting, Bibliographies, Statistics

GEPGYARTASTECHNOLOGIAI ES SZERSZAMGEPIPARI SZAKIRODALMI TAJEKOZTATO/MECHANICAL ENGINEERING & MACHINE TOOL ABSTRACTS. see ENGINEERING — Abstracting, Bibliographies, Statistics

624 016 FR
P A S C A L FOLIO. F 10: MECANIQUE ET ACOUSTIQUE ET TRANSFERT DE CHALEUR. 1984. 10/yr. 1275 F. Centre National de la Recherche Scientifique, Institut de l'Information Scientifique et Technique, B.P. 54, 54514 Vandoeuvre-Les-Nancy Cedex, France. TEL 83-50-46-00. abstr.; index, cum.index. (also avail. in microform from MIM)
Formerly: P A S C A L Folio. F 10: Mecanique et Acoustique (ISSN 0761-1730); Supersedes in part (1961-1984): Bulletin Signaletique. Part 130: Physique Mathematique, Optique, Acoustique, Mecanique, Chaleur (ISSN 0397-7757); Which was formerly: Bulletin Signaletique. Part 130: Physique (ISSN 0007-5345); Supersedes (1961-1984): Bulletin Signaletique. Part 891: Industries Mecaniques (ISSN 0223-4246); Which supersedes in part (since 1980): Bulletin Signaletique. Part 890: Industries Mecaniques-Batiment-Travaux Public-Transports (ISSN 0398-995X) Formerly: P A S C A L Folio. Part 10: Mecanique et Acoustique.

620 621 016 PL ISSN 0032-3713
QA801 CODEN: PBAMA6
POLSKA BIBLIOGRAFIA ANALITYCZNA MECHANIKI/POLISH SCIENTIFIC ABSTRACTS ON MECHANICS. (Contents page and captions in English) 1953. q. (Polska Akademia Nauk, Instytut Podstawowych Problemow Techniki) Panstwowe Wydawnictwo Naukowe, Miodowa 10, 00-251 Warsaw, Poland. (Dist. by: Ars Polona, Krakowskie Przedmiescie 7, 00-068 Warsaw, Poland) Ed. M. Sokolowski. bk.rev.; abstr.; circ. 350. **Indexed:** Appl.Mech.Rev., Math.R.

621.6 016 UK ISSN 0302-2870
TJ900
PUMPS AND OTHER FLUIDS MACHINERY ABSTRACTS. 1971. q. $250 (foreign £140). S T I Ltd., 4 Kings Meadow, Ferry Hinksey Rd., Oxford OX2 0DU, England. TEL 0865-798898. FAX 0865-798788. (Dist. in U.S. by: Air Science Co., P.O. Box 143, Corning, NY 14830. TEL 607-962-5591) Ed. Lindsay Gale. bk.rev.; abstr.; index, cum.index.
●Also available online. Vendor(s): DIALOG (File no.96/FLUIDEX), European Space Agency (File no.48/FLUIDEX).
Description: Design, development, manufacture, operation and performance of pumps and other fluids handling machines.

REFERATIVNYI ZHURNAL. GORNOE I NEFTEPROMYSLOVOE MASHINOSTROENIE. see MINES AND MINING INDUSTRY — Abstracting, Bibliographies, Statistics

REFERATIVNYI ZHURNAL. MASHINOSTROITEL'NYE MATERIALY, KONSTRUKTSII I RASCHET DETALI MASHIN. GIDROPRIVOD. see ENGINEERING — Abstracting, Bibliographies, Statistics

REFERATIVNYI ZHURNAL. NASOSOSTROENIE I KOMPRESSOROSTROENIE. KHOLODIL'NOE MASHINOSTROENIE. see ENGINEERING — Abstracting, Bibliographies, Statistics

385.1 016 RU ISSN 0034-2556
REFERATIVNYI ZHURNAL. PROMYSHLENNYI TRANSPORT. 1963. 12/yr. 63 Rub. (67 Rub. including index). Vsesoyuznyi Institut Nauchno-Tekhnicheskoi Informatsii (VINITI), Baltiiskaya ul., 14, Moscow A-219, Russia. (Subscr. to: Mezhdunarodnaya Kniga, Dimitrova ul. 39, 113095 Moscow, Russia)

621 016 RU ISSN 0034-2599
CODEN: RZTMBK
REFERATIVNYI ZHURNAL. TEKHNOLOGIYA MASHINOSTROENIYA. 1956. m. 224 Rub. (including index 235.60 Rub.). Vsesoyuznyi Institut Nauchno-Tekhnicheskoi Informatsii (VINITI), Baltiiskaya ul., 14, Moscow A-219, Russia. (Subscr. to: Mezhdunarodnaya Kniga, Dimitrova ul. 39, 113095 Moscow, Russia)

REFERATIVNYI ZHURNAL. TRAKTORY I SEL'SKOKHOZYAISTVENNYE MASHINY I ORUDIYA. see AGRICULTURE — Abstracting, Bibliographies, Statistics

621.9 US ISSN 0039-615X
TJ1
SURPLUS RECORD; index of available capital equipment. 1924. m. $30. Surplus Record, Inc., 20 N. Wacker Dr., Chicago, IL 60606. TEL 312-372-9077. FAX 312-372-6537. Ed. Thomas Scanlan. adv.; bk.rev.; bibl.; illus.; stat.; circ. 70,000 (controlled).
●Also available online.
Description: Lists over 35,000 items of used and surplus machine tools, chemical equipment, motors, transformers, generators, and circuit breakers. Approximately 600 dealers are listed throughout the US and Canada.

MACHINERY — Computer Applications

INSIDE F M S; the comprehensive buying reference for factory automation. see COMPUTERS — Automation

621.8 001.6 UK ISSN 0957-6061
TS155.6 CODEN: IMSYEY
INTEGRATED MANUFACTURING SYSTEMS. vol.3, no.1, 1985. q. £129.95($329.95) M C B University Press Ltd., 62 Toller Ln., Bradford, W. Yorks BD8 9BY, England. TEL 0274-499821. FAX 0274-547143. TELEX 51317 MCBUNI G. Ed. Dr. David Bennett. adv. **Indexed:** A.I.Abstr., CAD CAM Abstr., Robomat., Sci.Abstr.
—BLDSC shelfmark: 4531.816060.
Formerly: F M S Magazine (ISSN 0263-9777)
Description: For technologists and flexible manufacturing system professionals. Includes information on system planning, automation, design, software, technological developments and applications.

621.8 US
N C - C I M GUIDEBOOK. (Numerical Control Computer Integrated Manufacturing); modern machine shop. 1970. a. $10 (effective Dec. 1990). Gardner Publications, Inc., 6600 Clough Pike, Cincinnati, OH 45244-4090. TEL 513-231-8020. FAX 513-231-2818. Ed. Kenneth M. Gettelman. adv.; circ. 70,000 (controlled). (also avail. in microform from UMI; back issues avail.; reprint service avail.)
Formerly: Modern Machine Shop N C Guidebook and Directory (ISSN 0076-9991)
Description: For numerical control (NC) equipment users and those considering other computer-aided manufacturing, programming, hardware and software.

MACROECONOMICS

see Business and Economics–Macroeconomics

MANAGEMENT

see Business and Economics–Management

MARITIME LAW

see Law–Maritime Law

MARKETING AND PURCHASING

see Business and Economics–Marketing and Purchasing

MATHEMATICS

510 DK ISSN 0105-8533
AARHUS UNIVERSITET. MATEMATISK INSTITUT. DATALOGISK AFDELING. DAIMI FN. 1973. irreg. price varies. Aarhus Universitet, Matematisk Institut, Datalogisk Afdeling, Ny Munkegade, Bygning 540, DK-8000 Aarhus C, Denmark.

510 DK ISSN 0106-9969
AARHUS UNIVERSITET. MATEMATISK INSTITUT. DATALOGISK AFDELING. DAIMI IR. 1973. irreg. price varies. Aarhus Universitet, Matematisk Institut, Datalogisk Afdeling, Bygn. 540, Ny Munkegade, 8000 Aarhus C, Denmark.

510 DK ISSN 0105-8525
AARHUS UNIVERSITET. MATEMATISK INSTITUT. DATALOGISK AFDELING. DAIMI MD. 1973. irreg. price varies. Aarhus Universitet, Matematisk Institut, Datalogisk Afdeling, Ny Munkegade, 8000 Aarhus C, Denmark.

510 DK ISSN 0105-8517
AARHUS UNIVERSITET. MATEMATISK INSTITUT. DATALOGISK AFDELING. DAIMI PB. 1972. irreg. price varies. Aarhus Universitet, Matematisk Institut, Datalogisk Afdeling, Ny Munkegade, 8000 Aarhus C, Denmark.

510 DK ISSN 0106-8997
AARHUS UNIVERSITET. MATEMATISK INSTITUT. ELEMENTAERAFDELING. 1957. irreg. price varies. Aarhus Universitet, Matematisk Institut, 8000 Aarhus C, Denmark. illus.

510 DK ISSN 0065-017X
AARHUS UNIVERSITET. MATEMATISK INSTITUT. LECTURE NOTES SERIES. 1963. irreg. no.60, 1990. price varies. Aarhus Universitet, Matematisk Institut, Ny Munkegade, 8000 Aarhus C, Denmark.

510 DK
AARHUS UNIVERSITET. MATEMATISK INSTITUT. MEMOIRS. 1973. irreg. no.11, 1988. Aarhus Universitet, Matematisk Institut, Bygning 530, Ny Munkegade, DK-8000 Aarhus C, Denmark.

MATHEMATICS

510   DK   ISSN 0065-0188
AARHUS UNIVERSITET. MATEMATISK INSTITUT. VARIOUS PUBLICATIONS SERIES. 1962. irreg., no.38, 1988. price varies. Aarhus Universitet, Matematisk Institut, Ny Munkegade, 8000 Aarhus C, Denmark.
—BLDSC shelfmark: 9146.650000.

510   NR   ISSN 0001-3099
QA1   CODEN: ABCSB6
ABACUS. 1960. a. NC.5. Mathematical Association of Nigeria, c/o Department of Education, University of Nigeria, Nsukka, Nigeria. Ed. R.O. Ohuche. bk.rev.

ACADEMIA DE CIENCIAS FISICAS MATEMATICAS Y NATURALES. BOLETIN. see *SCIENCES: COMPREHENSIVE WORKS*

510   CH
ACADEMIA SINICA. INSTITUTE OF MATHEMATICS. BULLETIN/CHUNG YANG YEN CHIU YUAN SHU HSUEH YEN CHIU SO T'UNG PAO. 1973. q. $30. Academia Sinica, Institute of Mathematics - Chung Yang Yen Chiu Yuan Shu Hsueh Yen Chiu So, Nankang, Taipei Hsien, Taiwan 11529, Republic of China. TEL 02-7851211. FAX 02-7827432. Ed.Bd. circ. 500.

510   FR   ISSN 0764-4442
Q2   CODEN: CASMEI
ACADEMIE DES SCIENCES. COMPTES RENDUS. SERIE 1: MATHEMATIQUES. (Text and summaries in English, French) 1835. 28/yr. 4200 F. (Academie des Sciences) Gauthier-Villars, 15 rue Gossin, 92543 Montrouge Cedex, France. TEL 33-1-40-92-65-00. FAX 33-1-40-92-65-97. TELEX 270 004. (Subscr. to: Centrale des Revues, 11 rue Gossin, 92543 Montrouge Cedex, France. TEL 33-1-46-56-52-66) Eds. Paul Germain, Francois Gros. charts; illus.; s-a. index; circ. 3,200. (also avail. in microform from MIM,PMC) **Indexed:** Appl.Mech.Rev., Biol.Abstr., Chem.Abstr., Compumath, Curr.Cont., Deep Sea Res.& Oceanogr.Abstr., Eng.Ind., Geo.Abstr., Ind.Med., INIS Atomind., Int.Aerosp.Abstr., Math.R., Met.Abstr., Meteor.& Geoastrophys.Abstr., Nutr.Abstr., Sci.Abstr, Zent.Math.
—BLDSC shelfmark: 3370.042000.
Formerly: Academie des Sciences. Comptes Rendus Hebdomadaires des Seances. Series A-B: Sciences Mathematiques (ISSN 0151-0509); Formed by the merger of: Academie des Sciences. Comptes Rendus Hebdomadaires des Seances. Serie A. Sciences Mathematiques (ISSN 0302-8429); Academie des Sciences. Comptes Rendus Hebdomadaires des Seances. Serie B. Sciences Physiques (ISSN 0302-8437).
Description: Covers set theory, number theory, linear algebra, complex analysis, calculus of variations, topology, numerical analysis and more.

510 500 520   YU
ACADEMIE SERBE DES SCIENCES ET DES ARTS. CLASSE DES SCIENCES MATHEMATIQUES ET NATURELLES. BULLETIN. SCIENCES MATHEMATIQUES. (Text in English, French, Russian) 1952. a. price varies. Srpska Akademija Nauka i Umetnosti - Serbian Academy of Sciences and Arts, Knez Mihailova 35, 11001 Belgrade, Serbia, Yugoslavia. FAX 38-11-182-825. TELEX 72593 SANU YU. (Dist. by: Prosveta, Terazije 16, Belgrade, Serbia, Yugoslavia) circ. 500. **Indexed:** Chem.Abstr, Math.R.
Supersedes in part: Academie Serbe des Sciences et des Arts. Classe des Sciences Mathematiques et Naturelles. Bulletin. Nouvelle Serie (ISSN 0001-4184)

510   US   ISSN 0001-4346
QA1   CODEN: MTHNB2
ACADEMY OF SCIENCES OF THE U S S R. MATHEMATICAL NOTES. English translation of: Matematicheskie Zametki (RU ISSN 0025-567X) 1950. m. (2 vols./yr.). $1075 (foreign $1260)(effective 1992). (Akademiya Nauk S.S.S.R., RU) Plenum Publishing Corp., Consultants Bureau, 233 Spring St., New York, NY 10013-1578. TEL 212-620-8468. FAX 212-463-0742. TELEX 23-421139. Ed. V.P. Maslov. charts; illus. (back issues avail.) **Indexed:** Appl.Mech.Rev., Comput.& Info.Sys., Curr.Cont., Ind.Sci.Rev., Math.R., Phys.Ber., Zent.Math.
—BLDSC shelfmark: 0415.815000.
Refereed Serial

ACCADEMIA DELLE SCIENZE DI TORINO. ATTI. PART 1. CLASSE DI SCIENZE FISICHE, MATEMATICHE E NATURALI. see *SCIENCES: COMPREHENSIVE WORKS*

ACCADEMIA DELLE SCIENZE DI TORINO. MEMORIE. PART 1. CLASSE DI SCIENZE FISICHE, MATEMATICHE E NATURALI. see *SCIENCES: COMPREHENSIVE WORKS*

ACCADEMIA NAZIONALE DEI LINCEI. CLASSE DI SCIENZE FISICHE MATEMATICHE E NATURALI. RENDICONTI. see *PHYSICS*

510 500 600   FI   ISSN 0001-5105
    CODEN: AAAMA4
ACTA ACADEMIAE ABOENSIS, SERIES B: MATHEMATICA ET PHYSICA. (Text in English, German and Swedish) 1922. irreg., vol.50, 1990. price varies. Aabo Akademis Foerlag, Kaskisgatan 2 C 14, 20700 Aabo, Finland. FAX 258-21-654497. Ed. Goeran Hoegnas. charts; index; circ. 600. **Indexed:** Abstr.Bull.Inst.Pap.Chem., Biol.Abstr., Curr.Adv.Ecol.Sci., Deep Sea Res.& Oceanogr.Abstr., Math.R.

510   NE   ISSN 0167-8019
QA1   CODEN: AAMADV
ACTA APPLICANDAE MATHEMATICAE; international survey journal on applying mathematics and mathematical applications. (Text and summaries in English) 1983. 12/yr. $518. Kluwer Academic Publishers, Postbus 17, 3300 AA Dordrecht, Netherlands. TEL 078-334911. FAX 078-334254. TELEX 29245. (Dist. by: Kluwer Academic Publishers Group, P.O. Box 322, 3300 AH Dordrecht, Netherlands; N. America dist. addr.: Box 358, Accord Station, Hingham, MA 02018-0358. TEL 617-871-6600) Ed. Michiel Hazewinkel. adv.; bk.rev.; index. (reprint service avail. from WSWZ) **Indexed:** Appl.Mech.Rev., ASCA, Compumath, Curr.Cont., Math.R.
—BLDSC shelfmark: 0595.970000.

510   PL   ISSN 0065-1036
QA3   CODEN: AARIA9
ACTA ARITHMETICA. (Text in English, French, German and Russian) 1936. irreg., vol.56, 1990. $60 per vol. (Polska Akademia Nauk, Instytut Matematyczny) Panstwowe Wydawnictwo Naukowe, Ul. Miodowa 10, 00-251 Warsaw, Poland. (Dist. by: Ars Polona, Krakowskie Przedmiescie 7, 00-068 Warsaw, Poland) Ed. A. Schinzel. bibl.; charts. (reprint service avail. from SWZ) **Indexed:** ASCA, Compumath, GeoRef, Math.R.
—BLDSC shelfmark: 0596.600000.

510   SW   ISSN 0001-5962
QA1   CODEN: ACMAA8
ACTA MATHEMATICA. 1882. q. (2 vols/yr.). $200. Institut Mittag-Leffler - Mittag-Leffler Institute, Auravaegen 17, S-182 62 Djursholm, Sweden. TEL 4-46-08-755-18-09. FAX 46-08-755-9971. index, cum.index: vols.1-100. (also avail. in microfilm from PMC; back issues avail.; reprint service avail. from SWZ) **Indexed:** ASCA, Compumath, Ind.Sci.Rev., Math.R., Sci.Cit.Ind.
—BLDSC shelfmark: 0630.000000.

510   HU   ISSN 0236-5294
QA1
ACTA MATHEMATICA HUNGARICA. (Text in English, French, German, Russian) 1950. 4/yr. (in 2 vols.). $68. (Magyar Tudomanyos Akademia) Akademiai Kiado, Publishing House of the Hungarian Academy of Sciences, P.O. Box 24, H-1363 Budapest, Hungary. Eds. K. Tandori, J. Szabados. bibl.; index. **Indexed:** ASCA, Compumath, Curr.Cont., Ind.Sci.Rev., Math.R., Sci.Cit.Ind.
Formerly: Academia Scientiarum Hungarica. Acta Mathematica (ISSN 0001-5954)

510   CC   ISSN 1000-9574
ACTA MATHEMATICA SINICA, NEW SERIES. Chinese edition: Shuxue Xuebao (ISSN 0583-1431) (Text in English) 1985. q. $150 to individuals; institutions $250. Kexue Chubanshe, 16 Donghuangchenggen Beijie, Beijing 100707, People's Republic of China. TEL 4010642. FAX 4012180. TELEX 210247 SPBJ CB. (US office: Science Press New York, Ltd., 63-117 Alderton St., Rego Park, NY 11374. TEL 718-459-4638; Co-publisher: V S P, P.O. Box 346, 3700 AH Zeist, Netherlands. TEL 03404-25790) Ed. Wang Yuan. adv.; circ. 6,000. (back issues avail.)
—BLDSC shelfmark: 0632.010000.
Description: Examines all branches of pure and applied mathematics.
Refereed Serial

510   VN   ISSN 0251-4184
ACTA MATHEMATICA VIETNAMICA. (Text mainly in English; occasionally in French, German and Russian) 1964. s-a. exchange basis. National Center for Scientific Research, Institute of Mathematics, P.O. Box 631, Bo Ho, 10000 Hanoi, Socialist Republic of Vietnam. Ed. Hoang Tuy. charts; illus.; stat. **Indexed:** Math.R.
—BLDSC shelfmark: 0632.100000.
Formerly (until 1976): Acta Scientiarum Vietnamicarum.
Description: Original papers in pure and applied mathematics.

510   CC   ISSN 0168-9673
QA1   CODEN: AASIEI
ACTA MATHEMATICAE APPLICATAE SINICA/CHINESE JOURNAL OF APPLIED MATHEMATICS. Chinese edition: Yingyong Shuxue Xuebao (ISSN 0254-3079) 1985. q. $165 to individuals; institutions $275. (Chinese Mathematics Society) Science Press, Marketing and Sales Department, 16 Donghuangchenggen Beijie, Beijing 100707, People's Republic of China. (US office: Science Press New York, Ltd., 63-117 Alderton St., Rego Park, NY 11374. TEL 718-459-4638; Co-publisher: Allerton Press, Inc., 150 Fifth Ave., New York, NY 10011, U.S.A.. TEL 212-924-3950) Ed. Yue Minyi. adv.; bk.rev.; index; circ. 6,000. (back issues avail.) **Indexed:** Math.R., Sci.Abstr.
—BLDSC shelfmark: 0632.205000.
Description: Covers applied mathematics research in China, including control theory and stochastic processes.
Refereed Serial

ACTA STEREOLOGICA. see *BIOLOGY*

510 530   CS   ISSN 0001-7140
    CODEN: AUMMBZ
ACTA UNIVERSITATIS CAROLINAE: MATHEMATICA ET PHYSICA. (Text in English, French, German or Russian; summaries in Czech, English, Russian) 1959. s-a. 20 Kcs.($11) Universita Karlova, Fakulta Matematiky a Fysiky, Ovocny Trh 5, Prague 1, Czechoslovakia. (Subscr. to: Artia, Ve Smeckach 30, 111 27 Prague 1, Czechoslovakia) Ed. E. Klier. bibl.; charts; illus.; circ. 600. **Indexed:** Astron.& Astrophys.Abstr., Math.R., Ref.Zh., Zent.Math.
—BLDSC shelfmark: 0584.519000.

510 370   PL   ISSN 0208-6204
ACTA UNIVERSITATIS LODZIENSIS: FOLIA MATHEMATICA. (Text in Polish; summaries in various languages) 1955-1974; N.S. 1987. irreg. Wydawnictwo Uniwersytetu Lodzkiego, Ul. Jaracza 34, Lodz, Poland. (Dist. by: Ars Polona-Ruch, Krakowskie Przedmiescie 7, Warsaw, Poland)
Supersedes in part: Uniwersytet Lodzki. Zeszyty Naukowe. Seria 2: Nauki Matematyczno-Przyrodnicze (ISSN 0076-0366)
Description: Papers concerning various branches of theoretical mathematics mainly real functions, compound analysis, functional analysis and teaching mathematics.

510   HU   ISSN 0001-6969
ACTA UNIVERSITATIS SZEGEDIENSIS DE ATTILA JOZSEF NOMINATAE. ACTA SCIENTIARUM MATHEMATICARUM. (Text in English, French, German, Italian and Russian) 1922. a. exchange basis. Attila Jozsef University, c/o E. Szabo, Exchange Librarian, Dugonics ter 13, P.O. Box 393, Szeged H-6701, Hungary. (Subscr. to: Kultura, Box 149, H-1389 Budapest, Hungary) Ed. Laszlo Leindler. adv.; bk.rev.; index; circ. 1,000. **Indexed:** Compumath, Curr.Cont., Math.R., Ref.Zh., Zent.Math.
—BLDSC shelfmark: 0663.100000.
Description: Original papers in the field of pure mathematics.

510   SI
ADVANCED SERIES IN DYNAMICAL SYSTEMS. (Text in English) 1986. irreg., vol.9, 1991. price varies. World Scientific Publishing Co. Pte. Ltd., Farrer Rd., P.O. Box 128, Singapore 9128, Singapore. TEL 3825663. FAX 3825919. TELEX RS 28561 WSPC. (UK addr.: 73 Lynton Mead, Totteridge, London N20 8DH, England. TEL 44-81-4462461; US addr.: 1060 Main St., Ste. 1B, River Edge, NJ 07661. TEL 800-227-7562) Ed. K. Shiraiwa.

ADVANCED SERIES IN MATHEMATICAL PHYSICS. see *PHYSICS*

MATHEMATICS

510 UK ISSN 0884-0016
ADVANCED STUDIES IN CONTEMPORARY MATHEMATICS. 1986. irregr., vol.7, 1990. Gordon & Breach Science Publishers, P.O. Box 90, Reading, Berkshire RG1 8JL, England. TEL 0734-560-080. FAX 0734-568-211. TELEX 849870 SCIPUB G. (US addr.: Box 786, Cooper Sta., New York, NY 10276. TEL 212-206-8900) Ed. R.V. Gamkrelidze. (also avail. in microfiche; microfilm)
Refereed Serial

510 JA
ADVANCED STUDIES IN PURE MATHEMATICS. (Text in English, French, German) 1983. irreg. (Mathematical Society of Japan) Kinokuniya Company Ltd., 17-7 Shinjuku 3-chome, Shinjuku-ku, Tokyo 160, Japan. FAX 81-52-781-4437.

510 US ISSN 0196-8858
QA1
ADVANCES IN APPLIED MATHEMATICS. 1980. q. $136 (foreign $172). Academic Press, Inc., Journal Division, 1250 Sixth Ave., San Diego, CA 92101. TEL 619-230-1840. FAX 619-699-6800. TELEX 181726. Ed. Gian-Carlo Rota. adv. (back issues avail.) Indexed: Compumath, Ind.Sci.Rev., Int.Aerosp.Abstr., Math.R.
—BLDSC shelfmark: 0698.950000.
Description: Features articles on continuum mechanics, mathematical physics, statistics, mathematical biology, mathematical economics, communication theory, and computer science.
Refereed Serial

510 620.1 UK
ADVANCES IN APPLIED MATHEMATICS AND MECHANICS IN CHINA. (Text in English) irreg. Pergamon Press plc, Headington Hill Hall, Oxford OX3 0BW, England. TEL 0865-794141. FAX 0865-743911. TELEX 83171 PERGAP G.

519 UK ISSN 0001-8678
QA273 CODEN: AAPBBD
ADVANCES IN APPLIED PROBABILITY. 1969. q. £30($53) to individuals; institutions £90($159). Applied Probability Trust, Department of Probability and Statistics, The University, Sheffield S3 7RH, England. TEL 0742-768555. FAX 0742-729782. Ed. C.C. Heyde. adv.; index. cum.index; circ. 1,100. Indexed: Anim.Breed.Abstr., Biol.Abstr., Biostat., Compumath, Curr.Cont., GeoRef., Ind.Sci.Rev., J.Cont.Quant.Meth., Math.R., Oper.Res.Manage.Sci., Qual.Contr.Appl.Stat., Ref.Zh., Sci.Abstr., Sci.Cit.Ind.
—BLDSC shelfmark: 0699.200000.

510 US ISSN 0001-8708
QA1 CODEN: ADMTA4
ADVANCES IN MATHEMATICS. 1967. m. $687 (foreign $829). Academic Press, Inc., Journal Division, 1250 Sixth Ave., San Diego, CA 92101. TEL 619-230-1840. FAX 619-699-6800. TELEX 181726. Ed. Gian-Carlo Rota. adv.; charts. (back issues avail.) Indexed: Compumath, Curr.Cont., Ind.Sci.Rev., Math.R., Sci.Cit.Ind.
Description: Provides research mathematicians with an effective medium for communicating important recent developments in their areas of specialization to colleagues and to scientists in related disciplines.
Refereed Serial

510 US
ADVANCES IN PROBABILITY AND RELATED TOPICS. 1971. irregr., vol.7, 1984. price varies. Marcel Dekker, Inc., 270 Madison Ave., New York, NY 10016. TEL 212-696-9000. FAX 212-685-4540. TELEX 421419. Eds. Peter Ney, Sidney Port.
Indexed: Math.R.
Formerly: Advances in Probability (ISSN 0065-3217)
Refereed Serial

510 SZ ISSN 0001-9054
QA1 CODEN: AEMABN
AEQUATIONES MATHEMATICAE. (Text in English) 1968. 6/yr. 418 Fr.($284) (University of Waterloo, Faculty of Mathematics, CN) Birkhaeuser Verlag, P.O. Box 133, CH-4010 Basel, Switzerland. TEL 061-737740. FAX 061-737950. TELEX 963475 BIRKH CH. (Dist. in N. America by: Springer-Verlag New York, Inc., Journal Fulfillment Services, Box 2485, Secaucus, NJ 07096-2491, USA. TEL 201-348-4033) Ed. A.M. Ostrowski. abstr.; bibl.; charts; index. Indexed: Math.R., Ref.Zh.

AICHI KYOIKU DAIGAKU KENKYU HOKOKU. SHIZEN KAGAKU/AICHI UNIVERSITY OF EDUCATION. NATURAL SCIENCE BULLETIN. see *SCIENCES: COMPREHENSIVE WORKS*

510 PL ISSN 0860-2727
AKADEMIA GORNICZO-HUTNICZA IM. STANISLAWA STASZICA. ZESZYTY NAUKOWE. OPUSCULA MATHEMATICA. (Text in English; summaries in Polish) 1985. irreg., no.11, 1991. price varies. Wydawnictwo A G H, Al. Mickiewicza 30, paw. B-5, 30-059 Krakow, Poland. (Dist. by: Ars Polona, Krakowskie Przedmiescie 7, 00-068 Warsaw, Poland) Ed. Z. Kleczek. illus.; circ. 300.

510 PL ISSN 0137-169X
AKADEMIA ROLNICZA, POZNAN. ROCZNIKI. ALGORYTMY BIOMETRYCZNE I STATYSTYCZNE. (Text in Polish; summaries in English, Russian) 1972. irreg. price varies. Akademia Rolnicza, Poznan, Ul. Wojska Polskiego 28, 60-637 Poznan, Poland. FAX 68-414-110-22. TELEX 04-33-22. Indexed: Bibl.Agri.
Description: Publications on procedures and programmes employing biometric methods, one-multidimensional methods for statistical concluding on the basis of experimental results.

510 530 GW
AKADEMIE DER WISSENSCHAFTEN IN GOETTINGEN. ABHANDLUNGEN. MATHEMATISCH-PHYSIKALISCHE KLASSE. DRITTE FOLGE. 1937. irreg. Vandenhoeck und Ruprecht, Robert-Bosch-Breite 6, Postfach 3753, 3400 Goettingen, Germany.
TEL 0551-6959-0. FAX 0551-695917. Ed.Bd. (reprint service avail. from KTO)

510 GW
AKADEMIE DER WISSENSCHAFTEN IN GOETTINGEN. ABHANDLUNGEN. MATHEMATISCH-PHYSIKALISCHE KLASSE. DRITTE FOLGE SONDERHEFTE. 1951. irreg. Vandenhoeck und Ruprecht, Robert-Bosch-Breite 6, Postfach 3753, 3753 Goettingen, Germany.
TEL 0551-6959-0. FAX 0551-695917. Ed.Bd. (reprint service avail. from KTO)

510 530 GW ISSN 0065-5295
AS182 CODEN: NAAKA5
AKADEMIE DER WISSENSCHAFTEN IN GOETTINGEN. NACHRICHTEN 2. MATHEMATISCH-PHYSIKALISCHE KLASSE. (Text in English, German; occasionally in French) 1893. irreg. price varies. Vandenhoeck und Ruprecht, Robert-Bosch-Breite 6, Postfach 37 53, 3400 Goettingen, Germany. TEL 0551-6959-0. FAX 0551-695917. index. (reprint service avail. from KTO) Indexed: GeoRef, Math.R.
—BLDSC shelfmark: 6001.950000.

510 AI ISSN 0002-3043
CODEN: IZMAAJ
AKADEMIYA NAUK ARMYANSKOI S.S.R. IZVESTIYA. SERIYA MATEMATIKA. English translation: Soviet Journal of Contemporary Mathematical Analysis (US ISSN 0735-2719) (Text in Russian; summaries in Armenian) 1965. bi-m. 13.20 Rub. Akademiya Nauk Armyanskoi S.S.R., Ul. Barekamutian, 24, Erevan, Armenia. index. Indexed: Math.R., World Alum.Abstr.

510 AJ ISSN 0002-3078
CODEN: DAZRA7
AKADEMIYA NAUK AZERBAIDZHANSKOI S.S.R. DOKLADY. (Text in Azerbaijani and Russian) 1945. m. 22.20 Rub. Izdatel'stvo Elm, Ul. Narimanova, 31, Baku 370073, Azerbaijan. (Subscr. to: Mezhdunarodnaya Kniga, Moscow, G-200, Russia) Ed. G. Abdullaev. charts; illus.; index; circ. 770. Indexed: Biol.Abstr., Chem.Abstr., Dairy Sci.Abstr., Field Crop Abstr., GeoRef, Hort.Abstr., INIS Atomind., Math.R., Met.Abstr., Seed Abstr., Soils & Fert., Triticale Abstr., Vet.Bull., World Alum.Abstr.
—BLDSC shelfmark: 0053.400000.

AKADEMIYA NAUK AZERBAIDZHANSKOI S.S.R. IZVESTIYA. SERIYA FIZIKO-TEKHNICHESKIKH I MATEMATICHESKIKH NAUK. see *PHYSICS*

AKADEMIYA NAUK KAZAKHSKOI S.S.R. IZVESTIYA. SERIYA FIZIKO - MATEMATICHESKAYA. see *PHYSICS*

AKADEMIYA NAUK MOLDAVSKOI S.S.R. IZVESTIYA. SERIYA FIZIKO-TEKHNICHESKIKH I MATEMATICHESKIKH NAUK. see *PHYSICS*

510 RU ISSN 0002-3361
AKADEMIYA NAUK S.S.S.R. IZVESTIYA. SERIYA MATEMATICHESKAYA. 1937. bi-m. 57.60 Rub. Izdatel'stvo Nauka, Fizmatlit, Leninskii prospekt, 15, 117071 Moscow, V-71, Russia. (Subscr. to: Mezhdunarodnaya Kniga, ul. Dimitrova D.39, 113095 Moscow, Russia) Ed. I.M. Vinogradov. bibl.; index; cum.index: vol.1-20 (in 2 vols.); circ. 2,135. Indexed: Comput.Rev., INIS Atomind., Math.R.

500 TK ISSN 0002-3469
AS581 CODEN: DANTAL
AKADEMIYA NAUK TADZHIKSKOI S.S.R. DOKLADY. (Text in Russian; titles of papers in English; summaries in Tadzhik) 1951. m. 30.60 Rub. Akademiya Nauk Tadzhikskoi S.S.R., Ul. Aym, 121, Dushanbe, Tajikistan. Ed. K.T. Poroshin. illus.; index; circ. 700. Indexed: Biol.Abstr., Chem.Abstr., Cott.& Trop.Fibr.Abstr., Crop Physiol.Abstr., Field Crop Abstr., GeoRef, INIS Atomind., Math.R., Met.Abstr., Triticale Abstr., World Alum.Abstr.
—BLDSC shelfmark: 0054.050000.

AKADEMIYA NAUK TADZHIKSKOI S.S.R. IZVESTIYA. OTDELENIE FIZIKO-MATEMATICHESKIKH I GEOLOGO-KHIMICHESKIKH NAUK. see *PHYSICS*

AKADEMIYA NAUK UKRAINSKOI S.S.R. DOKLADY. SERIYA A. FIZIKO-MATEMATICHESKIE I TEKHNICHESKIE NAUKI; nauchnyi zhurnal. see *PHYSICS*

AKADEMIYA NAUK UZBEKSKOI S.S.R. IZVESTIYA. SERIYA FIZIKO-MATEMATICHESKIKH NAUK. see *PHYSICS*

AKADEMIYA NAVUK BELARUSSKAI S.S.R. VESTSI. SERIYA FIZIKA-MATEMATYCHNYKH NAVUK. see *PHYSICS*

510 JA
AKITA DAIGAKU KYOIKUGAKUBU KENKYU KIYO/AKITA UNIVERSITY. COLLEGE OF EDUCATION. MEMOIRS. (Text in English and Japanese) 1950. a. Akita University, College of Education - Akita Daigaku Kyoikugakubu, 1-1, Tegata Gakuen-machi, Akita-shi, Akita-ken 010, Japan.
Formerly (until 1987): Akita University. Faculty of Education. Memoirs (ISSN 0365-1649)

512 511 US ISSN 0002-5232
QH150 CODEN: ALLOA6
ALGEBRA AND LOGIC. English translation of: Algebra i Logika. 1968. bi-m. $765 (foreign $895)(effective 1992). (Russian Academy of Sciences, RU) Plenum Publishing Corp., Consultants Bureau, 233 Spring St., New York, NY 10013-1578.
TEL 212-620-8468. FAX 212-463-0742. TELEX 23-421139. Ed. Yu.L. Ershov. (also avail. in microfilm from JSC) Indexed: Comput.& Info.Sys., Math.R., Zent.Math.
—BLDSC shelfmark: 0404.620000.
Refereed Serial

510 RU ISSN 0234-0852
ALGEBRA I ANALIZ. 1989. 6/yr. 2.30 Rub. per issue. (Akademiya Nauk S.S.S.R., Otdelenie Matematiki) Izdatel'stvo Nauka, Leningradskoe Otdelenie, Mendeleevskaya liniya 1, 199034 St. Petersburg B-34, Russia. TEL 218-36-12. Ed. D.K. Fadeev. circ. 972.
—BLDSC shelfmark: 0006.315000.

510 UK ISSN 1041-5394
ALGEBRA, LOGIC AND APPLICATIONS. 1989. s-m. Gordon & Breach Science Publishers, P.O. Box 90, Reading, Berkshire RG1 8JL, England. TEL 0734-560-080. FAX 0734-568-211. TELEX 849870 SCIPUB G. (US addr.: Box 786, Cooper Sta., New York, NY 10276. TEL 212-206-8900) Eds. R. Gobel, A. MacIntyre. (also avail. in microfilm; microfiche)
—BLDSC shelfmark: 0787.107000.
Refereed Serial

512 SZ ISSN 0002-5240
QA251 CODEN: AGUVA9
ALGEBRA UNIVERSALIS. (Text mainly in English) 1971. 4/yr. 358 Fr.($244) (University of Manitoba, CN) Birkhaeuser Verlag, P.O. Box 133, CH-4010 Basel, Switzerland. TEL 061-737740. FAX 061-737950. TELEX 963475 BIRKH CH. (Dist. in N. America by: Springer-Verlag New York, Inc., Journal Fulfillment Services, Box 2485, Secaucus, NJ 07096-2491, USA. TEL 201-348-4033) Ed.Bd. adv.; index. Indexed: Compumath, Math.R.

M

MATHEMATICS

510   YU
ALGEBRAIC CONFERENCE. PROCEEDINGS. 1980. irreg. $25. Institut za Matematiku, Prirodno-Matematicki Fakultet, Ul. Dr. Ilije Duricica 4, 21000 Novi Sad, Yugoslavia. TEL 38-21-58-136.
FAX 38-21-350-458. (Subscr. to: "FORUM", Izvozno Odelenje, ul. Vojvode Misica 1, 21000 Novi Sad, Yugoslavia)

510   US
ALGORITHMS AND COMBINATORICS; study and research text. 1986. irreg., vol.8, 1989. price varies. Springer-Verlag, 175 Fifth Ave., New York, NY 10010. TEL 212-460-1500. (Also: Berlin, Heidelberg, Tokyo, Vienna) (reprint service avail. from ISI)

510 530   HU   ISSN 0133-3399
QA1   CODEN: AMLAD8
ALKALMAZOTT MATEMATIKAI LAPOK. 1951. q. $12. (Magyar Tudomanyos Akademia, Matematikai es Fizikai Tudomanyok Osztalya) Akademiai Kiado, Publishing House of the Hungarian Academy of Sciences, P.O. Box 24, H-1363 Budapest, Hungary. Ed. K. Tandori. adv.; bk.rev.; index. **Indexed:** Appl.Mech.Rev., Chem.Abstr, Math.R., Sci.Abstr.
Formerly: Magyar Tudomanyos Akademia. Matematikai es Fizikai Tudomanyok Osztalya. Kozlemenyek (ISSN 0025-035X)

510 373   GW   ISSN 0002-6395
ALPHA-MATHEMATISCHE SCHUELERZEITSCHRIFT. 1967. bi-m. DM.15. Volk und Wissen Verlag GmbH, Lindenstr. 54A, 1086 Berlin, Germany. TEL 0372-20343-0. Ed. Johannes Lehmann. abstr.

510 310   US   ISSN 0196-6324
T55.4   CODEN: AMMSDX
AMERICAN JOURNAL OF MATHEMATICAL AND MANAGEMENT SCIENCES. 1981. q. $215. American Sciences Press, Inc., 20 Cross Rd., Syracuse, NY 13224-2144. Ed. Edward J. Dudewicz. adv.; bk.rev.; charts; illus.; stat.; index. (back issues avail.) **Indexed:** Biostat., Curr.Cont., Curr.Ind.Stat., Int.Abstr.Oper.Res., J.Cont.Quant.Meth., Math.R., Oper.Res.Manage.Sci., Qual.Contr.Appl.Stat, Ref.Zh., Stat.Theor.Meth.Abstr.
—BLDSC shelfmark: 0826.980000.
Description: Focuses on new work in the various areas of the mathematical and management sciences.

510   US   ISSN 0002-9327
QA1   CODEN: AJMAAN
AMERICAN JOURNAL OF MATHEMATICS. 1878. 6/yr. $52 to individuals (foreign $62.70); institutions $150 (foreign $159.70). Johns Hopkins University Press, Journals Publishing Division, 701 W. 40th St., Ste. 275, Baltimore, MD 21211.
TEL 410-516-6980. FAX 410-516-6998. Eds. Jun-Ichi Igusa, J.H. Sampson. adv.; bibl.; index; circ. 1,437. (also avail. in microform from UMI,PMC; back issues avail.; reprint service avail. from KTO,UMI) **Indexed:** Compumath, Curr.Cont., Ind.Sci.Rev., Math.R., Sci.Cit.Ind, SSCI.
—BLDSC shelfmark: 0827.000000.
Description: Presents pioneering work in applied and pure mathematics.

510   US   ISSN 0002-9890
QA1   CODEN: AMMYAE
AMERICAN MATHEMATICAL MONTHLY. 1894. 10/yr. $128. Mathematical Association of America, 1529 Eighteenth St., N.W., Washington, DC 20036. TEL 202-387-5200. Ed. Herbert Wilf. adv.; bk.rev.; index. cum.index: vols. 1-80; circ. 20,000. (also avail. in microfiche from UMI; reprint service avail. from UMI) **Indexed:** Biol.Abstr., C.I.J.E, Compumath, Curr.Cont., Gen.Sci.Ind., Ind.Sci.Rev., INIS Atomind., Math.R., Sci.Cit.Ind.
—BLDSC shelfmark: 0842.000000.
Description: Expository articles on all components of mathematics, pure and applied, old and new, with regular columns devoted to basic and complex problems and reviews.

510   US   ISSN 0192-5857
QA1
AMERICAN MATHEMATICAL SOCIETY. ABSTRACTS OF PAPERS PRESENTED.. 1979. 6/yr. $62 to non-members. American Mathematical Society, Box 1571, Annex Sta., Providence, RI 02901-9930. TEL 401-455-4000. circ. 4,400. **Indexed:** Math.R.
—BLDSC shelfmark: 0566.010000.
Refereed Serial

510   US   ISSN 0273-0979
QA1
AMERICAN MATHEMATICAL SOCIETY. BULLETIN. NEW SERIES. 1894; N.S. 1979. 4/yr. $202 (individual members $121; institutional members $162). American Mathematical Society, Box 1571, Annex Sta., Providence, RI 02901-9930.
TEL 401-455-4000. Ed. Edgar Lee Stout. bk.rev.; abstr.; cum.index vols. 71-84 (1965-1978) in 8 vols.; circ. 27,000. (also avail. in microfiche from UMI; microfilm from PMC) **Indexed:** Compumath, Curr.Cont., Ind.Sci.Rev., INIS Atomind., Math.R., Sci.Cit.Ind.
Supersedes: American Mathematical Society. Bulletin. (ISSN 0002-9904)
Description: Contains expository articles, book reviews and research announcements.
Refereed Serial

510   US   ISSN 0160-7642
QA1
AMERICAN MATHEMATICAL SOCIETY. C B M S REGIONAL CONFERENCE SERIES IN MATHEMATICS. 1970. irreg. price varies. American Mathematical Society, Box 1571, Annex Sta., Providence, RI 02901-9930. TEL 401-455-4000.
—BLDSC shelfmark: 7336.580000.
Refereed Serial

510   US   ISSN 0065-9258
AMERICAN MATHEMATICAL SOCIETY. COLLOQUIUM PUBLICATIONS. 1905. irreg. price varies. American Mathematical Society, Box 1571, Annex Sta., Providence, RI 02901-9930. TEL 401-455-4000. index in each vol. **Indexed:** Math.R., Zent.Math.
—BLDSC shelfmark: 3316.200000.
Refereed Serial

510   US   ISSN 0894-0347
QA1
AMERICAN MATHEMATICAL SOCIETY. JOURNAL. 1988. 4/yr. $136 to non-members; individual members $82; institutional members $109. American Mathematical Society, Box 1571, Annex Sta., Providence, RI 02901-9930. TEL 401-455-4000. circ. 1,000. **Indexed:** Math.R.
—BLDSC shelfmark: 4688.200000.
Refereed Serial

510   US   ISSN 0065-9266
QA3   CODEN: MAMCAU
AMERICAN MATHEMATICAL SOCIETY. MEMOIRS. 1950; N.S. 1975. bi-m. $292 non-members; institutional members $234. American Mathematical Society, Box 1571, Annex Sta., Providence, RI 02901-9930. TEL 401-455-4000. circ. 1,200. **Indexed:** Compumath, Math.R., Zent.Math.
—BLDSC shelfmark: 5577.000000.
Description: Devoted to research in pure and applied mathematics.

510   US   ISSN 0002-9920
CODEN: AMNOAN
AMERICAN MATHEMATICAL SOCIETY. NOTICES. 1953. 10/yr. $131 to non-members; individual members $79; institutional members $105. American Mathematical Society, Box 1571, Annex Sta., Providence, RI 02901-9930. TEL 401-455-4000. Ed. James A. Voytuk. index; circ. 28,000. (also avail. in microform from UMI; reprint service avail. from UMI) **Indexed:** Comput.Rev., Math.R.
—BLDSC shelfmark: 6170.500000.

510   US   ISSN 0002-9939
QA1   CODEN: PAMYAR
AMERICAN MATHEMATICAL SOCIETY. PROCEEDINGS. 1950. m. $508 to non-members; individual members $305; institutional members $406. American Mathematical Society, Box 1571, Annex Sta., Providence, RI 02901-9930.
TEL 401-455-4000. Ed. Paul S. Muhly. index; 10-yr. cum.index; circ. 1,900. (also avail. in microfiche from AMS) **Indexed:** Compumath, Curr.Cont., Math.R.
—BLDSC shelfmark: 6627.000000.

510   US   ISSN 0082-0717
AMERICAN MATHEMATICAL SOCIETY. PROCEEDINGS OF SYMPOSIA IN PURE MATHEMATICS. 1959. irreg. price varies. American Mathematical Society, Box 1571, Annex Sta., Providence, RI 02901-9930. TEL 401-455-4000. **Indexed:** Compumath.
—BLDSC shelfmark: 6849.620000.

510   US   ISSN 0160-7634
AMERICAN MATHEMATICAL SOCIETY. SYMPOSIA IN APPLIED MATHEMATICS. PROCEEDINGS. irreg. price varies. American Mathematical Society, Box 1517, Annex Sta., Providence, RI 02901-9930. TEL 401-455-4000.
—BLDSC shelfmark: 6849.440000.
Refereed Serial

510   US   ISSN 0002-9947
QA1   CODEN: TAMTAM
AMERICAN MATHEMATICAL SOCIETY. TRANSACTIONS. 1900. m. $842 to non-members; institutional members $674. American Mathematical Society, Box 1571, Annex Sta., Providence, RI 02901-9930. TEL 401-455-4000. Ed. Lance W. Small. bibl.; index; circ. 1,700. (also avail. in microform from UMI,PMC) **Indexed:** Compumath, Curr.Cont., Eng.Ind., Math.R.
—BLDSC shelfmark: 8892.000000.
Description: Devoted to research in pure and applied mathematics.
Refereed Serial

510   US   ISSN 0065-9290
QA3
AMERICAN MATHEMATICAL SOCIETY. TRANSLATIONS. SERIES 2. (Supersedes Series 1) 1955. irreg. price varies. American Mathematical Society, Box 6248, Providence, RI 02901-9930. TEL 401-455-4000. Ed. Ben Silver. cum.index: 1966-1973.
—BLDSC shelfmark: 0842.250000.

510   GW   ISSN 0174-4747
ANALYSIS; international mathematical journal of analysis and its applications. (Text in English) 1981. q. DM.258. R. Oldenbourg Verlag GmbH, Rosenheimerstr. 145, Postfach 801360, 8000 Munich 80, Germany. Ed.Bd. adv. (back issues avail.)
Description: Publication devoted to original research and survey articles in the field of classical analysis and its applications, and analytic number theories.

510   HU   ISSN 0133-3852
QA300   CODEN: ANMADK
ANALYSIS MATHEMATICA. (Text in English and Russian) 1975. q. $230. (Magyar Tudomanyos Akademia) Akademiai Kiado, Publishing House of the Hungarian Academy of Sciences, P.O. Box 24, H-1363 Budapest, Hungary. (Dist. in Western countries by: Pergamon Press, Inc., Maxwell House, Fairview Park, Elmsford, NY 10523 USA. TEL 914-592-7700) (Co-sponsor: Akademiya Nauk S.S.S.R., (UR)) Eds. S.M. Nikolsky, B. Szokefalvi-Nagy. (also avail. in microform from MIM) **Indexed:** Math.R., Sci.Abstr.

510   FI   ISSN 0066-1953
QA1   CODEN: AAFMAT
ANNALES ACADEMIAE SCIENTIARUM FENNICAE. SERIES A, I: MATHEMATICA. (Text in English, French, German) 1941. a. $60. Suomalainen Tiedeakatemia - Academia Scientiarum Fennica, Mariankatu 5, 00170 Helsinki, Finland. (Orders to: The Bookstore Tiedekirja, Kirkkokatu 14, SF-00170 Helsinki, Finland) Ed. Olli Lehto. index, cum.index: 1941-1967 in vol. 400; 1967-1975 in vol. 600; circ. 725. (also avail. in microform; back issues avail.; reprint service avail. from UMI) **Indexed:** Bull.Signal., Compumath, Math.R., Phys.Abstr., Ref.Zh., Sci.Abstr, Sci.Cit.Ind., Zent.Math.
—BLDSC shelfmark: 0914.390000.

510   FI   ISSN 0355-0087
QA1   CODEN: AAFMAT
ANNALES ACADEMIAE SCIENTIARUM FENNICAE. SERIES A, I: MATHEMATICA DISSERTATIONES. (Text in English, French and German) 1975. irreg. price varies. Suomalainen Tiedeakatemia - Academia Scientiarum Fennica, Mariankatu 5, 00170 Helsinki, Finland. (Orders to: Bookstore Tiedekirja, Kirkkokatu 14, SF-00170 Helsinki) Ed. Olli Lehto. circ. 725. (also avail. in microform; back issues avail.; reprint service avail. from UMI) **Indexed:** Bull.Signal., Math.R., Phys.Abstr., Ref.Zh., Sci.Cit.Ind., Zent.Math.

510   PL   ISSN 0066-2216
QA1   CODEN: APNMA4
ANNALES POLONICI MATHEMATICI. (Text in various languages) 1954. irreg., vol.51, 1990. $45 per vol. (Polska Akademia Nauk, Instytut Matematyczny) Panstwowe Wydawnictwo Naukowe, Ul. Miodowa 10, 00-251 Warsaw, Poland. (Dist. by: Ars Polona, Krakowskie Przedmiescie 7, 00-068 Warsaw, Poland) Eds. Jozef Siciak, St. Lojasiewicz. bibl. (reprint service avail. from SWZ) **Indexed:** Math.R.
—BLDSC shelfmark: 0993.500000.

510   PL   ISSN 0032-3799
ANNALES SOCIETATIS MATHEMATICAE POLONAE. SERIA 1: COMMENTATIONES MATHEMATICAE. (Text in English, French and German) 1955. s-a. price varies. Polskie Towarzystwo Matematyczne, Ul. Sniadeckich 8, 00-950 Warsaw, Poland. Eds. W. Orlicz & J. Musielak. bibl.; circ. 2,300. **Indexed:** Math.R.
Formerly: Polskie Towarzystwo Matematyczne. Prace. Matematyczne.

510   PL
ANNALES SOCIETATIS MATHEMATICAE POLONAE. SERIA 3: MATEMATYKA STOSOWANA. 1973. irreg. (3-4/yr.). 24 Zl. Polskie Towarzystwo Matematyczne, Ul. Sniadeckich 8, 00-950 Warsaw, Poland. Ed. Robert Bartoszynski. circ. 1,300. **Indexed:** Math.R.
Formerly: Polskie Towarzystwo Matematyczne. Roczniki. Seria 3: Matematyka Stosowana.

510   PL   ISSN 0365-1029
QA1.L8   CODEN: ACAMAI
ANNALES UNIVERSITATIS MARIAE CURIE-SKLODOWSKA. SECTIO A. MATHEMATICA. (Text in English, French, German, Polish) 1946. a. price varies. Uniwersytet Marii Curie-Sklodowskiej, Wydawnictwo, Pl. M. Curie-Sklodowskiej 5, 20-031 Lublin, Poland. TEL 48-81-375304. FAX 48-81-336699. TELEX 0643223. Eds. J. Krzyz, A. Bielecki. circ. 650. **Indexed:** Math.R.
—BLDSC shelfmark: 0956.000000.

510   IT   ISSN 0003-4622
ANNALI DI MATEMATICA; pura ed applicata. (Text in English, French, German and Italian) 1850. irreg. (approx. 2-4/yr.). L.50000 per no. Nicola Zanichelli Editore, Via Irnerio 34, Bologna 40126, Italy. TEL 051-293-111. FAX 051-249-782. bibl.; charts; circ. 700. (reprint service avail. from SWZ) **Indexed:** Math.R.

510   US   ISSN 1050-5164
QA273.A1
▼**ANNALS OF APPLIED PROBABILITY.** 1991. q. $70. Institute of Mathematical Statistics, Business Office, 3401 Investment Blvd., Ste. 7, Hayward, CA 94545. TEL 510-783-8141. Ed. J. Michael Steele.
—BLDSC shelfmark: 1038.190000.

510   NE
ANNALS OF DISCRETE MATHEMATICS. 1977. irreg., vol.50, 1991. price varies. Elsevier Science Publishers B.V., Books Division, P.O. Box 211, 1000 AE Amsterdam, Netherlands. TEL 020-5803911. FAX 020-5803705. TELEX 18582 ESPA NL. (Subscr. in U.S. and Canada to: Elsevier Science Publishing Co., Inc., Box 882, Madison Sq. Sta., New York, NY 10159. TEL 212-989-5800) (also avail. in microform from RPI) **Indexed:** Comput.Rev., Int.Abstr.Oper.Res., Math R, Zent.Math.
Refereed Serial

510   GW   ISSN 0232-704X
ANNALS OF GLOBAL ANALYSIS AND GEOMETRY. 3/yr. $161.50. VEB Deutscher Verlag der Wissenschaften, Johannes-Dieckmann-Str. 10, 1080 Berlin, Germany. (Dist. by: Kluwer Academic Publishers Group, P.O. Box 322, 3300 AH Dordrecht, Netherlands) Eds. Th. Friedrich, R. Sulanke. (reprint service avail. from SWZ)

510   US   ISSN 0003-486X
QA1   CODEN: ANMAAH
ANNALS OF MATHEMATICS. 1884. bi-m. $60 for individuals; institutions $180. (Princeton University) Johns Hopkins University Press, Journals Publishing Division, 701 W. 40th St., Ste. 275, Baltimore, MD 21211. TEL 410-516-6980. FAX 410-516-6998. (Co-sponsor: Institute for Advanced Study) Ed.Bd. charts; index; circ. 1,585. (also avail. in microform from UMI,PMC; reprint service avail. from KTO,UMI) **Indexed:** Compumath, Curr.Cont., Ind.Sci.Rev., Math.R.
—BLDSC shelfmark: 1043.000000.

ANNALS OF MATHEMATICS AND ARTIFICIAL INTELLIGENCE. see COMPUTERS — *Artificial Intelligence*

510   US
ANNALS OF MATHEMATICS STUDIES. irreg., no.124, 1990. price varies. Princeton University Press, 3175 Princeton Pike, Lawrenceville, NJ 08648. TEL 609-896-1344. FAX 609-895-1081. (reprint service avail. from KTO) **Indexed:** Compumath, Math.R.

510   US   ISSN 0091-1798
HA1   CODEN: APBYAE
ANNALS OF PROBABILITY. 1973. q. $18. Institute of Mathematical Statistics, Business Office, 3401 Investment Blvd., Ste. 7, Hayward, CA 94545. TEL 510-783-8141. Ed. Burgess Davis. adv.; circ. 3,100. (also avail. in microfilm from UMI) **Indexed:** Biostat., Compumath, Curr.Cont., Curr.Ind.Stat., Ind.Sci.Rev., J.Cont.Quant.Meth., Math.R., Oper.Res.Manage.Sci., Qual.Contr.Appl.Stat., Sci.Cit.Ind.
—BLDSC shelfmark: 1043.550000.
Refereed Serial

511.3 160   NE   ISSN 0168-0072
QA1   CODEN: APALD7
ANNALS OF PURE AND APPLIED LOGIC. (Text in English) 1969. 15/yr.(in 5 vols.; 3 nos./vol.). fl.1680 (effective 1992). (Association for Symbolic Logic) North-Holland (Subsidiary of: Elsevier Science Publishers B.V.), P.O. Box 211, 1000 AE Amsterdam, Netherlands. TEL 020-5803911. FAX 020-5803598. TELEX 18582 ESPA NL. (Subscr. in U.S. and Canada to: Elsevier Science Publishing Co., Inc., Box 882, Madison Sq. Sta., New York, NY 10159. TEL 212-989-5800) Ed. D.O. van Dalen. adv.; circ. 700. (also avail. in microform from RPI; back issues avail.; reprint service avail. from SWZ) **Indexed:** Compumath, Math R., Phil.Ind., Sci.Abstr.
Formerly (until 1983): Annals of Mathematical Logic (ISSN 0003-4843)
Description: Publishes papers and short monographs on topics of current interest in pure and applied logic.
Refereed Serial

APERIODICITY AND ORDER. see *PHYSICS*

510   US   ISSN 0003-6811
QA300   CODEN: APANCC
APPLICABLE ANALYSIS; an international journal. 1970. 16/yr. (in 4 vols., 4 nos./yr.). $263. Gordon and Breach Science Publishers, 270 Eighth Ave., New York, NY 10011. TEL 212-206-8900. FAX 212-645-2459. TELEX 236735 GOPUB UR. (Subscr. to: Box 786, Cooper Sta., New York, NY 10276. TEL 800-545-8398; UK subscr. to: P.O. Box 90, Reading, Berkshire RG1 8JL, England. TEL 0734-560-080) Ed. Robert P. Gilbert. adv.; index. (also avail. in microform from MIM) **Indexed:** Appl.Mech.Rev., Compumath, Math.R., Sci.Abstr.
—BLDSC shelfmark: 1570.450000.
Refereed Serial

519   US   ISSN 0862-7940
QA1   CODEN: APMTEO
APPLICATIONS OF MATHEMATICS. (Text and summaries in Czech, English, French, German, Russian, Slovak) 1956. bi-m. $415 (foreign $485)(effective 1992). (Czechoslovak Academy of Sciences, Mathematical Institute, CS) Plenum Publishing Corp., 233 Spring St., New York, NY 10013-1578. TEL 212-620-8000. FAX 212-463-0742. TELEX 23-421139. (Co-publisher: Academia, CS) Ed. Zbynek Sidak. bk.rev.; abstr.; bibl.; charts; illus.; index; circ. 1,150. **Indexed:** Appl.Mech.Rev., Comput.Rev., Math.R., Sci.Abstr.
—BLDSC shelfmark: 1571.172000.
Former titles (until 1991): Aplikace Matematiky - Applied Mathematics (ISSN 0373-6725); Aplikace Matematiky (ISSN 0003-6501)
Description: Papers dealing with the application of mathematics and computer algorithms in all branches of science, particularly in the technical sciences.

510   US   ISSN 0172-4568
             CODEN: APMADY
APPLICATIONS OF MATHEMATICS. 1975. irreg., vol.21, 1990. price varies. Springer-Verlag, 175 Fifth Ave., New York, NY 10010. TEL 212-460-1500. (Also: Berlin, Heidelberg, Tokyo and Vienna) Eds. A.V. Balakrishnan, W. Hildenbrand. (reprint service avail. from ISI) **Indexed:** Math.R.

510   US   ISSN 0066-5452
QA1   CODEN: AMSCDF
APPLIED MATHEMATICAL SCIENCES. (Text in English) 1972. irreg., vol.84, 1980. price varies. Springer-Verlag, 175 Fifth Ave., New York, NY 10010. TEL 212-460-2500. (Also: Berlin, Heidelberg, Tokyo and Vienna) (reprint service avail. from ISI) **Indexed:** Math.R.

510   UK   ISSN 0888-479X
APPLIED MATHEMATICS. 1987. irreg., latest vol.1. Gordon & Breach Science Publishers, P.O. Box 90, Reading, Berkshire RG1 8JL, England. TEL 0734-560-080. FAX 0734-568-211. TELEX 849870 SCIPUB G. (US addr.: Box 786, Cooper Sta., New York, NY 10276. TEL 212-206-8900) Ed. M. Blanc. (also avail. in microfilm; microfiche)
Refereed Serial

510   US   ISSN 0096-3003
QA1   CODEN: AMHCBQ
APPLIED MATHEMATICS AND COMPUTATION. 1975. 18/yr.(in 6 vols.; 3 nos./vol.). $876 (foreign $939)(effective 1992). Elsevier Science Publishing Co., Inc. (New York), 655 Ave. of the Americas, New York, NY 10010. TEL 212-989-5800. FAX 212-633-3965. TELEX 420643 AEP UI. Eds. John L. Casti, Melvin Scott. (also avail. in microform from RPI; reprint service avail. from SWZ) **Indexed:** Appl.Mech.Rev., Biol.Abstr., CAD CAM Abstr., Compumath, Comput.Cont., Comput Dtbs., Curr.Cont., Ind.Sci.Rev., Math.R., Robomat., Sci.Abstr., Sci.Cit.Ind.
—BLDSC shelfmark: 1573.731000.
Description: Addresses work at the interface between applied mathematics, numerical computation, and applications of systems-oriented ideas to the physical, biological, social, and behavioral sciences.
Refereed Serial

510 531   US   ISSN 0066-5479
APPLIED MATHEMATICS AND MECHANICS; an international series of monographs. vol.2, 1957. irreg., vol.18, 1986. Academic Press, Inc., 1250 Sixth Ave., San Diego, CA 92101. TEL 619-231-0926. FAX 619-699-6715. Eds. F.N. Frenkiel, G. Temple. (reprint service avail. from ISI) **Indexed:** Appl.Mech.Rev., Math.R., Sci.Abstr.
Refereed Serial

510 531   SZ   ISSN 0253-4827
QA1   CODEN: AMMEEQ
APPLIED MATHEMATICS AND MECHANICS. (Text in English) 1980. m. 769 Fr. J.C. Baltzer AG, Scientific Publishing Company, Wettsteinplatz 10, CH-4508 Basel, Switzerland. TEL 061-6918925. FAX 061-6924262. Ed. Chien Wei-zang. **Indexed:** Sci.Abstr.
—BLDSC shelfmark: 1573.747000.

510   US   ISSN 0095-4616
QA402.5   CODEN: AMOMBN
APPLIED MATHEMATICS AND OPTIMIZATION; an international journal. (Text mainly in English) 1974. 6/yr. $260. Springer-Verlag, Journals, 175 Fifth Ave., New York, NY 10010. TEL 212-460-1500. (Also Berlin, Heidelberg, Tokyo and Vienna) Ed. G. Kallianpur. (also avail. in microform from UMI; reprint service avail. from ISI) **Indexed:** Compumath, Curr.Cont., Eng.Ind., Ind.Sci.Rev., Math.R., Sci.Cit.Ind, Zent.Math.
—BLDSC shelfmark: 1573.800000.

510   US   ISSN 0893-9659
QA1   CODEN: AMLEEL
APPLIED MATHEMATICS LETTERS; an international journal of rapid publication. 1988. 6/yr. £195 (effective 1992). Pergamon Press, Inc., Journals Division, 660 White Plains Rd., Tarrytown, NY 10591-5153. TEL 914-524-9200. FAX 914-333-2444. (And: Headington Hill Hall, Oxford OX3 0BW, England. TEL 0865-794141) Ed. Ervin Y. Rodin. (also avail. in microform; back issues avail.) **Indexed:** Biostat.
—BLDSC shelfmark: 1573.880000.
Description: Provides a forum for short articles and research announcements.
Refereed Serial

MATHEMATICS

510   AT
APPLIED MATHEMATICS PROBLEMS. a. Aus.$39.95. Mathematical Association of South Australia, 163a Greenhill Rd., Parkside, S.A. 5066, Australia. TEL 8-3624332. FAX 8-3629288.
Description: A collection of problems generated and implemented at senior secondary level in Australian schools.

510   UK   ISSN 8755-0024
QA274.A1   CODEN: ASMAEM
APPLIED STOCHASTIC MODELS AND DATA ANALYSIS. 1985. q. $275 (effective 1992). John Wiley & Sons Ltd., Journals, Baffins Lane, Chichester, Sussex PO19 1UD, England. TEL 0243 779777. FAX 0243-775878. TELEX 86290 WIBOOK G. Ed. J. Janssen. (reprint service avail. from SWZ) **Indexed:** Biostat., Curr.Cont., Oper.Res.Manage.Sci., Qual.Contr.Appl.Stat.
—BLDSC shelfmark: 1580.062000.
Description: Interfaces the theoretical aspects of applied probability and data analysis and their applications in the real world.

511.4   CC   ISSN 1000-9221
APPROXIMATION THEORY AND ITS APPLICATIONS/BIJINLUN; an international mathematics journal. Short title: A T A. (Text in English) 1984. q. $60 individuals; institutions $120. (Nanjing Daxue - Nanjing University) Nanjing Daxue Chubanshe - Nanjing University Press, Nanjing, Jiangsu 210008, People's Republic of China. (Co-sponsors: Beijing University; Huazhong University of Science and Technology) Eds. M.T. Cheng, C.K. Chui. circ. 500. (back issues avail.)
—BLDSC shelfmark: 1581.532000.
Description: Focuses on approximation and expansions, Fourier and harmonic analysis, numerical approximation and applications, as well as other related areas of research.

ARAB GULF JOURNAL OF SCIENTIFIC RESEARCH. see *SCIENCES: COMPREHENSIVE WORKS*

510 519   IT   ISSN 0003-8369
QA1
ARCHIMEDE; rivista per gli insegnanti e i cultori di matematiche pure e applicate. 1949. q. L.50000($50) (effective 1992). Editoriale e Finanziaria Le Monnier, S.p.a., Via A. Meucci 2, Casella Postale 202, 50100 Florence, Italy. Ed.Bd. bk.rev.; index; circ. 3,700. **Indexed:** Math.R.
—BLDSC shelfmark: 1597.500000.
Description: Covers various applications and didactic problems involved with the teaching of mathematics, articles include current issues in the field of mathematics and computers.

510   SZ   ISSN 0003-889X
QA1   CODEN: ACVMAL
ARCHIV DER MATHEMATIK/ARCHIVES OF MATHEMATICS/ARCHIVES MATHEMATIQUES. (Text in English and German) 1948. m. 764 Fr.($520) Birkhaeuser Verlag, P.O. Box 133, CH-4010 Basel, Switzerland. TEL 061-737740. FAX 061-737950. TELEX 963475 BIRKH CH. (Dist. in N. America by: Springer-Verlag New York, Inc., Journal Fulfillment Services, Box 2485, Secaucus, NJ 07096-2491, USA. TEL 201-348-4033) Ed. E. Lamprecht. adv.; charts; illus.; index. **Indexed:** Appl.Mech.Rev., Compumath, Curr.Cont., Ind.Sci.Rev., Math.R., Sci.Cit.Ind.
—BLDSC shelfmark: 1616.000000.

ARCHIVE FOR HISTORY OF EXACT SCIENCES. see *SCIENCES: COMPREHENSIVE WORKS*

511.3   GW   ISSN 0933-5846
QA9.A1   CODEN: AMLOEH
ARCHIVE FOR MATHEMATICAL LOGIC. (Text in English and German) 1950. s-a. DM.198. Springer-Verlag, Postfach 105280, 6900 Heidelberg, Germany. FAX 06221-43982. TELEX 461723. Ed.Bd. adv.; bibl.; charts; index. (also avail. in microform; reprint service avail. from KTO) **Indexed:** Math.R., Phil.Ind., Sci.Abstr.
—BLDSC shelfmark: 1637.415000.
Formerly (until 1987): Archiv fuer Mathematische Logik und Grundlagenforschung (ISSN 0003-9268)

510 530   GW   ISSN 0003-9527
QA801.A7   CODEN: AVRMAW
ARCHIVE FOR RATIONAL MECHANICS AND ANALYSIS. (Text in English, French, German, Italian or Latin) 1957. 20/yr. DM.1,890($827) Springer-Verlag, Heidelberger Platz 3, D-1000 Berlin 33, Germany. TEL 030-8207-1. Ed. A. Antman. adv.; bibl.; charts; index. (also avail. in microform from UMI; reprint service avail. from ISI) **Indexed:** Appl.Mech.Rev., Chem.Abstr., Compumath, Eng.Ind., Fluidex, Ind.Sci.Rev., INIS Atomind., Math.R., Phys.Ber., Sci.Abstr., Sci.Cit.Ind, Zent.Math.
—BLDSC shelfmark: 1640.650000.
Description: Covers the discipline of mechanics as a deductive, mathematical science. Promotes pure analysis, particularly in contexts of application of continuum mechanics, thermodynamics, non-linear phenomena, and dynamic systems.

510   CS   ISSN 0044-8753
QA1   CODEN: ARVMAO
ARCHIVUM MATHEMATICUM. (Text in English, French, German, Russian) 1965. q. 40 Kcs. exchange basis. Universita J. E. Purkyne, Janackovo Nam. 2a, 662 95 Brno, Czechoslovakia. Ed.Bd. circ. 500. **Indexed:** Math.R.

513 370   US   ISSN 0004-136X
QA135
ARITHMETIC TEACHER. 1954. m. (Sep.-May). $40 to individuals; institutions $45. National Council of Teachers of Mathematics, 1906 Association Dr., Reston, VA 22091. TEL 703-620-9840. FAX 703-476-2970. Ed. Harry B. Tunis. adv.; bk.rev.; bibl.; illus.; index. cum.index: 1954-1973; 1974-1983; circ. 51,470. (also avail. in microform from UMI,MIM; reprint service avail. from UMI) **Indexed:** Acad.Ind., Biog.Ind., C.I.J.E., Cont.Pg.Educ., Educ.Ind., Except.Child.Educ.Abstr., Jun.High.Mag.Abstr., LAMP, Media Rev.Dig.
—BLDSC shelfmark: 1668.427000.
Description: Articles, teaching ideas, and features of interest to teachers of mathematics in kindergarten through the middle grades.

510 536   FI   ISSN 0004-1920
    CODEN: AKMDA5
ARKHIMEDES. (Text in English, Finnish, Swedish; summaries in English) 1949. q. FIM 135. Suomen Fyysikkoseura - Finnish Physical Society, Siltavuorenpenger 20 M, SF-00170 Helsinki 17, Finland. (Co-sponsor: Finnish Mathematical Society) Ed. Risto Nieminen. adv.; bk.rev.; circ. 2,000. **Indexed:** Chem.Abstr., INIS Atomind., Math.R.
—BLDSC shelfmark: 1672.000000.

510   SW   ISSN 0004-2080
QA3   CODEN: AKMTAJ
ARKIV FOER MATEMATIK. (Text in English, French and German) 1952. 2/yr. $90. Institut Mittag-Leffler - Mittag-Leffler Institute, Auravaegen 17, S-182 62 Djursholm, Sweden. TEL 08-7551809. (also avail. in microfilm from PMC; back issues avail.; reprint service avail. from SWZ) **Indexed:** Compumath, Math.R., Sci.Abstr.
—BLDSC shelfmark: 1679.000000.
Formerly: Arkiv foer Matematik, Astronomi och Fysik.

510   CN   ISSN 0381-7032
    CODEN: ACOMDN
ARS COMBINATORIA. 1976. 2/yr. $56. Charles Babbage Research Centre, P.O. Box 272, St. Norbert Postal Station, Winnipeg, Man. R3V 1L6, Canada. (Co-sponsor: University of Waterloo, Faculty of Mathematics, Department of Combinatorics and Optimization) Ed. Dr. W.L. Kocay. circ. 400. **Indexed:** Compumath, Int.Abstr.Oper.Res., Math.R.
—BLDSC shelfmark: 1697.360000.

510   RU
ASIMPTOTICHESKIE METODY V TEORII SISTEM. 1971. irreg. 1 Rub. Irkutskii Gosudarstvennyi Universitet im. A.A. Zhdanova, Ul. Karla Marksa, 1, Irkutsk, Russia. Ed. A.N. Panchenkov. circ. 600.

ASSOCIATION FOR WOMEN IN MATHEMATICS. NEWSLETTER. see *WOMEN'S INTERESTS*

510   FR   ISSN 0303-1179
ASTERISQUE. (Text and summaries in English, French) 1973. m. 1155 F.($194) Societe Mathematique de France, Ecole Normale Superieure, Tour L, 1 rue Maurice Arnoux, 92120 Montrouge, France. TEL 1-40-84-80-54. FAX 1-40-84-80-52. (Dist. in North America by: A M S, Box 6248, Providence, RI 02940.) circ. 1,300. **Indexed:** Compumath, Math.R., Zent.Math.
—BLDSC shelfmark: 1747.045000.
Description: Covers the whole spectrum of mathematics.
Refereed Serial

510   NE   ISSN 0921-7134
    CODEN: ASANEZ
ASYMPTOTIC ANALYSIS. (Text in English, French) 1988. 6/yr. fl.436 (effective 1992). North-Holland (Subsidiary of: Elsevier Science Publishers B.V.), P.O. Box 211, 1000 AE Amsterdam, Netherlands. TEL 020-5803911. FAX 020-5803598. TELEX 18582 ESPA NL. (Subscr. in U.S. and Canada to: Elsevier Science Publishing Co., Inc., Box 882, Madison Sq. Sta., New York, NY 10159. TEL 212-989-5800) Ed. L.S. Frank. (back issues avail.)
—BLDSC shelfmark: 1765.335800.
Description: Original mathematical results in the asymptotic theory of problems.
Refereed Serial

510   AT   ISSN 0004-9727
QA1   CODEN: ALNBAB
AUSTRALIAN MATHEMATICAL SOCIETY. BULLETIN. 1969. 6/yr. Aus.$196($151) (effective 1992). Australian Mathematical Society, c/o Dept. of Mathematics, University of Queensland, Queensland, 4072, Australia. Ed. Dr. A.S. Jones. index. (back issues avail.) **Indexed:** Appl.Mech.Rev., Biol.Abstr., Compumath, INIS Atomind., Math.R, Sci.Abstr.
Description: Aims at quick publication of original research in all branches of mathematics.

510   AT   ISSN 0263-6115
    CODEN: JAMADS
AUSTRALIAN MATHEMATICAL SOCIETY. JOURNAL. SERIES A. PURE MATHEMATICS AND STATISTICS. 1959. 6/yr. Aus.$215($166) (effective 1992). Australian Mathematical Society, c/o Dept. of Mathematics, University of Queensland, Queensland, 4072, Australia. Ed. Dr. J.R.J. Groves. index. (also avail. in microfilm from PMC; back issues avail.) **Indexed:** Appl.Mech.Rev., Compumath, Math.R.
—BLDSC shelfmark: 4707.520500.
Formerly (until 1979): Australian Mathematical Society, Journal. Series A. Pure Mathematics (ISSN 0334-3316); Supersedes (in 1975): Australian Mathematical Society. Journal (ISSN 0004-9735)
Description: Publication of papers on pure mathematics and statistics.

510   AT   ISSN 0334-2700
    CODEN: JAMMDU
AUSTRALIAN MATHEMATICAL SOCIETY. JOURNAL. SERIES B. APPLIED MATHEMATICS. 1975. 4/yr. Aus.$131($101) (effective 1992). Australian Mathematical Society, c/o Dept. of Mathematics, University of Queensland, Queensland, 4072, Australia. Ed. E.O. Tuck. stat.; index. (back issues avail.) **Indexed:** Appl.Mech.Rev., Compumath, INIS Atomind., Math.R., Sci.Abstr.
—BLDSC shelfmark: 4707.521000.
Description: Publication of papers in any field of applied mathematics and related mathematical sciences, excluding statistics.

510   AT   ISSN 0311-0729
AUSTRALIAN MATHEMATICAL SOCIETY GAZETTE. 1974. 6/yr. Aus.$39($30) (effective 1992). Australian Mathematical Society, c/o Dept. of Mathematics, University of Queensland, Queensland, 4072, Australia. Ed. Dr. B. Sims. **Indexed:** Math.R.
—BLDSC shelfmark: 1814.145000.
Description: Carries news items, mathematical articles of general interest and articles on tertiary mathematical teaching.

BALSKRISHNAN - NEUSTADT SERIES. see *TECHNOLOGY: COMPREHENSIVE WORKS*

| 510 610 | US | ISSN 1045-5523 |
RA407
▼**BASIC AND CLINICAL BIOSTATISTICS.** 1990. 3/yr. $29.95. Appleton & Lange (Subsidiary of: Simon & Schuster Company), 25 Van Zant St., Box 5630, Norwalk, CT 06856. TEL 203-838-4400. Ed. Beth Dawson-Saunders.
   Description: Covers the study of statistics applied to medicine, including biostatistics and quantitative methods in epidemiology.

| 510 | JA | ISSN 0386-6319 |
BASIC SUGAKU. (Text in Japanese) 1969. m. Gendai Sugaku-sha, 1, Shishigatani Nishi-teranomae-cho, Sakyo-ku, Kyoto-shi, Kyoto-fu 606, Japan.

BAYERISCHE AKADEMIE DER WISSENSCHAFTEN. MATHEMATISCH-NATURWISSENSCHAFTLICHE KLASSE. SITZUNGBERICHTE. see *SCIENCES: COMPREHENSIVE WORKS*

| 510 | GW | ISSN 0138-4821 |
BEITRAEGE ZUR ALGEBRA UND GEOMETRIE. 1971. irregr. DM.25. VEB Deutscher Verlag der Wissenschaften, Postfach 1216, 1080 Berlin, Germany. Ed.Bd. **Indexed:** Math.R.

| 510 | PL | ISSN 0519-8356 |
BIBLIOTEKA MATEMATYCZNA. 1953. irreg., vol.40, 1980. Panstwowe Wydawnictwo Naukowe, Miodowa 10, 00-251 00-251 Warsaw, Poland. (Dist. by: Ars Polona, Krakowskie Przedmiescie 7, 00-068 Warsaw, Poland) bibl. **Indexed:** Math.R.

BIOMATHEMATICS. see *BIOLOGY*

BIOMETRICS. see *STATISTICS*

BLACKJACK FORUM. see *SPORTS AND GAMES*

| 510 | BL | |
BOLETIM DE ANALISE E LOGICA MATEMATICA. 1969. irreg. Universidade Federal Fluminense, Instituto de Matematica, Niteroi, Brazil.

| 510 | IT | ISSN 0392-4432 |
QA21
BOLLETTINO DI STORIA DELLE SCIENZE MATEMATICHE. 1981. s-a. L.40000. (Unione Matematica Italiana) Editrice Compositori s.r.l., Via Stalingrado 97-2, 40128 Bologna, Italy. TEL 51-327811. Ed. Enrico Giusti. **Indexed:** Math.R.

| 510 | GW | ISSN 0524-045X |
QA1
BONNER MATHEMATISCHE SCHRIFTEN. (Text in German; occasionally in English) 1957. 10/yr. DM.7.50 per no. Universitaet Bonn, Mathematisches Institut, Wegelerstr. 10, 5300 Bonn 1, Germany. Ed.Bd. circ. 260. **Indexed:** Math.R., Zent.Math.

| 510 | FR | ISSN 0007-4497 |
| | | CODEN: BSMQA9 |
BULLETIN DES SCIENCES MATHEMATIQUES. (Text and summaries in English, French) 1870. q. 1165 F. Gauthier-Villars, 15 rue Gossin, 92543 Montrouge Cedex, France. TEL 33-1-40-92-65-00. FAX 33-1-40-92-65-97. TELEX 270 004. (Subscr. to: Centrale des Revues, 11 rue Gossin, 92543 Montrouge Cedex, France. TEL 33-1-76-56-52-66) Ed. P. Malliavin. adv.; bk.rev.; circ. 750. (also avail. in microfilm from MIM,PMC; reprint service avail. from SWZ) **Indexed:** Compumath, Curr.Cont., Ind.Sci.Rev., Math.R., Sci.Cit.Ind, Zent.Math.
   Description: Covers all branches of pure mathematics.

| 510 | RM | ISSN 0007-4691 |
BULLETIN MATHEMATIQUE. (Text in French, English, German, Russian) 1908. q. 100($52) Societatea de Stiinte Matematice, Str. Academiei 14, 70109 Bucharest, Rumania. (Subscr. to: ILEXIM, Str. 13 Decembrie Nr. 3, P.O. Box 136-137, Bucharest, Rumania) Ed. Prof. Dr. N. Teodorescu. bk.rev.; index; circ. 800. **Indexed:** Appl.Mech.Rev., Math.R.
—BLDSC shelfmark: 2869.090000.

| 519.5 | JA | ISSN 0286-522X |
QA276
BULLETIN OF INFORMATICS AND CYBERNETICS. (Text and summaries in English) vol.4, 1950. a. $78. Tokei Kagaku Kenkyukai - Research Association of Statistical Sciences, c/o Kyushu University 33, 10-1, Hakozaki 6-chome, Higashi-ku, Fukuoka 812, Japan. TEL 092-641-1101. FAX 092-611-2668. Ed. T. Kitagawa. bibl.; charts; circ. 600. **Indexed:** JCT, JTA, Math.R., Sci.Abstr, Zent.Math.
—BLDSC shelfmark: 2862.118000.
   Formerly (until vol.19, 1981): Bulletin of Mathematical Statistics (ISSN 0007-4993)
   Description: Offers scholarly papers on information sciences. Contains tests of statistical processes, theoretical computer science, games informatics, machine learning, logics, robotics, linguistics and mathematics.

BULLETIN OF MATHEMATICAL BIOLOGY. see *BIOLOGY*

| 510 | AG | |
BULLETIN OF NUMBER THEORY AND RELATED TOPICS/BOLETIN DE TEORIA DE NUMEROS Y TEMAS CONEXOS. (Text in English) 1975. a. $100. Rodriguez Pena 640, 1020 Buenos Aires, Argentina. TEL 854-8045. Ed. Aldo Peretti. adv.; bk.rev.; circ. 100. **Indexed:** Math.R., Ref.Zh., Zent.Math.

| 510 | II | ISSN 0970-6577 |
QA1
BULLETIN OF PURE & APPLIED SCIENCES. SECTION E: MATHEMATICS. 1982. 2/yr. Rs.40($8) to individuals; institutions Rs.80($12). Dr. A.K. Sharma, Ed. & Pub., P.O. Box 38, Modinagar 201 204, India. adv.; bk.rev.; circ. 300.
—BLDSC shelfmark: 2884.508000.

| 510 | CN | |
C M S NOTES. (Text in English and French) 1969. irreg. (8-9/yr.). Can.$15. Canadian Mathematical Society - Societe Mathematique du Canada, 577 King Edward, Ottawa, Ont. K1N 6N5, Canada. TEL 613-564-2223. Ed. Graham P. Wright. adv.; circ. 1,100.
   Formerly: Canadian Mathematical Congress. Notes, News and Comments (ISSN 0045-5164)

| 510 | NE | |
C W I. TRACTS. (Text in English) 1963. irreg., no.74, 1990. Stichting Mathematisch Centrum, Centrum voor Wiskunde en Informatica, P.O. Box 4079, 1009 AB Amsterdam, Netherlands. TEL 020-59240005. FAX 020-5924199. TELEX 12571 MACTR NL. Ed. M. Hazewinkel. circ. 300.
   Formerly (until 1984): Mathematical Centre Tracts.
   Description: Contains theses and scientific research by members and non-members. Also includes CWI Conference proceedings on mathematical and computer science.

| 510 | IT | ISSN 0008-0624 |
QA75.5 | | CODEN: CALOBK |
CALCOLO. (Text in English and Italian) 1964. q. $100. (Consiglio Nazionale delle Ricerche, Istituto di Elaborazione della Informazione) Giardini Editori e Stampatori in Pisa, Via S. Bibbiana, 28, 56100 Pisa, Italy. Ed. Gianfranco Capriz. adv.; charts; illus.; stat. **Indexed:** Comput.Rev., Math.R., Sci.Abstr.
—BLDSC shelfmark: 2954.300000.

| 510 | II | ISSN 0008-0659 |
QA1 | | CODEN: BCMSA5 |
CALCUTTA MATHEMATICAL SOCIETY. BULLETIN. (Text in English) 1908. bi-m. Rs.250($100) Calcutta Mathematical Society, AE-374, Sector-1, Salt Lake City, Calcutta 700 064, India. Ed.Bd. bibl.; index; circ. 1,000. (also avail. in microform from BHP) **Indexed:** Appl.Mech.Rev., INIS Atomind., Math.R., Ref.Zh., Sci.Abstr.

CAMBRIDGE MONOGRAPHS ON MATHEMATICAL PHYSICS. see *PHYSICS*

CAMBRIDGE MONOGRAPHS ON MECHANICS AND APPLIED MATHEMATICS. see *PHYSICS — Mechanics*

| 510 530 | UK | ISSN 0305-0041 |
Q41 | | CODEN: MPCPCO |
CAMBRIDGE PHILOSOPHICAL SOCIETY. MATHEMATICAL PROCEEDINGS. 1843. 6/yr. (in 2 vols., 3 nos./vol.). $299. Cambridge University Press, Edinburgh Bldg., Shaftesbury Rd., Cambridge CB2 2RU, England. TEL 0223-312393. FAX 0223-315052. TELEX 851817256. (North American orders to: Cambridge University Press, Journals Dept., 40 W. 20th St., New York, NY 10011) Ed. J.S. Wilson. bibl.; charts; illus.; index; cum.index vols.1-50. (also avail. in microform from UMI,PMC) **Indexed:** Appl.Mech.Rev., ASCA, Chem.Abstr., Compumath, Curr.Cont., Deep Sea Res.& Oceanogr.Abstr., Eng.Ind., GeoRef, Math.R., Met.Abstr., Sci.Abstr., Sci.Cit.Ind., Zent.Math.
—BLDSC shelfmark: 5402.576600.
   Formerly: Cambridge Philosophical Society. Proceedings. Mathematical and Physical Sciences (ISSN 0008-1981)

| 510 530.15 | UK | |
CAMBRIDGE TRACTS IN MATHEMATICS. 1905. irreg., no.88, 1986. price varies. Cambridge University Press, Edinburgh Bldg., Shaftesbury Rd., Cambridge CB2 2RU, England. TEL 0223-312393. FAX 0223-315052. TELEX 851817256. Ed.Bd. **Indexed:** Math.R
   Formerly: Cambridge Tracts in Mathematics and Mathematical Physics (ISSN 0068-6824)

| 510 | US | |
▼**CANADIAN APPLIED MATHEMATICS QUARTERLY.** 1992. q. Can.$102.50($87.50) to individuals; institutions Can.$205 ($175). (Canadian Mathematical Society, CN - Societe Canadienne de Mathematiques Appliquees) Rocky Mountain Mathematics Consortium, Dept. of Mathematics, Arizona State University, Tempe, AZ 85287-1904. (In Canada subscr. to: CAMQ, AMI, University of Alberta, Edmonton, Alta. T6G 2G1.) (Co-sponsor: University of Alberta, Applied Mathematics Institute) Eds. Herbert I. Freedman, T. Bryant Moodie.
   Description: Publishes original research articles relating mathematics to the physical, medical, biological and engineering sciences.

| 510 | CN | ISSN 0008-414X |
QA1 | | CODEN: CJMAAB |
CANADIAN JOURNAL OF MATHEMATICS/JOURNAL CANADIEN DE MATHEMATIQUES. (Text in English, French) 1945. bi-m. Can.$280 to non-members; members Can.$70. Canadian Mathematical Society, 577 King Edward, Ottawa, Ont. K1N 6N5, Canada. TEL 613-564-2223. (Subscr. to: University of Toronto Press, 5201 Dufferin St., Downsview, Ont. M3H 5T8, Canada) Eds. D. Dawson, V. Dlab. adv.; bibl.; index; circ. 1,400. (also avail. in microfilm from PMC) **Indexed:** Compumath, Curr.Cont., Ind.Sci.Rev., Math.R., Sci.Cit.Ind
—BLDSC shelfmark: 3032.000000.

| 510 | CN | ISSN 0008-4395 |
CANADIAN MATHEMATICAL BULLETIN/BULLETIN CANADIEN DE MATHEMATIQUES. (Text in English, French) 1958. q. Can.$140 to non-members; members Can.$35. Canadian Mathematical Society - Societe Mathematique du Canada, 577 King Edward, Ottawa, Ont. K1N 6N5, Canada. TEL 613-564-2223. (Subscr. to: University of Toronto Press, 5201 Dufferin St., Downsview, Ont. M3H 5T8, Canada) Eds. D. Sjerve, J. Fournier. adv.; bk.rev.; bibl.; charts; index; circ. 900. (also avail. in microfilm from UMI) **Indexed:** Compumath, Math.R.

| 510 | US | ISSN 0731-1036 |
CANADIAN MATHEMATICAL SOCIETY. CONFERENCE PROCEEDINGS. 1981. irreg. price varies. (Canadian Mathematical Society, CN) American Mathematical Society, Box 1571, Annex Sta., Providence, RI 02901-9930. TEL 401-455-4000.
—BLDSC shelfmark: 3409.768000.

MATHEMATICS

510   CS   ISSN 0528-2195
QA1   CODEN: CPMTA8
CASOPIS PRO PESTOVANI MATEMATIKY/JOURNAL FOR THE CULTIVATION OF MATHEMATICS. (Text, contents page and summaries in Czech, English, French, German, Russian, Slovak) 1872. q. DM.218. (Czechoslovak Academy of Sciences, Mathematical Institute) Academia, Publishing House of the Czechoslovak Academy of Sciences, Vodickova 40, 112 29 Prague 1, Czechoslovakia. TEL 22-66-01. (Dist. in Western countries by: Kubon & Sagner, P.O. Box 34 01 08, 8000 Munich, Germany) Ed. S. Schwabik. bk.rev.; index; circ. 800. **Indexed:** Comput.Rev., Math.R.
    Description: Presents mathematical research and expository papers, news and notices, and problems.

CENTAURUS; international magazine of the history of mathematics, science and technology. see *SCIENCES: COMPREHENSIVE WORKS*

510   SZ
CENTRE DE RECHERCHES EN MATHEMATIQUES PURES. P 1.* 1958. a. 24 Fr. Schweizerische Mathematische Gesellschaft, Matematische Institut Universitaet Freiburg, 1700 Freiburg-Perolles, Switzerland. cum.index. **Indexed:** Math.R.
    Formerly: Universite de Neuchatel. Seminaire de Geometrie. Publications. Serie 1. Courtes Publications (ISSN 0077-7641)

510   SZ
CENTRE DE RECHERCHES EN MATHEMATIQUES PURES. PUBLICATIONS. SERIE 2. MONOGRAPHIES.* 1966. irreg. price varies. Schweizerische Mathematische Gesellschaft, Matematische Institut Universitaet Freiburg, 1700 Freiburg-Perolles, Switzerland. **Indexed:** Math.R.
    Continues: Universite de Neuchatel. Seminaire de Geometrie. Publications. Serie 2. Monographies (ISSN 0077-765X)

510   SZ
CENTRE DE RECHERCHES EN MATHEMATIQUES PURES. PUBLICATIONS. SERIE 3. OEUVRES.* irreg. (Centre de Recherches en Mathematiques Pures) Schweizerische Mathematische Gesellschaft, Matematische Institut Universitaet Freiburg, 1700 Freiburg-Perolles, Switzerland. **Indexed:** Math.R.

510   SZ
CENTRE DE RECHERCHES EN MATHEMATIQUES PURES. PUBLICATIONS. SERIE 4. CONFERENCES COMMUNICATIONS.* a. 41.50 Fr. (Centre de Recherches en Mathematiques Pures) Schweizerische Mathematische Gesellschaft, Matematische Institut Universitaet Freiburg, 1700 Freiburg-Perolles, Switzerland. **Indexed:** Math.R.

510   CN
CENTRE FOR RESEARCH IN ALGEBRA AND NUMBER THEORY. 1987. irreg. price varies. Carleton University, Department of Mathematics and Statistics, Ottawa, Ont. K1S 5B6, Canada. TEL 613-788-2155. FAX 613-788-3536.
    Formerly (until 1991): Centre for Research in Algebra and Related Fields.

CHANTIERS DE PEDAGOGIE MATHEMATIQUE. see *EDUCATION — Teaching Methods And Curriculum*

510   US   ISSN 0960-0779
Q172.5.C45
▼**CHAOS, SOLITONS AND FRACTALS;** applications in science and engineering. 1991. 6/yr. £245 (effective 1992). Pergamon Press, Inc., Journals Division, 660 White Plains Rd., Tarrytown, NY 10591-5153. TEL 914-524-9200. FAX 914-333-2444. (And: Headington Hill Hall, Oxford OX3 OBW, England. TEL 0865-794141) Ed. M. El Naschie. (also avail. in microform; back issues avail.)
    —BLDSC shelfmark: 3129.716000.
    Description: Covers bifurcation and singularity theory, deterministic chaos and fractals; stability theory, soliton and coherent phenomena; formation of pattern, evolution and complexity theory.
    Refereed Serial

510   US   ISSN 0069-3286
CHICAGO LECTURES IN MATHEMATICS. 1964. irreg., latest 1984. price varies. University of Chicago Press, 5801 S. Ellis Ave., Chicago, IL 60637. TEL 312-702-7899. Ed. Irving Kaplansky. (reprint service avail. from UMI,ISI) **Indexed:** Math.R.
    Refereed Serial

510   US
CHINESE ANNALS OF MATHEMATICS. SERIES A. q. (Chinese Mathematical Society, CC) Allerton Press, Inc., 150 Fifth Ave., New York, NY 10011. TEL 212-924-3950. Ed. Su Buqing.
    Supersedes in part (in 1983): Shuxue Niankan (ISSN 0253-6137)

510   SZ   ISSN 0252-9599
QA1
CHINESE ANNALS OF MATHEMATICS. SERIES B. (Text in English) 1980. q. 436.50 Fr. (Chinese Mathematical Society, CC) J.C. Baltzer AG, Scientific Publishing Company, Wettsteinplatz 10, CH-4058 Basel, Switzerland. TEL 061-6918925. FAX 061-6924262. Ed. Su Buqing. (back issues avail.) **Indexed:** Curr.Cont.
    —BLDSC shelfmark: 3180.271200.
    Supersedes in part (in 1983): Shuxue Niankan (ISSN 0253-6137)

510   US   ISSN 0898-5111
QA1
CHINESE JOURNAL OF CONTEMPORARY MATHEMATICS. 1988. q. $290. (Chinese Mathematical Society, CC) Allerton Press, Inc., 150 Fifth Ave., New York, NY 10011. TEL 212-924-3950. Ed. Su Buqing. (back issues avail.)
    —BLDSC shelfmark: 3180.311500.
    Description: Covers contemporary mathematical research in China, including both pure and applied mathematics.

510   US   ISSN 0899-4358
QA297
CHINESE JOURNAL OF NUMERICAL MATHEMATICS AND APPLICATIONS. 1988. q. $290. (Academia Sinica - Chinese Academy of Sciences, Computing Center, CC - Zhongguo Kexueyuan Jisuan Zhongxin) Allerton Press, Inc., 150 Fifth Ave., New York, NY 10011. TEL 212-924-3950. Ed. Feng Kang. (back issues avail.)
    —BLDSC shelfmark: 3180.438600.
    Description: Covers mathematics research in China, including numerical linear and nonlinear algebra, and analysis.

510   JA   ISSN 0287-802X
CHOSEN SHOGAKKAI GAKUJUTSU RONBUNSHU/KOREAN SCHOLARSHIP ASSOCIATION IN JAPAN. SCIENCE REPORT. (Text and summaries in English, Japanese) 1971. a. Korean Scholarship Association in Japan - Chosen Shogakkai, 8-1, Nishi-shinjuku, 1-chome, Shinjuku-ku, Tokyo 160, Japan.
    —BLDSC shelfmark: 2600.390000.

510   CC
CHUZHONGSHENG SHUXUE FUDAO/MATHEMATICS TUTORING FOR JUNIOR HIGH SCHOOL STUDENTS. (Text in Chinese) m. Jiangsu Jiaoyu Chubanshe, 165 Zhongyang Lu, Nanjing, Jiangsu 210009, People's Republic of China. TEL 631836. Ed. He Zhenbang.

510   CR
▼**CIENCIAS MATEMATICAS.** (Text in Spanish; abstracts in English, Spanish) 1990. s-a. Col.500($10) Editorial de la Universidad de Costa Rica, Apdo. 75-2060, Ciudad Universitaria Rodrigo Facio, 2050 San Pedro de Montes de Oca, San Jose, Costa Rica. TEL 506-25-3133. FAX 506-24-9367. TELEX UNICORI 2544. Dir. Manuel Barahona Droguett. bibl.; charts.

510   IT   ISSN 0009-725X
                CODEN: RCMMAR
CIRCOLO MATEMATICO DI PALERMO. RENDICONTI. (In 2 Series) (Text in English, French, German and Italian) 1887. q. L.100000. Circolo Matematico di Palermo, Via Archirafi 34, 90123 Palermo, Italy. bk.rev.; circ. 1,000. (also avail. in microfiche from BHP) **Indexed:** Appl.Mech.Rev., Math.R.

CLASSICAL AND QUANTUM GRAVITY. see *PHYSICS*

510   US   ISSN 0743-9199
CLASSICS OF SOVIET MATHEMATICS. irreg., latest vol.2. Gordon and Breach Scientific Publishers, 270 Eighth Ave., New York, NY 10011. TEL 212-206-8900. FAX 212-645-2459. TELEX 236735 GOPUB UR. (Subscr. to: Box 786, Cooper Sta., New York, NY 10276. TEL 800-545-8398; UK subscr. to: P.O. Box 90, Reading, Berkshire RG1 8JL, England. TEL 0734-560-080)
    Refereed Serial

510   SP   ISSN 0010-0757
QD1   CODEN: COLMBA
COLLECTANEA MATHEMATICA. (Text in English, French, German, Italian, Portuguese and Spanish) 1948. q. 1000 ptas.($45) Universidad de Barcelona, Facultad de Ciencias, Seminario Matematico, Barcelona, Spain. FAX 343-412-1935. Ed. Joan Cerda. circ. 300. **Indexed:** Ind.SST, Math.R., Zent.Math.
    —BLDSC shelfmark: 3299.800000.

510   FR
COLLECTION FORMATION DES ENSEIGNANTS ET FORMATION CONTINUE. 1973. irreg. Editions Hermann, 293 rue Lecourbe, 75015 Paris, France. TEL 45-57-45-40. illus.
    Formerly: Collection Formation des Enseignants.

510 378.1   US   ISSN 0746-8342
QA11.A1
COLLEGE MATHEMATICS JOURNAL. 1970. 5/yr. $85. Mathematical Association of America, 1529 18th St. N.W., Washington, DC 20036. TEL 202-387-5200. Eds. William and Ann Watkins. adv.; bk.rev.; illus.; circ. 10,000. (also avail. in microfilm from UMI; reprint service avail. from UMI) **Indexed:** ASCA, C.I.J.E., Cont.Pg.Educ., Educ.Ind., Gen.Sci.Ind., Math.R.
    —BLDSC shelfmark: 3311.172000.
    Formerly (until 1983): Two-Year College Mathematics Journal (ISSN 0049-4925)
    Description: Articles on mathematics, curriculum and pedagogy, problems and solutions, classroom notes, and a special section on computers, focusing on the earlier years of college-level mathematics.
    Refereed Serial

510   NE
COLLOQUIA MATHEMATICA SOCIETATIS JANOS BOLYAI. vol.25, 1981. irreg., vol.59, 1992. price varies. Elsevier Science Publishers B.V., Books Division, P.O. Box 211, 1000 AE Amsterdam, Netherlands. TEL 020-5803911. FAX 020-5803705. TELEX 18582 ESPA NL. (Subscr. in U.S. and Canada to: Elsevier Science Publishing Co., Inc., Box 882, Madison Sq. Sta., New York, NY 10159. TEL 212-989-5800) (back issues avail.)
    Refereed Serial

510   PL   ISSN 0010-1354
QA1
COLLOQUIUM MATHEMATICUM. (Text in various languages) 1947. irreg., vol.58, 1990. $45 per vol. (Polska Akademia Nauk, Instytut Matematyczny) Panstwowe Wydawnictwo Naukowe, Ul. Miodowa 10, 00-251 Warsaw, Poland. (Dist. by: Ars Polona, Krakowskie Przedmiescie 7, 00-068 Warsaw, Poland) Ed. R. Duda. bibl.; circ. 900. (reprint service avail. from SWZ) **Indexed:** GeoRef., Math.R.

510   HU   ISSN 0209-9683
QA164   CODEN: COMBDI
COMBINATORICA. (Text in English) 1981. 4/yr. DM.298($183) (effective 1992). (Janos Bolyai Mathematical Society) Akademiai Kiado, Publishing House of the Hungarian Academy of Sciences, P.O. Box 24, H-1363 Budapest, Hungary. (Dist. by: Springer-Verlag, Postfach 10-52-80, D-6900, Heidelberg, Germany) Eds. P. Erdos, L. Lovasz. index. (back issues avail.; reprint service avail. from SWZ) **Indexed:** Compumath, Curr.Cont., Int.Abstr.Oper.Res., Math.R., Sci.Abstr., Zent.Math.
    —BLDSC shelfmark: 3324.750000.

510   SZ   ISSN 0010-2571
QA1   CODEN: COMHAX
COMMENTARII MATHEMATICI HELVETICI. (Text in English, French, German and Italian) 1929. 4/yr. 268 Fr.($188) (Schweizerischen Mathematischen Gesellschaft - Swiss Mathematical Society) Birkhaeuser Verlag, P.O. Box 133, CH-4010 Basel, Switzerland. TEL 061-737740. FAX 061-737950. TELEX 963475-BIRKH-CH. (Dist. in N. America by: Springer-Verlag New York, Inc. Journal Fulfillment Services, Box 2485, Secaucus, NJ 07096-2491, USA) Ed. H. Kraft. adv.; bk.rev.; illus.; tr.lit.; index. **Indexed:** Compumath, Ind.Sci.Rev., Math.R., Sci.Cit.Ind.
    —BLDSC shelfmark: 3333.000000.

510   JA   ISSN 0010-258X
QA1   CODEN: COMAAC
COMMENTARII MATHEMATICI UNIVERSITATIS SANCTI PAULI/RIKKYO DAIGAKU SUGAKU ZASSHI.* (Text and summaries in English) 1952. s-a. (Rikkyo Daigaku, Rigakubu Sugaku Kyoshitsu - Rikkyo University, Faculty of Science, Department of Mathematics) Kinokuniya Shoten - Kinokuniya Co., Ltd., 17-7 Shinjuku 3-chome, Shinjuku-ku, Tokyo 160, Japan. (Subscr. in US to: 1581 Webster St., San Francisco, CA 94115) Ed. Setsuya Seki. index. **Indexed:** Math.R.

510   CS   ISSN 0010-2628
QA1   CODEN: CMUCAA
COMMENTATIONES MATHEMATICAE UNIVERSITATIS CAROLINAE. (Text in English) 1960. q. exchange basis. Universita Karlova, Matematicky Ustav, Sokolovska 83, 18600 Prague 8, Czechoslovakia. (Dist. by: Messrs. Galloway and Porter Ltd., 30 Sidney St., Cambridge CB2 3HS, England) Ed. J. Danes. abstr.; charts; index; circ. 600. (also avail. in microform from SWZ; reprint service avail. from SWZ) **Indexed:** Math.R., Ref.Zh., Zent.Math.

COMMENTATIONES PHYSICO-MATHEMATICAE ET CHEMICO-MEDICAE. see PHYSICS

510   US   ISSN 0092-7872
QA150   CODEN: COALDM
COMMUNICATIONS IN ALGEBRA. 1974. 12/yr. $1095. Marcel Dekker Journals, 270 Madison Ave., New York, NY 10016. TEL 212-696-9000. FAX 212-685-4540. TELEX 421419. (Subscr. to: Box 10018, Church St. Sta., New York, NY 10249) Ed. Earl Taft. adv.; bibl.; charts; illus.; index. (also avail. in microform from RPI) **Indexed:** Compumath, Curr.Cont., Ind.Sci.Rev., Math.R., Sci.Cit.Ind.
—BLDSC shelfmark: 3359.200000.
Refereed Serial

510 624   UK   ISSN 0748-8025
TA335   CODEN: CANMER
COMMUNICATIONS IN APPLIED NUMERICAL METHODS. 1985. 12/yr. $375 (effective 1992). John Wiley & Sons Ltd., Journals, Baffins Lane, Chichester, Sussex PO19 1UD, England. TEL 0243 779777. FAX 0243-775878. TELEX 86290 WIBOOK G. Eds. Roland W. Lewis, Graham F. Carey. (reprint service avail. from SWZ) **Indexed:** Compumath, Curr.Cont.
—BLDSC shelfmark: 3359.338000.
Description: Contains short contributions describing significant developments in numerical methods and the applications of such techniques to the solution of practical engineering problems.
Refereed Serial

COMMUNICATIONS IN MATHEMATICAL PHYSICS. see PHYSICS

350   US   ISSN 0360-5302
QA377   CODEN: CPDIDZ
COMMUNICATIONS IN PARTIAL DIFFERENTIAL EQUATIONS. 1976. 12/yr. $650. Marcel Dekker Journals, 270 Madison Ave., New York, NY 10016. TEL 212-696-9000. FAX 212-685-4540. TELEX 421419. (Subscr. to: Box 10018, Church St. Sta., New York, NY 10249) Eds. M. Crandall, J. Ralston. (also avail. in microform from RPI) **Indexed:** Compumath, INIS Atomind., Math.R.
—BLDSC shelfmark: 3362.300000.
Refereed Serial

510 519   US   ISSN 0010-3640
QA1   CODEN: CPMAMV
COMMUNICATIONS ON PURE AND APPLIED MATHEMATICS. 1939. 10/yr. $550 to institutions (foreign $675). (Courant Institute of Mathematical Sciences) John Wiley & Sons, Inc., Journals, 605 Third Ave., New York, NY 10158-0012. TEL 212-850-6000. FAX 212-685-6088. TELEX 12-7063. Ed. Natascha A. Brunswick. bibl.; illus.; author index; circ. 1,400. (also avail. in microform from RPI; back issues avail.; reprint service avail. from KTO) **Indexed:** Appl.Mech.Rev., Compumath, Curr.Cont., Ind.Sci.Rev., Int.Aerosp.Abstr., Math.R., Sci.Cit.Ind.
—BLDSC shelfmark: 3363.000000.
Description: Examines developments in applied mathematics, mathematical physics, and mathematical analysis.
Refereed Serial

510   US   ISSN 0278-1077
QA331   CODEN: CVTADV
COMPLEX VARIABLES: THEORY AND APPLICATION; an international journal. 1982. 8/yr. (in 2 vols., 4 nos./vol.) $217. Gordon and Breach Science Publishers, 270 Eighth Ave., New York, NY 10011. TEL 212-206-8900. FAX 212-645-2459. TELEX 236735 GOPUB UR. (Subscr. to: Box 786, Cooper Sta., New York, NY 10276. TEL 800-545-8398; UK subscr. to: P.O. Box 90, Reading, Berkshire RG1 8JL, England. TEL 0734-560-080) Eds. Robert P. Gilbert, Klaus Habetha. (also avail. in microform) **Indexed:** Math.R.
—BLDSC shelfmark: 3364.585000.
Refereed Serial

510   NE   ISSN 0010-437X
QA1   CODEN: CMPMAF
COMPOSITIO MATHEMATICA. (Text mainly in English) 1933. m. $628. Kluwer Academic Publishers, Postbus 17, 3300 AA Dordrecht, Netherlands. TEL 078-334911. FAX 078-334254. TELEX 29245. (Dist. by: Kluwer Academic Publishers Group, P.O. Box 322, 3300 AH Dordrecht, Netherlands; N. America dist. addr.: Box 358, Accord Station, Hingham, MA 02018-0358. TEL 617-871-6600) Ed. J.H.M. Steenbrink. adv.; index; circ. 617. (also avail. in microform from MIM; back issues avail.; reprint service avail. from KTO,SWZ) **Indexed:** Compumath, Curr.Cont., Ind.Sci.Rev., Math.R, Sci.Cit.Ind.

COMPUTATIONAL GEOMETRY; theory and applications. see COMPUTERS

COMPUTATIONAL MATERIALS SCIENCE. see ENGINEERING — Engineering Mechanics And Materials

COMPUTATIONAL MATHEMATICS AND MODELING. see MATHEMATICS — Computer Applications

510   AG   ISSN 0010-5147
CONCEPTOS DE MATEMATICA; revista para el maestro, el profesor y el estudiante. 1967. q. Arg.$120($6) c/o Jose Banfi, 1949 Paraguay, Buenos Aires, Argentina. adv.; bk.rev.; bibl.; charts; illus.; circ. 5,000.
Supersedes: Elementos.

510   CN   ISSN 0384-9864
QA1
CONGRESSUS NUMERANTIUM; a conference journal on numerical themes. 1970. irreg. (approx. 5/yr.). $32 per vol. Utilitas Mathematica Publishing Inc., Box 7, University Centre, University of Manitoba, Winnipeg, Man. R3T 2N2, Canada. TEL 204-474-8675. Ed. Ralph G. Stanton. circ. 400. **Indexed:** Math.R., Zent.Math.
—BLDSC shelfmark: 3417.547000.
Incorporates (in 1971): Manitoba Conference on Numerical Mathematics and Computing. Proceedings; (in 1970): Southeastern Conference on Combinatorics, Graph Theory and Computing Proceedings.

CONNECT (BRATTLEBORO); the newsletter of practical science and math for K-8 teachers. see EDUCATION — Teaching Methods And Curriculum

510   US   ISSN 0176-4276
CONSTRUCTIVE APPROXIMATION. 1985. 4/yr. $125. Springer-Verlag, Journals, 175 Fifth Ave., New York, NY 10010. TEL 212-460-1500. (Subscr. to: 44 Hartz Way, Secaucus, NJ 07094) Eds. Ronald A. DeVore, Edward B. Saff. (also avail. in microform from UMI; back issues avail.; reprint service avail. from ISI) **Indexed:** Compumath, Curr.Cont., Math.R., Zent.Math.
—BLDSC shelfmark: 3422.627500.

510   US   ISSN 0271-4132
CONTEMPORARY MATHEMATICS. 1980. irreg. American Mathematical Society, Box 1571, Annex Sta., Providence, RI 02901-9930. TEL 401-455-4000. **Indexed:** Math.R.
—BLDSC shelfmark: 3425.191400.

510 620   JA   ISSN 0911-0704
QA402.3
CONTROL; theory and advanced technology. (Text and summaries in English) 1985. q. 30900 Yen($160) Mita Press, Ochanomizu Center Bldg. 8F, 2-12, Hongo-3, Bunkyo-ku, Tokyo 113, Japan. FAX 03-3818-1016. TELEX 2722813-MITA-PS-J. Eds. Y. Sunahara, D.P. Atherton. bk.rev.; circ. 1,300.
—BLDSC shelfmark: 3463.017000.
Description: Deals with control systems, information sciences and related areas.

510 375   AT
CROSS SECTION. 1989. 3/yr. Aus.$22. Mathematical Association of Western Australia, P.O. Box 492, Subiaco, W.A. 6008, Australia.
Formed by the 1989 merger of: Rhombus (ISSN 0313-4504) & Sigma (ISSN 0314-7606)

510   CN   ISSN 0705-0348
CRUX MATHEMATICORUM. (Text in English, French) 1975. 10/yr. Can.$20 to members; non-members Can.$40. Canadian Mathematical Society - Societe Mathematique du Canada, 577 King Edward, Ottawa, Ont. K1N 6N5, Canada. TEL 613-564-2223. Ed. George Sands. bk.rev.; circ. 700.
Formerly (until Mar. 1978): Eureka (ISSN 0700-558X)
Description: Problems solving journal at the senior secondary and university undergraduate levels.

510 652.8 US   ISSN 0161-1194
Z102.5   CODEN: CRYPE6
CRYPTOLOGIA; a quarterly journal devoted to all aspects of cryptology. 1977. q. $34 (foreign $40). Rose-Hulman Institute of Technology, Department of Mathematics, Terre Haute, IN 47803. TEL 812-877-8412. Ed. Brian J. Winkel. adv.; bk.rev.; illus.; pat.; stat.; circ. 1,000. (also avail. in microform from UMI; reprint service avail. from UMI; back issues avail.) **Indexed:** Comput.Cont., Math.R.
—BLDSC shelfmark: 3490.155480.
Description: Scholarly journal on aspects of cryptology including computer security, mathematics, codes, cryptanalysis, history, and ancient languages.

512   SP
CUADERNOS DE ALGEBRA. 1985. irreg., no.7, 1987. price varies. Universidad de Granada, Servicio de Publicaciones, Antiguo Colegio Maximo, Campus de Cartuja, 18071 Granada, Spain. TEL 281356.

510   UK   ISSN 0732-4405
QA1
CURRENT TOPICS IN CHINESE SCIENCE. SECTION C: MATHEMATICS. 1982. irreg., vol.3, 1985. Gordon & Breach Science Publishers, P.O. Box 90, Reading, Berkshire RG1 8JL, England. TEL 0734-560-080. FAX 0734-568-211. TELEX 849870 SCIPUB G. (US addr.: P.O. Box 786, Cooper Sta., New York, NY 10276. TEL 800-545-8398) (also avail. in microfilm)
Refereed Serial

510   US   ISSN 0011-4642
QA1
CZECHOSLOVAK MATHEMATICAL JOURNAL. (Text in English, French, German, Russian) 1951. q. $495 (foreign $580)(effective 1992). (Czechoslovak Academy of Sciences, Mathematical Institute, CS) Plenum Publishing Corp., 233 Spring St., New York, NY 10013-1578. TEL 212-620-8000. FAX 212-463-0742. TELEX 23-421139. (Co-publisher: Academia, CS) Ed. Miroslav Fiedler. bk.rev.; bibl.; index; circ. 1,200. (reprint service avail. from SWZ) **Indexed:** Appl.Mech.Rev., Compumath, Comput.Rev., Math.R.
Formerly: Jednota Ceskoslovenskych Matematiku a Fysiku. Casopis pro Pestovani Matematiky a Fysiky.
Description: Presents mathematical research papers, news and notices.
Refereed Serial

510   DK   ISSN 0106-6366
D C A M M REPORT. 1970. irreg. free. Danmarks Tekniske Hoejskole, Danish Center for Applied Mathematics and Mechanics, Department of Solid Mechanics, Technical University of Denmark, Lyngby, Denmark. circ. 500.

MATHEMATICS

510   DK   ISSN 0106-9306
DANMARKS TEKNISKE HOEJSKOLE. MATEMATISK INSTITUT. MAT - P R. no. 2, 1984. irreg. Danmarks Tekniske Hoejskole, Matematisk Institut, 2800 Lyngby, Denmark. TEL 02-883699.
FAX 45-42-88-13-99. TELEX 37529-DTHDIA-DK. Ed. V. Lundsgaard Hansen. circ. 100.
Description: Presents old and new results from all fields of mathematics.

510 530   PL
DELTA (WARSAW); matematyczno-fizyczny miesiecznik popularny. 1974. m. 60 Zl.($5.50) (Polskie Towarzystwo Matematyczne) Wydawnictwo Wspolczesne R S W "Prasa-Ksiazka-Ruch", Ul. Wiejska 12, 00-420 Warsaw, Poland.
TEL 48-22-285330. (Dist. by: Ars Polona-Ruch, Krakowskie Przedmiescie 7, Warsaw, Poland) (Co-sponsor: Polskie Towarzystwo Fizyczne) Ed. M. Kordos. circ. 20,000.

510   US   ISSN 0925-1022
▼**DESIGN, CODES AND CRYPTOGRAPHY.** 1991. q. $169. Kluwer Academic Publishers, 101 Philip Dr., Norwell, MA 02061. TEL 617-871-6600.
FAX 617-871-6528. (Subscr. to: Box 358, Accord Sta., Hingham, MA 02018-0358; Dist. in Europe by: Kluwer Academic Publishers Group, P.O. Box 322, 3300 AH Dordrecht, Netherlands.
TEL 078-334911) Ed. Scott A. Vanstone.
—BLDSC shelfmark: 3560.314000.
Description: Provides both theoretical and practical papers that bridge the gap between design theory, coding theory, and cryptography.

510   GW   ISSN 0012-0456
QA1   CODEN: JDMVA7
DEUTSCHE MATHEMATIKER VEREINIGUNG. JAHRESBERICHT. 1890. 4/yr. DM.128. B.G. Teubner GmbH, Industriestr. 15, 7000 Stuttgart 80, Germany. TEL 0711-78901-0.
FAX 0711-78901-10. Ed. W.-D. Geyer. adv.; bk.rev.; illus.; index; circ. 2,400. (back issues avail.; reprint service avail. from SWZ,UMI) **Indexed:** Math.R.
—BLDSC shelfmark: 4633.940000.

510   GW
DEUTSCHE MATHEMATIKER VEREINIGUNG. MITTEILUNGEN. 1890. q. Deutsche Mathematiker Vereinigung, Albertstr. 24, 7800 Freiburg, Germany. FAX 0761-272698. circ. 2,650.

DEVELOPMENTS IN GEOMATHEMATICS. see *EARTH SCIENCES — Geophysics*

510 793.73   II   ISSN 0300-4309
DHANDHA. (Text in Bengali) 1972. m. Rs.3($5) Mukherjee Library, 1 Gopi Mohan Dutta Lane, Calcutta 700003, India. Ed. Biswanath Bose. adv.; bibl.; illus.; circ. 1,500.
Description: Features recreational mathematics.

DIDAKTIK DER MATHEMATIK. see *EDUCATION — Teaching Methods And Curriculum*

DIDATTICA DELLE SCIENZE E INFORMATICA NELLA SCUOLA. see *EDUCATION — Teaching Methods And Curriculum*

510   US   ISSN 0893-4983
DIFFERENTIAL AND INTEGRAL EQUATIONS. 1988. bi-m. $226. Ohio University, Department of Mathematics, Athens, OH 45701. TEL 614-593-1268. Ed. Reza Aftabizadeh.
—BLDSC shelfmark: 3584.134000.

512   US   ISSN 0012-2661
QA371   CODEN: DIEQAN
DIFFERENTIAL EQUATIONS. English translation of: Differentsial'nye Uravneniya. 1965. m. $1125 (foreign $1315)(effective 1992). (Akademiya Navuk Belarusskai S.S.R., UR) Plenum Publishing Corp., Consultants Bureau, 233 Spring St., New York, NY 10013-1578. TEL 212-620-8468.
FAX 212-463-0742. TELEX 23-421139. Ed. E.I. Grudo. (also avail. in microfilm from JSC; back issues avail.) **Indexed:** Appl.Mech.Rev., Compumath, Comput.& Info.Sys., Zent.Math.
—BLDSC shelfmark: 0411.094000.
Refereed Serial

510   NE   ISSN 0926-2245
▼**DIFFERENTIAL GEOMETRY AND ITS APPLICATIONS.** (Text in English) 1991. 4/yr. fl.306 (effective 1992). North-Holland (Subsidiary of: Elsevier Science Publishers B.V.), P.O. Box 211, 1000 AE Amsterdam, Netherlands. TEL 020-5803911.
FAX 020-5803598. TELEX 18582 ESPA NL. (Subscr. in U.S. and Canada to: Elsevier Science Publishing Co., Inc., Box 882, Madison Sq. Sta., New York, NY 10159. TEL 212-989-5800) Ed. D. Krupka. (back issues avail.)
—BLDSC shelfmark: 3584.220000.
Description: Publishes original research papers and survey papers in differential geometry and in all interdisciplinary areas in mathematics which use differential geometric methods and investigate geometrical structures.
Refereed Serial

510 370   FI   ISSN 0782-6648
DIMENSIO. (Text in Finnish; summaries in English, Finnish and Swedish) 1937. 9/yr. FIM 135. Matemaattisten Aineiden Opettajien Liitto, Akavatalo, Rautatielaisenkatu 6, 00520 Helsinki 52, Finland. Ed. Kaisa-Liisa Korhonen. adv.; bk.rev.; charts; illus.; index; circ. 5,000.
Formerly: Matemaattisten Aineiden Aikakauskirja (ISSN 0025-5149)
Description: Presents study and teaching methods.

510 001.6 621.381   US   ISSN 0179-5376
QA440   CODEN: DCGEER
DISCRETE AND COMPUTATIONAL GEOMETRY. 1986. 6/yr. $175. Springer-Verlag, Journals, 175 Fifth Ave., New York, NY 10010. TEL 212-460-1500. (Subscr. to: Journal Fulfillment Services, Box 2485, Secaucus, NJ 07094) Eds. J.E. Goodman, R. Pollack. (back issues avail.) **Indexed:** Compumath, Curr.Cont., Eng.Ind., Math.R., Zent.Math.
—BLDSC shelfmark: 3597.024000.
Description: Articles for mathematicians and computer scientists in the areas of combinatorial geometry, and design and analysis of geometric algorithms.

510   NE   ISSN 0166-218X
QA1   CODEN: DAMADU
DISCRETE APPLIED MATHEMATICS; combinatorial operations research and computer science. (Text in English and French) 1979. 18/yr.(in 6 vols.; 3 nos./vol.). fl.1746 (combined subscr. with Discrete Mathematics fl.4518)(effective 1992). North-Holland (Subsidiary of: Elsevier Science Publishers B.V.), P.O. Box 211, 1000 AE Amsterdam, Netherlands. TEL 020-5803911. FAX 020-5803598. TELEX 18582 ESPA NL. (Subscr. in U.S. and Canada to: Elsevier Science Publishing Co., Inc., Box 882, Madison Sq. Sta., New York, NY 10159. TEL 212-989-5800) Ed. Peter L. Hammer. abstr.; illus.; index. (also avail. in microform from RPI; back issues avail.) **Indexed:** Compumath, Curr.Cont., Cyb.Abstr., Eng.Ind., Ind.Sci.Rev., Int.Abstr.Oper.Res., Math R., Sci.Abstr., Sci.Cit.Ind., Zent.Math.
—BLDSC shelfmark: 3597.025000.
Description: Brings together research in different areas of applied combinatorics and demonstrates the unity of the mathematical tools used in a variety of fields and applications.
Refereed Serial

510   NE   ISSN 0012-365X
                         CODEN: DSMHA4
DISCRETE MATHEMATICS. (Text in English) 1971. 36/yr.(in 12 vols.; 3 nos./vol.). fl.3492 (combined subscr. with Discrete Applied Mathematics fl.4518)(effective 1992). North-Holland (Subsidiary of: Elsevier Science Publishers B.V.), P.O. Box 211, 1000 AE Amsterdam, Netherlands.
TEL 020-5803911. FAX 020-5803598. TELEX 18582 ESPA NL. (Subscr. in U.S. and Canada to: Elsevier Science Publishing Co., Inc., Box 882, Madison Sq. Sta., New York, NY 10159. TEL 212-989-5800) Ed. P.L. Hammer. adv.; bk.rev.; circ. 2,000. (also avail. in microform from RPI; back issues avail.; reprint service avail. from SWZ) **Indexed:** Compumath, Comput.Rev., Curr.Cont., Cyb.Abstr., Int.Abstr.Oper.Res., Sci.Abstr., Sci.Cit.Ind.
—BLDSC shelfmark: 3597.030000.
Description: Publishes research papers, notes, communications, and research problems in the field of discrete mathematics.
Refereed Serial

510   NE   ISSN 0924-9265
▼**DISCRETE MATHEMATICS AND APPLICATIONS.** English translation of: Diskretnaya Matematika (RU ISSN 0234-0860) 1991. bi-m. DM.970($423) (effective 1992). V S P, P.O. Box 346, 3700 AH Zeist, Netherlands. TEL 03404-25790.
FAX 03404-32081. TELEX 40217 VSP NL. Ed. V.Y. Kozlov. bk.rev.
—BLDSC shelfmark: 3597.032000.
Description: Covers topics in discrete mathematics, with original articles in addition to translations.

510   RU   ISSN 0234-0860
                         CODEN: DIMAEJ
DISKRETNAYA MATEMATIKA. English translation: Discrete Mathematics and its Applications (NE ISSN 0924-9265) 4/yr. 6 Rub. (Akademiya Nauk S.S.S.R.) Izdatel'stvo Nauka, Fizmatlit, Leninskii prospekt, 15, 117071 Moscow, Russia. Ed. Yu. Khodan.
—BLDSC shelfmark: 0053.268700.

510   HU   ISSN 0070-671X
DISQUISITIONES MATHEMATICAE HUNGARICAE. (Text in English, French, German or Hungarian) 1970. irreg., vol.14, 1987. price varies. (Magyar Tudomanyos Akademia) Akademiai Kiado, Publishing House of the Hungarian Academy of Sciences, P.O. Box 24, H-1363 Budapest, Hungary.

510   PL   ISSN 0012-3862
                         CODEN: DSMAAH
DISSERTATIONES MATHEMATICAE/ROZPRAWY MATEMATYCZNE. (Text in English, French, German, Russian; summaries in English and Russian) 1952. irreg., vol.316, 1992. price varies. Polska Akademia Nauk, Instytut Matematyczny - Polish Academy of Sciences, Institute of Mathematics, Ul. Sniadeckich 8, P.O. Box 137w, 00-950 Warsaw, Poland. (Dist. by: Ars Polona, Krakowskie Przedmiescie 7, 00-068 Warsaw, Poland) Eds. B. Bojarski, W. Zelazko. bibl. **Indexed:** Math.R.

DIVREI HA-AKADEMIA HA-LEUMIT HA-YISRAELIT LEMADAIM-HA-HATIVA LE-MADAEI HA-TEVA. see *SCIENCES: COMPREHENSIVE WORKS*

510   TU   ISSN 1010-7622
DOGA TURKISH JOURNAL OF MATHEMATICS/DOGA TURK MATEMATIK DERGISI. (Text in English, Turkish) 1976. 3/yr. $20. Scientific and Technical Research Council of Turkey - Turkiye Bilimsel ve Teknik Arastirma Kurumu, Ataturk Bulvari, No. 221, Kavaklidere, 06100 Ankara, Turkey. TEL 1673657. FAX 1277489. TELEX 43186 BTAK TR. Ed. Tosun Terzioglu.
—BLDSC shelfmark: 3614.642500.
Supersedes in part (in 1986): Doga Bilim Dergisi. Serie A: Basic Sciences.

510   UK   ISSN 0260-4884
DOZENAL JOURNAL. 1959. irreg., no.8, 1990. £4. Dozenal Society of Great Britain, Millside, Mill Rd., Denmead, Hampshire PO7 6PA, England. Ed. Donald Hammond. bk.rev.; index; circ. 200. (tabloid format)
—BLDSC shelfmark: 3620.158000.
Former titles (until winter 1980): Dozenal Review (ISSN 0309-8648); (until 1977): Duodecimal Review.
Description: Advocacy of investigation into base twelve numeration and rational measure.

510   US   ISSN 0012-7094
QA1   CODEN: DUMJAO
DUKE MATHEMATICAL JOURNAL. 1935. 9/yr. $264 to individuals (foreign $288); institutions $528 (foreign $552). Duke University Press, 6697 College Station, Durham, NC 27708.
TEL 919-684-2173. FAX 919-684-8644. Ed. Morris Weisfeld. bibl.; charts; index, cum.index every 10 yrs; circ. 1,200. (also avail. in microform from MIM,UMI,KTO; reprint service avail. from ISI,UMI) **Indexed:** Compumath, Curr.Cont., Ind.Sci.Rev., Math.R., Sci.Cit.Ind.
—BLDSC shelfmark: 3631.000000.
Refereed Serial

MATHEMATICS

513.56 US ISSN 0046-0826
QA141
DUODECIMAL BULLETIN. 1945. 2/yr. $12. Dozenal Society of America, c/o Math Department, Nassau Community College, Garden City, NY 11530. TEL 516-669-0273. Ed. Patricia Zirkel. adv.; bk.rev.; circ. 230.
—BLDSC shelfmark: 3631.200000.
Description: Contains articles, news, and society announcements.
Refereed Serial

DYNAMATH. see *CHILDREN AND YOUTH — For*

510 500 FR ISSN 0012-9593
CODEN: ASENAH
ECOLE NORMALE SUPERIEURE. ANNALES SCIENTIFIQUES. (Text in English and French) 1864. 6/yr. 1340 F. Gauthier-Villars, 15 rue Gossin, 92543 Montrouge Cedex, France. TEL 33-1-40-92-65-00. FAX 33-1-40-92-65-97. TELEX 270 004. (Subscr. to: Centrale des Revues, 11 rue Gossin, 92543 Montrouge Cedex, France. TEL 33-1-46-56-52-66) Ed. B. Teissier. adv.; bk.rev.; charts; circ. 1,000. (reprint service avail. from KTO) **Indexed:** Appl.Mech.Rev., Compumath, Curr.Cont., Math.R., Sci.Abstr., Zent.Math.
Description: Covers all areas of mathematics.

ECUADOR. DIRECCION DE AVIACION CIVIL. MATHEMATICS. see *TRANSPORTATION — Air Transport*

510 370 NE ISSN 0013-1954
QA1 CODEN: EDSMAN
EDUCATIONAL STUDIES IN MATHEMATICS. 1968. bi-m. $74 to individuals; institutions $219.50. Kluwer Academic Publishers, Postbus 17, 3300 AA Dordrecht, Netherlands. TEL 078-334911. FAX 078-334254. TELEX 29245. (Dist. by: Kluwer Academic Publishers Group, P.O. Box 322, 3300 AH Dordrecht, Netherlands; N. America dist. addr.: Box 358, Accord Station, Hingham, MA 02018-0358. TEL 617-871-6600) Ed. Willibald Doerfler. adv.; bk.rev.; charts; illus.; index. (reprint service avail. from SWZ) **Indexed:** Br.Educ.Ind., C.I.J.E., Cont.Pg.Educ., Curr.Cont., Educ.Ind., Educ.Tech.Abstr., High.Educ.Curr.Aware.Bull., Math.R., Ref.Zh., Res.High.Educ.Abstr., Sci.Abstr., Stud.Wom.Abstr.
—BLDSC shelfmark: 3662.523000.

EEST TEADUSTE AKADEEMIA. TOIMETISED. FUUSIKA. MATEMAATIKA/ESTONIAN ACADEMY OF SCIENCES. PROCEEDINGS. PHYSICS. MATHEMATICS. see *PHYSICS*

510 FR ISSN 1161-059X
QA1
ELECTRICITE DE FRANCE. DIRECTION DES ETUDES ET RECHERCHES. COLLECTION DE NOTES INTERNES. MATHEMATIQUES, INFORMATIQUE, TELECOMMUNICATIONS. (Text and summaries in English, French) 1968. irreg. 3000 F. Electricite de France (EDF), Direction des Etudes et des Recherches, 1 av. du General de Gaulle, 92141 Clamart Cedex, France. TEL 1-47-65-43-21. FAX 1-47-65-31-24. TELEX 204,347 F. Ed. Ph. Esclangon. charts; illus.; cum.index; circ. 1,500. **Indexed:** GeoRef., INIS Atomind., Math.R., Sci.Abstr.
Supersedes (in 1992): Electricite de France. Direction des Etudes et Recherches. Bulletin. Serie C: Mathematiques-Informatique (ISSN 0013-4511)

510 SZ ISSN 0013-6018
QA1 CODEN: ELMMAF
ELEMENTE DER MATHEMATIK/REVUE DE MATHEMATIQUES ELEMENTAIRES/RIVISTA DI MATEMATICA ELEMENTARE. (Text in English, French and German) 1946. bi-m. 69 Fr.($48) Birkhaeuser Verlag, P.O. Box 133, CH-4010 Basel, Switzerland. TEL 061-737740. FAX 061-737950. TELEX 963475 BIRKH CH. (Dist. in N. America by: Springer-Verlag New York, Inc., Journal Fulfillment Services, Box 2485, Secaucus, NJ 07096-2491, USA. TEL 201-348-4033) Ed. M. Jeger. adv.; bk.rev.; bibl.; charts; illus.; tr.lit.; index. **Indexed:** Math.R.
—BLDSC shelfmark: 3728.000000.

510 US ISSN 0163-3287
EMPLOYMENT INFORMATION IN THE MATHEMATICAL SCIENCES. no.88, 1987. 6/yr. $146 to non-members; members $88; students or unemployed $34. American Mathematical Society, Box 1571, Annex Sta., Providence, RI 02901-9930. TEL 401-455-4000. circ. 750.
●Also available online. Vendor(s): Human Resources Information Network.

ENROLLED ACTUARIES REPORT. see *INSURANCE*

510 SZ ISSN 0013-8584
QA1 CODEN: ENMAAR
ENSEIGNEMENT MATHEMATIQUE. (Text in English, French, German and Italian) 1899. q. 150 Fr. Universite de Geneve, Section de Mathematiques, 2-4, rue du Lievre, Case Postale 240, CH-1211 Geneva 24, Switzerland. Ed. Pierre Jeanquartier. adv.; bk.rev.; circ. 900. (also avail. in microfiche from BHP; reprint service avail. from SWZ) **Indexed:** Math.R.
—BLDSC shelfmark: 3776.300000.

510 US ISSN 0071-1136
ERGEBNISSE DER MATHEMATIK UND IHRER GRENZGEBIETE. NEUE FOLGE. (Text in German or English; occasionally French or Italian) 1955; 3rd series 1984. irreg. price varies. Springer-Verlag, 175 Fifth Ave., New York, NY 10010. TEL 212-460-1500. (Also: Berlin, Heidelberg, Tokyo and Vienna) Ed. P.Z. Hilton. circ. 2,000. (reprint service avail. from ISI) **Indexed:** Math.R.

515.42 UK ISSN 0143-3857
QA611.5
ERGODIC THEORY AND DYNAMICAL SYSTEMS. 1981. q. $275. Cambridge University Press, Edinburgh Bldg., Shaftesbury Rd., Cambridge CB2 2RU, England. TEL 0223-312393. FAX 0223-315052. TELEX 851817256. (North American orders to: Cambridge University Press, 40 W. 20th St., New York, NY 10011) Ed. J. Franks. bk.rev.; circ. 450. (also avail. in microform from UMI; reprint service avail. from SWZ) **Indexed:** ASCA, Compumath, Math.R.
—BLDSC shelfmark: 3808.330000.
Description: Discusses applications of ergodic theory to differential geometry, statistical mechanics, number theory and operator algebras.

ETGAR (REHOVOT). see *CHILDREN AND YOUTH — For*

510 NE
EUCLIDES; maandblad voor de didactiek van de wiskunde. 1925. 10/yr. fl.52. (Nederlandse Vereniging van Wiskundeleraren) Wolters-Noordhoff B.V., Damsport 157, 9728 PS Groningen, Netherlands. TEL (050)226922. (Subscr. to: Postbus 58, 9700 MB Groningen, Netherlands) Ed. W. Kleijne. adv.; bk.rev.; index; circ. 4,000. **Indexed:** Math.R.

510 530.15 UK ISSN 0071-2248
EUREKA: THE ARCHIMEDEAN'S JOURNAL. 1939. a. £2.50 to individuals; institutions £3.50. Cambridge University, Mathematical Society, Archimedeans, c/o Arts School, Bene't St., Cambridge CB2 3PY, England. Ed. M.A. Wainwright. adv.; bk.rev.; circ. 800. **Indexed:** Met.Abstr.
—BLDSC shelfmark: 3829.000000.
Description: Contains articles by many leading mathematicians.

510 UK ISSN 0956-7925
QA1
▼**EUROPEAN JOURNAL OF APPLIED MATHEMATICS.** 1990. q. $155. Cambridge University Press, Edinburgh Bldg., Shaftesbury Rd., Cambridge CB2 2RU, England. TEL 0223-312-393. FAX 0223-315052. TELEX 851817256. (U.S. addr.: Cambridge University Press, 40 W. 20th St., New York, NY 10011) Ed. John Ockendon.
—BLDSC shelfmark: 3829.722207.
Description: Focuses on applied mathematics with real world applications, as well as the development of theoretical methods.

510 UK ISSN 0195-6698
QA164 CODEN: EJOCDI
EUROPEAN JOURNAL OF COMBINATORICS/JOURNAL EUROPEEN DE COMBINATOIRE/EUROPAEISCHE ZEITSCHRIFT FUER KOMBINATORIK. 1980. bi-m. $284. Academic Press Ltd., 24-28 Oval Rd., London NW1 7DX, England. TEL 071-267-4466. FAX 071-482-2293. TELEX 25775 ACPRES G. Ed.Bd. **Indexed:** Compumath, Curr.Cont., Int.Abstr.Oper.Res., Math.R., Sci.Abstr.
—BLDSC shelfmark: 3829.728200.
Description: Internationl journal of pure mathematics, specializing in theories arising from combinatorial problems.

510 GW ISSN 0723-0869
EXPOSITIONES MATHEMATICAE; international journal of pure and applied mathematics. (Text in English, French and German; summaries in German) 1982. q. DM.394. Bibliographisches Institut und F.A. Brockhaus AG, Postfach 100311, 6800 Mannheim 1, Germany. TEL 0621-3901-01. FAX 0621-3901-389. TELEX 462107. Ed. S.D. Chatherji.
—BLDSC shelfmark: 3843.352000.

510 PL ISSN 0044-4413
QA1 CODEN: FMPMDH
FASCICULI MATHEMATICI. (Text and summaries in English, French and Russian) irreg. price varies. Politechnika Poznanska, Pl. Curie Sklodowskiej 5, Poznan, Poland. (Dist. by: Ars Polona, Krakowskie Przedmiescie 7, Box 1001, 00-068 Warsaw, Poland) illus.; circ. 180. **Indexed:** Math.R., Ref.Zh.
Formerly: Politechnika Poznanska. Zeszyty Naukowe. Matematyka (ISSN 0079-452X)
Description: Mathematical analysis and probability.

510 US ISSN 0015-0517
QA1 CODEN: FIBQAU
FIBONACCI QUARTERLY; a journal devoted to the study of integers with special properties. 1963. q. $35 to individuals; libraries $40. (Fibonacci Association) South Dakota State University, Computer Science Department, Box 2201, Brookings, SD 57007-0194. Ed. G.E. Bergum. index; circ. 900. (also avail. in microform from UMI) **Indexed:** Compumath, Curr.Cont., Ind.Sci.Rev., Math.R., Sci.Cit.Ind.
—BLDSC shelfmark: 3914.700000.

FIZIKO-MATEMATICHESKO SPISANIE. see *PHYSICS*

510 371.9 US ISSN 0272-8893
QA11.A1
FOCUS ON LEARNING PROBLEMS IN MATHEMATICS. 1979. 4/yr. Center for Teaching - Learning of Mathematics, Box 3149, Framingham, MA 01701. Ed. Mahesh Sharma. circ. 2,000.
—BLDSC shelfmark: 3964.216800.
Description: Covers research on issues in mathematics learning from diffrent disciplines, including mathematics, special education, psychology, and neurology.

510 CS
FORMATOR SYMPOSIUM ON MATHEMATICAL METHODS FOR THE ANALYSIS OF LARGE-SCALE SYSTEMS. (Text in English) irreg., 4th 1983, Prague. (Czechoslovak Academy of Sciences, Institute of Information Theory and Automation) Academia, Publishing House of the Czechoslovak Academy of Sciences, Vodickova 40, 112 29 Prague 1, Czechoslovakia. TEL 221-413.

510 GW ISSN 0933-7741
QA1 CODEN: FOMAEF
FORUM MATHEMATICUM. (Text mainly in English) 1989. bi-m. DM.408($255) Walter de Gruyter & Co., Genthinerstr. 13, 1000 Berlin 30, Germany. TEL 030-26005-0. FAX 030-26005-251. TELEX 184027. Ed.Bd. adv.; illus.; index. (back issues avail.) **Indexed:** Math.R., Zent.Math.
—BLDSC shelfmark: 4024.087900.
Description: Original research articles in all fields of pure and applied mathematics, including mathematical physics.

MATHEMATICS

510   **FR**
FRANCE. MINISTERE DE LA RECHERCHE ET DE L'INDUSTRIE. REPERTOIRE NATIONAL DES LABORATOIRES; LA RECHERCHE UNIVERSITAIRE; SCIENCES EXACTES ET NATURELLES. TOME 4: MATHEMATIQUES, SCIENCES DE L'ESPACE ET DE LA TERRE. 1966. irreg. price varies. (Centre National de la Recherche Scientifique) Documentation Francaise, 29-31 Quai Voltaire, 75007 Paris, France. TEL 1-40-15-70-00.
Formerly: France. Delegation Generale a la Recherche Scientifique et Technique. Repertoire National des Laboratoires; la Recherche Universitaire; Sciences Exactes et Naturelles. Tome 4: Mathematiques, Sciences de l'Espace et de la Terre (ISSN 0071-8564)

510   **US**
FRONTIERS IN APPLIED MATHEMATICS. 1984. irreg. Society for Industrial and Applied Mathematics, Customer Service, 3600 University City Science Ctr., Philadelphia, PA 19104-2688. TEL 215-382-9800. FAX 215-386-7999.
Refereed Serial

510   **CC**
FUJIAN ZHONGXUE SHUXUE/FUJIAN MIDDLE SCHOOL MATHEMATICS. (Text in Chinese) bi-m. Y4.15. Fujian Shifan Daxue, Shuxue Xi - Fujian Normal University, Mathematics Department, Fuzhou, Fujian 350007, People's Republic of China. TEL 541616. (Dist. overseas by: Jiangsu Publications Import & Export Corp., 56 Gao Yun Ling, Nanjing, Jiangsu, P.R.C.) (Co-sponsor: Fujian Mathematics Association) Ed. Lin Zhangyan.
Description: Explores the teaching methods of middle school mathematics.

510   **JA**   ISSN 0386-6262
FUKUI-KENRITSU TANKI DAIGAKU KENKYU KIYO/FUKUI PREFECTURAL COLLEGE. BULLETIN. (Text in Japanese; summaries in English, Japanese) 1976. a. Fukui Prefectural College - Fukui-kenritsu Tanki Daigaku, 97-21-3, Obatake-cho, Fukui-shi, Fukui-ken 910, Japan.

510   **JA**   ISSN 0386-118X
Q4   CODEN: FDRSDG
FUKUOKA DAIGAKU RIGAKU SHUHO/FUKUOKA UNIVERSITY. CENTRAL RESEARCH INSTITUTE. SCIENCE REPORTS. (Text in English and Japanese; summaries in English) 1972. s-a. Fukuoka University, Central Research Institute - Fukuoka Daigaku Sogo Kenkyujo, 19-1, Nanakuma, 8-chome, Jonan-ku, Fukuoka-shi, Fukuoka-ken 814-01, Japan.
Description: Contains original papers.

510   **JA**   ISSN 0287-0002
FUKUOKA DAIGAKU SOGO KENKYUJO. SHIZEN KAGAKU HEN/FUKUOKA UNIVERSITY. CENTRAL RESEARCH INSTITUTE. BULLETIN. (Text in Japanese; summaries in English) 1977. irreg. Fukuoka University, Central Research Institute - Fukuoka Daigaku Sogo Kenkyujo, 19-1, Nanakuma, 8-chome, Jonan-ku, Fukuoka-shi, Fukuoka-ken 814-01, Japan.

FUKUOKA KYOIKU DAIGAKU KIYO. DAI-3-BUNSATSU. SUGAKU, RIKA, GIJUTSUKA HEN/FUKUOKA UNIVERSITY OF EDUCATION. BULLETIN. PART 3: MATHEMATICS, NATURAL SCIENCES AND TECHNOLOGY. see *SCIENCES: COMPREHENSIVE WORKS*

510   **AT**   ISSN 0313-6825
FUNCTION. 1977. 5/yr. Aus.$17. Monash University, Department of Mathematics, Wellington Road, Clayton, Vic. 3168, Australia. FAX 565-44-03. TELEX MONASH AA 32691. Ed. M.A.B. Deakin. adv.; bk.rev.; circ. 300. (back issues avail.)
Description: A journal of school mathematics.

515   **US**   ISSN 0016-2663
CODEN: FAAPBZ
FUNCTIONAL ANALYSIS AND ITS APPLICATIONS. English translation of: Funktsional'nyi Analiz i ego Prilozheniya. 1967. q. $795 (foreign $930)(effective 1992). (Russian Academy of Sciences, RU) Plenum Publishing Corp., Consultants Bureau, 233 Spring St., New York, NY 10013-1578. TEL 212-620-8468. FAX 212-463-0742. TELEX 23-421139. Ed. A.K. Kirillov. (also avail. in microfilm from JSC; back issues avail.) **Indexed:** Compumath, Curr.Cont., Math.R., Zent.Math.
—BLDSC shelfmark: 0411.763000.
Refereed Serial

510   **PL**   ISSN 0208-6573
QA331
FUNCTIONES ET APPROXIMATIO COMMENTARII MATHEMATICI. (Text in English) 1974. irreg., vol.18, 1989. $16. (Uniwersytet im. Adama Mickiewicza w Poznaniu, Instytut Matematyki) Adam Mickiewicz University Press, Nowowiejskiego 55, 61-734 Poznan, Poland. TEL 699 221. TELEX 413260 UAM PL. Eds. J. Musielak, A. Alexiewicz. circ. 600. (also avail. in microfiche) **Indexed:** Math.R.
Description: Contains papers on the theory of real functions and mathematical analysis with particular emphasis on the theory of approximation.

510   **PL**   ISSN 0016-2736
QA1
FUNDAMENTA MATHEMATICAE. (Text in various languages) 1920. irreg., vol.135, 1990. $45 per no. (Polska Akademia Nauk, Instytut Matematyczny) Panstwowe Wydawnictwo Naukowe, Miodowa 10, 00-251 Warsaw, Poland. (Dist. by: Ars Polona, Krakowskie Przedmiescie 7, 00-068 Warsaw, Poland) Ed. R. Engelking. (also avail. in microfiche from BHP; reprint service avail. from SWZ) **Indexed:** Compumath, Math.R.

510   **JA**   ISSN 0532-8721
QA431   CODEN: FESIAT
FUNKCIALAJ EKVACIOJ, SERIO INTERNACIA. (Text in English and French) 1958. 3/yr. Nihon Sugakkai, Kansu Hoteishiki - Mathematical Society of Japan, Division of Functional Equations, c/o Kobe Daigaku Rigakubu, Sugaku Kyoshitsu, Rokkodai-cho, Nada-ku, Kobe-shi, Hyogo-ken 657, Japan.
—BLDSC shelfmark: 4058.120000.

515   **RU**   ISSN 0016-285X
FUNKTSIONAL'NYI ANALIZ I EGO PRILOZHENIYA. 1967. q. 16.80 Rub. (Akademiya Nauk S.S.S.R.) Izdatel'stvo Nauka, Fazmatlit, Attn: Mr. V.A. Kulyamin, Editor-in-Chief, Leninskii prospekt, 15, 117071 Moscow, V-71, Russia. **Indexed:** Math.R.

510   **NE**   ISSN 0165-0114
QA248   CODEN: FSSYD8
FUZZY SETS AND SYSTEMS. (Text in English) 1978. 24/yr.(in 8 vols.; 3 nos./vol.). fl.2688 (effective 1992). (International Fuzzy Systems Association (IFSA)) North-Holland (Subsidiary of: Elsevier Science Publishers B.V.), P.O. Box 211, 1000 AE Amsterdam, Netherlands. TEL 020-5803911. FAX 020-5803598. TELEX 18582 ESPA NL. (Subscr. in U.S. and Canada to: Elsevier Science Publishing Co., Inc., Box 882, Madison Sq. Sta., New York, NY 10159. TEL 212-989-5800) Ed. H.J. Zimmermann. adv.; bk.rev. (also avail. in microform from RPI; back issues avail.; reprint service avail. from SWZ) **Indexed:** A.I.Abstr., Biostat., Compumath, Curr.Cont., Cyb.Abstr., Int.Abstr.Oper.Res., Math.R., Oper.Res.Manage.Sci., Qual.Contr.Appl.Stat., Robomat., Sci.Abstr.
—BLDSC shelfmark: 4060.740000.
Description: Encourages communication between scientists and practitioners interested in research and applications in fuzzy sets and systems.
Refereed Serial

510   **RM**
GAMMA. (Text and summaries in English and Rumanian) 1978. a. 10 lei. (Number Theory Company, US) Gamma Company, Str. Harmanului Nr. 22, Sacele, Rumania. TEL 011-40-22-71032. (US addr.: Box 42561, Phoenix, AZ 85080) Eds. Mihail Bencze, Florentin Smarandache. bk.rev.; circ. 1,000. (looseleaf format; back issues avail.)

510   **II**   ISSN 0046-5402
QA1   CODEN: GNTAAG
GANITA. (Text in English) 1950. s-a. Rs.150($20) (effective 1992). Bharata Ganita Parisad, University of Lucknow, Department of Mathematics and Astronomy, Lucknow, Uttar Pradesh, India. Ed. Dr. Kamala D. Singh. bk.rev.; circ. 500. **Indexed:** Math.R., Zent.Math.
Formerly: Benares Mathematical Society. Proceedings.

510   **II**   ISSN 0970-0307
QA21
GANITA BHARATI. 1979. q. Rs.100($50) to non-members; members Rs.25($25). Indian Society for History of Mathematics, Delhi University, Delhi 110 007, India. (Subscr. to: Dr. Man Mohan, Dept. of Math., Ramjas College, Delhi 110 007, India) Ed. R.C. Gupta.

510   **CC**   ISSN 1000-081X
QA1
GAODENG XUEXIAO JISUAN SHUXUE XUEBAO. (Text in Chinese) q. Nanjing Daxue - Nanjing University, Hankou Lu, Nanjing, Jiangsu 210008, People's Republic of China. TEL 637651. Ed. He Xuechu.
—BLDSC shelfmark: 6184.693700.

510   **CC**
GAOXIAO YINGYONG SHUXUE XUEBAO/JOURNAL OF APPLIED MATHEMATICS IN HIGHER EDUCATION. (Text in Chinese) q. Zhejiang Daxue - Zhejiang University, Zheda Lu, Hangzhou, Zhejiang 310027, People's Republic of China. TEL 572244. Ed. Dong Guangchang.

GAUSS - GESELLSCHAFT. MITTEILUNGEN. see *ASTRONOMY*

510   **RM**
GAZETA MATEMATICA; publicatie lunara pentu tineret. 1895. m. 24 lei($20) Societatea de Stiinte Matematice, Str. Academiei 14, 70109 Bucharest, Rumania. (Subscr. to: ILEXIM, Str. 13 Decembrie Nr. 3, P.O. Box 136-137, Bucharest, Rumania) Ed. N. Teodorescu. bk.rev.; index. **Indexed:** Math.R.
Formed by the merger of: Gazeta Matematica. Serie A (ISSN 0016-5433); Gazetta Matematica. Serie B (ISSN 0016-5441)

510 500   **PL**
GDANSKIE TOWARZYSTWO NAUKOWE. WYDZIAL 3. NAUK MATEMATYCZNO-FIZYCZNO-CHEMICZNYCH. PRACE. (Text in Polish; summaries in English and Russian) 1964. irreg. price varies. Ossolineum, Publishing House of the Polish Academy of Sciences, Rynek 9, 50-106 Wroclaw, Poland. TELEX 0712771 OSS PL. (Dist. by: Ars Polona-Ruch, Krakowskie Przedmiescie 7, Warsaw, Poland) Ed. Ryszard Piekos.
Formerly: Gdanskie Towarzystwo Naukowe. Wydzial 3. Nauk Matematyczno-Przyrodniczych. Rozprawy (ISSN 0072-0445)
Description: Dissertations on mathematical, physical and chemical problems.

516   **NE**   ISSN 0046-5755
QA440   CODEN: GEMDAT
GEOMETRIAE DEDICATA. (Text in English, French or German) 1972. m. $654. Kluwer Academic Publishers, Postbus 17, 3300 AA Dordrecht, Netherlands. TEL 078-334911. FAX 078-334254. TELEX 29245. (Dist. by: Kluwer Academic Publishers Group, P.O. Box 322, 3300 AH Dordrecht, Netherlands; N. America dist. addr.: Box 358, Accord Station, Hingham, MA 02018-0358. TEL 617-871-6600) Eds. K. Strambach, F.D. Veldkamp. adv.; bk.rev. (reprint service avail. from SWZ) **Indexed:** Compumath, Math.R.

510   **SZ**   ISSN 1016-443X
QA440
▼**GEOMETRIC AND FUNCTIONAL ANALYSIS.** (Text in English) 1991. 4/yr. 198 Fr.($138) Birkhaeuser Verlag, P.O. Box 133, CH-4010 Basel, Switzerland. TEL 061-737740. FAX 061-737950. TELEX 963475 BIRKH CH. (Dist. in N. America by: Springer-Verlag New York, Inc., Journal Fulfillment Services, Box 2485, Secaucus, NJ 07096-2491, USA) Ed.Bd. **Indexed:** Curr.Cont., Math.R.
—BLDSC shelfmark: 4147.581000.
Description: Covers geometry and analysis interactions, including elliptic operators of manifolds; global variational calculus; concentration phenomenon and geometric inequalities; and other pertinent subjects.

510   **UK**   ISSN 0017-0895
QA1   CODEN: GLMJAS
GLASGOW MATHEMATICAL JOURNAL. (Text mainly in English; occasionally French and German) 1952. 3/yr. £50($105) (Glasgow Mathematical Society) Oxford University Press, Oxford Journals, Pinkhill House, Southfield Road, Eynsham, Oxford OX8 1JJ, England. TEL 0865-882283. FAX 0865-882890. TELEX 837330-OXPRES-G. adv.; charts; illus.; index; circ. 600. **Indexed:** Compumath, Math.R.
—BLDSC shelfmark: 4183.700000.
Formerly: Glasgow Mathematical Association Proceedings.
Description: Original work in pure mathematics. Includes papers on applied mathematics.

MATHEMATICS 3037

510   CI   ISSN 0017-095X
QA1   CODEN: GLMAB2
GLASNIK MATEMATICKI. (Text in English, French, German, Russian and Serbocroatian) N.S. 1966. s-a. $20. Drustvo Matematicara i Fizicara SR Hrvatske, Marulicev Trg. 19, Zagreb, Croatia. Ed. Ivan Ivansic. bk.rev.; charts; illus.; index; circ. 1,000. **Indexed:** Chem.Abstr., Math.R., Ref.Zh., Sci.Abstr., Zent.Math.
—BLDSC shelfmark: 4187.980000.
   Formerly: Glasnik Matematicko-Fizicki i Astronomski.

510   US   ISSN 0072-5285
GRADUATE TEXTS IN MATHEMATICS. (Text in English) 1971. irreg., vol.111, 1986. price varies. Springer-Verlag, 175 Fifth Ave., New York, NY 10010. TEL 212-460-1500. (Also: Berlin, Heidelberg, Tokyo and Vienna) Ed.Bd. (reprint service avail. from ISI) **Indexed:** Math.R.

510   GR   ISSN 0072-7466
GREEK MATHEMATICAL SOCIETY. BULLETIN/HELLENIKE MATHEMATIKE HETAIREIA. DELTION. (Text in English, French, German, and Italian) 1960. a. $30. Greek Mathematical Society, 34, E. Venizelou St., GR-10679 Athens, Greece. TEL 3617784. FAX 30-1-3641025. Ed.Bd. circ. 1,000. **Indexed:** Math.R., Zent.Math.

510   US
GRUNDLEHREN DER MATHEMATISCHEN WISSENSCHAFTEN. (Text in English, occasionally in French and German) 1957. irreg., vol.286, 1987. price varies. Springer-Verlag, 175 Fifth Ave., New York, NY 10010. TEL 212-460-1500. (Also Berlin, Heidelberg, Tokyo and Vienna) (reprint service avail. from ISI) **Indexed:** Math.R.
   Formerly: Grundlehren der Mathematischen Wissenschaften in Einzeldarstellungen (ISSN 0072-7830)

510 310   TU
HACETTEPE BULLETIN OF NATURAL SCIENCES AND ENGINEERING. (Series A: Biology; Series B: Mathematics and Statistics; Series C: Chemistry, Physics, and Engineering) (Text in English, summaries in Turkish) a. TL.10000($8) Hacettepe University, Faculty of Science - Hacettepe Universitesi, Fen Fakultesi, 06532 Beytepe, Ankara, Turkey. Ed. Suleyman Gunay. bk.rev.
   Description: Publishes short to medium length original research papers.

510   II   ISSN 0073-2281
HINDU ASTRONOMICAL AND MATHEMATICAL TEXT SERIES. (Text in English and Sanskrit; summaries in English) 1957. irreg. price varies. Bharata Ganita Parisad, University of Lucknow, Department of Mathematics and Astronomy, Lucknow, Uttar Pradesh, India. Ed. Ram Ballabh. **Indexed:** Math.R.

510   JA   ISSN 0018-2079
QA1   CODEN: HMTJAD
HIROSHIMA MATHEMATICAL JOURNAL. (Text in English, French and German) 1971. 3/yr. exchange basis only. Hiroshima Daigaku, Rigakubu, Sugaku Kyoshitsu - Hiroshima University, Faculty of Science, Department of Mathematics, Higashisenda-cho 1-chome, Naka-ku, Hiroshima-shi, Hiroshima-ken 730, Japan. circ. 700. (also avail. in microform from MIM) **Indexed:** Math.R., World Alum.Abstr.
—BLDSC shelfmark: 4315.608000.
   Supersedes: Hiroshima University. Journal of Science. Series A. Section 1: Mathematics.

510   US   ISSN 0315-0860
QA21   CODEN: HIMADS
HISTORIA MATHEMATICA. 1974. q. $100 (foreign $123). (International Commission on the History of Mathematics) Academic Press, Inc., Journal Division, 1250 Sixth Ave., San Diego, CA 92101. TEL 619-230-1840. FAX 619-699-6800. TELEX 181726. Eds. Eberhard Knobloch, David E. Rowe. adv.; bk.rev.; index. (back issues avail.) **Indexed:** Amer.Hist.& Life, Bull.Signal., Compumath, Hist.Abstr., Math.R., Ref.Zh., Zent.Math.
   Description: Concerned with the history of all aspects of the mathematical sciences in all parts of the world and all historical periods. Publishes occasional biographies of mathematicians and historians, studies of organizations and institutions, essays on historiography, and articles on the interactions among all facets of mathematical activity and other aspects of culture and society.
   Refereed Serial

510   US   ISSN 0899-2428
HISTORY OF MATHEMATICS. 1988. irreg. price varies. American Mathematical Society, Box 1517, Annex Sta., Providence, RI 02901-9930.
TEL 401-455-4000.

510   GW   ISSN 0073-2842
HOCHSCHULBUECHER FUER MATHEMATIK. 1955. irreg. price varies. VEB Deutscher Verlag der Wissenschaften, Postfach 1216, 1080 Berlin, Germany. Ed.Bd. **Indexed:** Math.R.

510 530   JA   ISSN 0367-5939
Q77   CODEN: HKDSAE
HOKKAIDO KYOIKU DAIGAKU KIYO. DAI-2-BU, A. SUGAKU, BUTSURI, KAGAKU, KOGAKU-HEN/HOKKAIDO UNIVERSITY OF EDUCATION. JOURNAL. SECTION 2 A. MATHEMATICS, PHYSICS, CHEMISTRY, ENGINEERING. (Text and summaries in English and Japanese) 1949. s-a. exchange basis. Hokkaido University of Education - Hokkaido Kyoiku Daigaku, Ainosato 5-jou, 3-chome, Kita-ku, Sapporo-shi 002, Hokkaido, Japan. **Indexed:** Jap.Per.Ind., Math.R.

510   JA   ISSN 0385-4035
QA1   CODEN: HMAJDN
HOKKAIDO MATHEMATICAL JOURNAL. (Text in English, French, German) 1972. 3/yr. $222. Hokkaido Daigaku, Rigakubu Sugaku Kyoshitsu - Hokkaido University, Faculty of Science, Department of Mathematics, Nishi-8-chome, Kita-10-jo, Kita-ku, Sapporo 060, Japan. FAX 11-727-3705. TELEX 932510-HOKUSC-J. (Subscr. to: Kinokuniya Co. Ltd., 17-7 Shinjuku 3-chome, Shinjuku-ku, Tokyo 160-91, Japan) Ed. Y. Okabe. circ. 720. (back issues avail.) **Indexed:** Math.R.
—BLDSC shelfmark: 4322.268000.
   Formerly: Hokkaido University. Faculty of Science. Journal. Series 1: Mathematics (ISSN 0018-3482)

510   US   ISSN 0362-1588
QA1   CODEN: HJMADZ
HOUSTON JOURNAL OF MATHEMATICS.* 1975. q. $85 (foreign $90). (University of Houston, Central Campus) Arte Publico Press, Houston, TX 77004. TEL 713-749-2112. Ed. G. Johnson. circ. 450. **Indexed:** Compumath, Math.R., Sci.Abstr.

510 519   UK   ISSN 0272-4960
QA1   CODEN: IJAMDM
I M A JOURNAL OF APPLIED MATHEMATICS. 1981. 6/yr. £160($360) (Institute of Mathematics and its Applications) Oxford University Press, Oxford Journals, Pinkhill House, Southfield Road, Eynsham, Oxford OX8 1JJ, England. TEL 0865-882283. FAX 0865-882890. TELEX 837330 OXPRES G. (U.S. addr.: 200 Madison Ave., New York, NY 10016) Eds. D.A. Spence, J.R. Okendon. adv.; index; circ. 1,200. (back issues avail.) **Indexed:** Appl.Mech.Rev., Chem.Abstr., Compumath, Cyb.Abstr., Excerp.Med., Fluidex, Ind.Sci.Rev., Int.Aerosp.Abstr., Math.R., Sci.Abstr., Sci.Cit.Ind.
—BLDSC shelfmark: 4368.755000.
   Supersedes in part (as of 1981): Institute of Mathematics and its Applications. Journal (ISSN 0020-2932)
   Description: Papers in all areas of the application of mathematics, including analytic and numerical treatments of both physical and non-physical applied mathematical problems arising in industry.

510   UK   ISSN 0265-0754
I M A JOURNAL OF MATHEMATICAL CONTROL & INFORMATION. 1984. q. £85($185) (Institute of Mathematics and its Applications) Oxford University Press, Oxford Journals, Pinkhill House, Southfield Road, Eynsham, Oxford OX8 1JJ, England. TEL 0865-882283. FAX 0865-56646. TELEX 837330 OXPRES G. Eds. C.J. Harris, J.E. Marshall. adv. **Indexed:** Compumath, Math.R.
   Description: Presents original papers in mathematical control theory, systems theory, and allied information sciences.

510   UK   ISSN 0953-0061
HD30.25   CODEN: IMJIE9
I M A JOURNAL OF MATHEMATICS APPLIED IN BUSINESS AND INDUSTRY. 1986. q. £70($160) (Institute of Mathematics and its Applications) Oxford University Press, Oxford Journals, Pinkhill House, Southfield Road, Eynsham, Oxford OX8 1JJ, England. TEL 0865-882283. FAX 0865-882890. TELEX 8373300 OXPRES G. Eds. R.S. Stainton, L. Thomas. adv. **Indexed:** Math.R.
—BLDSC shelfmark: 4368.758500.
   Formerly: I M A Journal of Mathematics in Management (ISSN 0268-1129)
   Description: Disseminates new mathematical theories related to any class of management problems and practical case studies involving substantial analytical argument.

510   UK   ISSN 0265-0746
   CODEN: IJMBEG
I M A JOURNAL OF MATHEMATICS APPLIED IN MEDICINE & BIOLOGY. 1984. q. £85($185) (Institute of Mathematics and its Applications) Oxford University Press, Oxford Journals, Pinkhill House, Southfield Road, Eynsham, Oxford OX8 1JJ, England. TEL 0865-882283. FAX 0865-882890. TELEX 837330 OXPRES G. Ed. R.W. Hiorns. adv.; index. **Indexed:** Bio-Contr.News & Info., Biol.Abstr., Compumath, Curr.Cont., Excerp.Med., Math.R., Sci.Cit.Ind.
—BLDSC shelfmark: 4368.759000.
   Description: Uses of mathematics in medical and biological research with emphasis on the special insights and enhanced understanding which arise from these uses.

510   UK   ISSN 0272-4979
QA297   CODEN: IJNADH
I M A JOURNAL OF NUMERICAL ANALYSIS. 1981. 4/yr. £105($230) (Institute of Mathematics and its Applications) Oxford University Press, Oxford Journals, Pinkhill House, Southfield Road, Eynsham, Oxford OX8 1JJ, England. TEL 0865-882283. FAX 0865-882890. TELEX 837330 OXPRES G. Eds. I.S. Duff, G.A. Watson. adv.; index. **Indexed:** Appl.Mech.Rev., Compumath, Comput.Abstr., Curr.Cont., Fluidex, Int.Aerosp.Abstr., Math.R., Sci.Abstr., Sci.Cit.Ind.
—BLDSC shelfmark: 4368.760000.
   Supersedes in part (as of 1981): Institute of Mathematics and its Applications. Journal (ISSN 0020-2932)
   Description: Covers theoretical and practical aspects of numerical analysis.

510   US
I M A VOLUMES IN MATHEMATICS AND ITS APPLICATIONS. 1986. irreg. price varies. Springer-Verlag, 175 Fifth Ave., New York, NY 10010. TEL 212-460-1500. (Also: Berlin, Heidelberg, Tokyo, Vienna) (reprint service avail. from ISI)

510   US
I M S LECTURE NOTES. MONOGRAPH SERIES. 1981. irreg. Institute of Mathematical Statistics, Business Office, 3401 Investment Blvd., Ste. 7, Hayward, CA 94545. TEL 510-783-8141. Ed. Robert J. Serfling.

510   AT   ISSN 0311-0621
I M U CANBERRA CIRCULAR. 1972. 4/yr. free. (International Mathematical Union) B.H. Neumann, Ed. & Pub., Mathematics Research Section, Australian National University, G.P.O. Box 4, Canberra A.C.T. 2601, Australia.
FAX 61-6-490759. TELEX AA62620. Ed. B.H. Neumann. circ. 930.
   Description: Covers international and Australasian mathematical meetings, deaths of mathematicians, honors awarded, and visits of mathematicians to Australia and New Zealand.

510   JA   ISSN 0579-3068
IBARAKI UNIVERSITY. FACULTY OF SCIENCE. BULLETIN. SERIES A: MATHEMATICS/IBARAKI DAIGAKU RIGAKUBU KIYO. SUGAKU. (Text and summaries in English) 1968. a. exchange basis only. Ibaraki Daigaku, Rigakubu Sugaku Kyoshitsu - Ibaraki University, Faculty of Science, Department of Mathematics, 1-1, Bunkyo 2-chome, Mito-shi, Ibaraki-ken 310, Japan. FAX 0292-27-8040. circ. 350. **Indexed:** Math.R.
—BLDSC shelfmark: 2509.030000.

M

MATHEMATICS

510   US   ISSN 0019-2082
QA1   CODEN: IJMTAW
ILLINOIS JOURNAL OF MATHEMATICS. (Text in English, French and German) 1957. q. $90. (University of Illinois at Urbana-Champaign, Department of Mathematics) University of Illinois Press, 54 E. Gregory Dr., Champaign, IL 61820. TEL 217-333-0950. FAX 217-244-8082. Ed. Gerald Janusz. charts; illus.; stat.; index; circ. 1,100. (also avail. in microform from MIM,SWZ,UMI; reprint service avail. from SWZ,UMI) **Indexed:** Compumath, Curr.Cont., Math.R., Sci.Cit.Ind.
—BLDSC shelfmark: 4365.300000.
Refereed Serial

510   NE   ISSN 0019-3577
QA1   CODEN: IMTHBJ
INDAGATIONES MATHEMATICAE. (Text in English) 1937; N.S. 1990. q. fl.343 (effective 1992). (Koninklijke Nederlandse Akademie van Wetenschappen - Royal Netherlands Academy of Sciences) North-Holland (Subsidiary of: Elsevier Science Publishers B.V.), P.O. Box 211, 1000 AE Amsterdam, Netherlands. TEL 020-5803911. FAX 020-5803598. TELEX 18582 ESPA NL. (Subscr. in U.S. and Canada to: Elsevier Science Publishing Co., Inc., Box 882, Madison Sq. Sta., New York, NY 10159. TEL 212-989-5800) charts; illus.; index; circ. 1,500. (also avail. in microform from SWZ; back issues avail.; reprint service avail. from SWZ) **Indexed:** Chem.Abstr., Compumath, Curr.Cont., Math.R.
—BLDSC shelfmark: 4375.700000.
Incorporates (in 1990): Koninklijke Nederlandse Akademie van Wetenschappen. Series A, Mathematical Sciences. Proceedings (ISSN 0023-3358)
Refereed Serial

510   II   ISSN 0970-5120
QA1
INDIAN ACADEMY OF MATHEMATICS. JOURNAL. (Text in English) 1979. s-a. Rs.40($15) to individuals; institutions Rs.80($20)(effective 1991). Indian Academy of Mathematics, 46 Shankarbag, Indore 452 006, India. Ed. V.M. Bhise. circ. 250. **Indexed:** Math.R., Zent.Math.

510   II   ISSN 0253-4142
QA11.A1   CODEN: PIAMDO
INDIAN ACADEMY OF SCIENCES. PROCEEDINGS. MATHEMATICAL SCIENCES. (Text in English) 1934. 3/yr. Rs.75($75) Indian Academy of Sciences, C.V. Raman Ave., P.O. Box 8005, Bangalore, India. TEL 342546. FAX 91-812-346094. TELEX 0845-2178-ACAD-IN. Eds. S.G. Dani, A. Ramanathan. bibl.; illus.; index; circ. 1,000. (also avail. in microfilm from UMI; reprint services avail. from ISI,UMI) **Indexed:** Compumath, Curr.Cont.

510 620   II   ISSN 0304-9884
TA329
INDIAN JOURNAL OF ENGINEERING MATHEMATICS. (Text in English) 1968. s-a. Rs.20($5) Ram Prasad & Sons, Hospital Rd., Agra 3, India. Ed. G. Paria. adv.; bk.rev.; illus. (back issues avail.)

510 519   II   ISSN 0019-5588
QA1   CODEN: IJMHAU
INDIAN JOURNAL OF PURE AND APPLIED MATHEMATICS. (Text in English) 1970. m. Rs.400 (foreign 693.50 Fr.). Indian National Science Academy, Bahadur Shah Zafar Marg, New Delhi 110 002, India. TEL 61-6918925. FAX 61-6924262. TELEX 963475. (Dist. outside Sub-continent area by: J.C. Baltzer A.G., Wettsteinplatz 10, CH-4058 Basel, Switzerland) **Indexed:** Compumath, Curr.Cont., Ind.Sci.Rev., INIS Atomind., Math.R., Sci.Abstr., Sci.Cit.Ind.
—BLDSC shelfmark: 4420.600000.

510   II   ISSN 0019-5839
CODEN: JIMTA2
INDIAN MATHEMATICAL SOCIETY. JOURNAL. (Text in English) 1909; N.S. 1934. a. $70. Indian Mathematical Society, Meerut University, Department of Mathematics, Meerut 250 005, India. Ed. I.B.S. Passi. bk.rev.; bibl.; pat.; tr.lit.; index; circ. 1,200. **Indexed:** Cyb.Abstr., Math.R.

510 620   US   ISSN 0022-2518
QA1   CODEN: IUMJAB
INDIANA UNIVERSITY MATHEMATICS JOURNAL. (Text in English, French) 1952. q. $95. Indiana University, Department of Mathematics, Swain Hall East 222, Bloomington, IN 47405. TEL 812-855-2252. FAX 812-855-0046. Ed.Bd. bibl.; charts; index. (back issues avail.) **Indexed:** Compumath, Curr.Cont., Eng.Ind., Math.R., Sci.Cit.Ind., Zent.Math.
Formerly: Journal of Mathematics and Mechanics (ISSN 0095-9057)
Refereed Serial

510 600   US   ISSN 0019-8528
TA350   CODEN: IMTHAI
INDUSTRIAL MATHEMATICS. 1950. s-a. $15 to non-members. Industrial Mathematics Society, Box 159, Roseville, MI 48066. TEL 313-771-0403. Ed. Dr. Robert Schmidt. adv.; bk.rev.; illus.; circ. 600. (also avail. in microform from UMI; reprint service avail. from UMI) **Indexed:** Appl.Mech.Rev., Eng.Ind., Math.R., Sci.Abstr.
—BLDSC shelfmark: 4457.800000.

510.78   PL   ISSN 0542-9951
INFORMATYKA. 1965. m. $61. (Polski Komitet Automatycznego Przetwarzania Informacji NOT) Wydawnictwo Czasopism i Ksiazek Technicznych SIGMA - NOT, Ul. Biala 4, 00-950 Warsaw, Poland. (Dist. by: SIGMA NOT Ltd., Ul. Bartycka 20, 00-716 Warsaw, Poland) (Co-sponsor: Krajowe Biuro Informatyki) circ. 5,250. **Indexed:** Cyb.Abstr., INIS Atomind., Sci.Abstr.
—BLDSC shelfmark: 4496.915000.

510 371.3   IT
INSEGNAMENTO DELLA MATEMATICA E DELLE SCIENZE INTEGRATE. 1978. m. (plus q. supp.). L.20000. (Centro Ricerche Didattiche "Ugo Morin") Giovanni Battagin Editore, Via dell' Artigianato, 2, 31020 San Zenone degli Ezzelini (Treviso), Italy. TEL 0423 567300. FAX 0423-567750. Ed. Candido Sitia. adv.; bk.rev.; bibl.; illus.; stat.; circ. 2,500.
Description: For elementary and secondary teachers; presents methods of improving teaching techniques in mathematics and related fields.

510   FR   ISSN 0073-8301
QA1   CODEN: PMIHA6
INSTITUT DES HAUTES ETUDES SCIENTIFIQUES, PARIS. PUBLICATIONS MATHEMATIQUES. 1959. s-a. 980 F. to individuals; institutions 1350 F. Presses Universitaires de France, Departement des Revues, 14 Avenue du Bois-de-l'Epine, B.P.90, 91003 Evry Cedex, France. TEL 1-60-77-82-05. FAX 1-60-79-20-45. TELEX PUF 600 474 F. (U.S. Subscr. to: Springer-Verlag, 175 Fifth Ave., New York, NY 10010) Ed. Jean Dieudonne. charts; illus.; index. (back issues avail.; reprint service avail. from KTO) **Indexed:** Compumath, Math.R.
—BLDSC shelfmark: 7131.400000.

510 530   FR   ISSN 0294-1449
INSTITUT HENRI POINCARE. ANNALES: ANALYSE NON LINEAIRE. (Text in English) 1983. 6/yr. 1715 F. Gauthier-Villars, 15 rue Gossin, 92543 Montrouge Cedex, France. TEL 33-1-40-92-65-00. FAX 33-1-40-92-65-97. TELEX 270 004. (Subscr. to: Centrale des Revues, 11 rue Gossin, 92543 Montrouge Cedex, France. TEL 33-1-46-56-52-66) Ed. P.L. Lions. adv.; abstr.; bibl.; circ. 650. **Indexed:** Compumath, Curr.Cont., INIS Atomind., Math.R.
Description: Covers theoretical and numerical aspects of non-linear analysis, including applications to PDEs, mechanics, physics, economics.

519   FR   ISSN 0246-0203
QA273.A1   CODEN: AHPBAR
INSTITUT HENRI POINCARE. ANNALES. PROBABILITES ET STATISTIQUES. (Text in English and French) 1930. q. 1180 F. (Institut Henri Poincare) Gauthier-Villars, 15 rue Gossin, 92543 Montrouge Cedex, France. TEL 33-1-40-92-65-00. FAX 33-1-40-92-65-97. TELEX 270 004. (Subscr. to: Centrale des Revues, 11 rue Gossin, 92543 Montrouge Cedex, France. TEL 33-1-46-56-52-66) Ed. J. Neveu. adv.; circ. 800. (also avail. in microfilm from UMI) **Indexed:** Chem.Abstr., Compumath, Curr.Cont., INIS Atomind., INSPEC, Math.R., Sci.Abstr., Sci.Cit.Ind., Zent.Math.
—BLDSC shelfmark: 0921.320270.
Description: Concerned with stochastic processes, mathematical statistics and contiguous domains.

INSTITUT HENRI POINCARE. ANNALES. SECTION A: PHYSIQUE THEORIQUE. see *PHYSICS*

510   FR
INSTITUT HENRI POINCARE. GROUPE D'ETUDE D'ANALYSE ULTRAMETRIQUE. EXPOSES. 1974. a. 60 Fr. Institut Henri Poincare, Secretariat Mathematique, 11 rue Pierre et Marie Curie, F-75231 Paris Cedex 05, France. (Subscr. to: Offilib, 48 rue Gay Lussac, F-75240 Paris Cedex 05, France) Ed. Paul Belgodere. circ. 200. (back issues avail.) **Indexed:** Math.R., Ref.Zh., Zent.Math.

526 510   US
INSTITUTE OF MATHEMATICAL GEOGRAPHY. MONOGRAPH SERIES. 1986. irreg., no.15, 1991. price varies. Institute of Mathematical Geography, 2790 Briarcliff, Ann Arbor, MI 48105-1429. TEL 313-761-1231. Ed. Sandra Lach Arlinghaus. charts; illus.; stat. (back issues avail.)
Description: Scholarly research and conference proceedings on topics in mathematics and geography.
Refereed Serial

510 530   II
INSTITUTE OF MATHEMATICAL SCIENCES, MADRAS. REPORTS. (Text in English) 1962. irreg. $20. Institute of Mathematical Sciences, Madras 600 113, India. TEL 044-2352267. FAX 044-2351856. TELEX 041 21060 PCO IN PP WDT 20.
Formerly (until 1970): Symposia on Theoretical Physics and Mathematics (ISSN 0082-075X)

510   US   ISSN 0146-3942
QA276.A1
INSTITUTE OF MATHEMATICAL STATISTICS. BULLETIN. 1972. 6/yr. $50. Institute of Mathematical Statistics, Business Office, 3401 Investment Blvd., Ste. 7, Hayward, CA 94545. TEL 510-783-8141. Ed. George Styan. circ. 4,000. (also avail. in microform from UMI; reprint service avail. from UMI)
—BLDSC shelfmark: 2580.891000.

510   UK   ISSN 0950-5628
CODEN: IMTABW
INSTITUTE OF MATHEMATICS AND ITS APPLICATIONS. BULLETIN. 1965. 8/yr. £65 to non-members. Institute of Mathematics and its Applications, 16 Nelson St., Southend-on-Sea, Essex SS1 1EF, England. TEL 0702-354020. FAX 0702-354111. Ed. Catherine Richards. adv.; bk.rev.; circ. 7,000. **Indexed:** Math.R.
Description: Papers of general interest to mathematicians, conference reports, forthcoming meetings.

510   UK
INSTITUTE OF MATHEMATICS AND ITS APPLICATIONS. PROCEEDINGS. irreg. price varies. Institute of Mathematics and its Applications, 16 Nelson St., Southend-on-Sea, Essex SS1 1EF, England. TEL 0702-354020. FAX 0702-354111.

519.5 310   JA   ISSN 0020-3157
QA276   CODEN: AISXAD
INSTITUTE OF STATISTICAL MATHEMATICS. ANNALS. (Text and summaries in English) 1949. 4/yr. 28000 Yen($275) (Institute of Statistical Mathematics) Kluwer Academic Publishers, Tokyo, 303 Jiyugaoka Komatsu Bldg., 24-17, Midorigaoka 2-chome, Meguro-ku, Tokyo 152, Japan. TEL 03-718-4405. FAX 03-718-4406. (Dist. by: Kluwer Academic Publishers Group, P.O. Box 322, 3300 AH Dordrecht, Netherlands; N. America dist. addr.: Box 358, Accord Station, Hingham, MA 02018-0358. TEL 617-871-6600) Ed. H. Akaike. stat.; circ. 1,500. **Indexed:** Compumath, J.Cont.Quant.Meth., Jap.Per.Ind., Math.R., Sci.Cit.Ind.
Refereed Serial

510   AG   ISSN 0326-0690
INSTITUTO DE MATEMATICA BEPPO LEVI. CUADERNOS. 1971. irreg. exchange basis. Universidad Nacional de Rosario, Avenida Pellegrini 250, 2000 Rosario, Argentina. TEL 041-217998. TELEX 41817 CIROS AR. Ed.Bd. circ. 500. **Indexed:** Appl.Mech.Rev., Math.R., Zent.Math.

510   RM
INSTITUTUL DE SUBINGINERI ORADEA. LUCRARI STIINTIFICE: SERIA MATEMATICA. (Text in Rumanian, occasionally in English or French; summaries in English, French, German, Rumanian) 1967. a. Institutul de Subingineri Oradea, Calea Armatei Rosii Nr. 5, 3700 Oradea, Rumania.
    Formerly: Institutul Pedagogic Oradea. Lucrari Stiintifice: Seria Matematica; which continues in part (in 1973): Institutul Pedagogica Oradea. Lucrari Stiintifice: Seria Matematica, Fizica, Chimie; which superseded in part (in 1971): Institutul Pedagogica Oradea. Lucrari Stiintifice: Seria A and Seria B; which was formerly (until 1969): Institutul Pedagogica Oradea. Lucrari Stiintifice.

530 520   RM
INSTITUTUL POLITEHNIC "GHEORGHE ASACHI" DIN IASI. BULETINUL. SECTIA I: MECANICA MATEMATICA, FIZICA. (Text in English, French, German and Russian) 1946. q. exchange basis. Institutul Politehnic "Gheorghe Asachi" din Iasi, Calea 23 August 11, 6600 Jassy, Rumania. TEL 46577. (Subscr. to: Rompresfilatelia, PO Box 12-201, Bucharest, Rumania) Ed. Prof. Dr. D. Mangeron. adv.; bk.rev.; bibl.; circ. 450. **Indexed:** Appl.Mech.Rev., Math.R, Ref.Zh., Sci.Abstr.
    Formerly: Institutul Politehnic Iasi. Buletinul. Sectia I: Matematica, Mecanica Teoretica, Fizica (ISSN 0304-5188)

INSURANCE: MATHEMATICS & ECONOMICS. see *INSURANCE*

510   SZ   ISSN 0378-620X
QA431
INTEGRAL EQUATIONS AND OPERATOR THEORY. (Text in English) 1978. bi-m. 438 Fr.($298) Birkhaeuser Verlag, P.O. Box 133, CH-4010 Basel, Switzerland. TEL 061-737740. FAX 061-737950. TELEX 963475 BIRKH CH. (Dist. in N. America by: Springer-Verlag New York, Inc., Journal Fulfillment Services, Box 2485, Secaucus, NJ 07096-2491, USA. TEL 201-248-4033) Ed. I. Gohberg. **Indexed:** Compumath, Math.R.

515   US
INTERNATIONAL CONFERENCE ON COMPUTING FIXED POINTS WITH APPLICATIONS. PROCEEDINGS. 1977. irreg., 1st, 1974, Clemson University (pub. 1977). Department of the Navy, Office of Naval Research, Arlington, VA 22217. TEL 202-545-6700. (Co-sponsor: U.S. Army Research Office)

INTERNATIONAL JOURNAL FOR NUMERICAL METHODS IN ENGINEERING. see *ENGINEERING*

510   SI   ISSN 0218-1967
QA150   CODEN: IACOEA
▼**INTERNATIONAL JOURNAL OF ALGEBRA AND COMPUTATION.** 1991. q. $95 to individuals and developing countries; institutions $205. World Scientific Publishing Co. Pte. Ltd., Farrer Rd., P.O. Box 128, Singapore 9128, Singapore. TEL 3825663. FAX 3825919. TELEX RS-28561-WSPC. (UK addr.: 73 Lynton Mead, Totteridge, London N20 8DH, England. TEL 44-81-4462461; US addr.: 1060 Main St., Ste. 1B, River Edge, NJ 07661. TEL 800-227-7562) Ed. J. Rhodes.
  —BLDSC shelfmark: 4542.005000.
    Description: Publishes original papers in mathematics in general, but giving a preference to those in the areas of mathematics represented by the editorial board.

510 330.1 320   GW   ISSN 0020-7276
QA269   CODEN: IJGTA2
INTERNATIONAL JOURNAL OF GAME THEORY. (Text in English) 1971. 4/yr. DM.378. Physica-Verlag GmbH und Co., Tiergartenstr. 17, Postfach 105280, 6900 Heidelberg 1, Germany. TEL 030-8207-424. FAX 030-8207-448. (Subscr. to: Springer Verlag GmbH, Postfach 311340, 1000 Berlin 31, Germany; Dist. in N. America by: Springer-Verlag New York Inc., 175 Fifth Ave., New York, NY 10010, U.S.A.. TEL 212-460-1500) adv.; bk.rev.; bibl.; charts; index. (back issues avail. from SWZ) **Indexed:** Compumath, Comput.Cont., Cyb.Abstr., Int.Abstr.Oper.Res., J.Cont.Quant.Meth., J.of Econ.Lit., Math.R., Sci.Abstr.
  —BLDSC shelfmark: 4542.261000.
    Description: Publishes original articles on the theory of games and its applications.

510 370   UK   ISSN 0020-739X
                            CODEN: IJMEBM
INTERNATIONAL JOURNAL OF MATHEMATICAL EDUCATION IN SCIENCE AND TECHNOLOGY. 1970. bi-m. £176($302) Taylor & Francis Ltd., Rankine Rd., Basingstoke, Hants RG24 0PR, England. TEL 0256-840366. FAX 0256-479438. TELEX 858540. Ed. Dennis Walker. adv.; bk.rev.; index. **Indexed:** C.I.J.E., Cont.Pg.Educ., Educ.Ind., Educ.Tech.Abstr., High.Educ.Curr.Aware.Bull., Intl.Civil Eng.Abstr., Math.R., Mid.East: Abstr.& Ind., Sci.Abstr., Soft.Abstr.Eng.
  —BLDSC shelfmark: 4542.337000.
    Description: Provides a medium by which a wide range of experience in mathematical education can be presented, assimilated and eventually adapted to everyday needs in schools, colleges, polytechnics, universities, industry and commerce.
    Refereed Serial

510   SI   ISSN 0129-167X
QA1
▼**INTERNATIONAL JOURNAL OF MATHEMATICS.** (Text in English) 1990. bi-m. $130 to individuals and developing countries; institutions $280. World Scientific Publishing Co. Pte. Ltd., Farrer Rd., P.O. Box 128, Singapore 9128, Singapore. TEL 3825663. FAX 3825919. TELEX RS-28561-WSPC. (US addr.: 1060 Main St., Ste. 1B, River Edge, NJ 07661. TEL 800-227-7562; UK addr.: 73 Lynton Mead, Totteridge, London N20 8DH, England. TEL 44-81-4462461) Eds. A. Casson, S. Kobayashi. circ. 100.
  —BLDSC shelfmark: 4542.337500.

510   II   ISSN 0161-1712
QA1
INTERNATIONAL JOURNAL OF MATHEMATICS AND MATHEMATICAL SCIENCES. (Text in English) 1978. q. $60. Calcutta Mathematical Society, AE-374, Sector-1, Salt Lake City, Calcutta 700 064, India. (Subscr. to: University of Central Florida, Orlando, Florida 32816, U.S.A.) circ. 200. (back issues avail.) **Indexed:** Math.R.

INTERNATIONAL JOURNAL OF NON-LINEAR MECHANICS. see *ENGINEERING — Engineering Mechanics And Materials*

INTERNATIONAL JOURNAL OF NUMERICAL MODELLING: ELECTRONIC NETWORKS, DEVICES AND FIELDS. see *ENGINEERING — Computer Applications*

510   AU   ISSN 0020-7926
                            CODEN: IMTNA2
INTERNATIONAL MATHEMATICAL NEWS. (Text in English, French and German) 1947. 3/yr. S.200. Oesterreichische Mathematische Gesellschaft, Technische Universitaet, Wiedner Hauptstr. 8-10, A-1040 Vienna, Austria. Ed. P. Flor. adv.; bk.rev.; bibl.; circ. 1,500. **Indexed:** Math.R.
  —BLDSC shelfmark: 4544.000000.
    Description: News about mathematical events around the world, including reviews of mathematical books.

510 530   II   ISSN 0074-705X
INTERNATIONAL MONOGRAPHS ON ADVANCED MATHEMATICS AND PHYSICS. (Text in English) 1961. irreg. Hindustan Publishing Corp., 6-U.B. Jawahar Nagar, Delhi 110007, India. FAX 6863511.

INTERNATIONAL SOCIETY OF PARAMETRIC ANALYSTS. CONFERENCE PROCEEDINGS. see *BUSINESS AND ECONOMICS — Accounting*

510   GW   ISSN 0020-9910
QA1   CODEN: INVMBH
INVENTIONES MATHEMATICAE. (Text mainly in English; occasionally in French or German) 1966. 12/yr. DM.2896($1560) Springer-Verlag, Heidelberger Platz 3, D-1000 Berlin 33, Germany. TEL 030-8207-1. (Also Heidelberg, Tokyo, Vienna, and New York) Ed. M. Berger. charts; illus.; stat. (also avail. in microform from UMI; back issues avail.; reprint service avail. from ISI) **Indexed:** Compumath, Curr.Cont., Ind.Sci.Rev., Math.R., Sci.Cit.Ind., Zent.Math.
  —BLDSC shelfmark: 4557.660000.
    Description: Forum for papers in mathematics.
    Refereed Serial

IOWA STATE UNIVERSITY. STATISTICAL LABORATORY. ANNUAL REPORT. see *MATHEMATICS — Abstracting, Bibliographies, Statistics*

511   IR
IRANIAN MATHEMATICAL SOCIETY. BULLETIN/ANJOMAN-I RIYAZI-I IRAN. BULETAN-I. (Text in English) 1973. s-a. $20 to non-members. Iranian Mathematical Society, P.O. Box 13145-418, Teheran, Iran. TELEX SHU 332169. Ed. M. Radjabalipour. bk.rev.; circ. 1,000. **Indexed:** Math.R.
    Description: Publishes research or expository articles in mathematical sciences.

510   IS   ISSN 0021-2172
QA1   CODEN: ISJMAP
ISRAEL JOURNAL OF MATHEMATICS. (Text in English) 1951. 12/yr. (in 4 vols., 3 nos./vol.). $30. Weizmann Science Press of Israel, P.O. Box 801, Jerusalem 91007, Israel. TEL 783203. FAX 783784. TELEX 26144-BXJM-IL-7086. Ed. A. Lubotzky. charts; illus.; index; circ. 950. (also avail. in microform from SWZ; reprint service avail. from SWZ) **Indexed:** Compumath, Comput.Rev., Curr.Cont., Ind.Sci.Rev., Math.R., Sci.Abstr., Sci.Cit.Ind.

ISSLEDOVANIIA PO TEORII ALGORIFMOV I MATEMATICHESKOI LOGIKE. see *PHILOSOPHY*

510   RU
ISTORIKO-MATEMATICHESKIE ISSLEDOVANIYA. vol.22, 1977. irreg. price varies. (Akademiya Nauk S.S.S.R., Institut Istorii Estestvoznaniya i Tekhniki) Izdatel'stvo Nauka, Fizmatlit, Leninskii prospekt, 15, 117071 Moscow, Russia. TEL 234-05-84. (Dist. by: Mezhdunarodnaya Kniga, ul. Dimitrova D.39, 113095 Moscow, Russia) Ed. A.P. Yushkevich. abstr.; bibl.; illus.; circ. 1,500. **Indexed:** Math.R.

510   RU   ISSN 0202-7445
QA1
ITOGI NAUKI I TEKHNIKI: ALGEBRA - TOPOLOGIYA - GEOMETRIYA. irreg., vol.27, 1989. 8 Rub. Vsesoyuznyi Institut Nauchno-Tekhnicheskoi Informatsii (VINITI), Baltiiskaya ul. 14, Moscow A-219, Russia. (Subscr. to: Mezhdunarodnaya Kniga, Dimitrova ul. 39, 113095 Moscow, Russia)
  —BLDSC shelfmark: 0006.340000.

510   RU   ISSN 0202-7453
QA300
ITOGI NAUKI I TEKHNIKI: MATEMATICHESKII ANALIZ. irreg., vol.27, 1989. 8 Rub. Vsesoyuznyi Institut Nauchno-Tekhnicheskoi Informatsii (VINITI), Baltiiskaya ul. 14, Moscow A-219, Russia. (Subscr. to: Mezhdunarodnaya Kniga, Dimitrova ul. 39, 113095 Moscow, Russia)
  —BLDSC shelfmark: 0100.970000.

516   RU   ISSN 0202-7461
QA443
ITOGI NAUKI I TEKHNIKI: PROBLEMY GEOMETRII. irreg., vol.21, 1989. 8 Rub. Vsesoyuznyi Institut Nauchno-Tekhnicheskoi Informatsii (VINITI), Baltiiskaya ul. 14, Moscow A-219, Russia. (Subscr. to: Mezhdunarodnaya Kniga, Dimitrova 39, 113095 Moscow, Russia)
  —BLDSC shelfmark: 0133.196500.

510 001.53   RU   ISSN 0202-7488
QA273
ITOGI NAUKI I TEKHNIKI: TEORIYA VEROYATNOSTEJ - MATEMATICHESKAYA STATISTIKA-TEORETICHESKAYA KIBERNETIKA. (Text in Russian) 1965. irreg., vol.27, 1989. 8 Rub. Vsesoyuznyi Institut Nauchno-Tekhnicheskoi Informatsii (VINITI), Baltiiskaya ul. 14, Moscow A-219, Russia. (Subscr. to: Mezhdunarodnaya Kniga, Dimitrova ul. 39, 113095 Moscow, Russia)
  —BLDSC shelfmark: 0178.040000.

510   RU   ISSN 0021-3446
QA1   CODEN: IVUMBY
IZVESTIYA VYSSHIKH UCHEBNYKH ZAVEDENII. SERIYA MATEMATIKA. English translation: Soviet Mathematics - Iz. V U Z (US ISSN 0197-7156) 1957. m. 54 Rub. Kazanskii Universitet, Ul. Lenina, 4-5, 420008 Kazan, Russia. Ed. A.P. Norden. charts; illus.; circ. 2,000. **Indexed:** Compumath, Math.R., Sci.Abstr.
  —BLDSC shelfmark: 0077.530000.

MATHEMATICS

510   JA   ISSN 0386-2194
QA1   CODEN: PJAADT
JAPAN ACADEMY. PROCEEDINGS. SERIES A: MATHEMATICAL SCIENCES/NIPPON GAKUSHIIN KIYO A. (Text in English, French, German) 1919. 10/yr. $125. Nippon Gakushiin - Japan Academy, 7-32 Ueno Koen, Taito-ku, Tokyo 110, Japan. (Order from: Maruzen Co., Ltd., 3-10 Nihonbashi 2-chome, Chuo-ku, Tokyo 103, Japan; or Import and Export Department, Box 5050, Tokyo International, Tokyo 100-31, Japan) Ed.Bd. bibl.; charts; illus.; index, cum.index. **Indexed:** Anim.Breed.Abstr., Biol.Abstr., Chem.Abstr., Compumath, Curr.Cont., Field Crop Abstr., Herb.Abstr., Math.R., Met.Abstr., Sci.Abstr., Sci.Cit.Ind., World Alum.Abstr.
—BLDSC shelfmark: 6742.050000.
Supersedes in part and continues numbering of (vol.53): Japan Academy. Proceedings (ISSN 0021-4280)

510   JA   ISSN 0910-2043
QA1
JAPAN JOURNAL OF APPLIED MATHEMATICS. (Text and summaries in English) 1984. 3/yr. 35000 Yen. Kinokuniya Shoten - Kinokuniya Co., Ltd., 17-7, Shinjuku 3-chome, Shinjuku-ku, Tokyo 160, Japan.

510   JA   ISSN 0289-2316
QA1   CODEN: JJMAAK
JAPANESE JOURNAL OF MATHEMATICS. (Text in English) 1924; N.S. 1975. s-a. available on exchange. (Nihon Sugakkai - Mathematical Society of Japan) Kinokuniya Shoten - Kinokuniya Co., Ltd., 17-7, Shinjuku 3-chome, Shinjuku-ku, Tokyo 160, Japan. **Indexed:** Math.R.

510   CC   ISSN 0254-7791
QA297
JISUAN SHUXUE/MATHEMATICA NUMERICA SINICA. English edition: Chinese Journal of Computational Mathematics (ISSN 0254-9409) (Text in Chinese) 1964. q. $8 per no. (Chinese Academy of Sciences, Computer Centre) Science Press, Marketing and Sales Department, 16 Donghuangchenggen Beijie, Beijing 100707, People's Republic of China. TEL 4010642. FAX 4012180. TELEX 210247-SPBJ-CN. adv.; circ. 11,000. **Indexed:** Sci.Abstr.
—BLDSC shelfmark: 5399.870000.
Description: Contains original research papers on computational mathematics, such as numerical linear and non-linear algebra, numerical optimization and approximations, computational geometry, statistics and probability, Monte Carlo methods, numerical methods for ordinary, integral, and partial differential equations, and computational math problems in science and engineering.
Refereed Serial

510   JA   ISSN 0914-3378
JOCHI DAIGAKU SUGAKU KOKYUROKU/SOPHIA KOKYUROKU IN MATHEMATICS. (Text in Japanese) 1977. a. Sophia University, Department of Mathematics - Jochi Daigaku Sugaku Kyoshitsu, 7-1, Kioi-cho, Chiyoda-ku, Tokyo 102, Japan.

510   IS   ISSN 0021-7670
QA1   CODEN: JOAMAV
JOURNAL D'ANALYSE MATHEMATIQUE. (Text in English) 1951. s-a. $60 per vol. Weizmann Science Press of Israel, P.O. Box 801, Jerusalem 91007, Israel. TEL 783203. FAX 783784. TELEX 26144-BXJM-IL-7086. Ed. L. Zalcman. bibl.; charts; circ. 750. (reprint service avail. from SWZ) **Indexed:** Compumath, Curr.Cont., Ind.Sci.Rev., Math.R., Sci.Cit.Ind.

510 519   FR   ISSN 0021-7824
QA1   CODEN: JMPAAM
JOURNAL DE MATHEMATIQUES PURES ET APPLIQUEES. (Text in English, French) 1836. 6/yr. 1560 F. Gauthier-Villars, 15 rue Gossin, 92543 Montrouge Cedex, France. TEL 33-1-40-92-65-00. FAX 33-1-40-92-65-97. TELEX 270 004. (Subscr. to: Centrale des Revues, 11 rue Gossin, 92543 Montrouge Cedex, France. TEL 33-1-46-56-52-66) Ed. J.L. Lions. adv.; bk.rev.; circ. 1,000. (also avail. in microfilm from UMI; reprint service avail. from KTO,UMI) **Indexed:** Appl.Mech.Rev., Compumath, Curr.Cont., Ind.Sci.Rev., INIS Atomind., Math.R., Sci.Cit.Ind., Zent.Math.
Description: Covers all branches of pure mathematics.

510.07 378   US   ISSN 0021-8251
QA11.A1   CODEN: JRMEDN
JOURNAL FOR RESEARCH IN MATHEMATICS EDUCATION. 1970. 5/yr. $45. National Council of Teachers of Mathematics, 1906 Association Dr., Reston, VA 22091. TEL 703-620-9840. FAX 703-476-2970. Ed. Thomas P. Carpenter. adv.; index every 2 yrs.; circ. 8,870. (also avail. in microform from UMI,MIM; reprint service avail. from UMI) **Indexed:** C.I.J.E., Cont.Pg.Educ., Educ.Ind., Psychol.Abstr.
—BLDSC shelfmark: 5052.015000.
Description: Research reports and reviews on the teaching and learning of mathematics at all levels.

510   GW   ISSN 0075-4102
QA1   CODEN: JRMAA8
JOURNAL FUER DIE REINE UND ANGEWANDTE MATHEMATIK. (Text in English, German, and French) 1826. 10/yr. $1499. Walter de Gruyter und Co., Genthiner Str. 13, 1000 Berlin 30, Germany. TEL 030-26005-0. FAX 030-26005251. TELEX 184027. (U.S. addr.: Walter de Gruyter, Inc., 200 Saw Mill Rd., Hawthorne, N.Y. 10532) Ed.Bd. adv. (also avail. in microform from UMI; reprint service avail. from UMI) **Indexed:** Compumath, Math.R., Sci.Cit.Ind.
—BLDSC shelfmark: 5049.000000.

510 370   GW   ISSN 0173-5322
JOURNAL FUER MATHEMATIK-DIDAKTIK; Zeitschrift der Gesellschaft fuer Didaktik der Mathematik. 1980. q. DM.44. Ferdinand Schoeningh, Juehenplatz 1-3, 4790 Paderborn, Germany. TEL 05251-29010. FAX 05251-2901-35. TELEX 936929-FS-PB. Ed. Werner Blum. adv.; circ. 700. (back issues avail.)
—BLDSC shelfmark: 5013.830000.

512   US   ISSN 0021-8693
                                  CODEN: JALGA4
JOURNAL OF ALGEBRA. 1964. 18/yr. $1085 (foreign $1280). Academic Press, Inc., Journal Division, 1250 Sixth Ave., San Diego, CA 92101. TEL 619-230-1840. FAX 619-699-6800. TELEX 181726. Ed. Walter Feit. adv.; bibl.; index. (back issues avail.) **Indexed:** Compumath, Curr.Cont., Ind.Sci.Rev., Math.R., Sci.Cit.Ind.
—BLDSC shelfmark: 4926.750000.
Description: Presents articles concerning original research in the field of algebra.
Refereed Serial

510   US   ISSN 1056-3911
▼**JOURNAL OF ALGEBRAIC GEOMETRY.** 1991. q. $138. American Mathematical Society, Box 1571, Annex Sta., Providence, RI 02901-9930. TEL 401-455-4000. Ed. Stephen S.-T. Yau.
Description: Provides a forum for work in algebraic geometry, the study of singularities, and related fields.

510   UK   ISSN 0883-7252
HB139   CODEN: JAECET
JOURNAL OF APPLIED ECONOMETRICS. 1986. 5/yr. $250 (effective 1992). John Wiley & Sons Ltd., Journals, Baffins Lane, Chichester, Sussex PO19 1UD, England. TEL 0243-779777. FAX 0243-775878. TELEX 86290 WIBOOK G. Ed. M. Hashem Pesaran. (reprint service avail. from SWZ) **Indexed:** Curr.Cont., J.of Econ.Lit., Oper.Res.Manage.Sci., Qual.Contr.Appl.Stat.
—BLDSC shelfmark: 4942.520000.
Description: Articles dealing with the application of econometric techniques to a wide variety of problems in economics and related subjects: covering topics in measurement, estimation, testing, forecasting, and policy analysis.

JOURNAL OF APPLIED MATHEMATICS AND MECHANICS. see ENGINEERING — Engineering Mechanics And Materials

519   UK   ISSN 0021-9002
QA276   CODEN: JPRBAM
JOURNAL OF APPLIED PROBABILITY. 1964. q. £30($53) to individuals; institutions £90($159). Applied Probability Trust, Dept. of Probability and Statistics, The University, Sheffield S3 7RH, England. TEL 0742-768555. FAX 0742-729782. Ed. C.C. Heyde. adv.; stat.; charts; index; cum.index; circ. 1,500. **Indexed:** Anim.Breed.Abstr., Biol.Abstr., Biostat., Compumath, Curr.Cont., Cyb.Abstr., Field Crop Abstr., Ind.Sci.Rev., INIS Atomind., J.Cont.Quant.Meth., Math.R., Oper.Res.Manage.Sci., Qual.Contr.Appl.Stat., Ref.Zh., Sci.Abstr., Sci.Cit.Ind., Stat.Theor.Meth.Abstr.
—BLDSC shelfmark: 4946.700000.

JOURNAL OF APPLIED STATISTICS. see STATISTICS

510   US   ISSN 0021-9045
QA221   CODEN: JAXTAZ
JOURNAL OF APPROXIMATION THEORY. (Text and summaries in English and German) 1968. m. $486 (foreign $570). Academic Press, Inc., Journal Division, 1250 Sixth Ave., San Diego, CA 92101. TEL 619-230-1840. FAX 619-699-6800. TELEX 181726. Eds. Paul Nevai, Allan Pinkus. adv.; charts; stat. (back issues avail.) **Indexed:** Compumath, Curr.Cont., Ind.Sci.Rev., Math.R., Sci.Abstr., Sci.Cit.Ind.
Description: Devoted to new advances in pure and applied approximation theory and related areas.
Refereed Serial

510   US   ISSN 0176-4268
JOURNAL OF CLASSIFICATION. 1984. 2/yr. $73.50 includes CLASS - Classification Literature Automated Search Service. (Classification Society of North America) Springer-Verlag, Journals, 175 Fifth Ave., New York, NY 10010. (Also: Berlin, Heidelberg, Tokyo, Vienna) Ed. Phipps Arabie. **Indexed:** ASCA, Biol.Abstr., Biostat., Compumath, Curr.Cont., Curr.Ind.Stat., J.Cont.Quant.Meth., Math.R., Psychol.Abstr., Zent.Math.
—BLDSC shelfmark: 4958.369550.

510   US   ISSN 0097-3165
QA164   CODEN: JCBTA7
JOURNAL OF COMBINATORIAL THEORY. SERIES A. 1966. bi-m. $387 (foreign $473). Academic Press, Inc., Journal Division, 1250 Sixth Ave., San Diego, CA 92101. TEL 619-230-1840. FAX 619-699-6800. TELEX 181726. Eds. Basil Gordon, Bruce Rothschild. adv.; charts; illus.; index. (back issues avail.) **Indexed:** Compumath, Curr.Cont., Excerp.Med., Ind.Sci.Rev., Int.Abstr.Oper.Res., Math.R., Sci.Abstr., Sci.Cit.Ind.
—BLDSC shelfmark: 4960.510000.
Supersedes in part: Journal of Combinatorial Theory (ISSN 0021-9800)
Description: Publishes original mathematical research concerned with theoretical and physical aspects of the study of finite and discrete structures in all branches of science. Series A is primarily concerned with structure, design, and applications of combinatorics.
Refereed Serial

510   US   ISSN 0095-8956
QA166   CODEN: JCBTB8
JOURNAL OF COMBINATORIAL THEORY. SERIES B.. 1966. bi-m. $342 (foreign $413). Academic Press, Inc., Journal Division, 1250 Sixth Ave., San Diego, CA 92101. TEL 619-230-1840. FAX 619-699-6800. TELEX 181726. Eds. Adrian Bondy, U.S.R. Murty. adv.; charts; illus.; index. (back issues avail.) **Indexed:** Compumath, Curr.Cont., Ind.Sci.Rev., Math.R., Sci.Abstr., Sci.Cit.Ind.
—BLDSC shelfmark: 4960.520000.
Supersedes in part: Journal of Combinatorial Theory (ISSN 0021-9800)
Description: Publishes original mathematical research dealing with theoretical and physical aspects of the study of finite and discrete structures in all branches of science. Series B is primarily concerned with graph theory and matroid theory.
Refereed Serial

510   II   ISSN 0250-9628
QA164
JOURNAL OF COMBINATORICS, INFORMATION & SYSTEM SCIENCES. (Text in English, French and German) 1976. q. Rs.200($60) Forum for Interdisciplinary Mathematics, F-9-12 Model Town, Delhi 110009, India. (Dist. by: Prints India, 11 Darya Ganj, New Dehli 110 002, India.) Ed. Bhu Dev Sharma. adv.; bk.rev.; circ. 200. **Indexed:** Cyb.Abstr., Math.R.
—BLDSC shelfmark: 4960.600000.

510   NE   ISSN 0377-0427
QA1   CODEN: JCAMDI
JOURNAL OF COMPUTATIONAL AND APPLIED MATHEMATICS. (Text in English) 1975. 15/yr.(in 5 vols.; 3 nos./vol.). fl.1580 (effective 1992). (Computational and Applied Mathematics Group) North-Holland (Subsidiary of: Elsevier Science Publishers B.V.), P.O. Box 211, 1000 AE Amsterdam, Netherlands. TEL 020-5803911. FAX 020-5803598. TELEX 18582 ESPA NL. (Subscr. in U.S. and Canada to: Elsevier Science Publishing Co., Inc., Box 882, Madison Sq. Sta., New York, NY 10159. TEL 212-989-5800) Ed.Bd. bk.rev.; bibl.; charts; index. (back issues avail.; reprint service avail. from SWZ) **Indexed:** Appl.Mech Rev., BMT, Compumath, Comput.Abstr., Cyb.Abstr., Int.Abstr.Oper.Res., Int.Aerosp.Abstr., Math.R., Sci.Abstr.
—BLDSC shelfmark: 4963.450000.
Description: Publishes original papers discribing new computational techniques for solving scientific problems.
Refereed Serial

510   CC   ISSN 0254-9409
               CODEN: JCMMEB
JOURNAL OF COMPUTATIONAL MATHEMATICS. Chinese edition: Jisuan Shuxue (ISSN 0254-7791) (Text in English) 1983. q. DM.399. Science Press, Marketing and Sales Department, 16 Donghuangchenggen Beijie, Beijing 100707, People's Republic of China. TEL 4010642. FAX 4012180. TELEX 210247-SPBJ-CN. (US office: Science Press New York, Ltd., 63-117 Alderton St., Rego Park, NY 11374. TEL 718-459-4638; Co-publisher: V S P, P.O. Box 346, NE-3700 AH Zeist, Netherlands] (Co-publisher: V S P, P.O. Box 346, NE-3700 AH Zeist, Netherlands) Ed. Feng Kang. (back issues avail.)
—BLDSC shelfmark: 4963.480000.
Description: Presents numerical methods, analysis and applications.
Refereed Serial

510   US   ISSN 0022-0396
QA371   CODEN: JDEQAK
JOURNAL OF DIFFERENTIAL EQUATIONS. 1965. m. $759 (foreign $892). Academic Press, Inc., Journal Division, 1250 Sixth Ave., San Diego, CA 92101. TEL 619-230-1840. FAX 619-699-6800. TELEX 181726. Ed. Jack K. Hale. adv.; charts. (back issues avail.) **Indexed:** Appl.Mech.Rev., Compumath, Curr.Cont., Ind.Sci.Rev., Math.R., Sci.Abstr., Sci.Cit.Ind.
—BLDSC shelfmark: 4969.500000.
Description: Covers the theory and application of differential equations.
Refereed Serial

516   US   ISSN 0022-040X
QA641   CODEN: JDGEAS
JOURNAL OF DIFFERENTIAL GEOMETRY. 1967. 6/yr. $190 to non-members; members $48. Lehigh University, Box F 13, Bethlehem, PA 18015. TEL 215-865-1522. Ed. Prof. C.C. Hsiung. bk.rev.; circ. 950. (back issues avail.) **Indexed:** Compumath, Math.R.

510   US   ISSN 1040-7294
QA370   CODEN: JDDEEH
JOURNAL OF DYNAMICS AND DIFFERENTIAL EQUATIONS. 1989. 4/yr. $135 (foreign $160)(effective 1992). Plenum Publishing Corp., 233 Spring St., New York, NY 10013-1578. TEL 212-620-8000. FAX 212-463-0742. TELEX 23-421139. Ed. George R. Sell. adv. (also avail. in microfilm from JSC; back issues avail.)
—BLDSC shelfmark: 4970.650000.
Description: Original papers covering topics including attractors, bifurcation theory, dichotomies, ergodic theory, finite and infinite dimensional systems.
Refereed Serial

JOURNAL OF ENGINEERING MATHEMATICS. see *ENGINEERING*

510   US   ISSN 1058-6458
▼**JOURNAL OF EXPERIMENTAL MATHEMATICS.** 1992. q. $130. Jones and Bartlett Publishers, 20 Park Plaza, Ste. 1435, Boston, MA 02116. TEL 617-482-3900. Ed. David B.A. Epstein.
Description: Publishes experimental work intended to develop mathematical theory and insight.

515   US   ISSN 0022-1236
QA320   CODEN: JFUAAW
JOURNAL OF FUNCTIONAL ANALYSIS. (Text in English, French) 1967. 16/yr. $890 (foreign $1044). Academic Press, Inc., Journal Division, 1250 Sixth Ave., San Diego, CA 92101. TEL 619-230-1840. FAX 619-699-6800. TELEX 181726. Ed. Irving Segal. (back issues avail.) **Indexed:** Compumath, Curr.Cont., Ind.Sci.Rev., Math.R., Sci.Abstr., Sci.Cit.Ind.
Description: Presents original research papers in all scientific disciplines in which functional analysis plays a role.
Refereed Serial

516   SZ   ISSN 0047-2468
QA443
JOURNAL OF GEOMETRY. (Text in English and German) 1971. 6/yr. 297 Fr.($198) Birkhaeuser Verlag, P.O. Box 133, CH-4010 Basel, Switzerland. TEL 061-737740. FAX 061-737950. TELEX 963475 BIRKH CH. (Dist. in N. America by: Springer-Verlag New York, Inc., Journal Fulfillment Services, Inc., Box 2485, Secaucus, NJ 07096-2491, USA. TEL 201-348-4033) Ed.Bd. abstr.; index; circ. 1,000. (reprint service avail. from SWZ) **Indexed:** Math.R.

510 536   NE   ISSN 0393-0440
JOURNAL OF GEOMETRY AND PHYSICS. (Text in English) 1984-1987; resumed in 1991. 8/yr.(in 2 vols.). fl.562($278) North-Holland (Subsidiary of: Elsevier Science Publishers B.V.), P.O. Box 211, 1000 AE Amsterdam, Netherlands. TEL 020-5803911. FAX 020-5803598. TELEX 18582 ESPA NL. (Subscr. in U.S. and Canada to: Elsevier Science Publishing Co., Inc., Box 882, Madison Sq. Sta., New York, NY 10159. TEL 212-989-5800) Ed. Marco Modugno. (back issues avail.)
—BLDSC shelfmark: 4994.700000.
Description: Designed to promote interaction between geometry and physics. Includes articles on mathematical physics, pure geometry and physics.
Refereed Serial

511.5   US   ISSN 0364-9024
QA166   CODEN: JGTHDO
JOURNAL OF GRAPH THEORY. 1976. bi-m. $275 to institutions (foreign $350). John Wiley & Sons, Inc., Journals, 605 Third Ave., New York, NY 10158-0012. TEL 212-850-6000. FAX 212-850-6088. TELEX 12-7063. Eds. Fan Chung, Carsten Thomassen. adv.; index; circ. 700. (also avail. in microform from RPI; back issues avail.) **Indexed:** Compumath, Comput.& Contr.Abstr., Curr.Cont., Elec.& Electron.Abstr., Ind.Sci.Rev., Int.Abstr.Oper.Res., Math.R., Sci.Abstr., Sci.Cit.Ind.
—BLDSC shelfmark: 4996.450000.
Description: Covers a variety of topics in graph structures, as well as graph algorithms, with theoretical emphasis. Also covers related areas in combinatorics and other math sciences.
Refereed Serial

510 001.539   II   ISSN 0252-2667
QA75.5   CODEN: JIOSDC
JOURNAL OF INFORMATION & OPTIMIZATION SCIENCES. (Text in English) 1980. 3/yr. Rs.400($72) (typically set in Oct.). Analytic Publishing Co., F-23 Model Town, Delhi-110009, India. Ed. Bal Kishan Dass. bk.rev.; circ. 250. (back issues avail.) **Indexed:** Biostat., INSPEC, Int.Abstr.Oper.Res., Math.R., Oper.Res.Manage.Sci., Qual.Contr.Appl.Stat., Sci.Abstr., Zent.Math.
—BLDSC shelfmark: 5006.745000.
Description: Devoted to advances in information sciences, optimization sciences, and related aspects.

510   SI   ISSN 0218-2165
▼**JOURNAL OF KNOT THEORY AND ITS RAMIFICATIONS.** (Text in English) 1992. q. $86 to individuals and developing countries; institutions $185. World Scientific Publishing Co. Pte. Ltd., Farrer Rd., P.O. Box 128, Singapore 9128, Singapore. TEL 3826553. FAX 3825919. TELEX RS 28561 WSPC. (UK addr.: 73 Lynton Mead, Totteridge, London N20 8DH, England. TEL 44-81-4462461)
Description: Provides a forum for new developments in knot theory, particularly developments that create connections between knot theory and other aspects of mathematics and natural sciences.

515   US   ISSN 0022-247X
QA1   CODEN: JMANAK
JOURNAL OF MATHEMATICAL ANALYSIS AND APPLICATIONS. 1960. 18/yr. $1424.25 (foreign $1670.25). Academic Press, Inc., Journal Division, 1250 Sixth Ave., San Diego, CA 92101. TEL 619-230-1840. FAX 619-699-6800. TELEX 181726. Eds. Ralph P. Boas, George Leitmann. adv.; charts; index. (back issues avail.) **Indexed:** Appl.Mech.Rev., Compumath, Curr.Cont., Eng.Ind., Ind.Sci.Rev., INIS Atomind., Int.Abstr.Oper.Res., Math.R., Risk Abstr., Sci.Abstr., Sci.Cit.Ind.
—BLDSC shelfmark: 5012.350000.
Description: Presents mathematical papers that treat classical analysis and its numerous applications.
Refereed Serial

510 530   II   ISSN 0047-2557
QC20   CODEN: JMPSB9
JOURNAL OF MATHEMATICAL AND PHYSICAL SCIENCES. (Text in English) 1967. bi-m. Rs.120($20) to individuals; institutions Rs.300($50). Indian Institute of Technology, Madras, Humanities and Sciences Building, Room No. HsB 249, First Floor, Madras 600 036, India. TEL 419329. Ed. P. Achuthan. bk.rev. (back issues avail.) **Indexed:** Appl.Mech.Rev., Curr.Cont., INIS Atomind., Int.Aerosp.Abstr., Math.R., Sci.Abstr., Zent.Math.

510   US   ISSN 0732-3123
QA11.A1
JOURNAL OF MATHEMATICAL BEHAVIOR. 1984. q. $40 to individuals; institutions $110. Ablex Publishing Corporation, 355 Chestnut St., Norwood, NJ 07648. TEL 201-767-8450. FAX 201-767-6717. TELEX 135-393. Ed. Robert B. Davis. index; circ. 400. **Indexed:** Psychol.Abstr.
—BLDSC shelfmark: 5012.372000.
Refereed Serial

JOURNAL OF MATHEMATICAL BIOLOGY. see *BIOLOGY*

JOURNAL OF MATHEMATICAL CHEMISTRY. see *CHEMISTRY*

JOURNAL OF MATHEMATICAL ECONOMICS. see *BUSINESS AND ECONOMICS — Economic Systems And Theories, Economic History*

JOURNAL OF MATHEMATICAL PHYSICS. see *PHYSICS*

JOURNAL OF MATHEMATICAL PSYCHOLOGY. see *PSYCHOLOGY*

510   JA   ISSN 0075-4293
QA1   CODEN: JMTUBZ
JOURNAL OF MATHEMATICS. (Text in English) 1967. a. exchange basis. Tokushima Daigaku, Sogo Kagakubu - Tokushima University, Faculty of Integrated Arts and Sciences, 1-1, Minami-Josanjima-cho, Tokushima-shi, Toshima-ken 770, Japan. **Indexed:** Math.R.
—BLDSC shelfmark: 5012.490000.

519.53   US   ISSN 0047-259X
QA278   CODEN: JMVAAI
JOURNAL OF MULTIVARIATE ANALYSIS; an international journal. (Text in English, French, German) 1971. 8/yr. $436 (foreign $532). Academic Press, Inc., Journal Division, 1250 Sixth Ave., San Diego, CA 92101. TEL 619-230-1840. FAX 619-699-6800. TELEX 181726. Ed. C.R. Rao. adv. (back issues avail.) **Indexed:** Compumath, Curr.Cont., Eng.Ind., Ind.Sci.Rev., J.Cont.Quant.Meth., Math.R., Sci.Abstr.
—BLDSC shelfmark: 5021.080000.
Description: Presents articles on fundamental theoretical aspects of multivariate analysis as well as on other aspects concerned with applications of new theoretical methods.
Refereed Serial

JOURNAL OF NATURAL SCIENCES AND MATHEMATICS. see *SCIENCES: COMPREHENSIVE WORKS*

JOURNAL OF NONLINEAR BIOLOGY. see *BIOLOGY — Biophysics*

MATHEMATICS

510   US   ISSN 0022-314X
QA241   CODEN: JNUTA9
JOURNAL OF NUMBER THEORY. 1969. 9/yr. $408 (foreign $505). Academic Press, Inc., Journal Division, 1250 Sixth Ave., San Diego, CA 92101. TEL 619-230-1840. FAX 619-699-6800. TELEX 181726. Ed. Hans Zassenhaus. adv. (back issues avail.) **Indexed:** Compumath, Curr.Cont., Ind.Sci.Rev., Math.R., Sci.Abstr.
Description: Features selected research articles that represent the broad spectrum of interest in contemporary number theory and allied areas.
Refereed Serial

510   SI   ISSN 0129-3281
▼**JOURNAL OF NUMERICAL LINEAR ALGEBRA WITH APPLICATIONS.** (Text in English) 1992. q. $86 to individuals and developing countries; institutions $185. World Scientific Publishing Co. Pte. Ltd., Farrer Rd., P.O. Box 128, Singapore 9128, Singapore. TEL 3825663. FAX 3825919. TELEX RS 28561 WSPC. (UK addr.: 73 Lynton Mead, Totteridge, London N20 8DH, England. TEL 44-81-4462461)
Description: Directed at researchers in numerical analysis, computer science and natural sciences, engineers and economists who either take part in the development of methods in numerical linear algebra or use such methods in their research.

510   RM
JOURNAL OF OPERATOR THEORY. (Text in English, French, German or Russian) 1983. 4/yr. $80. (Increst, Department of Mathematics) Editura Academiei Romane, Calea Victoriei 125, 79717 Bucharest, Rumania. (Dist. by: Rompresfilatelia, Calea Grivitei 64-66, P.O. Box 12-201, 78104 Bucharest, Rumania) Ed.Bd. **Indexed:** Compumath, Math.R.

JOURNAL OF PARAMETRICS. see *BUSINESS AND ECONOMICS — Accounting*

510   US   ISSN 1000-940X
QA370
JOURNAL OF PARTIAL DIFFERENTIAL EQUATIONS.* 1988. 4/yr. (Zhengzhou University, Institute of Mathematics, CC) International Academic Publishers (IAP), Xizhimenwai Dajie, Beijing Exhibition Centre, Beijing 100044, People's Republic of China. TEL 8316677. FAX 4015664. TELEX 22313 CPC CN. Ed. Jiang Lishang. (also avail. in microform; back issues avail.)
—BLDSC shelfmark: 5029.280000.

512 519   NE   ISSN 0022-4049
QA150   CODEN: JPAAA2
JOURNAL OF PURE AND APPLIED ALGEBRA. 1971. 21/yr.(in 7 vols.; 3 nos./vol.) fl.2107 (effective 1992). North-Holland (Subsidiary of: Elsevier Science Publishers B.V.), P.O. Box 211, 1000 AE Amsterdam, Netherlands. TEL 020-5803911. FAX 020-5803598. TELEX 18582 ESPA NL. (Subscr. in U.S. and Canada to: Elsevier Science Publishing Co., Inc., Box 882, Madison Sq. Sta., New York, NY 10159. TEL 212-989-5800) Ed.Bd. cum.index: vols. 1-10, 1977. (also avail. in microform from RPI; back issues avail.; reprint service avail. from SWZ) **Indexed:** Compumath, Curr.Cont., Ind.Sci.Rev., Math.R., Zent.Math.
—BLDSC shelfmark: 5043.675000.
Description: Publishes papers in algebra of general mathematical interest.
Refereed Serial

510   US   ISSN 0022-412X
QA95   CODEN: JRMAB9
JOURNAL OF RECREATIONAL MATHEMATICS. 1968. q. $18.95 individuals; institutions $74. Baywood Publishing Co., Inc., 26 Austin Ave., Box 337, Amityville, NY 11701. TEL 516-691-1270. FAX 516-691-1770. Ed. Joseph S. Madachy. bk.rev.; charts; illus. (back issues avail.) **Indexed:** Gen.Sci.Ind., Math.R.
—BLDSC shelfmark: 5048.180000.
Description: Contains thought-provoking, stimulating, wit-sharpening games, puzzles, and articles.

JOURNAL OF REGIONAL CRITICISM. see *ART*

JOURNAL OF SCIENCE AND MATHEMATICS EDUCATION IN SOUTHEAST ASIA. see *EDUCATION — Teaching Methods And Curriculum*

510   US   ISSN 0090-4104
QA1   CODEN: JOSMAR
JOURNAL OF SOVIET MATHEMATICS. 1973. 30/yr. (in 4 vols.). $2650 (foreign $3100)(effective 1992). (Russian Academy of Sciences, Mathematical Institute - V.A. Steklova, RU) Plenum Publishing Corp., Consultants Bureau, 233 Spring St., New York, NY 10013-1578. TEL 212-620-8468. FAX 212-463-0742. TELEX 23-421139. Ed. R.V. Gamkrelidze. (also avail. in microfilm from JSC; back issues avail.) **Indexed:** Comput.& Info.Sys., INIS Atomind., Math.R., Zent.Math.
—BLDSC shelfmark: 5066.080000.
Description: English translation from several Soviet mathematical journals.
Refereed Serial

JOURNAL OF STATISTICAL PLANNING AND INFERENCE. see *STATISTICS*

JOURNAL OF SYMBOLIC LOGIC. see *PHILOSOPHY*

510   US   ISSN 1055-789X
▼**JOURNAL OF TECHNOLOGY IN MATHEMATICS.** 1992. 4/yr. $150 (foreign $181). Academic Press, Inc., Journal Division, 1250 Sixth Ave., San Diego, CA 92101. TEL 619-230-1840. FAX 619-699-6800. TELEX 181726. Ed. John G. Harvey.
Description: Focuses on research related to the use of existing and future technologies in mathematics research, instruction, and learning.
Refereed Serial

510   US   ISSN 0894-9840
QA273.A1   CODEN: JTPREO
JOURNAL OF THEORETICAL PROBABILITY. 1988. q. $175 (foreign $205)(effective 1992). Plenum Publishing Corp., 233 Spring St., New York, NY 10013-1578. TEL 212-620-8000. FAX 212-463-0742. TELEX 23-421139. Ed. A. Mukherjea. adv. (also avail. in microfilm from JSC; back issues avail.)
—BLDSC shelfmark: 5069.075700.
Refereed Serial

510 378   US   ISSN 0022-5339
QA1
JOURNAL OF UNDERGRADUATE MATHEMATICS. 1969. s-a. $3 to individuals; libraries $6. Guilford College, Department of Mathematics, Greensboro, NC 27410. Ed. J. R. Boyd. index.
Refereed Serial

510   FI   ISSN 0075-4641
JYVASKYLAN YLIOPISTO. MATEMATIIKAN LAITOS. REPORT. 1967. irreg. exchange basis only. University of Jyvaskyla, Department of Mathematics - Jyvaskylan Yliopisto, P.O. Box 35, SF-40351 Jyvaskyla, Finland. FAX 358-41-602701. Ed. Olli Martio. **Indexed:** Math.R., Zent.Math.
Description: Publication including studies in the whole field of mathematics. Each issue devoted to one single topic.

510   NE   ISSN 0920-3036
QA612.33   CODEN: KTHEEO
K - THEORY; interdisciplinary journal for the development, application and influence of K-theory in the mathematical sciences. (Text in English) 6/yr. $131 to individuals; institutions $239.50. Kluwer Academic Publishers, Postbus 17, 3300 AA Dordrecht, Netherlands. TEL 078-334911. FAX 078-334254. TELEX 29245. (Dist. by: Kluwer Academic Publishing Group, P.O. Box 322, 3300 AH Dordrecht, Netherlands; N. America dist. addr.: Box 358, Accord Station, Hingham, MA 02018-0358. TEL 617-871-6600) Ed.Bd. (reprint service avail. from SWZ)
—BLDSC shelfmark: 5079.080000.

KAGOSHIMA DAIGAKU RIGAKUBU KIYO. SUGAKU, BUTSURIGAKU, KAGAKU/KAGOSHIMA UNIVERSITY. FACULTY OF SCIENCE. REPORTS. MATHEMATICS, PHYSICS, CHEMISTRY. see *SCIENCES: COMPREHENSIVE WORKS*

510   JA
KEIO UNIVERSITY. FACULTY OF SCIENCE AND TECHNOLOGY. DEPARTMENT OF MATHEMATICS. RESEARCH REPORT. (Text and summaries in English) irreg. Keio Gijuku Daigaku, Rikogakubu, Suri Kagakka - Keio University, Faculty of Science and Technology, Department of Mathematics, 14-1, Hiyoshi 3-chome, Kohoku-ku, Yokohama-shi, Kanagawa-ken 223, Japan.

KEIRYO KOKUGOGAKU/MATHEMATICAL LINGUISTICS. see *LINGUISTICS*

KEISANKI TOKEIGAKU/BULLETIN OF THE COMPUTATIONAL STATISTICS OF JAPAN. see *STATISTICS*

510   KR
KHAR'KOVSKII GOSUDARSTVENNYI UNIVERSITET. MATEMATIKA I MEKHANIKA. (Subseries of: Khar'kovskii Gosudarstvennyi Universitet. Vestnik) 1965. irreg. 1 Rub. per issue. Izdatel'stvo Vysshaya Shkola, Khar'kovskoe Otdelenie, Universitetskaya 16, 310003 Kharkov, Ukraine. Ed. I. Tarapov. circ. 500.

510   JA   ISSN 0289-9051
QA1
KOBE JOURNAL OF MATHEMATICS. (Text in English) 1984. s-a. Kobe Daigaku, Kyoyobu Sugaku Kyoshitsu - Kobe University, College of Liberal Arts, Department of Mathematics, 2-1, Tsurukabuto 1-chome, Nada-ku, Kobe-shi, Hyogo-ken 657, Japan.
—BLDSC shelfmark: 5100.579700.

510   JA   ISSN 0389-0252
QA1
KOCHI UNIVERSITY. FACULTY OF SCIENCE. MEMOIRS. SERIES A, MATHEMATICS/KOCHI DAIGAKU RIGAKUBU KIYO. SUGAKU. (Text in English) 1980. a. Kochi Daigaku, Rigakubu - Kochi University, Faculty of Science, 5-1, Akebono-cho 2-chome, Kochi-shi, Kochi-ken 780, Japan.
—BLDSC shelfmark: 5597.830000.

510   JA   ISSN 0386-5991
KODAI MATHEMATICAL JOURNAL. (Text mainly in English, occasionally in German and French) 1949. 3/yr. 25000 Yen($221) Tokyo Kogyo Daigaku, Rigakubu Sugaku Kyoshitsu - Tokyo Institute of Technology, Faculty of Science, Department of Mathematics, 12-1 Ookayama 2-chome, Meguro-ku, Tokyo 152, Japan. (Subscr. to: Kinokuniya Company Ltd., Shinjuku 3-chome, Shinjuku-ku, Tokyo 160-91, Japan) Ed.Bd. circ. 520. **Indexed:** Math.R.
Formerly (until 1978): Kodai Mathematical Seminar Reports (ISSN 0023-2599)

KOEBENHAVNS UNIVERSITET. INSTITUT FOR ANVENDT OG MATEMATISK LINGVISTIK. SKRIFTER. see *LINGUISTICS*

510 530   DK   ISSN 0023-3323
AS28   CODEN: KDVSAK
KONGELIGE DANSKE VIDENSKABERNES SELSKAB. MATEMATISK - FYSISKE MEDDELELSER. (Text in English, French, German) 1919. irreg., vol.42, no.4, 1990. price varies. Kongelige Danske Videnskabernes Selskab - Royal Danish Academy of Sciences and Letters, H.C. Andersens 35, DK-1553 Copenhagen V, Denmark. TEL 33128570, FAX 33129387. (Dist. by: Munksgaard Export and Subscription Service, P.O. Box 2148, Noerre Soegade 35, DK-1060 Copenhagen K, Denmark) bibl.; charts; illus.; index. **Indexed:** Chem.Abstr., Math.R., Met.Abstr., Sci.Abstr.
—BLDSC shelfmark: 5392.000000.

510   UZ
KRAEVYE ZADACHI DLYA DIFFERENTSIAL'NYKH URAVNENII. 1971. irreg. 1.10 Rub. Akademiya Nauk Uzbekskoi S.S.R., Institut Matematiki im. V.I. Romanovskogo, Astronomicheskii tup., 11, Tashkent, Uzbekistan.

510 530 540   JA   ISSN 0914-675X
QA1   CODEN: KJMAEZ
KUMAMOTO JOURNAL OF MATHEMATICS. (Text in English) vol.9, 1972. s-a. Kumamoto Daigaku, Rigakubu Sugaku Kenkyujo - Kumamoto University, Faculty of Science, Department of Mathematics, 39-1, Kurokami 2-chome, Kumamoto-shi, Kumamoto-ken 860, Japan. FAX 096-345-4196. Ed. M. Hitsuda. charts; stat. **Indexed:** GeoRef., JTA, Math.R., Sci.Abstr.
—BLDSC shelfmark: 5121.685000.
Formerly: Kumamoto Journal of Science. Mathematics (ISSN 0385-6763); Supersedes in part: Kumamoto Journal of Science. Series A: Mathematics, Physics and Chemistry (ISSN 0023-5318)

MATHEMATICS

510   KU
KUWAIT UNIVERSITY. CONFERENCE ON ALGEBRA AND GEOMETRY. PROCEEDINGS. (Text in English) 1982. irreg. free. Kuwait University, Department of Mathematics, Kuwait. (Co-sponsor: Kuwait Foundation for the Advancement of Sciences) Ed.Bd. charts.
Description: Presents results of research papers to mathematicians for reading and further development.

510 500   JA   ISSN 0023-6101
KYOTO KYOIKU DAIGAKU KIYO. B. SHIZEN KAGAKU/KYOTO UNIVERSITY OF EDUCATION. BULLETIN. SERIES B: MATHEMATICS AND NATURAL SCIENCE. (Text in English, Japanese) 1951. s-a. exchange basis. Kyoto University of Education - Kyoto Kyoiku Daigaku, 1 Fukakusa Fujinomori-cho, Fushimi-ku, Kyoto 612, Japan. Ed.Bd. bibl.; charts; circ. 700. **Indexed:** Biol.Abstr., Chem.Abstr., INIS Atomind., Math.R.
Formerly: Kyoto Gakugei University. Bulletin. Series B: Mathematics and Natural Science.

510   JA   ISSN 0023-608X
QA1   **CODEN: JMKYAZ**
KYOTO UNIVERSITY. JOURNAL OF MATHEMATICS/KYOTO DAIGAKU RIGAKUBU SUGAKU KIYO. (Text in European languages) 1961. 3/yr. price varies. Kyoto University, Department of Mathematics - Kyoto Daigaku Rigakubu Sugaku Kyoshitsu, Oiwake-cho, Kitashirakawa, Sakyo-ku, Kyoto-shi, Kyoto-fu 606, Japan. (Dist. by: Kinokuniya Bookstore Co. Ltd, 3-17-7 Shinjuku, Shinjuku-ku, Tokyo 160, Japan) circ. 900. **Indexed:** Compumath, Math.R., Sci.Cit.Ind.
—BLDSC shelfmark: 5012.460000.

510   JA   ISSN 0287-9980
KYUSHU DAIGAKU KYOYOBU SUGAKU ZASSHI/KYUSHU UNIVERSITY. COLLEGE OF GENERAL EDUCATION. MATHEMATICAL REPORTS. (Text and summaries in English) a. Kyushu University, College of General Education, Department of Mathematics - Kyushu Daigaku Kyoyobu Sugaku Kyoshitsu, 2-1, Ropponmatsu 4-chome, Chuo-ku, Fukuoka-shi, Fukuoka-ken 810, Japan. TEL 092-731-8745. FAX 092-771-4161.

510 500   JA   ISSN 0454-8221
Q4   **CODEN: BKTMAA**
KYUSHU INSTITUTE OF TECHNOLOGY. BULLETIN: MATHEMATICS, NATURAL SCIENCE/KYUSHU KOGYO DAIGAKU KENKYU HOKOKU. SHIZEN KAGAKU. (Text in European languages) 1955. a. exchange basis. Kyushu Institute of Technology - Kyushu Kogyo Daigaku, Tobata, Kitakyushu 804, Japan. **Indexed:** Math.R., Sci.Abstr.
—BLDSC shelfmark: 2601.530000.

511   JA   ISSN 0373-6385
QA1   **CODEN: MFKAAF**
KYUSHU UNIVERSITY. FACULTY OF SCIENCE. MEMOIRS. SERIES A: MATHEMATICS/KYUSHU DAIGAKU RIGAKUBU KIYO A. SUGAKU. (Text in English, French, German) 1940. s-a. exchange basis. Kyushu University, Faculty of Science, Department of Mathematics - Kyushu Daigaku Rigakubu Sugaku Kyoshitsu, 10-1, Hakozaki 6-chome, Higashi-ku, Fukuoka-shi, Fukuoka-ken 812, Japan. circ. 700. **Indexed:** Deep Sea Res.& Oceanogr.Abstr., JCT, JTA, Met.Abstr., Sci.Abstr.
—BLDSC shelfmark: 5598.000000.

510 574   US   ISSN 0341-633X
                                 CODEN: LNBMAH
LECTURE NOTES IN BIOMATHEMATICS. 1974. irreg. price varies. Springer-Verlag, 175 Fifth Ave., New York, NY 10010. TEL 212-460-1500. (Also: Berlin, Heidelberg, Tokyo and Vienna) Ed. S. Levin. (reprint service avail. from ISI) **Indexed:** Biol.Abstr., Chem.Abstr.

510 330   US   ISSN 0075-8442
LECTURE NOTES IN ECONOMICS AND MATHEMATICAL SYSTEMS; operations research, computer science, social science. 1968. irreg. price varies. Springer-Verlag, 175 Fifth Ave., New York, NY 10010. TEL 212-460-1500. (Also: Berlin, Heidelberg, Tokyo and Vienna) Eds. M. Beckmann, W. Krelle. cum.index nos. 1-170. (reprint service avail. from ISI) **Indexed:** Compumath, Cyb.Abstr., Sci.Abstr., SSCI.
—BLDSC shelfmark: 5180.195000.
Formerly (until 1971): Lecture Notes in Operations Research and Mathematical Systems; Which supersedes (1967-1968): Lecture Notes in Operations Research and Mathematical Economics; Lecture Notes in Operations Research and Mathematical Systems.

510   US   ISSN 0075-8434
QA3   **CODEN: LNMAA2**
LECTURE NOTES IN MATHEMATICS. (Text in English; occasionally in German and French) 1964. irreg. price varies. Springer-Verlag, 175 Fifth Ave., New York, NY 10010. TEL 212-460-1500. (Also Berlin, Heidelberg, Tokyo, and Vienna) Eds. A. Dold, B. Eckmann. (reprint service avail. from ISI) **Indexed:** Compumath, Math.R.
—BLDSC shelfmark: 5180.200000.

510   CN
LECTURE NOTES IN MATHEMATICS. 1972. irreg. price varies. Carleton University, Department of Mathematics and Statistics, Ottawa, Ont. K1S 5B6, Canada. TEL 613-788-2155. FAX 613-788-3536. **Indexed:** Math.R.
Former titles (until 1992): Carleton-Ottawa Mathematical Lecture Note Series (ISSN 0827-3669); (until 1985): Carleton Lecture Note Series (ISSN 0318-6288)

510   US   ISSN 0075-8469
LECTURE NOTES IN PURE AND APPLIED MATHEMATICS. 1971. irreg., vol.137, 1991. price varies. Marcel Dekker, Inc., 270 Madison Ave., New York, NY 10016. TEL 212-696-9000. FAX 212-685-4540. TELEX 421419. Ed.Bd.
—BLDSC shelfmark: 5180.370000.

510   US   ISSN 0075-8485
LECTURES IN APPLIED MATHEMATICS. 1959. irreg. price varies. American Mathematical Society, Box 1572, Annex Sta., Providence, RI 02901-9930. TEL 401-455-4000. **Indexed:** Biol.Abstr., Math.R., Zent.Math.
—BLDSC shelfmark: 5179.870000.

510 570   US   ISSN 0075-8523
                                 CODEN: LMLSAA
LECTURES ON MATHEMATICS IN THE LIFE SCIENCES. 1968. irreg. price varies. American Mathematical Society, Box 1571, Annex Sta., Providence, RI 02901-9930. TEL 401-455-4000. **Indexed:** Biol.Abstr., Chem.Abstr., Math.R., Zent.Math.
—BLDSC shelfmark: 5179.980000.

510 370   GW
LEHRBUECHER UND MONOGRAPHIEN ZUR DIDAKTIK DER MATHEMATIK. 1985. irreg. price varies. Bibliographisches Institut und F.A. Brockhaus AG, Dudenstr. 6, Postfach 100311, 6800 Mannheim 1, Germany. TEL 0621-3901-01. FAX 0621-3901-389. Eds. N. Knoche, H. Scheid.

510   US   ISSN 1048-9924
QA150
▼**LENINGRAD MATHEMATICAL JOURNAL.** 1990. bi-m. $848. American Mathematical Society, Box 1571, Annex Sta., Providence, RI 02901-9930. TEL 401-455-4000. (Subscr. to: Box 6248, Providence, RI 02940-6248) Ed. A.N. Andrianov. bk.rev.
—BLDSC shelfmark: 0415.562000.

510 520   RU   ISSN 0024-0850
AS262   **CODEN: VMMAA3**
LENINGRADSKII UNIVERSITET. VESTNIK. SERIYA MATEMATIKA, MEKHANIKA I ASTRONOMIYA. (Text in Russian; contents page and summaries in English) 1946. q. 18.60 Rub. Leningradskii Universitet, Universitetskaya Nab., 7-9, St. Petersburg V-164, Russia. (Subscr. to: Mezhdunarodnaya Kniga, Moscow, G-200, Russia) Ed. N.N. Polyakov. abstr.; illus.; index; circ. 1,300. **Indexed:** Chem.Abstr., Int.Aerosp.Abstr., Math.R.
—BLDSC shelfmark: 0030.000000.

LETTERS IN MATHEMATICAL PHYSICS; a journal for the rapid dissemination of short contributions in the field of mathematical physics. see *PHYSICS*

LEUVEN NOTES IN MATHEMATICAL AND THEORETICAL PHYSICS. SERIES A, MATHEMATICAL PHYSICS. see *PHYSICS*

510   US   ISSN 0278-5307
QA1
LIBERTAS MATHEMATICA. (Text in English, French, Rumanian) 1981. a. $20 to individuals; institutions $40. (American Romanian Academy of Arts and Sciences) A R A Publication, Department of French and Italian, University of California, Sproul Hall, Davis, CA 95616. TEL 916-752-6442. Ed. Constantin Corduneanu. bibl.; illus.; stat.; circ. 250. (back issues avail.)
—BLDSC shelfmark: 5186.762500.

512   US   ISSN 0024-3795
QA251   **CODEN: LAAPAW**
LINEAR ALGEBRA AND ITS APPLICATIONS. 1968. 54/yr.(in 18 vols.). $1674 (foreign $1769)(effective 1992). Elsevier Science Publishing Co., Inc. (New York), 655 Ave. of the Americas, New York, NY 10010. TEL 212-989-5800. FAX 212-633-3965. TELEX 420643 AEP UI. Eds. Richard Brualdi, Hans Schneider. adv.; bk.rev.; charts; illus.; index. (also avail. in microform from RPI; reprint service avail. from SWZ) **Indexed:** Compumath, Curr.Cont., Eng.Ind., Ind.Sci.Rev., INIS Atomind., Int.Aerosp.Abstr., Math.R., Ref.Zh., Sci.Abstr.
—BLDSC shelfmark: 5221.110000.
Description: Provides information on the analytic, algebraic, combinatorial, and numerical aspects of linear algebra and matrix theory.
Refereed Serial

510   US   ISSN 0308-1087
QA184   **CODEN: LNMLAZ**
LINEAR AND MULTILINEAR ALGEBRA. 12/yr. (in 3 vols., 4 nos./vol.). $269. Gordon and Breach Science Publishers, 270 Eighth Ave., New York, NY 10011. TEL 212-206-8900. FAX 212-645-2459. TELEX 236735 GOPUB UR. (Subscr. to: Box 786, Cooper Sta., New York, NY 10276. TEL 800-545-8398; UK subscr. to: P.O. Box 90, Reading, Berkshire RG1 8JL, England. TEL 0734-560-080) Ed. William E. Watkins. adv.; bk.rev. (also avail. in microform from MIM) **Indexed:** Int.Abstr.Oper.Res., Math.R.
Refereed Serial

510   US   ISSN 0363-1672
QA1   **CODEN: LMJTD6**
LITHUANIAN MATHEMATICAL JOURNAL. English translation of: Akademiya Nauk Litovskoi S.S.R. Litovskii Matematicheskii Sbornik (LI ISSN 0132-2818) 1973. q. $675 (foreign $790)(effective 1992). Plenum Publishing Corp., Consultants Bureau, 233 Spring St., New York, NY 10013-1578. TEL 212-620-8468. FAX 212-463-0742. TELEX 23-421139. Ed. J. Kubilius. (also avail. in microfilm from JSC; back issues avail.) **Indexed:** Math.R.
—BLDSC shelfmark: 0415.590000.
Former titles: Lithuanian Mathematical Transactions (ISSN 0148-8279); Academy of Sciences of the Lithuanian S.S.R. Mathematical Transactions (ISSN 0094-1719)
Refereed Serial

510   LI   ISSN 0132-2818
LITOVSKII MATEMATICHESKII SBORNIK/LIETUVOS MOKSLU AKADEMIJA. LIETUVOS MATEMATIKOS RINKINYS. English translation: Lithuanian Mathematical Journal (US ISSN 0363-1672) (Text in Russian; summaries in English and Lithuanian) 1961. q. 1.80 Rub. per issue. (Akademiya Nauk Litvi, Institut Matematiki i Kibernetiki - Lithuanian Academy of Sciences, Institute of Mathematics and Information Science) Leidykla Mokslas, Zvaigzdziu 23, 232050 Vilnius, Lithuania. TEL 45-85-26. TELEX 261107 LMOK. Ed. P. Kubilius. circ. 1,050. **Indexed:** M.L.A.
—BLDSC shelfmark: 0098.100000.
Description: Articles on probability theory and mathematical statistics, differential equations and theory of functions.

MATHEMATICS

510 — UK — ISSN 0024-6093
QA1 — CODEN: LMSBBT
LONDON MATHEMATICAL SOCIETY. BULLETIN. 1969. 6/yr. $236. London Mathematical Society, Burlington House, Piccadilly, London W1V 0NL, England. FAX 071-439-4629. (Subscr. to: Cambridge University Press, 40 W. 20th St., New York, NY 10011-4211. TEL 212-924-3900) Eds. J.H. Rawnsley, J.S. Jones. bk.rev.; bibl.; index; circ. 1,850. (also avail. in microform from UMI) **Indexed:** Compumath, Curr.Cont., Math.R., Sci.Cit.Ind., Zent.Math.

510 — UK — ISSN 0024-6107
QA1 — CODEN: JLMSAK
LONDON MATHEMATICAL SOCIETY. JOURNAL. 1926. 6/yr. (in 2 vols.). $440. Cambridge University Press, Edinburgh House, Shaftesbury Rd., Cambridge CB2 2RU, England. TEL 0223-312393. FAX 01-439-4629. TELEX 851817256. (N. American addr.: 40 W. 20th St., New York, NY 10011) Eds. I.N. Barker, G.D. James. (back issues avail.) **Indexed:** Compumath.
—BLDSC shelfmark: 4818.000000.
Description: Covers number theory, algebra, analysis, differential equations, geometry, topology.

510 — UK — ISSN 0076-0552
LONDON MATHEMATICAL SOCIETY. LECTURE NOTE SERIES. 1971. irreg., no.128, 1987. price varies. Cambridge University Press, Edinburgh Bldg., Shaftesbury Rd., Cambridge CB2 2RU, England. TEL 0223-312393. FAX 0223-315052. TELEX 851817256. Ed. J.W.S. Cassels. index. **Indexed:** Math.R.

510 — US
LONDON MATHEMATICAL SOCIETY. MONOGRAPHS. 1970. irreg., latest 1985. Academic Press, Inc., 1250 Sixth Ave., San Diego, CA 92101. TEL 619-231-0926. FAX 619-699-6715. Eds. P.M. Cohn, Barry E. Johnson. (reprint service avail. from ISI) **Indexed:** Math.R.
Supersedes (1970-1985): L M S Monographs (ISSN 0076-0560)
Refereed Serial

510 — UK — ISSN 0024-6115
QA1 — CODEN: PLMTAL
LONDON MATHEMATICAL SOCIETY. PROCEEDINGS. 1865. 6/yr. £240($480) Oxford University Press, Oxford Journals, Pinkhill House, Southfield Road, Oxford OX8 1JJ, England. TEL 0865-882283. FAX 0865-882890. TELEX 837330 OXPRES G. Ed. W.D. Evans, J. Wiegold. bibl.; circ. 1,400. (also avail. in microform from UMI) **Indexed:** Appl.Mech.Rev., Compumath, Curr.Cont., Math.R., Sci.Cit.Ind., Stat.Theor.Meth.Abstr.
—BLDSC shelfmark: 6751.000000.
Description: Presents research papers in the fields of real and complex analysis, differential equations and related areas, topology, geometry, logic, probability and statistics, algebra, number theory, and combination theory.

510 370 — US
M A A FOCUS. 1981. 6/yr. membership only. Mathematical Association of America, 1529 18th St., N.W., Washington, DC 20036. TEL 202-387-5200. Ed. Peter Renz. circ. 26,000.

510 530 — US — ISSN 0275-7265
M M I PRESS POLYMER MONOGRAPH SERIES. irreg. Harwood Academic Publishers, 270 Eighth Ave., New York, NY 10011. TEL 212-206-8900. FAX 212-645-2459. TELEX 236735 GOPUB UR. (Subscr. to: Box 786, Cooper Sta., New York, NY 10276. TEL 800-545-8398; UK subscr. to: Box 90, Reading, Berkshire RG1 8JL, England. TEL 0734-560-080) Ed. R. Breitmaier. (also avail. in microform)
—BLDSC shelfmark: 5879.793200.
Refereed Serial

510 530 — US — ISSN 0195-3966
CODEN: MPSSDC
M M I PRESS SYMPOSIUM SERIES. 1980. irreg., vol.4, 1983. Harwood Academic Publishers, 270 Eighth Ave., New York, NY 10011. TEL 212-206-8900. FAX 212-645-2459. TELEX 236735 GOPUB UR. (Subscr. to: Box 786, Cooper Sta., New York, NY 10276. TEL 800-545-8398; UK subscr. to: Box 90, Reading, Berkshire RG1 8JL, England. TEL 0734-560-080) Ed. H.G. Elias. (also avail. in microform) **Indexed:** Chem.Abstr.
—BLDSC shelfmark: 5879.794000.
Refereed Serial

510 — US
M S U MATHEMATICS NEWSLETTER. 1958. 3/yr. $5. Montana State University, Mathematical Sciences Department, Bozeman, MT 59717. TEL 406-994-3601. Ed David A. Thomas. bk.rev.; circ. controlled. (processed)
Formerly (until 1978): M S U Mathematics Letter (ISSN 0024-8479)

MAKEDONSKA AKADEMIJA NA NAUKITE I UMETNOSTITE. ODDELENIE ZA MATEMATICKI I TEHNICKI NAUKI. PRILOZI/MACEDONIAN ACADEMY OF SCIENCES AND ARTS. SECTION OF MATHEMATICAL AND TECHNICAL SCIENCES. CONTRIBUTIONS. see *SCIENCES: COMPREHENSIVE WORKS*

510 — MY — ISSN 0126-6705
QA1
MALAYSIAN MATHEMATICAL SOCIETY. BULLETIN. (Text in English) 1970. 2/yr. $20 to individuals; institutions $50. Malaysian Mathematical Society, c/o Department of Mathematics, University of Malaya, 59100 Kuala Lumpur, Malaysia. Ed. Chin Seong Tah. adv.; circ. 500. **Indexed:** Math.R.

510 — GW — ISSN 0025-2611
QA1 — CODEN: MSMHB2
MANUSCRIPTA MATHEMATICA. (Text in English, French, German) 1969. 16/yr. DM.1192($553) Springer-Verlag, Heidelberger Platz 3, D-1000 Berlin 33, Germany. TEL 030-8207-1. (Also Heidelberg, Tokyo, Vienna, and New York) Ed. M. Barner. adv.; bibl.; illus. (also avail. in microform from UMI; back issues avail.; reprint service avail. from ISI) **Indexed:** Compumath, Curr.Cont., Ind.Sci.Rev., Math R., Zent.Math.
—BLDSC shelfmark: 5368.300000.
Description: Provides a forum for the rapid publication of advances in mathematical research.

510 500 — GW
MARTIN-LUTHER-UNIVERSITAETT HALLE-WITTENBERG. WISSENSCHAFTLICHE ZEITSCHRIFT. MATHEMATISCH-NATURWISSENSCHAFTLICHE REIHE. 1951. bi-m. DM.29.25 per no. Martin-Luther-Universitaet Halle-Wittenberg, August-Bebel-Str. 13, 4010 Halle, Germany. bk.rev.; bibl.; charts; illus.; index; circ. 1,000. **Indexed:** Biol.Abstr., Chem.Abstr., Ind.Vet., Math.R., Plant Breed.Abstr., Vet.Bull., VITIS, World Agri.Econ.& Rural Sociol.Abstr.

510 — CS
MASARYK UNIVERSITY. FACULTY OF SCIENCES. SCRIPTA MATHEMATICA. (Text in English, French, German and Russian) 1971. irreg. (1-2/yr.). 6.50 Kcs. per no. Masarykova Universita, Prirodovedecka Fakulta - Masaryk University, Faculty of Sciences, Kotlarska 2, 611 37 Brno, Czechoslovakia. **Indexed:** Math.R.
Former titles: Scripta Facultatis Scientiarum Naturalium Universitatis Masarykianae Brunensis: Mathematica; Scripta Facultatis Scientiarum Naturalium Universitatis Purkynianae Brunensis: Mathematica.

MATCH; communications in mathematical chemistry. see *CHEMISTRY*

MATEKON; translations of Russian and East European mathematical economics. see *BUSINESS AND ECONOMICS*

510 — IT
MATEMATICA E LA SUA DIDATTICA. 3/yr. L.35000. Casa Editrice Armando s.r.l., Piazza S. Sonnino 13, Rome 00153, Italy. TEL 06-581-7245. FAX 05-5818554. Dir. Bruno D'Amore.

510 530 — KR
MATEMATICHESKAYA FIZIKA I FUNKTSIONAL'NYI ANALIZ. (Text in Russian; summaries in English) irreg. 1 Rub. Akademiya Nauk Ukrainskoi S.S.R., Fiziko-Tekhnicheskii Institut Nizkikh Temperatur, Pr. Lenina 47, Kharkov, Ukraine.

510 — KR — ISSN 0233-7568
QC19.2
MATEMATICHESKAYA FIZIKA I NELINEINAYA MEKHANIKA; respublikanskiy mezhvedomstvennyi sbornik nauchnykh trudov. 1964. s-a. (Akademiya Nauk Ukrainskoi S.S.R., Institut Matematiki) Izdatel'stvo Naukova Dumka, c/o Yu.A. Khramov, Dir, Ul. Repina, 3, Kiev 252 601, Ukraine. (Subscr. to: Mezhdunarodnaya Kniga, Moscow, G-200, Russia) Ed. Yu.A. Mitropol'skii. **Indexed:** Int.Aerosp.Abstr., Math.R., Phys.Abstr., Sci.Abstr.
—BLDSC shelfmark: 0100.515000.
Formerly (until 1984): Matematicheskaya Fizika (ISSN 0542-9986)

510 — KR — ISSN 0130-9420
QC19.2 — CODEN: MMFPDJ
MATEMATICHESKIE METODY I FIZIKO-MEKHANICHESKIE POLYA; respublikanskii mezhvedomstvennyi sbornik nauchnykh trudov. (Text in Russian) 1975. s-a. (Akademiya Ukrainskoi S.S.R., Institut Prikladnykh Problem Mekhaniki i Matematiki) Izdatel'stvo Naukova Dumka, c/o Yu.A. Khramov, Dir, Ul. Repina, 3, Kiev 252 601, Ukraine. (Subscr. to: Mezhdunarodnaya Kniga, Moscow, G-200, Russia) Ed. Y.S. Podstrigach. **Indexed:** Math.R.
—BLDSC shelfmark: 0100.830000.

510 — RU — ISSN 0025-567X
MATEMATICHESKIE ZAMETKI. English translation: Academy of Sciences of the U S S R Mathematical Notes (US ISSN 0001-4346) 1967. m. 39.60 Rub. (Akademiya Nauk S.S.S.R.) Izdatel'stvo Nauka, Fizmatlit, Leninskii prospekt, 15, 117071 Moscow, V-71, Russia. bk.rev.; tr.lit.; circ. 380,000. (also avail. in microfiche from BHP) **Indexed:** INIS Atomind.
—BLDSC shelfmark: 0100.600000.

510 — RU — ISSN 0025-5157
MATEMATICHESKII SBORNIK. English translation: Mathematics of the U S S R - Sbornik (US ISSN 0025-5734) 1866. m. 66 Rub. (Akademiya Nauk S.S.S.R., Institut Matematiki) Izdatel'stvo Nauka, Fizmatlit, Leninskii prospekt, 15, 117071 Moscow, V-71, Russia. (Co-sponsor: Moskovskoe Matematicheskoe Obshchestvo) Ed. I.G. Petrovski. bibl.; illus.; index; circ. 2,285. (reprint service avail. from KTO) **Indexed:** Chem.Abstr., INIS Atomind., Math.R.

510 — YU — ISSN 0025-5165
QA1 — CODEN: MVNSAQ
MATEMATICKI VESNIK. (Text in Serbo-Croatian and international languages) vol.14, 1977. q. 7000 din.($20) Drustvo Matematicara S R Srbije, Knez Mihailova 35-IV, Belgrade, Yugoslavia. (Co-sponsor: Drustvo Matematicara, Fizicara i Astronoma Yugoslavije) Ed. Dusan Adnadjevic. bk.rev.; circ. 600. **Indexed:** Appl.Mech.Rev., Math.R., Ref.Zh.
—BLDSC shelfmark: 0101.040000.
Formerly: Vesnik Drustva Matematicara i Fizicara SR Srbije.

MATEMATIKA A FYZIKA VE SKOLE. see *EDUCATION*

510 370 — RU — ISSN 0025-5181
MATEMATIKA V SHKOLE. 1934. bi-m. 7.50 Rub. Izdatel'stvo Pedagogica, Ul. Pavla Korchagina 7, Moscow, Russia. (Co-sponsor: Academy of Pedagogical Scinces) Ed. R.S. Cherkasov. bk.rev.; tr.lit.; circ. 430,000.

510 — HU — ISSN 0025-519X
QA1 — CODEN: MTLPAR
MATEMATIKAI LAPOK/MATHEMATICAL PAPERS. (Text in Hungarian; summaries in English and Russian) 1892. q. $24.50. (Bolyai Janos Matematikai Tarsulat) Akademiai Kiado, Publishing House of the Hungarian Academy of Sciences, P.O. Box 24, H-1363 Budapest, Hungary. Ed. A. Csaszar. adv.; bk.rev.; charts; index. **Indexed:** Math.R., Sci.Abstr.
—BLDSC shelfmark: 5391.500000.

510 — PL
MATEMATYKA (POZNAN). 1963. irreg., no.10, 1988. price varies. Adam Mickiewicz University Press, Nowowiejskiego 55, 61-734 Poznan, Poland. TEL 527-380. FAX 61-52625.
Formerly: Uniwersytet im. Adama Mickiewicza w Poznaniu. Wydzial Matematyki, Fizyki i Chemii. Prace. Seria Matematyka (ISSN 0551-6625)
Description: Each volume contains current research results of one author in the field of mathematics, their Ph.D. works and other monographs.

510   PL   ISSN 0137-8848
QA1
MATEMATYKA (WARSAW); czasopismo dla nauczycieli matematyki. 1948. bi-m. $12. (Ministerstwo Edukacji Narodowej) Wydawnictwa Szkolne i Pedagogiczne, Pl. Dabrowskiego 8, 00-950 Warsaw, Poland. TEL 48 22 26-89-71. (Dist. by: Ars Polona-Ruch, Krakowskie Przedmiescie 7, Warsaw, Poland) circ. 17,052.
—BLDSC shelfmark: 5392.270000.
Description: Publishes articles dealing with teaching mathematics, descriptions of lessons, discusses new lesson techniques, and presents other research useful for mathematics teachers.

510   AT
MATH MATH WORLD. 1976. 4/yr. Aus.$10. Mathematical Association of Western Australia, P.O. Box 492, Subiaco, W.A. 6008, Australia.
Formerly: It's a Math Math World (ISSN 0159-9976)

510 371.9   US
MATH NOTEBOOK. 1979. m. Center for Teaching - Learning of Mathematics, Box 3149, Framingham, MA 01701. Ed. Mahesh Sharma. circ. 2,000.
Description: Improving mathematics instruction in regular and special education courses.

301.412   US
MATH SCIENCE NETWORK BROADCAST. 1978. q. $25 membership. Math Science Network, 678 13th St., Ste. 100, Oakland, CA 94612-1241. bk.rev.
Description: Encourages the participation and advancement of women in the fields of mathematics, science, and technology.

510   RM   ISSN 0025-5505
QA1   CODEN: MTHCA2
MATHEMATICA; revue d'analyse numerique et de theorie de l'approximation. (Text in English, French, German, Italian and Russian) 1929. s-a. 40 lei($50) (Academia Romana) Editura Academiei Romane, Calea Victoriei nr.125, sectorul 1, R-79717 Bucharest, Rumania. (Dist. by: Rompresfilatelia, Calea Grivitei 64-66, P.O. Box 12-201, 78104 Bucharest, Rumania) Ed. E. Popoviciu. abstr.; charts; illus.; index. **Indexed:** Appl.Mech.Rev., Math.R.

510   GW   ISSN 0170-1541
MATHEMATICA DIDACTICA. 1978. q. DM.41.50. Verlag B. Franzbecker, Mozartstr. 3, 3202 Bad Salzdetfurth, Germany. Ed.Bd. adv.; bk.rev.; circ. 350.
—BLDSC shelfmark: 5399.580000.

510   JA   ISSN 0025-5513
QA1   CODEN: MAJAA9
MATHEMATICA JAPONICA. (Text in English and European languages) 1948. bi-m. $330. Suri Kagaku Gakkai - Japanese Association of Mathematical Sciences, Shin Sakai-Higashi Bldg., 2-1-18 Minami-Hanadaguchi, Sakai-shi, Osaka-fu 590, Japan. FAX 0722-22-7987. (Co-sponsors: Osaka Joshi Daigaku; Osaka Kyoiku Daigaku; Osaka Daigaku; Osaka-kenritsu Daigaku) Ed.Bd. bibl.; charts; index; circ. 850. **Indexed:** Math.R.
—BLDSC shelfmark: 5399.800000.

510   DK   ISSN 0025-5521
QA1   CODEN: MTSCAN
MATHEMATICA SCANDINAVICA. (Text in English, French and German) 1953. 4/yr. (in 2 vols., 2 nos./vol.). DKK 890 (typically set in Sep.). (Mathematical Societies in Scandinavia) Aarhus Universitet, Matematisk Institut, Ny Munkegade Bldg.530, 8000 Aarhus C, Denmark. TEL 45-86-127188. FAX 45-86-135725. TELEX MSCAND@MI.AU.DK. Ed. Joergen Vesterstroem. circ. 1,000. (back issues avail.) **Indexed:** Compumath, Ind.Sci.Rev., Math.R.
—BLDSC shelfmark: 5400.000000.

510   CS   ISSN 0025-5173
QA1   CODEN: MACAB9
MATHEMATICA SLOVACA. (Text in English, French, German, Russian; summaries in English, Russian) 1951. q. 100 Kcs.($25) (Slovenska Akademia Vied) Veda, Publishing House of the Slovak Academy of Sciences, Klemensova 19, 814 30 Bratislava, Czechoslovakia. (Dist. by: Slovart, Gottwaldovo nam. 6, 817 64 Bratislava, Czechoslovakia) Ed. Stefan Schwarz. bibl.; charts; illus.; index; circ. 1,000.
Indexed: Math.R., Sci.Abstr.
Former titles: Matematicky Casopis; Matematicko-Fyzikalny Casopis.
Description: Publishes original scientific papers of Czechoslovak as well as foreign authors on various mathematical disciplines. The contributions are mainly from algebra, theory of numbers, graphs, differential equations, real functions, functional analysis, harmonic analysis and mathematical statistics.

510   AG   ISSN 0025-553X
QA1   CODEN: MANOA3
MATHEMATICAE NOTAE. (Text in English, French, German, Italian and Spanish) 1941. a. exchange basis. (Instituto de Matematica Beppo Levi) Universidad Nacional de Rosario, Avenida Pellegrini 250, 2000 Rosario, Argentina. TEL 041-217998. TELEX 41817 CIROS AG. Ed.Bd. bk.rev.; circ. 500.
Indexed: Appl.Mech.Rev., Math.R, Zent.Math.

510   US   ISSN 0895-7177
QA401   CODEN: MCMOEG
MATHEMATICAL AND COMPUTER MODELLING; an international journal. 1980. 13/yr. £735 (effective 1992). (International Association for Mathematical and Computer Modelling) Pergamon Press, Inc., Journals Division, 660 White Plains Rd., Tarrytown, NY 10591-5153. TEL 914-524-9200. FAX 914-333-2444. (And: Headington Hill Hall, Oxford OX3 0BW, England. TEL 0865-794141) Ed. Ervin Y. Rodin. (also avail. in microform from MIM,UMI) **Indexed:** Abstr.Bull.Inst.Pap.Chem., Biostat., Compumath, Curr.Adv.Ecol.Sci., Curr.Cont., Cyb.Abstr., Excerp.Med., Fluidex, Irr.& Drain.Abstr., Math.R., Oper.Res.Manage.Sci., Qual.Contr.Appl.Stat., Robomat., Sci.Abstr., Soils & Fert.
—BLDSC shelfmark: 5401.350000.
Formerly: Mathematical Modelling (ISSN 0270-0255)
Description: Publishes papers on the utilization of mathematical modelling as a theoretical or practical working tool.
Refereed Serial

510 530   UA
MATHEMATICAL AND PHYSICAL SOCIETY OF EGYPT. PROCEEDINGS. (Text in English; summaries in Arabic and English) 1937. s-a. $30. (Mathematical and Physical Society of Egypt, Research Department) National Information and Documentation Centre (NIDOC), Tahrir Street, Dokki, Awqaf P.O., Cairo, Egypt. Ed. M. El-Nady. charts; illus.; circ. 1,000.

MATHEMATICAL APPROACHES TO GEOPHYSICS. see EARTH SCIENCES — Geophysics

510   II   ISSN 0025-5556
QA11.A1
MATHEMATICAL ASSOCIATION OF INDIA. BULLETIN. (Text in English) 1969. q. Rs.40($8) per no. Mathematical Association of India, Indian Institute of Technology Kanpur, Mathematics Department, Kanpur, India. Ed. Prof. J. N. Kapur. adv.; bk.rev.; circ. 500. **Indexed:** Math.R.

MATHEMATICS   3045

510 500   US   ISSN 0025-5564
QH324   CODEN: MABIAR
MATHEMATICAL BIOSCIENCES; an international journal. 1967. 10/yr.(in 5 vols.; 2 nos./vol.). $735 to institutions (foreign $773)(effective 1992). Elsevier Science Publishing Co., Inc. (New York), 655 Ave. of the Americas, New York, NY 10010. TEL 212-989-5800. FAX 212-633-3965. TELEX 420643 AEP UI. Ed. John A. Jacquez. adv.; bk.rev.; abstr.; bibl.; charts; illus.; index; circ. 1,000. (also avail. in microform from RPI; reprint service avail. from SWZ) **Indexed:** Appl.Mech.Rev., Biol.Abstr., Biostat., Chem.Abstr., Compumath, Curr.Adv.Ecol.Sci., Curr.Cont., Deep Sea Res.& Oceanogr.Abstr., Eng.Ind., Excerp.Med., Helminthol.Abstr., Ind.Sci.Rev., Ind.Vet., INIS Atomind., Math.R., Risk Abstr., Sci.Abstr.
—BLDSC shelfmark: 5401.700000.
Description: Publishes research and expository papers on the formulation, analysis and solution of mathematical models in the biosciences.
Refereed Serial

MATHEMATICAL CHEMISTRY. see CHEMISTRY

510 370   KO
MATHEMATICAL EDUCATION. (Text and summaries in English and Korean) 1962. s-a. 2500 Won($4) Korea Society of Mathematical Education, c/o College of Education, Seoul National University, Seoul, South Korea. Ed. Han Shick Park. adv.; bk.rev.; abstr.; bibl.; charts; illus.; stat.; circ. 500. (back issues avail.)

510   NE   ISSN 0169-121X
MATHEMATICAL ENGINEERING IN INDUSTRY. (Text in English) q. DM.290. V S P, P.O. Box 346, 3700 AH Zeist, Netherlands. TEL 03404-25790. FAX 03404-32081. TELEX 40217 VSP NL. Ed. F.A. Goldsworthy.
—BLDSC shelfmark: 5401.960000.
Description: Academic and practical papers covering new mathematical applications in industry.

MATHEMATICAL FINANCE; an international journal of mathematics, statistics and financial theory. see BUSINESS AND ECONOMICS — Banking And Finance

510   UK   ISSN 0025-5572
QA1   CODEN: MAGAAS
MATHEMATICAL GAZETTE. 1894. 4/yr. £30 to non-members; membership $27. Mathematical Association, 259 London Rd., Leicester LE2 3BE, England. TEL 0533 703877. Ed. N. Mackinnon. adv.; bk.rev.; charts; index; circ. 5,000. (also avail. in microform; reprint service avail. from UMI) **Indexed:** Ind.Sci.Rev., Math.R.
—BLDSC shelfmark: 5402.000000.

510   US   ISSN 0343-6993
QA1   CODEN: MAINDC
MATHEMATICAL INTELLIGENCER. 1978. 4/yr. $39. Springer-Verlag, Journals, 175 Fifth Ave., New York, NY 10010. TEL 212-460-1500. (Also Berlin, Heidelberg, Tokyo and Vienna) Ed. S. Axler. adv.; bk.rev.; charts; illus.; index. (also avail. in microform from UMI; back issues avail.; reprint service avail. from ISI) **Indexed:** Curr.Cont., Gen.Sci.Ind., Ind.Sci.Rev., Math.R., Phys.Ber., Zent.Math.
—BLDSC shelfmark: 5402.250000.

510   JA   ISSN 0030-1566
QA1   CODEN: MJOKAP
MATHEMATICAL JOURNAL OF OKAYAMA UNIVERSITY. (Text in English, French, German) 1952. s-a. exchange basis. Okayama Daigaku, Rigakubu Sugaku Kyoshitsu - Okayama University, Faculty of Science, Department of Mathematics, 3-1-1 Tsushima-Naka, Okayama-shi, Okayama-ken 700, Japan. Ed.Bd. charts; index; circ. 700. **Indexed:** Bull.Signal., Math.R., Zent.Math.

510   US   ISSN 0025-5580
MATHEMATICAL LOG. 1957. 4/yr. $2 (foreign $3.50). Mu Alpha Theta, 601 Elm St., Rm. 423, Norman, OK 73019. TEL 405-325-4489. Ed. Thomas Butts. bk.rev.; charts; illus.; circ. 25,000 (controlled).

MATHEMATICS

510   UK   ISSN 0170-4214
QA1   CODEN: MMSCDB
MATHEMATICAL METHODS IN THE APPLIED SCIENCES. (Text in English) 1979. 9/yr. $525 (effective 1992). John Wiley & Sons Ltd., Journals, Baffins Lane, Chichester, Sussex PO19 1UD, England. Eds. S.B. Brosowski, G.F. Roach. adv.; bk.rev.; circ. 1,000. **Indexed:** Appl.Mech.Rev., Compumath, Curr.Cont., Eng.Ind., Int.Aerosp.Abstr., Math.R.
—BLDSC shelfmark: 5402.530000.
Description: Concerned with mathematical methods which could be necessary for the further understanding and eventual solution of problems in the applied sciences.

510   SI   ISSN 0218-2025
QA401   CODEN: MMMSEU
▼**MATHEMATICAL MODELS AND METHODS IN APPLIED SCIENCES.** (Text in English) 1991. q. $100 to individuals and developing countries; institutions $210. World Scientific Publishing Co. Pte. Ltd., Farrer Rd., P.O. Box 128, Singapore 9128, Singapore. TEL 3825663. FAX 3825919. TELEX RS 28561 WSPC. (UK addr.: 73 Lynton Mead, Totteridge, London N20 8DH, England. TEL 44-81-4462461; US addr.: 1060 Main St., Ste. 1B, River Edge, NJ 07661. TEL 800-227-7562) Eds. Nicola Bellomo, Franco Brezzi.
—BLDSC shelfmark: 5402.549000.
Description: Provides a medium of exchange for scientists engaged in applied sciences where there exists a non-trivial interplay between mathematics, mathematical modelling of real systems, and mathematical and computer methods oriented towards the qualitative and quantitative analysis of real physical systems.

510   US
MATHEMATICAL NOTES (PRINCETON). 1966. irreg., no.39, 1991. price varies. Princeton University Press, 3175 Princeton Pike, Lawrenceville, NJ 08648. TEL 609-896-1344. FAX 609-895-1081. (Co-publisher: University of Tokyo Press) (also avail. in microfilm from JSC; reprint service avail. from UMI) **Indexed:** Compumath, Math.R.

519 530.15   NE
MATHEMATICAL PHYSICS AND APPLIED MATHEMATICS. 1976. irreg. price varies. Kluwer Academic Publishers, Spuiboulevard 50, P.O. Box 17, 3300 AA Dordrecht, Netherlands. TEL 078-334911. FAX 078-334254. TELEX 29245. (Dist. by: Kluwer Academic Publishers Group, P.O. Box 322, 3300 AH Dordrecht; U.S. address: P.O. Box 358, Accord Station, Hingham, MA 02018-0358) Eds. M. Flato, R. Raczka. **Indexed:** Math.R.

MATHEMATICAL PHYSICS STUDIES. see *PHYSICS*

510 370   UK   ISSN 0025-5602
MATHEMATICAL PIE. 1951. 3/yr. 120p. per 3 issues. Mathematical Association, 259 London Rd., Leicester LE2 3BE, England. TEL 0533-703 877. Ed. G. Fowler. bibl.; charts; illus.; circ. 12,000.
Description: Presents study and teaching methods.

MATHEMATICAL POPULATION STUDIES; an international journal of mathematical demography. see *POPULATION STUDIES*

510   CN
MATHEMATICAL PREPRINTS. (Text in English and French) 1971. irreg. price varies. Carleton University, Department of Mathematics and Statistics, Ottawa, Ont. K1S 5B6, Canada. TEL 613-788-2155. FAX 613-788-3536. **Indexed:** Math.R.
Formerly (until 1991): Carleton Mathematical Series (ISSN 0069-0600)

510   US   ISSN 0275-7214
MATHEMATICAL REPORTS. a. $122. Harwood Academic Publishers, 270 Eighth Ave., New York, NY 10011. TEL 212-206-8900. FAX 212-645-2459. TELEX 236735 GOPUB UR. (Subscr. to: Box 786, Cooper Sta., New York, NY 10276. TEL 800-545-8398; UK subscr. to: P.O. Box 90, Reading, Berkshire RG1 8JL, England. TEL 0734-560-080) adv. (also avail. in microform) **Indexed:** Math.R.
Refereed Serial

510   US
MATHEMATICAL SCIENCES RESEARCH INSTITUTE PUBLICATIONS. 1984. irreg. price varies. Springer-Verlag, 175 Fifth Ave., New York, NY 10010. TEL 212-460-1500. (Also Berlin, Heidelberg, Tokyo, Vienna) (reprint service avail. from ISI)

510   UK   ISSN 0312-3685
QA1
MATHEMATICAL SCIENTIST. 1976. s-a. £8($14) Applied Probability Trust, Department of Probability and Statistics, The University, Sheffield S3 7RH, England. TEL 0742-768555. FAX 0742-729782. Ed. J. Gani. circ. 750. (back issues avail.) **Indexed:** Curr.Ind.Stat., J.Cont.Quant.Meth., Math.R., Oper.Res.Manage.Sci., Qual.Contr.Appl.Stat.
—BLDSC shelfmark: 5403.350000.

510 300   NE   ISSN 0165-4896
     CODEN: MSOSDD
MATHEMATICAL SOCIAL SCIENCES. (Text in English) 1980. 6/yr.(in 2 vols.; 3 nos./vol.). fl.688 (effective 1992). North-Holland (Subsidiary of: Elsevier Science Publishers B.V.), P.O. Box 211, 1000 AE Amsterdam, Netherlands. TEL 020-5803911. FAX 020-5803598. TELEX 18582 ESPA NL. (Subscr. in U.S. and Canada to: Elsevier Science Publishing Co., Inc., Box 882, Madison Sq. Sta., New York, NY 10159. TEL 212-989-5800) Ed. Ki Hang Kim. adv.; bk.rev. (also avail. in microform from RPI; back issues avail.) **Indexed:** Compumath, Curr.Cont., Cyb.Abstr., J.Cont.Quant.Meth., J.of Econ.Lit., Lang.& Lang.Behav.Abstr., Math.R., Sage Fam.Stud.Abstr., Sci.Abstr., Sociol.Abstr., SSCI.
—BLDSC shelfmark: 5403.400000.
Description: Publishes original research, as well as survey papers, short notes, news items, a calendar of meetings which are of broad interest in the mathematical social sciences.
Refereed Serial

510   JA   ISSN 0025-5645
QA1   CODEN: NISUBC
MATHEMATICAL SOCIETY OF JAPAN. JOURNAL. (Text in European languages) 1885. q. 16000 Yen. Nihon Sugakkai - Mathematical Society of Japan, 25-9-203, Hongo 4-chome, Bunkyo-ku, Tokyo 113, Japan. **Indexed:** Compumath, Curr.Cont., Jap.Per.Ind., Math.R., Sci.Cit.Ind.

510   JA   ISSN 0549-4540
MATHEMATICAL SOCIETY OF JAPAN. PUBLICATIONS. (Text in English and European languages) 1955. irreg. Nihon Sugakkai - Mathematical Society of Japan, 25-9-203, Hongo 4-chome, Bunkyo-ku, Tokyo 113, Japan.

510   UK   ISSN 0025-5653
QA1   CODEN: MSPEB8
MATHEMATICAL SPECTRUM. 1968. 4/yr. £7($13) Applied Probability Trust, Department of Probability and Statistics, The University, Sheffield S3 7RH, England. TEL 0742-768555. FAX 0742-729782. Ed. D.W. Sharpe. adv.; bk.rev.; circ. 2,000. (back issues avail.) **Indexed:** Cont.Pg.Educ., Fluidex, Math.R., Oper.Res.Manage.Sci., Qual.Contr.Appl.Stat., Ref.Zh, Sci.Abstr.
—BLDSC shelfmark: 5403.500000.

510   US
MATHEMATICAL SURVEYS & MONOGRAPHS. 1943. irreg. price varies. American Mathematical Society, Box 1571, Annex Sta., Providence, RI 02901-9930. TEL 401-455-4000. (Street addr.: 201 Charles St., Providence, RI 02904) **Indexed:** Math.R., Zent.Math.
Formerly (until 1950): Mathematical Surveys (ISSN 0076-5376)
Description: Covers current topics in mathematical research.

MATHEMATICAL SYSTEMS IN ECONOMICS. see *BUSINESS AND ECONOMICS — Economic Systems And Theories, Economic History*

510   US   ISSN 0025-5661
QA1   CODEN: MASTBA
MATHEMATICAL SYSTEMS THEORY. 1966. q. $115. Springer-Verlag, Journals, 175 Fifth Ave., New York, NY 10010. TEL 212-460-1500. Ed. S.A. Greibach. adv. (also avail. in microform from UMI; reprint service avail. from ISI) **Indexed:** Compumath, Curr.Cont., Ind.Sci.Rev., Math.R., Sci.Abstr., Zent.Math.
—BLDSC shelfmark: 5404.200000.
Description: Devoted to current research in the theories of both discrete and continuous systems.

MATHEMATICS AND COMPUTER EDUCATION. see *MATHEMATICS — Computer Applications*

510   UK   ISSN 0543-0941
MATHEMATICS AND ITS APPLICATIONS. 1962. irreg., vol.16, 1988. price varies. Gordon & Breach Science Publishers, P.O. Box 90, Reading, Berkshire RG1 8JL, England. TEL 0734-560-080. FAX 0734-568-211. TELEX 849870 SCIPUB G. (US addr.: Box 786, Cooper Sta., New York, NY 10276. TEL 800-545-8398) Eds. Jacob T. Schwartz, Maurice Levy. (also avail. in microform) **Indexed:** Math.R.
—BLDSC shelfmark: 5405.150000.
Formerly (until 1971): Notes on Mathematics and Its Applications.
Refereed Serial

510   NE
MATHEMATICS AND ITS APPLICATIONS. 1977. irreg., latest 1991. Kluwer Academic Publishers, Postbus 17, 3300 AA Dordrecht, Netherlands. TEL 078-334911. FAX 078-334254. TELEX 29245. (Dist. by: Kluwer Academic Publishers Group, P.O. Box 322, 3300 AH Dordrecht, Netherlands; N. America dist. addr.: Box 358, Accord Station, Hingham, MA 02018-0358. TEL 617-871-6600) Ed. M. Hazewinkel. **Indexed:** Math.R.

510   NE
MATHEMATICS AND ITS APPLICATIONS: EAST EUROPEAN SERIES. 1982. irreg. price varies. Kluwer Academic Publishers, Spuiboulevard 50, P.O. Box 17, 3300 AA Dordrecht. TEL 078-334911. FAX 078-334254. TELEX 29245. (Dist. by: Kluwer Academic Publishers Group, P.O. Box 322, 3300 AH Dordrecht, Netherlands; U.S. addr.: P.O. Box 358, Accord Station, Hingham, MA 02018-0358) Ed. M. Hazewinkel. **Indexed:** Math.R.

510   NE
MATHEMATICS AND ITS APPLICATIONS: JAPANESE SERIES. 1983. irreg. price varies. Kluwer Academic Publishers, Spuiboulevard 50, P.O. Box 17, 3300 AA Dordrecht, Netherlands. TEL 078-334911. FAX 078-334254. TELEX 29245. (Dist. by: Kluwer Academic Publishers Group, P.O. Box 322, 3300 AH Dordrecht, Netherlands; U.S. addr.: P.O. Box 358, Accord Station, Hingham, MA 02018-0358) Ed. M. Hazewinkel.

510   NE
MATHEMATICS AND ITS APPLICATIONS: SOVIET SERIES. 1984. irreg., latest 1991. price varies. Kluwer Academic Publishers, Postbus 17, 3300 AA Dordrecht, Netherlands. TEL 078-334911. FAX 078-334254. TELEX 29245. (Dist. by: Kluwer Academic Publishers Group, P.O. Box 322, 3300 AH Dordrecht, Netherlands; N. America dist. addr.: Box 358, Accord Station, Hingham, MA 02018-0358. TEL 617-871-6600) Ed. M. Hazewinkel. **Indexed:** Math.R.

510 370   II   ISSN 0047-6269
QA1
THE MATHEMATICS EDUCATION. (Text in English) 1967. q. Rs.300 (effective 1992). Nirala Nagar, Siwan, Bihar, India. Ed. J.B. Prasad. adv.; bk.rev.; bibl.; charts; index. **Indexed:** Math.R.
—BLDSC shelfmark: 5405.900000.
Description: Presents research and teaching methods in pure and applied mathematics.

MATHEMATICS EDUCATION LIBRARY. see *EDUCATION*

MATHEMATICS EDUCATION RESEARCH JOURNAL. see *EDUCATION — Teaching Methods And Curriculum*

510   UK   ISSN 0305-7259
MATHEMATICS IN SCHOOL. 1972. 5/yr. £36($65) (Mathematical Association) Longman Group UK Ltd., Westgate House, The High, Harlow, Essex CM20 1YR, England. TEL 0279-429655. Ed. D. Neal. adv.; bk.rev.; illus.; index; circ. 6,000. **Indexed:** C.I.J.E., Cont.Pg.Educ.
—BLDSC shelfmark: 5406.500000.
Description: Presents study and teaching methods.

510 620   US   ISSN 0076-5392
MATHEMATICS IN SCIENCE AND ENGINEERING; series of monographs and textbooks. 1961. irreg., vol.184, 1990. Academic Press, Inc., 1250 Sixth Ave., San Diego, CA 92101. TEL 619-231-0926. FAX 619-699-6715. Ed. William F. Ames. (reprint service avail. from ISI) **Indexed:** Math.R.
—BLDSC shelfmark: 5406.600000.
  Refereed Serial

510   US   ISSN 0025-570X
                        CODEN: MAMGA8
MATHEMATICS MAGAZINE. 1926. bi-m. (Sep.-Jun.). $68. Mathematical Association of America, 1529 Eighteenth St., N.W., Washington, DC 20036. TEL 202-387-5200. Ed. Gerald Alexanderson. adv.; bk.rev.; index, cum.index vols.1-50; circ. 14,000. (also avail. in microfiche from UMI; reprint service avail. from UMI) **Indexed:** Gen.Sci.Ind., Ind.Sci.Rev., Math.R.
—BLDSC shelfmark: 5406.000000.
  Incorporates (in 1976): Delta (Washington) (ISSN 0011-801X)
  Description: Articles, mathematical problems, and book reviews of interest to undergraduate students and faculty, focusing on the history and contemporary application of mathematics.

510   II
MATHEMATICS NEWSLETTER.* (Text in English) 1971. every 6 weeks. Rs.2. Mathematical Society, Central College, Bangalore 1, India. Ed. F.J. Noronha. adv.; charts.

510   US   ISSN 0025-5718
QA47   CODEN: MCMPAF
MATHEMATICS OF COMPUTATION. 1943. 4/yr. $221 to non-members; individual members $133; institutional members $177. American Mathematical Society, Box 1571, Annex Sta., Providence, RI 02940-9930. TEL 401-455-4000. (Street addr.: 201 Charles St., Providence, RI 02901-9930) Ed. Walter Gautschi. adv.; bk.rev.; abstr.; cum.index: vols.1-23; circ. 2,200. (also avail. in microfilm from UMI; microfiche from AMS) **Indexed:** A.S.& T.Ind., Abstr.Bull.Inst.Pap.Chem., Appl.Mech.Rev., Compumath, Curr.Cont., Cyb.Abstr., Ind.Sci.Rev., INIS Atomind., Int.Aerosp.Abstr., Math.R., Sci.Abstr.
—BLDSC shelfmark: 5405.800000.
  Description: Covers all aspects of numerical mathematics, tables and technical notes.
  Refereed Serial

MATHEMATICS OF OPERATIONS RESEARCH. see *COMPUTERS*

510   US   ISSN 0025-5726
QA1   CODEN: MUSIAE
MATHEMATICS OF THE U S S R - IZVESTIYA. English translation of: Izvestiya Akademii Nauk SSR Seriya Matematicheskaya. 1967. bi-m. $714 to non-members; institutional members $571. American Mathematical Society, Box 1571, Annex Sta., Providence, RI 02940-9930. TEL 401-455-4000. (Street addr.: 201 Charles St., Providence, RI 02901-9930) Ed. Lev J. Leifman. index; circ. 700. (also avail. in microfiche from AMS; microfilm) **Indexed:** Compumath, Curr.Cont., Ind.Sci.Rev., Math.R.
—BLDSC shelfmark: 0415.825000.
  Refereed Serial

510   US   ISSN 0025-5734
                        CODEN: MUSBBS
MATHEMATICS OF THE U S S R - SBORNIK. English translation of: Matematicheskii Sbornik (UR ISSN 0025-5157) 1967. bi-m. $865 to non-members; institutional members $692. American Mathematical Society, Box 1571, Annex Sta., Providence, RI 02901-9930. TEL 401-455-4000. (Street addr.: 201 Charles St., Providence, RI 02904) Ed. Lev J. Leifman. index; circ. 700. (also avail. in microfiche from AMS) **Indexed:** Compumath, Curr.Cont., Ind.Sci.Rev., Math.R.
—BLDSC shelfmark: 0415.827000.

510   UK   ISSN 0957-1280
▼**MATHEMATICS REVIEW**. 1990. q. £15.95 (foreign £19). Philip Allan Publishers Ltd., Deddington, Oxfordshire OX15 0SE, England. TEL 0869-38652. FAX 0869-38803.

510 370   II   ISSN 0025-5742
QA1   CODEN: MTHSBH
MATHEMATICS STUDENT. 1933. q. $60. Indian Mathematical Society, Meerut University, Department of Mathematics, Meerut 250 005, India. Ed. A.M. Vaidya. bk.rev.; circ. 1,200. **Indexed:** Math.R.
—BLDSC shelfmark: 5407.000000.
  Description: Presents study and teaching methods and research papers.

510 370   US   ISSN 0025-5769
QA1
MATHEMATICS TEACHER. 1908. m. (Sep.-May). $40 to individuals; institutions $45. National Council of Teachers of Mathematics, 1906 Association Dr., Reston, VA 22091. TEL 703-620-9840. FAX 703-476-2970. Ed. Harry B. Tunis. adv.; bk.rev.; bibl.; illus.; index, cum.index: 1908-1965, 1966-1975, 1976-1985; circ. 52,845. (also avail. in microform from UMI,MIM; reprint service avail. from UMI) **Indexed:** Biog.Ind., C.I.J.E., Cont.Pg.Educ., Educ.Ind., Except.Child.Educ.Abstr., LAMP, Math.R., Yrbk.Assoc.Educ.& Rehab.Blind.
—BLDSC shelfmark: 5407.200000.
  Description: Articles and features on the improvement of mathematics instruction in junior and senior high schools, two-year colleges, and teacher education colleges.

510 370   UK   ISSN 0025-5785
MATHEMATICS TEACHING. 1956. q. £30.50 to individual members; institutional members £46; including "Micromath". Association of Teachers of Mathematics, 7 Shaftesbury St., Derby DE3 8YB, England. TEL 0332 46599. Eds. L. Brown, A. Brown. adv.; bk.rev.; circ. 6,000. (controlled). (tabloid format; also avail. in microfilm from UMI; reprint service avail. from UMI) **Indexed:** C.I.J.E., Cont.Pg.Educ., Educ.Ind., High.Educ.Curr.Aware.Bull., Res.High.Educ.Abstr.
  Description: Presents study and teaching methods.

510   II
MATHEMATICS TODAY. m. H-2A, Green Park Extension, New Delhi 110 016, India. TEL 664119.
  Description: Devoted to mathematics education in India.

510   GW   ISSN 0543-100X
MATHEMATIK FUER NATURWISSENSCHAFT UND TECHNIK. 1957. irreg. price varies. VEB Deutscher Verlag der Wissenschaften, Postfach 1216, 1080 Berlin, Germany. Eds. H. Heinrich, H. Schubert.

371 510   GW   ISSN 0465-3750
MATHEMATIK IN DER SCHULE. 1963. m. DM.40. Volk und Wissen Verlag GmbH, Lindenstr. 54A, 1086 Berlin, Germany. TEL 0372-20343-0. bk.rev.; bibl.; index; circ. 16,000.
—BLDSC shelfmark: 5407.600000.

MATHEMATIK LEHREN. see *EDUCATION — Teaching Methods And Curriculum*

510   GW   ISSN 0233-1063
MATHEMATIK UND IHRE ANWENDUNGEN IN PHYSIK UND TECHNIK. (Text in English, German) 1927. a. Akademische Verlagsgesellschaft Geest & Portig K.-G., Sternwartenstrasse 8, 7010 Leipzig, Germany. Ed.Bd. adv.

510 519   UK   ISSN 0025-5793
QA1   CODEN: MTKAAB
MATHEMATIKA; a journal of pure and applied mathematics. 1954. s-a. £48. (University College London, Department of Mathematics) J.W. Arrowsmith Ltd., 71 Winterstoke Road, Bristol BS3 2NT, England. FAX 637829. Ed.Bd. bk.rev.; bibl.; charts; index; circ. 750. **Indexed:** Appl.Mech.Rev., Compumath, Curr.Cont., Ind.Sci.Rev., Math.R., Zent.Math.
—BLDSC shelfmark: 5408.000000.

510 371   GW   ISSN 0025-5807
DER MATHEMATIKUNTERRICHT; Beitraege zu seiner wissenschaftlichen und methodischen Gestaltung. 1955. 6/yr. DM.111.70 (foreign DM.118). Erhard Friedrich Verlag GmbH, Im Brande 15, Postfach 100150, 3016 Seelze-Velber, Germany. TEL 0511-40004-0. Ed.Bd. index, cum.index; circ. 5,100. **Indexed:** Math.R.
—BLDSC shelfmark: 5408.070000.

510   GW   ISSN 0025-5831
QA1   CODEN: MAANA3
MATHEMATISCHE ANNALEN. (Text in English, French or German) 1868. 12/yr. DM.2580($1681) Springer-Verlag, Heidelberger Platz 3, D-1000 Berlin 33, Germany. TEL 030-8207-1. (Also Heidelberg, Tokyo, Vienna, and New York) Ed. H. Amann. adv.; charts; illus. (also avail. in microform from UMI; back issues avail.; reprint service avail. from ISI) **Indexed:** Compumath, Curr.Cont., Ind.Sci.Rev., Math.R., Zent.Math.
—BLDSC shelfmark: 5410.000000.
  Description: Covers mathematics, especially complex analysis, algebraic geometry, algebraic number theory, modular forms, differential geometry, and functional analysis.

510 531   GW
MATHEMATISCHE FORSCHUNG/MATHEMATICAL RESEARCH. 1972. irreg., vol.58, 1989. price varies. (Akademie der Wissenschaften der DDR, Karl-Weierstrass-Institut fuer Mathematik) Akademie-Verlag Berlin, Leipziger Str. 3-4, 1086 Berlin, Germany. TELEX 114420-AVERL-DD. Ed.Bd. **Indexed:** Math.R.
  Former titles: Mathematische Forschung. Schriftenreihe (ISSN 0138-3019); Zentralinstitut fuer Mathematik und Mechanik. Schriftenreihe.

510   GW   ISSN 0076-5422
MATHEMATISCHE LEHRBUECHER UND MONOGRAPHIEN. ABTEILUNG 1: MATHEMATISCHE LEHRBUECHER. 1951. irreg., vol.40, 1989. price varies. (Akademie der Wissenschaften der DDR, Karl-Weierstrass-Institut fuer Mathematik) Akademie-Verlag Berlin, Leipziger Str. 3-4, 1086 Berlin, Germany. TELEX 114420-AVERL-DD.

510   GW   ISSN 0076-5430
MATHEMATISCHE LEHRBUECHER UND MONOGRAPHIEN. ABTEILUNG 2: MATHEMATISCHE MONOGRAPHIEN. 1952. irreg., vol.72, 1989. price varies. (Akademie der Wissenschaften der DDR, Karl-Weierstrass-Institut fuer Mathematik) Akademie-Verlag Berlin, Leipziger Str. 3-4, 1086 Berlin, Germany. TELEX 114420-AVERL-DD.
—BLDSC shelfmark: 5410.300000.

510   GW   ISSN 0543-1042
MATHEMATISCHE MONOGRAPHIEN. 1958. irreg. price varies. VEB Deutscher Verlag der Wissenschaften, Postfach 1216, 1080 Berlin, Germany. Eds. W. Groebner, H. Reichardt.

510   GW   ISSN 0025-584X
QA1   CODEN: MTMNAQ
MATHEMATISCHE NACHRICHTEN. (Text in English, French, German; summaries in English) 1948. 5/yr. DM.114.80 per no. (Akademie der Wissenschaften der DDR, Karl-Weierstrass-Institut fuer Mathematik) Akademie-Verlag Berlin, Leipziger Str. 3-4, 1086 Berlin, Germany. TELEX 114420-AVERL-DD. Ed. H. Koch. adv.; charts; illus. (reprint service avail. from SWZ) **Indexed:** Compumath, Curr.Cont., Ind.Sci.Rev., Math.R.

510   GW   ISSN 0076-5449
MATHEMATISCHE SCHUELERBUECHEREI. 1956. irreg. price varies. VEB Deutscher Verlag der Wissenschaften, Postfach 1216, 1080 Berlin, Germany. **Indexed:** Math.R.

510   GW   ISSN 0720-728X
MATHEMATISCHE SEMESTERBERICHTE; zur Foerderung der Mathematik in Unterricht und Kultur. 1932. s-a. DM.62. Springer-Verlag, Heidelberger Platz 3, 1000 Berlin 33, Germany. Ed. N. Knoche. adv.; bk.rev.; charts; illus.; index; circ. 580. **Indexed:** Math.R.
—BLDSC shelfmark: 5410.720000.
  Formerly: Mathematisch-Physikalische Semesterberichte (ISSN 0340-4897)

510 500 370   GW   ISSN 0025-5866
                        CODEN: MNWUAL
DER MATHEMATISCHE UND NATURWISSENSCHAFTLICHE UNTERRICHT. 1948. 8/yr. DM.72. Ferd. Duemmlers Verlag, Postfach 1480 Kaiserstr. 31-37, D-5300 Bonn 1, Germany. Ed. D.H. Noack. adv.; bk.rev.; illus.; index; circ. 8,000. **Indexed:** Chem.Abstr., Excerp.Med., Math.R.
—BLDSC shelfmark: 5410.800000.

510　　　　　　　GW　ISSN 0025-5874
QA1　　　　　　　　　CODEN: MAZEAX
MATHEMATISCHE ZEITSCHRIFT. (Text in English, French, German) 1918. 12/yr. DM.2298($1143) Springer-Verlag, Heidelberger Platz 3, D-1000 Berlin 33, Germany. TEL 030-8207-1. (Also Heidelberg, Tokyo, Vienna, and New York) Ed. W.P. Barth. adv.; bibl.; index. (also avail. in microform from UMI; back issues avail.; reprint service avail. from ISI) **Indexed:** Chem.Abstr., Compumath, Curr.Cont., Ind.Sci.Rev., Math.R., Zent.Math.
Description: Covers a variety of topics in modern mathematics, from algebra to analysis and applied disciplines.

510　　　　　　　GW　ISSN 0340-4358
　　　　　　　　　　　CODEN: MNGBAK
MATHEMATISCHEN GESELLSCHAFT IN HAMBURG. MITTEILUNGEN. 1881. s-a. DM.48. Mathematischen Gesellschaft in Hamburg, Bundesstr. 55, 2000 Hamburg 13, Germany. TEL 040-41235153. Ed. R. Carlsson. adv.; index; circ. 800. (back issues avail.)

510　　　　　　　GW　ISSN 0373-8221
　　　　　　　　　　　CODEN: MMUGAU
MATHEMATISCHEN SEMINAR GIESSEN. MITTEILUNGEN. (Text in English and German) 1921. 6/yr. DM.100. Mathematisches Seminar Giessen, Arndtstr. 2, 6300 Giessen, Germany. Eds. Dieter Gaier, F. Timmesfeld. (back issues avail.)
—BLDSC shelfmark: 5878.360000.

MECHANICS. see *PHYSICS — Mechanics*

510　　　　　　　　　NE
MECHANICS AND MATHEMATICAL METHODS - SERIES OF HANDBOOKS. 1983. irreg., vol.3, 1989. price varies. Elsevier Science Publishers B.V., Books Division, P.O. Box 211, 1000 AE Amsterdam, Netherlands. TEL 020-5803911. FAX 020-5803705. TELEX 18582 ESPA NL. (Subscr. in U.S. and Canada to: Elsevier Science Publishing Co., Inc., Box 882, Madison Sq. Sta., New York, NY 10159. TEL 212-989-5800) Ed. J.D. Achenbach.
Refereed Serial

510　　　　　　　MY　ISSN 0126-9003
MENEMUI MATEMATIK. (Text in English and Malay) 1979. 3/yr. $20. Malaysian Mathematical Society, c/o Department of Mathematics, University of Malaya, 59100 Kuala Lumpur, Malaysia. Ed. Ng Boon Yian.
—BLDSC shelfmark: 5678.442500.

510 530　　　　　　GW
METHODEN UND VERFAHREN DER MATHEMATISCHEN PHYSIK. 1969. irreg., no.37, 1991. price varies. (Bibliographisches Institut) Verlag Peter Lang GmbH, Eschborner Landstr. 42-50, 6000 Frankfurt a.M. 90, Germany. TEL 069-7807050. FAX 069-785893. Eds. Bruno Brosowski, Erich Martensen.

510　　　　　　　US　ISSN 0026-2285
QA1
MICHIGAN MATHEMATICAL JOURNAL. (Text in English, French) 1952. 3/yr. $30 to individuals; institutions $60 (typically set in Jan.). University of Michigan, Department of Mathematics, Ann Arbor, MI 48109-1003. TEL 313-764-0337. FAX 313-763-0937. Ed. Douglas G. Dickson. index; circ. 1,200. **Indexed:** Compumath, Curr.Cont., Ind.Sci.Rev., Math.R.

510　　　　　　　UK　ISSN 0267-5501
MICROMATH. 1985. 3/yr. £23($48) (Association of Teachers of Mathematics) Basil Blackwell Ltd., 108 Cowley Rd., Oxford OX4 1JF, England. TEL 0865-791100. (Subscr. addr.: c/o Marston Book Services, P.O. Box 87, Oxford OX2 0DT, England) Eds. Janet Ainley, Ronnie Goldstein. adv.; bk.rev.; circ. 6,000. (also avail. in microform; reprint service avail. from SWZ) **Indexed:** Cont.Pg.Educ.
—BLDSC shelfmark: 5759.190000.

510　　　　　　　US　ISSN 1047-5982
▼**MODERN LOGIC**; international journal of the history of mathematical logic, set theory, and foundation of mathematics. 1990. q. $100. Irving H. Anellis, Ed. & Pub., Box 1036, Welch Ave. Sta., Ames, IA 50010-1036.
—BLDSC shelfmark: 5888.500000.
Description: Publishes expository surveys and historical studies of 19th- and 20th-century mathematical logic, set theory, and foundation of mathematics.

510　　　　　　　US　ISSN 0026-9255
　　　　　　　　　　　CODEN: MNMTA2
MONATSHEFTE FUER MATHEMATIK. (Text in English and German) 1890. 8/yr. $367. Springer-Verlag, Journals, 175 Fifth Ave., New York, NY 10010. TEL 212-460-1500. (Also Berlin, Heidelberg, Tokyo and Vienna) Ed. S. Graber. adv.; bk.rev.; charts; illus.; index. (also avail. in microfiche from UMI; reprint service avail. from ISI) **Indexed:** Compumath, Curr.Cont., Ind.Sci.Rev., Math.R., Zent.Math.

510　　　　　　　BL
MONOGRAFIAS DE MATEMATICA. 1969. irreg., no.47, 1990. Cr.$15.00. Instituto de Matematica Pura e Aplicada, Estrada Dona Castorna, 110 Jardim Botanico, CEP 22460 Rio de Janeiro, Brazil. TEL 021-294-9032. FAX 55-5124115. TELEX 21-21145 IAMP. circ. 600. **Indexed:** Math.R.

510　　　　　　　PL　ISSN 0077-0507
MONOGRAFIE MATEMATYCZNE. (Text in English, French, German and Polish) 1932. irreg., vol.61, 1982. price varies. (Polska Akademia Nauk, Instytut Matematyczny) Panstwowe Wydawnictwo Naukowe, Miodowa 10, 00-251 Warsaw, Poland. (Dist. by: Ars Polona, Krakowskie Przedmiescie 7, 00-068 Warsaw, Poland) **Indexed:** Math.R.

510　　　　　　　RM
MONOGRAFII MATEMATICE. 1973. irreg. 120 lei($5) Universitatea din Timisoara, Facultatea de Matematica, Bd. Vasile Pirvan Nr. 4, Timisoara, Rumania. Ed. Dumitru Gaspar. circ. 150. **Indexed:** Math.R.

510　　　　　　　US
MONOGRAPHS, ADVANCED TEXTS AND SURVEYS IN PURE AND APPLIED MATHEMATICS. no.2, 1976. irreg. John Wiley and Sons, Inc., 605 Third Ave., New York, NY 10158-0012. Ed.Bd.
Formerly (until vol.25, 1986): Monographs and Studies in Mathematics.

510　　　　　　　US
MONOGRAPHS ON NUMERICAL ANALYSIS. irreg. price varies. Oxford University Press, 200 Madison Ave., New York, NY 10016. TEL 212-679-7300. Eds. J. Walsh, L. Fox. **Indexed:** Math.R.
Refereed Serial

510.8　　　　　　US　ISSN 0077-1554
QA1　　　　　　　　　CODEN: TMMSD4
MOSCOW MATHEMATICAL SOCIETY. TRANSACTIONS. English translation of: Moskovskoe Matematicheskoe Obshchestvo. Trudy. 1978. a. $222 to non-members; institutional members $178. American Mathematical Society, Box 1571, Annex Sta., Providence, RI 02901-9930. TEL 401-455-4000. (Street addr.: 201 Charles St., Providence, RI 02904) (Co-sponsor: London Mathematical Society) Ed. Ben Silver. circ. 600. **Indexed:** Math.R.
—BLDSC shelfmark: 0427.800000.

510　　　　　　　US　ISSN 0027-1322
　　　　　　　　　　　CODEN: MUMBA
MOSCOW UNIVERSITY MATHEMATICS BULLETIN. English translation of: Moskovskii Universitet. Vestnik. Seriya 1: Matematika i Mekhanika. 1966. bi-m. $640. (Moskovskii Universitet, RU) Allerton Press, Inc., 150 Fifth Ave., New York, NY 10011. TEL 212-924-3950. Ed. O.B. Lupanov. bk.rev.; abstr.; bibl.; charts; illus.; index. **Indexed:** Appl.Mech.Rev., Math.R.
—BLDSC shelfmark: 0416.239000.

510 531　　　　　　RU
MOSKOVSKII UNIVERSITET. VESTNIK. SERIYA 1: MATEMATIKA I MEKHANIKA. English translation: Moscow University Mathematics Bulletin (US ISSN 0027-1322) bi-m. 22.80 Rub. Moskovskii Universitet, Ul. Gertsena 5-7, 103009 Moscow, Russia. bk.rev.; bibl.; index. **Indexed:** Int.Aerosp.Abstr., Math.R.

510　　　　　　　RU
MOSKOVSKOE MATEMATICHESKOE OBSHCHESTVO. TRUDY. English translation: Moscow Mathematical Society. Transactions (US ISSN 0077-1554) vol.34, 1977. irreg. 2.90 Rub. per no. Moskovskii Universitet, Moskovskoe Matematicheskoe Obshchestvo, Universitetskii Prospekt, 13, Moscow V-234, Russia. Ed. O. Oleinik. bibl.; illus.; circ. 1,270. **Indexed:** Int.Aerosp.Abstr., Math.R.

510　　　　　　　UK　ISSN 0269-0780
N A G NEWSLETTER. 1979. s-a. Numerical Algorithms Group Ltd., Wilkinson House, Jordan Hill Rd., Oxford OX2 8DR, England. TEL 0865-511245. FAX 0865-310139. TELEX 83354 NAG UK G. bk.rev.; circ. 3,000. (back issues avail.)
Description: Reviews current NAG products and their applications.

510 500　　　　　　NE
N A T O ADVANCED SCIENCE INSTITUTES SERIES C: MATHEMATICAL AND PHYSICAL SCIENCES. (Text in English) irreg., latest 1991. price varies. (North Atlantic Treaty Organization, Scientific Affairs Division, BE) Kluwer Academic Publishers, Postbus 17, 3300 AA Dordrecht, Netherlands. TEL 078-334911. FAX 078-334254. TELEX 29245. (Dist. by: Kluwer Academic Publishing Group, P.O. Box 322, 3300 AH Dordrecht, Netherlands; N. America dist. addr.: Box 358, Accord Station, Hingham, MA 02018-0358. TEL 617-871-6600) **Indexed:** GeoRef., Phys.Ber.
●Also available online. Vendor(s): European Space Agency (File no.128).

N C T M NEWS BULLETIN. (National Council of Teachers of Mathematics) see *EDUCATION — Teaching Methods And Curriculum*

510　　　　　　　JA　ISSN 0027-7630
QA1　　　　　　　　　CODEN: NGMJA2
NAGOYA MATHEMATICAL JOURNAL/NAGOYA SUGAKU ZASSHI. (Text in English, French, German) 1950. q. $214 (effective 1991). Nagoya Daigaku Rigakubu, Sugaku Kyoshitsu - Nagoya University, School of Science, Department of Mathematics, Chikusa-ku, Nagoya 464-01, Japan. FAX 52-781-4437. (Subscr. to: Kinokuniya Shoten - Kinokuniya Co., Ltd., 17-7, Shinjuku 3-chome, Shinjuku-ku, Tokyo 160, Japan; Subscr. in US to: Kinokuniya Book Stores of America Co., Ltd., West Bldg., Japanese Cultural and Trade Center, 1581 Webster St., San Francisco, CA 94115) Ed. Y. Shikata. charts; index, cum.index: vols.1-40, 41-70; also vols. 1-100, 1985; vols.101-110, 1988; vols.111-120, 1990; circ. 1,250 (controlled). **Indexed:** Compumath, Curr.Cont., Ind.Sci.Rev., Math.R., Sci.Cit.Ind.
Description: Primarily publishes research papers, also features invited papers on mathematics.

510　　　　　　　JA　ISSN 0288-500X
NANZAN UNIVERSITY. NANZAN ACADEMIC SOCIETY. BULLETIN. (Text and summaries in English, Japanese) 1983. irreg. Nanzan University, Nanzan Academic Society - Nanzan Daigaku Nanzan Gakkai, 18, Yamazato-cho, Showa-ku, Nagoya-shi, Aichi-ken 466, Japan.

510 370　　　　　　US
NATIONAL COUNCIL OF TEACHERS OF MATHEMATICS. PROFESSIONAL REFERENCE SERIES. 1980. irreg. National Council of Teachers of Mathematics, 1906 Association Dr., Reston, VA 22091. TEL 703-620-9840. FAX 703-476-2970. (reprint service avail. from UMI)
Description: Scholarly monographs on topics of interest to mathematics teachers and educators.

510 370　　　　　　US　ISSN 0077-4103
QA1
NATIONAL COUNCIL OF TEACHERS OF MATHEMATICS. YEARBOOK. 1926. a. $18. National Council of Teachers of Mathematics, 1906 Association Dr., Reston, VA 22091. TEL 703-620-9840. FAX 703-476-2970. circ. controlled. (also avail. in microform from UMI; back issues avail.; reprint service avail. from UMI) **Indexed:** Educ.Ind.
—BLDSC shelfmark: 9391.000000.
Description: Scholarly papers of interest to mathematics teachers and educators.

NATIONAL INSTITUTE OF STANDARDS AND TECHNOLOGY. JOURNAL OF RESEARCH. see *METROLOGY AND STANDARDIZATION*

510　　　　　　　KR
NELINEINYE GRANICHNYE ZADACHI; respublikanskii mezhvedomstvennyi sbornik nauchnykh trudov. 1989. a. (Akademiya Nauk Ukrainskoi S.S.R., Institut Prikladnoi Matematiki i Mekhaniki) Izdatel'stvo Naukova Dumka, c/o Yu.A. Khramov, Dir., Ul. Repina 3, Kiev 252601, Ukraine. (Subscr. to: Mezhdunarodnaya Kniga, Moscow G-200, Russia) Ed. I.V. Skripnik.

NEW PARADIGMS NEWSLETTER. see *SCIENCES: COMPREHENSIVE WORKS*

MATHEMATICS 3049

510 UN ISSN 0077-8893
QA11.A1
NEW TRENDS IN MATHEMATICS TEACHING. (Editions in English, French and Spanish) 1966. irreg., latest no.4. $13. Unesco, 7-9 Place de Fontenoy, 75700 Paris, France. TEL 577-16-10. (Dist. in U.S. by: Unipub, 4611-F Assembly Dr., Lanham, MD 20706-4391)

510 NZ
QA1 CODEN: MTHCB3
NEW ZEALAND JOURNAL OF MATHEMATICS. 1969. s-a. NZ.$25 to individuals; institutions NZ.$50. New Zealand Journal of Mathematics Committee, Private Bag, Auckland, New Zealand. (Co-sponsors: University of Auckland, Department of Mathematics and Statistics; New Zealand Mathematical Society) Ed. D.B. Gauld. bibl.; charts; cum.index vols: 1-10; circ. 300. Indexed: Math.R.
  Formerly (until vol.20, 1991): Mathematical Chronicle (ISSN 0581-1155)
  Description: Publishes research papers and expository or survey articles in pure and applied mathematics.

510 NE ISSN 0028-9825
QA1
NIEUW ARCHIEF VOOR WISKUNDE. (Text in English; occasionally in Dutch, French, German) 1875. 3/yr. fl.97.50 (foreign fl.117.50). Stichting Mathematisch Centrum, Kruislaan 413, 1098 SJ Amsterdam, Netherlands. TEL 020-592-9333. FAX 020-592-4199. TELEX 12571 MATCTR NL. (Subscr. to: Stichting Mathematisch Centrum, Postbus 4079, 1009 AB Amsterdam, Netherlands) (Co-sponsor: Wiskundig Genootschap) Eds. M. Hazewinkel, M. Bart. adv.; bk.rev.; index; circ. 2,000. (reprint service avail. from SWZ) Indexed: Math.R., Ref.Zh., Zent.Math.
  —BLDSC shelfmark: 6111.000000.

511 JA ISSN 0369-576X
QA1 CODEN: NSMABQ
NIIGATA UNIVERSITY. FACULTY OF SCIENCE. SCIENCE REPORTS. SERIES A: MATHEMATICS/NIIGATA DAIGAKU RIGAKUBU KENKYU HOKOKU. A-RUI, SUGAKU. (Text in European languages) 1964. a. exchange basis. Niigata Daigaku, Rigakubu - Niigata University, Faculty of Science, 8050, Igarashi-Nino-cho, Niigata-shi, Niigata-ken 950-21, Japan. Indexed: Math.R.

510 UK
NONLINEAR SCIENCE: THEORY AND APPLICATIONS. 1985. irreg. price varies. John Wiley & Sons, Baffins Lane, Chichester, W. Sussex PO19 1UD, England. TEL 061-273 5539. FAX 061-274-3346. TELEX 666517-UNIMAN. Ed. A.V. Holden.

510 530 UK ISSN 0951-7715
QA427 CODEN: NONLE5
NONLINEARITY. 1988. 6/yr. £269($536) (effective 1992). (London Mathematical Society) I O P Publishing, Techno House, Redcliffe Way, Bristol BS1 6NX, England. TEL 0272 297481. FAX 0272-294318. TELEX 449149. (U.S. addr.: American Institute of Physics, Subscr. Serv., 500 Sunnyside Blvd., Woodbury, NY 11797-2999) (Co-sponsor: Institute of Physics) Eds. J.D. Gibbon, D.A. Rand. index. (also avail. in microform; microfiche; back issues avail.)
  —BLDSC shelfmark: 6117.320500.
  Description: Publishes papers on a wide range of nonlinear mathematics, mathematical and experimental physics and other areas in the sciences where nonlinear phenomena are of fundamental importance.

510 NO ISSN 0801-3500
QA1
NORMAT: NORDISK MATEMATISK TIDSKRIFT; Scandinavian journal on mathematics. (Text in Scandinavian languages; summaries in English) 1953. q. $39 to individuals; institutions $51. Universitetsforlaget, P.O. Box 2959-Toeyen, N-0608 Oslo 1, Norway. (U.S. addr.: Publications Expediting Inc., 200 Meacham Ave., Elmont, NY 11003) Ed. Jon Reed. bibl.; index; circ. 1,500. Indexed: Math.R.
  Supersedes (1973-1979): Nordisk Matematisk Tidskrift (ISSN 0029-1412)

510 NE
NORTH-HOLLAND MATHEMATICAL LIBRARY. 1971. irreg., vol.47, 1991. price varies. Elsevier Science Publishers B.V., Books Division, P.O. Box 211, 1000 AE Amsterdam, Netherlands. TEL 020-5803911. FAX 020-5803705. TELEX 18582 ESPA NL. (Subscr. in U..S and Canada to: Elsevier Science Publishing Co., Inc., Box 882, Madison Sq. Sta., New York, NY 10159. TEL 212-989-5800)
  Refereed Serial

510 NE
NORTH-HOLLAND MATHEMATICS STUDIES. 1970. irreg., vol.172, 1992. price varies. Elsevier Science Publishers B.V., Books Division, P.O. Box 211, 1000 AE Amsterdam, Netherlands. TEL 020-5803911. FAX 020-5803705. TELEX 18582 ESPA NL. (Subscr. in U.S. and Canada to: Elsevier Science Publishing Co., Inc., Box 882, Madison Sq. Sta., New York, NY 10159. TEL 212-989-5800)
  Refereed Serial

620 510 NE ISSN 0066-5460
NORTH-HOLLAND SERIES IN APPLIED MATHEMATICS AND MECHANICS. 1967. irreg., vol.36, 1990. price varies. Elsevier Science Publishers B.V., Books Division, P.O. Box 211, 1000 AE Amsterdam, Netherlands. TEL 020-5803911. FAX 020-5803705. TELEX 18582 ESPA NL. (Subscr. in U.S. and Canada to: Elsevier Science Publishing Co., Inc., Box 882, Madison Sq. Sta., New York, NY 10159. TEL 212-989-5800) Ed.Bd. Indexed: Math.R.
  Refereed Serial

510 AG ISSN 0078-2009
NOTAS DE ALGEBRA Y ANALISIS. (Text in English, French and Spanish) 1966. irreg., no.17, 1991. price varies. Universidad Nacional del Sur, Instituto de Matematica, Avda. Alem 1253, 8000 Bahia Blanca, Argentina. circ. 1,000. Indexed: Math.R., Zent.Math.
  —BLDSC shelfmark: 6153.270000.

510 AG ISSN 0325-8963
NOTAS DE GEOMETRIA Y TOPOLOGIA. 1980. irreg. Universidad Nacional del Sur, Instituto de Matematica, Avda. Alem 12530, 8000 Bahia Blanca, Argentina. circ. 750.

510 AG ISSN 0078-2017
NOTAS DE LOGICA MATEMATICA. (Text in English, French, Portuguese, Spanish) 1963. irreg., no.37, 1989. price varies. Universidad Nacional del Sur, Instituto de Matematica, Avda. Alem 1253, 8000 Bahia Blanca, Argentina. abstr.; charts; stat.; circ. 1,000. Indexed: Math.R., Zent.Math.
  Description: Covers research in the mathematical sciences.

510 AG ISSN 0326-1336
NOTAS DE MATEMATICA DISCRETA. 1982. irreg. Universidad Nacional del Sur, Instituto de Matematica, Avda. Alem 1253, 8000 Bahia Blanca, Argentina. charts; illus. Indexed: Math.R.

510 BL ISSN 0085-5413
NOTAS E COMUNICACOES DE MATEMATICA. (Text in English, French, Portuguese, Spanish) 1965. irreg., vol. 148, 1987. price varies. Universidade Federal de Pernambuco, Departamento de Matematica, Cidade Universitaria, 50.739 Recife, PE, Brazil. FAX 00550812711833. Ed. Sostenes Lins. circ. 125.

510 CL
NOTAS MATEMATICAS. English edition: Mathematical Notes. 1972. a. free. Universidad Catolica de Chile, Instituto de Matematicas, Casilla 114-D, Santiago, Chile. (Subscr. to: Instituto de Matematica, Vicuna Mackenna 4860, Santiago, Chile) Ed. Alvaro Cofre. circ. 200.

510 AT
NOTES ON PURE MATHEMATICS. 1974. irreg., no.13, 1986. price varies. Australian National University, Department of Mathematics, I A S, G.P.O Box 4, Canberra, A.C.T. 2601, Australia. FAX 61-62-490759. Ed. M.F. Newman. circ. 200.

511.3 160 US ISSN 0029-4527
BC1 CODEN: NDJFAM
NOTRE DAME JOURNAL OF FORMAL LOGIC. 1960. q. $25 to individuals; institutions $45. University of Notre Dame, Box 5, Notre Dame, IN 46556. TEL 219-239-6157. FAX 219-239-8609. Ed.Bd. adv.; bk.rev.; index, cum.index; circ. 825. (back issues avail.) Indexed: Math.R., Phil.Ind., Sci.Abstr.
  Description: Focuses on philosophical and mathematical logic.

510 SZ ISSN 1017-1398
QA297 CODEN: NUALEG
▼**NUMERICAL ALGORITHMS.** 1991. 8/yr. 296.50 Fr. J.C. Baltzer AG, Scientific Publishing Company, Wettsteinplatz 10, CH-4058 Basel, Switzerland. TEL 061-6918925. FAX 061-6924262. Ed. Claude Brezinski.
  —BLDSC shelfmark: 6184.671000.

510 US ISSN 0163-0563
QA320 CODEN: NFAODL
NUMERICAL FUNCTIONAL ANALYSIS AND OPTIMIZATION; an international journal for rapid publication. 1979. 6/yr. $152.50 to individuals; institutions $305. Marcel Dekker Journals, 270 Madison Ave., New York, NY 10016. TEL 212-696-9000. FAX 212-685-4540. TELEX 421419 MARDEEK. (Subscr. to: Box 10018, Church St. Sta., New York, NY 10249) Ed. M. Z. Nashed. (also avail. in microform from RPI) Indexed: Compumath, Curr.Cont., Math.R., Sci.Abstr.
  —BLDSC shelfmark: 6184.692000.
  Refereed Serial

510 US ISSN 0749-159X
QA377 CODEN: NMPDEB
NUMERICAL METHODS FOR PARTIAL DIFFERENTIAL EQUATIONS: AN INTERNATIONAL JOURNAL. 1985. bi-m. $285 to institutions (foreign $360). John Wiley & Sons, Inc., Journals, 605 Third Ave., New York, NY 10158-0012. TEL 212-850-6000. FAX 212-850-6088. TELEX 12-7063. Ed. George F. Pinder. (also avail. in microform from RPI) Indexed: Appl.Mech.Rev.
  —BLDSC shelfmark: 6184.696600.
  Description: Focuses on technique rather than application. Topics include applied numerical analysis, computational methods.
  Refereed Serial

510 GW ISSN 0029-599X
QA76.5 CODEN: NUMMA7
NUMERISCHE MATHEMATIK. (Text mainly in English; occasionally French and German) 1959. 16/yr. DM.1420($649) Springer-Verlag, Heidelberger Platz 3, D-1000 Berlin 33, Germany. TEL 030-8207-1. (Also Heidelberg, Tokyo, Vienna, and New York) Ed. R.S. Varga. adv. (also avail. in microform from UMI; back issues avail.; reprint service avail. from ISI) Indexed: Appl.Mech.Rev., Compumath, Comput.Abstr., Curr.Cont., Ind.Sci.Rev., Math.R., Sci.Abstr., Zent.Math.
  —BLDSC shelfmark: 6184.700000.
  Description: Aids international dissemination of contributions on mathematical topics arising in contemporary numerical computation, including optimization of parallel computers.

500 510 US ISSN 0379-0207
AS142 CODEN: AMNDBP
OESTERREICHISCHE AKADEMIE DER WISSENSCHAFTEN, VIENNA. MATHEMATISCH-NATURWISSENSCHAFTLICHE KLASSE. DENKSCHRIFTEN. (Text in German) irreg. price varies. Springer-Verlag, 175 Fifth Ave., New York, NY 10010. TEL 212-460-1500. (Also Berlin, Heidelberg, Tokyo and Vienna) (reprint service avail. from ISI) Indexed: Biol.Abstr., Math.R.
  —BLDSC shelfmark: 3552.000000.
  Formerly: Oesterreichische Akademie der Wissenschaften, Vienna. Mathematisch-Naturwissenschaftliche Klasse. Anzeiger (ISSN 0065-535X)

510 UK ISSN 0261-1023
OKIKIOLU SCIENTIFIC AND INDUSTRIAL ORGANIZATION. BULLETIN OF MATHEMATICS. 1981. q. £24. Okikiolu Scientific and Industrial Co., 377 Edgware Rd., London W2 1BT, England. Ed. Dr. G.O. Okikiolu. Indexed: Math.R., Zent.Math.
  Description: Scholarly research papers on the results of new mathematics analysis.

MATHEMATICS

510   CN   ISSN 0030-3011
ONTARIO MATHEMATICS GAZETTE. 1962. 3/yr. Can.$30. Ontario Association for Mathematics Education, University of Western Ontario, 1137 Western Rd., London, Ont. N6G 1G7, Canada. TEL 519-661-2086. Eds. Eric Wood, Barry Onslow. bk.rev.; charts; circ. 1,700.
—BLDSC shelfmark: 6262.040000.

OPERATIONS RESEARCH. see *COMPUTERS*

519   RU
OPTIMIZATSIYA. irreg. (5-6/yr.). 1 Rub. Akademiya Nauk S.S.S.R., Sibirskoe Otdelenie, Institut Matematiki, Novosibirsk, Akademgorodok, Russia. Ed. L.V. Vantorovich. **Indexed:** Math.R.

510   NE   ISSN 0167-8094
QA171.48   CODEN: ORDER5
ORDER; a journal on the theory of ordered sets and its applications. 1984. q. $95.50 to individuals; institutions $170.50. Kluwer Academic Publishers, Postbus 17, 3300 AA Dordrecht, Netherlands. TEL 078-334911. FAX 078-334254. TELEX 29245. (Dist. by: Kluwer Academic Publishers Group, P.O. Box 322, 3300 AH Dordrecht, Netherlands; N. America dist. addr.: Box 358, Accord Station, Hingham, MA 02018-0358. TEL 617-871-6600) adv.; bk.rev.; charts; index. (reprint service avail. from SWZ) **Indexed:** Math.R.
—BLDSC shelfmark: 6278.859000.

510   US   ISSN 0078-6330
ORGANIZATION OF AMERICAN STATES. DEPARTMENT OF SCIENTIFIC AFFAIRS. SERIE DE MATEMATICA: MONOGRAFIAS. no.2, 1965. irreg., no.22, 1979. $3.50 per no. Organization of American States, Department of Publications, 1889 F St., N.W., Washington, DC 20006. TEL 703-941-1617.

510 658   SA   ISSN 0259-191X
ORION. (Text and summaries in Afrikaans, English) 1985. s-a. $40 (effective 1992). Operations Research Society of South Africa, P.O. Box 3982, Johannesburg 2000, South Africa. Ed. M. Sinclair. adv.; circ. 450. **Indexed:** Int.Abstr.Oper.Res.
—BLDSC shelfmark: 6291.279000.
Description: Features success stories, case studies, and methodological reviews in operations research.
Refereed Serial

510   JA   ISSN 0030-6126
QA1   CODEN: OJMAA7
OSAKA JOURNAL OF MATHEMATICS. (Text in English, French, German) 1964. 4/yr. $257. Osaka Daigaku, Rigakubu Sugaku Kyoshitsu - Osaka University, Faculty of Science, Department of Mathematics, 1-1 Machikaneyama-cho, Toyonaka-shi, Osaka-fu 560, Japan. FAX 06-845-1163. (Subscr. to: Kinokuniya Co. Ltd., 17-7 Shinjuku 3-chome, Shinjuku-ku, Tokyo 160-91, Japan) (Co-sponsor: Osaka-shiritsu Daigaku Sugaku Kyoshitsu - Osaka City University, Department of Mathematics) Ed. Mitsuru Ikawa. cum.index: vols.1-15. (reprint service avail.) **Indexed:** Compumath, Math.R., Sci.Cit.Ind.
Formed by the merger of (1949-1963): Osaka Mathematical Journal; (1950-1963): Journal of Mathematics.

510   US
OXFORD MATHEMATICAL MONOGRAPHS. irreg. price varies. Oxford University Press, 200 Madison Ave., New York, NY 10016. TEL 212-679-7300. **Indexed:** Math.R.
Refereed Serial

OYO TOKEIGAKU/JAPANESE JOURNAL OF APPLIED STATISTICS. see *STATISTICS*

510   US   ISSN 0030-8730
QA1   CODEN: PJMAAI
PACIFIC JOURNAL OF MATHEMATICS. 1951. m. (5 vols./yr.). $200. American Mathematical Society, Pacific Journal of Mathematics, c/o V.S. Varadarajan, Ed., Mathematics Department, University of California, Los Angeles, CA 90024-1555. FAX 213-206-6673. bibl.; charts; index; circ. 1,600. (back issues avail.; reprint service avail. from KTO) **Indexed:** Compumath, Curr.Cont., Math.R., Zent.Math.
—BLDSC shelfmark: 6330.000000.
Refereed Serial

500   GW
PAEDAGOGISCHE HOCHSCHULE KARL FRIEDRICH WILHELM WANDER. WISSENSCHAFTLICHE ZEITSCHRIFT. MATHEMATISCH-NATURWISSENSCHAFTLICHE REIHE; mathematisch-naturwissenschaftliche Reihe and thematische Reihe. (Text in German; summaries in English, German and Russian) 1967. q. DM.60. Paedagogische Hochschule Karl Friedrich Wilhelm Wander, Dresden, PSF 365, 8060 Dresden, Germany. (Dist. by: Buchexport, Leninstr. 16, 7010 Leipzig, Germany) circ. 500.
Supersedes in part: Paedagogische Hochschule Karl Friedrich Wilhelm Wander. Wissenschaftliche Zeitschrift (ISSN 0138-1520)

PARAMETRIC WORLD. see *BUSINESS AND ECONOMICS — Accounting*

510   US   ISSN 1054-6618
▼**PATTERN RECOGNITION AND IMAGE ANALYSIS;** advances in mathematical theory and applications in the USSR. (English translation of Soviet title) 1991. q. $140 to individuals (outside N. America $150); institutions $200 (outside N. America $210). New Soviet Sciences Press (USA), c/o Allen Press, Inc., Dist., Box 1897, Lawrence, KS 66044-8897. TEL 913-843-1235. FAX 913-843-1274. Ed. Yuri Zhuravlev.
—BLDSC shelfmark: 0416.679700.
Refereed Serial

510 530   CS
PEDAGOGICKA FAKULTA V OSTRAVE. MATEMATIKA, FYZIKA. (Subseries of its Sbornik Praci: Rada A) (Text in Czech; summaries in English, German, Russian) 1971. irreg. Statni Pedagogicke Nakladatelstvi, Ostrovni 30, 113 01 Prague 1, Czechoslovakia. (Subscr.to: c/o Dr. Lubojacza, Dekanat P F Ostrava, Dvorakova c.7, 701 03 Ostrava 1, Czechoslovakia) illus.
Supersedes in part: Prirodni Vedy a Matematika.

510   US   ISSN 0031-4870
QA1
PENTAGON; a mathematics magazine for students. 1940. s-a. $3 (foreign $5). Kappa Mu Epsilon, c/o Sharon Kunoff, Bus. Manager, Department of Mathematics, C W Post - Long Island University, Brookville, NY 11548. Ed. Andrew M. Rockett. adv.; bk.rev.; index; circ. 3,000. (also avail. in microform from UMI; back issues avail.; reprint service avail. from UMI)

510   NE   ISSN 0031-5303
QA1   CODEN: PMHGAW
PERIODICA MATHEMATICA HUNGARICA. (Text in English, French, German; summaries in English) 1970. 6/yr. $259. (Janos Bolyai Mathematical Society) Kluwer Academic Publishers, Postbus 17, 3300 AA Dordrecht, Netherlands. TEL 078-334911. FAX 078-334254. TELEX 29245. (Dist. by: Kluwer Academic Publishers Group, P.O. Box 322, 3300 AH Dordrecht, Netherlands; N. America dist. addr.: Box 358, Accord Station, Hingham, MA 02018-0358. TEL 617-871-6600) (Co-sponsor: Akademiai Kiado, Budapest) Ed. P. Erdos. adv.; bk.rev.; circ. 550. (back issues avail.) **Indexed:** Math.R., Sci.Abstr.
—BLDSC shelfmark: 6425.200000.

510   US   ISSN 0172-6641
PERSPECTIVES IN MATHEMATICAL LOGIC. 1975. irreg. price varies. Springer-Verlag, 175 Fifth Ave., New York, NY 10010. TEL 212-460-1500. (reprint service avail. from ISI) **Indexed:** Math.R.

510   US
PERSPECTIVES IN MATHEMATICS. 1986. irreg., vol.13, 1990. Academic Press, Inc., 1250 Sixth Ave., San Diego, CA 92101. TEL 619-231-6616. FAX 619-699-6715. Eds. John Coates, Sigurdur Helhason. (back issues avail.)
Refereed Serial

510 541.3 621.3   UK   ISSN 0165-5817
Q1   CODEN: PHJRD9
PHILIPS JOURNAL OF RESEARCH. (Text in English) vol.33, 1978. bi-m. £79 (effective 1992). (Philips Corporate Research Laboratories, NE) Elsevier Science Publishers Ltd., Crown House, Linton Rd., Barking, Essex IG11 8JU, England. TEL 081-594-7272. FAX 081-594-5942. TELEX 896950 APPSCI G. (Subscr. in U.S. and Canada to: Elsevier Science Publishing Co., Inc., Box 882, Madison Sq. Sta., New York, NY 10159. TEL 212-989-5800) Ed. M. Vincken. circ. 2,200. **Indexed:** Br.Ceram.Abstr., CAD CAM Abstr., Cadscan, Chem.Abstr., Curr.Cont., Eng.Ind., Excerp.Med., Lead Abstr., Mass Spectr.Bull., Math.R., Met.Abstr., Phys.Abstr., Sci.Abstr., Sci.Cit.Ind., World Alum.Abstr., Zincscan.
Formerly: Philips Research Reports.
Description: Findings of industrial researchers in many fields including mathematics, physics, chemistry and information technology.
Refereed Serial

510   US   ISSN 0031-8019
QA9   CODEN: PHMAB5
PHILOSOPHIA MATHEMATICA. (Text in English, French and German) 1964-1981 (vol.18); N.S. 1986. s-a. $35. Box 206, Wood Crossroad, VA 23190. TEL 804-440-4738. Ed. Joong J. Fang. adv.; bk.rev.; circ. 500. **Indexed:** Math.R., Phil.Ind., Zent.Math.
—BLDSC shelfmark: 6461.500000.
Description: Philosophical study in the nature of mathematics.

PHYSICS - MATHEMATICS INFORMATION REVIEW. see *PHYSICS*

510   US   ISSN 0031-952X
QA1   CODEN: PMEJBR
PI MU EPSILON JOURNAL. 1949. s-a. $8 to members; non-members $12. Pi Mu Epsilon, St. Norbert College, De Pere, WI 54115. TEL 414-337-3198. Ed. Richard Poss. adv.; bk.rev.; charts; illus.; cum.index every 5 yrs.; circ. 5,000. (also avail. in microform from UMI; back issues avail.; reprint service avail. from UMI) **Indexed:** Math.R.
—BLDSC shelfmark: 6498.000000.
Description: Research articles, chapter reports and news items submitted by members.

510 520 530   PL   ISSN 0239-7269
QA1   CODEN: BAPMAN
POLISH ACADEMY OF SCIENCES. BULLETIN. MATHEMATICAL SCIENCES. (Text in English, French, German and Russian) 1953. q. $100. Polska Akademia Nauk, Centrum Upowszechniania Nauki, Palac Kultury i Nauki, Pietro XXIII, pok.23-10, 00-901 Warsaw, Poland. (Dist. by: Ars Polona, Krakowskie Przedmiescie 7, 00-068 Warsaw, Poland) Ed. A. Pelczynski. bibl.; charts; illus.; circ. 520. (also avail. in microform from UMI; reprint service avail. from UMI) **Indexed:** Chem.Abstr., Math.R., Met.Abstr., Phys.Ber., Sci.Abstr.
Formerly (until 1983): Academie Polonaise des Sciences. Bulletin. Serie des Sciences Mathematiques, Astronomiques et Physiques (ISSN 0001-4117)

510   PL   ISSN 0137-6934
     CODEN: BCPUEU
POLISH ACADEMY OF SCIENCES. MATHEMATICAL INSTITUTE. BANACH CENTER PUBLICATIONS. (Text in various languages) 1976. irreg., vol.21, 1989. price varies. Panstwowe Wydawnictwo Naukowe, Miodowa 10, 00-251 Warsaw, Poland. (Dist. by: Ars Polona, Krakowskie Przedmiescie 7, 00-068 Warsaw, Poland) Ed. Czeslaw Olech.
—BLDSC shelfmark: 1861.525000.

510   PL   ISSN 0072-0372
POLITECHNIKA GDANSKA. ZESZYTY NAUKOWE. MATEMATYKA. (Text in Polish and English; summaries in Russian and one West-European language) 1963. irreg. price varies. Politechnika Gdanska, Majakowskiego 11-12, 81-952 Gdansk 6, Poland. (Dist. by: Osrodek Rozpowszechniania Wydawnictw Naukowych PAN, Palac Kultury i Nauki, 00-901 Warsaw, Poland) bibl.; charts; illus.

510 PL ISSN 0137-2572
POLITECHNIKA LODZKA. ZESZYTY NAUKOWE. MATEMATYKA. (Text in various languages; summaries in Polish and Russian) 1972. irreg. price varies. Wydawnictwo Politechniki Lodzkiej, Ul. Wolczanska 219, 93-085 Lodz, Poland. (Dist. by: Ars Polona-Ruch, Krakowskie Przedmiescie 7, Warsaw, Poland) Ed. Janusz Matkowski. circ. 166. **Indexed:** Math.R.
Description: Focuses on applied mathematics.

510 PL ISSN 0239-488X
POLITECHNIKA POZNANSKA. ZESZYTY NAUKOWE. GEOMETRIA. (Text in English, French) irreg. price varies. Politechnika Poznanska, Pl. Curie-Sklodowskiej 5, Poznan, Poland. (Dist. by: Ars Polona, Krakowskie Przedmiescie 7, PO Box 1001, 00-068 Warsaw, Poland) Ed. Eugeniusz Korczak.
Formerly: Politechnika Poznanska. Zeszyty Naukowe. Geometria Wykreslna.
Description: Papers dealing with foundations of geometry, geometry of incidence, non-Euclidean geometries and geometrical transformations.

510 530 PL ISSN 0072-470X
QA1 CODEN: PSMFBT
POLITECHNIKA SLASKA. ZESZYTY NAUKOWE. MATEMATYKA - FIZYKA. (Text in Polish; summaries in English, German, Russian) 1961. irreg. price varies. Politechnika Slaska, Katowicka 4, 44-100 Gliwice, Poland. FAX 371655. TELEX 036304. (Dist. by: Ars Polona, Krakowskie Przedmiescie 7, 00-068 Warsaw, Poland) Ed. Boguslaw Nosowicz. circ. 205.
Indexed: Chem.Abstr., Math.R.

510 PL ISSN 0137-6268
POLITECHNIKA WROCLAWSKA. INSTYTUT MATEMATYKI. PRACE NAUKOWE. KONFERENCJE. 1977. irreg., no.2, 1986. price varies. Politechnika Wroclawska, Wybrzez Wyspianskiego 27, 50-370 Wroclaw, Poland. FAX 22-36-64. TELEX 712559 PWRPL.

510 PL ISSN 0324-9603
TJ260.A1 CODEN: PNMMEI
POLITECHNIKA WROCLAWSKA. INSTYTUT MATEMATYKI. PRACE NAUKOWE. MONOGRAFIE. (Text in Polish; summaries in English and Russian) 1974. irreg., no.6, 1990. price varies. Politechnika Wroclawska, Wybrzeze Wyspianskiego 27, 50-370 Wroclaw, Poland. FAX 22-36-64. TELEX 712559 PWRPL. (Dist. by: Ars Polona-Ruch, Krakowskie Przedmiescie 7, Warsaw, Poland) circ. 475. **Indexed:** Math.R.

510 530 PL ISSN 0324-9611
TJ260.A1
POLITECHNIKA WROCLAWSKA. INSTYTUT MATEMATYKI. PRACE NAUKOWE. STUDIA I MATERIALY. (Former Name of Institute: Instytut Matematyki i Fizyki Teoretycznej) (Text in Polish; summaries in English and Russian) 1970. irreg., no.15, 1980. price varies. Politechnika Wroclawska, Wybrzeze Wyspianskiego 27, 50-370 Wroclaw, Poland. FAX 22-36-64. TELEX 712559 PWRPL. (Dist. by: Ars Polona-Ruch, Krakowskie Przedmiescie 7, Warsaw, Poland) **Indexed:** Math.R.

510 PL ISSN 0373-8299
QA1 CODEN: RPTPAQ
POLSKIE TOWARZYSTWO MATEMATYCZNE. ROCZNIKI. SERIA 1: COMMENTATIONES MATHEMATICAE. PRACE MATEMATYCZNE. (Text in English, French, German, Polish or Russian; summaries in English, French or Russian) 1955. irreg., vol.29, 1990. Panstwowe Wydawnictwo Naukowe, Ul. Miodowa 10, 00-251 Warsaw, Poland. (Dist. by: Ars Polona, Krakowskie Przedmiescie 7, 00-068 Warsaw, Poland) Ed. Wladyslaw Orlicz. bibl.; index. **Indexed:** Math.R.
—BLDSC shelfmark: 8007.000000.

510 PL ISSN 0079-3698
POLSKIE TOWARZYSTWO MATEMATYCZNE. ROCZNIKI. SERIA 2: WIADOMOSCI MATEMATYCZNE. 1955. irreg. (3-4 yr.). 35 Zl.($3.50) per volume. Polskie Towarzystwo Matematyczne, Ul. Sniadeckich 8, 00-950 Warsaw, Poland. (Dist. by: Ars Polona-Ruch, Krakowskie Przedmiescie 7, Warsaw, Poland) Ed. Zbigniew Semadeni. bk.rev.; bibl.; index; circ. 2,750.

510 PO ISSN 0032-5155
QA1 CODEN: POMAAJ
PORTUGALIAE MATHEMATICA. (Text in English, French, German, Italian and Portuguese) 1937. q. $95 in Europe; elsewhere $100. Sociedade Portuguesa de Matematica, Avenida da Republica 37-4o, 1000 Lisbon, Portugal. TEL 77-32-51. Ed. A. Pereira Gomes. index; circ. 700. **Indexed:** Math.R.
—BLDSC shelfmark: 6557.000000.

POZNANSKIE TOWARZYSTWO PRZYJACIOL NAUK. KOMISJA MATEMATYCZNO-PRZYRODNICZA. PRACE. see PHYSICS

510 GW ISSN 0032-7042
QA1
PRAXIS DER MATHEMATIK. 1959. bi-m. DM.86.40 (foreign DM.94.80). Aulis-Verlag Deubner und Co. KG, Antwerpener Str. 6-12, 5000 Cologne 1, Germany. TEL 0221-518051. FAX 0221-518443. TELEX 8883068-AVD. Ed.Bd. adv.; bk.rev.; bibl.; charts; illus. (reprint service avail. from KTO) **Indexed:** Math.R.
—BLDSC shelfmark: 6603.172000.

510 600 RU ISSN 0032-8235
QA801 CODEN: PMAMAF
PRIKLADNAYA MATEMATIKA I MEKHANIKA. (Text in English, French or German) 1933. bi-m. 47.40 Rub. (Akademiya Nauk S.S.S.R.) Izdatel'stvo Nauka, Fizmatlit, Leninskii prospekt, 15, 117071 Moscow, Russia. Ed. L.A. Galin. bibl.; charts; index; circ. 3,015. (reprint service avail. from KTO) **Indexed:** Appl.Mech.Rev., Eng.Ind., Geotech.Abstr., Int.Aerosp.Abstr., Math.R., Sci.Abstr.
—BLDSC shelfmark: 0132.000000.

510 PP
PRIME. s-a. K.3 per no. Mathematics and Statistics Department, Private Mail Bag, Lae, Papua New Guinea. Ed. G.R. Baird.

510 US ISSN 1051-1970
QA11.A1
▼**PRIMUS**; problems, resources, and issues in mathematics undergraduate studies. 1991. q. $34 (foreign $40). Rose-Hulman Institute of Technology, Department of Mathematics, Terre Haute, IN 47803. TEL 812-877-8412. Ed. Brian J. Winkel.
—BLDSC shelfmark: 6612.930850.
Description: Provides a forum for discussion of all aspects of collegiate mathematics education.
Refereed Serial

510 US ISSN 0079-5194
PRINCETON MATHEMATICAL SERIES. 1946. irreg., no.39, 1990. price varies. Princeton University Press, 3175 Princeton Pike, Lawrenceville, NJ 08648. TEL 609-896-1344. FAX 609-895-1081. (back issues avail.; reprint service avail. from UMI)
Refereed Serial

519 US ISSN 0079-5607
PROBABILITY AND MATHEMATICAL STATISTICS; a series of monographs and textbooks. 1967. irreg., latest 1988. Academic Press, Inc., 1250 Sixth Ave., San Diego, CA 92101. TEL 619-231-0926. FAX 619-699-6715. Eds. Z.W. Birnbaum, E. Lukacs. **Indexed:** Math.R.
Refereed Serial

510 US
PROBABILITY: PURE AND APPLIED. 1984. irreg., vol.9, 1991. price varies. Marcel Dekker, Inc., 270 Madison Ave., New York, NY 10016. TEL 212-696-9000. FAX 212-685-4540. TELEX 421419. Ed. Marcel Neuts.

510 GW ISSN 0178-8051
QA273 CODEN: PTRFEU
PROBABILITY THEORY AND RELATED FIELDS. (Text mainly in English; ocassionally in French, German) 1962. 16/yr. DM.2440($1122) Springer-Verlag, Heidelberger Platz 3, D-1000 Berlin 33, Germany. TEL 030-8207-1. (Subscr. to: 44 Hartz Way, Secaucus, NJ 07094) Ed. H. Rost. adv.; charts; illus. (also avail. in microform from UMI; back issues avail.; reprint service avail. from ISI) **Indexed:** Compumath, Curr.Cont., Math.R., Zent.Math.
—BLDSC shelfmark: 6617.223500.
Supersedes: Zeitschrift fuer Wahrscheinlichkeitstheorie und Verwandte Gebiete (ISSN 0044-3719)

510 US
PROBLEM BOOKS IN MATHEMATICS. 1981. irreg. price varies. Springer-Verlag, 175 Fifth Ave., New York, NY 10010. TEL 212-460-1500. (And Berlin, Heidelberg, Tokyo and Vienna) Ed. P. Halmos.

510 RU
PROBLEMY ISTORII MATEMATIKI I MEKHANIKI. 1972. irreg. 1 Rub. Moskovskii Universitet, Ul. Gertsena 5-7, 103009 Moscow, Russia. illus.

510 CL ISSN 0716-0917
PROYECCIONES; revista de matematica. (Text in English, French, Spanish) 1982. s-a. $20 per no. or exchange basis. Universidad Catolica del Norte, Departamento de Matematicas, Avda. Angamos 0610, Casilla 1280, Antofagasta, Chile. TEL 241148. FAX 241724. TELEX 225097 UNORTE CL. Ed. Julio Pena Rodriguez. circ. 500.
Description: Publishes papers from all areas of mathematics.

510 YU ISSN 0350-1302
PUBLICATIONS DE L'INSTITUT MATHEMATIQUE. (Text in English, French, German, Russian) 1932. s-a. $100. Matematicki Institut, Knez Mihailova 35, p.p. 367, 11001 Belgrade, Yugoslavia. TEL 011-630-170. FAX 011-186-105. TELEX 72593 SANU YU. (Subscr. to: Kubon & Sagner, Buchexport-Import GMBH, Hesstr. 39-41, Posfach 34 01 08, D-3000 Munich 34, Germany) Ed. Slobodan Aljancic. circ. 600. (back issues avail.) **Indexed:** Math.R., Zent.Math.
—BLDSC shelfmark: 7077.500000.

510 PK
PUNJAB UNIVERSITY JOURNAL OF MATHEMATICS. (Text in English) 1967. a. $12. University of the Punjab, Department of Mathematics, New Campus, Lahore 54590, Pakistan. Ed. Abdul Majeed. circ. 500.
Indexed: Math.R.
Formerly: University of the Punjab. Department of Mathematics. Journal.

510 US ISSN 0079-8169
QA3
PURE AND APPLIED MATHEMATICS; a series of monographs and textbooks. 1949. irreg., vol.137, 1989. Academic Press, Inc., 1250 Sixth Ave., San Diego, CA 92101. TEL 619-231-0926. FAX 619-699-6715. Ed.Bd. (reprint service avail. from ISI) **Indexed:** Math.R.
Refereed Serial

510 US
PURE AND APPLIED MATHEMATICS: A WILEY INTERSCIENCE SERIES OF TEXTS, MONOGRAPHS AND TRACTS. 1948. irreg., latest 1990. price varies. John Wiley & Sons, Inc., Wiley Interscience Journals, 605 Third Ave., New York, NY 10158-0012. TEL 212-850-6418. Ed. L. Bers. **Indexed:** Math.R.
Formed by the merger of: Interscience Tracts in Pure and Applied Mathematics (ISSN 0074-994X); Pure and Applied Mathematics; a Series of Texts and Monographs (ISSN 0079-8185)
Refereed Serial

510 US ISSN 0079-8177
PURE AND APPLIED MATHEMATICS SERIES. 1970. irreg., vol.157, 1992. price varies. Marcel Dekker, Inc., 270 Madison Ave., New York, NY 10016. TEL 212-696-9000. FAX 212-685-4540. TELEX 421419. Ed. S. Kobayashi.
—BLDSC shelfmark: 7161.452000.
Refereed Serial

510.5 001.6
621.381 II ISSN 0379-3168
PURE AND APPLIED MATHEMATIKA SCIENCES. (Text in English) 1974. s-a. Rs.250($150) Mathematika Sciences Society of India, M.S. College, Department of Mathematics, P.O. Box 65, Saharanpur, India. TEL 25407. Ed. P.L. Maggu. adv.; bk.rev.; illus. (back issues avail.) **Indexed:** Math.R., Math.R., Zent.Math.
Formerly: Mathematika Sciences.

510 UK ISSN 0260-0781
QARCH. 1980. irreg. £1($2) Cambridge University, Mathematical Society, Archimedeans, c/o The Art's School, Bene't St., Cambridge CB2 3PY, England. Ed. Paul Balister. charts; circ. 1,000. (back issues avail.)
Description: Solved and unsolved mathematical problems.

QINGBAO KEXUE/INFORMATION SCIENCE. see *COMPUTERS — Information Science And Information Theory*

QUANTUM (WASHINGTON); the student magazine of math and science. see *SCIENCES: COMPREHENSIVE WORKS*

MATHEMATICS

510 UK ISSN 0033-5606
QA1 CODEN: QJMAAT
QUARTERLY JOURNAL OF MATHEMATICS. (Oxford Second Series) 1930. q. £70($125) (effective Jan. 1991). Oxford Journals, Pinkhill House, Southfield Road, Eynsham, Oxford OX8 1JJ, England. TEL 0865-882283. FAX 0865-882890. TELEX 837330-OXPRES-G. Eds. R.G. Haydon, W.B. Stewart. adv.; bibl.; index; circ. 1,200. (also avail. in microform from SWZ,UMI; reprint service avail. from SWZ) **Indexed:** Compumath, Curr.Cont., Math.R., Sci.Cit.Ind., Stat.Theor.Meth.Abstr.
—BLDSC shelfmark: 7192.000000.
Description: Addresses original contributions to pure mathematics as well as the main branches of algebra, analysis, combinatorics and topology.

510 620.1 UK ISSN 0033-5614
QA1 CODEN: QJMMAV
QUARTERLY JOURNAL OF MECHANICS AND APPLIED MATHEMATICS. 1948. q. £84($165) Oxford University Press, Oxford Journals, Pinkhill House, Southfield Rd., Eynsham, Oxford OX8 1JJ, England. TEL 0865-882283. FAX 0865-882890. TELEX 837330 OXPRES G. Ed.Bd. adv.; index; circ. 1,400. (also avail. in microform from UMI) **Indexed:** Appl.Mech.Rev., Br.Ceram.Abstr., Chem.Abstr., Compumath, Curr.Cont., Deep Sea Res.& Oceanogr.Abstr., Eng.Ind., Fluidex, Int.Aerosp.Abstr., Math.R., Met. Abstr., Phys.Abstr., Sci.Cit.Ind., Sh.& Vib.Dig.
—BLDSC shelfmark: 7193.000000.
Description: Addresses original articles in the general field of mechanics, particularly theoretical mechanics, classical electromagnetism, nonlinear dynamics and combined fields such as magnetohydro-numerical methods.

519 US ISSN 0033-569X
QA1 CODEN: QAMAAY
QUARTERLY OF APPLIED MATHEMATICS. 1943. q. $50. Brown University, Providence, RI 02912. TEL 401-831-5037. Ed. Walter F. Freiberger. adv.; bk.rev.; index; circ. 1,600. (also avail. in microform from UMI; reprint service avail. from UMI) **Indexed:** Appl.Mech.Rev., Biol.Abstr., Chem.Abstr., Compumath, Curr.Cont., Eng.Ind., Int.Aerosp.Abstr., Math.R., Petrol.Abstr., Sci.Abstr.
—BLDSC shelfmark: 7170.000000.
Refereed Serial

510 CN ISSN 0079-8797
QUEEN'S PAPERS IN PURE AND APPLIED MATHEMATICS. (Text in English and French) 1966. irreg. price varies. Queen's University, Department of Mathematics and Statistics, Kingston, Ont. K7L 3N6, Canada. TEL 613-545-2390. Ed. Grace Orzech. **Indexed:** Math.R.
—BLDSC shelfmark: 7211.500000.
Formerly: Queen's University at Kingston. Department of Mathematics. Research Report.

510 FR ISSN 0764-583X
QA1 CODEN: RMMAEV
R A I R O - M 2 A N MATHEMATICAL MODELLING AND NUMERICAL ANALYSIS. (Revue Francaise d'Automatique d'Informatique et de Recherche Operationelle) 1966. 7/yr. 2450 F. (Association Francaise des Sciences et Technologies de l'Information et des Systemes) Dunod, 15 rue Gossin, 92543 Montrouge Cedex, France. TEL 33-1-40-92-65-00. FAX 33-1-40-92-65-97. TELEX 270 004. (Subscr. to: Centrale des Revues, 11 rue Gossin, 92543 Montrouge Cedex, France. TEL 33-1-46-56-52-66) Ed. R. Temam. adv.; bibl.; charts; circ. 1,150. (also avail. in microfilm from UMI) **Indexed:** Compumath, Curr.Cont., Math.R., Sci.Abstr.
—BLDSC shelfmark: 5402.548000.
Formerly (1977-1985): R A I R O Analyse Numerique - Numerical Analysis (ISSN 0399-0516)
Description: Presents original research and survey papers of high scientific level in numerical analysis and mathematical modelling.

R E C S A M NEWS. (Regional Centre for Education in Science and Mathematics) see *EDUCATION — Teaching Methods And Curriculum*

510 II ISSN 0079-9602
QA1
RANCHI UNIVERSITY MATHEMATICAL JOURNAL. (Text in English) 1970. a. Rs.40($10) Ranchi University, Department of Mathematics, Ranchi 834008, Bihar, India. TEL 22914. Ed. R.C. Choudhary. circ. 150. **Indexed:** Math.R.

510 NE ISSN 0926-6364
▼**RANDOM OPERATORS AND STOCHASTIC EQUATIONS.** (Text in English) 1992. q. DM.650 (effective 1992). V S P, P.O. Box 346, 3700 AH Zeist, Netherlands. TEL 03404-25790. FAX 03404-32081. TELEX 40217 VSP NL. Eds. V. Girko, A. Skorokhod.

510 US ISSN 1042-9832
▼**RANDOM STRUCTURES & ALGORITHMS.** 1990. q. $145 (foreign $195). John Wiley & Sons, Inc., Journals, 605 Third Ave., New York, NY 10158-0012. TEL 212-850-6000. FAX 212-850-6088. TELEX 12-7063. Ed. Michal Karonski.
—BLDSC shelfmark: 7254.411950.
Description: Covers the latest research on discrete random structures and the applications of probablistic techniques to problem solving in various areas of mathematics, computer science, and operations research.

510 US ISSN 0147-1937
QA331.5
REAL ANALYSIS EXCHANGE. (Text in English; occasionally in French or German) 1976. s-a. $33. Michigan State University, Department of Mathematics, East Lansing, MI 48824-1027. TEL 517-353-8489. Ed. Clifford E. Weil. circ. 425. (back issues avail.) **Indexed:** Math.R.
—BLDSC shelfmark: 7303.245000.
Description: Contains surveys, research articles, inroads and queries concerning this branch of mathematics.

510 FR ISSN 0246-9367
RECHERCHES EN DIDACTIQUE DES MATHEMATIQUES. (Text in English and French; summaries in English and Spanish) 3/yr. 240 F. to individuals; institutions 340 F. Pensee Sauvage Editions, B.P. 141, F-38002 Grenoble cedex, France.

519 IT ISSN 0034-4427
CODEN: RNMTAN
RENDICONTI DI MATEMATICA. (Text in English, French, Italian; summaries in English and Italian) 1913. q. DM.200.00 plus postage. (Istituto Matematico G. Castlenuovo) Edizioni Scientifiche Inglesi Americane, Via Palestro, 30, 00185 Rome, Italy. (Co-sponsors: Istituto di Alta Mathematica; Istituto Mathematica Applicata) Ed. G. Roghi. index; circ. 1,000. **Indexed:** Appl.Mech.Rev., Math.R.

REPORTS ON MATHEMATICAL LOGIC. see *PHILOSOPHY*

510 JA ISSN 0034-5318
CODEN: KRMPBV
RESEARCH INSTITUTE FOR MATHEMATICAL SCIENCES. PUBLICATIONS/KYOTO DAIGAKU SURI KAISEKI KENKYUJO KIYO. (Text in English and European languages) 1965. bi-m. 36000 Yen($318) Kyoto University, Research Institute for Mathematical Sciences - Kyoto Daigaku Suri Kaiseki Kenkyujo, Kita-Shirakawa Oiwake-cho, Sakyo-ku, Kyoto-shi, Kyoto-fu 606, Japan. TEL 03-3439-0162. (Dist. by: Kinokuniya Company Ltd., 17-7, Shinjuku 3-chome, Shinjuku-ku, Tokyo 160, Japan) Ed.Bd. circ. 1,100. **Indexed:** Compumath, JTA, Math.R., Sci.Cit.Ind.
—BLDSC shelfmark: 7107.919000.
Formerly (until vol.4, 1969): Kyoto University. Research Institute for Mathematical Sciences. Publications: Series A (ISSN 0454-7845)

516 JA
RESEARCH NOTES AND MEMORANDA OF APPLIED GEOMETRY FOR PREVENIENT NATURAL PHILOSOPHY. (Text in English; summaries in English and Japanese) 1973. m. 4000 Yen. Post-R A A G Library, c/o Mr. Kazuo Kondo, 1570 Yotsukaido, Yotsukaido-shi, Chiba-ken 284, Japan. TEL 0434-22-2839.

510 US
RESEARCH NOTES IN MATHEMATICS. 1975. irreg., no.257, 1992. John Wiley & Sons, Inc., Journals, 605 Third Ave., New York, NY 10158-0012. TEL 212-850-6000. FAX 212-850-6088. TELEX 12-7063. **Indexed:** Math.R.
Refereed Serial

RESEARCH REPORTS ON INFORMATION SCIENCES. SERIES A, MATHEMATICAL SCIENCE. see *COMPUTERS — Information Science And Information Theory*

510 SZ ISSN 0378-6218
QA1
RESULTS IN MATHEMATICS/RESULTATE DER MATHEMATIK. (Text in English and German) 1978. 8/yr. 478 Fr.($326) Birkhaeuser Verlag, P.O. Box 133, CH-4010 Basel, Switzerland. TEL 061-737740. FAX 061-737950. TELEX 963475 BIRKH CH. (Dist. in N. America by: Springer-Verlag New York, Inc., Journal Fulfillment Services, Box 2485, Secaucus, NJ 07096-2491, USA. TEL 201-348-4033) Ed. H.J. Arnold. **Indexed:** Math.R.
—BLDSC shelfmark: 7782.500000.

REVIEWS IN MATHEMATICAL PHYSICS. see *PHYSICS*

510 CK ISSN 0034-7426
QA1 CODEN: RCMABQ
REVISTA COLOMBIANA DE MATEMATICAS. (Text in English, French, Portuguese and Spanish) 1952. q. $22. Sociedad Colombiana de Matematicas, Apdo. Aereo No. 25-21, Bogota, Colombia. FAX 2686465. Ed. Xavier Caicedo. bk.rev.; bibl.; index; circ. 800. **Indexed:** Math.R.
—BLDSC shelfmark: 7851.402000.
Formerly: Revista de Matematicas Elementales.
Refereed Serial

510 CU ISSN 0256-5374
REVISTA CUBANA DE CIENCIAS MATEMATICAS. (Text in Spanish; summaries in English, Spanish) 1980. 3/yr. C.$4.50($18) Universidad de La Habana, Direccion de Informacion Cientifica y Tecnica, Havana 4, Cuba. (Dist. by: Ediciones Cubanas, Obispo 527, Apdo. 605, Havana, Cuba) (back issues avail.)

510 BL ISSN 0102-0811
CODEN: RMAEDG
REVISTA DE MATEMATICA E ESTATISTICA. (Abstracts in English and Portuguese) 1983. a. $30 or exchange basis. Universidade Estadual Paulista, Av. Vicente Ferreira 1278, Caixa Posta 603, 17.500 Marilia SP, Brazil. TEL 0144-33-1844. FAX 0144-22-2504. TELEX 111 9016 UJME BR. abstr.; bibl.; charts; stat. **Indexed:** Math R.
Description: Cover original articles and research in the field of mathematics and statistics.

510 SP ISSN 0213-2230
QA1
REVISTA MATEMATICA IBEROAMERICANA. 1985. 3/yr. $45 to individuals; institutions $180. Consejo Superior de Investigaciones Cientificas, Real Sociedad Matematica Espanola, c/o Departamento de Matematicas, Universidad Autonoma de Madrid, 28049 Madrid, Spain. TELEX 91-397-4987. bk.rev.; illus.; index. **Indexed:** Math.R.
—BLDSC shelfmark: 7864.020000.
Supersedes (1919-1982): Revista Matematica Hispano-Americana (ISSN 0373-0999)

510 574 FR ISSN 0035-1024
QH323.5 CODEN: RBIMBZ
REVUE DE BIO-MATHEMATIQUE/BIOMATHEMATICS REVIEW. (Text in English and French) 1962. q. 120 F. (International Society of Mathematical Biology) Editions Europeennes, 11 bis Ave. de la Providence, 92160 Antony, France. Ed. Frances Collot. adv.; bk.rev.; circ. 1,000. **Indexed:** Biol.Abstr., Chem.Abstr., Math.R.

510 FR ISSN 0035-1504
QA1
REVUE DE MATHEMATIQUES SPECIALES. 1890. 10/yr. 420 F. Librairie Vuibert, 63 bd. Saint-Germain, 75005 Paris, France. FAX 43-25-75-86. Ed.Bd. adv.; bk.rev.; index; circ. 3,000.
—BLDSC shelfmark: 7930.000000.
Description: General survey of the entrance examination to the French "Grandes Ecoles": Ecole Polytechnique, Ecole Normale Superieure.

510 RM ISSN 0035-3965
QA1 CODEN: RRMPB6
REVUE ROUMAINE DE MATHEMATIQUES PURES ET APPLIQUEES. (Text in English, French, German, Russian and Spanish) 1956. 10/yr. 400 lei($110) (Academia Romana) Editura Academiei Romane, Calea Victoriei 125, 79717 Bucharest, Rumania. (Dist. by: Rompresfilatelia, Calea Grivitei 64-66, P.O. Box 12-201, 78104 Bucharest, Rumania) adv.; bk.rev.; abstr.; bibl.; charts; index. **Indexed:** Appl.Mech.Rev., Biostat., Chem.Abstr., Compumath, Int.Aerosp.Abstr., Math.R., Oper.Res.Manage.Sci., Qual.Contr.Appl.Stat.

510   IT   ISSN 0035-5038
CODEN: RCMTAE
RICERCHE DI MATEMATICA. 1952. s-a. L.60000 per vol. Universita degli Studi di Napoli, Istituto di Matematica, Via Mezzocannone 8, Naples, Italy. (Orders to: Libreria Liguori, Via Mezzocannone 23, 80134 Naples, Italy) Ed. Prof. Carlo Miranda. charts; circ. 750. **Indexed:** Curr.Cont., Math.R.

510   US   ISSN 0272-4332
T174.5   CODEN: RIANDF
RISK ANALYSIS. 1980. q. $240 (foreign $280)(effective 1992). (Society for Risk Analysis) Plenum Publishing Corp., 233 Spring St., New York, NY 10013-1578. TEL 212-620-8000. FAX 212-463-0742. TELEX 23-421139. Ed. Curtis C. Travis. adv.; bk.rev.; illus.; index. (also avail. in microfilm from JSC; back issues avail.) **Indexed:** Curr.Cont., Dok.Arbeitsmed., Energy Ind., Energy Info.Abstr., Eng.Ind., Environ.Abstr., I D A, INSPEC, Psychol.Abstr., Ref.Zh., Risk Abstr., W.R.C.Inf.
—BLDSC shelfmark: 7972.583000.
Refereed Serial

510   IT
RIVISTA DI MATEMATICA PER LE SCIENZE ECONOMICHE E SOCIALI. (Text and summaries in English and Italian) 1978. s-a. L.40000. Associazione per la Matematica Applicata alle Scienze Economiche e Sociali, Via Conservatorio 7, 20122 Milan, Italy. Ed. Lorenzo Peccati. adv.; bk.rev; circ. 2,000. (back issues avail.) **Indexed:** Math.R.

510   US   ISSN 0035-7596
QA1   CODEN: RMJMAE
ROCKY MOUNTAIN JOURNAL OF MATHEMATICS. 1971. q. $175 to individuals; institutions $350. Rocky Mountain Mathematics Consortium, Arizona State University, Department of Mathematics, Tempe, AZ 85287. TEL 602-965-3788. Ed. John McDonald. index; circ. 600. (back issues avail.) **Indexed:** Compumath, Math.R., Sci.Abstr.
—BLDSC shelfmark: 8002.630000.
Refereed Serial

500   IE
ROYAL IRISH ACADEMY. PROCEEDINGS. SECTION A: MATHEMATICAL AND PHYSICAL SCIENCES. 1836. 2/yr. price varies. Royal Irish Academy, 19 Dawson St., Dublin 2, Ireland. TEL 01-762570. FAX 01-762346. Ed. B. Young. index. cum.index; circ. 500. **Indexed:** Art & Archaeol.Tech.Abstr., Chem.Abstr., Curr.Cont., Field Crop Abstr., GeoRef., Herb.Abstr., Ind.Vet., Intl.Civil Eng.Abstr., Math.R, Phys.Abstr., Phys.Ber., RILA, Sci.Abstr., Soft.Abstr.Eng., Vet.Bull., Zent.Math.
Formerly: Royal Irish Academy. Proceedings. Section A: Mathematical, Astronomical and Physical Science (ISSN 0035-8975)

510   UK   ISSN 0308-2105
Q41
ROYAL SOCIETY OF EDINBURGH. PROCEEDINGS. SECTION A (MATHEMATICS). 1832. 6/yr. £155 (foreign £175). Royal Society of Edinburgh, 22 George Street, Edinburgh, EH2 2PQ, Scotland. TEL 031-225 6057. FAX 031-220-6889. Ed. J.M. Ball. circ. 1,000. (also avail. in microfiche from BHP) **Indexed:** Appl.Mech.Rev., Biol.Abstr., Chem.Abstr., Compumath, Curr.Cont., Eng.Ind., Math.R., Met.Abstr., Nucl.Sci.Abstr., Sci.Abstr.
—BLDSC shelfmark: 6803.000000.
Formerly: Royal Society of Edinburgh. Proceedings. Section A. Mathematical and Physical Sciences (ISSN 0080-4541)
Description: Publishes papers of international standard across the whole spectrum of mathematics.

ROYAL SOCIETY OF LONDON. PHILOSOPHICAL TRANSACTIONS. SERIES A. PHYSICAL SCIENCES AND ENGINEERING. see *PHYSICS*

500 510   UK   ISSN 0080-4630
QA   CODEN: PRLAAZ
ROYAL SOCIETY OF LONDON. PROCEEDINGS. SERIES A. MATHEMATICAL AND PHYSICAL SCIENCES. 1832. m. £360 (foreign £384). Royal Society of London, 6 Carlton Terrace, London SW1Y 5AG, England. TEL 071-839-5561. FAX 071-976-1837. TELEX 917876. Ed. J.E. Enderby. circ. 1,620. (reprint service avail. from ISI) **Indexed:** Appl.Mech.Rev., Br.Archaeol.Abstr., Chem.Abstr., Curr.Cont., Deep Sea Res.& Oceanogr.Abstr., Eng.Ind., Excerp.Med., Fluidex, Forest Prod.Abstr., GeoRef, Mass Spectr.Bull., Math.R., Met.Abstr., Petrol.Abstr., Sci.Abstr.
—BLDSC shelfmark: 6804.500000.
Refereed Serial

ROZHLEDY MATEMATICKO-FYZIKALNI. see *EDUCATION*

510   UK   ISSN 0036-0279
QA1
RUSSIAN MATHEMATICAL SURVEYS. English translation of: Uspekhi Matematicheskikh Nauk (RU ISSN 0042-1316) vol.15, 1960. 6/yr. £304. British Library, Distribution Centre, Blackhorse Rd., Letchworth, Herts SG6 1HW, England. TEL 0937-843434. FAX 0937-546333. TELEX 557381. (Co-sponsor: London Mathematical Society) bibl.; index. (also avail. in microform from MIM) **Indexed:** Compumath, Math.R.
—BLDSC shelfmark: 0420.766000.

510   US   ISSN 0080-5084
CODEN: SAMPBY
S I A M - A M S PROCEEDINGS. 1969. irreg. price varies. (Society for Industrial and Applied Mathematics) American Mathematical Society, Box 1571, Annex Sta., Providence, RI 02901-9930. TEL 401-455-4000. (Street addr.: 201 Charles St., Providence, RI 02904) Ed.Bd. index in each vol. **Indexed:** Math.R., Zent.Math.
Formerly: American Mathematical Society. Proceedings of Symposia in Applied Mathematics.
Refereed Serial

519   US   ISSN 0036-1399
QA1   CODEN: SMJMAP
S I A M JOURNAL ON APPLIED MATHEMATICS. 1953. bi-m. $210 to non-members; members $48. Society for Industrial and Applied Mathematics, Attn: M. Lafferty, 3600 University City Science Center, Philadelphia, PA 19104-2688. TEL 215-382-9800. FAX 215-386-7999. TELEX 446-715. Ed. James P. Keener. adv.; index; circ. 2,424. (also avail. in microform from IAM; back issues avail.) **Indexed:** A.S.& T.Ind., Abstr.Bull.Inst.Pap.Chem., Appl.Mech.Rev., Appl.Mech.Rev., ASCA, Biostat., Chem.Abstr., Compumath, Comput.Cont., Comput.Rev., Cyb.Abstr., Deep Sea Res.& Oceanogr.Abstr., Eng.Ind., Int.Abstr.Oper.Res., Int.Aerosp.Abstr., Math.R., Oper.Res.Manage.Sci., Qual.Contr.Appl.Stat., Sci.Abstr., Sh.& Vib.Dig.
—BLDSC shelfmark: 8271.350000.
Formerly: Society for Industrial and Applied Mathematics. Journal.
Description: Contains research articles in mathematical methods and their applications in the physical, engineering, biological, and medical sciences.
Refereed Serial

519 600   US   ISSN 0363-0129
QA402.3   CODEN: SJCODE
S I A M JOURNAL ON CONTROL AND OPTIMIZATION. 1963. bi-m. $242 to non-members; members $48. Society for Industrial and Applied Mathematics, Attn: M. Lafferty, 3600 University City Science Center, Philadelphia, PA 19104-2688. TEL 215-382-9800. FAX 215-386-7999. TELEX 446-715. Ed. Jan C. Willems. adv.; index; circ. 1,799. (also avail. in microform; back issues avail.) **Indexed:** A.S.& T.Ind., Appl.Mech.Rev., ASCA, Compumath, Comput.Cont., Comput.Rev., Cyb.Abstr., INSPEC, Int.Abstr.Oper.Res., Int.Aerosp.Abstr., Math.R., Sci.Abstr.
—BLDSC shelfmark: 8271.355200.
Formerly: S I A M Journal on Control (ISSN 0036-1402)
Description: Contains research articles in the mathematical theory of control and its applications and the associated areas of systems theory and optimization, the theories of games and differential games, and the topics in mathematical analysis, algebra, differential geometry, probability, statistics, and stochastics that apply to control, systems theory, and optimization.
Refereed Serial

510   US   ISSN 0895-4801
QA76.9.M35   CODEN: SJDMEC
S I A M JOURNAL ON DISCRETE MATHEMATICS. 1980. q. $188 to non-members; members $40. Society for Industrial and Applied Mathematics, Attn: P. Clifford, 3600 University City Science Center, Philadelphia, PA 19104-2688. TEL 215-382-9800. FAX 215-386-7998. TELEX 446-715. Ed. Clyde Monma. adv.; index; circ. 1,017. (also avail. in microform from IAM; back issues avail.) **Indexed:** Biostat., Compumath, Int.Abstr.Oper.Res., Math.R., Oper.Res.Manage.Sci., Qual.Contr.Appl.Stat.
—BLDSC shelfmark: 8271.355400.
Supersedes in part (in 1987): S I A M Journal on Algebraic and Discrete Methods (ISSN 0196-5212)
Description: Contains research articles on a broad range of topics from pure and applied mathematics including combinatorics and graph theory, discrete optimization and operations research, theoretical computer science, coding and communication theory, and game theory and mathematical modeling.
Refereed Serial

515   US   ISSN 0036-1410
QA300   CODEN: SJMAAH
S I A M JOURNAL ON MATHEMATICAL ANALYSIS. 1970. bi-m. $305 to non-members; members $48. Society for Industrial and Applied Mathematics, Attn: M. Lafferty, 3600 University City Science Center, Philadelphia, PA 19104-2688. TEL 215-382-9800. FAX 215-386-7999. TELEX 446-715. Ed. J.L. Bona. adv.; index; circ. 1,342. (also avail. in microform from IAM; back issues avail.) **Indexed:** Appl.Mech.Rev., ASCA, Compumath, Comput.Rev., Int.Aerosp.Abstr., Math.R., Sci.Abstr.
—BLDSC shelfmark: 8271.356000.
Description: Focuses on those parts of classical and modern analysis that have direct or potential application to the natural sciences and engineering. Papers fall into two broad categories, the first being those that analyse interesting problems associated with realistic mathematical models for natural phenomena. The second category includes those papers which contribute in a substantial way to the general, analytical information and techniques which are like to bear upon such models.
Refereed Serial

519   US   ISSN 0895-4798
QA188   CODEN: SJMAEL
S I A M JOURNAL ON MATRIX ANALYSIS AND APPLICATIONS. 1980. q. $150 to non-members; members $40. Society for Industrial and Applied Mathematics, Attn: P. Clifford, 3600 University City Science Ctr., Philadelphia, PA 19104-2688. TEL 215-382-9800. FAX 215-386-7999. TELEX 446-715. Ed. Gene Golub. adv.; index; circ. 1,165. (also avail. in microform from IAM)
—BLDSC shelfmark: 8271.356300.
Supersedes in part (in 1987): S I A M Journal on Algebraic and Discrete Methods (ISSN 0196-5212)
Description: Contains research articles on the application of matrix analysis to areas such as Markov chains, networks, signal processing, systems and control theory, mathematical programming, economic and biological modeling, and statistics and operations research.
Refereed Serial

515 600   US   ISSN 0036-1429
CODEN: SJNAAM
S I A M JOURNAL ON NUMERICAL ANALYSIS. 1964. bi-m. $220 to non-members; members $48. Society for Industrial and Applied Mathematics, Attn.: M. Lafferty, 3600 University City Science Center, Philadelphia, PA 19104-2688. TEL 215-382-9800. FAX 215-386-7999. TELEX 446-715. Ed. M.L. Luskin. adv.; charts; index; circ. 2,408. (also avail. in microform from IAM; back issues avail.) **Indexed:** A.S.& T.Ind., Appl.Mech.Rev., ASCA, Compumath, Comput.Abstr., Comput.Rev., INSPEC, Math.R., Sci.Abstr.
—BLDSC shelfmark: 8271.357000.
Description: Contains research articles on the development and anlysis of numerical methods including their convergence, stability, and error analysis, as well as related results in functional analysis and approximation theory. Computational experiments and new types of numerical applications are also included.
Refereed Serial

MATHEMATICS

519 600   US   ISSN 1052-6234
QA402.5
▼**S I A M JOURNAL ON OPTIMIZATION.** 1991. q. $160 to non-members; members $40. Society for Industrial and Applied Mathematics, Attn: P. Clifford, 3600 University City Science Ctr., Philadelphia, PA 19104. TEL 215-382-9800. FAX 215-386-7999. TELEX 446-715. Ed. John E. Dennis, Jr. adv.; index; circ. 730.
—BLDSC shelfmark: 8271.357100.
Description: Research and expository articles on the theory and practice of optimization, and papers that link optimization theory with computational practice and applications.
Refereed Serial

S I A M JOURNAL ON SCIENTIFIC AND STATISTICAL COMPUTING. see *STATISTICS*

510 600   US
S I A M NEWS. 1968. bi-m. $18. Society for Industrial and Applied Mathematics, Attn: M. Lafferty, 3600 University City Science Center, Philadelphia, PA 19104-2688. TEL 215-382-9800. FAX 215-386-7999. TELEX 446-715. Ed. I.E. Block. adv.; circ. 10,441. **Indexed:** Math.R.
Formerly: S I A M Newsletter (ISSN 0036-1437)
Refereed Serial

510   US   ISSN 0036-1445
QA1   CODEN: SIREAD
S I A M REVIEW. 1959. q. $129 to non-members. Society for Industrial and Applied Mathematics, Attn: M. Lafferty, 3600 University City Science Center, Philadelphia, PA 19104-2688. TEL 215-382-9800. FAX 215-386-7999. TELEX 446-715. Ed. P. Davis. adv.; bk.rev.; index; circ. 9,998. (also avail. in microform from IAM; back issues avail.) **Indexed:** A.S.& T.Ind., Appl.Mech.Rev., ASCA, Biostat., Compumath, Comput.Rev., Deep Sea Res.& Oceanogr.Abstr., Int.Abstr.Oper.Res., Math.R., Oper.Res.Manage.Sci., Qual.Contr.Appl.Stat., Risk Abstr.
—BLDSC shelfmark: 8271.360000.
Description: Contains primarily expository and survey papers as well as occcasional essays on topics of interest to applied mathematicians. Other features are classroom notes, problems and solutions.
Refereed Serial

510   CN   ISSN 0316-5779
S M T S JOURNAL - NEWSLETTER. 3/yr. Can.$25 for 2 yrs. (Saskatchewan Mathematics Teachers' Society) Saskatchewan Teachers' Federation, Box 1108, Saskatoon, Sask. S7K 3N3, Canada. Ed. Don Kapoor.

S S M ARRT. (School Science & Mathematics Association, Inc.) see *EDUCATION — Teaching Methods And Curriculum*

510   JA
QA1
S U T JOURNAL OF MATHEMATICS. (Text and summaries in English) 1965. s-a. Science University of Tokyo - Tokyo Rika Daigaku, 1-3, Kagurazaka, Shinjuku-ku, Tokyo 162, Japan.
Formerly: T R U Mathematics (ISSN 0496-6597)

SACHUNTERRICHT UND MATHEMATIK IN DER GRUNDSCHULE. see *EDUCATION — Teaching Methods And Curriculum*

SAECHSISCHE AKADEMIE DER WISSENSCHAFTEN, LEIPZIG. MATHEMATISCH-NATURWISSENSCHAFTLICHE KLASSE. ABHANDLUNGEN. see *SCIENCES: COMPREHENSIVE WORKS*

SAECHSISCHE AKADEMIE DER WISSENSCHAFTEN, LEIPZIG. MATHEMATISCH-NATURWISSENSCHAFTLICHE KLASSE. SITZUNGSBERICHTE. see *SCIENCES: COMPREHENSIVE WORKS*

SAGA DAIGAKU RIKOGAKUBU SHUHO/SAGA UNIVERSITY. FACULTY OF SCIENCE AND ENGINEERING. REPORTS. see *ENGINEERING*

SAINS MALAYSIANA: JERNAL SAINS ALAM SEMULA; jadi. see *SCIENCES: COMPREHENSIVE WORKS*

500   JA   ISSN 0387-9313
    CODEN: SDSKD4
SAITAMA DAIGAKU KIYO. KYOIKUGAKUBU. SUGAKU, SHIZEN KAGAKU/SAITAMA UNIVERSITY. JOURNAL: MATHEMATICS AND NATURAL SCIENCES. (Text and summaries in English and Japanese) 1952. a. Saitama Daigaku, Kyoikugakubu - Saitama University, Faculty of Education, 255 Shimo-Okubo, Urawa-shi, Saitama-ken 338, Japan.

510 530 540   JA   ISSN 0289-0739
QA1
SAITAMA MATHEMATICAL JOURNAL. (Text in English) 1952. a. exchange basis. Saitama Daigaku, Rigakubu, Sugaku Kyoshitsu - Saitama University, Faculty of Science, Department of Mathematics, 255, Shimo-Okubo, Urawa-shi, Saitama-ken 338, Japan. FAX 048-857-4560. Ed. Takashi Kako. circ. 500. **Indexed:** Math.R., Sci.Abstr.
—BLDSC shelfmark: 8070.438000.
Former titles (until 1983): Saitama University. Science Reports. Series A: Mathematics; Saitama University. Science Reports. Series A: Mathematics, Physics and Chemistry (ISSN 0558-2431)

510   US   ISSN 0198-8379
SCHOLASTIC MATH. 1980. 14/yr. (Sept.-May). $5.25. Scholastic Inc., 730 Broadway, New York, NY 10003. TEL 212-505-3000. Ed. Rachel Maizes. circ. 311,000. (also avail. in microform from UMI; reprint service avail. from UMI, BLH)
Description: Activities and features focusing on consumer math, math on the job, computation to problem solving practice.

SCHOOL SCIENCE AND MATHEMATICS; journal for all science and mathematical teachers. see *EDUCATION*

SCIEN TECH/SAGA DAIGAKU RIKOGAKUBU KOHO. see *ENGINEERING*

510 530   IT
SCUOLA NORMALE SUPERIORE DI PISA. ANNALI. CLASSE DI SCIENZE. (Text in English, French, German, Italian) 1871; N.S. 1973. q. $80. Scuola Normale Superiore di Pisa, Piazza dei Cavalieri 7, 56100-Pisa, Italy. TEL 050-597111. FAX 050-563513. TELEX 590548. Ed. Edoardo Vesentini. index. cum.index; circ. 1,300. (also avail. in microfilm from BHP) **Indexed:** Appl.Mech.Rev., INIS Atomind., Math.R.
Formerly: Scuola Normale Superiore di Pisa. Annali. Scienze, Fisiche e Matematiche (ISSN 0036-9918)

SEIKEN N S T SHINPOJUMU KOEN RONBUNSHU. see *COMPUTERS — Computer Simulation*

510   SZ   ISSN 0272-9903
QA1   CODEN: SMSODB
SELECTA MATHEMATICA SOVIETICA. 1981. 4/yr. 428 Fr.($292) Birkhaeuser Verlag, P.O. Box 133, CH-4010 Basel, Switzerland. TEL 061-737740. FAX 061-737950. TELEX 963475 BIRKH CH. (Dist. in N. America by: Springer-Verlag New York, Inc., Journal Fulfillment Services, Box 2485, Secaucus, NJ 07096-2491, USA. TEL 201-348-4033) Ed. R.P. Boas. index; circ. 800. (back issues avail.) **Indexed:** Math.R., Sci.Abstr.
—BLDSC shelfmark: 8231.600000.

519.5   US   ISSN 0094-8837
QA276.25
SELECTED TABLES IN MATHEMATICAL STATISTICS. 1970. irreg. American Mathematical Society, Box 1571, Annex Sta., Providence, RI 02901-9930. TEL 401-455-4000. (Street addr.: 201 Charles St., Providence, RI 02904)
Refereed Serial

510 519   US   ISSN 0065-9274
QA273   CODEN: SMSRB
SELECTED TRANSLATIONS IN MATHEMATICAL STATISTICS AND PROBABILITY. 1961. irreg. price varies. (Institute of Mathematical Statistics) American Mathematical Society, Box 1571, Annex Sta., Providence, RI 02901-9930. TEL 401-455-4000. (Street addr.: 201 Charles St., Providence, RI 02904) Ed. Ben Silver. cum.index 1966-1973.

510   US   ISSN 0037-1912
QA171   CODEN: SMGFAN
SEMIGROUP FORUM. 1970. 6/yr. $192. Springer-Verlag, Journals, 175 Fifth Ave., New York, NY 10010. TEL 212-460-1500. (Also Berlin, Heidelberg, Tokyo, and Vienna) Ed. K.H. Hofmann. bk.rev. (also avail. in microform from UMI; reprint service avail. from ISI) **Indexed:** ASCA, Compumath, Curr.Cont., Math.R., Zent.Math.
Description: Encompasses algebraic, topological, partially ordered, and transformation semigroups, semigroups of measures, harmonic analysis of semigroups, semigroups of operators, and applications of semigroup theory to other topics such as ring theory, category theory, automata, and logic.

510   RM
SEMINAR ARGHIRIADE. (Text in English, French, Rumanian, Russian) 1974. irreg. 50 lei($2) Universitatea din Timisoara, Facultatea de Matematica, Bd. Vasile Pirvan Nr. 4, Timisoara, Rumania. Ed. Achim Dragomir. circ. 250. **Indexed:** Math.R, Zent.Math.

515.74
SEMINAR ON APPLIED FUNCTIONAL ANALYSIS. (Text in English) 1978. a. Oyo Kansu Kaisekigaku Kenkyukai - Society of Applied Functional Analysis, c/o Mr. Hisaharu Umegaki, Tokyo Kogyo Daigaku Rigakubu, 12-1, Ookayama 2-chome, Meguro-ku, Tokyo 152, Japan.

510   JA
SEMINAR ON MATHEMATICAL SCIENCES. (Text in Japanese) 1980. irreg. Keio Gijuku Daigaku, Rikogakubu, Suri Kagakka - Keio University, Faculty of Science and Technology, Department of Mathematics, 14-1, Hiyoshi 3-chome, Kohoku-ku, Yokohama-shi, Kanagawa-ken 223, Japan.

510   BU   ISSN 0204-4110
QA1   CODEN: SERDDJ
SERDIKA; BULGARSKO MATEMATICHESKO SPISANIE/SERDICA; BULGARICAE MATHEMATICAE PUBLICATIONES. (Text in English, German, Russian) 1975. q. 2.70 lv. per no. (Bulgarska Akademiia na Naukite) Publishing House of the Bulgarian Academy of Sciences, Acad. G. Bonchev St., Bldg. 6, 1113 Sofia, Bulgaria. (Dist. by: Hemus, 6, Rouski Blvd., 1000 Sofia, Bulgaria) Ed. L. Iliev. charts. **Indexed:** Math.R.
—BLDSC shelfmark: 0164.087800.

510 530
SERIE DI MATEMATICA E FISICA. PROBLEMI. 1978. irreg., no.6, 1982. price varies. Liguori Editore s.r.l., Via Mezzocannone 19, 80134 Naples, Italy. TEL 081-5227139. Ed. Livio C. Piccinini.
Formerly: Serie di Matematica e Fisica. Problemi Risolti.

510 530
SERIE DI MATEMATICA E FISICA. TESTI. 1974. irreg., no.11, 1988. price varies. Liguori Editore s.r.l., Via Mezzocannone 19, 80134 Naples, Italy. TEL 081-5227139. Ed. G. Vidossich.
Formerly: Serie di Matematica e Fisica (ISSN 0391-3252)

510   SI
SERIES IN PURE MATHEMATICS. (Text in English) 1984. irreg., vol. 13, 1991. price varies. World Scientific Publishing Co. Pte. Ltd., Farrer Rd., P.O. Box 128, Singapore 9128, Singapore. TEL 3825663. FAX 3825919. TELEX RS 28561 WSPC. (UK addr.: 73 Lynton Mead, Totteridge, London N20 8DH, England. TEL 44-81-4462461; US addr.: 1060 Main St., Ste. 1B, River Edge, NJ 07661. TEL 800-227-7562) Ed. C.C. Hsiung.

510   SI
SERIES IN REAL ANALYSIS. (Text in English) 1988. irreg., vol. 4, 1992. price varies. World Scientific Publishing Co. Pte. Ltd., Farrer Rd., P.O. Box 128, Singapore 9128, Singapore. TEL 3825663. FAX 3825919. TELEX RS 28561 WSPC. (UK addr.: 73 Lynton Mead, Totteridge, London N20 8DH, England. TEL 44-81-4462461; US addr.: 1060 Main St., Ste. 1B, River Edge, NJ 07661. TEL 800-227-7562)

510 SI
▼SERIES ON ADVANCES IN MATHEMATICS FOR APPLIED SCIENCES. (Text in English) 1990. irreg., vol. 12, 1992. price varies. World Scientific Publishing Co. Pte. Ltd., Farrer Rd., P.O. Box 128, Singapore 9128, Singapore. TEL 3825663. FAX 3825919. TELEX RS 28561 WSPC. (UK addr.: 73 Lynton Mead, Totteridge, London N20 8DH, England. TEL 44-81-4462461; US addr.: 1060 Main St., Ste. 1B, River Edge, NJ 07661. TEL 800-227-7562) Ed. N. Bellomo.

510 SI
▼SERIES ON KNOTS AND EVERYTHING. (Text in English) 1991. irreg. price varies. World Scientific Publishing Co. Pte. Ltd., Farrer Rd., P.O. Box 128, Singapore 9128, Singapore. TEL 3825663. FAX 3825919. TELEX RS 28561 WSPC. (UK addr.: 73 Lynton Mead, Totteridge, London N20 8DH, England. TEL 44-81-4462461; US addr.: 1060 Main St., Ste. 1B, River Edge, NJ 07661. TEL 800-227-7562) Ed. L.H. Kauffman.

510 SI
▼SERIES ON SOVIET AND EAST EUROPEAN MATHEMATICS. (Text in English) 1991. irreg., vol. 12, 1992. price varies. World Scientific Publishing Co. Pte. Ltd., Farrer Rd., P.O. Box 128, Singapore 9128, Singapore. TEL 3825663. FAX 3825919. TELEX RS 28561 WSPC. (UK addr.: 73 Lynton Mead, Totteridge, London N20 8DH, England. TEL 44-81-4462461; US addr.: 1060 Main St., Ste. 1B, River Edge, NJ 07661. TEL 800-227-7562)

510 RU ISSN 0321-3005
QE1 CODEN: ISTVAY
SEVERO-KAVKAZSKII NAUCHNYI TSENTR VYSSHEI SHKOLY. ESTESTVENNYE NAUKI. IZVESTIYA/NORTH-CAUCASUS SCIENTIFIC CENTER OF HIGH SCHOOL. NATURAL SCIENCES. NEWS. 4/yr. 7.20 Rub. Rostovski Universitet, Ul. Pushkinskaia 160, 344 700 Rostov-na-Donu, Russia. TEL 8-863-536411. TELEX 123520 NAUKA.
—BLDSC shelfmark: 0082.321500.

510 370 CC
SHANGHAI ZHONGXUE SHUXUE/SHANGHAI SECONDARY SCHOOL MATHEMATICS. (Text in Chinese) bi-m. Shanghai Shifan Daxue, Shuxue Xi - Shanghai Normal University, Mathematics Department, 10 Guilin Lu, Shanghai 4362223, People's Republic of China. Ed. Ying Zhiyi.

SHINSHU UNIVERSITY. FACULTY OF TEXTILE SCIENCE AND TECHNOLOGY. JOURNAL. SERIES F: PHYSICS AND MATHEMATICS. see PHYSICS

510 CC ISSN 1000-0984
SHUXUE DE SHIJIAN YU RENSHI/MATHEMATICS IN PRACTICE AND COGNITION. (Text in Chinese) 1984. q. Y7.60($7) per no. (Chinese Academy of Sciences, Institute of Systems Science) Science Press, Marketing and Sales Department, 16 Donghuangchenggen Beijie, Beijing 100707, People's Republic of China. TEL 4010642. FAX 4012180. TELEX 210247-SPBJ-CN. adv.; bk.rev.; circ. 16,000. Indexed:
 Description: Carries articles on results attained in the application of theories and methods of mathematics. Includes efficient mathematical methods, lectures, academic developments, history of mathematics, practical mathematic questions to be solved, and news.
 Refereed Serial

SHUXUE JIAOXUE/MATHEMATICS TEACHING. see EDUCATION — Teaching Methods And Curriculum

510 CC
SHUXUE JIAOXUE TONGXUN/MATHEMATICS TEACHING BULLETIN. (Text in Chinese) bi-m. Xinan Shifan Daxue, Shuxue Xi - Southwest Normal University, Mathematics Department, 1, Tiansheng Lu, Beipei, Chongqing, Sichuan 630715, People's Republic of China. TEL 630715. Ed. Zhou Zhongqun.

510 CC ISSN 0488-7395
SHUXUE TONGXUN/MATHEMATICS BULLETIN. (Text in Chinese) m. Wuhan Shi Shuxue Xuehui, Huazhong Shifan Daxue, Guizishan, Wuchang-qu, Wuhan, Hubei 430070, People's Republic of China. TEL 715601. Ed. Li Xiumu.

510 530 CC
SHUXUE WULI XUEBAO. English edition: Acta Mathematica Scientia (ISSN 0252-9602) (Text in Chinese) 1981. q. Y14($8) per no.; English edition $10 per no. Science Press, Marketing and Sales Department, 16 Donghuangchenggen Beijie, Beijing 100707, People's Republic of China. TEL 4010642. FAX 4012180. TELEX 210247-SPBJ-CN. adv.; circ. 6,000. (reprint service avail. from KTO) Indexed: ASCA, Compumath, Math.R.
 Description: Aims to present important new achievements in the mathematical sciences. Publishes original expository papers in areas bordering on both mathematics and the physical sciences.

510 CC ISSN 0583-1431
SHUXUE XUEBAO. English edition: Acta Mathematica Sinica, New Series (ISSN 1000-9574) (Text in Chinese; summaries in English) 1936. bi-m. $10 per no. (Chinese Academy of Science, Institute of Mathematics) Science Press, Marketing and Sales Department, 16 Donghuangchenggen Beijie, Beijing 100707, People's Republic of China. TEL 4010642. FAX 4012180. TELEX 210247-SPBJ-CN. adv.; bibl.; index; circ. 24,000. (reprint service avail. from KTO) Indexed: Math.R.
—BLDSC shelfmark: 0632.000000.
 Description: Contains original papers on pure mathematics.
 Refereed Serial

510 CC
SHUXUE YILIN. (Text in Chinese) q. Zhongguo Kexueyuan, Shuxue Yanjiusuo - Chinese Academy of Sciences, Institute of Mathematics, Zhongguancun, Beijing 100080, People's Republic of China. TEL 283376. Ed. Tian Fangzeng.

SHUZHI JISUAN YU JISUANJI YINGYONG/JOURNAL ON NUMERICAL METHODS AND COMPUTER APPLICATIONS. see SCIENCES: COMPREHENSIVE WORKS — Computer Applications

510 US ISSN 1055-1344
▼SIBERIAN ADVANCES IN MATHEMATICS. 1991. q. $345. (Russian Academy of Sciences, Institute of Mathematics, Siberian Branch, RU) Allerton Press, Inc., 150 Fifth Ave., New York, NY 10011. TEL 212-924-3950. Ed. A.A. Borovkov.
—BLDSC shelfmark: 8271.374900.
 Description: Covers both pure and applied mathematics, reflecting achievements of mathematicians in the eastern part of Russia.

510 US ISSN 0037-4466
QA1 CODEN: SMTJAW
SIBERIAN MATHEMATICAL JOURNAL. English translation of: Sibirskii Matematicheskii Zhurnal (RU ISSN 0037-4474) 1966. bi-m. $1215 (foreign $1420)(effective 1992). (Russian Academy of Sciences, Siberian Division, RU) Plenum Publishing Corp., Consultants Bureau, 233 Spring St., New York, NY 10013-1578. TEL 212-620-8468. FAX 212-463-0742. TELEX 23-421139. Ed. M.M. Lavrent'ev. (also avail. in microfilm from JSC; back issues avail.) Indexed: Compumath, Comput.& Info.Sys., Curr.Cont., Math.R., Zent.Math.
—BLDSC shelfmark: 0420.810000.
 Refereed Serial

510 RU ISSN 0037-4474
SIBIRSKII MATEMATICHESKII ZHURNAL. English translation: Siberian Mathematical Journal (US ISSN 0037-4466) 1960. bi-m. 56.70 Rub. Akademiya Nauk S.S.S.R., Sibirskoe Otdelenie, Prospekt Nauki, 21, Novosibirsk, Russia. Ed. A.I. Mal'tzev. index. (tabloid format)
—BLDSC shelfmark: 0164.120000.

510 BE ISSN 0037-5454
QA1 CODEN: SSWNAX
SIMON STEVIN; a quarterly journal of pure and applied mathematics. 1904. q. 1500 BEF. Natuur- en Geneeskundige Vennootschap, Krijgslaan 281, B-9000 Ghent, Belgium. Ed. J. Thas. bk.rev.; index; circ. 600. Indexed: Math.R., Sci.Abstr., Zent.Math.

510 US ISSN 1053-4792
QA246
▼SMARANDACHE FUNCTION JOURNAL. 1990. a. $9.99. Number Theory Publishing Company, Box 42561, Phoenix, AZ 85080. Ed. Mihail Bencze. bk.rev.; circ. 1,000.
 Description: Publishes solved and unsolved problems, notes and articles on research about the Smarandache Function in number theory, i.e., m(n) is the smallest integer m such that m! is divisible by n.

510 MX ISSN 0037-8615
QA1 CODEN: BSMXAU
SOCIEDAD MATEMATICA MEXICANA. BOLETIN. (Text in English, French and Spanish) 1944. 2/yr. Mex.$800($16) Sociedad Matematica Mexicana, Apdo. Postal 14-170, Mexico 14, D.F., Mexico 07000. Ed. Jose Adem. circ. 3,000. (reprint service avail. from ISI) Indexed: Math.R.
 Description: Presents original papers on mathematics.

510 BL ISSN 0037-8712
SOCIEDADE PARANAENSE DE MATEMATICA. BOLETIM. 1958. 2/yr. $40. Sociedade Paranaense de Matematica, Caixa Postal 1261, 80001 Curitiba, Parana, Brazil. (Subscr. to: Editora UFPR, Trav. Alfredo Bufrem, 140, 3a andar, 80020 Curitiba PR, Brazil) Ed. Jair M. Abe. adv.; bk.rev.; charts; illus.; circ. 600. Indexed: Math.R., Zent.Math.

510 BL ISSN 0102-3292
SOCIEDADE PARANAENSE DE MATEMATICA. MONOGRAFIAS. 1984. irreg. $10. Sociedade Paranaense de Matematica, Caixa Postal 1261, 80001 Curitiba, Parana, Brazil. Ed. Jair M. Abe. bibl. Indexed: Math.R., Zent.Math.

510 BE ISSN 0037-9476
SOCIETE MATHEMATIQUE DE BELGIQUE. BULLETIN. (Text in English or French) 1948. q. 1350 Fr.($36) Societe Mathematique de Belgique, c/o Guy Hirsch, 317 Av. Charles Woeste, 1090 Brussels, Belgium. adv.; bk.rev.; index; circ. 1,400. Indexed: Math.R.

510 FR
QA1 CODEN: BSMFAA
SOCIETE MATHEMATIQUE DE FRANCE. BULLETIN ET MEMOIRES. (Text and summaries in English, French) 1873. q. 840 F. (foreign 1060 F.) Societe Mathematique de France, Ecole Normale Superieure, Tour L, 1 rue Maurice Arnoux, France. TEL 33-40-84-80-54. FAX 33-40-84-80-52. (Dist. by: Centrale des Revues, 11 rue Gossin, 92543 Montrouge Cedex, France. TEL 1-46-56-52-66) Ed.Bd. bibl.; circ. 1,400. (also avail. in microfilm from BHP) Indexed: Compumath, Curr.Cont., Eng.Ind., INIS Atomind., Math.R., Ref.Zh., Sci.Cit.Ind, Zent.Math.
 Formerly: Societe de Mathematique de France. Bulletin (ISSN 0037-9484)
 Description: Covers the range of pure mathematics.
 Refereed Serial

510 FR
SOCIETE MATHEMATIQUE DE FRANCE. SUPPLEMENTS. (Text in English, French; summaries in English) 4/yr. (Societe Mathematique de France) Gauthier-Villars, 15 rue Gossin, 92543 Montrouge Cedex, France. TEL 33-1-40-92-65-00. FAX 33-1-40-92-65-97. TELEX 270 004. (Subscr. to: Centrale des Revues, 11 rue Gossin, 92543 Montrouge Cedex, France. TEL 33-1-46-56-52-66) Ed.Bd.

510 BU ISSN 0081-1858
QA1 CODEN: GSUMDR
SOFIISKI UNIVERSITET. FAKULTET PO MATEMATIKA I MEKHANIKA. GODISHNIK/UNIVERSITE DE SOFIA. FACULTE DES MATHEMATIQUES ET DE MECANIQUE. ANNUAIRE. (Text in Bulgarian and English) irreg. vol.67, 1972/73. price varies. Publishing House of the Bulgarian Academy of Sciences, Acad. G. Bonchev St., Bldg. 6, 1113 Sofia, Bulgaria. Ed. M. Pecheva. circ. 550. Indexed: Chem.Abstr., Math.R.

MATHEMATICS

526 510   US   ISSN 1059-5325
▼**SOLSTICE: AN ELECTRONIC JOURNAL OF GEOGRAPHY AND MATHEMATICS.** 1990. 2/yr. $15.95 for print edition (effective 1992). Institute of Mathematical Geography, 2790 Briarcliff, Ann Arbor, MI 48105-1429. TEL 313-761-1231. Ed. Sandra Lach Arlinghaus. charts; illus.; stat. (back issues avail.)
●Also available online.
Description: Publishes papers discussing the interactions between geography and mathematics, in which elements of one discipline shed light on the other. Disseminates original scientific research in electronic format.
Refereed Serial

510 500   CH   ISSN 0250-3255
QA1
SOOCHOW JOURNAL OF MATHEMATICS. 1975. q. $20 per no. Soochow University, Soochow University Library, Wai Shuang Hsi, Shih Lin, Taipei, Taiwan, Republic of China. FAX 886-02-8829310. (reprint service avail.) **Indexed:** Math.R. Key Title: Dongwu Shuli Xuebao.
—BLDSC shelfmark: 8328.016000.
Former titles: Soochow Journal of Mathematical and Natural Sciences; (until 1978): Soochow Journal of Mathematics.

510   US   ISSN 0172-6315
SOURCES IN THE HISTORY OF MATHEMATICS AND PHYSICAL SCIENCES. 1976. irreg. price varies. Springer-Verlag, 175 Fifth Ave., New York, NY 10010. TEL 212-460-1500. (Also Berlin, Heidelberg, Tokyo, Vienna) (reprint service avail. from ISI)

SOUTH AFRICAN STATISTICAL JOURNAL/SUID-AFRIKAANSE STATISTIESE TYDSKRIF. see *STATISTICS*

510   SI   ISSN 0218-0006
SOUTHEAST ASIAN BULLETIN OF MATHEMATICS. 1977. s-a. $40. (Southeast Asian Mathematical Society) World Scientific Publishing Co. Pte. Ltd., Farrer Rd., P.O. Box 128, Singapore 9128, Singapore. TEL 3825663. FAX 3825919. TELEX RS-28561-WSPC. (US addr.: 1060 Main St., Ste. 1B, River Edge, NJ 07661. TEL 800-227-7562; UK addr.: 73 Lynton Mead, Totteridge, London N20 8DH, England. TEL 44-81-4462461) Eds. R.F. Turner-Smith, P.Y. Lee. bk.rev.; circ. 150. **Indexed:** Math.R.
—BLDSC shelfmark: 8352.294000.

510   US   ISSN 0735-2719
QA297
SOVIET JOURNAL OF CONTEMPORARY MATHEMATICAL ANALYSIS. English translation of: Akademiya Nauk Armyanskoi S.S.R. Izvestiya. Seriya Matematika (AI ISSN 0002-3043) 1979. bi-m. $625. (Armenian Academy of Sciences, Al) Allerton Press, Inc., 150 Fifth Ave., New York, NY 10011. TEL 212-924-3950. Ed. M.M. Dzhrbashyan. **Indexed:** Math.R.
—BLDSC shelfmark: 0422.855000.

510   NE   ISSN 0169-2895
SOVIET JOURNAL OF NUMERICAL ANALYSIS AND MATHEMATICAL MODELLING. (Text in English) 1986. bi-m. DM.970. V S P, P.O. Box 346, 3700 AH Zeist, Netherlands. TEL 03404-25790. FAX 03404-32081. TELEX 40217 VSP NL. Ed. G.I. Marchuk. adv. (back issues avail.)
Description: Provides English translations of Soviet research on theoretical aspects of numerical analysis as well as application of mathematical methods to simulation and modelling.

510   US   ISSN 0197-6788
QA1
SOVIET MATHEMATICS - DOKLADY. English translation of: Akademii Nauk S.S.S.R. Doklady. 1960. bi-m. $650 to non-members; members $390; institutions $520. American Mathematical Society, Box 1571, Annex Sta., Providence, RI 02901-9930. TEL 401-455-4000. (Street addr.: 201 Charles St., Providence, RI 02904) Ed. Lev J. Leifman. adv.; bibl.; index; circ. 1,000. (also avail. in microfiche from AMS) **Indexed:** Math.R., Sci.Abstr.
—BLDSC shelfmark: 0423.850000.

510   US   ISSN 0197-7156
QA1   CODEN: SOMADL
SOVIET MATHEMATICS - IZ. V U Z. English translation of: Izvestiya Vysshikh Uchebnykh Zavedenii. Seriya Matematika (RU ISSN 0021-3446) 1974. m. $750. (Ministerstvo Visshego i Srednego Spetsialnogo Obrazovaniya, RU) Allerton Press, Inc., 150 Fifth Ave., New York, NY 10011. TEL 212-924-3950. Ed. A.V. Sul'din. charts; index. **Indexed:** Math.R.
—BLDSC shelfmark: 0423.900000.

SOVIET SCIENTIFIC REVIEWS. SECTION C: MATHEMATICAL PHYSICS REVIEWS. see *PHYSICS*

SPECTRUM; natural science journal for teachers and lecturers. see *SCIENCES: COMPREHENSIVE WORKS*

510   US
SPRINGER SERIES IN COMPUTATIONAL MATHEMATICS. 1983. irreg. price varies. Springer-Verlag, 175 Fifth Ave., New York, NY 10010. TEL 212-460-1500. (Also Berlin, Heidelberg, Tokyo, Vienna) (reprint service avail. from ISI)

510   US
SPRINGER SERIES IN SOVIET MATHEMATICS. 1983. irreg. price varies. Springer-Verlag, 175 Fifth Ave., New York, NY 10010. TEL 212-460-1500. (Also Berlin, Heidelberg, Tokyo, Vienna) (reprint service avail. from ISI)

510 530   GW   ISSN 0081-4113
STAATLICHE MATHEMATISCH-PHYSIKALISCHE SALONS, DRESDEN. VEROEFFENTLICHUNGEN. 1960. irreg. price varies. VEB Deutscher Verlag der Wissenschaften, Postfach 1216, 1080 Berlin, Germany. Ed. H. Groetzsch.

510   GW   ISSN 0721-2631
STATISTICS AND DECISIONS; an international mathematical journal for stochastic methods and models. (Text in English) 1982. q. DM.258. R. Oldenbourg Verlag GmbH, Postfach 801360, 8000 Munich 80, Germany. Ed.Bd. adv. **Indexed:** Math.R.
—BLDSC shelfmark: 8453.516600.
Description: Covers classical and multiple statistical decision procedures, asymptotic and nonparametric statistical procedures, including sequential analysis, abstract and applied statistical inference for stochastic processes.

STATISTICS & PROBABILITY LETTERS. see *STATISTICS*

510   US   ISSN 0081-5438
QA1
STEKLOV INSTITUTE OF MATHEMATICS. PROCEEDINGS. (English translation of the original Russian) 1967. q. since 1979. $518 to non-members; institutional members $414. American Mathematical Society, Box 1572, Annex Sta., Providence, RI 02901-9930. TEL 401-455-4000. (Street addr.: 201 Charles St., Providence, RI 02904) Ed. Ben Silver. circ. 550. **Indexed:** Math.R.
—BLDSC shelfmark: 0420.401500.

510   US   ISSN 0736-2994
QA274.2   CODEN: SAAPDA
STOCHASTIC ANALYSIS AND APPLICATIONS. 1983. 5/yr. $212.50 to individuals; institutions $425. Marcel Dekker Journals, 270 Madison Ave., New York, NY 10016. TEL 212-696-9000. FAX 212-685-4540. TELEX 421419 MARDEEK. (Subscr. to: Box 10018, Church St. Sta., New York, NY 10249) Eds. V. Lakshmikantham, G.S. Ladde. charts; stat.; index. (also avail. in microform from RPI) **Indexed:** ASCA, Compumath, Math.R.
—BLDSC shelfmark: 8465.250000.
Refereed Serial

STOCHASTIC PROCESSES AND THEIR APPLICATIONS. see *SCIENCES: COMPREHENSIVE WORKS*

510   US   ISSN 1045-1129
QA274.A1   CODEN: SSTREY
STOCHASTICS AND STOCHASTICS REPORTS. (Text in English; occasionally in French and German) 1978. 16/yr. (in 4 vols., 4 nos./vol.). $333. Gordon and Breach Science Publishers, 270 Eighth Ave., New York, NY 10011. TEL 212-206-8900. FAX 212-645-2459. TELEX 236735 GOPUB UR. (Subscr. to: Box 786, Cooper Sta., New York, NY 10276. TEL 800-545-8398; UK subscr. to: P.O. Box 90, Reading, Berkshire RG1 8JL, England. TEL 0734-560-080) Ed. Mark H.A. Davis. adv.; index. (also avail. in microform from MIM) **Indexed:** Math.R., Sci.Abstr.
—BLDSC shelfmark: 8465.331000.
Formerly: Stochastics (ISSN 0090-9491)
Refereed Serial

510   US   ISSN 0275-5785
STOCHASTICS MONOGRAPHS. 1985. irreg., vol.6, 1990. Gordon & Breach Science Publishers, 270 Eighth Ave., New York, NY 10011. TEL 212-206-8900. FAX 212-645-2459. TELEX 236735 GOPUB UR. (Subscr. to: Box 786, Cooper Sta., New York, NY 10276. TEL 800-545-8398; UK addr.: P.O. Box 90, Raeding, Berkshire RG1 8JL, England. TEL 0734-560-080) Ed. M. Davis. (also avail. in microform)
—BLDSC shelfmark: 8465.333000.
Refereed Serial

510   CN   ISSN 0085-6800
STUDENT MATHEMATICS. 1970. a. Can.$0.20. c/o S.K. Harburn, Ed., Faculty of Education, Rm. 373, University of Toronto, 371 Bloor St. West, Toronto, Ont. M5S 2R7, Canada. TEL 416-978-2011. bk.rev.; circ. 3,000.

510   PL   ISSN 0039-3223
QA1   CODEN: SMATAZ
STUDIA MATHEMATICA. (Text in various languages) 1929. irreg., no.96, 1990. $45 per vol. (Polska Akademia Nauk, Instytut Matematyczny) Panstwowe Wydawnictwo Naukowe, Ul. Miodowa 10, 00-251 Warsaw, Poland. (Dist. by: Ars Polona, Krakowskie Przedmiescie 7, 00-068 Warsaw, Poland) Ed.Bd. bibl.; index; circ. 1,100. (reprint service avail. from SWZ) **Indexed:** ASCA, Compumath, Math.R.

510   HU   ISSN 0081-6906
STUDIA SCIENTIARUM MATHEMATICARUM HUNGARICA. (Text in English, French, German, Russian) 1966. q. $68. (Magyar Tudomanyos Akademia) Akademiai Kiado, Publishing House of the Hungarian Academy of Sciences, P.O. Box 24, H-1363 Budapest, Hungary. Ed. A. Hajnal. **Indexed:** Math.R.
—BLDSC shelfmark: 8483.205000.

510   RM
STUDIA UNIVERSITATIS "BABES-BOLYAI". MATHEMATICA. (Text in English, French, German, Rumanian) 1958. q. exchange basis. Universitatea "Babes-Bolyai", Biblioteca Centrala Universitara, Str. Clinicilor Nr. 2, Cluj-Napoca, Rumania. charts; illus. **Indexed:** Math.R.
Formerly: Studia Universitatis "Babes-Bolyai". Series Mathematica - Physica (ISSN 0039-3436)

510 378   GW
STUDIENFUEHRER MATHEMATIK. 1973. a. free. Technical University Berlin, Department of Mathematics, Strasse des 17.Juni 135, 1000 Berlin 12, Germany. FAX 030-31421110. illus; circ. 400.

519   US   ISSN 0022-2526
QA1   CODEN: SAPMB6
STUDIES IN APPLIED MATHEMATICS. 1922. 8/yr.(in 2 vols.; 4 nos./vol.). $272 (foreign $306)(effective 1992). (Massachusetts Institute of Technology, Applied Mathematics Group) Elsevier Science Publishing Co., Inc. (New York), 655 Ave. of the Americas, New York, NY 10010. TEL 212-989-5800. FAX 212-633-3965. TELEX 420643 AEP UI. Ed. D.J. Benney. charts. (also avail. in microform from RPI; back issues avail.) **Indexed:** A.S.& T.Ind., Appl.Mech.Rev., Compumath, Curr.Cont., Deep Sea Res.& Oceanogr.Abstr., Eng.Ind., Math.R., Sci.Abstr., Sci.Cit.Ind.
—BLDSC shelfmark: 8489.480000.
Formerly: Journal of Mathematics and Physics.
Description: Reports results involving core concepts: propagation, equilibrium, stability, optimization as well as discrete and random processes.
Refereed Serial

511 NE ISSN 0049-237X
STUDIES IN LOGIC AND THE FOUNDATIONS OF MATHEMATICS. 1954. irreg., vol.130, 1991. price varies. Elsevier Science Publishers B.V., Books Division, P.O. Box 211, 1000 AE Amsterdam, Netherlands. TEL 020-5803911. FAX 020-5803705. TELEX 18582 ESPA NL. (Subscr. in U.S. and Canada to: Elsevier Science Publishing Co., Inc., Box 882, Madison Sq. Sta., New York, NY 10159. TEL 212-989-5800) Ed.Bd.
Refereed Serial

STUDIES IN MATHEMATICAL AND MANAGERIAL ECONOMICS. see *BUSINESS AND ECONOMICS — Management*

510 US ISSN 0081-8208
STUDIES IN MATHEMATICS (WASHINGTON). Variant title: M A A Studies in Mathematics. 1962. irreg., no.26, 1987. Mathematical Association of America, 1529 Eighteenth St., N.W., Washington, DC 20036. TEL 202-387-5200. Ed. C.W. Curtis. (reprint service avail. from UMI)
Refereed Serial

510 NE
STUDIES IN MATHEMATICS AND ITS APPLICATIONS. 1975. irreg., vol.25, 1992. price varies. Elsevier Science Publishers B.V., Books Division, P.O. Box 211, Amsterdam, Netherlands. TEL 020-5803911. FAX 020-5803705. TELEX 18582 ESPA NL. (Subscr. in U.S. and Canada to: Elsevier Science Publishing Co., Inc., Box 882, Madison Sq. Sta., New York, NY 10159. TEL 212-989-5800) Ed.Bd. bibl. **Indexed:** Math.R.
Refereed Serial

510 US ISSN 1040-6441
STUDIES IN THE DEVELOPMENT OF MODERN MATHEMATICS. irreg., latest vol.2. Gordon and Breach Scientific Publishers, 270 Eighth Ave., New York, NY 10011. TEL 212-206-8900. FAX 212-645-2459. TELEX 236735 GOPUB UR. (Subscr. to: Box 786, Cooper Sta., New York, NY 10276. TEL 800-545-8398; UK subscr. to: P.O. Box 90, Reading, Berkshire RG1 8JL, England. TEL 0734-560-080) Ed. Yu. I. Manin.
Refereed Serial

509 US ISSN 0172-570X
CODEN: SHMSDQ
STUDIES IN THE HISTORY OF MATHEMATICS AND PHYSICAL SCIENCES. 1975. irreg. price varies. Springer-Verlag, 175 Fifth Ave., New York, NY 10010. TEL 212-460-1500. (And Berlin, Heidelberg, Tokyo and Vienna) Eds. M.J. Klein, G.J. Toomer. (reprint service avail. from ISI) **Indexed:** Biol.Abstr., Math.R.
Refereed Serial

510 RM ISSN 0039-4068
QA1
STUDII SI CERCETARI MATEMATICE. (Text in Rumanian; summaries in English, French, German or Spanish) 1950. 6/yr. 180 lei($72) (Academia Romana) Editura Academiei Romane, Calea Victoriei 125, 79717 Bucharest, Rumania. (Dist. by: Rompresfilatelia, Calea Grivitei 64-66, P.O. Box 12-201, 78104 Bucharest, Rumania) adv.; bk.rev.; abstr.; charts; index. (reprint service avail. from SWZ) **Indexed:** Appl.Mech.Rev., Math.R.

510 JA ISSN 0039-470X
CODEN: SUGKAQ
SUGAKU/MATHEMATICS. English translation: Sugaku Expositions (US ISSN 0898-9583) (Text in Japanese) 1947. q. 3500 Yen. (Nihon Sugakkai - Mathematical Society of Japan) Iwanami Shoten Publishers, 5-5, Hitotsubashi 2-chome, Chiyoda-ku, Tokyo 101-02, Japan. FAX 03-3239-9618. (Dist. overseas by: Japan Publications Trading Co., Ltd., Box 5030, Tokyo International, Tokyo 100-31, Japan; Or: 1255 Howard St., San Francisco, CA 94103) Ed.Bd. bk.rev. **Indexed:** Jap.Per.Ind., Math.R.

510 US ISSN 0898-9583
QA1
SUGAKU EXPOSITIONS. English translation of: Sugaku (JA ISSN 0039-470X) 1988. s-a. $87 to non-members (individual members $52; institutional members $70). (Mathematical Society of Japan, JA) American Mathematical Society, Box 1571, Annex Sta., Providence, RI 02901-9930. TEL 401-455-4000. (Street addr.: 201 Charles St., Providence, RI 02904) circ. 950. **Indexed:** Math.R.
—BLDSC shelfmark: 8509.910000.

510 JA ISSN 0912-7569
SUGAKU OCHIKOBORE TSUSHIN. (Text in Japanese) 1986. s-a. (Sugaku Ochikobore Semina - Enjoy Mathematics Seminar) Scientist Inc. - Saientisutosha, 3-2, Kanda Surugadai, Chiyoda-ku, Tokyo 101, Japan.

510 JA ISSN 0386-4960
SUGAKU SEMINA/SUGAKU SEMINAR. (Text in Japanese) 1962. s-a. Nippon Hyoronsha Co., Ltd., 10-10, Minami-Otsuka 3-chome, Toshima-ku, Tokyo 170, Japan.

510.92 JA ISSN 0386-9555
QA27.J3
SUGAKUSHI KENKYU/JOURNAL OF THE HISTORY OF MATHEMATICS, JAPAN. (Text in Japanese) 1962. q. Nihon Sugakushi Gakkai - History of Mathematics Society of Japan, Fuji Tanki Daigaku, 7-7, Shimo-Ochiai 1-chome, Shinjuku-ku, Tokyo 161, Japan. **Indexed:** Jap.Per.Ind.

510 II
SUGANITAM. (Text in English or Gujarati) 1963. bi-m. Rs.15($4) Suganitam Trust, Department of Mathematics, Gujarat University, Ahmedabad 380009, India. Ed. A.M. Vaidya. adv.; bk.rev.; illus.; circ. 1,000.

510 JA
SUGEI PAZURU. (Text in Japanese) 1964. bi-m. Sugei Pazuru Aikokai, c/o Mr. Akio Suzuki, 9-1, Tsutsui 2-chome, Higashi-ku, Nagoya-shi, Aichi-ken 461, Japan.
Description: Contains mathematical puzzles.

SUHAKKWA MULLI. see *PHYSICS*

510 UK ISSN 0958-6709
▼**SUMMIT G C S E MATHEMATICS REVIEW.** 1990. 3/yr. £12.50 (foreign £20). Philip Allan Publishers Ltd., Deddington, Oxfordshire OX15 0SE, England. TEL 0869-38652. FAX 0869-38803.

510 JA ISSN 0386-2240
Q172 CODEN: SUKADJ
SURI KAGAKU/MATHEMATICAL SCIENCES. (Text in Japanese) 1963. m. (Suri Kagakusha) Saiensu-sha Co., Ltd., 2-4, Kanda Suda-cho, Chiyoda-ku, Tokyo 101, Japan. **Indexed:** Chem.Abstr., Jap.Per.Ind.
—BLDSC shelfmark: 5403.200000.

510 JA
SURI KAISEKI KENKYUJO DAYORI. (Text in Japanese) s-a. Kyoto University, Research Institute for Mathematical Sciences - Kyoto Daigaku Suri Kaiseki Kenkyujo, Oiwake-cho, Kita-Shirakawa, Sakyo-ku, Kyoto-shi, Kyoto-fu 606, Japan.
Description: Contains news of the Institute.

510 001.642 JA
SURI KEIKAKU SHINPOJUMU RONBUNSHU/MATHEMATICAL PROGRAMMING SYMPOSIUM, JAPAN. PROCEEDINGS. (Text in English and Japanese; summaries in English) 1980. a. Suri Keikaku Shinpojumu linkai - Committee of Mathematical Programming Symposium, Japan, c/o Mr. Masao Iri, Tokyo Daigaku Kogakubu Keisu Kogakka, 3-1, Hongo 7-chome, Bunkyo-ku, Tokyo 113, Japan.

510 US
SURVEYS & REFERENCE WORKS IN MATHEMATICS. 1979. irreg., no.9, 1983. John Wiley and Sons, Inc., 605 Third Avenue, New York, NY 10158-0012. TEL 212-850-6000. FAX 212-850-6088. TELEX 12-7063. **Indexed:** Math.R.
Refereed Serial

510 AU ISSN 0938-1953
▼**SURVEYS ON MATHEMATICS FOR INDUSTRY.** 1991. q. S.1680. Springer-Verlag, Sachsenplatz 4-6, Postfach 89, A-1201 Vienna, Austria. TEL 0222-3302415-0. Ed.Bd.
—BLDSC shelfmark: 8550.545000.

512.92 JA ISSN 0288-4046
SUSHIKI SHORI TSUSHIN/COMMUNICATIONS FOR SYMBOLIC AND ALGEBRAIC MANIPULATION. (Text in English and Japanese) 1983. 3/yr. Scientist Inc. - Saientisutosha, 3-2, Kanda Surugadai, Chiyoda-ku, Tokyo 101, Japan.

510 US ISSN 0082-0725
SYMPOSIA MATHEMATICA. (Contributions in English, French, German and Italian) 1969. irreg., vol.31, 1991. (Istituto Nazionale di Alta Matematica Francesco Severi) Academic Press, Inc., 1250 Sixth Ave., San Diego, CA 92101. TEL 619-231-0926. FAX 619-699-6715. (reprint service avail. from ISI) **Indexed:** Math.R., Zent.Math.
Refereed Serial

SYMPOSIUM ON COMPUTER ARITHMETIC. PROCEEDINGS. see *COMPUTERS — Cybernetics*

512.4 JA
SYMPOSIUM ON RING THEORY. PROCEEDINGS. (Text in English) 1968. a. Okayama Daigaku - Okayama University, 1-1, Tsushima Naka 1-chome, Okayama-shi, Okayama-ken 700, Japan.

510 GW ISSN 0232-9298
CODEN: SAMSEC
SYSTEMS ANALYSIS MODELLING SIMULATION; journal of mathematical modelling and simulation in systems analysis. (Text in English) 1984. m. DM.382.40. (Akademie der Wissenschaften der D.D.R., Zentralinstitut fuer Kybernetik und Informationsprozesse) Akademie-Verlag Berlin, Leipzigstr. 3-4, 1086 Berlin, Germany. TELEX 114420-AVERL-DD. Ed. A. Sydow. bk.rev.; illus.; index. **Indexed:** Compumath, Cyb.Abstr.
—BLDSC shelfmark: 8589.287500.

SYSTEMS SCIENCE. see *ENGINEERING*

510 001.6 US ISSN 1000-9590
Q295
SYSTEMS SCIENCE AND MATHEMATICAL SCIENCES. Chinese edition: Xitong Kexue yu Shuxue (ISSN 1000-0577) 1988. q. $260. (Chinese Academy of Sciences, Institute of Systems Science) Allerton Press, Inc., 150 Fifth Ave., New York, NY 10011. TEL 212-924-3950. (Co-publisher: Science Press, 16 Donghuangchenggen Beijie, Beijing 100707, People's Republic of China) Ed. Chen Hanfu. adv.; circ. 6,000. (back issues avail.)
—BLDSC shelfmark: 8589.432000.
Description: Presents original papers in mathematics from mainland China, including systems theory, system modeling, and system control.
Refereed Serial

SZIGMA; mathematics in economical science. see *BUSINESS AND ECONOMICS — Economic Systems And Theories, Economic History*

510 CH ISSN 0049-2930
TAMKANG JOURNAL OF MATHEMATICS. (Text in English) 1970. q. $50. (Tamkang University, Graduate School of Mathematics) Tamkang University Press, Tamsui, Taipei Hsien 25137, Taiwan, Republic of China. Ed. Bit-Shun Tam. circ. 300. **Indexed:** Math.R., Zent.Math.
—BLDSC shelfmark: 8601.610000.
Description: Covers pure and applied mathematics.

510 375 TZ ISSN 0856-065X
TANZANIAN MATHEMATICAL BULLETIN. (Text in English and Swahili) 1966. 2/yr. Sh.500($15) Mathematical Association of Tanzania - Chama Cha Hisabati Tanzania, PO Box 35062, Dar es Salaam, Tanzania. TEL 49192-2046. Ed. C.B. Alphonce. bk.rev.; index; circ. 300. (looseleaf format)
Formerly (until 1970): Mathematical Association of Tanzania. Bulletin (ISSN 0047-6250)
Description: Covers all mathematics topics relevant to primary, secondary and university education.

510 US
TATA INSTITUTE LECTURES ON MATHEMATICS. 1979. irreg. price varies. (Tata Institute of Fundamental Research, II) Springer-Verlag, 175 Fifth Ave., New York, NY 10010. TEL 212-460-1500. (Also Berlin, Heidelberg, Tokyo and Vienna) Eds. K.G. Ramanathan, B.V. Sreekantan. (reprint service avail. from ISI) **Indexed:** Math.R.
Formerly: Tata Institute Lecture Notes; Which supersedes: Tata Institute of Fundamental Research. Lectures on Mathematics and Physics. Physics (ISSN 0496-9472) & Tata Institute of Fundamental Research. Lectures on Mathematics and Physics. Mathematics (ISSN 0406-6987)

MATHEMATICS

510   **US**
TATA INSTITUTE STUDIES IN MATHEMATICS. 1978? irreg. price varies. (Tata Institute of Fundamental Research, Il) Springer-Verlag, 175 Fifth Ave., New York, NY 10010. TEL 212-460-1500. (Also Berlin, Heidelberg, Tokyo and Vienna) Ed. K.G. Ramanathan. (reprint service avail. from ISI)

510   **GS**   **ISSN 0320-9512**
QA1
TBILISSKII UNIVERSITET. INSTITUT PRIKLADNOI MATEMATIKI. SEMINAR. DOKLADI. (Text in Russian; summaries in English and Georgian) 1969. irreg., no.21, 1990. price varies. Tbilisskii Universitet, Institut Prikladnoi Matematiki - University of Tbilisi, Institute of Applied Mathematics, Chavchavadze Ave. 14, 380028 Tbilisi, Georgia. Ed. D. Gordeziani. circ. 300.
Formerly: Tbilisskii Universitet. Institut Prikladnoi Matematiki. Seminar. Annotatsii Dokladov (ISSN 0082-2191)

510   **UK**
TEACHING MATHEMATICS AND ITS APPLICATIONS. 1982. 4/yr. £32($64) Oxford University Press, Oxford Journals, Pinkhill House, Southfield Road, Eynsham, Oxford OX8 1JJ, England. TEL 0865-882283. FAX 0865-882890. TELEX 837330-OXPRES-G. Ed. David Burghes. adv.; bk.rev.
Description: Provides teaching aids for mathematics teachers in secondary and tertiary education.

TECHNICAL UNIVERSITY OF DENMARK. INSTITUTE OF MATHEMATICAL STATISTICS AND OPERATIONS RESEARCH. RESEARCH REPORTS. see *STATISTICS*

510   **NE**
TECHNISCHE UNIVERSITEIT EINDHOVEN. FACULTEIT DER WISKUNDE EN INFORMATICA. E U T REPORTS - W S K. 1968. irreg. Technische Universiteit Eindhoven, Faculteit de Wiskunden Informatica - Eindhoven University of Technology, Department of Mathematics and Computing Science, Postbus 513, 5600 MB Eindhoven, Netherlands. Ed. J. Boersma. circ. 100. **Indexed:** Math.R., Ref.Zh., Zent.Math.
Former titles: Technische Hogeschool Eindhoven. Onderafdeling der Wiskunde en Informatica. E U T Reports - W S K; Technische Hogeschool Eindhoven. Onderafdeling der Wiskunde. E U T Reports - W S K; Technische Hogeschool Eindhoven. Onderafdeling der Wiskunde. T H Report W S K.

510 530   **DK**   **ISSN 0106-6242**
TEKSTER FRA I M F U F A. no.50, 1982. irreg. Roskilde Universitetscenter, Institut for Studiet af Matematik og Fysik Samt Deres Funktioner i Undervisning Forskning og Anvendelse, Postbus 260, 4000 Roskilde, Denmark. TEL 02-757711. illus.

510 600   **JA**   **ISSN 0040-3504**
QA1   **CODEN: TNSRAZ**
TENSOR. (Text in English, French, German and Italian) 1938. 3/yr. 26000 Yen($250) Tensor Society - Tenzoru Gakkai, Kawaguchi Sukenkyujo - Kawaguchi Institute of Mathematical Sciences, 7-15, Matsu-ga-oka 2-chome, Chigasaki-shi, Kanagawa-ken 253, Japan. Ed. T. Kawaguchi. illus.; index; circ. 1,000. **Indexed:** INIS Atomind., Math.R.

510   **KR**   **ISSN 0321-4427**
QA331
TEORIYA FUNKTSII, FUNKTSIONAL'NYI ANALIZ I IKH PRILOZHENIYA. 1965. s-a. 1.40 Rub. per issue. (Khar'kovskii Gosudarstvennyi Universitet) Izdatel'stvo Vysshaya Shkola, Khar'kovskoe Otdelenie, Ul. Universitetskaya 16, 310003 Kharkov, Ukraine. Ed. V. Marchenko. abstr.; charts. **Indexed:** Math.R.
—BLDSC shelfmark: 0178.500000.
Description: Presents articles on the theory of function of many complex variables.

510   **RU**
TEORIYA FUNKTSII KOMPLEKSNOGO PEREMENNOGO I KRAEVYE ZADACHI. 1972. irreg. 0.80 Rub. Chuvashskii Gosudarstvennyi Universitet, Moskovskii prospekt, 15, Cheboksary, Chuvash A.R., Russia.

510   **KR**   **ISSN 0321-3900**
QA274.A1
TEORIYA SLUCHAINYKH PROTSESSOV; respublikanskii mezhvedomstvennyi sbornik nauchnykh trudov. 1973. a. 1.38 Rub. (Akademiya Nauk Ukrainskoi S.S.R., Institut Prikladnoi Matematiki i Mekhaniki) Izdatel'stvo Naukova Dumka, c/o Yu.A. Khramov, Dir, Ul. Repina, 3, Kiev 252 601, Ukraine. (Subscr. to: Mezhdunarodnaya Kniga, Moscow, G-200, Russia) Ed. Yu.N. Lin'kov. circ. 1,400.
—BLDSC shelfmark: 0178.420000.

510   **RU**   **ISSN 0040-361X**
QA273   **CODEN: TVPRA8**
TEORIYA VEROYATNOSTEI I EE PRIMENENIE. (Text in Russian; summaries in English) 1956. q. $32.40. (Akademiya Nauk S.S.S.R., Institut Matematiki) Izdatel'stvo Nauka, Fizmatlit, Leninskii prospekt, 15, 117071 Moscow, Russia. Ed. A.N. Kolmogorov. bk.rev.; charts; index; circ. 2,515. **Indexed:** Chem.Abstr., Math.R., Sci.Abstr.
—BLDSC shelfmark: 0178.000000.

510   **GW**   **ISSN 0233-0962**
TEUBNER-ARCHIV ZUR MATHEMATIK. 1984. 2/yr. B.G. Teubner Verlagsgesellschaft mbH, Sternwartenstr. 8, 7010 Leipzig, Germany. TEL 293158.

510   **GW**   **ISSN 0138-502X**
TEUBNER-TEXTE ZUR MATHEMATIK. (Text in English, German) 1976. 10/yr. B.G. Teubner Verlagsgesellschaft KG, Sternwartenstr. 8, 7010 Leipzig, Germany. TEL 293158. Ed.Bd.

TEXTS AND MONOGRAPHS IN ECONOMICS AND MATHEMATICAL SYSTEMS. see *BUSINESS AND ECONOMICS — Economic Systems And Theories, Economic History*

THEORETICAL AND MATHEMATICAL PHYSICS. see *PHYSICS*

519   **US**   **ISSN 0040-585X**
QA273   **CODEN: TPRBAU**
THEORY OF PROBABILITY AND ITS APPLICATIONS. English translation of: Teoriya Veroyatnostei i ee Primeneniya. 1956. q. $320 to non-members; members $99. Society for Industrial and Applied Mathematics, Attn: P. Clifford, 3600 University City Science Center, Philadelphia, PA 19104-2688. TEL 215-382-9800. FAX 215-386-7999. TELEX 446-715. Ed. Natasha Brunswick. adv.; circ. 1,978. (also avail. in microform from IAM; back issues avail.) **Indexed:** Appl.Mech.Rev., ASCA, Compumath, Comput.Rev., Curr.Cont., Math.R., Sci.Abstr.
—BLDSC shelfmark: 0427.000000.
Description: Contains papers on the theory and application of probability, statistics, and stochastic processes.
Refereed Serial

510   **US**   **ISSN 0094-9000**
QA273.A1   **CODEN: TPMSCO**
THEORY OF PROBABILITY AND MATHEMATICAL STATISTICS. English translation of: Teoriya Veroyatnostei i Matematicheskaya Statistika. 1970. 2/yr. $297 to non-members; institutional members $238. (Kievskii Universitet, UR) American Mathematical Society, Box 1571, Annex Sta., Providence, RI 02901-9930. TEL 401-455-4000. (Street addr.: 201 Charles St., Providence, RI 02904) Ed. Ben Silver. charts; stat.; circ. 250. **Indexed:** J.Cont.Quant.Meth., Math.R.
—BLDSC shelfmark: 0427.120000.

510   **UK**   **ISSN 0953-0738**
THETA. 1987. s-a. £5. Crewe & Alsager College of Higher Education, Crewe, Cheshire CW1 1DU, England. TEL 0270-500661. FAX 0270-583433. Ed.Bd. adv.; bk.rev.; circ. 1,500.
Description: Journal of general mathematics for all who teach, learn, practice and enjoy mathematics.

510 370   **JA**   **ISSN 0913-221X**
TOHOKU - HOKURIKU SUGAKU KYOIKU KISOTEKI KENKYU HOKOKU. (Text and summaries in Japanese) 1973. s-a. Tohoku - Hokuriku Sugaku Kyoiku Kisoteki Kenkyukai - Study Group on the Mathematics Education in Tohoku-Hokuriku District, c/o Iwate Daigaku Kyoikugakubu, Saeki Kenkyushitsu, 18-33, Ueda 3-chome, Morioka-shi, Iwate-ken 020, Japan.
Description: Reports on mathematics education in the district.

510   **JA**   **ISSN 0040-8735**
QA1   **CODEN: TOMJAM**
TOHOKU MATHEMATICAL JOURNAL/TOHOKU SUGAKU ZASSHI. (Text in English, French, German) 1911. q. $187 or exchange basis. Tohoku Daigaku, Suugaku Kyoushitsu - Tohoku University, Mathematical Institute, Aramaki aza Aoba, Aoba-ku, Sendai-shi, Miyagi-ken 980, Japan. FAX 022-263-6793. (Subscr. to: Maruzen Co., Ltd., P.O. Box 5050, Tokyo International, Tokyo 100-31, Japan) Ed. Tadao Oda. circ. 1,100. (also avail. in microform from BHP) **Indexed:** ASCA, Compumath, JCT, JTA, Math.R., Sci.Cit.Ind., Zent.Math.
—BLDSC shelfmark: 8862.300000.

TOKEI. see *STATISTICS*

510 310   **JA**
TOKEI SURI KENKYUJO KENKYU RIPOTO/JAPAN. INSTITUTE OF STATISTICAL MATHEMATICS. RESEARCH REPORTS, GENERAL SERIES. (Text in Japanese) 1955. irreg. Tokei Suri Kenkyujo - Institute of Statistical Mathematics, 4-6-7, Minami-Azabu, Minato-ku, Tokyo 106, Japan.

510   **JA**   **ISSN 0387-3870**
TOKYO JOURNAL OF MATHEMATICS. (Text and summaries in English) 1978. 2/yr. $159. (Sophia University, Department of Mathematics - Jochi Daigaku Sugaku Kyoshitsu) Kinokuniya Shoten - Kinokuniya Co., Ltd., Publishing Dept., 38-1 Sakuragaoka 5-chome, Setagaya-ku, Tokyo 156, Japan. circ. 170.

250   **US**   **ISSN 0040-9383**
QA611   **CODEN: TPLGAF**
TOPOLOGY; an international journal of mathematics. (Text in English, French, German or Italian) 1962. 4/yr. £330 (effective 1992). Pergamon Press, Inc., Journals Division, 660 White Plains Rd., Tarrytown, NY 10591-5153. TEL 914-524-9200. FAX 914-333-2444. (And: Headington Hill Hall, Oxford OX3 0BW, England. TEL 0865-794141) Ed.Bd. adv.; bk.rev.; charts; illus.; index; circ. 1,500. (also avail. in microform from MIM,UMI) **Indexed:** ASCA, Compumath, Curr.Cont., Math.R.
Description: Publishes mathematical papers with a special emphasis on subjects pertaining to topology and geometry.
Refereed Serial

514   **NE**   **ISSN 0166-8641**
QA611.A1   **CODEN: TIAPD9**
TOPOLOGY AND ITS APPLICATIONS; a journal devoted to general, geometric, set-theoretic and algebraic topology. (Text in English) 1971. 18/yr.(in 6 vols.; 3 nos./vol.) fl.1806 (effective 1992). North-Holland (Subsidiary of: Elsevier Science Publishers B.V.), P.O. Box 211, 1000 AE Amsterdam, Netherlands. TEL 020-5803911. FAX 020-5803598. TELEX 18582 ESPA NL. (Subscr. in U.S. and Canada to: Elsevier Science Publishing Co., Inc. Box 882, Madison Sq. Sta., New York, NY 10159. TEL 212-989-5800) Eds. Richard B. Sher, Jerry E. Vaughan. adv.; index; circ. 700. (also avail. in microform from RPI; back issues avail. from SWZ) **Indexed:** ASCA, Compumath, Math.R.
—BLDSC shelfmark: 8867.710000.
Formerly: General Topology and Its Applications (ISSN 0016-660X)
Refereed Serial

510   **US**   **ISSN 0146-4124**
QA611.A1
TOPOLOGY PROCEEDINGS. 1976. a. $70. Auburn University, Mathematics Department, Auburn, AL 36830. TEL 205-844-6566. FAX 205-887-3799. Ed.Bd. circ. 300. **Indexed:** Math.R.
—BLDSC shelfmark: 8867.720000.
Refereed Serial

510   **JA**   **ISSN 0916-6009**
QA1   **CODEN: MJTUEG**
TOYAMA UNIVERSITY. MATHEMATICS JOURNAL. (Text in English) 1978. a. Toyama University, Department of Mathematics, 3190, Gofuku, Toyama 930, Japan. **Indexed:** Sci.Abstr.
—BLDSC shelfmark: 5405.951000.
Formerly (until 1990): Toyama University. Mathematics Reports (ISSN 0386-832X)

TRAITEMENT DU SIGNAL. see *PHYSICS*

510 620 US
TRANSLATION SERIES IN MATHEMATICS AND ENGINEERING. 1984. irreg. price varies. Springer-Verlag, 175 Fifth Ave., New York, NY 10010. TEL 212-460-1500. (Also Berlin, Heidelberg, Tokyo, Vienna) (reprint service avail. from ISI)

510 US ISSN 0065-9282
TRANSLATIONS OF MATHEMATICAL MONOGRAPHS. (Chiefly from Russian sources) 1962. irreg. price varies. American Mathematical Society, Box 1571, Annex Sta., Providence, RI 02901-9930. TEL 401-455-4000. (Street addr.: 201 Charles St., Providence, RI 02904) Ed. Ben Silver. circ. 400. **Indexed:** Math.R.
—BLDSC shelfmark: 9024.895000.
  Description: Contains works of advanced mathematical research and exposition.

510 FR
TRAVAUX EN COURS. 1983. irreg. Editions Hermann, 293 rue Lecourbe, 75015 Paris, France. TEL 45-57-45-40. FAX 40-60-12-93. TELEX 200595.

510 AT
TRIGON; school maths journal. 4/yr. Aus.$16. Mathematical Association of South Australia, 163a Greenhill Rd., Parkside, S.A. 5066, Australia. TEL 8-370-2174. FAX 8-370-2674.
  Description: Contains problems and puzzles for secondary school students.

510 JA ISSN 0387-4982
QA1
TSUKUBA JOURNAL OF MATHEMATICS. (Text and summaries in English) 1930. s-a. 30000 Yen. Tsukuba Daigaku, Sugakukei - University of Tsukuba, Institute of Mathematics, 1-1, Tennoda 1-chome, Tsukuba-shi, Ibaraki-ken 305, Japan. FAX 298-53-6501.
—BLDSC shelfmark: 9067.785000.

510 US ISSN 0197-3622
QA11.A1
U M A P JOURNAL. (Undergraduate Mathematics Applications Project); the journal of undergraduate mathematics and its applications. 1980. q. $51 to individuals; institutions $148. Consortium for Mathematics and Its Applications, 57 Bedford St., Ste. 210, Lexington, MA 02173-4428. TEL 617-862-7878. FAX 617-643-1295. TELEX 9102504757. Ed. P.J. Campbell. adv.; bk.rev.; circ. 1,109. **Indexed:** Educ.Ind.
—BLDSC shelfmark: 9082.819000.

510 530 US ISSN 0041-5553
QA297 CODEN: CMMPA9
U S S R COMPUTATIONAL MATHEMATICS AND MATHEMATICAL PHYSICS. English translation of: Zhurnal Vychislitel'noi Matematiki i Matematicheskoi Fiziki (RU ISSN 0044-4669) 1962. 12/yr. £935 (effective 1992). Pergamon Press, Inc., Journals Division, 660 White Plains Rd., Tarrytown, NY 10591-5153. TEL 914-524-9200. FAX 914-333-2444. (And: Headington Hill Hall, Oxford OX3 0BW, England. TEL 0865-794141) Ed. R. Glass. adv.; bk.rev.; charts; illus.; index; circ. 1,000. (also avail. in microform from MIM,UMI; back issues avail.) **Indexed:** Appl.Mech.Rev., Compumath, Curr.Cont., Math.R., Sci.Abstr.
  Description: Publishes mathematical papers from all fields of science as well as papers of a purely mathematical nature.
  Refereed Serial

510 US ISSN 0041-5995
QA1 CODEN: UKMJB6
UKRAINIAN MATHEMATICAL JOURNAL. English translation of: Ukrainskii Matematicheskii Zhurnal (KR ISSN 0041-6053) 1967. m. $1125 (foreign $1315)(effective 1992). (Ukrainian Academy of Sciences, Mathematical Institute, KR) Plenum Publishing Corp., Consultants Bureau, 233 Spring St., New York, NY 10013-1578. TEL 212-620-8468. FAX 212-463-0742. TELEX 23-421139. Ed. Yu.A. Mitropol'skii. (also avail. in microform from JSC; back issues avail.) **Indexed:** Comput.& Info.Sys., Math.R., Zent.Math.
—BLDSC shelfmark: 0428.950000.
  Refereed Serial

510 KR ISSN 0041-6053
QA1 CODEN: UMZHAA
UKRAINSKII MATEMATICHESKII ZHURNAL/UKRAINS'KYI MATEMATYCHNYI ZHURNAL; nauchnyi zhurnal. English translation: Ukrainian Mathematical Journal (US ISSN 0041-5995) (Text in Russian) 1949. m. 16.80 Rub.($19.80) (Akademiya Nauk Ukrainskoi S.S.R., Institut Matematiki) Izdatel'stvo Naukova Dumka, c/o Yu.A. Khramov, Dir, Ul. Repina, 3, Kiev 252 601, Ukraine. TEL 224-45-64. Ed. Yu.A. Mitropol'skii. index; circ. 1,352. **Indexed:** Chem.Abstr., Math.R.

510 US ISSN 0172-6056
UNDERGRADUATE TEXTS IN MATHEMATICS. 1974. irreg. price varies. Springer-Verlag, 175 Fifth Ave., New York, NY 10010. TEL 212-460-1500. (Also Berlin, Heidelberg, Tokyo and Vienna) (reprint service avail. from ISI)

510 AG ISSN 0041-6932
QA1 CODEN: RMAFAG
UNION MATEMATICA ARGENTINA. REVISTA. (Text in English and Spanish) 1936. 2/yr. $40. Union Matematica Argentina, Pema-Intec, Guemes 3450, 3000 Santa Fe, Argentina. TEL 42-20024. FAX 42-50944. TELEX 48186 INTEC AR. Ed.Bd. bk.rev.; bibl.; index; circ. 2,000. **Indexed:** Math.R., Zent.Math.
—BLDSC shelfmark: 7834.900000.
  Formerly: Union Matematica Argentina y Associacion Fisica Argentina Revista.
  Description: Original papers in pure and applied mathematics.

519.5 JA ISSN 0034-4842
HA1 CODEN: RARJAT
UNION OF JAPANESE SCIENTISTS AND ENGINEERS. REPORTS OF STATISTICAL APPLICATION RESEARCH. (Text in English) 1951. q. 8700 Yen. Union of Japanese Scientists and Engineers, 5-10-11, Sendagaya, Shibuya-ku, Tokyo 151, Japan. Ed. T. Okuno. adv.; index; circ. 1,000. **Indexed:** Chem.Abstr., JTA, Math.R.

510 IT ISSN 0041-7084
QA1 CODEN: BLUMAM
UNIONE MATEMATICA ITALIANA. BOLLETTINO. (In 4 sections; supplements avail.) (Text in French, Italian and Spanish) 1922. bi-m. L.180000 (foreign L.230000)(effective 1992). Zanichelli Editore S.p.A., Via Irnerio 34, 40126 Bologna, Italy. TEL 051-293111. FAX 051-249782. Ed. Prof. Giovanni Ricci. bk.rev.; index. **Indexed:** Appl.Mech.Rev., Compumath, Math.R.

510 CU ISSN 0257-4306
T57.6.A1
UNIVERSIDAD DE LA HABANA. DIRECCION DE INFORMACION CIENTIFICA Y TECNICA. INVESTIGACION OPERACIONAL. 1980. 3/yr. C.$21($21) Universidad de la Habana, Direccion de Informacion Cientifica y Tecnica, Havana 4, Cuba. (Dist. by: Ediciones Cubanas, Vice Direccion de Exportacion, Obispo 461, Apdo. 605, Havana, Cuba) (back issues avail.)

570 CU
UNIVERSIDAD DE LA HABANA. ESCUELA DE MATEMATICA. INVESTIGACION OPERACIONAL. 1968. q. exchange basis. Universidad de la Habana, Departamento de Matematica Aplicada, Centro de Informacion Cientifico Tecnica, Calle L y San Lazaro, Havana, Cuba. TEL 537-322757. Eds. Sina Allende, Juan Cue. adv.; bk.rev.; circ. 2,000. **Indexed:** Math.R., Ref.Zh.

510 UY
UNIVERSIDAD DE LA REPUBLICA. FACULTAD DE HUMANIDADES Y CIENCIAS. REVISTA. SERIE CIENCIAS EXACTAS. 1980. irreg. exchange basis. Universidad de la Republica, Facultad de Humanidades y Ciencias, Seccion Revista, Tristan Narvaja 1674, Montevideo, Uruguay. Dir. Beatriz Martinez Osorio.
  Supersedes in part: Universidad de la Republica. Facultad de Humanidades y Ciencias. Revista.

510 MX ISSN 0185-0644
UNIVERSIDAD NACIONAL AUTONOMA DE MEXICO. INSTITUTO DE MATEMATICAS. ANALES. 1950. a. $15 per no. Universidad Nacional Autonoma de Mexico, Instituto de Matematicas, Area de la Investigacion Cientifica, Circuito Exterior, Ciudad Universitaria, Mexico 04510, DF, Mexico. TEL 548-20-07. FAX 548-94-99. bk.rev.; cum.index 1961-1986 vols.1-26; circ. 500. **Indexed:** Math.R.

510 MX ISSN 0187-4780
UNIVERSIDAD NACIONAL AUTONOMA DE MEXICO. INSTITUTO DE MATEMATICAS. MONOGRAFIAS. 1975. irreg., no.23, 1991. $15 per vol. Universidad Nacional Autonoma de Mexico, Instituto de Matematicas, Area de la Investigacion Cientifica, Circuito Exterior, Ciudad Universitaria, Mexico 04510, DF, Mexico. TEL 548-20-07. FAX 548-94-99. **Indexed:** Math.R.
—BLDSC shelfmark: 5911.650000.

510 BL
UNIVERSIDADE FEDERAL DO RIO DE JANEIRO. INSTITUTO DE MATEMATICA. ESTUDOS E COMUNICACOES. (Text in English, French, Portuguese, Spanish; summaries in English) 1983. irreg., no.42, 1991. $3 to institutions; free to individuals. Universidade Federal do Rio de Janeiro, Instituto de Matematica, C.P. 68530, 21944 Rio de Janeiro, RJ, Brazil. circ. controlled.
  Description: Articles in mathematics, statistics and computer science.

510 BL
UNIVERSIDADE FEDERAL DO RIO DE JANEIRO. INSTITUTO DE MATEMATICA. TEXTOS DE METODOS MATEMATICOS. (Text in language of author) 1972. irreg., no.23, 1991. $5 institutions; free to individuals. Universidade Federal do Rio de Janeiro, Instituto de Matematica, C.P. 68.530, 21944 Rio de Janeiro, RJ, Brazil.
  Formerly: Universidade Federal do Rio de Janeiro. Instituto de Matematica. Notas de Matematica Fisica.
  Description: Expository monographs dedicated to graduate students in mathematics.

510 530 IT ISSN 0041-8986
CODEN: ASMMAK
UNIVERSITA DEGLI STUDI DI MODENA. SEMINARIO MATEMATICO E FISICO. ATTI. Variant title: Universita di Modena. Seminario Matematico e Fisico. Atti. (Text and summaries in English and Italian) 1947. s-a. exchange basis only. Universita degli Studi di Modena, Seminario Matematico e Fisico, Via Campi 213-b, 41100 Modena, Italy. FAX 059-370513. Dir. Calogero Vinti. bk.rev.; bibl.; charts; circ. 450. **Indexed:** Appl.Mech.Rev., Math.R., Sci.Abstr.
—BLDSC shelfmark: 1786.370000.
  Description: Presents original papers in mathematics and physics.

510 IT ISSN 0035-6298
UNIVERSITA DEGLI STUDI DI PARMA. RIVISTA DI MATEMATICA. (Text in English, French, German, Italian and Spanish) 1950. a. L.90000($70) Universita degli Studi di Parma, Rivista di Matematica, Via Universita 12, 43100 Parma, Italy. FAX 0521-2053500. Dir. Bianca Manfredi. bk.rev.; bibl.; charts; index; circ. 500. **Indexed:** Appl.Mech.Rev., Math.R.
—BLDSC shelfmark: 7989.400000.

510 IT
QA1 CODEN: RIMTDP
UNIVERSITA DEGLI STUDI DI TRIESTE. DIPARTIMENTO DI SCIENZE MATEMATICHE. RENDICONTI. (Text in English, French, German, Italian; summaries in English and Italian) 1969. s-a. exchange basis. Universita degli Studi di Trieste, Dipartimento di Scienze Matematiche, Piazzale Europa 1, Trieste, Italy. FAX 040-5603256. Ed. Arno Predonzan. index; circ. 300. **Indexed:** Math.R., Ref.Zh., Zent.Math.
  Formerly: Universita degli Studi di Trieste. Istituto di Matematica. Rendi Conti. (ISSN 0049-4704)

510 IT ISSN 0041-8994
QA1
UNIVERSITA DI PADOVA. SEMINARIO MATEMATICO. RENDICONTI. (Text in English, French and Italian) 1929. 3/yr. L.80000. Levrotto e Bella, Cso Vitt. Emanuele 26-F, 10123 Turin, Italy. (Subscr. to: Rosenberg & Sellier, Via Andrea Doria 14, 10123 Turin, Italy) Dir. Franco Fava. **Indexed:** Appl.Mech.Rev.
—BLDSC shelfmark: 7361.050000.

510 IT ISSN 0373-1243
UNIVERSITA E POLITECNICO DI TORINO. SEMINARIO MATEMATICO. RENDICONTI. q. L.143000 (Europe L.180000; elsewhere L.270000). Rosenberg & Sellier, Via Andrea Doria, 14, 10123 Turin, Italy. TEL 011-561-39-07. FAX 011-532188.
—BLDSC shelfmark: 7361.100000.

MATHEMATICS

510   GW   ISSN 0025-5858
QA1   CODEN: AMHAAJ
UNIVERSITAET HAMBURG. MATHEMATISCHES SEMINAR. ABHANDLUNGEN. 1922. a. DM.136. Vandenhoeck und Ruprecht, Theaterstr. 13, Postfach 3753, 3400 Goettingen, Germany. TEL 0551-6959-22. FAX 0551-695917. Eds. R. Ansorge, O. Riemenschneider. adv.; tr.lit.; circ. 410. **Indexed:** Compumath, Math.R.
—BLDSC shelfmark: 0544.068000.

510   AU
UNIVERSITAET INNSBRUCK. MATHEMATISCHE STUDIEN. (Subseries of: Universitaet Innsbruck. Veroeffentlichungen) 1974. irreg. price varies. Oesterreichische Kommissionsbuchhandlung, Maximilian Str. 17, A-6020 Innsbruck, Austria. Ed. Roman Liedl.

510   RM
UNIVERSITATAE DIN TIMISOARA. FACULTATAE DE STIINTE ALE NATURII. SEMINARUL DE ECUATII FUNCTIONALE. (Text in English, French) 1972. irreg. 20 lei. Universitatae din Timisoara, Facultatae de Stiinte ale Naturii, Bd. Vasile Parvan, no.4, Timisoara, Rumania. Ed. Mircea Reghis.

510   RM
UNIVERSITATAE DIN TIMISOARA. FACULTATAE DE STIINTE ALE NATURII. SEMINARUL DE OPERATORI LINIARI SI ANALIZA ARMONICA. (Text in English) 1978. irreg. 20 lei. Universitatae din Timisoara, Facultatae de Stiinte ale Naturii, Bd. Vasile Parvan no.4, Timisoara, Rumania. Ed. Dumitru Gaspar.

510   RM   ISSN 0041-9109
QA1   CODEN: AUZMAV
UNIVERSITATEA "AL. I. CUZA" DIN IASI. ANALELE STIINTIFICE. SECTIUNEA 1A: MATEMATICA. (Text in English, French, German, Italian, Russian, Spanish) 1900; N.S. 1955. 4/yr. 40 lei. Universitatea "Al. I. Cuza" din Iasi, Calea M. Eminescu 11, Jassy, Rumania. (Subscr. to: ILEXIM, Str. 13 Decembrie Nr. 3, P.O. Box 136-137, Bucharest, Rumania) Eds. Adolf Haimovici, D. Iesan. bk.rev.; abstr.; charts; illus.; circ. 500. (also avail. in microfilm; back issues avail.) **Indexed:** Bull.Signal., Chem.Abstr., Math.R., Ref.Zh.
—BLDSC shelfmark: 0869.600000.
Description: Papers in all fields of pure and applied mathematics, and informatics.

510 530   RM
UNIVERSITATEA DIN CRAIOVA. ANALE. SERIA: MATEMATICA, FIZICA-CHIMIE. (Text in English, French and German) a. Universitatea din Craiova, Str. A.I. Cuza Nr. 13, Craiova, Rumania. **Indexed:** Math.R.

510   RM
UNIVERSITATEA DIN TIMISOARA. FACULTATEA DE MATEMATICA. ANALELE: STIINTE MATEMATICE. (Text and summaries in English, French, Rumanian and Russian) 1963. 3/yr. 200 lei($8) per no. Universitatea din Timisoara, Facultatea de Matematica, Bd. Vasile Pirvan Nr. 4, Timisoara, Rumania. Ed. Dr. Papuc I. Dan. bk.rev.; index; circ. 400. **Indexed:** Math.R., Ref.Zh., Zent.Math.
Formerly: Universitatea din Timisoara. Facultatea de Stiinte ale Naturii. Analele: Stiinte Matematice.

514 516   RM
UNIVERSITATEA DIN TIMISOARA. FACULTATEA DE MATEMATICA. LUCRARILE SEMINARULUI DE GEOMETRIE SI TOPOLOGIE. (Text in English, French, German and Rumanian) 1972. irreg. 50 lei($2) Universitatea din Timisoara, Facultatea de Matematica, Bd. Vasile Pirvan Nr.4, Timisoara, Rumania. Ed. Dan I. Papuc. circ. 250.
Formerly: Universitatea din Timisoara. Facultatea de Stiinte ale Naturii. Lucrarile Seminarului de Geometrie si Topologie.

510   RM
UNIVERSITATEA DIN TIMISOARA. FACULTATEA DE MATEMATICA. SEMINARUL DE MECANICA. (Text in English, French) 1987. irreg. 50 lei($2) Universitatea din Timisoara, Facultatea de Matematica, Bd. Vasile Parvan Nr. 4, Timisoara, Rumania. Ed. V. Obadeanu. circ. 250.
Formerly: Universitatea din Timisoara. Facultatea de Stiinte ale Naturii. Seminarul de Mecanica.

510   RM
UNIVERSITATEA DIN TIMISOARA. FACULTATEA DE MATEMATICA. SEMINARUL DE TEORIA STRUCTURILOR. (Text in English, French, German, and Rumanian) 1971. irreg. 50 lei($2) Universitatea din Timisoara, Facultatea de Matematica, Bd. Vasile Pirvan Nr. 4, Timisoara, Rumania. Ed. Constantin Popa. circ. 250.
Formerly: Universitatea din Timisoara. Facultatea de Stiinte ale Naturii. Seminarul de Teoria Structurilor.

510   RM
UNIVERSITATEA DIN TIMISOARA. FACULTATEA DE STIINTE ALE NATURII. SEMINARUL DE TEORIA PROBABILITATILOR SI APLICATII. (Text in English, French, German, Rumanian) 1973. irreg. 50 lei($2) Universitatea din Timisoara, Facultatea de Matematica, Bd. Vasile Pirvan Nr.4, Timisoara, Rumania. Ed. Gh. Constantin. circ. 250.
Former titles: Universitatea din Timisoara. Facultatea de Stiinte ale Naturii. Seminarul de Teoria Probabilitatilor si Aplicatii; (until 1980, no.51): Universitatea din Timisoara. Facultatea de Stiinte ale Naturii. Seminarul de Teoria Functiilor si Matematici Aplicate. A: Spatii Metrice Probabiliste.

510   RM
UNIVERSITATEA DIN TIMISOARA. SECTIA MATEMATICA INFORMATICA. SEMINARUL DE INFORMATICA SI ANALIZA NUMERICA. (Text in English, French, German, Rumanian) 1975. irreg. 20 lei. Universitatea din Timisoara, Sectia Matematica Informatica, Bd. Vasile Pirvan Nr.4, Timisoara, Rumania. Ed. S. Maruster. circ. 250.
Formerly (until 1981): Universitatea din Timisoara. Facultatea de Stiinte ale Naturii. Seminarul de Teoria Functiilor si Matematici Aplicate. B: Analiza Numerica.

510 530 570   RM
UNIVERSITATEA TRANSILVANIA DIN BRASOV. BULETINUL. SERIA C. MATEMATICA, FIZICA, CHIMIE. (Text in English, French and German) 1956. a. price varies. Universitatea din Brasov, Bd. Eroiltor, Nr. 29, Brasov R-2200, Rumania. bibl.; charts; stat. **Indexed:** Chem.Abstr., Math.R.
Former titles: Universitatea din Brasov. Buletinul. Seria C. Matematica, Fizica, Chimie; Universitatea din Brasov. Buletinul. Seria C. Stiinte Ale Naturri si Pedagogie; Universitatea din Brasov. Buletinul. Seria C. Matematica, Fizica, Chimie.

510   BE
UNIVERSITE CATHOLIQUE DE LOUVAIN. INSTITUT DE MATHEMATIQUE. RAPPORT DE MATHEMATIQUE. (Text and summaries in French, English) 1978. irreg., latest no.144. price varies. Chemin du Cyclotron, 2, 1348 Louvain-la-Neuve, Belgium. bibl.; charts.
Formerly: Universite Catholique de Louvain. Institut de Mathematique Pure et Appliquee. Rapport.

510   FR   ISSN 0076-1656
UNIVERSITE CLAUDE BERNARD. DEPARTEMENT DE MATHEMATIQUES. PUBLICATIONS. 1964. q. 80 F. Universite de Lyon I, Departement de Mathematiques, 43, Boulevard du 11 November 1918, 69622 Villeurbanne, France. **Indexed:** Compumath, Math.R.

510   AE   ISSN 0002-5321
UNIVERSITE D'ALGER. PUBLICATIONS SCIENTIFIQUES. SERIE A: MATHEMATIQUES.* 1954. s-a. 15 fr.per no. Universite d'Alger, 2 rue Didouche-Mourad, Algiers, Algeria. **Indexed:** Math.R.

510   FR   ISSN 0069-472X
UNIVERSITE DE CLERMONT-FERRAND II. ANNALES SCIENTIFIQUES. SERIE MATHEMATIQUE. 1962. irreg., latest no.95, 1991. price varies. Universite de Clermont-Ferrand II, Departement de Mathematiques, 63177 Aubiere, France. circ. 250. (back issues avail.)

510   FR
UNIVERSITE DE CLERMONT-FERRAND II. ANNALES SCIENTIFIQUES. SERIE PROBABILITES ET APPLICATIONS. irreg. price varies. Universite de Clermont-Ferrand II, Departement de Mathematiques, 63177 Aubiere, France.

UNIVERSITE DE MADAGASCAR. ETABLISSEMENT D'ENSEIGNEMENT SUPERIEUR DES SCIENCES. ANNALES: SERIE SCIENCES DE LA NATURE ET MATHEMATIQUES. see *SCIENCES: COMPREHENSIVE WORKS*

510   FR
UNIVERSITE PAUL SABATIER. FACULTE DES SCIENCES. ANNALES; mathematiques. (Text in English and French) 1887. q. 700 F. (foreign 900 F.). Universite Paul Sabatier, 118 route de Narbonne, 31062 Toulouse cedex, France. Ed. Paul Sabatier. adv. (also avail. in microfilm from BHP) **Indexed:** Math.R., Sci.Abstr., Zent.Math.
Formerly: Universite de Toulouse. Faculte des Sciences. Annales (ISSN 0240-2955)

510   FR   ISSN 0373-0956
Q46   CODEN: AIFUA7
UNIVERSITE SCIENTIFIQUE ET MEDICALE DE GRENOBLE. INSTITUT FOURIER. ANNALES. (Text and summaries in English, French) 1949. a. 900 F. (foreign 1150 F.). Association des Annales de l'Institut Fourier, Universite Scientifique , Technologique et Medicale de Grenoble, B.P. 74, 38402 Saint-Martin d'Heres cedex, France. Ed.Bd. adv.; circ. 1,000. **Indexed:** Compumath, INIS Atomind., Math.R., Zent.Math.
—BLDSC shelfmark: 0920.000000.

510 530   US   ISSN 0172-5939
UNIVERSITEXTS. 1973. irreg. price varies. Springer-Verlag, 175 Fifth Ave., New York, NY 10010. TEL 212-460-1500. (reprint service avail. from ISI)

510   US
UNIVERSITY OF ARKANSAS. LECTURE NOTES IN THE MATHEMATICAL SCIENCES. irreg., vol.13, 1992. John Wiley & Sons, Inc., 605 Third Ave., New York, NY 10158-0012. TEL 212-850-6000. FAX 212-850-6088. TELEX 12-7063. bibl.; index. **Indexed:** Math.R.
Refereed Serial

510   NZ   ISSN 0110-4152
UNIVERSITY OF AUCKLAND. DEPARTMENT OF MATHEMATICS AND STATISTICS. REPORT SERIES. 1971. irreg., no.262, 1991. free to individuals or on exchange. University of Auckland, Department of Mathematics & Statistics, Private Bag, Auckland, New Zealand. circ. 175.

510   NO   ISSN 0084-778X
UNIVERSITY OF BERGEN. DEPARTMENT OF APPLIED MATHEMATICS. REPORT. (Text in English) 1964. irreg. exchange basis. University of Bergen, Department of Applied Mathematics, Allegate 55, 5007 Bergen, Norway. TEL 47-5-21-28-38. circ. 100. (processed)
—BLDSC shelfmark: 7620.854000.

510   CN
UNIVERSITY OF CALGARY. DEPARTMENT OF MATHEMATICS AND STATISTICS. RESEARCH PAPERS. 1966. irreg. free. University of Calgary, Department of Mathematics and Statistics, Calgary, Alta. T2N 1N4, Canada. TEL 403-220-7456. FAX 403-282-5150. Ed. P. Zvengrowski. circ. 40.
Formerly: University of Calgary. Department of Mathematics and Computing Science. Research Papers (ISSN 0575-206X)

311   DK
UNIVERSITY OF COPENHAGEN. INSTITUTE OF MATHEMATICAL STATISTICS. ANNUAL REPORT. (Text in English) a. Koebenhavns Universitet, Institut for Matematisk Statistik, 5, Universitetsparken, DK-2100 Copenhagen OE, Denmark.

510   US   ISSN 0076-5341
UNIVERSITY OF NOTRE DAME. DEPARTMENT OF MATHEMATICS. MATHEMATICAL LECTURES. 1941. irreg., vol.11, 1989. price varies. University of Notre Dame Press, Notre Dame, IN 46556. TEL 219-239-6346.

510 375   AT   ISSN 1036-0697
▼**UNIVERSITY OF TECHNOLOGY, SYDNEY. FACULTY OF MATHEMATICAL & COMPUTING SCIENCES HANDBOOK.** 1990. a. Aus.$5 (foreign $10). University of Technology, Sydney, P.O. Box 123, City Campus, Broadway, N.S.W. 2007, Australia. TEL 02-330-1990. FAX 02-330-1551.

MATHEMATICS

510   JA   ISSN 0286-9640
Q4   CODEN: BCSRDZ
UNIVERSITY OF THE RYUKYUS. COLLEGE OF SCIENCE. BULLETIN/RYUKYU DAIGAKU RIGAKUBU KIYO. (Text in English, Japanese; summaries in English) 1957. irreg. University of the Ryukyus, College of Science - Ryukyu Daigaku Rigakubu, 1 Senbaru, Nishihara-cho, Nakagami-gun, Okinawa-ken 903-01, Japan.
—BLDSC shelfmark: 2448.730000.

510   JA   ISSN 0040-8980
QA1   CODEN: JFTMAT
UNIVERSITY OF TOKYO. FACULTY OF SCIENCE. JOURNAL. SECTION 1A: MATHEMATICS/TOKYO DAIGAKU RIGAKUBU KIYO, DAI-1-RUI A, SUGAKU. (Text in English, French, German) 1925. 3/yr. price varies. University of Tokyo, Faculty of Science - Tokyo Daigaku Rigakubu, Hongo, Tokyo, Japan. TEL 03-3812-2111. (Order from: Maruzen Co., Ltd., 3-10, Nihonbashi 2-chome, Chuo-ku, Tokyo 103, Japan; or their Import and Export Department, P.O. Box 5050, Tokyo International, Tokyo 100-31, Japan) Ed. Yukio Matsumoto. illus.; circ. 850. **Indexed:** Chem.Abstr., JCT, JTA, Math.R., Sci.Abstr.
—BLDSC shelfmark: 4750.010000.
Supersedes in part: University of Tokyo. Faculty of Science. Journal. Section 1: Mathematics, Astronomy, Physics, Chemistry.

510   YU   ISSN 0352-0900
Q1.A1
UNIVERZITET U NOVOM SADU. PRIRODNO-MATEMATICKI FAKULTET. ZBORNIK RADOVA. SERIJA ZA MATEMATIKU. (Text in English, French, German and Russian) 1971. 2/yr. $60. Institut za Matematiku, Prirodno-Matematicki Fakultet - Institute of Mathematics, Dr. Ilije Djuricica 4, 21000 Novi Sad, Yugoslavia. TEL 38-21-58-136. FAX 38-21-350-458. (Subscr. to: "FORUM", Izvozno Odelenje, 21000 Novi Sad, ul. Vojvode Misica 1, Yugoslavia) Ed. Olga Hadzic. circ. 650. **Indexed:** Math.R., Nutr.Abstr., Ref.Zh.

510   PL   ISSN 0072-0402
UNIWERSYTET GDANSKI. WYDZIAL MATEMATYKI, FIZYKI I CHEMII. ZESZYTY NAUKOWE. MATEMATYKA. (Text in Polish; summaries in English) 1972. irreg. price varies. Uniwersytet Gdanski, Wydzial Matematyki, Fizyki i Chemii, c/o Biblioteka Glowna, Ul. Armii Krajowej 110, 81-824 Sopot, Poland. TEL 51-0061. TELEX 051 2247 BMOR PL. (Dist. by: Acta Polona-Ruch, Krakowskie Przedmiescie 7, 00-680 Warsaw, Poland) illus.; circ. 250.
Description: Covers operational calculus, topology, real functions, geometry, differential equations, mathematical foundation of computer science, didactics of mathematics, set theory, and probability calculus.

510   PL
UNIWERSYTET JAGIELLONSKI. ZESZYTY NAUKOWE. ACTA MATEMATICA. (Text in Polish; summaries in French, English, Russian) no.5, 1959. irreg. price varies. Panstwowe Wydawnictwo Naukowe, Miodowa 10, 00-251 Warsaw, Poland. (Dist. by: Ars Polona, Krakowskie Przedmiescie 7, 00-068 Warsaw, Poland) **Indexed:** Math.R.
Formerly (until 1984): Uniwersytet Jagiellonski. Zeszyty Naukowe. Prace Matematyczne (ISSN 0083-4386); Which superseded in part: Seria Nauk Matematyczno-Przyrodniczych. Matematyka, Fizyka, Chemia.

510   PL
UNIWERSYTET SLASKI W KATOWICACH. PRACE NAUKOWE. ANNALES MATHEMATICAE SILESIANAE. (Text in English) 1969. irreg. price varies. Wydawnictwo Uniwersytetu Slaskiego, Ul. Bankowa 14, 40-007 Katowice, Poland. TEL 48-32-599-915. FAX 48-32-599-605. TELEX 0315584 USKPL. (Dist. by: CHZ Ars Polona, P.O. Box 1001, 00-950 Warsaw, Poland)
Formerly: Uniwersytet Slaski w Katowicach. Prace Matematyczne (ISSN 0208-5410)
Description: Covers all aspects of pure and applied mathematics in general, in particular: algebra and theory of numbers, differential equations and dynamical systems, functional and real analysis, functional equations, geometry, topology.

510   RU   ISSN 0042-1316
QA1   CODEN: UMANA5
USPEKHI MATEMATICHESKIKH NAUK. English translation: Russian Mathematical Surveys (UK ISSN 0036-0279) 1936. bi-m. 47.40 Rub. (Akademiya Nauk S.S.S.R.) Izdatel'stvo Nauka, Fizmatlit, Leninskii prospekt, 15, 117071 Moscow, Russia. (Dist. by: Mezhdunarodnaya Kniga, ul. Dimitrova D.39, 113095 Moscow, Russia) (Co-sponsor: Moskovskoe Matematicheskoe Obshchestvo) Ed. P.S. Aleksandrov. bk.rev.; bibl.; charts; circ. 3,120. (also avail. in microfiche from BHP; reprint service avail. from KTO) **Indexed:** Chem.Abstr., Math.R., Sci.Abstr.
—BLDSC shelfmark: 0385.900000.

510   CN   ISSN 0382-0718
VECTOR. 1968. irreg. Can.$45 to non-members; members Can.$30; students Can.$15. (B.C. Association of Mathematics Teachers) B.C. Teachers' Federation, 2235 Burrard St., Vancouver, B.C. V6J 3H9, Canada. TEL 604-731-8121. illus.; circ. 650. **Indexed:** Can.Educ.Ind.
Formerly: British Columbia Association of Mathematics Teachers. Newsletter (ISSN 0382-0726)

510   US   ISSN 0146-924X
QA1
VESTNIK LENINGRAD UNIVERSITY: MATHEMATICS. (English translation of mathematics section of Vestnik Leningradskogo Universiteta) 1984. q. $500. Allerton Press, Inc., 150 Fifth Ave., New York, NY 10011. TEL 212-924-3950. circ. 150. **Indexed:** Chem.Abstr., Math.R.
—BLDSC shelfmark: 0429.570000.

510 372   AT   ISSN 0157-759X
VINCULUM. 1963. 4/yr. membership (foreign Aus.$61). Mathematical Association of Victoria, 61 Blight St., Brunswick, Vic. 3056, Australia. TEL 03-380-2399. FAX 03-840-8243. Ed. Roy James. adv.; bk.rev.; circ. 1,200. **Indexed:** Aus.Educ.Ind.
—BLDSC shelfmark: 9236.852600.

510   JA   ISSN 0913-0195
WASEDA DAIGAKU KYOIKUGAKUBU GAKUJUTSU KENKYU. SUGAKU HEN/WASEDA UNIVERSITY. SCHOOL OF EDUCATION. SCIENTIFIC RESEARCHES: MATHEMATICS. (Text in English and Japanese) 1952. a. Waseda Daigaku, Kyoikugakubu - Waseda University, School of Education, 6-1, Nishi-Waseda 1-chome, Shinjuku-ku, Tokyo 160, Japan. **Indexed:** Jap.Per.Ind.

510   US   ISSN 0043-082X
WASHINGTON STATE UNIVERSITY. MATHEMATICS NOTES. 1958. irreg. free. (Washington State University, Department of Pure and Applied Mathematics) Washington State University, Pullman, WA 99164-3113. TEL 509-335-8518. Ed. Jack Robertson. bk.rev.; circ. 1,400.

530 510   GW   ISSN 0084-098X
WISSENSCHAFTLICHE TASCHENBUECHER. REIHE MATHEMATIK - PHYSIK. 1965. irreg. price varies. Akademie-Verlag Berlin, Leipziger Str. 3-4, 1086 Berlin, Germany. TELEX 114420-AVERL-DD. **Indexed:** Biol.Abstr., Math.R.
Description: Single-topic introductory studies in mathematics and physics.

510   US   ISSN 0512-2740
QA30
WORLD DIRECTORY OF MATHEMATICIANS. 1958. quadrennial, 9th ed., 1990. $40. (International Mathematical Union) American Mathematical Society, Box 1571, Annex Sta., Providence, RI 02901-9933. TEL 401-455-4000. (Street addr.: 201 Charles St., Providence, RI 02904) Ed. G.D. Mostow. circ. 2,000.
Description: Contains names and addresses of about 40,000 mathematicians from 83 countries.

510   PL   ISSN 0239-7978
WYZSZA SZKOLA PEDAGOGICZNA IM. KOMISJI EDUKACJI NARODOWEJ W KRAKOWIE. ROCZNIK NAUKOWO-DYDAKTYCZNY. PRACE MATEMATYCZNE. 1954. irreg., no.12, 1987. free. Wydawnictwo Naukowe W S P, Ul. Karmelicka 41, 31-128 Krakow, Poland. TEL 33-78-20. (Co-sponsor: Ministerstwo Edukacji Narodowej)

510   PL
WYZSZA SZKOLA PEDAGOGICZNA IM. KOMISJI EDUKACJI NARODOWEJ W KRAKOWIE. ROCZNIK NAUKOWO-DYDAKTYCZNY. PRACE Z DYDAKTYKI MATEMATYKI. 1974. irreg., no.3, 1986. price varies. Wydawnictwo Naukowe W S P, Ul. Karmelicka 41, 31-128 Krakow, Poland. TEL 33-78-20. (Co-sponsor: Ministerstwo Edukacji Narodowej)

730   PL   ISSN 0860-6994
WYZSZA SZKOLA PEDAGOGICZNA IM. KOMISJI EDUKACJI NARODOWEJ W KRAKOWIE. ROCZNIK NAUKOWO-DYDAKTYCZNY. PRACE Z RACHUNKU PRAWDOPODOBIENSTWA I JEGO DYDAKTYKI. 1987. irreg. price varies. Wydawnictwo Naukowe W S P, Ul. Karmelicka 41, 31-129 Krakow, Poland. TEL 33-78-20. (Co-sponsor: Ministerstwo Edukacji Narodowej)

510   PL   ISSN 0078-5431
WYZSZA SZKOLA PEDAGOGICZNA, OPOLE. ZESZYTY NAUKOWE. SERIA A. MATEMATYKA. (Text in Polish; summaries in English) 1961. irreg., vol.27, 1990. available on exchange. Wyzsza Szkola Pedagogiczna, Opole, Oleska 48, 45-951 Opole, Poland. TEL 48 77 383-87. (Dist. by: Ars Polona-Ruch, Krakowskie Przedmiescie 7, Warsaw, Poland) **Indexed:** Math.R.
—BLDSC shelfmark: 9512.478980.

510 371.3   CC
XIAOXUE SHUXUE JIAOSHI/ARITHMETIC TEACHER. (Text in Chinese) bi-m. $17.60. Shanghai Jiaoyu Chubanshe - Shanghai Education Publishers, 123 Yongfu Road, Shanghai 200031, People's Republic of China. TEL 4377165. (Dist. in US by: China Books & Periodicals, Inc., 2929 24th St., San Francisco, CA 94110. TEL 415-282-2994) Ed. Chen He.
Description: For elementary school arithmetic teachers.

XITONG KEXUE YU SHUXUE. see COMPUTERS — Computer Systems

510   CC
YINGYONG SHUXUE/APPLIED MATHEMATICS. (Text in Chinese) q. Huazhong Ligong Daxue, Shuxue Xi - Central-China University of Science and Engineering, Department of Mathematics, Yujiashan, Wuchang-qu, Wuhan, Hubei 430074, People's Republic of China. TEL 701152. Ed. Chen Qingyi.

510   CC   ISSN 0254-3079
QA1   CODEN: YYSPDS
YINGYONG SHUXUE XUEBAO. English edition: Acta Mathematicae Applicatae Sinica (ISSN 0168-9673) (Text in Chinese; summaries in English) 1976. q. $10 per no. (Chinese Mathematics Society) Science Press, Marketing and Sales Department, 16 Donghuangchenggen Beijie, Beijing 100707, People's Republic of China. TEL 4010642. FAX 4012180. TELEX 210247-SPBJ-CN. adv.; circ. 11,000.
—BLDSC shelfmark: 0632.200000.
Description: Covers mathematics research in China and abroad, including control theory and stochastic processes.
Refereed Serial

510 531   CC   ISSN 1000-0887
YINGYONG SHUXUE YU LIXUE/APPLIED MATHEMATICS AND MECHANICS. (Text in Chinese) m. Chongqing Jiaotong Xueyuan, 107, Dahuang Lu, Daping, Chongqing, Sichuan 630042, People's Republic of China. TEL 813708. Ed. Qian Weichang.
Refereed Serial

510   JA   ISSN 0044-0523
QA1
YOKOHAMA MATHEMATICAL JOURNAL. (Text and summaries in English) 1953. s-a. exchange basis. Yokohama City University, 22-2 Seto, Kanazawa-ku, Yokohama 236, Japan. TEL 045-787-2311. FAX 045-787-2202. Ed. Hiroshi Asano. **Indexed:** Math.R., Zent.Math.
—BLDSC shelfmark: 9419.000000.

YUGOSLAV JOURNAL OF OPERATIONS RESEARCH; an international journal dealing with theoretical and computational aspects of operations research, systems science, and management science. see COMPUTERS

Z O R - METHODS AND MODELS OF OPERATIONS RESEARCH. see COMPUTERS

519 PL ISSN 0044-1899
QA1 CODEN: ZAMTAK
ZASTOSOWANIA MATEMATYKI/APPLICATIONES MATHEMATICAE. (Text in English, French, German or Russian; summaries in Polish) 1960. 3/yr. price varies. (Polska Akademia Nauk, Instytut Matematyczny) Panstwowe Wydawnictwo Naukowe, Ul. Miodowa 10, 00-251 Warsaw, Poland. (Dist. by: Ars Polona, Krakowskie Przedmiescie 7, 00-068 Warsaw, Poland) Eds. J. Lukaszewicz, S. Paszkowski. bibl.; charts; illus.; index; circ. 540. **Indexed:** Appl.Mech.Rev., Math.R., Ref.Zh.

ZAVODSKAYA LABORATORIYA; zhurnal po analiticheskoi khimii, fizicheskim, matematicheskim i mekhanicheskim metodam issledovaniya materialov. see CHEMISTRY — Analytical Chemistry

510 GW ISSN 0232-2064
QA300
ZEITSCHRIFT FUER ANALYSIS UND IHRE ANWENDUNGEN. (Text in English, German and Russian) 1982. bi-m. DM.310.20. VEB Deutscher Verlag der Wissenschaften, Postfach 1216, 1080 Berlin, Germany. **Indexed:** Math.R.
—BLDSC shelfmark: 9446.980000.

519 620 GW ISSN 0044-2267
TA3 CODEN: ZAMMAX
ZEITSCHRIFT FUER ANGEWANDTE MATHEMATIK UND MECHANIK; applied mathematics and mechanics. Abbreviated title: Z A M M. (Text in English and German; summaries in English, German and Russian) 1921. m. DM.500.40. (Akademie der Wissenschaften der DDR, Institut fuer Mechanik) Akademie-Verlag Berlin, Leipziger Str. 3-4, 1086 Berlin, Germany. TELEX 114420-AVERL-DD. Ed. G. Schmidt. adv.; charts; illus.; index. (reprint service avail. from SWZ) **Indexed:** Appl.Mech.Rev., Chem.Abstr., Compumath, Curr.Cont., Eng.Ind., Int.Aerosp.Abstr., Math.R., Met.Abstr., Sci.Abstr., Sh.& Vib.Dig.
—BLDSC shelfmark: 9449.000000.

519 530 SZ ISSN 0044-2275
QA1 CODEN: ZAMPDB
ZEITSCHRIFT FUER ANGEWANDTE MATHEMATIK UND PHYSIK/JOURNAL OF APPLIED MATHEMATICS AND PHYSICS/JOURNAL DE MATHEMATIQUES ET DE PHYSIQUE APPLIQUEES. Short title: Z A M P. (Text and summaries in English, French, German and Italian) 1950. bi-m. 668 Fr.($455) Birkhaeuser Verlag, P.O. Box 133, CH-4010 Basel, Switzerland. TEL 061-737740. FAX 061-737750. TELEX 963475 BIRKH CH. (Dist. in N. America by: Springer-Verlag New York, Inc., Journal Fulfillment Services, Box 2485, Secaucus, NJ 07096-2491. TEL 201-348-4033) Ed.Bd. adv.; bk.rev.; bibl.; charts; illus.; index; circ. 1,000. **Indexed:** Appl.Mech.Rev., Chem.Abstr., Compumath, Curr.Cont., Deep Sea Res.& Oceanogr.Abstr., Eng.Ind., Int.Aerosp.Abstr., Math.R., Met.Abstr., Phys.Ber., Sci.Abstr.
—BLDSC shelfmark: 9449.050000.

511.3 519 GW ISSN 0044-3050
QA1 CODEN: ZMLGAQ
ZEITSCHRIFT FUER MATHEMATISCHE LOGIK UND GRUNDLAGEN DER MATHEMATIK. ZEITSCHRIFT. (Text in English, French, German and Russian) 1955. bi-m. DM.220.20. (Humboldt-Universitaet zu Berlin, Institut fuer Mathematische Logik) VEB Deutscher Verlag der Wissenschaften, Johannes-Dieckmann-Str. 10, 1080 Berlin, Germany. Eds. Prof. Asser, Prof. Schroeter. adv.; bk.rev.; charts; illus.; index. **Indexed:** Compumath, Math.R, Sci.Abstr.
—BLDSC shelfmark: 9469.700000.

510 371 GW ISSN 0044-4103
ZENTRALBLATT FUER DIDAKTIK DER MATHEMATIK. 1969. bi-m. DM.260. Fachinformationszentrum Karlsruhe, Gesellschaft fuer wissenschaftlich-technische Information mbH, 7514 Eggenstein-Leopoldshafen 2, Germany. TEL 07247-808-0. FAX 07247-808-666. TELEX 724710-FIZKA. (Co-sponsor: Zentrum fuer Didaktik der Mathematik) Ed. Gerhard Koenig. bk.rev.; abstr.; bibl.; index. cum.index; circ. 660.
●Also available online. Vendor(s): STN International.
—BLDSC shelfmark: 9504.800000.

ZHONGXUESHENG SHU-LI-HUA (GAOZHONG BAN). see EDUCATION — Teaching Methods And Curriculum

510 028.5 CC
ZHONGXUESHENG SHUXUE/MATHEMATICS FOR MIDDLE SCHOOL STUDENTS. (Text in Chinese) bi-m. Zhongguo Shuxuehui, Puji Gongzuo Weiyuanhui - Chinese Mathematics Association, Popularization Commission, 50 Sanlihe Lu, Fuxingmenwai, Beijing 100045, People's Republic of China. TEL 863901. Ed. Mei Xiangming.

510 530 RU ISSN 0044-4669
QA297 CODEN: ZVMFAN
ZHURNAL VYCHISLITEL'NOI MATEMATIKI I MATEMATICHESKOI FIZIKI. English translation: U S S R Computational Mathematics and Mathematical Physics (US ISSN 0041-5553) 1961. m. 55.20 Rub. (Akademiya Nauk S.S.S.R.) Izdatel'stvo Nauka, Fizmatlit, Leninskii prospekt, 15, 117071 Moscow, Russia. TEL 234-05-84. Ed. A.A. Dorodnitzyn. adv.; bk.rev.; charts; illus.; index; circ. 2,100. **Indexed:** Appl.Mech.Rev., Chem.Abstr., Int.Aerosp.Abstr., Math.R., Sci.Abstr.
—BLDSC shelfmark: 0060.700000.

ZUGAKU KENKYU/JOURNAL OF GRAPHIC SCIENCE OF JAPAN. see ART

MATHEMATICS — Abstracting, Bibliographies, Statistics

510 GW ISSN 0933-9663
ABSTRACTS AND REVIEWS FROM ZENTRALBLATT FUER MATHEMATIK. (Text in English, French, German) 1981. m. DM.168($135) Fachinformationszentrum Karlsruhe, D-7514 Eggenstein-Leopoldshafen, Germany. TEL 030-2611585. (U.S. subscr. to: Scientific Information Service Inc., 7 Woodland Avenue, Larchmont, NY 10538) bk.rev.; circ. 300. (looseleaf format)
●Also available online.
—BLDSC shelfmark: 0553.842010.

500 016 BU ISSN 0204-9449
Q4
ABSTRACTS OF BULGARIAN SCIENTIFIC LITERATURE. MATHEMATICAL AND PHYSICAL SCIENCES. Russian edition (ISSN 0204-9430) (Editions in English and Russian) 1963. q. 20 lv.($20) Bulgarska Akademiia na Naukite, 7 Noemvri St., 1, 1040 Sofia, Bulgaria. (Dist. by: RP, Klokotnica St., no.2A, 1202 Sofia, Bulgaria) Ed.Bd. abstr.; index; circ. 300. **Indexed:** Chem.Abstr.
Formerly: Abstracts of Bulgarian Scientific Literature. Mathematics, Physics, Astronomy, Geophysics, Geodesy (ISSN 0001-351X)

APPLIED STOCHASTIC MODELS AND DATA ANALYSIS. see MATHEMATICS

BIOSTATISTICA. see BIOLOGY — Abstracting, Bibliographies, Statistics

510 310 US ISSN 0163-9439
C B M S. N S F. REGIONAL CONFERENCE SERIES IN APPLIED MATHEMATICS. 1971. irreg., no.60, 1990. Society for Industrial and Applied Mathematics, Conference Board of the Mathematical Sciences, Attn: P. Manning, 3600 University City Science Center, Philadelphia, PA 19104-2688. TEL 215-382-9800. FAX 215-386-7999. (Co-sponsor: National Science Foundation) **Indexed:** Appl.Mech.Rev.
Formerly: Conference Board of the Mathematical Sciences. Regional Conference Series in Applied Mathematics (ISSN 0097-4455)
Refereed Serial

510 001.6 US ISSN 0730-6199
Z6653
COMPUMATH CITATION INDEX. Short title: C M C I. (Includes: Source Index, Research Front Speciality Index, Citation Index, Permuterm Subject Index, and Corporate Index) 3/yr. $1645. Institute for Scientific Information, 3501 Market St., Philadelphia, PA 19104. TEL 215-386-0100. FAX 215-386-2991. (And: 132 High St., Uxbridge, Middx. UB8 1DP, England) cum.index: 1976-80. (also avail. in magnetic tape)
●Also available online. Vendor(s): BRS.
Description: A multidisciplinary index to the journal literature of computer science, mathematics, applications and chemistry and engineering, plus other related disciplines such as mathematical physics and econometrics.

016 311 US ISSN 0364-1228
QA276.A1
CURRENT INDEX TO STATISTICS; applications-methods-theory. 1976. a. $60. American Statistical Association, 1429 Duke St., Alexandria, VA 22314-3402. TEL 703-684-1221. FAX 703-684-2037. (Co-sponsor: Institute of Mathematical Statistics) index; circ. 2,000.
●Also available online. Vendor(s): BRS (MATH), DIALOG, European Space Agency.

510 016 US ISSN 0361-4794
Z6653 CODEN: CUMPBW
CURRENT MATHEMATICAL PUBLICATIONS. 1969. 17/yr. $339 to non-members; individual members $203; institutional members $271; reviewer $136. American Mathematical Society, Box 1571, Annex Sta., Providence, RI 02901-9930. TEL 401-455-4000. (Street addr.: 201 Charles St., Providence, RI 02904) Ed. Robert G. Bartle. abstr.; circ. 1,600. **Indexed:** Math.R.
●Also available online. Vendor(s): BRS, DIALOG, European Space Agency.
Also available on CD-ROM. Producer(s): SilverPlatter (MathDisc).
Formed by the 1975 merger of: American Mathematical Society. New Publications (ISSN 0002-9912); Contents of Contemporary Mathematical Journals (ISSN 0010-759X)

510 GW ISSN 0343-639X
FACHBUCHVERZEICHNIS MATHEMATIK - PHYSIK (YEAR). 1900. a. DM.5.50. Fr. Weidemanns Buchhandlung (H.Witt), Georgstr. 11, Postfach 6406, 3000 Hannover 1, Germany. TEL 0511-16382-0. FAX 0511-1638266. Ed. Kaethe Deichmann. circ. 20,000.

510 016 US ISSN 0019-3917
Z6653
INDEX OF MATHEMATICAL PAPERS. Variant title: Mathematical Reviews Annual Index. (Special issue of Mathematical Reviews (ISSN 0025-5629)) 1971. a. price varies. American Mathematical Society, Box 1571, Annex Sta., Providence, RI 02901-9930. TEL 401-455-4000. (Street addr.: 201 Charles St., Providence, RI 02904) circ. 3,500.

510 US
IOWA STATE UNIVERSITY. STATISTICAL LABORATORY. ANNUAL REPORT. 1945. a. free. Iowa State University of Science and Technology, Statistical Laboratory, 102 Snedecor Hall, Ames, IA 50011. TEL 515-294-3440. FAX 515-294-4040. Ed. Jauvanta M. Walker. bk.rev.; abstr.; bibl.; illus.; circ. 2,050. (back issues avail.) **Indexed:** Biol.Abstr.

JOURNAL OF APPLIED ECONOMETRICS. see MATHEMATICS

JOURNAL OF MATHEMATICAL SOCIOLOGY. see SOCIOLOGY

510 519 US ISSN 0022-3239
QA402.5 CODEN: JOTABN
JOURNAL OF OPTIMIZATION THEORY AND APPLICATIONS. m. (3 vols./yr.). $775 (foreign $905)(effective 1992). Plenum Publishing Corp., 233 Spring St., New York, NY 10013-1578. TEL 212-620-8000. FAX 212-463-0742. TELEX 23-421139. Ed. Angelo Miele. adv.; bibl.; charts; illus. (also avail. in microfilm from JSC; back issues avail.) **Indexed:** Appl.Mech.Rev., Compumath, Comput.& Contr.Abstr., Comput.Cont., Curr.Cont., Cyb.Abstr., Ind.Sci.Rev., INIS Atomind., Int.Aerosp.Abstr., Math.R., Sci.Abstr., Sci.Cit.Ind., Zent.Math.
—BLDSC shelfmark: 5026.370000.
Refereed Serial

512 016 RU
KOL'TSA; bibliografiya. irreg. 0.45 Rub. single issue. Akademiya Nauk S.S.S.R., Sibirskoe Otdelenie, Institut Matematiki, Novosibirsk, Akademgorodok, Russia.

510 016 US ISSN 0025-5€29
QA1 CODEN: MAREAR
MATHEMATICAL RFVIEWS; a reviewing journal covering the world literature of mathematical research. (Text in English, French, German and Italian) 1940. m. $4331 (individual members $520; institutional members $3565; reviewer $346. American Mathematical Society, Box 1571, Annex Sta., Providence, RI 02901-9930. TEL 401-455-4000. (Street addr.: 201 Charles St., Providence, RI 02904) Ed. Robert G. Bartle. bk.rev.; index; circ. 2,400. (also avail. in microfiche from AMS) **Indexed:** Appl.Mech.Rev., Math.R.
●Also available online. Vendor(s): BRS (MATH), DIALOG, European Space Agency (File no.80/MATHSCI).
Also available on CD-ROM. Producer(s): SilverPlatter (MathDisc).
—BLDSC shelfmark: 5403.000000.
Refereed Serial

NIHON KODO KEIRYO GAKKAI TAIKAI HAPPYO RONBUN SHOROKUSHU. see *PSYCHOLOGY — Abstracting, Bibliographies, Statistics*

510 JA
NIHON SUGAKKAI KOEN ABUSUTORAKUTO. DAISU BUNKAKAI. (Text in Japanese) 2/yr. Nihon Sugakkai - Mathematical Society of Japan, 25-9-203, Hongo 4-chome, Bunkyo-ku, Tokyo 113, Japan. abstr.
Description: Contains abstracts of speeches from the society's conference on algebra.

510 JA
NIHON SUGAKKAI KOEN ABUSUTORAKUTO. JITSUKANSURON BUNKAKAI. (Text in Japanese) 2/yr. Nihon Sugakkai - Mathematical Society of Japan, 25-9-203, Hongo 4-chome, Bunkyo-ku, Tokyo 113, Japan. abstr.
Description: Contains abstracts of speeches from the society's conference on real variable functions.

510 JA
NIHON SUGAKKAI KOEN ABUSUTORAKUTO. KANSU HOTEISHIKIRON BUNKAKAI. (Text in Japanese) 2/yr. Nihon Sugakkai - Mathematical Society of Japan, 25-9-203, Hongo 4-chome, Bunkyo-ku, Tokyo 113, Japan. abstr.
Description: Contains abstracts of speeches from the society's conference on functional equations.

510 JA
NIHON SUGAKKAI KOEN ABUSUTORAKUTO. KANSU KAISEKIGAKU BUNKAKAI. (Text in Japanese) 2/yr. Nihon Sugakkai - Mathematical Society of Japan, 25-9-203, Hongo 4-chome, Bunkyo-ku, Tokyo 113, Japan. abstr.
Description: Contains abstracts of speeches from the society's conference on functional analysis.

510 JA
NIHON SUGAKKAI KOEN ABUSUTORAKUTO. KANSURON. (Text in Japanese) 2/yr. Nihon Sugakkai - Mathematical Society of Japan, 25-9-203, Hongo 4-chome, Bunkyo-ku, Tokyo 113, Japan. abstr.
Description: Contains abstracts of speeches from the society's conference on the theory of functions.

510 JA
NIHON SUGAKKAI KOEN ABUSUTORAKUTO. KIKAGAKU BUNKAKAI. (Text in Japanese) 2/yr. Nihon Sugakkai - Mathematical Society of Japan, 25-9-203, Hongo 4-chome, Bunkyo-ku, Tokyo 113, Japan. abstr.
Description: Contains abstracts of speeches from the society's conference on geometry.

510 JA
NIHON SUGAKKAI KOEN ABUSUTORAKUTO. OYO SUGAKKAI BUNKAKAI. (Text in Japanese) 2/yr. Nihon Sugakkai - Mathematical Society of Japan, 25-9-203, Hongo 4-chome, Bunkyo-ku, Tokyo 113, Japan. abstr.
Description: Contains abstracts of speeches from the society's conference on applied mathematics.

510 JA
NIHON SUGAKKAI KOEN ABUSUTORAKUTO. SUGAKU KISORON BUNKAKAI. (Text in Japanese) 2/yr. Nihon Sugakkai - Mathematical Society of Japan, 25-9-203, Hongo 4-chome, Bunkyo-ku, Tokyo 113, Japan. abstr.
Description: Contains abstracts of speeches from the society's conference on basic mathematical theory.

510 310 JA
NIHON SUGAKKAI KOEN ABUSUTORAKUTO. TOKEI SUGAKU BUNKAKAI. (Text in Japanese) 2/yr. Nihon Sugakkai - Mathematical Society of Japan, 25-9-203, Hongo 4-chome, Bunkyo-ku, Tokyo 113, Japan. abstr.
Description: Contains abstracts of speeches from the society's conference on mathematical statistics.

510 JA
NIHON SUGAKKAI KOEN ABUSUTORAKUTO. TOPOROJI BUNKAKAI. (Text in Japanese) 2/yr. Nihon Sugakkai - Mathematical Society of Japan, 25-9-203, Hongo 4-chome, Bunkyo-ku, Tokyo 113, Japan. abstr.
Description: Contains abstracts of speeches from the society's conference on topology.

510 GW
OPTIMIZATION; a journal of mathematical programming and operations research. (Text in English, French, German, Russian) 1970. 6/yr. DM.232.20. (Technische Hochschule Ilmenau, Sektion Mathematik, Rechentechnik und Oekenomische Kybernetik) Akademie-Verlag Berlin, Leipziger Str. 3-4, 1086 Berlin, Germany. TELEX 114420-AVERL-DD. Ed. K.H. Elster. illus.; index. **Indexed:** Int.Abstr.Oper.Res., J.Cont.Quant.Meth., Math.R., Sci.Abstr.
Formerly: Series Optimization (ISSN 0233-1934); Supersedes in part (from 1977): Mathematische Operationsforschung und Statistik (ISSN 0047-6277)

510 311.2 PL ISSN 0208-4147
QA273.A1
PROBABILITY AND MATHEMATICAL STATISTICS. (Text in various languages) 1980. s-a. $42. (Uniwersytet Wroclawski - University of Wroclaw) Wydawnictwo Uniwersytetu Wroclawskiego, Pl. Uniwersytecki 9-13, 50-137 Wroclaw, Poland. TEL 48 71 21-15-00. (Dist. by Ars Polona-Ruch, Krakowskie Przedmiescie 7, Warsaw, Poland) (Co-sponsors: Polska Akademia Nauk, Technical University of Wroclaw) Ed. Kazimierz Urbanik. circ. 1,000. **Indexed:** Math.R.
—BLDSC shelfmark: 6617.220000.

510 016 RU ISSN 0034-2467
QA1
REFERATIVNYI ZHURNAL. MATEMATIKA. 1953. m. 226 Rub. (300 Rub. including index). Vsesoyuznyi Institut Nauchno-Tekhnicheskoi Informatsii (VINITI), Baltiiskaya ul., 14, Moscow A-219, Russia. (Subscr. to: Mezhdunarodnaya Kniga, Dimitrova ul. 39, 113095 Moscow, Russia) Ed. R.V. Gamkrelidze. circ. 2,296. (also avail. in microfiche from BHP)
—BLDSC shelfmark: 0145.000000.

S S O R YOKOSHU/PROCEEDINGS OF S S O R. (Summer Symposium of Operation Research) see *COMPUTERS — Abstracting, Bibliographies, Statistics*

SEIKEN N S T SHINPOJUMU KOEN KOGAISHU. see *COMPUTERS — Abstracting, Bibliographies, Statistics*

513.028 JA
SHUZAN KENKYU RONBUN SHIRYO MOKUROKUSHU. (Text in Japanese) 1963. 4/yr. Zenkoku Shuzan Kyoiku Renmei, 28, Higashi-Hieijo-cho, Nishi-9-jo, Minami-ku, Kyoto-shi, Kyoto-fu 601, Japan. bibl.; abstr.
Description: Bibliography of papers about calculation on abacus.

STATISTICAL THEORY AND METHOD ABSTRACTS. see *STATISTICS*

STATISTICS; a journal of theoretical and applied statistics. see *COMPUTERS — Abstracting, Bibliographies, Statistics*

510 JA ISSN 0912-6112
TOKEI SURI/PROCEEDINGS OF THE INSTITUTE OF STATISTICAL MATHEMATICS. (Text in Japanese; summaries in English) 1953. s-a. free. Institute of Statistical Mathematics, 4-6-7 Minami-Azabu, Minato-ku, Tokyo 106, Japan. TEL 03-3446-1501. Ed. T. Suzuki. stat.; circ. 700. (back issues avail.)
—BLDSC shelfmark: 6718.000000.

530 510 US
U S S R REPORT: PHYSICS AND MATHEMATICS. irreg., approx. 10/yr. $7 per no. (foreign $14 per no.). U.S. Joint Publications Research Service, Box 12507, Arlington, VA 22209. TEL 703-487-4630. (Orders to: NTIS, Springfield, VA 22161)
Formerly: U S S R and Eastern Europe Scientific Abstracts: Physics and Mathematics; Which was formed by the merger of: U S S R Scientific Abstracts: Physics and Mathematics; East European Scientific Abstracts: Physics and Mathematics.

510 310 BL
UNIVERSIDADE FEDERAL DO RIO DE JANEIRO. INSTITUTO DE MATEMATICA. MEMORIAS DE MATEMATICA. (Text in English, French, Portuguese, Spanish; summaries in English) 1971. irreg., no.148, 1987. $4 to institutions; free to individuals. Universidade Federal do Rio de Janeiro, Instituto de Matematica, C.P. 68530, 21944 Rio de Janeiro, RJ, Brazil. Ed.Bd. circ. controlled.
Description: Original articles accepted for publication in journals or proceedings of scientific meetings.

310 FR ISSN 0041-9184
UNIVERSITE DE PARIS VI (PIERRE ET MARIE CURIE). INSTITUT DE STATISTIQUE. PUBLICATIONS. 1952. 3/yr. 220 F. Universite de Paris VI (Pierre et Marie Curie), Institut de Statistique, 4, Place Jussieu, 75230 Paris Cedex 05, France. Ed. M.J. Geffroy. charts; stat.; circ. 650. **Indexed:** Math.R.

510 016 GW ISSN 0044-4235
QA1
ZENTRALBLATT FUER MATHEMATIK UND IHRE GRENZGEBIETE/MATHEMATICS ABSTRACTS. (Text in English, French, German) 1931. 30/yr. DM.6360($2689) (Deutsche Akademie der Wissenschaften zu Berlin) Springer-Verlag, Heidelberger Platz 3, D-1000 Berlin 33, Germany. TEL 030-8207-1. (Also Heidelberg, Tokyo, Vienna, and New York) (Co-sponsor: Heidelberger Akademie der Wissenschaften) Ed. B. Wegner. cum.index: vols.1-25; 26-41; 60-61; 77-100; 221-249; 251-299; 301-349; 351-399. (also avail. in microform from UMI; reprint service avail. from ISI) **Indexed:** Appl.Mech.Rev., Math.R.
●Also available online. Vendor(s): STN International (MATH).

510 CC ISSN 1001-1919
ZHONGGUO SHUXUE WENZHAI/CHINESE MATHEMATICS ABSTRACTS. (Text in Chinese) q. Zhongguo Kexueyuan, Wenxian Qingbao Zhongxin - Chinese Academy of Sciences, Documentation Information Center, 27 Wangfujing Dajie, Beijing 100710, People's Republic of China. TEL 556180. Ed. Shen Xinyao.

MATHEMATICS — Computer Applications

A C M TRANSACTIONS ON MATHEMATICAL SOFTWARE. see *COMPUTERS — Software*

510 FR
A M S E NEWS. (Text mainly in English) q. membership. (International Association for the Advancement of Modelling and Simulation Techniques in Enterprises) A M S E Press, 16 av. de Grange Blanche, 69160 Tassin-la-Demi-Lune, France. TEL 78-34-36-04. FAX 78-34-54-17. TELEX 389 000. Ed. G. Mesnard.

ACTA POLYTECHNICA SCANDINAVICA. MATHEMATICS AND COMPUTER SCIENCE SERIES. see *COMPUTERS*

510 332.1 US
ADVANCES IN MATHEMATICAL PROGRAMMING AND FINANCIAL PLANNING. a research annual. 1987. a. $63.50 to institutions. J A I Press Inc., 55 Old Post Rd., No. 2, P.O. Box 1678, Greenwich, CT 06836-1678. Ed. Kenneth D. Lawrence.

MATHEMATICS — COMPUTER APPLICATIONS

510 FR
ADVANCES IN MODELLING & ANALYSIS. (Text mainly in English) irreg. 95 F.($19) per no. (International Association for the Advancement of Modelling and Simulation Techniques in Enterprises) A M S E Press, 16 av. de Grange Blanche, 69160 Tassin-la-Demi-Lune, France. TEL 78-34-36-04. FAX 78-34-54-17. TELEX 389 000. Ed. G. Mesnard. (back issues avail.)
Description: Centers on the methodological aspects of signals, data and systems problems.
Refereed Serial

510 US
▼**ADVANCES IN THE THEORY OF COMPUTATION AND COMPUTATIONAL MATHEMATICS.** 1992. irreg. price varies. Ablex Publishing Corporation, 355 Chestnut St., Norwood, NJ 07648. TEL 201-767-8450. FAX 201-767-6717. TELEX 135-393. Ed. Lee Keener.

ANNALS OF MATHEMATICS AND ARTIFICIAL INTELLIGENCE. see *COMPUTERS — Artificial Intelligence*

510 SZ ISSN 0254-5330
ANNALS OF OPERATIONS RESEARCH. (Text and summaries in English) 1984. 6 vols./yr. 305 Fr. per vol. J.C. Baltzer AG, Scientific Publishing Company, Wettsteinplatz 10, CH-4058 Basel, Switzerland. TEL 061-6918925. FAX 061-6924262. Ed. Peter L. Hammer. **Indexed:** Cyb.Abstr., Oper.Res.Manage.Sci., Qual.Contr.Appl.Stat.
—BLDSC shelfmark: 1043.330000.
Description: Presentation of trends in specific areas of operations research.

510 GW ISSN 0938-1279
CODEN: AAECEW
▼**APPLICABLE ALGEBRA IN ENGINEERING, COMMUNICATION AND COMPUTING.** 1990. q. DM.190. Springer-Verlag, Heidelberg Platz 3, D-1000 Berlin 33, Germany. (Also Heidelberg, Tokyo, Vienna, and New York) Ed. J. Calmet.
Description: Publishes mathematically rigorous, original research papers reporting on algebraic methods and techniques relevant to all domains concerned with computers, intelligent systems and communications.

651.8 510 US ISSN 0307-904X
QA1 CODEN: AMMODL
APPLIED MATHEMATICAL MODELLING; simulation & computation for engineering & environmental systems. 1976. m. $495 (foreign $560). Butterworth - Heinemann Ltd. (Subsidiary of: Reed International PLC), 80 Montvale Ave., Stoneham, MA 02180. TEL 617-438-8464. FAX 617-438-1479. TELEX 880052. Ed. Mark Cross. adv.; bk.rev.; abstr.; bibl.; charts; illus.; stat.; index. (also avail. in microform from UMI; back issues avail.) **Indexed:** Abstr.J.Earthq.Eng., Appl.Mech.Rev., BMT, Br.Tech.Ind., CAD CAM Abstr., Compumath, Curr.Cont., Energy Ind., Energy Info.Abstr., Eng.Ind., Environ.Abstr., Excerp.Med., Fluidex, Geo.Abstr., GeoRef, Intl.Civil Eng.Abstr., J.of Ferroc., Math.R., Risk Abstr., Sci.Abstr., Sel.Water Res.Abstr., Soft.Abstr.Eng., W.R.C.Inf.
—BLDSC shelfmark: 1573.715000.
Description: Research on all aspects of mathematical modelling pertinent to practical systems analysis.
Refereed Serial

510 NE ISSN 0168-9274
QA297
APPLIED NUMERICAL MATHEMATICS. (Text in English) 1985. 12/yr.(in 2 vols.; 6 nos./vol.) fl.922 (combined with Mathematics and Computer in Simulation fl.1203)(effective 1992). (International Association for Mathematics and Computers in Simulation) North-Holland (Subsidiary of: Elsevier Science Publishers B.V.), P.O. Box 211, 1000 AE Amsterdam, Netherlands. TEL 020-5803911. FAX 020-5803598. TELEX 18582 ESPA NL. (Subscr. in U.S. and Canada to: Elsevier Science Publishing Co., Inc., Box 882, Madison Sq. Sta., New York, NY 10159. TEL 212-989-5800) Eds. R. Vichnevetsky, J.E. Flaherty. (back issues avail.) **Indexed:** Appl.Mech.Rev., Compumath, Comput.Abstr.
—BLDSC shelfmark: 1576.234000.
Description: Devoted to contemporary problems in numerical computing.
Refereed Serial

610 NE
C W I. MONOGRAPHS. (Text in English) 1984. irreg., no.7, 1988. Stichting Mathematisch Centrum, Centrum voor Wiskunde en Informatica, P.O. Box 4079, 1009 AB Amsterdam, Netherlands. TEL 020-5924005. FAX 020-5924199. TELEX 12571 MACTR NL. (Subscr. to: Elsevier Science Publishers B.V., Books Division, P.O. Box 211, 1000 AE Amsterdam, Netherlands. TEL 020-5803911; Subscr. in U.S. and Canada to: Elsevier Science Publishing Co., Inc., Box 882, Madison Sq. Sta., New York, NY 10159. TEL 212-989-5800) (Co-publisher: North-Holland) Ed.Bd.
Description: Covers mathematics and computer science.
Refereed Serial

610 NE
C W I. PUBLICATIONS. (Text in Dutch, English) 1981. irreg. price varies. Stichting Mathematisch Centrum, Centrum voor Wiskunde en Informatica, P.O. Box 4079, 1009 AB Amsterdam, Netherlands. TEL 020-5924005. FAX 020-5924199. TELEX 12571 MACTR NL. Ed.Bd.
Description: Disseminates research and theories on mathematics and computer science.

610 NE
C W I. SYLLABI. (Text in English) 1969. irreg., no.27, 1990. price varies. Stichting Mathematisch Centrum, Centrum voor Wiskunde en Informatica, P.O. Box 4079, 1009 AB Amsterdam, Netherlands. TEL 020-5924005. FAX 020-5924199. TELEX 12571 MACTR NL. Ed.Bd.
Formerly (until 1984): Mathematical Centre Syllabi.
Description: Details seminar reports, course manuals, and lecture notes revisions on mathematics and computer science.

CHAOS, SOLITONS AND FRACTALS; applications in science and engineering. see *MATHEMATICS*

510 US ISSN 0963-5483
▼**COMBINATORICS, PROBABILITY & COMPUTING.** 1992. q. $148. Cambridge University Press, 40 W. 20th St., New York, NY 10011-4211. TEL 212-924-3900. FAX 212-691-3239. (UK addr.: Cambridge University Press, Edinburgh Bldg., Shaftesbury Rd., Cambridge CB2 2RU, England. TEL 0223-312393) Ed. Bela Bollobas.
Description: Encompasses combinatorics in a broad sense, including classical and algebraic graph theory, extremal set theory, matriod theory, and other theories.

510 620 UK ISSN 0332-1649
TK1.A1 CODEN: CODUDU
COMPEL; the international journal for computation and mathematics in electrical and electronic engineering. 1982. q. £110($190) James & James, 5 Castle Rd., London NW1 8PR, England. TEL 071-284-3833. FAX 071-284-3737. (Dist. by: Taylor & Francis Ltd., Rankine Rd., Basingstoke, Hants. RG24 OPR, England. TEL 0256-840366; Alt N. America addr.: Taylor & Francis, 1900 Frost Rd., Ste. 101, Bristol, PA 19007-1598. TEL 215-785-5800) Ed. J. Penman. adv.; bk.rev. **Indexed:** Compumath, INSPEC, Sci.Abstr.
—BLDSC shelfmark: 3363.924000.

COMPLEXITY; an international journal of complex and adaptive systems. see *ENGINEERING — Computer Applications*

510 SZ ISSN 1016-3328
▼**COMPUTATIONAL COMPLEXITY.** (Text in English) 1991. 4/yr. 298 Fr.($198) Birkhaeuser Verlag, P.O. Box 133, CH-4010 Basel, Switzerland. TEL 061-737740. FAX 061-737950. TELEX 963475 BIRKH CH. (Dist. in N. America by: Springer-Verlag New York, Inc., Journal Fulfillment Services, Box 2485, Secaucus, NJ 07096-2491, USA. TEL 201-348-4033) Ed. J. von zur Gathen. **Indexed:** Comput.Rev., Curr.Cont., Math.R.
—BLDSC shelfmark: 3390.580000.
Description: Interface between mathematics and theoretical computer science.

510 US ISSN 1046-283X
QA76.95 CODEN: CMMOEA
▼**COMPUTATIONAL MATHEMATICS AND MODELING.** 1991. q. $375 (foreign $440)(effective 1992). Plenum Publishing Corp., Consultants Bureau, 233 Spring St., New York, NY 10013. TEL 212-620-8000. FAX 212-463-0742. TELEX 23-421139. Eds. W.A. Light, A.N. Tikhonov. (also avail. in microfilm from JSC; back issues avail.)
—BLDSC shelfmark: 0411.054000.
Description: Contains current USSR mathematical articles in translation covering discrete mathematics, numerical analysis, and computational number theory.
Refereed Serial

COMPUTER SCIENCE AND SCIENTIFIC COMPUTING. see *COMPUTERS*

651.8 510 US ISSN 0898-1221
QA76 CODEN: CMAPDK
COMPUTERS & MATHEMATICS WITH APPLICATIONS. 1975. 24/yr. £805 (effective 1992). Pergamon Press, Inc., Journals Division, 660 White Plains Rd., Tarrytown, NY 10591-5153. TEL 914-524-9200. FAX 914-333-2444. (And: Headington Hill Hall, Oxford OX3 0BW, England. TEL 0865-794141) Ed. Ervin Y. Rodin. adv.; bk.rev.; charts; illus.; index; circ. 1,125. (also avail. in microform from MIM,UMI) **Indexed:** Appl.Mech.Rev., Biostat., Compumath, Comput.Abstr., Comput.Cont., Comput.Rev., Curr.Cont., Fluidex, Ind.Sci.Rev., Int.Abstr.Oper.Res., Intl.Civil Eng.Abstr., Math.R., Sci.Abstr., Sci.Cit.Ind., Soft.Abstr.Eng.
Formed by the 1987 merger of: Computers & Mathematics with Applications. Part A (ISSN 0886-9553); Computers & Mathematics with Applications. Part B (ISSN 0886-9561); Which superseded (in 1986): Computers & Mathematics with Applications (ISSN 0097-4943)
Description: Covers computers in mathematical research, mathematical models of computer systems and interactive applications.
Refereed Serial

510 621.381 UK ISSN 0269-9184
ELECTROSOFT. q. $210. Elsevier Science Publishers Ltd., Crown House, Linton Rd., Barking, Essex IG11 8JU, England. TEL 081-594-5942. FAX 081-594-7272. TELEX 896950 APPSCI G. (N. America dist. addr.: Elsevier Science Publishing Co., Inc., Box 882, Madison Sq. Sta., New York, NY 10159. TEL 212-989-5800) Eds. R. Magureanu, Charles P. Neuman.
—BLDSC shelfmark: 3707.506000.
Description: For engineers, researchers and educators; covers the entire spectrum of computational algorithms, techniques and developments in numerical methods, modelling and software for electrical, control and electronic engineerng, and signal processing.
Refereed Serial

GAMES AND ECONOMIC BEHAVIOR. see *PSYCHOLOGY*

510 GW ISSN 0911-0119
CODEN: GRCOE5
GRAPHS AND COMBINATORICS. 1985. 4/yr. DM.368($214) Springer-Verlag, Heidelberger Platz 3, D-1000 Berlin 33, Germany. TEL 030-8207-1. (Subscr. to: 44 Hartz Way, Secaucus, NJ 07094, USA; or 37-3 Hongo 3-chome, Bunkyo-ku, Tokyo 113, Japan) Ed. Hoon Heng Teh. (also avail. in microform from UMI; back issues avail.; reprint service avail. from ISI) **Indexed:** Compumath, Math.R., Sci.Abstr., Zent.Math.

510 SZ ISSN 1012-2435
I M A C S ANNALS ON COMPUTING AND APPLIED MATHEMATICS. (Text in English) 1989. 2/yr. 311.50 Fr. per vol. J.C. Baltzer AG, Scientific Publishing Company, Wettsteinplatz 10, CH-4508 Basel, Switzerland. TEL 061-6918925. FAX 061-6924262. Ed. R. Vichnevetsky.
—BLDSC shelfmark: 4368.833000.

IMPACT OF COMPUTING IN SCIENCE AND ENGINEERING. see *ENGINEERING — Computer Applications*

INTERNATIONAL JOURNAL OF ALGEBRA AND COMPUTATION. see *MATHEMATICS*

MATHEMATICS — COMPUTER APPLICATIONS

510   SI   ISSN 0218-1959
QA448.D38   CODEN: IJCAEV
▼**INTERNATIONAL JOURNAL OF COMPUTATIONAL GEOMETRY AND APPLICATIONS.** 1991. q. $195 to institutions; individuals and developing countries $95. World Scientific Publishing Co. Pte. Ltd., Farrer Rd., P.O. Box 128, Singapore 9128, Singapore. TEL 3825633. FAX 3825919. TELEX RS-28561-WSPC. (US addr.: 1060 Main St., Ste. 1B, River Edge, NJ 07661. TEL 800-227-7562; UK addr.: 73 Lynton Mead, Totteridge, London N20 8DH, England. TEL 44-81-4462461) Ed. D.T. Lee.
—BLDSC shelfmark: 4542.173710.
    Description: Covers the design and analysis of algorithms, and its applications to various fields including computer-aided geometry design, computer graphics, constructive solid geometry, operations research, pattern recognition, robotics, solid modelling, and others.

510   US   ISSN 0020-7160
QA76   CODEN: IJCMAT
INTERNATIONAL JOURNAL OF COMPUTER MATHEMATICS. 1964. 16/yr. (in 4 vols., 4 nos./vol.). $269. Gordon and Breach Science Publishers, 270 Eighth Ave., New York, NY 10011. TEL 212-206-8900. FAX 212-645-2459. TELEX 236735 GOPUB UR. (Subscr. to: Box 786, Cooper Sta., New York, NY 10276. TEL 800-545-8398; UK subscr. to: P.O. Box 90, Reading, Berkshire RG1 8JL, England. TEL 0734-560-080) Ed. David J. Evans. adv.; abstr.; charts; illus.; index. (also avail. in microform from MIM) Indexed: Appl.Mech.Rev., CAD CAM Abstr., Compumath, Comput.Rev., Curr.Cont., Cyb.Abstr., Eng.Ind., Ind.Sci.Rev., INIS Atomind., Math.R., Sci.Abstr., Sci.Cit.Ind.
—BLDSC shelfmark: 4542.175000.
    Description: Research papers on the theory and development of programming languages and their translators.
    Refereed Serial

510 620 621.381   UK   ISSN 0266-5611
                                 CODEN: INPEEY
INVERSE PROBLEMS; inverse problems, inverse methods and computerized inversion of data. 1985. 6/yr. £315($630) (effective 1992). (Institute of Physics) I O P Publishing, Techno House, Redcliffe Way, Bristol BS1 6NX, England. TEL 0272-297481. FAX 0272-294318. TELEX 449149-INSTP-G. (U.S. and Canadian addr.: American Institute of Physics, Subscr. Services, 500 Sunnyside Blvd., Woodbury, NY 11797-2999) Ed. M. Bertero. (also avail. in microfiche; microfilm; back issues avail.) Indexed: Compumath, Curr.Cont., Deep Sea Res.& Oceanogr.Abstr.
—BLDSC shelfmark: 4557.703170.

510   US   ISSN 0196-6774
QA76.6   CODEN: JOALDV
JOURNAL OF ALGORITHMS. 1980. q. $155 (foreign $189). Academic Press, Inc., Journal Division, 1250 Sixth Ave., San Diego, CA 92101. TEL 619-230-1840. FAX 619-699-6800. TELEX 181726. Ed.Bd. adv. (back issues avail.) Indexed: Compumath, Comput.Cont., Int.Abstr.Oper.Res., Math.R., Sci.Abstr.
—BLDSC shelfmark: 4926.800000.
    Description: Presents papers on algorithms that are inherently discrete and finite and that have some definite mathematical content in a natural way, either in their objective or in their analysis.
    Refereed Serial

510   US   ISSN 0885-064X
QA267   CODEN: JOCOEH
JOURNAL OF COMPLEXITY. 1985. q. $121 (foreign $146). Academic Press, Inc., Journal Division, 1250 Sixth Ave., San Diego, CA 92101. TEL 619-230-1840. FAX 619-699-6800. TELEX 181726. Ed. Joesph F. Traub. (back issues avail.)
—BLDSC shelfmark: 4963.393000.
    Description: Publishes original research papers that contain mathematical results on complexity as broadly received.
    Refereed Serial

510 500 371.3 500   US   ISSN 0731-9258
QA20.C65   CODEN: JCMTDV
JOURNAL OF COMPUTERS IN MATHEMATICS AND SCIENCE TEACHING. Variant title: J C M S T. 1981. q. $45 to individuals (foreign $60); institutions $68 (foreign $83). Association for the Advancement of Computing in Education, Box 2966, Charlottesville, VA 22902-2966. TEL 804-973-3987. Ed. Gary H. Marks. adv.; bk.rev.; circ. 3,500. (also avail. in microfiche; back issues avail.) Indexed: C.I.J.E., Comput.Dtbs., Cont.Pg.Educ., Educ.Ind., Educ.Tech.Abstr., ERIC, Microcomp.Ind., Sci.Abstr.
—BLDSC shelfmark: 4963.760000.
    Description: For mathematics and science teachers of all levels. Articles cover various aspects of computer literacy, ideas and experiences of instruction with computers and the characteristics of mathematics-science teachers and students using computers.
    Refereed Serial

510   US   ISSN 0924-9907
▼**JOURNAL OF MATHEMATICAL IMAGING AND VISION.** 1991. q. $150. Kluwer Academic Publishers, 101 Philip Dr., Norwell, MA 02061. TEL 617-871-6600. FAX 617-871-6528. (Subscr. to: Box 358, Accord Sta., Hingham, MA 02018-0358; Dist. in Europe by: Kluwer Academic Publishers Group, P.O. Box 322, 3300 AH Dordrecht, Netherlands. TEL 078-334911) Ed. Gergard X. Ritter.
    Description: Covers all aspects of mathematical imagery, including medical, industrial, military, and geophysical.

510   US   ISSN 1052-0600
▼**JOURNAL OF MATHEMATICAL SYSTEMS, ESTIMATION AND CONTROL.** 1991. 4/yr. $164 (foreign $174). Birkhaeuser Boston, Inc., 675 Massachusetts Ave., Cambridge, MA 02139-3309. FAX 201-348-4505. (Dist. by: Springer-Verlag New York, Inc., Journal Fulfillment Services, Box 2485, Secaucus, NJ 07096-2491. TEL 201-348-4033)
—BLDSC shelfmark: 5012.452000.
    Description: For researchers in numeric analysis, the computer sciences, or the natural sciences; presents new methods in numerical linear algebra.

JOURNAL OF STATISTICAL COMPUTATION AND SIMULATION. see COMPUTERS — Computer Simulation

510   UK   ISSN 0747-7171
QA76.95
JOURNAL OF SYMBOLIC COMPUTATION. 1985. m. (2 vols./yr.). $326. Academic Press Ltd., 24-28 Oval Rd., London NW1 7DX, England. TEL 071-267-4466. FAX 071-482-2293. TELEX 25775 ACPRES G. Ed. B. Buchberger. index. Indexed: Compumath.
—BLDSC shelfmark: 5067.900000.
    Description: Directed to mathematicians and computer scientists who have a particular interest in symbolic computation.

519   BL   ISSN 0101-8205
MATEMATICA APLICADA E COMPUTACIONAL/COMPUTATIONAL AND APPLIED MATHEMATICS. (Text in English, French, Portuguese) 1982. 3/yr. $105 to individuals; institutions $153 (effective 1992). (Sociedade Brasileira de Matematica Aplicada e Computacional) Editora Campus Ltda. (Subsidiary of: Elsevier Science Publishers B.V.), Rua Barao de Itapagipe, 55 Rio Comprido, 20261 Rio de Janeiro-RJ, Brazil. TEL 021-293-6443. FAX 021-293-5683. TELEX 21-32606 EDCP BR. Ed. Carlos A. de Moura. Indexed: Compumath, INSPEC, Math.R., Zent.Math.
—BLDSC shelfmark: 5390.820000.
    Description: Articles on all areas of applied mathematics using a computational approach. Includes a special issue on heuristic procedures, numerical, non-numerical and statistical techniques designed to solve scientific and technical problems with the aid of computers.
    Refereed Serial

550 001.6   RU   ISSN 0301-6897
MATEMATICHESKIE PROBLEMY GEOFIZIKI. 1969. irreg. 1.41 Rub. (Akademiya Nauk S.S.S.R., Vychislitel'nyi Tsentr) Izdatel'stvo Nauka, Fizmatlit, Leninskii prospekt, 15, 117071 Moscow, Russia. TEL 234-05-84. illus.

MATHEMATICAL AND COMPUTER MODELLING; an international journal. see MATHEMATICS

510   US   ISSN 1054-6634
▼**MATHEMATICAL MODELING (SOVIET).** (English translation of Soviet title) 1991. m. $130 to individuals (outside N. America $160); institutions $330 (outside N. America $350). (U S S R Academy of Sciences, Department of Information, Computer Technology and Automation, RU) New Soviet Sciences Press (USA), c/o Allen Press, Inc. Dist., Box 1897, Lawrence, KS 66044-8897. TEL 913-843-1235. FAX 913-843-1274. Ed. A.A. Samarskii.

510   NE   ISSN 0025-5610
QA264   CODEN: MHPGA4
MATHEMATICAL PROGRAMMING. (In 2 series: A and B) 1971. 15/yr.(in 5 vols.; 3 nos./vol.). fl.1400 (effective 1992). (Mathematical Programming Society) North-Holland (Subsidiary of: Elsevier Science Publishers B.V.), P.O. Box 211, 1000 AE Amsterdam, Netherlands. TEL 020-5803911. FAX 020-5803598. TELEX 18582 ESPA NL. (Subscr. in U.S. and Canada to: Elsevier Science Publishing Co., Inc., Box 882, Madison Sq. Sta., New York, NY 10159. TEL 212-989-5800) Eds. R. Bixby, W.R. Pulleyblank. cum.index: 1976-1981. (also avail. in microform from RPI; back issues avail.; reprint service avail. from SWZ) Indexed: Compumath, Comput.Rev., Curr.Cont., Cyb.Abstr., Ind.Sci.Rev., Int.Abstr.Oper.Res., J.Cont.Quant.Meth., Math.R., Oper.Res.Manage.Sci., Qual.Contr.Appl.Stat., Sci.Abstr.
—BLDSC shelfmark: 5402.577000.
    Description: Publishes original articles dealing with every aspect of mathematical programming.
    Refereed Serial

570   UK   ISSN 0960-1295
▼**MATHEMATICAL STRUCTURES IN COMPUTER SCIENCE.** 1991. 3/yr. $135. Cambridge University Press, The Edinburgh Bldg., Shaftesbury Rd., Cambridge CB2 2RU, England. TEL 0223-312393. FAX 0223-31505. TELEX 851817256. (North American addr.: Cambridge University Press, 40 W. 20th St., New York, NY 10011-4211. TEL 212-924-3900) Ed. G. Longo.
—BLDSC shelfmark: 5403.620000.
    Description: Journal of theoretical computer science which focuses on the application of ideas from the structural side of mathematics and mathematical logic to computer science.

510   US   ISSN 0730-8639
QA13   CODEN: MCEDDA
MATHEMATICS AND COMPUTER EDUCATION. 1967. 3/yr. $23 to individuals (foreign $29); institutions $55 (foreign $66). M A T Y C Journal, Inc., Box 158, Old Bethpage, NY 11804. TEL 516-822-5475. Ed. George M. Miller. adv.; bk.rev.; illus.; circ. 2,000. (also avail. in microform from UMI; reprint service avail. from UMI) Indexed: C.I.J.E., Comput. & Info. Sys., Comput.Lit.Ind., Comput.Rev., Cont.Pg.Educ., Educ.Tech.Abstr., Math R., Sci.Abstr.
—BLDSC shelfmark: 5405.175000.
    Formerly (until 1982): M A T Y C Journal (ISSN 0092-1424)
    Description: For high school and college educators. Articles cover computers in education, mathematical applications, remedial instruction and teaching ideas and methods.

MATHEMATICS AND COMPUTERS IN SIMULATION. see COMPUTERS — Computer Simulation

510 620   CN
MICRO CONTROL JOURNAL. 1989. 6/yr. Can.$17.50($17.50) Micro Control Journal, 27 Penrith Crescent, London, Ont. N6G 4M8, Canada. TEL 519-434-6904. FAX 519-668-1450. Ed. S. Gupta. adv.; bk.rev.; circ. 5,000. (back issues avail.)
    Description: Covers applications of computers to real time control systems, data acquisitions, sensors and motor controls.

510   FR
MODELLING, MEASUREMENT AND CONTROL. (Text mainly in English) irreg. 95 F.($19) per no. (International Association for the Advancement of Modelling and Simulation Techniques in Enterprises) A M S E Press, 16 av. de Grange Blanche, 69160 Tassin-la-Demi-Lune, France. TEL 78-34-36-04. FAX 78-34-54-17. TELEX 389 000. Ed. G. Mesnard. (back issues avail.)
    Description: Provides examples of signals, data and systems problems in all areas of activity.
    Refereed Serial

MATRIMONY

510   US   ISSN 0028-3045
CODEN: NTWKAA
NETWORKS: AN INTERNATIONAL JOURNAL. 1970. 7/yr. $390 (foreign $477.50). John Wiley & Sons, Inc., Journals, 605 Third Ave., New York, NY 10158-0012. TEL 212-850-6000. FAX 212-850-6088. TELEX 12-7063. Ed. F.T. Boesch. adv.; bk.rev.; charts; illus.; index; circ. 950. (also avail. in microform from RPI; back issues avail.; reprint service avail. from RPI) **Indexed:** Commun.Abstr., Compumath, Comput.Abstr., Comput.& Contr.Abstr., Comput.Cont., Curr.Cont., Cyb.Abstr., Eng.Ind., Int.Abstr.Oper.Res., J.Cont.Quant.Meth., Math.R., Sci.Abstr., Tel.Abstr.
—BLDSC shelfmark: 6077.205000.
Description: Applications and theory for innovations in design and use of computer networks, telecommunications, transportation systems, power grids, distributions systems and other networks.

PRINCIPLES OF COMPUTER SCIENCE SERIES. see *ENGINEERING — Computer Applications*

510 621.381   US   ISSN 0097-5397
QA76   CODEN: SMJCAT
S I A M JOURNAL ON COMPUTING. 1972. bi-m. $198 to non-members; members $48. Society for Industrial and Applied Mathematics, Attn: P. Clifford, 3600 University City Science Center, Philadelphia, PA 19104-2688. TEL 215-382-9800. FAX 215-386-7999. TELEX 446-715. Ed. lvi Galil. adv.; circ. 1,982. (also avail. in microform from IAM; back issues avail.) **Indexed:** A.S.& T.Ind., Appl.Mech.Rev., ASCA, Compumath, Comput.Abstr., Comput.Rev., Cyb.Abstr., INSPEC, Math.R., Sci.Abstr.
—BLDSC shelfmark: 8271.353000.
Description: For mathematicians, scientific and computer professionals and members of the society. Contains research articles in the application of mathematics to the problems of computer science and the nonnumerical aspects of computing.
Refereed Serial

S I A M JOURNAL ON DISCRETE MATHEMATICS. (Society for Industrial and Applied Mathematics) see *MATHEMATICS*

510   US   ISSN 0163-5778
QA297   CODEN: SNEWD6
S I G N U M NEWSLETTER. 1965. q. $23 to non-members; members $15; students $7.50. Association for Computing Machinery, Special Interest Group on Numerical Mathematics, 1515 Broadway, 17th Fl., New York, NY 10036. TEL 212-869-7440. Ed. P.W. Gafney. charts; stat.; circ. 1,800 (controlled). (back issues avail.) **Indexed:** Sci.Abstr.

510   US   ISSN 0163-5824
QA155.7.E4   CODEN: SIGSBZ
S I G S A M BULLETIN. q. $20 to non-members; members $15 (students $5). Association for Computing Machinery, Special Interest Group on Symbolic and Algebraic Manipulation, 1515 Broadway, 17th Fl., New York, NY 10036. TEL 212-869-7440. Ed. Robert Grossman. **Indexed:** Sci.Abstr.

SHUZHI JISUAN YU JISUANJI YINGYONG/JOURNAL ON NUMERICAL METHODS AND COMPUTER APPLICATIONS. see *SCIENCES: COMPREHENSIVE WORKS — Computer Applications*

510   NE   ISSN 0169-1015
CODEN: SPVIEU
SPATIAL VISION. (Text in English) 1985. q. DM.150 to individuals; institutions DM 250. V S P, P.O. Box 346, 3700 AH Zeist, Netherlands. TEL 03404-25790. FAX 03404-32081. TELEX 40217 VSP NL. Eds. D.H. Foster, A. Reeves. adv. (back issues avail.) **Indexed:** Psychol.Abstr.
—BLDSC shelfmark: 8361.785700.
Description: International psychophysical, perceptual and cognitive research on the visual processing of spatial information.

510   UK   ISSN 0275-5815
TOPICS IN COMPUTER MATHEMATICS. 1983. irreg., vol.3, 1986. Gordon & Breach Science Publishers, P.O. Box 90, Reading, Berkshire RG1 8JL, England. TEL 0734-560-080. FAX 0734-568-211. TELEX 849870 SCIPUB G. (US addr.: Box 786, Cooper Sta., New York, NY 10276. TEL 800-545-8398) Ed. D.J. Evans. (also avail. in microform)
—BLDSC shelfmark: 8867.433500.
Refereed Serial

ZASTOSOWANIA MATEMATYKI/APPLICATIONES MATHEMATICAE. see *MATHEMATICS*

ZENTRALBLATT FUER DIDAKTIK DER MATHEMATIK. see *MATHEMATICS*

MATRIMONY

Includes: divorce.

see also *Home Economics*

305.412 338   US   ISSN 1053-9107
A B C DIALOGUE. 1981. bi-m. membership. Association of Bridal Consultants, 200 Chestnutland Rd., New Milford, CT 06776-2521. TEL 203-355-0464. Ed. Gerard J. Monaghan. adv.; circ. 1,500.

306.8   US   ISSN 0272-7897
HQ536
ANNUAL EDITIONS: MARRIAGE AND FAMILY. 1974. a. $10.95. Dushkin Publishing Group, Inc., Sluice Dock, Guilford, CT 06437-9989. TEL 203-453-4351. FAX 203-453-6000. Ed. Ollie Pocs. illus.
Formerly: Annual Editions: Readings in Marriage and Family (ISSN 0095-6155)
Refereed Serial

301.4157 155.3   AT   ISSN 1034-652X
HQ1
AUSTRALIAN JOURNAL OF MARRIAGE AND FAMILY. 1980. 3/yr. Aus.$25 to individuals; institutions and libraries Aus.$30; foreign Aus.$30. Family Life Movement of Australia, P.O. Box 143, Concord, N.S.W. 2137, Australia. TEL 02-736-2117. FAX 02-736-2663. Ed. Alan H. Craddock. adv.; bk.rev.; index; circ. 700. (back issues avail.) **Indexed:** Psychol.Abstr., Sage Fam.Stud.Abstr.
—BLDSC shelfmark: 1810.220000.
Formerly: (until vol.10, 1989): Australian Journal of Sex, Marriage and Family (ISSN 0159-1487)
Description: For academics, researchers, administrators, educators and clinicians in the helping professions.

051   US
BLUSHING BRIDE. 1989. q. $3 per no. Baker - Brown Enterprise, Inc., 11402 Merrick Blvd., Jamaica, NY 11434-1335. TEL 718-739-1296. circ. 10,000.
Description: Bridal magazine for blacks. Covers wedding planning.

BRIDAL APPAREL NEWS. see *CLOTHING TRADE — Fashions*

745.5
▼**BRIDAL CRAFTS.** 1991. q. $14.97. Clapper Communications Companies, 701 Lee St., Ste. 1000, Des Plaines, IL 60016-4570. TEL 708-297-7400. FAX 708-297-8328. Ed. Julie Stephani. adv.: B&W page $1200. circ. 110,000.
Description: Aimed at women who wish to customize their wedding through hand-made items.

301.42   US
BRIDAL GUIDE; the how to for "I do". 1982. bi-m. $18.95. Globe Communications Corp. (New York), 441 Lexington Ave., New York, NY 10017. TEL 800-472-7744. adv.; circ. 225,000.

301.412   US
BRIDAL TRENDS. m. Meridian Publishing, Inc., Box 10010, Ogden, UT 84409. TEL 801-394-9446. Ed. Marjorie Rice.
Formerly: Bridal Fair.

305   US
BRIDE AND GROOM. 1981. s-a. Chevalier Associates, Inc., 2 Westborough Business Park, Westborough, MA 01581-5001. TEL 508-366-1476. FAX 508-366-1480. adv.: B&W page $960, color page $1440; trim 8 3/8 x 11. circ. 20,000.
Description: For the central New England bride, groom and wedding party.

640   CN
BRIDE & GROOM MAGAZINE. 1973. 6/yr. Can.$18. A.T.E. Publishing Co. Ltd., Box 175, Downsview, Ont. M3M 3A3, Canada. TEL 416-881-3070. Ed. Gabriel Erem. adv.; illus.

640   UK   ISSN 0006-9787
BRIDES & SETTING UP HOME. 1955. bi-m. £18.60 (foreign £22.60). Conde Nast Publications Ltd., Vogue House, Hanover Square, London W1R OAD, England. (Subscr. to: Quadrant Subscription Services, Oakfield House, Perrymount Rd., Haywards Heath, W. Sussex RH16 3DH, England) Ed. Sandra Boler. adv.; bk.rev.; illus.; circ. 69,821.

051   US
BRIDE'S & YOUR NEW HOME. 1934. 6/yr. $12. Conde Nast Publications Inc., Bride's Magazine, 350 Madison Ave., New York, NY 10017. TEL 212-880-8800. FAX 212-880-8331. (Subscr. to: Box 2886, Boulder, CO 80322) Ed. Barbara Donovan Tober. adv.; bk.rev.; bibl.; charts; illus.; stat.; circ. 436,069. (also avail. in microform from UMI; reprint service avail. from UMI) **Indexed:** PMR.
Former titles (until Nov. 1991): Bride's (ISSN 0161-1992); Bride's Magazine (ISSN 0006-9795)
Description: Features articles on all aspects of planning a wedding, honeymoon travel, and advice for new homeowners.

306.8   UK
BRIDES OF BRITAIN SERIES. 1988. s-a. £1.50. Brides of Britain Magazines Ltd., Highfield House, 2 Highfield Ave., Newbury, Berkshire RG14 5DS, England. TEL 0635-38888. FAX 0635-528638. Ed. Alison Moore. circ. 8,000.
Description: Regional bridal magazine for many areas of Britain.

051   US
▼**BRIDES TODAY.** 1991. q. $3.95 per no. H & S Publications, 3400 Dundee Rd., Northbrook, IL 60062. TEL 708-498-0618. Ed. Andrew Sawyer. adv.: B&W page $3000, color page $4600. circ. 100,000.
Description: For African-American brides and grooms; planning guide for brides, grooms and their families.

746.92   CN
CANADA'S ORIGINAL BRIDAL BUYERS' GUIDE. 1986. 4/yr. Network Direct, 1360 Danforth Rd., Ste. 1406, Scarborough, Ont. M1J 1G4, Canada. TEL 416-264-3535. (Subscr. to: P.O. Box 2216, Sta. B., Scarborough, Ont. M1N 2E9, Canada) Ed. Anne Fitterer. circ. 30,000.

CANADIAN ALPINE JOURNAL. see *SPORTS AND GAMES — Outdoor Life*

391   US
CHICAGOLAND WEDDING GUIDE. 1983. s-a. $2.50. P B Communications, Inc., 874 Green Bay Rd., Winnetka, IL 60093. TEL 708-441-7892. Ed. Asher J. Birnbaum. adv.; circ. 55,000.
Description: Guide to weddings and special events.

301.412   US
COLUMBUS BRIDE AND GROOM. 1985. 2/yr. $9.90. National Bridal Publications Inc., 303 E. Livingston Ave., Columbus, OH 43215. TEL 614-224-1992. Ed. Marvin Brown. adv.; circ. 15,000. (back issues avail.)

305   US
ELEGANT BRIDE. 1988. bi-m. $30. Pace Communications Inc., 1301 Carolina St., Greensboro, NC 27401. TEL 919-378-6065. FAX 919-275-2864. adv.; circ. 164,885.
Formerly: Southern Bride.
Description: National bridal service book featuring photography of bridal gowns, wedding traditions and honeymoon travel.

FAMILY THERAPY NEWS. see *PSYCHOLOGY*

659.152 640   US
▼**FOR THE BRIDE BY DEMITRIOS.** 1991. q. $4.50 per no. 'D J E Publications, 222 W. 37th St., 12th Fl., New York, NY 10018. TEL 212-967-5222. Ed. Gerald Magit. adv.; circ. 210,000. (back issues avail.)
Description: Features Demetrios bridal gowns.

301.412 305.3   US
GREATER CINCINNATI - NORTHERN KENTUCKY BRIDE & GROOM MAGAZINE. s-a. C O N A Publishing Corp., 707 Race St., Ste. 708, Cincinnati, OH 45202-4316. TEL 513-651-2662. Ed. Sheree Mancini Brown. adv.; circ. 20,000.

HEADPIECE. see *CLOTHING TRADE*

053.1　　　　　　GW　ISSN 0720-7301
HOCHZEIT; die Zeitschrift fuer Brautpaare. 1966. 6/yr. DM.72. Terra Verlag GmbH, Postfach 102144, 7750 Konstanz, Germany. TEL 07531-54031. FAX 07531-50083. Ed. Christel Poensgen. adv.; bk.rev.; circ. 70,800.
　Description: Information on wedding clothes, fashion accessories, ceramics, glass and pottery, wedding gifts, furnishings.

640　　　　　　　　US
HUNYIN YU JIATING/MARRIAGE & FAMILY. (Text in Chinese) m. $41.30. China Books & Periodicals, Inc., 2929 24th St., San Francisco, CA 94110. TEL 415-282-2994. FAX 415-282-0994.

I T MAGAZINE. (Irish Tatler) see *GENERAL INTEREST PERIODICALS — Ireland*

INVENTORY OF MARRIAGE AND FAMILY LITERATURE. see *SOCIOLOGY — Abstracting, Bibliographies, Statistics*

301.428　　　　US　ISSN 1050-2556
K10　　　　　　　　CODEN: JDREEJ
JOURNAL OF DIVORCE & REMARRIAGE; clinical studies and research in family therapy, family mediation, family studies and family law. 1977. q. $40 to individuals; institutions $95; libraries $190. Haworth Press, Inc., 10 Alice St., Binghamton, NY 13904. TEL 800-342-9678. FAX 607-722-1424. Ed. Craig A. Everett. adv.; bk.rev.; circ. 511. (also avail. in microfiche from HAW; reprint service avail. from HAW) **Indexed:** Adol.Ment.Hlth.Abstr., Bull.Signal., C.I.J.E., Chicago Psychoanal.Lit.Ind, Curr.Cont., Human Resour.Abstr., Past.Care & Couns.Abstr., Psychol.Abstr., Sage Fam.Stud.Abstr., Soc.Work Res.& Abstr., SSCI, Stud.Wom.Abstr. —BLDSC shelfmark: 4969.910000.
　Formerly (until 1990): Journal of Divorce (ISSN 0147-4022)
　Description: Presents current interdisciplinary findings on all aspects of divorce, from clinical practice, to theory, to research.
　Refereed Serial

JOURNAL OF MARITAL AND FAMILY THERAPY. see *PSYCHOLOGY*

JOURNAL OF MARRIAGE AND THE FAMILY. see *SOCIOLOGY*

LOVING MORE. see *SOCIOLOGY*

310.412　　　　　　　US
MAHAGONE BRIDE.* 1987. bi-m. Gold Starr Publishing, Inc., 780 Crescent St., Brockton, MA 02402-3343. TEL 617-584-5136. Ed. Jan Nargi. circ. 65,000.

640　　　　　　　FR　ISSN 0025-2980
MARIAGES. 1960. q. $25. Editions Rusconi, 8 rue Halevy, 75009 Paris, France. Eds. Piere Louchel, Andre Thiebaut. adv.; illus.; circ. 40,000.

MARRIAGE AND FAMILY LAW AGREEMENTS. see *LAW — Family And Matrimonial Law*

MARRIAGE & FAMILY REVIEW. see *SOCIOLOGY*

360 376　　　　　　　US
MARRIAGE MAGAZINE. 1972. m. (except July-Aug.). $15 (foreign $20). International Marriage Encounters, Inc., 955 Lake Dr., St. Paul, MN 55120. TEL 612-454-6434. FAX 612-454-7947. Ed. Kyrsta Eryn Kavenaugh. adv.: B&W page $480. bk.rev.; film rev.; music rev.; circ. 7,600. (back issues avail.)
　Formerly: Marriage Encounter (ISSN 0734-0052)
　Description: Focuses on healthy, intimate, committed marriages; individual empowerment and spiritual growth.

301.412　　　　　US　ISSN 0897-5469
MARRIAGE PARTNERSHIP. q. $14.95. Christianity Today, Inc., 465 Gundersen Dr., Carol Stream, IL 60188. TEL 708-260-6200. Ed. Ron Lee. circ. 60,000.
　Formerly: Partnership (ISSN 0747-9190)

306.8 646　　　　　　AT
MODE BRIDES. 1955. q. Aus.$29. Australian Consolidated Press, 54-58 Park St., Sydney, N.S.W. 2000, Australia. Ed. Sandra Larkin. adv.; illus.; circ. 21,100.
　Formerly: Australian Bride Magazine (ISSN 0004-8771)

306.8　　　　　　　US　ISSN 0026-7546
HQ1
MODERN BRIDE; a complete guide for the bride to be. 1949. 6/yr. $17.97 (Canada $24.54; Mexico $22.97; elsewhere $25.97). Cahners Publishing Company (New York), Consumer and Entertainment Division (Subsidiary of: Reed International PLC), Division of Reed Publishing (USA) Inc., 249 W. 17th St., New York, NY 10011. TEL 212-337-7000. FAX 212-545-5400. (Dist. by: Neodata Services, Box 2971, Boulder, CO 80329) Ed. Cele Lalli. adv.; illus.; tr.lit.; circ. 360,000. (also avail. in microform from UMI) **Indexed:** Mag.Ind., PMR.
　●Also available online. Vendor(s): DIALOG.
　Description: Complete bridal guide to wedding planning; the honeymoon; the first apartment. Covers fashion, home furnishings.

306.8　　　　　　　US　ISSN 0744-6861
NEW ENGLAND BRIDE. 1972. m. $24. New England Publishing Group, Inc., 215 Newbury St., Peabody, MA 01960. TEL 508-535-4186. Ed. Jane Lindley. adv.; bk.rev.; circ. 15,300.
　Description: Complete guide to help newly engaged men and women plan their weddings. Includes honeymoon travel, table top purchases, invitations and bridal fashions.

301.412　　　　　　　US
NEW JERSEY BRIDE. 1988. s-a. $3.95 per no. Tomlinson Enterprises, 55 Park Place, Box 920, Morristown, NJ 07960-0920. TEL 201-539-8230. FAX 201-538-2953. Ed. Leah Rosch. adv.; circ. 40,000.
　Description: Provides information about getting married in New Jersey.

392 640　　　　　　　US
NORTH COAST BRIDE AND GROOM. 1988. s-a. $4.90. P I M Publishing, 1360 W. 9th, No. 30, Cleveland, OH 44113. TEL 216-696-2766. Ed. James J. Ondrey. adv.; circ. 12,000. (back issues avail.)
　Description: Covers wedding preparations.

301.412　　　　　　　US
▼REVISTA PARA NOVIAS. 1992. 3/yr. $4.50 per no. White Lace (Subsidiary of: Welcome Publishing Co.), Box 630518, N. Miami, FL 33163. TEL 305-944-9444. FAX 305-949-0544. adv.: B&W page $3165, color $4689; trim 8 1/2 x 10 7/8. circ. 65,000.
　Description: Guide for Hispanic brides and grooms-to-be. Contains information on planning stages, budgets, customs, ceremonies and receptions.

SINGLE AGAIN. see *SINGLES' INTERESTS AND LIFESTYLES*

640　　　　　　　　SA
SOUTH AFRICAN BRIDE TO BE: FIRST HOME. (Text in English) s-a. R.3 per no. Cotswold Publications, 208 Gale St., P.O. Box 1925, Durban 4000, South Africa. TEL 031-3055974. FAX 031-3015926. Ed. Sue Miles. adv.

640　　　　　　　　IT　ISSN 0038-8319
SPOSA. 1962. s-a. L.20000($28) Edizioni Moderne Internazionali, Via Burlamacchi, 11, 20135 Milan, Italy. Ed. A. Maria Pietraccini. adv.; circ. 45,000.

301.412　　　　　　　CN
SPOSA 2000; the bilingual wedding planner. s-a. Word - Picture Advertising, Inc., 77 Mowat Ave., Ste. 413, Toronto, Ont. M6K 3E3, Canada. TEL 416-534-1851. FAX 416-534-0527. Ed. Ross Skoggard. circ. 10,000.

MECHANICS 3067

659.152　　　　　IT　ISSN 0394-3682
SPOSABELLA. 1973. s-a. L.20000. Casa Editrice Moda Italiana S.p.A., Viale Umbria 52, 20135 Milan, Italy. FAX 025458285. TELEX 332082 MODAIT I. Ed. Rita Rabassi. adv.; circ. 95,000.

646.3　　　　　　　AT　ISSN 1031-9115
STUDIO BRIDES. s-a. Aus.$82. Buying Systems Australia Pty. Ltd., Level 3, 101-111 William St., Sydney, N.S.W. 2011, Australia. TEL 02-360-1422. FAX 02-360-9742.

640　　　　　　　　CN
TODAY'S BRIDE. 1979. s-a. Family Communications, Inc., 37 Hanna Ave., Toronto, Ont. M6K 3E3, Canada. circ. 100,000.

305.412 640　　　　UK
ULSTER BRIDE. 1970. s-a. £2 per no. Ulster Journals Ltd., 39 Boucher Rd., Belfast BT12 6UT, N. Ireland. Ed. P. Rainey. adv.; illus.

U.S. NATIONAL CENTER FOR HEALTH STATISTICS. VITAL AND HEALTH STATISTICS. SERIES 21. DATA ON NATALITY, MARRIAGE, AND DIVORCE. see *PUBLIC HEALTH AND SAFETY — Abstracting, Bibliographies, Statistics*

UTAH MARRIAGE AND DIVORCE ANNUAL REPORT. see *POPULATION STUDIES — Abstracting, Bibliographies, Statistics*

055.1 659.152　　　IT　ISSN 1120-7809
VOGUE SPOSA. 1981. q. L.26000 (foreign L.52000). Edizioni Conde Nast S.p.A., Piazza Castello 27, 20121 Milan, Italy. TEL 02-85611. FAX 02-870686. Ed. I. Monti. adv.; circ. 40,000.

640　　　　　　　　UK　ISSN 0307-6474
WEDDING AND HOME. 1975. bi-m. £4. Headway, Home and Law Publishing, Greater London House, Hampstead Rd., London NW1 7QQ, England. FAX 01-387-9518. TELEX 269470. Ed. Debbie Djordjevic. adv.; bk.rev.; circ. 50,000.
　Formerly: Wedding Day and First Home.

MECHANICAL ENGINEERING

see *Engineering–Mechanical Engineering*

MECHANICS

see *Physics–Mechanics*

MEDICAL SCIENCES

see also Medical Sciences–Allergology and Immunology; Medical Sciences–Anaesthesiology; Medical Sciences–Cancer; Medical Sciences–Cardiovascular Diseases; Medical Sciences–Chiropractic, Homeopathy, Osteopathy; Medical Sciences–Communicable Diseases; Medical Sciences–Computer Applications; Medical Sciences–Dentistry; Medical Sciences–Dermatology and Venereology; Medical Sciences–Endocrinology; Medical Sciences–Experimental Medicine, Laboratory Technique; Medical Sciences–Forensic Sciences; Medical Sciences–Gastroenterology; Medical Sciences–Hematology; Medical Sciences–Hypnosis; Medical Sciences–Nurses and Nursing; Medical Sciences–Obstetrics and Gynecology; Medical Sciences–Ophthalmology and Optometry; Medical Sciences–Orthopedics and Traumatology; Medical Sciences–Pediatrics; Medical Sciences–Psychiatry and Neurology; Medical Sciences–Radiology and Nuclear Medicine; Medical Sciences–Respiratory Diseases; Medical Sciences–Rheumatology; Medical Sciences–Sports Medicine; Medical Sciences–Surgery; Medical Sciences–Urology and Nephrology; Drug Abuse and Alcoholism; Gerontology and Geriatrics; Hospitals; Men's Health; Nutrition and Dietetics; Pharmacy and Pharmacology; Physical Fitness and Hygiene; Public Health and Safety; Women's Health

617   CN
CODEN: AAACEC
A A C: AUGMENTATIVE AND ALTERNATIVE COMMUNICATION. q. $58 to individuals; institutions $105. (International Society for Augmentative and Alternative Communication) Decker Periodicals, One James St. S., P.O. Box 620, LCD 1, Hamilton, Ont. L8N 3K7, Canada. TEL 416-522-7017. FAX 416-522-7839. (US addr.: Box 785, Lewiston, NY 14092-0785) Ed. Lyle L. Lloyd. adv.; circ. 1,600. (also avail. in microfilm; back issues avail.) **Indexed:** Psychol.Abstr.
Description: Articles on systems and devices for speech- and language-impaired individuals for speech-language specialists, special educators, rehabilitation engineers.

610   US
A A F P REPORTER. 1974. m. membership. American Academy of Family Physicians, 8880 Ward Pkwy., Kansas City, MO 64114. TEL 816-333-9700. FAX 816-822-0580. Ed. Paula Binder. circ. 75,000.
Description: News and features covering information specific to family physicians. Covers all medical-socioeconomic matters affecting medicine.

A A M C CURRICULUM DIRECTORY. (Association of American Medical Colleges) see *EDUCATION — Teaching Methods And Curriculum*

A A M C DIRECTORY OF AMERICAN MEDICAL EDUCATION. (Association of American Medical Colleges) see *EDUCATION — School Organization And Administration*

610.28   US
A A M I ANNUAL MEETING. PROCEEDINGS.. a. $49 to non-members; members $25. Association for the Advancement of Medical Instrumentation, c/o Elizabeth Tilly, 3330 Washington Blvd., Ste. 400, Arlington, VA 22201-4598. TEL 703-525-4890. FAX 703-276-0793.
Description: Papers presented at the association's annual meeting.

610   US   ISSN 8750-9687
A A P S NEWS. 1943. m. $35 includes membership. Association of American Physicians & Surgeons, Inc., 1601 N. Tucson Blvd., Ste. 9, Tucson, AZ 85716-3405. FAX 602-290-9674. Ed. Dr. Jane M. Orient. circ. 2,000.
Formerly: A A P S News Letter (ISSN 0001-0170)
Description: Covers socio-economic aspects of medical practice.

610   US   ISSN 0884-1543
R729.5.S6
A B M S COMPENDIUM OF CERTIFIED MEDICAL SPECIALISTS. 1986. biennial. $250 (includes supplement). American Board of Medical Specialties, One Rotary Center, Ste. 805, Evanston, IL 60201. TEL 708-491-9091. FAX 708-328-3596. Ed. Dr. J. Lee Dockery.

610   US   ISSN 0742-0366
RC86
A B M S DIRECTORY OF CERTIFIED EMERGENCY PHYSICIANS. 1983. biennial. $24.95. American Board of Medical Specialties, One Rotary Center, Ste. 805, Evanston, IL 60201. TEL 708-491-9091. FAX 708-328-3596. Ed. Dr. J. Lee Dockery.

610   US   ISSN 0884-643X
R712.A1
A B M S DIRECTORY OF CERTIFIED FAMILY PHYSICIANS. 1985. biennial. $39.95. American Board of Medical Specialties, One Rotary Center, Ste. 805, Evanston, IL 60201. TEL 708-491-9091. FAX 708-328-3596. Ed. Dr. J. Lee Dockery.

610   US   ISSN 0884-6448
R712.A1
A B M S DIRECTORY OF CERTIFIED INTERNISTS. 1985. biennial. $59.95. American Board of Medical Specialties, One Rotary Center, Ste. 805, Evanston, IL 60201. TEL 708-491-9091. FAX 708-328-3596. Ed. Dr. J. Lee Dockery.

610   US   ISSN 0883-2986
RM697.U5
A B M S DIRECTORY OF CERTIFIED PHYSICAL MEDICINE & REHABILITATION PHYSICIANS. 1985. biennial. $24.95. American Board of Medical Specialties, One Rotary Center, Ste. 805, Evanston, IL 60201. TEL 708-491-9091. FAX 708-328-3596. Ed. Dr. J. Lee Dockery.

610   US   ISSN 0883-2978
RA423.5
A B M S DIRECTORY OF CERTIFIED PREVENTIVE MEDICINE SPECIALISTS. 1985. biennial. $24.95. American Board of Medical Specialties, One Rotary Center, Ste. 805, Evanston, IL 60201. TEL 708-491-9091. FAX 708-328-3596. Ed. Dr. J. Lee Dockery.

610 617   US   ISSN 0884-1462
RD10.U6
A B M S DIRECTORY OF CERTIFIED THORACIC SURGEONS. 1983. biennial. $24.95. American Board of Medical Specialties, One Rotary Center, Ste. 805, Evanston, IL 60201. TEL 708-491-9091. FAX 708-328-3596. Ed. Dr. J. Lee Dockery.

610   US
A B M S RECORD. 1981. 8/yr. American Board of Medical Specialties, One Rotary Center, Ste. 805, Evanston, IL 60201. TEL 708-491-9091. FAX 708-328-3596. Ed. Dr. J. Lee Dockery. circ. 1,200. (looseleaf format)
Description: Covers graduate medical education, specialty certification, evaluation of physician performance, and legislation.

610.7   CN   ISSN 0836-3463
A C M C FORUM. (Text in English and French) 1968. bi-m. Can.$30 (effective 1992). Association of Canadian Medical Colleges, 151 Slater St., Ottawa, Ont. K1P 5N1, Canada. TEL 613-237-0070. FAX 613-594-3364. Ed. H. Barkun. adv.; bk.rev.; circ. 1,100. (processed)
Formerly (until vol.7, no.2, 1974): A C M C Newsletter (ISSN 0001-0774)

610 614.44   US
A C P M NEWS. 1957. q. $25. American College of Preventive Medicine, 1015 15th St., N.W., Ste. 403, Washington, DC 20005. TEL 202-789-0003. FAX 202-289-8274. Ed. Emily Slough. adv.; bk.rev.; charts; circ. 3,000. (also avail. in microform from UMI)
Formerly: American College of Preventive Medicine Newsletter (ISSN 0002-8029)

A D T A NEWSLETTER. (American Dance Therapy Association, Inc.) see *EDUCATION — Special Education And Rehabilitation*

610   US
A F I P ATLAS OF RADIOLOGIC-PATHOLOGIC CORRELATION. a. $50 (foreign $59). (Armed Forces Institute of Pathology) Hanley & Belfus, Inc., 210 S. 13th St., Philadelphia, PA 19107. TEL 215-546-7293. FAX 215-790-9330. Ed. Dr. Alan J. Davidson.
Refereed Serial

610 500 600   FR
A F P SCIENCES; information scientifique, technique, medicale. 1976. w. 5760 F. (foreign 6312 F.). Agence France-Presse, 13 Place de la Bourse, B.P. 20, 75061 Paris Cedex 2, France. TEL 40-41-46-46. TELEX 210064 AFPA.

610   US   ISSN 0269-9370
RC607.A26   CODEN: AIDSET
A I D S. (Acquired Immune Deficiency Syndrome) (Suppl. avail.: A I D S (Year)) 1987. m. $130 to individuals; institutions $255; residents $91. Current Science, 20 N. Third St., Philadelphia, PA 19106. TEL 800-552-5866. FAX 215-574-2270. Ed.Bd. adv.; bibl.; illus.; circ. 3,500. (also avail. on diskette)
●Also available on CD-ROM.
—BLDSC shelfmark: 0773.083000.
Description: Publishes original papers on all aspects of acquired immunodeficiency syndrome, AIDS. Features rapid publication of the latest in the clinical and scientific aspects of the disease.

610 616   AT
A I M S NEWSLETTER. 6/yr. Aus.$12 to non-members. Australian Institute of Medical Scientists, P.O. Box 450, Toowong, Qld. 4066, Australia. TEL 07-371-3370. FAX 07-870-4857.
Former titles: A I M L S Newsletter; A I M T Newsletter (ISSN 0311-1253)
Description: Discusses interests, legislation and meetings pertaining to medical laboratory science. Continuing education material and details are included.

610   AT   ISSN 0813-6394
A M A VICTORIA BRANCH NEWS. m. Aus.$20. Australian Medical Association, Victoria Branch, 293 Royal Parade, Parkville, Vic. 3052, Australia. FAX 03-347-9871. adv.; illus.; circ. controlled.
Formerly: Australian Medical Association. Victoria Branch. Monthly Paper.

A M C R A'S MANAGED CARE MONITOR. (American Managed Care & Review Association) see *HOSPITALS*

610   US
A M I NEWS. 1958. bi-m. $25 (foreign $30). Association of Medical Illustrators, 1819 Peachtree St. N.E., Ste. 560, Atlanta, GA 30309-1851. TEL 404-350-7900. Ed. Charlotte Bauer. adv.; bk.rev.; illus.; circ. 850. **Indexed:** Ind.Med.
Formerly: A M I Newsletter (ISSN 0001-1916)

610   US
A M P R A REVIEW. 1984. q. $75 to non-members. American Medical Peer Review Association, 810 First St., N.E., Ste. 410, Washington, DC 20002. TEL 202-371-5610. FAX 202-371-8954. circ. 1,200. (looseleaf format; back issues avail.)

MEDICAL SCIENCES

610 301.16 US
A M W A JOURNAL. 1972. q. $35. American Medical Writers Association, 9650 Rockville Pike, Bethesda, MD 20814. TEL 301-493-0003. Ed. Ronald J. Sanchez. adv.; bk.rev.; circ. 3,500.
Formerly: Medical Communications (ISSN 0090-046X); Which supersedes: American Medical Writers Association. Bulletin (ISSN 0002-9971)

A N A D: WORKING TOGETHER. (National Association of Anorexia Nervosa and Associated Disorders) see PSYCHOLOGY

A N R E D ALERT. (Anorexia Nervosa & Related Eating Disorders, Inc.) see PSYCHOLOGY

617.5 US
A P M A NEWS. m. American Podiatric Medical Association, 9312 Old Georgetown Rd., Bethesda, MD 20814-1646. TEL 301-571-9200. FAX 301-530-2752. Ed. David Zych.

A P M I S. see BIOLOGY

610 US ISSN 0889-7190
RD130 CODEN: ASATEJ
A S A I O TRANSACTIONS. 1955. q. $115 to individuals; institutions $165. (American Society of Artificial Internal Organs) J.B. Lippincott Co., E. Washington Sq., Philadelphia, PA 19105. TEL 215-238-4200. Ed. Eli A. Friedman. **Indexed:** INIS Atomind.

610 340 US ISSN 1052-7893
A S C P WASHINGTON REPORT ON NATIONAL AND STATE ISSUES. 1983. fortn. $96. American Society of Clinical Pathologists, 2100 W. Harrison St., Chicago, IL 60612. TEL 312-738-4890. FAX 312-738-1619. Ed.Bd.
Description: Offers current information on the most relevant laboratory legislative topics.

A S H A. (American Speech - Language - Hearing Association) see HANDICAPPED — Hearing Impaired

A U L INSIGHTS. (Americans United for Life) see LAW

A U L STUDIES IN LAW, MEDICINE & SOCIETY. (Americans United for Life) see LAW

610 AT ISSN 0310-8341
ABORIGINAL MEDICAL SERVICE. NEWSLETTER. 1973. m. Aboriginal Medical Service, 36 Turner St., Redfern, N.S.W. 2016, Australia.

610 CL
ACADEMIA CHILENA DE MEDICINA. BOLETIN ANUAL. 1967. a. $25. Academia Chilena de Medicina, Clasificador 1349, Santiago 1, Chile. Eds. Dr. Amador Neghme, Dr. Alberto Donoso. index; circ. 1,000. (back issues avail.) **Indexed:** Ind.Med.
Formerly: Academia de Medicina. Boletin.

610 BL ISSN 0001-3838
ACADEMIA NACIONAL DE MEDICINA. BOLETIM. (Text in Portuguese; summaries in English) 1831. m. Academia Nacional de Medicina, Caixa Postal 459, Rio de Janeiro, Brazil. charts; bibl.; illus. **Indexed:** Biol.Abstr., Chem.Abstr., Helminthol.Abstr.
Formerly: Academia Nacional de Medicina Revista.

610 PL ISSN 0303-4135
CODEN: AAMGBD
ACADEMIAE MEDICAE GEDANENSIS. ANNALES. (Text in English, Polish; summaries in English, Russian) 1971. a. 13000 Zl.($20) Academia Medyczna w Gdansku, Ul. Marii Sklodowskiej-Curie 3a, 80-210 Gdansk, Poland. FAX 58-316-115. Ed. Stefan Raszeja. index; circ. 300. (back issues avail.) **Indexed:** Biol.Abstr., Ind.Med.
—BLDSC shelfmark: 0914.263000.
Description: Details medical research and includes historical aspects.

610.7 US ISSN 1040-2446
R11 CODEN: ACMEEO
ACADEMIC MEDICINE. 1926. m. $60. Association of American Medical Colleges, One Dupont Circle, N.W., Washington, DC 20036. TEL 202-828-0590. FAX 202-785-5027. Ed. Addeane S. Caelleigh. adv.; bk.rev.; bibl.; illus.; stat.; index; circ. 5,800. (also avail. in microform from PMC,UMI; reprint service avail. from UMI) **Indexed:** Abstr.Health Care Manage.Stud., Biol.Abstr., C.I.J.E., Chem.Abstr., CINAHL, Cont.Pg.Educ., Crim.Just.Abstr., Curr.Cont., Curr.Lit.Fam.Plan., Educ.Tech.Abstr., Excerp.Med., FAMLI, Hosp.Lit.Ind., Ind.Med., Ind.Sci.Rev., Int.Nurs.Ind., Med.Care Rev., Psychol.Abstr., Res.High.Educ.Abstr., Sci.Cit.Ind., SRI, Stud.Wom.Abstr., Trop.Dis.Bull.
—BLDSC shelfmark: 0570.513500.
Former titles (until 1988): Journal of Medical Education (ISSN 0022-2577); (until 1951): Medical Education.
Refereed Serial

610 FR ISSN 0001-4079
CODEN: BANMAC
ACADEMIE NATIONALE DE MEDECINE. BULLETIN. 1836. 9/yr. 580 F. Academie Nationale de Medecine, 16 rue Bonaparte, 75006 Paris cedex 06, France. FAX 40-46-87-55. Ed. A. Lemaire. bk.rev.; charts; circ. 1,300. (also avail. in microfilm from BHP) **Indexed:** Abstr.Hyg., B.R.I., Biol.Abstr., Bull.Signal, C.I.S. Abstr., Chem.Abstr., Curr.Adv.Ecol.Sci., Curr.Cont., Excerp.Med., Helminthol.Abstr., Ind.Med., Ind.Vet., Nutr.Abstr., Pig News & Info., Trop.Dis.Bull., Vet.Bull.
—BLDSC shelfmark: 2367.300000.
Formerly: Academie de Medicine. Memoirs.

610 BE ISSN 0377-8231
R41 CODEN: BMABDZ
ACADEMIE ROYALE DE MEDECINE DE BELGIQUE. BULLETIN ET MEMOIRES. 1841. m. 3000 BEF. Academie Royale de Medecine de Belgique, Palais des Academies, Rue Ducale 1, B-1000 Brussels, Belgium. **Indexed:** Biol.Abstr., Chem.Abstr., Dent.Ind., Excerp.Med., Ind.Med., INIS Atomind.
—BLDSC shelfmark: 2853.600500.
Formed by the merger of: Academie Royale de Medecine de Belgique. Memoires. (ISSN 0065-0595); Academie Royale de Medecine de Belgique. Bulletin (ISSN 0001-4168)

610 SI ISSN 0304-4602
CODEN: AAMSCG
ACADEMY OF MEDICINE, SINGAPORE. ANNALS. 1972. bi-m. S.$90($50) Academy of Medicine, Singapore, 16 College Road, 01-01 College of Medicine Bldg., Singapore 0316, Singapore. TEL 2245166. FAX 2255155. TELEX RS 40173 ACAMED. Ed. Dr. Tan Ngoh Chuan. adv.; bk.rev.; bibl.; charts; illus.; circ. 1,000. **Indexed:** Dent.Ind., Excerp.Med., Ind.Med. ●Also available online. Vendor(s): National Library of Medicine.
—BLDSC shelfmark: 1018.300000.
Description: Published to help young writers improve in medical and scientific writing.

610 CN ISSN 0001-4311
ACADEMY OF MEDICINE, TORONTO. BULLETIN. 1927. m. Can.$12.50. Academy of Medicine, Toronto, 288 Bloor St. W., Toronto, Ont. M5S 1V8, Canada. TEL 416-922-1134. Ed. H.F. Robertson. adv.; bk.rev.; charts; index; circ. 2,700.

610 IT
ACCADEMIA DELLA SCIENZE MEDICHE. ATTI. (Text in Italian; summaries in English, French) 1889. a. Accademia della Scienze Mediche, Via L. Giuffre 5, 90127 Palermo, Italy. TEL 091-217938. Ed. Giuseppe di Gesu.

610 IT ISSN 0390-7783
CODEN: AFISAT
ACCADEMIA DELLE SCIENZE DI SIENA DETTA DE FISIOCRITICI. ATTI. 1760; currently series 15. a. L.25000. Accademia delle Scienze di Siena Detta de Fisiocritici, Piazza S. Agostino 5, 53100 Siena, Italy. **Indexed:** Biol.Abstr.
—BLDSC shelfmark: 1772.815000.
Formerly: Accademia dei Fisiocritici, Siena. Sezione Medico-Fisica (ISSN 0065-0722)

610 IT ISSN 0001-4427
CODEN: AAMLAR
ACCADEMIA MEDICA LOMBARDA. ATTI. (Issued in 2 vols.) 1862. a. L.50000 (foreign L.100000). Accademia Medica Lombarda, III Clinica Chirurgica, Policlinico - Pad. Monteggia, Via Francesco Sforza 35, 20122 Milan, Italy. Ed. E. Trabucchi. bibl.; illus.; index,cum.index; circ. 500. **Indexed:** Biol.Abstr., Chem.Abstr., Excerp.Med., Ind.Med., INIS Atomind.

610 IT
ACCADEMIA MEDICA PISTOIESE "FILIPPO PACINI". BOLLETTINO. 1928. a. L.5000($20) Accademia Medica Pistoiese "Filippo Pacini", Via della Rosa, Pistoia, Italy. Ed. Collatino Cantieri. adv.

610 AT ISSN 0817-1351
ACCESS (TOORAK). 1976. q. Aus.$40 to non-members. Victorian Medical Postgraduate Foundation, Inc., P.O. Box 27, Parkville, Vic. 3052, Australia. adv.; circ. 1,200.
Description: Diary of postgraduate medical events in Australia and overseas.

610 CN
ACCESS (TORONTO). (Text in English and French) bi-m. membership. Canadian Rehabilitation Council, 45 Sheppard Ave. E., Ste.801, Willowdale, Ont. M2N 5W9, Canada. TEL 416-250-7490. FAX 416-229-1371. circ. 800.

610 FR
ACOPSIS.* 1972. bi-m. 35 F. I R F A, 42 rue Boileau, 75106 Paris, France. Ed. Francois Anger. adv.; circ. 15,000. (also avail. in microfilm)

611 574.87 SZ ISSN 0001-5180
QL801 CODEN: ACATA5
ACTA ANATOMICA; international archives of anatomy, histology, embryology and cytology. (Text in English, French, and German; summaries in English and original language) 1945. m. (in 3 vols.). 637 Fr.($425) per vol. S. Karger AG, Allschwilerstr. 10, P.O. Box, CH-4009 Basel, Switzerland. TEL 061-3061111. FAX 061-3061234. TELEX CH 962652. Eds. W. Lierse, A.W. English. adv.; abstr.; illus.; index; circ. 1,200. (also avail. in microform from PMC,RPI; reprint service avail. from ISI,SWZ) **Indexed:** Abstr.Anthropol., Anim.Breed.Abstr., ASCA, Biol.Abstr., Chem.Abstr., Curr.Adv.Ecol.Sci., Curr.Cont., Dairy Sci.Abstr., Dent.Ind., Excerp.Med., Ind.Med., Ind.Sci.Rev., Ind.Vet., Pig News & Info., Poult.Abstr., Sci.Cit.Ind., Small Anim.Abstr., Vet.Bull.
—BLDSC shelfmark: 0594.000000.

ACTA ANATOMICA NIPPONICA/KAIBOGAKU ZASSHI. see BIOLOGY

610 GW ISSN 0722-4192
ACTA BIOLOGICA; Zeitschrift fuer angewandte Homoeo-Phytotherapie, Ganzheitsbehandlungen und Sondermethoden der Medizin. 1962. s-a. Pascoe Pharmazeutische Praeparate GmbH, Schiffenberger Weg 55, Postfach 61 40, D-6300 Giessen, Germany. TEL 0641-7960-0. FAX 0641-77333. circ. 7,500.

610 BE
ACTA BIOMEDICA LOVANIENSIA. 1988. irreg., (8-10/yr.), vol.51, 1992. price varies. Leuven University Press, Krakenstraat 3, B-3000 Leuven, Belgium. TEL 016-284175. FAX 016-284176. (Dist. by: Editions Peeters s.p.r.l., Bondgenotenlaan 153, B-3000 Leuven, Belgium. TEL 016-235170)
Description: Research monographs on topics in the bio-medical sciences.

ACTA BIOQUIMICA CLINICA LATINOAMERICANA. see BIOLOGY — Biological Chemistry

610 CI ISSN 0065-1206
CODEN: AFMFBB
ACTA FACULTATIS MEDICAE FLUMINENSIS. (Text in Croatian or English) 1963. s-a. 250 din. to individuals; institutions 1000 din.(foreign $50). Sveuciliste u Rijeci, Medicinski Fakultet, Olge Ban 20-22, 51000 Rijeka, Croatia. TEL 051-513-222. FAX 051-514-915. (Co-sponsor: Republicka Zajednica za Znanstveni Rad) Ed. Juraj Sepcic. adv.; bk.rev.; circ. 700. **Indexed:** Biol.Abstr., Chem.Abstr., Excerp.Med., Ref.Zh.
Description: Publishes leading articles, original scientific and professional papers, preliminary communications, review articles, reports on scientific meetings and congresses, and other contributions.

M

MEDICAL SCIENCES

610   CS
ACTA FACULTATIS MEDICAE UNIVERSITATIS BRUNENSIS. (Text and summaries in Czech, English, Russian) 1958. irreg. price varies. Masarykova Univerzita, Lekarska Fakulta - Masaryk University, Medical Faculty, Komenskeho nam.2, 66243 Brno, Czechoslovakia. Ed. M. Dokladal. bk.rev.; circ. 800. **Indexed:** Biol.Abstr., Excerp.Med.

575.1   IT   ISSN 0001-5660
CODEN: AGMGAK
ACTA GENETICAE MEDICAE ET GEMELLOLOGIAE: TWIN RESEARCH; international quarterly of twin research. 1952. q. $300. Gregor Mendel Institute for Medical Genetics and Twin Studies, Piazza Galeno 5, 00162 Rome, Italy. TEL 396-8552055. FAX 396-8555179. (Co-sponsor: International Society for Twin Studies) Ed. Luigi Gedda. adv.; bk.rev.; abstr.; bibl.; charts; illus.; index. (also avail. in microfilm; reprint service avail. from ISI) **Indexed:** A.I.C.P., Abstr.Anthropol., ASCA, Biol.Abstr., Curr.Adv.Ecol.Sci., Curr.Cont., Dairy Sci.Abstr., Dent.Ind., Excerp.Med., Helminthol.Abstr., Ind.Med., Ind.Sci.Rev., INIS Atomind., Psychol.Abstr., Sci.Cit.Ind.
—BLDSC shelfmark: 0618.000000.
Formerly (until 1978): Acta Geneticae Medicae et Gemellologiae.

574   GW   ISSN 0065-1281
CODEN: AHISA9
ACTA HISTOCHEMICA; Zeitschrift fuer histologische Topochemie. (Text in English, French, German; summaries in English) 1954. irreg.(4-6/yr.). DM.404 (foreign DM.406). Gustav Fischer Verlag Jena, Villengang 2, Postfach 176, 6900 Jena, Germany. TEL 03778-27332. FAX 03778-22638. TELEX 18069-588676. Ed. J.-H. Scharf. bk.rev.; bibl.; charts; illus.; index. (also avail. in microform from PMC,SWZ; reprint service avail. from ISI) **Indexed:** ASCA, Biol.Abstr., Chem.Abstr., Curr.Adv.Ecol.Sci., Curr.Cont., Dairy Sci.Abstr., Dent.Ind., Excerp.Med., Helminthol.Abstr., Ind.Med., Ind.Sci.Rev., Ind.Vet., INIS Atomind., Nutr.Abstr., Ref.Zh., Sci.Cit.Ind., Vet.Bull.
—BLDSC shelfmark: 0624.000000.

ACTA HISTORICA LEOPOLDINA. see *SCIENCES: COMPREHENSIVE WORKS*

610   MX   ISSN 0001-5997
R21   CODEN: ACMDBI
ACTA MEDICA. (Text in Spanish; summaries in English, Spanish) 1965. q. Mex.$500($20) Instituto Politecnico Nacional, Escuela Superior de Medicina, Prolongacion de Diaz Miron y Plan de San Luis, 2 piso, C.P. 11340, Apdos. Postales 42-161 y 42-200 (Z.P.), Mexico 17, D.F., Mexico. Ed. Carlos de la Vega Lezama. adv.; bk.rev.; bibl.; charts; illus. **Indexed:** Biol.Abstr.
—BLDSC shelfmark: 0632.640000.

610   AU   ISSN 0303-8173
CODEN: AMAUBB
ACTA MEDICA AUSTRIACA. (Text in German or English; summaries in English) 1920. 5/yr. S.890. (Oesterrichische und Wiener Gesellschaft fuer Innere Medizin) Blackwell Medizinische Zeitschriftenverlagsgesellschaft mbH, Feldgasse 13, A-1238 Vienna, Austria. TEL 0222-8893646. FAX 0222-889364724. (Co-sponsors: Oesterreichische Gesellschaft fuer Innere Medizin; Oesterreichische Nuklearmedizinische Gesellschaft; Austro-Transplant) Ed.Bd. adv.; bk.rev.; illus.; stat.; index; circ. 1,500. (reprint service avail. from ISI) **Indexed:** ASCA, Biol.Abstr., Chem.Abstr., Dent.Ind., Dok.Arbeitsmed., Excerp.Med., Ind.Med., Ind.Sci.Rev., INIS Atomind., Nutr.Abstr., Sci.Cit.Ind.
—BLDSC shelfmark: 0633.100000.
Formerly: Wiener Zeitschrift fuer Innere Medizin und ihre Grenzgebiete. (ISSN 0043-5376)

610   CR   ISSN 0001-6012
CODEN: ATCTAW
ACTA MEDICA COSTARRICENSE. (Text in Spanish; summaries in English) 1957. 3/yr. Cr.$25. Colegio de Medicos y Cirujanos, Apdo. 548-1000, San Jose, Costa Rica. Ed.Bd. adv.; abstr.; charts; illus.; index; circ. 2,000. **Indexed:** Biol.Abstr., Chem.Abstr., Excerp.Med., Trop.Dis.Bull.

616.07 614.49   CI
ACTA MEDICA CROATICA. (Text in English, French, German and Serbo-Croatian; summaries in English and Serbo-Croatian) 1946. 5/yr. 12000 din.($150) Medical Academy of Coatia, Subiceva 29, 41000 Zagreb, Croatia. FAX 38-41-419-446. Ed. Prof. Nikola Persic. adv.; index; circ. 800. **Indexed:** Biol.Abstr., Chem.Abstr., Dent.Ind., Excerp.Med., Ind.Med., INIS Atomind.
Formerly (until 1991): Acta Medica Yugoslavica (ISSN 0375-8338)

610   DR   ISSN 0379-4857
ACTA MEDICA DOMINICANA. 1979. bi-m. RD.$80($20) Jose Contreras no. 8, Santo Domingo, Dominican Republic. TEL 809-688-4010. Eds. Julio M. Rodriguez, Mariano Defillo. adv.; bk.rev.; bibl.; charts; illus.

610 574   JA   ISSN 0567-7734
CODEN: AMBNAS
ACTA MEDICA ET BIOLOGICA/IGAKU SEIBUTSUGAKU KENKYU KIYO. (Text in English and European languages) 1953. q. exchange basis. Niigata Daigaku, Igakubu - Niigata University, School of Medicine, Ichiban-cho, Asahicho-dori, Niigata 951, Japan. Ed. Shoichi Imai. **Indexed:** Biol.Abstr., Chem.Abstr., Excerp.Med., INIS Atomind., Nutr.Abstr.
—BLDSC shelfmark: 0634.000000.

610   HU   ISSN 0236-5286
CODEN: AMEHDS
ACTA MEDICA HUNGARICA. (Text in English, French, German, Russian) 1950. q. $56. (Magyar Tudomanyos Akademia) Akademiai Kiado, Publishing House of the Hungarian Academy of Sciences, P.O. Box 24, H-1363 Budapest, Hungary. Ed. E. Stark. adv.; bk.rev.; bibl.; charts; illus.; index. **Indexed:** ASCA, Biol.Abstr., Chem.Abstr., Curr.Adv.Ecol.Sci., Curr.Cont., Excerp.Med., Helminthol.Abstr., Ind.Med., INIS Atomind.
Formerly: Academia Scientiarum Hungarica. Acta Medica (ISSN 0001-5989)

610   IR   ISSN 0044-6025
CODEN: AMEIAS
ACTA MEDICA IRANICA. (Text in English, French or German; summaries in English and French) 1957. q. Rs.400($20) Medical Sciences University of Teheran, School of Medicine, Enghelab Ave., Teheran 14-174, Iran. TEL 021-6112743. FAX 0098-21-6404377. Ed. Parviz Jabal-Ameli. charts; illus.; index; circ. 2,000. **Indexed:** Abstr.Hyg., Biol.Abstr., Chem.Abstr., Excerp.Med., Nutr.Abstr., Rev.Med.& Vet.Mycol., Trop.Dis.Bull.
Refereed Serial

610   JA   ISSN 0386-6092
ACTA MEDICA KINKI UNIVERSITY. (Text and summaries in English) 1976. s-a. 2000 Yen($30) Kinki University Medical Association - Kinki Daigaku Igakkai, 2-377, Ohno-Higashi, Osaka-Sayama, Osaka 589, Japan. TEL 0723-66-0221. FAX 0723-66-0206. Ed.Bd. index; circ. 1,300. (back issues avail.) **Indexed:** Chem.Abstr., Excerp.Med.
Description: Covers original articles, reviews and care reports of inventive work on medical services.

610   YU   ISSN 0365-4478
CODEN: AMMNCH
ACTA MEDICA MEDIANAE. 1962. 8/yr. 40 din. Srpsko Lekarsko Drustvo, Podruznica u Nisu, 18000 Nis, Yugoslavia. Ed. Radoslav Zivic. adv.; bk.rev.; circ. 700. **Indexed:** Biol.Abstr., Chem.Abstr.

610   JA   ISSN 0001-6055
ACTA MEDICA NAGASAKIENSIA. (Text in English) 1939. q. exchange basis. Nagasaki Daigaku, Igakubu - Nagasaki University, School of Medicine, 12-4 Sakamoto-machi, Nagasaki 852, Japan. Ed.Bd. charts; illus.; index; circ. 370. **Indexed:** Abstr.Hyg., Biol.Abstr., Chem.Abstr., Excerp.Med., Ind.Med., INIS Atomind., Trop.Dis.Bull.
—BLDSC shelfmark: 0635.150000.

610   JA   ISSN 0386-300X
CODEN: AMOKAG
ACTA MEDICA OKAYAMA. (Text in English and European languages) 1928. bi-m. free or exchange basis. Okayama Daigaku, Igakubu - Okayama University, School of Medicine, 2-5-1 Shikata-cho, Okayama 700, Japan. Ed. Takuzo Oda. bk.rev.; bibl.; charts; illus.; index, cum.index; circ. controlled. (back issues avail.; reprint service avail. from ISI) **Indexed:** ASCA, Biol.Abstr., C.I.S. Abstr., Chem.Abstr., Curr.Adv.Cancer Res., Curr.Adv.Cell & Devel.Biol., Curr.Adv.Ecol.Sci., Curr.Cont., Dairy Sci.Abstr., Dent.Ind., Excerp.Med., Helminthol.Abstr., Ind.Med., Ind.Sci.Rev., Ind.Vet., INIS Atomind., Nutr.Abstr., Sci.Cit.Ind., Small Anim.Abstr., Vet.Bull.
—BLDSC shelfmark: 0635.155000.
Formerly: Acta Medicinae Okayama (ISSN 0001-6152)

610   PE
ACTA MEDICA PERUANA. (Text in Spanish; summaries in English) 1972. q. S.250($6) Colegio Medico del Peru, Malecon Armendarir 791, Miraflores, Lima, Peru. Ed. Dr. Fausto Garmendia. adv.; abstr.; charts; illus.; index; circ. 10,000. **Indexed:** Biol.Abstr., Curr.Cont.

610   PH   ISSN 0001-6071
ACTA MEDICA PHILIPPINA. 1938. q. P.120($40) University of the Philippines, College of Medicine, P.O. Box 593, Manila, Philippines. (Co-sponsor: College of Public Health) Ed. Dr. Romeo R. Gutierrez. adv.; bk.rev.; charts; illus.; index; circ. 2,000. **Indexed:** Abstr.Hyg., Biol.Abstr., Chem.Abstr., Excerp.Med., Ind.Med., INIS Atomind.
Incorporates: University of the Philippines. College of Medicine. Proceedings.

610   PL   ISSN 0001-608X
CODEN: AMDPAA
ACTA MEDICA POLONA. (Text in English, French, German, Italian, Russian or Spanish) 1960. q. $40. (Polska Akademia Nauk, Wydzial Nauk Medycznych) Ossolineum, Publishing House of the Polish Academy of Sciences, Ul. Rynek 9-11, 50-106 Wroclaw, Poland. TELEX 0712771 OSS PL. (Dist. by: Ars Polona-Ruch, Krakowskie Przedmiescie 7, 00-068 Warsaw, Poland) Ed. Franciszek Kokot. bk.rev.; charts; illus.; index; circ. 600. (reprint service avail. from UMI) **Indexed:** Abstr.Hyg., ASCA, Biol.Abstr., Chem.Abstr., Curr.Cont., Excerp.Med., Helminthol.Abstr., Ind.Med., INIS Atomind., Nutr.Abstr., Trop.Dis.Bull.
—BLDSC shelfmark: 0635.200000.
Formerly: Polska Akademia Nauk. Wydzial Nauk Medycznych. Annals (ISSN 0048-4733)
Description: Contains original articles from various fields of medicine.

610   IT   ISSN 0001-6098
CODEN: AMROBA
ACTA MEDICA ROMANA. (Text in English) 1963. q. L.200000($153) (effective 1992). (Universita Cattolica del Sacro Cuore, Facolta di Medicina e Chirurgia) Vita e Pensiero, Largo Gemelli 1, 20123 Milan, Italy. TEL 02-8856310. FAX 02-8856260. TELEX 321033 UCATMI 1. Ed. Ermanno Manni. adv.; bk.rev.; abstr.; bibl.; charts; illus.; stat.; index. **Indexed:** Biol.Abstr., Chem.Abstr., Excerp.Med.
—BLDSC shelfmark: 0635.250000.
Description: Publishes original research in psychology, biology, medicine and surgery.

610   IT   ISSN 0065-1389
ACTA MEDICAE HISTORIAE PATAVINA. (Text in Italian or language of contributor; summaries in English, French, German and Italian) 1955. a. L.35000($30) Universita degli Studi di Padova, Istituto di Storia della Medicina, Via Fallopia 50, 35121 Padua, Italy. Ed. Loris Premuda. index in vols. 10,20,30; circ. 250.

574.4   HU   ISSN 0236-5391
QP1   CODEN: AMHUDE
ACTA MORPHOLOGICA HUNGARICA. (Text in English, French, German, Russian) 1951. q. $62. (Magyar Tudomanyos Akademia) Akademiai Kiado, Publishing House of the Hungarian Academy of Sciences, P.O. Box 24, H-1363 Budapest, Hungary. Ed. K. Lapis. adv.; bk.rev.; charts; illus.; index. **Indexed:** Abstr.Bulg.Sci.Med.Lit., ASCA, Biol.Abstr., Chem.Abstr., Curr.Adv.Ecol.Sci., Curr.Cont., Excerp.Med., Helminthol.Abstr., Ind.Med., INIS Atomind., Sci.Cit.Ind., Vet.Bull.
—BLDSC shelfmark: 0639.150000.
Formerly: Academia Scientiarum Hungarica. Acta Morphologica (ISSN 0001-6217)

616.07 574.2   JA   ISSN 0001-6632
                                CODEN: APJAAG
ACTA PATHOLOGICA JAPONICA. (Text in English) 1950. m. 18000 Yen for members outside Japan; $250 for non-members (effective Jan. 1991). Japanese Society of Pathology - Nihon Byori Gakkai, c/o Clinical Laboratory Division, National Cancer Center Hospital, 1-1, Tsukiji 5-chome, Chuo-ku, Tokyo 104, Japan. FAX 03-3545-3567. (Overseas distributor: Japan Publications Trading Co., Ltd., P.O. Box 5030, Tokyo International, Tokyo 100-31, Japan; or 1255 Howard St., San Francisco, CA 94103, USA) Ed. Yukio Shimosato. adv.; bk.rev.; charts; illus.; circ. 3,700. (reprint service avail. from ISI) **Indexed:** ASCA, Biol.Abstr., Chem.Abstr., Curr.Adv.Cell & Devel.Biol., Curr.Adv.Ecol.Sci., Curr.Adv.Genetics & Molec.Biol., Curr.Cont., Excerp.Med., Helminthol.Abstr., Ind.Med., Ind.Sci.Rev., INIS Atomind., Rev.Med.& Vet.Mycol., Sci.Cit.Ind.
—BLDSC shelfmark: 0644.100000.
  Description: Presents original papers on human and experimental pathology.

ACTA PHYSIOLOGICA PHARMACOLOGICA ET THERAPEUTICA LATINOAMERICANA; fisiologia, farmacologia, bioquimica y ciencias afines. see *BIOLOGY — Physiology*

ACTA PHYSIOLOGICA SCANDINAVICA. see *BIOLOGY — Physiology*

ACTA STEREOLOGICA. see *BIOLOGY*

610 340   IT   ISSN 1121-2098
▼**ACTA TECNOLOGIAE ET LEGIS MEDICAMENTI.** 1990. 3/yr. L.50000 (foreign L.10000)(effective 1992). C E M Casa Editoriale Maccari, Via Trento 53, 43100 Parma, Italy. FAX 39-521-771268. circ. 1,000.

610   CS   ISSN 0567-8250
                                CODEN: AUCMBJ
ACTA UNIVERSITATIS CAROLINAE: MEDICA. (Text in English) 8/yr. 25 Kcs.($66) Universita Karlova, Fakulta Vseobecneho Lekarstvi, Katerinska 32, 121 08 Prague 2, Czechoslovakia. TEL 29 62 63. (Dist. by: Artia, Ve Smeckach 30, 111 27 Prague 1, Czechoslovakia) **Indexed:** Biol.Abstr., C.I.S. Abstr., Chem.Abstr., Dent.Ind., Excerp.Med., Ind.Med.
—BLDSC shelfmark: 0584.522000.
  Description: Summarizes results in studies of anatomy.

610   FI   ISSN 0355-3221
                                CODEN: AUODDK
ACTA UNIVERSITATIS OULUENSIS. SERIES D. MEDICA. (Text in English) 1972. irreg. price varies. University of Oulu, Publications Committee, P.O. Box 191, SF-90101 Oulu, Finland. FAX 81-363-135. TELEX 81-32256. Ed. Heikki Ruskoaho. cum.index; circ. 450. **Indexed:** Biol.Abstr., Curr.Adv.Cell & Devel.Biol., Curr.Adv.Ecol.Sci., Curr.Adv.Genetics & Molec.Biol., Psychol.Abstr.
—BLDSC shelfmark: 0585.290000.

610   CS   ISSN 0301-2514
                                CODEN: AUPMAF
ACTA UNIVERSITATIS PALACKIANAE OLOMUCENSIS. FACULTATIS MEDICAE. (Text in English) 1955. q. 460 Kcs.($70) Univerzita Palackeho, Olomouc, Lekarska Fakulta - Medical Faculty of the Palacky University, Olomouc, S. Allende 3, 775 15 Olomouc, Czechoslovakia. FAX 42-68-414541. (Subscr. to: ARTIA, Ve Smeckach 30, Prague 1, Czechoslovakia) Ed. Dr. Vilim Simanek. bk.rev.; charts; illus.; circ. 400. **Indexed:** Biol.Abstr., C.I.S. Abstr., Chem.Abstr., Dent.Ind., Excerp.Med., Helminthol.Abstr., Ind.Med., INIS Atomind.
—BLDSC shelfmark: 0585.450000.
  Formerly: Acta Universitatis Palackianae, Facultatis Medicae (ISSN 0001-7167)

ACTA UNIVERSITATIS UPSALIENSIS. see *SCIENCES: COMPREHENSIVE WORKS*

610   FR   ISSN 0044-6149
ACTUALITE DE LA MEDECINE OFFICIELLE ET MEDECINE NATURELLE. 1963. bi-m. 120 F. Editions Andrillon, 6 Avenue du General Leclerc, B.P. 80, 02202 Soissons cedex, France. Ed. Eric Andrillon. bk.rev.; circ. 20,000.

615.89 615.845   US   ISSN 0360-1293
RM184   CODEN: AEREDS
ACUPUNCTURE AND ELECTRO-THERAPEUTICS RESEARCH; the international journal. 1976. q. £240 (effective 1992). (International College of Acupuncture and Electro-Therapeutics) Pergamon Press, Inc., Journals Division, 660 White Plains Rd., Tarrytown, NY 10591-5153. TEL 914-524-9200. FAX 914-333-2444. (And: Headington Hill Hall, Oxford OX3 0BW, England. TEL 0865-794141) Ed. Dr. Yoshiaki Omura. adv.; bk.rev.; abstr.; bibl.; charts; illus.; stat.; index; circ. 1,000. (also avail. in microform from MIM,UMI) **Indexed:** Bioeng.Abstr., Biol.Abstr., Chem.Abstr., CINAHL, Curr.Adv.Ecol.Sci., Curr.Cont., Dent.Ind., Excerpt.Med., Ind.Med., Psychol.Abstr., Sci.Cit.Ind.
—BLDSC shelfmark: 0677.930000.
  Description: Covers developments in basic and clinical research in acupuncture, electro-therapeutics and related fields. Fosters efforts to understand and improve these treatments and their use in diagnosis, prognosis, treatment and prevention of diseases in both Western and Oriental medicine.
  Refereed Serial

636.089 610   AT   ISSN 0065-1907
ADELAIDE. INSTITUTE OF MEDICAL AND VETERINARY SCIENCE. ANNUAL REPORT OF THE COUNCIL. 1937. a. free. Institute of Medical and Veterinary Science, Frome Rd., Adelaide, S.A., Australia. TEL 08-228-7317. FAX 08-2287538. Ed. Dr. R.J. Kimber. circ. 500.

ADLER MUSEUM BULLETIN. see *MUSEUMS AND ART GALLERIES*

610 658   US
ADMINISTRATION & MANAGEMENT; special interest section newsletter. (Consists of 7 sections: Administration and Management; Developmental Disabilities; Gerontology; Mental Health; Physical Disabilities; Sensory Integration; Work Programs) vol.5, no.4, 1989. q. $15. American Occupational Therapy Association, Inc., 1383 Piccard Dr., Box 1725, Rockville, MD 20850-0822.
TEL 301-948-9626. FAX 301-948-5512.

614.58   US   ISSN 0894-587X
RA790.A1   CODEN: APMHEM
ADMINISTRATION AND POLICY IN MENTAL HEALTH. 1972. bi-m. $195 (foreign $230). Human Sciences Press, Inc. (Subsidiary of: Plenum Publishing Corp.), 233 Spring St., New York, NY 10013-1578. TEL 212-620-8000. FAX 212-463-0742. Ed. Saul Feldman. adv.; bk.rev.; abstr.; bibl. (reprint service avail. from ISI,UMI) **Indexed:** Abstr.Health Care Manage.Stud., Abstr.Soc.Work., C.I.J.E., Curr.Cont., Educ.Admin.Abstr., Excerp.Med., Hosp.Lit.Ind., PSI, Psychol.Abstr., Sage Pub.Admin.Abstr., Soc.Work Res.& Abstr., SSCI, SSSCI.
—BLDSC shelfmark: 0681.956200.
  Formerly (until 1988): Administration in Mental Health (ISSN 0090-1180)
  Description: Intended to improve effectiveness of mental health and related human service programs.
  Refereed Serial

610   US   ISSN 0044-6335
ADOLESCENT MEDICINE (WASHINGTON); report for the health professionals with teenage patients. 1969. m. $69 (foreign $72). 821 Delaware Ave., S.W., Washington, DC 20024. TEL 202-488-7533. Ed. Nathaniel Polster. bk.rev.; stat.

610   US
ADULT'S HEALTH ADVISER. q. Whittle Communications L.P., 333 Main Ave., Knoxville, TN 37902. TEL 615-595-5300. Ed. Margot Leske.
  Description: Provides medical information designed to enhance the well-being of adult patients, and to support and reaffirm an internist's own advice.

610   US   ISSN 0741-9783
RC49
ADVANCES (KALAMAZOO). 1983. q. $40. Fetzer Institute, 9292 West KL Ave., Kalamazoo, MI 49009. TEL 616-375-2000. FAX 616-372-2163. Ed. Harris Dienstfrey. adv.; bk.rev.; abstr.; bibl.; charts; illus.; circ. 4,000. (back issues avail.) **Indexed:** Psychol.Abstr.
—BLDSC shelfmark: 0697.060000.
  Description: Studies mind-body interactions and their use in health care and health promotion.

MEDICAL SCIENCES 3071

616.075   NE   ISSN 0925-5206
                                CODEN: ADECEJ
▼**ADVANCES IN ECHO-CONTRAST.** (Text in English) 1991. 4/yr. fl.100($56.50) Kluwer Academic Publishers, Postbus 17, 3300 AA Dordrecht, Netherlands. TEL 078-334911. FAX 078-334254. TELEX 29245. (Dist. by: Kluwer Academic Publishers Group, P.O. Box 322, 3300 AH Dordrecht, Netherlands; N. America dist. addr.: Box 358, Accord Station, Hingham, MA 02018-0358. TEL 617-871-6600) Ed.Bd.
—BLDSC shelfmark: 0704.480000.

612.015 574.192   US   ISSN 0065-2571
QP601.A1   CODEN: AEZRA2
ADVANCES IN ENZYME REGULATION. 1963. 1/yr. £195 (effective 1992). Pergamon Press, Inc., Journals Division, 660 White Plains Rd., Tarrytown, NY 10591-5153. TEL 914-524-9200. FAX 914-333-2444. (And: Headington Hill Hall, Oxford OX3 0BW, England. TEL 0865-794141) Ed. George Weber. adv. (also avail. in microform from MIM,UMI) **Indexed:** Biol.Abstr., Chem.Abstr., Curr.Adv.Ecol.Sci., Ind.Med., Ind.Sci.Rev., Sci.Cit.Ind.
  Description: Evaluates topics including metabolic regulation, inborn errors of metabolism, metabolic diseases, diabetes, and cancer in the light of new research results.
  Refereed Serial

ADVANCES IN EXPERIMENTAL MEDICINE AND BIOLOGY. see *BIOLOGY*

610   US   ISSN 0197-8322
                                CODEN: ADIRDF
ADVANCES IN INFLAMMATION RESEARCH. 1979. irreg., latest vol.12. price varies. Raven Press, 1185 Ave. of the Americas, New York, NY 10036. TEL 212-930-9500. FAX 212-869-3495. TELEX 640073. Ed. Gerald Weissmann. **Indexed:** Biol.Abstr., Chem.Abstr., Curr.Adv.Ecol.Sci., Curr.Cont.
—BLDSC shelfmark: 0709.130000.
  Refereed Serial

616.026   US   ISSN 0065-2822
RC46   CODEN: AIMNAL
ADVANCES IN INTERNAL MEDICINE. 1954. a. $59.95. Mosby - Year Book, Inc. (Chicago) (Subsidiary of: Times Mirror Company), 200 N. LaSalle St., Chicago, IL 60601-1080. TEL 312-726-9733. FAX 312-726-6075. TELEX 206155. (Subscr. to: 11830 Westline Industrial Dr., St. Louis, MO 63146. TEL 800-325-4177) Ed. G.H. Stollerman, MD. (also avail. in microfilm from UMI; reprint service avail. from UMI) **Indexed:** Biol.Abstr., Chem.Abstr., Curr.Adv.Ecol.Sci., Curr.Adv.Genetics & Molec.Biol., Dent.Ind., Ind.Med., Ind.Sci.Rev., INIS Atomind., Sci.Cit.Ind.
—BLDSC shelfmark: 0709.250000.
  Description: Presents a collection of original fully referenced clinical reviews from the experts in the field.

ADVANCES IN MEDICAL SOCIAL SCIENCE; health and illness as view by anthropology, geography, history, psychology and sociology. see *SOCIAL SCIENCES: COMPREHENSIVE WORKS*

ADVANCES IN PAIN RESEARCH AND THERAPY. see *MEDICAL SCIENCES — Psychiatry And Neurology*

616.07   US
RB1
ADVANCES IN PATHOLOGY AND LABORATORY MEDICINE. 1988. a. $59.95. Mosby - Year Book, Inc. (Chicago) (Subsidiary of: Times Mirror Company), 200 N. LaSalle St., Chicago, IL 60601-1080. TEL 312-726-9733. FAX 312-726-6075. TELEX 206155. (Subscr. to: 11830 Westline Industrial Dr., St. Louis, MO 63146. TEL 800-325-4177) Ed. Dr. Cecilia M. Fenoglio-Preiser.
  Formerly: Advances in Pathology (ISSN 0889-3969)
  Description: Presents a collection of original, fully referenced clinical reviews and articles in pathology.

610   BE
ADVANCES IN PROTEIN PHOSPHATASES. 1985. irreg., vol.6, 1991. 2300 BEF. Leuven University Press, Krakenstraat 3, B-3000 Leuven, Belgium. TEL 016-284175. FAX 016-284176. (Dist. by: Editions Peeters s.p.r.l., Bondgenotenlaan 153, B-3000 Leuven, Belgium. TEL 016-235170) Eds. W. Merlevede, J. DiSalvo.

M

MEDICAL SCIENCES

ADVANCES IN THE BIOSCIENCES. see *BIOLOGY*

615.1 610   UK   ISSN 0044-6394
CODEN: ADRBBA
ADVERSE DRUG REACTION BULLETIN. (Editions in English, Italian) 1966. bi-m. £10($25) (elsewhere £13.75). 45 Woodland Grove, Weybridge, Surrey KT13 9EQ, England. TEL 0932-847629. FAX 0932-858035. Ed. D.M. Davies. index; circ. 30,000. (looseleaf format; also avail. in microfilm from UMI; back issues avail.) **Indexed:** Biol.Abstr., Curr.Adv.Ecol.Sci., Excerp.Med., I.P.A., Ind.Med.
—BLDSC shelfmark: 0712.232000.

615.1 610   UK
CODEN: ADRRE
ADVERSE DRUG REACTIONS AND TOXICOLOGICAL REVIEWS. 1982. q. £80($160) (effective 1992). Oxford University Press, Oxford Journals, Pinkhill House, Southfield Rd., Eynsham, Oxford OX8 1JJ, England. TEL 0865-882283. FAX 0865-882890. TELEX 837330-OXPRES-G. (U.S. subscr. to: Journals Fulfillment, 2001 Evans Rd., Cary, NC 25713. TEL 919-677-0977) Eds. D.M. Davies, H. de Glanville. circ. 750. **Indexed:** Biol.Abstr., Chem.Abstr., Curr.Adv.Ecol.Sci., Curr.Cont., Excerp.Med., Ind.Med., Ind.Sci.Rev., NRN, Sci.Cit.Ind., SSCI.
Formerly (until 1991): Adverse Drug Reactions and Acute Poisoning Reviews (ISSN 0260-647X)
Description: Covers developments in the field of adverse drug reactions and acute poisoning.

610.6   GW
AE K - K V W L AKTUELL; berufspolitische Informationen fuer die Aerzte in Westfalen-Lippe. m. (Aerztkammer Westfalen-Lippe, Kassenaerztliche Vereinigung Westfalen-Lippe) Aschendorffsche Verlagsbuchhandlung GmbH, Soester Str. 13, D-4400 Muenster, Germany. TEL 0251-3750-0. (Subscr. to: Aerztliche Pressestelle Westfalen-Lippe, Kaiser-Wilhelm-Ring 4-6, D-4400 Muenster, Germany) adv.; stat.; circ. 22,800.
Description: Information about legislation affecting doctors in Westfalen-Lippe.

610   US
AEROMEDICAL & TRAINING DIGEST; a quarterly newsletter discussing the current issues in aerospace medicine and training. 1986. q. free. Environmental Tectonics Corporation, 125 James Way, County Line Industrial Park, Southampton, PA 18966. TEL 215-355-9100. FAX 215-357-4000. TELEX 244926 ETC UR. (Co-publisher: AeroMedical Training Institute) Ed. Robert A.G. Montgomery III. circ. 4,683.

610 011   ISSN 0175-5811
AERZTE ZEITUNG; die Tagesinformation fuer den Aerzt. 1982. d. DM.140. Aerzte Zeitung Verlagsgesellschaft mbH, Am Forsthaus Gravenbruch 5, 6078 Neu-Isenburg 2, Germany. (Subscr. to: Postfach 101047, 6072 Dreieich, Germany) Ed. Gerald Kosaris, Ruediger Hennigs. adv.; bk.rev.; circ. 45,000.

610   GW   ISSN 0720-3489
AERZTEBLATT BADEN-WUERTTEMBERG. 1946. m. DM.164.40 (foreign DM.187.20). (Landesaerztekammer Baden-Wuerttemberg) A.W. Gentner Verlag, Forststr. 131, Postfach 101742, 7000 Stuttgart 10, Germany. TEL 0711-63672-0. FAX 0711-6367211. Ed. Juergen Dreher. adv.; bk.rev.; illus.; index; circ. 40,300. (back issues avail.) **Indexed:** Chem.Abstr.

610   GW   ISSN 0001-9488
AERZTEBLATT RHEINLAND-PFALZ. 1948. m. DM.132. (Landesaerztekammer Rheinland-Pfalz) Verlag Kirchheim und Co. GmbH, Kaiserstr. 41, Postfach 2524, 6500 Mainz, Germany. TEL 06131-671081. Ed. Prof. Dr. W. Ohler. adv.; bk.rev.; abstr.; illus.; index, cum.index; circ. 15,600.
—BLDSC shelfmark: 1738.240000.
Description: Publication for physicians and specialists. Covers various medical issues, public health, medical research and news from local medical institutions.

610   GW   ISSN 0938-8478
AERZTEBLATT SACHSEN. m. DM.138 (foreign DM.156). A.W. Gentner Verlag, Forststr. 131, Postfach 101742, 7000 Stuttgart 10, Germany. TEL 0711-63672-0. FAX 0711-6367211.

610   GW   ISSN 0863-5412
▼**AERZTEBLATT THUERINGEN.** 1990. m. DM.104 (foreign DM.109). Gustav Fischer Verlag Jena, Villengang 2, Postfach 176, 6900 Jena, Germany. TEL 03778-27332. FAX 03778-22638. TELEX 18069-588676. Ed. E. Beleites. adv.; bk.rev.; bibl.; charts; illus.; index.

616.98   GW   ISSN 0930-6900
AERZTEBUCH; Fachaddressbuch des gesamten Gesundheitswesens Deutschland. (Text in German; summaries in English, French, German and Italian) 1977. a. DM.135. Aerztebuch Verlag GmbH, Postfach 360129, 1000 Berlin 36, Germany. TEL 030-6123049. circ. 8,500.

615.8   GW   ISSN 0720-6003
AERZTEZEITSCHRIFT FUER NATURHEILVERFAHREN. (Text mainly in German; summaries in English and French) 1963. m. DM.106 (students DM.79.50). (Zentralverband der Aerzte fuer Naturheilverfahren e.V.) Medizinisch-Literarische Verlagsgesellschaft mbH, Postfach 1151-1152, 3110 Uelzen 1, Germany. TEL 0581-808-151. FAX 0581-808158. TELEX 91326-AZ-D. Ed. K.C. Schimmel. adv.; bk.rev.; charts; illus.; index, cum.index; circ. 7,800. (tabloid format; back issues avail.) **Indexed:** Excerp.Med.
—BLDSC shelfmark: 1738.250000.
Formerly: Physikalische Medizin und Rehabilitation (ISSN 0031-9287)

610   GW   ISSN 0341-2458
AERZTIN. 1953. m. DM.42. (Deutscher Aerztinnenbund e.V.) Deutscher Aerzte-Verlag GmbH, Dieselstr. 2, Postfach 400265, 5000 Cologne 40, Germany. TEL 02234-7011-0. FAX 02234-7011444. circ. 3,000.

616.1   GW   ISSN 0001-9534
AERZTLICHE PRAXIS; Die Zeitung des Arztes in Klinik und Praxis. 1948. s-w. DM.103. Werk-Verlag Dr. Edmund Banaschewski GmbH, Hans-Cornelius-Str.4, 8032 Munich-Graefelfing, Germany. TEL 089-855021. FAX 089-853799. TELEX 522451. Ed. Edmund Banaschewski. adv.; bk.rev.; abstr.; bibl.; charts; illus.; stat.; index. (newspaper) **Indexed:** C.I.S. Abstr., INIS Atomind.

610   GW   ISSN 0722-866X
AERZTLICHES MITTEILUNGSBLATT MITTELFRANKEN. 1976. m. DM.60. Demeter Verlag, Wuermstr. 13, 8032 Graefelfing, Germany. TEL 089-852033. Ed. Dr. Klaus Dehler. circ. 6,700.

610   GW   ISSN 0723-8010
AERZTLICHES MITTEILUNGSBLATT SCHWABEN. 1980. bi-m. DM.36. Demeter Verlag, Wuermstr. 13, 8032 Graefelfing, Germany. TEL 089-852033. FAX 089-8543347. Ed. Dr. Klaus Hellmann. circ. 5,500.

610   UK   ISSN 0141-9536
AFRICA HEALTH. 1978. bi-m. £37 (foreign $98) to individuals; institutions £33.30 (foreign $88.20). F S G Communications Ltd., 57-59 Whitechapel Rd., London E1 1DU, England. TEL 071-377-8413. FAX 071-375-0371. adv.; bk.rev. **Indexed:** ASSIA, Trop.Dis.Bull.
—BLDSC shelfmark: 0732.157700.

610   UK   ISSN 0951-8266
AFRICA HEALTH MARKETLETTER. 10/yr. £210 to individuals (foreign $375); institutions £189 (foreign $337.50). F S G Communications Ltd., 57-59 Whitechapel Rd., London E1 1DU, England. TEL 071-377-8413. FAX 071-375-0371.

610   KE
AFRICA MEDICINE AND HEALTH. (Text in English) 1978. m. EAs.360($25) Oryx Publications Limited, P.O. Box 40106, Nairobi, Kenya. Ed. Peter Moll. adv.; illus.; circ. 5,000.

610   UK   ISSN 0309-3913
CODEN: AJMSDC
AFRICAN JOURNAL OF MEDICINE & MEDICAL SCIENCES. 1970. q. £81.50($148) Blackwell Scientific Publications Ltd., Osney Mead, Oxford OX2 0EL, England. TEL 0865-240201. FAX 0865-721205. TELEX 83355-MEDBOK-G. Ed. Prof. O.A. Ladipo. adv.; circ. 490. (back issues avail.; reprint service avail. from ISI) **Indexed:** Abstr.Hyg., Biol.Abstr., Chem.Abstr., Curr.Adv.Ecol.Sci., Curr.Cont., Excerp.Med., Helminthol.Abstr., Ind.Med., Trop.Dis.Bull.
—BLDSC shelfmark: 0732.530000.
Formerly: African Journal of Medical Sciences (ISSN 0002-0028)

610   FR   ISSN 0299-3007
AFRIQUE MEDECINE ET SANTE. 1986. m. 300 F. S A P E F, 11 rue de Teheran, 75008 Paris, France. Ed. Michel de Breteuil. adv.; bk.rev.; circ. 7,750.

610   SG   ISSN 0002-0516
AFRIQUE MEDICALE. (Text in French) 1958. 11/yr. 220 F.($41) (foreign 260 F.). B.P. 1826, Dakar, Senegal. TEL 23-48-80. FAX 22-56-30. TELEX 1300 ATT AFRICA. Ed. P. Correa. adv.; charts; illus.; circ. 7,500. **Indexed:** Abstr.Hyg., Biol.Abstr., Nutr.Abstr., Rev.Med.& Vet.Mycol., Trop.Dis.Bull.

610   KE
AFYA. q. P.O. Box 30125, Nairobi, Kenya. TEL 501301. FAX 506-112. TELEX 23254.
Description: Contains information for and about medical and health workers.

610   IT   ISSN 0392-3002
AGGIORNAMENTO DEL MEDICO; rivista mensile di cultura e pratica medica. 1982. m. (10/yr.). L.40000 (foreign $50). Editrice Kurtis s.r.l., Via L. Zoja, 30, 20153 Milan, Italy. TEL 02-48202740. FAX 02-48201219. Ed. C. Fuse. adv.; circ. 80,000.
—BLDSC shelfmark: 0736.280600.
Description: Presents research papers and articles on a wide variety of topics in modern medicine. Includes diagrams and statistical data.

612 615   FR   ISSN 0002-1148
BF575.A3   CODEN: AGSOA6
AGRESSOLOGIE; revue internationale de physiobiologie et de pharmacologie appliquees aux effets de l'agression. (Text in English, French, German, Russian, Spanish) 1959. m. $170. (Hopital Lariboisiere, Departement d'Anesthesie Reanimation) S P E I, 14 rue Droust, 75009 Paris, France. Ed. G. Nedjar. adv.; bk.rev.; charts; illus.; index; circ. 550. (also avail. in microform from UMI) **Indexed:** Biol.Abstr., Biotech.Abstr., Chem.Abstr., Excerp.Med., Ind.Med., Nutr.Abstr.
—BLDSC shelfmark: 0738.750000.

610   IR
AHWAZ UNIVERSITY OF MEDICAL SCIENCES. SCIENTIFIC MEDICAL JOURNAL/MAJALLEH ELMI PESESHKI DANESHGAHE ELOME PEZESHKI AHWAZ. (Text in Persian; summaries in English) 1971. s-a. Ahwaz University of Medical Sciences, P.O. Box 189, Ahwaz, Iran. Ed. Dr. S. Zahedi.

610   JA   ISSN 0301-0902
CODEN: AIDZAC
AICHI MEDICAL UNIVERSITY ASSOCIATION. JOURNAL. (Text in English and Japanese; summaries in English) 1973. q. 3000 Yen. Aichi Medical University Association, 21, Karimata, Yazako, Nagakute-cho, Aichi-gun, Aichi-ken 480-11, Japan. Ed. Kazumi Takeya. circ. 1,700. **Indexed:** Excerp.Med., INIS Atomind.

610   UA   ISSN 0002-2144
CODEN: AIMJA9
AIN SHAMS MEDICAL JOURNAL. 1949. bi-m. Ain Shams University, University Hospital, Abbassia, Cairo, Egypt. (Co-sponsor: Ain Shams Clinical and Scientific Society) Ed. Ahmed Ghareeb. adv.; bk.rev.; abstr.; charts; illus.; stat; circ. 2,000. **Indexed:** Biol.Abstr., C.I.S. Abstr., Chem.Abstr., Excerp.Med., Helminthol.Abstr., Trop.Dis.Bull.

610   PL   ISSN 0067-6489
                CODEN: RJMBA9
AKADEMIA MEDYCZNA W BIALYMSTOKU. ROCZNIKI/ANNALES ACADEMIAE MEDICAE BIALOSTOCENSIS. (Text in English, German, Polish; summaries in English, Polish, Russian) 1955. irreg. exchange basis. Akademia Medyczna w Bialymstoku, Ul. Kilinskiego 1, 15-089 Bialystok, Poland. TEL 48-85-21705. FAX 48-85-24907. TELEX 2200 AMPL. Ed. Andrzej Rozanski. (back issues avail.) **Indexed:** Ind.Med.

610   RU   ISSN 0002-3027
                CODEN: VAMNAQ
AKADEMIYA MEDITSINSKIKH NAUK S.S.S.R. VESTNIK/ACADEMY OF MEDICAL SCIENCES OF THE U.S.S.R. ANNALS. (Text in Russian; summaries in English) 1946. m. $27.60. (Akademiya Meditsinskikh Nauk S.S.S.R.) Izdatel'stvo Meditsina, Petroverigskii pereulok 6-8, 101838 Moscow, Russia. Ed. N.P. Bochkov. bk.rev.; charts; illus.; index. **Indexed:** Biol.Abstr., Chem.Abstr., Dent.Ind., Ind.Med.
—BLDSC shelfmark: 0025.400000.
  Description: Publishes original scientific papers and review articles on the important problems of medical science and public health practice.

AKADEMIYA NAUK S.S.S.R. SIBIRSKOE OTDELENIE. IZVESTIYA. SERIYA BIOLOGICHESKIKH I MEDITSINSKIKH NAUK. see *BIOLOGY*

610   IR
AKHBAR-E PEZESHKI. w. Dr. T. Foruzin, Ed. & Pub., 86 Ghaem Magham Farahani Ave., Teheran, Iran.

610   JA   ISSN 0002-368X
AKITA JOURNAL OF RURAL MEDICINE/AKITA-KEN NOSON IGAKKAI ZASSHI. 1954. irreg. 1000 Yen($3.) Akita Association of Rural Medicine - Akita-ken Noson Igakkai, c/o Akita-ken Kosei Nogyo Kyodo Kumiai Rengokai, 3 Omachi, Akita-shi 010, Japan. Ed. Masakazu Tatsumi, M. D. adv.; abstr.; charts; illus.; stat.; cum.index.

AKTUELLE ERNAEHRUNGSMEDIZIN; Klinik und Praxis. see *NUTRITION AND DIETETICS*

615.89   GW   ISSN 0340-3130
AKUPUNKTUR: THEORIE UND PRAXIS. 1973. q. DM.65 (students DM.49). (Deutsche Aerztegesellschaft fuer Akupunktur e.V.) Medizinisch-Literarische Verlagsgesellschaft mbH, Postfach 1151-1152, 3110 Uelzen 1, Germany. TEL 0581-808151. FAX 0581-808158. TELEX 91326-AZD. Ed. Dr. R. Pothmann. adv.; bk.rev.; circ. 5,200. (back issues avail.) **Indexed:** Excerp.Med.
  Description: Articles on scientific research in acupuncture. Includes lists of courses and events.

615.89   GW   ISSN 0172-9322
DER AKUPUNKTURARZT - AURIKULOTHERAPEUT. 1980. q. DM.79. (Deutsche Akademie fuer Akupunktur und Aurikulo-Medizin) Friedr. Vieweg und Sohn Verlagsgesellschaft mbH, Postfach 5829, 6200 Wiesbaden, Germany. TEL 0611-160230. FAX 0611-160229. TELEX 4186928-VWVD. Ed. Dr. F.R. Bahr. adv.; bk.rev. (back issues avail.)

610   US   ISSN 0738-4947
ALABAMA MEDICINE. 1931. m. $30. Medical Association of the State of Alabama, 19 S. Jackson St., Montgomery, AL 36104. TEL 205-263-6441. Ed. Dr. Claude R. Brown, Jr. adv.; bk.rev.; bibl.; illus.; index; circ. 4,600. **Indexed:** Chem.Abstr., Excerp.Med., Ind.Med., INIS Atomind., Rev.Med.& Vet.Mycol.
—BLDSC shelfmark: 0786.522920.
  Formerly: Medical Association of the State of Alabama. Journal (ISSN 0025-7044)

610   US   ISSN 0002-4414
ALAMEDA-CONTRA COSTA MEDICAL ASSOCIATION. BULLETIN. 1945. m. membership. Alameda-Contra Costa Medical Association, 6230 Claremont Ave., Oakland, CA 94618. TEL 510-654-5383. FAX 510-654-8959. Ed. Dr. Julien M. Goodman. adv.; circ. 2,950.

610   US   ISSN 0002-4538
ALASKA MEDICINE. 1959. q. $30. Alaska State Medical Association, American Society for Circumpolar Health, 4107 Laurel St., Anchorage, AK 99508. TEL 907-562-2662. FAX 907-561-2063. Ed. Donald Rogers. adv.; index; circ. 1,400. (reprint service avail. from UMI)

610   UA   ISSN 1010-6324
ALEXANDRIA FACULTY OF MEDICINE BULLETIN. (Text in English) 1965. q. £E50. University of Alexandria, Faculty of Medicine, 22 Sharia al-Gaish, Al-Shatby, Alexandria, Egypt. Ed. Nahmoud Naim. bibl.; illus. **Indexed:** Biol.Abstr., Chem.Abstr., Soils & Fert.

610   UA   ISSN 0516-5849
ALEXANDRIA MEDICAL JOURNAL. (Text in Arabic, English, French) 1955. q. Alexandria Medical Association, 4 G. Carducci St., Alexandria, Egypt. Ed. Amin Rida. circ. 1,500. **Indexed:** Biol.Abstr., C.I.S. Abstr., Excerp.Med., Nutr.Abstr.

612 574   DK   ISSN 0105-3639
                CODEN: ABSYB2
ALFRED BENZON SYMPOSIUM. PROCEEDINGS. 1969. irreg. price varies. Munksgaard International Publishers Ltd., Journals Division, 35 Noerre Soegade, P.O. Box 2148, DK-1016 Copenhagen K, Denmark. TEL 33-127030. FAX 33-129387. TELEX 19431-MUNKS-DK. (Dist. in the U.S. by: Yearbook Medical Publishers, Inc., 200 N. LaSalle St., Chicago, IL 60601-1080) **Indexed:** Biol.Abstr., Chem.Abstr.
—BLDSC shelfmark: 0786.991000.

610   AE
ALGERIE MEDICALE. 1964. 2/yr. Union Medicale Algerienne, 3 bd. Zirout Youcef, Algiers, Algeria. adv.; circ. 3,000. **Indexed:** Biol.Abstr.

610   IT   ISSN 0392-9116
ALGOLOGIA. (Includes supplements) (Text in Italian; summaries in English and Italian) 1982. s-a. L.30000. Istituto per lo Studio e la Terapia del Dolore (I.S.T.D.), Via del Pergolino 4-6, 50139 Florence, Italy. TEL 055-416081. Ed. Pierluigi Zucchi. adv.; bk.rev.; charts; illus.; circ. 5,000. (back issues avail.) **Indexed:** Ind.Med., Ref.Zh.
—BLDSC shelfmark: 0787.328000.
  Description: Features worldwide research papers on the study of pain. Covers neurology, psychoanalysis and cardiology.

610   US   ISSN 0098-3772
ALLEGHENY COUNTY MEDICAL SOCIETY. BULLETIN. 1911. s-m. (except July and Aug.) $35 to profit organizations; non-profit organizations $25. Allegheny County Medical Society, 713 Ridge Ave., Pittsburgh, PA 15212. TEL 412-321-5030. FAX 412-321-5323. Ed. Dr. Jack E. Wilberger. adv.; bk.rev.; charts; illus.; index; circ. 3,400 (paid); 3,400 (controlled) 90,031. (back issues avail.)

616.07   GW   ISSN 0172-7249
DER ALLGEMEINARZT. q. DM.72 (students DM.45). (Fachverbandes Deutscher Allgemeinarzte e.V.) Verlag Kirchheim und Co. GmbH, Kaiserstr. 41, Postfach 2524, 6500 Mainz, Germany. TEL 06131-671081. Ed.Bd. adv.; charts; illus.

610   GW   ISSN 0257-3199
ALLGEMEINMEDIZIN; Zeitschrift fuer Forschung und Methodik in der hausaerztlichen Primaerversorgung. 1985. 4/yr. DM.128($82) (Societas Internationalis Medicinae Generalis) Springer-Verlag, Heidelberger Platz 3, D-1000 Berlin 33, Germany. TEL 030-8207-1. (Subscr. to: Journal Fulfillment Services, Springer-Verlag New York, Inc., 44 Hartz Way, Secaucus, NJ 07094) Eds. M. Kohle, E. Hesse. (also avail. in microform from UMI; back issues avail.; reprint service avail. from ISI) **Indexed:** Excerp.Med.
  Description: Research and methodology in general practice.

ALLIANCE (CHARLESTON). see *COLLEGE AND ALUMNI*

610 574   US   ISSN 0589-1019
R856   CODEN: CEMBAD
ALLIANCE FOR ENGINEERING IN MEDICINE AND BIOLOGY. PROCEEDINGS OF THE ANNUAL CONFERENCE. vol. 1, covering 12th conference, 1959. a. $35 to non-members; members $28. Alliance for Engineering in Medicine & Biology, 1101 Connecticut Ave., N.W., Ste. 700, Washington, DC 20036. TEL 202-857-1199. circ. 1,500. **Indexed:** Chem.Abstr., Eng.Ind.

ALLIED HEALTH EDUCATION DIRECTORY. see
EDUCATION — Guides To Schools And Colleges

ALLIED HEALTH EDUCATION NEWSLETTER. see
EDUCATION

MEDICAL SCIENCES   3073

ALZHEIMER'S ASSOCIATION NEWSLETTER. see
GERONTOLOGY AND GERIATRICS

610   US   ISSN 0897-554X
AMBULATORY MEDICINE LETTER. 1988. s-m. $75. J.B. Lippincott Co., E. Washington Sq., Philadelphia, PA 19105. TEL 215-238-4200. (Subscr. to: Downville Pike, Rte. 3, Box 20-B, Hagerstown, MD 21740)
  Description: Devoted exclusively to summarizing and interpreting the latest advances in outpatient medicine.

610   US   ISSN 0893-7400
AMERICAN ACADEMY OF PHYSICIAN ASSISTANTS. JOURNAL. 1988. 10/yr. $35 to individuals (foreign $50); institutions $52 (foreign $67). Mosby - Year Book, Inc. (Subsidiary of: Times Mirror Company), 11830 Westline Industrial Dr., St. Louis, MO 63146. TEL 800-325-4117. FAX 314-432-1380. TELEX 44-2402. Ed. Leslie A. Kole. adv.; bk.rev.; abstr.; charts; illus.; circ. 25,782. (also avail. in microform from UMI; back issues avail.)
—BLDSC shelfmark: 4683.732500.
  Description: Focuses on the clinical conditions seen in the primary care and specialty settings where physician assistants practice.
  Refereed Serial

610   US   ISSN 8756-6095
AMERICAN ASSOCIATION OF BLOOD BANKS. NEWS BRIEFS. 1981. m. membership only. American Association of Blood Banks, 1117 N. 19th St., Ste. 600, Arlington, VA 22209. TEL 703-528-8200. FAX 703-527-8036. Ed. John F. Horrell. circ. 10,000.

610   US   ISSN 0270-2673
AMERICAN ASSOCIATION OF TISSUE BANKS NEWSLETTER. 1976. q. membership. American Association of Tissue Banks, 1350 Beverly Rd., Ste. 220A, McLean, VA 22101. TEL 703-827-9582. FAX 703-356-2198. Ed. J. Mowe. circ. 1,000 (controlled).

610   US   ISSN 0272-9741
R729.5.S6
AMERICAN BOARD OF MEDICAL SPECIALTIES. ANNUAL REPORT & REFERENCE HANDBOOK. 1970. a. free. American Board of Medical Specialties, One Rotary Center, Ste. 805, Evanston, IL 60201. TEL 708-491-9091. FAX 708-328-3596. Ed. Dr. J. Lee Dockery. circ. 6,000.
  Formerly: American Board of Medical Specialties. Annual Report (ISSN 0146-5872)

610
AMERICAN BOARD OF PRACTICE. JOURNAL. 6/yr. Massachusetts Medical Society, 1440 Main St., Waltham, MA 02154. TEL 617-893-3800. FAX 617-893-0413. Ed. John Geyman. circ. 39,000.

616.98   US   ISSN 0065-7778
                CODEN: TACCAN
AMERICAN CLINICAL AND CLIMATOLOGICAL ASSOCIATION. TRANSACTIONS. 1881. a. $35. American Clinical and Climatological Association, c/o James C. Allen, M.D., Sec.-Treas., Medical University of South Carolina, Rm. 803CSB, 171 Ashley Ave., Charleston, SC 29425. TEL 803-792-2914. circ. 500. **Indexed:** Biol.Abstr., Excerp.Med., Ind.Med.

610
AMERICAN COLLEGE OF MEDICAL QUALITY NEWSLETTER. 1973. m. $70 to libraries; others $75. American College of Medical Quality, 1531 S. Tamiani Trail, Ste. 703, Venice, FL 34292. TEL 813-497-3340. FAX 813-497-5573. Ed. Ralph H. Rosenblum. adv.; bk.rev.; circ. 1,700. (tabloid format; back issues avail.)
  Formerly: American College of Utilization Review Physicians Newsletter.
  Description: Covers quality assurance, utilization review, risk management, cost containment, seminar announcements, and news briefs.

610   US   ISSN 0279-9529
AMERICAN COLLEGE OF PHYSICIANS OBSERVER. 1981. m. $12. American College of Physicians, Independence Mall W., Sixth St. at Race, Philadelphia, PA 19106. TEL 215-351-2400. Ed. Robert Spanier. adv.; circ. 53,000 (controlled). (tabloid format)

AMERICAN COLLEGE OF TOXICOLOGY. JOURNAL. PART A. see *ENVIRONMENTAL STUDIES — Toxicology And Environmental Safety*

MEDICAL SCIENCES

AMERICAN COLLEGE OF TOXICOLOGY. JOURNAL. PART B; acute toxicity data. see PHARMACY AND PHARMACOLOGY

610 US ISSN 0002-838X
R11
AMERICAN FAMILY PHYSICIAN. 1950. m. $60 (foreign $80) to individuals; institutions $75 (foreign $95); students, residents $40 (foreign $60). American Academy of Family Physicians, 8880 Ward Pkwy., Kansas City, MO 64114. TEL 816-333-9700. FAX 816-822-0580. adv.; bk.rev.; charts; illus.; mkt.; pat.; tr.lit.; cum.index every 6 mos.; circ. 148,000. (also avail. in microfilm from UMI; reprint service avail. from UMI) **Indexed:** A.D.& D., Adol.Ment.Hlth.Abstr., Bus.Ind., C.I.S. Abstr., Chem.Abstr., Curr.Cont., Dent.Ind., Dok.Arbeitsmed., Excerp.Med., FAMLI, Gen.Sci.Ind., Helminthol.Abstr., Hlth.Ind., Ind.Med., Ind.Sci.Rev., Med.Care Rev., NRN, Nutr.Abstr., Protozool.Abstr., Rev.Med.& Vet.Mycol., Sci.Cit.Ind., Tr.& Indus.Ind.
●Also available online. Vendor(s): BRS, Mead Data Central.
Also available on CD-ROM.
—BLDSC shelfmark: 0814.700000.
Formerly (until 1970): G P (ISSN 0016-3600)
Description: Provides continuing medical education for doctors involved with primary care.
Refereed Serial

614.8 340 US
AMERICAN GROUP PRACTICE ASSOCIATION. EXECUTIVE NEWS SERVICE. 1980. 22/yr. membership. American Group Practice Association, 1422 Duke St., Alexandria, VA 22314. TEL 703-838-0033. FAX 703-548-1890. Ed. Brent Miller. circ. 2,200. (looseleaf format; back issues avail.)
Description: Current federal legislation and regulations and health law affecting physicians, hospitals and clinics with emphasis on Medicare reimbursement, health politics, and quality of care.

610 US ISSN 0098-2377
RA977
AMERICAN GROUP PRACTICE ASSOCIATION DIRECTORY. 1952. a. $125. American Group Practice Association, 1422 Duke St., Alexandria, VA 22314. TEL 703-838-0033. FAX 703-548-1890. adv.; circ. 2,500.
Formerly: American Association of Medical Clinics. Directory (ISSN 0569-2679)

610 US
RA976
AMERICAN HEALTH INFORMATION MANAGEMENT ASSOCIATION. JOURNAL. 1929. m. $60. American Health Information Management Association, 919 N. Michigan Ave., Ste. 1400, Chicago, IL 60611-1601. TEL 312-787-2672. adv.; bk.rev.; charts; illus.; stat.; index; circ. 31,000. **Indexed:** Abstr.Health Care Manage.Stud., CINAHL, Curr.Cont., Excerp.Med, Hosp.Lit.Ind.
Former titles: American Medical Record Association. Journal (ISSN 0273-9976); Medical Record News (ISSN 0025-7486)

610 534 US
AMERICAN INSTITUTE OF ULTRASOUND IN MEDICINE. ANNUAL SCIENTIFIC CONFERENCE. PROCEEDINGS. a. membership. American Institute of Ultrasound in Medicine, Attn. James Packer, Ph.D., 11200 Rockville Pike, Ste. 205, Rockville, MD 20852-3139. TEL 301-881-2486. FAX 301-881-7303. adv.; bk.rev.; circ. 8,000.
Formerly: American Institute of Ultrasound in Medicine. Annual Scientific Conference. Program (ISSN 0065-8871)

AMERICAN INTERNATIONAL JOURNAL OF ARTS, SCIENCES, ENGINEERING AND MEDICINE. see ART

610 US ISSN 0091-3960
CODEN: AJAPB9
AMERICAN JOURNAL OF ACUPUNCTURE. 1972. q. $60 to individuals; institutions $90. 1840 41st Ave., Ste. 102, Box 610, Capitola, CA 95010. TEL 408-475-1700. FAX 408-475-1700. adv.; bk.rev.; abstr.; charts; illus.; circ. 4,800. (back issues avail.; reprint service avail. from ISI) **Indexed:** Biol.Abstr., Curr.Cont., Dent.Abstr., Excerp.Med., Ind.Vet., Med. Care Rev., Oral Res.Abstr., Pig News & Info., Sci.Cit.Ind., Vet.Bull.
—BLDSC shelfmark: 0820.945000.
Description: Explains the theoretical and practical basis of specific acupuncture and electroacupuncture techniques used in diagnosis and treatment of every conceivable condition.

610 US
AMERICAN JOURNAL OF ALZHEIMER'S CARE AND RELATED DISORDERS AND RESEARCH. 1986. bi-m. $48 to individuals; institutions $58; libraries $68. Prime National Publishing Corp., 470 Boston Post Rd., Weston, MA 02193. TEL 617-899-4311. FAX 617-899-4361. Ed. Nancy Stone Hindlian. adv.; bk.rev.; abstr.; bibl.; charts; illus.; circ. 3,000. (back issues avail.) **Indexed:** Abstr.Soc.Geront.
Formerly: American Journal of Alzheimer's Care and Related Disorders (ISSN 0888-4897)
Description: Covers Alzheimer's disease for medical professionals.
Refereed Serial

610 US ISSN 0192-415X
R601 CODEN: AJCMBA
AMERICAN JOURNAL OF CHINESE MEDICINE. 1973. 3/yr. (in 4 vols.). $75. Institute for Advanced Research in Asian Science and Medicine, Box 555, Garden City, NY 11530. TEL 516-292-2767. FAX 516-248-0930. Ed. Dr. Frederick F. Kao. bk.rev. **Indexed:** Biol.Abstr., Curr.Adv.Ecol.Sci., Curr.Cont., Excerp.Med., Helminthol.Abstr., Ind.Med., Med. Care Rev., Psychol.Abstr.
Former titles (until 1978): Comparative Medicine East and West (ISSN 0147-2917); (until 1977): American Journal of Chinese Medicine (ISSN 0090-2942)
Description: Covers basic science and clinical research in indigenous medical techniques and therapeutic procedures, medicinal plants, and traditional medicine.

AMERICAN JOURNAL OF CLINICAL NUTRITION; a journal reporting the practical application of our world-wide knowledge of nutrition. see NUTRITION AND DIETETICS

616.07 574.2 US ISSN 0002-9173
RB1 CODEN: AJCPAI
AMERICAN JOURNAL OF CLINICAL PATHOLOGY. (Supplement avail.: Pathology Patterns) 1931. m. $105 to individuals (foreign $150); institutions $140(foreign $175). (American Society of Clinical Pathologists) J.B. Lippincott Co., E. Washington Sq., Philadelphia, PA 19105. TEL 215-238-4200. Ed. Dr. Mark R. Wick. adv.; illus.; index, cum.index; circ. 15,000. (also avail. in microform from UMI) **Indexed:** Biol.Abstr., Biotech.Abstr., C.I.S. Abstr., Cadscan, Chem.Abstr., Curr.Adv.Cancer Res., Curr.Adv.Ecol.Sci., Curr.Adv.Genetics & Molec.Biol., Curr.Cont., Dairy Sci.Abstr., Dent.Ind., Dok.Arbeitsmed., Excerp.Med., Helminthol.Abstr., Hosp.Lit.Ind., Ind.Med., Ind.Sci.Rev., Ind.Vet., INIS Atomind., Lead Abstr., Protozool.Abstr., Rev.Med.& Vet.Mycol., Sci.Cit.Ind., SSCI, Zincscan.
—BLDSC shelfmark: 0824.000000.
Description: Helps pathologists and other clinical laboratory scientists keep their professional knowledge current. Publishes original investigations and observation in clinical pathology, the articles cover a broad spectrum of subspecialty topics.
Refereed Serial

610 US ISSN 0002-9262
CODEN: AJEPAS
AMERICAN JOURNAL OF EPIDEMIOLOGY. 1921. s-m. (2 vols./yr.). $190. (Society for Epidemiologic Research) Johns Hopkins University, School of Hygiene and Public Health, 2007 E. Monument St., Baltimore, MD 21205. TEL 301-955-3441. Ed. Moyes Szklo. adv.; illus.; index, cum.index; circ. 5,800. (also avail. in microform from MIM; microfilm from WWS) **Indexed:** Abstr.Health Care Manage.Stud., Abstr.Hyg., Bibl.Dev.Med.& Child Neur., Biol.Abstr., Biol.Dig., Biostat., C.I.S. Abstr., Chem.Abstr., Curr.Adv.Cancer Res., Curr.Adv.Ecol.Sci., Curr.Cont., Dairy Sci.Abstr., Dok.Arbeitsmed., Excerp.Med., Helminthol.Abstr., Ind.Med., Ind.Sci.Rev., Ind.Vet., INIS Atomind., Lab.Haz.Bull., NRN, Nutr.Abstr., Poult.Abstr., Protozool.Abstr., Rev.Appl.Entomol., Rev.Med.& Vet.Mycol., Rev.Plant Path, Risk Abstr., Sci.Cit.Ind., Small Anim.Abstr., So.Pac.Per.Ind., SSCI, Trop.Dis.Bull., Vet.Bull., W.R.C.Inf.
—BLDSC shelfmark: 0824.600000.
Former titles: American Journal of Hygiene; Journal of Hygiene (ISSN 0096-5294)
Refereed Serial

AMERICAN JOURNAL OF HYPERTENSION. see MEDICAL SCIENCES — Cardiovascular Diseases

AMERICAN JOURNAL OF LAW & MEDICINE. see LAW

AMERICAN JOURNAL OF MEDICAL GENETICS. see BIOLOGY — Genetics

610 US ISSN 0002-9343
RC60 CODEN: AJMEAZ
AMERICAN JOURNAL OF MEDICINE. 1946. m. $57 to individuals (foreign $125); institutions $100 (foreign $150)(effective Mar. 1992). Cahners Publishing Company (New York), Medical-Health Care Group, Yorke Medical Journals (Subsidiary of: Reed International PLC), Division of Reed Publishing (USA) Inc., 249 W. 17th St., New York, NY 10011-5301. TEL 212-463-6460. FAX 212-463-6470. (Subscr. to: Box 173306, Denver, CO 80217-3306. TEL 800-662-7776) Eds. Dr. J. Claud Bennett, Monica Schmidt. adv.; bibl.; illus.; index; circ. 57,000. (also avail. in microform from RPI; back issues avail.) **Indexed:** Abstr.Hyg., Abstr.Inter.Med., Behav.Med.Abstr., Biol.Abstr., Biol.Dig., Biostat., Biotech.Abstr., C.I.S. Abstr., Chem.Abstr., Curr.Adv.Biochem., Curr.Adv.Cancer Res., Curr.Adv.Cell & Devel.Biol., Curr.Adv.Ecol.Sci., Curr.Adv.Genetics & Molec.Biol., Curr.Cont., Dairy Sci.Abstr., Dent.Ind., Dok.Arbeitsmed., Excerp.Med., Helminthol.Abstr., I.P.A., Ind.Med., Ind.Sci.Rev., INIS Atomind., Lead Abstr., Nutr.Abstr., Protozool.Abstr., Rev.Plant Path., Risk Abstr., Sci.Cit.Ind., Telegen, Trop.Dis.Bull.
●Also available online. Vendor(s): BRS, Mead Data Central.
—BLDSC shelfmark: 0828.100000.
Description: Contains the original output of clinical investigators worldwide. Includes case reports and clinical-pathologic conferences, symposia, and essays and editorials on medicine, science and society.
Refereed Serial

615.85 US ISSN 0272-9490
RM735.A1 CODEN: AJOTAM
AMERICAN JOURNAL OF OCCUPATIONAL THERAPY. 1947. 12/yr. $25 to individuals; institutions $100; foreign $110. American Occupational Therapy Association, Inc., 1383 Piccard Dr., Box 1725, Rockville, MD 20850-0882. TEL 301-948-9626. FAX 301-948-5512. Ed. Elaine Viseltear. adv.; bk.rev.; abstr.; bibl.; charts; illus.; index; circ. 45,000. (also avail. in microform from UMI) **Indexed:** Abstr.Soc.Geront., ASSIA, Bibl.Dev.Med.& Child Neur., Biol.Abstr., C.I.J.E., CLOA, Curr.Cont., Dent.Ind., Dok.Arbeitsmed., Except.Child.Educ.Abstr., Excerp.Med., Hosp.Lit.Ind., Ind.Med., Psychol.Abstr., Rehabil.Lit., SSCI.
—BLDSC shelfmark: 0828.750000.
Former titles (until 1978): A J O T: The American Journal of Occupational Therapy (ISSN 0161-326X); (until 1977): American Journal of Occupational Therapy (ISSN 0002-9386)
Refereed Serial

616.07 US ISSN 0002-9440
RB1 CODEN: AJPAA4
AMERICAN JOURNAL OF PATHOLOGY. 1901. m. $145 to individuals (foreign $205); institutions $205 (foreign $265). (American Association of Pathologists) J.B. Lippincott Co., E. Washington Sq., Philadelphia, PA 19105. TEL 215-238-4200. Ed. Vincent T. Marchesi, M.D. adv.; illus.; circ. 5,218. (also avail. in microform from UMI) **Indexed:** Biol.Abstr., Biol.Dig., Biotech.Abstr., Chem.Abstr., Curr.Adv.Cancer Res., Curr.Adv.Cell & Devel.Biol., Curr.Adv.Ecol.Sci., Curr.Adv.Genetics & Molec.Biol., Curr.Cont., Dok.Arbeitsmed., Excerp.Med., Helminthol.Abstr., Ind.Med., Ind.Sci.Rev., Ind.Vet., INIS Atomind., Maize Abstr., Poult.Abstr., Protozool.Abstr., Sci.Cit.Ind., SSCI, Vet.Bull.
—BLDSC shelfmark: 0829.600000.
Formerly: Journal of Medical Research (ISSN 0097-3599)
Refereed Serial

615.8 US ISSN 0894-9115
RM735.A1 CODEN: AJPREP
AMERICAN JOURNAL OF PHYSICAL MEDICINE AND REHABILITATION. 1921. bi-m. $55 to individuals; institutions $87. (Association of Academic Physiatrists) Williams & Wilkins, 428 E. Preston St., Baltimore, MD 21202. TEL 301-528-4000. FAX 301-528-4312. Ed. Dr. Ernest W. Johnson. adv.; bk.rev.; charts; illus.; tr.lit.; circ. 3,400. (also avail. in microform; microfilm from WWS) **Indexed:** Bibl.Dev.Med.& Child Neur., Bioeng.Abstr., Biol.Abstr., Chem.Abstr., CINAHL, Curr.Cont., Ergon.Abstr., Excerp.Med., Ind.Med., INIS Atomind., Int.Sci.Rev., Nutr.Abstr., Psychol.Abstr., Rehabil.Lit., Sci.Abstr., Sci.Cit.Ind., Sportsearch (1988-).
●Also available online. Vendor(s): Mead Data Central.
—BLDSC shelfmark: 0832.160000.
  Formerly: American Journal of Physical Medicine (ISSN 0002-9491)
  Description: Examines acute problems of rehabilitation, their treatment, new methods and equipment.
  Refereed Serial

AMERICAN JOURNAL OF PHYSIOLOGY. see *BIOLOGY — Physiology*

610 614.8 US ISSN 0749-3797
RA421 CODEN: AJPMEA
AMERICAN JOURNAL OF PREVENTIVE MEDICINE. 1984. bi-m. $70 to individuals; institutions $140. (American College of Preventive Medicine) Oxford University Press, Journals, 200 Madison Ave., New York, NY 10016. TEL 212-679-7300. FAX 212-725-2972. TELEX 6859654. (Subscr. to: Journals Fulfillment, 2001 Evans Rd, Cary, NC 27513. TEL 919-677-0977) (Co-sponsor: Association of Teachers of Preventive Medicine) adv.; bk.rev.; charts; illus.; circ. 3,000. (back issues avail.) **Indexed:** Abstr.Health Care Manage.Stud., Curr.Cont., Excerp.Med., Ind.Med., NRN.
—BLDSC shelfmark: 0834.370000.
  Description: Original articles and correspondence on all aspects of practice, teaching, and research in preventive medicine.
  Refereed Serial

AMERICAN JOURNAL OF SURGICAL PATHOLOGY. see *MEDICAL SCIENCES — Surgery*

610 US ISSN 0002-9629
R11 CODEN: AJMSA9
AMERICAN JOURNAL OF THE MEDICAL SCIENCES. 1820. m. $90 to individuals (foreign $110); institutions $110 (foreign $170). J.B. Lippincott Co., E. Washington Sq., Philadelphia, PA 19105. TEL 215-238-4200. Ed. Suzanne Oparil. bibl.; illus.; s-a. index; circ. 2,391. (also avail. in microform from UMI;PMC) **Indexed:** Abstr.Hyg., Biol.Abstr., Chem.Abstr., Curr.Adv.Ecol.Sci., Ergon.Abstr., Excerp.Med., Helminthol.Abstr., I.P.A., Ind.Med., Ind.Sci.Rev., Ind.Vet., INIS Atomind., NRN, Nutr.Abstr., Sci.Cit.Ind., Small Anim.Abstr., Vet.Bull.
—BLDSC shelfmark: 0828.000000.
  Refereed Serial

615.8 US
AMERICAN JOURNAL OF THERAPY. 1974. m. $28. McMahon Publishing Co., 83 Peaceable St., West Redding, CT 06896. TEL 203-544-9343. (Subscr. to: 121 S. Gertrude Ave., Paramus, NJ 07652) Ed. Jack Phillips. (back issues avail.)
  Refereed Serial

610 US
AMERICAN MEDICAL ASSOCIATION. COUNCIL ON ETHICAL AND JUDICIAL AFFAIRS. CURRENT OPINIONS. 1981. irreg. $15. American Medical Association, Council on Ethical and Judicial Affairs, 515 N. State St., Chicago, IL 60610. TEL 312-464-0183. FAX 312-464-5834. Ed. David Orentlicher. circ. 20,000.
  Formerly: American Medical Association. Judicial Council. Current Opinions.

610 US
AMERICAN MEDICAL DIRECTORY. 1906. irreg., 31st ed., 1988. $495 for 4 vols. American Medical Association, 515 N. State St., Chicago, IL 60610. TEL 312-464-5000.
  Former titles: American Medical Directory of Physicians; American Medical Directory (ISSN 0065-9339)

610 US ISSN 0001-1843
AMERICAN MEDICAL NEWS. 1958. w. $60. American Medical Association, 515 N. State St., Chicago, IL 60610. TEL 312-464-0183. FAX 312-464-5834. Ed. Dick Walt. adv.; bk.rev.; charts; illus.; s-a. index; circ. 366,000. (also avail. in microform from UMI; microfiche) **Indexed:** Bus.Ind., Chic.Per.Ind., Hlth.Ind., Hosp.Lit.Ind., Med.Care Rev., MEDSOC, Tr.& Indus.Ind.
  Formerly: A M A News.

610 US ISSN 0098-8421
R15
AMERICAN MEDICAL WOMEN'S ASSOCIATION. JOURNAL. 1915. bi-m. $35. American Medical Women's Association, Inc., 801 N. Fairfax St., Ste. 400, Alexandria, VA 22314. TEL 703-838-0500. Ed. Dr. Kathryn E. McGoldrick. adv.; bk.rev.; bibl.; illus.; index; circ. 11,000. (also avail. in microform from UMI; reprint service avail. from UMI) **Indexed:** Biol.Abstr., Ind.Med., Stud.Wom.Abstr. **Key Title:** Journal of the American Medical Women's Association.
—BLDSC shelfmark: 4689.100000.
  Formerly: Woman Physician (ISSN 0002-7103)

610 US ISSN 0162-3907
AMERICAN PHYSICAL THERAPY ASSOCIATION. PROGRESS REPORT. 1972. 11/yr. $20 to non-members. American Physical Therapy Association, 1111 N. Fairfax St., Alexandria, VA 22314. TEL 703-684-2782. Ed. Ellen Woods. adv.; charts; illus.; stat; tr.lit.; circ. 50,584. (tabloid format; reprint service avail. from UMI)

AMERICAN REHABILITATION. see *SOCIAL SERVICES AND WELFARE*

616.132
AMERICAN SOCIETY OF HYPERTENSION. SYMPOSIUM SERIES. 1987. irreg., latest vol.3. price varies. Raven Press, 1185 Ave. of the Americas, New York, NY 10036. TEL 212-930-9500. FAX 212-869-3495.

610
AMP. 1920. m. $15. National Amputation Foundation, 12-45 150th St., Whitestone, NY 11357. TEL 718-767-0596. Ed. Don Sloss. adv.; bk.rev.; circ. 2,500.

610 SP ISSN 0569-9894
  CODEN: AANOA7
ANALES DE ANATOMIA. (Text in Spanish; summaries in English) 1952. 2/yr. $100. Universidad de Zaragoza, Facultad de Medicina, Departamento de Ciencias Morfologicas, E-50009, Zaragoza, Spain. TEL 010-34-76-359593. Ed. Jose Escobar Garcia. adv.; bk.rev. **Indexed:** Chem.Abstr., Excerp.Med.
—BLDSC shelfmark: 0887.900000.

610 SP ISSN 0003-2530
ANALES DEL INSTITUTO CORACHAN. * vol.23, 1971. q. free. Instituto Corachan, Buigas 19, Barcelona, Spain. adv.; bk.rev.; charts; illus.; stat. **Indexed:** Chem.Abstr., Excerp.Med.

610 AT ISSN 1033-8810
ANALGESIC GUIDELINES. 1988. biennial. Aus.$10. Victorian Medical Postgradute Foundation Inc., Therapeutic Committee, Chelsea House, Level 3, 55 Flemingron Rd., N. Melbourne, Vic. 3051, Australia. TEL 03-329-1566. FAX 03-326-5632. circ. 8,000.
  Description: Covers clinical aspects of the management of pain for doctors, nurses and pharmacists.

610 CI ISSN 0301-2255
ANALI KLINICKE BOLNICE "DR. M. STOJANOVIC". (Includes two monographic supplements per volume) (Text in Croatian; summaries in English) 1962. q. 10000 din.($20) to individuals; institutions 25000 Din. Klinicka Bolnica "Dr. M. Stojanovic" u Zagrebu, Vinogradska 29, 41000 Zagreb, Croatia. Ed. V Hudolin. adv.; bk.rev.; bibl.; illus.; circ. 1,000. **Indexed:** Biol.Abstr., Excerp.Med.
  Formerly: Anali Bolnice "Dr. M. Stojanovic".

610 SP ISSN 0212-4572
ANALISIS CLINICOS. (Supplement avail.: Actualidades en el Laboratorio Clinico (ISSN 0212-4564)) 1975. 8/yr. 7300 ptas.($100) (Asociacion Espanola de Farmaceuticos Analistas) Editorial Garsi, S.A., Londres, 17, 28028 Madrid, Spain. TEL 256-08-00. FAX 361-10-07. Ed. J.M. Guardiola Vicente. circ. 3,500.

MEDICAL SCIENCES 3075

ANATOMICAL RECORD. see *BIOLOGY*

ANATOMICAL SOCIETY OF INDIA. JOURNAL. see *BIOLOGY*

574.4 611 GW ISSN 0066-1562
  CODEN: VHAGAS
ANATOMISCHE GESELLSCHAFT. VERHANDLUNGEN. (Supplement to: Anatomischer Anzeiger) 1887. a. price varies. Gustav Fischer Verlag, Villengang 2, Postfach 176, 6900 Jena, Germany. TEL 27332. TELEX 588676. (reprint service avail. from ISI) **Indexed:** Biol.Abstr., Chem.Abstr., Excerp.Med., Ind.Med.
—BLDSC shelfmark: 9162.800000.

574.4 611 GW ISSN 0003-2786
QL801 CODEN: ANANAU
ANATOMISCHER ANZEIGER; Zentralblatt fuer die gesamte wissenschaftliche Anatomie. (Text in English, French and German; summaries in English) 1886. 6/yr. DM.550 (foreign DM.553). Gustav Fischer Verlag Jena, Villengang 2, Postfach 176, 6900 Jena, Germany. TEL 03778-27332. FAX 03778-22638. TELEX 18069-588676. Ed. G.-H. Schumacher. adv.; bk.rev.; bibl.; charts; illus.; index, cum.index: vols.1-100. (also avail. in microfilm from PMC; reprint service avail. from ISI) **Indexed:** Biol.Abstr., Chem.Abstr., Curr.Adv.Cell & Devel.Biol., Curr.Adv.Ecol.Sci., Curr.Cont., Dairy Sci.Abstr., Dent.Ind., Excerp.Med., Ind.Med., Ind.Sci.Rev., Ind.Vet., INIS Atomind., Ref.Zh., Sci.Cit.Ind., Vet.Bull.
—BLDSC shelfmark: 0899.000000.

ANATOMY AND EMBRYOLOGY. see *BIOLOGY — Physiology*

610 IT
ANCH'IO. 1978. m. free. Associazione Laziale Motulesi (A.L.M.), Via Laurentina 5, 00142 Rome, Italy. TEL 5406705. Ed. Carmello Pelle. illus.
  Description: Covers news and events for and about the handicapped.

610 II ISSN 0257-7941
R605
ANCIENT SCIENCE OF LIFE. (Text in English) 1981. q. Rs.140($37) International Institute of Ayurveda, P.B. No. 7102, Ramanathapuram, Coimbatore 641 045, India. TEL 23188. Ed. S. Vijayan. adv.; bk.rev.; circ. 2,000. **Indexed:** Forest.Abstr., Forest Prod.Abstr., Hort.Abstr., Rev.Med.& Vet.Mycol.
—BLDSC shelfmark: 0900.325500.
  Description: Publishes research papers on Ayurveda, the Indian system of medicine, and allied disciplines. Also acts as an interdisciplinary medium on all aspects of medical health care.

610 GW ISSN 0303-4569
  CODEN: ANDRDQ
ANDROLOGIA. (Text and summaries in English or German) 1969. bi-m. DM.223.50 (foreign DM.252). (Deutsche Gesellschaft fuer Andrologie) Blackwell Publishing Co., Meinekestr. 4, 1000 Berlin 15, Germany. Ed. Dr. C. Schirren. index; circ. 1,800. (reprint service avail. from UMI) **Indexed:** Anim.Breed.Abstr., Biol.Abstr., Biotech.Abstr., Chem.Abstr., Curr.Adv.Cell & Devel.Biol., Curr.Adv.Ecol.Sci., Curr.Adv.Genetics & Molec.Biol., Curr.Cont., Dok.Arbeitsmed., Excerp.Med., Ind.Med., Ind.Sci.Rev., Ind.Vet., Nutr.Abstr., Pig News & Info., Sci.Cit.Ind., Small Anim.Abstr.
—BLDSC shelfmark: 0900.443000.
  Formerly: Andrologie.

610 340 US ISSN 0738-1018
KF2910.A53
ANESTHESIOLOGY MALPRACTICE REPORTER. 1981. bi-m. $78. Public Reporting Services, Inc., 496A Hudson St., Ste. 424, New York, NY 10014. TEL 212-989-8303. Ed. Natalie Kaplan.

610 CC ISSN 1000-1492
ANHUI YIKE DAXUE XUEBAO/ANHUI UNIVERSITY OF MEDICAL SCIENCES. JOURNAL. (Text in Chinese) q. Anhui Yike Daxue - Anhui University of Medical Sciences, Meishan Lu, Hefei, Anhui 230032, People's Republic of China. TEL 336600. Ed. Gong Xiyu.

610 CC ISSN 1000-0399
ANHUI YIXUE/ANHUI MEDICAL SCIENCES. (Text in Chinese) bi-m. Anhui Yixue Qingbao Yanjiusuo - Anhui Institute of Medical Information, 1 Yonghong Lu, Hefei, Anhui 230061, People's Republic of China. TEL 277688. Ed. Lu Yayi.

MEDICAL SCIENCES

610   CC   ISSN 1000-2219
ANHUI ZHONGYI XUEYUAN XUEBAO/ANHUI INSTITUTE OF TRADITIONAL CHINESE MEDICINE. JOURNAL. (Text in Chinese) q. Anhui Zhongyi Xueyuan - Anhui Institute of Traditional Chinese Medicine, Meishan Lu, Hefei, Anhui 230038, People's Republic of China. TEL 331006. Ed. Liu Zhongben.

ANIMALS FOR RESEARCH - A DIRECTORY OF SOURCES. see BIOLOGY — Zoology

610   TU   ISSN 0365-8104
ANKARA UNIVERSITESI. TIP FAKULTESI. MECMUASI.* (Supplement avail. (ISSN 0365-2238)) (Text in Turkish; summaries in English) q. free. Ankara Universitesi, Tip Fakultesi - Anakara University, Faculty of Medicine, Tandogan, Ankara, Turkey. FAX 4-2236370. circ. 1,000. **Indexed:** Biol.Abstr., Chem.Abstr., Helminthol.Abstr., Nutr.Abstr.

610   PL   ISSN 0066-1945
                                      CODEN: RPMKAA
ANNALES ACADEMIAE MEDICAE STETINENSIS/ROCZNIKI POMORSKIEJ AKADEMII MEDYCZNEJ W SZCZECINIE. (Supplements avail.) 1951. a. price varies. (Pomorska Akademia Medyczna w Szczecinie) Panstwowy Zaklad Wydawnictw Lekarskich, Ul. Dluga 38-40, Warsaw 1, Poland. TEL 31-42-81. (Dist. by: Ars Polona-Ruch, Krakowskie Przedmiescie 7, 00-068 Warsaw, Poland) **Indexed:** Dent.Ind., Ind.Med.

610   FI   ISSN 0066-1996
ANNALES ACADEMIAE SCIENTIARUM FENNICAE. SERIES A, V: MEDICA. (Text in English, French, German) 1945. irreg. price varies. Suomalainen Tiedeakatemia - Academia Scientiarum Fennica, Mariankatu 5, 00170 Helsinki, Finland. (Orders to: The Bookstore Tiedekirja, Kirkkokatu 14, SF-00170 Helsinki, Finland) Ed. Matti Bergstrom. circ. 400. (also avail. in microform; back issues avail.; reprint service avail. from UMI) **Indexed:** Biol.Abstr., Bull.Signal, Chem.Abstr., Curr.Adv.Ecol.Sci., Excerp.Med., Ind.Med., INIS Atomind., Ref.Zh.

610   BE   ISSN 0003-3863
ANNALES COLLEGII MEDICI ANTVERPIENSIS. 1946. m. (10/yr.). 350 Fr. Koninklijke Geneeskundige Kring van Antwerpen, Louizastraat 8, 2000 Antwerp, Belgium. adv.; bk.rev.; circ. 1,000.
—BLDSC shelfmark: 0914.690000.

ANNALES DE BIOLOGIE CLINIQUE. see BIOLOGY

615.8   FR   ISSN 0302-427X
ANNALES DE KINESITHERAPIE. 1974. 8/yr. 97 ECU($121) (Societe de Kinesitherapie) Masson, 120 bd. St. Germain, 75280 Paris Cedex 06, France. TEL 1-46-34-21-60. FAX 1-45-87-29-99. TELEX 202 671 F. Ed. E. Viel. adv.; bk.rev.; charts; illus.; circ. 3,800. (also avail. in microform from UMI; reprint service avail. from ISI) **Indexed:** Biol.Abstr., Curr.Cont., Sportsearch (1974-).
—BLDSC shelfmark: 0981.040000.
Formed by the merger of: Revue de Kinesitherapie (ISSN 0035-1172); Journal de Kinesitherapie (ISSN 0021-7751)
Description: Focuses on physical therapy and rehabilitation.

616.026   FR   ISSN 0003-410X
                                      CODEN: AMDIBO
ANNALES DE MEDECINE INTERNE. 1848. 8/yr. 23 ECU($295) (typically set in Jan.). (Societe Medicale des Hopitaux de Paris) Masson, 120 bd. Saint-Germain, 75280 Paris Cedex 06, France. TEL 1-46-34-21-60. FAX 1-45-87-29-99. TELEX 202 671 F. Ed.Bd. adv.; index; circ. 1,500. (also avail. in microform from UMI; reprint service avail. from ISI) **Indexed:** Biol.Abstr., Bull.Signal., C.I.S. Abstr., Chem.Abstr., Curr.Cont., Dent.Ind., Excerp.Med., Helminthol.Abstr., Ind.Med., INIS Atomind., Protozool.Abstr., Rev.Med.& Vet.Mycol., Rev.Plant Path., Sci.Cit.Ind.
—BLDSC shelfmark: 0981.800000.
Supersedes: Societe Medicale des Hopitaux de Paris. Bulletins et Memoires.

ANNALES DE PATHOLOGIE. see BIOLOGY

615.8 362   FR   ISSN 0168-6054
                                      CODEN: ARMPEQ
ANNALES DE READAPTATION ET DE MEDECINE PHYSIQUE. (Text mainly in French; summaries in English, French) 1957. 6/yr. 945 F.($178) (foreign 1050 F.)(effective 1992). (Societe Francaise de Reeducation Fonctionnelle de Readaptation et de Medecine Physique) Editions Scientifiques Elsevier, 29, rue Buffon, 75005 Paris, France. TEL 47-07-11-22. FAX 43-36-80-93. TELEX 202 400 F. (Subscr. in U.S. and Canada to: Elsevier Science Publishing Co., Inc., Box 882, Madison Sq. Sta., New York, NY 10159. TEL 212-989-5800) Ed. M. Perrigot. adv.; bk.rev.; index; circ. 3,000. (also avail. in microform from RPI) **Indexed:** Biol.Abstr., Bull.Signal., Excerp.Med.
—BLDSC shelfmark: 0995.170000.
Formerly (until 1983): Annales de Medecine Physique (ISSN 0402-4621)
Description: Publishes clinical, paraclinical and basic research papers pertaining to all aspects of the medicine of readaptation and rehabilitation.
Refereed Serial

ANNALES MEDICO-PSYCHOLOGIQUES. see PSYCHOLOGY

610   PL   ISSN 0066-2240
B6   CODEN: AUMKAS
ANNALES UNIVERSITATIS MARIAE CURIE-SKLODOWSKA. SECTIO D. MEDICINA. (Text in English or Polish; summaries and table of contents in English) 1946. a. price varies. Uniwersytet Marii Curie-Sklodowskiej, Wydawnictwo, Pl. M. Curie-Sklodowskiej 5, 20-031 Lublin, Poland. TEL 48-81-375304. FAX 48-81-336699. TELEX 0643223. Ed. Stanislaw Bryc. circ. 600. **Indexed:** Biol.Abstr., Chem.Abstr., Curr.Adv.Ecol.Sci., Excerp.Med., Field Crop Abstr., Herb.Abstr., Ind.Med., Ind.Vet., INIS Atomind., Rev.Appl.Entomol., Vet.Bull.
—BLDSC shelfmark: 0958.995000.

610   GW   ISSN 0173-6973
ANNALES UNIVERSITATIS SARAVIENSIS. MEDICINAE. 1953-1976; resumed 1980. 2/yr. DM.35. (Universitaet des Saarlandes, Medizinische Fakultaet) Verlag Ermer KG, Postfach 1155, 6650 Homburg-Saar, Germany. TEL 06841-78186. FAX 06841-72257. Ed. E. Wenzel. adv.; bk.rev.; bibl.; charts; illus.; index; circ. 8,000. **Indexed:** Biol.Abstr., C.I.S. Abstr., Chem.Abstr., Excerp.Med., Ind.Med.
—BLDSC shelfmark: 0962.989000.
Formerly: Annales Universitatis Saraviensis. Reihe: Medizin (ISSN 0003-4533)

616.98   IT   ISSN 0003-4630
ANNALI DI MEDICINA NAVALE. (Text in Italian; summaries in English and Italian) 1895. 3/m. L.20000. Ministero Difensa - Marina, Lungo Tevere delle Navi, 00196 Rome, Italy. bk.rev.; circ. 500. **Indexed:** Abstr.Hyg., Biol.Abstr., C.I.S. Abstr., Chem.Abstr., Excerp.Med., Helminthol.Abstr., Ind.Med., INIS Atomind., Trop.Dis.Bull.
—BLDSC shelfmark: 1015.450000.
Description: Features items on military medicine.

617   SP   ISSN 0210-7465
ANNALS DE MEDICINA. 1878. m. (10/yr.). 4000 ptas. (effective Jan. 1991). (Academia de Ciencies Mediques de Catalunya i de Balears) Ediciones Doyma S.A., Travesera de Gracia, 17-21, 08021 Barcelona, Spain. TEL 200-07-11. FAX 209-11-36. TELEX 51963 INK E. Ed. Goncal Lloveras i Valles. adv.: page 140000 ptas.; trim 210 x 280; adv. contact: Ana Ma. Alfonso. bk.rev.; circ. 15,000. **Indexed:** Biol.Abstr., Nutr.Abstr.
Formed by the merger of: Anales de Medicina. Medicina (ISSN 0517-6824) & Anales de Medicina. Cirugia (ISSN 0517-6816) & Anales de Medicina. Especialidades (ISSN 0517-6832); Which were formerly (until 1972): Anales de Medicina (ISSN 0003-2514)
Description: Contains news of the activities and research of the academy.

616.07   US   ISSN 0883-6612
R726.5   CODEN: ABMEEH
ANNALS OF BEHAVIORAL MEDICINE. 1979. q. $125 (foreign $150) (effective 1992). Society of Behavioral Medicine, 103 South Adams St, Rockville, MD 20850. TEL 301-251-2790. FAX 301-279-6749. Ed. Francis J. Keefe. adv.; bk.rev.; circ. 3,000. (also avail. in microfilm from WWS,PMC; back issues avail.) **Indexed:** Behav.Abstr., Behav.Med.Abstr., Biol.Abstr., Excerp.Med., Psychol.Abstr., Soc.Work Res.& Abstr., Sociol.Abstr.
—BLDSC shelfmark: 1038.700000.
Incorporates (in 1991): Behavioral Medicine Abstracts (ISSN 0197-7717); Formerly: Behavioral Medicine Update.
Description: Covers behavioral advances across the spectrum of health care disciplines.

ANNALS OF BIOMEDICAL ENGINEERING. see BIOLOGY — Bioengineering

ANNALS OF EMERGENCY MEDICINE. see MEDICAL SCIENCES — Orthopedics And Traumatology

610   US   ISSN 1047-2797
RA648.5   CODEN: ANNPE3
▼**ANNALS OF EPIDEMIOLOGY.** 1990. 6/yr. $150 (foreign $178)(effective 1992). (American College of Epidemiology) Elsevier Science Publishing Co., Inc. (New York), 655 Ave. of the Americas, New York, NY 10010. TEL 212-989-5800. FAX 212-633-3965. TELEX 420643 AEP UI. Eds. Charles H. Hennekens, Julie E. Buring. **Indexed:** Excerp.Med. (1992-).
—BLDSC shelfmark: 1040.470000.
Description: Provides reports of original research in epidemiology of chronic and acute diseases that are of interest to clinicians as well as public health researchers.
Refereed Serial

616.026   US   ISSN 0003-4819
R11   CODEN: AIMEAS
ANNALS OF INTERNAL MEDICINE. (Bi-monthly supplement avail.: ACP Journal Club) 1922. s-m. $79. American College of Physicians, Independence Mall W., Sixth St. at Race, Philadelphia, PA 19106-1572. TEL 215-351-2400. Eds. Drs. Suzanne W. Fletcher, Robert H. Fletcher. adv.; bk.rev.; charts; illus.; index, cum.index; circ. 95,000. (also avail. in microform from UMI,PMC) **Indexed:** Abstr.Health Care Manage.Stud., Abstr.Hyg., Abstr.Inter.Med., Behav.Med.Abstr., Biol.Abstr., Biotech.Abstr., C.I.S. Abstr., Chem.Abstr., CINAHL, Curr.Adv.Cancer Res., Curr.Adv.Ecol.Sci., Curr.Cont., Dairy Sci.Abstr., Dent.Ind., Dok.Arbeitsmed., Excerp.Med., FAMLI, Helminthol.Abstr., Hosp.Lit.Ind., I.P.A., Ind.Med., Ind.Sci.Rev., INIS Atomind., Int.Nurs.Ind., Med.Care Rev, NRN, Nutr.Abstr., Protozool.Abstr., Rev.Med.& Vet.Mycol., Rev.Plant Path., Risk Abstr., Sci.Cit.Ind, Trop.Dis.Bull.
●Also available online. Vendor(s): BRS, BRS/Saunders Colleague.
—BLDSC shelfmark: 1041.200000.
Refereed Serial

ANNALS OF MEDICINE. see MEDICAL SCIENCES — Experimental Medicine, Laboratory Technique

610   SU   ISSN 0256-4947
                                      CODEN: ANSMEJ
ANNALS OF SAUDI MEDICINE. (Text in English; summaries in Arabic) 1981. bi-m. free. King Faisal Specialist Hospital and Research Centre, P.O. Box 3354, Riyadh 11211, Saudi Arabia. FAX 442-7237. Ed. Dr. Mohammed Akhtar. adv.; bk.rev.; circ. 14,000 (controlled). (back issues avail.) **Indexed:** Abstr.Hyg., Curr.Adv.Ecol.Sci., Curr.Cont., Excerp.Med., Protozool.Abstr., Rev.Med.& Vet.Mycol.
—BLDSC shelfmark: 1043.925000.
Formerly: King Faisal Specialist Hospital Medical Journal (ISSN 0253-4770)
Description: A multidisciplinary medical journal dealing with aspects of clinical, academic, investigative medicine and research.

610   FR   ISSN 0066-3298
ANNUAIRE MEDICAL DE L'HOSPITALISATION FRANCAISE.. 1949. a. 620 Fr. (effective 1991). Edi-Publi-France, 10, rue Vineuse, 75116 Paris, France. TEL 1-45-20-93-36. FAX 1-45-20-81-74. adv.
Description: Provides names and adresses of care-giving facilities, the number of beds, types of specializations and medical equipment and methods of payment.

MEDICAL SCIENCES

610 FR
ANNUAIRE MEDICAL DU DR. PORCHERON ET PROF. G. BELTRAMI. 1912. a. 120 F. SO-GE-CO-PRO S.A.R.L, 20-26 rue Caisserie, 13235 Marseille Cedex 1, France. adv.

ANNUAL BOOK OF A S T M STANDARDS. VOLUME 13.01. MEDICAL DEVICES. see *ENGINEERING — Engineering Mechanics And Materials*

ANNUAL EDITIONS: HUMAN DEVELOPMENT. see *BIOLOGY — Physiology*

610 US ISSN 0066-4219
CODEN: ARMCAH
ANNUAL REVIEW OF MEDICINE: SELECTED TOPICS IN THE CLINICAL SCIENCES. 1950. a. $44 (foreign $49)(effective Jan. 1992). Annual Reviews Inc., 4139 El Camino Way, Box 10139, Palo Alto, CA 94303-0897. TEL 415-493-4400. TELEX 910-290-0275. Ed. William P. Creger. bibl.; index, cum.index. (also avail. in microfilm from PMC; back issues avail.; reprint service avail. from ISI) **Indexed:** Biol.Abstr., Chem.Abstr., Curr.Adv.Cancer Res., Curr.Adv.Ecol.Sci., Curr.Cont., Dent.Ind., Helminthol.Abstr., Ind.Med., Ind.Sci.Rev., Ind.Vet., M.M.R.I, Nutr.Abstr., Protozool.Abstr., Psychol.Abstr., Sci.Cit.Ind., Vet.Bull.
—BLDSC shelfmark: 1522.700000.
Description: Original reviews of critical literature and current developments in medicine.
Refereed Serial

610 IT
ANTHOLOGIA MEDICA SANTORIANA. a. price varies. Giardini Editori e Stampatori, Via Santa Bibbiana 28, 56100 Pisa, Italy. TEL 050 502531. Ed. Marcello Comel.

610 AT ISSN 0729-218X
ANTIBIOTIC GUIDELINES. 1978. biennial. Aus.$12($10) Victorian Medical Postgraduate Foundation Inc, Therapeutics Committee, Chelsea House, Level 3, 55 Flemington Rd., N. Melbourne, Vic. 3051, Australia. TEL 03-329-1566. FAX 03-326-5632. (Co-sponsor: Victorian Drug Usage Advisory Committee) bk.rev.; circ. 25,000.
Description: Disease-oriented guide to therapeutic use of microbial agents for doctors, nurses and pharmacists.

610 CK ISSN 0044-8389
ANTIOQUIA MEDICA. (Text in Spanish; summaries in English, Spanish) 1950. 10/yr. Col.$100($7.50) Universidad de Antioquia, Facultad de Medicina-Academia de Medicina, Apdo. Aereo 52278, Medellin, Colombia. Ed. Jose Luis Ramirez Castro. bk.rev.; abstr.; index; circ. 1,200. (looseleaf format) **Indexed:** Biol.Abstr., Chem.Abstr., Excerp.Med., Ind.Vet., Rev.Plant Path., Trop.Dis.Bull., Vet.Bull.

610 CL
ANUARIO ENFERMEDADES DE NOTIFICACION OBLIGATORIA. 1947. a. $5. Ministerio de Salud, Departamento de Control y Evaluacion, Santiago, Chile.

APHASIE; Presseorgan fuer Sprachgestoerte (Aphasiker). see *EDUCATION — Special Education And Rehabilitation*

APPLIED CARDIOPULMONARY PATHOPHYSIOLOGY; the interface between laboratory and clinical practice. see *BIOLOGY — Physiology*

610 SJ ISSN 0254-9492
ARAB MEDICAL BULLETIN. (Text in Arabic or English) 1979. m. $200 to individuals; institutions SL.100. P.O. Box 1882, Khartoum, Sudan. Ed. T.A. Rahman. adv.; bk.rev.; circ. 1,500. **Indexed:** Abstr.Hyg., Excerp.Med.
Formerly: Sudan Medical Bulletin.

610 GW ISSN 0723-5100
ARAB MEDICO; alam al tubb wa al-saydazah. (Text in Arabic) 1983. bi-m. DM.58($90) Beta Publishing, Postfach 140121, 5300 Bonn 1, Germany. TEL 0228-25206-1. FAX 0228-252067. TELEX 869536-BETA-D. Ed. Taleb Ulama. adv.; charts; illus.; circ. 15,900. (back issues avail.)

ARBEITSMEDIZIN, SOZIALMEDIZIN, PRAEVENTIVMEDIZIN; Zeitschrift fuer Praxis, Klinik, Forschung, Begutachtung. see *PUBLIC HEALTH AND SAFETY*

614 613.62 BE
ARCHIVES BELGES DE MEDECINE SOCIALE ET D'HYGIENE. (Summaries in English, Flemish, French) 1938. 6/yr. 1200 F.($38) Archives de Medecine Sociale et d'Hygiene, Cite Administrative de l'Etat, Quartier Esplanade, No.6, 1010 Brussels, Belgium. bk.rev.; abstr.; bibl.; charts; index. **Indexed:** Abstr.Hyg., Biol.Abstr., C.I.S. Abstr., Chem.Abstr., Dairy Sci.Abstr., Excerp.Med., Food Sci.& Tech.Abstr., Ind.Med., INIS Atomind., Biotech.Abstr., Trop.Dis.Bull.
Formerly: Archives Belges de Medecine Sociale, Hygiene, Medecine du Travail et Medecine Legale (ISSN 0003-9578)

ARCHIVES D'ANATOMIE, D'HISTOLOGIE ET D'EMBRYOLOGIE; normales et experimentales. see *BIOLOGY*

616.07 FR ISSN 0395-501X
ARCHIVES D'ANATOMIE ET DE CYTOLOGIE PATHOLOGIQUES. 1953. 6/yr. 1050 F. to individuals (foreign 1400 F.); students 525 F. (foreign 720 F.). (Semaine des Hopitaux) Expansion Scientifique, 15 rue Saint-Benoit, 75278 Paris Cedex 06, France. Ed. Chomette. **Indexed:** Biol.Abstr., C.I.S. Abstr., Chem.Abstr., Curr.Cont., Dent.Ind., Excerp.Med., Helminthol.Abstr., Ind.Med.
—BLDSC shelfmark: 1630.970000.
Formerly: Archives d'Anatomie Pathologique (ISSN 0003-9608)

610 FR ISSN 0003-9845
ARCHIVES MEDITERRANEENNES DE MEDECINE. 1923. 3/mo. 50 F. (S.D.M.S.) Sud-Regie, 58 Ave. de la Marne, 92600 Asnieres, France. Ed. Prof. M. Audier. adv.; bk.rev.; charts; illus.; circ. 1,000. **Indexed:** Chem.Abstr., Ind.Med.
Formerly: Archives de Medecine Generale et Tropicale.

610 US ISSN 0148-5016
QP253 CODEN: ARANDR
ARCHIVES OF ANDROLOGY; an international journal. 1978. bi-m. $375. Hemisphere Publishing Corporation (Subsidiary of: Taylor & Francis Group), 1900 Frost Rd., Ste. 101, Bristol, PA 19007-1598. TEL 215-785-5800. FAX 215-785-5515. Ed. E.S.E. Hafez. bk.rev. (back issues avail.; reprint service avail. from UMI) **Indexed:** Anim.Breed.Abstr., Biol.Abstr., Chem.Abstr., Curr.Adv.Ecol.Sci., Curr.Cont., Excerp.Med., Ind.Med., Ind.Sci.Rev., Pig News & Info., Sci.Cit.Ind.
—BLDSC shelfmark: 1631.220000.
Description: Reproduction, fertility and regulation; infertility in the human and animal male.
Refereed Serial

614.7 016 US ISSN 0003-9896
RC963 CODEN: AEHLAU
ARCHIVES OF ENVIRONMENTAL HEALTH. 1950. bi-m. $90. (Helen Dwight Reid Educational Foundation) Heldref Publications, 1319 Eighteenth St., N.W., Washington, DC 20036-1802. TEL 202-296-6267. FAX 202-296-5149. Ed. Patricia McCready Meyer. adv.; bk.rev.; charts; illus.; index; circ. 2,800. (also avail. in microform; reprint service avail.) **Indexed:** A.S.& T.Ind., Abstr.Hyg., Acid Pre.Dig., API Abstr., API Catal., API Hlth.& Environ., API Oil., API Pet.Ref., API Pet.Subst., API Transport, Biodet.Abstr., Biol.Abstr., Biotech.Abstr., Br.Ceram.Abstr., C.I.S. Abstr., Cadscan, Chem.Abstr., Curr.Adv.Cancer Res., Curr.Adv.Ecol.Sci., Curr.Cont., Dairy Sci.Abstr., Dent.Ind., Energy Info.Abstr., Energy Rev., Environ.Abstr., Environ.Ind., Environ.Per.Bibl., Environ.Per.Bibl., Excerp.Med., Fuel & Energy Abstr., G.Soc.Sci.& Rel.Per.Lit., Gas Abstr., Helminthol.Abstr., Hosp.Lit.Ind., Ind.Hyg.Dig., Ind.Med., Ind.Sci.Rev., Ind.Vet., INIS Atomind., Lab.Haz.Bull., Lead Abstr., NRN, Nutr.Abstr., Pollut.Abstr., Rev.Plant Path., Risk Abstr., Sci.Cit.Ind., Sel.Water Res.Abstr., Small Anim.Abstr., Vet.Bull., W.R.C.Inf., Zincscan.
—BLDSC shelfmark: 1634.250000.
Refereed Serial

ARCHIVES OF HISTOLOGY AND CYTOLOGY/NIHON SOSHIKIGAKU KIROKU. see *BIOLOGY — Cytology And Histology*

616.026 US ISSN 0003-9926
CODEN: AIMDAP
ARCHIVES OF INTERNAL MEDICINE. 1908. m. $65. American Medical Association, 515 N. State St., Chicago, IL 60610. TEL 312-464-0183. FAX 312-464-5834. Ed. Dr. James E. Dalen. adv.; bk.rev.; charts; illus.; index; circ. 100,000. (also avail. in microform from UMI,PMC) **Indexed:** Abstr.Health Care Manage.Stud., Abstr.Hyg., Abstr.Inter.Med., Biol.Abstr., Biotech.Abstr., C.I.S. Abstr., Chem.Abstr., Curr.Adv.Cancer Res., Curr.Adv.Ecol.Sci., Curr.Cont., Curr.Lit.Fam.Plan., Dairy Sci.Abstr., Dent.Ind., Dok.Arbeitsmed., Excerp.Med., Helminthol.Abstr., Hosp.Lit.Ind., I.P.A., Ind.Hyg.Dig., Ind.Med., Ind.Sci.Rev., Ind.Vet., INIS Atomind., Int.Nurs.Ind., NRN, Nutr.Abstr., Poult.Abstr., Protozool.Abstr., Rev.Med.& Vet.Mycol., Rev.Plant Path., Sci.Cit.Ind, Trop.Dis.Bull., Vet.Bull.
●Also available online. Vendor(s): Mead Data Central.
—BLDSC shelfmark: 1634.850000.
Refereed Serial

616.98 IT ISSN 0003-9934
ARCHIVES OF MEDICAL HYDROLOGY. (Text in English, French, German, Italian) 1928. irreg. (3-4/yr.). $5. International Society of Medical Hydrology and Climatology, Via Rovereto 11, 00198 Rome, Italy. bibl.; circ. 550. **Indexed:** Chem.Abstr.
Description: Covers climatological medicine.

610 FR ISSN 0750-6244
ARCHIVES OF OTOLARYNGOLOGY/JOURNAL D'O.R.L. 1981. 4/yr. 230 F. (foreign 400 F.). Publications Medicales Internationales, 24 bis bd. Verd de Saint-Julien, 92190 Meudon, France. Ed. Michelle Deker.

616.07 US ISSN 0363-0153
RB1 CODEN: ARPAAQ
ARCHIVES OF PATHOLOGY & LABORATORY MEDICINE. 1926. m. $72. American Medical Association, 515 N. State St., Chicago, IL 60610. TEL 312-464-0183. FAX 312-464-5834. Ed. Dr. William W. McLendon. adv.; bk.rev.; charts; illus.; index; circ. 15,500. (also avail. in microform from UMI,PMC) **Indexed:** Abstr.Hyg., Biol.Abstr., C.I.S. Abstr., Chem.Abstr., Curr.Adv.Cancer Res., Curr.Adv.Ecol.Sci., Curr.Adv.Genetics & Molec.Biol., Curr.Cont., Dent.Ind., Dok.Arbeitsmed., Excerp.Med., Helminthol.Abstr., Ind.Med., Ind.Sci.Rev., Ind.Vet., INIS Atomind., Nutr.Abstr., Protozool.Abstr., Rev.Med.& Vet.Mycol., Rev.Plant Path., Sci.Cit.Ind., Trop.Dis.Bull., Vet.Bull.
●Also available online. Vendor(s): Mead Data Central.
Formerly: Archives of Pathology (ISSN 0003-9985)
Refereed Serial

615.8 362 US ISSN 0003-9993
RM845 CODEN: APMHAI
ARCHIVES OF PHYSICAL MEDICINE AND REHABILITATION. 1921. m. $110 to individuals (foreign $135); institutions $135 (foreign $145). (American Congress of Rehabilitation Medicine) W.B. Saunders Co., Journals Department, Independence Sq. W., Philadelphia, PA 19106. TEL 215-238-7824. FAX 215-238-7883. (Co-sponsor: American Academy of Physical Medicine and Rehabilitation) Ed. Marvin A. Schroder. adv.; charts; illus.; index; circ. 8,600. (also avail. in microform from UMI; reprint service avail. from UMI,ISI) **Indexed:** Abstr.Health Care Manage.Stud., Bibl.Dev.Med.& Child Neur., Biol.Abstr., C.I.S. Abstr., Chem.Abstr., CINAHL, Curr.Cont., Dent.Ind., Excerp.Med., Hosp.Lit.Ind., Ind.Med., Ind.Sci.Rev., INIS Atomind., JAMA, Lang.& Lang.Behav.Abstr., Phys.Ed.Ind., Rehabil.Lit., Sci.Cit.Ind., Sportsearch (1974-).
—BLDSC shelfmark: 1639.000000.
Description: Covers physiotherapy and rehabilitation.
Refereed Serial

610 US ISSN 0004-0002
HQ1 CODEN: ASXBA8
ARCHIVES OF SEXUAL BEHAVIOR. 1971. 6/yr. $295 (foreign $345)(effective 1992). Plenum Publishing Corp., 233 Spring St., New York, NY 10013-1578. TEL 212-620-8000. FAX 212-463-0742. TELEX 23-421139. Ed. Dr. Richard Green. adv.; bk.rev. (back issues avail.) **Indexed:** Abstr.Crim.& Pen., Adol.Ment.Hlth.Abstr., Biol.Abstr., Chem.Abstr., Curr.Adv.Ecol.Sci., Curr.Cont., Curr.Lit.Fam.Plan., Excerp.Med., Ind.Med., Mid.East: Abstr.& Ind., Psychol.Abstr., Ref.Zh., SSCI, Stud.Wom.Abstr.
—BLDSC shelfmark: 1643.128000.
Refereed Serial

MEDICAL SCIENCES

610   IT   ISSN 0004-010X
ARCHIVIO DI MEDICINA INTERNA. 1949. bi-m. L.60000 (foreign L.120000)(effective 1992). Casa Editrice Maccari, Via Trento 53, 43100 Parma, Italy. FAX 039-521-771268. circ. 1,400. **Indexed:** Excerp.Med.
—BLDSC shelfmark: 1647.650000.

616.07   IT   ISSN 0004-0193
                           CODEN: AMPCAV
ARCHIVIO E. MARAGLIANO DI PATOLOGIA E CLINICA.* vol.28, 1972. bi-m. L.5000. Universita degli Studi di Genova, Istituto Scientifico di Medicina Interna, 16132 Genoa, Italy. **Indexed:** Biol.Abstr., Chem.Abstr., Excerp.Med., Ind.Med.

ARCHIVIO ITALIANO DI ANATOMIA E DI EMBRIOLOGIA. see *BIOLOGY*

610   BO   ISSN 0004-0525
ARCHIVOS BOLIVIANOS DE MEDICINA. 1943. 3/yr. free. Universidad Mayor, Real y Pontificia de San Francisco Xavier de Chuquisaca, Facultad de Ciencias de la Salud, Calle Colon No. 235, Casilla Coreo 460, Sucre, Bolivia. Eds. Antonio Dubravcic L., Alberto Aquirre. adv.; bk.rev.; bibl.; charts; illus.; circ. 650.

ARCHIVOS DE BIOLOGIA ANDINA. see *BIOLOGY*

610   MX   ISSN 0066-6769
                           CODEN: AIMSC4
ARCHIVOS DE INVESTIGACION MEDICA. (Supplements avail.) (Text in English and Spanish) 1970. q. $25. Instituto Mexicano del Seguro Social, Oficina de Bibliotecas y Divulgacion, Apdo. Postal 12976, 03001 Mexico D.F., Mexico. Ed. Dr. Juan Somolinos-Palencia. circ. 5,000. (also avail. in microform from UMI) **Indexed:** Abstr.Hyg., Biol.Abstr., Chem.Abstr., Curr.Cont., Excerp.Med., Helminthol.Abstr., Ind.Med., Ind.Sci.Rev., Nutr.Abstr., Sci.Cit.Ind., Trop.Dis.Bull.

616 574.29   PL   ISSN 0004-069X
                           CODEN: AITEAT
ARCHIVUM IMMUNOLOGIAE ET THERAPIAE EXPERIMENTALIS. (Text in English) 1953. bi-m. $72. (Polska Akademia Nauk, Instytut Immunologii i Terapii Doswiadczalnej) Ossolineum, Publishing House of the Polish Academy of Sciences, Rynek 9-11, 50-106 Wroclaw, Poland. TELEX 0712771 OSS PL. (Dist. by: Ars Polona, Krakowskie Przedmiescie 7, 00-068 Warsaw, Poland) Ed. Jerzy Gieldanowski. charts; illus.; index; circ. 790. (also avail. in microfilm from PMC; reprint service avail. from ISI, UMI) **Indexed:** Abstr.Hyg., C.I.S. Abstr., Chem.Abstr., Curr.Adv.Cell & Devel.Biol., Curr.Adv.Ecol.Sci., Curr.Adv.Genetics & Molec.Biol., Curr.Cont., Dent.Ind., Excerp.Med, Helminthol.Abstr., Ind.Med., Ind.Sci.Rev., Ind.Vet., INIS Atomind., Sci.Cit.Ind, Trop.Dis.Bull.
—BLDSC shelfmark: 1659.500000.
Description: Publishes papers containing original results of scientific research and experiments that make a contribution to immunology or experimental therapy.

610   PL   ISSN 0860-1844
R131
ARCHIWUM HISTORII I FILOZOFII MEDYCYNY. (Text in Polish; summaries in English and Russian) 1924. q. $32. (Polskie Towarzystwo Historii Medycyny - Polish Society of History of Medicine) Ossolineum, Publishing House of the Polish Academy of Sciences, Ul. Rynek 9-11, 50-106 Wroclaw, Poland. TELEX 0712771 OSS PL. (Dist. by: Ars Polona-Ruch, Krakowskie Przedmiescie 7, 00-068 Warsaw, Poland) Ed. Andrzej Srodka. bk.rev.; index; circ. 860. (reprint service avail. from UMI) **Indexed:** Amer.Hist.& Life, Biol.Abstr., Hist.Abstr., Ind.Med.
—BLDSC shelfmark: 1661.045000.
Formerly (until 1985): Archiwum Historii Medycyny (ISSN 0004-0762)
Description: Provides papers to Polish scholars in medicine, medical societies, evolution of medical research and results.

610 236   FI   ISSN 0782-226X
RC955   CODEN: AMRSEP
ARCTIC MEDICAL RESEARCH. 1972. q. free. Nordic Council for Arctic Medical Research, Aapistie 3, SF-90220 Oulu, Finland. FAX 358-81-334765. (Co-sponsor: International Union for Circumpolar Health) Eds. J.P.Hart Hansen, B. Harvald. bk.rev.; circ. 1,400 (controlled). (back issues avail.)
—BLDSC shelfmark: 1663.152000.

610   IT
▼**ARGOMENTI DI CHEMIOANTIBIOTICOTERAPIA.** 1991. q. Masson Italia Periodici, Via Statuto 2-4, 20121 Milan, Italy. TEL 02-6367-1. FAX 02-6367-211. Ed. Franco Fraschini.

ARIZONA POISON CONTROL SYSTEM NEWSLETTER. see *PHARMACY AND PHARMACOLOGY*

ARKANSAS. DIVISION OF REHABILITATION SERVICES. ANNUAL REPORT. see *EDUCATION — Special Education And Rehabilitation*

610   US   ISSN 0004-1858
                           CODEN: JAMSAB
ARKANSAS MEDICAL SOCIETY. JOURNAL. 1890. m. $22 (foreign $27). Arkansas Medical Society, Box 5776, Little Rock, AR 72215-5776. FAX 501-224-6489. adv.; bk.rev.; abstr.; bibl.; charts; illus.; stat.; index; circ. 3,400. **Indexed:** Chem.Abstr., Dent.Ind., Ind.Med., INIS Atomind., Nutr.Abstr.
—BLDSC shelfmark: 4700.850000.

ARKHIV ANATOMII, GISTOLOGII I EMBRIOLOGII/ARCHIVES OF ANATOMY, HISTOLOGY AND EMBRYOLOGY. see *BIOLOGY*

616.07   RU   ISSN 0004-1955
                           CODEN: ARPTAF
ARKHIV PATOLOGII/ARCHIVES OF PATHOLOGY. (Text in Russian; summaries in English) 1935. m. 45.60 Rub.($22.20) (Akademiya Meditsinskikh Nauk S.S.S.R.) Izdatel'stvo Meditsina, Petroverigskii pereulok 6-8, 101838 Moscow, Russia. (Subscr. to: Mezhdunarodnaya Kniga, Moscow, G-200, Russia) (Co-sponsor: Vsesoyuznoe Nauchnoe Obshchestvo Patologanatomov) Ed. A.V. Smol'iyannikov. bk.rev.; index. **Indexed:** Biol.Abstr., Biotech.Abstr., Chem.Abstr., Dent.Ind., Excerp.Med., Helminthol.Abstr., Ind.Med., Ind.Vet., INIS Atomind., Nutr.Abstr., Protozool.Abstr., Rev.Med.& Vet.Mycol., Vet.Bull.
—BLDSC shelfmark: 0009.800000.
Description: Deals with original investigation on pressing problems of general pathology and pathologic anatomy, performed with the help of the newest research methods and describing major provisions of the theory and practice of different human diseases, as well as problems of experimental, comparative and geographic pathology.

ARMY MEDICAL SERVICES MAGAZINE. see *MILITARY*

AROGYA; a journal of health sciences. see *PHYSICAL FITNESS AND HYGIENE*

616.07   PO   ISSN 0004-2714
                           CODEN: APALA4
ARQUIVO DE PATOLOGIA. vol.43, 1971. 3/yr. Esc.150. Instituto Portugues de Oncologia de Francisco Gentil, Palhava, Lisbon, Portugal. circ. 800. **Indexed:** Biol.Abstr., Chem.Abstr., Excerp.Med., Ind.Med.

610   BL   ISSN 0365-0723
ARQUIVOS BRASILEIROS DE MEDICINA. (Text in Portuguese; summaries in English) 1911. bi-m. Cr.$3500($60) Editora Cientifica Nacional Ltda., Ave. Almirante Barroso 97-1.205-1210, CEP 20031 Rio de Janeiro, RJ, Brazil. adv.; bk.rev.; index, cum.index; circ. 20,000. **Indexed:** Biol.Abstr., Excerp.Med., Ind.Med.
—BLDSC shelfmark: 1695.220000.

610   BL   ISSN 0004-2773
ARQUIVOS CATARINENSES DE MEDICINA. (Text in Portuguese; summaries in English) 1967. q. Cr.$40.000($40) (Asociacao Catarinense de Medicina) Artes Graficas Ltda., Rua Jeronimo Coelho 359, Andar 4, 88000 Florianopolis SC, Brazil. Ed. Mario Jose da Conceicao. adv.; bk.rev.; bibl.; charts; index; circ. 5,000. (back issues avail.) **Indexed:** Biol.Abstr., Ind.Med.

616.07   PO   ISSN 0066-7854
ARQUIVOS DE PATOLOGIA GERAL E ANATOMIA PATOLOGICA. (Text in Portuguese; summaries in English and French) 1913. a. exchange basis. Universidade de Coimbra, Instituto de Anatomia Patologica, Faculdade de Medicina, 3049 Coimbra Codex, Portugal. Ed. Renato Trincao. bk.rev.; circ. 400. **Indexed:** Biol.Abstr., Excerp.Med.

ARQUIVOS DOS HOSPITAIS E DA FACULDADE DE CIENCIAS MEDICAS DA SANTA CASA DE SAO PAULO. see *HOSPITALS*

610   SZ   ISSN 0004-2897
ARS MEDICI; Zeitschrift fuer praktische Medizin. 1910. m. 66 Fr. Verlag Mosse Annoncen, PO Box 206, 8025 Zurich, Switzerland. FAX 01-2526855. adv.; bk.rev.; index; circ. 4,000. **Indexed:** Biol.Abstr., Excerp.Med.
—BLDSC shelfmark: 1697.636000.

617.95   NE   ISSN 0924-3054
▼**ARTIFICIAL ORGANS TODAY.** (Text in English) 1991. q. DM.360($234) (Japan Society for Artificial Organs, JA) V S P, P.O. Box 346, 3700 AH Zeist, Netherlands. TEL 03404-25790. FAX 03404-32081. TELEX 40217 VSP NL. Ed. T. Agishi.
—BLDSC shelfmark: 1735.053000.
Description: Covers international research and practical information on artificial organs.

610   BE
ARTSENPRAKTIJK. (Supplement avail.) (Text in Flemish) s-m. 3286 Fr. C E D Samson (Subsidiary of: Wolters Samson Belgie n.v.), Louizalaan 485, B-1050 Brussels, Belgium. TEL 02-7231111. FAX 02-6498480. TELEX CEDSAM 64130. index.
Description: Provides fiscal and administrative advice for doctors in regards to their practices.

ARUT PERUM JOTHI. see *RELIGIONS AND THEOLOGY — Buddhist*

614   AU   ISSN 0004-4180
ARZT IN NIEDEROESTERREICH. 1965. m. $1. Ueberparteilicher Aerzteverband Niederoesterreichs, Klostergasse 6-8, A-3100 St. Poelten, Austria. Ed. Dr. Erich Klier. adv.; bk.rev.; abstr.; film rev.; illus.; stat.; circ. 3,000.

610 338.3   GW   ISSN 0341-4434
ARZT UND AUTO; der kraftfahrende Arzt. 1924. m. DM.30. K V D A Verlag, Johanna-Melber-Weg 8, 6000 Frankfurt a.M. 70, Germany. TEL 069-622007. FAX 069-622496. Ed. Dr. A. Becker. adv.; bk.rev.; circ. 10,000.
Formerly (until 1971): Kraftfahrende Arzt.

610 170   GW   ISSN 0403-3884
ARZT UND CHRIST; Vierteljahresschrift fuer medizinisch-ethische Grundsatzfragen. 1955. q. DM.79. Schwaben Verlag AG, Senefelderstr. 12, 7302 Ostfildern 1, Germany. TEL 0711-4406160. FAX 0711-4406101. Ed. Dr. W. Mueller-Hartburg. adv.; bk.rev.
—BLDSC shelfmark: 1738.150000.

610 340   GW   ISSN 0343-5733
ARZTRECHT; Kompendium des Gesamten Rechtes der Medizin. 1965. m. DM.60. Verlag fuer Arztrecht, Schinnrainstr. 15, 7500 Karlsruhe 41, Germany. TEL 0721-402904. Ed. Dr. Manfred Andreas. adv.; bk.rev.; circ. controlled.
Description: Examines the role of the law in medical practice.

610 572   SP   ISSN 0210-4466
R131.A1
ASCLEPIO; archivo iberoamericano de historia de la medicina. 1949. s-a. 3300 ptas. (foreign 4950 ptas.). Consejo Superior de Investigaciones Cientificas (C.S.I.C.), Centro de Estudios Historicos, Departamento de Historia de la Medicina, Vitruvio, 8, 28006 Madrid, Spain. Ed. Pedro Lain Entralgo. bk.rev.; bibl.; cum.index: 1949-1973. **Indexed:** A.I.C.P., Ind.Med.Esp.
—BLDSC shelfmark: 1739.250000.
Description: Contains original studies and researches in the fields of medical history, science, and medical anthropolgy.

610   HK   ISSN 1011-596X
ASIAN HOSPITAL. 1987. q. $25. Techni-Press Asia Ltd., P.O. Box 20494, Hennessy Road, Hong Kong. FAX 527-8399. circ. 5,108.
Description: Clinical articles and news about all aspects of hospitals in Asia.

610   HK   ISSN 0250-3328
ASIAN MEDICAL NEWS. (Text and summaries in English) 1979. s-m. HK.$250($65) MediMedia Pacific Ltd., Unit 1216, Seaview Estate, 2-8 Wastson Rd., North Point, Hong Kong. TEL 5700708. FAX 5705076. TELEX HX-63267. Ed. J. Fox. adv.; bk.rev.; index; circ. 34,635.
—BLDSC shelfmark: 1742.700200.

MEDICAL SCIENCES

610   BL
ASOCIACAO MEDICA BRASILEIRA. BOLETIM. 1962. irreg. Asociacao Medica Brasileira, Sao Carlos Pinhal 324, Sao Paulo, SP, Brazil. Ed. Pedro Kassab. adv.; circ. 45,000. **Indexed:** Soils & Fert.

610   PR   ISSN 0004-4849
ASOCIACION MEDICA DE PUERTO RICO. BOLETIN. (Text in English and Spanish) 1903. m. $40. Asociacion Medica de Puerto Rico, Avenida Fernandez Juncos, No. 1305, Apdo. de Correo 9387, Santurce, PR 00908. Ed.Bd. adv.; bk.rev.; bibl.; illus.; index; circ. 3,500. **Indexed:** Abstr.Hyg., Bio-Contr.News & Info., Biol.Abstr., Chem.Abstr., CINAHL, Dent.Ind., Ind.Med., Nutr.Abstr., Trop.Dis.Bull.
—BLDSC shelfmark: 2160.850000.

610.7   MX   ISSN 0004-4857
ASOCIACION MEXICANA DE FACULTADES Y ESCUELAS DE MEDICINA. BOLETIN. 1962. irreg. free. Asociacion Mexicana de Facultades y Escuelas de Medicina, Queretaro No. 147, Oficinas 501 y 502, Apdo. Postal 12927, 06760 Mexico, D.F., Mexico. Ed. Dr. Manuel Loria-Mendez. bibl.; charts; illus.; index; circ. 750.

610   MX   ISSN 0004-489X
ASOCIACION PARA EVITAR LA CEGUERA EN MEXICO. ARCHIVOS. 1956. q. free. Asociacion para Evitar la Ceguera en Mexico, Vicente Garcia Torres 46, Coyoacan 21, 04330 Mexico D.F, Mexico. Ed. Dr. Teodulo M. Agundis. adv.; bibl.; charts; illus.

610 378   US
ASSEMBLY ON EDUCATION NETWORK. 1985. q. $15. American Health Information Management Association, 919 N. Michigan Ave., Ste. 1400, Chicago, IL 60611-1601. TEL 312-787-2672. Ed. Linda Bergen. circ. 750. (back issues avail.)
Formerly: Medical Record Educator.
Description: Focuses on academic issues and research related to medical record education. Articles cover field research, grants and funding, recruitment and retention, creative classroom and teaching methods, joint ventures and international news.

610   IS   ISSN 0334-3871
ASSIA. English edition: Assia - Jewish Medical Ethics. (Text in Hebrew) 1970. irreg. $30 per 4 nos. (English ed. $25 for 2 nos.). Shaare Zedek Medical Center, Falk Schlesinger Institute for Medical Halachic Research, P.O. Box 3235, Jerusalem 91031, Israel. TEL 555266. Ed. Rabbi Mordechai Halperin. adv.; bk.rev.; abstr.; circ. 1,700. **Indexed:** Ind.Heb.Per.
●Also available on CD-ROM.

ASSISTIVE TECHNOLOGY. see *EDUCATION — Special Education And Rehabilitation*

610   BL   ISSN 0004-5233
ASSOCIACAO MEDICA BRASILEIRA. JORNAL.* w. Cr.$5.($5.) Associacao Medica Brasileira, Rua Sao Carlos do Pinhal 324, CEP 01333 Sao Paulo, Brazil. Ed. Dr. Pedro Kassab. adv.; bk.rev.; charts; illus.; circ. 30,000.

610   BL   ISSN 0004-5241
ASSOCIACAO MEDICA BRASILEIRA. REVISTA. (Text in Portuguese; summaries in English and French) 1954. m. Associacao Medica Brasileira, Sao Carlos Pinhal 324, CEP 01333 Sao Paulo, SP, Brazil. Ed. Abrao Rapoport. adv.; bk.rev.; abstr.; charts; illus.; index; circ. 40,000. **Indexed:** Biol.Abstr., Chem.Abstr., Excerp.Med., Ind.Med.

610   BL   ISSN 0004-525X
               CODEN: RAMMDG
ASSOCIACAO MEDICA DE MINAS GERAIS. REVISTA. (Text in Portuguese; summaries in English) 1949. q. Cr.$400($30) (Associacao Medica de Minas Gerais) Edicao & Mercado, Av. Men de Sa, 801 St. Efigenia, 30000 Belo Horizonte Minas Gerais, Brazil. Dir. Jose Netto. adv.; bk.rev.; bibl.; charts; illus.; stat.; index; circ. 5,000. (also avail. in microfilm) **Indexed:** Biol.Abstr., Nutr.Abstr.

611 574.4   FR   ISSN 0066-8915
ASSOCIATION DES ANATOMISTES. BULLETIN. 1899. q. 650 F. (foreign 770 F.). Association des Anatomistes, Faculte Medecine, B.P. 184, 54505 Vandoeuvre les Nancy Cedex, France. TEL 33-83-59-28-33. adv.; circ. 1,100. **Indexed:** Biol.Abstr., Bull.Signal., Dent.Ind., Excerp.Med., Ind.Med.
Formerly: Association des Anatomistes. Comptes Rendus.

610   CN   ISSN 0004-539X
ASSOCIATION DES MEDECINS DE LANGUE FRANCAISE DU CANADA. BULLETIN. 1967. m. membership. Association des Medecins de Langue Francaise du Canada, 1440 St. Catherine St. West, Ste. 210, Montreal, Que. H3G 2P9, Canada. TEL 514-866-2053. bk.rev.; illus.; circ. 12,744. (looseleaf format; reprint service avail. from UMI)

ASSOCIATION FOR PSYCHOANALYTIC MEDICINE. BULLETIN. see *PSYCHOLOGY*

388.3 610   US   ISSN 0892-6484
ASSOCIATION FOR THE ADVANCEMENT OF AUTOMOTIVE MEDICINE. PROCEEDINGS.* 1959. a. $40 to US and Canada; Europe $50; others $55. Association for the Advancement of Automotive Medicine, c/o Associated Life Inst., 446 E. Ontario, 7 Fl., Chicago, IL 60611. TEL 312-390-8927. circ. 1,000. (also avail. in microform) **Indexed:** Psychol.Abstr.
—BLDSC shelfmark: 1082.217000.
Formerly (until 1987): American Association for Automotive Medicine. Proceedings (ISSN 0401-6351)

610   FR   ISSN 0004-5519
ASSOCIATION GENERALE DES MEDECINS DE FRANCE. BULLETIN. 1858. m. 24 F. Association Generale des Medecins de France, 30 bd. Pasteur, 75740 Paris Cedex 15, France. Dir. Dr. Jean Fassy. adv.; bk.rev.; film rev.; illus.; play rev.; stat.; circ. 43,649.

610   US
ASSOCIATION OF AMERICAN INDIAN PHYSICIANS NEWSLETTER.* q. Association of American Indian Physicians, 10013 S. Penn, No. G, Oklahoma City, OK 73159-6995.

610   US   ISSN 0066-9458
R15   CODEN: TAAPAI
ASSOCIATION OF AMERICAN PHYSICIANS. TRANSACTIONS. 1886. a. $44 (foreign $50). Waverly Press, Inc. (Subsidiary of: Williams & Wilkins), 428 E. Preston St., Baltimore, MD 21202. Ed. Dr. R.W. Schrier. circ. 1,000. (also avail. in microfilm from BHP) **Indexed:** Chem.Abstr., Excerp.Med., Ind.Med.
—BLDSC shelfmark: 8902.700000.
Description: Manuscripts of abstracts presented at the annual national meeting of the Association of American Physicians.

610   US   ISSN 0884-8424
RD701
ASSOCIATION OF CHILDREN'S PROSTHETIC-ORTHOTIC CLINICS. JOURNAL. 1961. q. $35 for 2 years. Association of Children's Prosthetic-Orthotic Clinics, 222 S. Prospect Ave., Park Ridge, IL 60068. TEL 708-698-1694. FAX 708-823-0536. Ed. Dr. John Fisk. adv.; bk.rev.; abstr.; bibl.; charts; illus.; stat.; index; circ. 500. **Indexed:** Curr.Cont., Except.Child Educ.Abstr., Excerp.Med., Rehabil.Lit.
—BLDSC shelfmark: 4702.897000.
Formerly (until Apr. 1985): New York University Post-Graduate Medical School. Inter-Clinic Information Bulletin.
Description: Contains articles relating to the prosthetic-orthotic treatment of orthopaedically disabled children.
Refereed Serial

ASSOCIATION OF LIFE INSURANCE MEDICAL DIRECTORS OF AMERICA. TRANSACTIONS. see *INSURANCE*

610   US
ASSOCIATION OF MEDICAL REHABILITATION ADMINISTRATORS. JOURNAL.* 1956. s-a. membership. Association of Medical Rehabilitation Administrators (AMRA), Box 1964, Parkersburg, WV 26102-1964. adv.; bk.rev.; circ. 250.
Formerly: Association of Medical Rehabilitation Directors and Coordinators. Quarterly Bulletin.

610   US
ASSOCIATION OF MEDICAL REHABILITATION ADMINISTRATORS. NEWSLETTER.* q. membership. Association of Medical Rehabilitation Administrators (AMRA), Box 1964, Parkersburg, WV 26012-1964. TEL 304-485-5842. adv.; bk.rev.; circ. 250.

610   II   ISSN 0004-5772
               CODEN: JPHIAR
ASSOCIATION OF PHYSICIANS OF INDIA. JOURNAL. vol.28, 1980. m. Rs.450. Association of Physicians of India, Laud Mansion, 3rd Fl., 21 M. Karve Rd., Bombay 400 004, India. Ed. Dr. V.R. Joshi. adv.; bk.rev.; circ. 5,500. **Indexed:** Chem.Abstr., Dent.Ind., Ind.Med., Nutr.Abstr., Trop.Dis.Bull.
—BLDSC shelfmark: 4705.120000.

610   MX   ISSN 0185-6235
ATENCION MEDICA. 1970. m. Mex.$120000($80) Intersistemas, S.A. de C.V., Fernando Alencastre No. 110 Lomas de Virreyes, 11000 Mexico D.F., Mexico. Ed. Pedro Vera C. adv.; circ. 15,500.

610   BO
ATENEO DE MEDICINA. 6/yr. Casilla 549, La Paz, Bolivia. adv.

610 574   IT   ISSN 0004-6531
ATENEO PARMENSE. ACTA BIO-MEDICA. (Text and summaries in English and Italian) 1929. bi-m. L.20000 (foreign L.25000). (Societa di Medicina e Scienze Naturali di Parma) Ateneo Parmense, Via Gramsci 14, 43100 Parma, Italy. TEL 0521-290370. Ed. Paolo Bobbio. adv.; bk.rev.; bibl.; charts; illus.; stat.; index, cum.index; circ. 550. **Indexed:** Biol.Abstr., Chem.Abstr., Excerp.Med., Ind.Med., INIS Atomind., Nutr.Abstr.
—BLDSC shelfmark: 0603.000000.
Description: Research papers covering a variety of medical topics.

610 309   IO
ATMA JAYA RESEARCH CENTRE. SOCIO-MEDICAL RESEARCH REPORT/PUSAT PENELITIAN ATMA JAYA. PENELITIAN TENTANG KEBUTUHAN KESEHATAN MASYARAKAT DAN SISTEM PELEYANAN KESEHATAN DI KECAMATAN PENJARINGAN. 1978. irreg. Atma Jaya Research Centre - Pusat Penelitian Atma Jaya, Jalan Jenderal Sudirman 57, P.O. Box 2639, Jakarta 10001, Indonesia.

616   US   ISSN 0748-8947
AUDIO-DIGEST EMERGENCY MEDICINE. 1984. s-m. $168. Audio-Digest Foundation (Subsidiary of: California Medical Association), 1577 E. Chevy Chase Dr., Glendale, CA 91206. TEL 213-245-8505. FAX 818-240-7379. (audio cassette)
Refereed Serial

610   US   ISSN 0271-1362
AUDIO-DIGEST FAMILY PRACTICE. 1953. w. & s-m. $336 w. edition; s-m. edition $168. Audio-Digest Foundation (Subsidiary of: California Medical Association), 1577 E. Chevy Chase Dr., Glendale, CA 91206. TEL 213-245-8505. FAX 818-240-7379. (audio cassette)
Formerly: Audio-Digest General Practice (ISSN 0571-8619)
Refereed Serial

616.026 016   US   ISSN 0271-1303
AUDIO-DIGEST INTERNAL MEDICINE. 1954. s-m. $168. Audio-Digest Foundation (Subsidiary of: California Medical Association), 1577 E. Chevy Chase Dr., Glendale, CA 91206. TEL 213-245-8505. FAX 818-240-7379. Ed. Claron L. Oakley. index; circ. controlled. (audio cassette)
Refereed Serial

AUDIOLOGISCH AKUSTIK/AUDIOLOGICAL ACOUSTICS. see *PHYSICS — Sound*

AUSTRALASIAN HEALTH & HEALING; journal of alternative medicine. see *NUTRITION AND DIETETICS*

610   AT   ISSN 0811-6199
AUSTRALIA. NATIONAL HEALTH AND MEDICAL RESEARCH COUNCIL. DEPARTMENT OF HEALTH. MEDICAL RESEARCH. 1968. a. free. Australian Government Publishing Service, G.P.O. Box 84, Canberra, A.C.T. 2601, Australia. Ed. A. Charlton. circ. 1,000. (back issues avail.)
—BLDSC shelfmark: 5531.620000.

MEDICAL SCIENCES

610   AT   ISSN 0728-6910
AUSTRALIA. NATIONAL HEALTH AND MEDICAL RESEARCH COUNCIL. DEPARTMENT OF HEALTH. REPORT. 1935. s-a. free. Australian Government Publishing Service, G.P.O. Box 84, Canberra, A.C.T. 2601, Australia. Ed. A. Charlton. circ. 1,000. (back issues avail.)
—BLDSC shelfmark: 7672.088000.

616.98   AT
AUSTRALIAN ACUPUNCTURE ASSOCIATION. NEWSLETTER. 1977. q. Australian Acupuncture Association, 25 Marshall Rd., Holland Park, Qld. 4121, Australia.

610   AT   ISSN 0004-8291
                           CODEN: ANZJB8
AUSTRALIAN AND NEW ZEALAND JOURNAL OF MEDICINE. 1952. bi-m. Aus.$160 (effective 1992). (Royal Australasian College of Physicians) Adis Press Australasia Pty. Ltd., 404 Sydney Rd., Balgowlah, N.S.W. 2093, Australia. FAX 02-949-5007. Ed. Graham MacDonald. adv.; bk.rev.; charts; illus.; index; circ. 5,500. (also avail. in microform from PMC) **Indexed:** Abstr.Hyg., Biol.Abstr., Biotech.Abstr., Chem.Abstr., Curr.Adv.Ecol.Sci., Curr.Cont., Dairy Sci.Abstr., Dok.Arbeitsmed., Excerp.Med., Helminthol.Abstr., I.P.A., Ind.Med., Ind.Sci.Rev., INIS Atomind., NRN, Nutr.Abstr., Protozool.Abstr., Rev.Plant Path., Sci.Cit.Ind., Trop.Dis.Bull.
●Also available online.
—BLDSC shelfmark: 1796.888000.
Formerly: Australasian Annals of Medicine.

610 028.5   AT   ISSN 0157-9789
AUSTRALIAN ASSOCIATION FOR ADOLESCENT HEALTH. NEWSLETTER. 1978. irreg. Aus.$25. Canberra College of Advanced Education, P.O. Box 1, Belconnen, A.C.T. 2616, Australia. Ed. Murray Williams. bk.rev.; circ. 500. (back issues avail.)

616.07   AT   ISSN 0726-3139
AUSTRALIAN CLINICAL REVIEW. 1979. q. Aus.$110($110) Blackwell Scientific Publications (Australia) Pty. Ltd., P.O. Box 378, Carlton, Vic. 3053, Australia. TEL 03-347-0300. FAX 03-347-5001. TELEX 10716421. Ed. Joh Duggan. bk.rev.; illus.; index; circ. 850. (back issues avail.) **Indexed:** Ind.Med.
—BLDSC shelfmark: 1798.164100.
Description: Reference data designed to keep health professionals informed about quality assurance developments in Australia and abroad.

610   AT   ISSN 0814-6012
AUSTRALIAN DR WEEKLY. 1984. w. Aus.$96. Reed Business Publishing Pty. Ltd., 1-5 Railway St., Chatswood, N.S.W. 2067, Australia. TEL 02-372-5222. FAX 02-419-7533. Ed. Kathryn Ryan. circ. 20,000. (tabloid format; back issues avail.)
Description: Examines the clinical, socio-economic and leisure aspects of the medical professional.

610   AT   ISSN 0300-8495
                           CODEN: AFPHCX
AUSTRALIAN FAMILY PHYSICIAN. 1956. m. Aus.$100 (foreign Aus.$135). Royal Australian College of General Practitioners, 4th Fl., 70 Jolimont St., Jolimont, Vic. 3002, Australia. TEL 03-654-3000. FAX 03-650-5723. Ed. Susan Kaye. adv.; bk.rev.; abstr.; charts; illus.; index; circ. 18,500. (tabloid format; back issues avail.) **Indexed:** Curr.Adv.Cancer Res., Curr.Adv.Ecol.Sci., Dent.Ind., Dok.Arbeitsmed., Excerp.Med., FAMLI, Ind.Med.
—BLDSC shelfmark: 1798.922000.
Formerly: Annals of General Practice (ISSN 0003-4789)

610 616   AT   ISSN 0158-4960
                           CODEN: AJMLDP
AUSTRALIAN JOURNAL OF MEDICAL SCIENCE. 4/yr. Aus.$50 to non-members (foreign Aus.$65). Australian Institute of Medical Scientists, P.O. Box 450, Toowong, Qld. 4066, Australia. TEL 07-371-3370. FAX 07-870-4857. **Indexed:** Chem.Abstr., Excerp.Med., INIS Atomind.
—BLDSC shelfmark: 1810.270000.
Formerly: Australian Journal of Medical Technology.
Description: Scientific and technological papers relating to clinical laboratory practice.

615.8   AT   ISSN 0004-9514
AUSTRALIAN JOURNAL OF PHYSIOTHERAPY. 1954. q. Aus.$55 (overseas Aus.$80)(effective 1992). Australian Physiotherapy Association, 141 St. Georges Rd., N. Fitzroy, Vic. 3068, Australia. TEL 03-482-1044. FAX 03-482-2348. Ed. Margaret Wyrill. adv.; bk.rev.; index; circ. 8,300 (controlled). **Indexed:** Excerp.Med.
—BLDSC shelfmark: 1811.100000.

AUSTRALIAN JOURNAL OF PSYCHOTHERAPY. see *PSYCHOLOGY*

610   AT   ISSN 0727-3851
AUSTRALIAN MEDLINER; news bulletin for medical and hospital librarians. 1976. q. Aus.$30. National Library of Australia, Publications Section, Public Programs, Parkes Place, Canberra, A.C.T. 2600, Australia. TEL 06-262-1365. FAX 06-273-4493. circ. 650.

615.8   AT   ISSN 0045-0766
AUSTRALIAN OCCUPATIONAL THERAPY JOURNAL. 1951. q. Aus.$54. Australian Association of Occupational Therapists, 17 Anchorage St., St. Clair, N.S.W. 2759, Australia. TEL 02-670 6268. Ed. Gwynnyth Llewellyn. adv.; bk.rev.; index; circ. 4,000. (back issues avail.) **Indexed:** Excerp.Med.
—BLDSC shelfmark: 1815.950000.
Formerly: Australian Association of Occupational Therapists. Journal.

615.8   AT   ISSN 0728-490X
AUSTRALIAN REHABILITATION DIGEST. 1977. q. free. (National Advisory Council for the Handicapped) Australian Government Publishing Service, G.P.O. Box 84, Canberra, A.C.T. 2601, Australia. Ed. L.H. Costello. bk.rev.; bibl.; illus.; stat.; cum.index; circ. 1,500.
Former titles: National Rehabilitation Digest (ISSN 0314-111X); Rehabilitation Research and Development Digest.

610   US   ISSN 0891-6934
QR188.3   CODEN: AUIMEI
AUTOIMMUNITY. 12/yr. (in 3 vols., 4 nos./vol.). $98. Harwood Academic Publishers, 270 Eighth Ave., New York, NY 10011. TEL 212-206-8900. FAX 212-645-2459. TELEX 236735 GOPUB UR. (Subscr. to: Box 786, Cooper Sta., New York, NY 10276. TEL 800-545-8398; UK subscr. to: P.O. Box 90, Reading, Berkshire RG1 8JL, England. TEL 0734-560-080) Ed. Terence J. Wilkin. (also avail. in microform)
—BLDSC shelfmark: 1828.345000.
Refereed Serial

AUTONOMIC NERVOUS SYSTEM. see *BIOLOGY — Physiology*

610   DK
AUTORISEREDE LAEGER I DANMARK. 1982. irreg. DKK 80. Sundhedsstyrelsen, Amaliegade 13, 1012 Copenhagen K, Denmark. (Subscr. to: Statens Informationtjeneste, P.O. Box 1103, Copenhagen K, Denmark) circ. 900.
Former titles (until 1992): Autoriserede Laeger, Tandlaeger, Dyrlaeger i Danmark (ISSN 0108-4739); Fortegnelse over Autoriserede Laeger, Tandlaeger, Dyrlaeger i Danmark (ISSN 0106-7354)

AVIATION MEDICAL EDUCATION SERIES. see *AERONAUTICS AND SPACE FLIGHT*

610 629.132   II   ISSN 0250-5045
AVIATION MEDICINE. (Text in English) 1951. s-a. Rs.100. Aero Medical Society of India, Medical Directorate, Air Headquarters, R.K. Puram West, Block 6, New Delhi 110 006, India. TEL 60661. Ed. Ari Cude Pe Chatterje. adv.; bk.rev.; index; circ. 700.

616.98   US   ISSN 0095-6562
RC1050   CODEN: ASEMCG
AVIATION, SPACE, AND ENVIRONMENTAL MEDICINE. 1930. m. $100 (foreign $110). Aerospace Medical Association, 320 S. Henry St., Alexandria, VA 22314-3579. TEL 703-739-2240. Ed. David R. Jones, M.D. adv.; bk.rev.; index; circ. 5,100. (also avail. in microfiche from UMI) **Indexed:** Air Un.Lib.Ind., Biol.Abstr., C.I.S. Abstr., Chem.Abstr., CINAHL, Curr.Adv.Ecol.Sci., Curr.Cont., Dent.Ind., Ergon.Abstr., Excerp.Med., Ind.Med., Ind.Sci.Rev., INIS Atomind., Noise Pollut.Publ.Abstr., Nutr.Abstr., Psychol.Abstr., Psycscan, Risk Abstr., Sci.Cit.Ind.
—BLDSC shelfmark: 1838.640000.
Formerly (until 1975): Aerospace Medicine (ISSN 0001-9402)
Refereed Serial

610   IT
L'AVVENIRE MEDICO. a. price varies. Giardini Editori e Stampatori, Via Santa Bibbiana 28, 56100 Pisa, Italy. TEL 050 502531.

610   II   ISSN 0005-2469
R606
AYU. (Text in English, Gujarati, Hindi and Sanskrit) 1964. m. Rs.15. Gujarat Ayurved University, Institute of Post Graduate Teaching and Research, Jamnagar, P.O. Box 511, Gujarat, India. Ed.Bd. adv.; bk.rev.; bibl.; charts; circ. 225.

610   II   ISSN 0005-2493
AYURVEDA DOOT. (Text in English, Hindi) 1969. w. Rs.10.50. Rajasthan Ayurvedic Research Laboratories, Ayurveddoot Karyalaya 4, Dhamani Market, Sawai Mansingh Highway, Jaipur 3, India. Ed. Dhan Kumar Jain.

610   AJ   ISSN 0005-2523
                           CODEN: AZMZA6
AZERBAIDZHAN TIBB ZHURNALY/AZERBAIDZHANSKII MEDITSINSKII ZHURNAL. (Text in Azerbaijani and Russian) vol.53, 1976. m. 21 Rub. Izdatel'stvo Akademiya Nauk Azerbaidzhanskoi S.S.R., Poselok Musabekova, 571, Baku, Azerbaijan. (Dist. by: Mezhdunarodnaya Kniga, Moscow, G-200, Russia) **Indexed:** Biol.Abstr., Chem.Abstr.
—BLDSC shelfmark: 0005.300000.

616.39 575.1   NE   ISSN 0925-4439
B B A - MOLECULAR BASIS OF DISEASE. (Section of: Biochimica et Biophysica Acta (ISSN 0006-3002)) 8/yr.(in 2 vols.; 4 nos./vol.). fl.676 (effective 1992). Elsevier Science Publishers B.V., P.O. Box 211, 1000 AE Amsterdam, Netherlands. TEL 020-5803911. FAX 020-5803598. TELEX 18582 ESPA NL. (Subscr. in U.S. and Canada to: Elsevier Science Publishing Co., Inc., Box 882, Madison Sq. Sta., New York, NY 10159. TEL 212-989-5800) Ed.Bd.
Description: Focuses on a fundamental biochemical and genetic approach to understanding dysfunction in human disease states and their models.
Refereed Serial

610 382   US   ISSN 1049-4316
                           CODEN: BBNWEJ
THE B B I NEWSLETTER. 1978. 12/yr. $625 (foreign $690). Biomedical Business International (Subsidiary of: Maxwell - Macmillan Company), 1524 Brookhollow Dr., Santa Ana, CA 92705-5426. TEL 714-755-5757. FAX 714-755-5704. Ed. Mike Gibb.
●Also available online. Vendor(s): Data-Star, DIALOG.
—BLDSC shelfmark: 1871.362500.
Description: Includes tracking and analysis of healthcare technology and market trends.

610   CN
B C M A NEWS. 1970. 6/yr. B C Medical Association, 1665 W. Broadway, Ste. 115, Vancouver, B.C. V6J 5A4, Canada. TEL 604-736-5551. FAX 604-736-4566. Ed. Bob Young. adv.; bk.rev.; circ. 6,200.

610   UK   ISSN 0306-5472
B M A NEWS REVIEW. m. £36. (British Medical Association) Professional and Scientific Publications, B M A House, Tavistock Sq., London WC1H 9JR, England. circ. 86,000. **Indexed:** Curr.Adv.Ecol.Sci.
—BLDSC shelfmark: 2116.035000.
Description: Articles on medical politics.

MEDICAL SCIENCES 3081

610   US
B M E S BULLETIN. 1976. q. $25. Biomedical Engineering Society, Box 2399, Culver City, CA 90231. TEL 310-618-9322. Eds. Jerry Collins, Rita M. Schaffer. adv.; circ. 1,800.

610 340   US   ISSN 1049-7986
▼**B N A'S MEDICARE REPORT.** 1990. fortn. $568. The Bureau of National Affairs, Inc., 1231 25th St., N.W., Washington, DC 20037. TEL 202-452-4200. FAX 202-822-8092. TELEX 285656 BNAI WSH. (Subscr. to: 9435 Key West Ave., Rockville, MD 20850. TEL 800-372-1033) Ed. Mary Davis. (back issues avail.)
Description: Notification service covering legislative, regulatory, and legal developments affecting or pertaining to the Medicare program.

610   US   ISSN 0746-9489
BACK PAIN MONITOR. 1983. m. $269. American Health Consultants, Inc., Six Piedmont Center, Ste. 400, 3525 Piedmont Rd., N.E., Atlanta, GA 30305. TEL 404-262-7436. FAX 800-284-3291. (Subscr. to: Department L100, Box 740056, Atlanta, GA 30374-9822. TEL 800-688-2421) Ed. Debra Golden. circ. 1,004. (back issues avail.; reprint service avail.)
●Also available online. Vendor(s): Mead Data Central.

610   BA   ISSN 1012-7666
CODEN: BMBUEU
BAHRAIN MEDICAL BULLETIN. (Text in English) 1979. q. P.O. Box 32159, Manama, Bahrain. TEL 279472. Ed. Jaffar al-Ibriq. circ. 1,750.

614.88   UK
BAILLIERE'S HANDBOOK OF FIRST AID. 1958. irreg., vol.7, 1987. £6.95. Bailliere Tindall, 24-28 Oval Rd., London NW1 7DX, England.

610   CC   ISSN 0253-3707
BAIQIU'EN YIKE DAXUE XUEBAO/BAIQIU'EN UNIVERSITY OF MEDICAL SCIENCES. JOURNAL. (Text in Chinese) bi-m. Baiqiu'en Yike Daxue, Xuebao Bianjibu, 6, Xinmin Dajie, Changchun, Jilin 130021, People's Republic of China. TEL 885911. Ed. Liu Shushu.
—BLDSC shelfmark: 4833.735000.

615.853   CS   ISSN 0302-8070
RM801   CODEN: BLBHAE
BALNEOLOGIA BOHEMICA. (Text in German; summaries in Czech, English, French, Russian) 1972. q. free. (Vyzkumny Ustav Balneologicky) Avicenum, Czechoslovak Medical Press, Malostranske nam. 28, 118 02 Prague 1, Czechoslovakia. Ed. J. Benda. bk.rev.; abstr.; illus.; index; circ. 1,000. **Indexed:** Biol.Abstr., Excerp.Med., Ind.Med.

615.8   PL   ISSN 0005-4402
CODEN: BAPOBT
BALNEOLOGIA POLSKA. (Text in Polish; summaries in English, Polish) 1950. a. $20 per no. Polskie Towarzystwo Balneoklimatologii, Bioklimatologii i Medycyny Fizykalnej, Szamarzewskiego 84, Poznan, Poland. FAX 411-547. Ed. Gerard Straburzynski. adv.; bk.rev.; illus.; index. **Indexed:** Biol.Abstr.
—BLDSC shelfmark: 1861.300000.
Formerly: Wiadomosci Uzdrowiskowe.

610   BG   ISSN 0301-035X
BANGLADESH MEDICAL JOURNAL. Short title: B.M.J. (Text in English) 1972. q. $20. Bangladesh Medical Association, B.M.A. House, 15-2 Topkhana Rd., Dhaka 2, Bangladesh. Ed. Nazrul Islam. adv.; bk.rev.; bibl.; charts; illus.; circ. 6,000. **Indexed:** Abstr.Hyg., Excerp.Med., Trop.Dis.Bull.
Supersedes: East Pakistan Medical Journal (ISSN 0424-1401)

610   BG   ISSN 0377-9238
CODEN: BMRBDI
BANGLADESH MEDICAL RESEARCH COUNCIL BULLETIN. (Text in English) 1976. 3/yr. Tk.300($30) Bangladesh Medical Research Council, Mokakhali, Dhaka 1212, Bangladesh. Ed. S.M. Keramat Ali. adv.; index; circ. 1,000. **Indexed:** Abstr.Hyg., Excerp.Med., Ind.Med., Nutr.Abstr., Trop.Dis.Bull.

BASIC AND APPLIED HISTOCHEMISTRY. see *BIOLOGY — Biological Chemistry*

BASIC AND CLINICAL BIOSTATISTICS. see *MATHEMATICS*

610 574   SZ   ISSN 0067-4524
R131.A1
BASLER VEROEFFENTLICHUNGEN ZUR GESCHICHTE DER MEDIZIN UND DER BIOLOGIE. 1953. irreg., no.35, 1985. price varies. Schwabe und Co. AG, Steinentorstr. 13, CH-4010 Basel, Switzerland. TEL 061-2725523. FAX 061-2725573. Eds. Heinrich Buesst, Ulrich Troehler. index.

610   US   ISSN 0067-4672
BAYER-SYMPOSIEN. (Text in English) 1969. irreg., vol.9, 1985. price varies. (Bayer AG, GW) Springer-Verlag, 175 Fifth Ave., New York, NY 10010. TEL 212-460-1500. (Also: Berlin, Heidelberg, Tokyo and Vienna) (reprint service avail. from ISI) **Indexed:** Biol.Abstr.
—BLDSC shelfmark: 1871.140000.

610   GW   ISSN 0005-7126
BAYERISCHES AERZTEBLATT. 1946. m. DM.5 per no. Bayerische Landesaerztekammer, Muehlbaurstr. 16, 8000 Munich 80, Germany. TEL 089-4147-1. (Co-sponsor: Kassenaerztliche Vereinigung Bayerns) Ed.Bd. adv.; bk.rev.; bibl.; charts; illus.; stat.; upd. 27 92104; circ. 47,000.
—BLDSC shelfmark: 1871.185000.

610   US
BAYLOR MEDICINE. vol.23, no.2, 1992. 11/yr. Baylor College of Medicine, One Baylor Plaza, Houston, TX 77030. Ed. B.J. Almond.

BAYLOR PROGRESS. see *HOSPITALS*

BEHAVIOR GENETICS; an international journal devoted to research in the inheritance of behavior in animals and man. see *BIOLOGY — Genetics*

610   CC   ISSN 1000-1530
BEIJING YIKE DAXUE XUEBAO/BEIJING UNIVERSITY OF MEDICAL SCIENCES. JOURNAL. (Text in Chinese) bi-m. Beijing Yike Daxue - Beijing University of Medical Sciences, Xueyuan Lu, Beijing 100083, People's Republic of China. TEL 2017601. Ed. Feng Chuanhan.
Refereed Serial

630   CC   ISSN 0253-9713
BEIJING YIXUE/BEIJING MEDICAL SCIENCES. (Text in Chinese) bi-m. Zhonghua Yixuehui, Beijing Fenhui - Chinese Society of Medical Sciences, Beijing Chapter, A-7 Dongdan Santiao, Beijing 100005, People's Republic of China. TEL 5127766. Ed. Gao Shouzheng.

613.7   CC   ISSN 0476-0247
BEIJING ZHONGYI/BEIJING TRADITIONAL CHINESE MEDICINE. (Text in Chinese) bi-m. (Beijing Zhongyi Xuehui) Beijing Zhongyi Zazhishe, A-7 Dongdan Santiao, Beijing 100005, People's Republic of China. TEL 6127766.

613.7   CC   ISSN 0258-8811
BEIJING ZHONGYI XUEYUAN XUEBAO/BEIJING INSTITUTE OF TRADITIONAL CHINESE MEDICINE. JOURNAL. (Text in Chinese) bi-m. Beijing Zhongyi Xueyuan - Beijing Institute of Traditional Chinese Medicine, Hepingjie Beikou, Beijing 100029, People's Republic of China. TEL 4212731. Ed. Liu Duzhou.
—BLDSC shelfmark: 4707.885000.

610   SZ   ISSN 1011-6974
CODEN: BEINEM
BEITRAEGE ZU INFUSIONSTHERAPIE. 1978. irreg. price varies. S. Karger AG, Allschwilerstr. 10, P.O. Box, CH-4009 Basel, Switzerland. TEL 061-3061111. FAX 061-3061234. TELEX CH 962652. Ed.Bd. (back issues avail.) **Indexed:** Biol.Abstr., Chem.Abstr., Curr.Cont., Ind.Med.
Formerly: Beitraege zu Infusionstherapie und Klin. Ernaehrung (ISSN 0378-8679)

616.02   SZ   ISSN 0254-8275
BEITRAEGE ZUR INTENSIV- UND NOTFALLMEDIZIN. (Text in German) 1983. irreg. price varies. S. Karger AG, Allschwilerstr. 10, P.O. Box, CH-4009 Basel, Switzerland. TEL 061-3061111. FAX 061-3061234. TELEX CH 962652. Ed. G. Kalff.
—BLDSC shelfmark: 1884.403300.

610   GW
BEITRAEGE ZUR NATIONALSOZIALISTISCHEN GESUNDHEITS- UND SOZIALPOLITIK. 1985. s-a. price varies. Rotbuch Verlag, Potsdammerstr. 98, 1000 Berlin 30, Germany. TEL 030-261196. FAX 030-2626182. bk.rev.; circ. 2,500. (back issues avail.)

BEITRAEGE ZUR PSYCHOLOGIE UND SOZIOLOGIE DES KRANKEN MENSCHEN. see *PSYCHOLOGY*

610   II   ISSN 0005-8793
BENGAL MEDICAL JOURNAL. (Text in English) 1962. m. Rs.12. Indian Medical Association, Bengal State Branch, 67 Dharmatola St., Calcutta 13, India. Ed. Dr. Amiya Kumar Bose. circ. 5,500.

BERICHTE NATURWISSENSCHAFTLICH-MEDIZINISCHEN VEREINS IN INNSBRUCK. see *BIOLOGY*

610   MY
BERITA M M A/M M A NEWSLETTER. (Text in English) m. free. Malaysian Medical Association, 4th Fl., MMA House, 124 Jalan Pahang, 53000 Kuala Lumpur, Malaysia. TEL 03-6340324.

610   GW
BERLINER AERZTE. 1964. m. DM.78. (Aerztekammer Berlin) Deutscher Aerzte-Verlag GmbH, Dieselstr. 2, Postfach 40 02 65, 5000 Cologne 40, Germany. TEL 02234-7011-0. FAX 02234-7011444. illus.; circ. 18,500.
Formerly: Berliner Aerztekammer (ISSN 0568-0743)

610   GW
BERLINER AERZTEBLATT. 1887. s-m. DM.96. CB Verlag Carl Boldt, Baseler Str. 80, 1000 Berlin 45, Germany. FAX 030-8339125. Ed. Peter Gesellius. adv.; bk.rev.; index, cum.index; circ. 18,500 (controlled). (back issues avail.)

BIBLIOTEK FOR LAEGER. see *LIBRARY AND INFORMATION SCIENCES*

611 574.4   SZ   ISSN 0067-7833
CODEN: BIANA6
BIBLIOTHECA ANATOMICA. (Text in English) 1961. irreg. (approx. a.). price varies. S. Karger AG, Allschwilerstr. 10, P.O. Box, CH-4009 Basel, Switzerland. TEL 061-3061111. FAX 061-3061234. TELEX CH 962652. Ed. W. Lierse. (reprint service avail. from ISI, back issues avail.) **Indexed:** Biol.Abstr., Chem.Abstr., Curr.Cont., Ind.Med.
—BLDSC shelfmark: 2017.920000.
Incorporates: European Conference on Microcirculation. Proceedings.

BIBLIOTHECA MEDICA CANADIANA. see *LIBRARY AND INFORMATION SCIENCES*

610   US
BILL OF HEALTH. m. $125 to non-members; members $75. Pennsylvania Chamber of Business and Industry, 222 N. Third St., Harrisburg, PA 17101. TEL 800-326-3252. FAX 717-255-3298.
Description: Covers developments affecting health care benefits, including legislative updates, health care statistics, and cost containment issues.

BIO-MEDICAL MATERIALS AND ENGINEERING; an international journal. see *BIOLOGY — Bioengineering*

BIO-NYT; biologi, medicin, natur, miljoe. see *BIOLOGY*

BIO-TECHNOLOGY; the international monthly for industrial biology. see *BIOLOGY — Biotechnology*

BIOCHEMICAL MEDICINE AND METABOLIC BIOLOGY; an international journal. see *BIOLOGY — Biological Chemistry*

BIOCHEMISTRY OF DISEASE. see *BIOLOGY — Biological Chemistry*

M

MEDICAL SCIENCES

570   US   ISSN 0197-8462
QP82.2.E43   CODEN: BLCTDO
BIOELECTROMAGNETICS. 1980. bi-m. $295 (foreign $370). (Bioelectromagnetics Society) John Wiley & Sons, Inc., Journals, 605 Third Ave., New York, NY 10158. TEL 212-850-6000. FAX 212-850-6088. TELEX 12-7063. Ed. Don R. Justesen. adv.; bibl.; charts; illus.; index. **Indexed:** Biol.Abstr., Chem.Abstr., Curr.Adv.Ecol.Sci., Curr.Cont., Dent.Ind., Excerp.Med, Ind.Med., Ind.Sci.Rev., INIS Atomind., Sci.Abstr., Sci.Cit.Ind.
●Also available online.
—BLDSC shelfmark: 2072.009000.
Description: Devoted to research on biological systems as they are infulenced by natural or manufactued electric and - or magnetic fields at frequencies from DC to visible light.
Refereed Serial

BIOENGINEERING NEWS. see *BIOLOGY — Bioengineering*

BIOETHICS. see *PHILOSOPHY*

615   US
BIOFEEDBACK CLINICIANS. Variant title: A A B C Newsletter. 1976. q. $16. American Association of Biofeedback Clinicians, 2424 Dempster Ave., Des Plaines, IL 60016. TEL 312-827-0440. Eds. Joseph Sargent, Charles Sheridan. adv. **Indexed:** Excerp.Med., Psychol.Abstr.
Formerly: American Association of Biofeedback Clinicians. News.

BIOLOGICAL RHYTHMS. see *BIOLOGY — Physiology*

BIOLOGICAL STRUCTURES AND MORPHOGENESIS. see *BIOLOGY*

BIOLOGICAL THERAPIES IN DENTISTRY. see *MEDICAL SCIENCES — Dentistry*

610.28   UK   ISSN 0142-9612
R857.M3   CODEN: BIMADU
BIOMATERIALS. 1980. 9/yr. £370 in U.K. and Europe; elsewhere £400. Butterworth - Heinemann Ltd. (Subsidiary of: Reed International PLC), Linacre House, Jordan Hill, Oxford OX2 8DP, England. TEL 0865-310366. FAX 0865-310898. TELEX 83111 BHPOXF G. (Subscr. to: Turpin Transactions Ltd., Distribution Centre, Blackhorse Rd., Letchworth, Herts SG6 1HN, England. TEL 0462-672555) Ed.Bd. adv.; bk.rev.; charts; illus.; index. (also avail. in microform from UMI; back issues avail.) **Indexed:** Biol.Abstr., Br.Tech.Ind., Chem.Abstr., Curr.Adv.Ecol.Sci., Curr.Cont, Curr.Leather Lit., Curr.Tit.Dent., Dent.Ind., Excerp.Med., Ind.Med., Ind.Sci.Rev., Sci.Abstr, Telegen.
—BLDSC shelfmark: 2087.715000.
Description: Focuses on the structure, properties, interactions, functions and applications of biomaterials. For bio-materials and materials scientists, clinicians, biochemists and pharmacologists.
Refereed Serial

BIOMEDICA BIOCHIMICA ACTA; Zeitschrift fuer funktionelle Biowissenschaften. see *BIOLOGY*

614.49 615.9   CC   ISSN 0895-3988
                    CODEN: BESCE5
BIOMEDICAL AND ENVIRONMENTAL SCIENCES. (Text in English) 1988. q. $112. Zhongguo Yufang Kexue Yanjiuyuan - Chinese Academy of Preventive Medicine, 207 Ruijin 2 Lu, Shanghai 200025, People's Republic of China. TEL 4377008. FAX 619-699-6800. TELEX 181726. (Dist. by: Academic Press, Inc., Journal Division, 1250 Sixth Ave., San Diego, CA 92101, USA. TEL 619-230-1840) Eds. Frederick Coulston, Chen Chunming. (back issues avail.)
—BLDSC shelfmark: 2087.753700.
Description: Provides a forum for the publication of epidemiological studies in China that confirm toxicological findings obtained in animals, identify etiologic factors for specific health effects observed among certain population groups, or better estimate the acceptable levels of toxic agents.
Refereed Serial

610.28   US   ISSN 0006-3398
R856   CODEN: BIOEAF
BIOMEDICAL ENGINEERING. English translation of: Meditsinskaya Tekhnika. 1967. bi-m. $795 (foreign $930)(effective 1992). (Ministerstvo Zdravookhraneniya, UR) Plenum Publishing Corp., Consultants Bureau, 233 Spring St., New York, NY 10013-1578. TEL 212-620-8468. FAX 212-463-0742. TELEX 23-421139. Ed. V.A. Viktorov. (also avail. in microfilm from JSC; back issues avail.) **Indexed:** Appl.Mech.Rev., Biol.Abstr., Eng.Ind., Excerp.Med., Ind.Med., INIS Atomind.
—BLDSC shelfmark: 0406.050000.
Refereed Serial

BIOMEDICAL ENGINEERING AND INSTRUMENTATION SERIES. see *BIOLOGY — Bioengineering*

610.28   US   ISSN 0899-8205
R856.A1   CODEN: BITYE2
BIOMEDICAL INSTRUMENTATION & TECHNOLOGY. 1967. bi-m. $60 to individuals (foreign $70); institutions $85 (foreign $95). (Association for the Advancement of Medical Instrumentation) Hanley & Belfus, Inc., 210 S. 13th St., Philadelphia, PA 19107. TEL 215-546-7293. FAX 215-790-9330. (Alt. addr.: 3330 Washington Blvd., Ste. 400, Arlington, VA 22201-4598) Ed. Michael Kallock. adv. contact: Diane R. Sherel. bk.rev.; charts; illus.; index; circ. 6,000. (also avail. in microform; back issues avail.) **Indexed:** Abstr.Health Care Manage.Stud., Bioeng.Abstr., Biol.Abstr., CINAHL, Curr.Adv.Ecol.Sci., Curr.Cont., Excerp.Med., Ind.Med., INIS Atomind., Ref.Zh., Sci.Abstr., Sci.Cit.Ind.
—BLDSC shelfmark: 2087.830500.
Former titles (until 1989): Medical Instrumentation (ISSN 0090-6689); Biomedical Technology Today; Incorporating: Clinical Engineering; Which was formerly: Medical Instrumentation Journal; Association for the Advancement of Medical Instrumentation. Journal (JAAMI) (ISSN 0004-5446)
Description: Covers the development, use and maintenance of medical instrumentation, including testing, evaluation, and purchasing.
Refereed Serial

BIOMEDICAL LETTERS; a prestige international biomedical journal for the rapid publication of biomedical communications. see *BIOLOGY — Cytology And Histology*

610   UK   ISSN 0955-7717
                    CODEN: BMATEM
BIOMEDICAL MATERIALS; an international newsletter. 1975. m. £291 (effective 1992). Elsevier Science Publishers Ltd., Crown House, Linton Rd., Barking, Essex IG11 8JU, England. TEL 081-594-7272. FAX 081-594-5942. TELEX 896950 APPSCI G. (N. America dist. addr.: Elsevier Science Publishing Co., Inc., Box 882, Madison Sq. Sta., New York, NY 10159. TEL 212-989-5800) Eds. P. Read, Richard Juniper. bk.rev.; charts; stat. (back issues avail.)
●Also available online. Vendor(s): Data-Star, DIALOG.
—BLDSC shelfmark: 2087.838000.
Formerly (until 1988): Biomedical Polymers (ISSN 0267-5439)
Description: Provides coverage of design, production and research management in the fibre and polymer industries, and in related research departments and institutes. Also provides a survey for senior general management, serving to highlight new trends and possibilities, market gaps and business opportunities.

681.761 610.28   US   ISSN 0192-1266
BIOMEDICAL PRODUCTS. 1976. m. $12. Gordon Publications, Inc., 301 Gibraltar Dr., Morris Plains, NJ 07950. TEL 201-292-5100. FAX 201-898-9281. Ed. Steve Ernst. adv.; circ. 75,000. (tabloid format) **Indexed:** Curr.Pack.Abstr.

610   UK   ISSN 0955-9701
R31   CODEN: BSCHE4
▼**BIOMEDICAL SCIENCE.** 1990. m. £190. Royal Society of Chemistry, Thomas Graham House, Science Park, Milton Rd., Cambridge CB4 4WF, England. (Dist. by: Turpin Transactions Ltd., The Distribution Centre, Blackhorse Rd., Letchworth, Hertfordshire SG6 1HN, England) (Co-publishers: Academy of Sciences of the USSR; Pion Ltd.) Eds. Rem Petrov, Bernard Donovan.
—BLDSC shelfmark: 2087.879000.
Refereed Serial

610   US   ISSN 1051-2020
R856.A1
▼**BIOMEDICAL SCIENCE AND TECHNOLOGY;** a review journal. 1991. q. $95 (foreign $112). Academic Press, Inc., Journal Division, 1260 Sixth Ave., San Diego, CA 92101. TEL 619-230-1840. FAX 619-699-6800. TELEX 181726. Ed. Robert D. Gold.
—BLDSC shelfmark: 2087.879500.
Description: Covers the development and production of devices and instruments used in medical practice.

610.28   US   ISSN 0067-8856
R856   CODEN: BMSIA7
BIOMEDICAL SCIENCES INSTRUMENTATION. 1963. a. price varies. Instrument Society of America, 67 Alexander Dr., Box 12277, Research Triangle Park, NC 27709. TEL 919-549-8411. FAX 919-549-8288. TELEX 802540 ISA DURM. (also avail. in microform from UMI; reprint service avail. from ISI,UMI) **Indexed:** Appl.Mech.Rev., Biol.Abstr., Chem.Abstr., Dent.Ind., Eng.Ind., Excerp.Med., Ind.Med.
—BLDSC shelfmark: 2087.880000.
Refereed Serial

610   US   ISSN 0147-2682
                    CODEN: BTISE6
BIOMEDICAL TECHNOLOGY INFORMATION SERVICE. 1974. s-m. (m. in Jan. & Aug.). $195 (foreign $233). Quest Publishing Co., 1351 Titan Way, Brea, CA 92621. TEL 714-738-6400. FAX 714-525-6258. Ed. Allan F. Pacela. bk.rev.; index. (looseleaf format; back issues avail.)
Formed by the merger of: Advanced Biomedical Technology (ISSN 0094-0100); Biomedical Inventions Reporter (ISSN 0094-0119); Government Documents Review (ISSN 0094-0127); Health Care Statistics Report (ISSN 0094-0135)
Description: Covers advances in medical device technology and biomedical engineering, including latest biomedical inventions and federal regulations.

610 574   FR   ISSN 0753-3322
                    CODEN: BIPHEX
BIOMEDICINE AND PHARMACOTHERAPY. (Text and summaries in English, French) 1956. 10/yr. 1340 F. (foreign 1570 F.)(effective 1992). Editions Scientifiques Elsevier, 29, rue Buffon, 75005 Paris, France. TEL 47-07-11-22. FAX 43-36-80-93. TELEX 202400F. (Subscr. in U.S. and Canada to: Elsevier Science Publishing Co., Inc., Box 882, Madison Sq. Sta., New York, NY 10159. TEL 212-989-5800) Ed. G. Mathe. adv.; bk.rev.; bibl.; illus.; index; circ. 2,000. (also avail. in microform from UMI; reprint service avail. from ISI) **Indexed:** Biol.Abstr., Chem.Abstr., Dairy Sci.Abstr., Excerp.Med., Helminthol.Abstr., Ind.Med., Ind.Vet., INIS Atomind., Vet.Bull.
—BLDSC shelfmark: 2087.883300.
Former titles: Biomedicine (ISSN 0300-0893); Revue Europeenne d'Etudes Cliniques et Biologiques (ISSN 0035-3019)
Description: Discusses medical ailments with an emphasis on how they relate to pharmacological drugs and subsequent treatments.
Refereed Serial

610.28   GW   ISSN 0013-5585
R856.A1   CODEN: BMZTA7
BIOMEDIZINISCHE TECHNIK/BIOMEDICAL ENGINEERING. 1955. m. (10/yr.). DM.442. (Deutsche Gesellschaft fuer Biomedizinische Technik - German Association on Bio-Medical Engineering) Fachverlag Schiele und Schoen GmbH, Markgrafenstr. 11, 1000 Berlin 61, Germany. TEL 030-2516029. FAX 030-2517248. Eds. M. Schaidach, U. Boenick. adv.; bk.rev.; abstr.; bibl.; charts; circ. 1,500. **Indexed:** Biol.Abstr., C.I.S. Abstr., Chem.Abstr., Curr.Adv.Ecol.Sci., Excerp.Med., Helminthol.Abstr., Ind.Med., Ind.Sci.Rev., INIS Atomind., Sci.Abstr, Sci.Cit.Ind, Vet.Bull.
—BLDSC shelfmark: 2087.890000.
Formerly: Elektromedizin.

610   GW   ISSN 0933-2871
BIOMEDIZINSCHE FORSCHUNG - INFORMATIONEN. 1987. s-a. DM.34. Demeter Verlag, Wuermstr. 13, 8032 Graefelfing, Germany. TEL 089-852033. FAX 089-8543347. circ. 1,500.
—BLDSC shelfmark: 2087.888000.

610 574   GW   ISSN 0934-9235
BIOMETRIE AND INFORMATIK. (Text in English or German) 1970. q. DM.273 (foreign DM.274). Gustav Fischer Verlag, Wollgrasweg 49, Postfach 720143, 7000 Stuttgart 70, Germany. TEL 0711-458030. FAX 0711-4580334. TELEX 7111488-FIBUCH. (U.S. addr.: Gustav Fischer New York Inc., 220 East 23rd St., Ste. 909, New York, NY 10010) Ed.Bd. circ. 1,000. Indexed: Biol.Abstr., Comput.Rev., Forest.Abstr., VITIS.
—BLDSC shelfmark: 2088.990000.
  Formerly: E D V in Medizin und Biologie - E D V in Medicine and Biology (ISSN 0300-8282)

BIOORGANIC & MEDICINAL CHEMISTRY LETTERS; for rapid dissemination of preliminary communications on all aspects of bioorganic chemistry, medicinal chemistry and related disciplines. see *CHEMISTRY — Organic Chemistry*

BIOPSYCHE; rivista di scienze antropologiche. see *PSYCHOLOGY*

BIOTECHNOLOGY ADVANCES. see *BIOLOGY — Biotechnology*

BIOTECHNOLOGY AND GENETIC ENGINEERING REVIEWS. see *BIOLOGY — Biotechnology*

BIOTHERAPY; an international journal on biological agents. see *MEDICAL SCIENCES — Cancer*

BIRMINGHAM HEALTHCARE REVIEW & FORECAST ANNUAL. see *HOSPITALS*

616.043   US
BIRTH DEFECTS INSTITUTE. SYMPOSIA. 1971. irreg. Academic Press, Inc., 1250 Sixth Ave., San Diego, CA 92101. TEL 619-231-0926. FAX 619-699-6715. Ed. Ian H. Porter. (reprint service avail. from ISI)
  Refereed Serial

BISHVILEI HAREFUAH. see *RELIGIONS AND THEOLOGY — Judaic*

610   UK   ISSN 0045-2084
BLACK BAG. 1898. irreg. Galenicals Society, Bristol University Medical School, Dolphin House, Bristol Royal Infirmary, Bristol 2, England. Ed. Paul T. Johns. adv.; bk.rev.; film rev.; illus.; circ. 1,000 (controlled).

BLACK HEALTH. see *ETHNIC INTERESTS*

610   UK
BLACK'S MEDICAL DICTIONARY. 1906. irreg. (every 2-3 yrs.) £17.50. A & C Black (Publishers) Ltd., Howard Rd., Eaton Socon, Huntingdon, Cambs PE19 3EZ, England. TEL (0480) 212666. FAX 0480-405014. TELEX 32524. Ed. Dr. C.W.H. Havard.
  Description: Comprehensive medical dictionary for lay people and specialists.

610   AT
BLOOD AND ITS PRODUCTS. triennial. Aus.$5.80. Victorian Medical Postgraduate Foundation Inc., P.O. Box 27, Parkville, Vic. 3052, Australia. TEL 03-347-9633. FAX 03-347-4547. circ. 5,000.
  Description: Comprehensive guide to correct handling and usage of blood and its products.

610   US   ISSN 0747-2420
BLOOD BANK WEEK. 1984. w. $128 to non-members (foreign $150); members $98 (foreign $130). American Association of Blood Banks, 1117 N. 19th St., Ste. 600, Arlington, VA 22209. TEL 703-528-8200. FAX 703-527-8036. Ed. Joel Solomon. circ. 1,400. (looseleaf format; back issues avail.)

610   US
BLUE BOOK DIGEST OF H M O'S. 1983. a. $59.50. (National Association of Employers on Health Care Action) Blue Book, Inc., Box 220, Key Biscayne, FL 33149. TEL 305-361-2810. FAX 305-361-2842. Ed. Ruth H. Stack. adv.; circ. 2,000. (back issues avail.)
  Description: Lists names, addresses, key executives, profit status, chain, operational dates, federal qualifications, enrollments, employer contracts and data reports.

610   US
BLUE BOOK DIGEST OF P P O'S. 1985. a. $59.50. (National Association of Employers on Health Care Action, Preferred Provided Organization) Blue Book, Inc., Box 220, Key Biscayne, FL 33149. TEL 305-361-2810. FAX 305-361-2842. Ed. Ruth H. Stack. adv.; circ. 2,000. (back issues avail.)
  Description: Lists names, addresses, key officers, profit status, Preferred Provided Organization sponsors, number of physicians, hospitals, subscriber and subscriber groups.

BOLETIN DE BIOTECNOLOGIA. see *BIOLOGY — Biotechnology*

610 574   MX   ISSN 0067-9666
R21   CODEN: BEMBA2
BOLETIN DE ESTUDIOS MEDICOS Y BIOLOGICOS. (Some articles in English) 2/yr. $50. Universidad Nacional Autonoma de Mexico, Instituto de Investigaciones Biomedicas, Ciudad Universitaria, Coyoacan, Mexico 04510, D.F., Mexico. Ed. Dr. Alfonso Escobar. bk.rev. Indexed: Biol.Abstr., Excerp.Med., Ind.Med.
—BLDSC shelfmark: 2203.870000.

610   CU
BOLETIN DE MEDICIANA TRADICIONAL GRUPO "JUAN TOMAS ROIG". a. Academia de Ciencias, Instituto de Documentacion e Informacon Cientifico-Tecnica (I D I C T), Capitolio Nacional, Prado y San Jose, La Habana 2, Havana, Cuba.

610   IT   ISSN 0007-5787
BOLLETTINO DELLE SCIENZE MEDICHE. 1823. 4/yr. L.20000. Societa Medica Chirurgica di Bologna-Archiginnasio, Piazza Galvani, 1, 40100 Bologna, Italy. Ed. Michele Fiorentino. adv.; bk.rev. Indexed: Biol.Abstr., Chem.Abstr.
—BLDSC shelfmark: 2927.250000.

BOLLETTINO DI MICROBIOLOGIA ED INDAGINI DI LABORATORIO. see *BIOLOGY — Microbiology*

610   II   ISSN 0524-0182
BOMBAY HOSPITAL JOURNAL. (Text in English) 1959. q. Rs.100. Bombay Hospital Institute of Medical Sciences, 16th Floor, 12 Marine Lines, Bombay 400 020, India. Ed. Dr. O.P. Kapoor. adv.; bk.rev.; charts; illus.; index; circ. 5,000. Indexed: Biol.Abstr., Indian Sci.Abstr., INIS Atomind.
—BLDSC shelfmark: 2245.800000.

BONE AND MINERAL RESEARCH ANNUAL. see *MEDICAL SCIENCES — Orthopedics And Traumatology*

616.7   US
BONING UP ON OSTEOPOROSIS. 1987. irreg., latest 1991. $2. National Osteoporosis Foundation, 2100 M St., N.W., Ste. 602, Washington, DC 20037. TEL 202-223-2226. FAX 202-223-2237.
  Description: Covers prevention, diagnosis and treatment of osteoporosis for the general public.

610   GW   ISSN 0935-8013
BONNER AERZTLICHE NACHRICHTEN. 1967-1984; resumed 198? q. DM.12. (Bonner Aerzte-Verein e.V.) Asgard-Verlag Dr. Werner Hippe KG, Postfach 1465, 5205 St. Augustin, Germany. TEL 02241-3164-0. adv.; bk.rev.; illus.; circ. 3,800.

610   US   ISSN 0894-4024
RA1190
BOSTON BULLETIN ON CHEMICALS AND DISEASE;* objective reports on the health effects of chemicals. 1985. q. $20 to individuals; students $15; non-profit libraries $30; corporations $50. ChemoPathology ResourCenter, Inc., 30 Worthington St., Boston, MA 02120-1605. TEL 617-864-7838. Ed. S. Szabo. bk.rev.; circ. 2,000. (back issues avail.)
  Description: Contains summaries, mini-reviews, and brief news items about how chemicals effect our health.

BRAILLE JOURNAL OF PHYSIOTHERAPY. see *HANDICAPPED — Visually Impaired*

BRAIN DYSFUNCTION. see *MEDICAL SCIENCES — Psychiatry And Neurology*

610   US
BRANDEIS UNIVERSITY. BIGEL INSTITUTE FOR HEALTH POLICY. RESEARCH NEWS. 1986. s-a. Brandeis University, Bigel Institute for Health Policy, 415 South St., Waltham, MA 02254-9110. TEL 617-736-3910. FAX 617-736-3905. Ed. Jacqueline M. Davidson. circ. 1,000. (back issues avail.)
  Description: Includes public policy articles on long-term care, substance abuse, medicare, county health policy, and state policy.

610   BL   ISSN 0006-9205
BRASIL-MEDICO;* revista de medicina e cirurgia. (Text in English, French, Portuguese or Spanish) 1887. bi-m. Policlinica Geral do Rio de Janeiro, Av. Nilo Pecanha 38, Rio de Janeiro, Brazil. adv.; bk.rev.; abstr.; bibl.; illus.; index. Indexed: Biol.Abstr., Chem.Abstr.

610   BL   ISSN 0524-2053
BRASILIA MEDICA. 1968. s-a. Cz.$1000($30) Associacao Medica de Brasilia, EQS 713-913, Modulo E, 70930 Brasilia, D.F., Brazil. TEL 061-245-1408. FAX 061-245-2501. Ed. Denis M. Brandao. adv.; bk.rev.; circ. 5,000. Indexed: Ind.Med.

610   CS   ISSN 0006-9248
                CODEN: BLLIAX
BRATISLAVSKE LEKARSKE LISTY. (Text in Slovak; summaries in Russian and Slovak) 1921. m. 300 Kcs.($55) (Slovenska Akademia Vied) Veda, Publishing House of the Slovak Academy of Sciences, Klemensova 19, 814 30 Bratislava, Czechoslovakia. (Dist. by: Slovart, Nam. Slobody 6, 817 64 Bratislava, Czechoslovakia) Ed. Dr. Jozef Pogady. bk.rev.; charts; illus.; s-a. index, cum.index: 1921-1950, 1951-1955. Indexed: Biol.Abstr., C.I.S. Abstr., Chem.Abstr., Dent.Ind., Dok.Arbeitsmed., Excerp.Med., Ind.Med., INIS Atomind., Protozool.Abstr.
—BLDSC shelfmark: 2275.500000.
  Description: Presents original works written by domestic and foreign authors covering experimental and clinical medicine, public health, therapy and practical spheres as well as reviews and studies of history.

610   US   ISSN 0888-6008
RC280.B8
BREAST DISEASES (NEW YORK); an international journal. 1987. 4/yr. $150 to institutions (foreign $172)(effective 1992). Elsevier Science Publishing Co., Inc. (New York), 655 Ave. of the Americas, New York, NY 10010. TEL 212-989-5800. FAX 212-633-3965. TELEX 420643 AEP UI. Ed. Dr. Douglas J. Marchant. Indexed: Excerp.Med.
—BLDSC shelfmark: 2277.494070.
  Description: Provides information on all aspects of human breast disease - benign and malignant - to help improve the health care and management of patients.
  Refereed Serial

610   GW   ISSN 0340-5362
BREMER AERZTEBLATT. 1948. m. DM.60. (Aerztekammer Bremen) Carl Ed. Schuenemann KG, Zweite Schlachtpforte 7, Postfach 106067, 2800 Bremen 1, Germany. TEL 0421-36903-72. FAX 0421-36903-39. Ed. W. Arens. circ. 3,900. Indexed: Excerp.Med.
—BLDSC shelfmark: 2277.850000.

610   CN
BRITISH COLUMBIA MEDICAL ASSOCIATION. NEWS. 6/yr. membership. British Columbia Medical Association, 115-1665 West Broadway, Vancouver, B.C. V6J 5A4, Canada. TEL 604-736-5551. FAX 604-736-4566. Ed. Dr. Robert Young.

610   CN   ISSN 0007-0556
BRITISH COLUMBIA MEDICAL JOURNAL. 1959. m. Can.$50 (foreign $65). British Columbia Medical Association, 115-1665 West Broadway, Vancouver, B.C. V6J 5A4, Canada. TEL 604-736-5551. FAX 604-733-7317. Ed. W. Alan Dodd. adv.; bk.rev.; charts; illus.; stat.; index; circ. 6,800. (back issues avail.) Indexed: Med.Care Rev.
—BLDSC shelfmark: 2297.100000.

MEDICAL SCIENCES

615.89   UK   ISSN 0143-4977
BRITISH JOURNAL OF ACUPUNCTURE. 1977. 2/yr. £8 (foreign £13). British Acupuncture Association & Register, 34 Alderney St., London SW1V 4EW, England. TEL 071-834-6229. Ed. R. Newman Turner. circ. 700.
—BLDSC shelfmark: 2303.860000.

610   UK   ISSN 0007-0947
R11   CODEN: BJCPAT
BRITISH JOURNAL OF CLINICAL PRACTICE. 1947. q. £52($105) (elsewhere £57). Medicom UK Ltd., The Quandrant, 118 London Rd., Kingston-upon-Thames KT2 6QJ, England. TEL 081-541-5666. FAX 081-541-4746. Ed. Graham Jackson. adv.; bk.rev.; bibl.; illus.; index; circ. 6,000. **Indexed:** Abstr.Hyg., Biotech.Abstr., Chem.Abstr., Curr.Adv.Ecol.Sci., Curr.Cont., Excerp.Med., Helminthol.Abstr., I.P.A., Ind.Med., Ind.Sci.Rev., NRN, Nutr.Abstr., Sci.Cit.Ind., Sp.Ed.Needs Abstr., Trop.Dis.Bull.
●Also available online.
—BLDSC shelfmark: 2307.200000.
Refereed Serial

610   UK   ISSN 0961-1053
▼**BRITISH JOURNAL OF CLINICAL RESEARCH.** (Supplement avail.) 1992. s-m. £60 (Europe £65; elsewhere £70). Brookwood Medical Publications Ltd., 3 Jenner Rd., Guildford, Surrey GU1 3AQ, England. TEL 0483-797975. FAX 0483-797915. (Subscr. to: Orchard House, Brookwood, Surrey GU24 0AT, England)
—BLDSC shelfmark: 2307.235000.
Description: Covers research on new drugs, devices and other products, clinical trials phases I to IV, including papers showing negative results, clinical pharmacology, preclinical studies, drug metabolism.

610   UK   ISSN 0960-1643
CODEN: BJGPEJ
BRITISH JOURNAL OF GENERAL PRACTICE.. 1958. m. (foreign £90). Royal College of General Practitioners, 12 Queen Street, Edinburgh EH2 1JE, Scotland. TEL 031-225-7629. (Bailey Bros and Swinfen Ltd., Warner House, Folkestone, Kent CT19 6PH, England) Ed. Dr. E.G. Buckley. adv.; bk.rev.; charts; illus.; stat.; index; circ. 17,000. (back issues avail.) **Indexed:** Abstr.Hyg., CINAHL, Curr.Adv.Ecol.Sci., Dok.Arbeitsmed., Geo.Abstr., Helminthol.Abstr., Ind.Med., Med.Care Rev., Nutr.Abstr., Protozool.Abstr., Trop.Dis.Bull.
—BLDSC shelfmark: 2308.360000.
Formerly: Royal College of General Practitioners. Journal. (ISSN 0035-8797)

610   UK   ISSN 0007-1064
CODEN: BJHMAB
BRITISH JOURNAL OF HOSPITAL MEDICINE. Spanish edition (ISSN 0210-0258) 1966. m. £42. Mark Allen Publishing Ltd., 288 Croxted Rd., London SE24 9DA, England. Ed. Jack Tinker. adv.; bk.rev.; bibl.; charts; illus.; stat.; index. (processed; also avail. in microform from UMI; reprint service avail. from UMI) **Indexed:** Biol.Abstr., Chem.Abstr., Curr.Adv.Cancer Res., Curr.Adv.Ecol.Sci., Curr.Cont., Dent.Ind., Excerp.Med., Helminthol.Abstr., Ind.Med., Ind.Sci.Rev., Ind.Vet., Nutr.Abstr., Pig News & Info., Sci.Abstr., Trop.Dis.Bull., Vet.Bull.
—BLDSC shelfmark: 2309.500000.
Formerly: Hospital Medicine.

610 657.832   UK   ISSN 0962-1423
▼**BRITISH JOURNAL OF MEDICAL ECONOMICS.** 1992. s-m. £60 (Europe £65; elsewhere £70). Brookwood Medical Publications Ltd., 3 Jenner Rd., Guildford, Surrey GU1 3AQ, England. TEL 0483-797975. FAX 0483-797915. (Subscr. to: Orchard House, Brookwood, Surrey GU24 0AT, England)
—BLDSC shelfmark: 2311.370000.
Description: Publishes papers on aspects of health economics.

615.85   UK   ISSN 0308-0226
BRITISH JOURNAL OF OCCUPATIONAL THERAPY. 1937. m. £40. College of Occupational Therapists Ltd., 6-8 Marshalsea Rd., Southwark, London SE1 1HL, England. TEL 071-357-6480. FAX 071-378-8095. Ed.Bd. adv.; bk.rev.; charts; illus.; index; circ. 13,500. **Indexed:** Abstr.Health Care Manage.Stud., ASSIA, Curr.Adv.Ecol.Sci., Psychol.Abstr., Rehabil.Lit.
—BLDSC shelfmark: 2312.700000.

616.742 362   UK   ISSN 0263-7103
CODEN: BJRHDF
BRITISH JOURNAL OF RHEUMATOLOGY. (Supplements avail.: Abstracts from B S R Scientific Meetings) 1952. bi-m. $220. (British Association of Rheumatology) Bailliere Tindall, 24-28 Oval Rd., London NW1 7DX, England. Ed. Terry Gibson. adv.; bk.rev.; bibl.; illus.; index. (also avail. in microform from UMI; reprint service avail. from UMI) **Indexed:** Abstr.Inter.Med., Biol.Abstr., Biotech.Abstr., Chem.Abstr., CINAHL, Curr.Adv.Ecol.Sci., Curr.Adv.Ecol.Sci., Curr.Cont., Dent.Ind., Excerp.Med., Ind.Med., Ind.Sci.Rev., Sci.Cit.Ind.
●Also available online. Vendor(s): BRS.
—BLDSC shelfmark: 2324.320000.
Former titles: Rheumatology and Rehabilitation (ISSN 0300-3396); Rheumatology and Physical Medicine (ISSN 0003-4908)
Description: Devoted to clinical and laboratory rheumatology worldwide.

610   UK   ISSN 0301-5572
CODEN: BJMEDF
BRITISH JOURNAL OF SEXUAL MEDICINE. Abbreviated title: B J S M. 1974. 6/yr. £42 (foreign £48). Hayward Medical Communications, Hayward House, 1 Threshers Yard, Kingham, Oxon OX2 67F, England. TEL 0608-6595955. Ed. Dr. Paul Wooley. adv.; bk.rev.; circ. 22,000. **Indexed:** Biol.Abstr., Curr.Adv.Cancer Res., Curr.Adv.Ecol.Sci., Excerp.Med.
—BLDSC shelfmark: 2324.600000.

BRITISH JOURNAL OF SPECIAL EDUCATION. see
EDUCATION — Special Education And Rehabilitation

610   UK   ISSN 0007-1420
R31   CODEN: BMBUAQ
BRITISH MEDICAL BULLETIN. 1943. 4/yr. £105($200) (British Council, Medical Department) Churchill Livingstone Medical Journals, Robert Stevenson House, 1-3 Baxter's Pl., Leith Walk, Edinburgh EH1 3AF, Scotland. TEL 031-556-2424. FAX 031-558-1278. TELEX 727511. (Subscr. to: Longman Group, Journals Subscr. Dept., P.O. Box 77, Fourth Ave., Harlow, Essex CM19 5AA, England; U.S. subscr. to: Churchill Livingstone, 650 Ave. of the Americas, New York, NY 10011. TEL 212-206-5000) adv.; charts; illus.; index; circ. 3,300. (also avail. in microform from UMI; reprint service avail. from UMI) **Indexed:** Abstr.Hyg., Anim.Breed.Abstr., Bibl.Dev.Med.& Child Neur., Biol.Abstr., Biotech.Abstr., C.I.S. Abstr., Chem.Abstr., Curr.Adv.Ecol.Sci., Curr.Cont., Dairy Sci.Abstr., Excerp.Med., Helminthol.Abstr., I.P.A., Ind.Med., Ind.Sci.Rev., Ind.Vet., Nutr.Abstr., Rev.Plant Path., Sci.Cit.Ind., Vet.Bull.
●Also available online.
—BLDSC shelfmark: 2329.000000.

610   UK   ISSN 0007-1447
R31   CODEN: BMJOAE
BRITISH MEDICAL JOURNAL. 1832. w. £154. B M J Publishing Group, B.M.A. House, Tavistock Sq., London WC1H 9JR, England. TEL 071-387-4499. Ed. Richard Smith. adv.; bk.rev.; abstr.; bibl.; charts; illus.; index. (also avail. in microform from UMI,PMC; reprint service avail. from UMI) **Indexed:** Abstr.Health Care Manage.Stud., Abstr.Hyg., Abstr.Inter.Med., Anal.Abstr., ASSIA, Behav.Med.Abstr., Bibl.Dev.Med.& Child Neur., Biol.Abstr., Biotech.Abstr., C.I.S. Abstr., Cadscan, Chem.Abstr., CINAHL, Curr.Adv.Cancer Res., Curr.Adv.Ecol.Sci., Curr.Adv.Genetics & Molec.Biol., Curr.Cont., Curr.Lit.Fam.Plan., Dairy Sci.Abstr., Dent.Ind., Dok.Arbeitsmed., Excerp.Med., FAMLI, Food Sci.& Tech.Abstr., Helminthol.Abstr., High.Educ.Curr.Aware.Bull., HRIS, I.P.A., Ind.Hyg.Dig., Ind.Med., Ind.Sci.Rev., Ind.Vet., INIS Atomind., Lab.Haz.Bull., Lead Abstr., Med.Care Rev., NRN, Nutr.Abstr., Popul.Ind., Potato Abstr., Protozool.Abstr., Res.High.Educ.Abstr., Rev.Appl.En tomol., Rev.Plant Path., Risk Abstr., Sci.Cit.Ind, Sp.Ed.Needs Abstr., Stud.Wom.Abstr., Trop.Dis.Bull., Vet.Bull., W.R.C.Inf., Zincscan.
●Also available online. Vendor(s): BRS, BRS/Saunders Colleague.
Also available on CD-ROM.
—BLDSC shelfmark: 2330.000000.

610   SP   ISSN 0213-3954
BRITISH MEDICAL JOURNAL. EDICION ESPANOLA. 1986. m. 4900 ptas. Salvat Publicaciones Cientificas, S.A., Muntaner, 263, 6o, 08021 Barcelona, Spain. TEL 2010911. FAX 2015911. TELEX 53132 SAEDI E. (Subscr. to: Cempro, Plaza Conde Valle Suchil 20, 28015 Madrid, Spain) Ed. Joan Rodes. adv.; bk.rev.; index; circ. 15,000. (back issues avail.; reprint service avail.)

610   US
BRONX MEDICINE. vol.45, 1967. 4/yr. $10. Bronx County Medical Society, 2600 Netherland Ave., Bronx, NY 10463. TEL 212-548-4401. FAX 212-549-6681. Ed. John P. Albanese, M.D. adv.; illus.; circ. 1,800. **Indexed:** Med.Care Rev.
Formerly: Bronx County Medical Society. Bulletin (ISSN 0007-2257)

410   AA
BULETINI I SHKENCAVE MJEKESORE/BULLETIN DES SCIENCES MEDICALES. (Text in Albanian; summaries in French) s-a. $3.85. Enver Hoxha Universitet, Tirana, Albania. Ed. Ylvi Vehbiu. **Indexed:** Chem.Abstr.

610   JA   ISSN 0007-4705
BULLETIN MEDICAL FRANCO-JAPONAIS/NICHI-FUTSU IGAKU. (Text in French and Japanese) 1954. q. 800 Yen. Societe Franco-Japonaise de Medecine - Nichi-Futsu Igakkai, 2-3 Kanda Surugadai, Chiyoda-ku, Tokyo 101, Japan. Ed. Tatsuo Kobayashi. adv.; bk.rev.; charts; illus.; circ. 250. (also avail. in microform)

BULLETIN OF EXPERIMENTAL BIOLOGY AND MEDICINE. see *BIOLOGY*

610 581   II
BULLETIN OF MEDICO-ETHNO-BOTANICAL RESEARCH. (Text in English; summaries in Hindi) 1980. q. Rs.60. Central Council for Research in Ayurveda and Siddha, Dharma Bhawan, S-10, Green Park Extn. Market, New Delhi 110 016, India. TEL 11-669315. Ed. V.N. Pandey. adv.; bk.rev.; bibl.; charts; illus.; circ. 300. **Indexed:** Hort.Abstr.
Description: Covers folk medicine, pharmacognosy, and phytochemistry. Examines the correlation between ancient insights and modern scientific thought.

610   US   ISSN 0007-5140
R11
BULLETIN OF THE HISTORY OF MEDICINE. 1933. q. $26 to individuals (foreign $33.50); institutions $53 (foreign $59.50). (American Association for the History of Medicine) Johns Hopkins University Press, Journals Publishing Division, 701 W. 40th St., Ste. 275, Baltimore, MD 21211. TEL 410-516-6987. FAX 410-516-6998. (Co-sponsor: Johns Hopkins Institute of the History of Medicine) Eds. Gert H. Brieger, Jerome J. Bylebyl. adv.; bk.rev.; bibl.; illus.; index, cum.index vols.1-56; circ. 4,432. (also avail. in microform from UMI,PMC; microfiche; back issues avail.; reprint service avail. from UMI) **Indexed:** Amer.Bibl.Slavic & E.Eur.Stud., Amer.Hist.& Life, Arts & Hum.Cit.Ind., Biol.Abstr., Chem.Abstr., Curr.Cont., Excerp.Med., Hist.Abstr., Ind.Med., Ind.Sci.Rev., Sci.Cit.Ind., SSCI, Trop.Dis.Bull.
—BLDSC shelfmark: 2856.000000.
Description: Presents articles that analyze advances in medical science, examine changes in clinical practices, and explore how the response of societies to health care needs have varied with times and cultures.

610   US
BULLETIN OF THE MEDICAL SOCIETY OF THE COUNTY OF QUEENS AND THE ACADEMY OF MEDICINE OF QUEENS. 1925. 10/yr. $10. Medical Society of the County of Queens, 112-25 Queens Blvd., Forest Hills, NY 11375. FAX 718-268-6918. (Co-sponsor: Academy of Medicine of Queens County) Ed. Dr. Lorraine Maria Giordano. adv.; illus.; tr.lit.; circ. 2,000.

BULLETIN SCIENTIFIQUE. SECTION A: SCIENCES NATURELLES, TECHNIQUES ET MEDICALES. see
MEDICAL SCIENCES — Abstracting, Bibliographies, Statistics

BUNDESARBEITSGEMEINSCHAFT HILFE FUER BEHINDERTE. BERICHTE. JAHRESSPIEGEL. see
EDUCATION — Special Education And Rehabilitation

610   BR   ISSN 0007-6295
BURMA MEDICAL JOURNAL.* vol.12, 1964. q. Burma Medical Association, 249 Theinbyu Rd., Yangon, Union of Myanmar. **Indexed:** Chem.Abstr.

BYULLETEN' EKSPERIMENTAL'NOI BIOLOGII I MEDITSINY. see *BIOLOGY*

MEDICAL SCIENCES

610　　　US　　ISSN 0891-1525
C A P TODAY; pathology-laboratory medicine-laboratory management. 1987. m. $15 to non-members; free to qualified personnel. College of American Pathologists, 325 Waukegan Rd., Northfield, IL 60093-2750. TEL 708-446-8800.
FAX 708-446-8807. Ed. Gordon Briggs. adv.; circ. 42,000. (tabloid format)

610　　　DK　　ISSN 0901-067X
C A S NYT. 1979. q. free. Statens Seruminstitut, Centrale Afdeling for Sygehushygiejne, Artillerivej 5, DK-2300 Copenhagen S, Denmark.
TEL 32-68-32-68. FAX 32-68-38-77. TELEX 31316 SERUM DK. Ed. O.B. Jepsen. bk.rev.; circ. 5,000.

616.15 011　　　IT
C C S S. FEDERAZIONE DELLE SOCIETA MEDICO-SCIENTIFICHE. ITALIANE BOLLETTINO CONGRESSI (YEAR). (Text in English, Italian) 1978. a. free. (Comitato per la Collaborazione tra Societa Medico-Scientifiche Italiane, Federazione delle Societa Medico-Scientifiche) Centro Trasfusionale e di Immunologia dei Trapianti, Ospedale Policlinico, Via Francesco Sforza 35, 20122 Milan, Italy.
TEL 02-55181346. FAX 02-5458129. adv.; charts; illus.; circ. 8,000.
Formerly: C C S S.
Description: Lists international medical and scientific conferences.

C H A C INFO/INFO A C C S. (Catholic Health Association of Canada) see HOSPITALS

C H A C REVIEW. see HOSPITALS

610 029　　　CN
C H R A PROGRESS NOTES. (Text in English, French) 1949. 6/yr. membership. Canadian College of Health Record Administrators, Canadian Health Record Association., 250 Ferrand Dr., Ste. 909, Don Mills, Ont. M3C 3G8, Canada. TEL 416-429-5835. FAX 416-429-2967. Ed. Diana Kellington. adv.; bk.rev.; charts; illus.; circ. 3,000. **Indexed:** Hosp.Lit.Ind.
Former titles: C C H R A - C H R A Progress Notes; (until 1984): C C H E A - C H R A Bulletin; (until 1979): Canadian Health Record Association. Bulletin (ISSN 0227-3748); C A M R L Recorder; Canadian Association of Medical Record Librarians. Bulletin (ISSN 0045-4397)

614.88 384.5　　　IT
C.I.R.M.. (Text in English) 1935. a. free. Centro Internazionale Radio-Medico, Via Architettura 41, 00144 Rome, Italy. TEL 06-5923331-2. TELEX 612068 CIRM I. charts; illus.
Description: Covers news, activities and services of the medical center.

610　　　US
C I R NEWS. 1971. q. $12 to individuals; institutions $24. Committee of Interns and Residents, 386 Park Ave. S., New York, NY 10016. TEL 212-725-5500. Ed. Michael Yellin. adv.; bk.rev.; circ. 15,000. (tabloid format; back issues avail.)
Former titles: C I R Bulletin; Committee of Interns and Residents Bulletin (ISSN 0090-1660)

610 200　　　US
C M D S. bi-m. free to members. Christian Medical & Dental Society, 1616 Gateway Blvd., Box 830689, Richardson, TX 75083-0689. TEL 214-783-8384. Ed. Juanita McGinnis. circ. 7,900 (controlled).
Formerly: Christian Medical and Dental Society News and Report.
Description: Informs members about society's activities and other like-minded organizations.

610　　　SA
C M E; South Africa's continuing medical education monthly - Suid Afrika se maandblad van voortgesette mediese onderrig. (Text in Afrikaans, English) 1983. m. R.175. Medical Association of South Africa, Private Bag X1, Pinelands 7430, South Africa. TEL 531-3081. FAX 531-4126. Ed. Dr. F.N. Sanders. adv.; bk.rev.; index; circ. 13,900. (also avail. in microfiche; back issues avail.) **Indexed:** Ind.S.A.Per.

610 378　　　CN
C M E - CONTINUING MEDICAL EDUCATION. m. S T A Communications Inc., 955 St. John's Blvd., Ste. 306, Pointe Claire, Que. H9R 5K3, Canada.
TEL 514-695-7623. FAX 514-695-8554. Ed. Paul Brand. circ. 30,082.

362.1　　　US　　ISSN 0007-8808
C O P H BULLETIN. 1960. q. $2. National Congress of Organizations of the Physically Handicapped, Inc., 6106 N. 30th St., Arlington, VA 22207. Ed. Rose A. Wilson. adv.; bk.rev.; illus.; circ. 2,500. (tabloid format) **Indexed:** Rehabil.Lit.

610　　　US　　ISSN 0276-8283
RB115
C P T. (Physicians' Current Procedural Terminology) 1966. irreg., 4th ed., 1988. $34 (floppy disk $175). American Medical Association, 515 N. State St., Chicago, IL 60610. TEL 312-464-0183.
FAX 312-464-5834. (also avail. in microfiche)
●Also available online.
Formerly (1st & 2nd eds.): Current Procedural Terminology (ISSN 0065-9312)

610　　　FR　　ISSN 0007-9480
CADUCEE. 1961. m. 170 F. B.C. Savy, 18, Avenue de la Marne, 92600 Asnieres, France. adv.; abstr.; bibl.; illus.; stat.; cum.index; circ. 15,000.

CADUCEUS: A MUSEUM JOURNAL FOR THE HEALTH SCIENCES. see MUSEUMS AND ART GALLERIES

610　　　FR
CAHIERS D'ETUDES ET DE RECHERCHES FRANCOPHONES SANTE. 6/yr. 380 F. to individuals; institutions 650 F.; students 250 F. John Libbey Eurotext, 6 rue Blanche, 92120 Montrouge, France. TEL 1-47-35-85-52. FAX 1-46-57-10-09.
Description: Aims to establish the medical research of the francophone world and expose the research of developing countries.

610.28　　　FR　　ISSN 0575-0563
CAHIERS DE BIOTHERAPIE. 1964. q. 450 F. (foreign 500 F.). (Societe Medicale de Biotherapie) Editions Similia, 71 rue Beaubourg, 75003 Paris, France. TEL 42-71-68-66. adv.; bk.rev.; circ. 6,000.

610　　　FR
CAHIERS DE GEOGRAPHIE DE LA SANTE/JOURNAL OF GEOGRAPHY OF HEALTH. Short title: GEOS. irreg. Universite de Montpellier (Universite Paul Valery), B.P. 5043, 34032 Montpellier Cedex 1, France.
TEL 67-14-20-00.
Description: Covers the research done at the university level by geographers, either in the form of excerpts, digests or research positions. Covers the geographical study of illness, health care and health care services.

610　　　FR　　ISSN 0007-9936
CAHIERS DE MEDECINE INTERPROFESSIONNELLE. 1961. q. 261 F. (Association Interprofessionnelle des Centres Medicaux et Sociaux de la Region Parisienne) Editions Docis, 31 rue Mederic, 75832 Paris Cedex 17, France. Ed.Bd. bk.rev.; circ. 1,250. **Indexed:** C.I.S. Abstr.
—BLDSC shelfmark: 2949.740000.

612　　　FR
CAHIERS DE SEXOLOGIE CLINIQUE.* bi-m. 300 F. (students 200 F.). Nouvelles Editions Medicales Francaises, P.B. 451, 95005 Clergy Poutoise Cedex, France. **Indexed:** Biol.Abstr.

610　　　SZ　　ISSN 0409-8757
CAHIERS MEDICO-SOCIAUX. 1956. 4/yr.
65 SFr.($46.50) Editions Medecine et Hygiene, 78 Av. de la Roseraie, Case Postale 456, CH-1211 Geneva 4, Switzerland. TEL 022-469355.
FAX 022-475610. Ed. O. Jeanneret.
—BLDSC shelfmark: 2949.784000.

610　　　II　　ISSN 0008-0667
R97　　　CODEN: CMJRAY
CALCUTTA MEDICAL JOURNAL. (Text in English) 1906. m. Rs.12($4.) Calcutta Medical Club, 91-B Chittaranjan Ave., Calcutta 12, India. Ed. K.K. Sen-Gupta. adv.; bk.rev.; abstr.; charts; illus. **Indexed:** Biol.Abstr., Chem.Abstr., Excerp.Med., Helminthol.Abstr., Ind.Med., Nutr.Abstr.
—BLDSC shelfmark: 2948.950000.

CALENDAR OF CONGRESSES OF MEDICAL SCIENCES. see MEETINGS AND CONGRESSES

610　　　US　　ISSN 0410-2894
CALIFORNIA F P. 1950. bi-m. $35. California Academy of Family Physicians, 114 Sansome St. K No.1305, San Francisco, CA 94104-3824.
FAX 415-394-9119. Ed. Sheri L. Cardo. adv.; circ. 6,900 (controlled). (also avail. in microform from UMI; reprint service avail. from UMI)
Formerly: California G P.
Description: Covers socioeconomic issues of relevance to family physicians.

616.98 338.476　　　US　　ISSN 8750-1813
CALIFORNIA PHYSICIAN. 1984. m. $30 to non-members. California Medical Association, 221 Main St., San Francisco, CA 94105.
TEL 415-882-5118. (Subscr. to: Box 7690, San Francisco, CA 94120-7690) Ed. Kelly Guncheon. circ. 33,000. (back issues avail.)
Description: Non-clinical medical publication. Covers economic, legal, social and political issues affecting medical practice in California.

610　　　UK
CAMBRIDGE MEDICINE. 1981. 2/yr. £4.50. Cambridge Clinical School, Cambridge Medical Committee, Cambridge, England. Ed. M. Goodman. adv.; bk.rev.; circ. 1,000.

CAMBRIDGE UNIVERSITY MEDICAL LIBRARY BULLETIN. see LIBRARY AND INFORMATION SCIENCES

610　　　CN　　ISSN 0008-2791
CODEN: CAMHA3
CANADA'S MENTAL HEALTH. French edition: Sante Mentale au Canada (ISSN 0701-9602) (Supplements avail.) (Editions in English, French) 1953. q. free in Canada; Can.$10 elsewhere. Department of National Health and Welfare, Health Services & Promotion Branch, Ottawa, Ont. K1A 1B4, Canada. TEL 613-954-8642.
FAX 613-957-1406. (Dist. by: Supply and Services Canada, Canadian Government Publishing Centre, Ottawa, Ont. K1A 0S9) Ed. Thomas Lips. bk.rev.; abstr.; bibl.; index; circ. 43,000. (also avail. in microfilm from CML) **Indexed:**
Abstr.Hosp.Manage.Stud., ASSIA, Can.Educ.Ind., Can.Per.Ind., Chicago Psychoanal.Lit.Ind., CMI, Except.Child.Educ.Abstr., Hosp.Lit.Ind., Mid.East: Abstr.& Ind., P.A.I.S., Psychol.Abstr., Pt.de Rep., Rehabil.Lit., Sage Fam.Stud.Abstr., Soc.Work Res.& Abstr.

CANADIAN ASSOCIATION OF ANATOMISTS. BULLETIN. see BIOLOGY

616.07　　　CN　　ISSN 0703-8372
CANADIAN ASSOCIATION OF PATHOLOGISTS. NEWSLETTER. (Text in English, French) 1969. bi-m. membership. Canadian Association of Pathologists, c/o Dr. John Jacques, Ed., Dept. of Laboratory Medicine, Royal Hospital, Edmonton, Alta. T5H 3V9, Canada. FAX 403-477-4715. bk.rev.; circ. 800.

610　　　CN　　ISSN 0823-2105
R461
CANADIAN BULLETIN OF MEDICAL HISTORY/BULLETIN CANADIEN D'HISTOIRE DE LA MEDECINE. (Text and summaries in English, French) 1984. 2/yr. Can.$25 (foreign Can.$30). (Canadain Society for the History of Medicine - Societe Canadienne d'Histoire de la Medicine) Wilfrid Laurier University Press, Waterloo, Ont. N2L 3C5, Canada. TEL 519-884-1970. Ed. Jim Connor. bk.rev. (back issues avail.) **Indexed:** Hist.Abstr. (1990-).
—BLDSC shelfmark: 3017.900000.
Description: Presents articles, notes, review articles and book reviews.
Refereed Serial

610　　　CN　　ISSN 0826-6778
CANADIAN CRITICAL CARE NURSING JOURNAL. 1984. 4/yr. Can.$15($20) Health Media Inc., 14453 29A Ave., White Rock, B.C. V4A 9K8, Canada.
TEL 604-535-7933. Ed. Agnes Forster. adv.; circ. 3,000. **Indexed:** CINAHL.
—BLDSC shelfmark: 3019.818000.

610　　　CN　　ISSN 0008-3429
CANADIAN DOCTOR. 1935. m. $53. Health Care Communications, 9030 Leslie St., Ste. 300, Richmond Hill, Ont. L4B 1J2, Canada.
TEL 416-882-0999. Ed. Marc J. Charette. adv.; bk.rev.; bibl.; illus.; circ. 29,000. (also avail. in microform from UMI) **Indexed:** CMI.

MEDICAL SCIENCES

610   CN   ISSN 0008-350X
CANADIAN FAMILY PHYSICIAN/MEDECIN DE FAMILLE CANADIEN. 1954. m. Can.$55($55) College of Family Physicians of Canada, 4000 Leslie St., Willowdale, Ont. M2K 2R9, Canada. TEL 416-493-7513. Ed. Tony Dixon. adv.; bk.rev.; abstr.; bibl.; charts; illus.; stat.; index; circ. 27,000. **Indexed:** CMI, Curr.Cont., Excerp.Med., FAMLI, Helminthol.Abstr., Protozool.Abstr.
—BLDSC shelfmark: 3022.100000.
Formerly: College of General Practice Journal.
Description: Aimed at practicing, teaching and research for family physicians and general practitioners.

CANADIAN HEALTH CARE MANAGEMENT. see *INSURANCE*

610 340   CN
▼**CANADIAN HEALTH CASE LAW DIGEST.** 1990. 3/yr. Can.$160. Butterworths Canada Ltd., 75 Clegg Rd., Markham, Ont. L6G 1A1, Canada. TEL 800-668-6481. FAX 416-479-2826. Ed.Bd. (looseleaf format)
Description: Collection of case summaries concerning a wide variety of health-related matters. Provides insights as to how the law deals with various cases.

610   CN
CANADIAN JOURNAL OF DIAGNOSIS. 1984. m. $5.50. S T A Communications Inc., 955 boul. St. Jean, Ste. 306, Pointe-Claire, Que. H9R 5K3, Canada. TEL 514-695-7623. FAX 514-695-8554. Ed. Paul F. Branel. adv.; circ. 33,849.
Formerly: Diagnosis.

362   CN   ISSN 0008-4174
CANADIAN JOURNAL OF OCCUPATIONAL THERAPY/REVUE CANADIENNE D'ERGOTHERAPIE. (Text mainly in English, occasionally in French) 1933. 5/yr. Can.$35($50) Canadian Association of Occupational Therapists, 110 Eglinton Ave. West, 3rd fl., Toronto, Ont. M4R 1A3, Canada. TEL 416-487-5404. FAX 416-487-0480. Ed. Geraldine Moore. adv.; bk.rev.; bibl.; illus.; index; circ. 5,800. (reprint service avail. from UMI) **Indexed:** CINAHL, Excerp.Med., Ind.Med., Rehabil.Lit.
—BLDSC shelfmark: 3033.600000.

CANADIAN JOURNAL OF VETERINARY RESEARCH/REVUE CANADIENNE DE RECHERCHE VETERINAIRE. see *VETERINARY SCIENCE*

610.28   CN   ISSN 0384-1820
CANADIAN MEDICAL AND BIOLOGICAL ENGINEERING SOCIETY. NEWSLETTER/SOCIETE CANADIENNE DE GENIE BIOMEDICAL. BULLETIN. vol.15, 1981. 4/yr. Can.$35 membership only. Canadian Medical and Biological Engineering Society Inc. - Societe Canadienne de Genie Biomedical, Rm. 307, Bldg. M-50, National Research Council, Ottawa, Ont. K1A 0R8, Canada. TEL 613-993-1686. FAX 613-954-2216. TELEX 053 3145 NRCADMINOTT.

610   CN   ISSN 0008-4409
CODEN: CMAJAX
CANADIAN MEDICAL ASSOCIATION JOURNAL/ASSOCIATION DES MEDICINS DU CANADA. JOURNAL. (Text in English, French) 1911. s-m. Can.$76($91) Canadian Medical Association, 1867 Alta Vista Dr., Box 8650, Ottawa, Ont. K1G 0G8, Canada. TEL 613-731-9331. FAX 613-731-0937. TELEX 053-3152. Ed. Dr. Bruce P. Squires. adv.; bibl.; charts; illus.; index; circ. 55,800. (also avail. in microform from UMI; reprint service avail. from UMI) **Indexed:** Abstr.Health Care Manage.Stud., Abstr.Hyg., Bibl.Dev.Med.& Child Neur., Biol.Abstr., Biol.Dig., Biotech.Abstr., C.I.S. Abstr., Can.Per.Ind., Chem.Abstr., CINAHL, Curr.Adv.Biochem., Curr.Adv.Ecol.Sci., Curr.Adv.Genetics & Molec.Biol., Curr.Cont, Dairy Sci.Abstr., Dent.Ind., Dok.Arbeitsmed., Excerp.Med., FAMLI, Helminthol.Abstr., I.P.A., Ind.Med., Ind.Sci.Rev., INIS Atomind., Lab.Haz.Bull., Med.Care Rev., NRN, Nutr.Abstr., Protozool.Abstr., Rev.Plant Path., Risk Abstr., Sci.Cit.Ind, Sportsearch, Trop.Dis.Bull.
●Also available online. Vendor(s): BRS.
—BLDSC shelfmark: 3038.000000.

610   CN   ISSN 0068-9203
CANADIAN MEDICAL DIRECTORY. 1955. a. Can.$174.41($163) Southam Business Communications Inc. (Subsidiary of: Southam Inc.), 1450 Don Mills Rd., Don Mills, Ont. M3B 2X7, Canada. TEL 416-445-6641. FAX 416-442-2261.

615.8   CN
CANADIAN PHYSIOTHERAPY ASSOCIATION. SPORTS PHYSIOTHERAPY DIVISION. NEWSLETTER. bi-m. Canadian Physiotherapy Association, Sports Physiotherapy Division - Association Canadienne de Physiotherapie, 890 Yonge St., 9th Fl., Toronto, Ont. M4W 3P4, Canada. TEL 416-924-5312. FAX 416-924-7335. **Indexed:** Sportsearch (1981-).

610   CN   ISSN 0382-7453
CANADIAN PRACTITIONER AND REVIEW. 1883. m. Bryant Press Ltd., 260 Bartley Dr., Toronto, Ont., Canada. illus.
Formerly: Canadian Practitioner (ISSN 0382-7437)

616.04   CN
CANDID FACTS/A PROPOS. (Text in English and French) 1960. q. free. Canadian Cystic Fibrosis Foundation, 2221 Yonge St., Ste 601, Toronto, Ont. M4S 2B4, Canada. TEL 416-485-9149. FAX 416-485-0960. Ed. Carol Hill. circ. 7,000.

610   IT
CARDARELLI; medicina - chirugia - specialita. q. free to members. Scuola Medica Ospedaliera, Casella Postale 1102, 80100 Naples, Italy. Ed. R. Sessa. adv.
Description: Publishes original works on clinical and experimental subjects.

610   US   ISSN 1053-5500
CASE MANAGEMENT ADVISOR. m. $169. American Health Consultants, Six Piedmont Center, Ste. 400, 3525 Piedmont Rd., N.E., Atlanta, GA 30305. TEL 404-262-7436. FAX 800-284-3291. (Subscr. to: Department L100, Box 740056, Atlanta, GA 30374-9822. TEL 800-688-2421) circ. 1,500.

610 368.382   US
▼**CASE MANAGER.** 1990. q. $25. (Individual Case Management Association, Inc.) Systemedic Corporation, 10809 Executive Center Dr., Ste. 105, Little Rock, AR 72211. TEL 501-227-5553. FAX 501-227-8362. Ed. Tom Strickland. adv.: B&W page $1650; color page $2050; trim 8 3/8 x 10 7/8. circ. 16,250.
Description: Provides education, marketing and networking support to medical case managers who coordinate and manage services involving large or serious claims in the health and compensation industry.

610   CS   ISSN 0008-7335
CODEN: CLCEAL
CASOPIS LEKARU CESKYCH. (Text mainly in Czech or Slovak; summaries in English, French, German, Russian) 1862. 52/yr. $114.70. (Ceskoslovenska Lekarska Spolecnost J. Ev. Purkyne) Avicenum, Czechoslovak Medical Press, Malostranske nam. 28, 118 02 Prague 1, Czechoslovakia. (Subscr. to: Artia, Ve Smeckach 30, 111 27 Prague 1, Czechoslovakia) Ed. J. Petrasek. adv.; bk.rev.; bibl.; charts; illus.; index. **Indexed:** Abstr.Hyg., Biol.Abstr., C.I.S. Abstr., Chem.Abstr., Curr.Adv.Ecol.Sci., Dent.Ind., Excerp.Med., Ind.Med., INIS Atomind., Nutr.Abstr., Trop.Dis.Bull.
—BLDSC shelfmark: 3061.400000.

362.1   CN   ISSN 0828-5748
CATHOLIC HEALTH ASSOCIATION OF CANADA. DIRECTORY. Short title: C H A C Directory. (Text in English and French) 1968. biennial. Can.$20 to non-members. Catholic Health Association of Canada, 1247 Kilborn Pl., Ottawa, Ont. K1H 6K9, Canada. TEL 613-731-7148. FAX 613-731-7797. Ed. Freda Fraser. circ. 975.
Formerly: Catholic Hospital Association of Canada. Directory (ISSN 0380-8475)

610 200   UK   ISSN 0008-8226
CATHOLIC MEDICAL QUARTERLY. 1923. q. Guild of Catholic Doctors, Ed. Dr. Peter Doherty, 60 Grove End Road, London NW8 9NH, England. adv.; bk.rev.; bibl.; index; circ. 2,500.
—BLDSC shelfmark: 3093.078500.

610   KO
CATHOLIC UNIVERSITY MEDICAL COLLEGE JOURNAL. (Text in English or Korean; summaries in English) 1957. q. free. Catholic University, Graduate School, Bampo-dong, Kannam-ku, Seoul 137, S. Korea. TEL 02-593-5141. FAX 02-532-3112. Ed. Dr. Yong Whee Bahk. circ. 1,000 (controlled). **Indexed:** Biol.Abstr., Chem.Abstr.
Formerly: Catholic Medical College Journal.

CELL BIOCHEMISTRY AND FUNCTION. see *BIOLOGY — Biological Chemistry*

CELL CALCIUM (EDINBURGH). see *BIOLOGY — Cytology And Histology*

CELL CALCIUM (SHEFFIELD). see *BIOLOGY — Biological Chemistry*

CELL MEMBRANES. see *BIOLOGY — Cytology And Histology*

CELL NUCLEUS. see *BIOLOGY — Cytology And Histology*

610   US   ISSN 1051-6794
CODEN: CEMAEE
▼**CELLS AND MATERIALS.** 1991. q. $75 (foreign $90). Scanning Microscopy International, Inc., Box 66507, AMF O'Hare, Chicago, IL 60666-0507. TEL 708-529-6677. FAX 708-980-6698. Ed. Dr. A. Jay Wasserman.
—BLDSC shelfmark: 3097.913000.
Description: The scope of topics covered includes cardiovascular, ocular, and orthopedic prostheses, drug delivery systems, and related topics. Emphasis is on morphological aspects of replaceable tissues, and their subsequent fortification or substitution by a biomaterial.
Refereed Serial

CELLULAR SIGNALLING. see *BIOLOGY — Cytology And Histology*

616   JA   ISSN 0078-6632
CENTER FOR ADULT DISEASES, OSAKA. ANNUAL REPORT. (Text in English) 1961. a. free. Center for Adult Diseases, Osaka, 1-3-3 Nakamichi, Higashinari-ku, Osaka 537, Japan. Ed. Nobuyuki Senda, M.D. **Indexed:** Biol.Abstr., Excerp.Med.
—BLDSC shelfmark: 1141.050000.

610   US
CENTERSCOPE. 3/yr. Boston University, School of Medicine, Office of Publication Services, 80 E. Concord St., Boston, MA 02118. Ed. Owen McNamara. circ. 13,000.
Description: Informs alumni and friends of research and events at the School of Medicine.

610   RH   ISSN 0008-9176
CODEN: CAJMA3
CENTRAL AFRICAN JOURNAL OF MEDICINE. 1955. m. $40. P.O. Box A195, Avondale, Harare, Zimbabwe. TEL 791631. Ed. H.M. Chinyanga. adv.; bk.rev.; charts; illus.; index; circ. 1,500. (reprint service avail. from ISI) **Indexed:** Abstr.Hyg., Biol.Abstr., Chem.Abstr., Curr.Adv.Ecol.Sci., Curr.Cont., Dairy Sci.Abstr., Dent.Ind., Excerp.Med., Helminthol.Abstr., Ind.Med., Ind.S.A.Per., NRN, Nutr.Abstr., Protozool.Abstr., Rev.Appl.Entomol., Rev.Plant Path., Trop.Dis.Bull.

610   US   ISSN 0008-946X
CENTRAL NEW YORK ACADEMY OF MEDICINE. BULLETIN. 1936. bi-m. $4. Central New York Academy of Medicine, 210 Clinton Rd., New Hartford, NY 13413. TEL 315-735-2204. (Co-sponsors: Medical Societies of the Counties of Oneida, Herkimer, Madison and Chenango) Ed. Dr. Edwin P. Russell, Jr. adv.; charts; illus.; stat.; circ. 2,475.

610   FR   ISSN 0338-7070
CENTRE LYONNAIS D'ACUPUNCTURE DE SAINT-LUC. BULLETIN DE LIAISON. 1975. 2/yr. Hopital St. Luc, 20 Quai Claude-Bernard, 69007 Lyon, France. Ed. Dr. Castro. (processed)

610   US   ISSN 1047-3211
QP383
▼**CEREBRAL CORTEX.** 1991. bi-m. $95 to individuals; institutions $190. Oxford University Press, Journals, 200 Madison Ave., New York, NY 10016. TEL 212-679-7300. FAX 212-725-2972. TELEX 6859654. (Subscr. to: Journals Fulfillment, 2001 Evans Rd. Cary, NC 27513. TEL 919-677-0977) Eds. Patricia Goldman-Rakic, Pasko Rakic. circ. 500.
—BLDSC shelfmark: 3120.027550.
Description: Interdisciplinary journal covering all of the issues of modern neuroscience including development, evolution, plasticity, perception, learning, memory, as well as neurological and psychiatric disorders.
Refereed Serial

MEDICAL SCIENCES 3087

610   TU   ISSN 0376-7833
CODEN: CTFDDO
CERRAHPASA MEDICAL FACULTY. JOURNAL/CERRAHPASA TIP FAKULTESI DERGISI. (Annual supplement avail.: Cerrahpasa Medical Review) (Text in Turkish; summaries in English) vol.12, 1982. q. University of Istanbul, Cerrahpasa Medical Faculty, Cerrahpasa Tip Fakultesi, Aksaray, 34303 Istanbul, Turkey. TEL 588-4800-1175. Ed. Vural Solok. abstr.; bibl.; charts; illus.; index.
Description: Contains research studies of the Cerrahpasa Medical Faculty.

610   TU
CERRAHPASA MEDICAL REVIEW. (Supplement to: Cerrahpasa Medical Faculty. Journal) 1982. a. TL.220($2) free to medical libraries. University of Istanbul, Cerrahpasa Medical Faculty, Dergi Kurulu, Cerrahpasa Tip Fakultesi, Aksaray, Istanbul, Turkey. Ed. Altan Onat. bibl.; charts; illus.

CESKOSLOVENSKA FYSIOLOGIE/CZECHOSLOVAK PHYSIOLOGY. see BIOLOGY — Physiology

616.07 574.2   CS   ISSN 0009-0611
CODEN: CPSLAE
CESKOSLOVENSKA PATOLOGIE. (Includes: Soudni Lekarstvi) (Text in Czech; summaries in English and Russian) 1965. 4/yr. $31.20. (Ceskoslovenska Spolecnost Patologicka) Avicenum, Czechoslovak Medical Press, Malostranske nam. 28, 118 02 Prague 1, Czechoslovakia. (Dist. by: Artia, Ve Smeckach 30, 111 27 Prague 1, Czechoslovakia) (Co-sponsor: Ceskoslovenska Lekarska Spolecnost J. Ev. Purkyne) Ed. Dr. B. Bednar. bk.rev.; index; circ. 1,000. **Indexed:** Biol.Abstr., Chem.Abstr., Curr.Adv.Ecol.Sci., Excerp.Med., Ind.Med., INIS Atomind.
—BLDSC shelfmark: 3122.475000.

610   CE   ISSN 0011-2232
CEYLON JOURNAL OF MEDICAL SCIENCE. (Text in English) 1949. 2/yr. $5 per no. University of Colombo, Faculty of Medicine, Kynsey Rd., Colombo 8, Sri Lanka. TEL 01-698449. Ed. T.W. Wikramanayake. bk.rev.; charts; illus.; circ. 700. (back issues avail.) **Indexed:** Biol.Abstr., Chem.Abstr., Helminthol.Abstr., Ind.Med., Rev.Appl.Entomol., Sri Lanka Sci.Ind., Trop.Dis.Bull.
—BLDSC shelfmark: 3125.000000.
Description: Covers all branches of medical, dental, and veterinary sciences.

610   CE   ISSN 0009-0875
CEYLON MEDICAL JOURNAL. (Text in English) 1887. q. $80. Sri Lanka Medical Association, Wijerama House, 6 Wijerama Mawatha, Colombo 7, Sri Lanka. TEL 6-93324. Eds. Dr. C.G. Uragoda, C. Goonaratna. adv.; bk.rev.; charts; illus.; circ. 1,200. **Indexed:** Abstr.Hyg., Biol.Abstr., Chem.Abstr., Excerp.Med., Helminthol.Abstr., Ind.Med., Nutr.Abstr., Sri Lanka Sci.Ind., Trop.Dis.Bull.
—BLDSC shelfmark: 3128.200000.

610 658   US
CHANGING MEDICAL MARKETS; the international monthly newsletter for executives in the healthcare and biotechnology industries. 1978. m. $195. Theta Corporation, Theta Bldg., Middlefield, CT 06455. TEL 203-349-1054. FAX 203-349-1227. Ed. Phyllis Klaben. circ. controlled. (back issues avail.)
Description: Comprehensive coverage of corporate activities, new products and services, emerging opportunities around the world, technology assessment, the impact of legislation and news from healthcare associations.

610 658   GW   ISSN 0232-7090
CHARITE ANNALEN. NEUE FOLGE. 1981. a. Akademie-Verlag Berlin, Leipziger Str. 3-4, 1086 Berlin, Germany. Ed. Jurgen Grosser.

610   US
CHECK SAMPLE. (Subject areas offered include: Anatomic Pathology, Cytopathology, Forensic Pathology, Chemistry, Hematopathology, Immunopathology, Microbiology, and Transfusion Medicine) 1949. bi-w. $1,788 for complete series; price varies for individual subject area. American Society of Clinical Pathologists, 2100 W. Harrison St., Chicago, IL 60612. TEL 312-738-4890. FAX 312-738-1619. Ed. Raymond Gambino. circ. 1,000.
Formerly (until 1958): Institute for Clinical Science. Proficiency Test Service. Report (ISSN 0073-8638)
Description: Each series consists of exercise which present patient cases for diagnosis or other laboratory study supplemented with kodachromes or specimen analytic materials.

610   TH   ISSN 0125-5983
CODEN: CMMBB2
CHIANG MAI MEDICAL BULLETIN. (Text in English and Thai) 1961. q. B.80($40) to individuals; institutions $100. Chiang Mai University, Faculty of Medicine, 110 Intavaroros Street, Chiang Mai 50002, Thailand. TEL 52-221122. FAX 53-217144. Ed. Dr. Watana Navacharoen. adv.; bk.rev.; abstr.; charts; illus.; stat.; circ. 1,000 (controlled). **Indexed:** Chem.Abstr.

610   JA   ISSN 0303-5476
CODEN: CIZAAZ
CHIBA IGAKU ZASSHI/CHIBA MEDICAL JOURNAL. (Text in Japanese; contents page and summaries in English) 1923. bi-m. 4000 Yen($29) Chiba Igakkai - Chiba Medical Society, c/o Chiba Daigaku Igakubu, 8-1 Inohana 1-chome, Chiba-shi 280, Japan. TEL 0472-22-7171. FAX 0472-22-7853. Ed. Yoshio Nakajima. adv.; bk.rev.; circ. 3,200. **Indexed:** Biol.Abstr., Chem.Abstr., Excerp.Med., INIS Atomind.
Formerly: Chiba Medical Society. Journal (ISSN 0009-3459)
Description: Presents review articles, original papers, case reports, laboratory findings, and news of the society.

CHICAGO HISTORY OF SCIENCE AND MEDICINE. see HISTORY

610   US   ISSN 0009-3637
CHICAGO MEDICINE. 1902. s-m. $10 to non-members; members $5. Chicago Medical Society, 515 N. Dearborn, Chicago, IL 60610. TEL 312-670-2550. FAX 312-670-3646. Ed. J. Gregory Wiezorek. adv.; bk.rev.; charts; illus.; index; circ. 11,000. **Indexed:** Med.Care Rev.
—BLDSC shelfmark: 3172.691000.
Description: Provides a forum for the discussion of medical, ethical, legal, socioeconomic, and other concerns affecting physicians in Chicago and Cook County.

610   II
CHIKITSAK BARTA. (Supplements avail.) (Text in Bengali) 1973. fortn. Rs.10($3) Amal Ghosh-hajra, Ed. & Pub., 240 Diamond Harbour Rd., Behala, Calcutta 700060, West Bengal, India. adv.; bk.rev.; abstr.; bibl.; stat.; index; circ. 15,000.

610   II   ISSN 0009-3858
CHIKITSAK SAMAJ. (Supplements avail.) (Text in several languages) 1969. m. Rs.15. Amal Ghosh-hajra, Ed. & Pub., 240 Diamond Harbour Rd., Behala, Calcutta 700060, West Bengal, India. adv.; bk.rev.; abstr.; bibl.; film rev.; play rev.; stat.; index; circ. 5,500.

610   US   ISSN 0069-3685
CHINA MEDICAL BOARD OF NEW YORK. ANNUAL REPORT.* 1951. a. membership. China Medical Board of New York, 750 Third Ave., New York, NY 10003. TEL 212-682-8000. circ. 300.

610   CC
▼**CHINESE ANDROLOGY.** (Text in Chinese) 1991. s-a. $14. China Ocean Press, International Cooperation Department, Haimao Dalou, 1 Fuxingmenwai Dajie, Beijing 100860, People's Republic of China. TEL 868941. FAX 862209. TELEX 22536 NBO CN. (Co-publisher: C H L (H.K.) Co.) Ed. Wang Qi.
Description: Focuses on traditional Chinese andrology, including the essence of ancient and modern therapeutics in the illness of the male. Discusses Chinese sexual hygiene in a scholarly manner.
Refereed Serial

CHINESE JOURNAL OF PHYSIOLOGY/CHUNG-KUO SHENG LI HSUEH TSA CHIH. see BIOLOGY — Physiology

610   CC   ISSN 0366-6999
CODEN: CMJODS
CHINESE MEDICAL JOURNAL/ZHONGHUA YIXUE ZAZHI YINGWEN BAN. Chinese edition: Zhonghua Yixue Zazhi (ISSN 0376-2491) (Text in English) 1887-1966; resumed 1975. m. £85 (effective 1992). Chinese Medical Association - Zhonghua Yixuehui, 42 Dongsi Xidajie, Beijing 100710, People's Republic of China. TEL 546231-292. (Dist. outside China by: Pergamon Press plc, Headington Hill Hall, Oxford OX3 0BW, England. TEL 0865-794141; In U.S.: 660 White Plains Rd., Tarrytown, NY 10591-5153. TEL 914-524-9200) Ed. Feng Chuan-han. abstr.; bibl.; charts; illus.; circ. 5,000. (also avail. in microform from UMI; back issues avail.) **Indexed:** Abstr.Hyg., Biol.Abstr., Chem.Abstr., Curr.Adv.Ecol.Sci., Curr.Cont., Dairy Sci.Abstr., Dent.Abstr., Dent.Ind., Excerp.Med. (1983-), Helminthol.Abstr., I.P.A., Ind.Med., Ind.Sci.Rev., Med.Care Rev., Nutr.Abstr., Protozool.Abstr., Rehabil.Lit., Rev.Plant Path., Sci.Cit.Ind., Trop.Dis.Bull.
●Also available online.
—BLDSC shelfmark: 3180.990000.
Formerly (until 1932): China Missionary Medical Journal.
Description: Introduces advances and research results in China's medical sciences and technology, serving primarily senior medical clinicians and research personnel of high academic level.
Refereed Serial

610   CC   ISSN 1001-9294
CODEN: CMSJEP
CHINESE MEDICAL SCIENCES JOURNAL. (Text in English) 1986. q. Y20 (foreign £60;$105). Chinese Academy of Medical Sciences (CAMS) - Zhongguo Yixue Kexueyuan, 9 Dong Dan San Tiao, Beijing 100730, People's Republic of China. TEL 5133074. FAX 5124876. TELEX 222689-CAMS-CN. (Subscr. to: Taylor & Francis Ltd., Rankine Rd., Basingstoke, Hants. RG24 0PR, England. TEL 0256-840366) Ed. Li Zongyan. adv.; bk.rev.; bibl.; charts; index; circ. 2,000. (back issues avail.) **Indexed:** Excerp.Med., Ind.Med.
—BLDSC shelfmark: 3181.012000.
Formerly (until 1991): Chinese Academy of Medical Sciences and Peking Union Medical College. Proceedings - Zhongguo Yixue Kexueyuan, Zhongguo Xiehe Yike Daxue Xuebao (ISSN 0258-8757)
Description: Presents recent advances in medical research. Includes information on clinical medicine, pharmacology, as well as traditional Chinese medicine.

610   GW   ISSN 0930-2786
CHINESISCHE MEDIZIN; theoretische Grundlagen, Diagnostik, Akupunktur, Arzneimittel, Taiji, Qigong. 1986. q. DM.120 (foreign DM.140). (Societas Medicinae) Urban und Vogel, Lindwurmstr. 95, 8000 Munich 2, Germany. TEL 089-53292-0. FAX 089-53292-100. Eds. E. Stueder-Wobmann, C.H. Hempen. circ. 1,500.

610   CC   ISSN 1000-7911
CHONGQING YIYAO/CHONGQING MEDICINE. bi-m. (Chongqingshi Weishengju - Chongqing Public Health Bureau) Chongqing Yiyao Bianjibu, 44 Qingnian Lu, Chongqing, Sichuan 630010, People's Republic of China.
—BLDSC shelfmark: 3181.559300.

610   US
CHRISTIAN MEDICAL & DENTAL SOCIETY JOURNAL. 1949. q. $20. Christian Medical & Dental Society, 1616 Gateway Blvd., Box 830689, Richardson, TX 75083-0689. TEL 214-783-8384. Ed. Sidney Macaulay. adv.; bk.rev.; circ. 8,275. **Indexed:** Chr.Per.Ind.
Formerly: Christian Medical Society Journal (ISSN 0009-546X)

610   II   ISSN 0009-5451
CHRISTIAN MEDICAL COLLEGE VELLORE ALUMNI JOURNAL. (Text in English) 1967. q. Rs.40 per no. to non-members; members Rs.25($6). Christian Medical College, Alumni Association, Vellore 632 002, Tamil Nadu, India. TEL 22603. TELEX 405-202 CMCH IN. Ed. Dr. Thomas Sen Bhanu. adv.; bk.rev.; abstr.; bibl.; charts; illus.; circ. 1,700 (controlled).
Description: Provides updated material of scientific interest to doctors.

MEDICAL SCIENCES

CHRONOBIOLOGY INTERNATIONAL; a journal about biological rhythm research. see *BIOLOGY*

610　　　　　US　　ISSN 0084-8786
CIBA COLLECTION OF MEDICAL ILLUSTRATIONS. 1953. irreg., vol.8, Pt.2, 1990. price varies. Ciba Geigy Corporation, Medical Education Division, 14 Henderson Dr., W. Caldwell, NJ 07006. TEL 201-882-4700. TELEX 131411. Ed. Gina Dingle. illus. (avail. on slides) **Indexed:** Biol.Abstr.
　Description: Presents series of anatomical atlases for each body system.

610　　　　　SP　　ISSN 0212-6052
CIENCIA MEDICA; para la practica diaria. 6/yr. 5500 ptas.($55) Alpe Editores, S.A., Pedro Rico, 27, 28029 Madrid, Spain. TEL 733 88 11. FAX 315-96-52. Ed. Dr. J. Abascal Morte.
　—BLDSC shelfmark: 3196.509000.

610　　　　　US　　ISSN 0163-0075
CINCINNATI MEDICINE. 1978. q. $12. Academy of Medicine of Cincinnati, 320 Broadway, Cincinnati, OH 45202. TEL 513-421-7010. Ed. Pam Fairbanks. adv.; bk.rev.; bibl.; illus.; index, cum.index; circ. 3,400. **Indexed:** Chem.Abstr., Ind.Med.
　—BLDSC shelfmark: 3198.570000.
　Supersedes (1921-1978): Cincinnati Journal of Medicine (ISSN 0009-6873)

610　　　　　US
THE CIVIL ABOLITIONIST. 1986. q. $5. Civitas, Box 26, Swain, NY 14884. TEL 607-545-6213. Ed. Bina Robinson. bk.rev.; circ. 2,600.
　Former titles: Civitas Abolitionist; (until vol.3, no.3, 1988): Civitas.
　Description: Aims to promote better human health care (as opposed to sickness care), by abolishing the practice of vivisection, i.e. animal experimentation.

616.98　　　　　US
CLAUSTROPHOBIA; life expansion news. 1977. m. $24. H T Communications, 1402 S.W. Upland Dr., Portland, OR 97221-2649. TEL 503-245-4763. Ed. Eric Geislinger. adv.; bk.rev.; circ. 500. (back issues avail.)

610　　　　　US　　ISSN 0891-1150
R11　　　　　　　　　CODEN: CCJMEL
CLEVELAND CLINIC JOURNAL OF MEDICINE. 1931. 6/yr. $30 to individuals; institutions and foreign $40. Cleveland Clinic Educational Foundation, 9500 Euclid Ave., Cleveland, OH 44195-5058. TEL 216-444-2662. FAX 216-444-9385. Ed. James S. Taylor, M.D. adv.; bk.rev.; bibl.; charts; illus.; index; circ. 10,000 (paid); 88,000 (controlled). (also avail. in microfilm from UMI) **Indexed:** Biol.Abstr., Curr.Adv.Cancer Res., Curr.Adv.Genetics & Molec.Biol., Curr.Cont., Dok.Arbeitsmed., Excerp.Med., Ind.Med., Ind.Sci.Rev., INIS Atomind., Sci.Cit.Ind.
　—BLDSC shelfmark: 3278.649800.
　Formerly (until 1987): Cleveland Clinic Quarterly (ISSN 0009-8787)
　Description: Original contributions, case reports, and timely reviews on subjects of interest to physicians in clinical practice.
　Refereed Serial

610　　　　　US
CLEVELAND PHYSICIAN. 1920. m. $24. (Academy of Medicine of Cleveland) Academy Graphic Communication, 1000 Brookpark, Cleveland, OH 44109. Ed. George Reitz. adv.; bk.rev.; illus.; circ. 4,800.
　Formerly: Academy of Medicine of Cleveland. Bulletin (ISSN 0001-4281)

610.28　　　　　UK　　ISSN 0144-7777
　　　　　　　　　　　CODEN: CLNCD5
CLINICA; world medical device & diagnostic news. 1980. w. £345($595) P J B Publications Ltd., 18-20 Hill Rise, Richmond, Surrey TW10 6UA, England. TEL 081-948-3262. FAX 081-948-6866. TELEX 8951042. Ed. Peter Charlish. adv.; bk.rev.; circ. 2,300. **Indexed:** ABC, PROMT, Psychol.Abstr.
　●Also available online. Vendor(s): BRS, Data-Star, DIALOG.
　—BLDSC shelfmark: 3286.170000.
　Description: News for the medical device and diagnostic industry.

615.19　　　　　NE　　ISSN 0009-8981
RB1　　　　　　　　　CODEN: CCATAR
CLINICA CHIMICA ACTA; international journal of clinical chemistry and medical biochemistry. (Text in English) 1956. 27/yr.(in 9 vols.; 3 nos./vol.). fl.3006 (effective 1992). Elsevier Science Publishers B.V., P.O. Box 211, 1000 AE Amsterdam, Netherlands. TEL 020-5803911. FAX 020-5803598. TELEX 18582 ESPA NL. (Subscr. in U.S. and Canada to: Elsevier Science Publishing Co., Inc., Box 882, Madison Sq. Sta., New York, NY 10159. TEL 212-989-5800) Ed.Bd. adv.; charts; illus.; index. (also avail. in microform from RPI; reprint service avail. from ISI) **Indexed:** Anal.Abstr., Biol.Abstr., Biotech.Abstr., Chem.Abstr., Curr.Adv.Biochem., Curr.Adv.Cancer Res., Curr.Adv.Ecol.Sci., Curr.Adv.Genetics & Molec.Biol., Curr.Chem.React, Curr.Cont., Dairy Sci.Abstr., Dent.Ind., Excerp.Med., Helminthol.Abstr., Ind.Chem., Ind.Med., Ind.Sci.Rev., Ind.Vet., INIS Atomind., Int.Abstr.Biol.Sci., Mass Spectr.Bull., Nutr.Abstr., Potato Abstr., Sci.Cit.Ind, Triticale Abstr., Vet.Bull., Weed Abstr.
　—BLDSC shelfmark: 3286.200000.
　Description: Publishes information leading to a better understanding of biological mechanisms of human diseases, their diagnosis and treatment.
　Refereed Serial

610　　　　　IT
▼**CLINICA E TERAPIA.** 1990. q. L.50000 (foreign L.120000)(effective 1992). C E M Casa Editoriale Maccari, Via Trento 53, 43100 Parma, Italy. FAX 039-521-771268. circ. 1,000.

610　　　　　IT　　ISSN 0009-9007
　　　　　　　　　　　CODEN: CLEUAB
CLINICA EUROPEA; attualita di medicina. 1962. bi-m. L.80000($64) Edizioni Clinica Europea, Via Concordia 20, 00183 Rome, Italy. TEL 75.76.475. Ed. Fausto Federici. adv.; bk.rev.; circ. 2,000. **Indexed:** Excerp.Med., Ind.Med.
　—BLDSC shelfmark: 3286.205000.

610　　　　　IT　　ISSN 0393-7585
CLINICA MEDICA DEL NORD AMERICA. bi-m. L.130000($160) Piccin Editore, Via Altinate 107, 35100 Padua, Italy. TEL 049-655566. TELEX 432074 PICCIN I. (reprint service avail. from UMI)

610　　　　　SP
CLINICA; PORTAVOZ DEL INTERNADO. 1989. a. 400 ptas. Universidad de Valladolid, Secretariado de Publicaciones, Facultad de Medicina, Avda. de Ramon y Cajal, 7, 47005 Valladolid, Spain. TEL 983-423000. FAX 983-423003. TELEX 26357.

615.5　　　　　IT　　ISSN 0009-9074
　　　　　　　　　　　CODEN: CLTEA4
CLINICA TERAPEUTICA. (Text in Italian; summaries in English, Italian) 1951. s-m. L.120000. Societa Editrice Universo, Via G.B. Morgagni 1, 00161 Rome, Italy. Ed. Prof. Michele De Martiis. adv.; bk.rev.; abstr.; bibl.; index; circ. 10,000. (tabloid format; back issues avail.) **Indexed:** Biol.Abstr., Biotech.Abstr., Chem.Abstr., Excerp.Med., Ind.Med., Nutr.Abstr.
　—BLDSC shelfmark: 3286.237000.

615.8　　　　　IT
CLINICA TERMALE. bi-m. L.18000. (Associazione Italiana di Idroclimatologia, Talassologia e Terapia Fisica) Societa Editrice Universo, Via G.B. Morgagni 1, 00161 Rome, Italy. Ed. Mariano Messini.

CLINICAL AND BIOCHEMICAL ANALYSIS. see *BIOLOGY — Biological Chemistry*

610　　　　　US　　ISSN 0730-0077
RC685.H8　　　　　　CODEN: CEHADM
CLINICAL AND EXPERIMENTAL HYPERTENSION. PART A: THEORY AND PRACTICE. 1978. 6/yr. $750 (Parts A and B combined $1045). Marcel Dekker Journals, 270 Madison Ave., New York, NY 10016. TEL 212-696-9000. FAX 212-685-4540. TELEX 421419. (Subscr. to: Box 10018, Church St. Sta., New York, NY 10249) Ed. J.P. Buckley. adv.; bk.rev.; index. (also avail. in microform from RPI; back issues avail.) **Indexed:** Biol.Dig., Biotech.Abstr., Chem.Abstr., Curr.Adv.Cell & Devel.Biol., Curr.Adv.Ecol.Sci., Curr.Adv.Genetics & Molec.Biol., Curr.Cont., Dent.Ind., Excerp.Med., Ind.Med., Ind.Sci.Rev., NRN, Sci.Cit.Ind.
　—BLDSC shelfmark: 3286.250600.
　Supersedes in part: Clinical and Experimental Hypertension (ISSN 0148-3927)
　Refereed Serial

610　　　　　US　　ISSN 0730-0085
RG580.H9　　　　　　CODEN: CEHBDP
CLINICAL AND EXPERIMENTAL HYPERTENSION. PART B: HYPERTENSION IN PREGNANCY. 1982. 3/yr. $295 (Parts A and B combined $1045). (International Society for the Study of Hypertension in Pregnancy) Marcel Dekker Journals, 270 Madison Ave., New York, NY 10016. TEL 212-696-9000. FAX 212-685-4540. TELEX 421419. (Subscr. to: Box 10018, Church St. Sta., New York, NY 10249) W.M. Barron, H.C.S Wallenburg. (also avail. in microform from RPI) **Indexed:** Biol.Dig., Biotech.Abstr., Chem.Abstr., Curr.Adv.Ecol.Sci., Excerp.Med., Ind.Sci.Rev., Sci.Cit.Ind.
　—BLDSC shelfmark: 3286.250620.
　Supersedes in part: Clinical and Experimental Hypertension (ISSN 0148-3927)
　Refereed Serial

610　　　　　CN　　ISSN 0147-958X
　　　　　　　　　　　CODEN: CNVMDL
CLINICAL AND INVESTIGATIVE MEDICINE/MEDECINE CLINIQUE ET EXPERIMENTALE. 1978. q. Can.$65 to individuals; institutions Can.$150. Canadian Society for Clinical Investigation, Montreal General Hospital, 1650 Cedar Ave., Montreal, Que. H3G 1A4, Canada. TEL 514-485-9550. Ed. C. Goresky. adv.; abstr.; bibl.; charts; illus.; stat.; index; circ. 1,384. (also avail. in microform from MIM,UMI; back issues avail.) **Indexed:** Biol.Abstr., Chem.Abstr., Curr.Adv.Cancer Res., Curr.Adv.Ecol.Sci., Curr.Cont., Dairy Sci.Abstr., Dok.Arbeitsmed., Excerp.Med., Helminthol.Abstr., Ind.Med., Nutr.Abstr., Risk Abstr.
　—BLDSC shelfmark: 3286.253000.
　Formerly: Medical Sciences Quarterly.

610　　　　　UK　　ISSN 0959-9851
▼**CLINICAL AUTONOMIC RESEARCH.** 1991. bi-m. £155($275) (Clinical Autonomic Research Society) Rapid Communications of Oxford Ltd., The Old Malthouse, Paradise St., Oxford OX1 1LD, England. TEL 0865-790447. FAX 0865-244012. Ed. Christopher Mathias. (reprint service avail.)
　—BLDSC shelfmark: 3286.259900.

CLINICAL BIOCHEMISTRY (TARRYTOWN). see *BIOLOGY — Biological Chemistry*

610　　　　　US　　ISSN 0191-7870
CLINICAL BIOMECHANICS. 1971. irreg. Clinical Biomechanics Corp., Box 35185, Los Angeles, CA 90035.

615.19　　　　　US　　ISSN 0009-9147
RB1　　　　　　　　　CODEN: CLCHAU
CLINICAL CHEMISTRY; clinical chemistry reference edition (the institutional edition). 1955. m. $95 to individuals (foreign $125); institutions $195 (foreign $235). American Association for Clinical Chemistry, Inc., 2029 K St. N.W., 7th fl., Washington, DC 20006. TEL 800-892-1400. FAX 202-887-5093. TELEX 251925 AACC UR. Ed. David E. Bruns. adv.; bk.rev.; abstr.; bibl.; charts; illus.; index. cum.index; circ. 14,000. (also avail. in microfiche; microfilm; back issues avail.; reprint service avail.) **Indexed:** Anal.Abstr., Biodet.Abstr., Biol.Abstr., C.I.S. Abstr., Chem.Abstr., Curr.Adv.Cancer Res., Curr.Adv.Ecol.Sci., Curr.Cont., Dairy Sci.Abstr., Dent.Ind., Excerp.Med., Ind.Med., Ind.Sci.Rev., Ind.Vet., INIS Atomind., Mass Spectr.Bull., Nutr.Abstr., Sci.Cit.Ind., So.Pac.Per.Ind., Vet.Bull.
　—BLDSC shelfmark: 3286.268000.
　Refereed Serial

610   US   ISSN 0161-9640
CLINICAL CHEMISTRY NEWS. 1978. m. $30 (foreign $70; free to qualified personnel). American Association for Clinical Chemistry, Inc., 2029 K St. N.W., 7th fl., Washington, DC 20006. TEL 800-892-1400. FAX 202-887-5093. TELEX 251925 AACC UR. Ed. Cherlyn Kirk. adv.; bk.rev.; circ. 30,000. Indexed: Chem.Abstr.

616.07   CN
▼**CLINICAL DIAGNOSTICS TODAY.** 1990. 8/yr. Can.$28 (foreign Can.$40). Intermac Publishing Inc., 60 W. Wilmot St., Richmond Hill, Ont. L4B 1M6, Canada. TEL 416-886-4141. FAX 416-886-4616. adv.; circ. 11,437.

610.28   US
CLINICAL ENGINEERING SERIES. 1972. irreg., vol.5, 1981. Academic Press, Inc., 1250 Sixth Ave., San Diego, CA 92101. TEL 619-231-0926. FAX 619-699-6715. Ed. Cesar A. Caceres. (reprint service avail. from ISI)
Description: Details research in the biomedical fields.
Refereed Serial

610   GW
CLINICAL INVESTIGATION. (Text in English, German) 1922. 12/yr. DM.568($368) (effective 1992). (Gesellschaft Deutscher Naturforscher und Aerzte) Springer-Verlag, Heidelberger Platz 3, D-1000 Berlin 33, Germany. TEL 030-8207-1. (Also Heidelberg, Tokyo, Vienna, and New York) Ed N. Zoellner. adv.; bibl.; charts; illus.; index. (also avail. in microform from UMI; back issues avail.; reprint service avail. from ISI) Indexed: Biol.Abstr., Biotech.Abstr., Chem.Abstr., Curr.Adv.Cancer Res., Curr.Adv.Ecol.Sci., Curr.Cont., Dairy Sci.Abstr., Dent.Ind., Excerp.Med., Helminthol.Abstr., Ind.Med., Ind.Sci.Rev., INIS Atomind., Nutr.Abstr., Protozool.Abstr., Risk Abstr., Sci.Cit.Ind., Trop.Oil Seeds Abstr.
Formerly (until 1991): Klinische Wochenschrift (ISSN 0023-2173)

CLINICAL LABORATORY MANAGEMENT REVIEW. see BUSINESS AND ECONOMICS — Management

610   US   ISSN 0894-959X
CLINICAL LABORATORY SCIENCE. 1988. bi-m. $40 to individuals; institutions $60; foreign $80. American Society of Medical Technology, Inc., 2021 L St., N.W., Ste. 400, Washington, DC 20036. TEL 202-785-3311. FAX 202-466-2254. Ed. L. Michael Posey. adv.; bk.rev.; circ. 20,000. (also avail. in microform from UMI; back issues avail.)
—BLDSC shelfmark: 3286.295880.
Description: Written for all medical technologists, including senior management, mid-level supervisors, and staff technologists. Editorial is based on the common body of knowledge that unites all clinical laboratory scientists, and articles cover all subspecialties of medical technology.

615.8   US
CLINICAL MANAGEMENT. 1981. bi-m. $35 to non-members; foreign $50. American Physical Therapy Association, 1111 N. Fairfax St., Alexandria, VA 22314. TEL 703-684-2782. Ed. Jan P. Reynolds. adv.; circ. 50,584.
Formerly: Clinical Management in Physical Therapy (ISSN 0276-8038)

610   UK   ISSN 0267-6605
                       CODEN: CLNME2
CLINICAL MATERIALS. 1986. 12/yr.(in 3 vols.). £285 (effective 1992). Elsevier Science Publishers Ltd., Crown House, Linton Rd., Barking, Essex IG11 8JU, England. TEL 081-594-7272. FAX 081-594-5942. TELEX 896950 APPSCI G. (Subscr. in U.S. and Canada to: Elsevier Science Publishing Co., Inc., Box 882, Madison Sq. Sta., New York, NY 10159. TEL 212-989-5800) Ed.Bd. adv.: B&W page £ 345; 192 x 258; adv. contact: Claire Coakley.
—BLDSC shelfmark: 3286.299000.
Description: For those involved in the development and application of materials for use in the medical environment.
Refereed Serial

610   US   ISSN 0196-4399
                       CODEN: CMNEEJ
CLINICAL MICROBIOLOGY NEWSLETTER. 1979. s-m. $135 to institutions (foreign $187)(effective 1992). Elsevier Science Publishing Co., Inc. (New York), 655 Ave. of the Americas, New York, NY 10010. TEL 212-989-5800. FAX 212-633-3965. TELEX 420643 AEP UI. Ed.Bd. Indexed: Abstr.Hyg., Excerp.Med., Trop.Dis.Bull.
—BLDSC shelfmark: 3286.305600.
Description: For clinical microbiologists, clinical pathologists, laboratory technologists and technicians.

CLINICAL NUTRITION. see NUTRITION AND DIETETICS

610 530   UK   ISSN 0143-0815
                       CODEN: CPPMD5
CLINICAL PHYSICS AND PHYSIOLOGICAL MEASUREMENT. 1980. 4/yr. £142($249) (effective 1992). Institute of Physical Sciences in Medicine, P.O. Box 303, York YO1 2WR, England. TEL 0904-610821. FAX 0904-612279. (U.S. address: American Institute of Physics, 335 E. 45th St., New York, N.Y. 10017) (Co-sponsors: Hospital Physicists' Association; European Federation of Organizations for Medical Physics; German Society for Medical Physics) Eds. A. Murray, D.J. Wheatley. adv.; bk.rev.; bibl.; illus.; charts; circ. 730. (also avail. in microfiche; microfilm; back issues avail., reprint service avail.) Indexed: Biol.Abstr., Curr.Adv.Ecol.Sci., Curr.Cont., Dent.Ind., Excerp.Med., Ind.Med., Ind.Sci.Rev., Sci.Abstr., Sci.Cit.Ind.
—BLDSC shelfmark: 3286.331700.
Description: Covers the applications of physics and physical measurement to clinical practice and investigation.

612   UK   ISSN 0144-5979
RB113   CODEN: CLPHDU
CLINICAL PHYSIOLOGY. 1981. bi-m. £142.50 (foreign £160). (Scandinavian Society of Clinical Physiology) Blackwell Scientific Publications Ltd., Osney Mead, Oxford OX2 OEL, England. TEL 0865-240201. FAX 0865-721205. TELEX 83355-MEDBOK-G. Ed. B. Parnow. Indexed: ASCA, Biol.Abstr., Chem.Abstr, Curr.Adv.Biochem., Curr.Adv.Ecol.Sci., Curr.Cont., Excerp.Med., Ind.Med., Ind.Sci.Rev., Sci.Cit.Ind
—BLDSC shelfmark: 3286.332500.

610   UK   ISSN 0269-2155
                       CODEN: CEHAEN
CLINICAL REHABILITATION. 1987. q. £60($87) to individuals; institutions £107.50($165). Edward Arnold (Subsidiary of: Hodder & Stoughton), Mill Road, Dunton Green, Sevenoaks, Kent TN13 2YA, England. TEL 0732-450111. FAX 0732-461321. (Dist. in U.S. and Canada by: Cambridge University Press, 40 W. 20th St., New York, NY 10011) adv.; bk.rev.
—BLDSC shelfmark: 3286.351500.
Description: Provides a forum for the exchange of ideas and information for all those concerned with rehabilitation.

610 574   UK   ISSN 0143-5221
                       CODEN: CSCIAE
CLINICAL SCIENCE. 1909. m. £195($380) Portland Press, Box 32, Commerce Way, Colchester, Essex CO2 8HP, England. TEL 0206-46351. FAX 0206-549331. (Co-sponsor: Medical Research Society) Ed. M. Brown. adv.; bibl.; illus.; index. (back issues avail.) Indexed: Biol.Abstr., Biotech.Abstr., Chem.Abstr, Curr.Adv.Ecol.Sci., Curr.Cont., Dairy Sci.Abstr., Dent.Ind., Excerp.Med., Helminthol.Abstr., Ind.Med., Ind.Sci.Rev., INIS Atomind., NRN, Sci.Cit.Ind, Trop.Dis.Bull.
—BLDSC shelfmark: 3286.375000.
Formerly: Heart.
Description: Studies of clinical science with emphasis on biochemical, physiological and metabolic approaches.

610   US   ISSN 0009-9295
R11
CLINICAL SYMPOSIA. 1948. 4/yr. $27.97. Ciba Geigy Corporation, Medical Education Division, 14 Henderson Dr., W. Caldwell, NJ 07006. TEL 201-882-4700. Ed. Maria Erdelyi-Brown. adv.; charts; illus.; circ. 330,000. Indexed: Biol.Abstr., C.I.N.L., Ind.Med.
—BLDSC shelfmark: 3286.399000.
Formerly (1950-1956): Ciba Clinical Symposia.

610   US   ISSN 0149-2918
RM260   CODEN: CLTHDG
CLINICAL THERAPEUTICS; the international journal of drug therapy. 1978. bi-m. $67.50 (foreign $78.75)(effective 1992). Excerpta Medica, Inc., Core Publishing Division (Subsidiary of: Elsevier Science Publishers B.V.), 105 Raider Blvd., Belle Mead, NJ 08502-1510. TEL 908-874-8550. FAX 908-874-5633. Ed. Dr. Arthur Krosnick. charts; illus.; index; circ. 1,050. Indexed: Biol.Abstr., Chem.Abstr., Curr.Adv.Cancer Res., Excerp.Med., Helminthol.Abstr., I.P.A., Ind.Med., Nutr.Abstr.
—BLDSC shelfmark: 3286.399450.
Refereed Serial

610 616.9   US
CLINICAL TOPICS IN INFECTIOUS DISEASE. 1986. irreg. price varies. Springer-Verlag, 175 Fifth Ave., New York, NY 10010. TEL 212-460-1500. (Also Berlin, Heidelberg, Tokyo, Vienna) (reprint service avail. from ISI)

610   NE
                       CODEN: CLTJAJ
CLINICAL TRIALS AND META-ANALYSIS; an international publication of scientific and clinical investigations. (Text in English; summaries in French, German, Italian, Russian, Spanish) 1964. 6/yr. fl.152 (effective 1992). Elsevier Science Publishers B.V., P.O. Box 211, 1000 AE Amsterdam, Netherlands. FAX 020-5803911. TELEX 18582 ESPA NL. (Subscr. in U.S. and Canada to: Elsevier Science Publishing Co., Inc., Box 882, Madison Sq. Sta., New York, NY 10159. TEL 212-989-5800) Ed. Dr. Stuart Phillips. adv.; bk.rev.; abstr.; illus.; stat.; index; circ. 10,000. Indexed: Biol.Abstr., Biotech.Abstr., Curr.Adv.Ecol.Sci., Curr.Cont., Excerp.Med., I.P.A., Telegen.
Formerly (until 1991): Clinical Trials Journal (ISSN 0009-9325); Incorporates: British Journal of Geriatrics and Psychogeriatrics; Orthopaedic Medicine Surgery (ISSN 0030-5855); New Products Medical - Surgical (ISSN 0047-9845)
Description: Provides a professional reflection of the quality and effectiveness of new drugs and techniques.
Refereed Serial

610   SP
CLINICAS DE MEDICINA DE URGENCIAS DE NORTEAMERICA. 4/yr. 13992 ptas. (effective 1990). Interamericana de Espana, S.A., Division de Ciencias de la Salud de McGraw-Hill, Manuel Ferrero, 13, 28036 Madrid, Spain. TEL 315-0340. FAX 733-6627.

610 790.1   SP
CLINICAS DE MEDICINA DEPORTIVA DE NORTEAMERICA. 4/yr. 15900 ptas. (effective 1990). Interamericana de Espana, S.A., Division de Ciencias de la Salud de McGraw-Hill, Manuel Ferrero, 13, 28036 Madrid, Spain. TEL 315-0340. FAX 733-6627.

610   SP
CLINICAS DE PERINATOLOGIA DE NORTEAMERICA. Spanish translation of: Clinics in Perinatology. 1974. 4/yr. 14204 ptas.($104) (effective 1990). Interamericana de Espana, S.A., Division de Ciencias de la Salud de McGraw-Hill, Calle Manuel Ferrero, 13, 28036 Madrid, Spain. TEL 315-0340. FAX 733-6627. charts; illus.; cum.index.

610   SP
CLINICAS MEDICAS DE NORTEAMERICA. Spanish translation of: Medical Clinics of North America. 1959. 6/yr. 18126 ptas.($133) (effective 1990). Interamericana de Espana, S.A., Division de Ciencias de la Salud de McGraw-Hill, Calle Manuel Ferrero, 13, 28036 Madrid, Spain. TEL 315-0340. FAX 733-6627. charts; illus.; cum.index.

610   II   ISSN 0009-9341
                       CODEN: CLCNBF
CLINICIAN; monthly journal of medical science and news. (Text in English) 1936. m. $6. Cosme Matias Menezes Pvt. Ltd., Rua de Ourem, P.O. Box 12, Panjim-Goa, India. Ed.Bd. adv.; bk.rev.; circ. 5,000. Indexed: Chem.Abstr., Curr.Cont., Excerp.Med., Helminthol.Abstr.

616.07   CN
CLINICIEN. 1986. 12/yr. S T A Communications Inc., 955 Boul. St. Jean, Ste. 306, Pointe-Claire, Que. H9R 5K3, Canada. TEL 514-695-7623. FAX 514-695-8554. Ed. Paul Brand. adv.; circ. 14,494.

MEDICAL SCIENCES

610 US ISSN 0891-8422
RD563
CLINICS IN PODIATRIC MEDICINE & SURGERY. 1984. q. $73. W.B. Saunders Co., Curtis Center, Independence Square W., Philadelphia, PA 19106. TEL 215-238-7800. (Subscr. to: Journals, 6277 Sea Harbor Dr., 4th Fl., Orlando, FL 32891) Ed. Melissa Mitchell. circ. 3,500. (also avail. in microfilm; back issues avail.) **Indexed:** Excerp.Med., INIS Atomind.
Formerly (until 1986): Clinics in Podiatry (ISSN 0742-0668)

610 FR ISSN 0009-935X
CLINIQUE;* revue du medecin practicien. 1906. m. 100 F. (Societe Medicale des Praticiens) Editions de Medecine Pratique, 4, rue Louis-Armand, 92600 Asnieres, France. bibl.; index. **Indexed:** Ind.Med.

610 NE ISSN 0045-7183
CLIO MEDICA. (Text in English, French and German) 1966. irreg. price varies. Editions Rodopi B.V., Keizersgracht 302-304, 1016 EX Amsterdam, Netherlands. TEL 020-6227507. FAX 020-6380948. (US and Canada subscr. to: 233 Peachtree St. N.E., Ste. 404, Atlanta, GA 30303-1504. TEL 800-225-3998) Ed. A.M. Luyendijk-Elshout. adv.; bk.rev.; illus.; index; circ. 550. (tabloid format) **Indexed:** Amer.Hist.& Life, Biol.Abstr., Hist.Abstr., Ind.Med.
—BLDSC shelfmark: 3286.650000.
Description: Explores history of medicine.

610 SP
COLECCION CIENCIAS MEDICAS DE BOLSILLO. 1977. irreg., no.17, 1984. price varies. (Universidad de Navarra, Facultad de Medicina) Ediciones Universidad de Navarra, S.A., Apdo. 396, 31080 Pamplona, Spain. TEL 94 825 6850.

610 SP
COLECCION LIBROS DE MEDICINA. 1974. irreg., no.24, 1989. price varies. (Universidad de Navarra, Facultad de Medicina) Ediciones Universidad de Navarra, S.A., Apdo. 396, 31080 Pamplona, Spain. TEL 94 825 6850.
Formerly: Coleccion Medicina.

610 ES ISSN 0010-0641
COLEGIO MEDICO DE EL SALVADOR. ARCHIVAS. (Text in Spanish; summaries in English) 1947. q. $3.50. Colegio Medico de El Salvador, Final Pasaje 10, Col. Miramonte, San Salvador, El Salvador. Ed. Dr. Ramon Lucio Fernandez. adv.; bibl.; charts; illus.; index. **Indexed:** Biol.Abstr., Ind.Med.

610 SA
COLIMPEX MEDICAL EXECUPAD. (Text in Afrikaans and English) a. free to qualified personnel. Colimpex Africa (Pty) Ltd., P.O. Box 5838, Johannesburg 2000, South Africa. adv.

610 SA ISSN 0375-3220
COLLEGE OF MEDICINE OF SOUTH AFRICA. TRANSACTIONS. (Text and summaries in Afrikaans, English) 1957. s-a. R.15. College of Medicine of South Africa, 17 Milner Rd., Rondebosch, Cape Town 7700, South Africa. TEL 021-689-9533. FAX 021-685-3766. Ed. P.J. Commerford. adv.; charts; illus.; circ. 4,000. **Indexed:** Biol.Abstr., Ind.S.A.Per.
Formerly: College of Physicians, Surgeons and Gynecologists of South Africa. Transactions (ISSN 0010-1095)

610 CN
COLLEGE OF PHYSICIANS AND SURGEONS OF BRITISH COLUMBIA. ANNUAL REPORT. a. membership. College of Physicians and Surgeons of British Columbia, 1807 W. 10th Ave., Vancouver, B.C. V6J 2A9, Canada. TEL 604-736-5551.

610 CN ISSN 0069-5726
COLLEGE OF PHYSICIANS AND SURGEONS OF BRITISH COLUMBIA. MEDICAL DIRECTORY. a. Can.$28. College of Physicians and Surgeons of British Columbia, 1807 W. 10th Ave., Vancouver, B.C. V6J 2A9, Canada. TEL 604-736-5551.

610 US ISSN 0010-1087
R15 CODEN: TSCPAI
COLLEGE OF PHYSICIANS OF PHILADELPHIA. TRANSACTIONS & STUDIES. 1793. q. $35 per no. College of Physicians of Philadelphia, 19 S. 22nd St., Philadelphia, PA 19103. TEL 215-563-3737. FAX 215-561-6477. Ed. Caroline Hannaway. bk.rev.; bibl.; charts; illus.; index; circ. 2,300. (also avail. in microfilm from BHP) **Indexed:** Biol.Abstr., Chem.Abstr., Ind.Med.
—BLDSC shelfmark: 9020.210000.

610 GW ISSN 0174-2450
COLO-PROCTOLOGY. (Editions in English and German; summaries in French and Spanish) 1979. bi-m. DM.179($70) Edition Nymphenburg GmbH & Co. KG, Prinzregentenstr. 121, 8000 Munich 80, Germany. TEL 089-4708279. Ed.Bd. adv.; bk.rev.; index; circ. 10,000. (back issues avail.)
—BLDSC shelfmark: 3320.408800.
Formerly: Proctology.
Description: Covers case reports and techniques in proctology. Includes new product information, calendar of events and reviews of journal articles.

610 CK
COLOMBIA MEDICA. 1970. 4/yr. Col.$3,000($15) Corporacion Editora Medica del Valle, Apdo. Aereo 8025, Cali, Colombia. TEL 564504-08-10. (Co-sponsors: Academia de Medicina del Valle del Cauca; Asosciacion Colombiana de Medicina Interna; Sociedad Colombiana de Epidemiologia) Ed. Dr. Francisco Falabella. adv.; bk.rev.; illus.; stat.; circ. 2,000. (also avail. in microfilm from UMI) **Indexed:** Chem.Abstr.
Former titles: Acta Medica Colombiana; Acta Medica del Valle (ISSN 0044-6017)
Description: Original research papers and articles in all areas of medicine.

610 US ISSN 0199-7343
R11
COLORADO MEDICINE. 1903. m. $30. Colorado Medical Society, 7800 E. Dorado Pl., Englewood, CO 80111. TEL 303-779-5455. FAX 303-779-8775. (Subscr. to: Box 17550, Denver, CO 80217-0550) Ed. William Pierson. adv.; bk.rev.; charts; illus.; tr.lit.; index; cum.index; circ. 4,700. (also avail. in microform from UMI; reprint service avail. from UMI) **Indexed:** Biol.Abstr., C.I.S. Abstr., Chem.Abstr., Curr.Cont., Dent.Ind., Excerp.Med., Ind.Med., Med.Care Rev.
—BLDSC shelfmark: 3321.630000.
Supersedes in part: Rocky Mountain Medical Journal (ISSN 0035-760X); Formed by the merger of: Colorado Medicine; Utah State Medical Journal.
Refereed Serial

COMMENTATIONES PHYSICO-MATHEMATICAE ET CHEMICO-MEDICAE. see *PHYSICS*

COMMENTS ON TOXICOLOGY. see *ENVIRONMENTAL STUDIES — Toxicology And Environmental Safety*

COMMUNIQUE (ITHACA). see *COLLEGE AND ALUMNI*

COMMUNITY HEALTH FUNDING REPORT. see *PUBLIC ADMINISTRATION*

360 UK ISSN 0262-8759
COMMUNITY OUTLOOK. 1977. £30. Macmillan Magazines Ltd., 4 Little Essex St., London WC2R 3LF, England. TEL 01-379-0970. FAX 01-379-4204. Ed. Sue Smith. circ. 15,000. **Indexed:** CINAHL.

615 US ISSN 0098-8243
R11
COMPREHENSIVE THERAPY. 1975. m. $139 (foreign $159). (American Society of Contemporary Medicine and Surgery) International Publishing Group, 4959 Commerce Pkwy., Cleveland, OH 44128. TEL 800-342-6237. FAX 216-464-1835. Ed. Dr. John G. Bellows. bk.rev.; circ. 1,400. **Indexed:** Biol.Abstr., CINAHL, Dent.Ind., Excerp.Med., Ind.Med., INIS Atomind., Lang.& Lang.Behav.Abstr., NRN.
—BLDSC shelfmark: 3366.390700.
Refereed Serial

615.8 FR ISSN 0293-9908
CODEN: CRTCD9
COMPTES RENDUS DE THERAPEUTIQUE ET DE PHARMACOLOGIE CLINIQUE. 1982. m. (11/yr.). 200 F. (students 130 F. foreign 360 F.). D & D Medical, 6 rue Emile Verhaeren, B.P. 4 92210 Saint-Cloud, France. TEL 1-47-71-27-18. FAX 1-46-02-72-55. Ed. Serge Dard. adv.; bk.rev.; circ. 3,500. **Indexed:** Chem.Abstr, Excerp.Med.

COMUNICACIONES BIOLOGICAS. see *BIOLOGY*

610 US
CONCERN (ANAHEIM). 1984. 4/yr. $15 to non-members (foreign $25). Society of Critical Care Medicine, 8101 E. Kaiser Blvd., Anaheim, CA 92808-2214. TEL 714-282-6000. FAX 714-282-6050. Ed. Deborah Kincade-Branch. adv.; circ. 6,000. (back issues avail.)
Description: Non-scientific articles and activities of the Society's members.

610 FR ISSN 0010-5309
CODEN: COMEAO
CONCOURS MEDICAL. 1879. w. 465 F.($77) 37 rue de Bellefond, 75441 Paris, France. Ed. Dr. Francois Mignon. adv.; bk.rev.; bibl.; charts; illus.; index; circ. 57,000. **Indexed:** Biol.Abstr., C.I.S. Abstr., Chem.Abstr., Excerp.Med., Ind.Med., INIS Atomind.
—BLDSC shelfmark: 3399.480000.

610.28 US
CONFERENCE ON ENGINEERING IN MEDICINE AND BIOLOGY. RECORD. a. Alliance for Engineering in Medicine and Biology, 1101 Connecticut Ave., N.W., Ste. 700, Washington, DC 20036. TEL 202-857-1199.
Formerly: Engineering in Medicine and Biology Conference. Record (ISSN 0071-0334)
Description: Covers biomedical engineering.

616.043 JA ISSN 0914-3505
CONGENITAL ANOMALIES. (Text in English) 1960. q. 8000 Yen. Nihon Senten Ijo Gakkai - Japanese Teratology Society, Kinki University School of Medicine, Osaka-Sayama-Shi, Osaka 589, Japan. TEL 0723-66-0221. FAX 0723-66-0206. Ed. Mineo Yasuda. adv.; bk.rev.; abstr.; bibl.; charts; illus.; index; circ. 1,700. (processed) **Indexed:** Biol.Abstr., Chem.Abstr., Excerp.Med.
Former titles (until 1987): Senten Ijo (ISSN 0037-2285); (until 1963): Nihon Senten Ijo Gakkai Kaiho.
Description: Reports studies in all areas of abnormal development and related fields.

610 US ISSN 0010-6178
CONNECTICUT MEDICINE. 1936. m. $25 (foreign $40). Connecticut State Medical Society, 160 St. Ronan St., New Haven, CT 06511. TEL 203-865-0587. FAX 203-865-4997. Ed. Robert U. Massey. adv.; bk.rev.; bibl.; illus.; index; circ. 3,800. **Indexed:** Biol.Abstr., C.I.S. Abstr., Chem.Abstr., CINAHL, Curr.Cont., Dent.Ind., Excerp.Med., Ind.Med., INIS Atomind., Med.Care Rev.
—BLDSC shelfmark: 3417.655000.
Formerly (1940-1958): Connecticut State Medical Journal (ISSN 0096-0179)

610 CN ISSN 0828-301X
CONNECTIONS/CONNEXIONS. (Editions in English and French) 1984. q. free. Muscular Dystrophy Association of Canada, 150 Eglington Ave. E., Toronto, Ont. M4P 1E8, Canada. TEL 416-488-0030. FAX 416-488-7523. Ed. Liz Guccione. bk.rev.; illus.; circ. 11,500. (back issues avail.)
Description: Covers fund raising, lient profiles and disability issues.

610 US ISSN 0010-7069
R11
CONSULTANT (GREENWICH); consultants in primary care. 1961. 12/yr. $65. Cliggott Publishing Co., 55 Holly Hill Ln., Box 4010, Greenwich, CT 06830. TEL 203-661-0600. Ed. Charles F. Williams. adv.; charts; illus.; circ. 125,339. (also avail. in microform from UMI; reprint service avail. from UMI) **Indexed:** C.I.N.L, Hlth.Ind., Tr.& Indus.Ind.
—BLDSC shelfmark: 3423.760000.
Description: Practical clinical information on diagnosis and therapy.

MEDICAL SCIENCES

615.8 FR ISSN 0751-7718
CONSULTATION. 1983. fortn. 200 F. (students 130 F.; foreign 360 F.) D & D Medical, 6 rue Emile Verhaeren, B.P. 4 92210 Saint-Cloud, France. TEL 1-47-71-27-18. FAX 1-46-02-72-55. Ed. S. Dard. adv.; circ. 33,500.

610 JO ISSN 0254-7147
CONSULTING MEDICAL LABORATORIES. BULLETIN. (Text in English) 1983. q. $20. Consulting Medical Laboratories, P.O. Box 35198, Amman, Jordan. FAX 962-6-644414. TELEX 21207 JOR HTL JO. Ed. Yahia F. Dajani. circ. 2,000. (back issues avail.)

CONTACT. see RELIGIONS AND THEOLOGY

610 US ISSN 1042-9646
CONTEMPORARY INTERNAL MEDICINE. 1989. 10/yr. $70. Aegean Communications, Inc., 411 W. Putnam, Ste. 109, Greenwich, CT 06830. TEL 203-629-2201. FAX 203-629-9475. Ed. Lucy H. Labson. adv.; circ. 90,000 (controlled).
  Description: Provides clinically practical and authoritative information in areas of high interest to internists and specialist physicians.

610 US ISSN 1050-9623
  CODEN: CMCCEQ
▼**CONTEMPORARY MANAGEMENT IN CRITICAL CARE.** 1991. q. $65 to individuals (foreign $80); institutions $85 (foreign $105). Churchill Livingstone Medicals Journals, 650 Ave. of the Americas, New York, NY 10011. TEL 212-206-5040. FAX 212-727-7808. TELEX 662266. (Dist. by: Transaction Publishers, Department 3091, Rutgers University, New Brunswick, NJ 08903. TEL 908-932-2280) Eds. Dr. Ake Grenvik, Dr. Martin Tobin. **Indexed:** Excerp.Med. (1992-).
  —BLDSC shelfmark: 3425.191150.

610 US
CONTEMPORARY MANAGEMENT SERIES. (Consists of: Contemporary Management in Internal Medicine; Contemporary Management in Obstetrics and Gynecology; Contemporary Management in Critical Care) q. and bi-m. Churchill Livingstone Medical Journals, 650 Ave. of the Americas, New York, NY 10011. TEL 212-206-4050. TELEX 662266. (Dist. by: Transaction Publishers, Department 3091, Rutgers University, New Brunswick, NJ 08903. TEL 908-932-2280)
  Description: Provides current and practical information in clinical specialities.

610 US ISSN 0886-8220
CONTRIBUTIONS IN MEDICAL STUDIES. 1978. irreg., no.36, 1992. price varies. Greenwood Press, Inc. (Subsidiary of: Greenwood Publishing Group Inc.), 88 Post Rd. W., Box 5007, Westport, CT 06881-5007. TEL 203-226-3571. FAX 203-222-1502. Ed. John Burnham.
  —BLDSC shelfmark: 3459.900000.
  Formerly: Contributions in Medical History (ISSN 0147-1058)

612 SZ ISSN 0301-4193
  CODEN: CHDEDZ
CONTRIBUTIONS TO HUMAN DEVELOPMENT. (Text in English) 1962. irreg. (approx. 1/yr.). price varies. S. Karger AG, Allschwilerstr. 10, CH-4009 Basel, Switzerland. TEL 061-3061111. FAX 061-3061234. TELEX CH 962652. Ed. D. Kuhn. (reprint service avail. from ISI) **Indexed:** Biol.Abstr., Chem.Abstr., Curr.Cont., Ind.Med., Psychol.Abstr.
  —BLDSC shelfmark: 3458.630000.
  Formerly: Bibliotheca Vita Humana.

610 SZ ISSN 0250-3220
  CODEN: BEONDH
CONTRIBUTIONS TO ONCOLOGY/BEITRAEGE ZUR ONKOLOGIE. (Text in English and German) 1979. irreg. price varies. S. Karger AG, Allschwilerstr. 10, CH-4009 Basel, Switzerland. TEL 061-3061111. FAX 061-3061234. TELEX CH 962652. Eds. J.H. Holzner, W. Queisser. index. **Indexed:** Biol.Abstr., Chem.Abstr., Curr.Cont.
  —BLDSC shelfmark: 1887.090000.

610 SP ISSN 0213-8328
CONTROL DE CALIDAD ASISTENCIAL. 1987. q. 5500 ptas.($65) (Sociedad Espanola de Control de Calidad) Editorial Garsi, S.A., Londres, 17, 28028 Madrid, Spain. TEL 256-08-00. FAX 361-10-07. Ed. A. Esteban de la Torre. circ. 1,600.

610 NE
COPING WITH MEDICAL ISSUES. 1981. irreg., vol.3, 1982. price varies. Elsevier Science Publishers B.V., Books Division, P.O. Box 211, 1000 AE Amsterdam, Netherlands. TEL 020-5803911. FAX 020-5803705. TELEX 18582 ESPA NL. (Subscr. in U.S. and Canada to: Elsevier Science Publishing Co., Inc. Box 882, Madison Sq. Sta., New York, NY 10159. TEL 212-989-5800)
  Refereed Serial

610 365 US
CORHEALTH. 1975. bi-m. $45. American Correctional Health Services Association, Box 2307, Dayton, OH 45401-2307. TEL 513-223-9630. FAX 513-223-6307. Ed. Rebecca Craig. adv.; bk.rev.; circ. 1,700.
  Description: Covers health care in correctional institutions.

610 378 US ISSN 0010-8898
CORNELL UNIVERSITY MEDICAL COLLEGE ALUMNI QUARTERLY. vol.41, 1978. q. free. Cornell University Medical College, Alumni Association, Inc., 1300 York Ave., New York, NY 10021. TEL 212-746-6546. Ed. C. Richard Minick. adv.; bk.rev.; illus.; circ. 8,000.
  Formerly: Cornell University Medical College Alumni Bulletin.

610 614 US
CORNHUSKER FAMILY PHYSICIAN. q. Nebraska Academy of Family Physicians, 401 N. 117th St., No. 202, Omaha, NE 68154. Ed. David H. Filipi, M.D. adv.

610 CN ISSN 0315-226X
CORPORATION PROFESSIONNELLE DES MEDECINS DU QUEBEC. ANNUAIRE MEDICAL. a. Can.$50. Corporation Professionnelle des Medecins du Quebec, 1440 Ouest rue St. Catherine, Ste 914, Montreal, Que. H3G 1S5, Canada. TEL 514-878-4441.
  Description: List of physicians appearing on the roll of the Corporation Professionnelle des Medecins du Quebec.

610 CN ISSN 0315-2979
CORPORATION PROFESSIONNELLE DES MEDECINS DU QUEBEC. BULLETIN. 1961. irreg. (4-6/yr.). free. Corporation Professionnelle des Medecins du Quebec, 1440 Ouest rue St. Catherine, Ste 914, Montreal, Que. H3G 1S5, Canada. TEL 514-878-4441. **Indexed:** Pt.de Rep.
  Formerly: College des Medecins et Chirurgiens de la Province de Quebec. Bulletin (ISSN 0069-5599)

610 GW ISSN 0070-0347
R126.A1
CORPUS MEDICORUM GRAECORUM. 1958. irreg., vol.27, 1988. price varies. (Akademie der Wissenschaften der DDR, Zentralinstitut fuer Alte Geschichte und Archaeologie) Akademie-Verlag Berlin, Leipziger Str. 3-4, 1086 Berlin, Germany. TELEX 114420-AVERL-DD. (Co-sponsors: Koenigliche Daenische Akademie; Saechsische Akademie der Wissenschaften, Leipzig)

610 US ISSN 1048-5791
CORTLANDT FORUM. m. Cortlandt Group, Inc., 500 Executive Blvd., Ste. 302, Ossining, NY 10562. TEL 914-762-0647. FAX 914-762-8820.

610 668.5 US
COSMETIC SCIENCE AND TECHNOLOGY SERIES. 1984. irreg., vol.11, 1991. price varies. Marcel Dekker, Inc., 270 Madison Ave., New York, NY 10016. TEL 212-696-9000. FAX 212-685-4540. TELEX 421419. Ed. Eric Jungerman.
  Refereed Serial

610.6 US ISSN 0196-2434
R729.5.G6
COST AND PRODUCTION SURVEY REPORT. 1970. a. $185. Medical Group Management Association, 104 Inverness Terrace E., Enlgewood, CO 80112. TEL 303-799-1111. Ed.Bd. charts; stat.; circ. 7,500. (back issues avail.)

616.865 US ISSN 0361-1612
R850.A1
COUNCIL FOR TOBACCO RESEARCH, U.S.A. REPORT. a. Council for Tobacco Research, U.S.A. Inc., 900 Third Ave., New York, NY 10022. TEL 212-421-8885. abstr. Key Title: Report of the Council for Tobacco Research - U.S.A., Inc.
  —BLDSC shelfmark: 7411.355000.

610 US
CRANIO: JOURNAL OF CRANIOMANDIBULAR PRACTICE. Variant title: Cranio. 1982. q. $47 to individuals; institutions $85. Williams & Wilkins, 428 E. Preston St., Baltimore, MD 21202. TEL 301-528-4000. FAX 301-528-4312. Ed. Riley H. Lunn, D.D.S. adv.; bk.rev.; circ. 4,500. **Indexed:** Curr.Tit.Dent., Dent.Abstr., Dent.Ind., Excerp.Med.
  Formerly: Journal of Craniomandibular Practice (ISSN 0734-5410)
  Description: Discusses diagnosis and treatment of craniomandibular disorders for dentists, physicians and physical therapists.
  Refereed Serial

610 US ISSN 0749-0704
RC86 CODEN: CCCLEH
CRITICAL CARE CLINICS. 1985. q. $78. W.B. Saunders Co., Curtis Center, Independence Square W., Philadelphia, PA 19106. TEL 215-238-7800. (Subscr. to: Journals 6277 Sea Harbor Dr., 4th Fl., Orlando FL 32891) Ed. Mary Mulroy. circ. 3,650. (also avail. in microfilm; back issues avail.) **Indexed:** Excerp.Med.
  —BLDSC shelfmark: 3487.450700.

610 US ISSN 0090-3493
RC86 CODEN: CCMDC7
CRITICAL CARE MEDICINE. 1973. m. $80 to individuals; institutions $120. (Society of Critical Care Medicine) Williams & Wilkins, 428 E. Preston St., Baltimore, MD 21202. TEL 301-528-4000. FAX 301-528-4312. Ed. Bart C. Lernow, M.D. illus.; circ. 11,000. (also avail. in microform) **Indexed:** Abstr.Health Care Manage.Stud., CINAHL, Curr.Adv.Ecol.Sci., Curr.Cont., Excerp.Med., Ind.Med., Ind.Sci.Rev., INIS Atomind., Sci.Cit.Ind.
  ●Also available online. Vendor(s): Mead Data Central. Also available on CD-ROM.
  —BLDSC shelfmark: 3487.451000.
  Description: Cross-disciplinary news for hospital-based specialists who treat patients in the ICU and CCU, including anesthesiologists and critical care nurses.
  Refereed Serial

610 US
CRITICAL CARE REPORT. 1989-1991 (Jan.). 3/yr. $52.50 (foreign $58.50). Mosby - Year Book, Inc. (Subsidiary of: Times Mirror Company), 11830 Westline Industrial Dr., St. Louis, MO 63146. TEL 800-325-4117. FAX 314-432-1380. TELEX 44-2402. Ed. Dr. Mark C. Rogers. illus.

610 US ISSN 0748-5204
  CODEN: CCRBES
CRITICAL REVIEWS IN BIOCOMPATIBILITY. $149. Elsevier Science Publishing Co., Inc. (New York), 655 Ave. of the Americas, New York, NY 10010. TEL 212-989-5800. FAX 212-633-3965. TELEX 420643 AEP UI. Ed. David F. Williams.

CRITICAL REVIEWS IN BIOMEDICAL ENGINEERING. see BIOLOGY — Bioengineering

616.07 US ISSN 1040-8363
RB37 CODEN: CRCLBH
CRITICAL REVIEWS IN CLINICAL LABORATORY SCIENCES. 1970. q. $99.95 to individuals; institutions $225. C R C Press, Inc., 2000 Corporate Blvd., N.W., Boca Raton, FL 33431. TEL 407-994-0555. FAX 407-998-9784. Eds. Drs. John Batsakis, John Savory. bibl.; charts; illus.; circ. 530. (back issues avail.) **Indexed:** Biol.Abstr., Chem.Abstr., Curr.Cont., Dent.Ind., Helminthol.Abstr., Ind.Med., Ind.Sci.Rev., INIS Atomind., Nutr.Abstr., Sci.Cit.Ind.
  Formerly: C R C Critical Reviews in Clinical Laboratory Sciences (ISSN 0590-8191)
  Refereed Serial

610 US ISSN 0896-2960
CRITICAL REVIEWS IN PHYSICAL & REHABILITATION MEDICINE. 1989. q. $79.95 to individuals; institutions $225. C R C Press, Inc., 2000 Corporate Blvd., N.W., Boca Raton, FL 33431. TEL 407-994-0555. FAX 407-998-9784. Eds. Martin Grabois, Ernest J. Henley.
  —BLDSC shelfmark: 3487.479800.

MEDICAL SCIENCES

610 500   SP   ISSN 0011-2577
CUADERNOS VALENCIANOS DE HISTORIA DE LA MEDICINA Y DE LA CIENCIA. (Text in Spanish and classical languages) 1962. irreg. (2-3/yr.). price varies. Universidad de Valencia, C.S.I.C., Instituto de Estudios Documentales e Historicos sobre la Ciencia, Avda. Blasco Ibanez 17, Valencia 10, Spain. FAX 96-331-39-75. Ed.Bd. charts; illus.; circ. 500. (reprint service avail.)

CULTURE, MEDICINE AND PSYCHIATRY; an international journal of comparative cross-cultural research. see *ANTHROPOLOGY*

616.97   US
CUMITECHS. (Cumulative Techniques and Procedures in Clinical Microbiology) 1974. irreg. (2-3/yr.). $7.50 per no. American Society for Microbiology, 1325 Massachusetts Ave., N.W., Washington, DC 20005. TEL 202-737-3600. Ed. Steven C. Specter.

610   IT   ISSN 0391-8904
CUORE E VASI. 10/yr. L.15000($15) C I C Edizioni Internazionali s.r.l., Via L. Spallenzani, 11, 00161 Rome, Italy. TEL 06-8412673. FAX 06-8443365. TELEX 622099 CIC.

610   US
CURANDERO NEWSLETTER. 1980. s-a. $2. (Boricua Health Organization) University of Medicine and Dentistry of New Jersey, 100 Bergen St., Newark, NJ 07103. TEL 201-456-4300. Ed.Bd. adv.; bk.rev.; bibl.; charts; illus.; stat.; circ. 2,000. (also avail. in Braille; talking book)

CURRENT ADVANCES IN CLINICAL CHEMISTRY. see *CHEMISTRY — Abstracting, Bibliographies, Statistics*

CURRENT ADVANCES IN TOXICOLOGY. see *PHARMACY AND PHARMACOLOGY — Abstracting, Bibliographies, Statistics*

610 574   UK
CURRENT AWARENESS. S D I SERVICE. (Text in English, French, German and Italian) 1962. w. £20. Scientific Documentation Centre Ltd., Halbeath House, Dunfermline, Fife KY12 0TZ, Scotland.

616.4   NE
CURRENT CLINICAL PRACTICE. 1982. irreg., vol.59, 1991. price varies. Elsevier Science Publishers B.V., Books Division, P.O. Box 211, 1000 AE Amsterdam, Netherlands. TEL 020-5803911. FAX 020-5803705. TELEX 18582 ESPA NL. (Subscr. in U.S. and Canada to: Elsevier Science Publishing Co., Inc., Box 882, Madison Sq. Sta., New York, NY 10159. TEL 212-989-5800) (back issues avail.)
Refereed Serial

616.5 616.362   US   ISSN 0198-8093
RC845   CODEN: CUHEDA
CURRENT HEPATOLOGY. 1980. a. $79.95. Mosby - Year Book, Inc. (Subsidiary of: Times Mirror Company), 200 N. LaSalle St., Chicago, IL 60601-1080. TEL 312-726-9733. FAX 312-726-6075. TELEX 206155. (Subscr. to: 11830 Westline Industrial Dr., St. Louis, MO 63146. TEL 800-325-4117) Ed. Gary L. Gitnick, M.D.
—BLDSC shelfmark: 3497.430000.
Description: Surveys developments in hepatology and provides synopses of the past twelve months of medical literature.

610   US   ISSN 0092-8682
RC71
CURRENT MEDICAL DIAGNOSIS AND TREATMENT. 1962. a. price varies. Appleton & Lange (Subsidiary of: Simon & Schuster Company), 25 Van Zant St., Box 5630, Norwalk, CT 06856. TEL 203-838-4400. Ed.Bd.
—BLDSC shelfmark: 3500.220000.
Formerly: Current Diagnosis and Treatment.

610   II   ISSN 0011-3700
    CODEN: CMDPAW
CURRENT MEDICAL PRACTICE. 1956. m. Rps.50($15) Current Technical Literature Co. Pvt. Ltd., Malhotra House, P.O. Box 1374, Bombay 1, India. Ed. B.S. Singhal. adv.; bk.rev.; abstr.; illus.; circ. 2,500. (also avail. in microform from UMI; reprint service avail. from UMI) **Indexed:** Biol.Abstr., Chem.Abstr.

610 615   UK   ISSN 0300-7995
    CODEN: CMROCX
CURRENT MEDICAL RESEARCH AND OPINION. (Supplement avail. (ISSN 0141-9951)) 1972. irreg. $60. Clayton-Wray Publications Ltd., 1A High St., Alton, Hants GU34 1BA, England. TEL 0420-87293. Ed. N.B. Clayton. index; circ. 6,000. (also avail. in microform from UMI; back issues avail.; reprint service avail. from UMI) **Indexed:** Abstr.Hyg., Biotech.Abstr., Chem.Abstr, Curr.Adv.Ecol.Sci., Curr.Cont., Excerp.Med., Helminthol.Abstr., Ind.Med., Ind.Sci.Rev., NRN, Nutr.Abstr., Rev.Plant Path., Sci.Cit.Ind, Trop.Dis.Bull.
—BLDSC shelfmark: 3500.301000.

610   US   ISSN 0011-393X
    CODEN: CTCEA9
CURRENT THERAPEUTIC RESEARCH; clinical and experimental. 1960. m. $105 (effective 1992). Excerpta Medica, Inc., Core Publishing Division (Subsidiary of: Elsevier Science Publishers B.V.), 105 Raider Blvd., Belle Mead, NJ 08502-1510. TEL 908-874-8550. FAX 908-874-5633. Ed. Charles R. Ream. circ. 1,200. **Indexed:** Biotech.Abstr., Chem.Abstr., Curr.Adv.Ecol.Sci., Curr.Cont., Dairy Sci.Abstr., Excerp.Med., Helminthol.Abstr., I.P.A., Ind.Sci.Rev., Int.Nurs.Ind., Nutr.Abstr., Psychol.Abstr., Rev.Plant Path., Sci.Cit.Ind.
—BLDSC shelfmark: 3504.600000.
Description: Publishes results of original research in the broad field of medical therapy and related areas.
Refereed Serial

610   UK   ISSN 0732-4448
R97   CODEN: CGMSDD
CURRENT TOPICS IN CHINESE SCIENCE. SECTION G: MEDICAL SCIENCE. 1982. irreg., vol.3, 1985. Gordon & Breach Science Publishers, P.O. Box 90, Reading, Berkshire RG1 8JL, England. TEL 0734-560-080. FAX 0734-568-211. TELEX 849870 SCIPUB G. (US addr.: Box 786, Cooper Sta., New York, NY 10276. TEL 800-545-8398) (also avail. in microfilm; microfiche)
Refereed Serial

616.07 574.2   US   ISSN 0070-2188
    CODEN: CTPHBG
CURRENT TOPICS IN PATHOLOGY. irreg. price varies. Springer-Verlag, 175 Fifth Ave., New York, NY 10010. TEL 212-460-1500. (Also Berlin, Heidelberg, Tokyo and Vienna) (reprint service avail. from ISI) **Indexed:** Biol.Abstr., Chem.Abstr., Ind.Med., Ind.Vet., Vet.Bull.
—BLDSC shelfmark: 3504.895000.
Formerly: Ergebnisse der Allgemeinen Pathologie und Pathologischen Anatomie.

610   IE
CYSTIC FIBROSIS NEWS. 1979. m. Cystic Fibrosis Association of Ireland, Dublin, Ireland. **Indexed:** Curr.Adv.Ecol.Sci.

610   DK   ISSN 0901-4500
CYSTISK FIBROSE. 1980. 4/yr. free. Landsforeningen til Bekaempelse af Cystisk Fibrose, Hyrdebakken 246, 8800 Viborg, Denmark. TEL 06-674422. FAX 45-86676666. adv.; illus.; circ. 1,300.
Formerly: Hej (ISSN 0108-5409)

CYTOBIOS; a prestige international biomedical research journal of cell biology. see *BIOLOGY — Cytology And Histology*

CYTOGENETICS AND CELL GENETICS. see *BIOLOGY — Genetics*

CYTOKINES. see *BIOLOGY — Microbiology*

610   CS
CZECHOSLOVAK MEDICINE. (Editions in English, Russian) 1978. 4/yr. 120 Kcs. (Ceskoslovenska Lekarska Spolecnost J. Ev. Purkyne) Avicenum, Czechoslovak Medical Press, Malostranske nam. 28, 118 02 Prague 1, Czechoslovakia. (Dist. by: Karger Libri A.G., Petersgr. 31, 4011 Basel, Switzerland) Ed. Dr. S. Fiala. adv.; bk.rev.; abstr.; charts; illus.; stat.; index. **Indexed:** Abstr.Hyg., Chem.Abstr., Curr.Adv.Cancer Res., Dent.Abstr., Dent.Ind., Dok.Arbeitsmed., Excerp.Med., Ind.Med., INIS Atomind., Nutr.Abstr., Trop.Dis.Bull.
Formerly: Review of Czechoslovak Medicine (ISSN 0034-6497)

610   GW
D G F MITTEILUNGSBLATT. q. Deutsche Gesellschaft fuer Fachkrankenpflege e.V., Langenbeckstr. 1, D-6500 Mainz, Germany. TEL 173237.

610   DK   ISSN 0108-7320
D I M S BULLETIN. 1981. 3/yr. free. Dansk Idraetsmedicinsk Selskab, Idraettens Hus, Broendby Stadion, DK-2605 Broendby, Denmark. Ed. Jens H. Kristensen. adv.; bk.rev.

610   US   ISSN 0011-5029
R11
D M. (Disease-a-Month) 1954. m. $65 to individuals (foreign $90); institutions $100 (foreign $125); students $45 (foreign $70) (effective Jan. 1992). Mosby - Year Book, Inc. (Subsidiary of: Times Mirror Company), 11830 Westline Industrial Dr., St. Louis, MO 63146. TEL 800-325-4177. Ed. Dr. Roger C. Bone. charts; illus.; stat.; cum.index; circ. 4,606. (also avail. in microform from UMI; back issues avail.; reprint service avail. from UMI) **Indexed:** Curr.Cont., Excerp.Med., Ind.Med., NRN.
—BLDSC shelfmark: 3598.100000.
Description: For the general internist. Each issue is a single topic discussion that focuses on the integrated management of a particular disease.

D W D NEWSLETTER. (Death with Dignity) see *LAW*

610   SG
DAKAR MEDICAL. 1959. s-a. 25000 Fr.CFA. Societe Medicale d'Afrique Noire de Langue Francaise - Medical Society of the French Speaking Zone of Black Africa, B.P. 450, Dakar, Senegal. Ed. Agrege P. Ndiaye. adv.; bk.rev.; illus.; circ. 1,300. **Indexed:** Abstr.Hyg., Biol.Abstr., Dent.Ind., Excerp.Med., Helminthol.Abstr., Ind.Med., Rev.Plant Path., Trop.Dis.Bull.
Former titles (until 1980): Societe Medicale d'Afrique Noire de Langue Francaise. Bulletin (ISSN 0049-1101); A.O.F. Bulletin Medical.

610   CC   ISSN 1000-5676
DALIAN YIXUEYUAN XUEBAO/DALIAN MEDICAL INSTITUTE. JOURNAL. (Text in Chinese) q. Dalian Yixueyuan - Dalian Medical Institute, 465 Zhongshan Lu, Dalian, Liaoning 116023, People's Republic of China. TEL 491802. Ed. Jin Yongxi.

610   UA
DALIL AL-AHRAM AL-TIBBI/AL-AHRAM MEDICAL GUIDE. 1989. a. Mu'assasat al-Ahram, Sharia al-Galaa, Cairo, Egypt. TEL 02-758333. FAX 02-745888. TELEX 92001.

610   US   ISSN 0011-586X
DALLAS MEDICAL JOURNAL. 1914. m. membership. Dallas County Medical Society, Box 4680, Sta. A, Dallas, TX 75208. TEL 214-948-3622. FAX 214-946-5805. Ed. Linda C. Chandler. adv.; circ. 4,000. **Indexed:** Ind.Med.

DANCE AUSTRALIA. see *DANCE*

610   IR
DANESHKADE PEZESHKI. 1947. 10/yr. Teheran Medical Sciences University, Faculty of Medicine, Enghelab Ave., Teheran 14-714, Iran. TEL 021-6112743. Ed. Hassan Arefi. adv.; circ. 1,500.

610   DK   ISSN 0011-6092
    CODEN: DMBUAE
DANISH MEDICAL BULLETIN. 1954. irreg. (6-8/yr.). DKK 250 (free to medical institutions on request). Almindelige Danske Laegeforening - Danish Medical Association, Trondhjemsgade 9, DK-2100 Copenhagen, Denmark. (Subscr. to: Laegeforeningens Forlag, Esplanaden 8 A, DK-1263 Copenhagen K, Denmark) Eds. John Christiansen, Erik Juhl. adv.; charts; illus.; circ. 5,300. (also avail. in microform from UMI; reprint service avail. from UMI) **Indexed:** Abstr.Hyg., Biol.Abstr., Chem.Abstr., Curr.Adv.Cancer Res., Curr.Adv.Ecol.Sci., Curr.Adv.Genetics & Molec.Biol., Curr.Cont., Dairy Sci.Abstr., Excerp.Med., Ind.Med., Ind.Sci.Rev., NRN, Nutr.Abstr., Rehabil.Lit., Risk Abstr., Sci.Cit.Ind, Trop.Dis.Bull.
—BLDSC shelfmark: 3519.400000.

610 DK ISSN 0084-9588
R539
DANSK MEDICINHISTORISK AARBOG/YEARBOOK OF DANISH MEDICAL HISTORY. (Text in Danish; summaries in English) 1972. a. DKK 130. Medical History Societies in Denmark, H.P. Hanssensgade 42, DK-6200 Aabenraa, Denmark. Ed. Tage Grodum. adv.; circ. 900. **Indexed:** NAA.

610 DK ISSN 0105-0648
DANSKE FYSIOTERAPEUTER. 1918. 23/yr. DKK 550. Danske Fysioterapeuters Organisation, Norre Voldgade 90, 1358 Copenhagen K, Denmark. TEL 33-13-82-11. FAX 33938214. Ed. Inga Wolf. adv.; bk.rev.; circ. 6,300.

610 TZ
DAR ES SALAAM MEDICAL JOURNAL. 1969. s-a. University of Dar es Salaam, Faculty of Medicine, Nuhimbili Medical Centre, P.O. Box 65007, Dar es Salaam, Tanzania. Ed. Ernest Komba. adv.; bk.rev.; bibl.; illus. **Indexed:** Biol.Abstr.

610 378
DARTMOUTH MEDICINE. 1976. q. free to qualified personnel. Dartmouth Medical School, Hanover, NH 03756. TEL 603-646-7815. FAX 603-646-6103. Ed. Dana Cook Grossman. adv.; bk.rev.; charts; illus.; circ. 15,000. (back issues avail.)
  Formerly: Dartmouth Medical School Alumni Magazine.

610 US
DATA CENTRUM. 1984. m. $32 (free to qualified personnel). Whitmore Jenson Publishers, 100 Greene St., New York, NY 10012-3813. TEL 212-586-4287. Ed. Stu Chapman. adv.; circ. 127,500.

610 LH ISSN 0011-7005
DATENJOURNAL. (Text and summaries in English and German) 1969. q. 80 Fr. (International Society for Prospective Medicine) Mecudo Aktiengesellschaft, Vaduz, Liechtenstein. (Subscr. to: Dr. Josef Schmid, Walfischgasse 10, 1010 Vienna, Austria) adv.; abstr.; bibl.; charts; illus.; stat.; circ. 2,000. (tabloid format; also avail. in cards) **Indexed:** Biol.Abstr.
  Description: Features latest in medical electronics.

610 CC ISSN 1000-8470
DAZHONG YIXUE/POPULAR MEDICINE. (Text in Chinese) 1948. m. $1 per no. Shanghai Scientific and Technical Publishers, Journal Department, 450 Ruijin 2 Lu, Shanghai 200020, People's Republic of China. (Dist. outside China by: China International Book Trading Corp., P.O. Box 399, Beijing, P.R.C.)

610 GW ISSN 0931-8305
DE NATURA RERUM; international medical review for documentation and information. (Text in English, French, German, Italian and Spanish) q. DM.70 to individuals; students DM.52. (C.E.I.A. Benelux) Karl F Haug Verlag GmbH, Fritz-Frey-Str. 21, Postfach 102840, 6900 Heidelberg 1, Germany. TEL 06221-4062-0. FAX 06221-400727. TELEX 461683-HVVFMD. Ed. Dr. Eric Reymond.
  —BLDSC shelfmark: 3535.947200.

610 US
DEAR DOCTOR; written by health-care professionals for your family's well-being. 1989. bi-m. $27 (foreign $30). Dear Doctor, Inc., Rt. 6, Box 81, Brewster, NY 10509. TEL 914-279-7510. Ed. Marion Roach.

610 US ISSN 0011-7781
DELAWARE MEDICAL JOURNAL. 1929. m. $20 (foreign $25). Medical Society of Delaware, 1925 Lovering Ave., Wilmington, DE 19806-2147. TEL 302-658-3957. FAX 302-571-1876. Eds. Dr. Wayne Martz, Dr. Virginia U. Collier. adv.; bk.rev.; bibl.; illus.; index; circ. 1,400. (also avail. in microfilm from UMI; reprint service avail. from UMI) **Indexed:** Chem.Abstr., Curr.Cont., Ind.Med., INIS Atomind.
  —BLDSC shelfmark: 3547.500000.

610 II ISSN 0011-7854
DELHI MEDICAL JOURNAL. (Text in English) vol.4, 1969. s-a. Rs.4. Delhi Medical Association, House Daryaganj, Delhi 6, India. Ed. Dr. Kili Tuli. adv.; abstr.; charts.

DEMETER KONGRESS KALENDER MEDIZIN. see MEETINGS AND CONGRESSES

610 US
DETROIT MEDICAL NEWS. w. Wayne County Medical Society, 1010 Antietam, Detroit, MI 48207-2832. TEL 313-567-1640. Ed. Susan Adelman. circ. 4,500.

610 GW ISSN 0011-9873
DER DEUTSCHE ARZT. 1951. 20/yr. DM.144. Hartmannbund - Verband der Aerzte Deutschlands e.V., Godesberger Allee 54, D-5300 Bonn - Bad Godesberg, Germany. TEL 02234-7011-0. Ed. K. Kieselbach. adv.; bk.rev.; circ. 45,000. **Indexed:** Excerp.Med.
  Description: Contains news and information of interest to all German physicians. Features new medical research, public health issues, political and economical issues. Includes readers' comments.

362 618.92 GW ISSN 0939-4702
DEUTSCHE BEHINDERTENZEITSCHRIFT. Abbreviated title: D B Z. 1964. bi-m. DM.27. Reha-Verlag GmbH, Roonstr. 30, 5300 Bonn 2, Germany. TEL 0228-352328. Ed. L. Sparty. adv.: adv.: B&W page DM.1500; trim 210 x 297. bk.rev.; circ. 10,000.
  Former titles: Behindertenzeitschrift (ISSN 0175-5854) & Behinderte Kind (ISSN 0005-7991)

610 GW ISSN 0027-7460
DEUTSCHE GESELLSCHAFT FUER GESCHICHTE DER MEDIZIN, NATURWISSENSCHAFT UND TECHNIK. NACHRICHTENBLATT. 1951. 3/yr. DM.50 membership. Deutsche Gesellschaft fuer Geschichte der Medizin, Naturwissenschaft und Technik e.V., Werbachstr. 17, 2900 Oldenburg, Germany. Ed. Dr. Claus Priesner. adv.; circ. 650.
  —BLDSC shelfmark: 6007.300000.

616.02 US ISSN 0070-4067
CODEN: VDGIA2
DEUTSCHE GESELLSCHAFT FUER INNERE MEDIZIN. VERHANDLUNGEN. 44th congress, 1932. irreg., 90th congress, 1984. price varies. Springer-Verlag, 175 Fifth Ave., New York, NY 10010. TEL 212-460-1500. (Also Berlin, Heidelberg, Tokyo and Vienna) Ed. B. Schlegel. (also avail. in microfiche from BHP; reprint service avail. from ISI) **Indexed:** Biol.Abstr.

616.07 574.2 GW ISSN 0070-4113
CODEN: VDGPAN
DEUTSCHE GESELLSCHAFT FUER PATHOLOGIE. VERHANDLUNGEN. a. price varies. Gustav Fischer Verlag, Wollgrasweg 49, Postfach 720143, 7000 Stuttgart 70, Germany. TEL 0711-458030. FAX 0711-4580334. TELEX 7111-488-FIBUCH. (U.S. address: Gustav Fischer New York Inc., 220 East 23rd St., Suite 909, New York, NY 10010) **Indexed:** Biol.Abstr., Chem.Abstr., Ind.Med.
  —BLDSC shelfmark: 9163.310000.

610 GW ISSN 0177-3747
DEUTSCHE GESELLSCHAFT FUER UNFALLHEILKUNDE. MITTEILUNGEN UND NACHRICHTEN. 1978. s-a. DM.24. Demeter Verlag, Wuermstr. 13, 8033 Graefelfing, Germany. TEL 089-852033. FAX 089-8543347. Ed. Dr. A. Pannike.

610 GW ISSN 0012-0472
CODEN: DMWOAX
DEUTSCHE MEDIZINISCHE WOCHENSCHRIFT/GERMAN MEDICAL WEEKLY. (Editions in English, German, Greek, Italian, Spanish; summaries in English, German, Spanish) 1875. w. DM.243 (students DM.84). Georg Thieme Verlag, Ruedigerstr. 14, Postfach 104853, 7000 Stuttgart 10, Germany. TEL 0711-8931-0. Ed.Bd. adv.; bk.rev.; abstr.; bibl.; illus.; stat.; index; circ. 38,200. (also avail. in microform from UMI; reprint service avail. from UMI) **Indexed:** Abstr.Hyg., Biol.Abstr., Biotech.Abstr., C.I.S. Abstr., Chem.Abstr., Curr.Adv.Ecol.Sci., Curr.Adv.Genetics & Molec.Biol., Curr.Cont., Dairy Sci.Abstr., Dent.Ind., Excerp.Med., Forest Prod.Abstr., Helminthol.Abstr., Ind.Med., Ind.Sci.Rev., INIS Atomind., Nutr.Abstr., Protozool.Abstr., Rev.Plant Path., Risk Abstr., Sci.Cit.Ind, Small Anim.Abstr., Trop.Dis.Bull.
  —BLDSC shelfmark: 3573.000000.

MEDICAL SCIENCES 3093

615.89 GW ISSN 0415-6412
DEUTSCHE ZEITSCHRIFT FUER AKUPUNKTUR; Zeitschrift fuer die wissenschaftliche Erforschung und praktische Anwendung der Akupunktur in Klinik und Praxis. (Text in German; summaries in English) bi-m. DM.106 (students DM.86). (Oesterreichische Gesellschaft fuer Akupunktur and Auriculotherapie) Karl F. Haug Verlag GmbH, Fritz-Frey-Str. 21, Postfach 102840, 6900 Heidelberg 1, Germany. TEL 06221-4062-0. FAX 06221-400727. TELEX 461683-HVVFMD. Ed. Johannes Bischko. adv. **Indexed:** Excerp.Med.
  —BLDSC shelfmark: 3575.720000.

610 GW ISSN 0940-4783
DEUTSCHER FORSCHUNGSDIENST. BERICHTE AUS DER WISSENSCHAFT - AUSWAHL MEDIZIN. m. DM.72. Deutscher Forschungsdienst, Ahrstr. 45, 5300 Bonn 2, Germany. TEL 0228-302210. FAX 0228-302270.

610 GW ISSN 0012-1207
DEUTSCHES AERZTEBLATT; aerztliche Mitteilungen. 1903. w. DM.483 (students DM.112). (Bundesaerztekammer) Deutscher Aerzte-Verlag GmbH, Dieselstr. 2, Postfach 40 02 65, 5000 Cologne 40, Germany. TEL 02234-7011-0. FAX 02234-7011444. (Co-sponsor: Kassenaerztliche Bundesvereinigung) Ed. Ernst Roemer. adv.; bk.rev.; circ. 276,000. **Indexed:** Excerp.Med., INIS Atomind.
  —BLDSC shelfmark: 3576.285000.

DEVELOPMENT. see BIOLOGY

DEVELOPMENTAL AND COMPARATIVE IMMUNOLOGY; ontogeny - phylogeny - aging. see MEDICAL SCIENCES — Allergology And Immunology

DEVELOPMENTAL DYNAMICS. see BIOLOGY

610 SZ ISSN 1015-8154
DEVENIR. 1989. q. 78 SFr. to individuals; institutions 110 SFr. Editions Medecine et Hygiene, Case Postale 456, CH-1211 Geneva 4, Switzerland. TEL 022-469355. FAX 022-475610.

610 US ISSN 0098-7573
DEVICES & DIAGNOSTICS LETTER. 1974. w. $577. Washington Business Information, Inc., c/o Karen Harrington, 1117 N. 19th St., Ste. 200, Arlington, VA 22209. TEL 703-247-3434. FAX 703-247-3421. Ed. Jerome Boin. bk.rev. (looseleaf format)
  ●Also available online. Vendor(s): BRS (DIOG), Data-Star, DIALOG.
  Description: For business leaders concerned with government regulation of medical devices and in vitro diagnostics. Covers compliance and inspection programs, defect reporting, labeling and testing rules.

610 AG ISSN 0012-1762
DIA MEDICO. (Supplements avail.) 1928. m. Tucuman 2012, 4th Fl., Buenos Aires, Argentina. Ed.Bd. adv.; bk.rev.; charts; illus.; index; circ. 8,000. **Indexed:** Biol.Abstr., Ind.Med.

610 US ISSN 0145-7217
RC660.A1 CODEN: DIEDEM
DIABETES EDUCATOR. 1975. bi-m. $35 to non-members. American Association of Diabetes Educators, 500 N. Michigan Ave., Ste. 1400, Chicago, IL 60611. FAX 312-661-0769. Ed. James A. Fain. adv.; bk.rev.; circ. 6,000. (back issues avail.) **Indexed:** CINAHL, Ind.Med., Int.Nurs.Ind.
  —BLDSC shelfmark: 3579.600650.

612 616.4 UK ISSN 0263-7294
DIABETES MELLITUS. s-m. £75. Sheffield University Biomedical Information Service (SUBIS), The University, Sheffield S10 2TN, England. TEL 0742-768555. FAX 0742-739826. TELEX 547216 UGSHEF G. (looseleaf format; back issues avail.)
  Description: Current awareness service for researchers in clinical and life sciences.

DIABETES SELF-MANAGEMENT. see MEDICAL SCIENCES — Endocrinology

610 IT
DIAGNOSIS; ricerca e tecnologie diagnostiche. 1989. q. L.45000($67) (effective 1991). Masson Italia Periodici, Via Statuto 2-4, 20121 Milan, Italy. TEL 02-6367-1. FAX 02-6367-211. Ed. Mario Ghione. circ. 5,000. **Indexed:** Ind.Med.

M

MEDICAL SCIENCES

610   US
DIAGNOSTIC IMAGING SCAN. 1987. s-m. $557. Miller Freeman, Inc. (Subsidiary of: United Newspapers), 600 Harrison St., San Francisco, CA 94107. TEL 415-905-2200. FAX 415-905-2232. TELEX 278273. Ed. Roger Lindahl.

610   US
▼**DIAGNOSTIC MOLECULAR PATHOLOGY.** 1992. q. $75 to individuals; institutions $85. Raven Press, 1185 Ave. of the Americas, New York, NY 10036. TEL 212-930-9500. FAX 212-869-3495. TELEX 640073. Ed. Dr. Stephen S. Sternberg. adv.; bk.rev.; charts; illus.
Description: Publishes contributions on molecular probes for diagnosis, such as tumor suppressor genes, oncogenes, the polymerase chain reaction, and in situ hybridization.
Refereed Serial

610   FR
DIAGNOSTICS. 1965. 22/yr. 140 F. 12 bis Place Henri Bergson, 75008 Paris, France. (Subscr.to: Office Universitarie de Presse, 15 rue Tiphaine, 75015 Paris, France) adv.; circ. 22,500 (controlled).

DIAGNOSTICS INTELLIGENCE. see *PHARMACY AND PHARMACOLOGY*

616.075   PL   ISSN 0012-1932
CODEN: DLJNAQ
DIAGNOSTYKA LABORATORYJNA. 1964. bi-m. $96. (Polskie Towarzystwo Diagnostyki Laboratoryjnej) Panstwowe Zaklad Wydawnictw Lekarskich, Ul. Dluga 38-40, 00-068 Warsaw, Poland. TEL 31-42-81. (Dist. by: Ars Polona-Ruch, Krakowskie Przedmiescie 7, Warsaw, Poland) Ed. Dr. Stefan Angielski. adv.; bk.rev.; circ. 1,450. Indexed: Biol.Abstr., Chem.Abstr., Excerp.Med., INIS Atomind.
Description: Examines clinical chemistry, cytomorphology, parasitology and serology.

DIARIO DE CONGRESOS MEDICOS. see *MEETINGS AND CONGRESSES*

DIMENSIONE SALUTE. see *PHYSICAL FITNESS AND HYGIENE*

610   US   ISSN 0891-947X
R835
DIRECTORY OF AUDIO-VISUAL PROGRAMS FOR THE HEALTH SCIENCES AND RELATED FIELDS.* 1987. a. $35. Med-Av Publishing Co. Inc., 32 Bellport Pl., Garfield, NJ 07026-1421. TEL 201-423-3330. Ed. Charles M. Murtaugh. circ. 1,000. (back issues avail.)

614.88 616.02   UK
DIRECTORY OF EMERGENCY AND SPECIAL CARE UNITS (YEAR). a. £40. C M A Medical Data Ltd., Cambridge Research Laboratories, 181A Huntingdon Rd., Cambridge CB3 0DJ, England. TEL 0223-277709. FAX 0223-276444.
Description: Contains detailed information on emergency and special care units and services throughout the British Isles.

DIRECTORY OF GRADUATE MEDICAL EDUCATION. see *EDUCATION — Higher Education*

DIRECTORY OF INDEPENDENT HOSPITALS AND HEALTH SERVICES; a comprehensive guide to the independent health care sector in the U.K. see *HOSPITALS*

610   US
DIRECTORY OF MEDICAL INSTITUTIONS CONDUCTING CLINICAL RESEARCH AND SERVICES FOR PERSONS WITH THE MARFAN SYNDROME AND RELATED CONNECTIVE TISSUE DISORDERS. 1985. biennial. National Marfan Foundation, 382 Main St., Port Washington, NY 11050. TEL 516-883-8712. Ed. Priscilla Cillariello. circ. 150.
Description: Provides access to knowledgeable treatment and diagnosis, and promotes communication in the research community.

610 378.0025   US
DIRECTORY OF MEDICAL SCHOOLS WORLDWIDE. irreg., 4th ed. 1988. $29.95. U S Directory Service, 655 N.W., 128th St., Box 68-1700, Miami, FL 33168. TEL 305-769-1700. FAX 305-769-0548.
Description: Comprehensive listing of 1,200 medical schools from over 100 countries. Detailed introduction provides facts and information on admissions, statistics, language and curricula.

610   US   ISSN 0070-5829
R712.A1
DIRECTORY OF MEDICAL SPECIALISTS. (Supplement avail.) 1940. biennial, 25th ed., 1992. $295 for 3-vol. set. Marquis Who's Who, A Reed Reference Publishing Company, Division of Reed Publishing (USA) Inc., 121 Chanlon Rd., New Providence, NJ 07974. TEL 800-521-8110. FAX 908-665-6688. TELEX 138 755. (Subscr. to: R.R. Bowker, Order Dept., Box 31, New Providence, NJ 07974) (also avail. in magnetic tape)
Description: Presents current professional and biographical information on more than 400,000 practicing specialists, as well as profiles of nearly 35,000 newly board-certified physicians.

616.07 574.2   US   ISSN 0070-6086
DIRECTORY OF PATHOLOGY TRAINING PROGRAMS (YEAR). 1968. a. $55. Intersociety Committee on Pathology Information, 4733 Bethesda Ave., Ste. 700, Bethesda, MD 20814. TEL 301-656-2944. FAX 301-656-3179. Ed. Eileen Lavine. circ. 2,500.
Description: Describes residency programs and post-graduate subspecialty fellowships in anatomic and clinical pathology in the U.S. and Canada.

613.7   US
DIRECTORY OF U.S. BASED AGENCIES INVOLVED IN INTERNATIONAL HEALTH ASSISTANCE. 1980. biennial. $60 to non-members; members $30. National Council for International Health, 1701 K St., N.W., Ste. 600, Washington, DC 20006. TEL 202-833-5900. FAX 202-833-0075. Ed. Tom Zakin. adv.; bk.rev.; circ. 1,000.
Description: Provides a comprehensive listing of all major U.S. organizations supporting international health.

610 340   US
DISABILITIES REGULATION NEWS. fortn. $457. Buraff Publications (Subsidiary of: Millin Publications, Inc.), 1350 Connecticut Ave. N.W., Ste. 1000, Washington, DC 20036. TEL 202-862-0990. FAX 202-862-0999.

612   UK   ISSN 0963-8288
CODEN: DREHET
DISABILITY AND REHABILITATION. (Text in English) 1979. q. £68($119) Taylor & Francis Ltd., Rankine Road, Basingstoke, Hants. RG24 0PR, England. TEL 0256-840366. FAX 0256-479438. TELEX 858540. Ed. P. Wood. adv.; bk.rev.; circ. 1,000. Indexed: Excerp.Med., Ind.Med.
—BLDSC shelfmark: 3595.420300.
Former titles (until 1991): International Disability Studies (ISSN 0259-9147); (until 1987): International Rehabilitation Medicine (ISSN 0379-0797)
Refereed Serial

610 617   IT
DISEASES OF THE ESOPHAGUS. (Text in English) 1988. 3/yr. L.55000($83) (effective 1992). (International Society for Diseases of the Esophagus) Masson Italia Periodici, Via Statuto 2-4, 20121 Milan, Italy. TEL 02-6367-1. FAX 02-6367211. Ed. Sergio Stipa. circ. 1,000. Indexed: Excerp.Med.

616.748   IT   ISSN 0012-4087
DISTROFIA MUSCOLARE. 1962. q. free. Unione Italiana Lotta alla Distrofia Muscolare, Via P.P. Vergerio 17, 35126 Padua, Italy. TEL 049-757361. FAX 049-757033. Ed. Franco Bomprezzi. adv.; bk.rev.; bibl.; charts; illus.; circ. 27,000.
Description: Presents research papers from various doctors interested in the field of muscular dystrophy. Also features articles on how to deal with victims of this illness as well as how to make their lives easier and more autonomous.

DIVERSION (NEW YORK). see *SPORTS AND GAMES*

613   UA   ISSN 0012-4435
AD-DOCTOR; health education magazine. (Text in Arabic) 1947. m. £E1($4) 8 Sharia Hoda Shaarawy, Cairo, Egypt. Ed. Dr. Ahmad M. Kamal. bibl.; index; cum.index; circ. 30,000.

610   UK   ISSN 0046-0451
DOCTOR. 1971. w. £65 (free to qualified personnel). Reed Business Publishing Group, Reed Healthcare Communications (Subsidiary of: Reed International PLC), Quadrant House, The Quadrant, Sutton, Surrey SM2 5AS, England. TEL 081-661-3500. FAX 081--661-3500. Ed. Helena Sturidge. adv.; bk.rev.; abstr.; charts; illus.; circ. 36,000. (tabloid format; also avail. in microfilm from UMI)
—BLDSC shelfmark: 3606.400000.
Description: Provides general practitioners with latest news on medicine, political subjects, clinical developments and innovations.

610   JA
DOCTOR. (Text in Japanese) 1966. w. 2000 Yen. Yakuji Nyususha, c/o Indo Bldg., Dosho-machi, Higashi-ku, Osaka 541, Japan. stat.

610   US
DOCTORS FOR DISASTER PREPAREDNESS NEWSLETTER. Short title: D D P. 1984. bi-m. $10. Doctors for Disaster Preparedness, Box 272, 2509 N. Campbell, Tucson, AZ 85719. TEL 904-964-5397. Ed. Jane Orient. adv.; circ. 500. (back issues avail.)
Formerly: Triage!

610   US   ISSN 0733-2262
DOCTOR'S OFFICE. 1982. m. $96. Wentworth Publishing Company, 1858 Charter Ln., Box 10488, Lancaster, PA 17605-0488. TEL 800-822-1858. Ed. Ann Mead Ash. Indexed: Hlth.Ind.
Description: Provides information to clarify insurance regulations, collections techniques, marketing ideas and other practice management techniques.

DOCTOR'S REVIEW; leisure-time journal for physicians. see *TRAVEL AND TOURISM*

610   US
DOCTOR'S SHOPPER. 1983. q. $5 per no. Marketing Communications, Inc., 1086 Remsen Ave., Brooklyn, NY 11236. TEL 718-257-8484. FAX 718-257-8845. Ed. Ralph Selitzek. adv.; bk.rev.; illus.; pat.; stat.; tr.lit.; circ. 208,000 (controlled).

610   TU   ISSN 1010-7584
DOGA TURKISH JOURNAL OF MEDICAL SCIENCES/DOGA TURK SAGLIK BILIMLERI DERGISI. (Text in English, Turkish) 1976. 4/yr. $20. Scientific and Technical Research Council of Turkey - Turkiye Bilimsel ve Teknik Arastirma Kurumk, Ataturk Bulvari, No. 221, Kavaklidere, 06100 Ankara, Turkey. TEL 1673657. FAX 1277489. TELEX 43186 BTAK TR. Ed. Sinasi Ozsoylu. Indexed: Biol.Abstr., Chem.Abstr, Excerp.Med.
—BLDSC shelfmark: 3614.642510.
Former titles (until 1988): Doga Turkish Journal of Medicine and Pharmacy; Doga Bilim Dergisi. Series C: Medicine.

610   NR   ISSN 0046-0508
DOKITA. 1960. s-a. £N2.40($5) to individuals; $3 to students. (University of Ibadan Medical Students' Association, Dept. of Medicine) Ibadan University Press, University of Ibadan, Ibadan, Nigeria. A. Ibe Otuka. adv.; bk.rev.; charts; illus.; circ. 1,000. (looseleaf format) Indexed: Biol.Abstr.

610   JA   ISSN 0385-5023
CODEN: DJMSDB
DOKKYO JOURNAL OF MEDICAL SCIENCES. (Text in English) 1974. s-a. exchange basis. Dokkyo University School of Medicine, Dokkyo Medical Society - Dokkyo Daigaku Igakubu Dokkyo Igakkai, Mibu, Tochigi 321-02, Japan. FAX 0282-86-6214. TELEX 3562118. Ed. Sohei Makino. circ. 1,100. Indexed: Biol.Abstr., Chem.Abstr., Excerp.Med., Ind.Med., INIS Atomind.
—BLDSC shelfmark: 3614.950000.

610   JA   ISSN 0288-1829
DONAN IGAKUKAI. 1948. a. Hakodate-shi Medical Association, 33-19, Motomachi, Hakodate-shi, Japan. Ed.Bd. circ. 850.
—BLDSC shelfmark: 4824.160000.

MEDICAL SCIENCES 3095

610 US
DORLAND'S MEDICAL DIRECTORY. EASTERN PENNSYLVANIA AND SOUTHERN NEW JERSEY EDITION. 1952. a. $70.85. Legal Communications, Ltd., 1617 JFK Blvd., Ste. 1245, Philadelphia, PA 19103. TEL 215-563-9000. FAX 215-563-4911. Ed. Debra Silverman Shain. adv.; circ. 6,500.
Former titles: Dorland's Medical Directory. Delaware Valley Edition; Dorland's Medical Directory. Philadelphia Metropolitan Area.
Description: Listings of physicians, health care organizations, hospitals and specialists in the greater Philadelphia metropolitan area.

610 SZ ISSN 1011-288X
DOULEUR ET ANALGESIE. q. 65 SFr. to individuals; institutions 115 SFr. Editions Medecine et Hygiene, Case Postale 456, CH-1211 Geneva 4, Switzerland. TEL 022-469355. FAX 022-475610.
—BLDSC shelfmark: 3619.931800.

610 US
DR. ALEXANDER GRANT'S HEALTH GAZETTE; a monthly digest of medical facts and news. 1978. m. (10/yr.) $21.95 (effective Jan. 1992). Alexander Grant and Associates, Inc., Box 1786, Indianapolis, IN 46206. FAX 317-253-8582. Ed. Dr. Alexander Grant. cum.index; circ. 40,000. (looseleaf format; back issues avail.)
Formerly: Healthwise (ISSN 0740-1086)

610 615.19 GW ISSN 0173-430X
DR. MED. MABUSE. 1976. 6/yr. DM.48 (foreign DM.48). Mabuse Verlag GmbH, Kasselerstr. 1A, Postfach 900647, 6000 Frankfurt a.M. 90, Germany. TEL 069-705053. FAX 069-704132. Ed. Hermann Loeffler, M.D. adv.; bk.rev.; circ. 13,000. (back issues avail.)
Description: Publication for those working in the health field. Features a broad variety of health and medical issues worldwide. Includes readers' letters, list of events and positions available.

610 US
DRUG ENFORCEMENT ADMINISTRATION REGISTRATION FILE - ACTIVE. Short title: D.E.A Registration File - Active. q. $3600 in US, Canada, Mexico; elsewhere $7200. (Department of Treasury, Drug Enforcement Administration) U.S. National Technical Information Service, 5825 Port Royal Rd., Springfield, VA 22161. TEL 703-487-4630. (magnetic tape)
Description: Lists all those registered under the Controlled Substance Act who are doing business registered in their own name rather than that of a business name.

612.39 615 US ISSN 0360-2532
CODEN: DMTRAR
DRUG METABOLISM REVIEWS. 1972. 4/yr. $775. Marcel Dekker Journals, 270 Madison Ave., New York, NY 10016. TEL 212-696-9000. FAX 212-685-4540. TELEX 421419. (Subscr. to: Box 10018, Church St. Sta., New York, NY 10249) Ed. Frederick J. DiCarlo. (also avail. in microform from RPI) Indexed: Abstr.Inter.Med., Biol.Abstr., Biotech.Abstr., Chem.Abstr., Curr.Adv.Biochem., Curr.Adv.Ecol.Sci., Curr.Cont., Dairy Sci.Abstr., Excerp.Med., I.P.A., Ind.Med., Ind.Sci.Rev., Ind.Vet., Pig News & Info., Poult.Abstr., Sci.Cit.Ind, Vet.Bull.
—BLDSC shelfmark: 3629.330000.
Refereed Serial

DRUGS IN RESEARCH. see PHARMACY AND PHARMACOLOGY

DRUGS IN USE. see PHARMACY AND PHARMACOLOGY

610 FI ISSN 0012-7183
CODEN: DUODAG
DUODECIM; laaketieteellinen aikakauskirja. 1885. s-m. FIM 590. Finnish Medical Society Duodecim, Kalevankatu 11 A, 00100 Helsinki, Finland. TEL 90-611050. Ed. Kimmo Kontula. adv.; bk.rev.; film rev.; bibl.; charts; illus.; index. cum.index; circ. 17,500. Indexed: Biol.Abstr., Chem.Abstr., Curr.Adv.Ecol.Sci., Dent.Ind., Excerp.Med., Ind.Med., INIS Atomind.
—BLDSC shelfmark: 3631.195000.

610 SP ISSN 0211-9536
R131.A1
DYNAMIS; acta hispanica ad medicinae scientiarumque historiam illustrandam. 1981. a. 1800 ptas.($18) Universidad de Granada, Departamento de Historia de la Medicina, Servicio de Publicaciones, Antiguo Colegio Maximo, Campus de Cartuja, 18071 Granada, Spain. TEL 281356. Ed.Bd. bk.rev.; circ. 150. Indexed: Amer.Hist.& Life, Bull.Signal, Hist.Abstr., Ind.Med.Esp.
—BLDSC shelfmark: 3637.146000.

611 US ISSN 0179-051X
CODEN: DYSPE2
DYSPHAGIA; an international multidisciplinary journal devoted to swallowing and its disorders. 1986. 4/yr. $113. Springer-Verlag, Journals, 175 Fifth Ave., New York, NY 10010. TEL 212-460-1500. (Also Berlin, Heidelberg, Tokyo, Vienna) Ed. M.W. Donner. Indexed: Excerp.Med.
—BLDSC shelfmark: 3637.270000.

610 US
DYSTONIA DIALOGUE. 1976. q. free. Dystonia Medical Research Foundation, 8383 Wilshire Blvd., Ste. 800, Beverly Hills, CA 90211. TEL 213-852-1630. Ed. Dana Klosner.
Description: Helps to build awareness of dystonia in the medical and lay community.

610 US ISSN 0897-0297
THE E M S LEADER. 1984. 10/yr. $34 (Canada $40). Cornell Communications, 330 Garfield Ave., Eau Claire, WI 54701. TEL 715-834-6046. FAX 715-834-0212. Ed. Dixie Cornell. circ. 400.
Description: Management information for managers, directors, supervisors of emergency medical service systems. Covers leadership issues, performance appraisal, volunteer service, motivation, and dealing with people.

610 KE ISSN 0012-835X
R98 CODEN: EAMJAV
EAST AFRICAN MEDICAL JOURNAL. 1923. m. EAs.3600($145) (effective Jan. 1991). Kenya Medical Association House, Chyulu Rd., P.O. Box 41632, Nairobi, Kenya. Ed. E.G. Kasili. adv.; bk.rev.; index; circ. 4,000. Indexed: Abstr.Hyg., Biodet.Abstr., Biol.Abstr., Chem.Abstr., Curr.Cont., Dent.Ind., Dok.Arbeitsmed., Excerp.Med., Helminthol.Abstr., HRIS, Ind.Med., Ind.Sci.Rev., Ind.Vet., Med.Abstr., NRN, Nutr.Abstr., Protozool.Abstr., Rev.Appl.Entomol., Rev.Plant Path., Sci.Cit.Ind, Sp.Ed.Needs Abstr., Trop.Dis.Bull., Vet.Bull.

610 US
EAST TEXAS MEDICINE. 1989. bi-m. $20. P.O. Box 8583, Tyler, TX 75711-8583. TEL 214-592-8533. FAX 903-593-0494. Ed. Dr. Gary D. Boyd. adv.; circ. 5,000.
Description: Forum for physicians in the East Texas area. Presents doctors' case studies and research.

610 UK ISSN 0260-3934
EDINBURGH MEDICINE. 1980. 6/yr. £12 (overseas £15). Hermiston Publications Ltd., 2 Hill Sq., Edinburgh EH8 9DR, Scotland. TEL 031-668-3753. Ed. Dr. Ian H. McKee. adv.; bk.rev.; illus.; circ. 4,000.

EDUCACION MEDICA Y SALUD. see EDUCATION — Guides To Schools And Colleges

EDUCATION AND HEALTH. see EDUCATION — School Organization And Administration

352.3 US ISSN 0145-2037
RA396.A3
EDUCATIONAL COMMISSION FOR FOREIGN MEDICAL GRADUATES. ANNUAL REPORT. 1958. a. free. Educational Commission for Foreign Medical Graduates, 3624 Market St., 4th Fl., Philadelphia, PA 19104-2685. TEL 215-386-5900. FAX 215-387-9963. Ed.Bd. circ. 5,000.
Formerly: Educational Council for Foreign Medical Graduates. Annual Report (ISSN 0422-6690)
Description: Provides information to foreign medical graduates regarding entry into graduate medical education and health care systems in the United States.

610 HU ISSN 0013-2268
CODEN: EGESAQ
EGESZSEGTUDOMANY. (Text in Hungarian; Summaries in English, German and Russian) q. $29. Ifjusagi Lap-es Konyvkiado Vallalat, Revay u. 16, 1374 Budapest 6, Hungary. (Subscr. to: Kultura, PO Box 149, H-1389 Budapest, Hungary) Ed. Dr. Tibor Bartha. bk.rev.; abstr.; bibl.; charts; illus. Indexed: Abstr.Hyg., C.I.S. Abstr., Chem.Abstr., Food Sci.& Tech.Abstr., INIS Atomind., Nutr.Abstr., Trop.Dis.Bull.

614 HU ISSN 0013-2276
EGESZSEGUGYI GAZDASAGI SZEMLE. (Text in Hungarian; summaries in English, German and Russian) 1963. q. $22. (Egeszsegugyi Miniszterium - Ministry of Health) Egeszsegugyi Miniszterium Szervezesi Tervezesi es Informacios Kozpontja, PO Box 1, H-1361 Budapest, Hungary. (Co-sponsor: Egeszsegugyi Dolgozok Szakszervezete) Ed. E. Kovesi. adv.; bk.rev.; circ. 1,300. Indexed: Excerp.Med., Hosp.Abstr.
—BLDSC shelfmark: 3664.195000.

610 UA ISSN 0013-2411
EGYPTIAN MEDICAL ASSOCIATION. JOURNAL. (Text in Arabic and English) 1917. m. membership. Egyptian Medical Association, Dar El-Hekma, 42 Kasr-El Aini St., Cairo, Egypt. Ed. Prof. Dr. M. Ibrahim. adv.; bk.rev.; charts; illus.; index. Indexed: Biol.Abstr., C.I.S. Abstr., Chem.Abstr., Excerp.Med., Helminthol.Abstr., Ind.Med., Nutr.Abstr., Rev.Plant Path., Trop.Dis.Bull.

610 GW ISSN 0934-9820
CODEN: EICOEM
EICOSANOIDS. 1989. 4/yr. DM.250($149) Springer-Verlag, Heidelberger Platz 3, D-1000 Berlin 33, Germany. TEL 030-8207-1. Ed.Bd. Indexed: Excerp.Med. (1992-).
—BLDSC shelfmark: 3664.840000.

EINSTEIN QUARTERLY JOURNAL OF BIOLOGY AND MEDICINE. see BIOLOGY

610 IS ISSN 0334-3928
EITANIM; monthly of health issues. (Text in Hebrew) 1948. m. IS.35($17.50) Merkaz Kupat Holim, P.O. Box 16250, Tel Aviv 62098, Israel. FAX 03-433500. Ed. David Taggar. adv.; bk.rev.; index; circ. 20,000. Indexed: Ind.Heb.Per.

610 US ISSN 0070-959X
ELDRIDGE REEVES JOHNSON FOUNDATION FOR MEDICAL PHYSICS. COLLOQUIUM. PROCEEDINGS. 1963. irreg., 5th 1969. price varies. University of Pennsylvania, Eldridge Reeves Johnson Foundation for Medical Physics, D501 Richards Bldg., 37th & Hamilton Walk, Philadelphia, PA 19104-6089. TEL 215-898-4342. FAX 216-898-0465.

610 UK
ELECTRO MEDICAL TRADE ASSOCIATION. PRODUCTS DIRECTORY. (Text in English; summaries in French, German and Spanish) 1965. irreg. free to qualified personnel. (Electro Medical Trade Association Ltd.) A B H I, Consort House, 26-28 Queensway, London W2 3RX, England. Ed. J.W. Christopher. circ. 500.

615.845 GW ISSN 0340-5389
ELECTROMEDICA. English edition (ISSN 0013-4724); French edition (ISSN 0341-650X); Spanish edition (ISSN 0341-6518) 1932. q. DM.6. per no. Siemans Verlag AG, Postfach 3240, 8520 Erlangen 2, Germany. Indexed: Excerp.Med., INIS Atomind., Sci.Abstr.
Formerly: Siemans Electromedica (ISSN 0037-4660)
Description: Covers medical electronics.

616.8 612 BE ISSN 0301-150X
RC77.5 CODEN: EMCNA9
ELECTROMYOGRAPHY AND CLINICAL NEUROPHYSIOLOGY. (Text in English) 1961. 8/yr. $100. Editions Nauwelaerts S.A., Rue de l'Eglise St. Suplice 19, B-1320 Beauvechain, Belgium. Eds. N. Rosselle, W. T. Liberson. abstr.; bibl.; charts; illus.; index. Indexed: Biol.Abstr., Excerp.Med., Ind.Med., Sci.Abstr.
—BLDSC shelfmark: 3699.720000.
Formerly: Electromyography (ISSN 0013-4732)

EMERGENCY DEPARTMENT LAW; bi-weekly news and analysis for health professionals, administrators, and counsel. see LAW

MEDICAL SCIENCES

610   US
EMERGENCY DEPARTMENT MANAGEMENT. m. $219. American Health Consultants, Inc., Six Piedmont Center, Ste. 400, 3525 Piedmont Rd., N.E., Atlanta, GA 30305. TEL 404-262-7436.
FAX 800-284-3291. (Subscr. to: Department L100, Box 740056, Atlanta, GA 30374-9822. TEL 800-688-2421) Ed. David Penley. circ. 1,200.
Incorporates (in 1991): Reports in Emergency Nursing.

610 340   US
EMERGENCY MEDICAL TECHNICIAN LEGAL BULLETIN. 1977. q. $15. Med-Law Publishers, Inc., Box 293, Westville, NJ 08093. Ed. James E. George, M.D. Indexed: CINAHL.

610   US   ISSN 1054-0725
EMERGENCY MEDICINE NEWS; the news magazine for the emergency care professional. 1979. m. $50 to individuals (foreign $60); institutions $75 (foreign $85). J.B. Lippincott Co., E. Washington Sq., Philadelphia, PA 19105. TEL 215-238-4270. (Subscr. to: Downsville Pike, Rte. 3, Box 20-B, Hagerstown, MD 21740) Ed. Lisa Hoffman. adv.; circ. 21,000. (tabloid format)
—BLDSC shelfmark: 3733.190450.
Former titles: Emergency Medicine and Ambulatory Care News; (until Aug. 1986): Emergency Department News.
Description: Disseminates information in all areas of emergency medicine, as well as emergency departments and ambulatory care centers.

610   US   ISSN 0746-2506
EMERGENCY MEDICINE REPORTS; the practical journal for primary care physicians. 1980. fortn. $189. American Health Consultants, Inc., Six Piedmont Center, Ste. 400, 3525 Piedmont Rd., N.E., Atlanta, GA 30305. TEL 404-262-7436.
FAX 404-262-7837. (Subscr. to: Box 740056, Atlanta, GA 30374. TEL 800-688-2421) Ed. Dr. Phil Fontanarosa. circ. 6,800.
●Also available online. Vendor(s): BRS.
—BLDSC shelfmark: 3733.190700.
Incorporates (1983-1990): Advanced Clinical Updates; Which was formerly (until 1985): Family Medicine Reports; E R Reports (Emergency Room Reports).

610 340   US
EMERGENCY MEDICINE REPORTS LEGAL BRIEFINGS. m. $130. American Health Consultants, Inc., Six Piedmont Center, Ste. 400, 3525 Piedmont Rd., N.E., Atlanta, GA 30305. TEL 404-262-7436. FAX 800-284-3291. (Subscr. to: Box 740056, Atlanta, GA 30374-9822. TEL 800-688-2421) Ed. Deborah Lydon. circ. 900.

610 340   US   ISSN 0098-1524
EMERGENCY PHYSICIAN LEGAL BULLETIN. Abbreviated title: E P L B. 1975. q. $25. Med-Law Publishers, Inc., Box 293, Westville, NJ 08093. Ed. James E. George, M.D.

610   US   ISSN 0891-7043
EMORY UNIVERSITY JOURNAL OF MEDICINE. 1987. q. free to health care professionals. Emory University, 1462 Clifton Rd., N.E., Ste. 301, Atlanta, GA 30322. TEL 404-727-3530. FAX 404-727-3309. Ed. Dr. J. Willis Hurst. adv. (also avail. in microform from UMI)
—BLDSC shelfmark: 3733.563000.
Description: Reports clinical and basic science research of interest to medical professionals.
Refereed Serial

610   US
EMPLOYER'S GUIDE PURCHASING MANAGED HEALTH CARE SERVICES. 1988. a. $49.50. (National Association of Employers on Health Care Action) Blue Book, Inc., Box 220, Key Biscayne, FL 33149. TEL 305-361-2810. FAX 305-361-2842. Ed. Ruth H. Stack. circ. 1,000.
Description: Educates the employer on how to purchase health care services using the industrial quality model.

610   US
ENDOSCOPY REVIEW. bi-m. Island Publishing Group, Inc., Box 598, Lawrence, NY 11559-0598. TEL 516-295-3188. FAX 516-295-0648. Ed. Harold Jacob. circ. 10,219.

ENTWICKLUNGSLAENDER-STUDIEN; Bibliographie entwicklungslaenderbezogener Forschungsarbeiten. see BUSINESS AND ECONOMICS — Abstracting, Bibliographies, Statistics

614   US   ISSN 0196-0598
ENVIRONMENTAL HEALTH LETTER. 1961. fortn. $267.54 (effective Sep. 1992). Business Publishers, Inc., 951 Pershing Dr., Silver Spring, MD 20910-4464. TEL 301-587-6300.
FAX 301-585-9075. Ed. Kathleen Hart. (looseleaf format)
●Also available online. Vendor(s): NewsNet.

ENVIRONMENTAL MANAGEMENT & HEALTH. see ENVIRONMENTAL STUDIES

610   JA   ISSN 0287-0517
ENVIRONMENTAL MEDICINE. (Text in English) 1951. a. exchange basis. Nagoya Daigaku, Kankyo Igaku Kenkyujo - Nagoya University, Research Institute of Environmental Medicine, Furo-cho, Chikusa-ku, Nagoya 464-01, Japan. TEL 052-781-5111.
FAX 052-781-9117. Ed. Takao Kumazawa. circ. 400. Indexed: Biol.Abstr., Chem.Abstr., Excerp.Med., INIS Atomind.
—BLDSC shelfmark: 3791.522500.
Formerly (until vol.25, 1980): Nagoya University. Research Institute of Environmental Medicine. Annual Report (ISSN 0469-4759)

616.3   IT   ISSN 0013-9475
CODEN: EPATA4
EPATOLOGIA. vol.12, 1966. bi-m. L.18000. Societa Editrice Universo, Via G. B. Morgagni 1, 00161 Rome, Italy. Ed. Mariano Messini. Indexed: Biol.Abstr., Chem.Abstr., Excerp.Med.
—BLDSC shelfmark: 3793.335000.

614.49   EC
EPIDEMIOLOGIA CIENTIFICA: TEORIA Y PRACTICA. 1979. irreg. $6. Centro de Estudios y Asesoria en Salud, Roca No. 549-Dpto. 602, Quito, Ecuador. circ. 1,000.

610   US   ISSN 0193-936X
RA648.5   CODEN: EPIRD7
EPIDEMIOLOGIC REVIEWS. 1979. a. $19. Johns Hopkins University, School of Hygiene & Public Health, 2007 E. Monument St., Baltimore, MD 21205. TEL 301-955-3441. Ed. Haroutune K. Armenian. Indexed: Abstr.Hyg., Biol.Dig., Biostat., Curr.Adv.Ecol.Sci., Excerp.Med., Helminthol.Abstr., Ind.Med., Ind.Sci.Rev., Ind.Vet., Sci.Cit.Ind, Trop.Dis.Bull., Vet.Bull.
—BLDSC shelfmark: 3793.540000.

610 614   CE
EPIDEMIOLOGICAL BULLETIN. (Text in English) 1960. q. free. Department of Health, Epidemiological Unit, N.T.I. Building, 385 Dean's Road, Colombo 10, Sri Lanka. Ed. Charles A.L. Forbes. circ. 750. Indexed: IIS, Ind.Vet., Trop.Dis.Bull., Vet.Bull.

610   US   ISSN 1044-3983
RA648.5   CODEN: EPIDEY
EPIDEMIOLOGY. 6/yr. $80 to individuals; institutions $110. Epidemiology Resources Inc., Box 339, Chestnut Hill, MA 02167. TEL 617-734-9100.
—BLDSC shelfmark: 3793.574000.

610   US   ISSN 0744-0898
CODEN: EPMOEJ
EPIDEMIOLOGY MONITOR. 1980. m. price varies. 2560 Whisper Wind Ct., Roswell, GA 30076.
TEL 404-594-1613. Ed. Roger H. Bernier. circ. 1,900. (tabloid format; back issues avail.)
Description: Covers preventive medicine, public health and epidemiology.

610   CU
EQUIPOS Y PRODUCTOS. BIOMEDICINA. m. Academia de Ciencias, Instituto de Documentacion e Informacion Cientifico-Tecnica (I D I C T), Capitolio Nacional, Prado y San Jose, Havana 2, Havana, Cuba.

610   GW   ISSN 0014-0082
CODEN: ERFAAK
ERFAHRUNGSHEILKUNDE/ACTA MEDICA EMPIRICA; Zeitschrift fuer die aerztliche Praxis. (Text in German; summaries in English) 1951. m. DM.196 (students DM.162). (Gesellschaft der Aerzte fuer Erfahrungsheilkunde e.V.) Karl F. Haug Verlag GmbH, Fritz-Frey-Str. 21, 6900 Heidelberg 1, Germany. TEL 06221-4062-0.
FAX 06221-400727. TELEX 461683-HVVFMD. Ed. Dr. Gyoergy Irmey. adv.; bk.rev.; abstr.; charts; illus.; circ. 7,500. Indexed: Chem.Abstr, Dok.Arbeitsmed.
—BLDSC shelfmark: 3801.500000.

616.026   US   ISSN 0071-111X
ERGEBNISSE DER INNEREN MEDIZIN UND KINDERHEILKUNDE. NEW SERIES/ADVANCES IN INTERNAL MEDICINE AND PEDIATRICS. (Text in German; occasionally in English) 1949. irreg. price varies. Springer-Verlag, 175 Fifth Ave., New York, NY 10010. TEL 212-460-1500. (Also Berlin, Heidelberg, Tokyo and Vienna) (reprint service avail. from ISI) Indexed: Ind.Med.
—BLDSC shelfmark: 0709.253000.
Description: Covers internal medicine.

615.8   DK   ISSN 0105-8282
ERGOTERAPEUTEN. 1939. 22/yr. DKK 427. Ergoterapeutforeningen - Danish Organisation of Occupational Therapists, Norre Voldgade 90, 1358 Copenhagen K, Denmark. FAX 33-938214. Ed. Esther Boserup. adv.; bk.rev.; circ. 4,400.
Description: News on occupational therapy.

ERNAERINGSNYT. see NUTRITION AND DIETETICS

ESCALPELO. see COLLEGE AND ALUMNI

611   US
ESO MONOGRAPHS. 1986. irreg. price varies. Springer-Verlag, 175 Fifth Ave., New York, NY 10010. TEL 212-460-1500. (Also Berlin, Heidelberg, Tokyo, Vienna) (reprint service avail. from ISI)

610   US   ISSN 0014-0937
ESSEX COUNTY MEDICAL SOCIETY. BULLETIN. vol.314, 1970. 9/yr. membership only. Essex County Medical Society, 80 Pompton Ave., Verona, NJ 07044. TEL 201-239-9392. Ed. Enio Callouri, M.D. adv.; illus.

610 574   MX   ISSN 0020-3858
ESTUDIOS MEDICOS Y BIOLOGICOS. BOLETIN. (Text in English and Spanish) 1942. q. free to qualified personnel. Universidad Nacional Autonoma de Mexico, Instituto de Investigaciones Biomedicas, Apartado Postal 70228, Circuito Interior, Delegacion Coyoacan 04510, Ciudad Universitaria Mexico DF, Mexico. (Co-sponsor: Biblioteca Nacional) Ed. Dr. Alfonso Escobar. bk.rev.; charts; illus.; index; circ. 1,800. Indexed: Biol.Abstr., Chem.Abstr., Ind.Med., INIS Atomind.
Formerly: Instituto de Estudios Medicos y Biologicos. Boletin.

610   UK
ETHICS AND MEDICINE. 3/yr. £8.25. Paternoster Press, 3 Mount Radford Crescent, Exeter EX2 4JW, England. Ed. N.M. de S. Cameron. Indexed: Rel.& Theol.Abstr. (1985-).

ETHICS AND MEDICS. see PHILOSOPHY

ETHIK IN DER MEDIZIN. see PHILOSOPHY

610   ET   ISSN 0014-1755
CODEN: EMDJA2
ETHIOPIAN MEDICAL JOURNAL. 1962. 4/yr. Eth.$36($40) Ethiopian Medical Association, P.O. Box 3472, Addis Ababa, Ethiopia. TEL 158174. Ed. Abrehet Habtemariam. adv.; bk.rev.; illus.; circ. 500. Indexed: Abstr.Hyg., Biol.Abstr., Curr.Adv.Ecol.Sci., Curr.Adv.Genetics & Molec.Biol., Curr.Cont., Dairy Sci.Abstr., Dent.Ind., Excerp.Med., Helminthol.Abstr., Ind.Med., MEDSOC, Nutr.Abstr., Protozool.Abstr., Sci.Cit.Ind., Triticale Abstr., Trop.Dis.Bull.

MEDICAL SCIENCES 3097

610   US   ISSN 1049-510X
RA652   CODEN: ETDIEI
▼ETHNICITY & DISEASE. 1991. q. $40 to individuals (foreign $48); institutions $90 (foreign $98). (Loyola University, Department of Preventive Medicine and Epidemiology) International Society on Hypertension in Blacks, 69 Butler St. S.E., Atlanta, GA 30303. FAX 708-216-4117. Ed. Richard S. Cooper. adv.; bk.rev.
—BLDSC shelfmark: 3814.840500.
Description: Covers population differences in disease patterns and provides a comprehensive source of information on causal relationships in the etiology of common illnesses through the study of ethnic patterns of disease.

362   IT   ISSN 0014-2573
EUROPA MEDICOPHYSICA. (Text in English, Italian) 1965. q. L.60000($70) (European Federation of Physical and Rehabilitation Medicine and of the Italian Society) Edizioni Minerva Medica, Corso Bramante 83-85, 10126 Turin, Italy. (Dist. in U.S. by: J.B. Lippincott Company, E. Washington Square, Philadelphia, PA 19105) (Co-sponsor: Italian Society of Physical and Rehabilitation Medicine) Ed. S. Boccardi. adv.; bk.rev.; bibl.; charts; illus.; index; circ. 3,000.
—BLDSC shelfmark: 3829.319500.

EUROPEAN JOURNAL OF APPLIED PHYSIOLOGY AND OCCUPATIONAL PHYSIOLOGY. see *BIOLOGY — Physiology*

EUROPEAN JOURNAL OF BIOCHEMISTRY. see *BIOLOGY — Biological Chemistry*

610   UK   ISSN 0014-2972
R850.A1   CODEN: EJCIB8
EUROPEAN JOURNAL OF CLINICAL INVESTIGATION. 1971. bi-m. £135 (foreign £149). (European Society for Clinical Investigation) Blackwell Scientific Publications Ltd., Osney Mead, Oxford OX2 0EL, England. TEL 0865-240201. FAX 0865-721205. TELEX 83355-MEDBOK-G. Ed.Bd. adv.; abstr.; bibl.; charts; illus.; index; circ. 1,770. (back issues avail.: reprint service avail. from ISI) **Indexed:** ASCA, Biol.Abstr., Biotech.Abstr., Chem.Abstr, Curr.Adv.Biochem., Curr.Adv.Ecol.Sci., Curr.Cont., Dairy Sci.Abstr., Excerp.Med., Helminthol.Abstr., Ind.Med., Ind.Sci.Rev., INIS Atomind., NRN, Nutr.Abstr., Sci.Cit.Ind, Soyabean Abstr., Telegen.
—BLDSC shelfmark: 3829.727100.

610   UK   ISSN 0961-3692
▼**EUROPEAN JOURNAL OF CLINICAL RESEARCH.** (Supplement avail.) 1992. s-m. £60 (Europe £65; elsewhere £70). Brookwood Medical Publications Ltd., 3 Jenner Rd., Guilford, Surrey GU1 3AQ, England. TEL 0483-797975. FAX 0483-797915. (Subscr. to: Orchard House, Brookwood, Surrey GU24 0AT, England)
—BLDSC shelfmark: 3829.728120.
Description: Covers clinical and medical research on drugs, devices and environmental pollutants.

610 617   GW
EUROPEAN JOURNAL OF EPIDEMIOLOGY. (Text in English) 1985. m. DM.420 (foreign DM.472). Gustav Fischer Verlag, Wollgrasweg 49, Postfach 720143, 7000 Stuttgart 70, Germany. TEL 0711-458030. FAX 0711-4580334. TELEX 7111488-FIBUCH. adv.; bk.rev.; index. **Indexed:** Curr.Cont., Excerp.Med., Ind.Med., Protozool.Abstr.

610   NE   ISSN 0924-3860
QL799   CODEN: EJMOEB
EUROPEAN JOURNAL OF MORPHOLOGY. (Text in English, French and German) 1956. 4/yr. $190. Swets Publishing Service (Subsidiary of: Swets en Zeitlinger B.V.), Heereweg 347, 2161 CA Lisse, Netherlands. TEL 31-2521-35111. FAX 31-2521-15888. TELEX 41325. (Dist. in N. America by: Swets & Zeitlinger, Box 517, Berwyn, PA 19312. TEL 215-644-4944) Ed. Dr. J. Drukker. adv.; bk.rev.; bibl.; charts; index; circ. 600. (also avail. in microform from SWZ; reprint avail. from SWZ) **Indexed:** Anim.Breed.Abstr., ASCA, Biol.Abstr., Chem.Abstr, Curr.Adv.Ecol.Sci., Curr.Cont., Dent.Ind., Excerp.Med., Helminthol.Abstr., Ind.Med., Ind.Sci.Rev., Sci.Cit.Ind, Vet.Bull.
—BLDSC shelfmark: 3829.731660.
Formerly: Acta Morphologica Neelando-Scandinavica (ISSN 0001-6225)

610   GW   ISSN 0939-6365
CODEN: EJPAE
EUROPEAN JOURNAL OF PAIN. q. DM.108 (students DM.85). Verlag fuer Medizin Dr. Ewald Fischer GmbH, Fritz-Frey-Str. 21, Postfach 105767, 6900 Heidelberg 1, Germany. TEL 06221-4062-0. Ed. Dr. W. Nix. adv. **Indexed:** Excerp.Med.
Formerly: Schmerz (Heidelberg) (ISSN 0174-4895)

615.8   AU   ISSN 1017-6721
EUROPEAN JOURNAL OF PHYSICAL MEDICINE AND REHABILITATION. 1978. 6/yr. S.1100. (Royal Belgian Society of Physical Medicine and Rehabilitation) Blackwell Medizinische Zeitschriftenverlagsgesellschaft mbH, Feldgasse 13, A-1238 Vienna, Austria. TEL 0222-8893646. FAX 0222-889364724. adv.; bk.rev.; circ. 1,500. **Indexed:** Biol.Abstr., Excerp.Med., Ind.Med.
—BLDSC shelfmark: 3829.734700.
Former titles: Acta Belgica - Medica Physica; Journal Belge de Medecine Physique et de Rehabilitation.

610   US   ISSN 0163-2787
RA399.A1
EVALUATION AND THE HEALTH PROFESSIONS. 1978. q. $42 to individuals; institutions $115. Sage Publications, Inc., 2455 Teller Rd., Newbury Park, CA 91320. TEL 805-499-0721. FAX 805-499-0871. (And: Sage Publications, Ltd., 6 Bonhill St., London EC2A 4PU, England) Ed. R. Barker Bausell. adv.; bk.rev.; bibl.; charts; stat.; index; circ. 900. (back issues avail.) **Indexed:** Abstr.Health Care Manage.Stud., Biostat., C.I.J.E., Excerp.Med., Med.Care Rev., Mid.East: Abstr.& Ind., Psychol.Abstr., Risk Abstr., Sage Pub.Admin.Abstr.
—BLDSC shelfmark: 3830.564000.

616.07   US   ISSN 0014-4800
RB1   CODEN: EXMPA6
EXPERIMENTAL AND MOLECULAR PATHOLOGY. 1962. bi-m. $334 (foreign $410). Academic Press, Inc., Journal Division, 1250 Sixth Ave., San Diego, CA 92101. TEL 619-230-1840. FAX 619-699-6800. TELEX 181726. Eds. Frederick Coulston, Wilbur A. Thomas. adv.; bibl.; charts; illus.; index. (back issues avail.) **Indexed:** Biol.Abstr., Chem.Abstr., Curr.Adv.Cancer Res., Dairy Sci.Abstr., Dent.Ind., Excerp.Med., Helminthol.Abstr., Ind.Med., Ind.Sci.Rev., Ind.Vet., INIS Atomind., Nutr.Abstr., Sci.Cit.Ind, Vet.Bull., Weed Abstr.
—BLDSC shelfmark: 3838.700000.
Description: Presents articles on disease processes in relation to structural and biochemical alterations in mammalian tissues and fluids and on the application of the newer techniques of analytical chemistry, histochemistry, pharmacology, toxicology, and electronic microscopy to problems of pathology in humans and animals.
Refereed Serial

EXPERIMENTAL CELL RESEARCH. see *BIOLOGY — Cytology And Histology*

EXPERIMENTAL PHYSIOLOGY. see *BIOLOGY — Physiology*

EXPERIMENTELLE UND KLINISCHE HYPNOSE. see *PSYCHOLOGY*

610   SP   ISSN 0210-8852
F A C: REVISTA PRACTICA DE MEDICINA. 1969. irreg. (4-5/yr.). free to qualified personnel. Laboratorio Alonga, S.A., Avda. Aragon, 18, 28027 Madrid, Spain. Ed. Francisco Llagostera Campillo. adv.; bk.rev.; circ. 30,000.
Formerly: F A C: Revista Practica del Estudiante de Medicina.

610   US
F M A TODAY (JACKSONVILLE). 1985. m. $15.90. Florida Medical Association, 760 Riverside Ave., Jacksonville, FL 32204. TEL 940-356-1571. FAX 904-353-1247. (Subscr. to: Box 2411, Jacksonville, FL 32203) Ed. Dr. R.G. Lacsamana. adv.; tr.lit.; circ. 17,000. (tabloid format)
Description: Covers association news, members' achievements, upcoming and past meetings, health issues, and health-related legislation.

610   US   ISSN 0888-5656
RA396.A3
F S M B HANDBOOK. a. $15 to non-members. Federation of State Medical Boards, 6000 Western Pl., Ste. 707, Fort Worth, TX 76107-4618. TEL 817-735-8445. FAX 817-738-6629. Ed. Dale G. Breaden.

610   US   ISSN 0163-0512
FACETS (CHICAGO). 1939. 6/yr. $5. American Medical Association, Auxiliary, 515 N. State St., Chicago, IL 60610. TEL 312-464-0183. FAX 312-464-5834. Ed. Kathleen T. Jordan. adv.; bk.rev.; abstr.; charts; illus.; stat.; circ. 90,000.
Former titles (until 1978): M D'S Wife (ISSN 0024-807X); (until 1965): American Medical Association Auxiliary. Bulletin (ISSN 0098-3748)

362   FR   ISSN 0014-6951
FAIRE FACE. 1933. m. 100 F. (typically set in Jan.). Association des Paralyses de France, 17 bd. Auguste Blanqui, 75013 Paris, France. TEL 40-78-69-00. FAX 45-89-40-57. Ed.Bd. adv.; bk.rev.; illus.; circ. 50,000.
Description: Features rehabilitation techniques.

610   US
FAMILY CARE.* 1989. q. $14.95. HealthTeam Interactive Communications, Inc., 274 Madison Ave., No. PH, New York, NY 10016-0701. adv.

610   US
FAMILY HEALTH ADVISER. q. Whittle Communications L.P., 333 Main Ave., Knoxville, TN 37902. TEL 615-595-5300. Ed. Margot Leake.
Description: Helps family members to better understand how the family unit influences health (emotionally and physically) and provides a wide spectrum of health information and medical news that speaks to all age groups, sexes, and health interests.

610 370   US   ISSN 0742-3225
FAMILY MEDICINE. 1967. 8/yr. $50 to individuals; institutions $75. Society of Teachers of Family Medicine, Box 8729, 8880 Ward Pkwy., Kansas City, MO 64114. TEL 816-333-9700. FAX 816-333-3884. (Co-sponsor: North American Primary Care Research Group) Ed. Barry Weiss. adv.; bk.rev.; bibl.; charts; illus.; cum.index (1981-1986); circ. 4,000. **Indexed:** Excerp.Med., FAMLI, Ind.Med.
—BLDSC shelfmark: 3865.567450.
Former titles: Family Medicine Teacher; Family Medicine Times.
Description: Presents research studies and teaching methods.

610   AT
FAMILY MEDICINE PROGRAMME. R.A.C.G.P. VICTORIA NEWSLETTER. 1977. m. (Royal Australian College of General Practitioners) New Lithographics Pty. Ltd., 63 Sunbury Crescent, Surrey Hills, Vic. 3127, Australia. FAX 03-824-2023. adv.; bk.rev.; circ. 2,800.

610   US   ISSN 0014-732X
FAMILY PHYSICIAN. 1951. bi-m. $30 to members (foreign $48); non-members $5 per no. Illinois Academy of Family Physicians, 1101 Perimeter Dr., Ste. 730, Schaumburg, IL 60173. TEL 708-240-5522. FAX 708-240-5887. Ed. Cynthia J. Straub. adv.; circ. 5,000. (tabloid format) **Indexed:** Biol.Abstr.
Description: Includes news of academy programs and articles about issues related to the practice of family medicine in Illinois. It does not contain scientific abstracts or research articles.

610   UK   ISSN 0263-2136
FAMILY PRACTICE. 1984. q. £60($120) Oxford University Press, Oxford Journals, Pinkhill House, Southfield Road, Eynsham, Oxford OX9 1JJ, England. TEL 0865-882283. FAX 0865-882890. TELEX 837330 OXPRES G. Ed. J.G.R. Howie. adv.; bk.rev. (also avail. in microform) **Indexed:** Curr.Cont., Excerp.Med.
—BLDSC shelfmark: 3865.574700.
Description: Intends to serve as a means of broadening the international base of family medicine in general practice. Covers health care delivery, epidemiology, public health and medical sociology.

MEDICAL SCIENCES

610 CN
FAMILY PRACTICE. 1989. 48/yr. Can.$48.15 (foreign Can.$69.55). Fam Pra Publications Inc., 2000 Argentia Rd., Plaza 4, Ste. 401, Mississauga, Ont. L5N 1W1, Canada. TEL 416-858-1312. FAX 416-858-7769. Ed. Steven Manners. adv.; bk.rev.; circ. 24,000. (tabloid format)

610 US ISSN 0300-7073
FAMILY PRACTICE NEWS. 1971. s-m. $96. International Medical News Group, 12230 Wilkins Ave., Rockville, MD 20852. TEL 301-770-6170. Ed. William Rubin. circ. 72,900. (tabloid format; also avail. in microform from UMI)

610 US ISSN 0163-6642
R11
FAMILY PRACTICE RECERTIFICATION. 1979. m. $60. (Medical Recertification Associates) M R A Publications, Inc., 3 Greenwich Office Park, Greenwich, CT 06831-5154. TEL 203-629-3550. FAX 203-629-2536. Eld. Diann Peterson, Dr. Paul Dishart. adv.; bk.rev.; index; circ. 83,365 (controlled). **Indexed:** FAMLI.
—BLDSC shelfmark: 3865.574750.
Description: Directed towards physicians associated with family medicine; includes articles on new developments in medicine, clinical issues and family practice skills.
Refereed Serial

610 US ISSN 0270-2304
CODEN: FPRJD5
FAMILY PRACTICE RESEARCH JOURNAL. 1981. q. $110 (foreign $130). (American Academy of Family Physicians) Human Sciences Press, Inc. (Subsidiary of: Plenum Publishing Corp.), 233 Spring St., New York, NY 10013-1578. TEL 212-620-8000. FAX 212-463-0742. Ed. Leif Solberg. adv.; bk.rev.; abstr. (also avail. in microfiche; microfilm; reprint service avail. from UMI) **Indexed:** CINAHL, FAMLI, Psychol.Abstr., Soc.Work Res.& Abstr.
—BLDSC shelfmark: 3865.574800.
Description: Fosters clinical research in family practice and encourages the training of family physicians in research philosophy, methodology, and research.
Refereed Serial

610 US ISSN 0736-1718
FAMILY SYSTEMS MEDICINE. 1983. q. $35 to individuals (foreign $41); institutions $70 (foreign $76). Box 6542, Syracuse, NY 13217. TEL 212-879-4900. (And: 149 E. 78th St., New York, NY 10021) Ed. Donald Bloch. adv.; bk.rev.; circ. 1,500. (also avail. in microfilm; reprint service avail. from SWZ) **Indexed:** Excerp.Med., FAMLI, Lang.& Lang.Behav.Abstr., Psychol.Abstr., Sociol.Abstr.
—BLDSC shelfmark: 3865.576300.

610 US
FANLIGHT NEWS. 1985. s-a. free. Fanlight Productions, 47 Halifax St., Boston, MA 02130. TEL 617-524-0980. FAX 617-524-8838. Ed. Ben Achtenberg. bk.rev.; film rev.; circ. 20,000.
Description: Describes new media resources and general information of interest to medical professionals, educators, librarians and administrators.

610 VE ISSN 0533-0327
FEDERACION PANAMERICANA DE ASOCIACIONES DE FACULTADES DE MEDICINA. BOLETIN. 1963. bi-m. free. (Federacion Panamericana de Asociaciones de Facultades de Medicina - Panamerican Federation of Associations of Medical Schools) Editorial Fepafem, Apdo. 60411, Caracas 1060-A, Venezuela. FAX 58-2-934275. Ed. Dr. Roberto Rondon Morales. bk.rev.; bibl.; circ. 2,000. **Indexed:** FAMLI.

FEDERAL HEALTH MONITOR, see *PUBLIC HEALTH AND SAFETY*

610 CN
FEDERATION DES MEDECINS RESIDENTS DU QUEBEC. BULLETIN. 1977. 4/yr. Can.$5 to non-members. Federation des Medecins Residents du Quebec, 445 Sherbrooke West, Montreal, Que. H3A 1B6, Canada. TEL 514-282-0256. FAX 514-282-0471. adv.; circ. 2,000.
Formerly: Federation des Medecins Residents et Internes du Quebec. Bulletin.

610 US ISSN 0888-5648
RA396.A3
FEDERATION EXCHANGE. a. $60. Federation of State Medical Boards, 6000 Western Pl, Ste. 707, Fort Worth, TX 76107-4618. TEL 817-735-8445. FAX 817-738-6629.

610.7 US ISSN 0014-9306
FEDERATION OF STATE MEDICAL BOARDS OF THE UNITED STATES. FEDERATION BULLETIN. 1914. m. $25 (effective 1992). Federation of State Medical Boards, 6000 Western Pl., Ste. 707, Fort Worth, TX 76107-4618. TEL 817-735-8445. FAX 817-738-6629. Ed. Dr. Ray L. Casterline. bk.rev.; charts; index; circ. 4,000. (also avail. in microform from UMI; reprint service avail. from UMI) **Indexed:** Ind.Med.
Incorporates (1981-1991): F S M B Newsletter (ISSN 0888-5664)
Description: Presents study and teaching methods.

610 IT ISSN 0014-9500
FEDERAZIONE MEDICA. 1921. m. free. Federazione Nazionale degli Ordini dei Medici, Piazza Cola di Rienzo 80-A, 00192 Rome, Italy. Ed.Bd. adv.; bk.rev.; charts; illus.; bibl.; index; circ. 200,000. **Indexed:** C.I.S. Abstr.

610 IT ISSN 0014-9659
FEGATO. vol.24, 1978. 3/yr. L.5000. Societa Terme di Chianciano, S.p.A., 5302 Chianciano Terme, Italy. Ed. Piero Valori. bk.rev. **Indexed:** Chem.Abstr, Excerp.Med.
—BLDSC shelfmark: 3902.600000.

610 UK ISSN 0305-9324
FELLOWSHIP FOR FREEDOM IN MEDICINE. NEWSLETTER. 1948. 2/yr. £2 to non-members. Fellowship for Freedom in Medicine, Stockbury House, Church St., Storrington, Sussex RH20 4LD, England. Ed. L.S. Carstairs.
Formerly: Fellowship for Freedom in Medicine. Bulletin (ISSN 0014-9829)

611 US
FIDIA RESEARCH SERIES. 1986. irreg. price varies. Springer-Verlag, 175 Fifth Ave., New York, NY 10010. TEL 212-460-1500. (reprint service avail. from ISI)

610 FJ
FIJI MEDICAL JOURNAL. 1960. m. F.$10. Fiji Medical Association, Box 1116, Suva, Fiji. Ed. Dr. K.D. Sharma. adv.; bk.rev.; circ. 1,000. **Indexed:** So.Pac.Per.Ind.

FINLAND. KANSANELAKELAITOS. JULKAISUJA. SARJA AL. see *INSURANCE*

FINLAND. KANSANELAKELAITOS. JULKAISUJA. SARJA EL. see *INSURANCE*

FINLAND. KANSANELAKELAITOS. JULKAISUJA. SARJA ML. see *INSURANCE*

610 617.6 FI
FINLAND. LAAKINTOHALLITUS. LAAKARIT, HAMMASLAAKARIT - LAKARE, TANDLAEKARE. (Text in Finnish and Swedish) 1976. a. FIM 58. Valtion Painatuskeskus, Annankatu 44, 00100 Helsinki 10, Finland.
Formerly: Finland. Laakintohallitus. Laakarit, Hammaslaakarit, Sairaalat (ISSN 0430-5299)

FINLAND. TILASTOKESKUS. KUOLEMANSYYT/FINLAND. STATISTIKCENTRALEN. DOEDSORSAKER/FINLAND. CENTRAL STATISTICAL OFFICE. CAUSES OF DEATH IN FINLAND. see *BUSINESS AND ECONOMICS — Abstracting, Bibliographies, Statistics*

610 FI ISSN 0015-2501
FINSKA LAEKARESAELLSKAPET. HANDLINGAR. (Text in Swedish; summaries in English) 1841. 4/yr. FIM 160. Finska Laekaresaellskapet - Medical Society of Finland, Snellmansgatan 9-11, 00170 Helsinki 17, Finland. Ed. Henrik Riska. adv.; charts; illus.; circ. 15,000. **Indexed:** Biol.Abstr., Chem.Abstr., Curr.Adv.Ecol.Sci., Excerp.Med.
Description: Covers basic, experimental and clinical medical sciences. Includes original articles, association news, obituaries.

614.88 US
FIRST AIDER. 8/yr. Cramer Products, Inc., Box 1001, Gardner, KS 66030. **Indexed:** Sportsearch (1979-).

FISIOPATOLOGIA DELLA RIPRODUZIONE. see *BIOLOGY*

610 UK
FITZHUGH DIRECTORY OF INDEPENDENT HOSPITALS AND PROVIDENT ASSOCIATIONS. 1986. a. Health Care Information Services (Subsidiary of: W A F Health Care Consultant Ltd.), Euston House, 81-103 Euston St., London NW1 2ET, England. TEL 01-221-1527. FAX 01-383-4515. TELEX 262562-CALRIM-G.

FIZIOLOGICHESKII ZHURNAL (KIEV); nauchno-teoreticheskii zhurnal. see *BIOLOGY — Physiology*

FIZIOLOGICHESKII ZHURNAL (MOSCOW). see *BIOLOGY — Physiology*

610 US ISSN 0015-4067
FLORIDA FAMILY PHYSICIAN. 1953. q. membership. (Florida Academy of Family Physicians) Publication Strategies, 4905 Pine Cone Dr., Durham, NC 27707. TEL 919-489-1916. FAX 919-489-4767. (Subscr. to: Florida Academy of Family Physicians, 1627 Rogero Rd., Jacksonville, FL 32211. TEL 904-743-6304) Ed. Dr. R. Edward Dodge. adv.; charts; illus.; circ. 18,000.
—BLDSC shelfmark: 3956.005000.
Formerly: Florida Academy of General Practice Journal.

610 US ISSN 0015-4148
CODEN: JFMAAQ
FLORIDA MEDICAL ASSOCIATION. JOURNAL. 1914. m. $25 (foreign $30). Florida Medical Association, Inc., Box 2411, Jacksonville, FL 32203. TEL 904-356-1571. FAX 904-353-1247. Ed. Dr. Jacques R. Caldwell. adv.; bk.rev.; bibl.; charts; illus.; stat.; index; circ. 16,300. (also avail. in microform from UMI; reprint service avail. from UMI) **Indexed:** Chem.Abstr., Curr.Cont., Dent.Ind., Excerp.Med., Helminthol.Abstr., Ind.Med., INIS Atomind., Nutr.Abstr.
—BLDSC shelfmark: 4754.200000.
Refereed Serial

616.9 US ISSN 0015-4857
FLYING PHYSICIAN. 1955. q. $15 (foreign $20). Flying Physician Association, c/o Carol Laurie, Exec. VP, Box 17841, Kansas City, MO 64134. TEL 816-763-9336. Ed. Dr. George M. Gumbert, Jr. adv.; bk.rev.; illus.; circ. 5,000.
Description: Discusses aerospace medicine.

610 US
FOCUS (NEW YORK, 1978). 1978. m. during academic year. free. State University of New York, Health Science Center at Brooklyn, 450 Clarkson Ave., Brooklyn, NY 11203. Ed. M. Ellen Griffin. circ. controlled.
Incorporates: State University of New York. Downstate Medical Center. Faculty Briefs (ISSN 0039-0208); Former titles: Downstate Medical Center; Downstate Examiner; Supersedes (1969-1978): What's News.

610 GW
FOCUS M U L; Zeitschrift fuer Wissenschaft, Forschung und Lehre an der medizinische Universitaet zu Luebeck. q. DM.70. (Medizinischen Universitaet zu Luebeck) Hansisches Verlagskontor H. Scheffler, Mengstr. 16, Postfach 2051, 2400 Luebeck 1, Germany. TEL 0451-1605-0. Eds. H.F. Piper, R. Labahn. adv. contact: Ulrike Plath. circ. 5,000.

610 DK ISSN 0107-3362
FODPLEJEREN. 1976. q. Sammenslutningen af Danske Fodplejere, c/o Hartvig Pedersen, Tegelvaerksvej 20, Brundby, 8791 Tranebjerg, Denmark.
Formerly: Fodspecialisten (ISSN 0107-4148)

610 BL ISSN 0015-5454
FOLHA MEDICA. (Text in Portuguese; summaries in English and Portuguese) 1920. m. $180. Cidade - Editora Cientifica Ltda., Rua Mexico 90-2 Andar, 20031 Rio de Janeiro RJ, Brazil. Ed. Fernando Moyses. adv.; bk.rev.; abstr.; bibl.; charts; illus.; index; circ. 15,000. **Indexed:** Biol.Abstr., Chem.Abstr., Excerp.Med., Ind.Med., INIS Atomind.
—BLDSC shelfmark: 3965.400000.

MEDICAL SCIENCES

610   BN   ISSN 0352-9657
FOLIA ANATOMICA IUGOSLAVICA. (Text in Serbo-Croatian; summaries in English) 1972. a. $14. Savez Drustava Anatoma Jugoslavije, Mose Pijade 6, 71000 Sarajevo, Bosnia Hercegovina. Ed. M. Scepovic. bk.rev.; circ. 600. **Indexed:** Excerp.Med. (until 1992).
—BLDSC shelfmark: 3966.100000.

610   CS
FOLIA FACULTATIS MEDICAE UNIVERSITATIS COMENIANAE BRATISLAVIENSIS. (Text in English, German, Russian, Slovak) 1970. s-a. (Rektorat Univerzity Komenskeho) Vydavatel'stvo Osveta, Osloboditelov 21, 036 54 Martin, Czechoslovakia. FAX 0842-350-36. Ed.Bd. **Indexed:** Biol.Abstr., Excerp.Med., INIS Atomind., Trop.Dis.Bull.

610   PL   ISSN 0015-5616
CODEN: FMCRAW
FOLIA MEDICA CRACOVIENSIA. (Text in Polish; summaries in English and Russian) 1959. 4/yr. price varies. (Polska Akademia Nauk, Oddzial w Krakowie) Ossolineum, Publishing House of the Polish Academy of Sciences, Ryne 9, Wroclaw, Poland. TELEX 0712771 OSS PL. (Dist. by: Ars Polona-Ruch, Krakowskie Przedmiescie 7, 00-068 Warsaw, Poland) Ed. Dr. Zdzislaw Mach. bibl.; charts; illus.; index. **Indexed:** Biol.Abstr., Chem.Abstr, Excerp.Med., Ind.Med.
—BLDSC shelfmark: 3971.405000.
Description: Presents both clinical and experimental research and discusses the mechanisms of pathogenesis of various diseases.

FOOD AND CHEMICAL TOXICOLOGY. see ENVIRONMENTAL STUDIES — Toxicology And Environmental Safety

610   US   ISSN 1049-6742
FOR THE RECORD (VALLEY FORGE). 1989. w. free. Valley Forge Press, 1200 Valley Forge Rd., Box 1135, Valley Forge, PA 19481. TEL 215-935-1296. FAX 215-935-3072. Ed. Eileen Moran. bk.rev.; charts; illus.
Description: Items of general interest to medical record professionals, including legislation, software, and management issues.

610   CH   ISSN 0371-7682
CODEN: TIHHAH
FORMOSAN MEDICAL ASSOCIATION. JOURNAL/TAIWAN I HSUEH HUI TSA CHIH. (Includes supplement) (Text and summaries mainly in English; partly in Chinese) vol.44, 1945. m. NT.$800($30) (non-members $90). Formosan Medical Association, National Taiwan University Hospital, 1 Chang-Te St., Taipei 10016, Taiwan, Republic of China. TEL 02-3810367. FAX 02-3896716. Ed. Dr. Tsu-pei Hung. adv.; charts; illus.; circ. 5,200. (reprints avail. from ISC) **Indexed:** Abstr.Hyg., Biol.Abstr., Chem.Abstr., Dent.Ind., Excerp.Med., Helminthol.Abstr., Ind.Med., Trop.Dis.Bull. Key Title: Taiwan Yixuehui Zazhi.
—BLDSC shelfmark: 4754.900000.
Description: Covers basic, experimental, and clinical medical sciences. Includes original articles, case reports, brief communications, review articles, association news, announcements of meetings, etc. Supplement issues include programs and abstracts of meetings.

610   GW
FORSCHUNG UND PRAXIS IM DIALOG. irreg., vol.12, 1990. price varies. Ferdinand Enke Verlag, Postfach 101254, 7000 Stuttgart 10, Germany. TEL 0711-8931-0. FAX 0711-8931-419. TELEX 07252275-GTV-D.

FORSKNING I GROENLAND-TUSAAT. see EARTH SCIENCES

610   GW   ISSN 0938-9407
▼**FORTSCHRITTE DER DIAGNOSTIK;** Zeitschrift fuer die gesamte Diagnostik in der aerztlichen Praxis. 1990. q. DM.40. Urban und Vogel, Lindwurmstr. 95, Postfach 152209, 8000 Munich 2, Germany. TEL 089-53292-0. FAX 089-53292-100. circ. 10,000.
—BLDSC shelfmark: 4021.135000.

610   GW   ISSN 0015-8178
CODEN: FMDZAR
FORTSCHRITTE DER MEDIZIN; Internationale Zeitschrift fuer die gesamte Heilkunde. (Text in German, summaries in English) 1882. 3/m. DM.164 (foreign DM.212). Verlag Urban und Vogel, Postfach 15 22 09, 8000 Munich 15, Germany. TEL 089-53292-0. FAX 089-53292-100. adv.; bk.rev.; abstr.; bibl.; charts; illus.; stat.; index; circ. 48,500 (controlled). **Indexed:** Biol.Abstr., Chem.Abstr., Curr.Adv.Cancer Res., Curr.Adv.Ecol.Sci., Curr.Cont., Dent.Ind., Excerp.Med., Helminthol.Abstr., Ind.Med., INIS Atomind., Nutr.Abstr.
—BLDSC shelfmark: 4021.950000.
Description: Publication for physicians, covering all fields of medicine. Features current research and technology, news, and reports of events.

610   GW   ISSN 0930-925X
FORTSCHRITTE IN DER ARTHROSKOPIE. 1985. irreg., vol.7, 1991. price varies. Ferdinand Enke Verlag, Postfach 101254, 7000 Stuttgart 10, Germany. TEL 0711-8931-0. FAX 0711-8931-419. TELEX 07252275-GTV-D. Eds. H. Hofer, W. Glinz.

610   GW   ISSN 0939-7256
FORUM (MUNICH); des praktischen und Allgemein-Arztes. 1962. m. DM.24. Verlag Neuer Merkur GmbH, Ingolstaedter Str. 63a, Postfach 460805, 8000 Munich 46, Germany. TEL 089-318905-0. FAX 089-318905-38.

610   GW   ISSN 0015-850X
FORUM DES PRAKTISCHEN ARZTES. 1962. m. DM.40. (Vereinigung der Praktischen Aerzte Bayerns e.V.) Verlag A. Fruehmorgen, Schwindstr. 5, 8000 Munich 40, Germany. Ed. A. Fruhmorgen. adv.; bk.rev.; illus.; circ. 20,000. (tabloid format)

610   IT   ISSN 0015-9271
CODEN: FRACAC
FRACASTORO. 1907. 3/yr. L.10000 per no. Istituti Ospitalieri Verona, Via Bassini 1, Verona, Italy. FAX 45-8301200. Ed. G. Mastella. adv.; bk.rev.; circ. 4,000. **Indexed:** Biol.Abstr., Chem.Abstr., Curr.Adv.Ecol.Sci., Excerp.Med., Ind.Med.
—BLDSC shelfmark: 4030.600000.

610   FR   ISSN 0763-7098
FRANCE. INSTITUT NATIONAL DE LA SANTE ET DE LA RECHERCHE MEDICALE. COLLOQUES. 1971. irreg. price varies. Institut National de la Sante et de la Recherche Medicale, 101 rue de Tolbiac, 75654 Paris Cedex 13, France.

FRANCE. INSTITUT NATIONAL DE LA SANTE ET DE LA RECHERCHE MEDICALE. INSERM ACTUALITES. see PUBLIC HEALTH AND SAFETY

610   GW   ISSN 0938-7463
▼**FRAUENAERZTLICHES SEMINAR.** 1990. q. DM.25. Berliner Medizinische Verlagsanstalt GmbH, Kurfuerstenstr. 112-113, 1000 Berlin 30, Germany. TEL 030-219909-0. FAX 030-219909-10. Ed. Dr. Fritz Bella. circ. 7,000.

FREEWHEELER. see SOCIAL SERVICES AND WELFARE

610   IT   ISSN 0016-1535
IL FRIULI MEDICO. (Text in Italian; summaries in English) 1946. bi-m. L.40000 (foreign L.50000). (Societa Medica del Friuli) Tipografia A. Pellegrini (Udine), Via della Vigna 26, 33100 Udine, Italy. TEL 0432-502612. Ed. Pietro Carnielli. adv.; bk.rev.; bibl.; charts; illus.; stat.; index. cum.index; circ. 1,000. **Indexed:** Biol.Abstr., Chem.Abstr., Excerp.Med., Ind.Med.
—BLDSC shelfmark: 4040.200000.
Description: Features research papers on a wide variety of topics in medicine. Includes much research done in the north western region of Italy (Friuli).

610   IT
FRONTE SANITARIO; quindicinale dei medici Italiani. 1944. fortn. (22/yr.). L.2500. Dr. Paolo Ardoino, Ed. & Pub., Via Galata 20-A, 16121 Genoa, Italy. adv.; circ. 45,000.

616.072   US
FRONTIERS IN HEADACHE RESEARCH. 1991. irreg. price varies. Raven Press, 1185 Ave. of the Americas, New York, NY 10036. TEL 212-930-9500. FAX 212-869-3495.

FRONTIERS OF HEALTH SERVICES MANAGEMENT. see HOSPITALS

610.28   NE   ISSN 0921-3775
CODEN: FMBEEQ
FRONTIERS OF MEDICAL AND BIOLOGICAL ENGINEERING. (Text in English) 1988. q. DM.360. (Japan Society of Medical Electronics and Biomedical Engineering, JA) V S P, P.O. Box 346, 3700 AH Zeist, Netherlands. TEL 03404-25790. FAX 03404-32081. TELEX 40217 VSP NL. Ed. M. Saito.
—BLDSC shelfmark: 4042.037000.

FUJIAN YIYAO ZAZHI/FUJIAN MEDICAL AND PHARMACOLOGICAL JOURNAL. see PHARMACY AND PHARMACOLOGY

615.89 619   CC   ISSN 0427-7074
FUJIAN ZHONGYI YAO/FUJIAN JOURNAL OF TRADITIONAL CHINESE MEDICINE. (Text in Chinese) bi-m. $0.80 per no. Fujian Zhongyi Xueyuan, 53 Wusi Beilu, Fuzhou, Fujian 350003, People's Republic of China. TEL 571708. (Dist. overseas by: China International Book Trading Corporation, Chegongzhuang Xilu 21, P.O. Box 399, Beijing, P.R.C.) (Co-sponsor: Zhonghua Quanguo Zhongyi Xuehui Fujian Fenhui) Ed. Yu Changrong.

610   JA   ISSN 0016-254X
CODEN: FKIZA4
FUKUOKA ACTA MEDICA/FUKUOKA IGAKU ZASSHI. (Text in Japanese; summaries in English) 1907. m. 3000 Yen($6.70) Fukuoka Medical Society - Fukuoka Igakkai, c/o Kyushu Daigaku Igakubu, Igaku Toshokan, Maidashi 3-1-1, Higashi-ku, Fukuoka 812, Japan. FAX 092-631-2794. Ed. Kazunobu Amako. adv.; charts; mkt.; index; circ. 1,100. **Indexed:** Biol.Abstr., Chem.Abstr, Curr.Adv.Cancer Res., Curr.Adv.Ecol.Sci., Dent.Ind., Excerp.Med., Ind.Med., INIS Atomind.
—BLDSC shelfmark: 4054.896200.

610   JA   ISSN 0016-2590
CODEN: FJMSAU
FUKUSHIMA JOURNAL OF MEDICAL SCIENCE. (Text in English) 1954. s-a. membership. Fukushima Society of Medical Science, Fukushima Medical College Library, 1, Hikariga-oka, Fukushima 960-12, Japan. FAX 81-245-48-2535. Ed. Yukihiko Kayama. charts; illus.; index; circ. 1,600. **Indexed:** Abstr.Hyg., Biol.Abstr., Chem.Abstr., Curr.Adv.Ecol.Sci., Excerp.Med., Ind.Med., INIS Atomind., Nutr.Abstr., Trop.Dis.Bull.
—BLDSC shelfmark: 4055.000000.

610   JA   ISSN 0016-2582
CODEN: FSIZAQ
FUKUSHIMA MEDICAL JOURNAL/FUKUSHIMA IGAKU ZASSHI. (Text in Japanese; summaries in English) 1951. q. membership. Fukushima Society of Medical Science, Fukushima Medical College Library, 1, Hikariga-oka, Fukushima 960-12, Japan. FAX 81-245-48-2535. Ed. Yukihiko Kayama. charts; illus.; index; circ. 1,330. **Indexed:** Biol.Abstr., Chem.Abstr., Excerp.Med., INIS Atomind.
—BLDSC shelfmark: 4055.200000.

FUNCTIONAL AND DEVELOPMENTAL MORPHOLOGY. see BIOLOGY

FUNCTIONS OF THE NERVOUS SYSTEM. see MEDICAL SCIENCES — Psychiatry And Neurology

FUNDACAO SERVICOS DE SAUDE PUBLICA. REVISTA. see PUBLIC HEALTH AND SAFETY

610   SP   ISSN 0016-2698
FUNDACION JIMENEZ DIAZ. BOLETIN.* 1968. m. $32. Fundacion Jimenez Diaz, Av. de los Reyes Catolicos 2, Madrid 3, Spain. Dir. Eloy Lopez Garcia. adv.; bk.rev.; bibl.; charts; illus.; circ. 43,251 (controlled).

610   SP
FUNDACION PUIGVERT. ANALES. (Text in Spanish; summaries in English) 1971. q. ($12) (Fundacion Puigvert) Editorial ECO, S.A., Calle de la Cruz 44, Barcelona 17, Spain. adv.; bk.rev.; bibl.; illus.; circ. 2,500. (back issues avail.) **Indexed:** Excerp.Med., Ind.Med.Esp.

FUNDAMENTAL AND APPLIED TOXICOLOGY. see ENVIRONMENTAL STUDIES — Toxicology And Environmental Safety

MEDICAL SCIENCES

610 GW
FUTURA. (Text in English and German) 1986. q. (Boehringer Ingelheim Fonds, Stiftung fuer Medizinische Grundlagenforschung) Hippokrates Verlag GmbH, Ruedigerstr. 14, Postfach 102263, 7000 Stuttgart 30, Germany. TEL 0711-89310. circ. 2,200.

610 DK
FYNSKE LAEGER. 1981. bi-m. DKK 150. Laegekredsforeningen for Fyns Amt, Sankt Anne Plads 2, 5000 Odense C, Denmark. Ed. Niels Mayerhofer. adv.; bk.rev.; illus.; circ. 1,750.
Formerly: Laegekredsforeningen Fyns Amt (ISSN 0109-5439)

615.8 NO ISSN 0016-3384
FYSIOTERAPEUTEN. 1933. 16/yr. NOK 640. Norske Fysioterapeuters Forbund, Pilestredet 56, P.O. Box 7009 Homansbyen, 0306 Oslo 3, Norway. TEL 02-697800. FAX 02-565825. Ed. Gerd Vidje. adv.; bk.rev.; illus.; circ. 6,000.

615.8 FI
FYSIOTERAPIA. (Text in Finnish, Swedish; summaries in English) 1954. 8/yr. FIM 305. Suomen Laakintavoimistelijaliitto - Finnish Physical Therapy Association, Asemamiehenkatu 4, 00520 Helsinki, Finland. TEL 90-1496034. FAX 90-1483054. Ed. Marja-Helena Rajala. adv.; bk.rev.; charts; illus.; circ. 7,850.
Former titles: Laakintavoimistelija (ISSN 0039-5579) & Suomen Laakintavoimistelija.
Description: Covers physiotherapy, movement and health, rehabilitation.

610 SP ISSN 0304-4858
CODEN: GCMBA9
GACETA MEDICA DE BILBAO. (Text in Spanish; summaries in English and Spanish) 1895. m. 1000 ptas.($30) Academia de Ciencias Medicas de Bilbao, Lersundi 11, Bilbao 9, Spain. Ed. Angel Arrien Echevarri. adv.; circ. 5,000. (back issues avail.) Indexed: Excerp.Med., Ind.Med.Esp.

610 VE
GACETA MEDICA DE CARACAS. 1893. q. free. Academia Nacional de Medicina, Apdo. Postal 804, Caracas 1010-A, Venezuela. (Co-sponsor: Congreso Venezolano de Ciencias Medicas) Ed. Dr. Oscar Aguero. bk.rev.; bibl.; illus.; circ. 1,000. Indexed: Abstr.Hyg., Chem.Abstr., Excerp.Med., Trop.Dis.Bull.

610 MX ISSN 0016-3813
R21 CODEN: GMMEAK
GACETA MEDICA DE MEXICO. (Text in Spanish; summaries in English) 1864. bi-m. Mex.$300000($100) Academia Nacional de Medicina, Unidad de Congresos del Centro Medico Nacional, Bloque B, Av. Cuauhtemoc 330, 06741 Mexico D.F., Mexico. TEL 578-20-44. FAX 5784271. (Co-sponsor: Instituto Mexicano del Seguro Social) Ed. Juan Somolinos. bk.rev.; bibl.; illus.; index; circ. 40,000. (also avail. in microform from UMI; reprint service avail. from UMI) Indexed: Biol.Abstr., Chem.Abstr., Ind.Med., Ind.Vet., Small Anim.Abstr., Soils & Fert., Trop.Dis.Bull.
—BLDSC shelfmark: 4066.080000.

610 US
GAP CONFERENCE REPORTS. 1975. a. Cystic Fibrosis Foundation, 6931 Arlington Rd., Ste. 200, Bethesda, MD 20814-5205. (back issues avail.)

GASETA SANITARIA. see PUBLIC HEALTH AND SAFETY

610 616.39 US
GATHERED VIEW. 1975. bi-m. $20 to individuals; families $25; professionals $30. Prader-Willi Syndrome Association, 6490 Excelsior Blvd., E102, St. Louis Park, MN 55426. TEL 612-926-1947. FAX 612-928-9133. Ed. Teresa Schaefer. bk.rev.; circ. 1,800. (back issues avail.)
Description: Intended to educate anyone interested in caring for persons with Prader-Willi syndrome.

610 US
GAUCHER'S DISEASE NEWSLETTER. bi-m. $25. (National Gaucher Foundation) L G T Associates, 4801 Monticello Ave., Silver Spring, MD 20902. Ed. Karen A. Cohen. circ. 2,500. (back issues avail.)

610 US
GAZETTE INTERNATIONAL NETWORKING INSTITUTE. PROCEEDINGS. irreg., 3rd, 1985. $8 (foreign $9.35). Gazette International Networking Institute, 5100 Oakland Ave., Ste. 206, St. Louis, MO 63110-1441. TEL 314-534-0475. Eds. Gini Laurie, Judith Raymond.

610 FR ISSN 0016-5557
GAZETTE MEDICALE DE FRANCE. (Text in English and French) 1892. w. 100 F. 123 Rue de Tocqueville, 75017 Paris, France. Ed. D. Testard. adv.; bk.rev.; abstr.; bibl.; charts; illus.; index; circ. 45,000. (also avail. in microform from UMI; back issues avail.; reprint service avail.from UMI) Indexed: Biol.Abstr., C.I.S. Abstr., Curr.Adv.Cancer Res., Curr.Adv.Ecol.Sci., Curr.Cont., Excerp.Med., Helminthol.Abstr., Ind.Med, Nutr.Abstr.
Formerly: Gazette Medicale de France et Science Medicale Pratique.

610 MG
GAZETY MEDIKALY. 1965. m. Lot 12 B, Ampahibe, 101 Antananarivo, Malagasy Republic. TEL 27898. Ed. Paul Ratsimiseta. circ. 2,000. (newspaper)

610 IT
GAZZETTA MEDICA ITALIANA ARCHIVIO PER LE SCIENZE MEDICHE. m. L.70000($90) Edizioni Minerva Medica, Corso Bramante 83-85, Turin 10126, Italy. TEL 011-678282. Dir. Alberto Oliaro. Indexed: Biol.Abstr., C.I.S. Abstr., Chem.Abstr., Excerp.Med., Ind.Med., INIS Atomind.
Formed by the merger of: Archivio per le Scienze Mediche (ISSN 0004-0312) & Gazzetta Medica Italiana - Aggiornamenti Clinicoterapeutici; Which was formed by the merger of: Gazzetta Medica Italiana (ISSN 0016-5670); Aggiornamenti Clinicoterapeutici (ISSN 0002-0907)

610 IT ISSN 0016-5697
GAZZETTA SANITARIA. 1948. q. free. Carlo Erba S.p.A., Via Imbonati 24, 20159 Milan, Italy. Ed. Corrado Scagliarini. adv.; bk.rev.; bibl.; charts; illus.; circ. 280,000. Indexed: Biol.Abstr., Chem.Abstr., Excerp.Med.

GEGENBAURS MORPHOLOGISCHES JAHRBUCH. see BIOLOGY

610 SA ISSN 0016-643X
CODEN: GENEB4
GENEESKUNDE. (Text in Afrikaans) 1957. m. R.77. Medpharm Publications, Noodhulpliga Centre, 3rd Fl., 204B HF Verwoerd Dr., Randburg 2194, South Africa. FAX 011-787-4981. Ed. R. van Rooyen. adv.; bk.rev.; charts; illus.; index; circ. 4,000. Indexed: Chem.Abstr., Ind.S.A.Per., INIS Atomind.
Description: Contains scientific articles written by South African doctors for South Africa.

GENEESKUNDE EN SPORT. see MEDICAL SCIENCES — Sports Medicine

610 NE
GENEESKUNDIG ADRESBOEK NEDERLAND. a. fl.220. Nijgh Periodieken B.V., Postbus 122, 3100 AC Schiedam, Netherlands. TEL 010-4274100. FAX 010-4739911. TELEX 22680. circ. 11,500.
Supersedes in part: Geneeskundig Jaarboekje.

610 NE
GENEESKUNDIG JAARBOEK MEDICIJNEN. a. fl.48.50. Nijgh Periodieken B.V., Postbus 122, 3100 AC Schiedam, Netherlands. TEL 010-4274100. FAX 010-4739911. TELEX 22680. circ. 10,000.
Supersedes in part: Geneeskundig Jaarboekje.

610 UK
GENERAL MEDICAL COUNCIL. ANNUAL REPORT. 1859. a. General Medical Council, 44 Hallam St., London W1N 6AE, England. TEL 01-580 7642. FAX 01-436-1383.

610 UK ISSN 0072-0763
GENERAL MEDICAL COUNCIL. MEDICAL REGISTER. 1859. a. £90. General Medical Council, 44 Hallam St., London W1N 6AE, England. TEL 01-580-7642. FAX 01-436-1383.

610.6 UK
GENERAL MEDICAL COUNCIL. MINUTES. 1858. a. £42.50. General Medical Council, 44 Hallam St., London W1N 6AE, England. TEL 01-580-7642. FAX 01-436-1383.

610 UK ISSN 0046-5607
GENERAL PRACTITIONER. 1963. w. £85. Haymarket Medical Publications Ltd., 30 Lancaster Gate, London W2 3LP, England. (Subscr. to: Tower Publishing, 3-4 Harwick St., London EC1R 4RY) Ed. Stephen Lederer. adv.; circ. 43,635.
●Also available online. Vendor(s): Data-Star (GPGP).
—BLDSC shelfmark: 4107.840000.

610 FR ISSN 0183-4568
GENERALISTE. 1975. s-w. 110 Fr. Editions du Medecin Generaliste, 11 bd. de Sebastopol, 75001 Paris, France. Ed. Dr. Christine Pasquet. adv.

610 US
GENESEE COUNTY MEDICAL SOCIETY BULLETIN. 1927. m. $60. Genesee County Medical Society, 80 Tuuri Place, Flint, MI 48503. TEL 313-238-3781. FAX 313-238-3792. Ed. Dr. Willys F. Mueller, Jr. adv.; circ. 610. (back issues avail.)
Description: Contains information and articles of interest to the members.

610 FR ISSN 0016-6839
GENIE MEDICAL; symbiose medico-artistique. 1949. m. 25 F. E.S.T.E.C., 127 bd. Saint Michel, 75005 Paris, France. Ed. Dr. H. Drouin. adv.; bk.rev.; film rev.; illus.; tr.lit.; circ. 23,500.

GEOGRAPHIA MEDICA; international journal on geography of health - journal international de la geographie de la sante. see GEOGRAPHY

610 US ISSN 0016-8106
R11 CODEN: GTMBAQ
GEORGETOWN MEDICAL BULLETIN. q. $6. 3900 Reservoir Rd., N.W., Washington, DC 20007. Ed. Karen Jones. bk.rev.; circ. 10,000. Indexed: Biol.Abstr., Chem.Abstr.

GERIATRIC NEPHROLOGY AND UROLOGY. see MEDICAL SCIENCES — Urology And Nephrology

610 SZ ISSN 0016-9161
GESNERUS; die medizin-wissenschaftliche Zeitschrift der medizinischen und naturwissenschaftlichen Forschung. (Text in English, French, German and Italian) 1943. 2/yr. 80 Fr. to non-members. (Schweizerische Gesellschaft fuer Geschichte der Medizin und der Naturwissenschaften) Verlag Sauerlaender, Laurenzenvorstadt 89, CH-5001 Aarau, Switzerland. TEL 064-268626. FAX 064-245780. TELEX 981195 SAG CH. Eds. H.H. Walser, H. Balmer. adv.; bk.rev.; illus.; index; cum.index; circ. 650. Indexed: Biol.Abstr., Chem.Abstr., Excerp.Med., Ind.Med.
—BLDSC shelfmark: 4163.000000.

GEZONDHEIDSZORG, BELEID EN ORGANIZATIE. see HOSPITALS

610 GH ISSN 0855-0328
GHANA MEDICAL JOURNAL. 1962. q. $5. Ghana Medical Association, P.O. Box 1596, Accra, Ghana. Ed. S.K. Arthur. adv.; bk.rev.; abstr.; bibl.; charts; illus.; stat.; circ. 1,000. Indexed: Biol.Abstr., Curr.Cont., Excerp.Med., Ind.Med., INIS Atomind., Nutr.Abstr.

610 JA ISSN 0072-4521
CODEN: GDIKAN
GIFU UNIVERSITY. SCHOOL OF MEDICINE. ARCHIVES/GIFU DAIGAKU IGAKUBU KIYO/ACTA SCHOLAE MEDICINALIS UNIVERSITATIS IN GIFU. (Text mainly in Japanese; occasionally in English or German) 1953. bi-m. free. Gifu University, School of Medicine, 40 Tsukasa-machi, Gifu 500, Japan. Ed.Bd. circ. 370. Indexed: Chem.Abstr, Dairy Sci.Abstr., Excerp.Med., INIS Atomind.
—BLDSC shelfmark: 0582.720000.

GIORNALE DEI CONGRESSI MEDICI. see MEETINGS AND CONGRESSES

610 IT
GIORNALE DEL MEDICO; bisettimanale di informazione per il medico pratico. 1985. s-w. L.14500 (effective 1991). Masson Italia Periodici, Via Statuto 2-4, 20121 Milan, Italy. TEL 02-6367-1. FAX 02-6367-211. Ed. Carlo Grassi. circ. 85,000.

MEDICAL SCIENCES 3101

616.07   IT   ISSN 0017-0275
CODEN: GCMEAI
GIORNALE DI CLINICA MEDICA. (Text in Italian; summaries in English, French, German) 1920. m. L.70000($110) Piccin Editore, Via Altinate 107, 35100 Padua, Italy. TEL 049-655566. TELEX 432074 PICCIN I. Ed. Prof. Luciano Campanacci. adv.; bk.rev.; charts; illus.; index. **Indexed:** Biol.Abstr., Chem.Abstr., Excerp.Med., Ind.Med.

616.98   IT   ISSN 0017-0364
CODEN: GMMIAW
GIORNALE DI MEDICINA MILITARE. 1851. bi-m. L.50000($60) Comando del Corpo di Sanita dell' Esercito, Via S. Stefano Rotondo, n.4, 00184 Rome, Italy. adv.; bk.rev.; abstr.; illus.; index; circ. 3,000. **Indexed:** C.I.S. Abstr., Chem.Abstr., Excerp.Med., Ind.Med.
●Also available online.

GIORNALE ITALIANO DI CHIMICA CLINICA. see
BIOLOGY — Biological Chemistry

616.98   IT   ISSN 0391-9889
CODEN: GIMLDG
GIORNALE ITALIANO DI MEDICINA DEL LAVORO. (Text in English and Italian; summaries in English) 1979. bi-m. L.80000($100) Giardini Editori e Stampatori, Via Santa Bibbiana 28, 56100 Pisa, Italy. TEL 050 502531. Ed. Francesco Candura. adv.; bk.rev.; index. cum.index; circ. 1,500. (back issues avail.) **Indexed:** Biol.Abstr., Chem.Abstr, Dent.Ind., Excerp.Med., Ind.Med.
—BLDSC shelfmark: 4178.230000.
Description: Features research papers on various topics of occupational health.

616.07   IT   ISSN 0393-5957
GIORNALE ITALIANO DI RICERCHE CLINICHE E TERAPEUTICHE. (Text and summaries in English, Italian) 1979. bi-m. L.20000($4.85) E S I Stampa Medica s.r.l., Casella Postale 42, Lgo. Volontari del Sangue 10, 22097 S. Donato, Milan, Italy. TEL 02-5274241. FAX 02-5274775. TELEX 324894. adv.; bk.rev.; circ. 25,000. (back issues avail.)
—BLDSC shelfmark: 4178.244000.
Description: Covers clinical medicine.

610   IT   ISSN 0391-9056
CODEN: GISEDP
GIORNALE ITALIANO DI SENOLOGIA. (Text in Italian; summaries in English) q. L.50000($50) (Societa Italiana di Senologia) C I C Edizioni Internazionali s.r.l., Via L. Spallanzani 11, 00161 Rome, Italy. TEL 06-8412673. FAX 06-8443365. TELEX 622099 CIC. **Indexed:** Excerp.Med.
—BLDSC shelfmark: 4178.247000.

610   PL   ISSN 0017-1344
GLOWNA BIBLIOTEKA LEKARSKA. BIULETYN. 1952. m. 300 Zl.($46.20) Glowna Biblioteka Lekarska - Central Medical Library, Ul. Chocimska 22, Warsaw, Poland. (Dist. by: Ars Polona - Ruch, Krakowskie Przedmiescie 7, 00-068 Warsaw, Poland) Ed. Feliks Widy-Wirski. adv.; bk.rev.; bibl.; index; circ. 625. **Indexed:** Excerp.Med.

GOLD INSTITUTE. INTERNATIONAL CONFERENCE ON GOLD & SILVER IN MEDICINE. PROCEEDINGS. see
MINES AND MINING INDUSTRY

610   GW
GOLDENE GESUNDHEIT. 1976. m. DM.30. Bastei-Verlag Gustav H. Luebbe GmbH und Co., Scheidtbachstr. 23-31, D-5060 Bergisch Gladbach 2, Germany. TEL 02202-121-0. Eds. Stephan Vogel, Gudrun Stehr.

GOLFER'S COMPANION. see *SPORTS AND GAMES — Ball Games*

610   CC   ISSN 1001-814X
GONGQI YIKAN/ENTERPRISE MEDICAL JOURNAL. (Text in Chinese) q. Harbin Gongchang Qiye Yiyuan Guanli Weiyuanhui - Harbin Enterprise-owned Hospital Management Committee, 34, Siwu Daojie, Daoli-qu, Harbin, Heilongjiang 150010, People's Republic of China. TEL 413165. Ed. Mu Rui.

610   GW   ISSN 0177-3941
GOURMED; magazine for doctors. 1984. m. DM.53.50. Medizinische Praxis-Verlagsgesellschaft mbH, Basler Str. 19, 7812 Bad Krozingen, Germany. TEL 07633-14081. circ. 50,000.

610.6   CE
GOVERNMENT MEDICAL OFFICERS' ASSOCIATION. NEWSLETTER. q. Government Medical Officers' Association, 6 Wijerama Mawatha, Colombo 7, Sri Lanka.

610   US
GRAY SHEET. w. F D C Reports, Inc., 5550 Friendship Blvd., Chevy Chase, MD 20815-7201. TEL 301-657-9830. FAX 301-656-3094. Ed. Timothy Harrington.

GREAT BRITAIN. GENERAL REGISTER OFFICE. STUDIES ON MEDICAL AND POPULATION SUBJECTS. see
POPULATION STUDIES

610   UK   ISSN 0141-2256
GREAT BRITAIN. MEDICAL RESEARCH COUNCIL. ANNUAL REPORT (YEAR). a. £8. Medical Research Council, 20 Park Crescent, London W1N 4AL, England. TEL 071-636-5422. FAX 071-436-6179. TELEX 24897.
—BLDSC shelfmark: 1340.190000.
Formerly (until 1965): Great Britain. Medical Research Council. Report (ISSN 0072-6567)

610   UK   ISSN 0309-0132
R854.G7
GREAT BRITAIN. MEDICAL RESEARCH COUNCIL. HANDBOOK (YEAR). a. £8. Medical Research Council, 20 Park Crescent, London W1N 4AL, England. TEL 071-636-5422. FAX 071-436-6179. TELEX 24897.

610   US   ISSN 0894-508X
GREATER KANSAS CITY MEDICAL BULLETIN. 1907. m. $7 to non-members; members $5. Metropolitan Medical Society of Greater Kansas City, Metropolitan Medical Society, 3036 Gillham Rd., Kansas City, MO 64108. TEL 816-531-8432. Ed. Dr. John H. Renner. adv.; bk.rev.; circ. 3,100.

362 610   US   ISSN 0199-5103
GROUP PRACTICE JOURNAL. 1951. bi-m. $65. American Group Practice Association, 1422 Duke St., Alexandria, VA 22314. TEL 703-838-0033. FAX 703-549-1890. Ed. Charles Honaker. adv.; circ. 40,000. **Indexed:** Abstr.Health Care Manage.Stud., Excerp.Med., Hosp.Lit.Ind., Med.Care Rev., MEDSOC.
—BLDSC shelfmark: 4220.182100.
Formerly: Group Practice (ISSN 0017-4726)
Description: Focuses on business and financial management of medical group practices including medical marketing, managed care and computers in health care.

610   US
GROUP PRACTICE MANAGED HEALTHCARE NEWS. 1986. 12/yr. $48. Medical Communique Inc., c/o Stuart G. Mann, 240 Cedar Knolls Rd., Ste. 220, Cedar Knolls, NJ 07927. TEL 201-285-0855. FAX 201-285-1472. Ed. Alfred Saint-Jacques. adv.; bk.rev.; circ. 61,538.
Formerly: Group Practice News (ISSN 0279-4942)
Description: Presents useful information in a cogent, timely fashion on topics of interest to those associated with the managed healthcare field.

612.6   US   ISSN 1041-1232
QH511.A1   CODEN: GDAGE9
GROWTH, DEVELOPMENT & AGING; devoted to problems of normal and abnormal growth. 1937. q. $90 to non-members (foreign $110); members $40 (foreign $50). Growth Publishing Co., Inc., Box 42, Bar Harbor, ME 04609-0042. TEL 207-288-3533. FAX 207-288-5079. Ed. Dr. D.E. Harrison. bk.rev.; bibl.; charts; illus.; index; circ. 750. (also avail. in microform from UMI; reprint service avail. from UMI,ISI) **Indexed:** Abstr.Anthropol., Anim.Breed.Abstr., Biol.Abstr., Biol.& Agr.Ind., Chem.Abstr, Curr.Adv.Ecol.Sci., Curr.Cont., Dairy Sci.Abstr., Dent.Ind., Excerp.Med., Ind.Med., Ind.Sci.Rev., Ind.Vet., INIS Atomind., Mid.East: Abstr.& Ind., Nutr.Abstr, Sci.Cit.Ind., Vet.Bull., W.R.C.Inf.
Formerly (until 1987): Growth (ISSN 0017-4793)
Refereed Serial

610   CC
GUANGDONG YIXUE/GUANGDONG MEDICAL SCIENCE. (Text in Chinese) bi-m. Guangdong Yixue Qingbao Yanjiusuo - Guangdong Medical Information Institute, No. 2, Jinbuli, Huifu Xilu, Guangzhou, Guangdong 510180, People's Republic of China. TEL 884610. Ed. Zhu Fumin.

610   CC
GUANGXI ZHONGYI YAO/GUANGXI TRADITIONAL CHINESE MEDICINE. (Text in Chinese) bi-m. Guangxi Zhongyi Xueyuan - Guangxi Institute of Traditional Chinese Medicine, 21 Mingxiu Donglu, Nanning, Guangxi 530001, People's Republic of China. TEL 32101. (Co-sponsor: Zhonghua Quanguo Zhongyi Xuehui, Guangxi Fenhui) Ed. Ban Qiuwen.

610   CC
GUANGZHOU ZHONGYI XUEYUAN XUEBAO/GUANGZHOU INSTITUTE OF TRADITIONAL CHINESE MEDICINE. JOURNAL. (Text in Chinese) q. Guangzhou Zhongyi Xueyuan - Guangzhou Institute of Traditional Chinese Medicine, Sanyuanli, Guangzhou, Guangdong 510407, People's Republic of China. TEL 661233. Ed. Ou Ming.

610   SP   ISSN 0214-4689
GUIA DE CONGRESOS MEDICOS JANO. 1987. 3/yr. free to qualified personnel. Ediciones Doyma S.A., Travesera de Gracia, 17-21, 08021 Barcelona, Spain. TEL 200-07-11. FAX 209-11-36. TELEX 51964 INK E. Ed. C. Ribera Banus. adv.; page 290000 ptas.; trim 230 x 295; adv. contact: Francisco Torras. circ. 25,000.
Description: Offers information on congresses, courses, reunions, symposiums, and round tables at national and international levels.

GUIA DEL EQUIPAMIENTO HOSPITALARIO. see
INSTRUMENTS

610   FR
GUIDE ROSENWALD: ANNUAIRE MEDICAL. 1887. a. 1130 F.($200) (typically set in Dec.). I C Publications, 10 rue Vineuse, 75116 Paris, France. TEL 45-20-93-36. FAX 45-20-81-74. adv.; circ. 10,000.
Formerly: Guide Rosenwald: Annuaire Medical et Pharmaceutique (ISSN 0072-8209)

610   US   ISSN 0888-6768
RA396.A3
GUIDE TO THE ESSENTIALS OF A MODERN MEDICAL PRACTICE ACT. triennial. $10. Federation of State Medical Boards, 6000 Western Pl., Ste. 707, Fort Worth, TX 76107-4618. TEL 817-735-8445. FAX 817-738-6629. Ed. Dale G. Breaden.

GUIDELINES FOR HEALTH SUPERVISION II. see
HOSPITALS

610   UK   ISSN 0952-0643
▼**GULLET.** 1990. 4/yr. £118($129) Churchill Livingstone Medical Journals, Robert Stevenson House, 1-3 Baxter's Pl., Leith Walk, Edinburgh EH1 3AF, Scotland. TEL 031-556-2424. FAX 031-558-1278. TELEX 727511. (Subscr. to: Longman Group, Journals Subscr. Dept., P.O. Box 77, Fourth Ave., Harlow, Essex CM19 5AA, England; U.S. subscr. to: Churchill Livingstone, 650 Ave. of the Americas, New York, NY 10011. TEL 212-206-5000) Eds. J.R. Bennet, G.G. Jamieson. adv.; bk.rev. **Indexed:** Excerp.Med. (1992-).
—BLDSC shelfmark: 4230.518000.
Description: Explores original and review material covering all aspects of oesophagal disorders, their aetiology, investigation and diagnosis, and both medical and surgical treatment.

610   JA   ISSN 0386-0760
CODEN: GRMSBU
GUNMA REPORTS ON MEDICAL SCIENCES/GUNMA REPOTO. (Text in English and European languages) 1952. s-a. Gunma University, School of Medicine - Gunma Daigaku Igakubu, 39-22 Showa-machi, Maebashi, Gunma-ken 371, Japan. Ed.Bd. illus.; circ. 700. **Indexed:** Biol.Abstr., Chem.Abstr.
Supersedes (in Jan. 1970): Gunma Journal of Medical Sciences (ISSN 0017-565X)

612.015   CC
GUOWAI YIXUE (LINCHUANG SHENGWU HUAXUE YU JIANYAN FENCE/FOREIGN MEDICAL SCIENCE (CLINICAL BIOCHEMISTRY AND INSPECTION). (Text in Chinese) bi-m. Chongqing Yixue Qingbao Yanjiusuo - Chongqing Medical Science Information Research Institute, 44 Qingnian Lu, Chongqing, Sichuan 630010, People's Republic of China. TEL 41978.

MEDICAL SCIENCES

610 CC
GUOWAI YIXUE - NEIKEXUE FENCE/FOREIGN MEDICAL SCIENCE - INTERNAL MEDICINE. (Text in Chinese) m. Zhongshan Yike Daxue - Sun Yat-sen Medical University, 74 Zhongshan Erlu, Guangzhou, Guangdong 510089, People's Republic of China. TEL 778223. Ed. Liang Sudi.

610 US ISSN 0882-696X
GUTHRIE JOURNAL. vol.40, 1970. q. free. Donald Guthrie Foundation for Medical Research, Sayre, PA 18840. TEL 717-888-6666. Ed. Dr. Ralph D. Zehr. bk.rev.; charts; illus.; index; circ. 6,400. **Indexed:** C.I.S. Abstr., Chem.Abstr., Excerp.Med.
Former titles (until vol.55, 1985): Guthrie Bulletin (ISSN 0735-4592); Guthrie Clinic Bulletin (ISSN 0017-5838)

H C E A EXHIBITORS ADVISORY COUNCIL'S ACTION MEMO. (Healthcare Convention & Exhibitors Association) see *MEETINGS AND CONGRESSES*

610 US ISSN 0891-6624
H M O PRACTICE. 1987. q. $50 to individuals (foreign $65); institutions $70 (foreign $80). H M O Group, 900 Guaranty Bldg., Buffalo, NY 14202. TEL 716-857-6361. Ed. Dr. Leonard A. Katz. adv.; circ. 25,322. (also avail. in microform from UMI)
—BLDSC shelfmark: 4319.370000.
Description: Focuses on issues of concern to physicians and clinical health professionals practicing in HMOs. Includes clinical practice and research, management of prepaid healthcare, and the impact of the health care environment on the HMO delivery system.

HADASHOT KUPOT HOLIM. see *INSURANCE*

362 JA ISSN 0017-6605
HAGEMI/ENCOURAGEMENT; a journal for the guidance of the parents with crippled children. (Text in Japanese) 1955. bi-m. 3100 Yen. Japanese Society for Disabled Children - Nihon Shitai Fujiyuji Kyokai, 1-7, 1-chome, Komone, Itabashi-ku, Tokyo 173, Japan. Ed.Bd. adv.; bk.rev.; charts; illus.; stat.; circ. 10,000.
Description: Medical and educational facts for parents and rehabilitation workers involved with the disabled.

610 CC
HAINAN YIXUE/HAINAN MEDICAL SCIENCE. (Text in Chinese) q. Hainan Sheng Yixuehui - Hainan Medical Society, No. 42, Haifu Dadao, Haikou, Hainan 570003, People's Republic of China. TEL 32513. Ed. Zheng Jianchao.

610 GW
HAMBURG-MANNHEIMER-STIFTUNG FUER INFORMATIONSMEDIZIN. SCHRIFTENREIHE. 1985. irreg., vol.5, 1991. price varies. (Hamburg-Mannheimer Stiftung fuer Informationsmedizin) Ferdinand Enke Verlag, Postfach 101254, 7000 Stuttgart 10, Germany. TEL 0711-8931-0. FAX 0711-8931-419. TELEX 07252275-GTV-D.

610 PK ISSN 0250-7188
HAMDARD MEDICUS; journal of science and medicine. (Text in English) 1957. q. Rs.120($20) Hamdard Foundation, Nazimabad No. 3, Karachi 18, Pakistan. Ed. Hakim Mohammed Said. adv.; bk.rev.; charts; circ. 2,000. (back issues avail.) **Indexed:** Abstr.Hyg., Biol.Abstr., Curr.Adv.Ecol.Sci., Trop.Dis.Bull.
Former titles: Hamdard; Hamdard Medical Digest (ISSN 0017-7024)

610 NE ISSN 0167-5567
RB131
HANDBOOK OF INFLAMMATION. 1979. irreg., vol.6, 1989. Elsevier Science Publishers B.V., Books Division, P.O. Box 211, 1000 AE Amsterdam, Netherlands. TEL 020-5803911. FAX 020-5803705. TELEX 18582 ESPA NL. (Subscr. in U.S. and Canada to: Elsevier Science Publishing Co., Inc., Box 882, Madison Sq. Sta., New York, NY 10159. TEL 212-989-5800) Ed.Bd.
Refereed Serial

HANDBOOK OF MEDICAL EDUCATION. see *EDUCATION — Guides To Schools And Colleges*

616.02 US ISSN 0072-9841
HANDBOOK OF MEDICAL TREATMENT.* 1949. biennial. $7.50. Jones Medical Publications, 355 Los Cerros Dr., Greenbrae, CA 94904. Ed. Milton J. Chatton.

610 615.9 US
HANDBOOK OF NATURAL TOXINS. 1983. irreg., vol.6, 1991. Marcel Dekker, Inc., 270 Madison Ave., New York, NY 10016. TEL 212-696-9000. FAX 212-685-4540. TELEX 421419.
Refereed Serial

610 UK
▼**HANDBOOK OF PRACTICE TREATMENT.** 1992. 4/yr. Churchill Livingstone Medical Journals, Robert Stevenson House, 1-3 Baxter's Pl., Leith Walk, Edinburgh EH1 3AF, Scotland. TEL 031-556-2424. FAX 031-558-1278. TELEX 727511. (Subscr. to: Longman Group, Journals Subscr. Dept., P.O. Box 77, Fourth Ave., Harlow, Essex CM19 5AA, England; U.S. subscr. to: Churchill Livingstone, 650 Ave. of the Americas, New York, NY 10011. TEL 212-206-5000) Ed. Dr. J. Hasler.
Description: Provides updates to help practice managers and partners cope with the demands of general practice in the 90s.

612 US ISSN 0072-9906
HANDBOOK OF SENSORY PHYSIOLOGY. (Supplement avail.: Foundations of Sensory Science) 1971. irreg., vol.9, 1984. price varies. Springer-Verlag, 175 Fifth Ave., New York, NY 10010. TEL 212-460-1500. (Also Berlin, Heidelberg, Tokyo, Vienna) (reprint service avail. from ISI)

610 US
HANDBOOK OF THE SPINAL CORD. 1983. irreg., vol.5, 1987. Marcel Dekker, Inc., 270 Madison Ave., New York, NY 10016. TEL 212-696-9000. FAX 212-685-4540. TELEX 421419.
Refereed Serial

610 GW
HANDBUCH FUER DAS GESUNDHEITSWESEN IN SCHLESWIG-HOLSTEIN. 1948. a. DM.43.50. Boettcher und Buelter, Justus-von-Liebig-Str. 2-4, 2350 Neumuenster, Germany. FAX 4321-5042. adv.; circ. 5,000.
Description: Listing of doctors, dentists, hospitals, etc. in Schleswig-Holstein.

610.73 AU ISSN 0073-0181
R500
HANDBUCH FUER DIE SANITAETSBERUFE OESTERREICH. 1950. a. S.720. Verlag Dieter Goeschl GmbH, Andergasse 10, A-1170 Vienna, Austria. TEL 0222-464240. FAX 0222-454902. Ed. K.H. Kux. adv.; index; circ. 7,200.

616.9 575.1 US
HARVARD A I D S INSTITUTE SERIES ON GENE REGULATION OF HUMAN RETROVIRUSES. 1991. irreg. price varies. Raven Press, 1185 Ave. of the Americas, New York, NY 10036. TEL 212-930-9500. FAX 212-869-3495.

HARVARD MEDICAL ALUMNI BULLETIN. see *COLLEGE AND ALUMNI*

610 US ISSN 0073-0874
R111.H33 CODEN: HALEAA
HARVEY LECTURES. 1953. irreg., vol.79, 1985. Academic Press, Inc., 1250 Sixth Ave., San Diego, CA 92101. TEL 619-231-0926. FAX 619-699-6715. cum.index: series 1-50 in series 50 (1956). (reprint service avail. from ISI) **Indexed:** Biol.Abstr., Chem.Abstr, Curr.Adv.Ecol.Sci., Ind.Med., Ind.Sci.Rev., Sci.Cit.Ind.
Refereed Serial

610 100 US ISSN 0093-0334
R724 CODEN: HSCRAS
HASTINGS CENTER REPORT. 1971. bi-m. $52 to individuals; libraries and institutions $65; students and senior citizens $40. Hastings Center, 255 Elm Rd., Briarcliff Manor, NY 10510. TEL 914-762-8500. Ed. Bette Crigger. bk.rev.; bibl.; index; circ. 11,700. (also avail. in microform from RPI; reprint service avail. from UMI) **Indexed:** Acad.Ind., Biol.Abstr., Curr.Cont., Curr.Lit.Fam.Plan., Fut.Surv., Gen.Sci.Ind., Hlth.Ind., Ind.Med., Med.Care Rev., P.A.I.S., Phil.Ind., Rel.Ind.One, Soc.Sci.Ind., Soc.Work Res.& Abstr., SSCI. Key Title: Report - Hastings Center.
—BLDSC shelfmark: 4273.019000.
Formerly: Hastings Center Studies (ISSN 0093-3252)

610 GW ISSN 0934-3164
HAUSARZT IN HESSEN. bi-m. DM.52. (Berufsverband der Praktischen Aerzte) Berliner Medizinische Verlagsanstalt, Kurfuerstenstr. 112, 1000 Berlin 30, Germany. TEL 030-219909-0. FAX 030-21990910. (Co-sponsor: Aerzte fuer Allgemeinmedizin Deutschlands e.V.) Ed. Dr. Wolfgang Weber. adv.; bk.rev.; circ. 5,000. (back issues avail.; reprint service avail. from UMI)

610 GW
HAUSARZT IN THUERINGEN. 1989. bi-m. DM.52. (Landesverband Thueringen in B P A) Berliner Medizinische Verlagsanstalt GmbH, Kurfuerstenstr. 112-113, 1000 Berlin 30, Germany. TEL 030-219909-0. FAX 030-219909-10. circ. 3,000.

610 US ISSN 0017-8594
CODEN: HWMJAE
HAWAII MEDICAL JOURNAL. 1941. m. $18. Hawaii Medical Association, 1360 S. Beretania St., 2nd Fl., Honolulu, HI 96814. TEL 808-536-7702. FAX 808-528-2376. Ed. J. Frederick Reppun, MD. adv.; bk.rev.; charts; illus.; index; circ. 1,600. (also avail. in microform from ISI,UMI) **Indexed:** Abstr.Hyg., Biol.Abstr., Chem.Abstr., Curr.Adv.Cancer Res., Curr.Adv.Ecol.Sci., Curr.Cont., Excerp.Med., Ind.Med., Soc.Work Res.& Abstr., Trop.Dis.Bull.
—BLDSC shelfmark: 4273.903000.

HAWAII'S NATIONAL GAY COMMUNITY NEWS; Hawaii and Western States. see *HOMOSEXUALITY*

610 CN
HEAD TO TOE. 1983. q. free. British Columbia Medical Association, 115-1665 W. Broadway, Vancouver, B.C. V6J 5A4, Canada. TEL 604-736-5551. FAX 604-736-4566. Ed. Avrill Peters. circ. 30,000. (back issues avail.)

610 US
▼**HEADACHE QUARTERLY**; current treatment and research. 1990. q. $45 to individuals (foreign $60); institutions $65 (foreign $90). International Universities Press, Inc., Journal Department, 59 Boston Post Rd., Box 1524, Madison, CT 06443-1524. TEL 203-245-4000. FAX 203-245-0775. (Co-sponsors: Diamond Headache Foundation, Inpatient Headache Unit of Weiss Memorial Hospital) Ed. Dr. Seymour Diamond. adv.; bk.rev.; abstr.; charts.
Description: Reports on current research, futuristic therapies and headache theories. Covers histamines, serotonin, prostaglandins, radiological and diagnostic advances and behavioral medicine.
Refereed Serial

610 US
HEADLINES; the brain injury magazine. q. New Medico Head Injury System, 14 Central Ave., Lynn, MA 01901-9963. TEL 617-596-4914. FAX 617-596-1670. Ed. Ann Saydah. circ. 300,000.
Description: Studies the many facets of brain injury and presents new research.

HEALTH ACTION. see *HOSPITALS*

610 US
HEALTH ACTION NEWSLETTER. 1985. bi-m. $49.50. (National Association of Employers on Health Care Action) Blue Book, Inc., Box 220, Key Biscayne, FL 33149. TEL 305-361-2810. FAX 305-361-2842. Ed. Ruth H. Stack. circ. 500.

HEALTH & HEALING. see *PHYSICAL FITNESS AND HYGIENE*

HEALTH & MEDICAL HORIZONS. see *PHYSICAL FITNESS AND HYGIENE*

610 US
HEALTH & WEALTH GUARDIAN. 1988. q. $18. Health & Wealth Guardian, Ltd., 462 S. Gilbert Rd., Mesa, AZ 85204. TEL 602-829-8888. FAX 602-835-5741. (European addr.: Island Resources National House, Santon, Isle of Man, British Isles) Ed. Phillip Fry. adv.; bk.rev.; circ. 5,000. (back issues avail.)
Formerly: International Medical Advances Now!
Description: Reports advances and news about health, medicine, tax planning and asset protection in Europe and N. America.

MEDICAL SCIENCES 3103

610 362 UK ISSN 0374-8014
CODEN: HBHSA5
HEALTH BULLETIN. 1941. bi-m. £6. H.M.S.O., Scottish Home and Health Department, St. Andrew's House, Edinburgh EH1 3DE, Scotland. FAX 031-2442683. TELEX 72202. Ed. Dr. J. Forrester. index; circ. 11,500. (back issues avail.) **Indexed:** Abstr.Health Care Manage.Stud., Abstr.Hyg., ASSIA, Biol.Abstr., CINAHL, Curr.Adv.Ecol.Sci., Dent.Ind., Excerp.Med., Ind.Med., Med. Care Rev, Nutr.Abstr., Trop.Dis.Bull. —BLDSC shelfmark: 4274.935400.

610 US
HEALTH BUSINESS. w. $595. Faulkner & Gray, Healthcare Information Center (Subsidiary of: J P T Publishing Group), 1133 15th St., N.W., Ste. 450, Washington, DC 20005. TEL 202-828-4150. FAX 202-828-2352. Ed. John Reichard.
Description: Covers financial and economic aspects of the US health care industry.

362.1 US ISSN 0195-8631
RA410.53
HEALTH CARE FINANCING REVIEW. (Annual supplement avail.) 1979. q. $19 (foreign $23.75). U.S. Health Care Financing Administration, Department of Health and Human Services, Oak Meadows Bldg., Rm. 1A9, 6325 Security Blvd., Baltimore, MD 21207. TEL 410-966-6572. (Dist. by: Supt. of Documents, Washington, DC 20402) Ed. Linda F. Wolf. (also avail. in microform from UMI) **Indexed:** ABI Inform, Abstr.Health Care Manage.Stud., Amer.Stat.Ind., CLOA, Excerp.Med., Hosp.Lit.Ind., Ind.U.S.Gov.Per., Med.Care Rev., MEDOC, PROMT, Soc.Work Res.& Abstr., World Bibl.Soc.Sec.
Description: Includes statistics and projections on health expenditures; research articles on health care financing and delivery; policy and legislation affecting the Medicare and Medicaid programs.

HEALTH CAREER POST. see *HOSPITALS*

HEALTH CONSEQUENCES OF SMOKING. see *DRUG ABUSE AND ALCOHOLISM*

610 US
▼**HEALTH DEVICES INSPECTION & PREVENTIVE MAINTENANCE SYSTEM.** 1990. a. $695. (Emergency Care Research Institute) E C R I, 5200 Butler Pike, Plymouth Meeting, PA 19462. TEL 215-825-6000. FAX 215-834-1275. Ed. Susan Bastnagel.
Refereed Serial

681 US ISSN 0278-3452
R856.48
HEALTH DEVICES SOURCEBOOK. 1979. a. $245 (foreign $265). (Emergency Care Research Institute) E C R I, 5200 Butler Pike, Plymouth Meeting, PA 19462. TEL 215-825-6000. FAX 215-834-1275. Ed. Dorothy Wood.
●Also available online. Vendor(s): DIALOG (File no.188).
Description: Directory of medical device manufacturers and their product lines. Includes service firms which lease or repair equipment, and which buy and sell used equipment.
Refereed Serial

610 US
HEALTH DIGEST. q. Whittle Communications L.P., 333 Main Ave., Knoxville, TN 37902. TEL 615-595-5300. Ed. Ron King.
Description: Presents factual information about gastroenterology procedures and medications, tips on relieving common symptoms and discomforts, and advice for reducing stress that may complicate an ailment.

338.476 UK ISSN 1057-9230
CODEN: HEECEZ
▼**HEALTH ECONOMICS.** 1992. q. $145. John Wiley & Sons Ltd., Journals, Baffins Lane, Chichester, Sussex PO19 1UD, England. TEL 0243-779777. FAX 0243-775878. TELEX 86290-WIBOOK-G. Eds. Alan Maynard, John Hutton.
Description: Contains articles on all aspects of health economics: theoretical contributions, empirical studies, economic evaluations and analyses of health policy from the economic perspective.

610 US ISSN 0195-8402
RA440.A1 CODEN: HEQUDC
HEALTH EDUCATION QUARTERLY. 1957-1978; resumed 1980. q. $165 (foreign $215). (Society for Public Health Education) John Wiley & Sons, Inc., Journals, 605 Third Ave., New York, NY 10158-0012. TEL 212-692-6000. Ed. Noreen M. Clark. adv.; circ. 2,200. (also avail. in microform from RPI; reprint service avail. from RPI) **Indexed:** Cont.Pg.Educ., Excerp.Med., NRN, Phys.Ed.Ind., Psychol.Abstr., Risk Abstr., Soc.Work Res.& Abstr., Sociol.Abstr.
—BLDSC shelfmark: 4275.011400.
Supersedes (in 1980): Health Education Monographs (ISSN 0073-1455)
Description: Discusses the promotion of public health by elevating the quality of health education, improving medical practice, and stimulating research.
Refereed Serial

HEALTH EDUCATION RESEARCH; theory and practice. see *SOCIAL SERVICES AND WELFARE*

610 US ISSN 0742-8081
HEALTH EXCHANGE. 1984. q. Medical Group Management Association, 104 Inverness Terrace E., Englewood, CO 80112. TEL 303-799-1111. Ed. Brenda Hull. (back issues avail.)
Description: Covers health maintenance and wellness topics used as a marketing tool by group practices. Geared toward the education of patients.

610 US
HEALTH INDUSTRY BUYERS GUIDE. 1940. a. $105. S - N Publications, Inc., 103 N. Second St., Ste. 200, W. Dundee, IL 60118. TEL 708-426-6100. FAX 708-426-6416. Ed. Mike Kennedy. adv.; circ. 4,000. (also avail. in microform from UMI)
Formerly: Surgical Trade Buyers Guide (ISSN 0081-9654)

610 ISSN 0745-4678
CODEN: HITOD3
HEALTH INDUSTRY TODAY. 1938. m. $277 to individuals (foreign $295). Business Word, 770 LaSalle St., Ste. 701, Chicago, IL 60610-3541. FAX 312-943-9682. Ed. Donald E.L. Johnson. adv.; bk.rev.; illus.; stat.; index; circ. 1,600. (also avail. in microform from UMI; reprint service avail. from UMI) **Indexed:** PROMT.
—BLDSC shelfmark: 4275.016700.
Formerly (until 1982): Surgical Business (ISSN 0039-6095)

HEALTH INFORMATION AND LIBRARIES; international journal for medical, health and welfare librarians and information officers. see *LIBRARY AND INFORMATION SCIENCES*

610 UK ISSN 0268-5973
HEALTH INFORMATION SERVICE. 1983. m. £60. (Newcastle-upon-Tyne Polytechnic Library) Newcastle-upon-Tyne Polytechnic Products Ltd., Ellison Place, Newcastle-upon-Tyne NE1 8ST, England. TEL 091-235 8148.

610 KE
HEALTH INFORMATION SYSTEM. 1977. q. Ministry of Health, Division of Health Information System, P.O. Box 20781, Nairobi, Kenya. TEL 501341.

610 658 US
HEALTH LABOR RELATIONS ALERT.* 1981. m. $119. National Health Publishing, 428 E. Preston St., Baltimore, MD 21202-3923. TEL 301-363-6400. circ. 175.
Incorporates (in Jan. 1990): Director of Nursing Labor Alert (ISSN 0272-636X)
Description: Information on effective management of labor.

HEALTH LAWYER. see *LAW*

HEALTH LAWYERS NEWS REPORT. see *LAW*

614 US ISSN 0899-8965
KF3821.A15
HEALTH LEGISLATION AND REGULATION. 1975. w. (50/yr.). $595. Faulkner & Gray, Healthcare Information Center (Subsidiary of: J P T Publishing Group), 1133 15th St., N.W., Ste. 450, Washington, DC 20005. TEL 202-828-4150. FAX 202-828-2352. Ed. Jeanine Mjoseth. index. (looseleaf format; back issues avail.) **Indexed:** Med.Care Rev.
Former titles (until 1986): Washington Report on Health Legislation and Regulation (ISSN 0740-7793); (until 1983): Washington Report on Health Legislation (ISSN 0098-2512)
Description: Covers health care related legislative issues at the federal and congressional level.

610 650 US ISSN 0882-598X
HEALTH LETTER (WASHINGTON). 1985. m. $18. Public Citizen Health Research Group, 2000 P St. N.W., Washington, DC 20036. TEL 202-872-0320. FAX 202-785-3584. Ed. Sidney M. Wolfe. bk.rev.; circ. 35,000.
Description: Information on common health problems as well as information pried from tightly sealed government and industry files.

610 US
HEALTH MANAGER'S UPDATE. 1986. bi-w. $215. Faulkner & Gray, Inc. (New York), 11 Penn Plaza, 17th Fl., New York, NY 10001. TEL 212-967-7000. FAX 212-967-7155. Ed. Susan Namovicz.
Description: Provides timely briefings on the latest legislative, regulatory, and business developments.

610 CN ISSN 0821-3925
HEALTH NEWS (TORONTO); your authoritative guide to current health issues. French edition: Action Sante (ISSN 1180-1050) 1983. bi-m. Can.$14.95($18.95) University of Toronto, Faculty of Medicine, Medical Sciences Bldg., Toronto, Ont. M5S 1A8, Canada. TEL 416-978-5411. FAX 416-978-7552. Ed. Dr. June V. Engel. illus.; circ. 24,000. (back issues avail.) **Indexed:** Can.Per.Ind.
●Also available online. Vendor(s): Information Access Company.
Description: General health publication dealing with wellness, fitness, good eating habits, diseases, psychosocial topics.

610 US ISSN 1042-2781
HEALTH NEWS DAILY. 1989. d. $1,087 (effective Jan. 1991). F-D-C Reports, Inc., 5550 Friendship Blvd., Ste. One, Chevy Chase, MD 20815. TEL 301-657-9830. FAX 301-656-3094. Ed. John Zakotnik.
●Also available online. Vendor(s): BRS (HNDY), Data-Star, DIALOG, NewsNet.
Description: Information service for executives and decision-makers in the health industries.

610 614 US ISSN 0440-5609
R711 .H4
HEALTH ORGANIZATIONS OF THE U.S., CANADA AND THE WORLD; a directory of voluntary associations, professional societies and other groups concerned with health and related fields. 1961. irreg., 5th ed., 1981. $90. Gale Research Inc., 835 Penobscot Bldg., Detroit, MI 48226. TEL 313-961-2242. FAX 313-961-6083. TELEX 810-221-7086. Eds. Paul Wasserman, Marek Kaszubski.
Description: Directory of volunteer and professional health organizations worldwide.

HEALTH - P A C BULLETIN. (Health Policy Advisory Center) see *PUBLIC HEALTH AND SAFETY*

610 CN
HEALTH PERSONNEL IN CANADA/PERSONNEL DE LA SANTE AU CANADA. (Text in English and French) 1969. a. free. Department of National Health and Welfare, Health Information Division, Brooke Claxton Bldg., Ottawa, Ont. K1A 0K9, Canada. TEL 613-957-1372. FAX 613-952-0271. stat.; circ. 1,400.
Formerly (until 1988): Canada Health Manpower Inventory (ISSN 0381-2561)
Description: Provides year-end statistics for 38 occupational groups of health care practitioners over an 11-year period.

M

MEDICAL SCIENCES

610　　　　　　　US　　ISSN 0017-9078
QH505.A1　　　　　　　CODEN: HLTPAO
HEALTH PHYSICS; the radiation protection journal. 1958. m. (2 vols./yr.). $99 to individuals; institutions $475. (Health Physics Society) Williams & Wilkins, 428 E. Preston St., Baltimore, MD 21202. TEL 301-528-4000. FAX 301-528-4321. Ed. Richard Vetter. adv.; charts; illus.; stat.; index; circ. 6,800. (also avail. in microform from MIM,UMI; reprint service avail. from UMI; back issues avail.)
Indexed: Abstr.Health Care Manage.Stud., Abstr.Hyg., Appl.Mech.Rev., Biol.Abstr., C.I.S. Abstr., Chem.Abstr., Curr.Adv.Ecol.Sci., Curr.Cont., Dairy Sci.Abstr., Deep Sea Res.& Oceanogr.Abstr., Dent.Ind., Dok.Arbeitsmed., Energy Info.Abstr., Energy Rev., Environ.Abstr., Environ.Per.Bibl., Excerp.Med., Food Sci.& Tech.Abstr., Ind.Med., Ind.Vet., INIS Atomind., Int.Aerosp.Abstr., Nutr.Abstr., Ocean.Abstr., Pollut.Abstr., Poult.Abstr., Risk Abstr., Sci.Abstr., Sci.Cit.Ind, So.Pac.Per.Ind., Soils & Fert., Vet.Bull., W.R.C.Inf.
—BLDSC shelfmark: 4275.100000.
Refereed Serial

HEALTH PHYSICS SOCIETY. NEWSLETTER. see *MEDICAL SCIENCES — Radiology And Nuclear Medicine*

610　　　　　　　US　　ISSN 0162-3605
　　　　　　　　　　　　　CODEN: DRRSAL
HEALTH POLICY & BIOMEDICAL RESEARCH: THE BLUE SHEET. 1957. w. $340 (foreign $415). F-D-C Reports, Inc., 5550 Friendship Blvd., Ste. One, Chevy Chase, MD 20815. TEL 301-657-9830. FAX 301-656-3094. (looseleaf format; back issues avail.) **Indexed:** P.N.I., Rehabil.Lit.
•Also available online. Vendor(s): Mead Data Central.
Formerly: Drug Research Reports: The Blue Sheet (ISSN 0012-6608)
Description: Includes issues relating to Medicare, Medicaid, public health, health professions education and supply, health planning, and federal programs affecting the nation's health care system and industry.

HEALTH PSYCHOLOGY. see *PSYCHOLOGY*

610　　　　　　　CN
HEALTH SCIENCES INFORMATION IN CANADA: ASSOCIATIONS/INFORMATION EN SCIENCES DE LA SANTE AU CANADA: ASSOCIATIONS. irreg. Can.$18. (National Research Council of Canada - Conseil National de Recherches du Canada) C.I.S.T.I. Health Sciences Resource Centre, Ottawa, Ont. K1A 0S2, Canada. TEL 613-993-1604.

610　　　　　　　CN
HEALTH SCIENCES INFORMATION IN CANADA: LIBRARIES/INFORMATION EN SCIENCES DE LA SANTE AU CANADA: BIBLIOTHEQUES. irreg. Can.$20. (National Research Council of Canada - Conseil National de Recherches du Canada) C.I.S.T.I. Health Sciences Resource Centre, Ottawa, Ont. K1A 0S2, Canada. TEL 613-993-1604.

610.6　　　　UK　　ISSN 0951-4848
HEALTH SERVICES MANAGEMENT RESEARCH. 1988. 3/yr. £64($112) (University of Birmingham, Health Services Management Centre) Longman Group UK Ltd., Westgate House, The High, Harlow, Essex CM20 1YR, England. TEL 0279-442601. Ed. Peter Spurgeon. circ. 400.
—BLDSC shelfmark: 4275.108200.
Description: Current research and its implications for management.

610 614　　　　US　　ISSN 0017-9124
RA960　　　　　　　　　CODEN: HESRA
HEALTH SERVICES RESEARCH. 1965. bi-m. $50 (foreign $60). (Foundation of the American College of Healthcare Executives) Health Administration Press, 1021 E. Huron St., Ann Arbor, MI 48104-9990. TEL 312-943-0544. FAX 708-450-1618. (Subscr. to: Order Processing Center, 1951 Cornell Ave., Melrose Park, IL 60160-1001) (Co-sponsors: Association for Health Services Research, Hospital Research and Educational Trust) Ed. Gordon DeFriese. circ. 2,600. (also avail. in microform from UMI; reprint service avail. from UMI) **Indexed:** ABI Inform, Abstr.Health Care Manage.Stud., Abstr.Hyg., BPIA, Bus.Ind., CINAHL, Curr.Cont, Excerp.Med., Hosp.Lit.Ind., I.P.A., Ind.Med., Int.Nurs.Ind., Manage.Cont., Med.Care Rev., MEDSOC, SSCI, Tr.& Indus.Ind., Trop.Dis.Bull.
—BLDSC shelfmark: 4275.120000.
Description: Provides those engaged in research, public policy formulation, health care administration, education, and practice with advance information on new trends and the latest techniques of research and evaluation, enabling them to take advantage of current and significant research.
Refereed Serial

610 600　　　　US
HEALTH TECHNOLOGY MANAGEMENT. a. $315 (Canada $335; elsewhere $325). (Emergency Care Research Institute) E C R I, 5200 Butler Pike, Plymouth Meeting, PA 19462. TEL 215-825-6000. FAX 215-834-1275. Ed. Michael Argentieri.
Refereed Serial

610 614　　　　UK　　ISSN 0017-9132
RA485　　　　　　　　　CODEN: HETBAT
HEALTH TRENDS. 1969. q. £10. Departments of Health and Social Security, Hannibal House, Elephant and Castle, London SE1 6TE, England. (Subscr. to: H.M.S.O. Publications Centre, 51, Nine Elms Lane, London SW8 5DP, England) Ed. Valerie M. Willcocks. **Indexed:** Abstr.Health Care Manage.Stud., Abstr.Hyg., ASSIA, Biol.Abstr., Curr.Adv.Ecol.Sci., Excerp.Med., Trop.Dis.Bull.
—BLDSC shelfmark: 4275.240000.

610 331.1　　　　US
HEALTH WAGE MONITOR. q. $150. D R I - McGraw-Hill, 24 Hartwell Ave., Lexington, MA 02173. TEL 617-563-5100. FAX 617-860-6332. TELEX 200285.

610 658.8　　　　US　　ISSN 0894-9980
HEALTHCARE COMMUNITY RELATIONS & MARKETING LETTER. 1987. 12/yr. $197. Health Resources Publishing, Brinley Professional Plaza, 3100 Hwy. 138, Box 1442, Wall Township, NJ 07719-1442. TEL 908-681-1133. FAX 908-681-0490. Ed. Robert K. Jenkins. (back issues avail.)
Description: Provides current news and innovations for the public and community relations and marketing professionals.

610　　　　　　　US
HEALTHCARE ENVIRONMENTAL MANAGEMENT SYSTEM. (Includes monthly updates) a. $695. (Emergency Care Research Institute) E C R I, 5200 Butler Pike, Plymouth Meeting, PA 19462. TEL 215-825-6000. FAX 215-834-1275. Ed. Paul Segal.
Refereed Serial

610 330　　　　US
HEALTHCARE TECHNOLOGY & BUSINESS OPPORTUNITIES. 1980. m. $325 (foreign $370). Biomedical Business International, 1524 Brookhollow Dr., Santa Ana, CA 92705-5426. TEL 714-755-5757. FAX 714-755-5704. (back issues avail.)
Formerly: Medical Product Development.
Description: Includes listing of technologies available for license and transfer, business opportunities, US, Japanese and European patent activity, and resources.

HEALTHCARE TRENDS AND TRANSITION. see *OCCUPATIONS AND CAREERS*

HEALTHDOCS. see *LIBRARY AND INFORMATION SCIENCES*

614　　　　　　　US　　ISSN 0738-811X
HEALTHFACTS. 1976. m. $21 (Canada and Mexico $24; Asia and Europe $33). Center for Medical Consumers, 237 Thompson St., New York, NY 10012. TEL 212-674-7105. FAX 212-674-7100. Ed. Maryann Napoli. bk.rev.; index. cum.index; circ. 12,000. (back issues avail.) **Indexed:** CHNI, Hlth.Ind.
—BLDSC shelfmark: 4275.247975.
Description: Designed for informed medical decision-making.

610 617.6　　　　US
HEALTHSTATE. 1982. q. University of Medicine and Dentistry of New Jersey, 100 Bergen St., Rm. 121, Newark, NJ 07103.

610　　　　　　　CC　　ISSN 1000-1581
HEBEI YIXUE YUAN XUEBAO/HEBEI ACADEMY OF MEDICAL SCIENCES. JOURNAL. (Text in Chinese) bi-m. Hebei Yixue Yuan - Hebei Academy of Medical Sciences, 5 Chang'an Xilu, Shijiazhuang, Hebei 050017, People's Republic of China. TEL 44121. Ed. Wu Shenchun.

610　　　　　　　CC
HEBEI ZHONGYI/HEBEI TRADITIONAL MEDICINE. (Text in Chinese) bi-m. Hebei Yixue Kexueyuan, Qingbao Yanjiusuo, Zhongyi Fenhui - Hebei Academy of Medical Sciences, Information Institute, Department of Traditional Medicine, 62 Qingyuan Jie, Shijiazhuang, Hebei 050021, People's Republic of China. TEL 612687. Ed. Xia Jintang.

613　　　　　　　GW　　ISSN 0017-9604
DIE HEILBERUFE; Magazin fuer Kranken-, Kinderkranken- und Altenpflege, Gesundheitserziehung und Rehabilitation. 1949. m. DM.33.60. Verlag Gesundheit GmbH, Neue Gruenstr. 18, 1020 Berlin, Germany. TEL 030-2700516. FAX 030-2754983. TELEX 114488. Ed. F. Dietze. adv.; bk.rev.; charts; illus.; index; circ. 60,000. **Indexed:** Excerp.Med.
—BLDSC shelfmark: 4284.190000.

610　　　　　　　CC　　ISSN 1000-9906
HEILONGJIANG ZHONGYIYAO/HEILONGJIANG TRADITIONAL CHINESE MEDICAL SCIENCE. (Text in Chinese) bi-m. Heilongjiang Zhongyi Yanjiuyuan - Heilongjiang Institute of Traditional Chinese Medicine, 72, Sanfu Jie, Xiangfang-qu, Harbin, Heilongjiang 150036, People's Republic of China. TEL 53086. Ed. Zhang Qi.
—BLDSC shelfmark: 4284.195780.

HEIM UND ANSTALT. see *FOOD AND FOOD INDUSTRIES*

610　　　　　　　II　　ISSN 0017-9922
HELAN MEDICAL MAGAZINE. (Text in Tamil) 1960. m. Rs.6. Thilaga Medical Publications, 28 Melaponnagaram, 8th St., Madurai 10, India. Ed. Dr. N. Thankaraj. adv.; pat.; circ. 1,000.

610　　　　　　　FI　　ISSN 0437-2468
HELSINGIN LAAKARILEHTI. 1954. 9/yr. FIM 160. Helsingin Laakariyhdistys r.y., Museokatu 13 A 2, 00100 Helsinki 10, Finland. TEL 90-490-403. FAX 358-0-408170. Ed. Dr. Olli Seppala. adv.; bk.rev.; circ. 13,500.
Description: Explores doctors' jobs, relations with the government, free time, education and pensions.

610 362.8 340　　　　US　　ISSN 0742-5376
R726
HEMLOCK QUARTERLY. 1980. q. $25. Hemlock Society, Box 11830, Eugene, OR 97440. TEL 503-342-5748. FAX 503-345-2751. Eds. Derek Humphry, Kris Larsen. circ. 50,000. (also avail. in looseleaf format; back issues avail.)

610　　　　　　　US　　ISSN 0883-2285
HEMOCHROMATOSIS AWARENESS; a quarterly update on hereditary and acquired iron-overload. 1982. q. free. Hemochromatosis Research Foundation, Inc., Box 8569, Albany, NY 12008. TEL 518-489-0972. Ed. Dr. Margit A. Krikker. bk.rev.; tr.lit.; circ. 1,500. (looseleaf format)
Description: Discusses all aspects of heriditary hemochromatosis, a disorder of iron metabolism, in which dietary iron absorption exceeds body needs. Reviews relevent literature and relevant public policy and food regulatory issues.

HENRY FORD HOSPITAL MEDICAL JOURNAL. see *HOSPITALS*

MEDICAL SCIENCES 3105

610 US ISSN 0270-9139
RC845 CODEN: HPTLD9
HEPATOLOGY (ST. LOUIS). 1981. m. $179 to individuals (foreign $215); institutions $279 (foreign $315); trainees $60 (foreign $96). (American Association for the Study of Liver Diseases) Mosby - Year Book, Inc. (Subsidiary of: Times Mirror Company), 11830 Westline Industrial Dr., St. Louis, MO 63146. TEL 800-325-4117. FAX 314-432-1380. TELEX 44-2402. Ed. Paul D. Berk. adv.; circ. 4,384. (also avail. in microform; back issues avail.) **Indexed:** Curr.Adv.Cancer Res., Curr.Adv.Ecol.Sci., Curr.Cont., Excerp.Med., Ind.Med., Ind.Sci.Rev., Ind.Vet., INIS Atomind., Poult.Abstr., Risk Abstr., Sci.Cit.Ind, Vet.Bull.
—BLDSC shelfmark: 4295.836000.
Description: Examines hepatitis, gallstone formation, drug injury, liver physiology and disease. For gastroenterologists and internists.
Refereed Serial

616.07 GW
HESSISCHES AERZTEBLATT. m. DM.132. Verlag Kirchheim und Co. GmbH, Kaiserstr. 41, Postfach 2524, 6500 Mainz, Germany. TEL 06131-671081. Ed.Bd. adv.; charts; illus.

616.07 615.8 IT ISSN 1120-7000
▼**HIP PATHOLOGY**; the journal of clinical and experimental research on hip pathology and therapy. 1991. q. L.140000($140) (effective 1992). Wichtig Editore s.r.l., Via Friuli, 72-74, 20135 Milan, Italy. TEL 02-5452306. FAX 02-5451843.

610 US ISSN 1050-9631
CODEN: HIPPEL
▼**HIPPOCAMPUS.** 1991. q. $79 to individuals (foreign $95); institutions $150 (foreign $166). Churchill Livingstone Medical Journals, 650 Ave. of the Americas, New York, NY 10011. TEL 212-206-5040. FAX 212-727-7808. TELEX 662266. (Dist. by: Transaction Publishers, Department 3091, Rutgers University, New Brunswick, NJ 08903. TEL 908-932-2280) Eds. Dr. David Amaral, Dr. Menno Witter.
—BLDSC shelfmark: 4315.255000.

610 US ISSN 0892-2977
RA773
HIPPOCRATES. 1987. bi-m. free to qualified personnel. Hippocrates Partners, 301 Howard St., 18th Fl., San Francisco, CA 94105-2252. TEL 415-512-9100. Ed. Eric W. Schrier. adv.; circ. controlled. **Indexed:** Hlth.Ind.
●Also available online.
Description: For medical professionals.

610 616.1 JA ISSN 0910-0377
HIROSAKI DAIGAKU IGAKUBU EISEIGAKU KYOSHITSU GYOSEKISHU. (Text in Japanese; summaries in English) 1954. irreg. Hirosaki Daigaku, Igakubu - Hirosaki University, School of Medicine, 5 Zaifu-cho, Hirosaki-shi, Aomori-ken 036, Japan. Ed. Naosuke Sasaki. circ. 90.

610 574 JA ISSN 0439-1721
CODEN: HIRIA6
HIROSAKI MEDICAL JOURNAL. (Text in English and Japanese, summaries in English) 1950. q. Hirosaki Daigaku, Igakubu - Hirosaki University, School of Medicine, 5 Zaifu-cho, Hirosaki-shi, Aomori-ken 036, Japan. circ. 400. **Indexed:** Excerp.Med.
—BLDSC shelfmark: 4315.570000.

610 JA ISSN 0018-2087
CODEN: HDIZAB
HIROSHIMA DAIGAKU IGAKU ZASSHI. English edition: Hiroshima University Journal of Medical Sciences (ISSN 0018-2052) (Text in Japanese; summaries in English) 1952. bi-m. 5000 Yen. Hiroshima University, School of Medicine - Hiroshima Daigaku Igakubu, 1-2-3 Kasumi, Hiroshima 734, Japan. Ed. Yoshiyasu Matsuo. bibl.; charts; illus.; index; circ. 450. **Indexed:** Biol.Abstr., Chem.Abstr, INIS Atomind.
—BLDSC shelfmark: 5527.820000.

610 JA ISSN 0018-2052
CODEN: HIJMAC
HIROSHIMA JOURNAL OF MEDICAL SCIENCES. Japanese edition: Hiroshima Daigaku Igaku Zasshi (ISSN 0018-2087) (Text in English) 1951. q. $20. Hiroshima University, School of Medicine - Hiroshima Daigaku Igakubu, 1-2-3 Kasumi, Hiroshima 734, Japan. Ed. Yoshiyasu Matsuo. bibl.; charts; illus.; index; circ. 600. (also avail. in microform from UMI; reprint service avail. from UMI) **Indexed:** Biol.Abstr., Chem.Abstr., Curr.Adv.Ecol.Sci., Curr.Cont., Dairy Sci.Abstr., Dent.Ind., Excerp.Med., Helminthol.Abstr., Ind.Med., Ind.Sci.Rev., INIS Atomind., Sci.Cit.Ind.
—BLDSC shelfmark: 4315.600000.

610 JA ISSN 0018-2044
CODEN: HIRIA6
HIROSHIMA MEDICAL ASSOCIATION. JOURNAL/HIROSHIMA IGAKU. (Text in Japanese) 1896. m. 1700 Yen($13) Hiroshima Medical Association - Hiroshima Igakkai, 1-1-1 Kannonhon-machi, Hiroshima 733, Japan. FAX 082-293-3363. Ed. Dr. Sumio Sugimoto. adv.; bibl.; charts; illus.; index; circ. 5,700 (controlled). **Indexed:** C.I.S. Abstr., Chem.Abstr., INIS Atomind.

610 SP ISSN 0018-2125
HISPALIS MEDICA; revista Sevillana de medicina y cirugia. 1944. m. $50. Miguel y Rafael Rios Mozo, Eds. & Pubs., Gravina 29, Seville, Spain. adv.; bk.rev.; abstr.; bibl.; illus.; index. cum.index; circ. 1,000. **Indexed:** Chem.Abstr., Dent.Ind., Ind.Med.Esp., Nutr.Abstr.
—BLDSC shelfmark: 4315.750000.

610 JA
HOKKAIDO JOURNAL OF MEDICAL SCIENCE. (Text in English, Japanese) 1923. bi-m. 6000 Yen. Hokkaido Medical Society - Hokkaido Daigaku Igakubu, Nishi 7-chome, Kita-15-jo, Kita-ku, Sapporo-shi 060, Japan. Ed. Masamichi Kato. adv.; circ. 1,200. (back issues avail.)

610 CN
HOLOGRAM.* 1983. 6/yr. $5 per no. Canadian Holistic Medical Association, 420 MacDonnell St., Toronto, Ont. K7L 4E4, Canada. TEL 613-542-5663. Ed. Zoltan Rona. circ. 600.

610 US
HOLOS PRACTICE REPORT. 1985. bi-m. $25. Holos Institute of Health, 1328 E. Evergreen, Springfield, MO 65803. TEL 417-865-5940. Ed. Dr. C. Norman Shealy. bk.rev.; index; circ. 250. (looseleaf format; back issues avail.)
Description: Covers alternative approaches to medical and psychological treatments.

HOMBRE Y TRABAJO; boletin de medicina, seguridad e higiene. see *PUBLIC HEALTH AND SAFETY*

612 CN
HOME HEALTH CARE. 1988. bi-m. Home Health Care Publishing Inc., 26 Dorchester Ave., Toronto, Ont. M8Z 4W3, Canada. TEL 416-253-9963. FAX 416-253-4506. adv.; circ. 12,597.

610 US ISSN 0884-741X
CODEN: HHNUEJ
HOME HEALTHCARE NURSE. 1970-1985; resumed 1987. bi-m. $30 to individuals (foreign $40); institutions $40 (foreign $80). J.B. Lippincott Co., E. Washington Sq., Philadelphia, PA 19105. (Subscr. to: National Fulfillment Services, 100 Pine Ave, Holmes, PA, 19043. TEL 800-345-8112) adv.; bk.rev.; illus.; stat.; tr.lit.; circ. 10,200. (also avail. in microfilm from UMI; back issues avail.; reprint service avail. from UMI) **Indexed:** CINAHL, Int.Nurs.Ind., Nurs.Abstr.
Former titles: Home Healthcare Business (ISSN 0744-4923); Patient Aid Digest.

610 HK ISSN 1010-8424
CODEN: JHKAEY
HONG KONG MEDICAL ASSOCIATION. JOURNAL. (Text in English) 1948. q. $50 to non-members. Hong Kong Medical Association, Duke of Windsor Bldg., 15 Hennessy Rd., 5th Fl., Hong Kong. FAX 865-0943. Ed. Dr. E.K. Yeoh. adv.; circ. 4,000. (back issues avail.) **Indexed:** Excerp.Med.
—BLDSC shelfmark: 4758.568000.
Formerly (until 1985): Hong Kong Medical Association. Bulletin.

HOSPICE TODAY. see *SOCIAL SERVICES AND WELFARE*

610 PO ISSN 0046-8037
HOSPITAIS CIVIS DE LISBOA. BOLETIM CLINICO. vol.35, 1974. 4/yr. Esc.150. Livraria Sa da Costa Editora, Praca Luis de Camoes, 22-4, 1294 Lisbon, Portugal. TEL 3607215. TELEX 15574 SACOST. Ed. Dr. Fernando Nogueira. bibl.; charts; illus.

658 US ISSN 0018-5485
EL HOSPITAL (CINCINNATI). (Includes Buyer's Guide) (Text in Spanish) 1944. bi-m. $35 to non-qualified personnel (foreign $50). Gregory Loomis, Ed. & Pub., 5790 Eaglesridge Lane, Cincinnati, OH 45230. TEL 513-232-0511. FAX 513-232-0662. adv.; bk.rev.; film rev.; charts; illus.; stat.; tr.lit.; index, cum.index; circ. 14,680. (back issues avail.)
Description: Reports on latest developments in medical technology, equipment and supplies.
Refereed Serial

610 UK ISSN 0262-3145
HOSPITAL DOCTOR. 1967. w. £48. Reed Business Publishing Group, Reed Healthcare Communications (Subsidiary of: Reed International PLC), Quadrant House, The Quadrant, Sutton, Surrey SM2 5AS, England. TEL 081-661-3500. FAX 081-661-8946. Ed. Simon Warne. adv.; bk.rev.; circ. 34,000. (tabloid format)
—BLDSC shelfmark: 4333.148000.
Incorporates (in Apr. 1981): On Call.

610 618.92 CN ISSN 0082-5034
HOSPITAL FOR SICK CHILDREN, TORONTO. RESEARCH INSTITUTE. ANNUAL REPORT. (Text in English) 1969. a. Hospital for Sick Children, 555 University Ave., Toronto, Ont. M5G 1X8, Canada. TEL 416-597-1500. Ed. Dr. A. Rothstein. circ. 500.

HOSPITAL INFECTION CONTROL. see *HOSPITALS*

610 UA ISSN 0046-8010
HOSPITAL MEDICAL PRACTICE. (Text in Arabic and English) 1971. q. £E1($3.) Scientific Society of the Medical Care Organization, 375 Ramses St., Abbassieh, Cairo, Egypt. Ed. Mohammed Sadek Sabbour. adv.; bk.rev.; abstr.; bibl.; charts; illus.; pat.; index; circ. 5,000.

610 US ISSN 0441-2745
R11
HOSPITAL MEDICINE; journal of clinical problems encountered in office and hospital. 1965. m. $33 (foreign $75); students $20. Cahners Publishing Company (New York), Health Care Group (Subsidiary of: Reed International PLC), Division of Reed Publishing (USA) Inc., 249 W. 17th St., New York, NY 10011. TEL 212-645-0067. FAX 914-878-4158. (Subscr. to: Box 338, Brewster, NY 10509-0338. TEL 800-722-2346) Ed. Marian Berger. adv.; illus.; circ. 134,488. **Indexed:** CINAHL.
—BLDSC shelfmark: 4333.205800.
Description: For primary care physicians who are office and hospital based. Editorial covers cardiovascular, GI, respiratory, arthritis and all other areas of medical interest to the primary care physician.
Refereed Serial

610 US ISSN 0018-5795
CODEN: HOPYA
HOSPITAL PHYSICIAN. 1957. m. Turner White Communications, 353 W. Lancaster Ave., Wayne, PA 19087. TEL 215-975-4541. adv.; charts; illus.; circ. 90,000. (also avail. in microform from UMI; reprint service avail. from UMI) **Indexed:** Med.Care Rev.
Supersedes (in 1965): R I S S; National Magazine for Residents, Interns, and Senior Students (ISSN 0485-8182)

MEDICAL SCIENCES

610 US ISSN 8750-2836
R11 CODEN: HOPRBW
HOSPITAL PRACTICE. 1966. 18/yr. $54 (free to qualified physicians). H P Publishing Co. (Subsidiary of: Maclean Hunter Ltd.), 55 Fifth Ave., New York, NY 10003-6903. TEL 212-989-2100. FAX 212-727-7316. Ed. David Fisher. adv.; bk.rev.; charts; illus.; index; circ. 172,300. (also avail. in microfilm from UMI; reprint service avail. from UMI) **Indexed:** Biol.Abstr., C.I.N.L., Curr.Adv.Cancer Res., Curr.Adv.Ecol.Sci., Curr.Cont., Curr.Lit.Fam.Plan., Dent.Ind., Excerp.Med., Hosp.Lit.Ind., I.P.A., Ind.Med., Ind.Sci.Rev., INIS Atomind., Med.Care Rev., Nutr.Abstr., Sci.Cit.Ind.
●Also available online.
Incorporates: Clinical Experience.
Description: Review articles with information on problem areas in medicine and clinical research.
Refereed Serial

610 SP ISSN 0213-4845
HOSPITAL PRACTICE (EDICION ESPANOLA). 1986. m. (10/yr.). 5300 ptas.($55) (free to qualified personnel). Ediciones Doyma, S.A., Travesera de Gracia, 17-21, 08021 Barcelona, Spain. TEL 200 07 11. FAX 209-11-36. TELEX 51964 INK-E. Dir. R. Carmena Rodriguez. adv.: page 195000 ptas.; trim 210 x 280; adv. contact: Ana Ma. Alfonso. circ. 10,200. (reprint service avail. from UMI) **Indexed:** Ind.Med.
Description: For physicians who practice in hospitals. Covers physiopathology, diagnosis and therapeutics. Includes case studies, editorials and essays.

HOSPITAL UPDATE; the journal of continuing education for hospital doctors. see *HOSPITALS*

HOSPITAL UPDATE. see *HOSPITALS*

610 VE ISSN 0018-5884
HOSPITAL VARGAS. ARCHIVOS.* vol.9, 1967. q. Hospital Vargas, Caracas, Venezuela. Ed.Bd. illus. **Indexed:** Abstr.Hyg., Biol.Abstr., Chem.Abstr, Trop.Dis.Bull.

610 US
HOSPITAL'S MEDICARE POLICY & PAYMENT REPORT. 1989. m. $199 (includes Physician's Coding Strategist). American Health Consultants, Inc., Six Piedmont Center, Ste. 400, 3525 Piedmont Rd., N.E., Atlanta, GA 30305. TEL 404-262-7436. FAX 800-284-3291. (Subscr. to: Box 740056, Atlanta, GA 30374-9822. TEL 800-688-2421) Ed. Reba Griffith. circ. 2,000.
Formerly (until 1992): Physician's Payment Update; Incorporates (in 1992): Ophthalmology Alert; Formerly (until 1991): Physician's Payment Advisory.

610 US ISSN 0889-0358
HOUSTON MEDICINE. 1969. q. $30 (foreign $60). St. Joseph Hospital Foundation, 1919 LaBranch, Houston, TX 77002. TEL 713-757-7552. Ed. Dr. Herbert L. Fred. adv.; circ. 3,000. (back issues avail.)
Former titles: Houston Medical Journal; (until Nov. 1985): St. Joseph Hospital. Medical Journal.
Description: Contains articles pertaining to all aspects of clinical medicine.

610 612 AT ISSN 0314-6162
HOWARD FLOREY INSTITUTE OF EXPERIMENTAL PHYSIOLOGY & MEDICINE. ANNUAL REPORT AND NOTICE OF MEETING. 1974. a. Howard Florey Institute of Experimental Physiology & Medicine, Parkville, Vic., Australia. FAX 03-348-1707. illus.; circ. 3,000.

610 CC ISSN 0257-7712
CODEN: HYDXET
HUAXI YIKE DAXUE XUEBAO/WEST CHINA UNIVERSITY OF MEDICAL SCIENCES. JOURNAL. (Text in Chinese; summaries, captions, table of contents in English) 1959. q. Y8 (foreign Y80 or $16). West China University of Medical Sciences - Huaxi Yike Daxue, Renmin Nanlu Sec. 3, No. 17, Chengdu, Sichuan 610044, People's Republic of China. FAX 583252. TELEX 60251-WCUMS-CN. (Dist. overseas by: China International Book Trading Corporation, P.O. Box 2820, Beijing 100044, P.R.C.) Ed. Yang Guanghua. abstr.; bibl.; charts; illus.; stat.; index; circ. 2,500. (back issues avail.) **Indexed:** Biol.Abstr., Chem.Abstr., Excerp.Med., Ind.Med.
—BLDSC shelfmark: 4915.650000.
Formerly (until 1985): Sichuan Yixueyuan Xuebao - Acta Academiae Medicinae Sichuan (ISSN 0253-4290)

610 CC ISSN 1002-0179
HUAXI YIXUE/WEST CHINA MEDICAL JOURNAL. (Text in Chinese; summaries in Chinese and English) 1986. q. Y9.6 (foreign $16). Huaxi Yike Daxue, Fushu Diyi Yiyuan - West China University of Medical Sciences, 1st University Hospital, No. 37, Guoxue Xiang, Chengdu, Sichuan 610041, People's Republic of China. TEL 551255-258. FAX 011-86-28-582944. Ed. Tang Xiaoda. adv.; abstr.; bibl.; charts; illus.; stat.; index; circ. 5,000. (also avail. in microfilm; microfiche; back issues avail.)

610 GW ISSN 0179-7581
HUFELAND - JOURNAL; Zeitschrift der Hufelandgesellschaft fuer Gesamtmedizin. 1986-1987; resumed 1991. q. DM.70 (students DM.52). Karl F. Haug Verlag GmbH, Fritz-Frey-Str. 21, Postfach 102840, 6900 Heidelberg 1, Germany. TEL 06221-4062-0. FAX 06221-400727. TELEX 461683-HVVFM-D. Ed. Dr. Franz Schmid.
—BLDSC shelfmark: 4335.841810.

610 NE ISSN 0018-7070
HUISARTS EN WETENSCHAP. (Text in Dutch; summaries in Dutch, English) 1950. m. fl.175. (Nederlands Huisartsengenootschap) Bohn Stafleu van Loghum B.V., P.O. Box 246, 3990 GA Houten, Netherlands. TEL 03403-95711. Ed. F.J. Meyman. adv.; bk.rev.; circ. 5,075. **Indexed:** Excerp.Med., FAMLI.
—BLDSC shelfmark: 4335.850000.
Refereed Serial

610 US ISSN 1045-2729
HUMAN ECOLOGY & ENERGY BALANCING SCIENTIST. 1987. q. $14.95. Human Ecology Balancing Sciences, Inc., Box 737, Mahopac, NY 10541-0737. TEL 914-228-4162. Eds. Steven Rochlitz, Irene Yaychuk. adv.; bk.rev.; index; circ. 500. (back issues avail.)
Formerly (until 1989): Human Ecology Balancing Scientist (ISSN 0896-7164)
Description: Covers human ecology, learning problems, nutrition, kinesiology, and integration of brain-heart-acupuncture meridians.

HUMAN FACTORS & AVIATION MEDICINE. see *AERONAUTICS AND SPACE FLIGHT*

615.8 NE ISSN 0167-9457
QP303 CODEN: HMSCDO
HUMAN MOVEMENT SCIENCE; journal devoted to pure and applied research on human movement. (Text in English) 1982. bi-m. fl.471 (effective 1992). North-Holland (Subsidiary of: Elsevier Science Publishers B.V.), P.O. Box 211, 1000 AE Amsterdam, Netherlands. TEL 020-5803911. FAX 020-5803598. TELEX 18582 ESPA NL. (Subscr. in U.S. and Canada to: Elsevier Science Publishing Co., Inc., Box 882, Madison Sq. Sta., New York, NY 10159. TEL 212-989-5800) Ed. H.T.A. Whitting. bk.rev. (back issues avail.) **Indexed:** Sportsearch (1987-).
—BLDSC shelfmark: 4336.210000.
Description: Consists of empirical reports, overviews, methodologies as well as announcements of seminars, conferences and research programs relevant to the study of human movement.
Refereed Serial

616.07 US ISSN 0046-8177
CODEN: HPCQA4
HUMAN PATHOLOGY. 1970. m. $94 to individuals; institutions $121; residents $59; foreign $152. W.B. Saunders Co., Curtis Center, Independence Square W., Philadelphia, PA 19106. TEL 215-238-7800. Ed. Fred Gorstein, M.D. (also avail. in microform from MIM,UMI; reprint service avail. from ISI,SWZ,UMI,) **Indexed:** Biol.Abstr., Chem.Abstr., Curr.Adv.Cancer Res., Curr.Adv.Ecol.Sci., Curr.Cont., Excerp.Med., Helminthol.Abstr., Ind.Med., Ind.Sci.Rev., INIS Atomind., Rev.Plant Path., Sci.Cit.Ind.
—BLDSC shelfmark: 4336.260000.
Refereed Serial

610 CN ISSN 0828-7090
HUMANE MEDICINE; a journal of the art and science of medicine. 1985. q. Can.$47.50 to individuals (foreign $58); institutions Can.$100 (foreign $110). Canadian Medical Association, P.O. Box 8650, Ottawa, Ont. K1G 0G8, Canada. TEL 613-731-9331. FAX 613-523-0937. Eds. Dr. D.G. Oreopoulos, Dr. J.O. Godden. adv.; circ. 56,000. (also avail. in microfilm from UMI; reprint service avail. from UMI) **Indexed:** Curr.Cont.
—BLDSC shelfmark: 4336.472600.
Description: Provides a vehicle for communication among all those who have something to share about ministry to the whole person - to body, mind and spirit.
Refereed Serial

610 GW ISSN 0172-3790
CODEN: HYGMED
HYGIENE & MEDIZIN. 1976. m. DM.132. M H P Verlag GmbH, Ostring 13, 6200 Wiesbaden-Nordenstadt, Germany. FAX 06122-76331. Ed. Margrit Werner. adv.; bk.rev. **Indexed:** Excerp.Med.
—BLDSC shelfmark: 4352.267000.

610 JA ISSN 0385-7638
CODEN: HIDZDO
HYOGO IKA DAIGAKU IGAKKAI ZASSHI. (Text in Japanese; summaries in English) 1976. 3/yr. 2000 Yen. Hyogo Ika Daigaku Igakkai - Medical Society of Hyogo College of Medicine, 1-1 Mukogawa-cho, Nishinorniya-shi, Hyogo 663, Japan. TEL 0798-45-6289. FAX 0798-48-8045. Ed. Yasumasa Hayashi. circ. 1,400. (back issues avail.) **Indexed:** Chem.Abstr., Excerp.Med., INIS Atomind.
—BLDSC shelfmark: 0635.020000.

610 AT ISSN 0819-9558
I A A H NEWSLETTER. 1987. q. $25. International Association for Adolescent Health, Health Center University of Canberra, P.O. Box 1, Belconnen, A.C.T. 2616, Australia. TEL 062-522351. FAX 06-282-3618. Ed. M. Williams. adv.; bk.rev.; circ. 450.
Description: Contains reports and discussion of all topics relevant to adolescent health, health education and madical care.

I A L NEWS. (International Association of Laryngectomees) see *EDUCATION — Special Education And Rehabilitation*

610 PL
I B - 1. INFORMACJA BIEZACA; przeglad zawartosci obcojezycznych czasopism medycznych. (Text in various languages) s-m. $62.40. Glowna Biblioteka Lekarska, Ul. Chocimska 22, Warsaw, Poland. (Dist. by: Ars Polona-Ruch, Krakowskie Przedmiescie 7, 00-068 Warsaw, Poland)

610 614 PL
I B - 2. INFORMACJA BIEZACA; przeglad zawartosci czasopism polskich i obcojezycznych z zakresu medycyny spolecznej i organizacji ochrony zdrowia. (Text in various languages) q. 60 Zl.($10.40) Glowna Biblioteka Lekarska, Ul. Chocimska 22, Warsaw, Poland. (Dist. by: Ars Polona-Ruch, Krakowskie Przedmiescie 7, 00-068 Warsaw, Poland) Ed. Feliks Widy-Wirski.

I C H P E R CONGRESS PROCEEDINGS. (International Council on Health, Physical Education and Recreation) see *PHYSICAL FITNESS AND HYGIENE*

610 JA ISSN 0287-1785
I C M R ANNALS. 1979. a. International Center for Medical Research, Kobe University, School of Medicine, 5-1 Kusunoki-cho 7-chome, Chuo-ku, Kobe 650, Japan. TEL 078-341-7451. FAX 078-351-6709. Ed. Matsuto Mochizuki.
—BLDSC shelfmark: 4362.048580.

610 II ISSN 0377-4910
I C M R BULLETIN. (Text in English) 1971. m. free. (Indian Council of Medical Research, Division of Publication & Information) Shri J.N. Mathur, P.O. Box 4508, Ansari Nagar, New Delhi 110 029, India. TELEX 031-63067. Ed. Dr. N. Medappa. abstr.; index; circ. 6,200 (controlled). (back issues avail.)
Description: Medical research articles, seminar and training program calendars.

I E E E ENGINEERING IN MEDICINE AND BIOLOGY MAGAZINE. see BIOLOGY — Bioengineering

I E E E TRANSACTIONS ON BIOMEDICAL ENGINEERING. see BIOLOGY — Bioengineering

610.28 US ISSN 0278-0062
RC78.A1 CODEN: ITMID4
I E E E TRANSACTIONS ON MEDICAL IMAGING. 1982. q. $110 to non-members. Institute of Electrical and Electronics Engineers, Inc., 345 E. 47th St., New York, NY 10017-2394. TEL 212-705-7366. FAX 212-705-7682. (Subscr. to: Box 1331, 445 Hoes Lane, Piscataway, NJ 08855-1331. TEL 908-562-3948} (Co-sponsors: I E E E Acoustics, Speech, and Signal Processing Society; Engineering in Medicine and Biology Society; Nuclear and Plasma Sciences Society; Ultrasonics, Ferroelectrics and Frequency Control Society) Ed. Dr. A. Bertrand Brill. (also avail. in microform from UMI,EEE) **Indexed:** Bioeng.Abstr., Ergon.Abstr., Sci.Abstr.
—BLDSC shelfmark: 4363.204500.
Description: Explores ultrasonics, x-ray imaging and tomography, image processing by computers, microwave and nuclear magnetic resonance imaging.

I M A JOURNAL OF MATHEMATICS APPLIED IN MEDICINE & BIOLOGY. see MATHEMATICS

610 UK ISSN 0267-2928
I M L S GAZETTE. 1951. m. £40. Institute of Medical Laboratory Sciences, 12 Queen Anne St., London W1M 0AU, England. TEL 071-636-8192. circ. 14,000. **Indexed:** CINAHL.
—BLDSC shelfmark: 4369.625000.
Former titles: Institute of Medical Laboratory Sciences. Gazette (ISSN 0307-5656); Institute of Medical Laboratory Technology. Gazette (ISSN 0020-2959)
Description: Professional information for medical laboratory scientists.

610 US
I V U N NEWS. 1987. s-a. $8 to individuals (foreign $10); health professionals and institutions $20 (foreign $22). (International Ventilator Users Network) Gazette International Networking Institute, 5100 Oakland Ave., Ste. 206, St. Louis, MO 63110-1441. TEL 314-534-0475. Eds. Judith Raymond Fischer, Joan Headley. circ. 2,000. (back issues avail.)
Description: Shares information of ventilator users and health care professionals experienced in home mechanical ventilation. Discusses topics such as equipment, breathing techniques, travel and family life.

610 GR ISSN 0019-0942
IATRIKA PEPRAGMENA. (Text in Greek; summaries in English and French) 1964. s-a. free. Army Pension Share Hospital, Athens, Greece. abstr.; bibl.; charts; illus.; stat.; circ. 900.

610 GR ISSN 0019-0950
IATRIKI. (Text in Greek; summaries in English) 1962. m. Dr.5000. (Society for Medical Studies) Beta Medical Arts, 5 Sisini Str., 115 28 Athens, Greece. Ed. Dr. Nicholas P. Zissis. adv.; bk.rev.; abstr.; bibl.; stat.; index. cum.index; circ. 6,000. (back issues avail.)

610.6 US
IATROFON; the voice of Iatros. 1981. q. $5 free to qualified personnel. Iatros, 10 E. Charles, Oelwein, IA 50662. TEL 319-283-3491. FAX 319-283-4985. Ed. Dr. Robert S. Jaggard. circ. 1,000.
Description: Newsletter for private and independent doctors.

610 360 US
ICARUS FILE. 1980. q. $4 (foreign $10). Phoenix Society, Inc., 11 Rust Hill Rd., Levittown, PA 19056. TEL 215-946-2876. FAX 215-946-4788. Ed. Alan Jeffry Breslau. adv.; bk.rev.; circ. 6,500. (back issues avail.)

610 JA ISSN 0019-1574
IGAKU HYORON/JAPANA MEDICINA REVUO. (Text in Japanese) 1950. s.a. 540. Yen($1.50) Shin Nihon Ishi Kyokai - New Japanese Doctors' Association, Hidaka Bldg., 1-10-2 Nishi-Ikebukuro, Toshima-ku, Tokyo 171, Japan. Ed. Sadatoshi Yoshida. circ. 1,200.
—BLDSC shelfmark: 4650.500000.

610 JA ISSN 0039-2359
CODEN: IGAYAY
IGAKU NO AYUMI. 1946. w. 600 Yen per wk. Ishiyaku Publishers, Inc., 7-10 Honkomagome 1-chome, Bunkyo-ku, Tokyo 113, Japan. Ed. Hiroshi Miura. adv.; bk.rev.; charts; illus.; index every 3 mos.; circ. 8,800. **Indexed:** C.I.S. Abstr., INIS Atomind.
—BLDSC shelfmark: 4363.381000.

610 JA ISSN 0019-1582
IGAKU TO FUKUIN/MEDICINE AND GOSPEL. (Text in Japanese) vol.40, 1988. m. 400 Yen($3) Japan Christian Medical Association - Nihon Kirisutosha Ika Renmei, 2-3-18-23, Nishi-Waseda, Shinjuku-ku, Tokyo 169, Japan. FAX 03-3232-6922. Ed. Dr. Kiyosumi Nakamura. bk.rev.; circ. 1,200.

610 574 JA ISSN 0019-1604
IGAKU TO SEIBUTSUGAKU/MEDICINE AND BIOLOGY. (Text in Japanese) 1942. m. 12000 Yen. Ogata Institute for Medical and Chemical Research, 2-10-14 Higashi-Kanda, Chiyoda-ku, Tokyo 101, Japan. FAX 03-3865-7510. Ed. Kan Suzuki. adv.; abstr.; charts; illus.; index; circ. 1,200. **Indexed:** C.I.S. Abstr., Chem.Abstr., Dairy Sci.Abstr., Food Sci.& Tech.Abstr., Ind.Med., INIS Atomind.
—BLDSC shelfmark: 5534.005000.

IGAKU TOSHOKAN. see LIBRARY AND INFORMATION SCIENCES

610 JA ISSN 0019-1612
IGAKUSHI KENKYU/STUDIES ON HISTORY OF MEDICINE. (Text in Japanese) 1961. a. 1500 Yen($10.) (Collegium Ad Studium Historiae Medicae - Igakushi Kenkyukai) Osaka University Medical School, Department of Hygiene, 4-3 Nakanoshima, Kita-ku, Osaka 530, Japan. Ed. Hiroshi Maruyama. adv.; bk.rev.; abstr.; bibl.; illus.; cum.index 1961-1968; circ. 700. **Indexed:** Curr.Cont.

610 IT
IGEA MEDICA. 1978. q. L.15000. Casa Editrice Menna, Via C.so Vittorio Emanuele 123, 83100 Avellino, Italy. Ed. Luigi Tulimiero. adv.; circ. 3,000.

610 GW
IHR ARZT AN SIE. 1970. a. DM.120. Verlag A. Fruehmorgen, Schwindstr. 5, 8000 Munich 40, Germany. TEL 089-526083. Ed. A. Fruehmorgen. circ. 10,000.
Description: Magazine for medical waiting rooms.

610 JA ISSN 0019-1728
IKAI JIHO. 1957. 3/m. 10 Yen($1.66) Kanehara & Co., Ltd., 2-31-14 Yushima, Bunkyo-ku, Tokyo 113, Japan. Ed. Hideo Kanehara. adv.; bk.rev.; circ. 100,000.

IKAKIKAI GAKU ZASSHI/JOURNAL OF MEDICAL INSTRUMENTS. see INSTRUMENTS

610 US
CODEN: IMJOAN
ILLINOIS MEDICINE. 1899. fortn. $12 to non-members; foreign $19. Illinois State Medical Society, 20 N. Michigan Ave., Ste. 700, Chicago, IL 60602. TEL 312-782-1654. FAX 312-782-2023. Ed. Mark M. Hagland. adv.; charts; illus.; s-a. index; circ. 17,500. (also avail. in microfilm from UMI) **Indexed:** Biol.Abstr., Excerp.Med., Helminthol.Abstr., HRIS, Ind.Med., INIS Atomind., Lang.& Lang.Behav.Abstr., Med.Care Rev., Rehabil.Lit.
Formerly (until no.6, vol.174, 1988): Illinois Medical Journal (ISSN 0019-2120)
Description: Covers health care issues and professional concerns. Circulation to community leaders is intended to stimulate dialogue and articulate timely, relevant information on public policy matters.

ILLUSTRATED DIRECTORY OF HANDICAPPED PRODUCTS. see BUSINESS AND ECONOMICS — Trade And Industrial Directories

610 AT
IMAGING GUIDELINES. biennial. Aus.$12. Victorian Medical Postgraduate Foundation Inc., P.O. Box 27, Parkville, Vic. 3052, Australia. TEL 03-347-9633. FAX 03-347-4547. circ. 5,000.
Description: Assisting medical practitioners to make the best possible use of available imaging facilities.

610 378 US
IMPACT (OMAHA). 1983. q. University of Nebraska Medical Center, 600 S. 42nd St., Omaha, NE 68198-5230. TEL 402-559-4353. FAX 402-559-4103. Ed. Sandy Goetzinger. circ. 7,000.
Description: Covers issues associated with education, research, and medical care at the center.

330 610 US ISSN 0733-1398
IN VIVO; the business and medicine report. 1983. m. $460 (typically set in Jan.). Windhover Information, Inc., 50 Washington St., 3rd. Fl., South Norwalk, CT 06864. TEL 203-838-4401. FAX 203-838-3214. (Subscr. to: P.O. Box 360 South Norwalk, CT 06856-0360) Ed. Roger Longman. adv. (back issues avail.)
Description: Reports about the medical industry and its effect on business. Features range from industry trends and new products to controversial issues in the medical field as they relate to business.

615.8 II
INDIAN ASSOCIATION OF PHYSIOTHERAPISTS. JOURNAL. 1965. a. membership. Indian Association of Physiotherapists, c/o Mrs. S.M. Sanghavi, 35 Chowpaty Sea Face, 3rd Fl., Bombay 400007, India. adv.; bk.rev.; circ. 500.

610 II
INDIAN INSTITUTE OF HISTORY OF MEDICINE. BULLETIN (MADRAS). (Text in English) 1956. n.8. Indian Institute of the History of Medicine, 497 Poonamalee, Madras 7, India. Ed. Dr. K. Bhasker Rao. adv.; bk.rev.; bibl.; illus.; cum.index every 10 yrs.; circ. 500.
Formerly: Indian Journal of the History of Medicine (ISSN 0019-5677)

610 II ISSN 0304-9558
R605
INDIAN INSTITUTE OF HISTORY OF MEDICINE. BULLETIN (NEW DELHI). (Text in English; summaries in Hindi) 1971. a. Rs.60. Central Council for Research in Ayurveda and Siddha, Dharma Bhawan, S-10, Green Park Extn. Market, New Delhi 110 016, India. TEL 11-669315. (Co-sponsor: Indian Institute of Medicine) Ed. Momin Ali. adv.; bk.rev.; abstr.; bibl.; charts; illus.; circ. 300.
Former titles: Osmania Medical College. Institute of History of Medicine. Bulletin (ISSN 0304-9566); Osmania Medical College. Department of History of Medicine. Bulletin (ISSN 0011-8877)
Description: Publishes original articles on the history of all systems of medicine in India: ayurveda, unani, yoga, siddha, homeopathy, allopathy, and naturopathy. Includes lists and descriptions of medical manuscripts, notes on archeological evidences, and news of medico-historical activities in India and abroad.

610 II ISSN 0970-6666
INDIAN JOURNAL OF AEROSPACE MEDICINE. (Text in English) 1951. s-a. Indian Society of Aerospace Medicine, Medical Directorate, Air Headquarters, Rk Puram West, New Delhi 110 066, India. TEL 3010231-1176. Ed. Surjit Singh. circ. 800.
Formerly: Journal of Aeromedical Society of India.
Description: Includes original articles, topical reviews and other scientific information in the field of aerospace medicine and allied sciences.

616.1 II ISSN 0377-9343
INDIAN JOURNAL OF CHEST DISEASES AND ALLIED SCIENCES. (Text in English) 1959. q. Rs.200($50) University of Delhi, Valladhbhai Patel Chest Institute, P.O. Box 2101, Delhi 110 007, India. TEL 2517027. (Co-sponsor: National College of Chest Physicians) Ed. Dr. A.S. Paintal. adv.; B&W page Rs.900; trim 19 1/2 x 13. bk.rev.; circ. 1,000. **Indexed:** Biol.Abstr., Chem.Abstr., Curr.Cont., Dent.Ind., Dok.Arbeitsmed., Excerp.Med., Helminthol.Abstr., Ind.Med.
—BLDSC shelfmark: 4410.710000.
Formerly (until vol.18, Jan. 1976): Indian Journal of Chest Diseases.
Description: Covers internal medicine.

MEDICAL SCIENCES

613.62   II   ISSN 0019-5278   CODEN: IJIDAW
INDIAN JOURNAL OF INDUSTRIAL MEDICINE. Variant title: Indian Association of Occupational Medicine. Journal. (Text in English) 1949. q. Rs.20($5.) Indian Association of Occupational Health, 82-B Shakespeare Sarani, Calcutta 700017, India. Ed. Dr. B.B. Chatterjee. bk.rev.; abstr.; bibl.; charts; illus.; stat.; index, cum.index; circ. 1,000. **Indexed:** Biol.Abstr., C.I.S. Abstr.

610   II   ISSN 0367-8326   CODEN: IJMAA9
INDIAN JOURNAL OF MALARIOLOGY. (Text in English) 1947-1963; resumed 1981. q. Rs.75($20) Indian Council of Medical Research, Malaria Research Center, 22, Sham Nath Marg, Delhi 110 054, India. TEL 2528455. FAX 7234234. TELEX 31-65518 MRC IN. bk.rev.
—BLDSC shelfmark: 4416.000000.

INDIAN JOURNAL OF MEDICAL PHOTOGRAPHY. see *PHOTOGRAPHY*

610   II   ISSN 0019-5340
R97   CODEN: IJMRAQ
INDIAN JOURNAL OF MEDICAL RESEARCH. (Issued in two sections: Section A - Infectious Diseases, Section B - Biomedical Research Other Than Infectious Diseases) (Text in English) 1913. m. Rs.1500($90) for both sections and supplements; for one section Rs.750($45). Indian Council of Medical Research, PO Box 4508, Ansari Nagar, New Delhi 110029, India. TELEX 031-63067. Ed. Dr. G.V. Satyavati. adv.; bk.rev.; bibl.; charts; illus.; index; circ. 1,000 (controlled). (reprint service avail. from ISI, UMI) **Indexed:** Abstr.Hyg., Agri.Eng.Abstr., Anim.Breed.Abstr., Bio-Contr.News & Info., Biol.Abstr., Chem.Abstr., Curr.Adv.Cancer Res., Curr.Adv.Ecol.Sci., Curr.Adv.Genetics & Molec.Biol., Curr.Cont., Dairy Sci.Abstr., Dent.Ind., Dok.Arbeitsmed., Excerp.Med., Helminthol.Abstr., Ind.Med., Ind.Sci.Rev., Ind.Vet., INIS Atomind., Nutr.Abstr., Pig News & Info., Potato Abstr., Poult.Abstr., Protozool.Abstr., Rev.Appl.Entomol., Rev.Plant Path., Rice Abstr., Sci.Cit.Ind., Trop.Dis.Bull., Vet.Bull.

610   II   ISSN 0367-9012
INDIAN JOURNAL OF MEDICAL RESEARCH. SUPPLEMENT. (Text in English) 1922. irreg. Rs.1500($90) (subscr. includes Journal). Indian Council of Medical Research, PO Box 4508, Ansari Nagar, New Delhi 110029, India. TELEX 031-63067. Ed. Dr. G.V. Satyavati. bk.rev.; bibl.; charts; circ. 1,000. (reprint service avail. from ISI, UMI) **Indexed:** Biol.Abstr., Chem.Abstr., Curr.Cont., Ind.Med., Nutr.Abstr., Sci.Cit.Ind, Trop.Dis.Bull.

610   II   ISSN 0019-5359   CODEN: INJMAO
INDIAN JOURNAL OF MEDICAL SCIENCES. (Text in English) 1947. m. Rs.450. Indian Journal of Medical Sciences Trust, c/o J.C. Patel, Back Bay View, New Queen's Rd., Bombay 4, India. Ed. Dr. J.C. Patel. adv.; bk.rev.; abstr.; charts; illus.; index; circ. 3,000. **Indexed:** Abstr.Hyg., Biol.Abstr., Chem.Abstr., Curr.Adv.Cancer Res., Curr.Adv.Ecol.Sci., Excerp.Med., Ind.Med., INIS Atomind., NRN, Nutr.Abstr., Rev.Plant Path., Trop.Dis.Bull.
—BLDSC shelfmark: 4416.550000.
Incorporates: Medical Bulletin.

615.8   II   ISSN 0445-7706
INDIAN JOURNAL OF OCCUPATIONAL THERAPY. 1955. 3/yr. $12. All India Occupational Therapists' Association, O.T. School & Centre, D.B. Orthopaedic Centre, Opp.Tata Cancer Hospital, Parel, Bombay 400 012, India. Ed. G.H. Purohit. adv.; bk.rev.; circ. 450. **Indexed:** Indian Psychol.Abstr.

616.07 576   II
INDIAN JOURNAL OF PATHOLOGY & MICROBIOLOGY. (Text in English) 1958. q. Rs.250. Indian Association of Pathologists and Microbiologists, Nizam's Institute of Medical Sciences, Panjagutta, Hyderabad 500 482, India. TELEX 0425-6478. (Subscr. to: Dr. K.R. Harilal, Treasurer, Prof. of Pathology, Medical College, Kottayam 686 008 (Kerala) India) Ed. Dr. K.S. Ratnakar. adv.; bk.rev.; abstr.; bibl.; charts; illus.; index; circ. 2,000. **Indexed:** Biol.Abstr., Chem.Abstr., Curr.Adv.Ecol.Sci., Dent.Ind., Excerp.Med., Ind.Med., Ind.Vet., Nutr.Abstr., Rev.Plant Path., Vet.Bull.
Formerly: Indian Journal of Pathology and Bacteriology (ISSN 0019-5448)

INDIAN JOURNAL OF VETERINARY ANATOMY. see *VETERINARY SCIENCE*

610   II   ISSN 0019-5847   CODEN: JIMAAD
INDIAN MEDICAL ASSOCIATION. JOURNAL. (Supplement) (Text in English) 1931. m. Rs.455. Indian Medical Association, I.M.A House, 53 Creek Row, Calcutta 700 014, India. TEL 26-3598. adv.; bk.rev.; abstr.; charts; illus.; circ. 56,000. (reprint service avail. from UMI) **Indexed:** Abstr.Hyg., Biol.Abstr., Chem.Abstr., Dent.Ind., Excerp.Med., Helminthol.Abstr., Ind.Med., Nutr.Abstr., Rev.Plant Path., Trop.Dis.Bull.
—BLDSC shelfmark: 4767.400000.

610   II   ISSN 0019-5855
INDIAN MEDICAL FORUM; devoted to the advancement of medical science. (Text in English) 1950. m. $2.27. Thornes (Private) Ltd., 13 Ezra Mansions, PO Box 2361, Calcutta 1, India. Ed. S. Chatterjee. adv. **Indexed:** Chem.Abstr.

INDIAN MEDICAL GAZETTE. see *MEDICAL SCIENCES — Surgery*

610   II   ISSN 0019-6169
THE INDIAN PRACTITIONER; a monthly journal of medicine, surgery & public health. (Text in English) 1947. m. Rs.300($30) Indian Practitioner Group, 101, Lawrence Apartments-2, 1st Floor, Vidyanagari Marg, Opp. Lakhbir Petrol Pump, Kalina, Santa Cruz (E), Bombay 400 098, India. TEL 6116170. Ed. V. Godinho. adv.; bk.rev.; circ. 43,967. (reprint service avail.) **Indexed:** Biol.Abstr., Chem.Abstr., Dent.Ind., Ind.Med.
—BLDSC shelfmark: 4427.900000.

610   US   ISSN 0746-8288
R15
INDIANA MEDICINE. 1908. bi-m. $15 to individuals (foreign $18); medical libraries $14 (foreign $16); medical students $7. Indiana State Medical Association, 322 Canal Walk, Indianapolis, IN 46202-3252. TEL 317-261-2060. FAX 317-261-2076. adv.; bk.rev.; abstr.; charts; illus.; index; circ. 7,000. (also avail. in microform from UMI; reprint service avail. from UMI) **Indexed:** Biol.Abstr., Chem.Abstr., Excerp.Med., Hosp.Lit.Ind., Ind.Med., INIS Atomind.
—BLDSC shelfmark: 4431.769300.
Formerly (until 1984): Indiana State Medical Association. Journal (ISSN 0019-6770)

INDUSTRIAL HEALTH & HAZARDS UPDATE. see *PUBLIC HEALTH AND SAFETY*

INDUSTRIAL HEALTH FOUNDATION. MEDICAL SERIES. BULLETINS. see *OCCUPATIONAL HEALTH AND SAFETY*

610   US   ISSN 0073-5639
INFACT MEDICAL SCHOOL INFORMATION SYSTEM. 1967. 3/yr. $195 (Canada $205; Europe $225)(effective 1992). Dataflow Systems Inc., 7758 Wisconsin Ave., Bethesda, MD 20814. TEL 301-654-9133. Ed. J.B. Malcom. index; circ. 100. (microfiche)
Description: Indexed collection of current U.S. and Canadian medical school catalogs on microfiche.

610   GW   ISSN 0300-8126   CODEN: IFTNAL
INFECTION; journal for the clinical study and treatment of infections /Zeitschrift fuer Klinik und Therapie der Infektionen. (Text in English and German) 1973. 6/yr. DM.240. (Deutsche Gesellschaft fuer Infektiologie) M M V Medizin Verlag, Neumarkter Str. 18, Postfach 801246, 8000 Munich 80, Germany. Ed. W. Marget. adv.; bk.rev.; circ. 3,000. **Indexed:** Abstr.Hyg., Biol.Abstr., Biotech.Abstr., Chem.Abstr., Curr.Adv.Ecol.Sci., Curr.Cont., Dent.Ind., Excerp.Med., Helminthol.Abstr., Ind.Med., Ind.Sci.Rev., Ind.Vet., INIS Atomind., Sci.Cit.Ind., Trop.Dis.Bull., Vet.Bull.
—BLDSC shelfmark: 4478.710000.

INFECTION CONTROL YEARBOOK. see *MEDICAL SCIENCES — Nurses And Nursing*

INFECTIOUS DISEASE NEWS. see *MEDICAL SCIENCES — Communicable Diseases*

610   US   ISSN 0162-6493
INFECTIOUS DISEASE PRACTICE. 1977. m. $77 (foreign $97). International Publishing Group, 4959 Commerce Pkwy., Cleveland, OH 44128. TEL 216-464-1210. FAX 216-464-1835. Dr. Louis Weinstein. circ. 700. (back issues avail.)
Description: For physicians in practice or research. Each issue focuses on a specific disease presenting symptoms, differential diagnosis, clinical course, management, and treatment or prevention.

610   US
▼**INFECTIOUS DISEASES IN CLINICAL PRACTICE.** 1991. bi-m. $73. Williams & Wilkins, 428 E. Preston St., Baltimore, MD 21202-3993. TEL 410-528-4000. FAX 410-528-4452. Ed. Sherwood Gorbach. adv.: B&W page $650, color page $1400; trim 8 1/8 x 10 7/8. circ. 5,500.
Description: For physicians who treat patients with infectious diseases.

INFECTIOUS WASTES NEWS. see *ENVIRONMENTAL STUDIES — Waste Management*

616.07   GW   ISSN 0178-9090
INFEKTIONEN UND KLINIKHYGIENE; Kongressberichte und Referate aus dem internationalen Schrifttum. 1982. bi-m. DM.58. Friedr. Vieweg und Sohn Verlagsgesellschaft mbH, Postfach 5829, 6200 Wiesbaden 1, Germany. TEL 0611-160230. FAX 0611-160229. TELEX 4186928-VWVD. Ed. I. Braveny. circ. 10,000. (back issues avail.)
Description: Congress reports and lectures on infection and clinical hygiene selected from international medical literature.

610   FR
INFIRMIERE MAGAZINE; revue d'enseignment technique et de developpement professionnel. 1923. 11/yr. 580 F. to individuals; institutions 685 F. Editions Lamarre-Poinat, 47 rue St. Andre des Arts, 75006 Paris, France. FAX 46-34-75-01. Ed. Thierry Verret. adv.; illus.; circ. 70,000. **Indexed:** Int.Nurs.Ind.
Formerly: Infirmiere Francaise (ISSN 0019-9613)

610   US   ISSN 0360-3997
RB131   CODEN: INFLD4
INFLAMMATION. 1975. bi-m. $225 (foreign $300)(effective 1992). Plenum Publishing Corp., 233 Spring St., New York, NY 10013-1578. TEL 212-620-8000. FAX 212-463-0742. TELEX 23-421139. Ed. Gerald Weissmann. adv.; illus. (also avail. in microfilm from JSC; back issues avail.) **Indexed:** Biol.Abstr., Biotech.Abstr., Chem.Abstr., Curr.Adv.Biochem., Curr.Adv.Ecol.Sci., Curr.Cont., Excerp.Med., Ind.Med., Ind.Sci.Rev., Ind.Vet., INIS Atomind., Ref.Zh., Vet.Bull.
—BLDSC shelfmark: 4478.845000.
Refereed Serial

INFLAMMOPHARMACOLOGY. see *PHARMACY AND PHARMACOLOGY*

610   GW   ISSN 0931-2358
INFORMATION MEDIZIN; das Periodikum fuer den naturheilkundlich interessierten Arzt. 1986. irreg. DM.16. Spitta Verlag GmbH und Co. KG, Wasserwiesen 42, Postfach 100963, 7460 Balingen, Germany. TEL 07433-381474. FAX 07433-20461. TELEX 763-683-SPIVA-D. adv.; bk.rev.; circ. 5,000. (back issues avail.)

610.6   SP
INFORMATIVO MEDICO. no.131, 1974. m. Colegios Medicos de Espana, Consejo General, Villaneuva 11, Madrid 1, Spain. adv.; bk.rev.; circ. 108,000.
Formerly: Colegios Medicos de Espana. Consejo General. Boletin Informativo.

610   IT   ISSN 0020-0743
INFORMATORE MEDICO-SOCIALE. 1964. fortn. Istituto Italiano di Medicina Sociale, Via Pasquale Stanislao Mancini 28, Rome, Italy. Marafioti Renzi.
Description: Covers issues in social medicine.

MEDICAL SCIENCES 3109

615.7   US   ISSN 0160-757X
INFUSION. 1977. q. $52 (foreign $69)(effective Jan. 1991). Shugar Publishing, 32 Mill Rd., Westhampton Beach, NY 11978. TEL 516-288-4404. FAX 516-288-4435. Ed. Douglas Scheckelhoff. adv.; bk.rev.; abstr.; bibl.; charts; illus.; stat.; index; circ. 9,043. **Indexed:** I.P.A.
●Also available online.
—BLDSC shelfmark: 4499.540000.
Description: Information on intravenous therapy to all sectors of the health-care delivery system. Covers parenteral and enteral nutrition, infectious diseases, pediatric I.V. therapy, chemotherapy, adverse drug reactions, home care I.V. therapy and new product developments.

610   GW   ISSN 0720-0722
INFUSIONS-JOURNAL. 1978. s-a. free. (Boehringer Mannheim) P M I Verlag GmbH, August-Schanz-Str. 21, 6000 Frankfurt a.M. 50, Germany. TEL 069-548000-0. FAX 069-548000-77. TELEX 412952-PMI-D. Ed. Peter Hoffmann. (tabloid format; back issues avail.)
Description: A seminar paper journal, containing summaries of original articles and interviews.

610   GW   ISSN 0303-4305
INNERE MEDIZIN; Zeitschrift fuer die gesamte Innere Medizin in Klinik und Praxis. 1974. 6/yr. DM.113.40 (foreign DM.117.60). Richard Pflaum Verlag GmbH und Co. KG, Lazarettstr. 4, Postfach 190737, 8000 Munich 19, Germany. TEL 089-12607-0. FAX 089-12607-281. Ed. B. Kommerell. adv.; bk.rev.; circ. 12,000. **Indexed:** Curr.Cont., Excerp.Med., Helminthol.Abstr., INIS Atomind., Nutr.Abstr.
—BLDSC shelfmark: 4515.455000.

614 362   US   ISSN 0046-9580
RA410.A1   CODEN: INQYA
INQUIRY (CHICAGO); the journal of health care organization, provision and financing. 1963. q. $40 to individuals; institutions $45; foreign $55. Blue Cross and Blue Shield Association, 676 N. St. Clair St., Chicago, IL 60611. TEL 312-440-5575. FAX 312-440-5705. (Subscr. to: Box 527, Glenview, IL 60025) Ed. Jack Hadley. bk.rev.; charts; index, cum.index: 1963-1973, 1974-1978; circ. 3,500. (tabloid format; also avail. in microform from UMI; back issues avail.; reprint service avail. from UMI) **Indexed:** A.B.C.Pol.Sci., Abstr.Health Care Manage.Stud., Abstr.Hyg., Acad.Ind., B.P.I., BPIA, Bus.Ind., Curr.Cont., Excerp.Med., Hosp.Abstr., Hosp.Lit.Ind., Ind.Med., J.of Econ.Lit., Med.Care Rev., Mid.East: Abstr.& Ind., P.A.I.S., PHRA, Soc.Sci.Ind., SSCI, Tr.& Indus.Ind., Trop.Dis.Bull.
—BLDSC shelfmark: 4516.100000.
Refereed Serial

INSIGHT (ATLANTA). see *MEETINGS AND CONGRESSES*

610   FR   ISSN 0020-2142
INSTANTANES MEDICAUX. At head of title: E M C Encyclopedie Medico Chirurgicale. 1949. m. (Encyclopedie Medico Chirurgicale) Editions Techniques, 123 rue d'Alesia, 75014 Paris, France. TEL 45-39-22-91. FAX 45428155. TELEX EDITEC 270737 F. Ed.Bd. adv.; bk.rev.; charts; pat.; circ. 68,800. **Indexed:** C.I.S. Abstr., INIS Atomind.

362   CN
INSTITUT DE READAPTATION DE MONTREAL. BULLETIN. (Text in English, French) 1967. 4/yr. free. Institut de Readaptation de Montreal, Communications Branch, 6300 Ave. Darlington, Montreal, Que. H3S 2J4, Canada. TEL 514-340-2085. FAX 514-340-2149. Ed. Solange-Marie Gagnon. adv.; bk.rev.; illus.; circ. 7,000.
Formerly: Rehabilitation Institute of Montreal. Bulletin (ISSN 0316-4454)

610   CX
INSTITUT PASTEUR DE BANGUI. RAPPORT BISANNUEL. 1961. a. $25. Institut Pasteur de Bangui, B.P. 923, Bangui, Central African Republic. FAX 236-610109. TELEX 5312 RC. adv.; circ. 200. **Indexed:** Biol.Abstr.
Formerly (until 1984): Institut Pasteur de Bangui. Rapport Annuel.

610 613   UK   ISSN 0307-3289
INSTITUTE OF HEALTH EDUCATION. JOURNAL. 1962. q. £12 to non-members. Institute of Health Education, 9 Elm Ridge Dr., Hale Barns, Altrincham, Cheshire WA15 0JE, England. TEL 0742-660790. FAX 061-980-7446. Ed. F.St.D. Rowntree. adv.; bk.rev.; film rev.; circ. controlled. **Indexed:** Abstr.Hyg., Curr.Adv.Ecol.Sci., Trop.Dis.Bull.
—BLDSC shelfmark: 4776.200000.

610   MK
INSTITUTE OF HEALTH SCIENCES. QUARTERLY MEDICAL NEWS BULLETIN. q. Ministry of Health, Institute of Health Sciences, P.O. Box 6720, Ruwi, Muscat, Sultanate of Oman. TEL 560066. TELEX 5465.

610   NP   ISSN 0259-0972
INSTITUTE OF MEDICINE. JOURNAL. (Text in English) 1979. q. $12 per no. Institute of Medicine, P.O. Box 2533, Kathmandu, Nepal. Ed. Hemang Dixit. adv.; bk.rev.; charts; illus.; circ. 500. **Indexed:** Abstr.Hyg., Excerp.Med., Protozool.Abstr.
—BLDSC shelfmark: 4776.980000.

610   US   ISSN 0091-746X
                         CODEN: PMICAP
INSTITUTE OF MEDICINE OF CHICAGO. PROCEEDINGS. 1916. q. $22. Institute of Medicine of Chicago, 332 S. Michigan Ave., Chicago, IL 60604. TEL 312-663-0040. FAX 312-663-9058. Ed. Robert L. Schmitz. bk.rev.; circ. 4,500. **Indexed:** Biol.Abstr.

INSTITUTION OF MECHANICAL ENGINEERS. PROCEEDINGS. PART H: JOURNAL OF ENGINEERING IN MEDICINE. see *BIOLOGY — Bioengineering*

610   BO
INSTITUTO MEDICO "SUCRE". REVISTA. 1905. a. free. Instituto Medico "Sucre", Calle San Alberto No. 30, Casilla Correo 82, Sucre, Bolivia. TEL 2-1956. Dr. Jaime Sanchez Porcel.
Description: Information on all aspects of health and medicine in Bolivia.

616.98   PL
INSTYTUT MEDYCYNY PRACY. ZESZYTY METODYCZNO-ORGANIZACYJNE. (Text in Polish; summaries in English) 1982. irreg. (3-4/yr.) price varies. Instytut Medycyny Pracy im. Jerzego Nofera - Nofer's Institute of Occupational Medicine, Ul. Teresy 8, P.O. Box 199, 90-950 Lodz, Poland. TEL 48-42-552505. FAX 48-42-348331. Ed. Lech Dawydzik. abstr.; bibl.; charts; illus.; stat.; tr.; lit.; circ. 300. (back issues avail.)
Formerly: Instytut Medycyny Pracy w Przemysle Wlokienniczym i Chemicznym. Zeszyty Metodyczno-Organizacyjne (ISSN 0209-1186)
Description: Covers methodology of medical care, organization and management of industrial medicine, organization of prophylaxis and its evaluation, educational and specialization problems.

610   GW
                         CODEN: NTNSDQ
INTENSIV- UND NOTFALLBEHANDLUNG. 1976. q. DM.90($60) Dustri-Verlag Dr. Karl Feistle, Bahnhofstr. 9, 8024 Deisenhofen, Germany. TEL 089-613861-0. FAX 089-613-5412. Ed. Dr. B. Landauer. **Indexed:** Biol.Abstr., Curr.Adv.Ecol.Sci., Curr.Cont., Excerp.Med.
Formerly: Intensivbehandlung (ISSN 0341-3063)

610   UK   ISSN 0265-5241
INTENSIVE & CRITICAL CARE DIGEST. q. King & Wirth Publishing Co. Ltd., Hillside, Arnolds Lane, Hinxworth, Baldock, Hertfordshire SG7 5HR, England. TEL 44-46274-2580. FAX 44-46274-2986. Ed. Dr. Simon Bursztein.
Description: Articles about state-of-the-art intensive and critical care medicine.

610   GW   ISSN 0342-4642
                         CODEN: ICMED9
INTENSIVE CARE MEDICINE. 1974. 8/yr. DM.462($246) (European Society of Intensive Care Medicine) Springer-Verlag, Heidelberger Platz 3, D-1000 Berlin 33, Germany. TEL 030-8207-1. (Also Heidelberg, Tokyo, Vienna, and New York) Ed. F. Lemarre. (also avail. in microform from UMI; back issues avail.; reprint service avail. from ISI) **Indexed:** Curr.Cont., Excerp.Med., Ind.Med., Ind.Sci.Rev., INIS Atomind., Sci.Cit.Ind.
—BLDSC shelfmark: 4531.837000.
Formerly: European Journal of Intensive Care Medicine.

610 542   UK   ISSN 0266-7037
INTENSIVE CARE WORLD. 1984. q. $60. King & Wirth Publishing Co. Ltd., Hillside, Arnolds Ln., Hinxworth, Baldock, Herts SG7 5HR, England. TEL 44-46274-2580. FAX 44-46274-2986. Ed. Geoffrey Dobb. adv.; bk.rev.; abstr.; bibl.; illus.; circ. 19,898. **Indexed:** Curr.Adv.Ecol.Sci.
Description: Articles about state-of-the-art intensive and critical care medicine.

610   GW   ISSN 0175-3851
                         CODEN: INNOEK
INTENSIVMEDIZIN UND NOTFALLMEDIZIN. (Text in German; summaries in English) 1961. 8/yr. DM.340. Dr. Dietrich Steinkopff Verlag, Saalbaustr. 12, Postfach 111442, 6100 Darmstadt 11, Germany. TEL 06151-26538. FAX 06151-20849. Ed.Bd. adv.; bk.rev.; circ. 2,500. **Indexed:** Biol.Abstr., Curr.Cont., Excerp.Med.
—BLDSC shelfmark: 4531.845000.
Former titles: Intensivmedizin (ISSN 0303-6251); Wiederbelebung-Organersatz-Intensivmedizin (ISSN 0043-5252)

610   NG   ISSN 0534-4735
INTER-AFRICAN CONFERENCE ON MEDICAL CO-OPERATION. MEETING.* Title varies slightly; some issues called reports. irreg.; 1955 3rd. (Commission for Technical Co-Operation in Africa South of the Sahara) Maison de l'Afrique, B.P. 878, Niamey, Niger.

610   SP
INTERCON. Spanish edition of: Vademecum. 1967. a. 5500 ptas. Editores Medicos, S.A., Paseo de la Castellana, 53, 28046 Madrid, Spain. TEL 442-86-56. FAX 422-80-43. circ. 40,000.

INTERFACE (CHICAGO). see *LIBRARY AND INFORMATION SCIENCES*

INTERFACES: LINGUISTICS, PSYCHOLOGY AND HEALTH THERAPEUTICS; an international journal of research, notes and commentary. see *LINGUISTICS*

610   SZ   ISSN 0026-9212
INTERKANTONALE KONTROLLSTELLE FUER HEILMITTEL. MONATSBERICHT/OFFICE INTERCANTONAL DE CONTROLE DE MEDICAMENTS. BULLETIN MENSUEL/UFFICIO INTERCANTONALE DI CONTROLLO DEI MEDICAMENTI. BOLLETTINO MENSILE. (Text in French, German, Italian) 1947. m. 85 Fr. (foreign 100 Fr.). Interkantonale Kontrollstelle fuer Heilmittel, Erlachstr. 8, CH-3000 Bern 9, Switzerland. FAX 031-240654. adv.; index; circ. 3,000.

616   JA
INTERNAL MEDICINE/NAIKA. (Text in Japanese) 1958. m. 29800 Yen (foreign 36303 Yen). Nankodo Co., Ltd., 42-6, Hongo 3-chome, Bunkyo-ku, Tokyo 113, Japan. TEL 03-3811-7239. FAX 03-3811-7230. Ed. Tsuneaki Sugimoto. adv.; charts; illus.; s-a. index; circ. 13,000. **Indexed:** Biol.Abstr., Curr.Adv.Cancer Res.
Formerly: Journal of Internal Medicine (ISSN 0022-1961)
Description: Covers internal medicine.

616.02   US   ISSN 0195-315X
INTERNAL MEDICINE ALERT. 1979. s-m. $96. American Health Consultants, Inc., Six Piedmont Center, Ste. 400, 3525 Piedmont Rd., N.E., Atlanta, GA 30305. TEL 404-262-7436. FAX 800-284-3291. (Subscr. to: Box 740056, Atlanta, GA 30374-9822. TEL 800-688-2421) Ed. Dr. Stephen A. Brunton. index; circ. 8,800. (also avail. in audio cassette; reprint service avail.)
Incorporates (1985-1991): Diagnostic Testing Alert (ISSN 8756-7474)

616   US   ISSN 0274-5542
INTERNAL MEDICINE NEWS & CARDIOLOGY NEWS. 1968. s-m. $96. International Medical News Group, 12230 Wilkins Ave., Rockville, MD 20852. TEL 301-770-6170. Ed. William Rubin. adv.; bk.rev.; circ. 81,600. (tabloid format; also avail. in microform from UMI)
Former titles (until 1980): Internal Medicine News (ISSN 0099-152X); Internal Medicine and Diagnosis News (ISSN 0012-1908); Diagnosis News.
Description: Covers internal medicine.

M

MEDICAL SCIENCES

610 US
▼INTERNAL MEDICINE RESIDENT. 1992. bi-m. Slack, Inc., 6900 Grove Rd., Thorofare, NJ 08086. TEL 609-848-1000. FAX 609-853-5991. Ed. Laura Ronge. adv.; circ. 21,900.
Description: Contains information on career, lifestyle and business issues facing residents.

616.02 US
INTERNAL MEDICINE WORLD REPORT. 21/yr. Medical World Business Press, Inc., 322-D Englishtown Rd., No. 201, Old Bridge, NJ 08857. TEL 908-251-9400. FAX 908-251-9468. Ed. Dena Manulkin. circ. 95,000.

611 574.4 RU ISSN 0074-1353
INTERNATIONAL ANATOMICAL CONGRESS. PROCEEDINGS. (Text in English, French and German) 1905. quinquennial, 1970, 9th, Leningrad. International Anatomical Congress, c/o Prof. Dr. Shdanow, Karl Marx Prospekt 18, Moscow K-9, Russia. TEL 203-74-09.

610 FR ISSN 0074-1760
INTERNATIONAL ASSOCIATION OF THALASSOTHERAPY. CONGRESS REPORTS. (Proceedings published by organizing committee) 1954. triennial; 1975, 16th, Opatija, Yugoslavia. International Association of Thalasso-Therapy, c/o Professeur D. Leroy, 6, rue Lafayette, 35000 Rennes, France.
Description: Covers marine medicine.

610 UK
INTERNATIONAL BACK PAIN NEWS. 1986. 3/yr. £30. (International Back Pain Society) Congress Team International (U.K.) Ltd., 15 Bedford Rd., Northwood, Middlesex HA6 2BA, England. TEL 081 206 0426. FAX 081-206-0427.

615 US ISSN 0020-6571
INTERNATIONAL DRUG THERAPY NEWSLETTER. 1966. m. (Sep.-Jun.). $45. Ayd Medical Communications, 1130 E. Cold Spring Ln., Baltimore, MD 21239. TEL 301-433-9220. FAX 301-532-5419. Ed. Frank J. Ayd, Jr., M.D. bk.rev.; circ. 7,000. Indexed: I.P.A.
—BLDSC shelfmark: 4539.749000.
Description: Psychoactive drug therapy.

610 NE ISSN 0074-6037
INTERNATIONAL FEDERATION OF MEDICAL STUDENTS' ASSOCIATIONS. MINUTES AND REPORTS OF THE GENERAL ASSEMBLY. 1951. a. free. International Federation of Medical Students' Associations, Faculty of Medicine A M C, Meibergdreef 15, 1105 AZ Amsterdam, Netherlands. FAX 020-566-4440. TELEX 11944 AZUA NL. circ. 150.

610 BE
INTERNATIONAL HOSPITAL EQUIPMENT. 1975. 9/yr. $70 (free to qualified personnel). Pan European Publishing Co., Rue Verte 216, B-1210 Brussels, Belgium. TEL 02-242-29-92. FAX 02-242-71-11. TELEX 25828. Ed. Thomas Clark. adv.; illus.; circ. 30,010 (controlled). (tabloid format) Indexed: Key to Econ.Sci.
Description: Reports on hospital products and equipment in the diagnostic, therapeutic and patient handling fields from manufacturers worldwide.

610 619 IT ISSN 0391-3988
RD130 Db .I576 CODEN: IJAODS
INTERNATIONAL JOURNAL OF ARTIFICIAL ORGANS. 1978. m. L.340000($300) (effective 1992). Wichtig Editore s.r.l., Via Friuli, 72-74, 20135 Milan, Italy. TEL 02-5452306. FAX 02-5451843. Ed. Diego Brancaccio. adv.; bk.rev.; circ. 2,000. Indexed: Chem.Abstr, Curr.Cont., Excerp.Med., Ind.Med., Ind.Sci.Rev., Protozool.Abstr., Sci.Cit.Ind.
—BLDSC shelfmark: 4542.105000.
Incorporates: Life Support Systems (ISSN 0261-989X)
Description: Provides the most current information available on clinical and experimental developments in the field of artificial organs. Automated therapeutic aids and devices are covered in occasional articles.

610 700 US ISSN 1057-4263
▼INTERNATIONAL JOURNAL OF ARTS MEDICINE. 1991. s-a. $20. (International Arts Medicine Association) I J A M, M M B Music, Inc., 10370 Page Industrial Blvd., St. Louis, MO 63132. (Co-sponsor: International Society for Music in Medicine) Ed. Rosalie Rebollo Pratt.
Description: Contains theoretical, clinical, and philosophical articles that pertain to arts medicine and arts therapies.
Refereed Serial

INTERNATIONAL JOURNAL OF BIOMETEOROLOGY. see METEOROLOGY

614.4 UK ISSN 0300-5771
RA651 CODEN: IJEPBF
INTERNATIONAL JOURNAL OF EPIDEMIOLOGY. 1972. q. £99($180) (International Epidemiological Association) Oxford University Press, Oxford Journals, Pinkhill House, Southfield Rd., Eynsham, Oxford OX8 1JJ, England. TEL 0865-882283. FAX 0865-882890. TELEX 837330 OXPRES G. Ed. Charles du Ve Florey. adv.; bk.rev.; illus.; index; circ. 1,800. (also avail. in microform from UMI; reprint service avail. from UMI) Indexed: Abstr.Hyg., Bibl.Dev.Med.& Child Neur., Biol.Abstr., C.I.S. Abstr., Curr.Adv.Cancer Res., Curr.Adv.Ecol.Sci., Curr.Cont., Dairy Sci.Abstr., Dent.Ind., Excerp.Med., Helminthol.Abstr., Ind.Med., Ind.Sci.Rev., Ind.Vet., INIS Atomind., Lab.Haz.Bull., Nutr.Abstr., Protozool.Abstr., Risk Abstr., Sci.Cit.Ind, Small Anim.Abstr., SSCI, Trop.Dis.Bull., Vet.Bull., W.R.C.Inf.
—BLDSC shelfmark: 4542.244000.
Description: Epidemiology of infectious and non-infectious diseases. Includes research results, new methods, statistical or otherwise, for the analysis of data used by those who practice social and preventive medicine.

616.07 UK ISSN 0959-9673
RB1 CODEN: IJEPEI
INTERNATIONAL JOURNAL OF EXPERIMENTAL PATHOLOGY. 1920. bi-m. £115 (foreign £127.50). Blackwell Scientific Publications Ltd., Osney Mead, Oxford OX2 0EL, England. TEL 0865-240201. FAX 0865-721205. TELEX 83355-MEDBOK-G. Ed. R.M. Hicks. adv.; bibl.; illus.; index; circ. 1,600. (also avail. in microform from UMI,PMC; reprint service avail. from UMI) Indexed: Abstr.Hyg., Biol.Abstr., Biotech.Abstr., Chem.Abstr., Curr.Adv.Cancer Res., Curr.Adv.Ecol.Sci., Curr.Cont., Dairy Sci.Abstr., Dent.Ind., Excerp.Med., Helminthol.Abstr., Ind.Med., Ind.Sci.Rev., Ind.Vet., Lab.Haz.Bull., Nutr.Abstr., Protozool.Abstr., Rev.Plant Path., Sci.Cit.Ind, Trop.Dis.Bull., Vet.Bull.
—BLDSC shelfmark: 4542.244820.
Formerly: British Journal of Experimental Pathology (ISSN 0007-1021)

612.6 574.16 US ISSN 0020-725X
QP251 CODEN: INJFA3
INTERNATIONAL JOURNAL OF FERTILITY. 1956. bi-m. $50 (foreign $60). (U S International Foundation for Studies in Reproduction, Inc.) M S P (Medical Science Publishing) International, Inc., 403 Main St., Port Washington, NY 11050. TEL 516-944-7340. FAX 516-944-8663. (Co-sponsors: Scandinavian Association for Studies in Fertility; Fallopius International Society; International Society of Reproductive Medicine) Ed. Kathleen M. Yasas. adv.; bibl.; charts; illus.; index; circ. 25,000. (reprint service avail.) Indexed: Anim.Breed.Abstr., Biol.Abstr., Biotech.Abstr., Chem.Abstr., Curr.Adv.Ecol.Sci., Curr.Cont., Curr.Lit.Fam.Plan., Dairy Sci.Abstr., Dent.Ind., Excerp.Med., Helminthol.Abstr., Ind.Med., Ind.Sci.Rev., Ind.Vet., Sci.Cit.Ind, Vet.Bull.
—BLDSC shelfmark: 4542.250000.
Description: Scholarly articles on medical treatments, surgery, and pathology pertaining to human reproduction.

610 UK ISSN 0952-6862
INTERNATIONAL JOURNAL OF HEALTH CARE QUALITY ASSURANCE. 6/yr. $429.95. M C B University Press Ltd., 62 Toller Ln., Bradford, W. Yorks BD8 9BY, England. TEL 0274-499821. FAX 0274-547134. TELEX 51317-MCBUNI-G. (N. American subscr. to: M C B University Press Limited, Box 1943, Birmingham, AL 35202) Ed. Robin Gourlay. (reprint service avail. from SWZ)
—BLDSC shelfmark: 4542.275000.
Incorporates: Health Care Management (ISSN 0269-2104)
Description: Theory and practice of quality assurance: measuring quality and customer satisfaction, alternative methodologies for implementing programs.

610 NE ISSN 0924-2287
▼INTERNATIONAL JOURNAL OF HEALTH SCIENCES. (Text in English) 1990. q. fl.165. (Northern Centre for Health Care Research and Education) Van Gorcum en Co. B.V., P.O. Box 43, 9400 AA Assen, Netherlands. TEL 05920-46846. FAX 05920-72064. Ed. W.J.A. vanden Heuvel. adv.; bk.rev.; circ. 1,200.
—BLDSC shelfmark: 4542.277900.

610 US ISSN 0167-6865
QP106.6 CODEN: IMCEDT
INTERNATIONAL JOURNAL OF MICROCIRCULATION: CLINICAL & EXPERIMENTAL. 1982. q. fl.200($105) to individuals; institutions fl.311 ($158.50). Kluwer Academic Publishers, 101 Philip Dr., Norwell, MA 02061. TEL 617-871-6600. FAX 617-871-6528. TELEX 200190. (Subscr. to: Box 358, Accord Sta., Hingham, MA 02018-0358) Eds. B. Farrell, K. Messmer. adv.; bk.rev. (back issues avail.; reprint service avail. from SWZ,UMI) Indexed: Chem.Abstr., Curr.Adv.Ecol.Sci., Curr.Cont., Excerp.Med., Ind.Sci.Rev., Sci.Cit.Ind.
—BLDSC shelfmark: 4542.354000.
Refereed Serial

INTERNATIONAL JOURNAL OF PEPTIDE & PROTEIN RESEARCH. see BIOLOGY — Biological Chemistry

610 617.6 150
615.19 US ISSN 0884-8297
CODEN: IJOPEY
INTERNATIONAL JOURNAL OF PSYCHOSOMATICS. 1954. q. $50 foreign $60. International Psychosomatics Institute, Box 1296, Philadelphia, PA 19105. TEL 215-565-1964. Ed. Dr. Arnold H. Gessel. adv.; bk.rev.; abstr.; bibl.; charts; illus.; index; circ. 1,000. (also avail. in microform from UMI) Indexed: Behav.Med.Abstr., Biol.Abstr., Dent.Ind., Excerp.Med., Ind.Med., Psychol.Abstr.
Formerly (until 1984): American Society of Psychosomatic Dentistry and Medicine. Journal (ISSN 0003-1194)

371.9 UK ISSN 0342-5282
RM695 CODEN: IJRRDK
INTERNATIONAL JOURNAL OF REHABILITATION RESEARCH. (Text in English, French and German; summaries in English, French, German and Spanish) 1977. q. £25 to individuals (US & Canada $45); institutions £55 (US & Canada $95). (Rehabilitation International, US) Chapman & Hall, 2-6 Boundary Row, London SE1, England. TEL 071-865-0066. (Dist. by: International Thomson Publishing Services, Ltd., N. Way, Andover, Hampshire SP10 5BE, England. TEL 0264-33-2424; US addr.: Chapman & Hall, 29 W. 35th St., New York, NY 10001-2291. TEL 212-244-3336) Ed. Paul Cornes. adv.; bk.rev.; charts; circ. 3,500. Indexed: Biol.Abstr., C.I.J.E., Child Devel.Abstr., Crim.Just.Abstr., Ergon.Abstr., Excerp.Med., Ind.Med., Lang.& Lang.Behav.Abstr., Psychol.Abstr., Rehabil.Lit., SSCI, Yrbk.Assoc.Educ.& Rehab.Blind.
—BLDSC shelfmark: 4542.526000.
Description: An interdisciplinary forum for research into disability and handicaps experienced by people in both developed and developing societies.
Refereed Serial

MEDICAL SCIENCES

610 NE ISSN 0924-6479
CODEN: IJMDEM
▼**INTERNATIONAL JOURNAL OF RISK AND SAFETY IN MEDICINE**; side effects of drugs - devices - surgery - prevention - liability. 1990. 6/yr. fl.396 (effective 1992). Elsevier Science Publishers B.V., P.O. Box 211, 1000 AE Amsterdam, Netherlands. TEL 020-5803911. FAX 020-5803598. TELEX 18582 ESPA NL. (Subscr. in U.S. and Canada to: Elsevier Science Publishing Co., Inc., Box 882, Madison Sq. Sta., New York, NY 10159. TEL 212-989-5800) Ed. M.N.G. Dukes. bk.rev. (back issues avail.) Indexed: Excerp.Med. (1992-).
—BLDSC shelfmark: 4542.538200.
Description: Covers medical science, pharmacology, public health and safety.
Refereed Serial

610 BE
INTERNATIONAL ORGANIZATION FOR COOPERATION IN HEALTH CARE. GENERAL ASSEMBLY. REPORT. 1979. a. free. Medicus Mundi International, Rue du Marteau 19, 1040 Brussels, Belgium. TEL 02-2199588.
Supersedes: International Organization for Medical Cooperation. General Assembly. Report (ISSN 0579-3912)

362 US ISSN 0020-8477
CODEN: IRERB
INTERNATIONAL REHABILITATION REVIEW. 1949. 3/yr. $30. Rehabilitation International, 25 E. 21st St., 4th Fl., New York, NY 10010. TEL 212-420-1500. FAX 212-505-0871. TELEX 446412. Ed. Barbara Duncan. adv.; bk.rev.; film rev.; play rev.; illus.; circ. 20,000. (tabloid format; back issues avail.) Indexed: CINAHL, Except.Child.Educ.Abstr., Excerp.Med., Rehabil.Lit., Soc.Work Res.& Abstr.
—BLDSC shelfmark: 4545.797000.
Formerly: Rehabilitation International Newsletter.
Description: Issues and developments in disability prevention and rehabilitation worldwide.

616.07 US ISSN 0074-7718
RB6 CODEN: IRXPAT
INTERNATIONAL REVIEW OF EXPERIMENTAL PATHOLOGY. 1962. irreg., vol.32, 1991. Academic Press, Inc., 1250 Sixth Ave., San Diego, CA 92101. TEL 619-231-0926. FAX 619-699-6715. Ed. G.W. Richter. index. (reprint service avail. from ISI) Indexed: Abstr.Hyg., Biol.Abstr., Chem.Abstr., Curr.Adv.Cell & Devel.Biol., Excerp.Med., Ind.Med., Ind.Sci.Rev., Ind.Vet., Sci.Cit.Ind, Trop.Dis.Bull., Vet.Bull.
—BLDSC shelfmark: 4547.150000.
Refereed Serial

INTERNATIONAL UNION OF SCHOOL AND UNIVERSITY HEALTH AND MEDICINE. CONGRESS REPORTS. see *EDUCATION*

616 GW ISSN 0020-9554
CODEN: INTEAG
DER INTERNIST. (Text mainly in German) 1960. 12/yr. DM.312($167) (Berufsverband Deutscher Internisten) Springer-Verlag, Heidelberger Platz 3, D-1000 Berlin 33, Germany. TEL 030-8207-1. (Also Heidelberg, Tokyo, Vienna, and New York) Ed. G. Budelmann. adv.; bk.rev.; charts; illus.; index, cum.index. (also avail. in microform from UMI; back issues avail.; reprint service avail. from ISI) Indexed: Biol.Abstr., Biotech.Abstr., Curr.Cont., Excerp.Med., Ind.Med., Ind.Sci.Rev., Nutr.Abstr.
—BLDSC shelfmark: 4557.200000.

610 SA
INTERNIST.* (Text in Afrikaans and English) 1980. q. R.6($8) (Association of Specialist Physicians) Melton Publications (Pty) Ltd., P.O. Box 3445, Randburg 2125, South Africa. Ed. Sue Smith. adv.; bk.rev.; circ. 900.

616 330.9 US
INTERNIST: HEALTH POLICY IN PRACTICE. 1959. 10/yr. $24 to non-members (foreign $30). American Society of Internal Medicine, 2011 Pennsylvania Ave., N.W., Ste. 800, Washington, DC 20006-1808. TEL 202-835-2746. Ed. C. Burns Roehrig, M.D. adv.; charts; illus.; stat; circ. 29,500. (also avail. in microform from UMI; reprint service avail. from UMI) Indexed: C.I.S. Abstr., Chem.Abstr, Hosp.Lit.Ind., Med.Care Rev., Sci.Cit.Ind.
Formerly (until 1986): Internist (ISSN 0020-9546)
Description: Analysis and reports on current health policy, medical socioeconomic trends and issues affecting the practice of medicine.

616 GW ISSN 0020-9570
CODEN: INPXAJ
INTERNISTISCHE PRAXIS; taegliche Praxis der gesamten Inneren Medizin. 1961. 4/yr. DM.268. Hans Marseille Verlag, Buerkleinstr. 12, 8000 Munich 22, Germany. TEL 089-227988. Ed. H. Feiereis. bk.rev.; abstr.; bibl.; charts; illus.; index. cum.index every 5 yrs.; circ. 4,800. (also avail. in microfilm from UMI; reprint service avail. from UMI) Indexed: Biol.Abstr., Excerp.Med., Ind.Med.
—BLDSC shelfmark: 4557.220000.
Description: Practical information of interest to specialists in internal medicine. Features the latest research in the field. Includes questions and answers.

616.02 GW ISSN 0344-4201
DIE INTERNISTISCHE WELT. 1978. 5/yr. DM.228($150.30) F.K. Schattauer Verlagsgesellschaft mbH, Lenzhalde 3, Postfach 104545, 7000 Stuttgart 10, Germany. TEL 0711-22987-0. FAX 0711-22987-50. Ed. G. Oehler. Indexed: Excerp.Med.
—BLDSC shelfmark: 4557.220200.

610 US ISSN 0164-6419
INTERNIST'S INTERCOM. m. membership only. American Society of Internal Medicine, 2011 Pennsylvania Ave., N.W., Ste. 800, Washington, DC 20006-1808. TEL 202-835-2746. circ. 29,500.
Description: Covers the socioeconomics of internal medicine practice.

574 610 VE ISSN 0535-5133
CODEN: ICLIAD
INVESTIGACION CLINICA. (Supplements avail.) (Text and summaries in English and Spanish) 1960. q. $40. Universidad del Zulia, Instituto de Investigaciones Clinicas, Facultad de Medicina, Apdo. Postal 1151, Maracaibo, Venezuela. Ed. Dra. Elena Ryder. bibl.; charts; circ. 2,000. Indexed: Abstr.Hyg., Biol.Abstr., Chem.Abstr., Curr.Cont., Excerp.Med., Helminthol.Abstr., Nutr.Abstr., Trop.Dis.Bull.
—BLDSC shelfmark: 4557.720000.

610 GW ISSN 0938-0922
▼**INVITRO DIAGNOSTIKA NACHRICHTEN**. 1990. m. DM.112. Berliner Medizinische Verlagsanstalt GmbH, Kurfuerstenstr. 112-113, 1000 Berlin 30, Germany. TEL 030-219909-0. FAX 030-219909-10. circ. 7,000.

610 US ISSN 0746-8709
R15
IOWA MEDICINE. 1910. m. $20. Iowa Medical Society, 1001 Grand Ave., W. Des Moines, IA 50265. TEL 515-223-1401. Ed. Tina Preftakes. adv.; bk.rev.; charts; illus.; index; circ. 4,300. (back issues avail.) Indexed: Biol.Abstr., Chem.Abstr., Ind.Med., INIS Atomind., Med.Care Rev.
—BLDSC shelfmark: 4566.400000.
Formerly (until 1984): Iowa Medical Society. Journal (ISSN 0021-0587)
Description: Scientific and socioeconomic medical journal.

610 IR ISSN 0253-0716
CODEN: IJMSDW
IRANIAN JOURNAL OF MEDICAL SCIENCES. (Text and summaries in English) 1970. irreg., vol.14 no.2 1989. Rs.1600($20) Shiraz University of Medical Sciences, Nemazee Hospital, Shiraz, Iran. TELEX 332169 SHU IR. Ed. Dr. K. Vessal. adv.; bk.rev.; charts; illus.; stat.; circ. 2,500. (also avail. in microform from MIM,UMI; reprint service avail. from UMI) Indexed: Biol.Abstr., Biotech.Abstr., Chem.Abstr., Chem.Abstr, Curr.Cont., Excerp.Med., Helminthol.Abstr., Ind.Med., Nutr.Abstr., Trop.Dis.Bull.
—BLDSC shelfmark: 4567.528900.
Formerly: Pahlavi Medical Journal (ISSN 0030-9427)
Description: Aims to provide a medium of scientific communication for Iranian physicians, biomedical investigators, and medical and health educators in the world scientific community.

610 IQ ISSN 0021-0927
IRAQI MEDICAL PROFESSIONS' ASSOCIATION. JOURNAL.* (Text in Arabic and English) vol.13, 1965. 3/yr. Iraqi Medical Professions' Association, Republican Hospital, Baghdad, Iraq. Ed. Dr. F.H. Ghali. adv.; charts; illus.; stat. Indexed: Biol.Abstr., Ind.Med.

610 UK ISSN 0374-8405
CODEN: IPSJB7
IRISH COLLEGES OF PHYSICIANS AND SURGEONS. JOURNAL. 1971. q. £55 (foreign £60). Macmillan Press Ltd., Houndmills, Basingstoke, Hampshire RG2 2XS, England. TEL 0256-29242. FAX 0256-810526. (Co-Sponsors: Royal Colleges of Physicans and Surgeons) Ed. Eoin O'Brien. adv.; bk.rev.; charts; illus.; index; circ. 3,500. Indexed: Biol.Abstr., Curr.Adv.Ecol.Sci., Curr.Cont., INIS Atomind.
—BLDSC shelfmark: 4802.780000.
Supersedes: Royal College of Surgeons in Ireland. Journal (ISSN 0035-8827)

610 IE ISSN 0021-1265
CODEN: IJMSAT
IRISH JOURNAL OF MEDICAL SCIENCES. 1832. m. £48 (foreign £60). Royal Academy of Medicine in Ireland, 6 Kildare St., Dublin 2, Ireland. FAX 611684. Ed. Thomas F. Gorey. adv.; bk.rev.; circ. 1,500. (also avail. in microfilm; reprint service avail. from UMI) Indexed: Biol.Abstr., Chem.Abstr., Curr.Adv.Cancer Res., Dent.Ind., Excerp.Med., Helminthol.Abstr., Ind.Med., Ind.Sci.Rev., INIS Atomind., NRN, Nutr.Abstr., Rev.Plant Path., Sci.Cit.Ind.
—BLDSC shelfmark: 4572.000000.

610 IE ISSN 0332-3102
CODEN: IMDJBD
IRISH MEDICAL JOURNAL. 1937-1987 (Dec.); resumed 1988 (Sep.). q. £35 (foreign £45). Irish Medical Organization, 10 Fitzwilliam Place, Dublin 2, Ireland. TEL 01-767273. FAX 01-612758. Ed. John Murphy. adv.; bk.rev.; charts; illus.; s-a. index; circ. 5,000. Indexed: Biol.Abstr., Chem.Abstr., Curr.Cont., Dent.Ind., Dok.Arbeitsmed., Excerp.Med., Helminthol.Abstr., Ind.Med., INIS Atomind., NRN, Nutr.Abstr.
—BLDSC shelfmark: 4572.910000.
Former titles: Irish Medical Organization & Irish Medical Association. Journal (ISSN 0021-129X)
Description: Forum for all aspects of Irish medicine.

610 IE
IRISH MEDICAL NEWS. 1974. w. £50 to non-members. Winstone Publishing, 10 Fitzwilliam Place, Dublin 2, Ireland. TEL 01-767273. FAX 01-612758. Ed. John Gibbons. adv.; bk.rev.; circ. 5,000.
Formerly (until 1984): I M J Appointments.

610 UK ISSN 0047-147X
IRISH MEDICAL TIMES. 1967. w. £45. Medical Publications Ltd., 30 Lancaster Gate, London W2 3LP, England. (Subscr. to: 12-14 Ansdell St., London W8 5TR, England) Ed. Dr. John F. O'Connell. adv.; bk.rev.; circ. controlled. (tabloid format; also avail. in microfilm from UMI; reprint service avail. from UMI)

610 JA ISSN 0910-6030
IRYO (YEAR). 1985. m. 13200 Yen. Medical Friend Co. Ltd. - Mejikaru Furendo-Sha, 2-4, 3-chome, Kudan-Kita, Chiyoda-ku, Tokyo 102, Japan. FAX 03-3261-6602. Ed. Kazuhazu Ogura. adv.; bk.rev.; circ. 30,000. (back issues avail.) Indexed: Excerp.Med.
Description: Analyzes and discusses health service trends.

ISLAMIC ACADEMY OF SCIENCES. JOURNAL. see *SCIENCES: COMPREHENSIVE WORKS*

ISOTOPE NEWS. see *BIOLOGY — Biological Chemistry*

MEDICAL SCIENCES

610   IS   ISSN 0021-2180
R97   CODEN: IJMDAI
ISRAEL JOURNAL OF MEDICAL SCIENCES. (Text in English) 1965. m. $100 to individuals; institutions $150 (effective 1992). Israel Journal of Medical Sciences, 2 Etzel St., French Hill, Jerusalem 97853, Israel. TEL 02-817727. FAX 02-815722. (Co-sponsors: National Council for Research and Development; Israel Medical Association) Ed. Dr. Moshe Prywes. adv.; bk.rev.; bibl.; charts; illus.; index; circ. 5,000. (also avail. in microform from UMI; reprint service avail. from UMI) **Indexed:** Abstr.Hyg., Biol.Abstr., Biotech.Abstr., Chem.Abstr., Curr.Adv.Cancer Res., Curr.Cont., Dairy Sci.Abstr., Dent.Ind., Dok.Arbeitsmed., Excerp.Med., Helminthol.Abstr., Ind.Med., Ind.Sci.Rev., Ind.Vet., INIS Atomind., Int.Abstr.Biol.Sci, Int.Nurs.Ind., NRN, Nutr.Abstr., Pig News & Info., Poult.Abstr., Rev.Plant Path., Sci.Cit.Ind., Small Anim.Abstr., Soyabean Abstr., Vet.Bull.
—BLDSC shelfmark: 4583.812000.
Incorporates: Israel Journal of Experimental Medicine; Israel Medical Journal.

615.8   IS   ISSN 0021-2199
ISRAEL JOURNAL OF PHYSIOTHERAPY. (Text in English and Hebrew) irreg. (3-4/yr.) membership. National Union of Physiotherapy in Israel, 93 Arlozorov St., Tel Aviv, Israel. TEL 03-431111. Ed.Bd. adv.; bk.rev.; charts; illus.; circ. 500.

610   IS
ISRAEL MEDICAL ASSOCIATION. QUARTERLY MEDICAL REVIEW. (Editions in English, French, Spanish) q. membership. Fraser, 17 Bugrashov St., Tel Aviv, Israel. Ed. Yehuda Shoefeld. adv.; illus.
Formerly: Israel Medical Association. Quarterly Review. (ISSN 0021-2253)

ISSUES IN BIOMEDICINE. see *BIOLOGY*

ISSUES IN LAW AND MEDICINE. see *LAW*

610   TU   ISSN 0374-1656
R97.7.T8   CODEN: TFMEAC
ISTANBUL MEDICAL FACULTY. MEDICAL BULLETIN/ISTANBUL TIP FAKULTESI. MECMUASI. Cover title: Istanbul Universitesi. Istanbul Tip Fakultesi. Mecmuasi. (Text in English; summaries in English, French, German) 1919; N.S. 1938. biennial. free. Istanbul University, Istanbul Medical Faculty - Istanbul Universitesi. Istanbul Tip Fakultesi, Beyazit, 34390 Istanbul, Turkey. illus.; circ. 1,000. **Indexed:** Biol.Abstr., Chem.Abstr., Excerp.Med. (1992-), Ind.Med., Nutr.Abstr.
Formerly: Istanbul Universitesi. Tip Fakultesi. Tip Fakultesi Mecmuasi (ISSN 0047-1623)

ISTITUTO SUPERIORE DI SANITA. ANNALI. see *PUBLIC HEALTH AND SAFETY*

610   JA   ISSN 0021-3284
CODEN: IIZAAX
IWATE IGAKU ZASSHI/IWATE MEDICAL ASSOCIATION. JOURNAL. (Text in Japanese; Index partly in English) 1945. bi-m. 5000 Yen. Iwate Igakkai - Iwate Medical Association, c/o Iwate Medical University, 19-1 Uchimaru, Morioka-shi, Iwate-ken 020, Japan. TEL 0196-51-5111.2224. FAX 0196-25-0547. Ed. Takeshi Kashimoto. adv.; abstr.; bibl.; charts; illus.; index; circ. 1,400. **Indexed:** Biol.Abstr., Chem.Abstr., Excerp.Med., INIS Atomind.
—BLDSC shelfmark: 4803.200000.
Description: Compilation of original medical research reports.

610   SP
J A M A EN COLOMBIA. (Journal of the American Medical Association) 1977. m. 1800 ptas.($42) Editorial ECO, S.A., Calle de la Cruz 44, Barcelona 17, Spain. Ed. Cesar A. Pantoja, M.D. circ. 7,500.

610   SP
J A M A EN ESPANOL. (Journal of the American Medical Association) 1975. m. 1800 ptas.($23) Editorial ECO, S.A., Calle de la Cruz 44, Barcelona 17, Spain. Ed. Dr. J. Ferre Fuentes. adv.; charts; illus.; stat.; index; circ. 35,000 (controlled). **Indexed:** Dok.Arbeitsmed., Nutr.Abstr.

610   SP
J A M A EN VENEZUELA. (Journal of the American Medical Association) 1977. m. Bol.$130($30) Editorial ECO, S.A., Calle de la Cruz 44, Barcelona 34, Spain. Ed. Francisco Kerdel, M.D. adv.; charts; illus.; stat.; index; circ. 7,000.

610   FR
J A M A - FRANCE. (Journal of the American Medical Association) 1980. s-m. 270 F.($30) to individuals (foreign 480 F.); students 210 F. (foreign 370 F.). Publications Medicales Internationales, 24 bis bd. Verd de Saint-Julien, 92190 Meudon, France. Ed. Jean Pascal Huve. adv.; circ. 32,000.

610   US   ISSN 0098-7484
R15   CODEN: JAMAAP
J A M A: THE JOURNAL OF THE AMERICAN MEDICAL ASSOCIATION. Chinese translation: Meiguo Yixuehui Zazhi (Zhongwen Ban) (CC ISSN 1000-842X) 1848. w. $79. American Medical Association, 515 N. State St., Chicago, IL 60610. TEL 312-464-0183. FAX 312-464-5834. Ed. Dr. George D. Lundberg. adv.; bk.rev.; abstr.; bibl.; charts; illus.; index in last no. of each vol.(2 vols. per year); circ. 372,000. (also avail. in microform from UMI,PMC; reprint service avail. from UMI) **Indexed:** Abstr.Anthropol., Abstr.Health Care Manage.Stud., Abstr.Hyg., Acad.Ind., Adol.Ment.Hlth.Abstr., Behav.Med.Abstr., Bibl.Dev.Med.& Child Neur., Biol.Abstr., Biostat., Biotech.Abstr., C.I.S. Abstr., CAD CAM Abstr., Chem.Abstr., Curr.Adv.Cancer Res., Curr.Cont., Dairy Sci.Abstr., Deep Sea Res.& Oceanogr.Abstr., Dent.Abstr., Dent.Ind., Environ.Abstr., Excerp.Med., FAMLI, Food Sci.& Tech.Abstr., Gen.Sci.Ind., Helminthol.Abstr., Hlth.Ind., I.P.A., Ind.Hyg.Dig., Ind.Med., Ind.Vet., INIS Atomind., Int.Nurs.Ind., Lab.Haz.Bull., Mag.Ind., Med.Care Rev., NRN, Nutr.Abstr., Protozool.Abstr., Rev.Appl.Entomol, Rev.Plant Path., Risk Abstr., Sci.Cit.Ind, Small Anim.Abstr., Telegen, Tr.& Indus.Ind., Trop.Dis.Bull., Vet.Bull.
●Also available online. Vendor(s): BRS (JWAT), Mead Data Central.
—BLDSC shelfmark: 4689.000000.
Formerly: American Medical Association. Journal (ISSN 0002-9955)
Refereed Serial

610   IT   ISSN 0393-554X
J A M A: THE JOURNAL OF THE AMERICAN MEDICAL ASSOCIATION (ITALIAN EDITION). 1989. m. (10/yr.). L.50000. E S I Stampa Medica s.r.l., Casella Postale 42, Lgo. Volontari del Sangue 10, 20097 S. Donato, Milan, Italy. TEL 02-5274241. FAX 02-5274775. TELEX 324894. Ed. Bruno Pieroni. adv.; bk.rev.; circ. 8,000.

610   FR   ISSN 0299-3953
J A M I F. (Journal Association des Medecins Israelites de France) 1952. 10/yr. 100 F.($75) (effective Jan. 1990). Association des Medecins Israelites de France, 11 ave. de la Republique, 94260 Fresnes, France. Ed. Dr. D. Bellaiche. adv.; bk.rev.; abstr.; film rev.; play rev.; circ. 8,500 (controlled).
Former titles: Association des Medecins Israelites de France. Revue Medicale (ISSN 0298-2900); A M I F (ISSN 0400-132X)

610   US   ISSN 0197-2510
J E M S. (Journal of Emergency Medical Services) 1975. m. $21.97. Jems Publishing Co., Inc., Box 2789, Carlsbad, CA 92018. TEL 619-431-9797. FAX 619-431-8176. Ed. Keith Griffiths. adv.; bk.rev.; charts; illus.; stat.; circ. 22,187. (also avail. in microform; back issues avail.)
—BLDSC shelfmark: 4663.525000.

J O P S O M. (Journal of Preventive and Social Medicine) see *PUBLIC HEALTH AND SAFETY*

JACKSON LABORATORY SCIENTIFIC REPORT. see *BIOLOGY — Genetics*

610   US
JACKSONVILLE MEDICINE JOURNAL. m. $25. Duval County Medical Society, 515 Lomax St., Jacksonville, FL 32204. TEL 904-355-6561. FAX 904-353-5848. Ed. A. Allen Seals, M.D. adv.; circ. 1,800. (back issues avail.)
Formerly: Jacksonville Medicine Bulletin.

610   CE
JAFFNA MEDICAL JOURNAL. (Text in English) 1953. s-a. Rs.100($20) Jaffna Medical Association, General Hospital, Jaffna, Sri Lanka. TEL 222661. Ed. Dr. N. Sivarajah. adv.; bk.rev.; circ. 700. **Indexed:** Sri Lanka Sci.Ind.

610   SP   ISSN 0210-220X
JANO "MEDICINA Y HUMANIDADES". 1971. w. (45/yr.). 6900 ptas.($87) (free to qualified personnel). Ediciones Doyma S.A., Travesera de Gracia 17-21, 08021 Barcelona, Spain. TEL 200-07-11. FAX 209-11-36. TELEX 51964 INK-E. Ed. Celia Ribera Banus. adv.: page 355000 ptas.; trim 230 x 295; adv. contact: Francisco Torras. circ. 40,000. (reprint service avail. from UMI)
Description: Covers topics in clinical medicine, diagnosis and treatment, to support the continuing education of postgraduates. Includes cultural topics in history, the arts, literature, music, films and theater.

JANUS; revue internationale de l'histoire des sciences, de la medecine, de la pharmacie et de la technique. see *SCIENCES: COMPREHENSIVE WORKS*

610   JA   ISSN 0385-9215
JAPAN MEDICAL JOURNAL. (Text in Japanese) 1921. w. 30500 Yen. Nihon Iji Shimposha, 2-9 Kanda Surugadai, Chiyoda-ku, Tokyo 101, Japan. FAX 03-3292-1550. Ed. Shinji Umezawa. circ. 45,000. (back issues avail.)
Description: Published mainly for family physicians.

610   JA   ISSN 0021-4515
JAPAN MEDICAL NEWS. (Text in English) 1959. bi-m. free. Japan Pharmaceutical, Medical & Dental Supply Exporter's Association - Nihon Iyakuryohin Yushutsu Kumiai, Ninjin Building, 7-1 Nihonbashi-Honcho 4-chome, Chuo-ku, Tokyo 103, Japan. TEL 81-3-3241-2106. FAX 81-3-3241-2109. Ed. Kuniichiro Ohno. adv.; bk.rev.; abstr.; charts; illus.; circ. 2,300. (tabloid format)

610 658   US   ISSN 0914-0255
JAPAN MEDICAL REVIEW; a monthly report on the Japanese healthcare industry. 1986. m. 80,000 Yen($450) Japan Publications, Inc., 150 Post St., Ste. 500, San Francisco, CA 94108. TEL 415-772-5555. FAX 415-772-5659. Ed. S. Nakamura. s-a index. (back issues avail.)

616   JA   ISSN 0021-4809
CODEN: NAHOAI
JAPANESE ARCHIVES OF INTERNAL MEDICINE/NAIKAHOKAN. (Text in Japanese; summaries in English) 1954. m. $30. Kyoto University, Medical Faculty, Department of Internal Medicine - Kyoto Daigaku Igakubu, 54 Shogoin, Kawara-machi, Kyoto 606, Japan. TEL 075-751-3153. FAX 075-771-2309. Ed. Dr. Tadashi Kano. adv.; bk.rev.; abstr.; charts; illus.; circ. 500. **Indexed:** Chem.Abstr, Dent.Ind., Excerp.Med., Ind.Med.
—BLDSC shelfmark: 4650.600000.

610 615.329   JA   ISSN 0368-2781
CODEN: JJANAX
JAPANESE JOURNAL OF ANTIBIOTICS. (Text in Japanese; summaries in English) 1947. m. $97. Japan Antibiotics Research Association - Nihon Koseibusshitsu Gakujutsu Kyogikai, 2-20-8 Kamiosaki, Shinagawa-ku, Tokyo 141, Japan. TEL 03-3491-0181. FAX 03-3491-0179. Ed. Kenji Maeda; adv.; bibl.; charts; index; circ. 1,500. (also avail. in microform from UMI; back issues avail.; reprint service avail. from UMI) **Indexed:** Biotech.Abstr., Chem.Abstr., Curr.Chem.React, Curr.Cont., Dent.Ind., Excerp.Med., Ind.Chem, Ind.Med., Mass Spectr.Bull.
—BLDSC shelfmark: 4650.845000.
Formerly: Journal of Antibiotics. Series B.

610   JA   ISSN 0047-1852
JAPANESE JOURNAL OF CLINICAL MEDICINE/NIPPON RINSHO. (Text in Japanese) 1943. m. Nippon Rinsho Co., Inc., 3-1 Dosho-machi, Higashi-ku, Osaka 541, Japan. illus. **Indexed:** Curr.Cont., Ind.Med.
—BLDSC shelfmark: 4651.375000.

615.845 610.28   JA   ISSN 0021-3675
JAPANESE JOURNAL OF MEDICAL ELECTRONICS AND BIOLOGICAL ENGINEERING/IYO DENSHI TO SEITO KOGAKU (NIHON M-E GAKKAI ZASSHI). (Text in Japanese; summaries in English) 1963. bi-m. 6000 Yen($20) (Japan Society of Medical Electronics and Biological Engineering - Nihon M-E Gakkai) Corona Publishing Co., Ltd., 4-46-10 Sengoku, Bunkyo-ku, Tokyo 112, Japan. Ed. Dr. Ippei Hatakeyama. adv.; bk.rev.; bibl.; charts; illus.; stat.; index. **Indexed:** Dent.Ind., Excerp.Med., Ind.Med., JCT, JTA, Sci.Abstr.

MEDICAL SCIENCES 3113

610 574   JA   ISSN 0021-5112
R97   CODEN: JJMCAQ
JAPANESE JOURNAL OF MEDICAL SCIENCE AND BIOLOGY. (Text in English) 1948. bi-m. $78 (effective 1990). National Institute of Health, 2-10-35 Kamiosaki, Shinagawaku, Tokyo 141, Japan. Ed. Tohru Tokunaga. bk.rev.; charts; illus.; circ. 1,100. **Indexed:** Abstr.Hyg., Biol.Abstr., Chem.Abstr., Curr.Cont., Dairy Sci.Abstr., Dent.Ind., Excerp.Med., Helminthol.Abstr., Ind.Med., Ind.Sci.Rev., Ind.Vet., INIS Atomind., NRN, Nutr.Abstr., Protozool.Abstr., Sci.Cit.Ind., Trop.Dis.Bull., Vet.Bull.
—BLDSC shelfmark: 4656.320000.
Description: Publishes full and short communications, reviews, epidemiological reports and reports dealing with fundamental aspects of medical science and biology.

610   JA   ISSN 0021-5120
JAPANESE JOURNAL OF MEDICINE. (Text in English) 1962. q. 9000 Yen to non-members; members 7000 Yen (foreign 413.50 Fr.). Japanese Society of Internal Medicine - Nihon Naika Gakkai, Hongo Daiichi Bldg., 34-3, 3-Chome, Bunkyo-ku, Tokyo 113, Japan. TEL 61-3691-8925. FAX 61-3692-4262. TELEX 963475. (Dist. outside Japan by: J.C. Baltzer A.G., Wettsteinplatz 10, CH-4058 Basel, Switzerland) Ed. Hiroshi Oka. abstr.; charts; illus.; circ. 1,000. **Indexed:** Biol.Abstr., Chem.Abstr., Curr.Cont., Excerp.Med., Helminthol.Abstr., Ind.Med., INIS Atomind., Nutr.Abstr.
—BLDSC shelfmark: 4656.449000.

JAPANESE JOURNAL OF PHYSIOLOGY. see *BIOLOGY — Physiology*

610 574   JA
JAPANESE MATRIX (COLLAGEN) CLUB. PROCEEDINGS OF THE ANNUAL MEETING. (Text in Japanese; summaries in English) 1959. a. 3000 Yen($15) Japanese Matrix (Collagen) Club, c/o Tokyo Medical and Dental University, Department of Tissue Physiology, Kanda Surugadai 2-3-10, Chiyoda-ku, Tokyo 101, Japan. TEL 03-3291-9573. Ed. Yutaka Nagai. adv.; circ. 300. (back issues avail.)
Formerly: Japanese Collagen Club. Proceedings of the Annual Meeting.
Description: Investigates the structure, function and metabolism of extracellular matrix macromolecules, especially collagen.

610   JA
JAPANESE MEDICAL RESEARCHERS DIRECTORY. (Text in English and Japanese) 1959. a. 33000 Yen. Igaku-Shoin Ltd., 5-24-3 Hongo, Bunkyo-ku, Tokyo 113-91, Japan. TEL 03-3817-5721. Ed. Hiromasa Kita. circ. 4,000. **Indexed:** Biol.Abstr.

616   JA   ISSN 0021-5384
                              CODEN: NNGAAS
JAPANESE SOCIETY OF INTERNAL MEDICINE. JOURNAL/NIHON NAIKA GAKKAI ZASSHI. (Text in Japanese) 1913. m. 9000 Yen to non-members. Japanese Society of Internal Medicine - Nihon Naika Gakkai, Hongo Daiichi Bldg., 34-3, 3 chome, Bunkyo-ku, Tokyo 113, Japan. Ed. Hiroshi Oka. adv.; charts; illus.; index. cum.index; circ. 25,300. **Indexed:** Biol.Abstr., Curr.Cont., Dent.Ind., Ind.Med.
—BLDSC shelfmark: 4809.460000.
Description: Covers internal medicine.

610   II   ISSN 0379-1653
JASLOK HOSPITAL & RESEARCH CENTRE. BULLETIN. (Text in English) 1976. a. Rs.25. Jaslok Hospital & Research Centre, 15 Dr. G. Deshmukh Marg, Bombay 400026, India. FAX 4948008. TELEX 011-75743-JASH-IN. Ed. S. Sadikot. adv.: B&W page Rs.5000; trim 21 x 15. bk.rev.; circ. 1,500.

610   II
JEEVAK. (Text in English, Hindi, and Sanskrit) q. Rs.41. Jeevak Anshathlya, Sahitya Marg, Barnalla, India. adv.; bk.rev.; abstr.; tr.lit.; index; circ. 1,500. (also avail. in record; microform)

610   US   ISSN 0021-5821
JEFFERSON MEDICAL COLLEGE ALUMNI BULLETIN. vol.19, 1970. q. free to alumni. Jefferson Medical College, Alumni Association, 1020 Locust St., Philadelphia, PA 19107. TEL 215-298-7750. Ed. Nancy S. Groseclose. circ. 13,000.

610   CC   ISSN 1001-7321
JIAMUSI YIXUEYUAN XUEBAO/JIAMUSI MEDICAL INSTITUTE. JOURNAL. (Text in Chinese) q. Jiamusi Yixueyuan, Xuebao Bianjibu, Jiamusi, Heilongjiang 154002, People's Republic of China. TEL 32949. Ed. Liu Fangzhen.

610   CC   ISSN 0529-0414
JIANGSU ZHONGYI/JIANGSU TRADITIONAL CHINESE MEDICINE. (Text in Chinese) m. Jiangsu Sheng Weisheng-ting - Jiangsu Provincial Bureau of Public of Health, 42 Zhongyang Lu, Nanjing, Jiangsu 210008, People's Republic of China. TEL 711580. Ed. Zhang Huaqiang.

JIANKANG BAO/HEALTH GAZETTE. see *PHYSICAL FITNESS AND HYGIENE*

610   CC   ISSN 1001-0203
JIATING YIXUE/FAMILY MEDICINE. (Text in Chinese) m. Zhonghua Yufang Yixuehui (Zhengzhou) - China Preventive Medical Society (Zhengzhou), No. 3, Wei 5 Lu, Zhengzhou, Henan 450003, People's Republic of China. TEL 558367. Ed. Wang Jian.

610   CC
JICHU YIXUE YU LINCHUANG/BASIC MEDICAL SCIENCE AND CLINICS. (Text in Chinese) bi-m. Zhongguo Yixue Kexueyuan, Jichu Yixue Yanjiusuo - Chinese Academy of Medical Sciences, Institute of Basic Medical Science, 5 Dongdan Santiao, Beijing 100730, People's Republic of China. TEL 5127733. Ed. Cheng Mengqin.

610   JA   ISSN 0021-6968
                              CODEN: JMEJAS
JIKEIKAI MEDICAL JOURNAL. (Text in English) 1954. q. exchange basis. Jikei University School of Medicine - Tokyo Jikeikai Ika Daigaku, 3-25-8 Nishi Shinbashi, Minato-ku, Tokyo 105, Japan. Ed. Kenji Sakurai. charts; illus.; stat.; index; circ. 1,000. **Indexed:** Abstr.Hyg., Biol.Abstr., Chem.Abstr., Excerp.Med., INIS Atomind., Trop.Dis.Bull.
—BLDSC shelfmark: 4669.000000.

610   CC
JILIN ZHONGYIYAO/JILIN TRADITIONAL CHINESE MEDICINE. (Text in Chinese) bi-m. Changchun Zhongyiyuan - Changchun Institute of Traditional Chinese Medicine, 15, Gongnong Dalu, Changchun, Jilin 130021, People's Republic of China. Ed. Gao Guangzhen.

610 616.6   JA   ISSN 0385-2156
JIN TO TOSEKI. 1976. m. 35,000 Yen($272) Tokyo Igaku-sha, 35-4, 3-chome, Hongo, Bunkyo-ku, Tokyo 113, Japan. Ed.Bd. circ. 6,000.
—BLDSC shelfmark: 5094.210000.

JINAN LIYI XUEBAO/JINAN UNIVERSITY. JOURNAL: MEDICAL & NATURAL SCIENCE AND TECHNOLOGY EDITION. see *SCIENCES: COMPREHENSIVE WORKS*

610   JO   ISSN 0446-9283
                              CODEN: JOMJAE
JORDAN MEDICAL JOURNAL/MAJALLAT AL-TIBBIYYA AL-URDANIYYA. (Text in Arabic and English) 1965. s-a. $20. Jordan Medical Association, P.O. Box 915, Amman, Jordan. (Co-sponsor: Royal Jordanian Medical Services) Ed. Mahmoud M. Abu-Khalaf. adv.; circ. 4,000. **Indexed:** Abstr.Hyg., Biol.Abstr., Excerp.Med., Nutr.Abstr., Trop.Dis.Bull.
—BLDSC shelfmark: 4673.670000.
Description: Contains original papers, reviews, case reports, and brief communications.

610   BL   ISSN 0047-2077
                              CODEN: JBRMAP
JORNAL BRASILEIRO DE MEDICINA. Cover title: J B M. (Text in Portuguese; summaries in English) 1959. m. Editora de Publicacoes Cientificas Ltda., Rua Major Suckow, 30 a 36, P.O. Box 20.911, Rio de Janeiro, RJ, Brazil. TEL 021-201-3722. FAX 021-261-3749. Ed. Ismar C. de Silveira. adv.; bk.rev.; abstr.; bibl.; charts; illus.; cum.index; circ. 30,000. **Indexed:** Biol.Abstr., Chem.Abstr.
—BLDSC shelfmark: 4663.438000.

610   PO
                              CODEN: JCMEE
JORNAL DAS CIENCIAS MEDICAS. 1834. m. (Sociedade das Ciencias Medicas de Lisboa) Edicoes Recipe, Calcada do Monte 23 r-c, 1100 Lisbon, Portugal. TEL 1-874847. **Indexed:** Excerp.Med.
Formerly: Sociedade das Ciencias Medicas. Jornal.

610   PO   ISSN 0021-7573
                              CODEN: JOMEAX
JORNAL DO MEDICO. 1940. w. Esc.3900. Empresa Editora de Estudos Medicos, Ltda., Rua de Sa da Bandeira 245-2, Porto, Portugal. (Subscr. to: Praca da Alegria 58-1 A, 1200 Lisbon, Portugal) Ed. Dr. Cidrais Rodrigues. adv.; bk.rev.; abstr.; bibl.; charts; illus.; index; circ. 3,500. **Indexed:** Biol.Abstr., Ind.Med.
—BLDSC shelfmark: 4674.750000.

616.02   FR   ISSN 0245-5552
JOURNAL D'ECHOGRAPHIE ET DE MEDECINE PAR ULTRASONS. 1980. bi-m. 110 ECU($133) (typically set in Jan.). Masson, 120 bd. St. Germain, 75280 Paris Cedex 06, France. TEL 1-46-34-21-60. FAX 1-45-87-29-99. TELEX 202 671 F. Ed. Plainfosse. circ. 2,500. (also avail. in microform from UMI) **Indexed:** Excerp.Med., INIS Atomind.
—BLDSC shelfmark: 4663.550000.

610 640.73   FR   ISSN 0294-0736
JOURNAL D'ECONOMIE MEDICALE. (Text in French; summaries in English) 1983. 8/yr. 136 ECU($160) (typically set in Jan.). (Association Lyonnaise de Medecine Legale) Masson, 120 bd. St. Germain, 75280 Paris Cedex 06, France. TEL 1-46-34-21-60. FAX 1-45-87-29-99. TELEX 202 671 F. Ed. L. Roche. adv.; bk.rev.; index; circ. 3,183. (back issues avail.) **Indexed:** Excerp.Med., World Bibl.Soc.Sec.
—BLDSC shelfmark: 4973.095500.

616.07   FR   ISSN 0249-6550
JOURNAL D'ERGOTHERAPIE. 1979. q. 70 ECU($85) (typically set in Jan.). Masson, 120 bd. Saint Germain, 75280 Paris Cedex 6, France. TEL 1-46-34-21-60. FAX 1-45-87-29-99. TELEX 202 671 F. Ed. Darnault. circ. 1,400. (also avail. in microform from UMI)
—BLDSC shelfmark: 4979.540000.
Description: Discusses physiotherapy techniques.

610   FR   ISSN 0021-7883
                              CODEN: JMLYA6
JOURNAL DE MEDECINE DE LYON;* organe de professeurs, agreges, medecins des hopitaux et medicins practiciens de Lyon. (Text in French; summaries in English) 1920. m. 95 F. 38 rue Pascal, 75013 Paris, France. Ed.Bd. adv.; bk.rev.; illus.; index. **Indexed:** Biol.Abstr., Chem.Abstr., Excerp.Med., Ind.Med., Nutr.Abstr.
—BLDSC shelfmark: 5017.015000.

610   FR   ISSN 0021-7905
                              CODEN: JMSTBR
JOURNAL DE MEDECINE DE STRASBOURG. 1970. 10/yr. 365 F. to individuals (foreign 525 F.); students 180 F. (foreign 315 F.). (Faculte de Medecine et de la Communaute Medicale d'Alsace et de Moselle) Expansion Scientifique, 15 rue Saint-Benoit, 75278 Paris Cedex 06, France. Ed. Dr. Paul Rohmer. adv.; bk.rev.; circ. 6,500. (also avail. in microform) **Indexed:** Biol.Abstr., Chem.Abstr., Chem.Abstr, Curr.Cont., Helminthol.Abstr., Nutr.Abstr.
—BLDSC shelfmark: 5017.040000.

JOURNAL DE MYCOLOGIE MEDICALE. see *BIOLOGY — Botany*

JOURNAL DE PHYSIOLOGIE. see *BIOLOGY — Physiology*

JOURNAL DE TOXICOLOGIE CLINIQUE ET EXPERIMENTALE. see *ENVIRONMENTAL STUDIES — Toxicology And Environmental Safety*

610   FR   ISSN 0021-8111
                              CODEN: JSMLAE
JOURNAL DES SCIENCES MEDICALES DE LILLE. 1882. m. 30 F.($7.50) 8, rue Nicolas Leblanc, 59-Lille, France. Ed.Bd.; charts; illus.; index. **Indexed:** Biol.Abstr., Chem.Abstr., Dent.Ind., Excerp.Med., Ind.Med.

610   FR   ISSN 0993-9857
JOURNAL EUROPEEN DES URGENCES/EUROPEAN JOURNAL OF EMERGENCIES. (Text in English, French) 1988. q. 105 ECU($125) Masson, 120 Bd. Saint-Germain, 75280 Paris Cedex 06, France. TEL 1-46-34-21-60. FAX 1-45-87-29-99. TELEX 202 671 F. (Subscr. to: SPPIF, S.I. Vineuil, B.P. 22, 41350 Vineuil, France) Ed. Patrick Barriot. adv.; circ. 1,500. (back issues avail.)
Description: Includes original articles, brief reviews, clinical cases and letters.

MEDICAL SCIENCES

610　　　　　　　US　　ISSN 1054-139X
RJ550　　　　　　　　　　CODEN: JADHE5
JOURNAL OF ADOLESCENT HEALTH. 1980. 8/yr. $220 to institutions (foreign $254)(effective 1992). (Society for Adolescent Medicine) Elsevier Science Publishing Co., Inc. (New York), 655 Ave. of the Americas, New York, NY 10010. TEL 212-989-5800. FAX 212-633-3965. TELEX 420643 AEP UI. Ed. H. Verdain Barnes. (also avail. in microform from RPI) **Indexed:** Adol.Ment.Hlth.Abstr., ASSIA, Biol.Abstr., CINAHL, Curr.Cont., Curr.Lit.Fam.Plan., Energy Ind., Energy Info.Abstr., Excerp.Med., Ind.Med., NRN, Psychol.Abstr., Risk Abstr., Soc.Sci.Ind., SSCI.
—BLDSC shelfmark: 4918.942800.
Formerly (until 1991): Journal of Adolescent Health Care (ISSN 0197-0070)
Refereed Serial

610　　　　　　　US　　ISSN 0894-5888
　　　　　　　　　　　　CODEN: JAMEE7
JOURNAL OF ADVANCEMENT IN MEDICINE. 1988. q. $150 (foreign $175). (American College of Advancement in Medicine) Human Sciences Press, Inc. (Subsidiary of: Plenum Publishing Corp.), 233 Spring St., New York, NY 10013-1578. TEL 212-620-8000. FAX 212-463-0742. Ed. Derrick Lonsdale. adv. (reprint service avail. from UMI)
—BLDSC shelfmark: 4918.947950.
Description: Presents information about innovative, emerging, and non-traditional advances in preventive medicine, nutrition, risk factors, and modification of harmful life-style.
Refereed Serial

616.98　　　　　　US
JOURNAL OF AIR MEDICAL TRANSPORT. 1986. bi-m. $19.95. Howard Collett, Ed. & Pub., 270 W. Center, Orem, UT 84057. TEL 801-226-5555. adv.; bk.rev.; illus.; circ. 10,000.
Formerly (until 1989): AeroMedical Journal (ISSN 0894-8321)
Description: News and continuing educational material for professionals involved in emergency air care services.

610　　　　　　　US　　ISSN 1055-324X
RA395.A3
▼**JOURNAL OF AMERICAN HEALTH POLICY.** 1991. bi-m. $125. Faulkner & Gray, 1133 15th St., N.W., Ste. 450, Washington, DC 20005. TEL 202-828-4148. FAX 202-828-2352. Ed. Richard Sorian.
Description: Provides the latest information on all aspects of health policy developments and debate. Contains articles, analyses, investigative reports, interviews, and up-to-date data on federal, regional, and state health policy issues and trends.

JOURNAL OF ANATOMY. see *BIOLOGY*

610　　　　　　　US　　ISSN 0196-3635
QP253　　　　　　　　　　CODEN: JOAND3
JOURNAL OF ANDROLOGY. 1980. bi-m. $165 to individuals (foreign $180); institutions $215 (foreign $230). (American Society of Andrology) J.B. Lippincott Co., E. Washington Sq., Philadelphia, PA 19105. TEL 215-238-4200. Ed. Marie-Claire Orgebin-Crist. adv.; illus.; index.; circ. 1,300. (also avail. in microform from UMI) **Indexed:** Anim.Breed.Abstr., Biol.Abstr., Chem.Abstr., Curr.Adv.Cell & Devel.Biol., Curr.Cont., Excerp.Med., Ind.Med., Ind.Sci.Rev., Sci.Cit.Ind., SSCI.
—BLDSC shelfmark: 4935.340000.
Refereed Serial

615.329　　　　　JA　　ISSN 0021-8820
　　　　　　　　　　　　CODEN: JANTAJ
JOURNAL OF ANTIBIOTICS; an international journal devoted to research on bioactive microbial products. (Text in English) 1947. m. $230. Japan Antibiotics Research Association - Nihon Koseibusshitsu Gakujutsu Kyogikai, 2-20-8 Kamiosaki, Shinagawa-ku, Tokyo 141, Japan. TEL 03-3491-0181. FAX 03-3491-0179. Ed. Morimasa Yagisawa. adv.; bibl.; charts; index; circ. 2,000. (also avail. in microform from UMI; reprint service avail. from UMI) **Indexed:** Biol.Abstr., Biotech.Abstr., Chem.Abstr., Curr.Adv.Genetics & Molec.Biol., Curr.Biotech.Abstr., Curr.Cont., Excerp.Med., Helminthol.Abstr., Ind.Chem., Ind.Med., Ind.Sci.Rev., Rev.Plant Path., Sci.Cit.Ind.
—BLDSC shelfmark: 4937.900000.
Formerly: Journal of Antibiotics. Series A.

610　　　　　　　JA
JOURNAL OF APPLIED MEDICINE/OYO IGAKU. (Text in English, Japanese and European languages) 1960. q. membership. Society of Applied Medicine - Nihon Oyo Igakkai, 108 Shimogamo Miyazakai-cho, Sakyo-ku, Kyoto 606, Japan. abstr. **Indexed:** Chem.Abstr.

610　　　　　　　II　　ISSN 0377-0400
　　　　　　　　　　　　CODEN: JAMED6
JOURNAL OF APPLIED MEDICINE. (Text in English) 1975. m. Rs.96. Living Media India Pvt. Ltd., F-14, Connaught Place, New Delhi 110001, India. TEL 3313076. Ed. R.S. Hoon. adv.; bk.rev.; bibl.; illus.
—BLDSC shelfmark: 4943.030000.

JOURNAL OF APPLIED PHYSIOLOGY. see *BIOLOGY — Physiology*

610 574　　　　　UK　　ISSN 0140-511X
　　　　　　　　　　　　CODEN: JAUMD2
JOURNAL OF AUDIOVISUAL MEDIA IN MEDICINE. 1951. q. £64 in U.K. & Europe £58; elsewhere £762. (Institute of Medical & Biological Illustration) Butterworth - Heinemann Ltd. (Subsidiary of: Reed International PLC), Linacre House, Jordan Hill, Oxford OX2 8DP, England. TEL 0865-310366. FAX 0865-310898. TELEX 83111 BHPOXF G. (Subscr. to: Turpin Transactions Ltd., Distribution Centre, Blackhorse Rd., Letchworth, Herts SG6 1HN, England. TEL 0462-672555) Ed. K.P. Duguid. adv.; bk.rev.; film rev.; abstr.; charts; illus.; index. (also avail. in microform from UMI; reprint service avail.; back issues avail.) **Indexed:** Abstr.Hyg., Art & Archaeol.Tech.Abstr., Biol.Abstr., Chem.Abstr., Curr.Cont., Dent.Ind., Educ.Tech.Abstr., Geo.Abstr., Ind.Med., Ind.Vet., Res.High.Educ.Abstr., Sci.Cit.Ind, Trop.Dis.Bull., Vet.Bull.
—BLDSC shelfmark: 4949.350000.
Formerly: Medical and Biological Illustration (ISSN 0025-6978)
Description: Presents information and ideas on the development, implementation and use of audiovisual media for education, recording and research purposes in all areas of the health sciences.
Refereed Serial

610.28　　　　　　US　　ISSN 0094-2499
R118
JOURNAL OF BIOCOMMUNICATION. 1974. 4/yr. $28 individuals; institutions $35; students $22. Journal of Biocommunication, Inc., 170 Pomfret Rd., Box 217, Brooklyn, CT 06234. (Co-sponsors: Association of Biomedical Communications Directors; Association of Medical Illustrators; Health Sciences Communications Association) bk.rev.; film rev.; illus.; circ. 2,000. (also avail. in microform from UMI; back issues avail.; reprint service avail. from UMI) **Indexed:** B.R.I., Biol.Abstr., C.I.J.E., Dent.Abstr., Hosp.Lit.Ind., Ind.Med., Mid.East: Abstr.& Ind.
Supersedes: Medical Art (ISSN 0076-5902) Which was formerly (1953-1964): Association of Medical Illustrators. Journal (ISSN 0098-8456); Graphics.

JOURNAL OF BIOMECHANICAL ENGINEERING. see *BIOLOGY — Bioengineering*

JOURNAL OF BIOMEDICAL ENGINEERING. see *BIOLOGY — Bioengineering*

JOURNAL OF BIOMEDICAL MATERIALS RESEARCH. see *BIOLOGY — Biotechnology*

614.88　　　　　US　　ISSN 0273-8481
　　　　　　　　　　　　CODEN: JBCRD2
JOURNAL OF BURN CARE AND REHABILITATION. 1980. bi-m. $41 to individuals (foreign $52); institutions $68 (foreign $79); students $23 (foreign $34). (American Burn Association) Mosby - Year Book, Inc. (Subsidiary of: Times Mirror Company), 11830 Westline Industrial Dr., St. Louis, MO 63146. TEL 800-325-4117. FAX 314-432-1380. TELEX 44-2402. Ed. Dr. Charles R. Baxter. adv.; bk.rev.; index; circ. 3,236. (also avail. in microform from UMI; back issues avail.) **Indexed:** Chem.Abstr., CINAHL, Excerp.Med.
—BLDSC shelfmark: 4954.640000.
Refereed Serial

JOURNAL OF CELLULAR PHYSIOLOGY. see *BIOLOGY — Physiology*

JOURNAL OF CHILD NEUROLOGY. see *MEDICAL SCIENCES — Psychiatry And Neurology*

JOURNAL OF CLINICAL ENGINEERING. see *BIOLOGY — Bioengineering*

616.9　　　　　　US　　ISSN 0895-4356
RB156　　　　　　　　　　CODEN: JCEPEE
JOURNAL OF CLINICAL EPIDEMIOLOGY; devoted to the problems and management of chronic illness in all age groups. 1955. m. £405 (effective 1992). Pergamon Press, Inc., Journals Division, 660 White Plains Rd., Tarrytown, NY 10591-5153. TEL 914-524-9200. FAX 914-333-2444. (And: Headington Hill Hall, Oxford OX3 0BW, England. TEL 0865-794141) Eds. Alvan R. Feinstein, Walter O. Spitzer. adv.; bk.rev.; bibl.; charts; illus.; index; circ. 2,200. (also avail. in microform from MIM,UMI; reprint service avail. from UMI) **Indexed:** Abstr.Health Care Manage.Stud., Abstr.Hyg., Biol.Abstr., C.I.S. Abstr., Chem.Abstr., CINAHL, Curr.Cont., Dent.Ind., Dok.Arbeitsmed., Excerp.Med., Helminthol.Abstr., Hosp.Lit.Ind., I.P.A., Ind.Med., Ind.Sci.Rev., INIS Atomind., Int.Nurs.Ind., Med.Care Rev., NRN, Nutr.Abstr., Psychol.Abstr., Risk Abstr., Sci.Cit.Ind, Trop.Dis.Bull.
●Also available online.
—BLDSC shelfmark: 4958.435000.
Formerly: Journal of Chronic Diseases (ISSN 0021-9681)
Refereed Serial

610 340　　　　　US　　ISSN 1046-7890
R724
▼**JOURNAL OF CLINICAL ETHICS.** 1990. q. $55 to individuals; institutions $105. University Publishing Group, Inc., 107 E. Church St., Frederick, MD 21701. TEL 301-694-8531. Ed. Dr. Edmund G. Howe. bk.rev. (also avail. in microfilm; back issues avail.) **Indexed:** Ind.Med.
—BLDSC shelfmark: 4958.440000.
Description: Addresses the complex ethical, legal, and social issues in clinical medicine and direct patient care.
Refereed Serial

610　　　　　　　US　　ISSN 0021-9738
R11　　　　　　　　　　　CODEN: JCINAO
JOURNAL OF CLINICAL INVESTIGATION. 1924. m. $250 (effective 1992). (American Society for Clinical Investigation) Rockefeller University Press, 222 E. 70th St., New York, NY 10021. TEL 212-570-8572. FAX 212-570-7944. (Subscr. to: Box 5108, Church Street Sta., New York, NY 10249) Ed. Ajit Varki. adv.; bibl.; charts; illus.; index; circ. 6,360. (also avail. in microform from UMI; microfiche from UMI; reprint service avail. from ISI, UMI) **Indexed:** Abstr.Hyg., Biol.Abstr., Biotech.Abstr., C.I.S. Abstr., Chem.Abstr., Curr.Adv.Biochem., Curr.Adv.Cancer Res., Curr.Adv.Cell & Devel.Biol., Curr.Adv.Genetics & Molec.Biol., Curr.Cont., Dairy Sci.Abstr., Excerp.Med., Food Sci.& Tech.Abstr., Helminthol.Abstr., Ind.Med., Ind.Sci.Rev., Ind.Vet., INIS Atomind., NRN, Nutr.Abstr., Protozool.Abstr., Rev.Plant Path., Sci.Cit.Ind, Small Anim.Abstr., Soyabean Abstr., Trop.Dis.Bull., Vet.Bull.
●Also available online. Vendor(s): BRS.
—BLDSC shelfmark: 4958.500000.
Description: Provides a forum for research that links basic science to clinical practice. Includes brief summaries of newly emerging avenues of investigation.
Refereed Serial

616.07　　　　　US　　ISSN 0748-1977
　　　　　　　　　　　　CODEN: JCMOEH
JOURNAL OF CLINICAL MONITORING. 1985. q. $95 for individuals (foreign 135); institutions $125 (foreign $160); resident $68 (foreign $82)(effective Nov. 1991). (Society for Technology in Anesthesia) Little, Brown and Company, Medical Journals, 34 Beacon St., Boston, MA 02108. TEL 617-859-5500. FAX 617-859-0629. Ed.Bd. adv.; bk.rev.; abstr.; charts; illus.; stat.; index; circ. 2,692. (also avail. in microform from UMI; back issues avail.; reprint service avail. from UMI) **Indexed:** Curr.Cont., Excerp.Med., Ind.Med.
—BLDSC shelfmark: 4958.572000.
Description: Contains original articles on the latest monitoring techniques, research findings, new developments, updates on monitoring equipment, analyses of monitoring procedures, case reports and clinical controversies.
Refereed Serial

MEDICAL SCIENCES 3115

616.07 UK ISSN 0021-9746
CODEN: JCPAAK
JOURNAL OF CLINICAL PATHOLOGY. 1947. m. £161. (Association of Clinical Pathologists) British Medical Association, B.M.A. House, Tavistock Sq., London WC1H 9JR, England. TEL 071-387-4499. Ed. J. Lilleyman. adv.; bk.rev.; abstr.; charts; illus.; index. (also avail. in microform from UMI; reprint service avail. from UMI) **Indexed:** Abstr.Hyg., Biol.Abstr., Biotech.Abstr., C.I.S. Abstr., Chem.Abstr., CINAHL, Curr.Adv.Biochem., Curr.Adv.Cancer Res., Curr.Adv.Genetics & Molec.Biol., Curr.Cont., Dent.Ind., Dok.Arbeitsmed., Excerp.Med., Helminthol.Abstr., Ind.Med., Ind.Sci.Rev., Ind.Vet., INIS Atomind., Lab.Haz.Bull., Nutr.Abstr., Protozool.Abstr., Rev.Plant Path., Sci.Cit.Ind, Trop.Dis.Bull., Vet.Bull., W.R.C.Inf.
●Also available online. Vendor(s): BRS, BRS/Saunders Colleague.
—BLDSC shelfmark: 4958.650000.

610 US
JOURNAL OF CLINICAL PRACTICE IN SEXUALITY. vol.4, 1988. m. Gordon L. Deal, Inc., 3 Bunker Hill Run, E. Brunswick, NJ 08816. Ed. Dr. Alan J. Wabrek.

JOURNAL OF CLINICAL ULTRASOUND. see PHYSICS — Sound

610 614 US ISSN 0094-5145
RA421 CODEN: JCMHB
JOURNAL OF COMMUNITY HEALTH; the publication for health promotion and disease prevention. 1975. bi-m. $195 (foreign $230). Human Sciences Press, Inc. (Subsidiary of: Plenum Publishing Corp.), 233 Spring St., New York, NY 10013-1578. TEL 212-620-8000. FAX 212-463-0742. Ed. Pascal J. Imperato. adv.; bk.rev.; index. (also avail. in microform from UMI; reprint service avail. from ISI,UMI) **Indexed:** Abstr.Health Care Manage.Stud., Abstr.Hyg., Acad.Ind., Adol.Ment.Hlth.Abstr., C.I.J.E., CINAHL, Community Ment.Health Rev., Except.Child.Educ.Abstr., Excerp.Med., FAMLI, Gen.Sci.Ind., Hlth.Ind., Hosp.Lit.Ind., Human Resour.Abstr., Ind.Med., INIS Atomind., Lang.& Lang.Behav.Abstr., Med.Care Rev., Nurs.Abstr., Nutr.Abstr., Saf.Sci.Abstr., Sage Urb.Stud.Abstr., Soc.Work Res.& Abstr., Sociol.Abstr., Trop.Dis.Bull.
—BLDSC shelfmark: 4961.720000.
Description: Covers new community health information, including the areas of preventive medicine, new forms of health manpower, analysis of environmental factors, delivery of health care services, and the study of health maintenance and health insurance programs.
Refereed Serial

610 340 US ISSN 0882-1046
JOURNAL OF CONTEMPORARY HEALTH LAW AND POLICY. 1985. a. $10. Catholic University of America, Columbus School of Law, Washington, DC 20064. TEL 202-319-5732. Ed.Bd. (also avail. in microform from WSH; reprint service avail. from WSH) **Indexed:** C.L.I., Leg.Per.
—BLDSC shelfmark: 4965.229500.
Refereed Serial

610 US
JOURNAL OF CONTINUING MEDICAL EDUCATION INTERNATIONAL. 1975. q. $50. Association for International Medical Study, Inc., 1040 E. McDonald St., Lakeland, FL 33801. Ed. Dr. Ben H. McConnell. adv.; charts; illus.; stat.; circ. 500,000.

JOURNAL OF CRANIOMANDIBULAR DISORDERS. see MEDICAL SCIENCES — Dentistry

610 US ISSN 0883-9441
CODEN: JCCAER
JOURNAL OF CRITICAL CARE. 1986. q. $87 to individuals; institutions $124; foreign $139. W.B. Saunders Co. (Subsidiary of: Harcourt Brace Jovanovich, Inc.), Curtis Center, Independence Square W., Philadelphia, PA 19106. TEL 215-238-7800. (Subscr. to: 6277 Sea Harbor Dr., 4th Fl. Orlando FL 32891) Ed. Michael R. Pinsky, M.D. adv.; abstr.; bibl.; charts; illus.; index. **Indexed:** Excerp.Med.
—BLDSC shelfmark: 4965.630000.
Refereed Serial

610 US ISSN 1040-0257
JOURNAL OF CRITICAL ILLNESS. 1986. m. $65. Cliggott Publishing Co., 55 Holly Hill Lane, Box 4010, Greenwich, CT 06830. TEL 203-661-0600. Ed. Ellen M. Rosen. circ. 81,642. (reprint service avail.)
—BLDSC shelfmark: 4965.635000.
Description: Presents practical information on clinical management of critically ill patients. Includes original review articles and instructions on specific procedures used.

JOURNAL OF CYTOLOGY AND GENETICS. see BIOLOGY — Genetics

JOURNAL OF DEVELOPMENTAL PHYSIOLOGY. see MEDICAL SCIENCES — Obstetrics And Gynecology

610 US ISSN 8756-4793
JOURNAL OF DIAGNOSTIC MEDICAL SONOGRAPHY. 1985. bi-m. $55 to individuals (foreign $70); institutions $85 (foreign $100). (Society of Diagnostic Medical Sonographers) J.B. Lippincott Co., E. Washington Sq., Philadelphia, PA 19105. TEL 215-238-4200. Ed. Dale R. Cyr. adv.; illus.; index.; circ. 6,567. (also avail. in microform) **Indexed:** Excerp.Med.
Refereed Serial

JOURNAL OF DISABILITY POLICY STUDIES. see LAW

JOURNAL OF ELECTRON MICROSCOPY. see BIOLOGY — Microscopy

610 US ISSN 0736-4679
JOURNAL OF EMERGENCY MEDICINE. 1983. bi-m. $250 (effective 1992). Pergamon Press, Inc., Journals Division, 660 White Plains Rd., Tarrytown, NY 10591-5153. TEL 914-524-9200. FAX 914-333-2444. (And: Headington Hill Hall, Oxford OX3 0BW, England. TEL 0865-794141) Ed. Peter Rosen. (also avail. in microform; back issues avail.) **Indexed:** Excerp.Med., Ind.Med.
—BLDSC shelfmark: 4977.250000.
Refereed Serial

614.44 UK ISSN 0141-7681
CODEN: JECHDR
JOURNAL OF EPIDEMIOLOGY & COMMUNITY HEALTH. 1947. bi-m. £92. B M J Publishing Group, B.M.A. House, Tavistock Sq., London WC1H 9JR, England. TEL 071-387-4499. Ed. J.R.T. Colley. adv.; bk.rev.; bibl.; charts; illus.; index. (also avail. in microform from UMI; reprint service avail. from UMI) **Indexed:** Abstr.Hyg., Bibl.Dev.Med.& Child Neur., Biol.Abstr., Biostat., C.I.S. Abstr., Chem.Abstr., Curr.Adv.Cancer Res., Curr.Lit.Fam.Plan., Dairy Sci.Abstr., Dent.Ind., Dok.Arbeitsmed., Excerp.Med., Helminthol.Abstr., Hosp.Lit.Ind., Ind.Med., Ind.Sci.Rev., INIS Atomind., Lab.Haz.Bull., Nutr.Abstr., Psychol.Abstr., Risk Abstr., Sci.Cit.Ind, SSCI, Stud.Wom.Abstr., Trop.Dis.Bull.
Former titles: Journal of Epidemiology and Community Medicine; (until Dec. 1977): British Journal of Preventive and Social Medicine (ISSN 0007-1242)

JOURNAL OF EXPOSURE ANALYSIS AND ENVIRONMENTAL EPIDEMIOLOGY. see ENVIRONMENTAL STUDIES

610 US ISSN 0022-1058
QP110.A7 CODEN: JEXCBD
JOURNAL OF EXTRA-CORPOREAL TECHNOLOGY. 1968. q. $40 (foreign $55). American Society of Extra-Corporeal Technology, Inc., 11480 Sunset Hills Rd., Ste. 100E, Reston, VA 22090. TEL 703-435-8556. FAX 703-435-0056. Ed. Phyllis Palmer. bk.rev.; circ. 2,800. (back issues avail.) **Indexed:** Excerp.Med.
—BLDSC shelfmark: 4983.300000.

610 US ISSN 0094-3509
R11
JOURNAL OF FAMILY PRACTICE. 1974. m. $73 to individuals (foreign $85); institutions $96 (foreign $107); students $55 (foreign $67). Appleton & Lange, Journal Division (Subsidiary of: Simon & Schuster Company), 25 Van Zant St., Box 5630, Norwalk, CT 06855. TEL 203-838-4400. (Subscr. to: Dept. FP, Box 3000, Denville, NJ 07834) Ed. Dr. Paul M. Fischer. adv.; bk.rev.; charts; illus.; stat.; s-a index; circ. 76,000. (also avail. in microform from UMI; back issues avail.; reprint service avail. from UMI) **Indexed:** Abstr.Health Care Manage.Stud., Adol.Ment.Hlth.Abstr., Biol.Abstr., CINAHL, Curr.Adv.Cancer Res., Curr.Cont., Dent.Ind., Dok.Arbeitsmed., Excerp.Med., FAMLI, Helminthol.Abstr., HRIS, I.P.A., Ind.Med., Ind.Sci.Rev., Ind.Vet., INIS Atomind., Med.Care Rev., Nutr.Abstr., Psychol.Abstr., Sci.Cit.Ind, Small Anim.Abstr.
●Also available online.
—BLDSC shelfmark: 4983.730000.
Description: Contains original research articles, clinical reviews, case reports, editorials, and technology reviews that have clinical applications in family medicine.
Refereed Serial

616.02 US ISSN 0884-8734
R11 CODEN: JGIMEJ
JOURNAL OF GENERAL INTERNAL MEDICINE. bi-m. $70 to individuals (foreign $82); institutions $85 (foreign $95). (American College of Physicians, Society for General Internal Medicine) Hanley & Belfus, Inc., 210 S. 13th St., Philadelphia, PA 19107. TEL 215-546-4995. FAX 215-790-9330. Ed. Dr. David Dale. circ. 4,000. **Indexed:** Excerp.Med.
—BLDSC shelfmark: 4987.827000.
Description: Focuses on the training and practice of the general internist.
Refereed Serial

610 II ISSN 0970-566X
JOURNAL OF GENERAL MEDICINE; a quarterly for the family physician. (Supplement avail.: The Indian Practitioner) 1988. q. Rs.85($25) Indian Practitioner Group, 101, Lawrence Apartments-2, Ist Floor, Vidyanagari Marg, Opp. Lakhbir Petrol Pump, Kalina, Santa Cruz (E), Bombay 400 098, India. TEL 273809. Ed. Joan Godinho. adv.; abstr.; bibl.; charts; illus.; stat.; circ. 33,413. (reprint service avail.)
—BLDSC shelfmark: 4987.950000.

JOURNAL OF GENERAL PHYSIOLOGY. see BIOLOGY — Physiology

610 US ISSN 0894-1130
JOURNAL OF HAND THERAPY. 1987. q. $48 to individuals (foreign $58); institutions $58 (foreign $68). (American Society of Hand Therapists) Hanley & Belfus, Inc., 210 S. 13th St., Philadelphia, PA 19107. TEL 215-546-7293. FAX 215-790-9330. Ed. Evelyn Mackin. circ. 5,000.
—BLDSC shelfmark: 4996.623500.
Description: Concerned with post-traumatic and post-surgical rehabilitation of the hand.
Refereed Serial

JOURNAL OF HEALTH & HEALING. see PHYSICAL FITNESS AND HYGIENE

610 340 US
JOURNAL OF HEALTH AND HOSPITAL LAW. m. $125. (DePaul University, College of Law) American Academy of Hospital Attorneys, 840 N. Lake Shore Dr., Chicago, IL 60611. TEL 312-280-6600. (Subscr. to: 25 E. Jackson Blvd., Chicago, IL 60604) Ed. Donald H.J. Hermann. index; circ. 3,000. (back issues avail.)
Formerly: Hospital Law.
Description: News for physicians, attorneys, hospitals on long and short-term care facilities and current court decisions.

M

MEDICAL SCIENCES

610 US ISSN 1049-2089
CODEN: JHCUEK
▼JOURNAL OF HEALTH CARE FOR THE POOR AND UNDERSERVED. 1990. q. $35 to individuals; institutions $60; students $15. Institute on Health Care for the Poor and Underserved, Meharry Medical College, 1005 D B Todd Blvd., Nashville, TN 37208. Ed. Kirk A. Johnson. bk.rev.; illus. Indexed: Soc.Work Res.& Abstr.
Description: Focuses on the health of underserved communities. Explores health problems of the poor, elderly, rural and inner-city residents, and the uninsured and underinsured.
Refereed Serial

610 UK
JOURNAL OF HEALTH INFORMATION & MEDICAL RECORDS OFFICERS. 1948. q. £16. Association of Health Care Information & Medical Records Officers, c/o Mr. N.A. Campion, Wrexham Maelor Hospital, Clwyd LL13 7TD, Wales. adv.; bk.rev.; charts; illus.; stat.; index. cum.index: 1965-1972; circ. 1,500. Indexed: Excerp.Med., Hosp.Lit.Ind.
Former titles: A M R O; Medical Record (ISSN 0025-7478)

320 340 US ISSN 0361-6878
RA395.A3 CODEN: JHPLDN
JOURNAL OF HEALTH POLITICS, POLICY AND LAW. 1976. q. $40 to individuals (foreign $48); institutions $76 (foreign $84); students $20 (foreign $28). (Duke University, Department of Health Administration) Duke University Press, 6697 College Station, Durham, NC 27708. TEL 919-684-2173. FAX 919-684-8644. Ed. Jim Morone. adv.; bk.rev.; circ. 2,000. (also avail. in microfilm from UMI,WSH; microfiche from WSH; back issues avail.) Indexed: ABI Inform, Abstr.Bk.Rev.Curr.Leg.Per., Abstr.Health Care Manage.Stud., Abstr.Hyg., Adol.Ment.Hlth.Abstr., Biol.Abstr., C.L.I., Curr.Cont., Dent.Ind., Excerp.Med., Fut.Surv., Hlth.Ind., Hosp.Abstr., Hosp.Lit.Ind., Ind.Med., Int.Polit.Sci.Abstr., L.R.I., Lang.& Lang.Behav.Abstr., Leg.Per., Med.Care Rev., P.A.I.S., PSI, Risk Abstr., Sage Pub.Admin.Abstr., Sociol.Abstr., SSCI, Trop.Dis.Bull.
—BLDSC shelfmark: 4996.870000.
Refereed Serial

JOURNAL OF HERBS, SPICES & MEDICINAL PLANTS. see GARDENING AND HORTICULTURE

JOURNAL OF HUMAN ERGOLOGY. see BUSINESS AND ECONOMICS — Labor And Industrial Relations

JOURNAL OF HUMAN MOVEMENT STUDIES. see PSYCHOLOGY

614.49 615.37 576 CS ISSN 0022-1732
RA421 CODEN: JHEMA2
JOURNAL OF HYGIENE, EPIDEMIOLOGY, MICROBIOLOGY AND IMMUNOLOGY. Russian edition: Zhurnal Gigieny, Epidemiologii, Mikrobiologii i Immunologii. (Text in English, French, German, Spanish) 1956. 4/yr. 174 Fr. (Institut Hygieny a Epidemiologie) Avicenum, Czechoslovak Medical Press, Malostranske nam. 28, 118 02 Prague 1, Czechoslovakia. (Dist. in Western countries by: Petersgraben 31, 4011 Basel, Switzerland) (Co-sponsor: Ministerstvo Zdravotinctvi Ceske Socialisticke Republiky) Ed. Dr. B. Rosicky. adv.; bk.rev.; bibl.; charts; illus.; index; circ. 900. Indexed: Abstr.Hyg., Biol.Abstr., Biotech.Abstr., C.I.S. Abstr., Chem.Abstr., Curr.Adv.Ecol.Sci., Curr.Cont., Dairy Sci.Abstr., Excerp.Med., Helminthol.Abstr., Ind.Med., Ind.Vet., INIS Atomind., Poult.Abstr., Protozool.Abstr., Rev.Appl.Entomol., Rev.Plant Path., Soils & Fert., Trop.Dis.Bull., Vet.Bull.
—BLDSC shelfmark: 5004.050000.
Description: Covers epidemiology and immunology.

JOURNAL OF HYPERBARIC MEDICINE. see SCIENCES: COMPREHENSIVE WORKS

616.02 US ISSN 1053-8550
RM270 CODEN: JOIME7
JOURNAL OF IMMUNOTHERAPY. 1982. 8/yr. $176 to individuals; institutions $306. (Society for Biological Therapy) Raven Press, 1185 Ave. of the Americas, New York, NY 10036. TEL 212-930-9500. FAX 212-869-3495. TELEX 640073. Ed. Steven A. Rosenberg. adv.; bk.rev.; illus.; index; circ. 1,300. (back issues avail.) Indexed: Chem.Abstr., Excerp.Med., Ind.Med., Ind.Sci.Rev., INIS Atomind., Sci.Cit.Ind.
Formerly (until 1991): Journal of Biological Response Modifiers (ISSN 0732-6580)
Description: Publishes laboratory, preclinical, and clinical reports on mechanisms and methods in immunotherapy.
Refereed Serial

JOURNAL OF INSURANCE MEDICINE. see INSURANCE

610 US ISSN 0885-0666
JOURNAL OF INTENSIVE CARE MEDICINE. 1986. bi-m. $59 to individuals (foreign $85); institutions $82 (foreign $106); residents $39 (foreign $58). Blackwell Scientific Publications Inc., Three Cambridge Center, Ste. 208, Cambridge, MA 02142-1413. Ed. Dr. James M. Rippe. bk.rev.; charts; illus.; index; circ. 1,900. (back issues avail.)
—BLDSC shelfmark: 5007.539000.
Refereed Serial

574.4 573.21 US ISSN 0197-8357
QR187.5 CODEN: JIREDJ
JOURNAL OF INTERFERON RESEARCH. 1981. bi-m. $275 (foreign $330). (International Society for Interferon Research) Mary Ann Liebert, Inc., 1651 Third Ave., New York, NY 10128. TEL 212-289-2300. FAX 212-289-4697. Ed. Philip I. Marcus. adv.; circ. 1,000. (reprint service avail. from ISI; back issues avail.) Indexed: Anim.Breed.Abstr., Biol.Abstr., Chem.Abstr, Curr.Adv.Cancer Res., Curr.Adv.Cell & Devel.Biol., Curr.Adv.Ecol.Sci., Curr.Adv.Genetics & Molec.Biol., Curr.Biotech.Abstr., Excerp.Med., Ind.Med., Ind.Sci.Rev., Ind.Vet., Pig News & Info., Sci.Cit.Ind, Telegen, Vet.Bull.
—BLDSC shelfmark: 5007.548300.
Description: Publishes original articles on varied aspects of interferon research and clinical applications.
Refereed Serial

610 UK ISSN 0954-6820
CODEN: JINMEO
JOURNAL OF INTERNAL MEDICINE. (Supplements avail.) 1869. m. £140($255) incl. supplements. Blackwell Scientific Publications Ltd., Osney Mead, Oxford OX2 0EL, England. TEL 0865-240201. FAX 0865-721205. TELEX 83355-MEDBOK-G. Ed. Lars-Erik Boettiger. adv.; charts; illus.; index. cum.index: vols.52-140; circ. 2,900. (also avail. in microfilm from PMC) Indexed: Abstr.Inter.Med., ASCA, Biol.Abstr., Biotech.Abstr., C.I.S. Abstr., Chem.Abstr., Curr.Adv.Ecol.Sci., Curr.Cont., Dairy Sci.Abstr., Dent.Ind., Energy Ind., Energy Info.Abstr., Excerp.Med., Helminthol.Abstr., Ind.Med., Ind.Sci.Rev., NRN, Nutr.Abstr., Risk Abstr., Sci.Cit.Ind.
—BLDSC shelfmark: 5007.548700.
Formerly (until 1989): Acta Medica Scandinavica (ISSN 0001-6101)

610 UK ISSN 0300-0605
CODEN: JIMRBV
JOURNAL OF INTERNATIONAL MEDICAL RESEARCH. (Supplements avail.) 1972. bi-m. £55($110) Cambridge Medical Publications Ltd., 3 Liverpool Gardens, Worthing, West Sussex BN11 1TF, England. TEL 0903-205884. FAX 0903-34862. TELEX 878372-PPSLTD. Ed.Bd. bk.rev.; circ. 2,500. (also avail. in microfiche from UMI) Indexed: Abstr.Hyg., Biol.Abstr., Biotech.Abstr., Chem.Abstr., Curr.Adv.Ecol.Sci., Curr.Cont., Dent.Ind., Excerp.Med., Helminthol.Abstr., HRIS, Ind.Med., Int.Sci.Rev., Nutr.Abstr., Rev.Plant Path., Sci.Cit.Ind, Trop.Dis.Bull.
—BLDSC shelfmark: 5007.674000.
Description: Original papers and reviews in clinical and medical research. Topics include animal and clinical pharmacology, pharmacokinetics and drug metabolism, toxicology, teratology and clinical trials.
Refereed Serial

610 II ISSN 0022-2054
JOURNAL OF J.J. GROUP OF HOSPITALS AND GRANT MEDICAL COLLEGE. (Text in English) 1956. q. Rs.20($6) Research Society, Grant Medical College and J.J. Group of Hospitals, Main Bldg., 1st Fl., Ward IX, J.J. Hospital, Byculla, Bombay 400 008, India. TEL 22-860943. Ed. Dr. H.B. Chandalia. adv.; bk.rev.; abstr.; bibl.; charts; illus.; index; circ. 600. Indexed: Chem.Abstr., Ind.Med., Nutr.Abstr.

JOURNAL OF LAW AND HEALTH. see LAW

JOURNAL OF LEARNING DISABILITIES. see EDUCATION — Special Education And Rehabilitation

610 340 US ISSN 0194-7648
K10
JOURNAL OF LEGAL MEDICINE. 1979. q. $105. Hemisphere Publishing Corporation (Subsidiary of: Taylor & Francis Group), 1900 Frost Rd., Ste.101, Bristol, PA 19007-1598. TEL 215-785-5800. FAX 215-785-5515. Ed. Theodore R. Leblanc. bk.rev. (also avail. in microfilm from UMI,WSH; reprint service avail. from WSH) Indexed: Abstr.Bk.Rev.Curr.Leg.Per., C.L.I., Excerp.Med., Hlth.Ind., Ind.Med., L.R.I., Leg.Cont., Leg.Per., Risk Abstr., SSCI.
—BLDSC shelfmark: 5010.270300.
Description: Articles, comments and essays on topics of interest in legal medicine: health law and policy, professional liability, hospital law, food and drug law, medical-legal research and education, and history of legal medicine.
Refereed Serial

616.026 US ISSN 0741-5400
QP185 CODEN: JLBIE7
JOURNAL OF LEUKOCYTE BIOLOGY. 1967. m. (2 vols./yr.). subscr. information by request only. (Society for Leukocyte Biology) John Wiley & Sons, Inc., Journals, 605 Third Ave., New York, NY 10158. TEL 212-850-6000. FAX 212-850-6088. TELEX 12-7063. Ed. Carleton C. Stewart. adv.; charts; illus.; index. (back issues avail.) Indexed: ASCA, Biol.Abstr., Chem.Abstr., Curr.Adv.Cancer Res., Curr.Adv.Cell & Devel.Biol., Curr.Adv.Ecol.Sci., Curr.Cont., Dairy Sci.Abstr., Dent.Ind., Excerp.Med., Ind.Med., Ind.Sci.Rev., Ind.Vet., INIS Atomind., Int.Aerosp.Abstr., Pig News & Info., Sci.Cit.Ind, Small Anim.Abstr., Vet.Bull.
●Also available online.
—BLDSC shelfmark: 5010.305000.
Formerly (until 1984): R E S Reticuloendothelial Society. Journal (ISSN 0033-6890)
Description: Presents manuscripts of original investigations on the origins, developmental biology, and functions of granulocytes, lymphocytes, and monuclear phagocytes.

616 NE ISSN 0921-8319
CODEN: JLMEEG
JOURNAL OF LIPID MEDIATORS. (Text in English) 1989. 6/yr.(in 2 vols.; 3 nos./vol.). fl.842 (effective 1992). Elsevier Science Publishers B.V., P.O. Box 211, 1000 AE Amsterdam, Netherlands. TEL 020-5803911. FAX 020-5803598. TELEX 18582 ESPA NL. (Subscr. in U.S. and Canada to: Elsevier Science Publishing Co., Inc., Box 882, Madison Sq. Sta., New York, NY 10159. TEL 212-989-5800) Ed. B.B. Vargaftig. (back issues avail.) Indexed: Curr.Cont., Excerp.Med.
—BLDSC shelfmark: 5010.495000.
Description: Publishes articles on the chemistry, biophysics, biochemistry, pharmacology, toxicology, pathology, immunology and clinical aspects of lipid mediators in general.
Refereed Serial

610 US ISSN 1040-2152
JOURNAL OF LITHOTRIPSY & STONE DISEASE. 1989. q. $82 (foreign $100). Futura Publishing Company, Inc., 2 Bedford Ridge Rd., Box 330, Mt. Kisco, NY 10549. TEL 800-877-8761. FAX 914-666-0993. Ed. Dr. Laurence B. Kandel. adv.; circ. 1,126. (back issues avail.)
Description: Articles on extracorporeal mechanical disintegration of stones in the urinary and biliary tracts, endoscopic techniques, chemical dissolution, metabolic evaluations, ESWL applications and open surgical procedures.

JOURNAL OF LONG-TERM CARE ADMINISTRATION. see HOSPITALS

610 GW ISSN 0935-6339
JOURNAL OF MANUAL MEDICINE. 1983. 4/yr.
DM.116($71) (Federation Internationale de
Medicine Manuelle) Springer-Verlag, Heidelberger
Platz 3, D-1000 Berlin 33, Germany.
TEL 030-8207-1. (Also Heidelberg, Tokyo, Vienna,
and New York) Ed. J. Dvorak. (also avail. in
microform from UMI; reprint service avail. from ISI)
—BLDSC shelfmark: 5011.605000.
Formerly: Manual Medicine (ISSN 0254-9522)

JOURNAL OF MATERIALS SCIENCE: MATERIALS IN
MEDICINE. see ENGINEERING — Engineering
Mechanics And Materials

JOURNAL OF MEDICAL AND PHARMACEUTICAL
MARKETING. see BUSINESS AND ECONOMICS —
Marketing And Purchasing

610.28 UK ISSN 0309-1902
R856.A1 CODEN: JMTEDN
JOURNAL OF MEDICAL ENGINEERING & TECHNOLOGY.
1965. bi-m. £96($165) Taylor & Francis Ltd.,
Rankine Rd., Basingstoke, Hants RG24 0PR,
England. TEL 0256-840366. FAX 0256-479438.
TELEX 858540. Ed. R.E. Trotman. adv.; bk.rev.;
abstr.; illus.; pat.; tr.lit.; tr.mkt.; index. Indexed:
Agri.Eng.Abstr., Appl.Mech.Rev., Biol.Abstr.,
Br.Tech.Ind., Chem.Abstr., Curr.Adv.Ecol.Sci.,
Curr.Cont., Eng.Ind., Ergon.Abstr., Excerp.Med.,
Ind.Med., Ind.Sci.Rev., Ind.Vet., Sci.Abstr, Vet.Bull.
—BLDSC shelfmark: 5017.057000.
Formerly: Biomedical Engineering (ISSN
0006-2898)
Description: An international journal providing
information on the application of engineering and
technology in medical research and clinical medicine.
Articles cover treatment techniques, instrument
design and development, and evaluation of
equipment.
Refereed Serial

610 UK ISSN 0306-6800
CODEN: JMETDR
JOURNAL OF MEDICAL ETHICS. 1975. q. £69. B M J
Publishing Group, B.M.A. House, Tavistock Square,
London WC1H 9JR, England. TEL 071-387-4499.
(Co-sponsors: Institute of Medical Ethics) Ed. R.
Gillon. adv.; bk.rev.; index. Indexed: Biol.Abstr.,
CERDIC, Curr.Adv.Ecol.Sci., Curr.Cont., Excerp.Med.,
Ind.Med., Phil.Ind., SSCI.
—BLDSC shelfmark: 5017.062000.

JOURNAL OF MEDICAL GENETICS. see BIOLOGY —
Genetics

100 174 US ISSN 1041-3545
R724 CODEN: JMHBEN
JOURNAL OF MEDICAL HUMANITIES. 1976. q. $115
(foreign $135). Human Sciences Press, Inc.
(Subsidiary of: Plenum Publishing Corp.), 233
Spring St., New York, NY 10013-1578.
TEL 212-620-8000. FAX 212-463-0742. Ed.
Charles Perakis. adv.; circ. 400. (also avail. in
microform from UMI; reprint service avail. from
ISI,UMI) Indexed: Curr.Adv.Ecol.Sci., Phil.Ind.,
Psychol.Abstr.
—BLDSC shelfmark: 5017.070500.
Former titles (until 1991): Journal of Medical
Humanities and Bioethics (ISSN 0882-6498); (until
vol.6, 1985): Journal of Bioethics (ISSN
0278-9523); (until 1982): Bioethics Quarterly
(ISSN 0163-9803); Bioethics Northwest (ISSN
0362-0824)
Description: Highlights the relationship between
medicine and art, ethics, history, literature,
philosophy, sociology, economics, and jurisprudence.
Refereed Serial

616.01 UK ISSN 0022-2615
QR46 CODEN: JMMIAV
JOURNAL OF MEDICAL MICROBIOLOGY. 1968. 12/yr.
£189($377.50) (Pathological Society of Great
Britain and Ireland) Churchill Livingstone Medical
Journals, Robert Stevenson House, 1-3 Baxter's Pl.,
Leith Walk, Edinburgh EH1 3AF, Scotland.
TEL 031-556-2424. FAX 031-558-1278. TELEX
727511. (Subscr. to: Longman Group, Journals
Subscr. Dept., P.O. Box 77, Fourth Ave., Harlow,
Essex CM19 5AA, England; U.S. subscr. to: Churchill
Livingstone, 650 Ave. of the Americas, New York,
NY 10011. TEL 212-206-5000) Ed. B.I. Duerden.
bk.rev.; bibl.; charts; illus. (also avail. in microform
from UMI; back issues avail.) Indexed: Abstr.Hyg.,
Biol.Abstr., Biotech.Abstr., Chem.Abstr.,
Curr.Adv.Ecol.Sci., Curr.Adv.Genetics & Molec.Biol.,
Curr.Cont., Dairy Sci.Abstr., Excerp.Med.,
Helminthol.Abstr., Ind.Med., Ind.Sci.Rev., Ind.Vet.,
INIS Atomind., Nutr.Abstr., Pig News & Info.,
Poult.Abstr., Protozool.Abstr., Rev.Plant Path.,
Vet.Bull.
—BLDSC shelfmark: 5017.079000.

610 US
JOURNAL OF MEDICAL PRACTICE MANAGEMENT. 1985.
q. $59 to individuals; institutions $77. Williams &
Wilkins, 428 E. Preston St., Baltimore, MD 21202.
TEL 301-528-4000. FAX 301-528-4312. Ed.
Marcel Frenkel, M.D. circ. 2,200. (also avail. in
microfilm)
Formerly: Medical Practice Management (ISSN
8755-0229)
Description: Perspectives on legislation, litigation,
office management and other issues that affect the
medical practice of office-based physicians and
health care professionals.

616.01 US ISSN 0146-6615
RC114.5 CODEN: JMVIDB
JOURNAL OF MEDICAL VIROLOGY. 1977. m. $696
(foreign $846). John Wiley & Sons, Inc., Journals,
605 Third Ave., New York, NY 10158.
TEL 212-850-6000. FAX 212-850-6088. TELEX
12-7063. Ed. Arie J. Zuckerman. charts; illus.
(reprint service avail. from ISI) Indexed: Abstr.Hyg.,
Biol.Abstr., Chem.Abstr., Curr.Adv.Ecol.Sci.,
Curr.Adv.Genetics & Molec.Biol., Curr.Cont., Dairy
Sci.Abstr., Dent.Ind., Excerp.Med., Ind.Med.,
Ind.Sci.Rev., Ind.Vet., INIS Atomind., Sci.Cit.Ind,
Trop.Dis.Bull., Vet.Bull.
●Also available online.
—BLDSC shelfmark: 5017.095000.
Description: Covers the structure and composition
of viruses, epidemiology, humoral and cell-mediated
immune responses, and clinical features of infection.
Refereed Serial

610 US
CODEN: JNMDBO
JOURNAL OF MEDICINE (CLINICAL, EXPERIMENTAL AND
THEORETICAL). 1970. bi-m. $110 (foreign $135). P
J D Publications Ltd., Box 966, Westbury, NY
11590. TEL 516-626-0650. Ed. Julian L. Ambrus,
M.D. adv.; bk.rev.; charts; illus.; stat.; index. (reprint
service avail.) Indexed: Biol.Abstr., Biotech.Abstr.,
C.I.S. Abstr., Chem.Abstr, CINAHL, Curr.Adv.Ecol.Sci.,
Curr.Cont., Curr.Lit.Fam.Plan., Excerp.Med.,
Helminthol.Abstr., Ind.Med., INIS Atomind., L.R.I.,
Nutr.Abstr., Sci.Cit.Ind.
Former titles (1974-1975): Journal of Medicine,
Experimental and Clinical; (until 1974): Journal of
Medicine (ISSN 0025-7850)
Description: Articles on all areas of medicine and
medical science.
Refereed Serial

610 174 NE ISSN 0360-5310
R723 CODEN: JMPHDC
JOURNAL OF MEDICINE AND PHILOSOPHY. 1976. bi-m.
fl.280($159) (Baylor College of Medicine, Center for
Ethics, Medicine, and Public Issues, US) Kluwer
Academic Publishers, Postbus 17, 3300 AA
Dordrecht, Netherlands. TEL 078-334911.
FAX 078-334254. TELEX 29245. (Dist. by: Kluwer
Academic Publishers Group, P.O. Box 322, 3300
AH Dordrecht, Netherlands; N. America dist. addr.:
Box 358, Accord Station, Hingham, MA
02018-0358. TEL 617-871-6600) (Co-sponsors:
Society for Health and Human Values, US;
Association for Philosophical and Ethical Research in
Medicine, JA; European Society for Philosophy of
Medicine and Health Care) Ed. H. Tristram
Engelhardt, Jr. adv.; bk.rev.; bibl.; index. Indexed:
Biol.Abstr., Curr.Cont., Dent.Ind., Excerp.Med.,
G.Soc.Sci.& Rel.Per.Lit., Hum.Ind., Ind.Med., Lang.&
Lang.Behav.Abstr., Phil.Ind., Sociol.Abstr., SSCI.
—BLDSC shelfmark: 5017.385000.

JOURNAL OF MICROENCAPSULATION. see PHARMACY
AND PHARMACOLOGY

JOURNAL OF MORPHOLOGY. see BIOLOGY

612 UK ISSN 0142-4319
CODEN: JMRMD3
JOURNAL OF MUSCLE RESEARCH AND CELL MOTILITY.
1980. bi-m. £55 to individuals (US & Canada $99);
institutions £275 (US & Canada $495). Chapman
& Hall, 2-6 Boundary Row, London SE1 8HN,
England. TEL 071-865-0066. FAX 071-522-9623.
TELEX 290164-CHAPMAG. (Dist. by: International
Thomson Publishing Services, Ltd., N. Way, Andover,
Hampshire SP10 5BE, England. TEL
0264-33-2424; US addr.: Chapman & Hall, 29 W.
35th St., New York, NY 10001-2291.
TEL 212-244-3336) Ed.Bd. adv.; bk.rev.; bibl.; illus.;
index. (reprint service avail. from ISI, UMI) Indexed:
Biol.Abstr., Chem.Abstr, Curr.Adv.Ecol.Sci., Dent.Ind.,
Excerp.Med., Ind.Med., Ind.Sci.Rev.
—BLDSC shelfmark: 5021.120000.
Description: Presents Original research papers on
any aspect of muscle, contractive mechanisms and
cell motility.

610 US ISSN 1043-609X
R850.A1 CODEN: JNREEL
JOURNAL OF N I H RESEARCH. 1989. m. $69 to
individuals; institutions $119. (National Institutes of
Health) William M. Miller, 2101 L Steet, N.W., Ste.
207, Washington, DC 20037. TEL 202-785-5333.
FAX 202-872-7738. Ed. Dr. Deborah Barnes. adv.:
B&W page $3175; trim 8 1/9 x 10 7/8. circ.
2,000 (paid); 28,000 (controlled).
—BLDSC shelfmark: 5022.817000.
Description: Covers life science, research, and lab
techniques.

JOURNAL OF NUTRITION, GROWTH AND CANCER. see
NUTRITION AND DIETETICS

610 US ISSN 0096-1736
RC963 CODEN: JOCMA7
JOURNAL OF OCCUPATIONAL MEDICINE. 1959. m. $77
to individuals; institutions $107. (American College
of Occupational Medicine) Williams & Wilkins, 428
E. Preston St., Baltimore, MD 21202.
TEL 301-528-4000. FAX 301-528-4312. Ed. Lloyd
B. Tepper, M.D. adv.; bk.rev.; abstr.; bibl.; charts;
index. cum.index; circ. 8,900. (also avail. in
microfiche from UMI; reprint service avail. from UMI)
Indexed: Abstr.Hyg., Biol.Abstr., Bus.Ind., C.I.S. Abstr.,
Cadscan, Chem.Abstr., Curr.Cont., Dent.Ind.,
Environ.Per.Bibl., Ergon.Abstr, Excerp.Med.,
Helminthol.Abstr., Hlth.Ind., Ind.Med., Ind.Sci.Rev.,
Ind.Vet., INIS Atomind., Lab.Haz.Bull., Lead Abstr.,
Noise Pollut.Publ.Abstr., Sci.Cit.Ind, Stud.Wom.Abstr.,
Tr.& Indus.Ind., Trop.Dis.Bull., World Surf.Coat.,
Zincscan.
—BLDSC shelfmark: 5026.100000.
Former titles: J O M: Journal of Occupational
Medicine (ISSN 0022-3212); (until 1968): Journal
of Occupational Medicine.
Description: Original articles on occupational
medical practice including epidemiology, toxicology,
health screening, ergonomics, assessment,
rehabilitation, health education, and administration.
Refereed Serial

MEDICAL SCIENCES

615.8   US   ISSN 1053-0487
RC964   CODEN: JOCTEW
▼**JOURNAL OF OCCUPATIONAL REHABILITATION.** 1991. q. $150 (foreign $175)(effective 1992). Plenum Publishing Corp., 233 Spring St., New York, NY 10013-1578. TEL 212-620-8000. FAX 212-463-0742. TELEX 23-421139. Ed. Michael Feuerstein. adv. (back issues avail.)
—BLDSC shelfmark: 5026.125000.
Description: Multidisciplinary forum for the publication of original research, theoretical papers, review articles, and case studies related to the mechanism and management of work-related disabilities.
Refereed Serial

JOURNAL OF ORTHOPAEDIC AND SPORTS PHYSICAL THERAPY. see *MEDICAL SCIENCES — Sports Medicine*

610   642   CN   ISSN 0825-8597
JOURNAL OF PALLIATIVE CARE. 1985. q. Can.$60 to individuals (foreign Can.$640); institutions Can.$95 (foreign Can.$99). Center for Bioethics, Clinical Research Institute of Montreal, 110 Pine Ave. W., Montreal, Que. H2W 1R7, Canada. TEL 514-987-5619. FAX 514-987-5695. Ed. D.J. Roy. adv.; bk.rev.; circ. 880. (also avail. in microfilm from MML; back issues avail.) **Indexed:** Can.Per.Ind., CINAHL, Ind.Med., PSI, Psychol.Abstr.
—BLDSC shelfmark: 5028.260000.
Description: Publishes up-to-date scientific research in the field of palliative-Hospice care, combining scientific validation with humanistic concerns.

616.07   UK   ISSN 0022-3417
CODEN: JPTLAS
JOURNAL OF PATHOLOGY. 1892. m. $345 (effective 1992). (Pathological Society of Great Britain and Ireland) John Wiley & Sons Ltd., Baffins Lane, Chichester, Sussex PO19 1UD, England. TEL 0243-779777. FAX 0243-775878. TELEX 86290 WIBOOK G. Ed.Bd. adv.; bk.rev.; bibl.; charts; illus.; cum.index: vols.1-90. (back issues avail.) **Indexed:** Abstr.Hyg., Biol.Abstr., C.I.S. Abstr., Chem.Abstr., Curr.Adv.Cancer Res., Curr.Adv.Cell & Devel.Biol., Curr.Adv.Ecol.Sci., Curr.Adv.Genetics & Molec.Biol., Curr.Cont., Dairy Sci.Abstr., Dent.Ind., Excerp.Med., Helminthol.Abstr., Ind.Med., Ind.Sci.Rev., Ind.Vet., Nutr.Abstr., Pig News & Info., Rev.Plant Path., Sci.Cit.Ind, Trop.Dis.Bull., Vet.Bull.
—BLDSC shelfmark: 5029.900000.
Incorporates (in Jan. 1984): Diagnostic Histopathology (ISSN 0272-7749); Which was formerly: Investigative and Cell Pathology (ISSN 0146-7611)
Description: Covers the field of experimental pathology, relevent to the understanding of human disease, and includes papers on the use of techniques such as immunology and molecular biology to elucidate disease mechanisms.

JOURNAL OF PHARMACEUTICAL AND MEDICAL SCIENCES. see *PHARMACY AND PHARMACOLOGY*

JOURNAL OF PHYSIOLOGY. see *BIOLOGY — Physiology*

610   II   ISSN 0022-3859
CODEN: JPMDA3
JOURNAL OF POSTGRADUATE MEDICINE. (Text in English) 1955. q. Rs.40($30) Seth G.S. Medical College and K.E.M. Hospital, Staff Society, Dept. of Physiology, Bombay 400012, India. Ed. S.D. Bhandarkar. adv.; bk.rev.; charts; illus.; stat.; index; circ. 700. **Indexed:** Biol.Abstr., Chem.Abstr. Dent.Ind., Ind.Med., Nutr.Abstr.
—BLDSC shelfmark: 5041.150000.

610   US   ISSN 0731-8332
HV8833   CODEN: JPJHD3
JOURNAL OF PRISON AND JAIL HEALTH; medicine, law, corrections and ethics. 1980. s-a. $80 (foreign $95). (National Commission on Correctional Health Care) Human Sciences Press, Inc. (Subsidiary of: Plenum Publishing Corp.), 233 Spring St., New York, NY 10013-1578. TEL 212-620-8000. FAX 212-463-0742. Ed. Nancy Neveloff Dubler. adv. (also avail. in microform from UMI; back issues avail.) **Indexed:** Crim.Just.Abstr., Excerp.Med., Med.Care Rev., Psychol.Abstr., Sociol.Abstr.
—BLDSC shelfmark: 5042.410000.
Formerly (until 1981): Journal of Prison Health (ISSN 0192-7051)
Description: Provides a forum for professionals to share information which can help to improve the level of health care provided in prisons and jails.
Refereed Serial

JOURNAL OF PRODUCTS LIABILITY. see *LAW*

610   US   ISSN 1040-8800
RD130
JOURNAL OF PROSTHETICS AND ORTHOTICS. 1970. q. $50 (foreign $60). American Academy of Orthotists and Prosthetists, 1650 King St., Ste. 500, Alexandria, VA 22314. TEL 703-836-7116. FAX 703-836-0838. Ed. John W. Michael. adv.; bk.rev.; circ. 4,200. (also avail. in microfilm from UMI)
—BLDSC shelfmark: 5042.910000.
Formerly (until 1988): Clinical Prosthetics and Orthotics (ISSN 0279-6910)
Description: Presents articles and reports from professionals on current topics in orthotics and prosthetics.
Refereed Serial

610   US   ISSN 0197-5110
QH603.C43   CODEN: JRERDM
JOURNAL OF RECEPTOR RESEARCH. 1980. 4/yr. $197.50 to individuals; institutions $395. Marcel Dekker Journals, 270 Madison Ave., New York, NY 10016. TEL 212-696-9000. FAX 212-685-4540. TELEX 421419 MARDEEK. (Subscr. to: Box 10018, Church St. Sta., New York, NY 10249) Eds. R. Mikkelsen, V. Pliska. (also avail. in microform from RPI) **Indexed:** Biol.Abstr., Chem.Abstr, Curr.Adv.Ecol.Sci., Curr.Cont., Dairy Sci.Abstr., Excerp.Med., Ind.Med., Ind.Sci.Rev., Protozool.Abstr.
—BLDSC shelfmark: 5047.850000.
Refereed Serial

JOURNAL OF REHABILITATION. see *SOCIAL SERVICES AND WELFARE*

JOURNAL OF REHABILITATION ADMINISTRATION. see *BUSINESS AND ECONOMICS — Management*

JOURNAL OF REPRODUCTION AND FERTILITY (INDIA). see *BIOLOGY*

610   II
JOURNAL OF RESEARCH IN AYURVEDA AND SIDDHA. (Text in English; summaries in Hindi) 1966. q. Rs.60($4) Central Council for Research in Ayurveda and Siddha, Dharma Bhawan, S-10, Green Park Extn. Market, New Delhi 110 016, India. TEL 11-669315. Ed. Dr. V.N. Pandey. adv.; bk.rev.; abstr.; bibl.; charts; illus.; stat.; index; circ. 300. (processed) **Indexed:** Biol.Abstr., Chem.Abstr.
Formerly (until 1980): Journal of Research in Indian Medicine (ISSN 0022-4286)
Description: Covers work on fundamental anthropological and behavioral details referred to in clinical and literary studies of medicinal systems.

616.07   US   ISSN 0890-765X
RA771.A1
JOURNAL OF RURAL HEALTH. 1985. q. $35 to individuals; institutions $90. (Center for Rural Studies) National Rural Health Association, 301 E. Armour Blvd., Ste. 420, Kansas City, MO 64111. TEL 816-756-3140. FAX 816-756-3144. Ed. Michael K. Miller. adv.; bk.rev.; abstr.; circ. 1,700.
—BLDSC shelfmark: 5052.128850.
Description: Covers rural health research.

JOURNAL OF SCIENTIFIC RESEARCH IN PLANTS & MEDICINES. see *PHARMACY AND PHARMACOLOGY*

JOURNAL OF SEX RESEARCH. see *PSYCHOLOGY*

610   UK   ISSN 0959-2431
▼**JOURNAL OF SMOKING-RELATED DISORDERS.** 1991. 2/yr. £55($100) Gardiner - Caldwell Communications Ltd., Old Ribbon Mill, Pitt Street, Macclesfield, Cheshire SK11 7PT, England. TEL 0625-618507. FAX 0625-610260.
—BLDSC shelfmark: 5064.711000.

610   JA   ISSN 0374-3527
CODEN: JSMRE
JOURNAL OF SMOOTH MUSCLE RESEARCH. (Text in English) 1965. q. (Nihon Heikatsukin Gakkai - Japanese Society of Smooth Muscle Research) Journal of Smooth Muscle Research, 5 Zaifucho, Hirosaki-shi, Aomori 036, Japan. Ed.Bd. adv.; bk.rev.; abstr.; charts; illus.; index; circ. 950. **Indexed:** Biol.Abstr., Excerp.Med., Ind.Med.
—BLDSC shelfmark: 4658.800000.
Formerly (until 1991): Nihon Heikatsukin Gakkai Zasshi - Japanese Journal of Smooth Muscle Research (ISSN 0029-0238)

610   US   ISSN 0022-5045
R131.A1   CODEN: JHMAA6
JOURNAL OF THE HISTORY OF MEDICINE AND ALLIED SCIENCES. 1946. q. $45 to individuals; institutions $65. Journal of the History of Medicine and Allied Sciences, Inc., 333 Cedar St., New Haven, CT 06510. TEL 203-785-4341. (Subscr. to: 1017 Turnpike St., Canton, MA 02021) Ed. Dr. Stanley W. Jackson. adv.; bk.rev.; charts; illus.; index: vols.1-30, 1946-75; circ. 1,500. (also avail. in microform from UMI; reprint service avail. from UMI) **Indexed:** Amer.Hist.& Life, Biol.Abstr., Chem.Abstr., Curr.Adv.Ecol.Sci., Curr.Cont., Dent.Ind., Excerp.Med., Hist.Abstr., Ind.Med., Ind.Sci.Rev., Mid.East: Abstr.& Ind., Sci.Cit.Ind., SSCI.
—BLDSC shelfmark: 5001.000000.

610   II   ISSN 0022-507X
JOURNAL OF THE INDIAN MEDICAL PROFESSION. (Text in English) 1954. m. Rs.15($4.50) United Asia Publications Pvt. Ltd., 12 Rampart Row, Bombay 1, India. Ed. Dr. R.M. Rajpal. adv.; charts; illus. (tabloid format) **Indexed:** Chem.Abstr., Ind.Med.

610   IO   ISSN 0126-1312
JOURNAL OF THE MEDICAL SCIENCES/BERKALA ILMU KEDOKTERAN. (Text and summaries in English and Indonesian) 1969. q. Rps.8000($20) Gadjah Mada University, College of Medicine, Department of Physical Anthropology - Universitas Gadjah Mada, Fakultas Kedokteran, Sekip, Yogyakarta, Indonesia. Ed. Teuku Jacob. adv.; bk.rev.; charts; illus.; stat.; circ. 1,200. **Indexed:** Chem.Abstr.
Formerly: Gadjah Mada Journal of the Medical Sciences.

610   JA   ISSN 0022-5207
JOURNAL OF THERAPY/CHIRYO. (Text in Japanese) vol.52, 1970. m. $21.50. Nanzando Co., Ltd., 4-1-11 Yushima, Bunkyoku, Tokyo 113-91, Japan. Ed. Masatsugu Suzuki. adv.; circ. 12,000. **Indexed:** Chem.Abstr.
Formed by the merger of: Chiryo Oyobi Shono & Naika Oyobi Shonika.

610   US
JOURNAL OF THORACIC IMAGING. 1985. q. $135. Aspen Publishers, Inc., 200 Orchard Ridge Dr., Gaithersburg, MD 20878. TEL 301-417-7500. FAX 301-417-7550. **Indexed:** Curr.Adv.Cancer Res., INIS Atomind.

JOURNAL OF TRACE ELEMENTS AND ELECTROLYTES IN HEALTH AND DISEASE; analytical methods - metabolism: biochemistry, pathobiochemistry - nutrition - toxicology - epidemiology - clinical application: diagnosis therapy. see *BIOLOGY — Biological Chemistry*

616.98   US
JOURNAL OF TRADITIONAL ACUPUNCTURE. 3/yr. Traditional Acupuncture Institute, American City Bldg., Ste. 100, Columbia, MD 21044. TEL 301-596-6006. Ed. M.E. Zorbaugh.

MEDICAL SCIENCES

610 534   US   ISSN 0278-4297
                      CODEN: JUMEDA
JOURNAL OF ULTRASOUND IN MEDICINE. 1982. m. American Institute for Ultrasound in Medicine, 4405 East-West Hwy, Ste. 504, Bethesda, MD 20814. Ed. Dr. George R. Leopold. adv.; bk.rev.; abstr.; bibl.; charts; illus.; index; circ. 9,500. (also avail. in microform from UMI; reprint service avail. from UMI) **Indexed:** Curr.Cont., Dent.Ind., Excerp.Med., Ind.Med., Ind.Sci.Rev., Sci.Cit.Ind.
—BLDSC shelfmark: 5071.455000.
Refereed Serial

JOURNAL OF VESTIBULAR RESEARCH: EQUILIBRIUM AND ORIENTATION. see *BIOLOGY — Physiology*

610   US   ISSN 0896-7210
JOURNAL WATCH. 1987. s-m. $65. Massachusetts Medical Society, 1440 Main St., Waltham, MA 02154. TEL 617-893-3800. FAX 617-893-8103.

JUNDI SHAPUR UNIVERSITY. FACULTY OF MEDICINE. LIBRARY BULLETIN/DANESHGAH-E JONDISHAPUR. DANESHKADE-YE PEZESAKI. BULTAN-E KETABKHANEH. see *LIBRARY AND INFORMATION SCIENCES*

610   JA   ISSN 0022-6769
                      CODEN: JUIZAG
JUNTENDO MEDICAL JOURNAL/JUNTENDO IGAKU. (Text in Japanese) 1887. q. 4000 Yen. Juntendo Medical Society - Juntendo Igakkai, 2-1-1 Hongo, Bunkyo-ku, Tokyo 113, Japan. Ed. Yoshiro Fukuda. adv.; abstr.; index; circ. 1,800. **Indexed:** Chem.Abstr., INIS Atomind.
—BLDSC shelfmark: 5075.550000.

610   JA   ISSN 0075-4579
JUNTENDO UNIVERSITY. MEDICAL ULTRASONICS RESEARCH CENTER. ANNUAL REPORT.* (Text in English) a. Juntendo University, School of Medicine, Medical Ultrasonics Research Center, 2-1-2 Hongo, Bunkyo-ku, Tokyo 113, Japan.

610   MY   ISSN 0127-1075
JURNAL PERUBATAN U K M. (Text in English and Malay) 1979. s-a. $15 per no. Penerbit Universiti Kebangsaan Malaysia, 43600 UKM Bangi, Selangor, Malaysia.

610   JA   ISSN 0022-7226
                      CODEN: JUZIAG
JUZEN IGAKKAI ZASSHI/JUZEN MEDICAL SOCIETY. JOURNAL. (Text in English and Japanese) 1896. 6/yr. 3000 Yen($20) Kanazawa Daigaku Igakubu, Juzen Igakkai - Kanazawa University, School of Medicine, Juzen Medical Society, 13-1 Takara-machi, Kanazawa-shi, Ishikawa-ken 920, Japan. adv.; abstr.; bibl.; illus. **Indexed:** Biol.Abstr., C.I.S. Abstr., Chem.Abstr, INIS Atomind.
—BLDSC shelfmark: 4810.100000.

610   US   ISSN 0090-5089
K A F P JOURNAL. 1956. q. membership. Kentucky Academy of Family Physicians, Medical Arts Bldg., 1169 Eastern Pkwy., Louisville, KY 40217. TEL 502-451-0370. FAX 502-451-5914. Eds. Drs. Walter Zukof, James E. Redmon, Jr. adv.; circ. 2,000.
Formerly: K A G P Journal (ISSN 0022-7250)
Description: Articles and essays focusing on the practical issues that affect the health and welfare of families, and on conferences, activities, and issues relevant to contemporary family physicians.

610   US   ISSN 0886-4772
K C M S BULLETIN. 1921. 6/yr. $2.50 (non-members $15). Medical Society County of Kings, 1313 Bedford Ave., Brooklyn, NY 11216. TEL 718-467-9000. FAX 718-778-0380. (Co-publisher: Academy of Medicine of Brooklyn) Ed. Sol Mora. adv.; bk.rev.; charts; tr.lit.; index; circ. 2,800. (back issues avail.)
Formerly: Medical Society of the County of Kings and Academy of Medicine of Brooklyn. Bulletin (ISSN 0025-7532)

610   JA   ISSN 0368-5063
                      CODEN: KDIZAA
KAGOSHIMA DAIGAKU IGAKU ZASSHI/MEDICAL JOURNAL OF KAGOSHIMA UNIVERSITY. 1945. q. Kagoshima Daigaku, Igakubu - Kagoshima University, Faculty of Medicine, 8-35-1, Sakuragaoka, Kagoshima 890, Japan. **Indexed:** INIS Atomind.
—BLDSC shelfmark: 5527.830000.

610.6   JA
KANAGAWA MEDICAL PREFECTURE ASSOCIATION. JOURNAL. 1973. Kanagawa Medical Prefecture Association - Kanagawa Igakkai Zasshi, 4-104 Nishi-ku, Yokohama City, Japan. Ed. Kinzo Kiyokawa.
Formerly: Kanagawa Medical Association. Journal.

610   CC
KANG FU/REHABILITATION. (Text in Chinese) bi-m. Y7.20. (Shanghai Yike Daxue, Jiaoyu Yanjiu Zhongxin - Shanghai University of Medical Sciences, Educational Research Center) Kang Fu Zazhishe, No. 5, Alley 733, Huaihai Zhonglu, Shanghai 200020, People's Republic of China. TEL 3235326. Ed. Yang Zhonghua.

610.7   JA
KANSAI MEDICAL UNIVERSITY. JOURNAL/KANSAI IKA DAIGAKU. ZASSHI. (Text and summaries in English, German and Japanese) 1948. q. 1000 Yen($2.80) Kansai Medical University, 1 Fumizono-cho, Moriguchi 570, Japan. adv.; abstr.; bibl.; charts; illus.; index. **Indexed:** Biol.Abstr., Chem.Abstr, Excerp.Med., INIS Atomind.
Formerly: Kansai Medical School. Journal (ISSN 0022-8400)

610   US   ISSN 8755-0059
R15   CODEN: KAMEEI
KANSAS MEDICINE. 1901. m. $45 (foreign $50). Kansas Medical Society, 1300 Topeka Ave., Topeka, KS 66612. TEL 913-235-2383. Ed. David E. Gray, M.D. adv.; bibl.; charts; illus.; tr.lit.; index; circ. 3,600. (also avail. in microform from UMI; reprint service avail. from UMI) **Indexed:** Dent.Ind., Hosp.Lit.Ind., Ind.Med., INIS Atomind.
—BLDSC shelfmark: 5085.647000.
Formerly: Kansas Medical Society. Journal (ISSN 0022-8699)

610   CH   ISSN 0257-5655
                      CODEN: KHHCE2
KAOHSIUNG JOURNAL OF MEDICAL SCIENCES. (Text in Chinese and English) 1985. m. NT.$1000($50) Kaohsiung Medical College, 100 Shih-Chuan 1st Rd., Kaohsiung 80708, Taiwan, Republic of China. TEL 07-3121101. FAX 07-3210564. Ed. Eng-Rin Chen. adv.; charts; illus.; index; circ. 1,500. (back issues avail.) **Indexed:** Chem.Abstr., Excerp.Med., Nutr.Abstr., Soyabean Abstr. Key Title: Gaoxiong Yixue Kexue Zazhi.
—BLDSC shelfmark: 5085.674500.
Description: Scientific papers in all fields of medicine; review articles, and case reports.

610 616.1   GW   ISSN 0724-9187
KARDIO; Erkrankungen von Herz, Kreislauf und Gefaessen. 1983. 12/yr. DM.150. P M I Verlag GmbH, August-Schanz-Str. 21, 6000 Frankfurt a.M. 50, Germany. TEL 069-548000-0. FAX 069-548000-77. TELEX 412952-PMI-D. Ed.Bd. circ. 20,000.

610   II   ISSN 0377-9378
KARNATAKA MEDICAL JOURNAL. (Text in English) 1939. q. Rs.20($2) Indian Medical Association, Karnataka State Branch, IMA House, Alur Venkata Rao Rd., Bangalore 560018, India. Ed. Dr. K.V. Ghorpade. adv.; bk.rev.; circ. 5,000. **Indexed:** Biol.Abstr.
Continues (Oct.-Dec. 1974): Mysore Medical Association. Journal.

610   US
KAROLINSKA INSTITUTE. NOBEL CONFERENCE SERIES. 1980. irreg., latest 1990. price varies. Raven Press, 1185 Ave. of the Americas, New York, NY 10036. TEL 212-930-9500. FAX 212-869-3495.

610   VE   ISSN 0075-5222
KASMERA. (Text in Spanish; abstracts in English) 1962. a. exchange basis. Universidad del Zulia, Departamento de Microbiologia y Patologia Tropical, Apdo. 526, 4011 Maracaibo, Venezuela. Ed. Dr. Ricardo Soto Urribarri. bibl.; charts; illus.; stat.; circ. 1,000. (also avail. in microform) **Indexed:** Abstr.Hyg., Biol.Abstr., Trop.Dis.Bull.
Description: Publishes research by the Faculty of Medicine in areas of bacteriology, immunology, parasitology and other topics.

610   GW
KATHOLISCHER BERUFSVERBAND FUER PFLEGEBERUFE. MITTEILUNGSBLATT. bi-m. Katholischer Berufsverband fuer Pflegeberufe e.V., Kaiserstr. 42, D-6500 Mainz 1, Germany. TEL 06131-232340.

610   JA   ISSN 0386-5924
KAWASAKI IGAKKAI SHI. (Text in Japanese; summaries in English and Japanese) 1975. q. 10000 Yen. Kawasaki Medical Society, 577 Matsushima, Kurashiki-Shi, Okayama 701-01, Japan. FAX 0864-62-1199. Eds. Toshitami Sawayama, Moto Matsumura. bk.rev.; illus.; circ. 1,200. **Indexed:** INIS Atomind.
—BLDSC shelfmark: 5088.096000.

610   JA   ISSN 0385-0234
                      CODEN: KAMJDW
KAWASAKI MEDICAL JOURNAL. (Text in English; summaries in Japanese) 1975. q. 20000 Yen. Kawasaki Medical Society, 577 Matsushima, Kurashiki-Shi, Okayama 701-01, Japan. FAX 0864-62-1199. Eds. Yoshihito Yawata, Fumihiko Kajiya. bk.rev.; illus.; circ. 800. **Indexed:** Abstr.Hyg., Biol.Abstr., Chem.Abstr., Excerp.Med., INIS Atomind., Trop.Dis.Bull.
—BLDSC shelfmark: 5088.097000.

610   JA   ISSN 0022-9717
                      CODEN: KJMEA9
KEIO JOURNAL OF MEDICINE. (Text in English) 1952. q. $90. Keio Gijuku Daigaku, Igakubu - Keio University, School of Medicine, 35 Shinano-machi, Shinjuku-ku, Tokyo 160, Japan. TEL 03-3353-1211. FAX 03-3353-2077. Ed. Toyomi Fujino. circ. 1,400. **Indexed:** Abstr.Hyg., Biol.Abstr., Chem.Abstr., Excerp.Med., Ind.Med., Nutr.Abstr., Trop.Dis.Bull.
—BLDSC shelfmark: 5089.000000.

950 615.89   JA
KEIRAKU SHINRYO. 1969. m. 8400 Yen (effective Apr. 1991). Toyo Hari Igakkai - Toyo HariMedical Association, Royaru Hainesu 1 F 111, Takadanobaba 1-18-26, Shinjuku-ku, Tokyo 160, Japan. Ed. Kenji Fukushima. adv.; bk.rev.; index; circ. 800. (Braille; also avail. in magnetic tape; back issues avail.)
Description: Concerns "hari", traditional Japanese medicine based on pulse diagnosis.

170 610   US
KENNEDY INSTITUTE OF ETHICS. SCOPE NOTE. 1982. q. $5 (in U.S., Canada and Mexico; elsewhere $8). Kennedy Institute of Ethics, National Reference Center for Bioethics Literature, Georgetown University, Washington, DC 20057. TEL 202-687-3885. FAX 202-687-6770. Ed. Doris Goldstein. circ. 2,000. **Indexed:** Vert.File.Ind.
Formerly: Kennedy Institute of Bioethics. Scope Note.
Description: Presents current viewpoints related to specific topics in biomedical ethics. Intended specifically for scholars, journalists, medical and legal practitioners, students and interested laypersons.

610   US   ISSN 0023-0294
                      CODEN: JKMAB5
KENTUCKY MEDICAL ASSOCIATION. JOURNAL.* 1903. m. $25. Kentucky Medical Association, 301 N. Hurstbourne Ln., Ste. 200, Louisville, KY 40222-5142. TEL 502-459-9790. FAX 502-459-9796. Ed. A. Evan Overstreet. adv.; bk.rev.; bibl.; illus.; index; circ. 5,200. (also avail. in microform from UMI) **Indexed:** Biol.Abstr., Chem.Abstr., Curr.Cont., Excerp.Med., Helminthol.Abstr., Ind.Med., Rev.Plant Path.
—BLDSC shelfmark: 4810.740000.
Refereed Serial

610   KE
KENYA. MINISTRY OF HEALTH. ANNUAL REPORT. a. Ministry of Health, P.O. Box 52, Homa Bay, Kenya.

610   KE   ISSN 1010-576X
KENYA MEDICAL RESEARCH INSTITUTE. PROCEEDINGS OF THE ANNUAL MEDICAL SCIENTIFIC CONFERENCE. (Text and summaries in English) 1980. a. EAs.100. Kenya Medical Research Institute (KEMRI), P.O. Box 54840, Nairobi, Kenya. FAX 720039. TELEX 25696. circ. 1,000. (back issues avail.)
Formerly: Kenya Medical Research Institute. Proceedings of the Annual Medical Research Conferences.

610   II   ISSN 0301-4827
KERALA MEDICAL JOURNAL. (Text in English) 1959. m. membership. Indian Medical Association, Kerala State Branch, Cochin 682 016, India. Ed. I.S. Menon. adv.; bk.rev.; bibl.; charts; film rev.; illus.; circ. 4,500.

M

MEDICAL SCIENCES

610   JA
KETSUEKI JIGYO NO GENKYO. 1865. a. free. Niigata kaen Niigatashi, Sinkocho 4-1, Niigata-shi, Japan.

616.07   FR
KINESITHERAPIE ACTUALITE.* 42/yr. 505 Fr. Societe de Presse et d'Edition de la Kinesitherapie, 24 rue des Petits-Hotels, 75010 Paris, France.
Formerly: Kine Loisirs.

615.8   FR   ISSN 0023-1576
CODEN: KNTSAC
KINESITHERAPIE SCIENTIFIQUE.* 1965. m. (except Aug.). 520 F. Societe de Presse et d'Edition de la Kinesitherapie, 24 rue des Petits Hotels, 75010 Paris, France. adv.; charts, illus. **Indexed:** Biol.Abstr.
—BLDSC shelfmark: 5096.070000.
Formerly: Kinesitherapie.

610   US
KING COUNTY MEDICAL SOCIETY. BULLETIN. 1916. m. $12.95 memberhip. (King County Medical Society) Journal and Bulletin Agency, Box 10249, Bainbridge Island, WA 98110. TEL 206-682-7813. adv.; circ. 3,600.

610   UK   ISSN 0085-2546
KING'S GAZETTE; the journal of King's College Hospital. 1921. s-a. £2.75. Kings College Hospital Medical School, Denmark Hill, London SE5 8RX, England. Ed. Sarah Hawxwell. adv.; bk.rev.; illus.; circ. 1,500.

615.8   CN   ISSN 0709-8227
KINO - NOUVELLES. bi-m. Ministere du Loisir, de la Chasse et de la Peche, Direction des Communications - Department of Recreation, Fish and Game, 150 bd. Saint-Cyrille est, Quebec, Que. G1R 4Y1, Canada. **Indexed:** Sportsearch (1980-).

610   JA   ISSN 0023-1908
CODEN: KKAIA2
KITAKANTO MEDICAL JOURNAL/KITAKANTO IGAKU. (Text in Japanese; summaries in English) 1951. bi-m. 3600 Yen. Kitakanto Medical Society - Kitakanto Igakkai, c/o Gumma Daigaku Igakubu, 3-39-22 Showa-machi, Maebashi-shi 371, Japan. Ed. Katsuhiro Shibata. abstr.; charts; illus. **Indexed:** Biol.Abstr., Chem.Abstr., INIS Atomind.

610   JA   ISSN 0023-1916
CODEN: KBYKAV
KITANO HOSPITAL JOURNAL OF MEDICINE.* (Text in Japanese and European languages; summaries and table of contents in English) 1955. q. Tazuke Kofukai Foundation, Medical Research Institute, 13-3 Kamiyama-cho, Kita-ku, Osaka 530, Japan. charts; illus.; stat.; circ. 500. **Indexed:** Biol.Abstr., Excerp.Med.
—BLDSC shelfmark: 5098.150000.

610   RU   ISSN 0023-2149
R.91   CODEN: KLMIAZ
KLINICHESKAYA MEDITSINA/CLINICAL MEDICINE. (Text in Russian; summaries in English) 1920. m. 31.80 Rub.($27.60) (Ministerstvo Zdravookhraneniya S.S.S.R.) Izdatel'stvo Meditsina, Petroverigskii pereulok 6-8, 101838 Moscow, Russia. (Subscr. to: Mezhdunarodnaya Kniga, Moscow, G-200, Russia) Ed. F.I. Komarov. bk.rev.; index. **Indexed:** Biol.Abstr., Biotech.Abstr., Chem.Abstr., Curr.Cont., Dent.Ind., Excerp.Med., Helminthol.Abstr., Ind.Med., Ind.Sci.Rev., INIS Atomind., Nutr.Abstr.
—BLDSC shelfmark: 0089.240000.
Description: Discusses principal issues of clinical medicine, dealing mainly with matters of diagnosis, pathogenesis, prophylaxis, treatment and clinical course. Includes original essays on the scientific developments of Soviet medicine and surveys of modern theoretical medicine abroad.

610   GW   ISSN 0341-2350
KLINIKARZT; Medizin im Krankenhaus. 1972. m. DM.72. Perimed Verlag Dr. D. Straube, Weinstr. 70, Postfach 3740, 8520 Erlangen, Germany. TEL 09131-609-1. FAX 09131-609217. TELEX 629851-PEMEDD. adv.; bk.rev.; index; circ. 25,000.
—BLDSC shelfmark: 5099.284900.

616.07   GW
KLINIKKALENDER. 1972. a. DM.18. Perimed Verlag Dr. D. Straube, Weinstr. 70, 8520 Erlangen, Germany. TEL 09131-609-1. Ed. Dr. D. Straube.

615.8   GW   ISSN 0173-6647
KLINISCHE CHEMIE; Mitteilungen. bi-m. DM.60. (Deutsche Gesellschaft fuer Klinische Chemie) Demeter Verlag, Wuermstr. 13, 8032 Graefelfing, Germany. TEL 089-852033. FAX 089-8543347. Ed. Dr. W.G. Guder. circ. 1,600.

616.3   GW
KLOPFZEICHEN; eine Informationszeitschrift rund um CF. 1981. s-a. free. Cystic Fibrosis Selbsthilfe Bundesverband, Muehlenstr. 13, 3121 Gross Oesingen, Germany. TEL 05838-571. adv.; bk.rev.; circ. 5,000.

610   JA   ISSN 0075-6431
CODEN: KDIKAX
KOBE DAIGAKU IGAKUBU KIYO/KOBE UNIVERSITY. MEDICAL JOURNAL. (Formerly: Kobe Ika Daigaku. Kiyo) (Table of contents and summaries in English) 1949. a. free. (Kobe Daigaku Igakkai - Kobe University Medical Society) Kobe Daigaku, Igakubu, 5-1, Kusunoki-cho 7-chome, Chuo-ku, Kobe-shi, Hyogo-ken 650, Japan. Ed. Kazushi Hirohata. **Indexed:** Biol.Abstr., Ind.Med., INIS Atomind.
—BLDSC shelfmark: 5527.840000.

610   JA   ISSN 0023-2513
CODEN: KJMDA6
KOBE JOURNAL OF MEDICAL SCIENCES. (Text and summaries in English, French, German) 1951. bi-m. 6000 Yen. Kobe Daigaku, Igakubu - Kobe University, School of Medicine, 5-1, Kusunoki-cho 7-chome, Chuo-ku, Kobe-shi, Hyogo-ken 650, Japan. (Subscr. to: Executive Editor, c/o Department of Medical Zoology, Kobe University School of Medicine, 5-1, Kusunoki-cho 7-chome, Chuo-ku, Kobe-shi, Hyogo-ken 650, Japan) Ed. Takeo Matsumura. abstr.; charts; illus.; index; circ. 650. (back issues avail.) **Indexed:** Abstr.Hyg., Biol.Abstr., Chem.Abstr., Excerp.Med., Ind.Med., INIS Atomind., Trop.Dis.Bull.
—BLDSC shelfmark: 5100.580000.

610   DK   ISSN 0105-4139
KOEBENHAVNS UNIVERSITET. INSTITUT FOR SOCIAL MEDICIN. PUBLIKATIONER. no.13, 1981. irregr. price varies. Foreningen af Danske Laegestuderendes Forlag, Prinsesse Charlottesgade 29, st.tv., 2200 Copenhagen N, Denmark. TEL 31-356287. FAX 35-366229. TELEX 16698 UNBOG. illus.; circ. 500.

616.98   JA   ISSN 0023-2858
KOKU IGAKU JIKKENTAI HOKOKU/JAPAN AIR SELF DEFENSE FORCE. AEROMEDICAL LABORATORY. REPORTS. (Text in Japanese; summaries in English) 1958. q. exchange basis. Japan Air Self Defense Force, Aeromedical Laboratory - Kokujieitai Koku Igaku Jikkentai, 2-10, Sakae-cho 1-chome, Tachikawa-shi, Tokyo, Japan. Ed.Bd. bibl.; charts; illus.; circ. 500. **Indexed:** Biol.Abstr., INIS Atomind., Int.Aerosp.Abstr., Psychol.Abstr.
—BLDSC shelfmark: 7368.740000.

KOKUTETSU CHUO HOKEN KANRIJOHO; health control. see *PUBLIC HEALTH AND SAFETY*

610   HU   ISSN 0075-6792
CODEN: KSTUAJ
KORANYI SANDOR TARSASAG. TUDOMANYOS ULESEK. 1961. irreg. price varies. Akademiai Kiado, Publishing House of the Hungarian Academy of Sciences, P.O. Box 24, H-1363 Budapest, Hungary.

610   KO   ISSN 0023-4028
KOREAN MEDICAL ASSOCIATION. JOURNAL.* (Text in Korean; summaries in English) 1908. m. free. Korean Medical Association, Box 2062, Seoul, S. Korea. Ed. Dr. Hee Young Lee. adv.; abstr.; charts; illus.; stat.; index. **Indexed:** Excerp.Med., Ind.Med., INIS Atomind. Key Title: Taehan Uihak Hyophoe Chi.
—BLDSC shelfmark: 4812.340000.

610   IS   ISSN 0023-4109
KOROTH (HAIFA); a journal devoted to the history of medicine and science. (Text in Hebrew; summaries in English) 1952. a. $15. Israel Society of the History of Medicine and Science, Maon Harofe, 37 Gedaljahu St., Nave Shaanan, Haifa, Israel. (Co-sponsor: Israel Institute of Medical History) Ed.Bd. adv.; bk.rev.; abstr.; bibl.; illus.; index; circ. 2,000. **Indexed:** Amer.Hist.& Life, Hist.Abstr., Ind.Heb.Per.

610   IT   ISSN 0393-2095
KOS. 1983. bi-m. L.50000. Franco Maria Ricci Editore s.p.a., Via Durini, 19, 20122 Milan, Italy. TEL (2) 7702. Ed. Gianni Guadalupi. adv.; circ. 15,000.

616.98   RU   ISSN 0321-5040
RC1050   CODEN: KBAMAJ
KOSMICHESKAYA BIOLOGIYA I AVIAKOSMICHESKAYA MEDITSINA/SPACE BIOLOGY AND AEROSPACE MEDICINE. English translation: U S S R Report: Space Biology and Aerospace Medicine. (Text in Russian; summaries in English) 1967. bi-m. 23.70 Rub.($10.20) (Ministerstvo Zdravookhraneniya S.S.S.R.) Izdatel'stvo Meditsina, Petroverigskii pereulok 6-8, 101838 Moscow, Russia. (Subscr. to: Mezhdunarodnaya Kniga, Moscow, G-200, Russia) Ed. A.I. Grigor'ev. bk.rev.; abstr.; bibl.; charts; illus.; index. **Indexed:** Biol.Abstr., Chem.Abstr., Curr.Adv.Ecol.Sci., Curr.Cont., Dairy Sci.Abstr., Dent.Ind., Dok.Arbeitsmed., Excerp.Med., Field Crop Abstr., Ind.Med., Ind.Sci.Rev., INIS Atomind., Nutr.Abstr., Psychol.Abstr., Triticale Abstr.
—BLDSC shelfmark: 0092.490000.
Formerly: Kosmicheskaya Biologiya i Meditsina (ISSN 0023-4192)
Description: Articles both of scientific and applied character on a wide range of problems in the field of aerospace medicine and biology. Includes physiology and hygiene of flight, psychophysiological peculiarities of flight activity, psychological screening and medical examination for flight fitness.

616.39   DK   ISSN 0904-3764
KOST OG ALLERGI NYT. bi-m. free. Sundhedsministeriet, Levnedsmiddelsesstyrelsen, Moerkehoej Bygade 19, DK-2860 Soeborg, Denmark. TEL 39-69-66-00. Ed.Bd.

615.8   GW   ISSN 0023-4494
KRANKENGYMNASTIK; Zeitschrift fuer Physikalische Therapie, Bewegungstherapie, Massage, Praevention und Rehabilitation. 1948. m. DM.128.40 (foreign DM.139.20). (Deutscher Verband fuer Physiotherapie - Zentralverband der Krankengymnasten (ZvK) e.V.) Richard Pflaum Verlag GmbH und Co. KG, Lazarettstr. 4, Postfach 190737, 8000 Munich 19, Germany. TEL 089-12607-0. FAX 089-12607-281. Ed. Antje Hueter-Becker. adv.; bk.rev.; abstr.; charts; illus.; index. **Indexed:** Excerp.Med.
—BLDSC shelfmark: 5118.137000.

610 614.8   GW   ISSN 0341-0943
KRITISCHE MEDIZIN IM ARGUMENT. 1976. s-a. DM.33 to individuals. Argument-Verlag GmbH, Rentzelstr. 1, 2000 Hamburg 13, Germany. TEL 040-456018. circ. 2,000.
Description: Discusses economic and world politics, peace research, feminism, critical studies of medicine and psychology, international socialism, Marxism, culture, racism, literary studies.

610   JA
KUMAMOTO DAIGAKU TAISHITSU IGAKU KENKYUJO HOKOKU/KUMAMOTO UNIVERSITY. INSTITUTE OF CONSTITUTIONAL MEDICINE. REPORT. (Text in Japanese) 1950. q. exchange basis. Kumamoto Daigaku, Taishitsu Igaku Kenkyujo - Kumamoto University, Institute of Constitutional Medicine, 24-1 Kuhonji 4-chome, Kumamoto 862, Japan.

610   JA
KUMAMOTO IGAKKAI ZASSHI/KUMAMOTO MEDICAL SOCIETY. JOURNAL. (Text in Japanese; summaries in English) 1925. m. Kumamoto Igakkai - Kumamoto Medical Society, c/o Kumamoto Daigaku Igakubu, 2-1, Honjo 2-chome, Kumamoto-shi, Kumamoto-ken 860, Japan. Ed. Katsuhide Nishi. **Indexed:** INIS Atomind.

610   JA   ISSN 0023-5326
CODEN: KUMJAX
KUMAMOTO MEDICAL JOURNAL. (Text in English) 1938-1942; resumed 1951. q. free. (Ministry of Education, Science and Culture) Kumamoto Daigaku Igakubu, 2-1 Honjo 2-chome, Kumamoto-shi, Kumamoto-ken 860, Japan. FAX 096-372-6140. Ed.Bd. abstr.; charts; illus.; index; circ. 450. **Indexed:** Biol.Abstr., Chem.Abstr., Excerp.Med., Ind.Med., INIS Atomind., Nutr.Abstr.
—BLDSC shelfmark: 5122.000000.
Description: Contains original papers from the medical school.

MEDICAL SCIENCES

610 JA ISSN 0023-530X
CODEN: KDTIAE
KUMAMOTO UNIVERSITY. INSTITUTE OF CONSTITUTIONAL MEDICINE. BULLETIN/KUMAMOTO DAIGAKU TAISHITSU IGAKU KENKYUJO HOKOKU. (Annual supplement in English) (Text in Japanese; summaries in English or German) 1950. q. exchange basis. Kumamoto Daigaku, Taishitsu Igaku Kenkyujo - Kumamoto University, Institute of Constitutional Medicine, 24-1, Kuhonji 4-chome, Kumamoto-shi, Kumamoto-ken 862, Japan. Ed. Yoshio Sawada. charts; stat.; circ. 400. **Indexed:** Biol.Abstr., C.I.S. Abstr., Chem.Abstr.

610 JA ISSN 0075-7217
KUMAMOTO UNIVERSITY. INSTITUTE OF CONSTITUTIONAL MEDICINE. BULLETIN. SUPPLEMENT. (Text in English or European languages; summaries in English) 1951. a. exchange basis. Kumamoto Daigaku, Taishitsu Igaku Kenkyujo - Kumamoto University, Institute of Constitutional Medicine, 24-1, Kuhonzi 4-chome, Kumamoto-shi, Kumamoto-ken 862, Japan.

610 JA
KURUME MEDICAL ASSOCIATION. JOURNAL/KURUME IGAKKAI ZASSHI. (Text in Japanese; summaries in European languages) 1936. m. Kurume Medical Association - Kurume Igakkai, c/o Kurume University School of Medicine, 67 Asahi-machi, Kurume 830, Japan. **Indexed:** Biol.Abstr., C.I.S. Abstr., INIS Atomind.

610 JA ISSN 0023-5679
CODEN: KRMJAC
KURUME MEDICAL JOURNAL. (Text in English) 1954. q. 5800 Yen or exchange basis. Kurume University School of Medicine - Kurume Daigaku Igakubu, c/o Dept. of Physiology, 67 Asahi-machi, Kurume 830, Japan. Ed. S. Nishi. charts; illus.; circ. 550. **Indexed:** Abstr.Hyg., Biol.Abstr., Chem.Abstr., Excerp.Med., Ind.Med., INIS Atomind., Nutr.Abstr., Trop.Dis.Bull.
—BLDSC shelfmark: 5131.420000.

610 KU ISSN 0023-5776
CODEN: KMAJAJ
KUWAIT MEDICAL ASSOCIATION. JOURNAL. (Text in English) 1967. q. 6 din. Kuwait Medical Association, c/o Executive Secretary, Jabriyah, Box 1202, Safat 13013, Kuwait. TEL 531-7972. FAX 533-3276. Ed. Abdulla A. Al-Rashed. adv.; bk.rev.; abstr.; bibl.; charts; illus.; index; circ. 4,000. **Indexed:** Abstr.Hyg., Biol.Abstr., Curr.Adv.Ecol.Sci., Curr.Cont., Excerp.Med., Helminthol.Abstr., Nutr.Abstr., Rev.Plant Path., Trop.Dis.Bull.
—BLDSC shelfmark: 4812.800000.
Description: Collection of review articles, original articles, case reports in all areas within the medical sciences as well as general information concerning the Association.

610 618.97 JA ISSN 0368-5829
CODEN: KIZSB8
KYORIN IGAKKAI ZASSHI/KYORIN MEDICAL SOCIETY. JOURNAL. (Text in Japanese; summaries in English) 1970. q. 4000 Yen. Kyorin Medical Society, Kyorin University, 20-2, 6-chome, Shinkawa, Mitaka-shi, Tokyo 181, Japan. FAX 0422-40-7281. Ed. Nobuo Watanabe. adv.; index; circ. 1,800. (back issues avail.) **Indexed:** Chem.Abstr., INIS Atomind.

KYOTO DAIGAKU. REICHORUI KENKYUJO NENPO/KYOTO UNIVERSITY. PRIMATE RESEARCH INSTITUTE. ANNUAL REPORT. see ANTHROPOLOGY

610 JA ISSN 0023-6012
KYOTO PREFECTURAL UNIVERSITY OF MEDICINE. MEDICAL SOCIETY. JOURNAL/KYOTO-FURITSU IKA DAIGAKU ZASSHI. (Text in Japanese and English; summaries in English) 1927. m. 6000 Yen($40) Kyoto Prefectural University of Medicine, Kyoto Foundations for the Promotion of Medical Science - Kyoto-furitsu Ika Daigaku, Hirokoji, Kawara-machi, Kamigyo-ku, Kyoto 602, Japan. FAX 075-211-7093. Ed. Taketoshi Morimoto. adv.; abstr.; index; circ. 1,350 (controlled). **Indexed:** Biol.Abstr., Chem.Abstr, INIS Atomind.
—BLDSC shelfmark: 4812.857000.

610 US ISSN 0162-7163
L A C M A PHYSICIAN. 1871. 20/yr. $30 to non-members; members $15. Los Angeles County Medical Association, Box 3465, Los Angeles, CA 90051-1465. TEL 213-483-1581. FAX 213-484-1699. Ed. Janice M. Nagano. adv.; bk.rev.; circ. 10,500. (processed) **Indexed:** CINAHL.
Formerly: Los Angeles County Medical Association. Bulletin (ISSN 0047-5076)

610 US
L E R S MONOGRAPH SERIES. 1983. irreg., latest vol.7. price varies. (Laboratoires d'Etudes et de Recherches Synthelabo) Raven Press, 1185 Ave. of the Americas, New York, NY 10036. TEL 212-930-9500. FAX 212-869-3495.

613.2 DK ISSN 0904-5198
L S T NYT. 1988. irreg. (4-6/yr.). DKK 60. Sundhedsministeriet, Levnedsmiddelstyrelsen, Moerkehoej Bygade 19, DK-2860 Soeborg, Denmark. TEL 39-69-66-00. Ed. Joergen Hoejmark Jensen.
Description: Focuses on current activities of the National Food Agency of Denmark; features articles on toxicology, chemical contaminants in food, nutrition, and law dealing with food administration.

610 US ISSN 1045-7313
LAB REPORT; a monthly update on laboratory diagnosis. 1972. m. $75 (effective Jan. 1992). G & R Publications, Inc., c/o Rosse Enterprises Ltd., 155 Federal St., No. 16, Boston, MA 02110-1727. TEL 617-723-1840. FAX 617-723-4785. Ed. Dr. Raymond Gambino. bibl.; charts; index; circ. 2,500. (looseleaf format; back issues avail.; reprint service avail.)
Formerly (until Sep. 1989): Lab Report for Physicians Newsletter (ISSN 0278-5161)

610 RU ISSN 0023-6748
RB1 CODEN: LABDAZ
LABORATORNOE DELO/LABORATORY TECHNIQUE. 1955. m. 16.80 Rub.($15) (Vsesoyuznoe Nauchnoe Obshchestvo Vrachei-Laborantov) Izdatel'stvo Meditsina, Petroverigskii pereulok 6-8, 101838 Moscow, Russia. (Co-publisher: Ministerstvo Zdravookhraneniya S.S.S.R.) Ed. V.V. Men'shikov. bk.rev.; bibl. **Indexed:** Anal.Abstr., Biol.Abstr., Chem.Abstr., Dent.Ind., Ind.Med., INIS Atomind., Nutr.Abstr.
Description: Covers clinical laboratory diagnosis - hematology, cytology, coagulation, biochemistry, immunology.

616.07 US ISSN 0007-5027
RB37.A1 CODEN: LBMEBX
LABORATORY MEDICINE. 1965. m. $40 to individuals (foreign $55); institutions $45 (foreign $60). American Society of Clinical Pathologists, 2100 W. Harrison St., Chicago, IL 60612. TEL 312-738-4890. FAX 312-738-1619. Ed. Dr. Paul Phillip Sher. adv.; bk.rev.; charts; illus.; stat.; circ. 160,000. (also avail. in microform from UMI; reprint service avail. from UMI) **Indexed:** C.I.S. Abstr., Chem.Abstr., Curr.Adv.Cell & Devel.Biol., Curr.Adv.Ecol.Sci., Curr.Adv.Genetics & Molec.Biol., Curr.Cont., Excerp.Med.
—BLDSC shelfmark: 5140.400000.
Formerly (until 1970): Bulletin of Pathology; Incorporates: Technical Improvement Service Bulletin.
Description: Devoted to the continuing education of laboratory professionals. Presents original scientific articles from laboratory professionals containing both theoretical and practical information on the most recent ideas and the latest research.
Refereed Serial

610 DK
LAEGEFORENINGENS VEJVISER. 1976. a. DKK 320. (Almindelige Danske Laegeforening) Laegeforeningens Forlag, Esplanaden 8A, DK-1263 Copenhagen K, Denmark.
Formerly: Almindelige Danske Laegeforening (ISSN 0105-1830)

610 DK
LAEGEN. a. Forlaget John Vaboe A-S, Birkedommervej 27, 3, DK-2400 Copenhagen NV, Denmark. TEL 38-33-80-00. FAX 38-33-82-80. adv.; circ. 5,200.

610 SW ISSN 0023-7205
LAEKARTIDNINGEN. (Text in Swedish; summaries in English) 1904. w. SEK 655. Sveriges Laekarfoerbund - Swedish Medical Association, Box 5610, S-114 86 Stockholm, Sweden. FAX 08-907435. Ed. Bosse Tolander. adv.; bk.rev.; bibl.; charts; illus.; index; circ. 30,000. (back issues avail.) **Indexed:** C.I.S. Abstr., Chem.Abstr., Dok.Arbeitsmed., Ind.Med, INIS Atomind., Protozool.Abstr.
—BLDSC shelfmark: 5143.920000.

610 IC ISSN 0023-7213
LAEKNABLADID. 1915. m. $20. Icelandic Medical Association, Domus Medica, 101 Reykjavik, Iceland. Ed. Oern Bjarnason. circ. 1,500.
—BLDSC shelfmark: 5143.650000.

610 UK ISSN 0140-6736
R31 CODEN: LANCAO
LANCET. 1823. w. £62($95) Lancet Ltd., 46 Bedford Square, London WC1B 3SL, England. TEL 01-436-4981. FAX 01-436-7550. TELEX 291785. Ed. Robin Fox. adv.; bk.rev.; s-a. index; circ. 30,000. (also avail. in microform from UMI; back issues avail.) **Indexed:** Abstr.Health Care Manage.Stud., Abstr.Hyg., Acad.Ind., ASSIA, Bibl.Dev.Med.& Child Neur., Biol.Abstr, Biol.Dig., Biotech.Abstr., C.I.S.Abstr., CAD CAM Abstr., Cadscan, Chem.Abstr, Curr.Adv.Cancer Res., Curr.Adv.Ecol.Sci., Curr.Adv.Genetics & Molec.Biol., Curr.Cont., Curr.Lit.Fam.Plan., Curr.Tit.Dent., Dairy Sci.Abstr., Deep Sea Res.& Oceanogr.Abstr., Dent.Ind., Dok.Arbeitsmed., Environ.Abstr., FAMLI, Food Sci.& Tech.Abstr., Geo.Abstr, Helminthol.Abstr., High.Educ.Curr.Aware.Bull., Hlth.Ind., Hosp.Lit.Ind, I.P.A., Ind.Hyg.Dig., Ind.Med, Ind.Sci.Rev., Ind.Vet., INIS Atomind., Int.Nurs.Ind, Lab.Haz.Bull., Lead Abstr., Med.Care Rev., Nutr.Abstr., Popul.Ind., Protozool.Abstr., Res.High.Educ.Abstr., Rev.Appl.Entomol., Rev.Plant Path., Risk Abstr., Small Anim.Abstr., Stud.Wom.Abstr., Telegen, Trop.Dis.Bull., Vet.Bull., W.R.C.Inf., Zincscan.
●Also available online. Vendor(s): BRS, BRS/Saunders Colleague.
Also available on CD-ROM.
—BLDSC shelfmark: 5146.000000.

610 SP ISSN 0212-0151
LANCET (EDICION ESPANOLA). 1982. m. (2 vols./yr.). 6500 ptas.($68) Ediciones Doyma, S.A., Travesera de Gracia, 17-21, 08021 Barcelona, Spain. TEL 200 07 11. FAX 209-11-36. TELEX 51694 INK-E. Dir. M. Foz i Sala. adv.; page 210000 ptas.; trim 210 x 280; adv. contact: Jordi Grau. circ. 12,000. (reprint service avail. from UMI)
Description: Contains translations of the English edition's articles on clinical observations, physiopathological interpretations, descriptions of new syndromes, diagnostic methodology.

610 FR ISSN 0923-7577
LANCET (EDITION FRANCAISE). 1989. 12/yr. 475 F. (foreign 550 F.)(effective 1992). Editions Scientifiques Elsevier, 29, rue Buffon, 75005 Paris, France. (Subscr. in U.S. and Canada to: Elsevier Science Publishing Co., Inc., Box 882, Madison Sq. Sta., New York, NY 10159. TEL 212-989-5800) Ed. P. Brenier.
Description: Covers all aspects of the medical field.
Refereed Serial

610 IT ISSN 0393-0637
LANCET (EDIZIONE ITALIANA). 1984. m. (10/yr.). L.75000 (effective 1992). Masson Italia Periodici, Via Statuto 2-4, 20121 Milan, Italy. TEL 02-6367-1. FAX 02-6367211. Ed. Carlo Zanussi. circ. 18,000.

616.02 US ISSN 0099-5355
R31
LANCET (NORTH AMERICAN EDITION). 1826. w. $90 to individuals; institutions $120(typically set in Jan.). Williams & Wilkins, 428 E. Preston St., Baltimore, MD 21202. TEL 301-528-4000. FAX 301-528-4312. Ed. Robin Fox. adv.; circ. 14,000. (also avail. in microfilm)
Description: Covers major developments in general medicine and clinical research worldwide.
Refereed Serial

LANGUAGE AND SPEECH. see LINGUISTICS

MEDICAL SCIENCES

610   900   IT   ISSN 0393-7445
LANTERNINO; bimestrale di storia della medicina e medicina sociale. 1978. bi-m. free. Claudio Bevilacqua, Ed. & Pub., Via Rossetti 25, Trieste, Italy. TEL 040-360332. circ. 2,000.

610   UK   ISSN 0898-5901
CODEN: LATHE5
LASER THERAPY; an international journal of low level laser therapy and photobioactivation. 1989. q. $195 (effective 1992). John Wiley & Sons Ltd., Journals, Baffins Lane, Chichester, Sussex PO19 1UD, England. TEL 0243-779777. FAX 0243-775878. TELEX 86290 WIBOOK G. Ed. T. Ohshiro. bk.rev.
—BLDSC shelfmark: 5156.651000.
Description: Links an international outlook in the field of laser therapy with academic contents; contains clinical and basic scientific studies in the use of low level laser therapy.

610 535.58   UK   ISSN 0268-8921
CODEN: LMSCEZ
LASERS IN MEDICAL SCIENCE. 1986. q. $134. (European Laser Association) Bailliere Tindall, 24-28 Oval Rd., London NW1 7DX, England. TEL 071-267-4466. FAX 071-482-2293. TELEX 25775-ACPRES-G. Ed.Bd. **Indexed**: Curr.Adv.Ecol.Sci.
—BLDSC shelfmark: 5156.680800.
Description: Brings together the work of clinicians and basic scientists in the field of the medical applications of lasers.

LAWYERS' MEDICAL DIGEST. see *LAW*

610   LE   ISSN 0023-9852
CODEN: LMJJA7
LEBANESE MEDICAL JOURNAL/JOURNAL MEDICAL LIBANAIS. (Text and title in English and French) 1948. bi-m. £L3000($10) Order of Physicians in Lebanon, Bechara el-Khoury, Box 640, Beirut, Lebanon. Ed.Bd. adv.; bk.rev.; abstr.; bibl.; charts; illus.; index; circ. 3,500. **Indexed**: Biol.Abstr., Chem.Abstr., Curr.Cont., Excerp.Med., Ind.Med.

610   US   ISSN 0172-7788
LECTURE NOTES IN MEDICAL INFORMATICS. 1978. irreg. price varies. Springer-Verlag, 175 Fifth Ave., New York, NY 10010. TEL 212-460-1500. (Also: Berlin, Heidelberg, Tokyo and Vienna) Eds. D.A.B. Lindberg, P.L. Reichertz. (reprint service avail. from ISI) **Indexed**: Cyb.Abstr.

610.7   SA   ISSN 0377-9696
THE LEECH. (Text in English) 1929. 3/yr. R.15 (foreign R.45). University of the Witwatersrand Medical School, 7 York Rd., Parktown 2193, South Africa. TEL 011-643-4318. FAX 011-647-2451. Ed. Manfred Spanger. adv.; bk.rev.; circ. 7,000.
—BLDSC shelfmark: 5181.200000.
Supersedes: Auricle (ISSN 0004-8070)
Description: Contains research articles, drug reviews, conference information, coverage of changing trends in health care, and departmental news for students and graduates of the University of the Witwatersrand Medical School.
Refereed Serial

340   US
LEGAL MEDICINE: LEGAL DYNAMICS OF MEDICAL ENCOUNTERS. 1988. irreg., 2nd ed., 1991. $95. (American College of Legal Medicine) Mosby - Year Book, Inc. (Subsidiary of: Times Mirror Company), 11830 Westline Industrial Dr., St. Louis, MO 63146. TEL 800-325-4117. FAX 314-432-1380. TELEX 44-2402.

LEGAL QUARTERLY DIGEST OF MINE SAFETY AND HEALTH DECISIONS. see *MINES AND MINING INDUSTRY*

610   CS   ISSN 0075-8736
LEKARSKE PRACE. (Text mainly in Slovak; occasionally in English, German or Russian; summaries in one or two of the other languuages) 1961. irreg. (approx. s-a.); vol.10, no.2, 1973. (Slovenska Akademia Vied) Veda, Publishing House of the Slovak Academy of Sciences, Klemensova 19, 814 30 Bratislava, Czechoslovakia. (Dist. by: Slovart, Nam. Slobody 6, 817 64 Bratislava, Czechoslovakia) **Indexed**: Biol.Abstr., Ind.Med.
—BLDSC shelfmark: 5182.315000.

610 615.19   CS
LEKARSKY OBZOR. (Text in Czech or Slovak; summaries in English, German, Russian) m. $78. (Ministry of Health Care of the Slovak Socialist Republic, Institute of Further Education of Physicians and Pharmaceutists in Bratislava) Obzor, Ceskoslovenskej Armady 35, 815 85 Bratislava, Czechoslovakia. **Indexed**: C.I.S. Abstr., Chem.Abstr., INIS Atomind.

610   PL
LEKARZ KOLEJOWY. 1965. bi-m. $8.40. Polskie Koleje Panstwowe, Dyrekcja Gneralna, Dyrekcja Kolejowej Sluzby Zdrowia, Chalubinskiego 3-4, Warsaw, Poland. (Dist. by: Ars Polona-Ruch, Krakowskie Przedmiescie 7, Warsaw, Poland) Ed. Dr. Eleonora Czerpinska-Gajek. charts; illus.; circ. 3,100. **Indexed**: C.I.S. Abstr.
Formerly: Komunikacyjna (ISSN 0025-861X)

616.98   PL   ISSN 0024-0745
CODEN: LEKWAT
LEKARZ WOJSKOWY. m. $8.40. Szefostwo Sluzby Zdrowia MON, Warsaw, Poland. **Indexed**: Excerp.Med., INIS Atomind.

610   FR   ISSN 0153-4742
LETTRE MEDICALE. 1975. 10/yr. $31. Lettre Medicale, 27, rue du Fg, St. Jacques, 75674 Paris Cedex 14, France. TEL 42341684. Ed. M. Detilleux. circ. 3,000.

610 615.328   CC   ISSN 1000-1719
R97.7.C5
LIAONING ZHONGYI ZAZHI/LIAONING JOURNAL OF TRADITIONAL CHINESE MEDICINE. (Text in Chinese) 1979. m. $0.70 per no. Liaoning Zhongyi Xueyuan - Liaoning College of Traditional Chinese Medicine, 79 Congshan Donglu, Shenyang, Liaoning 110032a, People's Republic of China. (Dist. outside China by: China International Book Trading Corporation, P.O. Box 399, Beijing, P.R.C.) (Co-sponsor: Zhonghua Quanguo Zhongyi Xuehui Liaoning Fenhui) **Indexed**: Dent.Ind., Ind.Med.
—BLDSC shelfmark: 5186.247500.

610   AU
LIEFERKATALOG FUER KRANKENHAUS, ARZT, APOTHEKE UND LABOR; Lieferfirmen- und Bezugsquellennachweis. 1974. a. S.240. Verlag Dieter Goeschl GmbH, Andergasse 10, A-1170 Vienna, Austria. TEL 0222-464240. FAX 0222-454902. adv.; circ. 13,500.

616.04   UK
LIFT; the magazine for young ASBAH. 1985. q. free to qualified personnel. Association for Spina Bifida and Hydrocephalus, 42 Park Rd., Peterborough PE1 2UQ, England. TEL 0733-555985. FAX 0733-555985. Ed. Gill Winfield. adv.; circ. 2,400.

610   FR   ISSN 0981-1095
CODEN: LIMEEH
LILLE MEDICAL. (Summaries in English, French) vol.11, 1966. 10/yr. 375 Fr. (Facultes de Medecine de Lille) Medi-Presse, 1 Place de Verdun, 59045 Lille Cedex, France. adv.; abstr.; charts; illus.; stat.; tr.lit. **Indexed**: Biol.Abstr., C.I.S. Abstr., Chem.Abstr., Curr.Cont., Dent.Ind., Dok.Arbeitsmed., Excerp.Med., Helminthol.Abstr., Ind.Med., Nutr.Abstr.
Former titles: L A R C Medical; Lille Medical (ISSN 0024-3507); Echo Medical du Nord.

610   US   ISSN 0024-3639
R15
LINACRE QUARTERLY. 1932. q. $24. National Federation of Catholic Physicians Guilds, 850 Elm Grove Rd., Elm Grove, WI 53122. TEL 414-784-3435. FAX 414-782-8788. Ed. Dr. John P. Mullooly. adv.; bk.rev.; abstr.; bibl.; index; circ. 11,150. (also avail. in microfilm from UMI; back issues avail.) **Indexed**: Cath.Ind., CERDIC.
—BLDSC shelfmark: 5220.170000.
Description: Journal of the philosophy and ethics of medical practice.

610   CC
LINCHUANG HUICUI/CLINICAL FOCUS; daneike. (Text in Chinese) m. Y14.40. Hebei Yixue Yuan - Hebei Academy of Medical Sciences, 5 Chang'an Xilu, Shijiazhuang, Hebei 050017, People's Republic of China. TEL 44121. Ed. Du Benfa.

610   CC   ISSN 1001-7399
LINCHUANG YU SHIYAN BINGLIXUE ZAZHI/JOURNAL OF CLINICAL AND EXPERIMENTAL PATHOLOGY. (Text in Chinese) q. Anhui Yike Daxue - Anhui University of Medical Sciences, Meishan Lu, Hefei, Anhui 230032, People's Republic of China. TEL 336600. Ed. Zheng Guohao.

616.04   UK
LINK (LONDON, 1966); the magazine for people with spina bifida and/or hydrocephalus. 1966. bi-m. £3.30 (foreign £5.60). Association for Spina Bifida and Hydrocephalus, 42 Park Rd., Peterborough PE1 2UQ, England. TEL 0733-555988. FAX 0733-555985. Ed. Gill Winfield. adv.; bk.rev.; circ. 7,000. (back issues avail.)

LITERATURE & MEDICINE. see *LITERATURE*

616.02   US
LIVER UPDATE. irreg.(2-4/yr.). American Liver Foundation, 1425 Pompton Ave., Cedar Grove, NJ 07009-1043. TEL 201-256-2550. Ed. Nathan Bass. circ. 70,000.

610 360   UK
LONDAM. 1966. q. free to qualified personnel. London Ambulance Service, LAS HQ, 220 Waterloo Rd., London SE1 8SD, England. Ed. Kathy Nye. circ. 3,500. (back issues avail.)

610   US
LOOSE CONNECTIONS. 1986. q. $20 includes membership. Ehlers-Danlos National Foundation, Box 1212, Southgate, MI 48195. TEL 313-282-0180. FAX 313-282-2793. Ed. Gerald J. Rogowski. bk.rev.; circ. 1,200.
Description: Provides emotional support and information to those who suffer from Ehlers Danlos Syndrome, and serves as communication link with the medical community.

610   US   ISSN 0024-6921
CODEN: JLSMAW
LOUISIANA STATE MEDICAL SOCIETY. JOURNAL.* 1844. m. $12. Journal of the Louisiana State Medical Society, Inc., 3501 N. Causeway Blvd., Ste. 800, Metatrie, LA 70002-3625. TEL 504-561-1033. Ed. Conway S. Magee. adv.; bk.rev.; bibl.; illus.; index; circ. 6,300. (also avail. in microform from UMI; reprint service avail. from UMI) **Indexed**: Biol.Abstr., C.I.S. Abstr., Chem.Abstr., Dent.Ind., Ind.Med., INIS Atomind.
—BLDSC shelfmark: 4818.700000.

610   BE   ISSN 0024-6956
CODEN: LOMEAL
LOUVAIN MEDICAL. (Text in French; summaries in English and French) 1966. m. (except Jul.-Aug. combined). 2000 Fr.($14) 52, Ave. E. Mounier, B-1200 Brussels, Belgium. adv.; bk.rev.; abstr.; index; circ. 3,000. (back issues avail.) **Indexed**: Biol.Abstr., Chem.Abstr., Curr.Adv.Ecol.Sci., Curr.Cont., Excerp.Med., Helminthol.Abstr., Nutr.Abstr.
—BLDSC shelfmark: 5296.350000.
Formerly: Revue Medicale de Louvain et Recipe.

610   AT   ISSN 1033-2480
LUPUS ASSOCIATION OF NEW SOUTH WALES. NEWSLETTER. 1979. bi-m. Aus.$15. Lupus Association of New South Wales Inc., P.O. Box 89, North Sydney, N.S.W. 2113, Australia. TEL 02-878-6055. (Subscr. to: P.O. Box 271, Cammeray, N.S.W. 2062, Australia) Ed. Leslie McAllister. bk.rev.; circ. 1,000. (back issues avail.)
Description: News from the Association, a self-help organization for sufferers of systemic Lupus Erythematosus and related diseases.

610   US
LYCOMING MEDICINE. 1910. m. $20. Lycoming County Medical Society, 777 Rural Ave., Williamsport, PA 17701-3198. TEL 717-321-2000. Ed. Paul John. adv.; bk.rev.; circ. 325.

610   FR   ISSN 0766-5466
LYON MEDITERRANEE MEDICAL - MEDECINE DU SUD EST. m. 240 F. to individuals (foreign 330 F.); students 210 F. (foreign 300 F.). Galliena Promotions, 58 A, Rue du Dessous des Berges, 75013 Paris, France. TEL 45-84-97-66. FAX 45-84-92-56.
Formerly: Lyon Mediterranee Medical (ISSN 0399-032X)

LYSOSOMES IN BIOLOGY AND PATHOLOGY. see *BIOLOGY*

M A P NEWS. (Medical Aid for Palestine) see *SOCIAL SERVICES AND WELFARE*

610   BU   ISSN 0324-119X
RM1
M B I. (Medico-Biologic Information) (Editions in English and Russian) 1967. bi-m. free. Pharmachim, 16, Iliensko Chaussee, 1220 Sofia, Bulgaria. Ed. A. Damyanov. adv.; illus.; circ. 2,000 (English edt.). **Indexed:** Biol.Abstr., Curr.Adv.Ecol.Sci., Excerp.Med.

610   US   ISSN 0047-6471
M C G TODAY.* 1970. q. free to alumni and donors. Medical College of Georgia Foundation, Inc., Alumni Center, 919 15th St., Augusta, GA 30912. TEL 404-721-4421. Ed. Christine Deriso. circ. 15,000.

616.748   US   ISSN 8750-2321
RC935.M7
M D A NEWSMAGAZINE. 1952. q. free. Muscular Dystrophy Association, Inc., 3561 E. Sunrise Dr., Tucson, AZ 85718. TEL 602-529-2000. FAX 602-529-5300. Ed. P. Settle Madden. bk.rev.; illus.; circ. 90,000. **Indexed:** CHNI, Rehabil.Lit.
Former titles: M D A News (ISSN 0279-0742); Muscular Dystrophy News (ISSN 0027-3759)
Description: Presents patient profiles, instructive articles, research and association news, resource listings, and helpful articles of special interest to those with neuromuscular diseases and their families.

610   MX   ISSN 0024-8002
M D EN ESPANOL. 1963. m. Mex.$150000. Mundo Medico, S.A., Matias Romero 116, Col. del Valle, 03100 Mexico D.F., Mexico. TEL 559-27-55. circ. 15,000.

610   US
M D MAGAZINE. 1957. m. $40 (free to physicians). M D Publications, Inc., 55 Fifth Ave., New York, NY 10003. TEL 212-989-2100. adv.; bk.rev.; illus.; index; circ. 125,000. (reprint service avail. from UMI)
Former titles: M D: Medical Newsmagazine; Medical Newsmagazine (ISSN 0024-8010)

610 640.73   US   ISSN 0890-7587
M D R WATCH. (Medical Device Reporting); an independent guide to medical device reporting. 1986. m. $577. Washington Business Information, Inc., c/o Karen Harrington, 1117 N. 19th St., Ste. 200, Arlington, VA 22209. TEL 703-247-3434. FAX 703-247-3427. Ed. Zaira Steele. stat. (back issues avail.)
Description: Monitors compliance with FDA's MDR regulation, with charts by: manufacturer and product, company, product, "top 10" products and "top 10" firms filing reports, details of each death report. Includes current and year-to-date figures.

610   JA   ISSN 0025-8830
M E J. (Medical Equipment Journal of Japan); monthly information on medical, surgical, scientific and dental instruments and drugs. (Text in English) 1957. m. 9490 Yen($85) Genyosha Publications Inc., 18-2, Shibuya 3-chome, Shibuya-ku, Tokyo 150, Japan. TEL 03-3407-7521. FAX 03-3407-7902. Ed. Naru Sakano. adv.; circ. 6,984. (tabloid format) **Indexed:** JTA.

610 370   US   ISSN 0046-9122
M E R P MEMO. (Medical Education Resources Program) 1970. q. free. Indiana University, School of Medicine, 1100 W. Michigan St., Indianapolis, IN 46202. TEL 317-264-8157. Ed. Margaret R. Thomson. illus.; circ. 1,000 (controlled). (looseleaf format)
Incorporates: V I R Playback.

610   US
M F M C REVIEW. q. Mississippi Foundation for Medical Care, 735 Riverside Dr., Jackson, MS 39202-1166. TEL 601-354-0304. FAX 601-948-8917. Ed. Carole Kelly. circ. 5,000.

M H H - INFO. (Medizinische Hochschule Hannover) see *COLLEGE AND ALUMNI*

M H L A NEWS. (Manitoba Health Libraries Association) see *LIBRARY AND INFORMATION SCIENCES*

610   SA
M I M S COMPANION. 1981. irreg. price varies. M.I.M.S. (Subsidiary of: Times Media Ltd.), P.O. Box 2059, Pretoria 0001, Transvaal, South Africa. TEL 012-3485010. FAX 012-477716. Ed. R. van Rooyen. adv.; circ. 3,000.
Formerly: M I M S Medical Memory Aids.
Description: Examines symptoms, clinical signs, investigations, pathology, treatments and syndromes for medical professions.

610   AT
M I M S COMPANION. a? Aus.$35. M I M S Australia, 48 Albany St., Crows Nest, N.S.W. 2065, Australia.
Description: Guide to symptoms, clinical signs, investigations, pathology, diagnosis, treatment and prognosis.

610   US   ISSN 0543-2774
M L A DIRECTORY (YEAR). 1959. a. $95. Medical Library Association, Six N. Michigan Ave., Ste. 300, Chicago, IL 60602. TEL 312-419-9094. circ. 5,000.

610 026   US   ISSN 0541-5489
Z675.M4
M L A NEWS (CHICAGO). 1961. 10/yr. $46 (foreign $58.50). Medical Library Association, Six N. Michigan Ave., Ste. 300, Chicago, IL 60602. TEL 312-419-9094. adv.; circ. 5,400. (reprint service avail. from UMI, ISI)
—BLDSC shelfmark: 5879.715400.

610 614   GW   ISSN 0340-8183
M M G. (Medizin-Mensch-Gesellschaft) 1976. q. DM.86. Ferdinand Enke Verlag, Postfach 101254, 7000 Stuttgart 10, Germany. TEL 0711-8931-0. FAX 0711-8931-419. TELEX 07252275-GTV-D. Ed.Bd. **Indexed:** Biol.Abstr., Excerp.Med.
—BLDSC shelfmark: 5534.900000.

610   US
M M NEWS. 10/yr. $15. New York County Medical Society, 40 W. 57th St., New York, NY 10019. FAX 212-399-9041. Ed. Cheryl Malone. adv.; circ. 6,200. (looseleaf format)
Formerly: New York County Medical Society Newsletter.

616.8   CN   ISSN 0707-0934
M S ONTARIO. 1977. q. Can.$10 membership. Multiple Sclerosis Society of Canada, Ontario Division, 250 Bloor St. E., Ste. 820, Toronto, Ont. M4W 3P9, Canada. TEL 416-922-6065. FAX 416-922-7538. Ed. Deanna Groetzinger. adv.; bk.rev.; circ. 12,000.

618   GW   ISSN 0930-4622
                      CODEN: MTAAEX
M T A - FACHZEITSCHRIFT FUER TECHNISCHE ASSISTENTEN DER MEDIZIN. (Medizinisch-Technische Assistenten); Monatsschrift fuer MTA's, Labormediziner, Fachleute Radio-Diagnostik, Lehrer und Studenten. (Includes supplement: Gelernt-Vergessen) m. DM.103.80 (students DM.79.80). Umschau Verlag Breidenstein GmbH, Stuttgarter Str. 18-24, 6000 Frankfurt a.M. 1, Germany. TEL 069-2600-0. FAX 069-2600-609. TELEX 411964. Ed. Ruth Nitz. circ. 23,500.
Formerly: M T A - Journal.

616.02   SP   ISSN 0212-1514
M T A MEDICINA INTERNA. (Metodos Terapeutico-diagnosticos de Actualidad) 1983. m. 6890 ptas.($50) J.R. Prous, S.A. International Publishers, Apdo. de Correos 540, 08080 Barcelona, Spain. TEL 343-258-5250. FAX 343-258-1535. TELEX 98270 PROU E. Ed. A. Urbano Marquez. adv.; index; circ. 2,500. (back issues avail.)

610   GW   ISSN 0935-137X
M T DIALOG. (Medizin-Technischer) 1975. m. DM.237. M T D - Verlag GmbH und Co., Wangener Str. 12, 7989 Amtzell, Germany. TEL 07520-6611. FAX 07520-6911. Ed. Klaus Witzer. adv.

610   IS
MABAT LAMERPAOT. 1987. q. Association of Kupat Cholim Doctors, 6 Tel Hai St., Tel Aviv, Israel. TEL 03-280118. Ed. Dr. Dor Michael.

610 350   US   ISSN 1047-8922
MCGRAW-HILL'S WASHINGTON REPORT ON MEDICINE AND HEALTH. Short title: Medicine and Health. (Includes: Medicine and Health Perspectives) 1946. w. $450. Faulkner & Gray, Healthcare Information Center (Subsidiary of: J P T Publishing Group), 1133 15th St., N.W., Ste. 450, Washington, DC 20005. TEL 202-828-4150. FAX 202-828-2352. Ed. Janet Firshein. index.
Former titles (until 1986): Washington Report on Medicine and Health (ISSN 0043-0730); (until 1968): Washington Report on the Medical Sciences (ISSN 1047-8876)
Description: Covers current developments in the health care industry, including legislative matters, with in-depth coverage of selected specific topics.

610   GW   ISSN 0720-597X
MADE IN EUROPE - MEDICAL EQUIPMENT AND SUPPLY GUIDE. (Text in English) 1981. a. DM.50($33) Made in Europe Marketing Organization GmbH, Hahnstr. 70, 6000 Frankfurt a.M. 71, Germany. TEL 069-6668266. FAX 069-6668276. Ed. Veronique Schaufelberger. adv.; index; circ. 18,000. (back issues avail.)

610   IS   ISSN 0334-4169
MAEDA LEROFEI; periodical on problems in medicine. q. Kupat Cholim Central Management House, Rehov Arlozorov 101, Tel Aviv 62 098, Israel. TEL 03-433269. Ed. Dr. Noach Kaplinski.

362.1   UK   ISSN 0047-5475
MAGIC CARPET. 1948. q. £8 single; joint £12. Disabled Drivers' Association, Registered Office, The Hall, Ashwellthorpe, Nr. Norwich, NR16 1EX, England. Ed. Michael Elmore. adv.; bk.rev.; illus.; circ. 17,000.
—BLDSC shelfmark: 5334.770000.
Description: Concerned with the welfare of disabled people; encourages greater independence through mobility.

MAGNESIUM BULLETIN. see *CHEMISTRY — Analytical Chemistry*

610   HU   ISSN 0133-5464
MAGYAR BELORVOSI ARCHIVUM. (Summaries in English, German and Russian) 1945. bi-m. $31. Ifjusagi Lap-es Konyvkiado Vallalat, Revay u. 16, 1374 Budapest 6, Hungary. (Subscr. to: Kultura, Box 149, H-1389 Budapest, Hungary) Ed. Dr. Dezso Lehoczky. bk.rev.; bibl.; charts; illus. **Indexed:** Chem.Abstr., Ind.Med., INIS Atomind.
—BLDSC shelfmark: 5340.325000.
Supersedes (since 1955): Magyar Belorovosi Archivum es Ideggyogyaszati Szemle (ISSN 0301-7850); **Formerly (until 1951):** Magyar Belorvosi Archivum (ISSN 0025-0066)

610   IO   ISSN 0377-1121
MAJALAH KEDOKTERAN INDONESIA; the journal of the Indonesian Medical Association. (Text in English) 1950. m. Rps.35,000($17.75) (effective Jan. 1992). Indonesian Medical Association, Yayasan penerbitan IDI, Jl. Dr. Samratulangi No. 29, Jakarta 10350, Indonesia. TEL 62-021-337910. Ed. Chicf Tjokronegoro. adv.; circ. 18,000. (back issues avail.)

610   IO   ISSN 0303-7932
R97.7.I5
MAJALAH KEDOKTERAN SURABAYA. (Text in Indonesian; summaries in English) 1964. q. Rps.1000. Airlangga University, School of Medicine, Jalan Dharmahusada No. 47, Surabaya, Indonesia. Ed. Soedarso Djojonegoro. adv.; bk.rev.; circ. 4,000.
Former titles: Madjalah Kedokteran Surabaja (ISSN 0024-9564); Madjalah Research Kedokteran, Surabaja.

610   SY
MAJALLA AL-TOUBIYA AL-ARABIYA. m. Arab Medical Commission, Al-Jala St., Damascus, Syria. Ed. Adnan Takriti.

MAKEDONSKA AKADEMIJA NA NAUKITE I UMETNOSTITE. ODDELENIE ZA BIOLOSKI I MEDICINSKI NAUKI. PRILOZI/MACEDONIAN ACADEMY OF SCIENCES AND ARTS. SECTION OF BIOLOGICAL AND MEDICAL SCIENCES. CONTRIBUTIONS. see *BIOLOGY*

610   UG   ISSN 0025-1119
MAKERERE MEDICAL JOURNAL. 1957. a. $5.75. Makerere University Medical Students' Association, Box 7072, Kampala, Uganda. adv.; bk.rev.; charts; illus.; circ. 1,000. **Indexed:** Biol.Abstr., Chem.Abstr., Trop.Dis.Bull.

MEDICAL SCIENCES

616.07 MY ISSN 0126-8635
MALAYSIAN JOURNAL OF PATHOLOGY. 1978. s-a. $15 per no. Malaysian Society of Pathologists, Department of Pathology, c/o University of Malaysia, Faculty of Medicine, 59100 Kuala Lumpur, Malaysia. FAX 603-7573661. TELEX UNIMAL-MA-39845. Ed. L.M. Looi. adv.; bk.rev.; circ. 500. **Indexed:** Ind.Med.
—BLDSC shelfmark: 5356.068500.

610 340 US ISSN 0738-1026
KF2905.3.A15
MALPRACTICE REPORTER; comprehensive reporting of malpractice issues for the medical, legal, health services, and insurance communities. 1981. bi-m. $89. Public Reporting Services, Inc., 496A Hudson St., Ste. 424, New York, NY 10014. TEL 212-989-8303. Ed. Neil Fabricant. circ. 2,500.

610 340 US ISSN 0738-1956
KF3825.3.A59
MALPRACTICE REPORTER. HOSPITALS EDITION. 1981. bi-m. $89. Public Reporting Services, Inc., 496A Hudson St., Ste. 424, New York, NY 10014. TEL 212-989-8303. Ed. Natalie Kaplan.

610 340 US ISSN 0749-3495
MALPRACTICE REPORTER. PODIATRY EDITION. 1983. bi-m. $89. Public Reporting Services, Inc., 496A Hudson St., Ste. 424, New York, NY 10014. TEL 212-989-8303. Ed. Natalie Kaplan. (back issues avail.)

658 US ISSN 1042-4091
KF1183.A15
MANAGED CARE LAW OUTLOOK. m. $381 (foreign $393). Capitol Publications Inc., 1101 King St., Ste. 444, Alexandria, VA 22314. TEL 703-683-4100. FAX 703-739-6517. Ed. Russ Jackson.
●Also available online. Vendor(s): NewsNet.
Description: Briefings and analyses of legal issues affecting HMOs, PPOs and benefit options. Covers court cases, decisions and legal and legislative trends involving managed care systems.

658 US ISSN 0896-6567
RA413.5.U5
MANAGED CARE OUTLOOK; the insider's business briefing on managed health care. bi-w. $399 (foreign $423). Capitol Publications Inc., 1101 King St., Ste. 444, Alexandria, VA 22314. TEL 703-683-4100. FAX 703-739-6517. Ed. Mary Kahn.
●Also available online. Vendor(s): NewsNet.
Incorporates (in 1990): Managed Care Report.
Description: Includes reports on new business, industry trends, regional happenings, legal and policy news, conference coverage, case studies.

610 658 US ISSN 0196-9455
MANAGEMENT UPDATE (DENVER). vol.20, 1981. m. membership. Medical Group Management Association, 104 Inverness Terrace E., Englewood, CO 80112. TEL 303-799-1111. (tabloid format)

610 CN ISSN 0832-6096
MANITOBA MEDICINE. 1929. 4/yr. Can.$20. University of Manitoba, Faculty of Medicine, 750 Bannatyne Ave., Winnipeg, Man. R3E 0W3, Canada. TEL 204-788-6660. FAX 204-788-6499. Ed. Ian Carr. adv.; bk.rev.; circ. 3,500. (back issues avail.)
—BLDSC shelfmark: 5360.660000.
Formerly (until 1987): University of Manitoba. Medical Journal (ISSN 0076-4108)

610 DK ISSN 0107-9190
MANUEL MEDICIN. 1981. q. free. (Dansk Selskab for Manuel Medicin) Dadl Service Afdeling, Aarhus Amtssygehus, 8000 Aarhus C, Denmark. FAX 66-13-28-54. Ed. Dr. Johannes Fossgreen. adv.; bk.rev.; circ. 950.

615.8 GW ISSN 0025-2514
MANUELLE MEDIZIN; Interdisziplinaere Zeitschrift fuer Arthrologie, Kinesiologie und Chirotherapie. 1963. 6/yr. DM.492($68) (Deutsche Gesellschaft fuer Manuelle Medizin) Springer-Verlag, Heidelberger Platz 3, D-1000 Berlin 33, Germany. TEL 030-8207-1. (Also Heidelberg, Tokyo, Vienna, and New York) Eds. H. Baumgartner, H.D. Wolff. adv.; bk.rev.; index. (also avail. in microform from UMI; reprint service avail. from ISI) **Indexed:** Excerp.Med.
—BLDSC shelfmark: 5365.766000.
Description: Covers physiotherapy.

610 US ISSN 0886-0572
R11 CODEN: MMJRA8
MARYLAND MEDICAL JOURNAL. 1952. m. $35 to non-members (foreign $42) (typically set in June). Medical and Chirurgical Faculty of Maryland, 1211 Cathedral St, Baltimore, MD 21201. TEL 410-539-0872. FAX 410-547-0915. Ed. Dr. Victor R. Hrehorovich. adv.; bk.rev.; bibl.; charts; illus.; index; circ. 7,500. (also avail. in microform from UMI; reprint service avail. from ISI) **Indexed:** Biol.Abstr., Chem.Abstr., CINAHL, Curr.Cont., Ind.Med., INIS Atomind., Med. Care Rev.
Formerly (until 1985): Maryland State Medical Journal (ISSN 0025-4363)

615.8 AU
MASSEUR. 1985. 4/yr. S.120. (Internationale Vereinigung der oesterreichischen Masseure) Anna Pichler Verlag, Marchettigasse 6, A-1060 Vienna, Austria. TEL 0222-5970275. FAX 0222-5870984.

610 PL ISSN 0025-5246
CODEN: MMDPA6
MATERIA MEDICA POLONA; the Polish journal of medicine and pharmacy. (Text in English) 1969. q. $60. (Centrum Medyczne Ksztalcenia Podyplomowego) AGPOL - Polexportpress, Ul. Marszalkowska 124, 00-950 Warsaw, Poland. TELEX 813567 AGPOL PL. Ed. Edward Ruzyllo. adv.; bk.rev.; index; circ. 3,000. **Indexed:** Abstr.Hyg., Biol.Abstr., Dent.Ind., Excerp.Med., Ind.Med., Nutr.Abstr., Trop.Dis.Bull.
—BLDSC shelfmark: 5392.600000.

610 GW ISSN 0934-8832
QP552.C6 CODEN: MTRXEH
MATRIX; clinical and experimental. (Text in English) bi-m. DM.478. Gustav Fischer Verlag, Wollgrasweg 49, Postfach 720143, 7000 Stuttgart 70, Germany. TEL 0711-458030. FAX 0711-4580334. TELEX 7111488-FIBUCH. (U.S. address: Gustav Fischer New York Inc., 220 East 23rd St., Suite 909, New York, NY 10010) Eds. S. Gay, E.J. Miller. **Indexed:** Biol.Abstr., Chem.Abstr., Curr.Adv.Ecol.Sci., Curr.Cont., Curr.Leather Lit., Dent.Ind., Excerp.Med., Ind.Med., Ind.Sci.Rev., Sci.Cit.Ind.
—BLDSC shelfmark: 5411.990000.
Formerly (until 1988): Collagen and Related Research (ISSN 0174-173X)

610 617.6 JA ISSN 0385-1613
CODEN: MATSDE
MATSUMOTO SHIGAKU/MATSUMOTO DENTAL COLLEGE SOCIETY. JOURNAL. (Text in Japanese; summaries in English) 1975. 3/yr. 3500 Yen($18) Matsumoto Dental College Society - Matsumoto Shika Daigaku Gakkai, 1780, Gobara, Hiroka, Shojiri-shi 399-07, Japan. FAX 0263-53-3285. Ed. Shigeo Kobayashi. adv.; circ. 2,000.
—BLDSC shelfmark: 5413.245000.

610 US
MAUDSLEY MONOGRAPHS. irreg. price varies. Oxford University Press, 200 Madison Ave, New York, NY 10016. TEL 212-679-7300. Ed.Bd.

610 US
MAYO ALUMNUS. 1965. q. free. Mayo Foundation, Mayo Alumnus, Rochester, MN 55905. Ed. Rosemary Cashman. circ. 14,000 (controlled).
Description: Directed to the physicians, scientists and medical educators who trained at Mayo.

612 US ISSN 0741-6245
MAYO CLINIC HEALTH LETTER; reliable information for a healthier life. 1983. m. $24. Mayo Foundation, Rochester, MN 55905. TEL 507-284-4730. FAX 507-284-5410. Ed. David E. Swanson. circ. 375,000. **Indexed:** Hlth.Ind.
Description: Presents timely facts and findings on a broad variety of health issues.

610 US ISSN 0025-6196
CODEN: MACPAJ
MAYO CLINIC PROCEEDINGS. 1926. m. $70. (Mayo Clinic) Mayo Foundation for Medical Education and Research, Rochester, MN 55905. TEL 507-284-2154. FAX 507-284-0796. Ed. P.J. Palumbo. adv.; bk.rev.; abstr.; charts; illus.; index; circ. 108,000. (also avail. in microform from MIM) **Indexed:** Abstr.Hyg., Biol.Abstr., Chem.Abstr., Child Devel.Abstr., CINAHL, Curr.Adv.Biochem., Curr.Adv.Cancer Res., Curr.Adv.Ecol.Sci., Curr.Cont., Excerp.Med., Helminthol.Abstr., Ind.Med., Ind.Sci.Rev., INIS Atomind., Nutr.Abstr., Rehabil.Lit., Rev.Plant Path., Risk Abstr., Sci.Cit.Ind., Trop.Dis.Bull.
Description: Articles on the results of medical research and technology, including abstracts, editorials, subject reviews, case reports and announcements for the medical community.

610 GW ISSN 0934-3148
MED - REPORT. irreg. DM.108. (Aerztliche Fortbildungskongresse) Berliner Medizinische Verlagsanstalt GmbH, Kuerfuerstenstr. 112-113, 1000 Berlin 30, Germany. TEL 030-219909-0. FAX 030-219909-10. Ed. Barbara Braatz. circ. 3,000.

MEDDELELSER OM GROENLAND, MAN & SOCIETY. see *ANTHROPOLOGY*

610 CN ISSN 0025-6692
MEDECIN DU QUEBEC. (Text in French, summaries in English) 1965. m. Can.$75 (effective Jan. 1991). Federation des Medecins Omnipraticiens du Quebec - Federation of General Practitioners of Quebec, 1440 W. St. Catherine St., Ste. 1100, Montreal, Que. H3G 1R8, Canada. TEL 514-878-1911. FAX 514-878-4455. Ed. Dr. Georges Boileau. adv.; bk.rev.; bibl.; index; circ. 18,500 (controlled). (back issues avail.) **Indexed:** Anim.Breed.Abstr., Pt.de Rep. (1983-).

616.98 FR ISSN 0294-0817
MEDECINE AERONAUTIQUE ET SPATIALE. (Summaries in English, French) 1962. 4/yr. $30 (foreign 450 F.) C M P C A A Paris 15 Air, 26 bvd. Victor, 75731 Paris Cedex 15, France. TEL 1-45-52-67-91. FAX 1-45-52-65-90. Ed. J.R. Galle-Tessonneau. adv.; bk.rev.; abstr.; bibl.; charts; illus.; index. **Indexed:** Chem.Abstr., Excerp.Med.
Former titles: Medecine Aeronautique et Spatiale - Medecine Subaquatiqe et Hyperbare (ISSN 0399-6417); (until 1976): Revue de Medecine Aeronautique et Spatiale (ISSN 0035-1520); (until 1965): Revue de Medecine Aeronautique.

610 FR ISSN 0543-2243
MEDECINE DE L'HOMME. 1968. 2/yr. 300 F. Centre Catholique des Medecins Francais, 5 ave. de l'Observatoire, 75006 Paris, France. TEL 4634-3915. Ed. Claude Laroche. adv.; bk.rev.; circ. 4,376.
—BLDSC shelfmark: 5487.733500.

616.98 FR ISSN 0300-4937
CODEN: MDARC4
MEDECINE ET ARMEES. 1973. 8/yr. 220 F. (foreign 290 F.). Association pour le Developpement et la Diffusion de l'Information Militaire, 6 rue Saint Charles, 75015 Paris, France. TEL 45-77-03-76. adv.; bk.rev.; charts; illus.; index; circ. 6,000. **Indexed:** Biol.Abstr., C.I.S. Abstr., Chem.Abstr., Curr.Cont., Excerp.Med., Helminthol.Abstr., Ind.Med, Nutr.Abstr.
Supersedes: Revue des Corps de Sante des Armees (ISSN 0035-1954)

610 613 SZ ISSN 0025-6749
CODEN: MEHGAB
MEDECINE ET HYGIENE. (Text in French and German) 1943. w. 140 SFr.($100) Editions Medecine et Hygiene, Case Postale 456, CH-1211 Geneva 4, Switzerland. TEL 022-469455. FAX 022-475610. Ed. Dr. Pierre Rentchnick. adv.; bk.rev.; bibl.; charts; illus.; index; circ. 7,500. (reprint service avail. from UMI) **Indexed:** Biol.Abstr., C.I.S. Abstr., Chem.Abstr., Dent.Ind., Excerp.Med.
—BLDSC shelfmark: 5487.730000.

MEDECINE ET NUTRITION. see *NUTRITION AND DIETETICS*

610　　　　　　　FR　ISSN 0767-0974
CODEN: MSMSE4
MEDECINE - SCIENCES. 10/yr. 395 F. to individuals; institutions 700 F.; students 250 F. John Libbey Eurotext, 6 rue Blanche, 92120 Montrouge, France. TEL 1-47-35-85-52. FAX 1-46-57-10-09. (Dist. by: Gauthier-Villars, 11 rue Gossin, 92543 Montrouge Cedex, France. TEL 1-46-56-52-66) Ed. A. Khan.
—BLDSC shelfmark: 5980.840100.
Description: Studies the biology of today and the medicine of tomorrow.

610　　　　　　　FR　ISSN 0025-6838
MEDECINS DE GROUPE. 1967. m. and w. 200 F. Societe d'Edition de Publications Medicales, 80620 Domart-en-Ponthieu, France. Ed. Dr. Guiheneuf. adv.; bk.rev.; charts; circ. 21,000.

610　　　　　　　UK　ISSN 0144-4271
MEDECONOMICS. 1980. m. £53. Haymarket Medical Publications Ltd., 30 Lancaster Gate, London W2 3LP, England. (Subscr. addr.: Tower Publishing, 3-4 Hardwick St, London EC1R4RY, England) Ed. Ann Warburter. adv.; circ. 31,442.
●Also available online. Vendor(s): Data-Star.
—BLDSC shelfmark: 5488.060000.

610　　　　　　　AU　ISSN 0253-7419
MEDEQUIP. 1982. a. S.300. Blackwell Medizinische Zeitschriftenverlagsgesellschaft mbH, Feldgasse 13, A-1238 Vienna, Austria. TEL 0222-8893646. FAX 0222-889364724. Ed. Dr. H. Kurz. adv.; circ. 8,000.

610　　　　　　　US　ISSN 0740-1892
RA440.55
MEDIA PROFILES: HEALTH SCIENCES EDITION. 1974. q. $135. Olympic Media Information, Box 190, West Park, NY 12493. TEL 914-384-6563. Ed. Walt Carroll. film rev.; abstr.; index. cum.index every 2 yrs.; circ. 1,000. (looseleaf format; also avail. in microfiche; back issues avail.) Indexed: Media Rev.Dig.
Formerly: Hospital - Health Care Training Media Profiles (ISSN 0095-0580)
Description: Reference resource of films, videos and media based courses of interest to libraries and learning resource centers serving healthcare professionals who teach medical and nursing students and patients.

610　　　　　　　UK　ISSN 0962-9351
▼**MEDIATORS OF INFLAMMATION.** 1992. bi-m. £198($355) Rapid Communications of Oxford Ltd., The Old Malthouse, Paradise St., Oxford OX1 1LD, England. TEL 0865-790447. FAX 0865-244012. Ed. I. Bonta. (reprint service avail.)
—BLDSC shelfmark: 5525.385100.

MEDICAID FRAUD REPORT. see LAW

MEDICAID RECIPIENT CHARACTERISTICS AND UNITS OF SELECTED MEDICAL SERVICES. see SOCIAL SERVICES AND WELFARE

610 614　　　　　　US
MEDICAL ADMINISTRATION EXECUTIVE. bi-m. $60. American Academy of Medical Administrators, 30555 Southfield Rd., Ste. 150, Southfield, MI 48076. TEL 313-540-4310. FAX 313-645-0590. Ed. Thomas R. O'Donovan. adv.; bk.rev.; circ. 3,000.
Formerly: A A M A Executive (ISSN 0065-6879)

MEDICAL & BIOLOGICAL ENGINEERING & COMPUTING. see BIOLOGY — Bioengineering

610　　　　　　　BS
MEDICAL AND DENTAL ASSOCIATION OF BOTSWANA. JOURNAL. (Text in English) 1971. q. $11. Medical and Dental Association of Botswana, P.O. Box 798, Gaborone, Botswana. adv.; charts; circ. 200. (back issues avail.) Indexed: Ind.S.A.Per.

610　　　　　　　US　ISSN 0363-0366
R5
MEDICAL AND HEALTH ANNUAL. 1976. a. $30.95. Encyclopaedia Britannica, Inc., 310 S. Michigan Ave., Chicago, IL 60604. TEL 312-347-7000. FAX 312-347-7914. TELEX 190203. Ed. Ellen Bernstein. index.
—BLDSC shelfmark: 5525.954000.
Description: For lay readers, covers broad areas of medicine and health including in-depth articles. Reviews important developments in the medical specialties.

MEDICAL AND HEALTHCARE MARKETPLACE GUIDE. see BUSINESS AND ECONOMICS — Trade And Industrial Directories

MEDICAL ANTHROPOLOGY; cross-cultural studies in health and illness. see ANTHROPOLOGY

MEDICAL ANTHROPOLOGY QUARTERLY; international journal for the cultural and social analysis of health. see ANTHROPOLOGY

610　　　　　　　US　ISSN 0025-7028
R15
MEDICAL ASSOCIATION OF GEORGIA. JOURNAL. 1911. m. $40 in Georgia; other states $60. Medical Association of Georgia, 938 Peachtree St., N.E., Atlanta, GA 30309. TEL 404-876-7535. FAX 404-874-8651. Ed. Dr. Charles R. Underwood. adv.; bk.rev.; bibl.; charts; illus.; index; circ. 7,000. (also avail. in microform) Indexed: Chem.Abstr., Dent.Ind., Ind.Med., INIS Atomind.
—BLDSC shelfmark: 4824.130000.

610　　　　　　　TH　ISSN 0025-7036
CODEN: JMTHBU
MEDICAL ASSOCIATION OF THAILAND. JOURNAL. (Text in English; summaries in Thai) 1917. m. $40. Medical Association of Thailand, 67-9 Soi Soonvichai, New Pechburi Rd., Bangkok 10, Thailand. Ed. Dr. Prasert Thongcharoen. adv.; abstr.; charts; illus.; index; circ. 3,500. Indexed: Abstr.Hyg., Biol.Abstr., Chem.Abstr., Curr.Adv.Ecol.Sci., Curr.Cont., Dairy Sci.Abstr., Excerp.Med., Helminthol.Abstr., Ind.Med., Maize Abstr., Protozool.Abstr., Rev.Plant Path., Seed Abstr., Soyabean Abstr., Trop.Dis.Bull.

MEDICAL AUDIT NEWS. see BUSINESS AND ECONOMICS — Accounting

MEDICAL BENEFITS. see INSURANCE — Abstracting, Bibliographies, Statistics

MEDICAL BUSINESS REVIEW; medical business analysis for the doctor-executive. see BUSINESS AND ECONOMICS — Management

610 614　　　　　　US　ISSN 0025-7079
RA1　　　　　　　CODEN: MDLCBD
MEDICAL CARE. 1967. m. $80 to individuals (foreign $100); institutions $115 (foreign $135). (American Public Health Association, Medical Care Section) J.B. Lippincott Co., E. Washington Sq., Philadelphia, PA 19105. TEL 215-238-4200. Ed. Dr. Duncan Neuhauser. index; circ. 3,200. (also avail. in microform from UMI) Indexed: Abstr.Health Care Manage.Stud., Curr.Cont., Dent.Ind., Dok.Arbeitsmed., Excerp.Med., Hosp.Lit.Ind., Ind.Med., Ind.Sci.Rev., Int.Nurs.Ind., Psychol.Abstr., Risk Abstr., Sci.Cit.Ind., SSCI.
—BLDSC shelfmark: 5526.900000.
Refereed Serial

610　　　　　　　US
▼**MEDICAL CARE INTERNATIONAL.** (Text in English; summaries in French, German, Italian, Spanish) 1991. bi-m. $95. Globetech Publishing, 30 Cannon Rd., Wilton, CT 06897. TEL 203-762-3432. FAX 203-762-8640. Ed. Dr. Roy Barnett. adv.; circ. 30,000.

610　　　　　　　US
MEDICAL CARE PRODUCTS. 1982. 7/yr. Gordon Publications, Inc., 301 Gibraltar Dr., Morris Plains, NJ 07950. TEL 201-292-5100. FAX 201-898-9281. circ. 87,500. (tabloid format)

610　　　　　　　AT　ISSN 0812-7077
MEDICAL CAREERS IN AUSTRALIA. 1984. triennial. Aus.$12. Victorian Medical Postgraduate Foundation Inc., P.O. Box 27, Parkville, Vic. 3052, Australia. TEL 03-347-9633. FAX 03-347-4547. Ed. Dr. N.D. Yeomans. circ. 5,000. (back issues avail.)
Description: Career advice in medicine for undergraduates and recent graduates.

610　　　　　　　UK　ISSN 0025-7095
MEDICAL CENTRE JOURNAL. 1967. 3/yr. free. (Bedfordshire District Health Authority) Luton & Dunstable Hospital, Medical Centre, Luton, Bedfordshire, England. Ed. D.I.M. Siegler. circ. 600.

610　　　　　　　HK
MEDICAL CHINA NEWSFILE. 1987. fortn. $475. (People's Medical Publishing House, CC) Medical China Ltd., 44-F China Resources Building, 26 Harbour Road, Wanchai, Hong Kong. TEL 573-6211. FAX 8913831. (Distr. in U.S. by: McGraw-Hill, Inc., 1221 Ave. of the Americas, New York, NY 12292. TEL 212-512-2000) Ed. Derek Dickins.
Description: News and information on the Chinese healthcare market.

610　　　　　　　SA　ISSN 0025-7117
MEDICAL CHRONICLE. 1964. m. Newspaper Representations (S.A.) (Pty.), Box 549, Johannesburg, South Africa. Eds. L.P. Thomas, B.S. Unterhalter. adv.; bk.rev.; film rev.; illus.; tr.lit.; circ. 13,695. (tabloid format)

MEDICAL CLIENT NEWSLETTER. see BUSINESS AND ECONOMICS — Accounting

610　　　　　　　US　ISSN 0025-7125
RC60　　　　　　　CODEN: MCNAA9
MEDICAL CLINICS OF NORTH AMERICA. 1916. bi-m. $66. W.B. Saunders Co., Curtis Center, Independence Square W., Philadelphia, PA 19106. TEL 215-238-7800. Ed. Naina Chohan. bibl.; charts; illus.; index, cum.index. (also avail. in microform from MIM,UMI; reprint service avail. from UMI,ISI) Indexed: Biol.Abstr., Biotech.Abstr., Chem.Abstr., Curr.Adv.Ecol.Sci., Curr.Cont., Dairy Sci.Abstr., Excerp.Med., Helminthol.Abstr., I.P.A., Ind.Med., Ind.Sci.Rev., INIS Atomind., Int.Nurs.Ind., Nutr.Abstr., Risk Abstr.
●Also available online. Vendor(s): BRS, BRS/Saunders Colleague.
—BLDSC shelfmark: 5527.000000.
Formerly: Medical Clinics.

610　　　　　　　II　ISSN 0025-7133
MEDICAL COLLEGE AND HOSPITAL, CALCUTTA. BULLETIN. (Text in English) 1967. Rs.12. Medical College and Hospital, Department of Medicine, 88 College St., Calcutta 12, India. Ed. Dr. Nalini Ranjan Konar. adv.; charts; illus.; circ. 600.

616.98　　　　　　GW　ISSN 0179-1826
MEDICAL CORPS INTERNATIONAL; forum for military medicine and pharmacy. (Text in English; summaries in English, French and Spanish) a. $28. Beta Publishing, Postfach 140121, 5300 Bonn 1, Germany. TEL 0228-252061. FAX 0228-252067. TELEX 8869536 BETA D. Ed. Dr. Karl-Wilhem Wedel. adv.; circ. 14,000. (back issues avail.)
—BLDSC shelfmark: 5527.045000.
Description: Aimed at doctors, pharmacists and scientists in the Medical Corps.

610　　　　　　　IR
MEDICAL COUNCIL OF IRAN. PUBLICATION/NEZAM PEZESHKI-YE IRAN. NASHRIYEH.* (Text in Persian) 1970. irreg. free to physicians. Medical Council of Iran, 40 Shirin Ave., Hafez Ave., P.O. Box 11365-8759, Teheran, Iran. Ed. Mohammad Ali Hafizi.

610　　　　　　　US　ISSN 0272-989X
CODEN: MDMADE
MEDICAL DECISION MAKING; an international journal. 1980. q. $82 to individuals (foreign $92); institutions $92 (foreign $102). (Society for Medical Decision Making, Inc.) Hanley & Belfus, Inc., 210 S. 13th St., Philadelphia, PA 19107. TEL 215-546-7293. FAX 215-790-9330. Ed. Robert Beck. illus.; charts; stat.; index; circ. 2,000. (back issues avail.) Indexed: Abstr.Health Care Manage.Stud., Abstr.Hyg., Excerp.Med., Ind.Med., Ind.Sci.Rev.
—BLDSC shelfmark: 5527.053500.
Description: Concerned with the quantitative science of decision-making in medicine.
Refereed Serial

610　　　　　　　US　ISSN 1048-6690
▼**MEDICAL DEVICE TECHNOLOGY.** 1990. 9/yr. $59 (foreign $117). Aster Publishing Corporation, 859 Willamette St., Box 10955, Eugene, OR 97440. TEL 503-343-1200. FAX 503-343-3641. TELEX 510-597-0365. Ed. Chris Young. circ. 20,000 (controlled).
—BLDSC shelfmark: 5527.055420.
Description: For professionals in the European medical device and diagnostics market. Includes information on regulatory and legal affairs.

MEDICAL SCIENCES

615 US ISSN 0163-2426
CODEN: MDDIDR
MEDICAL DEVICES, DIAGNOSTICS & INSTRUMENTATION REPORTS: THE GRAY SHEET. Short title: M D D I Reports. 1975. w. $520 (foreign $595). F-D-C Reports, Inc., 5550 Friendship Blvd., Ste. One, Chevy Chase, MD 20815. TEL 301-657-9830. FAX 301-656-3094. (back issues avail.)
●Also available online. Vendor(s): Data-Star, DIALOG (File no.187), Mead Data Central.
—BLDSC shelfmark: 5413.519050.
Description: Provides coverage of the medical devices, diagnostics and instrumentation industries. Includes regulatory agency and congressional activities, industry developments, investor and financial news.

610 US
MEDICAL DEVICES REPORTER. 1976. irreg. $515. Commerce Clearing House, Inc., 4025 W. Peterson Ave., Chicago, IL 60646. TEL 312-583-8500. Ed. D. Newquist.

610 UK ISSN 0305-3342
MEDICAL DIRECTORY; an alphabetical listing of medical practitioners registered in Britain. a. £125. Longman Group UK Ltd., Westgate House, The High, Harlow, Essex CM20 2JE, England. TEL 0279-442601.
—BLDSC shelfmark: 5527.070000.

610 US
MEDICAL DIRECTORY OF NEW YORK STATE. biennial. $100. Medical Society of the State of New York, 420 Lakeville Rd., Lake Success, NY 11042.

610 US ISSN 0739-6554
MEDICAL DOCUMENTATION UPDATE. 1983. 10/yr. $125 (foreign $150). Medical Records Institute, 567 Walnut St., Newtonville, MA 02160. TEL 617-964-3923. FAX 617-964-3926. Ed. C. Peter Waegemann. (back issues avail.)

610 US ISSN 0025-7206
R723.5
MEDICAL ECONOMICS. 1923. fortn. $94 (foreign $148). Medical Economics Publishing Co., Five Paragon Dr., Montvale, NJ 07645. TEL 201-358-7200. FAX 201-573-1045. Ed. Steve Murata. adv.; charts; illus.; stat.; index; circ. 173,000. (also avail. in microform from RPI) **Indexed:** Abstr.Health Care Manage.Stud., Account.Ind. (1974-), BPIA, Bus.Ind., CINAHL, Curr.Lit.Fam.Plan., Hlth.Ind., Med.Care Rev., P.A.I.S., Tr.& Indus.Ind.
●Also available online. Vendor(s): DIALOG.
—BLDSC shelfmark: 5527.160000.
Description: Publishes original articles designed to help the physician manage his practice, his professional relations and his personal and financial affairs.

610.7 UK ISSN 0308-0110
R735.A1
MEDICAL EDUCATION. 1966. bi-m. £90 (foreign £99). (Association for the Study of Medical Education) Blackwell Scientific Publications Ltd., Osney Mead, Oxford OX2 0EL, England. TEL 0865-240201. FAX 0865-721205. TELEX 83355-MEDBOK-G. Ed. H.J. Walton. adv.; bk.rev.; circ. 1,800. (also avail. in microfilm; back issues avail.; reprint service avail. from ISI) **Indexed:** Abstr.Health Care Manage.Stud., Abstr.Hyg., ASCA, Biol.Abstr., Cont.Pg.Educ., Curr.Adv.Ecol.Sci., Curr.Cont., Dent.Ind., Educ.Tech.Abstr., Excerp.Med., FAMLI, High.Educ.Curr.Aware.Bull., Ind.Med., Ind.Sci.Rev., Mid.East: Abstr.& Ind., Psychol.Abstr., Res.High.Educ.Abstr., Sci.Cit.Ind., Trop.Dis.Bull.
—BLDSC shelfmark: 5527.166000.
Formerly: British Journal of Medical Education (ISSN 0007-1110)
Description: Covers medical education.

615.845 US
MEDICAL ELECTRONICS. 1970. bi-m. $22. Measurements & Data Corp., 2994 W. Liberty Ave., Pittsburgh, PA 15216. TEL 412-343-9666. Ed. Harish Saluja. adv.; charts; illus.; tr.lit.; circ. 100,000. (also avail. in microform from UMI; reprint service avail. from UMI) **Indexed:** Biol.Abstr., Comput.Lit.Ind.
Incorporates: American Journal of Electromedicine (ISSN 0894-8291); **Former titles:** Medical Electronics and Data (ISSN 0098-3446); M E D (ISSN 0024-810X)
Description: Covers medical electronics.

615.845 US
MEDICAL ELECTRONICS AND EQUIPMENT NEWS. 1961. 6/yr. $35 (free to qualified personnel). Reilly Publishing Co., 532 Busse Hwy., Park Ridge, IL 60068. TEL 312-693-3773. FAX 312-696-0946. Ed. Marianne Schmidt. adv.; bk.rev.; abstr.; charts; illus.; stat.; tr.lit.; circ. 52,615. (tabloid format) **Indexed:** Excerp.Med.
Formerly: Medical Electronics News (ISSN 0025-7230)
Description: Covers medical electronics.

MEDICAL EQUIPMENT DESIGNER. see *INSTRUMENTS*

610 JA
MEDICAL EQUIPMENT JOURNAL OF JAPAN. 12/yr. $95. Intercontinental Maketing Corp., I.P.O. Box 5056, Tokyo 100-31, Japan. FAX 81-3-3667-9646.

610 340 170 US ISSN 0886-0653
MEDICAL ETHICS ADVISOR. 1985. m. $228. American Health Consultants, Inc., Six Piedmont Center, Ste. 400, 3525 Piedmont Rd., N.E., Atlanta, GA 30305. TEL 404-262-7436. FAX 800-284-3291. (Subscr. to: Box 740056, Atlanta, GA 30374-9822. TEL 800-688-2421) Ed. Anne Corner. (reprint service avail.)

610 II
MEDICAL EXPRESS; newspaper of the medical profession. (Text in English) 1974. fortn. Rs.12($6) Amal Ghosh-Hajra, Ed. & Pub., 240 Diamond Harbour Rd., Behala, Calcutta 700060, West Bengal, India. adv.; bk.rev.; abstr.; bibl.; index; circ. 10,500.

610 PK
MEDICAL GAZETTE. (Text in English) vol.2, 1971. s-m. Pakistan Medical Association, P.M.A. House, Garden Rd., Karachi 74400, Pakistan.

658 US ISSN 0025-7257
R729.5.G6
MEDICAL GROUP MANAGEMENT. JOURNAL. 1953. bi-m. $41. Medical Group Management Association, 104 Inverness Terrace E., Englewood, CO 80112. TEL 303-799-1111. Ed. Dr. Fred E. Graham II. adv.; charts; illus.; stat.; index; circ. 19,000. (also avail. in microform from UMI) **Indexed:** Abstr.Health Care Manage.Stud., Hosp.Lit.Ind, Med.Care Rev.
—BLDSC shelfmark: 5527.432000.

610 US ISSN 1040-2330
R729.5.G6
MEDICAL GROUP MANAGEMENT ASSOCIATION. DIRECTORY. 1961. a. $250. Medical Group Management Association, 104 Inverness Terrace E., Englewood, CO 80112. TEL 303-799-1111. Ed. Dennis Barnhardt. circ. 12,000.
Formerly: Medical Group Management Association. International Directory (ISSN 0094-9604)

610 US
THE MEDICAL HERALD. m. Medical Herald Publishing Co., Inc., 211 E. 43rd St., Ste. 908, New York, NY 10017. TEL 212-983-3525. FAX 212-922-9211. Ed. Hugh Wyatt. circ. 50,000.

610 UK ISSN 0025-7273
R131.A1 CODEN: MDHIAA
MEDICAL HISTORY; devoted to the history and bibliography of medicine and the related sciences. 1957. q. £44 to individuals; institutions £56. (Wellcome Institute for the History of Medicine) Professional & Scientific Publications, Tavistock House East, Tavistock Square, London WC1H 9JR, England. Eds. W.F. Bynum, V. Nutton. adv.; bk.rev.; bibl.; illus.; index; circ. 1,000. **Indexed:** Abstr.Hyg., Amer.Hist.& Life, Biol.Abstr., Br.Archaeol.Abstr., Curr.Adv.Ecol.Sci., Curr.Cont., Dairy Sci.Abstr., Excerp.Med., Hist.Abstr., Ind.Med., Ind.Sci.Rev., Ind.Vet., Nutr.Abstr., Trop.Dis.Bull., Vet.Bull.
—BLDSC shelfmark: 5527.500000.

MEDICAL HUMANITIES REVIEW. see *HUMANITIES: COMPREHENSIVE WORKS*

610 UK ISSN 0306-9877
R5 CODEN: MEHYDY
MEDICAL HYPOTHESES. 1975. m. £295($569) Churchill Livingstone Medical Journals, Robert Stevenson House, 1-3 Baxter's Pl., Leith Walk, Edinburgh EH1 3AF, Scotland. TEL 031-556-2424. FAX 031-558-1278. TELEX 727511. (Subscr. to: Longman Group, Journals Subscr. Dept., P.O. Box 77, Fourth Ave., Harlow, Essex CM19 5AA, England; U.S. subscr. to: Churchill Livingstone, 650 Ave. of the Americas, New York, NY 10011. TEL 212-206-5000) Ed. Dr. D.F. Horrobin. adv.; bk.rev.; circ. 500. (also avail. in microform from UMI; back issues avail.) **Indexed:** Anim.Breed.Abstr., Biol.Abstr., C.I.S. Abstr., Chem.Abstr., Curr.Adv.Cancer Res., Curr.Adv.Cell & Devel.Biol., Curr.Adv.Ecol.Sci., Curr.Adv.Genetics & Molec.Biol., Curr.Cont., Dairy Sci.Abstr., Dok.Arbeitsmed., Excerp.Med., Helminthol.Abstr., Ind.Med., Ind.Sci.Rev., Ind.Vet., Nutr.Abstr., Protozool.Abstr., Psychol.Abstr., Small Anim.Abstr., Vet.Bull., Weed Abstr.
—BLDSC shelfmark: 5527.530000.

610 AT
MEDICAL IMAGING AND MONITORING. q. Aus.$40 free to qualified personnel. Reed Business Publishing Pty. Ltd., 1-5 Railway St., Chatswood, N.S.W. 2067, Australia. Ed. L. Lange. adv.; illus.; circ. 2,999. (tabloid format)
Former titles: Imaging and Monitoring News & Medical Electronics News.

610 US
▼**MEDICAL INDUSTRY EXECUTIVE.** 1992. bi-m. Medical Industry Publications, Inc., 1190 Hightower Trail, Atlanta, GA 30350. TEL 404-998-9797. FAX 404-594-6998. Ed. Elizabeth Porter. adv.: B&W page $4695. circ. 40,000 (controlled).
Description: Focuses on reports and analyses of market trends, business, issues, regulatory requirements, product development and technology research for executives in the medical equipment, device and supply industry.

610 US ISSN 0896-4831
MEDICAL INTERFACE. 1988. m. $45 to individuals (foreign $65); institutions (foreign $80). Medicom International, Inc., 66 Palmer Ave., Ste. 49, Bronxville, NY 10708. TEL 914-337-7878. FAX 914-337-5023. Ed. Stanton R. Mehr. adv.; circ. 25,686.
Description: Open forum for the managed health-care industry.

616.98 II
MEDICAL JOURNAL ARMED FORCES, INDIA. (Text in English) 1945. q. Rs.200($60) (effective Jan. 1990). Armed Forces Medical College, Pune 411 040, Maharashtra, India. TEL 673290. Ed. Col. M.M. Arora. adv.; bk.rev.; charts; illus.; stat.; circ. 5,000. **Indexed:** Biol.Abstr., Excerp.Med., Trop.Dis.Bull.
Formerly (until 1974): Armed Forces Medical Journal, India (ISSN 0004-2218)

610 AT ISSN 0025-729X
CODEN: MJAUAJ
MEDICAL JOURNAL OF AUSTRALIA. 1914. s-m. Aus.$210 (foreign Aus.$280). (Australian Medical Association) Australasian Medical Publishing Co., P.O. Box 410, Kingsgrove, N.S.W. 2208, Australia. FAX 02-502-3626. adv.: B&W page Aus.$1115, color page Aus.$1,750. bk.rev.; abstr.; bibl.; illus.; s-a. index; circ. 22,846. (also avail. in microform from MIM,UMI; reprint service avail. from UMI) **Indexed:** A.D.& D., Abstr.Hyg., Aus.P.A.I.S., Aus.Rd.Ind., Bibl.Dev.Med.& Child Neur., Biol.Abstr., Biotech.Abstr., C.I.S. Abstr., Chem.Abstr., CINAHL, Curr.Adv.Cancer Res., Curr.Adv.Ecol.Sci., Curr.Cont., Dent.Ind., Dok.Arbeitsmed., Excerp.Med., Helminthol.Abstr., HRIS, I.P.A., Ind.Med., Ind.Sci.Rev., Ind.Vet., INIS Atomind., Int.Nurs.Ind., Lab.Haz.Bull., Med.Care Rev., Nutr.Abstr., Protozool.Abstr., Rev.Plant Path., Risk Abstr., Trop.Dis.Bull.
●Also available online.
—BLDSC shelfmark: 5529.000000.

MEDICAL SCIENCES 3127

610   MY   ISSN 0300-5283
CODEN: MJMLAI
MEDICAL JOURNAL OF MALAYSIA. q. M.$120.
Malaysian Medical Association, 124 Jalan Pahang, 53000 Kuala Lumpur, Malaysia. Ed. Prof. Victor Lim. adv.; bk.rev.; charts; illus.; stat. **Indexed:** Abstr.Hyg., Biol.Abstr., Chem.Abstr., CINAHL, Dent.Ind., Excerp.Med., Helminthol.Abstr., Ind.Med., Nutr.Abstr., Protozool.Abstr., Rev.Appl.Entomol., Soyabean Abstr., Trop.Dis.Bull.
Formerly: Medical Journal of Malaya (ISSN 0025-7303)

610   ZA   ISSN 0047-651X
CODEN: MJZAAG
MEDICAL JOURNAL OF ZAMBIA.* 1967. bi-m. Zambia Medical Association, P.O. Box 717, Ndola, Zambia. Ed. M.N. Lowenthal. adv.; bk.rev.; index; circ. 1,700. **Indexed:** Abstr.Hyg., Biol.Abstr., Curr.Cont., Excerp.Med., Helminthol.Abstr., Ind.Med., Ind.Vet., Nutr.Abstr., Protozool.Abstr., Trop.Dis.Bull, Vet.Bull.

MEDICAL LASER INDUSTRIAL REPORT. see *PHYSICS — Optics*

610   026   US   ISSN 0025-7338
CODEN: BMLAAG
MEDICAL LIBRARY ASSOCIATION. BULLETIN. 1911. q. $130 (foreign $165). Medical Library Association, Six N. Michigan Ave., Ste. 300, Chicago, IL 60602. TEL 312-419-9094. Ed. Naomi Broering. adv.; bk.rev.; bibl.; index, cum.index; circ. 6,400. (also avail. in microform from UMI; reprint service avail. from UMI,ISI,KTO) **Indexed:** Abstr.Health Care Manage.Stud., Abstr.Hyg., Biol.Abstr., C.I.N.L., Curr.Adv.Ecol.Sci., Dent.Ind., Dent.Ind., Excerp.Med., Hosp.Lit.Ind., I.P.A., Ind.Med., Int.Nurs.Ind., LHTN, Lib.Lit., LISA, Nutr.Abstr., Sci.Abstr., Sci.Cit.Ind., SSCI, Telegen, Trop.Dis.Bull.
—BLDSC shelfmark: 2612.090000.

MEDICAL MALPRACTICE: BASES OF LIABILITY. see *LAW — Civil Law*

MEDICAL MALPRACTICE DEFENSE AND HEALTH CARE COUNSEL DIRECTORY. see *LAW — Civil Law*

MEDICAL MALPRACTICE DEFENSE REPORTER. see *LAW — Civil Law*

MEDICAL MALPRACTICE LAW & STRATEGY. see *LAW — Civil Law*

MEDICAL MALPRACTICE - OB-GYN LITIGATION REPORTER; the monthly national journal of record reporting general medical malpractice, obstetrical and gynecological litigation. see *LAW — Civil Law*

MEDICAL MALPRACTICE REPORTS. see *LAW — Civil Law*

MEDICAL MALPRACTICE VERDICTS, SETTLEMENTS & EXPERTS. see *LAW — Civil Law*

610   AT
MEDICAL MARKET PLACE. 1974. 3/yr. free. Permail Pty. Ltd., P.O. Box 56, Artarmon, N.S.W. 2064, Australia. adv.; circ. 36,950.

MEDICAL MICROBIOLOGY LETTERS. see *BIOLOGY — Microbiology*

610   US   ISSN 0025-7397
MEDICAL-MORAL NEWSLETTER. 1964. 10/yr. $25. Ayd Medical Communications, 1130 E. Cold Spring Ln., Baltimore, MD 21239. TEL 301-433-9120. FAX 301-532-5419. Ed. Dr. Frank J. Ayd, Jr. bk.rev.; circ. 1,000.
Formerly: Medical Newsletter for Religious.
Description: Discusses medical ethics.

610   368.382   US   ISSN 0895-4313
MEDICAL OFFICE REPORT. 1988. m. $156 (typically set in Jan.). Dennis W. Washington G - 2 Reports, 1111 14th St. N.W., Ste. 711, Washington, DC 20005. TEL 202-789-1034. FAX 202-289-4062. Ed. D.J. Curren. charts; stat.; circ. 1,000. (also avail. in tabloid format; back issues avail.)
Description: Offers the latest Medicare reimbursement and policy information for the office physician.

MEDICAL ONCOLOGY & TUMOR PHARMACOTHERAPY. see *MEDICAL SCIENCES — Cancer*

530   610   US   ISSN 0094-2405
R895.A1   CODEN: MPHYA6
MEDICAL PHYSICS. 1970. bi-m. $250 (foreign $265). (American Association of Physicists in Medicine) American Institute of Physics, 335 E. 45th St., New York, NY 10017. TEL 212-661-9404. Ed. J. Laughlin. adv.; bk.rev.; abstr.; cum.index: vols. 1-10, 1985. (also avail. in microform; microfiche; back issues avail.) **Indexed:** Abstr.Health Care Manage.Stud., Appl.Mech.Rev., Biol.Abstr., C.P.I., Chem.Abstr., Curr.Cont., Dent.Ind., Excerp.Med., Gen.Phys.Adv.Abstr., Ind.Med., Ind.Sci.Rev., INIS Atomind., Phys.Ber., Sci.Abstr.
—BLDSC shelfmark: 5531.130000.
Formerly: A.A.P.M. Quarterly Bulletin (ISSN 0001-0162)
Refereed Serial

610   530   US   ISSN 0076-5953
MEDICAL PHYSICS SERIES. 1969. irreg, vol.8, 1985. Academic Press, Inc., 1250 Sixth Ave., San Diego, CA 92101. TEL 619-231-0926. FAX 619-699-6715. Ed. P.N.T. Wells. (reprint service avail. from ISI)
Refereed Serial

610   CN   ISSN 0025-7435
MEDICAL POST. 1965. fortn. Can.$41. Maclean-Hunter Ltd., Business Publication Division, Maclean-Hunter Bldg., 777 Bay St., Toronto, Ont. M5W 1A7, Canada. TEL 416-596-5770. TELEX 062-19547. Ed. Derek Cassels. adv.; bk.rev.; abstr.; charts; illus.; circ. 37,000. (tabloid format)
—BLDSC shelfmark: 5531.150000.
Description: Covers clinical, political and social news for physicians.

610   SZ   ISSN 1011-7571
MEDICAL PRINCIPLES AND PRACTICE. 1989. q. 256 Fr.($171) (Kuwait University, Health Science Center, KU) S. Karger AG, Allschwilerstr. 10, P.O. Box, CH-4009 Basel, Switzerland. TEL 061-3061111. FAX 061-3061234. TELEX CH 962652. Ed. M. Khogali.
—BLDSC shelfmark: 5531.260000.
Description: Concentrates on the recent advances made in basic medical sciences, clinical practice and associated disciplines within human medicine.

610   780   US   ISSN 0885-1158
CODEN: MPPAEC
MEDICAL PROBLEMS OF PERFORMING ARTISTS. 1986. q. $46 to individuals (foreign $56); institutions $56 (foreign $66). Hanley & Belfus, Inc., 210 S. 13th St., Philadelphia, PA 19107. TEL 215-546-7293. FAX 215-790-9330. Ed. Linda C. Belfus. adv.; bk.rev.; index; circ. 2,000. (back issues avail.)
—BLDSC shelfmark: 5531.280000.
Description: Concerned with medical and surgical problems deriving from artistic performance in dance, music and theater.
Refereed Serial

MEDICAL PRODUCTS DISTRIBUTORS. see *BUSINESS AND ECONOMICS — Trade And Industrial Directories*

610   380.1   JA
MEDICAL PRODUCTS OF JAPAN; medical equipment directory. (Text in English) no.7, 1983. irreg., no.13, 1991. 6000 Yen($76) Genyosha Publications, Inc., 18-2, Shibuya 3-chome, Shibuya-ku, Tokyo 150, Japan. TEL 03-3407-7521. FAX 03-3407-7902. adv.; circ. 7,500.

610   681   US   ISSN 0279-4802
MEDICAL PRODUCTS SALES. 1970. m. $49.95. (Health Industry Distributors Association) McKnight Medical Communications Co., 1419 Lake Cook Rd., Deerfield, IL 60015. TEL 708-949-0345. Ed. Bill Briggs. adv.; bk.rev.; illus.; circ. 24,400. (back issues avail.)
Formerly (until 1981): Medical Products Salesman (ISSN 0192-432X)

610   HK
MEDICAL PROGRESS. 1974. m. $40 to individuals; students $20. Medpro Pacific Ltd., 19F Tung Sun Commerical Centre, 200 Lockhart Rd., Wanchai, Hong Kong. TEL 5-8920638. FAX 5-8345330. Ed. Graeme S. Avery. adv. (back issues avail.) **Indexed:** Abstr.Hyg., Chem.Abstr.

MEDICAL PROGRESS THROUGH TECHNOLOGY. see *BIOLOGY — Biotechnology*

610   UK   ISSN 0076-5961
MEDICAL PROTECTION SOCIETY. ANNUAL REPORT. 1892. a. membership. Medical Protection Society Ltd., 50 Hallam Street, London W1N 6DE, England. TEL 44 71 637-0541. FAX 44-71-636-0690. TELEX 8952848 MEDPRO G. adv.; circ. 120,000 (controlled).

610   MW
MEDICAL QUARTERLY. (Text in English) 1980. q. (Medical Association of Malawi) Centraf Associates Ltd., PO Box 30462, Chichiri, Blantyre 3, Malawi. **Indexed:** Rural Devel.Abstr., Rural Ext.Educ.& Tr.Abstr.

MEDICAL RECORD RISKS: CLAIMS & LITIGATION. see *INSURANCE*

610   CN
MEDICAL REFORM. 1979. bi-m. $25. Medical Reform Group, P.O. Box 366, Sta. J, Toronto, Ont. M4J 4Y8, Canada. TEL 416-588-9167. Ed. Dr. Haresh Kirpolomi. adv.; bk.rev.; circ. 300. (back issues avail.)
Description: Covers the social, economic and political dimensions of health care provision.

610   US
MEDICAL REHABILITATION REVIEW. 1982. w. membership. National Association of Rehabilitation Review, Box 17675, Washington, DC 20041. TEL 703-648-9300. FAX 703-648-8646. Ed. Carolyn Zollar. circ. 1,000 (controlled).

610   KE   ISSN 0076-5988
MEDICAL RESEARCH CENTRE, NAIROBI. ANNUAL REPORT. 1966. a. free. Medical Research Centre, Nairobi, PO Box 20752, Nairobi, Kenya. (Affiliate: Koninklijk Instituut voor de Tropen, Netherlands) **Indexed:** Biol.Abstr.

610   UK
MEDICAL RESEARCH CENTRES; a world directory of organizations and programmes. irreg., 9th ed. 1990. £290. Longman Group UK Ltd., Westgate House, The High, Harlow, Essex CM20 2JE, England. TEL 0279-442601. (Dist. in U.S. and Canada by: Gale Research Inc., 10 Penobscot Bldg., Detroit, MI 48226)
Formerly: Medical Research Index (ISSN 0076-6003)

610   GH
MEDICAL RESEARCH CENTRES IN GHANA: CURRENT RESEARCH PROJECTS. 1973. irreg. free. Council for Scientific and Industrial Research, PO Box M32, Accra, Ghana. Ed. D.K. Opare-Sem. (back issues avail.)

610   CN   ISSN 0047-6560
MEDICAL RESEARCH COUNCIL NEWSLETTER/CONSEIL DE RECHERCHES MEDICALES. ACTUALITES. (Text in English and French) 1970. q. free. Medical Research Council of Canada, Tunney's Pasture, Ottawa, Ont. K1A 0W9, Canada. TEL 613-954-1806. circ. 4,500 (controlled).

610   CN
MEDICAL RESEARCH COUNCIL OF CANADA. GRANTS AND AWARDS GUIDE/GUIDE DE SUBVENTIONS ET BOURSES. (Text and summaries in English and French) a. Medical Research Council of Canada, Tunney's Pasture, Ottawa, Ont. K1A 0W9, Canada. TEL 613-954-1806. charts; circ. 7,400.

610.6   CN
MEDICAL RESEARCH COUNCIL OF CANADA. REFERENCE LIST OF HEALTH SCIENCE RESEARCH IN CANADA. (Text in English and French) 1968. a. free. Medical Research Council of Canada, Tunney's Pasture, Ottawa, Ont. K1A 0W9, Canada. TEL 613-954-1806. circ. 1,000.

610   CN
MEDICAL RESEARCH COUNCIL OF CANADA. REPORT OF THE PRESIDENT. (Text in English, French) 1960. a. free. Medical Research Council of Canada, Tunney's Pasture, Ottawa, Ont. K1A 0W9, Canada. TEL 613-954-1806. charts; illus.; stat.; index; circ. 2,300 (controlled).

MEDICAL RESEARCH FUNDING BULLETIN. see *SOCIAL SERVICES AND WELFARE*

MEDICAL SCIENCES

610 378   US
▼**MEDICAL RESEARCH FUNDING NEWS.** (Includes: Medical Grants Monitor) 1990. fortn. $345. Faulkner & Gray, Healthcare Information Center (Subsidiary of: J P T Publishing Group), 1133 15th St., N.W., Ste. 450, Washington, DC 20005. TEL 202-828-4150. FAX 202-828-2352. Ed. Catherine Tokarski.
  Description: Covers availability of government and private research funding and relevant policy developments, with a comprehensive listing of medical research grants awarded by the National Institutes of Health and private sources.

616.98   US
MEDICAL RESEARCH IN THE V.A.. 1957. a. $0.40. U.S. Veterans Administration, Medical Research Service, 810 Vermont Ave., N.W., Washington, DC 20420. TEL 202-745-8000. (Subscr. to: Supt. of Documents, Government Printing Office, Washington, DC 20402) Ed. Russell D. Bowman.
  Formerly: Highlights of V A Medical Research (ISSN 0073-2141)

MEDICAL SCHOOL ADMISSION REQUIREMENTS, UNITED STATES AND CANADA. see EDUCATION — Higher Education

610   UK   ISSN 0269-8951
               CODEN: MSCREJ
MEDICAL SCIENCE RESEARCH. 24/yr. $590. Science and Technology Letters, P.O. Box 81, Northwood, Middlesex HA6 3DN, England. TEL 09274-23586. FAX 09274-25066. Ed. S. Johnson. adv.; bk.rev. **Indexed:** Anim.Breed.Abstr., Curr.Adv.Cancer Res., Dairy Sci.Abstr., Ind.Vet., Pig News & Info., Poult.Abstr., Psychol.Abstr., Vet.Bull.
●Also available online. Vendor(s): BRS, BRS/Saunders Colleague, DIMDI, Data-Star.
—BLDSC shelfmark: 5531.892000.
  Formed by the 1986 merger of: I R C S Medical Science: Anatomy and Human Biology (ISSN 0305-6686); I R C S Medical Science: Biochemistry (ISSN 0305-6708); I R C S Medical Science: Biomedical Technology (ISSN 0305-6716); I R C S Medical Science: Cancer (ISSN 0305-6724); I R C S Medical Science: Cardiovascular System (ISSN 0305-6732) I R C S Medical Science: Cell and Molecular Biology; Which incorporates: I R C S Medical Science: Cell and Membrane Biology (ISSN 0305-6740) and I R C S Medical Science: Key Reports in Cell and Molecular Biology (ISSN 0142-484X); I R C S Medical Science: Clinical Biochemistry (ISSN 0309-1481); I R C S Medical Science: Clinical Medicine and Surgery.

MEDICAL SCIENCES BULLETIN; focus on pharmacology: theory and practice. see PHARMACY AND PHARMACOLOGY

MEDICAL SCIENCES INTERNATIONAL WHO'S WHO. see BIOGRAPHY

610   IR
MEDICAL SCIENCES UNIVERSITY OF TEHRAN. SCHOOL OF MEDICINE. JOURNAL/MAJALLEH DANESHKADEH PEZESHKI. (Text in Persian) 1944. 10/yr. Rs.200. Medical Sciences University of Tehran, School of Medicine, Enghelab Ave., Teheran, Iran. Ed.Bd.
  Formerly: University of Tehran. Faculty of Medicine. Journal.

610   UK   ISSN 0076-6011
MEDICAL SOCIETY OF LONDON. TRANSACTIONS. 1773. a. £15. Medical Society of London, 11 Chandos Street, Cavendish Square, London, W1N OEB, England. Ed. P.S. London. bk.rev.; circ. 550. **Indexed:** Excerp.Med., Ind.Med.

MEDICAL STAFF LAW MANUAL. see LAW — Civil Law

610   US   ISSN 0565-811X
Z695.1.M48
MEDICAL SUBJECT HEADINGS (BLACK BOOK). (Also issued as Part 2 of Jan Index Medicus) 1960. a. $37 (foreign $46.25). U.S. National Library of Medicine, 8600 Rockville Pike, Bethesda, MD 20894. TEL 301-496-6308. FAX 301-496-4450. (Orders to: Supt. of Documents, Washington, DC 20402) circ. 8,000.
  Description: An alphabetized and categorized list of all of the subject descriptors used to analyze the biomedical literature in the National Library of Medicine.

610   UK   ISSN 0142-159X
MEDICAL TEACHER. 1979. q. $98 to individuals; institutions $240. Carfax Publishing Co., P.O. Box 25, Abingdon, Oxfordshire OX14 3UE, England. TEL 0235-555335. FAX 0235-553559. (U.S. subscr. addr.: Carfax Publishing Co., Box 2025, Dunnellon, FL 32630) Ed. R.M. Harden. adv.; bk.rev.; charts; cum.index. (also avail. in microfiche; back issues avail.) **Indexed:** Curr.Adv.Ecol.Sci., Educ.Tech.Abstr.
—BLDSC shelfmark: 5531.965000.
  Description: Covers study and teaching.

610   UK   ISSN 0309-2666
MEDICAL TECHNOLOGIST AND SCIENTIST. 1971. m. £14 (foreign £16.50)(effective Jan. 1992). A.E. Morgan Publications Ltd., Stanley House, 9 West St., Epsom, Surrey KT18 7RL, England. TEL 0372-741411. FAX 0372-744493. Ed. Roy Goodall. bk.rev.; film rev.; circ. 7,000. (tabloid format) **Indexed:** ABC.
—BLDSC shelfmark: 5532.020000.
  Former titles: Medical Technologist (ISSN 0300-5879); Medical Technician (ISSN 0300-3868)
  Description: Articles and news of products and developments in the medical laboratory field.

610.28   UK
MEDICAL TECHNOLOGIST DIARY & CLASSIFIED BUYER'S GUIDE. a. A.E. Morgan Publications Ltd., Stanley House, 9 West St., Epsom, Surrey, England. TEL 0372-741411. FAX 0372-744493.
  Description: Lists products available for the laboratory technician.

MEDICAL TECHNOLOGY STOCK LETTER. see BUSINESS AND ECONOMICS — Investments

610   UK   ISSN 0266-2078
MEDICAL TEXTILES. 1984. m. £219 (effective 1992). Elsevier Science Publishers Ltd., Crown House, Linton Rd., Barking, Essex IG11 8JU, England. TEL 081-594-7272. FAX 081-594-5942. TELEX 896950 APPSCI G. (N. America dist. addr.: Elsevier Science Publishing Co., Inc., Box 882, Madison Sq. Sta., New York, NY 10159. TEL 212-989-5800) (Co-publisher: British Textile Technology Group) Eds. Peter Lennon-Kerr, Edward Love. bk.rev.; charts; stat. (back issues avail.)
●Also available online. Vendor(s): Data-Star, DIALOG.
—BLDSC shelfmark: 5532.028700.
  Description: Provides coverage of design, production and research management in the fiber and polymer industries and in related research departments and institutes. Also provides a survey of this whole area for senior general management, serving to highlight new trends and possibilities, market gaps and business opportunities.

MEDICAL TRIAL TECHNIQUE QUARTERLY. see LAW — Civil Law

610   IT   ISSN 0392-7199
MEDICAL TRIBUNE. 1982. w. (42/yr.). L.20000. E S I Stampa Medica s.r.l., Casella Postale 42, Lgo. Volontari del Sangue 10, 20097 S. Donato, Milan, Italy. TEL 02-5274241. FAX 02-5274775. TELEX 3248944. Ed. Bruno P. Pieroni. adv.; bk.rev.; circ. 70,000.

610   US   ISSN 0279-9340
R5
MEDICAL TRIBUNE (1980); world news of medicine and its practice. 1960. 26/yr. $75 (free to qualified personnel) (typically set in Oct). Medical Tribune, Inc., 257 Park Ave. South, New York, NY 10010. TEL 212-674-8500. FAX 212-529-8490. Ed. William Ingram. adv.; bk.rev.; charts; illus.; stat.; circ. 136,000 (controlled). **Indexed:** Curr.Lit.Fam.Plan.
  Former titles (until vol.21, 1980): Medical Tribune and Medical News (ISSN 0098-6240); (until vol.3, 1963): Medical Tribune (ISSN 0025-7605)

610   US   ISSN 0734-1970
MEDICAL UTILIZATION REVIEW. 1973. fortn. $385. Faulkner & Gray, Healthcare Information Center (Subsidiary of: J P T Publishing Group), 1133 15th St., N.W., Ste. 450, Washington, DC 20005. TEL 202-828-4150. FAX 202-828-2352. Ed. Spencer Vibbert. (looseleaf format; back issues avail.; reprint service avail. from UMI)
  Formerly: P S R O Letter.

610   IT
MEDICAL VIDEO FLASH. 1976. 8/yr. Editoriale Dumas S.p.A., Via Grandi 5-7, 20089 Rozzano (Mi), Italy. Ed. Gianni Mazzocchi. adv.; circ. 108,000.

MEDICAL WASTE NEWS. see ENVIRONMENTAL STUDIES — Waste Management

610   UK   ISSN 0025-7621
MEDICAL WORLD. 1913. m. £2.10. Association of Scientific, Technical and Managerial Staffs, 10-26 Jamestown Rd., London NW1 7DT, England. Ed. Alan Brown. adv.; bk.rev.; charts; illus.; stat.; index; circ. 15,000. **Indexed:** Chem.Abstr., I.P.A., Ind.Med., Psychol.Abstr.
●Also available online.
  Incorporates: Journal of Hospital Pharmacy (ISSN 0022-1619)

610   US   ISSN 0025-763X
R11   CODEN: MDWNA
MEDICAL WORLD NEWS; the newsmagazine of medicine. 1936. m. $55 (free to qualified physicians). Medical Tribune, Inc., 257 Park Ave. S., New York, NY 10010. TEL 212-674-8500. FAX 212-529-8490. TELEX 278273. Ed. Nicholas K. Ziffell. adv.; bk.rev.; charts; illus.; circ. 95,000. (also avail. in microform from UMI; reprint service avail. from UMI) **Indexed:** Biol.Abstr., Biol.Dig., CINAHL, Curr.Lit.Fam.Plan., Hlth.Ind., I.P.A., PROMT.
●Also available online.
—BLDSC shelfmark: 5532.150000.

MEDICARE ADVISOR. see INSURANCE

MEDICARE COMPLIANCE ALERT. see INSURANCE

MEDICARE REVIEW. see INSURANCE

610   AG   ISSN 0025-7680
R21   CODEN: MEDCAD
MEDICINA; Buenos Aires. (Text in English, Spanish; summaries in English, Spanish) 1939. bi-m. Arg.$600000($70) in Latin America; elsewhere $90(effective 1992). (Instituto de Investigaciones Medicas) Fundacion Medicina, Donato Alvarez 3150, 1427 Buenos Aires, Argentina. TEL 51-3336. (Co-sponsor: Sociedad Argentina de Investigacion Clinica) Ed.Bd. adv.; bk.rev.; abstr.; bibl.; illus.; stat.; index; circ. 5,000. (also avail. in microfilm from UMI) **Indexed:** Abstr.Hyg., Biol.Abstr., Chem.Abstr., Curr.Cont., Dent.Ind., Excerp.Med., Helminthol.Abstr., Ind.Med., INIS Atomind., Nutr.Abstr., Protozool.Abstr., Sci.Cit.Ind., Trop.Dis.Bull.
—BLDSC shelfmark: 5532.390000.
  Description: Original papers in clinical research.

610   JA   ISSN 0025-7699
MEDICINA; journal of internal medicine. (Text in Japanese; title in English) 1964. m. 25230 Yen($194) Igaku-Shoin Ltd., 5-24-3 Hongo, Bunkyo-ku, Tokyo 113-91, Japan. TEL 03-3817-5717. adv.; charts; illus.; index; circ. 19,000. **Indexed:** Chem.Abstr.
—BLDSC shelfmark: 5532.400000.

610   CI   ISSN 0025-7729
MEDICINA. (Supplement avail.: Acta Facultatis Medicae Fluminensis) (Text in Croatian; summaries in English) 1964. q. 15000 din.($30) Hrvatski Lijecnicki Zbor, Podruznica Rijeka, Borisa Kidrica 40-II, 51000 Rijeka, Croatia. TEL 051-34-542. Ed. Mladen Persic. adv.; bk.rev.; circ. 2,000. **Indexed:** Abstr.Hyg., Biol.Abstr., Biol.Abstr., Chem.Abstr., Excerp.Med., Ref.Zh., Trop.Dis.Bull.
  Description: Publishes original scientific papers, professional papers on all aspects of medicine.

610   BL   ISSN 0076-6046
MEDICINA. (Summaries in English and Portuguese) 1961. q. Universidade de Sao Paulo, Faculdade de Medicina de Ribeirao Preto, Hospital das Clinicas, Campus Universitario, Av. Bandeirantes, 3900, 14049 Ribeirao Preto, Sao Paulo, Brazil. FAX 016-6331144. TELEX 016-583. Ed. Dr. Juan Stuardo Yazlle Rocha. adv.; bk.rev.; bibl.; charts; illus.; circ. 2,000. **Indexed:** Biol.Abstr., Curr.Adv.Genetics & Molec.Biol., Excerp.Med. (1992-) Ind.Med.

MEDICAL SCIENCES

610   SP   ISSN 0025-7753
CODEN: MCLBA2
MEDICINA CLINICA. (Summaries in English) 1943. w. (40/yr.). 6500 ptas.($90) Ediciones Doyma, S.A., Travesera de Gracia 17-21, 08021 Barcelona, Spain. TEL 200 07 11. FAX 209-11-36. TELEX 51694 INK-E. (Co-sponsors: Hospitales y Sociedades Medicas de Barcelona) Ed. C. Rozman Borstnar. adv.: page 180000 ptas.; trim 210 x 280; adv. contact: Roberto Garcia. bk.rev.; abstr.; charts; illus.; circ. 8,000. (reprint service avail. from UMI) **Indexed:** Biol.Abstr., Chem.Abstr., Curr.Cont., Dent.Ind., Dok.Arbeitsmed., Excerp.Med., Helminthol.Abstr., Ind.Med., Ind.Med.Esp., Ind.Vet., Nutr.Abstr., Protozool.Abstr.
—BLDSC shelfmark: 5532.600000.
Description: Contains works of original research and articles for the continuing education of practicing professionals in clinical medicine.

610   BL   ISSN 0103-2690
MEDICINA DA PONTIFICIA UNIVERSIDADE CATOLICA DO RIO GRANDE DO SUL. REVISTA. 1988. 4/yr. Cr.$15($19) Editora da P U C R S, Caixa Postal 12001, 90620 Porto Alegre RS, Brazil. Ed. Leonel Lerner. circ. 3,000.

610   YU   ISSN 0025-7796
MEDICINA DANAS; casopis za strucno usavrsavanje lekara. 1965. 6/yr. 30 din.($16.70) Institut za Strucno Usavrsavanje i Specijalizaciju Zdravstvenih Radnika Srbije, Nusiceva 25-I, Belgrade, Yugoslavia. Ed. Ljubisa Sablic. circ. 5,000.

610   BL
MEDICINA DE HOJE. 1975. m. Bloch Editores S.A., Rua do Russel 804, CEP 22210 Rio de Janeiro, RJ, Brazil. Ed. Walter Benevides. adv.; bk.rev.; charts; illus. **Indexed:** Biol.Abstr.

610   SP
MEDICINA INTEGRAL; medicina preventiva y asistencial en el medio rural. 1980. bi-w. 6050 ptas. Ediciones Idepsa, Travesera de Gracia, 17-21, 08021 Barcelona, Spain. FAX 563-23-93. Dir. J.M. Sanchez Tapias. adv.; circ. 20,000. **Indexed:** Ind.Med.Esp.

610   SP
MEDICINA INTENSIVA. bi-m. 2000 ptas.($20) (Sociedad Espanola de Medicina Intensiva y Unidades Coronarias) I.D.E.P.S.A., Principes de Verguia, 112-114, Madrid-2, Spain. Dir. A. Tomasa Torrallardona, M.D. **Indexed:** Ind.Med.Esp.
Description: Covers intensive care medicine.

616.02   IT
MEDICINA INTERNA. ANNALI ITALIANI. q. $80. Edizioni Luigi Pozzi s.r.l., Via Panama, 68, 00198 Rome, Italy. TEL 06-8553548. FAX 06-8554105.

610   IT   ISSN 0394-2627
MEDICINA MODERNA OGGI/MODERN MEDICINE TODAY. (Text in English, Italian) 1985. s-a. L.10000($6) Amorosino Editore Roma, Via Francesco Salata, 18, 00177 Rome, Italy. TEL 06-274040.

610   RM
MEDICINA MUNCII SI MEDICINA SOCIALA. vol.38, 1990. bi-m. Uniunea Societatilor de Stiinte Medicale din Romania, Str. Progresului 8-10, Bucharest, Sector 1, Rumania. TEL 13-89-73. (Subscr. to: Rompresfilatelia, P.O. Box 12-201, Bucharest, Rumania)

610   IT
MEDICINA NATURALE. bi-m. L.40000 (foreign L.110000)(effective 1992). Tecniche Nuove s.p.a., Via C. Menotti, 14, 20129 Milan, Italy. TEL 02-75701. FAX 02-7570205.

610   IT   ISSN 0394-9001
R5   CODEN: MDSCAD
MEDICINA NEI SECOLI: ARTE E SCIENZA; rivista storico medica. (Text in English or Italian) 1964; N.S. 1989. 3/yr. L.40000($40) Universita degli Studi di Roma, Dipartimento di Medicina Sperimentale, Medicina Nei Secoli, Viale Regina Elena, 324, 00161 Rome, Italy. TEL 4461974. FAX 4454820. bk.rev.; circ. 500. (also avail. in microfiche) **Indexed:** Biol.Abstr., Ind.Med.
Formerly: Medicina nei Secoli (ISSN 0025-7877); Supersedes: Pagine di Storia della Medicina (ISSN 0030-9400)

610   IT   ISSN 0392-4548
MEDICINA OGGI; periodico di attualita in medicina e chirurgia. (Supplement avail.) q. L.50000($85) (effective 1992). Casa Editrice Idelson, Via A. DeGasperi, 55, 80133 Naples, Italy. TEL 081-5524733. FAX 081-5518295. Ed. Lucio Zarrilli. bibl. (back issues avail.) **Indexed:** Excerp.Med.
Description: Includes a wide variety of topics in medicine, current trends in surgery, and extensive research.

610   IT   ISSN 0391-7231
MEDICINA OSPEDALIERA ROMANA. (Text in Italian; summaries in English and Italian) 1980. q. L.20000($13) (Societa di Medicina Ospedaliera) Edizioni Medicina Ospedaliera Romana, Via Marco Papio 47, 00175 Rome, Italy. Ed. Salvatore Pasquale. adv.; bk.rev.; circ. 500. (back issues avail.)

616.988   IT   ISSN 0580-9320
CODEN: MTCLD7
MEDICINA TERMALE E CLIMATOLOGIA. (Includes: Osservatorio Lariano di Climatologia Applicata. Bolletino and Societa Italiana per le Scienze Ambientali. Notiziario) (Summaries in English) 1969. q. L.1500. (Universita degli Studi di Milano, Centro di Ricerche de Bioclimatologia Medica) Edizioni Libreria Dello Studente di F. Lucisano, Viale Romagna 37, 20133 Milan, Italy. Ed. R. Gualtierotti. adv.; bk.rev.
Description: Covers climatological medicine.

610 540   US   ISSN 1054-2523
RS400   CODEN: MCREEB
▼**MEDICINAL CHEMISTRY RESEARCH;** an international journal for rapid communications on design and mechanisms of action of biologically active agents. 1991. bi-m. $75 to individuals in N. America ($85 outside N. America); $215 to institutions in N. America ($225 outside N. America). Birkhaeuser Boston, Inc., 675 Massachusetts Ave., Cambridge, MA 02139-3309. FAX 201-348-4505. (Dist. by: Springer-Verlag New York, Inc., Journal Fulfillment Services, Box 2485, Secaucus, NJ 07096-2491. TEL 201-348-4033) Ed. Alfred Burger.
Description: Includes papers on novel experimental achievements in the many facets of drug design, drug discovery, and the elucidation of mechanisms of action of biologically active compounds.
Refereed Serial

610   US
MEDICINAL RESEARCH SERIES. 1967. irreg., vol.12, 1989. price varies. Marcel Dekker, Inc., 270 Madison Ave., New York, NY 10016. TEL 212-696-9000. FAX 212-658-4540. TELEX 421419. Ed. Gary Grunewald. **Indexed:** Biol.Abstr.
Formerly: Medicinal Research: A Series of Monographs (ISSN 0076-6062)
Refereed Serial

610   US   ISSN 0025-7974
R11   CODEN: MEDIAV
MEDICINE (BALTIMORE); analytical reviews of general medicine, neurology, psychiatry, dermatology and pediatrics. 1922. bi-m. $55 to individuals; institutions $97. Williams & Wilkins, 428 E. Preston St., Baltimore, MD 21202. TEL 301-528-4000. FAX 301-528-4312. TELEX 87669. Ed. Dr. Victor A. McKusick. adv.; bibl.; charts; illus.; circ. 5,100. (also avail. in microform) **Indexed:** Biol.Abstr., Chem.Abstr., Curr.Adv.Ecol.Sci., Curr.Adv.Genetics & Molec.Biol., Dairy Sci.Abstr., Excerp.Med., Helminthol.Abstr., Ind.Med., Ind.Sci.Rev., INIS Atomind., Nutr.Abstr., Rev.Plant Path.
●Also available online. Vendor(s): BRS, BRS/Saunders Colleague, Mead Data Central.
—BLDSC shelfmark: 5534.000000.
Refereed Serial

610   UK   ISSN 0748-8009
RC970   CODEN: MEWAE4
MEDICINE AND WAR. 1965. q. £25($40) to individuals; institutions £65($95). (Medical Association for Prevention of War) Frank Cass & Co. Ltd., Gainsborough House, 11 Gainsborough Rd., London E11 1RS, England. TEL 081-530-4226. FAX 081-530-7795. Eds. Donald Holdstock, Nevin Hughes Jones. adv.; bk.rev.; stat.; index, cum.index (1965-1969); circ. 2,000. (tabloid format; also avail. in microfilm from UMI; back issues avail.) **Indexed:** Curr.Adv.Ecol.Sci., Curr.Cont., P.A.I.S., Peace Res.Abstr.
—BLDSC shelfmark: 5534.008500.
Former titles (until 1985): Medical Association for Prevention of War. Journal (ISSN 0265-2196); (until Autumn 1982): Medical Association for Prevention of War. Proceedings (ISSN 0025-701X)

610   UK   ISSN 0140-9158
MEDICINE DIGEST. (Editions for: Caribbean, Middle East, English-speaking Africa, French-speaking Africa, South East Asia.) (Editions in English and French) 1974. m. £25($36) (Anglophone Africa £15; Caribbean £10; Middle East £25). Medicine Digest Ltd., 11-12 Bouverie St., London EC4Y 8DP, England. TEL 071-353-0585. FAX 071-353-0614. Ed. Dr. Hugh de Glanville. adv.; bk.rev.; circ. 88,785. **Indexed:** Abstr.Hyg., Trop.Dis.Bull.

612.2   US   ISSN 1057-9354
▼**MEDICINE, EXERCISE, NUTRITION AND HEALTH.** 1992. bi-m. $95 (effective 1992). Blackwell Scientific Publications Inc., Three Cambridge Center, Ste. 208, Cambridge, MA 02142-1413. TEL 617-225-0401. FAX 617-225-0412. Ed. Dr. James Rippe.
Description: Discusses scientific and medical information on the relationship between nutrition, exercise and long-term health.

MEDICINE - HEALTH INFORMATION REVIEW. see *HOSPITALS*

610   UK   ISSN 0144-0438
MEDICINE INTERNATIONAL. MIDDLE EASTERN EDITION. 1981; N.S. 1984; N.S. 1988. m. £40. Medical Education (International) Ltd., Publishing House, 62 Stert St., Abingdon, Oxon, England. TEL 0235-555770. FAX 0235-554691. adv.; charts; illus.
Description: Covers all aspects of medicine.

610   UK   ISSN 0144-0411
MEDICINE INTERNATIONAL. QUARTERLY EDITION. 1981; N.S. 1984; N.S. 1988. q. £40. Medical Education (International) Ltd., Publishing House, 62 Stert St., Abingdon, Oxon OX14 3UQ, England. TEL 0235-555770. FAX 0235-554691. Ed.Bd. adv.; illus.
Description: Covers all aspects of medicine.

610   SA   ISSN 0260-2334
MEDICINE INTERNATIONAL. SOUTHERN AFRICAN EDITION. m. R.96.63 (effective 1992). Medicine Group (S A) (Pty) Ltd., P.O. Box 1930, Randburg 2125, South Africa. TEL 011-789-4010. FAX 011-789-4028. adv.; circ. 5,500.
Formerly (until 1981): Medicine S.A.

610   UK   ISSN 0144-0403
MEDICINE INTERNATIONAL. U K EDITION. 1981; N.S. 1984; N.S. 1988. m. £66. Medical Education (International) Ltd., Publishing House, 62 Stert St., Abingdon OXON 3UQ, England. TEL 0235-555770. FAX 0235-554691. Ed. Margaret Stearn. adv.; charts; illus.; stat.; cum.index; circ. 250,000. **Indexed:** Curr.Adv.Ecol.Sci., Helminthol.Abstr.
—BLDSC shelfmark: 5534.066000.
Description: Covers all aspects of medicine.

610   CN   ISSN 0225-3895
MEDICINE NORTH AMERICA. 1980. m. Can.$48($52) C. M. E. Publishing Ltd., 640 St. Paul St. W., Suite 302, Montreal, Que. H3C 1L9, Canada. TEL 514-397-9393. Ed. Dr. Ian Hart. adv.; charts; illus.; index, cum.index; circ. 34,000. (back issues avail.) **Indexed:** FAMLI.
—BLDSC shelfmark: 5534.091000.

610   DK   ISSN 0461-6308
MEDICINSK AARBOG. 1957. a. price varies. Munksgaard International Publishers Ltd., Journals Division, 35 Noerre Soegade, P.O. Box 2148, DK-1016 Copenhagen K, Denmark. TEL 33-127030. FAX 33-129387. TELEX 19431-MUNKS-DK. illus.

M

MEDICAL SCIENCES

610   XN   ISSN 0065-1214
CODEN: GZMSAH
MEDICINSKA MISLA/ACTA FACULTATIS MEDICINAE SKOPIENSIS; godisen zbornik na medicinskiot fakultet vo Skopje. (Text in Macedonian and-or English) 1954. s-a. 500 din.($30) to institutions; students 50 din. Univerzitet vo Skoplje, Medicinski Fakultet, Central Library, Vodnjanska bb, 91000 Skopje, Macedonia. Ed. Avram Sadikario. **Indexed:** Biol.Abstr., Ind.Med.
—BLDSC shelfmark: 4197.700000.

610   YU   ISSN 0025-8091
MEDICINSKI GLASNIK. vol.20, 1966. m. 50 din.($5.75) Savez Lekarskih Drustava SFR Jugoslavije, Zeleni Venac 1-I, Belgrade, Yugoslavia. Ed. Lazar Stanojevic. **Indexed:** Biol.Abstr., C.I.S. Abstr., Dent.Ind., Ind.Med.

610   YU   ISSN 0369-1527
MEDICINSKI PODMLADAK. (Text in Serbo-Croatian; summaries in English) 1948. q. 1000 din.($26) Medicinski Podmladak, Dr. Subotica 8, 11000 Belgrade, Yugoslavia. Ed. Snezana D. Andrejevic. bk.rev.; circ. 1,000. (back issues avail.)
—BLDSC shelfmark: 5534.167000.

610   YU   ISSN 0025-8105
CODEN: MEPEAB
MEDICINSKI PREGLED. (Text in Serbian; abstracts in English) 1948. bi-m. $60. Drustvo Lekara Vojvodine - Serbian Medical Society of Vojvodina, Vase Stajica 9, Novi Sad, Vojvodina, Yugoslavia. TEL 021-28767. Ed. Vojislav Nikolic. adv.; bk.rev.; circ. 1,500. **Indexed:** Biol.Abstr., Chem.Abstr., Dent.Ind., Ind.Med., Nutr.Abstr.
—BLDSC shelfmark: 0106.400000.
Description: Covers clinical medicine of all specialities.

610   XV   ISSN 0025-8121
CODEN: MRAZAM
MEDICINSKI RAZGLEDI. (Text in Slovenian; summaries and contents page in English) 1961. q. $6. Univerza v Ljubljani, Medicinska Fakulteta, Korytkova 2, 61105 Ljubljana, Slovenia. TEL 442-356. (Co-sponsor: Raziskovalna Skupnost Slovenije) Ed. Igor Cabrian. adv.; bk.rev.; index; circ. 3,200. **Indexed:** Biol.Abstr., Chem.Abstr., Nutr.Abstr.
Description: Medical practice, research and review articles.

610   PO   ISSN 0461-6375
MEDICO; semanario de assuntos medicos e paramedicos. (Text in Portuguese; summaries in English and French) 1950. w. $230. Sociedade de Publicacoes e Iniciativas Medicas, Lda., Rua do Heroismo, 354-1o, P-4300 Porto, Portugal. adv.; bk.rev.; circ. 5,250. (also avail. in talking book; back issues avail.) **Indexed:** Biol.Abstr., Chem.Abstr.
—BLDSC shelfmark: 5534.175000.

610   IT   ISSN 0025-8148
MEDICO D'ITALIA. 1964. d. free. Federazione Nazionale degli Ordini dei Medici, Piazza Cola di Rienzo 80-A, 00192 Rome, Italy. TEL 06-6874034. FAX 06-6876739. Ed. Dr. Andrea Sertionti. adv.; bk.rev.; charts; illus.; stat.; circ. 200,000. (tabloid format)

610   IT
MEDICO E PAZIENTE. 1975. 2/m. (18/yr.) Edifarm S.p.A., Viale Sabotino 19-2, 20135 Milan, Italy. adv.; circ. 110,000.

616.07   US   ISSN 0278-9779
MEDICO INTERAMERICANO. 1981. m. $25. Interamerican College of Physicians and Surgeons, 299 Madison Ave., New York, NY 10017-6218. TEL 212-697-3175. FAX 212-986-2252. Ed. Charles H. Messina. adv.; circ. 32,500.

MEDICO-LEGAL ADVISOR. see *LAW — Civil Law*

MEDICO-LEGAL SOCIETY OF VICTORIA. PROCEEDINGS. see *LAW — Civil Law*

610   SP   ISSN 1130-6416
MEDICO PRACTICO. m. 4400 ptas.($72) Editorial Garsi, S.A., Londres, 17, 28028 Madrid, Spain. TEL 256-08-00. FAX 361-10-07. Dir. Dr. Portugal Alvarez. circ. 35,000.

610   SP
EL MEDICO, PROFESION Y HUMANIDADES. w. Saned, Apolonio Morales 6, 28036 Madrid, Spain. TEL 91-4035014. Dir. Fernando Gimenez. circ. 40,000.

MEDICOLEGAL LIBRARY. see *LAW — International Law*

610   KE
MEDICOM; African Journal of hospital medicine. 1979. bi-m. EAs.200($12.50) Update Publishers Ltd., Box 73824, Nairobi, Kenya. Ed. Dr. Peter A. Odhiambo. adv.; bk.rev.; circ. 1,000. (back issues avail.)

610   AU
MEDICUM. 1989. m. S.500. Manstein Zeitschriften Verlag Ges.m.b.H., Wiedner Hauptstr. 61, 1040 Vienna, Austria. FAX 0222-5053620-34. Ed. H.J. Manstein. circ. 27,000.

MEDIGRAM. see *ADVERTISING AND PUBLIC RELATIONS*

610 615.329 614.8   GW   ISSN 0171-3876
MEDIKAMENT & MEINUNG; Zeitschrift fuer Arzneimittel- und Gesundheitswesen. 1978. m. free. Bundesverband der Pharmazeutischen Industrie, Karlstr. 21, 6000 Frankfurt a.M. 1, Germany. FAX 069-237813. Ed. Thomas Postina. bk.rev.; circ. 55,000. (back issues avail.)

MEDINDEX. see *INSTRUMENTS*

MEDIPHARM. see *PHARMACY AND PHARMACOLOGY*

610   NR   ISSN 0794-3733
CODEN: MEMJEF
MEDIPHARM MEDICAL JOURNAL. (Text in English) q. $50 to individuals; institutions $60. Literamed Nigeria Ltd., Plot 45, Alausa, Oregun Village, P.M.B. 21068, Ikeja, Lagos, Nigeria. Ed. Oladapo A. Ashiru. adv.; circ. 2,000.

610   NE   ISSN 0025-8245
MEDISCH CONTACT. 1945. w. membership. (Koninklijke Nederlandsche Maatschappij tot Bevordering der Geneeskunst) Wegener Tijl Tijdschriften Groep B.V., Postbus 9943, 1006 AP Amsterdam, Netherlands. TEL 020-5182828. FAX 020-5182843. Ed.Bd. adv.; illus.; circ. 25,000. **Indexed:** Excerp.Med., Key to Econ.Sci.
—BLDSC shelfmark: 5534.400000.

610   UK   ISSN 0261-7099
MEDISCOPE; Manchester Medical School gazette. 1898. 3/yr. £5 to individuals; libraries £9. University of Manchester, Medical School, Manchester M13 9PT, England. TEL 061-275 5532. Ed. J. Cooke. adv.; bk.rev.; charts; illus.; circ. 2,000. **Indexed:** Ind.Med.
—BLDSC shelfmark: 5534.510000.
Formerly: Manchester Medical Gazette (ISSN 0025-2018)

610   FR
MEDISCOPE. m. 13 rue Beethoven, 75016 Paris, France. Ed. Guy Job. adv.; circ. 1,500. **Indexed:** Chem.Abstr.

610   FR   ISSN 0302-9263
CODEN: MDTMBF
MEDITERRANEE MEDICALE. 1955. 3/m. 170 F. includes 30 additional numbers yearly. (Faculte de Medecine de Marseille) Sud-Regie, 58 Avenue de la Marne, 92600 Asnieres, France. Dir. N. Ambrosini. **Indexed:** Abstr.Hyg., Biol.Abstr., C.I.S. Abstr., Excerp.Med., Trop.Dis.Bull.
—BLDSC shelfmark: 5534.760000.
Formerly: Corse Mediterranee Medicale (ISSN 0045-8686)

610   RU   ISSN 0025-8318
MEDITSINSKAYA GAZETA. 1938. s-w. $7.20. Ministerstvo Meditsinskoi i Microbiologicheskoi Promyshlennosti, c/o Triokhprudnyi pereulok, 11-13, 103301 Moscow, Russia. Ed. N.I. Sinko. index; circ. 1,200,000. (also avail. in microform from MIM) **Indexed:** Biol.Abstr., Curr.Dig.Sov.Press.

610   RU   ISSN 0025-8075
CODEN: MEDTBV
MEDITSINSKAYA TEKHNIKA/MEDICAL ENGINEERING. 1967. bi-m. 16.20 Rub.($7.20) (Vsesoyuznoe Nauchnoe Mediko-Tekhnicheskoe Obshchestvo) Izdatel'stvo Meditsina, Petroverigskii pereulok 6-8, 101838 Moscow, Russia. (Dist. by: Mezhdunarodnaya Kniga, Moscow, G-200, Russia) (Co-sponsor: Ministerstvo Zdravookhraneniya S.S.S.R.) Ed. V.A. Viktorov. adv.; bk.rev.; circ. 5,000. **Indexed:** Biol.Abstr., Chem.Abstr., Dent.Ind., Ind.Med., INIS Atomind., Sci.Abstr.
—BLDSC shelfmark: 0106.100000.
Description: Deals with theoretical and practical problems of the development of medical engineering and its application in public health practice.

610   UZ   ISSN 0025-830X
MEDITSINSKII ZHURNAL UZBEKISTANA. 1948. m. $9.20. Izdatel'stvo Meditsina, Otdelenie v Uzbekistane, Ul. Navoi, 30, Tashkent, Uzbekistan. Ed. K.C. Zaupoe. **Indexed:** Biol.Abstr., Chem.Abstr., Nutr.Abstr.
—BLDSC shelfmark: 0106.500000.

610   GW   ISSN 0323-5386
MEDIZIN AKTUELL; das Aerztemagazin. 1975. m. DM.84. Verlag Gesundheit GmbH, Neue Grunstr. 18, 1020 Berlin, Germany. TEL 030-2700516. FAX 030-2754983. TELEX 114488. Ed. H. Grosse-Nordhaus. circ. 20,000. **Indexed:** INIS Atomind.
—BLDSC shelfmark: 5534.798000.

MEDIZIN IN RECHT UND ETHIK. see *LAW — Civil Law*

610   AU
MEDIZIN POPULAER. bi-m. free. Oesterreichische Aerztekammer, Pressestelle und Verlag, Weihburggasse 10-12, A-1010 Vienna, Austria. TEL 512-44-86. FAX 513-19-25-24. adv.

610   GW   ISSN 0025-8431
R131.A1
MEDIZINHISTORISCHES JOURNAL. (Text in English, French and German) 1966. 4/yr. DM.127. (Akademie der Wissenschaften und der Literatur, Mainz, Kommission fuer Geschichte der Medizin und der Naturwissenschaften) Gustav Fischer Verlag, Wollgrasweg 49, Postfach 720143, 7000 Stuttgart 70, Germany. TEL 0711-458030. FAX 0711-4580334. TELEX 7111488-FIBUCH. (U.S. address: Gustav Fischer New York Inc., 220 East 23rd St., Suite 909, New York, NY 10010) Ed. G. Mann. adv.; bk.rev.; index; circ. 1,000. **Indexed:** Biol.Abstr., Chem.Abstr.

610   GW   ISSN 0070-721X
MEDIZINISCHE AKADEMIE "CARL GUSTAV CARUS" DRESDEN. SCHRIFTEN. 1959. irreg., vol.20, 1984. price varies. Medizinische Akademie "Carl Gustav Carus", Zentralbibliothek, Fiedlerstr. 27, 8019 Dresden, Germany. circ. 500.

610   US   ISSN 0342-4103
MEDIZINISCHE INFORMATIK UND STATISTIK. (Text in German) 1976. irreg. price varies. Springer-Verlag, 175 Fifth Ave., New York, NY 10010. TEL 212-460-1500. (Also Berlin, Heidelberg, Tokyo and Vienna) Ed.Bd. (reprint service avail. from ISI)

610   GW   ISSN 0723-5003
MEDIZINISCHE KLINIK. 1906. m. DM.180 (foreign DM.198). (Deutsche Gesellschaft fuer Innere Medizin) Urban und Vogel, Lindwurmstr. 95, Postfach 152209, 8000 Munich 15, Germany. TEL 089-53292-0. FAX 089-53292-100. circ. 10,500 (controlled). **Indexed:** Biol.Abstr., Biotech.Abstr., C.I.S. Abstr., Chem.Abstr., Curr.Cont., Excerp.Med., Helminthol.Abstr., Ind.Med, Ind.Sci.Rev., INIS Atomind., Nutr.Abstr.
—BLDSC shelfmark: 5535.080000.

610   US   ISSN 0076-6151
MEDIZINISCHE LAENDERKUNDE. GEOMEDICAL MONOGRAPH SERIES. Short title: Geomedical Monograph Series. (Text in German) 1967. irreg. price varies. Springer-Verlag, 175 Fifth Ave., New York, NY 10010. TEL 212-460-1500. (Also Berlin, Heidelberg, Vienna) (reprint service avail. from ISI)
—BLDSC shelfmark: 4147.270000.

MEDICAL SCIENCES

610 GW ISSN 0342-9601
CODEN: MMPHDB
MEDIZINISCHE MONATSSCHRIFT FUER PHARMAZEUTEN.
1947. m. DM.132.60 (DM.61.20 to students and subscribers to Deutsche Apotheker Zeitung and Oesterreichische Apotheker Zeitung). Deutscher Apotheker Verlag, Postfach 101061, 7000 Stuttgart 10, Germany. TEL 0711-2582-0. FAX 0711-2582290. TELEX 723636-DAZ-D. (Co-publisher: Wissenschaftliche Verlagsgesellschaft mbH) Eds. W. Wessinger, Susanne Heinzl. adv.; bk.rev.; illus.; tr.lit.; circ. 15,000. **Indexed:** Biol.Abstr., Biotech.Abstr., Chem.Abstr., Excerp.Med., Ind.Med.
—BLDSC shelfmark: 5535.108000.
Formerly: Medizinische Monatsschrift (ISSN 0025-8474)

610 GW ISSN 0025-8490
DER MEDIZINISCHE SACHVERSTAENDIGE. 1904. bi-m. DM.193.80 (foreign DM.217.20). A.W. Gentner Verlag, Forststr. 131, Postfach 101742, 7000 Stuttgart 10, Germany. TEL 0711-63672-0. FAX 0711-6367211. Ed. H.H. Rauschelbach. adv.; bk.rev.; abstr.; charts; illus.; index; circ. 1,300. **Indexed:** C.I.S. Abstr., Chem.Abstr.

610 GW ISSN 0025-8512
CODEN: MEWEAC
DIE MEDIZINISCHE WELT. 1950. m. DM.268.40($190) F.K. Schattauer Verlagsgesellschaft mbH, Lenzhalde 3, Postfach 104545, 7000 Stuttgart 10, Germany. TEL 0711-22987-0. FAX 0711-22987-50. adv.; bk.rev.; bibl.; charts; illus.; index; circ. 28,000. **Indexed:** Biol.Abstr., Biotech.Abstr., C.I.S. Abstr., Chem.Abstr., Curr.Adv.Ecol.Sci., Curr.Cont., Dent.Ind., Excerp.Med., Helminthol.Abstr., Ind.Med., INIS Atomind., Nutr.Abstr.
—BLDSC shelfmark: 5535.200000.

610 GW ISSN 0344-9416
CODEN: MDZNDG
MEDIZINTECHNIK. 1881. bi-m. DM.117 (foreign DM.131.20). A.W. Gentner Verlag, Forstr. 131, Postfach 101742, 7000 Stuttgart 10, Germany. TEL 0711-63672-0. FAX 0711-6367211. Ed. R.D. Boeckmann. adv.; bk.rev.; record rev.; charts; illus.; pat.; index; circ. 3,200. **Indexed:** Chem.Abstr., Excerp.Med., INIS Atomind.
Formerly: Medizinische Technik (ISSN 0025-8504)

610 US
MEDPRO MONTH. m. Medical Data Institute, 335 Centennial Way, Box 3804, Tustin, CA 92861. TEL 714-573-0344. FAX 714-573-0346. Ed. Cornelia Van Kleef.

MEDYCYNA DOSWIADCZALNA I MIKROBIOLOGIA. see BIOLOGY — Microbiology

610 PL ISSN 0465-5893
CODEN: MEPAAX
MEDYCYNA PRACY. (Text in Polish; summaries in English) 1950. bi-m. $90. Instytut Medycyny Prace im. Jerzego Nofera - Nofer's Institute of Occupational Medicine, Ul. Teresy 8, P.O. Box 199w, 90-950 Lodz, Poland. TEL 31-47-18. (Dist. by: Ars Polona - Ruch, Krakowskie Przedmiescie 7, 00-068 Warsaw, Poland) Ed. Janusz Indulski. index. **Indexed:** Abstr.Hyg., Biol.Abstr., C.I.S. Abstr., Chem.Abstr., Dent.Ind., Excerp.Med., Fuel & Energy Abstr., Ind.Med., INIS Atomind., Trop.Dis.Bull.
—BLDSC shelfmark: 5536.020000.
Description: Explores occupational hygiene, pathologies, epidemiology, physiology and psychology of health care organizations.

610 PL ISSN 0025-8636
MEDYCYNA WIEJSKA/RURAL MEDICINE. (Text in English, Polish, and Russian) 1953. q. $60. (Instytut Medycyny Wsi) Panstwowy Zaklad Wydawnictw Lekarskich, Dluga 38-40, 00-238 Warsaw, Poland. (Dist. by: Ars Polona - Ruch, Krakowskie Przedmiescie 7, 00-068 Warsaw, Poland) Ed. Maciej Latalski. index; circ. 2,000. **Indexed:** Agri.Eng.Abstr., C.I.S. Abstr.

610 PL ISSN 0867-3055
MEDYK/PHYSICIAN. 1953. s-m. 60000 Zl. Medyk Ltd., Foksal 11, Warsaw, Poland. TEL 48-22-263250. (Dist. by: Centrala Kolportazu Prasy i Wydawnictw, ul. Towarowa 28, 00-958 Warsaw, Poland) Ed. Andrzej Doroba. adv.; bk.rev.; circ. 25,000.
Formerly: Nowy Medyk (ISSN 0137-7175)

610 US
MEIJI COLLEGE OF ORIENTAL MEDICINE. NEWSLETTER.
q. Meiji College of Oriental Medicine, 1426 Fillmore St., Ste. 301, San Francisco, CA 94115.
TEL 415-771-1019. FAX 415-771-1036.

MEIKAI UNIVERSITY SCHOOL OF DENTISTRY. JOURNAL.
see MEDICAL SCIENCES — Dentistry

MEMBRANE PROTEINS. see BIOLOGY — Biological Chemistry

616.988 NE ISSN 0025-9063
MEMISA NIEUWS; medische editie. 1934. bi-m. free to qualified personnel. Memisa, Eendrachtsweg 48, 3012 LD Rotterdam, Netherlands.
FAX 010-4047319. TELEX 24541 MEMIS NL. bk.rev.; abstr.; charts; illus.; index; circ. 5,000 (controlled). (tabloid format)
Description: Covers tropical medicine.

610 FR ISSN 0301-6366
MENSUEL DU MEDECIN ACUPUNCTEUR. 1973. m. 400 F. Nguyen Van Nghi, Ed. & Pub., 27 bd. d'Athenes, 13001 Marseille, France. adv.; bibl.; illus.
—BLDSC shelfmark: 7904.201000.

610 US ISSN 0076-6526
RC55
MERCK MANUAL: A HANDBOOK OF DIAGNOSIS AND THERAPY. 1899. irreg., 15th ed., 1987. $21.50. Merck and Co., Inc., Attn: Michele Stotz, FTA-230, Box 2000, Rahway, NJ 07065.
TEL 201-855-4558. Ed. Dr. Robert Berkow.

610 US
MERGERS & ACQUISITIONS HEALTHCARE SOURCEBOOK; a comprehensive review of the deals, the companies, and the people reshaping the healthcare industry today. (Includes annual deal directory) 1987. a. $495. M L R Publishing Company (Subsidiary of: M L R Enterprises, Inc.), 229 S. 18th St., Philadelphia, PA 19103. TEL 215-790-7000.
FAX 215-790-7005. Ed. Robert Smith.
Description: Analyzes merger and acquisition activity in the healthcare industry.

610 299.93 GW ISSN 0935-798X
DER MERKURSTAB. 1950. bi-m. DM.90. Gesellschaft Anthroposophischer Aerzte in Deutschland, Trossingerstr. 53, Postfach 750221, 7000 Stuttgart 75, Germany. TEL 0711-471501. FAX 0711-4780186. bk.rev.

610 US ISSN 0885-7490
RC394.M48 CODEN: MBDIEE
METABOLIC BRAIN DISEASE. 1986. q. $225 (foreign $265)(effective 1992). Plenum Publishing Corp., 233 Spring St., New York, NY 10013-1578.
TEL 212-620-8000. FAX 212-463-0742. TELEX 23-421139. Ed. David W. McCandless. adv.; bk.rev.; charts; illus. (also avail. in microfilm from JSC; back issues avail.) **Indexed:** Curr.Adv.Biochem., Curr.Adv.Cell & Devel.Biol., Curr.Cont.
—BLDSC shelfmark: 5683.266500.
Refereed Serial

616.07 SZ ISSN 0076-681X
RB125 CODEN: MAEPBU
METHODS AND ACHIEVEMENTS IN EXPERIMENTAL PATHOLOGY. (Text in English) 1965. irreg. price varies. S. Karger AG, Allschwilerstr. 10, P.O. Box, CH-4009 Basel, Switzerland. TEL 061-3061111. FAX 061-3061234. TELEX CH 962652. Ed. G. Jasmin. (reprint service avail. from ISI) **Indexed:** Biol.Abstr., Chem.Abstr., Curr.Cont., Ind.Med.
—BLDSC shelfmark: 5746.600000.

610 029 GW ISSN 0026-1270
R51 CODEN: MIMCAI
METHODS OF INFORMATION IN MEDICINE; journal of methodology in medical research, information and documentation. 1962. q. DM.216($142) to individuals; institutions DM.292($190). F.K. Schattauer Verlagsgesellschaft mbH, Lenzhalde 3, Postfach 104545, 7000 Stuttgart 10, Germany. TEL 0711-22987-0. FAX 0711-22987-50. Ed. J.H. van Bemmel. adv.; bibl.; charts; illus.
Indexed: Abstr.Health Care Manage.Stud., Biol.Abstr., Curr.Cont., Cyb.Abstr., Excerp.Med., Ind.Med., Ind.Sci.Rev., Sci.Abstr., Telegen.
—BLDSC shelfmark: 5748.100000.
Description: Covers methodology of medical research, documentation, information science and medical informatics.

610 US ISSN 0026-2293
R15
MICHIGAN MEDICINE. 1902. m. $40. Michigan State Medical Society, 120 W. Saginaw, East Lansing, MI 48823. TEL 517-337-1351. FAX 517-337-2490. Ed. Betty Jeanne McNerney. adv.; illus.; index; circ. 11,000. (also avail. in microfilm from UMI; reprint service avail. from UMI) **Indexed:** C.I.S. Abstr., CINAHL, Ind.Med., Med. Care Rev., Mich.Mag.Ind.
—BLDSC shelfmark: 5755.400000.
Formerly (until 1964): Michigan State Medical Society. Journal (ISSN 0098-7522); Incorporates: Michigan State Medical Society. Transactions.
Description: Dedicated to providing information for Michigan physicians about actions of the Michigan State Medical Society. Covers contemporary issues, with special emphasis on socio-economics legislation and news about medicine.

MICROBIOS; a prestige international biomedical research journal of chemical and general microbiology. see BIOLOGY — Microbiology

026 US
MIDDLE ATLANTIC PERSPECTIVE. 1983. bi-m. free to qualified personnel. Middle Atlantic Regional Medical Library Program, New York Academy of Medicine, 2 E. 103rd St., New York, NY 10029.
TEL 212-876-8763. charts; stat.; circ. 2,100 (controlled).
Supersedes in part (in 1991): Greater Northeastern Regional Medical Library Program Newsletter; **Formerly (until 1983):** New York and New Jersey Regional Medical Library News.
Description: News items, information, and announcements pertaining to the National Library of Medicine Regional Library Program, which serves New York, New Jersey, Pennsylvania and Delaware.

610 JA ISSN 0026-3532
CODEN: MMJJAI
MIE MEDICAL JOURNAL. (Text in European languages) 1950. 3/yr. free. Mie Daigaku, Igakubu - Mie University, School of Medicine, 2-174 Edobashi, Tsu-shi, Mie-ken 514, Japan. Ed.Bd. charts; illus.; stat.; index; circ. 850. **Indexed:** Abstr.Hyg., Biol.Abstr., Chem.Abstr., Dent.Abstr., Dent.Ind., Excerp.Med., Ind.Med., Nutr.Abstr., Rev.Appl.Entomol., Trop.Dis.Bull.
—BLDSC shelfmark: 5761.450000.
Description: Multidisciplinary papers on medicine.

610 IS ISSN 0026-363X
MIKHTAV LEHAVER. 1940. m. Israel Medical Association, 39 Shaul Hamelech Blvd., Tel Aviv, Israel. FAX 03-6956103. Ed. Dr. M. Zangen. adv.; charts; illus.
Description: Contains organization news.

410 GW
MIKROBIELLE UMWELT UND ANTIMIKROBIELLE MASSNAHMEN; Schriftenreihe fuer Theorie und Praxis in Medizin, Pharmazie und Wirtschaft. 1977. irreg. price varies. Johann Ambrosius Barth Verlag, Leipzig - Heidelberg, Salomonstr. 18b, 7010 Leipzig, Germany. TEL 70131. Ed.Bd.

MIKROBIOLOGI-NYT. see VETERINARY SCIENCE

616.98 US ISSN 0026-4075
RD1 CODEN: MMEDA9
MILITARY MEDICINE. 1891. m. $35 (foreign $40). Association of Military Surgeons of the U S, 9320 Old Georgetown Rd., Bethesda, MD 20814.
TEL 301-897-8800. Ed. Dr. John C. Duffy. adv.; bk.rev.; bibl.; charts; illus.; stat.; index, cum.index; circ. 16,755. (also avail. in microfilm; back issues avail.; reprint service avail. from UMI) **Indexed:** Abstr.Health Care Manage.Stud., Abstr.Hyg., Biol.Abstr., C.I.S. Abstr., Chem.Abstr., CINAHL, Curr.Cont., Dent.Ind., Excerp.Med., Helminthol.Abstr., Hosp.Lit.Ind., Ind.Med., Ind.Vet., Nutr.Abstr., Protozool.Abstr., Psychol.Abstr., Small Anim.Abstr., Trop.Dis.Bull., Vet.Bull.
—BLDSC shelfmark: 5768.150000.
Description: Supports knowledge concerning medical activities of the Federal Medical Services, including developments in medical technology, education, management and research.

610 UK
MIMS. 1959. m. £53. Haymarket Medical Publication Ltd., 30 Lancaster Gate, London W2 3LP, England. (Subscr. to: Tower Publishing, 3-4 Hardwick St, London EC1R 4RY) Ed. Colin Duncan. adv.; circ. 58,412.

MEDICAL SCIENCES

610 UK
MIMS IRELAND. 1960. m. £48. Medical Publications Ltd., 30 Lancaster Gate, London W2 3LP, England. (Subscr. address: 12-14 Ansdell St., London W8 5TR, England) Ed. Dr. John F. O'Connell. adv.; circ. 3,460.

610 UK
MIMS MAGAZINE. 1974. fortn. £33. Haymarket Medical Publications, Ltd, 30 Lancaster Gate, London W2 3LP, England. (Tower Publishing, 3-4 Hardwick St, London, EC1R 4RY) Ed. Peter Chambers. adv.; charts; illus.; circ. 41,990. (back issues avail.)
●Also available online. Vendor(s): Data-Star.

MIND: THE MEETINGS INDEX. see *TECHNOLOGY: COMPREHENSIVE WORKS*

MINDENER KLINIKSCHRIFTEN. see *MEDICAL SCIENCES — Nurses And Nursing*

612.39 574.133 SZ ISSN 0378-0392
CODEN: MELMDI
MINERAL AND ELECTROLYTE METABOLISM. (Text in English) 1978. bi-m. 558 Fr.($372) per vol. S. Karger AG, Allschwilerstr. 10, P.O. Box, CH-4009 Basel, Switzerland. TEL 061-3061111. FAX 061-3061234. TELEX CH 962652. Ed. S.G. Massry. adv.; illus.; index; circ. 850. (also avail. in microfilm from RPI; back issues avail.) **Indexed:** Chem.Abstr., Curr.Adv.Cell & Devel.Biol., Curr.Adv.Ecol.Sci., Curr.Cont., Dent.Ind., Excerp.Med., Ind.Med.
—BLDSC shelfmark: 5776.710000.

616.98 IT ISSN 0026-4709
MINERVA AEROSPAZIALE. 1969. s-a. L.50000($60) or included in subscr. to: Minerva Medica. Edizioni Minerva Medica, Corso Bramante 83-85, 10126 Turin, Italy. Ed. T. Lomonaco. adv.; bk.rev.; bibl.; charts; illus.; index; circ. 2,000.
Description: Covers aerospace medicine.

610 IT ISSN 0026-4806
R61 CODEN: MIMEAO
MINERVA MEDICA. (In 10 parts) (Text in Italian; summaries in English, Italian) 1909. m. L.70000($100) Edizioni Minerva Medica, Corso Bramante 83-85, 10126 Turin, Italy. TEL 011-678282. Ed. Alberto Oliaro. bibl.; illus.; circ. 8,000. **Indexed:** Biol.Abstr., Biotech.Abstr., C.I.S. Abstr., Chem.Abstr., Curr.Adv.Cancer Res., Curr.Adv.Ecol.Sci., Curr.Cont., Dent.Ind., Dok.Arbeitsmed., Excerp.Med., Helminthol.Abstr., Ind.Med., Nutr.Abstr.
—BLDSC shelfmark: 5794.250000.

610 IT
MINERVA MEDICOPRATICA. m. $60. Edizioni Minerva Medica, Corso Bramante 83-85, 10126 Turin, Italy.

610 IT
MINERVA MESOTERAPEUTICA. s-a. L.50000($60) Edizioni Minerva Medica, Corso Bramante 83, 10126 Turin, Italy. TEL 011-67 82 82.

378 US ISSN 0085-3488
R745
MINORITY STUDENT OPPORTUNITIES IN UNITED STATES MEDICAL SCHOOLS. 1970. biennial. $10. Association of American Medical Colleges, One Dupont Circle, N.W., Washington, DC 20036. TEL 202-828-4572. FAX 202-785-5027. (reprint service avail. from UMI)

MIRKACHTEN. see *PHARMACY AND PHARMACOLOGY*

MISSISSIPPI ACADEMY OF SCIENCE. JOURNAL. see *SCIENCES: COMPREHENSIVE WORKS*

610 US ISSN 0026-6396
CODEN: MSMJB8
MISSISSIPPI STATE MEDICAL ASSOCIATION. JOURNAL. 1960. m. $35 (foreign $45). Mississippi State Medical Association, 735 Riverside Dr., Box 5229, Jackson, MS 39296-5229. TEL 601-354-5433. Ed. Myron W. Lockey. adv.; bk.rev.; charts; illus.; stat.; tr.lit.; index; circ. 2,800. (also avail. in microform from UMI; reprint service avail. from UMI) **Indexed:** Ind.Med., INIS Atomind.
—BLDSC shelfmark: 4828.210000.

610 US ISSN 0026-6620
MISSOURI MEDICINE. 1904. m. $20 to non-members. Missouri State Medical Association, Box 1028, 113 Madison St., Jefferson City, MO 65102. TEL 314-636-5151. FAX 314-636-8552. Ed. DR. J. Regan Thomas. adv.; bk.rev.; charts; illus.; index; circ. 7,000. (also avail. in microfilm) **Indexed:** Biol.Abstr., Chem.Abstr., Curr.Cont., Dent.Ind., Excerp.Med., Helminthol.Abstr., Ind.Med.
Description: Prints scientific articles, editorials on medical issues. Includes medical school news, classifieds, and information on new members, deaths, continuing medical education courses, and practice management.

610 360 GW
MITEINANDER. 1977. 3/yr. Deutsches Aussaetzigen Hilfswerk e.V., Postfach 110462, 8700 Wuerzburg 11, Germany. TEL 0931-50784. FAX 0931-51358. TELEX 68583-DAHW-D. Ed. Peter Schweiger. bk.rev.; circ. 80,000. (back issues avail.)
Description: Leprosy aid and health problems in developing countries.

MITOCHONDRIA. see *BIOLOGY — Cytology And Histology*

610 US ISSN 0888-6792
MODEL FOR THE PREPARATION OF A GUIDEBOOK ON MEDICAL DISCIPLINE. triennial. $8. Federation of State Medical Boards, 6000 Western Pl., Ste. 707, Fort Worth, TX 76107-4618. TEL 817-735-8445. FAX 817-738-6629. Ed. Dale G. Breaden.

610 US ISSN 0026-8070
R11
MODERN MEDICINE. 1932. m. $35. Avanstar Communications, Inc., 7500 Old Oak Blvd., Cleveland, OH 44130. TEL 216-826-2839. FAX 216-891-2726. (Subscr. to: 1 E. First St., Duluth, MN 55802) Ed. Martin M. Stevenson. adv.; abstr.; illus.; circ. 119,690. **Indexed:** Chem.Abstr., Curr.Lit.Fam.Plan., Med. Care Rev., Nutr.Abstr.
—BLDSC shelfmark: 5889.810000.
Incorporates: Quarterly Journal of Geriatrics.
Description: Professional journal on diagnosis and therapy, clinical techniques, highlights from medical meetings.
Refereed Serial

610 AT ISSN 1030-3782
MODERN MEDICINE OF AUSTRALIA. 1957. m. Aus.$90. Modern Medicine of Australia Pty. Ltd., 3-5 Grosvenor St., Neutral Bay, N.S.W. 2089, Australia. TEL 61-2-908-2155. FAX 61-2-908-1961. Ed. Dr. John Ellard. adv.; bk.rev.; illus.; index; circ. 26,000. **Indexed:** Curr.Adv.Ecol.Sci., Helminthol.Abstr., Nutr.Abstr.
Former titles: Modern Medicine (ISSN 0312-875X); Modern Medicine of Australia (ISSN 0026-8089)

610 UK
MODERN MEDICINE OF IRELAND. 1972. m. Findlay Publications Ltd., Franks Hall, Horton Kirby, Kent DA4 9LL, England. Ed. W.F. O'Dwyer. adv.; circ. 3,100.

610 SA
MODERN MEDICINE OF SOUTH AFRICA. 1976. 12/yr. R.84. National Publishing (Pty) Ltd., P.O. Box 2735, Johannesburg 2000, South Africa. TEL 011-835-2221. FAX 011-835-1943. TELEX 82735 SA. Ed. Dr. Issy Levy. adv.; abstr.; illus.; index; circ. 7,530.

616.07 574.2 US ISSN 0893-3952
RB37.A1 CODEN: MODPEO
MODERN PATHOLOGY. 1988. bi-m. $75 to individuals; institutions $120. (U S and Canadian Academy of Pathology) Williams & Wilkins, 428 E. Preston St., Baltimore, MD 21202. TEL 301-528-4000. FAX 301-528-4312. Ed. Dr. Bernard M. Wagner. adv.; bk.rev.; index, cum.index; circ. 5,000. (also avail. in microform; back issues avail.)
—BLDSC shelfmark: 5890.767000.
Description: Provides a forum for the presentation of advances in the understanding of pathological processes. It is practice-oriented and concentrates on diagnostic human pathology.
Refereed Serial

MODERNE GERIATRIE/GERIATRIE MODERNE. see *GERONTOLOGY AND GERIATRICS*

MOLECULAR ASPECTS OF MEDICINE; an interdisciplinary review journal. see *MEDICAL SCIENCES — Radiology And Nuclear Medicine*

630 MP
MONGOLYN ANAGAAKH UKHAAN/MONGOLIAN MEDICAL SCIENCES. (Text in Mongolian; summaries in English) 1970. q. 160 tugrik($4) Ministry of Health, Ulan Bator, Mongolia. (Co-sponsor: Scientific Society of Physicians) Ed. P. Nymadawa. circ. 3,000.

610 574.87 SZ ISSN 0077-0809
MONOGRAPHS IN CLINICAL CYTOLOGY. (Text in English) 1965. irreg. (approx. 1/yr.). price varies. S. Karger AG, Allschwilerstr. 10, P.O. Box, CH-4009 Basel, Switzerland. TEL 061-3061111. FAX 061-3061234. TELEX CH 962652. Ed. G.L. Wied. **Indexed:** Biol.Abstr., Chem.Abstr., Curr.Cont., Ind.Med.
—BLDSC shelfmark: 5915.410000.

610 US ISSN 0883-0266
MONTHLY PRESCRIBING REFERENCE. 1985. m. $75 to individuals; institutions $95. Prescribing Reference, Inc., 53 Park Pl., New York, NY 10007. TEL 212-766-7200. FAX 212-732-2360. Ed. Susan DiGeorgio. adv.; circ. 114,000.
Description: Provides up-to-date information to prescribing physicians on the latest Federal Drug Administration drug approvals.

610 IQ ISSN 0027-1446
CODEN: ACMMBB
MOSUL UNIVERSITY. COLLEGE OF MEDICINE. ANNALS. Cover title: Annals of the College of Medicine, Mosul. (Text in Arabic and English) 1966. s-a. $4. Mosul University, College of Medicine, Mosul, Iraq. Ed.Bd. adv.; bk.rev.; charts; illus.; index; circ. 2,000. **Indexed:** Chem.Abstr., Excerp.Med.
Description: Review articles, papers on laboratory and clinical research. preliminary communications and clinical case reports.

362 610 US ISSN 0027-2507
R11 CODEN: MSJMAZ
MOUNT SINAI JOURNAL OF MEDICINE. 1934. 6/yr. $60 (foreign $70). Mount Sinai Hospital, Committee on Medical Education and Publications, 19 E. 98th St., Box 1094, New York, NY 10029. TEL 212-241-6108. FAX 212-722-6386. Ed. Sherman Kupfer. adv.; index; circ. 3,000. (also avail. in microform from UMI) **Indexed:** Biol.Abstr., Chem.Abstr., Curr.Cont., Curr.Lit.Fam.Plan., Dent.Ind., Excerp.Med., Helminthol.Abstr., Ind.Med., Ind.Sci.Rev., Int.Nurs.Ind., Nutr.Abstr.
●Also available online. Vendor(s): DIALOG.
—BLDSC shelfmark: 5978.750000.
Formerly (until 1970): Mount Sinai Hospital. Journal.

610 IT
MOVIMENTO. 4/yr. $60. Edizioni Luigi Pozzi s.r.l., Via Panama, 68, 00198 Rome, Italy. TEL 06-8553548. FAX 06-8554105. **Indexed:** Psychol.Abstr.

610 CC ISSN 1001-7550
MUDANJIANG YIXUEYUAN XUEBAO/MUDANJIANG MEDICAL INSTITUTE. JOURNAL. (Text in Chinese) q. Mudanjiang Yixueyuan, Xuebao Bianjibu, Tongxiang Lu, Aimin-qu, Mudanjiang, Heilongjiang 157011, People's Republic of China. TEL 26156.

610 GW ISSN 0341-3098
CODEN: MMMWD7
MUENCHENER MEDIZINISCHE WOCHENSCHRIFT. Short title: M M W. (Text in German; summaries in English and German) 1853. w. DM.144. M M V Medizin Verlag, Neumarkter Str. 18, Postfach 801246, 8000 Munich 80, Germany. TEL 089-43189647. FAX 089-43189633. Ed. Heinrich Holzgreve. adv.; bk.rev.; bibl.; illus.; index; circ. 43,000. (back issues avail.) **Indexed:** Biol.Abstr., Biotech.Abstr., C.I.S. Abstr., Chem.Abstr., Curr.Cont., Helminthol.Abstr., Ind.Med., Nutr.Abstr., Protozool.Abstr., Rev.Plant Path., Trop.Dis.Bull.
—BLDSC shelfmark: 5983.720000.

610 SP
MUENCHNER MEDIZINISCHE WOCHENSCHRIFT EN ESPANOL. (Text in Spanish; summaries in English, Spanish) 1962. m. 840 ptas.($12) Editorial ECO, S.A., Calle de la Cruz 44, Barcelona 34, Spain. Eds. Dr. D. Ruano, Dr. J. Bragulat. adv.; charts; illus.; stat.; index; circ. 25,000 (controlled). **Indexed:** Curr.Cont., Dent.Ind., Excerp.Med., Ind.Sci.Rev.

MEDICAL SCIENCES

610 US
MULTIPLE SCLEROSIS RESEARCH REPORT. 1987. q. $35 (effective 1992). (International Federation of Multiple Sclerosis Societies) Demos Publications, Inc., 386 Park Ave. S., Ste.201, New York, NY 10016-8804. TEL 212-683-0072. FAX 212-683-0118. Ed.Bd.

610 MX
MUNDO MEDICO. 1973. m. Mex.$150,000. Mundo Medico, S.A., Matias Romero 116, Col. del Valle, 03100 Mexico, D.F., Mexico. TEL 559-27-55. FAX 559-28-21. Ed. Beatriz Elizalde. adv.; bk.rev.; circ. 15,000.

610 US ISSN 0148-639X
RC925.A1 CODEN: MUNEDE
MUSCLE & NERVE. 1979. m. $375 to institutions (foreign $525). John Wiley & Sons, Inc., Journals, 605 Third Ave., New York, NY 10158-0012. TEL 212-850-6000. FAX 212-850-6088. TELEX 12-7063. Ed. Jun Kimura. adv.; circ. 3,500. (also avail. in microform from RPI) **Indexed:** Bibl.Dev.Med.& Child Neur., Biol.Abstr., Chem.Abstr., Curr.Adv.Biochem., Curr.Adv.Ecol.Sci., Curr.Adv.Genetics & Molec.Biol., Dent.Ind., Excerp.Med., Ind.Med., Ind.Sci.Rev., Poult.Abstr., Risk Abstr.
—BLDSC shelfmark: 5986.493000.
Description: Covers muscle, the peripheral motor and sensory neurons, and the neuromuscular junction in both health and disease.

610 616.891 GW
MUSIK-, TANZ- UND KUNSTTHERAPIE. 1988. q. DM.76. Georg Thieme Verlag, Ruedigerstr. 14, Postfach 104853, 7000 Stuttgart 10, Germany. TEL 0711-8931-0. FAX 0711-8931-298. Ed. Karl Hoermann.

610 JA ISSN 0454-7586
CODEN: KYIHAZ
MUTUAL AID ASSOCIATION. MEDICAL JOURNAL. (Text and summaries in English and Japanese) 1951. q. Kyosai Iho Kokka komuin kyosai Kumiai Rengokai, Takebashi Kaikan 1-4-1, Otamachi Chiyodaku, Tokyo 100, Japan. Ed. Toyozo Aizawa. index; circ. 1,660. (back issues avail.) **Indexed:** INIS Atomind.
—BLDSC shelfmark: 5527.900000.

610 GW ISSN 0027-5557
QR145 CODEN: MYKSAW
MYCOSES. (Text in English; summaries in German) 1957. m. DM.199 (foreign DM.210). (Deutschsprachige Mykologische Gesellschaft e.V.) Blackwell Publishing Co., Meinekestr. 4, 1000 Berlin 15, Germany. Ed. J. Mueller. adv.; bk.rev.; charts; illus.; tr.lit.; index; circ. 1,600. **Indexed:** Biol.Abstr., Biotech.Abstr., Chem.Abstr., Curr.Adv.Ecol.Sci., Curr.Cont., Excerp.Med., Hort.Abstr., Ind.Med., Ind.Sci.Rev., Ind.Vet., Poult.Abstr., Rev.Plant Path., Rice Abstr., Soils & Fert., Vet.Bull.

616.743 BE
MYOPATHIE. (Editions in Dutch and French) 1964. q. 300 Fr. Ligue Nationale Belge Contre la Myopathie et la Myasthenie - Nationale Belgische Liga Tegen Myopathie en Myasthenie, Boulevard de Waterloo 115, B-1000 Brussels, Belgium. Ed. Madeleine Lemaire. adv.; bk.rev.; illus.
Description: Covers myositis and myasthenia gravis.

610 US
N A A C L S NEWS. 1970. 3/yr. $15 (includes Agency's Annual Report). National Accrediting Agency for Clinical Laboratory Sciences, 8410 W. Bryn Mawr, Ste. 670, Chicago, IL 60631. TEL 312-714-8880. FAX 312-714-8886. Ed. Megan M. Hennessy-Eggert. adv.; circ. 2,000. (back issues avail.)
Description: Current industry news in allied health education and accreditation, NAACLS employee news of interest to clinical laboratory officials in the U.S.

610 US
N A E M T NEWS. 1980. m. $25. National Association of Emergency Medical Technicians, 9140 Ward Pkwy., Kansas City, MO 64114. TEL 816-444-3500. FAX 816-444-0330. Ed. Lottie Thomas. adv.; circ. 5,000.
Formerly: N A E M T Newsletter.

610.6 US
N A H C REPORT. 1983. w. $325. National Association for Home Care, 519 C St., N.E., Washington, DC 20002-5809. TEL 202-547-7424. FAX 202-547-3540. adv.; circ. 3,508.
Description: Covers legislative, regulatory, operational, and financial developments affecting the home care industry.

N A R I STETHOSCOPE. (National Association of Residents and Interns) see *BUSINESS AND ECONOMICS — Investments*

610 FR ISSN 0301-6374
N G M. (Nouveau Genie Medical) 1974. bi-m. 25 F. E S T E C, 127 bd. St-Michel, 75005 Paris, France. Ed. Christian Damois. adv.; bk.rev.; circ. 15,250.

610.6 US
N I H RECORD. fortn. National Institutes of Health, Bldg. 31, Rm. 2B03, Bethesda, MD 20892. TEL 301-496-2125. Ed. Richard McManus. circ. 16,000.

610 AT
N S W A M H NEWS. 1974. q. Aus.$25 to individuals; institutions $35. New South Wales Association for Mental Health, 62 Victoria Rd., Gladesville, N.S.W. 2111, Australia. TEL 02-816-1611. FAX 02-816-4056. Ed. Jonine Penrose-Wall. bk.rev.; circ. 350. (back issues avail.)
Formerly: New South Wales Association for Mental Health. Newsletter (ISSN 0813-1724)

610 US
N T S A NEWSLETTER. 1975. q. $20 membership includes: Tuberous Sclerosis Resources. National Tuberous Sclerosis Association, 8000 Corporate Dr., Ste. 120, Landover, MD 20785-2239. TEL 800-225-6872. FAX 301-459-0394. Ed. Ann Kinsella. bk.rev.; circ. 6,000. (looseleaf format; back issues avail.)
Description: Includes current research developments, fund raising efforts and other Association news.

610 NZ ISSN 0110-022X
CODEN: NZFPDJ
N Z FAMILY PHYSICIAN. 1974. q. NZ.$48 (foreign NZ.$60)(effective Sep. 1991). Royal New Zealand College of General Practitioners, c/o Dr. S.R. West, Ed., 33 MacPherson St., Auckland 5, New Zealand. TEL 64-9-521-5602. adv.; bk.rev.; circ. 3,000.
—BLDSC shelfmark: 6091.400000.
Description: Contains original papers, news, academic commentary and College reports of interest to NZ and international general practioners, trainees and students.

610 II ISSN 0027-7576
NAGARJUN. (Text and summaries in English) 1957. m. Rs.150. O.N. Pandeya, 105-C Block F, New Alipore, Calcutta 700053, India. Ed. L.K. Pandeya.
Description: Covers medicine and health.

610 JA ISSN 0369-3228
CODEN: NAGZAC
NAGASAKI IGAKKAI ZASSHI/NAGASAKI MEDICAL JOURNAL. (Text in Japanese; summaries in English) 1923. q. 2000 Yen($20) (Nagasaki Medical Association) Fujiki Publishing Co., 5-13 Yorozuya-machi, Nagasaki 850, Japan. TEL 0978-47-2111. FAX 0958-47-8514. (Subscr. to: Nagasaki University School of Medicine, Department of Pathology, 12-4 Sakamoto-machi, Nagasaki 852, Japan) Ed. Takayoshi Ikeda. adv.; index; circ. 900. **Indexed:** Biol.Abstr.
Description: Contains papers on the specific diseases of the district and abstracts of local scientific meetings.

610 JA ISSN 0027-7622
R97 CODEN: NJMSAG
NAGOYA JOURNAL OF MEDICAL SCIENCE. (Text in European languages) 1923. q. Nagoya Daigaku, Igakubu - Nagoya University, School of Medicine, 65 Tsuruma-cho, Showa-ku, Nagoya 466, Japan. FAX 052-741-1654. Ed.Bd. circ. 750. **Indexed:** Abstr.Hyg., Biol.Abstr., Chem.Abstr., Curr.Adv.Ecol.Sci., Excerp.Med., Ind.Med., Nutr.Abstr., Trop.Dis.Bull.
—BLDSC shelfmark: 6014.000000.

610 JA ISSN 0027-7649
CODEN: NMJOAA
NAGOYA MEDICAL JOURNAL. (Text in European languages) 1953. q. free. Nagoya-shiritsu Daigaku, Igakubu - Nagoya City University, Medical School, Kawasumi, Mizuho-cho, Mizuho-ku, Nagoya 467, Japan. FAX 052-842-0863. Ed. Tomohiro Matsuda. bk.rev.; bibl.; charts; illus.; index; circ. 800. **Indexed:** Abstr.Hyg., Biol.Abstr., C.I.S. Abstr., Chem.Abstr., Curr.Adv.Ecol.Sci., Excerp.Med., Ind.Med., Rev.Appl.Entomol., Trop.Dis.Bull.
—BLDSC shelfmark: 6015.050000.
Description: Presents original articles in all branches of the medical sciences.

610 JA ISSN 0027-7606
CODEN: NASDA6
NAGOYA-SHIRITSU DAIGAKU IGAKKAI ZASSHI/NAGOYA CITY UNIVERSITY. MEDICAL ASSOCIATION. JOURNAL. (Text in Japanese) 1950. q. membership. Nagoya-shiritsu Daigaku, Igakkai - Nagoya City University, Medical Association, Kawasumi, Mizuho-cho, Mizuho-ku, Nagoya 467, Japan. Ed. Norio Abematsu. adv.; charts; illus.; index; circ. 1,200. **Indexed:** Chem.Abstr., Excerp.Med.

610 CC ISSN 1001-7275
NANJING TIEDAO YIXUEYUAN XUEBAO/NANJING RAILWAY INSTITUTE OF MEDICAL SCIENCES. JOURNAL. (Text in Chinese) q. Nanjing Tiedao Yixueyuan - Nanjing Railway Institute of Medical Sciences, 87 Dingjiaqiao, Nanjing, Jiangsu 210009, People's Republic of China. TEL 301509. Ed. Zhou Yujiao.

610 CC ISSN 1000-5331
NANJING YIXUEYUAN XUEBAO/NANJING INSTITUTE OF MEDICAL SCIENCES. JOURNAL. (Text in Chinese) q. Nanjing Yixueyuan - Nanjing Institute of Medical Sciences, 140 Hanzhong Lu, Nanjing, Jiangsu 210029, People's Republic of China. TEL 649141. Ed. Wang Jingliang.
—BLDSC shelfmark: 0579.715000.

610 CC ISSN 1000-5005
NANJING ZHONGYI XUEYUAN XUEBAO/NANJING INSTITUTE OF TRADITIONAL CHINESE MEDICINE. JOURNAL. (Text in Chinese) q. Nanjing Zhongyi Xueyuan - Nanjing Institute of Traditional Chinese Medicine, 282 Hanzhong Lu, Nanjing, Jiangsu 210029, People's Republic of China. TEL 649121. Ed. Zhou Zhongying.

610 CC ISSN 1000-2057
NANTONG YIXUEYUAN XUEBAO/NANTONG INSTITUTE OF MEDICAL SCIENCES. JOURNAL. (Text in Chinese) q. Nantong Yixueyuan - Nantong Institute of Medical Sciences, 19 Qixiu Lu, Nantong, Jiangsu 216001, People's Republic of China. TEL 517191. Ed. Meng Xianyong.

610 JA ISSN 0469-5550
CODEN: NAIZAM
NARA IGAKU ZASSHI/NARA MEDICAL ASSOCIATION. JOURNAL. (Text in Japanese and European languages) 1950. bi-m. 3000 Yen. Nara Igakkai - Nara Medical Association, Nara Medical University, Kashihara 634, Nara, Japan. TEL 07442-2-3051. Ed. Dr. Yasunori Enoki. index; circ. controlled. **Indexed:** Biol.Abstr., C.I.S. Abstr., Chem.Abstr., Excerp.Med., Ind.Med., Nutr.Abstr.
—BLDSC shelfmark: 4828.700000.

NASE LIECIVE RASTLINY. see *BIOLOGY — Botany*

610 II
NATIONAL ACADEMY OF INDIAN MEDICINE. ANNALS. (Text in English) s-a. Rs.100($100) National Academy of Indian Medicine, Department of Shalya-Shalakya, Institute of Medical Sciences, Banaras Hindu University, Varanasi 221 005, India.

610 II ISSN 0379-038X
CODEN: ANAIDI
NATIONAL ACADEMY OF MEDICAL SCIENCES. ANNALS. (Text and summaries in English) 1965. q. Rs.50($10) National Academy of Medical Sciences, Nams House, Ansari Nagar, Mahatma Gandhi Marg, New Delhi 110 029, India. Ed. Dr. Somnath Roy. adv.; bk.rev.; charts; circ. 755. **Indexed:** Biol.Abstr., Chem.Abstr., Curr.Cont., Excerp.Med., Nutr.Abstr.
Formerly: Indian Academy of Medical Sciences. Annals (ISSN 0019-4263)
Description: Technical articles on many aspects of medical science; news of the Academy.

MEDICAL SCIENCES

612   US
NATIONAL COMMITTEE ON THE TREATMENT OF INTRACTABLE PAIN. NEWSLETTER.* 1978. 2/yr. donation. National Committee on the Treatment of Intractable Pain, c/o Carol Rilley, 5500 Beech Ave., Bethesda, MD 20814. Ed. Jeffrey Finn. circ. 6,500.

616.98   JA   ISSN 0006-5528
NATIONAL DEFENSE MEDICAL JOURNAL/BOEI EISEI. (Text in Japanese; summaries in English) 1954. m. 5000 Yen. National Defense Medical Society - Boei Eisei Kyokai, c/o Boei-cho, Eisei-kyoku, Eisei-ka, 9-7-45 Akasaka, Minato-ku, Tokyo 107, Japan. Ed. Dr. Hiroshi Kobayashi. adv.; bk.rev.; circ. 3,200. **Indexed:** Chem.Abstr., INIS Atomind.
—BLDSC shelfmark: 6021.872000.

174.2   US
NATIONAL FEDERATION OF CATHOLIC PHYSICIANS' GUILDS. NEWSLETTER. q. National Federation of Catholic Physicians Guilds, 850 Elm Grove Rd., Elm Grove, WI 53122. TEL 414-784-3435.

616.1   AT
NATIONAL HEART NEWS. 1981. irreg. free. National Heart Foundation of Australia, Royal Insurance Building, 25 London Circuit, Canberra, A.C.T. 2601, Australia. TEL 06-247-7100. Ed. Linda Norton. bk.rev.; circ. 20,000.

610   UK   ISSN 0141-2116
NATIONAL INSTITUTE FOR MEDICAL RESEARCH. REPORT. 1973. a. free. Medical Research Council, Mill Hill, London NW7 1AA, England. circ. 500. **Indexed:** Biol.Abstr.
Formerly: National Institute for Medical Research. Scientific Report (ISSN 0307-076X)

NATIONAL INSTITUTE OF POLAR RESEARCH. MEMOIRS. SERIES E: BIOLOGY AND MEDICAL SCIENCE. see *BIOLOGY*

610   US   ISSN 0149-9939
R835
NATIONAL LIBRARY OF MEDICINE. AUDIOVISUALS CATALOG. (Includes 4th q. a. cumulation) 1978. q. (with a. cum.). $52 for quarterly; price of annual cumulation varies. U.S. National Library of Medicine, 8600 Rockville Pike, Bethesda, MD 20894. TEL 301-496-6308. FAX 301-496-4450. (Orders to: Supt. of Documents, Washington, D.C. 20402) **Description:** Annual cumulations of the NLM audiovisuals Catalog quarterly, and contains subject, name or title and procurement of source sections.

NATIONAL LIBRARY OF MEDICINE NEWS. see *LIBRARY AND INFORMATION SCIENCES*

610 617.6   US   ISSN 0027-9676
NATIONAL MEDICAL AND DENTAL ASSOCIATION. BULLETIN. (Text mainly in English; occasionally in Polish) 1926. a. $15. (National Medical and Dental Association of America) Polstar Publishing Corp., c/o Raymond S. Dziejma, Ed., 72-41 Grand Ave., Maspeth, NY 11378. TEL 718-478-3333. adv.; bk.rev.; illus.; circ. 3,000.

610   US   ISSN 0027-9684
R15   CODEN: JNMAAE
NATIONAL MEDICAL ASSOCIATION. JOURNAL. 1908. m. $60 to individuals; institutions $75; students $35. Slack, Inc., 6900 Grove Rd., Thorofare, NJ 08086. TEL 609-848-1000. FAX 609-853-5991. Ed. Dr. Calvin C. Sampson. adv.; bk.rev.; abstr.; bibl.; charts; illus.; stat.; index; circ. 26,800. (back issues avail.) **Indexed:** Biol.Abstr., Chem.Abstr., Chic.Per.Ind., Curr.Adv.Cancer Res., Curr.Cont., Dent.Ind., Excerp.Med., Hosp.Lit.Ind., I.P.A., Ind.Med., INIS Atomind., Int.Nurs.Ind., Med. Care Rev., Nutr.Abstr., Psychol.Abstr.
●Also available online.

610   US
NATIONAL MEDICAL FELLOWSHIPS NEWSLETTER. 3/yr. free. National Medical Fellowships Inc., 254 W. 31st St., 7th Fl., New York, NY 10001-2813. Ed. Paul E. Cothran. circ. 11,000.

610   II   ISSN 0970-258X
R97   CODEN: NMJIEU
NATIONAL MEDICAL JOURNAL OF INDIA. 1988. 6/yr. Rs.150 to individuals; institutions Rs.300 (UK £22; N. America $43;elsewhere $25). (All India Institute of Medical Sciences) Oxford University Press, Journals Subscription Department, YMCA Bldg., Jai Singh Rd., New Delhi 110 001, India. TEL 11-350490. TELEX 61108-OXON. (Or: Oxford University Press, Journals Subscription Dept., Walton St., Oxford OX2 6DP, England) Ed. Samiran Nundy. adv.; bk.rev.; index; circ. 2,000. **Indexed:** Excerp.Med., Trop.Dis.Bull.
—BLDSC shelfmark: 6027.090000.
Description: Provides a forum for Indian doctors in India or abroad. Publishes original and review articles relevant to clinical practice. Also encourages discussion of social and political problems.

610   US
NATIONAL PERINATAL ASSOCIATION. BULLETIN. q. $15 to non-members. National Perinatal Association, 3500 E. Fletcher Ave., Ste. 525, Tampa, FL 33613-4733. TEL 813-971-1008. FAX 813-974-5172. Ed. Julie A. Leachman. adv.; bk.rev.; circ. 5,000. (tabloid format)
Description: Information for association members.

610   US
NATIONAL STUDENT MEDICAL ASSOCIATION. JOURNAL. 1980. q. $8. Spectrum Unlimited, 3330 N. Causeway Blvd., Ste. 428, Metairie, LA 70001. TEL 504-830-4785. adv.; circ. 10,000.
Description: Reports on specialized research activities of its members. Includes articles on social, legal, financial and academic issues.

610   CH   ISSN 0028-0275
NATIONAL TAIWAN UNIVERSITY. COLLEGE OF MEDICINE. MEMOIRS. 1947. a. National Taiwan University, College of Medicine, No. 1 Jen-Ai Rd. Sec. 1, Taipei, Taiwan, Republic of China. Ed.Bd. bibl.; charts; illus.; stat.; circ. 1,500. **Indexed:** Abstr.Hyg., Anim.Breed.Abstr., Biol.Abstr., Trop.Dis.Bull. Key Title: Guoli Taiwan Daxue Yixueyuan Yanjiu Baogao.

610   GW   ISSN 0934-7909
NATUR- UND GANZHEITSMEDIZIN, WISSENSCHAFT UND PRAXIS. 1989. m. DM.108($84) F.K. Schattauer Verlagsgesellschaft mbH, Lenzhalde 3, Postfach 104545, 7000 Stuttgart 10, Germany. TEL 0711-22987-0. FAX 0711-22987-50.

610   GW   ISSN 0931-1513
NATURA MED; Aerztzeitschrift fuer praktische Therapien. 1986. 11/yr. DM.72($49) (Natura Med Verlagsgesellschaft mbH) Verlag Kirchheim, Postfach 2524, 6500 Mainz, Germany. TEL 06131-671081. FAX 06131-638843. adv.; bk.rev.; illus.; charts. (back issues avail.)
—BLDSC shelfmark: 6036.580000.
Description: New therapies for general practicioners.

615.89   AT   ISSN 1031-6965
NATURAL THERAPIST. bi-m. (Australian Natural Therapists Association) Research Publications Pty. Ltd., 27A Boronia Rd., Vermont, Vic. 3133, Australia. TEL 03-873-1450. FAX 03-873-1450.

610   GW   ISSN 0028-0941
NATURHEILPRAXIS; Fachzeitschrift fuer Naturheilkunde, Erfahrungsheilkunde und biologische Heilverfahren. (Supplement avail.: Heilpraktiker) 1947. m. DM.115.20 (foreign DM.124). Richard Pflaum Verlag GmbH und Co. KG, Lazarettstr. 4, 8000 Munich 19, Germany. TEL 089-12607-0. FAX 089-12607-281. Ed. K.F. Liebau. adv.; bk.rev.; illus.; index; circ. 12,000.

610   YU   ISSN 0352-5856
NAUCNI PODMLADAK: MEDICINSKE NAUKE; strucni casopis studenata Univerziteta u Nisu. (Text in Serbo-Croatian; summaries in English) 1969. q. 4000 din.($5) Univerzitet u Nisu, Strucno Udruzenje Studenata, Sumatovacka bb, 1800 Nis, Serbia, Yugoslavia. TEL 018 22-226. Ed. Milorad Pavlovic. adv.; circ. 1,300.
• **Supersedes in part (as of 1971):** Naucni Posmladak: Tehnicka Nauke. Drustvene Nauki.

NAUKOVE TOVARYSTVO IMENI SHEVCHENKA. PROCEEDINGS OF THE SECTION OF CHEMISTRY, BIOLOGY AND MEDICINE. see *CHEMISTRY*

616.98   US
R11
NAVY MEDICINE. vol.56, 1970. bi-m. $6.50 (foreign $8.15). U.S. Navy, Bureau of Medicine and Surgery, Washington, DC 20372. TEL 202-653-1297. FAX 202-653-1280. (Dist. by: Supt. of Documents, Washington, DC 20402) Ed. Jan Kenneth Herman. bk.rev.; s-a. index; circ. 175,000. (also avail. in microfiche) **Indexed:** Curr.Cont., Dent.Abstr., Dent.Ind., Ind.U.S.Gov.Per., MEDOC.
Former titles (until Mar. 1987): U.S. Navy Medicine (ISSN 0364-6807) & U.S. Navy Medical Newsletter (ISSN 0041-7998)

610   US   ISSN 0091-6730
                      CODEN: NBMJAZ
NEBRASKA MEDICAL JOURNAL. 1916. m. $20 (foreign $22). Nebraska Medical Association, 1512 First Tier Bank Bldg., Lincoln, NE 68508. TEL 402-474-4472. FAX 402-474-2198. Ed. Dr. Benjamin Gelber. adv.; bk.rev.; index; circ. 2,000. (also avail. in microform from UMI; reprint service avail. from UMI) **Indexed:** Biol.Abstr., Chem.Abstr., Dent.Ind., Ind.Med.
—BLDSC shelfmark: 6068.280000.
Formerly: Nebraska State Medical Journal.

610   NE   ISSN 0028-2162
                      CODEN: NETJAN
NEDERLANDS TIJDSCHRIFT VOOR GENEESKUNDE. 1856. w. fl.186 to individuals; students fl.93. Bohn Stafleu Van Loghum B.V., P.O. Box 246, 3990 GA Houten, Netherlands. TEL 03403-95711. FAX 03403-50903. Ed.Bd. adv.; bk.rev.; abstr.; bibl.; charts; illus.; index; circ. 30,000. **Indexed:** Abstr.Hyg., Biol.Abstr., Biotech.Abstr., Chem.Abstr., Dairy Sci.Abstr., Dent.Ind., Excerp.Med., Ind.Med., Nutr.Abstr., Ornam.Hort., Potato Abstr., Protozool.Abstr., Trop.Dis.Bull.
—BLDSC shelfmark: 6071.850000.

610   CC
NEI JING. (Text in Chinese) q. Zhonghua Yixuehui, Nanjing Fenhui - Chinese Society of Medical Sciences, Nanjing Chapter, 291 Zhongshan Lu, Nanjing, Jiangsu 210008, People's Republic of China. TEL 307361.

610   NP   ISSN 0028-2715
NEPAL MEDICAL ASSOCIATION. JOURNAL. Running title: J N M A. (Text in English) 1963. q. $24. Nepal Medical Association, Siddhi Sadan, Exhibition Road, G.P.O. Box 189, Kathmandu, Nepal. Ed. Neelam Adhikari. adv.; bk.rev.; abstr.; charts; illus.; index; circ. 1,250. **Indexed:** Trop.Dis.Bull.

610   NE   ISSN 0300-2977
NETHERLANDS JOURNAL OF MEDICINE. (In two editions: Netherlands & International) (Text in English) 1958. 12/yr.(in 2 vols.; 6 nos./vol.). fl.532 for Netherlands ed.; int'l ed. fl.802 (effective 1992). (Nederlandse Internisten Vereniging - Netherlands Association of Internal Medicine) Elsevier Science Publishers B.V., P.O. Box 211, 1000 AE Amsterdam, Netherlands. TEL 020-5803911. FAX 020-5803598. TELEX 18582 ESPA NL. (Subscr. in U.S. and Canada to: Elsevier Science Publishing Co., Inc., Box 882, Madison Sq. Sta., New York, NY 10159. TEL 212-989-5800) Ed. P.W. De Leeuw. adv.; bk.rev.; bibl.; charts; illus.; circ. 1,600. **Indexed:** Biol.Abstr., Chem.Abstr., Curr.Adv.Biochem., Curr.Cont., Excerp.Med., Helminthol.Abstr., Ind.Med., Nutr.Abstr.
—BLDSC shelfmark: 6077.003000.
Formerly (until 1973): Folia Medica Neerlandica (ISSN 0015-5624)
Description: Publishes original articles and reviews in all relevant fields of internal medicine.
Refereed Serial

NETWORK (DENVILLE). see *CONSUMER EDUCATION AND PROTECTION*

610   GW   ISSN 0300-8371
NEUE MUENCHNER BEITRAEGE ZUR GESCHICHTE DER MEDIZIN UND NATURWISSENSCHAFTEN. MEDIZINHISTORISCHE SERIE. 1970. irreg., vol.8, 1978. price varies. (Werner Fritsch Verlag) Theodor Ackermann, Ludwigstr. 7, D-8000 Munich 22, Germany. TEL 284787. Eds. Heinz Goerke, Joern Wolf. index. **Indexed:** Ind.Med.

610   US
NEVADA STATE MEDICAL ASSOCIATION. BULLETIN. 1973. bi-m. $30. Nevada State Medical Association, 3660 Baker Ln., Reno, NV 89509. Ed.Bd. adv.; circ. 1,250.

MEDICAL SCIENCES 3135

610   CN
NEW BRUNSWICK MEDICAL SOCIETY. NEWSLETTER.
12/yr. membership. New Brunswick Medical Society, 176 York St., Fredericton, N.B. E3B 3N8, Canada. TEL 506-458-8860. circ. 800.

610.73 301   AT   ISSN 0313-2153
NEW DOCTOR. 1976. q. Aus.$27. Doctors' Reform Society, P.O. Box 14, 4 Goulburn St., Sydney, N.S.W. 2000, Australia. FAX 02-267-4393. Ed. A.M. Liebhold. adv.; bk.rev.; circ. 2,000. (back issues avail.) **Indexed:** Aus.P.A.I.S.
  Description: Concerns with the wider sociological, political and environmental issues of health care provision and medical practice in modern society.

610   US   ISSN 0028-4793
R11   CODEN: NEJMAG
NEW ENGLAND JOURNAL OF MEDICINE. 1812. w. $93 (effective 1992). Massachusetts Medical Society, 1440 Main St., Waltham, MA 02254. TEL 617-734-9800. (Subscr. to: Box 1940, Waltham, MA 02254. TEL 800-843-6356; Or Attn.: Peter Cole, Saxon Way, Royston, Herts SG8 6NJ, England. TEL 07-6326-2368) Ed. Jerome Kassirer. adv.; bk.rev.; bibl.; charts; illus.; stat.; s-a. index; circ. 228,000. (also avail. in microform from UMI; reprint service avail. from UMI) **Indexed:** Abstr.Health Care Manage.Stud., Abstr.Hyg., Abstr.Soc.Geront., Acad.Ind., Behav.Med.Abstr., Bibl.Dev.Med.& Child Neur., Biol.Abstr., Biol.Dig., Biotech.Abstr., C.I.S. Abstr., Cadscan, Chem.Abstr., CINAHL, Crim.Just.Abstr., Curr.Adv.Cancer Res., Curr.Adv.Ecol.Sci., Curr.Cont., Curr.Lit.Fam.Plan, Curr.Tit.Dent., Dairy Sci.Abstr., Deep Sea Res.& Oceanogr.Abstr., Dent.Ind., Dent.Ind., Environ.Abstr., Environ.Ind., Excerp.Med., FAMLI, Food Sci.& Tech.Abstr., Fut.Surv., Gen.Sci.Ind., Helminthol.Abstr., Hlth.Ind., Hosp.Lit.Ind., I.P.A., Ind.Hyg.Dig., Ind.Med., Ind.Sci.Rev., Ind.Vet., Int.Nurs.Ind., Lang.& Lang.Behav.Abstr., Lead Abstr., Mag.Ind., Med.Care Rev., Nurs.Abstr., Nutr.Abstr., Protozool.Abstr., Psychol.Abstr., Rehabil.Lit., Rev.Plant Path., Risk Abstr., Sci.Cit.Ind., Soc.Work Res.& Abstr., Telegen, Tr.& Indus.Ind., Trop.Dis.Bull., Vet.Bull., W.R.C.Inf., Yrbk.Assoc.Educ.& Rehab.Blind, Zincscan.
  ●Also available online. Vendor(s): BRS (NEJM), BRS/Saunders Colleague.
  —BLDSC shelfmark: 6084.000000.
  Description: Presents original articles and interpretive reviews of a variety of developments in the major aspects of medicine, its science, its art and practice and its position in today's society.
  Refereed Serial

610   US
NEW ENGLAND JOURNAL OF MEDICINE (INTERNATIONAL EDITION). w. Massachusetts Medical Society, 1440 Main St., Waltham, MA 02154. TEL 617-893-3800. Ed. Dr. Arnold S. Relman. adv.; circ. 42,934.
  Description: Presents original articles and reviews of new developments in science, art, medical practices; including its positition in today's socio-political structure.

616   US
NEW HORIZONS IN THERAPEUTICS: SMITH, KLINE & FRENCH LABORATORIES RESEARCH SYMPOSIA SERIES. 1984. irreg., latest 1990. price varies. Plenum Publishing Corp., 233 Spring St., New York, NY 10013-1578. TEL 212-620-8000. FAX 212-463-0742. TELEX 23-421139. Eds. George Poste, Stanley T. Crooke.
  Formerly: New Horizons in Therapeutics.
  Refereed Serial

610   US
NEW JERSEY MEDICINE. 1904. m. $35. Medical Society of New Jersey, 2 Princess Rd., Trenton, NJ 08648. TEL 609-896-1766. Ed. Dr. Howard D. Slobodien. adv.; bk.rev.; abstr.; bibl.; charts; illus.; index; circ. 10,018. (also avail. in microfilm from UMI) **Indexed:** Excerp.Med., Ind.Med., INIS Atomind.
  Formerly (until 1985): Medical Society of New Jersey. Journal (ISSN 0025-7524)

617.8   US   ISSN 0028-5935
NEW JERSEY SPEECH AND HEARING ASSOCIATION. JOURNAL.* 1963. s-a. $10. New Jersey Speech and Hearing Association, c/o Auriemma, 6 Crest Ln., Warren, NJ 07059-5110. adv.; bk.rev.; circ. 1,100 (controlled).

610   US   ISSN 0028-6451
NEW PHYSICIAN. 1952. m. (9/yr.). $22 to non-members. American Medical Student Association, 1890 Preston White Dr., Reston, VA 22091. TEL 703-620-6600. FAX 703-620-5873. Ed. Richard Camer. adv.; bk.rev.; circ. 30,000. (also avail. in microform from UMI; reprint service avail. from UMI) **Indexed:** Biol.Abstr., Hosp.Lit.Ind., I.P.A., Med. Care Rev., Phys.Ber.
  —BLDSC shelfmark: 6084.980000.

610   US
NEW PRACTICE PLANNING. 1987. bi-m. $30. Health Care Publications & Research, Inc., 17 Larchdell Way, Mountain Lakes, NJ 07046. TEL 201-316-6873. adv.: B&W page $3400; trim 11 x 14 1/4. circ. 37,300.
  Description: Provides useful practice management and planning information for post-resident practice.

610 174   US   ISSN 0361-6347
Z6675.E8
NEW TITLES IN BIOETHICS. 1975. m. $20 (foreign $30). Kennedy Institute of Ethics, National Reference Center for Bioethics Literature, Georgetown University, Washington, DC 20057. TEL 202-687-3885. FAX 202-687-6770. Ed. Lucinda Fitch-Huttlinger. circ. 1,700.
  Description: Includes the Kampelman Collection of Jewish Ethics, the Shriver Collection of Christian Ethics and updates to the Syllabus Exchange catalog.

610.6   US
NEW YORK ACADEMY OF MEDICINE. ANNUAL REPORT. a. New York Academy of Medicine, 2 E. 103rd St., New York, NY 10029. TEL 212-876-8200. FAX 212-876-6620.

610   US   ISSN 0028-7091
R15   CODEN: BNYMAM
NEW YORK ACADEMY OF MEDICINE. BULLETIN. 1925. 6/yr. $18 (foreign $20). New York Academy of Medicine, 2 E. 103rd St., New York, NY 10029. TEL 212-876-8200. FAX 212-876-6620. Ed. Dr. William D. Sharpe. bk.rev.; charts; illus.; stat.; index; circ. 3,500. (also avail. in microform from UMI; back issues avail.; reprint service avail. from UMI) **Indexed:** Abstr.Health Care Manage.Stud., Abstr.Hyg., Biol.Abstr., Biotech.Abstr., Chem.Abstr., CINAHL, Curr.Adv.Ecol.Sci., Curr.Cont., Dairy Sci.Abstr., Excerp.Med., Helminthol.Abstr., Hosp.Lit.Ind., Ind.Med., INIS Atomind., Int.Nurs.Ind., NRN, Numis.Lit, Nutr.Abstr., Sci.Cit.Ind, Trop.Dis.Bull.
  —BLDSC shelfmark: 2650.000000.

610   US   ISSN 0898-6401
NEW YORK DOCTOR; the newsmagazine for New York physicians. 1988. 12/yr. $65 (free to qualified personnel). Chase Communications Group, Ltd., 25-35 Beechwood Ave., Box 9001, Mt. Vernon, NY 10552-9001. TEL 914-699-2020. FAX 914-664-1503. Ed. Michelle Eldredge. adv.; circ. 15,000 (controlled).
  Description: Covers hospital politics, malpractice cases, medical ethics, insurance, legislation, regulation and commercial real estate.

610   US   ISSN 0028-7628
R11   CODEN: NYSJAM
NEW YORK STATE JOURNAL OF MEDICINE. 1901. m. $40. Medical Society of the State of New York, 420 Lakeville Rd., Lake Success, NY 11042. TEL 516-488-6100. FAX 516-488-1267. Ed. Dr. Pascal James Imperato. adv.; bk.rev.; abstr.; bibl.; illus.; index; circ. 28,252. (also avail. in microform from UMI; reprint service avail. from UMI) **Indexed:** Biol.Abstr., Biotech.Abstr., C.I.S. Abstr., Chem.Abstr., CINAHL, Curr.Cont., Dent.Ind., Dok.Arbeitsmed., Excerp.Med., Helminthol.Abstr., Hosp.Lit.Ind., Ind.Med., Int.Nurs.Ind., Med.Care Rev., Nutr.Abstr., Psychol.Abstr., Rev.Plant Path.
  —BLDSC shelfmark: 6089.750000.
  Description: Research papers, case reports and original essays on the practice of medicine, medical education, public health, the history of medicine, medicolegal matters, legislation, ethics, the mass media and socioeconomic issues in health care.

610   US
NEW YORK STATE MEDICAL NEWS. m. Schueler Communications, Inc., 208 N. Townsend St., Syracuse, NY 13203-2339. TEL 315-472-6948. FAX 315-472-0217. Ed. Alaric Levin. circ. 42,000.

610.28   US
NEW YORK UNIVERSITY BIOMEDICAL ENGINEERING SERIES. 1987. irreg. price varies. New York University Press, 70 Washington Square S., New York, NY 10012. TEL 212-998-2575. FAX 212-995-3833. TELEX 235128 NYU UR. Ed. Walter Welkowitz.

610   NZ   ISSN 0114-2550
NEW ZEALAND GENERAL PRACTICE. (Supplement avail.: New Zealand General Practice, Business Management (ISSN 1170-327X)) 1984. fortn. NZ.$66.50 (effective 1991). Adis International Ltd., 41 Centorian Dr., Private Bag, Mairangi Bay, Auckland 10, New Zealand. TEL 479-8100. FAX 479-8066. Ed. Lyndsey Swan. adv.; circ. 4,500. (tabloid format; back issues avail.)
  Formerly (until 1988): Journal of General Practice (ISSN 0112-2541)
  Description: For general practitioners covering health news and issues, medicopolitical comment and lifestyle pages.

610 658   NZ   ISSN 1170-327X
NEW ZEALAND GENERAL PRACTICE, BUSINESS MANAGEMENT. (Supplement to: New Zealand General Practice (ISSN 0114-2550)) 1989. m. Adis International Ltd., 41 Centorian Dr., Private Bag, Mairangi Bay, Auckland 10, New Zealand. TEL 479-8100. FAX 479-8066.

615.8   NZ   ISSN 0303-7193
NEW ZEALAND JOURNAL OF PHYSIOTHERAPY. 1940? 3/yr. $45. New Zealand Society of Physiotherapists (Inc.), P.O. Box 27386, Wellington, New Zealand. FAX 801-5571. bk.rev.; abstr.; charts; illus.; circ. 1,500 (controlled). **Indexed:** CINAHL.
  —BLDSC shelfmark: 6094.640000.

610   NZ   ISSN 0028-8446
         CODEN: NZMJAX
NEW ZEALAND MEDICAL JOURNAL. 1887. s-m. $135. (New Zealand Medical Association) Southern Colour Print, P.O. Box 920, Dunedin, New Zealand. TEL 03-455-0554. FAX 03-455-0303. Ed. R.G. Robinson. adv.; bk.rev.; charts; illus.; index, cum.index; circ. 5,800. (also avail. in microform from UMI; reprint service avail. from UMI) **Indexed:** Abstr.Hyg., Bibl.Dev.Med.& Child Neur., Biol.Abstr., Biotech.Abstr., C.I.S. Abstr., Chem.Abstr., CINAHL, Curr.Adv.Cancer Res., Curr.Adv.Ecol.Sci., Curr.Cont., Dairy Sci.Abstr., Dent.Ind., Excerp.Med., Helminthol.Abstr., HRIS, Ind.Med., Ind.Sci.Rev., Ind.Vet., Nutr.Abstr., Pig News & Info., Rev.Plant Path., So.Pac.Per.Ind., Trop.Dis.Bull., Vet.Bull.
  —BLDSC shelfmark: 6096.100000.

610   CN   ISSN 0078-0316
NEWFOUNDLAND MEDICAL DIRECTORY. 1961. a. free. Newfoundland Medical Board, Registrar, 15 Rowan St., St. John's, Nfld., A1B 2X2, Canada. TEL 709-726-8546. circ. 700.

610   US
NEWS CAPSULE. vol.37, no.9, 1990. 10/yr. $10 to non-members. Fairfield County Medical Association, 60 Katona Dr., Fairfield, CT 06430. TEL 203-334-5168. FAX 203-330-0093. Ed. Leonard R. Tomcat. adv.; circ. 2,000.

610   US   ISSN 0028-9264
NEWS OF NEW YORK; news of New York in depth. 1945. s-m. $20. Medical Society of the State of New York, 420 Lakeville Rd., Lake Success, NY 11042. Ed. Colleen A. O'Brien. adv.; charts; illus.; circ. 29,000. (reprint service avail. from UMI)
  Formerly: Medical Society of the State of New York. News Letter.
  Description: Contains organization news.

610.2   US   ISSN 0048-0282
         CODEN: NBSSB
NEWSLETTER OF BIOMEDICAL SAFETY & STANDARDS. 1971. s-m (m. in Jan. & Aug.). $184 (foreign $222). Quest Publishing Co., 1351 Titan Way, Brea, CA 92621. TEL 714-738-6400. FAX 714-525-6258. Ed. Allan F. Pacela. bk.rev.; index. (looseleaf format; back issues avail.)
  Description: Covers medical device safety and standards, hazards, recalls, legal actions, legislation and regulations, BMET and CE activities and meetings.

M

MEDICAL SCIENCES

610   JA   ISSN 0029-0424
CODEN: NICHAS
NICHIDAI IGAKU ZASSHI/NIHON UNIVERSITY. JOURNAL OF MEDICINE. (Supplements avail.) (Text in Japanese; summaries in English) 1937. m. 5000 Yen. Nihon Daigaku Igakkai - Nihon University Medical Association, 30 Oyaguchi Kami-cho, Itabashi-ku, Tokyo 173, Japan. (Co-sponsor: Nihon University School of Medicine) Ed. Dr. Yukiyasu Sezai. adv.; bk.rev.; illus.; index; circ. 500. **Indexed:** Biol.Abstr., C.I.S. Abstr., Chem.Abstr., Excerp.Med.
—BLDSC shelfmark: 4833.390000,

610   GW   ISSN 0468-1746
DER NIEDERGELASSENE ARZT. 1952. m. DM.102. N A V - Verband der Niedergelassenen Aertze Deutschlands e.V., Belfortstrasse 9V, 5000 Cologne 1, Germany. TEL 0221-727072. FAX 0221-7391239. adv.; bk.rev.; circ. 50,000.

610   GW   ISSN 0028-9795
NIEDERSAECHSISCHES AERZTEBLATT. 1927. s-m. DM.192. (Aerztekammer Niedersachsen) Deutscher Aerzte-Verlag GmbH, Dieselstr. 2, Postfach 40 02 65, 5000 Cologne 40, Germany. TEL 02234-70110. FAX 02234-7011444. adv.; bk.rev.; abstr.; stat.; index; circ. 24,500.

610   NE   ISSN 0168-9827
NIEUWE NEDERLANDSE BIJDRAGEN TOT DE GESCHIEDNIS DER GENEESKUNDE EN DER NATUURWETENSCHAPPEN. (Text in Dutch, English, French and German) 1978. irreg. price varies. Editions Rodopi B.V., Keizersgracht 302-304, 1016 EX Amsterdam, Netherlands. TEL 020-6227507. FAX 020-6380948. (US and Canada subscr. to: 233 Peachtree St. N.E., Ste. 404, Atlanta GA 30303-1504. TEL 800-225-3998) Ed. M.J. van Lieburg. circ. 500.

610   NR   ISSN 0300-1652
CODEN: NGMDAI
NIGERIAN MEDICAL JOURNAL. 1971. q. $136 (typically set in Jan.). Nigerian Medical Association, P.O. Box 1108, Lagos, Nigeria. Ed. A.E. Ohwovoriole. adv.; bk.rev.; circ. 4,500. **Indexed:** Biol.Abstr., Helminthol.Abstr., Ind.Med., Nutr.Abstr., Trop.Dis.Bull.
Formerly: Nigerian Medical Association. Journal.

615.8   NR   ISSN 0331-3735
NIGERIAN SOCIETY OF PHYSIOTHERAPY. JOURNAL.* (Text in English) 1972. s-a. £N10($10) University of Ife, Department of Medical Rehabilitation, c/o V.A. Obajuluwa, Ile-Ife, Nigeria. Ed. V.C.B. Nwuga. adv.; circ. 1,000.

615.8   JA   ISSN 0029-0343
NIHON ONSEN KIKO BUTSURI IGAKKAI ZASSHI/JAPANESE ASSOCIATION OF PHYSICAL MEDICINE, BALNEOLOGY, AND CLIMATOLOGY. JOURNAL. (Text in Japanese; summaries in English) 1935. s-a. 2000 Yen($7.60) Nihon Onsen Kiko Butsuri Igakkai - Japanese Association of Physical Medicine, Balneology, and Climatology, c/o Japan Health and Research Institute, 1-5-20 Ishizuka Yaesu Bldg., Yaesu, Chuo-ku, Tokyo, Japan. FAX 03-274-5833. Ed. Terumasa Miyamoto. adv.; bk.rev.; bibl.; charts; illus.; index, cum.index; circ. 1,300. **Indexed:** Excerp.Med.
—BLDSC shelfmark: 4809.050000.
Description: Includes physiotherapy techniques.

610   JA   ISSN 0029-0440
CODEN: NIGZAY
NIIGATA IGAKKAI ZASSHI/NIIGATA MEDICAL JOURNAL. (Text in Japanese) 1887. m. 6500 Yen. Niigata Igakkai - Niigata Medical Society, c/o Niigata Daigaku Igakubu, Asahimachi Library, Asahi-machi 1, Niigata 951, Japan. adv.; bibl.; charts; illus.; mkt.; stat.; index; circ. 1,000. (also avail. in microform) **Indexed:** C.I.S. Abstr., Chem.Abstr.
—BLDSC shelfmark: 6113.170000.

NIKKEI HEALTH BUSINESS. see *HOSPITALS*

NIKKEI HEALTHCARE. see *HOSPITALS*

610   JA   ISSN 0385-1699
NIKKEI MEDICAL/NIKKEI MEDIKARU. (Text in Japanese) 1972. 15/yr. 5100 Yen for doctors. Nikkei Business Publications, Inc., 3-3-23, Misakicho, Chiyoda-ku, Tokyo 101, Japan. TEL 03-5210-8502. FAX 03-5210-8119. (Subscr. to: Nikkei Business Pub. Inc., Reader Service Center, P.O. Box 20, Kasai Post Office, Tokyo 134, Japan) Ed. Hitoshi Sawai. adv.; circ. 108,000 (controlled). **Indexed:** JTA.
Description: Contains specialized reports for clinicians, offering insight into both clinical and economic aspects of medicine.

610   JA   ISSN 0048-0444
CODEN: NIDZAJ
NIPPON MEDICAL SCHOOL. JOURNAL/NIPPON IKA DAIGAKU ZASSHI. (Text in English and Japanese) 1927. 6/yr. $60. Nippon Medical School, Medical Association - Nippon Ika Daigaku Igakkai, 1-1-5 Sendagi, Bunkyo-ku, Tokyo 113, Japan. FAX 03-3822-8575. TELEX 03-3822-2131-314. Ed. Kozo Yokomuro. adv.; bk.rev.; circ. 2,600 (controlled). **Indexed:** Biol.Abstr., C.I.S. Abstr., Chem.Abstr, Dent.Ind., Ind.Med.
●Also available online. Vendor(s): JICST.
—BLDSC shelfmark: 4833.600000.
Description: Covers developments in medical science from the association.

610   IR
NIZAM PEZESHKI JOMHURIYE ISLAMIYE IRAN. MAJALLEH/MEDICAL COUNCIL OF THE ISLAMIC REPUBLIC OF IRAN. JOURNAL. (Text in Persian; summaries in English or French) 1969. q. free to qualified personnel. Nizam Pezeshki Jomhuriye Islamiye Iran - Medical Council of the Islamic Republic of Iran, 40 Shirin Ave., Hafez Ave., P.O. Box 11365-8759, Teheran, Iran. TEL 821111. FAX 836522. adv.; circ. 18,000.
Formerly: Medical Council of Iran. Journal - Nezam Pezeshki-ye Iran. Majalleh.

610   DK   ISSN 0029-1420
NORDISK MEDICIN. (Text in Danish, Norwegian and Swedish; summaries in English) 1929. 10/yr. DKK 230. (Almindelige Danske Laegeforening - Danish Medical Association) Laegeforeningens Forlag, Esplanaden 8A, DK-1263 Copenhagen K, Denmark. adv.; bk.rev.; index; circ. 60,000. **Indexed:** Abstr.Hyg., Biol.Abstr., C.I.S. Abstr., Chem.Abstr., Dent.Ind., Ind.Med., Nutr.Abstr., Trop.Dis.Bull.
—BLDSC shelfmark: 6122.500000.

610   SW   ISSN 0078-1061
NORDISK MEDICINHISTORISK AARSBOK. (Text in Swedish; summaries in English) 1953. a. SEK 120. Medicinhistoriska Museet - Museum of Medical History, Aasoegatan 146, 116 32 Stockholm, Sweden. TEL 08-6-642-41-66. FAX 08-644-02-86. Ed. Lars Thoren. adv.; circ. 1,000. **Indexed:** Amer.Hist.& Life, Hist.Abstr.
Formerly: Medicinhistorisk Aarsbok.

610   DK   ISSN 0108-271X
NORDISK SEXOLOGI. (Text in Danish, Norwegian or Swedish; abstracts in English) 1983. 4/yr. DKK 370 (students DKK 280; foreign DKK 303.27). Dansk Psykologisk Forlag, Hans Knudsens Plads 1A, 2100 Copenhagen Oe, Denmark. TEL 31-18-27-57. FAX 31-18-57-58. Ed. Soeren Buus Jensen. adv.; bk.rev.; abstr.; charts; illus.; upd. 27 91344; circ. 900. **Indexed:** Psychol.Abstr.
—BLDSC shelfmark: 6122.785000.

616.026   GW   ISSN 0029-1609
NORDWESTDEUTSCHE GESELLSCHAFT FUER INNERE MEDIZIN. KONGRESSBERICHT. 1953. s-a. DM.10($6) Hansisches Verlagskontor H. Scheffler, Mengstr. 16, Postfach 2051, 2400 Luebeck 1, Germany. Ed. Prof. Dr. A. Doenhardt. adv.; illus.; circ. 1,800.
Description: Covers internal medicine.

616.98   NO   ISSN 0803-2394
NORSK TIDSKRIFT FOR ARBEJDSMEDISIN/NORWEGIAN JOURNAL OF OCCUPATIONAL MEDICINE. 1980. 6/yr. NOK 180. Norsk Bedriftslegeforening - Norwegian Association of Industrial Physicians, Postboks 1122, Blindern, N-0317 Oslo 3, Norway. TEL 02-854111. FAX 02-854004. (Subscr. to: S. Fekene, Den norske laegeforening Lagaasen, Fjellveien 5, N-1324 Lysaker, Norway) Ed. Dr. Oeivind Larsen. adv.; bk.rev.; circ. 1,783.
Formerly: Norsk Bedriftshelsetjeneste (ISSN 0333-0249)
Description: Covers industrial and occupational medicine, as well as general preventive medicine.

610   NO   ISSN 0029-2001
CODEN: TNLAAH
NORSKE LAEGEFORENING. TIDSSKRIFT/NORWEGIAN MEDICAL ASSOCIATION. JOURNAL; tidsskrift for praktisk medisin. (Supplements avail.) (Text in Norwegian; summaries in English) 1881. 3/m. NOK 720. Norske Laegeforening - Norwegian Medical Association, Fjellveien 5, N-1324 Lysaker, Norway. TEL 02-124600. FAX 02-124800. Ed. Magne Nylenna. adv.; bk.rev.; abstr.; charts; illus.; index, cum.index; circ. 15,200. **Indexed:** Biol.Abstr., Chem.Abstr., Excerp.Med., Ind.Med., Protozool.Abstr.
—BLDSC shelfmark: 8822.350000.

610   US   ISSN 0029-2559
R11
NORTH CAROLINA MEDICAL JOURNAL. 1940. m. $12. North Carolina Medical Society, Box 27167, Raleigh, NC 27611. TEL 919-684-5728. Ed. Eugene A. Stead, Jr. M.D. adv.; bk.rev.; illus.; index; circ. 8,300. (also avail. in microfilm from UMI) **Indexed:** C.I.S. Abstr., Chem.Abstr., CINAHL, Curr.Cont., Dent.Ind., Excerp.Med., Helminthol.Abstr., Ind.Med.
—BLDSC shelfmark: 6149.080000.

610   II
NORTH EASTERN DOCTORS CALLING. 1984. bi-m. Rs.35 to individuals (foreign Rs.80); institutions Rs.60 (foreign Rs.130). Indian Medical Association, Chaiduar Branch, c/o Dr. Ranjib Baruah, Secr., Hoogrijan 786 601, Assam, India. Ed.Bd. adv.; bk.rev.; abstr.; bibl.; charts; stat.
Description: Examines current professional, academic and related trends of interest to those in medical professions.
Refereed Serial

610   US   ISSN 0029-3334
NORTHWEST COMMUNITY HOSPITAL MEDICAL BULLETIN; practice of medicine in a community hospital. 1964. 3/yr. $3. Northwest Community Hospital, 800 W. Central, Arlington Heights, IL 60005. TEL 708-259-1000. Ed. Constantine S. Soter. bk.rev.; charts; illus.; circ. 2,000.

610 370   US
NORTHWESTERN UNIVERSITY MEDICAL CENTER MAGAZINE. 1963. 3/yr. free. Northwestern University Alumni Association, Medical Division, 303 E. Chicago Ave., Chicago, IL 60611. TEL 312-649-8012. Ed. Dr. David Shoch. bk.rev.; illus.; stat.; circ. 7,000.
#**Formerly:** Northwestern University Medical School Magazine (ISSN 0029-358X)
Description: Presents study and teaching methods.

610   GW   ISSN 0177-2309
DER NOTARZT; notfallmedizinische Informationen. 1985. bi-m. DM.76. Georg Thieme Verlag, Ruedigerstr. 14, Postfach 104853, 7000 Stuttgart 10, Germany. TEL 0711-8931-0. FAX 0711-8931298. Ed. M. Marloff. circ. 6,400.
—BLDSC shelfmark: 6152.910000.

610   SP   ISSN 0029-4225
NOTICIAS MEDICAS; el periodico de la medicina espanola. 1967. w. $100 (supplement $60). Paseo de la Castellana 53, 28046 Madrid, Spain. TEL 4428856. Ed. Adolfo Berzosa Blanco. adv.; bk.rev.; charts; illus.; circ. 50,000.

610   SP
NOTICIAS MEDICAS. English edition: Medical News. 1967. w. 8500 ptas. Editores Medicos, S.A., Paseo de la Castellana, 53, 28046 Madrid, Spain. TEL 442-86-56. FAX 422-80-43. circ. 50,000.

610   FR   ISSN 0292-384X
NOUVEAU CENTRE DE SANTE. vol.21, 1977. 10/yr. 275 F. (foreign 350 F.). Union des Syndicats de Medecins de Centres de Sante, Centre de Sante, 23 rue de Leningrad, 75008 Paris, France. TEL 45-22-21-40.
Formerly: Revue de Medecine Moderne (ISSN 0035-1539)

610   FR
NOUVELLES QUESTIONS.* 20/yr. 540 F. includes subscription to Vie Medicale. Editions de la Vie Medicale, c/o O.D.M. - V.M., 6, rue des Bateliers, 92 110 Clichy, France. circ. 13,500.
Formerly (until 1982): Questions Internat (ISSN 0033-636X)

MEDICAL SCIENCES

610 CN ISSN 0838-2638
NOVA SCOTIA MEDICAL JOURNAL. 1922. bi-m. $20. Medical Society of Nova Scotia, City of Lakes Business Park, 5 Spectacle Lakes Dr., Dartmouth, N.S. B3B 1X7, Canada. TEL 902-468-1866. FAX 902-568-6578. Ed. Dr. John F. O'Connor. adv.; bk.rev.; charts; illus.; index; circ. 2,025. **Indexed:** Chem.Abstr., Excerp.Med., Ind.Med.
—BLDSC shelfmark: 6179.460000.
Formerly (until 1988): Nova Scotia Medical Bulletin (ISSN 0029-5094)

NOVOSTI FARMATSII I MEDITSINY/NEWS IN PHARMACOLOGY AND MEDICINE. see *PHARMACY AND PHARMACOLOGY*

610 US
NUCLEUS SCIENCE JOURNAL. 1957. a. $10. Queens College, Kissena & Melbourne Ave., Flushing, NY 11367. TEL 718-520-7000. Ed. Kenneth M. Simckes. adv.; bk.rev.; bibl.; charts; illus.; stat.; index; circ. 7,000. (back issues avail.)

610 574 JA ISSN 0469-2071
NUKADA INSTITUTE FOR MEDICAL AND BIOLOGICAL RESEARCH. REPORTS. (Text in English) irreg. exchange basis. Nukada Institute for Medical and Biological Research - Nukada Igaku Seibutsugaku Kenkyujo, 5-18 Inage-cho, Chiba-shi 280, Japan.

NURSING RESEARCH ABSTRACTS. see *MEDICAL SCIENCES — Abstracting, Bibliographies, Statistics*

NUTRITION & THE M.D.; a continuing education service for physicians and nutritionists. see *NUTRITION AND DIETETICS*

610 613.2 CN
NUTRITION REVIEW. a. M P I Medical Publishing Inc., 14 Ronan Ave., Toronto, Ont. M4N 2X9, Canada. TEL 416-481-6384.

610 CM ISSN 0255-5352
O C E A C BULLETIN DE LIAISON ET DE DOCUMENTATION. q. 7500 Fr.CFA. Organisation de Coordination pour la Lutte Contre les Endemies en Afrique Centrale, BP 288, Yaounde, Cameroun. FAX 237-23-00-61. TELEX 8411KN. Ed. Henri Gelas. adv.; bk.rev. **Indexed:** Excerp.Med.

610 US
O H S U VIEWS. 1979. q. $25. Oregon Health Sciences University, 3181 S.W. Sam Jackson Park Rd., Portland, OR 97201. TEL 503-494-8231. FAX 503-494-8246. Ed. Marlys Levin. charts; illus.; stat.; circ. 30,000.
Formerly (until Nov. 1988): Oregon Health Sciences University News.

610 SP
O M C. 1989. 10/yr. free. (Organizacion Medica Colegial de Espana) Ediciones Doyma S.A., Travesera de Gracia, 17-21, 08021 Barcelona, Spain. TEL 200-07-11. FAX 209-11-36. TELEX 51964 INK E. Dir. Jose Farnes. circ. 100,000.
Description: Covers the socio-economic aspects of being a physician in Spain.

610 US
OAK RIDGE ASSOCIATED UNIVERSITIES. MEDICAL SCIENCES DIVISION. RESEARCH REPORT. 1951. a. free. Oak Ridge Associated Universities, Inc., Office of Communications Resources, Box 117, Oak Ridge, TN 37831-0117. TEL 615-576-3146. Ed. Fred L. Snyder. circ. 2,500. (also avail. in microform from NTI; reprint service avail. from NTI)
Formerly: Oak Ridge Institute for Nuclear Studies. Medical Division. Research Report (ISSN 0078-2890)

574.2 616 BU ISSN 0324-1998
CODEN: OSPADK
OBSTA I SRAVNITELNA PATOLOGIIA. (Text in various languages) 1976. s-a. price varies. (Bulgarska Akademiia na Naukite) Publishing House of the Bulgarian Academy of Sciences, Acad. G. Bonchev St., Bldg. 6, 1113 Sofia, Bulgaria. circ. 500. **Indexed:** Abstr.Bulg.Sci.Med.Lit., Biol.Abstr., BSL Biol., Chem.Abstr., Excerp.Med., Ind.Vet., Poult.Abstr., Vet.Bull.
—BLDSC shelfmark: 0126.705200.

OCCUPATIONAL HEALTH MANAGEMENT. see *OCCUPATIONAL HEALTH AND SAFETY*

613.62 UK
OCCUPATIONAL MEDICINE. 1951. q. £67 in U.K. & Europe; elsewhere £80. (Society of Occupational Medicine) Butterworth - Heinemann Ltd. (Subsidiary of: Reed International PLC), Linacre House, Jordan Hill, Oxford OX2 8DP, England. TEL 0865-310366. FAX 0865-310898. TELEX 83111 BHPOXF G. (Subscr. to: Turpin Transactions Ltd., Distribution Centre, Blackhorse Rd., Letchworth, Herts SG6 1HN, England. TEL 0462-672555) Ed. D. D'Auria. adv.; bk.rev.; illus.; index. (also avail. in microform from UMI; back issues avail.) **Indexed:** Abstr.Hyg., Biol.Abstr., C.I.S. Abstr., Chem.Abstr., Curr.Adv.Ecol.Sci., Curr.Cont., Excerp.Med., Ind.Med., INIS Atomind., Lab.Haz.Bull., Trop.Dis.Bull.
Former titles (until 1991): Society of Occupational Medicine. Journal (ISSN 0301-0023); Society of Occupational Medicine Transactions (ISSN 0037-9972)
Description: Covers original and review articles on all aspects of occupational health.
Refereed Serial

610 US
OCCUPATIONAL THERAPY FORUM. w. (50/yr.). Forum Publishing, Inc., 251 W. Dekalb Pike, Ste. A-115, King of Prussia, PA 19406. TEL 215-337-0381. FAX 215-337-3979. adv.; circ. 38,233.
Description: Covers new methodology, equipment, research trends and practical and philosophical aspects of the profession.

615.8 US ISSN 0738-0577
CODEN: OTHCES
OCCUPATIONAL THERAPY IN HEALTH CARE; a journal of contemporary practice. 1984. q. $36 to individuals; institutions $48; libraries $90. Haworth Press, Inc., 10 Alice St., Binghamton, NY 13904. TEL 800-342-9678. FAX 607-722-1424. TELEX 4932599. Ed. Susan Cook-Merrill. adv.; bk.rev.; circ. 174. (also avail. in microfiche from HAW; reprint service avail. from HAW) **Indexed:** Arts & Hum.Cit.Ind., CLOA, Curr.Cont., Except.Child Educ.Abstr., Excerp.Med., Hosp.Abstr., Soc.Work Res.& Abstr.
—BLDSC shelfmark: 6231.254000.
Description: Provides answers to clinical questions of current concern to occupational therapy practitioners.
Refereed Serial

OCCUPATIONAL THERAPY IN MENTAL HEALTH; a journal of psychosocial practice and research. see *MEDICAL SCIENCES — Psychiatry And Neurology*

610 US ISSN 0276-1599
RM735.A1 CODEN: OTJRDE
OCCUPATIONAL THERAPY JOURNAL OF RESEARCH. Abbreviated title: O T J R. 1981. bi-m. $80 to non-members; members $55. (American Occupational Therapy Foundation, Inc.) Slack, Inc., 6900 Grove Rd., Thorofare, NJ 08086-9447. TEL 609-848-1000. FAX 609-853-5991. Ed. Dr. Kenneth J. Ottenbacher. adv.; bk.rev.; abstr.; charts; bibl.; illus.; index; circ. 900. (back issues avail.)
Indexed: CIJE, Excerp.Med., Psychol.Abstr., SSCI.
—BLDSC shelfmark: 6231.255000.
Refereed Serial

615.85 US
OCCUPATIONAL THERAPY WEEK. 1939. m. $80 to individuals; institutions $175; foreign $200. American Occupational Therapy Association, Inc., 1383 Piccard Dr., Box 1725, Rockville, MD 20850-0822. TEL 301-948-9626. FAX 301-948-5512. adv.; charts; illus.; circ. 42,000. (tabloid format) **Indexed:** Rehabil.Lit.
Former titles: Occupational Therapy Newspaper; Occupational Therapy; American Occupational Therapy Association. Newsletter.

610 AU ISSN 0029-8786
OESTERREICHISCHE AERZTEZEITUNG. 1945. bi-m. S.710. Oesterreichische Aerztekammer, Pressestelle und Verlag, Weihburggasse 10-12, A-1010 Vienna, Austria. TEL 512-44-86. FAX 513-19-25-24. Ed. Martin Stickler. adv.; bk.rev.; illus.; index; circ. 31,000. **Indexed:** C.I.S. Abstr.
Description: Covers politics, laws and regulations, medical news, economics, educational material in all fields of medicine, and culture. Includes announcements of events, foreign news, reports and letters.

610 AU ISSN 0029-8875
DER OESTERREICHISCHE ARZT. 1950. 8/yr. S.200. (Vereinigung Oesterreichischer Aerzte) Steiger-Werbung Verlags- und Werbegesellschaft mbH, Hermanngasse 25, A-1070 Vienna, Austria. Ed. Franz-Josef Feichtenberger. adv.; bk.rev.; circ. 20,000.

610 GW ISSN 0938-9261
▼**OFFIZIELLES AERZTEBLATT FUER SACHSEN-ANHALT.** 1990. m. DM.54. (Landesaerzte Kammer Sachsen-Anhalt) Deutscher Aerzte-Verlag GmbH, Dieselstr. 2, Postfach 400265, 5000 Cologne 40, Germany. TEL 02234-70110.
FAX 02234-7011444. circ. 8,000.

610 US ISSN 0030-0888
OHIO FAMILY PHYSICIAN NEWS. 1955. m. $2. Ohio Academy of Family Physicians, 4075 N. High St., Columbus, OH 43214. TEL 614-267-7867. Ed. Dr. Robert D. Gillette. adv.; circ. 3,900.

610 US
OHIO MEDICINE. 1905. m. $25 to non-members (effective 1992). Ohio State Medical Association, 1500 Lakeshore Dr., Columbus, OH 43204-3824. TEL 614-486-2401. FAX 614-486-3130. Ed. Karen Edwards. adv. contact: George Quigley. bk.rev.; bibl.; illus.; index; circ. 12,000. (tabloid format) **Indexed:** Biol.Abstr., Dent.Ind., Excerp.Med., Ind.Med.
Formerly: Ohio State Medical Journal (ISSN 0030-1124)
Description: Covers legislative, legal and reimbursement issues for Ohio physicians, with association news and reports on trends in science and medical education.

610 US ISSN 0030-1132
OHIO STATE UNIVERSITY. COLLEGE OF MEDICINE. JOURNAL. 1947. q. Ohio State University, College of Medicine, 941 Chatham Ln., Columbus, OH 43221. TEL 614-459-3909. FAX 614-293-3666. Ed. Ernest W. Johnson. bk.rev.; bibl.; charts; illus.; stat.; circ. 13,700 (controlled).

OKAJIMA'S FOLIA ANATOMICA JAPONICA/OKAJIMA FORIA ANATOMIKA YAPONIKA. see *BIOLOGY*

610 JA ISSN 0030-1558
CODEN: OIZAAV
OKAYAMA IGAKKAI ZASSHI/MEDICAL ASSOCIATION OF OKAYAMA. JOURNAL. (Text in Japanese; summaries in English) vol.87, 1975. m. Okayama Igakkai - Medical Association of Okayama, c/o Okayama University Medical School, 5-1 Shikata-cho 2-chome, Okayama 700, Japan. Ed. Isamu Nisida. adv.; abstr.; charts; illus.; stat.; index; circ. 500. **Indexed:** Biol.Abstr., C.I.S. Abstr., Chem.Abstr.
—BLDSC shelfmark: 6252.830000.

610 US ISSN 0030-1876
OKLAHOMA STATE MEDICAL ASSOCIATION. JOURNAL. 1908. m. $30. Oklahoma State Medical Association, 601 N.W. Expressway, Oklahoma City, OK 73118. TEL 405-843-9571. Ed. Dr. Ray V. McIntyre. adv.; bk.rev.; abstr.; bibl.; illus.; stat.; index; circ. 4,400. (also avail. in microfilm from UMI) **Indexed:** Biol.Abstr., Chem.Abstr., Dent.Ind., Ind.Med, INIS Atomind., Nutr.Abstr.
—BLDSC shelfmark: 4835.300000.

615.5 IT ISSN 0030-2260
CODEN: OMDTA6
OMNIA MEDICA ET THERAPEUTICA.* 1949. q. L.3500. Edizioni Omnia Medica, Via S. Michele degli Scalzi 63, I-56100 Pisa, Italy. bk.rev.; abstr.; bibl.; illus.; index. **Indexed:** Biol.Abstr., Chem.Abstr., Excerp.Med., Ind.Med.

ON THE BEAM. see *HANDICAPPED — Visually Impaired*

362 US
ONE-IN-TEN. (Text in Arabic, English, French, Spanish) 1980. q. free. Rehabilitation International, 25 E. 21st St., New York, NY 10010.
TEL 212-420-1500. FAX 212-505-0871. TELEX 446412. (Co-sponsor: U N I C E F) Ed. Susan Hammerman. circ. 10,000.
Description: Covers childhood disabilities, their prevention and rehabilitation.

MEDICAL SCIENCES

610 CN ISSN 0030-302X
ONTARIO MEDICAL REVIEW. 1922. m. Can.$45 to non-members (in U.S. Can.$52; elsewhere Can.$68). Ontario Medical Association, 525 University Ave., Ste. 300, Toronto, Ont. M5G 2K7, Canada. TEL 416-599-2580. FAX 416-599-9309. Ed. R.D. Fletcher. adv.; bk.rev.; bibl.; charts; illus.; index; circ. 19,600. (back issues avail.) Indexed: Chem.Abstr.
—BLDSC shelfmark: 6262.050000.

610 CN
ONTARIO MEDICINE. 24/yr. Can.$49. Maclean-Hunter Ltd., Maclean-Hunter Bldg., 777 Bay St., Toronto, Ont. M5W 1A7, Canada.

610 SW ISSN 0030-414X
CODEN: OPMEAR
OPUSCULA MEDICA. (Text in Swedish; summaries in English) 1956. 4/yr. $15. Foereningen Opuscula Medica, Soedersjukhuset, 100 64 Stockholm 38, Sweden. Ed. Matts Halldin. adv.; bk.rev.; abstr.; charts; illus.; index; circ. 19,000. Indexed: Abstr.Hyg., Biol.Abstr., C.I.S. Abstr., Chem.Abstr., Excerp.Med., Trop.Dis.Bull.

610 PO ISSN 0030-4506
ORDEM DOS MEDICOS. BOLETIM. m. free to qualified personnel. Medical Association of Portugal, Ave. de Liberdade 65, Lisbon, Portugal.

610 IT
ORDINE DEI MEDICI DELLA PROVINCIA DI VENEZIA. NOTIZIARIO. 1957. bi-m. free to members. Ordine dei Medici, S. Polo 625, 30125 Venice, Italy. adv.; circ. 2,500.

610 FR ISSN 0030-4565
ORDRE NATIONAL DES MEDECINS. BULLETIN. 1941. 11/yr. 30 ECU($35) (typically set in Jan.). Masson, 120 bd. Saint-Germain, 75280 Paris Cedex 06, France. TEL 1-46-34-21-60. FAX 1-45-87-29-99. TELEX 202 671 F. circ. 70,000. (reprint service avail. from ISI)

610 US
ORGANIZATION OF TEACHERS OF ORAL DIAGNOSIS. NEWSLETTER. Also known as: Organization of Teachers of Oral Diagnosis. News. 1963. q. membership. (Organization of Teachers of Oral Diagnosis) University of Texas Dental School, 7703 Floyd Curl Dr., San Antonio, TX 78284. TEL 512-567-3333. Ed. James A. Cottone. bk.rev.; illus.; circ. 150. (looseleaf format)

610 US ISSN 0030-5669
ORLEANS PARISH MEDICAL SOCIETY. BULLETIN. 1935. bi-m. membership. Orleans Parish Medical Society, 1800 Canal St., New Orleans, LA 70112. TEL 504-523-2474. Ed. Dr. Russell C. Klein. adv.; circ. 2,019 (controlled). (tabloid format)

616 619 US ISSN 0887-0306
ORPHAN DISEASE UPDATE. 1983. 3/yr. $25. National Organization for Rare Disorders, Inc., Box 8923, New Fairfield, CT 06812. TEL 203-746-6518. FAX 203-746-6481. Ed. Abbey S. Meyers. charts; illus.; circ. 35,000. (tabloid format; back issues avail.)
●Also available online. Vendor(s): CompuServe Consumer Information Service (GO NORD).
Description: Information on orphan drugs and diseases. Covers medical advances, biomedical research, patient coping strategies, and legislative issues related to the field.

610 HU ISSN 0030-6002
R96.H8
ORVOSI HETILAP. (Text in Hungarian; summaries in English) 1857. w. $40. (Markusovszky Lajos Foundation) Springer Hungarica Kiado Ltd., Wesselenyi u. 28, 1410 Budapest 7, Hungary. (Subscr. to: Kultura, Box 149, 1389 Budapest, Hungary) Ed. Dr. Janos Feherseni. adv.; bk.rev.; illus.; index. Indexed: Biol.Abstr., Chem.Abstr., Dent.Ind., Dok.Arbeitsmed., Excerp.Med., Ind.Med., Nutr.Abstr., Protozool.Abstr.
—BLDSC shelfmark: 6296.500000.

610.7 HU ISSN 0030-6037
R91 **CODEN: ORVOAE**
ORVOSKEPZES. (Summaries in English and Russian) 1911. 6/yr. $30. Ifjusagi Lap-es Konyvkiado Vallalat, Revay u. 16, 1374 Budapest 6, Hungary. (Subscr. to: Kultura, Box 149, H-1389 Budapest, Hungary) Ed. Dr. Frigyes Kulka. adv.; index; circ. 3,200. Indexed: Biol.Abstr., Excerp.Med.
—BLDSC shelfmark: 6296.520000.
Description: Covers medical training.

610 HU ISSN 0010-3551
ORVOSTORTENETI KOZLEMENYEK/COMMUNICATIONS DE HISTORIA ARTIS MEDICINAE. (Text occasionally in English, French, German and Russian) 1955. q. $8. Semmelweis Orvostorteneti Muzeum, Konyvtar es Leveltar, Torok u. 12, 1023 Budapest, Hungary. (Subscr. to: Kultura, Box 149, 1389 Budapest, Hungary) (Co-sponsors: Magyar Orvostortenelmi Tarsasag; Springer Hungarica) Ed. Jozsef Antall. adv.; bk.rev.; cum.index; circ. 1,000. Indexed: Numis.Lit.
—BLDSC shelfmark: 6296.530000.

610 JA ISSN 0386-4103
OSAKA CITY MEDICAL JOURNAL. (Text in European languages) 1951. 2/yr. 7000 Yen($35) Osaka City Medical Center - Osaka-shi Igakkai, 1-4-54 Asahi-machi, Abeno-ku, Osaka 545, Japan. Ed. Shushi Matsuura. charts; illus.; stat.; circ. 1,200. (back issues avail.) Indexed: Biol.Abstr., C.I.S. Abstr., Chem.Abstr., Excerp.Med., Ind.Med., Nutr.Abstr.
—BLDSC shelfmark: 4838.000000.

610 JA ISSN 0387-446X
OSAKA DAIGAKU IRYO GIJUTSU TANKI DAIGAKUBU KENKYU KIYO. SHIZEN KAGAKU IRYO KAGAKU HEN/OSAKA UNIVERSITY. COLLEGE OF BIO-MEDICAL TECHNOLOGY AND NURSING. STUDIES IN NATURAL SCIENCE AND HEALTH TECHNOLOGY. (Text in Japanese; summaries in English and Japanese) 1968. a. Osaka Daigaku, Iryo Gijutsu Tanki Daigakubu - Osaka University. College of Bio-Medical Technology and Nursing, 1-1 Machikaneyama-cho, Toyonaka-shi, Osaka-fu 560, Japan.

610 JA ISSN 0030-6142
CODEN: BUOSA5
OSAKA MEDICAL COLLEGE. BULLETIN. (Text in English and European languages) 1954. s-a. free to medical institutions; exchange basis. Osaka Medical College - Osaka Ika Daigaku, 2-7 Daigaku-machi, Takatsuki, Osaka 569, Japan. Ed. Hideo Matsumoto. charts; illus.; index. Indexed: Biol.Abstr., Excerp.Med., Ind.Med.

610 JA ISSN 0030-6118
CODEN: OIDZAU
OSAKA MEDICAL COLLEGE. JOURNAL/OSAKA IKA DAIGAKU ZASSHI. (Text in Japanese; summaries in English) 1932. q. 1000 Yen. Osaka Medical College - Osaka Ika Daigaku, 2-7 Daigaku-machi, Takatsuki, Osaka 569, Japan. Ed. Hiroaki Takahashi. bk.rev. Indexed: Biol.Abstr., Chem.Abstr.
—BLDSC shelfmark: 4839.200000.

610 JA ISSN 0030-6169
CODEN: MJOUAL
OSAKA UNIVERSITY. MEDICAL JOURNAL/OSAKA DAIGAKU OBUN IGAKU ZASSHI. (Text in European languages) vol.24, 1973. q. Osaka Daigaku, Igakubu - Osaka University Medical School, 33 Joan-cho, Kita-ku, Osaka 530, Japan. Ed. Tadayasu Ban. charts; illus.; stat.; index. Indexed: Abstr.Hyg., Biol.Abstr., C.I.S. Abstr., Excerp.Med., Ind.Med., INIS Atomind., Mass Spectr.Bull., Nutr.Abstr., Trop.Dis.Bull.

OSLER LIBRARY NEWSLETTER. see LIBRARY AND INFORMATION SCIENCES

OSPEDALE AL MARE. ARCHIVIO. see HOSPITALS

610 UK ISSN 0937-941X
CODEN: OSINEP
OSTEOPOROSIS INTERNATIONAL. 1990. 6/yr. £120($212) (effective 1992). (European Foundation for Osteoporosis) Springer-Verlag, Springer House, 8 Alexandra Rd., London SW19 7JZ, England. TEL 081-947-1280. FAX 081-947-1274. (Co-sponsor: National Osteoporosis Foundation, US) Eds. Robert Lindsay, Pierre J. Meunier. (also avail. in microform from UMI) Indexed: Excerp.Med. (1992-).
—BLDSC shelfmark: 6303.873500.

616.7 US
OSTEOPOROSIS REPORT. 1985. q. $25 to individuals; institutions $125. National Osteoporosis Foundation, 2100 M St., N.W., Ste. 602, Washington, DC 20037. TEL 202-223-2226. FAX 202-223-2237. Ed. Sandra C. Raymond. circ. 6,000.
Description: Covers clinical updates, reports on activities, programs, and consumer articles.

610 US ISSN 0030-6517
OSTOMY QUARTERLY. 1963. q. $25. United Ostomy Association, Inc., 36 Executive Park, Ste. 120, Irvine, CA 92714-6744. FAX 714-660-9262. Ed. David Blum. adv.; bk.rev.; index; circ. 48,000. Indexed: Hlth.Ind., Rehabil.Lit.
—BLDSC shelfmark: 6312.375000.

610 UK ISSN 0030-7661
OXFORD MEDICAL SCHOOL GAZETTE. 1949. 3/yr. £4.50. University of Oxford Medical School, John Radcliffe Hospital, Headington, Oxford, England. adv.; bk.rev.; charts; illus.; stat.; circ. 1,000.

610 575 US
OXFORD MONOGRAPHS ON MEDICAL GENETICS. irreg. price varies. Oxford University Press, 200 Madison Ave., New York, NY 10016. TEL 212-679-7300. Ed.Bd.
Refereed Serial

610 US
P & S JOURNAL. (Physicians and Surgeons) 1955. 2/yr. free to qualified personnel. Columbia University, College of Physicians and Surgeons, Alumni Association, 630 W. 168 St., New York, NY 10032. TEL 212-305-3900. FAX 212-305-4521. Ed. Dr. Donald F. Tapley. illus.; circ. 20,000. (also avail. in microfilm from UMI; reprint service avail. from UMI)
Formerly (until 1981): P and S Quarterly (ISSN 0030-7831)

P B S BULLETIN. (Philippine Biochemical Society) see BIOLOGY — Biological Chemistry

610 GW ISSN 0722-477X
P M D - PRAXIS MEDIZINISCHER DOKUMENTATION. 1980. q. DM.40. P W D Presseverlag GmbH, Goethestr. 21, 8000 Munich 2, Germany. TEL 089-595261. Ed. Ulli Hoffmann. adv.; bk.rev.; circ. 2,000. (back issues avail.)
Description: Contains articles about medical documentation and record keeping. Also includes health care information, association news and reports, international news, events, and positions available.

616.02 GW ISSN 0938-9016
RB127
▼PAIN DIGEST. 1991. q. DM.240. Springer-Verlag, Heidelberger Platz 3, 1000 Berlin 33, Germany. TEL 030-8207-1. Ed. P. Prithvi Raj.
—BLDSC shelfmark: 6333.799000.
Description: Contains up-to-date knowledge of the research, evaluation methods, and techniques of pain management.

615 610.73 US ISSN 0896-9132
CODEN: PAIME9
PAIN MANAGEMENT. 1988. bi-m. Excerpta Medica, Inc., Core Publishing Division (Subsidiary of: Elsevier Science Publishers B.V.), 105 Raider Blvd., Belle Mead, NJ 08052. TEL 908-874-8550. FAX 908-874-0700. Ed. C. David Tollison. adv.; circ. 12,000.
—BLDSC shelfmark: 6333.805000.

610 US
PAIN SERIES. 1968. irreg. price varies. F.A. Davis Company, 1915 Arch St., Philadelphia, PA 19103. TEL 800-523-4049. TELEX 83-4837. Ed. Rene Cailliet.

610 UK
PAIN SOCIETY OF GREAT BRITAIN AND IRELAND. JOURNAL. 1987. s-a. £30($60) Pain Society of Great Britain and Ireland, 9 Bedford Square, London WC1B 3RA, England. Ed. R. Johnsbone. adv.; bk.rev.; circ. 600. (back issues avail.)
Formerly: Intractable Pain Society of Great Britain and Ireland. Journal.

MEDICAL SCIENCES 3139

610   PK   ISSN 0030-9842
PAKISTAN JOURNAL OF MEDICAL RESEARCH. 1961. q. $50. Pakistan Medical Research Council, National Health Research Complex, Shaikh Zayed Hospital, Lahore 54600, Pakistan. TEL 042-864230. FAX 042-864220. TELEX 47177 SZPMI PK. Ed. Dr. N. Rehan. adv.; bk.rev.; charts; illus.; stat.; index; circ. 1,000. (also avail. in microfilm from UMI; reprint service avail. from UMI) **Indexed:** Abstr.Hyg., Biol.Abstr., Nutr.Abstr.
—BLDSC shelfmark: 6341.550000.

610   PK   ISSN 0030-9982
                           CODEN: JJPAD4
PAKISTAN MEDICAL ASSOCIATION. JOURNAL. Abbreviated title: J P M A. (Text in English) 1950. m. Rs.200($75) Pakistan Medical Association, P.M.A. House, Garden Rd., Karachi 74400, Pakistan. Ed. Dr. S.J. Zuberi. adv.; bk.rev.; charts; illus.; stat.; circ. 6,000. (also avail. in microform from UMI; reprint service avail. from UMI) **Indexed:** Abstr.Hyg., Excerp.Med., Ind.Med., Trop.Dis.Bull.
—BLDSC shelfmark: 4839.497000.

610   UK   ISSN 0269-2163
                          CODEN: PAMDE2
PALLIATIVE MEDICINE. 1987. q. £67.50($105) to individuals; institutions £118($175). Edward Arnold (Subsidiary of: Hodder & Stoughton), Mill Road, Dunton Green, Sevenoaks, Kent TN13 2YA, England. TEL 0732-450111. FAX 0732-461321. (Dist. in U.S. and Canada by: Cambridge University Press, 40 W. 20th St., New York, NY 10011) adv.; bk.rev.
—BLDSC shelfmark: 6345.562060.
Description: Dedicated to improving knowledge and clinical practice in the care of patients with advanced diseases.

610   IT
PANMINERVA MEDICA - EUROPA MEDICA; monthly review of Italian medicine. (Text in English) 1959. q. L.60000($70) (Italian Medical Association) Edizioni Minerva Medica, Corso Bramante 83-85, 10126 Turin, Italy. (Dist. in U.S. by: J.B. Lippincott Company, E. Washington Square, Philadelphia, PA 19105) Ed. Alberto Oliaro. adv.; bk.rev.; abstr.; bibl.; charts; illus.; circ. 12,000. (also avail. in microfilm from UMI; reprint service avail. from UMI) **Indexed:** Biol.Abstr., Chem.Abstr., Curr.Cont., Dent.Ind., Helminthol.Abstr., Ind.Med., Nutr.Abstr.
Formed by the merger of: Panminerva Medica (ISSN 0031-0808) & Europa Medica (ISSN 0014-2557)

610   MX
PANORAMA MEDICO. 1971. m. free to doctors in Mexico. Dr. Javier Aranda Apellaniz, Ed. & Pub., Avda. Coyocan 1025, Edificio A no. 2, Condominio Jardin del Valle, Mexico 12, D.F., Mexico. adv.; circ. 15,000.

615.89   GW
PANTA. q. DM.46 (students DM.30). (Internationale Medizinische Gesellschaft fuer Elektroakupunktur) Karl F. Haug Verlag GmbH, Fritz-Frey-Str. 21, Postfach 102840, 6900 Heidelberg 1, Germany. TEL 06221-4062-0. FAX 06221-400727. TELEX 461683-HVVFM-D. Ed. Dr. G. Hanzl.

610   PP   ISSN 0256-2901
                          CODEN: MSPREG
PAPUA NEW GUINEA INSTITUTE OF MEDICAL RESEARCH. MONOGRAPH SERIES. 1970. irreg. price varies. Papua New Guinea Institute of Medical Research, P.O. Box 60, Goroka, Papua New Guinea. TEL 721469. FAX 675-721998. TELEX NE 72654. Ed. Dr. M.P. Alpers. bibl.; charts; illus.; circ. 1,000.
Description: A series of monographs on topics related to health and medical science in Papua New Guinea and elsewhere.

610   PP   ISSN 0031-1480
                          CODEN: PGMJBP
PAPUA NEW GUINEA MEDICAL JOURNAL. 1955. q. $60. Medical Society of Papua New Guinea, P.O. Box 60, Goroka, EHP, Papua New Guinea. FAX 721998. TELEX NE 72654. Ed. M. Alpers. adv.; bk.rev.; abstr.; bibl.; charts; illus.; index every 3 yrs.; circ. 500. (also avail. in microfilm from UMI; back issues avail.; reprint service avail. from UMI) **Indexed:** Abstr.Hyg., Biol.Abstr., Curr.Cont., Helminthol.Abstr., Ind.Med., Ind.Vet., Nutr.Abstr., Protozool.Abstr., Rev.Appl.Entomol., Rural Devel.Abstr., Rural Ext.Educ.& Tr.Abstr., Trop.Dis.Bull., Vet.Bull.
—BLDSC shelfmark: 6404.514000.

615.8   GW   ISSN 0723-5070
PARAPLEGIKER; das Nachrichtenmagazin der Querschnittgelaehmten. q. DM.28. Verlag fuer Medizin Dr. Ewald Fischer GmbH, Fritz-Frey-Str. 21, Postfach 105767, 6900 Heidelberg 1, Germany. TEL 06221-4062-0. Ed. Peter Mand.

610 636.089   UK   ISSN 0169-4758
                          CODEN: PATOE2
PARASITOLOGY TODAY; international review journal in the field of medical and veterinary parasites. Reference edition: Parsitology Today (ISSN 0169-4707) 1985. m. £239 (effective 1992). Elsevier Science Publishers Ltd., Crown House, Linton Rd, Barking, Essex IG11 8JU, England. TEL 081-594-7272. FAX 081-594-5942. TELEX 896950 APPSCI G. (Subscr. in U.S. and Canada to: Elsevier Science Publishing Co., Inc., Box 882, Madison Sq. Sta., New York, NY 10159. TEL 212-989-5800) Ed. Caroline Ash. adv.; bk.rev.; illus.; index; circ. 2,000. (back issues avail.) **Indexed:** Anim.Breed.Abstr., Biol.Abstr., Curr.Adv.Ecol.Sci., Curr.Cont., Dairy Sci.Abstr., Excerp.Med., Ind.Vet., Poult.Abstr., Protozool.Abstr., Trop.Dis.Bull., Vet.Bull.
Description: Interdisciplinary forum for communications in all aspects of current field and laboratory research in parasitology from molecular biology to ecology.
Refereed Serial

610   US
PARENT'S HEALTH ADVISER. m. Whittle Communications L.P., 333 Main Ave., Knoxville, TN 37902. TEL 615-595-5300. Ed. Margot Leske.
Description: Serves as a guide to parents by offering practical, comprehensive health care information about children.

610   US
PARK-NICOLLET MEDICAL FOUNDATION BULLETIN. 1956. q. free to qualified personnel. (Park Nicollet Medical Foundation) Park Nicollet Medical Center, 5000 W. 39th St, Minneapolis, MN 55416. TEL 612-927-3123. Ed. R.C. Woellner. charts; illus.; cum.index; circ. 6,500. **Indexed:** Ind.Med.
Formerly: St. Louis Park Medical Center. Bulletin (ISSN 0036-2980)
Description: Articles on diseases and treatment for physicians in primary care.

610   IT   ISSN 0031-2312
PARMAMEDICA;* bollettino dell'ordine dei medici. vol.15, 1967. m. L.2000 (free to qualified personnel). Ordine dei Medici della Provincia di Parma, Borgo al Collegio Maria Luigia 17, Parma, Italy. Ed. Carlo Molinari. adv.

PART B NEWS. see *INSURANCE*

616.07 576 574.8   SZ   ISSN 1015-2008
RB125   CODEN: PATHEF
PATHOBIOLOGY; journal of immunopathology, molecular and cellular biology. (Text in English) 1938. bi-m. 676 Fr.($451) S. Karger AG, Allschwilerstr. 10, P.O. Box, CH-4009 Basel, Switzerland. TEL 061-3061111. FAX 061-3061234. TELEX CH-962652. Ed. J.M. Cruse. adv.; bibl.; charts; illus.; index, cum.index; circ. 1,050. (also avail. in microform from RPI; back issues avail.) **Indexed:** Abstr.Hyg., ASCA, Biol.Abstr., Biotech.Abstr., C.I.S. Abstr., Chem.Abstr., Curr.Adv.Cancer Res., Curr.Adv.Cell & Devel.Biol., Curr.Adv.Ecol.Sci., Curr.Cont., Dairy Sci.Abstr., Dent.Ind., Excerp.Med., Helminthol.Abstr., Ind.Med., Ind.Sci.Rev., Ind.Vet., Nutr.Abstr., Rev.Plant Path., Sci.Cit.Ind., Trop.Dis.Bull., Vet.Bull.
—BLDSC shelfmark: 6412.738000.
Formed by the merger of: Experimental Cell Biology (ISSN 0304-3568) & Pathology and Immunopathology Research (ISSN 0257-2761); Experimental Cell Biology; Which was formerly: Pathologia et Microbiologia; Schweizerische Zeitschrift fuer Allgemeine Pathologie und Bakteriologie (ISSN 0031-2959) Pathology and Immunopathology Research; Which was formerly: Survey and Synthesis of Pathology Research (ISSN 0253-438X).

616.07   GW   ISSN 0172-8113
DER PATHOLOGE; pathologie und klinik. 1979. 6/yr. DM.296($181) (Deutsche Gesellschaft fuer Pathologie) Springer-Verlag, Heidelberger Platz 3, 1000 Berlin 33, Germany. TEL 030-8207-1. (Also Heidelberg, Tokyo, Vienna, and New York) (Co-sponsors: Internationale Academie fuer Pathologie - Pathologen e.V.; Oesterreichische Gesellschaft fuer Pathologie) Ed. V. Becker. (also avail. in microform from UMI; reprint service avail. from ISI) **Indexed:** Curr.Adv.Cell & Devel.Biol., Curr.Adv.Ecol.Sci., Curr.Cont., Excerp.Med., Ind.Med.
—BLDSC shelfmark: 6412.747000.

616.07   IT   ISSN 0031-2983
                          CODEN: PATHAB
PATHOLOGICA. (Text in English, French, Italian; summaries in English and Italian) 1908. bi-m. L.50000. E.O. Ospedali Galliera, Cappuccine 14, I-16128 Genoa, Italy. Eds. Pier Augusto Gemignani, Marco Canepa. adv.; bk.rev.; index; circ. 850. (back issues avail.) **Indexed:** Biol.Abstr., Excerp.Med., Ind.Med.
—BLDSC shelfmark: 6412.780000.

616.07 574.2   FR   ISSN 0031-3009
                          CODEN: PTBIAN
PATHOLOGIE BIOLOGIE. 1953. 10/yr. 1160 F. to individuals (foreign 1530 F.); students 580 F. (foreign 830 F.). (Semaine des Hopitaux) Expansion Scientifique, 15 rue St. Benoit, 75278 Paris Cedex 06, France. TEL 1-45-48-42-60. FAX 1-45-44-81-55. Ed. M. Boiron. adv. **Indexed:** Biol.Abstr., Chem.Abstr., Curr.Adv.Ecol.Sci., Curr.Cont., Dairy Sci.Abstr., Excerp.Med., Helminthol.Abstr., Ind.Med., Ind.Vet., Nutr.Abstr., Protozool.Abstr., Rev.Plant Path., Risk Abstr., Vet.Bull.

616.07 574.2   AT   ISSN 0031-3025
                          CODEN: PTLGAX
PATHOLOGY. 1969. q. Aus.$90. (Royal College of Pathologists of Australasia) Modern Medicine Australia Pty. Ltd., Ste. 33, 15 Grosvenor St., Neutral Bay, N.S.W. 2089, Australia. TEL 02-331-1431. Ed. B.A. Warren. adv.; bk.rev.; charts; illus.; index; circ. 1,800. **Indexed:** Abstr.Hyg., Biol.Abstr., Chem.Abstr., Curr.Adv.Ecol.Sci., Curr.Cont., Dairy Sci.Abstr., Excerp.Med., Helminthol.Abstr., Ind.Med., Ind.Vet., Nutr.Abstr., Rev.Plant Path., Risk Abstr., So.Pac.Per.Ind., Trop.Dis.Bull., Vet.Bull.
—BLDSC shelfmark: 6412.810000.

610   US   ISSN 1041-3480
PATHOLOGY; state of the art reviews. s-a. $60 (foreign $70). Hanley & Belfus, Inc., 210 S. 13th St., Philadelphia, PA 19107. TEL 215-546-7293. FAX 215-790-9330.
Refereed Serial

616.07 574.2   US   ISSN 0079-0184
RB1   CODEN: PATABP
PATHOLOGY ANNUAL. 1966. s-a. price varies. Appleton & Lange, Journal Division (Subsidiary of: Simon & Schuster Company), 25 Van Zant St., Box 5630, Norwalk, CT 06856. TEL 203-838-4400. Eds. Dr. Peter Rosen, Dr. Robert E. Fechner. bibl.; charts; illus. **Indexed:** Curr.Adv.Ecol.Sci., Excerp.Med., Ind.Med., Ind.Sci.Rev.
—BLDSC shelfmark: 6412.820000.
Description: Original articles written by an international contingent of scientists for practicing pathologists.
Refereed Serial

616.07 574.2   US
PATHOLOGY PATTERNS. (Suppl. to: American Journal of Clinical Pathology, ISSN 0002-9173) s-a. (American Society of Clinical Pathologists) J.B. Lippincott Co., E. Washington Sq., Philadelphia, PA 19105. TEL 800-638-3030. Ed. Dr. William T. Lockard, Jr.
Description: Provides current developments in the field of pathology and laboratory medicine.

MEDICAL SCIENCES

616.07   GW   ISSN 0344-0338
CODEN: PARPDS
PATHOLOGY, RESEARCH AND PRACTICE. (Text in English, German and French) 1886. irreg. (8 nos./vol.). DM.906. (European Society of Pathology) Gustav Fischer Verlag, Wollgrasweg 49, Postfach 720143, 7000 Stuttgart 70, Germany. TEL 0711-458030. FAX 0711-4580334. TELEX 7111488-FIBUCH. (US addr.: Gustav Fischer New York Inc., 220 E. 23rd St., Ste. 909, New York, NY 10010) Ed. Dr. E. Grundmann. adv.; bk.rev. **Indexed:** Biol.Abstr., Chem.Abstr., Curr.Adv.Cancer Res., Curr.Adv.Cell & Devel.Biol., Curr.Adv.Ecol.Sci., Curr.Cont., Dent.Ind., Dok.Arbeitsmed., Helminthol.Abstr., Ind.Med., Ind.Vet., Nutr.Abstr., Vet.Bull.
—BLDSC shelfmark: 6412.827000.
Former titles: Pathology and Practice; Beitraege zur Pathologie (ISSN 0005-8165)

610   US   ISSN 0031-305X
R11
PATIENT CARE. 1967. 20/yr. $72 (foreign $105). Medical Economics Publishing Co., Five Paragon Dr., Montvale, NJ 07645. TEL 201-358-7200. FAX 201-573-1045. Ed. Robert L. Edsall. adv.; charts; illus.; cum.index; circ. 117,000. (also avail. in microform from RPI; reprint service avail. from RPI) **Indexed:** Bus.Ind., C.I.N.L., FAMLI, Hlth.Ind., Tr.& Indus.Ind.
●Also available online. Vendor(s): DIALOG.
—BLDSC shelfmark: 6412.861200.
Description: Focuses on the diagnosis and treatment of problems encountered by the office-based, primary care physician.

610.2   AT   ISSN 0314-660X
PATIENT MANAGEMENT (AUSTRALIA); a journal of practical patient care. 1972. m. Aus.$96 (effective 1992). Adis Press Australasia Pty. Ltd., 404 Sydney Rd., Balgowlah, N.S.W. 2093, Australia. FAX 02-949-5007. Ed. Roger Olney. adv.; circ. 17,000.

610   CN
PATIENT UPDATE. q. Can.$10. Ontario Medical Association, 525 University Ave., Toronto, Ont. M5G 2K7, Canada. TEL 416-599-2580. FAX 416-599-9309.
Description: Covers such topics as family and sports medicine, women's health issues, lifestyle and preventive health care, medical research and advances in technology, diagnostic procedures and treatments, medications and physician profiles.

610   II   ISSN 0031-3084
CODEN: PAJMAA
PATNA JOURNAL OF MEDICINE. (Text in English) 1925. m. Rs.55 per no. Indian Medical Association, Bihar State Branch, Medical Association Bldg., Patna 800004, India. TEL 55295. (Co-sponsor: Patna Medical Association) Ed. Dr. A.M. Chatterjee. adv.; bk.rev.; charts; illus.; stat.; index; circ. 6,500 (controlled). (also avail. in microform) **Indexed:** Biol.Abstr.
Description: Aims to promote and advance medical and allied sciences, and the improvement of public health and medical education in Bihar and India.

PATOLOGIA. see BIOLOGY

616.07 574.2   PL   ISSN 0031-3114
CODEN: PAPOAC
PATOLOGIA POLSKA. 1950. q. $56. (Polskie Towarzystwo Anatomopatologow - Polish Society of Anatomo-Pathologists) Ossolineum, Publishing House of the Polish Academy of Sciences, 9 Rynek, 50-106 Wroclaw, Poland. TEL 386-25. (Dist. by: Ars Polona-Ruch, Krakowskie Przedmiescie 7, 00-068 Warsaw, Poland) Ed. Anna Urban. bk.rev.; illus.; index; circ. 1,020. **Indexed:** Biol.Abstr., Chem.Abstr., Excerp.Med., Ind.Med.
—BLDSC shelfmark: 6412.900000.
Description: Papers reporting of experimental research on pathology.

616.07 574.2   RU   ISSN 0031-2991
RB1   CODEN: PAFEAY
PATOLOGICHESKAYA FIZIOLOGIYA I EKSPERIMENTAL'NAYA TERAPIYA/PATHOLOGICAL PHYSIOLOGY AND EXPERIMENTAL THERAPY. (Text in Russian; summaries in English) 1957. bi-m. 25.20 Rub.($13.20) (Akademiya Meditsinskikh Nauk S.S.S.R.) Izdatel'stvo Meditsina, Petroverigskii pereulok 6-8, 101838 Moscow, Russia. (Subscr. to: Mezhdunarodnaya Kniga, Moscow, G-200, Russia) (Co-sponsor: Vsesoyuznoe Nauchnoe Obshchestvo Patofiziologov) Ed. B.B. Moroz. bk.rev.; illus.; index. **Indexed:** Biol.Abstr., Biotech.Abstr., Chem.Abstr., Dent.Ind., Excerp.Med., Ind.Med., Int.Aerosp.Abstr., Nutr.Abstr.
—BLDSC shelfmark: 0129.200000.
Description: Publishes materials on pressing problems of modern theoretical medicine - the etiology, pathogenesis of disease processes and individual nosological forms of the disease.

PEDIATRIC PHYSICAL THERAPY. see MEDICAL SCIENCES — Pediatrics

610   US   ISSN 0031-4595
R11   CODEN: PNMDAL
PENNSYLVANIA MEDICINE. 1897. m. $20. Pennsylvania Medical Society, Box 8820, Harrisburg, PA 17105-8820. Ed. Dr. John W. Mills. adv.; abstr.; bibl.; illus.; circ. 20,000. (also avail. in microfilm) **Indexed:** Biol.Abstr., C.I.S. Abstr., Chem.Abstr., CINAHL, Curr.Cont., Excerp.Med., Helminthol.Abstr., Ind.Med., Med. Care Rev.
—BLDSC shelfmark: 6421.745000.
Formerly: Pennsylvania Medical Journal.

PEOPLE'S MEDICAL SOCIETY NEWSLETTER. see CONSUMER EDUCATION AND PROTECTION

618   US   ISSN 0747-3079
RD598.35.A77
PERFUSION LIFE. 1973. m. (11/yr.) $35 (foreign $60). American Society of Extra-Corporeal Technology, Inc., 11480 Sunset Hills Rd., Ste. 100E, Reston, VA 22090. TEL 703-435-8556. Ed. John Patterson. circ. 2,400.

PERIODICUM BIOLOGORUM. see BIOLOGY

610 616.6   CN   ISSN 0896-8608
PERITONEAL DIALYSIS INTERNATIONAL. 1980. q. $50 to nurses; physicians $60; institutions $160. (International Society for Peritoneal Dialysis) Multimed, Inc., 1120 Finch Ave., W., Ste. 601, Toronto, Ont. M3J 3H7, Canada. TEL 416-650-0610. FAX 416-650-0639. Ed. Dimitrios Oreopoulos. index. (also avail. in microform from UMI; back issues avail.) **Indexed:** Curr.Cont., Excerp.Med.
—BLDSC shelfmark: 6426.459000.
Formerly: Peritoneal Dialysis Bulletin.

PERSONAL INJURY REVIEW (YEAR). see LAW

610 570   US   ISSN 0031-5982
QH301   CODEN: PBMEA8
PERSPECTIVES IN BIOLOGY AND MEDICINE. 1957. q. $35 to individuals; institutions $50; students $15. University of Chicago Press, Journals Division, 5720 S. Woodlawn Ave., Chicago, IL 60637. TEL 312-753-3347. FAX 312-702-0694. TELEX 25-4603. (Orders to: Box 37005, Chicago, IL 60637) Ed. Richard L. Landau. adv.; bk.rev.; bibl.; charts; index; circ. 3,500. (also avail. in microform from MIM,UMI; reprint service avail. from UMI,ISI) **Indexed:** Biol.Abstr., Biol.& Agr.Ind., Biol.Dig., Chem.Abstr., Curr.Adv.Cancer Res., Curr.Adv.Ecol.Sci., Curr.Cont., Deep Sea Res.& Oceanogr.Abstr., Dent.Abstr., Dent.Ind., Excerp.Med., Helminthol.Abstr., Ind.Med., Ind.Vet., Lang.& Lang.Behav.Abstr., Psychol.Abstr., Sci.Cit.Ind., Small Anim.Abstr., Vet.Bull.
—BLDSC shelfmark: 6428.138200.
Refereed Serial

610   CN
PERSPECTIVES IN EMERGENCY MEDICINE. 1986. q. S T A Communications Inc., 955 boul. St. Jean, Ste. 306, Pointe-Claire, Que. H9R 5K3, Canada. TEL 514-695-7623. FAX 514-695-8554. adv.; circ. 22,000.

616.132   US
PERSPECTIVES IN HYPERTENSION SERIES. 1987. irreg., latest vol.3. price varies. Raven Press, 1185 Ave. of the Americas, New York, NY 10036. TEL 212-930-9500. FAX 212-869-3495. Ed.Bd.

PERSPECTIVES IN PEDIATRIC PATHOLOGY. see MEDICAL SCIENCES — Pediatrics

610 614.8   PE
PERU. POLICIA NACIONAL. REVISTA DE LA SANIDAD. (Text in Spanish; abstracts in English, Spanish) 1940. s-a. $60. Ministerio del Interior, Direccion de Sanidad de las Fuerzas Policiales, Casilla 1683, Lima 100, Peru. (Subscr. to: Ave. Arequipa 4849 Miraflores Lima 18, Peru) Eds. Dr. Raul Morales Soto, Dr. Guillermo Quiros Jara. adv.; bk.rev.; abstr.; bibl.; charts; illus.; index; circ. 3,000. **Indexed:** Chem.Abstr., Excerp.Med.
Former titles: Peru. Fuerzas Policiales. Revista de la Sanidad & Peru. Direccion de Sanidad. Revista de la Sanidad; Instituto de Investigaciones Medicas de la Fuerza Armada y Fuerzas Policiales del Peru; Revista de la Sanidad de las Fuerzas Policiales del Peru; Revista de la Sanidad de Policia (ISSN 0034-8430)

610   BL   ISSN 0048-3567
PESQUISA MEDICA. (Text in Portuguese; summaries in English) 1965. s-a. Cr.$20000($25) Fundacao Faculdade Federal de Ciencias Medicas de Porto Alegre, Centro Academico XXII de Marco, Rua Sarmento Leite, 245, 90050 Porto Alegre RS, Brazil. TEL 0512-24-8822. FAX 0512-26-7913. Ed. Dr. Ligia M.B. Coutinho. adv.; bibl.; illus.; index; circ. 1,000 (controlled). **Indexed:** Biol.Abstr., Chem.Abstr.

612   GW   ISSN 0031-6768
QP1   CODEN: PFLABK
PFLUEGERS ARCHIV; European journal of physiology. (Text mainly in English; occasionally in French, German) 1868. 12/yr. DM.2160($1101) Springer-Verlag, Heidelberger Platz 3, D-1000 Berlin 33, Germany. TEL 030-8207-1. (Also Heidelberg, Tokyo, Vienna, and New York) Ed. Dr. F. Kreuzer. adv.; charts; illus. (also avail. in microform from UMI,BHP; back issues avail.; reprint service avail. from ISI) **Indexed:** Biol.Abstr., C.I.S. Abstr., Chem.Abstr., Curr.Adv.Ecol.Sci., Curr.Cont., Dairy Sci.Abstr., Excerp.Med., Ind.Med., Ind.Vet., Nutr.Abstr., Phys.Ber., Vet.Bull.
—BLDSC shelfmark: 6440.999000.
Formerly: Pfluegers Archiv fuer die Gesamte Physiologie des Menschen und der Tiere.
Description: Covers original research on the most current developments in areas of specialization, in interdisciplinary work, and in the physiological sciences as a whole.

PHARMACEUTICAL MEDICINE (HOUNDMILLS). see PHARMACY AND PHARMACOLOGY

610 615   UK   ISSN 0142-1581
PHARMACEUTICAL MEDICINE (WORTHING); symposium proceedings. 1979. irreg. Cambridge Medical Publications Ltd., 3 Liverpool Gardens, Worthing, West Sussex BN11 1TF, England. TEL 0903-205884. FAX 0903-34862. TELEX 878372-PPSLTD. **Indexed:** Curr.Adv.Ecol.Sci.

610   UK   ISSN 0308-051X
CODEN: PHARDW
PHARMATHERAPEUTICA. (Text and summaries in various languages) 1976. irreg. $60. Clayton-Wray Publications Ltd., 1A High St., Alton, Hants. GU34 1BA, England. Ed. Nigel Clayton. circ. 5,500. **Indexed:** Abstr.Hyg., Biol.Abstr, Biotech.Abstr., Chem.Abstr., Curr.Adv.Ecol.Sci., Curr.Cont., Dent.Ind., Excerp.Med., Helminthol.Abstr., Ind.Med., Nutr.Abstr.
—BLDSC shelfmark: 6447.640000.

610   US   ISSN 0031-7179
LJ105.A6
PHAROS (MENLO PARK). 1938. q. $10 to non-members. Alpha Omega Alpha Honor Medical Society, 525 Middlefield Rd., Ste. 130, Menlo Park, CA 94025. TEL 415-329-0291. FAX 415-329-1618. Ed. Dr. Robert J. Glaser. bk.rev.; bibl.; charts; circ. 70,000. **Indexed:** Ind.Med., RILA.
—BLDSC shelfmark: 6449.120000.

610   US   ISSN 0031-7306
PHILADELPHIA MEDICINE. 1906. m. $10.50. Philadelphia County Medical Society, 2100 Spring Garden St., Philadelphia, PA 19130. TEL 215-563-5343. FAX 215-563-3627. Ed. Dr. William Weiss. adv.; circ. 5,000.
—BLDSC shelfmark: 6449.600000.

MEDICAL SCIENCES

610   PH   ISSN 0031-7748
CODEN: JPMEA6
PHILIPPINE MEDICAL ASSOCIATION. JOURNAL. 1928. q. $20. P M A Press, P M A House, North Ave., Diliman, Quezon City, Philippines. Ed. Conrado Dayrit. adv.; bk.rev.; charts; illus.; stat.; index; circ. 13,000. **Indexed:** Biol.Abstr., C.I.S. Abstr., Chem.Abstr, INIS Atomind., Trop.Dis.Bull.

PHILOSOPHY AND MEDICINE. see *PHILOSOPHY*

616.20   GW   ISSN 0939-978X
CODEN: PHLBE
PHLEBOLOGIE. 1972. 6/yr. DM.150($102) to individuals; institutions DM.192($122.40). (German and Swiss Society of Phlebology) F.K. Schattauer Verlagsgesellschaft mbH, Lenzhalde 3, Postfach 104545, 7000 Stuttgart 10, Germany. TEL 0711-22987-0. FAX 0711-2298750. adv.; bk.rev. **Indexed:** Excerp.Med.
Formerly (until 1991): Phlebologie und Proktologie (ISSN 0340-305X)

610   GW
PHOTOMED. q. DM.178 (foreign DM.188). Quintessenz Verlags GmbH, Ifenpfad 2-4, 1000 Berlin 42, Germany. TEL 030-74006-0. FAX 030-7415080.

610 530   IT   ISSN 1120-1797
PHYSICA MEDICA. vol.5, no.1, 1989. (Italian Association of Biomedical Physicists) Acta Medica Edizioni e Congressi, Via Gian Giacomo Porro 5, 00197 Rome, Italy. TEL 06-805005. FAX 06-854164. Ed. A. Del Guerra.
—BLDSC shelfmark: 6475.070000.
Incorporates: Fisica in Medicina.

610   US   ISSN 0888-7357
RD755
PHYSICAL MEDICINE & REHABILITATION; state of the art reviews. Short title: P M & R. 3/yr. $68 (foreign $80). Hanley & Belfus, Inc., 210 S. 13th St., Philadelphia, PA 19107. TEL 215-546-7293. FAX 215-790-9330. circ. 2,000. (back issues avail.)
—BLDSC shelfmark: 6475.635000.
Refereed Serial

615.8   US   ISSN 0031-9023
RM695   CODEN: PTHEA
PHYSICAL THERAPY. 1921. m. $55 to non-members. American Physical Therapy Association, 1111 N. Fairfax St., Fairfax, VA 22314. TEL 703-684-2782. Ed. Jules Rothstein. adv.; bk.rev.; abstr.; charts; illus.; index; circ. 53,771. (also avail. in microform from UMI; reprint service avail. from UMI) **Indexed:** Abstr.Health Care Manage.Stud., Bibl.Dev.Med.& Child Neur., CINAHL, Curr.Cont., Except.Child Educ.Abstr, Excerp.Med., Hlth.Ind., Hosp.Lit.Ind., Ind.Med., Int.Nurs.Ind., Phys.Ed.Ind., Sportsearch (1980-).
●Also available online. Vendor(s): BRS, BRS/Saunders Colleague, Central Institute for Scientific & Technical Information, Information Access Company.
—BLDSC shelfmark: 6476.350000.
Formerly: American Physical Therapy Association. Journal.

615.8   US   ISSN 0742-9711
PHYSICAL THERAPY IN HEALTH CARE; the contemporary journal of clinical practice. 1986. q. $25 to individuals; institutions $32; libraries $60. Haworth Press, Inc., 10 Alice St., Binghamton, NY 13904. TEL 800-342-9678. FAX 607-722-1424. TELEX 4932599. Eds. Eleanor Branch, Mary Singleton. adv.; bk.rev.; circ. 147. (also avail. in microfiche)
—BLDSC shelfmark: 6476.350300.
Description: Provides practical information on the management of problems encountered in practice of physical therapy in health care.
Refereed Serial

615.8   US   ISSN 1059-096X
PHYSICAL THERAPY PRODUCTS. bi-m. Novicom, Inc., 3510 Torrance Blvd., Ste. 315, Torrance, CA 90503. TEL 310-316-8112. FAX 310-316-8422. Ed. Patricia Bennett. circ. 50,000.
Description: Covers the introductions of new physical therapy products, with advisory columns discussing new procedures, and other topics of interest to professionals.

615.8   US   ISSN 1042-2579
PHYSICAL THERAPY TODAY. 1956. q. $40 to individuals; institutions $52. (American Physical Therapy Association, Private Practice Section) Williams & Wilkins, 428 Preston St., Baltimore, MD 21202. TEL 301-528-4000. FAX 301-528-4312. TELEX 87669. Ed. Kay Schaefer. adv.; bk.rev.; illus.; circ. 4,600.
Formerly: Whirlpool.
Description: Addresses business and clinical concerns of physical therapists in private practice.

610 658   US
PHYSICIAN & PATIENT. 1982. m. D & G Publishing Corp., Box 377, 32 North Cottenet St., Irvington-on-Hudson, NY 10533.

610   US
PHYSICIAN ASSISTANT. 1976. m. $60. Excerpta Medica, Inc., Core Publishing Division (Subsidiary of: Elsevier Science Publishers B.V.), 105 Raider Blvd., Belle Mead, NJ 08502. TEL 908-874-8550. FAX 908-874-0700. illus.; circ. 18,000. (also avail. in microfilm from UMI; reprint service avail. from UMI) **Indexed:** CINAHL.
Former titles (1979-1982): Physician Assistant - Health Practitioner (ISSN 0197-713X); (1978-1979): Health Practitioner, Physician Assistant (ISSN 0192-7310); Which was formed by the merger of: Physician Assistant; (1977-1978): Health Practitioner (ISSN 0149-6549)

610   US   ISSN 1051-600X
R847.5
PHYSICIAN ASSISTANT PROGRAMS DIRECTORY. 1975. biennial. $15. Association of Physician Assistant Programs, 950 N. Washington St., Alexandria, VA 22314-1534. TEL 703-836-2272. FAX 703-684-1924. Ed.Bd. circ. 10,000.
Former titles (until 1989): Physician Assistant Programs, A National Directory; National Health Practitioner Program Profile (ISSN 0277-3376); National New Health Practitioner Program Profile (ISSN 0145-3793)
Description: Contains summary charts detailing the PA program and postgraduate PA program entrance requirements, fees, deadlines, program length, and credentials awarded.

PHYSICIAN EXECUTIVE REVIEW; journal of management. see *BUSINESS AND ECONOMICS — Management*

610   US
PHYSICIAN MANAGER. m. Atlantic Information Services, Inc., 1050 17th St., N.W., Ste. 480, Washington, DC 20036. TEL 202-775-9008. FAX 202-331-9542. Ed. Michael Carbine.

610   US
PHYSICIAN'S CODING STRATEGIST. Issued with: Physician's Payment Advisory. 1989. m. American Health Consultants, Inc., 67 Peachtree Park Dr., N.E., Atlanta, GA 30309-1397. TEL 404-351-4523.

610   US   ISSN 0093-4461
RS75
PHYSICIANS' DESK REFERENCE. 1947. a. $54.95 (foreign $94.95)(effective 1992). Medical Economics Publishing Co., Five Paragon Dr., Montvale, NJ 07645. TEL 201-357-7200. FAX 201-573-1045. (Subscr. to: P D R, Box 10689, Des Moines, IA 50336) circ. 485,000 (controlled).
●Also available online.
Also available on CD-ROM.
Formerly: Physicians' Desk Reference to Pharmaceutical Specialties and Biologicals (ISSN 0093-447X)
Description: Contains prescription drug information.

610   US   ISSN 1044-1395
RM671.A1
PHYSICIANS' DESK REFERENCE FOR NONPRESCRIPTION DRUGS. 1980. a. $35.95 (foreign $55.95)(effective 1992). Medical Economics Publishing Co., Five Paragon Dr., Montvale, NJ 07645. TEL 201-358-7200. FAX 201-573-1045. (Subscr. to: P D R, Box 10689, Des Moines, IA 50336) circ. 315,000 (controlled).
●Also available online.
Also available on CD-ROM.
Description: Covers over-the-counter drugs.

PHYSICIANS FINANCIAL NEWS. see *BUSINESS AND ECONOMICS — Banking And Finance*

610   US   ISSN 0079-192X
RC55
PHYSICIAN'S HANDBOOK. 1941. irreg., 21st ed., 1985. Appleton & Lange (Subsidiary of: Simon & Schuster Company), 25 Van Zant St., Box 5630, Norwalk, CT 06856. TEL 203-838-4400.
Description: Essential medical facts include diagnostic tests, patient examination, laboratory tests, emergency medical examination, drugs and hormones.

PHYSICIANS LIFESTYLE MAGAZINE. see *GENERAL INTEREST PERIODICALS — United States*

610   US   ISSN 0031-9066
R728
PHYSICIAN'S MANAGEMENT; the doctor's business journal. 1961. m. $40 (effective 1992). Avanstar Communications, Inc., 7500 Old Oak Blvd., Cleveland, OH 44130. TEL 216-826-2839. FAX 216-891-2726. (Subscr. to: 1 E. First St., Duluth, MN 55802. TEL 800-346-0085) Ed. Bob Feigenbaum. adv.; illus.; stat.; index; circ. 110,393. **Indexed:** Account.Ind. (1987-).
Description: Covers management techniques and economic factors affecting the doctor's practice.

610 658   CN   ISSN 0705-6311
PHYSICIAN'S MANAGEMENT MANUALS. 1976. m. Can.$81. Maclean-Hunter Ltd., Business Publication Division, Maclean-Hunter Bldg., 777 Bay St., Toronto, Ont. M5W 1A7, Canada. TEL 416-596-5724. Ed. William Koteff. adv.; circ. 41,500. **Indexed:** Can.B.P.I.
Description: Information for Canadian doctors on practice management and investment.

610   US   ISSN 1042-2625
PHYSICIANS MARKETING & MANAGEMENT. m. $157 to individuals; institutions $197. American Health Consultants, Inc., Six Piedmont Center, Ste. 400, 3525 Piedmont Rd., N.E., Atlanta, GA 30305. TEL 404-262-7436. FAX 800-284-3291. (Subscr. to: Box 740056, Atlanta, GA 30374-9822. TEL 800-688-2421) Ed. Kim Putnam. charts; illus.; tr.lit.; index; circ. 2,000. (back issues avail.)
Incorporates (1986-1992): Practice Personel Bulletin (ISSN 0888-9066); **Formerly:** Physician's Marketing.
Description: Covers all aspects of private practice management, including personnel, capital and risk management, and how-to marketing methods.

616.7   US
PHYSICIAN'S RESOURCE MANUAL ON OSTEOPOROSIS; a decision making guide. 1987. irreg., latest 1991. $7.50. National Osteoporosis Foundation, 2100 M St., N.W., Ste 602, Washington, DC 20037. TEL 202-223-2226. FAX 202-223-2237. Ed. Dr. W.A. Peck. circ. 25,000.
Description: Covers biology of the bone, pathogenesis of fracture, prevention and treatment.

610   US
PHYSICIAN'S WEEKLY. 48/yr. Whittle Communications L.P., 333 Main Ave., Knoxville, TN 37902. TEL 615-595-5300. Ed. Mark Blume.
Description: Offers highlights and analyses of medical news about a wide range of specialties.

574.191 610   UK   ISSN 0031-9155
QH505   CODEN: PHMBA7
PHYSICS IN MEDICINE AND BIOLOGY. (Text in English; abstracts in English, French, German) 1956. m. £315($630) (effective 1991). (Institute of Physics) I O P Publishing, Techno House, Redcliffe Way, Bristol BS1 6NX, England. TEL 0272-297481. FAX 0272-294318. TELEX 449149-INSTP-G. (U.S. Address: American Institute of Physics, Dept. N/M, 335 E. 45th St., New York, NY 10017) (Co-sponsors: Hospital Physicists Association, UK; International Organization for Medical Physics; European Federation of Organizations for Medical Physics) Ed. S.C. Lillicrap. adv.; bk.rev.; bibl.; charts; illus.; index. (also avail. in microform; microfiche; back issues avail.) **Indexed:** Biol.Abstr., Chem.Abstr., Curr.Adv.Ecol.Sci., Curr.Cont., Dairy Sci.Abstr., Dok.Arbeitsmed., Excerp.Med., Ind.Med., Nutr.Abstr., Sci.Abstr.
—BLDSC shelfmark: 6478.800000.

MEDICAL SCIENCES

615.8   GW   ISSN 0940-6689
CODEN: PMRKE
PHYSIKALISCHE MEDIZIN REHABILITATIONSMEDIZIN KURORTMEDIZIN. (Text in German; summaries in English, German and Russian) 1949. irreg. (approx. 6/yr.). DM.102. Georg Thieme Verlag, Ruedigerstr. 14, Postfach 104853, 7000 Stuttgart 10, Germany. TEL 0711-8931-0. FAX 0711-8931298. Eds. Prof. H. Jordan, Dr. J.C. Cordes. adv.; bk.rev.; abstr.; charts; illus.; circ. 1,100. **Indexed:** Biol.Abstr., Chem.Abstr., Excerp.Med., Ind.Med.
—BLDSC shelfmark: 6482.280000.
   Former titles (until 1991): Zeitschrift fuer Physiotherapie (ISSN 0003-9357); Archiv fuer Physikalische Therapie, Balneologie und Klimatologie.

615.8   CN   ISSN 0706-4284
PHYSIO-QUEBEC. 1975. q. Can.$20($25) Corporation Professionnelle des Physiotherapeutes du Quebec, 1100 Beaumont, No. 530, Mount-Royal, Que. H3P 3E5, Canada. FAX 514-737-6431. Ed. Johanne Sabourin. adv.; bk.rev.; circ. 2,800.

PHYSIOLOGICAL RESEARCH. see *BIOLOGY — Physiology*

PHYSIOLOGICAL REVIEWS. see *BIOLOGY — Physiology*

PHYSIOLOGICAL SOCIETY OF JAPAN. JOURNAL/NIHON SEIRIGAKU ZASSHI. see *BIOLOGY — Physiology*

PHYSIOLOGIST. see *BIOLOGY — Physiology*

612 574.1   CN   ISSN 0822-9058
PHYSIOLOGY CANADA. (Text in English and French) 1969. 3/yr. Can.$11.50 (foreign $16). Canadian Physiological Society, Department of Physiology, University of Western Ontario, London, Ont. N6A 5C1, Canada. TEL 519-661-3480. FAX 519-661-3827. Ed. D.L. Jones. adv.; bk.rev.; circ. 700. **Indexed:** Biol.Abstr.
—BLDSC shelfmark: 6488.350000.

615.8   SZ
PHYSIOTHERAPEUT/PHYSIOTHERAPEUTE. (Text in French and German) 1933. m. 80 F. Schweizerischer Physiotherapeuten-Verband, Postfach, CH-6204 Sempach-Stadt, Switzerland. FAX 041-993388. Ed. Verena Ruegg. adv.; bk.rev.; charts; illus.; stat.; circ. 4,300.

615.8   UK   ISSN 0031-9406
PHYSIOTHERAPY. 1915. m. £45 (typically set in Jan.). Chartered Society of Physiotherapy, 14 Bedford Row, London WC1R 4ED, England. FAX 071-831-4509. Ed. Jill Whitehouse. adv.; bk.rev.; illus.; index; circ. 29,000. **Indexed:** Bibl.Dev.Med.& Child Neur., CINAHL, Dok.Arbeitsmed., Excerp.Med., Ind.Med.
—BLDSC shelfmark: 6489.000000.

615.8   CN   ISSN 0300-0508
CODEN: PTHCAZ
PHYSIOTHERAPY CANADA. (Text in English, French) 1923. 6/yr. Can.$35($50) Canadian Physiotherapy Association, 890 Yonge St, 9th Fl., Toronto, Ont. M4W 3P4, Canada. TEL 416-924-5312. FAX 416-924-7335. Ed. Diane Charter. adv.; bk.rev.; index; circ. 6,500. (also avail. in microform from UMI; reprint service avail. from UMI) **Indexed:** Biol.Abstr., C.I.N.L., Excerp.Med., Hosp.Lit.Ind, Rehabil.Lit.
—BLDSC shelfmark: 6489.100000.
   Formerly: Canadian Physiotherapy Association Journal - Association Canadienne de Physiotherapie Revue (ISSN 0008-4751)

610 613.7   UK   ISSN 0959-3985
CODEN: PTHPEA
PHYSIOTHERAPY THEORY AND PRACTICE; an international journal of physical therapy. 1985. 4/yr. £33($74) to individuals; institutions £66($135). Lawrence Erlbaum Associates Ltd., 27 Palmeira Masions, Church Rd., Hove, E. Sussex BN3 2FA, England. TEL 0273-207411. FAX 0273-205612. Ed. Hilary Baddeley. bk.rev.
—BLDSC shelfmark: 6489.140000.
   Description: Forum for recent developments and current research in physiotherapy.
   Refereed Serial

610   CN
PHYSIOTHERAPY TODAY. 1980. bi-m. $25 to non-members. Ontario Physiotherapy Association, 29 Gervais Drive, Ste. 303, Don Mills, Ont. M3C 1Y9, Canada. TEL 416-391-4700. FAX 416-391-4702. Ed. Carolyn F. Strutt. adv.; circ. 3,000 (controlled).
   Formerly: Taking Care of O P A Business.

610   GW   ISSN 0931-9069
PHYSIS; Medizin und Naturwissenschaften. 1984. m. DM.40. Urban und Vogel, Lindwurmstr. 95, Postfach 152209, 8000 Munich 2, Germany. TEL 089-53292-0. FAX 089-53292-100. circ. 48,500 (controlled).

PHYTOTHERAPY RESEARCH; an international journal devoted to medical and scientific research on plants and plant products. see *BIOLOGY — Botany*

610   IT
PIEMONTE MEDICO. 1953. m. free. Federazione Regionale Ordini dei Medici Chirurghi e degli Odontoiatri, Via Caboto 35, 10129 Turin, Italy. Ed. Luigi Triberti. adv.; circ. 20,150.
   Formerly: Ordine dei Medici. Bollettino (ISSN 0471-7708)

610   LE   ISSN 0032-0404
PJICHK.* (Text in Armenian) 1956. m. £L12.($5.) Atlas Publishing Co., Spears St., Beirut, Lebanon. Eds. Dr. V. Sahakian, Dr. A. Kazandian.

610.69   CN
PLACE OF GRADUATION FOR SELECTED HEALTH OCCUPATIONS. 1975. biennial. free. University of British Columbia, Centre for Health Services and Policy Research, No. 429 - 2194 Health Sciences Mall, Vancouver, B.C. V6T 1Z3, Canada. TEL 604-822-4810. FAX 604-822-5690. circ. 100 (controlled).
   Description: Provides an analysis by province or country of graduation for each of the groups represented.

610   US
PODIATRY MANAGEMENT MAGAZINE. 1982. 9/yr. $30. Kane Communications, Inc., 7000 Terminal Square, Ste. 210, Upper Darby, PA 19082. TEL 215-734-2420. Ed. Dr. Barry Block. adv.; bk.rev.; pat.; stat.; circ. 12,500. (back issues avail.)

610   IT   ISSN 0048-4717
POLICLINICO. SEZIONE MEDICA. 1893. q. (includes Policlinico. Sezione Pratica). Edizioni Luigi Pozzi s.r.l., Via Panama 68, 00198 Rome, Italy. TEL 06-8553548. FAX 06-8554105. Ed.Bd. adv.; illus.; circ. 1,900. **Indexed:** Chem.Abstr., Excerp.Med., Ind.Med.
—BLDSC shelfmark: 6543.302000.

610   IT   ISSN 0032-2644
POLICLINICO. SEZIONE PRATICA. (Text in Italian; summaries in English, French and Italian) 1893. fortn. $140 (includes Policlinico. Sezione Medica). Edizioni Luigi Pozzi s.r.l., Via Panama 68, 00198 Rome, Italy. TEL 06-8553548. FAX 06-8554105. adv.; bk.rev.; charts; illus.; stat.; index; circ. 11,500. **Indexed:** Chem.Abstr., Dent.Ind., Excerp.Med.
   Description: Covers internal medicine.

610   US
POLIO NETWORK NEWS. q. $12 to individuals (foreign $16); health professionals and institutions $20 (foreign $24). (International Polio Network) Gazette International Networking Institute, 5100 Oakland Ave., Ste. 206, St. Louis, MO 63110-1441: TEL 314-534-0475. Ed. Joan Headley. circ. 5,000.
   Description: Serves as a communications network for polio survivors, support groups and health professionals. Highlights the late effects of polio (post-polio syndrome) - cause, treatment, and current research.

610 327   UK   ISSN 0730-9384
JA80
POLITICS AND THE LIFE SCIENCES. 1982. s-a. £45($65) to individuals (foreign $26); libraries $40 (foreign $46). (Northen Illinois University) Beech Tree Publishing, 10 Watford Close, Guildford, Surrey GU1 2EP, England. TEL 44-0483-67497. Ed. Garry Johnson. adv.; bk.rev.; bibl.; charts; illus.; circ. 350. (back issues avail.) **Indexed:** A.B.C.Pol.Sci., Biol.Abstr., Biol.Dig., Curr.Cont., Int.Polit.Sci.Abstr., SSCI.
—BLDSC shelfmark: 6543.941850.
   Description: Provides a forum for scholars interested in both the methods and the findings of research in the life sciences that relates to the study of politics and public policy.

610   PL   ISSN 0079-3558
POLSKA AKADEMIA NAUK. WYDZIAL NAUK MEDYCZNYCH. ROZPRAWY. (Text in Polish; summaries in English and Russian) 1956. irreg. price varies. Ossolineum, Pulishing House of the Polish Academy of Sciences, Ul. Rynek 9-11, 50-106 Wroclaw, Poland. (Dist. by: Ars Polona-Ruch, Krakowskie Przedmiescie 7, 00-068 Warsaw, Poland) Ed. Witold Orlowski.

610   PL   ISSN 0032-3756
POLSKI TYGODNIK LEKARSKI. (Text in Polish; summaries in English and Russian) 1946. w. $221. Panstwowy Zaklad Wydawnictw Lekarskich, Ul. Dluga 38-40, Warsaw, Poland. TEL 31-42-81. (Dist. by: Ars Polona-Ruch, Krakowskie Przedmiescie 7, 00-068 Warsaw, Poland) Ed. Jan Taton. adv.; bk.rev.; abstr.; charts; illus.; s-a. index; circ. 9,200. **Indexed:** Biol.Abstr., C.I.S. Abstr., Chem.Abstr., Dent.Ind., Dok.Arbeitsmed., Excerp.Med., Ind.Med., Nutr.Abstr., Protozool.Abstr., Rev.Plant Path.
—BLDSC shelfmark: 6545.950000.
   Description: Presents papers, editorials and case reports on radiodiagnosis, nuclear medicine, medical disciplines, social hygiene, deontology and ethics.

616.026   PL   ISSN 0032-3772
CODEN: PAMWAL
POLSKIE ARCHIWUM MEDYCYNY WEWNETRZNEJ/POLISH ARCHIVES OF INTERNAL MEDICINE. (Text in Polish; summaries in English) 1923. m. $144. (Towarzystwo Internistow Polskich) Panstwowy Zaklad Wydawnictw Lekarskich, Ul. Dluga 38-40, Warsaw, Poland. TEL 31-42-81. (Dist. by: Ars Polona- Ruch, Krakowskie Przedmiescie 7, 00-068 Warsaw, Poland) Ed. J. Szajewski. adv.; bk.rev.; charts; illus.; index; circ. 4,100. (back issues avail.) **Indexed:** Biol.Abstr., Chem.Abstr., Dent.Ind., Excerp.Med., Ind.Med.
—BLDSC shelfmark: 6546.500000.
   Description: Covers internal medicine.

610   IT
IL POLSO. 1969. 18/yr. Masson Italia Periodici, Via Statuto 2-4, 20121 Milan, Italy. TEL 02-63671. Ed. Gabriele Bianchi Porro.

POST MARKETING SURVEILLANCE. see *PHARMACY AND PHARMACOLOGY*

610   US
POST-POLIO DIRECTORY. a. $3 to individuals (foreign $4); health professionals and institutions $6 (foreign $7). (International Polio Network) Gazette International Networking Institute, 5100 Oakland Ave., St. Louis, MO 63110-1441. TEL 314-534-0475.
   Description: Lists self-identified clinics, health professionals, and support groups knowledgeable about the late effects of polio.

610   PL   ISSN 0137-8465
POSTEPY FIZYKI MEDYCZNEJ. (Text in Polish; summaries in English and Russian) q. $20. (Polish Association of Medical Physics) Ossolineum, Publishing House of the Polish Academy of Sciences, Rynek 9, 50-106 Wroclaw, Poland. TEL 386-25. (Dist. by: Ars Polona, Krakowskiw Przedmiescie 7, 00-068 Warsaw, Poland) Ed. Waldemar Scharf.

MEDICAL SCIENCES   3143

610   PL   ISSN 0032-5449
CODEN: PHMDAD
POSTEPY HIGIENY I MEDYCYNY DOSWIADCZALNEJ. (Text in Polish; summaries in English and Russian) 1949. bi-m. $74. (Polska Akademia Nauk, Instytut Immunologii i Terapii Doswiadczalnej - Polish Academy of Science, Institute of Immunology and Experimental Therapy) Ossolineum, Publishing House of the Polish Academy of Sciences, 9 Rynek, 50-106 Wroclaw, Poland. TEL 31-42-81. (Dist. by: Ars Polona-Ruch, Krakowskie Przedmiescie 7, 00-068 Warsaw, Poland) Ed. M. Mordarski. charts; illus.; index; circ. 980. (reprint service avail. from ISI) **Indexed:** Abstr.Hyg., Biol.Abstr., Chem.Abstr., Curr.Adv.Ecol.Sci., Ind.Med., Nutr.Abstr., Rev.Plant Path., Trop.Dis.Bull.
Description: Reports of experimental medical research, proceedings of scientific conferences on immunology and experimental medicine.

610   UK   ISSN 0142-7946
POSTGRADUATE DOCTOR: AFRICA; the journal of prevention, diagnosis and treatment. 1979. 6/yr. £28 (foreign £35). Barker Publications Ltd., Barker House, 539 London Rd., Isleworth, Middlesex TW7 4DA, England. TEL 081-847-1774. Ed. Dr. David Harvey. adv.; bk.rev.; charts; illus.; circ. 9,300. (back issues avail.) **Indexed:** Abstr.Hyg., Nutr.Abstr., Trop.Dis.Bull.
—BLDSC shelfmark: 6563.851800.

610   UK   ISSN 0267-0275
POSTGRADUATE DOCTOR: CARIBBEAN; the journal of prevention, diagnosis and treatment. 1985. 6/yr. £18 (foreign £25). Barker Publications Ltd., Barker House, 539 London Rd., Isleworth, Middlesex TW7 4DA, England. TEL 081-874-1774. Ed. Dr. David Harvey. adv.; bk.rev.; charts; illus.; circ. 3,000. (back issues avail.) **Indexed:** Nutr.Abstr.

610   UK   ISSN 0140-7724
POSTGRADUATE DOCTOR: MIDDLE EAST; the journal of prevention, diagnosis & treatment. 1978. 12/yr. £55 (foreign £70). Barker Publications Ltd., Barker House, 539 London Rd., Isleworth, Middlesex TW7 4DA, England. TEL 081-847-1774. Ed. Dr. David Harvey. adv.; bk.rev.; charts; illus.; circ. 19,500. (back issues avail.) **Indexed:** Abstr.Hyg., Nutr.Abstr., Trop.Dis.Bull.
—BLDSC shelfmark: 6563.852000.

610 378   UK   ISSN 0959-4299
▼**POSTGRADUATE EDUCATION FOR GENERAL PRACTICE.** 1990. 3/yr. £45. Radcliffe Medical Press Ltd., 15 Kings Meadow, Ferry Hinksey Rd., Oxford OX2 ODP, England. TEL 0865-790-696. FAX 0865-244651. Ed. Declan Dwyer. adv.; bk.rev.; circ. 5,000. (back issues avail.)
—BLDSC shelfmark: 6563.855000.
Description: Postgraduate education in family practice, general practice for trainers and all others interested.

610   II   ISSN 0302-2404
CODEN: BPIRD8
POSTGRADUATE INSTITUTE OF MEDICAL EDUCATION AND RESEARCH, CHANDIGARH. BULLETIN. (Text in English) 1967. q. Rs.50($25) to individuals; libraries Rs.100. Postgraduate Institute of Medical Education and Research, Chandigarh, Chandigarh 160012, India. TEL 45157. TELEX 395-315 PGI IN. Ed. P.L. Sharma. adv.; bk.rev.; bibl.; illus.; circ. 550. **Indexed:** Abstr.Hyg., Biol.Abstr., Chem.Abstr., Excerp.Med, Ind.Sci.Rev., INIS Atomind., Trop.Dis.Bull.
Description: Contains articles contributed by faculty and students of the Institute. Includes editorial and research articles, case reports, and a Clinico-Pathological Conference report.

610   UK   ISSN 0032-5473
CODEN: PGMJAO
POSTGRADUATE MEDICAL JOURNAL. 1924. m. £118. (Fellowship of Postgraduate Medicine) Macmillan Press Ltd., Scientific & Medical Division, Houndmills, Basingstoke, Hampshire RG2 2XS, England. TEL 0256-29242. FAX 0256-810526. Ed. B.I. Hoffbrand. adv.; bk.rev.; bibl.; charts; illus.; stat.; index; circ. 2,000. (also avail. in microform from SWZ,UMI; back issues avail.; reprint service avail. from ISI) **Indexed:** Abstr.Health Care Manage.Stud., Abstr.Hyg., ASCA, Biol.Abstr., Biotech.Abstr., Chem.Abstr., Curr.Adv.Cancer Res., Curr.Adv.Ecol.Sci., Curr.Cont., Dent.Ind., Excerp.Med., Food Sci.& Tech.Abstr., Helminthol.Abstr., I.P.A., Ind.Med., Nutr.Abstr., Sci.Cit.Ind., Trop.Dis.Bull.
●Also available online.
—BLDSC shelfmark: 6563.860000.
Description: Current clinical research and practice, surveys and case reports.

610   US   ISSN 0032-5481
R11   CODEN: POMDAS
POSTGRADUATE MEDICINE; the journal of applied medicine for physicians providing primary care. 1947. 16/yr. $56 (Canada $66.50; elsewhere $115). McGraw-Hill, Inc., 1221 Ave. of the Americas, New York, NY 10020. TEL 212-512-2000. (Subscr. to: 4530 W. 77th St., Minneapolis, MN 55435) Ed. Glen C. Griffin. adv.; bk.rev.; charts; illus.; s-a. index; circ. 125,161. (also avail. in microfilm from UMI; reprint service avail. from UMI) **Indexed:** Biol.Abstr., C.I.S. Abstr., Chem.Abstr., CINAHL, Curr.Adv.Cancer Res., Curr.Adv.Ecol.Sci., Curr.Cont., Dent.Ind., Excerp.Med., FAMLI, Helminthol.Abstr., Ind.Med., Int.Nurs.Ind., Nutr.Abstr.
—BLDSC shelfmark: 6563.900000.
Description: Presents original clinical articles stressing the diagnosis and treatment of problems encountered in general medical practice.
Refereed Serial

613.62 616.9803   CS   ISSN 0032-6291
CODEN: PRLFAG
PRACOVNI LEKARSTVI. (Text in Czech or Slovak; summaries in English and Russian) 1948. 10/yr. $55.50. (Ceskoslovenska Spolecnost pro Pracovni Lekarstvi) Avicenum, Czechoslovak Medical Press, Malostranske nam. 28, 118 02 Prague 1, Czechoslovakia. (Dist. by: Artia, Ve Smeckach 30, 111 27 Prague 1, Czechoslovakia) (Co-sponsor: Ceskoslovenska Lekarska Spolecnost J. Ev. Purkyne) Ed. Dr. A. Zeleny. adv.; bk.rev.; abstr.; index; circ. 1,200. **Indexed:** Abstr.Hyg., Biol.Abstr., C.I.S. Abstr., Chem.Abstr., Ergon.Abstr., Excerp.Med., Ind.Med., Trop.Dis.Bull.
—BLDSC shelfmark: 6593.500000.
Description: Covers industrial medicine.

PRACTICAL GUIDE TO PREVENTING LEGAL MALPRACTICE. see *LAW*

610   UK
▼**PRACTICE;** clinical management in general practice. 1992. 2/yr. Churchill Livingstone Medical Journals, Robert Stevenson House, 1-3 Baxter's Pl., Leith Walk, Edinburgh EH1 3AF, Scotland. TEL 031-556-2424. FAX 031-558-1278. TELEX 727511. (Subscr. to: Longman Group, Journals Subscr. Dept., P.O. Box 77, Fourth Ave., Harlow, Essex CM19 5AA, England; U.S. subscr. to: Churchill Livingstone, 650 Ave. of the Americas, New York, NY 10011. TEL 212-206-5000) Ed.Bd.
Description: Provides updates on sensible approaches to common symptoms and problems of patients.

610   DK   ISSN 0109-2235
PRACTICUS. vol.8, 1984. bi-m. free. (Dansk Selskab for Almen Medecin) Tidsskrift for Praktisk Laegegerning, Stockholmsgade 55, DK-2100 Copenhagen Oe, Denmark. TEL 35-43-36-73. FAX 35-43-36-73. illus.
Formerly: D S A M Orientering (ISSN 0108-0717)

610   UK   ISSN 0032-6518
PRACTITIONER. 1868. 12/yr. $98. Morgan-Grampian (Professional Press) Ltd., 30 Calderwood St., London SE18 6QH, England. Ed. Howard Griffiths. adv.; bk.rev.; illus.; pat.; index; circ. 37,923. (also avail. in microform from UMI; back issues avail.; reprint service avail. from UMI) **Indexed:** Abstr.Health Care Manage.Stud., Biol.Abstr., Biotech.Abstr., Chem.Abstr., CINAHL, Curr.Adv.Cancer Res., Curr.Adv.Ecol.Sci., Dent.Ind., Dok.Arbeitsmed., Excerp.Med., Helminthol.Abstr., Ind.Med., Int.Nurs.Ind., Nutr.Abstr., Rev.Plant Path., Trop.Dis.Bull.
—BLDSC shelfmark: 6598.000000.

DER PRAEPARATOR. see *CONSERVATION*

610   GW
PRAEVENTION UND REHABILITATION. 1989. q. DM.90($60) Dustri-Verlag Dr. Karl Feistle, Bahnhofstr. 9, 8024 Deisenhofen, Germany. TEL 089-613861-0. FAX 089-6135412. Ed. J. Lecheler.

PRAKRITI VANI; the voice of nature. see *MEDICAL SCIENCES — Chiropractic, Homeopathy, Osteopathy*

610   CS   ISSN 0032-6739
CODEN: PRLEAD
PRAKTICKY LEKAR. (Text in Czech or Slovak) 1920. 2/yr. (plus q. supplements). $65.50. (Ceskoslovenska Lekarska Spolecnost J. Ev. Purkyne) Avicenum, Czechoslovak Medical Press, Malostranske nam. 28, 118 02 Prague 1, Czechoslovakia. (Dist. by: Artia, Ve Smeckach 30, 111 27 Prague 1, Czechoslovakia) Ed. Dr. J. Strejcek. adv.; bk.rev.; abstr.; bibl.; illus.; stat.; index, cum.index; circ. 9,000. **Indexed:** Biol.Abstr., C.I.S. Abstr., Chem.Abstr.

610   AU   ISSN 0048-5128
DER PRAKTISCHE ARZT; Oesterreichische Zeitschrifft fuer Allgemeinmedizin. 1946. 21/yr. S.275. Verlag der Praktische Arzt, Trude Schmitt, Kleine Sperlgasse 1, A-1020 Vienna, Austria. FAX 352166. TELEX 111267-SMITR. Ed. O. Hartz. adv.; bk.rev.; circ. 5,800. (tabloid format) **Indexed:** Biol.Abstr.
—BLDSC shelfmark: 6599.700000.

610   FR
PRATICIEN DU SUD OUEST. (Text in French; summaries in English) 1824. 20/yr. 360 F. 153 rue de Pessac, 33000 Bordeaux, France. Ed. J. Aubertin. adv.; bk.rev.; abstr.; illus.; index; circ. 7,000. **Indexed:** Abstr.Hyg., Biol.Abstr., C.I.S. Abstr., Chem.Abstr., Excerp.Med., Ind.Med., Trop.Dis.Bull.

610   GW
PRAXIS - DEPESCHE. 1987. bi-m. DM.34. Gesellschaft fuer Medizinische Information, Baumkirchnerstr. 53a, 8000 Munich 80, Germany. TEL 089-4361066. FAX 089-437971. Ed. H. Spude. adv.; circ. 50,000.

PRAXIS DER KLINISCHEN VERHALTENSMEDIZIN UND REHABILITATION. see *EDUCATION — Special Education And Rehabilitation*

614.8   US   ISSN 1049-023X
PREHOSPITAL AND DISASTER MEDICINE; an international journal. (Text in English) 1981. q. $48 to individuals (foreign $68); institutions $78 (foreign $98). (World Association for Emergency and Disaster Medicine) Jems Publishing Co., Inc., Box 2789, Carlsbad, CA 92018. TEL 619-431-9797. FAX 619-431-8176. (Co-sponsors: National Association of Emergency Medical Service Physicians; Acute Care Foundation; National Association of State Emergency Medical Services Directors) Ed. Dr. Marvin L. Birnbaum. adv.; bk.rev.; abstr.; bibl.; stat.
Former titles (until 1989): Journal of Prehospital Medicine; (until 1987): World Association for Emergency and Disaster Medicine. Journal (ISSN 0882-7397)
Description: Establishes, maintains, and promulgates the sciences associated with the delivery of emergency services to one or multiple victims of sudden illness or injury through the stimulation and dissemination of quality research in the areas of prehospital emergency medical care and disaster medicine.
Refereed Serial

M

MEDICAL SCIENCES

610   US
▼**PREHOSPITAL CARE REPORTS.** 1991. m. $89. American Health Consultants, Inc., Six Piedmont Center, Ste. 400, 3525 Piedmont Rd., N.E., Atlanta, GA 30305. TEL 404-262-7436. FAX 800-284-3291. (Subscr. to: Box 740056, Atlanta, GA 30374-9822. TEL 800-688-2421) Ed. Shelly McLain. circ. 200.
   Description: Practical journal for clinical summaries of emergency treatment for paramedics and EMTs.

610   BO
PRENSA MEDICA. 6/yr. Casilla 891, La Paz, Bolivia. Ed. Dr. Santiago Medeiros. adv.

610   VE
PRENSA MEDICA (CARACAS). 1975. m. Editorial TERSEG C.A., Edif. San Jose 1o, Avda. Prinicipal Mariperez, Caracas, Venezuela. circ. 8,000.

610   AG   ISSN 0032-745X
                CODEN: PMARAU
PRENSA MEDICA ARGENTINA. (Text in Spanish; summaries in English) 1914. m. $120. Prensa Medica Argentina s.r.l., Junin 845, Buenos Aires, Argentina. TEL 961-9793. Ed. Dr. Pablo A. Lopez. adv.; bk.rev.; charts; illus.; index; circ. 8,000. (also avail. in microform from UMI; back issues avail.; reprint service avail. from UMI) **Indexed:** Biol.Abstr., Curr.Cont., Excerp.Med., Helminthol.Abstr., Nutr.Abstr.
   —BLDSC shelfmark: 6607.700000.

610   FR   ISSN 0755-4982
LA PRESSE MEDICALE. (Summaries in English) 1893. w. 215 ECU($255) (typically set in Jan.). Masson, 120 bd. Saint-Germain, 75280 Paris Cedex 06, France. TEL 1-46-34-21-60. FAX 1-45-87-29-99. TELEX 202 671 F. Eds. J. Cambier, Ph. Letonturier. adv.; bk.rev.; abstr.; illus.; circ. 16,000. (also avail. in microform from UMI; microfiche from BHP; reprint service avail. from ISI) **Indexed:** Biol.Abstr., Biotech.Abstr., C.I.S. Abstr., Chem.Abstr., Curr.Adv.Cancer Res., Curr.Adv.Ecol.Sci., Curr.Cont., Dairy Sci.Abstr., Dent.Ind., Dok.Arbeitsmed., Excerp.Med., Helminthol.Abstr., Ind.Med., Ind.Sci.Rev., Nutr.Abstr., Protozool.Abstr., Rev.Plant Path., Risk Abstr.
   —BLDSC shelfmark: 6612.500000.
   Former titles (until 1982): Nouvelle Presse Medicale (ISSN 0301-1518); (until 1972): Presse Medicale (ISSN 0032-7867)

610   IT   ISSN 0393-0653
LA PRESSE MEDICALE: EDIZIONE ITALIANA. 1984. m. (10/yr.). L.7000. Masson Italia Periodici, Via Statuto 2-4, 20121 Milan, Italy. TEL 02-6367-1. FAX 02-6367211. Ed. Claudio Ortolani. circ. 15,000. **Indexed:** Dairy Sci.Abstr.

615.8   FR   ISSN 0032-7875
                CODEN: PTCLA3
PRESSE THERMALE ET CLIMATIQUE. 1864. 4/yr. 260 F. to individuals (foreign 330 F.); students 135 F. (foreign 200 F.). (Societe Francaise d'Hydrologie) Expansion Scientifique, 15 rue Saint-Benoit, 75278 Paris Cedex 06, France. Eds. J. Cottet, R. Flurin. adv.; bk.rev.; circ. 2,000. (also avail. in microform) **Indexed:** Biol.Abstr., Chem.Abstr., Dent.Ind., Excerp.Med.
   —BLDSC shelfmark: 6612.510000.

610   US   ISSN 0889-0242
PRESSURE (BETHESDA). 1972. bi-m. $25. Undersea and Hyperbaric Medical Society, Inc., 9650 Rockville Pike, Bethesda, MD 20814. TEL 301-571-1818. FAX 301-571-1815. Ed. G.S. Makulowich. bk.rev.; abstr.; bibl.; circ. 3,000.
   Formerly: Hyperbaric Medicine Newsletter (ISSN 0018-831X)

610   US
PREVENTION'S MEDICAL CARE YEARBOOK. a. $19.95. Rodale Press, Inc., Prevention Magazine, 33 E. Minor St., Emmaus, PA 18098. TEL 215-967-5171. FAX 215-967-3044. Ed. Mark Bricklin.
   Formerly: Medical Care Yearbook.

614.44 610   US   ISSN 0091-7435
RA421   CODEN: PVTMA3
PREVENTIVE MEDICINE; an international journal devoted to practice and theory. 1972. bi-m. $198 (foreign $238). (American Society of Preventive Oncology) Academic Press, Inc., Journal Division, 1250 Sixth Ave., San Diego, CA 92101. TEL 619-230-1840. FAX 619-699-6800. TELEX 181726. Ed. Ernst L. Wynder. index. (back issues avail.) **Indexed:** Abstr.Hyg., Biol.Abstr., C.I.S. Abstr., Chem.Abstr., Curr.Adv.Cancer Res., Curr.Adv.Ecol.Sci., Curr.Cont., Dent.Ind., Excerp.Med., Helminthol.Abstr., Ind.Med., Nutr.Abstr., Trop.Dis.Bull.
   —BLDSC shelfmark: 6612.790000.
   Refereed Serial

PREVISIONS GLISSANTES DETAILLEES EN PERSPECTIVES SECTORIELLES (VOL.35): SANTE. see BUSINESS AND ECONOMICS — Economic Situation And Conditions

610   JA   ISSN 0914-8426
PRIMARY CARE; Japanese journal of primary care. (Text in Japanese; summaries in English and Japanese) 1977. q. 6000 Yen($48) (Japanese Medical Society of Primary Care) Kyowakikakutsusin Ltd., 2-20, Shimbashiekimae Bldg., Shinbashi, Minatoku, Tokyo 105, Japan. FAX 03-3575-4748. Ed. Dr. Katsumi Jijima. adv.; bk.rev.; index; circ. 2,500. (back issues avail.)
   Formerly (until vol.11, no.1): Japanese Journal of Primary Care (ISSN 0387-3501)

610   US   ISSN 0095-4543
R11
PRIMARY CARE: CLINICS IN OFFICE PRACTICE. 1974. 4/yr. $67. W.B. Saunders Co., Curtis Center, Independence Square W., Philadelphia, PA 19106. TEL 215-238-7800. Ed. Melissa Mitchell. (also avail. in microform from MIM,UMI; reprint service avail. from ISI,UMI) **Indexed:** Curr.Cont., Dent.Ind., Excerp.Med., FAMLI, Ind.Med.
   —BLDSC shelfmark: 6612.908000.

610   UK   ISSN 0960-250X
▼**PRIMARY HEALTH CARE MANAGEMENT.** 1991. m. £38.50($77) Churchill Livingstone Medical Journals, Robert Stevenson House, 1-3 Baxter's Pl., Leith Walk, Edinburgh EH1 3AF, Scotland. TEL 031-556-2424. FAX 031-558-1278. (Subscr. to: Longman Group, Journals Subscr. Dept., P.O. Box 77, Fourth Ave., Harlow, Essex CM19 5AA, England; U.S. subscr. to: Churchill Livingstone, 650 Ave. of the Americas, New York, NY 10011. TEL 212-206-5000) Eds. M. Powell, L. Reed-Harding.
   —BLDSC shelfmark: 6612.908970.
   Description: Explores a range of policy and practical issues affecting primary care from different organizational and professional perspectives.

610   US   ISSN 0032-891X
R11
PRIVATE PRACTICE.* 1969. m. $18. Congress of County Medical Societies (CCMS) Publishing Co., Box 1485, Shawnee, OK 74802-1485. Ed. Karen Murphy. adv.; bk.rev.; index; circ. 190,000. (also avail. in microform from UMI; reprint service avail. from UMI)

610   US
PRIVATE SECTOR CONFERENCE. 1984. irreg. Duke University, 6697 College Station, Durham, NC 27708. TEL 919-684-2173. FAX 919-684-8644. Ed. Duncan Yaggy.

615.5   GW
PROBATUM EST; Informationen fuer den Arzt. 1950. 10/yr. Wissenschaft und Werbung, Freiburger Str. 23, 7844 Nuernberg, Germany. Ed. Rolf Nipken. adv.; pat.; index; circ. controlled.
   Former titles: Probatum Est Therapeutica Nova; Therapeutica Nova (ISSN 0049-3716)

610   US   ISSN 0889-4701
RC86
PROBLEMS IN CRITICAL CARE. 1987. q. $70 to individuals (foreign $90); institutions $95 (foreign $110). J.B. Lippincott Co., E. Washington Sq., Philadelphia, PA 19105. TEL 215-238-4200. Eds. Dr. Robert R. Kirby, Dr. Robert W. Taylor. (also avail. in microform from UMI)
   —BLDSC shelfmark: 6617.880200.

610   US
PROCEEDINGS OF THE STRAUB PACIFIC HEALTH FOUNDATION. vol.36, 1970. 3/yr. free to physicians and librarians. Straub Pacific Health Foundation, 846 S. Hotel St., Ste. 303, Honolulu, HI 96813. TEL 808-524-6755. FAX 808-531-0123. Ed. Dr. Bo Eliot. adv.; bk.rev.; charts; illus.; index; circ. 2,500. (also avail. in microfiche; reprint service avail. from UMI)
   Former titles: Straub Foundation Proceedings; Straub Proceedings; Straub Clinic Proceedings (ISSN 0039-2251)

610.69   CN
PRODUCTION; a status report on the production of health and human services personnel in the province of British Columbia. 1975. biennial. free. University of British Columbia, Centre for Health Services and Policy Research, No. 429 - 2194 Health Sciences Mall, Vancouver, B.C. V6T 1Z3, Canada. TEL 604-822-4810. FAX 604-822-5690. circ. 250 (controlled).
   Description: Offers a status report on the current and projected number of entrants into and graduates from health education programs in B.C.

610.6   CN
PROFESSIONAL CORPORATION OF PHYSICIANS OF QUEBEC. BULLETIN. (Text in English and French) 1961. 5/yr. free. Professional Corporation of Physicians of Quebec - Corporation Professionnelle des Medecins du Quebec, 1440 St. Catherine St. W., Ste. 914, Montreal, Que. H3G 1S5, Canada. TEL 514-878-4441. FAX 514-878-4379. bk.rev.; circ. 20,000.

610   US   ISSN 0033-0140
R728.8
PROFESSIONAL MEDICAL ASSISTANT. 1956. bi-m. $20. American Association of Medical Assistants, 20 N. Wacker Dr., Ste. 1575, Chicago, IL 60606. Ed. Karen S. Rodd. adv.; bk.rev.; illus.; index; circ. 15,000. (also avail. in microform) **Indexed:** CINAHL.
   Formerly: A A M A Bulletin.
   Description: Educational articles of interest to medical assistants in the office, hospital, clinic or school setting.

610   FR   ISSN 0339-3666
PROFILS MEDICO-SOCIAUX. 1972. m. 170 F. (Union Nationale pour l'Avenir de la Medecine) B.C. Savy, 18, avenue de la Marne, 92600 Asnieres, France. adv.; bk.rev.; circ. 45,000.

PROGRESS & CARE; at the Medical Center Hospital. see HOSPITALS

610   US   ISSN 0361-7742
                CODEN: PCBRD2
PROGRESS IN CLINICAL AND BIOLOGICAL RESEARCH. 1975. irreg., vol.333, 1990. price varies. Wiley-Liss, Inc., 41 E. 11th St., New York, NY 10003. TEL 212-475-7700. (reprint service avail. from ISI) **Indexed:** Biol.Abstr., Chem.Abstr., Chic.Per.Ind., Dent.Ind., Dok.Arbeitsmed., Excerp.Med., Ind.Med., Ind.Vet., Vet.Bull.
   —BLDSC shelfmark: 6867.400000.
   Refereed Serial

PROGRESS IN MEDICINAL CHEMISTRY. see CHEMISTRY

612   US   ISSN 0721-9156
QP431   CODEN: PSPYDZ
PROGRESS IN SENSORY PHYSIOLOGY. 1981. irreg. price varies. Springer-Verlag, 175 Fifth Ave., New York, NY 10010. TEL 212-460-1500. (Also Berlin, Heidelberg, Tokyo and Vienna) (reprint service avail. from ISI)

610   US
PROGRESS REPORT. 11/yr. 1111 N. Fairfax St., Alexandria, VA 22314. TEL 703-684-2782. FAX 703-684-7343. Ed. Ellen Woods. circ. 51,000.

616.07   IT   ISSN 0393-7658
PROGRESSI CLINICI: MEDICINA. 1985. bi-m. L.130000($160) Piccin Editore, Via Altinate 107, 35100 Padua, Italy. TEL 049-655566. TELEX 432074 PICCIN I. circ. 3,000.

610 IT ISSN 0370-1514
CODEN: PRMOAE
IL PROGRESSO MEDICO. (Text in Italian; summaries in English) bi-m. L.150000. Lombardo Editore, Via Verona, 22, 00161 Rome, Italy. TEL 06-428905. FAX 06-428543. Ed. M. Condorelli. adv.; index. (also avail. in microform) Indexed: Excerp.Med.
—BLDSC shelfmark: 6924.672000.

610 FR ISSN 0033-1392
PROPOS UTILES AUX MEDECINS. 1950. w. 490 F. Editions Marigny, 6 rue Montalivet, 75008 Paris, France. Ed. Pierre Duchesne de Lamotte. adv.; index; circ. 12,000.

PROSPECTIVE PAYMENT SURVIVAL. see HOSPITALS

616.99 US ISSN 0270-4137
RC899 CODEN: PRSTDS
THE PROSTATE. 1980. 8/yr. $376 (foreign $476). John Wiley & Sons, Inc., Journals, 605 Third Ave., New York, NY 10158. TEL 212-850-6000. FAX 212-850-6088. TELEX 1207063. Eds. Avery A. Sandberg, Gerald P. Murphy. adv.; bibl.; charts; illus.; index. Indexed: Biol.Abstr., Chem.Abstr., Curr.Cont., Excerp.Med., Ind.Med.
●Also available online.
—BLDSC shelfmark: 6935.194000.
Description: Serves as an international medium presenting comprehensive coverage of clinical, anatomic, embryologic, physiologic, endocrinologic, and biochemical studies.

610 DK ISSN 0309-3646
CODEN: POIND7
PROSTHETICS AND ORTHOTICS INTERNATIONAL. (Text in English) 1977. 3/yr. £60 (typically set in July). International Society for Prosthetics and Orthotics, Borgervaenget 5, DK-2100 Copenhagen OE, Denmark. TEL 31-20-72-60. Ed.Bd. adv.; bk.rev.; illus.; index; circ. 2,800 (controlled). Indexed: Bibl.Dev.Med.& Child Neur., Biol.Abstr., Curr.Cont., Excerp.Med., Ind.Med.
—BLDSC shelfmark: 6935.500000.
Description: Publishes scientific articles on prosthetics, orthotics and related topics.

610 PL ISSN 0033-2240
CODEN: PRLKAV
PRZEGLAD LEKARSKI. (Text in Polish; summaries in English and Russian) 1862. m. $180. Panstwowy Zaklad Wydawnictw Lekarskich, Ul. Dluga 38-40, Warsaw, Poland. TEL 31-42-81. (Dist. by: Ars Polona-Ruch, Krakowskie Przedmiescie 7, 00-068 Warsaw, Poland) Ed. Dr. Jan Sznajd. index. Indexed: Abstr.Hyg., Biol.Abstr., C.I.S. Abstr., Chem.Abstr., Dok.Arbeitsmed., Excerp.Med., Ind.Med., Trop.Dis.Bull.
—BLDSC shelfmark: 6942.800000.

610 UK ISSN 0033-2585
PSIONIC MEDICINE. 1969. s-a. £9.50($20) Psionic Medical Society, Hindhead, Surrey, England. Ed. Dr. C.W. Upton. bk.rev.; bibl.; circ. 500 (controlled). (tabloid format)
Description: Techniques for diagnosing the cause of disease dynamically.

PSYCHOLOGIA A PATOPSYCHOLOGIA DIETATA. see PSYCHOLOGY

152 612 US ISSN 0048-5772
QP351 CODEN: PSPHAF
PSYCHOPHYSIOLOGY. 1964. bi-m. $44 to individuals; libraries $68. Society for Psychophysiological Research, 2101 Winchester Dr., Champaign, IL 61821. TEL 217-398-6969. FAX 217-244-5876. Ed. Michael G.H. Coles. adv.; bk.rev.; abstr.; charts; illus.; index; circ. 2,300. (also avail. in microfilm from UMI; back issues avail.; reprint service avail. from UMI) Indexed: Bibl.Dev.Med.& Child Neur., Biol.Abstr., Curr.Adv.Ecol.Sci., Curr.Cont., Excerp.Med., Ind.Med., Psychol.Abstr.
—BLDSC shelfmark: 6946.552000.
Formerly: Psychophysiology Newsletter.
Description: Concerns the relationships between human autonomic and central nervous system behavior on the one hand, and cognitive performance, personality and emotions on the other. Studies effects of stress, individual differences, aging, anxiety, and psychosomatic and psychiatric disease.
Refereed Serial

614 610 UK ISSN 0033-3506
CODEN: PUHEAE
PUBLIC HEALTH. 1888. 6/yr. £102. (Society of Community Medicine) Macmillan Press Ltd., Scientific & Medical Division, Houndmills, Basingstoke, Hampshire RG2 2XS, England. TEL 0256-29242. FAX 0256-810526. Ed. M.W. Beaver. adv.; bk.rev.; charts; illus.; stat.; index; circ. 1,500. Indexed: Abstr.Hyg., ASSIA, Biol.Abstr., C.I.S. Abstr., Chem.Abstr., Curr.Adv.Cancer Res., Curr.Adv.Ecol.Sci., Curr.Cont., Dent.Ind., Excerp.Med., Helminthol.Abstr., Ind.Med., Ind.Vet., Nutr.Abstr., SSCI, Trop.Dis.Bull., Vet.Bull.
Description: Covers all aspects of community health and medicine, including preventive medicine and epidemiology.

PUBLIKATIONEN ZU WISSENSCHAFTLICHEN FILMEN. SEKTION MEDIZIN. see MOTION PICTURES

360 613 PR
PUERTO RICO. DEPARTMENT OF HEALTH. INFORME DEL REGISTRO DE PROFESIONALES DE LA SALUD. (Text in Spanish) 1979. biennial. free. Department of Health, Health Facilities and Services Administration, Office of Health Statistics, Box 9342, Santurce, PR 00908. TEL 809-721-4050. circ. 500.

610 574 PR ISSN 0738-0658
CODEN: PRHJDB
PUERTO RICO HEALTH SCIENCES JOURNAL. (Text in English, Spanish) 1982. 3/yr. $25 to individuals; institutions $35 (effective 1992). University of Puerto Rico, Office of the Dean for Academic Affairs, Medical Sciences Campus, Box 365067, San Juan, PR 00936-5067. TEL 809-758-2525. FAX 809-764-2470. Ed. Dr. Rafael Villavicencio. bk.rev.; index; circ. 400. (back issues avail.) Indexed: Chem.Abstr., Ind.Med.
●Also available on CD-ROM.
Description: Covers medical, dental, pharmaceutical and biosocial sciences. Discusses historical, philosophical and ethical matters of health sciences.

610 UK ISSN 0048-6000
PULSE. 1959. w. $145. Morgan-Grampian (Professional Press) Ltd., Morgan-Grampian House, 30 Calderwood St., London SE18 6QH, England. Ed. Howard Griffiths. adv.; bk.rev.; illus.; circ. 38,319. (tabloid format)
—BLDSC shelfmark: 7160.070000.

610 CN ISSN 1182-5405
▼PUNCH DIGEST FOR CANADIAN DOCTORS. 1990. 6/yr. Can.$25 (in US Can.$40; elsewhere Can.$60)(effective Jan. 1991). Punch Digest for Canadian Doctors Inc., 14845 Yonge St., Ste. 300, Aurora, Ont. L4G 6H8, Canada. TEL 416-841-5607. FAX 416-841-5688. Ed. Simon Hally. adv.; circ. 36,000 (controlled).
Description: A humor and lifestyle magazine for physicians.

610 II ISSN 0033-4340
PUNJAB MEDICAL JOURNAL.* (Text in English) 1951. m. Rs.10.($4) Partap Nagar, Jullundur 1, India. Ed. Dr. R. R. Laroia. adv.; bk.rev.; abstr.; charts; illus.; index. Indexed: Biol.Abstr., Chem.Abstr., Excerp.Med., Nucl.Sci.Abstr.

610 US ISSN 1040-2950
Q A SECTION CONNECTION. 1983. bi-m. membership only. American Health Information Management Association, Quality Assurance Section, 919 N. Michigan Ave., Ste. 1400, Chicago, IL 60611-1601. TEL 312-787-2672. Ed. Patrice Spath. bk.rev.; index; circ. 3,000. (tabloid format; back issues avail.)
Description: Devoted to articles helpful to quality assurance professionals working in inpatient and outpatient health care facilities.

610 CC ISSN 1001-4047
QINGDAO YIXUEYUAN XUEBAO/QINGDAO MEDICAL INSTITUTE. JOURNAL. (Text in Chinese) m. Qingdao Yixueyuan, No. 10, Huangtai Lu, Qingdao, Shandong 266012, People's Republic of China. TEL 228106. Ed. Li Juesheng.

QUADERNI DI ANATOMIA PRATICA. see BIOLOGY

MEDICAL SCIENCES 3145

610 US ISSN 1049-7323
RA440.85 CODEN: QHREEM
▼QUALITATIVE HEALTH RESEARCH. 1991. q. $39 to individuals; institutions $85. Sage Publications, Inc., 2455 Teller Rd., Newbury Park, CA 91320. TEL 805-499-0721. FAX 805-499-0871. Ed. Janice M. Morse. adv.; bk.rev.; circ. 1,000.
—BLDSC shelfmark: 7168.124200.
Description: Provides an interdisciplinary forum that will enhance health care and further the development and understanding of qualitative research methods in health care settings.

QUALITY & RISK MANAGEMENT IN HEALTH CARE; an information service. see HOSPITALS

610 US ISSN 1040-6166
RA399.A1 CODEN: QAHCEJ
QUALITY ASSURANCE IN HEALTH CARE. 1989. 4/yr. £80 (effective 1992). (International Society for Quality Assurance in Health Care) Pergamon Press, Inc., Journals Division, 660 White Plains Rd., Tarrytown, NY 10591-5153. TEL 914-524-9200. FAX 914-333-2444. (And: Headington Hill Hall, Oxford OX3 0BW, England. TEL 0865-794141) Ed. Peter Reizenstein. (also avail. in microform; back issues avail.)
—BLDSC shelfmark: 7168.139360.
Description: Seeks to make more widely available the results of quality assessment studies and quality assurance activities.
Refereed Serial

610 UK ISSN 0962-9343
▼QUALITY OF LIFE RESEARCH. 1992. bi-m. £195($350) Rapid Communications of Oxford Ltd., The Old Malthouse, Paradise St., Oxford OX1 1LD, England. TEL 0865-790447. FAX 0865-244012. Ed. M. Staquet. (reprint service avail.)

610 US
▼QUALITY SOURCE. 1991. q. membership. (Baxter International Inc.) American Group Practice Association, 1422 Duke St., Alexandria, VA 22314. TEL 703-838-0033. FAX 703-548-1890. (Co-sponsor: Ernest & Young) Ed. Julie Sanderson-Austin. circ. controlled.

610 UK ISSN 0033-5622
CODEN: QJMEA7
QUARTERLY JOURNAL OF MEDICINE. 1907. m. £105($210) (Association of Physicians of Great Britain and Ireland) Oxford University Press, Oxford Journals, Pinkhill Road, Southfield Road, Eynsham, Oxford OX2 1JJ, England. TEL 0865-882283. FAX 0865-882890. TELEX 837330 OXPRES G. Ed. J.S. Cameron. adv.; bibl.; charts; illus.; cum.index every 20 vols.; circ. 3,300. (also avail. in microform from UMI) Indexed: Abstr.Hyg., Adol.Ment.Hlth.Abstr., Biol.Abstr., Chem.Abstr., Curr.Adv.Ecol.Sci., Curr.Cont., Dairy Sci.Abstr., Excerp.Med., I.P.A., Ind.Med., Nutr.Abstr., Protozool.Abstr., Sci.Cit.Ind., Trop.Dis.Bull.
●Also available online. Vendor(s): BRS.
—BLDSC shelfmark: 7194.000000.
Description: Covers the whole field of medicine with emphasis on internal medicine.

610 II ISSN 0481-2158
QUARTERLY MEDICAL REVIEW. (Text in English) 1949. q. free to qualified personnel. Raptakos, Brett & Co., Ltd, Dr. Annie Besant Rd., Worli, Bombay 400025, India. Ed. Dr. G.B. Ramasarma. adv.; circ. 70,000. Indexed: Ind.Med.

610 UK ISSN 0033-6033
QUEENS MEDICAL MAGAZINE. vol.62, 1970. 3/yr. £10. (Birmingham Medical Society) Birmingham Medical and Dental Schools, Birmingham 15, England. Ed. Clive Meanwell. adv.; bk.rev.; charts; illus.; stat.; tr.lit.; circ. 5,000.

610 CN ISSN 0079-8789
QUEEN'S MEDICAL REVIEW. 1951. a. Aesculapian Society, Queen's University, Kingston, Ont., Canada. TEL 613-545-2542. Ed.Bd. adv.; circ. 1,000.

616.98 950 US
QUINTESSENCE. 4/yr. membership. Traditional Acupuncture Institute, American City Bldg., Ste. 100, Columbia, MD 21044. TEL 301-596-6006. FAX 410-944-3544. Ed. Edna M. Brandt. bk.rev.; circ. 5,000.
Description: Informs acupuncture patients and the general public about acupuncture, self-health care and the development of Oriental medicine in America.

MEDICAL SCIENCES

610   AG   ISSN 0325-2345
QUIRON. (Text in Spanish; summaries in English and French) 1970. q. $25 (foreign $45). (Fundacion Dr. Jose Maria Mainetti para el Progreso de la Medicina) Editorial Quiron, Calle 508 entre 16 y 18, 1897 M. B. Gonnet, Buenos Aires, Argentina. TEL 021-84-2616. FAX 54-21-5346. Ed. Dr. Alberto Mainetti. adv.; bk.rev.; charts; bibl.; illus.; circ. 3,000. (reprint service avail. from IRC) **Indexed:** Ind.Med.

610   UK   ISSN 0954-237X
R A D A R BULLETIN. m (11/yr.). £6.50 (foreign £7). Royal Association for Disability and Rehabilitation, 25 Mortimer St., London W1N 8AB, England. TEL 01-637-5400. FAX 01-637-1827. Ed. Gordon Rockett. circ. 4,000.
Formerly: Royal Association for Disability and Rehabilitation.

R V S FEE SCHEDULE. (Relative Value Scale) see *INSURANCE*

362.3   NE   ISSN 0166-4298
RAAKPUNT. 1957. 8/yr. fl.25($15) Vereniging van Ouders en Verwanten van Mensen met een Verstandelijke Handicap V O G G, Postbus 85274, 3508 AG Utrecht, Netherlands. TEL 030-363744. FAX 030-313054. Ed. S.J. Overbeek. adv.; bk.rev.; illus.; circ. 30,000. (processed)
Formerly: Zorgenkind (ISSN 0044-5339)
Description: Contains news and information for parents and relatives of persons with mental disabilities.

RADIOISOTOPES. see *BIOLOGY — Biological Chemistry*

610   UK   ISSN 0481-6722
RADIONIC QUARTERLY; an approach to health and harmony. 1954. q. membership only. Radionic Association Ltd., Baerlein House, Goose Green, Deddington, Banbury OX15 0SZ, England. TEL 0869-38852. Ed. V. Roberts. adv.; bk.rev.; circ. 500.
Formerly (until 1957): Radionic Therapy.
Description: Discusses distant healing practice using instruments and radiesthesia.

610   II   ISSN 0485-9561
RAJASTHAN MEDICAL JOURNAL. (Text in English) 1961. q. Rs.40. Government of Rajasthan, Medical Health and Family Planning Department, S.M.S. Medical College, Rajasthan, Jaipur 302 004, India. TEL 60291. Ed. Dr. V.M. Bhandari. adv.; bk.rev.; charts; circ. 1,400. **Indexed:** Biol.Abstr., Excerp.Med.
—BLDSC shelfmark: 7253.258000.
Description: Guides post doctors in rural areas on latest medical developments.

616.6   IT   ISSN 0033-992X
RASSEGNA DI UROLOGIA E NEFROLOGIA. (Text in Italian; summaries in English) 1963. q. L.60000 (foreign L.120000)(effective 1992). C E M Casa Editrice Maccari, Via Trento, 53, 43100 Parma, Italy. FAX 039-521-771268. Ed.Bd. adv.; bk.rev.; circ. 1,000. **Indexed:** Excerp.Med.

610   IT   ISSN 0033-9695
RASSEGNA INTERNAZIONALE DI CLINICA E TERAPIA. 1920. bi-m. L.25000($30) Bruno Buonomo La Rossa, Ed. & Pub., Pallonetto S. Chiara 8, 80134 Naples, Italy. TEL 081-5520424. adv.; bk.rev.; abstr.; bibl.; charts; illus.; index; circ. 15,000. (also avail. in microform from UMI; reprint service avail. from UMI) **Indexed:** Biol.Abstr., Chem.Abstr., Excerp.Med., Ind.Med.
—BLDSC shelfmark: 7294.240000.

RAUM UND ZEIT; die neue Dimension der Wissenschaft. see *NEW AGE PUBLICATIONS*

610   PK
RAWAL MEDICAL JOURNAL. (Text in English) 1976. q. Rs.60($60) Pakistan Medical Association, Rawalpindi-Islamabad Branch, Rawalpindi, Pakistan. adv.; bk.rev.; circ. 1,500.

REACHING OUT; a parents' guide to CdLS. see *HANDICAPPED*

610   SP   ISSN 0034-0634
REAL ACADEMIA NACIONAL DE MEDICINA. ANALES. 1879. q. 800 ptas.($11) Real Academia Nacional de Medicina, Prof. Dr. D. Valentin Matilla y Gomez, Arrieta 12, Madrid, Spain. illus.; circ. 600. **Indexed:** Biol.Abstr., Chem.Abstr., Ind.Med.
—BLDSC shelfmark: 0882.150000.

610   FR   ISSN 0765-5290
                     CODEN: RMDUA8
REANIMATION, SOINS INTENSIFS, MEDECINE D'URGENCE. 1968. 6/yr. 975 F. to individuals (foreign 1260 F.); students 485 F. (foreign 830 F.). (Societe de Reanimation de Langue Francaise) Expansion Scientifique, 15 rue St. Benoit, 75278 Paris Cedex 06, France. circ. 4,000.
—BLDSC shelfmark: 7303.555000.
Formerly: Reanimation et Medecine d'Urgence (ISSN 0246-1234)

613   US   ISSN 0306-7548
                     CODEN: RAORD7
RECENT ADVANCES IN OBESITY RESEARCH. 1977. irreg. price varies. Technomic Publishing Co., Inc., 851 New Holland Ave., Box 3535, Lancaster, PA 17604. TEL 717-291-5609. FAX 717-295-4538. TELEX 203-753565 (TECHNOMIC UD). Eds. Dr. Alan N. Howard, Dr. George A. Bray. illus. **Indexed:** Chem.Abstr.
Refereed Serial

610   IT   ISSN 0034-1193
                     CODEN: RPMDAN
RECENTI PROGRESSI IN MEDICINA. (Text and summaries in English, Italian) 1946. m. L.60000($180) to individuals; institutions L.100000. Pensiero Scientifico Editore s.r.l., Via Panama 48, Rome, Italy. TEL 06 855-36-33. Ed. Lorenzo Bonomo. adv.; bk.rev.; abstr.; bibl.; illus.; index; circ. 5,000. **Indexed:** Biol.Abstr., Chem.Abstr., Dent.Ind., Dok.Arbeitsmed., Excerp.Med., Ind.Med.
—BLDSC shelfmark: 7305.100000.

RECEPTOR. see *BIOLOGY — Biological Chemistry*

610   GW   ISSN 0937-9819
▼**RECHTSMEDIZIN.** 1991. 4/yr. DM.210. (Deutsche Gesellschaft fuer Rechtsmedizin) Springer-Verlag, Heidelberger Platz 3, 1000 Berlin 33, Germany. TEL 030-8207-0. FAX 030-8214091. adv. contact: E. Lueckermann.
—BLDSC shelfmark: 7309.453000.

RECOMBINANT D N A. see *BIOLOGY — Genetics*

617.8   FR   ISSN 0034-222X
REEDUCATION ORTHOPHONIQUE. 1963. 4/yr. 480 F. (foreign 550 F.). Bibliotheque ARPLOEV (Association pour la Reeducation de la Parole, du Langage Oral et Ecrit, et de la Voix), 10 rue de l'Arrivee, 75015 Paris, France. TEL 45-44-48-85. adv.; bk.rev.; bibl.; charts; illus.; stat.; tr.lit.; circ. 2,000.
—BLDSC shelfmark: 7331.430040.
Description: Covers hearing, speech and voice disorders.

610   IS   ISSN 0017-7768
                     CODEN: HAREA6
HA-REFUAH. (Text in Hebrew; summaries in English) 1930. fortn. $250. Israel Medical Association, 39 Shaul Hamelech Blvd., Tel Aviv, Israel. FAX 03-6956103. Ed. Y. Rotem. adv.; bk.rev.; abstr.; bibl.; charts; illus.; stat.; index. **Indexed:** Biol.Abstr., Chem.Abstr., Curr.Cont., Dent.Ind., Excerp.Med., Ind.Med., INIS Atomind., Psychol.Abstr.
—BLDSC shelfmark: 4264.000000.

REGAN REPORT ON MEDICAL LAW. see *LAW*

610   SA
REGISTER OF MEDICAL PRACTITIONERS, INTERNS AND DENTISTS FOR THE REPUBLIC OF SOUTH AFRICA. (Text and summaries in Afrikaans, English) a. (with m. supplements). R.55 (plus R.13 for m. supplements). South African Medical & Dental Council, P.O. Box 205, Pretoria 0001, South Africa. TEL 012-28-6680. FAX 012-28-5120.

615.8   US
REHAB MANAGEMENT. 1988. bi-m. $5 per no. Curant Communications, Inc., 4676 Admiralty Way, Ste. 202, Marina Del Rey, CA 90292-6603. TEL 213-479-1769. FAX 213-301-3329. Ed. Tony Ramos. adv.; circ. 20,000.
Description: Directed toward physical therapists, directors and managers of rehabilitation hospitals, and occupational therapists. Features the business aspects of rehabilitation, plus case histories.

615   CS   ISSN 0033-8680
REHABILITACIA/REHABILITATION. (Supplements avail.) (Text in Czech or Slovak; summaries in English, French, German, Russian) 1967. 8/yr. $36. (Institut pre Dalsie Vzdelavanie Lekarov a Farmaceutov - Institute of Further Education of Physicians and Pharmaceutists) Obzor, Ceskoslovenskej Armady 35, 815 85 Bratislava, Czechoslovakia. (Dist. by: Slovart, Gottwaldovo nam. 48, 805 32 Bratislava, Czechoslovakia) (Co-sponsor: Ministry of Health Care of the Slovak Socialist Republic) Ed. Dr. Miroslav Palat. bk.rev.; film rev.; bibl.; charts; illus.; index; circ. 2,500. (tabloid format; back issues avail.) **Indexed:** Biol.Abstr., Excerp.Med.

615.8 371.9   SP   ISSN 0048-7120
REHABILITACION. (Text in Spanish; summaries in English and Spanish) 1967. bi-m. 6700 ptas.($87) (Sociedad Espanola de Rehabilitacion) Editorial Garsi, S.A., Londres, 17, 28028 Madrid, Spain. TEL 255680827. FAX 91-361-10-07. TELEX 47124 GARSI. Ed. Dr. I. Bori de Fortuny. adv.; bk.rev.; abstr.; bibl.; illus.; stat.; index; circ. 1,000. (tabloid format) **Indexed:** Excerp.Med.

615.8   SP
REHABILITACION FISICA XXI; revista ciencia sobre temas de rehabilitacion fisica. 6/yr. 5000 ptas.($95) Prensa XXI, S.A., Avda Paral.lel, 180, Apdo. No. 350 F.D., 08015 Barcelona, Spain. TEL 93-325-53-50. FAX 93-425-28-80. circ. 5,000.

362.4   US
REHABILITACION: PREVENCION Y INTEGRACION. (Text in Spanish) 1982. 2/yr. Rehabilitation International, 25 E. 21st St., New York, NY 10010. TEL 212-420-1500. FAX 212-505-0871. TELEX 446412. (Co-sponsor: I N S E R S O) Eds. Luis Reguera, Barbara Duncan. bk.rev.; circ. 6,000.
Description: Covers disability and rehabilitation in Latin America, Spain and Portugal.

362   GW   ISSN 0034-3536
DIE REHABILITATION; Zeitschrift fuer alle Fragen der medizinischen, schulisch-beruflichen und sozialen Eingliederung. (Text in German; summaries in English, German) 1961. q. DM.120. (Deutsche Vereinigung fuer die Rehabilitation Behinderter) Georg Thieme Verlag, Ruedigerstr. 14, Postfach 104853, 7000 Stuttgart 10, Germany. TEL 0711-8931-0. FAX 0711-8931298. Ed.Bd. adv.; bk.rev.; bibl.; charts; illus.; stat.; index; circ. 1,800. (also avail. in microform from UMI; reprint service avail. from UMI) **Indexed:** Curr.Cont., Excerp.Med., Ind.Med.
—BLDSC shelfmark: 7350.210000.

REHABILITATION DER ENTWICKLUNGSGEHEMMTEN. see *EDUCATION — Special Education And Rehabilitation*

REHABILITATION DIGEST. see *EDUCATION — Special Education And Rehabilitation*

362   US   ISSN 0172-6412
REHABILITATION UND PRAEVENTION. 1977. irreg. price varies. Springer-Verlag, 175 Fifth Ave., New York, NY 10010. TEL 212-460-1500. (Also Berlin, Heidelberg, Tokyo and Vienna) (reprint service avail. from ISI)

RELAX; the travel magazine for practicing physicians. see *TRAVEL AND TOURISM*

612.015   IT   ISSN 0048-7198
RELAZIONI CLINICO SCIENTIFICHE.* (Text in Italian; summaries in English) 1948. bi-m. free to medical doctors. Istituto Ganassini di Ricerche Biochimiche, Via Gaggia 16, Milan, Italy. adv.; bk.rev.; abstr.; bibl.; illus.; index, cum.index; circ. 13,000. **Indexed:** Chem.Abstr.

REMEDIA. see *BIBLIOGRAPHIES*

610   CN
RENAL FAMILY. 1979. q. $12 (foreign $14). Multimed Inc., 1120 Finch Ave., W., Ste. 201, Toronto, Ont. M3J 3H7, Canada. TEL 416-650-0610. FAX 416-650-0639. adv.: B&W page Can.$1200; trim 8 1/8 x 10 7/8. circ. 8,786.

MEDICAL SCIENCES 3147

610 NE
REPERTORIUM. 1967. a. fl.69.50. Dutch Association of the Pharmaceutical Industry (NEFARMA), Postbus 9193, 3506 GD Utrecht, Netherlands. FAX 30-614554. (Dist. by: S D U, Postbus 30446, 2500 GK the Hague, Netherlands. TEL 070-3429700) Ed.Bd. adv.; abstr.; cum.index; circ. 40,000.
●Also available online.
  Former titles: Repertorium Farmaceutische Specialites Periodiek Overzicht voor Artsen; Repertorium Verpakte Geneesmiddelen Periodiek Overzicht voor Artsen (ISSN 0034-463X)

610 AG
REPORTERO MEDICO. m. Editorial Artes y Ciencias, Santa Fe 2436, segundo, Buenos Aires, Argentina. Ed. Dr. Rufino J. Flores Belaunde. adv.

610 574 CH ISSN 0255-6596
Q72.5 CODEN: PNBSEF
REPUBLIC OF CHINA. NATIONAL SCIENCE COUNCIL. PROCEEDINGS. PART B: LIFE SCIENCES. (Text in English) 1984. q. NT.$240($16) National Science Council of the Republic of China, 106, Ho-ping E. Rd. Sec.2, Taipei, Taiwan 106, Republic of China. TEL 2-737-7594. FAX 2-737-7248. Ed. Jong-Ching Su. circ. 2,750. (also avail. in microfiche) **Indexed:** Anim.Breed.Abstr., Field Crop Abstr., Plant Grow.Reg.Abstr.
—BLDSC shelfmark: 6769.884600.

610 IT ISSN 0014-8784
RES MEDICAE. 1935. bi-m. L.6000. (Ordine Ospedaliero di S. Giovanni di Dio) Fatebenefratelli, Via S. Vittore 12, 20123 Milan, Italy. adv.; bk.rev.; bibl.; charts; illus.; stat.; index; circ. 6,000.

614.88 US ISSN 1041-0651
RESCUE (CARLSBAD); magazine of rescue professionals. 1981. bi-m. $14.95. Jems Publishing Co., Inc., Box 2789, Carlsbad, CA 92018. TEL 619-431-9797. FAX 619-431-8176. Ed. Lee Reeder. adv.; bk.rev.; circ. 25,000. (also avail. in microfiche)
  Formerly: Response (Solana Beach) (ISSN 0197-5676)

RESEARCH AND CLINICAL CENTER FOR CHILD DEVELOPMENT. ANNUAL REPORT. see CHILDREN AND YOUTH — About

610 UK ISSN 0143-3083
CODEN: RCLFD4
RESEARCH AND CLINICAL FORUMS. 1979. irreg. Wells Medical Ltd., Chapel Place, Tunbridge Wells, Kent TN1 1BP, England. FAX 0892-511400. circ. 50,000. **Indexed:** Chem.Abstr., Curr.Adv.Ecol.Sci.
—BLDSC shelfmark: 7714.445000.
  Description: Presents materials discussed at medico-scientific and medico-therapeutic congresses and symposia.

616.07 615 US ISSN 0034-5164
RM1 CODEN: RCOCB8
RESEARCH COMMUNICATIONS IN CHEMICAL PATHOLOGY AND PHARMACOLOGY. 1970. m. $195 (foreign $225). P J D Publications Ltd., Box 966, Westbury, NY 11590. TEL 516-626-0650. Ed.Bd. adv.; bk.rev.; abstr.; charts; illus.; index; circ. 1,000. (reprint service avail. from ISI) **Indexed:** Biol.Abstr., Biotech.Abstr., Chem.Abstr., Curr.Adv.Biochem., Curr.Adv.Ecol.Sci., Curr.Cont., Dairy Sci.Abstr., Dent.Ind., Excerp.Med., Ind.Med., Ind.Vet., Nutr.Abstr., Poult.Abstr., Rev.Plant Path., Vet.Bull.
—BLDSC shelfmark: 7736.500000.
  Description: Articles on all areas of pathology, pharmacology, toxicology in their basic and clinical aspects.
  Refereed Serial

610 IT
RESEARCH IN CLINIC AND LABORATORY. (Text in English) 1975. q. (with supplements). L.250000($180) Casa Editrice Il Ponte, Casella Postale 1071, 20100 Milan, Italy. TEL 00390-2 31072676. Ed.Bd. adv.; bk.rev.; abstr.; bibl.; illus.; index; circ. 6,000. (also avail. in microform from UMI; reprint service avail. from UMI) **Indexed:** Biol.Abstr., Bull.Signal., Chem.Abstr., Curr.Adv.Ecol.Sci., Curr.Cont., Dent.Ind., Excerp.Med., Ind.Med., Ref.Zh.
  Formerly: Ricerca in Clinica e in Laboratorio (ISSN 0390-5748)

610 US ISSN 0891-4222
HV1570.5.U65 CODEN: RDDIEF
RESEARCH IN DEVELOPMENTAL DISABILITIES; a multidisciplinary journal. 1981. 6/yr. £120 (effective 1992). Pergamon Press, Inc., Journals Division, 660 White Plains Rd., Tarrytown, NY 10591-5153. TEL 914-524-9200. FAX 914-333-2444. (And: Headington Hill Hall, Oxford OX3 0BW, England. TEL 0865-794141) Ed. Johnny L. Matson. (also avail. in microform from MIM,UMI) **Indexed:** Biol.Abstr., C.I.J.E., Chic.Per.Ind., Curr.Adv.Ecol.Sci., Curr.Cont., Dent.Ind., Ind.Med., Psychol.Abstr., SSCI, Yrbk.Assoc.Educ.& Rehab.Blind.
—BLDSC shelfmark: 7738.450000.
  Formed by the merger of: Applied Research in Mental Retardation (ISSN 0270-3092) & Analysis and Intervention in Developmental Disabilities (ISSN 0270-4684)
  Refereed Serial

614.8 US ISSN 0275-4959
RA418
RESEARCH IN THE SOCIOLOGY OF HEALTH CARE; a research annual. 1980. a. $58.50 to institutions. J A I Press Inc., 55 Old Post Rd., No. 2, Box 1678, Greenwich, CT 06836-1678. TEL 203-661-7602. Ed. Julius A. Roth. **Indexed:** Lang.& Lang.Behav.Abstr., Sociol.Abstr. (1980-).
—BLDSC shelfmark: 7770.720000.

612 NE
RESEARCH MONOGRAPHS IN CELL AND TISSUE PHYSIOLOGY. irreg., vol.17, 1991. price varies. Elsevier Science Publishers B.V., Books Division, P.O. Box 211, 1000 AE Amsterdam, Netherlands. TEL 020-5803911. FAX 020-5803705. TELEX 18582 ESPA NL. (Subscr. in U.S. and Canada to: Elsevier Science Publishing Co., Inc., Box 882, Madison Sq. Sta., New York, NY 10159. TEL 212-989-5800) Ed. J.T. Dingle.
  Refereed Serial

610 US ISSN 0160-807X
RESEARCH RESOURCES REPORTER. 1977. m. $9. U.S. National Institutes of Health, National Center for Research Resources, Westwood Bldg., Rm. 10A15, 5333 Westbard Ave., Bethesda, MD 20892. TEL 301-496-5545. Ed. Ole Henriksen. index; circ. 13,500. (back issues avail.) **Indexed:** Ind.U.S.Gov.Per., MEDOC.
—BLDSC shelfmark: 7769.585200.
  Description: Describes current biomedical research studies.

RESIDENT AND STAFF PHYSICIAN. see HOSPITALS

RESPIRATION PHYSIOLOGY. see BIOLOGY — Physiology

614.88 GW ISSN 0178-2525
RETTUNGSDIENST; Zeitschrift fuer praektische Notfallmedizin. (Text in German; summaries in English) 1978. m. DM.69. Stumpf Kossendey Verlag GmbH, Postfach 1153, 2905 Edewecht, Germany. TEL 04405-7073. FAX 04405-7744. circ. 14,000.

REVIEWS IN MEDICAL MICROBIOLOGY. see BIOLOGY — Microbiology

610 BL
REVISTA A M R I G S. (Text in Portuguese; summaries in English, Portuguese) 1957. q. Cr.$600($20) Associacao Medica do Rio Grande do Sul, Av. Ipiranga, 5311, 90620 Porto Alegre, Brazil. adv.; bk.rev.; illus.; circ. 7,000. **Indexed:** Biol.Abstr., Excerp.Med., Ind.Med.
  Formerly: Associacao Medica do Rio Grande do Sul. Revista (ISSN 0004-5268)

610 BL ISSN 0100-3232
CODEN: CLTRDC
REVISTA BRASILEIRA DE CLINICA E TERAPEUTICA. Short title: C T. (Includes: Booklet of Abstracts) (Text in Portuguese; summaries in English and Portuguese) m. Cr.$112000($100) Moreira Jr. Editora Ltda., Rua Herique Martins, 493, 04504 Sao Paulo SP, Brazil. TEL 011-884-9911. FAX 011-884-9993. Eds. Dr. Flavio F. Vormittag, Dr. Jose Abu Assali. adv.; bk.rev.; abstr.; bibl.; charts; illus.; index; circ. 30,000. (back issues avail.) **Indexed:** Abstr.Hyg., Biol.Abstr., Chem.Abstr., Excerp.Med., Ind.Med.
—BLDSC shelfmark: 7844.157000.
  Description: Presents results of medical research.

610 BL ISSN 0034-7264
CODEN: RBMEAU
REVISTA BRASILEIRA DE MEDICINA. Short title: R B M. (Table of contents and summaries in English and Portuguese) 1943. m. Cr.$112000($250) Moreira Jr. Editora Ltda., Rua Henrique Martins, 493, 04504 Sao Paulo, Brazil. TEL 011-884-9911. FAX 011-884-9993. Dir. Dr. Joaquim Prado P. de Moraes. adv.; bk.rev.; abstr.; bibl.; charts; illus.; stat.; index; circ. 30,000. (back issues avail.) **Indexed:** Abstr.Hyg., Biol.Abstr., Chem.Abstr., Curr.Cont., Excerp.Med., Helminthol.Abstr., Microbiol.Abstr., Trop.Dis.Bull.
—BLDSC shelfmark: 7845.275000.
  Description: Presents studies in all fields of medicine.

616.07 BL ISSN 0034-7302
CODEN: RBPTBN
REVISTA BRASILEIRA DE PATOLOGIA CLINICA. (Text in Portuguese; abstracts in English) 1950. q. Cr.$6500($60) Sociedade Brasileira de Patologia Clinica - Brazilian Clinical Pathology Society, Rua Sampaio Viana, 92, Rio de Janeiro, RJ 20261, Brazil. TEL 021-293-3848. FAX 021-2932041. (Co-sponsor: Associacao Latino-Americana de Patologia Clinica - Latin-American Clinical Pathology Association) Ed. Lucia Simas Parentoni. adv.; bk.rev.; abstr.; bibl.; charts; illus.; stat.; index; circ. 3,000. (tabloid format; back issues avail.) **Indexed:** Biol.Abstr., Chem.Abstr., Ind.Med.
●Also available on CD-ROM.
—BLDSC shelfmark: 7845.440000.
  Description: Original papers in laboratory medicine.

610 574 BL ISSN 0100-879X
CODEN: BJMRDK
REVISTA BRASILEIRA DE PESQUISAS MEDICAS E BIOLOGICAS/BRAZILIAN JOURNAL OF MEDICAL AND BIOLOGICAL RESEARCH. (Text in English) 1968. m. Cr.$6200($60) c/o Eduardo Moacy Krieger, Faculdade de Medicina de Ribeirao Preto, Campus de Ribeirao Preto, 14049 Ribeirao Preto SP, Brazil. FAX 016-633-2119. TELEX 0166-354. Ed.Bd. adv.; bk.rev.; bibl.; charts; illus.; circ. 5,000. (also avail. in microform from UMI; reprint service avail. from UMI, ISI) **Indexed:** Abstr.Hyg., Biol.Abstr., Chem.Abstr., Curr.Adv.Biochem., Curr.Adv.Cancer Res., Curr.Adv.Cell & Devel.Biol., Curr.Adv.Ecol.Sci., Curr.Adv.Genetics & Molec.Biol., Curr.Cont., Dairy Sci.Abstr., Dent.Ind., Excerp.Med., Helminthol.Abstr., Ind.Med., Ind.Sci.Rev., Ind.Vet., Nutr.Abstr., Protozool.Abstr., Sci.Cit.Ind., Trop.Dis.Bull., Vet.Bull.
—BLDSC shelfmark: 2277.419500.

610 SP ISSN 0014-2565
CODEN: RCESA5
REVISTA CLINICA ESPANOLA. (Text in Spanish; summaries in English) 1940. s-m. 4500 ptas.($60) Internacional de Ediciones y Publicaciones, S.A. (I D E P S A), Principe de Vergara, 112 - 1st Fl., 28002 Madrid, Spain. Ed. M. Jimenez Casado. adv.; bk.rev.; illus.; circ. 8,000. **Indexed:** Biol.Abstr., Chem.Abstr., Curr.Cont., Dent.Ind., Excerp.Med., Helminthol.Abstr., Ind.Med.Esp., Ind.Med., Nutr.Abstr., Rev.Plant Path.
—BLDSC shelfmark: 7851.170000.
  Incorporates: Europa Medica (ISSN 0375-8869)

610 CR ISSN 0253-2948
CODEN: RCCMEF
REVISTA COSTARRICENSE DE CIENCIAS MEDICAS. (Text in Spanish; abstracts in English) 1979. 4/yr. $15 free to qualified personnel. Caja Costarricense de Seguro Social, Centro de Docencia e Investigacion en Salud y Seguridad Social, Apdo. 10105, San Jose, Costa Rica. FAX 506-338359. Ed. Jessie M. Orlich. adv.; bk.rev.; circ. 2,000. **Indexed:** Biol.Abstr., Excerp.Med., Ind.Med.
●Also available on CD-ROM.
—BLDSC shelfmark: 7852.070000.

REVISTA CUBANA DE INVESTIGACIONES BIOMEDICAS. see BIOLOGY

M

MEDICAL SCIENCES

610   CU   ISSN 0034-7523
CODEN: RCBMA6
REVISTA CUBANA DE MEDICINA. (Text in Spanish; summaries in English, French, Spanish) 1962. 3/yr. $21 in N. America; S. America $23; Europe $28. Ministerio de Salud Publica, Centro Nacional de Informacion de Ciencias Medicas, Calle E No. 452, e-19 y 21, Plaza de la Revolucion, Apdo. 6520, Havana, Cuba. TEL 809-32-5338. (Dist. by: Ediciones Cubanas, Obispo No. 527, Apdo. 605, Havana, Cuba) Dir. Dr. Ignacio Macias Castro. bibl.; charts; illus.; index; circ. 2,300. **Indexed:** Abstr.Hyg., Bio-Contr.News & Info., Biol.Abstr., Chem.Abstr., Curr.Adv.Ecol.Sci., Excerp.Med., Trop.Dis.Bull.
—BLDSC shelfmark: 7852.120000.

610   CU   ISSN 0864-2125
REVISTA CUBANA DE MEDICINA GENERAL INTEGRAL. (Text in Spanish; summaries in English, French, Spanish) 1985. 4/yr. $24 in N. America; S. America $28; Europe $35. Ministerio de Salud Publica, Centro Nacional de Informacion de Ciencias Medicas, Calle E No. 452, e-19 y 21, Plaza de la Revolucion, Apdo. 6520, Havana, Cuba. TEL 809-32-5338. (Dist. by: Ediciones Cubanas, Obispo No. 527, Apdo. 605, Havana, Cuba) Dir. Vicente Osorio Acosta. abstr.; bibl.; charts; illus.; index; circ. 6,200. ●Also available online.
Description: Covers preventive medicine, primary health care, diabetes mellitus, community medicine, emergency medical service, and the family physician.

REVISTA DE CHIRURGIE, ONCOLOGIE, RADIOLOGIE, O.R.L., OFTALMOLOGIE, STOMATOLOGIE. ONCOLOGIE. see *MEDICAL SCIENCES — Cancer*

610   BL   ISSN 0101-322X
CODEN: RCBIDV
REVISTA DE CIENCIAS BIOMEDICAS. (Text in Portuguese; summaries in English and Portuguese) 1980. a. $30 or exchange basis. Universidade Estadual Paulista, Av. Vicente Ferreira 1278, Caixa Postal 603, 17500 Marilia SP, Brazil. TEL 0144-33-1844. FAX 0144-22-2504. TELEX 111-9016-UJME BR. abstr.; bibl.; charts; illus.; stat. **Indexed:** Biol.Abstr., Bull.Signal., Chem.Abstr., Ind.Med., Ind.Vet., Protozool.Abstr.
—BLDSC shelfmark: 7851.031000.
Description: Presents biomedical research results.

616.075   SP   ISSN 0034-7973
REVISTA DE DIAGNOSTICO BIOLOGICO. 1970. bi-m. 7700 ptas.($130) (Asociacion Espanola de Biopatologia Clinica) Editorial Garsi, S.A., Londres, 17, 28028 Madrid, Spain. TEL 256 08 00. Ed. Justo Aznar. bk.rev.; bibl.; charts; illus.; circ. 1,500. **Indexed:** Biol.Abstr., Biol.Abstr., Chem.Abstr., Ind.Med.Esp.
—BLDSC shelfmark: 7852.500000.

REVISTA DE IGIENA, BACTERIOLOGIE, VIRUSOLOGIE, PARAZITOLOGIE, PNEUMOFTIZIOLOGIE. IGIENA. see *PHYSICAL FITNESS AND HYGIENE*

610   MX   ISSN 0034-8376
CODEN: RICLAG
REVISTA DE INVESTIGACION CLINICA. (Text and summaries in English and Spanish) 1948. q. Mex.$25000($30) Instituto Nacional de la Nutricion "Salvador Zubiran", Av. San Fernando y Viaducto Tlalpan, Mexico 22, D.F., Mexico. TEL 5-655-1076. Eds. Ruben Lisker, Alvar Loria. adv.; bk.rev.; bibl.; charts; illus.; stat.; index; circ. 1,100. **Indexed:** Biol.Abstr., Chem.Abstr., Curr.Cont., Helminthol.Abstr., Ind.Med., Nutr.Abstr.
—BLDSC shelfmark: 7862.010000.

610 615.53   SP   ISSN 1130-4405
▼**REVISTA DE LA MEDICINA TRADICIONAL CHINA.** 1990. q. 5000 ptas.($90) Sinomed s.l., Veracruz, 4, 28036 Madrid, Spain. TEL 91-361-12-66. adv.; circ. 4,000.

610   BL   ISSN 0034-8554
REVISTA DE MEDICINA. (Text in Portuguese; summaries in English) 1916. q. free. Universidade de Sao Paulo, Faculdade de Medicina, Centro Academico "Oswaldo Cruz", Av. Dr. Arnaldo 455, Sao Paulo CEP 01246, Brazil. Ed. Sylvia Massue Iriya. adv.; bk.rev.; bibl.; charts; illus.; tr.lit.; tr.mk.; index; circ. 2,000. (processed; also avail. in microform from UMI; reprint service avail. from UMI) **Indexed:** Biol.Abstr., Excerp.Med., Ind.Med., Trop.Dis.Bull.
—BLDSC shelfmark: 7864.470000.

610   SP   ISSN 0556-6177
REVISTA DE MEDICINA. (Text in Spanish; summaries in English and Spanish) 1957. 4/yr. free. (Universidad de Navarra, Facultad de Medicina) Servicio de Publicaciones de la Universidad de Navarra, S.A., Apdo. 177, 31080 Pamplona, Spain. TEL 94 25 2700. Eds. Diego Martinez Caro, Eduardo Alegria. adv.; bk.rev.; bibl.; charts; illus.; stat.; circ. 12,000. (back issues avail.) **Indexed:** Biol.Abstr., Chem.Abstr., Excerp.Med., Ind.Med., Psychol.Abstr.
—BLDSC shelfmark: 7864.450000.

616.026   RM   ISSN 0025-7869
CODEN: MINTA6
REVISTA DE MEDICINA INTERNA, NEUROLOGIE, PSICHIATRIE, NEURO-CHIRURGIE, DERMATO-VENEROLOGIE. MEDICINA INTERNA. (Text in Rumanian; summaries in English, French, German, Russian) 1949. 6/yr. $20. Uniunea Societatilor de Stiinte Medicale din Republica Socialista Rumania, Str. Progresului No. 8, Bucharest, Rumania. (Subscr. to: ILEXIM, Str. 13 Decembrie Nr. 3, P.O. Box 136-137, Bucharest, Rumania) Ed.Bd. adv.; bk.rev.; abstr.; bibl.; charts; illus. **Indexed:** Biol.Abstr., Chem.Abstr., Dent.Ind., Ind.Med.
Description: Covers internal medicine.

610   CU
REVISTA DE MEDICINA MILITAR. 3/yr. Ministerio de las Fuerzas Armadas Revolucionarias, Instituto Superior de Medicina Militar, Ave. Monumental, Habana del Esta, Zona Postal 17, Havana, Cuba.

610 355   RM
REVISTA DE MEDICINA MILITARA. q? Calea Plevnei 134, 77103 Bucharest, Rumania.
Formerly (until 1989): Revista Sanitara Militara.

610   RM
CODEN: REMTAS
REVISTA DE MEDICINA SI FARMACIE/ORVOSI ES GYOGYSZERESZETI SZEMLE. (Text in Hungarian, Rumanian; abstracts in English, French, German) 1955. s-a. 48 lei($20) Universita de Medicina si Farmacie din Tirgu Mures, Str. Gh. Marinescu Nr. 38, 4300 Tirgu-Mures, Rumania. TEL 40-954-13127. FAX 40-954-30804. (Subscr. to: Rodipet S.A., Piata Presei Libere Nr.1, 71341 Bucharest, Rumania) Ed. Ion Pascu. bk.rev.; abstr.; bibl.; charts; illus.; circ. 500. (also avail. in microfilm from UMI; reprint service avail. from UMI) **Indexed:** Chem.Abstr., Excerp.Med.
Formerly (until 1991): Revista Medicala - Medical Review (ISSN 0034-995X)
Description: For medical and pharmaceutical practitioners and researchers.

610 574   EC   ISSN 0034-9313
CODEN: REMBA8
REVISTA ECUATORIANA DE MEDICINA Y CIENCIAS BIOLOGICAS. (Text in Spanish; summaries in English) 1963. q. $20. Casa de la Cultura Ecuatoriana, Avda. 6 de Diciembre 332, Casilla 67, Quito, Ecuador. Ed. Dr. Plutarco Naranjo. adv.; bk.rev.; charts; illus.; index; circ. 2,500. **Indexed:** Biol.Abstr., C.I.S. Abstr., Chem.Abstr.
—BLDSC shelfmark: 7852.800000.

REVISTA ESPANOLA DE FISIOLOGIA. see *BIOLOGY — Physiology*

610   BL   ISSN 0034-9585
REVISTA GOIANA DE MEDICINA. (Text in Portuguese; table of contents and summaries in English and Portuguese) 1955. q. Cr.$150000($100) to non-members. (Associacao Medica de Goias) Imprensa da Universidade Federal de Goias, Av. Portugal, Esq. Av. Mutirao Sector Bueno, Caixa Postal 254, 74000 - Goiania, Goias, Brazil. TEL 251-1422. (Co-sponsor: Faculdade de Medicina da Universidade Federal de Goias) Ed. Joffre M. DeRezende. adv.; bk.rev.; abstr.; bibl.; charts; illus.; cum.index; circ. 3,000. (also avail. in microform from UMI; reprint service avail. from UMI) **Indexed:** Abstr.Hyg., Chem.Abstr., Excerp.Med., Helminthol.Abstr., Ind.Med., Protozool.Abstr., Trop.Dis.Bull.
—BLDSC shelfmark: 7858.270000.
Description: Original papers and research in all branches of medicine, with emphasis on surgery.

REVISTA IBEROAMERICANA DE MICOLOGIA. see *BIOLOGY — Botany*

610   BO
REVISTA MEDICA (LA PAZ). 1977. q. Caja Nacional de Seguridad Social, La Paz, Bolivia. illus.

616.98 358.4   BL   ISSN 0370-6141
CODEN: RMABE8
REVISTA MEDICA DA AERONAUTICA DO BRASIL. s-a. Diretoria de Saude da Aeronautica, Av. Churchill 157-5oA, Castelo, RJ, 20020, Brazil. TEL 061-248-3040. charts; illus.; stat.

610   CL   ISSN 0034-9887
CODEN: RMCHAW
REVISTA MEDICA DE CHILE. 1872. m. $132. Sociedad Medica de Santiago, Clasificador 1, Correo 27, Santiago, Chile. FAX 56-02-2128510. Ed. Alejandro Goic. adv.; bk.rev.; abstr.; bibl.; charts; illus.; stat.; index; circ. 2,000. **Indexed:** Abstr.Hyg., Biol.Abstr., Chem.Abstr., Curr.Cont., Dent.Ind., Helminthol.Abstr., Ind.Med., Ind.Vet., Nutr.Abstr., Protozool.Abstr., Rev.Plant Path., Trop.Dis.Bull., Vet.Bull.
—BLDSC shelfmark: 7864.250000.

610   CR   ISSN 0034-9909
REVISTA MEDICA DE COSTA RICA. 1933. q. $20 or exchange basis. Dr. Manuel Zeledon, Ed. & Pub., Apdo. 978, 1000 San Jose, Costa Rica. TEL 21-69-52. FAX 35-75-93. adv.; bk.rev.; charts; illus.; circ. 4,000. (reprint service avail. from UMI) **Indexed:** Biol.Abstr.

610   MZ
REVISTA MEDICA DE MOCAMBIQUE. 1982. 3/yr. Ministerio da Saude, Instituto Nacional de Saude, Universidade Eduardo Mondland, Faculdade de Medicina, C.P. 264, Maputo, Mozambique. TEL 427131. Dir. Joao Schwalbach.

610   CL   ISSN 0034-9917
REVISTA MEDICA DE VALPARAISO. (Text in Spanish; summaries in English) 1948. q. $15. Sociedad Medica de Valparaiso, Av. Brazil 1689, Valparaiso, Chile. Ed. Dr. Antonio Barbera. adv.; bibl.; charts; illus.; circ. 1,000. **Indexed:** Chem.Abstr.
—BLDSC shelfmark: 7864.350000.

610   MX   ISSN 0034-9925
REVISTA MEDICA DEL HOSPITAL GENERAL DE MEXICO S.S.A. 1938. m. Mex.$1400($26) Sociedad Medica del Hospital General de Mexico, S.S.A., Dr. Balmis 148, Auditorio Abraham Ayala Gonzalez, Mexico, D.F. 06726, Mexico. Ed. Dr. Patricia Alonso de Ruiz. adv.; bk.rev.; illus.; circ. 3,000. **Indexed:** Chem.Abstr., Excerp.Med., Ind.Med.

610   PY   ISSN 0034-9933
REVISTA MEDICA DEL PARAGUAY. (Text in Spanish; summaries in Spanish and English) 1955. q. 500 g.($5) Sociedad de Pediatria y Puericultura del Paraguay, 25 de Mayo y Tacuai, Asuncion, Paraguay. adv.; bibl.; charts; illus.; stat.; index; circ. 800. (tabloid format) **Indexed:** Biol.Abstr.

610   BL   ISSN 0100-0195
REVISTA MEDICA DO ESTADO DO RIO DE JANEIRO. (Text in English, French and Portuguese) 1941; N.S. 1977. 3/yr. free. Secretaria de Estado de Saude, Centro de Informacao Cientifica para a Saude, Secao de Editoracao, Rua Moncorvo Filho, 100-2 Andar, Rio de Janeiro CEP 20211, Brazil. Ed. Henrique Antunes Franco. bk.rev.; abstr.; index; circ. 3,000. **Indexed:** Biol.Abstr., Chem.Abstr., Excerp.Med.
Formerly (until vol.42, no.2, 1975): Revista Medica do Estado da Guanabara (ISSN 0034-9941)

610 617   RM   ISSN 0048-7848
REVISTA MEDICO-CHIRURGICALA. (Text mainly in Rumanian, occasionally in English, French, German; summaries in English) 1887. q. 600 lei($52) Societatea de Medici si Naturalisti din Iasi - Society of Physicians and Naturalists, Bd. Independentei 16, P.O. Box 25, 6600 Iasi, Rumania. Ed. Gr. Teodorovici. adv.; bk.rev.; illus.; circ. 3,000. (also avail. in microform from UMI) **Indexed:** Biol.Abstr., Bull.Signal., Chem.Abstr., Dent.Ind., Excerp.Med., Ind.Med., Ref.Zh.
—BLDSC shelfmark: 7865.300000.

REVISTA MEXICANA DE MICOLOGIA. see *BIOLOGY — Botany*

610   AA   ISSN 0255-6790
REVISTA MJEKESORE. bi-m. Ministria e Shendetesise - Ministry of Health, Tirana, Albania. TELEX 4205.

MEDICAL SCIENCES

610   BL   ISSN 0035-0362
REVISTA PAULISTA DE MEDICINA. (Text in English) 1932. bi-m. $70. Associacao Paulista de Medicina, Av. Brigadeiro Luiz Antonio, 278, andar 8, 01318 Sao Paulo SP, Brazil. FAX 011-366773. TELEX 7136. adv.; bibl.; charts; illus.; circ. 2,500. **Indexed:** Biol.Abstr., Chem.Abstr., Dent.Ind., Excerp.Med., Ind.Med.
—BLDSC shelfmark: 7869.570000.

616.98   PO   ISSN 0482-7171
CODEN: RPMMAG
REVISTA PORTUGUESA DE MEDICINA MILITAR; orgao dos servicos de saude do exercito, marinha e forca aerea. (Text in English, French, Portuguese) 1953. q. Esc.2.200($40) Escola do Servico de Saude Militar, Rua Infantaria, 16, n. 30, 1200 Lisbon, Portugal. TEL 687869. Ed. Carlos Manuel Vieira Reis. adv.; index; circ. 2,000. (back issues avail.)

610   FR   ISSN 0035-2330
REVUE D'HISTOIRE DE LA MEDECINE HEBRAIQUE.* (Text in French, Hebrew) 1948. q. 75 F.($12) Societe d'Histoire de la Medecine Hebraique, 177 bd. Malesherbes, 75017 Paris, France. Ed. Isidore Simon. adv.; bk.rev.; bibl.; illus.; index, cum.index; circ. 1,000.

REVUE DE LARYNGOLOGIE - OTOLOGIE - RHINOLOGIE.
see MEDICAL SCIENCES — Otorhinolaryngology

610   FR
REVUE DE MEDECINE DE TOURS. 8/yr. 260 F. (foreign 270 F.)(effective 1991). Editions La Simarre, Z.I. No. 2 - rue Joseph-Cugnot, 37300 Joue-les-Tours, France. TEL 47-53-53-66. FAX 47-67-45-05.

616.026   FR   ISSN 0248-8663
CODEN: RMEIDE
REVUE DE MEDECINE INTERNE. 1962. 4/yr. 390 F. (Societe Francaise de Medecine Interne) J.B. Bailliere et Fils, 10 rue Thenard, 75005 Paris, France. Ed. Dr. Michel Roux-Dessarps. adv.; bk.rev.; illus.; index; circ. 5,000. **Indexed:** Biol.Abstr., C.I.S. Abstr., Chem.Abstr., Curr.Adv.Ecol.Sci., Curr.Cont., Excerp.Med., Ind.Med., Nutr.Abstr.
—BLDSC shelfmark: 7930.940000.
Formerly (until 1980): Coeur et Medecine Interne (ISSN 0010-0234)
Description: Covers internal medicine.

610   FR
REVUE DE PHYTOTHERAPY PRATIQUE. q. (foreign 300 F.). (Institut National de Phytotherapie) Groupe des Revue Associes, 25, rue Dagorno, 75012 Paris, France. FAX 43-47-30-80. (Co-Sponsor: College Francais des Medecines de Terrain et Science Appliquees) adv.
Formerly: Phytotherapy (ISSN 0292-9406)

610   FR   ISSN 0484-8594
REVUE DE PODOLOGIE. bi-m. Federation Nationale des Podologues, 163 rue St. Honore, 75001 Paris, France. Ed. L. Olie. adv.

610   FR   ISSN 0035-2640
REVUE DU PRATICIEN. 1951. 60/yr. 850 F. J.B. Bailliere et Fils, 10 rue Thenard, 75005 Paris, France. Ed. Dr. Gerard Roux-Dessarps. adv.; bk.rev.; charts; illus.; pat.; index; circ. 60,000. **Indexed:** Biol.Abstr., C.I.S. Abstr., Curr.Cont., Dent.Ind., Dok.Arbeitsmed., Excerp.Med., Helminthol.Abstr., Ind.Med., Nutr.Abstr.
—BLDSC shelfmark: 7942.600000.

610 551.46   FR   ISSN 0035-3493
RA600   CODEN: RVOMAY
REVUE INTERNATIONALE D'OCEANOGRAPHIE MEDICALE. (Text in English, French) 1966. q. 443.10 F. (Institut National de la Sante et de la Recherche Medicale) Centre d'Etudes et de Recherches de Biologie et d'Oceanographie Medicale (C.E.R.B.O.M.), Parc de la Cote, 1 av. Jean-Lorrain, 06300 Nice, France. TEL 93-89-72-49. FAX 93-26-62-27. Ed.Bd. adv.; bk.rev.; circ. 2,000. **Indexed:** Aqua.Sci.& Fish.Abstr., Biol.Abstr., Bull.Signal., Chem.Abstr., Curr.Adv.Ecol.Sci., Curr.Cont., Deep Sea Res.& Oceanogr.Abstr., Excerp.Med., Geo.Abstr., Helminthol.Abstr., Ocean.Abstr., Pollut.Abstr., W.R.C.Inf., Water Pollut.Abstr.
—BLDSC shelfmark: 7925.117000.
Description: Specializes itself in the presentation of scientific work and research with a special orientation towards a number of themes that define the links existing between man and the sea.

610   BE   ISSN 0035-3639
CODEN: RMBRDQ
REVUE MEDICALE DE BRUXELLES. 1944. 10/yr. 2000 BEF. Universite Libre de Bruxelles, Association des Medecins Anciens Etudiants, Route de Lennik 808, Bte. 612, B-1070 Brussels, Belgium. TEL 02-555-6062. FAX 02-555-6117. Ed. Charles Toussaint. adv.; bk.rev.; abstr.; bibl.; charts; illus.; stat.; tr.lit.; circ. 3,000 (controlled). **Indexed:** Biol.Abstr., C.I.S. Abstr., Dent.Ind., Excerp.Med., Ind.Med.

610   SZ   ISSN 0035-3655
CODEN: RMSRA6
REVUE MEDICALE DE LA SUISSE ROMANDE. 1880. m. 95 Fr. Societe Medicale de la Suisse Romande, 2 Bellefontaine, CH-1003 Lausanne, Switzerland. FAX 021-239737. Ed. E.C. Bonard. adv.; bk.rev.; charts; illus.; stat.; index; circ. 4,000. **Indexed:** Biol.Abstr., C.I.S. Abstr., Chem.Abstr., Dent.Ind., Excerp.Med., Ind.Med.
—BLDSC shelfmark: 7932.300000.

610   BE   ISSN 0035-3663
REVUE MEDICALE DE LIEGE; journal du praticien. 1946. m. 2000 Fr. (foreign 2800 Fr.). (Universite de Liege) Institut de Medecine, 13 rue Alex Bouvy, 4020 Liege, Belgium. TEL 041-437572. Ed. H. Kulbertus. adv.; bk.rev.; abstr.; bibl.; charts; illus.; index; circ. 3,000. (also avail. in microform from UMI; reprint service avail. from UMI) **Indexed:** Biol.Abstr., C.I.S. Abstr., Chem.Abstr., Dent.Ind., Excerp.Med., Ind.Med., Ind.Vet., Protozool.Abstr.
—BLDSC shelfmark: 7932.080000.
Description: Technical journal of interest to physicians covering all aspects of the medical profession.
Refereed Serial

610 614   RW
REVUE MEDICALE RWANDAISE. 1968. 4/yr. Ministere de la Sante Publique, B.P. 84, Kigali, Rwanda. Ed. Dr. Butera. adv.

616.026   RM
REVUE ROUMAINE DE MEDECINE INTERNE/ROMANIAN JOURNAL OF INTERNAL MEDICINE. (Text in English, French, German or Russian) 1964. 4/yr. 200 lei($55) (Academia de Stiinte Medicale) Editura Academiei Romane, Calea Victoriei 125, 79717 Bucharest, Rumania. (Dist. by: Rompresfilatelia, Calea Grivitei 64-66, P.O. Box 12-201, 78104 Bucharest, Rumania) Ed. Prof. S. Purice. bk.rev.; charts; illus.; index; circ. 1,500. (also avail. in microform from UMI; reprint service avail. from UMI) **Indexed:** Biol.Abstr., Chem.Abstr., Curr.Cont., Excerp.Med., Helminthol.Abstr., Ind.Med., Nutr.Abstr.
Former titles: Revue Roumaine de Medecine. Serie Medecine Interne; (until 1975): Revue Roumaine de Medecine Interne (ISSN 0035-3973)
Description: Contains reviews, articles, results of experimental studies and new book information.

REVUE ROUMAINE DE MORPHOLOGIE ET D'EMBRYOLOGIE/ROMANIAN JOURNAL OF MORPHOLOGY AND EMBRYOLOGY. see BIOLOGY

REVUE ROUMAINE DE PHYSIOLOGIE/RUMANIAN JOURNAL OF PHYSIOLOGY. see BIOLOGY — Physiology

610   GW   ISSN 0035-4481
RHEINISCHES AERZTEBLATT. 1946. s-m. DM.156. (Aerztekammer Nordrhein) Deutscher Aerzte-Verlag GmbH, Dieselstr. 2, Postfach 40 02 65, 5000 Cologne 40, Germany. TEL (02234)7011-0. FAX 02234-7011444. (Co-sponsor: Kassenaerztliche Vereinigung Nordrhein) Ed.Bd. adv.; illus.; circ. 34,500.

610   GW   ISSN 0720-390X
RHEUMA; Therapeutische Richtlinien-Diagnosehilfen. bi-m. DM.95 (students DM.80). Verlag fuer Medizin Dr. Ewald Fischer GmbH, Fritz-Frey-Str. 21, Postfach 105767, 6900 Heidelberg 1, Germany. TEL 06221-4062-0. Eds. Dr. Otto Bergsmann, Dr. Matthias Heinitz.
—BLDSC shelfmark: 7960.613000.

610   US   ISSN 0363-7913
RHODE ISLAND MEDICAL JOURNAL. 1917. m. $20 (foreign $25). Rhode Island Medical Society, 106 Francis St., Providence, RI 02903. TEL 401-331-3207. Ed. Dr. Stanley M. Aronson. adv.; bk.rev.; bibl.; illus.; index; circ. 1,700. (also avail. in microform from UMI; reprint service avail. from UMI) **Indexed:** A.D.& D., Chem.Abstr., CINAHL, Curr.Cont., Dent.Ind., Excerp.Med., Helminthol.Abstr., Ind.Med.

362   IT   ISSN 0557-9430
RIABILITAZIONE; rivista di medicina fisica e riabilitazione. 1968. q. L.74500($100) (effective 1992). (Istituto di Terapia Fisica e Riabilitazione) Masson Italia Periodici, Via Statuto 2-4, 20121 Milan, Italy. TEL 02-6367-1. FAX 02-6367211. Ed. Ivano Colombo. adv.; circ. 2,000. **Indexed:** Biol.Abstr., Excerp.Med.
—BLDSC shelfmark: 7963.560000.

610 371.9   IT
RIABILITAZIONE E APPRENDIMENTO. q. L.60000($90) (effective 1992). Casa Editrice Idelson, Via A. De Gasperi 55, 80133 Naples, Italy. TEL 081-5524733. FAX 081-5518295. Ed. Carlo Perfetti.

610 615   IT
RICERCA & PRACTICA. 1985. bi-m. L.45000 to individuals; institutions L.60000($80). (Istituto di Ricerche Farmacologiche Mario Negri) Pensiero Scientifico Editore s.r.l., Via Panama 48, 00198 Rome, Italy. TEL 06-863633. Ed. Daniele Coen. bibl.; index; circ. 3,000.

610   IT   ISSN 0035-5259
CODEN: RIMEAB
LA RIFORMA MEDICA. (Text in Italian; summaries in English) 1885. m. L.70000($90) Edizioni Minerva Medica, Corso Bramante 83-85, 10126 Turin, Italy. Ed. Emilio Marmo. adv.; bk.rev.; charts; illus.; stat.; index; circ. 4,000. **Indexed:** Biol.Abstr., C.I.S. Abstr., Chem.Abstr., Dent.Ind., Excerp.Med., Ind.Med.
—BLDSC shelfmark: 7970.600000.

610   JA   ISSN 0034-351X
RIHABIRITESHON IGAKU/JAPANESE JOURNAL OF REHABILITATION MEDICINE. (Text in Japanese) 1964. bi-m. 8000 Yen($66.90) Japanese Association of Rehabilitation Medicine - Nippon Rihabiriteshon Igakkai, 1-39-11-502 Higashi-Ikebukuro, Toshima-ku, Tokyo 170, Japan. TEL 03-3981-6153. FAX 03-5396-0477. Ed.Bd. adv.; index; circ. 6,000.
●Also available online. Vendor(s): JICST.
—BLDSC shelfmark: 4658.600000.

610   JA   ISSN 0389-1887
CODEN: METCDS
RINSHO KENSAGAKU ZASSHI/MEDICAL TECHNOLOGY. (Text in Japanese) 1973. m. 650 Yen per no. Ishiyaku Publishers, Inc., 7-10 Honkomagome 1-chome, Bunkyo-ku, Tokyo 113, Japan. Ed. Hiroshi Miura. circ. 14,500. **Indexed:** Chem.Abstr.
—BLDSC shelfmark: 5532.028300.

610   IT   ISSN 0392-4858
RIVISTA DEL MEDICO PRATICO. 1981. w. (44/yr.). L.38000. (Associazione del Medico Practico) Masson Italia Periodici, Via Statuto 2-4, 20121 Milan, Italy. TEL 02-6367-1. FAX 02-6367211. Ed. Carlo Grassi. circ. 85,000.

616.992 616.07
574.2   IT   ISSN 0048-8364
RIVISTA DI ANATOMIA PATOLOGICA E DI ONCOLOGIA. 1948. 3/yr. L.80000($110) (Universita degli Studi di Messina, Istituto di Anatomia e Istologia Patologica) Piccin Editore, Via Altinate 107, 35100 Padua, Italy. TEL 049-655566. TELEX 432074 PICCIN I. illus. (reprint service avail. from UMI) **Indexed:** Biol.Abstr., Ind.Med.
—BLDSC shelfmark: 7980.800000.

616.98   IT   ISSN 0035-631X
CODEN: RMDSA2
RIVISTA DI MEDICINA AERONAUTICA E SPAZIALE. 1938. q. L.30000 (foreign L.45000). Corps Sanitario Aeronautico, Via P. Gobetti 2, Rome, Italy. FAX 06-49865611. Ed. L. Spuri. adv.; bk.rev.; abstr.; bibl.; charts; illus.; stat.; index; circ. 1,300. **Indexed:** Biol.Abstr., C.I.S. Abstr., Chem.Abstr., Excerp.Med., Ind.Med.
Description: Covers aerospace medicine.

MEDICAL SCIENCES

610 616   IT
RIVISTA DI MEDICINA E CHIRURGIA. 1979. q. Giardini Editori e Stampatori, Via Santa Bibbiana 28, 56100 Pisa, Italy. TEL 050 502531. Ed.Bd.

616.07   IT   ISSN 0394-0772
RIVISTA DI PATOLOGIA DELL'APPARATO LOCOMOTORE. s-a. L.60000($70) (effective 1992). (Societa Italiana di Patologia dell'Apparato Locomotore) Casa Editrice Idelson, Via A. De Gasperi, 55, 80133 Naples, Italy. TEL 081-552-4733. FAX 081-5518295. Dir. Maurizio Monteleone. Indexed: Excerp.Med.
   Description: Research papers that contribute to a better knowledge of the structure, function and pathology of the locomotor apparatus.

616.07   IT   ISSN 0035-6417
RIVISTA DI PATOLOGIA E CLINICA. (Text in Italian; summaries in English and Italian) 1946. bi-m. L.60000 (foreign L.120000)(effective 1992). Casa Editrice Maccari, Via Trento 53, 43100 Parma, Italy. FAX 039-521-771268. adv.; charts; illus.; stat.; index; circ. 1,600. Indexed: Chem.Abstr., Excerp.Med.
   —BLDSC shelfmark: 7992.325000.

616.07   IT   ISSN 0394-4549
                        CODEN: RPSCEK
RIVISTA DI PATOLOGIA E SPERIMENTAZIONE CLINICA. 1960. q. L.70000($100) Piccin Editore, Via Altinate 107, 35100 Padua, Italy. TEL 049-655566. TELEX 432074 PICCIN I. Ed. Prof. Giovanni Lanza. adv.; charts; illus. (reprint service avail. from UMI) Indexed: Biol.Abstr., Excerp.Med.
   —BLDSC shelfmark: 7992.340000.
   Formerly: Rivista di Patologia Clinica e Sperimentale (ISSN 0035-6409)

610   IT   ISSN 0393-9715
RIVISTA INTERNAZIONALE DI CHIRURGIA VERTEBRALE E DEI NERVI PERIFERICI; mensile di chirurgia e branche affini. (Text in Italian; summaries in English) 1986. w. L.20000. Casa Editrice l' Antologia, Via E. Suarez, 5, 80129 Naples, Italy. Ed. Alfredo Tedeschi. bk.rev.
   Formerly (until 1986): Antologia Medica Italiana (ISSN 0393-0726)

610   IT
RIVISTA ITALIANA DI AGOPUNTURA.* 1973. 3/yr. L.9000. Societa Italiana di Agopuntura, Via Diaz 5, 21047 Saronno, Italy. Ed. Dr. U. Lanza. adv.; bk.rev.; bibl.; charts; illus.; circ. 1,000.

610 574   IT
RIVISTA ITALIANA DI BIOLOGIA E MEDICINA. q. L.60000($70) Edizioni Minerva Medica, Corso Bramante 83-85, 10126 Turin, Italy. Ed.Bd. Indexed: Excerp.Med.

610   IT   ISSN 0394-9109
RIVISTA ITALIANA DI COLON-PROCTOLOGIA.* q. L.90000 includes supplement. Promo Leader Service s.r.l., Borgo Pinti, 68, 50121 Florence, Italy.
   —BLDSC shelfmark: 7987.293300.

610   IT   ISSN 0025-7915
RIVISTA ITALIANA DI MEDICINA SOCIALE. 1951. s-a. L.40000 (foreign L.80000)(effective 1992). C E M Casa Editoriale Maccari, Via Trento 53, 43100 Parma, Italy. FAX 039-521-771268. Ed. C. Palenzona. adv.; bk.rev.; charts; illus.; index; circ. 1,000.

610   IT
RIZA PSICOSOMATICA. m. L.76000. Edizioni Riza, Via Luigi Anelli 1, 20122 Milan, Italy. TEL 02-55185411.

610 613   US   ISSN 0091-3472
RA440.6
ROBERT WOOD JOHNSON FOUNDATION. ANNUAL REPORT. 1971. a. free. Robert Wood Johnson Foundation, Box 2316, Princeton, NJ 08543-2316. TEL 609-452-8701. Ed. Thomas P. Gore, II. illus.; circ. 20,000. Indexed: Med.Care Rev. Key Title: Annual Report - Robert Wood Johnson Foundation.

610   US
ROCKEFELLER UNIVERSITY, NEW YORK. SCIENTIFIC AND EDUCATIONAL PROGRAMS. 1979. a. free. Rockefeller University Press, 222 E. 70th St., New York, NY 10021. TEL 212-570-8568. FAX 212-570-7944. circ. 9,000. (reprint service avail. from ISI,UMI)
   Supersedes (1955-1979): Rockefeller University, New York. Annual Report (ISSN 0080-3405)

614.88   US
▼ROCKY MOUNTAIN E M S. (Emergency Medical Service); dedicated to the region's pre-hospital professionals. 1991. m. Woodland Publications, Inc., Box 6280, Woodland Park, CO 80866-6280. TEL 719-687-6870. FAX 719-687-2835. Ed. Ann Lamkin. adv.; circ. 5,000.
   Description: For paramedics, EMTs, fire fighters, search and rescue personnel, police and sheriffs, ski patrols, and hospital emergency room staff.

610   IS   ISSN 0374-776X
ROFEI HA-MISHPACHA/FAMILY PHYSICIAN. (Text in Hebrew; summaries in English) 1969. 3/yr. free. Kupat Holim Health Insurance Institution, 101 Arlosoroff St., P.O. Box 16250, Tel Aviv, Israel. TEL 03-433388. FAX 03-433474. Ed. Max R. Polliack. bk.rev.; circ. 4,500. Indexed: Abstr.Hyg., Biol.Abstr., C.I.S. Abstr., Excerp.Med., FAMLI, Ind.Heb.Per.
   —BLDSC shelfmark: 3865.568000.

610.69   CN   ISSN 0707-3542
ROLLCALL; a status report of health personnel in the province of British Columbia. 1974. biennial. free. University of British Columbia, Centre for Health Services and Policy Research, No. 400-2194 Health Sciences Mall, Vancouver, B.C. V6T 1Z6, Canada. TEL 604-822-4810. FAX 604-822-5690. illus.; circ. 200.
   Description: Describes the distribution of health personnel in British Columbia by regional hospital district.

610   US   ISSN 1040-8487
▼ROUNDSMANSHIP (YEAR). 1990. a. $19.95. Mosby - Year Book, Inc. (Chicago) (Subsidiary of: Times Mirror Company), 200 N. LaSalle St., Chicago, IL 60601-1080. TEL 312-726-9733. FAX 312-726-6075. TELEX 206155. Ed. Dr. Bruce Dan. illus.
   ●Also available online. Vendor(s): BRS.
   Description: Presents abstracts and commentaries on journal literature of value to medical students and residents studying for board examinations.

610   UK
ROYAL COLLEGE OF GENERAL PRACTITIONERS. OCCASIONAL PAPERS. 1976. irreg., no.54, 1991. price varies. Royal College of General Practitioners, 9 Marlborough Rd., Exeter EX2 4TJ, England. TEL 0392-57938. FAX 0392-413449. Ed. D.J. Pereira Gray. adv.; bk.rev.; circ. 1,500. Indexed: Excerp.Med., Ind.Med.

ROYAL COLLEGE OF GENERAL PRACTITIONERS. OFFICIAL REFERENCE BOOK. see COLLEGE AND ALUMNI

616.07 574.2   AT
ROYAL COLLEGE OF PATHOLOGISTS OF AUSTRALASIA. BROADSHEETS. 1967. irreg. Aus.$5 membership. Royal College of Pathologists of Australasia, 207 Albion St., Surry Hills, N.S.W. 2010, Australia. FAX 02-331-1431. Ed. V. Stoermer. circ. 1,800.
   Formerly: Royal College of Pathologists of Australia. Broadsheets.

610   CN   ISSN 0035-8800
R15
ROYAL COLLEGE OF PHYSICIANS AND SURGEONS OF CANADA. ANNALS/COLLEGE ROYAL DES MEDECINS ET CHIRURGIENS DU CANADA. ANNALES. (Text in English, French) 1968. 7/yr. Can.$40 (Can.$50 in U.S; elsewhere Can.$60)(effective Jan. 1992). Royal College of Physicians & Surgeons of Canada - College Royal des Medecins et Chirurgiens du Canada, 74 Stanley Ave., Ottawa, Ont. K1M 1P4, Canada. TEL 613-746-8177. FAX 613-746-8833. Ed. Lynne Quon-Mak. adv.; bk.rev.; bibl.; charts; illus.; stat.; index; circ. 27,000. (also avail. in microform from AMP; back issues avail.) Indexed: Biol.Abstr., Curr.Cont, Excerp.Med.
   —BLDSC shelfmark: 1031.530000.
   Description: Covers continuing medical education, medical history, biomedical ethics, internal medicine and surgery.
   Refereed Serial

610   UK
ROYAL COLLEGE OF PHYSICIANS OF EDINBURGH. DIRECTORY. 1910. irreg. Royal College of Physicians of Edinburgh, 9 Queen Street, Edinburgh EH2 1JQ, Scotland. TEL 031-225-7324. FAX 031-220-3939. circ. controlled.
   Formerly: Royal College of Physicians of Edinburgh. Yearbook and Calendar.

616.98   UK   ISSN 0035-9033
                        CODEN: JRNMAF
ROYAL NAVAL MEDICAL SERVICE. JOURNAL. 1915. 3/yr. £15. Institute of Naval Medicine, Alverstoke PO12 2DL, England. TEL 0705-822351. FAX 0705-822351. Ed. F.R. Wilkes. adv.; bk.rev.; bibl.; illus.; index; circ. 1,000. (also avail. in microform from UMI; reprint service avail. from UMI) Indexed: Abstr.Hyg., Biol.Abstr., C.I.S. Abstr., Curr.Adv.Ecol.Sci., Excerp.Med., Ind.Med., Trop.Dis.Bull.
   —BLDSC shelfmark: 4862.150000.

ROYAL NETHERLANDS ACADEMY OF SCIENCES. PROCEEDINGS. see SCIENCES: COMPREHENSIVE WORKS

610   UK   ISSN 0144-8676
R35
ROYAL SOCIETY OF MEDICINE. ANNUAL REPORT OF THE COUNCIL. (Previously issued in the Society's Calendar) 1959. a. free. Royal Society of Medicine Services Ltd., 1 Wimpole St., London W1M 8AE, England. TEL 071-408 2119. FAX 071-355-3198. circ. 17,500. (reprint service avail. from ISI,UMI)
   —BLDSC shelfmark: 1423.500000.

610   UK   ISSN 0142-2367
                        CODEN: RMISDU
ROYAL SOCIETY OF MEDICINE. INTERNATIONAL CONGRESS AND SYMPOSIUM SERIES. 1978. irreg., vol.178, 1991. Royal Society of Medicine Services Ltd., 1 Wimpole St., London W1M 8AE, England. TEL 071-408-2119. FAX 071-355-3198. Ed. Lord Walton.
   —BLDSC shelfmark: 4538.996000.

610   UK   ISSN 0141-0768
R35   CODEN: JRSMD9
ROYAL SOCIETY OF MEDICINE. JOURNAL. 1907. m. £85($180) Royal Society of Medicine Services Ltd., 1 Wimpole St., London W1M 8AE, England. TEL 071-408 2119. FAX 071-355-3198. Ed. A.J. Harding Rains. adv.; bk.rev.; bibl.; charts; illus.; index; circ. 19,000. (also avail. in microform from UMI; reprint service avail. from ISI,UMI) Indexed: Abstr.Hyg., Anim.Breed.Abstr., Biol.Abstr., Biotech.Abstr., C.I.S. Abstr., Chem.Abstr., CINAHL, Curr.Adv.Cancer Res., Curr.Adv.Ecol.Sci., Curr.Cont., Curr.Tit.Dent., Dairy Sci.Abstr., Dent.Abstr., Dent.Ind., Dok.Arbeitsmed., Ergon.Abstr., Excerp.Med., Helminthol.Abstr., Hort.Abstr., I.P.A., Ind.Med., Ind.Vet., INIS Atomind., Int.Nurs.Ind., Lab.Haz.Bull., Nutr.Abstr., Res.High.Educ.Abstr., Risk Abstr., Trop.Dis.Bull., Vet.Bull.
   ●Also available online.
   —BLDSC shelfmark: 4864.550000.
   Formerly (until vol.70, 1978): Royal Society of Medicine. Proceedings (ISSN 0035-9157)
   Description: Publishes clinical research and reviews across the range of specialties for general medicine.

610   UK   ISSN 0268-3091
ROYAL SOCIETY OF MEDICINE. ROUND TABLE SERIES. 1980. irreg. Royal Society of Medicine Services Ltd., 1 Wimpole St., London W1M 8AE, England. TEL 071-408 2119. FAX 071-355-3198.
   —BLDSC shelfmark: 8025.870000.
   Formerly: Royal Society of Medicine. Forum Series (ISSN 0144-5618)

610   US
RUTGERS MIND AND MEDICINE SERIES. 1989. irreg., latest 1990. price varies. Rutgers University Press, 109 Church St., New Brunswick, NJ 08901. TEL 908-932-7762. FAX 908-932-7039. (Dist. by: Rutgers University Press Distribution Center, Box 4869, Hampden Sta., Baltimore, MD 21211. TEL 410-516-6947)

360   CN
S A S C H NEWSLETTER. 1960. 4/yr. Can.$1. Saskatchewan Association of Special Care Homes, 1540 Albert St., No. 2, Regina, Sask. S4P 2S4, Canada. TEL 306-565-0744. FAX 306-565-2404. Ed. John F. Carter. adv.; bk.rev.; circ. 900.
   Formerly: Saskatchewan Care (ISSN 0048-9166)

610   PH
S L U JOURNAL OF MEDICINE. (Text in English) 1979. q. free. Saint Louis University, PO Box 71, Baguio City 2600, Philippines. TEL 442-3043. Ed. Robert Legaspi. circ. 4,000.

MEDICAL SCIENCES 3151

610   AT   ISSN 0813-1988
S P U M S JOURNAL. 1972. q. Aus.$50. South Pacific Underwater Medicine Society Incorporated, 80 Wellington Parade, East Melbourne, Vic. 3002, Australia. FAX 03-417-5155. Ed. John Knight. adv.; bk.rev.; circ. 1,000. (back issues avail.)
—BLDSC shelfmark: 8425.050700.

610   US
S T F M MESSENGER. 1968. bi-m. membership. Society of Teachers of Family Medicine, Box 8729, 8880 Ward Pkwy., Kansas City, MO 64114. TEL 816-333-9700. circ. 3,600.
Formerly: S T F M Newsletter.
Description: News of concern to family medicine educators, society meetings and organizational information.

610   GW   ISSN 0340-644X
SAARLAENDISCHES AERZTEBLATT. 1947. m. DM.78. (Aerztekammer Saarland) Deutscher Aerzte-Verlag GmbH, Dieselstr. 2, Postfach 40 02 65, D-5000 Cologne 40, Germany. TEL 02234-7011-0. FAX 02234-7011444. adv.; circ. 5,600.

SAINT GEORGE'S HOSPITAL GAZETTE. see *HOSPITALS*

610   II   ISSN 0970-4221
ST. JOHN'S JOURNAL OF MEDICINE. (Text in English) 1988. q. Rs.100($20) St. John's Medical College, Alumni Association, (Subsidiary of: Catholic Bishop's Conference of India Society for Medical Education), c/o Dr. S.V. Srikishna, Gen. Sec., Robert Koch Bhavan, 1st Fl., St. John's Medical College, Bangalore 560 034, India. TEL 565435. Ed. Dr. Ashley D'Cruz. adv.; bibl.; charts; illus.; circ. 1,500. (back issues avail.)
Refereed Serial

610   UK   ISSN 0036-312X
ST. MARY'S HOSPITAL GAZETTE. 1890. 8/yr. £2($2.40) St. Mary's Hospital Medical School Students' Union, Paddington, London WC2, England. adv.; bk.rev.; bibl.; charts; illus.; stat.; index; circ. 1,500.

610 370.15   CR   ISSN 1018-4430
▼**SALUD Y FAMILIA.** 1990. bi-m. Col.1500($15) Ediciones Creativas de Costa Rica, S.A., Urb. Jose Maria Zeledon, P.O. Box 146-2300, Curridabat, San Jose, Costa Rica. TEL 506-24-7930. FAX 506-24-9086. Ed. Arkadio Vargas Vazquez. adv.; circ. 25,000.
Description: General information on family health and psychological topics.

616.98   VE   ISSN 0036-3642
SALUS MILITIAE. 1965. s-a. free. Hospital Central de las Fuerzas Armadas, San Martin, Caracas-1060, Venezuela. (Subscr. to: Apdo. Postal 16.297, Caracas, Venezuela) Ed. Luis Martinez Iturriza. abstr.; bibl.; charts; illus.; circ. 1,000 (controlled).

610   US
SAN ANTONIO M.D. q. Republic of Texas Publishing Co., Box 1836, Helotes, TX 78023. TEL 512-670-1836. Ed. Paul Carr. circ. 10,000.

610   US   ISSN 0036-4061
SAN DIEGO PHYSICIAN. 1915. m. $20. San Diego County Medical Society, 3702 Ruffin Rd., Box 23581, San Diego, CA 92193. TEL 619-565-8888. FAX 619-569-1334. Ed.Bd. adv.; charts; illus.; tr.lit.; circ. 3,200.
Formerly: San Diego County Medical Society. Bulletin.

610   US
SAN FRANCISCO MEDICINE. 1928. m. $30. San Francisco Medical Society, 1409 Satter St., San Francisco, CA 94109. TEL 415-561-0850. Ed. Dr. Judith L. Mates. adv.; bk.rev.; circ. 3,200.
Formerly: San Francisco Medical Society. Bulletin (ISSN 0036-4142)

610   IT   ISSN 0393-6414
SAN MARTINO. 1984. q. free. (Ospedali Civili) U S L, 13-GE4, Viale Benedetto XV, 16132 Genoa, Italy. Ed. Salvatore Serrano. adv.; bk.rev.; illus.; circ. 3,000.
Formerly: Pammatone (ISSN 0031-0549)

610   PH   ISSN 0115-1126
SANTO TOMAS JOURNAL OF MEDICINE. (Includes supplement: Medical Gazette) (Text in English) 1973. q. P.300 (students P.200; foreign $50). University of Santo Tomas, Faculty of Medicine and Surgery, Rm. 207, St. Martin de Porres Bldg., Espana St., Manila, Philippines. TEL 02-731-3101.224. FAX 632-731-3126. Ed. Benjamin G. Co. adv.; bk.rev.; abstr.; circ. 3,500.
Indexed: Biol.Abstr., Chem.Abstr., Excerp.Med.

610   JA   ISSN 0036-472X
CODEN: SIZSAR
SAPPORO IGAKU ZASSHI/SAPPORO MEDICAL JOURNAL. (Text in English, Japanese; contents page and summaries in English) 1950. bi-m. exchange basis. Sapporo Ika Daigaku - Sapporo Medical College, Nishi-17-chome, Minami-1-jo, Chuo-ku, Sapporo-shi, Hokkaido 060, Japan. Ed.Bd. bibl.; charts; illus.; stat.; index; circ. 500. *Indexed:* Biol.Abstr., C.I.S. Abstr., Chem.Abstr., Curr.Adv.Ecol.Sci., Excerp.Med.
—BLDSC shelfmark: 8075.800000.

610   CN
SASKATCHEWAN MEDICAL JOURNAL. 1970. 4/yr. Can.$25. University of Saskatchewan, Continuing Medical Education, Saskatoon, Sask. S7N 0W0, Canada. TEL 306-966-7787. (Co-sponsor: Saskatchewan Medical Association) Eds. Mona Chappell, Dr. Murray Flotre. adv.; circ. 1,900. (back issues avail.)
Formerly: C M E News.

610   SU   ISSN 0379-5284
CODEN: SAMJDI
SAUDI MEDICAL JOURNAL. (Text in English; summaries in Arabic, English) 1979. bi-m. SRI.10 per no. Saudi Arabian Armed Forces Ministry of Defence and Aviation, Medical Services Department, P.O. Box 7897, Riyadh 11159, Saudi Arabia. TEL 4777714. FAX 478-8033. TELEX 401645 RKHPA SJ. Ed. Dr. Saleh al-Deeb. adv.; bk.rev.; index; circ. 24,000. (back issues avail.) *Indexed:* Curr.Cont.
—BLDSC shelfmark: 8076.975000.
Description: Covers a broad range of medical problems with emphasis on Saudi Arabia and Middle East.

610   BU   ISSN 0562-7192
CODEN: SUMEA4
SAVREMENNA MEDICINA. (Text in Bulgarian; summaries in English and Russian) 1950. m. 32 lv.($14) (Ministerstvo na Narodnoto Zdrave) Izdatelstvo Meditsina i Fizkultura, 11, Pl. Slaveikov, Sofia, Bulgaria. (Dist. by: Hemus, 6, Rouski Blvd., 1000 Sofia, Bulgaria) Ed. A. Maleev. circ. 2,003. *Indexed:* Abstr.Bulg.Sci.Med.Lit., BSL Biol., Chem.Abstr.
—BLDSC shelfmark: 0161.570000.

610   CS   ISSN 0036-5327
CODEN: SBLEA2
SBORNIK LEKARSKY. (Text in Czech; summaries in English and Russian) 1898. m. 43.20 Kcs.($28.60) Universita Karlova, Fakulta Vseobecneho Lekarstvi, Katerinska 32, 121 08 Prague 2, Czechoslovakia. TEL 29 62 63. (Dist. by: Artia, Ve Smeckach 30, 111 27 Prague 1, Czechoslovakia) Ed. F. Macholda. bibl.; charts; illus.; index. *Indexed:* ASCA, Biol.Abstr., Chem.Abstr., Curr.Adv.Ecol.Sci., Curr.Cont., Dent.Ind., Excerp.Med., Helminthol.Abstr., Ind.Med., Nutr.Abstr.

SCANDINAVIAN AUDIOLOGY. see *HANDICAPPED — Hearing Impaired*

610   SW
SCANDINAVIAN JOURNAL OF CARING SCIENCES. (Text in English) 1987. q. SEK 460. (Gothenburg College of Nursing and Paramedical Education) Almqvist & Wiksell Periodical Company, PO Box 638, S-101 28 Stockholm, Sweden.

SCANDINAVIAN JOURNAL OF CLINICAL & LABORATORY INVESTIGATION. see *MEDICAL SCIENCES — Experimental Medicine, Laboratory Technique*

SCANDINAVIAN JOURNAL OF CLINICAL AND LABORATORY INVESTIGATION. SUPPLEMENT. see *MEDICAL SCIENCES — Experimental Medicine, Laboratory Technique*

SCANDINAVIAN JOURNAL OF MEDICINE & SCIENCE IN SPORTS. see *MEDICAL SCIENCES — Sports Medicine*

610   SW   ISSN 0107-833X
CODEN: SJPCD7
SCANDINAVIAN JOURNAL OF PRIMARY HEALTH CARE. 1983. q. SEK 510. Almqvist & Wiksell Periodical Company, P.O. Box 638, S-101 28 Stockholm, Sweden. Ed. Harold Siem. adv.; bk.rev.; circ. 4,500. *Indexed:* FAMLI, Ind.Med.

362   SW   ISSN 0036-5505
CODEN: SJRMAA
SCANDINAVIAN JOURNAL OF REHABILITATION MEDICINE. (Supplements avail.) (Text in English) 1969. q. SEK 415 incl. supplements. Almqvist & Wiksell Periodical Company, Box 638, S-101 28 Stockholm, Sweden. Ed. Dr. Olle Hook. adv.; bk.rev.; charts; illus.; circ. 1,200. *Indexed:* Bibl.Dev.Med.& Child Neur., Biol.Abstr., CINAHL, Curr.Cont., Ergon.Abstr., Except.Child.Educ.Abstr., Excerp.Med., Ind.Med., Psychol.Abstr.
—BLDSC shelfmark: 8087.530000.

610 360   SW   ISSN 0300-8037
CODEN: SJSMAF
SCANDINAVIAN JOURNAL OF SOCIAL MEDICINE. (Supplements avail.) (Text in English) 1973. 4/yr. SEK 540($65) (Nordisk Socialmedicinsk Foerening - Scandinavian Association for Social Medicine) Almqvist & Wiksell Periodical Company, Box 638, S-101 28 Stockholm, Sweden. Ed. Lars-Olov Bygren. adv.; charts; circ. 900. *Indexed:* Abstr.Hyg., ASCA, Biol.Abstr., C.I.S. Abstr., CINAHL, Curr.Cont., Dent.Ind., Excerp.Med., Ind.Med., Risk Abstr., SSCI, Trop.Dis.Bull.
—BLDSC shelfmark: 8087.548000.
Formerly: Acta Socio-Medica Scandinavica (ISSN 0044-6041)

616.98   GW   ISSN 0080-679X
SCHIFFAHRTMEDIZINISCHES INSTITUT DER MARINE, KIEL. VEROEFFENTLICHUNGEN. 1969. irreg. free. Schiffahrtmedizinisches Institut der Marine, Kopperpahler Allee 120, 2300 Kiel-Kronshagen, Germany. Ed. B. Greiner. adv.; bk.rev.; circ. 2,000.

610   GW   ISSN 0341-8707
SCHLESWIG-HOLSTEINISCHES AERZTEBLATT. 1947. m. DM.78. Deutscher Aerzte-Verlag GmbH, Dieselstr. 2, PF 40 02 65, 5000 Cologne 40, Germany. TEL 02234-7011-0. FAX 02234-7011444. adv.; circ. 10,800.

610   GW   ISSN 0932-433X
DER SCHMERZ; Konzepte, Klinik und Forschung. 4/yr. DM.108($71) Springer-Verlag, Heidelberger Platz 3, D-1000 Berlin 33, Germany. TEL 030-8207-1.
—BLDSC shelfmark: 8090.965000.

610   SZ   ISSN 0036-7486
SCHWEIZERISCHE AERZTEZEITUNG/BULLETIN DES MEDECINS SUISSES/BOLLETTINO DEI MEDICI SVIZZERI. (Text in French, German and Italian) 1919. w. 150 Fr. (Schweizerische Aerzteorganisation - Federation of Swiss Physicians) Verlag Hans Huber, Laenggasstr. 76, CH-3000 Berne 9, Switzerland. TEL 031-24-25-33. FAX 031-24-33-80. TELEX 911886-HAHU. adv.; bk.rev.; bibl.; charts; stat.; index; circ. 25,300. *Indexed:* Biol.Abstr., C.I.S. Abstr.
—BLDSC shelfmark: 8113.300000.

610   SZ   ISSN 0036-7672
CODEN: SMWOAS
SCHWEIZERISCHE MEDIZINISCHE WOCHENSCHRIFT. (Text in French and German; summaries in original languages and English) 1871. w. 125 Fr. Schwabe und Co. AG, Steinentorstr. 13, CH-4010 Basel, Switzerland. TEL 061-2725523. FAX 061-2725573. Ed.Bd. adv.; bk.rev.; abstr.; bibl.; charts; illus.; index; circ. 5,500. (back issues avail.) *Indexed:* Abstr.Hyg., ASCA, Biol.Abstr., Biotech.Abstr., C.I.S. Abstr., Chem.Abstr., Curr.Adv.Ecol.Sci., Curr.Cont., Dairy Sci.Abstr., Dent.Ind., Excerp.Med., Helminthol.Abstr., Ind.Med., Nutr.Abstr., Protozool.Abstr., Risk Abstr., Sci.Cit.Ind., Trop.Dis.Bull.
—BLDSC shelfmark: 8118.570000.
Description: Publishes original research across many medical disciplines; includes continuing education courses for the Swiss Society of Internal Medicine.

MEDICAL SCIENCES

610 SZ
SCHWEIZERISCHE MEDIZINISCHE WOCHENSCHRIFT (SUPPLEMENTUM). (Text in French, German; summaries in English) 1975. irreg. price varies. Schwabe und Co. AG, Steinentorstr. 13, CH-4010 Basel, Switzerland. TEL 061-2725523. FAX 061-2725573. adv.; circ. 4,500. (back issues avail.) **Indexed:** Ind.Med.

610 SZ
SCHWEIZERISCHE RUNDSCHAU FUER MEDIZIN PRAXIS/REVUE SUISSE DE MEDECINE. (Text in French and German; summaries in English, French and German) 1911. w. 165 Fr. (foreign 219 Fr.). Hallwag AG, Nordring 4, CH-3001 Berne, Switzerland. TEL 031-423131. FAX 031-414133. TELEX 912 661 CH. adv.; bk.rev.; abstr.; bibl.; illus.; circ. 3,745. **Indexed:** Biotech.Abstr., C.I.S. Abstr., Curr.Cont., Dent.Ind., Excerp.Med., Ind.Med.

616.98 SZ ISSN 0377-8347
SCHWEIZERISCHE ZEITSCHRIFT FUER MILITAER- UND KATASTROPHENMEDIZIN/REVUE SUISSE DE MEDECINE MILITAIRE ET DE CATASTROPHES. (Text in French, German and Italian) q. 70 SFr.($50) (Schweizerische Gesellschaft der Offiziere der Sanitatstruppen) Editions Medecine et Hygiene, Case Postale 456, CH-1211 Geneva 4, Switzerland. TEL 022-469355. FAX 022-475610. Ed.Bd. adv.; bk.rev.; charts; circ. 3,200. **Indexed:** Excerp.Med. **Former titles:** Schweizerische Zeitschrift fuer Militaermedizin (ISSN 0036-8024); Vierteljahrsschrift fuer Schweizerische Sanitats-Offiziere.

610 SZ
SCHWEIZERISCHER MEDIZINALKALENDER UND ARZNEIMITTELUEBERSICHT. (Text in German) 1878. a. 55 Fr. Schwabe und Co. AG, Steinentorstr. 13, CH-4010 Basel, Switzerland. TEL 061-2725523. FAX 061-2725573. adv.; index; circ. 6,000. **Formerly:** Schweizerischer Medizinalkalender (ISSN 0251-1762) **Description:** Provides information for medical students and pharmacists on pharmacology, anaesthetics, antidotes as well as narcotics and dosages.

610 SZ ISSN 0080-7400
SCHWEIZERISCHES MEDIZINISCHES JAHRBUCH. (Text in French and German) 1968. a. 125 Fr. (Schweizerische Aerzteorganisation - Federation of Swiss Physicians) Schwabe und Co. AG, Steinentorstr. 13, CH-4010 Basel, Switzerland. TEL 061-2725523. FAX 061-2725573. adv.; index; circ. 5,000. **Description:** Comprised of, in part, a directory of personnel and institutions.

610 FR ISSN 0048-9727
SCIENCES MEDICALES; revue des universites nouvelles. vol.3, 1972. 6/yr. 205 F. "R" Rhumatologie, 15 rue Turgot, 78100 St. Germain en Laye, France. (also avail. in microform from UMI; reprint service avail. from UMI) **Indexed:** Chem.Abstr., Excerp.Med.

SCIENCES ORGONOMIQUES; revue des lois de la vie. see *BIOLOGY*

610 UK ISSN 0261-3921
SCOTTISH MEDICINE. 1981-1989; resumed 1991. bi-m. free. Hermiston Publications Ltd., 2 Hill Sq., Edinburgh EH8 9DR, Scotland. adv.; bk.rev.; illus.; circ. 5,000 (controlled).

610 US ISSN 1049-5614
▼**SCRIPPS CLINIC PERSONAL HEALTH LETTER.** 1990. m. $29. Phillips Publishing, Inc., Consumer Publishing, 7811 Montrose Rd., Potomac, MD 20854. TEL 301-340-2100. FAX 301-309-3847. Ed. Dr. Donald J. Dalessio. **Description:** Promotes good health and ways to overcome and solve medical problems.

610 US
SCRIPPS RESEARCH INSTITUTE. SCIENTIFIC REPORT. 1974. a. free. Scripps Research Institute, 10666 N. Torrey Pines Rd., La Jolla, CA 92037. TEL 619-455-8263. FAX 619-554-6357. Ed. Dennis Blakeslee. circ. 5,000 (controlled). **Former titles (until 1990):** Research Institute of Scripps Clinic. Scientific Report; Scripps Clinic and Research Foundation. Research Institute. Scientific Report; (until 1977): Scripps Clinic and Research Foundation. Scientific Report (ISSN 0361-3054)

610 CS ISSN 0036-9721
CODEN: SCMEBF
SCRIPTA MEDICA. (Text mainly in English, occasionally in German or Russian; summaries in Czech, English, Russian) 1922. 8/yr. 80 Kcs. or exchange basis. Masarykova Univerzita, Lekarska Fakulta - Masaryk University, Medical Faculty, Komenskeho nam. 2, 662 43 Brno, Czechoslovakia. Ed. Dr. Milan Dokladal. bk.rev.; charts; illus.; index; circ. 900. **Indexed:** Biol.Abstr., C.I.S. Abstr., Chem.Abstr., Excerp.Med., Ind.Med., Nutr.Abstr. **Description:** Examines scientific research in medical fields.

616.748 UK
SEARCH (LONDON, 1957). 1957. 2/yr. free. Muscular Dystrophy Group of Great Britain and Northern Ireland, 35 Macaulay Rd., London SW4 0QP, England. TEL 071-720-8055. FAX 071-498-0670. Ed. Alex Duncan. adv.; bk.rev.; circ. controlled. **Indexed:** Rehabil.Lit. **Formerly (until 1987):** Muscular Dystrophy Journal (ISSN 0027-3740)

170 US ISSN 0890-1570
R724
SECOND OPINION (CHICAGO). 1986. 4/yr. $45. Park Ridge Center, 676 N. St. Clair, Ste. 450, Chicago, IL 60611. TEL 312-266-2222. FAX 312-266-6086. Ed. Martin E. Marty. bk.rev.; index; circ. 2,000.
●Also available online. Vendor(s): Information Access Company.
Description: Stimulates interdisciplinary conversations between members of fields relating to health, faith, and ethics.

610 US
SECOND SOURCE IMAGING. m. Satellite Publishing Company, 2900 E. Carolina Center, Charlotte, NC 28208. TEL 704-391-9306. FAX 704-394-8060. Ed. Jack Spears. circ. 12,000.

610 GW
SEIBT MEDIZINISCHE TECHNIK. (Text in English, French, German, Spanish) 1955. a. DM.45. Seibt Verlag GmbH, Leopoldstr. 208, 8000 Munich 40, Germany. TEL 089-363067. FAX 089-364317. TELEX 5214853-SEIB-D. circ. 8,200.

610 GW ISSN 0582-4877
SELECTA; das Wochenmagazin des Arztes. 1959. w. DM.96. Selecta-Verlag, Pasinger Str. 8, 8033 Planegg, Germany. TEL 857030. Ed. Ildar Idris. adv.; bk.rev.; circ. controlled.
—BLDSC shelfmark: 8230.900000.
Incorporates: Praxis-Kurier (ISSN 0030-8056)

610 FR
SEMAINE DES HOPITAUX. 1925. w. 1640 F. to individuals (foreign 2100 F.); students 840 F. (foreign 1410 F.). (Semaine des Hopitaux) Expansion Scientifique, 15, rue Saint-Benoit, 75278 Paris Cedex 06, France. adv.; circ. 16,808. **Indexed:** ASCA, Biol.Abstr., Biotech.Abstr., C.I.S. Abstr., Chem.Abstr., Curr.Adv.Cancer Res., Curr.Cont., Dent.Ind., Dok.Arbeitsmed., Excerp.Med., Helminthol.Abstr., Nutr.Abstr., Protozool.Abstr.

610 AG
SEMANA MEDICA. 1894. m. Arenales 3574, 1425 Buenos Aires, Argentina. TEL 824-5673. Ed. Dr. Eduardo F. Mele. circ. 7,000.

610 616.07 US ISSN 0740-2570
SEMINARS IN DIAGNOSTIC PATHOLOGY. 1984. q. $87 to individuals; institutions $120; foreign $132. W.B. Saunders Co. (Subsidiary of: Harcourt Brace Jovanovich, Inc.), Curtis Center, Independence Square W., Philadelphia, PA 19106. TEL 215-238-7800. (Subscr. to: 6277 Sea Harbor Dr., 4th Fl., Orlando FL 32891) Ed. Dr. Daniel J. Santa Cruz. adv.; abstr.; bibl.; charts; illus.; index. **Indexed:** Curr.Cont.
●Also available online.
—BLDSC shelfmark: 8239.448900.

615.8 371.9 US
SENSORY INTEGRATION; special interest section newsletter. (Consists of 7 sections: Administration and Management; Developmental Disabilities; Gerontology; Mental Health; Physical Disabilities; Sensory Integration; Work Programs) vol.12, no.4, 1989. q. $15. American Occupational Therapy Association, Inc., 1383 Piccard Dr., Box 1725, Rockville, MD 20850-0822. TEL 301-948-9626. FAX 301-948-5512.

610 KO ISSN 0582-6802
R97.7.K68 CODEN: SUICAC
SEOUL JOURNAL OF MEDICINE/SEOUL UIDAE HAKSULJI. (Text in English; summaries in Korean) 1960. q. $20. Seoul National University, College of Medicine, 28 Yunkeon-dong, Chongro-gu, Seoul, S. Korea. Ed. Soon-Hyung Lee. index; circ. controlled. (tabloid format) **Indexed:** Abstr.Hyg., Biol.Abstr., Excerp.Med., Helminthol.Abstr., Nutr.Abstr., Trop.Dis.Bull. Key Title: Sehur Ruidaihagsurji.
—BLDSC shelfmark: 8241.810000.

610 615 KO
SEOUL NATIONAL UNIVERSITY. FACULTY PAPERS..* (Text in English; summaries in Korean) 1972. a. Seoul National University, Research Committee, Seoul, S. Korea. Ed. Byong Seol Seo.

610 YU ISSN 0370-8179
SERBIAN ARCHIVES OF GENERAL MEDICINE. (Text in Serbo-Croatian; summaries in English, French and German) 1872. m. 400 din. Serbian Medical Association, Ulica Narodnog Fronta No. 1-3, P.O. Box 838, 11112 Belgrade, Yugoslavia. (Co-sponsor: Serbian Science and Culture Council) Ed. Dr. Ratibor Micic. adv.; bk.rev.; circ. 3,000.
—BLDSC shelfmark: 0166.680000.

610 IT
SERENO SYMPOSIA REVIEW. irreg., no.15, 1988. Ares - Serono Symposia, Via Ravenna 8, Rome, Italy.

610 US
SERONO CLINICAL COLLOQUIA ON REPRODUCTION SERIES. 1980. irreg., vol.3, 1983. Academic Press, Inc., 1250 Sixth Ave., San Diego, CA 92101. TEL 619-231-0962. FAX 619-699-6715.

610 US
SERONO FOUNDATION SYMPOSIA. 1973. irreg., vol.51, 1983. Academic Press, Inc., 1250 Sixth Ave., San Diego, CA 92101. TEL 619-231-0926. FAX 619-699-6715. (reprint service avail. from ISI) **Indexed:** Chem.Abstr.

SEXUAL AND MARITAL THERAPY. see *PSYCHOLOGY*

610 US ISSN 0146-1044
HQ30.5 CODEN: SDISDC
SEXUALITY AND DISABILITY; a journal devoted to the study of sex in psychological and medical aspects of sexuality in rehabilitation and community settings. 1978. q. $110 (foreign $130). Human Sciences Press, Inc. (Subsidiary of: Plenum Publishing Corp.), 233 Spring St., New York, NY 10013-1578. TEL 212-620-8000. FAX 212-463-0742. Ed. Stanky H. Ducharme. adv. (also avail. in microform from UMI; reprint service avail. from ISI,UMI) **Indexed:** ASCA, Biol.Abstr., CINAHL, Curr.Cont., Curr.Lit.Fam.Plan., Excerp.Med., Past.Care & Couns.Abstr., Psychol.Abstr., Rehabil.Lit., Sociol.Abstr., SSCI, Stud.Wom.Abstr.
—BLDSC shelfmark: 8254.485200.
Description: Provides a forum for clinical and research developments in the area of sexuality as it relates to a wide range of physical and mental illnesses and disabling conditions.
Refereed Serial

610 GW
SEXUALMEDIZIN. m. Medical Tribune Verlagsgesellschaft mbH, Rheinstr. 19, Postfach 4240, 6200 Wiesbaden, Germany. TEL 0611-1705-0. FAX 0611-300365. TELEX 4186160-MTWI-D. adv.; circ. 40,000.

610 CC
SHAANXI ZHONGYI XUEYUAN XUEBAO/SHAANXI INSTITUTE OF TRADITIONAL CHINESE MEDICINE. JOURNAL. (Text in Chinese) q. Y3. Shaanxi Zhongyi Xueyuan - Shaanxi Institute of Traditional Chinese Medicine, Xianyang, Shaanxi 712083, People's Republic of China. **Description:** Presents theoretical research, emphasizing clinical applications. Also covers clinical medicine, pharmacy, experimental research, and education.

SHAFTESBURY REVIEW. see *SOCIAL SERVICES AND WELFARE*

610   CC   ISSN 1000-0496
SHANDONG YIKE DAXUE XUEBAO/SHANDONG UNIVERSITY OF MEDICAL SCIENCES. JOURNAL. (Text in Chinese) q. Shandong Yike Daxue, Xuebao Bianjibu, No. 44, Wenhua Xilu, Jinan, Shandong 250012, People's Republic of China. TEL 612424. Ed. Xi Xiaosheng.

610 615   CC
SHANDONG YIYAO/SHANDONG MEDICINE. (Text in Chinese) m. Shandong Sheng Weisheng Ting - Shandong Provincial Bureau of Public Health, No. 1, Qingnian Donglu, Jinan, Shandong 250011, People's Republic of China. TEL 26921. Ed. Xu Jia'an.

610   CC   ISSN 0257-8131
                                  CODEN: SYDXEE
SHANGHAI YIKE DAXUE XUEBAO/SHANGHAI UNIVERSITY OF MEDICAL SCIENCES. JOURNAL. (Text in Chinese; abstracts in English) 1956. bi-m. $13.32. (Shanghai Yike Daxue - Shanghai University of Medical Sciences) Shanghai Scientific and Technical Publishers, Journal Department, 450 Ruijin 2 Lu, Shanghai 200020, People's Republic of China. Ed. Wu Jue.
Description: Covers original contributions in experimental, clinical studies in general medicine, public health, pharmacy and the related fields.

610   CC   ISSN 0253-9934
SHANGHAI YIXUE/SHANGHAI JOURNAL OF MEDICAL SCIENCE. (Text in Chinese) m. Zhonghua Yixuehui, Shanghai Fenhui - Chinese Society of Medical Sciences, Shanghai Chapter, 1623 Beijing Xilu, Shanghai 200040, People's Republic of China. TEL 2531885. Ed. Wu Mengchao.
—BLDSC shelfmark: 8254.589900.

615.89 615.328   CC
SHANGHAI ZHONGYIYAO ZAZHI/SHANGHAI JOURNAL OF TRADITIONAL CHINESE MEDICINE. (Text in Chinese) m. $0.80 per no. Guoji Shudian, Qikan Bu, Chegongzhuang Xilu 21, P.O. Box 399, Beijing 100044, People's Republic of China.

610   CC   ISSN 1000-7156
SHANXI ZHONGYI/SHANXI TRADITIONAL MEDICINE. (Text in Chinese) bi-m. Shanxi Sheng Weisheng-ting - Shanxi Provincial Bureau of Public Health, 23 Donghua Men, Taiyuan, Shanxi 030013, People's Republic of China. TEL 382791. Ed. Cui Tianyue.

SHENGLI KEXUE JINZHAN/PROGRESS IN PHYSIOLOGICAL SCIENCES. see *BIOLOGY — Physiology*

610.28   CC   ISSN 1001-5515
SHENGWU YIXUE GONGCHENGXUE ZAZHI/JOURNAL FOR BIOMEDICAL ENGINEERING. (Text in Chinese, English) 1984. q. $80. Sichuan Society for Biomedical Engineering, Chengdu Kexue Jishu Daxue, Chengdu, Sichuan 610065, People's Republic of China. TEL 581554. (Dist. outside China by: Guoji Shudian - China Interantional Book Trading Corp., P.O. Box 399, Beijing, P.R.C. TEL 8414284) (Co-sponsors: West China University of Medical Sciences; Chengdu University of Science and Technology; Sichuan Biomedical Engineering Research and Development Center) Ed. Le Yilun.
Description: Interdisciplinary journal that covers original research papers, review articles, and brief notes on biomaterials, artificial organs, biomechanics and computer applications to medical systems.

SHEPARD'S MEDICAL MALPRACTICE CITATIONS. see *LAW — Civil Law*

610   JA   ISSN 0037-3699
                                 CODEN: SKIZAB
SHIKOKU IGAKU ZASSHI/SHIKOKU ACTA MEDICA. (Text in Japanese; summaries in English) 1950. bi-m. exchange basis. Tokushima Igakkai - Tokushima Medical Association, c/o Tokushima Daigaku Igakubu, Kuramoto-cho 3-chome, Tokushima-shi, Tokushima-ken 770, Japan. FAX 0886-33-0771. Ed. Shigeo Daikoku. adv.; tr.lit.; index; circ. 800. **Indexed:** Abstr.Hyg., Biol.Abstr., Chem.Abstr., Excerp.Med., Nutr.Abstr., Trop.Dis.Bull.
—BLDSC shelfmark: 8256.600000.

500   JA   ISSN 0387-9097
SHIMANE IKA DAIGAKU KIYO/SHIMANE MEDICAL UNIVERSITY. BULLETIN. (Text mainly in Japanese; abstracts, contents page and some articles in English) 1978. a. Shimane Ika Daigaku - Shimane Medical University, 89-1 En'ya-cho, Izumo-shi, Shimane-ken 693, Japan. FAX 0583-21-1731. Ed.Bd.
Description: Contains research articles on medicine, as well as articles on anthropology, computers, linguistics, history, and translations of literature.

610   JA   ISSN 0386-5959
                               CODEN: SJSCDM
SHIMANE JOURNAL OF MEDICAL SCIENCE. (Text and summaries in English) 1977. s-a. free. Shimane Ika Daigaku - Shimane Medical University, 89-1 En'ya-cho, Izumo-shi, Shimane-ken 693, Japan. Ed.Bd. (back issues avail.) **Indexed:** Biol.Abstr., Chem.Abstr.

610   JA   ISSN 0037-3826
                               CODEN: SIZAA7
SHINSHU MEDICAL JOURNAL/SHINSHU IGAKU ZASSHI. (Text in Japanese; contents page in English) 1952. 6/yr. 7000 Yen($30) Shinshu University, School of Medicine, 3-1-1 Asahi-machi, Matsumoto, Nagano 390, Japan. Ed. Dr. S. Chiba. adv.; charts; illus.; circ. 1,200. **Indexed:** Biol.Abstr., Chem.Abstr., Excerp.Med., Ind.Med.
—BLDSC shelfmark: 8256.870000.

610.73   JA   ISSN 0385-1982
SHINSHU UNIVERSITY. SCHOOL OF ALLIED MEDICAL SCIENCES. TREATISES AND STUDIES. (Text in Japanese; summaries in English) 1975. a. free. Shinshu Daigaku, Iryo Gijutsu Tanki Daigakubu, 3-1-1, Asahi, Matsumoto-shi 390, Japan. Ed.Bd. circ. 300. (back issues avail.)

610   CC   ISSN 1001-084X
SHIYONG NEIKE ZAZHI/JOURNAL OF PRACTICAL INTERNAL MEDICINE. (Text in Chinese) 1981. m. $15. Shiyong Yixue Zazhishe, 44-1, Jixian Jie, Heping Qu, Shenyang, Liaoning 110005, People's Republic of China. TEL 364398. Ed. Yu Runhong.

630   CC
SHIYONG ZHONGXIYI JIEHE ZAZHI. (Text in Chinese) m. Changzhi Yixueyuan - Changzhi Medical Institute, 46, Yan'an Lu, Changzhi, Shanxi 046000, People's Republic of China. TEL 33322. Ed. Wong Weiliang.
Description: Discusses the combined application of traditional Chinese medicine and Western medicine.

SHONI NO HOKEN/HEALTH FOR CHILDREN. see *CHILDREN AND YOUTH — About*

630   CC   ISSN 1000-0305
SHOUDU YIXUEYUAN XUEBAO/CAPITAL INSTITUTE OF MEDICAL SCIENCES. JOURNAL. (Text in Chinese) q. Shoudu Yixueyuan - Capital Institute of Medical Sciences, You'anmenwai, Beijing 100054, People's Republic of China. TEL 3014433. Ed. Xu Qunyuan.
Refereed Serial

610   JA
SHUKAN IGAKKAI SHINBUN/NEW MEDICAL WORLD WEEKLY. (Text in Japanese) 1950. w. 5000 Yen. Igaku-Shoin Ltd., 5-24-3 Hongo, Bunkyo-ku, Tokyo 113-91, Japan. TEL 03-817-5694. circ. 50,000.

610   CC   ISSN 1000-3649
SICHUAN ZHONGYI/SICHUAN JOURNAL OF TRADITIONAL CHINESE MEDICINE. (Text in Chinese) m. Zhonghua Quanguo ZhongYi Xuehui, Sichuan Fenhui - Chinese National Society for Traditional Chinese Medicine, Sichuan Branch, 80, Wenmiao Xijie, Chengdu, Sichuan 610041, People's Republic of China. TEL 26595. Ed. Jin Jiajun.
—BLDSC shelfmark: 8271.627500.

SIDE EFFECTS OF DRUGS ANNUAL. see *PHARMACY AND PHARMACOLOGY*

610 617.6   SL   ISSN 0253-8482
SIERRA LEONE MEDICAL AND DENTAL ASSOCIATION. JOURNAL. 1973. a. $25. Sierra Leone Medical and Dental Association, Box 850, Freetown, Sierra Leone. Ed. Dr. E.C. Gooding. adv.; bk.rev.; circ. 1,000. **Indexed:** Abstr.Hyg., Trop.Dis.Bull.
Formerly (until vol.3, no.1): Sierra Leone Medical and Dental Association. Bulletin.
Description: Publishes articles on disease patterns in the country and in the West African subregion.

MEDICAL SCIENCES   3153

SIGNAL TRANSDUCTION & CYCLIC NUCLEOTIDES. see *BIOLOGY — Biological Chemistry*

610   SI   ISSN 0037-5675
                                 CODEN: SIMJA3
SINGAPORE MEDICAL JOURNAL. (Text in English) 1960. bi-m. S.$240. Singapore Medical Association, Level 2, Alumni Medical Centre, 2 College Rd., Singapore 0316, Singapore. TEL 2231264. FAX 2247827. Ed. Dr. Chee Yam Cheng. adv.; bk.rev.; circ. 3,600. **Indexed:** Abstr.Hyg., Biol.Abstr., Biol.Abstr., Chem.Abstr., CINAHL, Dent.Ind., Excerp.Med., Helminthol.Abstr., Ind.Med., Ind.Vet., Pig News & Info., Protozool.Abstr., Rev.Appl.Entomol., Trop.Dis.Bull., Vet.Bull.
—BLDSC shelfmark: 8285.480000.

615.8   SW   ISSN 0037-6019
SJUKGYMNASTEN. 1943. 11/yr. SEK 430. Legitimerade Sjukgymnasters Riksfoerbund, Box 3196, S-103 63 Stockholm, Sweden. TEL 08-241490. FAX 08-217931. Ed. Lena Lindstroem. adv.; bk.rev.; illus.; index; circ. 9,973.
—BLDSC shelfmark: 8294.830300.

SMITH FUNDING REPORT; the quarterly guide to research-project grant opportunities offered by private and corporate foundations for education and health institutions. see *EDUCATION — Higher Education*

615.89   UK   ISSN 0951-631X
R131.A1
SOCIAL HISTORY OF MEDICINE. 1970. 3/yr. £40($78) (Society for the Social History of Medicine) Oxford University Press, Oxford Journals, Pinkhill House, Southfield Road, Eynsham, Oxford OX8 1JJ, England. TEL 0865-882283. FAX 0865-882890. TELEX 837330 OXPRES G. Eds. Drs. Ann Digby, Richard Smith. adv.; bk.rev.; abstr.; bibl.; cum.index: 1970-1977; circ. 100. (back issues avail.)
—BLDSC shelfmark: 8318.099000.
Formerly (until 1987): Society for the Social History of Medicine. Bulletin (ISSN 0307-6792)
Description: Covers all aspects of health, illness and medical treatment, as well as biological aspects of normal life.

SOCIAL RESPONSIBILITY: BUSINESS, JOURNALISM, LAW, MEDICINE. see *PHILOSOPHY*

610 301   US   ISSN 0277-9536
RA418   CODEN: SSMDEP
SOCIAL SCIENCE & MEDICINE. 1978. 24/yr. (in 2 vols., 12 nos./vol.). £825 (effective 1992). Pergamon Press, Inc., Journals Division, 660 White Plains Rd., Tarrytown, NY 10591-5153. TEL 914-524-9200. FAX 914-333-2444. (And: Headington Hill Hall, Oxford OX3 0BW, England. TEL 0865-794141) Ed. P.J.M. McEwan. adv.; bk.rev.; index; circ. 1,800. (also avail. in microform from MIM,UMI; back issues avail.) **Indexed:** Abstr.Anthropol., Abstr.Health Care Manage.Stud., Abstr.Hyg., Adol.Ment.Hlth.Abstr., ASCA, ASSIA, Behav.Med.Abstr., Bibl.Dev.Med.& Child Neur., Biol.Abstr., Chic.Per.Ind., CINAHL, Curr.Adv.Ecol.Sci., Curr.Cont., Curr.Lit.Fam.Plan., Dairy Sci.Abstr., Dent.Ind., E.I., Excerp.Med., FAMLI, I D A, Ind.Med., Int.Nurs.Ind., Lang.& Lang.Behav.Abstr., Med.Care Rev., Mid.East: Abstr.& Ind., Nutr.Abstr., Popul.Ind., Protozool.Abstr., Psychol.Abstr., Res.High.Educ.Abstr., Rice Abstr., Risk Abstr., Rural Devel.Abstr., Rural Ext.Educ.& Tr.Abstr., Soc.Sci.Ind., SSCI, Stud.Wom.Abstr., Trop.Dis.Bull., World Agri.Econ.& Rural Sociol.Abstr.
●Also available online.
—BLDSC shelfmark: 8318.157000.
Formed by the merger of: Social Science and Medicine. Part A: Medical Sociology (ISSN 0271-7123); Social Science and Medicine. Part B: Medical Anthropology (ISSN 0160-7987); Social Science and Medicine. Part C: Medical Economics (ISSN 0160-7995); Social Science and Medicine. Part D: Medical Geography (ISSN 0160-8002); Social Science and Medicine. Part E: Medical Psychology (ISSN 0271-5384) Social Science and Medicine. Part F: Medical Ethics (ISSN 0271-5392); Which were formerly (until 1980): Ethics in Science and Medicine (ISSN 0306-4581); (until 1976): Science, Medicine and Man (ISSN 0300-9955).
Description: International forum for exchange among social scientists, medical researchers and practitioners, and health administrators and planners.
Refereed Serial

MEDICAL SCIENCES

610   SW   ISSN 0037-833X
SOCIALMEDICINSK TIDSKRIFT. 1924. m. (10/yr.). SEK 215. 172 83 Sundbyberg, Sweden. Ed. Dr. C.G. Westrin. adv.; bk.rev.; abstr.; charts; illus.; index; circ. 4,500. **Indexed:** C.I.S. Abstr., Excerp.Med., Ind.Med.

610   SP   ISSN 0213-3601
SOCIEDAD DE ESTUDIOS VASCOS. CUADERNOS DE SECCION. CIENCIAS MEDICAS. 1984. irreg. Eusko Ikaskuntza, S.A., Legazpi, 10-1, 20004 Donostia-San Sebastian, Spain. TEL 425 111.

610   SP   ISSN 0583-7480
SOCIEDAD ESPANOLA DE HISTORIA DE LA MEDICINA. BOLETIN. vol.14, 1974. a. Sociedad Espanola de Historia de la Medicina, Duque de Medinaceli 4, Madrid-14, Spain. bibl.

616.07   FR   ISSN 0037-9085
SOCIETE DE PATHOLOGIE EXOTIQUE ET DE SES FILIALES. BULLETIN. (Text in French; summaries in English) 1908. 5/yr. 100 ECU($120) (typically set in Jan.). Masson, 120 bd. Saint-Germain, 75280 Paris Cedex 06, France. TEL 1-46-34-21-60. FAX 1-45-87-29-99. TELEX 202 671 F. Ed. A. Dodin. adv.; bk.rev.; bibl.; charts; illus.; maps; index; circ. 1,350. (reprint service avail. from ISI) **Indexed:** Abstr.Hyg., Biol.Abstr., Chem.Abstr., Curr.Adv.Ecol.Sci., Excerp.Med., Helminthol.Abstr., Ind.Med., Ind.Vet., Nutr.Abstr., Protozool.Abstr., Rev.Appl.Entomol., Rev.Plant Path., So.Pac.Per.Ind., Trop.Dis.Bull., Vet.Bull.
—BLDSC shelfmark: 2747.380000.

610   LU   ISSN 0037-9247
                    CODEN: BMGLAO
SOCIETE DES SCIENCES MEDICALES DU GRAND-DUCHE DE LUXEMBOURG. BULLETIN. (Text in English, French, German) 1863. irreg. (approx. 2-3/yr.). free to institutions. (Societe des Sciences Medicales, Institut Grand-Ducal) Imprimerie Saint Paul, Centre Hospitalier de Luxembourg, 4 rue Barble, Luxembourg, Luxembourg. FAX 00352-458762. Ed. Dr. M. Dicato. adv.; bk.rev.; bibl.; charts; illus.; circ. 1,200. **Indexed:** Biol.Abstr., Chem.Abstr., Dent.Ind., Excerp.Med., Ind.Med.
    Description: Collection of research papers covering a variety of topics in medicine.

610   MG
SOCIETE DU CORPS MEDICAL MALAGACHE. BULLETIN. (Text in Malagasy) m. Imprimerie Volamahitsy, 101 Antananarivo, Malagasy Republic. Ed. Dr. Rakotomalala.

SOCIETE FRANCAISE DE MYCOLOGIE MEDICALE. BULLETIN. see BIOLOGY — Botany

SOCIETY FOR ENVIRONMENTAL THERAPY. NEWSLETTER. see NUTRITION AND DIETETICS

SOCIETY NEWSLETTER. see PSYCHOLOGY

615.8 371.9   JA   ISSN 0386-9822
SOGO REHABILITATION. (Text in Japanese) 1973. m. 20640 Yen($159) Igaku-Shoin Ltd., 5-24-3 Hongo, Bunkyo-ku, Tokyo 113-91, Japan. TEL 03-817-5704. Ed.Bd. circ. 6,000.
—BLDSC shelfmark: 8321.560000.
    Description: Studies rehabilitation medicine and related medical fields.

SOURCEBOOK ON ASBESTOS DISEASES. see LAW

SOURCEBOOK ON ASBESTOS DISEASES CASE LAW QUARTERLY. see LAW

610 574   SA
SOUTH AFRICAN INSTITUTE FOR MEDICAL RESEARCH. PUBLICATION. (Text in English) 1917. irreg. South African Institute for Medical Research, P.O. Box 1038, Johannesburg 2000, South Africa. FAX 011-725-2319. TELEX 4-22211. circ. 150. (back issues avail.)

615.8   SA   ISSN 0038-2337
SOUTH AFRICAN JOURNAL OF OCCUPATIONAL THERAPY. (Text in Afrikaans, English) 1949. s-a. R.20 (foreign R.45)(effective 1992). South African Association of Occupational Therapists, Box 145, Rondebosch 7700, South Africa. TEL 790-1009. FAX 790507. TELEX 95-527943 SA. Eds. Valerie Claxton, Hilary Henderson. adv.; bk.rev.; abstr.; bibl.; charts; illus.; pat.; stat.; circ. 900 (controlled). **Indexed:** Ind.S.A.Per.
—BLDSC shelfmark: 8339.305000.

615.8   SA   ISSN 0379-6175
SOUTH AFRICAN JOURNAL OF PHYSIOTHERAPY. (Text in English) 1925. q. R.55 to non-members (foreign R.90). (South African Society of Physiotherapy - Suid-Afrikaanse Fisiotherapie Vereiniging) Mara Communications, P.O. Box 695, Evandale 1610, South Africa. TEL 011-453-2746. FAX 011-453-1689. Ed. J. Beenhakker. adv.; bk.rev.; circ. 2,700. (back issues avail.) **Indexed:** Ind.S.A.Per.
—BLDSC shelfmark: 8339.700000.

610 360   SA
SOUTH AFRICAN MEDICAL AND DENTAL COUNCIL. REGISTER OF SUPPLEMENTARY HEALTH SERVICES PROFESSIONS. a. (with m. supplements). R.90 (plus R.6 for supplements). South African Medical and Dental Council, P.O. Box 205, Pretoria 0001, South Africa. TEL 012-28-6680. FAX 012-28-5120.
    Description: Provides names and addresses of all supplementary health services personnel registered with the council.

610   SA   ISSN 0038-2469
R98   CODEN: SAMJAF
SOUTH AFRICAN MEDICAL JOURNAL/SUID-AFRIKAANSE MEDIESE TYDSKRIF. (Text in Afrikaans, English) 1884. s-m. R.300. Medical Association of South Africa, Private Bag X1, Pinelands 7430, South Africa. TEL 531-3081. FAX 531-4126. Ed. N.C. Lee. adv.; bk.rev.; bibl.; illus.; index; circ. 13,600. **Indexed:** Abstr.Hyg., ASCA, Bibl.Dev.Med.& Child Neur., Biol.Abstr., Biotech.Abstr., C.I.S. Abstr., Chem.Abstr., CINAHL, Curr.Adv.Cancer Res., Curr.Adv.Ecol.Sci., Curr.Cont., Dairy Sci.Abstr., Dent.Ind., Dok.Arbeitsmed., Excerp.Med., Food Sci.& Tech.Abstr., Helminthol.Abstr., Ind.Med., Ind.S.A.Per., Ind.Vet., Nutr.Abstr., Protozool.Abstr., Rev.Plant Path., Rural Devel.Abstr., Trop.Dis.Bull., Vet.Bull., W.R.C.Inf., World Agri.Econ.& Rural Sociol.Abstr.
—BLDSC shelfmark: 8341.700000.
    Incorporating (as special issue, from vol.11, 1973): South African Journal of Obstetrics and Gynecology (ISSN 0038-2329)

610   SA   ISSN 0375-1880
R854.S6
SOUTH AFRICAN MEDICAL RESEARCH COUNCIL. ANNUAL REPORT. 1969. a. South African Medical Research Council, P.O. Box 19070, Tygerberg 7505, South Africa.
    Supersedes in part (in 1989): South African Medical Research Council. Research Report (ISSN 0081-248X)

SOUTH AFRICAN SOCIETY OF PATHOLOGISTS. CONGRESS BROCHURE. see MEETINGS AND CONGRESSES

610   US   ISSN 0038-3139
                 CODEN: JSCMAZ
SOUTH CAROLINA MEDICAL ASSOCIATION. JOURNAL. 1905. m. $25 to non-members; members $15. South Carolina Medical Association, Box 11188, Columbia, SC 29211. TEL 803-798-6207. FAX 803-772-6783. Ed. Dr. Charles S. Bryan. adv.; bk.rev.; charts; illus.; index; circ. 4,200 (controlled). (also avail. in microform from UMI; reprint service avail. from UMI) **Indexed:** Biol.Abstr., Chem.Abstr., Ind.Med., INIS Atomind.
—BLDSC shelfmark: 4902.110000.

610   US   ISSN 0038-3317
                 CODEN: SDMEAL
SOUTH DAKOTA JOURNAL OF MEDICINE. 1946. m. $15. South Dakota State Medical Association, 1323 S. Minnesota Ave., Sioux Falls, SD 57105. TEL 605-336-1965. FAX 605-336-0270. Ed. Dr. Robert E. Van Demark. adv.; bk.rev.; abstr.; illus.; index; circ. 1,300. **Indexed:** Biol.Abstr., Chem.Abstr., Ind.Med.
—BLDSC shelfmark: 8350.900000.

610   US   ISSN 0038-4348
R11   CODEN: SMJOAV
SOUTHERN MEDICAL JOURNAL. 1906. m. $55. Southern Medical Association, 35 Lakeshore Dr., Box 190088, Birmingham, AL 35219-0088. TEL 205-945-1840. FAX 205-945-1548. Ed. Dr. John B. Thomison. adv.; bibl.; charts; illus.; index; circ. 31,000. (also avail. in microform from UMI; reprint service avail. from UMI) **Indexed:** Adol.Ment.Hlth.Abstr., ASCA, Biol.Abstr., Biotech.Abstr., C.I.S. Abstr., Chem.Abstr., CINAHL, Curr.Adv.Cancer Res., Curr.Cont., Curr.Lit.Fam.Plan., Dent.Ind., Dok.Arbeitsmed., Excerp.Med., Helminthol.Abstr., Hosp.Lit.Ind., HRIS, Ind.Med., Nutr.Abstr., Protozool.Abstr., Rehabil.Lit., Rev.Plant Path., Trop.Dis.Bull.
—BLDSC shelfmark: 8354.400000.
    Description: Geared toward practicing physicians and surgeons. Presents original articles and papers in clinical medicine.
    Refereed Serial

610   RU   ISSN 0038-5077
                 CODEN: SOMEAU
SOVETSKAYA MEDITSINA/SOVIET MEDICINE. 1937. m. 30 Rub. (Ministerstvo Zdravookhraneniya R.S.F.S.R.) Izdatel'stvo Meditsina, Petroverigskii pereulok 6-8, 101838 Moscow, Russia. (Subscr. to: Mezhdunarodnaya Kniga, Moscow, G-200, Russia) Ed. I.I. Sivkov. **Indexed:** ASCA, Biol.Abstr., C.I.S. Abstr., Dairy Sci.Abstr., Dent.Ind., Helminthol.Abstr., Ind.Med., Int.Aerosp.Abstr., Nutr.Abstr., World Bibl.Soc.Sec.
—BLDSC shelfmark: 0164.600000.
    Description: Discusses problems of the clinical picture, diagnosis and treatment of chronic, infectious, obstetrical-gynecological, neurological and other diseases which are of interest to practitioners and scientific workers.

610   US   ISSN 1054-6596
▼**SOVIET ARCHIVES OF INTERNAL MEDICINE.** (English translation of Soviet title) 1991. bi-m. $120 to individuals (outside N. America $135); institutions $330 (outside N. America $345). (Soviet Archives of Internal Medicine, UR) New Soviet Sciences Press (USA), c/o Allen Press, Inc., Dist., Box 1897, Lawrence, KS 66044-8897. TEL 913-843-1235. FAX 913-843-1274. Ed. Eugene Chazov.
    Description: Each issue of the journal is dedicated to one common subject: cardiology, hematology, etc. Some general areas addressed are cancer, tumors, respiration, AIDS, circulation, medication, the immune system, stomach disorders, toxical complications, heart attacks, chemotherapy and genetics.

614.44   SZ
SOZIAL- UND PRAEVENTIVMEDIZIN/MEDECINE SOCIALE ET PREVENTIVE. (Text and summaries in English, French and German) bi-m. 168 Fr.($114) (Schweizerische Gesellschaft fuer Sozial und Praeventivmedizin - Swiss Society of Social and Preventive Medicine) Birkhaeuser Verlag, P.O. Box 133, CH-4010 Basel, Switzerland. TEL 061-737740. FAX 061-737950. TELEX 963475 BIRKH CH. (Dist. in N. America by: Springer-Verlag New York, Inc., Journal Fulfillment Services, Box 2485, Secaucus, NJ 07096-2491. TEL 201-348-4033) Ed. Fred Paccaud. adv.; bk.rev.; abstr.; bibl.; charts; illus.; index. **Indexed:** Abstr.Hyg., ASCA, Biol.Abstr., C.I.S. Abstr., Chem.Abstr, Excerp.Med., Helminthol.Abstr., Ind.Med., Trop.Dis.Bull.
    Formerly: Zeitschrift fuer Praeventivmedizin (ISSN 0044-3379)

616.07   US   ISSN 0081-3699
SPEZIELLE PATHOLOGISCHE ANATOMIE. 1966. irreg. price varies. Springer-Verlag, 175 Fifth Ave., New York, NY 10010. TEL 212-460-1500. (Also Berlin, Heidelberg, Tokyo and Vienna) (reprint service avail. from ISI)

610   UK   ISSN 0038-741X
SPHINCTER. (Supplement avail.: Sphincter Minimi) 1937. 2/yr. £0.50. University of Liverpool, Medical School, Royal Liverpool Hospital, Box 147, Liverpool L69 3BX, England. Ed. Callum Pearce. adv.; bk.rev.; circ. 900 (controlled).

610   US   ISSN 0160-9475
SPINA BIFIDA THERAPY. 1978. q. Eterna International, Inc., 27 W. 560 Warrenville Rd., Warrenville, IL 60555. TEL 708-393-2930. Ed. Stephen B. Parrish. bk.rev. **Indexed:** Psychol.Abstr.
—BLDSC shelfmark: 8413.883000.

610 GW ISSN 0932-0555
SPORTVERLETZUNG - SPORTSCHADEN. 1987. q. DM.114. Georg Thieme Verlag, Ruedigerstr. 14, Postfach 104853, 7000 Stuttgart 10, Germany. TEL 0711-8931-0. FAX 0711-8931298. Eds. W. Puhl, E. Beck. circ. 3,000.
—BLDSC shelfmark: 8419.860600.

610 YU ISSN 0081-3966
CODEN: SUGMAW
SRPSKA AKADEMIJA NAUKA I UMETNOSTI. ODELJENJE MEDICINSKIH NAUKA. GLAS. (Text in Serbo-Croatian; summaries in English, French, German or Russian) 1949, N.S. irreg. price varies. Srpska Akademija Nauka i Umetnosti, Knez Mihailova 35, 11001 Belgrade, Serbia, Yugoslavia. (Dist. by: Prosveta, Terazije 16, Belgrade, Serbia, Yugoslavia) circ. 1,000. **Indexed:** Excerp.Med., Ind.Med.
—BLDSC shelfmark: 0050.130000.

610 YU ISSN 0081-4016
SRPSKA AKADEMIJA NAUKA I UMETNOSTI. ODELJENJE MEDICINSKIH NAUKA. POSEBNA IZDANJA. (Text in Serbo-Croatian; summaries in English, French, German or Russian) 1950. irreg. price varies. Srpska Akademija Nauka i Umetnosti, Knez Mihailova 35, 11001 Belgrade, Serbia, Yugoslavia. FAX 38-11-182-825. TELEX 72593 SANU YU. (Dist. by: Prosveta, Terazije 16, Belgrade, Serbia, Yugoslavia) circ. 1,000. **Indexed:** Chem.Abstr, Excerp.Med., Ind.Med.

610 YU ISSN 0049-0210
SRPSKI ARHIV ZA CELOKUPNO LEKARSTVO/SERBIAN ARCHIVES OF ENTIRE MEDICINE. (Text in Serbo-Croatian, written in Cyrillic alphabet; title and some summaries in English, French, German) 1872. m. 2000 din. Srpsko Lekarsko Drustvo, Dzordza Vasingtona 19, Belgrade, Yugoslavia. Ed. Vladimir Slavkovic. illus. **Indexed:** Biol.Abstr., Dent.Ind., Excerp.Med., Ind.Med., Nutr.Abstr.

614 IT ISSN 0038-9323
STAMPA MEDICA. 1959. s-m. (21/yr.). L.20000. E S I Stampa Medica s.r.l., Casella Postale 42, Lgo. Volontari del Sangue 10, 20097 S. Donato Milan, Italy. TEL 02-5274241. FAX 02-5274775. TELEX 324894. Ed. Bruno P. Pieroni. adv.; bk.rev.; circ. 150,000.

STATE HEALTH NOTES. see *PUBLIC HEALTH AND SAFETY*

STEROIDS: STRUCTURE, FUNCTION AND REGULATION. see *BIOLOGY — Biological Chemistry*

STRITCH M.D.. see *COLLEGE AND ALUMNI*

610 DK ISSN 0039-2634
STUD. MED.. 1936. 4/yr. DKK 100. Danish Medical Students Association, Blegdamsvej 3, 2200 Copenhagen N, Denmark. Ed.Bd. bk.rev.; illus.; pat.; circ. 5,000 (controlled).

610 IT ISSN 0371-3172
CODEN: SSSEAK
STUDI SASSARESI. (Text in Italian; summaries in English) 1932. q. L.40000. Societa Sassarese di Scienze Mediche e Naturali, Vale Mancini 1, Piazza Universita, 07100 Sassari, Italy. (Subscr. to: Institute of Human Physiology, Via Muroni 23A, 07100 Sassari, Italy) Ed. Pierangelo Catalano. adv.; index; circ. 1,000. (back issues avail.) **Indexed:** Biol.Abstr., Excerp.Med., Food Sci.& Tech.Abstr.

STUDIA I MATERIALY Z DZIEJOW NAUKI POLSKIEJ. SERIA B. HISTORIA NAUK BIOLOGICZNYCH I MEDYCZNYCH. see *BIOLOGY*

610 PL ISSN 0860-9594
STUDIA SOCIETATIS SCIENTIARUM TORUNENSIS. SECTIO H. MEDICINA. 1989. irreg. price varies. Towarzystwo Naukowe w Toruniu, Ul. Wysoka 16, 87-100 Torun, Poland. TEL 48-56-23941. TELEX 552388 FSBH PL. Ed. Lech Bieganowski. circ. 220.
—BLDSC shelfmark: 8482.100000.

610 GW ISSN 0081-7333
CODEN: SMNJA2
STUDIEN ZUR MEDIZINGESCHICHTE DES NEUNZEHNTEN JAHRUNDERTS. 1963. irreg., vol.9, 1979. Vandenhoeck und Ruprecht, Robert-Bosch-Breite 6, Postfach 37 53, 3400 Goettingen, Germany. TEL 0551-6959-0. FAX 0551-695917.
Description: Studies medical history of the nineteenth century.

610 US
STUDIES IN AFRICAN HEALTH & MEDICINE. irreg., latest no.6. $39.95 per no. Edwin Mellen Press, 240 Portage Rd., Box 450, Lewiston, NY 14092. TEL 716-754-8566. FAX 716-754-4335.

610.09 NE ISSN 0925-1421
STUDIES IN ANCIENT MEDICINE. 1990. irreg., vol.4, 1992. price varies. E.J. Brill, P.O. Box 9000, 2300 PA Leiden, Netherlands. TEL 071-312624. FAX 071-317532. TELEX 39296 BRILL NL. (In N. America: E.J. Brill, 24 Hudson St., Kinderhook, NY 12106. TEL 800-962-4406) Ed. John Scarborough.
Description: Scholarly monographs on historical figures and topics in ancient medicine.

610 II ISSN 0970-5562
STUDIES IN HISTORY OF MEDICINE AND SCIENCE. (Text in English) 1977. q. Rs.100($25) Jamia Hamdard, Department of History of Medicine and Science - Hamdard University, Hamdard Nagar, New Delhi 110 062, India. Ed. Hakim Abdul Hameed. bk.rev.; circ. 600.
Formerly (until 1984): Studies in History of Medicine (ISSN 0379-3915)

610 US
STUDIES IN MEDICAL ETHICS. irreg. Peter Lang Publishing, Inc., 62 W. 45th St., 4th Fl., New York, NY 10036. TEL 212-302-6740. FAX 212-302-7574. Ed. Frank H. Marsh.

610 614 UK ISSN 0473-8837
STUDIES ON CURRENT HEALTH PROBLEMS. 1962. irreg. price varies. (Association of the British Pharmaceutical Industry) Office of Health Economics, 12 Whitehall, London SW1A 2DY, England. FAX 071-976-1962. Ed.Bd. charts; circ. 15,000.
—BLDSC shelfmark: 8490.320000.

STURZA'S MEDICAL INVESTMENT LETTER. see *BUSINESS AND ECONOMICS — Investments*

610 SJ ISSN 0491-4481
SUDAN MEDICAL JOURNAL. (Text in English) vol.12, 1974. q. $10. (Sudan Medical Association) Khartoum University Press, P.O. Box 321, Khartoum, Sudan. Ed. D.M.Y. Sukkar. adv.; charts; illus.; index; circ. 2,000. **Indexed:** C.I.S. Abstr.

610 II
SUDHANIDHI. (Text in Hindi) 1973. m. Rs.35. Dhanvantari Karyalaya, Aligarha, India. Ed. Sri Raghivir Prasad Trivedi. adv.; bk.rev.; circ. 12,000.

610 500 GW ISSN 0039-4564
CODEN: SZWBAC
SUDHOFFS ARCHIV; Zeitschrift fuer Wissenschaftsgeschichte. (Text in English, French, and German) 1908. s-a. DM.120 (supplements individually priced). Franz Steiner Verlag Wiesbaden GmbH, Birkenwaldstr. 44, Postfach 101526, 7000 Stuttgart 1, Germany. TEL 0711-2582-0. FAX 0711-2582290. TELEX 723636-DAZD. Ed.Bd. adv.; bk.rev.; bibl.; illus.; index; circ. 500. (back issues avail.) **Indexed:** Chem.Abstr., Excerp.Med., Hist.Abstr., Ind.Med., Math.R.
—BLDSC shelfmark: 8509.150000.
Formerly: Sudhoffs Archiv fuer Geschichte der Medizin und der Naturwissenschaften.

610 500 GW ISSN 0341-0773
SUDHOFFS ARCHIV. BEIHEFTE. irreg., vol.30, 1992. price varies. Franz Steiner Verlag Wiesbaden GmbH, Birkenwaldstr. 44, Postfach 101526, 7000 Stuttgart 1, Germany. TEL 0711-2582-0. FAX 0711-2582290. TELEX 723636-DAZD. Ed.Bd. **Indexed:** GeoRef., Ind.Med.

610 FI ISSN 0039-5560
SUOMEN LAAKARILEHTI/FINLANDS LAEKARTIDNING/FINNISH MEDICAL JOURNAL. 1946. 33/yr. Fmk.675 (outside Scandinavia Fmk.830). Suomen Laakariliitto - Finnish Medical Association, Makelankatu 2, 00500 Helsinki, Finland. TEL 90-393-091. Ed. Taito Pekkarinen. adv.; bk.rev.; bibl.; illus.; index; circ. 21,000 (controlled). **Indexed:** Biol.Abstr., Ind.Med.
—BLDSC shelfmark: 8543.700000.
Description: Covers general medical topics relating to diagnostics, treatment and rehabilitation, pharmaceutical advances, research results and more. The emphasis is on practical applications for physicians.
Refereed Serial

MEDICAL SCIENCES 3155

610 US
SURGICAL PRODUCTS. 1980. 9/yr. $12. Gordon Publications, Inc., 301 Gibraltar Dr., Box 50, Morris Plains, NJ 07950. TEL 201-292-5100. FAX 201-539-3476. adv.; circ. 76,000. (tabloid format)

610 CC ISSN 1000-5749
SUZHOU YIXUEYUAN XUEBAO/SUZHOU INSTITUTE OF MEDICAL SCIENCES. JOURNAL. (Text in Chinese) q. Suzhou Yixueyuan - Suzhou Institute of Medical Sciences, 48 Renmin Lu, Suzhou, Jiangsu 215007, People's Republic of China. TEL 225696. Ed. Du Ziwei.

610 SW ISSN 0284-5342
SVENSK MEDICIN. 1988. irreg. (approx. 8/yr.). SEK 600. Sjukvaardens och Socialvaardens Planerings och Rationaliseringsinstitut (SPRI), Box 70487, S-107 26 Stockholm, Sweden. TEL 08-7024600. FAX 08-7024799. (Co-sponsor: Svenska Laekaresaellskapet)

610 CI ISSN 0033-8575
SVEUCILISTE U ZAGREBU. MEDICINSKI FAKULTET. RADOVI/ACTA FACULTATIS MEDICAE ZAGRABIENSIS. (Text in Croatian; summaries in English) 1953-1976 (vol.24); resumed 1984 (vol.25). 4/yr. 1000 din.($28) Sveuciliste u Zagrebu, Medicinski Fakultet, Salata 3b, 41000 Zagreb, Croatia. Ed. V. Mandic. adv.; bk.rev.; charts; illus.; index. **Indexed:** Biol.Abstr., Chem.Abstr., Excerp.Med., Ind.Med.

610 SW ISSN 0346-6000
SWEDEN. SOCIALSTYRELSEN. FOERFATTNINGSSAMLING: MEDICAL. irreg. (approx. 30/yr.). SEK 350. Socialstyrelsen - National Board of Health and Welfare, 106 30 Stockholm, Sweden. FAX 48-783-36-54. TELEX 16773 NBHWS. Ed. Anne-Marie Svedin. index; circ. 8,000. (looseleaf format)
Supersedes in part (1883-1976): Sweden. Medicinalvaesendet. Foerfattningssamling (ISSN 0346-5837)

610 SW ISSN 0345-0171
SWEDEN. SOCIALSTYRELSEN. LEGITIMERADE LAEKARE/SWEDEN. NATIONAL BOARD OF HEALTH AND WELFARE. AUTHORIZED PHYSICIANS. a. Allmaenna Foerlaget, 106 47 Stockholm, Sweden. TEL 08-739-9630. FAX 08-739-9548. index; circ. 10,000.

SWITZERLAND. BUNDESAMT FUER SOZIALVERSICHERUNG. SPEZIALITAETENLISTE - LISTE DES SPECIALITES - ELENCO DELLE SPECIALITA. see *PHARMACY AND PHARMACOLOGY*

610 NE
SYMPOSIA FOUNDATION MERIEUX. Running title: Transplantation and Clinical Immunology. 1979. irreg., no.17, 1991. price varies. Elsevier Science Publishers B.V., Books Division, P.O. Box 211, 1000 AE Amsterdam, Netherlands. TEL 020-5803911. FAX 020-5803705. TELEX 18582 ESPA NL. (Subscr. in U.S. and Canada to: Elsevier Science Publishing Co., Inc., Box 882, Madison Sq. Sta., New York, NY 10159. TEL 212-989-5800) (back issues avail.)
Refereed Serial

610 BE
SYNDIKALE KAMER. 1963. s-a. membership. Sindikale Kamer der Geneesheren der Provincies Oost & West Vlaanderen, 2 Henri Beyaertstraet, B-8500 Kortrijk, Belgium. Ed. L. van Steenberge. bk.rev.; circ. 5,100.

610 PL ISSN 0082-125X
CODEN: SZTNBY
SZCZECINSKIE TOWARZYSTWO NAUKOWE. WYDZIAL NAUK LEKARSKICH. PRACE. (Text in Polish; summaries in English, Polish and Russian) 1959. irreg. price varies. Panstwowy Zaklad Wydawnictw Lekarskich, Dluga 38-40, Warsaw, Poland. TEL 31-42-81. (Dist. by: Ars Polona-Ruch, Krakowskie Przedmiescie 7, 00-068 Warsaw, Poland)

610 IT
T C. (Terapia del Comportamento) 1984. q. L.50000. Bulzoni Editore, Via dei Liburni n.14, 00185 Rome, Italy. TEL 06-4455207. FAX 06-4450355. Ed. Paolo Meazzini.

MEDICAL SCIENCES

610   US   ISSN 0885-9191
T M J UPDATE: A CURRENT REVIEW OF TEMPOROMANDIBULAR JOINT DEVELOPMENTS. 1983. bi-m. $59 to individuals (foreign $74); institutions $69 (foreign $84). Anadem Publishing, Inc., 3620 N. High St., Columbus, OH 43214. TEL 614-262-2539. index. (looseleaf format)
Description: Summarizes medical and dental journal articles about TMJ disorders and carniofacial pain.

610   AT
T S TODAY. 1982. q. Aus.$20 (membership). Australasian Tuberous Sclerosis Society Inc., 22 Mason St., Thirroul, N.S.W. 2515, Australia. TEL 042-673992. Eds. Lynn McKinnon, Beth Wilson. circ. 350. (back issues avail.)
Formerly: Lynn's Letter.
Description: Covers tuberous sclerosis and related subjects.

610   UA
TABIBAK AL-KHASS. 1969. m. £60. Dar Al-Hilal, 16 Sharia Muhammad Ezz el-Arab, Cairo, Egypt. TEL 02-27954. TELEX 92703. Ed. Abdel Rahman Nour El Dine. adv.; bk.rev.; circ. 133,000.

610   LE
TABIBOK/YOUR DOCTOR. (Text in Arabic) 1956. m. £L4800($55) Scientific Publications Ltd., P.O. Box 90434, Beirut, Lebanon. TEL 963-11-711316. TELEX 411513 MEDEQ SY. Ed. Sami Kabbani. adv.; bk.rev.; circ. 85,221. (back issues avail.)
Description: Provides up-to-date medical and health information and advice for a general audience.

610   IR
TABRIZ UNIVERSITY OF MEDICAL SCIENCES. MEDICAL JOURNAL. (Text in English, Farsi, French) 1960. q. Rs.200. Tabriz University of Medical Sciences, Faculty of Medicine, Tabriz, Iran. TEL 041-30081. FAX 041-34013. TELEX 412045. Ed. Dr. M. Chakoshian. adv.; abstr.; bibl.; charts; illus.; stat.; circ. 1,000. (looseleaf format)
Former titles: University of Azarabadegan. Faculty of Medicine. Journal - Daneshkaden Pezeshki Azarabadegan. Majallah; Daneshkaden Pezeshki Tabriz. Majalleh.

610   GW   ISSN 0494-464X
TAEGLICHE PRAXIS; Zeitschrift fuer Praktisch Taetigen Arzt. 4/yr. DM.215. Hans Marseille Verlag, Buerkleinstr. 12, 8000 Munich 22, Germany. TEL 089-227988.
—BLDSC shelfmark: 8598.402500.

610 100   US
TAKING SIDES: CLASHING VIEWS ON CONTROVERSIAL BIOETHICAL ISSUES. irreg., 4th ed., 1991. $11.95. Dushkin Publishing Group, Inc., Sluice Dock, Guilford, CT 06437-9989. TEL 203-453-4351. FAX 203-453-6000. Ed. Carol Levine. illus.

610   US   ISSN 1040-1334
TEACHING AND LEARNING IN MEDICINE; an international journal. 1989. q. $37 to individuals (foreign $52.50); institutions $125 (foreign $140). Lawrence Erlbaum Associates, Inc., 365 Broadway, Hillsdale, NJ 07642. TEL 201-666-4110. FAX 201-666-2394. Ed. Terrill A. Mast.
—BLDSC shelfmark: 8614.004000.
Description: Addresses practical issues in the conduct of medical education, providing the analysis and empirical research needed to facilitate decision-making about the education of medical professionals.
Refereed Serial

610   US
▼**TEAM REHAB REPORT.** 1990. bi-m. $24 (free to qualified personnel). Miramar Publishing Co., Box 3640, Culver City, CA 90231-3640. TEL 213-337-9717. FAX 213-337-1041. Ed. Andria Segedy. adv.; bk.rev.; tr.lit.; circ. 12,000 (controlled). (reprint service avail.)
Description: Covers rehabilitation in the areas of orthopedics, chiropractics, pediatrics, sports medicine, and hearing and sight impairment.

362   JA   ISSN 0040-0734
TEASHI NO FUJIYUUNA KODOMOTACHI/CRIPPLED CHILDREN. (Text in Japanese) 1958. m. 720 Yen. Japanese Society for Disabled Children - Nihon Shitai Fujiyuuji Kyokai, 1-7, 1-chome, Komone, Itabashi-ku, Tokyo 173, Japan. circ. 6,000.
Description: Focuses on rehabilitation practices.

610   IR
TEBB-O DARU. q? Inqilab Ave., P.O. Box 3033, Teheran, Iran. Ed. Dr. S.A. Zadeh.

610   US
TECH SAMPLE. (Subject areas offered include: Chemistry, Immunology, Hematology, Immunohematology, Microbiology, Education and Management, Histotechnology, Cytotechnology and Generalist) 1979. bi-w. $450 for complete series; price varies for individual subject. American Society of Clinical Pathologists, 2100 W. Harrison St., Chicago, IL 60612. TEL 312-738-4890. FAX 312-738-1619. Ed. Dr. Deanna Klosinski. circ. 3,800.
Description: Each series consists of exercises which present patient or laboratory-related problems for workup.

610   NE   ISSN 0169-622X
TECHNIEK IN DE GEZONDHEIDSZORG; beheer en toepassing. 1985. m. fl.73($60) Noordervliet B.V., Mississippidreef 85, 3565 CE Utrecht, Netherlands. Ed. M.A. Romijn. index; circ. 3,500. (back issues avail.)

610   US   ISSN 0892-7332
TECHNOLOGY FOR LABORATORY MEDICINE. 1987. m. $90 (Canada $100; elsewhere $120). (Emergency Care Research Institute) E C R I, 5200 Butler Pike, Plymouth Meeting, PA 19462. TEL 215-825-6000. FAX 215-834-1275. Ed. Robert Hockchild.
Refereed Serial

610   US   ISSN 8756-8608
TECHNOLOGY FOR MATERIALS MANAGEMENT. 1980. m. $90 (Canada $100; elsewhere $120). (Emergency Care Research Institute) E C R I, 5200 Butler Pike, Plymouth Meeting, PA 19462. TEL 215-825-6000. FAX 215-834-1275. Ed. Robert Hochschild. bk.rev.
Formerly: Health Devices Update: Materials Management.
Refereed Serial

610 615.9   UK
TECHNOMARK REGISTER. CONTRACT RESEARCH ORGANISATIONS. 1988. irreg. £160($275) Technomark Consulting Services Ltd., King House, 5-11 Westbourne Grove, London W2 4UA, England. TEL 071-229-9239. FAX 071-229-3549. Ed. R.G. Hughes. circ. 250. (looseleaf format)
Description: Listing of Contract Research Organizations in UK.

610   IT   ISSN 0492-6749
HC391
TEMPO MEDICO. 1959. w. L.45000. Editiemme s.r.l., Via Lanino 5, 20144 Milan, Italy. TEL 024227946. FAX 024120287. Ed. Roberto Satolli. adv.; bk.rev.; circ. 80,000.

610   US   ISSN 0040-3318
TENNESSEE MEDICAL ASSOCIATION. JOURNAL. 1902. m. $20. Tennessee Medical Association, Box 120909, 2301 21st Ave. S., Nashville, TN 37212-0909. TEL 615-385-2100. FAX 615-383-5918. Ed. Dr. John B. Thomison. adv.; bk.rev.; abstr.; bibl.; illus.; index; circ. 6,700. **Indexed:** Dent.Ind., Excerp.Med., Ind.Med., INIS Atomind.
—BLDSC shelfmark: 4907.200000.
Formerly: Tennessee State Medical Association Journal.

TENNESSEE MEDICO-LEGAL REPORTER. see *LAW*

610   RU   ISSN 0040-3660
                           CODEN: TEARAI
TERAPEVTICHESKII ARKHIV/THERAPEUTIC ARCHIVES. (Text in Russian; summaries in English) 1923. m. 37.80 Rub.($27.60) (Vsesoyuznoe Nauchnoe Obshchestvo Terapevtov) Izdatel'stvo Meditsina, Petroverigskii pereulok 6-8, 101838 Moscow, Russia. (Co-sponsor: Ministerstvo Zdravookhraneniya S.S.S.R.) Ed. E.I. Chazov. bk.rev. **Indexed:** ASCA, Biol.Abstr., Biotech.Abstr., Chem.Abstr., Dent.Ind., Excerp.Med., Helminthol.Abstr., Ind.Med., Nutr.Abstr., Protozool.Abstr.
—BLDSC shelfmark: 0180.000000.
Description: Presents clinical and clinico-experimental studies, as well as reviews and articles on all pressing problems concerning the diseases of the internal organs.

TERAPIA FAMILIARE. see *PSYCHOLOGY*

610   IT   ISSN 0040-3695
                           CODEN: TPMDAB
TERAPIA MODERNA. English edition: Modern Treatment. (Text in Italian; summaries in English) 1965. bi-m. L.130000($160) to individuals; institutions L.150000. Pensiero Scientifico Editore s.r.l., Via Panama 48, 00198 Rome, Italy. TEL 06 855-36-33. Ed. Vincenzo Lo Cascio. adv.; bibl.; illus.; index, cum.index: 1965-1968; circ. 2,000.

610   IT
TERAPIA OGGI. 1982. m. L.26000. Massimo Picasso, Ed. & Pub., Via Sabotino 19-2, 20135 Milan, Italy. adv.; circ. 70,000.

570   US   ISSN 0270-3211
                           CODEN: TCMUD8
TERATOGENESIS, CARCINOGENESIS, AND MUTAGENESIS. 1980. bi-m. $216 (foreign $369). John Wiley & Sons, Inc., Journals, 605 Third Ave., New York, NY 10158. TEL 212-850-6000. FAX 212-850-6088. TELEX 12-7063. Ed. Philippe Shubick. **Indexed:** ASCA, Biol.Abstr., Biotech.Abstr., C.I.S. Abstr., Chem.Abstr., Curr.Adv.Ecol.Sci., Curr.Cont., Dent.Ind., Dok.Arbeitsmed., Excerp.Med., Ind.Med., Lab.Haz.Bull., Risk Abstr.
●Also available online.
—BLDSC shelfmark: 8792.130000.
Description: Contains reports of original research and methods concerned with the detection, classification, and evaluation of risks associated with exposure to environmentally induced agents; serves as a forum for comments on controversial issues in biological risk assessment.
Refereed Serial

TERATOLOGY; the international journal of abnormal development. see *BIOLOGY*

610   US
TEXAS D O. 1945. m. $5. Texas Osteopathic Medical Association, 226 Bailey, Fort Worth, TX 76107. TEL 817-336-0549. Ed. Tex Roberts. adv.; circ. 2,650.
Formerly: Association: Journal of Texas Osteopathic Medical Association.

TEXAS HEALTH LAW REPORTER. see *LAW*

610   US   ISSN 0040-4470
R11   CODEN: TXMDAX
TEXAS MEDICINE. 1905. m. $40 to non-members; members $20. Texas Medical Association, 401 W. 1st St., Austin, TX 78701. TEL 512-370-1300. Ed. Kathryn Trombatore. adv.; charts; illus.; index; circ. 31,000. (also avail. in microform from UMI) **Indexed:** ASCA, Biol.Abstr., C.I.S. Abstr., CINAHL, Curr.Adv.Cancer Res., Curr.Cont., Dent.Ind., Dok.Arbeitsmed., Excerp.Med., Helminthol.Abstr., Ind.Med., Med.Care Rev., Nutr.Abstr., Rehabil.Lit.
—BLDSC shelfmark: 8799.550000.
Formerly: Texas State Journal of Medicine.

610 100   NE   ISSN 0167-9902
R723   CODEN: THMEDT
THEORETICAL MEDICINE; an international journal for the philosophy and methodology of medical research and practice. (Text in English) 1980. q. fl.266($151) Kluwer Academic Publishers, Postbus 17, 3300 AA Dordrecht, Netherlands. TEL 078-334911. FAX 078-334254. TELEX 29245. (Dist. by: Kluwer Academic Publishers Group, P.O. Box 322, 3300 AH Dordrecht, Netherlands; N. America dist. addr.: Box 358, Accord Station, Hingham, MA 02018-0358. TEL 617-871-6600) Ed. David Thomasma. adv.; bk.rev.; index. (reprint service avail. from SWZ) **Indexed:** Phil.Ind.
—BLDSC shelfmark: 8814.561500.
Former titles: Metamedicine (ISSN 0166-2031); Metamed (ISSN 0342-6866)

610   GW   ISSN 0935-3194
THERAPEUTIKON; Zeitschrift fuer die gesamte Medizin. m. DM.95. Verlag G. Braun, Karl-Friedrich-Str. 14-18, Postfach 1709, 7500 Karlsruhe 1, Germany. TEL 0721-165-0. FAX 0721-165-227.
—BLDSC shelfmark: 8814.679000.

MEDICAL SCIENCES 3157

610   FR   ISSN 0396-7107
THERAPEUTIQUES NATURELLES; revue francaise de vulgarisation. 1975. bi-m. 120 F. Groupement National pour l'Organisation de la Medecine Auxiliaire, 3 bis, rue Bleue, 75009 Paris, France. FAX 62-27-22-63. Dir. J.M. Girardin. adv.; bk.rev. (audio cassette)
   Formerly: Groupement National pour l'Organisation de la Medecine Auxiliaire. Bulletin de Liaison (ISSN 0396-7115)

610   HU   ISSN 0040-5949
THERAPIA HUNGARICA. English edition: Hungarian Medical Journal (ISSN 0133-3909) 1953. 4/yr. free. Medicina Kiado, Beloiannisz u. 8, 1054 Budapest, Hungary. Ed.Bd. adv.; bk.rev.; abstr.; bibl.; charts; illus.; circ. 20,000. **Indexed:** Biol.Abstr., Biotech.Abstr., Chem.Abstr., Excerp.Med., Ind.Med.

610   FR   ISSN 0040-5957
    CODEN: THERAP
THERAPIE. (Text in French; summaries in English, French) 1866. 6/yr. 910 F. (foreign 1020 F.). (Societe Francaise de Therapeutique et de Pharmacodynamie) Doin Editeurs, 8 Place de l'Odeon, 75006 Paris, France. adv.; bk.rev.; bibl.; charts; illus. **Indexed:** ASCA, Biol.Abstr., Biotech.Abstr., Chem.Abstr., Curr.Adv.Ecol.Sci., Curr.Cont., Dairy Sci.Abstr., Dent.Ind., Excerp.Med., Helminthol.Abstr., Ind.Med., Protozool.Abstr.
—BLDSC shelfmark: 8814.750000.

610   GW   ISSN 0040-5965
    CODEN: THGEAU
THERAPIE DER GEGENWART; Zeitschrift fuer praktische Medizin. 1860. m. DM.134 (foreign DM.175). Urban und Vogel, Lindwurmstr. 95, Postfach 152209, 8000 Munich 15, Germany. TEL 089-53292-0. FAX 089-53292-100. circ. 48,500. (also avail. in microfiche from BHP) **Indexed:** Biol.Abstr., Biotech.Abstr., Chem.Abstr., Excerp.Med., Ind.Med., Nutr.Abstr.
—BLDSC shelfmark: 8814.755000.

610   GW   ISSN 0040-5973
    CODEN: THEWA6
THERAPIEWOCHE. (Text in English) 1950. w. DM.129. Verlag G. Braun GmbH, Karl-Friedrich-Str. 14, Postfach 1709, 7500 Karlsruhe 1, Germany. TEL 0721-165-0. FAX 0721-165-227. TELEX 7826-904-VGB-D. Ed. R.G. Sommer. adv.; bk.rev.; film rev.; abstr.; charts; illus.; index; circ. 40,000. **Indexed:** Biol.Abstr., Biotech.Abstr., Chem.Abstr., Excerp.Med., Ind.Med.
—BLDSC shelfmark: 8814.760000.

610   GW   ISSN 0934-8395
THERMO MED. 1985. q. DM.96. (Deutsche Gesellschaft fuer Thermographie e.V.) Hippokrates Verlag, Ruedigerstr. 14, Postfach 102263, 7000 Stuttgart 10, Germany. TEL 0711-8931-0. FAX 0711-8931-298. TELEX 7252275-GTV-D. Eds. R. Berz, J. Engel.

610 658   US
THETA MARKET REPORTS. 1970. irreg. price varies. Theta Corporation, c/o Phyllis Klaben, Theta Building, Middlefield, CT 06455.
TEL 203-349-1054. FAX 203-349-1227. Ed.Bd.
   Description: Provides comprehensive coverage of new market research in healthcare.

610   UK   ISSN 0040-6376
    CODEN: THORA7
THORAX. 1946. m. £146. B M J Publishing Group, B.M.A. House, Tavistock Sq., London WC1H 9JR, England. TEL 071-387-4499. Ed. S. Spiro. adv.; bk.rev.; charts; illus.; index. (also avail. in microform from UMI; reprint service avail. from UMI) **Indexed:** Abstr.Hyg., ASCA, Biol.Abstr., C.I.S. Abstr., Chem.Abstr., Curr.Adv.Cancer Res., Curr.Adv.Ecol.Sci., Curr.Cont., Dent.Ind., Dok.Arbeitsmed., Excerp.Med., Helminthol.Abstr., Ind.Med., Ind.Vet., Lab.Haz.Bull., Rev.Plant Path., Trop.Dis.Bull.
●Also available online. Vendor(s): BRS.
—BLDSC shelfmark: 8820.250000.

THYROID HORMONES. see MEDICAL SCIENCES — Endocrinology

610   II   ISSN 0970-1257
TIBETAN MEDICINE. 1980. irreg. $3 per no. Library of Tibetan Works and Archives, Dharamshala 176 215, India. TELEX TF 2467. (back issues avail.)
   Description: Provides an international forum for the study of Tibetan medicine.

TIDSKRIFT FOER YNGRE LAEKARE. see BUSINESS AND ECONOMICS — Labor And Industrial Relations

610   SP   ISSN 0210-9999
TIEMPOS MEDICOS. 1973. fortn. 8500 ptas. Editores Medicos, S.A., Paseo de la Castellana, 53, 28046 Madrid, Spain. TEL 442-86-56. FAX 422-80-43. Dir. M. Serrano Rios. adv.; illus.; index, cum.index; circ. 35,000. (back issues avail.)

610   BE   ISSN 0005-8440
TIJDSCHRIFT VOOR GENEESKUNDE. Variant title: Belgisch Tijdschrift voor Geneeskunde. (Text in Dutch) 1945. s-m. 1200 Fr. Tijdschrift voor Geneeskunde A.S.B.L., De Pintelaan 185, B-9000 Ghent, Belgium. TEL 091-40-33-30. FAX 091-40-33-90. Ed. I. Leusen-Laurweyns. adv.; bk.rev.; abstr.; illus.; index; circ. 9,000. **Indexed:** Biotech.Abstr., Chem.Abstr., Excerp.Med., Ind.Med.

610   NE   ISSN 0920-0517
TIJDSCHRIFT VOOR SOCIALE GEZONDHEIDSZORG. (Text mainly in Dutch; occasionally in English, French and German; summaries in English) 1923. fortn. fl.148 to non-members. (Vereniging voor Volksgezondheid en Wetenschap) Begeerscie. TSG, P.A. N I P G - T N O, Postbus 124, 2300 AC Leiden, Netherlands. TEL 071-181817. FAX 071-176382. Ed. Dr. Ir. G.A. Zielhuis. adv.; bk.rev.; abstr.; bibl.; charts; circ. 3,800. **Indexed:** Chem.Abstr., Ergon.Abstr., Excerp.Med., HRIS, World Bibl.Soc.Sec.
   Formerly: Tijdschrift voor Sociale Geneeskunde (ISSN 0040-7607)

610 574   DK   ISSN 0001-2815
QR180   CODEN: TSANA2
TISSUE ANTIGENS. (Text in English) 1971. 10/yr. DKK 1635. Munksgaard International Publishers Ltd., 35 Noerre Soegade, P.O. Box 2148, DK-1016 Copenhagen K, Denmark. TEL 33-127030. FAX 33-129387. TELEX 19431-MUNKS-DK. Ed. Bo Dupont. adv.; bk.rev.; circ. 900. (also avail. in microform from SWZ; reprint service avail. from SWZ) **Indexed:** Abstr.Hyg., Anim.Breed.Abstr., ASCA, Biol.Abstr., Chem.Abstr., Curr.Adv.Cancer Res., Curr.Adv.Ecol.Sci., Curr.Cont., Excerp.Med., Helminthol.Abstr., Ind.Med., Ind.Vet., Protozool.Abstr., So.Pac.Per.Ind., Trop.Dis.Bull., Vet.Bull.
—BLDSC shelfmark: 8858.690000.

610   US
TODAY IN MEDICINE. 10/yr. Data Centrum Communications, Inc., 110 Greene St., New York, NY 10012. TEL 212-226-5252. Ed. Heidi Greene.

610   JA   ISSN 0040-8670
    CODEN: TOIZAG
TOHO UNIVERSITY MEDICAL SOCIETY. JOURNAL/TOHO IGAKKAI ZASSHI. (Text in English, Japanese, and European Languages) 1954. bi-m. 6000 Yen. Toho University Medical Society - Toho Daigaku Igakkai, c/o Library, School of Medicine, 5-21-16 Omori Nishi, Ota-ku, Tokyo 143, Japan. FAX 764-1642. Ed. Setsuo Takeuchi. adv.; bk.rev.; illus.; stat.; circ. 1,200. (processed) **Indexed:** Biol.Abstr., Chem.Abstr., Excerp.Med.
●Also available online.
—BLDSC shelfmark: 4824.300000.

610   JA   ISSN 0040-8700
    CODEN: THIZAZ
TOHOKU MEDICAL JOURNAL/TOHOKU IGAKU ZASSHI. (Text in Japanese; summaries in English and Japanese) 1916. s-a. 3000 Yen. Tohoku Medical Society - Tohoku Igakkai, 2-1 Seiryo-machi, Sendai 980, Japan. Ed.Bd. adv.; bibl.; charts; illus.; mkt.; index, cum.index; circ. 1,200. **Indexed:** Biol.Abstr., Chem.Abstr., Curr.Cont., Excerp.Med., Ind.Med.

610   JA   ISSN 0371-2761
    CODEN: SRTCAC
TOHOKU UNIVERSITY. SCIENCE REPORTS OF THE RESEARCH INSTITUTES. SERIES C: MEDICINE/TOHOKU DAIGAKU KENKYUJO HOKOKU, C-SHU, IGAKU. 1949. 4/yr. exchange basis. Tohoku Daigaku, Kenkyujo Rengokai - Tohoku University, Association of the Research Institutes, 4-1 Seiryo-machi, Aoba-ku, Sendai-shi, Miyagi-ken 980, Japan. FAX 022-264-7984. **Indexed:** Biol.Abstr., Chem.Abstr., Excerp.Med., Ind.Med.
—BLDSC shelfmark: 8156.555000.

610   JA   ISSN 0385-0005
    CODEN: TJEMDR
TOKAI JOURNAL OF EXPERIMENTAL AND CLINICAL MEDICINE. (Text and summaries in English) 1976. bi-m. 3000 Yen($15) (Tokai Daigaku, Igakubu - Tokai University, School of Medicine) Tokai Daigaku Shuppansha - Tokai University Press (Kanagawa), Boseidai, Isehara, Kanagawa 259-11, Japan. Ed. Tadao Mitsui. circ. 1,700. (back issues avail.) **Indexed:** Dairy Sci.Abstr.
—BLDSC shelfmark: 8862.705000.

610   JA   ISSN 0040-9022
    CODEN: TJIZAF
TOKYO JOSHI IKA DAIGAKU ZASSHI/TOKYO WOMEN'S MEDICAL COLLEGE. JOURNAL. (Text in Japanese; summaries in English) 1931. m. 6000 Yen($50) Tokyo Joshi Ika Daigaku Gakkai - Society of Tokyo Women's Medical College, c/o the Library, 8-1 Kawada-cho, Shinjuku-ku, Tokyo 162, Japan. TELEX 2322317-TWMLIB-J. Ed. Morimasa Yoshioka. adv.; index; circ. 1,750. **Indexed:** C.I.S. Abstr., Chem.Abstr., Excerp.Med.
—BLDSC shelfmark: 4909.050000.

610   JA   ISSN 0040-8921
    CODEN: BTMDAB
TOKYO MEDICAL AND DENTAL UNIVERSITY. BULLETIN/TOKYO IKA SHIKA DAIGAKU KIYO. (Text in European languages) 1954. q. exchange basis. Tokyo Medical and Dental University - Tokyo Ika Shika Daigaku, 1-5-45 Yushima, Bunkyo-ku, Tokyo 113, Japan. Ed. Sunao Nomoto. adv.; charts; illus.; circ. 1,000. **Indexed:** Abstr.Hyg., Biol.Abstr., Chem.Abstr., Curr.Adv.Ecol.Sci., Dent.Ind., Excerp.Med., Ind.Med., INIS Atomind., NRN, Nutr.Abstr., Trop.Dis.Bull.
—BLDSC shelfmark: 2781.000000.

610.28   JA   ISSN 0082-4739
    CODEN: IKKHBS
TOKYO MEDICAL AND DENTAL UNIVERSITY. INSTITUTE FOR MEDICAL AND DENTAL ENGINEERING. REPORTS/IYO KIZAI KENKYUJO HOKOKU. (Text in Japanese; table of contents and summaries in English) 1967. a. free. Tokyo Medical and Dental University, Institute for Medical and Dental Engineering - Tokyo Ika Shika Daigaku Iyo Kizai Kenkyujo, 3-10 Surugadai 2-chome, Kanda, Chiyoda-ku, Tokyo, Japan. TEL 03-3291-3721. FAX 03-3291-3727. Ed. Yoji Imai. **Indexed:** Dent.Ind.
—BLDSC shelfmark: 7520.950000.

610   JA   ISSN 0040-8905
    CODEN: TIDZAH
TOKYO MEDICAL COLLEGE. JOURNAL/TOKYO IKA DAIGAKU ZASSHI. (Text in English and Japanese; summaries in English) 1938. bi-m. 3000 Yen. Medical Society of Tokyo Medical College - Tokyo Ikadaigaku Igakukai, 1-1, Shinjuku 6-chome, Shinjuku-ku, Tokyo 160, Japan. Ed. Yuichi Otaka. adv.; index; circ. 1,400. **Indexed:** Biol.Abstr., C.I.S. Abstr., Chem.Abstr., Excerp.Med., Ind.Med.
—BLDSC shelfmark: 4908.950000.

610   JA   ISSN 0082-4771
    CODEN: TRENAF
TOKYO-TORITSU EISEI KENKYUJO KENKYU NENPO/TOKYO METROPOLITAN RESEARCH LABORATORY OF PUBLIC HEALTH. ANNUAL REPORT. (Text in Japanese; summaries occasionally in English) 1949. a. exchange basis. Tokyo-toritsu Eisei Kenkyujo - Tokyo Metropolitan Research Laboratory of Public Health, 24-1 Hyakunin-cho 3-chome, Shinjuku-ku, Tokyo 160, Japan. circ. 600. **Indexed:** Biodet.Abstr., Dairy Sci.Abstr., Food Sci.& Tech.Abstr., Rice Abstr.
—BLDSC shelfmark: 1471.740000.

610   US
TOLEDO MEDICINE. 1916. bi-m. $15. Academy of Medicine of Toledo and Lucas County, 4428 Secor Rd., Toledo, OH 43623. TEL 419-473-3200. FAX 419-475-6744. adv.; illus.; circ. controlled.
   Formerly (until 1987): Academy of Toledo and Lucas County. Bulletin (ISSN 0001-4303)

MEDICAL SCIENCES

610   CC   ISSN 0257-716X
CODEN: JTMUEI
TONGJI MEDICAL UNIVERSITY. JOURNAL. Chinese edition: Tongji Yike Daxue Xuebao (ISSN 0258-2090) (Text in English and German) 1981. q. $37. (Tongji Medical University - Tongji Yike Daxue) China National Publications Import & Export Corp., Export Department, P.O. Box 88, Beijing 100704, People's Republic of China. TEL 565811-327. FAX 4015664. TELEX 22313-CPC-CN. (Editorial addr.: c/o Prof. Liu Xunfang, Journal of Tongji Medical University, Wuhan, Hubei 430030, P.R.C.) Ed. Qiu Fazu. circ. 1,000. **Indexed:** Chem.Abstr., Ind.Med., Math.R.
—BLDSC shelfmark: 4909.158000.
   Incorporates (in 1985): Acta Academiae Medicinae Wuhan (ISSN 0253-3316); Which was formerly: Wuhan Yixueyuan Xuebao (ISSN 0510-9752)
   Description: Comprehensive journal of medical science. Includes basic and clinical medicine, public health, and forensic medicine.

TOO MUCH - UNIVERSITY COLLEGE HOSPITAL MAGAZINE. see *HOSPITALS*

610   GW   ISSN 0931-9522
TOP MEDIZIN; Zeitschrift fuer Internationale Medizin. 1987. m. DM.216. P M I Verlag GmbH, August-Schanz-Str. 21, 6000 Frankfurt a.M. 50, Germany. TEL 069-5480000. FAX 069-548000-77. Ed. Peter Hoffmann. adv.; bk.rev.; circ. 16,000. (tabloid format; back issues avail.)

610   US   ISSN 0164-2340
TOPICS IN EMERGENCY MEDICINE. 1979. q. $69. Aspen Publishers, Inc., 200 Orchard Ridge Dr., Gaithersburg, MD 20878. TEL 301-417-7500. FAX 301-417-7550. **Indexed:** CINAHL, Excerp.Med.
—BLDSC shelfmark: 8867.437400.

610 530   US   ISSN 0899-3459
CODEN: TMRIEY
TOPICS IN MAGNETIC RESONANCE IMAGING. 1988. 4/yr. $120. Aspen Publishers, Inc., 200 Orchard Ridge Dr., Gaithersburg, MD 20878. TEL 301-417-7500. FAX 301-417-7550.
—BLDSC shelfmark: 8867.459300.

610   US   ISSN 0882-5645
TOPICS IN PAIN MANAGEMENT; current concepts and treatment strategies. 1985. m. $65. Williams & Wilkins, 428 East Preston St., Baltimore, MD 21202. TEL 301-528-4000. FAX 301-528-4321. Ed. Dr. Joel R. Saper. circ. 1,300.
   Description: Contains reviews and abstracts from the international literature available on pain disorders and management.

TOXICOLOGIC PATHOLOGY. see *ENVIRONMENTAL STUDIES — Toxicology And Environmental Safety*

TOXICOLOGY IN VITRO. see *ENVIRONMENTAL STUDIES — Toxicology And Environmental Safety*

TOXICON; an international journal specialising in toxins. see *PHARMACY AND PHARMACOLOGY*

610   GW   ISSN 0174-7371
CODEN: TEMDE6
TRACE ELEMENTS IN MEDICINE. (Text in English) 1984. q. DM.164($86) Dustri-Verlag Dr. Karl Feistle, Bahnhofstr. 9, 8024 Deisenhofen, Germany. TEL 089-613861-0. FAX 089-613-5412. Ed. Dr. K.H. Rahn. bk.rev. **Indexed:** Curr.Adv.Ecol.Sci.
   Description: Covers developments in trace elements; intended for clinicians, as well as theoretical scientists (biologists, pharmacologists, physiologists).

TRACTRIX; yearbook for the history of science, medicine, technology, and mathematics. see *SCIENCES: COMPREHENSIVE WORKS*

610   II
TRADITIONAL MEDICAL SYSTEMS. 1979. 4/yr. Rs.410($45) K.K. Roy (Private) Ltd., 55 Gariahat Rd., P.O. Box 10210, Calcutta 700 019, India. Ed. Dr. K.K. Roy. adv.; abstr.; bibl.; index; circ. 2,100.

610   GW   ISSN 0934-0874
RD120.7
TRANSPLANT INTERNATIONAL. 1989. 4/yr. DM.240($144) Springer-Verlag, Heidelberger Platz 3, D-1000 Berlin 33, Germany. TEL 030-8207-1.
—BLDSC shelfmark: 9024.989000.

TRAUMA & EMERGENCY MEDICINE. see *MEDICAL SCIENCES — Orthopedics And Traumatology*

610   US
▼**TRAVEL MEDICINE ADVISOR.** 1991. bi-m. $248. American Health Consultants, Inc., Six Piedmont Center, Ste. 400, 3525 Piedmont Rd., N.E., Atlanta, GA 30305. TEL 404-262-7436. FAX 800-284-3291. (Subscr. to: Box 740056, Atlanta, GA 30374-9822. TEL 800-688-2421) Ed. Dr. Elaine Long. circ. 800.

610   UK
▼**TREATMENT.** 1992. 2/yr. Churchill Livingstone Medical Journals, Robert Stevenson House, 1-3 Baxter's Pl., Leith Walk, Edinburgh EH1 3AF, Scotland. TEL 031-556-2424. FAX 031-558-1278. TELEX 727511. (Subscr. to: Longman Group, Journals Subscr. Dept., P.O. Box 77, Fourth Ave., Harlow, Essex CM19 5AA, England; U.S. subscr. to: Churchill Livingstone, 650 Ave. of the Americas, New York, NY 10011. TEL 212-206-5000) Eds. M. Drury, Dr. Linda Beely.
   Description: Provides updates on drugs and the management and treatment of disease in general practice.

610   US
TREATMENT IN CLINICAL MEDICINE. 1984. irreg. price varies. Springer-Verlag, 175 Fifth Ave., New York, NY 10010. TEL 212-460-1500. (Also Berlin, Heidelberg, Tokyo, Vienna) (reprint service avail. from ISI)

TRENDS IN GENETICS; DNA, differentiation and development. see *BIOLOGY — Genetics*

610   SZ   ISSN 0041-2597
CODEN: TRGLAJ
TRIANGLE; the Sandoz journal of medical science. (Editions in English, French and Spanish) 1952. 3/yr. free. Sandoz Ltd., CH-4002 Basel, Switzerland. TEL (061) 24 43 79. Ed.Bd. charts; illus.; index; circ. 318,000. (also avail. in microfilm) **Indexed:** Chem.Abstr., Excerp.Med., Ind.Med.

610   SP   ISSN 0212-7512
TRIBUNA MEDICA. 1964. w. 4900 ptas.($75) Editorial Garsi, S.A, Londres, 17, 28028 Madrid, Spain. TEL 256-08-00. FAX 361-10-07. Ed. Jesus Ibanez Montoya. adv.; bk.rev.; index; circ. 35,000. (tabloid format; back issues avail.)

610   CK
TRIBUNA MEDICA. (Editions avail. for: Mexico, Central America, Colombia, Venezuela, Ecuador, Peru) 1961. 24/yr. Ediciones Lerner Ltda., Calle 8A No.68A-41, Bogota, Colombia. TEL 261-5047. FAX 262-4459. Ed. Salomon Lerner. adv.; circ. 50,000.

610   MX
TRIBUNA MEDICA. 1966. 24/yr. Jose Maria Rico 121, Desp. 604, Colonia del Valle 03100, Mexico 12, DF, Mexico. Ed. Ricardo Blaksley. circ. 20,000.

610   PE
TRIBUNA MEDICA. 1964. 24/yr. Ave. Angamos Oeste 371, Apto. 405, Miraflores, Lima, Peru. Ed. Jose Alva Neira. adv.; circ. 6,000.

610   VE
TRIBUNA MEDICA. 1963. 14/yr. $75. Tribuna Medica Venezolana C.A., Av. Principal los Ruices, Ofc. 319, Apartado 51064, Caracas, 10A, Venezuela. FAX 354456. TELEX 27326 TRIME VC. adv.; circ. 9,000.

610   CK
TRIBUNA MEDICA FOR CENTRAL AMERICA, PANAMA AND THE DOMINICAN REPUBLIC. 1969. 24/yr. Ediciones Lerner, Calle 8A, No. 68 a41, Bogota, Colombia. FAX 2624864. Ed. Eduardo Chegwin. adv.; circ. 10,000.

610   NE   ISSN 0041-3232
TROPICAL AND GEOGRAPHICAL MEDICINE. 1948. 4/yr. fl.94.50 to individuals; institutions fl.157.50. (Koninklijk Instituut voor de Tropen - Royal Tropical Institute) I C G Publications, P.O. Box 509, 3300 AM Dordrecht, Netherlands. TEL 078-510454. FAX 078-510972. (Co-sponsors: Netherlands Society of Tropical Medicine; Institute of Tropical Medicine) Ed. A. De Geus. (back issues avail.; reprint service avail. from SWZ) **Indexed:** Abstr.Hyg., ASCA, Biol.Abstr., Curr.Adv.Ecol.Sci., Dairy Sci.Abstr., Dent.Ind., Dok.Arbeitsmed., E.I., Helminthol.Abstr., Ind.Med., Ind.Vet., Nutr.Abstr., Pig News & Info., Protozool.Abstr., Rev.Appl.Entomol., Trop.Dis.Bull., Vet.Bull.
—BLDSC shelfmark: 9054.200000.

TROPICAL JOURNAL OF OBSTETRICS AND GYNAECOLOGY. see *MEDICAL SCIENCES — Obstetrics And Gynecology*

610   US
TUBEROUS SCLEROSIS RESOURCES; for scientists, physicians and other health professionals. s-a. $20 membership includes N T S A Newsletter. National Tuberous Sclerosis Association, 8000 Corporate Center Dr., Ste. 120, Landover, MD 20785-2239. TEL 800-225-6872. FAX 301-459-0394.
   Description: News for the medical community.

610   US
TULANE MEDICINE. 1969. 4/yr. free. Tulane University Medical Center, 1430 Tulane Ave., New Orleans, LA 70112. TEL 504-588-5221. Ed. Frances B. Simon. adv.; bk.rev.; abstr.; circ. 19,000.
   Formerly: Tulane Medicine: Faculty and Alumni (ISSN 0041-400X); Which superseded: Tulane University Medical Faculty. Bulletin.

610.6   US
TULSA MEDICINE.* 1935. m. $10. Tulsa County Medical Society, 2021 S. Lewis, No. 560, Tulsa, OK 74104-5758. Ed. Jack Spears. adv.; circ. 1,100.
   Formerly (until Oct. 1977): Tulsa County Medical Society. Bulletin.

610   TI   ISSN 0041-4131
LA TUNISIE MEDICALE. (Text in French; summaries in Arabic, English, French) 1911. 12/yr. 25 din.($40) Societe Tunisienne des Sciences Medicales, 16 Rue Touraine, 1002 Tunis - Belvedere, Tunisia. TEL 284-895. (Co-sponsor: Conseil de l'Ordre des Medecins) Ed. A. Chabbou. adv.; bk.rev.; charts; index; circ. 1,500. **Indexed:** Abstr.Hyg., Biol.Abstr., Chem.Abstr., Excerp.Med., Ind.Med., P.A.I.S.For.Lang.Ind., Trop.Dis.Bull.
   Formed by the merger of: Revue Tunisienne des Sciences Medicales & Bulletin de l'Hopital Sadiki.
   Description: Scientific journal featuring original papers and clinical cases in the medical sciences as well as updating reviews and state of the art discussions of medical questions.
   Refereed Serial

610   TU
TURK TIP DERNEGI DERGISI. (Text in Turkish; summaries and table of contents in English) 1965. m. Turkish Medical Society - Turk Tip Ernegi, Valikonagi Caddesi, Bizim Apt. 10-3, Nisantasi, Turkey. adv.; abstr.; bibl.; charts; stat.
   Formerly (until vol.39, no.9, 1973): Turkish Medical Association. Journal - Turk Tip Cemiyeti Mecmuasi (ISSN 0041-431X)

610   FI   ISSN 0355-9483
CODEN: TYJMDL
TURUN YLIOPISTO. JULKAISUJA. SARJA D. MEDICA - ODONTOLOGICA. (Latin title: Annales Universitatis Turkuensis) (Text in English) 1972. irreg. price varies. Turun Yliopisto - University of Turku, SF-20500 Turku 50, Finland. FAX 358-21-6335050. TELEX 62123 TYK SF. **Indexed:** Chem.Abstr.
—BLDSC shelfmark: 0963.354000.
   Description: Studies medicine and dentistry.

610   US   ISSN 0082-7134
CODEN: UCMSAA
U C L A FORUM IN MEDICAL SCIENCES. 1962. irreg. vol.28, 1988. (University of California, Los Angeles) Academic Press, Inc., 1250 Sixth Ave., San Diego, CA 92101. TEL 619-231-0926. FAX 619-699-6715. (reprint service avail. from ISI) **Indexed:** Biol.Abstr., Chem.Abstr., Ind.Med.
   Refereed Serial

MEDICAL SCIENCES

610   US
U C S F MAGAZINE. 1978. 3/yr. free. University of California, San Francisco, Department of News and Public Information Services, 513 Parnassus Ave., San Francisco, CA 94143-0462. TEL 415-476-8299. (Co-sponsors: U C S F Schools of Dentistry, Medicine, Nursing and Pharmacy) Ed. Michela Reichman. circ. 45,000. (back issues avail.)

610.25   US   ISSN 0091-8393
R712.A1
U S MEDICAL DIRECTORY. 1969. irreg., 8th ed. 1989-1990. $150. U S Directory Service, 665 N.W. 128th St., Box 68-1700, Miami, FL 33168. TEL 305-769-1700. FAX 305-769-0548. Ed. Stanley Alperin.
    Description: Information source of healthcare services: hospitals, nursing facilities, medical laboratories, medical doctors, medical libraries and more.

610   US   ISSN 0191-6246
U S MEDICINE; an independent national newspaper for physicians. 1965. m. $100. U S Medicine, Inc., 2033 M St., N.W., Ste. 505, Washington, DC 20036. TEL 202-463-6000. Ed. Nancy Tomich. adv.; bk.rev.; charts; illus.; circ. 31,000. (newspaper)

610 150 301.1   US
U S S R REPORT: LIFE SCIENCES. 1973. irreg. (approx. 20/yr.) $7 per no. (foreign $14 per no.). U.S. Joint Publications Research Service, Box 12507, Arlington, VA 22209. TEL 703-487-4630. (Orders to: NTIS, Springfield, VA 22161)
    Former titles: U S S R Report: Life Sciences, Biomedical and Behavioral Sciences; U S S R Report: Biomedical and Behavioral Sciences; U S S R and Eastern Europe Scientific Abstracts: Biomedical and Behavioral Sciences; U S S R and Eastern Europe Scientific Abstracts: Biomedical Sciences.

574 616.9   US
U S S R REPORT: SPACE BIOLOGY AND AEROSPACE MEDICINE. English translation of: Kosmicheskaya Biologiya i Aviakosmicheskaya Meditsina (UR ISSN 0321-5040) irreg. (approx. 6/yr.). $5 per no. U.S. Joint Publications Research Service, Box 12507, Arlington, VA 22209. TEL 703-487-4630. (Orders to NTIS, Springfield, VA 22161)
    Former titles: Space Biology and Aerospace Medicine; Space Biology and Medicine.
    Description: Translation of reports on Soviet technology in aerospace medicine.

610   DK   ISSN 0041-5782
                CODEN: UGLAAD
UGESKRIFT FOR LAEGER. (Text in Danish; summaries in English) 1839. w. DKK 1.420($116) Almindelige Danske Laegeforening - Danish Medical Association, Trondhjemsgade 9, DK-2100 Copenhagen, Denmark. TEL 31 38 55 00. FAX 31-15-28-58. (Subscr. to: Laegeforeningens Forlag, Esplanaden 8 A, DK-1263 Copenhagen K, Denmark) Eds. Povl Riis, Bente Hjelmar. adv.; bk.rev.; abstr.; bibl.; charts; illus.; stat.; cum.index; circ. 20,000. **Indexed:** Biol.Abstr., C.I.S. Abstr., Chem.Abstr., Dairy Sci.Abstr., Dent.Ind., Dok.Arbeitsmed., Excerp.Med., Ind.Med., Nutr.Abstr., Protozool.Abstr., Trop.Oil Seeds Abstr.

610   US   ISSN 0041-607X
UKRAINIAN MEDICAL ASSOCIATION OF NORTH AMERICA. JOURNAL. (Text in Ukrainian) vol.17, 1970. m. $20. Ukrainian Medical Association of North America, 2 E. 79th St., New York, NY 10027. TEL 212-535-8659. Ed. Dr. Paul J. Dzul. adv.; bk.rev.; circ. 1,000.

610   UK   ISSN 0041-6193
ULSTER MEDICAL JOURNAL. 1932. s-a. £30. Ulster Medical Society, c/o Queens University Medical Library, Institute of Clinical Science, Grosvenor Rd., Belfast BT12 6BJ, N. Ireland. TEL 0232-322043. FAX 0232-247068. TELEX 747578-QUBMED-G. Ed. Dr. D.R. Hadden. adv.; bk.rev.; bibl.; illus.; index; circ. 1,060. (also avail. in microfilm from UMI; reprint service avail. from UMI) **Indexed:** Abstr.Hyg., Chem.Abstr., Curr.Adv.Ecol.Sci., Curr.Cont, Excerp.Med., Helminthol.Abstr., Ind.Med., Sci.Cit.Ind., Trop.Dis.Bull.
    ●Also available on CD-ROM. Producer(s): SilverPlatter (MEDLINE).
    —BLDSC shelfmark: 9082.745000.

610   GW   ISSN 0172-4614
ULTRASCHALL IN DER MEDIZIN. 1980. bi-m. DM.195. (Deutsche Gesellschaft fuer Ultraschall in der Medizin) Georg Thieme Verlag, Ruedigerstr. 14, Postfach 104853, 7000 Stuttgart 10, Germany. TEL 0711-8931-0. FAX 0711-89312988. Ed.Bd. adv.; bk.rev.; abstr.; bibl.; charts; illus.; circ. 3,200. (reprint service avail. from UMI) **Indexed:** Curr.Cont., Excerp.Med., Ind.Med.
    —BLDSC shelfmark: 9082.786000.

610   GW   ISSN 0930-8040
ULTRASCHALL IN KLINIK UND PRAXIS. 4/yr. DM.136($87) Springer-Verlag, Heidelberger Platz 3, D-1000 Berlin 33, Germany. TEL 030-8207-1.
    —BLDSC shelfmark: 9082.785700.

610 500   US   ISSN 0161-7346
RC78.7.U4   CODEN: ULIMD4
ULTRASONIC IMAGING; an international journal. 1979. q. $98 (foreign $128). Academic Press, Inc., Journal Division, 1250 Sixth Ave., San Diego, CA 92101. TEL 619-230-1840. FAX 619-699-6800. TELEX 181726. Ed. Melvin Linzer. adv.; index. (back issues avail.) **Indexed:** Curr.Cont., Ind.Med., Sci.Abstr.
    —BLDSC shelfmark: 9082.787000.
    Description: Covers the development and application of ultrasonic techniques, with emphasis on medical diagnosis.

ULTRASOUND IN MEDICINE & BIOLOGY. see *BIOLOGY*

610   US   ISSN 0093-5387
RC1000   CODEN: UBMRAY
UNDERSEA BIOMEDICAL RESEARCH. 1974. 6/yr. $85. Undersea and Hyperbaric Medical Society, Inc., 9650 Rockville Pike, Bethesda, MD 20814. TEL 301-571-1818. FAX 301-571-1815. Ed. H. Van Liew. bk.rev.; index; circ. 2,000. **Indexed:** Biol.Abstr., Chem.Abstr., Curr.Adv.Ecol.Sci., Curr.Cont., Deep Sea Res.& Oceanogr.Abstr., Dent.Ind., Excerp.Med., Ind.Med., Ocean.Abstr., Pollut.Abstr., Psychol.Abstr.
    —BLDSC shelfmark: 9088.600000.
    Refereed Serial

610   US
UNIFORMED SERVICES ACADEMY OF FAMILY PHYSICIANS NEWSLETTER. q. membership. Phenix Corporation, 11508 Allecingie Pkwy., Ste. C, Richmond, VA 23235. TEL 804-794-2106. Ed. Dr. R. Dean Kirkham. adv.; circ. 2,600.

610   RM   ISSN 0041-6940
UNION MEDICALE BALKANIQUE. ARCHIVES. (Text in French; summaries in English) 1963. bi-m. $80. Union Medicale Balkanique, Str. Gabriel Peri Nr. 1, Bucharest, Rumania. (Subscr. to: ILEXIM, Str. 13 Decembrie Nr. 3, P.O. Box 136-137, Bucharest, Rumania) Ed. Prof. Popescu Buzeu. bk.rev.; abstr.; bibl.; charts; illus.; index; circ. 2,000 (controlled). **Indexed:** Biol.Abstr., Ind.Med., Nutr.Abstr.

610   CN   ISSN 0041-6959
                CODEN: UMCAAA
UNION MEDICALE DU CANADA. (Text in French; summaries in English and French) 1872. bi-m. Can.$40($55) Association des Medecins de Langue Francaise du Canada, 1440 St. Catherine St., W., Ste. 210, Montreal, Que. H3G 2P9, Canada. TEL 514-866-2053. Ed. Dr. Fernand Taras. adv.; bk.rev.; abstr.; bibl.; charts; illus.; index; circ. 13,446. (reprint service avail. from UMI) **Indexed:** Biol.Abstr., Chem.Abstr., Curr.Adv.Genetics & Molec.Biol., Curr.Cont., Dent.Ind., Dok.Arbeitsmed., Excerp.Med., Helminthol.Abstr., Ind.Med., Nutr.Abstr., Pt.de Rep. (1983-).
    —BLDSC shelfmark: 9090.750000.

616.98   TS
UNITED ARAB EMIRATES. AL-QIYADAH AL-AAMAH LIL-QUWWAT AL-MUSALLIHAH. MAJALLAH AL-TIBBIYYAH/UNITED ARAB EMIRATES. GENERAL COMMAND FOR THE ARMED FORCES. MEDICAL JOURNAL. (Text in Arabic) 1989. q. exchange basis. General Command for the Armed Forces, Medical Services Administration - Al-Qiyadah al-Aamah lil-Quwwat al-Musallihah, Mudiriyyah al-Khidamat al-Tibbiyyah, P.O. Box 4224, Abu Dhabi, United Arab Emirates. TEL 447999. Ed. Muhammad Farid. circ. 1,000.
    Description: Discusses topics in military medicine and medical concerns of the armed forces.

616.98   US
U.S. AIR FORCE. SCHOOL OF AEROSPACE MEDICINE. STANDARD TECHNICAL REPORT SERIES. 1958. irreg. free to qualified personnel. U.S. Air Force, School of Aerospace Medicine, Aeromedical Library (USAFSAM-TSKD), Brooks Air Force Base, TX 78235-5301. TEL 512-536-3322. (Orders to: National Technical Information Service (NTIS), Springfield, VA 22161) bk.rev. (also avail. in microfiche) **Indexed:** Excerp.Med., Ind.Med., Psychol.Abstr.
    Incorporates (in Oct. 1984): Aeromedical Reviews (ISSN 0065-3683)

610   US
U.S. DEPARTMENT OF VETERANS AFFAIRS. SUMMARY OF MEDICAL PROGRAMS. q. U.S. Department of Veterans Affairs, 810 Vermont Ave., N.W. (008B), Washington, DC 20420. TEL 202-233-3557.
    Formerly: U.S. Veterans Administration. Summary of Medical Programs.

U.S. LIBRARY OF CONGRESS. NATIONAL LIBRARY SERVICE FOR THE BLIND AND PHYSICALLY HANDICAPPED. NEWS. see *HANDICAPPED — Visually Impaired*

616.98   US   ISSN 0083-355X
U.S. VETERANS ADMINISTRATION. MEDICAL RESEARCH PROGRAM. 1957. a. $0.40. U.S. Veterans Administration, Medical Research Service, 810 Vermont Ave., N.W., Washington, DC 20420. TEL 202-745-8000. (Orders to: Supt. of Documents, Government Printing Office, Washington, DC 20402) Ed. Russell D. Bowman.

616.98   US   ISSN 0041-7491
RC1050
UNITED STATES AIR FORCE MEDICAL SERVICE DIGEST. 1950. q. $5. U.S. Air Force, Office of the Surgeon General, HQ USAF-SGI, Bolling AFB, DC 20332-6188. TEL 202-767-5046. FAX 202-767-6208. (Dist. by: Supt. of Documents, Washington, DC 20402) Ed. Elizabeth Taber. circ. 8,000.
    Description: Presents information about the people, programs and activities of the Air Force Medical Service.

610   EC   ISSN 0041-8412
UNIVERSIDAD DE GUAYAQUIL. FACULTAD DE CIENCIAS MEDICAS. REVISTA.* s-a. free. Universidad de Guayaquil, PO Box 3637, Guayaquil, Ecuador. Ed. Dr. Carlos Palan. charts; illus.; circ. 700.

610   SP   ISSN 0210-5527
UNIVERSIDAD DE OVIEDO. FACULTAD DE MEDICINA. ARCHIVOS. 1976. a. price varies. Universidad de Oviedo, Facultad de Medicina, Oviedo, Spain. (Subscr. to: Servicio de Publicaciones, Un. de Oviedo, Calle Jesus Arias de Velasco s-n, 33005 Oviedo, Spain) Ed. Bernardo Marin Fernandez. abstr.; illus.; circ. 500.

610   SP
                CODEN: AUHMDC
UNIVERSIDAD DE SEVILLA. SERIE: MEDICINA. 1949. irreg., latest no.49. Universidad de Sevilla, Servicio de Publicaciones, San Fernando, 4, 41004 Seville, Spain. TEL 954-22-8071. FAX 954-22-1315. charts; illus.
    Former titles: Universidad Hispalense. Anales. Serie: Medicina (ISSN 0586-9919); (Until 1967): Universidad Hispalense. Anales. Facultad de Medicina (ISSN 0210-7651)

610   VE   ISSN 0542-6375
UNIVERSIDAD DEL ZULIA. FACULTAD DE MEDICINA. REVISTA. (Text in Spanish; summaries in English) 1968. irreg. Bs.32($9.50) (or exchange). Universidad del Zulia, Facultad de Medicina, Apartado 526, Maracaibo, Venezuela. Ed. Ricardo Soto. bibl.; charts; illus.; stat.; index; circ. 1,000. **Indexed:** Abstr.Hyg., Biol.Abstr., Excerp.Med., Trop.Dis.Bull.

UNIVERSIDAD DEL ZULIA. REVISTAS. see *BIOLOGY*

UNIVERSIDAD INDUSTRIAL DE SANTANDER. REVISTA - INVESTIGACIONES. see *ENGINEERING*

MEDICAL SCIENCES

610   CK   ISSN 0121-0807
CODEN: RUIMDY
UNIVERSIDAD INDUSTRIAL DE SANTANDER. REVISTA - SALUD. (Text in Spanish; summaries in English, French, German and Spanish) 1959. s-a. Col.$2500($6) or exchange basis. Universidad Industrial de Santander, Facultad de Salud, Adpo. Aereo 678, Bucaramanga, Santander, Colombia. Ed. Myriam Orostegui Arenas. adv.; bk.rev.; bibl.; charts; illus.; stat.; cum.index: 1969-1987. (back issues avail.)
Formerly: Universidad Industrial de Santander. Revista - Medicina (ISSN 0120-0909); Which superseded in part (in 1969); Universidad Industrial de Santander. Revista (ISSN 0041-8587)
Description: Covers research and current issues on various topics in medical science and health.

610   CK   ISSN 0120-0011
UNIVERSIDAD NACIONAL DE COLOMBIA. FACULTAD DE MEDICINA. REVISTA. 1932. q. exchange basis. Universidad Nacional de Colombia, Facultad de Medicina, Aereo No. 14490, Bogota D.E., Colombia. Dir. Milton Arguello Jimenex. adv.; illus.; circ. 5,000. **Indexed:** Biol.Abstr.

610   AG   ISSN 0014-6722
UNIVERSIDAD NACIONAL DE CORDOBA. FACULTAD DE CIENCIAS MEDICAS. REVISTA. (Text in Spanish; summaries in English, French, German or Italian) 1943. q. $5. Universidad Nacional de Cordoba, Facultad de Ciencias Medicas, Ciudad Universitaria, Estafeta 32, 5000 Cordoba, Argentina. Ed. E.E. Tello. abstr.; charts; illus.; index. **Indexed:** Abstr.Hyg., Biol.Abstr., Dent.Ind., Excerp.Med., Ind.Med., Trop.Dis.Bull.

610   BL   ISSN 0041-8781
CODEN: RHCFAP
UNIVERSIDADE DE SAO PAULO. HOSPITAL DAS CLINICAS. REVISTA. (Text in English, Portuguese) 1946. bi-m. $35. Universidade de Sao Paulo, Faculdade de Medicina, Caixa Postal 8091, Sao Paulo, Brazil. Ed. Ruy G. Bevilacqua. adv.; charts; illus.; index. cum.index; circ. 10,000. **Indexed:** Abstr.Hyg., Excerp.Med., Ind.Med., Nutr.Abstr., Protozool.Abstr., Trop.Dis.Bull.
—BLDSC shelfmark: 7815.850000.

610   BL   ISSN 0100-1302
CODEN: RMUCD8
UNIVERSIDADE FEDERAL DO CEARA. CENTRO DE CIENCIAS DA SAUDE. REVISTA DE MEDICINA/FEDERAL UNIVERSITY OF CEARA SCHOOL OF MEDICINE. JOURNAL OF MEDICINE. (Text in Portuguese; summaries in English and Portuguese) 1961. s-a. free. Universidade Federal do Ceara, Centro de Ciencias da Saude, Rua Alexandre Barauna 1019, Caixa Postal 688, Porangabucu, 60000 Fortaleza-Ceara, Brazil.
FAX 085-243-95-13. TELEX 851077. Eds. Jose Murilo Martins, Manasses C. Fonteles. adv.; play rev.; charts; illus.; stat.; circ. controlled. (tabloid format) **Indexed:** Excerp.Med.
Formerly (until 1973): Universidade Federal do Ceara. Faculdade de Medicina. Revista (ISSN 0041-8889)

610   CS   ISSN 0049-5514
R95.P7   CODEN: SVLKAO
UNIVERSITA KARLOVA. FAKULTA VSEOBECNEHO LEKARSTVI. POBOCKA V HRADCI KRALOVE. SBORNIK VEDECKYCH PRACI. (Text in English; summaries in Czech, English and Russian) 1958. 5/yr. Universita Karlova, Fakulta Vseobecneho Lekarstvi, Pobocka v Hradci Kralove, Simkova 870, 500 38 Hradec Kralove, Czechoslovakia. TEL 22734. illus. **Indexed:** Ind.Med.

610   CS   ISSN 0049-5522
CODEN: SVKSA9
UNIVERSITA KARLOVA. FAKULTA VSEOBECNEHO LEKARSTVI. POBOCKA V HRADCI KRALOVE. SBORNIK VEDECKYCH PRACI: SUPPLEMENTUM. (Text in Czech; summaries in Czech, English and Russian) 1958. 5/yr. Universita Karlova, Fakulta Vseobecneho Lekarstvi, Pobocka v Hradci Kralove, Simkova 870, 500 38 Hradec Kralove, Czechoslovakia. TEL 22734. illus. **Indexed:** Ind.Med.

610   AU   ISSN 0579-7772
UNIVERSITAET INNSBRUCK. MEDIZINISCHE FAKULTAET. ARBEITEN. 1970. irreg. price varies. Oesterreichische Kommissionsbuchhandlung, Maximilianstrasse 17, A-6020 Innsbruck, Austria. Ed. Hans Schroecksnadel.

610   CK   ISSN 0041-9095
UNIVERSITAS MEDICA. (Text in Spanish; summaries in English and Spanish) 1951. q. Col.$1.500($30) to students. Pontificia Universidad Javeriana, Facultad de Medicina, Carrera 7a. N. 40-62 Piso 5, Hospital San Ignacio, Bogota, Colombia. TEL 571-2882166. FAX 571-285-6981. Ed. Dr. Jaime Alvarado B. adv.; bk.rev.; abstr.; bibl.; charts; illus.; stat.; index; circ. 3,000. **Indexed:** Chem.Abstr., Excerp.Med.
Description: Covers articles written on research done in medicine.

610   IQ   ISSN 0041-9419
CODEN: JFAQAE
UNIVERSITY OF BAGHDAD. FACULTY OF MEDICINE. JOURNAL. 1936. 4/yr. University of Baghdad, Medical College, Baghdad, Iraq. Ed. Dr. Fakhri al-Hadthy. adv.; bk.rev.; charts; circ. 1,500. **Indexed:** Biol.Abstr., Chem.Abstr., Helminthol.Abstr., Nutr.Abstr., Protozool.Abstr., Trop.Dis.Bull.

610   UA   ISSN 0045-3803
CODEN: MJCUDW
UNIVERSITY OF CAIRO. FACULTY OF MEDICINE. MEDICAL JOURNAL. (Supplement avail.) (Text in English) 1932. q. £E8($40) University of Cairo, Faculty of Medicine, Clinical Society Office, Manyal University Hospital, Kasr El-Aini Post, Cairo, Egypt. TEL 726-0595. Eds. Khairy A. Samrah, Mahmoud Khairy. adv.; bk.rev.; abstr.; index; circ. 400. (back issues avail.)
Formerly: University of Cairo. Faculty of Medicine. Gazette; Incorporates: Kasr El-Aini Clinical Society. Faculty of Medicine. Gazette.
Description: Presents original papers and research activities of medical school personnel. Features review articles, abstracts from current literature and historical notes.
Refereed Serial

610   II   ISSN 0008-0705
CODEN: BUYMA3
UNIVERSITY OF CALCUTTA. UNIVERSITY COLLEGE OF MEDICINE. BULLETIN. 1963. s-a. free. Calcutta University Press, Sri Sibendra Nath Kanjilal, 48 Hazra Rd., Calcutta 19, India. Ed. S.N. Sen. bibl.; charts; illus. **Indexed:** Biol.Abstr., Chem.Abstr., Excerp.Med.

UNIVERSITY OF CALIFORNIA. LAWRENCE BERKELEY LABORATORY. BIOLOGY AND MEDICINE DIVISION. ANNUAL REPORT. see *BIOLOGY — Biological Chemistry*

UNIVERSITY OF CHICAGO. PRITZKER SCHOOL OF MEDICINE. ALUMNI ASSOCIATION. MAGAZINE. see *COLLEGE AND ALUMNI*

610   IR
UNIVERSITY OF FERDOWSI. FACULTY OF MEDICINE. LETTERS/DANESHGAH-E FERDOWSI. DANESHKADE-YE PAZESHKI. NAMEH. (Text in Persian) 1956. bi-m. Rs.200. University of Ferdowsi, Faculty of Medicine, Ta'lifat Va Entesharat, Mashhad, Iran. Ed. Manuchehr Radpur.

610   LB
UNIVERSITY OF LIBERIA. A.M. DOGLIOTTI COLLEGE OF MEDICINE. ANNUAL REPORT OF THE DEAN.* a. University of Liberia, A.M. Dogliotti College of Medicine, Monrovia, Liberia.

610 010.7   UK   ISSN 0076-0854
UNIVERSITY OF LONDON. ROYAL POSTGRADUATE MEDICAL SCHOOL. ANNUAL REPORT. 1936. a. free. University of London, Royal Postgraduate Medical School, Hammersmith Hospital, Du Cane Rd., London W12 0NN, England. TEL 081-740-3200. FAX 081-740-3203. Ed. A.N. Smith. circ. 1,000 (controlled).

610   AT   ISSN 0312-6137
UNIVERSITY OF NEW SOUTH WALES. FACULTY HANDBOOKS: MEDICINE. a? Aus.$5. University of New South Wales, P.O. Box 1, Kensington, N.S.W. 2033, Australia. TEL 02-697-2840. FAX 02-662-2163.

UNIVERSITY OF OCCUPATIONAL AND ENVIRONMENTAL HEALTH. JOURNAL. see *OCCUPATIONAL HEALTH AND SAFETY*

UNIVERSITY OF ROCHESTER. SCHOOL OF MEDICINE AND DENTISTRY. EDWARD G. MINER LIBRARY. BULLETIN. see *LIBRARY AND INFORMATION SCIENCES*

UNIVERSITY OF SOUTH FLORIDA. INTERNATIONAL BIOMEDICAL SYMPOSIA SERIES. see *BIOLOGY*

UNIVERSITY OF TEHERAN. FACULTY OF MEDICINE. LIBRARY BULLETIN/DANESHGAH-E TEHRAN. DANESHKADE-YE PEZESHKI. NASHRIYE-YE KETABKHANEH. see *LIBRARY AND INFORMATION SCIENCES*

610   CN   ISSN 0042-0239
UNIVERSITY OF TORONTO MEDICAL JOURNAL. 1923. 3/yr. $25. University of Toronto, Medical Society, Medical Sciences Bldg., Toronto, Ont. M5S 1A8, Canada. TEL 613-978-8730. Eds. Owen Porwse, Corinne Fischer. adv.; bk.rev.; charts; illus.; circ. 2,000. (also avail. in microform from MML) **Indexed:** Biol.Abstr., Excerp.Med.

610   CN   ISSN 0042-0336
UNIVERSITY OF WESTERN ONTARIO MEDICAL JOURNAL. 1930. 4/yr. $6. University of Western Ontario, Medical School, Health Sciences Centre, London, Ont. N6A 5C1, Canada. TEL 519-885-1211. Ed.Bd. adv.; bk.rev.; bibl.; charts; illus.; stat.; circ. 1,200. **Indexed:** Biol.Abstr., Chem.Abstr.

610.7   UK   ISSN 0301-5718
UPDATE; the journal of postgraduate medical education. 1968. s-m. £75 (free to qualified personnel). Reed Business Publishing Group, Reed Healthcare Communications (Subsidiary of: Reed International PLC), Quadrant House, The Quadrant, Sutton, Surrey SM2 5AS, England. TEL 081-661-3500. FAX 081-661-8946. Ed. Andrew Baster. adv.; bk.rev.; charts; illus.; stat.; index; circ. 36,000. **Indexed:** Excerp.Med., FAMLI, Helminthol.Abstr., L.R.I., Rehabil.Lit.
—BLDSC shelfmark: 9121.900000.
Description: Covers the whole spectrum of medicine addressing the postgraduate needs of the general practitioner.

610   HK
UPDATE; modern medicine of Asia. 1979. m. Far East Trade Press Ltd., Kai Tak Commercial Bldg., 2nd Fl., 317 Des Voeux Rd., Centraly Bay, Hong Kong. TEL 5453028. FAX 5446979. TELEX 83434.

610   SA   ISSN 0258-929X
UPDATE; the journal of continuing education for general practitioners. (In South African and UK editions) (Text in English) 1986. m. R.104. George Warman Publications (Pty.) Ltd., 77 Hout St., P.O. Box 704, Cape Town 8000, South Africa. TEL 021-245320. FAX 021-261332. TELEX 521849 GWP CT SA. Ed. Anthea Barker. adv.; bk.rev.; illus.; index; circ. 7,700 (controlled). (back issues avail.)
Description: Publishes clinical articles on developments in all medical specializations of interest to the general practitioner.
Refereed Serial

610   SP
▼**UPDATE.** 1991. bi-m. Salvat Publicaciones Cientificas, S.A., Muntaner, 262, 6o, 08021 Barcelona, Spain. TEL 2010911. FAX 2015911. (Subscr. to: Cempro, Plaza Conde Valle Suchil 20, 28015 Madrid, Spain) Ed.Bd. adv.; bk.rev.; index. (back issues avail.)
Description: Covers internal medicine.

610   US
UPDATE IN INTENSIVE CARE AND EMERGENCY MEDICINE. 1986. irreg. price varies. Springer-Verlag, 175 Fifth Ave., New York, NY 10010. TEL 212-460-1500. (Also Berlin, Heidelberg, Tokyo, Vienna) (reprint service avail. from ISI)

610   UK
UPDATE POSTGRADUATE CENTRE SERIES. 1970. irreg. Reed Business Publishing Group, Reed Healthcare Communications (Subsidiary of: Reed International PLC), Quadrant House, The Quadrant, Sutton, Surrey SM2 5AS, England. TEL 081-661-3500. FAX 081-661-8946. Ed. Bronwyn Salter-Murison. adv.; circ. 11,500. (back issues avail.; reprint service avail.)
Description: Booklets written for United Kingdom's general practitioners.

MEDICAL SCIENCES 3161

610 SW ISSN 0300-9734
CODEN: UJMSAP
UPPSALA JOURNAL OF MEDICAL SCIENCES.
(Supplements avail.) (Text in English) 1865. 3/yr.
SEK 200 incl. supplements. (Uppsala
Laekareföerening - Uppsala Medical Society)
Almqvist & Wiksell Periodical Company, Box 638,
S-101 28 Stockholm, Sweden. Ed. Gunnar Ronquist.
charts; illus.; index; circ. 1,350. **Indexed:** Biol.Abstr.,
Chem.Abstr., Curr.Adv.Biochem., Curr.Adv.Ecol.Sci.,
Curr.Cont., Excerp.Med., Helminthol.Abstr., Ind.Med.,
Nutr.Abstr., Sci.Cit.Ind.
—BLDSC shelfmark: 9122.700000.
Formerly: Acta Societatis Medicorum Upsaliensis
(ISSN 0001-6985)

610 FR ISSN 0923-2524
CODEN: URGME3
URGENCES MEDICALES. (Text in French; summaries in
English, French) 1982. 6/yr. 690 F.($135) (foreign
720 F.)(effective 1992). (French Societe de
Medecine de Catastrophe) Editions Scientifiques
Elsevier, 29, rue Buffon, 75005 Paris, France.
TEL 47-07-11-22. FAX 43-36-80-93. TELEX
202400. (Subscr. in U.S. and Canada to: Elsevier
Science Publishing Co., Inc., Box 882, Madison Sq.
Sta., New York, NY 10159. TEL 212-989-5800)
Ed. P. Huguenard. adv.; circ. 3,000. (also avail. in
microform) **Indexed:** Curr.Cont.
—BLDSC shelfmark: 9124.170000.
Formerly: Convergences Medicales.
Description: Provides a forum for communication
and exchange between all disciplines connected with
emergency and natural disaster medicine:
anesthesiology, pathophysiology of aggression and
pharmacology.

V A MEDICAL CENTER DIRECTORY. see *HOSPITALS*

610 US ISSN 0883-5721
V A PRACTITIONER; the magazine for the health care
professionals of the Department of Veterans Affairs.
1984. 13/yr. (includes a. V A Medical Center
Directory). $44.95 (Canada $95.95; elsewhere
$89.95). Cahners Publishing Company (New York),
Medical-Health Care Group (Subsidiary of Reed
International PLC), Division of Reed Publishing (USA)
Inc., 249 W. 17th St., New York, NY 10011.
TEL 212-463-6522. FAX 212-463-6404. (Subscr.
to: 44 Cook St., Denver, CO 80286-5191. TEL
800-662-7776) Ed. Nina Tobier. adv.; index; circ.
25,854. (back issues avail.)
Description: An independent journal geared to the
needs of the health care professional working in the
VA medical system.

610 SW
VAARDFACKET. s-m. (22/yr.). Svenska Haelso- och
Sjukvaardens Tjaenstemannafoerbund, Box 3260,
103 65 Stockholm, Sweden. adv.; circ. 74,959.

610 VE
**VENEZUELA. HOSPITAL CENTRAL DE LA FUERZAS
ARMADAS. BOLETIN MEDICO.** 1970. q. free. Hospital
Central de las Fuerzas Armadas, San Martin,
Caracas, Venezuela. Ed. Dr. Leandro Potenza. abstr.;
bibl.; illus.; circ. 1,500.

610 GW ISSN 0174-738X
CODEN: VERDEJ
VERDAUUNGSKRANKHEITEN; gastroenterologische
Zeitschrift fuer Klinik und Praxis. 1983. bi-m.
DM.112($74.70) Dustri-Verlag Dr. Karl Feistle,
Bahnhofstr. 9, 8024 Deisenhofen, Germany.
TEL 089-613861-0. FAX 089-613-5412. Ed. Dr.
W. Bergemann. adv.
—BLDSC shelfmark: 9155.828000.

610 US
VERMONT STATE MEDICAL SOCIETY. REPORTER. 1949.
m. $35. Vermont State Medical Society, Box H,
Montpelier, VT 05602. TEL 802-223-7898. Ed.
Karen N. Meyer. adv.; circ. 1,100. (back issues
avail.)
Formerly: Vermont State Medical Society.
Newsletter.
Description: Provides non-technical information of
interest to practicing Vermont physicians.

610 GW ISSN 0340-241X
CODEN: VEPADX
VEROEFFENTLICHUNGEN AUS DER PATHOLOGIE. irreg.
price varies. Gustav Fischer Verlag, Wollgrasweg 49,
Postfach 720143, 7000 Stuttgart 70, Germany.
TEL 0711-458030. FAX 0711-4580334. TELEX
7111-488-FIBUCH. **Indexed:** Dent.Ind., Ind.Med.

610 GW ISSN 0933-4548
CODEN: VERSEU
VERSICHERUNGSMEDIZIN; Prognose Therapie
Begutachtung. 1949. bi-m. DM.22.43. (Verband der
Lebensversicherungsunternehmen e.V.) Verlag
Versicherungswirtschaft e.V., Klosestr. 20-24, 7500
Karlsruhe 1, Germany. Ed. O. Raestrup. adv.; bk.rev.;
abstr.; charts; tr.lit.; index; circ. 16,000. **Indexed:**
Biol.Abstr., Excerp.Med., Ind.Med.
—BLDSC shelfmark: 9195.570000.
Formerly: Lebensversicherungsmedizin (ISSN
0024-0044)

610 RM
VIATA MEDICALA - PENTRU MEDICI. (Text in Rumanian;
summaries in English, French, German, Russian)
1954. m. $25. Uniunea Societatilor de Stiinte
Medicale din Republica Socialista Rumania, Str.
Progresului No. 8, Bucharest, Rumania. (Subscr. to:
ILEXIM, Str. 13 Decembrie Nr. 3, P.O. Box 136-137,
Bucharest, Rumania) Ed.Bd. adv.; bk.rev.; abstr.
Indexed: Biol.Abstr., C.I.S. Abstr., Chem.Abstr.,
Ind.Med.
Formerly: Viata Medicala - Pentru Cadre
Superioare (ISSN 0042-5036)

610 FR ISSN 0042-5583
VIE MEDICALE.* 1919. 30/yr. 370 F. Editions de la Vie
Medicale, c/o O.D.M. - V.M., 6, rue des Bateliers, 92
110 Clichy, France. Ed. E. M. Vidal. adv.; bk.rev.; illus.;
circ. 30,000. **Indexed:** C.I.S. Abstr., Chem.Abstr.,
Helminthol.Abstr.

**VIRCHOWS ARCHIV. SECTION A: PATHOLOGICAL
ANATOMY AND HISTOPATHOLOGY.** see *BIOLOGY*

VIRCHOWS ARCHIV. SECTION B: CELL PATHOLOGY;
including molecular pathology. see *BIOLOGY — Cytology And Histology*

610 US
VIRGINIA MASON CLINIC BULLETIN. 1922. s-a. free to
hospitals, libraries and physicians. Virginia Mason
Clinic, 1100 Ninth Ave., Box 900, Seattle, WA
98111. TEL 206-223-6985. Ed. Dr. D.G. Fryer.
charts, illus, stat.; index; circ. 5,000.
Formerly (until 1987): Mason Clinic. Bulletin (ISSN
0025-4657)

610 US ISSN 1052-4231
VIRGINIA MEDICAL QUARTERLY. 1874. q. $24 (foreign
$30). Medical Society of Virginia, 4205 Dover Rd.,
Richmond, VA 23221. TEL 804-353-2721.
FAX 804-355-6189. Ed. Edwin L. Kendig, Jr., M.D.
adv.; bk.rev.; abstr.; charts; illus.; stat.; tr.lit.; index
annually; circ. 7,200. (also avail. in microfiche)
Indexed: Ind.Med.
Formerly (until July 1990): Virginia Medical.

VITA OSPEDALIERA. see *HOSPITALS*

610 US
VITAL SIGNS (FRESNO). 1949. m. $24. Fresno-Madera
Medical Society, 3425 N. First St., Box 31, Fresno,
CA 93707. TEL 209-224-4224.
FAX 209-227-1463. Ed.Bd. adv.; illus.; circ. 1,300.
Formerly: Fresno County Medical Society. Bulletin
(ISSN 0016-1160)

VITALITY MAGAZINE; Toronto's monthly wellness
journal. see *PHYSICAL FITNESS AND HYGIENE*

**VITAMINS AND HORMONES: ADVANCES IN RESEARCH
AND APPLICATIONS.** see *PHARMACY AND
PHARMACOLOGY*

610 RU
▼**VITAS.** 1991. irreg., (1-2/m.). 0.50 Rub. per issue.
Assotsiatsiya "Vitas", Ul. Pravdy 9, k.20, 630090
Novosibirsk, Russia. (Co-sponsor: Assotsiatsiya
Transaktnogo Analiza) circ. 100,000. (newspaper)

616.026 CS ISSN 0042-773X
CODEN: VNLEAH
VNITRNI LEKARSTVI. (Text in Czech; summaries in
Czech, English and Russian) 1955. 12/yr. $83.80.
(Ceskoslovenska Spolecnost pro Vnitrni Lekarstvi)
Avicenum, Czechoslovak Medical Press,
Malostranske nam. 28, 118 02 Prague 1,
Czechoslovakia. (Dist. by: Artia, Ve Smeckach 30,
111 27 Prague 1, Czechoslovakia) (Co-sponsor:
Ceskoslovenska Lekarska Spolecnost J. Ev. Purkyne)
Ed. Dr. D. Mrkos. adv.; bk.rev.; charts; illus.; stat.;
index. **Indexed:** C.I.S. Abstr., Chem.Abstr.,
Excerp.Med., Ind.Med., Nutr.Abstr.
—BLDSC shelfmark: 9250.300000.
Description: Covers internal medicine.

616.98 RU ISSN 0047-7397
VOENNO-MEDITSINSKII ZHURNAL. 1823. m.
17.40 Rub. Voenizdat, Bol'shoi Kiselnyi per., 14,
Moscow, Russia. **Indexed:** Biol.Abstr., Chem.Abstr.,
Dent.Ind., Ind.Med., Int.Aerosp.Abstr.
Description: Covers issues pertinent to military
medicine.

616.98 CS ISSN 0372-7025
VOJENSKE ZDRAVOTNICKE LISTY. (Text in Czech;
summaries in English, Russian) 1925. bi-m. 12 Kcs.
Vydavatelstvi Nase Vojsko, Vladislavova 26, 113 66
Prague 1, Czechoslovakia. (Co-sponsor: Ministerstvo
Narodni Obrany) Ed. Jaroslav Paces. bk.rev.; abstr.;
illus.; index. (also avail. in microfiche; back issues
avail.)
Description: Essays on military science, medical
sciences, veterinary sciences and pharmacology.

616.98 YU ISSN 0042-8450
**VOJNOSANITETSKI PREGLED/MILITARY MEDICAL AND
PHARMACEUTICAL REVIEW;** casopis lekara i
farmaceuta jugoslovenske narodne armije. (Text in
Serbo-Croatian; summaries in English, Russian)
1944. bi-m. 5000 din.($60) Savezni Sekretarijat za
Narodnu Odbranu, Sanitetska Uprava, P.O. Box
1003, 11000 Belgrade, Serbia, Yugoslavia.
FAX 669-689. Ed. Cedomir Markovic. adv.; bk.rev.;
abstr.; charts; illus.; stat.; index; circ. 2,000. **Indexed:**
Biol.Abstr., C.I.S. Abstr., Chem.Abstr., Dent.Ind.,
Ergon.Abstr., Excerp.Med., I.P.A., Ind.Med.,
Psychol.Abstr., Ref.Zh.
—BLDSC shelfmark: 9251.652000.

615.8 RU ISSN 0042-8787
CODEN: VKFLAL
**VOPROSY KURORTOLOGII, FIZIOTERAPII I LECHEBNOI
FIZICHESKOI KUL'TURY/PROBLEMS OF HEALTH
RESORTS, PHYSIOTHERAPY AND EXERCISE THERAPY.**
1923. bi-m. 10.80 Rub.($9.60) (Vsesoyuznoe
Nauchnoe Obshchestvo Fizioterapevtov i
Kurortologov) Izdatel'stvo Meditsina, Petroverigskii
pereulok 6-8, 101838 Moscow, Russia.
(Co-sponsors: Ministerstvo Zdravookhraneniya
S.S.S.R.; Vsesoyuznoe Nauchno-Meditsinskoe
Obshchestvo Vrachebnogo Kontrolya i Lechebnoi
Fizkul'tury) Ed. V.M. Bogolyubov. bk.rev.; illus.; index.
Indexed: Biol.Abstr., Chem.Abstr., Dent.Ind., Ind.Med.,
Int.Aerosp.Abstr.
—BLDSC shelfmark: 0043.000000.
Description: Examines the mechanisms of
physiological and therapeutic effects of physical and
health resort factors, methods and results of their
employment; also covers theoretical and practical
problems involved in the use of exercise therapy in
the complex treatment of different diseases.

610 KR ISSN 0049-6804
CODEN: VRDEA5
VRACHEBNOE DELO. (Some summaries in English)
1918. m. 25.80 Rub. Izdatel'stvo Zdorovya, Ul.
Yavarskaya, 1, Kiev 52, Ukraine. **Indexed:** Biol.Abstr.,
Chem.Abstr., Dent.Ind., Excerp.Med., Ind.Med.
—BLDSC shelfmark: 0045.830000.

610 US
W A NEWS. 1978. q. American Diabetes Association,
Washington Affiliate, Inc., 557 Roy St., Seattle, WA
98109. TEL 206-282-4616. FAX 206-282-4729.
Ed. Jack Fleming. circ. 6,500 (controlled). (tabloid
format)

610 UN ISSN 0512-3054
RA8 CODEN: WHOTAC
W H O TECHNICAL REPORT SERIES. (Editions in Arabic,
Chinese, English, French, Russian and Spanish)
1950. irreg., (approx. 15/yr), latest no.803. $80.
World Health Organization, Distribution and Sales,
CH-1211 Geneva 27, Switzerland.
TEL 022-791-2111. circ. 15,000 (combined).
Indexed: Abstr.Hyg., Biol.Abstr., Dent.Ind.,
Excerp.Med., Food Sci.& Tech.Abstr., I.P.A., Ind.Med.,
Ind.Vet., Med.Care Rev., Nutr.Abstr., Rural
Ext.Educ.& Tr.Abstr., Rural Recreat.Tour.Abstr.,
Trop.Dis.Bull., Vet.Bull., World Agri.Econ.& Rural
Sociol.Abstr.
Description: Summarizes current technical
knowledge on a given disease, health risk, medical
technology or research approach.

MEDICAL SCIENCES

610 574   JA   ISSN 0511-084X
CODEN: WKMRAH
WAKAYAMA MEDICAL REPORTS. (Text in English, French or German) 1953. q. exchange basis. Wakayama Medical College, Library - Wakayama-kenritsu Ika Daigaku Toshokan, Wakayama 640, Japan. FAX 0734-26-8308. TELEX 5542-488. Ed. Michio Koike. bibl.; charts; illus.; index; circ. 800. **Indexed:** Abstr.Hyg., Biol.Abstr., C.I.S. Abstr., Chem.Abstr., Excerp.Med., Nutr.Abstr., Trop.Dis.Bull.
—BLDSC shelfmark: 9261.400000.

610 574   JA   ISSN 0043-0013
CODEN: WKMIAO
WAKAYAMA MEDICINE/WAKAYAMA IGAKU. (Text in Japanese; summaries in English, French and German) 1950. q. 2000 Yen($20) Wakayama Medical Society - Wakayama Igakkai, c/o Wakayama Medical College, 9 Kyuban-cho, Wakayama 640, Japan. Ed. Hirotoshi Iwata. charts; illus.; stat.; circ. 1,200. **Indexed:** Biol.Abstr., Chem.Abstr., Excerp.Med., Jap.Per.Ind., Nutr.Abstr.
—BLDSC shelfmark: 4912.600000.

WARY CANARY; a news network for allergics, "sensitive birds," & environmental health advocates. see *ENVIRONMENTAL STUDIES*

610   US   ISSN 0164-1514
WASHINGTON HEALTH RECORD. 1983. w. $175. Faulkner & Gray, Healthcare Information Center (Subsidiary of: J P T Publishing Group), 1133 15th St., N.W., Ste. 450, Washington, DC 20005. TEL 202-828-4150. FAX 202-828-2352. Ed. Melissa Jee. (looseleaf format)

616.98   GW
WEHRMEDIZIN UND WEHRPHARMAZIE. 1976. q. DM.68. Beta Publishing, Postfach 140121, 5300 Bonn 1, Germany. TEL 0228-252061. FAX 0228-252067. TELEX 8869536 BETA D. Ed. Dr. Hannes Sauter. circ. 7,900. (back issues avail.)
Description: For doctors, pharmacists and scientists in the medical corps of Germany.

610   GW   ISSN 0043-2156
CODEN: WEMOBZ
WEHRMEDIZINISCHE MONATSSCHRIFT; Organ des Sanitaets- und Gesundheitswesen der Bundeswehr. (Text in German; summaries in English, German) 1956. m. DM.72. (Bundesministerium der Verteidigung) A. Bernecker Verlag, Unter dem Schoenenberg 1, 3508 Melsungen, Germany. (Co-sponsor: Deutsche Gesellschaft fuer Wehrmedizin und Wehrpharmazie) Ed. Dr. Wedel. adv.; bk.rev.; abstr.; charts; illus.; stat.; cum.index; circ. 5,300. **Indexed:** Biol.Abstr., Chem.Abstr.
—BLDSC shelfmark: 9288.120000.
Formerly: Wehrmedizinische Mitteilungen.

630   CC
WEISHENG DULIXUE ZAZHI. (Text in Chinese) q. Zhonghua Yufang Yixuehui - China Preventive Medical Society, 16, Hepingli Zhongjie, Beijing 100013, People's Republic of China. TEL 4218457. Ed. Liu Shijie.

610   CC
WEIZHONGBING JIJIU YIXUE. (Text in Chinese) q. Tianjin Shi Jijiu Yixue Yanjiusuo, 162, Munan Dao, Tianjin 300050, People's Republic of China. TEL 306917. Ed. Wang Jinda.

615.89   UK   ISSN 0143-7984
WELLCOME UNIT FOR THE HISTORY OF MEDICINE. RESEARCH PUBLICATIONS. 1979. irreg., latest issue 10. price varies. Wellcome Unit for the History of Medicine, University of Oxford, 45-47 Banbury Rd., Oxford OX2 6PE, England. TEL 0865-274600. FAX 0865-274605. bibl.; circ. 200. (back issues avail.)
—BLDSC shelfmark: 7759.155300.
Description: Contains bibliographical, documentary and research aids for the social history of medicine and health from the year 1500 to the present.

610   UK
WELSH MEDICAL GAZETTE. 1970. q. free to qualified personnel. Welsh Medical Press Ltd., 23 Blenheim Rd., Cardiff, Wales. Eds. Drs. Eric Payne, Bernard Knight. adv.; bk.rev.; illus.; circ. 5,000.

610   CC   ISSN 1000-2138
WENZHOU YIXUEYUAN XUEBAO/WENZHOU INSTITUTE OF MEDICAL SCIENCES. JOURNAL. (Text in Chinese) q. Wenzhou Yixueyuan - Wenzhou Institute of Medical Sciences, Wenzhou, Zhejiang 325003, People's Republic of China. TEL 34941.

610   UK
WEST ENGLAND MEDICAL JOURNAL. 1883. m. (Nuffield Hospitals) Clinical Press, 15 Bucklands Dr., Nailsea, Bristol BS19 2DJ, England.
Formerly (until 1990): Bristol Medico - Chirurgical Journal (ISSN 0960-6440)

610   JM   ISSN 0043-3144
CODEN: WIMJAD
WEST INDIAN MEDICAL JOURNAL. (Supplement avail.) 1951. q. $50. University of the West Indies, Faculty of Medical Sciences, Mona Campus, Kingston 7, Jamaica, W.I. TEL 809-92-71214. FAX 809-92-72556. Ed. Dr. Vasil Persaud. adv.; bk.rev.; charts, bibl.; illus.; circ. 2,000. (also avail. in microform; reprint service avail. from UMI, ISI) **Indexed:** Abstr.Hyg., Biol.Abstr., Chem.Abstr., Curr.Cont., Dent.Ind., Excerp.Med., Helminthol.Abstr., I.P.A., Ind.Med., Ind.Vet., Nutr.Abstr., Trop.Dis.Bull.
—BLDSC shelfmark: 9299.100000.
Description: Addresses areas of medical research of the greatest potential benefit to the people of the Commonwealth Caribbean. Contains articles covering those relevant medical topics.
Refereed Serial

610   US   ISSN 0043-3284
WEST VIRGINIA MEDICAL JOURNAL. 1906. m. $36. West Virginia State Medical Association, 4307 MacCorkle Ave., Box 4106, Charleston, WV 25364. TEL 304-925-0342. FAX 304-925-0345. Ed. Stephen D. Ward. adv.; bibl.; illus.; index; circ. 3,900. (also avail. in microform from UMI) **Indexed:** Biol.Abstr., Chem.Abstr., Curr.Cont., Dent.Ind., Excerp.Med., Helminthol.Abstr., Ind.Med., Med.Care Rev., Nutr.Abstr.
—BLDSC shelfmark: 9300.050000.
Refereed Serial

610   US
WESTCHESTER BULLETIN. vol.42, 1974. 10/yr. $2. Westchester Academy of Medicine, Purchase, NY 10577. TEL 914-948-4100. Ed. Mr. Zingaro. adv.; bk.rev.; circ. 2,000.

610   US   ISSN 0093-0415
R15   CODEN: WJMDA2
WESTERN JOURNAL OF MEDICINE. 1902. m. $40. California Medical Association, 221 Main St., San Francisco, CA 94105. TEL 415-882-5179. FAX 415-882-5116. (Co-sponsors: Medical Associations of Arizona, California, Idaho, Nevada State, New Mexico, Utah State, Washington State, and Wyoming) Ed. Dr. Linda Hawes Clever. adv.; bk.rev.; charts; illus.; s-a. index; circ. 55,238. (also avail. in microfilm from UMI; reprint service avail. from UMI) **Indexed:** Abstr.Health Care Manage.Stud., Biol.Abstr., C.I.S. Abstr., Chem.Abstr., CINAHL, Curr.Adv.Cancer Res., Curr.Adv.Ecol.Sci., Curr.Cont., Dairy Sci.Abstr., Dent.Ind., Dok.Arbeitsmed., Excerp.Med., Helminthol.Abstr., Hlth.Ind., Hosp.Lit.Ind., Ind.Med., Ind.Vet., Med.Care Rev., Nutr.Abstr., Protozool.Abstr., Small Anim.Abstr.
—BLDSC shelfmark: 9300.830000.
Incorporates (1944-1985): Arizona Medicine (ISSN 0004-1556); Former titles (1946-1973): California Medicine (ISSN 0008-1264); (1924-1946): California and Western Medicine (ISSN 0093-4038)
Refereed Serial

WHICH? WAY TO HEALTH. see *PHYSICAL FITNESS AND HYGIENE*

610   PL   ISSN 0043-5147
CODEN: WILEAR
WIADOMOSCI LEKARSKIE. (Text in Polish; summaries in English and Russian) 1948. bi-w. $216. Panstwowy Zaklad Wydawnictw Lekarskich, Dluga 38-40, 00-238 Warsaw, Poland. TEL 31-42-81. (Dist. by: Ars Polona-Ruch, Krakowskie Przedmiescie 7, Warsaw, Poland) Ed. Dr. Jan Dzieniszewski. **Indexed:** Biol.Abstr., Chem.Abstr., Dent.Ind., Dok.Arbeitsmed., Excerp.Med., Ind.Med., Protozool.Abstr.
—BLDSC shelfmark: 9313.800000.
Description: Explores clinical medicine and post-graduate education of physicians.

610   GW   ISSN 0179-3004
WIE GEHT'S HEUTE?; Ratschlaege und Informationen aus Ihrem Sanitaetsfachgeschaeft. 1985. 3/yr. DM.0.98. M T D Verlag GmbH und Co., Wangenerstr. 20, Postfach 50, 7989 Amtzell - Allgaeu, Germany. TEL 07520-6611. FAX 07520-6911. Eds. Klaus Witzer, Elisabeth Fetzer. adv. (back issues avail.)

610   US   ISSN 0043-5325
CODEN: WKWOAO
WIENER KLINISCHE WOCHENSCHRIFT. (Supplement avail.: Wiener Klinische Wochenschrift. Supplementum) (Text in German) 1887. 24/yr. DM.184($103) Springer-Verlag, Journals, 175 Fifth Ave., New York, NY 10010. TEL 212-460-1500. (Also Berlin, Heidelberg, Tokyo, Vienna) Eds. O. Kraupp, E. Deutsch. adv.; bk.rev.; charts; illus.; index. (also avail. in microform from UMI; reprint service avail. from ISI) **Indexed:** Biol.Abstr., Biotech.Abstr., C.I.S. Abstr., Chem.Abstr., Curr.Adv.Biochem., Curr.Adv.Cell & Devel.Biol., Curr.Cont., Dairy Sci.Abstr., Dent.Ind., Excerp.Med., Helminthol.Abstr., Ind.Med., Nutr.Abstr., Soyabean Abstr.
—BLDSC shelfmark: 9315.900000.

610   AU   ISSN 0043-5341
CODEN: WMWOA4
WIENER MEDIZINISCHE WOCHENSCHRIFT. (Text in German; summaries in English) 1851. bi-w. S.1350. Blackwell Medizinische Zeitschriftenverlagsgesellschaft mbH, Feldgasse 13, A-1238 Vienna, Austria. TEL 0222-8893646. FAX 0222-889364724. Ed.Bd. adv.; bk.rev.; abstr.; bibl.; illus.; index; circ. 4,150. (reprint service avail. from ISI) **Indexed:** Biol.Abstr., Biotech.Abstr., Chem.Abstr., Curr.Cont., Excerp.Med., Helminthol.Abstr., Ind.Med., Nutr.Abstr.
—BLDSC shelfmark: 9315.925000.

610   US
WILDERNESS MEDICINE LETTER. 1984. q. $90. Wilderness Medical Society, Box 397, Pt. Reyes Sta., CA 94956. TEL 415-663-9107. adv.; bk.rev.; circ. 2,500. (looseleaf format; back issues avail.)
Formerly: Wilderness Medicine.
Description: Covers research on human activities in wilderness environments.

610 636.089   US   ISSN 0736-6094
Z6674
WILDLIFE DISEASE REVIEW. 1983. m. $225 (foreign $255). P.O. Box 1522, Ft. Collins, CO 80522. TEL 303-484-6267. FAX 303-482-6184. TELEX 820567. Ed. B. Zimmerman. index; circ. 150.

610   GW
▼**WIRTSCHAFT FUER DEN ARZT.** 1990. 8/yr. (Verband Wirtschaft und Arzt e.V.) Berliner Medizinische Verlagsanstalt GmbH, Kurfuerstenstr. 112-113, 1000 Berlin 30, Germany. TEL 030-219909-0. FAX 030-219909-10. circ. 15,000.

610   US   ISSN 0043-6542
R11
WISCONSIN MEDICAL JOURNAL. 1903. m. $35. State Medical Society of Wisconsin, 330 E. Lakeside St., Box 1109, Madison, WI 53701. TEL 608-262-3266. FAX 608-283-5401. Ed. R.D. Sautter, M.D. adv.; bk.rev.; bibl.; illus.; index; circ. 7,000. **Indexed:** Biol.Abstr., Chem.Abstr., CINAHL, Curr.Cont., Dent.Ind., Excerp.Med., Helminthol.Abstr., Ind.Med., Nutr.Abstr., Rehabil.Lit.
—BLDSC shelfmark: 9325.800000.

WOHNUNG & GESUNDHEIT; Fachzeitschrift fuer oekologisches Bauen & Leben. see *ARCHITECTURE*

610   US
WOMAN'S HEALTH ADVISER. m. Whittle Communications L.P., 333 Main Ave., Knoxville, TN 37902. TEL 615-595-5300. Ed. Margot Leske.
Description: A guide to mind and body fitness for women. Topics vary from pregnancy to general health care.

610   US
WORCESTER MEDICINE. 1937. bi-m. $10. (Worcester District Medical Society) Cotton Communications, 321 Main St., Worcester, MA 01608. TEL 508-753-1579. Ed. J. Paul Lock. adv.; bk.rev.; circ. 2,100.
Formerly: Worcester Medical News (ISSN 0043-7905)

WORK PROGRAMS; special interest section newsletter. see *OCCUPATIONS AND CAREERS*

WORLD BIOLICENSING REPORT. see *BIOLOGY — Bioengineering*

WORLD BOOK HEALTH AND MEDICAL ANNUAL. see *ENCYCLOPEDIAS AND GENERAL ALMANACS*

610 UN ISSN 0251-2432
RA441 CODEN: WHFODN
WORLD HEALTH FORUM. (Editions in Arabic, Chinese, English, French, Italian, Russian, Spanish) 1980. q. 60 Fr.($48) World Health Organization, Distribution and Sales, CH-1211 Geneva 27, Switzerland. TEL 022-791-2111. circ. 33,000(combined). **Indexed:** Abstr.Hyg., Adol.Ment.Hlth.Abstr., ASSIA, Biol.Abstr., Curr.Adv.Ecol.Sci., Environ.Abstr., Environ.Per.Bibl., Excerp.Med., Geo.Abstr., Helminthol.Abstr., I D A, IIS, Med.Care Rev., Protozool.Abstr., Rural Devel.Abstr., Rural Ext.Educ.& Tr.Abstr., Rural Recreat.Tour.Abstr., Sage Pub.Admin.Abstr., Soc.Work Res.& Abstr., Telegen, W.R.C.Inf., World Agri.Econ.& Rural Sociol.Abstr., World Bibl.Soc.Sec.
—BLDSC shelfmark: 9356.040200.
Description: Practical information of public health policy and practice.

610 UN ISSN 0042-9686
R5 CODEN: BWHOA6
WORLD HEALTH ORGANIZATION. BULLETIN. (Supplements avail.) (Text in English or French; separate editions in Arabic, Chinese and Russian) 1947. 6/yr. ($104) World Health Organization, Distribution and Sales, CH-1211 Geneva 27, Switzerland. TEL 022-791-2111. Ed. A. Hussein. bibl.; charts; illus.; index; circ. 6,500. (back issues avail.) **Indexed:** Abstr.Hyg., Adol.Ment.Hlth.Abstr., ASSIA, Bio-Contr.News & Info., Biol.Abstr., Biotech.Abstr., Curr.Adv.Ecol.Sci., Curr.Cont., Dairy Sci.Abstr., Dent.Abstr., Dent.Ind., Environ.Per.Bibl., Excerp.Med., Helminthol.Abstr., I.P.A., IIS, Ind.Med., Ind.Vet., INIS Atomind., NRN, Nutr.Abstr., Ocean.Abstr., Pollut.Abstr., Poult.Abstr., Protozool.Abstr., Psychol.Abstr., Rev.Appl.Entomol., Rev.Plant Path., Sci.Cit.Ind, Sel.Water Res.Abstr., Trop.Dis.Bull., Vet.Bull., Weed Abstr.
—BLDSC shelfmark: 2819.000000.
Description: Presents original research findings selected on the basis of their immediate or potential relevance to problems of human health.

610 GW ISSN 0049-8122
R5
WORLD MEDICAL JOURNAL. 1954. bi-m. $18. (World Medical Association) Deutscher Aerzte-Verlag GmbH, Dieselstr. 2, Postfach 400265, 5000 Cologne 40, Germany. FAX 0221-7011-444. Ed. Iran M. Gillibrand. adv.; bk.rev.; abstr.; bibl.; charts; illus.; index; circ. 3,500. (tabloid format) **Indexed:** Biol.Abstr., Hosp.Lit.Ind., Med. Care Rev.
—BLDSC shelfmark: 9356.650000.

WORLD MEETINGS: MEDICINE. see *MEETINGS AND CONGRESSES*

610 CN ISSN 0742-535X
WORLD RIGHT-TO-DIE NEWSLETTER. 1979. s-a. free. World Federation of Right-to-Die Societies, 600 Eglinton Ave. E., Ste. 401, Toronto, Ont. M4P 1P3, Canada. FAX 416-423-7092. Ed. Marilynne Seguin. bk.rev.; circ. 100. (also avail. in looseleaf format)
Description: Features news of the society, such as meetings and conferences dealing with euthanasia and its growing support.

610 US ISSN 1044-7946
WOUNDS; a compendium of clinical research and practice. bi-m. $60 (foreign $96). Health Management Publications, Inc., 550 American Ave., King of Prussia, PA 19406. TEL 215-337-4466. FAX 215-337-0890.
—BLDSC shelfmark: 9364.529340.

610
WYOMING PHYSICIANS NEWSLETTER. 1962. bi-w. $24 to non-members. Wyoming State Medical Society, Box 4009, Cheyenne, WY 82001. TEL 307-635-3955. FAX 307-632-1793. Ed. Wendy P. Curran. circ. 550. (looseleaf format)
Former titles: Medical Wire; Pulse (ISSN 0043-9797)

610 CC
XIN YIXUE/NEW MEDICAL SCIENCE. (Text in Chinese) m. Zhongshan Yike Daxue - Sun Yat-sen Medical University, 74 Zhongshan Erlu, Guangzhou, Guangdong 510089, People's Republic of China. TEL 778223.

615.89 615.328 CC ISSN 0256-7415
XINZHONGYI/NEW JOURNAL OF TRADITIONAL CHINESE MEDICINE. (Text in Chinese) 1969. m. $1.50 per no. Guangzhou Zhongyi Xueyuan, Xinzhongyi Bianjibu - Guangzhou College of Traditional Chinese Medicine, Xinzhongyi Editorial Department, Jichang Lu, Sanyuanli, Guangzhou, Guangdong, People's Republic of China. TEL 6661233. (Dist. by: China International Book Trading Corporation, P.O. Box 339, Beijing, P.R.C.) Ed. Cheng Fang. adv.: B&W page $500. circ. 85,000.
—BLDSC shelfmark: 6084.322000.
Description: Covers theory and clinical practice of traditional Chinese medicine.

610 CC ISSN 1000-2065
XUZHOU YIXUEYUAN XUEBAO/XUZHOU INSTITUTE OF MEDICAL SCIENCES. JOURNAL. (Text in Chinese) q. Xuzhou Yixueyuan - Xuzhou Institute of Medical Sciences, 84 Huihai Xilu, Xuzhou, Jiangsu 221002, People's Republic of China. TEL 34650. Ed. Wang Pingyu.

610 574 US ISSN 0044-0086
R11 CODEN: YJBMAU
YALE JOURNAL OF BIOLOGY AND MEDICINE. 1928. bi-m. $50 to individuals; institutions $75. Yale Journal of Biology and Medicine, Inc., 333 Cedar St., New Haven, CT 06510. TEL 203-785-4251. Ed. Dr. Philip K. Bondy. adv.; bk.rev.; bibl.; charts; illus.; index; circ. 1,000. (also avail. in microform from UMI; reprint service avail. from KTO) **Indexed:** Biol.Abstr., Biol.Dig., Chem.Abstr., Curr.Adv.Ecol.Sci., Curr.Cont., Deep Sea Res.& Oceanogr.Abstr., Excerp.Med., Helminthol.Abstr., Ind.Med., Int.Aerosp.Abstr., JAMA, Nutr.Abstr., Risk Abstr., Vet.Bull.
—BLDSC shelfmark: 9370.000000.
Description: Original contributions and review articles in all fields of medicine and related sciences. *Refereed Serial*

YAMAGUCHI-KEN EISEI KOGAI KENKYU SENTA GYOSEKI HOKOKU. see *PUBLIC HEALTH AND SAFETY*

610 JA ISSN 0513-1812
CODEN: BYMSAN
YAMAGUCHI UNIVERSITY. SCHOOL OF MEDICINE. BULLETIN/YAMAGUCHI DAIGAKU IGAKUBU KIYO. (Text in English or German; summaries in English) 1953. 4/yr. exchange basis. Yamaguchi Daigaku, Igakubu - Yamaguchi University, School of Medicine, Kogushi, Ube-shi 755, Japan. Ed.Bd. circ. controlled. **Indexed:** Abstr.Hyg., Biol.Abstr., Chem.Abstr., Excerp.Med., INIS Atomind., Trop.Dis.Bull. Key Title: Bulletin of the Yamaguchi Medical School.
—BLDSC shelfmark: 2822.000000.

610 US ISSN 0734-3299
YEAR BOOK OF CRITICAL CARE MEDICINE. 1983. a. $51.95. Mosby - Year Book, Inc., Continuity Division, 200 N. LaSalle, Chicago, IL 60601. TEL 312-726-9733. Ed. Dr. Mark Rogers. illus. (reprint service avail.)
● Also available on CD-ROM. Producer(s): SilverPlatter (ClinMED-CD).
—BLDSC shelfmark: 9411.624360.

610 US ISSN 0147-1996
R101
YEAR BOOK OF FAMILY PRACTICE. 1977. a. $54.95. Mosby - Year Book, Inc., Continuity Division, 200 N. LaSalle, Chicago, IL 60601. TEL 312-726-9733. FAX 312-726-6075. TELEX 206155. Ed. Dr. Alfred O. Berg. illus. (reprint service avail.)
● Also available online. Vendor(s): BRS.

YEAR BOOK OF HAND SURGERY. see *MEDICAL SCIENCES — Surgery*

610 US ISSN 0084-3873
R101
YEAR BOOK OF MEDICINE. 1933. a. $57.95. Mosby - Year Book, Inc., Continuity Division, 200 N. LaSalle, Chicago, IL 60601. TEL 312-726-9733. FAX 312-726-6075. TELEX 206155. Ed. David E. Rogers, M.D. (reprint service avail.) **Indexed:** Curr.Adv.Ecol.Sci.
● Also available online. Vendor(s): BRS.
—BLDSC shelfmark: 9414.570000.

616.98 US ISSN 0899-8035
RC963.A1
▼**YEAR BOOK OF OCCUPATIONAL MEDICINE.** 1991. a. $59.95. Mosby - Year Book, Inc. (Chicago) (Subsidiary of: Times Mirror Company), 200 N. LaSalle St., Chicago, IL 60601-1080. TEL 312-726-9733. FAX 312-726-6075. TELEX 206155. Ed. Dr. Edward A. Emmett. illus.
● Also available online. Vendor(s): BRS.
—BLDSC shelfmark: 9414.655000.

616.07 US ISSN 0084-3946
YEAR BOOK OF PATHOLOGY AND CLINICAL PATHOLOGY. 1940. a. $57.95. Mosby - Year Book, Inc., Continuity Division, 200 N. LaSalle, Chicago, IL 60601. TEL 312-726-9733. FAX 312-726-6075. TELEX 206155. Ed. Dr. William Gardner. illus. (reprint service avail.) **Indexed:** Curr.Adv.Ecol.Sci.
● Also available online. Vendor(s): BRS.
—BLDSC shelfmark: 9414.700000.

YEAR BOOK OF ULTRASOUND. see *MEDICAL SCIENCES — Radiology And Nuclear Medicine*

650 616.1 US ISSN 0749-4041
RD598.5
YEAR BOOK OF VASCULAR SURGERY. a. $54.95. Mosby - Year Book, Inc., Continuity Division, 200 N. LaSalle, Chicago, IL 60601. FAX 312-726-9733. TELEX 312-726-6075. Ed. Dr. John Bergan.
● Also available online. Vendor(s): BRS.
—BLDSC shelfmark: 9417.580000.

610 CC
YICHUAN YU JIBING/HEREDITY AND DISEASE. (Text in Chinese) q. Huaxi Yike Daxue - West China University of Medical Sciences, 17, Renmin Nanlu 3 Duan, Chengdu, Sichuan 610041, People's Republic of China. TEL 581130. Ed. Liu Zudong.

610 CC ISSN 1001-7585
YIXUE LILUN YU SHIJIAN/MEDICAL THEORY AND PRACTICE. (Text in Chinese) q. Hebei Langfang Diqu Yixue Qingbaozhan, 8 Xinhua Lu, Langfang, Hebei 102800, People's Republic of China. TEL 23783. Ed. Zong Yuhua.

610 JA ISSN 0285-0877
YOBO IGAKU/HEALTH SERVICES JOURNAL. 1967. m. 3708 Yen (effective Jan. 1991). Japan Association of Health Services, c/o Hokenkaikan, 1-2 Sadohara-Cho, Ichigaya, Shinjuku-ku, Tokyo 162, Japan. TEL 03-3268-1800. FAX 03-3266-8767. Ed. Wataru Kunii. adv.; circ. 6,000. (back issues avail.)

610 JA ISSN 0044-0531
CODEN: YMBUA7
YOKOHAMA MEDICAL BULLETIN. (Text in English, French, German) 1950. 3/yr. exchange basis. Yokohama-shiritsu Daigaku, Igakubu - Yokohama City University, School of Medicine, 3-9 Fukuura, Kanazawa-ku, Yokohama 236, Japan. FAX 45-787-2560. Ed.Bd. bk.rev.; bibl.; charts; illus.; circ. 1,000. **Indexed:** Biol.Abstr., C.I.S. Abstr., Chem.Abstr., Excerp.Med., Helminthol.Abstr., Ind.Vet., Nutr.Abstr., Vet.Bull.
—BLDSC shelfmark: 9420.000000.

610 574 614.8 JA ISSN 0372-7726
CODEN: YKIGAK
YOKOHAMA MEDICAL JOURNAL. (Text in Japanese; summaries in English, French, German) 1948. bi-m. exchange basis. Yokohama-shiritsu Daigaku, Igakubu - Yokohama City University, School of Medicine, 3-9 Fukuura, Kanazawa-ku, Yokohama 236, Japan. FAX 45-787-2560. Ed.Bd. index; circ. 2,600. **Indexed:** Biol.Abstr.
—BLDSC shelfmark: 9420.100000.

610 JA ISSN 0513-5710
CODEN: YOAMAQ
YONAGO ACTA MEDICA. (Text in English and European languages) 1954. 3/yr. exchange basis. Tottori Daigaku, Igakubu - Tottori University, Faculty of Medicine, 86 Nishi-machi, Yonago 683, Japan. TEL 0859-34-8053. Ed. Kenzo Takeshita. circ. 700. **Indexed:** Biol.Abstr., Chem.Abstr., Curr.Cont., Dairy Sci.Abstr., Excerp.Med., Helminthol.Abstr., Ind.Med., Nutr.Abstr.
—BLDSC shelfmark: 9421.000000.

MEDICAL SCIENCES

610   JA   ISSN 0044-0558
YONAGO MEDICAL ASSOCIATION. JOURNAL/YONAGO IGAKU ZASSHI. (Text in Japanese; summaries in English and European languages) 1948. bi-m. 2000 Yen. Yonago Medical Association - Yonago Igakkai, Tottori University School of Medicine, 86 Nishi-machi, Yonago 683, Japan. Ed. Shiro Ikawa. adv.; bk.rev.; index; circ. 980. **Indexed:** Chem.Abstr.
—BLDSC shelfmark: 4917.730000.

610   KO
YONSEI JOURNAL OF MEDICAL SCIENCE. (Text in Korean; summaries in English) 1968. s-a. exchange basis. Yonsei University, College of Medicine, C.P.O. Box 8044, Seoul, S. Korea. TEL 392-0161. abstr.; bibl.; charts; illus.; stat. (tabloid format) **Indexed:** Biol.Abstr., Chem.Abstr.

610   KO   ISSN 0513-5796
                     CODEN: YOMJA9
YONSEI MEDICAL JOURNAL. (Text in English) 1960. q. exchange basis. Yonsei University, College of Medicine, C.P.O. Box 8044, Seoul, S. Korea. Ed. Dr. Jung Ho Suh. abstr.; charts; illus.; stat. (tabloid format) **Indexed:** Biol.Abstr., Chem.Abstr., Excerp.Med., Ind.Med.
—BLDSC shelfmark: 9421.100000.

615.89 615.328   CC   ISSN 0255-2914
YUNNAN ZHONGYI ZAZHI/YUNNAN JOURNAL OF TRADITIONAL CHINESE MEDICINE. (Text in Chinese) bi-m. $0.60 per no. Yunnan Sheng Zhongyi Zhongyao Yanjiusuo, Lianhua Chi, Kunming, Yunnan 650223, People's Republic of China. TEL 51957. (Dist. overseas by: Guoji Shudian - China International Book Trading Corp., P.O. Box 399, Beijing, People's Republic of China) Ed. Zhang Zhen.

610   GW   ISSN 0341-9835
Z F A MIT KARTEI DER PRAKTISCHEN MEDIZIN. (Zeitschrift fuer Allgemeinmedizin) 1924. 3/m. DM.148. (Vereinigung der Hochschullehrer und Lehrbeauftragten fuer Allgemeinmedizin) Hippokrates Verlag GmbH, Ruedigerstr. 14, Postfach 10 22 63, D-7000 Stuttgart 1, Germany. Ed.Bd. adv.; bk.rev.; bibl.; charts; illus.; index; circ. 40,000. **Indexed:** Dent.Ind., Excerp.Med., Ind.Med., Nutr.Abstr.
—BLDSC shelfmark: 9446.870000.
     Former titles: Z F A; Landarzt (ISSN 0023-7728)

610   XV   ISSN 0350-0063
ZDRAVSTVENI VESTNIK/JOURNAL OF SLOVENIA MEDICAL SOCIETY. (Text in Slovenian; summaries in English) 1929. m. 6000 din.($110) Slovensko Zdravnisko Drustvo, Komenskega 4, P.O. Box 26, 61001 Ljubljana, Slovenia. TEL 061-317-868. (Co-sponsors: Raziskovalna Skupnost Slovenije, Zdravstvena Skupnost Slovenije) Eds. Joze Drinovec, Martin Janko. adv.; bk.rev.; circ. 4,100. **Indexed:** Biol.Abstr., Curr.Cont., Excerp.Med.
—BLDSC shelfmark: 9439.100000.

610   GW   ISSN 0044-2178
ZEITSCHRIFT FUER AERZTLICHE FORTBILDUNG. 1904. s-m. DM.170 (foreign DM.207). Gustav Fischer Verlag Jena, Villengang 2, Postfach 176, 6900 Jena, Germany. TEL 03778-27332. FAX 03778-22638. TELEX 18069-588676. Ed. H. Berndt. adv.; bk.rev.; abstr.; bibl.; charts; illus.; index. (reprint service avail. from ISI) **Indexed:** Biol.Abstr., C.I.S. Abstr., Chem.Abstr., Dent.Ind., Excerp.Med., Ind.Med., Ref.Zh.
—BLDSC shelfmark: 9452.800000.

616.026   GW   ISSN 0044-2542
                     CODEN: ZGIMAL
ZEITSCHRIFT FUER DIE GESAMTE INNERE MEDIZIN UND IHRE GRENZGEBIETE; Klinik, Pathologie, Experiment. (Text in German; summaries in English, German and Russian) 1946. s-m. DM.117. Georg Thieme Verlag, Ruedigerstr. 14, Postfach 104853, 7000 Stuttgart 10, Germany. TEL 0711-8931-0. FAX 0711-8931298. Ed. H. Trenckmann. adv.; bk.rev.; bibl.; charts; illus.; index; circ. 2,500. **Indexed:** Biol.Abstr., C.I.S. Abstr., Chem.Abstr., Dent.Ind., Excerp.Med., Ind.Med., Nutr.Abstr.
—BLDSC shelfmark: 9462.875000.

616.98   GW   ISSN 0514-8782
RC970   CODEN: ZEMIAF
ZEITSCHRIFT FUER MILITAERMEDIZIN. 1960. 6/yr. DM.58.20. Militaerverlag der Deutschen Demokratischen Republik, Redaktion Zeitschrift fuer Militaermedizin, Box 16 157-E, 2200-Greifswald, Germany.

615.8   GW   ISSN 0720-9762
                     CODEN: ZPMKDX
ZEITSCHRIFT FUER PHYSIKALISCHE MEDIZIN, BALNEOLOGIE UND MEDIZINISCHE KLIMATOLOGIE; Praevention - Diagnostik - Therapie - Rehabilitation. (Text in German; summaries in English) 1972. bi-m. DM.86. (Deutsche Gesellschaft fuer Physikalische Medizin und Rehabilitation) Demeter Verlag, Wuermstr. 13, 8032 Graefelfing, Germany. TEL 089-852033. FAX 089-8543347. circ. 3,400.

610 155.3   GW   ISSN 0932-8114
HQ21
ZEITSCHRIFT FUER SEXUALFORSCHUNG. 1988. q. DM.84. (Deutsche Gesellschaft fuer Sexualforschung) Ferdinand Enke Verlag, Postfach 101254, 7000 Stuttgart 10, Germany. TEL 0711-8931-0. FAX 0711-8931-419. Ed.Bd.

610   SZ
ZEITSCHRIFT FUER UNFALLCHIRURGIE UND VERSICHERUNGSMEDIZIN. (Text in French and German) 1907. q. 110 Fr. Verlag Hans Huber, Laenggasstr. 76, CH-3000 Bern 9, Switzerland. TEL 031-24-25-33. FAX 031-24-33-80. TELEX 911886-HAHU. Ed. Dr. E. Frei. circ. 800. **Indexed:** Abstr.Hyg., Ind.Med.
     Formerly: Zeitschrift fuer Unfallchirurgie, Versicherungsmedizin und Berufskrankheiten (ISSN 0640-3603)

616.07 574.2   GW   ISSN 0863-4106
RB1   CODEN: ZEPAEA
ZENTRALBLATT FUER PATHOLOGIE. (Text and summaries in English and German) 1890. 6/yr. DM.344 (foreign DM.346). Gustav Fischer Verlag Jena, Villengang 2, Postfach 176, 6900 Jena, Germany. TEL 03778-27332. FAX 03778-22638. TELEX 18069-588676. Ed. W. Jaenisch. adv.; bk.rev.; abstr.; bibl.; charts; illus.; index. cum.index: vols.1-20. (also avail. in microfiche from BHP; reprint service avail. from ISI) **Indexed:** Biol.Abstr., Chem.Abstr., Dent.Ind., Excerp.Med., Ind.Med., Ind.Vet., Ref.Zh., Vet.Bull.
—BLDSC shelfmark: 9511.510000.
     Formerly: Zentralblatt fuer Allgemeine Pathologie und Pathologische Anatomie (ISSN 0044-4030)

ZENTRALINSTITUT FUER VERSUCHSTIERZUCHT. JAHRESBERICHT. see *BIOLOGY*

610   GW   ISSN 0932-0547
ZENTRALVERBAND FUER LOGOPAEDIE. FORUM DER MITGLIEDER. 1987. q. membership. (Zentralverband fuer Logopaedie) Deutscher-Aertze Verlag, Dieselstr. 2, 5000 Cologne 40, Germany. TEL 02234-7011-0. FAX 02234-49649. adv.; bk.rev.; index; circ. 2,500.

615.89 615.328   CC
ZHEJIANG ZHONGYI XUEYUAN XUEBAO/ZHEJIANG TRADITIONAL CHINESE MEDICAL COLLEGE. JOURNAL. (Text in Chinese) bi-m. $1.30 per no. Zhejiang Zhongyi Xueyuan - Zhejiang Traditional Chinese Medical College, Zhejiang, People's Republic of China. (Dist. by: Guoji Shudian (China Publications Centre), Chegongzhuang Xilu 21, P.O. Box 339, Beijing, P.R.C.)

615.89 615.328   CC   ISSN 0411-8421
ZHEJIANG ZHONGYI ZAZHI/ZHEJIANG JOURNAL OF TRADITIONAL CHINESE MEDICINE. (Text in Chinese) m. $1.90 per no. Zhejiang Sheng Zhongyiyao Yanjiusuo - Zhejiang Provincial Institute of Traditional Chinese Medicine, 26 Tianmushan Lu, Hangzhou, Zhejiang 310007, People's Republic of China. (Dist. overseas by: Guoji Shudian - China International Book Trading Corporation, P.O. Box 399, Beijing, P.R.C.)

610   CC
ZHIYE YIXUE/OCCUPATIONAL MEDICINE. (Text in Chinese) bi-m. Guangdong Sheng Zhiyebing Fangzhi Yuan - Guangdong Institute of Occupational Disease Prevention, No. 78, Yile Lu, Guangzhou, Guangdong 510260, People's Republic of China. TEL 558002. Ed. Tan Bingde.

ZHONG CAO YAO/CHINESE HERBAL MEDICINE. see *PHARMACY AND PHARMACOLOGY*

615.89   CC   ISSN 0254-9034
R97.7.C5
ZHONG-XIYI JIEHE ZAZHI/CHINESE JOURNAL OF INTEGRATED TRADITIONAL AND WESTERN MEDICINE. (Text in Chinese) bi-m. $1.20 per no. (Zhongyi Yanjiuyuan, Zhongguo Zhong-Xiyi Jiehe Yanjiuhui - Academy of Traditional Chinese Medicine, Chinese Association of the Integration of Traditional and Western Medicine) Guoji Shudian, Qikan Bu, Chegongzhuang Xilu 21, P.O. Box 399, Beijing 100044, People's Republic of China. **Indexed:** Dent.Ind., Ind.Med.

610   CC   ISSN 1000-4718
ZHONGGUO BINGLI SHENGLI ZAZHI/CHINESE JOURNAL OF PATHOLOGY AND PHYSIOLOGY. (Text in Chinese) bi-m. Zhongguo Bingli Shengli Xuehui - Chinese Society of Pathology and Physiology, Jinan Daxue, Shipai, Guangzhou, Guangdong 510632, People's Republic of China. TEL 516511. Ed. Li Chujie.
     Refereed Serial

610   CC   ISSN 1001-568X
ZHONGGUO CHUJI WEISHENG BAOJIAN/CHINESE PRIMARY HEALTH CARE. (Text in Chinese) m. Heilongjiang Sheng Weishengting - Heilongjiang Provincial Bureau of Health, 27, Xiangshun Jie, Xiangfang-qu, Harbin, Heilongjiang 150036, People's Republic of China. TEL 54637. Ed. Li Yihe.

610   CC   ISSN 1001-1889
ZHONGGUO DIFANGBING FANGZHI ZAZHI/CHINESE JOURNAL OF ENDEMIC DISEASE PREVENTION AND TREATMENT. (Text in Chinese) bi-m. Weisheng Bu, Difangbing Fangzhi Ju - Ministry of Health, Bureau of Endemic Disease Prevention and Treatment, 5, Chongqing Jie, Jilin, Jilin 132001, People's Republic of China. TEL 452118. Ed. Gao Shufen.

610   CC
ZHONGGUO JIJIU YIXUE/CHINESE FIRST AID MEDICAL SCIENCE. (Text in Chinese) bi-m. Heilongjiang Sheng Keji Qingbaosuo - Heilongjiang Institute of Science and Technology Information, 30, Yinhang Jie, Nangang-qu, Harbin, Heilongjiang 150001, People's Republic of China. TEL 33977. Ed. Pei Lizhong.

610   CC
ZHONGGUO KANGFU YIXUE ZAZHI/CHINESE JOURNAL OF RECOVERY. (Text in Chinese) bi-m. Zhongguo Kangfu Yixuehui - Chinese Medical Society of Recovery, Zhongri Youhao Yiyuan, Hepingjie Beikou, Beijing 100013, People's Republic of China. TEL 4221122. Ed. Gu Yingqi.

610   CC   ISSN 1000-629X
ZHONGGUO MAFENG ZAZHI/CHINESE JOURNAL OF LEPROSY. (Text in Chinese) q. Zhongguo Mafeng Fangzhi Xiehui - Chinese Association of Leprosy Prevention and Treatment, No. 2, Huifu Xilu, Guangzhou, Guangdong 510120, People's Republic of China. TEL 861996. Ed. Zhao Xiding.

630   CC
ZHONGGUO NONGCUN YIXUE/MEDICAL SCIENCE IN RURAL CHINA. (Text in Chinese) m. Renmin Weisheng Chubanshe - People's Health Publishing House, 10 Tiantan Xili, Beijing 100050, People's Republic of China. TEL 755431. Ed. Guo Yousheng.

630   CC
ZHONGGUO XIANGCUN YISHENG/CHINESE RURAL DOCTORS. (Text in Chinese) m. Jilin Kexue Jishu Chubanshe, 102, Stalin Street, Changchun, Jilin 130021, People's Republic of China. TEL 884778. Ed. Shan Shujian.

610   CC   ISSN 1001-7658
ZHONGGUO XIAODUXUE ZAZHI/CHINESE JOURNAL OF DISINFECTION. (Text in Chinese) 1984. q. $5.48 (foreign $18.17)(typically set in Oct.). Zhonghua Yufang Yixuehui - China Preventive Medical Society, A-23 Qilizhuang Lu, Fengtai, Beijing 100071, People's Republic of China. TEL 6888229. FAX 861-8213044. (Dist. outside China by: Guoji Shudian - China International Book Trading Corp., P.O. Box 399, Beijing, P.R.C.) Ed. Liu Yujing. adv.; bk.rev.; circ. 6,000.
     Formerly (until 1990): Disinfection and Sterilization.
     Description: Reports research achievements in area of disinfection sterilization in China, including mechanism of germicidal action, experimental techniques, administration and monitoring.
     Refereed Serial

610   CC   ISSN 1000-503X
ZHONGGUO YIXUE KEXUEYUAN XUEBAO/ACTA ACADEMIAE MEDICINAE SINICA. (Text in Chinese) bi-m. $4.30 per no. China Academy of Medical Sciences (CAMS) - Zhongguo Yixue Kexueyuan, 9 Dong Dan San Tiao, Beijing 100730, People's Republic of China. TEL 5127733. (Dist. by: China International Book Trading Corp., Chegongzhuang Xilu 21, P.O. Box 339, Beijing, P.R.C.) Ed. Gu Fangzhou. **Indexed:** Helminthol.Abstr.
—BLDSC shelfmark: 0579.723200.
  Refereed Serial

615.89   CC
ZHONGGUO ZHENJIU/CHINESE ACUPUNCTURE AND MOXIBUSTION. (Text mostly in Chinese, partly in English) 1981. bi-m. $2.40 per no. (China Academy of Traditional Chinese Medicine) Zhongguo Zhenjiu Zazhishe, Dongzhimennei, Beijing 100700, People's Republic of China. TEL 01-4014411. TELEX 210340. (Dist. overseas by: Zhongguo Guoji Shudian - China International Book Trading Corporation, P.O. Box 2820, Beijing, P.R.C.) (Co-sponsor: Chinese Society of Acupuncture and Moxibustion)

610   CC   ISSN 1000-6680
ZHONGHUA CHUANRANBING ZAZHI/CHINESE JOURNAL OF INFECTIOUS DISEASES. (Text in Chinese) q. Zhonghua Yixuehui, Shanghai Fenhui - Chinese Society of Medical Sciences, Shanghai Branch, 1623 Beijing Xilu, Shanghai 200040, People's Republic of China. TEL 2531885. Ed. Xu Zhaoming.
—BLDSC shelfmark: 3180.355000.

615.8   CC   ISSN 0254-1408
ZHONGHUA LILIAO ZAZHI/CHINESE JOURNAL OF PHYSICAL THERAPY. (Text in Chinese) q. $3 per no. Zhonghua Yixuehui - Chinese Society of Medical Sciences, Tang Gang Zi, Anshan, Liaoning 114048, People's Republic of China.
—BLDSC shelfmark: 3180.478000.

610   CC
ZHONGHUA LIUXINGBINGXUE ZAZHI/CHINESE JOURNAL OF EPIDEMIOLOGY. (Text in Chinese) bi-m. Zhonghua Yufang Yixuehui - China Preventive Medical Society, 16, Hepingli Zhongjie, Beijing 100013, People's Republic of China. TEL 4218457. Ed. He Guanqing.

616.02   CC
ZHONGHUA NEIKE ZAZHI/CHINESE JOURNAL OF INTERNAL MEDICINE. (Text in Chinese) m. $3 per no. Guoji Shudian, Qikan Bu, Chegongzhuang Xilu 21, P.O. Box 399, Beijing 100044, People's Republic of China. **Indexed:** Chem.Abstr, Ind.Med.

610 530   CC   ISSN 0254-1424
ZHONGHUA WULI YIXUE ZAZHI/CHINESE JOURNAL OF PHYSICAL MEDICINE. (Text in Chinese) q. $1.30 per no. Hebei Yixue Yuan - Hebei Academy of Medical Sciences, 5 Chang'an Xilu, Shijiazhuang, Hebei 050017, People's Republic of China. TEL 44121. (Dist. overseas by: Guoji Shudian - China International Book Trading Corporation, P.O. Box 399, Beijing, P.R.C.)
—BLDSC shelfmark: 3180.475000.

610   CC
ZHONGHUA YISHI ZAZHI/CHINESE JOURNAL OF MEDICAL HISTORY. (Text in Chinese) q. $3 per no. Guoji Shudian, Qikan Bu, Chegongzhuang Xilu 21, P.O. Box 399, Beijing 100044, People's Republic of China.

610   CC
ZHONGHUA YUFANG YIXUE ZAZHI/CHINESE JOURNAL OF PREVENTIVE MEDICINE. (Text in Chinese) bi-m. $3 per no. Guoji Shudian, Qikan Bu, Chegongzhuang Xilu 21, P.O. Box 399, Beijing 100044, People's Republic of China. **Indexed:** Chem.Abstr, Ind.Med.

630   CC   ISSN 1001-0025
ZHONGRI YOUHAO YIYUAN XUEBAO/SINO-JAPANESE FRIENDSHIP HOSPITAL JOURNAL. (Text in Chinese) q. Zhongri Youhao Yiyuan, Hepingjie Beikou, Beijing 100029, People's Republic of China. TEL 4221122. Ed. Bian Zhiqiang.

ZHONGYAO TONGBAO/CHINESE MEDICINE BULLETIN. see *PHARMACY AND PHARMACOLOGY*

610   CC   ISSN 1001-6910
ZHONGYI YANJIU/TRADITIONAL CHINESE MEDICINAL RESEARCH. (Text in Chinese, table of contents in English) q. Y3.20. Zhongyi Yanjiu Bianjibu, 7 Chengbei Lu, Zhengzhou, Henan 450004, People's Republic of China. TEL 22705. (Dist. overseas by: China International Book Trading Corporation - Guoji Shudian, P.O. Box 399, Beijing, P.R.C.)
—BLDSC shelfmark: 8881.070830.

615.89 615.328   CC
ZHONGYI ZAZHI/JOURNAL OF TRADITIONAL CHINESE MEDICINE. (Text in Chinese) m. $1.10 per no. (All-China Association of Workers of Traditional Chinese Medicine) Guoji Shudian, Qikan Bu, Chegongzhuang Xilu 21, P.O. Box 399, Beijing, People's Republic of China. **Indexed:** Helminthol.Abstr.

610   AI   ISSN 0013-3310
ZHURNAL EKSPERIMENTAL'NOI I KLINICHESKOI MEDITSINY. (Text in Armenian and Russian) 1952. bi-m. $8.40. Akademiya Nauk Armyanskoi S.S.R., Ul. Barekamutian, 24, Erevan, Armenia, U.S.S.R. **Indexed:** Biol.Abstr., Chem.Abstr., Ind.Med., Ind.Vet., Vet.Bull.

ZHURNAL MIKROBIOLOGII, EPIDEMIOLOGII I IMMUNOBIOLOGII/JOURNAL OF MICROBIOLOGY, EPIDEMIOLOGY AND IMMUNOBIOLOGY. see *BIOLOGY — Microbiology*

613   CI   ISSN 0350-7335
ZIVOT I ZDRAVIJE; obitelski casopis za proucavanje i promicanje prirodnih zdravstvenih nacela. (Editions in Croatian and Serbian) 1972. q. 50 din.($4) per issue. Centar za Proucavanje Prirodnih Zdravstvenih Nacela, Maksimirska 9, 41000 Zagreb, Croatia. TEL 041 217-264. Ed. Slavko Cop. circ. 6,500 Croatian ed.; 9,000 Serbian ed. (back issues avail.)

ZWISCHENSCHRITTE; Beitraege zu einer morphologischen Psychologie. see *PSYCHOLOGY*

MEDICAL SCIENCES — Abstracting, Bibliographies, Statistics

011 610.73   US   ISSN 1055-8349
▼**A A C N NURSING SCAN IN CRITICAL CARE.** 1991. bi-m. $35 to individuals; institutions $55. (American Association of Critical Care Nurses) Nursecom Inc., 1211 Locust St., Philadelphia, PA 19107. TEL 215-545-7222. Ed. Gayle Whitman.
  Description: Abstracts of articles from multidisciplinary literature that address topics in critical care nursing, with commentary on applications to nursing practice.

618   US   ISSN 0897-1471
A C O G CURRENT JOURNAL REVIEW. 1988. bi-m. $98 (foreign $126)(effective 1992). (American College of Obstetricians and Gynecologists) Elsevier Science Publishing Co., Inc. (New York), 655 Ave. of the Americas, New York, NY 10010. TEL 212-989-5800. FAX 212-633-3965. TELEX 420643 AEP UI. Ed. Dr. Albert B. Gerbie.
  Description: Designed to keep the reader up-to-date on issues in obstetrics and gynecology. Includes current abstracts of 28 medical journals published worldwide.
  Refereed Serial

616.9   US
A I D S (YEAR); a year in review. (Suppl. to: A I D S) 1988. a. $120 to individuals. Current Science, 20 N. Third St., Philadelphia, PA 19106. TEL 800-552-5866. FAX 215-574-2270. Ed.Bd. adv.; illus.; circ. 4,000.
  Description: Reviews all major developments during the preceding year. Topics include: virology; epidemiology; vaccines and immunology; clinical treatment; social, cultural and political aspects; and global statistics.

616.9   US   ISSN 0895-9331
Z6664.A27
A I D S BIBLIOGRAPHY. (Acquired Immune Deficiency Syndrome) a. price varies. Whitston Publishing Co. Inc., Box 958, Troy, NY 12181. TEL 518-283-4363.
  Description: World bibliography of the previous year's literature on AIDS.

616.9   UK   ISSN 0953-1580
A I D S INFORMATION. (Acquired Immune Deficiency Syndrome) 1985. m. £70 (foreign £75). Oncology Information Service, University of Leeds, Leeds LS2 9JT, England. TEL 0303-850501.
FAX 0303-850162. (Subscr. to: Bailey Management Services Ltd., 127 Sangate Rd., Folkestone CT20 2BL) Ed. S.P. Bates. adv.; circ. 1,000. (back issues avail.)
—BLDSC shelfmark: 0773.083430.
  Description: Provides full details of recently published papers on all aspects of AIDS and related animal and human retroviruses.

616.9   US   ISSN 0892-0125
A T I N: A I D S TARGETED INFORMATION NEWSLETTER. 1987. m. $225 to individuals; institutions $280. Williams & Wilkins, 428 E. Preston St., Baltimore, MD 21202. TEL 301-528-4000.
FAX 301-528-4312. Ed. Russell E. McDonald. circ. 1,000. (back issues avail.)
—BLDSC shelfmark: 1765.884670.
  Description: Compendium of the latest articles on medical knowledge and research about AIDS from over 300 journals.

610 016   US   ISSN 0001-3331
                    CODEN: AIXMA
ABRIDGED INDEX MEDICUS. 1970. m. $50. U.S. National Library of Medicine, 8600 Rockville Pike, Bethesda, MD 20894. TEL 301-496-6308. FAX 301-496-4450. (Orders to: Supt. of Documents, Washington, DC 20402) cum.index; circ. 4,700. (also avail. in microform from UMI) **Indexed:** MEDOC.
  Description: A bibliography of articles from 118 English language journals arranged in subject and author sections.

616.07 619 574.8   UK   ISSN 0268-4993
ABSTRACTS: CELLULAR PATHOLOGY. 1979. q. £13.50 (foreign £22.50). Charnlind Ltd., P.O. Box 29, Woking, Surrey GU21 1AE, England. Ed. R.E. Nunn. adv.; bk.rev.; circ. 3,000.
  Formerly (until 1986): Abstracts: Histopathology, Cytopathology (ISSN 0143-800X)

616.02   US
ABSTRACTS IN MEDICINE AND KEY WORD INDEX.* m. Medical Information Systems, Reference & Index Services, Inc., 3951 N. Meridian St., Ste. 100, Indianapolis, IN 46208-4011. TEL 317-923-1575.
●Also available online. Vendor(s): DIALOG (File 219).
  Formerly: Abstracts in Internal Medicine.

610 016   BU   ISSN 0001-3536
ABSTRACTS OF BULGARIAN SCIENTIFIC MEDICAL LITERATURE. (Editions in English and Russian) vol.9, 1970. a. 24 lv. Tsentur za Nauchno-Meditsinska Informatsiia - Medical and Public Health Scientific Information Centre, 1, Sveti Georgi Sofijski St., 1431 Sofia, Bulgaria. TEL 52-23-42. FAX 52-23-93. (Subscr. to: "Hemus", 7 Levski St., 1000 Sofia, Bulgaria) Ed. L. Sirakov. abstr.; index; circ. 540 (Eng. ed.). **Indexed:** Chem.Abstr.

616.98   UK   ISSN 0260-5511
RA421
ABSTRACTS ON HYGIENE AND COMMUNICABLE DISEASES. 1926. m. £80($150) to individuals; institutions £150($290). Bureau of Hygiene and Tropical Diseases, Keppel St., London WC1E 7HT, England. TEL 071-636-8636. FAX 071-580-6756. TELEX 8953474-LSHTML-G. Ed. D.W. FitzSimons. adv.; bk.rev.; abstr.; index; circ. 1,000. (also avail. in microform from UMI) **Indexed:** Biol.Abstr., C.I.S. Abstr., Ergon.Abstr., Ind.Vet., Nutr.Abstr., Rev.Appl.Entomol., Rev.Plant Path., Vet.Bull., World Text.Abstr.
●Also available online. Vendor(s): DIMDI.
—BLDSC shelfmark: 0564.407000.
  Former titles: Abstracts on Hygiene (ISSN 0001-3692); Bulletin of Hygiene.

MEDICAL SCIENCES — ABSTRACTING, BIBLIOGRAPHIES, STATISTICS

610 629.13   US   ISSN 0001-9410
Z6664.3
AEROSPACE MEDICINE AND BIOLOGY; a continuing bibliography. 1964. m. $19.50 (foreign $39) per no. U.S. National Aeronautics and Space Administration, Center for Aerospace Information, Box 8757, Baltimore - Washington International Airport, MD 21240. TEL 301-621-0153. (Dist. by: National Technical Information Service, 5285 Port Royal Rd., Springfield, VA 22161. TEL 703-487-4800) (Compiled by: U.S. Library of Congress and American Institute of Aeronautics and Astronautics) index. **Indexed:** Noise Pollut.Publ.Abstr.
   Formerly: Aerospace References in Medicine and Biology.

616.97   US
AMERICAN ACADEMY OF ALLERGY AND IMMUNOLOGY. ABSTRACT BOOK. (Published in Jan. issue of Journal of Allergy & Clinical Immunology and avail. separately) 1943. m. $9. (American Academy of Allergy and Immunology) Mosby - Year Book, Inc. (Subsidiary of: Times Mirror Company), 11830 Westline Industrial Dr., St. Louis, MO 63146. TEL 800-325-4117. FAX 314-432-1380. TELEX 44-2402. Ed. Burton Zweiman, M.D. adv.; bk.rev.; charts; illus.; stat.; index; cum.index; circ. 8,501. (back issues avail.)
   Description: Abstracts of papers presented at annual meeting of the Academy.

AMERICAN ASSOCIATION OF COLLEGES OF OSTEOPATHIC MEDICINE. ANNUAL STATISTICAL REPORT. see EDUCATION — *Abstracting, Bibliographies, Statistics*

616.1 011   US
AMERICAN COLLEGE OF CARDIOLOGY. ABSTRACTS. a. price varies. (American College of Cardiology) Elsevier Science Publishing Co., Inc. (New York), 655 Ave. of the Americas, New York, NY 10010. TEL 212-989-5800. FAX 212-633-3965. TELEX 420643 AEP UI.
   Refereed Serial

AMERICAN PSYCHIATRIC ASSOCIATION. SCIENTIFIC PROCEEDINGS IN SUMMARY FORM. see MEDICAL SCIENCES — *Psychiatry And Neurology*

610 013   PL   ISSN 0066-1937
ANNALES ACADEMIAE MEDICAE CRACOVIENSIS. INDEX DISSERTATIONUM EDITARUM. (Text in English, Polish and Russian) 1955. a. price varies. Akademia Medyczna, Krakow, Botaniczna 3, Krakow, Poland. (Dist. by: Ars Polona-Ruch, Krakowskie Przedmiescie 7, Warsaw, Poland) Ed. Dr. Mieczyslaw Goldsztajn. circ. 1,000.

616.1   US   ISSN 0952-0562
ANNUAL OF CARDIAC SURGERY. 1987. a. $160. Current Science, 20 N. Third St., Philadelphia, PA 19106. TEL 800-552-5866. FAX 215-574-2270. Ed. Magdi Yacoub. illus.; circ. 3,000.
   —BLDSC shelfmark: 1077.965000.
   Description: For cardiac surgeons, cardiologists and researchers involved with coronary artery disease. Reviews the year's research papers and presents invited reviews in featured areas such as pediatric and fetal cardiac surgery.

610 016   CS
ANNUAL OF CZECHOSLOVAK MEDICAL LITERATURE. (Text in English) 1956. a. free. Ustav Vedeckych Lekarskych Informaci, Sokolska 31, 121 32 Prague 2, Czechoslovakia. TEL 299956. index; circ. 400. (microfiche)

616.3   US   ISSN 0952-6293
ANNUAL OF GASTROINTESTINAL ENDOSCOPY. (Suppl. avail.: Slide Atlas of Gastrointestinal Endoscopy (Year)) 1988. a. $200. Current Science, 20 N. Third St., Philadelphia, PA 19106. TEL 800-552-5866. FAX 215-574-2270. Ed.Bd. illus.; circ. 7,500.
   —BLDSC shelfmark: 1085.673500.
   Description: For physicians, endoscopists, surgeons, radiologists and others interested in gastroenterology and gastrointestinal imaging or therapy.

617.6   US
ANNUAL REPORT ON ALLIED DENTAL HEALTH EDUCATION. 1967. a. American Dental Association, 211 E. Chicago Ave., Chicago, IL 60611. TEL 312-440-2674. Ed. Robert N. Czarnecki. **Indexed:** SRI.
   Formerly: Annual Report on Dental Auxillary Education (ISSN 0084-6554)

617.6   US   ISSN 0065-8030
ANNUAL REPORT ON DENTAL EDUCATION. 1967. a. American Dental Association, 211 E. Chicago Ave., Chicago, IL 60611. TEL 312-440-2674. Ed. Robert N. Czarnecki. **Indexed:** SRI.
   Formerly: Dental Students' Register (ISSN 0065-8049)

610   AT
▼**ASIAN MEDICAL EDUCATION INDEX.** 1991. irreg. (approx. 3/yr.). Aus.$298. Noyce Publishing, G.P.O. Box 2222T, Melbourne, Vic. 3001, Australia.

610   AT
▼**AUSTRALASIAN AND NEW ZEALAND MEDICAL EDUCATION INDEX.** 1991. irreg. (approx. 3/yr.). Aus.$298. Noyce Publishing, G.P.O. Box 2222T, Melbourne, Vic. 3001, Australia.
   Description: Indexes journal articles, monographic literature, theses, dissertations and conference papers on medical, nursing and health sciences education in Australia, New Zealand, Papua New Guinea and the South Pacific.

618 016   GW
BERICHTE GYNAEKOLOGIE - GEBURTSHILFE/GYNECOLOGY - OBSTETRICS. 13/yr. DM.1880($944) Springer-Verlag, Heidelberger Platz 3, D-1000 Berlin 33, Germany. TEL 030-8207-1. Ed. H. Ludwig. (also avail. in microform from UMI; reprint service avail. from ISI)
   Formerly: Berichte Gynaekologie und Geburtshilfe Sowie Deren Grenzgebiete (ISSN 0722-9852)
   Description: Abstracts articles in gynecology-obstetrics.

616.07 016   GW   ISSN 0722-9674
BERICHTE PATHOLOGIE/TRENDS IN PATHOLOGY. 1948. 26/yr. DM.2348($1263) Springer-Verlag, Heidelberger Platz 3, D-1000 Berlin 3, Germany. TEL 030-8207-1. (Also Heidelberg, Tokyo, Vienna, and New York) Ed. A. Bohle. (also avail. in microform from UMI; back issues avail.; reprint service avail. from ISI)
   Former titles: Pathologie; Berichte ueber die Allgemeine und Spezielle Pathologie (ISSN 0005-9056)
   Description: Abstracts articles in pathology.

617.643   BL   ISSN 0100-6266
BIBLIOGRAFIA BRASILEIRA DE ODONTOLOGIA. (Text in Portuguese; introduction and information in English) 1966. biennial. $6 to individuals; free to institutions. Universidade de Sao Paulo, Faculdade de Odontologia, Seccao de Documentacao Odontologica, Caixa Postal 8216, 01000 Sao Paulo, Brazil. circ. 700.

610 016   CI   ISSN 0067-6799
BIBLIOGRAFIJA MEDICINSKE PERIODIKE JUGOSLAVIJE/INDEX MEDICUS IUGOSLAVICUS. (Text in Serbo-Croatian; summaries in English, French, German and Russian) 1966. a. 150 din.($10) Opca Bolnica "Dr. Josip Kajfes", Miskine 64, Zagreb, Croatia.

610 016   CS   ISSN 0067-6802
BIBLIOGRAPHIA MEDICA CECHOSLOVACA. 1947. m. 840 Kcs. Ustav Vedeckych Lekarskych Informaci, Sokolska 31, 121 32 Prague 2, Czechoslovakia. TELEX 121293. Ed. M. Votipkova. index; circ. 110. (avail. on floppy disk)
   ●Also available online.
   —BLDSC shelfmark: 1963.400000.

610 011   US   ISSN 0896-6591
BIBLIOGRAPHIES AND INDEXES IN MEDICAL STUDIES. 1988. irreg. price varies. Greenwood Press, Inc. (Subsidiary of: Greenwood Publishing Group Inc.), 88 Post Rd. W., Box 5007, Westport, CT 06881-5007. TEL 203-226-3571. FAX 203-222-1502.

BIBLIOGRAPHIES IN THE HISTORY OF PSYCHOLOGY AND PSYCHIATRY. see PSYCHOLOGY — *Abstracting, Bibliographies, Statistics*

610 016   US   ISSN 0363-0161
Z6675.E8
BIBLIOGRAPHY OF BIOETHICS. 1975. a. price varies. Kennedy Institute of Ethics, National Reference Center for Bioethics Literature, Georgetown University, Washington, DC 20057. TEL 202-687-6738. FAX 202-687-6770. Eds. LeRoy Walters, Tamar Joy Kahn. circ. 1,500. **Indexed:** CERDIC.
   ●Also available online. Vendor(s): National Library of Medicine, Telesystemes - Questel (BIOETHICS).
   —BLDSC shelfmark: 2002.127000.

616.8 016   UK   ISSN 0067-7183
BIBLIOGRAPHY OF DEVELOPMENTAL MEDICINE AND CHILD NEUROLOGY. BOOKS AND ARTICLES RECEIVED. (Supplement to: Developmental Medicine and Child Neurology: ISSN 0012-1622) 1962. a. price varies. Mac Keith Press, 5A Netherhall Gardens, London NW3 5RN, England. TEL 01-794-9859. FAX 01-431-5183. (Dist. in U.S. by: Cambridge University Press, 110 Midland Ave, Port Chester, NY 10573-9864.) Ed. B. Hays. circ. 5,200. (reprint service avail. from UMI) **Indexed:** Nutr.Abstr.
   Description: Selected list of books and articles from the world medical literature, usually running 2400 listings, with subject and author indexes

BIBLIOGRAPHY OF REPRODUCTION; a classified monthly list of references compiled from research literature. see BIOLOGY — *Abstracting, Bibliographies, Statistics*

610 016   US   ISSN 0067-7280
Z6660
BIBLIOGRAPHY OF THE HISTORY OF MEDICINE. 1965. a., quinquennial cumulation. price varies. U.S. National Library of Medicine, 8600 Rockville Pike, Bethesda, MD 20894. TEL 301-496-6308. FAX 301-496-4450. (Orders to: Supt. of Documents, Washington, DC 20402)
   ●Also available online. Vendor(s): National Library of Medicine.
   Description: Bibliographic listing of citations dealing with the history of medicine and its related sciences and professions.

610 174.2   US
BIOETHICS LITERATURE REVIEW. m. $45 to individuals; institutions $65. University Publishing Group, Inc., 107 E. Church St., Frederick, MD 21701. TEL 800-654-8188.
   Description: Covers recent literature in bioethics and related subject areas; reviews hundreds of health, medical, and major law journals.

610   XV   ISSN 0352-8685
BIOMEDICINA IUGOSLAVICA; index medicus iugoslavicus. (Text in English) 1986. q. $50. Istitut za Biomedicinsko Informatiko, Medicinska Fakulteta, Vrazov trg 2, YU-61105 Ljubljana, Slovenia. TEL 061 313-233. FAX 38-61-311540. Ed. Stefan Adamic. circ. 250. (also avail. in magnetic tape; back issues avail.)

610   US
▼**BREAST DISEASES (ST. LOUIS).** 1990. q. $69 to individuals (foreign $83); institutions $89 (foreign $103); students $45 (foreign $59). Mosby - Year Book, Inc. (Subsidiary of: Times Mirror Company), 11830 Westline Industrial Dr., St. Louis, MO 63146. TEL 800-325-4117. FAX 314-432-1380. TELEX 44-2402. (also avail. in microform from UMI; reprint service avail. from UMI)
   Description: Provides an interdisciplinary perspective on advances in prevention, diagnosis, and management of breast diseases. Each issue includes more than 40 abstracts selected from 700 different journals worldwide.

649 016   US   ISSN 0896-4572
BREASTFEEDING ABSTRACTS. 1981. q. $9.50. La Leche League International, Inc., 9616 Minneapolis Ave., Box 1209, Franklin Park, IL 60131. TEL 708-455-7730. FAX 708-455-0125. Ed. Gwen Gotsch. bk.rev.; abstr.; circ. 1,100.
   —BLDSC shelfmark: 2277.494250.
   Description: Abstracts of medical journal articles related to breastfeeding.

MEDICAL SCIENCES — ABSTRACTING, BIBLIOGRAPHIES, STATISTICS

610   GW
BUECHER FUER DAS STUDIUM - MEDIZIN. a. Dr. Lothar Rossipaul Verlagsgesellschaft mbH, Menzingerstr. 37, 8000 Munich 19, Germany. TEL 089-179106-0. FAX 089-179106-22. Ed. Rainer Rossipaul. circ. 25,000.
Description: Bibliography of available medical books for students.

610   CI   ISSN 0350-1558
CODEN: BSYSA7
BULLETIN SCIENTIFIQUE. SECTION A: SCIENCES NATURELLES, TECHNIQUES ET MEDICALES. 1953. s-a. 700 din.($50) Jugoslavenska Akademija Znanosti i Umjetnosti - Yugoslav Academy of Sciences and Arts, Zrinski trg. 11, 41000 Zagreb, Croatia. TEL 41-433661. Ed. Zarko Dadic. index; circ. 1,000. (back issues avail.) **Indexed:** Biol.Abstr., Met.Abstr.

C A S BIOTECH UPDATES. ANTIBODY CONJUGATES. see CHEMISTRY — *Abstracting, Bibliographies, Statistics*

616.7   US   ISSN 1040-7111
CODEN: CAISEK
C A SELECTS. A I D S AND RELATED IMMUNODEFICIENCIES. 1989. s-w. $195. Chemical Abstracts Service (Subsidiary of: American Chemical Society), 2540 Olentangy River Rd., Box 3012, Columbus, OH 43210. TEL 614-447-3600. FAX 614-447-3713. TELEX 6842086.
Description: Covers etiology, pathophysiology, clinical manifestations, diagnosis, and therapy of AIDS and other immunodeficiencies.

616.97   US   ISSN 1047-8191
CODEN: CSAGE2
C A SELECTS. ALLERGY AND ANTIALLERGIC AGENTS. 1981. s-w. $195. Chemical Abstracts Service (Subsidiary of: American Chemical Society), 2540 Olentangy River Rd., Box 3012, Columbus, OH 43210. TEL 614-447-3600. FAX 614-447-3713. TELEX 6842086. (reprint service avail.)
Formerly (until 1989): BIOSIS CAS Selects: Allergy and Antiallergy (ISSN 0276-3095)
Description: Covers the pathogenesis, diagnosis, and biochemistry of various allergic conditions, including asthma, dermatitis, and allergies of food, drugs, and environmental agents.

616.8   US   ISSN 1047-8183
CODEN: CSDDE8
C A SELECTS. ALZHEIMER'S DISEASE & RELATED MEMORY DYSFUNCTIONS. 1986. s-w. $195. Chemical Abstracts Service (Subsidiary of: American Chemical Society), 2540 Olentangy River Rd., Box 3012, Columbus, OH 43210. TEL 614-447-3600. FAX 614-447-3713. TELEX 6842086.
Formerly (until 1989): BIOSIS CAS Selects: Alzheimer's Disease and Senile Dementias.
Description: Covers Alzheimer's Disease and related dementias; includes pathogenesis, diagnosis, and biochemistry of the disease as well as studies on drugs that control such dementias.

616.7   US   ISSN 0148-2394
CODEN: CSARDY
C A SELECTS. ANTI-INFLAMMATORY AGENTS AND ARTHRITIS. s-w. $195. Chemical Abstracts Service (Subsidiary of: American Chemical Society), 2540 Olentangy River Rd., Box 3012, Columbus, OH 43210. TEL 614-447-3600. FAX 614-447-3713. TELEX 6842086.
Description: Covers biochemistry of arthritis and rheumatism; effects and mechanism of action of inflammation inhibitors; and synthesis and structure-activity relationships of drugs with potential anti-inflammatory activity.

616.1   US   ISSN 1051-3892
CODEN: CANTEE
▼**C A SELECTS. ANTIARRHYTHMICS.** 1990. s-w. $195. Chemical Abstracts Service (Subsidiary of: American Chemical Society), 2540 Olentangy River Rd., Box 3012, Columbus, OH 43210. TEL 614-447-3600. FAX 614-447-3713. TELEX 6842086.
Description: Covers established and developmental drugs that ameliorate disorders of normal heart rhythms.

610   US   ISSN 1047-8175
CODEN: CSALEH
C A SELECTS. ANTICONVULSANTS & ANTIEPILEPTICS. 1986. s-w. $195. Chemical Abstracts Service (Subsidiary of: American Chemical Society), 2540 Olentangy River Rd., Box 3012, Columbus, OH 43210. TEL 614-447-3600. FAX 614-447-3713. TELEX 6842086.
Formerly (until 1989): BIOSIS CAS Selects: Anticonvulsants.
Description: Covers the anticonvulsant and antiepileptic activities of both established and developmental drugs. Includes synthesis, mechanism(s) of action, formulation, and structure-activity relationships.

610   US   ISSN 0148-2386
CODEN: CSAADH
C A SELECTS. ANTITUMOR AGENTS. s-w. $195. Chemical Abstracts Service (Subsidiary of: American Chemical Society), 2540 Olentangy River Rd., Box 3012, Columbus, OH 43210-0012. TEL 614-447-3600. FAX 614-447-3713. TELEX 6842086.
Description: Covers cytotoxic agents, antimetabolites, alkylating agents, neoplasm inhibitors; effect and mechanism of action; synthesis and structure-activity relationships of drugs with potential antitumor activity; and pharmacology of most common antitumor agents.

616.1   US   ISSN 0148-2378
CODEN: CASDDO
C A SELECTS. ATHEROSCLEROSIS & HEART DISEASE. s-w. $195. Chemical Abstracts Service (Subsidiary of: American Chemical Society), 2540 Olentangy River Rd., Box 3012, Columbus, OH 43210. TEL 614-447-3600. FAX 614-447-3713. TELEX 6842086.
Description: Covers atherosclerosis, arteriosclerosis, heart disease, hypertension, hypotension, embolic and thrombotic disorders, shock, pharmacology and treatment of cardiovascular disease.

616.8   US   ISSN 0162-7716
CODEN: CBASDK
C A SELECTS. BIOGENIC AMINES & THE NERVOUS SYSTEM. s-w. $195. Chemical Abstracts Service (Subsidiary of: American Chemical Society), 2540 Olentangy River Rd., Box 3012, Columbus, OH 43210. TEL 614-447-3600. FAX 614-447-3713. TELEX 6842086.
Description: Covers biogenic amines in the nervous system and neurotransmission.

616.15   US   ISSN 0162-7732
CODEN: CBCODI
C A SELECTS. BLOOD COAGULATION. s-w. $195. Chemical Abstracts Service (Subsidiary of: American Chemical Society), 2540 Olentangy River Rd., Box 3012, Columbus, OH 43210. TEL 614-447-3600. FAX 614-447-3713. TELEX 6842086.
Description: Covers blood-coagulation factors, vitamin K, anticoagulants; blood preservation and preservatives; and blood platelet biochemistry.

616.99   US   ISSN 0148-2408
CODEN: CSCTDG
C A SELECTS. CARCINOGENS, MUTAGENS & TERATOGENS. s-w. $195. Chemical Abstracts Service (Subsidiary of: American Chemical Society), 2540 Olentangy River Rd., Box 3012, Columbus, OH 43210. TEL 614-447-3600. FAX 614-447-3713. TELEX 6842086.
Description: Covers biological response to carcinogens, mutagens, and teratogens; mechanism of action and structural requirements for activity; detection and quantification in feed and food material; occupational exposure and resulting health hazard and safety requirements.

615.19   US   ISSN 1047-8205
C A SELECTS. DRUG INTERACTIONS. 1987. s-w. $195. Chemical Abstracts Service (Subsidiary of: American Chemical Society), 2540 Olentangy River Rd., Box 3012, Columbus, OH 43210. TEL 614-447-3600. FAX 614-337-3713. TELEX 6842086.
Formerly (until 1989): BIOSIS CAS Selects: Drug Interactions.
Description: Covers adverse, metabolic, and physicochemical drug interactions. Includes drug-drug, food-drug, and drug-alcohol interactions.

C A SELECTS. FORENSIC CHEMISTRY. see CHEMISTRY — *Abstracting, Bibliographies, Statistics*

610 612.015   US   ISSN 1051-3922
CODEN: CAHAET
▼**C A SELECTS. HYPERTENSION & ANTIHYPERTENSIVES.** 1990. s-w. $195. Chemical Abstracts Service (Subsidiary of: American Chemical Society), 2540 Olentangy River Rd., Box 3012, Columbus, OH 43210. TEL 614-447-3600. FAX 614-447-3713. TELEX 6842086.
Description: Covers etiology, pathophysiology, clinical manifestations, and diagnosis of hypertension.

616.97   US   ISSN 1048-874X
CODEN: CSIMEQ
C A SELECTS. IMMUNOCHEMICAL METHODS. 1981. s-w. $195. Chemical Abstracts Service (Subsidiary of: American Chemical Society), 2540 Olentangy River Rd., Box 3012, Columbus, OH 43210. TEL 614-447-3600. FAX 614-447-3713. TELEX 6842086. (reprint service avail.)
Formerly (until 1989): BIOSIS CAS Selects: Immunochemical Methods (ISSN 0276-3168)
Description: Covers use of antigen-antibody reactions in the detection, determination, and separation of sample components.

610 011   US   ISSN 1047-8094
CODEN: CMOAEC
C A SELECTS. MONOCLONAL ANTIBODIES. 1984. s-w. $195. Chemical Abstracts Service (Subsidiary of: American Chemical Society), 2540 Olentangy River Rd., Box 3012, Columbus, OH 43210. TEL 614-447-3600. FAX 614-447-3713. TELEX 6842086.
Formerly (until 1989): BIOSIS CAS Selects: Monoclonal Antibodies.
Description: Covers the preparation, characterization, and use of monoclonal antibodies and monoclonal antibody conjugates. Includes pathophysiology and hybridoma technology.

616.19 011   US   ISSN 1047-8116
C A SELECTS. NUTRITIONAL ASPECTS OF CANCER. 1985. s-w. $195. Chemical Abstracts Service (Subsidiary of: American Chemical Society), 2540 Olentangy River Rd., Box 3012, OH 43210. TEL 614-447-3600. FAX 614-447-3713. TELEX 6842086.
Formerly: BIOSIS CAS Selects: Cancer and Nutrition.
Description: Covers all aspects of cancer and nutrition; includes the role of nutrition in the development and control of neoplastic diseases.

610 011   US   ISSN 1047-8132
CODEN: CSOLEJ
C A SELECTS. OSTEOPOROSIS & RELATED BONE LOSS. 1989. s-w. $195. Chemical Abstracts Service (Subsidiary of: American Chemical Society), 2540 Olentangy River Rd., Box 3012, OH 43210. TEL 614-447-3600. FAX 614-447-3713. TELEX 6842086.
Formerly (until 1989): BIOSIS CAS Selects: Osteoporosis.
Description: Covers osteoporosis and related bone losses; includes the etiology, diagnosis, pathophysiology, biochemistry, and pharmacology of osteoporosis.

616.07   US   ISSN 1047-8159
CODEN: CSUIE6
C A SELECTS. ULCER INHIBITORS. 1986. s-w. $195. Chemical Abstracts Service (Subsidiary of: American Chemical Society), 2540 Olentangy River Rd., Box 3012, Columbus, OH 43210. TEL 614-447-3600. FAX 614-447-3713. TELEX 6842086.
Formerly: BIOSIS CAS Selects: Antiulcer Agents.
Description: Covers the digestive-tract antiulcer inhibitors of both established and developmental drugs; includes synthesis, mechanic(s) of action, formulation, and structure-activity relationship.

MEDICAL SCIENCES — ABSTRACTING, BIBLIOGRAPHIES, STATISTICS

616.8 011   US   ISSN 0141-7711
QP351
C S A NEUROSCIENCES ABSTRACTS. 1982. m. $635 (foreign $695). Cambridge Scientific Abstracts, 7200 Wisconsin Ave., 6th Fl., Bethesda, MD 20814. TEL 301-961-6750. FAX 301-961-6720. TELEX 910 2507547 CAMB MD. abstr.; index. (also avail. in magnetic tape; back issues avail.)
●Also available online. Vendor(s): BRS (CSAL), DIALOG (File no.76/LIFE SCIENCES COLLECTION). Also available on CD-ROM. Producer(s): Cambridge Scientific Abstracts (Compact Cambridge Life Sciences Collection).
Incorporates: Endocrinology Abstracts (ISSN 0749-8020)
Description: Covers all aspects of vertebrate and invertebrate neuroscience, with separate section on endocrinology.

016 610   CN   ISSN 0707-7629
Z6660
CANADIAN LOCATIONS OF JOURNALS INDEXED FOR MEDLINE/DEPOTS CANADIENS DES REVUES INDEXEES POUR MEDLINE. 1970. a. Can.$48. (National Research Council of Canada) Canada Institute for Scientific and Technical Information, Health Sciences Resource Centre, Ottawa, Ont. K1A 0S2, Canada. TEL 613-993-1601. circ. 300.
—BLDSC shelfmark: 3037.773000.
Formerly: Canadian Locations of Journals Indexed in Index Medicus (ISSN 0316-3938)

616.994 016   US
RC261
CANCERGRAM. 1962. m. $20. U.S. National Cancer Institute, International Cancer Information Center, Bethesda, MD 20892. TEL 301-496-7403. (Dist. by: Supt. of Documents, Washington, DC 20402) circ. 3,900.
Formerly: Carcinogenesis Abstracts (ISSN 0008-6258)

011 616.99 649   US
CANDLELIGHTERS CHILDHOOD CANCER FOUNDATION BIBLIOGRAPHY AND RESOURCE GUIDE. 1976. a. $5 (Canada $8; elsewhere $11). Candlelighters Childhood Cancer Foundation, 1312 18th St., N.W., Ste. 200, Washington, DC 20036-1808. TEL 202-659-5136. bk.rev.; circ. 3,000.
Former titles: Candlelighters Childhood Cancer Foundation Annotated Bibliography and Resource Guide; Candlelighters Foundation Bibliography and Resource Guide.

616.1 016   IT   ISSN 0008-6320
CARDIOLOGIA NEL MONDO; recensioni di riviste di cardiologia di tutto il mondo. 1950. m. L.50000($70) C N M s.r.l., Via Cimabue 28, 20032 Cormano (MI), Italy. FAX 6155-3239. TELEX 323126 FARSIM I. Dir. Prof. G. Marchetti. adv.; circ. 10,000.

617 016   GW   ISSN 0009-4722
DER CHIRURG; Zeitschrift fuer alle Gebiete der operativen Medizin. 1928. 12/yr. DM.354($190) (Berufsverband der Deutschen Chirurgen, e.V.) Springer-Verlag, Heidelberger Platz 3, D-1000 Berlin 33, Germany. TEL 030-8207-1. Ed. C. Herfarth. adv.; bk.rev.; abstr.; bibl.; charts; illus.; index. (also avail. in microform from UMI; back issues avail.; reprint service avail. from ISI) **Indexed:** Biol.Abstr., Biotech.Abstr., Chem.Abstr., Curr.Adv.Cancer Res., Curr.Cont., Dok.Arbeitsmed., Excerpt.Med., Helminthol.Abstr., Ind.Med., Ind.Sci.Rev., INIS Atomind., Nutr.Abstr., Sci.Cit.Ind.
—BLDSC shelfmark: 3181.150000.

610 011   US   ISSN 1043-3031
CODEN: CCTFEG
CLINICAL ABSTRACTS - CURRENT THERAPEUTIC FINDINGS. Short title: C A - C T F. vol.9, no.11, 1990. m. $32 to individuals; institutions $45; students $15. Harvey Whitney Books Company, Box 42696, Cincinnati, OH 45242. TEL 513-793-3555. FAX 513-793-3600. Ed.Bd.

616.07   NE   ISSN 0345-200X
CLINICAL CHEMISTRY LOOKOUT. (Text in English) 1974. 12/yr. fl.660 (effective 1992). (Swedish Society for Clinical Chemistry, SW) Elsevier Science Publishers B.V., P.O. Box 211, 1000 AE Amsterdam, Netherlands. TEL 020-5803911. FAX 020-5803598. TELEX 18582 ESPA NL. (Subscr. in U.S. and Canada to: Elsevier Science Publishing Co., Inc., Box 882, Madison Sq. Sta., New York, NY 10159. TEL 212-989-5800) Ed.Bd. adv.; index. cum.index. (reprint service avail. from ISI) **Indexed:** Excerp.Med.
Description: Contains classified and indexed abstracts and citations from more than 1000 international scientific and medical publications.
Refereed Serial

610 016   US   ISSN 0009-9279
CODEN: CLREAS
CLINICAL RESEARCH. 1953. 4/yr. $70 to non-members; institutions $100; foreign $75. (American Federation for Clinical Research) Slack, Inc., 6900 Grove Rd., Thorofare, NJ 08086. TEL 609-848-1000. FAX 609-853-5991. Ed. Dr. Joseph Craft. adv.; abstr.; illus.; index; circ. 11,675. (also avail. in microform from UMI) **Indexed:** Biol.Abstr., Biotech.Abstr., Chem.Abstr., Curr.Adv.Ecol.Sci., Curr.Cont., Excerp.Med., Helminthol.Abstr., Ind.Med., Ind.Sci.Rev., NRN, Risk Abstr., Sci.Cit.Ind., Telegen.
—BLDSC shelfmark: 3286.372000.
Refereed Serial

616.1   US   ISSN 0958-1650
▼**CLINICIAN'S MANUAL ON HYPERLIPIDEMIA (YEAR).** 1991. a. $30. Current Science, 20 N. Third St., Philadelphia, PA 19106. TEL 800-552-5866. FAX 215-574-2270. Ed. A.M. Gotto. illus.
Description: For the general practitioner. Focuses on hyperlipidemia, including diagnostic, treatment and screening concerns.

616.1   US   ISSN 0952-6307
▼**CLINICIAN'S MANUAL ON HYPERTENSION (YEAR).** 1990. a. $30. Current Science, 20 N. Third St., Philadelphia, PA 19106. TEL 800-552-5866. FAX 215-574-2270. Ed.Bd.
Description: For the general practitioner. Focuses on all aspects of hypertension treatment in a concise, easy-to-read format.

621.387 610   US
CLINMED - C D. (Compact Disc) bi-m. $850. SilverPlatter Information, Inc., 100 River Ridge Dr., Norwood, MA 02062. TEL 617-239-0306. FAX 617-235-1715. (UK addr.: 10 Barley Mow Passage, Chiswick, London W4 4PH, England)
●Available only on CD-ROM.
Description: A subset of the entire MEDLINE database focusing on clinical medicine encompassing citations from over 300 journals, primarily in English.

618   US   ISSN 0884-8092
COMBINED CUMULATIVE INDEX TO OBSTETRICS AND GYNECOLOGY. 1984. a. $125. Numarc Book Corporation, 60 Alcona Ave., Buffalo, NY 14226. TEL 716-834-1390. Ed. Carl W. Hepp. circ. 2,000. (back issues avail.)

618   US   ISSN 0190-4981
Z6671.5
COMBINED CUMULATIVE INDEX TO PEDIATRICS. 1979. a. $112.50. Numarc Book Corporation, 60 Alcona Ave., Buffalo, NY 14226. TEL 716-834-1390. Ed. Carl W. Hepp. circ. 2,000. (back issues avail.)

615.53 616.891
641.1   UK   ISSN 0950-6667
COMPLEMENTARY MEDICINE INDEX. m. £45 (foreign £62). Medical Information Service, The British Library, Boston Spa, Wetherby, W. Yorkshire LS23 7BQ, England. TEL 0937-546039. FAX 0937-546236. index.
●Also available online.
—BLDSC shelfmark: 3364.203720.
Description: Lists current index of literature for alternative medicine.

618.92   US
COMPREHENSIVE MANUALS IN PEDIATRICS. 1982. irreg. price varies. Springer-Verlag, 175 Fifth Ave., New York, NY 10010. TEL 212-460-1500. (Also Berlin, Heidelberg, Tokyo and Vienna) Eds. M. Katz, E.R. Stiehm.

617.75   US   ISSN 0885-9264
CONTACT LENS UPDATE. 1982. bi-m. $59 to individuals (foreign $74); institutions $69 (foreign $84). Anadem Publishing, Inc., 3620 N. High St., Columbus, OH 43214. TEL 614-262-2539. index. (looseleaf format)
Description: Summarizes medical and optometry journal articles about specialty contact lens practice.

617.7   US
CONTACTO. 1955. q. $125 to individuals (foreign $140); institutions $80 (foreign $85). National Eye Research Foundation, 910 Skokie Blvd., Ste. 207A, Northbrook, IL 60062. TEL 312-564-4652. Ed. Roy K.A. Wesley. adv.; bk.rev.; charts; illus.; index; circ. 500. **Indexed:** Excerp.Med.
Former titles: Contacto: Mini-Abstracts; Contacto (ISSN 0045-8317)
Description: Discusses contact lenses.

616.12   NE   ISSN 0165-9405
CODEN: CJCADW
CORE JOURNALS IN CARDIOLOGY. (Text in English) 1980. 11/yr. fl.435 (effective 1992). Elsevier Science Publishers B.V., P.O. Box 211, 1000 AE Amsterdam, Netherlands. TEL 020-5803911. FAX 020-5803598. TELEX 18582 ESPA NL. (Subscr. to: Excerpta Medica Core Journals, P.O. Box 85, Limerick, Ireland. TEL 061-61944; Subscr. in U.S. and Canada to: Elsevier Science Publishing Co., Inc., Box 882, Madison Sq. Sta., New York, NY 10159. TEL 212-989-5800) Ed.Bd.
—BLDSC shelfmark: 3470.620000.
Description: Abstracts of relevant articles in cardiology from the principal medical journals.
Refereed Serial

016 616.8   NE   ISSN 0165-1056
CORE JOURNALS IN CLINICAL NEUROLOGY. 1978. 11/yr. fl.435 (effective 1992). Elsevier Science Publishers B.V., P.O. Box 211, 1000 AE Amsterdam, Netherlands. TEL 020-5803911. FAX 020-5803598. TELEX 18582 ESPA NL. (Subscr. to: Excerpta Medica Core Journals, P.O. Box 85, Limerick, Ireland. TEL 061-61944; Subscr. in U.S. and Canada to: Elsevier Science Publishing Co., Inc., Box 882, Madison Sq. Sta., New York, NY 10159. TEL 212-989-5800)
Description: Current awareness service reporting relevant developments in clinical neurology from the principal medical journals.
Refereed Serial

616.5   NE   ISSN 0167-5796
CORE JOURNALS IN DERMATOLOGY. (Text in English) 1982. 11/yr. fl.435 (effective 1992). Elsevier Science Publishers B.V., P.O. Box 211, 1000 AE Amsterdam, Netherlands. TEL 020-5803911. FAX 020-5803598. TELEX 18582 ESPA NL. (Subscr. to: Excerpta Medica Core Journals, P.O. Box 85, Limerick, Ireland. TEL 061-61944; Subscr. in U.S. and Canada to: Elsevier Science Publishing Co., Inc., Box 882, Madison Sq. Sta., New York, NY 10159. TEL 212-989-5800) Ed.Bd.
Description: Current awareness service reporting important developments in dermatology from the principal medical journals.
Refereed Serial

616.3   NE   ISSN 0165-8719
CODEN: CJGADI
CORE JOURNALS IN GASTROENTEROLOGY. (Text in English) 1980. 11/yr. fl.435 (effective 1992). Elsevier Science Publishers B.V., P.O. Box 211, 1000 AE Amsterdam, Netherlands. TEL 020-5803911. FAX 020-5803598. TELEX 18582 ESPA NL. (Subscr. to: Excerpta Medica Core Journals, P.O. Box 85, Limerick, Ireland. TEL 061-61944; Subscr. in U.S. and Canada to: Elsevier Science Publishing Co., Inc., Box 882, Madison Sq. Sta., New York, NY 10159. TEL 212-989-5800) Ed.Bd.
Description: Current awareness service providing abstracts of recent papers in gastroenterology from the principal medical journals.
Refereed Serial

MEDICAL SCIENCES — ABSTRACTING, BIBLIOGRAPHIES, STATISTICS

618 016 NE ISSN 0376-5059
CODEN: CJOGD8
CORE JOURNALS IN OBSTETRICS - GYNECOLOGY. 1977. 11/yr. fl.435 (effective 1992). Elsevier Science Publishers B.V., P.O. Box 211, 1000 AE Amsterdam, Netherlands. TEL 020-5803911. FAX 020-5803598. TELEX 18582 ESPA NL. (Subscr. to: Excerpta Medica Core Journals, P.O. Box 85, Limerick, Ireland. TEL 061-61944; Subscr. in U.S. and Canada to: Elsevier Science Publishing Co., Inc., Box 882, Madison Sq. Sta., New York, NY 10159. TEL 212-989-5800)
Description: Current awareness service providing abstracts of recent articles relevant to obstetrics and gynecology from the principal medical journals.
Refereed Serial

016 617.7 NE ISSN 0165-1005
CORE JOURNALS IN OPHTHALMOLOGY. 1978. 11/yr. fl.435 (effective 1992). Elsevier Science Publishers B.V., P.O. Box 211, 1000 AE Amsterdam, Netherlands. TEL 020-5803911. FAX 020-5803598. TELEX 18582 ESPA NL. (Subscr. to: Excerpta Medica Core Journals, P.O. Box 85, Limerick, Ireland. TEL 061-61944; Subscr. in U.S. and Canada to: Elsevier Science Publishing Co., Inc., Box 882, Madison Sq. Sta., New York, NY 10159. TEL 212-989-5800)
Description: Current awareness service providing abstracts of recent papers in ophthalmology from the principal medical journals.
Refereed Serial

618.92 016 NE ISSN 0376-5040
CODEN: CJPED7
CORE JOURNALS IN PEDIATRICS. 1978. 11/yr. fl.435 (effective 1992). Elsevier Science Publishers B.V., P.O. Box 211, 1000 AE Amsterdam, Netherlands. TEL 020-5803911. FAX 020-5803598. TELEX 18582 ESPA NL. (Subscr. to: Excerpta Medica Core Journals, P.O. Box 85, Limerick, Ireland. TEL 061-61944; Subscr. in U.S. and Canada to: Elsevier Science Publishing Co., Inc. Box 882, Madison Sq. Sta., New York, NY 10159. TEL 212-989-5800)
Description: Current awareness service providing abstracts of current papers from the principal medical journals on topics pertaining to pediatrics.
Refereed Serial

616.1 US ISSN 0954-6928
RC685.C6 CODEN: CADIEX
▼**CORONARY ARTERY DISEASE.** 1990. bi-m. $125 to individuals; institutions $200. Current Science, 10 N. Third St., Philadelphia, PA 19106. TEL 800-552-5866. FAX 215-574-2270. Ed. Dr. Burton E. Sobel. adv.; illus.; circ. 1,500. (also avail. on diskette)
—BLDSC shelfmark: 3472.049000.
Description: Presents original research and clinical investigations in the expanding field of coronary artery research; includes reviews with annotated references. Each issue features a bibliography of the current world literature published during the previous year.

610 016 US ISSN 0090-1377
Z6660
CUMULATED ABRIDGED INDEX MEDICUS. a. price varies. U.S. National Library of Medicine, 8600 Rockville Pike, Bethesda, MD 20894. TEL 301-496-6308. FAX 301-496-4450. (Orders to: Supt. of Documents, Washington, DC 20402) circ. 1,500.
Description: An annual cumulation in one volume of the citations appearing in the monthly "Abridged Index Medicus." Contains author and subject sections.

610 016 US ISSN 0090-1423
Z6660
CUMULATED INDEX MEDICUS. a. price varies. U.S. National Library of Medicine, 8600 Rockville Pike, Bethesda, MD 20894. TEL 301-496-6308. FAX 301-496-4450. (Orders to: Supt. of Documents, Washington, DC 20402) circ. 5,000. (also avail. in microfilm from UMI; microfiche; reprint service avail. from UMI) **Indexed:** MEDOC.
—BLDSC shelfmark: 4382.500000.
Supersedes: Quarterly Cumulated Index Medicus.
Description: A sixteen-volume cumulation of the citations appearing in "Index Medicus" for the previous year.

610.73 016 US ISSN 0146-5554
Z6675.N7
CUMULATIVE INDEX TO NURSING & ALLIED HEALTH LITERATURE. Short title: C I N A H L. 1961. bi-m. and a. $220 (includes 5 bi-m. issues). (C I N A H L) C I N H A L Information Systems, Box 871, Glendale, CA 91209-0871. TEL 818-409-8005. FAX 818-546-5679. Ed. DeLauna Lockwood. adv.; cum.index: 1956 to date; circ. 5,300. (also avail. in microform from UMI; reprint service avail. from UMI)
●Also available online. Vendor(s): BRS (NAHL), Data-Star, DIALOG (File no. 218).
Also available on CD-ROM. Producer(s): C I N A H L, SilverPlatter.
—BLDSC shelfmark: 3492.190000.
Incorporates: Nursing and Allied Health Index (ISSN 0744-8732); Which was formerly (1956-1976): Nursing Literature Index; (until 1977): Cumulative Index to Nursing Literature (ISSN 0011-3018); Incorporates: C I N A H L'S List of Subject Headings; Which was formerly (until 1977): Cumulative Index to Nursing Literature, Nursing Subject Headings (ISSN 0070-1793)

616.9 UK ISSN 0952-8075
CURRENT A I D S LITERATURE. 1986. m. £135($230) to individuals; institutions £225($390). Bureau of Hygiene and Tropical Diseases, Keppel St., London WC1E 7HT, England. TEL 071-636-8636. FAX 071-580-6756. TELEX 8953474-LSHTML-G. Ed. D.W. Fitzsimons. adv.; bk.rev.; illus.; circ. 900.
—BLDSC shelfmark: 3494.125000.
Formerly: A I D S and Retroviruses Update.
Description: Features information on every paper published on AIDS in the previous month in 1,400 journals. Includes brief summaries of every paper, commentary, literature overview, correspondence, addresses of authors, statistical data, and a cumulative author index.

616.994 US ISSN 0895-9803
CURRENT ADVANCES IN CANCER RESEARCH. 1988. m. £420 (effective 1992). Pergamon Press, Inc., Journals Division, 660 White Plains Rd., Tarrytown, NY 10591-5153. TEL 914-524-9200. FAX 914-333-2444. (And: Headington Hill Hall, Oxford OX3 0BW, England. TEL 0865-794141) Ed. H. Smith. (also avail. in microform; back issues avail.)
●Also available online. Vendor(s): BRS (CABS).
—BLDSC shelfmark: 3494.061500.
Description: Provides a current awareness service in the sphere of cancer research. Lists titles of cancer research papers published throughout the world and classified into 38 main areas, with a comprehensive list of review articles.
Refereed Serial

612 US ISSN 0964-8720
CURRENT ADVANCES IN ENDOCRINOLOGY & METABOLISM. 1984. m. £400 (effective 1992). Pergamon Press, Inc., Journals Division, 660 White Plains Rd., Tarrytown, NY 10591-5153. TEL 914-524-9200. FAX 914-333-2444. (And: Headington Hill Hall, Oxford OX3 0BW, England. TEL 0865-794141) Ed. H. Smith. adv. (also avail. in microfilm from MIM,UMI) **Indexed:** Curr.Cont.
●Also available online. Vendor(s): BRS (CABS).
—BLDSC shelfmark: 3494.063700.
Formerly (until 1992): Current Advances in Physiology (ISSN 0741-1693)
Description: Provides current awareness service in the fields of endocrinology and metabolic studies. Gives listings of titles of these papers published throughout the world classified into 149 main areas and provides a comprehensive listing of review articles.
Refereed Serial

616.97 US ISSN 0964-8747
Z6663.I4
CURRENT ADVANCES IN IMMUNOLOGY & INFECTIOUS DISEASES. 1984. m. £400 (effective 1992). Pergamon Press, Inc., Journals Division, 660 White Plains Rd., Tarrytown, NY 10591-5153. TEL 914-524-9200. FAX 914-333-2444. (And: Headington Hill Hall, Oxford OX3 0BW, England. TEL 0865-794141) Ed. H. Smith. adv.; abstr.; bibl. (also avail. in microform from MIM,UMI) **Indexed:** Curr.Cont.
●Also available online. Vendor(s): BRS (CABS).
—BLDSC shelfmark: 3494.064220.
Formerly (until 1992): Current Advances in Immunology (ISSN 0741-1650)
Description: Provides a current awareness service in the sphere of immunology and infectious diseases. Gives listings of titles of immunological papers published throughout the world classified into 271 main areas and provides a comprehensive listing of review articles.
Refereed Serial

616.8 US ISSN 0741-1677
QP351
CURRENT ADVANCES IN NEUROSCIENCE. 1984. m. £400 (effective 1992). Pergamon Press, Inc., Journals Division, 660 White Plains Rd., Tarrytown, NY 10591-5153. TEL 914-524-9200. FAX 914-333-2444. (And: Headington Hill Hall, Oxford OX3 0BW, England. TEL 0865-794141) Ed. H. Smith. adv. (also avail. in microform from MIM,UMI) **Indexed:** Curr.Cont.
●Also available online. Vendor(s): BRS (CABS).
—BLDSC shelfmark: 3494.064340.
Description: Provides a current awareness service in the sphere of neuroscience. Gives listings of titles of neuroscientific papers published throughout the world classified into 28 main areas and provides a comprehensive listing of review articles.
Refereed Serial

617 016 US ISSN 0149-5348
CURRENT BIBLIOGRAPHY OF PLASTIC & RECONSTRUCTIVE SURGERY.* 1973. bi-m. $45. Plastic Surgery Education Foundation, c/o American Society of Plastic Surgeons, 444 E. Algonquin Rd., Arlington Heights, IL 60005. TEL 301-252-4022. (Subscr. to: Creative Products, Inc., 23 Pinewood Farm Ct., Owings Mills, MD 21117) bibl.; circ. 1,000. (looseleaf format; back issues avail.)
●Also available online. Vendor(s): National Library of Medicine.
Formerly (until 1976): Ongoing Current Bibliography of Plastic and Reconstructive Surgery (ISSN 0360-1722)
Description: Covers plastic surgery.

610 016 US
CURRENT CONTENTS: CLINICAL MEDICINE. Short title: C C: C M. (Includes Author Index and Address Directory, Current Book Contents and Title Word Index) 1973. w. $360. Institute for Scientific Information, 3501 Market St., Philadelphia, PA 19104. TEL 215-386-0100. FAX 215-386-2991. (And: 132 High St., Uxbridge, Middlesex, UB8 1DP, England) (also avail. in magnetic tape; also avail. on diskette) **Indexed:** Compumath, Curr.Lit.Fam.Plan., Ind.Sci.Rev., Sci.Cit.Ind.
●Also available online. Vendor(s): BRS (CCON,CLIN), DIALOG (File no.440).
Formerly: Current Contents: Clinical Pratice (ISSN 0091-1704)
Description: Tables of contents of the world's most important publications covering clinical medicine.

CURRENT CONTENTS: LIFE SCIENCES. see *BIOLOGY — Abstracting, Bibliographies, Statistics*

616.6 US
CURRENT LITERATURE IN NEPHROLOGY, HYPERTENSION AND TRANSPLANTATION. 1982. m. $52 (foreign $64). Current Literature Publications, Inc., 1513 E St., Bellingham, WA 98225. TEL 206-676-2298. FAX 206-676-8814. Ed. Jon C. Ransom, M.D. adv.; index; circ. 1,400.
Formerly: Current Literature in Nephrology (ISSN 0743-8036)
Description: Bibliography of clinical nephrology.

MEDICAL SCIENCES — ABSTRACTING, BIBLIOGRAPHIES, STATISTICS

617.96 US ISSN 0952-7907
CURRENT OPINION IN ANAESTHESIOLOGY. 1988. bi-m. $145 to individuals; institutions $255; residents $102. Current Science, 20 N. Third St., Philadelphia, PA 19106. TEL 800-552-5866. FAX 215-574-2270. Eds. C. Prys-Roberts, J.G. Reves. illus.; circ. 3,300. (also avail. on diskette)
—BLDSC shelfmark: 3500.772000.
Description: Directed toward researchers and practicing anesthesiologists. Presents review articles followed by annotated bibliographies of references consulted. Includes a bibliography of the current world literature published during the previous year.

616.2 US ISSN 0268-4705
CODEN: COPCE3
CURRENT OPINION IN CARDIOLOGY. 1986. bi-m. $100 to individuals; institutions $170; residents $70. Current Science, 20 N. 3rd St., Philadelphia, PA 19106. TEL 800-552-5866. FAX 215-574-2270. Ed. Burton E. Sobel. illus.; circ. 6,750. (also avail. on diskette)
—BLDSC shelfmark: 3500.773000.
Description: Directed toward clinicians and surgeons in cardiology. Presents review articles followed by annotated bibliographies of references consulted. Includes a bibliography of the current world literature published during the previous year.

617.6 011 US ISSN 1046-0764
▼**CURRENT OPINION IN DENTISTRY.** 1991. bi-m. $100 to individuals; institutions $170. Current Science, 20 N. Third St., Philadelphia, PA 19106. TEL 800-552-5866. FAX 215-574-2270. Ed. Steven T. Sonis. (also avail. on diskette)
—BLDSC shelfmark: 3500.774000.
Description: Directed toward researchers and practicing dentists. Presents review articles followed by annotated bibliographies of references consulted. Includes a bibliography of the current world literature published during the previous year.

616.3 US ISSN 0267-1379
CODEN: COGAEK
CURRENT OPINION IN GASTROENTEROLOGY. 1985. bi-m. $100 to individuals; institutions $170; residents $70. Current Science, 20 N. 3rd St., Philadelphia, PA 19106. TEL 215-4574-2270. Ed. Robert M. Donaldson, Jr. illus.; circ. 8,600. (also avail. on diskette) **Indexed:** Curr.Adv.Cancer Res.
—BLDSC shelfmark: 3500.775000.
Description: Directed toward clinicians, surgeons and endoscopists. Presents review articles followed by annotated bibliographies of references consulted. Includes a bibliography of the current world literature published during the previous year.

616.97 US ISSN 0952-7915
CODEN: COPIEL
CURRENT OPINION IN IMMUNOLOGY. 1988. bi-m. $120 to individuals; institutions $275; residents $84. Current Science, 20 N. 3rd St., Philadelphia, PA 19106. TEL 800-552-5866. FAX 215-574-2270. Ed.Bd. adv.; illus.; circ. 850. (also avail. on diskette)
—BLDSC shelfmark: 3500.775300.
Description: Directed toward researchers, educators, and students in immunology. Presents review articles followed by annotated bibliographies of references consulted. Includes a bibliography of the current world literature published during the previous year.

616.9 US ISSN 0951-7375
RC109 CODEN: COIDE5
CURRENT OPINION IN INFECTIOUS DISEASES. 1988. bi-m. $100 to individuals; institutions $170; residents $70. Current Science, 10 N. 3rd St., Philadelphia, PA 19106. TEL 800-552-5866. FAX 215-574-2270. Eds. H.P. Lambert, J.P. Sanford. illus.; circ. 3,250. (also avail. on diskette)
—BLDSC shelfmark: 3500.775500.
Description: Directed toward clinicians and researchers in infectious diseases, both general and specialized. Presents review articles followed by annotated bibliographies of references consulted. Includes a bibliography of the current world literature published during the previous year.

616.1 US ISSN 0957-9672
QP751 CODEN: COPLEU
▼**CURRENT OPINION IN LIPIDOLOGY.** 1990. bi-m. $125 to individuals; institutions $195. Current Science, 20 N. Third St., Philadelphia, PA 19106. TEL 800-552-5866. FAX 215-574-2270. Ed. Dr. G.R. Thompson. illus.; circ. 4,000. (also avail. on diskette)
—BLDSC shelfmark: 3500.775800.
Description: Directed toward cardiologists involved with lipids in research and clinical practice. Presents reviews and updates on the latest developments in all areas of lipidology. Each issue features a bibliography of the current world literature published during the previous year.

616.8 US ISSN 0951-7383
CODEN: CNENE8
CURRENT OPINION IN NEUROLOGY & NEUROSURGERY. 1988. bi-m. $145 to individuals; institutions $255; redents $102. Current Science, 20 N. 3rd St., Philadelphia, PA 19106. TEL 800-552-5866. FAX 215-574-2270. Eds. R.T. Johnson, Lord Walton. illus.; circ. 4,000. (also avail. on diskette)
—BLDSC shelfmark: 3500.776000.
Description: Directed toward clinicians, surgeons and researchers in the field. Presents review articles followed by annotated bibliographies of references consulted. Includes a bibliography of the current world literature published during the previous year.

618 011 US ISSN 1040-872X
RG1 CODEN: COOGEA
CURRENT OPINION IN OBSTETRICS & GYNECOLOGY. 1989. bi-m. $125 to individuals; institutions $215; residents $88. Current Science, 20 N. 3rd St., Philadelphia, PA 19106. TEL 800-552-5866. FAX 215-574-2270. Ed. Edward E. Wallach. bibl.; illus.; circ. 1,000. (also avail. on diskette)
—BLDSC shelfmark: 3500.776200.
Description: Directed toward researchers and practicing obstetricians and gynecologists. Presents review articles followed by annotated bibliographies of references consulted. Includes a bibliography of the current world literature published during the previous year.

616.99 011 US ISSN 1040-8746
RC254.A1 CODEN: CUOOE8
CURRENT OPINION IN ONCOLOGY. 1989. bi-m. $145 to individuals; institutions $270; residents $102. Current Science, 20 N. 3rd St., Philadelphia, PA 19106. TEL 800-552-5866. FAX 215-427-4399. Ed. Martin D. Abeloff. bibl.; illus.; circ. 1,500. (also avail. on diskette)
—BLDSC shelfmark: 3500.776400.
Description: Directed toward researchers and practicing oncologists. Presents review articles followed by annotated bibliographies of references consulted. Includes a bibliography of the current world literature published during the previous year.

617.7 011 US ISSN 1040-8738
CODEN: COOTEF
▼**CURRENT OPINION IN OPHTHALMOLOGY.** (Suppl. avail.: Slide Atlas of Current Optomology (Year)) 1990. bi-m. $195 to individuals; institutions $340; residents $137. Current Science, 20 N. Third St., Philadelphia, PA 19106. TEL 800-552-5866. FAX 215-574-2270. Ed. George W. Weinstein. bibl.; illus.; circ. 500. (also avail. on diskette)
—BLDSC shelfmark: 3500.776500.
Description: Directed toward researchers and practicing ophthalmologists. Presents review articles followed by annotated bibliographies of references consulted. Includes a bibliography of the current world literature published during the previous year.

617.3 011 US ISSN 1041-9918
▼**CURRENT OPINION IN ORTHOPAEDICS.** (Suppl. avail.: Slide Atlas of Current Orthopaedics (Year)) 1990. bi-m. $145 to individuals; institutions $290; residents $102. Current Science, 20 N. 3rd St., Philadelphia, PA 19106. TEL 800-552-5866. FAX 215-574-2270. Ed. William R.J. Rennie. bibl.; illus.; circ. 1,500. (also avail. on diskette)
—BLDSC shelfmark: 3500.776600.
Description: Directed toward researchers and practicing orthopedists. Presents review articles followed by annotated bibliographies of references consulted. Includes a bibliography of the current world literature published during the previous year.

618.92 011 US ISSN 1040-8703
RJ1 CODEN: COPEE9
CURRENT OPINION IN PEDIATRICS. 1989. bi-m. $100 to individuals; institutions $170; residents $70. Current Science, 20 N. 3rd St., Philadelphia, PA 19106. TEL 800-552-5866. FAX 215-574-2270. Ed. David G. Nathan. bibl.; illus.; circ. 1,500. (also avail. on diskette)
—BLDSC shelfmark: 3500.776800.
Description: Directed toward researchers and practicing pediatricians. Presents review articles followed by annotated bibliographies of references consulted. Includes a bibliography of the current world literature published during the previous year.

616.8 US ISSN 0951-7367
CODEN: COPPE8
CURRENT OPINION IN PSYCHIATRY. 1988. bi-m. $145 to individuals; institutions $230; residents $102. Current Science, 20 N. 3rd St., Philadelphia, PA 19106. TEL 800-552-5866. FAX 215-574-2270. Eds. H.L. Freeman, D.J. Kuper. illus.; circ. 4,500. (also avail. on diskette)
—BLDSC shelfmark: 3500.777000.
Description: Directed toward practicing psychiatrists and researchers. Presents review articles followed by annotated bibliographies of references consulted. Includes a bibliography of the current world literature published during the previous year.

615.842 011 US ISSN 1040-869X
RC78.A1 CODEN: CORAE7
CURRENT OPINION IN RADIOLOGY. (Suppl. avail.: Slide Atlas of Current Radiology (Year)) 1989. bi-m. $145 to individuals; institutions $290; residents $102. Current Science, 20 N. 3rd St., Philadelphia, PA 19106. TEL 800-552-5866. FAX 215-574-2270. Ed. Alexander R. Margulis. bibl.; illus.; circ. 1,250. (also avail. on diskette)
—BLDSC shelfmark: 3500.777500.
Description: Directed toward researchers and practicing radiologists. Presents review articles followed by annotated bibliographies of references consulted. Includes a bibliography of the current world literature published during the previous year.

616.7 011 US ISSN 1040-8711
RC925.A1 CODEN: CORHES
CURRENT OPINION IN RHEUMATOLOGY. 1989. bi-m. $100 to individuals; institutions $170; residents $70. Current Science, 20 N. 3rd St., Philadelphia, PA 19106. TEL 800-552-5866. FAX 215-574-2270. Ed. Daniel J. McCarty. bibl.; illus. (also avail. on diskette)
—BLDSC shelfmark: 3500.778000.
Description: Directed toward researchers and practicing rheumatologists. Presents review articles followed by annotated bibliographies of references consulted. Includes a bibliography of the current world literature published during the previous year.

617.6 016 DK ISSN 0903-3483
CURRENT TITLES IN DENTISTRY. (Text in English, German, French) m. DKK 940. Munksgaard International Publishers Ltd., 35 Noerre Soegade, P.O. Box 2148, DK-1016 Copenhagen K, Denmark. TEL 33-127030. FAX 33-129387. TELEX 19431-MUNKS-DK. Ed. Preben Junker Jacobsen. circ. 400.

610 016 UK ISSN 0011-3999
CURRENT WORK IN THE HISTORY OF MEDICINE; an international bibliography. 1954. q. £20 to individuals; institutions £30. (Wellcome Institute for the History of Medicine) Professional & Scientific Publications, Tavistock House East, Tavistock Square, London WC1H 9JR, England. bibl.; circ. 750. **Indexed:** A.I.C.P.
—BLDSC shelfmark: 3505.000000.
Description: Covers the history of medicine.

610 016 CC ISSN 0178-3351
DEGUO YIXUE/DEUTSCHE MEDIZIN. (Text in Chinese) q. DM.98($66) Tongji Yike Daxue - Tongji University of Medical Sciences, No. 515, Jiefang Dadao, Hankou, Hubei 430030, People's Republic of China. TEL 566641. (Dist. overseas by: Springer-Verlag, Heidelberger Platz 3, D-1000 Berlin 33, Germany. TEL 030-8207-1)
Description: Selected articles from German medical periodicals.

MEDICAL SCIENCES — ABSTRACTING, BIBLIOGRAPHIES, STATISTICS

617.6 016 US ISSN 0011-8486
RK1
DENTAL ABSTRACTS. 1956. m. $40 to individuals (foreign $55); institutions $75 (foreign $90). (American Dental Association) Mosby - Year Book, Inc. (Subsidiary of: Times Mirror Company), 11830 Westline Industrial Dr., St. Louis, MO 63146. TEL 800-325-4177. FAX 314-432-1380. TELEX 44-2402. Ed. Tracy Briggs. adv.; bk.rev.; abstr.; charts; illus.; stat.; index; circ. 8,000. (also avail. in microform from UMI; reprint service avail. from UMI) **Indexed:** Biol.Abstr.
—BLDSC shelfmark: 3553.240000.
  Description: Presents articles from more than 100 dental and medical journals.

617.6 US
DENTAL STATISTICS HANDBOOK. irreg. (every 3-4 yrs.). $7.50 to non-member; members $5. American Dental Association, Bureau of Economic and Behavioral Research, 211 E. Chicago Ave., Chicago, IL 60611. TEL 312-440-2500.

610 616.3 FR ISSN 1011-8594
DIARRHOEAL DISEASES/MALADIES DIARRHEIQUES. (Text in English, French) 1982. 2/yr. 240 F. for 2 yrs. Centre International de l'Enfance - International Children's Center, Chateau de Longchamp, Bois de Boulogne, 75016 Paris, France. TEL 1-45-20-79-92. FAX 1-45-25-73-67.
  Description: Abstracts on epidemiology, etiology, immunology and physiopathology, planification and evaluation of programs for combating diarrhoeal diseases, prevention and treatment, research and oral rehydration.

616.8 016 US ISSN 0012-2769
DIGEST OF NEUROLOGY & PSYCHIATRY. 1932. bi-m. $25. Institute of Living, 400 Washington St., Hartford, CT 06106. TEL 203-241-6824. Ed. Dr. William L. Webb, Jr. bk.rev.; abstr.; index; circ. 6,000. (also avail. in microform from UMI; reprint service avail. from UMI) **Indexed:** Rehabil.Lit.
—BLDSC shelfmark: 3588.150000.

DIRECTORY OF BIOMEDICAL AND HEALTH CARE GRANTS. see EDUCATION — Abstracting, Bibliographies, Statistics

610 016 016 GW ISSN 0342-0795
DOKUMENTATION MEDIZIN IM UMWELTSCHUTZ. 1977. 4/yr. DM.40. Institut fuer Dokumentation und Information, Sozialmedizin und Oeffentliches Gesundheitswesen, Westerfeldstr. 15, Postfach 201012, 4800 Bielefeld 1, Germany. TEL 0521-86033. Ed. Christiane Kelm-Dirkmorfeld. bk.rev.; cum.index; circ. 330.

614 016 GW ISSN 0932-5387
DOKUMENTATION SOZIALMEDIZIN, OEFFENTLICHER GESUNDHEITSDIENST, GESUNDHEITSERZIEHUNG. (Abstracts and summaries in English and German) 1969. 8/yr. DM.50. Institut fuer Dokumentation und Information, Sozialmedizin und Oeffentliches Gesundheitswesen, Westerfeldstr. 35-37, Postfach 201012, 4800 Bielefeld 1, Germany. TEL 0521-86033. Ed. Christiane Kelm-Dirkmorfeld. bk.rev.; abstr.; cum.index; circ. 620.
  Incorporates: Dokumentation Oeffentliches Gesundheitswesen, Sozialhygiene-Sozialmedizin; Formerly (until 1984): Dokumentation Sozialmedizin, Oeffentlicher Gesundheitsdienst, Arbeitsmedizin (ISSN 0012-513X)

011 610.73 US
▼**E N A NURSING SCAN IN EMERGENCY CARE.** 1991. bi-m. $35 to individuals; institutions $55. (Emergency Nurses Association) Nursecom Inc., 1211 Locust St., Philadelphia, PA 19107. TEL 215-545-7222. Ed. Margaret Miller.
  Description: Abstracts of articles from multidisciplinary literature that address topics in emergency care nursing, with commentary on applications to nursing practice.

616.99 310 GR ISSN 0302-9697
RC279.G75
ETESIA STATISTIKE. EREVNA TOU KARKINOU/ANNUAL STATISTICAL SURVEY OF CANCER. 1967. biennial. $5. National Statistical Service of Greece, Statistical Information and Publications Division, 14-16 Lycourgou St., 10166 Athens, Greece. TEL 3244-748. FAX 3222205. TELEX 216734 ESYE GR. circ. 1,000.

616.3 US ISSN 0954-691X
CODEN: EJGHES
EUROPEAN JOURNAL OF GASTROENTEROLOGY AND HEPATOLOGY. 1989. bi-m. $130 to individuals; institutions $255; residents $91. Current Science, 20 N. 3rd St., Philadelphia, PA 19106. TEL 800-552-5866. FAX 215-574-2270. Ed. J.J. Misiewicz. illus.; circ. 1,250. (also avail. on diskette) —BLDSC shelfmark: 3829.729400.
  Description: Directed toward practicing gastroenterologists, hepatologists and researchers. Presents review articles followed by annotated bibliographies of references consulted. Includes a bibliography of the current world literature published during the previous year.

610 011 NE ISSN 0921-822X
EXCERPTA MEDICA ABSTRACT JOURNALS. (Consists of 41 Sections) 1947. 794/yr. (in 94 vols., 6-10 nos./vol.). fl.41161 (includes s-a. cum. on CD-ROM)(effective 1992). Excerpta Medica (Subsidiary of: Elsevier Science Publishers B.V.), P.O. Box 548, 1000 AM Amsterdam, Netherlands. TEL 020-5803911. FAX 020-5803222. TELEX 18582 ESPA NL. (Dist. by: Elsevier Science Publishers Ireland Ltd., P.O. Box 85, Limerick, Ireland. TEL 061-61944; Subscr. in U.S. and Canada to: Elsevier Science Publishing Co., Inc., Box 882, Madison Sq. Sta., New York, NY 10159. TEL 212-989-5800) Ed.Bd. abstr.; index. cum.index. (back issues avail.)
  ●Also available online. Vendor(s): BRS, DIMDI, Data-Star, DIALOG, JICST.
  Also available on CD-ROM. Producer(s): SilverPlatter (Excerpta Medica Library Service).
  Description: Comprehensive medical abstract service providing relevant abstracts and bibliographic data from more than 3,500 international biomedical journals covered by the EMBASE Excerpta Medica Database.

574.92 016 NE ISSN 0014-4053
CODEN: AAEHA9
EXCERPTA MEDICA. SECTION 1: ANATOMY, ANTHROPOLOGY, EMBRYOLOGY & HISTOLOGY. 1947. 16/yr. (in 2 vols., 8 nos./vol.). fl.1358 (effective 1992). Excerpta Medica (Subsidiary of: Elsevier Science Publishers B.V.), P.O. Box 548, 1000 AM Amsterdam, Netherlands. TEL 020-5803911. FAX 020-5803222. TELEX 18582 ESPA NL. (Dist. by: Elsevier Science Publishers Ireland Ltd., P.O. Box 85, Limerick, Ireland. TEL 061-61944; Subscr. in U.S. and Canada to: Elsevier Science Publishing Co., Inc., Box 882, Madison Sq. Sta., New York, NY 10159. TEL 212-989-5800) adv.; abstr.; index. cum.index. **Indexed:** A.I.C.P., Chem.Abstr., Lab.Haz.Bull.
  ●Also available online. Vendor(s): BRS, DIMDI, Data-Star, DIALOG, JICST.
  Also available on CD-ROM. Producer(s): SilverPlatter.
  —BLDSC shelfmark: 3835.812000.

612 016 NE ISSN 0014-4061
CODEN: PHSGA
EXCERPTA MEDICA. SECTION 2: PHYSIOLOGY. 1948. 30/yr.(in 3 vols., 10 nos./vol.). fl.1995 (effective 1992). Excerpta Medica (Subsidiary of: Elsevier Science Publishers B.V.), P.O. Box 548, 1000 AM Amsterdam, Netherlands. TEL 020-5803911. FAX 020-5803222. TELEX 18582 ESPA NL. (Dist. by: Elsevier Science Publishers Ireland Ltd., P.O. Box 85, Limerick, Ireland. TEL 061-61944; Subscr. in U.S. and Canada to: Elsevier Science Publishing Co., Inc., Box 882, Madison Sq. Sta., New York, NY 10159. TEL 212-989-5800) adv.; abstr.; charts; index. cum.index. **Indexed:** Chem.Abstr.
  ●Also available online. Vendor(s): BRS, DIMDI, Data-Star, DIALOG, JICST.
  Also available on CD-ROM. Producer(s): SilverPlatter.

616.4 016 NE ISSN 0014-407X
CODEN: EEXCA
EXCERPTA MEDICA. SECTION 3: ENDOCRINOLOGY. 1947. 24/yr.(in 3 vols.; 8 nos./vol.) fl.1796 (effective 1992). Excerpta Medica (Subsidiary of: Elsevier Science Publishers B.V.), P.O. Box 548, 1000 BM Amsterdam, Netherlands. TEL 020-5803911. FAX 020-5803222. TELEX 18582 ESPA NL. (Dist. by: Elsevier Science Publishers Ireland Ltd., P.O. Box 85, Limerick, Ireland. TEL 061-61944; Subscr. in U.S. and Canada to: Elsevier Science Publishing Co., Inc., Box 882, Madison Sq. Sta., New York, NY 10159. TEL 212-989-5800) adv.; abstr.; charts; index. cum.index. **Indexed:** Chem.Abstr., Excerp.Med.
  ●Also available online. Vendor(s): BRS, DIMDI, Data-Star, DIALOG, JICST.
  Also available on CD-ROM. Producer(s): SilverPlatter.
  —BLDSC shelfmark: 3835.830000.

576 016 NE ISSN 0927-2771
EXCERPTA MEDICA. SECTION 4: MICROBIOLOGY: BACTERIOLOGY, MYCOLOGY, PARASITOLOGY AND VIROLOGY. 1948. 32/yr.(in 4 vols.; 8 nos./vol.). fl.2291 (effective 1992). Excerpta Medica (Subsidiary of: Elsevier Science Publishers B.V.), P.O. Box 548, 1000 AM Amsterdam, Netherlands. TEL 020-5803911. FAX 020-5803222. TELEX 18582 ESPA NL. (Dist. by: Elsevier Science Publishers Ireland Ltd., P.O. Box 85, Limerick, Ireland. TEL 061-61944; Subscr. in U.S. and Canada to: Elsevier Science Publishing Co., Inc., Box 882, Madison Sq. Sta., New York, NY 10159. TEL 212-989-5800) adv.; abstr.; index. cum.index. **Indexed:** Chem.Abstr.
  ●Also available online. Vendor(s): BRS, DIMDI, Data-Star, DIALOG, JICST.
  Also available on CD-ROM. Producer(s): SilverPlatter.
  Incorporates (1971-1991): Excerpta Medica. Section 47: Virology (ISSN 0304-4084); Former titles (until 1992): Excerpta Medica. Section 4: Microbiology: Bacteriology, Mycology and Parasitology; Excerpta Medica. Section 4: Microbiology: Bacteriology, Virology, Mycology and Parasitology (ISSN 0014-4088)
  Description: Covers general aspects of infectious diseases, diagnosis, treatment, epidemiology and prevention of diseases. Includes bacteriology, parasitology, mycology, algae and sexually transmitted diseases.

616.07 016 574.2 NE ISSN 0014-4096
RB1 CODEN: GPPABB
EXCERPTA MEDICA. SECTION 5: GENERAL PATHOLOGY AND PATHOLOGICAL ANATOMY. 1948. 24/yr.(in 3 vols.; 8 nos./vol.). fl.2046 (effective 1992). Excerpta Medica (Subsidiary of: Elsevier Science Publishers B.V.), P.O. Box 548, 1000 AM Amsterdam, Netherlands. TEL 020-5803911. FAX 020-5803222. TELEX 18582 ESPA NL. (Dist. by: Elsevier Science Publishers Ireland Ltd., P.O. Box 85, Limerick, Ireland. TEL 061-61944; Subscr. in U.S. and Canada to: Elsevier Science Publishing Co., Inc., Box 882, Madison Sq. Sta., New York, NY 10159. TEL 212-989-5800) adv.; abstr.; index. cum.index. **Indexed:** Chem.Abstr.
  ●Also available online. Vendor(s): BRS, DIMDI, Data-Star, DIALOG, JICST.
  Also available on CD-ROM. Producer(s): SilverPlatter.
  —BLDSC shelfmark: 3835.832000.

616.026 016 NE ISSN 0014-410X
CODEN: IMDCBQ
EXCERPTA MEDICA. SECTION 6: INTERNAL MEDICINE. 1947. 24/yr.(in 3 vols.; 8 nos./vol.). fl.1846 (effective 1992). Excerpta Medica (Subsidiary of: Elsevier Science Publishers B.V.), P.O. Box 548, 1000 AM Amsterdam, Netherlands. TEL 020-5803911. FAX 020-5803222. TELEX 18582 ESPA NL. (Dist. by: Elsevier Science Publishers Ireland Ltd., P.O. Box 85, Limerick, Ireland. TEL 061-61944; Subscr. in U.S. and Canada to: Elsevier Science Publishing Co., Inc., Box 882, Madison Sq. Sta., New York, NY 10159. TEL 212-989-5800) Ed.Bd. adv.; abstr.; index. cum.index. **Indexed:** Chem.Abstr.
  ●Also available online. Vendor(s): BRS, DIMDI, Data-Star, DIALOG, JICST.
  Also available on CD-ROM. Producer(s): SilverPlatter.
  —BLDSC shelfmark: 3835.844000.

MEDICAL SCIENCES — ABSTRACTING, BIBLIOGRAPHIES, STATISTICS

618.92 016   NE   ISSN 0373-6512
CODEN: PPSUDH
EXCERPTA MEDICA. SECTION 7: PEDIATRICS AND PEDIATRIC SURGERY. 1947. 24/yr.(in 3 vols.; 8 nos./vol.). fl.2067 (effective 1992). Excerpta Medica (Subsidiary of: Elsevier Science Publishers B.V.), P.O. Box 548, 1000 AM Amsterdam, Netherlands. TEL 020-5803911.
FAX 020-5803222. TELEX 18582 ESPA NL. (Dist. by: Elsevier Science Publishers Ireland Ltd., P.O. Box 85, Limerick, Ireland. TEL 061-61944; Subscr. in the U.S. and Canada to: Elsevier Science Publishing Co., Inc., Box 882, Madison Sq. Sta., New York, NY 10159. TEL 212-989-5800) adv.; abstr.; index. cum.index. **Indexed:** Excerp.Med.
●Also available online. Vendor(s): BRS, DIMDI, Data-Star, DIALOG, JICST.
Also available on CD-ROM. Producer(s): SilverPlatter.
—BLDSC shelfmark: 3835.866500.
  Formerly: Excerpta Medica. Section 7: Pediatrics (ISSN 0014-4118)
  Description: Covers all aspects of development and organic disease in neonates, children and adolescents, including surgery.

616.8 016   NE   ISSN 0014-4126
CODEN: NLNSB
EXCERPTA MEDICA. SECTION 8: NEUROLOGY AND NEUROSURGERY. 1948. 32/yr.(in 4 vols.; 8 nos./vol.). fl.2420 (effective 1992). Excerpta Medica (Subsidiary of: Elsevier Science Publishers B.V.), P.O. Box 548, 1000 AM Amsterdam, Netherlands. TEL 020-5803911.
FAX 020-5803222. TELEX 18582 ESPA NL. (Dist. by: Elsevier Science Publishers Ireland Ltd., P.O. Box 85, Limerick, Ireland. TEL 061-61944; Subscr. in U.S. and Canada to: Elsevier Science Publishing Co., Inc., Box 882, Madison Sq. Sta., New York, NY 10159. TEL 212-989-5800) Ed.Bd. adv.; abstr.; index. cum.index.
●Also available online. Vendor(s): BRS, DIMDI, Data-Star, DIALOG, JICST.
Also available on CD-ROM. Producer(s): SilverPlatter.
—BLDSC shelfmark: 3835.854000.
  Description: Covers clinical neurology and neurosurgery, including epilepsy and neuromuscular disorders.

617 016   NE   ISSN 0014-4134
CODEN: EMSGAY
EXCERPTA MEDICA. SECTION 9: SURGERY. 1947. 24/yr.(in 3 vols., 8 nos./vol.). fl.2037 (effective 1992). Excerpta Medica (Subsidiary of: Elsevier Science Publishers B.V.), P.O. Box 548, 1000 AM Amsterdam, Netherlands. TEL 020-5803911.
FAX 020-5803222. TELEX 18582 ESPA NL. (Dist. by: Elsevier Science Publishers Ireland Ltd., P.O. Box 85, Limerick, Ireland. TEL 061-61944; Subscr. in U.S. and Canada to: Elsevier Science Publishing Co., Inc., Box 882, Madison Sq. Sta., New York, NY 10159. TEL 212-989-5800) adv.; abstr.; index. cum.index. **Indexed:** Chem.Abstr., Excerp.Med.
●Also available online. Vendor(s): BRS, DIMDI, Data-Star, DIALOG, JICST.
Also available on CD-ROM. Producer(s): SilverPlatter.
—BLDSC shelfmark: 3835.881000.
  Description: Covers general, abdominal, thoracic and peripheral vascular surgery, cosmetic, plastic and reconstructive surgery, microsurgery, pre- and post-operative care and surgical aspects of intensive care medicine.

618 016   NE   ISSN 0014-4142
CODEN: EMOGAE
EXCERPTA MEDICA. SECTION 10: OBSTETRICS AND GYNECOLOGY. 1948. 20/yr.(in 2 vols.; 10 nos./vol.). fl.1493 (effective 1992). Excerpta Medica (Subsidiary of: Elsevier Science Publishers B.V.), P.O. Box 548, 1000 AM Amsterdam, Netherlands. TEL 020-5803911.
FAX 020-5803222. TELEX 18582 ESPA NL. (Dist. by: Elsevier Science Publishers Ireland Ltd., P.O. Box 85, Limerick, Ireland. TEL 061-61944; Subscr. in U.S. and Canada to: Elsevier Science Publishing Co., Inc., Box 882, Madison Sq. Sta., New York, NY 10159. TEL 212-989-5800) Ed.Bd. adv.; abstr.; index. cum.index. **Indexed:** Chem.Abstr., Excerp.Med.
●Also available online. Vendor(s): BRS, DIMDI, Data-Star, DIALOG, JICST.
Also available on CD-ROM. Producer(s): SilverPlatter.
—BLDSC shelfmark: 3835.858000.
  Description: Covers human obstetrics and gynecology, including female infertility, fetal monitoring, anticonception in women, and neonatal care of normal children.

616.21 016   NE   ISSN 0014-4150
RF1   CODEN: ORLGA8
EXCERPTA MEDICA. SECTION 11: OTORHINOLARYNGOLOGY. 1948. 16/yr.(in 2 vols.; 8 nos./vol.). fl.1293 (effective 1992). Excerpta Medica (Subsidiary of: Elsevier Science Publishers B.V.), P.O. Box 548, 1000 AM Amsterdam, Netherlands. TEL 020-5803911.
FAX 020-5803222. TELEX 18582 ESPA NL. (Dist. by: Elsevier Science Publishers Ireland Ltd., P.O. Box 85, Limerick, Ireland. TEL 061-61944; Subscr. in U.S. and Canada to: Elsevier Science Publishing Co., Inc., Box 882, Madison Sq. Sta., New York, NY 10159. TEL 212-989-5800) adv.; abstr.; index. cum.index. **Indexed:** Chem.Abstr., Excerp.Med.
●Also available online. Vendor(s): BRS, DIMDI, Data-Star, DIALOG, JICST.
Also available on CD-ROM. Producer(s): SilverPlatter.
—BLDSC shelfmark: 3835.864000.
  Description: Covers all aspects of diseases of the ear, nose, and throat, and includes phonetics and speech disorders, craniofacial disorders, vestibular disorders, surgery, stomatology and audiology.

617.7 016   NE   ISSN 0014-4169
CODEN: OPHYAS
EXCERPTA MEDICA. SECTION 12: OPHTHALMOLOGY. 1947. 16/yr.(in 2 vols.); 8 nos./vol.). fl.1293 (effective 1992). Excerpta Medica (Subsidiary of: Elsevier Science Publishers B.V.), P.O. Box 548, 1000 AM Amsterdam, Netherlands.
TEL 020-5803911. FAX 020-5803222. TELEX 18582 ESPA NL. (Dist. by: Elsevier Science Publishers Ireland Ltd., P.O. Box 85, Limerick, Ireland. TEL 061-61944; Subscr. in U.S. and Canada to: Elsevier Science Publishing Co., Inc., Box 882, Madison Sq. Sta., New York, NY 10159. TEL 212-989-5800) adv.; abstr.; index. cum.index. **Indexed:** Chem.Abstr.
●Also available online. Vendor(s): BRS, DIMDI, Data-Star, DIALOG, JICST.
Also available on CD-ROM. Producer(s): SilverPlatter.
—BLDSC shelfmark: 3835.860000.
  Description: Covers both surgical and non-surgical aspects of eye disease and vision disorders and includes articles on the anatomy, physiology and biochemistry of the eye, orbit and visual system.

616.5 016   NE   ISSN 0014-4177
CODEN: DVENB4
EXCERPTA MEDICA. SECTION 13: DERMATOLOGY AND VENEREOLOGY. 1947. 16/yr. (in 2 vols.; 8 nos/vol.). fl.1638 (effective 1992). Excerpta Medica (Subsidiary of: Elsevier Science Publishers B.V.), P.O. Box 548, 1000 AM Amsterdam, Netherlands.
TEL 020-5803911. FAX 020-5803222. TELEX 18582 ESPA NL. (Dist. by: Elsevier Science Publishers Ireland Ltd., P.O. Box 85, Limerick, Ireland. TEL 061-61944; Subscr. in U.S. and Canada to: Elsevier Science Publishing Co., Inc., Box 882, Madison Sq. Sta., New York, NY 10159. TEL 212-989-5800) adv.; abstr.; index. **Indexed:** Chem.Abstr.
●Also available online. Vendor(s): BRS, DIMDI, Data-Star, DIALOG, JICST.
Also available on CD-ROM. Producer(s): SilverPlatter.
—BLDSC shelfmark: 3835.826000.
  Description: Covers all aspects of skin and venereal diseases, and includes microbiology, sexually transmitted diseases, immunology, allergy and skin toxicology, skin physiology and biochemistry.

615.842 016   NE   ISSN 0014-4185
CODEN: RDGYA6
EXCERPTA MEDICA. SECTION 14: RADIOLOGY. 1947. 24/yr.(in 3 vols.; 8 nos./vol.). fl.1996 (effective 1992). Excerpta Medica (Subsidiary of: Elsevier Science Publishers B.V.), P.O. Box 548, 1000 AM Amsterdam, Netherlands. TEL 020-5803911.
FAX 020-5803222. TELEX 18582 ESPA NL. (Dist. by: Elsevier Science Publishers Ireland Ltd., P.O. Box 85, Limerick, Ireland. TEL 061-61944; Subscr. in U.S. and Canada to: Elsevier Science Publishing Co., Inc., Box 882, Madison Sq. Sta., New York, NY 10159. TEL 212-989-5800) adv.; abstr.; index. cum.index. **Indexed:** Chem.Abstr., Excerp.Med.
●Also available online. Vendor(s): BRS, DIMDI, Data-Star, DIALOG, JICST.
Also available on CD-ROM. Producer(s): SilverPlatter.
—BLDSC shelfmark: 3835.878000.
  Description: Covers articles on radiodiagnosis, radiotherapy and radiobiology, including ultrasound diagnosis, thermography, adverse reactions to radiotherapy, as well as techniques and apparatus.

616.2 016   NE   ISSN 0014-4193
RC306   CODEN: CDTSA
EXCERPTA MEDICA. SECTION 15: CHEST DISEASES, THORACIC SURGERY AND TUBERCULOSIS. 1948. 20/yr.(in 2 vols.) 10 nos./vol.). fl.1373 (effective 1992). Excerpta Medica (Subsidiary of: Elsevier Science Publishers B.V.), P.O. Box 548, 1000 AM Amsterdam, Netherlands. TEL 020-5803911.
FAX 020-5803222. TELEX 18582 ESPA NL. (Dist. by: Elsevier Science Publishers Ireland Ltd., P.O. Box 85, Limerick, Ireland. TEL 061-61944; Subscr. in U.S. and Canada to: Elsevier Science Publishing Co., Inc., Box 882, Madison Sq. Sta., New York, NY 10159. TEL 212-989-5800) adv.; abstr.; index. cum.index. **Indexed:** Chem.Abstr.
●Also available online. Vendor(s): BRS, DIMDI, Data-Star, DIALOG, JICST.
Also available on CD-ROM. Producer(s): SilverPlatter.
—BLDSC shelfmark: 3835.824000.
  Description: Covers all aspects of lung and respiratory tract diseases, thoracic surgery and tuberculosis, including respiratory infections, mediastical and pleural diseases, chronic chest diseases, allergy and bronchial asthma, and neoplastic disease.

616.994 016   NE   ISSN 0014-4207
CODEN: CEXCA3
EXCERPTA MEDICA. SECTION 16: CANCER. 1953. 32/yr.(in 4 vols.; 8 nos./vol.). fl.2420 (effective 1992). Excerpta Medica (Subsidiary of: Elsevier Science Publishers B.V.), P.O. Box 548, 1000 AM Amsterdam, Netherlands. TEL 020-5803911.
FAX 020-5803222. TELEX 18582 ESPA NL. (Dist. by: Elsevier Science Publishers Ireland Ltd., P.O. Box 85, Limerick, Ireland. TEL 061-61944; Subscr. in U.S. and Canada to: Elsevier Science Publishing Co., Inc. Box 882, Madison Sq. Sta., New York, NY 10159. TEL 212-989-5800) adv.; abstr.; index. cum.index. **Indexed:** Chem.Abstr.
●Also available online. Vendor(s): BRS, DIMDI, Data-Star, DIALOG, JICST.
Also available on CD-ROM. Producer(s): SilverPlatter.
—BLDSC shelfmark: 3835.820000.
  Description: Covers both experimental and clinical aspects of malignant neoplastic disease, including research in cancer immunology, oncogenes, viral and chemical carcinogenesis, and cancer chemotherapeutic agents.

EXCERPTA MEDICA. SECTION 17: PUBLIC HEALTH, SOCIAL MEDICINE & EPIDEMIOLOGY. see *PUBLIC HEALTH AND SAFETY — Abstracting, Bibliographies, Statistics*

616.1 016   NE   ISSN 0014-4223
CODEN: CDCSA
EXCERPTA MEDICA. SECTION 18: CARDIOVASCULAR DISEASES AND CARDIOVASCULAR SURGERY. 1957. 24/yr.(in 3 vols.; 8 nos./vol.). fl.1796 (effective 1992). Excerpta Medica (Subsidiary of: Elsevier Science Publishers), P.O. Box 548, 1000 AM Amsterdam, Netherlands. TEL 020-5803911.
FAX 020-5803222. TELEX 18582 ESPA NL. (Dist. by: Elsevier Science Publishers Ireland Ltd., P.O. Box 85, Limerick, Ireland. TEL 061-61944; Subscr. in U.S. and Canada to: Elsevier Science Publishing Co., Inc., Box 882, Madison Sq. Sta., New York, NY 10159. TEL 212-989-5800) adv.; abstr.; index. cum.index.
●Also available online. Vendor(s): BRS, DIMDI, Data-Star, DIALOG, JICST.
Also available on CD-ROM. Producer(s): SilverPlatter.
—BLDSC shelfmark: 3835.822000.
  Description: Covers both surgical and non-surgical aspects of cardiovascular disease, including cardiovascular aspects of hypertension.

MEDICAL SCIENCES — ABSTRACTING, BIBLIOGRAPHIES, STATISTICS

612 016   NE   ISSN 0014-4231
CODEN: RHPMA
EXCERPTA MEDICA. SECTION 19: REHABILITATION AND PHYSICAL MEDICINE. 1958. 8/yr. fl.843 (effective 1992). Excerpta Medica (Subsidiary of: Elsevier Science Publishers), P.O. Box 548, 1000 AM Amsterdam, Netherlands. TEL 020-5803911. FAX 020-5803222. TELEX 18582 ESPA NL. (Dist. by: Elsevier Science Publishers Ireland Ltd., P.O. Box 85, Limerick, Ireland. TEL 061-61944; Subscr. in U.S. and Canada to: Elsevier Science Publishing Co., Inc., Box 882, Madison Sq. Sta., New York, NY 10159. TEL 212-989-5800) adv.; abstr.; index. cum.index.
●Also available online. Vendor(s): BRS, DIMDI, Data-Star, DIALOG, JICST.
Also available on CD-ROM. Producer(s): SilverPlatter.
—BLDSC shelfmark: 3835.879000.
Description: Covers all aspects of the rehabilitation of somatic and mental disorders using physiotherapy and other therapeutic techniques.

EXCERPTA MEDICA. SECTION 20: GERONTOLOGY AND GERIATRICS. see *GERONTOLOGY AND GERIATRICS — Abstracting, Bibliographies, Statistics*

574 016 616   NE   ISSN 0014-4258
CODEN: DBITA
EXCERPTA MEDICA. SECTION 21: DEVELOPMENTAL BIOLOGY AND TERATOLOGY. 1961. 16/yr. (in 2 vols.; 8 nos./vol.) fl.1638 (effective 1992). Excerpta Medica (Subsidiary of: Elsevier Science Publishers), P.O. Box 548, 1000 AM Amsterdam, Netherlands. TEL 020-5803911. FAX 020-5803222. TELEX 18582 ESPA NL. (Dist. by: Elsevier Science Publishers Ireland Ltd., P.O. Box 85, Limerick, Ireland. TEL 061-61944; Subscr. in U.S. and Canada to: Elsevier Science Publishing Co., Box 882, Madison Sq. Sta., New York, NY 10159. TEL 212-989-5800) adv.; abstr.; index. cum.index.
●Also available online. Vendor(s): BRS, DIMDI, Data-Star, DIALOG, JICST.
Also available on CD-ROM. Producer(s): SilverPlatter.
—BLDSC shelfmark: 3835.828000.
Description: Covers both experimental and clinical aspects of embryology and fetal, neonatal development.

EXCERPTA MEDICA. SECTION 22: HUMAN GENETICS. see *BIOLOGY — Abstracting, Bibliographies, Statistics*

615.842 016   NE   ISSN 0014-4274
CODEN: NUMEAH
EXCERPTA MEDICA. SECTION 23: NUCLEAR MEDICINE. 1964. 20/yr.(in 2 vols.; 10 nos./vol.). fl.1373 (effective 1992). Excerpta Medica (Subsidiary of: Elsevier Science Publishers), P.O. Box 548, 1000 AM Amsterdam, Netherlands. TEL 020-5803911. FAX 020-5803222. TELEX 18582 ESPA NL. (Dist. by: Elsevier Science Publishers Ireland Ltd., P.O. Box 85, Limerick, Ireland. TEL 061-61944; Subscr. in U.S. and Canada to: Elsevier Science Publishing Co., Inc., Box 882, Madison Sq. Sta., New York, NY 10159. TEL 212-989-5800) adv.; abstr.; index. cum.index. Indexed: Chem.Abstr.
●Also available online. Vendor(s): BRS, DIMDI, Data-Star, DIALOG, JICST.
Also available on CD-ROM. Producer(s): SilverPlatter.
—BLDSC shelfmark: 3835.856000.
Description: Covers the diagnostic and therapeutic applications of radioisotopes in biomedicine, including the radiobiology of isotopes, aspects of radiohygiene, new labelling techniques and tracer applications.

617.96 016   NE   ISSN 0014-4282
CODEN: ATSYA
EXCERPTA MEDICA. SECTION 24: ANESTHESIOLOGY. 1966. 10/yr. fl.836 (effective 1992). Excerpta Medica (Subsidiary of: Elsevier Science Publishers), P.O. Box 548, 1000 AM Amsterdam, Netherlands. TEL 020-5803911. FAX 020-5803222. TELEX 18582 ESPA NL. (Dist. by: Elsevier Science Publishers Ireland Ltd., P.O. Box 85, Limerick, Ireland. TEL 061-61944; Subscr. in U.S. and Canada to: Elsevier Science Publishing Co., Inc., Box 882, Madison Sq. Sta., New York, NY 10159. TEL 212-989-5800) adv.; abstr.; index. cum.index.
●Also available online. Vendor(s): BRS, DIMDI, Data-Star, DIALOG, JICST.
Also available on CD-ROM. Producer(s): SilverPlatter.
—BLDSC shelfmark: 3835.814000.
Description: Covers both clinical and experimental aspects of anesthesiology, and includes resuscitation and intensive care medicine, pharmacology of anesthetic agents, spinal, epidural and caudal anesthesia, and acupuncture used as an anaesthetic procedure.

616.15 016   NE   ISSN 0014-4290
CODEN: HEMYA
EXCERPTA MEDICA. SECTION 25: HEMATOLOGY. 1967. 24/yr.(in 3 vols.; 8 nos./vol.). fl.1996 (effective 1992). Excerpta Medica (Subsidiary of: Elsevier Science Publishers), P.O. Box 548, 1000 AM Amsterdam, Netherlands. TEL 020-5803911. FAX 020-5803222. TELEX 18582 ESPA NL. (Dist. by: Elsevier Science Publishers Ireland Ltd., P.O. Box 85, Limerick, Ireland. TEL 061-61944; Subscr. in U.S. and Canada to: Elsevier Science Publishing Co., Inc., Box 882, Madison Sq. Sta., New York, NY 10159. TEL 212-989-5800) Ed.Bd. adv.; abstr.; index. cum.index.
●Also available online. Vendor(s): BRS, DIMDI, Data-Star, DIALOG, JICST.
Also available on CD-ROM. Producer(s): SilverPlatter.
—BLDSC shelfmark: 3835.836000.
Description: Covers all aspects of blood cell biology and disorders of the blood, its cells and the lymphatic tissues.

615.37 016   NE   ISSN 0014-4304
CODEN: ISTNB
EXCERPTA MEDICA. SECTION 26: IMMUNOLOGY, SEROLOGY AND TRANSPLANTATION. 1967. 32/yr.(in 4 vols.; 8 nos./vol.). fl.2295 (effective 1992). Excerpta Medica (Subsidiary of: Elsevier Science Publishers), P.O. Box 548, 1000 AM Amsterdam, Netherlands. TEL 020-5803911. FAX 020-5803222. TELEX 18582 ESPA NL. (Dist. by: Elsevier Science Publishers Ireland Ltd., P.O. Box 85, Limerick, Ireland. TEL 061-61944; Subscr. in U.S. and Canada to: Elsevier Science Publishing Co., Inc., Box 882, Madison Sq. Sta., New York, NY 10159. TEL 212-989-5800) adv.; abstr.; index. cum.index.
●Also available online. Vendor(s): BRS, DIMDI, Data-Star, DIALOG, JICST.
Also available on CD-ROM. Producer(s): SilverPlatter.
—BLDSC shelfmark: 3835.842000.
Description: Covers both clinical and experimental immunology and includes humoral immunity and associated factors.

610.28 016   NE   ISSN 0014-4312
CODEN: BBMIA
EXCERPTA MEDICA. SECTION 27: BIOPHYSICS, BIO-ENGINEERING AND MEDICAL INSTRUMENTATION. 1967. 10/yr. fl.948 (effective 1992). Excerpta Medica (Subsidiary of: Elsevier Science Publishers), P.O. Box 548, 1000 AM Amsterdam, Netherlands. TEL 020-5803439. FAX 020-5803222. TELEX 18582 10159. (Dist. by: Elsevier Science Publishers Ireland Ltd., P.O. Box 85, Limerick, Ireland. TEL 061-61944; Subscr. in U.S. and Canada to: Elsevier Science Publishing Co., Inc., Box 882, Madison Sq. Sta., New York, NY 10159. TEL 212-989-5800) adv.; abstr.; index. cum.index.
●Also available online. Vendor(s): BRS, DIMDI, Data-Star, DIALOG, JICST.
Also available on CD-ROM. Producer(s): SilverPlatter.
—BLDSC shelfmark: 3835.818000.
Description: Covers the application of biophysical principles to the development of instrumentation, the use of automation in biomedicine, biomechanics and bioengineering.

616.6 016   NE   ISSN 0014-4320
CODEN: URNLA
EXCERPTA MEDICA. SECTION 28: UROLOGY AND NEPHROLOGY. 1967. 20/yr.(in 2 vols.; 10 nos./vol.) fl.1373 (effective 1992). Excerpta Medica (Subsidiary of: Elsevier Science Publishers), P.O. Box 548, 1000 AM Amsterdam, Netherlands. TEL 020-5803911. FAX 020-5803222. TELEX 18582 ESPA NL. (Dist. by: Elsevier Science Publishers Ireland Ltd., P.O. Box 85, Limerick, Ireland. TEL 061-61944; Subscr. in U.S. and Canada to: Elsevier Science Publishing Co., Inc., Box 882, Madison Sq. Sta., New York, NY 10159. TEL 212-989-5800) Ed.Bd. adv.; abstr.; index. cum.index.
●Also available online. Vendor(s): BRS, DIMDI, Data-Star, DIALOG, JICST.
Also available on CD-ROM. Producer(s): SilverPlatter.
—BLDSC shelfmark: 3835.883000.
Description: Covers both clinical and experimental aspects of nephrological and urological disorders in either sex, kidney transplantation and dialysis, and the male reproductive system, including male fertility and the prostate.

574.192 016   NE   ISSN 0927-278X
EXCERPTA MEDICA. SECTION 29: CLINICAL AND EXPERIMENTAL BIOCHEMISTRY. 1948. 40/yr.(in 4 vols.; 10 nos./vol.). fl.2491 (effective 1992). Excerpta Medica (Subsidiary of: Elsevier Science Publishers B.V.), P.O. Box 548, 1000 AM Amsterdam, Netherlands. TEL 020-5803911. FAX 020-5803222. TELEX 18582 ESPA NL. (Dist. by: Elsevier Science Publishers Ireland Ltd., P.O. Box 85, Limerick, Ireland. TEL 061-61944; Subscr. in U.S. and Canada to: Elsevier Science Publishing Co., Inc., Box 882, Madison Sq. Sta., New York, NY 10159. TEL 212-989-5800) adv.; bk.rev.; abstr.; charts; index. cum.index. Indexed: Chem.Abstr.
●Also available online. Vendor(s): BRS, DIMDI, Data-Star, DIALOG, JICST.
Also available on CD-ROM. Producer(s): SilverPlatter.
Former titles (until 1992): Excerpta Medica. Section 29: Clinical Biochemistry (ISSN 0300-5372); Excerpta Medica. Section 29: Biochemistry (ISSN 0014-4339)
Description: Covers both clinical chemistry and general biochemistry and includes analytical methods, chemical function tests, enzyme assay, enzyme mode of action studies, biochemical roles in disease, metabolic biochemistry, nutritional analysis and molecular transport.

EXCERPTA MEDICA. SECTION 30: CLINICAL AND EXPERIMENTAL PHARMACOLOGY. see *PHARMACY AND PHARMACOLOGY — Abstracting, Bibliographies, Statistics*

616.742 016   NE   ISSN 0014-4355
RC933.A1   CODEN: EXARB
EXCERPTA MEDICA. SECTION 31: ARTHRITIS AND RHEUMATISM. 1965. 8/yr. fl.843 (effective 1992). Excerpta Medica (Subsidiary of: Elsevier Science Publishers), P.O. Box 548, 1000 AM Amsterdam, Netherlands. TEL 020-5803911. FAX 020-5803222. TELEX 18582 ESPA NL. (Dist. by: Elsevier Science Publishers Ireland Ltd., P.O. Box 85, Limerick, Ireland. TEL 061-61944; Subscr. in U.S. and Canada to: Elsevier Science Publishing Co., Inc., Box 882, Madison Sq. Sta., New York, NY 10159. TEL 212-989-5800) adv.; abstr.; index. cum.index.
●Also available online. Vendor(s): BRS, DIMDI, Data-Star, DIALOG, JICST.
Also available on CD-ROM. Producer(s): SilverPlatter.
—BLDSC shelfmark: 3835.815000.
Description: Covers both clinical and experimental aspects of arthritis, rheumatism, bone and joint pathology, and includes spine disorders, connective tissue disorders and rheumatic fever.

MEDICAL SCIENCES — ABSTRACTING, BIBLIOGRAPHIES, STATISTICS

616.89 016   NE   ISSN 0014-4363
                                       CODEN: PSCYA
EXCERPTA MEDICA. SECTION 32: PSYCHIATRY. 1948. 20/yr.(in 2 vols.; 10 nos./vol.). fl.1497 (effective 1992). Excerpta Medica (Subsidiary of: Elsevier Science Publishers), P.O. Box 548, 1000 AM Amsterdam, Netherlands. TEL 020-5803911. FAX 020-5803222. TELEX 18582 ESPA NL. (Dist. by: Elsevier Science Publishers Ireland Ltd., P.O. Box 85, Limerick, Ireland. TEL 061-61944; Subscr. in U.S. and Canada to: Elsevier Science Publishing Co., Inc., Box 882, Madison Sq. Sta., New York, NY 10159. TEL 212-989-5800) adv.; abstr.; index. cum.index.
●Also available online. Vendor(s): BRS, DIMDI, Data-Star, DIALOG, JICST.
Also available on CD-ROM. Producer(s): SilverPlatter.
—BLDSC shelfmark: 3835.874000.
   Description: Covers all aspects of medical psychology and psychiatry, including the psychological aspects of addiction, alcoholism, sexual behavior and suicide.

617.3 016   NE   ISSN 0014-4371
RD701   CODEN: OSUGA
EXCERPTA MEDICA. SECTION 33: ORTHOPEDIC SURGERY. 1956. 10/yr. fl.898 (effective 1992). Excerpta Medica (Subsidiary of: Elsevier Science Publishers), P.O. Box 548, 1000 AM Amsterdam, Netherlands. TEL 020-5803911. FAX 020-5803222. TELEX 18582 ESPA NL. (Dist. by: Elsevier Science Publishers Ireland, P.O. Box 85, Limerick, Ireland. TEL 061-61944; Subscr. in U.S. and Canada to: Elsevier Science Publishing Co., Inc., Box 882, Madison Sq. Sta., New York, NY 10159. TEL 212-989-5800) adv.; abstr.; index. cum.index.
●Also available online. Vendor(s): BRS, DIMDI, Data-Star, DIALOG, JICST.
Also available on CD-ROM. Producer(s): SilverPlatter.
—BLDSC shelfmark: 3835.862000.
   Description: Covers the general, diagnostic and surgical aspects of orthopedics, and includes surgical aspects of other bone diseases, bone tumors, trauma of the musculoskeletal system and biomechanics of the musculoskeletal system.

613.62 016   NE   ISSN 0014-4398
RC963   CODEN: EMOHAH
EXCERPTA MEDICA. SECTION 35: OCCUPATIONAL HEALTH AND INDUSTRIAL MEDICINE. 1971. 16/yr.(in 2 vols., 8 nos./vol.). fl.1547 (effective 1992). Excerpta Medica (Subsidiary of: Elsevier Science Publishers), P.O. Box 548, 1000 AM Amsterdam, Netherlands. TEL 020-5803911. FAX 020-5803222. TELEX 18582 ESPA NL. (Dist. by: Elsevier Science Publishers Ireland Ltd., P.O. Box 85, Limerick, Ireland. TEL 061-61944; Subscr. in U.S. and Canada to: Elsevier Science Publishing Co., Inc., Box 882, Madison Sq. Sta., New York, NY 10159. TEL 212-989-5800) adv.; abstr.; index. cum.index. **Indexed:** Ergon.Abstr.
●Also available online. Vendor(s): BRS, DIMDI, Data-Star, DIALOG, JICST.
Also available on CD-ROM. Producer(s): SilverPlatter.
—BLDSC shelfmark: 3835.859000.
   Description: Covers the health aspects of work and the working environment, and includes ergonomics, sports medicine, the influence of life style and psychosocial aspects.

EXCERPTA MEDICA. SECTION 36: HEALTH POLICY, ECONOMICS AND MANAGEMENT. see *HOSPITALS — Abstracting, Bibliographies, Statistics*

610 016   NE   ISSN 0001-8848
                                    CODEN: ADRTA
EXCERPTA MEDICA. SECTION 38: ADVERSE REACTIONS TITLES. 1966. 12/yr. fl.9950 (effective 1992). Excerpta Medica (Subsidiary of: Elsevier Science Publishers), P.O. Box 548, 1000 AM Amsterdam, Netherlands. TEL 020-5803911. FAX 020-5803222. TELEX 18582 ESPA NL. (Dist. by: Elsevier Science Publishers Ireland Ltd., P.O. Box 85, Limerick, Ireland. TEL 061-61944; Subscr. in U.S. and Canada to: Elsevier Science Publishing Co., Inc., Box 882, Madison Sq. Sta., New York, NY 10159. TEL 212-989-5800) adv.; index. cum.index.
●Also available online. Vendor(s): BRS, DIMDI, Data-Star, DIALOG, JICST.
Also available on CD-ROM. Producer(s): SilverPlatter.
—BLDSC shelfmark: 3835.805000.

016 613.83   NE   ISSN 0925-5958
                                    CODEN: DRDPA
EXCERPTA MEDICA. SECTION 40: DRUG DEPENDENCE, ALCOHOL ABUSE AND ALCOHOLISM. 1973. 6/yr. fl.843 (effective 1992). Excerpta Medica (Subsidiary of: Elsevier Science Publishers), P.O. Box 548, 1000 AM Amsterdam, Netherlands. TEL 020-5803911. FAX 020-5803222. TELEX 18582 ESPA NL. (Dist. by: Elsevier Science Publishers Ireland Ltd., P.O. Box 85, Limerick, Ireland. TEL 061-61944; Subscr. in U.S. and Canada to: Elsevier Science Publishing Co., Inc., Box 882, Madison Sq. Sta., New York, NY 10159. TEL 212-989-5800) Ed.Bd. adv.; abstr.; index. cum.index.
●Also available online. Vendor(s): BRS, DIMDI, Data-Star, DIALOG, JICST.
Also available on CD-ROM. Producer(s): SilverPlatter.
—BLDSC shelfmark: 3835.828920.
   Formerly: Excerpta Medica. Section 40: Drug Dependence (ISSN 0304-4041)
   Description: Covers all aspects of the abuse of drugs, alcohol and organic solvents and includes material relating to experimental pharmacology of addiction.

EXCERPTA MEDICA. SECTION 46: ENVIRONMENTAL HEALTH AND POLLUTION CONTROL. see *ENVIRONMENTAL STUDIES — Abstracting, Bibliographies, Statistics*

616.3 016   NE   ISSN 0031-3580
                                  CODEN: EMGSA
EXCERPTA MEDICA. SECTION 48: GASTROENTEROLOGY. 1971. 20/yr.(in 2 vols.) ; 10 nos./vol.). fl.1393 (effective 1992). Excerpta Medica (Subsidiary of: Elsevier Science Publishers), P.O. Box 548, 1000 AM Amsterdam, Netherlands. TEL 020-5803911. FAX 020-5803222. TELEX 18582 ESPA NL. (Dist. by: Elsevier Science Publishers Ireland Ltd., P.O. Box 85, Limerick, Ireland. TEL 061-61944; Subscr. in U.S. and Canada to: Elsevier Science Publishing Co., Inc., Box 882, Madison Sq. Sta., New York, NY 10159. TEL 212-989-5800) adv.; bk.rev.; abstr.; index. cum.index.
●Also available online. Vendor(s): BRS, DIMDI, Data-Star, DIALOG, JICST.
Also available on CD-ROM. Producer(s): SilverPlatter.
—BLDSC shelfmark: 3835.831000.
   Description: Covers all aspects of digestive system disease and includes disorders of the mouth and pharynx, the hepatobiliary system, the exocrine pancreas, the peritoneum, mesentery and omentum.

340.6 016   NE   ISSN 0303-8459
                                    CODEN: FSABD
EXCERPTA MEDICA. SECTION 49: FORENSIC SCIENCE ABSTRACTS. 1975. 6/yr. fl.909 (effective 1992). Excerpta Medica (Subsidiary of: Elsevier Science Publishers), P.O. Box 548, 1000 AM Amsterdam, Netherlands. TEL 020-5803911. FAX 020-5803222. TELEX 18582 ESPA NL. (Dist. by: Elsevier Science Publishers Ireland Ltd., P.O. Box 85, Limerick, Ireland. TEL 061-61944; Subscr. in U.S. and Canada to: Elsevier Science Publishing Co., Inc., Box 882, Madison Sq. Sta., New York, NY 10159. TEL 212-989-5800) adv.
●Also available online. Vendor(s): BRS, DIMDI, Data-Star, DIALOG, JICST.
Also available on CD-ROM. Producer(s): SilverPlatter.
—BLDSC shelfmark: 3835.830500.
   Formerly: Excerpta Medica. Section 49: Forensic Science.
   Description: Covers all aspects of biomedicine and science of relevance to criminal investigation or coroners.

616.853 016   NE   ISSN 0031-0743
RA1001   CODEN: EMEPA
EXCERPTA MEDICA. SECTION 50: EPILEPSY ABSTRACTS. 1968. 6/yr. fl.718 (effective 1992). Excerpta Medica (Subsidiary of: Elsevier Science Publishers), P.O. Box 548, 1000 AM Amsterdam, Netherlands. TEL 020-5803911. FAX 020-5803222. TELEX 18582 ESPA NL. (Dist. by: Elsevier Science Publishers Ireland Ltd., P.O. Box 85, Limerick, Ireland. TEL 061-61944; Subscr. in U.S. and Canada to: Elsevier Science Publishing Co., Inc., Box 882, Madison Sq. Sta., New York, NY 10159. TEL 212-989-5800) adv.; bk.rev.; abstr.; index. cum.index. **Indexed:** Excerp.Med.
●Also available online. Vendor(s): BRS, DIMDI, Data-Star, DIALOG, JICST.
Also available on CD-ROM. Producer(s): SilverPlatter.
—BLDSC shelfmark: 3835.830700.
   Formerly: Excerpta Medica. Section 50: Epilepsy.
   Description: Covers both clinical and experimental aspects of epilepsy and brain seizures, and includes psychosocial aspects of epilepsy and electoencephalography (EEG).

EXCERPTA MEDICA. SECTION 52: TOXICOLOGY. see *PHARMACY AND PHARMACOLOGY — Abstracting, Bibliographies, Statistics*

610 016   CN   ISSN 0227-2393
F A M L I. (Family Medicine Literature Index) 1980. a. Can.$60 (foreign $70). College of Family Physicians of Canada, 4000 Leslie St., Willowdale, Ont. M2K 2R9, Canada. TEL 416-493-7513. Ed. Lynn Dunikowski. cum.index; circ. 400. (back issues avail.)
●Also available online. Vendor(s): National Library of Medicine.
—BLDSC shelfmark: 3865.576620.
   Description: Comprehensive annual index to the literature of family medicine.

FIRE STATISTICS UNITED KINGDOM. see *FIRE PREVENTION — Abstracting, Bibliographies, Statistics*

617.643   US   ISSN 0015-4725
QP535.F1   CODEN: FLUOA4
FLUORIDE. 1968. q. $30. International Society for Fluoride Research, Box 692, Warren, MI 48090. Ed.Bd. bk.rev.; abstr.; bibl.; charts; illus.; stat.; circ. 600. (also avail. in microform from UMI; reprint service avail. from ISI,UMI) **Indexed:** Biol.Abstr., C.I.S. Abstr., Cadscan, Chem.Abstr., Curr.Adv.Ecol.Sci., Curr.Cont., Dairy Sci.Abstr., Excerp.Med., Field Crop Abstr., Food Sci.& Tech.Abstr., Ind.Sci.Rev., Ind.Vet., INIS Atomind., Lead Abstr., Nutr.Abstr., Ocean.Abstr., Pollut.Abstr., Sci.Cit.Ind., Soils & Fert., Vet.Bull., Zincscan.
—BLDSC shelfmark: 3962.262800.

617   FR
FRANCE. SERVICE D'ETUDE DES STRATEGIES ET DES STATISTIQUES INDUSTRIELLES. RESULTATS TRIMESTRIELS DES ENQUETES DE BRANCHE. FABRICATION DE MATERIEL MEDICO-CHIRURGICAL ET DES PROTHESES. q. 180 F. (foreign 210 F.)(effective 1991). Service d'Etude des Strategies et des Statistiques Industrielles (SESSI), 85 Bd. du Montparnasse, 75270 Paris Cedex 06, France. TEL 45-56-42-34. FAX 45-56-40-71. stat.
   Description: Provides detailed industry-wide performance statistics for comparative evaluations.

FRITZ-HUESER-INSTITUT FUER DEUTSCHE UND AUSLAENDISCHE ARBEITERLITERATUR. INFORMATIONEN. see *LITERATURE — Abstracting, Bibliographies, Statistics*

616.3 016   GW   ISSN 0863-1743
                                     CODEN: GAJOEN
GASTROENTEROLOGISCHES JOURNAL. 1938. 4/yr. DM.64. Johann Ambrosius Barth Verlag, Leipzig - Heidelberg, Salomonstr. 18b, 7010 Leipzig, Germany. TEL 70131. Ed. K.-U Schentke. adv.; bk.rev.; abstr.; bibl.; charts; illus.; index. **Indexed:** Chem.Abstr., Excerp.Med., Ind.Med., INIS Atomind.
—BLDSC shelfmark: 4088.993000.
   Formerly: Deutsche Zeitschrift fuer Verdauungs- und Stoffwechselkrankheiten (ISSN 0012-1053)

MEDICAL SCIENCES — ABSTRACTING, BIBLIOGRAPHIES, STATISTICS

619 US
GENERAL CLINICAL RESEARCH CENTERS; a research resources directory. 1978. biennial. free. U.S. National Institutes of Health, National Center for Research Resources, Westwood Bldg., Rm. 10A15, 5333 Westbard Ave., Bethesda, MD 20892. TEL 301-496-5545. circ. 9,000.
Description: Directory of clinical research centers.

GESUNDHEITSFOERDERUNG. see *PHYSICAL FITNESS AND HYGIENE — Abstracting, Bibliographies, Statistics*

616.1 US
▼**HANDBOOK OF HYPERLIPIDEMIA.** 1990. a. $35. Current Science, 20 N. Third St., Philadelphia, PA 19106. TEL 800-552-5866. FAX 215-574-2270. Ed. G.R. Thompson. illus.
Description: For lipid and cardiovascular specialists as well as the general practitioner. Covers all aspects of hyperlipidemia including pathophysiology, classification and clinical practice.

610 US ISSN 0163-0458
HEALTH DEVICES ALERTS; a summary of reported problems, hazards, recalls, and updates. (Includes: Health Devices Alerts Action Items; Health Devices Alerts Abstracts; Health Devices Alerts F D A Data; Health Devices Alerts Implants; Health Devices Alerts Hazards Bulletin) 1976. w. $530 to non-members. (Emergency Care Research Institute) E C R I, 5200 Butler Pike, Plymouth Meeting, PA 19462. TEL 215-825-6000. FAX 215-834-1275. abstr. (back issues avail.)
●Also available online. Vendor(s): DIALOG (File no.198).
Also available on CD-ROM.
—BLDSC shelfmark: 4274.963500.
Description: Series of four newsletters containing information on reported problems, hazards, and recalls of medical devices; also includes selections from FDA device problem databases.
Refereed Serial

HEALTH DEVICES SOURCEBOOK. see *MEDICAL SCIENCES*

610.73 016 US
HEALTH INDEX. (Not avail. in printed format) updated m. $80 per hour on BRS and DIALOG; $94.80 on Data-Star. Information Access Company, 362 Lakeside Dr., Foster City, CA 94404. TEL 800-227-8431. FAX 415-378-5499.
●Also available online. Vendor(s): BRS (HEAL), Data-Star (HLTH), DIALOG (File no.149).
Also available on CD-ROM.

610 015 US ISSN 0162-0843 CODEN: HSSED4
HEALTH SCIENCES SERIALS. 1979. q. $15 (foreign $18.75). U.S. National Library of Medicine, 8600 Rockville Pike, Bethesda, MD 20894. TEL 301-496-6308. FAX 301-496-4450. (Orders to: Supt. of Documents, Washington, DC 20402) (microfiche) **Indexed:** MEDOC.
●Also available online. Vendor(s): National Library of Medicine.
—BLDSC shelfmark: 4275.106710.

610 016 HU ISSN 0441-4438
HUNGARIAN MEDICAL BIBLIOGRAPHY; abstracts. (Text in English) 1961. s-a. 700 Ft.($30) Orszagos Orvostudomanyi Informacios Intezet es Konyvtar - National Institute for Medical Information and Library of Medicine, Szentkiralyi u. 21, 1088 Budapest, Hungary. TEL 361-117-6352. Ed. Akos Terebessy. circ. 300.

610 016 PL ISSN 0033-2321
I.B. INFORMACJA BIEZACA; przeglad pismiennictwa lekarskiego polskiego. 1963. m. 420 Zl.($46.20) Glowna Biblioteka Lekarska - Central Medical Library, Chocimska 22, Warsaw, Poland. (Dist. by: Ars Polona-Ruch, Krakowskie Przedmiescie 7, 00-068 Warsaw, Poland) Ed. Feliks Widy-Wirski. bibl.; index; circ. 1,200. **Indexed:** Excerp.Med.

616.99 016 US
I C R D B CANCERGRAM: ANTITUMOR AND ANTIVIRAL AGENTS - MECHANISM OF ACTION. (International Cancer Research Data Bank) 1977. m. $28. U.S. National Cancer Institute, International Cancer Information Center, Bldg. 82, Bethesda, MD 20892. TEL 301-496-7403. FAX 301-480-8105. (Dist. by: Supt. of Documents, Washington, DC 20402)

616.99 016 US
I C R D B CANCERGRAM: BREAST CANCER - DIAGNOSIS, TREATMENT, PRECLINICAL BIOLOGY. (International Cancer Research Data Bank) 1977. m. $28. U.S. National Cancer Institute, International Cancer Information Center, Bldg. 82, Bethesda, MD 20892. TEL 301-496-7403. FAX 301-480-8105. (Dist. by: Supt. of Documents, Washington, DC 20402)

616.99 016 US
I C R D B CANCERGRAM: C N S MALIGNANCIES - DIAGNOSIS, TREATMENT. (International Cancer Research Data Bank) 1977. m. $19. U.S. National Cancer Institute, International Cancer Information Center, Bldg. 82, Bethesda, MD 20892. TEL 301-496-7403. FAX 301-480-8105. (Dist. by: Supt. of Documents, Washington, DC 20402)

616.99 016 US
I C R D B CANCERGRAM: CANCER DETECTION AND MANAGEMENT - BIOLOGICAL MARKERS. (International Cancer Research Data Bank) 1977. m. $18. U.S. National Cancer Institute, International Cancer Information Center, Bldg. 82, Bethesda, MD 20892. TEL 301-496-7403. FAX 301-480-8105. (Dist. by: Supt. of Documents, Washington, DC 20402)

616.99 615.8 016 US
I C R D B CANCERGRAM: CANCER DETECTION AND MANAGEMENT - DIAGNOSTIC RADIOLOGY. (International Cancer Research Data Bank) 1977. m. $23. U.S. National Cancer Institute, International Cancer Information Center, Bldg. 82, Bethesda, MD 20892. TEL 301-496-7403. FAX 301-480-8105. (Dist. by: Supt. of Documents, Washington, DC 20402)

616.99 615.8 016 US
I C R D B CANCERGRAM: CANCER DETECTION AND MANAGEMENT - NUCLEAR MEDICINE. (International Cancer Research Data Bank) 1977. m. $19. U.S. National Cancer Institute, International Cancer Information Center, Bldg. 82, Bethesda, MD 20892. TEL 301-496-7403. FAX 301-480-8105. (Dist. by: Supt. of Documents, Washington, DC 20402)

616.99 615.8 016 US
I C R D B CANCERGRAM: CLINICAL TREATMENT OF CANCER - RADIATION THERAPY. (International Cancer Research Data Bank) 1977. m. $24. U.S. National Cancer Institute, International Cancer Information Center, Bldg. 82, Bethesda, MD 20892. TEL 301-496-7403. FAX 301-480-8105. (Dist. by: Supt. of Documents, Washington, DC 20402)

616.99 016 US
I C R D B CANCERGRAM: COLORECTAL CANCER - DIAGNOSIS, TREATMENT. (International Cancer Research Data Bank) 1977. m. $19. U.S. National Cancer Institute, International Cancer Information Center, Bldg. 82, Bethesda, MD 20892. TEL 301-496-7403. FAX 301-480-8105. (Dist. by: Supt. of Documents, Washington, DC 20402)

616.99 016 US
I C R D B CANCERGRAM: ENDOCRINE TUMORS - DIAGNOSIS, TREATMENT, PATHOPHYSIOLOGY. (International Cancer Research Data Bank) 1977. m. $19. U.S. National Cancer Institute, International Cancer Information Center, Bldg. 82, Bethesda, MD 20892. TEL 301-496-7403. FAX 301-480-8105. (Dist. by: Supt. of Documents, Washington, DC 20402)

616.99 016 US
I C R D B CANCERGRAM: GENITOURINARY CANCERS - DIAGNOSIS, TREATMENT. (International Cancer Research Data Bank) 1977. m. $23. U.S. National Cancer Institute, International Cancer Information Center, Bldg. 82, Bethesda, MD 20892. TEL 301-496-7403. FAX 301-480-8105. (Dist. by: Supt. of Documents, Washington, DC 20402)

616.99 618.1 016 US
I C R D B CANCERGRAM: GYNECOLOGICAL TUMORS - DIAGNOSIS, TREATMENT. (International Cancer Research Data Bank) 1977. m. $19. U.S. National Cancer Institute, International Cancer Information Center, Bldg. 82, Bethesda, MD 20892. TEL 301-496-7403. FAX 301-480-8105. (Dist. by: Supt. of Documents, Washington, DC 20402)

616.15 016 US
I C R D B CANCERGRAM: LEUKEMIA AND MULTIPLE MYELOMA - DIAGNOSIS, TREATMENT. (International Cancer Research Data Bank) 1977. m. $19. U.S. National Cancer Institute, International Cancer Information Center, Bldg. 82, Bethesda, MD 20892. TEL 301-496-7403. FAX 301-480-8105. (Dist. by: Supt. of Documents, Washington, DC 20402)
Incorporates: I C R D B Cancergram: Acute and Chronic Leukemia - Diagnosis, Treatment; I C R D B Cangergram: Clinical Evaluation and Treatment of Multiple Myeloma and other Gammopathies.

616.99 016 US
I C R D B CANCERGRAM: LUNG CANCER - DIAGNOSIS, TREATMENT. (International Cancer Research Data Bank) 1977. m. $19. U.S. National Cancer Institute, International Cancer Information Center, Bldg. 82, Bethesda, MD 20892. TEL 301-496-7403. FAX 301-480-8105. (Dist. by: Supt. of Documents, Washington, DC 20402)

616.99 016 US
I C R D B CANCERGRAM: LYMPHOMAS - DIAGNOSIS, TREATMENT. (International Cancer Research Data Bank) 1977. m. $19. U.S. National Cancer Institute, International Cancer Information Center, Bldg. 82, Bethesda, MD 20892. TEL 301-496-7403. FAX 301-480-8105. (Dist. by: Supt. of Documents, Washington, DC 20402)

616.99 016 US
I C R D B CANCERGRAM: MELANOMA AND OTHER SKIN CANCER - DIAGNOSIS, TREATMENT. (International Cancer Research Data Bank) 1977. m. $19. U.S. National Cancer Institute, International Cancer Information Center, Bldg. 82, Bethesda, MD 20892. TEL 301-496-7403. FAX 301-480-8105. (Dist. by: Supt. of Documents, Washington, DC 20402)

616.99 016 US
I C R D B CANCERGRAM: NEOPLASIA OF THE HEAD AND NECK - DIAGNOSIS, TREATMENT. (International Cancer Research Data Bank) 1977. m. $23. U.S. National Cancer Institute, International Cancer Information Center, Bldg. 82, Bethesda, MD 20892. TEL 301-496-7403. FAX 301-480-8105. (Dist. by: Supt. of Documents, Washington, DC 20402)

616.99 618.92 016 US
I C R D B CANCERGRAM: PEDIATRIC ONCOLOGY. (International Cancer Research Data Bank) 1977. m. $19. U.S. National Cancer Institute, International Cancer Information Center, Bldg. 82, Bethesda, MD 20892. TEL 301-496-7403. FAX 301-480-8105. (Dist. by: Supt. of Documents, Washington, DC 20402)

616.99 371.9 016 US
I C R D B CANCERGRAM: REHABILITATION AND SUPPORTIVE CARE. (International Cancer Research Data Bank) 1977. m. $19. U.S. National Cancer Institute, International Cancer Information Center, Bldg. 82, Bethesda, MD 20892. TEL 301-496-7403. FAX 301-480-8105. (Subscr. to: Supt. of Documents, Washington, DC 20402)

616.99 016 US
I C R D B CANCERGRAM: SARCOMAS AND RELATED TUMORS - DIAGNOSIS, TREATMENT. (International Cancer Research Data Bank) 1977. m. $19. U.S. National Cancer Institute, International Cancer Information Center, Bldg. 82, Bethesda, MD 20892. TEL 301-496-7403. FAX 301-480-8105. (Dist. by: Supt. of Documents, Washington, DC 20402)

616.99 016 US
I C R D B CANCERGRAM: UPPER GASTROINTESTINAL TUMORS - DIAGNOSIS, TREATMENT. (International Cancer Research Data Bank) 1977. m. $19. U.S. National Cancer Institute, International Cancer Information Center, Bldg. 82, Bethesda, MD 20892. TEL 301-496-7403. FAX 301-480-8105. (Dist. by: Supt. of Documents, Washington, DC 20402)

610 FR ISSN 1011-8624
IMMUNIZATIONS/VACCINATIONS/VACUNACIONES. (Text in English, French, Spanish) 1977. 3/yr. 360 F. for 2 yrs. Centre International de l'Enfance - International Children's Center, Chateau de Longchamp, Bois de Boulogne, 75016 Paris, France. TEL 1-45-20-79-92. FAX 1-45-25-73-67.
Description: Abstracts on program evaluation, investigation of new vaccines, immunization policies, epidemiological impact, technical aspects: vaccinal associations, schedules, cold chain, logistics.

M

MEDICAL SCIENCES — ABSTRACTING, BIBLIOGRAPHIES, STATISTICS

615.37 016   US   ISSN 0307-112X
QR180
IMMUNOLOGY ABSTRACTS. 1976. m. $815 (foreign $845). Cambridge Scientific Abstracts, 7200 Wisconsin Ave., 6th Fl., Bethesda, MD 20814. TEL 301-961-6750. FAX 301-961-6720. TELEX 910 2507547 CAMB MD. Ed.Bd. adv.; abstr.; index. (also avail. in magnetic tape; back issues avail.) **Indexed:** Cal.Tiss.Abstr., Chemorec.Abstr., Comput.& Info.Sys., Oncol.Abstr., Pollut.Abstr.
●Also available online. Vendor(s): BRS (CSAL), DIALOG (File no.76/LIFE SCIENCES COLLECTION). Also available on CD-ROM. Producer(s): Cambridge Scientific Abstracts (Compact Cambridge Life Sciences Collection).
—BLDSC shelfmark: 4369.701000.
Description: Covers immune systems in humans and animals, both basic research and clinical applications.

610 016   US   ISSN 0019-3879
Z6660
INDEX MEDICUS. (Medical Subject Headings (MSH) is published as Part 2 of the January Index Medicus) 1960. m. $319 includes List of Journals Indexed in Index Medicus and Medical Subject Headings. U.S. National Library of Medicine, 8600 Rockville Pike, Bethesda, MD 20894. TEL 301-496-6308. FAX 301-496-4450. (Orders to: Supt. of Documents, Washington, DC 20402) circ. 6,000. (also avail. in microform from MIM,UMI) **Indexed:** JAMA, MEDOC, Popul.Ind.
●Also available online. Vendor(s): BRS (MESH, MESZ), DIALOG (File nos.154 & 155/MEDLINE), National Library of Medicine, STN International (MEDLINE).
Also available on CD-ROM. Producer(s): Cambridge Scientific Abstracts (Compact Cambridge MEDLINE), Dialog Information Services (DIALOG OnDisc MEDLINE), SilverPlatter (MEDLINE).

016 610   BL   ISSN 0100-4743
Z6661.L29
INDEX MEDICUS LATINOAMERICANO. (Text in English, Portuguese and Spanish) 1979. q. $150 in Latin America; elsewhere $200. (Panamerican Health Organization-World Health Organization) Latin American and Caribbean Center on Health Sciences Information (BIREME), Rua Botucatu, 862, Caixa Postal 20.381, V. Clementino, 04023 Sao Paulo, Brazil. TEL (011) 5492611. FAX 5511-5711919. TELEX (11) 22143 OPAS BR. abstr.; bibl.; circ. 500. (back issues avail.)
●Also available on CD-ROM.
—BLDSC shelfmark: 4382.661000.
Description: Bibliography containing abstracts of articles from more than 650 Latin American titles.

610   RU   ISSN 0206-0515
INDEX OF CURRENT MEDICAL LITERATURE IN THE U S S R; including the medical demographic statistics of the U S S R. s-m. N P O Soyuzmedinform, Moskvoretskaya Nab 2A, 109240 Moscow, Russia.
—BLDSC shelfmark: 4377.680000.
Description: Covers all publications in the biomedical sciences in the USSR.

617.6 016   US   ISSN 0019-3992
Z6668
INDEX TO DENTAL LITERATURE; an alphabetical author and subject index to dental literature. q. (annual cumulation). $175 (including bound vol.). American Dental Association, Bureau of Library Services, 211 E. Chicago Ave., Chicago, IL 60611. TEL 312-440-2500. index; circ. 1,100. (also avail. in microform from UMI; reprint service avail. from UMI)
●Also available online. Vendor(s): BRS (MESH, MESZ), DIALOG (File nos.154 & 155/MEDLINE), National Library of Medicine, STN International (MEDLINE).
Also available on CD-ROM. Producer(s): Cambridge Scientific Abstracts (Compact Cambridge MEDLINE), Dialog Information Services (DIALOG OnDisc MEDLINE), SilverPlatter (MEDLINE).
—BLDSC shelfmark: 4377.800000.

617.6 016   AG   ISSN 0325-0679
INDICE DE LA LITERATURA DENTAL EN CASTELLANO. 1950. a. $40. Asociacion Odontologica Argentina, Junin 959, Buenos Aires, Argentina. bibl.; circ. 300.
●Also available on CD-ROM.
Supersedes: Indice de la Literatura Dental Periodica en Castellano y Portugues.

610 016   SP   ISSN 0019-7068
INDICE MEDICO ESPANOL. 1965. q. 4400 ptas. to individuals; institutions 5500 ptas.(foreign 6500 ptas.). (Centro de Documentacion e Informatica Biomedica) Universidad de Valencia, Facultad de Medicina, Avda. Blasco Ibanez - 17, 46010 Valencia, Spain. FAX 3613975. Dir. Maria-Luz Terrada Ferrandis. circ. 5,000. (reprint service avail.) **Indexed:** Nutr.Abstr.
●Also available online.
Also available on CD-ROM.

INFUSIONS-JOURNAL. see MEDICAL SCIENCES

340.6 016   US   ISSN 0098-2393
INTERNATIONAL BIBLIOGRAPHY OF THE FORENSIC SCIENCES. 1975. biennial. $25. International Reference Organization in Forensic Medicine and Sciences, c/o William G. Eckert, M.D., Ed., Box 8282, Wichita, KS 67208. TEL 316-268-5000.

617.11 016   US   ISSN 0090-0575
Z6667.B8
INTERNATIONAL BIBLIOGRAPHY ON BURNS. 1969. a., latest 1985. $25. National Institute for Burn Medicine, 909 E. Ann St., Ann Arbor, MI 48104. TEL 313-769-9000. Ed. Dr. Irving Feller. circ. 1,000.

610.73 016   US   ISSN 0020-8124
Z6675.N7
INTERNATIONAL NURSING INDEX. 1966. q. $250. (American Nurses' Association) American Journal of Nursing Co., 555 W. 57th St., New York, NY 10019. TEL 212-582-8820. Ed. Frederick W. Pattison. index; circ. 1,917. (also avail. in microform from UMI; reprint service avail. from UMI) **Indexed:** JAMA.
●Also available online. Vendor(s): BRS, DIALOG (File nos.154 & 155/MEDLINE), National Library of Medicine, STN International (MEDLINE).
Also available on CD-ROM. Producer(s): Cambridge Scientific Abstracts (Compact Cambridge MEDLINE), Dialog Information Services (DIALOG OnDisc MEDLINE), SilverPlatter (MEDLINE).
—BLDSC shelfmark: 4544.449000.
Description: Covers over 270 international nursing journals.

INTERNATIONAL RARE BOOK PRICES - SCIENCES & MEDICINE. see PUBLISHING AND BOOK TRADE — Abstracting, Bibliographies, Statistics

610 362   JA   ISSN 0911-8411
JAPAN. MINISTRY OF HEALTH AND WELFARE. STATISTICS AND INFORMATION DEPARTMENT. REPORT ON ACTIVITIES OF PUBLIC HEALTH CENTERS. a. 2500 Yen. Ministry of Health and Welfare, Statistics and Information Department - Kosei-sho Daijin Kanbo Tokei Joho-bu, 7-3 Ichigaya-Honmura cho, Shinjuku-ku, Tokyo 162, Japan. TEL 03-260-3181. (Order from: Health & Welfare Statistics Association, 5-13-14 Roppongi, Minato-ku, Tokyo, Japan) Key Title: Hokenjo Un'ei Hokoku.
Formerly (until 1960): Hokenjo Un'ei Hokoku Nenpo (ISSN 0437-6633)

616.9 312.3   JA   ISSN 0911-8489
JAPAN. MINISTRY OF HEALTH AND WELFARE. STATISTICS AND INFORMATION DEPARTMENT. STATISTICAL REPORT ON COMMUNICABLE DISEASES. (Text in English and Japanese) a. 1900 Yen. Ministry of Health and Welfare, Statistics and Information Department - Kosei-sho Daijin Kanbo Tokei Joho-bu, 7-3 Ichigaya Honmura-cho, Shinjuku-ku, Tokyo 162, Japan. TEL 03-260-3181. (Order from: Health & Welfare Statistics Association, 5-13-14 Roppongi, Minato-ku, Tokyo, Japan) Key Title: Densenbyo Tokei.
Supersedes in part (in 1981): Japan. Ministry of Health and Welfare. Statistics and Information Department. Statistical Report on Communicable Diseases and Food Poisonings.

616.9 312.3   JA   ISSN 0911-8497
JAPAN. MINISTRY OF HEALTH AND WELFARE. STATISTICS AND INFORMATION DEPARTMENT. STATISTICAL REPORT ON FOOD POISONINGS. (Text in English and Japanese) a. 1500 Yen. Ministry of Health and Welfare, Statistics and Information Department - Kosei-sho Daijin Kanbo Tokei Joho-bu, 7-3 Ichigaya-Honmura Cho, Shinjuku-ku, Tokyo 162, Japan. TEL 03-260-3181. (Subscr. to: Health and Welfare Statistics Association, 5-13-14 Roppongi, Minato-ku, Tokyo, Japan) Key Title: Shokuchudoku Tokei.
Supersedes in part (in 1981): Japan. Ministry of Health and Welfare. Statistics and Information Department. Statistical Report on Communicable Diseases and Food Poisonings.

JATROS DERMATOLOGIE. see MEDICAL SCIENCES — Dermatology And Venereology

JATROS GYNAEKOLOGIE. see MEDICAL SCIENCES — Obstetrics And Gynecology

JATROS H N O. see MEDICAL SCIENCES — Otorhinolaryngology

JATROS NEUROLOGIE - PSYCHIATRIE. see MEDICAL SCIENCES — Psychiatry And Neurology

JATROS ORTHOPAEDIE. see MEDICAL SCIENCES — Orthopedics And Traumatology

JATROS PAEDIATRIE. see MEDICAL SCIENCES — Pediatrics

JATROS UROLOGIE. see MEDICAL SCIENCES — Urology And Nephrology

616.1   US   ISSN 0263-6352
                                                 CODEN: JOHYD3
JOURNAL OF HYPERTENSION. 1982. m. $135 to individuals; institutions $255; residents $95. (International Society of Hypertension) Current Science, 20 N. Third St., Philadelphia, PA 19106. TEL 800-552-5866. FAX 215-574-2270. Ed. J.L. Reid. adv.; bibl.; illus.; circ. 5,750. (back issues avail.; also avail. on diskette) **Indexed:** Curr.Adv.Biochem., Curr.Adv.Cancer Res., Excerp.Med.
—BLDSC shelfmark: 5004.510000.
Description: Publishes original papers ranging from studies in clinical care to basic investigation of experimental hypertension. Presents review articles followed by annotated bibliographies of references consulted. Includes a bibliography of the current world literature published during the previous year.

610 016   GW   ISSN 0022-9113
KARTEI DER PRAKTISCHEN MEDIZIN; unabhaengige Referatenzeitschrift des in- und auslaendischen Fachschrifttums. 1927. s-m. DM.58. Deutscher Kartei-Verlag, 7971 Aitrach, Germany. Ed. Dr. R. F. Weiss. bk.rev.; abstr.; illus.; index. (cards)

618   US
KEY OBSTETRICS AND GYNECOLOGY. 1988. q. $69 to individuals (foreign $83); institutions $89 (foreign $103); students $45 (foreign $59). Mosby - Year Book, Inc. (Subsidiary of: Times Mirror Company), 11830 Westline Industrial Dr., St. Louis, MO 63146. TEL 800-325-4177. FAX 314-432-1380. TELEX 44-2402.
Description: Provides abstracts from the world's scientific literature covering new diagnostic techniques, new therapeutic approaches, and new issues, trends, discoveries, and developments.

618.92 016   GW   ISSN 0340-5877
DER KINDERARZT. 1953. bi-m. DM.150. (Berufsverband der Kinderaerzte Deutschlands e.V.) Hansisches Verlagskontor H. Scheffler, Mengstr. 16, Postfach 2051, 2400 Luebeck 1, Germany. Ed. T. Hellbruegge. **Indexed:** Dok.Arbeitsmed.
—BLDSC shelfmark: 5095.580000.

610 016   KO   ISSN 0047-360X
KOREAN MEDICAL ABSTRACTS. (Text in English) 1971. q. $25. Korea Institute for Economics and Technology, P.O. Box 250, 206-9 Cheongryangri-Dong, Dongdaimun-Ku, S. Korea. abstr.; index; circ. 400. (also avail. in microfilm; reprint service avail. from UMI)
—BLDSC shelfmark: 5113.592000.

MEDICAL SCIENCES — ABSTRACTING, BIBLIOGRAPHIES, STATISTICS

610 016   IS
KOROTH (JERUSALEM); a bulletin devoted to the history of medicine and science. (Text in English, Hebrew) 1952. a. $17. Israel Institute of the History of Medicine, Box 432, Jerusalem, Israel. Eds. Joshua O. Leibowitz, Samuel S. Kottek. bk.rev.; circ. 250.
Formerly: Jerusalem Historical Medical Publications (ISSN 0449-4881)

616   US   ISSN 1050-9658
▼**LABORATORY MEDICINE ABSTRACT AND COMMENT.** 1991. 10/yr. $55 to individuals (foreign $78); institutions $85 (foreign $108). Churchill Livingstone Medical Journals, 650 Ave. of the Americas, New York, NY 10011. TEL 212-819-5440. FAX 212-727-7808. TELEX 662266. (Dist. by: Transaction Publishers, Department 3091, Rutgers University, New Brunswick, NJ 08903. TEL 908-932-2280) Ed. Dr. Calvin Strand.
Description: Presents summaries of articles on clinical pathology and related specialties.

535.58 621.329   NE
▼**LASERS IN MEDICINE.** (Text in English) 1991. m. (except June-July combined). fl.205 to individuals; institutions fl.308 (effective 1992). Excerpta Medica (Subsidiary of: Elsevier Science Publishers B.V.), P.O. Box 548, 1000 AM Amsterdam, Netherlands. TEL 020-5803911. FAX 020-5803222. TELEX 18582 ESPA NL. (Subscr. to: Elsevier Scientific Publishers Ireland Ltd., P.O. Box 85, Limerick, Ireland. TEL 061-61944; Subscr. in U.S. and Canada to: Elsevier Science Publishing Co., Inc., Box 882, Madison Sq. Sta., New York, NY 10159. TEL 212-989-5800) Ed.Bd. cum.index.
●Also available online. Vendor(s): BRS, DIMDI, Data-Star, DIALOG.
Description: Covers international literature on developments regarding lasers and their applications in medicine and biomedicine.
Refereed Serial

616.15   US   ISSN 0887-6924
CODEN: LEUKED
LEUKEMIA. 1987. m. $90 to individuals; institutions $340. (Leukemia Society of America) Macmillan Publishing Company, Macmillan Research, 866 Third Ave., New York, NY 10022. TEL 212-319-1216. (Co-sponsor: Leukemia Research Fund, U.K.) Eds. Dr. C. Nicole Muller-Berat, Sven-Aage Killman. adv.; circ. 800. (also avail. in microform) **Indexed:** Curr.Adv.Cell & Devel.Biol., Curr.Adv.Genetics & Molec.Biol., Telegen.
—BLDSC shelfmark: 5185.249000.
Description: Articles on leukemia, germane diseases and normal hemopoiesis by specialists.
Refereed Serial

LIFE SCIENCE NETWORK NEWS. see *BIOLOGY — Abstracting, Bibliographies, Statistics*

610 016   SW   ISSN 0075-9813
LIST BIO-MED; BIOMEDICAL SERIALS IN SCANDINAVIAN LIBRARIES. (Text in English) 1965. irreg. SEK 300. Karolinska Institutets Bibliotek och Informationscentral, P.O. Box 60201, S-104 01 Stockholm, Sweden. FAX 46-8-348793. circ. 500.

011 610   PR
LIST OF CURRENT SERIAL PUBLICATIONS BEING RECEIVED AT THE UNIVERSITY OF PUERTO RICO MEDICAL SCIENCES CAMPUS LIBRARY. a. free. Universidad de Puerto Rico, Medical Sciences Campus Library, G.P.O. Box 5067, San Juan, PR 00936. (processed)

610 011   NE   ISSN 0923-5582
LIST OF JOURNALS ABSTRACTED (YEAR). Cover title: EMBASE List of Journals Abstracted. (Text in English) 1978? a. Excerpta Medica (Subsidiary of: Elsevier Science Publishers B.V.), P.O. Box 548, 1000 AM Amsterdam, Netherlands. TEL 020-5803911. FAX 020-5803222. TELEX 18582 ESPA NL. (Subscr. in U.S. and Canada to: Elsevier Science Publishing Co., Inc., Box 882, Madison Sq. Sta., New York, NY 10159. TEL 212-989-5800) bibl.; index. (back issues avail.)
Description: Complete listing of more than 3500 biomedical journals which are included in the Excerpta Medica and are screened for items for EMBASE and the other Excerpta Medica services, with full journal title, EMBASE abbreviation, ISSN and CODEN, and telephone and complete address.

610   US   ISSN 0093-3821
Z6660
LIST OF JOURNALS INDEXED IN INDEX MEDICUS. 1960. a. $12 (foreign $15). U.S. National Library of Medicine, 8600 Rockville Pike, Bethesda, MD 20894. TEL 301-496-6308. FAX 301-496-4450. (Orders to: Supt. of Documents, Washington, DC 20402) circ. 3,500.
—BLDSC shelfmark: 5233.400000.
Description: An annual listing of the 3,000 journals being indexed for Index Medicus as of January 1990.

610 015   US   ISSN 0736-7139
Z6660
LIST OF SERIALS INDEXED FOR ONLINE USERS. 1980. a. $22 (foreign $44). U.S. National Library of Medicine, 8600 Rockville Pike, Bethesda, MD 20894. TEL 301-496-6308. FAX 301-496-4450. (Orders to: NTIS, Springfield, VA 22161)
●Also available online. Vendor(s): National Library of Medicine.
Formerly: List of Serials and Monographs Indexed for Online Users (ISSN 0196-755X)
Description: Provides complete bibliographic information on serials and congress proceedings. Contains about 7,342 titles listed in alphabetical by abbreviated title followed full title.

LUNGE UND ATMUNG. see *MEDICAL SCIENCES — Respiratory Diseases*

610 011   AT   ISSN 1035-5693
M I M S DISEASE INDEX. a? Aus.$64. M I M S Australia, 48 Albany St., Crows Nest, N.S.W. 2065, Australia.

610 016   SA   ISSN 0580-6755
M I M S MEDICAL SPECIALITIES. 1960. m. M.I.M.S. (Subsidiary of: Times Media Ltd.), P.O. Box 2059, Pretoria 0001, South Africa. TEL 012-3485010. FAX 012-477716. Eds. Deo Botha, Dieter Brandt. adv.; index; cum.index; circ. 8,028. **Indexed:** Curr.Adv.Ecol.Sci.
Formerly: M I M S (ISSN 0027-0431)
Description: An index containing medicines available in South Africa in pharmacological order for humans.

610 016   HU   ISSN 0025-0252
MAGYAR ORVOSI BIBLIOGRAFIA; bibliographia medica Hungarica. 1957. bi-m. 2450 Ft. Orszagos Orvostudomanyi Informacios Intezet es Konyvtar - National Institute for Medical Information and Library of Medicine, Szentkiralyi u. 21, 1088 Budapest, Hungary. TEL 361-117-6352. Ed. Akos Terebessy. bibl.; index; circ. 350.

MAKERERE UNIVERSITY. ALBERT COOK LIBRARY. LIBRARY BULLETIN AND ACCESSION LIST. see *LIBRARY AND INFORMATION SCIENCES — Abstracting, Bibliographies, Statistics*

MEDEXPRES. see *PUBLIC HEALTH AND SAFETY — Abstracting, Bibliographies, Statistics*

613.7 614.8   US   ISSN 0730-7810
Discard
MEDICAL ABSTRACTS NEWSLETTER; your direct pipeline to the latest breakthroughs in health care. 1981. m. $24.95. Communi-T Publications, Box 2170, Teaneck, NJ 07666. TEL 201-836-5030. Ed. Toni L. Goldfarb. bk.rev. **Indexed:** CHNI.

610 016   US   ISSN 0000-085X
Z6658
MEDICAL AND HEALTH CARE BOOKS AND SERIALS IN PRINT; an index to literature in health sciences. (Issued in 2 vols.) 1972. a. $175. R.R. Bowker, A Reed Reference Publishing Company, Division of Reed Publishing (USA) Inc., 121 Chanlon Rd., New Providence, NJ 07974. TEL 800-521-8110. FAX 908-665-7974. TELEX 138 755. (Subscr. to: Order Dept., Box 31, New Providence, NJ 07974) (also avail. in magnetic tape)
●Also available online. Vendor(s): BRS, DIALOG. Also available on CD-ROM.
—BLDSC shelfmark: 5525.955000.
Former titles: Medical Books and Serials in Print (ISSN 0000-0574); Medical Books in Print (ISSN 0076-5929)
Description: Comprehensive, reference to currently published books and international serials in the biomedical and specialized health sciences, for professionals, students, librarians and others in the health sciences community. Provides bibliographic and ordering information, book classifications by subject, author and title, with an index to publishers and distributors; serial publications are classified by subject and title.

016.61   II   ISSN 0025-7060
MEDICAL BOOK NEWS; a guide to new books. (Text in English) 1967. bi-m. Rs.200($50) Medical Publications, 6 Owners Court, Near Strand Cinema, Colaba, Bombay 400 005, India. TEL 022-233962. FAX 022-202-2267. TELEX 11-2466-5863-KTKIN. Ed. Dr. Champaklal K. Parikh. adv.; bk.rev.; circ. 3,000.
Description: To be used by institutions as a basis for selection of books to be purchased.

MEDICAL CARE REVIEW. see *PUBLIC HEALTH AND SAFETY — Abstracting, Bibliographies, Statistics*

610 016   II   ISSN 0025-7109
MEDICAL CHECKLIST. 1966. bi-m. Rs.150($30) K.K. Roy (Private) Ltd., 55 Gariahat Rd., P.O. Box 10210, Calcutta 700 019, India. Ed. K.K. Roy. adv.; bk.rev.; bibl.; index; circ. 1,750. (looseleaf format)

MEDICAL COMPANIES GUIDE TO JAPAN. see *PHARMACY AND PHARMACOLOGY — Abstracting, Bibliographies, Statistics*

610   II   ISSN 0250-4367
MEDICINAL AND AROMATIC PLANTS ABSTRACTS. (Text in English) 1979. bi-m. Rs.300($125) Council of Scientific and Industrial Research, Publications & Information Directorate, Hillside Rd., New Delhi 110 012, India. TEL 11-5726014. Ed. H.C. Jain. adv.; bk.rev.; circ. 400. **Indexed:** Hort.Abstr.

618   DK   ISSN 0904-1966
MEDICINSK FOEDSELSSTATISTIK OG MISDANNELSESSTATISTIK. (Included in the series: Vitalstatistik) 1973. biennial. DKK 60. Sundhedsstyrelsen, Amaliegade 13, 1012 Copenhagen K, Denmark. (Subscr. to: Statens Informationtjeneste, P.O. Box 1103, 1009 Copenhagen K, Denmark)
Formerly: Medicinsk Foedselsstatistik (ISSN 0107-7597)

610 016   GW   ISSN 0025-8482
MEDIZINISCHE NEUERSCHEINUNGEN; Buch- und Zeitschriften-Erscheinungen. 1922. bi-m. DM.28.20. Theodor Oppermann Verlag, Ostfeldstr. 46, Postfach 710140, 3000 Hannover 71, Germany. adv.; bk.rev.; bibl.; circ. 4,500.

610 011   GW
MEDIZINISCHER LITERATUR ANZEIGER; bibliographische Zeitschrift fuer medizinische Neuerscheinungen. 1950. bi-m. DM.22.80. Dustri-Verlag, Bahnhofstr. 9, 8024 Deisenhofen, Germany. TEL 089-6138610. FAX 089-6135412. Ed. Joerg Feistle. circ. 6,000.
Description: Bibliography of new medical books.

610   US   ISSN 0097-9732
MEDOC: INDEX TO U S GOVERNMENT PUBLICATIONS IN THE MEDICAL AND HEALTH SCIENCES. 1975. q. $95 (foreign $100). Spencer S. Eccles Health Sciences Library, University of Utah, Bldg. 589, Salt Lake City, UT 84112. TEL 801-581-5268. FAX 801-581-3632. Ed. Michael Thelin. bk.rev.; circ. 400. (also avail. in microfiche)
—BLDSC shelfmark: 5535.570000.
Description: Includes abstracts of selected documents.

M

MEDICAL SCIENCES — ABSTRACTING, BIBLIOGRAPHIES, STATISTICS

616.89   UK   ISSN 0260-5252
RA790.7.G7
MENTAL HEALTH STATISTICS FOR WALES. 1981. a. £5. Welsh Office, Economic and Statistical Services Division, New Crown Bldg., Cathays Park, Cardiff CF1 3NQ, Wales. TEL 0222-825044. FAX 0222-825350. TELEX 498228. Ed. E. Swires-Hennessy. stat.; circ. 550.
—BLDSC shelfmark: 5678.589000.
Description: Specifics on mental illness and mental handicap services in Wales.

011   US   ISSN 1055-3533
N A A C O G'S WOMEN'S HEALTH NURSING SCAN. 1987. bi-m. $35 to individuals (foreign $47); institutions $55 (foreign $67). (Organization for Obstetric, Gynecologic and Neonatal Nurses) Nursecom Inc., 1211 Locust St., Philadelphia, PA 19107. TEL 215-545-7222. Ed. Shannon Perry. (also avail. in microform from UMI)
Former titles (until 1991): Women's Health Nursing Scan (ISSN 0895-3481); Nursing Scan in Women's Health.
Description: Abstracts from multidisciplinary literature on topics in women's health nursing, with commentary on application to nursing practice.

610.28 016   US
N T I S ALERTS: BIOMEDICAL TECHNOLOGY & HUMAN FACTORS ENGINEERING. w. $125 (foreign $175). U.S. National Technical Information Service, 5285 Port Royal Rd., Springfield, VA 22161. TEL 703-487-4630. FAX 703-321-8547. TELEX 64616. abstr.; index, cum.index. (back issues avail.)
Former titles: Abstract Newsletter: Biomedical Technology and Human Factors Engineering (ISSN 0163-1497); Weekly Abstract Newsletter: Biomedical Technology and Human Factors Engineering; Weekly Government Abstracts. Biomedical Technology and Human Factors Engineering; Weekly Government Abstracts. Biomedical Technology and Engineering (ISSN 0364-4952)

N T I S ALERTS: MEDICINE & BIOLOGY. see BIOLOGY — Abstracting, Bibliographies, Statistics

016 610   US
NATIONAL LIBRARY OF MEDICINE. CURRENT BIBLIOGRAPHIES IN MEDICINE. 1966. irreg. (approx. 20/yr.). $52 (foreign $65). U.S. National Library of Medicine, Reference Section, 8600 Rockville Pike, Bethesda, MD 20894. TEL 301-496-6308. FAX 301-496-4450. (Orders to: Supt. of Documents, Washington, DC 20402) circ. 1,000.
Formerly: National Library of Medicine. Literature Search Series (ISSN 0083-2251)
Description: Documents approximately 20 bibliographies per year on a variety of biomedical topics, excluding AIDS (see AIDS Bibliography) similar to those found in the NLM Literature Search Series.

610 016   US   ISSN 0027-9641
NATIONAL LIBRARY OF MEDICINE. CURRENT CATALOG. (Also issued: NLM Current Catalog Quarterly) 1966. q. with annual cumulation. q. & a. cum. price varies. U.S. National Library of Medicine, 8600 Rockville Pike, Bethesda, MD 20894. TEL 301-496-6308. FAX 301-496-4450. (Orders to: Supt. of Documents, Washington, DC 20402) **Indexed:** MEDOC, Popul.Ind.
Incorporates (1965-1980): Notes for Medical Catalogers (ISSN 0078-2025)
Description: A bibliographic listing of monographs and serials cataloged by the Library. Contains listings by subject and name.

610 020   US
NEW ENGLAND SOUNDING LINE. 1991. q. free. National Network of Libraries of Medicine, New England Region, Lyman Maynard Stowe Library, University of Connecticut Health Center, MC5370, Farmington, CT 06030. TEL 203-679-4500. FAX 203-679-4046. Ed. Linda Walton.
Description: Covers acquisitions and activities of the New England regional medical library program, including document loan projects.

312.3   NZ
NEW ZEALAND. HEALTH STATISTICAL SERVICES. CANCER DATA: NEW REGISTRATIONS AND DEATHS. a. NZ.$30. Health Statistical Services, c/o Josephine Ryan, 133 Molesworth St., P.O. Box 5013, Wellington, New Zealand. TEL 04-496-2000. FAX 04-496-2050. stat.; circ. controlled.
Formerly: Cancer Data: Deaths and Cases Reported (ISSN 0548-9415)

618.92 319.4   NZ
NEW ZEALAND. HEALTH STATISTICAL SERVICES. FETAL AND INFANT DEATHS. 1964. a. NZ.$30. Health Statistical Services, c/o Josephine Ryan, 133 Molesworth St., P.O. Box 5013, Wellington, New Zealand. TEL 04-496-2000. FAX 04-496-2050. circ. controlled.
Formerly: New Zealand. National Health Statistics Centre. Fetal and Infant Deaths (ISSN 0111-8617)

616.8   NZ   ISSN 0548-992X
RC451.N4
NEW ZEALAND. HEALTH STATISTICAL SERVICES. MENTAL HEALTH DATA. a. NZ.$30. Health Statistical Services, c/o Josephine Ryan, 133 Molesworth St., P.O. Box 5013, Wellington, New Zealand. TEL 04-496-2000. FAX 04-496-2050. circ. controlled.

617.6   US
NORTHWESTERN UNIVERSITY. DENTAL SCHOOL LIBRARY ACQUISITIONS LISTS. 1949. bi-m. free. Northwestern University, Dental School Library, 311 E. Chicago Ave., Chicago, IL 60611-3008. TEL 312-503-6896. Ed. Mary Kreinbring. circ. 350. (looseleaf format)

617.6   US
NORTHWESTERN UNIVERSITY. DENTAL SCHOOL LIBRARY. CURRENT SUBSCRIPTIONS LIST. 1970. a. free. Northwestern University, Dental School Library, 311 E. Chicago Ave., Chicago, IL 60611-3008. TEL 312-503-6896. bibl.; circ. 350. (looseleaf format)

610   NO   ISSN 0800-403X
NORWAY. STATISTISK SENTRALBYRAA. HELSEPERSONELLSTATISTIKK. (Subseries of: Norges Offisielle Statistikk) 1979. biennial. Statistisk Sentralbyraa, Box 8131-Dep., 0033 Oslo 1, Norway. TEL 02-864500. FAX 02-864973. circ. 2,000.
Supersedes: Norway. Statistisk Sentralbyraa. Legestatistikk (ISSN 0377-8886)

610 016   CS   ISSN 0029-5205
Z6660
NOVINKY LITERATURY: ZDRAVOTNICTVI. 1955. 10/yr. 50 Kcs. Ustav Vedeckych Lekarskych Informaci, Sokolska 31, 121 32 Prague 2, Czechoslovakia. TEL 299956. TELEX 121293. (Dist. by: Artia, Ve Smeckach 30, 111 27 Prague 1, Czechoslovakia) Ed. O. Pinkas. circ. 500. (tabloid format)

016 610.73   US   ISSN 0195-3354
NURSING ABSTRACTS. 1979. bi-m. $340 in N. America; elsewhere $385. Nursing Abstracts Co., Inc., Box 295, Forest Hills, NY 11375. Ed. Diana Dolgins. index. (back issues avail.)
Description: Abstracts of articles appearing in 82 nursing journals. Geared to all health professionals, educators, students and researchers.

610.73 016   UK   ISSN 0300-9947
NURSING BIBLIOGRAPHY. 1972. m. £40. Royal College of Nursing, Library, 20 Cavendish Sq., London W1M 0AB, England. TEL 071-409-3333. FAX 071-355-1379. circ. 700.
—BLDSC shelfmark: 6187.039000.

610.73   UK   ISSN 0141-3899
NURSING RESEARCH ABSTRACTS. 1978. q. £14. Departments of Health and Social Security, Hannibal House, Elephant and Castle, London SE1 6TE, England. (Subscr. to: DHSS (Leaflets), P.O. Box 21, Stanmore, Middlesex HA7 1AY, England) Ed. Debra Unsworth.
—BLDSC shelfmark: 6187.112000.

011 610.73   US   ISSN 0888-6288
NURSING SCAN IN ADMINISTRATION. 1986. bi-m. $35 to individuals; institutions $55. Nursecom Inc., 1211 Locust St., Philadelphia, PA 19107. TEL 215-545-7222. Eds. Beverly McElmurry, D. Faan. circ. 3,000.
Description: Contains abstracts from mulitdisciplinary literature on topics relating to administration, with commentary on applications to nursing practice.

011 610.73   US
NURSING SCAN IN RESEARCH: APPLICATION FOR CLINICAL PRACTICE. 1988. bi-m. $35 to individuals (foreign $40); institutions $55 (foreign $60). Nursecom Inc., 1211 Locust St., Philadelphia, PA 19107. TEL 215-545-7222. Eds. Judy Bealy, Carol Love. circ. 2,500.
Description: Contains abstracts of current research articles on topics related to nursing practice with critical evaluations of the methodology and commentary.

615.8   UK   ISSN 0950-6675
OCCUPATIONAL THERAPY INDEX. m. £45 (foreign £62). Medical Information Service, The British Library, Boston Spa, Wetherby, W. Yorkshire LS23 7BQ, England. TEL 0937-546039. FAX 0937-546236. index.
●Also available online.
—BLDSC shelfmark: 6231.254500.
Description: Current awareness service for occupational therapy journals.

616.4 011   US   ISSN 1043-8963
RC268.42
ONCOGENES AND GROWTH FACTORS ABSTRACTS. 1989. q. $185 (foreign $195). Cambridge Scientific Abstracts, 7200 Wisconsin Ave., 6th Fl., Bethesda, MD 20814. TEL 301-961-6750. FAX 301-961-6720. TELEX 910 2507547 CAMB MD. abstr.; index. (also avail. in magnetic tape; back issues avail.)
●Also available online. Vendor(s): BRS (CSAL), DIALOG (File no.76).
Also available on CD-ROM. Producer(s): Cambridge Scientific Abstracts (Compact Cambridge Life Sciences Collection).
Description: Covers worldwide research into the molecular basis of malignant transformation.

617.7   CN   ISSN 1180-0984
OPHTHALMIC ABSTRACT JOURNAL. q. Can.$136. Medicopea International Inc., 212 - 8200 Decarie Blvd., Montreal, Que. H4P 2P5, Canada. TEL 514-340-9157. FAX 514-342-5783. TELEX 055-62171.

617.7 016   UK   ISSN 0030-3720
Z6669
OPHTHALMIC LITERATURE. 1947. q. £70($195) Institute of Ophthalmology, Judd St., London WC1H 9QS, England. Ed. J.H. Kelsey. adv.; bk.rev.; abstr.; index. (also avail. in microform from UMI; reprint service avail. from UMI)

617.7   US
▼**OPTOMETRY;** current literature in perspective. 1991. q. $69 to individuals (foreign $83); institutions $89 (foreign $103); students $45 (foreign $59). Mosby - Year Book, Inc. (Subsidiary of: Times Mirror Company), 11830 Westline Industrial Dr., St. Louis, MO 63146. TEL 800-325-4177. FAX 314-432-1380. TELEX 44-2402.
Description: Keeps optometrists current with developments affecting their and the state of the eye care industry.

610   JA   ISSN 0913-4751
OSAKA UNIVERSITY. RESEARCH INSTITUTE FOR MICROBIAL DISEASES. ANNUAL REPORTS. a. Osaka Daigaku, Biseibutsubyo Kenkyujo - Osaka University, Research Institute for Microbial Diseases, 3-1 Yamadaoka, Suita-shi, Osaka 565, Japan. Ed. Hajime Fujio. abstr.
—BLDSC shelfmark: 1410.645000.
Description: Provides abstracts of papers published in the previous year from various departments of the institute.

OUT-OF-PRINT SCIENTIFIC, MEDICAL AND TECHNICAL BOOKS. see SCIENCES: COMPREHENSIVE WORKS — Abstracting, Bibliographies, Statistics

MEDICAL SCIENCES — ABSTRACTING, BIBLIOGRAPHIES, STATISTICS

616.4 016　　　　FR　　ISSN 0761-2168
P A S C A L EXPLORE. E 64: ENDOCRINOLOGIE HUMAINE ET EXPERIMENTALE. ENDOCRINOPATHIES. 1984. 10/yr. 1465 F. Centre National de la Recherche Scientifique, Institut de l'Information Scientifique et Technique, B.P. 54, 54514 Vandoeuvre-Les-Nancy Cedex, France. TEL 83-50-46-00.
　Formerly: P A S C A L Explore. Part 64: Endocrinologie Humaine et Experimentale. Endocrinopathies; Supersedes in part: Bulletin Signaletique. Part 361: Reproduction. Gynecologie. Obstetrique. Embryologie. Endocrinologie (ISSN 0245-9884)

150 616.89 016　　FR　　ISSN 0761-2176
Z7203
P A S C A L EXPLORE. E 65: PSYCHOLOGIE, PSYCHOPATHOLOGIE, PSYCHIATRIE. 1984. 10/yr. 1345 F. (foreign 1430 F.). Centre National de la Recherche Scientifique, Institut de l'Information Scientifique et Technique, Chateau du Montet, 54514 Vandoeuvre-Les-Nancy Cedex, France. (Subscr. to: I N I S T - Science, Technologie, Medecine- Service des Abonnements, 26 rue Boyer, 75971 Paris cedex 20, France) abstr.; index, cum.index. (also avail. in microform from MIM)
　Formerly: P A S C A L Explore. Part 65: Psychologie, Psychopathologie, Psychiatrie; Which supersedes (1961-1984): Bulletin Signaletique. Part 390: Psychologie. Psychopathologie. Psychiatrie (ISSN 0007-5531)

617.7 016　　　　FR　　ISSN 0761-2184
P A S C A L EXPLORE. E 71: OPHTALMOLOGIE. 1984. 10/yr. 980 F. Centre National de la Recherche Scientifique, Institut de l'Information Scientifique et Technique, B.P. 54, 54514 Vandoeuvre-Les-Nancy Cedex, France. TEL 83-50-46-00. abstr.; index, cum.index.
　Formerly: P A S C A L Explore. Part 71: Ophtalmologie; Which supersedes (1972-1984): Bulletin Signaletique. Part 346: Ophtalmologie (ISSN 0301-3324); Which supersedes in part: Bulletin Signaletique. Part 350. Pathologie Generale et Experimentale.

616.21 016　　　FR　　ISSN 0761-2192
P A S C A L EXPLORE. E 72: OTORHINOLARYNGOLOGIE. STOMATOLOGIE. PATHOLOGIE CERVICOFACIALE. 1984. 10/yr. 995 F. Centre National de la Recherche Scientifique, Institut de l'Information Scientifique et Technique, B.P. 54, 54514 Vandoeuvre-Les-Nancy, France. TEL 83-50-46-00. abstr.; bibl.; index, cum.index.
　Formerly: P A S C A L Explore. Part 72: Otorhinolaryngologie. Stomatologie. Pathologie Cervicofaciale; Which superseded (1972-1984): Bulletin Signaletique. Part 347: Oto-Rhino-Laryngologie, Stomatologie, Pathologie Cervicofaciale (ISSN 0301-3375); Which supersedes in part: Bulletin Signaletique. Part 350. Pathologie Generale et Experimentale.

616.5 016　　　　FR　　ISSN 0761-2206
P A S C A L EXPLORE. E 73: DERMATOLOGIE. MALADIES SEXUELLEMENT TRANSMISSIBLES. 1984. 10/yr. 1010 F. Centre National de la Recherche Scientifique, Institut de l'Information Scientifique et Technique, B.P. 54, 54514 Vandoeuvre-Les-Nancy, France. TEL 83-50-46-00. abstr.; index, cum.index.
　Formerly: P A S C A L Explore. Part 73: Dermatologie. Maladies Sexuellement Transmissibles; Which superseded (1972-1984): Bulletin Signaletique. Part 348: Dermatologie - Venerologie (ISSN 0301-3383); Which supersedes in part: Bulletin Signaletique. Part 350. Pathologie Generale et Experimentale.

616.2 016　　　　FR　　ISSN 0761-2214
P A S C A L EXPLORE. E 74: PNEUMOLOGIE. 1984. 10/yr. 1025 F. Centre National de la Recherche Scientifique, Institut de l'Information Scientifique et Technique, B.P. 54, 54514 Vandoeuvre-Les-Nancy Cedex, France. TEL 83-50-46-00. abstr.; index, cum.index. (also avail. in microform from MIM)
　Formerly: P A S C A L Explore. Part 74: Pneumologie; Which superseded in part (1973-1984): Bulletin Signaletique. Part 362: Maladies de l'Appareil Respiratoire du Coeur et des Vaisseaux. Chirurgie Thoracique et Vasculaire (ISSN 0301-3391); Which supersedes in part: Bulletin Signaletique. Part 350. Pathologie Generale et Experimentale.

616.2 016　　　　FR　　ISSN 0761-2222
P A S C A L EXPLORE. E 75: CARDIOLOGIE ET APPAREIL CIRCULATOIRE. 1984. 10/yr. 1510 F. Centre National de l'Information Scientifique et Technique, B.P. 54, 54514 Vandoeuvre-Les-Nancy Cedex, France. TEL 83-50-46-00.
　Formerly: P A S C A L Explore. Part 75: Cardiologie et Appareil Circulatoire; Which superseded in part: Bulletin Signaletique. Part 352: Maladies de l'Appareil Respiratoire, du Coeur et des Vaisseaux. Chirurgie Thoracique et Vasculaire.

616.3 617 016　　FR　　ISSN 0761-2230
P A S C A L EXPLORE. E 76: GASTROENTEROLOGIE, FOIE, PANCREAS, ABDOMEN. 1973. 10/yr. 1510 F. Centre National de la Recherche Scientifique, Institut de l'Information Scientifique et Technique, B.P. 54, 54514 Vandoeuvre-Les-Nancy Cedex, France. TEL 83-50-46-00. abstr.; index, cum.index. (also avail. in microform from MIM)
　Formerly: P A S C A L Explore. Part 76: Gastroenterologie, Foie, Pancreas, Abdomen; Which superseded (in 1984): Bulletin Signaletique. Part 354: Maladies de l'Appareil Digestif. Chirurgie Abdominale (ISSN 0301-3405); Which supersedes in part: Bulletin Signaletique. Part 350. Pathologie Generale et Experimentale.

616.6 016 617　　FR　　ISSN 0761-2249
P A S C A L EXPLORE. E 77: NEPHROLOGIE. VOIES URINAIRES. 1973. 10/yr. 995 F. Centre National de la Recherche Scientifique, Institut de l'Information Scientifique et Technique, B.P. 54, 54514 Vandoeuvre-Les-Nancy Cedex, France. TEL 83-50-46-00. abstr.; index, cum.index. (also avail. in microform from MIM)
　Formerly: P A S C A L Explore. Part 77: Nephrologie. Voies Urinaires; Which superseded (in 1984): Bulletin Signaletique. Part 355: Maladies des Reins et des Voies Urinaires - Chirurgie de l'Appareil Urinaire; Which was formerly: Bulletin Signaletique. Part 355: Maladies des Reins et des Voies Urinaires. Chirurgie (ISSN 0301-3413); Supersedes in part: Bulletin Signaletique. Part 350. Pathologie Generale et Experimentale.

616.8 016　　　　FR　　ISSN 0761-2257
P A S C A L EXPLORE. E 78: NEUROLOGIE. 1973. 10/yr. 1640 F. Centre National de la Recherche Scientifique, Institut de l'Information Scientifique et Technique, B.P. 54, 54514 Vandoeuvre-Les-Nancy Cedex, France. TEL 83-50-46-00. abstr.; index, cum.index. (also avail. in microform from MIM)
　Formerly: P A S C A L Explore. Part 78: Neurologie; Supersedes (in 1984): Bulletin Signaletique. Part 356: Maladies du Systeme Nerveux Myopathies-Neurochirurgie (ISSN 0301-3421); Which supersedes in part: Bulletin Signaletique. Part 350. Pathologie Generale et Experimentale.

617.3 016　　　　FR　　ISSN 0761-2265
P A S C A L EXPLORE. E 79: PATHOLOGIE ET PHYSIOLOGIE OSTEOARTICULAIRES. 1973. 10/yr. 1050 F. Centre National de la Recherche Scientifique, Institut de l'Information Scientifique et Technique, B.P. 54, 54514 Vandoeuvre-Les-Nancy Cedex, France. TEL 83-50-46-00. abstr.; index, cum.index. (also avail. in microform from MIM)
　Formerly: P A S C A L Explore. Part 79: Pathologie et Physiologie Osteoarticulaires; Which supersedes (in 1984): Bulletin Signaletique. Part 357: Maladies des Os et des Articulations. Chirurgie Orthopedique. Traumatologie (ISSN 0301-343X); Which superseded in part: Bulletin Signaletique. Part 350. Pathologie Generale et Experimentale.

616.15 016　　　FR　　ISSN 0761-2273
P A S C A L EXPLORE. E 80: HEMATOLOGIE. 1973. 10/yr. 1105 F. Centre National de la Recherche Scientifique, Institut de l'Information Scientifique et Technique, B.P. 54, 54514 Vandoeuvre-Les-Nancy Cedex, France. TEL 83-50-46-00. (also avail. in microform from MIM)
　Formerly: P A S C A L Explore. Part 80: Hematologie; Supersedes (in 1984): Bulletin Signaletique. Part 359: Maladies du Sang (ISSN 0301-3448); Which supersedes in part: Bulletin Signaletique. Part 350. Pathologie Generale et Experimentale.

616.462 016　　　FR　　ISSN 0761-2281
P A S C A L EXPLORE. E 81: MALADIES METABOLIQUES. 1972. 10/yr. 850 F. Centre National de la Recherche Scientifique, Institut de l'Information Scientifique et Technique, B.P. 54, 54514 Vandoeuvre-Les-Nancy Cedex, France. TEL 83-50-46-00. abstr.; index, cum.index. (also avail. in microform from MIM) **Indexed:** Nutr.Abstr.
　Former titles: P A S C A L Explore. Part 81: Maladies Metaboliques; Supersedes (in 1984): Bulletin Signaletique. Part 362: Diabete. Maladies Metaboliques; Which was formerly: Bulletin Signaletique. 362: Diabete. Obesite. Maladies. (ISSN 0007-5507).

616.4 016　　　　FR　　ISSN 0761-229X
P A S C A L EXPLORE. E 82: GYNECOLOGIE. OBSTETRIQUE. ANDROLOGIE. 1984. 10/yr. 1225 F. Centre National de la Recherche Scientifique, Institut de l'Information Scientifique et Technique, B.P. 54, 54514 Vandoeuvre-Les-Nancy Cedex, France. TEL 83-50-46-00.
　Formerly: P A S C A L Explore. Part 82: Gynecologie. Obstetrique. Andrologie; Supersedes in part: Bulletin Signaletique. Part 361: Reproduction. Gynecologie. Obstetrique. Embryologie. Endocrinologie (ISSN 0245-9884)

617.96 016　　　FR　　ISSN 0761-2303
P A S C A L EXPLORE. E 83: ANESTHESIE ET REANIMATION. 1972. 10/yr. 1030 F. Centre National de la Recherche Scientifique, Institut de l'Information Scientifique et Technique, B.P. 54, 54514 Vandoeuvre-Les-Nancy Cedex, France. TEL 83-50-46-00. abstr.; index, cum.index. (also avail. in microform from MIM)
　Formerly: P A S C A L Explore. Part 83: Anesthesie et Reanimation; Supersedes (in 1984): Bulletin Signaletique. Part 349: Anesthesie. Reanimation (ISSN 0301-133X); Bulletin Signaletique. Part 350. Pathologie Generale et Experimentale (ISSN 0007-5469)

610 016 574　　　FR　　ISSN 0761-2311
P A S C A L EXPLORE. E 84: GENIE BIOMEDICAL. INFORMATIQUE BIOMEDICALE. 1972. 10/yr. 740 F. Centre National de la Recherche Scientifique, Institut de l'Information Scientifique et Technique, B.P. 54, 54514 Vandoeuvre-Les-Nancy Cedex, France. TEL 83-50-46-00. abstr.; index, cum.index. (also avail. in microform from MIM)
　Formerly: P A S C A L Explore. Part 84: Genie Biomedical. Informatique Biomedicale; Supersedes (in 1984): Bulletin Signaletique. Part 310: Genie Biomedical. Informatique Biomedicale. Physique Biomedicale (ISSN 0398-9941)

616.4 016　　　　FR　　ISSN 0761-1919
P A S C A L FOLIO. F 54: REPRODUCTION DES VERTEBRES. EMBRYOLOGIE DES VERTEBRES ET DES INVERTEBRES. 1985. 10/yr. 805 F. Centre National de la Recherche Scientifique, Institut de l'Information Scientifique et Technique, B.P. 54, 54514 Vandoeuvre-Les-Nancy Cedex, France. TEL 83-50-46-00. (also avail. in microform from MIM)
　Formerly: P A S C A L Folio. Part 54: Reproduction des Vertebres. Embryologie des Vertebres et des Invertebres; Which superseded in part (1961-1984): Bulletin Signaletique. Part 361: Reproduction. Gynecologie. Obstetrique. Embryologie. Endocrinologie (ISSN 0245-9884); Which was formerly: Bulletin Signaletique. Part 361: Reproduction. Embryologie. Endocrinologie (ISSN 0180-9989); Bulletin Signaletique. Part 361. Endocrinologie et Reproduction (ISSN 0007-5493)

610 574　　　　　FR　　ISSN 0761-165X
P A S C A L THEMA. T 215: BIOTECHNOLOGIES (EDITIONS FRANCAISE). 1982. 10/yr. 1300 F. Centre National de la Recherche Scientifique, Institut de l'Information Scientifique et Technique, Chateau du Montet, 54514 Vandoeuvre-Les-Nancy Cedex, France. (Subscr. to: I N I S T - Science, Technologie, Medecine- Service des Abonnements, 26 rue Boyer, 75971 Paris Cedex 20, France) Ed.Bd. abstr.; index, cum.index. (also avail. in microform)
　●Also available online. Vendor(s): European Space Agency, Telesystemes - Questel.
　Formerly: P A S C A L Thema. Part 215. Biotechnologies (Editions Francaises); Which superseded (in 1984): Bulletin Signaletique. Part 215: Biotechnologies (French Edition) (ISSN 0245-954X)

MEDICAL SCIENCES — ABSTRACTING, BIBLIOGRAPHIES, STATISTICS

610 616.07   FR   ISSN 0761-1676
P A S C A L THEMA. T 235: MEDECINE TROPICALE. 1982. 10/yr. 1050 F. Centre National de la Recherche Scientifique, Institut de l'Information Scientifique et Technique, B.P. 54, 54514 Vandoeuvre-Les-Nancy Cedex, France. TEL 83-50-46-00. abstr.; index, cum.index.
●Also available online. Vendor(s): European Space Agency, Telesystemes - Questel.
Formerly: P A S C A L Thema. Part 235: Medecine Tropicale; Which superseded (in 1984): Bulletin Signaletique. Part 233: Medecine Tropicale (ISSN 0245-9558).

P H L S LIBRARY BULLETIN. (Public Health Laboratory Service Board) see *MEDICAL SCIENCES — Communicable Diseases*

610   UK   ISSN 0961-4591
PALLIATIVE CARE INDEX. m. £45 (foreign £62). Medical Information Service, The British Library, Document Supply Centre, Boston Spa, Wetherby, W. Yorkshire LS23 7BQ, England. TEL 0937-546039. FAX 0937-546236. index.
—BLDSC shelfmark: 6345.562055.
Formerly: Terminal Care Index (ISSN 0953-6779)
Description: Features abstracts on terminal and palliative care, hospice, symptom control, legal and ethical aspects of death, bereavement and psychosocial apsects of palliative care.

610   UK   ISSN 0957-4190
▼**PAPILLOMAVIRUS REPORT.** 1990. bi-m. £40($90) to individuals; institutions £48($108). (Oncology Information Service) Royal Society of Medicine Services Ltd., 1 Wimpole St., London W1M 8AE, England. TEL 071-408-2119. FAX 071-355-3198. TELEX 298902. Ed. C. Lacey.
—BLDSC shelfmark: 6403.165000.
Description: Bibliograhic information, including abstracts and authors' addresses, for papers on all aspects of papillomavirus infection in humans and animals published worldwide.

618.92   US   ISSN 1059-0870
PEDIATRIC EMERGENCY & CRITICAL CARE; a clinical update for those who care for infants and children. 1988. m. $55 to individuals; institutions $85; residents and nurses $28. Riverpress, Inc., Box 23, Jersey City, NJ 07303-0023. TEL 201-434-5073. FAX 201-434-7230. Ed. Douglas W.E. Wagner. circ. 950. (looseleaf format)
Formerly (until vol.5, 1992): Pediatric Trauma and Acute Care (ISSN 0894-1122)
Description: Digest of clinically useful literature and papers; each abstract has an expert's comment focusing on the clinical point.

618.92   US   ISSN 0893-6218
PEDIATRIC THERAPEUTICS & TOXICOLOGY; practical pediatrics for the pediatric practitioner. 1987. m. $45 to individuals; institutions $80; residents and nurses $23. Riverpress, Inc., Box 23, Jersey City, NJ 07303-0023. TEL 201-434-5073. FAX 201-434-7230. Ed. Douglas W.E. Wagner. (looseleaf format; back issues avail.)
Description: Digest of clinically useful articles; each abstract has an expert's comment focusing on the clinical point.
Refereed Serial

610 790.1 016   US   ISSN 0163-2582
Z6664.6
PHYSICAL FITNESS - SPORTS MEDICINE; a bibliographic service encompassing exercise physiology, sports injuries, physical conditioning and the medical aspects of exercise. 1978. q. $9. U.S. Department of Health and Human Services, President's Council on Physical Fitness & Sports, 450 5th St., N.W., Ste. 7130, Washington, DC 20001. TEL 202-272-3421. (Subscr. to: Supt. of Documents, Washington, DC 20402) Ed Clifford A. Bachrach, M.D. circ. 1,700. (back issues avail.)
Indexed: MEDOC.
●Also available online. Vendor(s): National Library of Medicine.
—BLDSC shelfmark: 6475.613000.

610   US   ISSN 0731-0315
RA410.7
PHYSICIAN CHARACTERISTICS & DISTRIBUTION IN THE U S. 1943. a. $75. American Medical Association, 515 N. State St., Chicago, IL 60610. TEL 312-464-0183. FAX 312-464-5834. Ed. G.A. Roback. Indexed: SRI.
Former titles: Physician Characteristics and Distribution; Physician Distribution and Medical Licensure in the U S (ISSN 0364-6610); Distribution of Physicians in the U S (ISSN 0146-4558); Distribution of Physicians, Hospital, Hospital Beds in the U S (ISSN 0419-4357)

610   UK   ISSN 0950-6659
PHYSIOTHERAPY INDEX. m. £45 (foreign £62). Medical Information Service, The British Library, Boston Spa, Wetherby, W. Yorkshire LS23 7BQ, England. TEL 0937-546039. FAX 0937-546236. index.
●Also available online.
—BLDSC shelfmark: 6489.107000.
Description: Current awareness service for physical therapy journals.

617.96 011   US
PLEXUS: ANNUAL MEDICAL SPECIALTY UPDATES. 1984. a. $72. (Methodist Hospital Graduate Medical Center of Indianapolis) References & Index Services, Inc., 3951 N. Meridian St., Ste. 100, Indianapolis, IN 46208-4011. TEL 317-923-1575.
Formerly: Medical Information Systems: Anesthesiology.

610 631   AT
RECENT LITERATURE ON MEDICINAL PLANTS. 1988. biennial. Noyce Publishing, G.P.O. Box 2222T, Melbourne, Vic. 3001, Australia. (back issues avail.)

616.97 016   RU   ISSN 0202-9154
REFERATIVNYI ZHURNAL. IMMUNOLOGIYA - ALLERGOLOGIYA. 1978. m. 69.40 Rub. (78.80 Rub. with index). Vsesoyuznyi Institut Nauchno-Tekhnicheskoi Informatsii (VINITI), Baltiiskaya ul. 14, Moscow A-219, Russia. (Subscr. to: Mezhdunarodnaya Kniga, Dimitrova ul. 39, 113095 Moscow, Russia)

610 016   RU   ISSN 0034-2475
REFERATIVNYI ZHURNAL. MEDITSINSKAYA GEOGRAFIYA. m. 27.80 Rub. (31.50 Rub. including index). Vsesoyuznyi Institut Nauchno-Tekhnicheskoi Informatsii (VINITI), Baltiiskaya ul. 14, Moscow A-219, Russia. (Subscr. to: Mezhdunarodnaya Kniga, Dimitrova ul. 39, 113095 Moscow, Russia)

REFERATIVNYI ZHURNAL. OBSHCHIE VOPROSY PATOLOGICHESKOI ANATOMII. see *BIOLOGY — Abstracting, Bibliographies, Statistics*

616.992 016   RU   ISSN 0202-9197
REFERATIVNYI ZHURNAL. ONKOLOGIYA. 1961. m. 168 Rub. (210 Rub. including index). Vsesoyuznyi Institut Nauchno-Tekhnicheskoi Informatsii (VINITI), Baltiiskaya ul. 14, Moscow A-219, Russia. (Subscr. to: Mezhdunarodnaya Kniga, Dimitrova ul. 39, 113095 Moscow, Russia)

574.19 016   RU   ISSN 0131-355X
QH652.A1   CODEN: RZRBDD
REFERATIVNYI ZHURNAL. RADIATSIONNAYA BIOLOGIYA. 1973. m. 56 Rub. (60 Rub. including index). Vsesoyuznyi Institut Nauchno-Tekhnicheskoi Informatsii (VINITI), Baltiiskaya ul., 14, Moscow A-219, Russia. (Subscr. to: Mezhdunarodnaya Kniga, Dimitrova ul. 39, 113095 Moscow, Russia) Indexed: Chem.Abstr.

617.96 016   CS   ISSN 0034-2688
REFERATOVY VYBER Z ANESTESIOLOGIE A RESUSCITACE/ABSTRACTS OF ANESTHESIOLOGY AND RESUSCITATION. 1954. bi-m. 90 Kcs. Ustav Vedeckych Lekarskych Informaci, Sokolska 31, 121 32 Prague 2, Czechoslovakia. TEL 299956. Ed. J. Drabkova. circ. 1,270.

617 016   CS   ISSN 0034-2696
REFERATOVY VYBER Z CHIRURGIE/ABSTRACTS OF SURGERY. 1969. bi-m. 90 Kcs. Ustav Vedeckych Lekarskych Informaci, Sokolska 31, 121 32 Prague 2, Czechoslovakia. TEL 299956. Ed. M. Klika. circ. 590.

616.9 016   CS   ISSN 0034-270X
REFERATOVY VYBER Z CHOROB INFEKCNICH/ABSTRACTS OF INFECTIOUS DISEASES. 1960. q. 60 Kcs. Ustav Vedeckych Lekarskych Informaci, Sokolska 31, 121 32 Prague 2, Czechoslovakia. TEL 299956. Ed. J. Vanista. circ. 455.

616.5 616.6 016   CS   ISSN 0034-2718
REFERATOVY VYBER Z DERMATOVENEROLOGIE/ABSTRACTS OF DERMATOLOGY AND VENEROLOGY. 1959. q. 60 Kcs. Ustav Vedeckych Lekarskych Informaci, Sokolska 31, 121 32 Prague 2, Czechoslovakia. TEL 299956. Ed. T. Frej. circ. 460.

616.3 016   CS   ISSN 0034-2742
REFERATOVY VYBER Z GASTROENTEROLOGIE/ABSTRACTS OF GASTROENTEROLOGY. 1965. q. 60 Kcs. Ustav Vedeckych Lekarskych Informaci, Sokolska 31, 121 32 Prague 2, Czechoslovakia. TEL 299956. Ed. V. Nerad. circ. 410.

616.1 016   CS   ISSN 0034-2769
REFERATOVY VYBER Z KARDIOLOGIE, FYSIOLOGIE A PATOLOGIE OBEHOVEHO USTROJI/ABSTRACTS OF CARDIOLOGY AND PHYSIOLOGY AND PATHOLOGY OF THE CIRCULATION SYSTEM. 1960. bi-m. 90 Kcs. Ustav Vedeckych Lekarskych Informaci, Sokolska 31, 121 32 Prague 2, Czechoslovakia. TEL 299956. Ed. J. Pokorny. bk.rev.; circ. 620. (tabloid format)

616.8 016   CS   ISSN 0034-2793
REFERATOVY VYBER Z NEUROLOGIE/ABSTRACTS OF NEUROLOGY. 1969. q. 60 Kcs. Ustav Vedeckych Lekarskych Informaci, Sokolska 31, 121 32 Prague 2, Czechoslovakia. TEL 299956. Ed. J. Simek. circ. 490.

617.7 016   CS   ISSN 0034-2807
REFERATOVY VYBER Z OFTALMOLOGIE/ABSTRACTS OF OPHTHALMOLOGY. 1969. q. 60 Kcs. Ustav Vedeckych Lekarskych Informaci, Sokolska 31, 121 32 Prague 2, Czechoslovakia. TEL 299956. Ed. J. Obenberger. bk.rev.; circ. 440.

617.3 016 016   CS   ISSN 0034-2823
REFERATOVY VYBER Z ORTOPEDIE, TRAUMATOLOGIE A PRIBUZNYCH OBORU/ABSTRACTS OF ORTHOPEDICS, TRAUMATOLOGY AND RELATED SUBJECTS. 1957. bi-m. 90 Kcs. Ustav Vedeckych Lekarskych Informaci, Sokolska 31, 121 32 Prague 2, Czechoslovakia. TEL 299956. Ed. R. Pavlansky. bk.rev.; circ. 690.

618.92 016   CS   ISSN 0034-2858
REFERATOVY VYBER Z PEDIATRIE/ABSTRACTS OF PEDIATRICS. 1959. bi-m. 90 Kcs. Ustav Vedeckych Lekarskych Informaci, Sokolska 31, 121 32 Prague 2, Czechoslovakia. TEL 299956. Ed. Maria Strakova. circ. 615.

616.246 016   CS   ISSN 0034-2890
REFERATOVY VYBER Z PNEUMOLOGIE A TUBERKULOSY/ABSTRACTS OF PNEUMOLOGY AND TUBERCULOSIS. 1956. q. 60 Kcs. Ustav Vedeckych Lekarskych Informaci, Sokolska 31, 121 32 Prague 2, Czechoslovakia. TEL 299956. Ed. I. Palkova. circ. 375.

618 016   CS   ISSN 0034-2866
REFERATOVY VYBER Z PORODNICTVI A GYNEKOLOGIE/ABSTRACTS OF OBSTETRICS AND GYNECOLOGY. 1962. bi-m. 90 Kcs. Ustav Vedeckych Lekarskych Informaci, Sokolska 31, 121 32 Prague 2, Czechoslovakia. TEL 299956. Ed. V. Trnka. circ. 715.

615.842 016   CS   ISSN 0034-2874
REFERATOVY VYBER Z RENTGENOLOGIE/ABSTRACTS OF RADIOLOGY. 1955. q. 60 Kcs. Ustav Vedeckych Lekarskych Informaci, Sokolska 31, 121 32 Prague 2, Czechoslovakia. FAX 299956. Ed. S. Vesin. circ. 340.

616.742 016   CS   ISSN 0034-2882
REFERATOVY VYBER Z REVMATOLOGIE/ABSTRACTS OF RHEUMATOLOGY. 1961. q. 60 Kcs. Ustav Vedeckych Lekarskych Informaci, Sokolska 31, 121 32 Prague 2, Czechoslovakia. TEL 299956. Ed. O. Vojtisek. bk.rev.; circ. 380.

MEDICAL SCIENCES — ABSTRACTING, BIBLIOGRAPHIES, STATISTICS

616.6   CS   ISSN 0139-9322
REFERATOVY VYBER Z UROLOGIE/ABSTRACTS OF UROLOGY. 1979. q. 60 Kcs. Ustav Vedeckych Lekarskych Informaci, Sokolska 31, 121 32 Prague 2, Czechoslovakia. TEL 299-956. Ed. M. Hanus. circ. 500.

617.1 790 016   CS
REFERATOVY VYBER ZE SPORTOVNI MEDICINY A LECEBNE REHABILITACE/ABSTRACTS OF SPORTS MEDICINE AND REHABILITATION. 1964. q. 60 Kcs. Ustav Vedeckych Lekarskych Informaci, Sokolska 31, 121 32 Prague 2, Czechoslovakia. TEL 299956. Ed. M. Pribil. circ. 495.
   Formerly: Referatovy Vyber ze Sportovni Mediciny - Abstracts of Sports Medicine (ISSN 0034-2904)
   Description: Abstracts of medical journal articles from around the world.

610   UK   ISSN 0955-0984
REHABILITATION INDEX. 1988. m. £45 (foreign £62). Medical Information Service, The British Library, Document Supply Centre, Boston Spa, Wetherby, W. Yorkshire LS23 7BQ, England. TEL 0937-546039. FAX 0937-546236. index.
   ●Also available online.
   —BLDSC shelfmark: 7350.243000.
   Description: Current awareness index of rehabilitation professional journals.

619   US
RESOURCES FOR COMPARATIVE BIOMEDICAL RESEARCH; a research resources directory. 1978. biennial. free. U.S. National Institutes of Health, National Center for Research Resources, Westwood Bldg. Rm. 10A15, 5333 Westbard Ave., Bethesda, MD 20892. TEL 301-496-5545. circ. 9,000.
   Formerly: Animal Resources.
   Description: Source directory of animals used for research purposes.

618.202   UK   ISSN 0260-5848
ROYAL COLLEGE OF MIDWIVES. CURRENT AWARENESS SERVICE; recent literature on midwifery. 1980. q. £15 to individuals; institutions £25; foreign £25(effective 1992). Royal College of Midwives Trust, Library, 15 Mansfield St, London W1M 0BE, England. FAX 01-436-3951. Ed. Mrs. Jan Ayres. circ. 450.

SELECTED ABSTRACTS ON OCCUPATIONAL DISEASES. see *OCCUPATIONAL HEALTH AND SAFETY — Abstracting, Bibliographies, Statistics*

610   US
SELECTED PERIODICALS FOR THE MEDICAL LIBRARY. 1967. a. free to qualified personnel. Ebsco Industries, Inc., Box 1943, Birmingham, AL 35201-1943. Ed. Erdeal Moore. adv.; tr.lit.; circ. 18,000.

610 011   US   ISSN 1041-2832
Z6664.A1
SICKNESS AND WELLNESS PUBLICATIONS. 1989. s-a. $89.50. John Gordon Burke Publishers, Inc., Box 1492, Evanston, IL 60204-1492. TEL 708-866-8625.
   ●Also available online.
   Description: Directory of newsletters indexed by type of disease and medical condition written for the layperson who has an interest in a specific disease or medical condition.

616.1   RU   ISSN 0234-9760
SIGNAL'NAYA INFORMATSIYA. ISHEMICHESKAYA BOLEZN' SERDTSA. 1987. m. 6.60 Rub. Vsesoyuznyi Institut Nauchno-Tekhnicheskoi Informatsii (VINITI), Baltiiskaya ul. 14, A-219 Moscow, Russia.

610   RU   ISSN 0234-9752
SIGNAL'NAYA INFORMATSIYA. NEIROPEPTIDY. 1987. m. 6.80 Rub. Vsesoyuznyi Institut Nauchno-Tekhnicheskoi Informatsii (VINITI), Baltiiskaya ul. 14, A-219 Moscow, Russia.

617.7   US
SLIDE ATLAS OF CURRENT OPTOMOLOGY (YEAR). (Suppl. to: Current Opinion in Ophthalmology) bi-m. £175($300) Current Science, 20 N. Third St., Philadelphia, PA 19106. TEL 800-552-5866. FAX 215-574-2270. (looseleaf format)

617.3   US
SLIDE ATLAS OF CURRENT ORTHOPAEDICS (YEAR). (Suppl. to: Current Opinion in Orthopaedics) bi-m. £225($375) Current Science, 20 N. Third St., Philadelphia, PA 19106. TEL 800-552-5866. FAX 215-574-2270. (looseleaf format)

615.842   US
SLIDE ATLAS OF CURRENT RADIOLOGY (YEAR). (Suppl. to: Current Opinion in Radiology) bi-m. £225($375) Current Science, 20 N. Third St., Philadelphia, PA 19106. TEL 800-552-5866. FAX 215-574-2270. (looseleaf format)

616.3   US
SLIDE ATLAS OF GASTROINTESTINAL ENDOSCOPY (YEAR). (Suppl. to: Annual of Gastrointestinal Endoscopy) bi-m. £120($200) Current Science, 20 N. Third St., Philadelphia, PA 19106. TEL 800-552-5866. FAX 215-574-2270. (looseleaf format)

610 011   GW   ISSN 0932-5034
SOZIALMEDIZIN. (Text in English and French) 1987. irreg. DM.10 per no. Institut fuer Dokumentation und Information, Sozialmedizin und Oeffentliches Gesundheitswesen, Westerfeldstr. 35-37, Postfach 20 10 12, D-4800 Bielefeld 1, Germany. TEL 0521-86033. circ. 350.

610 016   UK   ISSN 0277-6715
RA409   CODEN: SMEDDA
STATISTICS IN MEDICINE. 16/yr. $550 (effective 1992). John Wiley & Sons Ltd., Journals, Baffins Ln., Chichester, Sussex PO19 1UD, England. TEL 0243-779777. FAX 0243-775878. TELEX 86290 WIBOOK G. Ed.Bd. adv.; bk.rev.; charts; illus.; stat.; index. (reprint service avail. from SWZ,UMI) **Indexed:** Abstr.Hyg., ASCA, Biostat., Curr.Cont., Dok.Arbeitsmed., Excerp.Med., Ind.Med., Oper.Res.Manage.Sci., Qual.Contr.Appl.Stat.
   —BLDSC shelfmark: 8453.576000.
   Description: Covers all aspects of the collection, analysis, presentation and interpretation of medical data.

616.863 310   UK
STATISTICS OF THE MISUSE OF DRUGS IN THE UNITED KINGDOM: SEIZURES AND OFFENDERS DEALT WITH. 1978. a. Home Office, 50 Queen Anne's Gate, London SW1H 9AT, England.
   Formerly (until 1986): Great Britain. Home Office. Statistics of the Misuse of Drugs in the United Kingdom, Supplementary Tables.

610.73   DK   ISSN 0108-9714
STATISTIK OM SUNDHEDSPLEJERSKERNES VIRKSOMHED. (Subseries of: Primaer Sundhedstjenestestatistik) 1983. irreg. DKK 75. Sundhedsstyrelsen, Amaliegade 13, 1012 Copenhagen K, Denmark. (Subscr. to: Statens Informationstjeneste, P.O. Box 1103, 1009 Copenhagen K, Denmark) illus.

610 016   CS
STATNI VEDECKA KNIHOVNA. VYBER NOVINEK. SERIE B: LEKARSTVI. 1974. 6/yr. 18 Kcs. Statni Vedecka Knihovna, Kounicova 5-7, 601 87 Brno, Czechoslovakia. circ. 300.

SURGERY, GYNECOLOGY & OBSTETRICS. see *MEDICAL SCIENCES — Surgery*

617.96 016   US   ISSN 0039-6206
RD81.A1   CODEN: SANEA5
SURVEY OF ANESTHESIOLOGY. 1957. bi-m. $57 to individuals; institutions $75. Williams & Wilkins, 428 E. Preston St., Baltimore, MD 21202. TEL 301-528-4000. FAX 301-528-4312. Ed. Burnell R. Brown, Jr., M.D. adv.; bk.rev.; abstr.; circ. 3,800. (also avail. in microform) **Indexed:** Curr.Adv.Ecol.Sci.
   —BLDSC shelfmark: 8548.834400.
   Description: Abstracts of anesthesiology-related literature from around the world.

617.7 016   US   ISSN 0039-6257
   CODEN: SUOPAD
SURVEY OF OPHTHALMOLOGY. 1956. bi-m. $55 to individuals (foreign $95); institutions $65 (foreign $95)(typically set in Jan.). Survey of Ophthalmology, Inc., 7 Kent St., Ste. 4, Brookline, MA 02146. TEL 617-566-2138. FAX 617-566-4019. Ed. Dr. Bernard Schwartz. adv.; bk.rev.; abstr.; charts; illus.; index; circ. 9,773. (also avail. in microform from MIM,UMI; reprint service avail. from UMI) **Indexed:** ASCA, Biol.Abstr., Chem.Abstr., Curr.Adv.Cancer Res., Curr.Cont., Excerp.Med., Ind.Med., Ophthal.Lit., Rev.Plant Path.
   —BLDSC shelfmark: 8550.770000.

SWEDEN. STATISTISKA CENTRALBYRAAN. STATISTISKA MEDDELANDEN. SUBGROUP HS (PUBLIC HEALTH AND MEDICAL CARE). see *PUBLIC HEALTH AND SAFETY — Abstracting, Bibliographies, Statistics*

616.988   UK   ISSN 0041-3240
TROPICAL DISEASES BULLETIN. 1912. m. £60($115) to individuals; institutions £115($220). Bureau of Hygiene and Tropical Diseases, Keppel St., London WC1E 7HT, England. TEL 071-636-8636. FAX 071-580-6756. TELEX 8953474-LSHTML-G. Ed. C.A. Brown. adv.; bk.rev.; abstr.; index; circ. 1,200. **Indexed:** Biol.Abstr., Curr.Adv.Ecol.Sci., Helminthol.Abstr., Ind.Med., Ind.Vet., Nutr.Abstr., Rev.Appl.Entomol., Rev.Plant Path., Vet.Bull.
   ●Also available online. Vendor(s): DIMDI.
   —BLDSC shelfmark: 9056.000000.

TUMOUR MARKER UPDATE. see *MEDICAL SCIENCES — Cancer*

016.6   US   ISSN 0276-7570
U C M P QUARTERLY. 1973. q. $220 to non-participants; participants $190. Medical Library Center of New York, 5 E. 102nd St., 7th Fl., New York, NY 10029-5288. FAX 212-876-6697. Ed. Robert Dempsey. circ. 720. (microfiche)
   Incorporates (1966-1976): Union Catalog of Medical Periodicals (ISSN 0090-0672)

614   TS
UNITED ARAB EMIRATES. WIZARAT AL-SIHHAH. AL-KITAB AL-IHSA'I AL-SANAWI/UNITED ARAB EMIRATES. MINISTRY OF HEALTH. STATISTICAL YEARBOOK. (Text in Arabic) 1977. a. Wizarat al-Sihhah, Idarat al-Takhtit - Ministry of Health, Planning Department, P.O. Box 838, Abu Dhabi, United Arab Emirates. TEL 214100. circ. 1,000 (controlled).
   Description: Provides comprehensive information on the activities, projects and plans of the Ministry of Health, including decisions affecting public and international health care concerns.

619   US
R854.U5
U.S. NATIONAL INSTITUTES OF HEALTH. NATIONAL CENTER FOR RESEARCH RESOURCES. PROGRAM HIGHLIGHTS. 1978. a. free. U.S. National Institutes of Health, National Center for Research Resources, Westwood Bldg., Rm. 10A15, 5333 Westbard Ave., Bethesda, MD 20892. TEL 301-496-5545. circ. 11,000.
   Formerly: U.S. National Institutes of Health. Division of Research Resources. Program Highlights (ISSN 0278-5374)
   Description: Annual report of the National Center for Research Resources.

616.92 016 576.64   US   ISSN 0896-5919
QR360
VIROLOGY AND A I D S ABSTRACTS. 1967. m. $715 (foreign $795). Cambridge Scientific Abstracts, 7200 Wisconsin Ave., 6th Fl., Bethesda, MD 20814. TEL 301-961-6750. FAX 301-961-6720. TELEX 910 2507547 CAMB MD. Ed.Bd. adv.; abstr.; index. (also avail. in magnetic tape; back issues avail.) **Indexed:** Cal.Tiss.Abstr., Chemorec.Abstr., Comput.& Info.Sys., Oncol.Abstr., Pollut.Abstr.
   ●Also available online. Vendor(s): BRS (CSAL), DIALOG (File no.76/LIFE SCIENCES COLLECTION). Also available on CD-ROM. Producer(s): Cambridge Scientific Abstracts (Compact Cambridge Life Sciences Collection).
   Formerly: Virology Abstracts (ISSN 0042-6830)
   Description: Covers viruses of humans, animals and plants, with emphasis on AIDS.

MEDICAL SCIENCES — ABSTRACTING, BIBLIOGRAPHIES, STATISTICS

617.6   US   ISSN 0048-3389
WESTERN SOCIETY OF PERIODONTOLOGY. JOURNAL. PERIODONTAL ABSTRACTS. 1957. q. $60 (Canada, Mexico $70; foreign $75). Western Society of Periodontology, 9010 Reseda Blvd., Ste. 204, Northridge, CA 91324-3921. TEL 818-993-5093. Ed. Thomas N. Sims. adv.; bk.rev.; circ. 2,200.
Indexed: Curr.Tit.Dent., Dent.Ind.
Formerly: Periodontal Abstracts.

616.9   UN   ISSN 1013-0845
WORLD HEALTH ORGANIZATION A I D S TECHNICAL BULLETIN. (Editions in English, French, Spanish) 1989. m. free. World Health Organization, Distribution and Sales, CH-1211 Geneva 27, Switzerland. TEL 791-2111. FAX 22-788-0401. TELEX 415416. (Co-sponsor: Bureau of Hygiene and Tropical Diseases) abstr.; stat.
—BLDSC shelfmark: 0773.096100.

610   CC
YIXUE WENZHAI/MEDICAL ABSTRACTS. (Text in Chinese) bi-m. Guangxi Yixue Qingbao Yanjiusuo - Guangxi Institute of Medical Information, 20 Gucheng Lu, Nanning, Guangxi 530022, People's Republic of China. TEL 29823. Ed. Ma Banghai.

616.21 016   GW   ISSN 0340-5214
ZENTRALBLATT HALS-, NASEN- UND OHRENHEILKUNDE, PLASTISCHE CHIRURGIE AN KOPF UND HALS/OTO-RHINO-LARYNGOLOGY, PLASTIC SURGERY OF HEAD AND NECK. 13/yr. DM.1950($1173) (effective 1992). (Deutsche Gesellschaft fuer Hals,- Nasen-, Ohrenheilkunde, Kopf- und Halschirurgie) Springer-Verlag, Heidelberger Platz 3, D-1000 Berlin 33, Germany. TEL 030-8207-1. (Also Heidelberg, Tokyo, Vienna, and New York) Eds. H.J. Denecke, U.F. Denecke-Singer. (also avail. in microform from UMI; reprint service avail. from ISI)
Formerly: Zentralblatt fuer Hals-, Nasen- und Ohrenheilkunde Sowie Deren Grenzgebiete (ISSN 0044-4200)

616.5 016   GW   ISSN 0343-3048
ZENTRALBLATT HAUT- UND GESCHLECHTSKRANKHEITEN/DERMATOLOGY, VENEROLOGY, ANDROLOGY. 1921. 26/yr. DM.4780($2726) (effective 1992). (Deutsche Dermatologische Gesellschaft) Springer-Verlag, Heidelberger Platz 3, D-1000 Berlin 33, Germany. TEL 030-8207-1. (Also Heidelberg, Tokyo, Vienna, and New York) (Co-sponsor: Vereinigung Deutschsprachiger Dermatologen) Eds. R. Clorius, G. Landes. (also avail. in microform from UMI; reprint service avail. from ISI)
Formerly (until 1977): Zentralblatt fuer Haut- und Geschlechtskrankheiten Sowie Deren Grenzgebiete (ISSN 0044-4219)

618.92 016   GW   ISSN 0722-8953
ZENTRALBLATT KINDERHEILKUNDE/PEDIATRICS. 26/yr. (in 2 vols., 13 nos/vol.). DM.4300($2458) (effective 1992). (Deutsche Gesellschaft fuer Kinderheilkunde) Springer-Verlag, Heidelberger Platz 3, D-1000 Berlin 33, Germany. TEL 030-8207-1. (Also Heidelberg, Tokyo, Vienna, and New York) Ed. O. Linderkamp. (also avail. in microform from UMI; reprint service avail. from ISI)
Formerly: Zentralblatt fuer die Gesamte Kinderheilkunde (ISSN 0044-4111)

616.8 016   GW   ISSN 0722-3064
ZENTRALBLATT NEUROLOGIE - PSYCHIATRIE/NEUROLOGY - PSYCHIATRY. (Text in English or German) 39/yr. DM.6750($3896) (effective 1992). (Archiv fuer Psychiatrie und Nervenkrankheiten) Springer-Verlag, Heidelberger Platz 3, D-1000 Berlin 33, Germany. TEL 030-8207-1. (Also Heidelberg, Tokyo, Vienna, and New York) (Co-sponsor: Gesamtverbande Deutscher Nervenaerzte) Eds. O. Hallen, G. Huber. (also avail. in microform from UMI; reprint service avail. from ISI)
Formerly: Zentralblatt fuer die Gesamte Neurologie und Psychiatrie (ISSN 0044-412X)

617.7 016   GW   ISSN 0722-9933
ZENTRALBLATT OPHTHALMOLOGIE/OPHTHALMOLOGY. (Text in English or German) 13/yr. DM.2260($1317) (effective 1992). Springer-Verlag, Heidelberger Platz 3, D-1000 Berlin 33, Germany. TEL 030-8207-1. (Also Heidelberg, Tokyo, Vienna, and New York) Ed. O. Kaefer. (also avail. in microform from UMI; reprint service avail. from ISI)
Formerly: Zentralblatt fuer die Gesamte Ophthalmologie und ihre Grenzgebiete (ISSN 0044-4138)

615.842 016   GW   ISSN 0722-3072
ZENTRALBLATT RADIOLOGIE/RADIOLOGY. (Text in English or German) 1926. 26/yr. (in 2 vols., 13 nos./vol.). DM.4780($2756) (effective 1992). (Deutsche Roentgengesellschaft) Springer-Verlag, Heidelberger Platz 3, D-1000 Berlin 33, Germany. TEL 030-8207-1. (Also Heidelberg, Tokyo, Vienna, and New York) Eds. C. Wieland, U. Weischedel. (also avail. in microform from UMI; back issues avail.; reprint service avail. from ISI)
Formerly: Zentralblatt fuer die Gesamte Radiologie (ISSN 0044-4146)

614.19 016   GW   ISSN 0722-3056
RA1001
ZENTRALBLATT RECHTSMEDIZIN/LEGAL MEDICINE. 1970. 26/yr. DM.3980($2283) (effective 1992). (Deutsche Gesellschaft fuer Rechtsmedizin) Springer-Verlag, Heidelberger Platz 3, D-1000 Berlin 33, Germany. TEL 030-8207-1. (Also Heidelberg, Tokyo, Vienna, and New York) Ed. J.B. Dalgaard. (also avail. in microform from UMI; back issues avail.; reprint service avail. from ISI) Indexed: Ind.Med.
Formerly: Zentralblatt fuer die Gesamte Rechtsmedizin und ihre Grenzgebiete (ISSN 0044-4154); Which supersedes: Deutsche Zeitschrift fuer die Gesamte Gerichtliche Medizin. Abstract Section.

617 016   GW   ISSN 0722-6985
ZENTRALORGAN CHIRURGIE/SURGERY. 26/yr. DM.2840($1643.75) (effective 1992). (Deutsche Gesellschaft fuer Chirurgie) Springer-Verlag, Heidelberger Platz 3, D-1000 Berlin 33, Germany. TEL 030-8207-1. (Also Heidelberg, Tokyo, Vienna, and New York) Ed. G. Heberer. (also avail. in microform from UMI; reprint service avail. from ISI)
Formerly: Zentralorgan fuer die Gesamte Chirurgie und ihre Grenzgebiete (ISSN 0044-4308)

610   CC
ZHONGGUO YIXUE WENZHAI (ERKEXUE)/CHINA MEDICAL ABSTRACTS (PEDIATRICS). (Text in Chinese) bi-m. $3.80 per no. Liaoning Yixue Qingbao Yanjiusuo - Liaoning Medical Information Institute, 79 Jixian Jie, Heping-qu, Shenyang, Liaoning 110005, People's Republic of China. TEL 362837. Ed. Yang Xiaoxin.

618   CC   ISSN 1001-1315
ZHONGGUO YIXUE WENZHAI (JIHUA SHENGYU, FUCHAN KEXUE)/CHINA MEDICAL ABSTRACTS (BIRTH CONTROL AND GYNECOLOGY). (Text in Chinese) q. Sichuan Yixue Qingbao Yanjiusuo - Sichuan Medical Science Information Research Institute, 34, Wangjiaguai Jie, Chengdu, Sichuan 610041, People's Republic of China. TEL 28790. Ed. Song Wenli.

617.6   CC
ZHONGGUO YIXUE WENZHAI (KOUQIANG YIXUE)/CHINA MEDICAL ABSTRACTS (STOMATOLOGY). (Text in Chinese) q. Nanjing Yixueyuan - Nanjing Institute of Medical Sciences, 140 Hanzhong Lu, Nanjing, Jiangsu 210029, People's Republic of China. TEL 649141. Ed. Yin Liqiao.

610   CC   ISSN 1001-4136
ZHONGGUO YIXUE WENZHAI (NEIKE XUE). English edition: China Medical Abstracts (Internal Medicine). (Text in Chinese) bi-m. $26. Guangxi Yixue Kexue Qibaosuo - Guangxi Institute of Medical Science Information, 20 Gucheng Lu, Nanning, Guangxi 530022, People's Republic of China. TEL 29818. (Dist. outside China by: Guoji Shudian - China International Book Trading Corp., P.O. Box 399, Beijing, P.R.C.) Ed. Lin Zhongchang.

MEDICAL SCIENCES — Allergology And Immunology

616.97   AT   ISSN 0817-1300
A A A NEWS. 1982. q. Aus.$30. Allergy Association Australia - Victoria Inc., P.O. Box 298, Ringwood, Vic. 3134, Australia. TEL 03-888-1382. circ. 700. (back issues avail.)

616.97   US
A A O A NEWS. 1981. q. free. American Academy of Otolaryngic Allergy, 8455 Colesville Rd., Ste. 745, Silver Spring, MD 20910. Ed. Dr. Richard L. Mabay. adv.; tr.lit.; circ. 12,000. (back issues avail.)
Description: Developments in otolaryngic allergy for physicians and allied health practitioners.

616.97   US   ISSN 0883-2994
RC583
A B M S DIRECTORY OF CERTIFIED ALLERGISTS AND IMMUNOLOGISTS. (Individual directories are published biennially for each of 24 medical specialties) 1985. biennial. $24.95. American Board of Medical Specialties, One Rotary Center, Ste. 805, Evanston, IL 60201. TEL 708-491-9091. FAX 708-328-3596. Ed. Dr. J. Lee Dockery. circ. 2,000.

A I D S ALERT. see *MEDICAL SCIENCES — Communicable Diseases*

A I D S RESEARCH AND HUMAN RETROVIRUSES. see *MEDICAL SCIENCES — Communicable Diseases*

ADVANCES IN HOST DEFENSE MECHANISMS. see *MEDICAL SCIENCES — Communicable Diseases*

616.97   US   ISSN 0065-2776
QR180   CODEN: ADIMAV
ADVANCES IN IMMUNOLOGY. 1961. irreg., vol.51, 1991. Academic Press, Inc., 1250 Sixth Ave., San Diego, CA 92101. TEL 619-231-0926. FAX 619-699-6715. Eds. W.H. Taliaferro, J.H. Humphrey. index. (reprint service avail. from ISI)
Indexed: Abstr.Hyg., Anim.Breed.Abstr., Biol.Abstr., Chem.Abstr., Curr.Adv.Ecol.Sci., Dairy Sci.Abstr., Excerp.Med., Helminthol.Abstr., Ind.Med., Ind.Sci.Rev., Ind.Vet., Nutr.Abstr., Sci.Cit.Ind, Telegen, Trop.Dis.Bull., Vet.Bull.
—BLDSC shelfmark: 0709.100000.

616.97   UK   ISSN 0960-5428
                             CODEN: ADNIEE
▼**ADVANCES IN NEUROIMMUNOLOGY.** 1991. 4/yr. $210 (effective 1992). Pergamon Press plc, Headington Hill Hall, Oxford OX3 0BW, England. TEL 0865-794141. FAX 0865-743911. TELEX 83177 PERGAP. (And: 660 White Plains Rd., Tarrytown, NY 10591-5153. TEL 914-524-9200) Eds. George B. Stefano, Eric M. Smith. (also avail. in microform)
—BLDSC shelfmark: 0709.479000.
Description: Publishes comprehensive reviews on significant research into the interactions between the nervous and immune systems, from both basic and clinical standpoints.
Refereed Serial

AGING: IMMUNOLOGY & INFECTIOUS DISEASE. see *GERONTOLOGY AND GERIATRICS*

616.97   MX   ISSN 0002-5151
                             CODEN: ALEGAF
ALERGIA. (Text in Spanish; summaries in English) 1953. bi-m. $90. Sociedad Mexicana de Alergia e Inmunologia, A.C., Fuente Emperador 6, Tecamachalco, Deleg. Naucalpan, 53950 Edo. de Mexico, Mexico. Ed. Jesus Perez Martin. adv.; bk.rev.; circ. 3,000. Indexed: Biol.Abstr., Chem.Abstr., Dent.Ind., Ind.Med.
—BLDSC shelfmark: 7840.857000.
Description: Original research articles in clinical case studies on allergy and immunology.

615.37 616.97   FR
ALLERGIE ET IMMUNOLOGIE.* 1969. q. 300 F. (students 200 F.). Nouvelles Editions Medicales Francaises, B.P. 451, 95005 Clergy Poutoise Cedex, France. Ed. G.M. Halpern. adv.; bk.rev.; circ. 5,000. Indexed: Biol.Abstr., Excerp.Med., Ind.Med., Nutr.Abstr.

MEDICAL SCIENCES — ALLERGOLOGY AND IMMUNOLOGY

616.97 615.37   GW   ISSN 0323-4398
CODEN: ALIMCL
ALLERGIE UND IMMUNOLOGIE. 1955. 4/yr. DM.72. (Gesellschaft fuer Klinische und Experimentelle Immunologie) Johann Ambrosius Barth Verlag, Leipzig - Heidelberg, Salomonstr. 18bg, 7010 Leipzig, Germany. TEL 70131. Ed. H. Ambrosius. adv.; bk.rev.; abstr.; bibl.; charts; illus.; index; circ. 650. **Indexed:** Biol.Abstr., Chem.Abstr., Curr.Adv.Ecol.Sci., Excerp.Med., Ind.Med., INIS Atomind., Nutr.Abstr.
—BLDSC shelfmark: 0790.910000.
Formerly: Allergie und Asthma.

616.97 615.37   SP   ISSN 0301-0546
CODEN: AGIMBJ
ALLERGOLOGIA ET INMUNOPATHOLOGIA. (Supplement avail. (ISSN 0211-6448)) (Text in English, Spanish) 1972. bi-m. 8000 ptas.($130) Editorial Garsi, S.A., Londres, 17, 28028 Madrid, Spain. TEL 256-08-00. FAX 361-10-07. Dir. A. Bosambo. circ. 3,000. **Indexed:** Biol.Abstr., Chem.Abstr., CINAHL, Curr.Adv.Ecol.Sci., Dent.Ind., Excerp.Med., Helminthol.Abstr., Ind.Med., Ind.Med.Esp., Nutr.Abstr., Protozool.Abstr., Rev.Med.& Vet.Mycol.
—BLDSC shelfmark: 0790.930000.

616.97   SZ   ISSN 0065-6372
ALLERGOLOGICUM; TRANSACTIONS OF THE COLLEGIUM INTERNATIONALE. (Supplement to: International Archives of Allergy and Applied Immunology) (Text in English) 1955. a. Collegium Internationale Allergologicum, c/o Dr. Alain de Week, Institut fuer Klinische Immunologie, Inseksital, CH-3010 Berne, Switzerland. Ed. Basel Karger. **Indexed:** Curr.Cont.

616.97   GW   ISSN 0344-5062
CODEN: ALLRDI
ALLERGOLOGIE. 1978. m. DM.210($140) Dustri-Verlag Dr. Karl Feistle, Bahnhofstr. 9, 8024 Deisenhofen, Germany. TEL 089-613861-0. FAX 089-6135412. Ed. Dr. E. Fuchs. **Indexed:** Biol.Abstr., Chem.Abstr., Curr.Adv.Ecol.Sci., Curr.Cont., Excerp.Med., Rev.Med.& Vet.Mycol.
—BLDSC shelfmark: 0790.940000.

616.97   GW
ALLERGOTHEK. q. DM.24. (Allergie Vereins in Europa) Karl F. Haug Verlag GmbH, Fritz-Frey-Str. 21, Postfach 102840, 6900 Heidelberg 1, Germany. TEL 06221-4062-0. FAX 06221-400727. TELEX 461683-HVVFM-D. Ed. R. Zienczyk-Beckert.

616.97   DK   ISSN 0105-4538
CODEN: LLRGDY
ALLERGY. (Text in English) 1948. 6/yr. DKK 1610 includes supplements. (European Academy of Allergology and Clinical Immunology) Munksgaard International Publishers Ltd., P.O. Box 2148, DK-1016 Copenhagen K. TEL 33-127030. FAX 33-129387. TELEX 19431-MUNKS-DK. Ed. Gunnar Bendixen. adv.; bk.rev.; bibl.; charts; illus.; index; circ. 1,100. (also avail. in microform from SWZ; reprint service avail. from ISI) **Indexed:** Biol.Abstr., Biotech.Abstr., C.I.S. Abstr., Chem.Abstr., Curr.Adv.Ecol.Sci., Curr.Adv.Genetics & Molec.Biol., Curr.Cont., Dairy Sci.Abstr., Dent.Ind., Dok.Arbeitsmed., Excerp.Med., Helminthol.Abstr., Ind.Med., Ind.Sci.Rev., INIS Atomind., NRN, Nutr.Abstr., Rev.Med.& Vet.Mycol., Risk Abstr., Sci.Cit.Ind., Weed Abstr.
—BLDSC shelfmark: 0790.945000.
Formerly: Acta Allergologica (ISSN 0001-5148)

616.97   DK   ISSN 0108-1675
CODEN: ALSUE
ALLERGY. SUPPLEMENTUM. (Text in English) 1950. irreg. (European Academy of Allergology and Clinical Immunology) Munksgaard International Publishers Ltd., 35 Noerre Soegade, P.O. Box 2148, DK-1016 Copenhagen K, Denmark. TEL 33-127030. FAX 33-129387. TELEX 19431-MUNKS-DK. adv. (reprint service avail. from ISI) **Indexed:** Biol.Abstr., Curr.Cont., Excerp.Med.
—BLDSC shelfmark: 0790.946000.
Formerly: Acta Allergologica. Supplementum (ISSN 0065-096X)

616.97   CN   ISSN 0824-1333
ALLERGY ALERT. 1980. q. Can.$12. Allergy Foundation of Canada, Box 1904, Saskatoon, Sask. S7K 3S5, Canada. TEL 306-652-1608. Ed. Sandy Woynarski. bk.rev.; circ. 550.

616.97   CN   ISSN 0838-1925
ALLERGY & CLINICAL IMMUNOLOGY NEWS. Short title: A C I News. 1989. bi-m. Can.$44 to members; non-members Can.$56. (International Association of Allergology and Clinical Immunology) Hogrefe & Huber Publishers, 14 Bruce Park Ave., Toronto, Ont. M4P 2S3, Canada. TEL 416-482-6339. FAX 416-484-42006. Ed. A.L. de Weck. adv. (back issues avail.)
—BLDSC shelfmark: 0791.040000.
Description: Includes clinical trends and practice, research trends and notes, reports on meetings, forum, people and calendar of events.

616.97   US   ISSN 1046-9354
CODEN: ALPRE5
ALLERGY PROCEEDINGS. 1980. bi-m. $65 to individuals; institutions $75. Ocean Side Publications, Inc., 95 Pitman St., Providence, RI 02906. TEL 401-331-2510. FAX 401-331-5183. Ed. Dr. Guy A. Settipane. adv.; circ. 3,000. (back issues avail.) **Indexed:** Chem.Abstr, Curr.Adv.Ecol.Sci., Curr.Cont., Ind.Med., Ind.Vet., Small Anim.Abstr.
—BLDSC shelfmark: 0791.081000.
Former titles: New England and Regional Allergy Proceedings; New England Society of Allergy. Proceedings (ISSN 0276-7511)

616.97   US
AMERICAN ACADEMY OF ALLERGY. POLLEN AND MOLD COMMITTEE. STATISTICAL REPORT. 1973. a. free. Ross Laboratories, 625 Cleveland Ave., Columbus, OH 43216. TEL 614-227-3333. Ed. Bill Rohn. circ. 100. **Indexed:** Biol.Abstr., Nutr.Abstr.

AMERICAN ACADEMY OF ALLERGY AND IMMUNOLOGY. ABSTRACT BOOK. see *MEDICAL SCIENCES — Abstracting, Bibliographies, Statistics*

616.97 618.92   US   ISSN 0899-7411
AMERICAN JOURNAL OF ASTHMA & ALLERGY FOR PEDIATRICIANS. 1987. q. $55 to individuals; institutions $70; foreign $100. Slack, Inc., 6900 Grove Rd., Thorofare, NJ 08086-9447. TEL 609-848-1000. FAX 609-853-5991. Ed. Dr. Jacob Hen, Jr. adv.; circ. 800.
—BLDSC shelfmark: 0821.700000.
Refereed Serial

616.97 618   DK   ISSN 8755-8920
QP252.5   CODEN: AJRMEK
AMERICAN JOURNAL OF REPRODUCTIVE IMMUNOLOGY AND MICROBIOLOGY. (Text in English) 1980. 8/yr. $309. (American Society for the Immunology of Reproduction, US) Munksgaard International Publishers Ltd., P.O. Box 2148, DK-1016 Copenhagen K, Denmark. TEL 45-33-12-70-30. FAX 45-33-12-93-87. TELEX 19431 MUNKS DK. (Co-sponsor: International Coordination Committee for Immunology of Reproduction) Ed. Norbert Gleicher. adv.; bibl.; charts; illus.; index. **Indexed:** Anim.Breed.Abstr., Biol.Abstr., Chem.Abstr., Curr.Adv.Ecol.Sci., Curr.Cont., Dairy Sci.Abstr., Excerp.Med., Ind.Med., Ind.Sci.Rev., Ind.Vet., INIS Atomind., Pig News & Info., Sci.Cit.Ind.
● Also available online.
Formerly (until 1985): American Journal of Reproductive Immunology (ISSN 0271-7352)
Refereed Serial

616.97   US   ISSN 0003-4738
CODEN: ANAEA3
ANNALS OF ALLERGY. 1943. m. $42.50. American College of Allergists, 800 E. Northwest Hwy., Ste. 1080, Palatine, IL 60067-6516. FAX 708-821-2042. Ed. Dr. R. Michael Sly. adv.; bk.rev.; bibl.; charts; illus.; index; circ. 11,000. (also avail. in microfilm from UMI) **Indexed:** Abstr.Inter.Med., Biol.Abstr., Biotech.Abstr., C.I.S. Abstr., Chem.Abstr., Curr.Adv.Ecol.Sci., Curr.Cont., Dairy Sci.Abstr., Dent.Ind., Dent.Ind., Excerp.Med., Food Sci.& Tech.Abstr., Helminthol.Abstr., Ind.Med., Ind.Sci.Rev., NRN, Nutr.Abstr., Potato Abstr., Rev.Appl.Entomol., Rev.Med.& Vet.Mycol., Rev.Plant Path., Sci.Cit.Ind., Soyabean Abstr.
—BLDSC shelfmark: 1036.000000.

616.97   US   ISSN 0732-0582
QR180   CODEN: ARIMDU
ANNUAL REVIEW OF IMMUNOLOGY. 1983. a. $45 (foreign $50)(effective Jan. 1992). Annual Reviews Inc., 4139 El Camino Way, Box 10139, Palo Alto, CA 94303-0897. TEL 415-493-4400. FAX 415-855-9815. TELEX 910-290-0275. Ed. William E. Paul. bibl.; index. cum.index. (also avail. in microform from UMI) **Indexed:** Abstr.Hyg., Anim.Breed.Abstr., Biol.Abstr., Chem.Abstr., Curr.Adv.Ecol.Sci., Ind.Sci.Rev., Ind.Vet., Protozool.Abstr., Sci.Cit.Ind.
—BLDSC shelfmark: 1522.565800.
Description: Original reviews of critical literature and current developments in immunology.
Refereed Serial

ANTIBODY, IMMUNOCONJUGATES, AND RADIOPHARMACEUTICALS. see *MEDICAL SCIENCES — Cancer*

616.97 616.2   JA   ISSN 0287-0185
ARERUGIA. 1968. irreg. free. Japan Allergy Foundation, 6-8 Minamidai, Sagamihara, Kanagawa Prefecture, Japan. Ed. Prof. A. Kumagai. circ. 4,500.

616.97   US
ASTHMA AND ALLERGY ADVOCATE. 1985. q. $70. American Academy of Allergy and Immunology, 611 E. Wells St., Milwaukee, WI 53202. TEL 414-272-6071. Ed. S.E. Kaluzny. bk.rev.; charts; illus.; stat.; circ. 75,000. (looseleaf format)
Description: Patient newsletter with information in the field.

616.97   US
▼**ASTHMA RESOURCES DIRECTORY.** 1990. irreg. (every 2-3 yrs.). $29.95. Allergy Publications, Inc., Box 640, Menlo Park, CA 94026-0640. TEL 415-322-1663. Ed. Carol Rudoff. adv.
Description: Presents information on allergens that may trigger asthma symptoms, organizations and programs that provide support, information, education or products and services to asthma patients, doctors and treatment centers for asthma, and libraries or organizations with allergy specialty departments, databases and publications on asthma.

616.97   NO   ISSN 0801-3799
ASTMA ALLERGI. 1961. 6/yr. NOK 160. Norges Astma- og Allergiforbund, Industrigt. 36, 0357 Oslo 3, Norway. TEL 02-460613. FAX 02-698152. Eds. Ernst Pettersen, Tove T. Tveit. adv.; bk.rev.; illus.; pat.; circ. 25,000.
Formerly: Astma- og Allergi-Nytt (ISSN 0004-6086)

616.97   DK   ISSN 0900-4262
ASTMA ALLERGI BLADET. 1971. q. DKK 100. Danmarks Astma - Allergiforbund, Hurlufsholmvej 37, 2720 Vanlose, Denmark. adv.; bk.rev.; circ. 15,000.

616.97 616.7   UK   ISSN 0142-8365
AUTOIMMUNE DISEASES. s-m. £100. Sheffield University Biomedical Information Service (SUBIS), The University, Sheffield S10 2TN, England. TEL 0742-768555. FAX 0742-739826. TELEX 547216 UGSHEF G. (looseleaf format; back issues avail.)
Description: Current awareness service for researchers in clinical and life sciences.

615.37   SZ   ISSN 0301-3782
QR180
BASEL INSTITUTE FOR IMMUNOLOGY. ANNUAL REPORT. (Text in English) 1972. a. free to libraries and immunologists. Basel Institute for Immunology, Grenzacherstrasse 487, CH-4058 Basel, Switzerland. FAX 41-61-601-1353. Ed. C.M. Steinberg. circ. 5,500. **Indexed:** Biol.Abstr.
Description: Presents research reports on all aspects of immunology.

M

MEDICAL SCIENCES — ALLERGOLOGY AND IMMUNOLOGY

616.97   US   ISSN 0889-1591
QP356.47   CODEN: BBIMEW
BRAIN, BEHAVIOR, AND IMMUNITY. 1987. q. $128 (foreign $149). Academic Press, Inc., Journal Division, 1250 Sixth Ave., San Diego, CA 92101. TEL 619-230-1840. FAX 619-699-6800. TELEX 181726. Ed. Robert Ader. (back issues avail.)
—BLDSC shelfmark: 2268.101000.
Description: Concerned with the interaction between the nervous system and the immune system at the molecular, cellular, and organismic levels. Addresses the relationships among behavioral, neural, and immunoregulatory processes.
Refereed Serial

C A SELECTS. ALLERGY AND ANTIALLERGIC AGENTS. see *MEDICAL SCIENCES — Abstracting, Bibliographies, Statistics*

C A SELECTS. IMMUNOCHEMICAL METHODS. see *MEDICAL SCIENCES — Abstracting, Bibliographies, Statistics*

615.37   CN   ISSN 0068-9653
CANADIAN SOCIETY FOR IMMUNOLOGY. BULLETIN. (Text in English, French) 1967. q. membership. Canadian Society for Immunology, c/o Department of Immunology, University of Manitoba, 730 William Ave., Winnipeg, Man. R3E 0W3, Canada. TEL 204-788-6509. FAX 204-772-7924. Ed. Dr. Kent T. Hayglass. adv.; bk.rev.; circ. 500. (also avail. in microform from UMI; reprint service avail. from UMI)

615.37 574.8   US   ISSN 0008-8749
QR185.C4   CODEN: CLIMB8
CELLULAR IMMUNOLOGY. 1970. 14/yr. $910 (foreign $1105). Academic Press, Inc., Journal Division, 1250 Sixth Ave., San Diego, CA 92101. TEL 619-230-1840. FAX 619-699-6800. TELEX 181726. Ed. H. Sherwood Lawrence. index. (back issues avail.) **Indexed:** Abstr.Hyg., Anim.Breed.Abstr., Biol.Abstr., Chem.Abstr., Curr.Adv.Cancer Res., Curr.Adv.Ecol.Sci., Curr.Cont., Dairy Sci.Abstr., Dent.Ind., Excerpt.Med., Helminthol.Abstr., Ind.Med., Ind.Sci.Rev., Ind.Vet., INIS Atomind., Protozool.Abstr., Rev.Plant Path., Small Anim.Abstr., Trop.Dis.Bull., Vet.Bull.
—BLDSC shelfmark: 3097.930000.
Description: Publishes original investigations concerned with the immunological activities of cells in experimental or clinical situations.
Refereed Serial

616.97   SZ   ISSN 1015-0145
CODEN: CHMIEP
CHEMICAL IMMUNOLOGY. (Text in English) 1939. irreg. (approx. 1/yr.). price varies. S. Karger AG, Allschwilerstr. 10, P.O. Box, CH-4009 Basel, Switzerland. TEL 061-3061111. FAX 061-3061234. TELEX CH 962652. Ed.Bd. (back issues avail.) **Indexed:** Biol.Abstr., Chem.Abstr., Curr.Adv.Ecol.Sci., Curr.Cont., Excerp.Med., Ind.Med., Ind.Sci.Rev.
—BLDSC shelfmark: 3146.750000.
Formerly (until 1989): Progress in Allergy (ISSN 0079-6034)

CHINESE JOURNAL OF MICROBIOLOGY AND IMMUNOLOGY. see *BIOLOGY — Microbiology*

616.97   UK   ISSN 0954-7894
CODEN: CLEAEN
CLINICAL AND EXPERIMENTAL ALLERGY. 1971. bi-m. £160 (foreign £175). (British Society for Allergy & Clinical Immunology) Blackwell Scientific Publications Ltd., Osney Mead, Oxford OX2 OEL, England. TEL 0865-240201. FAX 0865-721205. TELEX 83355-MEDBOK-G. Eds. Prof. A.B. Kay, Dr. S.T. Holgate. adv.; bk.rev.; illus.; index; circ. 1,420. (also avail. in microform from MIM; back issues avail; reprint service avail. from ISI) **Indexed:** Abstr.Hyg., ASCA, Biol.Abstr., Biotech.Abstr., C.I.S. Abstr., Chem.Abstr., Curr.Adv.Ecol.Sci., Curr.Cont., Dairy Sci.Abstr., Dok.Arbeitsmed., Excerp.Med., Helminthol.Abstr., Ind.Med., Ind.Sci.Rev., INIS Atomind., Lab.Haz.Bull., NRN, Rev.Appl.Entomol., Sci.Cit.Ind., Trop.Dis.Bull.
—BLDSC shelfmark: 3286.249700.
Formerly (until Jan. 1989): Clinical Allergy (ISSN 0009-9090)

615.37   UK   ISSN 0009-9104
RC583   CODEN: CEXIAL
CLINICAL AND EXPERIMENTAL IMMUNOLOGY. (Supplement avail. (ISSN 0964-2536)) 1966. m. £299.50 (foreign £340). (British Society for Immunology) Blackwell Scientific Publications Ltd., Osney Mead, Oxford OX2 OEL, England. TEL 0865-240201. FAX 0865-721205. TELEX 83355-MEDBOK-G. Ed. J.L. Turk. adv.; bibl.; charts; illus.; index; circ. 1,900. (also avail. in microform from MIM; back issues avail.; reprint service avail. from ISI) **Indexed:** Abstr.Hyg., Anim.Breed.Abstr., ASCA, Biol.Abstr., Biotech.Abstr., Chem.Abstr., Curr.Adv.Cancer Res., Curr.Adv.Ecol.Sci., Curr.Adv.Genetics & Molec.Biol., Curr.Cont., Dairy Sci.Abstr., Dent.Ind., Excerpt.Med., Helminthol.Abstr., Ind.Med., Ind.Sci.Rev., Ind.Vet., Nutr.Abstr., Protozool.Abstr., Rev.Plant Path., Sci.Cit.Ind, Telegen, Trop.Dis.Bull., Vet.Bull.
—BLDSC shelfmark: 3286.251000.

615.37   US   ISSN 0090-1229
RC583   CODEN: CLIIAT
CLINICAL IMMUNOLOGY AND IMMUNOPATHOLOGY. 1972. m. $552 (foreign $677). Academic Press, Inc., Journal Division, 1250 Sixth Ave., San Diego, CA 92101. TEL 619-230-1840. FAX 619-699-6800. TELEX 181726. Ed. Noel Rose. adv.; illus.; index. (back issues avail.) **Indexed:** Biol.Abstr., Chem.Abstr., Curr.Adv.Ecol.Sci., Curr.Adv.Genetics & Molec.Biol., Curr.Cont., Dairy Sci.Abstr., Dent.Ind., Excerpt.Med., Helminthol.Abstr., Ind.Med., Ind.Sci.Rev., Ind.Vet., INIS Atomind., Nutr.Abstr., Sci.Cit.Ind., Vet.Bull.
—BLDSC shelfmark: 3286.293000.
Description: Publishes original research on the molecular and cellular bases of immunological diseases.

616.97   US   ISSN 0197-1859
CODEN: CIMNDC
CLINICAL IMMUNOLOGY NEWSLETTER. 1980. m. $145 to institutions (foreign $188)(effective 1992). Elsevier Science Publishing Co., Inc. (New York), 655 Ave. of the Americas, New York, NY 10010. TEL 212-989-5800. FAX 212-633-3965. TELEX 420643 AEP UI. Eds. Alan L. Landay, Henry Homburger. **Indexed:** Abstr.Hyg., Biol.Abstr., Excerpt.Med., Ind.Vet.
—BLDSC shelfmark: 3286.293400.
Description: For clinical immunologists, clinical patologists, microbiologists, and infectious desease physicians.
Refereed Serial

616.96   US   ISSN 0731-8235
CODEN: CRVADD
CLINICAL REVIEWS IN ALLERGY. 1983. q. $150. Humana Press Inc., Box 2148, Clifton, NJ 07015. TEL 201-256-1699. FAX 201-256-8341. Ed. M. Eric Gershwin. adv.; abstr.; bibl.; charts; illus.; index. (also avail. in microform from RPI; back issues avail.) **Indexed:** Biol.Abstr., Chem.Abstr., Curr.Adv.Ecol.Sci., Curr.Cont., Dok.Arbeitsmed., Excerp.Med., Ind.Med., Ind.Sci.Rev., Sci.Cit.Ind.
—BLDSC shelfmark: 3286.374500.
Description: Provides comprehensive coverage of subjects critical to the study of allergy. Each issue is thematic.
Refereed Serial

616.97   US   ISSN 0149-1148
CODEN: COIMDV
COMPREHENSIVE IMMUNOLOGY. irreg., latest vol.9. price varies. Plenum Publishing Corp., 233 Spring St., New York, NY 10013-1578. TEL 212-620-8000. FAX 212-463-0742. TELEX 23-421139. Eds. Robert A. Good, Stacey B. Day. **Indexed:** Biol.Abstr., Chem.Abstr.
Refereed Serial

616.97 574.2   US   ISSN 0093-4054
QR180   CODEN: CTIBBV
CONTEMPORARY TOPICS IN IMMUNOBIOLOGY. 1972. irreg., vol.15, 1985. price varies. Plenum Publishing Corp., 233 Spring St., New York, NY 10013-1578. TEL 212-620-8000. FAX 212-463-0742. TELEX 23-421139. **Indexed:** ASCA, Biol.Abstr., Ind.Med., INIS Atomind., Int.Sci.Rev., Sci.Cit.Ind.
—BLDSC shelfmark: 3425.310000.
Refereed Serial

615.37   US   ISSN 0090-8800
QR180   CODEN: CTMIB4
CONTEMPORARY TOPICS IN MOLECULAR IMMUNOLOGY. 1972. irreg., vol.15, 1985. price varies. Plenum Publishing Corp., 233 Spring St., New York, NY 10013-1578. TEL 212-620-8000. FAX 212-463-0742. TELEX 23-421139. Ed. F.P. Inman. **Indexed:** Biol.Abstr., Curr.Adv.Ecol.Sci., Ind.Med., Ind.Sci.Rev., Sci.Cit.Ind.
—BLDSC shelfmark: 3425.313000.
Refereed Serial

615.37 576   SZ   ISSN 0301-3081
CODEN: CMIMBF
CONTRIBUTIONS TO MICROBIOLOGY AND IMMUNOLOGY. (Text in English) 1973. irreg. (approx. 1/yr.). price varies. S. Karger AG, Allschwilerstr. 10, P.O. Box, CH-4009 Basel, Switzerland. TEL 061-3061111. FAX 061-3061234. TELEX CH 962652. Eds. J.M. Cruse, R.E. Lewis Jr. (reprint service avail. from ISI) **Indexed:** Biol.Abstr., Chem.Abstr., Curr.Cont., Ind.Med., Ind.Vet., Protozool.Abstr., Vet.Bull.
—BLDSC shelfmark: 3460.500000.
Supersedes: Bibliotheca Microbiologia (ISSN 0067-8058)

616.97   US   ISSN 1040-8401
QR180   CODEN: CCRIDE
CRITICAL REVIEWS IN IMMUNOLOGY. 1980. q. $99.95 to individuals; institutions $295. C R C Press, Inc., 2000 Corporate Blvd., N.W., Boca Raton, FL 33431. TEL 407-994-0555. FAX 407-998-9784. Ed. M.Z. Atassi. circ. 270. (back issues avail.) **Indexed:** Anim.Breed.Abstr., Biol.Abstr., Chem.Abstr., Curr.Adv.Ecol.Sci., Curr.Cont., Helminthol.Abstr., Ind.Med., Ind.Sci.Rev., Ind.Vet., Sci.Cit.Ind., Telegen.
—BLDSC shelfmark: 3487.477000.
Formerly: C R C Critical Reviews in Immunology (ISSN 0197-3355)
Refereed Serial

CURRENT ADVANCES IN IMMUNOLOGY & INFECTIOUS DISEASES. see *MEDICAL SCIENCES — Abstracting, Bibliographies, Statistics*

CURRENT OPINION IN IMMUNOLOGY. see *MEDICAL SCIENCES — Abstracting, Bibliographies, Statistics*

616.079 574.29   US   ISSN 0145-305X
QR180   CODEN: DCIMDQ
DEVELOPMENTAL AND COMPARATIVE IMMUNOLOGY; ontogeny - phylogeny - aging. Title originally announced as: Journal of Developmental and Comparative Immunology. 1977. 6/yr. £290 (effective 1992). (International Society of Developmental and Comparative Immunology) Pergamon Press, Inc., Journals Division, 660 White Plains Rd., Tarrytown, NY 10591-5153. TEL 914-524-9200. FAX 914-333-2444. (And: Headington Hill Hall, Oxford OX3 0BW, England. TEL 0865-794141) Ed. Edwin L. Cooper. adv.; bibl.; charts; illus.; index, cum.index; circ. 1,020. (also avail. in microform from MIM,UMI; back issues avail.; reprint service avail. from UMI) **Indexed:** Anim.Breed.Abstr., Biol.Abstr., Chem.Abstr., Curr.Adv.Ecol.Sci., Curr.Cont., Dairy Sci.Abstr., Excerp.Med., Helminthol.Abstr., Ind.Med., Ind.Sci.Rev., Ind.Vet., INIS Atomind., Poult.Abstr., Protozool.Abstr., Sci.Cit.Ind., Vet.Bull., W.R.C.Inf.
—BLDSC shelfmark: 3579.051000.
Description: Publishes original research addressing the development and maturation of the immune system in the broadest sense, emphasizing ontogenetic (including aging) and phylogenetic aspects, including recognitionmechanisms, cellular interactions, immunoglobins, and products of T cells and macrophages.
Refereed Serial

616.97   US   ISSN 1044-6672
QR184.5   CODEN: DEIME7
▼**DEVELOPMENTAL IMMUNOLOGY.** 1991. 4/yr. (in 1 vol., 4 nos./vol.). $75. Harwood Academic Publishers, 270 Eighth Ave., New York, NY 10011. TEL 212-206-8900. FAX 212-645-2459. TELEX 236735 GOPUB UR. (Subscr. to: Box 786, Cooper Sta., New York, NY 10276. TEL 800-545-8398; UK subscr. to: P.O. Box 90, Reading, Berkshire RG1 8JL, England. TEL 0734-560-080) Ed. Dr. Roland Scollay. (also avail. in microform)
—BLDSC shelfmark: 3579.054700.
Refereed Serial

MEDICAL SCIENCES — ALLERGOLOGY AND IMMUNOLOGY

616.97   IT   ISSN 0392-6699
CODEN: EOSSDJ
EOS; rivista di immunologia ed immunofarmacologia. (Text and summaries in English and Italian) 1981. q. L.90000($90) Sigma-Tau SpA, Via Pontina, Rm. 30,400, 00040 Pomezia, Rome, Italy. FAX 6-9108260. Ed. Claudio De Simone. bk.rev.; index; circ. 4,100. (back issues avail.) **Indexed:** Chem.Abstr., Curr.Cont., Excerp.Med., Sci.Cit.Ind.
—BLDSC shelfmark: 3793.030000.

615.37   GW   ISSN 0014-2980
QR180   CODEN: EJIMAF
EUROPEAN JOURNAL OF IMMUNOLOGY. (Text in English) 1970. m. DM.945. V C H Verlagsgesellschaft mbH, Postfach 101161, 6940 Weinheim, Germany. TEL 06201-602-0. FAX 06201-602328. TELEX 465516-VCHWH-D. (U.S. addr.: V C H Publishers Inc., 220 E. 23rd St., New York, NY 10010-4606) Ed. B. Kickhoefen. circ. 1,850. (also avail. in microfilm from VCI; reprint service avail. from ISI) **Indexed:** Abstr.Hyg., Anim.Breed.Abstr., Biol.Abstr., Biotech.Abstr., Chem.Abstr., Curr.Adv.Cell & Devel.Biol., Curr.Adv.Ecol.Sci., Curr.Adv.Genetics & Molec.Biol., Curr.Cont., Dairy Sci.Abstr., Excerp.Med., Helminthol.Abstr., Ind.Med., Ind.Sci.Rev., Ind.Vet., Pig News & Info., Poult.Abstr., Protozool.Abstr., Telegen, Trop.Dis.Bull., Vet.Bull.
—BLDSC shelfmark: 3829.730100.

EXCHANGE. see *MEDICAL SCIENCES — Dermatology And Venereology*

F E M S. MICROBIOLOGY IMMUNOLOGY. (Federation of European Microbiological Societies) see *BIOLOGY — Microbiology*

G AND B. see *MEDICAL SCIENCES — Cardiovascular Diseases*

615.37   GW   ISSN 0016-6006
DIE GELBEN HEFTE. 1961. q. DM.16. (Immunbiologische Informationen e.V.) Medizinische Verlagsgesellschaft mbH, Reitgasse, Postfach 1732, 3550 Marburg, Germany. Ed. Dr. Dietmar Nedde. illus.; cum.index; circ. 99,000.

616.97   IT   ISSN 1120-6373
▼**GIORNALE ITALIANO DI ALLERGOLOGIA E IMMUNOLOGIA CLINICA**. (Text in Italian; summaries in English, Italian) 1991. bi-m. L.100000($100) Editrice Kurtis s.r.l., Via L. Zoja, 30, 20153 Milan, Italy. TEL 02-48201219. FAX 02-48201219. Ed. G. Velsini.
Description: Publishes original studies on allergological and immunological subjects.

616   UK   ISSN 0964-7554
GROWTH FACTORS & CYTOKINES. 1985. s-m. £105. Sheffield University Biomedical Information Service (SUBIS), The University, Sheffield S10 2TN, England. TEL 0742-768555. FAX 0742-739826. TELEX 547216-UGSHEF-G.
Supersedes: Growth Factors (ISSN 0268-1595) & Cytokines (ISSN 0960-3212); Which was formerly (until 1990): Lymphokines (ISSN 0264-9586)
Description: Current awareness service for researchers in clinical and life sciences.

H I V PREVENTION NEWS. (Human Immunodeficiency Virus) see *MEDICAL SCIENCES — Communicable Diseases*

HOKKAIDO UNIVERSITY. INSTITUTE OF IMMUNOLOGICAL SCIENCE. BULLETIN. see *MEDICAL SCIENCES — Respiratory Diseases*

616.9   US   ISSN 0956-960X
QR185.8.H93   CODEN: HANHEX
▼**HUMAN ANTIBODIES AND HYBRIDOMAS**. 1990. q. $195 (foreign $225). Butterworth - Heinemann Ltd. (Subsidiary of: Reed International PLC), 80 Montvale Ave., Stoneham, MA 02180. TEL 617-438-8464. FAX 617-438-1479. TELEX 880052. Ed. Dr. Mark Glassy. (back issues avail.)
—BLDSC shelfmark: 4335.975000.
Description: Covers all aspects of human hybridomas and antibody technology, including fundamental research, applied science and clinical applications.
Refereed Serial

616.97   US   ISSN 0198-8859
QR180   CODEN: HUIMDQ
HUMAN IMMUNOLOGY. 1980. 12/yr.(in 3 vols.; 4 nos./vol.). $510 to institutions (foreign $555)(effective 1992). (American Society for Histocompatibility and Immunogenetics) Elsevier Science Publishing Co., Inc. (New York), 655 Ave. of the Americas, New York, NY 10010. TEL 212-989-5800. FAX 212-633-3965. TELEX 420643 AEP UI. Ed.Bd. (also avail. in microform from RPI) **Indexed:** Biol.Abstr., Chem.Abstr., Curr.Adv.Cancer Res., Curr.Adv.Genetics & Molec.Biol., Curr.Cont., Excerp.Med., Helminthol.Abstr., Ind.Med., Ind.Sci.Rev., Sci.Cit.Ind.
—BLDSC shelfmark: 4336.160000.
Description: Provides information on the immune system of man and the analogous systems of other vertebrates, emphasizing topics in histocompatibility and immunogenetics.
Refereed Serial

616.97 610   US   ISSN 0272-457X
QR185.8.H93   CODEN: HYBRDY
HYBRIDOMA; a journal of molecular immunology and experimental and clinical immunotherapy. 1981. bi-m. $210 (foreign $262). Mary Ann Liebert, Inc., 1651 Third Ave., New York, NY 10128. TEL 212-289-2300. FAX 212-289-4697. Ed. Dr. Zenon Steplewski. adv.; circ. 800. **Indexed:** Biol.Abstr., Biotech.Abstr., Chem.Abstr., Curr.Adv.Cancer Res., Curr.Adv.Ecol.Sci., Curr.Biotech.Abstr., Dairy Sci.Abstr., Excerp.Med., Ind.Med., Ind.Sci.Rev., Ind.Vet., Poult.Abstr., Sci.Cit.Ind., Telegen, Vet.Bull.
—BLDSC shelfmark: 4340.385000.
Description: Publishes research in molecular immunology and experimental and clinical immunotherapy. Includes papers on the application of monoclonal antibodies for diagnostics and therapy, and original articles on various aspects of hybridoma research.
Refereed Serial

615.37   GW   ISSN 0340-1162
CODEN: IMINDI
IMMUNITAET UND INFEKTION; Zeitschrift fuer Klinische Immunologie, Klinische Mikrobiologie. 1973. bi-m. DM.91.20 (foreign DM.95.70). (Deutsche Gesellschaft fuer Hygiene und Mikrobiologie) Richard Pflaum Verlag GmbH und Co. KG, Lazarettstr. 4, Postfach 190737, 8000 Munich 19, Germany. TEL 089-12607-0. FAX 089-12607-281. Eds. K. Federlin, H. Finger. adv.; bk.rev.; circ. 8,000. (also avail. in microform from UMI; back issues avail.; reprint service avail. from UMI) **Indexed:** Abstr.Hyg., Biol.Abstr., Chem.Abstr., Curr.Adv.Ecol.Sci., Curr.Adv.Genetics & Molec.Biol., Curr.Cont., Excerp.Med., Helminthol.Abstr., Ind.Med., INIS Atomind., Trop.Dis.Bull.
—BLDSC shelfmark: 4369.646000.

615.37   GW   ISSN 0171-2985
QR180   CODEN: IMMND4
IMMUNOBIOLOGY. (Text and summaries in English) 1909. irreg. (5 nos./vol.). DM.385 (foreign DM.387). Gustav Fischer Verlag, Wollgrasweg 49, Postfach 720143, 7000 Stuttgart 70, Germany. TEL 0711-458030. FAX 0711-4580334. TELEX 7111488-FIBUCH. (U.S. address: Gustav Fischer New York Inc., 220 E. 23rd St., Ste. 909, New York, NY 10010) Ed. D. Gemsa. circ. 900. **Indexed:** Anim.Breed.Abstr., Biol.Abstr., Chem.Abstr., Curr.Adv.Genetics & Molec.Biol., Excerp.Med., Ind.Med., Ind.Vet., Poult.Abstr., Vet.Bull.
—BLDSC shelfmark: 4369.656000.
Former titles: Zeitschrift fuer Immunitaetsforschung - Immunologie; Zeitschrift fuer Immunitaetsforschung, Experimentelle und Klinische Immunologie (ISSN 0300-872X)

616.97   US   ISSN 0893-5300
QR188.35   CODEN: IMMREH
IMMUNODEFICIENCY REVIEWS. 1988. 4/yr. (in 1 vol., 4 nos./vol.). $98. Harwood Academic Publishers, 270 Eighth Ave., New York, NY 10011. TEL 212-206-8900. FAX 212-645-2459. TELEX 236735 GOPUB UR. (Subscr. to: Box 786, Cooper Sta., New York, NY 10276. TEL 800-545-8398; UK subscr. addr.: P.O. Box 90, Reading, Berkshire RG1 8JL, England. TEL 0734-560-080) Eds. Fred Rosen, Maxime Seligmann. (also avail. in microform)
—BLDSC shelfmark: 4369.663800.
Refereed Serial

616.97 615.37   GW   ISSN 0093-7711
QR184   CODEN: IMNGBK
IMMUNOGENETICS. 1974. 12/yr. (in 2 vols., 6 nos./vol.). DM.956($537) Springer-Verlag, Heidelberger Platz 3, D-1000 Berlin 33, Germany. TEL 030-8207-1. Eds. J. Klein, J. Dausset. (also avail. in microform from UMI; reprint service avail. from ISI) **Indexed:** Anim.Breed.Abstr., Biol.Abstr., Biotech.Abstr., Chem.Abstr., Curr.Adv.Ecol.Sci., Curr.Adv.Genetics & Molec.Biol., Curr.Cont., Dent.Ind., Excerp.Med., Helminthol.Abstr., Ind.Med., Ind.Sci.Rev., Ind.Vet., Pig News & Info., Poult.Abstr., Sci.Cit.Ind., Small Anim.Abstr., Vet.Bull.
—BLDSC shelfmark: 4369.665000.

616.97   IT
IMMUNOLOGIA CLINICA; AIDS allergy and clinical immunology. (Text in Italian, English) 1982. q. L.78500($107) (Societa Italiana di Immunologia ed Immunoterapia) Masson Italia Periodici, Via Statuto 2-4, 20121 Milan, Italy. TEL 02-6367-1. FAX 02-6367211. Ed. Fernando Aiuti. circ. 1,500. **Indexed:** Excerp.Med.
Formerly: Immunologia Clinica e Sperimentale (ISSN 0392-6702)

615.37   PL   ISSN 0324-8534
QR180   CODEN: IMPODM
IMMUNOLOGIA POLSKA. (Text mainly in Polish; occasionally in English; summaries in English) 1969. q. $20. (Polskie Towarzystwo Immunologiczne) Panstwowe Wydawnictwo Naukowe, Miodowa 10, 00-251 Warsaw, Poland. (Dist. by: Ars Polona, Krakowskie Przedmiescie 7, 00-068 Warsaw, Poland) Ed. Irena Zimmermann-Gorska. bk.rev.; illus.; circ. 1,170. **Indexed:** Biol.Abstr., Biotech.Abstr., Chem.Abstr., Excerp.Med., INIS Atomind.
Formerly: Annals of Immunology (ISSN 0044-8338)

616.97   SZ   ISSN 0257-277X
CODEN: IMRSEB
IMMUNOLOGIC RESEARCH; a selective reference to current research and practice. (Text in English) 1982. q. 360 SFr.($240) S. Karger AG, Allschwilerstr. 10, P.O. Box, CH-4009 Basel, Switzerland. TEL 061-3061111. FAX 061-3061234. TELEX CH 962652. Ed. J.M. Cruse. circ. 800. (also avail. in microform from RPI; back issues avail.) **Indexed:** Anim.Breed.Abstr., ASCA, Chem.Abstr., Curr.Adv.Ecol.Sci., Dent.Ind., Excerp.Med., Ind.Med., Ind.Vet., Pig News & Info., Telegen.
—BLDSC shelfmark: 4369.677800.
Formerly: Survey of Immunologic Research (ISSN 0252-9564)

576   US   ISSN 0882-0139
QR180   CODEN: IMINEJ
IMMUNOLOGICAL INVESTIGATIONS; a journal of molecular and cellular immunology. 1972. 7/yr. $249.50 to individuals; institutions $499. Marcel Dekker Journals, 270 Madison Ave., New York, NY 10016. TEL 212-696-9000. FAX 212-685-4540. TELEX 421419. (Subscr. to: Box 10018, Church St. Sta., New York, NY 10249) Ed. Carel J. Van Oss. adv.; bk.; rev.; charts; illus.; index. (also avail. in microform from RPI) **Indexed:** Anim.Breed.Abstr., Biol.Abstr., Chem.Abstr., Curr.Adv.Cell & Devel.Biol., Curr.Adv.Ecol.Sci., Curr.Cont., Dairy Sci.Abstr., Excerp.Med., Helminthol.Abstr., Ind.Med., Ind.Sci.Rev., Ind.Vet., Sci.Cit.Ind., Telegen.
—BLDSC shelfmark: 4369.682500.
Formerly: Immunological Communications (ISSN 0090-0877); Incorporates (1982-1985): Clinical Immunology Reviews (ISSN 0277-9366)
Refereed Serial

617 612   DK   ISSN 0105-2896
CODEN: IMRED2
IMMUNOLOGICAL REVIEWS. (Text in English) 1969. bi-m. DKK 1800. Munksgaard International Publishers Ltd., 35 Noerre Soegade, P.O. Box 2148, DK-1016 Copenhagen K, Denmark. TEL 33-127030. FAX 33-129387. TELEX 19431-MUNKS-DK. Ed. Goeran Moeller. adv.; bk.rev.; circ. 2,300. (reprint service avail. from ISI) **Indexed:** Anim.Breed.Abstr., Biol.Abstr., Chem.Abstr., Curr.Adv.Ecol.Sci., Curr.Adv.Genetics & Molec.Biol., Curr.Biotech.Abstr., Curr.Cont., Excerp.Med., Helminthol.Abstr., Ind.Med., Ind.Sci.Rev., Sci.Cit.Ind., Telegen.
—BLDSC shelfmark: 4369.687000.
Formerly: Transplantation Reviews (ISSN 0082-5948)

MEDICAL SCIENCES — ALLERGOLOGY AND IMMUNOLOGY

616.97   RU   ISSN 0206-4952
CODEN: IMUNDA
IMMUNOLOGIYA/IMMUNOLOGY. English translation: Soviet Immunology (US ISSN 0739-8433) 1980. bi-m. 35.40 Rub. (Akademiya Meditsinskikh Nauk S.S.S.R.) Izdatel'stvo Meditsina, Petroverigskii pereulok 6-8, 101838 Moscow, Russia. Ed. N.V. Medunitsyn. **Indexed:** Biol.Abstr., Chem.Abstr, Excerp.Med., INIS Atomind.
—BLDSC shelfmark: 0086.168250.
Description: Publishes data on original investigations in immunogenetics, molecular and cellular immunology, immunochemistry, biochemistry of immunogenesis, immunomorphology, functional bases of immunity, immunology of allergic reaction, clinical immunology and immunopathology.

576   UK   ISSN 0019-2805
QR180   CODEN: IMMUAM
IMMUNOLOGY. 1958. m. £215 (foreign £245). (British Society for Immunology) Blackwell Scientific Publications Ltd., Osney Mead, Oxford OX2 OEL, England. TEL 0865-240201. FAX 0865-721205. TELEX 83355-MEDBOK-G. Ed. M.W. Steward. adv.; bk.rev.; bibl.; charts; illus.; index; circ. 2,400. (also avail. in microform from MIM; back issues avail.; reprint service avail. from ISI) **Indexed:** Abstr.Hyg., Anim.Breed.Abstr., Biol.Abstr., Biotech.Abstr., Chem.Abstr., Curr.Adv.Biochem., Curr.Adv.Ecol.Sci., Curr.Cont., Dairy Sci.Abstr., Dent.Ind., Excerp.Med., Helminthol.Abstr., Ind.Med., Ind.Sci.Rev., Ind.Vet., INIS Atomind., NRN, Nutr.Abstr., Pig News & Info., Sci.Cit.Ind., Telegen, Trop.Dis.Bull., Vet.Bull.
—BLDSC shelfmark: 4369.700000.

616.97   US   ISSN 0889-8561
IMMUNOLOGY AND ALLERGY CLINICS OF NORTH AMERICA. 1981. 3/yr. $74. W.B. Saunders Co., Curtis Center, Independence Square W., Philadelphia, PA 19106. TEL 215-238-7800. Ed. June Eberharter. **Indexed:** Chem.Abstr, Curr.Adv.Ecol.Sci., Excerp.Med., Helminthol.Abstr., Ind.Sci.Rev., Sci.Cit.Ind.
—BLDSC shelfmark: 4369.701500.
Formerly: Clinics in Immunology and Allergy (ISSN 0260-4639)

616.97   US   ISSN 0194-7508
RC581
IMMUNOLOGY AND ALLERGY PRACTICE. 1978. m. $55. (American Association for Clinical Immunology and Allergy) Macor Publishing Co., 116 W. 32nd St., New York, NY 10001. TEL 212-736-6688. FAX 212-564-1763. Ed. Dr. Sidney Frielander. adv. **Indexed:** Excerp.Med.
—BLDSC shelfmark: 4369.702000.
Description: Contains clinical, research, and review articles of interest to allergists and other related specialists.

616.97 574   AT   ISSN 0818-9641
QH301   CODEN: ICBIEZ
IMMUNOLOGY AND CELL BIOLOGY. 1924. bi-m. Aus.$199($180) Blackwell Scientific Publications (Australia) Pty. Ltd., P.O. Box 378, Carlton, Vic. 3053, Australia. TEL 03-347-0300. FAX 03-347-5001. TELEX 10716421. Ed. Chris Parish. charts; illus.; index; circ. 1,600. (also avail. in microfiche from JAI; microfilm from UMI,PMC) **Indexed:** Abstr.Hyg., Anim.Breed.Abstr., Biol.Abstr., Chem.Abstr., Curr.Adv.Cancer Res., Curr.Adv.Ecol.Sci., Curr.Biotech.Abstr., Curr.Cont., Dairy Sci.Abstr., Dent.Ind., Excerp.Med., Field Crop Abstr., Helminthol.Abstr., Herb.Abstr., Ind.Med., Ind.Sci.Rev., Ind.Vet., NRN, Nutr.Abstr., Protozool.Abstr., Sci.Cit.Ind., Trop.Dis.Bull., Vet.Bull.
—BLDSC shelfmark: 4369.702400.
Formerly: Australian Journal of Experimental Biology and Medical Science (ISSN 0004-945X)
Description: Covers original research, methods or concepts in the broad fields of immunology and cell biology.

IMMUNOLOGY AND INFECTIOUS DISEASES. see
MEDICAL SCIENCES — Communicable Diseases

616.97   NE   ISSN 0165-2478
CODEN: IMLED6
IMMUNOLOGY LETTERS; for the rapid publication of short reports in immunology. (Text in English) 1979. 15/yr.(in 5 vols.; 3 nos./vol.). fl.2055 (effective 1992). (European Federation of Immunological Societies (E.F.I.S.)) Elsevier Science Publishers B.V., P.O. Box 211, 1000 AE Amsterdam, Netherlands. TEL 020-5803911. FAX 020-5803598. TELEX 18582 ESPA NL. (Subscr. in U.S. and Canada to: Elsevier Science Publishing Co., Inc., Box 882, Madison Sq. Sta., New York, NY 10159. TEL 212-989-5800) Ed.Bd. adv.; bk.rev.; circ. 500. (also avail. in microform from RPI; back issues avail.) **Indexed:** Anim.Breed.Abstr., Biol.Abstr., Chem.Abstr., Curr.Adv.Cancer Res., Curr.Adv.Cell & Devel.Biol., Curr.Adv.Ecol.Sci., Curr.Adv.Genetics & Molec.Biol., Curr.Cont., Excerp.Med., Helminthol.Abstr., Ind.Med., Ind.Sci.Rev., Ind.Vet., Sci.Cit.Ind., Telegen, Vet.Bull.
—BLDSC shelfmark: 4369.705000.
Description: Publishes research articles and minireviews on all aspects of immunology.
Refereed Serial

616.97   US
IMMUNOLOGY SERIES. 1982. irreg., vol.56, 1991. price varies. Marcel Dekker, Inc., 270 Madison Ave., New York, NY 10016. TEL 212-696-9000. FAX 212-685-4540. TELEX 421419.
Refereed Serial

616.97   UK   ISSN 0167-4919
CODEN: IMTOD8
IMMUNOLOGY TODAY. (Text in English) 1980. m. £239. Elsevier Science Publishers Ltd., Crown House, Linton Rd., Barking, Essex IG11 8JU, England. TEL 081-594-7272. FAX 081-594-5942. TELEX 896950 APPSCI G. (Subscr. in U.S. and Canada to Elsevier Science Publishing Co., Inc., Box 882, Madison Sq. Sta., New York, NY 10159. TEL 212-989-5800) Ed. Richard Gallagher. adv.; bk.rev.; charts; illus.; index; circ. 4,000. (back issues avail.; reprint service avail. from SWZ) **Indexed:** Abstr.Hyg., Anim.Breed.Abstr., Biol.Abstr., Chem.Abstr., Curr.Cont., Dairy Sci.Abstr., Excerp.Med., Food Sci.& Tech.Abstr., Helminthol.Abstr., Ind.Sci.Rev., Ind.Vet., Protozool.Abstr., Sci.Cit.Ind., Telegen, Vet.Bull.
—BLDSC shelfmark: 4369.745000.
Description: For immunologists and transplantation researchers, and all other scientists with an interest in the theory, practice, applications and techniques of modern immunology.

616.97   US   ISSN 1058-6687
▼**IMMUNOMETHODS.** 1992. 3/yr. $66 (foreign $85). Academic Press, Inc., Journal Division, 1250 Sixth Ave., San Diego, CA 92101. TEL 619-230-1840. FAX 619-699-6800. TELEX 181726. Ed. John Langone.
Description: Provides focused, detailed, and authoritative reports on immunological techniques and procedures.
Refereed Serial

616.97   NE   ISSN 0162-3109
CODEN: IMMUDP
IMMUNOPHARMACOLOGY. 1979. 6/yr.(in 2 vols.; 3 nos./vol.). fl.788 (effective 1992). Elsevier Science Publishers B.V., P.O. Box 211, 1000 AE Amsterdam, Netherlands. TEL 020-5803911. FAX 020-5803598. TELEX 18582 ESPA NL. (Subscr. in U.S. and Canada to: Elsevier Science Publishing Co., Inc., Box 882, Madison Sq. Sta., New York, NY 10159. TEL 212-989-5800) Ed. Dr. J.R. Battisto. **Indexed:** Biol.Abstr., Biotech.Abstr., Chem.Abstr., Curr.Adv.Cancer Res., Curr.Adv.Ecol.Sci., Curr.Cont., Excerp.Med., Helminthol.Abstr., Ind.Med., Ind.Sci.Rev., Int.Abstr.Biol.Sci., Sci.Cit.Ind.
—BLDSC shelfmark: 4369.760000.
Description: Covers immunology, pharmacology and toxicology.
Refereed Serial

616.97   SZ   ISSN 1016-4901
CODEN: IENVEC
▼**INDOOR ENVIRONMENT.** (Text in English) 1992. 6/yr. $146.50 to individuals; institutions $293. (Indoor Air International) S. Karger AG, Allschwilerstr. 10, P.O. Box, CH-4009 Basel, Switzerland. TEL 061-3061111. FAX 061-3061234. Ed. D. Weetman.
—BLDSC shelfmark: 4438.047100.
Description: Publishes original reports on topics pertaining to the quality of indoor air and environment, and how these might affect the health, performance, efficiency and comfort of persons so exposed.

616.97   US   ISSN 0019-9567
QR1.A47   CODEN: INFIBR
INFECTION AND IMMUNITY. 1970. m. $350. American Society for Microbiology, 1325 Massachusetts Ave., N.W., Washington, DC 20005. TEL 202-737-3600. Ed. Vincent A. Fischetti. adv.; charts; stat.; index; circ. 6,577. (also avail. in microform from UMI,PMC; back issues avail.; reprint service avail. from UMI) **Indexed:** Abstr.Hyg., Anim.Breed.Abstr., Biol.Abstr., Biotech.Abstr., Chem.Abstr., Curr.Adv.Genetics & Molec.Biol., Curr.Cont., Curr.Tit.Dent., Dairy Sci.Abstr., Dent.Ind., Dok.Arbeitsmed., Excerp.Med., Food Sci.& Tech.Abstr., Helminthol.Abstr., Ind.Med., Ind.Sci.Rev., Ind.Vet., INIS Atomind., Nutr.Abstr., Pig News & Info., Poult.Abstr., Protozool.Abstr., Rev.Plant Path., Sci.Cit.Ind., Small Anim.Abstr., Soils & Fert., Telegen, Trop.Dis.Bull., Vet.Bull.
●Also available on CD-ROM.
—BLDSC shelfmark: 4478.720000.
Description: Directed toward immunologists, epidemiologists, pathologists, and clinicians.
Refereed Serial

616.97   SP   ISSN 0213-9626
INMUNOLOGIA. (Text in English, Spanish; summaries in English) 1982. q. 3500 ptas.($35) to non-members. (Sociedad Espanola de Inmunologia) Ediciones Doyma, S.A., Travesera de Gracia, 17-21, 08021 Barcelona, Spain. TEL 200 07 11. FAX 209-11-36. TELEX 51964 INK-E. Dir. F. Leyba Covian. adv.: page 125000 ptas.; trim 210 x 280; adv. contact: Jose L. Campos. circ. 2,000. (reprint service avail. from UMI) **Indexed:** Curr.Adv.Ecol.Sci., Curr.Adv.Genetics & Molec.Biol., Curr.Cont., Ind.Med.Esp., Ind.Sci.Rev., Sci.Cit.Ind
—BLDSC shelfmark: 4515.276000.
Former titles (until 1986): Revista Doyma de Inmunologia (ISSN 0213-540X); (until 1985): Inmunologia (ISSN 0212-5765)
Description: Covers the basic aspects and clinical application in immunology.

615.37 616.97   SZ   ISSN 1018-2438
RC583   CODEN: IAAAAM
INTERNATIONAL ARCHIVES OF ALLERGY AND IMMUNOLOGY. (Text in English) 1950. m. (3 vols./yr.). 623 Fr.($416) per vol. S. Karger AG, Allschwilerstr. 10, P.O. Box, CH-4009 Basel, Switzerland. TEL 061-3061111. FAX 061-3061234. TELEX CH 962652. Ed. G. Wick. adv.; bk.rev.; abstr.; bibl.; illus.; circ. 1,400. (also avail. in microform from RPI) **Indexed:** Anim.Breed.Abstr., Biol.Abstr., Biotech.Abstr., C.I.S. Abstr., Chem.Abstr., Curr.Adv.Ecol.Sci., Curr.Cont., Dairy Sci.Abstr., Dent.Ind., Dok.Arbeitsmed., Excerp.Med., Forest Prod.Abstr., Helminthol.Abstr., Ind.Med., Ind.Sci.Rev., Ind.Vet., NRN, Nutr.Abstr., Pig News & Info., Rev.Plant Path., Sci.Cit.Ind., Vet.Bull.
Formerly: International Archives of Allergy and Applied Immunology (ISSN 0020-5915)

616.97   UK   ISSN 0953-8178
CODEN: INIMEN
INTERNATIONAL IMMUNOLOGY. 1989. 6/yr. £170($295) Oxford University Press, Oxford Journals, Pinkhill House, Southfield Road, Eynsham, Oxford OX8 1JJ, England. TEL 0865-882283. FAX 0865-882890. TELEX 837330 OXPRES G. Ed. Tomio Tada. adv.; circ. 5,000.
—BLDSC shelfmark: 4541.038930.
Description: Publishes a broad range of experimental and theoretical studies in molecular and cellular immunology conducted in laboratories throughout the world.

616.97 615.19   IT
INTERNATIONAL JOURNAL OF IMMUNOPATHOLOGY AND PHARMACOLOGY. 3/yr. L.49000($49) to indiviudals; institutions L.190000 ($190). Biomedical Research Press, s.a.s., c/o Universita di Chieti, Depto. di Immunologia, Via dei Vestini, Italy. Ed. Dr. Pio Conti. **Indexed:** Excerp.Med.

MEDICAL SCIENCES — ALLERGOLOGY AND IMMUNOLOGY 3187

INTERNATIONAL JOURNAL OF IMMUNOPHARMACOLOGY. see *PHARMACY AND PHARMACOLOGY*

616.97   SZ   ISSN 0255-9625
CODEN: IJIMET
INTERNATIONAL JOURNAL OF IMMUNOTHERAPY. Short title: Immunotherapy. 1985. q. 250 SFr. Bioscience Ediprint Inc., Rue Alexandre-Gavard 16, CH-1227 Carouge-Geneva, Switzerland. TEL 022-3003383. FAX 022-3002489. TELEX 423355-BIOS-CH. Ed. Prof. A. Bertelli. (reprint service avail. from UMI) **Indexed:** Excerp.Med., Telegen.
—BLDSC shelfmark: 4542.302000.

616.97   US   ISSN 0883-0185
CODEN: IRIMEH
INTERNATIONAL REVIEWS IN IMMUNOLOGY. 1986. 8/yr. (in 2 vol., 4 nos./vol.). $118. Harwood Academic Publishers, 270 Eighth Ave., New York, NY 10011. TEL 212-206-8900. FAX 212-645-2459. TELEX 236735 GOPUB UR. (Subscr. to: Box 786, Cooper Sta., New York, NY 10276. TEL 800-545-8398; UK subscr. to: P.O. Box 90, Reading, Berkshire RG1 8JL, England. TEL 0734-560-080) Ed. Dr. Constantin Bona.
—BLDSC shelfmark: 4547.310000.
Refereed Serial

615.37 576   IT   ISSN 0021-2547
CODEN: BISMAP
ISTITUTO SIEROTERAPICO MILANESE. BOLLETTINO; archivio di microbiologia ed immunologia. (Text and summaries in English and Italian) vol.49, 1970. bi-m. L.20000. Istituto Sieroterapico Milanese, Via Darwin 20, 20143 Milan, Italy. Ed. Prof. Augusto De Barbieri. adv.; bk.rev.; charts; illus.; stat.; circ. 2,000. **Indexed:** Biol.Abstr., Curr.Adv.Ecol.Sci., Curr.Cont., Dairy Sci.Abstr., Excerp.Med., Helminthol.Abstr., Ind.Med., Ind.Vet., Nutr.Abstr., Protozool.Abstr., Sci.Cit.Ind, Trop.Dis.Bull., Vet.Bull.
—BLDSC shelfmark: 2226.000000.

616.97   US   ISSN 0724-6803
QR180   CODEN: JMCIDI
J M C I: JOURNAL OF MOLECULAR AND CELLULAR IMMUNOLOGY. 1983. bi-m. $110. Springer-Verlag, Journals, 175 Fifth Ave., New York, NY 10010. TEL 212-460-1500. Ed. C. Janeway. (also avail. in microfiche from UMI; reprint service avail. from ISI) **Indexed:** Anim.Breed.Abstr., Poult.Abstr.

616.97   JA   ISSN 0021-4884
CODEN: ARERAM
JAPANESE JOURNAL OF ALLERGOLOGY/ARERUGI. (Text in Japanese; captions, summaries in English) 1952. m. 15500 Yen. Japanese Society of Allergology - Nihon Arerugi Gakkai, Ishimizu Bldg., 7th Fl., 35-26 Hongo 1-chome, Bunkyo-ku, Tokyo, Japan. TEL 03-3816-0280. FAX 03-3816-0219. Ed. Minoru Okuda. adv.; bk.rev.; circ. 4,000. **Indexed:** Chem.Abstr., Dent.Ind., Excerp.Med., Ind.Med., INIS Atomind.

JAPANESE JOURNAL OF MEDICAL MYCOLOGY. see *BIOLOGY — Microbiology*

616.97 615.37   US   ISSN 0091-6749
CODEN: JACIBY
JOURNAL OF ALLERGY AND CLINICAL IMMUNOLOGY. (Supplement avail.: American Academy of Allergy and Immunology. Abstract Book) 1929. m. $80 to individuals (foreign $111); institutions $156 (foreign $187); students $38 (foreign $69). (American Academy of Allergy and Immunology) Mosby - Year Book, Inc. (Subsidiary of Times Mirror Company), 11830 Westline Industrial Dr., St. Louis, MO 63146. TEL 800-325-4117. FAX 314-432-1380. TELEX 44-2402. Ed. Dr. Burton Zweiman. adv.; abstr.; charts; illus.; index; circ. 8,501. (also avail. in microfilm from UMI; reprint service avail. from UMI) **Indexed:** ASCA, Biol.Abstr., Biol.Dig., Biotech.Abstr., Chem.Abstr., Curr.Cont., Dairy Sci.Abstr., Dok.Arbeitsmed., Excerp.Med., Fababean Abstr., Helminthol.Abstr., I.P.A., Ind.Med., Ind.Sci.Rev., Ind.Vet., INIS Atomind., NRN, Nutr.Abstr., Rev.Appl.Entomol., Rev.Plant Path., Sci.Cit.Ind., Seed Abstr., Small Anim.Abstr., Soyabean Abstr., Triticale Abstr., Weed Abstr.
●Also available online. Vendor(s): BRS.
—BLDSC shelfmark: 4927.100000.
Formerly: Journal of Allergy (ISSN 0021-8707); Incorporates: Allergy Abstracts.
Description: Articles on the clinical manifestations of allergies for the clinical allergist and immunologist, dermatologist, general practitioner, pediatrician and otolaryngologist.
Refereed Serial

616.97   UK   ISSN 0896-8411
QR188.3   CODEN: JOAUEP
JOURNAL OF AUTOIMMUNITY. 6/yr. $242. Academic Press Ltd., 24-28 Oval Rd., London NW1 7DX, England. TEL 071-267-4466. FAX 071-482-2293. TELEX 25775-ACPRES-G. Ed. J.F. Bach. index.
—BLDSC shelfmark: 4949.555000.
Description: Publishes papers on all aspects of autoimmunity and its diverse aspects.

616.97   UK   ISSN 0141-2760
CODEN: JLIMDJ
JOURNAL OF CLINICAL & LABORATORY IMMUNOLOGY. 1978. m. $180($465) Teviot Kimpton Publications, 2-3 Teviot Pl., Edinburgh EH1 2QZ, Scotland. Ed. Dr. W. James Irvine. adv.; bk.rev. **Indexed:** Chem.Abstr., Curr.Cont., Dairy Sci.Abstr., Excerp.Med., Helminthol.Abstr., Ind.Med., Ind.Sci.Rev., Ind.Vet., Sci.Cit.Ind., Vet.Bull.
—BLDSC shelfmark: 4958.380700.

616.97   US   ISSN 0736-4393
CODEN: JCLIES
JOURNAL OF CLINICAL IMMUNOASSAY. 1978. q. $60. (Clinical Ligand Assay Society) Kellner-McCaffery Associates, Inc., 150 Fifth Ave., Ste. 322, New York, NY 10011. TEL 212-741-0280. Ed. Gerald Nordblom. adv.; bk.rev.; circ. 1,600. (also avail. in microfilm; microfiche; microform from UMI) **Indexed:** Chem.Abstr.
—BLDSC shelfmark: 4958.489000.
Formerly: Ligand Quarterly.
Refereed Serial

616.97   US   ISSN 0271-9142
RC581   CODEN: JCIMDO
JOURNAL OF CLINICAL IMMUNOLOGY. 1981. bi-m. $260 (foreign $305)(effective 1992). Plenum Publishing Corp., 233 Spring St., New York, NY 10013-1578. TEL 212-620-8000. FAX 212-463-0742. TELEX 23-421139. Ed. Sudhir Gupta. adv.; bk.rev.; illus. (also avail. in microfilm from JSC; back issues avail.) **Indexed:** Biol.Abstr., Chem.Abstr., Curr.Adv.Cancer Res., Curr.Cont., Dent.Ind., Excerp.Med., Ind.Med., Ind.Sci.Rev., INIS Atomind., Sci.Cit.Ind.
—BLDSC shelfmark: 4958.490000.
Refereed Serial

JOURNAL OF HYGIENE, EPIDEMIOLOGY, MICROBIOLOGY AND IMMUNOLOGY. see *MEDICAL SCIENCES*

616 576.2   NE   ISSN 0022-1759
QR183   CODEN: JIMMBG
JOURNAL OF IMMUNOLOGICAL METHODS. (Text in English) 1971. 20/yr.(in 10 vols./2 nos./vol.). fl.3410 (effective 1992). Elsevier Science Publishers B.V., P.O. Box 211, 1000 AE Amsterdam, Netherlands. TEL 020-5803911. FAX 020-5803598. TELEX 18582 ESPA NL. (Subscr. in U.S. and Canada to: Elsevier Science Publishing Co., Inc., Box 882, Madison Sq. Sta., New York, NY 10159. TEL 212-989-5800) Eds. M. Turner, V. Nussenzweig. adv.; bk.rev.; illus.; index; circ. 2,500. (also avail. in microfilm from RPI; reprint service avail. from ISI,SWZ) **Indexed:** Abstr.Hyg., Anim.Breed.Abstr., Biol.Abstr., Chem.Abstr., Curr.Adv.Cancer Res., Curr.Adv.Cell & Devel.Biol., Curr.Adv.Ecol.Sci., Curr.Biotech.Abstr., Curr.Cont., Dairy Sci.Abstr., Dent.Ind., Excerp.Med., Helminthol.Abstr., Ind.Med., Ind.Sci.Rev., Ind.Vet., INIS Atomind., Nutr.Abstr., Poult.Abstr., Protozool.Abstr., Rev.Plant Path., Risk Abstr., Sci.Cit.Ind., Telegen, Trop.Dis.Bull., Vet.Bull.
—BLDSC shelfmark: 5004.600000.
Refereed Serial

615.37   US   ISSN 0022-1767
QR180   CODEN: JOIMA3
JOURNAL OF IMMUNOLOGY. 1916. s-m. $170 to individuals (foreign $247); institutions $300 (foreign $377); students $43 (foreign $120). American Association of Immunologists, 428 E. Preston St., Baltimore, MD 21202. TEL 301-530-7178. FAX 301-571-1831. Ed. Dr. Ethan M. Shevach. adv.; bibl.; illus.; circ. 8,600. (also avail. in microform from PMC) **Indexed:** Abstr.Hyg., Anim.Breed.Abstr., Biol.Abstr., Biotech.Abstr., Chem.Abstr., Curr.Adv.Biochem., Curr.Adv.Cancer Res., Curr.Adv.Cell & Devel.Biol., Curr.Adv.Ecol.Sci., Curr.Adv.Genetics & Molec.Biol., Curr.Biotech.Abstr., Dairy Sci.Abstr., Dent.Ind., Excerp.Med., Helminthol.Abstr., Ind.Med., Ind.Sci.Rev., Ind.Vet., INIS Atomind., Int.Aerosp.Abstr., Nutr.Abstr., Pig News & Info., Poult.Abstr., Protozool.Abstr., Rev.Appl.Entomol., Rev.Plant Path., Sci.Cit.Ind., Telegen, Trop.Dis.Bull., Vet.Bull.
—BLDSC shelfmark: 5005.000000.
Refereed Serial

JOURNAL OF NEUROIMMUNOLOGY. see *MEDICAL SCIENCES — Psychiatry And Neurology*

616.97   US   ISSN 1049-5150
QP141.A1   CODEN: JNUIEE
▼**JOURNAL OF NUTRITIONAL IMMUNOLOGY.** 1992. q. $32 to individuals; institutions $48; libraries $75. Haworth Press, Inc., 10 Alice St., Binghamton, NY 13904. TEL 800-342-9678. FAX 607-722-1424. TELEX 4932599. Ed. Jullian E. Spallholz. adv.; bk.rev. (also avail. in microfiche from HAW; reprint service avail. from HAW) **Indexed:** Biostat.
—BLDSC shelfmark: 5024.735000.
Description: Provides a forum for research scientists that bridges the disciplines of nutrition and immunology.
Refereed Serial

616.97 618   IE   ISSN 0165-0378
CODEN: JRIMDR
JOURNAL OF REPRODUCTIVE IMMUNOLOGY. (Text in English) 1979. 6/yr.(in 2 vols./3 nos./vol.). $362 (effective 1992). (International Society for Immunology of Reproduction) Elsevier Scientific Publishers Ireland Ltd., P.O. Box 85, Limerick, Ireland. TEL 061-61944. FAX 061-62144. TELEX 72191 ENH EI. (Subscr. in U.S. and Canada to: Elsevier Science Publishing Co., Inc., Box 882, Madison Sq. Sta., New York, NY 10159. TEL 212-989-5800) Eds. W.D. Billington, A.E. Beer. adv.; bk.rev. (also avail. in microform from RPI; reprint service avail. from SWZ) **Indexed:** Anim.Breed.Abstr., Biol.Abstr., Chem.Abstr., Curr.Adv.Ecol.Sci., Curr.Cont., Dairy Sci.Abstr., Excerp.Med., Ind.Med., Ind.Sci.Rev., Ind.Vet., INIS Atomind., Pig News & Info., Vet.Bull.
—BLDSC shelfmark: 5049.670000.
Refereed Serial

616.97 610   UK   ISSN 0142-8160
LEUCOCYTES. 1976. s-m. £115. Sheffield University Biomedical Information Service (SUBIS), The University, Sheffield S10 2TN, England. TEL 0742-768555. FAX 0742-739826. TELEX 547216-UGSHEF-G. bk.rev.
Description: Current awareness service for researchers. Covers leucocytes: structure, biochemistry, function, granulopoiesis, adherence and migration.

616.97   US   ISSN 0197-4041
CODEN: LRVWD8
LIGAND REVIEW; an international and independent publication. 1979. q. $20. Technical & Professional Services, Inc., Box 160095, San Antonio, TX 78280. Ed. Dr. Dean S. Skelley. adv.; bk.rev.; circ. 3,250. **Indexed:** Chem.Abstr.

616.97 611   UK   ISSN 0142-8179
LYMPHOCYTES. 1976. m. £65. Sheffield University Biomedical Information Service (SUBIS), The University, Sheffield S10 2TN, England. TEL 0742-768555. FAX 0742-739826. TELEX 547216 UGSHEF G.
Description: Current awareness service for researchers in clinical and life sciences. Covers helper and suppressor cells, transformation, T-lymphocytes, B-lymphocytes, T-cell receptors.

MEDICAL SCIENCES — ALLERGOLOGY AND IMMUNOLOGY

616.7   CN   ISSN 0315-1131
M S CANADA. 1974. q. Can.$10 (foreign Can.$12). Multiple Sclerosis Society of Canada, 250 Bloor St. E., Suite 820, Toronto, Ont. M4W 3P9, Canada. TEL 416-922-6065. FAX 416-922-7538. Ed. Deanna Groetzinger. bk.rev.; circ. 26,000.
   Description: Provides information on M S research, how to cope with multiple sclerosis, and activities of the Society.

616.97   UK   ISSN 0142-8195
MACROPHAGES. 1976. s-m. £100. Sheffield University Biomedical Information Service (SUBIS), The University, Sheffield S10 2TN, England. TEL 0742-768555. FAX 0742-739826. TELEX 547216-UGSHEF-G. bk.rev.
   Description: Current awareness service for researchers in clinical and life sciences. Covers the biochemistry, structure and function of monocytopoiesis, macrophages, monocytes.

616 615.37   GW   ISSN 0300-8584
                                            CODEN: MMIYAO
MEDICAL MICROBIOLOGY AND IMMUNOLOGY. (Text in English, French, German; summaries in English) 1886. 6/yr. DM.548($291) Springer-Verlag, Heidelberger Platz 3, D-1000 Berlin 33, Germany. TEL 030-8207-1. (Also Heidelberg, Tokyo, Vienna, and New York) Ed. R. Rott. (also avail. in microform from UMI; reprint service avail. from ISI) **Indexed:** Biol.Abstr., Chem.Abstr., Curr.Adv.Ecol.Sci., Curr.Cont., Excerp.Med., Helminthol.Abstr., Ind.Med., Ind.Sci.Rev., Ind.Vet., INIS Atomind., Rev.Plant Path., Telegen, Trop.Dis.Bull., Vet.Bull.
—BLDSC shelfmark: 5529.990000.
   Formerly: Zeitschrift fuer Medizinische Mikrobiologie und Immunologie (ISSN 0044-3077)
   Description: Covers a broad spectrum of the interrelationships between microorganisms and the human host, with special emphasis on medical virology and immunology, and how they relate to the mechanisms of pathogenesis.

616.97 576   UK   ISSN 0891-060X
QR171.A1   CODEN: MEHDE6
MICROBIAL ECOLOGY IN HEALTH & DISEASE. 1987. 6/yr. $275 (effective 1992). John Wiley & Sons Ltd., Journals, Baffins Ln., Chichester, W. Sussex PO19 1UD, England. TEL 0240-779777. FAX 0243-775878. Ed. S.P. Borriello. adv.; bk.rev. **Indexed:** Curr.Adv.Cancer Res., Ind.Med.
—BLDSC shelfmark: 5756.922000.
   Description: Draws together research on different human microbial ecosystems to increase understanding of their role in health and disease.
   Refereed Serial

MOLECULAR IMMUNOLOGY. see *BIOLOGY — Biological Chemistry*

616.97   UK   ISSN 0261-4960
MONOCLONAL ANTIBODIES. 1981. s-m. £105. Sheffield University Biomedical Information Service (SUBIS), The University, Sheffield S10 2TN, England. TEL 0742-768555. FAX 0742-739826. TELEX 547216-UGSHEF-G. bk.rev.
   Description: Current awareness service for researchers. Covers antibodies, molecules and cell types. Includes information on assays and separation techniques using MAB's.

616.97   SZ   ISSN 0077-0760
                                            CODEN: MOALAR
MONOGRAPHS IN ALLERGY. (Text in English) 1966. irreg. varies. S. Karger AG, Allschwilerstr. 10, P.O. Box, CH-4009 Basel, Switzerland. TEL 061-3061111. FAX 061-3061234. TELEX CH 962652. Eds. L.A. Hanson, F. Shakib. (reprint service avail. from ISI) **Indexed:** Biol.Abstr., Chem.Abstr., Curr.Cont., Dent.Ind., Ind.Med., Ind.Sci.Rev.
—BLDSC shelfmark: 5914.975000.

N O H A NEWS. (Nutrition for Optimal Health Association) see *NUTRITION AND DIETETICS*

NEW TRENDS IN LIPID MEDIATORS RESEARCH. see *PHARMACY AND PHARMACOLOGY*

616.97   US
NEWS & NOTES (MILWAUKEE). 1943. q. membership. American Academy of Allergy and Immunology, 611 E. Wells St., Milwaukee, WI 53202. TEL 414-272-6071. Ed. S.E. Kaluzny. adv.; charts; illus.; stat.; circ. 4,300.
   Description: Covers membership and educational activities.

ORAL MICROBIOLOGY AND IMMUNOLOGY. see *BIOLOGY — Microbiology*

PARASITE IMMUNOLOGY. see *MEDICAL SCIENCES — Communicable Diseases*

PEDIATRIC ASTHMA, ALLERGY & IMMUNOLOGY. see *MEDICAL SCIENCES — Pediatrics*

616.97   IT
PERSPECTIVES IN E.N.T. - IMMUNOLOGY. m. $45. Edizioni Luigi Pozzi s.r.l., Via Panama, 68, 00198 Rome, Italy. TEL 06-8553548. FAX 06-8554105.

615.37   US
PERSPECTIVES IN IMMUNOLOGY; a series of publications based on symposia. 1969. irreg., no.10, 1981. Academic Press, Inc., 1250 Sixth Ave., San Diego, CA 92101. TEL 619-231-0926. FAX 619-699-6715. (reprint service avail. from ISI)
Refereed Serial

616.97   CN   ISSN 0831-0998
PRACTICAL ALLERGY & IMMUNOLOGY; practical journal of allergy for the family practitioner. 1986. q. Can.$40($60) Medicopea International Inc., 8200 Decarie Blvd., Ste. 212, Montreal, Que. H4P 2P5, Canada. TEL 514-340-9157. FAX 514-342-5783. TELEX 055-62171. Ed. I. Gailis. adv.; bk.rev.; illus.; index; circ. 2,400. (back issues avail.)

616.97   US   ISSN 1045-2001
QP356.47
PROGRESS IN NEUROENDOCRIN IMMUNOLOGY. 1988. q. $49 to individuals; institutions $98. Thieme Medical Publishers, Inc., 381 Park Ave. S., New York, NY 10016. TEL 212-683-5088. FAX 212-779-9020. Ed. Robert M. MacLeod.
—BLDSC shelfmark: 6870.320000.
   Description: Highlights advances in interrelated disciplines: neuroscience, endocrinology, and immunology.
   Refereed Serial

615.37   FR   ISSN 0923-2494
                                            CODEN: RIMME5
RESEARCH IN IMMUNOLOGY. (Text in English) 1887. 9/yr. 1425 F.($265) (foreign 1545 F.)(effective 1992). (Institut Pasteur) Editions Scientifiques Elsevier, 29, rue Buffon, 75005 Paris, France. TEL 47-07-11-22. FAX 43-36-80-93. TELEX 202 400 F. (Subscr. in U.S. and Canada to: Elsevier Science Publishing Co., Inc., Box 882, Madison Sq. Sta., New York, NY 10159. TEL 212-989-5800) Eds. P. Kourilsky, P. Truffa-Bachi. index. (also avail. in microform from RPI; reprint service avail. from ISI) **Indexed:** Abstr.Hyg., Anim.Breed.Abstr., Biol.Abstr., Bull.Signal., Chem.Abstr., Curr.Adv.Ecol.Sci., Curr.Cont., Dairy Sci.Abstr., Dent.Ind., Excerp.Med., Helminthol.Abstr., Ind.Med., Ind.Sci.Rev., Ind.Vet., INIS Atomind., Pig News & Info., Rev.Med.& Vet.Mycol., Sci.Cit.Ind., Trop.Dis.Bull., Vet.Bull.
—BLDSC shelfmark: 7741.325000.
   Former titles (until 1988): Institut Pasteur. Annales. Immunologie (ISSN 0769-2625); (until 1985): Annales d'Immunologie (ISSN 0300-4910); Supersedes in part: Institut Pasteur. Annales (ISSN 0020-2444)
   Description: Publishes full-length articles on all aspects of immunology, including immunochemistry, cellular immunology, immunogenetics and transplantation immunopathology.
   Refereed Serial

616.97   NE
RESEARCH MONOGRAPHS IN IMMUNOLOGY. 1980. irreg., vol.12, 1989. price varies. Elsevier Science Publishers B.V., Books Division, P.O. Box 211, 1000 AE Amsterdam, Netherlands. TEL 020-5803911. FAX 020-5803705. TELEX 18582 ESPA NL. (Subscr. in U.S. and Canada to: Elsevier Science Publishing Co., Inc., Box 882, Madison Sq. Sta., New York, NY 10159. TEL 212-989-5800)
Refereed Serial

REVIEWS IN MEDICAL VIROLOGY. see *BIOLOGY — Microbiology*

REVISTA ARGENTINA DE MICROBIOLOGIA. see *BIOLOGY — Microbiology*

616.97   FR   ISSN 0335-7457
REVUE FRANCAISE D'ALLERGOLOGIE ET IMMUNOLOGIE CLINIQUE. 1961. 4/yr. 625 F. to individuals (foreign 820 F.); students 315 F. (foreign 420 F.). (Societe Francaise d'Allergologie) Expansion Scientifique, 15 rue Saint-Benoit, 75278 Paris Cedex 06, France. Ed. Dr. Sclafer. adv.; bk.rev.; abstr.; bibl.; charts; circ. 3,000. (also avail. in microform from UMI; reprint service avail. from UMI) **Indexed:** Biol.Abstr., C.I.S. Abstr., Chem.Abstr., Curr.Adv.Ecol.Sci., Curr.Cont., Ind.Med., Rev.Plant Path.
—BLDSC shelfmark: 7902.470000.
   Former titles: Revue Francaise d'Allergologie et Immunologie; Revue Francaise d'Allergologie (ISSN 0035-2845); Revue Francaise d'Allergie.

RHEUMATOLOGIA, BALNEOLOGIA, ALLERGOLOGIA. see *MEDICAL SCIENCES — Rheumatology*

616.07 576   RM
                                            CODEN: RAMIE
ROUMANIAN ARCHIVES OF MICROBIOLOGY AND IMMUNOLOGY. (Text in English and French; summaries in English, French, German, Russian) 1928. q. $55. Institutul Cantacuzino R A, P.O. Box 1-525, Spl. Independentei 103, 70100 Bucharest, Rumania. TEL 0-139720. bk.rev.; charts; illus.; index; circ. 1,000. (back issues avail.) **Indexed:** Abstr.Hyg., Biol.Abstr., Bull.Signal., Chem.Abstr., Excerp.Med., Ind.Med., Ind.Vet., INIS Atomind., Rev.Appl.Entomol., Trop.Dis.Bull., Vet.Bull.
   Formerly (until 1991): Archives Roumaines de Pathologie Experimentale et de Microbiologie (ISSN 0004-0037)

615.37   UK   ISSN 0300-9475
QR180   CODEN: SJIMAX
SCANDINAVIAN JOURNAL OF IMMUNOLOGY. 1972. m. £176($320) Blackwell Scientific Publications Ltd., Osney Mead, Oxford OX2 0EL, England. TEL 0865-240201. FAX 0865-721205. TELEX 83355-MEDBOK-G. Eds. M. Harboe, J.B. Natvig. adv.; circ. 1,110. (back issues avail.; reprint service avail. from ISI) **Indexed:** Anim.Breed.Abstr., ASCA, Biol.Abstr., Chem.Abstr., Curr.Adv.Biochem., Curr.Adv.Cancer Res., Curr.Adv.Cell & Devel.Biol., Curr.Adv.Ecol.Sci., Curr.Adv.Genetics & Molec.Biol., Curr.Cont., Dairy Sci.Abstr., Excerp.Med., Helminthol.Abstr., Ind.Med., Ind.Vet., Protozool.Abstr., Sci.Cit.Ind., Vet.Bull.
—BLDSC shelfmark: 8087.516800.

SEMINARS IN DIAGNOSTIC PATHOLOGY. see *MEDICAL SCIENCES*

SKIN AND PSORIASIS NEWSLETTER. see *MEDICAL SCIENCES — Dermatology And Venereology*

616.97   US   ISSN 0887-3488
QR180   CODEN: SMDREE
SOVIET MEDICAL REVIEWS. SECTION D: IMMUNOLOGY REVIEWS. a. $118. Harwood Academic Publishers, 270 Eighth Ave., New York, NY 10011. TEL 212-206-8900. FAX 212-645-2459. TELEX 236735 GOPUB UR. (Subscr. to: Box 786, Cooper Sta., New York, NY 10276. TEL 800-545-8398; UK subscr. to: P.O. Box 90, Reading, Berkshire RG1 8JL, England. TEL 0734-560-080) Ed. R.V. Petrov. (also avail. in microform)
Refereed Serial

616.97   US   ISSN 0896-601X
SOVIET MEDICAL REVIEWS SUPPLEMENT SERIES. SECTION B: IMMUNOLOGY. irreg. Harwood Academic Publishers, 270 Eighth Ave., New York, NY 10011. TEL 212-206-8900. FAX 212-645-2459. TELEX 236735 GOPUB UR. (Subscr. to: Box 786, Cooper Sta., New York, NY 10276. TEL 800-545-8398; UK subscr. to: Box 90, Reading, Berkshire RG1 8JL, England. TEL 0734-560-080) Ed. R.V. Petrov. (also avail. in microform)

616.97   GW   ISSN 0344-4325
                                          CODEN: SSIMDV
SPRINGER SEMINARS IN IMMUNOPATHOLOGY. 1978. 4/yr. DM.318($185.50) Springer-Verlag, Heidelberger Platz 3, D-1000 Berlin 33, Germany. TEL 030-8207-1. (Also Heidelberg, Tokyo, Vienna, and New York) Ed. P.A. Miescher. charts; illus.; index. (also avail. in microform from UMI; back issues avail.; reprint service avail. from ISI) **Indexed:** Abstr.Hyg., Anim.Breed.Abstr., ASCA, Chem.Abstr., Curr.Adv.Ecol.Sci., Curr.Adv.Genetics & Molec.Biol., Curr.Cont., Excerp.Med., Helminthol.Abstr., Ind.Med., Trop.Dis.Bull.
—BLDSC shelfmark: 8424.730000.

616.97   NE   ISSN 0165-6090
                          CODEN: THYMDB
THYMUS; international journal of thymology, immunobiology and clinical immunology. (Text in English) 1979. 8/yr. fl.448($255) Kluwer Academic Publishers, Postbus 17, 3300 AA Dordrecht, Netherlands. TEL 078-334911. FAX 078-334254. TELEX 29245. (Dist. by: Kluwer Academic Publishers Group, P.O. Box 322, 3300 AH Dordrecht, Netherlands; N. America dist. addr.: Box 358, Accord Station, Hingham, MA 02018-0358. TEL 617-871-6600) Ed. J. Touraine. adv.; circ. 1,000. (back issues avail.) Indexed: ASCA, Biol.Abstr., Chem.Abstr., Curr.Adv.Ecol.Sci., Curr.Cont., Excerp.Med., Ind.Med., Ind.Vet., Protozool.Abstr., Vet.Bull.
—BLDSC shelfmark: 8820.381500.

616.97   US   ISSN 0896-341X
                          CODEN: THUPEZ
THYMUS UPDATE. irreg. Harwood Academic Publishers, 270 Eighth Ave., New York, NY 10011. TEL 212-260-8900. FAX 212-645-2459. TELEX 236735 GOPUB UR. (Subscr. to: Box 786, Cooper Sta., New York, NY 10276. TEL 800-545-8398; UK subscr. to: Box 90, Reading, Berkshire RG1 8JL, England. TEL 0734-560-080) Eds. M.D. Kendall, M.A. Ritter. (also avail. in microform)
Refereed Serial

TRANSPLANTATION. see MEDICAL SCIENCES — Surgery

616.97   UK   ISSN 0264-410X
                          CODEN: VACCDE
VACCINE. 1983. 10/yr. £335 (foreign £365). Butterworth - Heinemann Ltd. (Subsidiary of: Reed International PLC), Linacre House, Jordan Hill, Oxford OX2 8DP, England. TEL 0865-310366. FAX 0865-310898. TELEX 83111 BHPOXF G. (Subscr. to: Turpin Transactions Ltd., Distribution Centre, Blackhorse Rd., Letchworth, Herts SG6 1HN, England. TEL 0462-672555) Ed. R.E. Spier. adv.; bk.rev.; abstr.; bibl.; charts; illus.; pat.; stat.; index. (also avail. in microform from UMI; back issues avail.) Indexed: Abstr.Hyg., Chem.Abstr., Curr.Adv.Ecol.Sci., Curr.Adv.Genetics & Molec.Biol., Curr.Biotech.Abstr., Curr.Cont., Dok.Arbeitsmed., Excerp.Med., Ind.Med., Ind.Vet., Poult.Abstr., Small Anim.Abstr., Telegen, Vet.Bull.
—BLDSC shelfmark: 9138.628000.
   Description: Research and development, production and use of both human and veterinary vaccines.
   Refereed Serial

616.96   US
VACCINES (YEAR). a. Cold Spring Harbor Laboratory Press, Publications Department, Box 100, Cold Spring Harbor, NY 11724. TEL 800-843-4388. FAX 516-349-1946. (reprint service avail.)

VETERINARY IMMUNOLOGY AND IMMUNOPATHOLOGY; an international journal of comparative immunology. see VETERINARY SCIENCE

616.97   US   ISSN 0882-8245
                          CODEN: VIIMET
VIRAL IMMUNOLOGY. vol.2, 1989. q. $142 (foreign $182). Mary Ann Liebert, Inc., 1651 Third Ave., New York, NY 10128. TEL 212-289-2300. FAX 212-289-4697. Ed.Bd. abstr.; charts; stat. (reprint service avail.)
—BLDSC shelfmark: 9237.876000.
   Description: Covers human and animal viral immunology. Includes research and development of viral vaccines. Features regular mini-reviews of all relevant literature.
   Refereed Serial

615.65   SZ   ISSN 0042-9007
                          CODEN: VOSAAD
VOX SANGUINIS; international journal of transfusion medicine. (Text in English) 1956. 8/yr. (2 vols./yr.). 243 SFr.($162) per vol. (International Society of Blood Transfusion) S. Karger AG, Allschwilerstr. 10, P.O. Box, CH-4009 Basel, Switzerland. TEL 061-3061111. FAX 061-3061234. TELEX CH 962652. (Co-sponsor: League of Red Cross Societies) Ed. C.P. Engelfriet. adv.; bibl.; charts; illus.; index; circ. 2,900. (also avail. in microform from RPI) Indexed: Abstr.Hyg., Anim.Breed.Abstr., Biol.Abstr., Chem.Abstr., Curr.Adv.Ecol.Sci., Curr.Cont., Dairy Sci.Abstr., Dent.Ind., Excerp.Med., Helminthol.Abstr., Ind.Med., Ind.Vet., Nutr.Abstr., Risk Abstr., Trop.Dis.Bull., Vet.Bull.
—BLDSC shelfmark: 9258.700000.

616.97   SZ   ISSN 0256-2308
QR180
YEAR IN IMMUNOLOGY. 1982. a. price varies. S. Karger AG, Allschwilerstr. 10, P.O. Box, CH-4009 Basel, Switzerland. TEL 061-3061111. FAX 061-3061234. TELEX CH 962652. Eds. J.M. Cruse, R.E. Lewis Jr. Indexed: Anim.Breed.Abstr., Biol.Abstr., Curr.Cont.
   Description: Provides updates on current developments of various aspects in immunologic research.

616.97   GW   ISSN 0343-8554
                          CODEN: ZELYDR
ZEITSCHRIFT FUER LYMPHOLOGIE; Ergebnisse aus Forschung, Klinik und Praxis. 1977. 2/yr. DM.95($60) (German Society of Lymphology) F.K. Schattauer Verlagsgesellschaft mbH, Lenzhalde 3, Postfach 104545, 7000 Stuttgart 10, Germany. TEL 0711-22987-0. FAX 0711-22987-50. Ed.Bd. adv.; bk.rev.
—BLDSC shelfmark: 5010.660000.

616.97   CC
ZHONGGUO MEIJIE SHENGWUXUE JI KONGZHI ZAZHI. (Text in Chinese) bi-m. Zhonghua Yufang Yixuehui - China Preventive Medical Society, 16, Hepingli Zhongjie, Beijing 100013, People's Republic of China. TEL 4218457. Ed. Wang Chengxin.

616.97   CC
ZHONGGUO MIANYIXUE ZAZHI/CHINESE JOURNAL OF IMMUNOLOGY. (Text in Chinese) bi-m. Jilin Sheng Weisheng Ting - Jilin Provincial Bureau of Health, Fu 2, Dong Minzhu Dajie, Changchun, Jilin 130061, People's Republic of China. TEL 825027. Ed. Xie Guangwen.
Refereed Serial

616.97   CC
ZHONGHUA WEISHENGWUXUE HE MIANYIXUE ZAZHI/CHINESE JOURNAL OF MICROBIOLOGY AND IMMUNOLOGY. (Text in Chinese) bi-m. Beijing Shengwu Zhipin Yanjiusuo - Beijing Institute of Biological Products, Sanjianfang, Beijing 100024, People's Republic of China. TEL 5009911. (Co-sponsor: Zhonghua Yixuehui - Chinese Society of Medical Sciences) Ed. Li Hemin. Indexed: Biodet.Abstr.

MEDICAL SCIENCES — Anaesthesiology

617.96   US   ISSN 0883-122X
RD78.62.U6
A B M S DIRECTORY OF CERTIFIED ANESTHESIOLOGISTS. 1985. biennial. $39.95. American Board of Medical Specialties, One Rotary Center, Ste. 805, Evanston, IL 60201. TEL 708-491-9091. FAX 708-328-3596. Ed. Dr. J. Lee Dockery.

617.96   US   ISSN 0363-471X
A S A REFRESHER COURSES IN ANESTHESIOLOGY. 1973. a. $19. (American Society of Anesthesiologists) J.B. Lippincott Co., E. Washington Sq., Philadelphia, PA 19105. TEL 215-238-4200. Ed. Dr. Paul G. Barash. (also avail. in microform from UMI)
—BLDSC shelfmark: 7333.765000.

617.96   BE   ISSN 0001-5164
                          CODEN: AABEAJ
ACTA ANAESTHESIOLOGICA BELGICA. (Supplements avail.) vol.17, 1966. 4/yr. 2200 BEF (foreign 2500 BEF)(effective 1992). Association des Societes Scientifiques Medicales Belges - Vereiniging van de Belgische Medische Wetenschappelijke Genootschappen, Av. Circulaire 138A, B-1180 Brussels, Belgium. TEL 02-374-5158. Ed. Dr. G. Rolly. Indexed: Biol.Abstr., Chem.Abstr., Dent.Ind., Excerp.Med., Ind.Med.
—BLDSC shelfmark: 0593.600000.

617.96   IT   ISSN 0374-4965
                          CODEN: AANIBO
ACTA ANAESTHESIOLOGICA ITALICA; rivista di anestesia e cure pre e post-operatorie. (Supplement avail: Anaesthesia and Intesive Care in Italy) (Summaries in English) 1949. q. L.120000 includes supplements. Tipografia Editrice la Garangola, Via Montona 4, 35137 Padua, Italy. FAX 049-8751743. adv.; abstr.; illus.; index. (back issues avail.) Indexed: Biol.Abstr., Chem.Abstr., Excerp.Med., Ind.Med.
—BLDSC shelfmark: 0593.620000.
   Formerly: Acta Anaesthesiologica.

617.96   DK   ISSN 0001-5172
                          CODEN: AANEAB
ACTA ANAESTHESIOLOGICA SCANDINAVICA. (Text and summaries in English) 1957. 8/yr. DKK 1045 includes supplements. Munksgaard International Publishers Ltd., Noerre Soegade, P.O. Box 2148, DK-1016 Copenhagen K, Denmark. TEL 33-127030. FAX 33-129387. TELEX 19431-MUNKS-DK. Ed. Jan Eklund. adv.; bibl.; charts; illus.; stat.; index; circ. 3,500. (reprint service avail. from ISI) Indexed: ASCA, Biol.Abstr., Biotech.Abstr., Chem.Abstr., Curr.Adv.Ecol.Sci., Curr.Cont., Curr.Tit.Dent., Dent.Ind., Dok.Arbeitsmed., Excerp.Med., Ind.Med., Ind.Sci.Rev., INIS Atomind., Sci.Cit.Ind.
—BLDSC shelfmark: 0593.650000.

617.96   DK   ISSN 0515-2720
                          CODEN: AASXAP
ACTA ANAESTHESIOLOGICA SCANDINAVICA. SUPPLEMENTUM. irreg. free with subcription to Acta Anaesthesiologica Scandinavica. Munksgaard International Publishers Ltd., Journals Division, 35 Noerre Soegade, P.O. Box 2148, DK-1016 Copenhagen K, Denmark. TEL 33-127030. FAX 33-129387. TELEX 19431-MUNKS-DK. Indexed: Biol.Abstr., Chem.Abstr., Curr.Adv.Ecol.Sci., Curr.Cont., Excerp.Med., Ind.Med., INIS Atomind.
—BLDSC shelfmark: 0593.651000.

617.96   US   ISSN 0737-6146
RD78.3
ADVANCES IN ANESTHESIA. 1982. a. $55.95. Mosby - Year Book, Inc. (Chicago) (Subsidiary of: Times Mirror Company), 200 N. LaSalle St., Chicago, IL 60601-1080. TEL 312-726-9733. FAX 312-726-6075. TELEX 206155. (Subscr. to: 11830 Westline Industrial Dr., St. Louis, MO 63146. TEL 800-325-4177) Ed. Robert K. Stoelting, M.D.
—BLDSC shelfmark: 0698.850000.
   Description: Presents a collection of original, fully referenced articles from experts in the field.

617.96   UK   ISSN 0003-2409
                          CODEN: ANASAB
ANAESTHESIA (LONDON). 1945. m. $259. (Association of Anaesthetists of Great Britain & Ireland) Academic Press Ltd., 24-28 Oval Rd., London NW1 7DX, England. TEL 071-267-4466. FAX 071-482-2293. TELEX 25775 ACPRES G. Ed. M. Morgan. adv.; bk.rev.; bibl.; illus.; index. (back issues avail.; reprint service avail. from ISI) Indexed: Biol.Abstr., Biotech.Abstr., Chem.Abstr., Curr.Adv.Ecol.Sci., Curr.Cont., Excerp.Med., Ind.Med., Ind.Sci.Rev., Int.Nurs.Ind., Nutr.Abstr., Rev.Plant Path., Sci.Cit.Ind.
—BLDSC shelfmark: 0859.900000.
   Description: Covers practical features of general and local anaesthesia, pre- and postoperative management, resuscitation and intensive care, acute and chronic pain therapy.

617.96   AT
ANAESTHESIA AND INTENSIVE CARE. 1972. q. Aus.$64 to individuals (foreign Aus.$90); institutions Aus.$90 (foreign Aus.$140) (effective 1992). Australian Society of Anaesthetists, P.O. Box 600, Edgecliff, N.S.W. 2027, Australia. TEL 61-2-327-4022. FAX 61-2-327-7666. Ed. J. Roberts. adv.; bk.rev.; bibl.; charts; illus.; index; circ. 3,800. (also avail. in microfiche from UMI; back issues avail.) Indexed: Biol.Abstr., CINAHL, Curr.Adv.Ecol.Sci., Curr.Cont., Excerp.Med., Ind.Med., Nutr.Abstr.
   Formerly: Anaesthesia and Intensive Care Journal (ISSN 0310-057X)
   Description: Presents original articles of scientific and clinical interest in the specialties of anaesthesia, intensive care, pain therapy and related disciplines.

617.96   IT
ANAESTHESIA AND INTENSIVE CARE IN ITALY. (Supplement to: Acta Anaesthesiologica Italica) vol.40, 1989. s-a. L.120000 includes Acta Anaesthesiologica Italica. Tipografia Editrice la Garangola, Via Montona, 4, 35137 Padua, Italy.

MEDICAL SCIENCES — ANAESTHESIOLOGY

617.96   JO   ISSN 0259-1162
CODEN: AESRE
ANAESTHESIA ESSAYS AND RESEARCHES. (Text in Arabic, English) 1985. a. $18. (Pan-Arabic Scientific Committee) Dar Ammar for Publication, P.O. Box 921691, Petra Market, Amman, Jordan. TEL 01-652437. TELEX 55545 JUST JO. Ed. Dr. M. Takrouri. adv.; bk.rev.; circ. 3,000. **Indexed:** Excerp.Med.
    Description: Specialized research journal published by the Arabic Scientific Committee on anaesthesia and intensive care.

617.96   GW   ISSN 0939-2661
CODEN: AISTE
ANAESTHESIE - INTENSIVTHERAPIE - NOTFALLMEDIZIN - SCHMERZTHERAPIE. (Summaries in English, German) 1966. bi-m. DM.280 (members DM.224). (Deutsche Gesellschaft fuer Anaesthesiologie und Intensivmedizin) Georg Thieme Verlag, Ruedigerstr. 14, Postfach 104853, 7000 Stuttgart 10, Germany. TEL 0711-8931-0. FAX 0711-8931298. Ed. O.H. Just. adv.; bk.rev.; bibl.; charts; illus.; stat.; index; circ. 3,900. (reprint service avail. from UMI) **Indexed:** Curr.Cont., Excerp.Med., Ind.Med., INIS Atomind., Sci.Cit.Ind.
—BLDSC shelfmark: 0897.895000.
    Former titles (until 1990): Anaesthesie - Intensivtherapie - Notfallmedizin (ISSN 0174-1837); (until 1980): Praktische Anaesthesie (ISSN 0302-7600); (until 1974): Zeitschrift fuer Praktische Anaesthesie, Wiederbelebung und Intensivtherapie (ISSN 0044-3387)

617   GW   ISSN 0170-5334
CODEN: ATIMDA
ANAESTHESIOLOGIE UND INTENSIVMEDIZIN. 1960. m. DM.72. (Deutsche Gesellschaft fuer Anaesthesiologie und Intensivmedizin, Berufsverband Deutscher Anaesthesisten) Perimed Verlag Dr. D. Straube, Weinstr. 70, Postfach 3740, 8520 Erlangen, Germany. TEL 09131-609-0. FAX 09131-609217. TELEX 629851-PEMEDD. Ed. H.W. Opderbecke. circ. 8,500. **Indexed:** Biol.Abstr., Chem.Abstr.
—BLDSC shelfmark: 0897.905000.
    Formerly: Anaesthesiologische Informationen.

617.96   US   ISSN 0171-1814
CODEN: ANIMD2
ANAESTHESIOLOGIE UND INTENSIVMEDIZIN/ANAESTHESIOLOGY AND INTENSIVE CARE MEDICINE. (Text in German; contributions in English and French) 1963. irreg., vol.212, 1989. price varies. Springer-Verlag, 175 Fifth Ave., New York, NY 10010. TEL 212-460-1500. (Also Berlin, Heidelberg, Tokyo and Vienna) (reprint service avail. from ISI)
—BLDSC shelfmark: 0859.909000.
    Formerly: Anaesthesiology and Resuscitation (ISSN 0066-1341)

617.96   GW   ISSN 0003-2417
CODEN: ANATAE
DER ANAESTHESIST. (Supplement avail.: Regional-Anaesthesie) 1952. 12/yr. DM.398($273) (effective 1992). (Deutsche Gesellschaft fuer Anaesthesie und Wiederbelebung) Springer-Verlag, Heidelberger Platz 3, D-1000 Berlin 33, Germany. TEL 030-8207-1. (Also Heidelberg, Tokyo, Vienna, and New York) (Co-sponsor: Oesterreichische und Schweizerische Gesellschaft fuer Anaesthesiologie und Reanimation) Ed. A. Doenicke. adv.; bk.rev.; abstr.; bibl.; charts; illus.; index. (also avail. in microform from UMI; back issues avail.; reprint service avail. from ISI) **Indexed:** Abstr.Health Care Manage.Stud., Biol.Abstr., Biotech.Abstr., Chem.Abstr., Curr.Cont., Dent.Ind., Excerp.Med., Ind.Med., Ind.Sci.Rev., INIS Atomind., Sci.Cit.Ind.
—BLDSC shelfmark: 0859.920000.

617.96   IT
ANESTESISTA. bi-m. Via Poliziano 69, 00184 Rome, Italy. Ed. Alessandro Pesce.

617   RU   ISSN 0201-7563
CODEN: AREAD8
ANESTEZIOLOGIYA I REANIMATOLOGIYA/ANAESTHESIOLOGY AND REANIMATOLOGY. 1956. bi-m. 24.60 Rub.($10.20) (Vsesoyuznoe Nauchnoe Obshchestvo Anesteziologov i Reanimatologov) Izdatel'stvo Meditsina, Petroverigskii pereulok 6-8, 101838 Moscow, Russia. (Dist. by: Mezhdunarodnaya Kniga, Moscow, G-200, Russia) (Co-sponsor: Ministerstvo Zdravookhraneniya S.S.S.R.) Ed. T.M. Darbinyan. bk.rev.; index. **Indexed:** Biol.Abstr., Chem.Abstr., Excerp.Med., Ind.Med.
—BLDSC shelfmark: 0006.650000.
    Formerly (until 1977): Eksperimental'naya Khirurgiya i Anesteziologiya (ISSN 0013-3329)
    Description: Covers general anaesthesiology in surgery, intensive treatment and resuscitation. Presents the progressive methods used in anesthesiology and reanimatology in obstetrics, gynecology, pediatrics, stomatology, otolaryngology, and surgery in the outpatient practice.

617.96   US   ISSN 0003-2999
RD81.A1   CODEN: AACRAT
ANESTHESIA AND ANALGESIA. (Supplement avail.) 1922. m. $150 to institutions (foreign $185) (effective 1992). (International Anesthesia Research Society) Elsevier Science Publishing Co., Inc. (New York), 655 Ave. of the Americas, New York, NY 10010. TEL 212-989-5800. FAX 212-633-3965. TELEX 420643 AEP UI. Ed. Dr. Nicholas M. Greene. adv.; bk.rev.; bibl.; charts; illus.; index; circ. 13,500. (also avail. in microfilm from PMC) **Indexed:** Abstr.Health Care Manage.Stud., Biol.Abstr., Biotech.Abstr., C.I.S Abstr., Chem.Abstr., CINAHL, Curr.Adv.Ecol.Sci., Curr.Cont., Dent.Abstr., Dent.Ind., Excerp.Med., Ind.Med., Ind.Sci.Rev., Sci.Cit.Ind.
● Also available online. Vendor(s): BRS.
—BLDSC shelfmark: 0900.500000.
    Formerly: Current Researches in Anesthesia and Analgesia.
    Description: Publishes original research and clinical articles, providing researchers, practicing physicians, and allied medical personnel in anesthesiology and related fields with a wealth of information to keep them up to date with the latest issues and advances in the field.
Refereed Serial

617.96   US
ANESTHESIA MALPRACTICE PROTECTOR. 1989. m. $189. American Health Consultants, Inc., Six Piedmont Center, Ste. 400, 3525 Piedmont Rd., N.E., Atlanta, GA 30305. TEL 800-688-2421. FAX 800-284-3291. Ed. Mark Lewyn.
    Incorporates (in 1991): Anesthesiology Alert.

ANESTHESIA PROGRESS; a journal for pain and anxiety control. see MEDICAL SCIENCES — Dentistry

617.96   US   ISSN 0003-3022
CODEN: ANESAV
ANESTHESIOLOGY. 1940. m. $100 to individuals (foreign $150); institutions $120 (foreign $180). (American Society of Anesthesiologists) J.B. Lippincott Co., E. Washington Sq., Philadelphia, PA 19105. TEL 215-238-4200. Ed. Dr. Lawrence J. Saidman. adv.; bk.rev.; illus.; cum.index; circ. 36,128. (also avail. in microform from UMI; reprint service avail. from UMI) **Indexed:** Biol.Abstr., Biotech.Abstr., Chem.Abstr., Curr.Adv.Ecol.Sci., Curr.Cont., Excerp.Med., Ind.Med., Ind.Sci.Rev., Ind.Vet., INIS Atomind., Int.Nurs.Ind., Pig News & Info., Risk Abstr., Sci.Cit.Ind., SSCI, Vet.Bull.
● Also available online. Vendor(s): BRS.
—BLDSC shelfmark: 0900.600000.
Refereed Serial

617.96   US
ANESTHESIOLOGY NEWS. 1975. m. $28. McMahon Publishing Co., 83 Peaceable St., West Redding, CT 06896. Ed. Kenneth J. Zeserson. circ. 17,500. (tabloid format)
    Formerly (until 1979?): Anesthesia Staff News.

617.96   US   ISSN 0093-4437
RD78.3
ANESTHESIOLOGY REVIEW. 1973. bi-m. $18.50. Excerpta Medica, Inc., Core Publishing Division (Subsidiary of: Elsevier Science Publishers B.V.), 105 Raider Blvd., Belle Mead, NJ 08520. TEL 908-874-8550. FAX 908-874-0700. Ed. Andrew Voynow. adv.; bk.rev.; charts; illus.; circ. 18,045 (controlled). **Indexed:** Excerp.Med.
—BLDSC shelfmark: 0900.800000.

617.96   FR   ISSN 0750-7658
CODEN: AFAREO
ANNALES FRANCAISES D'ANESTHESIE ET DE REANIMATION. 1965. bi-m 155 ECU($203) (typically set in Jan.). (Societe Francaise d'Anesthesie, d'Analgesie et de Reanimation) Masson, 120 bd. Saint-Germain, 75280 Paris Cedex 06, France. TEL 1-46-34-21-60. FAX 1-45-87-29-99. TELEX 202 671 F. Ed. Haberer. adv.; bk.rev.; abstr.; charts; illus.; circ. 5,800. (reprint service avail. from ISI) **Indexed:** Biol.Abstr., Biotech.Abstr., Chem.Abstr., Dent.Ind., Excerp.Med., Ind.Med., Nutr.Abstr.
—BLDSC shelfmark: 0973.800000.
    Formerly: Anesthesie, Analgesie, Reanimation (ISSN 0003-3014)

617.96 615.804   II   ISSN 0301-0368
CODEN: AAARDM
ASIAN ARCHIVES OF ANAESTHESIOLOGY AND RESUSCITATION. (Text in English) 1971. q. $75. National Association of Critical Care Medicine, 147, North Ave., New Delhi 110001, India. TEL 3014755. Ed. Dr. N.P. Singh. adv.; bk.rev.; bibl.; charts; illus.; circ. 2,000. (back issues avail.) **Indexed:** Biol.Abstr., Chem.Abstr.
    Formerly (1973): Archives of Anaesthesiology and Resuscitation.

617.96   US   ISSN 0271-1265
AUDIO-DIGEST ANESTHESIOLOGY. 1958. s-m. $168. Audio-Digest Foundation (Subsidiary of: California Medical Association), 1577 E. Chevy Chase Dr., Glendale, CA 91206. TEL 213-245-8505. FAX 818-240-7379. (audio cassette)
Refereed Serial

617.96   UK   ISSN 0950-3501
BAILLIERE'S CLINICAL ANAESTHESIOLOGY. 1986. 4/yr. $65. Grune & Stratton Ltd., Harcourt Brace Jovanovich, Publishers, 24-28 Oval Rd., London NW1, 7DX, England. (also avail. in microform from UMI) **Indexed:** Abstr.Health Care Manage.Stud., Curr.Adv.Ecol.Sci., Excerp.Med.
—BLDSC shelfmark: 1856.717000.
    Former titles: Anesthesiology Clinics (ISSN 0889-8537); (until 1986): Clinics in Anaesthesiology (ISSN 0261-9881)

617.96 610.73   US
BREATHLINE. bi-m. membership. Phenix Corporation, 11508 Allecingie Pkwy., Ste. C., Richmond, VA 23235. TEL 804-379-5516. bk.rev.

617.96   US
BRISTOL-MYERS - SQUIBB SYMPOSIUM ON PAIN RESEARCH SERIES. 1991. irreg. price varies. Raven Press, 1185 Ave. of the Americas, New York, NY 10036. TEL 212-930-9500. FAX 212-869-3495.

617.96   UK   ISSN 0007-0912
CODEN: BJANAD
BRITISH JOURNAL OF ANAESTHESIA. (Text in English; summaries in French, German, Spanish) 1923. m. £117. Professional & Scientific Publications, Tavistock House E., Tavistock Sq., London WC1H 9JR, England. Ed. G. Smith. adv.; bk.rev.; bibl.; charts; illus.; index; circ. 10,000. (also avail. in microform from UMI; reprint service avail. from SWZ) **Indexed:** Biol.Abstr., Biotech.Abstr., Chem.Abstr., Curr.Adv.Ecol.Sci., Curr.Cont., Dairy Sci.Abstr., Dent.Ind., Dok.Arbeitsmed., Excerp.Med., Helminthol.Abstr., Ind.Med., Ind.Sci.Rev., Ind.Vet., Nutr.Abstr., Risk Abstr., Sci.Cit.Ind., Small Anim.Abstr., Vet.Bull.
—BLDSC shelfmark: 2303.900000.

617.96 610.73   US
▼**C R N A: THE CLINICAL FORUM FOR NURSE ANESTHETISTS.** 1990. q. $49. W.B. Saunders Co., Curtis Center, Independence Sq. W., Philadelphia, PA 19106. TEL 215-238-7800. adv.; circ. 1,530.
    Description: Covers hands-on management and care of the anesthetized patient.

617.96   FR   ISSN 0007-9685
CODEN: CAANBU
CAHIERS D'ANESTHESIOLOGIE. 1953. 8/yr. 430 F. Librairie Arnette, 2 rue Casimir Delavigne, 75006 Paris, France. Ed. Lassner. adv.; bk.rev.; index; circ. 3,500. **Indexed:** Biol.Abstr., Excerp.Med., Ind.Med.
—BLDSC shelfmark: 2948.620000.

MEDICAL SCIENCES — ANAESTHESIOLOGY

617.96   CN   ISSN 0832-610X
CODEN: CJOAEP
CANADIAN JOURNAL OF ANAESTHESIA/JOURNAL CANADIEN D'ANESTHÉSIE. (Text in English and French) 1954. 10/yr. Can.$130 to individuals; institutions $170. Canadian Anaesthetists' Society - Societe Canadienne des Anesthesistes, 1 Eglinton Ave., E., Ste. 208, Toronto, Ont. M4P 3A1, Canada. TEL 416-480-0602. FAX 416-480-0320. Ed. Dr. David R. Bevan. adv.; bk.rev.; bibl.; charts; illus.; index; circ. 5,040. (also avail. in microform from UMI; back issues avail; reprint service avail. from UMI) **Indexed:** Biol.Abstr., Chem.Abstr, CINAHL, Curr.Adv.Ecol.Sci., Curr.Cont., Dent.Ind., Excerp.Med., Ind.Med., Ind.Sci.Rev., INIS Atomind., Sci.Cit.Ind.
—BLDSC shelfmark: 3028.300000.
   Formerly (until 1986): Canadian Anaesthetists' Society. Journal (ISSN 0008-2856)

CLINICAL JOURNAL OF PAIN. see *MEDICAL SCIENCES — Psychiatry And Neurology*

617.96   SP
▼**CLINICAS DE ANESTESIOLOGIA DE NORTEAMERICA.** 1991. 4/yr. 14416 ptas. (effective 1990). Interamericana de Espana, S.A., Manuel Ferrero, 13, 28036 Madrid, Spain. TEL 315-0340. FAX 733-6627.

617   UK
COLLEGE OF ANAESTHETISTS. NEWSLETTER. 1965. 4/yr. membership. College of Anaesthetists, 35-43 Lincoln's Inn Fields, London WC2A 3PN, England. TEL 071-405-3474. FAX 071-831-9019. circ. 6,000 (controlled).
   Former titles: Royal College of Surgeons of England. Faculty of Anaesthetists. Dean's Newsletter; Royal College of Surgeons of England. Faculty of Anaesthetists. Newsletter.
   Description: Report to Fellows and Members of College. Covers activities, events, and personalities.

617.96   UK   ISSN 0953-7112
CODEN: CCCAEI
CURRENT ANAESTHESIA AND CRITICAL CARE. 1989. 4/yr. £53($103) to individuals; institutions £99($190). Churchill Livingstone Medical Journals, Robert Stevenson House, 1-3 Baxter's Pl., Leith Walk, Edinburgh EH1 3AF, Scotland. TEL 031-556-2424. FAX 031-558-1278. TELEX 727511. (Subscr. to: Longman Group, Journals Subscr. Dept, P.O. Box 77, Fourth Ave., Harlow, Essex CM19 5AA, England; U.S. subscr. to: Churchill Livingstone, 650 Ave. of the Americas, New York, NY 10011. TEL 212-206-5000) Ed. B.J. Pollard.
—BLDSC shelfmark: 3494.128000.

CURRENT OPINION IN ANAESTHESIOLOGY. see *MEDICAL SCIENCES — Abstracting, Bibliographies, Statistics*

617.96   SP   ISSN 0071-2671
EUROPEAN CONGRESS OF ANAESTHESIOLOGY. PROCEEDINGS. (Proceedings published in host countries) 1962. quadrennial, 4th, Madrid, 1974. (World Federation of Societies of Anaesthesiologists) European Congress of Anaesthesiology, Inquire: Professor Arias, Arapiles 16, Madrid, Spain.

617.96   UK   ISSN 0265-0215
CODEN: EJANEG
EUROPEAN JOURNAL OF ANAESTHESIOLOGY. 1984. bi-m. £115($210) (European Academy of Anaesthesiology) Blackwell Scientific Publications Ltd., Osney Mead, Oxford OX2 0EL, England. TEL 0865-240201. FAX 0865-721205. TELEX 83355-MEDBOK-G. Eds. Prof. M.D. Vickers, Prof. E. Nilsson. adv.; bk.rev.; abstr.; bibl.; illus.; index. **Indexed:** Curr.Adv.Ecol.Sci., Excerp.Med.
—BLDSC shelfmark: 3829.722200.

EUROPEAN JOURNAL OF PAIN. see *MEDICAL SCIENCES*

617.96   IT   ISSN 0391-5670
GIORNALE DI ANESTESIA STOMATOLOGICA. 1972? q. L.68000($88) (effective 1992). (Associazione Italiana di Anestesia Odontostomatologica) Masson Italia Periodici, Via Statuto 2-4, 20121 Milan, Italy. TEL 02-6367-1. FAX 02-6367211. Ed. Mario Tiengo. circ. 1,000.
—BLDSC shelfmark: 4176.855000.

617.96   II   ISSN 0019-5049
INDIAN JOURNAL OF ANAESTHESIA.* (Text in English) 1953. q. $35. Indian Society of Anaesthetists, c/o Dr. D. Das Gupta, Department of Anaesthesia, K.E.M. Hospital, Parel, Bombay, India. adv.; bk.rev.; abstr.; bibl.; charts; illus.; stat.; index; circ. 2,000. (tabloid format) **Indexed:** Biol.Abstr.

617.96   US   ISSN 0020-5907
RD81.A1   CODEN: IACLAV
INTERNATIONAL ANESTHESIOLOGY CLINICS. 1963. q. $81 to individuals $99 (foreign $105); institutions $99 (foreign $129); residents $55 (foreign $75)(effective Nov. 1991). Little, Brown and Company, Medical Journals, 34 Beacon St., Boston, MA 02108. TEL 617-859-5500.
FAX 617-859-0629. Ed. Dr. Philip W. Lebowitz. charts; illus.; stat.; index; circ. 3,000. (also avail. in microform from UMI; reprint service avail. from UMI; back issues avail.) **Indexed:** Biol.Abstr., CINAHL, Curr.Cont., Dent.Ind., Excerp.Med., Ind.Med., Sci.Cit.Ind.
—BLDSC shelfmark: 4535.750000.
   Description: Focuses on a single topic in each issue. Presents discussions of physiology, pharmacology of the agents, clinical application of techniques, and causes and treatments of complications.

617.96 610   NE   ISSN 0167-9945
CODEN: IJMCEJ
INTERNATIONAL JOURNAL OF CLINICAL MONITORING AND COMPUTING. (Text and summaries in English) 1984. q. fl.273($155) Kluwer Academic Publishers, Postbus 17, 3300 AA Dordrecht, Netherlands. TEL 078-334911. FAX 078-334254. TELEX 29245. (Dist. by: Kluwer Academic Publishers Group, P.O. Box 322, 3300 AH Dordrecht, Netherlands; N. America dist. addr.: Box 358, Accord Station, Hingham, MA 02018-0358. TEL 617-871-6600) Ed. Omar Prakash. adv.; bk.rev. (reprint service avail. from SWZ) **Indexed:** Excerp.Med., Ind.Med.
—BLDSC shelfmark: 4542.170300.

617.96   UK   ISSN 0959-289X
INTERNATIONAL JOURNAL OF OBSTETRIC ANAESTHESIA. q. £55($102) to individuals; institutions £85($159). Churchill Livingstone Medical Journals, Robert Stevenson House, 1-3 Baxter's Pl., Leith Walk, Edinburgh EH1 3AF, Scotland. TEL 031-556-2424. FAX 031-558-1278. (Subscr. to: Longman Group, Journals Subscr. Dept., P.O. Box 77, Fourth Ave., Harlow, Essex CM19 5AA, England; U.S. subscr. to: Churchill Livingstone, 650 Ave. of the Americas, New York, NY 10011. TEL 212-206-5000) Eds. F. Reynolds, D.M. Dewan.
—BLDSC shelfmark: 4542.410500.
   Description: Presents research papers on obstetric anaesthesia, analgesia and related topics.
   Refereed Serial

617.96 616.1   US   ISSN 1053-0770
CODEN: JCVAEK
JOURNAL OF CARDIOTHORACIC AND VASCULAR ANESTHESIA. 1987. bi-m. $105 to individuals; institutions $132; foreign $152. W.B. Saunders Co. (Subsidiary of: Harcourt Brace Jovanovich, Inc.,) Curtis Center, Independence Square W., Philadelphia, PA 19106. TEL 215-238-7800. (Subscr. to: 6277 Sea Harbor Dr., 4th Fl., Orlando FL 32891) Ed. Joel A. Kaplan, M.D. adv.; bk.rev.; abstr.; bibl.; charts; illus.; index. **Indexed:** Excerp.Med.
—BLDSC shelfmark: 4954.864700.
   Formerly: Journal of Cardiothoracic Anesthesia (ISSN 0888-6296)
   Refereed Serial

617.96   US   ISSN 0952-8180
CODEN: JCLBE7
JOURNAL OF CLINICAL ANESTHESIA; an international journal of anesthesia practice. 1988. bi-m. $110 (foreign $145). Butterworth - Heinemann Ltd. (Subsidiary of: Reed International PLC), 80 Montvale Ave., Stoneham, MA 02180. TEL 617-438-8464. FAX 617-438-1479. TELEX 880052. Ed. Dr. Richard J. Kitz. adv.; bk.rev.; charts; illus.; index. (also avail. in microform from UMI; back issues avail.)
—BLDSC shelfmark: 4958.381070.
   Description: Serves as a forum for practical clinical information for the anesthesiologist from the resident level onward.
   Refereed Serial

617.96 617   US   ISSN 0898-4921
CODEN: JNANEV
JOURNAL OF NEUROSURGICAL ANESTHESIOLOGY. 1989. q. $98 to individuals; institutions $140. Raven Press, 1185 Ave. of the Americas, New York, NY 10036. TEL 212-930-9500.
FAX 212-869-3495. TELEX 640073. Ed. James E. Cottrell. adv.; charts; illus.; circ. 2,000.
—BLDSC shelfmark: 5022.150000.
   Description: Features articles on new drugs, equipment, and procedures, and presents reports of major clinical and laboratory research projects.
   Refereed Serial

615 610.73   US   ISSN 0885-3924
RB127
JOURNAL OF PAIN AND SYMPTOM MANAGEMENT. (Supplement avail.) 1982. 8/yr. $150 to institutions (foreign $184)(effective 1992). (University of Wisconsin-Madison, Department of Anesthesiology) Elsevier Science Publishing Co., Inc. (New York), 655 Ave. of the Americas, New York, NY 10010. TEL 212-989-5800.
FAX 212-633-3965. TELEX 420643 AEP UI. Eds. George Heidrich, Russell K. Portenoy. adv.; bk.rev.; index; circ. 3,200. (also avail. in microform from UMI; back issues avail.) **Indexed:** Child Devel.Abstr, CINAHL, Curr.Adv.Ecol.Sci., Excerp.Med, Int.Nurs.Ind., Nurs.Abstr, Psychol.Abstr.
—BLDSC shelfmark: 5027.790000.
   Formerly (until 1985): P R N Forum (ISSN 0743-345X)
   Description: Provides the professional with the results of important new research on pain and its clinical management.
   Refereed Serial

JOURNAL OF POST ANESTHESIA NURSING. see *MEDICAL SCIENCES — Nurses And Nursing*

617.96   CC
LINCHUANG MAZUIXUE ZAZHI/JOURNAL OF CLINICAL ANESTHESIOLOGY. (Text in Chinese) q. Zhonghua Yixuehui, Nanjing Fenhui - Chinese Society of Medical Sciences, Nanjing Chapter, 291 Zhongshan Lu, Nanjing, Jiangsu 210008, People's Republic of China. TEL 307361. Ed. Li Dexin.

617.96   BL
MEDISOM: ANAESTHESIOLOGY. 1982. bi-m. $90. Grupo Editorial Q B D Ltda, Rue Caravelas 326, Caixa Postal 30329, 01051 Sao Paulo, Brazil. FAX 55-11-572-5957. Ed. Dr. Philip Querido. adv. (audio cassette)

617.96   IT   ISSN 0026-4717
MINERVA ANESTESIOLOGICA. Variant title: Giornale Italiano di Anestesia e di Analgesia. (Text in Italian; summaries in English) 1935. m. L.70000($90) (Societa Italiana di Anestesia, Analgesia, Rianimazione e Terapia Intensiva) Edizioni Minerva Medica, Corso Bramante 83-85, 10126 Turin, Italy. Ed. G.P. Giron. adv.; bk.rev.; bibl.; charts; illus.; index; circ. 4,000. **Indexed:** Biol.Abstr., Chem.Abstr., Dent.Ind., Excerp.Med., Ind.Med.

617.96   NE   ISSN 0303-254X
CODEN: MOAND2
MONOGRAPHS IN ANAESTHESIOLOGY. 1974. irreg., vol.21, 1991. price varies. Elsevier Science Publishers B.V., Books Division, P.O. Box 211, 1000 AE Amsterdam, Netherlands. TEL 020-5803911. FAX 020-5803705. TELEX 18582 ESPA NL. (Subscr. in U.S. and Canada to: Elsevier Science Publishing Co., Inc., Box 882, Madison Sq. Sta., New York, NY 10159. TEL 212-989-5800) Ed. A.R. Hunter. (back issues avail.) **Indexed:** Biol.Abstr., Chem.Abstr.
   Refereed Serial

617.96   US   ISSN 0095-2273
N Y S S A SPHERE. 1948. q. $20. New York State Society of Anesthesiologists, Inc., 41 E. 42nd St., No. 1605, New York, NY 10017.
FAX 716-845-8518. Ed. Dr. Mark J. Lema. adv.; bk.rev.; abstr.; charts; illus.; tr.lit.; circ. 2,500 (controlled).
   Former titles: N Y S S A Bulletin (ISSN 0027-7169); New York State Society of Anesthesiologists. Bulletin (ISSN 0095-2265)
   Description: Articles and news of the industry on such topics as malpractice and state health codes. Includes budget and meeting news.

MEDICAL SCIENCES — CANCER

617.96 618.2   US   ISSN 0275-665X
                                           CODEN: OADIDS
OBSTETRIC ANESTHESIA DIGEST. 1981. q. $80. Obstetric Anesthesia Digest, Inc., Box 20057, Wichita, KS 67208-1057. TEL 316-733-5952. FAX 316-733-5952. Ed. Dr. Gerard M. Bassell. bk.rev.; abstr.; circ. 600.
—BLDSC shelfmark: 6208.155000.
Refereed Serial

617.96   NE   ISSN 0169-1112
                           CODEN: PACLEA
THE PAIN CLINIC. (Text in English) 1986. q. DM.237. V S P, P.O. Box 346, 3700 AH Zeist, Netherlands. TEL 03404-25790. FAX 03404-32081. TELEX 40217 VSP NL. Ed. Dr. G.M. Wyant. adv.; bk.rev. (back issues avail.)
—BLDSC shelfmark: 6333.798800.
Description: Focuses on the clinical methods used and the problems involved in the diagnosis and treatment of persistent and recurrent types of pain.

617.96 617.6   US   ISSN 0164-1700
RK1
PAIN CONTROL IN DENTISTRY. Represents: American Society for the Advancement of General Anesthesia in Dentistry. Proceedings. 1930. s-a. $70. American Society for the Advancement of Anesthesia in Dentistry, c/o Louis L. Zall, Ed., 11 Horseshoe Rd., Warren, NJ 07059-6912. TEL 908-356-8708. circ. 525. (back issues avail.)
Description: Pain control using sedation to perform all phases of dentistry.

617.96   GW   ISSN 0932-9196
PRAXIS DER ANAESTHESIOLOGIE UND INTENSIVMEDIZIN. 1988. irreg. price varies. Verlag Dr. Dieter Winkler, Katharinastr. 37, 4630 Bochum 1, Germany. TEL 0234-17508. Ed. Gholam Sehhati-Chafai. circ. 1,500. (back issues avail.)
Description: Covers standard methods and new developments in the fields of anaesthesiology and intensive care.

617.96   US   ISSN 0889-4698
RD82.5
PROBLEMS IN ANESTHESIA. 1987. q. $70 to individuals (foreign $90); institutions $95 (foreign $110). J.B. Lippincott Co., E. Washington Sq., Philadelphia, PA 19105. TEL 215-238-4200. Eds. Robert R. Kirby, David L. Brown. circ. 3,000. (also avail. in microform from UMI)
—BLDSC shelfmark: 6617.876900.

617.96   US   ISSN 0099-1546
                           CODEN: PRANDM
PROGRESS IN ANESTHESIOLOGY. 1975. irreg., latest vol.3. Raven Press, 1185 Ave. of the Americas, New York, NY 10036. TEL 212-930-9500. FAX 212-869-3495. TELEX 640073. **Indexed:** Biol.Abstr., Chem.Abstr.
Refereed Serial

617.96   US   ISSN 0146-521X
RD84   CODEN: RGANDZ
REGIONAL ANESTHESIA. 1975. bi-m. $70 to individuals (foreign $85); institutions $95 (foreign $115). (American Society of Regional Anesthesia) J.B. Lippincott Co., E. Washington Sq., Philadelphia, PA 19105. TEL 215-238-4200. Ed. Phillip O. Bridenbaugh, M.D. adv.; illus.; index.; circ. 5,200. (also avail. in microform from UMI; back issues avail.) **Indexed:** Excerp.Med.
—BLDSC shelfmark: 7336.572200.

RESUSCITATION; an exciting journal for the dissemination of clinical and basic science research relating to critical care and emergency medicine. see *MEDICAL SCIENCES — Respiratory Diseases*

617.96   BL   ISSN 0034-7094
REVISTA BRASILEIRA DE ANESTESIOLOGIA. (Annual English edition avail.) (Summaries in English, Portuguese and Spanish) 1951. bi-m. Cz.$51,64($120) (Sociedade Brasileira de Anestesiologia) Cidade - Editora Cientifica Ltda., c/o Dr. Antonio Leite Oliva Filho, Ed., Rua Professor Alfredo Gomes 36, 22251 Rio de Janeiro, Brazil. TEL 021-266-6324. adv.; bk.rev.; charts; illus.; stat.; circ. 4,500. (also avail. in microform from UMI; reprint service avail. from UMI) **Indexed:** Biol.Abstr., Chem.Abstr, Excerp.Med., Ind.Med.
—BLDSC shelfmark: 7843.300000.
Description: Original papers and articles on anaesthesiology.

617.96   BL
▼**REVISTA BRASILEIRA DE ANESTESIOLOGIA - INTERNATIONAL ISSUE.** (Text in English) 1990. a. $20. (Sociedade Brasileira de Anestesiologia) Editora Cientifica Ltda (CIDADE), c/o Dr. Antonio Leite Oliva Filho, Ed., Rua Professor Alfredo Gomes 36, 22251 Rio de Janeiro, Brazil. TEL 021-266-6324.
Description: Selcted articles translated from the previous year's issues.

617.96   CK   ISSN 0120-3347
REVISTA COLOMBIANA DE ANESTESIOLOGIA. 1973. q. $20. Sociedad Colombiana de Anestesiologia y Reanimacion, Apdo. Aereo 11206, Bogota, Colombia. TEL 2-883985. FAX 2-454481. Ed. Julio Enrique Pena. adv.; bk.rev.; circ. 1,000. (back issues avail.) **Indexed:** Hisp.Amer.Per.Ind.

617.96   SP   ISSN 0034-9356
                       CODEN: REANBJ
REVISTA ESPANOLA DE ANESTESIOLOGIA Y REANIMACION. (Text in Spanish; summaries in English) 1953. bi-m. 4400 ptas.($45) to non-members. (Sociedad Espanola de Anestesiologia - Reanimacion y Terapia del Dolor) Ediciones Doyma, S.A., Travesera de Gracia, 17-21, 08021 Barcelona, Spain. TEL 200-07-11. FAX 209-11-36. TELEX 51964 INK-E. Ed. R. Garcia Guasch. adv.: page 145000 ptas.; trim 210 x 280; adv. contact: Marta Cisa. bk.rev.; abstr.; charts; illus.; stat.; circ. 4,222. (reprint service avail. from UMI) **Indexed:** Biol.Abstr., Dent.Ind., Ind.Med., Ind.Med.Esp.
—BLDSC shelfmark: 7853.910000.
Formerly: Revista Espanola de Anestesiologia.
Description: Diffuses information on the clinical and experimental work of Spanish anesthesiologists.

617.96   GW   ISSN 0178-692X
SCHMERZDIAGNOSTIK UND THERAPIE. 1986. irreg., vol.4, 1991. price varies. Verlag Dr. Dieter Winkler, Katharinastr. 37, 4630 Bochum 1, Germany. TEL 0234-17508. Ed. Gholam Sehhati-Chafai. circ. 1,000. **Indexed:** Psychol.Abstr.
Description: Information for medical personnel involved in the diagnosis and therapy of pain.

617.96   US   ISSN 0277-0326
                       CODEN: SEANDW
SEMINARS IN ANESTHESIA. 1982. q. $62 to individuals; institutions $99; foreign $112. W.B. Saunders Co. (Subsidiary of: Harcourt Brace Jovanovich, Inc.), Curtis Center, Independence Square W., Philadelphia, PA 19106. TEL 215-238-7800. (Subscr. to: 6277 Sea Harbor Dr., 4th Fl., Orlando, FL 32891. TEL 800-543-9534) Ed. Dr. Ronald L. Katz. adv.; bibl.; charts; illus. **Indexed:** ASCA, Chem.Abstr., Curr.Cont., Sci.Cit.Ind.
●Also available online.
—BLDSC shelfmark: 8239.447600.

617.96   US   ISSN 8756-8578
TECHNOLOGY FOR ANESTHESIA. m. $90 (Canada $100; elsewhere $120). (Emergency Care Research Institute) E C R I, 5200 Butler Pike, Plymouth Meeting, PA 19462. TEL 215-825-6000. FAX 215-834-1275. Ed. Robert Hochschild.
Former titles: Technology of Anesthesiology; Health Devices Update: Anesthesiology.
Refereed Serial

617.96   US   ISSN 0084-3652
YEAR BOOK OF ANESTHESIA. 1961. a. $57.95. Mosby - Year Book, Inc., Continuity Division, 200 N. LaSalle, Chicago, IL 60601. TEL 312-726-9733. FAX 312-726-6075. TELEX 206155. Ed. Ronald D. Miller. illus. (reprint service avail.)
●Also available online. Vendor(s): BRS.
—BLDSC shelfmark: 9411.612000.

617.96   CC
ZHONGHUA MAZUIXUE ZAZHI/CHINESE JOURNAL OF ANAESTHESIOLOGY. q. $1.30 per no. Guoji Shudian, Qikan Bu, Chegongzhuang Xilu 21, P.O. Box 399, Beijing 100044, People's Republic of China. **Indexed:** Chem.Abstr.

MEDICAL SCIENCES — Cancer

616.99 340   US
A V A ADVISOR. 1980. q. $25 membership; reduced rate for asbestos victims. (Asbestos Victims of America) Publishers Press (Capitola), Box 569, Capitola, CA 95010. TEL 408-476-3646. Ed. H.R. Maurer. adv.; circ. 18,000. (looseleaf format; back issues avail.)
Description: Coverage of medical, legal, and social aspects of asbestos, including worker safety, scientific data, medical treatments, laws governing uses and exposure, legislative developments, and legal remedies.

ACOUSTIC NEUROMA ASSOCIATION NOTES. see *MEDICAL SCIENCES — Otorhinolaryngology*

616.994   PE   ISSN 1013-5545
ACTA CANCEROLOGICA. (Text in Spanish; summaries in English) 1960; resumed 1987. s-a. S/240($15) Peruvian Society of Cancerology, Av. Angamos Este 2520, Lima 34, Peru. Ed. Dr. Juvenal Sanchez. adv.; bibl.; charts; illus.; circ. 500. **Indexed:** Biol.Abstr.
Description: Covers the study and research of cancer.

616.994   IT   ISSN 0393-7542
ACTA ONCOLOGICA. (Consists of two sections published in alternative issues) (Editions in English, Italian) q. L.80000($110) (Italian Society for the Prevention and Diagnosis of Tumors) Piccin Editore, Via Altinate 107, 35100 Padua, Italy. TEL 049-655566. TELEX 432075 PICCIN I. (Co-sponsor: Italian Society for the Treatment of Tumors) Eds. C. Maltoni, L. Caldarola. (reprint service avail. from UMI) **Indexed:** Excerp.Med.

616.994   US   ISSN 0065-230X
RC267   CODEN: ACRSAJ
ADVANCES IN CANCER RESEARCH. 1953. irreg., vol.56, 1991. Academic Press, Inc., 1250 Sixth Ave., San Diego, CA 92101. TEL 619-231-0926. FAX 619-699-6715. Eds. George Klein, Sidney Weinhouse. (reprint service avail. from ISI) **Indexed:** Biol.Abstr., Biotech.Abstr., Chem.Abstr., Dent.Ind., Ind.Med., Ind.Sci.Rev., Ind.Vet., INIS Atomind., Sci.Cit.Ind, Telegen, Vet.Bull.
—BLDSC shelfmark: 0701.000000.
Refereed Serial

616.99   US
ADVANCES IN IMMUNITY AND CANCER THERAPY. 1985. irreg., vol.2, 1986. Springer-Verlag, 175 Fifth Ave., New York, NY 10010. TEL 212-460-1500. (Also Berlin, Heidelberg, Tokyo, Vienna) (reprint service avail. from ISI) **Indexed:** INIS Atomind.

616.99   US
ADVANCES IN VIRAL ONCOLOGY. 1982. irreg., latest vol.8. price varies. Raven Press, 1185 Ave. of the Americas, New York, NY 10036. TEL 212-930-9500. FAX 212-869-3495. Ed. George Klein.

616.99   JA
AICHI CANCER CENTER RESEARCH INSTITUTE. SCIENTIFIC REPORT. (Text in English) 1968. biennial. free. Aichi Cancer Center Research Institute, Kanakoden, Chikusa-ku, Nagoya, 464, Japan. FAX 052-763-5233. Ed. Akio Matsukaga. circ. 1,000.
Formerly: Aichi Cancer Center Research Institute. Annual Report (ISSN 0374-5295)

616.99   CC   ISSN 1000-467X
AIZHENG/CANCER. (Text in Chinese) bi-m. Zhongshan Yike Daxue, Zhongliu Yiyuan - Sun Yat-sen Medical University, Oncology Hospital, No. 651, Dongfeng Donglu, Guangzhou, Guangdong 510060, People's Republic of China. TEL 777136. Ed. Guan Zhongzhen.
—BLDSC shelfmark: 3180.297500.

616.99   US
AMERICAN INSTITUTE FOR CANCER RESEARCH NEWSLETTER. 1983. q. free to qualified personnel. American Institute for Cancer Research (AICR), 1759 R St., N.W., Washington, DC 20009. TEL 202-328-7744. FAX 202-328-7226. Ed. Christine Murray. bk.rev.; bibl.; charts; illus.; stat.; circ. 1,000,000 (controlled). (looseleaf format; back issues avail.)
Description: Covers diet, nutrition, and dietary guidelines for reducing cancer risk.

MEDICAL SCIENCES — CANCER

616.99   US   ISSN 0277-3732
CODEN: AJCODI
AMERICAN JOURNAL OF CLINICAL ONCOLOGY; cancer clinical trials. 1978. bi-m. $124 to individuals; institutions $158. Raven Press, 1185 Ave. of the Americas, New York, NY 10036.
TEL 212-930-9500. FAX 212-869-3495. TELEX 640073. Ed. Dr. Luther W. Brady. adv.; bk.rev.; charts; illus.; index; circ. 2,500. (also avail. in microform from MIM; back issues avail.) **Indexed:** Biol.Abstr., Biotech.Abstr., Chem.Abstr., Curr.Cont., Dent.Ind., Excerp.Med., Ind.Med., Ind.Sci.Rev., INIS Atomind., NRN, Sci.Cit.Ind., Telegen.
—BLDSC shelfmark: 0823.500000.
Formerly: Cancer Clinical Trials (ISSN 0190-1206)
Description: Presents pathologic, surgical, and clinical data related to all aspects of metastatic and neoplastic diseases and localized tumors.
Refereed Serial

AMERICAN JOURNAL OF PEDIATRIC HEMATOLOGY - ONCOLOGY. see MEDICAL SCIENCES — Pediatrics

616.99   UK   ISSN 0959-4973
CODEN: ANTDEV
▼**ANI-CANCER DRUGS;** international journal on anti-cancer agents. 1990. bi-m. £222($399) Rapid Communications of Oxford Ltd., The Old Malthouse, Paradise St., Oxford OX1 1LD, England.
TEL 0865-790447. FAX 0865-244012. Ed. Dr. Mels Sluyser. adv. contact: Nigel Olsen. (reprint service avail.) **Indexed:** Chem.Abstr., Ind.Med., Sci.Cit.Ind.

616.99   NE   ISSN 0923-7534
CODEN: ANONE2
▼**ANNALS OF ONCOLOGY.** 1990. 10/yr. fl.476($270) (European Society for Medical Oncology) Kluwer Academic Publishers, Postbus 17, 3300 AA Dordrecht, Netherlands. TEL 078-334911. FAX 078-334254. TELEX 29245. (Dist. by: Kluwer Academic Publishers Group, P.O. Box 322, 3300 AH Dordrecht, Netherlands; N. America dist. addr.: Box 358, Accord Sta., Hingham, MA 02018-0358. TEL 617-871-6600) Ed. F. Cavalli. (reprint service avail. from SWZ)
—BLDSC shelfmark: 1043.320000.

616.99   SW   ISSN 0348-8799
ANNUAL REPORT ON THE RESULTS OF TREATMENT IN GYNECOLOGICAL CANCER. 1937. triennial. $45. Annual Report, Radiumhemmet, S-104 01 Stockholm, Sweden. TEL 08-328752. Ed. Dr. Folke Pettersson. adv.; charts; circ. 2,000. **Indexed:** Excerp.Med.
—BLDSC shelfmark: 1515.880000.
Formerly (until 1979): Annual Report on the Results of Treatment in Carcinoma of the Uterus, Vagina, and Ovary.

616.994 612.015   UK   ISSN 0266-9536
CODEN: ACDDEA
ANTI-CANCER DRUG DESIGN. 1985. bi-m. £110 (foreign £121). (Cancer Research Campaign) Macmillan Press Ltd., Houndmills, Basingstoke, Hampshire RG21 2XS, England. TEL 0256-29242. FAX 0256-810526. Ad. Bd. index; cum.index. (also avail. in microfilm; back issues avail.) **Indexed:** Chem.Abstr., Curr.Adv.Ecol.Sci., Curr.Cont., Excerp.Med., Ind.Med., Telegen.
—BLDSC shelfmark: 1547.287000.

616.9   US   ISSN 0892-7049
RM282.I44
ANTIBODY, IMMUNOCONJUGATES, AND RADIOPHARMACEUTICALS. q. $129 (foreign $169). Mary Ann Liebert, Inc., 1651 Third Ave., New York, NY 10128. TEL 212-289-2300.
FAX 212-289-4697. Ed. Dr. Stanley E. Order.
—BLDSC shelfmark: 1547.271000.
Description: Contains papers and review articles in the new holistic science that involves the use of antibody and immunoconjugates in the diagnosis and treatment of cancer.
Refereed Serial

616.99   GR   ISSN 0250-7005
CODEN: ANTRD4
ANTICANCER RESEARCH; international journal of cancer research and treatment. (Text and summaries in English) 1981. bi-m. $290 to individuals (outside Europe $300); institutions $530 (outside Europe $560). John G. Delinassios, Ed. & Pub, 5 Argyropoulou St., Kato Patissia, Athens GR-111 45, Greece. TEL 8171209. FAX 2016380. adv.; bk.rev.; index; circ. 1,200. (back issues avail.) **Indexed:** Biol.Abstr., Chem.Abstr., Curr.Adv.Biochem., Curr.Adv.Cell & Devel.Biol., Curr.Adv.Ecol.Sci., Curr.Adv.Genetics & Molec.Biol., Curr.Cont., Excerp.Med., Ind.Med., Ind.Sci.Rev., NRN, Rev.Med.& Vet.Mycol., Sci.Cit.Ind., Telegen.
—BLDSC shelfmark: 1547.290000.

616.994   IT   ISSN 0004-0266
ARCHIVIO ITALIANO DI PATOLOGIA E CLINICA DEI TUMORI. (Text in English and Italian) vol.14, 1971. q. L.6000. Universita degli Studi di Milano, Istituto di Farmacologia, Via Vanvitelli 32, Milan, Italy. charts; illus. **Indexed:** Biol.Abstr., Chem.Abstr., Ind.Med.

616.9   SP
ASOCIACION ESPANOLA CONTRA EL CANCER. MEMORIA TECNICO-ADMINISTRATIVA. 1958. a. free. Asociacion Espanola Contra el Cancer, Amador de los Rios 5, Madrid 4, Spain. FAX 1-3190966. charts; stat.
Formerly: Asociacion Espanola Contra el Cancer. Memoria de la Assemblea General (ISSN 0066-8540)

616.994   NE   ISSN 0304-419X
QD1
B B A - REVIEWS ON CANCER. (Section of: Biochimica et Biophysica Acta (ISSN 0006-3002)) vol.605, 1977. 3/yr. fl.338 (effective 1992). Elsevier Science Publishers B.V., P.O. Box 211, 1000 AE Amsterdam, Netherlands. TEL 020-5803911. FAX 020-5803598. TELEX 18582 ESPA NL. (Subscr. in U.S. and Canada to: Elsevier Science Publishing Co., Inc., Box 882, Madison Sq. Sta., New York, NY 10159. TEL 212-989-5800) Ed.Bd. (also avail. in microform from RPI; reprint service avail. from ISI) **Indexed:** Curr.Adv.Ecol.Sci., Ind.Vet.
Description: Presents critical reviews on new developments in cancer investigation at the biochemical level.
Refereed Serial

616.99   IS
BAMAH; journal for health professionals in the field of cancer. irreg. free. Israel Cancer Association, Revivim 7, P.O. Box 437, Givatayim 51304, Israel.
TEL 03-5717234. FAX 03-5719578. Ed. Miri Ziv.

616.99   NE
BIOSYNTHETIC PRODUCTS FOR CANCER CHEMOTHERAPY. irreg., vol.6, 1989. price varies. Elsevier Science Publishers B.V., Books Division, P.O. Box 211, 1000 AE Amsterdam, Netherlands.
TEL 020-5803911. FAX 020-5803705. TELEX 18582 ESPA NL. (Subscr. in U.S. and Canada to: Elsevier Science Publishing Co., Inc., Box 882, Madison Sq. Sta., New York, NY 10159. TEL 212-989-5800) Ed.Bd. (reprint service avail. from ISI)
Refereed Serial

616.992 574   NE   ISSN 0921-299X
CODEN: BTHREW
BIOTHERAPY; an international journal on biological agents. 1988. q. fl.360($204.50) Kluwer Academic Publishers, Postbus 17, 3300 AA Dordrecht, Netherlands. TEL 078-334911. FAX 078-334254. TELEX 29245. (Dist. by: Kluwer Academic Publishers Group, P.O. Box 322, 3300 AH Dordrecht, Netherlands; N. America dist. addr.: Box 358, Accord Sta., Hingham, MA 02018-0358. TEL 617-871-6600) Ed. Huub Schellekens. (reprint service avail. from SWZ)
—BLDSC shelfmark: 2089.873800.

616.994   NE   ISSN 0167-6806
CODEN: BCTRD6
BREAST CANCER RESEARCH AND TREATMENT. 1981. q. fl.684($388.50) Kluwer Academic Publishers, Postbus 17, 3300 AA Dordrecht, Netherlands.
TEL 078-334911. FAX 078-334254. TELEX 29245. (Dist. by: Kluwer Academic Publishers Group, P.O. Box 322, 3300 AH Dordrecht, Netherlands; N. America dist. addr.: Box 358, Accord Sta., Hingham, MA 02018-0358. TEL 617-871-6600) Ed. William L. McGuire. adv.; bk.rev. (back issues avail.; reprint service avail. from SWZ) **Indexed:** Chem.Abstr., Curr.Adv.Cancer Res., Curr.Adv.Ecol.Sci., Curr.Cont., Excerp.Med., Ind.Med., Ind.Sci.Rev., INIS Atomind., Sci.Cit.Ind.
—BLDSC shelfmark: 2277.494000.
Formerly: Cancer Treatment and Research.

616.99   US
BRISTOL-MEYERS CANCER SYMPOSIA. PROCEEDINGS. 1979. irreg., vol.13, 1991. Academic Press, Inc., 1250 Sixth Ave., San Diego, CA 92101.
TEL 619-231-0926. FAX 619-699-6715. Eds. Stanley T. Cook, Maxwell Gordon. (reprint service avail. from ISI) **Indexed:** Chem.Abstr.

616.992   CN
BRITISH COLUMBIA CANCER RESEARCH CENTRE. ANNUAL REPORT. 1950. a. free. British Columbia Cancer Research Centre, 601 W. 10th Ave., Vancouver, B.C. V5Z 1L3, Canada.
TEL 604-877-6010. FAX 604-872-4596.
(Co-sponsors: Cancer Control Agency of British Columbia; British Columbia Cancer Foundation) Ed. D.S. Catton. circ. 6,000.
Formerly: British Columbia. Cancer Foundation. Annual Report (ISSN 0068-1423)

616.994   UK   ISSN 0007-0920
CODEN: BJCAAI
BRITISH JOURNAL OF CANCER. 1947. m. (2 vols./yr.). £310. (Cancer Research Campaign) Macmillan Press Ltd., Scientific & Medical Division, Houndmills, Basingstoke Hampshire RG2 2XS, England.
TEL 0256 29242. FAX 0256-810526. Ed. Dr. Peter Twentyman. adv.; bk.rev.; illus.; index; circ. 2,000. (also avail. in microform from UMI,PMC; reprint service avail. from UMI) **Indexed:** Abstr.Hyg., Anim.Breed.Abstr., Biol.Abstr., Biotech.Abstr., C.I.S. Abstr., Chem.Abstr., Curr.Adv.Biochem., Curr.Adv.Cell & Devel.Biol., Curr.Adv.Ecol.Sci., Curr.Adv.Genetics & Molec.Biol., Curr.Cont., Dairy Sci.Abstr., Dent.Ind., Dok.Arbeitsmed., Excerp.Med., Ind.Med., Ind.Sci.Rev., Ind.Vet., INIS Atomind., Nutr.Abstr., Rev.Plant Path., Risk Abstr., Sci.Cit.Ind., Small Anim.Abstr., Telegen, Trop.Dis.Bull., Vet.Bull.
Description: Clinical and experimental aspects of cancer research.

616.994   FR   ISSN 0007-4551
CODEN: BUCABS
BULLETIN DU CANCER. (Section avail.: Bulletin du Cancer - Radiotherapie (ISSN 0924-4212)) (Text and summaries in English, French) 1908. 12/yr. 1100 F.($228) (foreign 1,220 F.)(effective 1992). (Societe Francaise du Cancer) Editions Scientifiques Elsevier, 29, rue Buffon, 75005 Paris, France.
TEL 47-07-11-22. FAX 43-36-80-93. TELEX 202 400 F. (Subscr. in U.S. and Canada to: Elsevier Science Publishing Co., Inc., Box 882, Madison Sq. Sta., New York, NY 10159. TEL 212-989-5800) Ed.Bd. adv.; bk.rev.; illus.; index; circ. 3,500. (also avail. in microform; reprint service avail. from ISI) **Indexed:** Biol.Abstr., Chem.Abstr., Curr.Adv.Cancer Res., Curr.Adv.Ecol.Sci., Curr.Cont., Dent.Ind., Excerp.Med., Ind.Med., Ind.Sci.Rev., Ind.Vet., INIS Atomind., Nutr.Abstr., Sci.Cit.Ind., Vet.Bull.
—BLDSC shelfmark: 2837.970000.
Formerly: Association Francaise pour l'Etude du Cancer. Bulletin (ISSN 0004-5497)
Description: Publishes original articles on clinical oncology, basic cancer research and related fields. Includes review articles, editorials, brief notes, letters to the editor.
Refereed Serial

MEDICAL SCIENCES — CANCER

616.99 615.84   FR   ISSN 0924-4212
CODEN: BCRAEE
▼**BULLETIN DU CANCER - RADIOTHERAPIE.** (Section of: Bulletin de Cancer (ISSN 0007-4551)) (Text in French; summaries in English, French) 1990. 4/yr. 490 F. (foreign 550 F.)(effective 1992). (Societe Francaise de Radiotherapie Oncologique) Editions Scientifiques Elsevier, 29, rue Buffon, 75005 Paris, France. TEL 47-07-11-22. FAX 43-36-80-93. TELEX 202 400 F. (Subscr. in U.S. and Canada to: Elsevier Science Publishing Co., Inc., Box 882, Madison Sq. Sta., New York, NY 10159. TEL 212-989-5800) Ed.Bd. circ. 3,500. Indexed: Biol.Abstr., Curr.Cont., Excerp.Med., Ind.Med, Sci.Cit.Ind.
—BLDSC shelfmark: 2837.975000.
Description: Provides a forum within the field of oncology for the dissemination of knowledge in all areas relating to therapeutic radiation oncology: technology, radiophysics, radiobiology and clinical radiotherapy.
Refereed Serial

C A SELECTS. ANTITUMOR AGENTS. see *MEDICAL SCIENCES — Abstracting, Bibliographies, Statistics*

C A SELECTS. NUTRITIONAL ASPECTS OF CANCER. see *MEDICAL SCIENCES — Abstracting, Bibliographies, Statistics*

616.994   US   ISSN 0007-9235
RC261   CODEN: CAMCAM
CA - A CANCER JOURNAL FOR CLINICIANS. 1950. bi-m. free to qualified personnel. (American Cancer Society, Inc.) J.B. Lippincott Co. (New York), 1180 Ave. of the Americas, 6th Fl., New York, NY 10036. TEL 212-840-7760. FAX 212-840-7813. Ed. Dr. Gerard P. Murphy. adv.; bibl.; charts; illus.; index, cum.index: 1971-80; circ. 400,000. (also avail. in microform from UMI; reprint service avail. from UMI) Indexed: Biol.Abstr., CINAHL, Curr.Cont., Excerp.Med., Ind.Med., INIS Atomind.
—BLDSC shelfmark: 2943.180000.
Refereed Serial

CANADIAN ONCOLOGY NURSING JOURNAL/REVUE CANADIENNE DE NURSING ONCOLOGIQUE. see *MEDICAL SCIENCES — Nurses And Nursing*

616.994   US   ISSN 0008-543X
RC261   CODEN: CANCAR
CANCER. 1948. s-m. $95 to individuals; institutions $150. (American Cancer Society, Inc.) J.B. Lippincott Co., E. Washington Sq., Philadelphia, PA 19105. TEL 215-238-4200. Ed. Dr. Jonathan E. Rhoads. adv.; illus.; index; circ. 20,005. (also avail. in microform from UMI) Indexed: Biol.Abstr., Biotech.Abstr., Chem.Abstr., Curr.Adv.Cancer Res., Curr.Adv.Ecol.Sci., Curr.Adv.Genetics & Molec.Biol., Curr.Cont., Dent.Ind, Dok.Arbeitsmed., Excerp.Med., Helminthol.Abstr., Hosp.Lit.Ind., Ind.Med., Ind.Sci.Rev., Ind.Vet., INIS Atomind., NRR, Risk Abstr., Sci.Cit.Ind., Small Anim.Abstr., SSCI, Telegen, Vet.Bull.
●Also available on CD-ROM.
—BLDSC shelfmark: 3046.450000.
Refereed Serial

616.99   US
CANCER AND METASTASIS REVIEWS. 1981. q. fl.210($110) to individuals; to institutions fl.332 ($169). Kluwer Academic Publishers, 101 Philip Dr., Norwell, MA 02061. TEL 617-871-6600. FAX 617-871-6528. TELEX 200190. (Subscr. to: Box 358, Accord Sta., Hingham, MA 02018-0358) Ed. Isaiah J. Fidler, D.V.M. adv.; bk.rev. (back issues avail.; reprint service avail. from SWZ,UMI) Indexed: Chem.Abstr, Curr.Adv.Ecol.Sci., Curr.Adv.Genetics & Molec.Biol., Curr.Cont, Ind.Med., Ind.Sci.Rev., INIS Atomind., Sci.Cit.Ind.
Former titles: Cancer Metastasis Reviews (ISSN 0167-7659); Cancer Metastasis.

616.994   US   ISSN 0305-7232
RC261.A1   CODEN: CABCD4
CANCER BIOCHEMISTRY BIOPHYSICS. 1975. 4/yr. (in 1 vol., 4 nos./vol.) $232. Gordon and Breach Science Publishers, 270 Eighth Ave., New York, NY 10011. TEL 212-206-8900. FAX 212-645-2459. TELEX 236735 GOPUB UR. (Subscr. to: Box 786, Cooper Sta., New York, NY 10276. TEL 800-545-8398; UK subscr. to: P.O. Box 90, Reading, Berkshire RG1 8JL, England. TEL 0734-560-080) Ed. Harry Darrow Brown. adv. (also avail. in microform from MIM) Indexed: Biol.Abstr., Biotech.Abstr., Chem.Abstr., Curr.Adv.Ecol.Sci., Curr.Cont., Dairy Sci.Abstr., Excerp.Med., Helminthol.Abstr., Ind.Med., Ind.Sci.Rev., Sci.Cit.Ind.
—BLDSC shelfmark: 3046.456000.
Refereed Serial

616.99   UK   ISSN 0960-9768
▼**CANCER CARE.** 1992. q. £49($90) Churchill Livingstone Medical Journals, Robert Stevenson House, 1-3 Baxter's Pl., Leith Walk, Edinburgh EH1 3AF, Scotland. TEL 031-556-2424. FAX 031-558-1278. TELEX 727511. (Subscr. to: Longman Group, Journals Subscr. Dept., P.O. Box 77, Fourth Ave., Harlow, Essex CM19 5AA, England; U.S. subscr. to: Churchill Livingstone, 650 Ave. of the Americas, New York, NY 10011. TEL 212-206-5000) Eds. Ann Faulkner, Irene Scott. bk.rev.; bibl.
—BLDSC shelfmark: 4954.842800.
Description: Explores cancer care in hospitals, homes and hospices.

616.99   UK   ISSN 0957-5243
CODEN: CCCNEN
▼**CANCER CAUSES & CONTROL;** an international journal of studies of cancer in human populations. 1990. bi-m. £222. Rapid Communications of Oxford Ltd., The Old Malthouse, Paradise St., Oxford OX1 1LD, England. TEL 0865-790447. FAX 0865-244012. Ed. Brian MacMahon. adv. contact: Steve Harper. Indexed: Curr.Cont., Ind.Med.
—BLDSC shelfmark: 3046.464150.

616.99   US   ISSN 1042-2196
RC261.A1   CODEN: CCELER
CANCER CELLS; a monthly review. 1989. m. $75 to individuals; institutions $200. Cold Spring Harbor Laboratory Press, Publications Department, Box 100, Cold Spring Harbor, NY 11724. TEL 800-843-4388. FAX 516-349-1946. Ed. P. Kiberstis. (reprint service avail.)
—BLDSC shelfmark: 3046.464230.
Description: Surveys new ideas and experimental advances that shed light on the genesis and growth of neoplartic cells, and the application of these insights to the prevention, diagnosis and treatment of cancer.

616.99   NE
CANCER CHEMOTHERAPY AND BIOLOGICAL RESPONSE MODIFIERS. 1979. a. price varies. Elsevier Science Publishers B.V., Books Division, P.O. Box 211, 1000 AE Amsterdam, Netherlands. TEL 020-5803911. FAX 020-5803705. TELEX 18582 ESPA NL. (Subscr. in U.S. and Canada to: Elsevier Science Publishing Co., Inc., Box 882, Madison Sq. Sta., New York, NY 10159. TEL 212-989-5800) Ed. H. M. Pinedo. (back issues avail.)
Former titles (until vol.9, 1987): Cancer Chemotherapy Annual; (until vol.2, 1980): Cancer Chemotherapy.
Refereed Serial

616.99   GW   ISSN 0344-5704
CODEN: CCPHDZ
CANCER CHEMOTHERAPY AND PHARMACOLOGY. 1978. 12/yr. (in 2 vols., 6 nos./vol.). DM.1318($724) Springer-Verlag, Heidelberger Platz 3, D-1000 Berlin 33, Germany. TEL 030-8207-1. (Also Heidelberg, Tokyo, Vienna, and New York) Eds. A.H. Calvert, S.K. Carter. adv.; index. (also avail. in microform from UMI; reprint service avail. from ISI) Indexed: Biotech.Abstr., Chem.Abstr., Curr.Adv.Cancer Res., Curr.Adv.Ecol.Sci., Curr.Cont., Dent.Ind., Excerp.Med., Ind.Med., Ind.Sci.Rev., Ind.Vet., INIS Atomind., Sci.Cit.Ind.
—BLDSC shelfmark: 3046.467000.

616   US   ISSN 0191-3794
CANCER CONTROL JOURNAL. 1973. irreg. membership. Cancer Control Society, Cancer Book House, 2043 N. Berendo, Los Angeles, CA 90027. TEL 213-663-7801. Ed. Lorraine Rosenthal. bk.rev.; circ. 10,000. (back issues avail.)
—BLDSC shelfmark: 3046.472300.

616.99   US
▼**CANCER EPIDEMIOLOGY, BIOMARKERS & PREVENTION.** 1991. bi-m. American Association for Cancer Research, Inc., Public Ledger Bldg., 620 Chestnut St., Ste. 816, Philadelphia, PA 19106-3483. Ed. Pelayo Correa. adv.: B&W page $450, color page $1050; trim 8 3/8 x 10 7/8. circ. 800.
Description: Contains research on the causes and prevention of cancer in humans.

616.994   US   ISSN 0069-0147
CANCER FACTS AND FIGURES. 1951. a. free. American Cancer Society, Inc., 1599 Clifton Rd., N.E., Atlanta, GA 30329-4251. TEL 404-329-7911. FAX 404-325-2217. circ. 500,000. Indexed: SRI.

616.99   AT   ISSN 0311-306X
CANCER FORUM. 1974. 3/yr. free. Australian Cancer Society, Inc., P.O. Box 4708, G.P.O., Sydney, N.S.W. 2000, Australia. FAX 02-261-4123. Ed. L.A. Wright. adv.; bk.rev.; abstr.; circ. 3,000. Indexed: Biol.Abstr.
—BLDSC shelfmark: 3046.478200.

616.99   US   ISSN 0165-4608
RC268.4   CODEN: CGCYDF
CANCER GENETICS & CYTOGENETICS. 1979. 14/yr.(in 7 vols.; 2 nos./vol.). $1120 to institutions (foreign $1195)(effective 1992). Elsevier Science Publishing Co., Inc. (New York), 655 Ave. of the Americas, New York, NY 10010. TEL 212-989-5800. FAX 212-633-3965. TELEX 420643 AEP UI. Eds. A.A. Sandberg, H. van den Berghe. (also avail. in microform from RPI) Indexed: Biol.Abstr., Chem.Abstr., Curr.Adv.Cancer Res., Curr.Adv.Ecol.Sci., Curr.Adv.Genetics & Molec.Biol., Curr.Cont., Dent.Ind., Dok.Arbeitsmed., Excerp.Med., Ind.Med., Ind.Sci.Rev., Sci.Cit.Ind.
—BLDSC shelfmark: 3046.478400.
Description: Covers the cellular and molecular aspects of cancer research.
Refereed Serial

615 619   GW   ISSN 0340-7004
CODEN: CIIMDN
CANCER IMMUNOLOGY, IMMUNOTHERAPY; other biological response modifications. 1976. 12/yr. DM.1396($831) (effective 1992). Springer-Verlag, Heidelberger Platz 3, D-1000 Berlin 33, Germany. TEL 030-8207-1. (Also Heidelberg, Tokyo, Vienna, and New York) Ed. R.W. Baldwin. adv. (also avail. in microfiche from UMI; reprint service avail. from ISI) Indexed: Chem.Abstr., Curr.Adv.Cancer Res., Curr.Adv.Ecol.Sci., Curr.Cont., Excerp.Med., Helminthol.Abstr., Ind.Med., Ind.Sci.Rev., INIS Atomind., Sci.Cit.Ind., Telegen.
—BLDSC shelfmark: 3046.478600.

616.9   CN   ISSN 0315-9884
CANCER IN ONTARIO. 1946. a. free. Ontario Cancer Treatment and Research Foundation, 7 Overlea Blvd., Toronto, Ont. M4H 1A8, Canada. TEL 416-423-4240. Ed. J.O. Godden. circ. 20,000.
—BLDSC shelfmark: 3046.492000.
Formerly: Ontario Cancer Treatment and Research Foundation. Annual Report (ISSN 0078-4699)

616.9   PR   ISSN 0896-9035
CANCER IN PUERTO RICO. (Text in English and Spanish) 1950. a. free. (Department of Health, Cancer Control Program, NCI-BIO Branch) Cancer Registry of Puerto Rico, Department of Health, P.O. Box 9342, Santurce, PR 00657. TEL 809-764-7453. Ed. Dr. Isidro Martinez. adv.; bk.rev.; circ. 1,000. Indexed: Excerp.Med.

616.9   SW   ISSN 0069-0155
CANCER INCIDENCE IN SWEDEN. 1960. a. (Swedish Cancer Registry) Allmaenna Foerlaget, 106 47 Stockholm, Sweden. TEL 08-739-9690. FAX 08-739-9548. circ. 2,000.

616.994   JA
CANCER INSTITUTE SCIENTIFIC REPORT. 1976. a. free. Japanese Foundation for Cancer Research, Cancer Institute, 1-37-1 Kami-Ikebukuro, Toshima-ku, Tokyo 170, Japan. Ed. Dr. Tadashi Utakoji. circ. 1,500.

MEDICAL SCIENCES — CANCER

616.99　　　　　　US　　ISSN 0735-7907
RC261.A1　　　　　　　　CODEN: CINVD7
CANCER INVESTIGATION. 1983. 6/yr. $65 to individuals; institutions $399. (Inter-American Society for Chemotherapy, Cancer Section) Marcel Dekker Journals, 270 Madison Ave., New York, NY 10016. TEL 212-696-9000. FAX 212-685-4540. TELEX 421419. (Subscr. to: Box 10018, Church St. Sta., New York, NY 10049) (Co-sponsor: Chemotherapy Foundation) Ed. Y. Hirshaut. adv.; bk.rev.; charts; illus.; index. (also avail. in microform from RPI) **Indexed:** Biol.Abstr, Biol.Dig., Chem.Abstr., Curr.Adv.Ecol.Sci., Curr.Cont., Dok.Arbeitsmed., Excerp.Med., Ind.Med., Ind.Sci.Rev., NRN, Sci.Cit.Ind., Telegen.
—BLDSC shelfmark: 3046.479500.
Refereed Serial

616.994　　　　　　US　　ISSN 0096-3917
CANCER LETTER. (Includes monthly supplement: Cancer Economics) 1974. 48/yr. $215 (foreign $240). Cancer Letter Inc., Box 15189, Washington, DC 20003. TEL 202-543-7665. Ed. Kirsten B. Goldberg. bk.rev. **Indexed:** Curr.Adv.Biochem., Curr.Adv.Cancer Res., Curr.Adv.Cell & Devel.Biol.

616.994　　　　　IE　　ISSN 0304-3835
RC261.A1　　　　　　　CODEN: CALEDQ
CANCER LETTERS; an international journal providing a forum for original and pertinent contributions in cancer research. 1975. 27/yr.(in 9 vols.); 3 nos./vol.). $1458 (effective 1992). Elsevier Scientific Publishers Ireland Ltd., P.O. Box 85, Limerick, Ireland. TEL 061-61944. FAX 061-62144. TELEX 72191 ENH EI. (Subscr. in U.S. and Canada to: Elsevier Science Publishing Co., Inc., Box 882, Madison Sq. Sta., New York, NY 10159. TEL 212-989-5800) Ed.Bd. adv.; charts; illus.; index. (also avail. in microform from RPI; reprint service avail. from SWZ) **Indexed:** Biol.Abstr., Chem.Abstr., Curr.Adv.Biochem., Curr.Adv.Ecol.Sci., Curr.Cont., Dent.Ind., Excerp.Med., Ind.Med., Ind.Sci.Rev., Ind.Vet., INIS Atomind., NRN, Risk Abstr., Sci.Cit.Ind., Small Anim.Abstr., Telegen, Vet.Bull.
—BLDSC shelfmark: 3046.485000.
Description: Covers all areas of cancer research, including: molecular biology of cancer, oncogenes, carcinogenesis, hormones and cancer, viral oncology, chemotherapy, epidemiology, biology of cancer and metastasis.
Refereed Serial

616.994　　　　US　　ISSN 0008-5464
RC261　　　　　　　　CODEN: CANEAX
CANCER NEWS. 1947. 3/yr. free to qualified personnel. American Cancer Society, Inc., 1599 Clifton Rd., N.E., Atlanta, GA 30329. TEL 404-329-7936. FAX 404-325-2217. Ed. Jerie Jordan. bk.rev.; illus.; circ. 240,000. **Indexed:** Excerp.Med., Hlth.Ind.

CANCER NURSING; an international journal for cancer care. see MEDICAL SCIENCES — Nurses And Nursing

CANCER NURSING NEWS. see MEDICAL SCIENCES — Nurses And Nursing

616.99　　　　　US　　ISSN 1043-8491
RC268
▼**CANCER PREVENTION**; an international journal. 1990. q. $60 to individuals; institutions $95. Williams & Wilkins, 428 E. Preston St., Baltimore, MD 21202. TEL 301-528-4000. FAX 301-528-4321. Eds. Dr. Daniel W. Nixon, Dr. Myron Winick. circ. 500.
Description: Discusses malignant disease care management strategies, for oncologists, primary care physicians, nutritionists, epidemiologists, and biomedical researchers.
Refereed Serial

616.994　　　　　US　　ISSN 0008-5472
RC261　　　　　　　　CODEN: CNREA8
CANCER RESEARCH. 1941. m. $210. (American Association for Cancer Research) Waverly Press, Inc. (Subsidiary of: Williams & Wilkins), 428 E. Preston St., Baltimore, MD 21202. TEL 301-528-4000. Ed. Dr. Peter N. Magee. adv.; abstr.; bibl.; charts; illus.; index; circ. 7,000. (also avail. in microfilm from PMC) **Indexed:** ABC, Abstr.Hyg., Anim.Breed.Abstr., Biol.Abstr., Biotech.Abstr., Chem.Abstr., Curr.Adv.Biochem., Curr.Adv.Cancer Res., Curr.Adv.Cell & Devel.Biol., Curr.Adv.Ecol.Sci., Curr.Adv.Genetics & Molec.Biol., Curr.Biotech.Abstr., Curr.Cont., Dairy Sci.Abstr., Dent.Ind., Dok.Arbeitsmed., Excerp.Med., Helminthol.Abstr., I.P.A., Ind.Med., Ind.Sci.Rev., Ind.Vet., INIS Atomind., Lab.Haz.Bull., Maize Abstr., NRN, Nutr.Abstr., Pig News & Info., Poult.Abstr., Rev.Plant Path., Risk Abstr., Sci.Cit.Ind., Small Anim.Abstr., Telegen, Trop.Dis.Bull., Vet.Bull.
—BLDSC shelfmark: 3046.500000.
Refereed Serial

616.994　　　　　UK　　ISSN 0365-9623
RC261
CANCER RESEARCH CAMPAIGN. ANNUAL REPORT. 1924. a. free to medical & scientific institutions. Cancer Research Campaign, 2 Carlton House Terrace, London SW1Y 5AR, England. circ. controlled.

616.99　　　　　US
CANCER REVIEW.* 1980. 3/yr. (Cancer Center at Wadley) Wadley Institute of Molecular Medicine, Box 35988, 9000 Harry Hines, Dallas, TX 75235. TEL 214-351-8111. Ed. Christine Donovan. illus.; circ. 50,000.
Formerly: Quest (Dallas).

616.99　　　　　US　　ISSN 0261-2429
　　　　　　　　　　　　CODEN: CASUD7
CANCER SURVEYS; advances and prospects in clinical, epidemiological, and laboratory oncology. 1982. q. $162. Cold Spring Harbor Laboratory Press, Publications Department, Box 100, Cold Spring Harbor, NY 11724. TEL 800-843-4388. FAX 516-349-1946. Ed. L.M. Franks. (also avail. in microform from UMI) **Indexed:** Abstr.Hyg., Curr.Adv.Ecol.Sci., Curr.Cont., Excerp.Med., Ind.Sci.Rev., Ind.Vet., Poult.Abstr., Sci.Cit.Ind., Small Anim.Abstr., Telegen, Vet.Bull.
—BLDSC shelfmark: 3046.610000.
Description: Provides a comprehensive state and future developments in well-defined areas in occology. Each issues deals with a specific topic and has guest editors with a special knowledge of the subject.

616.99　　　　　US　　ISSN 0896-5080
RC261.A1　　　　　　　CODEN: CTCOE9
CANCER THERAPY AND CONTROL. 4/yr. (in 1 vol., 4 nos./vol.). $93. Harwood Academic Publishers, 270 Eighth Ave., New York, NY 10011. TEL 212-206-8900. FAX 212-645-2459. TELEX 236735 GOPUB UR. (Subscr. to: Box 786, Cooper Sta., New York, NY 10276. TEL 800-545-8398; UK subscr. to: P.O. Box 90, Reading, Berkshire RG1 8JL, England. TEL 0734-560-080) Ed. Samuel Gross. (also avail. in microform)
—BLDSC shelfmark: 3046.620300.

616.99　　　　　US
▼**CANCER THERAPY REPORTS.** 1991. bi-m. $75 to individuals; institutions $125. Williams & Wilkins, 428 E. Preston St., Baltimore, MD 21202. TEL 301-528-4000. FAX 301-528-4321. Ed. Dr. Joseph Aisner.
Description: For medical oncologists, hematologists, and radiation therapists. Provides early reports of clinical and preclinical trials covering all aspects of cancer treatment.

616.99　　　　　NE　　ISSN 0924-6533
CANCER THERAPY UPDATE. (Text in English) vol.10, 1990. 6/yr. fl.125($62.50) Kluwer Academic Publishers, Postbus 17, 3300 AA Dordrecht, Netherlands. TEL 078-334911. FAX 078-334254. TELEX 29245. (Dist. by: Kluwer Academic Publishers Group, P.O. Box 322, 3300 AH Dordrecht, Netherlands; N. America dist. addr.: Box 358, Accord Sta., Hingham, MA 02018-0358. TEL 617-871-6600) Eds. F.M. Muggia, K. Norris, Jr.

616.994　　　　　UK　　ISSN 0305-7372
　　　　　　　　　　　　CODEN: CTREDJ
CANCER TREATMENT REVIEWS. 1974. 4/yr. $119. Academic Press Ltd., 24-28 Oval Rd., London NW1 7DX, England. TEL 071-267-4466. FAX 071-482-2293. TELEX 25775 ACPRES G. Ed. K. Hellmann. adv.; illus.; index. **Indexed:** Biol.Abstr., Curr.Cont., Dent.Ind., Excerp.Med., Ind.Med., Ind.Sci.Rev., Sci.Cit.Ind.
—BLDSC shelfmark: 3046.630000.
Description: Devoted to important advances in the field of cancer treatment for oncologists and physicians.

616.994　　　　　US　　ISSN 0891-0766
CANCER VICTORS JOURNAL. 1964. q. $20 membership. International Association of Cancer Victors and Friends, Inc., 7740 W. Manchester Ave., Ste. 110, Playa del Rey, CA 90293. TEL 213-822-5032. FAX 213-822-5132. Ed. Ann Cinquina. adv.; bk.rev.; film rev.; illus.; stat.; circ. 5,000.
Formerly: Cancer News Journal (ISSN 0099-2372)

616.994　　　　　IT　　ISSN 0008-5480
CANCRO. (Summaries in English) vol.23, 1970. bi-m. L.4000. Istituto di Oncologia, Via Cavour 31, 10123 Turin, Italy. adv.; bk.rev.; charts; illus. **Indexed:** Biol.Abstr., Chem.Abstr., Dent.Ind., Ind.Med., INIS Atomind.

CANDLELIGHTERS CHILDHOOD CANCER FOUNDATION PROGRESS REPORTS. see CHILDREN AND YOUTH — For

618.92 616.99　　　　US
CANDLELIGHTERS CHILDHOOD CANCER FOUNDATION QUARTERLY NEWSLETTER. 1970. q. free. Candlelighters Childhood Cancer Foundation, 1312 18th St., N.W., Ste. 200, Washington, DC 20036-1808. TEL 202-659-5136. bk.rev.; circ. 30,000. **Indexed:** Rehabil.Lit.
Formerly: Candlelighters Foundation Quarterly Newsletter.

616.99 649
CANDLELIGHTERS CHILDHOOD CANCER FOUNDATION YOUTH NEWSLETTER. 1979. q. free. Candlelighters Childhood Cancer Foundation, 1312 18th St., N.W., Ste. 200, Washington, DC 20036-1808. TEL 202-659-5136. circ. 12,000.
Formerly: Candlelighters Foundation Youth Newsletter.

616　　　　　　UK　　ISSN 0143-3334
RC268.5　　　　　　　CODEN: CRNGDP
CARCINOGENESIS. 1980. m. $170 to individuals; institutions $460 (effective 1992). I R L Press Ltd., Pinkhill House, Southfield Road, Eynsham, Oxford OX8 1JJ, England. TEL 0865-882283. FAX 0865-882890. TELEX 837330-OXPRES-G. (U.S. subscr. to: I R L Press, Box Q, McLean, VA 22101. TEL 703-356-4301) Ed.Bd. adv.; bk.rev.; illus.; index. (back issues avail.; reprint service avail. from SWZ) **Indexed:** Curr.Adv.Cancer Res., Curr.Adv.Cell & Devel.Biol., Curr.Adv.Ecol.Sci., Curr.Adv.Genetics & Molec.Biol., Curr.Cont., Excerp.Med., Ind.Med., INIS Atomind., Sci.Cit.Ind.
—BLDSC shelfmark: 3051.007000.
Description: Multi-disciplinary research journal in the areas of viral, physical and chemical carcinogenesis and mutagenesis.

616　　　　　US　　ISSN 0147-4006
RC268.5　　　　　　　CODEN: CCSUDL
CARCINOGENESIS; a comprehensive survey. 1976. irreg., latest vol.11. price varies. Raven Press, 1185 Ave. of the Americas, New York, NY 10036. TEL 212-930-9500. FAX 212-869-3495. TELEX 640073. **Indexed:** Biol.Abstr., Chem.Abstr., Dairy Sci.Abstr., Dent.Ind., Dok.Arbeitsmed., Ind.Med., Rev.Plant Path., Risk Abstr., Sci.Cit.Ind.
—BLDSC shelfmark: 3051.005000.
Refereed Serial

CELL CONTACT PHENOMENA. see BIOLOGY — Cytology And Histology

M

MEDICAL SCIENCES — CANCER

616.99   US
CENTER NEWS. 1975. bi-m. Memorial Sloan-Kettering Cancer Center, Department of Public Affairs, 1275 York Ave., New York, NY 10021. TEL 212-639-3573. FAX 212-639-3576. Ed. Judith Friedman. circ. 250,000.
— Description: Lay language coverage of treatment advances, basic and clinical research, and other programs and activities at Memorial Sloan-Kettering Cancer Center.

616.99   CC   ISSN 1000-9604
CHINESE JOURNAL OF CANCER RESEARCH/ZHONGGUO AIZHENG YANJIU. (Text in English) 1989. q. Beijing Institute for Cancer Research, Da-Hong-Luo-Chang Street, Western District, Beijing, People's Republic of China. (Co-sponsor: China Anti-Cancer Association) Ed. Ling Qibo.
—BLDSC shelfmark: 3180.297700.
Refereed Serial

616   US
CHOICE (CHULA VISTA). 1975. 4/yr. $16. Committee for Freedom of Choice in Medicine, Inc., c/o American Biologics, 1180 Walnut St., Chula Vista, CA 91911. TEL 619-429-8200. FAX 619-429-8004. Ed. Michael L. Culbert. adv.; bk.rev.; circ. 10,000.
— Description: Devoted to news about medicine, medical politics, and "alternative" therapies.

616.99   UK   ISSN 0262-0898
CODEN: CEXMD2
CLINICAL AND EXPERIMENTAL METASTASIS. 1982. bi-m. £198($357) Rapid Communications of Oxford Ltd., The Old Malthouse, Paradise St., Oxford OX1 1LD, England. TEL 0865-790447. FAX 0865-244012. Ed. K. Hellmann. adv.; bk.rev.; index. Indexed: Chem.Abstr, Curr.Adv.Ecol.Sci., Curr.Cont., Excerp.Med., Ind.Med., Ind.Sci.Rev., Sci.Cit.Ind.
—BLDSC shelfmark: 3286.251400.
— Description: Focuses on the crucial process of dissemination and metastasis formation.

616.99   US   ISSN 0164-985X
CLINICAL CANCER LETTER. (Includes monthly supplement: Clinical Trials) 1978. m. $60 (foreign $72). Cancer Letter Inc., Box 15189, Washington, DC 20003. TEL 202-543-7665. Ed. Kirsten B. Goldberg.

616.99   UK   ISSN 0954-7495
CLINICAL CANCER MONOGRAPHS. 1989. Macmillan Press Ltd., Houndmills, Basingstoke, Hampshire RG2 2XS, England. (U.S. addr.: Stockton Press, 15 E. 26th St., New York, NY 10010) Ed. John Fielding.
—BLDSC shelfmark: 3286.264700.

616.99   US   ISSN 0886-7186
CLINICAL ONCOLOGY ALERT. 1986. m. $95. American Health Consultants, Inc., Six Piedmont Center, Ste. 400, 3525 Piedmont Rd., N.E., Atlanta, GA 30305. TEL 404-262-7436. FAX 800-284-3291. (Subscr. to: Department L100, Box 740056, Atlanta, GA 30374-9822. TEL 800-688-2421) Ed. Dr. Dan L. Longo. index; circ. 1,800. (also avail. in audio cassette; reprint service avail.)
Refereed Serial

CLINICAL RADIOLOGY. see *MEDICAL SCIENCES — Radiology And Nuclear Medicine*

616.99   US
▼**CONTEMPORARY ONCOLOGY.** 1991. 10/yr. $49. Medical Economics Publishing Co., 5 Paragon Dr., Montvale, NJ 07645. TEL 201-358-7200. FAX 201-573-8979. Ed. Judith M. Orvos. adv.: B&W page $1890, color page $3130; trim 7 7/8 x 10 3/4. circ. 22,944.
— Description: Contains reviews of the latest procedures, treatment and research.

616.99   US   ISSN 1043-8637
RC261.A1
COPING; living with cancer. 1986. q. $17. Media America, 2019 N. Carothers, Franklin, TN 37064. TEL 615-790-2400. FAX 615-791-4719. Ed. Randy O'Brien. adv.; bk.rev.; circ. 50,000. (back issues avail.)
— Description: Offers feature articles, news reports, profiles and current trend information on oncology prevention, research and issues for people living with cancer.

616.99   US   ISSN 0893-9675
CODEN: CRONEI
CRITICAL REVIEWS IN ONCOGENESIS. 1989. q. $79.95 to individuals; institutions $165. C R C Press, Inc., 2000 Corporate Blvd., N.W., Boca Raton, FL 33431. TEL 407-994-0555. FAX 407-998-9784. Eds. Enrique Pimentel, Manuel Perucho.
—BLDSC shelfmark: 3487.478900.

616.99 616.15   NE   ISSN 1040-8428
RC254.A1
CRITICAL REVIEWS IN ONCOLOGY - HEMATOLOGY. (Text in English) 1981. 6/yr. (in 2 vols., 3 nos./vol.). fl.782 (effective 1992). Elsevier Science Publishers B.V., P.O. Box 211, 1000 AE Amsterdam, Netherlands. TEL 020-5803911. FAX 020-5803598. TELEX 18582 ESPA NL. (Subscr. in U.S. and Canada to: Elsevier Science Publishing Co., Inc., Box 882, Madison Sq. Sta., New York, NY 10159. TEL 212-989-5800) Ed. Stephen Davis. Indexed: ASCA, Excerp.Med., Ind.Sci.Rev., Telegen.
—BLDSC shelfmark: 3487.479000.
Formerly: C R C Critical Reviews in Oncology - Hematology (ISSN 0737-9587)
— Description: Publishes scholarly, critical reviews in the fields of oncology and hematology.
Refereed Serial

CURRENT ADVANCES IN CANCER RESEARCH. see *MEDICAL SCIENCES — Abstracting, Bibliographies, Statistics*

CURRENT OPINION IN ONCOLOGY. see *MEDICAL SCIENCES — Abstracting, Bibliographies, Statistics*

616.99   US   ISSN 0147-0272
CODEN: CPRCDJ
CURRENT PROBLEMS IN CANCER. Short title: C P Ca. 1976. bi-m. $62 to individuals; institutions $87; students $39; (foreign $82; $107; $59). Mosby - Year Book, Inc. (Subsidiary of: Times Mirror Company), 11830 Westline Industrial Dr., St. Louis, MO 63146. Ed. Robert Ozols. index; circ. 1,928. (also avail. in microform from UMI; reprint service avail. from UMI) Indexed: Biol.Abstr., Curr.Cont., Dent.Ind., Dok.Arbeitsmed., Ind.Med., INIS Atomind.
—BLDSC shelfmark: 3501.345000.
— Description: A fully referenced monographic journal with information from recognized experts on practical clinical care.

616.99   US
CURRENT TREATMENT OF CANCER. 1986. irreg. price varies. Springer-Verlag, 175 Fifth Ave., New York, NY 10010. TEL 212-460-1500. (Also Berlin, Heidelberg, Tokyo, Vienna) (reprint service avail. from ISI)

362.1   US   ISSN 0095-6775
RC267
DAMON RUNYON - WALTER WINCHELL CANCER RESEARCH FUND. ANNUAL REPORT. 1973. a. free. Damon Runyon Walter Winchell Cancer Research Fund, 131 E. 36th St., New York, NY 10016-3404. circ. 1,000. Key Title: Annual Report, Damon Runyon - Walter Winchell Cancer Research Fund.
Continues: Damon Runyon Memorial Fund for Cancer Research. Report.

616.99   GW   ISSN 0932-7479
DEUTSCHE KREBSGESELLSCHAFT. MITTEILUNGEN. 1986. q. DM.60. (Deutsche Krebsgesellschaft) Demeter Verlag, Wuermstr. 13, 8032 Graefelfing, Germany. TEL 089-852033. FAX 089-8543347. circ. 2,400.

616.99   GW   ISSN 0931-0037
DEUTSCHE ZEITSCHRIFT FUER ONKOLOGIE/JOURNAL OF ONCOLOGY; journal of oncology. (Text in German; summaries in English) bi-m. DM.105 (students DM.87). (Deutsche Gesellschaft fuer Onkologie e.V.) Verlag fuer Medizin Dr. Ewald Fischer GmbH, Fritz-Frey-Str. 21, Postfach 105767, 6900 Heidelberg 1, Germany. TEL 06221-4062-0. Ed. Dr. E. Dieter Hager. circ. 5,000. (back issues avail.) Indexed: Excerp.Med.
—BLDSC shelfmark: 3575.830000.

616.9   GW   ISSN 0070-4229
DEUTSCHES KREBSFORSCHUNGSZENTRUM. VEROEFFENTLICHUNGEN. 1965. a. Deutsches Krebsforschungszentrum, Institut fuer Epidemiologie und Biometrie, Im Neuenheimer Feld 280, 6900 Heidelberg 1, Germany. FAX 06221-401271. TELEX 461562-DKFZ-D. circ. 1,000.

616.99   NE
DEVELOPMENTS IN CANCER RESEARCH. 1979. irreg., vol.7, 1982. price varies. Elsevier Science Publishers B.V., Books Division, P.O. Box 211, 1000 AE Amsterdam, Netherlands. TEL 020-5803911. FAX 020-5803705. TELEX 18582 ESPA NL. (Subscr. in U.S. and Canada to: Elsevier Science Publishing Co., Inc., Box 882, Madison Sq. Sta., New York, NY 10159. TEL 212-989-5800)
Refereed Serial

619.99   NE
DEVELOPMENTS IN ONCOLOGY. 1980. irreg. (5-6 vols./yr.). price varies. Kluwer Academic Publishers, P.O. Box 17, 3300 AA Dordrecht, Netherlands. TEL 078-334911. (Dist. by: Kluwer Academic Publishers Group, P.O. Box 322, 3300 AH Dordrecht) circ. 2,000. Indexed: Chem.Abstr.

616.99   SZ   ISSN 1013-8129
CODEN: DIONEY
▼**DIAGNOSTIC ONCOLOGY.** 1991. bi-m. 558 Fr.($372) S. Karger AG, Allschwilerstr. 10, P.O. Box, CH-4009 Basel, Switzerland. TEL 061-306-1111. FAX 061-306-1234. Ed. A. Malkin.
—BLDSC shelfmark: 3579.663500.
— Description: Forum for the latest developments in cancer diagnosis. Multidisciplinary in scope, the journal features clinically relevant contributions from the fields of medical, surgical and radiation oncology; pathology; tumor immunology; and diagnostic imaging.

616.99   FR
DIRECTORY OF ON-GOING RESEARCH IN CANCER EPIDEMIOLOGY. (Text in English) 1976. a. £42($90) International Agency for Research on Cancer, 150 cours Albert-Thomas, 69372 Lyon Cedex 08, France. TEL 72-73-84-85. FAX 72-73-85-75. TELEX 380023 CIRC F. (Subscr. to: Oxford University Press, Walton St., Oxford OX2 6DP, England) Eds. M.P. Coleman, J. Wahrendorf. circ. 2,300.
— Description: Compilation of current research projects in the field of cancer epidemiology.

616.99   UK   ISSN 0278-0240
CODEN: DMARD3
DISEASE MARKERS. 1982. bi-m. $365 (effective 1992). John Wiley & Sons Ltd., Journals, Baffins Ln., Chichester, Sussex PO19 1UD, England. TEL 0243 779777. FAX 0243-775878. TELEX 86290 WIBOOK G. Eds. C.M. Steel, R.A. Gatti. adv.; bk.rev.; charts; illus.; index. (reprint service avail. from SWZ) Indexed: Chem.Abstr., Curr.Adv.Ecol.Sci., Curr.Adv.Genetics & Molec.Biol., Curr.Cont., Excerp.Med., Telegen.
—BLDSC shelfmark: 3598.090000.
— Description: Addresses original research findings and reviews on the subject of the identification of markers associated with the disease process, whether or not they are an integral part of the pathlogical lesion.

616.99   KR   ISSN 0204-3564
CODEN: EKSODD
EKSPERIMENTAL'NAYA ONKOLOGIYA/EXPERIMENTAL ONCOLOGY; nauchno-tekhnicheskii zhurnal. (Text in Russian; summaries in English and Russian) 1979. bi-m. 6 Rub. (Akademiya Nauk Ukrainskoi S.S.R. Otdelenie Biokhimii, Fiziologii i Teoretiheskoi Meditsiny) Izdatel'stvo Naukova Dumka, c/o Yu.A. Khramov, Dir, Ul. Repina, 3, Kiev 252 601, Ukraine. TEL 224-40-68. (Subscr. to: Mezhdunarodnaya Kniga, Moscow, G-200, Russia) (Co-sponsor: Akademiya Nauk S.S.S.R., Otdelenie Fiziologii) Ed. V.G. Pinchuk. Indexed: Biol.Abstr., Chem.Abstr, Curr.Adv.Ecol.Sci., Excerp.Med., Ind.Med., Ind.Sci.Rev., INIS Atomind., Sci.Cit.Ind.
—BLDSC shelfmark: 0397.998500.

EMOTION; Wilhelm-Reich-Zeitschrift ueber Triebenergie, Charakterstruktur, Krankheit, Natur und Gesellschaft. see *ENERGY*

ETESIA STATISTIKE. EREVNA TOU KARKINOU/ANNUAL STATISTICAL SURVEY OF CANCER. see *MEDICAL SCIENCES — Abstracting, Bibliographies, Statistics*

MEDICAL SCIENCES — CANCER 3197

616.99　　　　　　NE　ISSN 0921-3732
　　　　　　　　　　　　CODEN: ECNEE5
EUROPEAN CANCER NEWS. 1988. 10/yr. fl.189($107.50) Kluwer Academic Publishers, Postbus 17, 3300 AA Dordrecht, Netherlands. TEL 078-334911. FAX 078-334254. TELEX 29245. (Dist. by: Kluwer Academic Publishers Group, P.O. Box 322, 3300 AH Dordrecht, Netherlands; N. America dist. addr.: Box 358, Accord Station, Hingham, MA 02018-0358. TEL 617-871-6600) Ed. J. Gordon McVie. (reprint service avail. from SWZ)

616.994　　　　　　US　ISSN 0964-1947
EUROPEAN JOURNAL OF CANCER PART A. 1965. 14/yr. £840($1525) includes Part B: Oral Oncology (effective 1992). (Federation of European Cancer Societies) Pergamon Press, Inc., Journals Division, 660 White Plains Rd., Tarrytown, NY 10591-5153. TEL 914-524-9200. FAX 914-333-2444. (And: Headington Hill Hall, Oxford OX3 0BW, England. TEL 0865-794141) (Co-sponsors: European Organization for Research & Treatment of Cancer; European School of Oncology; European Association for Cancer Research) Ed. M.J. Peckham. adv.; bk.rev.; charts; illus.; index; circ. 3,500. (also avail. in microform from MIM,UMI; back issues avail.) **Indexed:** Abstr.Health Care Manage.Stud., Biol.Abstr., Biotech.Abstr., Chem.Abstr., Curr.Adv.Biochem., Curr.Adv.Cancer Res., Curr.Adv.Cell & Devel.Biol., Curr.Adv.Ecol.Sci., Curr.Adv.Genetics & Molec.Biol., Curr.Cont., Dairy Sci.Abstr., Dent.Ind., Dok.Arbeitsmed., Excerp.Med., Ind.Med., Ind.Sci.Rev., Ind.Vet., INIS Atomind., NRN, Risk Abstr., Sci.Cit.Ind., Vet.Bull.
　Former titles (until 1989): European Journal of Cancer and Clinical Oncology (ISSN 0277-5379); (until vol.18, 1982): European Journal of Cancer (ISSN 0014-2964)
　Description: Provides an integrated forum for publication of clinical and laboratory research in all specializations of oncology.
　Refereed Serial

616.99　　　　　　UK　ISSN 0964-1955
▼**EUROPEAN JOURNAL OF CANCER PART B: ORAL ONCOLOGY**. 1992. 2/yr. £58($105) with Part A £840 ($1525)(effective 1992). Pergamon Press plc, Headington Hill Hall, Oxford OX3 0BW, England. TEL 0865-794141. FAX 0865-743911. TELEX 83177 PERGAP. (And: 660 White Plains Rd., Tarrytown, NY 10591-5153. TEL 914-524-9200) Ed. Crispian Scully. (also avail. in microform)
　Description: Discusses issues relating to aetiopathogenesis, epidemiology, prevention and management of oral cancer.
　Refereed Serial

616.99　　　　　　UK　ISSN 0959-8278
▼**EUROPEAN JOURNAL OF CANCER PREVENTION**. 1992. bi-m. £222($399) (European Cancer Prevention Organisation) Rapid Communications of Oxford Ltd., The Old Malthouse, Paradise St., Oxford OX1 1LD, England. TEL 0865-790447. FAX 0865-244012. Ed. M.J. Hill. (reprint service avail.)
　—BLDSC shelfmark: 3829.725400.

616.99 618.1　　　　IT　ISSN 0392-2936
　　　　　　　　　　　　CODEN: EJGODE
EUROPEAN JOURNAL OF GYNECOLOGICAL ONCOLOGY. (Text and summaries in English) 1980. q. $200 to individuals; institutions $300. Studi Ostetrico Ginecologici s.r.l., Galleria Storione 2-A, 35128 Padua, Italy. TEL 049-8758644. Ed. Antonio Onnis. adv.; bk.rev.; circ. 600. (back issues avail.) **Indexed:** Biol.Abstr., Excerp.Med., Ind.Med., NRN.
　—BLDSC shelfmark: 3829.729600.

616.994　　　　　　UK　ISSN 0748-7983
EUROPEAN JOURNAL OF SURGICAL ONCOLOGY. 1975. 6/yr. £220. (British Association of Surgical Oncology) Academic Press Ltd., 24-28 Oval Rd., London NW1 7DX, England. TEL 071-267-4466. FAX 071-482-2293. TELEX 25775 ACPRES G. Ed. Ian Burn. adv.; illus.; index. **Indexed:** Biol.Abstr., Curr.Adv.Cancer Res., Curr.Adv.Ecol.Sci., Curr.Adv.Genetics & Molec.Biol., Curr.Cont., Excerp.Med., Ind.Med., INIS Atomind., Nutr.Abstr.
　—BLDSC shelfmark: 3829.745500.
　Formerly: Clinical Oncology (ISSN 0305-7399)
　Description: Presents original articles and state-of-the-art reviews of interest to surgeons treating patients with cancer.

616　　　　　　　　US
EUROPEAN ORGANIZATION FOR RESEARCH ON TREATMENT OF CANCER. MONOGRAPH SERIES. Short title: E O R T C Monograph Series. 1975. irreg., latest vol.20. price varies. Raven Press, 1185 Ave. of the Americas, New York, NY 10036. TEL 212-930-9500. FAX 212-869-3495. TELEX 640073. **Indexed:** Biol.Abstr., Curr.Cont.
　Refereed Serial

616.994　　　　　　IT　ISSN 0392-047X
FOLIA ONCOLOGICA. (Text in English, Italian; summaries in English) 1978. q. L.50000($50) Istituto Scientifico Oncologico, c/o Mater Dei, Via Amendola 209, 70126 Bari, Italy. (Subscr. to: Libreria Editrice Universitaria Dr. C. Fortunato S.a.s., Via Garruba 19-19A, 70122 Bari, Italy) Ed. Luigi Marinaccio. bk.rev.; circ. 600. **Indexed:** Excerp.Med.
　—BLDSC shelfmark: 3971.790000.

FONDAMENTAL. see SOCIAL SERVICES AND WELFARE

616.99　　　　　　GW　ISSN 0323-5084
　　　　　　　　　　　　CODEN: FONKDF
FORTSCHRITTE DER ONKOLOGIE. (Text in English and German) 1975. irreg., vol.16, 1989. (Akademie der Wissenschaften der DDR, Zentralinstitut fuer Krebsforschung) Akademie-Verlag Berlin, Leipziger Str. 3-4, 1086 Berlin, Germany. TELEX 114420-AVERL-DD.
　—BLDSC shelfmark: 4022.600000.
　Description: Results of recent research in special fields of oncological science: tumor growth, liposomes, radiation pathology and tumor markers.

616.99 573.21　　　　US
FOX CHASE CANCER CENTER. SCIENTIFIC REPORT. 1948. a. free. Fox Chase Cancer Center, 7701 Burholme Ave., Philadelphia, PA 19111. Ed. Elizabeth C. Travaglini. circ. 9,000.
　Formerly: I.C.R. Scientific Report.

FRONTIERS OF RADIATION THERAPY AND ONCOLOGY. see MEDICAL SCIENCES — Radiology And Nuclear Medicine

616.9　　　　　　　　JA
GANN MONOGRAPHS ON CANCER RESEARCH. (Text in English) 1966. s-a. price varies. (Japanese Cancer Association) Japan Scientific Societies Press, 6-2-10 Hongo, Bunkyo-ku, Tokyo 113, Japan. bk.rev.; circ. 2,000. **Indexed:** Biol.Abstr., Chem.Abstr, Excerp.Med., INIS Atomind.
　Fomerly: Gann Monographs (ISSN 0072-0151)
　Description: Includes collected contributions on current topics in cancer problems and allied fields.
　Refereed Serial

616.99　　　　　　　IT　ISSN 0392-128X
GIORNALE ITALIANO DI ONCOLOGIA. (Text in Italian; summaries in English) q. L.50000($50) C I C Edizioni Internazionali s.r.l., Via L. Spallanzani 11, 00161 Rome, Italy. TEL 06-8412673. FAX 06-8443365. TELEX 622099 CIC. Dirs. L. Caldarola, C. Maltoni. **Indexed:** Excerp.Med.
　—BLDSC shelfmark: 4178.236000.

616.99　　　　　　　US
HEALTH VICTORY BULLETIN. 1975. m. $20. Arlin J. Brown Information Center, Inc., Box 251, Fort Belvoir, VA 22060. TEL 703-752-4324. Ed. Arlin J. Brown. bk.rev.; index; circ. 300. (back issues avail.)
　Formerly (until 1982): Cancer Victory Bulletin.
　Description: Covers current developments in cancer, health and nutrition with emphasis on practical information for the patient.

616.99　　　　　　　US　ISSN 0889-8588
RB145　　　　　　　　CODEN: HCNAEQ
HEMATOLOGY - ONCOLOGY CLINICS OF NORTH AMERICA. 1972. 4/yr. $93 to individuals; institutions $110. W.B. Saunders Co., Curtis Center, Independence Square W., Philadelphia, PA 19106. TEL 215-574-4700. Ed. Leslie Kramer. **Indexed:** Biol.Abstr., Chem.Abstr., Curr.Adv.Ecol.Sci., Excerp.Med., Helminthol.Abstr., Ind.Med., Ind.Sci.Rev., Nutr.Abstr., Sci.Cit.Ind.
　—BLDSC shelfmark: 4291.610000.
　Formed by the 1987 merger of: Clinics in Oncology (ISSN 0261-9873); Clinics in Haematology (ISSN 0308-2261)
　Description: Addresses a single topic in the management of patients with cancer and systemic disease.
　Refereed Serial

616.994　　　　　　UK　ISSN 0309-0167
　　　　　　　　　　　　CODEN: HISTDD
HISTOPATHOLOGY. 1977. m. £165 (foreign £190). (International Academy of Pathology) Blackwell Scientific Publications Ltd., Osney Mead, Oxford OX2 0EL, England. TEL 0865-240201. FAX 0865-721205. TELEX 83355-MEDBOK-G. Ed. R.N.M. MacSween. adv.; bk.rev.; illus.; index; circ. 2,300. (back issues avail.; reprint service avail. from ISI) **Indexed:** ASCA, Biol.Abstr., Curr.Adv.Cancer Res., Curr.Adv.Ecol.Sci., Curr.Cont, Dent.Ind., Dok.Arbeitsmed., Excerp.Med., Helminthol.Abstr., Ind.Med., Ind.Sci.Rev., Sci.Cit.Ind., Vet.Bull.
　—BLDSC shelfmark: 4316.027000.

HUMAN ANTIBODIES AND HYBRIDOMAS. see MEDICAL SCIENCES — Allergology And Immunology

616.994　　　　　　UK
I A QUARTERLY JOURNAL. 1956. q. £12. Ileostomy Association of Great Britain & Ireland, Amblehurst House, Black Scotch Ln., Mansfield, Notts NG18 4PF, England. TEL 0623-28099. adv.; pat.; stat.; circ. 11,000.

616.99　　　　　　　FR　ISSN 0250-8613
I A R C BIENNIAL REPORT. (Editions in English, French) 1987. biennial. 25 SFr. International Agency for Research on Cancer, 150, Cours Albert Thomas, 69372 Lyon Cedex 08, France. FAX 72-73-85-75. TELEX 380023. (Dist. by: World Health Organization, Distribution and Sales Service, 1211 Geneva 27, Switzerland)
　Formerly: I A R C Annual Report.

616.994　　　　　　UN
I A R C MONOGRAPHS ON THE EVALUATION OF CARCINOGENIC RISKS TO HUMANS. (Text in English) 1972. 3/yr. price varies. International Agency for Research on Cancer, 150 cours Albert-Thomas, 69372 Lyon Cedex 08, France. TEL 33-72738485. FAX 72-73-85-75. TELEX 380023. (Subscr. addr.: World Health Organization, Distribution and Sales Services,1211 Geneva 27, Switzerland) **Indexed:** Abstr.Hyg., Anal.Abstr., Biol.Abstr., Curr.Cont., Food Sci.& Tech.Abstr., Ind.Med., NRN, Trop.Dis.Bull.
　Formerly: I A R C Monographs on the Evaluation of Carcinogenic Risk of Chemicals to Man (ISSN 0250-9555)
　Description: Monographs comprise sections on physical and chemical data, technical products, use, occurrence and analysis, carcinogenicity in animals, other biological data and human epidemiological results.

616.994　　　　　　UN　ISSN 0300-5038
　　　　　　　　　　　　CODEN: IARCCD
I A R C SCIENTIFIC PUBLICATIONS. 1971. irreg., latest no.115. price varies. International Agency for Research on Cancer, 150 cours Albert-Thomas, 69372 Lyon Cedex 08, France. TEL 33-72738485. FAX 33-72738575. TELEX 380023. (U.S. subscr. to: Oxford University Press, 200 Madison Ave., New York, NY 10016) Ed. J. Cheney. **Indexed:** Abstr.Hyg., Anal.Abstr., Biol.Abstr., Chem.Abstr., Curr.Cont., Dent.Ind., Dok.Arbeitsmed., Excerp.Med., Food Sci.& Tech.Abstr., Ind.Med., Trop.Dis.Bull.
　—BLDSC shelfmark: 4359.537000.

I C R D B CANCERGRAM: ANTITUMOR AND ANTIVIRAL AGENTS - EXPERIMENTAL THERAPEUTICS, TOXICOLOGY, PHARMACOLOGY. (International Cancer Research Data Bank) see ENVIRONMENTAL STUDIES — Toxicology And Environmental Safety

I C R D B CANCERGRAM: ANTITUMOR AND ANTIVIRAL AGENTS - MECHANISM OF ACTION. (International Cancer Research Data Bank) see MEDICAL SCIENCES — Abstracting, Bibliographies, Statistics

I C R D B CANCERGRAM: BREAST CANCER - DIAGNOSIS, TREATMENT, PRECLINICAL BIOLOGY. (International Cancer Research Data Bank) see MEDICAL SCIENCES — Abstracting, Bibliographies, Statistics

I C R D B CANCERGRAM: C N S MALIGNANCIES - DIAGNOSIS, TREATMENT. (International Cancer Research Data Bank) see MEDICAL SCIENCES — Abstracting, Bibliographies, Statistics

I C R D B CANCERGRAM: CANCER DETECTION AND MANAGEMENT - BIOLOGICAL MARKERS. see MEDICAL SCIENCES — Abstracting, Bibliographies, Statistics

M

MEDICAL SCIENCES — CANCER

I C R D B CANCERGRAM: CANCER DETECTION AND MANAGEMENT - DIAGNOSTIC RADIOLOGY. see *MEDICAL SCIENCES — Abstracting, Bibliographies, Statistics*

I C R D B CANCERGRAM: CANCER DETECTION AND MANAGEMENT - NUCLEAR MEDICINE. see *MEDICAL SCIENCES — Abstracting, Bibliographies, Statistics*

I C R D B CANCERGRAM: CLINICAL TREATMENT OF CANCER - RADIATION THERAPY. see *MEDICAL SCIENCES — Abstracting, Bibliographies, Statistics*

I C R D B CANCERGRAM: COLORECTAL CANCER - DIAGNOSIS, TREATMENT. see *MEDICAL SCIENCES — Abstracting, Bibliographies, Statistics*

I C R D B CANCERGRAM: ENDOCRINE TUMORS - DIAGNOSIS, TREATMENT, PATHOPHYSIOLOGY. see *MEDICAL SCIENCES — Abstracting, Bibliographies, Statistics*

I C R D B CANCERGRAM: GENITOURINARY CANCERS - DIAGNOSIS, TREATMENT. see *MEDICAL SCIENCES — Abstracting, Bibliographies, Statistics*

I C R D B CANCERGRAM: GYNECOLOGICAL TUMORS - DIAGNOSIS, TREATMENT. see *MEDICAL SCIENCES — Abstracting, Bibliographies, Statistics*

I C R D B CANCERGRAM: LEUKEMIA AND MULTIPLE MYELOMA - DIAGNOSIS, TREATMENT. see *MEDICAL SCIENCES — Abstracting, Bibliographies, Statistics*

I C R D B CANCERGRAM: LUNG CANCER - DIAGNOSIS, TREATMENT. see *MEDICAL SCIENCES — Abstracting, Bibliographies, Statistics*

I C R D B CANCERGRAM: LYMPHOMAS - DIAGNOSIS, TREATMENT. see *MEDICAL SCIENCES — Abstracting, Bibliographies, Statistics*

I C R D B CANCERGRAM: MELANOMA AND OTHER SKIN CANCER - DIAGNOSIS, TREATMENT. see *MEDICAL SCIENCES — Abstracting, Bibliographies, Statistics*

I C R D B CANCERGRAM: NEOPLASIA OF THE HEAD AND NECK - DIAGNOSIS, TREATMENT. see *MEDICAL SCIENCES — Abstracting, Bibliographies, Statistics*

I C R D B CANCERGRAM: PEDIATRIC ONCOLOGY. see *MEDICAL SCIENCES — Abstracting, Bibliographies, Statistics*

I C R D B CANCERGRAM: REHABILITATION AND SUPPORTIVE CARE. see *MEDICAL SCIENCES — Abstracting, Bibliographies, Statistics*

I C R D B CANCERGRAM: SARCOMAS AND RELATED TUMORS - DIAGNOSIS, TREATMENT. see *MEDICAL SCIENCES — Abstracting, Bibliographies, Statistics*

I C R D B CANCERGRAM: UPPER GASTROINTESTINAL TUMORS - DIAGNOSIS, TREATMENT. see *MEDICAL SCIENCES — Abstracting, Bibliographies, Statistics*

616.99 362.1   GW   ISSN 0724-8016
I L C O PRAXIS. 1974. q. DM.27. Deutsche I L C O, Kepserstr. 50, 8050 Freising, Germany. FAX 08161-85521. Ed. Gerhard Englert. adv.; bk.rev.; circ. 11,000.

616.994   UK   ISSN 0306-4905
IMPERIAL CANCER RESEARCH FUND. SCIENTIFIC REPORT. 1973. a. free to qualified personnel. Imperial Cancer Research Fund, Lincoln's Inn Fields, London WC2A 3PX, England. TEL 071-242-0200. FAX 071-404-4182. Ed. Angela H. Aldam. circ. 1,900 (paid); 1,900 (controlled).
—BLDSC shelfmark: 8197.900000.

IN VITRO CELLULAR & DEVELOPMENTAL BIOLOGY - ANIMAL. see *BIOLOGY — Microbiology*

IN VITRO CELLULAR & DEVELOPMENTAL BIOLOGY - PLANT. see *BIOLOGY — Microbiology*

616.9   XV   ISSN 0079-9580
INCIDENCA RAKA V SLOVENIJI/CANCER INCIDENCE IN SLOVENIA. (Text in English and Slovenian) 1957. a. free. Onkoloski Institut, Zaloska C,2, 61105 Ljubljana, Slovenia. TEL 061 316 490. Ed. Vera Pompe Kirn. index; circ. 800.
Formerly: Rak v Sloveniji. Tabele.

616.994   II   ISSN 0019-509X
                          CODEN: IJCAAR
INDIAN JOURNAL OF CANCER. (Text in English) 1963. q. Rs.120($35) Indian Cancer Society, 74 Jerbai Wadia Rd., Parel, Bombay 400 012, India. TEL 22-412-5238. (Co-sponsor: Indian Association of Oncology) Ed. Dr. D.J. Jussawalla. adv.; bk.rev.; charts; illus.; stat.; circ. 1,500. (also avail. in microfilm from UMI; reprint service avail. from UMI) **Indexed:** Biol.Abstr., Chem.Abstr., Dent.Ind., Excerp.Med., Ind.Med, INIS Atomind., Vet.Bull.
—BLDSC shelfmark: 4410.550000.

616.994   MX   ISSN 0076-7131
INSTITUTO NACIONAL DE CANCEROLOGIA DE MEXICO. REVISTA. (Text in Spanish; summaries in English) 1954. 4/yr. Mex.$50,000($30) to individuals; institutions Mex.$60,000. Instituto Nacional de Cancerologia, Av. San Fernando 22, 14000 Mexico, D.F., Mexico. TEL 6551437. FAX 525-5733627. (Co-sponsors: Sociedad Mexicana de Estudios Oncologicos; Grupo de Estudios y Tratamiento Latinoamericano del Cancer) Ed. Dr. Jaime G. de la Garza Salazar. adv.; charts; illus.; stat.; circ. 1,000.
Indexed: Excerp.Med., Ind.Med.
Description: Provides original papers in cancer research.

616.994   US   ISSN 0020-7136
RC261   CODEN: IJCNAW
INTERNATIONAL JOURNAL OF CANCER. (Text in English, French) 1966. 18/yr. $1149. (International Union Against Cancer - Union Internationale Contre le Cancer) John Wiley & Sons, Inc., 605 Third Ave., New York, NY 10158. TEL 212-850-6000. FAX 212-850-6088. TELEX 12-7063. Ed. N. Odartchenko. adv.; bk.rev.; charts; illus.; s-a. index. (also avail. in microform from MIM; reprint service avail. from SWZ) **Indexed:** Abstr.Hyg., Biol.Abstr., Biotech.Abstr., C.I.S. Abstr., Chem.Abstr., Curr.Adv.Cell & Devel.Biol., Curr.Adv.Ecol.Sci., Curr.Adv.Genetics & Molec.Biol., Curr.Cont., Dairy Sci.Abstr., Dent. Ind., Dok.Arbeitsmed., Excerp.Med., Helminthol.Abstr., Ind.Med., Ind.Sci.Rev., Ind.Vet., NRN, Poult.Abstr., Risk Abstr., Sci.Cit.Ind., Small Anim.Abstr., Telegen, Trop.Dis.Bull., Vet.Bull.
—BLDSC shelfmark: 4542.156000.
Description: Examines all topics relevant to experimental and clinical cancer research, with an emphasis on fundamental studies that have relevance to the understanding of human cancer.
Refereed Serial

INTERNATIONAL JOURNAL OF GYNECOLOGICAL CANCER. see *MEDICAL SCIENCES — Obstetrics And Gynecology*

616.99   UK   ISSN 0265-6736
                          CODEN: IJHYEQ
INTERNATIONAL JOURNAL OF HYPERTHERMIA. bi-m. £215($368) (North American Hyperthermia Group) Taylor & Francis Ltd., Rankine Rd., Basingstoke, Hants. RG24 0PR, England. TEL 0256-840366. FAX 0256-479438. TELEX 858540. Ed. S.B. Field. **Indexed:** Curr.Adv.Cancer Res., Curr.Adv.Cell & Devel.Biol., Curr.Adv.Ecol.Sci., Excerp.Med., Sci.Abstr.
—BLDSC shelfmark: 4542.297000.
Description: Provides a forum for the publication of research and clinical papers on hyperthermia, which fall largely into the three main categories: clinical studies, biological studies and techniques of heat delivery and temperature measurement.
Refereed Serial

INTERNATIONAL JOURNAL OF PANCREATOLOGY. see *MEDICAL SCIENCES — Endocrinology*

616.99 574.191   UK   ISSN 0020-7616
QH652.   CODEN: IJRBA3
INTERNATIONAL JOURNAL OF RADIATION BIOLOGY. (Text and summaries in English, French, German) 1959. m. (2 vols./yr.). £421($724) Taylor & Francis Ltd., Rankine Rd., Basingstoke, Hants RG24 0PR, England. TEL 0256-840366. FAX 0256-479438. TELEX 858540. Ed. Jolyon H. Hendry. adv.; charts; illus.; index. (also avail. in microform from MIM) **Indexed:** Biol.Abstr., Chem.Abstr., Crop Physiol.Abstr., Curr.Adv.Biochem., Curr.Adv.Cancer Res., Curr.Adv.Cell & Devel.Biol., Curr.Adv.Genetics & Molec.Biol., Curr.Cont., Dairy Sci.Abstr., Excerp.Med., Field Crop Abstr., Helminthol.Abstr., Herb.Abstr., Hort.Abstr., Ind.Med., Ind.Vet., INIS Atomind., Nutr.Abstr., Poult.Abstr., Sci.Abstr., Sci.Cit.Ind., Seed Abstr., Vet.Bull.
Description: Contains original research and review papers on the effects of ionization, ultraviolet and visible radiation, accelerated particles, microwaves, ultrasound and heat and related modalities.
Refereed Serial

616.99   TU   ISSN 0259-840X
INTERNATIONAL QUARTERLY OF CANCER RESEARCH. (Text in English) 1987. q. $160. Tahsin Yazicioglu, P. Kutusu 1318, Sirkeci, Istanbul 34438, Turkey. Ed. Kenneth D. Tew. adv.; bk.rev. **Indexed:** Biol.Abstr., Chem.Abstr., Curr.Cont., Excerp.Med., Ref.Zh., Sci.Cit.Ind.

616.99   RU   ISSN 0202-7127
RC280.B6
ITOGI NAUKI I TEKHNIKI: ONKOLOGIYA. irreg., latest vol.18, 1989. 6.60 Rub. Vsesoyuznyi Institut Nauchno-Tekhnicheskoi Informatsii (VINITI), Baltiiskaya ul. 14, Moscow A-219, Russia. (Subscr. to: Mezhdunarodnaya Kniga, Dimitrova ul. 39, 113095 Moscow, Russia)
—BLDSC shelfmark: 0127.449000.

616.994   JA   ISSN 0021-4671
                          CODEN: NGCJAK
JAPAN SOCIETY FOR CANCER THERAPY. JOURNAL. (Text in English, Japanese) 1966. m. 10000 Yen. Japan Society for Cancer Therapy - Nihon Gan Chiryo Gakkai, c/o Kinki Invention Center, 14 Yoshida, Kawara-cho, Sakyo-ku, Kyoto 606, Japan. Ed.Bd. adv.; bk.rev.; abstr.; bibl.; charts; illus. **Indexed:** Biol.Abstr., Dent.Ind., Excerp.Med., Ind.Med.
—BLDSC shelfmark: 4806.500000.

616.9   JA   ISSN 0075-3327
JAPAN SOCIETY FOR CANCER THERAPY. PROCEEDINGS OF THE CONGRESS. (Text in English) 1963. a. 10000 Yen. Japan Society for Cancer Therapy - Nihon Gan Chiryo Gakkai, c/o Kinki Invention Center, 14 Yoshida, Kawara-cho, Sakyo-ku, Kyoto 606, Japan.

616.994   JA   ISSN 0021-4949
                          CODEN: GANRAE
JAPANESE JOURNAL OF CANCER CLINICS/GAN NO RINSHO. (Text in Japanese; summaries in English) 1954. m. 34820 Yen. Shinohara Publishers, Inc., Yaguchi Bldg., 2-11-7 Hongo 2-chome, Bunkyo-ku, Tokyo 113, Japan. TEL 03-3816-5311. FAX 03-3816-5314. Ed. Yoshikuni Shinohara. adv.; bk.rev.; abstr.; charts; illus.; index; circ. 3,800. **Indexed:** Chem.Abstr., Dent.Ind., Ind.Med., INIS Atomind., Telegen.
—BLDSC shelfmark: 4651.250000.

616.994   JA   ISSN 0910-5050
CODEN: JJCREP
JAPANESE JOURNAL OF CANCER RESEARCH. (Text and summaries in English) 1907. 12/yr. fl.727 (effective 1992). (Japanese Cancer Association) Japan Scientific Societies Press, 6-2-10 Hongo, Bunkyo-ku, Tokyo 113, Japan. TEL 3814-2001. FAX 3814-2002. TELEX 2722268 BCJSP J. (Dist. by: Business Center for Academic Societies Japan, Koshin Bldg., 6-16-3 Hongo, Bunkyo-ku, Tokyo 113, Japan; Dist. outside the Far East by: Elsevier Science Publishers B.V., P.O. Box 211, 1000 AE Amsterdam, Netherlands. TEL 020-5803911; Subscr. in U.S. and Canada to: Elsevier Science Publishing Co., Inc., Box 882, Madison Sq. Sta., New York, NY 10159. TEL 212-989-5800) Ed. Takashi Sugimura. adv.; illus.; index, cum.index; circ. 12,500. (also avail. in microform from UMI; back issues avail.; reprint service avail. from ISI) **Indexed:** Biol.Abstr., Chem.Abstr., Curr.Adv.Biochem., Curr.Adv.Cancer Res., Curr.Adv.Cell & Devel.Biol., Curr.Adv.Ecol.Sci., Curr.Adv.Genetics & Molec.Biol., Dairy Sci.Abstr., Excerp.Med., Ind.Med., Ind.Sci.Rev., Ind.Vet., INIS Atomind., Nutr.Abstr., Sci.Cit.Ind.
—BLDSC shelfmark: 4651.270000.
Formerly: Gann (ISSN 0016-450X)
Description: Provides an overview of state of the art cancer research in Japan.

616.994   JA   ISSN 0368-2811
CODEN: JJCOAC
JAPANESE JOURNAL OF CLINICAL ONCOLOGY. (Text in English) 1971. 6/yr. 10,000 Yen. Foundation for Promotion of Cancer Research, c/o National Cancer Center Hospital, 1-1, Tsukiji 5-chome, Chuo-ku, Tokyo 104, Japan. TEL 03-3542-2511. FAX 03-3542-2511. Ed. Dr. Takashi Sugimura. bk.rev.; bibl.; charts; illus.; circ. 1,100. (reprint service avail. from ISI) **Indexed:** Chem.Abstr., Curr.Cont., Dent.Ind., Excerp.Med., Ind.Med., INIS Atomind., NRN.
●Also available online. Vendor(s): JICST.
—BLDSC shelfmark: 4651.378000.

616.99   UK   ISSN 0885-8195
JOURNAL OF CANCER EDUCATION. 1986. q. $180 (effective 1992). (American Association for Cancer Education) Pergamon Press plc, Headington Hill Hall, Oxford OX3 0BW, England. TEL 0865-794141. FAX 0865-743911. TELEX 83177 PERGAP. (And: 660 White Plains Rd., Tarrytown, NY 10591-5153. TEL 914-524-9200) (Co-sponsor: European Association for Cancer Education) Ed. Richard F. Bakemeier. index; circ. 900. (also avail. in microform; back issues avail.) **Indexed:** Excerp.Med.
—BLDSC shelfmark: 4954.843000.
Refereed Serial

616.994   GW   ISSN 0171-5216
CODEN: JCROD7
JOURNAL OF CANCER RESEARCH AND CLINICAL ONCOLOGY. (Text in English, French, German; summaries in English) 1903. 6/yr. DM.1218($687) (Deutsche Krebsgesellschaft) Springer-Verlag, Heidelberger Platz 3, D-1000 Berlin 33, Germany. TEL 030-8207-1. (Also Heidelberg, Tokyo, Vienna, and New York) Ed. E. Grundmann. adv. (also avail. in microform from UMI; back issues avail.; reprint service avail. from ISI) **Indexed:** Biol.Abstr., Biotech.Abstr., C.I.S. Abstr., Chem.Abstr., Curr.Adv.Cancer Res., Curr.Cont., Dairy Sci.Abstr., Dok.Arbeitsmed., Excerp.Med., Ind.Med., Ind.Sci.Rev., Ind.Vet., INIS Atomind., NRN, Nutr.Abstr., Protozool.Abstr., Sci.Cit.Ind., Vet.Bull.
—BLDSC shelfmark: 4954.851000.
Formerly: Zeitschrift fuer Krebsforschung und Klinische Onkologie (ISSN 0084-5353)
Refereed Serial

616.99   US   ISSN 0732-183X
CODEN: JCONDN
JOURNAL OF CLINICAL ONCOLOGY. 1983. m. $169 to individuals; institutions $212; foreign $220. (American Society of Clinical Oncology) W.B. Saunders Co. (Subsidiary of: Harcourt Brace Jovanovich, Inc.), Curtis Center, Independence Square W., Philadelphia, PA 19106. TEL 215-238-7800. (Subscr. to: 6277 Sea Harbor Dr., 4th Fl., Orlando FL 32891) Ed. Dr. George P. Canellos. adv.; abstr.; bibl.; charts; illus.; index. **Indexed:** Abstr.Health Care Manage.Stud., Chem.Abstr., Curr.Cont., Dent.Ind., Excerp.Med., Ind.Med., Ind.Sci.Rev., INIS Atomind., NRN, Sci.Cit.Ind.
●Also available online.
—BLDSC shelfmark: 4958.615000.
Refereed Serial

JOURNAL OF DERMATOLOGIC SURGERY AND ONCOLOGY. see *MEDICAL SCIENCES — Surgery*

JOURNAL OF ENVIRONMENTAL SCIENCE AND HEALTH. PART C: ENVIRONMENTAL CARCINOGENESIS AND ECOTOXICOLOGY REVIEWS. see *ENVIRONMENTAL STUDIES — Toxicology And Environmental Safety*

616.99   US   ISSN 0167-594X
CODEN: JNODD2
JOURNAL OF NEURO-ONCOLOGY. 1983. bi-m. fl.420($201) to individuals; institutions fl.738 ($376.50). Kluwer Academic Publishers, 101 Philip Dr., Norwell, MA 02061. TEL 617-871-6600. FAX 617-871-6528. TELEX 200190. (Subscr. to: Box 358, Accord Sta., Hingham, MA 02018-0358) Ed. Dr. Michael D. Walker. adv.; bk.rev. (back issues avail.; reprint service avail. from SWZ,UMI) **Indexed:** Chem.Abstr., Curr.Adv.Biochem., Curr.Adv.Cell & Devel.Biol., Ind.Med., Ind.Sci.Rev.
—BLDSC shelfmark: 5021.650000.
Refereed Serial

616.9   US   ISSN 0734-7332
RC261.A1
JOURNAL OF PSYCHOSOCIAL ONCOLOGY. 1983. q. $35 to individuals; institutions $90; libraries $175. Haworth Press, Inc., 10 Alice St., Binghamton, NY 13904. TEL 800-342-9678. FAX 607-722-1424. TELEX 4932599. Ed. Grace H. Christ. adv.; bk.rev.; circ. 869. (also avail. in microfiche from HAW; back issues avail.; reprint service avail. from HAW) **Indexed:** CLOA, Excerp.Med., Past.Care & Couns.Abstr., Psychol.Abstr., Ref.Zh., Rehabil.Lit., Soc.Work Res.& Abstr., Sp.Ed.Needs Abstr., Stud.Wom.Abstr.
—BLDSC shelfmark: 5043.476000.
Description: Multidisciplinary journal published specifically for health professionals responsible for the psychosocial needs of cancer patients and their families.
Refereed Serial

JOURNAL OF SURGICAL ONCOLOGY. see *MEDICAL SCIENCES — Surgery*

JOURNAL OF TISSUE CULTURE METHODS. see *BIOLOGY — Microbiology*

JOURNAL OF TOXICOLOGY AND ENVIRONMENTAL HEALTH. see *ENVIRONMENTAL STUDIES — Toxicology And Environmental Safety*

616.99   US   ISSN 0886-3849
CODEN: JTMOEY
JOURNAL OF TUMOR MARKER ONCOLOGY. q. $120 (foreign $160). (International Academy of Tumor Marker Oncology) Mary Ann Liebert, Inc., 1651 Third Ave., New York, NY 10128. TEL 212-289-2300. FAX 212-289-4697. Ed. Dr. J.V. Klavins.
—BLDSC shelfmark: 5071.250000.
Description: Covers tumor markers and their applications in the diagnosis and treatment of malignant neoplasms. Includes new markers for clinical application, and basic research on their physiological behavior and role in malignant neoplasms.

KAZAKHSKII NAUCHNO-ISSLEDOVATEL'SKII INSTITUT ONKOLOGII I RADIOLOGII. TRUDY. see *MEDICAL SCIENCES — Radiology And Nuclear Medicine*

KOREAN JOURNAL OF GENETICS. see *BIOLOGY — Genetics*

LEUKEMIA AND LYMPHOMA. see *MEDICAL SCIENCES — Hematology*

616.99   US   CI
LEUKEMIA SOCIETY OF AMERICA. SOCIETY NEWS. 1983. q. free. Leukemia Society of America, Inc., 733 Third Ave., 14th Fl., New York, NY 10017. TEL 212-573-8484. FAX 212-972-5776. Ed. Tom Gibson. bk.rev.; circ. 18,000 (controlled). (back issues avail.; reprint service avail.)
Description: To inform patients, volunteers, grantees, and the public about the society's programs and advances in research.

616
LIBRI ONCOLOGICI; casopis kancerologa Jugoslavije. (Text in Serbo-Croatian; summaries in English) 1972. q. 150 din.($20) Sredisnji Institut za Tumore i Slicne Bolesti, Ilica 197, 41000 Zagreb, Croatia. Ed. Predrag Keros. **Indexed:** Chem.Abstr., Excerp.Med.

LIVEWELL. see *PHYSICAL FITNESS AND HYGIENE*

616.994   US
LIVINGRIGHT. 1970. 4/yr. free. American Cancer Society, Inc., Florida Division, 1001 S. MacDill Ave., Tampa, FL 33629. TEL 813-253-0541. FAX 813-254-5857. Ed. Sheila Buchert. circ. 20,000.
Formerly (until 1990): Florida Cancer News (ISSN 0015-3931)
Description: Health promotion and lifestyle information for the mature audience. Not cancer specific.

616.994   US   ISSN 0459-889X
LOUISIANA CANCER REPORTER. vol.23, 1974. q. free to qualified personnel. American Cancer Society, Inc., Louisiana Division, 837 Gravier St., Ste. 700, New Orleans, LA 70112. TEL 509-523-2029. Ed. Garrett G. Stearns. circ. 3,000.

616.99   NE   ISSN 0169-5002
LUNG CANCER. (Text in English) 1985. bi-m. fl.400 (effective 1992). (International Association for the Study of Lung Cancer) Elsevier Science Publishers B.V., P.O. Box 211, 1000 AE Amsterdam, Netherlands. TEL 020-5803911. FAX 020-5803598. TELEX 18582 ESPA NL. (Subscr. in U.S. and Canada to: Elsevier Science Publishing Co., Inc., Box 882, Madison Sq. Sta., New York, NY 10159. TEL 212-989-5800) Ed. H.H. Hansen. **Indexed:** Excerp.Med.
—BLDSC shelfmark: 5307.245000.
Description: Reports new findings and advances in therapy, etiology and related aspects.
Refereed Serial

616.9   US
M.D. ANDERSON CANCER CENTER. RESEARCH REPORT. 1955. biennial. free. University of Texas, M.D. Anderson Cancer Center, Scientific Publications, Box 234, 1515 Holcombe, Houston, TX 77030. TEL 713-792-3305. FAX 713-794-1370. Ed. Diane S. Rivera. circ. 5,500.
Formerly: M.D. Anderson Hospital and Tumor Institute. Research Report (ISSN 0066-1635)
Description: Compendium of research accomplishments at the center.

616.99   US   ISSN 0160-2454
M.D. ANDERSON CLINICAL CONFERENCES ON CANCER. 1978. a., latest 27th. (University of Texas System Cancer Center) Raven Press, 1185 Ave. of the Americas, New York, NY 10036. TEL 212-930-9500. FAX 212-869-3495. TELEX 640073. (Co-sponsor: M.D. Anderson Hospital and Tumor Institute)

616.99   US
M.D. ANDERSON SYMPOSIA IN FUNDAMENTAL CANCER RESEARCH. 1978. a., latest 37th. (University of Texas System Cancer Center) Raven Press, 1185 Ave. of Americas, New York, NY 10036. TEL 212-930-9500. FAX 212-869-3495. TELEX 640073. (Co-sponsor: M.D. Anderson Hospital and Tumor Insitute)

610   HU   ISSN 0025-0244
CODEN: MGONAD
MAGYAR ONKOLOGIA. (Summaries in English and Russian) 1957. q. $38.50. (Magyar Rakkutatok Tarsasaga) Ifjusagi Lap-es Konyvkiado Vallalat, Revay u. 16, 1374 Budapest 6, Hungary. (Subscr. to: Kultura, P.O. Box 149, H-1389 Budapest, Hungary) Ed. Dr. Gyorgy Gyenes. bk.rev.; bibl.; charts; illus.; circ. 500. **Indexed:** Biol.Abstr., Chem.Abstr., Excerp.Med., Ind.Med., INIS Atomind.

616.9   CN   ISSN 0076-3802
MANITOBA CANCER TREATMENT AND RESEARCH FOUNDATION. REPORT. 1957. a. free. Manitoba Cancer Treatment and Research Foundation, 100 Olivia St., Winnipeg, Man. R3E 0V9, Canada. TEL 204-787-2197. FAX 204-783-6875. circ. 1,000.

MEDICAL SCIENCES — CANCER

616.99 614.7   BE   ISSN 0302-0800
MEDECINE - BIOLOGIE - ENVIRONNEMENT/MEDICINE - BIOLOGY - ENVIRONMENT/GENEESKUNDE - BIOLOGIE - LEEFMILIEU. (Annual supplement avail.) (Text in Dutch, English, French) 1971. s-a. 1000 BEF($40) (effective 1992). European Institute of Ecology and Cancer, Belgian Section, 24 Bis, Rue des Fripiers, B-1000 Brussels, Belgium. TEL 2-219-0830. FAX 02-219-0636. Ed. Dr. Emile-Gaston Peeters. adv.; circ. 3,000.
Description: Disseminates information of relevance to medical biology and environmental studies.

616.994 618.92   US   ISSN 0098-1532
RC261.A1   CODEN: MPONDB
MEDICAL AND PEDIATRIC ONCOLOGY. 1975. bi-m. $271 (foreign $346). (International Society of Pediatric Oncology) John Wiley & Sons, Inc., Journals, 605 Third Ave., New York, NY 10158. TEL 212-850-6000. FAX 212-850-6088. TELEX 12-7063. Ed. Alvin M. Mauer. adv.; charts; illus.; index. (reprint service avail. from ISI) **Indexed:** Biol.Abstr., Curr.Adv.Ecol.Sci., Curr.Cont., Dent.Ind., Excerp.Med., Ind.Med., Ind.Sci.Rev., INIS Atomind.
●Also available online.
—BLDSC shelfmark: 5525.980000.
Description: Provides broad coverage of advances in clinical oncology in children and adults; presents original articles on the diagnosis and treatment of malignant diseases.
Refereed Serial

610   UK   ISSN 0736-0118
                             CODEN: MOTPE2
MEDICAL ONCOLOGY & TUMOR PHARMACOTHERAPY. 1984. 4/yr. $200. Science and Technology Letters, P.O. Box 81, Northwood, Middlesex HA6 3AA, England. TEL 0923-823586. FAX 0923-825066. (also avail. in microform from UMI,MIM) **Indexed:** ASCA, Curr.Adv.Cancer Res., Curr.Adv.Ecol.Sci.
—BLDSC shelfmark: 5531.041000.

616.99   BL
MEDISOM: CANCER. 1980. bi-m. $90. Grupo Editorial Q B D Ltda, Rua Caravelas 326, Caixa Postal 30329, 01051 Sao Paulo, Brazil. FAX 55-11-572-5957. Ed. Dr. Philip Querido. adv. (audio cassette)

616.99   UK   ISSN 0960-8931
▼**MELANOMA RESEARCH.** 1990. bi-m. £165($295) Rapid Communications of Oxford Ltd., The Old Malthouse, Paradise St., Oxford OX1 1LD, England. TEL 0865-790447. FAX 0865-244012. Ed.Bd. (reprint service avail.) **Indexed:** Excerp.Med.
—BLDSC shelfmark: 5536.813450.

616.99   US   ISSN 1060-233X
MESSAGE LINE. 1974. s-a. free. American Brain Tumor Association, 3725 N. Talman Ave., Chicago, IL 60618. TEL 312-286-5571. FAX 312-549-5561. Ed.Bd. circ. 31,000. (looseleaf format; back issues avail.)
Description: Updates on research advances in the treatment of brain tumors.

MICROBIOS; a prestige international biomedical research journal of chemical and general microbiology. see BIOLOGY — Microbiology

616.99 612.015   US   ISSN 0952-8172
RC271.I45   CODEN: MOLBEM
MOLECULAR BIOTHERAPY; the international journal for the application of biologicals in clinical or veterinary practice. 1988. q. $160 (foreign $200). Butterworth - Heinemann Ltd. (Subsidiary of: Reed International PLC), 80 Montvale Ave., Stoneham, MA 02180. TEL 617-438-8464. FAX 617-438-1479. TELEX 880052. Ed. Robert K. Oldham. adv.; bk.rev.; charts; illus.; index. (also avail. in microform from UMI; back issues avail.) **Indexed:** Telegen.
—BLDSC shelfmark: 5900.798500.
Description: Focuses on biological approaches to clinical cancer therapy.
Refereed Serial

616.99   US   ISSN 0899-1987
                           CODEN: MOCAE8
MOLECULAR CARCINOGENESIS. 8/yr. $350 (foreign $450). (University of Texas, M.D. Anderson Cancer Center) John Wiley & Sons, Inc., Journals, 605 Third Ave., New York, NY 10158. TEL 212-850-6000. FAX 212-850-6088. TELEX 12-7063. Eds. Thomas Slaga, Stuart H. Yuspa.
—BLDSC shelfmark: 5900.802000.
Description: Devoted to the study of the molecular aspects of mechanisms involved in chemical, physical and viral (biological) carcinogenesis.

616.99   US   ISSN 0896-7385
N C I CANCER WEEKLY; a complete weekly report privately circulated. Variant title: Cancer Weekly. 1988. w. (52/yr.). $916 (foreign $969). Charles W. Henderson, Ed. & Pub., Box 5528, Atlanta, GA 30307-0528. TEL 404-377-8895. FAX 205-991-1479. TELEX 3762848. (Subscr. to: Box 830409, Birmingham, AL 35283-0409)
●Also available online. Vendor(s): Data-Star, DIALOG, NewsNet.
Description: Comprehensive periodical on cancer.

616.99   US   ISSN 0270-7950
RC267
N C I FACT BOOK; national cancer institute. a. National Cancer Institute, Department of Health and Human Services, Bldg. 31, Rm. 10A16, Bethesda, MD 20892. TEL 301-496-5583.
Formerly: National Cancer Institute Fact Book.

616.9   JA
NATIONAL CANCER CENTER. ANNUAL REPORT/KOKURITSU GAN SENTA NENPO. 1967. a. free. National Cancer Center - Kokuritsu Gan Senta, 5-1-1 Tsukiji, Chuo-ku, Tokyo 104, Japan.

616.9   JA   ISSN 0077-3662
NATIONAL CANCER CENTER RESEARCH INSTITUTE. COLLECTED PAPERS/KOKURITSU GAN SENTA, TOKYO. COLLECTED PAPERS. (Text in English) 1966. a. free to medical libraries and researchers. National Cancer Center - Kokuritsu Gan Senta, 5-1-1 Tsukiji, Chuo-ku, Tokyo 104, Japan. author index; circ. 225.

616.994   US   ISSN 0027-8874
                         CODEN: JNCIEQ
NATIONAL CANCER INSTITUTE. JOURNAL. Short title: J N C I. 1940. fortn. $51. U.S. National Cancer Institute, 9030 Old Georgetown Rd., Rm. 213, Bethesda, MD 20814. TEL 301-496-4907. (Dist. by: Supt. of Documents, Washington, DC 20402) Ed. Dr. Daniel Ihde. bibl.; charts; illus.; index; circ. 4,100. (also avail. in microform from MIM,UMI) **Indexed:** Abstr.Hyg., Biol.Abstr., Biotech.Abstr., C.I.S. Abstr., Chem.Abstr., Chic.Per.Ind., Curr.Adv.Biochem., Curr.Adv.Cancer Res., Curr.Adv.Ecol.Sci., Curr.Adv.Genetics & Molec.Biol., Curr.Cont., Dent.Ind., Dok.Arbeitsmed., Excerp.Med., I.P.A., Ind.Med., Ind.U.S.Gov.Per., Ind.Vet., INIS Atomind., Nutr.Abstr., Poult.Abstr., Risk Abstr., Telegen, Triticale Abstr., Vet.Bull.
●Also available online. Vendor(s): BRS, BRS/Saunders Colleague, Mead Data Central.
—BLDSC shelfmark: 4830.000000.
Description: Contains original reports, articles, reviews and commentary on new findings in clinical and laboratory cancer research.
Refereed Serial

616.994   US   ISSN 1052-6773
                         CODEN: JNCME4
NATIONAL CANCER INSTITUTE. JOURNAL. MONOGRAPHS. 1959. irreg., latest no.10, 1990. price varies. U.S. National Cancer Institute, Department of Health and Human Services, 9030 Old Georgetown Rd., Bethesda, MD 20814. TEL 301-496-4907. (Subscr. to: Supt. of Documents, Washington, DC 20402) Ed. Dr. Daniel Ihde. circ. 3,000. (microfiche) **Indexed:** Biol.Abstr., Ind.Med.
—BLDSC shelfmark: 5914.670000.
Former titles: N C I Monographs (ISSN 0893-2190); National Cancer Institute. Monographs (ISSN 0083-1921)

616.9   CN   ISSN 0077-3689
NATIONAL CANCER INSTITUTE OF CANADA. ANNUAL REPORT. 1947. a. free. National Cancer Institute of Canada, 10 Alcorn Ave., Ste. 200, Toronto, Ont. M4V 3B1, Canada. TEL 416-961-7223. FAX 416-961-4189. Ed. Mrs. A. Vogel. circ. 1,000.

616.99   SP
NEOPLASIA; oncologia multidisciplinaria. 1984. bi-m. 4400 ptas.($45) (free to qualified personnel). Ediciones Doyma S.A., Travesera de Gracia, 17-21, 08021 Barcelona, Spain. TEL 200-07-11. FAX 209-11-36. TELEX 51964 INK E. Ed. J. Estape Rodriguez. adv.: page 125000 ptas.; trim 210 x 280; adv. contact: Cristina Garrote. circ. 2,000.
Description: For oncologists, epidemiologists, pathologists, surgeons, internists and specialists interested in oncology and neoplasia.

616.994   CS   ISSN 0028-2685
                         CODEN: NEOLA4
NEOPLASMA. (Text in English) 1954. bi-m. 240 Kcs.($32) (Slovenska Akademia Vied) Veda, Publishing House of the Slovak Academy of Sciences, Klemensova 19, 814 30 Bratislava, Czechoslovakia. (Dist. in Western countries by: Karger-Libri AG, Scientific Booksellers, Arnold-Bocklin-Strasse 25, CH-4000 Basel 11, Switzerland) Ed. Viliam Ujhazy. bk.rev.; charts; illus.; index. **Indexed:** Biol.Abstr., C.I.S. Abstr., Chem.Abstr., Curr.Adv.Cancer Res., Curr.Adv.Genetics & Molec.Biol., Curr.Cont., Dent.Ind., Excerp.Med., Ind.Med., Ind.Sci.Rev., Ind.Vet., Risk Abstr., Vet.Bull.
—BLDSC shelfmark: 6075.630000.
Description: Publishes original works of Czechoslovak and foreign authors in the fields of experimental and clinical oncology. Covers the biochemistry of tumors, the biology and genetics of oncology, and significant causistry. Includes statistics of oncology.

616   US
NORTHWESTERN UNIVERSITY. ROBERT H. LURIE CANCER CENTER. JOURNAL. (Not published 1988-1989) 1977. 3/yr. free. Northwestern University, Robert H. Lurie Cancer Center, Olson Pavilion 8250, 303 E. Chicago Ave., Chicago, IL 60611. TEL 312-908-5250. Ed. Dr. Steven T. Rosen. bk.rev.; charts; illus.; index; circ. 2,000.
Former titles (until vol.2, no.2., 1991): Northwestern University Cancer Center. Journal (ISSN 1049-6025); Supersedes (1977-1987): Cancer Focus (ISSN 0147-1155)
Refereed Serial

616.994   PL   ISSN 0029-540X
                         CODEN: NOWOAL
NOWOTWORY. (Text in Polish; summaries in English) 1923. q. $80. Maria Curie-Sklodowska Memorial Cancer Center and Institute of Oncology, Ul. Wawelska 15, 00-973 Warsaw, Poland. TEL 48-22-224831. FAX 48-22-222429. TELEX 812704 INONK. (Co-sponsor: Polskie Towarzystwo Onkologiczne) Ed. Jerzy Meyza. bk.rev.; index; circ. 2,000. (reprint service avail.) **Indexed:** Biol.Abstr., Chem.Abstr., Dent.Ind., Excerp.Med., Ind.Med.
—BLDSC shelfmark: 6180.479000.
Description: Highlights oncology, radio-chemotherapy and surgery, cancer biology, epidemiology and control.

616.39 616.99   US   ISSN 0163-5581
                         CODEN: NUCADQ
NUTRITION AND CANCER; an international journal. 1978. 6/yr., 2 vols. $120 to individuals (foreign $150); institutions $325 (foreign $360). Lawrence Erlbaum Associates, Inc., 365 Broadway, Hillsdale, NJ 07642. TEL 201-666-4110. FAX 201-666-2394. Ed. Dr. Gio B. Gori. bk.rev.; charts; illus.; circ. 500. (back issues avail.) **Indexed:** Biol.Abstr., Chem.Abstr., Dairy Sci.Abstr., Dent.Ind., Excerp.Med., Ind.Med., Maize Abstr., Nutr.Abstr., Triticale Abstr.
—BLDSC shelfmark: 6188.045000.
Description: Reports and reviews current findings on the effect of nutrition on the etiology, therapy, and prevention of cancer.
Refereed Serial

616.99 612.015   UK   ISSN 0950-9232
                         CODEN: ONCNES
ONCOGENE. 1987. m. £350 (foreign £380). Macmillan Press Ltd., Houndmills, Basingstoke, Hampshire RG21 2XS, England. TEL 0256-29242. FAX 0256-810526. Ed.Bd. adv.; index. (also avail. in microfilm from UMI; back issues avail.) **Indexed:** Anim.Breed.Abstr., Curr.Cont., Excerp.Med., Ind.Vet., Small Anim.Abstr., Telegen, Vet.Bull.
—BLDSC shelfmark: 6256.782000.
Description: Studies all aspects of oncogene research and relationships to cancer.

616.99　　　US　ISSN 0890-6467
CODEN: ONCGE7
ONCOGENE RESEARCH. 8/yr. (in 2 vols.; 4 nos./vol.). $111. Harwood Academic Publishers, 270 Eighth Ave., New York, NY 10011. TEL 212-206-8900. FAX 212-645-2459. TELEX 236735 GOPUB UR. (Subscr. to: Box 786, Cooper Sta., New York, NY 10276. TEL 800-545-8398; UK subscr. to: Box 90, Reading, Berkshire RG1 8JL, England. TEL 0734-560-080) (also avail. in microform)
—BLDSC shelfmark: 6256.783000.
Refereed Serial

616.994　575.1　　UK　ISSN 0950-0561
ONCOGENES. 1987. s-m. £100. Sheffield University Biomedical Information Service (SUBIS), The University, Sheffield S10 2TN, England. TEL 0742-768555. FAX 0742-739826. TELEX 547216-UGSHEF-G.
Description: Current awareness service for researchers. Covers oncogenes and neoplastic cell transformation.

616.99　　　SP　ISSN 0378-4835
CODEN: NCLGDV
ONCOLOGIA. 1976. m. 8500 ptas.($65) (Sociedad Espanola de Oncologia) Alpe Editores, S.A., Pedro Rico, 27, 28029 Madrid, Spain. TEL 733 88 11. FAX 315-96-52. Ed.Bd. adv.; charts; illus.; bibl. **Indexed:** Biol.Abstr., Chem.Abstr., Excerp.Med., Ind.Med.Esp.

616.994　　　SZ　ISSN 0030-2414
RC261　　CODEN: ONCOBS
ONCOLOGY; international journal of cancer research and treatment. (Text in English) 1948. m. 793 SFr.($529) S. Karger AG, Allschwilerstr. 10, P.O. Box, CH-4009 Basel, Switzerland. TEL 061-3061111. FAX 061-3061234. TELEX CH 962652. Ed.Bd. adv.; bk.rev.; abstr.; bibl.; charts; illus.; index; circ. 1,200. (also avail. in microform) **Indexed:** Biol.Abstr., Chem.Abstr., Curr.Adv.Ecol.Sci., Curr.Cont., Dairy Sci.Abstr., Dent.Ind., Excerp.Med., Ind.Med., Ind.Vet., Nutr.Abstr., Telegen, Vet.Bull.
—BLDSC shelfmark: 6256.900000.
Supersedes: Oncologia.

616.99　　　US　ISSN 1046-3356
ONCOLOGY ISSUES; the journal of cancer program management. 1986. q. $40 to individuals; institutions and libraries $60. Association of Community Cancer Centers, 11600 Nebel St., Ste. 201, Rockville, MD 20852. TEL 301-984-9496. FAX 301-770-1949. Ed. Marilyn M. Evans. adv.; circ. 17,000. (back issues avail.)
Description: Provides economic, health policy and planning information to United States cancer programs.

ONCOLOGY NURSING FORUM. see *MEDICAL SCIENCES — Nurses And Nursing*

616.99　　　US　ISSN 0965-0407
RC261.A1
ONCOLOGY RESEARCH. 1989. 12/yr. $415 (effective 1992). Pergamon Press, Inc., Journals Division, 660 White Plains Rd., Tarrytown, NY 10591-5153. TEL 914-524-9200. FAX 914-333-2444. (And: Headington Hill Hall, Oxford OX3 0BW, England. TEL 0865-794141) Ed. A.C. Sartorelli. (also avail. in microform; back issues avail.)
Formerly (until 1992): Cancer Communications (ISSN 0955-3541)
Refereed Serial

616.99　　　US　ISSN 0276-2234
ONCOLOGY TIMES; the independent newspaper for cancer specialists. 1979. m. $60 to individuals (foreign $70); insitutions $85 (foreign $95). Lippincott Healthcare Publications, 1180 Avenue of the Americas, 6th Fl., New York, NY 10036. TEL 212-532-9400. FAX 212-679-9716. (Subscr. to: Subscriber Services Dept., Downsville Pike, Rte.3, Box 20B, Hagerstown, MD 21740) Ed. Debra Lumpe. adv.; index; circ. 25,218. (back issues avail.)
—BLDSC shelfmark: 6256.984000.
Description: Covers all aspects of the diagnosis, treatment, and care of the cancer patient.

616　　　SZ　ISSN 0378-584X
CODEN: ONKOD2
ONKOLOGIE; Zeitschrift fuer Krebsforschung und -behandlung. (Text in English and German) bi-m. 124 SFr.($83) (Deutsche und Oesterreichische Gesellschaft fuer Haematologie und Onkologie) S. Karger AG, Allschwilerstr. 10, P.O. Box, CH-4009 Basel, Switzerland. TEL 061-3061111. FAX 061-3061234. TELEX CH 962652. (Co-sponsor: Oesterreichische Krebsgesellschaft-Krebsliga) Ed. W. Queisser, J.H. Holzner. adv.; illus.; index; circ. 20,000. (also avail. in microfilm; back issues avail.) **Indexed:** Biol.Abstr., Curr.Adv.Cancer Res., Curr.Adv.Ecol.Sci., Curr.Cont., Dent.Ind., Excerp.Med., Ind.Med.
—BLDSC shelfmark: 6260.650000.
Formerly: Oesterreichische Zeitschrift fuer Onkologie.

616　　　BU　ISSN 0369-7649
CODEN: ONKLAO
ONKOLOGIJA. (Text in Bulgarian; summaries in English and Russian) 1964. q. 10 lv.($6) (Ministerstvo na Narodnoto Zdrave) Izdatelstvo Meditsina i Fizkultura, 11, Pl. Slaveikov, Sofia, Bulgaria. (Dist. by: Hemus, 6, Rouski Blvd., 1000 Sofia, Bulgaria) (Co-sponsor: Nauchno Druzhestvo po Onkologija) Ed. T. Tchernozemski. circ. 713. **Indexed:** Abstr.Bulg.Sci.Med.Lit., Excerp.Med.
—BLDSC shelfmark: 0127.450000.

616　　　JA
OSAKA UNIVERSITY. INSTITUTE FOR CANCER RESEARCH. ANNUAL REPORT. (Text in English) irrege. exchange basis. Osaka Daigaku, Igakubu Fuzoku Gankenku Shisetsu - Osaka University, Institute for Cancer Research, 3-12 Dojimahama-dori, Fukushima-ku, Osaka-shi 553, Japan.

616.9　　　US
P P O UPDATE. (Principles and Practices of Oncology) 1987. m. $99. J.B. Lippincott Co., E. Washington Sq., Philadelphia, PA 19105. TEL 215-238-4200. FAX 215-238-4228. (Subscr. to: Downville Pike, Rt. 3, Box 20B, Hagerstown, MD 21740. TEL 800-638-3030) Ed.Bd. circ. 25,000 (controlled). (looseleaf format)
Description: Provides updated information for the textbook Principles and Practices of Oncology.

THE PAIN CLINIC. see *MEDICAL SCIENCES — Anaesthesiology*

PEDIATRIC HEMATOLOGY & ONCOLOGY. see *MEDICAL SCIENCES — Pediatrics*

PEDIATRIC HEMATOLOGY - ONCOLOGY SERIES. see *MEDICAL SCIENCES — Pediatrics*

PEDIATRIC PATHOLOGY. see *MEDICAL SCIENCES — Pediatrics*

616.994　　　IT　ISSN 0069-8520
CODEN: PPQCDL
PERUGIA QUADRENNIAL INTERNATIONAL CONFERENCES ON CANCER. PROCEEDINGS. 1957. quadrennial. price varies. Universita degli Studi di Perugia, Division of Cancer Research, P.O. Box 327, 06100 Perugia, Monteluce, Italy. Ed. Lucio Severi. index.

616.994　　　PH　ISSN 0031-7608
PHILIPPINE JOURNAL OF CANCER.* vol.12, 1970. q. P.10. Philippine Cancer Society, 310 San Rafael, Manila, Philippines. Ed. Dr. C.P. Manahan. charts; illus.; stat.; index; circ. 1,000. **Indexed:** Chem.Abstr., Ind.Med.

616.99　　　US　ISSN 0743-8176
RC261.A1
PRIMARY CARE & CANCER. 1981. m. $45. Dominus Publishing Company, Inc., 331 Willis Ave., Box 86, Williston Park, NY 11596. TEL 516-294-1880. Ed. James F. McCarthy. adv.; charts; illus.; stat.; circ. 91,000 (controlled). (also avail. in microform from UMI; reprint service avail. from UMI)
—BLDSC shelfmark: 6612.908100.
Formerly (until 1984): Your Patient and Cancer (ISSN 0272-6955)

616.994　　　CN　ISSN 0033-0604
PROGRESS AGAINST CANCER/PROGRES CONTRE LE CANCER. (Editions in English and French) 1948. q. free. Canadian Cancer Society, 10 Alcorn Ave., Ste. 200, Toronto, Ont. M4V 3B1, Canada. TEL 416-961-7223. Ed. Kerstin Ring. illus.; circ. 9,000 (8,000 English ed.; 1,000 French ed.).

616　　　US　ISSN 0145-3726
CODEN: PCRTDK
PROGRESS IN CANCER RESEARCH AND THERAPY. 1976. irreg., latest vol.35. price varies. Raven Press, 1185 Ave. of the Americas, New York, NY 10036. TEL 212-930-9500. FAX 212-869-3495. TELEX 640073. **Indexed:** Biol.Abstr., Chem.Abstr., Dairy Sci.Abstr., Hort.Abstr., Nutr.Abstr.
Refereed Serial

616.994　　　SZ　ISSN 0079-6263
RC254　　CODEN: PEXTAR
PROGRESS IN EXPERIMENTAL TUMOR RESEARCH. (Text in English) 1960. irreg. (approx. 1/yr.). price varies. S. Karger AG, Allschwilerstr. 10, P.O. Box, CH-4009 Basel, Switzerland. TEL 061-3061111. FAX 061-3061234. TELEX CH 962652. Ed. G. Nagel. (reprint service avail. from ISI, back issues avail.) **Indexed:** Biol.Abstr., Chem.Abstr., Curr.Cont., Ind.Med., Ind.Sci.Rev.

THE PROSTATE. see *MEDICAL SCIENCES*

616.99　　　UK　ISSN 1057-9249
CODEN: POJCEE
▼**PSYCHO-ONCOLOGY;** journal of the psychological, social and behavioral dimensions of cancer. 1992. q. $160. John Wiley & Sons Ltd., Journals, Baffins Ln., Chichester, Sussex PO19 1UD, England. TEL 0243-779777. FAX 0243-775878. TELEX 86290-WIBOOK-G. Eds. J. Holland, M. Watson.
Description: Concerned with the psychological, social, behavioral, and ethical aspects of cancer.

PUBLIC HEALTH REVIEWS; an international quarterly. see *PUBLIC HEALTH AND SAFETY*

RADIATION MEDICINE; medical imaging and radiation oncology. see *MEDICAL SCIENCES — Radiology And Nuclear Medicine*

616.994　　　US　ISSN 0080-0015
RC261　　CODEN: RRCRBU
RECENT RESULTS IN CANCER RESEARCH/FORTSCHRITTE DER KREBSFORSCHUNG. (Text in English; occasionally in French or German) 1965. irreg. price varies. Springer-Verlag, 175 Fifth Ave., New York, NY 10010. TEL 212-460-1500. Ed. P. Rentchnick. (reprint service avail. from ISI) **Indexed:** Biol.Abstr., Chem.Abstr., Dent.Ind., Excerp.Med., Ind.Med.
—BLDSC shelfmark: 7305.090000.

616.99　　　GW　ISSN 0935-0411
REGIONAL CANCER TREATMENT. 1989. 6/yr. DM.256($153) Springer-Verlag, Heidelberger Platz 3, D-1000 Berlin 33, Germany. TEL 030-8207-1. Ed.Bd.
—BLDSC shelfmark: 7336.572900.

616.99　　　NE
REVIEWS IN CANCER EPIDEMIOLOGY. 1980. irreg., vol.2, 1983. price varies. Elsevier Science Publishers B.V., Books Division, P.O. Box 211, 1000 AE Amsterdam, Netherlands. TEL 020-5803911. FAX 020-5803705. TELEX 18582 ESPA NL. (Subscr. in U.S. and Canada to: Elsevier Science Publishing Co., Inc., Box 882, Madison Sq. Sta., New York, NY 10159. TEL 212-989-5800)
Refereed Serial

616.994　　　BL　ISSN 0034-7116
CODEN: RVBCA7
REVISTA BRASILEIRA DE CANCEROLOGIA. (Summaries in English and Portuguese) 1947. bi-m. free to qualified personnel; exchange requested. Divisao Nacional de Doencas Cronico-Degenerativas, Praca Cruz Vermelha 23, sala 230, CEP 20230 Rio de Janeiro, RJ, Brazil. Ed. Jorge Wanderley. adv.; bibl.; charts; illus.; circ. 2,500. **Indexed:** Chem.Abstr, Excerp.Med., Ind.Med.

616.99　　　CU　ISSN 0864-0297
REVISTA CUBANA DE ONCOLOGIA. (Text in Spanish; summaries in English, French, Spanish) 1985. s-a. $10 in N. America; S. America $12; Europe $14. Ministerio de Salud Publica, Centro Nacional de Informacion de Ciencias Medicas, Calle E No. 452, e-19 y 21, Plaza de la Revolucion, Apdo. 605, Havana, Cuba. TEL 809-32-5338. (Dist. by: Ediciones Cubanas, Obispo No. 527, Apdo. 605, Havana, Cuba) Dir. Dr. Zoilo Marinello Vidaurreta. bibl.; charts; illus.; index; circ. 1,000. **Indexed:** Excerp.Med.

MEDICAL SCIENCES — CANCER

616.994   RM
REVISTA DE CHIRURGIE, ONCOLOGIE, RADIOLOGIE, O.R.L, OFTALMOLOGIE, STOMATOLOGIE. ONCOLOGIE. (Text in Rumanian; summaries in English, French, German, Russian) 1962. 4/yr. $20. Uniunea Societatilor de Stiinte Medicale din Republica Socialista Rumania, Str. Progresului No. 8-10, Sectorul 1, Bucharest 70754, Rumania. (Subscr. to: ILEXIM, Str. 13 Decembrie Nr. 3, P.O. Box 136-137, Bucharest, Rumania) Ed.Bd. adv.; bk.rev.; abstr.; bibl.; charts; illus.; index. **Indexed:** Biol.Abstr., Chem.Abstr.
   Supersedes in part: Oncologia si Radiologia (ISSN 0030-2406)

RIVISTA DI ANATOMIA PATOLOGICA E DI ONCOLOGIA. see MEDICAL SCIENCES

616.99 150   US
▼**S O L O.** (Surviving Our Leukemia on Our Own) 1992. m. $15. Spirit of Success Publishing Company, 704 Versailles, Mesquite, TX 75149. TEL 214-216-1962. Ed. Christine Michael.
   Description: Newsletter for cancer patients who have had their spouse or partner abandon them upon diagnosis.

616.994   JA   ISSN 0022-2119
SAIBOKAKU BYORIGAKU ZASSHI/JOURNAL OF KARYOPATHOLOGY; tumor and tumor virus. (Text in Japanese; summaries in English) 1953. irreg. $2. Okayama Daigaku, Igakubu Byorigaku Kyoshitsu - Okayama University, School of Medicine, Department of Pathology, 2-5-1 Shikata-cho, Okayama 700, Japan. Ed. Y. Hamazaki. adv. (reprint service avail. from ISI) **Indexed:** Biol.Abstr., Ind.Med.

616.99   BU   ISSN 0582-3250
   CODEN: SSCMBX
SCRIPTA SCIENTIFICA MEDICA. (Text in English; summaries in Russian) 1962. a. 10 lv. Izdatelstvo Meditsina i Fizkultura, Pl. Slaveikov 11, Sofia, Bulgaria. (Subscr. to: Higher Institute of Medicine, 55 Marin Drinov St., Varna 9002, Bulgaria) Ed. G. Marinov. (back issues avail.) **Indexed:** Abstr.Bulg.Sci.Med.Lit., Abstr.Hyg., Biol.Abstr., BSL Biol., Ref.Zh., Trop.Dis.Bull.
—BLDSC shelfmark: 8213.230000.

616.99   US   ISSN 1043-0733
   CODEN: SCTHES
SELECTIVE CANCER THERAPEUTICS. 1983. q. $142 (foreign $182). Mary Ann Liebert, Inc., 1651 Third Ave., New York, NY 10128. TEL 212-289-2300. FAX 212-289-4697. Ed. Eric G. Mayhew. **Indexed:** Chem.Abstr., Curr.Adv.Ecol.Sci., Excerp.Med., Telegen.
—BLDSC shelfmark: 8235.171800.
   Formerly (until 1989): Cancer Drug Delivery (ISSN 0732-9482)
   Description: Reports on research and advances in cancer therapy, including more selective delivery of drugs, biologicals, radiopharmaceuticals, and advances in delivery instrumentation and technology.
   Refereed Serial

SEMINARS IN CANCER BIOLOGY SERIES. see BIOLOGY — Biological Chemistry

574.8 616.994   US   ISSN 0093-7754
RC261   CODEN: SOLGAV
SEMINARS IN ONCOLOGY. 1974. bi-m. $98 to individuals; institutions $1136 foreign $154. W.B. Saunders Co. (Subsidiary of: Harcourt Brace Jovanovich, Inc.), Curtis Center, Independence Square W., Philadelphia, PA 19106. TEL 215-238-7800. (Subscr. to: 6277 Sea Harbor Dr., 4th Fl., Orlando FL 32891) Ed. Dr. John W. Yarbro. adv.; bibl.; charts; illus.; index. **Indexed:** ASCA, Biol.Abstr., C.I.S. Abstr., Chem.Abstr., Curr.Adv.Cell & Devel.Biol., Curr.Adv.Ecol.Sci., Curr.Adv.Genetics & Molec.Biol., Curr.Cont., Dent.Ind., Excerp.Med., Ind.Med., Sci.Cit.Ind.
●Also available online. Vendor(s): Mead Data Central.
—BLDSC shelfmark: 8239.456500.

SEMINARS IN ONCOLOGY NURSING. see MEDICAL SCIENCES — Nurses And Nursing

616.99   US
▼**SEMINARS IN RADIATION ONCOLOGY.** 1991. q. $80 per no. W.B. Saunders Co. (Subsidiary of: Harcourt Brace Jovanovich, Inc.), Curtis Center, Independence Sq. W., Philadelphia, PA 19106. TEL 215-238-7800. Ed. Dr. Joel E. Tepper. adv.; circ. 907.

616.99   US
SEMINARS IN SURGICAL ONCOLOGY. 1985. bi-m. $195 (foreign $270). John Wiley & Sons, Inc., Journals, 605 Third Ave., New York, NY 10158. TEL 212-850-6000. FAX 212-850-6988. TELEX 12-7063. Ed. Gerald P. Murphy. adv.
   Description: Offers invited review articles about topics in the field of surgical oncology; each issue focuses on a particular disease entity.

616.99   CC   ISSN 1001-1692
SHIYONG ZHONGLIU ZAZHI/JOURNAL OF APPLIED ONCOLOGY. (Text in Chinese) q. Zhejiang Yike Daxue - Zhejiang University of Medical Sciences, 157 Yan'an Lu, Hangzhou, Zhejiang 310006, People's Republic of China. TEL 722700. Ed. Zheng Shu.
   Refereed Serial

616.99   CC
SHIYONG ZHONGLIUXUE ZAZHI/JOURNAL OF APPLIED ONCOLOGY. (Text in Chinese) q. Heilongjiang Zhongliu Fangzhi Bangongshi - Heilongjiang Cancer Prevention and Treatment Office, Haping Lu, Harbin, Heilongjiang 150040, People's Republic of China. TEL 33977. Ed. Ding Li.

616.99   GW   ISSN 0721-6831
SIGNAL; Leben mit Krebs. 4/yr. DM.28. Verlag fuer Medizin Dr. Ewald Fischer GmbH, Fritz-Frey-Str. 21, Postfach 105767, 6900 Heidelberg 1, Germany. TEL 06221-4062-0. Ed. Arndt Kroedel. **Indexed:** Abstr.Engl.Stud.

616.9   US
SLOAN-KETTERING INSTITUTE: RESEARCH AND EDUCATIONAL PROGRAMS. 1949. biennial. free. Memorial Sloan-Kettering Cancer Center, 1275 York Ave., New York, NY 10021. TEL 212-639-5818. circ. 7,000.
   Former titles: Sloan-Kettering Institute for Cancer Research. Progress Report (ISSN 0081-0045); Memorial Sloan-Kettering Cancer Center. New York. Report.
   Description: Research activities of Sloan-Kettering Institute investigators in molecular biology, cell biology and genetics, immunology, molecular pharmacology and therapeutics, molecular biochemistry and biophysics. Includes the Institute's educational programs.

616.99   US   ISSN 0888-0700
RC261.A1   CODEN: SMFREO
SOVIET MEDICAL REVIEWS. SECTION F: ONCOLOGY REVIEWS. a. $118. Harwood Academic Publishers, 270 Eighth Ave., New York, NY 10011. TEL 212-645-2459. FAX 212-645-2459. TELEX 236735 GOPUB UR. (Subscr. to: Box 786, Cooper Sta., New York, NY 10276. TEL 800-545-8398; UK subscr. to: P.O. Box 90, Reading, Berkshire RG1 8JL, England. TEL 0734-560-080) Ed. N.N. Trapeznikov. (also avail. in microform)
—BLDSC shelfmark: 8359.616000.
   Refereed Serial

616.99   UK
▼**SURGICAL ONCOLOGY.** 1991. bi-m. £55 (foreign £63). Blackwell Scientific Publications Ltd., Osney Mead, Oxford OX2 OEL, England. TEL 0865-240201. FAX 0865-721205. TELEX 833355-MEDBOK-G. Ed.Bd. adv.; bk.rev.; illus.; index. (back issues avail.)

616.994   US   ISSN 0082-0733
SYMPOSIA ON FUNDAMENTAL CANCER RESEARCH. PAPERS. no.2, 1947. a. price varies. American Association for Cancer Research, Inc., 428 E. Preston St., Baltimore, MD 21202. TEL 301-528-4000. Eds. R.W. Cumley, J. McCay.

616.994   FI   ISSN 0356-3081
SYOPA/CANCER. (Text in Finnish, Swedish) 1969. 6/yr. FIM 120. Suomen Syopayhdistys - Cancer Society of Finland, Liisankatu 21 B, 00170 Helsinki 17, Finland. FAX 358-0-1351093. adv.; bk.rev.; circ. 140,000. **Indexed:** Risk Abstr.
   Former titles: Syovantorjunta - Kampen Mot Kraefta - Against Cancer; Terveystyo (ISSN 0049-2787)

T C A REPORT. (Tissue Culture Association) see BIOLOGY — Microbiology

TASK FORCE ON ENVIRONMENTAL CANCER AND HEART AND LUNG DISEASE. ANNUAL REPORT TO CONGRESS. see ENVIRONMENTAL STUDIES — Toxicology And Environmental Safety

TISSUE CULTURE ASSOCIATION. MONOGRAPH SERIES. see BIOLOGY — Microbiology

TISSUE CULTURE ASSOCIATION. PROCEEDINGS. see BIOLOGY — Microbiology

TUBERCULOSIS, LEPROSY AND CANCER. see MEDICAL SCIENCES — Communicable Diseases

616.99   SZ   ISSN 1010-4283
TUMOR BIOLOGY. (Text in English) 1980. bi-m. 317.10 SFr.($211.40) to individuals; institutions 453 SFr.($302). (International Society for Oncodevelopmental Biology and Medicine) S. Karger AG, Allschwilerstr. 10, P.O. Box, CH-4009 Basel, Switzerland. TEL 061-3061111. FAX 061-3061234. TELEX CH 962652. Eds. H. Hirai, A.M. Neville. **Indexed:** Curr.Adv.Biochem., Curr.Adv.Cancer Res., Curr.Adv.Cell & Devel.Biol.
—BLDSC shelfmark: 9070.645500.
   Former titles: Oncodevelopmental Biology and Medicine (ISSN 0167-1618); Tumour Biology (ISSN 0289-5447)

616.994   JA   ISSN 0041-4093
   CODEN: TUREA6
TUMOR RESEARCH: EXPERIMENTAL AND CLINICAL/GAN KENKYU, JIKKEN TO RINSHO. (Text in English and European languages) 1966. s-a. exchange basis. Sapporo Ika Daigaku, Fuzoku Gan Kenkyujo - Sapporo Medical College, Cancer Research Institute, Nishi-17-chome, Minami-1-jo, Chuo-ku, Sapporo-shi, Hokkaido 060, Japan. Ed. Kei Fujinaga. abstr.; bibl.; charts; illus.; stat.; circ. 550. (also avail. in microfilm from UMI) **Indexed:** Biol.Abstr., Chem.Abstr., Curr.Adv.Ecol.Sci., Excerp.Med.

616.99   GW   ISSN 0722-219X
TUMORDIAGNOSTIK & THERAPIE. bi-m. DM.120. Georg Thieme Verlag, Postfach 104853, Ruedigerstr. 14, 7000 Stuttgart 10, Germany. TEL 0711-8931-0. FAX 0711-8931298. Eds. M. Luethgens, S. Seeber. circ. 7,500.
—BLDSC shelfmark: 9070.675000.

616.994   IT   ISSN 0041-4352
TUMORI. (Text in English) 1911. bi-m. L.135000. (Istituto Nazionale Tumori) Casa Editrice Ambrosiana, Via Frua 6, 20146 Milan, Italy. FAX 2-236-2692. Dir. Umberto Veronesi. bk.rev.; bibl.; charts; illus.; index; cum.index; circ. 2,000. **Indexed:** Biol.Abstr., Chem.Abstr., Curr.Adv.Biochem., Curr.Adv.Cancer Res., Curr.Adv.Ecol.Sci., Curr.Adv.Genetics & Molec.Biol., Curr.Cont., Dent.Ind., Excerp.Med., Ind.Med., Ind.Vet., Risk Abstr., Vet.Bull.

616.99   UK   ISSN 0955-5102
TUMOUR MARKER UPDATE. 1989. bi-m. £45($90) to individuals; institutions £55($105). Oncology Information Service, University of Leeds, Leeds LS2 9JT, England. TEL 0303-850501. FAX 0303-850162. (Subscr. to: Bailey Management Services, Ltd., 127 Sandgate Rd., Folkestone CT20 2BL) Ed.Bd. circ. 500.
   Description: Locates and reports the scientific literature on circulating tumor markers from 1400 international biomedical titles.

U I C C INTERNATIONAL CALENDAR OF MEETINGS ON CANCER. (International Union Against Cancer) see MEETINGS AND CONGRESSES

616.99   SZ
U I C C INTERNATIONAL DIRECTORY OF CANCER INSTITUTES AND ORGANIZATIONS. 1976. quadrennial, 5th edition, 1990. 30 Fr. International Union Against Cancer, 3 rue de Conseil-General, 1205 Geneva, Switzerland. TEL 022-201811. FAX 022-201810.
   Formerly: International Directory of Specialized Cancer Research and Treatment Establishments.

ULTRASTRUCTURAL PATHOLOGY. see BIOLOGY — Cytology And Histology

616.99   US   ISSN 0272-2836
RC268.6
U.S. NATIONAL TOXICOLOGY PROGRAM. ANNUAL REPORT ON CARCINOGENS. 1980. a. U.S. National Toxicology Program, Box 12233, Research Triangle Park, NC 27709. TEL 919-541-3991.

616.994   US
UNIVERSITY OF TEXAS. M.D. ANDERSON CANCER CENTER. CANCER BULLETIN. 1948. bi-m. $40 (foreign $50). University of Texas, M.D. Anderson Cancer Center, 1515 Holcombe Blvd., Houston, TX 77030. TEL 713-792-6014. FAX 713-792-6014. Ed. Dr. Helmuth Goepfert. bk.rev.; illus.; index; circ. 39,000. **Indexed:** Biol.Abstr., Excerp.Med., Ind.Med.
   Former titles: M.D. Anderson Hospital and Tumor Institute at Houston. Cancer Bulletin (ISSN 0740-820X); Cancer Bulletin (ISSN 0008-5448)

UROLOGISCHE ONKOLOGIE. see *MEDICAL SCIENCES — Urology And Nephrology*

616.994   FR
VIVRE. 1923. q. 20 F. Ligue Nationale Francaise Contre le Cancer, 1 av. Stephen Pichon, 75013 Paris, France. Ed. Alain Froissard. adv.; bk.rev.; bibl.; charts; illus.; stat.; circ. 300,000. **Indexed:** Biol.Abstr., Ind.Med.
   Formerly: Lutte Contre le Cancer (ISSN 0024-7642)
   Description: Information on cancer research, prevention, and treatments.

616.994   RU   ISSN 0507-3758
CODEN: VOONAW
VOPROSY ONKOLOGII/PROBLEMS IN ONCOLOGY. (Text in Russian; summaries in English) 1955. m. 31.80 Rub.($27.60) (Vsesoyuznoe Nauchnoe Obshchestvo Onkologov) Izdatel'stvo Meditsina, Petroverigskii pereulok 6-8, 101838 Moscow, Russia. (Subscr. to: Mezhdunarodnaya Kniga, Moscow, G-200, Russia) (Co-sponsor: Ministerstvo Zdravookhraneniya S.S.S.R.) Ed. N.P. Napalkov. bk.rev.; abstr.; bibl.; charts; illus.; stat.; circ. 6,000. **Indexed:** Biol.Abstr., Biotech.Abstr., Chem.Abstr., Curr.Cont., Dent.Ind., Dok.Arbeitsmed., Excerp.Med., Ind.Med., Ind.Vet., Nutr.Abstr., Vet.Bull.
  —BLDSC shelfmark: 0043.630000.
   Description: Discusses problems of experimental and clinical oncology (origin, development, course, diagnosis and methods of treating neoplasms), the problems of the organization of oncological aid to the population, prevention and treatment of malignant tumours and precancerous diseases.

616.994   US   ISSN 1040-1741
RC261
YEAR BOOK OF ONCOLOGY. 1957. a. $54.95. Mosby - Year Book, Inc., Continuity Division, 200 N. LaSalle, Chicago, IL 60601. TEL 312-726-9733. FAX 312-726-6075. TELEX 206155. Ed. Dr. Robert C. Young, M.D. illus. (reprint service avail.)
  ●Also available online. Vendor(s): BRS.
  Also available on CD-ROM. Producer(s): SilverPlatter.
   Formerly: Year Book of Cancer (ISSN 0084-3679)

616.99   CC   ISSN 1000-8179
ZHONGGUO ZHONGLIU LINCHUANG/CHINESE JOURNAL OF CLINICAL ONCOLOGY. (Text in Chinese) 1963. bi-m. Y2.40 per no. Tianjin Zhongliu Yanjiusuo - Tianjin Cancer Institute, Huan-hu-xi Lu, Tiyuanbei, Hexi Qu, Tianjin 300060, People's Republic of China. TEL 319929. FAX 86-022-319984. Ed. Zhang Tian-ze. adv.: B&W page Y1200; adv. contact: Meng-Lan Li.

ZHONGHUA SHENJING WAIKE ZAZHI/CHINESE JOURNAL OF NEUROSURGERY. see *MEDICAL SCIENCES — Psychiatry And Neurology*

616.99   CC
ZHONGHUA ZHONGLIU ZAZHI/CHINESE JOURNAL OF ONCOLOGY. (Text in Chinese) bi-m. $3.50 per no. Guoji Shudian, Qikan Bu, Chegongzhuang Xilu 21, P.O. Box 399, Beijing 100044, People's Republic of China. **Indexed:** Biol.Abstr., Excerp.Med., Ind.Med., Maize Abstr.

MEDICAL SCIENCES — Cardiovascular Diseases

616.1   US
A C C E L; audio cassette journal of clinical cardiology. 1969. m. $150 to non-members; members $125. American College of Cardiology, 9111 Old Georgetown Rd., Bethesda, MD 20814. TEL 800-253-4636. FAX 301-897-9745. Ed. Dr. Sylvan L. Weinberg. index; circ. 7,500. (audio cassette) **Indexed:** Risk Abstr.
   Former titles: A C C E L for Physicians; A C C E S S (ISSN 0001-0626)

616.1   BE   ISSN 0001-5385
CODEN: ACCAAQ
ACTA CARDIOLOGICA; journal international de cardiologie - international journal of cardiology. (Supplements avail.) (Text in English) 1946. bi-m. 3100 BEF. Association des Societes Scientifiques Medicales Belges - Vereiniging van de Belgische Wetenschappelijke Genootschappen, Av. Circulaire, 138A, B-1180 Brussels, Belgium. TEL 02-375-58-92. FAX 02-374-96-28. Eds. J. Lequime, H. Kesteloot. adv.; bk.rev.; charts; illus.; index; circ. 900. **Indexed:** ASCA, Biol.Abstr., Biotech.Abstr., Chem.Abstr., Curr.Cont., Excerp.Med., Ind.Med.
   Description: Papers on fundamental, clinical, epidemiological and nutritional research in the field of cardiovascular disease.

616.1   IT   ISSN 0392-9698
ACTA CARDIOLOGICA MEDITERANEA. (Text in English, Italian) 1960. 3/yr. L.35000($35) Carbone Editore, Via G. Daita, 29, 90139 Palermo, Italy. TEL 091-321273. FAX 91-321782. adv.; abstr.; bibl.; illus.; stat.; index; circ. 3,000.
  —BLDSC shelfmark: 0608.403000.
   Description: Discusses and reviews clinical cases of cardiovascular diseases.

616.1   US
ADVANCED CARDIAC LIFE SUPPORT. m. $149. American Health Consultants, Inc., Six Piedmont Center, Ste. 400, 3525 Piedmont Rd., N.E., Atlanta, GA 30305. TEL 800-688-2421. FAX 800-284-3291. Ed. Dr. Mikel A. Rothenberg.
  Refereed Serial

616.1   US
ADVANCES IN CARDIAC SURGERY. 1989. a. $69.95. Mosby - Year Book, Inc. (Chicago) (Subsidiary of: Times Mirror Company), 200 N. LaSalle St., Chicago, IL 60601-1080. TEL 312-726-9733. FAX 312-726-6075. TELEX 206155. (Subscr. to: 11830 Westline Industrial Dr., St. Louis, MO 63146. TEL 800-325-4177) Ed. Robert B. Karp, M.D.
   Formerly: Advances in Cardiovascular Surgery (ISSN 0889-5074)
   Description: Presents a collection of original and fully referenced articles from experts in the field.

616.1   SZ   ISSN 0065-2326
RC681.A25   CODEN: ACDYB2
ADVANCES IN CARDIOLOGY. (Text in English) 1956. irreg. (approx. 2/yr). price varies. S. Karger AG, Allschwilerstr. 10, P.O. Box, CH-4009 Basel, Switzerland. TEL 061-3061111. FAX 061-3061234. TELEX CH 962652. Ed. J. Kellermann. (reprint service avail. from ISI) **Indexed:** Biol.Abstr., Chem.Abstr., CINAHL, Curr.Adv.Ecol.Sci., Curr.Cont., Excerp.Med., Ind.Med.
  —BLDSC shelfmark: 0702.300000.

616.1   SZ   ISSN 0378-6900
CODEN: ACAPDU
ADVANCES IN CARDIOVASCULAR PHYSICS. (Text in English) irreg. price varies. S. Karger AG, Allschwilerstr. 10, P.O. Box, CH-4009 Basel, Switzerland. TEL 061-3061111. FAX 061-3061234. TELEX CH 962652. Ed. D.N. Ghista. charts. (reprint service avail. from ISI) **Indexed:** Biol.Abstr., Chem.Abstr., Curr.Cont., Ind.Med.
  —BLDSC shelfmark: 0702.530000.

612 591   SZ   ISSN 0065-2938
QP101   CODEN: ADVMBT
ADVANCES IN MICROCIRCULATION. (Text in English) 1968. irreg. (approx. 1/yr). price varies. S. Karger AG, Allschwilerstr. 10, P.O. Box, CH-4009 Basel, Switzerland. TEL 061-3061111. FAX 061-3061234. TELEX CH 962652. Ed. B.M. Altura. (back issues avail.; reprint service avail. from ISI) **Indexed:** Biol.Abstr., Chem.Abstr., Curr.Cont., Ind.Med., Ind.Sci.Rev., Sci.Cit.Ind.
  —BLDSC shelfmark: 0709.427000.

616.1   RU   ISSN 0201-7369
AKADEMIYA MEDITSINSKIKH NAUK S.S.S.R. VSESOYUZNYI KARDIOLOGICHESKII NAUCHNYI TSENTR. BYULLETEN/ACADEMY OF MEDICAL SCIENCES OF THE U.S.S.R. ALL-UNION CARDIOLOGY RESEARCH CENTER. BULLETIN. (Text in Russian; summaries in English) 1978. s-a. (Akademiya Meditsinskikh Nauk S.S.S.R.) Izdatel'stvo Meditsina, Petroverigskii pereulok 6-8, 101838 Moscow, Russia. (Subscr. to: Mezhdunarodnaya Kniga, Moscow, G-200, Russia) (Co-sponsor: Ministerstvo Zdravookhraneniya S.S.S.R.) Ed. Yu.N. Belenkov.
   Description: Covers the substantial results of studies on theoretical and clinical cardiology at the center.

AMERICAN COLLEGE OF CARDIOLOGY. ABSTRACTS. see *MEDICAL SCIENCES — Abstracting, Bibliographies, Statistics*

616.12   US   ISSN 0735-1097
CODEN: JACCDI
AMERICAN COLLEGE OF CARDIOLOGY. JOURNAL. 14/yr.(in 2 vols.; 7 nos./vol.)(plus supplement). $140 to institutions (foreign $205)(effective 1992). (American College of Cardiology) Elsevier Science Publishing Co., Inc. (New York), 655 Ave. of the Americas, New York, NY 10010. TEL 212-989-5800. FAX 212-633-3965. TELEX 420643 AEP UI. Ed. Dr. Simon Dack. adv. (also avail. in microform from RPI; back issues avail.) **Indexed:** Biol.Abstr., Chem.Abstr., Curr.Cont., Dent.Ind., Excerp.Med., Ind.Med., INIS Atomind., NRN, Risk Abstr., Sci.Cit.Ind.
  ●Also available online. Vendor(s): BRS.
  —BLDSC shelfmark: 4685.500000.
   Description: Publishes original clinical and experimental reports on all aspects of cardiovascular disease.
  Refereed Serial

616.1   US
AMERICAN COLLEGE OF CARDIOLOGY. SYMPOSIA. (Suppl. to: American College of Cardiology. Journal) 1973. irreg. vol.14, no.3, 1989. price varies. (American College of Cardiology) Elsevier Science Publishing Co., Inc. (New York), 655 Ave. of the Americas, New York, NY 10010. TEL 212-989-5800. FAX 212-633-3965. TELEX 420643 AEP UI.

616.1   US
AMERICAN COLLEGE OF CARDIOLOGY ANNUAL SCIENTIFIC SESSION NEWS. 1982. 5/yr. American College of Cardiology, 9111 Old Georgetown Rd., Bethesda, MD 20814. TEL 301-897-2627. FAX 301-897-9745. Ed. Suzanne H. Howard. adv.; circ. 55,000 (controlled). (tabloid format; back issues avail.)
   Description: For attendees of the college's Annual Scientific Session. Highlights events and activities of the meetings as well as activities within the city.

616.1   US   ISSN 0065-8502
AMERICAN HEART ASSOCIATION. SCIENTIFIC SESSIONS. ABSTRACTS. 1927. a. $15 (foreign $25). American Heart Association, Committee on Scientific Sessions Program, 7272 Greenville Ave., Dallas, TX 75231-4596. TEL 214-706-1253. FAX 214-691-6342. adv.; index; circ. 40,000. (also avail. in microfiche; reprint service avail. from UMI)

616.6   US
AMERICAN HEART ASSOCIATION. SUPPLEMENTS. 1960. irreg. $10 (foreign $15). American Heart Association, 7272 Greenville Ave., Dallas, TX 75231-4596. TEL 214-706-1310. FAX 214-691-2704. (Subscr. to: Box 843543, Dallas, TX 75284-3543) (reprint service avail. from UMI) **Indexed:** Biol.Abstr., Ind.Med.
   Formerly: American Heart Association. Monographs (ISSN 0065-8499)
   Description: Provides proceedings of council meetings and significant research related to cardiovascular disease and cerebral circulation.
  Refereed Serial

MEDICAL SCIENCES — CARDIOVASCULAR DISEASES

616.1 US ISSN 0002-8703
RC681.A1 CODEN: AHJOA2
AMERICAN HEART JOURNAL; an international publication for the study of the circulation. 1925. m. $84 to individuals (foreign $112); institutions $160 (foreign $188); students $42 (foreign $70). Mosby - Year Book, Inc. (Subsidiary of: Times Mirror Company), 11830 Westline Industrial Dr., St. Louis, MO 63146. TEL 800-325-4117.
FAX 314-432-1380. TELEX 44-2402. Ed. Dr. Dean T. Mason. adv.; bibl.; charts; illus.; s-a. index; circ. 11,645. (also avail. in microfilm from PMC,UMI; reprint service avail. from UMI) **Indexed**: Abstr.Hyg., Abstr.Inter.Med., ASCA, Behav.Med.Abstr., Biol.Abstr., Biotech.Abstr., Chem.Abstr., Curr.Adv.Ecol.Sci., Curr.Cont., Dairy Sci.Abstr., Excerp.Med., Helminthol.Abstr., I.P.A., Ind.Med., Ind.Sci.Rev., INIS Atomind., NRN, Rev.Plant Path., Risk Abstr., Sci.Cit.Ind., Trop.Dis.Bull.
●Also available online. Vendor(s): BRS, BRS/Saunders Colleague.
—BLDSC shelfmark: 0817.000000.
Description: For those concerned with the diagnosis and management of cardiovascular disease.
Refereed Serial

616.1 US ISSN 0887-7971
CODEN: AJCIEZ
AMERICAN JOURNAL OF CARDIAC IMAGING. 1987. q. $69 to individuals; institutions $96 (foreign $106). W.B. Saunders Co. (Subsidiary of: Harcourt Brace Jovanovich, Inc.), Curtis Center, Independence Square W., Philadelphia, PA 19106.
TEL 215-238-7800. (Subscr. to: 6277 Sea Harbor Dr., 4th Fl., Orlando FL 32891) Ed. James V. Talano. adv.; bk.rev.; abstr.; bibl.; charts; illus.
Indexed: Excerp.Med.
—BLDSC shelfmark: 0822.475000.
Refereed Serial

616.1 US ISSN 0002-9149
RC681.A1 CODEN: AJCDAG
AMERICAN JOURNAL OF CARDIOLOGY. 1958. 24/yr. $66 to individuals (foreign $135); institutions $95 (foreign $150) (effective Mar. 1992). Cahners Publishing Company (New York), Medical-Health Care Group, Yorke Medical Journals (Subsidiary of: Reed International PLC), Division of Reed Publishing (USA) Inc., 249 W. 17th St., New York, NY 10011-5301. TEL 212-645-0067.
FAX 212-242-6987. (Subscr. to: Box 173306, Denver, CO 80217-3306. TEL 800-662-7776) Eds. Dr. William C. Roberts, Judy Wagner. adv.; bk.rev.; bibl.; charts; illus.; index; circ. 31,300. (also avail. in microform from RPI) **Indexed**: Abstr.Hyg., Abstr.Inter.Med., Biol.Abstr., Biotech.Abstr., C.I.S. Abstr., Curr.Adv.Ecol.Sci., Curr.Cont., Dent.Ind., Dok.Arbeitsmed., Excerp.Med., Helminthol.Abstr., I.P.A., Ind.Med., Ind.Sci.Rev., NRN, Nutr.Abstr., Risk Abstr., Sci.Cit.Ind., Trop.Dis.Bull.
●Also available online. Vendor(s): BRS, Mead Data Central.
—BLDSC shelfmark: 0822.500000.
Description: Explores and highlights advances in diagnosis and treatment of cardiovascular disease, stressing a practical, clinical approach to cardiology.
Refereed Serial

616.12 612.67 US
▼**AMERICAN JOURNAL OF GERIATRIC CARDIOLOGY**. 1992. bi-m. Cardiovascular Reviews & Reports, Inc., 47 Arch St., Greenwich, CT 06830.
TEL 203-625-0194. FAX 203-625-0393. Ed. Kenneth Lane. adv.: B&W page $2200, color page $3240; trim 7 7/8 x 10 3/4. circ. 20,000.
Description: Devoted to the study of heart disease in the elderly.
Refereed Serial

618 US ISSN 0895-7061
CODEN: AJHYE6
AMERICAN JOURNAL OF HYPERTENSION. 1988. 12/yr (plus supplement). $192 to institutions (foreign $238)(effective 1992). (American Society of Hypertension) Elsevier Science Publishing Co., Inc. (New York), 655 Ave. of the Americas, New York, NY 10010. TEL 212-989-5800.
FAX 212-633-3965. TELEX 420643 AEP UI. Ed. John H. Laragh. **Indexed**: Curr.Cont., Excerp.Med., Ind.Med.
—BLDSC shelfmark: 0826.400000.
Incorporates (1985-1987): Journal of Clinical Hypertension (ISSN 0748-450X)
Description: Offers wide coverage of experimental and clinical hypertension and related cardiovascular diseases.
Refereed Serial

616.12 SZ ISSN 0258-4425
CODEN: AJNCE4
AMERICAN JOURNAL OF NONINVASIVE CARDIOLOGY. (Text in English) 6/yr. 144.50 Fr.($96.60) to individuals; institutions 413 Fr.($276). S. Karger AG, Allschwilerstr. 10, P.O. Box, CH-4009 Basel, Switzerland. TEL 021-3061111.
FAX 061-3061234. TELEX CH 962652. (U.S. addr.: S. Karger, 79 Fifth Ave., New York, NY 10003) Ed. H.D. Spodick. circ. 950. (also avail. in microform) **Indexed**: Excerp.Med.
—BLDSC shelfmark: 0828.410000.

574.1 US ISSN 0363-6135
QP101.2
AMERICAN JOURNAL OF PHYSIOLOGY: HEART AND CIRCULATORY PHYSIOLOGY. 1977. m. $220 to individuals (Canada and Mexico $260); elsewhere $290); institutions $275 (Canada and Mexico $319; elsewhere $375); members $110. American Physiological Society, 9650 Rockville Pike, Bethesda, MD 20814. TEL 301-530-7071.
FAX 301-571-1814. Ed. V.S. Bishop. circ. 715. (also avail. in microform from UMI; reprint service avail. from UMI) **Indexed**: Abstr.Hyg., Biol.Abstr., Biol.& Agr.Ind., Biotech.Abstr., Chem.Abstr., Curr.Cont., Dent.Ind., Excerp.Med., Helminthol.Abstr., Ind.Med., Ind.Sci.Rev., Ind.Vet., Int.Abstr.Biol.Sci., Key Word Ind.Wildl.Res., Nutr.Abstr., Ref.Zh., Sci.Cit.Ind., Trop.Dis.Bull., Vet.Bull.
Description: Presents experimental and theoretical studies of cardiovascular function at all levels of organization ranging from the intact animal to the cellular, subcellular, and molecular levels.
Refereed Serial

616.1 US ISSN 0735-1283
AMERICAN REVIEW OF DIAGNOSTICS; journal of cardiac, vascular and pulmonary technologies and sciences. 1982. bi-m. $24 to individuals; institutions $36. Degram Communications, Inc., Box 617, Encino, CA 91426. TEL 818-501-6167. Ed. Dennis Schwesinger. adv.; bk.rev.; circ. 17,460.

616.01 US ISSN 0894-7317
CODEN: JSECEJ
AMERICAN SOCIETY OF ECHOCARDIOGRAPHY. JOURNAL. 1988. bi-m. $56 to individuals (foreign $67); institutions $73 (foreign $84); students $32 (foreign $43). (American Society of Echocardiography) Mosby - Year Book, Inc. (Subsidiary of: Times Mirror Company), 11830 Westline Industrial Dr., St. Louis, MO 63146. TEL 800-325-4117. FAX 314-432-1380. TELEX 44-2402. Ed. Dr. Harvey Feigenbaum. adv.; s-a index; circ. 5,607. (also avail. in microform from UMI; reprint service avail. from UMI)
—BLDSC shelfmark: 4692.680000.

616.1 574 FR ISSN 0003-3049
ANGEIOLOGIE. (Text in English or French; summaries in English, French) 1948. 8/yr. 520 F. (foreign 700 F.). Societe Francaise de Publications Angeiologiques, 3 rue Jacques-Dulud, 92200 Neuilly-sur-Seine, France. TEL 46-37-07-54. (Co-sponsor: Union Internationale d'Angeiologie) Ed.Bd. adv.; bk.rev.; circ. 3,800. **Indexed**: Excerp.Med.
—BLDSC shelfmark: 0900.900000.

616.13 SP ISSN 0003-3170
CODEN: ANGOAT
ANGIOLOGIA; publicacion dedicada al estudio de las enfermedades vasculares. (Text in Spanish; summaries in English) 1949. bi-m. 4600 ptas.($75) Editorial Rocas, Calaf. 29, 2-3, 08021 Barcelona, Spain. TEL 200 13 89.
FAX 202-19-58. Ed. Fernando Martorell. adv.; bk.rev.; abstr.; charts; illus.; index; circ. 2,500.
Indexed: Biol.Abstr., Chem.Abstr., Excerp.Med., Ind.Med.
—BLDSC shelfmark: 0902.650000.

616.1 US ISSN 0003-3197
RC691 CODEN: ANGIAB
ANGIOLOGY. 1950. m. $91. (American College of Angiology) Westminster Publications, Inc., 1044 Northern Blvd., Ste. 103, Roslyn, NY 11576. TEL 516-484-6882. FAX 516-625-1174. adv.; bk.rev.; circ. 6,028. **Indexed**: Biol.Abstr., Biotech.Abstr., Chem.Abstr., Curr.Adv.Ecol.Sci., Curr.Cont., Excerp.Med., Ind.Med., Ind.Sci.Rev., INIS Atomind., Nutr.Abstr., Sci.Cit.Ind.
—BLDSC shelfmark: 0902.700000.
Description: Original papers relating to cerebrovascular, cardiovascular and peripheral vascular diseases. Official journal of International College of Angiology.

616.13 FR ISSN 0003-3928
CODEN: ACAABH
ANNALES DE CARDIOLOGIE ET D'ANGEIOLOGIE. (Summaries in English) 1952. 10/yr. 740 F. to individuals (foreign 975 F.); students 370 F. (foreign 570 F.). Expansion Scientifique, 15 rue Saint Benoit, 75278 Paris Cedex 06, France. Eds. J.J. Welti, M. Grivaux. adv.; bk.rev.; abstr.; bibl.; illus.; circ. 2,800. (also avail. in microform) **Indexed**: Biol.Abstr., Chem.Abstr., Curr.Cont., Dent.Ind., Excerp.Med., Ind.Med., Ind.Sci.Rev., Sci.Cit.Ind.
—BLDSC shelfmark: 0969.500000.
Formerly: Actualities Cardiologiques et Angeiologiques Internationales.

617.41 FR ISSN 0066-2054
CODEN: ACSSBP
ANNALES DE CHIRURGIE THORACIQUE ET CARDIO-VASCULAIRE. (Supplement to: Annales de Chirurgie) (Text in English, French) 1962. 2/yr. (Societe de Chirurgie Thoracique de Langue Francaise) Expansion Scientifique, 15 rue St. Benoit, 75278 Paris Cedex 06, France.
TEL 1-45-48-42-60. FAX 1-45-44-81-55. adv.; bk.rev.; circ. 3,500. **Indexed**: Biol.Abstr., Curr.Cont., Ind.Med.

ANNALS OF VASCULAR SURGERY. see *MEDICAL SCIENCES — Surgery*

ANNUAL OF CARDIAC SURGERY. see *MEDICAL SCIENCES — Abstracting, Bibliographies, Statistics*

616.1 FR ISSN 0003-9683
CODEN: AMCVAN
ARCHIVES DES MALADIES DU COEUR ET DES VAISSEAUX. 1908. m. 665 F. J.B. Bailliere et Fils, 10 rue Thenard, 75005 Paris, France. Ed. Dr. Gerard Roux-Dessarps. adv.; bk.rev.; abstr.; charts; illus.; index; circ. 4,300. (also avail. in microform) **Indexed**: Biol.Abstr., C.I.S. Abstr., Chem.Abstr., Curr.Adv.Ecol.Sci., Excerp.Med., Helminthol.Abstr., Ind.Med., Ind.Sci.Rev., Nutr.Abstr., Sci.Cit.Ind.
—BLDSC shelfmark: 1637.370000.

ARCHIVIO DI CHIRURGIA TORACICA E CARDIOVASCOLARE. see *MEDICAL SCIENCES — Surgery*

616.12 IT
▼**ARGOMENTI DI CARDIOLOGIA**. 1990. q. L.8200($46) (effective 1991). Masson Italia Periodici, Via Statuto 2-4, 20121 Milan, Italy. TEL 02-6367-1. FAX 02-6367-211. Ed. Alberto Zanchetti. circ. 15,000.

616.12 BL ISSN 0066-782X
CODEN: ABCAAJ
ARQUIVOS BRASILEIROS DE CARDIOLOGIA. (Articles in several languages; summaries in English) 1948. m. $150. Arquivos Brasileiros de Cardiologia, Rua Itapeva, 574, 8, 01332 Sao Paulo, SP, Brazil. Ed. Joao Pimenta. adv.; bk.rev.; circ. 6,000. **Indexed**: Biol.Abstr., Chem.Abstr., Excerp.Med., Ind.Med., Protozool.Abstr.
—BLDSC shelfmark: 1695.160000.

MEDICAL SCIENCES — CARDIOVASCULAR DISEASES

616.1   FR   ISSN 0293-5090
ARTERES ET VEINES. 1982. 8/yr. 370 F. to individuals (foreign 440 F.); students 225 F. (foreign 300 F.) (Arteres et Veines) Publications Medicales A G C F, 34 bis rue Paul Eluard, 93200 Saint Denis, France. TEL 48-20-18-21. FAX 1-48-20-09-52. adv.; bk.rev.; illus.
—BLDSC shelfmark: 1733.492500.

616.136   US   ISSN 1049-8834
RC692   CODEN: ARTTE5
ARTERIOSCLEROSIS AND THROMBOSIS; a journal of vascular biology. 1981. -m. $108 to individuals (foreign $128); institutions $146 (foreign $166). American Heart Association, 7272 Greenville Ave., Dallas, TX 75231-4596. TEL 214-706-1310. FAX 214-691-6342. (Subscr. to: Box 843543, Dallas, TX 75284-3543) Ed. Dr. Alan M. Fogelman. adv.; index; circ. 1,740. (also avail. in microform from UMI; back issues avail.) **Indexed:** Biol.Abstr., Curr.Adv.Ecol.Sci., Curr.Adv.Genetics & Molec.Biol., Excerp.Med., Ind.Med., Ind.Sci.Rev., NRN, Poult.Abstr., Sci.Cit.Ind.
—BLDSC shelfmark: 1733.650000.
Formerly: Arteriosclerosis (ISSN 0276-5047)
Description: Relates original research and reviews on the biology, prevention, and impact of vascular diseases.
Refereed Serial

616.1   IO   ISSN 0587-5471
ASIAN PACIFIC CONGRESS OF CARDIOLOGY. SYMPOSIA.* irreg. Asian-Pacific Society of Cardiology, c/o Cardiac Centre, Jalan Diponegoro 69, Jakarta, Indonesia. (Symposia from 4th Congress: 1968, pub. by Academic Press, US) **Indexed:** Biol.Abstr.

616.1   IE   ISSN 0021-9150
                        CODEN: ATHSBL
ATHEROSCLEROSIS; international journal for research and investigation on atherosclerosis and related diseases. (Text mainly in English, occasionally in French and German; summaries in English, French and German) 1961. 18/yr.(in 6 vols.; 3 nos./vol.). $1203 (effective 1992). (International Atherosclerosis Society) Elsevier Scientific Publishers Ireland Ltd., P.O. Box 85, Limerick, Ireland. TEL 061-61944. FAX 061-62144. TELEX 72191 ENH EI. (Subscr. in U.S. and Canada to: Elsevier Science Publishing Co., Inc., Box 882, Madison Sq. Sta., New York, NY 10159. TEL 212-989-5800) Ed.Bd. adv.; charts; illus.; index. **Indexed:** Biol.Abstr., Chem.Abstr., Curr.Adv.Biochem., Curr.Cont., Excerp.Med., Ind.Med., INIS Atomind., NRN, Poult.Abstr., Rice Abstr., Vet.Bull.
—BLDSC shelfmark: 1765.874000.
Formerly: Journal of Atherosclerosis Research.
Description: Brings together research papers related to the focal accumulation of collagen, lipids, complex carbohydrates, blood and blood products, fibrous tissue and calcium deposits in the intima of arteris, its medical complications, related phenomena and diseases.
Refereed Serial

616.136   US   ISSN 0362-1650
RC692   CODEN: ATHEDF
ATHEROSCLEROSIS REVIEWS. 1975. irreg., latest vol.23. price varies. Raven Press, 1185 Ave. of the Americas, New York, NY 10036. TEL 212-930-9500. FAX 212-869-3495. TELEX 640073. Eds. Antonio Gotto, Jr., Rodolfo Paoletti. **Indexed:** Biol.Abstr., Chem.Abstr., Curr.Cont., Ind.Sci.Rev., Sci.Cit.Ind.
Refereed Serial

616.1   US
BASIC AND CLINICAL CARDIOLOGY SERIES. 1982. irreg., vol.11, 1988. price varies. Marcel Dekker, Inc., 270 Madison Ave., New York, NY 10016. TEL 212-696-9000. FAX 212-685-4540. TELEX 421419.
Refereed Serial

616.1   GW   ISSN 0300-8428
RC633.A1   CODEN: BRCAB7
BASIC RESEARCH IN CARDIOLOGY. (Text in English) 1938. bi-m. DM.672. Dr. Dietrich Steinkopff Verlag, Saalbaustr. 12, Postfach 111442, 6100 Darmstadt 11, Germany. TEL 06151-26538. FAX 06151-20849. (Subscr. in Austria to: Minerva Wissenschaftliche Buchhandlung GmbH, Sachsenplatz 4-6, A-1201; Subscr in Japan to: Eastern Book Service, Inc., 37-3, Hongo 3-chome, Bunkyo-ku, Tokyo 113, Japan; Subscr. in N. America to: Springer-Verlag, Journals, 175 Fifth Ave., New York, NY 10010; Subscr. in Switzerland to: Freihofer AG, Weinbergstr. 109, CH-8033 Zurich, Switzerland) Ed.Bd. adv.; charts; illus.; pat.; index; circ. 2,000. **Indexed:** Biol.Abstr., Chem.Abstr., Curr.Adv.Ecol.Sci., Curr.Cont., Excerp.Med., Ind.Med., Ind.Sci.Rev., INIS Atomind., Nutr.Abstr., Sci.Cit.Ind.
—BLDSC shelfmark: 1864.080000.

616.1   SZ   ISSN 0067-7906
                        CODEN: BCSCAL
BIBLIOTHECA CARDIOLOGICA. (Text in English) 1939. irreg. S. Karger AG, Allschwilerstr. 10, P.O. Box, CH-4009 Basel, Switzerland. TEL 061-3061111. FAX 061-3061234. TELEX CH 962652. Ed. A. Katz. (reprint service avail. from ISI) **Indexed:** Biol.Abstr., Chem.Abstr., Curr.Cont., Ind.Med.
—BLDSC shelfmark: 2018.400000.

BLOOD COAGULATION FACTORS; current awareness service for researchers in life sciences. see *MEDICAL SCIENCES — Hematology*

616.1   UK   ISSN 0007-0769
                        CODEN: BHJUAV
BRITISH HEART JOURNAL. 1939. m. £156 (combined subscr. with Cardiovascular Research £293). (British Cardiac Society) B M J Publishing Group, B.M.A. House, Tavistock Sq., London WC1H 9JR, England. TEL 071-387-4499. Ed. M.J. Davies. adv.; bk.rev.; abstr.; charts; illus.; index, cum.index: 1939-1955; 1956-1967. (also avail. in microform from UMI) **Indexed:** Abstr.Hyg., Behav.Med.Abstr., Biol.Abstr., Biotech.Abstr., C.I.S. Abstr., Chem.Abstr., Curr.Adv.Ecol.Sci., Curr.Cont., Dent.Ind., Excerp.Med., Helminthol.Abstr., Ind.Med., INIS Atomind., NRN, Nutr.Abstr., Risk Abstr., Sci.Cit.Ind., Trop.Dis.Bull.
●Also available online. Vendor(s): BRS, BRS/Saunders Colleague.
—BLDSC shelfmark: 2301.300000.

C A SELECTS. ANTIARRHYTHMICS. see *MEDICAL SCIENCES — Abstracting, Bibliographies, Statistics*

616.1   US
C P DIGEST. (Cardiovascular Pulmonary) bi-m. $35. National Society for Cardiovascular Technology - National Society for Pulmonary Technology, Inc., 1101 14th St., N.W., Ste. 1100, Washington, DC 20005. TEL 202-371-1267. FAX 202-371-109. Ed. Peggy McElgunn. adv.; circ. 3,000.

616.1   GW   ISSN 0940-8770
C V. (Cardiovascular); European journal of cardiovascular disease. (Text in English, French, German, Italian, Spanish) 1988. bi-m. DM.142. (Society for Advances in Cardiovascular Medicine e.V.) Miranda Communications GmbH, Guenterstalstr. 3, 7800 Freiburg, Germany. TEL 0761-74094. FAX 0761-75422. Ed. Dr. H.W. Heiss. adv.; bk.rev.; circ. 15,000. (back issues avail.)
Formerly (until 1991): C V World Report (ISSN 0934-0815)

616.1   CN   ISSN 0828-282X
                        CODEN: CJCAEX
CANADIAN JOURNAL OF CARDIOLOGY. 1985. 10/yr. Can.$105($95) (foreign $150) to individuals; institutions Can.$125 ($115)(foreign $175). Pulsus Group Inc., 2902 S. Sheridan Way, Oakville, Ont. L6J 7L6, Canada. TEL 416-829-4770. FAX 416-829-4799. Eds. Drs. R.E. Beamish, R.E. Blakley. adv.; bk.rev.; abstr.; bibl.; charts; illus.; index; circ. 16,000. (back issues avail.) **Indexed:** Biol.Abstr., Chem.Abstr., Curr.Cont., Excerp.Med., Ind.Med., NRN.
—BLDSC shelfmark: 3030.500000.
Description: Original studies in the area of cardiovascular medicine.
Refereed Serial

CANADIAN JOURNAL OF CARDIOVASCULAR NURSING. see *MEDICAL SCIENCES — Nurses And Nursing*

CARDIAC ALERT. see *PHYSICAL FITNESS AND HYGIENE*

616.1   NE   ISSN 0921-5166
CARDIAC IMAGING VIDEO JOURNAL. q. fl.495($275) Kluwer Academic Publishers, Postbus 17, 3300 AA Dordrecht, Netherlands. TEL 078-334911. FAX 078-334254. TELEX 29245. (Dist. by: Kluwer Academic Pub. Group, P.O. Box 322, 3300 AH Dordrecht, Netherlands; N. America dist. addr.: Box 358, Accord Station, Hingham, MA 02018-0358. TEL 617-871-6600) Ed. Dr. Andrew J. Buda. (avail. on video cassette only)
Description: Presents the latest imaging techniques and provides real-time studies in video-based format.

617   US   ISSN 0887-9850
RD598
CARDIAC SURGERY; state of the art reviews. 3/yr. $93 (foreign $103). Hanley & Belfus, Inc., 210 S. 13th St., Philadelphia, PA 19107. TEL 215-546-7293. FAX 215-790-9330.
—BLDSC shelfmark: 3051.130000.
Refereed Serial

616.1   US   ISSN 0742-9622
CARDIO. 1984. m. $85 (free to qualified personnel). Miller Freeman, Inc. (Subsidiary of: United Newspapers), 600 Harrison St., San Francisco, CA 94107. TEL 415-905-2200. FAX 415-905-2232. TELEX 278273. Ed. Joe Kornfeld. adv.; circ. 30,000. (also avail. in microform from UMI; reprint service avail. from UMI)
—BLDSC shelfmark: 3051.240000.

616.1   US
▼**CARDIO INTERVENTION.** 1991. q. Miller Freeman, Inc. (Subsidiary of: United Newspapers), 600 Harrison St., San Francisco, CA 94107. TEL 415-905-2200. FAX 415-905-2235. Ed. Steve Stiles. adv.: B&W page $2310, color page $3555; trim 8 1/8 x 10 7/8. circ. 10,000.
Description: Covers the field of interventional cardiology: angioplasty, angiography, and other therapeutic and diagnostic lab procedures.

616.1   IT
CARDIOLOGIA. (Summaries in English, French, German) 1955. m. $25. Societa Italiana di Cardiologia, Corso Francia 197, 00191 Rome, Italy. Ed. Antonio Strano. adv.; bk.rev.; charts; illus.; index; circ. 1,600. **Indexed:** Biol.Abstr., Chem.Abstr., Excerp.Med., Ind.Med.
Formerly: Societa Italiana di Cardiologia. Bollettino (ISSN 0037-878X)

616.12   FR   ISSN 0983-4532
CARDIOLOGIE. 1987. 6/yr. 230 Fr. Maloine Editeur, 27 rue de l'Ecole de Medecine, 75006 Paris, France. (Subscr. to: Publicite Batard, 38 rue Pascal, 75013 Paris, France) Ed. N. Gofstein. adv.; bk.rev.

CARDIOLOGIST'S COMPENDIUM OF DRUG THERAPY. see *PHARMACY AND PHARMACOLOGY*

616.1   SZ   ISSN 0008-6312
RC681.A1   CODEN: CAGYAO
CARDIOLOGY; international journal of cardiovascular medicine, surgery and pathology. (Text in English) 1937. m. (in 2 vols.). 439 SFr.($293) per vol. S. Karger AG, Allschwilerstr. 10, P.O. Box, CH-4009 Basel, Switzerland. TEL 061-3061111. FAX 061-3061234. TELEX CH 962652. Ed. J.S. Alpert. adv.; bk.rev.; charts; illus.; index; circ. 1,300. (also avail. in microfilm from PMC) **Indexed:** Biol.Abstr., Biotech.Abstr., Chem.Abstr., Curr.Adv.Ecol.Sci., Curr.Cont., Excerp.Med., Helminthol.Abstr., Ind.Med., Ind.Sci.Rev., Nutr.Abstr., Protozool.Abstr.
—BLDSC shelfmark: 3051.410000.
Formerly: Cardiologia.

616.1   US
CARDIOLOGY (BETHESDA). 1972. m. membership. American College of Cardiology, Communications Department, 9111 Old Georgetown Rd., Bethesda, MD 20814. TEL 301-897-5400. FAX 301-897-9745. Ed. Suzanne H. Howard. circ. 19,000. (looseleaf format; back issues avail.) **Indexed:** Protozool.Abstr.
Description: Describes the activities, services and products of the American College of Cardiology.

MEDICAL SCIENCES — CARDIOVASCULAR DISEASES

616.2   US   ISSN 0275-0066
RC681.A1
CARDIOLOGY (YEAR). 1981. a. $85. Butterworth-Heinemann Ltd. (Subsidiary of: Reed International PLC), 80 Montvale Ave., Stoneham, MA 02180. TEL 617-438-8464. FAX 617-438-1479. TELEX 880052. Ed.Bd. bibl.; charts; illus.; index. (also avail. in microform from UMI; back issues avail.) **Indexed:** Chem.Abstr, NRN, Protozool.Abstr., Sci.Cit.Ind.
—BLDSC shelfmark: 3051.415000.

616.12   US   ISSN 0888-8418
CARDIOLOGY BOARD REVIEW. 1984. m. $60. M R A Publications, Inc., 3 Greenwich Office Park, Greenwich, CT 06831-5154. TEL 203-629-3550. FAX 203-629-2536. Ed. Dr. Peter F. Cohn. adv.; bk.rev.; bibl.; charts; illus.; circ. 65,000 (controlled). (back issues avail.) **Indexed:** Excerp.Med.
—BLDSC shelfmark: 3051.416500.
Description: Revised and updated articles that originally appeared in the literature of cardiology.
Refereed Serial

616.12   US   ISSN 0733-8651
RC681.A1   CODEN: CACLE3
CARDIOLOGY CLINICS. 1983. 4/yr. $81. W.B. Saunders Co., Curtis Center, Independence Square W., Philadelphia, PA 19106. TEL 215-238-7800. Ed. Naina Chohan. (also avail. in microform from UMI) **Indexed:** Curr.Adv.Ecol.Sci., Excerp.Med., INIS Atomind.
●Also available online. Vendor(s): BRS, BRS/Saunders Colleague.
—BLDSC shelfmark: 3051.417000.

616.1   UK   ISSN 0262-5547
CARDIOLOGY IN PRACTICE. Abbreviated title: C I P. 1982. bi-m. £42 (foreign £48). Hayward Medical Communications, Hayward House, 1 Threshers Yard, Kingham, Oxon OX7 6YF, England. TEL 071-379-6005. FAX 071-379-6737. TELEX 266854-MEDTRB-G. Eds. Philip Poole-Wilson, Dr. Kim Fox. adv.; bk.rev.; circ. 21,000.
—BLDSC shelfmark: 3051.433000.

616.12   CN
CARDIOLOGY IN PRACTICE. m. $48. M P I Medical Publishing Inc., 14 Ronan Ave., Toronto, Ont. M4N 2X9, Canada. TEL 416-481-6384. Ed. Dr. Harry Rakowski. adv.; circ. 22,028. (tabloid format)

616.1   US   ISSN 0163-1675
RC681.A1
CARDIOLOGY UPDATE; reviews for physicians. 1979. a. price varies. Elsevier Science Publishing Co., Inc. (New York), 655 Ave. of the Americas, New York, NY 10010. TEL 212-989-5800. FAX 212-633-3965. TELEX 420643 AEP UI. Ed. E. Rapaport.
Refereed Serial

616.1   IT   ISSN 1015-5007
CODEN: CRDIEG
▼**CARDIOSCIENCE;** a service to cardiology. (Text in English) 1990. q. £55($95) Canal Press, S. Polo 2171, Venice 30125, Italy. (Subscr. to: Blackhorse Rd., Letchworth, Herts. SG6 1HN, England) **Indexed:** Curr.Cont., Excerp.Med.
—BLDSC shelfmark: 3051.437100.

616.1   IT   ISSN 0390-5403
CARDIOSTIMOLAZIONE. (Text in English and Italian) 1983. q. $100. (Italian Society of Cardiac Pacing) Edizioni Luigi Pozzi s.r.l., Via Panama 68, 00198 Rome, Italy. TEL 06-8553548. FAX 06-8554105. Ed. G.A. Feruglio. adv.; bk.rev.; circ. 2,200.
Description: Covers cardiology and cardiac pacing.

616.1   US
CARDIOTHORACIC SURGERY SERIES. 1986. irreg., vol.3, 1987. price varies. Marcel Dekker, Inc., 270 Madison Ave., New York, NY 10016. TEL 212-696-9000. FAX 212-685-4540. TELEX 421419.
Refereed Serial

616.1   US   ISSN 0174-1551
CODEN: CAIRDG
CARDIOVASCULAR AND INTERVENTIONAL RADIOLOGY; a journal of imaging in diagnosis and treatment. 1977. 6/yr. $139.50. (European College of Angiography) Springer-Verlag, Journals, 175 Fifth Ave., New York, NY 10010. TEL 212-460-1500. (Also Berlin, Heidelberg, Tokyo, and Vienna) (Co-sponsors: European Society of Cardiovascular and International Radiology; North American Society of Cardiac Radiology) Eds. K.E. Fellows, E. Zeitler. adv.; bk.rev.; illus. (also avail. in microform from UMI; reprint service avail. from ISI) **Indexed:** Curr.Cont., Excerp.Med., Ind.Med., INIS Atomind.
—BLDSC shelfmark: 3051.438000.
Formerly: Cardiovascular Radiology (ISSN 0342-7196)

616.6   US   ISSN 0069-0384
RC681.A1   CODEN: CCLIBG
CARDIOVASCULAR CLINICS. 1969. irreg. price varies. F.A. Davis Company, 1915 Arch St., Philadelphia, PA 19103. TEL 800-523-4049. TELEX 83-4837. Ed. Dr. Albert N. Brest. (reprint service avail. from UMI) **Indexed:** Curr.Adv.Ecol.Sci., Excerp.Med., Ind.Med., INIS Atomind.
—BLDSC shelfmark: 3051.440000.

616.1   US   ISSN 0920-3206
RM345   CODEN: CDTHET
CARDIOVASCULAR DRUGS AND THERAPY. 1987. bi-m. fl.250($110) to individuals; institutions fl.435 ($222.50). (International Society of Cardiovascular Pharmacotherapy) Kluwer Academic Publishers, 101 Philip Dr., Norwell, MA 02061. TEL 617-871-6300. FAX 617-871-6528. (Subscr. to: Box 358, Accord Sta., Hingham, MA 02018-0358) Eds. Lionel H. Opie, Elliot Rapaport. adv.; bk.rev. (back issues avail.; reprint service avail. from SWZ,UMI) **Indexed:** Curr.Cont., Excerp.Med.
—BLDSC shelfmark: 3051.462500.
Description: Articles on laboratory investigators and clinical studies related to cardiovascular drug therapy.
Refereed Serial

616.1   AT
▼**CARDIOVASCULAR GUIDELINES.** 1991. s-a. Aus.$12. Victorian Medical Postgraduate Foundation Inc., Therapeutics Committee, Chelsea House, Level 3, 55 Flemington Rd., N. Melbourne, Vic. 3051, Australia. TEL 03-329-1566. FAX 03-326-5632. (Co-sponsor: Victorian Drug Usage Advisory Committee) bk.rev.

616.1   US   ISSN 1054-8807
▼**CARDIOVASCULAR PATHOLOGY.** 1992. 4/yr. $157 (effective 1992). (Society for Cardiovascular Pathology) Elsevier Science Publishing Co., Inc. (New York), 655 Ave. of the Americas, New York, NY 10010. TEL 212-989-5800. FAX 212-633-3965. TELEX 42063 AEP UI. Ed. Dr. Stephen M. Factor.
—BLDSC shelfmark: 3051.470700.
Description: Papers on disease-oriented morphology and pathobiology from pathologists and investigators in the cardiovascular field.
Refereed Serial

616.1 615.7   UK   ISSN 0263-7243
CARDIOVASCULAR PHARMACOLOGY. s-m. £100. Sheffield University Biomedical Information Service (SUBIS), The University, Sheffield S10 2TN, England. TEL 0742-768555. FAX 0742-739826. TELEX 547216-UGSHEF-G.
Description: Current awareness service for researchers in clinical and life sciences. Studies anti-hypertensives, calcium channel blockers, vasoconstrictors, and vasodilators.

CARDIOVASCULAR PHYSIOLOGY. see *BIOLOGY — Physiology*

616.1   UK   ISSN 0008-6363
CODEN: CVREAU
CARDIOVASCULAR RESEARCH. 1967. m. £185 (combined subscr. with British Heart Journal £293). B M J Publishing Group, B.M.A. House, Tavistock Sq., London WC1H 9JR, England. TEL 071-387-4499. (Co-sponsor: British Cardiac Society) Ed. David J. Hearse. adv.; abstr.; index. (also avail. in microform from UMI; reprint service avail. from UMI) **Indexed:** Biol.Abstr., Biotech.Abstr., Chem.Abstr., Curr.Adv.Ecol.Sci., Curr.Cont., Excerp.Med., Helminthol.Abstr., Ind.Med., Ind.Sci.Rev., NRN, Nutr.Abstr., Sci.Cit.Ind.
—BLDSC shelfmark: 3051.490000.

616.1   US   ISSN 0197-3118
CARDIOVASCULAR REVIEWS & REPORTS. 1980. m. $60 to individuals(foreign $75); institutions $75(foreign $90). Cardiovascular Reviews & Reports, Inc., 47 Arch St., Greenwich, CT 06830. TEL 203-625-0194. FAX 203-625-0393. Ed. Dr. John H. Laragh. adv.; circ. 81,004. (back issues avail.) **Indexed:** Excerp.Med., NRN.
—BLDSC shelfmark: 3051.513000.
Refereed Serial

616.1   SP
CARDIOVASCULAR REVIEWS & REPORTS (EDICION ESPANOLA); actualidad internacional en enfermedades del cardiacas. 1980. m. 4820 ptas.($48) Haymarket, S.A., Aribau, 168-170, 08036 Barcelona, Spain. TEL 93-238-1742. Dir. F.B. Ferrer Ruscalleda, M.D. circ. 10,000.

616.12   SP   ISSN 1130-7501
▼**CARDIOVASCULAR RISK FACTORS;** an international journal. 1991. m. 10000 ptas.($135) to individiuals; institutions $200. Saned, Apolonio Morales, 6, 28036 Madrid, Spain. TEL 403-50-14. FAX 457-99-18. TELEX 47331 SNED E. Ed. A. Fernandez-Cruz.
—BLDSC shelfmark: 3051.514000.

617.41   US   ISSN 0069-0406
CARDIOVASCULAR SURGERY. (Subseries of: American Heart Association Journals) 1962. a. $10 (foreign $20). American Heart Association, Council on Cardiovascular Surgery, 7272 Greenville Ave., Dallas, TX 75231-4596. TEL 214-706-1310. FAX 214-691-6342. (Subscr. to: Box 843543, Dallas, TX 75284-3543) adv.; circ. 23,000. **Indexed:** Ind.Med.
Refereed Serial

616.1   US   ISSN 0098-6569
RC683   CODEN: CCDID
CATHETERIZATION AND CARDIOVASCULAR DIAGNOSIS. 1975. m. $447 (foreign $597). John Wiley & Sons, Inc., Journals, 605 Third Ave., New York, NY 10158. TEL 212-850-6000. FAX 212-850-6088. TELEX 12-7063. Ed. Dr. Frank J. Hildner. adv.; bibl.; charts; illus. (reprint service avail. from ISI) **Indexed:** Biol.Abstr, Curr.Cont., Excerp.Med., Ind.Med., Ind.Sci.Rev., INIS Atomind., Sci.Cit.Ind.
—BLDSC shelfmark: 3092.990000.
Description: Devoted to invasive cardiology; emphasizes angioplasty and the newest techniques of interventional cardiology.
Refereed Serial

616.1   GW
CEREBRO; Zerebrale und periphere Gefaesskrankheiten. 1985. 6/yr. DM.45. P M I Verlag GmbH, August-Schanz-Str. 21, 6000 Frankfurt a.M. 50, Germany. TEL 069-548000-0. FAX 069-548000-77. TELEX 412952-PMI-D. Ed. Peter Hoffmann. adv.; circ. 20,000. (back issues avail.)
Formerly: Arterien und Venen (ISSN 0178-7470)
Description: Seminar paper journal that includes short summaries of original publications targeted to general practitioners.

CHEST; the journal of circulation, respiration and related systems. see *MEDICAL SCIENCES — Respiratory Diseases*

616.12   US
CHOICES IN CARDIOLOGY. bi-m. C P G Inc., 129 Washington St., Hoboken, NJ 07030. TEL 201-792-1900. Ed. Alice Goodman.

MEDICAL SCIENCES — CARDIOVASCULAR DISEASES

616.1 016 US ISSN 0009-7322
RC681.A1 CODEN: CIRCAZ
CIRCULATION. 1950. m. $102 to individuals (foreign $182); institutions $133 (foreign $213). American Heart Association, 7272 Greenville Ave., Dallas, TX 75231-4596. TEL 214-706-1310. FAX 214-691-6342. (Subscr. to: Box 843543, Dallas, TX 75284-3543) Ed. Dr. John Ross Jr. adv.; abstr.; bibl.; illus.; index; circ. 25,000. (also avail. in microform from UMI,MIM; back issues avail.; reprint service avail. from UMI) **Indexed:** Abstr.Hyg., Abstr.Inter.Med., Behav.Med.Abstr., Biol.Abstr., Biotech.Abstr., C.I.S. Abstr., Chem.Abstr., Curr.Adv.Ecol.Sci., Curr.Cont., Excerp.Med., Ind.Med., Ind.Sci.Rev., Int.Nurs.Ind., NRN, Nutr.Abstr., Pig News & Info., Protozool.Abstr., Risk Abstr., Sci.Cit.Ind., Trop.Dis.Bull.
●Also available online. Vendor(s): BRS (JWAT).
—BLDSC shelfmark: 3265.200000.
Description: For cardiologists and internists; presents clinical and laboratory research relevant to cardiovascular diseases.
Refereed Serial

616.1 US ISSN 0009-7330
RC681.A1 CODEN: CIRUAL
CIRCULATION RESEARCH. 1953. m. $152 to individuals (foreign $212); institutions $207 (foreign $267). American Heart Association, 7272 Greenville Ave., Dallas, TX 75231-4596. TEL 214-706-1310. FAX 214-691-6342. (Subscr. to: Box 843543, Dallas, TX 75284-3543) Ed. Dr. Stephen Vather. adv.; charts; illus.; stat.; index; circ. 3,750. (also avail. in microform from UMI,MIM; back issues avail.; reprint service avail. from UMI) **Indexed:** Biol.Abstr., Biotech.Abstr., Chem.Abstr., Curr.Adv.Biochem., Curr.Adv.Cell & Devel.Biol., Curr.Adv.Ecol.Sci., Curr.Cont., Excerp.Med., Ind.Med., Ind.Sci.Rev., Ind.Vet., INIS Atomind., NRN, Nutr.Abstr., Sci.Cit.Ind., Vet.Bull.
●Also available online. Vendor(s): BRS.
—BLDSC shelfmark: 3265.300000.
Description: Documents research advances in basic science, research, and experimental medicine.
Refereed Serial

616.1 US ISSN 0092-6213
RC685.C18 CODEN: CRSHAG
CIRCULATORY SHOCK. 1974. m. $867 (foreign $1,017). (Shock Society) John Wiley & Sons, Inc., Journals, 605 Third Ave., New York, NY 10158. TEL 212-850-6000. FAX 212-850-6088. TELEX 12-7063. Ed. James P. Filkins. adv.; bibl.; illus.; index. **Indexed:** Biol.Abstr, Chem.Abstr, Curr.Adv.Ecol.Sci., Curr.Cont., Excerp.Med., Ind.Med., Ind.Sci.Rev., Ind.Vet., INIS Atomind., Sci.Cit.Ind, Small Anim.Abstr., Vet.Bull.
●Also available online.
—BLDSC shelfmark: 3265.320000.
Description: Devoted to basic and clinical research on shock and low-flow states.
Refereed Serial

616.1 IT ISSN 0392-1344
CLINICA & TERAPIA CARDIOVASCOLARE. (Summaries in English) 1980. q. L.50000($50) C I C Edizioni Internazionali s.r.l., Via L. Spallanzani 11, 00161 Rome, Italy. TEL 06-8412673. FAX 06-8443365. TELEX 622099 CIC. Dirs. A. Dagianti, G. Ricci. **Indexed:** Chem.Abstr, Excerp.Med.
—BLDSC shelfmark: 3286.203500.

616.1 SP ISSN 0212-1808
CODEN: CCAREP
CLINICA CARDIOVASCULAR. vol.4, 1986. 6/yr. 5500 ptas. (Universidad de Navarra (Pamplona)) Alpe Editores, S.A., Pedro Rico, 27, 28029 Madrid, Spain. TEL 733 88 11. FAX 315-96-52. Eds. Dr. O'Connor, Dr. Montero.
—BLDSC shelfmark: 3286.190000.

616.136 SP ISSN 0214-9168
CLINICA E INVESTIGACION EN ARTERIOSCLEROSIS. q. 3500 ptas.($35) to non-members. (Sociedad Espanola de Arteriosclerosis) Ediciones Doyma S.A., Travesera de Gracia, 17-21, 08021 Barcelona, Spain. TEL 200-07-11. FAX 209-11-36. TELEX 51964 INK E. Ed. R. Carmena Rodriguez. adv.: page 135000 ptas.; trim 210 x 280; adv. contact: Marta Cisa. circ. 3,000.
—BLDSC shelfmark: 3286.201500.
Description: Covers basic science aspects such as etiology, epidemiology, physiopathology, and the diagnosis and treatment of arteriosclerosis and related processes.

616.1 US ISSN 0160-9289
CLINICAL CARDIOLOGY; international journal for cardiovascular diseases. 1978. m. $80 (foreign $126.50). Clinical Cardiology Publishing Company, Inc., Box 832, Mahwah, NJ 07430-0832. TEL 201-818-1010. FAX 201-818-0086. TELEX 220883 TAUR. Ed. Dr. C.R. Conti. adv.; bk.rev.; circ. 30,035. **Indexed:** Biol.Abstr., Curr.Cont., Excerp.Med., Ind.Med., Ind.Sci.Rev., INIS Atomind., NRN, Sci.Cit.Ind.
—BLDSC shelfmark: 3286.265000.
Description: Provides a forum for the coordination of clinical research in cardiology and cardiovascular surgery; also publishes the results of experimental studies closely related to clinical problems.
Refereed Serial

616.1 US ISSN 0741-4218
CLINICAL CARDIOLOGY ALERT. 1982. m. $95. American Health Consultants, Inc., Six Piedmont Center, Ste. 400, 3525 Piedmont Rd., N.E., Atlanta, GA 30305. TEL 404-262-7436. FAX 800-284-3291. (Subscr. to: Department L100, Box 740056, Atlanta, GA 30374-9822. TEL 800-688-2421) Ed. Dr. Michael Crawford. index; circ. 2,700. (also avail. in audio cassette; reprint service avail.)
Formerly: Cardiology Alert.

616.1 SP
CLINICAS CARDIOLOGICAS DE NORTEAMERICA. Spanish translation of: Cardiology Clinics of North America. 1984. 4/yr. 13144 ptas.($80) Interamericana de Espana, S.A., Division de Ciencias de la Salud de McGraw-Hill, Calle Manuel Ferrero, 13, 28036 Madrid, Spain. TEL 315-0340. FAX 733-6627. charts; illus.; cum.index.

CLINICIAN'S MANUAL ON HYPERLIPIDEMIA (YEAR). see MEDICAL SCIENCES — Abstracting, Bibliographies, Statistics

CLINICIAN'S MANUAL ON HYPERTENSION (YEAR). see MEDICAL SCIENCES — Abstracting, Bibliographies, Statistics

COEUR ET SANTE. see PHYSICAL FITNESS AND HYGIENE

616.12 FR
COEUR 2000. 10/yr. 210 F. (foreign 400 F.). C M R, 58 av. de la Narne, 92600 Asnieres, France.

616.12 US ISSN 8756-9086
CONNECTIVE ISSUES. 1984. q. $25 membership. National Marfan Foundation, 382 Main St., Pt. Washington, NY 11050. TEL 516-883-8712. Ed. Joseph Kolman. circ. 8,000. (back issues avail.)
Description: Provides information on the Marfan syndrome, an inherited disorder of connective tissue that can cause heart disease, orthopedic problems and blindness.

616.1 CS ISSN 0010-8650
CODEN: COVAAN
COR ET VASA; international journal of cardiology. (Text in English, French, and German; separate edition in Russian) 1958. 6/yr. 90 Kcs. Avicenum, Czechoslovak Medical Press, Malostranske nam. 28, 118 02 Prague 1, Czechoslovakia. (Dist. in Western countries by: Karger Libri A G, Petersgraben 31, 4011 Basel, Switzerland) Ed. Dr. J. Widimsky. adv.; bk.rev.; index. **Indexed:** Biol.Abstr., Chem.Abstr., Curr.Adv.Ecol.Sci., Curr.Cont., Excerp.Med., Ind.Med., Nutr.Abstr.
—BLDSC shelfmark: 3470.250000.

CORE JOURNALS IN CARDIOLOGY. see MEDICAL SCIENCES — Abstracting, Bibliographies, Statistics

CORONARY ARTERY DISEASE. see MEDICAL SCIENCES — Abstracting, Bibliographies, Statistics

CURRENT OPINION IN CARDIOLOGY. see MEDICAL SCIENCES — Abstracting, Bibliographies, Statistics

CURRENT OPINION IN LIPIDOLOGY. see MEDICAL SCIENCES — Abstracting, Bibliographies, Statistics

616.12 US ISSN 0146-2806
CURRENT PROBLEMS IN CARDIOLOGY. Short title: C P C. 1976. m. $75 to individuals (foreign $100); institutions $100 (foreign $125); students $45 (foreign $70) (effective Jan. 1992). Mosby - Year Book, Inc. (Subsidiary of: Times Mirror Company), 11830 Westline Indusrial Dr., St. Louis, MO 63146. Ed. Robert A. O'Rourke. cum.index; circ. 3,708. (also avail. in microform from UMI; back issues avail.; reproduction service avail. from UMI) **Indexed:** Curr.Cont., Excerp.Med., Ind.Med., SSCI.
—BLDSC shelfmark: 3501.347000.
Description: A fully referenced monographic journal that consists of original review articles on practical clinical topics.

616.12 CN ISSN 0847-2157
DIAGNOSTIC CARDIOLOGY; information retrieval system. 1989. q. Can.$136. Medicopea International, Inc., 8200 Decarie Blvd., Ste. 212, Montreal, Que. H4P 2P5, Canada. TEL 514-340-9157. FAX 514-342-5783. TELEX 055-62171.

615.65 IT ISSN 0012-544X
DONO. 1959. 3/yr. free. Associazione Friulana Donatori di Sangue, Via Forni di Sotto, 33100 Udine, Italy. Ed. Giovanni Faleschini. illus.; stat.; circ. 15,000.
Description: Reports on blood transfusions.

616.12 GW ISSN 0170-8287
E E G LABOR. (Text in German; summaries in English and German) q. DM.119 (foreign DM.121). Gustav Fischer Verlag, Wollgrasweg 49, Postfach 720143, 7000 Stuttgart 70, Germany. TEL 0711-458030. FAX 0711-4580334. TELEX 7111488-FIBUCH. (U.S. address: Gustav Fischer New York Inc., 220 E. 23rd St., Suite 909, New York, NY 10010) **Indexed:** Excerp.Med.
—BLDSC shelfmark: 3663.395500.

616.12 US ISSN 0742-2822
ECHOCARDIOGRAPHY; a journal of cardiovascular ultrasound and allied techniques. 1984. bi-m. $110 (foreign $136). Futura Publishing Company, Inc., 2 Bedford Ridge Rd., Box 330, Mt. Kisco, NY 10549. TEL 800-877-8761. FAX 914-666-0993. Ed. Dr. Navin C. Nanda. bk.rev.; circ. 2,500.
—BLDSC shelfmark: 3647.572500.
Description: Contains articles on specific applications of diagnostic ultrasound and other related techniques. Includes case reports, panel discussions, news items and abstracts from non-English literature.

616.1 UK ISSN 0421-7527
EUROPEAN CONGRESS OF CARDIOLOGY. ABSTRACTS OF PAPERS. (Supplement to: European Heart Journal (ISSN 0195-668X)) (Text in English) 1952. a. (European Society of Cardiology) Academic Press Ltd., 24-28 Oval Rd., London NW1 7DX, England. TEL 071-267-4466. FAX 071-482-2293. TELEX 25775 ACPRES G.

616.1 UK ISSN 0423-7242
EUROPEAN CONGRESS OF CARDIOLOGY. (PROCEEDINGS). 1952. a. (European Society of Cardiology, SZ) Academic Press Ltd., 24-28 Oval Rd., London NW1 7DX, England.

616.1 UK ISSN 0195-668X
CODEN: EHJODF
EUROPEAN HEART JOURNAL. (Supplement avail.: European Congress of Cardiology. Abstracts of Papers (ISSN 0421-7527)) 1980. m. $297. (European Society of Cardiology) Academic Press Ltd., 24-28 Oval Rd., London NW1 7DX, England. TEL 071-267-4466. FAX 071-482-2293. TELEX 25775 ACPRES G. Ed. H.E. Kulbertus. adv.; illus.; index. **Indexed:** Biotech.Abstr., Chem.Abstr, Curr.Cont., Dok.Arbeitsmed., Excerp.Med., Ind.Med., Ind.Sci.Rev., Sci.Cit.Ind.
—BLDSC shelfmark: 3829.717500.
Description: Directed to practicing cardiologists publishing original papers on all aspects of cardiovascular medicine, surgery, and basic research.

616.1 GW ISSN 1010-7940
EUROPEAN JOURNAL OF CARDIO-THORACIC SURGERY. 1989. 12/yr. DM.296($149) Springer-Verlag, Heidelberger Platz 3, D-1000 Berlin 33, Germany. TEL 030-8207-1. (Also Heidelberg, Tokyo, Vienna, and New York)
—BLDSC shelfmark: 3829.725620.

MEDICAL SCIENCES — CARDIOVASCULAR DISEASES

616.1   UK   ISSN 0950-821X
EUROPEAN JOURNAL OF VASCULAR SURGERY. bi-m. $282. (European Society for Vascular Surgery) Academic Press Ltd., Grune & Stratton Ltd., 24-28 Oval Rd., London NW1 7DX, England. TEL 071-267-4466. FAX 071-482-2293. TELEX 25775-ACPRES-G. Ed. P.R.F. Bell. adv.; bk.rev. **Indexed:** Excerp.Med.
—BLDSC shelfmark: 3829.747300.
Description: Covers all aspects of diagnosis, investigation and management of vascular disorders. Includes papers on technical aspects of vascular surgery.

615.65   FR   ISSN 0253-1321
F I O D S REVUE. (Editions in English, French, Spanish) 1967. q. 70 F. (Federation Internationale des Organisations de Donneurs de Sang Benevoles - International Federation of Blood Donors Organizations) F I O D S, c/o Secretary Pierre Pelletier, 30 rue de Boichot, 39100 Dole, France. FAX 84-82-61-02. Ed. Maurice Trambouze. adv.; bk.rev.; illus.; circ. 5,000.
Formerly (until 1980): Don Universel du Sang (ISSN 0012-5407)

610   IT
G AND B. 1971. m. L.70000($110) Piccin Editore, Via Altinate 107, Padova, Italy. TEL 049-655566. TELEX 432074 PICCIN I. Ed. Prof. Mariano Ferrari. adv.; index; circ. 85,000. **Indexed:** Excerp.Med.
Formerly (until 1991): Basi Razionali della Terapia (ISSN 0393-7569)

616.136   IT   ISSN 0017-0224
CODEN: GIARA5
GIORNALE DELL'ARTERIOSCLEROSI. (Supplement to: Giornale de Gerontologia) (Text in Italian; summaries in English) 1965-1972; N.S. 1976. 3/yr. L.30000. (Societa Italiana di Gerontologia e Geriatria) Pacini Editore s.r.l., Via A. Gherardesca 1, 56014 Ospedaletto (PI), Italy. TEL 050-982439. FAX 050-983906. TELEX 501628 PACINI I. Ed. G. Gentili. adv.; bk.rev.; abstr.; bibl.; charts; illus.; index; circ. 5,000. **Indexed:** Chem.Abstr, Excerp.Med.
—BLDSC shelfmark: 4176.870000.
Description: Features original articles, reviews and letters on topics of physiopathology, clinics and the therapy of arteriosclerosis.

616.13   IT   ISSN 0392-1387
GIORNALE ITALIANO DI ANGIOLOGIA. (Text in Italian; summaries in English) 1981. q. L.50000($50) C I C Edizioni Internazionali s.r.l., Via L. Spallanzani 11, 00161 Rome, Italy. FAX 06-8443365. TELEX 622099 CIC. Dir. P. Pola. adv.; bk.rev. **Indexed:** Excerp.Med.
—BLDSC shelfmark: 4178.140000.

616.1   IT   ISSN 0046-5968
CODEN: GICDA7
GIORNALE ITALIANO DI CARDIOLOGIA. 1971. m. L.130000($180) Piccin Editore, Via Altinate 107, 35100 Padua, Italy. TEL 049-655566. TELEX 432074 PICCIN I. Ed. P.F. Fazzini. adv.; bk.rev.; illus.; circ. 4,000. **Indexed:** Biol.Abstr., Chem.Abstr, Excerp.Med., Ind.Med.
—BLDSC shelfmark: 4178.150000.
Formed by the merger of: Cuore e Circolazione & Folia Cardiologica & Malattie Cardiovascolari.

H L B NEWSLETTER; reporting on heart, lung and blood disease research program, policy development. see *MEDICAL SCIENCES — Experimental Medicine, Laboratory Technique*

616.15   SZ   ISSN 0301-0147
CODEN: HMTSB7
HAEMOSTASIS; international journal on haemostasis and thrombosis research. (Text in English) 1973. bi-m. 413 SFr.($276) per vol. S. Karger AG, Allschwilerstr. 10, P.O. Box, CH-4009 Basel, Switzerland. TEL 061-3061111. FAX 061-3061234. TELEX CH 962652. Ed. H.C. Hemker. adv.; bk.rev.; circ. 1,150. (also avail. in microform from RPI) **Indexed:** Biol.Abstr., Chem.Abstr., Curr.Adv.Biochem., Curr.Adv.Cancer Res., Curr.Adv.Cell & Devel.Biol., Curr.Adv.Ecol.Sci., Curr.Cont., Excerp.Med., Helminthol.Abstr., Ind.Med., Ind.Sci.Rev., Sci.Cit.Ind.
—BLDSC shelfmark: 4238.090000.
Formerly: Coagulation (ISSN 0009-9902)

HANDBOOK OF HYPERLIPIDEMIA. see *MEDICAL SCIENCES — Abstracting, Bibliographies, Statistics*

616.1   US
HEALTHY HEART. (In two eds.: Physicians' ed. and Patients' ed.) 1988. q. Medical Economics Publishing Co., Five Paragon Dr., Montvale, NJ 07645. TEL 201-358-7200. FAX 201-573-1045. circ. 10,000.

616.1   GW   ISSN 0179-342X
HEART & CIRCULATION; diseases of heart and cardiovascular system. (Text in English) 1986. q. P M I Verlag GmbH, August-Schanz-Str. 21, 6000 Frankfurt a.M. 50, Germany. TEL 069-5480000. FAX 069-54800077. Ed. Peter Hoffmann. circ. 20,000. (back issues avail.)

616.1   CN
HEART AND STROKE FOUNDATION OF CANADA. ANNUAL REPORT.* (Text in English, French) 1956. a. free. Heart and Stroke Foundation of Canada, 160 George St., Ste. 200, Ottawa, Ont. K1N 9M2, Canada. TEL 613-237-4361. FAX 613-234-3278. Ed. J.C. McCrea. circ. 5,000.
Formerly: Canadian Heart Foundation. Annual Report (ISSN 0068-8851)

616.1   JA   ISSN 0910-8327
CODEN: HEVEEO
HEART AND VESSELS; an international journal. (Text and summaries in English) 1985. q. 12800 Yen in Japan; N. America $114; elsewhere DM.182. (Heart Institute of Japan, Tokyo) Springer-Verlag Tokyo, Inc., 37-3 Hongo, 3-chome, Bunkyo-ku, Tokyo 113, Japan. TEL 03-3812-0331. FAX 03-3812-0719. (Co-publisher: Tokyo Women's Medical College) Ed. Atsuyoshi Takao. adv.; bk.rev.; index; circ. 1,000. (also avail. in microform from UMI; back issues avail.; reprint service avail. UMI) **Indexed:** Chem.Abstr., Excerp.Med., Ind.Med.
—BLDSC shelfmark: 4275.297000.
Description: Publishes research, ideas, methods, and techniques on cardiovascular diseases.

616.1   II   ISSN 0046-7111
HEART CARE. (Text in English) 1970. q. Rs.10($6) (Society for the Prevention of Heart Disease and Rehabilitation) Praga Publications, 43 Sundar Mahal, Churchgate, Bombay 400020, India. Ed. C.V. Shah. adv.; bk.rev.; charts; illus.; circ. 3,000.

616.1   US   ISSN 8755-7673
HEART FAILURE. 1984. bi-m. $45. (Albert Einstein College of Medicine) LeJacy Communications, Inc., 47 Arch St., Greenwich, CT 06830. TEL 203-625-0194. Ed. John E. Strobeck, M.D., Ph.D. adv.; bk.rev.; abstr.; bibl.; illus.; circ. 50,000.
—BLDSC shelfmark: 4275.340000.

616.12   US
HEARTBEAT (NEW YORK). 1988. q. $21.95. HealthTeam Interactive Communications, Inc., 274 Madison Ave., 19th Fl., New York, NY 10016-0701. TEL 212-689-1520. FAX 212-779-2094. Ed. John Nattoli. adv. contact: Paul Sisia.
Description: Provides patient education in cardiovascular matters.

616.135   US
HEARTBEAT (SAN FRANCISCO);* an emergency nursing Newsletter. q. Henderson Communications, 3476 21st St., San Francisco, CA 94110-2213. Ed. Estelle MacPhail. bk.rev.

616.1   US   ISSN 8755-5271
HEARTLINE. 1972. m. $20. Coronary Club, Inc., 9500 Euclid Ave., E4-15, Cleveland, OH 44195-5058. TEL 216-444-3690. (Co-sponsor: Cleveland Clinic Educational Foundation) Ed. Dr. Fredric J. Pashkow. index; circ. 10,000. (looseleaf format; back issues avail.)
Formerly (until 1985): Coronary Club Bulletin.

616.12   GW   ISSN 0340-9937
HERZ. 1976. bi-m. DM.180 (foreign DM.198). Urban und Vogel, Lindwurmstr. 95, Postfach 152209, 8000 Munich 15, Germany. TEL 089-53292-0. FAX 089-53292-100. Ed. Prof. W. Rudolph. **Indexed:** Curr.Cont., Excerp.Med., Ind.Med.
—BLDSC shelfmark: 4300.396000.

616.1   GW   ISSN 0046-7324
CODEN: HZKLAV
HERZ KREISLAUF; Zeitschrift fuer Kardiologie und Angiologie in Klinik und Praxis. 1969. m. DM.171.60 (foreign DM.180). (Deutsche Gesellschaft fuer Praevention und Rehabilitation von Herz-Kreislauf-Erkrankungen e.V.) Richard Pflaum Verlag GmbH und Co. KG, Lazarettstr. 4, Postfach 190737, 8000 Munich 19, Germany. TEL 089-12607-0. FAX 089-12607-281. Ed. K.W. Westermann. adv.; bk.rev.; bibl.; charts; illus.; circ. 32,000. **Indexed:** Chem.Abstr., Curr.Cont., Excerp.Med., Ind.Sci.Rev., INIS Atomind., Sci.Cit.Ind.
—BLDSC shelfmark: 4300.420000.

616.1   GW   ISSN 0720-0730
HERZ UND GEFAESSE; Zeitschrift fuer praktische Kardioangiologie. 1981. m. DM.48. Perimed Verlag Dr. D. Straube, Weinstr. 70, Postfach 3740, 8520 Erlangen, Germany. TEL 09131-609-1. FAX 09131-609217. TELEX 629851-PEMEDD. adv.; bk.rev.; index; circ. 30,000. **Indexed:** Excerp.Med.
—BLDSC shelfmark: 4300.430000.

616.1   GW
HERZ UND GESUNDHEIT. ceased 1986; resumed 1991. 4/yr. DM.24. (Deutschen Herzhilfe e.V.) Verlag fuer Medizin Dr. Ewald Fischer GmbH, Fritz-Frey-Str. 21, Postfach 105767, 6900 Heidelberg 1, Germany. TEL 06221-49974. Eds. A. Kroedel, P. Mand.

616.1   GW   ISSN 0938-7412
▼**HERZSCHRITTMACHERTHERAPIE UND ELEKTROPHYSIOLOGIE.** (Text in German; summaries in English) 1990. q. DM.140. Dr. Dietrich Steinkopff Verlag, Saalbaustr. 12, Postfach 111442, 6100 Darmstadt 11, Germany. TEL 06151-26538. FAX 06151-20849. Ed.Bd. adv. bk.rev.; bibl.; charts; illus.; circ. 1,500.

HIROSAKI DAIGAKU IGAKUBU EISEIGAKU KYOSHITSU GYOSEKISHU. see *MEDICAL SCIENCES*

616.1   DK   ISSN 0105-9785
HJERTEFORENINGEN. 1978. a. free. Hjerteforeningen, Hauser Plads 10, 1127 Copenhagen K, Denmark. illus.

616.1   DK   ISSN 0108-8904
HJERTENYT; orientering om sundhed og praeventiv medicin. 1982. irreg. free. Hjerteforeningen, Hauser Plads 10, 1127 Copenhagen K, Denmark.

616.1   GW   ISSN 0721-1465
HOCHDRUCK; Risikofaktor fuer Herz, Kreislauf und Gefaesse. 1983. 12/yr. DM.150. P M I Verlag GmbH, August-Schanz-Str. 21, 6000 Frankfurt a.M. 50, Germany. TEL 069-548000-0. FAX 069-548000-77. Ed. Peter Hoffmann. circ. 20,000. (back issues avail.)

616.1   US   ISSN 0194-911X
RC685.H8   CODEN: HPRTDN
HYPERTENSION. 1979. m. $106 to individuals (foreign $144); institutions $138 (foreign $176). American Heart Association, 7272 Greenville Ave., Dallas, TX 75231-4596. TEL 214-706-1310. FAX 214-691-6342. (Subscr. to: Box 843543, Dallas, TX 75284-3543) Ed. Dr. Allyn L. Mark. adv.; index; circ. 4,600. (also avail. in microform from UMI; back issues avail.; reprint service avail. from UMI) **Indexed:** Biol.Abstr., Biotech.Abstr., Curr.Adv.Genetics & Molec.Biol., Curr.Cont., Dent.Ind., Excerp.Med., Ind.Med., Ind.Sci.Rev., INIS Atomind., Risk Abstr.
—BLDSC shelfmark: 4352.629000.
Supersedes: Circulation Research.
Description: For cardiologists, internists, and researchers; reports clinical and laboratory investigations in hypertension.
Refereed Serial

616.1   UK   ISSN 0143-117X
HYPERTENSION. m. £65. Sheffield University Biomedical Information Service (SUBIS), The University, Sheffield S10 2TN, England. TEL 0742-768555. FAX 0742-739826. TELEX 547216 UGSHEF G. (looseleaf format; back issues avail.)
Description: Current awareness service for researchers in clinical and life sciences.

MEDICAL SCIENCES — CARDIOVASCULAR DISEASES

616.1 RC681 II ISSN 0019-4832
INDIAN HEART JOURNAL. (Text in English) 1949. bi-m. Rs.10($15) Cardiological Society of India, Bombay Mutual Terrace, 534 Sandhurst Bridge, Bombay 400007, India. Ed. Shantilal Shah. bk.rev.; abstr.; illus.; circ. 1,500. **Indexed:** Biol.Abstr., Chem.Abstr., Excerp.Med., Ind.Med., INIS Atomind., NRN.

616.12 FR ISSN 0220-2476
INFORMATION CARDIOLOGIQUE. 1978. 11/yr. 420 F. to individuals (foreign 490 F.); students 290 F. (foreign 360 F.). (Centre Cardiologique du Nord) Publications Medicales A G C F, Rue des Moulins Gemeaux, 93200 Saint Denis, France. TEL 48-20-18-21. (Subscr. to: Mme. L. Pino, 34 bis rue Paul Eluard, 93200 Saint Denis, France) Ed. Dr. A. Castillo Fenoy. adv.; bk.rev.; circ. 2,500.
—BLDSC shelfmark: 4485.640000.

616.1 MX ISSN 0020-3785
CODEN: AICMA2
INSTITUTO DE CARDIOLOGIA DE MEXICO. ARCHIVOS. (Text in Spanish; summaries in English and French) 1930. bi-m. Mex.$100($75) Instituto Nacional de Cardiologia, Sociedad Mexicana de Cardiologia - National Institute of Cardiology "Ignacio Chavez", Mexican Society of Cardiology, Oficina de Publicaciones, Juan Badiano No.1, Tlalpan, 14080 Mexico D.F., Mexico. Eds. Drs. F. Attie, A. de Micheli. adv.; bk.rev.; charts; illus.; stat.; index; circ. 2,500. **Indexed:** Biol.Abstr., Chem.Abstr., Curr.Adv.Ecol.Sci., Dent.Ind., Excerp.Med., Ind.Med.
—BLDSC shelfmark: 1651.500000.

616.12 US ISSN 0173-0282
INTERNATIONAL BOEHRINGER MANNHEIM. SYMPOSIA. 1976. irreg. price varies. Springer-Verlag, 175 Fifth Ave., New York, NY 10010. TEL 212-460-1500. (reprint service avail. from ISI)

616.13 IT ISSN 0074-347X
INTERNATIONAL CONGRESS OF ANGIOLOGY. PROCEEDINGS. 1952. irreg., 1976, 10th, Tokyo. International Union of Angiology, c/o Marcello Tesi, Via Bonifacio Lupi 11, 20129 Florence, Italy.

616.1 NE ISSN 0167-9899
INTERNATIONAL JOURNAL OF CARDIAC IMAGING. 1984. q. fl.280($159) Kluwer Academic Publishers, Postbus 17, 3300 AA Dordrecht, Netherlands. TEL 078-334911. FAX 078-334254. TELEX 29245. (Dist. by: Kluwer Academic Publishers Group, P.O. Box 322, 3300 AH Dordrecht, Netherlands; N. America dist. addr.: Box 358, Accord Station, Hingham, MA 02018-0358. TEL 617-871-6600) Eds. G.B. John Mancini, Johan H.C. Reiber. adv.; bk.rev. (reprint service avail. from SWZ) **Indexed:** Excerp.Med., Ind.Med.
—BLDSC shelfmark: 4542.157000.
Formerly: International Journal of Cardiovascular Imaging.

616.1 NE ISSN 0167-5273
CODEN: IJCDD5
INTERNATIONAL JOURNAL OF CARDIOLOGY. 1973. 12/yr.(in 4 vols.; 3 nos./vol.). fl.1392 (effective 1992). Elsevier Science Publishers B.V., P.O. Box 211, 1000 AE Amsterdam, Netherlands. TEL 020-5803911. FAX 020-5803598. TELEX 18582 ESPA NL. (Subscr. in U.S. and Canada to: Elsevier Science Publishing Co., Inc., Box 882, Madison Sq. Sta., New York, NY 10159. TEL 212-989-5800) Ed.Bd. bk.rev.; illus. (also avail. in microform from RPI; back issues avail.) **Indexed:** Biol.Abstr., Biotech.Abstr., Chem.Abstr, Curr.Adv.Ecol.Sci., Curr.Cont., Dent.Ind., Excerp.Med., Ind.Med., Ind.Sci.Rev., NRN, Sci.Cit.Ind.
—BLDSC shelfmark: 4542.158000.
Formerly: European Journal of Cardiology (ISSN 0301-4711); Incorporates: Association of European Paediatric Cardiologists. Proceedings (ISSN 0066-9547).
Description: For clinical practitioners and research workers in cardiovascular research and surgery, clinical cardiology and paediatric cardiology.
Refereed Serial

616.12 IT ISSN 0393-6066
INTERNATIONAL JOURNAL OF SPORTS CARDIOLOGY. 1984. s-a. L.50000($60) (Italian Society of Sports Cardiology) Edizioni Minerva Medica, Corso Bramante 83-85, 10126 Turin, Italy. Ed. Antonio Venerando. **Indexed:** Excerp.Med., NRN, Sportsearch (1984-).
—BLDSC shelfmark: 4542.681200.

616.1 SZ ISSN 1016-4723
INTERNATIONAL SOCIETY FOR APPLIED CARDIOVASCULAR BIOLOGY. (Text in English) 1989. irreg. price varies. S. Karger AG, Allschwilerstr. 10, P.O. Box, CH-4009 Basel, Switzerland. TEL 061-3061111. FAX 061-3061234. Ed. P. Zilla.

INTERNATIONAL SOCIETY OF BLOOD TRANSFUSION. PROCEEDINGS OF THE CONGRESS. see *MEDICAL SCIENCES — Hematology*

616.1 ISSN 0074-8765
INTERNATIONAL SYMPOSIUM ON ATHEROSCLEROSIS. PROCEEDINGS. irreg. price varies. Springer-Verlag, 175 Fifth Ave., New York, NY 10010. TEL 212-460-1500.

615.63 US
INTRAVENOUS THERAPY NEWS.* 1974. m. $14. McMahon Publishing Co., 83 Peaceable St., W. Redding, CT 06896. TEL 203-544-9343. (Subscr. to: 121 S. Gertrude Ave., Paramus, NJ 07652) Ed.Bd. adv.; illus. **Indexed:** CINAHL, Excerp.Med., I.P.A.
●Also available online.
Former titles: American Journal of Intravenous Therapy and Clinical Nutrition (ISSN 0195-0282); American Journal of Intravenous Therapy (ISSN 0161-3065); American Journal of I.V. Therapy (ISSN 0095-4012)

616.1 JA ISSN 0047-1828
RC681 CODEN: JCIRA2
JAPANESE CIRCULATION JOURNAL/NIHON JUNKANKIGAKUSHI. (Title varies: Nippon Journal of Angio-Cardiology) (Text in English) 1935. m. 15000 Yen. Japanese Circulation Society - Nihon Junkanki Gakkai, Kinki Invention Center, 14 Yoshida Kawahara-cho, Sakyo-ku, Kyoto 606, Japan. TEL 075-751-8643. FAX 075-771-3060. Ed. Kazuo Yamada. adv.; circ. 14,000. **Indexed:** Biol.Abstr., Chem.Abstr., Curr.Cont., Excerp.Med., Ind.Med., INIS Atomind., Nutr.Abstr., Sci.Cit.Ind.
—BLDSC shelfmark: 4650.750000.

616.1 JA
JAPANESE CIRCULATION JOURNAL SUPPLEMENT. (Text in Japanese) irreg. (2-3/yr.) Japanese Circulation Society - Nihon Junkanki Gakkai, Kinki Invention Center, 14 Yoshida Kawahara-cho, Sakyo-ku, Kyoto 606, Japan. TEL 075-751-8643. FAX 075-771-3060. Ed. Kazuo Yamada.

616.1 JA ISSN 0021-4868
CODEN: JHEJAR
JAPANESE HEART JOURNAL. (Text in English) 1960. bi-m. 15,000 Yen (foreign 357 SFr.). (University of Tokyo, Faculty of Medicine, Department of Internal Medicine - Tokyo Daigaku Igakubu Dai-2-Naika) Nankodo Co. Ltd., 42-6, Hongo 3-chome, Bunkyo-ku, Tokyo 113, Japan. TEL 03-3811-7239. FAX 03-3811-7230. TELEX 963475. (Dist. outside Japan by: J.C. Baltzer A.G., Wettsteinplatz 10, CH-4058 Basel, Switzerland) Ed. Hideo Ueda. adv.; bk.rev.; charts; illus.; index; circ. 1,000. (also avail. in microfilm from UMI; reprint service avail. from UMI) **Indexed:** Biol.Abstr., Chem.Abstr., Curr. Cont., Excerp.Med., Ind.Med., Ind.Sci.Rev., INIS Atomind., NRN, Sci.Cit.Ind.
—BLDSC shelfmark: 4650.770000.

616 FR ISSN 0398-0499
JOURNAL DES MALADIES VASCULAIRES. 1976. q. 135 ECU($155) (typically set in Jan.). (College Francais de Pathologie Vasculaire) Masson, 120 bd. St. Germain, 75280 Paris Cedex 06, France. TEL 1-46-34-21-60. FAX 1-45-87-29-99. TELEX 202 671 F. Ed. Vayssairat. circ. 2,100. (also avail. in microform from UMI; reprint service avail. from ISI) **Indexed:** Excerp.Med., Ind.Med., Ind.Sci.Rev., Sci.Cit.Ind.
—BLDSC shelfmark: 5010.850000.

JOURNAL OF AIR MEDICAL TRANSPORT. see *TRANSPORTATION — Air Transport*

616.1 UK ISSN 0951-1830
JOURNAL OF AMBULATORY MONITORING. 1988. q. £24.20($42.35) to individuals; institutions £88($154). Taylor & Francis Ltd., Rankine Rd., Basingstoke, Hants RG24 OPR, England. TEL 0256-840366. FAX 0256-479438. TELEX 858540. Eds. S.J. Meldrum, S. Stern.
—BLDSC shelfmark: 4927.230200.
Description: Covers ambulatory, or personal, monitoring in the broadest sense. In addition to the established field of ECG monitoring this will include blood pressure, oesophageal pH, EEG, and the emerging fields of radio and transtelephonic monitoring.
Refereed Serial

616.1 US ISSN 0886-0440
JOURNAL OF CARDIAC SURGERY. 1986. q. $85 (foreign $103). Futura Publishing Company, Inc., 2 Bedford Ridge Rd., Box 330, Mt. Kisco, NY 10549. TEL 800-877-8761. FAX 914-666-0993. Ed. Lawrence H. Cohn, M.D. adv.; bk.rev.; circ. 2,300. (back issues avail.) **Indexed:** Excerp.Med.
—BLDSC shelfmark: 4954.863500.
Refereed Serial

616.1 US ISSN 0883-9212
JOURNAL OF CARDIOPULMONARY REHABILITATION. m. $55 to individuals (foreign $65); institutions $75 (foreign $85). (American Association of Cardiovascular & Pulmonary Rehabilitation) J.B. Lippincott Co., E. Washington Sq., Philadelphia, PA 19105. TEL 215-238-4200. (Subscr. to: Downville Pike, Rte. 3, Box 20-B, Hagerstown, MD 21740) Ed. Dr. Mike Pollock. adv.; bk.rev.; circ. 16,200. (also avail. in microform from UMI; back issues avail.) **Indexed:** Phys.Ed.Ind.
—BLDSC shelfmark: 4954.864500.
Formerly: Journal of Cardiac Rehabilitation (ISSN 0275-1429)
Description: Covers articles in peripheral, vascular, and pulmonary rehabilitation.
Refereed Serial

JOURNAL OF CARDIOTHORACIC AND VASCULAR ANESTHESIA. see *MEDICAL SCIENCES — Anaesthesiology*

616.1 US ISSN 0893-2972
JOURNAL OF CARDIOVASCULAR AND PULMONARY TECHNOLOGY. 1970. s-a. $45. National Society for Cardiovascular Technology - National Society for Pulmonary Technology, Inc., 1101 14th St. N.W., Ste. 1100, Washington, DC 20005. TEL 202-371-1267. FAX 202-371-1090. Ed. Dr. John Cissik. adv.; index; circ. 3,200. (back issues avail.)
Formerly: C V Tech; Supersedes (in 1985): Analyzer (ISSN 0146-5449)

616.1 US ISSN 1045-3873
CODEN: JCELE2
▼**JOURNAL OF CARDIOVASCULAR ELECTROPHYSIOLOGY.** 1990. 6/yr. $75 (foreign $101). Futura Publishing Company, Inc., 2 Bedford Ridge Rd., Box 330, Mt. Kisco, NY 10549. TEL 800-877-8761. FAX 914-666-0993. Ed. Dr. Douglas P. Zipes.
—BLDSC shelfmark: 4954.866000.
Description: Devoted to the study of the electrophysiology of the heart and its blood vessels.

616.12 US
JOURNAL OF CARDIOVASCULAR MANAGEMENT. bi-m. Knolls Publishing Group, 240 Cedar Knolls Rd., Ste. 220, Cedar Knolls, NJ 07927. TEL 201-285-0855. FAX 201-285-1472. Ed. Alfred Saint-Jacques. circ. 11,366.

616.12 610.73 US ISSN 0889-4655
JOURNAL OF CARDIOVASCULAR NURSING. 1986. q. $57. Aspen Publishers, Inc., 200 Orchard Ridge Dr., Gaithersburg, MD 20878. TEL 301-417-7500. FAX 301-417-7550. **Indexed:** Nurs.Abstr.
—BLDSC shelfmark: 4954.867500.

JOURNAL OF CARDIOVASCULAR PHARMACOLOGY. see *PHARMACY AND PHARMACOLOGY*

M

MEDICAL SCIENCES — CARDIOVASCULAR DISEASES

616.1   IT   ISSN 0021-9509
CODEN: JCVSA2
JOURNAL OF CARDIOVASCULAR SURGERY. (Text in English) 1960. bi-m. L.80000($90) (International Cardiovascular Society) Edizioni Minerva Medica, Corso Bramante 83-85, 10126 Turin, Italy. TEL 11-678282. FAX 11-674502. (Dist. in U.S. by: J.B. Lippincott Company, E. Washington Sq., Philadelphia, PA 19105) Eds. S.S. Rose, J.E. Connolly. adv.; bk.rev.; bibl.; charts; illus.; index; circ. 4,000. (also avail. in microform from SWZ; back issues avail.) Indexed: Biol.Abstr., Chem.Abstr., Curr.Cont., Excerp.Med., Ind.Med.
—BLDSC shelfmark: 4954.870000.

616.1 619   US   ISSN 1043-4356
CODEN: JCATE6
JOURNAL OF CARDIOVASCULAR TECHNOLOGY. 1982. q. $160 (foreign $199). Mary Ann Liebert, Inc., 1651 Third Ave., New York, NY 10128. TEL 212-289-2300. FAX 212-289-4697. Ed. Dr. Myron R. Schoenfeld. adv.; bk.rev. (back issues avail.) Indexed: Curr.Cont., Excerp.Med.
—BLDSC shelfmark: 4954.872300.
Formerly (until 1989): Journal of Cardiovascular Ultrasonography (ISSN 0730-8396)
Description: Publishes articles on both diagnostic and therapeutic applications to cardiovascular disease.
Refereed Serial

JOURNAL OF CRITICAL CARE. see MEDICAL SCIENCES

616.1   US   ISSN 0022-0736
RC681.A1   CODEN: JECAB6
JOURNAL OF ELECTROCARDIOLOGY. 1968. q. $72 to individuals (foreign $95); institutions $120 (foreign $143). Churchill Livingstone Medical Journals, 650 Ave. of the Americas, New York, NY 10011. TEL 212-819-5400. FAX 212-727-7808. TELEX 662266. (Dist. by: Transaction Publishers, Department 3091, Rutgers University, New Brunswick, NJ 08903. TEL 908-932-2280) Ed. Ronald H. Selvester, M.D. adv.; bk.rev.; charts; illus.; index; circ. 5,291. (also avail. in microfilm from UMI; reprint service avail. from UMI, ISI) Indexed: Biol.Abstr., Curr.Cont., Excerp.Med., Ind.Med., Ind.Sci.Rev., INIS Atomind., Sci.Cit.Ind.
—BLDSC shelfmark: 4974.750000.
Description: Devoted to the clinical and experimental studies of the electrical activities of the heart.
Refereed Serial

616.1   UK   ISSN 0950-9240
RC685.H8
JOURNAL OF HUMAN HYPERTENSION. 1987. bi-m. £96 (foreign £106). Macmillan Press Ltd., Houndmills, Basingstoke, Hampshire RG21 2XS, England. TEL 0256-29242. FAX 0256-810526. Ed. D.G. Beevers. adv.; bk.rev.; index. (also avail. in microfilm from UMI; back issues avail.) Indexed: Curr.Cont., Excerp.Med., Ind.Med.
—BLDSC shelfmark: 5003.416000.

JOURNAL OF HYPERTENSION. see MEDICAL SCIENCES — Abstracting, Bibliographies, Statistics

616.1   US   ISSN 0896-4327
JOURNAL OF INTERVENTIONAL CARDIOLOGY. vol.2, 1989. q. $70 (foreign $88). Futura Publishing Company, Inc., 2 Bedford Ridge Rd., Box 330, Mt. Kisco, NY 10549. TEL 800-877-8761. FAX 914-666-0993.
—BLDSC shelfmark: 5007.696000.

616.1   US   ISSN 1042-3931
JOURNAL OF INVASIVE CARDIOLOGY. 1988. 9/yr. $90 (foreign $144). Health Management Publications, Inc., 550 American Ave., King of Prussia, PA 19406-1441. TEL 215-337-4466. FAX 215-337-0890. Ed. Dr. Richard Shaw. adv.
—BLDSC shelfmark: 5007.800000.
Description: Covers cardiac catheterization, coronary and peripheral angioplasty, including thrombolytic and associated therapy.

616.1   UK   ISSN 0022-2828
RC681.A1   CODEN: JMCDAY
JOURNAL OF MOLECULAR AND CELLULAR CARDIOLOGY. 1970. m. $591. (International Society for Heart Research) Academic Press Ltd., 24-28 Oval Rd., London NW1 7DX, England. TEL 071-267-4466. FAX 071-482-2293. TELEX 25775 ACPRES G. Ed. Arnold M. Katz. Indexed: Biol.Abstr., Biotech.Abstr., Chem.Abstr., Curr.Adv.Biochem., Curr.Adv.Cell & Devel.Biol., Curr.Adv.Ecol.Sci., Curr.Adv.Genetics & Molec.Biol., Dent.Ind., Excerp.Med., Helminthol.Abstr., Ind.Med., Ind.Sci.Rev.
—BLDSC shelfmark: 5020.690000.
Description: Provides a forum for research papers dealing with the molecular biology, physiology, pharmacology, and pathophysiology of the heart and cardiovascular system.

616.1 574   US   ISSN 1042-5268
JOURNAL OF VASCULAR MEDICINE AND BIOLOGY. 1988. bi-m. $150. Blackwell Scientific Publications Inc., Three Cambridge Center, Ste. 208, Cambridge, MA 02142-1413. TEL 617-225-0401. FAX 617-225-0412. Ed. V. Dzau.
—BLDSC shelfmark: 5072.268000.
Description: Focuses on the blood vessel - the biology and pathology - including the vascular wall and blood components.

JOURNAL OF VASCULAR SURGERY. see MEDICAL SCIENCES — Surgery

KARDIO; Erkrankungen von Herz, Kreislauf und Gefaessen. see MEDICAL SCIENCES

616.1   PL   ISSN 0022-9032
KARDIOLOGIA POLSKA. (Text in Polish; summaries in English) 1958. m. $120. Klinika Kardiologii CMKP, Ul. Grenadierow 51-59, 04-073 Warsaw, Poland. TEL 48-22-10-17-38. Ed. Leszek Ceremuzynski. adv.; bk.rev.; circ. 2,500. Indexed: Biol.Abstr, Chem.Abstr., Excerp.Med., Ind.Med., INIS Atomind.

616.1   RU   ISSN 0022-9040
CODEN: KARDA2
KARDIOLOGIYA/CARDIOLOGY. 1961. m. 37.20 Rub. (Vsesoyuznoe Nauchnoe Kardiologicheskoe Obshchestvo) Izdatel'stvo Meditsina, Petroverigskii pereulok 6-8, 101838 Moscow, Russia. (Dist. by: Mezhdunarodnaya Kniga, Moscow, G-200, Russia) (Co-sponsor: Ministerstvo Zdravookhraneniya S.S.S.R.) Ed. A.S. Smetnev. bk.rev.; bibl.; index. Indexed: Biol.Abstr., Chem.Abstr., Curr.Cont., Dok.Arbeitsmed., Excerp.Med., Ind.Med., Ind.Sci.Rev., INIS Atomind., Int.Aerosp.Abstr., Nutr.Abstr.
—BLDSC shelfmark: 0088.300000.
Description: Deals with the major problems of cardiovascular pathology in the clinical, morphological, biochemical and pathophysiological aspects. Including coronary heart disease, arterial hypertension, atherosclerosis, acquired and congenital disease of the heart, circulatory insufficiency, disorders of the cardiac rhythm.

LIVEWELL. see PHYSICAL FITNESS AND HYGIENE

616.1   BL
MEDISOM: CARDIOLOGY. 1976. bi-m. $90. Grupo Editorial Q B D Ltda, Rua Caravelas 326, Caixa Postal 30329, 01051 Sao Paulo, Brazil. FAX 55-11-572-5957. Ed. Dr. Philip Querido. adv. (audio cassette)

616.1   NE
METABOLIC ASPECTS OF CARDIOVASCULAR DISEASE. 1981. irreg., vol.3, 1984. price varies. Elsevier Science Publishers B.V., Books Division, P.O. Box 211, 1000 AE Amsterdam, Netherlands. TEL 020-5803911. FAX 020-5803705. TELEX 18582 ESPA NL. (Subscr. in U.S. and Canada to: Elsevier Science Publishing Co., Inc., Box 882, Madison Sq. Sta., New York, NY 10159. TEL 212-989-5800)
Refereed Serial

616.1   US   ISSN 0026-2862
RC681.A1   CODEN: MIVRA6
MICROVASCULAR RESEARCH; an international journal. 1968. bi-m. $330 (foreign $395). Academic Press, Inc., Journal Division, 1250 Sixth Ave., San Diego, CA 92101. TEL 619-230-1840. FAX 619-699-6800. TELEX 181726. Ed. David Shepro. adv.; charts; illus.; index. (back issues avail.) Indexed: Biol.Abstr., Chem.Abstr., Curr.Adv.Ecol.Sci., Curr.Cont., Dent.Ind., Excerp.Med., Ind.Med., Ind.Sci.Rev., Ind.Vet., Pig News & Info., Vet.Bull.
—BLDSC shelfmark: 5761.060000.
Description: Disseminates information related to the microvascular field.
Refereed Serial

616.1   IT   ISSN 0391-3627
MINERVA ANGIOLOGICA. q. L.60000($70) (Societa Italiana di Patologia Vascolare). Edizioni Minerva Medica, Corso Bramante 83-85, 10126 Turin, Italy.
—BLDSC shelfmark: 5794.050000.

616.1   IT   ISSN 0026-4725
MINERVA CARDIOANGIOLOGICA. (Text in Italian; summaries in English) 1953. m. L.47000($90) Edizioni Minerva Medica, Corso Bramante 83-85, 10126 Turin, Italy. Ed. F. Spadaccini. abstr.; bibl.; illus.; circ. 4,000. Indexed: Biol.Abstr., Chem.Abstr., Curr.Adv.Ecol.Sci., Curr.Cont., Dent.Ind., Excerp.Med., Ind.Med., Nutr.Abstr.
—BLDSC shelfmark: 5794.060000.

616.1   SZ   ISSN 0077-099X
CODEN: MOATAH
MONOGRAPHS ON ATHEROSCLEROSIS. (Text in English) 1969. irreg. (approx. 1/yr.) price varies. S. Karger AG, Allschwilerstr. 10, P.O. Box, CH-4009 Basel, Switzerland. TEL 061-3061111. FAX 061-3061234. TELEX CH 962652. Ed.Bd. (reprint service avail. from ISI) Indexed: Biol.Abstr., Chem.Abstr., Curr.Cont., Ind.Med.
—BLDSC shelfmark: 5915.250000.

616.1   DK   ISSN 0109-0690
MOTIONSBLADET; magazine for the Runners Club of the Danish Heart Foundation. 1974. bi-m. DKK 100. Hjerteforeningens Motionsklub, Paradisvejen 44, 8600 Silkeborg, Denmark. TEL 06-837114. Ed. Soeren Staehr. adv.; bk.rev.; illus.; circ. 6,000.
Formerly: Hjerteforeningens Motionsblad (ISSN 0109-0704)

616.1   AT
NATIONAL HEART FOUNDATION OF AUSTRALIA. ANNUAL REPORT (YEAR). a. National Heart Foundation of Australia, Royal Insurance Bldg., 25 London Circuit, Canberra, A.C.T. 2601, Australia. TEL 062-822-144. FAX 062-825-147.

616.1   AT   ISSN 0077-4685
NATIONAL HEART FOUNDATION OF AUSTRALIA. RESEARCH IN PROGRESS. 1962. a. free. National Heart Foundation of Australia, Royal Insurance Bldg., 25 London Circuit, Canberra, A.C.T. 2601, Australia. TEL 06-247-7100. Ed. Robert Hodge. circ. 2,000.

NATIONAL HEART NEWS. see MEDICAL SCIENCES

616.1   US
NEWSPAPER OF CARDIOLOGY. 1982. m. $46. McMahon Group, 148 W. 24th St., New York, NY 10011. TEL 212-620-4600. FAX 212-620-5928. Ed. William Dunnett. adv. contact: Ward Byrne. circ. 35,000. (tabloid format)
Formerly: Cardiovascular News.
Description: Features research developments.

616.1   GW   ISSN 0300-5224
CODEN: NIHOD9
NIEREN- UND HOCHDRUCKKRANKHEITEN. 1972. m. DM.210($140) Dustri-Verlag Dr. Karl Feistle, Bahnhofstr. 9, 8024 Deisenhofen, Germany. TEL 089-613861-0. FAX 089-613-5412. Ed. Dr. H. Brass. Indexed: Biol.Abstr., Chem.Abstr, Curr.Adv.Ecol.Sci., Curr.Cont., Excerp.Med.

OBESITY & HEALTH; journal of research, news, issues. see NUTRITION AND DIETETICS

MEDICAL SCIENCES — CARDIOVASCULAR DISEASES

616.1   US   ISSN 0147-8389
RC684.P3
P A C E. (Pacing and Clinical Electrophysiology) 1978. m. $148 (foreign $194). Futura Publishing Company, Inc., 2 Bedford Ridge Rd., Box 330, Mount Kisco, NY 10549. TEL 800-877-8761. FAX 914-666-0993. Ed. Dr. Seymour Furman. adv.; bk.rev.; abstr.; bibl.; charts; illus.; pat.; stat.; index, cum.index; circ. 6,300. **Indexed:** Biol.Abstr., Curr.Cont., Ind.Med.
—BLDSC shelfmark: 6328.210000.

616.1   PK   ISSN 0048-2706
PAKISTAN HEART JOURNAL. (Text in English) 1968. q. Rs.200($25) Pakistan Cardiac Society, c/o National Institute of Cardiovascular Diseases, Jinnah Hospital Rd., Karachi, Pakistan. Ed. Azhar M.A. Faruqui. adv.; bk.rev.; bibl.; charts; illus.; circ. 1,000.
—BLDSC shelfmark: 6340.842000.
Description: Covers cardiac science in Pakistan with original papers and review papers.

616.136   FR
PAROI ANTERIELLE. (Text in English, French) 1973. q. 300 F. Centre de Recherches Cardiologiques, Hopital Boucicaut, 78 rue de la Convention, 75730 Paris Cedex 15, France. Ed. L. Scebat. adv.; circ. 1,000. **Indexed:** Curr.Cont., Ind.Med.

618.92 616.12   US   ISSN 0172-0643
RJ421   CODEN: PECAD4
PEDIATRIC CARDIOLOGY. 1979. 4/yr. $105. Springer-Verlag, Journals, 175 Fifth Ave., New York, NY 10010. TEL 212-460-1500. (Also Berlin, Heidelberg, Tokyo, and Vienna) Ed. I. Carr. circ. 890. (also avail. in microform from UMI; reprint service avail. from ISI) **Indexed:** Curr.Cont., Dent.Ind., Excerp.Med., Ind.Med.
—BLDSC shelfmark: 6417.535000.
Description: Devoted exclusively to the diagnosis and management of heart disease in young people. Presents research reports and the latest clinical information from across the entire field.

616.1   UK   ISSN 0267-6591
                     CODEN: PERFER
PERFUSION. 1986. q. £68.50($100) to individuals; institutions £127.50($185). Edward Arnold (Subsidiary of: Hodder & Stoughton), Mill Rd., Dunton Green, Sevenoaks, Kent TN13 2YA, England. TEL 0732-450111. FAX 0732-461321. (Dist. in U.S. and Canada by: Cambridge University Press, 40 W. 20th St., New York, NY 10011) Ed. Prof. K.M. Taylor. adv.; bk.rev.; index.
—BLDSC shelfmark: 6425.020000.
Description: Dedicated to the advancement of knowledge and clinical practice in the field of extracorporeal circulation.

616.12   CN
PERSPECTIVES IN CARDIOLOGY. 1985. bi-m. S T A Communications Inc., 955 boul. St. Jean, Ste. 306, Pointe-Claire, Que. H9R 5K3, Canada. TEL 514-695-7623. FAX 514-695-8554. Ed. Paul Brand. adv.; circ. 22,000.

616.1   US   ISSN 0361-0527
                     CODEN: PCRED9
PERSPECTIVES IN CARDIOVASCULAR RESEARCH. 1976. irreg., latest vol.10. Raven Press, 1185 Ave. of the Americas, New York, NY 10036. TEL 212-930-9500. FAX 212-869-3495. TELEX 640073. Ed. Arnold M. Katz. **Indexed:** Chem.Abstr.
—BLDSC shelfmark: 6428.138800.
Refereed Serial

616.1   UK   ISSN 0268-3555
                     CODEN: PHLEEF
PHLEBOLOGY. 1986. q. £66 (foreign £72). (Union Internationale de Phlebology) Macmillan Press Ltd., Houndmills, Basingstoke, Hampshire RG21 2XS, England. TEL 0256 29242. FAX 0256-810526. Ed. David Negus. index; circ. 700. (back issues avail.) **Indexed:** Curr.Cont., Excerp.Med., Ind.Med.
—BLDSC shelfmark: 6465.101100.

616.1   US   ISSN 0361-3372
RC681.A1
PRACTICAL CARDIOLOGY. 1975. m. $60. Med Publishing, Inc., Office Center at Princeton Meadows, Bldg. 1000, Plainsboro, NJ 08536. TEL 609-275-1900. FAX 609-275-1909. Ed. Karen Rosenberg. circ. 134,000. **Indexed:** Excerp.Med.
—BLDSC shelfmark: 6593.974200.
Description: Diagnosis and management of cardiovascular and related diseases.

616.1   US   ISSN 0363-5104
RC681.A1   CODEN: PRCRDA
PRIMARY CARDIOLOGY; cardiovascular medicine for the primary care physician. 1975. m. $55. P W Communications, Inc., 400 Plaza Dr., Secaucus, NJ 07094. TEL 201-865-7500. Ed. Frederick Robin. illus. (also avail. in microfilm from UMI; reprint service avail. from UMI) **Indexed:** Excerp.Med.
—BLDSC shelfmark: 6612.907500.
Incorporates (as of 1986): Cardiovascular Medicine; Which was formerly titled: Journal of Cardiovascular Medicine (ISSN 0199-6614); (1976-1980): Cardiovascular Medicine (ISSN 0145-403X)
Refereed Serial

616.1   US
PRINCETON RESEARCH CONFERENCES ON CEREBROVASCULAR DISEASES. 1976. irreg., latest 16th. price varies. Raven Press, 1185 Ave. of the Americas, New York, NY 10036. TEL 212-930-9500. FAX 212-869-3495. TELEX 640073. index. **Indexed:** Chem.Abstr. Key Title: Cerebrovascular Diseases.
Former titles: Princeton Conference on Cerebrovascular Diseases (ISSN 0146-6917); (until 1976): Cerebral Vascular Diseases. Conference (ISSN 0069-2255)

616.1   SZ   ISSN 0254-5195
                     CODEN: MFKLDH
PROGRESS IN APPLIED MICROCIRCULATION. (Text in English and German) 1983. irreg. (1-2/yr.). price varies. S. Karger AG, Allschwilerstr. 10, P.O. Box, CH-4009 Basel, Switzerland. TEL 061-3061111. FAX 061-3061234. TELEX CH 962652. Ed. K. Messmer. **Indexed:** Chem.Abstr.
—BLDSC shelfmark: 6865.910100.

616.1   US   ISSN 0097-109X
RC681.A1   CODEN: PGCDAO
PROGRESS IN CARDIOLOGY; a series. 1972. s-a. $49.50. Lea & Febiger, 200 Chester Field Parkway, Malvern, PA 19355. TEL 800-444-1785. FAX 215-251-2229. Eds. Douglas P. Zipes, Derek J. Rowlands. illus. **Indexed:** Biol.Abstr., Curr.Adv.Ecol.Sci.
—BLDSC shelfmark: 6866.630000.
Refereed Serial

616.1   US   ISSN 0033-0620
                     CODEN: PCVDAN
PROGRESS IN CARDIOVASCULAR DISEASES. Italian translation: Progressi in Patologia Cardiovascolare (IT ISSN 0033-0701) (French and Spanish translations also avail.) 1958. bi-m. $89 to individuals; institutions $141 (foreign $167). W.B. Saunders Co. (Subsidiary of: Harcourt Brace Jovanovich, Inc.), Curtis Center, Independence Square W., Philadelphia, PA 19106. TEL 215-238-7800. (Subscr. to: 6277 Sea Harbor Dr., 4th Fl., Orlando FL 32891) Eds. Dr. Edmond H. Sonnenblick, Dr. Michael Lesch. adv.; bibl.; charts; illus.; index; circ. 5,000. **Indexed:** Biol.Abstr., Chem.Abstr., Curr.Adv.Ecol.Sci., Curr.Cont., Curr.Cont., Excerp.Med., Ind.Med., Ind.Sci.Rev., Nutr.Abstr., Sci.Cit.Ind.
●Also available online. Vendor(s): Mead Data Central.
—BLDSC shelfmark: 6866.650000.
Refereed Serial

616.12 610.73   US   ISSN 0889-7204
PROGRESS IN CARDIOVASCULAR NURSING. 1986. q. $30 to individuals (foreign $35); institutions $50 (foreign $55). Box 3000, Dpt. CN, Denville, NJ 07834. Ed. Julie A Shinn, RN.
—BLDSC shelfmark: 6866.660000.

616.1   US
PROGRESS IN CORONARY SINUS INTERVENTIONS. 1986. irreg. price varies. Springer-Verlag, 175 Fifth Ave., New York, NY 10010. TEL 212-460-1500. (Dist. in Germany by: Dr. Dietrich Steinkopff Verlag, Darmstadt, Germany) (reprint service avail. from ISI)

616.15   US
PROGRESS IN HEMOSTASIS AND THROMBOSIS. 1972. irreg., vol.7, 1985. price varies. W.B. Saunders Co. (Subsidiary of: Harcourt Brace Jovanovich, Inc.), Curtis Center, Independence Square W., Philadelphia, PA 19106. TEL 215-238-7800. Ed. Theodore H. Spaet, M.D. **Indexed:** Biol.Abstr., Chem.Abstr., Ind.Med., Ind.Sci.Rev.
Formerly: Progress in Hemostasis.
Refereed Serial

616.1 618.92   US   ISSN 1058-9813
▼**PROGRESS IN PEDIATRIC CARDIOLOGY.** 1992. q. $85 to individuals (foreign $110); institutions $115 (foreign $130). Andover Medical Publishers Inc., 125 Main St., Reading, MA 01867. TEL 617-944-8242. FAX 617-279-4851. TELEX 880052. (Dist. by: Butterworth - Heinemann Ltd., 80 Montvale Ave., Stoneham, MA 02180. TEL 800-366-2665) Ed. Dr. William W. Miller.
Description: Presents information and opinion important to the understanding and management of cardiovascular disease in children.

616.1   IT   ISSN 0033-0701
PROGRESSI IN PATOLOGIA CARDIOVASCOLARE. Italian translation of: Progress in Cardiovascular Disease (US ISSN 0033-0620) 1957. bi-m. L.80000 to individuals; institutions L.120000($170). Pensiero Scientifico Editore s.r.l., Via Panama 48, Rome, Italy. TEL 06 855-36-33. Ed. Piero Lega. adv.; bk.rev.; bibl.; charts; cum.index; circ. 3,000.

616.1   US
PULMONARY AND CRITICAL CARE MEDICINE. biennial. $55 (foreign $65). Hanley & Belfus, Inc., 210 S. 13th St., Philadelphia, PA 19107. TEL 215-546-7293. FAX 215-790-9330. Ed.Bd.
Refereed Serial

616.1   AG   ISSN 0034-6993
REVISTA ARGENTINA DE ANGIOLOGIA.* (Text in Spanish; summaries in English) 1967. q. Arg.$20($8) (Argentine Society of Angiology) Plantie Talleres Graficos S.A., Juan B. Alberdi 571, Buenos Aires, Argentina. Ed. Dr. Miguel Angel Lucas. adv.; bk.rev.; abstr.; bibl.; charts; illus.; circ. 1,500. (also avail. in microform from UMI; reprint service avail. from UMI) **Indexed:** Biol.Abstr.

616.12   CU
REVISTA CUBANA CARDIOLOGIA Y CIRUGIA CARDIOVASCULAR. 3/yr. Ministerio de Salud Publica, Centro Nacional de Informacion de Ciencias Medicas, Calle E, No. 452 e-19 y 21, Plaza de la Revolucion, Apdo. 6520, Havana, Cuba.
Formerly, until 1987: Boletin de Cardiologia y Cirugia Cardiovascular.

REVISTA DE NUTRICION Y ATEROSCLEROSIS. see *NUTRITION AND DIETETICS*

616.1   SP   ISSN 0300-8932
                     CODEN: RCDOAM
REVISTA ESPANOLA DE CARDIOLOGIA. (Summaries in English, Spanish) 1958. m. (10/yr.). 5500 ptas.($57) to non-members. (Sociedad Espanola de Cardiologia) Ediciones Doyma S.A., Travesera de Gracia, 17-21, 08021 Barcelona, Spain. TEL 200-07-11. FAX 209-11-36. TELEX 51964 INK E. Ed. Emilio Marin Huerta. adv.; page145000 ptas.; trim 210 x 180; adv. contact: Marta Cisa. bk.rev.; index; circ. 4,200. **Indexed:** Chem.Abstr., Excerp.Med, Ind.Med.Esp., Ind.Med.
—BLDSC shelfmark: 7853.930000.
Description: Covers cardiac physiopathology and the diagnostic and therapeutic resources applicable to heart disease.

616.1   SP   ISSN 0214-3941
REVISTA IBEROAMERICANA DE TROMBOSIS Y HEMOSTASIA. (Supplement avail. (ISSN 0214-395X)) 1988. q. 5200 ptas.($63) Editorial Garsi S.A., Londres, 17, 28028 Madrid, Spain. TEL 256-08-00. FAX 361-10-07. Ed. Justo Aznar. circ. 1,000.

REVUE DE PNEUMOLOGIE CLINIQUE; le poumon et le coeur. see *MEDICAL SCIENCES — Respiratory Diseases*

616.12   FR   ISSN 1146-6537
REVUE DU CARDIOLOGUE PRATICIEN. 1989. 8/yr. 100 ECU($120) (typically set in Jan.). Masson, 5 et 7, rue Laromiguiere, 75005 Paris, France. TEL 1-46-34-21-60. FAX 1-45-87-29-99. TELEX 202 671 F. Ed. Francois Jan. adv.; circ. 6,000.

SCRIPTA SCIENTIFICA MEDICA. see *MEDICAL SCIENCES — Cancer*

SEMINARS IN HEMATOLOGY. see *MEDICAL SCIENCES — Hematology*

SEMINARS IN THORACIC AND CARDIOVASCULAR SURGERY. see *MEDICAL SCIENCES — Surgery*

MEDICAL SCIENCES — CARDIOVASCULAR DISEASES

SEMINARS IN VASCULAR SURGERY. see *MEDICAL SCIENCES — Surgery*

SIGNAL'NAYA INFORMATSIYA. ISHEMICHESKAYA BOLEZN' SERDTSA. see *MEDICAL SCIENCES — Abstracting, Bibliographies, Statistics*

SMOOTH MUSCLE. see *BIOLOGY — Physiology*

616.1   FR   ISSN 0395-403X
SOCIETE FRANCAISE DE CARDIOLOGIE. BULLETIN D'INFORMATIONS. 1976. q. membership. Grou-Radenez-Joly, 19 rue des Saints Peres, 75006 Paris, France. Ed. Dr. A. Barrillon. adv.; circ. 1,800. **Indexed:** I.P.A.
●Also available online.

616.1   FR
SOCIETE FRANCAISE DE PHLEBOLOGIE. BULLETIN. 1948. 4/yr. 420 F. to individuals (foreign 565 F.); students 210 F. (foreign 300 F.). (Societe Francaise de Phlebologie) Expansion Scientifique, 15 rue Saint-Benoit, 75278 Paris Cedex 06, France. (Co-sponsor: Union Internationale de Phlebologie) Ed. J.P. Caille. adv.; bk.rev.; bibl.; charts; illus.; index, cum.index; circ. 2,700. (also avail. in microform) **Indexed:** Bibl.Cart., Biol.Abstr., Curr.Cont., Excerp.Med., Ind.Med.
Formerly: Phlebologie (ISSN 0031-8280)

616.1   US   ISSN 0888-0697
RC666   CODEN: SRAREY
SOVIET MEDICAL REVIEWS. SECTION A: CARDIOLOGY REVIEWS. a. $118. Harwood Academic Publishers, 270 Eighth Ave., New York, NY 10011. TEL 212-206-8900. FAX 212-645-2459. TELEX 236735 GOPUB UR. (Subscr. to: Box 786, Cooper Sta., New York, NY 10276. TEL 800-545-8398; UK subscr. to: P.O. Box 90, Reading, Berkshire RG1 8JL, England. TEL 0734-560-080) Eds. E.I. Chazov, V.N. Smirnov. (also avail. in microform)
Refereed Serial

616.1   US   ISSN 0888-0727
SOVIET MEDICAL REVIEWS SUPPLEMENT SERIES. SECTION A: CARDIOLOGY. irreg. Harwood Academic Publishers, 270 Eighth Ave., New York, NY 10011. TEL 212-206-8900. FAX 212-645-2459. TELEX 236735 GOPUB UR. (Subscr. to: Box 786, Cooper Sta., New York, NY 10276. TEL 800-545-8398; UK subscr. to: Box 90, Reading, Berkshire RG1 8JL, England. TEL 0734-560-080) Eds. E.L. Chazov, V.N. Smirnov. (also avail. in microform)

616.1   US   ISSN 0039-2499
RC388.5   CODEN: SJCCA7
STROKE; a journal of cerebral circulation. 1970. m. $102 to individuals (foreign $136); institutions $117 (foreign $151). American Heart Association, 7272 Greenville Ave., Dallas, TX 75231-4596. TEL 214-706-1310. FAX 214-691-6342. (Subscr. to: Box 843543, Dallas, TX 75284-3543) Ed. Dr. Mark Dyken. adv.; abstr.; charts; illus.; index; circ. 6,200. (also avail. in microform from UMI,MIM; back issues avail.; reprint service avail. from UMI) **Indexed:** ASCA, Biol.Abstr., Biotech.Abstr., Chem.Abstr., Curr.Adv.Ecol.Sci., Curr.Cont., Dent.Ind., Excerp.Med., Ind.Med., Nutr.Abstr., Rehabil.Lit.
●Also available online. Vendor(s): BRS.
—BLDSC shelfmark: 8474.900000.
Description: For neurologists and internists. Includes articles on prevention, diagnosis, treatment and rehabilitation of stroke victims.
Refereed Serial

616.1   FI   ISSN 0039-7571
SYDAN. (Text in Finnish, Swedish) 1958. 7/yr. FIM 70. Suomen Sydantautiliitto - Finnish Heart Association, Oltermanninttie 8, 00620 Helsinki, Finland. FAX 175085. Ed. Marjatta Karvinen. adv.; bk.rev.; circ. 115,000.

TASK FORCE ON ENVIRONMENTAL CANCER AND HEART AND LUNG DISEASE. ANNUAL REPORT TO CONGRESS. see *ENVIRONMENTAL STUDIES — Toxicology And Environmental Safety*

616.12   US   ISSN 8756-8586
TECHNOLOGY FOR CARDIOLOGY. m. $90 (Canada $100; elsewhere $120). (Emergency Care Research Institute) E C R I, 5200 Butler Pike, Plymouth Meeting, PA 19462. TEL 215-825-6000. FAX 215-834-1275. Ed. Robert Hochschild.
Formerly: Health Devices Update: Cardiology.
Refereed Serial

616.1   US   ISSN 0730-2347
   CODEN: THIJDO
TEXAS HEART INSTITUTE JOURNAL. 1974. q. $25 (foreign $35). Texas Heart Institute, Publications & Communications, Box 20345, Houston, TX 77225-0345. TEL 713-522-7060. FAX 713-630-0999. Ed. Dr. Robert J. Hall. adv.; bk.rev.; illus.; stat.; circ. 25,000. (also avail. in microform from UMI; back issues avail.) **Indexed:** ASCA, Biol.Abstr., Curr.Cont., Excerp.Med., Helminthol.Abstr.
—BLDSC shelfmark: 8798.865000.
Formerly: Cardiovascular Diseases (ISSN 0093-3546)

616.1   GW   ISSN 0340-6245
   CODEN: THHADQ
THROMBOSIS AND HAEMOSTASIS. 1957. 12/yr. DM.429.60($302.40) (International Society on Thrombosis and Haemostasis) F.K. Schattauer Verlagsgesellschaft mbH, Lenzhalde 3, Postfach 104545, 7000 Stuttgart 10, Germany. TEL 0711-22987-0. FAX 0711-22987-50. circ. 2,100. (also avail. in microform from SWZ; reprint service avail. from SWZ) **Indexed:** ASCA, Biol.Abstr., Biotech.Abstr., Chem.Abstr., Curr.Adv.Cancer Res., Curr.Adv.Ecol.Sci., Curr.Cont., Dairy Sci.Abstr., Dent.Ind., Helminthol.Abstr., Ind.Med., Ind.Vet., Nutr.Abstr., Vet.Bull.
—BLDSC shelfmark: 8820.344000.
Formerly: Thrombosis et Diathesis Haemorrhagica (ISSN 0040-6597)

616.1   US   ISSN 0049-3848
   CODEN: THBRAA
THROMBOSIS RESEARCH; an international journal on vascular obstruction, hemorrhage and hemostasis. (Text in English, French, German and Russian; summaries in English) 1972. 24/yr. (in 4 vols.). £725 (effective 1992). Pergamon Press, Inc., Journals Division, 660 White Plains Rd., Tarrytown, NY 10591-5153. TEL 914-524-9200. FAX 914-333-2444. (And: Headington Hill Hall, Oxford OX3 0BW, England. TEL 0865-794141) Eds. Birger Blombak, Calvin M. Redman. adv.; bk.rev.; charts; illus.; index; circ. 700. (also avail. in microform from MIM,UMI) **Indexed:** ASCA, Biol.Abstr., Biotech.Abstr., Chem.Abstr., Curr.Adv.Biochem., Curr.Adv.Cell & Devel.Biol., Curr.Adv.Ecol.Sci., Curr.Cont., Dairy Sci.Abstr., Dent.Ind., Excerp.Med., Ind.Med., Nutr.Abstr., Risk Abstr.
—BLDSC shelfmark: 8820.365000.
Description: Forum for the rapid dissemination of original research on thrombosis, hemostasis and fibrinolysis.
Refereed Serial

616.135   AU   ISSN 0934-9669
▼**THROMBOTIC AND HAEMORRHAGIC DISORDERS.** 1990. 4/yr. Springer-Verlag, Moelkerbastei 5, Postfach 367, A-1011 Vienna, Austria. TEL 1-5339614. (Also Berlin, Heidelberg, Tokyo and New York) Eds. E. Deutsch, M.R. Buchanan-Wien.
—BLDSC shelfmark: 8820.366050.
Description: Features experimental and clinical works. Information on advances provided through original research papers, short communications, and reviews.

615.65   US   ISSN 0041-1132
RC633.A1   CODEN: TRANAT
TRANSFUSION. 1961. 9/yr. $105 to individuals (foreign $125); institutions $145 (foreign $165). American Association of Blood Banks, 1117 N. 19th St., Ste. 600, Arlington, VA 22209. TEL 703-528-8200. FAX 703-527-8036. Ed. Jeffrey McCullough, M.D. adv.; illus.; index; circ. 12,700. (also avail. in microform from UMI) **Indexed:** Biol.Abstr., Chem.Abstr., Curr.Adv.Cell & Devel.Biol., Curr.Adv.Ecol.Sci., Curr.Cont., Dent.Ind., Excerp.Med., Helminthol.Abstr., Hosp.Lit.Ind., Ind.Med., Protozool.Abstr., Sci.Cit.Ind., SSCI.
—BLDSC shelfmark: 9020.704000.
Supersedes (1947-1960): American Association of Blood Banks. Bulletin (ISSN 0360-9197)

616.1   US   ISSN 1050-1738
   CODEN: TCMDEQ
▼**TRENDS IN CARDIOVASCULAR MEDICINE.** 1991. 6/yr. $135 (foreign $158)(effective 1992). Elsevier Science Publishing Co., Inc. (New York), 655 Ave. of Americas, New York, NY 10010. TEL 212-989-5800. FAX 212-633-3965. TELEX 420643 AEP UI. Ed.Bd. **Indexed:** Excerp.Med. (1992-).
—BLDSC shelfmark: 9049.549000.
Description: Designed to help clinical cardiologists and basic researchers keep up with advances in cardiovascular research.
Refereed Serial

616.13   IT
TROMBOSI E ATEROSCLEROSI. bi-m. L.60000($100) Piccin Editore, Via Altinate 107, 35121 Padua, Italy. TEL 049-655566. TELEX 432074 PICCIN I.

616.1   SZ   ISSN 0301-1526
   CODEN: VASAAH
VASA; Zeitschrift fuer Gefaesskrankheiten - journal of vascular diseases. (Text in English or German) 1972. q. 116 Fr. Verlag Hans Huber, Laenggassstr. 76, Postfach, CH-3000 Berne 9, Switzerland. TEL 031-24-25-33. FAX 031-24-33-80. TELEX 911886-HAHU. Ed. Dr. H.J. Leu. adv.; bk.rev.; abstr.; charts; illus.; index; circ. 1,300. **Indexed:** Biol.Abstr., Curr.Cont., Excerp.Med., Ind.Med.
—BLDSC shelfmark: 9148.300000.
Formerly: Zentralblatt fuer Phlebologie (ISSN 0044-426X)

616.1   UK   ISSN 0954-2582
   CODEN: VMEREI
▼**VASCULAR MEDICINE REVIEW.** 1990. biennial. £44.50($69) to individuals; institutions £64($99). Edward Arnold, Division of Hodder and Stoughton, Mill Rd., Dunton Green, Sevenoaks, Kent TN13 2YA, England. TEL 0732-450111. FAX 0732-461321. **Indexed:** Excerp.Med. (1992-).
—BLDSC shelfmark: 9148.852000.

VASCULAR SURGERY. see *MEDICAL SCIENCES — Surgery*

616.1   US   ISSN 1052-2174
VIDEO JOURNAL OF ECHOCARDIOGRAPHY. (Includes 4 video cassettes.) 1987. q. $225 (effective 1991). Dynamedia, Inc., 2 Fulham Court, Silver Spring, MD 20902-3016. TEL 301-649-6886. FAX 301-649-3447. Ed. S.B. Ritter. adv.; circ. 1,000. (back issues avail.)
—BLDSC shelfmark: 9234.208620.
Description: Covers ultrasound imaging. Consists of tutorials, reviews, case reports and original research.
Refereed Serial

VOX SANGUINIS; international journal of transfusion medicine. see *MEDICAL SCIENCES — Allergology And Immunology*

616.12   CC
XINXUEGUANBINGXUE JINZHAN/ADVANCES IN CARDIOVASCULAR DISEASE. (Text in Chinese) 1980. q. Chengdu Yixue Qingbao Yanjiusuo - Chengdu Medical Science Information Research Institute, 54 Tidu Jie, Chengdu, Sichuan 610016, People's Republic of China. TEL 673735. (Co-sponsor: Chengdu Xinxueguanbing Yanjiushi - Chengdu Cardiovascular Disease Research Office) Ed. Du Chuan-li. circ. 10,000.

616.1005   US   ISSN 0145-4145
RC681.A1
YEAR BOOK OF CARDIOLOGY. 1968. a. $54.95. Mosby - Year Book, Inc., Continuity Division, 200 N. LaSalle, Chicago, IL 60601. TEL 312-726-9733. FAX 312-726-6075. TELEX 206155. Ed. Robert C. Schlant, M.D. illus. (reprint service avail.)
●Also available online. Vendor(s): BRS.
Also available on CD-ROM. Producer(s): SilverPlatter (ClinMED-CD).
—BLDSC shelfmark: 9411.617000.
Former titles: Yearbook of Cardiovascular Medicine (ISSN 0360-6031); Yearbook of Cardiovascular Medicine and Surgery (ISSN 0084-3687); Supersedes in part title issued 1962-67 as: Yearbook of Cardiovascular and Renal Disease.

YEAR BOOK OF VASCULAR SURGERY. see *MEDICAL SCIENCES*

MEDICAL SCIENCES — CHIROPRACTIC, HOMEOPATHY, OSTEOPATHY

ZEITSCHRIFT FUER HERZ, THORAX- UND GEFAESSCHIRURGIE. see *MEDICAL SCIENCES — Surgery*

616.1 GW ISSN 0300-5860
CODEN: ZKRDAX
ZEITSCHRIFT FUER KARDIOLOGIE. (Text in German; summaries in English) 1909. m. DM.460. (Deutsche Gesellschaft fuer Herz- und Kreislaufforschung) Dr. Dietrich Steinkopff Verlag, Saalbaustr. 12, Postfach 111442, 6100 Darmstadt 11, Germany. TEL 06151-26538. FAX 06151-20849. Ed.Bd. adv.; bk.rev.; bibl.; charts; illus.; index; circ. 3,000. (back issues avail.) Indexed: Biol.Abstr., Biotech.Abstr., Chem.Abstr., Curr. Cont., Curr.Adv.Ecol.Sci., Excerp.Med., Ind.Med., Nutr.Abstr.
—BLDSC shelfmark: 9467.430000.
Formerly: Zeitschrift fuer Kreislaufforschung (ISSN 0044-295X)

616.12 CC
ZHONGHUA XIN-XUEGUANBING ZAZHI/CHINESE JOURNAL OF CARDIOLOGY. q. $3.50 per no. Guoji Shudian, Qikan Bu, Chegongzhuang Xilu 21, P.O. Box 399, Beijing 100044, People's Republic of China. Indexed: Biol.Abstr., Chem.Abstr., Excerp.Med., Ind.Med.

MEDICAL SCIENCES — Chiropractic, Homeopathy, Osteopathy

A A C O M ORGANIZATIONAL GUIDE. (American Association of Colleges of Osteopathic Medicine) see *EDUCATION — School Organization And Administration*

615.633 US
A A O A ACCENTS. 1941. q. (Auxiliary to the American Osteopathic Association) McVey Marketing & Advertising, Box 569, Flint, MI 48501-0569. TEL 313-735-7892. FAX 313-735-4226. (Subscr. to: 142 E. Ontario St., Chicago, IL 60611) Ed. Mary M. Balog. circ. 1,900.
Description: For spouses of osteopathic physicians. Covers issues pertinent to the osteopathic profession.

615.53 US
▼A A O NEWSLETTER. 1991. q. $25. American Academy of Osteopathy, 1127 Mt. Vernon Rd., Box 750, Newark, OH 43058-0750. TEL 614-366-7911. Ed. Raymond J. Hruby. adv. (back issues avail.)
Description: Includes clinically related articles that illustrate the art and science of osteopathic practice.

A F H H A INSIDER. (American Federation of Home Health Agencies) see *MEDICAL SCIENCES — Nurses And Nursing*

615.533 US
A O A YEARBOOK AND DIRECTORY OF OSTEOPATHIC PHYSICIANS. 1908. a. $50. American Osteopathic Association, 142 E. Ontario St., Chicago, IL 60611. TEL 312-280-5800. Ed. Thomas Wesley Allen. adv.; stat.; index; circ. 35,000. Indexed: SRI.
Formerly: Yearbook and Directory of Osteopathic Physicians (ISSN 0084-358X)

ACTA BIOLOGICA; Zeitschrift fuer angewandte Homoeo-Phytotherapie, Ganzheitsbehandlungen und Sondermethoden der Medizin. see *MEDICAL SCIENCES*

615.532 GW ISSN 0175-7881
ALLGEMEINE HOMOEOPATHISCHE ZEITUNG. 1832. 6/yr. DM.105 (students DM.57). (Deutscher Zentralverein Homoeopathischer Aerzte e.V.) Karl F. Haug Verlag GmbH, Fritz-Frey-Str. 21, 6900 Heidelberg 1, Germany. TEL 06221-4062-0. FAX 06221-400727. TELEX 461683-HVVFMD. Ed. Karl-Heinz Gebhardt. Indexed: Excerp.Med.

615.533 US ISSN 0732-703X
AMERICAN ACADEMY OF OSTEOPATHY YEARBOOK. Variant title: Yearbook of Selected Osteopathic Papers. 1943. a. $15. American Academy of Osteopathy, 1127 Mt. Vernon Rd., Box 750, Newark, OH 43058-0750. TEL 614-366-7911. illus.; cum.index 1972, 1977; circ. 1,100 (controlled).

615.53 612.3 US ISSN 0194-6536
AMERICAN CHIROPRACTOR. 1979. m. $56. (American Chiropractor Magazine) Busch Publishing, 5005 Rivera Ct., Ft. Wayne, IN 46825. TEL 219-484-9600. Ed. Jennifer H. Maxfield. adv.; bk.rev.; circ. 35,000. (also avail. in microform from UMI)
—BLDSC shelfmark: 0812.425000.

615.53 US ISSN 0002-8967
RX1
AMERICAN INSTITUTE OF HOMEOPATHY. JOURNAL. 1907. q. $35 (foreign $45). American Institute of Homeopathy, 1585 Glencoe, Denver, CO 80220. TEL 303-898-5477. Ed. Dr. George Guess. adv.; bk.rev.; index; circ. 550.
—BLDSC shelfmark: 4686.730000.
Description: Presents articles of historical interest, current research, and case studies. Includes listing of foreign and U.S. homeopathic organizations and upcoming homeopathic conferences and meetings.

AMERICAN JOURNAL OF NONINVASIVE CARDIOLOGY. see *MEDICAL SCIENCES — Cardiovascular Diseases*

ANNALES DE KINESITHERAPIE. see *MEDICAL SCIENCES*

615.53 619 II
AYURVEDA SAUKHYAM SERIES. (Text in English, Sanskrit) 1980. irreg. price varies. Concept Publishing Company, A 15-16, Commercial Block, Mohan Garden, New Delhi 110 059, India. TEL 5554-042. index.
Description: Includes fundamental principles of Ayurveda, anatomy, physiology, hygiene, various aspects of public health, and the treatment of diseases.

615.53 US
BEACON (IOWA). 1967. m. $20. Palmer Chiropractic College, 1000 Brady St., P C C Box 66, Davenport, IA 52803. Ed. Nils Heubach. circ. 3,000.

615.53 GW ISSN 0340-8671
BIOLOGISCHE MEDIZIN. 1962. bi-m. DM.20. Aurelia Verlag GmbH, Ruhrstr. 14, 7570 Baden-Baden, Germany. TEL 07221-50102. circ. 140,000.
—BLDSC shelfmark: 2083.700000.

615.532 UK ISSN 0007-0785
BRITISH HOMOEOPATHIC JOURNAL. 1911. q. £32($60) Royal London Homoeopathic Hospital, Faculty of Homoeopathy, Great Ormond St., London WC1N 3HR, England. TEL 071-833-1197. FAX 071-278-7900. (Subscr. to: Headley Brothers Ltd. Invicta Press, Queens Rd., Ashford, Kent TN24 8HH, England) Ed. P. Fisher. adv.; bk.rev.; index; circ. 1,400. (also avail. in microform from UMI; reprint service avail. from UMI) Indexed: Excerp.Med.
—BLDSC shelfmark: 2301.340000.
Description: Covers all works of homoeopathy with emphasis on scientific research, clinical homoeopathy, provings and historical articles.

615.53 UK ISSN 0959-6879
▼BRITISH JOURNAL OF PHYTOTHERAPY. 1990. q. £17. School of Phytotherapy, Bucksteep Manor, Bodle Street Green, Near Hailsham, E. Sussex BN27 4RJ, England. Ed. Hein Zeylstra.
—BLDSC shelfmark: 2319.300000.

CAHIERS DE KINESITHERAPIE; revue d'enseignement post-scolaire et de documentation technique. see *MEDICAL SCIENCES — Sports Medicine*

615.53 US ISSN 0899-0204
CALIFORNIA CHIROPRACTIC ASSOCIATION JOURNAL. m. $50. California Chiropractic Association, 7801 Folsom Blvd., Ste. 375, Sacramento, CA 95826. TEL 916-387-0177. FAX 916-325-4855. Ed. Don C. Meadows. adv.
Description: Promotes chiropractic and general health progress.
Refereed Serial

615.534 CN ISSN 0008-3194
CANADIAN CHIROPRACTIC ASSOCIATION. JOURNAL. Abbreviated title: J C C A (Journal of the Canadian Chiropractic Association). 1957. q. Can.$58 (foreign Can.$75). Canadian Chiropractic Association, 1396 Eglinton Ave. W., Toronto, Ont. M6C 2E4, Canada. TEL 416-781-5656. FAX 416-781-7344. Ed. Allan Gotlib. adv.; bk.rev.; charts; illus.; stat.; circ. 4,000. (reprint service avail. from UMI)
—BLDSC shelfmark: 4723.003000.

615.53 US ISSN 0897-6058
CHIROPRACTIC; the journal of chiropractic research, study and clinical investigation. 1988. q. $60. Busch Publishing, 5005 Riviera Court, Fort Wayne, IN 46825. TEL 219-484-9600. Ed. Dr. Paul A. Jaskoviak. adv.; bk.rev.; abstr.; index; circ. 4,000. (also avail. in microfiche; back issues avail.)
—BLDSC shelfmark: 3181.143000.
Description: Dedicated to the advancement of chiropractic health care principles and practice. Seeks to fulfill this purpose by the critical review and publication of original research and scholarly work relating to its scientific bases and clinical applications.

615.53 920 900 US ISSN 0736-4377
RZ221
CHIROPRACTIC HISTORY. 1981. s-a. $35. Association for the History of Chiropractic, 207 Grandview Dr., S., Pittsburgh, PA 15215. FAX 412-237-4512. Ed. Russell W. Gibbons. adv.; bk.rev.; circ. 680.
●Also available online. Vendor(s): National Library of Medicine.

615.53 US
CHIROPRACTIC JOURNAL. 1986. m. Chiropractic Journal, 2950 N. Dobson Rd., No.1, Chandler, AZ 85224. TEL 800-458-0178. FAX 602-732-9313. adv.; circ. 56,000.
Description: Includes information on practice enhancement, legislative developments, insurance regulations, medicine and other topics of professional interest.

615.534 AT ISSN 1036-0913
CHIROPRACTIC JOURNAL OF AUSTRALIA. 1966. q. Aus.$55 (foreign Aus.$70). Chiropractors' Association of Australia, P.O. Box 748, Wagga Wagga, N.S.W. 2650, Australia. TEL 61-69-21-3238. FAX 61-69-21-8869. Eds. Rolf E. Peters, Mary Ann Chance. adv.; bk.rev.; circ. 1,700. (also avail. in microform from UMI; back issues avail.) Indexed: Aus.P.A.I.S.
—BLDSC shelfmark: 3181.144050.
Formerly (until 1991): Australian Chiropractors Association. Journal (ISSN 0045-0359)
Description: Contains original investigations, case studies, literature reviews, clinical procedures, chiropractic history and commentary; seeks to cultivate professional dialogue and awareness in areas relevant to the practice of chiropractic in Australia.
Refereed Serial

615.53 US ISSN 1041-2360
CHIROPRACTIC PRODUCTS. 1985. 8/yr. $16 (free to qualified personnel). Novicom, Inc., 3510 Torrance Blvd., No.315, Torrance, CA 90503. TEL 310-316-8112. FAX 310-316-8422. Ed. Julie Craig. adv.; bk.rev.; charts; illus.; circ. 35,059 (controlled).
Description: Covers news of product releases, topics of interest to professionals in the field, and special features.

615.53 617.1 US ISSN 0889-6976
CODEN: CHSMEX
CHIROPRACTIC SPORTS MEDICINE. 1987. q. $50 to individuals; institutions $77. Williams & Wilkins, 428 E. Preston St., Baltimore, MD 21202. TEL 301-528-4000. FAX 301-528-4312. Ed. Robert H. Hazel, Jr., D.C. circ. 3,100. (also avail. in microform) Indexed: Excerp.Med.
—BLDSC shelfmark: 3181.144200.
Description: Covers chiropractic advances in sports injury treatment, athletic training and injury prevention.
Refereed Serial

615.543 US ISSN 0899-3467
CHIROPRACTIC TECHNIQUE. 1989. q. $48 to individuals; institutions $70. (National College of Chiropractic) Williams & Wilkins, 428 E. Preston St., Baltimore, MD 21202. TEL 301-528-4000. FAX 301-528-4312. Ed. Thomas F. Bergman. circ. 2,050.
—BLDSC shelfmark: 4958.195000.
Description: Focuses on traditional, time-tested procedures, as well as innovative concepts in manipulative and physiological therapeutics.
Refereed Serial

M

MEDICAL SCIENCES — CHIROPRACTIC, HOMEOPATHY, OSTEOPATHY

615.53   AT   ISSN 1037-8839
CHIROPRACTORS' ASSOCIATION OF AUSTRALIA. MEMBERSHIP DIRECTORY. 1938. a. Aus.$20. Chiropractors' Association of Australia, Editorial Office, P.O. Box 241, Springwood, N.S.W 2777, Australia. TEL 047-515644. FAX 047-515856. Ed. T. Sweaney. circ. 1,500.
   Formerly (until 1992): Australian Chiropractor's Association. Membership Directory (ISSN 0728-7291)
   Description: Listing of Australian and New Zealand practitioners.

615.53 200   US
CHRISTIAN CHIROPRACTOR. 1953. bi-m. membership. Christian Chiropractors Association, 3200 S. Lemay Ave., Fort Collins, CO 80525-3605. TEL 800-999-1970. FAX 303-482-1404. circ. 1,600.

615.53 200   US
CHRISTIAN CHIROPRACTORS ASSOCIATION JOURNAL. 1953. bi-m. membership. Christian Chiropractors Association, 3200 S. Lemay Ave., Fort Collins, CO 80525-3605. TEL 800-999-1970. FAX 303-482-1404. circ. 1,200.
   Formerly: Christian Chiropractors Association Bulletin.

615.532   GW   ISSN 0934-1854
CLASSICAL HOMEOPATHY QUARTERLY. (Text in English) 1988. q. DM.78($48) Karl F. Haug Verlag, Fritz-Frey-Str. 21, 6900 Heidelberg, Germany. TEL 06221-40620. FAX 06221-400727. TELEX 461683-HVVFM-D. adv.; bk.rev.; circ. 5,000. (back issues avail.)
   —BLDSC shelfmark: 3274.546000.

615.533   UK   ISSN 0268-0033   CODEN: CLBIEW
CLINICAL BIOMECHANICS. 1968. q. £88 in UK and Europe; elsewhere £96. (Osteopathic Association of Great Britain) Butterworth - Heinemann Ltd. (Subsidiary of: Reed International PLC), Linacre House, Jordan Hill, Oxford OX2 8DP, England. TEL 0865-310366. FAX 0865-310898. TELEX 83111 BHPOXF G. (Subscr. to: Turpin Transactions Ltd., Distribution Centre, Blackhorse Rd., Letchworth, Herts SG6 1HN, England. TEL 0462-672555) Ed. A. Kim Burton. adv.; bk.rev.; abstr.; illus.; index; circ. 750. (also avail. in microform from UMI; back issues avail.) Indexed: Curr.Adv.Ecol.Sci., Curr.Cont., Excerp.Med.
   —BLDSC shelfmark: 3286.262800.
   Formerly (until 1986): British Osteopathic Journal.
   Description: Multidisciplinary journal of original research papers, reviews and abstracts on clinical aspects of biomechanics related to dysfunction of the musculo-skeletal system.
   Refereed Serial

615.53   US
▼**CLINICAL CHIROPRACTIC REPORT**. 1991. q. $54.50 to individuals and institutions (foreign $62); students $27.25 (foreign $34.75). Mosby - Year Book, Inc. (Subsidiary of: Times Mirror Company), 11830 Westline Industrial Dr., St. Louis, MO 63146. TEL 800-325-4177. FAX 314-432-1380. Ed. Reed B. Phillips. (also avail. in microfilm from UMI; reprint service avail. from UMI)
   Description: Concentrates on a single clinical topic in each issue.

COLLEGE INFORMATION BOOKLET. see *EDUCATION — Higher Education*

615.53 616.15   UK   ISSN 0268-4055
COMPLEMENTARY MEDICAL RESEARCH. 1986. 3/yr. £35 (foreign £45). British Library, Document Supply Centre, Boston Spa, Wetherby, W. Yorkshire LS23 7BQ, England. TEL 0937-546077. FAX 0937-546333. TELEX 557381. Ed. Jill Turner. Indexed: Excerp.Med.
   —BLDSC shelfmark: 3364.203680.
   Description: Covers alternative medicine and therapies, homeopathy, chiropractic, acupuncture, herbalism, naturopathy and osteopathy.

615.533   US
CRANIAL LETTER. 1946. q. membership only. Cranial Academy, 1140 W. 8th St., Meridian, ID 83642. circ. 800.
   Formerly: Cranial Academy Newsletter (ISSN 0011-0825)

615.53 617.3   US   ISSN 1041-469X
D.C. TRACTS. 1989. bi-m. $225 to individuals; residents $95; institutions $325 (effective 1992; typically set in Dec.). Data Trace Chiropractic Publishers, Inc., 606 Baltimore Ave., Ste. 322, Baltimore, MD 21204. TEL 301-494-4994. FAX 301-494-0515. Ed. Bruce Gundersen.
   Description: Provides condensations of current chiropractic literature accompanied by in-depth commentaries written by experts on the editorial board. Each issue also includes either an audio tape or a video tape lecture.

615.533 340   US   ISSN 0011-5088
D.O. (Doctor of Osteopath); a publication for osteopathic physicians and surgeons. 1960. m. $20. American Osteopathic Association, 142 E. Ontario St., Chicago, IL 60611. TEL 312-280-5800. Ed. Thomas Wesley Allen. adv.; bk.rev.; stat.; circ. 38,000. Indexed: Chem.Abstr.
   —BLDSC shelfmark: 3605.780000.
   Supersedes: Forum of Osteopathy.
   Description: For practicing physicians. Contains articles on legislative developments and news of the profession and its members.

DEBTS AND CAREER PLANS OF OSTEOPATHIC MEDICAL STUDENTS. see *EDUCATION — Higher Education*

615.53   US   ISSN 0415-8407
DIGEST OF CHIROPRACTIC ECONOMICS. 1958. bi-m. $24. Chiropractic News Publishing Corp., 29229 W. 6 Mile Rd., Livonia, MI 48152. TEL 313-427-5720. FAX 313-427-2760. Ed. Keith Tosolt. adv.; bk.rev.; circ. 22,000. (back issues avail.)
   —BLDSC shelfmark: 3586.879500.
   Description: Business and practice management for the doctor of chiropractic.

615.53 617.7
DINSHAH HEALTH SOCIETY NEWSLETTER. 1980. s-a. membership. Dinshah Health Society, 100 Dinshah Dr., Malaga, NJ 08328. TEL 609-692-4686. Ed. Darius Dinshah. circ. 1,000. (back issues avail.)
   Description: Covers general health topics, including unorthodox methods of healing (primarily chromopathy).

615.53   US
DOCTOR'S PEOPLE. 1976. 12/yr. $24. Box 982, Evanston, IL 60204. FAX 708-328-1550. Ed. Vera Chatz.
   Formerly: People's Doctor.

615.53   US
DYNAMIC CHIROPRACTIC. 1983. fortn. free to qualified personnel. Non-Profit Motion Palpation Institute, 21541 Surveyor Circle, Box 6100, Huntington, CA 92646. TEL 714-960-6577. Ed. Donald M. Petersen, Jr. (tabloid format)

615.53   UK   ISSN 0263-9114
EUROPEAN JOURNAL OF CHIROPRACTIC. 1953. q. £45 (foreign £50). (European Chiropractors' Union) Blackwell Scientific Publications Ltd., Osney Mead, Oxford OX2 0EL, England. TEL 0865-240201. FAX 0865-721205. TELEX 83355-MEDBOK-G. Ed. S.M. Leyson. adv.; bk.rev.; bibl.; charts; illus.; circ. 820.
   —BLDSC shelfmark: 3829.725900.

615.532   II   ISSN 0015-0827
FIFTY MILLESIMAL NEWS LETTER; the journal of pure homoeopathy. (Text and summaries in English) 1969. q. Rs.6($2) Hahnemann Homoeopathic Pharmacy, Hahnemann House, College Rd., Kottayam, India. Ed. Dr. Ramanial P. Patel. adv.; bk.rev.; circ. 1,600.

615.53   GW   ISSN 0258-2015
DIE FUNKTIONSKRANKHEITEN DES BEWEGUNGSAPPARATES; Zeitschrift fuer interdisziplinaere Diagnostik und Therapie. 1986. irreg. (approx 2/yr.). DM.96. (Internationaler Arbeitskreis zur Erforschung der Funktionskrankheiten des Bewegungsapparates e.V.) Gustav Fischer Verlag, Wollgrasweg 49, Postfach 720143, 7000 Stuttgart 70, Germany. TEL 0711-458030. FAX 0711-4580334. TELEX 7111488-FIBUCH. (U.S. address: Gustav Fischer New York Inc., 220 East 23rd St., Suite 909, New York, NY 10010) Ed. Dr. A. Brueggen.
   —BLDSC shelfmark: 4058.372000.

615.53   GW   ISSN 0931-5527
GERMAN JOURNAL OF HOMEOPATHY. (Text in English) 1987. q. DM.93. Barthel & Barthel Publishing, Schatzlgasse 31, 8137 Berg 1, Germany. TEL 08151-51085. FAX 08151-51086. Ed. Dr. Michael Barthel. circ. 1,000.
   —BLDSC shelfmark: 4162.120730.

GOOD LIFE TIMES; choices in health, education and the arts. see *NEW AGE PUBLICATIONS*

615.53   US
H L Q WELLNESS DIRECTORY. 1980. a. $3.50. (H L Q Associates) Allen Goodman, Ed. & Pub., Box 86054, Pittsburgh, PA 15221-0054. TEL 412-731-5533. Ed. Linda Klapak. adv.; bk.rev.; circ. 10,000.
   Former titles: H L Q Wellness Calendar; H L Q Magazine; Holistic Learning Quarterly.
   Description: Focuses on personal health, social responsibility, and global awareness.

165.53   II   ISSN 0379-8151
HAHNEMANNIAN HOMOEOPATHIC SANDESH. 1977. m. Rs.30($10) Delhi Homoeopathic Medical Association, 4457 Pahari Dhiraj, Delhi 110 006, India. Ed. Phool Chand Jain. adv.; bk.rev.; circ. 1,500.

610   UK
HEALTH AND HOMOEOPATHY. 1980. q. £3. Hahnemann Society for the Promotion of Homoeopathy, Two Powis Pl., Great Ormond St., London WC1N 3HT, England. illus.
   Formerly: Homoeopathy Today (ISSN 0261-2828)

615.53   GW   ISSN 0017-9639
HEILKUNST. bi-m. DM.64 (students DM.52.80). Heilkunst Verlag GmbH, Angererstr. 4, D-8000 Munich 40, Germany. TEL 089-3004061. Ed. Dr. Victor Harth.
   —BLDSC shelfmark: 4284.195500.

615.53   GW   ISSN 0177-8617
HEILPRAXIS - MAGAZIN. 1982. m. DM.60. Medizinische Praxis-Verlagsgesellschaft mbH, Basler Str. 19, 7812 Bad Krozingen, Germany. TEL 07633-14081. circ. 6,500.

HERBA POLONICA. see *BIOLOGY — Botany*

615.53   US   ISSN 1060-2615
▼**HOLISTIC LIFE/VIDA HOLISTICA**; take control of your own health/ponga el control de su salud en usted mismo. (Text in English, Spanish) 1991. q. New York Institute for Holistic Life, Box 302, Bronx, NY 10458. TEL 212-923-7124.

615.53   US   ISSN 0898-6029
HOLISTIC MEDICINE. 1978. bi-m. $25. American Holistic Medical Association, 4101 Lake Boone Trl., Ste. 201, Raleigh, NC 27607-6518. TEL 919-787-5146. FAX 919-787-4916. adv.; bk.rev.; circ. 1,500. (back issues avail.) Indexed: Excerp.Med.
   Description: Essays on holistic medicine.

615.532   II   ISSN 0377-4902
HOMEOPATHIC HERALD. (Text in English) 1940. m. Rs.9. 73 Netaji Subhas Rd., Calcutta 700001, India.

615.532   FR   ISSN 0018-4225
HOMEOPATHIE FRANCAISE. (Text in French; summaries in English, French) 1912. 6/yr. 430 F. (Centre Homeopathique de France) Editions du Porphyre, 4 Place du 18 Juin 1940, 75006 Paris, France. Eds. Dr. Poitevin, Dr. Hustache. adv.; bk.rev.; bibl.; index.
   —BLDSC shelfmark: 4326.176390.

615.53   II   ISSN 0970-6038
HOMOEOPATHIC HERITAGE; monthly journal in homoeopathy. (Text in English) 1976. m. Rs.50($20) (foreign Rs. 300). B. Jain Publishers, 1921 Chuna Mandi, St. 10th, Pahar Ganj, New Delhi 110 055, India. TEL 11-770430. FAX 11-510471. (Subscr. to: P.O. Box 5775, New Delhi 110 055, India) Ed. Dr. S.P. Koppikar. adv.; bk.rev.; circ. 10,000. (back issues avail.)
   Description: Covers acupuncture and acupressure as well as homeopathic research on preventative and curative medicine.

615.532   II   ISSN 0046-7812
HOMOEOPATHIC WORLD. (Text in English) 1964. m. Rs.35. Sundar Homoeo Sadan, 113 Netaji Subhas Rd., Calcutta 1, India. TEL 387632. Ed. Sri Abinash Das. adv.; bk.rev.; circ. 1,500.

MEDICAL SCIENCES — CHIROPRACTIC, HOMEOPATHY, OSTEOPATHY

615.532　　　　　NE
HOMOEOPATHISCH TIJDSCHRIFT.* 1889. bi-m. fl.25. Vereniging tot Bevordering der Homoeopathie in Nederland, Nieuwe Gracht 46, 3512 LT Utrecht, Netherlands. Ed. J.W. Puttenstein. adv.; bk.rev.; abstr.; bibl.; illus.; stat.; index; circ. 7,900.
　Formerly: Homoeopathisch Maandblad (ISSN 0018-4489)

615.532　　II　　ISSN 0046-7820
HOMOEOPATHY; for health and life. (Text in English and Tamil) 1948. m. Rs.5($3) Indian Institute of Homoeopaths, c/o Dr. R.J. Murty, Murty Gardens, Srinagar Colony, Kumbakonam, India. Eds. Dr. R.J. Murty, Sri R. Srinivasan. circ. 2,000.

615.532　　　　　UK
HOMOEOPATHY. 1932. bi-m. £15. British Homoeopathic Association, 27a Devonshire St., London W1N 1RJ, England. Ed. Mrs. M.J. Munday. adv.; bk.rev.; circ. 5,500. **Indexed:** Curr.Adv.Ecol.Sci.

370　　　　　US
I C A REVIEW; international review of Chiropractic. 1944. bi-m. $50. International Chiropractors Association, 1110 N. Glebe Rd., Ste. 1000, Arlington, VA 22201. Ed. Molly Rangnath. adv.; bk.rev.; illus.; index; circ. 10,000.
　Description: Scientific and general articles on chiropractic and health-related issues.

IN TOUCH FOR HEALTH. see *PHYSICAL FITNESS AND HYGIENE*

615.532　　II　　ISSN 0019-4867
INDIAN HOMOEOPATHIC GAZETTE. 1961. q. Rs.4($1.50) Med-House, Chowghat, S. India. Ed. Dr. Mathews. adv.; bk.rev.; bibl.; index; circ. 3,000. **Indexed:** Hist.Abstr.

615.532　　II　　ISSN 0019-5243
INDIAN JOURNAL OF HOMOEOPATHIC MEDICINE. 1967. q. Rs.50($20) Homoeopathic Education Society, Gadkari Marg, Vile Parle (West), Bombay 400 056, India. Ed. Dr. Vishpala R. Parthasarathy. adv.; bk.rev.; abstr.; index; circ. 2,000.
　Absorbed: Indian Journal of Homoeopathy (ISSN 0537-202X) & Journal of Homoeopathic Medicine.

615.53　　II
INDIAN MEDICINE/INDIYAN MEDISIN. (Text in English and Telegu) vol.20, 1971. m. Rs.50. Indian Medicine Industries, Dubagunta Nivas, Vijayawada 520 002, India. Ed. Dr. D.L. Narayana. adv.; bk.rev.; charts; circ. 2,000.

615.533　　US　　ISSN 0098-6151
RZ301　　　　CODEN: JAOAAZ
J A O A: JOURNAL OF THE AMERICAN OSTEOPATHIC ASSOCIATION. 1901. m. $20. American Osteopathic Association, 142 E. Ontario St., Chicago, IL 60611. TEL 312-280-5800. FAX 312-280-5893. Ed. Thomas Wesley Allen. adv.; bk.rev.; abstr.; charts; illus.; index, cum.index 1901-1956; 1956-1965; circ. 38,000. (also avail. in microfilm from UMI; reprint service avail. from UMI) **Indexed:** Biol.Abstr., C.I.S. Abstr., Chem.Abstr., Curr.Cont., Dok.Arbeitsmed., Excerp.Med., Ind.Med., INIS Atomind., Med. Care Rev., Nutr.Abstr.
　—BLDSC shelfmark: 4689.400000.
　Formerly: American Osteopathic Association. Journal (ISSN 0003-0287)
　Refereed Serial

615 617.3　　　　　US
J M P T: JOURNAL OF MANIPULATIVE AND PHYSIOLOGICAL THERAPEUTICS. 1978. 9/yr. $68 to individuals; institutions $85. (National College of Chiropractic) Williams & Wilkins, 428 E. Preston St., Baltimore, MD 21202. TEL 301-528-4000. FAX 301-528-4312. Ed. Dana J. Lawrence, D.C. adv.; bk.rev.; circ. 4,400. (also avail. in microfilm; back issues avail.) **Indexed:** Biol.Abstr., Curr.Cont., Dent.Ind., Excerp.Med., Ind.Med.
　Formerly: Journal of Manipulative and Physiological Therapeutics (ISSN 0161-4754)
　Description: Chiropractic medicine issues such as manipulation, physical therapy and other conservative treatment methods.
　Refereed Serial

JOURNAL OF BACK AND MUSCULOSKELETAL REHABILITATION. see *MEDICAL SCIENCES — Orthopedics And Traumatology*

615.543　　US　　ISSN 0744-9984
JOURNAL OF CHIROPRACTIC. 1964. m. $80 (foreign $100). American Chiropractic Association, Inc., 8229 Maryland Ave., St. Louis, MO 63105. TEL 314-862-7800. FAX 314-721-5171. Ed. Irvin Davis. adv.; bk.rev.; charts; illus.; index; circ. 23,161. (also avail. in microform from UMI; reprint service avail. from UMI)
　—BLDSC shelfmark: 4958.179000.
　Formerly (1964-1981): A C A Journal of Chiropractic (ISSN 0044-7609); **Supersedes** (1930-1963): National Chiropractic Journal.
　Description: Discusses current procedures, research and developments in the field of chiropractic and in related fields of interest to chiropractors.
　Refereed Serial

615.33 616.8　　　　　UK
JOURNAL OF INTERPROFESSIONAL CARE. 1986. q. $56 to individuals; institutions $176 (effective 1992). (British Holistic Medical Association) Carfax Publishing Co., P.O. Box 25, Abingdon, Oxfordshire OX14 3UE, England. TEL 0235-555335. FAX 0235-553559. (U.S. subscr. addr.: Carfax Publishing Co., Box 2025, Dunnellon, FL 32630) (Co-sponsor: Marylebone Centre Trust) Ed. Dr. Patrick Pietroni. **Indexed:** Curr.Adv.Ecol.Sci., Curr.Cont., Excerp.Med.
　Formerly (until 1992): Holistic Medicine (ISSN 0884-3998)
　Description: Covers issues in personal care within the community, in primary health, hospital and other institutional settings.
　Refereed Serial

JOURNAL OF MUSCULOSKELETAL PAIN. see *MEDICAL SCIENCES — Orthopedics And Traumatology*

615.532　　II　　ISSN 0300-3957
KERALA HOMOEO JOURNAL. (Text and summaries in English) 1971. q. Rs.8. All Kerala Homeopathic Physicians Association, Kanjikuzhy, Kottayam 4, Kerala, India. (Co-sponsor: Indian Homoeo Chemists Federation) Ed. Dr. T.R. Sivan Tholoor. adv.; bk.rev.; abstr.; stat.; circ. 15,890.

615.53 378　　　　　US
LOS ANGELES COLLEGE OF CHIROPRACTIC. NEWS & ALUMNI REPORT. 1977. q. free. Los Angeles College of Chiropractic, 16200 E. Amber Valley Dr., Box 1166, Whittier, CA 90604-1166. TEL 310-947-8755. FAX 310-947-5724. Ed. Laura H. Arthur. adv.; circ. 6,000.
　Description: News, announcements, and notes on the activities and people associated with the College.

165.53　　GW　　ISSN 0340-577X
MODERNES LEBEN-NATUERLICHES HEILEN; Monatsblaetter fuer naturgemaesse Lebenspflege, Homoeopathie und Naturheilkunde. 1875. m. DM.23. Paracelsus Verlag (Subsidiary of: Hippokrates Verlag GmbH), Neckarstr. 121, Postfach 593, 7000 Stuttgart 1, Germany. Ed. Dr. Gunther Seng.

615.533　　US　　ISSN 0892-0249
N J A O P S JOURNAL. 1901. 8/yr. $15. New Jersey Association of Osteopathic Physicians and Surgeons, 1212 Stuyvesant Ave., Trenton, NJ 08618. TEL 609-393-8114. (Affiliate: American Osteopathic Association) Ed. Eleanore A. Farley. adv.; bk.rev.; illus.; circ. 1,650.
　Formerly: New Jersey Association of Osteopathic Physicians and Surgeons. Journal (ISSN 0028-5528)

NATIONAL DIRECTORY OF CHIROPRACTIC. see *BUSINESS AND ECONOMICS — Trade And Industrial Directories*

NURSES IN TRANSITION. see *MEDICAL SCIENCES — Nurses And Nursing*

615.53　　US　　ISSN 0888-9341
O H A I BULLETIN. 1976. q. $30. Oriental Healing Arts Institute, 1945 Palo Verde Ave., Ste. 208, Long Beach, CA 90815. TEL 213-431-3544. FAX 213-594-6513. Ed. Pi-Kwang Tsung. circ. 500. (back issues avail.)
　Former titles: Oriental Healing Arts International Bulletin; (until 1986): Oriental Healing Arts Institute of U S A. Bulletin.

615.53　　　　　FR
OFFICIEL DE L'HOMEOPATHIE ET DE L'ACUPUNCTURE. 1983. m. 220 F. (foreign 250 F.). Editions Similia, 71 rue Beaubourg, 75003 Paris, France. TEL 42-71-68-66. adv.; bk.rev.; circ. 1,400.

615.532　　II　　ISSN 0048-2242
ORISSA HOMOEOPATHIC BULLETIN; bilingual monthly magazine. (Text in English and Oriya) 1969. m. Rs.40($20) Natabar Naik, Ed. & Pub., Tilottame Homoeo House, P.O. Jagatsinghpur, Cuttack 754 103, Orissa, India. TEL 754103. adv.; bk.rev.; circ. 500. (also avail. in microform from UMI; reprint service avail. from UMI)

617.3　　US　　ISSN 0030-591X
ORTHOPOD.* 1960. 2/yr. free to qualified personnel. (American Osteopathic Academy of Orthopedics) Orthopedic Surgeons, 2500 Hollywood Blvd., No. 212, Hollywood, FL 33020-6615. TEL 513-274-7151. adv.; illus.; circ. 500. (processed)

615.533　　US　　ISSN 0092-9336
RZ301
OSTEOPATHIC ANNALS. 1973. m. $32. Ronald Park Davis Publishing Co., Inc., 45 Whitney Rd., Mahwah, NJ 07430. TEL 201-444-8660. (Subscr. to: 55 E. Washington St., Ste. 621, Chicago, IL 60602) Ed. Dr. J. Jerry Rodos. adv.; bk.rev.; illus.; index; circ. 20,100. (also avail. in microfilm from UMI; reprint service avail. from UMI) **Indexed:** Biol.Abstr., Excerp.Med.

OSTEOPATHIC MEDICAL EDUCATION: A HANDBOOK FOR MINORITY APPLICANTS. see *EDUCATION — Higher Education*

615.53　　　　　US
OSTEOPATHIC MEDICAL NEWS. m. Compendium Publishing Company Inc., 9 Pheasant Run, Newtown, PA 18940. TEL 215-860-9560. FAX 215-860-9558. Ed. Letha Strothers. circ. 31,494.

615.53　　US　　ISSN 0479-9534
PENNSYLVANIA OSTEOPATHIC MEDICAL ASSOCIATION. JOURNAL. 1945. 5/yr. membership only. Pennsylvania Osteopathic Medical Association, 1330 Eisenhower Blvd., Harrisburg, PA 17111. TEL 717-939-9318. Ed. Leonard H. Finkelstein, D.O. adv.; circ. 2,500.
　Description: Publishes articles on topics relating to the practice of osteopathic medicine.

615.53　　US　　ISSN 1054-8513
▼**PHYSICAL THERAPY PRACTICE.** 1992. q. $55 to individuals (foreign $70); institutions $82 (foreign $95). Andover Medical Publishers Inc., 125 Main St., Reading, MA 01867. TEL 617-438-8464. FAX 617-438-1479. TELEX 880052. (Dist. by: Butterworth - Heinemann Ltd., 80 Montvale Ave., Stoneham, MA 02180. TEL 800-366-2665) Ed. Dr. Susan J. Herdman. (back issues avail.)
　Description: Emphasizes assessment, diagnosis and treatment of problems commonly seen in daily practice. Includes guidelines for evaluation.

610　　II　　ISSN 0303-7967
PRAKRITI VANI; the voice of nature. (Text in English and Hindi) 1970. m. Rs.20. Nature Cure Research Association, Nature Cure Research Hospital, 51 Gwynne Rd., Lucknow 18, India. TEL 244552. Ed. S.J. Singh. adv.; bk.rev.; circ. 2,000.
　Formerly: Prakriti (ISSN 1508-1788)
　Description: Journal of naturopathy and related areas: yoga, chromotherapy, hydrotherapy, exercise-therapy, electro-therapy and iridology.

REVISTA DE LA MEDICINA TRADICIONAL CHINA. see *MEDICAL SCIENCES*

615.532　　BE　　ISSN 0035-0885
　　　　　　　　CODEN: RBHOD4
REVUE BELGE D'HOMOEOPATHIE. 1949. q. 2000 BEF. Societe Royale Belge d'Homoeopathie, 117 Bld. Louis Schmidt, B-1040 Brussels, Belgium. TEL 02-735-35-25. FAX 02-242-75-55. Ed. J.Cl. Gregoire. adv.; bk.rev.; bibl.; illus.; index; circ. 2,000.
　—BLDSC shelfmark: 7891.930000.

MEDICAL SCIENCES — COMMUNICABLE DISEASES

615.53 615.8   JA
RIGAKU RYOHO JANARU/JAPANESE JOURNAL OF PHYSICAL THERAPY. (Text in Japanese; summaries in English) 1967. m. 15980 Yen($123) Igaku-Shoin Ltd., 5-24-3 Hongo, Bunkyo-ku, Tokyo 113-91, Japan. TEL 03-3817-5703. Ed.Bd. circ. 7,500.
●Also available online. Vendor(s): JICST.
    Formerly: Rigaku Ryoho to Sagyo Ryoho - Japanese Journal of Physical Therapy and Occupational Therapy (ISSN 0386-9849)

SELECTED SOURCES OF FINANCIAL AID FOR OSTEOPATHIC MEDICAL STUDENTS. see *EDUCATION — Higher Education*

615.53   US
TEXAS JOURNAL OF CHIROPRACTIC. m. $36. Texas Chiropractic Association, 6448 Hwy., 290 E., No. D-110, Austin, TX 78723. TEL 512-454-4551. Ed. Dr. Chris Dalrymple. adv.; circ. 1,650.

615.543   US   ISSN 0091-2360
RZ201
TODAY'S CHIROPRACTIC. 1971. bi-m. $24. Life Chiropractic College, 1269 Barclay Circle, Marietta, GA 30060. TEL 404-424-0554. FAX 404-429-8359. Ed. Paul E. Gillette. adv.; bk.rev.; charts; illus.; circ. 33,000.
—BLDSC shelfmark: 8859.727800.

TRANSFORMATION TIMES; New Age journal. see *NEW AGE PUBLICATIONS*

615.533   US
TRIAD (FARMINGTON). 1989. 8/yr. $30. Michigan Association of Osteopathic Physicians and Surgeons, Inc., 33100 Freedom Rd., Farmington, MI 48336. TEL 313-476-2800. FAX 313-476-1834. Ed. Cathi A. Liebziet. adv.; bk.rev.; charts; illus.; circ. 3,200.
    Formerly (until Aug. 1989): Michigan Osteopathic Journal (ISSN 0026-2374)

615.53   US
VOICE OF NAPRAPATHY. 1955. irreg., vol.82, 1988. American Naprapathic Association, 5321 N. Central Ave., Chicago, IL 60630. TEL 312-685-6020. (Subscr. to: 5913 W. Montrose Ave., Chicago, IL 60634) (Co-sponsor: Illinois Naprapathic Association) Ed. Ray Webster. circ. 5,000. (back issues avail.)
    Description: A forum for practitioners of naprapathy, a system of manipulation administered by the hands.

615.532   GW   ISSN 0935-0853
ZEITSCHRIFT FUER KLASSISCHE HOMOEOPATHIE; kritisches Organ fuer Homoeopathie. (Text in German; summaries in English) 1957. 6/yr. DM.105 (students DM.57). Karl F. Haug Verlag GmbH, Fritz-Frey-Str. 21, 6900 Heidelberg 1, Germany. TEL 06221-4062-0. Ed. Dr. K.H. Gypser. adv.; bk.rev.; circ. 2,800.
—BLDSC shelfmark: 9467.719000.
    Former titles: Klassische Homoeopathie (ISSN 0301-1402); (until 1971): Acta Homeopathica (ISSN 0001-5881)

615.53   CC
ZHONGGUO ZHONGYI GUSHANGKE ZAZHI. (Text in Chinese) bi-m. Guangxi Zhongyi Gushangke Yanjiusuo, 32 Xinmin Lu, Nanning, Guangxi 530012, People's Republic of China. TEL 24732. (Co-sponsor: Zhonghua Quanguo Zhongyi Xuehui) Ed. Wei Mingzong.

MEDICAL SCIENCES — Communicable Diseases

A I D S. (Acquired Immune Deficiency Syndrome) see *MEDICAL SCIENCES*

616.9   GW   ISSN 0934-1129
A I D S; Informationen fuer Klinik und Praxis ueber HIV und andere Retroviren. 1988. bi-m. DM.56. Friedr. Vieweg und Sohn Verlagsgesellschaft mbH, Postfach 5829, 6200 Wiesbaden, Germany. TEL 0611-160230. FAX 0611-160229. TELEX 418928-VWV-D. Ed. I. Braveny. adv.; bk.rev.; circ. 10,000. (back issues avail.)

A I D S (YEAR); a year in review. see *MEDICAL SCIENCES — Abstracting, Bibliographies, Statistics*

616.9   US   ISSN 0887-0292
A I D S ALERT. (Acquired Immune Deficiency Syndrome) 1986. m. $219. American Health Consultants, Inc., Six Piedmont Center, Ste. 400, 3525 Piedmont Rd., N.E., Atlanta, GA 30305. TEL 404-262-7436. FAX 800-284-3291. (Subscr. to: Department L100, Box 740056, Atlanta, GA 30374-9822) Ed. Aura Bland. circ. 2,800. (reprint service avail.)
—BLDSC shelfmark: 0773.083070.
    Incorporates: A I D S Medical Report.
    Refereed Serial

A I D S & FLORIDA LAW. see *LAW*

616.9 340   US   ISSN 0887-3852
RA644.A25
A I D S & PUBLIC POLICY JOURNAL. (Acquired Immune Deficiency Syndrome) 1986. 4/yr. $45 to individuals; institutions $95. University Publishing Group, Inc., 107 E. Church St., Frederick, MD 21701. TEL 800-654-8188. Ed. Dr. Alvin Novick.
Indexed: Excerp.Med. (1992-).
—BLDSC shelfmark: 0773.083090.
    Description: Addresses the social, political, ethical, and legal issues in public health and health policy, especially as they relate to AIDS. Draws from a variety of disciplines and intellectual perspectives, including medicine, law, philosophy, business, and the social sciences.
    Refereed Serial

A I D S BIBLIOGRAPHY. see *MEDICAL SCIENCES — Abstracting, Bibliographies, Statistics*

616.9   GW
A I D S - BRIEF. 1988. m. DM.36. Hippokrates Verlag GmbH, Rudigerstrasse 14, 7000 Stuttgart 30, Germany. TEL 0711-8931-446. Ed. Dr. M.M. Kochen. circ. 2,500. (back issues avail.)

616.9   US
A I D S BULLETIN. irreg., 4th ed., 1990. $15. American Correctional Health Services Association, 11 W. Monument Ave., Box 2307, Dayton, OH 45401. TEL 513-223-9630.
    Description: Discusses CDC classification system for HTLV-III - LAV infections; the case definition of AIDS; CDC AIDS update; sample history and physical examination; guidelines for prevention of transmission of HIV and Hepatitis B virus to healthcare and public-safety workers.

616.9   UK   ISSN 0954-0121
RC607.A26   CODEN: AIDCEF
A I D S CARE; psychological and socio-medical aspects of AIDS-HIV. 1989. q. $88 to individuals; institutions $220. Carfax Publishing Co., P.O. Box 25, Abingdon, Oxfordshire OX14 3UE, England. TEL 0235-555335. FAX 0235-553559. (Subscr. addr. in U.S.: Carfax Publishing Co., Box 2025, Dunnellon, FL 32630) Ed.Bd. adv.; bk.rev. (also avail. in microfiche).
    Description: Provides a forum for publishing in one authoritative source. Research and reports from the many complementary disciplines involved in the AIDS-HIV field.

616.9   US   ISSN 1043-1543
A I D S CLINICAL CARE. 1989. m. $107 (foreign $117) (typically set in Jan.). Massachusetts Medical Society, Publishing Division, 1440 Main St., Waltham, MA 02254. TEL 800-843-6356. FAX 617-893-0413. (Co-sponsor: American Foundation for A I D S Research) Ed.Bd. charts; circ. 9,500. (back issues avail.)
—BLDSC shelfmark: 0773.083193.
    Description: Brings the latest developments on diagnosis and treatment of HIV-related diseases to the practicing clinician.

616.9   US   ISSN 0899-9546
RA644.A25   CODEN: AEPREO
A I D S EDUCATION AND PREVENTION. (Acquired Immune Deficiency Syndrome); an interdisciplinary journal. 1989. q. $30 to individuals; institutions $70. (International Society of AIDS Education) Guilford Publications, Inc., 72 Spring St., 4th Fl., New York, NY 10012. TEL 212-431-9800. FAX 212-966-6708. Ed. Dr. Francisco Sy. adv.
Indexed: Psychol.Abstr., Soc.Work Res.& Abstr.
—BLDSC shelfmark: 0773.083360.
    Description: Provides information on prevention of AIDS geared towards all professionals: epidemiologists, physicians, health educators, psychologists, social workers, counselors and legislators.
    Refereed Serial

616.9   US   ISSN 0898-5030
RC607.A26
A I D S - H I V TREATMENT DIRECTORY; experimental and approved agents and methods. 1987. q. $44 (foreign $66). American Foundation for A I D S Research, 733 Third Ave., 12th Ave., New York, NY 10017-3204. TEL 212-682-7440. FAX 212-682-9812. (Subscr. to: 6020 N. Lindbergh Blvd., St. Louis, MO 63042. TEL 314-731-4554) Eds. Drs. Donald I. Abrams, Michael H. Grieco.
    Description: Comprehensive source of information on treatments in development for AIDS-HIV infections and neoplasms.

616.9   UN   ISSN 1013-7785
A I D S HEALTH PROMOTION EXCHANGE. (Editions in English, French, Spanish) 1988. q. $16. World Health Organization, Distribution and Sales, 1211 Geneva 27, Switzerland. TEL 022-791-2111. circ. 2,000.
—BLDSC shelfmark: 0773.083415.
    Description: Communicates different educational approaches being used by different countries to inform the general public about the AIDS risk and measures for prevention.

A I D S INFORMATION. see *MEDICAL SCIENCES — Abstracting, Bibliographies, Statistics*

614 616.96   US
A I D S INFORMATION EXCHANGE. (Acquired Immune Deficiency Syndrome) 1984. bi-m. $50 for two years (free to qualified personnel). U S Conference of Mayors, 1620 Eye St., N.W., Washington, DC 20006. TEL 202-293-7330. FAX 202-293-2352. (Co-sponsor: U.S. Department of Health and Human Services) Ed. Alan E. Gambrell. bk.rev.; charts; illus.
    Description: Provides information on innovative and effective AIDS-related policies and programs.
    Refereed Serial

616.9   US   ISSN 1044-2138
RC607.A26
A I D S INFORMATION SOURCEBOOK. 1988. a. $39.95 (foreign $47.95). Oryx Press, 4041 N. Central at Indian School Rd., Phoenix, AZ 85012-3397. TEL 602-265-2651. FAX 602-265-6250. Ed. H. Robert Malinowski.
    Description: Lists over 900 testing, treatment, and counseling centers, as well as information sources, statistics, and reports of drugs in development.

610 340   US
A I D S LAW & LITIGATION REPORTER. (Acquired Immune Deficiency Syndrome) q. $1995. University Publishing Group, Inc., 107 E. Church St., Frederick, MD 21701. TEL 800-654-8188.
    Description: Presents complete, retrospective, full-text decisions from federal, state, and local courts, surveys proposed and enacted legislation. Provides an analysis of current thinking on crucial issues.

616.9   UK   ISSN 0952-7427
A I D S LETTER. (Acquired Immune Deficiency Syndrome) bi-m. £12($25) Royal Society of Medicine Services Ltd., 1 Wimpole St., London W1M 8AE, England. TEL 071-408-2119. FAX 071-355-3198. Ed. Dr. Victor G. Daniels.
—BLDSC shelfmark: 0773.083490.
    Description: Includes information about research and treatment for AIDS; and related political and social issues.

610   US   ISSN 0893-1526
A I D S LITERATURE & NEWS REVIEW. (Acquired Immune Deficiency Syndrome) m. $195 to individuals; institutions and libraries $225. University Publishing Group, Inc., 107 E. Church St., Frederick, MD 21701. TEL 800-654-8188.
    Description: Provides monthly coverage of AIDS-related articles, developments, and news from more than 500 journals and periodicals. Serves as a reference tool for physicians, attorneys, scientists, policy makers, researchers, health care professionals, administrators, and managers.

A I D S LITIGATION REPORTER; the national journal of record of AIDS-related litigation. see *LAW*

MEDICAL SCIENCES — COMMUNICABLE DISEASES

616.9   UK   ISSN 0268-8360
A I D S NEWSLETTER. (Acquired Immune Deficiency Syndrome) 1986. 17/yr. £75($155) Bureau of Hygiene and Tropical Diseases, Keppel St., London WC1E 7HT, England. TEL 071-636-8636. FAX 071-580-6756. TELEX 8953474-LSHTML-G. Eds. D.W. FitzSimons, C.J. Akehurst. circ. 1,800.
● Also available online. Vendor(s): DIMDI.
—BLDSC shelfmark: 0773.083800.

616   US   ISSN 0893-5068
RC607.A26   CODEN: APACEF
A I D S PATIENT CARE. 1987. bi-m. $79 (foreign $119). Mary Ann Liebert, Inc., 1651 Third Ave., New York, NY 10128. TEL 212-289-2300. FAX 212-289-4697. (back issues avail.) Indexed: Hlth.Ind., Telegen.
—BLDSC shelfmark: 0773.083870.
Description: Covers the full spectrum of health care for patients with AIDS and ARC. Provides guidelines and critical resources.
Refereed Serial

344.043   US   ISSN 0887-1493
KF3803.A54
A I D S POLICY AND LAW. (Acquired Immune Deficiency Syndrome); the bi-weekly newsletter on legislation, regulation, and litigation concerning AIDS. 1986. bi-w. $487 (foreign $509). Buraff Publications (Subsidiary of: The Bureau of National Affairs, Inc.), 1350 Connecticut Ave. N.W., Ste. 1000, Washington, DC 20036. TEL 202-862-0990. FAX 202-822-8092. TELEX 285656 BNAI WSH. Ed. Richard M. Hagan. index. (back issues avail.)
● Also available online. Vendor(s): Human Resources Information Network (Files CDD, HDD).
Description: Covers practical and legal issues of AIDS; the latest developments on the federal, state and local levels, fair employment practices, litigation, legislation, regulation, policy guidelines, case studies, and interviews.

616.9   US   ISSN 0893-5084
A I D S REPORT. 1987. m. $25 (effective Aug. 1991). Food & Nutrition Press, Inc., F N P Health Division, 2 Corporate Dr., Box 374, Trumbull, CT 06611. TEL 203-261-8587. FAX 203-261-9724. Ed. Gerald C. Melson. bk.rev. (reprint service avail. from ISI)
—BLDSC shelfmark: 0773.085500.

616.97   US   ISSN 0889-2229
RC607.A26   CODEN: ARHRE7
A I D S RESEARCH AND HUMAN RETROVIRUSES. 1983. m. $265 (foreign $335). Mary Ann Liebert, Inc., 1651 Third Ave., New York, NY 10128. TEL 212-289-2300. FAX 212-289-4697. Ed. Dani Bolognesi. adv. Indexed: Curr.Adv.Ecol.Sci., Protozool.Abstr., Rev.Med.& Vet.Mycol., Telegen.
—BLDSC shelfmark: 0773.089000.
Formerly (until 1987): A I D S Research (ISSN 0737-6006)
Description: Provides studies of new viruses pertaining to cancer, degenerative diseases, and the immune system.
Refereed Serial

616.9   US   ISSN 1052-4207
A I D S TREATMENT NEWS. 1986. s-m. $230 to individuals; institutions $100; low income HIV positive individuals $45. A T N Publications, Box 411256, San Francisco, CA 94141. TEL 415-255-0588. FAX 415-255-4659. Ed. John S. James. bk.rev.; circ. 6,000.
Description: Chronicles current developments in experimental and alternative treatments and deals with public policy issues.

616.9   CN
A I D S UPDATE. q. Ministry of Health, Centre for Disease Control, 828 W. 10th Ave., Vancouver, B.C. V5Z 1L8, Canada.

610 340   US
A I D S UPDATE (NEW YORK). (Acquired Immune Deficiency Syndrome) 1984. 6/yr. $50 to non-members; members $30; institutions $75. Lambda Legal Defense & Education Fund, Inc., 666 Broadway, New York, NY 10012-2317. TEL 212-995-8585. FAX 212-995-2306. Ed. Mike Isbell. circ. 7,000. (looseleaf format; back issues avail.)
Description: AIDS-related legal, legislative and policy developments.

616.9   US   ISSN 1042-4784
A I D S UPDATE (WASHINGTON). (Acquired Immuno Deficiency Syndrome) 1988. w. $235 (foreign $260). Cancer Letter Inc., Box 15189, Washington, DC 20003. TEL 202-543-7665. FAX 202-543-6879. Ed. Kirsten B. Goldberg. stat. (tabloid format; back issues avail.)
—BLDSC shelfmark: 0773.096200.
Description: Covers research, treatment and funding news about AIDS.

A T I N: A I D S TARGETED INFORMATION NEWSLETTER.
see *MEDICAL SCIENCES — Abstracting, Bibliographies, Statistics*

619.9   AT   ISSN 1031-4873
ACCENT. 1988. m. free. A I D S Council of South Australia, Inc., 20130 Carrington St., Adelaide, SA 5000, Australia. TEL 08-223-6322. FAX 08-232-0715. Ed. Kenton Penley. circ. 250.
Description: For staff, volunteers and general members of AIDS Council of SA. Includes current information about HIV infection and AIDS.

616.998   SZ   ISSN 0001-5938
   CODEN: ALEPA8
ACTA LEPROLOGICA; revue editee par le comite international executif de l'Ordre S.M. de Malte. (Text in English, French, Spanish) 1960. s-a. $50. Ordre de Malte pour l'Assistance aux Lepreux, 3 Place Claparede, Geneva, Switzerland. FAX 022-470861. Ed. J. Languillon. adv.; bk.rev.; bibl.; circ. 2,000. Indexed: Excerp.Med., Ind.Med.
—BLDSC shelfmark: 0629.100000.
Description: Technical journal devoted to leprosy research, its treatment and prevention, drug therapy and health education. Contains articles about survey methodology, and recent technological and medical developments. Also includes reports of events and list of courses.

616.9   IT   ISSN 0392-9515
ACTA MEDITERRANEA DI PATOLOGIA INFETTIVA E TROPICALE. (Text in English, Italian) 1960. 3/yr. L.35000($35) Carbone Editore, Via G. Daita, 29, 90139 Palermo, Italy. TEL 091-321-273. FAX 091-321782. adv.; abstr.; bibl.; illus.; stat.; index; circ. 3,000.
Description: Reviews clinical cases of communicable and tropical diseases.

616.988   NE   ISSN 0001-706X
Q3   CODEN: ACTRAQ
ACTA TROPICA; journal of biomedical sciences. (Text in English, French and German; summaries in English) 1944. 12/yr. (in 3 vols., 4 nos./vol.) fl.1083 (effective 1992). (Schweizerisches Tropeninstitut - Swiss Tropical Institute) Elsevier Science Publishers B.V., P.O. Box 211, 1000 AE Amsterdam, Netherlands. TEL 020-5803911. FAX 020-5803598. TELEX 18582 ESPA NL. (Subscr. in U.S. and Canada to: Elsevier Science Publishing Co., Inc., Box 882, Madison Sq. Sta., New York, NY 10159. TEL 212-989-5800) Ed. H. Hecker. adv.; bk.rev.; abstr.; charts; illus.; index. (back issues avail.) Indexed: Abstr.Hyg., Biol.Abstr., Biotech.Abstr., Chem.Abstr., Curr.Adv.Ecol.Sci., Curr.Cont., Excerp.Med., Helminthol.Abstr., Ind.Med., Ind.Sci.Rev., Ind.Vet., Key Word Ind.Wildl.Res., Nutr.Abstr., Plant Breed.Abstr., Protozool.Abstr., Rev.Appl.Entomol., Rice Abstr., Sci.Cit.Ind., Trop.Dis.Bull., Vet.Bull.
—BLDSC shelfmark: 0666.000000.
Description: Details every aspect of biomedical sciences relevant to humans, including veterinary medicine and biology in the tropics.
Refereed Serial

ACTA VIROLOGICA; international journal. see *BIOLOGY — Microbiology*

616.9
ADVANCES IN HOST DEFENSE MECHANISMS. 1983. irreg., latest vol.8. price varies. Raven Press, 1185 Ave. of the Americas, New York, NY 10036. TEL 212-930-9500. FAX 212-869-3495. Eds. John I. Gallin, Anthony S. Fauci.

616.9 618.92   US   ISSN 0884-9404
   CODEN: APIDEO
ADVANCES IN PEDIATRIC INFECTIOUS DISEASES. 1986. a. $59.95. Mosby - Year Book, Inc. (Chicago) (Subsidiary of: Times Mirror Company), 200 N. LaSalle St., Chicago, IL 60601-1080. TEL 312-726-9733. FAX 312-726-6075. TELEX 206155. (Subscr. to: 11830 Westline Industrial Dr., St. Louis, MO 63146. TEL 800-325-4177) Ed. Stephen C. Aronoff, M.D.
—BLDSC shelfmark: 0709.588500.
Description: Presents a collection of original, fully referenced clinical reviews and articles from the experts in the field.

ADVANCES IN VIRUS RESEARCH. see *BIOLOGY — Microbiology*

ALERT (LOS ANGELES). see *SOCIAL SERVICES AND WELFARE*

616.9   US
AM F A R REPORT. 1985. q. free. American Foundation for A I D S Research, 733 Third Ave., 12th Fl., New York, NY 10017-6204. TEL 212-682-7400. FAX 212-682-9812. (Los Angeles Office: 5900 Wilshire Blvd., 2nd Fl. E. Satellite, Los Angeles, CA 90036) circ. 60,000.

616.9   US   ISSN 0891-544X
AMERICAN ACADEMY OF TROPICAL MEDICINE & SURGERY. JOURNAL. 1987. s-a. $175 to non-members; members $150; institutions $200. American Academy of Tropical Medicine & Surgery, 16126 E. Warren, Detroit, MI 48224. TEL 313-882-5110. Ed. Ben Allie. adv.; bk.rev.
Description: Offers practical approaches to diagnosis and treatment of tropical diseases as a continuing education to physicians in tropical countries.

AMERICAN JOURNAL OF INFECTION CONTROL. see *MEDICAL SCIENCES — Nurses And Nursing*

616.988   US   ISSN 0002-9637
RC960   CODEN: AJTHAB
AMERICAN JOURNAL OF TROPICAL MEDICINE AND HYGIENE. 1921. m. membership. American Society of Tropical Medicine and Hygiene, 3088 Briarcliff Rd., Ste. 1A, Atlanta, GA 30329. TEL 404-636-3621. FAX 404-633-5737. Ed. Dr. William D. Tigertt. adv.; bk.rev.; bibl.; charts; illus.; circ. 2,800. Indexed: Abstr.Anthropol., Abstr.Hyg., Biol.Abstr., Biotech.Abstr., Chem.Abstr., Curr.Adv.Ecol.Sci., Curr.Adv.Genetics & Molec.Biol., Curr.Cont., Dairy Sci.Abstr., Dent.Ind., Excerp.Med., Helminthol.Abstr., I.P.A., Ind.Med., Ind.Sci.Rev., Ind.Vet., INIS Atomind., Nutr.Abstr., Pig News & Info., Poult.Abstr., Protozool.Abstr., Rev.Appl.Entomol., Sci.Cit.Ind., Small Anim.Abstr., So.Pac.Per.Ind., Trop.Dis.Bull., Vet.Bull.
—BLDSC shelfmark: 0839.000000.
Supersedes in part (in 1951): American Journal of Tropical Medicine (ISSN 0096-6746)

614.8   US
AMERICAN LEPROSY MISSIONS ANNUAL REPORT. a. American Leprosy Missions International, 1 ALM Way, Greenville, SC 29601. TEL 803-271-7040. FAX 803-271-7062.

616.96   GW   ISSN 0003-3162
QL757   CODEN: AWPAAR
ANGEWANDTE PARASITOLOGIE. (Text in English, German) 1960. q. DM.155 (foreign DM.157). Gustav Fischer Verlag Jena, Villengang 2, Postfach 176, 6900 Jena, Germany. TEL 03778-27332. FAX 03778-22638. TELEX 18069-588676. Ed. K. Odening. adv.; bk.rev.; bibl.; charts; illus.; index. (reprint service avail. from ISI) Indexed: Abstr.Hyg., Bio-Contr.News & Info., Biol.Abstr., Chem.Abstr., Dent.Ind., Excerp.Med., Helminthol.Abstr., Ind.Med., Ind.Vet., Protozool.Abstr., Ref.Zh., Rev.Appl.Entomol., Soils & Fert., Trop.Dis.Bull., Vet.Bull.
—BLDSC shelfmark: 0902.380000.

M

MEDICAL SCIENCES — COMMUNICABLE DISEASES

616.96 574.524   FR   ISSN 0003-4150
QL757   CODEN: APHCAC
ANNALES DE PARASITOLOGIE HUMAINE ET COMPAREE. (Text and summaries in English, French) 1923. bi-m. 245 ECU($304) Masson, 120 bd. Saint-Germain, 75280 Paris Cedex 06, France. TEL 1-46-34-21-60. FAX 1-45-87-29-99. TELEX 202 671 F. Ed. M.C. Durette-Desset. bk.rev.; illus.; index; circ. 700. (also avail. in microform from UMI; reprint service avail. from ISI) **Indexed:** Abstr.Hyg., Biol.Abstr., Chem.Abstr., Curr.Adv.Ecol.Sci., Curr.Cont., Dairy Sci.Abstr., Excerp.Med., Helminthol.Abstr., Ind.Med., Ind.Vet., Pig News & Info., Protozool.Abstr., Rev.Appl.Entomol., Rev.Med.& Vet.Mycol., Rev.Plant Path., Trop.Dis.Bull., Vet.Bull.
—BLDSC shelfmark: 0991.250000.

616.998   UK   ISSN 0003-4983
RC960   CODEN: ATMPA2
ANNALS OF TROPICAL MEDICINE AND PARASITOLOGY. 1907. 6/yr. $254. (Liverpool School of Tropical Medicine) Academic Press Ltd., 24-28 Oval Rd., London NW1 7DX, England. TEL 071-267-4466. Ed. Dr. W. Crewe. adv.; bibl.; illus.; index. (also avail. in microform from UMI,PMC; back issues avail.) **Indexed:** Abstr.Hyg., Biol.Abstr., Biotech.Abstr., Chem.Abstr., Curr.Adv.Ecol.Sci., Curr.Cont., Dairy Sci.Abstr., Dent.Ind., Excerp.Med., Helminthol.Abstr., Ind.Med., Ind.Sci.Rev., Ind.Vet., Nutr.Abstr., Protozool.Abstr., Rev.Appl.Entomol., Rev.Plant Path., Sci.Cit.Ind., Trop.Dis.Bull., Vet.Bull.
—BLDSC shelfmark: 1045.000000.
Description: Deals with tropical diseases and medical and veterinary parasitology in their broadest aspects.

616.9   US   ISSN 0738-1751
CODEN: ANNLDO
ANTIMICROBIC NEWSLETTER. 1984. m. $110 (foreign $153)(effective 1992). Elsevier Science Publishing Co., Inc. (New York), 655 Ave. of the Americas, New York, NY 10010. TEL 212-989-5800. FAX 212-633-3965. TELEX 420643 AEP UI. Ed. Daniel Amsterdam. **Indexed:** Abstr.Hyg., Excerp.Med.
—BLDSC shelfmark: 1549.250000.
Description: For professionals and researchers in clinical microbiology, infectious disease, clinical pharmacology, and clinical pharmacy.
Refereed Serial

616.9   US
ARCHIVES OF A I D S RESEARCH; an international journal. 4/yr. $110 to individuals (foreign $125); institutions $130 (foreign $150). Reproductive Health Center, 78 Surfsong Rd., Kiawah Island, SC 29455. TEL 803-768-5556. Ed.Bd. **Indexed:** Excerp.Med.
Refereed Serial

616.019 576.64   US   ISSN 0304-8608
QR360   CODEN: ARVIDF
ARCHIVES OF VIROLOGY. 1939. 24/yr. (in 6 vols., 4 nos./vol.). DM.1680($947) Springer-Verlag, Journals, 175 Fifth Ave., New York, NY 10010. TEL 212-460-1500. (Also Berlin, Heidelberg, Tokyo and Vienna) Ed. J.W. Almond. adv.; charts; illus.; index. (also avail. in microform from UMI; reprint service avail. from ISI) **Indexed:** Abstr.Hyg., Biol.Abstr., Biotech.Abstr., Chem.Abstr., Curr.Adv.Ecol.Sci., Curr.Cont., Dairy Sci.Abstr., Dent.Ind., Excerp.Med., Ind.Med., Ind.Sci.Rev., Ind.Vet., INIS Atomind., Pig News & Info., Poult.Abstr., Rev.Appl.Entomol., Sci.Cit.Ind., Small Anim.Abstr., Trop.Dis.Bull., Vet.Bull.
Formerly: Archiv fuer die Gesamte Virusforschung (ISSN 0003-9012)

610.73   US   ISSN 1055-3290
ASSOCIATION OF NURSES IN A I D S CARE. JOURNAL. Short title: J A N A C. 1989. q. $44 to individuals; institutions $55. Nursecom Inc., 1211 Locust St., Philadelphia, PA 19107. TEL 215-545-7222. Ed. Janine Kalinosi. Key Title: Journal of the Association of Nurses in AIDS Care.
Description: Articles focus on clinical practice, health services, education, research, and social issues related to the care of persons with HIV infection or AIDS.
Refereed Serial

AUSTRALIAN JOURNAL OF PUBLIC HEALTH. see *PUBLIC HEALTH AND SAFETY*

616.96 574.524   CL   ISSN 0006-6176
BOLETIN CHILENO DE PARASITOLOGIA. (Text in Spanish; abstracts in English) 1946. s-a. $15. Universidad de Chile, Departamento de Microbiologia y Parasitologia, Casilla No. 9183, Santiago, Chile. Ed. Hugo Schenone. adv.; bk.rev.; charts; illus.; index; circ. 1,000. **Indexed:** Abstr.Hyg., Biol.Abstr., Chem.Abstr., Excerp.Med., Helminthol.Abstr., Ind.Med., Ind.Vet., Protozool.Abstr., Rev.Appl.Entomol., Small Anim.Abstr., Trop.Dis.Bull., Vet.Bull.
—BLDSC shelfmark: 2203.000000.

BOLETIN EPIDEMIOLOGICO NACIONAL. see *PUBLIC HEALTH AND SAFETY*

610   IQ   ISSN 0007-4845
BULLETIN OF ENDEMIC DISEASES. 1954. s-a. ID.3000($12) Endemic Diseases Institute, Alwiyab, P.O. Box 1178, Baghdad, Iraq. TEL 719-2033. Ed. Najat Abbas Ali. adv.; circ. 1,000. **Indexed:** Abstr.Hyg., Biol.Abstr., Excerp.Med., Helminthol.Abstr., Ind.Med., Protozool.Abstr., Rev.Appl.Entomol., Trop.Dis.Bull.

C A SELECTS. A I D S AND RELATED IMMUNODEFICIENCIES. see *MEDICAL SCIENCES — Abstracting, Bibliographies, Statistics*

610 574 330   US   ISSN 0884-903X
C D C - A I D S WEEKLY. (Centers for Disease Control - Acquired Immune Deficiency Syndrome); a complete weekly report privately circulated. Variant title: A I D S Weekly. 1985. w. (52/yr.). $870 (foreign $969). Charles W. Henderson, Ed. & Pub., Box 5528, Atlanta, GA 30307-0528. TEL 404-377-8895. FAX 205-991-1479. TELEX 2762848. (Subscr. to: Box 830409, Birmingham, AL 35283-0409. TEL 800-633-4931) adv.; bk.rev.; index. (back issues avail.)
●Also available online. Vendor(s): Data-Star (PTS NEWSLETTER DATABASE), DIALOG (file no.636), NewsNet.
—BLDSC shelfmark: 0773.096900.
Incorporates (in 1988): Brown University S T D Update.
Description: Comprehensive newsletter on AIDS.

616.9   US
CALIFORNIA MORBIDITY; bi-weekly report from the Infectious Disease Branch. 1968. bi-w. Department of Health Services, Infectious Disease Branch, 2151 Berkeley Way, Berkeley, CA 94704-1011. TEL 510-540-2566. index; circ. 4,000.

616.9   US   ISSN 1188-0325
▼**CANADIAN A I D S NEWS/S I D A: REALITES;** the new facts of life - les faits. (Text in English, French) 1991. bi-m. free. Canadian Public Health Association, 1565 Carling Ave., Ste. 400, Ottawa, Ont. K1Z 8R1. TEL 613-725-3769. FAX 613-725-9826. Ed. Judy Redpath. circ. 10,000.
Formerly (until Dec. 1991): New Facts of Life.
Description: Covers issues related to schools, the workplace, health care workers, testing and innovative education strategies for AIDS education workers.

616.9   CN
▼**CANADIAN JOURNAL OF INFECTIOUS DISEASES.** 1990. q. Can.$67($58) (foreign $90) to individuals; institutions Can.$80($70)(foreign $117). Pulsus Group Inc., 2902 S. Sheridan Way, Oakville, Ont. L6J 7L6, Canada. TEL 416-829-4770. FAX 416-829-4799. adv.; bk.rev.; circ. 24,000.
Description: Provides experimental and original clinical papers, case reports, editorials, news and meeting announcements and reports.
Refereed Serial

616.9   CN
▼**CANADIAN JOURNAL OF INFECTIOUS DISEASES.** 1990. bi-m. Can.$67($58) (foreign Can.$103). Pulsus Group Inc., 2902 S. Sheridan Way, Oakville, Ont. L6J 7L6, Canada. TEL 416-829-4770. FAX 416-829-4799. adv.; B&W page Can.$2165; trim 8 1/8 x 10 7/8. circ. 20,500.
Formerly: Canadian Journal of Infection Control.
Refereed Serial

616.9   US
RC110
CLINICAL INFECTIOUS DISEASES. 1979. m. $81 to individuals; institutions $186. (Infectious Diseases Society of America) University of Chicago Press, Journals Division, 5720 S. Woodlawn Ave., Chicago, IL 60637. TEL 312-753-3347. FAX 312-702-0694. (Subscr. to: Box 37005, Chicago, IL 60637) Ed. Sidney H. Finegold. adv.; circ. 8,100. (also avail. in microform from UMI; reprint service avail. from UMI,ISI) **Indexed:** Abstr.Hyg., Biol.Dig., Chem.Abstr., Curr.Cont., Dent.Ind., Dok.Arbeitsmed., Excerp.Med., Helminthol.Abstr., Ind.Med., Ind.Vet., Pig News & Info., Protozool.Abstr., Sci.Cit.Ind., Trop.Dis.Bull., Vet.Bull.
Formerly (until 1991): Reviews of Infectious Diseases (ISSN 0162-0886)
Refereed Serial

CLINICAL TOPICS IN INFECTIOUS DISEASE. see *MEDICAL SCIENCES*

614.49   AT   ISSN 0725-3141
COMMUNICABLE DISEASES INTELLIGENCE. 1978. bi-w. free. Department of Community Services and Health, G.P.O. Box 9848, Canberra, A.C.T. 2601, Australia. TEL 06-289-7808. FAX 062-816-946. TELEX 61209. Ed. Robert Hall. stat.; index; circ. 2,920. (back issues avail.)
Description: Communicable disease epidemiology, surveillance and alert for health professionals.

COMPLICATIONS IN SURGERY. see *MEDICAL SCIENCES — Surgery*

CURRENT A I D S LITERATURE. see *MEDICAL SCIENCES — Abstracting, Bibliographies, Statistics*

CURRENT ADVANCES IN IMMUNOLOGY & INFECTIOUS DISEASES. see *MEDICAL SCIENCES — Abstracting, Bibliographies, Statistics*

616.9   UK   ISSN 0195-3842
RC111
CURRENT CLINICAL TOPICS IN INFECTIOUS DISEASES. 1980. a. $45. Blackwell Scientific Publications Ltd., Osney Mead, Oxford OX2 OEL, England. TEL 212-512-2000. (Dist. by: Mosby - Year Book, Inc., 11830 Westline Industrial Drive, St. Louis, MO 63146) Eds. Jack Remington, M.D., Morton Swartz, M.D. illus.
—BLDSC shelfmark: 3496.056000.

CURRENT OPINION IN INFECTIOUS DISEASES. see *MEDICAL SCIENCES — Abstracting, Bibliographies, Statistics*

DIAGNOSTIC MICROBIOLOGY AND INFECTIOUS DISEASE. see *BIOLOGY — Microbiology*

616.9   TZ
EAST AFRICAN INSTITUTE OF MALARIA AND VECTORBORNE DISEASES. ANNUAL REPORT. (Text in English) a. East African Institute of Malaria and Vectorborne Diseases, P.O. Box 4, Amani, Tanzania. **Indexed:** Biol.Abstr., Rev.Appl.Entomol.

616.988   UA   ISSN 0301-8849
CODEN: EJBLAB
EGYPTIAN JOURNAL OF BILHARZIASIS. (Text in English; summaries in Arabic and English) 1974. s-a. (Egyptian Society of Tropical Medicine and Parasitology, Research Department) National Information and Documentation Centre (NIDOC), Tahrir St., Dokki, Awqaf P.O., Cairo, Egypt. (Co-sponsor: General Society for Combat of Bilharziasis) Ed. A.A. El-Garem. adv.; charts; illus.; circ. 1,000. **Indexed:** Biol.Abstr., Chem.Abstr., Excerp.Med., Ind.Med.

616.9   UA   ISSN 0253-5890
EGYPTIAN SOCIETY OF PARASITOLOGY. JOURNAL. 1972. s-a. Egyptian Society of Parasitology, Tager Bldg, Ozoris St., Garden City, Cairo, Egypt. **Indexed:** Irr.& Drain.Abstr.

MEDICAL SCIENCES — COMMUNICABLE DISEASES

616.9   SP   ISSN 0213-005X
CODEN: EIMCE2
ENFERMEDADES INFECCIOSAS Y MICROBIOLOGIA CLINICA. (Text in Spanish; summaries in English) 1982. m. (10/yr). 5500 ptas.($57) to non-members. (Sociedad Espanola de Enfermedades Infecciosas y Microbiologia Clinica) Ediciones Doyma, S.A, Travesera de Gracia, 17-21, 08021 Barcelona, Spain. TEL 200 07 11. FAX 209-11-36. TELEX 51964 INK-E. Dir. R. Cisterna Cancer. adv.: page 155000 ptas.; trim 210 x 280; adv. contact: Marta Cisa. circ. 4,800. (reprint service avail. from UMI) **Indexed:** Ind.Med.Esp.
—BLDSC shelfmark: 3747.900500.
   Formerly: Enfermedades Infecciosas (ISSN 0212-5218)
   Description: Diffuses investigative works, clinical and microbiological, related to infectious pathology. Contributes to the continuing education of professionals.

616.9   BU   ISSN 0425-1482
EPIDEMIOLOGIJA, MIKROBIOLOGIJA I INFEKCIOZNI BOLESTI. (Text in Bulgarian; summaries in English, Russian) bi-m. 16 lv. (Ministerstvo na Narodnoto Zdrave) Izdatelstvo Meditsina i Fizkultura, 11 Pl. Slaveikov, Sofia, Bulgaria. (Dist. by: Hemus, 6 Rouski Blvd., 1000 Sofia, Bulgaria) (Co-sponsor: Nauchno Druzhestvo po Epidemiologija, Mikrobiologija, Virusologiji i Infekciozni Bolesti) Ed. L. Shindarov. circ. 653. **Indexed:** Abstr.Bulg.Sci.Med.Lit., BSL Biol.
—BLDSC shelfmark: 0057.320000.

616.9   UK   ISSN 0950-2688
RA421   CODEN: EPINEU
EPIDEMIOLOGY AND INFECTION. 1901. 6/yr. (in 2 vols., 3 nos./vol.). $245. Cambridge University Press, Edinburgh Bldg., Shaftesbury Rd., Cambridge CB2 2RU, England. TEL 0223-312393. FAX 0223-315052. TELEX 851817256. (N. American orders to: Cambridge University Press, 40 W. 20th St., New York, NY 10011) Ed. J.R. Pattison. adv.; charts; illus.; index. (also avail. in microform from UMI; reprint service avail. from UMI) **Indexed:** Abstr.Health Care Manage.Stud., Abstr.Hyg., Biodet.Abstr., Biol.Abstr., Biostat., Br.Tech.Ind., Chem.Abstr., Curr.Adv.Ecol.Sci., Curr.Adv.Genetics & Molec.Biol., Curr.Cont, Dairy Sci.Abstr., Excerp.Med., Food Sci.& Tech.Abstr., Geo.Abstr., Helminthol.Abstr., Ind.Med., Ind.Sci.Rev., Ind.Vet., Int.Abstr.Biol.Sci., Lab.Haz.Bull., Nutr.Abstr., Pig News & Info., Poult.Abstr., Protozool.Abstr., Rev.Appl.Entomol., Rev.Plant Path., Rice Abstr., Risk Abstr., Small Anim.Abstr., Trop.Dis.Bull., Vet.Bull., W.R.C.Inf.
—BLDSC shelfmark: 3793.600000.
   Formerly (until 1987): Journal of Hygiene (ISSN 0022-1724)
   Description: Original findings in microbiology and infectious disease. Emphasis on epidemiology, prevention and control.

616.96   US   ISSN 0014-4894
QL757   CODEN: EXPAAA
EXPERIMENTAL PARASITOLOGY. 1952. 8/yr. $342 (foreign $411). Academic Press, Inc., Journal Division, 1250 Sixth Ave., San Diego, CA 92101. TEL 619-230-1840. FAX 619-699-6800. TELEX 181726. Ed. Dyann F. Wirth. adv.; bibl.; illus.; index. (back issues avail.) **Indexed:** Abstr.Hyg., Bio-Contr.News & Info., Biol.Abstr., Biotech.Abstr., Chem.Abstr., Curr.Adv.Ecol.Sci., Curr.Cont., Dent.Ind., Excerp.Med., Helminthol.Abstr., Ind.Med., Ind.Sci.Rev., Ind.Vet., INIS Atomind., Nutr.Abstr., Pig News & Info., Poult.Abstr., Protozool.Abstr., Rev.Appl.Entomol., Sci.Cit.Ind., Small Anim.Abstr., Trop.Dis.Bull., Vet.Bull.
—BLDSC shelfmark: 3840.000000.
   Description: Emphasizes modern approaches to parasitology, including molecular biology and immunology.
   Refereed Serial

610   US   ISSN 1047-0719
FOCUS (SAN FRANCISCO); a guide to AIDS research & counseling. 1985. m. $36 to individuals (foreign $48); institutions $90 (foreign $110). AIDS Health Project, University of California, San Francisco, Box 0884, San Francisco, CA 94143-0884. TEL 415-476-6430. FAX 415-476-7996. Ed. Dr. James W. Dilley. bk.rev.; circ. 5,000.
●Also available online.
—BLDSC shelfmark: 3964.199500.
   Description: Places AIDS data and medical reports in a context that is meaningful, useful and accessible to anyone involved with talking to others about HIV issues.

616.96 574.524   CS   ISSN 0015-5683
CODEN: FPARA9
FOLIA PARASITOLOGICA. (Text mainly in English; occasionally in French or German; summaries in English and Russian) 1966. q. fl.299($170) (Czechoslovak Academy of Sciences, Parasitological Institute) Academia, Publishing House of the Czechoslovak Academy of Sciences, Vodickova 40, 112 29 Prague 1, Czechoslovakia. (Dist. in Western countries by: Kluwer Academic Publishers Group, P.O. Box 322, 3300 AH Dordrecht, Netherlands) bk.rev.; bibl.; charts; illus.; index; circ. 850. **Indexed:** Abstr.Hyg., Biol.Abstr., Chem.Abstr., Curr.Adv.Ecol.Sci., Curr.Cont., Excerp.Med., Helminthol.Abstr., Ind.Med., Ind.Sci.Rev., Ind.Vet., Pig News & Info., Poult.Abstr., Protozool.Abstr., Rev.Appl.Entomol., Sci.Cit.Ind., Soils & Fert., Trop.Dis.Bull., Vet.Bull.
—BLDSC shelfmark: 3971.850000.
   Formerly (until 1965): Ceskoslovenska Parasitologie.
   Description: Includes papers on human and veterinary parasitology and on the morphology, histology, histochemistry and ultrastructure, physiology and biochemistry of parasites.

616.96   IT   ISSN 0017-0321
GIORNALE DI MALATTIE INFETTIVE E PARASSITARIE. 1948. m. L.150000. (Societa Italiana per lo Studio delle Malattie Infettive e Parassitarie) Edizioni Arti Grafische Valsesiane s.a.s, Corso di Porta Vittoria 47, 20122 Milan, Italy. TEL 2-5455164. Ed. F. Colonnello. adv.; bk.rev.; abstr.; bibl.; charts; illus.; stat.; index, cum.index; circ. 1,350. **Indexed:** Abstr.Hyg., Biol.Abstr., Chem.Abstr., Curr.Adv.Ecol.Sci., Curr.Cont., Dent.Ind., Excerp.Med., Helminthol.Abstr., Ind.Vet., Protozool.Abstr., Trop.Dis.Bull.
—BLDSC shelfmark: 4178.330000.

616.9   US
H I V FUNDING WATCH. (Human Immunodeficiency Virus) s-m. free to Texas residents. Department of Health, H I V Division, 1100 West 49th St., Austin, TX 78756-3199. TEL 512-458-7684. circ. controlled.

616.9   US
H I V PREVENTION NEWS. (Human Immunodeficiency Virus) 1988. bi-m. free. Department of Health, H I V Division, 1100 W. 49th St., Austin, TX 78756. TEL 512-458-7304. FAX 512-458-7434. Ed. Dianne Green. circ. 3,000. (back issues avail.)
   Description: Statewide news on HIV and AIDS, resources for health education and risk reduction.

616.998   BL   ISSN 0100-3283
CODEN: HAINDP
HANSENOLOGIA INTERNATIONALIS. (Text in English, French, Italian, Portuguese or Spanish) 1976. s-a. exchange basis. Instituto de Saude, Biblioteca, Caixa Postal 8027, 01051 Sao Paulo, SP, Brazil. Ed. Teresa A.E. Kliemann. bk.rev.; bibl.; charts; illus.; stat.; circ. 2,000. **Indexed:** Biol.Abstr., Excerp.Med., Ind.Med., Trop.Dis.Bull.
—BLDSC shelfmark: 4262.280000.
   Supersedes (1933-1970): Revista Brasileira de Leprologia.
   Description: Articles, news, correspondence and more on Hanseniasis disease.

HARVARD A I D S INSTITUTE SERIES ON GENE REGULATION OF HUMAN RETROVIRUSES. see *MEDICAL SCIENCES*

HEALTH INFORMATION BULLETIN. see *PUBLIC HEALTH AND SAFETY*

616.9   US
THE HELPER. 1979. q. $20. Herpes Resource Center, (Subsidiary of: American Social Health Association), Box 13827, Research Triangle Park, NC 27709. FAX 919-361-8425. Ed. Charles Ebel. bk.rev.; circ. 12,000.
   Description: Offers current information on the treatment and psychosocial issues useful to people with herpes.

016.6   US   ISSN 0197-8160
RB155
HUMAN GENETICS, INFORMATIONAL AND EDUCATIONAL MATERIALS. SUPPLEMENT. 1980. a. U.S. Public Health Service, 5600 Fishers Lane, Rockville, MD 20857. TEL 301-444-6656.

616.9   NE
HUMAN PARASITIC DISEASES. 1985. irreg., vol.4, 1991. price varies. Elsevier Science Publishers B.V., Books Division, P.O. Box 211, 1000 AE Amsterdam, Netherlands. TEL 020-5803911. FAX 020-5803705. TELEX 18582 ESPA NL. (Subscr. in U.S. and Canada to: Elsevier Science Publishing Co., Inc., Box 882, Madison Sq. Sta., New York, NY 11059. TEL 212-989-5800)
   Refereed Serial

616.9   US   ISSN 0278-2316
I D N - INFECTIOUS DISEASES NEWSLETTER. 1982. m. $175 to institutions (foreign $218)(effective 1992). Elsevier Science Publishing Co., Inc. (New York), 655 Ave. of the Americas, New York, NY 10010. TEL 212-989-5800. FAX 212-633-3965. TELEX 420643 AEP UI. Ed. Charles W. Stratton. **Indexed:** Biol.Abstr., Excerp.Med.
—BLDSC shelfmark: 4478.729000.
   Description: Provides information on newly characterized diseases, syndromes, and treatment protocols, includes the latest in identification and diagnostic techniques.
   Refereed Serial

616.9 616.97   UK   ISSN 0959-4957
▼**IMMUNOLOGY AND INFECTIOUS DISEASES.** 1991. q. £190($340) Rapid Communications of Oxford Ltd., The Old Malthouse, Paradise St., Oxford OX1 1LD, England. TEL 0865-790447. FAX 0865-244012. Ed. R.K. Chandra. (reprint service avail.)
—BLDSC shelfmark: 4369.703500.

INDIAN JOURNAL OF DERMATOLOGY, VENEREOLOGY AND LEPROLOGY. see *MEDICAL SCIENCES — Dermatology And Venereology*

616.96 574.524   II   ISSN 0019-5227
OL386
INDIAN JOURNAL OF HELMINTHOLOGY. 1948. s-a. Rs.20($40) Helminthological Society of India, Prints India, 11 Darya Ganj, New Delhi 110 002, India. Ed. Dr. G.S. Thapar. illus. (back issues avail.) **Indexed:** Biol.Abstr., Helminthol.Abstr., Ind.Vet., Vet.Bull.

616.998   II   ISSN 0254-9395
RC154.7.I6
INDIAN JOURNAL OF LEPROSY. (Text in English) 1929. q. Rs.60($22) Indian Leprosy Association - Hind Kusht Nivaran Sangh, 1, Red Cross Road, New Delhi 110 001, India. TEL 3714748. Ed. Dr. H. Srinivasan. adv.; bk.rev.; abstr.; charts; illus.; stat.; index; circ. 1,750. **Indexed:** Abstr.Hyg., Biol.Abstr., Dent.Ind., Excerp.Med., Ind.Med., Indian Sci.Abstr., Trop.Dis.Bull.
—BLDSC shelfmark: 4415.850000.
   Formerly (until 1984): Leprosy in India (ISSN 0024-1024)

616.9   FR
INFECTIOLOGIE DU PRATICIEN. 10/yr. 200 F. (foreign 250 F.). Societe Francaise d'Editions Medicales, 22-24 rue du Chateau des Rentiers, 75013 Paris, France. TEL 45-83-50-54.

616.9   US   ISSN 0899-823X
RA969   CODEN: ICEPE3
INFECTION CONTROL & HOSPITAL EPIDEMIOLOGY. 1980. m. $70 to individuals; institutions $80. Slack, Inc., 6900 Grove Rd., Thorofare, NJ 08086. TEL 609-848-1000. FAX 609-853-5991. adv.; circ. 5,000. (also avail. in microform from UMI) **Indexed:** Biol.Abstr., Chem.Abstr., CINAHL, Curr.Adv.Ecol.Sci., Curr.Cont., Dok.Arbeitsmed., Helminthol.Abstr., Ind.Med., Int.Nurs.Ind., Nurs.Bull.
   Formerly: Infection Control (ISSN 0195-9417)
   Refereed Serial

616.9   US   ISSN 0749-6524
CODEN: INMDEG
INFECTIONS IN MEDICINE; infectious disease in medical and family practice. 1984. m. $50 to individuals; residents and students $30. S C P Communications, Inc., 134 W. 29th St., New York, NY 10001-5304. TEL 212-714-1740. adv.; circ. 61,693 (controlled).
—BLDSC shelfmark: 4478.721550.

MEDICAL SCIENCES — COMMUNICABLE DISEASES

616.9 576   US
▼**INFECTIOUS AGENTS AND DISEASE.** 1992. bi-m. $85 to individuals; institutions $119. Raven Press, 1185 Ave. of the Americas, New York, NY 10036. TEL 212-930-9500. FAX 212-869-3495. TELEX 640073. Ed. Bernard Roizman. adv.; bk.rev.; charts; illus.
Description: Publishes major interdisciplinary review articles in infectious disease and related disciplines, and commentaries on significant and controversial issues.
Refereed Serial

616.9   US   ISSN 0739-7348
INFECTIOUS DISEASE ALERT. 1981. s-m. $96. American Health Consultants, Inc., Six Piedmont Center, Ste. 400, 3525 Piedmont Rd., N.E., Atlanta, GA 30305. TEL 800-688-2421. FAX 800-284-3291. (Subscr. to: Box 740056, Atlanta, GA 30374-9822. TEL 800-688-2421) Ed. Dr. Jeffrey E. Galpin. index; circ. 3,400. (reprint service avail.)
Incorporates (in 1991): A I D S Clinical Digest.

616.9 610   US
INFECTIOUS DISEASE NEWS. m. $110 to individuals (foreign $146); institutions $120 (foreign $156). Slack, Inc., 6900 Grove Rd., Thorofare, NJ 08086-9447. TEL 609-848-1000. FAX 609-853-5991.

616.9 576   GW   ISSN 0934-8379
INFEKTIONS KLINIK. 1988. bi-m. DM.66. Universimed Verlag GmbH, August-Schanz-Str. 21, 6000 Frankfurt a.M. 50, Germany. TEL 069-5480000. Ed. Peter Hoffmann. circ. 9,500. (back issues avail.)
Description: Interviews, congress reports and patient information about communicable diseases.

616.01 589.9   FR   ISSN 0020-2452
R108   CODEN: BIPAA8
INSTITUT PASTEUR. BULLETIN. (Supplement avail.) (Text and summaries in English, French) 1903. 4/yr. 670 F.($125) (foreign 740 F.)(effective 1992). Editions Scientifiques Elsevier, 29, rue Buffon, 75005 Paris, France. (Subscr. in U.S. and Canada to: Elsevier Science Publishing Co., Inc., Box 882, Madison Sq. Sta., New York, NY 10159. TEL 212-989-5800) Ed. P. Meyer. adv.; bk.rev.; index; circ. 1,300. (also avail. in microform from RPI; reprint service avail. from ISI) **Indexed:** Abstr.Hyg., Biol.Abstr., Bull.Signal., Curr.Adv.Ecol.Sci., Curr.Cont., Dairy Sci.Abstr., Excerp.Med., Helminthol.Abstr., Ind.Vet., Trop.Dis.Bull., Vet.Bull.
—BLDSC shelfmark: 2575.000000.
Description: Presents reviews on all aspects of microbiology, immunology and infectious diseases, and aims at providing researchers and teaching staff in these fields.
Refereed Serial

616.01 576.64   AE   ISSN 0020-2460
INSTITUT PASTEUR D'ALGERIE. ARCHIVES. (Text in English and French) 1921. a. 30 din.($6) Institut Pasteur d'Algerie, Rue du Docteur Laveran, Algiers, Algeria. TEL 67-25-02. TELEX 65337. bibl.; charts; illus.; stat.; index; circ. 1,000. (also avail. in microfilm) **Indexed:** Bio-Contr.News & Info., Biol.Abstr., Dairy Sci.Abstr., Excerp.Med., Helminthol.Abstr., Ind.Med., Ind.Vet., Protozool.Abstr., Rev.Appl.Entomol., Trop.Dis.Bull., Vet.Bull.

INSTITUT PASTEUR DE LYON. REVUE. see *BIOLOGY — Microbiology*

INSTITUT PASTEUR DE MADAGASCAR. ARCHIVES. see *BIOLOGY — Microbiology*

616.01 574   TI   ISSN 0020-2509
                            CODEN: APTUAO
INSTITUT PASTEUR DE TUNIS. ARCHIVES. vol.47, 1970. q. Institut Pasteur de Tunis, 13 Place Pasteur, B.P. 74, 1002 Tunis Belvedere, Tunisia. FAX 791833. TELEX 14391 PAS TU. adv.; bk.rev.; circ. 700. **Indexed:** Abstr.Hyg., Bio-Contr.News & Info., Biol.Abstr., Cott.& Trop.Fibr.Abstr., Curr.Adv.Ecol.Sci., Excerp.Med., Helminthol.Abstr., Ind.Med., Ind.Vet., Protozool.Abstr., Rev.Appl.Entomol., Rev.Med.& Vet.Mycol., Small Anim.Abstr., Trop.Dis.Bull., Vet.Bull.
—BLDSC shelfmark: 1628.100000.

616.01 576   GR   ISSN 0004-6620
INSTITUT PASTEUR HELLENIQUE. ARCHIVES. (Text in French; summaries in English and Greek) 1923. a. free. Institut Pasteur Hellenique, 127 Ave. de la Reine Sophie, Athens 618, Greece. Dir. Charles Serie. adv.; circ. 1,500. **Indexed:** Abstr.Hyg., Biol.Abstr., Ind.Vet., Trop.Dis.Bull., Vet.Bull.

INSTITUTO DE HIGIENE E MEDICINA TROPICAL. ANAIS. see *PUBLIC HEALTH AND SAFETY*

616.988   BL   ISSN 0036-4665
                       CODEN: RMTSAE
INSTITUTO DE MEDICINA TROPICAL DE SAO PAULO. REVISTA. (Text and summaries in English, Portuguese and Spanish) 1959. bi-m. $200. Instituto de Medicina Tropical de Sao Paulo, Universidad de Sao Paulo, Ave. Dr. Eneias C. Aguiar 470, 05403 Sao Paulo, Brazil. Ed. Thales F. de Brito. adv.; bk.rev.; abstr.; illus.; index; circ. 1,300. (also avail. in microform from UMI; back issues avail.) **Indexed:** Abstr.Hyg., B.R.I., Biol.Abstr., Bull.Anal.Ent.Med.Vet., Curr.Adv.Ecol.Sci., Curr.Cont., Dent.Ind., Excerp.Med., Helminthol.Abstr., Ind.Med., Ind.Vet., Protozool.Abstr., Rev.Appl.Entomol., Rev.Plant Path., Sci.Cit.Ind., Trop.Dis.Bull., Vet.Bull.
—BLDSC shelfmark: 7819.850000.

616.988   PL
INSTYTUT MEDYCYNY MORSKIEJ I TROPIKALNEJ W GDYNI. BIULETIN/INSTITUTE OF MARITIME AND TROPICAL MEDICINE IN GDYNIA. BULLETIN. (Text in English; summaries in Polish and Russian) 1948. q. free. (Instytut Medycyny Morskiej i Tropikalnej w Gdyni) Panstwowy Zaklad Wydawnictw Lekarskich, Ul. Dluga 38-40, Warsaw, Poland. TEL 31-42-81. (Co-sponsor: Ministry of Health and Social Welfare) Ed. R. Dolmierski. adv.; bk.rev.; circ. 550. **Indexed:** Abstr.Hyg., Anal.Abstr., Biol.Abstr., C.I.S.Abstr., Chem.Abstr., Excerp.Med., Ind.Med., Protozool.Abstr., Rev.Appl.Entomol., Trop.Dis.Bull.
Formerly (until 1974): Instytut Medycyny Morskiej w Gdansku. Biuletyn - Institute of Marine Medicine in Gdansk. Bulletin (ISSN 0020-4463)
Description: Details bacteriology, virology, epidemiology, parasitology, maritime hygiene and occupational diseases related to the work of seamen and maritime ports personnel.

616.96   PL   ISSN 0074-3356
INTERNATIONAL COMMISSION ON TRICHINELLOSIS. PROCEEDINGS. (Published as a No. of "Wiadomosci Parazytologiczne") 1962. irreg. 130 Zl. Polskie Towarzystwo Parazytologiczne, Norwida 29, 50-375 Wroclaw, Poland. TEL 21-66-61. Ed. J. Zlotozycka. bk.rev.; circ. 800.

616.9   NE   ISSN 0074-4212
INTERNATIONAL CONGRESSES ON TROPICAL MEDICINE AND MALARIA. (PROCEEDINGS). (Proceedings issued at discretion of host country; none issued for 8th, Teheran.) 1948. quinquennial, latest 1988. International Congresses on Tropical Medicine and Malaria, c/o School of Tropical Medicine, University of Amsterdam, Amsterdam, Netherlands. circ. 1,500.

616.96 574.524   US   ISSN 0020-7519
QL757   CODEN: IJPYBT
INTERNATIONAL JOURNAL FOR PARASITOLOGY. 1971. 8/yr. £360 (effective 1992). (Australian Society for Parasitology, AT) Pergamon Press, Inc., Journals Division, 660 White Plains Rd., Tarrytown, NY 10591-5153. TEL 914-524-9200. FAX 914-333-2444. (And: Headington Hill Hall, Oxford OX3 0BW, England. TEL 0865-794141) Ed. J.F.A. Sprent. adv.; bk.rev.; circ. 1,250. (also avail. in microform from MIM,UMI; reprint service avail. from UMI) **Indexed:** Anim.Breed.Abstr., Chem.Abstr., Curr.Adv.Ecol.Sci., Dent.Ind., Excerp.Med., Helminthol.Abstr., Ind.Med., Ind.Sci.Rev., Ind.Vet., Ocean.Abstr., Poult.Abstr., Protozool.Abstr., Sci.Cit.Ind., Small Anim.Abstr., Vet.Bull.
—BLDSC shelfmark: 4542.449000.
Description: Serves as an international medium for the communication of scientific contributions in the field of parasitology.
Refereed Serial

616.998   US   ISSN 0148-916X
INTERNATIONAL JOURNAL OF LEPROSY AND OTHER MYCOBACTERIAL DISEASES. 1933. q. $100 to non-members; members $70. International Leprosy Association, One ALM Way, Greenville, SC 29601. TEL 803-271-4040. FAX 803-271-7062. Ed. Robert C. Hastings. bk.rev.; abstr.; index; illus.; index; circ. 1,400. (also avail. in microform from UMI; back issues avail.; reprint service avail. from UMI) **Indexed:** Abstr.Hyg., Biol.Abstr., Chem.Abstr., Curr.Adv.Ecol.Sci., Curr.Cont., Excerp.Med., Helminthol.Abstr., Ind.Med., Ind.Sci.Rev., Sci.Cit.Ind., Trop.Dis.Bull.
—BLDSC shelfmark: 4542.319000.
Formerly: International Journal of Leprosy (ISSN 0020-7349)

616.9   UK   ISSN 0956-4624
RC201.A1   CODEN: INSAE3
▼**INTERNATIONAL JOURNAL OF S T D & A I D S.** 1990. bi-m. £65($120) to individuals; institutions £85($155). Royal Society of Medicine Services Ltd., 1 Wimpole St., London W1M 8AE, England. TEL 071-408-2119. FAX 071-355-3198. TELEX 298902. Ed. W.W. Dinsmore. adv.; bk.rev.; illus.; index; circ. 900.
—BLDSC shelfmark: 4542.681350.
Description: Clinically oriented forum for papers on both the traditional sexually transmissible diseases (STD) and AIDS.
Refereed Serial

616.01   JA   ISSN 0021-4930
                        CODEN: NSKZAM
JAPANESE JOURNAL OF BACTERIOLOGY. (Text in English) 1944. bi-m. $145. (Japanese Society for Bacteriology) Japan Scientific Societies Press, 6-2-10 Hongo, Bunkyo-ku, Tokyo 113, Japan. TEL 3814-2001. FAX 3814-2002. TELEX 2722268 BCJSP J. (Dist. by: Business Center for Academic Societies Japan, Koshin Bldg., 6-16-3 Hongo, Bunkyo-ku, Tokyo 113, Japan; Dist. in U.S. by: International Specialized Book Services, Inc., 5602 N.E. Hassalo St., Portland, OR 97213; in Asia by: Toppan Company Pvt. Ltd., 38 Liu Fang Rd., Box 22 Jurong Town, Jurong, Singapore 2262, Singapore) adv.; bk.rev.; bibl.; charts; circ. 3,700. **Indexed:** Abstr.Hyg., Biol.Abstr., Chem.Abstr., Dairy Sci.Abstr., Excerp.Med., Food Sci.& Tech.Abstr., Hort.Abstr., Ind.Med., Rev.Plant Path., Trop.Dis.Bull.
—BLDSC shelfmark: 4651.000000.

616.998   JA   ISSN 0386-3980
                        CODEN: NRGZDW
JAPANESE JOURNAL OF LEPROSY. (Text mainly in Japanese; summaries in English) 1930. q. 5000 Yen($15) Japanese Leprosy Association - Nihon Rai Gakukai, 2-1, Aobacho 4-chome, Higashimurayama-shi, Tokyo 189, Japan. Ed. Dr. Masahide Abe. adv.; bk.rev.; charts; illus.; index; circ. 700. **Indexed:** Abstr.Hyg., Chem.Abstr., Excerp.Med., Ind.Med., Trop.Dis.Bull.
—BLDSC shelfmark: 4655.870000.
Formerly (until vol.46, no.1): Leppro (ISSN 0024-1008)

616.96   JA   ISSN 0021-5171
                        CODEN: KISZAR
JAPANESE JOURNAL OF PARASITOLOGY/KISEICHUGAKU ZASSHI. (Text in English or Japanese; summaries in English) 1951. bi-m. $128. (Japanese Society of Parasitology) Japan Scientific Societies Press, 6-2-10 Hongo, Bunkyo-ku, Tokyo 113, Japan. TEL 3814-2001. FAX 3814-2002. TELEX 2722268 BCJSP J. (Dist. by: Business Center for Academic Societies Japan, Koshin Bldg., 6-16-3 Hongo, Bunkyo-ku, Tokyo 113, Japan; Dist. in U.S. by: International Specialized Book Services, Inc., 5602 N.E. Hassalo St., Portland, OR 97213; in Asia by: Toppan Company Pvt. Ltd., 38 Liu Fang Rd., Box 22 Jurong Town, Jurong, Singapore 2262) adv.; charts; illus.; circ. 1,000. (also avail. in microform from UMI; reprint service avail. from UMI) **Indexed:** Abstr.Hyg., Biotech.Abstr., Chem.Abstr., Excerp.Med., Helminthol.Abstr., Ind.Med., Ind.Vet., INIS Atomind., Pig News & Info., Poult.Abstr., Trop.Dis.Bull., Vet.Bull.
—BLDSC shelfmark: 4656.900000.

MEDICAL SCIENCES — COMMUNICABLE DISEASES

616.988   JA   ISSN 0304-2146
JAPANESE JOURNAL OF TROPICAL MEDICINE AND HYGIENE. (Text in English) 1959. q. 7000 Yen. Japanese Society of Tropical Medicine - Nihon Nettai Igakkai, c/o Institute of Tropical Medicine, Nagasaki University, 12-4, Sakamoto-machi, Nagasaki 852, Japan. Ed. Hideyo Itakura. abstr.; circ. 700. (reprint service avail.) **Indexed:** Abstr.Hyg.
—BLDSC shelfmark: 4658.970000.
Formerly (until 1973): Japanese Journal of Tropical Medicine.

610   US   ISSN 0894-9255
RC607.A26   CODEN: JAISET
JOURNAL OF ACQUIRED IMMUNE DEFICIENCY SYNDROMES. 1988. m. $125 to individuals; institutions $250. Raven Press, 1185 Ave. of the Americas, New York, NY 10036. TEL 212-930-9500. FAX 212-869-3495. TELEX 640073. Ed.Bd. adv.; circ. 3,000.
—BLDSC shelfmark: 4918.933000.
Description: Provides results of clinical trials, case reports, reviews of current research, discussions of national policy issues and a literature citation index.
Refereed Serial

616.9   UK   ISSN 0305-7453
CODEN: JACHDX
JOURNAL OF ANTIMICROBIAL CHEMOTHERAPY. 1975. 12/yr. (2 vols./yr.) $375. (British Society for Antimicrobial Chemotherapy) Academic Press Ltd., 24-28 Oval Rd., London NW1 7DX, England. TEL 071-267-4466. FAX 071-482-2293. TELEX 25775 ACPRES G. Ed. R.G. Finch. adv.; illus.; charts; index. **Indexed:** Abstr.Hyg., Biol.Abstr., Biotech.Abstr., Chem.Abstr., Curr.Cont., Dairy Sci.Abstr., Dent.Ind., Excerp.Med., Helminthol.Abstr., I.P.A., Ind.Med., Ind.Sci.Rev., Ind.Vet., INIS Atomind., Protozool.Abstr., Rev.Plant Path., Sci.Cit.Ind., Trop.Dis.Bull., Vet.Bull.
—BLDSC shelfmark: 4939.100000.
Description: Presents original articles about laboratory and clinical aspects of the use of antimicrobials, including antibacterial, antiviral, antifungal, antihelminthic, and anti-protozoal agents; also includes reviews, articles, Working Party reports, and corresondence on related subjects.

610   II   ISSN 0019-5138
CODEN: JCDSBF
JOURNAL OF COMMUNICABLE DISEASES. (Text in English) 1969. q. Rs.40($10) Indian Society for Malaria and Other Communicable Diseases, 22 Alipur Rd., Delhi 110006, India. **Indexed:** Abstr.Hyg., Biol.Abstr., Excerp.Med., Helminthol.Abstr., I D A, Ind.Med., Ind.Vet., Protozool.Abstr., Rev.Appl.Entomol., Trop.Dis.Bull., Vet.Bull.

616.96   UK   ISSN 0022-149X
CODEN: JOHLAT
JOURNAL OF HELMINTHOLOGY. 1923. q. £85($170) Bureau of Hygiene and Tropical Diseases, Keppel St., London WC1E 7HT, England. TEL 071-636-8636. FAX 071-580-6756. TELEX 8953474-LSHTML-G. Fd. R. Muller. adv.; bk.rev.; charts; illus.; circ. 700. **Indexed:** Abstr.Hyg., Biol.Abstr., Biotech.Abstr., Chem.Abstr., Curr.Adv.Ecol.Sci., Curr.Cont., Excerp.Med., Helminthol.Abstr., Ind.Med., Ind.Sci.Rev., Ind.Vet., INIS Atomind., Nutr.Abstr., Pig News & Info., Poult.Abstr., Protozool.Abstr., Rev.Appl.Entomol., Sci.Cit.Ind., Small Anim.Abstr., Trop.Dis.Bull., Vet.Bull.
—BLDSC shelfmark: 4997.000000.

616.9   UK   ISSN 0195-6701
CODEN: JHINDS
JOURNAL OF HOSPITAL INFECTION. 1980. 12/yr. (3 vols./yr.) $305. (Hospital Infection Society) Academic Press Ltd., 24-28 Oval Rd., London NW1 7DX, England. TEL 071-267-4466. FAX 071-482-2293. TELEX 25775 ACPRES G. Ed. T.R. Rogers. adv.; bk.rev.; illus. **Indexed:** Abstr.Health Care Manage.Stud., Abstr.Hyg., ASCA, Curr.Adv.Ecol.Sci., Dent.Ind., Dok.Arbeitsmed., Excerp.Med., Ind.Med., Ind.Sci.Rev., Sci.Cit.Ind, Trop.Dis.Bull.
—BLDSC shelfmark: 5003.285000.
Description: Provides a forum for original observations of international significance in all aspects of hospital infection.

616.9   UK   ISSN 0163-4453
CODEN: JINFD2
JOURNAL OF INFECTION. 1979. 6/yr. (2 vols./yr.). $178. (British Society for the Study of Infection) Academic Press Ltd., 24-28 Oval Rd., London, NW1 7DX, England. TEL 071-267-4466. FAX 071-482-2293. TELEX 25775 ACPRES G. Ed. B.K. Mandal. adv.; bk.rev.; illus.; index. **Indexed:** Abstr.Hyg., Biotech.Abstr., Chem.Abstr., Curr.Adv.Cancer Res., Curr.Adv.Ecol.Sci., Curr.Cont., Dairy Sci.Abstr., Dent.Ind., Dok.Arbeitsmed., Excerp.Med., Helminthol.Abstr., I.P.A., Ind.Med., Ind.Sci.Rev., Ind.Vet., Protozool.Abstr., Sci.Cit.Ind., Trop.Dis.Bull., Vet.Bull.
● Also available online.
—BLDSC shelfmark: 5006.690000.
Description: Focuses on papers that reflect the diverse nature of infection and seeks to brings together the views of clinicians, micro-biologists, epidemiologists, molecular biologists, and other researchers working in the field of publication.

616.9   US   ISSN 0022-1899
CODEN: JIDIAQ
JOURNAL OF INFECTIOUS DISEASES. 1904. m. (2 vols./yr.). $81 to individuals; institutions $186. (Infectious Diseases Society of America) University of Chicago Press, Journals Division, 5720 S. Woodlawn Ave., Chicago, IL 60637. TEL 312-753-3347. FAX 312-702-0694. TELEX 25-4603. (Subscr. to: Box 37005, Chicago, IL 60637) Ed. Marvin Turck. adv.; bibl.; charts; illus.; index; circ. 9,900. (also avail. in microform from UMI; reprint service avail. from UMI,ISI) **Indexed:** Abstr.Health Care Manage.Stud., Abstr.Hyg., Biol.Abstr., Biol.Dig., Biotech.Abstr., Chem.Abstr., Curr.Adv.Ecol.Sci., Curr.Adv.Genetics & Molec.Biol., Curr.Cont., Dairy Sci.Abstr., Dent.Ind., Dok.Arbeitsmed., Excerp.Med., Helminthol.Abstr., I.P.A., Ind.Med., Ind.Sci.Rev., Ind.Vet., INIS Atomind., Int.Abstr.Biol.Sci., Nutr.Abstr., Protozool.Abstr., Risk Abstr., Sci.Cit.Ind., Small Anim.Abstr., Trop.Dis.Bull., Vet.Bull., W.R.C.Inf.
● Also available online. Vendor(s): BRS (JWAT).
—BLDSC shelfmark: 5006.700000.
Refereed Serial

616.9   UK   ISSN 0268-1218
RC117   CODEN: JMVMEO
JOURNAL OF MEDICAL & VETERINARY MYCOLOGY. (Text in English; summaries in French and German) 1963. bi-m. £135 (foreign £145). (International Society for Human and Animal Mycology) Blackwell Scientific Publications Ltd., Osney Mead, Oxford OX2 0EL, England. TEL 0865-240201. FAX 0865-721205. TELEX 833355-MEDBOK-G. Ed. Glyn Evans. bk.rev.; bibl.; charts; illus.; circ. 3,000. (also avail. in microfiche; back issues avail.) **Indexed:** Abstr.Hyg., Biol.Abstr., Curr.Adv.Ecol.Sci., Curr.Cont., Dairy Sci.Abstr., Dent.Ind., Excerp.Med., Ind.Med., Ind.Vet., Rev.Plant Path., Small Anim.Abstr., So.Pac.Per.Ind., Soils & Fert., Vet.Bull.
—BLDSC shelfmark: 5017.048200.
Formerly (until 1986): Sabouraudia: Journal of Medical and Veterinary Mycology (ISSN 0036-2174)

616.968   US   ISSN 0022-2585
RA639.5   CODEN: JMENA6
JOURNAL OF MEDICAL ENTOMOLOGY. 1964. bi-m. $75 to individuals (foreign $95); institutions $150 (foreign $170); members $25 (foreign $40). Entomological Society of America, 9301 Annapolis Rd., Lanham, MD 20706. TEL 301-731-4535. FAX 301-731-4538. (Subscr. to: Box 177, Hyattsville, MD 20781-0177) Eds. Drs. Cluff Hopla, William K. Reisen. bk.rev.; bibl.; charts; illus.; maps; index; circ. 1,600. (also avail. in microform from UMI; back issues avail.; reprint service avail. from UMI) **Indexed:** Abstr.Hyg., Bio-Contr.News & Info., Biol.Abstr., Biol.Dig., Biotech.Abstr., Chem.Abstr., Curr.Adv.Ecol.Sci., Curr.Cont., Dent.Ind., Entomol.Abstr., Excerp.Med., Helminthol.Abstr., Ind.Med., Ind.Sci.Rev., Ind.Vet., INIS Atomind., Poult.Abstr., Protozool.Abstr., Rev.Appl.Entomol., Sci.Cit.Ind., Small Anim.Abstr., So.Pac.Per.Ind., Trop.Dis.Bull., Vet.Bull., Zoo.Rec.
—BLDSC shelfmark: 5017.060000.
Description: Covers all phases of medical entomology.
Refereed Serial

616.96 574.524   US   ISSN 0022-3395
QL757   CODEN: JOPAA2
JOURNAL OF PARASITOLOGY. 1914. bi-m. $110 (foreign $115). American Society of Parasitologists, School of Biological Sciences, University of Nebraska, Lincoln, NE 68588-0118. TEL 402-472-2307. FAX 402-472-2083. Ed. Brent B. Nickol. adv.; bk.rev.; bibl.; illus.; index, cum.index; circ. 2,800. (also avail. in microform from UMI; reprint service avail. from UMI) **Indexed:** Abstr.Hyg., Bio-Contr.News & Info., Biol.Abstr., Biol.& Agr.Ind., Biotech.Abstr., Chem.Abstr., Curr.Adv.Ecol.Sci., Curr.Cont., Excerp.Med., Helminthol.Abstr., Ind.Med., Ind.Sci.Rev., Ind.Vet., INIS Atomind., Nutr.Abstr., Pig News & Info., Poult.Abstr., Protozool.Abstr., Rev.Appl.Entomol., Small Anim.Abstr., Soils & Fert., SSCI, Trop.Dis.Bull., Vet.Bull., W.R.C.Inf.
—BLDSC shelfmark: 5029.000000.
Description: Results of research, primarily on animal parasitology.

616.988   UK   ISSN 0022-5304
CODEN: JTMHA9
JOURNAL OF TROPICAL MEDICINE AND HYGIENE; devoted to medical, surgical and sanitary work in warm countries. 1898. bi-m. £90 (foreign £98). (London School of Hygiene & Tropical Medicine) Blackwell Scientific Publications Ltd., Osney Mead, Oxford OX2 0EL, England. TEL 0865-240201. FAX 0865-721205. TELEX 83355-MEDBOK-G. Ed. D.J. Bradley. adv.; bk.rev.; abstr.; bibl.; charts; illus.; index; circ. 900. (also avail. in microform from SWZ; reprint service avail. from SWZ) **Indexed:** Abstr.Hyg., ASCA, Biol.Abstr., Chem.Abstr., Curr.Adv.Ecol.Sci., Curr.Cont., Dairy Sci.Abstr., Dent.Ind., Excerp.Med., Helminthol.Abstr., Ind.Med., Ind.Sci.Rev., Ind.Vet., Int.Nurs.Ind., Nutr.Abstr., Protozool.Abstr., Rev.Appl.Entomol., Rev.Plant Path., Sci.Cit.Ind., So.Pac.Per.Ind., Trop.Dis.Bull., Vet.Bull.
—BLDSC shelfmark: 5071.000000.

614 616.998   JA   ISSN 0454-2029
KOKURITSU TAMA KENKYUJO NENPO/NATIONAL INSTITUTE FOR LEPROSY RESEARCH ANNUAL REPORT. (Text in Japanese) 1955. a. free. Kokuritsu Tama Kenkyujo - National Institute for Leprosy Research, 2-1 Aoba-cho 4-chome, Higashi-Murayama-shi, Tokyo 189, Japan. TEL 0423-91-8211. FAX 0423-94-9092.

616.96   KO   ISSN 0023-4001
QL757   CODEN: KSCHAV
KOREAN JOURNAL OF PARASITOLOGY. (Text in English and Korean) 1963. q. 20000 Won($30) Korean Society for Parasitology, c/o Dept. of Parasitology, College of Medicine, Seoul National University, Seoul 110 460, S. Korea. FAX 02-742-5947. Ed. Soon-Hyung Lee. abstr.; charts; illus.; circ. 1,000. (back issues avail.) **Indexed:** Abstr.Hyg., Biol.Abstr., Excerp.Med., Helminthol.Abstr., Ind.Vet., Protozool.Abstr., Rev.Appl.Entomol., Trop.Dis.Bull., Vet.Bull.
—BLDSC shelfmark: 5113.570000.
Description: Contains original papers of research articles, case records, and brief communications on parasites of humans or animals, and host-parasite relations.

LEARNING A I D S; an information resource directory. see *BIBLIOGRAPHIES*

616.9   UK
LEGIONNAIRES DISEASE - UPDATE SERVICE. 12/yr. £40($85) Bureau of Hygiene and Tropical Diseases, Keppel St., London WC1E 7HT, England. TEL 071-636-8636. FAX 071-580-6756.

616.998   AG   ISSN 0024-1016
LEPROLOGIA. vol.10, 1965. s-a. $5. Sociedad Argentina de Leprologia, P.O. Box 2899, Buenos Aires, Argentina. Ed. Dr. Luis M. Balina. **Indexed:** Biol.Abstr.

616.9   UK   ISSN 0305-7518
CODEN: LEREAA
LEPROSY REVIEW. 1927. q. £30($56) British Leprosy Relief Association, Fairfax House, Causton Rd., Colchester, Essex CO1 1PU, England. TEL 0206-562286. FAX 0206-762151. Ed. J.L. Turk. adv.; bk.rev.; circ. 1,800. (also avail. in microform from SWZ) **Indexed:** Abstr.Hyg., Biol.Abstr., Curr.Adv.Ecol.Sci., Curr.Cont., Ind.Med., Ind.Sci.Rev., Trop.Dis.Bull.
—BLDSC shelfmark: 5183.300000.

MEDICAL SCIENCES — COMMUNICABLE DISEASES

614.49 616.96   FR
MEDECINE ET MALADIES INFECTIEUSES; revue francaise d'epidemiologie, de pathologie infectieuse et parasitaire. (Text in French; summaries in English and French) 1971. m. 500 F. (foreign 650 F.). Societe Francaise d'Editions Medicales, 22-24 rue du Chateau des Rentiers, 75013 Paris, France. TEL 45-83-50-54. Ed. Colette Gallula. bk.rev.; bibl.; charts; illus.; index; circ. 5,000. (back issues avail.) **Indexed:** Bull.Signal., Curr.Adv.Cancer Res., Curr.Cont., Excerp.Med., Forest.Abstr., Forest Prod.Abstr., Helminthol.Abstr., Ind.Vet., Pig News & Info., Protozool.Abstr., Vet.Bull.

616.988   FR   ISSN 0025-682X
                  CODEN: METRA2
MEDECINE TROPICALE. (Summaries in English, French) 1941. q. 160 F. (foreign 180 F.). Institut de Medecine Tropicale, Parc du Pharo, 13007 Marseille, France. TEL 91-52-35-68. FAX 91-59-44-77. Ed. Dr. Ramaniraka. adv.; bk.rev.; bibl.; charts; illus.; stat.; index; circ. 1,500. **Indexed:** Abstr.Hyg., Biol.Abstr., Chem.Abstr., Excerp.Med., Helminthol.Abstr., Ind.Med., Nutr.Abstr., Protozool.Abstr., Rev.Appl.Entomol., Rev.Plant Path., Trop.Dis.Bull.
—BLDSC shelfmark: 5488.000000.

616.96   RU   ISSN 0025-8326
RC960   CODEN: MPPBAB
MEDITSINSKAYA PARAZITOLOGIYA I PARAZITARNYE BOLEZNI/MEDICAL PARASITOLOGY AND PARASITIC DISEASES. (Text in Russian; summaries in English) 1923. bi-m. 25.20 Rub.($15) (Vsesoyuznoe Nauchnoe Meditsinskoe Obshchestvo im. I.I. Mechnikova) Izdatel'stvo Meditsina, Petroverigskii pereulok 6-8, 101838 Moscow, Russia. (Co-sponsor: Ministerstvo Zdravookhraneniya S.S.S.R.) Ed. L.V. Yarotskii. bibl.; charts; illus.; index. **Indexed:** Abstr.Hyg., Bio-Contr.News & Info., Biol.Abstr., Biotech.Abstr., Chem.Abstr., Excerp.Med., Helminthol.Abstr., Ind.Med., Ind.Vet., Irr.& Drain.Abstr., Pig News & Info., Poult.Abstr., Protozool.Abstr., Rev.Appl.Entomol., Trop.Dis.Bull.
—BLDSC shelfmark: 0104.000000.
Description: Covers general and medical parasitology, results of elaborating, testing and introduction into public health practice of scientifically substantiated measures of the control of parasitic and transmissible diseases, as well as bloodsucking insects and ticks.

616.96   AG   ISSN 0524-952X
MUSEO ARGENTINO DE CIENCIAS NATURALES "BERNARDINO RIVADAVIA." INSTITUTO NACIONAL DE INVESTIGACION DE LAS CIENCIAS NATURALES. REVISTA. PARASITOLOGIA. 1968. irreg., vol.2, no.5, 1980. Museo Argentino de Ciencias Naturales "Bernardino Rivadavia", Instituto Nacional de Investigacion de las Ciencias Naturales, Avda. Angel Gallardo 470, Casilla de Correo 220-Sucursal 5, Buenos Aires, Argentina.

616.9   NO   ISSN 0332-5652
                  CODEN: NIAND5
N I P H ANNALS. (Text in English) 1978. s-a. NOK 100($20) National Institute for Public Health, Geitmyrsveien 75, N-0462 Oslo 4, Norway. FAX 47-2-353605. TELEX 72400 FOTEX N. Ed. Stian Erichsen. circ. 900. (back issues avail.) **Indexed:** Abstr.Hyg., Biol.Abstr., Chem.Abstr., Excerp.Med., Ind.Med., Trop.Dis.Bull.
—BLDSC shelfmark: 6113.247000.
Description: Covers public health and medical research in Norway.

616.9   AT   ISSN 1030-5289
NATIONAL A I D S BULLETIN; a monthly digest of news, information & comment. m. Australian Federation of A I D S Organisations Inc., G.P.O. Box 229, Canberra, A.C.T. 2601, Australia. TEL 06-257-3411. FAX 06-257-3086. Ed. Leanne Joyce.
Description: Provides news, research reports, reviews and feature articles for all groups and individuals concerned about AIDS and HIV infection.

616.9   US
NATIONAL COUNCIL OF LA RAZA. A I D S NEWSLETTER. q. free. National Council of La Raza, 810 First St., N.E., Ste. 300, Washington, DC 20002-4272. TEL 202-289-1380. FAX 202-289-8173. Ed. Miguel Serrez.
Description: Covers medical and legislative news of AIDS with a focus on the Hispanic community. Also disseminates news of the NCLR AIDS Center's activities.

616.998   UK
NEW DAY. 1896. 2/yr. free. Leprosy Mission, Goldhay Way, Orton Goldway, Peterborough PE2 OGZ, England. TEL 0733-3705052. FAX 0733-3709608. Ed. D. Chand. circ. 139,700.
Former titles: Leprosy Mission in Action; Without the Camp (ISSN 0043-7018)

616.9   UK   ISSN 0958-1316
P H L S H I V BULLETIN. 1989. m. £34 (foreign £56). Public Health Laboratory Service, 61 Colindale Ave., London NW9 5DF, England. TEL 081-200-1295. FAX 081-200-8130. circ. 500.
Description: Microbiological and epidemiological aspects of AIDS and HIV.

616.3 576 628   UK   ISSN 0267-6850
P H L S LIBRARY BULLETIN. 1948. w. £45 (foreign £110). Public Health Laboratory Service Board, 61 Colindale Ave., London NW9 5DF, England. TEL 081-200-1295. FAX 081-200-8130. Ed. Margaret Clennett. circ. 1,000.
Description: Compiled specifically with the public health and medical laboratory microbiologist in mind. Lists authors and titles of 350 relevant papers published in over 300 of the world's journals.

616.9 576 628   UK   ISSN 0265-3400
P H L S MICROBIOLOGY DIGEST. 1983. q. £16 (free with P H L S Library Bulletin). Public Health Laboratory Service Board, 61 Colindale Ave., London, NW9 5DF, England. TEL 081-200-1295. FAX 081-200-8130. Ed. M. McBride. adv.; bk.rev.; circ. 1,500. **Indexed:** Ind.Vet., Small Anim.Abstr., Vet.Bull.
—BLDSC shelfmark: 6465.101700.
Description: Written by specialists for both specialists and non-specialists. Focuses on communicable diseases.

P P O UPDATE. (Principles and Practices of Oncology) see MEDICAL SCIENCES — Cancer

616.9   US
P W A COALITION NEWSLINE. (People with AIDS) m. $35 (free to persons with AIDS or ARC). P W A Coalition Inc., 31 W. 26th St., 5th Fl., New York, NY 10010. TEL 212-532-0290. FAX 212-447-1508. circ. 10,000.
Description: Reports new developments dealing with the health crisis as well as alternative treatments.

616.9 574   UK   ISSN 0141-9838
                  CODEN: PAIMD8
PARASITE IMMUNOLOGY. 1979. bi-m. £165 (foreign £185). Blackwell Scientific Publications Ltd., Osney Mead, Oxford OX2 OEL, England. TEL 0865-240201. FAX 0865-721205. TELEX 83355-MEDBOK-G. Eds. G.A.T. Targett, B.M. Ogilvie. adv.; bibl.; charts; illus.; index; circ. 500. (back issues avail.; reprint service avail. from ISI) **Indexed:** Abstr.Hyg., ASCA, Biol.Abstr., Curr.Adv.Ecol.Sci., Curr.Adv.Genetics & Molec.Biol., Curr.Cont., Excerp.Med., Helminthol.Abstr., Ind.Med., Ind.Vet., Protozool.Abstr., Sci.Cit.Ind., Trop.Dis.Bull., Vet.Bull.
—BLDSC shelfmark: 6404.940000.

574.5   UK   ISSN 0031-1820
                  CODEN: PARAAE
PARASITOLOGY (CAMBRIDGE). (Supplement avail.) 1908. 6/yr. (in 2 vols., 3 nos./vol.) $150 to individuals; institutions $336. Cambridge University Press, Edinburgh Bldg., Shaftesbury Rd., Cambridge CB2 2RU, England. TEL 0223-312393. FAX 0223-315052. TELEX 851817256. (North American orders to: Cambridge University Press, 40 W. 20th St., New York, NY 10011) Eds. F.E.G. Cox, C. Arme. adv.; index. (also avail. in microfilm from UMI) **Indexed:** Abstr.Hyg., Anim.Breed.Abstr., Biol.Abstr., Biotech.Abstr., Chem.Abstr., Curr.Adv.Ecol.Sci., Curr.Cont., Dairy Sci.Abstr., Excerp.Med., Geo.Abstr., Helminthol.Abstr., Ind.Med., Ind.Vet., Int.Abstr.Biol.Sci, Nutr.Abstr., Potato Abstr., Rev.Appl.Entomol., Trop.Dis.Bull., Vet.Bull.
—BLDSC shelfmark: 6406.000000.
Description: Papers on all aspects of pure and applied parasitology including biochemical, immunological, physiological and ecological topics with emphasis on parasites and their control.

616.96 574.524   GW   ISSN 0932-0113
QL757   CODEN: PARREZ
PARASITOLOGY RESEARCH. (Text in English, French and German; summaries in English) 1928. 8/yr. DM.1340($656) (Deutsche Gesellschaft fuer Parasitologie) Springer-Verlag, Heidelberger Platz 3, D-1000 Berlin 33, Germany. TEL 030-8207-1. (Also Heidelberg, Tokyo, Vienna, and New York) Ed. B.M. Honigberg. adv.; charts; illus. (also avail. in microform from UMI; back issues avail.; reprint service avail. from ISI) **Indexed:** Abstr.Hyg., Biol.Abstr., Biotech.Abstr., Chem.Abstr., Curr.Adv.Ecol.Sci., Curr.Cont., Excerp.Med., Helminthol.Abstr., Ind.Med., Ind.Vet., Poult.Abstr., Protozool.Abstr., Rev.Appl.Entomol., Trop.Dis.Bull., Vet.Bull.
—BLDSC shelfmark: 6406.120000.
Formerly: Zeitschrift fuer Parasitenkunde (ISSN 0044-3255)
Description: Presents information on the latest developments in parasitology research, with special emphasis on practical aspects such as immunodiagnosis, chemotherapy, and epidemiology. Includes review articles that provide an overview of current advances.

616.96 574.524   IT   ISSN 0048-2951
QL757   CODEN: PSSGAR
PARASSITOLOGIA. (Text in English, French and Italian; summaries in English) 1959. 3/yr. L.120000. (Societa Italiana di Parassitologia) Lombardo Editore, Via Verona, 22, 00161 Rome, Italy. TEL 06-428905. FAX 06-428543. Ed. M. Coluzzi. adv.; index. (also avail. in microform) **Indexed:** Abstr.Hyg., Biol.Abstr., Chem.Abstr., Excerp.Med., Helminthol.Abstr., Ind.Med., Ind.Vet., Protozool.Abstr., Rev.Appl.Entomol., Trop.Dis.Bull., Vet.Bull.
—BLDSC shelfmark: 6406.130000.

616.96 574.524   RU   ISSN 0031-1847
QL757   CODEN: PAZGA4
PARAZITOLOGIYA/PARASITOLOGY. 1966. bi-m. 21.60 Rub. (Akademiya Nauk S.S.S.R.) Izdatel'stvo Nauka, 90 Profsoyuznaya ul., 117864 Moscow, Russia. index. (also avail. in microfiche from BHP) **Indexed:** Abstr.Hyg., Bio-Contr.News & Info., Biol.Abstr., Chem.Abstr., Curr.Adv.Ecol.Sci., Curr.Cont., Excerp.Med., Helminthol.Abstr., Ind.Med., Ind.Vet., Protozool.Abstr., Rev.Appl.Entomol., Trop.Dis.Bull., Vet.Bull.
—BLDSC shelfmark: 0129.130000.

616.998   UK   ISSN 0308-745X
PARTNERS. (Text in English and French) 1976. s-a. free. Leprosy Mission, 80 Windmill Road, Brentford, Middlesex TW8 OQH, England. TEL 081-569-7292. FAX 081-569-7808. TELEX 9312133925 LM G. Ed. P.J. Neville. circ. 34,500. **Indexed:** Abstr.Hyg., Curr.Adv.Ecol.Sci., Rehabil.Lit., Trop.Dis.Bull.

618.92   US   ISSN 1045-5418
RJ387.A25   CODEN: PAHIEQ
▼**PEDIATRIC A I D S AND H I V INFECTION: FETUS TO ADOLESCENT.** 1990. bi-m. $85 (foreign $125). Mary Ann Liebert, Inc., 1651 Third Ave., New York, NY 10128. TEL 212-289-2300. FAX 212-289-4697. Eds. Mhairi G. MacDonald, Dr. Harold M. Ginzburg.
—BLDSC shelfmark: 6417.525000.
Description: Covers methods of diagnosis and treatment of HIV infection. Includes epidemiology, molecular biology, clinical presentation, diagnosis and treatment, pathology, virology, reproductive, psychosocial, and relevant legal and community needs.

THE PEDIATRIC INFECTIOUS DISEASE JOURNAL. see MEDICAL SCIENCES — Pediatrics

PEDIATRIC PATHOLOGY. see MEDICAL SCIENCES — Pediatrics

616.998   PH
PHILIPPINE JOURNAL OF DERMATOLOGY AND LEPROSY. (Text and summaries in English) 1966. s-a. exchange basis. Dermatology Research and Training, Ministry of Health, Manila, Philippines. Ed. Perpetua D. Reyes Javier. bk.rev.; abstr.; illus.; circ. 500.
Formerly: Philippine Journal of Leprosy (ISSN 0031-7632)

616.9   AT   ISSN 1032-0229
PRIDE (COLLINGWOOD). q. Victorian Aids Council Inc., 117 Johnston St., Collingwood 3066, Australia. TEL 03-417-1759. FAX 03-419-7435. Ed. Leigh Holloway.

MEDICAL SCIENCES — COMMUNICABLE DISEASES

610 576.64　　　　SZ　　ISSN 0079-645X
RC114.5　　　　　　　　　CODEN: PMVIA6
PROGRESS IN MEDICAL VIROLOGY. (Text in English) 1958. irreg. (approx. 1/yr.). price varies. S. Karger AG, Allschwilerstr. 10, P.O. Box, CH-4009 Basel, Switzerland. TEL 061-3061111. FAX 061-3061234. TELEX CH 962652. Ed. J.L. Melnick. (reprint service avail. from ISI) **Indexed:** Abstr.Hyg., Biol.Abstr., Chem.Abstr., Curr.Adv.Ecol.Sci., Curr.Cont., Dent.Ind., Ind.Med., Ind.Sci.Rev., Ind.Vet., Vet.Bull.
—BLDSC shelfmark: 6868.960000.

616.9　　　　　　　　　US
PSYCHOSOCIAL EPIDEMIOLOGY SERIES. 1982. irreg., latest 1991. price varies. Rutgers University Press, 109 Church St., New Brunswick, NJ 08901. TEL 908-932-7399. FAX 908-932-7039. (Dist. by: Rutgers University Press Distribution Center, Box 4869, Hampden Sta., Baltimore, MD 21211. TEL 410-516-6947.)

616.9 614　　　　UK　　ISSN 0142-3517
PUBLIC HEALTH LABORATORY SERVICE BOARD. BIENNIAL REPORT. 1975. biennial. Public Health Laboratory Service Board, 61 Colindale Ave., London NW9 5DF, England. TEL 081-200-1295. FAX 081-200-8130. Ed. J. McBride. circ. 1,500. (also avail. in microform; MI)
Formerly: Public Health Laboratory Service Board. Year Book (ISSN 0306-1531)

616.9　　　　　　UK　　ISSN 0959-2946
PUBLIC HEALTH NEWS. m. £60($115) Bureau of Hygiene and Tropical Diseases, Keppel St., London WC1E 7HT, England. TEL 071-636-8636. FAX 071-580-6756.

616.9　　　　　　FR　　ISSN 0923-2516
　　　　　　　　　　　　CODEN: RESVEY
RESEARCH IN VIROLOGY. (Text in English) 1886. 6/yr. 895 F.($175) (foreign 1030 F.)(effective 1992). Editions Scientifiques Elsevier, 29, rue Buffon, 75005 Paris, France. (Subscr. in U.S. and Canada to: Elsevier Science Publishing Co., Inc., Box 882, Madison Sq. Sta., New York, NY 10159. TEL 212-989-5800) Ed. P. Tiollais. index. (also avail. in microform from RPI; back issues avail.) **Indexed:** Abstr.Hyg., Biol.Abstr., Bull.Signal., Chem.Abstr., Curr.Adv.Ecol.Sci., Curr.Adv.Genetics & Molec.Biol., Curr.Cont., Excerp.Med., Ind.Sci.Rev., Ind.Vet., INIS Atomind., Sci.Cit.Ind., Trop.Dis.Bull., Vet.Bull.
—BLDSC shelfmark: 7774.120000.
Former titles (until 1988): Institut Pasteur. Annales. Virologie (ISSN 0769-2617); Annales de Virologie (ISSN 0242-5017)
Description: Publishes editorials, full-length articles, technical and brief notes on molecular virology, virus-cell interactions, viral oncogenesis, medical virology and epidemiology.
Refereed Serial

616.9　　　　　　CN
RESPONDING TO H I V - A I D S IN CANADA. q. Can.$147. M P L Communications Inc., 700-133 Richmond St., W., Toronto, Ont. M5H 3M8, Canada. TEL 416-869-1177. FAX 416-869-0456. (looseleaf format)
Description: Provides information on how various governments and organizations in Canada have responded to HIV-AIDS.

RETROVIRUS; la revue du SIDA. see *BIOLOGY — Microbiology*

616.988　　　　　BL　　ISSN 0034-7256
RA644.M2
REVISTA BRASILEIRA DE MALARIOLOGIA E DOENCAS TROPICAIS. (Text in Portuguese; summaries in English and Portuguese) 1949. a. free to medical organizations. Ministerio da Saude, Esplanada dos Ministerios Bloco G, 7 Andar, 70058 Brasilia DF, Brazil. TEL 061-224-9457. TELEX 061-1603. Ed. Marcos A. Soares Porto. bk.rev.; abstr.; charts; illus.; stat.; index, cum.index; circ. 2,000. **Indexed:** Abstr.Hyg., Biol.Abstr., Chem.Abstr., Helminthol.Abstr., Ind.Med., Rev.Appl.Entomol., Trop.Dis.Bull.
—BLDSC shelfmark: 7845.260000.

616.988　　　　　CU
REVISTA CUBANA DE MEDICINA TROPICAL. (Summaries in English, French, Russian and Spanish) 1966. 3/yr. $17 in N. America; S. America $18; Europe $22. (Ministerio de Salud Publica, Centro Nacional de Informacion de Ciencias Medicas) Ediciones Cubanas, Calle 23 No. 177, e-N y O, La Rampa, Vedado, Apdo. 6520, Havana, Cuba. TEL 32-5556-60. (Dist. by: Ediciones Cubanas, Obispo No. 461, Apdo. 605, Havana, Cuba) bibl.; charts; illus.; index; circ. 1,500. **Indexed:** Abstr.Hyg., Biol.Abstr., Chem.Abstr., Curr.Adv.Ecol.Sci., Excerp.Med., Helminthol.Abstr., Ind.Med., Nutr.Abstr., Protozool.Abstr., Trop.Dis.Bull.
Formerly: Medicina Tropical (ISSN 0025-794X)

REVISTA DE IGIENA, BACTERIOLOGIE, VIRUSOLOGIE, PARAZITOLOGIE, PNEUMOFTIZIOLOGIE. BACTERIOLOGIE, VIRUSOLOGIE, PARAZITOLOGIE, EPIDEMIOLOGIE. see *BIOLOGY — Microbiology*

REVISTA DE IGIENA, BACTERIOLOGIE, VIRUSOLOGIE, PARAZITOLOGIE, PNEUMOFTIZIOLOGIE. see *MEDICAL SCIENCES — Respiratory Diseases*

616.988　　　　　EC　　ISSN 0048-7775
REVISTA ECUATORIANA DE HIGIENE Y MEDICINA TROPICAL. 1944. q. exchange basis. Instituto Nacional de Higiene y Medicina Tropical "Leopoldo Izquieta Perez", Casilla de Correos No. 3961, Guayaquil, Ecuador. Ed.Bd. illus.; circ. 3,500. (reprint service avail. from ISI) **Indexed:** Biol.Abstr., Ind.Med., Rev.Appl.Entomol.

616.96 574.524　　SP　　ISSN 0034-9623
QL757　　　　　　　　　CODEN: RIPAAE
REVISTA IBERICA DE PARASITOLOGIA.* (Text in Spanish; summaries in English and Spanish) 1940. 4/yr. 2800 ptas. (foreign 4200 ptas.). Consejo Superior de Investigaciones Cientificas (C.S.I.C.), Instituto de Parasitologia, "Lopez-Neyra", Ventanilla 11, 18001 Granada, Spain. TEL 91-2612833. FAX 91-4113077. TELEX 42182. (Co-sponsor: Asociacion de Parasitologos Espanoles) Ed. Jaime Gallego Berenguer. bk.rev.; abstr.; bibl.; charts; illus.; index; circ. 800. **Indexed:** Abstr.Hyg., Agrindex, Biol.Abstr., Bull.Signal., Chem.Abstr., Curr.Adv.Ecol.Sci., Excerp.Med., Geo.Abstr., Helminthol.Abstr., Ind.Med., Ind.Med.Esp., Ind.SST, Ind.Vet., Nutr.Abstr., Protozool.Abstr., Rev.Appl.Entomol., Trop.Dis.Bull., Vet.Bull.
—BLDSC shelfmark: 7858.800000.
Description: Publishes papers and original papers on every aspect of parasitology with emphasis related to the Iberian peninsula.

616.019 576.64　　RM
REVUE ROUMAINE DE VIROLOGIE/RUMANIAN JOURNAL OF VIROLOGY. (Text in English, French, German and Russian) 1964. 4/yr. 200 lei($55) (Academia de Stiinte Medicale) Editura Academiei Romane, Calea Victoriei 125, 79717 Bucharest, Rumania. TEL 50-76-80. (Dist. by: Rompresfilatelia, Calea Grivitei 64-66, P.O. Box 12-201, 78104 Bucharest, Rumania) Ed. N. Cajal. bk.rev.; circ. 800. **Indexed:** Abstr.Hyg., Biol.Abstr., Chem.Abstr., Excerp.Med., Ind.Vet., Poult.Abstr., Trop.Dis.Bull., Vet.Bull., Virol.Abstr.
Former titles: Revue Roumaine de Medecine. Serie Virologie; Revue Roumaine de Virologie; Revue Roumaine d'Inframicrobiologie (ISSN 0035-4082)

616.96 574.524　　IT　　ISSN 0035-6387
QL757　　　　　　　　　CODEN: RPSTAX
RIVISTA DI PARASSITOLOGIA. (Text in English, French, German, Italian and Spanish) 1937. 3/yr. $60. Istituto di Parassitologia, Universita di Messina, Via Cesare Battisti 48, 98100 Messina, Italy. TEL 090-673136. adv.; bk.rev.; charts; illus.; index; circ. 600. **Indexed:** Abstr.Hyg., Biol.Abstr., Chem.Abstr., Excerp.Med., Helminthol.Abstr., Ind.Vet., Rev.Appl.Entomol., Trop.Dis.Bull., Vet.Bull.
—BLDSC shelfmark: 7992.200000.

616.988　　　　　UK　　ISSN 0080-4711
ROYAL SOCIETY OF TROPICAL MEDICINE AND HYGIENE, LONDON. YEARBOOK. 1908. a. £15. Royal Society of Tropical Medicine and Hygiene, Manson House, 26 Portland Place, London, W1N 4EY, England. TEL 071-580-2127. FAX 071-436-1389. Ed. J.R. Baker. adv.; bk.rev.; circ. 3,500. **Indexed:** Curr.Cont.

616.988　　　　　UK　　ISSN 0035-9203
　　　　　　　　　　　　CODEN: TRSTAZ
ROYAL SOCIETY OF TROPICAL MEDICINE AND HYGIENE TRANSACTIONS. 1907. bi-m. £96. Royal Society of Tropical Medicine and Hygiene, Manson House, 26 Portland Pl., London W1N 4EY, England. TEL 071-580-2127. FAX 071-436-1389. Ed. Dr. J. Baker. adv.; bibl.; charts; illus.; index; circ. 3,800. **Indexed:** Abstr.Hyg., Biol.Abstr., Chem.Abstr., Curr.Adv.Cancer Res., Curr.Adv.Ecol.Sci., Curr.Adv.Genetics & Molec.Biol., Dairy Sci.Abstr., Dent.Ind., Excerp.Med., Helminthol.Abstr., Ind.Med., Ind.Vet., Nutr.Abstr., Protozool.Abstr., Rev.Appl.Entomol., Rev.Plant Path., Risk Abstr., So.Pac.Per.Ind., Trop.Dis.Bull., Vet.Bull.
—BLDSC shelfmark: 9003.000000.

616　　　　　　　SW　　ISSN 0036-5548
　　　　　　　　　　　　CODEN: SJIDB7
SCANDINAVIAN JOURNAL OF INFECTIOUS DISEASES. (Supplements free to subscribers) (Text in English) 1969. 6/yr. SEK 645. Almqvist & Wiksell Periodical Company, Box 638, S-101 28 Stockholm, Sweden. Eds. Folke Nordbring, Stellan Bengtsson. adv.; circ. 1,200. **Indexed:** Abstr.Hyg., ASCA, Biol.Abstr., Biol.Dig., Biotech.Abstr., Chem.Abstr., Curr.Adv.Ecol.Sci., Curr.Cont., Dent.Ind., Dok.Arbeitsmed., Excerp.Med., Helminthol.Abstr., Ind.Med., Ind.Vet., Protozool.Abstr., Rev.Plant Path., Trop.Dis.Bull., Vet.Bull.
—BLDSC shelfmark: 8087.517000.

SEMINARS IN DIAGNOSTIC PATHOLOGY. see *MEDICAL SCIENCES*

616.9　　　　　　UK　　ISSN 0888-0786
　　　　　　　　　　　　CODEN: SIIDE3
SERODIAGNOSIS AND IMMUNOTHERAPY. 1987. bi-m. £86($162) Academic Press Ltd., 24-28 Oval Rd., London NW1 7DX, England. FAX 071-482-2293. TELEX 25775 ACPRESS G. Ed. J.P. Burnie. **Indexed:** Vet.Bull.

616.988　　　　　BL　　ISSN 0037-8682
SOCIEDADE BRASILEIRA DE MEDICINA TROPICAL. REVISTA. (Text in Portuguese; summaries in English, French or German) 1967. bi-m. Cr.$35($15) Sociedade Brasileira de Medicina Tropical, Rua Laura de Araujo 36, P.O. Box 1859, Rio de Janeiro, Brazil. Ed. Dr. Lea Camillo-Coura. adv.; abstr.; bibl.; charts; index; circ. controlled. **Indexed:** Abstr.Hyg., Biol.Abstr., Excerp.Med., Trop.Dis.Bull.
—BLDSC shelfmark: 7834.200000.
Formerly: Jornal Brasileiro de Medicina Tropical.

616.988　　　　　BE　　ISSN 0365-6527
　　　　　　　　　　　　CODEN: ASBMAX
SOCIETE BELGE DE MEDECINE TROPICALE. ANNALES/BELGISCHE VEREINIGING VOOR TROPISCHE GENEESKUNDE. ANNALEN. (Text and summaries in English, French) 1920. q. 2800 Fr. Association des Societes Scientifiques Medicales Belges - Vereiniging van de Belgische Medische Wetenschappelijke Genootschappen, Av. Circulaire 138A, B-1180 Brussels, Belgium. TEL 02-374-5158. Ed. L. Eyckmans. adv.; bk.rev.; charts; illus.; index, cum.index: 1920-1969; circ. 900. (also avail. in microfilm) **Indexed:** Abstr.Hyg., Biol.Abstr., Chem.Abstr., Curr.Cont., Excerp.Med., Helminthol.Abstr., Ind.Med., Ind.Vet., Nutr.Abstr., Rev.Appl.Entomol., Rev.Med. & Vet.Mycol., Rev.Plant Path., Sci.Cit.Ind., Trop.Dis.Bull., Vet.Bull.
—BLDSC shelfmark: 0946.750000.
Formerly: Societes Belges de Medecine Tropicale, de Parasitologie et de Mycologie. Annales.
Description: Covers a variety of aspects of tropical medicine.

616.988　　　　　TH　　ISSN 0038-3619
　　　　　　　　　　　　CODEN: SJTMAK
SOUTHEAST ASIAN JOURNAL OF TROPICAL MEDICINE AND PUBLIC HEALTH. 1970. q. $24. Southeast Asian Ministers of Education Organisation (SEAMEO), Regional Tropical Medicine & Public Health Project (TROPMED), 420-6 Rajvithi Rd., Bangkok 10400, Thailand. Ed. D.C. Reynolds. adv.; bk.rev.; abstr.; bibl.; illus.; index; circ. 1,000. (also avail. in microform from UMI; reprint service avail. from UMI) **Indexed:** Abstr.Hyg., Biol.Abstr., Chem.Abstr., Excerp.Med., Helminthol.Abstr., Ind.Med., Ind.Vet., Nutr.Abstr., Protozool.Abstr., Rev.Appl.Entomol., Rev.Plant Path., Trop.Dis.Bull., Vet.Bull.

MEDICAL SCIENCES — COMPUTER APPLICATIONS

SPAIN. MINISTERIO DE AGRICULTURA, PESCA Y ALIMENTACION. BOLETIN DE SANIDAD VEGETAL: PLAGAS. see *AGRICULTURE — Crop Production And Soil*

616.9 US
SPOTLIGHT ON A I D S.* 1988? 12/yr. $20. Odyssey Institute Corporation, Concerned Physicians Network, 5 Hedley Rd., Westport, CT 06880.
Formerly: Odyssey Institute Journal.

616.96 US
STUDIES IN INFECTIOUS DISEASES RESEARCH. 1975. irreg., latest 1981. price varies. University of Chicago Press, 5801 S. Ellis Ave., Chicago, IL 60637. TEL 312-702-7899. (Subscr. to: 11030 Langley Ave., Chicago, IL 60628)
Refereed Serial

610 US ISSN 0171-2160
CODEN: TIDID3
TOPICS IN INFECTIOUS DISEASES. 1975. irreg. price varies. Springer-Verlag, 175 Fifth Ave., New York, NY 10010. TEL 212-460-1500. (And Berlin, Heidelberg, Tokyo and Vienna) (reprint service avail. from ISI) Indexed: Chem.Abstr.

616.9 US
TREATMENT ISSUES; newsletter of experimental AIDS therapies. 1987. 10/yr. $30 (foreign $40). (Gay Men's Health Crisis, Inc.) G M H C, Inc., Department of Medical Information, 129 W. 20th St., New York, NY 10011. FAX 212-337-1975. Ed. David Gold. circ. 18,000.
Description: Addresses the various medical aspects of AIDS (experimental treatments, descriptions of opportunistic infections often seen in AIDS, drug licensing issues, medical articles of general interest to people who are HIV-infected).

616.988 UK ISSN 0049-4755
RC960 CODEN: TPDCAV
TROPICAL DOCTOR; a journal of modern medical practice. 1971. q. £26($65) Royal Society of Medicine Services Ltd., 1 Wimpole St., London W1M 8AE, England. TEL 071-408 2119. FAX 071-355-3198. Ed.Bd. bk.rev.; illus.; circ. 2,000. (reprint service avail. from ISI) Indexed: Abstr.Hyg., Biol.Abstr., Curr.Adv.Ecol.Sci., Curr.Cont., Excerp.Med., Helminthol.Abstr., Ind.Med., Nutr.Abstr., Rice Abstr., So.Pac.Per.Ind., Trop.Dis.Bull.
—BLDSC shelfmark: 9056.060000.
Description: Publishes contributions on the prevention, management and treatment of prevalent diseases in developing countries and on the promotion of health.

616.988 JA ISSN 0041-3267
TROPICAL MEDICINE/NETTAI IGAKU. (Text in English and Japanese) 1959. q. exchange basis only. Nagasaki Daigaku, Nettai Igaku Kenkyujo - Nagasaki University, Institute of Tropical Medicine, 12-4 Sakamoto-machi, Nagasaki 852, Japan. Ed.Bd. abstr.; charts; illus.; index; circ. 450. Indexed: Abstr.Hyg., Biol.Abstr., Excerp.Med., Helminthol.Abstr., Ind.Vet., Protozool.Abstr., Rev.Appl.Entomol., Trop.Dis.Bull., Vet.Bull.
Formerly: Endemic Diseases Bulletin of Nagasaki University.

616.988 US ISSN 0041-3275
RC960 CODEN: TMHNAT
TROPICAL MEDICINE AND HYGIENE NEWS. 1952. bi-m. membership. American Society of Tropical Medicine and Hygiene (Washington), 6436 31st St., N.W., Washington, DC 20015. TEL 301-496-6721. FAX 202-362-6094. Ed. Dr. Karl A. Western. bk.rev.; circ. 2,400. Indexed: Abstr.Hyg., Biol.Abstr., Helminthol.Abstr., Protozool.Abstr., Trop.Dis.Bull.

616.988 574.524 GW ISSN 0177-2392
CODEN: TMPAEY
TROPICAL MEDICINE AND PARASITOLOGY. (Summaries in English and German) 1949. q. DM.260. (Deutsche Tropenmedizinische Gesellschaft) Georg Thieme Verlag, Ruedigerstr. 14, Postfach 104853, 7000 Stuttgart 10, Germany. TEL 0711-8931-0. FAX 0711-8931298. Ed.Bd. adv.; bk.rev.; abstr.; bibl.; charts; illus.; index; circ. 900. (reprint service avail. from UMI) Indexed: Abstr.Hyg., ASCA, Biol.Abstr., Biotech.Abstr., Chem.Abstr., Curr.Adv.Ecol.Sci., Curr.Cont., Dairy Sci.Abstr., Dent.Ind., Excerp.Med., Helminthol.Abstr., Ind.Med., Ind.Vet., Nutr.Abstr., Pig News & Info., Protozool.Abstr., Rev.Appl.Entomol., Sci.Cit.Ind., Trop.Dis.Bull., Vet.Bull.
—BLDSC shelfmark: 9056.405000.
Former titles: Tropenmedizin und Parasitologie (ISSN 0303-4208) & Zeitschrift fuer Tropenmedizin und Parasitologie (ISSN 0044-359X)

616.9 TH
TROPMED SEMINARS ON TROPICAL MEDICINE. PROCEEDINGS. (Text in English) irreg., no.29, 1986. $10. Southeast Asian Ministers of Education Organisation (SEAMEO), Regional Tropical Medicine & Public Health Project (TROPMED), 420-6 Rajvithi Road, Bangkok 10400, Thailand. circ. 500.
Former titles: Tropmed Seminars on Parasitology and Tropical Medicine. Proceedings; Southeast Asian Seminar on Parasitology and Tropical Medicine. Proceedings (ISSN 0085-6517)

616.2 616.994
616.998 JA
TUBERCULOSIS, LEPROSY AND CANCER. (Text in English) 1949, q. exchange basis. Tohoku Daigaku, Kosankinbyo Kenkyujo - Tohoku University, Research Institute for Tuberculosis, Leprosy, and Cancer, 4-12 Hirose-machi, Sendai 980, Japan.

610 US
U.S. ARMY MEDICAL RESEARCH INSTITUTE OF INFECTIOUS DISEASES. ANNUAL PROGRESS REPORT.. 1968. a. free. U.S. Army Medical Research Institute of Infectious Diseases, Fort Detrick, Frederick, MD 21701. TEL 301-663-8000. (Orders to: NTIS, Springfield, VA 22151) Ed. K. Kenyon. Key Title: Annual Progress Report - U.S. Army Medical Research Institute of Infectious Diseases.

616.9 US
U.S. CENTERS FOR DISEASE CONTROL. DIPHTHERIA SURVEILLANCE REPORT. 1962. irreg. U.S. Centers for Disease Control, Dept. of Health and Human Services, 1600 Clifton Rd., NE, Atlanta, GA 30333. TEL 404-329-3311. charts; stat. (looseleaf format)

616.998 US
U.S. CENTERS FOR DISEASE CONTROL. LEPROSY SURVEILLANCE REPORT. 1970. irreg., no.2, 1972. U.S. Centers for Disease Control, Dept. of Health and Human Services, 1600 Clifton Rd., N.E., Atlanta, GA 30333. TEL 404-329-3311. charts; stat.

616.9 US
U.S. CENTERS FOR DISEASE CONTROL. LISTERIOSIS SURVEILLANCE REPORT. irreg. U.S. Centers for Disease Control, Dept. of Health and Human Services, 1600 Clifton Rd., N.E., Atlanta, GA 30333. TEL 404-329-3311. charts; stat.

616.9 US ISSN 0501-8390
U.S. CENTERS FOR DISEASE CONTROL. MALARIA SURVEILLANCE REPORT. 1955. a. free. U.S. Centers for Disease Control, Dept. of Health and Human Services, 1600 Clifton Rd., N.E., Atlanta, GA 30333. TEL 404-329-3311. Ed. Dr. Myron G. Schultz. circ. 2,000.

VIROLOGY. see *BIOLOGY — Microbiology*

VIROLOGY MONOGRAPHS/VIRUSFORSCHUNG IN EINZELDARSTELLUNGEN. see *BIOLOGY — Microbiology*

VIRUS/UIRUSU. see *BIOLOGY — Microbiology*

616.9 UN ISSN 1011-5773
CODEN: WASEEA
W H O AIDS SERIES. (Editions in English, French, Spanish) 1988. irreg. World Health Organization, Distribution and Sales, 1211 Geneva 27, Switzerland. TEL 022-791-2111. circ. 4,000.
—BLDSC shelfmark: 9311.596000.
Description: Features documents and reports issued by the WHO Global Programme on AIDS.

WEEKLY EPIDEMIOLOGICAL RECORD. see *PUBLIC HEALTH AND SAFETY*

616.9 US
WISCONSIN A I D S UPDATE. m? Department of Health and Social Services, Division of Health, Box 309, Madison, WI 53702. TEL 608-267-5287.

614.8 US
WORD AND DEED. 1976. m. American Leprosy Missions International, 1 ALM Way, Greenville, SC 29601. TEL 803-271-7040. FAX 803-271-7062. Ed. James A. Gittings. circ. 70,000. (tabloid format; back issues avail.)
Formerly: Crossways.
Description: News and features on the international effort to fight leprosy.

616.9 US ISSN 0743-9261
RC109 CODEN: YBIDEK
YEAR BOOK OF INFECTIOUS DISEASES. 1986. a. $57.95. Mosby - Year Book, Inc. (Chicago) (Subsidiary of: Times Mirror Company), 200 N. LaSalle St., Chicago, IL 60601-1080. TEL 312-726-9733. FAX 312-726-6075. TELEX 206155. Ed. Dr. Sheldon M. Wolfe. illus.
●Also available online. Vendor(s): BRS.
—BLDSC shelfmark: 9413.450000.

610 KO
YONSEI REPORTS ON TROPICAL MEDICINE. (Text in English) 1970. a. exchange basis. Yonsei University, College of Medicine, C.P.O. Box 8044, Seoul, S. Korea. Ed. Chin-Thack Soh. adv.; abstr.; bibl.; charts; stat. (tabloid format) Indexed: Biol.Abstr., Excerp.Med., Protozool.Abstr.

616.96 574.524 GW ISSN 0934-8840
QR46 CODEN: ZEBAE8
ZENTRALBLATT FUER BAKTERIOLOGIE. irreg. (4 nos./vol.). DM.405 per no. Gustav Fischer Verlag, Wollgrasweg 49, Postfach 720143, 7000 Stuttgart 70, Germany. TEL 0711-458030. FAX 0711-4580334. TELEX 7111488-FIBUCH. (U.S. address: Gustav Fischer New York Inc., 220 East 23rd St., Ste. 909, New York, NY 10010) Ed. G. Henneberg. (also avail. in microfilm from VCI) Indexed: Biol.Abstr., Chem.Abstr., Dent.Ind., Helminthol.Abstr., Ind.Med., Poult.Abstr., Rev.Appl.Entomol.
—BLDSC shelfmark: 9500.970000.
Formerly: Zentralblatt fuer Bakteriologie, Parasitenkunde, Infektionskrankheiten und Hygiene. Series A: Medizinische Mikrobiologie und Parasitologie (ISSN 0174-3031)

MEDICAL SCIENCES — Computer Applications

ADVANCES IN CONNECTIONIST AND NEURAL COMPUTATION THEORY. see *COMPUTERS — Artificial Intelligence*

ADVANCES IN CONTROL NETWORKS AND LARGE SCALE PARALLEL DISTRIBUTED PROCESSING MODELS. see *COMPUTERS — Artificial Intelligence*

ADVANCES IN ECHO-CONTRAST. see *MEDICAL SCIENCES*

001.535 610 NE ISSN 0933-3657
CODEN: AIMEEW
ARTIFICIAL INTELLIGENCE IN MEDICINE. 1989. bi-m. fl.316 (effective 1992). Elsevier Science Publishers B.V., P.O. Box 211, 1000 AC Amsterdam, Netherlands. TEL 020-5803911. FAX 020-5803598. TELEX 18582 ESPA NL. (Subscr. in U.S. and Canada to: Elsevier Science Publishing Co., Inc., Box 882, Madison Sq. Sta., New York, NY 10159. TEL 212-989-5800) Eds. D.G. Bobrow, M. Brady. adv.; bk.rev.; circ. 1,500. (back issues avail.) Indexed: Excerp.Med. (1992-).
—BLDSC shelfmark: 1735.036800.
Description: Publishes original articles from a wide variety of interdisciplinary perspectives concerning the theory and practice of medical artificial intelligence.
Refereed Serial

MEDICAL SCIENCES — COMPUTER APPLICATIONS

610 001.6   US   ISSN 0095-0963
R858.A1   CODEN: AUMDC9
AUTOMEDICA; a multinational journal for automation in the medical sciences. 1974. 4/yr. (in 1 vol.). $245. Gordon and Breach Science Publishers, 270 Eighth Ave., New York, NY 10011. TEL 212-206-8900. FAX 212-645-2459. TELEX 236735 GOPUB UR. (Subscr. to: Box 786, Cooper Sta., New York, NY 10276. TEL 800-545-8398; UK subscr. to: P.O. Box 90, Reading, Berkshire RG1 8JL. TEL 0734-560-080) Ed. Barry W. Hyndman. adv.; bk.rev.; abstr.; bibl.; charts; illus.; index, cum.index. (also avail. in microform from MIM) **Indexed:** Bioeng.Abstr., Biol.Abstr., Chem.Abstr., Comput.Cont., Comput.Rev., Sci.Abstr.
—BLDSC shelfmark: 1831.770000.
Refereed Serial

610   UK   ISSN 0265-5217
BRITISH JOURNAL OF HEALTHCARE COMPUTING. 1984. 10/yr. £45 (foreign £50). B.J.H.C., 45 Woodland Grove, Weybridge, Surrey KT13 9EQ, England. FAX 0932-820305. Ed. Peter Brown. adv.; circ. 13,000.

COGNITIVE BRAIN RESEARCH. see *MEDICAL SCIENCES — Psychiatry And Neurology*

610.28 616   NE   ISSN 0169-2607
CODEN: CMPBEK
COMPUTER METHODS & PROGRAMS IN BIOMEDICINE; an international journal devoted to the development, implementation and exchange of computing methodology and software systems in biomedical research and medical practice. 1970. 12/yr. (in 3 vols.; 4 nos./vol.). fl.1272 (effective 1992). Elsevier Science Publishers B.V., P.O. Box 211, 1000 AE Amsterdam, Netherlands. TEL 020-5803911. FAX 020-5803598. TELEX 18582 ESPA NL. (Subscr. in U.S. and Canada to: Elsevier Science Publishing Co., Inc., Box 882, Madison Sq. Sta., New York, NY 10159. TEL 212-989-5800) Ed. W. Schneider. bk.rev.; charts. (also avail. in microform from RPI) **Indexed:** Biol.Abstr., Compumath, Comput.& Contr.Abstr., Curr.Adv.Ecol.Sci., Curr.Cont., Cyb.Abstr., Excerp.Med., Ind.Med., Ind.Sci.Rev., INSPEC, Sci.Abstr., Sci.Cit.Ind., Telegen.
—BLDSC shelfmark: 3394.095000.
Incorporates: Journal of Biomedical Measurement Informatics and Control; Formerly (until 1985): Computer Programs in Biomedicine (ISSN 0010-468X)
Description: For all life science researchers, clinicians, statisticians, health scientists, computer scientists, programmers and bio-engineers, engaged in applying and teaching biomedical information processing.
Refereed Serial

610   US   ISSN 0895-6111
CODEN: CMIGEY
COMPUTERIZED MEDICAL IMAGING AND GRAPHICS; the international journal on imaging and image archiving in all medical specialties. 1977. bi-m. £285 (effective 1992). Pergamon Press, Inc., Journals Division, 660 White Plains Rd., Tarrytown, NY 10591-5153. TEL 914-524-9200. FAX 914-333-2444. (And: Headington Hill Hall, Oxford OX3 0BW, England. TEL 0865-794141) Ed. Robert S. Ledley. adv.; circ. 1,500. (also avail. in microform from MIM,UMI) **Indexed:** Biol.Abstr., Comput.Cont., Curr.Cont., Dent.Ind., Excerp.Med., Ind.Med., Ind.Sci.Rev., INIS Atomind., Protozool.Abstr., Sci.Abstr., Sci.Cit.Ind.
—BLDSC shelfmark: 3394.586000.
Former titles (until 1988): Computerized Radiology (ISSN 0730-4862); (until 1982): Computerized Tomography (ISSN 0363-8235)
Refereed Serial

610.28 001.6   US   ISSN 0010-4809
CODEN: CBMRB7
COMPUTERS AND BIOMEDICAL RESEARCH. 1969. bi-m. $175 (foreign $221). (American Medical Informatics Association) Academic Press, Inc., Journal Division, 1250 Sixth Ave., San Diego, CA 92101. TEL 619-230-1840. FAX 619-699-6800. TELEX 181726. Ed. Homer R. Warner. adv.; charts; illus. (back issues avail.) **Indexed:** Abstr.Hyg., Anim.Breed.Abstr., Appl.Mech.Rev., Biol.Abstr., Biostat., Chem.Abstr., Compumath, Comput.Cont., Comput.Rev., Curr.Adv.Ecol.Sci., Curr.Cont., Excerp.Med., Ind.Med., Ind.Sci.Rev., Ind.Vet., INIS Atomind., Risk Abstr., Sci.Abstr., Sci.Cit.Ind., Trop.Dis.Bull., Vet.Bull.
—BLDSC shelfmark: 3394.660000.
Description: Provides researchers with current information concerning the use of computers in biomedicine.
Refereed Serial

610 001.6   US   ISSN 0163-0547
CODEN: CMPMDI
COMPUTERS AND MEDICINE (GLENCOE). 1972. m. $117. Medical Group News Inc., Box 36, Glencoe, IL 60022. TEL 708-446-3100. Ed. Carol Brierly. adv.; bk.rev.; charts; illus.; cum.index; circ. 4,000. (back issues avail.) **Indexed:** Comput.Lit.Ind., LAMP, Sci.Abstr.
—BLDSC shelfmark: 3394.740000.
Description: For medical personnel interested in computer applications. Articles cover current computer technology in medicine, medical education, practice management, and hospitals.

610.28 574   US   ISSN 0010-4825
R858.A1   CODEN: CBMDAW
COMPUTERS IN BIOLOGY AND MEDICINE. 1971. 6/yr. £275 (effective 1992). Pergamon Press, Inc., Journals Division, 660 White Plains Rd., Tarrytown, NY 10591-5153. TEL 914-524-9200. FAX 914-333-2444. (And: Headington Hill Hall, Oxford OX3 0BW, England. TEL 0865-794141) Ed. R.S. Ledley. adv.; bk.rev.; circ. 1,200. (also avail. in microform from MIM,UMI; back issues avail.) **Indexed:** Anim.Breed.Abstr., Appl.Mech.Rev., Bioeng.Abstr., Biol.Abstr., Biostat., Chem.Abstr., Compumath, Comput.Abstr., Comput.Cont., Comput.Dtbs., Curr.Adv.Ecol.Sci., Curr.Cont., Eng.Ind., Excerp.Med., Ind.Med., Ind.Sci.Rev., Risk Abstr., Sci.Abstr., Sci.Cit.Ind., Telegen.
—BLDSC shelfmark: 3394.880000.
Refereed Serial

621.3 616   US   ISSN 0276-6574
RC683.5.D36   CODEN: COCADX
COMPUTERS IN CARDIOLOGY. 1974. a. price varies. (Institute of Electrical and Electronics Engineers, Inc.) I E E E Computer Society Press, 10662 Los Vaqueros Circle, Los Alamitos, CA 90720-1264. TEL 714-821-8380. FAX 714-821-4010. (Co-sponsors: U.S. National Institutes of Health; European Society of Cardiology) **Indexed:** Sci.Abstr.
—BLDSC shelfmark: 3394.895000.
Description: Presents topics of mutual interest to computer scientists and cardiologists.

610 658   US   ISSN 0745-1075
COMPUTERS IN HEALTHCARE. 1980. m. $29 (foreign $42). Cardiff Publishing Co., 6300 S. Syracuse Way, Ste. 650, Englewood, CO 80111. TEL 303-220-0600. (Subscr. to: Box 6228, Duluth, MN 55806) Ed. Michael Stefanchik. adv.; bk.rev.; charts; illus.; stat.; circ. 17,545. (also avail. in microfiche; reprint service avail. from UMI) **Indexed:** ABI Inform., Abstr.Health Care Manage.Stud., Comput.Cont., Comput.Dtbs., I.P.A., Sci.Abstr.
●Also available online. Vendor(s): DIALOG.
—BLDSC shelfmark: 3394.920500.
Formerly (until 1982): Computers in Hospitals (ISSN 0274-631X)
Description: For healthcare systems professionals. Features articles on systems applications for hospitals and other health facilities.

610   US   ISSN 0736-8593
COMPUTERS IN NURSING. Abbreviated title: C I N. bi-m. $35 to individuals (foreign $45); institutions $70 (foreign $90). J.B. Lippincott Co., E. Washington Sq., Philadelphia, PA 19105. TEL 215-238-4200. Ed. Gary D. Hales. adv.; illus.; index.; circ. 6,000. (also avail. in microform from UMI) **Indexed:** CINAHL, Ind.Med., Int.Nurs.Ind., Nurs.Abstr.
—BLDSC shelfmark: 3394.925500.

610 621.381   US   ISSN 0739-6201
COMPUTERTALK DIRECTORY OF MEDICAL COMPUTER SYSTEMS. 1983. 3/yr. $50. ComputerTalk Associates, Inc., 482 Norristown Rd., Ste. 112, Blue Bell, PA 19422. TEL 215-825-7686. FAX 215-825-7641. Ed. Neil R. Bauman. adv.; circ. 195,521. (back issues avail.)
Formerly: ComputerTalk Directory of Medical Systems.
Description: A compilation of information on available medical computer systems. Information contained in product profiles written by vendors. Features articles on the applications of computer systems to medical practices.

COMPUTERTALK FOR THE PHARMACIST. see *PHARMACY AND PHARMACOLOGY*

COMPUTERTALK PHARMACY SYSTEMS BUYERS GUIDE. see *PHARMACY AND PHARMACOLOGY*

610 621.381
001.642   US
CYBERLOG; library of applied medical software. 1985. q. $99.95 per program (includes text and software). Cardinal Health Systems, Inc., 4600 W. 77th St., Ste. 150, Edina, MN 55435. TEL 800-328-0180. FAX 612-835-7141. Ed.Bd.
Description: Library and interactive software for physicians. Each program is devoted to a single topic, presented by prominent experts and organizations.

610   US
DECISIONS IN IMAGING ECONOMICS. q. Curant Communications, Inc., 1849 Sawtelle Blvd., Ste. 770, Los Angeles, CA 90025-7012. TEL 213-479-1769. FAX 213-479-6275. Ed. Roger Backlar. circ. 40,000.

610 621.381 617.6   US   ISSN 0738-9744
DENTAL COMPUTER NEWSLETTER. 1978. bi-m. $20. Andent, Inc., 1000 North Ave., Waukegan, IL 60085. TEL 708-223-5077. Ed. E.J. Neiburger. adv.; bk.rev.; illus.; circ. 2,800. **Indexed:** LAMP.
Description: For dentists and other medical practitioners interested in office computers. Offers notes on hardware, software, peripherals and integration with office personnel.

610   US
DENTISTS' COMPUTER NEWS. 1981. 12/yr. Charles Mann & Associates, Microcomputer Division, 55888 Yucca Trail, Box 2080, Yucca Valley, CA 92286-2080. TEL 619-365-9718. Ed. Ray Burr. bk.rev.; circ. 100,000.

610   US
HEALTHCARE INFORMATICS. 1984. m. $24. Health Data Analysis, Inc., Box 2830, Evergreen, CO 80439-2830. TEL 303-674-2774. Ed. Bill W. Childs. adv.; circ. 28,000 (controlled).
Former titles (until Jan. 1990): U S Healthcare; (until Aug. 1988): Healthcare Computing and Communications.
Description: Features on computer and communications for the healthcare field. Contains articles on new products, applications and systems market for healthcare administrators and medical professionals.

610 001.6   US
I E E E ENGINEERING IN MEDICINE AND BIOLOGY SOCIETY. INTERNATIONAL CONFERENCE. 1979. a. price varies. (I E E E, Engineering in Medicine and Biology Society) Institute of Electrical and Electronics Engineers, Inc., 345 E. 47th St., New York, NY 10017-2394. TEL 212-705-7900. FAX 212-705-7682. (Subscr. to: Box 1331, 445 Hoes Lane, Piscataway, NJ 08855-1331)
Former titles: I E E E Engineering in Medicine and Biology Society. Conference; (until 1984): Frontiers of Engineering and Computing in Health Care; Which was formed by the merger of (1981-1982): I E E E Frontiers of Computers in Medicine; (1979-1982): I E E E Frontiers of Engineering in Health Care.

610   US   ISSN 1048-0501
INTERACTIVE HEALTHCARE NEWSLETTER. 1985. m. $70 to non-members. Stewart Publishing Inc., 6471 Merrit Ct., Alexandria, VA 22312. TEL 703-354-8155. FAX 703-354-8155. Ed. Scott Alan Stewart.
Formerly (until 1989): MedicalDisc Reporter (ISSN 0882-4665)
Description: Covers the use of CD-ROM, DVI, and related technology in the health sciences.

MEDICAL SCIENCES — DENTISTRY

610 574 IE ISSN 0020-7101
CODEN: IJBCBT
INTERNATIONAL JOURNAL OF BIO-MEDICAL COMPUTING. 1970. 8/yr. (in 2 vols.; 4 nos./vol.). $425 (effective 1992). Elsevier Scientific Publishers Ireland Ltd., P.O. Box 85, Limerick, Ireland. TEL 061-61944. FAX 061-62144. TELEX 72191 ENH EI. (Subscr. in U.S. and Canada to: Elsevier Science Publishing Co., Inc. Box 882, Madison Sq. Sta., New York, NY 10159. TEL 212-989-5800) Eds. J.G. Llaurado, A. Hasman. charts; illus.; index. **Indexed:** Biol.Abstr., Biostat., Chem.Abstr., Compumath, Comput.Cont., Comput.Rev., Curr.Adv.Ecol.Sci., Curr.Cont., Excerp.Med., Ind.Med., Math.R., Sci.Abstr., Sci.Cit.Ind.
—BLDSC shelfmark: 4542.152000.
 Description: For those working in computing apppplied to the medical and life sciences.
Refereed Serial

INTERNATIONAL JOURNAL OF CLINICAL MONITORING AND COMPUTING. see *MEDICAL SCIENCES — Anaesthesiology*

610 US ISSN 0090-1091
CODEN: JCLCB
JOURNAL OF CLINICAL COMPUTING. 1971. bi-m. $30. Journal of Clinical Computing, Inc., 166 Morris Ave., Buffalo, NY 14214. Ed. E.R. Gabrielle. adv.; bk.rev.; circ. 700. (back issues avail.) **Indexed:** Comput.Cont., Cyb.Abstr., Excerp.Med., Sci.Abstr.
—BLDSC shelfmark: 4958.387000.

610 001.6 US ISSN 0148-5598
R858.A1 CODEN: JMSYDA
JOURNAL OF MEDICAL SYSTEMS. 1977. bi-m. $275 (foreign $320)(effective 1992). Plenum Publishing Corp., 233 Spring St., New York, NY 10013-1578. TEL 212-620-8000. FAX 212-463-0742. TELEX 23-421139. Ed. Dr. Ralph R. Grams. adv. (also avail. in microfilm from JSC; back issues avail.) **Indexed:** Biol.Abstr., CINAHL, Curr.Cont., Excerp.Med., Ind.Med., INIS Atomind., Med.Care Rev.
—BLDSC shelfmark: 5017.088000.
Refereed Serial

610 621.381 US ISSN 0738-8772
LABORATORY COMPUTER LETTER.* Variant title: L C L. 1981. 11/yr. $124 includes hotline consulting. Information Research, 15401 Cambay Lane, Huntington Beach, CA 92649. Ed. Phillip Good. bk.rev.; circ. 500.
 Description: For laboratory research executives, scientists, and health-care professionals. Provides evaluations and up-to-date information on micro-computer hardware and software for the laboratory.

610 621.381 US ISSN 0724-6811
R858.A1
M.D. COMPUTING (NEW YORK); computers in medical practice. 1983. 6/yr. $99. (American Association for Medical Systems and Informatics) Springer-Verlag, Journals, 175 Fifth Ave., New York, NY 10010. TEL 212-460-1500. Ed. W.V. Slack. adv. (also avail. in microfiche from UMI; reprint service avail. from ISI) **Indexed:** Comput.Dtbs., Comput.Lit.Ind., Curr.Cont., Excerp.Med., Ind.Med., Microcomp.Ind., Sci.Abstr.
—BLDSC shelfmark: 5413.509920.
 Supersedes (in July 1985): Medical Computer Journal; Formerly: Medcomp: Computers in Medicine.
 Description: Articles cover various uses of microcomputing in the medical field - from software to clinical applications.

M U M P S COMPUTING. (Massachusetts General Hospital Utility Multi-Programming System) see *COMPUTERS — Computer Programming*

M U M P S NEWS. (Massachusetts General Hospital Utility Multi-Programming Systems) see *COMPUTERS — Computer Programming*

610 UK ISSN 0307-7640
CODEN: MINFDZ
MEDICAL INFORMATICS/MEDECINE ET INFORMATIQUE. 1976. q. £144($249) Taylor and Francis Ltd., Rankine Rd., Basingstoke, Hants RG24 0PR, England. TEL 0256-840366. FAX 0256-479438. TELEX 858540. Ed. J.A. Newell. adv.; bk.rev. (back issues avail.) **Indexed:** Art.Int.Abstr., Biol.Abstr., CAD CAM Abstr., CINAHL, Comput.Lit.Ind., Curr.Cont., Excerp.Med., Helminthol.Abstr., Hosp.Lit.Ind., Ind.Med., Sci.Abstr.
—BLDSC shelfmark: 5527.553000.
 Description: Serves not only as a focus for most aspects of the application of computers to medicine, but promotes the application of analysis, inference and reasoning to medical information.
Refereed Serial

610 US
▼**MEDICAL INTELLIGENCE.** 1990. 12/yr. $745 in US and Canada; elsewhere $900. Gallifrey Publishing, Box 155, Vicksburg, MI 49097.
TEL 616-649-3772. Ed. Dr. Derek F. Stubbs.
 Description: For investors and researchers exploring the interrelationships between medicine and technology and current and future advances in medical therapy.

MEDICAL SOFTWARE DIRECTORY. see *COMPUTERS — Software*

610 IT
MEDICINA E INFORMATICA. (Text in Italian; summaries in English) 1984. 4/yr. L.50000($180) to individuals; institutions L.80000. Pensiero Scientifico Editore s.r.l., Via Panama 48, 00198 Rome, Italy. TEL 06 855-36-33. Eds. Amedeo Mencuccini, Sergio I. Magalini. adv.; bk.rev.; bibl.; circ. 2,000.

610 US
MICRO M D NEWSLETTER.* 1983. 12/yr. Micro M D Publishing, 170 University Ave. W, Waterloo, Ontario, Canada N2L 3E9. Ed. Terry Polevoy. adv.; bk.rev.; circ. 1,500.
●Also available online. Vendor(s): CompuServe Consumer Information Service, NewsNet.
 Formerly: Micro M D Journal.

610 621.381 US
MICRO MEDICAL NEWSLETTER. 1981. 12/yr. Charles Mann & Associates, Microcomputer Division, 55888 Yucca Trail, Box 2080, Yucca Valley, CA 92286-2080. TEL 619-365-9718. Ed. Ray Burr. bk.rev.; circ. 101,712.

610 US ISSN 0748-2051
MICROPSYCH NETWORK; computer applications in psychology. 1985. bi-m. $20 (foreign $30). (Professional Resource Exchange, Inc.) Human Technology Interface, Ink Press, 163 Wood Wedge Way, Sanford, NC 27330. Ed. Emory Sadler. adv.; bk.rev.; circ. 500. (back issues avail.)
 Description: Publishes computer-related material that psychologists will find useful; articles about using computers in clinical practice, the classroom, and research laboratory, and reviews of software and original programs.

MONOGRAFIAS DE DIAGNOSTICO POR IMAGEN. see *MEDICAL SCIENCES — Radiology And Nuclear Medicine*

610 US ISSN 0273-4974
NATIONAL REPORT ON COMPUTERS AND HEALTH. 1980. 25/yr. $427. United Communications Group, 11300 Rockville Pike, Ste. 1100, Rockville, MD 20852-3030. TEL 301-816-8950. Ed. Bob Gough. (back issues avail.) **Indexed:** Tel.Alert.
●Also available online. Vendor(s): Data-Star, DIALOG.
 Description: Features articles pertaining to new software, technologies in the fast changing field of hospital data processing and clinical information systems.

NEURAL COMPUTATION. see *COMPUTERS — Artificial Intelligence*

610 330 US ISSN 0882-8075
NODE; for hackers with soul. 1985. q. $12. Performing Arts Social Society, Inc., Box 421713, San Francisco, CA 94102-9991. TEL 415-759-4625. FAX 415-759-2490. Ed. Eve Furchgott. adv.; bk.rev.; circ. 36,000.

610 US
PHYSICIANS & COMPUTERS. 1982. m. $24. Physicians & Computers, Inc., 2333 Waukegan Rd., Ste. S-280, Bannockburn, IL 60015. TEL 708-940-8333. Ed. Al Anderson. adv.; tr.lit.; circ. 90,000. (reprint service avail.)
 Description: For physicians who have little or no computer experience. Articles cover applications to office management and clinical medicine environment.

610 GW
PHYSIS MEDIZIN COMPUTER. 1984. q. DM.15. Urban und Vogel, Lindwurmstr. 95, Postfach 152209, 8000 Munich 2, Germany. TEL 089-53292-0. FAX 089-53292-100. circ. 20,000.
 Formerly: Physis Computer (ISSN 0935-994X)

610 011 FR
▼**REPERTOIRE INTERNATIONAL DES BANQUES DE DONNEES BIOMEDICALES.** 1991. a. 370 F. Editions F L A Consultants, 27 rue de la Vistule, 75013 Paris, France. TEL 1-45-82-75-75. FAX 1-45-82-46-04. TELEX 205 231 FLA.
 Description: A tool for better use and understanding of French and foreign biomedical databases.

651.8 US
S I G B I O NEWSLETTER. 1970. q. $28 to non-members; members $20. Association for Computing Machinery, Special Interest Group on Biomedical Computing, 1515 Broadway, 17th Fl., New York, NY 10036. TEL 212-869-7440. FAX 212-302-5826. Ed. Cathy Rubens. bk.rev.; circ. 1,000. **Indexed:** Sci.Abstr.

610 GW ISSN 0934-5841
SOFTWARE KURIER; fuer Mediziner und Psychologen. 1989. 6/yr. DM.98($72) Springer-Verlag, Journals, Heidelberger Platz 3, D-1000 Berlin 33, Germany. TEL 030-8207-1.
—BLDSC shelfmark: 8321.451640.

001.6 610 US ISSN 0195-4210
R858.A2 CODEN: PCMCDC
SYMPOSIUM ON COMPUTER APPLICATIONS IN MEDICAL CARE. PROCEEDINGS. 1977. a. $50. S C A M C, Inc., c/o American Medical Informatics Association, 4915 St. Elmo Ave., Ste. 302, Bethesda, MD 20814. TEL 301-657-1291. FAX 301-657-1296. circ. 3,000.
—BLDSC shelfmark: 1534.946800.
Refereed Serial

MEDICAL SCIENCES — Dentistry

617.6 BL
A B E S P BOLETIM. 1972. q. Cr.$200($13) Associacao Brasileira de Endodontia, Seccao Sao Paulo, Praca Amadeu Amaral 47-8, Sao Paulo, SP, Brazil. Ed. Antonio Elias Makaron. adv.; circ. 2,500 (controlled).

617.6 CN ISSN 0820-5949
A C F D FORUM. (Text mainly in English; occasionally in French) 1968. q. membership. Association of Canadian Faculties of Dentistry, Central Office, Ste. 109, Alta Vista Dr., Ottawa, Ont. K1G 3Y6, Canada. TEL 604-228-3413. FAX 604-228-6698. Ed. R.M. Shah. bk.rev.; circ. 700. (processed)
 Formerly: Association of Canadian Faculties of Dentistry. Newsletter (ISSN 0044-9555)

617.6 US ISSN 0001-0855
RK1
A D A NEWS. 1970. 24/yr. $16 to non-members. American Dental Association, 211 E. Chicago Ave., Chicago, IL 60611. TEL 312-440-2500. adv.; circ. 140,000. (also avail. in microform from UMI)

617.6 CN
A D A NEWSLETTER. 1967. irreg. membership. Alberta Dental Association, 209-1610 37th S.W., Calgary, Alta. T3C 3P1, Canada. Ed. Dr. John Aitken. adv.; circ. 1,375.
 Formerly: A D A News Information (ISSN 0383-6355)

MEDICAL SCIENCES — DENTISTRY

617.6   MX   ISSN 0001-0944
A D M. 1943. bi-m. $70. Asociacion Dental Mexicana, A.C., Ezequiel Montes No. 92, Col. Revolucion, Delegacion Cuauhtemoc, Mexico, D.F. 06030, Mexico. TEL 566-61-33. FAX 705-4629.
(Co-sponsor: Federacion Nacional de Colegios de Cirujanos Dentistas) Ed. Elias Grego Samra. adv.; abstr.; charts; illus.; circ. 3,000. **Indexed:** Chem.Abstr., Ind.Med., INIS Atomind.
—BLDSC shelfmark: 7802.195000.

617.6   US   ISSN 0194-729X
A G D IMPACT. 1973. 11/yr. $20 to individuals; institutions $32. Academy of General Dentistry, 211 E. Chicago Ave., Ste. 1200, Chicago, IL 60611. TEL 312-440-4300. FAX 312-440-0559. Ed. Dr. William W. Howard. adv.; illus.; circ. 33,000.
Description: Features issues, controversies, legislation and trends that affect the practice of general dentistry.

617.6   IT   ISSN 0001-1908
A M D I BOLLETTINO.* vol.16, 1970. m. Associazione Medici Dentisti Italiani, Via Savoia 78, Rome, Italy. Ed. Ermano Ricci. adv.; charts.

617.6   US   ISSN 0277-3619
RK58.5
A S D A HANDBOOK. a. $10 to non-members; members $5; foreign $25. American Student Dental Association, 211 E. Chicago Ave., Ste. 840, Chicago, IL 60611. TEL 312-440-2795. adv.; circ. 23,000.

617.6   US   ISSN 0277-3627
A S D A NEWS (YEAR). 1971. m. (Sep.-May). $10 to non-members (foreign $20). American Student Dental Association, 211 E. Chicago Ave., Chicago, IL 60611. TEL 312-440-2795. Ed. Lisa Coghlan. adv.; circ. 15,000. **Indexed:** Dent.Abstr., Dent.Ind.
Former titles (until 1981): New Dentist; (until 1979): A S D A News; A S D A Newsletter (ISSN 0044-8052)

617.6   US
ACCESS (CHICAGO). 10/yr. American Dental Hygienists Association, 444 N. Michigan Ave., Ste. 3400, Chicago, IL 60611. TEL 312-440-8929. FAX 312-440-8900. Ed. Rosetta Gervasi. circ. 30,000.

617.6 618.92   DR   ISSN 0252-1032
ACTA DE ODONTOLOGIA PEDIATRICA. (Text in English and Spanish) 1980. s-a. $15 (free to qualified personnel). Centro de Odontologia Pediatrica, Jose Joaquin Perez No. 101 - Zona 1, Apartado Postal 2753, Santo Domingo, Dominican Republic. Ed. Dr. Fredrico Garcia-Godoy. adv.; bk.rev.; circ. 2,300. **Indexed:** Dent.Ind., Ind.Med.
—BLDSC shelfmark: 0641.624000.

617.6   NO   ISSN 0001-6357
                 CODEN: AOSCAQ
ACTA ODONTOLOGICA SCANDINAVICA. Scandinavian dental research journal. (Text in English) 1939. bi-m. $160. Universitetsforlaget, P.O. Box 2959-Toeyen, N-0608 Oslo 6, Norway. (Dist. by: Publications Expediting Inc., 200 Meacham Ave., Elmont, NY 11003) Ed. Gunnar E. Carlsson. adv.; bibl.; charts; illus.; index; circ. 1,000. (also avail. in microform from UMI; reprint service avail. SWZ) **Indexed:** Abstr.Health Care Manage.Stud., Biol.Abstr., Chem.Abstr., Curr.Adv.Ecol.Sci., Curr.Cont., Dent.Ind., Excerp.Med., Ind.Med., Ind.Sci.Rev., INIS Atomind., Sci.Cit.Ind.
—BLDSC shelfmark: 0641.630000.

617.6   BE   ISSN 0001-7000
                 CODEN: ASBEBA
ACTA STOMATOLOGICA BELGICA. (Text in Flemish and French; summaries in English, Flemish, French and German) vol.67, 1970. 4/yr. 1800 Fr. (foreign 2000 Fr.)(effective 1992). Association des Societes Scientifiques Medicales Belges - Vereiniging van de Belgische Medische Wetenschappelijke Genootschappen, Av. Circulaire 138A, B-1180 Brussels, Belgium. TEL 02-374-5158. bk.rev.; abstr.; bibl.; illus.; index. **Indexed:** Biol.Abstr., Dent.Ind., Excerp.Med., Ind.Med.
—BLDSC shelfmark: 0663.380000.

617.6   CI   ISSN 0001-7019
ACTA STOMATOLOGICA CROATICA. (Text in Croatian or English; summaries in English) 1966. q. 2500 din.($30) Zbor Lijecnika Hrvatske, Subiceva 9, Zagreb, Croatia. Ed. Zdenko Njemirovskij. adv.; bk.rev.; charts; illus.; circ. 2,000. **Indexed:** Biol.Abstr., Dent.Ind.

617.6   FR   ISSN 0001-7817
                 CODEN: ACOPAR
ACTUALITES ODONTO-STOMATOLOGIQUES. (Summaries in English, German, Italian, Portuguese, Russian and Spanish) 1946. 4/yr. 228 F. to individuals; students 162 F. Groupe C D P, 77 rue de Richelieu, 75002 Paris, France. **Indexed:** Biol.Abstr., Chem.Abstr., Curr.Cont., Dent.Ind., Ind.Med.

617.6   US   ISSN 0091-729X
RK91
ADMISSION REQUIREMENTS OF U S AND CANADIAN DENTAL SCHOOLS. 1963. a. $20 to non-members; members $15. American Association of Dental Schools, 1625 Massachusetts Ave., N.W., Washington, DC 20036-2212. TEL 202-667-9433. circ. 3,000. (reprint service avail.)
Formerly: Admission Requirements of American Dental Schools (ISSN 0065-1990)

617.6   US   ISSN 0895-9374
ADVANCES IN DENTAL RESEARCH. (Suppl. to: Journal of Dental Research (ISSN 0022-0345)) 1987. irreg. (2-6/yr.). free to qualified personnel. (International Association for Dental Research) American Association for Dental Research, 1111 14th St., N.W., Ste. 1000, Washington, DC 20005. TEL 202-898-1050. FAX 202-789-1033. Ed. Dr. Arthur R. Hand. cum.index every 3 yrs.; circ. 3,000. (also avail. in microform from UMI; back issues avail.; reprint service avail. from UMI) **Indexed:** Biol.Abstr., Chem.Abstr., Curr.Cont., Dairy Sci.Abstr., Dent.Abstr., Dent.Ind., Excerp.Med., Ind.Med., Ind.Sci.Rev., Met.Abstr., Nutr.Abstr., Sci.Cit.Ind., World Alum.Abstr.
—BLDSC shelfmark: 0704.242200.
Description: Proceedings of conferences, symposia, and workshops devoted to dental research.

617.6   JA   ISSN 0044-6912
                 CODEN: AGDSAB
AICHI-GAKUIN JOURNAL OF DENTAL SCIENCE. (Text in Japanese; summaries in English) 1964. q. 5000 Yen($20) per no. Aichi-Gakuin Society of Dental Science, School of Dentistry, Aichi-Gakuin University, 1-100 Kusumoto-cho, Chikusa-ku, Nagoya 464, Japan. Ed. Takuro Sakai. adv.; bk.rev.; abstr.; charts; stat.; circ. 4,000. **Indexed:** Biol.Abstr., Dent.Ind.
—BLDSC shelfmark: 0773.074200.

617.6   US   ISSN 0002-3701
AKRON DENTAL SOCIETY. BULLETIN. vol.29, 1970. 8/yr. $40 (foreign $60). Akron Dental Society, 440 Grant St., Akron, OH 44311. TEL 216-376-3551. Ed. James L. Colopy. adv.; circ. 450.

617.6   US   ISSN 0002-4198
ALABAMA DENTAL ASSOCIATION. JOURNAL. 1917. q. $24 (foreign $35). Alabama Dental Association, 3915 Old Shell Rd., Mobile, AL 36608. TEL 205-342-6410. Ed. Dr. John H. Mosteller. adv.; bk.rev.; bibl.; charts; illus.; circ. 1,650. (also avail. in microform from UMI; reprint service avail. from UMI) **Indexed:** Dent.Abstr., Dent.Ind.
—BLDSC shelfmark: 4683.030000.

617.6   UA
ALEXANDRIA DENTAL JOURNAL/MAGALLAT AL-ISKANDIRIYYAH LI-TIBB AL-ASNAN. vol.14, 1989. q. Alexandria University, Faculty of Dentistry, 22 Sharia al-Gaish, Al-Shatby, Alexandria, Egypt.

617.6   US   ISSN 0002-6417
ALPHA OMEGAN. 1908. q. $40. Alpha Omega International Fraternity, 347 Fifth Ave., New York, NY 10016. TEL 212-683-4155. FAX 212-683-0027. Ed. Dr. Roger Scott. adv.; bk.rev.; circ. 8,000. (back issues avail.)
—BLDSC shelfmark: 0802.091000.

617.6   US
AMERICAN ASSOCIATION FOR DENTAL AESTHETICS NEWSLETTER. 1980. s-a. membership. American Association for Dental Aesthetics, 635 Madison Ave., New York, NY 10022. TEL 212-371-4575. Ed. Michael M. Friedman. circ. 3,000 (controlled).
Description: Covers porcelain laminates, bonding, new dental materials and techniques presented on the post graduate level of advanced dentistry.

617.6   US   ISSN 0002-7421
AMERICAN ASSOCIATION OF DENTAL EXAMINERS. BOARD BULLETIN. 1965. q. $10. American Association of Dental Examiners, 211 E. Chicago Ave., Ste. 844, Chicago, IL 60611. TEL 312-440-7464. FAX 312-440-7494. Ed. Kathleen Kelly. illus.; circ. 1,100 (controlled).

617.6   US
AMERICAN ASSOCIATION OF WOMEN DENTISTS. CHRONICLE. 1964. 6/yr. $12. American Association of Women Dentists, 401 N. Michigan Ave., Chicago, IL 60611-4267. TEL 312-644-6610. Ed. Dr. Rhona Gissen-Stanley. adv.; bk.rev.; circ. 2,200 (controlled).
Former titles (until 1980): American Association of Women Dentists. Journal; (until 1978): Association of American Women Dentists. Newsletter.

617.6   US   ISSN 0002-7979
RK1
AMERICAN COLLEGE OF DENTISTS. JOURNAL. 1934. q. $30. American College of Dentists, 839-J Quince Orchard Blvd., Gaithersburg, MD 20878. TEL 301-986-0555. FAX 301-654-3275. Ed. Keith P. Blair. bk.rev.; index; circ. 4,600. (also avail. in microform from UMI; reprint service avail. from UMI) **Indexed:** Curr.Tit.Dent., Dent.Abstr., Dent.Ind., Ind.Med.
—BLDSC shelfmark: 4685.700000.
Refereed Serial

617.6   US   ISSN 0002-8177
RK1   CODEN: JADSAY
AMERICAN DENTAL ASSOCIATION. JOURNAL. 1913. m. $45 to non-members. A D A Publishers, Inc., 211 E. Chicago Ave., Chicago, IL 60611. TEL 312-440-2500. Ed. Dr. Lawrence Meskin. adv.; charts; illus.; tr.lit.; s-a. index; circ. 140,000. (also avail. in microform from UMI; reprint service avail. from UMI) **Indexed:** Abstr.Health Care Manage.Stud., Behav.Med.Abstr., Biol.Abstr., C.I.S.Abstr., Chem.Abstr., Curr.Adv.Ecol.Sci., Curr.Cont., Curr.Tit.Dent., Dent.Abstr., Dent.Ind., Dok.Arbeitsmed., Helminthol.Abstr., Hosp.Lit.Ind., Ind.Med., INIS Atomind., Med.Care Rev., NRN, Nutr.Abstr.
—BLDSC shelfmark: 4686.075000.
Refereed Serial

617.6   US
AMERICAN DENTAL ASSOCIATION. TRANSACTION SERIES: ANNUAL REPORTS AND RESOLUTIONS, SUPPLEMENTS ONE AND TWO, TRANSACTIONS. a. price varies. American Dental Association, 211 E. Chicago Ave., Chicago, IL 60611. TEL 312-440-2500.
Formerly: American Dental Association. Annual Reports and Resolutions (ISSN 0090-3329)

617.6   US   ISSN 0065-8073
RK37
AMERICAN DENTAL DIRECTORY. 1947. a. $100. American Dental Association, 211 E. Chicago Ave., Chicago, IL 60611. TEL 312-440-2500.

617.643   US   ISSN 0889-5406
RK1   CODEN: AJOOEB
AMERICAN JOURNAL OF ORTHODONTICS AND DENTOFACIAL ORTHOPEDICS. French edition (ISSN 1145-0541) 1915. m. $69 to individuals (foreign $91); institutions $141 (foreign $163); students $34 (foreign $56). (American Association of Orthodontists) Mosby - Year Book, Inc. (Subsidiary of: Times Mirror Company), 11830 Westline Industrial Dr., St. Louis, MO 63146. TEL 800-325-4117. FAX 314-432-1380. TELEX 44-2402. (Co-sponsor: American Board of Orthodontics) Ed. T.M. Graber, D.M.D. adv.; s-a. index; circ. 15,589. (also avail. in microfilm from UMI; reprint service avail. from UMI) **Indexed:** ASCA, Biol.Abstr., Curr.Cont., Curr.Tit.Dent., Dent.Ind., Excerp.Med., Ind.Med., Ind.Sci.Rev., INIS Atomind., Sci.Cit.Ind.
—BLDSC shelfmark: 0829.152000.
Formerly (until 1986): American Journal of Orthodontics (ISSN 0096-6347); Which incorporates: International Journal of Orthodontics (ISSN 0020-7500); (1937-1938): American Journal of Orthodontics and Oral Surgery (ISSN 0002-9416)
Description: International research covering all phases of orthodontic treatment.
Refereed Serial

MEDICAL SCIENCES — DENTISTRY

617.6   IT
AMERICAN JOURNAL OF ORTHODONTICS AND DENTOFACIAL ORTHOPEDICS: ITALIAN EDITION. bi-m. L.122000 (effective 1992). Masson Italia Periodici, Via Statuto 2-4, 20121 Milan, Italy. TEL 02-6367-1. FAX 02-6367211. Ed. Giorgio Nidoli.

617.6 618.97   US   ISSN 0003-1054
AMERICAN SOCIETY FOR GERIATRIC DENTISTRY. JOURNAL.* 1966. q. membership. Academy of Geriatric Dentistry, 891 Pleasant Ave., Highland Park, IL 60035. TEL 312-432-2341. (Affiliate: American Dental Association) Ed. Sidney Rafal. bk.rev.; abstr.; illus.; circ. 5,000. **Indexed:** Dent.Ind.
Refereed Serial

617.6   US
AMERICAN SOCIETY FOR THE ADVANCEMENT OF ANESTHESIA IN DENTISTRY. PROCEEDINGS. 1972. s-a. $40. American Society for the Advancement of Anesthesia in Dentistry, 475 White Plains Rd., Eastchester, NY 10707. TEL 914-961-8136. Ed. R. Antonio Reyes-Guerra. adv.; bk.rev.; circ. 650.

617.6   US   ISSN 0003-3006
                           CODEN: ANPRBG
ANESTHESIA PROGRESS; a journal for pain and anxiety control. 1957. bi-m. $120 to institutiorts (foreign $148)(effective 1992). (American Dental Society of Anesthesiology) Elsevier Science Publishing Co., Inc. (New York), 655 Ave. of the Americas, New York, NY 10010. TEL 212-989-5800.
FAX 212-633-3965. TELEX 420643 AEP UI. Ed. Raymond A. Dionne. adv.; bk.rev.; abstr.; bibl.; charts; illus.; stat.; index; circ. 4,000. (also avail. in microform from UMI) **Indexed:** Biol.Abstr., Curr.Tit.Dent., Dent.Abstr., Dent.Ind., Excerp.Med., Oral Res.Abstr.
—BLDSC shelfmark: 0900.520000.
Formerly: American Dental Society of Anesthesiology. Journal.
Description: Directed to practicing dentists. Devoted to the management of pain and anxiety in dental outpatients.
Refereed Serial

617.6   US   ISSN 0003-3219
                           CODEN: ANORA
ANGLE ORTHODONTIST. 1931. q. $40 (foreign $47). (Edward H. Angle Society of Orthodontists, Inc.) Angle Orthodontists Research & Education Foundation, Inc., Box 2577, Appleton, WI 54913-2577. Ed. Dr. John S. Kloehn. charts; illus.; index; circ. 5,000. (also avail. in microform; back issues avail.) **Indexed:** Curr.Cont., Curr.Tit.Dent., Dent.Abstr., Dent.Ind., Excerp.Med., Ind.Med., Ind.Sci.Rev., Sci.Cit.Ind.
—BLDSC shelfmark: 0902.750000.
Description: Covers all phases of orthodontic treatment as well as the basic sciences related to orthodontics.

617.6   US   ISSN 0003-4770
ANNALS OF DENTISTRY. 1934. s-a. $20 (foreign $22). New York Academy of Dentistry, 540 Hudson St., Box 522, Hackensack, NJ 07602. Ed. Murray A. Cantor. bk.rev.; charts; illus.; circ. 750. **Indexed:** Curr.Tit.Dent., Dent.Abstr., Dent.Ind., Ind.Med., NRN.
—BLDSC shelfmark: 1040.350000.

617.6   FR   ISSN 0066-2712
ANNUAIRE DENTAIRE. 1936. a. 450 F.($75) Editions de Chabassol, 30 rue de Gramont, 75002 Paris, France. TEL 42-97-50-30. FAX 42-86-02-81. Ed. B. Laloup. adv.; circ. 6,500.

618   US
ANNUAL REPORT ON ADVANCED DENTAL EDUCATION. 1972. a. free. American Dental Association, 211 E. Chicago Ave., Chicago, IL 60611.
TEL 312-440-2674. Ed. Robert N. Czarnecki. **Indexed:** SRI.

617.6   GW
ARAB DENTAL/ALAM TUB AL-ASSNAN. (Text in Arabic) 1989. q. $26. Beta Publishing, Postfach 140121, 5300 Bonn 1, Germany. TEL 0228-252061. FAX 0228-252067. TELEX 8869536 BETA D. Ed. Dr. Rabih Nahas. adv.: B&W page DM.4770; trim 250 x 178. charts; illus.; circ. 7,200.

617.6   US   ISSN 0003-9969
RK1   CODEN: AOBIAR
ARCHIVES OF ORAL BIOLOGY; multidisciplinary journal in oral research. (Text in English, French, and German) 1959. m. £575 (effective 1992). Pergamon Press, Inc., Journals Division, 660 White Plains Rd., Tarrytown, NY 10591-5153.
TEL 914-524-9200. FAX 914-333-2444. (And: Headington Hill Hall, Oxford OX3 0BW, England. TEL 0865-794141) Eds. D.B. Ferguson, Dr. Edward J. Kollar. adv.; bk.rev.; charts; illus.; index; circ. 1,250. (also avail. in microform from MIM,UMI; back issues avail.) **Indexed:** Abstr.Anthropol., Biol.Abstr., Chem.Abstr., Curr.Adv.Biochem., Curr.Adv.Cell & Devel.Biol., Curr.Adv.Ecol.Sci., Curr.Cont., Curr.Tit.Dent., Dairy Sci.Abstr., Dent.Ind., Excerp.Med., Ind.Med., Ind.Sci.Rev., Ind.Vet., INIS Atomind., NRN, Nutr.Abstr., Rev.Med.& Vet.Mycol., Rev.Plant Path., Sci.Cit.Ind., Small Anim.Abstr., Triticale Abstr., Vet.Bull.
—BLDSC shelfmark: 1638.475000.
Description: Publishes research results on every aspect of the oral and dental tissues and bone from the entire range of vertabrates.
Refereed Serial

617.6   SP   ISSN 0213-4144
ARCHIVOS DE ODONTOESTOMATOLOGIA. (Text in Spanish; summaries in English) 1985. m. 6400 ptas. Ediciones Ergon S.A., Muntaner, 262, 6o, 08021 Barcelona, Spain. TEL 2010911. FAX 2015911. (Subscr. to: Cempro, Plaza Conde Valle Suchil 20, 28015 Madrid, Spain) Ed. Jose Javier Echeverria. adv.; bk.rev.; index; circ. 2,000. (back issues avail.)

617.6   SP
ARCHIVOS DE ODONTOESTOMATOLOGIA PREVENTIVA Y COMUNITARIA. (Text in Spanish; summaries in English) 1989. s-a. 1800 ptas. Ediciones Ergon S.A., Muntaner, 262, 6o, 08021 Barcelona, Spain. TEL 2010911. FAX 2015911. (Subscr. to: Cempro, Plaza Conde Valle Suchil 20, 28015 Madrid, Spain) Eds. Dr. Carolina, Dr. Emilio Cuenca. adv.; bk.rev.; index; circ. 1,500. (back issues avail.)

617.6   US   ISSN 0004-1769
ARKANSAS DENTAL JOURNAL.* 1930. q. $5 to non-members; members $4. Arkansas State Dental Association, 920 W. 2nd St., Ste. 204, Little Rock, AR 72201-2125. Ed. R.L. Smith, Jr. adv.; bk.rev.; abstr.; illus.; circ. 1,100. (also avail. in microform from UMI) **Indexed:** Dent.Ind.
—BLDSC shelfmark: 1671.080000.

617.6   FR   ISSN 0571-1525
ART DENTAIRE LIBERAL. 1974. m. 400 F. Federation des Chirurgiens-Dentistes de France, 4 rue de la Vrilliere, 75001 Paris, France. FAX 1-60-20-99-83. (Subscr. to: 15 bis, av. Foch, 77500 Chelles, France. TEL 1-60-20-53-45) Ed P. Petit. adv.; bk.rev.; circ. 6,000.

617.6   US
ARTICULATOR. m. North Central Ohio Dental Society, 2355 W. State Rte. 18, Triffin, OH 44883.
TEL 419-447-0253. Ed. Robert J. Dornauer. circ. 108. (looseleaf format)

617.6   GW
DER ARTIKULATOR; Zeitschrift der Kritische Zahnmedizin. 1976. q. DM.7.50. Vereinigung Demokratische Zahnmedizin e.V., Koelnstr. 198, 5300 Bonn 1, Germany. TEL 0228-693327.

617.6   AG   ISSN 0004-4881
                           CODEN: RAOABM
ASOCIACION ODONTOLOGICA ARGENTINA. REVISTA. 1898. q. $45. Asociacion Odontologica Argentina, Junin 959, 1113 Buenos Aires, Argentina. Ed. Juan Ramon Castro. adv.; bk.rev.; abstr.; bibl.; charts; illus.; index; circ. 6,220. **Indexed:** Dent.Ind.
—BLDSC shelfmark: 7804.425000.

617.6   FR
ASSISTANCE ET LE PROTHESISTE DENTAIRES. bi-m. Syndicat National des Assistantes et Prothesistes Dentaires, 21 rue Defresne Bast, 95100 Argenteuil, France. Ed. M. Hachmanian. adv.

617.6   BL
ASSOCIACAO PAULISTA DE CIRURGIOES DENTISTAS. JOURNAL. 1957. m. free to members and qualified personnel. Associacao Paulista de Cirurgioes Dentistas - Sao Paulo State Dental Association, Rua Humaita 389, 01321 Sao Paulo (SP), Brazil. Ed. F. Tornelli. adv.; circ. 23,500 (controlled). (tabloid format; back issues avail.)

617.6   BL   ISSN 0004-5276
ASSOCIACAO PAULISTA DE CIRURGIOES DENTISTAS. REVISTA. 1947. bi-m. $15. Associacao Paulista de Cirurgioes Dentistas, Rua Humaita 389, C. P. 2523, Sao Paulo, Brazil. Ed. Julio Jorge D'Albuquerque Lossio. adv.; bk.rev.; cum.index; circ. 23,500. (also avail. in microfilm) **Indexed:** Dent.Ind.

618   AT
AUSTRALIAN DENTAL ASSOCIATION. DENTAL BULLETIN. 1964. 10/yr. Aus.$2. Australian Dental Association, Western Australian Branch, 14 Altona St., West Perth, W.A. 6005, Australia. Ed. P.J. Colgan.

617.6   AT   ISSN 0810-7440
AUSTRALIAN DENTAL ASSOCIATION. NEWS BULLETIN. 11/yr. Aus.$73. Australian Dental Association, 75 Lithgow St., St. Leonards, N.S.W. 2065, Australia. TEL 02-906-4412. FAX 02-906-4917. Ed. J. Campbell. adv.: B&W page $685, color page $1544; trim 177 x 236. circ. 7,600.

617.6   AT   ISSN 0045-0421
                           CODEN: ADEJA2
AUSTRALIAN DENTAL JOURNAL. 1956. bi-m. Aus.$96. Australian Dental Association, Inc., P.O. Box 520, St. Leonards, N.S.W. 2065, Australia.
FAX 02-906-4617. Ed. J.K. Harcourt. adv.; bk.rev.; index; circ. 7,200. (also avail. in microfilm from UMI; back issues avail.; reprint service avail. from UMI) **Indexed:** Biol.Abstr., C.I.S.Abstr., Chem.Abstr., Curr.Adv.Cancer Res., Curr.Adv.Ecol.Sci., Curr.Cont., Curr.Tit.Dent., Dent.Abstr., Dent.Ind., Excerp.Med., Ind.Med., Ind.Sci.Rev., NRN, Sci.Cit.Ind., So.Pac.Per.Ind.
—BLDSC shelfmark: 1798.450000.

617.6   AT   ISSN 0587-3908
AUSTRALIAN ORTHODONTIC JOURNAL. 1967. s-a. Aus.$34. c/o Dr. B. Mollenhauer, Ed., 299 Upper Heidelberg Rd., Ivanhoe, Vic. 3079, Australia. circ. 550. **Indexed:** Dent.Ind., NRN.
Description: Includes scientific and clinical articles.

617.6   AT   ISSN 0819-0887
AUSTRALIAN PROSTHODONTIC JOURNAL. 1971. a. Aus.$35 (foreign Aus.$40). Australian Prosthodontic Society, P.O. Box 140, Summer Hill, N.S.W. 2130, Australia. TEL 02-282-0292. FAX 02-633-2893. adv.; bk.rev.; circ. 1,000.
—BLDSC shelfmark: 1818.340000.
Formerly (until 1986): Australian Prosthodontic Society. Bulletin (ISSN 0816-4460)
Description: Covers all aspect of prosthodontics.

617.6   AT   ISSN 0313-7384
AUSTRALIAN SOCIETY OF ENDODONTOLOGY. NEWSLETTER. 1965. 3/yr. membership (Aus.$4 per no. for institutions only). Australian Society of Endodontology Inc., Ste. 301, 60 Park St., Sydney, N.S.W. 2000, Australia. Ed. Dr. Steven A. Cohn. adv.; bk.rev.; circ. 500.

617.6   GW   ISSN 0005-3473
B Z B. (Bayerisches Zahnaerzteblatt) 1961. m. DM.120. (Bayerische Landeszahnaerztekammer) Demeter Verlag, Wuermstr. 13, 8032 Graefelfing, Germany. TEL 089-852033. FAX 089-8543347. Ed. Ursel Meenzen. adv.; bk.rev.; abstr.; bibl.; illus.; index; circ. 11,300. **Indexed:** Dent.Ind.

617.6   US
BANDELETTE. 1968. m. $15 (foreign $20). International Association for Orthodontics, 211 E. Chicago Ave., No. 915, Chicago, IL 60611.
TEL 312-642-2602. FAX 312-642-4191. Ed. Joanna Carey. circ. 2,100. (tabloid format; back issues avail.)
Description: Contains news and concerns of Association members.

MEDICAL SCIENCES — DENTISTRY

617.6   US   ISSN 0005-7258
BAYLOR DENTAL JOURNAL. 1951. a. free to qualified personnel. Baylor College of Dentistry, Office of Alumni and Public Relations, 3302 Gaston Ave., Dallas, TX 75246. TEL 214-828-8214. FAX 214-828-8346. Ed. Dr. William Binnie. adv.; abstr.; illus.; circ. 5,000 (controlled). **Indexed:** Dent.Ind.

617.6   US   ISSN 0092-9832
BERGEN COUNTY DENTAL SOCIETY. NEWSLETTER. 1920. m. $12 (foreign $18). Bergen County Dental Society, 1060 Main St., River Edge, NJ 07661. Ed. Paul A. Barabas. adv.; circ. 700 (controlled). (back issues avail.) **Indexed:** Dent.Ind.
    Formerly: Bergen County Dental Society. Journal.
    Description: Provides Bergen county dentists with social, societal, political, and legislative information; includes scientific sessions.

617.6 610   US   ISSN 0882-1852
BIOLOGICAL THERAPIES IN DENTISTRY. 1985. bi-m. $40 to individuals (foreign $60); institutions $60 (foreign $80); students $25 (foreign $45); (effective Jan. 1992). Mosby - Year Book, Inc. (Subsidiary of: Times Mirror Company), 11830 Westline Industrial Dr., St. Louis, MO 63146. TEL 800-225-5020. FAX 508-486-9423. Ed. Sebastian G. Ciancio. circ. 322.
    Description: Keeps the dental profession up-to-date with current developments in dental therapeutics.

617.6   DK
RK55.C5
BOERNE- OG UNGDOMSTANDPLEJEN I DANMARK. (Subseries: Primaer Sundhedstjenestestatistik) 1983. irreg. DKK 60. Sundhedsstyrelsen, Amaliegade 13, 1012 Copenhagen K, Denmark. (Subscr. to: Statens information, P.O. Box 1103, 1009 Copenhagen K, Denmark)
    Formerly: Boernetandplejen i Danmark (ISSN 0108-6618)

617.6   BL   ISSN 0045-2378
BOLETIM DE MATERIAIS DENTARIOS.* (Summaries in English) 1969. s-a. Universidade Estadual de Campinas, Faculdade de Odontologia de Piracicaba, Sao Paulo, Brazil. illus. **Indexed:** Dent.Ind.

617.6   US   ISSN 8756-3282
                      CODEN: BONEDL
BONE. (Text in English and French) 1979. bi-m. £335 (effective 1992). Pergamon Press, Inc., Journals Division, 660 White Plains Rd., Tarrytown, NY 10591-5153. TEL 914-524-9200. FAX 914-333-2444. (And: Headington Hill Hall, Oxford OX3 0BW, England. TEL 0865-794141) Ed. Roland Baron. adv.; abstr.; illus.; circ. 1,200. (also avail. in microform; back issues avail.) **Indexed:** Biol.Abstr., Chem.Abstr., Curr.Adv.Ecol.Sci., Curr.Cont., Dairy Sci.Abstr., Dent.Ind., Excerp.Med., Ind.Med., Ind.Sci.Rev., NRN.
    —BLDSC shelfmark: 2247.330000.
    Formerly: Metabolic Bone Disease and Related Research (ISSN 0221-8747)
    Description: Provides an interdisciplinary forum for rapid publication of original experimental or clinical studies and review articles.
    Refereed Serial

617.6   UK   ISSN 0007-0610
                      CODEN: BDJOHJ
BRITISH DENTAL JOURNAL. 1880. s-m. £160. British Dental Association, 64 Wimpole St., London W1M 8AL, England. FAX 071-224-0603. Ed. Margaret H. Seward. adv.; bk.rev.; abstr.; charts; illus.; s-a. index; circ. 18,000. (also avail. in microform from UMI) **Indexed:** Abstr.Hyg., Biol.Abstr., C.I.S.Abstr., Chem.Abstr., Curr.Adv.Cancer Res., Curr.Adv.Ecol.Sci., Curr.Cont., Curr.Tit.Dent., Dent.Abstr., Dent.Ind., Ind.Med., Ind.Sci.Rev., Met.Abstr., NRN, Nutr.Abstr., Risk Abstr., Sci.Cit.Ind., Trop.Dis.Bull., World Alum.Abstr.
    —BLDSC shelfmark: 2299.000000.

617.6   UK   ISSN 0007-0629
BRITISH DENTAL SURGERY ASSISTANT. vol.32, 1973. q. £25. Association of British Dental Surgery Assistants, DSA House, 29 London St., Fleetwood, Lancs., England. FAX 0253-773099. Ed. Sue Adams. adv.; bk.rev.; illus.; circ. 3,000. **Indexed:** Dent.Ind.
    —BLDSC shelfmark: 2299.100000.

617.6   UK   ISSN 0266-4356
BRITISH JOURNAL OF ORAL AND MAXILLOFACIAL SURGERY. 1963. 6/yr. £90($180) (British Association of Oral and Maxillofacial Surgeons) Churchill Livinginstone Medical Journals, Robert Stevenson House, 1-3 Baxter's Pl., Leith Walk, Endinburgh EH1 3AF, Scotland. TEL 031-556-2424. FAX 031-558-1278. TELEX 727511. (Subscr. to: Longman Group, Journals Subscr. Dept., P.O. Box 77, Fourth Ave., Harlow, Essex CM19 5AA, England; U.S. subscr: Churchill Livingstone, 650 Ave. of the Americas, New York, NY 10011. TEL 212-206-5000) Ed. J. Frame. adv.; bk.rev.; charts; illus.; index. (also avail. in microform from SWZ,UMI) **Indexed:** Biol.Abstr., Curr.Adv.Ecol.Sci., Curr.Cont., Curr.Tit.Dent., Dent.Abstr., Dent.Ind., Excerp.Med., Ind.Med., Ind.Sci.Rev., Res.High.Educ.Abstr., Sci.Cit.Ind.
    —BLDSC shelfmark: 2314.200000.
    Formerly: British Journal of Oral Surgery (ISSN 0007-117X)

617.643   UK   ISSN 0301-228X
BRITISH JOURNAL OF ORTHODONTICS. 1974. q. £45($95) (foreign £86). (British Society of the Study of Orthodontics) Oxford University Press, Oxford Journals, Pinkhill House, Southfield Road, Eynsham, Oxford OX8 1JJ, England. TEL 0865-882283. FAX 0865-882890. TELEX 837330 OXPRES G. (Co-sponsor: British Association of Orthodontists) Ed. B. Leighton. adv.; bk.rev.; index; circ. 1,800. (also avail. in microform from UMI) **Indexed:** Curr.Adv.Ecol.Sci., Curr.Tit.Dent., Dent.Abstr., Dent.Ind., Ind.Med.
    —BLDSC shelfmark: 2314.500000.
    Description: Contains original articles, reviews, critical commentaries, editorials, and correspondence on features of orthodontic practice and teaching and research.

617.6   UK
BRITISH SOCIETY OF DENTAL AND MAXILLOFACIAL RADIOLOGY. PROCEEDINGS. 1978. a. £20. British Society of Dental and Maxillofacial Radiology, University of Manchester Dental School, Radiology Dept., Higher Cambridge St., Manchester M15 6FH, England. TEL 061-275-6776. bk.rev.; circ. 150.

617.6   US   ISSN 0007-4837
BULLETIN OF DENTAL EDUCATION. 1959. m. $18 to non-members (foreign $24); members $12. American Association of Dental Schools, 1625 Massachusetts Ave. N.W., Washington, DC 20036-2212. TEL 202-667-9433. Ed. Owen R. Terry. circ. 3,800. (reprint service avail. from UMI) **Indexed:** Dent.Ind.

617.6   US   ISSN 0007-5132
BULLETIN OF THE HISTORY OF DENTISTRY. 1952. s-a. $35. American Academy of the History of Dentistry, c/o Dr. Hannelore T. Loevy, Ed., 5524 S. Harper Ave., Chicago, IL 60037. adv.; bk.rev.; bibl.; illus.; cum.index every 5 yrs.; circ. 800. (also avail. in microfilm from UMI; reprint service avail. from UMI; back issues avail.) **Indexed:** Curr.Tit.Dent., Dent.Abstr., Dent.Ind., Ind.Med.
    —BLDSC shelfmark: 2855.980000.
    Description: Covers all areas relating to dental history; includes bibliography.
    Refereed Serial

617.6   US   ISSN 0007-6007
BUR. 1896. s-a. free to alumni. Loyola University Chicago, School of Dentistry, Alumni Association, 820 N Michigan Ave., Chicago, IL 60611. TEL 708-216-6700. FAX 708-216-8199. (Subscr. to: 2160 S. First Ave., Maywood, IL, 60153) Ed. Janine Horne. bk.rev.; illus.; circ. 7,200 (controlled). (also avail. in microform; back issues avail.) **Indexed:** Dent.Ind.

617.6   CN   ISSN 0831-6279
C M T NEWSLETTER; published bimonthly by and for those with Charcot-Marie-Tooth disease. 1984. bi-m. donation. (Personal Muscular Atrophy International Association, Inc.) C M T International, 1 Springbank Dr., St. Catharine, Ont. L2S 2K1, Canada. TEL 416-687-3630. Ed. Linda D. Crabtree. index; circ. 2,400. (back issues avail.)
    Description: For people and health professionals interested in learning more about Charcot-Marie-Tooth disease, a progressive debilitating neuromuscular disorder.

617.6   US   ISSN 0008-0977
CALIFORNIA DENTAL ASSOCIATION. JOURNAL. 1918. m. $64.65 to non-members; members $25.83; foreign $43.10. California Dental Association, Box 13749, Sacramento, CA 95853. TEL 916-443-0505. FAX 916-443-2943. Ed. Jack Conley. adv.; bk.rev.; charts; illus.; circ. 18,000. **Indexed:** Curr.Tit.Dent., Dent.Abstr., Dent.Ind., INIS Atomind.
    Incorporates (as of 1973): Southern California Dental Association. Journal (ISSN 0049-156X); Which was formerly (1934-1966): Southern California State Dental Association. Journal (ISSN 0098-7115); S C D A Newsletter; Composite.

617.6   CN   ISSN 0833-8264
CANADIAN DENTAL ASSISTANTS ASSOCIATION. JOURNAL. 1956. 3/yr. Can.$30 (foreign Can.$40). Canadian Dental Assistants Association, 869-871 Dundas St., London, Ont. N5W 2Z8, Canada. TEL 519-679-1582. FAX 519-679-8494. Ed. Diane Pike. adv.; bk.rev.; circ. 2,600. (back issues avail.)

617.6   CN   ISSN 0008-3372
                      CODEN: JCDAAS
CANADIAN DENTAL ASSOCIATION. JOURNAL/ASSOCIATION DENTAIRE CANADIENNE. JOURNAL. (Text in English, French) 1935. m. Can.$48($53) (foreign $58). Canadian Dental Association, 1815 Alta Vista Dr., Ottawa, Ont. K1G 3Y6, Canada. TEL 613-523-1770. FAX 613-523-7736. Ed. Dr. P.R. Crawford. adv.; bk.rev.; abstr.; charts; index; circ. 16,400. **Indexed:** Biol.Abstr., Chem.Abstr., Curr.Tit.Dent., Dent.Abstr., Dent.Ind., Dok.Arbeitsmed., Ind.Med., NRN, Nutr.Abstr.
    Description: Clinical and scientific articles directed toward general practitioners.
    Refereed Serial

617.6   CN   ISSN 0834-1494
CANADIAN DENTAL HYGIENISTS ASSOCIATION. PROBE. 1967. q. Can.$32.10 (foreign Can.$60). Canadian Dental Hygienists Association, 1018 Merivale Rd., Ste. 201, Ottawa, Ont. K1Z 6A5, Canada. TEL 613-728-8730. FAX 613-728-3788. (Subscr. to: Keith Health Care Communications, 4953 Dundas St. W., Ste. 105, Toronto, Ont. M9A 1B6, Canada) Ed. Marilyn Goulding. adv.; bk.rev.; charts; illus.; circ. 4,000. **Indexed:** Dent.Ind.
    —BLDSC shelfmark: 6617.275000.
    Formerly: Canadian Dental Hygienist (ISSN 0008-3380)

617.6   CN
CANADIAN DENTAL MANAGEMENT. 1977. m. Can.$30. Sentinel Business Publications, P.O. Box 14, Lachine, Que. H8S 4A5, Canada. TEL 514-333-1116. FAX 514-631-8858. Ed. Wayne Paterson. adv.

617.6   SZ   ISSN 0008-6568
                      CODEN: CAREBK
CARIES RESEARCH. (Text in English) 1967. bi-m. 545 Fr.($364) (European Organization for Caries Research) S. Karger AG, Allschwilerstr. 10, P.O. Box, CH-4009 Basel, Switzerland. TEL 061-3061111. FAX 061-3061234. TELEX CH 962652. Ed. J.M. ten Cate. adv.; bibl.; charts; illus.; index; circ. 1,450. (also avail. in microform from RPI; reprint service avail. from ISI) **Indexed:** Biol.Abstr., Chem.Abstr., Curr.Adv.Ecol.Sci., Curr.Cont., Curr.Tit.Dent., Dairy Sci.Abstr., Dent.Abstr., Dent.Ind., Excerp.Med., Food Sci.& Tech.Abstr., Ind.Med., Ind.Sci.Rev., NRN, Nutr.Abstr., Sci.Cit.Ind.
    —BLDSC shelfmark: 3053.200000.
    Description: Coverage of human and animal experimental work for the researcher; clinical trials of interest to the practicing dentist.

617.6   US
CASE WESTERN RESERVE UNIVERSITY SCHOOL OF DENTISTRY: ALUMNI MAGAZINE. 1985. s-a. free. Case Western Reserve University, School of Dentistry, 2123 Abington Rd., Cleveland, OH 44106. TEL 216-368-3480. FAX 216-368-3204. Ed. Mary Wirtz Juhnke. adv.; bk.rev.; illus.; circ. 3,500.
    Former titles: Case Western Reserve University School of Dentistry: Dental Alumni News; Case Western Reserve University School of Dentistry: Dental Alumni Newsletter; Case Western Reserve University School of Dentistry: Dental Alumni News; Case Western Reserve University. School of Dentistry. Dental Alumni Bulletin (ISSN 0043-4140); Western Reserve University Dental Alumni Bulletin.
    Description: Covers dental advancement and school status, university and alumni news.

MEDICAL SCIENCES — DENTISTRY

617.6 ES ISSN 0008-9907
CENTRO AMERICA ODONTOLOGICA. 1965. q. membership. Editorial Zavaleta, 23 Av. N. 1214, San Salvador, El Salvador. Ed. Dr. J. Benjamin Zavaleta. adv.; bk.rev.

617.6 CS ISSN 0009-0654
CESKOSLOVENSKA STOMATOLOGIE. (Text in Czech or Slovak; summaries in English and Russian) 1900. bi-m. $48.60. (Ceskoslovenska Stomatologicka Spolecnost) Avicenum, Czechoslovak Medical Press, Malostranske nam. 28, 118 02 Prague 1, Czechoslovakia. (Dist. by: Artia, Ve Smeckach 30, 111 27 Prague 1, Czechoslovakia) (Co-sponsor: Ceskoslovenska Lekarska Spolecnost J. Ev. Purkyne) Ed. Dr. J. Toman. adv.; bk.rev.; abstr.; charts; illus.; index, cum.index. **Indexed:** Chem.Abstr., Dent.Abstr., Dent.Ind., Ind.Med., INIS Atomind., Nutr.Abstr., Protozool.Abstr.
—BLDSC shelfmark: 3122.805000.

617.6 US ISSN 0091-1666
CHICAGO DENTAL SOCIETY REVIEW. 1920. m. $18. Chicago Dental Society, 401 N. Michigan Ave., Ste. 300, Chicago, IL 60611-4205.
TEL 312-836-7300. FAX 312-836-7337. Ed. Noel T. Maxson. adv.; illus.; circ. 10,000. (also avail. in microform from UMI; reprint service avail. from UMI) **Indexed:** Dent.Abstr., Dent.Ind.
Formerly: Chicago Dental Society Fortnightly Review (ISSN 0009-353X)

617.6 FR ISSN 0009-4838
CHIRURGIEN-DENTISTE DE FRANCE. vol.46, 1976. w. 235 F. Confederation Nationale des Syndicats Dentaires, 22 av. de Villiers, 75017 Paris, France. Ed. Guy Robert. adv.; bk.rev.; illus.; s-a. index; circ. 22,000. **Indexed:** Dent.Ind., Dok.Arbeitsmed.

617.6 AG ISSN 0325-7479
CIRCULO ARGENTINO DE ODONTOLOGIA. REVISTA. 1938. s-a. Circulo Argentino de Odontologia, Eduardo Acevedo 54, 1405 Buenos Aires, Argentina. circ. 3,000. **Indexed:** Dent.Ind.

617.6 AG ISSN 0045-6942
CIRCULO ODONTOLOGICO DE CORDOBA. REVISTA. 1936. 3/yr. free. Circulo Odontologico de Cordoba, Direccion y Administracion, 27 de Abril 887, T.E. 46207, Cordoba, Argentina. Ed. Dr. Ramon Ocanto. illus.; circ. 1,800. **Indexed:** Dent.Ind.

617.6 AG ISSN 0009-7357
CIRCULO ODONTOLOGICO DE ROSARIO. REVISTA. (Text in Spanish; summaries in English) 1929. q. membership or exchange basis. Circulo Odontologico de Rosario, Rioja 2471, Rosario, Argentina. Ed. Dr. Natalio Grynberg. adv.; bk.rev.; bibl.; illus.; circ. 1,000. (also avail. in microfiche) **Indexed:** Dent.Ind.

CLEFT PALATE - CRANIOFACIAL JOURNAL; an international journal of craniofacial anomalies. see *MEDICAL SCIENCES — Surgery*

617.6 IT ISSN 0393-7593
CLINICA ODONTOIATRICA DEL NORD AMERICA. 3/yr. L.90000($160) Piccin Editore, Via Altinate 107, 35100 Padua, Italy. TEL 049-655566. TELEX 432074 PICCIN I. (reprint service avail. from UMI) **Indexed:** Excerp.Med.

617.6 US
CLINICAL DENTAL BRIEFINGS; timesaving summaries of significant clinical literature. 1987. m. $108. Boston University, Goldman School of Graduate Dentistry, 100 E. Newton St., Boston, MA 02118.
TEL 617-638-4677. Ed. Abigail M. Obenchain. abstr.; tr.lit.; circ. 1,168. (back issues avail.)
Formerly (until 1991): Dental Watch (ISSN 0893-665X)
Description: Summaries of literature and dental news.

617.3 US ISSN 0163-9633
RK60.7 CODEN: CPRDDM
CLINICAL PREVENTIVE DENTISTRY. 1974. bi-m. $35 to individuals (foreign $45); institutions $55 (foreign $65). Stevens Publishing Corporation, 225 N. New Rd., Waco, TX 76710. TEL 817-776-9000.
FAX 817-775-9018. Ed. J.H. Manhold. adv.; illus.; index; circ. 2,100. (also avail. in microform from UMI) **Indexed:** Curr.Tit.Dent., Dent.Abstr., Dent.Ind., NRN.
—BLDSC shelfmark: 3286.334000.
Supersedes (1974-1978): Journal of Preventive Dentistry (ISSN 0096-2732)
Refereed Serial

617.6 SP
CLINICAS ODONTOLOGICAS DE NORTEAMERICA. Spanish translation of: Dental Clinics of North America. 1973. 4/yr. 15264 ptas.($113) (effective 1990). Interamericana de Espana, S.A., Division de Ciencias de la Salud de McGraw-Hill, Calle Manuel Ferrero, 13, 28036 Madrid, Spain. TEL 315-0340.
FAX 733-6627. charts; illus.; index.

617.6 US ISSN 0010-1559
COLORADO DENTAL ASSOCIATION. JOURNAL. 1922. 4/yr. $15 (foreign $25). Colorado Dental Association, 7535 E Hampden Ave., Ste. 505, Denver, CO 80231-4844. TEL 303-671-6600. FAX 303-671-6603. Ed. James H. Pearce, Jr. adv.; bk.rev.; circ. 1,850. **Indexed:** Dent.Abstr., Dent.Ind.
—BLDSC shelfmark: 4730.800000.

617.6 US
COMMUNICATOR (JOHNSTOWN). 1971. q. American Academy of Dental Practice Administration, First United Federal Bldg., 227 Franklyn St., Ste. 220, Johnstown, PA 15901. Ed. W.F. Hrin. circ. 1,100.

617.6 US
COMMUNIQUE (IOWA CITY). q. American Association of Public Health, c/o Marsha Cunningham, Ed., College of Dentistry, University of Iowa, Iowa City, IA 52242. (reprint service avail. from UMI)

617.6 UK ISSN 0265-539X
  CODEN: CDHEES
COMMUNITY DENTAL HEALTH. 4/yr. £77 to individuals; institutions £44. (British Association for the Study of Community Dentistry) Macmillan Press Ltd., Houndmills, Basingstoke, Hants RG12 2XS, England. Ed. P.M.C. James. **Indexed:** Curr.Adv.Ecol.Sci., Curr.Tit.Dent.
—BLDSC shelfmark: 3363.608900.

617.6 DK ISSN 0301-5661
  CODEN: CDOEAP
COMMUNITY DENTISTRY AND ORAL EPIDEMIOLOGY. (Text in English) 1973. bi-m. DKK 1060. Munksgaard International Publishers Ltd., 35 Noerre Soegade, P.O. Box 2148, DK-1016 Copenhagen K, Denmark. TEL 33-12-70-30. FAX 33-12-93-87. TELEX 19431 MUNKS DK. Ed. Ole Fejerskov. adv.; bk.rev.; circ. 1,000. (also avail. in microform from SWZ; reprint service avail. from ISI,SWZ) **Indexed:** Biol.Abstr., Curr.Cont., Curr.Tit.Dent., Dent.Abstr., Dent.Ind., Dok.Arbeitsmed., Excerp.Med., Ind.Med., Ind.Sci.Rev., NRN, Nutr.Abstr., Sci.Cit.Ind.
—BLDSC shelfmark: 3363.609000.

617.6 US ISSN 0196-1756
COMPENDIUM OF CONTINUING EDUCATION IN DENTISTRY. 1980. 12/yr. $48. (University of Pennsylvania, School of Dental Medicine) Dental Learning Systems Co., Inc., 9 Pheasant Run Rd., Newtown, PA 18940-1818. TEL 215-860-9595. adv.; bk.rev.; circ. 46,000. (back issues avail.) **Indexed:** Curr.Tit.Dent., Dent.Abstr., Dent.Ind.
Description: Published for generalists and specialists in private practice who wish to expand their knowledge in a variety of dental specialties.

617.6 AG
CONECTOR. 1971. q. Arg.$4500($45) Instituto de Implantodontologia, Callao 433-3e, Buenos Aires, Argentina. Ed. Carlos Alberto Rillos. adv.; bk.rev.; abstr.; bibl.; illus.; stat.; circ. 10,000. (back issues avail.)

617.6 US ISSN 0010-6232
CONNECTICUT STATE DENTAL ASSOCIATION. JOURNAL. vol.27, 1953. q. $15 to non-members; members $10 (typically set in Oct.). Connecticut State Dental Association, c/o Dr. Howard I. Mark, Ed., 62 Russ St., Hartford, CT 06106-1522. TEL 203-278-5550. FAX 203-522-6587. adv.; bk.rev.; charts; illus.; circ. 3,000. **Indexed:** Dent.Abstr., Dent.Ind.
—BLDSC shelfmark: 4731.900000.

617.6 US ISSN 0010-7301
RK97
CONTACT POINT. 1924. q. free. University of the Pacific, School of Dentistry, 2155 Webster St., San Francisco, CA 94115. TEL 415-929-6400. Ed. David W. Chambers. adv.; illus.; circ. 6,700. **Indexed:** Chem.Abstr., Dent.Ind.

617.6 AG ISSN 0069-9799
COOPERADOR DENTAL.* 1933. irreg. membership. Cooperativa Dental Argentina, M.T. de Alvear 2167, Buenos Aires, Argentina. Eds. H.B. Ferreri, Horacio Martinez. adv.; bk.rev.; circ. 6,000.

617.6 US ISSN 1045-4411
  CODEN: CROMEF
CRITICAL REVIEWS IN ORAL BIOLOGY AND MEDICINE. 1989. q. $79.95 to individuals; institutions $165. C R C Press, Inc., 2000 Corporate Blvd., N.W., Boca Raton, FL 33431. TEL 407-994-0555.
FAX 407-998-9784. Ed. Olav F. Alvares.
—BLDSC shelfmark: 3487.479500.

CURRENT OPINION IN DENTISTRY. see *MEDICAL SCIENCES — Abstracting, Bibliographies, Statistics*

617.643 610.28 UK
CURRENT PERSPECTIVES ON IMPLANTABLE DEVICES; a research annual. 1989. a. (University of Liverpool, Institute of Medical and Dental Bioengineering) J A I Press Ltd., 118 Pentonville Rd., London N1 9JN, England. (Subscr. in U.S. to: J A I Press, Inc., 55 Old Post Rd., No. 2, Greenwich, CT 06836) Ed. David F. Williams.

CURRENT TITLES IN DENTISTRY. see *MEDICAL SCIENCES — Abstracting, Bibliographies, Statistics*

617.6 PL ISSN 0011-4553
  CODEN: CZSTA6
CZASOPISMO STOMATOLOGICZNE. 1948. m. $132. Panstwowy Zaklad Wydawnictw Lekarskich, Ul. Dluga 38-40, Warsaw, Poland. TEL 31-42-81. (Dist. by: Ars Polona-Ruch, Krakowskie Przedmiescie 7, 00-068 Warsaw, Poland) Ed. Kazimierz Stawinski. **Indexed:** Biol.Abstr., Chem.Abstr., Dent.Abstr., Dent.Ind., Dok.Arbeitsmed., Excerp.Med., Ind.Med., INIS Atomind.
—BLDSC shelfmark: 3507.300000.

617.6 CN
DALHOUSIE DENTAL JOURNAL. 1961. a. free. Dalhousie Dental Students Society, Dalhousie University, Halifax, N.S. B3H 4H8, Canada.
TEL 902-424-2211. Ed. Heather Carr-Kinnear. adv.; circ. 1,000. (back issues avail.)

617.6 DK
DENS. 1910. m. Tandteknikenen Foereningen, Upsalagade 20B, DK-2100 Copenhagen OE, Denmark. FAX 009-45-35432104. adv.; circ. 800.

617.6 GW ISSN 0177-7483
DENT - TAX; Ratgeber fuer den Zahnarzt. 1980. q. DM.28. Pharmedtax Verlagsgesellschaft mbH, Marienburgerstr. 22, 5000 Cologne 51, Germany. TEL 0221-376950. Ed. Peter John von Freyend. adv.; bk.rev.; circ. 28,500.
—BLDSC shelfmark: 5915.905000.

617.6
DENTAL ADMISSION TESTING PROGRAM. 1951. a. free. American Dental Association, 211 E. Chicago Ave., Chicago, IL 60611. TEL 312-440-2500. Ed. Dr. Gene A. Kramer. circ. 110,000.

617.6 UK ISSN 0266-6073
RK1
DENTAL ANNUAL. 1985. a. £35. Butterworth - Heinemann Ltd. (Subsidiary of: Reed International PLC), Linacre House, Jordan Hill, Oxford OX2 8DP, England. TEL 0865-310366. FAX 0865-310898. TELEX 83111 BHPOXF G. (Subscr. to: Turpin Transactions Ltd., Distribution Centre, Blackhorse Rd., Letchworth, Herts SG6 1HN, England. TEL 0462-672555) Ed. Donald Derrick. index. (also avail. in microform from UMI; back issues avail.)

617.6 US ISSN 0733-9836
DENTAL ASEPSIS REVIEW. 1980. m. $10 (foreign $13). Indiana University School of Dentistry, Department of Oral Microbiology, 1121 W. Michigan St., Indianapolis, IN 46202. TEL 317-274-7461. FAX 317-274-5425. Eds. Chris H. Miller, Charles J. Palenik. bk.rev.; index; circ. 1,100. (looseleaf format; back issues avail.)

MEDICAL SCIENCES — DENTISTRY

617.6   US   ISSN 0011-8508
CODEN: DEASEJ
DENTAL ASSISTANT JOURNAL. 1931. q. $20 (foreign $24). American Dental Assistants Association, 919 N. Michigan Ave., Ste. 3400, Chicago, IL 60611. TEL 312-664-3327. FAX 312-664-5288. Ed. Douglas McDonough. adv.; abstr.; illus.; circ. 15,500. (also avail. in microform from UMI; reprint service avail. from UMI) **Indexed:** Curr.Tit.Dent., Dent.Abstr., Dent.Ind., Oral Res.Abstr.
—BLDSC shelfmark: 3553.255500.
   Description: Contains technical and theoretical articles specifically written for and directed to the dental assistant. Includes office management articles and news of advances in dentistry.

617.6   SA   ISSN 0011-8516
CODEN: DASJAG
DENTAL ASSOCIATION OF SOUTH AFRICA. JOURNAL/TANDHEELKUNDIGE VERENIGING VAN SUID AFRIKA. TYDSKRIF. (Text and summaries in Afrikaans, English) 1922. m. R.280($100) membership (effective 1992). Dental Association of South Africa, Private Bag 1, Houghton, Johannesburg 2041, South Africa. TEL 011-6424687. FAX 011-6425718. TELEX 5-21849 SA. Ed. Helmut Heydt. adv.; bk.rev.; charts; illus.; index; circ. 3,750. (back issues avail.) **Indexed:** Biol.Abstr., Dent.Abstr., Dent.Ind., I.P.A., Ind.S.A.Per., INIS Atomind.
   Description: Original scientific research articles of interest to association members.

617.6   TH   ISSN 0045-9917
DENTAL ASSOCIATION OF THAILAND. JOURNAL. 1949. bi-m. $30. Dental Association of Thailand, 107-58 Soi Prangthip, Lardprao, Bangkapi, Bangkok 10310, Thailand. (Mailing addr.: P.O. Box 355, Samsen Nai, Bangkok 10400, Thailand) Ed. Dr. Porjai Ruangsri. illus. **Indexed:** Dent.Ind.
—BLDSC shelfmark: 4732.750000.

617.6   IT   ISSN 0011-8524
DENTAL CADMOS; rivista quindicinale di odontoiatria e tecnica dentaria. 1933. bi-w. L.145000($198) (effective 1992). Masson Italia Periodici, Via Statuto 2-4, 20121 Milan, Italy. TEL 02-6367-1. FAX 02-6367211. Ed. Carlo Guastamacchia. adv.; bk.rev.; index; circ. 21,000. **Indexed:** Dent.Ind., Ind.Med.
—BLDSC shelfmark: 3553.260000.

617.6   US   ISSN 0011-8532
RK1   CODEN: DCNAAC
DENTAL CLINICS OF NORTH AMERICA. 1956. 4/yr. $69. W.B. Saunders Co., Curtis Center, Independence Square W., Philadelphia, PA 19106. TEL 215-238-7800. Ed. Susan Short. illus.; index; cum.index every 3 yrs. (also avail. in microform from MIM,UMI; reprint service avail. from ISI,UMI) **Indexed:** Curr.Cont., Dent.Ind., Excerp.Med., Ind.Med., INIS Atomind., Nutr.Abstr.
—BLDSC shelfmark: 3553.290000.

DENTAL COMPUTER NEWSLETTER. see *MEDICAL SCIENCES — Computer Applications*

617.6 355   GW
DENTAL CORPS INTERNATIONAL. 2/yr. DM.42($28) Beta Publishing, Postfach 140121, 5300 Bonn 1, Germany. TEL 0228-252061. FAX 0228-252067. TELEX 8869536 BETA D. Ed. Dr. Claus Schulz. circ. 6,450.
   Description: Provides an international forum for the exchange of information among military dentists.

617.6   II
DENTAL DIALOGUE. 1974. q. $5. Government Dental College & Hospital, Nagpur 440 003, India. Ed. Dr. V.K. Hazarey. circ. 1,500. **Indexed:** Dent.Ind.

617.6   GW   ISSN 0011-8575
DENTAL ECHO. (Text in English, French, German, Italian and Spanish) 1950. every 6 weeks. DM.137.69. Dental Echo Verlag GmbH, Wieblingerstr. 41, 6904 Eppelheim, Germany. FAX 06221-768592. Ed. Dr. Karlheinz Kimmel. adv.; bk.rev.; charts; illus.; circ. 4,500. **Indexed:** Biol.Abstr., Dent.Ind.
—BLDSC shelfmark: 3553.320000.

617.6   US   ISSN 0011-8583
RK1
DENTAL ECONOMICS. 1911. m. $50 (foreign $95). PennWell Publishing Co., Dental Economics Division, Box 3408, Tulsa, OK 74101. TEL 918-835-3161. FAX 918-831-9497. Ed. Dick Hale. adv.; illus.; index; circ. 112,000. **Indexed:** Account.Ind. (1987-), Dent.Abstr., Dent.Ind.
   Formerly: Oral Hygiene.
   Description: Serves the business concerns of practicing dentists.

DENTAL EQUIP; guia de equipamiento dental. see *INSTRUMENTS*

617.6   GW   ISSN 0935-8447
DENTAL EQUIPMENT AND SUPPLY GUIDE. 1989. a. DM.50($33) Made in Europe Marketing Organization GmbH, Hahnstr. 70, 6000 Frankfurt a.M. 71, Germany. TEL 069-6668266. FAX 069-6668276. Ed. Veronique Schaufelberger. adv.; circ. 18,000. (back issues avail.)

617.6   CN   ISSN 0070-3656
DENTAL GUIDE. 1965. a. Can.$10.70 (foreign $10). Southam Business Communications Inc. (Subsidiary of: Southam Inc.), 1450 Don Mills Rd., Don Mills, Ont. M3B 2X7, Canada. TEL 416-445-6641. FAX 416-442-2261. adv.; circ. 13,663.

617.6   US
DENTAL HEALTH ADVISER. q. Whittle Communications L.P., 333 Main Ave., Knoxville, TN 37902. TEL 615-595-5300. Ed. Wayne Christensen.
   Description: Provides information regarding diet, dental hygiene and other areas of concern for dental patients, such as gum disease, braces and infant dental care.

617.6   US   ISSN 0070-3664
DENTAL IMAGES. 1961. 3/yr. free. Marquette University, School of Dentistry, 604 N. 16th St., Milwaukee, WI 53233. TEL 414-288-7738. Ed. Dr. Prem S. Sharma. adv.; circ. 7,800. **Indexed:** Dent.Ind.
   Description: For alumni and friends. Covers the school, the university, and their alumni.

617.6   US
▼**DENTAL IMPLANTOLOGY UPDATE.** 1990. m. $197. American Health Consultants, Inc., Six Piedmont Center, Ste. 400, 3525 Piedmont Rd., N.E., Atlanta, GA 30305. TEL 404-262-7436. FAX 800-284-3291. (Subscr. to: Box 740056, Atlanta, GA 30374-9822. TEL 800-688-2421) Ed. Morton Perel. circ. 1,050.

617.6   US   ISSN 8750-9539
DENTAL LAB MANAGEMENT TODAY. 1984. 10/yr. $17 (foreign $75). Dental Lab Publications, Inc., 205 Liberty Square., E. Norwalk, CT 06855. TEL 203-866-3302. FAX 203-838-3454. Ed. Maribeth Marsico. adv.; tr.lit.; circ. 18,500 (controlled). (reprint service avail.)

617.6   US   ISSN 0146-9738
DENTAL LAB PRODUCTS; timely products, news and features for dental laboratories. 1976. bi-mo $12. Medical Economics Publishing Co., Five Paragon Dr., Montvale, NJ 07645. TEL 201-358-7200. FAX 201-573-1045. Ed. Jeanne K. Matson. adv.; bk.rev.; illus.; tr.lit.; circ. 20,983. (tabloid format)

617.6   GW   ISSN 0011-8656
DAS DENTAL-LABOR; internationales Fachblatt fuer die gesamte Zahntechnik und ihre Randgebiete. 1953. m. DM.114 (foreign DM.126). Verlag Neuer Merkur GmbH, Ingolstaedter Str. 63a, 8000 Munich 46, Germany. TEL 089-318905-0. FAX 089-31890538. TELEX 5215-520. Ed. Dr. Joerg Lingenberg. adv.; bk.rev.; charts; illus.; pat.; stat.; index; circ. 17,000. (tabloid format) **Indexed:** Curr.Tit.Dent., Dent.Ind.

617.6   DK   ISSN 0070-3672
DENTAL LABORATORIE BLADET. 1949. 4/yr. DKK 150. (Association of Dental Laboratories in Denmark - Danske Dental Laboratorier) D L B -Bladforlag A-S, Rentemestervej 64, DK-2400 Copenhagen NV, Denmark. TEL 31-10-76-83. FAX 38-33-16-07. Eds. Vibeke Fialla, Alf Rasmussen. adv.; bk.rev.; circ. 500.

617.6   UK   ISSN 0957-5138
DENTAL LABORATORY. 1975. m. £36. Dental Laboratories Association Ltd., Chapel House, Noel St., Nottingham NG7 6AS, England. TEL 0602-704321. FAX 0602-422675. Ed. Bill Courtney. adv.; bk.rev.; circ. 3,000.
   Description: The official journal of the Dental Laboratories Association. Articles of interest to dental labs, DLA news and more.

617.6   US
DENTAL LABORATORY CONFERENCE. NEWS & VIEWS.* 1976. q. membership. Dental Laboratory Conference, 111 Presidential Blvd., Ste. 154, Bala Cynwyd, PA 19004-1008. FAX 215-546-9595. Ed. Robert C. Gitman. adv.; circ. 700. (back issues avail.)

617.6   US   ISSN 0011-8664
DENTAL LABORATORY NEWS. 1939. bi-m. $10. Dental Laboratory Association of State of New York, 42-01 215th Pl., Bayside, NY 11361-2934. Ed. Janice Bagley. adv.; bk.rev.; illus.; stat.; circ. 10,000.

DENTAL LABORATORY REVIEW BUYER'S GUIDE. see *MEDICAL SCIENCES — Experimental Medicine, Laboratory Technique*

617.6   US   ISSN 0109-5641
CODEN: DEMAEP
DENTAL MATERIALS. 1985. q. $145 to non-members. (Academy of Dental Materials) International and American Associations for Dental Research, 1111 14th St., N.W., Ste. 1000, Washington, DC 20005. TEL 202-898-1050. FAX 202-789-1033. Ed. Victoria A. Marker. adv.; bk.rev.; circ. 850. (also avail. in microfilm from UMI; back issues avail.) **Indexed:** Curr.Tit.Dent., Dent.Abstr.
—BLDSC shelfmark: 3553.365800.
   Description: Devoted to the materials used in dentistry; covers all aspects of materials science, such as laboratory, clinical, and animal testing of materials and their components, as well as instruments and equipment; interactions of materials, testing methods, and protocols.

617.1   US
DENTAL OFFICE; today's magazine for the dental staff. 1981. m. $48. Stevens Publishing Corporation, 225 N. New Rd., Waco, TX 76710. TEL 817-776-9000. FAX 817-776-9018. Ed. Kathy Witherspoon. adv.; tr.lit.; circ. 7,000. **Indexed:** Dent.Ind.
   Formerly: Dental Assisting.

617.6   JA   ISSN 0011-8702
DENTAL OUTLOOK/SHIKAI TENBO. (Text in Japanese) 1921. m. 1300 Yen per no. Ishiyaku Publishers, Inc., 7-10 Honkomagome 1-chome, Bunkyo-ku, Tokyo 113, Japan. Ed. Hiroshi Miura. adv.; bk.rev.; abstr.; charts; illus.; s-a. index; circ. 24,500. **Indexed:** Dent.Ind.
—BLDSC shelfmark: 3553.370000.

617.6   UK   ISSN 0011-8710
DENTAL PRACTICE; the journal of modern techniques, equipment and materials. vol.2, 1970. s-m. £25 (foreign £35)(effective Jan. 1992). A.E. Morgan Publications Ltd., Stanley House, 9 West St., Epsom, Surrey KT18 7RL, England. TEL 0372-741411. FAX 0372-744493. Ed. H.C. Davis. adv.; bk.rev.; abstr.; charts; illus.; circ. 23,300. (tabloid format; also avail. in microform from UMI; reprint service avail. from UMI) **Indexed:** Curr.Tit.Dent., Dent.Ind.
—BLDSC shelfmark: 3553.372300.
   Incorporating: Dental News.
   Description: Entertaining and informative reading for dentists including up-to-date articles on products and news.

617.6 380.1   UK
DENTAL PRACTICE DIRECTORY. 1985. a. £7.10 (effective Jan. 1992). A.E. Morgan Publications Ltd., Stanley House, 9 West Street, Epsom, Surrey KT18 7RL, England. TEL 0372-741411. FAX 0372-744493. circ. 7,500.
   Description: Listing of suppliers and contacts to dental practitioners.

617.6 658   CN
DENTAL PRACTICE MANAGEMENT. 1985. q. Can.$16.85($19.50) (foreign $32). Southam Business Communications Inc. (Subsidiary of: Southam Inc.), 1450 Don Mills Rd., Don Mills, Ont. M3B 2X7, Canada. TEL 416-445-6641. FAX 416-442-2261. Ed. Janet Bonellie. circ. 16,910. (back issues avail.) **Indexed:** Dent.Abstr.

MEDICAL SCIENCES — DENTISTRY

617.6 US ISSN 0011-8737
CODEN: DPREE3
DENTAL PRODUCTS REPORT; trends in dentistry. 1967. 11/yr. $44. Medical Economics Company Inc., 680 Kinderkamack Rd., Oradell, NJ 07649. TEL 201-262-3030. FAX 201-262-5461. Ed. Jeanne K. Matson. adv.; bk.rev.; illus.; tr.lit.; circ. 147,801 (controlled). (tabloid format)
Formerly: Dental Products Annual Report (ISSN 0070-3702)

617.6 658 AT
DENTAL REPORTER. 1980. m. Aus.$95. Daber Holdings, P.O. Box 575, 98 Alfred St., Ste. 12, Milsons Point 2061, Australia. TEL 02 922-4477. FAX 02-922-2247. Ed. Peter Harrigan. adv.; bk.rev.; circ. 3,000. (back issues avail.)

617.6 PH
DENTAL SERVICE QUARTERLY. 4/yr. Philippines Dental Society, Armed Forces, 23 Zamboanga St., Diliman, Quezon City, Philippines. adv.; circ. 1,200.

617.6 US
DENTAL SOCIETY OF WESTERN PENNSYLVANIA. BULLETIN. 1900. bi-m. $36. Dental Society of Western Pennsylvania, 900 Cedar Ave., Pittsburgh, PA 15212. TEL 412-321-5810. Ed. Dr. V. Lynne Cochran. adv.; bk.rev.; charts; illus.; circ. 1,600. **Indexed**: Dent.Ind.
Formerly: Odontological Bulletin (ISSN 0029-8433)

617.6 CN
DENTAL STUDY CLUB; journal of dental continuing education. bi-m. Decker Periodicals, One James St. S., P.O Box 620, LCD 1, Hamilton, Ont. L8N 3K7, Canada. TEL 416-522-7017. FAX 416-522-7839. (U.S. addr.: Box 785, Lewiston, NY 14092) Ed. Dr. Willian F. Wathen. abstr.
Description: Presents abstracts and expert reviews from 60 dental journals.

617.6 US
DENTAL TEAMWORK. bi-m. American Dental Association, 211 E. Chicago Ave., Ste. 840, Chicago, IL 60611-2616. TEL 312-440-2500. FAX 312-440-2550. Ed. Linda Strouls. circ. 90,110.

617.6 UK ISSN 0011-8796
DENTAL TECHNICIAN. 1948. m. £12.50 (foreign £18)(effective Jan. 1992). A.E. Morgan Publications Ltd., Stanley House, 9 West St., Epsom, Surrey KT18 7RL, England. TEL 0372-741411. FAX 0372-744493. Ed. C. Lloyd. adv.; bk.rev.; illus.; circ. 3,500. **Indexed**: Br.Ceram.Abstr., Curr.Tit.Dent., Dent.Ind.
Description: Listing of suppliers and contacts for dental technicians.

617.6 UK
DENTAL TECHNICIAN YEARBOOK & DIRECTORY. 1979. a. £7.40 (effective Jan. 1992). A.E. Morgan Publications Ltd., Stanley House, 9 West St., Epsom, Surrey KT18 7RL, England. TEL 0372-741411. FAX 0372-744493. Ed. D. Ritchie. adv.

617.3 UK ISSN 0305-5000
DENTAL UPDATE. 1972. 10/yr. £32. Reed Business Publishing Group, Carew Division (Subsidiary of: Reed International PLC), Quadrant House, The Quadrant, Sutton, Surrey SM2 5AS, England. TEL 081-661-3500. Ed. A. Baxter. adv.; bk.rev.; cum.index; circ. 8,500. **Indexed**: Curr.Adv.Ecol.Sci., Curr.Tit.Dent., Dent.Ind.
—BLDSC shelfmark: 3553.515000.
Description: Provides dentists with in-depth clinical information on orthodontics, preventative, restorative and conservative dentistry.

617.6 SA ISSN 1011-5986
DENTAL UPDATE; the journal for the general dental practitioner. (South African and UK editions) (Text in English) 1987. m. R.75. George Warman Publications (Pty.) Ltd., P.O. Box 704, 77 Hout St., Cape Town 8000, South Africa. TEL 021-24-5320. FAX 021-261-332. TELEX 521849. Ed. A. Rademeyer. adv.; circ. 2,499. (back issues avail.)
Description: Clinical journal for the continuing education of dentist.

617.6 CN
DENTALETTER. 10/yr. Can.$89. M P L Communications Inc., 700-133 Richmond St. W., Toronto, Ont. M5H 3M8, Canada. TEL 416-869-1177. FAX 416-869-0456.
Description: Professional source letter for the dentist.

617.6 SA ISSN 0259-563X
DENTEKSA. (Text in Afrikaans, English) 1980. q. (Dental Laboratories Association of South Africa) M.I.M.S. (Subsidiary of: Times Media Ltd.), P.O. Box 2059, Pretoria 0001, South Africa. TEL 012-3485010. FAX 012-477716. Ed. A. Hacquebord. adv.; bk.rev.; charts; illus.; index; circ. 750. **Indexed**: Ind.S.A.Per.
Description: A journal for the dental technician.

617.6 UK ISSN 0266-3414
DENTIST. m. £29. Reed Business Publishing Group, Carew Division (Subsidiary of: Reed International PLC), Quadrant House, The Quadrant, Sutton, Surrey SM2 5AS, England. TEL 081-661-3500. Ed. Jennifer C. Dyer. (back issues avail.)

617.6 US
DENTIST (WACO). 1923. bi-m. $36. Stevens Publishing Corporation, 225 N. New Rd., Waco, TX 76710. FAX 817-776-9018. Ed. Mark Hartley. adv.; bk.rev.; illus.; circ. 110,000. (also avail. in microform from UMI; reprint service avail. from UMI) **Indexed**: Dent.Ind.
Former titles: Dental Student - Dentalpractice; Dental Student (ISSN 0011-877X); Dental Students' Magazine.
Description: Presents study and teaching methods.

617.6 US ISSN 0277-3635
CODEN: DENTEJ
DENTISTRY (YEAR). 1981. q. $8 (foreign $16). American Student Dental Association, 211 E. Chicago Ave., Ste. 840, Chicago, IL 60611. TEL 312-440-2795. adv.; circ. 15,000. (reprint service avail.)
—BLDSC shelfmark: 3553.544000.

617.6 JA ISSN 0070-3737
DENTISTRY IN JAPAN. (Text in English) 1968. a. membership. (Japanese Association for Dental Science - Nihon Shika Igakkai) Japan Dental Association, 4-1-20 Kudan-Kita, Chiyoda-ku, Tokyo 102, Japan. FAX 03-3262-9885. Ed. I. Ishikawa. circ. 1,300 (controlled).
—BLDSC shelfmark: 3553.545000.

617.6 US
DENTISTRY TODAY. 1982. 9/yr. $30. Dentistry Today, Inc., 26 Park St., Montclair, NJ 07042. TEL 201-783-3935. FAX 201-783-7112. Ed. Ted Fetner. adv.; tr.lit.; circ. 140,000.

DENTISTS' COMPUTER NEWS. see MEDICAL SCIENCES — Computer Applications

617.6 US ISSN 0011-9601
DETROIT DENTAL BULLETIN.* 1939. m. (10/yr.). $15 to non-members. Detroit District Dental Society, 7430 2nd Ave., Ste. 420, Detroit, MI 48202. TEL 313-871-3500. Ed. Dr. Wallin McMinn. adv.; bk.rev.; abstr.; circ. 1,900. **Indexed**: Dent.Ind.
—BLDSC shelfmark: 3561.500000.

617.6 GW ISSN 0012-1029
CODEN: DZZEA7
DEUTSCHE ZAHNAERZTLICHE ZEITSCHRIFT. (Summaries in English) 1946. m. DM.247.20. (Deutsche Gesellschaft fuer Zahn-, Mund- und Kieferheilkunde) Carl Hanser Verlag, Kolbergerstr. 22, Postfach 860420, 8000 Munich 80, Germany. TEL 089-926940. Ed.Bd. adv.; bk.rev.; abstr.; charts; illus.; circ. 6,300. **Indexed**: Biol.Abstr., Chem.Abstr., Curr.Cont., Curr.Tit.Dent., Dent.Ind., Ind.Med., INIS Atomind.
—BLDSC shelfmark: 3575.694000.

617.643 GW ISSN 0178-7276
DEUTSCHE ZEITSCHRIFT FUER BIOLOGISCHE ZAHNMEDIZIN; Archiv fuer ganzheitliche Stomatologie. q. DM.75 (students DM.57). Karl F. Haug Verlag GmbH, Fritz-Frey-Str. 21, Postfach 102840, 6900 Heidelberg 1, Germany. TEL 06221-4062-0. FAX 06221-400727. TELEX 461683-HVVFMD. Ed. Dr. Christoph Herrmann.

617.6 GW ISSN 0343-3137
DEUTSCHE ZEITSCHRIFT FUER MUND, KIEFER- UND GESICHTSCHIRURGIE. (Summaries in English) 1977. bi-m. DM.317.40. (Deutsche Gesellschaft fuer Mund- Kiefer- und Gesichtschirurgie) Carl Hanser Verlag, Kolbergerstr. 22, Postfach 860420, 8000 Munich 80, Germany. TEL 089-926940. (Co-sponsor: Berufsverband Deutscher Aerzte fuer Mund-Kiefer-Gesichtschirurgie e.V.) adv.; bk.rev.; abstr.; charts; illus.; circ. 1,350. **Indexed**: Curr.Tit.Dent.
—BLDSC shelfmark: 3575.815000.

DEUTSCHER KONGRESS KALENDER ZAHNMEDIZINER. see MEETINGS AND CONGRESSES

617.6 GW
DEUTSCHER ZAHNAERZTEKALENDER. 1941. a. DM.56. Carl Hanser Verlag, Kolbergerstr. 22, Postfach 860420, 8000 Munich 80, Germany. TEL 089-926940. Ed. Dr. Werner Ketterl. adv.; circ. 6,000.

617.5 MX
DICCIONARIO DE ESPECIALIDADES ODONTOLOGICAS. 1984. a. Ediciones P L M, S.A. de C.V., San Bernadino 17, Colonia del Valle, 03100 Mexico D.F., Mexico. TEL 687-1311. FAX 536-5027. TELEX 01772912 EPLM ME. Ed. Patricia Calderon. circ. 5,000.

617.6 378 US
DIRECTORY OF DENTAL EDUCATORS. 1966. biennial. $50 to non-members; members $30. American Association of Dental Schools, 1625 Massachusetts Ave., N.W., Washington, DC 20036-2212. TEL 202-667-9433. (reprint service avail. from UMI)
Former titles: Directory of Dental and Allied Dental Educators (ISSN 0271-8677); Directory of Dental Educators (ISSN 0090-0141); (until 1971): Directory of Dental Educators in the United States and Canada.

617.6 US
DISTRIBUTION OF DENTISTS IN THE U S. triennial. $22.50 to non-members; members $15. American Dental Association, Bureau of Economic and Behavioral Research, 211 E. Chicago Ave., Chicago, IL 60611. TEL 312-440-2500.

617.6 US
DISTRICT OF COLUMBIA DENTAL SOCIETY. NEWSLETTER. 1915. 10/yr. membership. District of Columbia Dental Society, 502 C St., N.E., Washington, DC 20002-5810. TEL 202-547-7613. FAX 202-546-1482. Ed. Kim Groover. adv.; circ. 1,000.

617.6 US ISSN 0012-8759
EASTERN DENTAL SOCIETY BULLETIN.* vol.11, 1968. m. membership. Eastern Dental Society, c/o Tim Wong, D.D.S., 85 4th Ave., New York, NY 10003. bk.rev.; illus.

617.6 UA ISSN 0070-9484
EGYPTIAN DENTAL JOURNAL. (Text in English; summaries in Arabic) 1955. q. $36. Egyptian Dental Association, Dar el Hekma, 42 Kasr el-Eini St., Cairo, Egypt. Ed. Dr. M. el Sadeek. **Indexed**: Biol.Abstr., Dent.Ind.

617.6 GR
ELLINIKI ODONTIATRIKI OMOSPONDIA. ENEMEROTIKO DELTIO/HELLENIC DENTAL ASSOCIATION. JOURNAL. (Text in Greek) 4/yr. free to qualified personnel. Hellenic Dental Association, Themistokleous 38, 106 78 Athens, Greece. TEL 36-13-380. Ed. Dimitrios Damoulis.

617.6 DK ISSN 0109-2502
CODEN: EDTRED
ENDODONTICS & DENTAL TRAUMATOLOGY. (Supplements avail.) (Text and summaries in English) 1985. bi-m. DKK 990. Munksgaard International Publishers Ltd., 35 Noerre Soegade, P.O. Box 2148, DK-1016 Copenhagen K, Denmark. TEL 33-127030. FAX 33-129387. TELEX 19431-MUNKS-DK. Ed. Leif Tronstad. adv.; circ. 800. (back issues avail.) **Indexed**: Chem.Abstr., Curr.Cont., Curr.Tit.Dent., Dent.Abstr., Excerp.Med.
—BLDSC shelfmark: 3743.120000.

MEDICAL SCIENCES — DENTISTRY

617.6   BL
EQUIPE DE ODONTOLOGIA SANITARIA. BOLETIM.* (Text in Portuguese; occasionally in Spanish) 1964. 4/yr. free. Departamento da Saude, Esplanada dos Ministerios, Bloco 11, 70058 Brasilia, D.F., Brazil. Ed. Dr. Antonio Motta Gimenez. bibl.; charts; stat.; circ. 1,000 (controlled). (looseleaf format)
   Formerly: Servico de Odontologia Sanitaria. Boletim (ISSN 0037-2722)

617.6   BL
ESPECIALIDADES ODONTOLOGICAS.* m. Cr.$15.($8) Pontificia Universidade Catolica do Rio de Janeiro, Instituto de Odontologia, Garca, Rua Marques de Sao Vicente 225, 22453 Rio de Janeiro, Brazil. Ed. Aristeo Leite. **Indexed:** I.P.A.
   Formerly: Revista de Farmacia e Odontologia (ISSN 0034-8201)

617.6   SP   ISSN 0212-4939
ESTOMODEO/STOMATOLOGY. 1983. 6/yr. 4500 ptas. Editores Medicos, S.A., Paseo de la Castellana, 53, 28046 Madrid, Spain. TEL 442-86-56. FAX 442-80-43. circ. 5,000.

617.6   UK   ISSN 0141-5387
EUROPEAN JOURNAL OF ORTHODONTICS. 1979. q. £80($145) (European Association of Orthodontics) Oxford University Press, Oxford Journals, Pinkhill House, Southfield Road, Eynsham, Oxford OX8 1JJ, England. TEL 0865-882283. FAX 0865-882890. TELEX 837330 OXPRES G. Ed. W.J.B. Houston. adv.; bk.rev.; circ. 2,000. **Indexed:** Biol.Abstr., Curr.Cont., Dent.Ind., Excerpt.Med., Ind.Med.
—BLDSC shelfmark: 3829.733300.
   Description: Presents research or clinical papers of interest to all orthodontists.

617.6   NE
EXKIES; vaktijdschrift voor tandartsen en tandtechnici. 1981. m. fl.105. Hofstad Vakpers B.V., Postbus 119, 2700 AC Zoetermeer, Netherlands. TEL 079-711811. FAX 079-711803. Ed. M.J.M. van Duijn. circ. 4,950.

617.6   US   ISSN 0894-7929
EXPLORER (FALLS CHURCH). 1974. m. $15 (foreign $20). National Association of Dental Assistants, 900 S. Washington St., Ste. G13, Falls Church, VA 22046. TEL 703-237-8616. Ed. S. Young. circ. 3,000.

617.6   US
EXPLORER (LAKE WORTH). 1972. s-a. free. Atlantic Coast District Dental Association, 5700 Lake Worth Rd., Ste. 206, Lake Worth, FL 33463. TEL 407-968-7714. Ed. Dr. John R. Jordan. adv.; tr.lit.; circ. 980. **Indexed:** Biol.Abstr., Biol.Dig., GeoRef.

617.6   UK   ISSN 0965-9986
F D I DENTAL WORLD. (Editions in English, French, German and Spanish) 1952. bi-m. £30 to non-members in Europe; elsewhere £35. (Federation Dentaire Internationale - International Dental Federation) F D I World Dental Press Ltd., 64 Wimpole St., London W1M 8AL, England. TEL 44-071-935-7852. FAX 44-071-486-0182. Ed. Dr. Stephen Hancocks. adv.; bk.rev.; illus.; circ. 17,000.
   Former titles (until 1992): F D I News; F D I Newsletter (ISSN 0014-5777)
   Description: Includes clinical articles, dental news from around the world, news of the F D I's activities, and the trade industry; also contains features and congress news.

617.6   US
FACETS (SAN DIEGO). 1930. m. $20. San Diego County Dental Society, 3942 Hancock St., San Diego, CA 92210-1562. TEL 619-223-5391. FAX 619-223-9947. Ed. Dr. Harriet Seldin. adv.; circ. 1,300. **Indexed:** Dent.Ind.
   Former titles: San Diego County Dental Society. News; San Diego County Dental Society. Bulletin (ISSN 0036-4010)

617.6   US   ISSN 0517-1024
RK58
FACTS ABOUT STATES FOR THE DENTIST SEEKING A LOCATION. 1953. irreg. (every 2-3 yrs.). $4.50 to non-members; members $3. American Dental Association, Bureau of Economic Research and Statistics, 211 E. Chicago Ave., Chicago, IL 60611. TEL 312-440-2500.

617.6   BL   ISSN 0048-3419
FACULDADE DE ODONTOLOGIA DE PERNAMBUCO. REVISTA. (Text in Portuguese; summaries in English, Portuguese) 1968. s-a. free. Faculdade de Odontologia de Pernambuco, Biblioteca, Av. General Newton Cavalcanti, 1650, Camarajibe, Pernambuco, Brazil. illus.; index. **Indexed:** Dent.Ind.

617.6   BL
FACULDADE DE ODONTOLOGIA DE PORTO ALEGRE. REVISTA.. (Text in Portuguese; summaries in English) 1958. irreg., vol.28, 1988. $100. Universidade Federal do Rio Grande do Sul, Faculdade de Odontologia, Ramiro Barcelos 2492, P.O. Box 1118, 90000 Porto Alegre, Brazil. TEL 0512-25-57-84. TELEX 051-1055. Eds. Jorge H. Brito, Pantelis Varvaki Rados. adv.; circ. 3,500. (back issues avail.) **Indexed:** Bibliogr.Bras.Odontol., Dent.Ind.
   Formerly: Universidade Federal do Rio Grande do Sul. Faculdade de Odontologia. Revista (ISSN 0477-6763)
   Description: Covers orthodontics, dental oclusion, pathology, preventive dentistry and dental care.

617.6   CK   ISSN 0046-354X
FEDERACION ODONTOLOGICA COLOMBIANA. REVISTA. 1950. 4/yr. Federacion Odontologica Colombiana, Calle 71 No. 11-10, Of 1101, Apdo. Aereo 52925, Bogota, Colombia. Ed. Edmundo Alberto Noguera. adv.; illus. **Indexed:** Dent.Ind., Ind.Med.

FINLAND. LAAKINTOHALLITUS. LAAKARIT, HAMMASLAAKARIT - LAKARE, TANDLAEKARE. see *MEDICAL SCIENCES*

617.6   FI   ISSN 0039-551X
                                   CODEN: PFDSAX
FINNISH DENTAL SOCIETY. PROCEEDINGS. (Text in English) 1904. 4/yr. FIM 480($110) Finnish Dental Society, Akavatalo, Rautatielaisenkatu 6, SF-00520 Helsinki 52, Finland. TEL 358-0-15021. FAX 358-0-143317. Ed. Matti Narhi. adv.; charts; illus.; index; circ. 5,800. (back issues avail.) **Indexed:** Biol.Abstr., Curr.Adv.Cancer Res., Curr.Adv.Ecol.Sci., Dent.Abstr., Dent.Ind., Ind.Med.
—BLDSC shelfmark: 6700.700000.
   Description: Presents original research reports, reviews, case studies, and short communications concerning the dental sciences and oral health.

617.6   FI   ISSN 0355-4651
FINNISH DENTAL SOCIETY. PROCEEDINGS. SUPPLEMENT. (Text in English) 1966. irreg. included in subscr. to Finnish Dental Society Proceedings. Finnish Dental Society, Akavatalo, Rautatielaisenkatu 6, SF-00520 Helsinki, Finland. TEL 08-015021. FAX 08-01496855. Ed. Matti Narhi. **Indexed:** Chem.Abstr.

614   US
FLUORIDATION CENSUS. 1954. quinquennial. U.S. Center for Prevention Services, Division of Oral Health, Program Services Branch, 1600 Clifton Rd., N.E., F-10, Atlanta, GA 30333. TEL 404-488-4451. FAX 404-488-4488.

FLUORIDE. see *MEDICAL SCIENCES — Abstracting, Bibliographies, Statistics*

617.6   US
FOCUS ON OHIO DENTISTRY. m. $30 to non-members. Ohio Dental Association, 1370 Dublin Rd., Columbus, OH 43215-1098. TEL 614-486-2700. (Subscr. to: Dept. 367, Box 182039, Columbus, OH 43218-2039)

617.6   HU   ISSN 0015-5314
FOGORVOSI SZEMLE. (Summaries in German and Russian) vol.70, 1976. m. $38.50. (Magyar Fogorvosok Egyesulete) Ifjusagi Lap-es Konyvkiado Vallalat, Revai u. 16, 1374 Budapest 6, Hungary. (Subscr. to: Kultura, P.O. Box 149, H-1389 Budapest, Hungary) Ed. Tibor Fabian. adv.; bk.rev.; illus.; index; circ. 2,400. **Indexed:** Biol.Abstr., Chem.Abstr., Dent.Ind., Ind.Med.
—BLDSC shelfmark: 3964.300000.

617.6   US   ISSN 0071-9285
LJ105.P75
FRATER OF PSI OMEGA. 1901. 4/yr. membership. Psi Omega Fraternity, 1030 Lincoln Ave., Prospect Park, PA 19076. TEL 215-532-2330. Ed. Christina E. Angott. circ. 8,500.

617.6   GW   ISSN 0340-1766
DER FREIE ZAHNARZT. 1958. m. DM.2.50. (Freier Verband Deutscher Zahnaerzte e.V.) Druck und Verlag Kern und Birner, Werrastr. 4, 6000 Frankfurt 90, Germany. Ed. Hanns Meenzen. adv.; bk.rev.; circ. 35,000. **Indexed:** Curr.Tit.Dent., Dent.Ind.
   Formerly: Monatschrift Deutscher Zahnaerzte (ISSN 0047-7842)

617.643   SZ   ISSN 0301-536X
                                   CODEN: FROPBK
FRONTIERS OF ORAL PHYSIOLOGY. (Text in English) 1974. irreg. price varies. S. Karger AG, Allschwilerstr. 10, P.O. Box, CH-4009 Basel, Switzerland. TEL 061-3061111. FAX 061-3061234. TELEX CH 962652. Ed. D.B. Ferguson. (reprint service avail. from ISI) **Indexed:** Biol.Abstr., Chem.Abstr., Ind.Med.
—BLDSC shelfmark: 4042.045000.

617.6   US   ISSN 8756-3150
FUNCTIONAL ORTHODONTIST; a journal of functional jaw orthopedics. vol.4, 1987. bi-m. $69. c/o The AAFO, 106 S. Kent St., Winchester, VA 22601. TEL 703-662-2200. Ed. Dr. Craig C. Stoner.
—BLDSC shelfmark: 4055.630000.

617.6   US   ISSN 0884-6898
G M D A BULLETIN. 1934. q. $30 (foreign $40). Greater Milwaukee Dental Association, 3953 N. 76th St., Milwaukee, WI 53222. TEL 414-461-0230. Ed. R.F. Johnson. adv.; charts; illus.; circ. 1,000. **Indexed:** Dent.Ind.
—BLDSC shelfmark: 4196.370000.
   Formerly: Greater Milwaukee Dental Bulletin (ISSN 0017-3754)

617.6   US
G P. m. $127. American Health Consultants, Inc., Six Piedmont Center, Ste. 400, 3525 Piedmont Rd., N.E., Atlanta, GA 30305. TEL 404-262-7436. FAX 404-262-7837. (Subscr. to: Box 740056, Atlanta, GA 30374-9822. TEL 800-688-2421) Ed. Fran W. Goldstein. circ. 4,000.
   Incorporates (in 1992): Cosmetic Dentistry for G Ps & Dental Practice Success; Which incorporates (in 1990): American Health Consultants. Press Report; Former titles: Dental Update on Practice Management; Dental Management Update. Incorporates (1990-1991): Dentist's Malpractice Protector; (1989-1991): Endodontics for G Ps; (1989-1991): Soft Tissue Care for G Ps.
   Description: Covers clinical topics of interest to the general dentist such as aesthetic dentistry, periodontics, endodontics, implant dentistry, pediatric dentistry and orthodontics.

617.6   UK   ISSN 0072-0674
GENERAL DENTAL COUNCIL. DENTISTS REGISTER. 1878. a. £18.50. General Dental Council, 37 Wimpole St., London W1M 8DQ, England. TEL 071-486-2171. FAX 071-224-3294. (back issues avail.)

617.6   UK   ISSN 0072-0682
GENERAL DENTAL COUNCIL. MINUTES OF THE PROCEEDINGS. 1956. a. £10. General Dental Council, 37 Wimpole St., London W1M 8DQ, England. TEL 071-486-2171. FAX 071-224-3294.

617.6   UK
▼**GENERAL DENTAL TREATMENT.** 1991. 2/yr. Churchill Livingstone Medical Journals, Robert Stevenson House, 1-3 Baxter's Pl., Leith Walk, Edinburgh EH1 3AF, Scotland. TEL 031-556-2424. FAX 031-558-1278. TELEX 727511. (Subscr. to: Longman Group, Journals Subscr. Dept., P.O. Box 77, Fourth Ave., Harlow, Essex CM19 5AA, England; U.S. subscr. to: Churchill Livingstone, 650 Ave. of the Americas, New York, NY 10011. TEL 212-206-5000) Eds. Dr. W.M. Tay, E. Lynch.
   Description: Provides updates on materials, techniques, and drugs commonplace in dentistry today.

MEDICAL SCIENCES — DENTISTRY

617.6 US ISSN 0363-6771
GENERAL DENTISTRY. 1952. bi-m. $25 to individuals; institutions $40. Academy of General Dentistry, 211 E. Chicago Ave., Ste. 1200, Chicago, IL 60611. TEL 312-440-4300. FAX 312-440-0559. Ed. Dr. William W. Howard. adv.; bk.rev.; illus.; index; circ. 45,000. (reprint service avail. from UMI) **Indexed:** Biol.Abstr., Dent.Ind., Energy Res.Abstr.
Former titles: Academy of General Dentistry. Journal (ISSN 0001-4265); Academy of General Dentistry. Bulletin (ISSN 0098-3810)
Description: Offers clinical data and management information for the general dentist.
Refereed Serial

617.6 IT
GIORNALE DELL'ODONTOIATRA; dental flash. 1984. 18/yr. L.3600($21) (effective 1991). Masson Italia Periodici, Via Statuto 2-4, 20121 Milan, Italy. TEL 02-6367-1. FAX 02-6367-211. circ. 25,000. (tabloid format)

617.643 IT
GIORNALE DI STOMATOLOGIA E DI ORTOGNATODONZIA. 1982. q. $50. Poliambulatorio Odontoiatrico Riunito S.r.l., P.za Castello, 9, 31046 Oderzo (TV), Italy. Dir. Dr. Lorenzo Favero. adv.; bk.rev.; circ. 5,000.

617.643 IT
GIOVANE ODONTOIATRIA. 1984. q. L.34000($42) (effective 1992). (Associazione Italiana Studenti in Odontoiatria) Masson Italia Periodici, Via Statuto 2-4, 20121 Milan, Italy. TEL 02-6367-1. FAX 02-6367211. circ. 4,200.
Formerly: Bollettino Nazionale A I S O.

616.7 BE ISSN 0303-7479
CODEN: BGEODI
GROUPEMENT INTERNATIONAL POUR LA RECHERCHE EN STOMATOLOGIE ET ODONTOLOGIE. BULLETIN. q. 2000 F. International Group for Research in Stomatology and Odontology, Institut de Stomatologie, Hospital Universitaire Saint-Pierre, Rue Haute 322, 1000 Brussels, Belgium. **Indexed:** Curr.Adv.Ecol.Sci., Excerp.Med., Ind.Med.

617.6 TU
HACETTEPE FACULTY OF DENTISTRY. JOURNAL/HACETTEPE DIS HEKIMLIGI FAKULTESI DERGISI. Variant title: Hacettepe Universitesi. Dis Hekimligi Fakultesi. Dergisi. (Text in Turkish; summaries in English, French or German) 1977. q. University of Hacettepe, Faculty of Dentistry - Hacettepe Universitesi, Dis Hekimligi Fakultesi, Ankara, Turkey. Ed. Aytekin Bilge.
Description: Keeps dentists informed on research being done in the field of dentistry and related areas.

617.6 US ISSN 0046-6891
HARVARD DENTAL ALUMNI BULLETIN. 1940. 2/yr. free. Harvard Dental Alumni Association, 188 Longwood Ave., Boston, MA 02115. TEL 617-732-2186. Ed. Richard S. Carroll. illus.; circ. 3,000. **Indexed:** Ind.Med.
Supersedes: Harvard Dental Record.
Description: Contains articles and news items on Harvard Dental alumni and on the teaching, research, and clinical activities of the Harvard School of Dental Medicine.

617.6 US
HARVARD DENTAL BULLETIN. s-a. Harvard School of Dental Medicine, 188 Longwood Ave., Boston, MA 02115. (Co-sponsor: Harvard Dental Alumni Association) Ed. Henry D. Epstein.

617.6 US ISSN 0073-1021
HAWAII DENTAL ASSOCIATION. TRANSACTIONS. a. (typically set in Jan.). Hawaii Dental Association, 1000 Bishop St., Ste. 805, Honolulu, HI 96813. TEL 808-536-2135. FAX 808-536-2137.

617.6 US
HAWAII DENTAL JOURNAL. 1967. m. $20 (foreign $25)(typically set in Jan.). Hawaii Dental Association, 1000 Bishop St., Ste. 805, Honolulu, HI 96813. TEL 808-536-2135. FAX 808-536-2137. Ed. Dr. Martin Nweeia. adv.; illus.; circ. 950 (controlled). **Indexed:** Dent.Abstr., Dent.Ind.
Formerly: Hawaii State Dental Association. Journal (ISSN 0017-8616)

617.3 US ISSN 0073-1404
HAYES DIRECTORY OF DENTAL SUPPLY HOUSES. 1935. a. $75. Edward N. Hayes, Ed. & Pub., 4229 Birch St., Newport Beach, CA 92660. TEL 714-756-9063.

HEALTHSTATE. see *MEDICAL SCIENCES*

617.6 GR
HELLENIC STOMATOLOGICAL REVIEW. (Text in Greek; summaries in English) 1957. q. Dr.1000($15) (students Dr.500). Hellenic Dental Association, 38 Themistocleous St, Athens 142, Greece. Ed.Bd. adv.; bk.rev.; bibl.; charts; illus.; index; circ. 5,000.
Former titles: Hellenic Stomatological Annals; Acta Stomatologica Hellenica.

617.6 JA ISSN 0046-7472
HIROSHIMA UNIVERSITY DENTAL SOCIETY. JOURNAL/HIROSHIMA DAIGAKU SHIGAKU ZASSHI. (Text in English or Japanese) 1969. s-a. $12. Hiroshima Daigaku Shigakkai - Hiroshima University Dental Society, Hiroshima Daigaku, 2-3 Kasumi 1-chome, Minami-ku, Hiroshima 734, Japan. Ed. Nobuo Nagasaka. adv.; illus. (also avail. in microform from UMI; reprint service avail. from UMI) **Indexed:** Chem.Abstr., Dent.Ind., INIS Atomind.
—BLDSC shelfmark: 4758.330000.

617.6 JA ISSN 0073-2915
HOKKAIDO DENTAL ASSOCIATION. JOURNAL/HOKKAIDO SHIKA ISHIKAISHI, DOSHIKAI TSUSHIN. (Text in Japanese) 1948. a. Hokkaido Dental Association - Hokkaido Shika Ishikai, 7-2 Odori Nishi, Chuo-ku, Sapporo 060, Japan.

617.6 CC ISSN 1000-1182
HUAXI KOUQIANG YIXUE ZAZHI/WEST CHINA JOURNAL OF STOMATOLOGY. (Text in Chinese; summaries in English) 1983. q. Y7.2. Huaxi Yike Daxue - West China University of Medical Sciences, 14, Remin Nanlu 3 Duan, Chengdu, Sichuan 610041, People's Republic of China. FAX 028-583252. (Co-sponsor: Sichuan Branch of the Chinese Medical Association) Ed. Wang Hanzhang.

617.6 US ISSN 0018-8875
I C D LETTERETTE. Alternate issues titled: I C D Newsletter. vol.2, 1970. membership. International College of Dentists, c/o Dr. William E. Hawkins, Ed., 320 W. Indian School Rd., Phoenix, AZ 85013. TEL 602-248-9445. circ. 6,000.

617.6 US ISSN 0019-1973
ILLINOIS DENTAL JOURNAL. 1905. bi-m. $30. Illinois State Dental Society, 524 S. Fifth St., Box 376, Springfield, IL 62705. TEL 217-525-1406. FAX 217-525-8872. Ed. Dr. Roger H. Scholle. adv.; illus.; index; circ. 6,000 (controlled). (also avail. in microform from UMI; reprint service avail.) **Indexed:** Chem.Abstr., Dent.Abstr., Dent.Ind.
—BLDSC shelfmark: 4365.120000.

617.6 US
▼**IMPLANT DENTISTRY.** 1992. q. $76. Williams & Wilkins, 428 E. Preston St., Baltimore, MD 21202. TEL 410-528-4000. Ed. Sheldon Winkler. adv.: B&W page $550, color page $1240; trim 8 1/8 x 10 7/8. circ. 3,500.
Description: Covers oral implantology, biomaterials, clinical reports, oral and maxillofacial surgery, oral pathology, periodontics, prosthodontics and research.
Refereed Serial

617.6 II ISSN 0019-4611
INDIAN DENTAL ASSOCIATION. JOURNAL. (Text in English) 1925. m. Rs.60($30) Indian Dental Association, 532, 10th Main, 5th Block, Jayanagar, Bangalore 560 041, India. TEL 643838. Ed. K.G. Ghorpade. adv.; B&W page Rs.2,500, color page Rs.5,000. bk.rev.; abstr.; charts; illus.; index; circ. 3,000. **Indexed:** Dent.Abstr., Dent.Ind.
—BLDSC shelfmark: 4764.500000.
Formerly: All India Dental Association. Journal.

617.6 US ISSN 0019-6568
CODEN: IDNJBY
INDIANA DENTAL ASSOCIATION. JOURNAL. vol.54, 1975. bi-m. $25 to non-members; members $8. Indiana Dental Association, 126 E. 86th St., Indianapolis, IN 46240. FAX 317-634-2612. Ed. Diane M. Buyer. adv.; charts; illus.; circ. 3,000. **Indexed:** Dent.Abstr., Dent.Ind.
—BLDSC shelfmark: 4769.070000.

617.6 US
INDIANAPOLIS DISTRICT DENTAL SOCIETY. NEWSLETTER. vol.11, 1957. bi-m. $25. Indianapolis District Dental Society, 3901 N. Meridian St., no.10, Indianapolis, IN 46208-4026. TEL 317-923-8421. Ed. Dr. Ted Reese. adv.; bk.rev.; circ. 725.
Formerly: Indianapolis District Dental Society. Journal (ISSN 0073-7135)

INDICE DE LA LITERATURA DENTAL EN CASTELLANO. see *MEDICAL SCIENCES — Abstracting, Bibliographies, Statistics*

617.6 FR ISSN 0020-0018
INFORMATION DENTAIRE; hebdomadaire independant. 1918. w. 645 F. Information Dentaire, 42, rue Vignon, 75009 Paris cedex 09, France. TEL 42-66-24-07. FAX 42-66-26-07. Dir. Yves Leroux. adv.; bk.rev.; abstr.; illus.; circ. 13,321. (reprint service avail. from ISI) **Indexed:** Biol.Abstr., Chem.Abstr., Curr.Tit.Dent., Dent.Ind., Dok.Arbeitsmed.
—BLDSC shelfmark: 4493.530000.

617.43 GW ISSN 0020-0336
INFORMATIONEN AUS ORTHODONTIE UND KIEFERORTHOPAEDIE. 1968. q. DM.198. Dr. Alfred Huethig Verlag GmbH, Im Weiher 10, Postfach 102869, 6900 Heidelberg 1, Germany. TEL 06221-489-281. FAX 06221-489279. TELEX 461727-HUEHDD. Ed.Bd. adv.; bk.rev.; illus.; circ. 2,000. **Indexed:** Dent.Ind.

617.6 US ISSN 0534-669X
INTERNATIONAL ASSOCIATION FOR DENTAL RESEARCH. ABSTRACTS OF THE GENERAL MEETING. Variant title: Program and Abstracts of Papers. 1919. a. $20. International Association for Dental Research, 1111 14th St., N.W., Ste. 1000, Washington, DC 20005. TEL 202-898-1050. FAX 202-789-1033. (Co-sponsor: American Association for Dental Research) Ed. Colin Dawes. adv.; circ. 6,500. (also avail. in microform from UMI) **Indexed:** Dent.Abstr.

617.6 UK
INTERNATIONAL COLLEGE OF DENTISTS. EUROPEAN SECTION. NEWSLETTER. 1956. a. membership. International College of Dentists, European Section, 2 Haigh Lawn, St. Margaret's Rd., Altrincham, Cheshire WA14 2AP, England. Ed. Dr. H.D. Norton. bk.rev.; circ. 600.

617.6 US ISSN 1057-5235
INTERNATIONAL COMMUNICATOR. 1976. 2/yr. Academy of Dentistry International, 5125 MacArthur Blvd., N.W., Washington, DC 20016-3315. TEL 202-364-8349. FAX 202-244-6244. Ed. Dr. Henry J. Sazima. circ. 1,600. (tabloid format)
Description: Informs membership of news, actions of the Board of Regents, and meetings.

617.6 US ISSN 0074-3216
INTERNATIONAL CONFERENCE ON ORAL BIOLOGY. PROCEEDINGS. (Special issue of Journal of Dental Research) triennial. American Association for Dental Research, 1111 14th St., N.W., Ste. 1000, Washington, DC 20005. TEL 202-898-1050. FAX 202-789-1033. Ed. Arthur Hand. circ. 7,000. (reprint service avail. from UMI) **Indexed:** Dent.Abstr., Oral Res.Abstr.
Description: In-depth reports on specific topics relevant to the oral cavity and its contiguous parts in health and disease.

617.6 UK ISSN 0020-6539
CODEN: IDJOAS
INTERNATIONAL DENTAL JOURNAL. (Text in English; abstracts in French, German, Spanish) 1950. bi-m. £75 (Europe £80; elsewhere £85). Federation Dentaire Internationale, 64 Wimpole St., London W1M 8AL. FAX 0865-310898. TELEX 83111 BHPOXF G. adv.; illus.; index. (also avail. in microfilm from UMI; reprint service avail. from UMI) **Indexed:** Biol.Abstr., Chem.Abstr., Curr.Adv.Ecol.Sci., Curr.Cont., Curr.Tit.Dent., Dent.Ind., Dok.Arbeitsmed., Ind.Med., Ind.Sci.Rev., NRN, Nutr.Abstr., Sci.Cit.Ind.
—BLDSC shelfmark: 4539.520000.
Description: Presents a selection of Transactions of FDI Annual World Dental Congresses and other suitable manuscripts of international interest and significance.
Refereed Serial

MEDICAL SCIENCES — DENTISTRY

617.6   UK   ISSN 0143-2885
              CODEN: IENJEA
INTERNATIONAL ENDODONTIC JOURNAL. vol.14, 1981. bi-m. £60 (foreign £66). (British Endodontic Society) Blackwell Scientific Publications Ltd., Osney Mead, Oxford OX2 OEL, England. TEL 0865-240201. FAX 0865-721205. TELEX 83355-MEDBOK-G. (Co-sponsors: Netherlands Society for Endodontology; European Society of Endodontology; Canadian Academy of Endodontics) Ed. T.R. Pitt Ford. circ. 1,250. (reprint service avail. from SWZ) **Indexed:** Curr.Tit.Dent., Dent.Ind.
—BLDSC shelfmark: 4539.975000.
Formerly (until 1980): British Endodontic Society Journal (ISSN 0007-0653)

617.6 617   US   ISSN 0742-1931
              CODEN: IAOSEE
INTERNATIONAL JOURNAL OF ADULT ORTHODONTICS AND ORTHOGNATHIC SURGERY. 1986. 4/yr. $82 (foreign $98). Quintessence Publishing Co., Inc., 551 Kimberly Dr., Carol Stream, IL 60188-1881. TEL 708-682-3223. FAX 708-682-3288. Eds. Dr. Robert Vanarsdall, Dr. Raymond White. adv.; charts; illus.; index; circ. 5,620. (back issues avail.) **Indexed:** Curr.Tit.Dent., Dent.Abstr., Dent.Abstr.
—BLDSC shelfmark: 4541.571000.
Description: Conveys advances in orthodontics and orthognathic surgery care of interest to general practitioners, orthodontists, oral surgeons and periodontists.
Refereed Serial

617.6   US   ISSN 0882-2786
              CODEN: IJOIED
INTERNATIONAL JOURNAL OF ORAL & MAXILLOFACIAL IMPLANTS. 1986. q. $84 (foreign $101). (Academy of Osseointegration) Quintessence Publishing Co., Inc., 551 Kimberly Dr., Carol Stream, IL 60188-1881. TEL 708-682-3223. FAX 708-682-3288. Ed. Dr. William Laney. adv.; charts; illus.; index; circ. 7,200. (back issues avail.) **Indexed:** Dent.Abstr., Excerp.Med.
—BLDSC shelfmark: 4542.429600.
Description: Tracks developments in reconstructive dentistry and implantology by compiling research, technology, clinical applications, symposia proceedings and review treatises.
Refereed Serial

617.6   DK   ISSN 0901-5027
              CODEN: IJOSE9
INTERNATIONAL JOURNAL OF ORAL & MAXILLOFACIAL SURGERY. (Text in English) 1972. bi-m. DKK 1415. (International Association of Oral Surgeons) Munksgaard International Publishers Ltd., 35 Noerre Soegade, P.O. Box 2148, DK-1016 Copenhagen K, Denmark. TEL 33-127030. FAX 33-129387. TELEX 19431-MUNKS-DK. Ed. P. Stoelinga. adv.; bk.rev.; circ. 2,500. (also avail. in microform from SWZ; reprint service avail. from ISI,SWZ) **Indexed:** Biol.Abstr., C.I.J.E., Chem.Abstr., Curr.Cont., Curr.Tit.Dent., Dent.Abstr., Dent.Ind., Excerp.Med., Ind.Med., Ind.Sci.Rev., Ind.Vet., INIS Atomind., Nutr.Abstr.
—BLDSC shelfmark: 4542.429800.
Formerly: International Journal of Oral Surgery (ISSN 0300-9785)

617.6   US
INTERNATIONAL JOURNAL OF ORAL IMPLANTOLOGY. 1976. s-a. $60 (foreign $75). International Congress of Oral Implantologists, Box 912, Upper Montclair, NJ 07043. TEL 201-783-6300. FAX 201-783-1175. Ed. Dr. Carl E. Misch. adv.; circ. 6,000.
Formerly: Implantologist (ISSN 0190-2024)
Description: Scientific, clinical and research articles pertaining to the field of oral implantology.
Refereed Serial

617.6   UK   ISSN 0960-7439
INTERNATIONAL JOURNAL OF PAEDIATRIC DENTISTRY. 1971. 3/yr. £78 (foreign £87). (British Paedodontic Society) Blackwell Scientific Publications Ltd., Osney Mead, Oxford OX2 OEL, England. TEL 0865-240201. FAX 0865-721205. TELEX 83355-MEDBOK-G. (Co-sponsor: International Association of Dentistry for Children) Ed. R.J. Andlaw. adv.; bk.rev.; abstr.; illus.; index.
—BLDSC shelfmark: 4542.440800.
Incorporating: International Association of Dentistry for Children. Journal (ISSN 0309-6858); Former titles: Journal of Paediatric Dentistry (ISSN 0267-2073); British Paedodontic Society. Proceedings (ISSN 0308-4922)

617.6   GW
INTERNATIONAL JOURNAL OF PERIODONTICS & RESTORATIVE DENTISTRY. German edition: Internationales Journal fuer Paradontologie & Restaurative Zahnheilkunde. (Text in English) bi-m. DM.280 (foreign DM.310). Quintessenz Verlags GmbH, Ifenpfad 2-4, 1000 Berlin 42, Germany. TEL 030-74006-0. FAX 030-7415080. TELEX 183815-QUNIT-D. (Subscr. for English ed.: Quintessence Publishing Co., 870 Oak Creek Dr., Lombard, IL 60148. TEL 708-620-4443) **Indexed:** Curr.Tit.Dent.

617.6 617   US   ISSN 0198-7569
INTERNATIONAL JOURNAL OF PERIODONTICS & RESTORATIVE DENTISTRY. (Editions in English, French, German, Italian, Japanese) 1981. bi-m. $160 (foreign $195). Quintessence Publishing Co., Inc., 551 Kimberly Dr., Carol Stream, IL 60188-1881. TEL 708-682-3223. FAX 708-682-3288. Eds. Dr. Gerald M. Kramer, Dr. Myron Nevins. adv.; charts; illus.; index; circ. 7,687. (back issues avail.) **Indexed:** Curr.Tit.Dent., Dent.Abstr.
—BLDSC shelfmark: 4542.452400.
Description: Clinically oriented coverage of the relationship between a healthy periodontium and precise restorations.
Refereed Serial

617.6   US   ISSN 0893-2174
              CODEN: IJLPEJ
INTERNATIONAL JOURNAL OF PROSTHODONTICS. 1988. 6/yr. $92 (foreign $114). (International College of Prosthodontists) Quintessence Publishing Co., Inc., 551 Kimberly Dr., Carol Stream, IL 60188-1881. TEL 708-682-3223. FAX 708-682-3288. Ed. Dr. Jack D. Preston. adv.; charts; illus.; index; circ. 5,000. (back issues avail.)
—BLDSC shelfmark: 4542.488000.
Description: Contains articles covering interrelated disciplines such as periodontics, oral and maxillofacial surgery, endodontics and orthodontics.
Refereed Serial

INTERNATIONAL JOURNAL OF PSYCHOSOMATICS. see *MEDICAL SCIENCES*

617.6   US   ISSN 0021-0498
IOWA DENTAL JOURNAL. vol.15, 1929. 4/yr. $30 (foreign $35). Iowa Dental Association, 333 Insurance Exchange Bldg., Des Moines, IA 50309. TEL 515-282-7250. FAX 515-282-7256. Ed. R.W. Harpster. adv.; bk.rev.; charts; illus.; stat.; circ. 2,250. **Indexed:** Curr.Tit.Dent., Dent.Abstr., Dent.Ind.
—BLDSC shelfmark: 4565.700000.

617.6   IE   ISSN 0021-1133
IRISH DENTAL ASSOCIATION. JOURNAL. vol.21, 1975. q. I£45. Irish Dental Association, 10 Richview Office Park, Clonskeagh Rd., Dublin 14, Ireland. TEL 01-2830499. FAX 01-2830515. Ed. Dr. N. Hayes. adv.; bk.rev.; abstr.; bibl.; charts; illus.; stat.; index; circ. 1,000. **Indexed:** Biol.Abstr., Curr.Tit.Dent., Dent.Abstr., Dent.Ind., INIS Atomind.
—BLDSC shelfmark: 4802.800000.

617.6   JA   ISSN 0385-1311
IWATE MEDICAL UNIVERSITY. DENTAL JOURNAL/IWATE IKA DAIGAKU SHIGAKU ZASSHI. (Text in Japanese; summaries in English) 1976. 3/yr. 4000 Yen($32) Iwate Medical University, Dental Society, c/o Iwate Ika Daigaku Shigakubu, 3-27, Chuo-dori 1-chome, Morioka 020, Japan. TEL 0196-51-5111. Ed. Dr. Tokio Nawa. circ. 900. (back issues avail.) **Indexed:** INIS Atomind.

617.7   IT   ISSN 0393-800X
J D : rivista d'informazione dentale. 1986. q. free. Imadent s.n.c., Via Locana 14-A, 10143 Turin, Italy. Ed. Federico Manassero. adv.; bk.rev.; illus.; index; circ. 21,000.

617.6   CN   ISSN 0845-9320
J D Q: JOURNAL DENTAIRE DU QUEBEC. (Text in English and French) 1963. m. Can.$42.80 (foreign Can.$60). Ordre des Dentistes du Quebec, 625, Rene-Levesque Ouest, 5th Floor, Montreal, Que. H3B 1R2, Canada. TEL 514-875-8511. FAX 514-875-9412. Ed. Jaques Richer. adv.; bk.rev.; charts; illus.; cum.index: 1963-1966; circ. 4,500. **Indexed:** Dent.Ind., Pt.de Rep. (1988-).
Formerly (until 1987): Journal Dentaire du Quebec (ISSN 0021-7999)

617.6   JM
JAMAICA DENTAL ASSOCIATION. NEWSLETTER. irreg. Jamaica Dental Association, P.O. Box 19, Kingston 5, Jamaica.

617.6   IR
JAME'E DANDANPEZESHKI IRAN. NAMAH-I/IRANIAN DENTAL ASSOCIATION. BULLETIN. m. (Iranian Dental Association) Hamid Adeli-Najafi, Ed. & Pub., 2 Ex-Shahi Alley, Shahid Dr. Abaspour St., Vali Asr Ave., P.O. Box 14155-3695, Teheran, Iran. TEL 021-686508. TELEX 212918.

617.6   JA   ISSN 0047-1763
              CODEN: NISIA9
JAPAN DENTAL ASSOCIATION. JOURNAL/NIHON SHIKA ISHIKAI ZASSHI. (Text in Japanese) 1948. m. 4320 Yen($50) Japan Dental Association - Nihon Shika Igakkai, 4-1-20 Kudan-Kita, Chiyoda-ku, Tokyo 102, Japan. Ed. Dr. Y. Tajime. adv.; illus.; index; circ. 58,000. (also avail. in microform from UMI; reprint service avail. from UMI) **Indexed:** Dent.Ind., Ind.Med.

617.643   JA   ISSN 0021-454X
JAPAN ORTHODONTIC SOCIETY. JOURNAL/NIHON KYOSEI SHIKA GAKKAI ZASSHI. (Text in Japanese; summaries in English) 1932. bi-m. 8000 Yen($18) Japan Orthodontic Society - Nihon Kyosei Shika Gakkai, c/o Oral health Association of Japan, 1-44-2 Komagome, Toshima-ku, Tokyo 170, Japan. Ed. Yoshii Suzuki. adv. **Indexed:** Dent.Ind.
—BLDSC shelfmark: 4805.670000.

617.6   FR   ISSN 0301-3952
              CODEN: JBBUA3
JOURNAL DE BIOLOGIE BUCCALE. (Text in English, French; summaries in English, French, German) 1973. q. 720 F. Societe d'Edition de l'Information Dentaire, 42 rue Vignon, 75442 Paris Cedex 09, France. Ed. R. Frank. adv.; bk.rev.; circ. 1,565. (reprint service avail. from ISI) **Indexed:** Biol.Abstr., Chem.Abstr., Curr.Cont., Dent.Ind., Excerp.Med., Helminthol.Abstr., Ind.Med., Ind.Sci.Rev., Nutr.Abstr., Sci.Cit.Ind.
—BLDSC shelfmark: 4953.440000.

617.643   US   ISSN 0022-3875
JOURNAL OF CLINICAL ORTHODONTICS. 1967. m. $97 (typically set in May). J C O Inc., 1828 Pearl St., Boulder, CO 80302. FAX 303-443-9356. Ed. Larry White. adv.; bk.rev.; circ. 11,000. **Indexed:** Curr.Tit.Dent., Dent.Abstr., Dent.Ind.
—BLDSC shelfmark: 4958.630000.
Refereed Serial

617.6 618.92   US   ISSN 1053-4628
RK55.C5   CODEN: JCPDEX
JOURNAL OF CLINICAL PEDIATRIC DENTISTRY. 1977. q. $79. Journal of Pedontics, Inc., Box C-259, Birmingham, AL 95283-0259. Ed. Dr. George E. White. index; circ. 2,600. (also avail. in microform from UMI,MIM; reprint service avail. from UMI) **Indexed:** Biol.Abstr., Chem.Abstr., Dent.Ind., Excerp.Med.
Formerly: Journal of Pedodontics (ISSN 0145-5508)

617.6   DK   ISSN 0303-6979
              CODEN: JCPEDZ
JOURNAL OF CLINICAL PERIODONTOLOGY. (Text in English; summaries in German and French) 1974. 10/yr. DKK 1115 includes supplements. Munksgaard International Publishers Ltd., 35 Noerre Soegade, P.O. Box 2148, DK-1016 Copenhagen K, Denmark. TEL 33-127030. FAX 33-129387. TELEX 19431-MUNKS-DK. Ed. Jan Lindhe. adv.; circ. 11,000. (also avail. in microform from SWZ; reprint service avail. from ISI,SWZ) **Indexed:** Biol.Abstr., Chem.Abstr., Curr.Cont., Curr.Tit.Dent., Dent.Abstr., Dent.Ind., Excerp.Med., Ind.Med., Ind.Sci.Rev., Sci.Cit.Ind.
—BLDSC shelfmark: 4958.672000.

MEDICAL SCIENCES — DENTISTRY

617.6 US ISSN 0890-2739
CODEN: JCDIEM
JOURNAL OF CRANIOMANDIBULAR DISORDERS. 1987. 4/yr. $64 (foreign $80). (American Academy of Craniomandibular Disorders) Quintessence Publishing Co., Inc., 551 Kimberly Dr., Carol Stream, IL 60188-1881. TEL 708-682-3223. FAX 708-682-3288. (Co-sponsor: European Academy of Craniomandibular Disorders) Ed. Dr. Harold T. Perry. adv.; charts; illus.; index. (back issues avail.) Indexed: Dent.Abstr.
—BLDSC shelfmark: 4965.478000.
  Description: Research, clinical material and treatment therapies on facial pain, headaches, occlusion, physiology and physical therapy.
  Refereed Serial

617.6 US ISSN 0022-0337
RK71
JOURNAL OF DENTAL EDUCATION. 1936. m. $50 (foreign $75). American Association of Dental Schools, 1625 Massachusetts Ave., N.W., Washington, DC 20036-2212. TEL 202-667-9433. Ed. Dr. James D. Bader. adv.; bk.rev.; charts; illus.; stat.; index; circ. 4,500. (also avail. in microform from MIM,UMI; reprint service avail. from UMI) Indexed: Biol.Abstr., C.I.J.E., Cont.Pg.Educ., Curr.Tit.Dent., Dent.Abstr., Dent.Ind., Ind.Med., Res.High.Educ.Abstr.
—BLDSC shelfmark: 4968.450000.
  Description: Presents study and teaching methods.

617.6 US ISSN 1043-254X
RK1
JOURNAL OF DENTAL HYGIENE. 1927. 9/yr. $40. American Dental Hygienists' Association, 444 N. Michigan Ave., Ste. 3400, Chicago, IL 60611. TEL 312-440-8900. FAX 312-440-8929. Ed. Nancy Sisty-LePeau. adv.; bk.rev.; abstr.; bibl.; charts; illus.; stat.; index; circ. 30,000. (also avail. in microform from UMI; reprint service avail. from UMI) Indexed: Biol.Abstr., Curr.Tit.Dent., Dent.Abstr., Dent.Ind.
  Former titles (until Oct. 1988): Dental Hygiene (ISSN 0091-3979); American Dental Hygienists Association. Journal (ISSN 0002-8185)
  Description: Scientific journal with articles pertaining to dental hygiene practice, education, and research.
  Refereed Serial

617.6 JA ISSN 0285-0508
JOURNAL OF DENTAL HYGIENE. (Text in Japanese) 1981. m. 850 Yen per no. Ishiyaku Publishers, Inc., 7-10 Honkomagome 1-chome, Bunkyo-ku, Tokyo 113, Japan. Ed. Hiroshi Miura. adv.; bk.rev.; charts; illus.; circ. 15,000.

617.6 US ISSN 0741-8620
JOURNAL OF DENTAL PRACTICE ADMINISTRATION. Abbreviated title: J D P A. 1984. q. $40 to individuals (foreign $50); institutions $55 (foreign $65). Stevens Publishing Corporation, 225 N. New Rd., Waco, TX 76710. TEL 718-776-9000. FAX 817-776-9018. (Co-sponsors: American Academy of Dental Group Practice; American Academy of Dental Practice Administration; Organization of Teachers of Dental Practice Administration) Ed. Dr. Arthur G. Williams. adv.; illus.; index.; circ. 3,000. (also avail. in microform from UMI) Indexed: Dent.Abstr., Dent.Ind.

617.6 US ISSN 0022-0345
RK1 CODEN: JDREAF
JOURNAL OF DENTAL RESEARCH. (Supplements avail.: Advances in Dental Research (ISSN 0895-9374)) 1919. m. $240 (foreign $250). (International Association for Dental Research) American Association for Dental Research, 1111 14th St., N.W., Ste. 1000, Washington, DC 20005. TEL 202-898-1050. FAX 202-789-1033. Ed. Dr. Colin Dawes. adv.; charts; illus.; stat.; index; circ. 7,237. (also avail. in microform from UMI; back issues avail.; reprint service avail. from UMI) Indexed: Biol.Abstr., Chem.Abstr., Curr.Cont., Curr.Tit.Dent., Dairy Sci.Abstr., Dent.Abstr., Dent.Ind., Excerp.Med., Ind.Med., Ind.Sci.Rev., INIS Atomind., Met.Abstr., NRN, Nutr.Abstr., Sci.Cit.Ind., World Alum.Abstr.
—BLDSC shelfmark: 4968.500000.
  Description: Original research on the oral cavity, its contiguous parts and its impact on the total human organism in health and disease.
  Refereed Serial

617.6 UK ISSN 0300-5712
CODEN: JDENAB
JOURNAL OF DENTISTRY. 1972. bi-m. £110 in U.K. & Europe; elsewhere £120. Butterworth - Heinemann Ltd. (Subsidiary of: Reed International PLC), Linacre House, Jordan Hill, Oxford OX2 8DP, England. TEL 0865-310366. FAX 0865-310898. TELEX 83111 BHPOXF G. (Dist. by: Turpin Transactions Ltd., Distirbution Centre, Blackhorse Rd., Letchworth, Herts. SG6 1HN, England) Ed. Nairn H.F. Wilson. bk.rev.; illus.; index. (also avail. in microform from UMI; reprint service avail. from UMI; back issues avail.) Indexed: Chem.Abstr., Curr.Cont., Curr.Tit.Dent., Dent.Ind., Ind.Med., Ind.Sci.Rev., NRN, Nutr.Abstr., Sci.Cit.Ind.
—BLDSC shelfmark: 4968.670000.
  Incorporates: Quarterly Dental Review (ISSN 0033-5479); Dental Practitioner and Dental Record (ISSN 0011-8729)
  Description: Reports on all issues relating to research, innovations and the practice of, in particular, restorative dentistry, including dental materials science.
  Refereed Serial

617.64 618.92 US ISSN 0022-0353
CODEN: JDCHAH
JOURNAL OF DENTISTRY FOR CHILDREN. 1933. bi-m. $65 to individuals (foreign $75); institutions $95 (foreign $105). American Society of Dentistry for Children, 211 E. Chicago Ave., Ste. 1430, Chicago, IL 60611. TEL 312-943-1244. FAX 312-943-5341. (Editorial addr.: 730 Blaney Dr., Dyer, IN 46311) Ed. Dr. George W. Teuscher. adv.; bk.rev.; abstr.; charts; illus.; stat.; index; circ. 10,000. (also avail. in microform from UMI; reprint service avail. from KTO,UMI) Indexed: Biol.Abstr., Chem.Abstr., Chic.Per.Ind., Curr.Tit.Dent., Dent.Abstr., Dent.Ind., Ind.Med., Ind.Sci.Rev., Nutr.Abstr., Sci.Cit.Ind.
—BLDSC shelfmark: 1739.600000.
  Refereed Serial

617.6 US ISSN 0099-2399
RK351
JOURNAL OF ENDODONTICS. 1975. m. $50 to individuals; institutions $76. (American Association of Endodontics) Williams & Wilkins, 428 E. Preston St., Baltimore, MD 21202. TEL 301-528-4000. FAX 301-528-4312. Ed. Dr. Henry J. Van Hassell. abstr.; illus.; index; circ. 6,000. (also avail. in microform; reprint service avail.) Indexed: Biol.Abstr., Curr.Tit.Dent., Dent.Abstr., Dent.Ind., Excerp.Med.
—BLDSC shelfmark: 4978.200000.
  Description: Explores methods of pulp conservation, root canal instrumentation and endodontic treatment.
  Refereed Serial

617.6 CN
JOURNAL OF ESTHETIC DENTISTRY. 1988. bi-m. $75 to individuals; institutions $110. Decker Periodicals, One James St. S., P.O. Box 620, LCD 1, Hamilton, Ont. L8N 3K7, Canada. TEL 416-522-7017. FAX 416-522-7839. (U.S. address: Box 785, Lewiston, NY 14092) adv.; circ. 30,000.
  Description: Provides information relative to the fields of esthetic and geriatric dentistry.

617.6 SP
▼**JOURNAL OF ESTHETIC DENTISTRY (EDICION ESPANOLA).** 1991. q. (Rhone-Poulenc Rorer) Ediciones Ergon S.A., Muntaner, 262, 6o, 08021 Barcelona, Spain. TEL 2010911. FAX 2015911. (Subscr. to: Cempro, Plaza Conde Valle Suchil 20, 28015 Madrid, Spain) Ed.Bd. adv.; bk.rev.; index. (back issues avail.)

617.643 US ISSN 1048-1990
▼**JOURNAL OF GENERAL ORTHODONTICS.** 1990. q. $40 (foreign $60). International Association for Orthodontics, 211 E. Chicago Ave., No. 915, Chicago, IL 60611. TEL 312-642-2602. FAX 312-642-4191. adv.; bk.rev.; circ. 3,500.
  Description: Contains scientific and clinical articles on orthodontic techniques.

617.6 US ISSN 0278-2391
RK1 CODEN: JOMSDA
JOURNAL OF ORAL AND MAXILLOFACIAL SURGERY. 1943. m. $72 to individuals; institutions $90; foreign $120. (American Association of Oral and Maxillofacial Surgeons) W.B. Saunders Co., Curtis Center, Independence Square W., Philadelphia, PA 19106. TEL 215-238-7800. Ed. Dr. Daniel Laskin. adv.; bk.rev.; abstr.; bibl.; charts; illus.; index; circ. 8,500. (also avail. in microform from UMI; reprint service avail. from UMI) Indexed: Biol.Abstr., Chem.Abstr., Curr.Cont., Curr.Tit.Dent., Dent.Abstr., Dent.Ind., Excerp.Med., Helminthol.Abstr., Ind.Med., Ind.Sci.Rev., INIS Atomind.
—BLDSC shelfmark: 5026.385000.
  Former titles (until 1982): Journal of Oral Surgery (ISSN 0022-3255); Journal of Oral Surgery, Anesthesia and Hospital Dental Service (ISSN 0095-9618)
  Description: Contains editorials, clinical and scientific articles, case reports, news and announcements.
  Refereed Serial

617.6 US ISSN 0160-6972
JOURNAL OF ORAL IMPLANTOLOGY. 1970. q. $75 to non-members. (American Academy of Implant Dentistry) International and American Associations for Dental Research, 1111 14th St., N.W., Ste. 1000, Washington, DC 20005. TEL 202-898-1050. FAX 202-789-1033. Ed. A. Norman Cranin. adv.; bk.rev.; illus.; circ. 3,000. (also avail. in microform from UMI; back issues avail.) Indexed: Dent.Ind.
  Formerly (until 1977): Oral Implantology (ISSN 0048-2064); Which incorporates: American Academy of Implant Dentistry. Newsletter.

617.6 DK ISSN 0904-2512
CODEN: JPMEEA
JOURNAL OF ORAL PATHOLOGY & MEDICINE. (Text in English) 1972. 10/yr. DKK 2400. (International Association of Oral Pathologists) Munksgaard International Publishers Ltd., 35 Noerre Soegade, P.O. Box 2148, DK-1016 Copenhagen K, Denmark. TEL 33-127030. FAX 33-129387. TELEX 19431-MUNKS-DK. Ed. Jens J. Pindborg. adv.; bk.rev.; charts; illus.; bibl.; circ. 800. (also avail. in microform from SWZ; reprint service avail. from ISI,SWZ) Indexed: Biol.Abstr., Chem.Abstr., Curr.Adv.Ecol.Sci., Curr.Cont., Curr.Tit.Dent., Dent.Abstr., Dent.Ind., Excerp.Med., Ind.Med., Ind.Sci.Rev., INIS Atomind., Nutr.Abstr., Rev.Plant Path.
—BLDSC shelfmark: 5026.435000.
  Formerly: Journal of Oral Pathology (ISSN 0300-9777)

617.6 UK ISSN 0305-182X
CODEN: JORHBY
JOURNAL OF ORAL REHABILITATION; clinical dental science and materials. 1974. bi-m. £148 (foreign £162.50). Blackwell Scientific Publications Ltd., Osney Mead, Oxford OX2 0EL, England. TEL 0865-240201. FAX 0865-721205. TELEX 83355-MEDBOK-G. Ed. A.S.T. Franks. circ. 500. (also avail. in microform from MIM; back issues avail.; reprint service avail. from ISI) Indexed: ASCA, Behav.Med.Abstr., Chem.Abstr., Curr.Cont., Curr.Tit.Dent., Dent.Abstr., Dent.Ind., Excerp.Med., Ind.Med., Ind.Sci.Rev., Sci.Cit.Ind.
—BLDSC shelfmark: 5026.440000.

617.632 DK ISSN 0022-3484
RK361.A1 CODEN: JPDRAY
JOURNAL OF PERIODONTAL RESEARCH. (Supplements avail.) (Text in English) 1966. bi-m. DKK 1510. Munksgaard International Publishers Ltd., 35 Noerre Soegade, P.O. Box 2148, DK-1016 Copenhagen K, Denmark. TEL 33-127030. FAX 33-129387. TELEX 19431-MUNKS-DK. Ed. Roy C. Page. adv.; bibl.; charts; illus.; circ. 1,200. (also avail. in microform from SWZ; reprint service avail. from ISI,SWZ) Indexed: Biol.Abstr., Chem.Abstr., Curr.Adv.Ecol.Sci., Curr.Cont., Curr.Tit.Dent., Dairy Sci.Abstr., Dent.Abstr., Dent.Ind., Excerp.Med., Ind.Med., Ind.Sci.Rev., INIS Atomind.
—BLDSC shelfmark: 5030.600000.

617.632 US ISSN 0022-3492
RK1.A512 CODEN: JOPRAJ
JOURNAL OF PERIODONTOLOGY. 1930. m. $80 in US and Canada; elsewhere $90. American Academy of Periodontology, 737 N. Michigan, Ste. 800, Chicago, IL 60611. TEL 312-787-5518.
FAX 312-787-3670. Ed. Robert Genco. adv.; abstr.; bibl.; illus.; index; circ. 8,000. (also avail. in microform from UMI; reprint service avail. from UMI) **Indexed:** Biol.Abstr., Chem.Abstr., Curr.Adv.Ecol.Sci., Curr.Cont., Curr.Tit.Dent., Dent.Abstr., Dent.Ind., Excerp.Med., Ind.Med., Ind.Sci.Rev., INIS Atomind., Nutr.Abstr.
—BLDSC shelfmark: 5030.700000.
Formerly: Journal of Periodontology - Periodontics.
Refereed Serial

617.69 US ISSN 0022-3913
RK1 CODEN: JPDEAT
JOURNAL OF PROSTHETIC DENTISTRY. 1951. m. $71 to individuals (foreign $96); institutions $134 (foreign $159); students $48 (foreign $73). (Academy of Denture Prosthetics) Mosby - Year Book, Inc. (Subsidiary of Times Mirror Company), 11830 Westline Industrial Dr., St. Louis, MO 63146. TEL 800-325-4117. FAX 314-432-1380. TELEX 44-2402. (Co-sponsors: American Prosthodontic Society; Pacific Coast Society of Prosthodontists) Ed. Dr. Glen P. McGivney. adv.; bk.rev.; charts; illus.; s-a. index; circ. 15,120. (also avail. in microform from UMI; back issues avail.; reprint service avail. from UMI) **Indexed:** ASCA, Biol.Abstr., Br.Ceram.Abstr., Ceram.Abstr., Chem.Abstr., Curr.Adv.Ecol.Sci., Curr.Cont., Curr.Tit.Dent., Dent.Abstr., Dent.Ind., Ind.Med., Ind.Sci.Rev., INIS Atomind., Sci.Cit.Ind.
—BLDSC shelfmark: 5042.900000.
Description: New techniques, evaluation of dental materials, and patient psychology relevant to practitioners of prosthetic dentistry.
Refereed Serial

617.6 IT
JOURNAL OF PROSTHETIC DENTISTRY (EDIZIONE ITALIANA). English edition (ISSN 0022-3913) 1989. bi-m. L.68900 (effective 1991). Masson Italia Periodici, Via Statuto 2-4, 20121 Milan, Italy. TEL 02-6367-1. FAX 02-6367-211. Ed. Manlio Quaranta. circ. 3,000.

617.6 614.8 US ISSN 0022-4006
RK52 CODEN: JPHDAC
JOURNAL OF PUBLIC HEALTH DENTISTRY. 1941. q. $55 (foreign $60). American Association of Public Health Dentistry, 10619 Jousting Ln., Richmond, VA 23235. Ed. Dennis Leverett. adv.; bk.rev.; bibl.; charts; illus.; stat.; circ. 1,200. (also avail. in microform from UMI; reprint service avail. from UMI) **Indexed:** Abstr.Health Care Manage.Stud., Biol.Abstr., Curr.Cont., Curr.Tit.Dent., Dent.Abstr., Dent.Ind., Excerp.Med., Ind.Med., Ind.Sci.Rev.
—BLDSC shelfmark: 5043.550000.
Former titles: Public Health Dentistry; American Association of Public Health Dentists. Bulletin.

617.6 JA ISSN 0385-1443
CODEN: BKDCD5
KANAGAWA DENTAL COLLEGE. BULLETIN. (Text in English) 1973. s-a. free. Kanagawa Dental College Society - Kanagawa Shika Daigaku Gakkai, 82 Inaoka-cho, Yokosuka, Kanagawa-ken, Japan. TEL 0468-25-1500. FAX 0468-23-9415. Ed. Akiya Yamanaka. circ. 1,000.
—BLDSC shelfmark: 2597.959000.

617.6 JA ISSN 0454-8302
KANAGAWA SHIGAKU/KANAGAWA ODONTOLOGICAL SOCIETY. JOURNAL. 1967. q. 1500 Yen. Kanagawa Dental College Society - Kanagawa Shika Daigaku Gakkai, 82 Inaoka-cho, Yokosuka, Kanagawa-ken, Japan. TEL 0468-25-1500. FAX 0468-23-9415. Ed. Tsugio Iwamoto. circ. 3,000. **Indexed:** INIS Atomind.
—BLDSC shelfmark: 4810.229000.

617.6 US
KANSAS DENTAL ASSOCIATION. JOURNAL.* vol.57, 1973. q. $5. Kansas Dental Association, 5200 S.W. Huntoon St., Topeka, KS 66604-2365. Ed. Dr. Ron Davies. adv.; illus.; circ. 1,200. **Indexed:** Dent.Abstr., Dent.Ind., Med. Care Rev.
Formerly (until July 1981): Kansas State Dental Association. Journal (ISSN 0022-8796)

617.6 US ISSN 0744-396X
KENTUCKY DENTAL ASSOCIATION. JOURNAL.* 1949. bi-m. $20. Kentucky Dental Association, 1725 Hillcrest Dr., Madisonville, KY 42431. Ed. Joe W. Jones, Jr. adv.; bk.rev.; illus.; circ. 1,900. **Indexed:** Dent.Abstr., Dent.Ind.

617.6 US
KERN COUNTY DENTAL SOCIETY OCCLUSAL REGISTER. 1967. bi-m. free. Kern County Dental Society, 1701 Westwind Dr., Ste. 209, Bakersfield, CA 93301. TEL 805-327-2666. FAX 805-327-1229. Ed. Dr. Karen Yoon. adv.; charts; illus.; stat.; circ. 180. (looseleaf format)
Formerly: Kern County Dental Society Newsletter (ISSN 0023-0634)

617.6 DK ISSN 0109-2294
KLINISKE TANDTEKNIKERE. 1982. 10/yr. membership. Landsforeningen af Kliniske Tandteknikere, Roedevej 3, 8800 Viborg, Denmark. illus.

617.6 JA ISSN 0023-2831
CODEN: KEGZA7
KOKU EISEI GAKKAI ZASSHI/JOURNAL OF DENTAL HEALTH. (Text mainly in Japanese; summaries in English) 1953. q. (Koku Eisei Gakkai - Japanese Society for Dental Health) Tokyo Medical and Dental University, School of Dentistry, Dept. of Preventive Dentistry, Yushima 1-chome, Bunkyo-ku, Tokyo 113, Japan. Ed. Masao Onisi. adv.; index. **Indexed:** Biol.Abstr., Chem.Abstr., Dent.Ind.
—BLDSC shelfmark: 4968.460000.

617.6 KO ISSN 0023-3927
KOREA RESEARCH SOCIETY FOR DENTAL MATERIALS. JOURNAL.* (Text in Korean; summaries and contents page in English) 1966. q. free. Seoul National University, College of Dentistry, 28-1, Yenkum-Dong, Chongro-Ku, Seoul, S. Korea. Ed. Dr. Yang-Shok Yoo. adv.; abstr.; bibl.; charts; illus.

617.6 KO
KOREAN DENTAL ASSOCIATION. JOURNAL. (Text in English and Korean) 1962. m. $60. Korean Dental Association, P.O. Box 41, Yongdungpo, Seoul 150-650, S. Korea. TEL 2-635-3351. FAX 2-671-3624. Ed. S.R. Lee. adv.; circ. 7,000. **Indexed:** Dent.Ind.

617.6 FI ISSN 0023-5717
KUSPI. 1961. q. FIM 50. Turun Hammaslaaketieteenkandidaattiseura, Lemminkaisenkatu 2, 20520 Turku 52, Finland. Ed. Riitta Saarikivi. adv.; bk.rev.; charts; illus.; circ. 2,600. (controlled).

617.6 RU
▼**KVINTESSENTSIYA;** mezhdunarodnyi stomatologicheskii zhurnal. (Text in Russian) 1991. 6/yr. 14 Rub. per issue. c/o Yu.E. Shirokov, Ed., Abonementnyi yashchik 212, 125190 Moscow, Russia. TEL 203-99-88.

617.6 US ISSN 0023-9062
LAVENDER BAND. 1961. bi-m. $15 to non-members. Iowa Dental Hygienists' Association, 321 E. Walnut, Ste. 320, Des Moines, IA 50309.
TEL 515-243-8680. adv.; circ. 575.

617.6 US ISSN 0024-6786
LOUISIANA DENTAL ASSOCIATION. JOURNAL. vol.23, 1966. q. $15. Louisiana Dental Association, 8510 Line Ave., Shreveport, LA 71106.
FAX 318-869-3111. (Or: Mng. Ed., Dr. David Austin, 230 Carroll, Shreveport, LA 71105) Ed. Dr. Gary L. Roberts. adv.; illus.; circ. 1,650. **Indexed:** Dent.Abstr., Dent.Ind.

617.6 US ISSN 0738-4556
M D S NEWS. 1964. 6/yr. $20. Massachusetts Dental Society, 83 Speen St., Natick, MA 01760-4125. TEL 508-651-7511. Ed. Peg Pollard. circ. 4,250. (looseleaf format; back issues avail.)

617.6 CN ISSN 0024-9025
MCGILL DENTAL REVIEW. 1934. irreg. free. McGill University, Faculty of Dentistry, 3640 University St., Montreal, Que. H3A 2B2, Canada. Ed. Andrea Berardelli. illus. **Indexed:** Dent.Ind.
Description: Communication vehicle for dentistry students and professionals.

617.6 IO ISSN 0024-9548
MADJALAH PERSATUAN DOKTER GIGI INDONESIA.* (Summaries in English) 1951. 4/yr. $10. Indonesian Dental Association, Jalan Prapatan 14, Jakarta, Indonesia. Ed. Geri Pandjaitan. circ. 1,000.

617.6 IR
MAJDA. (Text in Farsi; summaries in English) 1964. 3/yr. membership. (Iranian Dental Association) Hamid Adeli-Najafi, Ed. & Pub., 2 Ex-Shahi Alley, Shahid Dr. Abaspour St., Vali Asr Ave., P.O. Box 14155-3695, Teheran, Iran. TEL 021-686508. TELEX 212918.
Formerly: Iranian Dental Association. Journal - Jame'e-Ye Dandanpezeshkan-e Iran. Majalleh.

617.6 US ISSN 0025-4355
MARYLAND STATE DENTAL ASSOCIATION. JOURNAL. 1958. 4/yr. $24. Maryland State Dental Association, 1132 S. Charles St., Baltimore, MD 21230. TEL 301-964-2880. FAX 301-964-0583. Ed. Dr. Bernard Gordon. adv.; bk.rev.; charts; illus.; stat.; index; circ. 2,600. **Indexed:** Dent.Abstr., Dent.Ind.
—BLDSC shelfmark: 4821.310000.

617.6 US ISSN 0025-4800
MASSACHUSETTS DENTAL SOCIETY. JOURNAL. 1951. q. $12 to non-members; members $3. Massachusetts Dental Society, 83 Speen St., Natick, MA 01760-4125. TEL 508-651-7511. Ed. Dr. Norman Becker. adv.; bk.rev.; illus.; abstr.; circ. 4,166. **Indexed:** Dent.Ind.
—BLDSC shelfmark: 4821.600000.

MATSUMOTO SHIGAKU/MATSUMOTO DENTAL COLLEGE SOCIETY. JOURNAL. see *MEDICAL SCIENCES*

617.6 FR
MECANICIEN EN PROTHESE DENTAIRE. (Text in French) 1945. m. 163 rue Saint Honore, 75001 Paris, France. Ed. Louis Vergniavo. adv.; circ. 4,200.

617.6 GW ISSN 0940-2500
MED. DENT. MAGAZIN; der Wegbegleiter vom Studienanfaenger zum Praxisgruender. 1987. bi-m. DM.24. H.P. Kuechenmeister Hochschulverlag, Daldorferstr. 15, 2351 Rickling, Germany.
TEL 04328-208. FAX 04328-1516. Ed. Hans-Peter Kuechenmeister. adv.; bk.rev.; circ. 11,000.

MEDICAL AND DENTAL ASSOCIATION OF BOTSWANA. JOURNAL. see *MEDICAL SCIENCES*

MEDICAL MALPRACTICE: HANDLING DENTAL CASES, 2-E. see *LAW — Civil Law*

617.6 CI ISSN 0025-7966
MEDICINAR; strucni i znanstveni casopis Saveza Studenata. (Text in Croatian, English) 1946. 2/yr. $28. Sveuciliste u Zagrebu, Medicinski Fakultet, Salata 3b, 41000 Zagreb, Croatia. TEL 041 271-188. Ed. Dinka Pavicic. adv.; bk.rev.; abstr.; bibl.; charts; illus.; stat.; index; circ. 3,500.

617.6 610 JA ISSN 0916-0701
MEIKAI UNIVERSITY SCHOOL OF DENTISTRY. JOURNAL. (Text and summaries in English, Japanese) 1972. 3/yr. Josai Dental University, Sakado, Saitama 350-02, Japan. Ed. Nobuo Utsumi. circ. 1,000.
—BLDSC shelfmark: 4824.365000.
Formerly: Josai Shika Daigaku Kiyo (ISSN 0301-2662)
Description: Focuses on oral tumors, cleansing agents, head and neck cancer and osteotomy. Includes case reports.

617.6 US ISSN 0026-2102
MICHIGAN DENTAL ASSOCIATION. JOURNAL. 1919. 8/yr. $15 to college libraries; non-members $70. Michigan Dental Association, 230 N. Washington Sq., Ste. 208, Lansing, MI 48933.
TEL 517-372-9070. FAX 517-484-5460. Ed. Dr. Charles E. Owens. adv.; illus.; circ. 6,300. **Indexed:** Abstr.Health Care Manage.Stud., Biol.Abstr., Dent.Abstr., Dent.Ind.
Former titles (1951-1968): Michigan State Dental Association (ISSN 0098-7107); Michigan State Dental Society. Journal.

617.6 US ISSN 0047-7095
MICHIGAN DENTAL HYGIENIST ASSOCIATION. BULLETIN. 1973. q. $12 (foreign $18). Michigan Dental Hygienists Association, 1609 E. Kalamazoo St., Ste. 11, Lansing, MI 48912. TEL 517-484-1352. Ed. Pamela Zarkowski. adv.; bk.rev.; illus.; circ. 1,200. **Indexed:** Dent.Ind.

MEDICAL SCIENCES — DENTISTRY

617.6   US   ISSN 0026-3478
MIDWESTERN DENTIST. 1925. m. (except June, July, Aug.). $18. Greater Kansas City Dental Society, 17 W. Gregory Blvd., Kansas City, MO 64114. TEL 816-333-5454. Ed. Dr. William J. Carter. adv.; bk.rev.; circ. 800.
    Former titles (until 1959): Kansas City District Dental Society. Journal; (until 1947): Kansas City Dental Society Bulletin; (until 1932): Kansas City Dental Society. Monthly Bulletin.

617.6   IT   ISSN 0394-168X
MINERVA ORTOGNATODONTICA. q. $60. Edizioni Minerva Medica, Corso Bramante 83, 10126 Turin, Italy.
    —BLDSC shelfmark: 5794.307000.

617.6   IT   ISSN 0026-4970
MINERVA STOMATOLOGICA. (Text in Italian; summaries in English) 1952. m. L.80000($120) (Societa Italiana di Odontostomatologia e Chirurgia Maxillo-Facciale) Edizioni Minerva Medica, Corso Bramante 83-85, 10126 Turin, Italy. Ed. R. Modica. adv.; bk.rev.; abstr.; bibl.; charts; illus.; index; circ. 3,000. **Indexed:** Biol.Abstr., Chem.Abstr., Dent.Ind., Excerp.Med., Ind.Med.
    —BLDSC shelfmark: 5794.600000.

617.6   CE
MIRROR AND PROBE.* (Text in English; summaries in Sinhala and Tamil) 1963. a. Dental Students' Association, University of Sri Lanka, University Park, Peradeniya, Sri Lanka. adv.; charts; illus.; stat.; circ. controlled.

617.6   US
MISSOURI DENTAL JOURNAL. 1921. 6/yr. $12 to non-members; members $5 (foreign $18). Missouri Dental Association, 230 W. McCarty St., Box 1707, Jefferson City, MO 65102. TEL 314-634-3436. Ed. Dr. Elizabeth Ward. adv.; bk.rev.; illus.; circ. 2,700. (also avail. in microform from UMI; reprint service avail. from UMI) **Indexed:** Dent.Abstr., Dent.Ind., Med.Care Rev.
    Former titles: Missouri Dental Association Journal (ISSN 0273-3463); M D A Journal (ISSN 0199-6584); Missouri Dental Association. Journal (ISSN 0026-6523).

617.6   US
MOMENTUM (ROCHESTER). 1974. q. Eastman Dental Center, 625 Elmwood Ave., Rochester, NY 14620. TEL 716-275-5064. FAX 716-244-8772. Ed. Teresa A. O'Loughlin. circ. 1,800.

617.6   IT   ISSN 0391-2000
                        CODEN: MOORDG
MONDO ORTODONTICO. 1975. bi-m. L.119000($159) Masson Italia Periodici, Via Statuto 2-4, 20121 Milan, Italy. TEL 02-6367-1. FAX 02-6367211. circ. 3,100. **Indexed:** Biol.Abstr., Dent.Ind., Excerp.Med.
    —BLDSC shelfmark: 5908.235000.

617.6   SZ   ISSN 0077-0892
                        CODEN: MGUSCU
MONOGRAPHS IN ORAL SCIENCE. (Text in English) 1972. irreg. (approx. 1/yr.) price varies. S. Karger AG, Allschwilerstr. 10, P.O. Box, CH-4009 Basel, Switzerland. TEL 061-3061111. FAX 061-3061234. TELEX CH 962652. Ed. H.M. Myers. (reprint service avail. from ISI) **Indexed:** Biol.Abstr., Chem.Abstr., Curr.Cont., Ind.Med.
    —BLDSC shelfmark: 5915.830000.

617.6   US   ISSN 0027-0156
MONTGOMERY - BUCKS DENTAL SOCIETY. BULLETIN. 1955. 7/yr. membership. Montgomery - Bucks County Dental Society, 625 N. Charlotte St., Pottstown, PA 19464. TEL 215-326-3610. Ed. Dr. Jeffrey Sameroff. adv.; bk.rev.; bibl.; circ. 800. **Indexed:** Dent.Ind.

617.6   US
MOUTHPIECE (CHICAGO). 1983. q. $39 to non-members. American Dental Association, 211 E. Chicago Ave., Chicago, IL 60611. TEL 312-440-2602. Ed. Alanna Gordon. illus. **Indexed:** Sports Per.Ind.

617.6   US
MOUTHPIECE (SAN MATEO). 1965. m. $15. San Mateo County Dental Society, 1941 O'Farrel St., Ste. 9, San Mateo, CA 94403. TEL 415-345-5714. FAX 415-345-2820. Ed. Dr. Michael A. Njo. adv.; circ. 525.
    Formerly: San Mateo County Dental Society. Bulletin (ISSN 0080-598X)
    Description: General information for dentists with emphasis on local impact.

617.6   NO   ISSN 0047-8377
MUNNPLEIEN. 1916. 4/yr. NOK 300. Norsk Tannvern - Oral Health of Norway, Ullevaals vn. 11, 0165 Oslo 1, Norway. TEL 02-20-08-69. Ed. Johan R. Ringdal. adv.; bk.rev.; circ. 5,000. **Indexed:** Dent.Ind.
    —BLDSC shelfmark: 5985.470000.

617.6   US   ISSN 0027-6545
N H D S NEWSLETTER. 1939. bi-m. membership. New Hampshire Dental Society, Box 2229, Concord, NH 03301-1772. Ed. Dr. David G. Stahl. adv.; bk.rev.; illus.; stat.; circ. 600. **Indexed:** Dent.Abstr.

N S T A NEWSLETTER. (National Spasmodic Torticollis Association) see MEDICAL SCIENCES — Psychiatry And Neurology

617.6   US
NASSAU COUNTY DENTAL SOCIETY. NEWSLETTER.* 1949. m. $10. Tenth District Dental Society Headquarters, 377 Oak St., No. 205, Garden City, NY 11530-6543. TEL 516-764-9620. Ed. William L. O'Connell. adv.; bk.rev.; circ. 2,300.
    Former titles (until 1984): Nassau County Dental Society. Bulletin; (until 1981): Tenth District Dental Society of the State of New York. Bulletin (ISSN 0070-3729)

NATIONAL FLUORIDATION NEWS; covering reports on research into the toxicity of fluoride, news on accidents, election outcomes and general information on the issue. see ENVIRONMENTAL STUDIES

NATIONAL MEDICAL AND DENTAL ASSOCIATION. BULLETIN. see MEDICAL SCIENCES

617.6   NE   ISSN 0028-2200
                        CODEN: NTTAAX
NEDERLANDS TIJDSCHRIFT VOOR TANDHEELKUNDE. 1894. 11/yr. fl.151.50. Wegener Tijl Tijdschriften Groep B.V., P.B. 9943, 1006 AP Amsterdam, Netherlands. TEL 020-5182828. FAX 020-177143. TELEX 15230. Ed. Dr. I. van der Waal. adv.; bk.rev.; illus.; tr.lit.; index; circ. 5,900. **Indexed:** Biol.Abstr., Dent.Ind.

617.6   US   ISSN 0093-7347
NEW JERSEY DENTAL ASSOCIATION. JOURNAL. 1912. q. $50. New Jersey Dental Association, One Dental Plaza, N. Brunswick, NJ 08902. TEL 908-821-9400. FAX 908-821-1082. Ed. Dr. Harvey S. Nisselson. adv.; bk.rev.; bibl.; charts; illus.; stat.; circ. 5,000. **Indexed:** Dent.Abstr., Dent.Ind.
    —BLDSC shelfmark: 4832.200000.

617.6   US   ISSN 0028-7296
RK1
NEW YORK JOURNAL OF DENTISTRY. 1860. 8/yr. $12. (First District Dental Society) New York Journal of Dentistry, Inc., 295 Madison Ave., New York, NY 10017. TEL 212-889-8940. adv.; bk.rev.; illus.; circ. 5,525. **Indexed:** Chem.Abstr., Curr.Tit.Dent., Dent.Abstr., Dent.Ind., Dent.Ind., Ind.Med.
    —BLDSC shelfmark: 6089.318000.

617.6   US   ISSN 0028-7571
NEW YORK STATE DENTAL JOURNAL. N.S. 1933. m. (Oct.-May); bi-m. (June-Sep.). $40 to non-members; members $5; foreign $85 (effective in 1992). Dental Society of the State of New York, 7 Elk St., Albany, NY 12207-1066. TEL 518-465-0044. FAX 518-427-0461. Ed. Bernard P. Tillis. adv.; bk.rev.; bibl.; illus.; stat.; index; circ. 15,286. (also avail. in microform from UMI; reprint service avail. from UMI) **Indexed:** Biol.Abstr., Chem.Abstr., Curr.Tit.Dent., Dent.Abstr., Dent.Ind., Dok.Arbeitsmed., Excerp.Med., Ind.Med., Med.Care Rev.
    —BLDSC shelfmark: 6089.730000.
    Description: Features scientific articles covering research reports, case studies, and experiences with new techniques. Includes general and technical information of interest to dental practitioners.

617.6   NZ   ISSN 0028-8047
                        CODEN: NZDJAM
NEW ZEALAND DENTAL JOURNAL. 1905. q. NZ.$85. New Zealand Dental Association, P.O. Box 647, Dunedin, New Zealand. TEL 64-03-479-7115. FAX 64-03-479-0673. Ed. R.H. Brown. adv.; bk.rev.; abstr.; charts; illus.; index; circ. 1,660. **Indexed:** Biol.Abstr., Dent.Abstr., Dent.Ind., Excerp.Med., Ind.Med.
    —BLDSC shelfmark: 6089.970000.

617.632   NZ   ISSN 0111-1485
NEW ZEALAND SOCIETY OF PERIODONTOLOGY. JOURNAL. 1956. s-a. NZ.$80. New Zealand Society of Periodontology, P.O. Box 647, Dunedin, New Zealand. FAX 03-4790-673. Ed. Angela Pack. adv.; bk.rev.; stat.; circ. 600. **Indexed:** Curr.Tit.Dent., Dent.Ind.
    —BLDSC shelfmark: 4833.070000.
    Formerly: New Zealand Society of Periodontology. Bulletin (ISSN 0028-8705)

617.6   US
NEWS AND VIEWS (BETHESDA). 1972. q. membership. American College of Dentists, 839-J Quince Orchard Blvd., Bethesda, MD 20878. TEL 301-986-0555. FAX 301-654-3275. Ed. Gordon H. Rovelstad. (tabloid format; back issues avail.)
    Description: Covers the activities and projects of the College and its 41 sections.

617.6   JA   ISSN 0029-0297
                        CODEN: NKOGAV
NIHON KOKUKA GAKKAI ZASSHI/JAPANESE STOMATOLOGICAL SOCIETY. JOURNAL. (Text in Japanese) 1952. q. 5200 Yen($3.50) Nihon Kokuka Gakkai - Japanese Stomatological Society, Department of Oral Surgery, School of Medicine, University of Tokyo, 7-3-1 Hongo, Bunkyo-ku, Tokyo 113, Japan. Ad.Bd. circ. 1,900. **Indexed:** Chem.Abstr., Ind.Med.
    —BLDSC shelfmark: 4809.550000.

617.6   JA   ISSN 0385-0145
                        CODEN: NKOKDC
NIHON UNIVERSITY. JOURNAL OF ORAL SCIENCE/NICHIDAI KOKU KAGAKU. 1975. q. exchange basis. Nihon University, School of Dentistry at Matsudo, 870-1 Sakaecho, Nishi-2, Matsudo-shi, Chiba-ken 271, Japan. Ed. Tadamasa Iwasawa. index; circ. 900.
    —BLDSC shelfmark: 6113.150000.

617.6   JA   ISSN 0029-0432
                        CODEN: JNUDAT
NIHON UNIVERSITY. SCHOOL OF DENTISTRY. JOURNAL/NIHON DAIGAKU SHIGAKUBU OBUN ZASSHI. (Text in English) 1958. q. free to qualified personnel. Nihon University, School of Dentistry - Nihon Daigaku Shigakubu, 1-8-13 Kanda Surugadai, Chiyoda-ku, Tokyo 101, Japan. FAX 03-3219-8310. Ed. Itaru Moro. bk.rev.; abstr.; charts; illus.; index; circ. 1,200. **Indexed:** Biol.Abstr., Chem.Abstr., Curr.Tit.Dent., Dent.Ind., Ind.Med., INIS Atomind., Med.Abstr.
    —BLDSC shelfmark: 4833.400000.

617.6   JA   ISSN 0549-5245
NIPPON DENTAL UNIVERSITY. ANNUAL PUBLICATIONS. (Text in English) 1964. a. exchange basis. Society of the Nippon Dental University - Nihon Shika Daigaku Shigakkai, 9-20 Fujimi 1-chome, Chiyoda-ku, Tokyo 102, Japan. FAX 03-264-8745. Ed. Yoshiroh Katoh. circ. 2,000.
    Formerly: Society of Nippon Dental College. Annual Publications.

617.6   NO   ISSN 0029-2303
NORSKE TANNLEGEFORENINGS TIDENDE. (Text in Norwegian; summaries in English) 1890. 20/yr. NOK 850. Norske Tannlegeforening - Norwegian Dental Association, P.O.B. l873 Vika, 0124 Oslo 1, Norway. TEL 42-2-833400. FAX 47-2-831576. Eds. Gudrun Sangnes, Bente R. Try. adv.; bk.rev.; charts; illus.; stat.; index; tr.lit.; index; circ. 5,000. **Indexed:** Dent.Abstr., Dent.Ind., Ind.Med.
    —BLDSC shelfmark: 6147.800000.

MEDICAL SCIENCES — DENTISTRY   3239

617.6 US
NORTH CAROLINA DENTAL REVIEW. 1983. s-a. University of North Carolina, School of Dentistry, Brauer Hall, Rm. 410, CB 7450, Chapel Hill, NC 27599-7450. TEL 919-966-4563. FAX 919-839-8672. (Co-sponsor: U N C Dental Alumni Association) Ed. Sharon K. Graydon. circ. 6,000 (controlled).
Description: Supports the school's missions of dental education, patient care, research and service.

617.6 US
NORTHWEST DENTISTRY. 1930. bi-m. $20 to non-members. Minnesota Dental Association, 2236 Marshall Ave., St. Paul, MN 55104. TEL 612-646-7457. FAX 612-646-8246. (Co-sponsors: North Dakota Dental Association; South Dakota Dental Society) Ed. Richard A. Johnson. adv.; circ. 3,472. **Indexed:** Dent.Ind.

617.6 CN
NOVA SCOTIA DENTIST. 1985. bi-m. membership. Nova Scotia Dental Association, 5991 Spring Garden Road, Ste 604, Halifax, N.S. B3H 1Y6, Canada. TEL 902-420-0088. FAX 902-423-6537. Ed. D.V. Pamenter. adv.; circ. 1,000.
Formerly (until 1985): Nova Scotia Dental Association. Newsletter.

617.6 US
O D A NEWSLETTER. vol.17, 1987. q. $20 to non-members; members $15 (includes subscr. to Journal of the Oregon Dental Association). Oregon Dental Association, 17898 S.W. McEwan Rd., Portland, OR 97224. Ed. Dr. James P. Fratzke.

617.6 FR ISSN 0251-172X
ODONTO-STOMATOLOGIE TROPICALE/TROPICAL DENTAL JOURNAL. (Text in English, French) 1978. q. 250 F.($60) Universite de Bordeaux 2, Departement Sante et Developpement, c/o Jean-Louis Miquel, Universite de Bordeaux 2, 146, rue Leo-Saignat, F-33076 Bordeaux cedex, France. TEL 56-90-91-24. FAX 56-24-55-51. TELEX IN UB2 572 237 F. (Co-sponsor: Commonwealth Foundation) Ed. J.L. Miquel. adv.; bk.rev.; index; circ. 2,500. (back issues avail.; reprint service avail.) **Indexed:** Biol.Abstr., So.Pac.Per.Ind.
Formerly: Secretariat de Sante Dentaire de l'Afrique. Revue.
Description: Addresses numerous oral health problems in various tropical countries and efforts to treat them.

617.6 IT ISSN 0393-7631
ODONTOIATRIA OGGI. 1984. m. L.120000($160) Piccin Editore, Via Altinate 107, 35100 Padua, Italy. TEL 049-655566. TELEX 432074 PICCIN I. Ed. Prof. E. Gianni. circ. 5,000.

618 IT
ODONTOIATRIA PRATICA. 1966. q. L.8000. Sabatelli Editori, Piazza Diaz 11, 17100 Savona, Italy. Ed. Raffaello Rastelli. adv.; bk.rev.; abstr.; bibl.; illus.; circ. 1,500. (back issues avail.)

617.6 DK ISSN 0105-0141
ODONTOLOGI. (Text in Danish, Norwegian and Swedish) 1976. a. price varies. Munksgaard International Publishers Ltd., Journals Division, 35 Noerre Soegade, P.O. Box 2148, DK-1016 Copenhagen K, Denmark. TEL 33-127030. FAX 33-129387. TELEX 19431-MUNKS-DK. illus.

617.6 CL ISSN 0029-8417
ODONTOLOGIA CHILENA. 1954. s-a. free. (Colegio de Dentistas de Chile) Editorial Universitaria, Avda. Santa Maria 1990, Casila 3444 Correo Central, Santiago, Chile. Ed. Dr. Juan Montagna Concha. adv.; bibl.; charts; illus.; stat.; tr.mk.; circ. 3,500. **Indexed:** Dent.Ind.

617.6 UY ISSN 0029-8425
ODONTOLOGIA URUGUAYA. vol.21, 1965. s-a. membership. Asociacion Odontologica Uruguaya, Durazno 937-39, Montevideo, Uruguay. TEL 901572. Ed.Bd. adv.; bk.rev.; bibl.; charts; illus.; stat.; circ. 3,000.

617.6 FI ISSN 0078-3358
ODONTOLOGISKA SAMFUNDET I FINLAND. AARSBOK. 1946. a. Fmk.50. Odontologiska Samfundets i Finland, Bergmansg. 11 D 11, SF-00140 Helsinki 14, Finland. adv.; bk.rev.; circ. 500. **Indexed:** Biol.Abstr.
—BLDSC shelfmark: 6235.228000.

617.6 BL
ODONTOLOGO MODERNO; a revista dos cursos. 1973. 6/yr. Editora de Publicacoes Cientificas Ltda., Rua Major Suckow, 30 a 36, 20911 Rio de Janeiro RJ, Brazil. TEL 021-201-3722. FAX 021-261-3749. Ed. Almir L. de Fonseca. adv.; abstr.; bibl.; illus.; cum.index; circ. 15,000.

617.6 IT ISSN 0029-8492
ODONTOPROTESTI.* 1950. m. L.25000. Sindacato Nazionale Odontotecnici, Via Termopoli 12, 20127 Milan, Italy. Dir. Bonifacci Romano. adv.

617.6 IT ISSN 0391-3783
ODONTOSTOMATOLOGIA E IMPLANTOPROTESI. Spanish edition (ISSN 0213-9898) 1974. m. L.230000. Nuovo Odonto s.r.l., Via della Liberazione, 1, 20068 Peschiera Borromeo (MI), Italy. TEL 02-55-30-26-06. FAX 02-55-30-27-00. TELEX 321083. adv.; bk.rev.; circ. 20,000. **Indexed:** Dent.Ind.

617.6 GR ISSN 0029-8506
ODONTOSTOMATOLOGICAL PROGRESS. (Text in Greek; summaries in English) 1947. bi-m. $60. Society of Odontostomatological Research, 70 Micras Asias St., Athens 11527, Greece. Ed. B.G. Tsatsas. adv.; bk.rev.; charts; illus.; circ. 3,000.

617.6 AU ISSN 0029-9596
OESTERREICHISCHE ZAHNAERZTE - ZEITUNG. 1950. m. S.200. Bundesfachgruppe fuer Zahn-, Mund- und Kieferheilkunde, Weihburgstrasse 1012, A-1010 Vienna, Austria. adv.; bk.rev.; charts; stat.; circ. 2,500.
Incorporates (1949-1989): Oesterreichische Dentistenzeitschrift (ISSN 0029-9006)

617.6 AU
DAS OESTERREICHISCHE ZAHNTECHNIKERHANDWERK. 1955. q. S.280. (Bundesinnung der Zahntechniker) Oesterreichischer Wirtschaftsverlag, Nikolsdorfergasse 7-11, 1050 Vienna, Austria. TEL 0222-555585. TELEX 1-11669. Ed. Ingeborg Reisner. tr.lit.; circ. 1,000.
Former titles: Oesterreichische Zahntechniker; Oesterreichische Zahnprothetik; Oesterreichische Zahntechnikerhandwerk.

617.6 US ISSN 0030-087X
OHIO DENTAL JOURNAL. 1927. 2/yr. $30 to non-members. Ohio Dental Association, 1370 Dublin Rd., Columbus, OH 43215-1098. TEL 614-486-2700. (Subscr. to: Department 367, Box 182039, Columbus, OH 43218-2039) Ed. Donald F. Bowers. adv.; illus.; circ. 5,300 (controlled). **Indexed:** Dent.Abstr., Dent.Ind.
—BLDSC shelfmark: 6245.800000.

617.6 US ISSN 0164-9442
OKLAHOMA DENTAL ASSOCIATION JOURNAL. vol.64, 1973. q. $12 (foreign $18). Oklahoma Dental Association, 629 N.W. Expressway, Oklahoma City, OK 73118. TEL 405-848-8873. Ed. Jerome Miller. adv.; illus.; circ. 1,600. **Indexed:** Dent.Abstr., Dent.Ind.
Former titles: Your Oklahoma Dental Association. Journal; Oklahoma State Dental Association. Journal (ISSN 0030-1868)

617.6 US ISSN 0030-2201
OMAHA DISTRICT DENTAL SOCIETY. CHRONICLE. 1936. m. (10/yr.). $10. (Omaha District Dental Society) Barnhart Press, Dundee Professional Bldg., Ste. 403, 119 N. 51st St., Omaha, NE 68132. TEL 402-341-1322. Ed. Dr. Douglas O. deShazer. adv.; bk.rev.; abstr.; charts; illus.; circ. 2,600. **Indexed:** Dent.Ind.

617.6 CN ISSN 0300-5275
ONTARIO DENTIST. 1925. m. Can.$55. Ontario Dental Association, 4 New St., Toronto, Ont. M5R 1P6, Canada. TEL 416-922-3900. FAX 416-922-9005. Ed. Dr. James Shosenberg. adv.; bk.rev.; bibl.; illus.; circ. 6,500. **Indexed:** Dent.Abstr., Dent.Ind.
Formerly: Ontario Dental Association. Journal (ISSN 0030-2864)

617.6 US ISSN 0361-7734
RK501
OPERATIVE DENTISTRY. Variant title: Journal of Operative Dentistry. (Supplements avail.) 1976. bi-m. $55 to individuals (foreign $65); students $25 (foreign $34). (Academy of Operative Dentistry) University of Washington, School of Dentistry, SM-57, Seattle, WA 98195-0001. TEL 206-543-5913. FAX 206-543-7783. (Alt addr.: c/o R.J. Werner, Box 177, Menominie, WI 54751) (Co-sponsor: American Academy of Gold Foil Operators) Ed. David J. Bales. bk.rev.; illus.; circ. 2,000. (also avail. in microfilm from UMI; back issues avail.) **Indexed:** Curr.Cont., Curr.Tit.Dent., Dent.Abstr., Dent.Ind.
—BLDSC shelfmark: 6269.375000.
Supersedes: American Academy of Gold Foil Operators. Journal (ISSN 0002-7146)

617.6 US
ORACLE.* 1964. m. $2. Napa-Solano Dental Society, 4437 Central Pl., Suisun City, CA 94585-1669. Ed. Dr. Robert E. Sprott. adv.; circ. 195.
Formerly: Napa-Solano Dental Society. District Six. Newsletter (ISSN 0027-7800)
Description: Contains organization news.

ORAL AND MAXILLOFACIAL SURGERY CLINICS. see MEDICAL SCIENCES — Surgery

617.6 CN ISSN 0030-4204
ORAL HEALTH; clinical journal devoted to the advancement of the dental profession. 1911. m. Can.$41.19($44) (foreign $75). Southam Business Communications Inc. (Subsidiary of: Southam Inc.), 1450 Don Mills Rd., Don Mills, Ont. M3B 2X7, Canada. TEL 416-445-6641. FAX 416-442-2077. TELEX 069-66612. Ed. Janet Bonellie. adv.; bk.rev.; abstr.; illus.; circ. 15,000. **Indexed:** Chem.Abstr., Dent.Abstr., Dent.Ind.
—BLDSC shelfmark: 6277.500000.

617.6 US ISSN 0030-4220
RD1 CODEN: OSOMAE
ORAL SURGERY, ORAL MEDICINE AND ORAL PATHOLOGY. 1948. m. $67 to individuals (foreign $88); institutions $141 (foreign $162); students $34 (foreign $55). (American Academy of Oral Pathology) Mosby - Year Book, Inc. (Subsidiary of: Times Mirror Company), 11830 Westline Industrial Dr., St. Louis, MO 63146. TEL 800-325-4117. FAX 314-432-1380. TELEX 44-2402. (Co-sponsors: American Academy of Dental Radiology; American Institute of Oral Biology) Ed. Dr. Robert B. Shira. adv.; bk.rev.; abstr.; illus.; s-a. index; circ. 8,858. (also avail. in microfilm from UMI; reprint service avail. from UMI) **Indexed:** ASCA, Chem.Abstr., Curr.Adv.Cancer Res., Curr.Adv.Ecol.Sci., Curr.Cont., Curr.Tit.Dent., Dent.Abstr., Dent.Ind., Excerp.Med., Helminthol.Abstr., Ind.Med., Nutr.Abstr., Rev.Plant Path., Sci.Cit.Ind.
—BLDSC shelfmark: 6277.800000.
Description: Comprehensive coverage of the field including identification of abnormalities and use of specialized diagnostic techniques.
Refereed Serial

617.6 GW ISSN 0724-4991
ORALPROPHYLAXE. 1984. q. DM.32. (Verein fuer Zahnhygiene e.V.) Deutscher Aerzte-Verlag GmbH, Postfach 400265, 5000 Cologne 40, Germany. TEL 02234-7011-0. circ. 5,000.
—BLDSC shelfmark: 6277.808000.
Description: Contains current information and research concerning dental and mouth hygiene. Covers flouride, toothpaste research, and childrens' dental care.

617.6 FR
ORDRE NATIONAL DES CHIRURGIENS- DENTISTES. CONSEIL NATIONAL. BULLETIN OFFICIEL. 1976. q. 190 F. Ordre National des Chirurgiens- Dentistes, Conseil National, 22, rue Emile-Menier, 75116 Paris, France. TEL 45-53-40-05. Dir. M.A. Rochais. charts; illus.

M

MEDICAL SCIENCES — DENTISTRY

617.6 US ISSN 0030-4670
OREGON DENTAL ASSOCIATION. JOURNAL. 1930. q. $20 to non-members; members $15 (includes ODA newsletter). Oregon Dental Association, 17898 S.W. McEwan Rd., Portland, OR 97224. TEL 503-620-3230. Ed. Dr. James P. Fratzke. adv.; bk.rev.; charts; illus.; circ. 2,000. **Indexed:** Dent.Abstr., Dent.Ind.
—BLDSC shelfmark: 4837.450000.
Formerly: Oregon State Dental Journal.
Description: Covers the current news in the science of dentistry.

617.6 FR ISSN 0078-6608
ORTHODONTIE FRANCAISE. (1921-1962 called also Comptes Rendus du Congres Annuel) 1921. a. 1170 F. (effective Jan. 1992). Societe d'Information et de Diffusion, Librarie internationale, 49, bvd. du Lycee, F 92170 Vanves, France. TEL 33-1-645-53-11. (back issues avail.) **Indexed:** Ind.Med.

617.6 AG ISSN 0030-5936
ORTODONCIA. (Summaries in English, French, German and Spanish) 1937. s-a. $30. Sociedad Argentina de Ortodoncia, Montevideo 971, 1019 Buenos Aires, Argentina. Ed. Dr. Marcos M. Rose. adv.; bk.rev.; abstr.; bibl.; charts; illus.; stat.; index; circ. 1,500. **Indexed:** Biol.Abstr., Dent.Ind.

617.6 SP
ORTODONCIA ESPANOLA. (Text in Spanish; summaries in English) 1959. q. 3000 ptas. (Sociedad Espanola de Ortodoncia) Ediciones Ergon, S.A., Muntaner, 262, 6o, 08021 Barcelona, Spain. TEL 2010911. FAX 2015911. (Subscr. to: Cempro, Plaza Conde Valle Suchil 20, 28015 Madrid, Spain) adv.; bk.rev.; index; circ. 2,000. (back issues avail.)

617.6 BL ISSN 0030-5944
ORTODONTIA.* (Text in Portuguese; summaries in English) 1968. 3/yr. exchange basis. Sociedade Paulista de Ortodontia, R. do Livramento, 243, 01321 Sao Paulo, SP, Brazil. Dir. Dr. Julio W. Vigorito. adv.; bk.rev.; bibl.; charts; illus.; index; circ. 5,000. (also avail. in microform) **Indexed:** Dent.Ind.
Description: Presents results of research in orthodontics.

617.6 JA ISSN 0473-4629
CODEN: ODSZA2
OSAKA DAIGAKU SHIGAKU ZASSHI/OSAKA UNIVERSITY DENTAL SOCIETY. JOURNAL. (Text in Japanese) 1956. s-a. 3000 Yen. Osaka Daigaku Shigakkai - Osaka University Dental Society, 1-8 Yamadaoka, Suita, Osaka 565, Japan. TEL 06-876-5711. FAX 06-876-7931. Ed. Yoshio Shigenaga. adv.; circ. 1,700. **Indexed:** Dent.Ind., Excerp.Med.
—BLDSC shelfmark: 4839.370000.
Description: Contains mini-reviews, original articles, and case reports on dental science.

617.6 JA ISSN 0475-2058
CODEN: JODUA2
OSAKA DENTAL UNIVERSITY. JOURNAL. (Text and summaries in English) 1967. s-a. exchange basis. Osaka Dental University - Osaka Shika Daigaku, 5-31, Otemae 1-chome, Chuo-ku, Osaka 540, Japan. FAX 06-943-5656. Ed. Tetsuya Sakaki. abstr.; charts; illus.; stat.; tr.lit.; index. (back issues avail.) **Indexed:** Biol.Abstr., Chem.Abstr., Curr.Tit.Dent., Dent.Ind., Excerp.Med., Ind.Med., Oral Res.Abstr.
—BLDSC shelfmark: 4838.500000.

617.6 JA ISSN 0030-6150
OSAKA ODONTOLOGICAL SOCIETY. JOURNAL/SHIKA IGAKU. (Text in Japanese; summaries in English) 1930. bi-m. $6.50. Osaka Odontological Society - Osaka Shika Gakkai, 1-47 Kyobashi Higashiku, Osaka 540, Japan. adv.; charts; illus. **Indexed:** Biol.Abstr., Chem.Abstr.
—BLDSC shelfmark: 4839.300000.
Description: Contains numerous studies in dental research, including new technologies and treatments.

PAIN CONTROL IN DENTISTRY. see *MEDICAL SCIENCES — Anaesthesiology*

617.6 PK ISSN 0030-9710
CODEN: PKDRAV
PAKISTAN DENTAL REVIEW. (Text in English) 1951. q. $30. 26 Shahrah-e-Quaid-e-Azam, Lahore 54000, Pakistan. Ed. S. Eckbelle. adv.; bk.rev.; bibl.; charts; illus.; stat.; index; circ. 5,000. **Indexed:** Biol.Abstr., Dent.Ind.

PANKEY-GRAM. see *COLLEGE AND ALUMNI*

617.6 IT
PARODONTOLOGIA E STOMATOLOGIA NUOVA. (Summaries in English, French and German) vol.9, 1965. q. L.50000. Istituto Clinico di Odontostomatologia, Viale Benedetto 15, Genoa, Italy. Eds. I. Jonata, F. Torrielli. adv.; bk.rev.; charts; illus.; index. **Indexed:** Chem.Abstr.
Formerly: Stomatologica (ISSN 0039-1727)

617.6 GW
PARODONTOLOGIE. q. DM.158 (foreign DM.172). Quintessenz Verlags GmbH, Ifenpfad 2-4, 1000 Berlin 42, Germany. TEL 030-74006-0. FAX 030-7415080. **Indexed:** Curr.Tit.Dent.

617.6 US
PASSAIC COUNTY DENTAL SOCIETY NEWSLETTER. 1979. m. (Oct.-May). $40. Passaic County Dental Society, 642 Broad St., Clifton, NJ 07013. Ed. Dr. Barry Raphael. adv.; circ. 300. **Indexed:** Dent.Ind.
Formerly: (until 1981) Passaic County Dental Society. Bulletin (ISSN 0079-0125)

617.6 US ISSN 0164-1263
CODEN: PEDEDL
PEDIATRIC DENTISTRY. 1979. bi-m. $65 to individuals (foreign $95); institutions $80 (foreign $115)(effective July 1991). American Academy of Pediatric Dentistry, 211 E. Chicago Ave., Ste. 1036, Chicago, IL 60611-2616. TEL 312-337-2169. FAX 312-337-6329. Ed. Dr. Paul S. Casamassimo. adv.; bk.rev.; circ. 4,120. **Indexed:** Biol.Abstr., Curr.Tit.Dent., Dent.Abstr., Dent.Ind.
—BLDSC shelfmark: 6417.580000.
Description: Promotes the practice, education, and research of pediatric dentistry.
Refereed Serial

617.6 US ISSN 0031-4331
PENN DENTAL JOURNAL. 1897. s-a. $40 (typically set in Dec.). University of Pennsylvania, School of Dental Medicine, 4001 Spruce St., Philadelphia, PA 19104. TEL 215-898-8964. FAX 215-898-8964. Ed. John F. Zak. adv.; bk.rev.; bibl.; charts; illus.; index; circ. 7,500. (also avail. in microform from UMI) **Indexed:** Dent.Ind.
—BLDSC shelfmark: 6421.650000.
Description: A progressive, clinical journal of dentistry, containing articles by faculty and students.

617.6 US ISSN 0031-4439
RK1
PENNSYLVANIA DENTAL JOURNAL. 1933. 6/yr. $12 (foreign $36). Pennsylvania Dental Association, Box 3341, Harrisburg, PA 17105. TEL 717-234-5941. FAX 717-232-7169. Ed. Dr. Marvin Sniderman. adv.; B&W page $354.20, color page $600; 7 x 10. index; circ. 7,000. (also avail. in microfilm from UMI; reprint service avail. from UMI) **Indexed:** Dent.Abstr., Dent.Ind., Med.Care Rev.
—BLDSC shelfmark: 6421.705000.
Description: Covers topics of interest to members of the dental professions: dentistry techniques, breakthroughs, governmental regulations, and other items.

617.6 SP
▼**PERIODONCIA.** (Text in Spanish; summaries in English) 1991. q. 3000 ptas. (Sociedad Espanola de Periodoncia) Ediciones Ergon S.A., Muntaner, 262, 6o, 08021 Barcelona, Spain. TEL 2010911. FAX 2015911. (Subscr. to: Cempro, Plaza Conde Valle Suchil 20, 28015 Madrid, Spain) adv.; bk.rev.; index. (back issues avail.)

618 AT ISSN 0726-5247
PERIODONTOLOGY. 1967. s-a. Aus.$25. Australian Society of Periodontology, Dept. of Dentistry, University of Queensland, Brisbane, Qld. 4000, Australia. TEL 61-7-365-8111. FAX 61-7-365-8199. Ed. Mark Bartold. adv.; bk.rev.; circ. 400.
Formerly: (until 1980): A S P Newsletter.

617.6 US ISSN 0031-7268
PHILADELPHIA COUNTY DENTAL SOCIETY. BULLETIN. 1936. m. (Oct.-May). membership. Philadelphia County Dental Society, 225 E. Washington Square, Philadelphia, PA 19106. TEL 215-925-6050. Ed. Dr. James H. Dyen. adv.; illus.; circ. 2,600. **Indexed:** Dent.Ind., Med.Care Rev.

617.6 PH ISSN 0031-7497
PHILIPPINE DENTAL ASSOCIATION. JOURNAL. 1908. q. $20 to individuals; institutions $40; students $15. Philippines Dental Association, Ayala Ave. corner Kamagong St., Makati, Metro Manila, Philippines. Ed. Dr. Peciencia L. Miravite. adv.; bk.rev.; bibl.; illus.; index; circ. 5,000. (back issues avail.) **Indexed:** Dent.Ind.

617.6 GW ISSN 0174-5980
PHILLIP JOURNAL. 1983. bi-m. DM.180. Phillip Verlag, Maximilianstrasse 52, 8000 Munich 22, Germany. FAX 089-222268. (Dist. by: PAN-Adress Direktmarketing GmbH, Semmelweisstrasse 8, 8033 Planegg, Germany) Ed. Dr. J. Schmidseder. adv.; bk.rev.; circ. 6,500.
—BLDSC shelfmark: 6450.100000.
Formerly: Philip Journal fuer Restaurative Zahnmedizin.

617.6 BL ISSN 0102-9460
PONTIFICIA UNIVERSIDADE CATOLICA DO RIO GRANDE DO SUL. ODONTOCIENCIA. REVISTA. 1986. 2/yr. Cr.$10($20) Editora da P U C R S, c/o Antoninho M. Naime, Caixa Postal 12001, 90620 Porto Alegre RS, Brazil. circ. 1,000.
—BLDSC shelfmark: 6235.212500.

617.632 US
PRACTICAL PERIODONTICS AND AESTHETIC DENTISTRY. 1988. 9/yr. $65 (typically set in Jan.). Practical Periodontics and Aesthetic Dentistry, Inc., 600 Sylvan Ave., Englewood Cliffs, NJ 07632. TEL 201-568-5350. FAX 201-568-5890. adv.; circ. 54,000.
Description: Presents practical applications of soft tissue management and all aspects of restorative and aesthetic dentistry.

617.69 JA ISSN 0018-6341
PRACTICE IN PROSTHODONTICS/HOTETSU RINSHO. (Text in Japanese) 1968. bi-m. 1300 Yen per no. Ishiyaku Publishers, Inc., 7-10 Honkomagome 1-chome, Bunkyo-ku, Tokyo 113, Japan. Ed. Hiroshi Miura. adv.; bk.rev.; index; circ. 16,200. **Indexed:** Dent.Ind.
—BLDSC shelfmark: 6597.350000.

617.6 CS ISSN 0032-6720
PRAKTICKE ZUBNI LEKARSTVI. 1952. 10/yr. $45.10. (Ceskoslovenska Stomatologicka Spolecnost) Avicenum Czechoslovak Medical Press, Malostranske nam. 28, 118 02 Prague 1, Czechoslovakia. (Dist. by: Artia, Ve Smeckach 30, 111 27 Prague 1, Czechoslovakia) (Co-sponsor: Ceskoslovenska Lekarska Spolecnost J. Ev. Purkyne) Ed. Dr. V. Sicha. bk.rev.; abstr.
—BLDSC shelfmark: 3120.700000.

617.6 GW ISSN 0931-6965
PRAKTISCHE KIEFERORTHOPAEDIE; die Zeitschrift aus Praxis und Wissenschaft. 1987. q. DM.168 (foreign DM.178). Quintessenz Verlags GmbH, Ifenpfad 2-4, Postfach 420452, 1000 Berlin 42, Germany. TEL 030-74006-0. FAX 030-7415080. Eds. Prof. Rainer-Reginald Miethke, Prof. Ulrich-Georg Tammoscheit. circ. 3,000. (back issues avail.)
—BLDSC shelfmark: 6600.800000.
Description: Further education for dentists and orthodontists.

617.6 IT
PRATICA ODONTOIATRICA. m. L.50000($60) Edizioni Minerva Medica, Corso Bramante 83, 10126 Turin, Italy. TEL (011) 67 82 82.

617.6 IT
PREVENZIONE E ASSISTENZA DENTALE. 1975. bi-m. L.57000($87) (effective 1992). Masson Italia Periodici, Via Statuto 2-4, 20121 Milan, Italy. TEL 02-6367-1. FAX 02-6367211. Ed. Carlo Guastamacchia. circ. 5,000.
Formerly: Prevenzione Stomatologica.

617.6 UK ISSN 0032-9185
PROBE. 1959. m. £20. Mark Allen Publishing Ltd., Croxted Mews, 288 Croxted Rd., London SE24 9DA, England. FAX 081-671-7327. Ed. Jeremy Cowan. adv.; bk.rev.; circ. 20,000. **Indexed:** Dent.Ind.

617.6 AT ISSN 0079-5631
PROBE. 1949. a. Aus.$15. Adelaide University Dental Students Society (AUDSS), School of Dentistry, Undergraduate Mailbox, 5th Fl., Dental Hospital, Frome Rd., Adelaide, S.A. 5000, Australia. Eds. M. Bilski, K. Tabalotny. adv.; bk.rev.; circ. 220.

MEDICAL SCIENCES — DENTISTRY

617.6 GW ISSN 0932-4488
PRODENT; Zahntechnik-Gesundheit-Soziales-Arbeit. 1988. q. DM.180. Deutscher Zahntechniker Verband e.V., Bundesgeschaeftsstelle, Am Bach 6-8, 4800 Bielefeld, Germany. TEL 0521-179674. Ed. Dr. Ulrich Weisemann. adv.; bk.rev.; circ. 3,500. (back issues avail.)

617.6 US ISSN 0033-1236 RK1
PROOFS; the magazine of dental sales. 1918. 10/yr. $15 (foreign $55). PennWell Publishing Co., Dental Economics Division, Box 3408, Tulsa, OK 74101. TEL 918-835-3161. FAX 918-831-9497. Ed. Mary Elizabeth Good. adv.; illus.; circ. 7,000.
   Description: Directed to dental sales and marketing sales personnel and staff, and to key executives and marketing personnel of dental manufacturing firms.

617.6 613.7 US
PROPHYGRAM. 1982. 4/yr. $25. Florida Dental Hygienists' Association, Inc., Box 948113, Maitland, FL 32794-8113. Ed. Cynthia Macri. adv.; illus.; tr.lit.; circ. 2,300. (tabloid format; back issues avail.)

617.6 PL ISSN 0033-1783
PROTETYKA STOMATOLOGICZNA. 1965. bi-m. $87. Panstwowy Zaklad Wydawnictw Lekarskich, Dluga 38-40, Warsaw, Poland. TEL 31-42-81. (Dist. by: Ars Polona-Ruch, Krakowskie Przedmiescie 7, 00-068 Warsaw, Poland) Ed. E. Spiechowicz. adv.; bk.rev.; abstr.; charts; illus.; pat.; tr.mk.; index, cum.index; circ. 5,000. **Indexed:** Dent.Ind.
   —BLDSC shelfmark: 6936.195000.
   Description: Deals with clinical and laboratory prosthetics.

617.6 US ISSN 1060-1341
Q D T. (Editions in English, German, Italian and Japanese) 1976. a. $54. Quintessence Publishing Co., Inc., 551 Kimberly Dr., Carol Stream, IL 60188-1881. TEL 708-682-3223. FAX 708-682-3288. Ed.Bd. adv.; illus.; index. **Indexed:** Dent.Abstr., Dent.Ind.
   Former titles: Q D T Yearbook (ISSN 0896-6532); (until 1987): Quintessence of Dental Technology (ISSN 0362-0913)

617.6 US
QUEENS COUNTY DENTAL SOCIETY. BULLETIN. vol.8, 1970. 6/yr. $30. Queens County Dental Society, 86-90 188th St., Jamaica, NY 11423. TEL 718-454-8344. FAX 718-454-8818. Ed. Alan N. Queen. adv.; bk.rev.; illus.; circ. 1,500. **Indexed:** Dent.Ind.
   Formerly: Eleventh District Dental Society. Bulletin (ISSN 0013-6166)
   Description: Covers news of the Society and the dental profession.

617.6 SP ISSN 0214-0985
QUINTESSENCE (EDICION ESPANOLA); publicacion internacional de odontologia. 1988. m. (10/yr.). 9900 ptas.($100) (free to qualifed personnel). Ediciones Doyma S.A., Travesera de Gracia, 17-21, 08021 Barcelona, Spain. TEL 200-07-11. FAX 209-11-36. TELEX 51964 INK E. Dir. S. Campi Schoeller. adv.: page 165000 ptas.; trim 210 x 280; adv. contact: Jose Luis Campos. circ. 7,000.
   Description: Contains scientific and technical information from clinical centers in Europe and N. America. Covers hygiene and prophylaxis, implantology, periodontics, pediatric dentistry, maxofacial surgery and prothesis.

617.6 US ISSN 0033-6572
QUINTESSENCE INTERNATIONAL. (Text in English) 1969. m. $72 (foreign $107). Quintessence Publishing Co., Inc., 551 Kimberly Dr., Carol Stream, IL 60188-1881. TEL 708-682-3223. FAX 708-682-3288. Ed. Dr. Richard J. Simonsen. adv.; circ. 26,412. **Indexed:** Curr.Tit.Dent., Dent.Abstr., Dent.Ind.
   —BLDSC shelfmark: 7218.120000.
   Incorporates: Dental Digest (ISSN 0011-8567)
   Description: Targeted at general practitioners. Covers all areas of dentistry, including oral surgery, clinical communication, preventive and pediatric dentistry, practice administration, and clinical communication.
   Refereed Serial

617.6 SP
▼**QUINTESSENCE TECNICA (EDICION ESPANOLA)**; publicacion internacional de protesis dental. Spanish translation of: Quintessenz der Zahntechnik. 1990. bi-m. 6500 ptas.($66) Ediciones Doyma S.A., Travesera de Gracia, 17-21, 08021 Barcelona, Spain. TEL 200-07-11. FAX 209-11-36. TELEX 51964 INK E. Dir. G. Sierra del Hoyo. adv.: page 115000 ptas.; trim 150 x 210; adv. contact: Jose Luis Campos. circ. 3,500.
   Description: Covers dental prosthesis. Contains photographs and schematics of new techniques to facilitate their immediate practical application.

617.6 GW
DIE QUINTESSENZ; die Monatszeitschrift fuer den praktizierenden Zahnarzt. m. DM.208 (foreign DM.220). Quintessenz Verlags GmbH, Ifenpfad 2-4, 1000 Berlin 42, Germany. TEL 030-74006-0. FAX 030-7415080. TELEX 183815-QUINT-D.
   Indexed: Curr.Tit.Dent., Dok.Arbeitsmed.

617.6 GW
QUINTESSENZ DER ZAHNTECHNIK. m. DM.178 (foreign DM.188). Quintessenz Verlags GmbH, Ifenpfad 2-4, 1000 Berlin 42, Germany. TEL 030-74006-0. FAX 030-7415080. TELEX 183815-QUINT-D.
   Indexed: Curr.Tit.Dent., Dok.Arbeitsmed.

617.6 GW ISSN 0033-6599
QUINTESSENZ JOURNAL; Zeitschrift fuer die Zahnarzthelferin. 1971. m. DM.128 (foreign DM.136). Quintessenz Verlags GmbH, Ifenpfad 2-4, 1000 Berlin 42, Germany. TEL 030-74006-0. FAX 030-7415080. TELEX 183815-QUINT-D.
   Indexed: Dent.Ind., Dok.Arbeitsmed., So.Pac.Per.Ind.
   —BLDSC shelfmark: 7218.145000.

617.6 IT ISSN 0390-6841
QUINTESSENZA; rivista mensile di odontostomatologia pratica. 1970. m. L.110000($120) Piccin Editore, Via Altinate 107, 35100 Padua, Italy. Ed. Giorgio Borea. adv.; bk.rev.; illus.; index; circ. 5,000. (back issues avail.; reprint service avail. from UMI) **Indexed:** Chem.Abstr., Dent.Ind.

617.6 US
R D H; the national magazine for dental hygiene professionals. 1981. m. $40. Stevens Publishing Corporation, 225 N. New Rd., Waco, TX 76710. TEL 817-776-9000. Ed. Laura Albrecht. adv.; circ. 55,000.

617.6 IT ISSN 0048-6787
RASSEGNA ODONTOTECNICA.* 1954. bi-m. L.25000. Sindacato Nazionale Odontotecnici, Via Termopoli 12, 20127 Milan, Italy. Dir. Martinazzi Ermenegildo. **Indexed:** Dent.Ind.
   —BLDSC shelfmark: 7294.480000.

617.6 IT ISSN 0033-9911
RASSEGNA TRIMESTRALE DI ODONTOIATRIA. (Text in Italian; summaries in English, French and German) 1920. q. L.5000. Istituto Stomatologico Italiano, Via della Pace 21, 20122 Milan, Italy. Ed. Oscar Hoffer. adv.; charts; illus.; index. **Indexed:** Biol.Abstr., Ind.Med.

617.6 UK
RESTORATIVE DENTISTRY. 1962. q. £30 per no. to non-members. European Dental Society, c/o Dr. P. Wright, Dept. Prosthetic Dentistry, Dental School, London Hospital, Medical College, Turner St., London E1 2AD, England. (Co-sponsor: British Society for Restorative Dentistry) Ed. Gavin Pearson. adv.; bk.rev.; circ. 1,500. (tabloid format)
   Formerly: Anglo-Continental Dental Society. Journal (ISSN 0003-3324)
   Description: Contains professional articles on all aspects of prosthetics and periodontology.

617.6 BL ISSN 0034-7272
REVISTA BRASILEIRA DE ODONTOLOGIA. (Text in Portuguese; summaries in English and Portuguese) 1942. bi-m. Cr.$2000($15) Associacao Brasileira de Odontologia, Secao do Rio de Janeiro, Rua Barao de Sertorio, 75, CEP 20261, Rio de Janeiro RJ, Brazil. TEL 021-293-5322. FAX 021-293-3893. Ed. Francisco Nader. adv.; bk.rev.; abstr.; circ. 15,000. (back issues avail.) **Indexed:** Biol.Abstr.

617.6 CU ISSN 0034-7507
REVISTA CUBANA DE ESTOMATOLOGIA. (Text in Spanish; summaries in English, French, Spanish) 1965. s-a. $10 in N. America; S. America $12; Europe $14. Ministerio de Salud Publica, Centro Nacional de Informacion de Ciencias Medicas, Calle E No. 452, e-19 y 21, Plaza de la Revolucion, Apdo. 6520, Havana, Cuba. TEL 809-32-5338. (Dist. by: Ediciones Cubanas, Obispo No. 527, Apdo. 605, Havana, Cuba) Dir. Dr. Luis Delgado Mendez. bibl.; abstr.; charts; illus.; index; circ. 2,500. **Indexed:** Biol.Abstr., Dent.Ind., Ind.Med.
   —BLDSC shelfmark: 7852.105000.

617.6 SP ISSN 1130-0094
REVISTA DE ACTUALIDAD ODONTO ESTOMATOLOGICA ESPANOLA. 1954. m. (10/yr.). free. (Consejo General de Colegios de Odontologos y Estomatologos de Espana) Editorial Garsi, S.A., Londres, 17, 28028 Madrid, Spain. TEL 256-08-00. FAX 361-10-07. Dir. Jose A. del Pozo del Olmo. adv.; bk.rev.; bibl.; illus.; circ. 10,000. **Indexed:** Dent.Ind., Ind.Med.Esp.
   —BLDSC shelfmark: 7835.625000.
   Former titles (until 1990): Revista de Actualidades de Estomatologica Espanola (ISSN 0212-9701); (until 1983): Boletin de Informacion Dental (ISSN 0006-6311)

617.6 RM
REVISTA DE CHIRURGIE, ONCOLOGIE, RADIOLOGIE, O.R.L., OFTALMOLOGIE, STOMATOLOGIE. STOMATOLOGIE. (Text in Rumanian; summaries in English, French, German, Russian) 1954. 4/yr. $20. Uniunea Societatilor de Stiinte Medicale din Republica Socialista Rumania, Str. Progresului No. 8-10, Sectorul 1, Bucharest 70754, Rumania. (Subscr. to: ILEXIM, Str. 13 Decembrie Nr. 3, P.O. Box 136-137, Bucharest, Rumania) Ed.Bd. adv.; bk.rev.; abstr.; bibl.; charts; illus.; index. **Indexed:** Biol.Abstr., Chem.Abstr., Dent.Ind., Ind.Med.
   Supersedes: Stomatologia (ISSN 0039-1719)

REVISTA ESPANOLA DE CIRUGIA ORAL Y MAXILOFACIAL. see MEDICAL SCIENCES — Surgery

617.6 SP ISSN 0212-4688
REVISTA ESPANOLA DE ENDODONCIA. (Text in Spanish; summaries in English) 1982. q. 3000 ptas.($35) (Asociacion Espanola de Endodoncia) Ediciones Ergon, S.A., Muntaner, 262, 6o, 08021 Barcelona, Spain. TEL 2010911. FAX 2015911. (Subscr. to: Cempro, Plaza Conde Valle Suchil 20, 028015 Madrid, Spain) adv.; bk.rev.; index. (back issues avail.)

617.6 SP ISSN 0210-0576
REVISTA ESPANOLA DE ORTODONCIA. 1971. 3/yr. 4000 ptas. Dr. Eliseo Plasencia, Ed. & Pub., San Vicente, 95, 46007 Valencia, Spain. FAX 34-6-3410626. adv.; bk.rev.; abstr.; bibl.; circ. 1,000. (back issues avail.) **Indexed:** Dent.Abstr., Ind.Med.Esp.

617.6 BL ISSN 0034-9542
REVISTA GAUCHA DE ODONTOLOGIA. (Text in Portuguese; summaries in English) 1953. q. $21. Estrada da Ponta Grossa 5311, Porto Alegre, 9000 Rio Grande do Sul, Brazil. Ed. Ricardo Cauduro Neto. adv.; bk.rev.; abstr.; bibl.; illus.; index; circ. 22,680. **Indexed:** Dent.Ind.

617.6 CK ISSN 0120-2855
REVISTA ODONTOLOGIA. 1963. 3/yr. Universidad Nacional de Colombia, Facultad de Odontologia, Ciudad Universitaria, Bogota, Colombia. Ed. Oscar Monroy Vega. adv.; bibl.; illus.; circ. 2,000.
   Formerly: Odontologia (ISSN 0029-8409)

617.5 BL ISSN 0100-705X
REVISTA PAULISTA DE ODONTOLOGIA. 1979. 6/yr. Sindicato dos Odontologistas do Estado de Sao Paulo, Rua Humaita 349-1a, sobreloja, CEP 01321 Sao Paulo, Brazil. TEL 011-37-7567. FAX 011-37-0727. Ed. Henrique Motilinsky. circ. 10,000.

617.6 PO ISSN 0035-0397
REVISTA PORTUGUESA DE ESTOMATOLOGIA E CIRURGIA MAXILO-FACIAL. (Summaries in English and French) vol.12, 1971. q. Esc.2000. Sociedade Portuguesa de Estomatologia e Medicina Dentaria, Av. Rainha D. Amelia 36, 1600 Lisbon, Portugal. TEL 759-39-48. FAX 759-39-48. Ed. Antonio Mano Azul. adv.; bk.rev.; abstr.; bibl.; charts; illus.; stat.; index; circ. 1,200. **Indexed:** Biol.Abstr., Dent.Ind., Ind.Med.

MEDICAL SCIENCES — DENTISTRY

617.6   BE
REVUE BELGE DE MEDECINE DENTAIRE. Dutch edition: Belgisch Tijdschrift voor Tandheelkunde. (Text in French) 1946. q. 1600 Fr. (foreign 1800 Fr.). Societe Francophone Belge de Medecine Dentaire a.s.b.l., Bd. Gen. Jacques 221, B-1050 Brussels, Belgium. TEL 02-647-41-37. FAX 02-640-29-15. adv.; bk.rev.; index; circ. 3,500. **Indexed:** Ind.Med.

617.6   FR   ISSN 0300-9815
REVUE D'ODONTO-STOMATOLOGIE. (Text in French; summaries in English) 1954. bi-m. 920 Fr. (effective Jan. 1991). Societe Odontologique de Paris, 239 rue du Faubourg Saint-Martin, 75010 Paris, France. FAX 42-09-29-08. Eds. Gerard Mandel, Brigitte Di Crescenzo. adv.; bk.rev.; bibl.; charts; illus.; tr.lit.; index, cum.index: 1954-1961. **Indexed:** Chem.Abstr., Curr.Tit.Dent., Dent.Ind., Ind.Med.
—BLDSC shelfmark: 7938.710000.
Formerly: Revue Francaise d'Odonto-Stomatologie (ISSN 0035-3043)

617.6   FR   ISSN 0035-2470
REVUE D'ODONTO-STOMATOLOGIE DU MIDI DE LA FRANCE. (Text in French; summaries in English) 1937. 4/yr. $45. Faculte de Medecine, 3 ter. Place de la Victoire, 33076 Bordeaux Cedex, France. Ed. P. Benoit. adv.; bk.rev.; abstr.; bibl.; charts; circ. 2,000. **Indexed:** Dent.Ind.

617.6   FR   ISSN 0035-1768
CODEN: RSCMAL
REVUE DE STOMATOLOGIE ET DE CHIRURGIE MAXILLO-FACIALE. 1894. bi-m. 205 ECU($251) (typically set in Jan.). (Societe de Stomatologie et de Chirurgie Maxillo-Faciale de France) Masson, 120 bd. Saint-Germain, 75280 Paris Cedex 06, France. Eds. M. Grellet, P. Laudenbach. adv.; bk.rev.; illus.; index; circ. 1,600. (also avail. in microform from UMI; reprint service avail. from ISI) **Indexed:** Biol.Abstr., Curr.Adv.Cancer Res., Curr.Adv.Ecol.Sci., Curr.Cont., Curr.Tit.Dent., Dent.Ind., Excerp.Med., Ind.Med.
—BLDSC shelfmark: 7953.325000.
Formerly: Revue de Stomatologie.

617.6   FR   ISSN 0035-4147
REVUE STOMATO-ODONTOLOGIQUE DU NORD DE LA FRANCE.* vol.25, 1970. q. 25 F. Place de Verdun, 59 Lille, France. adv.; illus.; index. **Indexed:** Biol.Abstr.

617.6   US
RHODE ISLAND DENTAL ASSOCIATION. JOURNAL. 1968. q. $15. Rhode Island Dental Association, 200 Centerville Pl., Warwick, RI 02886. TEL 401-732-6833. Ed. Dr. Jan Feldman. adv.; bk.rev.; illus.; circ. 700. **Indexed:** Dent.Ind.
Formerly (until 1975): Rhode Island State Dental Society. Journal (ISSN 0035-4643)

617.6   US
RHODE ISLAND DENTAL ASSOCIATION. NEWSLETTER. 1972. s-a. membership only. Rhode Island Dental Association, 200 Centerville Pl., Warwick, RI 02886. TEL 401-732-6833. Ed. Valerie G. Donnelly. circ. 600.

617.6   JA   ISSN 0035-5488
RINSHO SHIKA/FOLIA ODONTOLOGICA PRACTICA. (Text in Japanese) 1929. q. 4000 Yen (effective 1991). Rinsho-Shika Sha, 29 Ishiicyo Nishinanajo, Shimogyo-ku, Kyoto, Japan. TEL 075-313-5811. Ed. Nanae Tsuge. adv.; abstr.; charts; illus. **Indexed:** Chem.Abstr.
—BLDSC shelfmark: 3971.680000.

617.6   IT
RIVISTA ITALIANA DEGLI ODONTOTECNICI; dental press. 1964. 9/yr. L.79000($122) (effective 1992). Masson Italia Periodici, Via Statuto 2-4, 20121 Milan, Italy. TEL 02-6367-1. FAX 02-6367211. 111 Fulvio Tonesi. adv.; bk.rev.; circ. 7,000. **Indexed:** Dent.Ind.

617.6 613.92
▼**RIVISTA ITALIANA DI ODONTOIATRIA INFANTILE.** 1990. q. L.53000($78) (effective 1991). Masson Italia Periodici, Via Statuto 2-4, 20121 Milan, Italy. TEL 02-6367-1. FAX 02-6367-211. Ed. Giovanni Dolci. circ. 1,500.

617.6   IT   ISSN 0035-6905
RIVISTA ITALIANA DI STOMATOLOGIA.* 1931. m. L.65000. (Associazione Medici Dentisti Italiani) Attualita Dentale S.r.l., Via L. da Viadana 9, 20122 Milan, Italy. bk.rev.; circ. 15,000. **Indexed:** Dent.Ind.
—BLDSC shelfmark: 7987.700000.

617.6   UK
ROLLS OF DENTAL AUXILIARIES. a. £8. General Dental Council, 37 Wimpole St., London W1M 8DQ, England. TEL 071-4862171. FAX 071-224-3294. (back issues avail.)
Formerly: Rolls of Ancilliary Dental Workers.

617.6   AT   ISSN 0158-1570
ROYAL AUSTRALASIAN COLLEGE OF DENTAL SURGEONS. ANNALS. 1967. irreg., vol.11, 1992. Aus.$40. Royal Australasian College of Dental Surgeons, 64 Castlereagh St., Sydney, N.S.W. 2000, Australia. TEL 02-232-3800. FAX 02-221-8108. Ed. John Harcourt. circ. 1,000.
Former titles: Royal Australian College of Dental Surgeons. Annals (ISSN 0312-7923); Australian College of Dental Surgeons. Annals. (ISSN 0004-8895)

617.6   UK   ISSN 0049-1160
S A A D DIGEST. 1970. q. £20. Society for the Advancement of Anaesthesia in Dentistry, 59 Summerlands Ave., London W3 6EW, England. TEL 01-993 6844. Ed. P. Sykes. adv.; bk.rev.; illus.; circ. 1,500. **Indexed:** Curr.Adv.Ecol.Sci.
—BLDSC shelfmark: 8055.110000.

SAARLAENDISCHES AERZTEBLATT. see *MEDICAL SCIENCES*

617.6   US   ISSN 0892-1334
ST. LOUIS METROPOLITAN MEDICINE. 1979. m. $50. St. Louis Metropolitan Medical Society, 3839 Lindell Blvd., St. Louis, MO 63108. TEL 314-371-5225. FAX 314-533-8601. Ed. Dr. Edmond B. Cabbabe. adv.; bk.rev.; index; circ. 3,100. (back issues avail.)

617.6   US
SAN ANTONIO DISTRICT DENTAL SOCIETY NEWSLETTER. 1970. m. $40. San Antonio District Dental Society, 202 W. French Pl., San Antonio, TX 78212. TEL 512-732-1264. Ed. Dr. Dave C. Bensh. adv.; illus.; circ. 1,100. **Indexed:** Dent.Ind.
Supersedes (1946-1970): San Antonio District Dental Society. Journal (ISSN 0036-3979)

617.6   DK   ISSN 0029-845X
CODEN: SJDRAN
SCANDINAVIAN JOURNAL OF DENTAL RESEARCH. (Text and summaries in English) 1893. 6/yr. DKK 1250. (Nordiska Odontologiska Foreningen) Munksgaard International Publishers Ltd., 35 Noerre Soegade, P.O. Box 2148, DK-1016 Copenhagen K, Denmark. TEL 33-127030. FAX 33-129387. TELEX 19431-MUNKS-DK. Ed. J.J. Pindborg. adv.; illus.; index; circ. 1,300. (also avail. in microform from SWZ; reprint service avail. from ISI,SWZ) **Indexed:** Biol.Abstr., Chem.Abstr., Curr.Adv.Ecol.Sci., Curr.Cont., Curr.Tit.Dent., Dent.Abstr., Dent.Ind., Excerp.Med., Ind.Med., Nutr.Abstr., Risk Abstr.
—BLDSC shelfmark: 8087.505500.

617.6   SZ   ISSN 1011-4203
CODEN: SMOZEP
SCHWEIZER MONATSSCHRIFT FUER ZAHNMEDIZIN. (Text in English, French, German and Italian) 1891. m. 250 SFr. Schweizerische Zahnaerztegesellschaft, Postfach, CH-3000 Bern 8, Switzerland. TEL 031-210377. FAX 031-223534. Ed.Bd. adv.; bk.rev.; abstr.; bibl.; charts; illus.; index; circ. 4,300. **Indexed:** Biol.Abstr., Chem.Abstr., Curr.Adv.Ecol.Sci., Curr.Tit.Dent., Dent.Ind., Excerp.Med., Ind.Med.
Formerly: Schweizerische Monatsschrift fuer Zahnheilkunde (ISSN 0036-7702); Which included: Helvetica Odontologica Acta (ISSN 0018-0211) & Helvetica Odontologica Acta. Supplementum (ISSN 0073-1803)

617.6   US   ISSN 0037-0452
SEATTLE - KING COUNTY DENTAL SOCIETY. JOURNAL. 1962. m. (Aug.-May). $12.95. Journal and Bulletin Agency, Box 10249, Bainbridge Island, WA 98110. TEL 206-682-7813. adv.; bk.rev.; circ. 1,300. **Indexed:** Dent.Ind.
Formerly: Seattle District Dental Society. Journal.

SELECTED READINGS IN ORAL AND MAXILLOFACIAL SURGERY. see *MEDICAL SCIENCES — Surgery*

617.6   IT
SELEZIONE ODONTOIATRICA. q. L.110000($120) Piccin Editore, Via Altinate 107, 35121 Padua, Italy. TEL 049-655566. TELEX 432074 PICCIN I.

617.6   IR
SHAHEED BEHESHTI UNIVERSITY. FACULTY OF DENTISTRY. JOURNAL. (Text in Farsi) 1968. q. Shaheed Beheshti University, Faculty of Dentistry, Shahid Chamran Ave., Evin, Teheran 19834, Iran. TEL 021-21411. TELEX 215464. Ed. Dr. Ali- A. Bahreman. adv.
Formerly (until 1983): National University of Iran. Dental School. Journal (ISSN 0011-8745)

617.6   JA   ISSN 0029-8484
SHIGAKU/ODONTOLOGY. (Text in Japanese; summaries in English) 1941. 6/yr. 8000 Yen. Society of the Nippon Dental University - Nihon Shika Daigaku Shigakkai, 9-20 Fujimi 1-chome, Chiyoda-ku, Tokyo 102, Japan. FAX 03-264-8745. Ed. Shigeo Aiyama. charts; illus.; circ. 2,650. **Indexed:** Biol.Abstr., Chem.Abstr., Dent.Ind., Hist.Abstr. (until 1992).
—BLDSC shelfmark: 6235.230000.

617.6   JA   ISSN 0037-3710
CODEN: SHGKA3
SHIKA GAKUHO/TOKYO DENTAL COLLEGE SOCIETY JOURNAL. (Text in English and Japanese) 1895. m. 5000 Yen($8.60) Tokyo Shika Daigaku Gakkai - Tokyo Dental College Society, Tokyo Dental College, 2-2 Masago 1-chome, Chiba 260, Japan. (Order from: Maruzen Co., Ltd., 2-3-10 Nihonbashi, Chuo-ku, Tokyo 103, Japan; or their Import and Export Department, P.O. Box 5050, Tokyo International, Tokyo 100-31, Japan) Ed. Dr. Tetsuya Kanatake. adv.; bk.rev.; abstr.; bibl.; charts; illus.; stat.; tr.lit.; index; circ. 4,600. **Indexed:** Biol.Abstr., Dent.Ind., Excerp.Med.
—BLDSC shelfmark: 4908.920000.

617.6   JA   ISSN 0389-1895
CODEN: SHGKD6
SHIKA GIKO/JOURNAL OF DENTAL TECHNICS. (Special issues avail.) (Text in Japanese) 1973. m. 1200 Yen per no. Ishiyaku Publishers, Inc., 7-10 Honkomagome 1-chome, Bunkyo-ku, Tokyo 113, Japan. Ed. Hiroshi Miura. adv.; bk.rev.; charts; illus.; circ. 20,000. **Indexed:** Chem.Abstr.

SIERRA LEONE MEDICAL AND DENTAL ASSOCIATION. JOURNAL. see *MEDICAL SCIENCES*

617.5   BL
SINDICATO DOS ODONTOLOGISTAS DO ESTADO DE SAO PAULO. NOTICIAS. 1981. 6/yr. Sindicato dos Odontologistas do Estado de Sao Paulo, Rua Humaita 349-1, sobreloja, CEP 01321 Sao Paulo, Brazil. TEL 011-37-7567. FAX 011-37-0727. Ed. Henrique Motilinsky. circ. 10,000.

617.6   US
SMILES IN DENTAL HEALTH. 1988. q. Dental Learning Systems Co., Inc., 9 Pheasant Run Rd., Newtown, PA 18940-1818. TEL 215-860-9595. Ed. Mathew T. Corso.
Description: Covers dental hygiene, preventive care, and nutrition for patients.

617.643   CK   ISSN 0037-8453
SOCIEDAD COLOMBIANA DE ORTODONCIA. REVISTA.* 1963. q. free. Sociedad Colombiana de Ortodoncia, Carrera 9a, No. 52A-46, Bogota D.E., Colombia. Ed. Dr. Carlos Perez Martinez. adv.; bk.rev.; charts; illus.; index; circ. 1,000.

617.6   SP   ISSN 0213-831X
SOPRODEN. 1985. q. 4300 ptas.($72) (Sociedad Espanola de Protesicos Dentales) Editorial Garsi, S.A., Londres, 17, 28028 Madrid, Spain. TEL 265-08-00. FAX 361-10-07. Ed. J. Tevar Montero. circ. 5,000.

617.6   US   ISSN 0038-3287
SOUTH DAKOTA DENTAL ASSOCIATION. NEWSLETTER. 1962. m. $20 to non-members. South Dakota Dental Association, 108 W. Missouri Ave., Box 1194, Pierre, SD 57501. TEL 605-224-9133. Ed. Trudy Feigum. adv.; circ. 500 (controlled).

MEDICAL SCIENCES — DENTISTRY

617.6   US   ISSN 0038-3945
SOUTHERN CALIFORNIA DENTAL LABORATORY ASSOCIATION. BULLETIN. 1944. bi-m. $5. Southern California Dental Laboratory Association, 3333 Glendale Blvd., Ste. 4, Los Angeles, CA 90039. TEL 213-661-2188. Ed. James C. Powell. adv.; illus.; circ. 2,000.
    Formerly: Southern California State Dental Laboratory Association Bulletin.

617.6   US   ISSN 0275-1879
RK55.H28
SPECIAL CARE IN DENTISTRY; managing special patients, settings, and situations. 1981. bi-m. $18. (Foundation of Special Care Organizations) American Dental Association, 211 E. Chicago Ave., Chicago, IL 60611. TEL 312-440-2500. **Indexed:** CINAHL, Curr.Tit.Dent., Dent.Abstr., Dent.Ind.
    —BLDSC shelfmark: 8365.680000.

617.6   NE
STANDBY; vaktijdschrift voor tandartsassistenten. 1988. 6/yr. fl.54.95. Hofstad Vakpers B.V., Postbus 119, 2700 AC Zoetermeer, Netherlands. TEL 079-711811. FAX 079-711803. Ed. S. Menheere. circ. 2,900.

617.6   IT   ISSN 1120-9402
STOMATOLOGIA MEDITERRANEA; rivista trimestrale di odontoiatria e chirurgia maxillo-facciale. (Text in Italian; summaries in English) 1981. q. L.70000($80) Via Emerico Amari 32, 90139 Palermo, Italy. TEL 091-32-82-69. Ed. Giuseppe Messina. adv.; bk.rev.; bibl.; charts; illus.; stat.; circ. 1,500.

617.6   BU   ISSN 0491-0982
CODEN: STMYAN
STOMATOLOGIJA. (Text in Bulgarian; summaries in English, Russian) 1951. bi-m. 16 lv. (Ministerstvo na Narodnoto Zdrave) Izdatel'stvo Meditsina i Fizkultura, 11 Pl. Slaveikov, Sofia, Bulgaria. (Distr. by: Hemus, 6 Rouski Bvld., 1000 Sofia, Bulgaria) (Co-sponsor: Nauchno Druzhestvo po Stomatologija) Ed. E. Atanassova. circ. 2,581. **Indexed:** Abstr.Bulg.Sci.Med.Lit.
    —BLDSC shelfmark: 0169.600000.

617.6   RU   ISSN 0039-1735
CODEN: STOAAT
STOMATOLOGIYA/STOMATOLOGY. 1922. bi-m. 14.40 Rub.($11.40) (Vsesoyuznoe Nauchnoe Obshchestvo Stomatologov) Izdatel'stvo Meditsina, Petroverigskii pereulok 6-8, 101838 Moscow, Russia. (Co-sponsor: Ministerstvo Zdravookhraneniya S.S.S.R.) Ed. V.F. Rud'ko. bk.rev.; index. **Indexed:** Biol.Abstr., Chem.Abstr., Dent.Ind., Excerp.Med., Ind.Med., Nutr.Abstr.
    —BLDSC shelfmark: 0169.500000.
    Description: Reports on theoretical and practical problems of therapeutic, operative and orthopedic stomatology, stomatology of childhood, the etiology, pathogenesis, prophylaxis and treatment of diseases of the teeth, oral cavity and the maxillofacial region.

617.6   YU   ISSN 0039-1743
CODEN: SGLSAB
STOMATOLOSKI GLASNIK SRBIJE. (Text in Serbian; summaries in English, French and German) 1954. bi-m. $25. Srpsko Lekarsko Drustvo, Dzordza Vasingtona 19, Belgrade, Yugoslavia. Ed. Dr. Miroslav Pajic. adv.; bk.rev.; charts; illus.; circ. 2,000. **Indexed:** Dent.Ind.
    —BLDSC shelfmark: 8465.920000.

617.6   US
SUFFOLK DENTISTRY. vol.16, 1970. 6/yr. $12. Suffolk County Dental Society, 850 Veterans Memorial Hwy., Hauppauge, NY 11788. TEL 516-265-6924. Ed. Charles S. Liebowitz, D.D.S. adv.; bk.rev.; circ. 1,100.
    Formerly: Suffolk County Dental Society. Bulletin (ISSN 0039-4688)

617.6   US
SURGICAL UPDATE. 1985. 3/yr. American Association of Oral and Maxillofacial Surgeons, 9700 W. Bryn Mawr Ave., Rosemont, IL 60018. TEL 708-678-6200. FAX 708-678-6286. Ed.Bd. circ. 150,000 (controlled). (back issues avail.)
    Description: Provides information on oral and maxillofacial surgery for general dentists.
    Refereed Serial

617.6   US
SURVEY OF DENTAL PRACTICE. a. $27.50 for set to non-members; members $25. American Dental Association, Bureau of Economic and Behavioral Research, 211 E. Chicago Ave., Chicago, IL 60611. TEL 312-440-2500.

617.6   SW   ISSN 0347-9994
CODEN: SDJOD5
SWEDISH DENTAL JOURNAL. (Text in English) 1908. bi-m. SEK 450($47) Sveriges Tandlaekarfoerbund - Swedish Dental Association, P.O. Box 5843, S-102 48 Stockholm, Sweden. Ed. Dr. Goeran Koch. adv.; bk.rev.; charts; illus.; index, cum.index: 1908-1953; circ. 11,000. **Indexed:** ASCA, Biol.Abstr., Chem.Abstr., Curr.Adv.Ecol.Sci., Curr.Cont., Curr.Tit.Dent., Dent.Abstr., Dent.Ind., Excerp.Med., Ind.Med.
    —BLDSC shelfmark: 8573.865000.
    Formed by the merger of: Odontologisk Revy (ISSN 0029-8441); Svensk Tandlaekare-Tidskrift (ISSN 0039-6745)

617.6   DK   ISSN 0039-9353
TANDLAEGEBLADET/DANISH DENTAL JOURNAL. 1897. 18/yr. DKK 945. Dansk Tandlaegeforening - Danish Dental Association, Amaliegade 17, Postboks 143, 1004 Copenhagen K, Denmark. Eds. J.J. Pindborg, Chr. Nissen. adv.; bk.rev.; index; circ. 6,925. **Indexed:** Dent.Ind., Ind.Med.

617.6   US   ISSN 0040-3385
CODEN: JTDAAB
TENNESSEE DENTAL ASSOCIATION. JOURNAL. 1919. q. $9.50 (Canada $20; foreign $25). Tennessee Dental Association, 2104 Sunset Pl., Box 120188, Nashville, TN 37212. TEL 615-383-8962. Ed. Stephen Brooks. adv.; bk.rev.; illus.; index; circ. 2,100. (back issues avail.) **Indexed:** Dent.Abstr., Dent.Ind.
    —BLDSC shelfmark: 4907.100000.
    Formerly: Tennessee State Dental Association. Journal.

617.6   US
TENTH TIMES. 1962. m. $15. Texas Dental Association, Tenth District Dental Society, 3303 Northland, No. 313, Austin, TX 78731. TEL 512-452-9296. Ed. Dr. Mark Sweeney. adv.; circ. 450 (controlled).
    Formerly: Austin Dental News (ISSN 0004-8267)

617.6   US
TEXAS DENTAL ASSISTANTS ASSOCIATION. BULLETIN. 1955? 3/yr. $10. Texas Dental Assistants Association, 6649 Murel, Watauga, TX 78148. TEL 817-281-3949. Ed. Dennise Jennings. adv.; illus.; circ. 500. **Indexed:** Dent.Ind.
    Former titles: Texas Dental Assistants Association. Newsletter; Texas Dental Assistants Association. Bulletin (ISSN 0049-3503)
    Description: Information for Association members.

617.6   US   ISSN 0040-4284
TEXAS DENTAL JOURNAL. 1883. m. $75. Texas Dental Association, 1946 S. Interregional, Austin, TX 78704. TEL 512-443-3675. FAX 512-443-3031. Ed. Dr. Douglas B. Willingham. adv.; bk.rev.; film rev.; charts; illus.; stat.; circ. 7,200. **Indexed:** Dent.Abstr., Dent.Ind.
    —BLDSC shelfmark: 8798.690000.

617.6   US
THIRTIETH DISTRICT DENTAL SOCIETY, FRESNO, CALIFORNIA. BULLETIN. 1953. 10/yr. Fresno-Madera Dental Society, 4747 N. First St., No. 123, Fresno, CA 93726-0517. FAX 209-224-1098. Ed. Dr. Richard Furze. adv.; circ. 600.
    Former titles: Thirteenth District Dental Society. Bulletin; Fifth District Dental Society. Bulletin (ISSN 0071-9544)

617.6   GW   ISSN 0939-5687
▼**THUERINGER ZAHNAERZTEBLATT.** 1991. m. DM.104 (foreign DM.109). Gustav Fischer Verlag Jena, Villengang 2, Postfach 176, 6900 Jena, Germany. TEL 003778-27332. FAX 003778-22638. TELEX 18069-588676.

617.6   US   ISSN 1048-5317
TODAY'S F D A. 1938. m. $30 (foreign $45). Florida Dental Association, 3021 Swann Ave., Tampa, FL 33609. TEL 813-877-7597. FAX 813-876-3225. Ed. Dr. Bert V. Dannheisser, Jr. adv.; bk.rev.; charts; illus.; circ. 6,800. **Indexed:** Dent.Ind.
    Incorporates (in July-Aug. 1989): Dental Team; Florida Dental Journal (ISSN 0360-1676); Which was formerly titled (1938-1967): Florida State Dental Society. Journal (ISSN 0015-3990); F D A Dental Times Dispatch. F D A Dispatch; F D A Intaglio.
    Description: Contains news, features commentary, and scientific information for the Florida dentist.

617.6   JA   ISSN 0040-8891
CODEN: BTDCAV
TOKYO DENTAL COLLEGE. BULLETIN/TOKYO SHIKA DAIGAKU OBUN KIYO. (Text in English) 1960. q. 6000 Yen. Tokyo Shika Daigaku - Tokyo Dental College, 2-2 Masago 1-chome, Chiba 260, Japan. Ed. Tetsuya Kanatake. adv.; illus.; circ. 1,000. (also avail. in microfiche) **Indexed:** Biol.Abstr., Curr.Adv.Ecol.Sci., Curr.Tit.Dent., Dent.Abstr., Dent.Ind., INIS Atomind.
    —BLDSC shelfmark: 2780.300000.

TOKYO MEDICAL AND DENTAL UNIVERSITY. BULLETIN/TOKYO IKA SHIKA DAIGAKU KIYO. see *MEDICAL SCIENCES*

TOKYO MEDICAL AND DENTAL UNIVERSITY. INSTITUTE FOR MEDICAL AND DENTAL ENGINEERING. REPORTS/IYO KIZAI KENKYUJO HOKOKU. see *MEDICAL SCIENCES*

617.6   FR   ISSN 0242-6862
TONUS DENTAIRE. 1977. bi-m. 200 F. Editions Tonus, 29 rue du Faubourg Poissonniere, 75009 Paris, France. FAX 42-46-31-38. TELEX 643-412. Ed. R.C. Borel. adv.; bk.rev.; circ. 15,000. (back issues avail.)

617.6   US
RK1.N28
TRENDS & TECHNIQUES IN THE CONTEMPORARY DENTAL LABORATORY. 1954. 6/yr. $40 (foreign $50). National Association of Dental Laboratories, 3801 Mt. Vernon Ave., Alexandria, VA 22305. TEL 703-683-5263. FAX 703-549-4788. Ed. Douglas W. Newcomb. adv.; bk.rev.; illus.; circ. 17,000. **Indexed:** Dent.Ind.
    Former titles: N A D L Journal (ISSN 0360-5361); N A C D L Journal (ISSN 0027-5735)

617.6   UY   ISSN 0083-4785
UNIVERSIDAD DE LA REPUBLICA. FACULTAD DE ODONTOLOGIA. ANALES. (Supplements accompany some numbers) 1955. irreg. exchange basis. Universidad de la Republica, Facultad de Odontologia, Gral. las Heras 1925, Montevideo, Uruguay. **Indexed:** Biol.Abstr., Dent.Ind.

617.6   VE
UNIVERSIDAD DE LOS ANDES. FACULTAD DE ODONTOLOGIA. REVISTA.* 1958. s-a. exchange basis. Universidad de Los Andes, Facultad de Odontologia, Via los Chorras de Milla, C.P. 5101, Merida, Venezuela. illus.
    Formerly: Revista Odontologica de Merida (ISSN 0035-0273)

617.6   AG   ISSN 0325-1071
UNIVERSIDAD NACIONAL DE CORDOBA. FACULTAD DE ODONTOLOGIA. REVISTA. (Text in Spanish; summaries in English, Spanish) 1966. s-a. exchange. Universidad Nacional de Cordoba, Facultad de Odontologia, Casilla de Correo 458, 5000 Cordoba, Argentina. Dir. Dr. Juan Carlos Albera. adv.; bk.rev.; bibl.; charts; illus.; circ. 350. **Indexed:** Dent.Ind., Ind.Med.
    Supersedes: Revista Odontologica (ISSN 0035-0257)

MEDICAL SCIENCES — DENTISTRY

617.6   **BL**
UNIVERSIDADE DE SAO PAULO. REVISTA DE ODONTOLOGIA. (Text in Portuguese; abstracts in English and Portuguese) 1967. 4/yr. Cr.$750($50) or exchange basis. Universidade de Sao Paulo, Faculdade de Odontologia de Bauru, Al. Otavio Pinheiro Brisola, 9-75, C.P. 73, 17100 Bauru, Sao Paulo, Brazil. Ed. Joao Adolfo Caldas Navarro. adv.; bk.rev.; abstr.; bibl.; charts; illus.; stat.; circ. 1,500. (reprint service avail. from UMI) **Indexed:** Biol.Abstr., Chem.Abstr., Dent.Ind.
    Formed by the 1979 merger of: Estomatologia e Cultura (ISSN 0014-1364); Faculdade de Odontologia de Ribeirao Preto. Revista (ISSN 0102-129X); Which was formerly (until 1983): Faculdade de Farmacia e Odontologia de Rebeirao Preto. Revista (ISSN 0006-9418); Universidade de Sao Paulo. Faculdade de Odontologia. Revista (ISSN 0581-6866); Which superseded in part (1939-1962): Universidade de Sao Paulo. Faculdade de Farmacia. Anais (ISSN 0365-2181)

617.6   **BL**   **ISSN 0101-1774**
    CODEN: ROUNDL
UNIVERSIDADE ESTADUAL PAULISTA. REVISTA DE ODONTOLOGIA. (Text in Portuguese; summaries in English and Portuguese) 1972. a. $30 or exchange basis. Universidade Estadual Paulista, Faculdade de Odontologia, Av. Vicente Ferreira, 1278, Caixa Postal 603, 17.500 Marilia SP, Brazil. TEL 0144 33-1844. FAX 0144-22-2504. TELEX 1119016 UJME BR. Ed.Bd. bibl.; charts; illus.; stat.; circ. 1,000 (controlled). (back issues avail.) **Indexed:** Bibliogr.Bras.Odontol., Bibliogr.Bras.Odontol., Biol.Abstr.
  —BLDSC shelfmark: 7869.080000.
    Formed by the 1979 merger of: Universidade Estadual Paulista. Faculdade de Odontologia de Aracatuba. Revista; Faculdade de Odontologia e Odontologia de Araraquara. Revista (ISSN 0014-6684); Faculdade de Odontologia de Sao Jose dos Campos. Revista.
    Description: Publishes original articles in the study and research of odontology.

617.6   **BL**   **ISSN 0004-2838**
    CODEN: ACECDB
UNIVERSIDADE FEDERAL DE MINAS GERAIS. CURSO DE ODONTOLOGIA. ARQUIVOS DO CENTRO DE ESTUDOS. (Text in Portuguese; summaries in English) 1964. s-a. Cr.$20 per no. or exchange basis. Universidade Federal de Minas Gerais, Faculdade de Odontologia, Rua Conde Linhares 141, 30000 Belo Horizonte, Minas Gerais, Brazil. Ed. Mario Lucio Jardim Parreira. bibl.; charts; illus. **Indexed:** Biol.Abstr., Chem.Abstr., Dent.Ind., Oral Res.Abstr.

617.6   **BL**
UNIVERSIDADE FEDERAL DE PERNAMBUCO. FACULDADE DE ODONTOLOGIA. ANAIS. (Text in Portuguese; summaries in English) 1960. a. Universidade Federal de Pernambuco, Faculdade de Odontologia, Recife, Pernambuco, Brazil.
    Continues (with vol.5): Universidade do Recife. Faculdade de Odontologia. Anais.

617.6   **BL**   **ISSN 0041-8919**
UNIVERSIDADE FEDERAL DO RIO DE JANEIRO. FACULDADE DE ODONTOLOGIA. ANAIS.* (Text in Portuguese; summaries in English) 1947. Universidade Federal do Rio de Janeiro, Faculdade de Odontologia, Ilha da Cidade Universitaria, Rio de Janeiro, Brazil. illus.; stat.; circ. controlled. **Indexed:** Biol.Abstr.

617.6   **SW**   **ISSN 0076-3438**
UNIVERSITY OF LUND. SCHOOL OF DENTISTRY. FACULTY OF ODONTOLOGY. ANNUAL PUBLICATIONS. Cover title: University of Lund. Faculty of Odontology. Annual Publications. (Text in English) 1958. a. free. University of Lund, Faculty of Odontology, School of Dentistry, 214 21 Malmoe, Sweden. FAX 46-40-92-53-59. Ed. Krister Nilner. bk.rev.; circ. 750.

617.6   **US**   **ISSN 0076-843X**
UNIVERSITY OF MICHIGAN. SCHOOL OF DENTISTRY. ALUMNI BULLETIN. 1937. a. University of Michigan, School of Dentistry, Ann Arbor, MI 48104. TEL 313-764-1817. Charles C. Kelsey. circ. 6,000. **Indexed:** Dent.Ind.

617.6   **CN**   **ISSN 0843-5812**
UNIVERSITY OF TORONTO DENTAL JOURNAL. 3/yr. Can.$15. University of Toronto, 124 Edward St., Toronto, Ont. M5G 1G6, Canada. TEL 416-979-4549. FAX 416-979-4566. **Indexed:** Curr.Tit.Dent., Dent.Ind.
  —BLDSC shelfmark: 9119.010000.

617.6   **CN**   **ISSN 0042-0255**
UNIVERSITY OF TORONTO UNDERGRADUATE DENTAL JOURNAL. 1964. a. $4 for 2 yrs. University of Toronto, Front Campus, Toronto, Ont. M5S 1A6, Canada. TEL 416-596-2552. Ed.Bd. adv.; bk.rev.; abstr.; charts; illus. **Indexed:** Curr.Tit.Dent.

617.6   **US**
UPDATE (GAINESVILLE). 1967. 3/yr. free to qualified personnel. University of Florida, College of Dentistry, Box J-405 JHMHC, Gainesville, FL 32610. TEL 904-392-4431. FAX 904-392-3070. Ed. Linda Mealiea. circ. 2,100.

617.6   **CN**
VANCOUVER & DISTRICT DENTAL SOCIETY PROGRAM. 1978. a. Naylor Communications Ltd., 920 Yonge St., 6th fl., Toronto, Ont. M4W 3C7, Canada. Ed. Jim Hutson. adv.; circ. 1,352.

617.6   **VE**   **ISSN 0042-3424**
VENEZUELA ODONTOLOGIA. 1934. bi-m. Colegio de Odontologos de Venezuela, Junta Directiva, Av. Guanare, Las Palmas, Apdo. 1341, Caracas 105, Venezuela. TEL 782.15.54. adv.; bk.rev.; charts; illus.; index; circ. 2,000. **Indexed:** Dent.Ind.

617.6   **US**   **ISSN 0049-6472**
VIRGINIA DENTAL JOURNAL. 1924. q. $6 to non-members. Virginia Dental Association, c/o Richard D. Wilson, DDS, Ed., Box 6906, Richmond, VA 23230. TEL 804-358-4927. FAX 804-353-7342. adv.; bk.rev.; illus.; circ. 2,900. **Indexed:** Dent.Ind., Ind.Med.
  —BLDSC shelfmark: 9238.400000.
    Continues: Virginia Dental Association. Bulletin.

617.6   **US**   **ISSN 0042-983X**
W S D A NEWS. 1960. m. $30 includes Annual Roster; foreign $40 (typically set in July). Washington State Dental Association, 2033 6th Ave., No. 333, Seattle, WA 98121. TEL 206-448-1914. adv.; illus.; circ. 3,260.

617.6   **JA**
WAY. 1975. Kawamura Dental Clinic, Matsuzakaya, 2-chome, Kyobashi, Higashi-ku, Osaka, Japan.

617.6   **US**   **ISSN 0043-3225**
WEST VIRGINIA DENTAL JOURNAL. vol.40, 1966. q. $10. West Virginia Dental Association, 300 Capitol St., K V Bldg., Ste. 1002, Charleston, WV 25301. TEL 304-925-7201. Ed. R.D. Smith. adv.; bk.rev.; illus.; circ. 1,100. **Indexed:** Dent.Abstr., Dent.Ind., Dent.Ind., Med.Care Rev.
  —BLDSC shelfmark: 9299.800000.

WESTERN SOCIETY OF PERIODONTOLOGY. JOURNAL. PERIODONTAL ABSTRACTS. see *MEDICAL SCIENCES — Abstracting, Bibliographies, Statistics*

617.6   **US**
WESTVIEWS. 1972. 8/yr. $10. Western Dental Society, 6242 Westchester Pkwy, No. 220, Los Angeles, CA 90045. FAX 213-641-3258. Ed. Victor Pineschi. adv.; circ. 910. (tabloid format)
    Formerly: Western Dental Society. Newsletter.

617.6   **US**
RK37
WHO'S WHO IN BLACK DENTISTRY IN AMERICA. triennial with a. supplements. $125. Aqua Dynamics Ltd., 1317 E. Bramblestone Ave., Norfolk, VA 23510. TEL 804-627-3100. FAX 804-627-2907. Ed. Lord Cecil Rhodes. stat.
    Formerly: Rhodes Directory of Black Dentists Registered in the United States (ISSN 0090-7995)

617.6   **US**   **ISSN 0091-4185**
    CODEN: JWDAE2
WISCONSIN DENTAL ASSOCIATION. JOURNAL. vol.49, 1973. 10/yr. $35 to libraries and dental agencies (foreign $65). Wisconsin Dental Association, St. 507, Clark Bldg., 633 W. Wisconsin Ave., Milwaukee, WI 53203. TEL 414-276-4520. Ed. Dr. Paul M. Mann. adv.; charts; illus.; circ. 3,400. (processed) **Indexed:** Dent.Abstr., Dent.Ind., Med.Care Rev.
    Formerly: Wisconsin State Dental Society. Journal (ISSN 0043-6674)

617.6   **US**
WORD OF MOUTH (SAN FRANCISCO). q. c/o Delta Dental Plan of CA, Box 7736, San Francisco, CA 94120. adv.

617.6   **US**   **ISSN 0049-8262**
XI PSI PHI QUARTERLY.* 1906. q. $6. Xi Psi Phi Fraternity, c/o Dr. Leighton A. Wier, Ed., 104 Magnolia Ave., San Antonio, TX 78212. TEL 512-733-1961. bk.rev.; illus.; circ. 3,000. **Indexed:** Dent.Ind.

617.6058   **US**   **ISSN 0084-3717**
RK16
YEAR BOOK OF DENTISTRY. 1936. a. $49.95. Mosby - Year Book, Inc., Continuity Division, 200 N. LaSalle, Chicago, IL 60601. TEL 312-726-9733. FAX 312-726-6075. TELEX 206155. Ed. Dr. Lawrence Meskin. illus. (reprint service avail.) **Indexed:** Curr.Adv.Ecol.Sci.
  ●Also available online. Vendor(s): BRS.
  —BLDSC shelfmark: 9411.625000.

617.6   **GW**
Z F N SEMINARPROGRAMM. a. Zahnaerztliches Fortbildungszentrum Niedersachsen, Hildesheimerstr. 35, Postfach 6643, 3000 Hannover 1, Germany. TEL 0511-8112-303. FAX 0511-8112-106. Ed. Herbert Buettner. adv.

617.6   **GW**   **ISSN 0044-166X**
Z W R. (Zahnaerztliche Welt Rundschau); das Deutsche Zahnaerzteblatt. 1891. m. DM.210. Dr. Alfred Huethig Verlag GmbH, Im Weiher 10, Postfach 102869, 6900 Heidelberg 1, Germany. TEL 06221-489-281. FAX 06221-489279. TELEX 461727-HUEHDD. Eds. Dr. Cornelia Gins, W. Pietsch. adv.; bk.rev.; illus.; index; circ. 22,166. **Indexed:** Biol.Abstr., Chem.Abstr., Curr.Tit.Dent., Dent.Ind., Ind.Med.
    Incorporates: Der Zahnarzt (ISSN 0044-1678); Stoma (ISSN 0039-1697); Which was formerly: Z W R - Zahnaerztliche Welt, Zahnaerztliche Rundschau (ISSN 0301-1607)

617.6   **GW**   **ISSN 0303-6464**
ZAHN- MUND- UND KIEFERHEILKUNDE; mit Zentralblatt. Title varies: Deutsche Zahn- Mund- und Kieferheilkunde. (Summaries in English, German) 1934. 8/yr. DM.160. Johann Ambrosius Barth Verlag, Leipzig - Heidelberg, Salomonstr. 18b, 7010 Leipzig, Germany. TEL 70131. Ed. Dr. A. Breustedt. adv.; bk.rev. **Indexed:** Biol.Abstr., Chem.Abstr., Dent.Abstr., Dent.Ind., Ind.Med.
    Incorporates: Zentralblatt fuer die Gesamte Zahn- Mund- und Kieferheilkunde.

617.6   **GW**   **ISSN 0340-3017**
ZAHNAERZTEBLATT BADEN-WUERTTEMBERG. 1973. m. DM.164.40 (foreign DM.187.20). (Landeszahnaerztekammer Baden-Wuerttemberg) A.W. Gentner Verlag, Forststr. 131, Postfach 101742, 7000 Stuttgart 10, Germany. TEL 0711-63672-0. FAX 0711-63672-11. Eds. H.-H. Holfeld, J. Glueck. circ. 9,900. **Indexed:** Dent.Ind.

617.6   **GW**   **ISSN 0938-8486**
ZAHNAERZTEBLATT SACHSEN. m. DM.92.40 (foreign DM.108). A.W. Gentner Verlag, Forststr. 131, Postfach 101742, 7000 Stuttgart 10, Germany. TEL 0711-63672-0. FAX 0711-6367211.

617.6   **GW**   **ISSN 0341-8995**
ZAHNAERZTLICHE MITTEILUNGEN. 1910. s-m. DM.240 (students DM.60). (Bundesverband der Deutschen Zahnaerzte e.V.) Deutscher Aerzte-Verlag GmbH, Dieselstr. 2, Postfach 40 02 65, 5000 Cologne, Germany. TEL 02234-7011-0. FAX 02234-7011444. adv.; bk.rev.; charts; illus.; stat.; tr.lit.; index; circ. 64,000. **Indexed:** Curr.Tit.Dent., Dent.Ind., Ind.Med.

617.6 GW ISSN 0044-1651
ZAHNAERZTLICHE PRAXIS. 1949. m. DM.96.
Werk-Verlag Dr. Edmund Banaschewski GmbH,
Hans-Cornelius Str. 4, 8032 Munich-Graefelfing,
Germany. Ed. Edmund Banaschewski. adv.; bk.rev.;
charts; illus.; index. **Indexed:** Curr.Tit.Dent., Dent.Ind.
—BLDSC shelfmark: 9425.720000.

617.6 GW ISSN 0027-3198
ZAHNAERZTLICHER ANZEIGER. 1953. fortn. DM.53.
(Zahnaerztlicher Bezirksverband Muenchen Stadt
und Land) Industrie- und Handelswerbung A.
Hanuschik, Ungererstr. 19-VI (Fuchsbau), 8000
Munich 40, Germany. adv.; bk.rev.; charts; illus.;
stat.; circ. 2,650.

617.6 SZ ISSN 0044-1686
ZAHNTECHNIK. (Text in French, German and Italian)
1942. 6/yr. 45 Fr. Schweizerische
Zahntechniker-Vereinigung, Heidenbuehlstr. 2, 8840
Einsiedeln, Switzerland. adv.; bk.rev.; abstr.; bibl.;
charts; illus.; stat.; cum.index; circ. 5,000. **Indexed:**
Curr.Tit.Dent., Dent.Ind.
—BLDSC shelfmark: 9425.905000.

617.6 AU ISSN 0175-7784
ZEITSCHRIFT FUER STOMATOLOGIE. 1903. irreg.
DM.196($126) Springer-Verlag, Sachsenplatz 4-6,
Postfach 89, A-1201 Vienna, Austria.
TEL 0222-3302415-0. FAX 0222-3302426.
TELEX 114506-SPRIW-A. (U.S. address:
Springer-Verlag New York, 175 Fifth Avenue, New
York, NY 10010) Eds. Drs. G. Watzek, M. Matejka.
adv.; bk.rev.; bibl.; illus.; index; circ. 3,500. (also
avail. in microform; back issues avail.) **Indexed:**
Biol.Abstr., Curr.Cont., Curr.Tit.Dent., Dent.Ind.
—BLDSC shelfmark: 9486.405000.
Formerly: Oesterreichische Zeitschrift fuer
Stomatologie (ISSN 0029-9642)

617.7 GW
ZEITSCHRIFT FUER ZAHNAERZTLICHE IMPLANTOLOGIE.
(Text in German; summaries in English) 1984. q.
DM.191. (Deutsche Gesellschaft fuer Zahn-, Mund-
und Kieferheilkunde) Carl Hanser Verlag,
Kolbergerstr. 22, Postfach 860420, 8000 Munich
80, Germany. TEL 089-92694-0. Ed.Bd. adv.;
bk.rev.; charts; illus.; circ. 1,500. **Indexed:**
Curr.Tit.Dent.
Formerly: Fortschritte der Zahnaerztliche
Implantologie (ISSN 0177-3348)

**ZHONGGUO YIXUE WENZHAI (KOUQIANG YIXUE)/CHINA
MEDICAL ABSTRACTS (STOMATOLOGY).** see *MEDICAL
SCIENCES — Abstracting, Bibliographies, Statistics*

617.6 XV ISSN 0044-4928
ZOBOZDRAVSTVENI VESTNIK. (Text in Slovenian;
summaries in English and German) 1946. bi-m.
100 din.($20.85) Drustvo Zobozdrastvenih Delavcev
Slovenije, Hrvatski trg 6, Ljubljana, Slovenia. Ed.
Rajko Sedej. adv.; bk.rev.; illus.; index; circ. 1,500.
Indexed: Chem.Abstr., Dent.Ind.
—BLDSC shelfmark: 9514.950000.

MEDICAL SCIENCES — Dermatology And Venereology

616.5 US ISSN 0884-1489
RL43
A B M S DIRECTORY OF CERTIFIED DERMATOLOGISTS.
1984. biennial. $29.95. American Board of Medical
Specialties, One Rotary Center, Ste. 805, Evanston,
IL 60201. TEL 708-491-9091.
FAX 708-328-3596. Ed. Dr. J. Lee Dockery.

A I D S INFORMATION EXCHANGE. see *MEDICAL
SCIENCES — Communicable Diseases*

616.5 616.95 SW ISSN 0001-5555
CODEN: ADVEA4
ACTA DERMATO-VENEREOLOGICA. (Supplements avail.)
(Text and summaries in English) 1920. 6/yr.
SEK 480($63) incl. supplements. Almqvist & Wiksell
Periodical Company, P.O. Box 638, S-101 28
Stockholm, Sweden. Ed. Lennart Juhlin. adv.; illus.;
index; circ. 1,600. **Indexed:** Abstr.Hyg., ASCA,
Biol.Abstr., Biotech.Abstr., C.I.S. Abstr., Chem.Abstr.,
Curr.Adv.Cancer Res., Curr.Adv.Ecol.Sci., Curr.Cont.,
Dairy Sci.Abstr., Dent.Ind., Dok.Arbeitsmed.,
Excerp.Med., Helminthol.Abstr., Ind.Med.,
Ind.Sci.Rev., Nutr.Abstr., Rev.Med.& Vet.Mycol.,
Rev.Plant Path., Sci.Cit.Ind., Trop.Dis.Bull.
—BLDSC shelfmark: 0612.320000.

616.5 JA ISSN 0065-1176
ACTA DERMATOLOGICA/HIFUKA KIYO. (Issues for
1923-1961 have title: Acta Dermatologica:
Dermatologia, Syphilidologia et Urologia) (Articles in
Japanese with some English; table of contents and
summaries in English) 1923. q. 3000 Yen or
exchange basis. Kyoto University, Faculty of
Medicine, Department of Dermatology - Kyoto
Daigaku Igakubu Hifuka Kyoshitsu, 53 Shogoin
Kawara-cho, Sakyo-ku, Kyoto 606, Japan. Ed. Sadao
Imamura. bk.rev.; circ. 1,000. **Indexed:** Biol.Abstr.,
Excerp.Med., INIS Atomind.
—BLDSC shelfmark: 0612.300000.

616 CI ISSN 0302-4466
ACTA DERMATOVENEROLOGICA IUGOSLAVICA. (Text in
Croatian, English, Serbian) 1974. q. $50. Udruzenje
Dermatovenerologa Jugoslavije - Association of
Yugoslavian Dermatovenerologists, Salata 4, 41000
Zagreb, Croatia. (Co-sponsor: SIZ za Znanost
Hrvatske) Ed. A. Kansky. adv.; bk.rev.; circ. 600.
Indexed: Biol.Abstr., Excerp.Med.

616.5 SP ISSN 0001-7310
ACTAS DERMOSIFILIOGRAFICAS. m. (10/yr.).
8200 ptas.($117) (Academia Espanola de
Dermatologia y Sifiologrfia) Editorial Garsi, S.A.,
Londres, 17, 28028 Madrid, Spain. TEL 256-08-00.
FAX 361-10-01. Ed. Dr. Miguel Armijo Moreno. adv.;
bk.rev.; illus.; index; circ. 1,500. **Indexed:**
Chem.Abstr., Dent.Ind., Excerp.Med., Ind.Med.Esp.,
Ind.Med., Rev.Med.& Vet.Mycol., Rev.Plant Path.
—BLDSC shelfmark: 0612.330000.

616.5 US ISSN 0882-0880
CODEN: ADDEEK
ADVANCES IN DERMATOLOGY. 1986. a. $59.95.
Mosby - Year Book, Inc. (Chicago) (Subsidiary of:
Times Mirror Company), 200 N. LaSalle St.,
Chicago, IL 60601-1080. TEL 312-726-9733.
FAX 312-726-6075. TELEX 206155. (Subscr. to:
11830 Westline Industrial Dr., St. Louis, MO 63146.
TEL 800-325-4177) Ed. Dr. Jeffrey P. Callen. illus.
—BLDSC shelfmark: 0704.242300.
Description: Presents a collection of fully
referenced articles from experts in dermatology.

616.5 GW ISSN 0340-2541
AKTUELLE DERMATOLOGIE; Andrologie - Phlebologie -
Proktologie - Venerologie - Allergologie - Mykologie.
1975. 10/yr. DM.220. Georg Thieme Verlag,
Ruedigerstr. 14, Postfach 104853, 7000 Stuttgart
10, Germany. Ed.Bd. adv.; index; circ. 2,700.
(reprint service avail. from UMI) **Indexed:** Biol.Abstr.,
Excerp.Med.
—BLDSC shelfmark: 0785.729700.

616.5 US ISSN 0190-9622
RL1 CODEN: JAADDB
AMERICAN ACADEMY OF DERMATOLOGY. JOURNAL.
1979. m. $93 to individuals (foreign $125);
institutions $167 (foreign $199); students $47
(foreign $79). (American Academy of Dermatology)
Mosby - Year Book, Inc. (Subsidiary of: Times Mirror
Company), 11830 Westline Industrial Dr., St. Louis,
MO 63146. TEL 800-325-4117.
FAX 314-432-1380. TELEX 44-2402. Ed. Dr.
Richard Dobson. adv.; bk.rev.; s-a. index; circ.
14,129. (also avail. in microfilm from UMI; reprint
service avail. from UMI) **Indexed:** ASCA, Biol.Abstr.,
Curr.Adv.Cancer Res., Curr.Cont., Dok.Arbeitsmed.,
Excerp.Med., Helminthol.Abstr., Ind.Med., INIS
Atomind., Lab.Haz.Bull., NRN, Protozool.Abstr.,
Sci.Cit.Ind., Small Anim.Abstr.
—BLDSC shelfmark: 4683.703000.
Description: Provides a clinical perspective on
manifestations of skin disease.
Refereed Serial

616.5 US
▼**AMERICAN JOURNAL OF CONTACT DERMATITIS.**
1990. q. W.B. Saunders Co., Curtis Center,
Independence Sq. W., Philadelphia, PA 19106.
TEL 215-238-7807. Ed. Dr. Robert M. Adams. adv.;
circ. 421.
Description: Covers diagnosing and treating
dermatologic conditions caused by irritants and
allergic reactions.

616.5 US ISSN 0193-1091
RL95 CODEN: AJODDB
AMERICAN JOURNAL OF DERMATOPATHOLOGY. 1979.
bi-m. $124 to individuals; institutions $168.
(International Society of Dermatopathology) Raven
Press, 1185 Ave. of the Americas, New York, NY
10036. TEL 212-930-9500. FAX 212-869-3495.
TELEX 640073. Ed. Clifton R. White, Jr. adv.;
bk.rev.; abstr.; charts; illus.; index; circ. 2,500. (also
avail. in microform from MIM; back issues avail.)
Indexed: Curr.Adv.Cancer Res., Curr.Cont., Dent.Ind.,
Excerp.Med., Ind.Med., Ind.Sci.Rev., Ind.Vet.,
Rev.Med.& Vet.Mycol., Sci.Cit.Ind., Small Anim.Abstr.
—BLDSC shelfmark: 0824.240000.
Refereed Serial

616.5 BL ISSN 0365-0596
CODEN: ABDEB3
ANAIS BRASILEIROS DE DERMATOLOGIA. (Text in
Portuguese; summaries in English, Portuguese)
1925. bi-m. Cr.$3500($60) or exchange basis.
(Sociedade Brasileira de Dermatologia) Editora
Cientifica Nacional Ltda., Av. Almirante Barroso
97-1205-1210, CEP 20031 Rio de Janeiro, RJ,
Brazil. TEL 2622825. (Orders to: ECN-Editora
Cientifica Nacional Ltda., Caixa Postal 590, 20001
Rio de Janeiro, Brazil) Ed. R.D. Azulay. adv.; bk.rev.;
abstr.; bibl.; charts; illus.; stat.; index, cum.index;
circ. 3,000. (also avail. in microform from UMI; back
issues avail.) **Indexed:** Abstr.Hyg., Biol.Abstr.,
Chem.Abstr., Curr.Cont., Excerp.Med., Ind.Med.,
Rev.Med.& Vet.Mycol., Trop.Dis.Bull.
—BLDSC shelfmark: 0869.027000.
Description: Original research papers in
dermatology.

616.5 616.951 FR ISSN 0151-9638
CODEN: ADVED7
ANNALES DE DERMATOLOGIE ET DE VENEREOLOGIE.
(Text in French; summaries in English) 1869. 11/yr.
190 ECU($230) (typically set in Jan.). (Societe
Francaise de Dermatologie et de Venereologie)
Masson, 120 bd. Saint-Germain, 75280 Paris
Cedex 06, France. TEL 1-46-34-21-60.
FAX 1-45-87-29-99. Ed. E. Grosshans. adv.; bk.rev.;
abstr.; illus.; index; circ. 3,900. (also avail. in
microform from UMI; reprint service avail. from ISI)
Indexed: Biol.Abstr., C.I.S. Abstr., Chem.Abstr.,
Curr.Adv.Ecol.Sci., Curr.Cont., Dent.Ind., Excerp.Med.,
Helminthol.Abstr., Ind.Med., Ind.Sci.Rev.,
Lab.Haz.Bull., Protozool.Abstr., Rev.Med.&
Vet.Mycol., Rev.Plant Path., Sci.Cit.Ind.
—BLDSC shelfmark: 0971.600000.
Former titles: Annales de Dermatologie et de
Syphiligraphie; Societe Francaise de Dermatologie et
de Syphiligraphie. Bulletin (ISSN 0003-3979)

616.5 IT ISSN 0003-4703
**ANNALI ITALIANI DI DERMATOLOGIA CLINICA E
SPERIMENTALE.** (Text in English, Italian) 1945. q.
L.70000($130) Pensiero Scientifico Editore s.r.l.,
Via Panama, 48, I-00198 Rome, Italy.
TEL 06-8549506. FAX 06-8841741. Ed. Maurizio
Binazzi. adv.; bk.rev.; circ. 1,000 (controlled).
Indexed: Biol.Abstr., Chem.Abstr., Excerp.Med.,
Ind.Med.
—BLDSC shelfmark: 1014.350000.

616.5 616.95 KO ISSN 1013-9087
CODEN: ANDEEM
ANNALS OF DERMATOLOGY. (Text in English) 1989.
s-a. Korean Dermatological Association, 401
Sindonga Jonghap-Sangka, 491 Suecho-dong,
Suecho-ku, Seoul 137-070, S. Korea.
TEL 02-567-0284. FAX 02-552-4203. (Editorial
addr.: c/o Department of Dermatology, St. Mary's
Hospital, 62 Yeido-dong, Youngdeungpo-ku, Seoul
150-010, S. Korea) Ed. Dr. Won Houh.
—BLDSC shelfmark: 1040.351000.

MEDICAL SCIENCES — DERMATOLOGY AND VENEREOLOGY

616.5   GW   ISSN 0340-3696
CODEN: ADMFAU
ARCHIVES OF DERMATOLOGICAL RESEARCH. 1869. 8/yr. DM.968($556) (Deutsche Dermatologische Gesellschaft) Springer-Verlag, Heidelberger Platz 3, D-1000 Berlin 33, Germany. TEL 030-8207-1. (Also Heidelberg, Tokyo, Vienna, and New York) Ed. E. Christophers. adv.; bibl.; charts; illus.; index. (also avail. in microfilm from UMI; back issues avail.; reprint service avail. from ISI) **Indexed:** Biol.Abstr., Biotech.Abstr., Chem.Abstr., Curr.Adv.Ecol.Sci., Curr.Cont., Dairy Sci.Abstr., Excerp.Med., Helminthol.Abstr., Ind.Med., Ind.Sci.Rev., NRN, Nutr.Abstr., Ornam.Hort., Rev.Appl.Entomol., Rev.Plant Path., Risk Abstr., Sci.Cit.Ind.
—BLDSC shelfmark: 1634.130000.
Former titles: Archiv fuer Dermatologische Forschung (ISSN 0003-9187); Archiv fuer Klinische und Experimentelle Dermatologie.

616.5   US   ISSN 0003-987X
CODEN: ARDEAC
ARCHIVES OF DERMATOLOGY. Spanish translation: Archives of Dermatology (Edicion Espanola) (SP ISSN 1130-1910) 1920. m. $73. American Medical Association, 515 N. State St., Chicago, IL 60610. TEL 312-464-0183. FAX 312-464-5834. Ed. Dr. Kenneth A. Arndt. bk.rev.; abstr.; charts; illus.; index; circ. 14,500. (also avail. in microfilm from UMI) **Indexed:** Abstr.Hyg., Abstr.Inter.Med., Biol.Abstr., Biotech.Abstr., C.I.S. Abstr., Chem.Abstr., Curr.Adv.Cancer Res., Curr.Adv.Ecol.Sci., Curr.Adv.Genetics & Molec.Biol., Curr.Cont., Dairy Sci.Abstr., Dent.Ind., Dok.Arbeitsmed., Excerp.Med., Helminthol.Abstr., I.P.A., Ind.Med., Ind.Sci.Rev., INIS Atomind., NRN, Nutr.Abstr., Protozool.Abstr., Rev.Appl.Entomol., Rev.Med.& Vet.Mycol., Sci.Cit.Ind., Trop.Dis.Bull.
●Also available online. Vendor(s): Mead Data Central.
—BLDSC shelfmark: 1634.150000.
Refereed Serial

616.5   SP   ISSN 1130-1910
ARCHIVES OF DERMATOLOGY (EDICION ESPANOLA). Spanish translation of: Archives of Dermatology (US ISSN 0003-987X) bi-m. 3500 ptas.($35) (American Medical Association, US) Ediciones Doyma S.A., Travesera de Gracia, 17-21, 08021 Barcelona, Spain. TEL 200-07-11. FAX 209-11-36. TELEX 51964 INK E. Ed. J.M. Mascaro Ballester. adv.; page 125000 ptas.; trim 210 x 280; adv. contact: Cristina Garrote. circ. 2,500. **Indexed:** Sci.Cit.Ind.
Description: Contains translations of articles on investigative dermatology from the American edition.

616.5   AG   ISSN 0066-6750
ARCHIVOS ARGENTINOS DE DERMATOLOGIA. (Text in Spanish; abstracts in English) 1951. bi-m. $60 (effective Jan. 1992). Paraguay 1307, 4 38, 1057 Buenos Aires, Argentina. Ed. Fernando M. Stengel. adv.; bk.rev.; circ. 1,600 (controlled). **Indexed:** Bull.Signal., Excerp.Med., Ind.Med.
—BLDSC shelfmark: 1654.150000.

616.5   IT
▼**ARGOMENTI DI DERMATOLOGIA.** 1992. 3/yr. Masson Italia Periodici, Via Statuto 2-4, 20121 Milan, Italy. TEL 02-63671. Ed. Benvenuto Giannotti.

616.5   US   ISSN 0360-4020
ASSOCIATION OF MILITARY DERMATOLOGISTS. JOURNAL. 1975. s-a. free. Interaction Projects, 25 Church Hill Rd., Box 305, Newtown, CT 06470. FAX 203-426-8500. Ed. Rebecca Skinner Borgatti. circ. 11,500. **Indexed:** Excerp.Med.
Formerly: Association of Military Dermatologists. Bulletin.

616.5   AT   ISSN 0004-8380
CODEN: AJDEBP
AUSTRALASIAN JOURNAL OF DERMATOLOGY. 1951. 3/yr. Aus.$20. Australasian College of Dermatologists, 271 Bridge Rd., Glebe, N.S.W. 2037, Australia. Ed. D.S. Nurse. adv.; bk.rev.; circ. 500. **Indexed:** Biol.Abstr., Chem.Abstr., Curr.Cont., Dent.Ind., Excerp.Med., Ind.Med., NRN, Nutr.Abstr., Rev.Plant.Path.
—BLDSC shelfmark: 1794.900000.
Formerly: Australian Journal of Dermatology.

616.5   616.951   HU   ISSN 0006-7768
BORGYOGYASZATI ES VENEROLOGIAI SZEMLE. (Text in Hungarian; summaries in English, German and Russian) 1924. bi-m. $36.50. Ifjusagi Lap-es Konyvkiado Vallalat, Revay u. 16, 1374 Budapest 6, Hungary. (Subscr. to: Kultura, Box 149, H-1389 Budapest, Hungary) Ed. Dr. Ibolya Torok. adv.; bk.rev.; charts; illus.; index. **Indexed:** Biol.Abstr., Chem.Abstr., Excerp.Med., INIS Atomind.
—BLDSC shelfmark: 2251.400000.

616.5   UK   ISSN 0007-0963
CODEN: BJDEAZ
BRITISH JOURNAL OF DERMATOLOGY. 1886. m. £119.50 (foreign £130). (British Association of Dermatologists) Blackwell Scientific Publications Ltd., Osney Mead, Oxford OX2 OEL, England. TEL 0865-240201. FAX 0865-721205. TELEX 83355-MEDBOK-G. Ed. R.M. Mackie. adv.; bk.rev.; abstr.; bibl.; illus.; index; circ. 4,100. (back issues avail.; reprint service avail. from ISI) **Indexed:** Abstr.Hyg., Abstr.Inter.Med., ASCA, Biol.Abstr., Biotech.Abstr., C.I.S. Abstr., Chem.Abstr., Curr.Adv.Cancer Res., Curr.Adv.Genetics & Molec.Biol., Curr.Cont., Dent.Ind., Excerp.Med., Helminthol.Abstr., I.P.A., Ind.Med., Ind.Sci.Rev., Ind.Vet., INIS Atomind., Lab.Haz.Bull., NRN, Nutr.Abstr., Pig News & Info., Rev.Plant Path., Sci.Cit.Ind, Triticale Abstr., Trop.Dis.Bull.
●Also available online.
—BLDSC shelfmark: 2307.400000.

616.5   UK   ISSN 0366-077X
CODEN: BJDSA9
BRITISH JOURNAL OF DERMATOLOGY. SUPPLEMENT. 1969. irreg. free. (British Association of Dermatologists) Blackwell Scientific Publications Ltd., Osney Mead, Oxford OX2 OEL, England. TEL 0865-240201. FAX 0865-721205. TELEX 83355-MEDBOK-G. Ed. R.M. Mackie. adv.; circ. 3,800. (also avail. in microfiche) **Indexed:** ASCA, Biol.Abstr., Chem.Abstr., Curr.Cont., Excerp.Med., Helminthol.Abstr., I.P.A., Ind.Med., Nutr.Abstr., Rev.Plant Path., Sci.Cit.Ind.
—BLDSC shelfmark: 2307.405000.

616.5   CN   ISSN 0843-4247
CANADIAN JOURNAL OF DERMATOLOGY; for primary care physicians and the specialist. 1986. 6/yr. Can.$60($67) Rodar Publishing Inc., 19180 Trans Canada Hwy., Baie d'Urfe, Que. H9X 3T9, Canada. TEL 514-457-2673. FAX 514-457-2679. Ed. Sonia Osario. adv.; bk.rev.; charts; illus.; index; circ. 9,640 (controlled). (also avail. in microfilm; back issues avail.) **Indexed:** CMI.
Formerly: Contemporary Dermatology.
Refereed Serial

616.5   CS   ISSN 0009-0514
CODEN: CEDEAB
CESKOSLOVENSKA DERMATOLOGIE. (Text in Czech or Slovak; summaries in English and Russian) 1925. 6/yr $48.60. (Ceskoslovenska Dermato-Venerologicka Spolecnost) Avicenum, Czechoslovak Medical Press, Malostranske nam. 28, 118 02 Prague 1, Czechoslovakia. (Dist. by: Artia, Ve Smeckach 30, 111 27 Prague 1, Czechoslovakia) (Co-sponsor: Ceskoslovenska Lekarska Spolecnost J. Ev. Purkyne) Ed. Z. Stava. adv.; bk.rev. **Indexed:** Biol.Abstr., C.I.S. Abstr., Chem.Abstr., Curr.Adv.Ecol.Sci., Excerp.Med., Ind.Med.
—BLDSC shelfmark: 3120.550000.

616.5   IT   ISSN 0011-1759
CHRONICA DERMATOLOGICA. (Text in Italian; summaries in English and Italian) 1946. bi-m. free to qualified personnel. Istituto Dermopatico dell'Immacolata, Via Monti di Creta, 106, 00167 Rome, Italy. FAX 06-6211746. Dir. Rino Cavalieri. adv.; bk.rev.; abstr.; bibl.; charts; illus.; stat.; index; circ. 7,000 (controlled). **Indexed:** Excerp.Med.
—BLDSC shelfmark: 3185.100000.
Formerly: I D I Cronache.

616.5   UK   ISSN 0307-6938
CODEN: CEDEDE
CLINICAL AND EXPERIMENTAL DERMATOLOGY. 1976. bi-m. £124 (foreign £136). Blackwell Scientific Publications Ltd., Osney Mead, Oxford OX2 OEL, England. TEL 0865-240201. FAX 0865-721205. TELEX 83355-MEDBOK-G. Ed. W.A.D. Griffiths. circ. 950. (back issues avail.; reprint service avail. from ISI) **Indexed:** ASCA, Biotech.Abstr., Chem.Abstr., Curr.Adv.Ecol.Sci., Curr.Cont., Dent.Ind., Dok.Arbeitsmed., Excerp.Med., Helminthol.Abstr., Ind.Med., Ind.Sci.Rev., Ind.Vet., NRN, Nutr.Abstr., Protozool.Abstr., Rev.Plant Path., Sci.Cit.Ind., Small Anim.Abstr.
—BLDSC shelfmark: 3286.250000.
Formerly (until 1976): St. John's Hospital Dermatological Society. Transactions (ISSN 0036-2891)

616.5   JA   ISSN 0018-1404
CLINICAL DERMATOLOGY/HIFUKA NO RINSHO. (Text in Japanese) 1959. m. 1950 Yen per no. Kanehara & Co., Ltd., 2-31-14 Yushima, Bunkyo-ku, Tokyo 113, Japan. Ed. Dr. Kenichi Ueno. bk.rev.; illus.; index; circ. 4,500. **Indexed:** INIS Atomind.
—BLDSC shelfmark: 7971.620000.

616.5   US   ISSN 0738-081X
CLINICS IN DERMATOLOGY. 1983. q. $140 to institutions (foreign $162)(effective 1992). Elsevier Science Publishing Co., Inc. (New York), 655 Ave. of the Americas, New York, NY 10010. TEL 212-989-5800. FAX 212-633-3965. TELEX 420643 AEP UI. Ed. Lawrence Charles Parish. illus.; index; circ. 1,500. (also avail. in microform from UMI) **Indexed:** Ind.Med.
—BLDSC shelfmark: 3286.548000.
Description: Provides information on the treatment and care of skin disorders.
Refereed Serial

616.5   DK   ISSN 0105-1873
CODEN: CODEDG
CONTACT DERMATITIS; environmental and occupational dermatitis. (Text in English) 1975. 10/yr. DKK 1280. (European Society of Contact Dematitis) Munksgaard International Publishers Ltd., 35 Noerre Soegade, P.O. Box 2148, DK-1016 Copenhagen K, Denmark. TEL 33-127030. FAX 33-129387. TELEX 19431-MUNKS-DK. Ed. Dr. Richard Rycroft. bk.rev.; circ. 1,800. (also avail. in microform from SWZ; reprint service avail. from ISI,SWZ) **Indexed:** Abstr.Hyg., Biol.Abstr., C.I.S.Abstr., Chem.Abstr., Curr.Adv.Ecol.Sci., Curr.Cont., Dent.Ind., Dok.Arbeitsmed., Excerp.Med., Hort.Abstr., Ind.Med., Ind.Sci.Rev., Lab.Haz.Bull., Sci.Cit.Ind., Trop.Dis.Bull.
—BLDSC shelfmark: 3424.960000.

CORE JOURNALS IN DERMATOLOGY. see *MEDICAL SCIENCES — Abstracting, Bibliographies, Statistics*

616.5   US
COSMETIC DERMATOLOGY. m. Knolls Publishing Group, 240 Cedar Knolls Rd., Ste. 220, Cedar Knolls, NJ 07927-1621. TEL 201-285-0855. FAX 201-285-1472. Ed. Alfred Saint-Jacques. circ. 15,004.

616.5   SZ   ISSN 0070-2064
CODEN: APDEBX
CURRENT PROBLEMS IN DERMATOLOGY. (Text in English) 1959. irreg., approx. a price varies. S. Karger AG, Allschwilerstr. 10, P.O. Box, CH-4009 Basel, Switzerland. TEL 061-3061111. FAX 061-3061234. TELEX CH 962652. Ed. H. Hoenigsmann. (reprint service avail. from ISI) **Indexed:** Biol.Abstr., Chem.Abstr., Curr.Cont., Dent.Ind., Ind.Med.
—BLDSC shelfmark: 3501.370000.
Description: Provides in-depth information on clinical problems in dermatology.

616.5   US   ISSN 1040-0486
CURRENT PROBLEMS IN DERMATOLOGY. 1989. bi-m. $65 to individuals (foreign $85); institutions $90 (foreign $110); students $39 (foreign $59) (effective Jan. 1992). Mosby Year - Book, Inc. (Subsidiary of: Times Mirror Company), 11830 Westline Industrial Dr., St. Louis, MO 63146. TEL 800-325-4177. Ed. William L. Weston. circ. 1,703.
Description: Covers current concerns of the dermatologist in everyday practice.

MEDICAL SCIENCES — DERMATOLOGY AND VENEREOLOGY

616.5 US ISSN 0011-4162
RL1 CODEN: CUTIB
CUTIS; cutaneous medicine for the practitioner. 1965. m. $70 to physicians (foreign $95); institutions $80; students $40 (foreign $80). Cahners Publishing Company (New York), Medical-Health Care Group (Subsidiary of: Reed International PLC), Division of Reed Publishing (USA) Inc., 249 W. 17th St., New York, NY 10011. TEL 212-645-0067. FAX 212-242-6987. (Subscr. to: 44 Cook St., Denver, CO 80206. TEL 800-662-7776) Ed. Sharon Finch. adv.; bk.rev.; charts; illus.; circ. 51,160. (also avail. in microform from RPI; reprint service avail. from UMI) **Indexed:** Abstr.Inter.Med., Curr.Cont., Dent.Ind., Excerp.Med., Helminthol.Abstr., Ind.Med., Ind.Sci.Rev., INIS Atomind., NRN, Nutr.Abstr., Protozool.Abstr., Sci.Cit.Ind.
 Description: Provides practical information on skin diseases and allergies, with clinical observations and discussions of therapeutic techniques.
 Refereed Serial

616.5 US ISSN 0898-1655
DECUBITUS; the journal of skin ulcers. 1988. q. $25 ($35 to Canada; elsewhere $45)(effective Jan. 1992). S - N Publications, Inc., 103 N. Second St., Ste. 200, W. Dundee, IL 60118. TEL 708-426-6100. FAX 708-426-6146. Ed. Roberta S. Abruzzese. adv.; tr.lit.; circ. 6,500.
 —BLDSC shelfmark: 3540.350000.
 Description: Examines medical and technical developments of interest to physicians, nurses, and specialists responsible for the treatment of pressure ulcers, with reports of current research, legal and professional issues.
 Refereed Serial

616.5 MX ISSN 0185-4038
DERMATOLOGIA; revista mexicana. (Text in Spanish; summaries in English, Spanish) 1956. bi-m. Mex.$60000($50) Sociedad Mexicana de Dermatologia, Dr. Vertiz 464, Mexico 7, D.F., Cod. 06780, Mexico. (Co-sponsor: Academia Mexicana de Dermatologia) Ed. Dr. Amado Saul. bk.rev.; cum.index: 1956-1981; circ. 3,000. (tabloid format) **Indexed:** Biol.Abstr., Excerp.Med., Trop.Dis.Bull.
 —BLDSC shelfmark: 3555.000000.

616.5 IT ISSN 0392-1395
DERMATOLOGIA CLINICA. (Text in Italian; summaries in English) q. L.50000($50) C I C Edizioni Internazionali s.r.l., Via L. Spallanzani 11, 00161 Rome, Italy. TEL 06-8412673. FAX 06-8443365. TELEX 622099 CIC. Dir. O.A. Carlesimo. **Indexed:** Excerp.Med.
 —BLDSC shelfmark: 3555.110000.

616.5 616.95 BU ISSN 0417-0792
 CODEN: DVENA3
DERMATOLOGIA I VENEROLOGIA. (Text in Bulgarian; summaries in Russian and English) 1962. q. 15 lv.($5) (Ministerstvo na Narodnoto Zdrave) Izdatelstvo Meditsina i Fizkultura, 11, Pl. Slaveikov, Sofia, Bulgaria. (Dist by: Hemus, 6, Rouski Blvd., 1000 Sofia, Bulgaria) (Co-sponsor: Nauchno Druzhestvo po Dermatologia) Ed. N.Z. Catkov. circ. 988. **Indexed:** Abstr.Bulg.Sci.Med.Lit., Biol.Abstr., C.I.S. Abstr., Chem.Abstr., Excerp.Med.
 —BLDSC shelfmark: 0053.120000.

616.5 IT ISSN 0394-2503
DERMATOLOGIA OGGI. 1986. q. L.20000. E S I Stampa Medica s.r.l., Casella Postale 42, Lgo. Volontari del Sangue 10, 20097 S. Donato, Milan, Italy. TEL 02-5274241. FAX 02-5274775. TELEX 324894. Ed. Bruno Pieroni. adv.; bk.rev.; circ. 8,000.
 —BLDSC shelfmark: 3555.127000.

616.5 US ISSN 0733-8635
RL1
DERMATOLOGIC CLINICS. 1983. 4/yr. $95. W.B. Saunders Co., Curtis Center, Independence Square W., Philadelphia, PA 19106. TEL 215-238-7800. Ed. Barton Dudlick. (also avail. in microform from UMI) **Indexed:** Excerp.Med., Ornam.Hort.
 —BLDSC shelfmark: 3555.138000.

616.5 SZ ISSN 0011-9075
 CODEN: DERAAC
DERMATOLOGICA; international journal for clinical and investigative dermatology. (Text in English) 1893. 8/yr. (in 2 vols.) 360 Fr.($240) per vol. N. S. Karger AG, Allschwilerstr. 10, P.O. Box, CH-4009 Basel, Switzerland. TEL 061-3061111. FAX 061-3061234. TELEX CH 962652. (Co-sponsors: Belgian Society for Dermatology and Syphiligraphy, Schweizerische Gesellschaft fuer Dermatologie und Venerologie) Ed. J.H. Saurat. adv.; bk.rev.; bibl.; illus.; index; circ. 2,250. (also avail. in microform from UMI) **Indexed:** Biol.Abstr., Biotech.Abstr., C.I.S. Abstr., Chem.Abstr., Curr.Adv.Ecol.Sci., Curr.Cont., Dent.Ind., Excerp.Med., Helminthol.Abstr., Ind.Med., Ind.Sci.Rev., NRN, Nutr.Abstr., Rev.Plant Path., Sci.Cit.Ind.

616.5 GW ISSN 0011-9083
 CODEN: DMONBP
DERMATOLOGISCHE MONATSSCHRIFT. 1892. m. DM.216. Johann Ambrosius Barth Verlag, Leipzig - Heidelberg, Salomonstr. 18b, 7010 Leipzig, Germany. TEL 70131. Ed. Prof. N. Sonnichsen. adv.; bk.rev.; bibl.; charts; illus.; stat.; index. **Indexed:** Biol.Abstr., C.I.S. Abstr., Chem.Abstr., Curr.Adv.Ecol.Sci., Dent.Ind., Excerp.Med., Hort.Abstr., Ind.Med., INIS Atomind., Rev.Plant Path.
 —BLDSC shelfmark: 3555.195000.
 Formerly: Dermatologische Wochenschrift.

616.5 IT
IL DERMATOLOGO. bi-m. L.15000($15) C I C Edizioni Internazionali s.r.l., Via L. Spallanzani 11, 00161 Rome, Italy. FAX 8443365. TELEX 622099 CIC. adv.; bk.rev.
 Formerly: Dermatologo Ospedaliero (ISSN 0391-8912)

616.5 US
DERMATOLOGY CLINICAL DIGEST SERIES. m. Bugamor Pharma Inc., 36 W. 44th St., Ste. 1412, New York, NY 10036. TEL 212-840-8480. FAX 212-840-9550. Ed. Paul Diamond. circ. 14,414.

616.5 US
DERMATOLOGY NURSING. bi-m. $28 to individuals; institutions $38. (Dermatology Nurses' Association) Anthony J. Jannetti, Inc., North Woodbury Road, Box 56, Pitman, NJ 08071. TEL 609-589-2319. **Indexed:** CINAHL.
 Refereed Serial

616.5 US
DERMATOLOGY SERIES. 1982. irreg., vol.7, 1986. price varies. Marcel Dekker, Inc., 270 Madison Ave., New York, NY 10016. TEL 212-696-9000. FAX 212-685-4540. TELEX 421419. Eds. Charles D. Calnan, Howard I. Mailbach.
 Refereed Serial

616.5 US ISSN 0196-6197
 CODEN: DETIEG
DERMATOLOGY TIMES. 1980. m. $60. Edgell Communications, 7500 Old Oak Blvd., Cleveland, OH 44130. TEL 216-826-2839. FAX 216-891-2726. (Subscr. to: 1 E. First St., Duluth, MN 55802) Ed. Dean Celia. circ. 6,765.
 Description: Industry news and developments, meeting announcements and classifieds for office-based and hospital-based dermatology professionals.

616.5 GW ISSN 0343-2432
 CODEN: DBUMDB
DERMATOSEN IN BERUF UND UMWELT. (Text in English and German; summaries in English, French and German) 1952. bi-m. DM.75. Editio Cantor, Postfach 1255, 7960 Aulendorf, Germany. TEL 07525-2060. FAX 07525-20680. Ed.Bd. adv.; bk.rev.; abstr.; bibl.; charts; illus.; index; circ. 6,850. (reprint service avail. from ISI; back issues avail.) **Indexed:** Abstr.Hyg., Biol.Abstr., C.I.S. Abstr., Chem.Abstr., Excerp.Med., Ind.Med., INIS Atomind., Protozool.Abstr., Trop.Dis.Bull.
 —BLDSC shelfmark: 3555.234000.
 Formerly: Berufs-Dermatosen (ISSN 0005-9498)

616.5 616.95 US
DIALOGUES IN DERMATOLOGY. 1977. m. $180 to non-members; members $130. American Academy of Dermatology, Box 3116, Evanston, IL 60204-3116. TEL 312-869-3954. FAX 312-869-4382. Ed. Dr. Richard K. Scher. bibl.; illus.; cum.index: 1977-present; circ. 2,500. (back issues avail.; avail. in audio cassette only)
 Description: Features interviews with experts on recent advances in the field of dermatology.

616.5 SA
DISEASES OF THE SKIN. vol.5, 1991. 4/yr. R.50. Helm Publishing Co. (Pty.) Ltd., P.O. Box 41706, Craighall 2024, South Africa. TEL 011-788-0612.

616.5 US
▼**DOCTORS' ORDERS;*** dermatology edition. 1990. q. HealthTeam Interactive Communications, Inc., 274 Madison Ave., No. PH, New York, NY 10016-0701. TEL 212-689-7971. FAX 212-779-2094. Ed. John Nittoli. adv.; circ. 10,000.
 Description: Comprised of patient sections on acne, seasonal skin care, dermatitis and psoriasis and written in laymen's terms for patient reading.

616.5 646.7 US
ELECTROLYSIS WORLD.* 1982. q. membership. American Electrolysis Association, 7332 E. Camelback Rd., No. D, Scottsdale, AZ 85251. TEL 602-945-4245. Ed. Gail J. Walker. circ. 1,700. (back issues avail.)

616 NE ISSN 0926-9959
▼**EUROPEAN ACADEMY OF DERMATOLOGY AND VENEREOLOGY. JOURNAL.** 1992. 4/yr. fl.350($173.50) (effective 1992). Elsevier Science Publishers B.V., P.O. Box 211, 1000 AE Amsterdam, Netherlands. TEL 020-5803911. FAX 020-5803598. TELEX 18582 ESPA NL. (N. America dist. addr.: Elsevier Science Publishing Co., Inc., Box 882, Madison Sq. Sta., New York, NY 10159. TEL 212-989-5800) Eds. T. Lotti, D. Freedman.
 Description: Broad-based articles of general relevance for the practicing dermato-venereologist.
 Refereed Serial

616.5 UK ISSN 0951-9785
EXCHANGE. 1976. q. £7. National Eczema Society, Tavistock House North, Tavistock Square, London WC1H 9SR, England. TEL 01-388-4097. Ed. Freda Houlton. adv.; bk.rev.; circ. 10,000.

616.5 616.95 US ISSN 0071-7932
FORTSCHRITTE DER PRAKTISCHEN DERMATOLOGIE UND VENEROLOGIE. 1952. irreg. price varies. Springer-Verlag, 175 Fifth Ave., New York, NY 10010. TEL 212-460-1500. (Also Berlin, Heidelberg, Tokyo and Vienna) (reprint service avail. from ISI)

616.951 UK
GENITOURINARY MEDICINE: THE JOURNAL OF SEXUAL HEALTH, STDS AND HIV. 1925. bi-m. £112. B M J Publishing Group, B.M.A. House, Tavistock Sq., London WC1H 9JR, England. TEL 071-387-4499. Ed. A. Mindel. adv.; bk.rev.; abstr.; charts; illus.; index. (also avail. in microform from UMI) **Indexed:** Abstr.Hyg., Biol.Abstr., Biotech.Abstr., Chem.Abstr., Curr.Adv.Ecol.Sci., Curr.Cont., Dent.Ind., Excerp.Med., Helminthol.Abstr., Ind.Med., Ind.Sci.Rev., Protozool.Abstr., Rev.Plant Path., Sci.Cit.Ind., Trop.Dis.Bull.
 ●Also available online. Vendor(s): BRS.
 Former titles: Genitourinary Medicine (ISSN 0266-4348); (until 1984): British Journal of Venereal Diseases (ISSN 0007-134X); **Incorporates:** International Union Against the Venereal Diseases and the Treponematoses. Proceedings of Assemblies (ISSN 0074-9230)

616.5 618.92 IT ISSN 1120-0499
GIORNALE INTERNAZIONALE DI DERMATOLOGIA PEDIATRICA. (Text in Italian; summaries in English) 1989. q. L.50000($50) C I C Edizioni Internazionali s.r.l., Via L. Spallanzani 11, 00161 Rome, Italy. TEL 06-8412673. FAX 06-8443365. TELEX 622099 CIC I. Dir. F. Rantuccio.
 —BLDSC shelfmark: 4178.115000.

MEDICAL SCIENCES — DERMATOLOGY AND VENEREOLOGY

616.5 616.951 IT ISSN 0533-7712
CODEN: GIDMB6
GIORNALE ITALIANO DI DERMATOLOGIA E VENEREOLOGIA. (Text in Italian; summaries in English) 1926. m. L.80000($120) (Societa Italiana di Dermatologia e Venereologia) Edizioni Minerva Medica, Corso Bramante 83-85, 10126 Turin, Italy. Eds. A.G. Bellome, G. Zina. abstr.; bibl.; charts; illus.; index; circ. 3,000. (also avail. in microform) **Indexed:** Biol.Abstr., C.I.S. Abstr., Chem.Abstr., Dent.Ind., Excerp.Med., Ind.Med., Soils & Fert.
Incorporates: Minerva Dermatologica (ISSN 0026-4741); Giornale Italiano di Cosmetologia; Dermosifilografo; Dermàtologia; Cosmetologia.

HANSENOLOGIA INTERNATIONALIS. see *MEDICAL SCIENCES — Communicable Diseases*

616.5 616.95 GW ISSN 0017-8470
CODEN: HAUTAW
DER HAUTARZT; Zeitschrift fuer Dermatologie, Allergologie, Venerologie und verwandte Gebiete. (Supplements avail.) (Text in German) 1950. 12/yr. DM.348($196) Springer-Verlag, Heidelberger Platz 3, D-1000 Berlin 33, Germany. TEL 030-8207-1. (Also Heidelberg, Tokyo, Vienna, and New York) Ed. O. Braun-Falco. adv.; bk.rev.; illus.; index. (also avail. in microform from UMI; back issues avail.; reprint service avail. from ISI) **Indexed:** Biol.Abstr., Biotech.Abstr., Chem.Abstr., Curr.Adv.Cancer Res., Curr.Cont., Dent.Ind., Dok.Arbeitsmed., Excerp.Med., Ind.Med., Nutr.Abstr., Protozool.Abstr., Sci.Cit.Ind.
—BLDSC shelfmark: 4273.760000.
Refereed Serial

616.5 GW ISSN 0933-7385
HAUTFREUND. 1986. bi-m. DM.38. (Deutscher Neurodermitiker Bund e.V.) Verlag fuer Medizin Dr. Ewald Fischer GmbH, Fritz-Frey-Str. 21, 6900 Heidelberg 1, Germany. TEL 06221-49974. Ed. E. Ruge. circ. 5,650. (back issues avail.)

616.5 GW ISSN 0930-7109
HAUTNAH; Dermatologie aus der Praxis. (Text in German; summaries in English and German) 1985. bi-m. DM.29. Medi-A-Derm Verlag GmbH, Postfach 100745, 2000 Hamburg 1, Germany. TEL 040-232334. Ed. Peter Baack. circ. 5,900.

I C R D B CANCERGRAM: MELANOMA AND OTHER SKIN CANCER - DIAGNOSIS, TREATMENT. see *MEDICAL SCIENCES — Abstracting, Bibliographies, Statistics*

616.5 US
ICHTHYOSIS FOCUS. 1981. q. $35 membership. Foundation for Ichthyosis and Related Skin Types, Inc., Box 20921, Raleigh, NC 27619-0921. TEL 800-545-3286. Ed. Ellen Rowe. circ. 2,500. (back issues avail.)
Description: Provides information on rare skin diseases for patients, physicians and health workers.

616.5 II ISSN 0019-5154
CODEN: IJDEAA
INDIAN JOURNAL OF DERMATOLOGY. (Text in English) 1955. q. $16. 78 Lenin Sarani, Calcutta 7000 013, India. Ed.Bd. adv.; bk.rev.; charts; illus.; circ. 1,000. **Indexed:** Biol.Abstr., Curr.Adv.Ecol.Sci., Excerp.Med., Ind.Med., Nutr.Abstr.

616.5 616.951 II ISSN 0378-6323
CODEN: IJDLDY
INDIAN JOURNAL OF DERMATOLOGY, VENEREOLOGY AND LEPROLOGY. (Text in English) 1935. bi-m. Rs.200($80) Indian Association of Dermatologists, Venereologists and Leprologists, c/o Dr. R.M. Parmanand, Ed., 76 Lokmanya Nagar, Babu Labhchand Chhajalani Marg, Indore 452 009, India. adv.; bk.rev.; charts; illus.; stat.; index; circ. 2,000. (also avail. in microform from UMI; reprint service avail. from UMI) **Indexed:** Biol.Abstr., Chem.Abstr., Excerp.Med., Indian Sci.Abstr., Rev.Plant Path.
Supersedes (in 1976): Indian Journal of Dermatology and Venereology (ISSN 0019-5162)

616.5 US ISSN 0011-9059
RL1 CODEN: IJDEBB
INTERNATIONAL JOURNAL OF DERMATOLOGY. 1962. 10/yr. $70 to individuals (foreign $85); institutions $95 (foreign $115). (International Society of Dermatology: Tropical, Geographic, and Ecologic) J.B. Lippincott Co., E. Washington Sq., Philadelphia, PA 19105. TEL 215-238-4200. Ed. Dr. Lawrence C. Parish. adv.; illus.; index; circ. 9,714. (also avail. in microform from UMI) **Indexed:** Biol.Abstr., Chem.Abstr., Curr.Adv.Ecol.Sci., Curr.Cont., Dent.Ind., Dok.Arbeitsmed., Excerp.Med., Helminthol.Abstr., Ind.Med., Ind.Sci.Rev., INIS Atomind., NRN, Protozool.Abstr., Sci.Cit.Ind, SSCI.
—BLDSC shelfmark: 4542.185000.
Formerly: Dermatologia Internationalis.
Refereed Serial

616.5 IT ISSN 0021-292X
ITALIAN GENERAL REVIEW OF DERMATOLOGY. (Text in English and Italian) vol.10, 1970. q. $60. (Centro Servizi Segreteria) Sigred S.r.l., Via Lapini 1, 50136 Florence, Italy. TEL 39-55670369. FAX 3955-660236. Ed. E. Panconesi. adv.; bk.rev.; abstr.; charts; illus.; circ. 3,300. **Indexed:** Excerp.Med., Ind.Med.
—BLDSC shelfmark: 4588.335000.

616.5 JA ISSN 0021-4973
JAPANESE JOURNAL OF CLINICAL DERMATOLOGY/RINSHO HIFUKA. (Text in Japanese) 1946. m. 30330 Yen($233) Igaku-Shoin Ltd., 5-24-3 Hongo, Bunkyo-ku, Tokyo 113-91, Japan. TEL 03-817-5716. Ed. Yoshio Sato. circ. 3,500.
—BLDSC shelfmark: 4651.373000.

616.5 JA ISSN 0021-499X
CODEN: NHKZAD
JAPANESE JOURNAL OF DERMATOLOGY: SERIES A/NIHON HIFUKA GAKKAI ZASSHI. 1901. m. 7000 Yen. Japanese Dermatological Association - Nihon Hifuka Gakkai, Taisei Bldg., 3-14-10 Hongo, Bunkyo-ku, Tokyo 113, Japan. Dir. M. Takenouchi. bk.rev.; charts; illus.; index. **Indexed:** Biol.Abstr., Chem.Abstr., Dent.Ind., Ind.Med.
—BLDSC shelfmark: 4651.550000.

616.5 JA
JAPANESE JOURNAL OF DERMATOLOGY: SERIES B/NIHON HIFUKA GAKKAI ZASSHI. 1963. bi-m. 5000 Yen. Japanese Dermatological Association - Nihon Hifuka Gakkai, Taisei Bldg., 3-14-10 Hongo, Bunkyo-ku, Tokyo 113, Japan. Dir. M. Takenouchi. bk.rev.; charts; illus.; index. **Indexed:** Biol.Abstr., Chem.Abstr., Dent.Ind., Ind.Med.

616.5 GW ISSN 0932-8661
JATROS DERMATOLOGIE. 1987. 12/yr. DM.150. P M I Verlag GmbH, August-Schanz-Str. 21, 6000 Frankfurt a.M. 50, Germany. TEL 069-5480000. Ed. Peter Hoffmann. circ. 3,000. (back issues avail.)
Description: A seminar paper journal containing summaries of dermatologic articles, interviews and Congress reports.

616.5 FR
JOURNAL EUROPEEN DE DERMATOLOGIE/EUROPEAN JOURNAL OF DERMATOLOGY. 8/yr. 123 ECU to individuals; institutions 215 ECU; students 61 ECU. John Libbey Eurotext, 6 rue Blanche, 92120 Montrouge, France. TEL 1-47-35-85-52. FAX 1-46-57-10-09.

616.5 IT ISSN 0392-8543
CODEN: JACOEL
JOURNAL OF APPLIED COSMETOLOGY; quarterly review of cosmetic dermatology. 1983. q. $50. International Ediemme, Via Innocenzo XI, 41, 00165 Rome, Italy. TEL 637-8788. Ed. P. Morganti. adv.; bk.rev.; circ. 5,000. **Indexed:** Excerp.Med.
—BLDSC shelfmark: 4942.380000.

616.5 US ISSN 0894-0061
▼**JOURNAL OF CUTANEOUS AGING & COSMETIC DERMATOLOGY.** 1990. q. $120 (foreign $160). Mary Ann Liebert, Inc., 1651 Third Ave., New York, NY 10128. TEL 212-289-2300. FAX 212-289-4697. Eds. Dr. James J. Leyden, Gary Grove.
—BLDSC shelfmark: 4965.956000.
Description: Covers intrinsic aging, photo-aging and other clinical aspects of the aging process, benign and malignant disorders, and disorders of hair, nails, and other cutaneous appendages.

616.5 DK ISSN 0303-6987
CODEN: JCUPBN
JOURNAL OF CUTANEOUS PATHOLOGY. (Text and summaries in English) 1974. bi-m. DKK 1412. (American Society for Dermatopathology, US) Munksgaard International Publishers Ltd., 35 Noerre Soegade, P.O. Box 2148, DK-1016 Copenhagen K, Denmark. TEL 33-127030. FAX 33-129387. TELEX 19431-MUNKS-DK. Ed. Philip Cooper. adv.; bibl.; charts; illus.; circ. 1,700. (reprint service avail. from ISI) **Indexed:** Biol.Abstr., Chem.Abstr., Curr.Adv.Biochem., Curr.Cont., Dent.Ind., Excerp.Med., Helminthol.Abstr., Ind.Med., Ind.Sci.Rev., INIS Atomind., Nutr.Abstr., Rev.Plant Path., Sci.Cit.Ind.
—BLDSC shelfmark: 4965.960000.

JOURNAL OF DERMATOLOGIC SURGERY AND ONCOLOGY. see *MEDICAL SCIENCES — Surgery*

616.5 NE ISSN 0923-1811
CODEN: JDSCEI
▼**JOURNAL OF DERMATOLOGICAL SCIENCE.** (Text in English) 1990. 6/yr. (in 2 vols., 3 nos./vol.). fl.588 (effective 1992). (Japanese Society for Investigative Dermatology, JA) Elsevier Science Publishers B.V., P.O. Box 211, 1000 AE Amsterdam, Netherlands. TEL 020-5803911. FAX 020-5803598. TELEX 18582 ESPA NL. (Subscr. in U.S. and Canada to: Elsevier Science Publishing Co., Inc., Box 882, Madison Sq. Sta., New York, NY 10159. TEL 212-989-5800) Ed. Hideoki Ogawa. adv.; bk.rev.; circ. 1,500. (back issues avail.)
—BLDSC shelfmark: 4968.766500.
Description: Publishes manuscripts covering the entire scope of dermatology, from molecular studies to clinical investigations.
Refereed Serial

616.5 UK ISSN 0954-6634
CODEN: JDTREY
JOURNAL OF DERMATOLOGICAL TREATMENT. 1989. 4/yr. £90 in Europe; elsewhere £100. Macmillan Press Ltd., Houndmills, Basingstoke, Hampshire RG21 2XS, England. TEL 0256-29242. FAX 0256-810526.
—BLDSC shelfmark: 4968.767000.
Description: All aspects of the treatment of skin disorders.

616.5 US ISSN 0022-202X
RL1 CODEN: JIDEAE
JOURNAL OF INVESTIGATIVE DERMATOLOGY. 1938. 12/yr.(in 2 vols.; 6 nos./vol.) plus supplement. $278 to institutions (foreign $324)(effective 1992). (Society of Investigative Dermatology, Inc.) Elsevier Science Publishing Co., Inc. (New York), 655 Ave. of the Americas, New York, NY 10010. TEL 212-989-5800. FAX 212-633-3965. TELEX 420643 AEP UI. (Co-sponsor: European Society for Dermatological Research) Ed. Dr. David Norris. adv.; bk.rev.; bibl.; illus.; index; circ. 4,800. (also avail. in microform from PMC) **Indexed:** Abstr.Hyg., Biol.Abstr., Biotech.Abstr., C.I.S. Abstr., Chem.Abstr, Curr.Adv.Biochem., Curr.Adv.Cancer Res., Curr.Adv.Cell & Devel.Biol., Curr.Adv.Ecol.Sci., Curr.Adv.Genetics & Molec.Biol., Curr.Cont., Dent.Ind., Excerp.Med., I.P.A., Ind.Med., Ind.Sci.Rev., Ind.Vet., INIS Atomind., Nutr.Abstr., Pig News & Info., Sci.Cit.Ind., Small Anim.Abstr., Vet.Bull.
●Also available online.
—BLDSC shelfmark: 5008.000000.
Description: Presents original papers and reviews pertinent to the normal and abnormal function of the skin.
Refereed Serial

JOURNAL OF TOXICOLOGY: CUTANEOUS AND OCULAR TOXICOLOGY. see *PHARMACY AND PHARMACOLOGY*

616.5 KO ISSN 0494-4739
KOREAN JOURNAL OF DERMATOLOGY. (Text mainly in Korean, occasionally in English; contents and summaries in English) 1960. bi-m. 20000 Won($40) Korean Dermatological Association - Taehan P'ibu Kwahakhoe, No. 401, Sindonga Jonghap-Sangka, 491 Suecho-dong, Suecho-ku, Seoul 137-070, S. Korea. TEL 02-567-0284. FAX 02-552-4203. Ed. Eil Soo Lee. adv.; bk.rev.; bibl.; charts; circ. 900. (back issues avail.) **Indexed:** Biol.Abstr., Excerp.Med. Key Title: Taehan P'ibu Kwahakhoe Chi.
—BLDSC shelfmark: 5113.530000.

MEDICAL SCIENCES — DERMATOLOGY AND VENEREOLOGY

616.5   CC   ISSN 1000-4963
LINCHUANG PIFUKE ZAZHI/JOURNAL OF CLINICAL DERMATOLOGY. (Text in Chinese) bi-m. Jiangsu Sheng Renmin Yiyuan - Jiangsu People's Hospital, 300 Guangzhou Lu, Nanjing, Jiangsu 210029, People's Republic of China. TEL 303836. Ed. Zhao Bian.
—BLDSC shelfmark: 4958.391000.

611   SP   ISSN 0210-5187
MEDICINA CUTANEA IBERO-LATINO-AMERICANA. 1973. bi-m. 7700 ptas.($105) in Europe; elsewhere $130. (Colegio Ibero-Latino-Americano de Dermatologia) Editorial Garsi, S.A., Londres, 17, 28028 Madrid, Spain. TEL 2560800. (Subscr. to: Prof. Jose M. Mascaro, Casanova 143, Barcelona 36, Spain) Ed. Jose Maria Mascaro. adv.; bk.rev.; circ. 3,000. Indexed: Biol.Abstr., Dent.Ind., Excerp.Med., Ind.Med.
Formed by the merger of: Medicina Cutanea (ISSN 0025-7788); Dermatologia Ibero Latino-Americano (ISSN 0011-9040)

616.5   BL
MEDISOM: DERMATOLOGY. 1982. bi-m. $90. Grupo Editorial Q B D Ltda, Rua Caravelas 326, Caixa Postal 30329, 01051 Sao Paulo, Brazil. FAX 55-11-572-5957. Ed. Dr. Philip Querido. adv. (audio cassette)

616.5   SZ   ISSN 0259-1340
CODEN: MODEEP
MODELS IN DERMATOLOGY. (Text in English) 1985. irreg. price varies. S. Karger AG, Allschwilerstr. 10, P.O. Box, CH-4009 Basel, Switzerland. TEL 061-3061111. FAX 061-3061234. TELEX CH 962652. Eds. H.I. Maibach, N.J. Lowe. Indexed: Biol.Abstr., Curr.Cont., Ind.Med.
—BLDSC shelfmark: 5883.539000.

616.5 616.4 646.7   US
NATIONAL ALOPECIA AREATA FOUNDATION NEWSLETTER. 1981. bi-m. $30. National Alopecia Areata Foundation, 710 C St., Ste. 11, San Rafael, CA 94901. TEL 415-456-4644. FAX 415-456-4274. Ed. Vicki Kalabokes. circ. 5,000. (back issues avail.)

616.5   US   ISSN 8756-2243
RL321
NATIONAL PSORIASIS FOUNDATION. ANNUAL REPORT. (Included in Bulletin) a. donation. National Psoriasis Foundation, 6443 S.W. Beaverton Hwy., No. 210, Portland, OR 97221. TEL 503-297-1545. FAX 503-292-9341. Ed. Sheri Decker. circ. 25,000.
Description: Provides a summary of the Foundation's major activities, programs, and research involvement, plus financial statements.

616.5   US   ISSN 1040-0060
NATIONAL PSORIASIS FOUNDATION. BULLETIN. (Includes Annual Report) 1968. bi-m. donation. National Psoriasis Foundation, 6443 S.W. Beaverton Hwy., No. 210, Portland, OR 97221. TEL 503-297-1545. FAX 503-292-9341. Ed. Sherith Decker. circ. 25,000.
Description: Provides information on psoriasis treatments and includes news of the Foundation's research and activities.

616.5   JA
NISHI NIHON JOURNAL OF DERMATOLOGY/NISHI NIHON HIFUKA. (Text in Japanese; summaries in English) 1934. bi-m. 8000 Yen. Kyushu University, Faculty of Medicine, Department of Dermatology, Maidashi 3-1-1, Higashi-ku, Fukuoka 812, Japan. Ed. Yoshiaki Hori. adv.; bk.rev.; bibl.; charts; illus.; circ. 3,500. Indexed: Biol.Abstr., Chem.Abstr., Excerp.Med., Ind.Med.
Formerly: Dermatology and Urology - Hifu to Hitsunyo (ISSN 0011-9091)

616.5   SW   ISSN 0345-9616
P S O AKTUELLT. 1963. q. SEK 100. Svenska Psoriasisfoerbundet, Roekerigatan 5, 121 62 Johanneshov, Sweden. TEL 08-6003636. FAX 08-6002284. Ed. Gunilla Qwerin. adv.; bk.rev.; circ. 30,000.

PARAPHARMEX. see *PHARMACY AND PHARMACOLOGY*

616.5 618.92   US   ISSN 0736-8046
PEDIATRIC DERMATOLOGY. 1983. q. $100 to individuals; institutions $180. (Society for Pediatric Dermatology) Blackwell Scientific Publications Inc., Three Cambridge Center, Ste. 208, Cambridge, MA 02142-1413. TEL 617-225-0401. FAX 617-225-0412. (Co-sponsor: International Society of Pediatric Dermatology) Eds. Dr. B. Esterly, Dr. Lawrence M. Solomon. adv.; bk.rev.; circ. 1,200. Indexed: Ind.Med.
—BLDSC shelfmark: 6417.582000.
Refereed Serial

616.5   SZ   ISSN 1011-291X
CODEN: PHSKEY
PHARMACOLOGY AND THE SKIN. (Text in English) 1987. irreg. price varies. S. Karger AG, Allschwilerstr. 10, P.O. Box, CH-4009 Basel, Switzerland. TEL 061-3061111. FAX 061-3061234. TELEX CH 962652. Eds. B. Shroot, H. Schaefer.
—BLDSC shelfmark: 6447.061500.

616.5   DK   ISSN 0905-4383
CODEN: PPPHEW
PHOTODERMATOLOGY, PHOTOIMMUNOLOGY & PHOTOMEDICINE. (Text and summaries in English) 1984. bi-m. DKK 1965. Munksgaard International Publishers Ltd., 35 Noerre Soegade, P.O. Box 2148, DK-1016 Copenhagen K, Denmark. TEL 33-127030. FAX 33-129387. TELEX 19431-MUNKS-DK. Ed. Paul Bergstresser. bk.rev.; circ. 700. Indexed: Chem.Abstr., Curr.Adv.Ecol.Sci., Curr.Cont., Excerp.Med., Ind.Med.
Formerly: Photodermatology (ISSN 0108-9684)

616.5   SP   ISSN 0213-9251
PIEL. 1986. m. (10/yr.) 5500 ptas.($57) (free to qualified personnel). Ediciones Doyma, S.A., Travesera de Gracia, 17-21, 08021 Barcelona, Spain. TEL 200-07-11. FAX 209-11-36. TELEX 51964 INK-E. Dir. Carlos Ferrandiz Foraster. adv.: page 165000 ptas.; trim 210 x 280; adv. contact: Ana Ma. Alfonso. circ. 6,000. (reprint service avail. from UMI) Indexed: Ind.Med.Esp.
Description: Offers articles for the continuing education of physicians concerned with dermatology.

616.5   US   ISSN 0033-0639
PROGRESS IN DERMATOLOGY.* 1966. 4/yr. membership. Dermatology Foundation, 1560 Sherman Ave., Ste. 302, Evanston, IL 60201-4802. Ed. Thomas Lawley, M.D. adv.; circ. 3,000 (controlled). (looseleaf format)

616.5   PL   ISSN 0033-2526
CODEN: PRDEA7
PRZEGLAD DERMATOLOGICZNY. (Text in Polish; summaries in English) bi-m. $120. (Polskie Towarzystwo Dermatologiczne) Panstwowy Zaklad Wydawnictw Lekarskich, Ul. Dluga 38-40, Warsaw, Poland. FAX 48-22-215180. (Dist. by: Ars Polona-Ruch, Krakowskie Przedmiescie 7, Warsaw, Poland) Ed. Maria Blaszczyk. bk.rev.; abstr.; charts; illus.; index. Indexed: Biol.Abstr., Chem.Abstr., Dent.Ind., Dok.Arbeitsmed., Excerp.Med., Ind.Med.
—BLDSC shelfmark: 6939.700000.
Description: Addresses skin problems and sexually transmitted diseases.

616.5   GW   ISSN 0931-1521
PSO MAGAZIN. 1974. 6/yr. membership. Deutscher Psoriasis Bund e.V., Oberaltenallee 20a, 2000 Hamburg 76, Germany. TEL 040-2270985. adv.
Formerly: Psoriasis Magazin.

616.5   US
PSORIASIS NEWSLETTER. 1980. s-a. Psoriasis Research Institute, 600 Town and Country Village, Palo Alto, CA 94301-2326. TEL 415-326-1848. Ed. Dr. Eugene M. Farber. circ. 14,000.
Description: Reports research advances in the field of dermatology relevant to psoriasis. Directed to the general public.

616.5   IT   ISSN 0033-9490
RASSEGNA DI DERMATOLOGIA E SIFILOGRAFIA. 1948. s-a. L.60000 (foreign L.120000)(effective 1992). Casa Editrice Maccari, Via Trento, 53, 43100 Parma, Italy. FAX 039-521-771268. circ. 1,000.

REVISTA DE MEDICINA INTERNA, NEUROLOGIE, PSIHIATRIE, NEURO-CHIRURGIE, DERMATO-VENEROLOGIE. see *MEDICAL SCIENCES — Psychiatry And Neurology*

616.9   JA
S T D: JAPANESE JOURNAL OF THE SEXUALLY TRANSMITTED DISEASES. (Text in Japanese) 1921. q. 2,000 Yen. Japanese Association for the Prevention of Venereal Diseases - Nihon Seibyo Yobo Kyokai, 3-14-10 Hongo, Bunkyo-ku, Tokyo 113, Japan. FAX 03-814-4117. Ed. Tadao Niijima. adv.; stat.; circ. 880.
Formerly (until vol.64, 1983): V D: Japanese Journal of Venereal Diseases.

616.5   US   ISSN 0278-145X
CODEN: SDERDN
SEMINARS IN DERMATOLOGY. 1982. q. $75 to individuals; institutions $104; foreign $121. W.B. Saunders Co. (Subsidiary of: Harcourt Brace Jovanovich, Inc.), Curtis Center, Independence Square W., Philadelphia, PA 19106. TEL 215-238-7800. (Subscr. to: 6277 Sea Harbor Dr., 4th Fl., Orlando FL 32891) Ed. Dr. Howard I. Maibach. adv.; bibl.; charts; illus.; stat.; index. (also avail. in microform from UMI; back issues avail.) Indexed: ASCA, Curr.Cont.
●Also available online.
—BLDSC shelfmark: 8239.448800.

616.951   US   ISSN 0148-5717
RC201.A1   CODEN: STRDDM
SEXUALLY TRANSMITTED DISEASES. 1974. q. $70 to individuals; institutions $100. (American Venereal Disease Association) J.B. Lippincott Co., E. Washington Sq., Philadelphia, PA 19105. TEL 215-238-4200. Ed. Dr. Michael F. Rein. adv.; illus.; index.; circ. 2,300. Indexed: Chem.Abstr., Curr.Adv.Ecol.Sci., Curr.Cont., Dent.Ind., Excerp.Med., Helminthol.Abstr., Ind.Med., Sci.Cit.Ind., SSCI.
●Also available online. Vendor(s): BRS, Mead Data Central.
—BLDSC shelfmark: 8254.486500.
Formerly: American Venereal Disease Association. Journal (ISSN 0095-148X)
Refereed Serial

616 312.39   CN
SEXUALLY TRANSMITTED DISEASES IN CANADA. French edition: Maladies Tranmises Sexuellement au Canada. 1972. a. free. Department of National Health and Welfare, Laboratory Centre for Disease Control, Ottawa, Ont. K1A 0L2, Canada. TEL 613-957-1785. illus.
Former titles: Venereal Diseases in Canada; Canada. Epidemiology Division. Venereal Disease in Canada (ISSN 0319-0382)

616.5   US   ISSN 0037-6337
CODEN: SKANB4
SKIN & ALLERGY NEWS. 1970. m. $60. International Medical News Group, 12230 Wilkins Ave., Rockville, MD 20852. TEL 301-770-6170. Ed. William Rubin. adv.; bk.rev.; circ. 32,300. (tabloid format; also avail. in microform from UMI)
—BLDSC shelfmark: 8295.910000.

616.5   AT   ISSN 1030-7257
SKIN AND PSORIASIS NEWSLETTER. 1979. a. free. Skin and Psoriasis Foundation, Dodgshun House, 9 Brunswick St., Fitzroy, Vic. 3065, Australia. TEL 03-471-4425. Ed. Joan Wishart. circ. 5,000. (back issues avail.)
Description: Articles by dermatologists directed to the general public.

616.5   US   ISSN 0898-6525
SKIN INC; business and science for skin care professionals. 1988. 6/yr. $42. Allured Publishing, Bldg. C, Ste. 1600, 2100 Manchester Rd., Box 318, Wheaton, IL 60189-0318. TEL 708-653-2155. FAX 708-653-2192. TELEX 910-253-2133. Ed. Jean Allured. adv.; bk.rev.; index; circ. 15,000. (back issues avail.)
Description: For the aesthetician and skin care professional. Includes treatments, physiology and business articles.

SKIN PHARMACOLOGY. see *PHARMACY AND PHARMACOLOGY*

616.5   JA   ISSN 0018-1390
SKIN RESEARCH/HIFU. (Text in Japanese; summaries in English) 1959. bi-m. 5000 Yen($35) Osaka Dermatological Association - Nihon Hifukagakkai Osaka Chihokai, c/o Osaka University School of Medicine, Dept. of Dermatology, 1-1-50 Fukushima, Fukushima-ku, Osaka 553, Japan. Ed. Dr. Minoru Yasuhara. adv.; index; circ. 1,050. Indexed: Biol.Abstr., Chem.Abstr., INIS Atomind.
—BLDSC shelfmark: 8295.940000.

MEDICAL SCIENCES — ENDOCRINOLOGY

616.5   SA
SOUTHERN AFRICAN JOURNAL OF EPIDEMIOLOGY AND INFECTION. 1982. q. membership. (Sexually Transmitted Diseases Society of Southern Africa) M.I.M.S. (Subsidiary of: Times Media Ltd.), P.O. Box 2059, Pretoria 0001, South Africa. TEL 012-348-5010. FAX 012-477716. (Subscr. to: P.O. Box 1038, Johnnesburg 2000, South Africa) (Co-sponsors: Epidemiological Society of Southern Africa; Infections Diseases Society of Southern Africa) Ed. H. Koornhoff. adv.; bk.rev.; charts; illus.; circ. 1,800. (back issues avail.)
    Incorporates: Southern African Journal of Sexually Transmitted Diseases.
    Description: Contains articles on infectious diseases, sexually transmitted diseases and epidemiology.

668.5 616.5   GW
           CODEN: AEKODN
T W DERMATOLOGIE; Fachzeitschrift fuer kosmetische Dermatologie. 1971. 6/yr. DM.80. Verlag G. Braun GmbH, Karl-Friedrich-Str. 14, Postfach 1709, 7500 Karlsruhe 1, Germany. TEL 0721-165-0. FAX 0721-165227. TELEX 7826904-VGB-D. Ed. Dr. Scheicher-Gottron. circ. 5,000. **Indexed:** Chem.Abstr., Excerp.Med.
    Former titles: Aerztliche Kosmetologie (ISSN 0340-5702); Kosmetologie.

TOILETRIES, FRAGRANCES AND SKIN CARE: THE ROSE SHEET. see *BEAUTY CULTURE — Perfumes And Cosmetics*

616.5 616.951   RU   ISSN 0042-4609
           CODEN: VDVEAV
VESTNIK DERMATOLOGII I VENEROLOGII/ANNALS OF DERMATOLOGY AND VENEREOLOGY. (Text in Russian; summaries in English) 1924. m. 22.20 Rub.($18.60) (Vsesoyuznoe Nauchnoe Obshchestvo Dermatologov i Venerologov) Izdatel'stvo Meditsina, Petroverigskii pereulok 6-8, 101838 Moscow, Russia. (Co-sponsor: Ministerstvo Zdravookhraneniya S.S.S.R.) Ed. N.D. Sheklakov. bk.rev.; bibl.; illus. **Indexed:** Abstr.Hyg., Biol.Abstr., Chem.Abstr., Curr.Cont., Dent.Ind., Dok.Arbeitsmed., Excerp.Med., Helminthol.Abstr., Ind.Med., Rev.Plant Path., Trop.Dis.Bull.
   —BLDSC shelfmark: 0033.000000.
    Description: Deals with experimental and clinical dermatology and venereology, control of skin and venereal diseases.

VETERINARY DERMATOLOGY; an international journal. see *VETERINARY SCIENCE*

616.5 617   US   ISSN 1059-0587
▼**YEAR BOOK OF DERMATOLOGIC SURGERY.** 1992. a. $59.95. Mosby - Year Book, Inc. (Chicago) (Subsidiary of: Times Mirror Company), 200 N. LaSalle St., Chicago, IL 60601. TEL 312-726-9733. Ed. Dr. Neil Swanson.
   ●Also available online. Vendor(s): BRS.

616.505   US   ISSN 0093-3619
RL26
YEAR BOOK OF DERMATOLOGY. 1933. a. $51.95. Mosby - Year Book, Inc., Continuity Division, 200 N. LaSalle, Chicago, IL 60601. TEL 312-726-9733. FAX 312-726-6075. TELEX 206155. Eds. Drs. Arthur Sober, Thomas B. Fitzpatrick. illus. (reprint service avail.) **Indexed:** Biol.Abstr., Curr.Adv.Ecol.Sci.
   ●Also available online. Vendor(s): BRS.
    Formerly: Yearbook of Dermatology and Syphilology (ISSN 0093-3627)

610   GW   ISSN 0301-0481
ZEITSCHRIFT FUER HAUTKRANKHEITEN H UND G. 1946. m. DM.272. Berliner Medizinische Verlagsanstalt GmbH, Kurfuerstenstr. 112-113, 1000 Berlin 30, Germany. TEL 219909-0. FAX 219909-10. Ed. G.K. Steigleder. adv.; bk.rev.; charts; illus.; tr.lit.; index; circ. 2,500. **Indexed:** A.D.&D., Biol.Abstr., Biotech.Abstr., Curr.Cont., Dent.Ind., Excerp.Med., Helminthol.Abstr., Ind.Med., Rev.Plant Path.
   —BLDSC shelfmark: 9464.322000.
    Formerly: Zeitschrift fuer Haut- und Geschlechtskrankheiten (ISSN 0044-2844)

616.5   CC
ZHONGGUO SHAOSHANG CHUANGSHANG ZAZHI/CHINESE JOURNAL OF BURNS AND WOUNDS. (Text in Chinese) q. Zhongguo Shaoshang Chuangshang Keji Zhongxin - Chinese Science and Technology Center for Burns and Wounds, 106 Yong'an Lu, Xuanwu-qu, Beijing 100050, People's Republic of China. TEL 2567733. Ed. Xu Rongxiang.

MEDICAL SCIENCES — Endocrinology

616.462   IT   ISSN 0001-5563
           CODEN: ADILAS
ACTA DIABETOLOGICA LATINA. (Text in English) 1964. q. L.250000($180) Casa Editrece Il Ponte, Casella Postale 1071, 20100 Milan, Italy. TEL (0039)-2 31072676. Ed. G. Pozza. bk.rev.; abstr.; bibl.; illus.; index; circ. 5,000. (also avail. in microfiche from UMI) **Indexed:** ASCA, Biol.Abstr., Bull.Signal., Chem.Abstr., Curr.Adv.Ecol.Sci., Curr.Cont., Diab.Lit.Ind., Excerp.Med., Ind.Med., Ind.Sci.Rev., Nutr.Abstr., Ref.Zh., Sci.Cit.Ind.
   —BLDSC shelfmark: 0612.400000.

616.4   NO
           CODEN: ACENA7
ACTA ENDOCRINOLOGICA. (Text in English) 1948. m. $350 includes supplements. Scandinavian University Press, P.O. Box 2959 Toeyen, N-0608 Oslo, Norway. TEL 47-2-677600. FAX 47-2-677575. Ed. Christian Binder. abstr.; charts; illus.; index; circ. 1,800. **Indexed:** Abstr.Inter.Med., Anim.Breed.Abstr., ASCA, Biol.Abstr., Biotech.Abstr., C.I.S. Abstr., Chem.Abstr., Curr.Adv.Cancer Res., Curr.Adv.Cell & Devel.Biol., Curr.Adv.Ecol.Sci., Curr.Adv.Genetics & Molec.Biol., Curr.Cont., Dairy Sci.Abstr., Dent.Ind., Excerp.Med., Ind.Med., Ind.Sci.Rev., Ind.Vet., INIS Atomind., Nutr.Abstr., Pig News & Info., Sci.Cit.Ind., Small Anim.Abstr., Vet.Bull.
    Description: Covers clinical as well as experimental endocrinology.
   Refereed Serial

616.4   AG   ISSN 0065-1192
ACTA ENDOCRINOLOGICA PANAMERICANA.* irreg. Panamerican Federation of Endocrine Societies, c/o Dr. Noe Altschuler, 25 de Mayo no. 648, Vicente Lopez, Buenos Aires, Argentina.

616.4 618.2 610.73   IT   ISSN 0001-6004
           CODEN: AMAXBK
ACTA MEDICA AUXOLOGICA. (Text in English, Italian) 1969. 3/yr. L.80000($54) Centro Auxologico Italiano, Corso Magenta, 96, 20123 Milan, Italy. TEL 02-48194588. (Subscr. to: Editrice Vita e Pensiero, Largo Gemelli, 1, 20123 Milan, Italy) Ed. Francesco Morabito. adv.; bk.rev.; abstr.; bibl.; illus.; index; circ. 3,000. **Indexed:** Biol.Abstr., Curr.Adv.Ecol.Sci., Curr.Cont., Excerp.Med., Ind.Med., Nutr.Abstr., Psychol.Abstr.
   —BLDSC shelfmark: 0633.200000.

616   US   ISSN 1049-6734
RC648.a1
▼**ADVANCES IN ENDOCRINOLOGY AND METABOLISM.** 1990. a. $59.95. Mosby - Year Book, Inc. (Chicago) (Subsidiary of: Times Mirror Company), 200 N. Lasalle St., Chicago, IL 60601-1080. TEL 312-726-9733. FAX 312-726-6075. TELEX 206155. (Subscr. to: 11830 Westline Industrial Dr., St. Louis, MO 63146. TEL 800-325-4177) Ed. Dr. Ernest L. Mazzaferri.
   —BLDSC shelfmark: 0705.250000.
    Description: Provides referenced articles that enable clinical endocrinologists to incorporate new data in the day-to-day management of endocrine and metabolic disease.

616.4   US   ISSN 0065-2903
RC620.A1   CODEN: AMTDAK
ADVANCES IN METABOLIC DISORDERS. 1964. irreg., vol.11, 1988. Academic Press, Inc., 1250 Sixth Ave., San Diego, CA 92101. TEL 619-231-0926. FAX 619-699-6715. (reprint service avail. from ISI) **Indexed:** Biol.Abstr., Curr.Adv.Ecol.Sci.
   —BLDSC shelfmark: 0709.400000.
    Supersedes: Advances in Metabolic Disorders. Supplements (ISSN 0587-4394)
   Refereed Serial

616.4   US
ADVANCES IN PROSTAGLANDIN, THROMBOXANE, AND LEUKOTRIENE RESEARCH. 1976. irreg., latest vol.21. price varies. Raven Press, 1185 Ave. of the Americas, New York, NY 10036. TEL 212-930-9500. FAX 212-869-3495. TELEX 640073. Eds. Bengt Samuelsson, Rodolfo Paoletti. **Indexed:** Anim.Breed.Abstr., Biol.Abstr., Chem.Abstr., Curr.Adv.Ecol.Sci., Curr.Cont., Ind.Med., Ind.Sci.Rev., Sci.Cit.Ind.
    Formerly: Advances in Prostaglandin and Thromboxane Research (ISSN 0361-5952)
   Refereed Serial

616.4   GW   ISSN 0172-4606
           CODEN: AENSDG
AKTUELLE ENDOKRINOLOGIE UND STOFFWECHSEL. 1980. q. DM.180. Georg Thieme Verlag, Ruedigerstr. 14, Postfach 104853, 7000 Stuttgart 10, Germany. Ed.Bd. adv.; bk.rev.; abstr.; bibl.; charts; circ. 1,000. (reprint service avail. from UMI) **Indexed:** Chem.Abstr., Excerp.Med., Nutr.Abstr.

AMERICAN JOURNAL OF KIDNEY DISEASES. see *MEDICAL SCIENCES — Urology And Nephrology*

616.4   FR   ISSN 0003-4266
           CODEN: ANENAG
ANNALES D'ENDOCRINOLOGIE. (Text and summaries in English, French) 1939. bi-m. 195 ECU($235) (typically set in Jan.). (Societe Francaise d'Endocrinologie) Masson, 120 bd. St. Germain, 75280 Paris Cedex 06, France. TEL 1-46-34-21-60. FAX 1-45-87-29-99. TELEX 202 671 F. Ed. L.M. Wolf. adv.; bk.rev.; illus.; index; circ. 1,500. (tabloid format; also avail. in microform from UMI; reprint service avail. from ISI) **Indexed:** Anim.Breed.Abstr., Biol.Abstr., Chem.Abstr., Curr.Adv.Ecol.Sci., Curr.Cont., Dairy Sci.Abstr., Excerp.Med., Ind.Med., Ind.Sci.Rev., Ind.Vet., INIS Atomind., Nutr.Abstr., Sci.Cit.Ind.
   —BLDSC shelfmark: 0972.000000.

616.4   BL   ISSN 0004-2730
           CODEN: ABENAY
ARQUIVOS BRASILEIROS DE ENDOCRINOLOGIA E METABOLOGIA. (Text in English, French, Portuguese and Spanish) 1951-1973; resumed 1978. q. free. Universidade de Sao Paulo, Faculdade de Medicina, Av. Dr. Arnaldo 455, Cx. Postal 8100, 01246 Sao Paulo, Brazil. Ed. Antonio Roberto Chacra. bk.rev.; bibl.; charts; illus.; index. **Indexed:** Biol.Abstr., Chem.Abstr., Excerp.Med., Ind.Med., Nutr.Abstr.

616.4 615   UK   ISSN 0268-1641
ATRIAL NATRIURETIC FACTORS. 1986. s-m. £95. Sheffield University Biomedical Information Service (SUBIS), The University, Sheffield S10 2TN, England. TEL 0742-768555. FAX 0742-739826. TELEX 547216-UGSHEF-G.
    Description: Current awareness service for researchers in clinical and life sciences. Studies atrial natriuretic factors: peptides, cardionatrin, atriopeptin, and cardiac endocrinology.

616.462   UK   ISSN 0005-4216
BALANCE. 1935. bi-m. membership. British Diabetic Association, 10 Queen Anne St., London W1M 0BD, England. FAX 01-637-3644. Ed. Lesley Hallett. adv.; bk.rev.; illus.; circ. 140,000.
    Description: For people with diabetes and their families: medical and dietary information and research news.

616.4   US
BASIC & CLINICAL ENDOCRINOLOGY. 1981. irreg., vol.9, 1987. Marcel Dekker, Inc., 270 Madison Ave., New York, NY 10016. TEL 212-696-9000. FAX 212-685-4540. TELEX 421419. **Indexed:** Chem.Abstr.
   Refereed Serial

MEDICAL SCIENCES — ENDOCRINOLOGY

616.4   NE   ISSN 0169-6009
CODEN: BOMIET
BONE AND MINERAL; an international journal of bone, mineral and calcium regulation research. (Text and summaries in English) 1986. 12/yr.(in 4 vols., 3 nos./vol.). fl.1344 (effective 1992). (International Conferences on Calcium Regulating Hormones, Inc.) Elsevier Science Publishers B.V., P.O. Box 211, 1000 AE Amsterdam, Netherlands.
TEL 020-5803911. FAX 020-5803598. TELEX 18582 ESPA NL. (Subscr. in U.S. and Canada to: Elsevier Science Publishing Co., Inc., Box 882, Madison Sq. Sta., New York, NY10159. TEL 212-989-5800) Ed. David V. Cohn. adv.; bk.rev. (back issues avail.; reprint service avail. from SWZ) **Indexed:** Chem.Abstr., Curr.Adv.Biochem., Excerp.Med., Ind.Vet., NRN, Small Anim.Abstr., Vet.Bull.
—BLDSC shelfmark: 2247.335000.
Description: Publishes basic and clinical papers on the structure and development of bone and other mineralized tissues and on the biochemistry and physiology of factors and hormones that regulate bone metabolism.
Refereed Serial

616.46   US
BOUNTY DIABETESCARE GUIDE. a. Bounty Group, 2425 Pennington Rd., Trenton, NJ 08535.
TEL 609-737-3700. FAX 609-737-1803. adv.; circ. 360,000.
Description: Covers the practical aspects of controlling and managing diabetes. Aimed at newly-diagnosed adults.

CHRONOBIOLOGIA. see *BIOLOGY*

616.46   US
CLINICAL DIABETES. 1983. bi-m. $15. American Diabetes Association, Inc., 1660 Duke St., Alexandria, VA 22314. TEL 703-549-1500. FAX 703-836-7439. TELEX 901132. Ed. Dr. Marvin Levin. circ. 70,000.
●Also available online. Vendor(s): BRS.
Refereed Serial

616.4   UK   ISSN 0300-0664
CODEN: CLECAP
CLINICAL ENDOCRINOLOGY. 1972. m. £190 (foreign £215). Blackwell Scientific Publications Ltd., Osney Mead, Oxford OX2 0EL, England.
TEL 0865-240201. FAX 0865-721205. TELEX 83355-MEDBOK-G. Eds. D.C. Anderson, J.S. Jenkins. adv.; bk.rev.; index; circ. 1,280. (also avail. in microform from MIM; back issues avail.; reprint service avail. from ISI) **Indexed:** Abstr.Inter.Med., ASCA, Biol.Abstr., Biotech.Abstr., Chem.Abstr., Curr.Adv.Ecol.Sci., Curr.Adv.Genetics & Molec.Biol., Curr.Cont., Dairy Sci.Abstr., Excerp.Med., Ind.Med., Ind.Sci.Rev., INIS Atomind., Nutr.Abstr., Sci.Cit.Ind.
—BLDSC shelfmark: 3286.278000.

616.462   US   ISSN 0149-5992
CLINICAL PRACTICE RECOMMENDATIONS. (Supplement to: Diabetes Care) a. $8. American Diabetes Association, Inc., 1660 Duke St., Alexandria, VA 22314. TEL 703-549-1500. FAX 703-836-7439. TELEX 901132.

616.4   US   ISSN 0160-242X
COMPREHENSIVE ENDOCRINOLOGY. 1978. irreg. Raven Press, 1185 Ave. of the Americas, New York, NY 10036. TEL 212-930-9500. FAX 212-869-3495. Ed. Luciano Martini.
Refereed Serial

616.4   SZ   ISSN 0255-7983
CONCEPTS IN IMMUNOPATHOLOGY; series in immunoregulation research. 1985. irreg. price varies. S. Karger AG, Allschwilerstr. 10, P.O. Box, CH-4009 Basel, Switzerland. TEL 061-3061111. FAX 061-3061234. TELEX CH-962652. Eds. J.M. Cruse, R.E. Lewis Jr.
—BLDSC shelfmark: 3399.413100.

616.4   US
CONTEMPORARY ENDOCRINOLOGY. 1976. irreg., vol.2, 1985. Plenum Publishing Corp., 233 Spring St., New York, NY 10013-1578. TEL 212-620-8000. FAX 212-463-0742. TELEX 23-421139. Ed. Sidney H. Ingbar. (back issues avail.) **Indexed:** Chem.Abstr.
Formerly: Year in Endocrinology.
Refereed Serial

616.4   US   ISSN 0193-340X
RC627.5   CODEN: CONMDM
CONTEMPORARY METABOLISM; analytical reviews of basic & clinical progress. 1976. irreg., vol.2, 1982. Plenum Publishing Corp., 233 Spring St., New York, NY 10013-1578. TEL 212-620-8000.
FAX 212-463-0742. TELEX 23-421139. Ed. Norbert Freinkel.
Formerly: Year in Metabolism (ISSN 0147-4189)
Refereed Serial

616.4   GW   ISSN 0933-002X
CORTISON SPIEGEL. 1988. q. p M I Verlag GmbH, August-Schanz-Str. 21, 6000 Frankfurt a.M. 50, Germany. TEL 069-5480000. Ed. E. Merck. circ. 60,000. (back issues avail.)

CURRENT ADVANCES IN ENDOCRINOLOGY & METABOLISM. see *MEDICAL SCIENCES — Abstracting, Bibliographies, Statistics*

616.4   NE
CURRENT ENDOCRINOLOGY. 1981. irreg., latest 1986. price varies. Elsevier Science Publishers B.V., Books Division, P.O. Box 211, 1000 AE Amsterdam, Netherlands. TEL 020-5803911.
FAX 020-5803705. TELEX 18582 ESPA NL. (Subscr. in U.S. and Canada to: Elsevier Science Publishing Co., Inc., Box 882, Madison Sq. Sta., New York, NY 10159. TEL 212-989-5800) (reprint service avail. from ISI)
Refereed Serial

CURRENT HEPATOLOGY. see *MEDICAL SCIENCES*

616.4   US   ISSN 0091-7397
RC648.A1   CODEN: CTEEAJ
CURRENT TOPICS IN EXPERIMENTAL ENDOCRINOLOGY. 1972. irreg., vol.5, 1983. Academic Press, Inc., 1250 Sixth Ave., San Diego, CA 92101.
TEL 619-231-0926. FAX 619-699-6715. Eds. L. Martini, V.H.T. James. (reprint service avail. from ISI) **Indexed:** Biol.Abstr., Curr.Adv.Ecol.Sci., Excerp.Med., Ind.Med.
—BLDSC shelfmark: 3504.883000.
Refereed Serial

CURRENT TOPICS IN NEUROENDOCRINOLOGY. see *MEDICAL SCIENCES — Psychiatry And Neurology*

616.4   NE
DEVELOPMENTS IN ENDOCRINOLOGY. 1977. irreg., vol.16, 1985. price varies. Elsevier Science Publishers B.V., Books Division, P.O. Box 211, 1000 AE Amsterdam, Netherlands. TEL 020-5803911. FAX 020-5803705. TELEX 18582 ESPA NL. (Subscr. in U.S. and Canada to: Elsevier Science Publishing Co., Inc., Box 882, Madison Sq. Sta., New York, NY 10159. TEL 212-989-5800) **Indexed:** Chem.Abstr.
Refereed Serial

616.46   IT   ISSN 0394-901X
DIABETE. 1989. q. L.80000($80) (Italian Society of Diabetology) Editrice Kurtis s.r.l., Via L. Zoja, 30, 20153 Milan, Italy. TEL 02-48202740.
FAX 02-48201219. Ed. Riccardo Vigneri.

616.462   FR   ISSN 0338-1684
CODEN: DIMEDU
DIABETE & METABOLISME. (Text in English, French) 1975. bi-m. 155 ECU($190) (typically set in Jan.). Masson, 120 bd. St-Germain, 75280 Paris Cedex 06, France. TEL 1-46-34-21-60.
FAX 1-45-87-29-99. TELEX 202 671 F. Ed. G. Reach. adv.; illus.; index; circ. 1,000. (also avail. in microform from UMI; reprint service avail. from ISI) **Indexed:** Biol.Abstr., Chem.Abstr., Curr.Adv.Ecol.Sci., Curr.Cont., Excerp.Med., Ind.Med., Ind.Sci.Rev., Nutr.Abstr., Risk Abstr., Sci.Cit.Ind.
—BLDSC shelfmark: 3579.585000.
Formerly: Diabete (ISSN 0012-1770)

616.462   FI   ISSN 0046-0192
DIABETES. 1948. 10/yr. FIM 130($32) Finnish Diabetes Association, Kirjaniementie 15, 33680 Tampere, Finland. TEL 358-31-600-333.
FAX 358-31-600-462. Ed. Leena Etu-Seppala. adv.; illus.; circ. 50,000. **Indexed:** Abstr.Inter.Med., Curr.Adv.Biochem., NRN.
Description: Directed to diabetics.

616.462   US   ISSN 0012-1797
RC660.A1   CODEN: DIAEAZ
DIABETES. 1952. m. $90. American Diabetes Association, Inc., 1660 Duke St., Alexandria, VA 22314. TEL 703-549-1500. FAX 703-836-7439. TELEX 901132. Ed. Dr. R. Paul Robertson. adv.; abstr.; charts; illus.; index; circ. 9,000. (also avail. in microform from UMI; reprint service avail. from UMI) **Indexed:** Abstr.Hyg., Abstr.Inter.Med., Biol.Abstr., Biotech.Abstr., Chem.Abstr., Curr.Adv.Biochem., Curr.Adv.Cancer Res., Curr.Adv.Cell & Devel.Biol., Curr.Adv.Ecol.Sci., Curr.Adv.Genetics & Molec.Biol., Excerp.Med., Ind.Med., Ind.Sci.Rev., INIS Atomind., Nutr.Abstr., Sci.Cit.Ind, So.Pac.Per.Ind., Trop.Dis.Bull.
●Also available online. Vendor(s): BRS.
—BLDSC shelfmark: 3579.600000.
Refereed Serial

616.4   DK   ISSN 0901-3652
DIABETES; tidskrift for sukkersyge. 1941. 5/yr. DKK 100 to individuals; retirees Kr.50. Diabetesforeningen - Danish Diabetes Association, Filosofgangen 24, 500 Odense C, Denmark. TEL 66-12-90-06. FAX 65-91-49-08. circ. 40,000.

616.4   NE
DIABETES ANNUAL. 1985. a., latest vol.6, 1991. price varies. Elsevier Science Publishers B.V., Books Division, P.O. Box 211, 1000 AE Amsterdam, Netherlands. TEL 020-5803911.
FAX 020-5803705. TELEX 18582 ESPA NL. (Subscr. in U.S. and Canada to: Elsevier Science Publishing Co., Inc., Box 882, Madison Sq. Sta., New York, NY 10159. TEL 212-989-5800) Eds. K.G.M.M. Alberti, L.P. Krall.
Refereed Serial

616.462   US   ISSN 0149-5992
RC660.A1   CODEN: DICAD2
DIABETES CARE. (Suppl. avail.: Clinical Practice Recommendations) 1978. 10/yr. $65. American Diabetes Association, Inc., 1660 Duke St., Alexandria, VA 22314. TEL 703-549-1500. FAX 703-836-7439. TELEX 901132. Ed. Dr. David C. Robbins. adv.; bk.rev.; charts; illus.; stat.; index; circ. 11,500. (also avail. in microform from UMI; reprint service avail. from UMI) **Indexed:** Abstr.Inter.Med., Chem.Abstr, CINAHL, Curr.Cont., Excerp.Med., Ind.Med., Ind.Sci.Rev., NRN, Sci.Cit.Ind.
●Also available online. Vendor(s): BRS.
—BLDSC shelfmark: 3579.600600.
Refereed Serial

616.4   US
DIABETES COUNTDOWN. 1982. q. $25. Juvenile Diabetes Foundation International, 432 Park Ave. S., New York, NY 10016. TEL 212-889-7575.
FAX 212-532-8791. Ed. Sandy Dylak. adv.; circ. 240,042.
Description: Offers the latest information in diabetes research and treatment, as the foundation strives for a cure.

616.462   CN   ISSN 0703-5764
DIABETES DIALOGUE. 1954. q. Can.$15 membership. Canadian Diabetes Association, 78 Bond St., Toronto, Ont. M5B 2J8, Canada.
TEL 416-362-4440. FAX 416-362-6849. Ed. Dr. Robert Silver. adv.; bk.rev.; illus.; circ. 59,398. (also avail. in audio cassette)
Formerly (until vol.24, 1977): C D A Newsletter (ISSN 0007-8018)
Description: News for and about people with diabetes: treatments and life styles.

616.462   US   ISSN 0095-8301
RC660.A1
DIABETES FORECAST. 1948. m. $24. American Diabetes Association, Inc., 1660 Duke St., Alexandria, VA 22314. TEL 703-549-1500.
FAX 703-836-7439. TELEX 901132. Ed. Dr. Philip Levy. adv.; bk.rev.; charts; illus.; circ. 225,000. (reprint service avail.) **Indexed:** CHNI, Hlth.Ind.
—BLDSC shelfmark: 3579.600670.
Formerly: A.D.A. Forecast (ISSN 0001-0847)

616.462   US   ISSN 0893-5939
DIABETES IN THE NEWS. 1962. 6/yr. $12. Miles Laboratories, Inc., Ames Education Service, 1201 N. Clark St., Chicago, IL 60610. FAX 312-664-9770. Ed. Morton B. Stone. adv.; bk.rev.; circ. 90,000.
Indexed: Hlth.Ind.
Former titles: D I T N: Diabetes in the News (ISSN 8750-1244); (Until 1972): Diabetes in the News (ISSN 0012-1800)

MEDICAL SCIENCES — ENDOCRINOLOGY

616.462   GW   ISSN 0341-8812
DIABETES-JOURNAL. 1951. m. DM.60. (Deutscher Diabetikerbund e.V.) Verlag Kirchheim und Co. GmbH, Kaiserstr. 41, Postfach 2524, 6500 Mainz, Germany. TEL 06131-671081. Ed. H. Mehnert. adv.; bk.rev.; charts; illus.; circ. 48,000. **Indexed:** Chem.Abstr.
—BLDSC shelfmark: 3579.600900.
Formerly: Diabetiker (ISSN 0012-1851)

DIABETES MELLITUS. see *MEDICAL SCIENCES*

616.4   UK   ISSN 0742-4221
CODEN: DMREEG
DIABETES - METABOLISM REVIEWS. 1985. q. $225 (effective 1992). John Wiley & Sons Ltd., Journals, Baffins Lane, Chichester, Sussex PO19 1UD, England. TEL 0243-779777. FAX 0423-775878. TELEX 86290-WIBOOK-G. Ed. D. Andreani. (also avail. in microform from RPI; reprint service avail. from SWZ) **Indexed:** Curr.Cont., Excerp.Med., INIS Atomind.
—BLDSC shelfmark: 3579.601900.
Description: Covers clinical and basic scientific advances in edocrinology, insulin secretion, resistance, ketone metabolism, obesity and lipid metabolism, pathogenesis and cellular action of insulin.

616.46 612.3   IT   ISSN 0394-3402
DIABETES, NUTRITION & METABOLISM, CLINICAL AND EXPERIMENTAL. (Text in English) 1988. q. L.80000($80) Editrice Kurtis s.r.l., Via. L. Zoja, 30, 20153 Milan, Italy. TEL 02-48202740. FAX 02-48201219. Ed. P. Brunetti.
—BLDSC shelfmark: 3579.601950.
Description: Publishes original papers on diabetes, nutrition and metabolism research.

616.4   NE   ISSN 0168-8227
CODEN: DRCPE9
DIABETES RESEARCH AND CLINICAL PRACTICE. (Text in English) 12/yr.(in 4 vols.; 3 nos./vol.) fl.1524 (effective 1992). (International Diabetes Federation) Elsevier Science Publishers B.V., P.O. Box 211, 1000 AE Amsterdam, Netherlands. TEL 020-5803911. FAX 020-5803598. TELEX 18582 ESPA NL. (Subscr. in U.S. and Canada to: Elsevier Science Publishing Co. Inc., Box 882, Madison Sq. Sta., New York, NY 10159. TEL 212-989-5800) Ed. S. Baba. (back issues avail.) **Indexed:** Excerp.Med., NRN.
—BLDSC shelfmark: 3579.603700.
Description: Covers diabetes research, experimental biology, molecular biology and immunology, clinical practice, epidemiology and diabetes education.
Refereed Serial

371.9 616.4 613.7   US   ISSN 0741-6253
CODEN: DSMAEL
DIABETES SELF-MANAGEMENT. 1983. bi-m. $14.97. R.A. Rapaport Publishing, Inc., 150 W. 22nd St., New York, NY 10011. TEL 212-989-0200. FAX 212-989-4786. (Subscr. to: Box 52890, Boulder, CO 80322-2890) Ed. James Hazlett. adv.; charts; illus.; circ. 180,000 (paid); 50,000 (controlled). (also avail. in audio cassette; back issues avail.)
Description: Practical and instructive "how-to" information for people with diabetes.

616.4   US   ISSN 1040-9165
RC660.A1
DIABETES SPECTRUM; from research to practice. 1988. bi-m. $30. American Diabetes Association, Inc., 1660 Duke St., Alexandria, VA 22314. TEL 703-549-1500. FAX 703-836-7439. TELEX 901132. Ed.Bd. adv.; bk.rev.; illus.; circ. 7,500.
Refereed Serial

616.462   US
DIABETES UPDATE. 1955. 4/yr. $10 to non-members (foreign $20). Greater Boston Diabetes Society Inc., 1330 Beacon St., Ste. 345, Brookline, MA 02146. TEL 617-731-2972. Ed. Thelma Gruenbaum. adv.; bk.rev.; circ. 4,000.
Former titles (until 1985): Diabetes Dialogue; Diabetes Newsletter (ISSN 0012-1827)
Description: News, information, and announcements pertaining to the members and activities of the Greater Boston Diabetes Society with medical and nutritional information on inhibiting and controlling the disorder and information about diet and exercise to help prevent or delay the onset of diabetes.

616.462   II   ISSN 0970-4035
DIABETIC ASSOCIATION OF INDIA. JOURNAL. (Text in English) 1960. q. Rs.50. Diabetic Association of India, Maneckji Wadia Bldg., 1st Fl., 127, Mahatma Gandhi Rd., Fort., Bombay 400 001, India. TEL 273813. Ed. R.D. Lele. adv.; bk.rev.; illus.; circ. 3,000. **Indexed:** Biol.Abstr., Excerp.Med.
—BLDSC shelfmark: 4734.541000.
Formerly (until 1974): Madhumeh (ISSN 0024-9424)

616.46 616.3   UK   ISSN 0742-3071
610.73 CODEN: DIMEEV
DIABETIC MEDICINE. 1984. 10/yr. $240 (effective 1992). (British Diabetic Association) John Wiley & Sons Ltd., Journals, Baffins Lane, Chichester, Sussex PO19 1UD, England. TEL 0243 779777. FAX 0243-775878. TELEX 86290 WIBOOK G. Ed. A. Boulton. adv.; bk.rev. (reprint service avail. from SWZ) **Indexed:** Behav.Med.Abstr., Curr.Adv.Ecol.Sci., Curr.Cont., Excerp.Med., Ind.Med., NRN, Triticale Abstr.
—BLDSC shelfmark: 3579.606000.
Description: Designed as an information exchange on all aspects of diabetes mellitus and aims to interest everyone helping diabetic patients whether through fundamental research or better health care.

616.46   NO   ISSN 0419-0505
DIABETIKEREN. 1950. 6/yr. NOK 180. Norges Diabetesforbund - Norwegian Diabetic Association, Ostensjoveien 29, 0661 Oslo 6, Norway. TEL 02-654550. FAX 02-630688. Ed. Georg Gramfjeld. adv.; bk.rev.; circ. 21,000.

616.462   GW   ISSN 0012-186X
RC660.A1 CODEN: DBTGAJ
DIABETOLOGIA; clinical and experimental diabetes and metabolism. 1965. 12/yr. DM.498($280) (European Association for the Study of Diabetes) Springer-Verlag, Heidelberger Platz 3, D-1000 Berlin 33, Germany. TEL 030-8207-1. (Also Heidelberg, Tokyo, Vienna, and New York) Ed. C. Hellerstroem. adv.; bibl.; charts; illus.; tr.lit. (also avail. in microform from UMI; back issues avail.; reprint service avail. from ISI) **Indexed:** Behav.Med.Abstr., Biol.Abstr., Biotech.Abstr., Chem.Abstr, Curr.Adv.Cell & Devel.Biol., Curr.Adv.Ecol.Sci., Curr.Adv.Genetics & Molec.Biol., Curr.Cont., Excerp.Med., Ind.Med., Ind.Sci.Rev., INIS Atomind., NRN, Nutr.Abstr., Sci.Cit.Ind., Small.Anim.Abstr.
—BLDSC shelfmark: 3579.615000.
Description: Reports of clinical and experimental work on all aspects of diabetes research and related medicine, metabolic diseases, and physiology.

616.46 619   CI   ISSN 0350-1892
DIABETOLOGIA CROATICA. (Text and summaries in Croatian, English) 1972. q. 300 din.($12) Vuk Vrhovac Institute for Diabetes, Endocrinology and Metabolic Diseases, Krijesnice b.b., 41000 Zagreb, Croatia. Ed. Zdenko Skrabalo. bk.rev.; circ. 1,000. **Indexed:** Biol.Abstr., Chem.Abstr, Excerp.Med.
—BLDSC shelfmark: 0050.533000.

616.4 636.089   US   ISSN 0739-7240
CODEN: DANEEE
DOMESTIC ANIMAL ENDOCRINOLOGY. 1984. q. $35 to individuals; institutions $75. (Auburn University, College of Veterinary Medicine) Butterworth - Heinemann Ltd. (Subsidiary of: Reed International PLC), 80 Montvale Ave., Stoneham, MA 02180. TEL 617-438-8464. FAX 617-279-4851. TELEX 880052. adv.; charts; illus.; stat.; index; circ. 320. **Indexed:** Anim.Breed.Abstr., Biol.Abstr., Chem.Abstr., Curr.Cont., Dairy Sci.Abstr., Ind.Vet., Pig News & Info., Poult.Abstr., Sci.Abstr., Small Anim.Abstr., Vet.Bull.
—BLDSC shelfmark: 3616.884000.
Refereed Serial

616.4   UA   ISSN 0070-9506
EGYPTIAN SOCIETY OF ENDOCRINOLOGY AND METABOLISM. JOURNAL.* (Text in English) 1955-1969; resumed 1971. irreg. Egyptian Society of Endocrinology and Metabolism, 42 Sharia Kasr el-Aini, Cairo, Egypt.

616.4   US   ISSN 1046-3976
ENDOCRINE PATHOLOGY. 1989. q. $250. Blackwell Scientific Publications Inc., Three Cambridge Center, Ste. 208, Cambridge, MA 02142-1413. TEL 617-225-0401. FAX 617-225-0412. Eds. S. Asa, K. Kovacs.
—BLDSC shelfmark: 3740.460000.
Description: Publishes articles on clinical and basic aspects of endocrine disorders. Concerned with histopathology and pathology of hormone producing cells.

616.4   CS
CODEN: EREGE
ENDOCRINE REGULATIONS. (Text and summaries in English) 1967. q. 90 Kcs.($19) (Slovenska Akademia Vied) Veda, Publishing House of the Slovak Academy of Sciences, Klemensova 19, 814 30 Bratislava, Czechoslovakia. (Dist. in Western countries by: Karger-Libri AG, Scientific Booksellers, Arnold-Bocklin-Strasse 25, CH-4000 Basel 11, Switzerland) Eds. L. Macho, P. Langer. bk.rev.; charts; illus.; stat.; index; circ. 800. **Indexed:** Biol.Abstr., Chem.Abstr., Curr.Adv.Ecol.Sci., Curr.Cont., Dairy Sci.Abstr., Endocrin.Ind., Excerp.Med., Ind.Med., Ind.Sci.Rev., Ind.Vet., INIS Atomind., Nutr.Abstr., Pig News & Info., Ref.Zh., Sci.Cit.Ind, Vet.Bull.
Formerly (until 1991): Endocrinologia Experimentalis (ISSN 0013-7200)
Description: Publishes original works that deal with the contemporary problems of experimental endocrinology of morphologic, physiologic, biochemical, pathophysiological or pharmacologic character.

616.4   US   ISSN 0743-5800
QP187.A1 CODEN: ENRSE8
ENDOCRINE RESEARCH. 1964. 4/yr. $310. Marcel Dekker Journals, 270 Madison Ave., New York, NY 10016. TEL 212-696-9000. FAX 212-685-4540. TELEX 421419. (Subscr. to: Box 10018, Church St. Sta., New York, NY 10249) Ed. Paul Davis. adv. (also avail. in microform from RPI) **Indexed:** Anim.Breed.Abstr., ASCA, Biol.Abstr., Chem.Abstr, Curr.Adv.Ecol.Sci., Curr.Cont., Dairy Sci.Abstr., Excerp.Med., Ind.Med., Ind.Sci.Rev., INIS Atomind., Nutr.Abstr., Pig News & Info., Sci.Cit.Ind.
Formerly: Endocrine Research Communications (ISSN 0093-6391); Supersedes: Endocrinological Communications.
Refereed Serial

616.4   US   ISSN 0163-769X
QP187.A1 CODEN: ERVIDP
ENDOCRINE REVIEWS. 1980. q. $65 to individuals; institutions $85. (Endocrine Society) Williams & Wilkins, 428 E. Preston St., Baltimore, MD 21202. TEL 301-528-4000. FAX 301-528-4312. Ed. Dr. Andres Negro Vilar. circ. 4,800. (also avail. in microform) **Indexed:** Anim.Breed.Abstr., Chem.Abstr, Curr.Adv.Ecol.Sci., Excerp.Med., Ind.Med., Ind.Sci.Rev., Pig News & Info., Poult.Abstr., Sci.Cit.Ind.
—BLDSC shelfmark: 3740.480000.
Description: Review articles explore clinical and experimental endocrinology topics.

616.4   AT   ISSN 0312-4738
ENDOCRINE SOCIETY OF AUSTRALIA. PROCEEDINGS. 1958. a. Aus.$5. Endocrine Society of Australia, c/o Endocrine Unit, Royal Adelaide Hospital, Adelaide, S.A. 5000, Australia. Ed. P.E. Harding. adv.; circ. 650. **Indexed:** Biol.Abstr., Excerp.Med.

616.4   SP   ISSN 0211-2299
ENDOCRINOLOGIA. (Text in Spanish; summaries in English) 1953. m. (10/yr). 5500 ptas.($57) to non-members (Sociedad Espanola de Endocrinologia) Ediciones Doyma S.A., Traversera de Gracia, 17-21, 08021 Barcelona, Spain. TEL 200 07 11. FAX 209-11-36. TELEX 51964 INK-E. Ed. E. Vilardell Vinas. adv.: page 135000 ptas.; trim 210 x 280; adv. contact: Marta Cisa. circ. 3,100. (reprint service avail. from UMI) **Indexed:** Excerp.Med., Ind.Med.Esp.
—BLDSC shelfmark: 3740.485000.
Description: Publishes clinical and experimental research in endocrinology.

MEDICAL SCIENCES — ENDOCRINOLOGY

616.4 618.92   XV   ISSN 0351-1677
ENDOCRINOLOGIA IUGOSLAVICA. (Text in Serbo-Croatian; summaries in English) 1977. s-a. 1800 din.($20) (Raziskovalna Skupnost Slovenija) Tiskarna Tone Tomsic, Gregorciceua 25a, 61000 Ljubljana, Slovenia. (Subscr. to: Nusa Bambic, Dispanzer za Diabetike, UKC Njegoseva 4, 61000 Ljubljana, Slovenia) Ed. Andreja Kocijancic. adv.; bk.rev.; circ. 400.
Description: Research reports on clinical endocrinology and diabetology for internists, endocrinologists, gynecologists and pediatricians.

616.4   JA   ISSN 0013-7219
CODEN: ECJPAE
ENDOCRINOLOGIA JAPONICA/NIHON NAIBUNPI GAKKAI. (Text in English) 1954. bi-m. 10000 Yen($100) Japan Endocrine Society - Nihon Naibunpi Gakkai, Department of Veterinary Physiology, Veterinary Medical Science, University of Tokyo, 1-1-1 Yayoi Bunkyo-ku, Tokyo 113, Japan. FAX 011-2-3-815-4266. (Overseas Dist. by: Japan Publications Trading Co., Ltd., P.O. Box 5030, Tokyo International, Tokyo 100-31, Japan) Michio Takahashi. adv.; bk.rev.; abstr.; charts; illus.; index; circ. 1,000. (back issues avail.) **Indexed:** Anim.Breed.Abstr., Biol.Abstr., Chem.Abstr., Curr.Adv.Ecol.Sci., Curr.Cont., Dairy Sci.Abstr., Dent.Ind., Excerp.Med., Ind.Med., Ind.Sci.Rev., Ind.Vet., INIS Atomind., Nutr.Abstr., Sci.Cit.Ind., Vet.Bull.
—BLDSC shelfmark: 3741.000000.

616.4   US   ISSN 1051-2144
▼**THE ENDOCRINOLOGIST.** 1991. bi-m. $65 to individuals; institutions $97. Williams & Wilkins, 428 E. Preston St., Baltimore, MD 21202. TEL 301-528-4000. FAX 301-528-4321. Ed. Dr. Lynn Loriaux.
—BLDSC shelfmark: 3741.750000.
Description: Directed exclusively to clinicians interested in practical applications of new discoveries in endocrinology, diabetes, and metabolism.
Refereed Serial

616.4   US   ISSN 0013-7227
QP187   CODEN: ENDOAO
ENDOCRINOLOGY. 1917. m. $110 to individuals; institutions $170. (Endocrine Society) Williams & Wilkins, 428 E. Preston St., Baltimore, MD 21202. TEL 301-528-4000. FAX 301-528-4312. Ed. P. Michael Conn. adv.; bibl.; charts; illus.; index; circ. 5,800. (also avail. in microform; reprint service avail.) **Indexed:** Anim.Breed.Abstr., Biol.Abstr., Biotech.Abstr., Chem.Abstr., Curr.Adv.Biochem., Curr.Adv.Cancer Res., Curr.Adv.Cell & Devel.Biol., Curr.Adv.Ecol.Sci., Curr.Adv.Genetics & Molec.Biol., Curr.Cont., Dairy Sci.Abstr., Dent.Ind., Excerp.Med., Ind.Med., Ind.Sci.Rev., Ind.Vet., INIS Atomind., Nutr.Abstr., Pig News & Info., Poult.Abstr., Sci.Cit.Ind., Small.Anim.Abstr., Soyabean Abstr., Trop.Dis.Bull., Vet.Bull.
—BLDSC shelfmark: 3742.000000.
Description: Covers all aspects of research on endocrine glands and their hormones.
Refereed Serial

616.4   US   ISSN 0889-8529
RC648.A1   CODEN: ECNAER
ENDOCRINOLOGY AND METABOLISM CLINICS. 1972. 4/yr. $84. W.B. Saunders Co., Curtis Center, Independence Square W., Philadelphia, PA 19106. TEL 215-238-7800. Ed. Mary Mulroy. **Indexed:** Biol.Abstr., Chem.Abstr., Curr.Adv.Ecol.Sci., Dent.Ind., Excerp.Med., Ind.Med., Ind.Sci.Rev., Nutr.Abstr., Sci.Cit.Ind.
—BLDSC shelfmark: 3743.052000. **Indexed:**
Formerly: Clinics in Endocrinology and Metabolism (ISSN 0300-595X)

616.4   GW   ISSN 0721-667X
ENDOKRINOLOGIE - INFORMATIONEN. (Text in German; summaries in English) 1977. bi-m. DM.60. (Deutsche Gesellschaft fuer Endokrinologie) Demeter Verlag, Wuermstr. 13, 8032 Graefelfing, Germany. TEL 089-852033. FAX 089-8543347. Ed. Dr. O.-A. Mueller. circ. 1,400.

616.4   PL   ISSN 0423-104X
CODEN: EDPKA2
ENDOKRYNOLOGIA POLSKA. (Text in Polish; summaries in English and Russian) 1951. bi-m. $30. (Polskie Towarzystwo Endokrynologiczne - Polish Endocrinological Association) Ossolineum, Publishing House of the Polish Academy of Sciences, Rynek 9, 50-106 Wroclaw, Poland. (Dist. by: Ars Polona, Krakowskie Przedmiescie 7, 00-068 Warsaw, Poland) Ed. Zbigniew Szybinski. adv.; bk.rev.; bibl.; charts; illus.; index. **Indexed:** Anim.Breed.Abstr., Biol.Abstr., Chem.Abstr., Dent.Ind., Excerp.Med., Ind.Med., INIS Atomind.
—BLDSC shelfmark: 3743.300000.
Description: Papers on practical and theoretical aspects of Polish research on endocrinology.

ENZYME; metabolism, experimental and clinical enzymology. see *BIOLOGY — Biological Chemistry*

616.4   GW   ISSN 0232-7384
QP187.A1   CODEN: EXCEDS
EXPERIMENTAL AND CLINICAL ENDOCRINOLOGY. 1928. 6/yr. DM.84. Johann Ambrosius Barth Verlag, Leipzig - Heidelberg, Salomonstr. 18b, 7010 Leipzig, Germany. TEL 70131. Ed. Guenter Doerner. adv.; abstr.; bibl.; charts; illus.; index. **Indexed:** Anim.Breed.Abstr., Biol.Abstr., Biotech.Abstr., Chem.Abstr., Curr.Adv.Cancer Res., Curr.Cont., Dairy Sci.Abstr., Dent.Ind., Dok.Arbeitsmed., Excerp.Med., Ind.Med., Ind.Sci.Rev., Ind.Vet., INIS Atomind., Nutr.Abstr., Pig News & Info., Sci.Cit.Ind., Vet.Bull.
—BLDSC shelfmark: 3838.630000.
Formerly: Endokrinologie (ISSN 0013-7251)

616.4   SZ   ISSN 0251-5342
CODEN: FDIADJ
FRONTIERS IN DIABETES. (Text in English) irreg. price varies. S. Karger AG, Allschwilerstr. 10, P.O. Box, CH-4009 Basel, Switzerland. TEL 061-3061111. FAX 061-3061234. TELEX CH 962652. Ed. F. Belfiore. (reprint service avail. from ISI) **Indexed:** Biol.Abstr.
—BLDSC shelfmark: 4042.003000.

616.4 616.8   US   ISSN 0532-7466
FRONTIERS IN NEUROENDOCRINOLOGY. q. $150 to individuals; institutions $195. Raven Press, 1185 Ave. of the Americas, New York, NY 10036. TEL 212-930-9500. FAX 212-869-3495. TELEX 640073. Eds. L. Martini, William F. Ganong. **Indexed:** Biol.Abstr., Chem.Abstr., Curr.Cont., Ind.Sci.Rev., Sci.Cit.Ind.
—BLDSC shelfmark: 4042.040000.
Description: Contains review coverage of major clinical issues.
Refereed Serial

616.4   SZ   ISSN 0301-3073
CODEN: FHRSA7
FRONTIERS OF HORMONE RESEARCH. (Text in English) 1972. irreg. price varies. S. Karger AG, Allschwilerstr. 10, P.O. Box, CH-4009 Basel, Switzerland. TEL 061-3061111. FAX 061-3061234. TELEX CH 962652. Ed. Tj.B. van Wimersma Greidanus. (reprint service avail. from ISI) **Indexed:** Biol.Abstr., Chem.Abstr., Curr.Cont., Ind.Med., Ind.Sci.Rev., Ind.Vet., Sci.Cit.Ind., Small Anim.Abstr., Vet.Bull.
—BLDSC shelfmark: 4042.025000.
Formerly: Monographs in Hormone Research (ISSN 0077-0868)

GASTROINTESTINAL RADIOLOGY; a journal of diagnostic imaging. see *MEDICAL SCIENCES — Radiology And Nuclear Medicine*

616.4   US   ISSN 0016-6480
QP187   CODEN: GCENA5
GENERAL AND COMPARATIVE ENDOCRINOLOGY; an international journal. 1961. m. $584 (foreign $672). Academic Press, Inc., Journal Division, 1250 Sixth Ave., San Diego, CA 92101. TEL 619-230-1840. FAX 619-699-6800. TELEX 181726. Eds. Aubrey Gorbman, Ian W. Henderson. adv.; bk.rev.; bibl.; charts; illus.; index. (back issues avail.) **Indexed:** Anim.Breed.Abstr., Biol.Abstr., Chem.Abstr., Curr.Adv.Cell & Devel.Biol., Curr.Adv.Ecol.Sci., Curr.Cont., Excerp.Med., Helminthol.Abstr., Ind.Med., Ind.Sci.Rev., INIS Atomind., Nutr.Abstr., Poult.Abstr., Rev.Appl.Entomol., Vet.Bull.
—BLDSC shelfmark: 4097.400000.
Description: Devoted to basic endocrinological research; emphasizes fundamental research; features occasional brief reviews that deals with a particular field or problem.
Refereed Serial

616.46   IT   ISSN 0391-7525
GIORNALE ITALIANO DI DIABETOLOGIA. (Text in Italian; summaries in English, Italian, Spanish) 1981. q. L.30000($35) (Boehringer Mannheim Italia S.p.A.) Pacini Editore s.r.l., Via Gherardesca 1, 56014 Ospedaletto (Pisa), Italy. TEL 050-982439. FAX 050-983906. TELEX 321339 BMM I. Ed. G. Gentili. adv.; bk.rev.; abstr.; charts; illus.; stat.; index; circ. 2,300. **Indexed:** Chem.Abstr., Excerp.Med.
—BLDSC shelfmark: 4178.214300.
Description: Features original articles, reviews and edited letters on topics of physiopathology, clinics, and the therapy of diabetic illnesses. Includes columns on domestic and international cultural, social and sanitary-political activities for the diabetic.

GROWTH FACTORS & CYTOKINES. see *MEDICAL SCIENCES — Allergology And Immunology*

GROWTH PROMOTING HORMONES. see *BIOLOGY — Biological Chemistry*

616.4   UK   ISSN 0956-523X
CODEN: GREGEP
▼**GROWTH REGULATION.** 1991. q. £79($166) to individuals; institutions £99($209). Churchill Livingstone Medical Journals, Robert Stevenson House, 1-3 Baxter's Pl., Leith Walk, Edinburgh EH1 3AF, Scotland. TEL 031-556-2424. FAX 031-558-1278. (Subscr. to: Longman Group UK, Ltd., Journals Dept. P.O. Box 77, Harlow, Essex CM19 5BQ, England. TEL 0279-623760; U.S. subscr. to: Churchill Livingstone, 650 Ave. of the Americas, New York, NY 10011. TEL 212-206-5000) Ed. D. Schuster.
—BLDSC shelfmark: 4223.047000.
Description: Publishes research articles and topical mini-reviews concerning all aspects of growth-promoting and growth-inhibiting hormones and factors, whether in whole animals or in tissues and cells.
Refereed Serial

616.4   JA   ISSN 0533-6724
QP187.A1   CODEN: GUSYAU
GUNMA SYMPOSIA ON ENDOCRINOLOGY. (Text in English) 1964. a. 5000 Yen. (Gunma University, Faculty of Medicine - Gunma Daigaku Igakubu) Center for Academic Publications, Japan, 2-4-16 Yayoi, Bunkyo-ku, Tokyo 113, Japan. FAX 03-817-5830. (Co-publisher: V S P, P.O. Box 346, 3700 AH Zeist, Netherlands) Ed.Bd. circ. 900. **Indexed:** Biol.Abstr.

616.46   US
HEALTH-O-GRAM. 1981. s-a. $6. Sugarfree Center for Diabetics, 13715 Burbank Blvd., Box 114, Van Nuys, CA 91408. TEL 818-994-1093. Eds. June Biermann, Barbara Toohey. adv.; bk.rev.; circ. 150,000.

616.4   US
HOMEOSTASIS QUARTERLY. 1971. q. $5. Hypoglycemia Foundation, Inc., Adrenal Metabolic Research Society, 153 Pawling Ave., Troy, NY 12180. Ed. Marilyn Hamilton Light. bk.rev.; circ. 5,000. (tabloid format)

MEDICAL SCIENCES — ENDOCRINOLOGY

616.4   GW   ISSN 0018-5043
QP801.H7   CODEN: HMMRA2
HORMONE AND METABOLIC RESEARCH. (Supplement Series (ISSN 0170-5903)) (Text in English, French and German; summaries in English) 1969. m. DM.360. (German Society of Endocrinology) Georg Thieme Verlag, Ruedigerstr. 14, Postfach 104853, 7000 Stuttgart 10, Germany. TEL 0711-8931-0. FAX 0711-8931298. Eds. E.F. Pfeiffer, G.M. Reaven. adv.; bibl.; charts; illus.; stat.; index; circ. 1,300. (also avail. in microform from UMI; reprint service avail. from UMI) **Indexed:** Anim.Breed.Abstr., Biol.Abstr., Biotech.Abstr., Chem.Abstr., Curr.Adv.Biochem., Curr.Adv.Cell & Devel.Biol., Curr.Adv.Ecol.Sci., Curr.Cont., Dairy Sci.Abstr., Dent.Ind., Excerp.Med., Ind.Med., Ind.Sci.Rev., Ind.Vet., INIS Atomind., Nutr.Abstr., Pig News & Info., Poult.Abstr., Risk Abstr., Sci.Cit.Ind., Vet.Bull.
—BLDSC shelfmark: 4327.300000.

616.4   SZ   ISSN 0301-0163
QP187.A1   CODEN: HRMRA3
HORMONE RESEARCH; international journal of experimental and clinical endocrinology. (Text in English) 1970. 12/yr.(2 vols.) 398 Fr.($266) per vol. S. Karger AG, Allschwilerstr. 10, P.O. Box, CH-4009 Basel, Switzerland. TEL 061-3061111. FAX 061-3061234. TELEX CH 962652. Ed. J. Girard. adv.; bk.rev.; bibl.; charts; stat.; circ. 1,000. (also avail. in microform from RPI) **Indexed:** Anim.Breed.Abstr., Biol.Abstr., Biotech.Abstr., Chem.Abstr., Curr.Adv.Ecol.Sci., Curr.Cont., Dairy Sci.Abstr., Dent.Ind., Excerp.Med., Ind.Med., Ind.Sci.Rev., Nutr.Abstr., Pig News & Info., Sci.Cit.Ind.
—BLDSC shelfmark: 4327.400000.
Incorporates: Hormones (ISSN 0018-5051); Steroids and Lipids Research (ISSN 0300-0621); Which was formerly: Steroidologica (ISSN 0049-2221)

616.4 156   US   ISSN 0018-506X
QP187.A1   CODEN: HOBEAO
HORMONES AND BEHAVIOR. 1969. q. $169 (foreign $213). Academic Press, Inc., Journal Division, 1250 Sixth Ave., San Diego, CA 92101. TEL 619-230-1840. FAX 619-699-6800. TELEX 181726. Ed. Robert W. Goy. adv. (back issues avail.) **Indexed:** Abstr.Anthropol., Anim.Breed.Abstr., Biol.Abstr., Chem.Abstr., Curr.Adv.Ecol.Sci., Curr.Cont., Dairy.Sci.Abstr., Excerp.Med., Ind.Med., Ind.Sci.Rev., Mid.East: Abstr.& Ind., Nutr.Abstr., Poult.Abstr., Psychol.Abstr.
—BLDSC shelfmark: 4328.050000.
Description: Publishes original articles concerned with behavioral systems that are known to be hormonally influenced.
Refereed Serial

HUMAN REPRODUCTION. see *MEDICAL SCIENCES — Obstetrics And Gynecology*

616.33   JA   ISSN 0289-2057
I-BUNPI KENKYUKAISHI/JAPANESE SOCIETY OF GASTRIC SECRETION RESEARCH. PROCEEDINGS. Variant title: I-bunpi Kenkyukai Kiroku. (Text in Japanese) 1971. a. 2000 Yen. Japanese Society of Gastric Secretion Research - I-bunpi Kenkyukai, c/o Tokyo Jikaijai Ika Daigaku Dai-2 Geka, 25-8, 3-chome, Nishi-Shinbashi, Minato-ku, Tokyo 105, Japan. TEL 03-433-1111. FAX 03-435-1922. Eds. Teruaki Aoki, Fusahiro Nagao. adv.; circ. 1,000. (back issues avail.)

I C R D B CANCERGRAM: ENDOCRINE TUMORS - DIAGNOSIS, TREATMENT, PATHOPHYSIOLOGY. see *MEDICAL SCIENCES — Abstracting, Bibliographies, Statistics*

616.462   BE   ISSN 0306-4980
CODEN: IDFBD6
I D F BULLETIN. 3/yr. $25 includes I D F Newsletter. International Diabetes Federation, 40 Rue Washington, 1050 Brussels, Belgium. TEL 02-647-4414. FAX 02-640-8565. TELEX 65080 INAC B. (Co-sponsor: American Diabetes Association) Ed.Bd. adv.; bk.rev.; circ. 8,500. (back issues avail.)
—BLDSC shelfmark: 4362.460100.

616.462   BE
I D F DIRECTORY. 2nd ed., 1991. triennial. $30. International Diabetes Federation, 40 Rue Washington, 1050 Brussels, Belgium. TEL 02-647-4414. FAX 02-640-8565. TELEX 65080 INAC B.

616.462   BE
I D F NEWS BULLETIN. q. $25 includes I D F Bulletin. International Diabetes Federation, 40 Rue Washington, 1050 Brussels, Belgium. TEL 02-647-4414. FAX 02-640-8565. TELEX 65080 INAC B. Ed.Bd. circ. 8,500.

616.4   UK   ISSN 0142-8144
INSULIN AND GLUCAGON. 1979. s-m. £75. Sheffield University Biomedical Information Service (SUBIS), The University, Sheffield S10 2TN, England. TEL 0742-768555. FAX 0742-739826. TELEX 547216-UGSHEF-G.
Description: Current awareness service for researchers. Studies insulin and glucagon: cellular and extracellular effects and receptors.

616.462   BE
INTERNATIONAL DIABETES FEDERATION. TRIENNIAL REPORT. 1952. triennial, latest Washington, DC, 1991. fl.196($81.75) International Diabetes Federation, 40 Rue Washington, 1050 Brussels, Belgium. TEL 02-647-4414. FAX 02-6408565. TELEX 65080 INAC B.
Formerly: International Diabetes Federation. Proceedings of Congress (ISSN 0074-4522)

616.3   US   ISSN 0169-4197
CODEN: IJPNEX
INTERNATIONAL JOURNAL OF PANCREATOLOGY. 1986. bi-m. $280. (International Association of Pancreatology) Humana Press Inc., Box 2148, Clifton, NJ 07015. TEL 201-256-1699. FAX 201-256-8341. Ed. Parviz M. Pour. adv.; bk.rev.; abstr.; bibl.; charts; illus.; index. (back issues avail.) **Indexed:** Biol.Abstr., Curr.Cont., Excerp.Med., Ind.Med., Sci.Cit.Ind.
—BLDSC shelfmark: 4542.441000.
Description: Multidisciplinary forum for original research on exocrine and endocrine pancreas.
Refereed Serial

616.462   JA   ISSN 0021-437X
CODEN: TONYA4
JAPAN DIABETES SOCIETY. JOURNAL/TONYOBYO. (Text in Japanese; summaries in English) 1958. m. 20550 Yen($65) Japan Diabetes Society - Nihon Tonyobyo Gakkai, Sky Bldg., Rm. 403, 3-38-11 Hongo, Bunkyo-ku, Tokyo 113, Japan. Ed. Dr. Y. Kanazawa. adv.; charts; index; circ. 4,800. **Indexed:** Biol.Abstr., Chem.Abstr, Excerp.Med.
—BLDSC shelfmark: 4804.840000.
Formerly: Japan Diabetic Society. Journal.

616.4 574   JA   ISSN 0913-9036
CODEN: PJSEEU
JAPAN SOCIETY FOR COMPARATIVE ENDOCRINOLOGY. PROCEEDINGS. (Text in English) 1986. irreg., no.5, 1990. 3000 Yen. Japan Society for Comparative Endocrinology, c/o Zoology Institute, Faculty of Science, University of Tokyo, Bunkyo-ku, Tokyo 113, Japan. TEL 03-3812-2111. FAX 81-3-3816-1965. Ed. Tetsuya Hirano. circ. 600. (back issues avail.)
—BLDSC shelfmark: 6742.312000.

616.462   US
JOSLIN MAGAZINE. 1985. 4/yr. $25. Joslin Diabetes Center, Inc., One Joslin Pl., Boston, MA 02215. TEL 617-732-2415. FAX 617-732-2664. Ed. Julie F. Rafferty. illus.; circ. 17,000. (back issues avail.)
Former titles: Joslin Diabetes Center Newsletter; Joslin Diabetes Foundation. Newsletter (ISSN 0021-7611)
Description: Covers articles on patient care and research on diabetics and its complications.

616.4   US   ISSN 0021-972X
CODEN: JCEMAZ
JOURNAL OF CLINICAL ENDOCRINOLOGY AND METABOLISM. 1941. m. $105 to individuals; institutions $150. (Endocrine Society) Williams & Wilkins, 428 E. Preston St., Baltimore, MD 21202. TEL 301-528-4000. FAX 301-528-4312. Ed. Dr. Lewis E. Braverman. adv.; charts; illus.; circ. 9,400. (also avail. in microform; reprint service avail.) **Indexed:** Behav.Med.Abstr., Biol.Abstr., Biotech.Abstr., Chem.Abstr., Curr.Adv.Biochem., Curr.Adv.Cancer Res., Curr.Adv.Cell & Devel.Biol., Curr.Adv.Genetics & Molec.Biol., Curr.Cont., Dairy Sci.Abstr., Dent.Ind., Excerp.Med., Food Sci.& Tech.Abstr., Helminthol.Abstr., Ind.Med., Ind.Sci.Rev., INIS Atomind., NRN, Nutr.Abstr., Risk Abstr., Sci.Cit.Ind.
—BLDSC shelfmark: 4958.400000.
Description: Information on the clinical applications of endocrine research.
Refereed Serial

616.4   US   ISSN 1056-8727
JOURNAL OF DIABETES AND ITS COMPLICATIONS. 1987. q. $150 to institutions (foreign $172)(effective 1992). Elsevier Science Publishing Co., Inc. (New York), 655 Ave. of the Americas, New York, NY 10010. TEL 212-989-5800. FAX 212-633-3965. TELEX 420643 AEP UI. Ed. Eli A. Friedman. (also avail. in microform from UMI)
—BLDSC shelfmark: 4969.407000.
Formerly (until 1992): Journal of Diabetic Complications (ISSN 0891-6632)
Description: Publishes original contributions developed from clinical investigation, as well as brief review articles.
Refereed Serial

616.4   IT   ISSN 0391-4097
CODEN: JEIND7
JOURNAL OF ENDOCRINOLOGICAL INVESTIGATION. (Text in English) 1978. 11/yr. L.140000 (foreign $140). (Società Italiana di Endocrinologia - Italian Society of Endocrinology) Editrice Kurtis s.r.l., Via L. Zoja, 30, 20153 Milan, Italy. TEL 02-48202740. FAX 02-48201219. Ed. Aldo Pinchera. adv.; charts; illus.; stat. **Indexed:** Curr.Adv.Biochem., Curr.Adv.Cell & Devel.Biol., Curr.Cont., Dairy Sci.Abstr., Excerp.Med., Excerp.Med., Ind.Med.
—BLDSC shelfmark: 4977.900000.
Description: Publishes original studies on clinical and experimental research in endocrinology and related fields.

616.4   UK   ISSN 0022-0795
QP187.A1   CODEN: JOENAK
JOURNAL OF ENDOCRINOLOGY. 1939. m. (4 vols. per year). $410. Journal of Endocrinology Ltd., 17-18 North Court, The Courtyard, Almondsbury, Bristol BS12 4NQ, England. TEL 0454-616046. FAX 0454-616071. (Dist. by: The Distribution Centre, Blackhorse Rd., Letchworth, Herts SG6 1HN, England) Ed. Dr. G.P. Vinson. adv.; bibl.; charts; illus.; index, cum.index: vols.1-20, 21-40; circ. 2,200. **Indexed:** Anal.Abstr., Anim.Breed.Abstr., Behav.Med.Abstr., Biol.Abstr., Biotech.Abstr., Chem.Abstr., Curr.Adv.Biochem., Curr.Adv.Cell & Devel.Biol., Curr.Adv.Genetics & Molec.Biol., Curr.Cont., Dairy Sci.Abstr., Dent.Ind., Excerp.Med., Ind.Med., Ind.Sci.Rev., Ind.Vet., INIS Atomind., Mass Spectr.Bull., NRN, Nutr.Abstr., Poult.Abstr., Sci.Cit.Ind, Vet.Bull.
—BLDSC shelfmark: 4978.000000.

616.4 618   IT
JOURNAL OF GYNAECOLOGICAL ENDOCRINOLOGY. (Included in: Clinical and Experimental Obstetrics and Gynecology) (Text and summaries in English) 1985. s-a. Studi Ostetrico Ginecologici s.r.l., Galleria Storione 2-A, 35123 Padua, Italy. TEL 049-8758644. Ed.Bd. adv.; bk.rev.; circ. 300.

JOURNAL OF GYNECOLOGIC SURGERY. see *MEDICAL SCIENCES — Obstetrics And Gynecology*

JOURNAL OF NEUROENDOCRINOLOGY. see *MEDICAL SCIENCES — Psychiatry And Neurology*

616.4 618.92   UK   ISSN 0334-018X
CODEN: JPENEV
JOURNAL OF PEDIATRIC ENDOCRINOLOGY. (Text in English) 1985. q. $160. Freund Publishing House Ltd., Suite 500, Chesham House, 150 Regent St., London W1R 5FA, England. (Alt. addr.: P.O. Box 35010, Tel Aviv, Israel. TEL 972-3-615335) Ed. H.J. Hirsch. adv.; bk.rev.; circ. 1,000. (back issues avail.) **Indexed:** Excerp.Med.
—BLDSC shelfmark: 5030.173000.

616.4   IS
JOURNAL OF PEDIATRIC ENDOCRINOLOGY. 1985. a. $100. Freund Publishing House, P.O. Box 35010, 61 Nachmani St., Tel Aviv, Israel. Ed. Dan Herness. **Indexed:** Curr.Adv.Ecol.Sci.

616.4   JA   ISSN 0289-4947
JOURNAL OF PRACTICAL DIABETES; practice. (Text in Japanese) 1984. q. 800 Yen per no. Ishiyaku Publishers, Inc., 7-10 Honkomagome 1-chome, Bunkyo-ku, Tokyo 113, Japan. Ed. Hiroshi Miura. adv.; bk.rev.; charts; illus.; circ. 10,000.
—BLDSC shelfmark: 6597.119700.

MEDICAL SCIENCES — ENDOCRINOLOGY

616.4   FR   ISSN 0075-4439
CODEN: JDBHAC
JOURNEES ANNUELLES DE DIABETOLOGIE DE L'HOTEL DIEU. 1961. a. price varies. (Hotel-Dieu, Clinique Medico-Sociale du Diabete et des Maladies Metaboliques) Flammarion Medecine Sciences, 4 rue Casimir Delavigne, 75006 Paris, France. (U.S. subscr. addr. S.F.P.A., c/o M. Benech, 14 E. 60 St., New York, NY 10022) Ed. Dr. Rathery. **Indexed:** Biol.Abstr., Chem.Abstr., Dent.Ind., Ind.Med.

616.4   574.133   US   ISSN 0026-0495
RB147   CODEN: METAAJ
METABOLISM: CLINICAL AND EXPERIMENTAL. vol.23, 1974. m. $140 to individuals; institutions $194; foreign $235. W.B. Saunders Co. (Subsidiary of: Harcourt Brace Jovanovich, Inc.), Curtis Center, Independence Square W., Philadelphia, PA 19106. TEL 215-238-7800. (Subscr. to: 6277 Sea Harbor Dr., 4th Fl., Orlando FL 32891) Ed. Dr. James B. Field. adv.; abstr.; bibl.; charts; illus.; index. **Indexed:** Abstr.Hyg., Biol.Abstr., Biotech.Abstr., Chem.Abstr., Curr.Adv.Biochem., Curr.Adv.Cell & Devel.Biol., Curr.Adv.Ecol.Sci., Curr.Cont., Excerp.Med., Helminthol.Abstr., Ind.Med., Ind.Vet., INIS Atomind., Nutr.Abstr., Pig News & Info., Trop.Dis.Bull.
●Also available online.
—BLDSC shelfmark: 5683.300000.
Description: Reports on research into the metabolic aspects of nutrition, endocrines, genetics, dystrophies, diabetes and gout.
Refereed Serial

616.4   IT   ISSN 0391-1977
CODEN: MNREDJ
MINERVA ENDOCRINOLOGICA. q. L.60000($70) Edizioni Minerva Medica, Corso Bramante 83-85, 10126 Turin, Italy. **Indexed:** Chem.Abstr., Ind.Med.

616.4   IE   ISSN 0303-7207
QP187.A1   CODEN: MCEND6
MOLECULAR AND CELLULAR ENDOCRINOLOGY; an international journal integrating all aspects related to the biochemical effects, synthesis and secretions of extracellular signals (hormones, neurotransmitters, etc.) and to the understanding of cellular regulatory mechanisms involved in hormonal control. 1974. 24/yr.(in 8 vols.; 3 nos./vol.) $1392 (effective 1992). Elsevier Scientific Publishers Ireland Ltd., P.O. Box 85, Limerick, Ireland. TEL 061-61944. FAX 061-62144. TELEX 72191 ENH EI. (Subscr. in U.S. and Canada to: Elsevier Science Publishing Co., Inc., Box 882, Madison Sq. Sta., New York, NY 10159. TEL 212-989-5800) Ed. B.A. Cooke. (also avail. in microform from RPI) **Indexed:** Anim.Breed.Abstr., Biol.Abstr., Chem.Abstr., Curr.Adv.Biochem., Curr.Adv.Cell & Devel.Biol., Curr.Adv.Ecol.Sci., Curr.Adv.Genetics & Molec.Biol., Curr.Cont., Dairy Sci.Abstr., Excerp.Med, Ind.Med., Ind.Sci.Rev., Nutr.Abstr., Poult.Abstr.
—BLDSC shelfmark: 5900.760000.
Refereed Serial

616.4   US   ISSN 0888-8809
QP187.3.M64   CODEN: MOENEN
MOLECULAR ENDOCRINOLOGY. m. $110 to individuals; institutions $170. Williams & Wilkins, 428 E. Preston St., Baltimore, MD 21202. TEL 301-528-4000. FAX 301-528-4312. TELEX 87669. Ed. Dr. E. Brad Thompson. circ. 1,900. (also avail. in microform; back issues avail.) **Indexed:** Anim.Breed.Abstr., Curr.Adv.Biochem., Curr.Adv.Cancer Res., Curr.Adv.Cell & Devel.Biol., Curr.Adv.Genetics & Molec.Biol., Poult.Abstr.
—BLDSC shelfmark: 5900.817390.
Description: Forum for molecular and cellular biologists investigating the molecular mechanisms of cellular regulatory processes.
Refereed Serial

616.4   US   ISSN 0077-1015
CODEN: MOENBK
MONOGRAPHS ON ENDOCRINOLOGY. 1967. irregr. price varies. Springer-Verlag, 175 Fifth Ave., New York, NY 10010. TEL 212-460-1500. (Also see Berlin, Heidelberg, Tokyo and Vienna) (reprint service avail. from ISI) **Indexed:** Biol.Abstr., Chem.Abstr., Ind.Med.
—BLDSC shelfmark: 5915.430000.

616.4   UK   ISSN 0047-8385
MURMUR. 1922. 3/yr. free to qualified medical students. Cambridge University Medical Society, Department of Anatomy, Cambridge University, Cambridge CB2 9DT, England. adv.; bk.rev.; circ. 750.

NATIONAL ALOPECIA AREATA FOUNDATION NEWSLETTER. see *MEDICAL SCIENCES — Dermatology And Venereology*

NEUROENDOCRINE PERSPECTIVES. see *MEDICAL SCIENCES — Psychiatry And Neurology*

616.4   616.8   SZ   ISSN 0028-3835
QP187.A1   CODEN: NUNDAJ
NEUROENDOCRINOLOGY; international journal for basic and clinical studies on neuroendocrine relationships. (Text in English) 1965. m. (2 vols./ yr.). 780 Fr.($520) per vol. (International Society of Neuroendocrinology) S. Karger AG, Allschwilerstr. 10, P.O. Box, CH-4009 Basel, Switzerland. TEL 061-3061111. FAX 061-3061234. TELEX CH 962652. Ed. S.M. McCann. adv.; illus.; circ. 1,650. (also avail. in microform from RPI) **Indexed:** Anim.Breed.Abstr., Biol.Abstr., Biotech.Abstr., Chem.Abstr., Curr.Adv.Cell & Devel.Biol., Curr.Adv.Ecol.Sci., Curr.Adv.Genetics & Molec.Biol., Curr.Cont., Dairy Sci.Abstr., Excerp.Med., Ind.Med., Ind.Sci.Rev., Ind.Vet., Int.Aerosp.Abstr., Poult.Abstr., Vet.Bull.
—BLDSC shelfmark: 6081.370000.

616.4   UK   ISSN 0143-4276
NEUROHYPOPHYSIAL HORMONES. 1980. s-m. £75. Sheffield University Biomedical Information Service (SUBIS), The University, Sheffield S10 2TN, England. TEL 0742-768555. FAX 0742-739826. TELEX 547216-UGSHEF-G.
Description: Current awareness service for researchers. Covers oxytocin, vasopressin and neurophysin.

616.46   IT
OBIETTIVO DIABETE. q. L.90000($150) (effective 1992). Casa Editrice Idelson, Via A. De Gasperi 55, 80133 Naples, Italy. TEL 081-5524733. FAX 081-5518295. Ed. Renato Carleo.

616.4   US   ISSN 0885-3177
CODEN: PANCE4
PANCREAS. 1986. bi-m. $234 to individuals; institutions $358. Raven Press, 1185 Ave. of the Americas, New York, NY 10036. TEL 212-930-9500. FAX 212-869-3495. TELEX 640073. Ed. Dr. Vay Liang W. Go. adv.; bk.rev.; charts; illus.; index; circ. 1,500. (back issues avail.) **Indexed:** Curr.Adv.Biochem., Curr.Adv.Cell & Devel.Biol.
—BLDSC shelfmark: 6357.351500.
Description: Publishes both basic and clinical work on the exocrine and endocrine pancreas, their interrelationship, and consequences in disease states.
Refereed Serial

PANCREATIC AND SALIVARY SECRETION. see *BIOLOGY — Physiology*

616.4   SZ   ISSN 0304-4254
CODEN: PAENDP
PEDIATRIC AND ADOLESCENT ENDOCRINOLOGY. (Text in English) 1976. irreg. price varies. S. Karger AG, Allschwilerstr. 10, P.O. Box, CH-4009 Basel, Switzerland. TEL 061-3061111. FAX 061-3061234. TELEX CH 962652. Ed. Z. Laron. (reprint service avail. from ISI) **Indexed:** Biol.Abstr., Chem.Abstr, Curr.Adv.Ecol.Sci.
—BLDSC shelfmark: 6417.528000.

616.4   574.8   UK   ISSN 0268-1552
PEPTIDE HORMONE RECEPTORS. 1986. m. £65. Sheffield University Biomedical Information Service (SUBIS), The University, Sheffield S10 2TN, England. TEL 0742-768555. FAX 0742-739826. TELEX 547216-UGSHEF-G.
Description: Current awareness service for researchers. Studies receptors for gastrointestinal hormones, hypothalamic and pituitary hormones, placental hormones, angiotensin, and growth factors.

616.462   CN   ISSN 0384-7810
PLEIN SOLEIL. 1958. q. Can.$20. Association du Diabete du Quebec Inc., 1160, rue Panet, Montreal, Que. H2L 2Y7, Canada. TEL 514-597-0555. FAX 514-597-0652. Ed.Bd. adv.; bk.rev.; circ. 25,000. (also avail. in audio cassette) **Indexed:** Pt.de Rep. (1979-).
Formerly: Survivre (ISSN 0562-7087).

616.5   UK   ISSN 0266-447X
PRACTICAL DIABETES; the journal for diabetes care team. (Supplement avail.: Introduction to Human Research) 1984. bi-m. £21 to individuals; students £12. (Newbourne Group) Home & Law Publishing Ltd., Greater London House, Hampstead Rd., London NW1 7QQ, England. TEL 01-388-3171. FAX 01-387-9518. TELEX 269470. Ed. A.K. Baksi.
—BLDSC shelfmark: 6593.980150.
Description: Delivers important educational service to all health professionals involved in diabetes care.
Refereed Serial

616.462   UK   ISSN 0960-8893
PRACTICAL DIABETES DIGEST. 1989. q. £27($50) F S G Communications Ltd., 57-59 Whitechapel Rd., London E1 1DU, England. TEL 071-377-8413. FAX 071-375-0371. Eds. G. Alberti, G. Gill.
Description: Contains original and review articles for physicians and others treating diabetes in the Middle East and Africa.

616.4   US   ISSN 0730-3491
PRACTICAL DIABETOLOGY. 1982. bi-m. $48 (effective 1992). R.A. Rapaport Publishing, Inc., 150 W. 22nd St., New York, NY 10011. TEL 212-989-0200. FAX 212-989-4786. Ed. Dr. Daniel L. Lorber. adv.; circ. 65,200 (controlled). (back issues avail.)
Description: Practical diabetes information for the busy physician and pharmacist.

616.4   612.405   RU   ISSN 0375-9660
CODEN: PROEAS
PROBLEMY ENDOKRINOLOGII/PROBLEMS OF ENDOCRINOLOGY. (Text in Russian; summaries in English) 1955. bi-m. 16.80 Rub.($15) (Vsesoyuznoe Nauchnoe Obshchestvo Endokrinologov) Izdatel'stvo Meditsina, Petroverigskii pereulok 6-8, 101838 Moscow, Russia. (Co-sponsor: Ministerstvo Zdravookhraneniya S.S.S.R.) Ed. V.P. Fedotov. bk.rev. (tabloid format) **Indexed:** Biol.Abstr., Biotech.Abstr., Chem.Abstr., Excerp.Med., Ind.Med., Int.Aerosp.Abstr., Nutr.Abstr.
—BLDSC shelfmark: 0133.980000.
Formerly: Problemy Endokrinologii i Gormonoterapii (ISSN 0032-9509)
Description: Covers the most pressing problems of modern endocrinology, such as chemical structure, biosynthesis and metabolism of hormones, the metabolism of their action at cellular and molecular levels, as well as the pathogenesis and clinical picture of endocrine diseases and new methods of their diagnosis and treatment.

616.4   US
PROGRESS IN ENDOCRINE RESEARCH AND THERAPY. 1984. irreg., latest vol.5. price varies. Raven Press, 1185 Ave. of the Americas, New York, NY 10036. TEL 212-930-9500. FAX 212-869-3495.

PROGRESS IN GROWTH FACTOR RESEARCH. see *BIOLOGY — Microscopy*

616.4   UK   ISSN 0142-8276
PROLACTIN. s-m. £75. Sheffield University Biomedical Information Service (SUBIS), The University, Sheffield S10 2TN, England. TEL 0742-768555. FAX 0742-739826. TELEX 547216 UGSHEF G. (looseleaf format; back issues avail.)
Description: Current awareness service for researchers in clinical and life sciences.

616.4   US   ISSN 0090-6980
QP801.P68   CODEN: PRGLBA
PROSTAGLANDINS. 1972. m. (2 vols./yr.). $290 (foreign $330). Butterworth - Heinemann Ltd. (Subsidiary of: Reed International PLC), 80 Montvale Ave., Stoneham, MA 02180. TEL 617-438-8464. FAX 617-438-1479. TELEX 880052. Ed. Peter W. Ramwell. (also avail. in microform from UMI; back issues avail.) **Indexed:** Anal.Abstr., Anim.Breed.Abstr., Biol.Abstr., Biotech.Abstr., Chem.Abstr., Curr.Adv.Biochem., Curr.Adv.Cancer Res., Curr.Adv.Cell & Devel.Biol., Curr.Adv.Ecol.Sci., Curr.Chem.React., Curr.Cont., Dairy Sci.Abstr., Dent.Ind., Excerp.Med., Helminthol.Abstr., Ind.Chem., Ind.Med., Ind.Vet., Mass Spectr.Bull., Nutr.Abstr., Pig News & Info., Telegen, Vet.Bull.
—BLDSC shelfmark: 6935.180000.
Description: Covers all areas of prostaglandin research, including chemistry, endocrinology, immunology, and oncology.
Refereed Serial

MEDICAL SCIENCES — EXPERIMENTAL MEDICINE, LABORATORY TECHNIQUE

616.4   UK   ISSN 0142-8284
PROSTAGLANDINS - BIOLOGY. 1979. s-m. £105. Sheffield University Biomedical Information Service (SUBIS), The University, Sheffield S10 2TN, England. TEL 0742-768555. FAX 0742-739826. TELEX 547216-UGSHEF-G.
Description: Current awareness service for researchers. Covers prostaglandin precursors, production, release, effects, medical uses and metabolism.

616.4   UK   ISSN 0952-3278
                                     CODEN: PLEAEU
PROSTAGLANDINS, LEUKOTRIENES AND MEDICINE. 1978. 15/yr. £725($1399) Churchill Livingstone Medical Journals, Robert Stevenson House, 1-3 Baxter's Pl., Leith Walk, Edinburgh EH1 3AF, Scotland. TEL 031-556-2424. FAX 031-558-1278. TELEX 727511. (Subscr. to: Longman Group, Journals Subscr. Dept., P.O. Box 77, Fourth Ave., Harlow, Essex CM19 5AA, England; U.S. subscr. to: Churchill Livingstone 650 Ave. of the Americas, New York, Ny 10011. TEL 212-206-5000) Ed. Dr. D.F. Horrobin. (also avail. in microform from UMI; back issues avail.) **Indexed:** Anim.Breed.Abstr., Chem.Abstr., Curr.Adv.Ecol.Sci., Curr.Cont., Dairy Sci.Abstr., Excerp.Med., Ind.Med., Poult.Abstr.
—BLDSC shelfmark: 6935.190900.
Formerly: Prostaglandins and Medicine (ISSN 0161-4630)

PSYCHONEUROENDOCRINOLOGY. see *MEDICAL SCIENCES — Psychiatry And Neurology*

616.4 574.192   US   ISSN 0079-9963
QP187   CODEN: RPHRA6
RECENT PROGRESS IN HORMONE RESEARCH. PROCEEDINGS OF THE LAURENTIAN HORMONE CONFERENCE. 1947. irreg., vol.46, 1990. Academic Press, Inc., 1250 Sixth Ave., San Diego, CA 92101. TEL 619-231-0926. FAX 619-699-6715. Ed. Roy O. Greep. index, cum.index: vols.1-10, 1947-1954; vol.11, 1955. (reprint service avail. from ISI) **Indexed:** Anim.Breed.Abstr., Biol.Abstr., Chem.Abstr., Dairy Sci.Abstr., Excerp.Med., Ind.Med., Ind.Vet., Nutr.Abstr., Vet.Bull.
—BLDSC shelfmark: 7305.000000.
Refereed Serial

616.4   UK   ISSN 0142-8314
RELEASING HORMONES. 1978. s-m. £75. Sheffield University Biomedical Information Service (SUBIS), The University, Sheffield S10 2TN, England. TEL 0742-768555. FAX 0742-739826. TELEX 547216-UGSHEF-G.
Description: Current awareness service for researchers. Explores buserelin, corticotropin releasing hormone, LH-ESH releasing hormone, somatotropin releasing hormone, and thyrotropin releasing hormone.

RENIN, ANGIOTENSIN & KININS. see *BIOLOGY — Physiology*

616.4   FR   ISSN 0048-8062
                                     CODEN: RECNAS
REVUE FRANCAISE D'ENDOCRINOLOGIE CLINIQUE, NUTRITION ET METABOLISME.* (Text in French; some summaries in English) 1960. bi-m. Editions de Medecine Pratique, 4 rue Louis-Armand, 92600 Asnieres, France. illus. **Indexed:** Biol.Abstr., C.I.S. Abstr., Chem.Abstr., Excerp.Med., Ind.Med.
—BLDSC shelfmark: 7903.800000.

616.4   RM
REVUE ROUMAINE D'ENDOCRINOLOGIE/ROMANIAN JOURNAL OF ENDOCRINOLOGY. (Text in English, French, German, Russian or Spanish) 1964. 4/yr. 200 lei($55) (Academia de Stiinte Medicale) Editura Academiei Romane, Calea Victoriei 125, 79717 Bucharest, Rumania. (Dist. by: Rompresfilatelia, Calea Grivitei 64-66, P.O. Box 12-201, 78104 Bucharest, Rumania) Ed. Marcela Pitis. adv.; bk.rev.; abstr.; bibl.; illus.; index; circ. 1,050. **Indexed:** Biol.Abstr., Chem.Abstr., Curr.Adv.Ecol.Sci., Curr.Cont., Excerp.Med., Ind.Med.
Former titles: Revue Roumaine de Medecine. Serie Endocrinologie (ISSN 0253-1801); Revue Roumaine d'Endocrinologie (ISSN 0035-4015)
Description: Original papers (studies and researches in experimental and clinical endocrinology), short articles on unusual cases and techniques, editorials and endocrinological news.

616.4   GW   ISSN 0720-065X
DIE SCHILDDRUESE. 1976. irreg. P M I Verlag GmbH, August-Schanz-Str. 6, 6000 Frankfurt a.M. 50, Germany. TEL 069-548000-0. FAX 069-548000-77. TELEX 412952-PMI-D. circ. 30,000.

616.4   US   ISSN 0882-5815
RC963.A1
SEMINARS IN REPRODUCTIVE ENDROCRINOLOGY. q. $72 to individuals; institutions $99. Thieme Medical Publishers, Inc., 381 Park Ave., So., Ste. 1501, New York, NY 10016. TEL 212-683-5088. Ed. Leon Speroff, M.D. adv.; abstr.; bibl.; illus. **Indexed:** Curr.Adv.Cell & Devel.Biol., Curr.Adv.Ecol.Sci., Curr.Adv.Genetics & Molec.Biol.
Formerly: Reproductive Endocrinology (ISSN 0734-8630)

SEMINARS IN RESPIRATORY INFECTIONS. see *MEDICAL SCIENCES — Respiratory Diseases*

616.4   CK   ISSN 0120-1182
SOCIEDAD COLOMBIANA DE ENDOCRINOLOGIA. REVISTA. (Text in Spanish; summaries in English and Spanish) 1958. s-a. $6. Sociedad Colombiana de Endocrinologia, Apdo. Aereo 29714, Bogota, D.E., Colombia. Ed. Dr. Alfredo F. Jacome. adv.; index; circ. 2,000. **Indexed:** Biol.Abstr.

STEROID RECEPTORS. see *BIOLOGY — Cytology And Histology*

616.44   US   ISSN 1050-7256
                                   CODEN: THYRER
▼**THYROID.** 1991. q. $132 (foreign $172). (American Thyroid Association) Mary Ann Liebert, Inc., 1651 Third Ave., New York, NY 10128. TEL 212-289-2300. FAX 212-289-4697. **Indexed:** Excerp.Med. (1992-).
—BLDSC shelfmark: 8820.383300.
Description: Covers all aspects of thyroid medicine, from the molecular biology of the cell to clinical managemnt of thyroid disorders.

616.4 610   UK   ISSN 0142-8349
THYROID HORMONES. 1976. s-m. £100. Sheffield University Biomedical Information Service (SUBIS), The University, Sheffield S10 2TN, England. TEL 0742-768555. FAX 0742-739826. TELEX 547216-UGSHEF-G.
Description: Current awareness service for researchers. Studies hormone synthesis and secretion, receptors, effects, and hypothalamic-pituitary control of thyroid function.

616.46   DK
TIDSSKRIFT FOR SUKKERSYGE. q. Landsforeningen for Sukkersyge, Skt. Anne Plads 4, 5000 Odense C, Denmark. adv.; circ. 20,000.
Description: Covers developments in diabetes.

616.46   US   ISSN 1043-2760
TRENDS IN ENDOCRINOLOGY AND METABOLISM. 10/yr. $160 (foreign $187)(effective 1992). Elsevier Science Publishing Co., Inc. (New York), 655 Ave. of the Americas, New York, NY 10010. TEL 212-989-5800. FAX 212-633-3965. TELEX 420643 AEP UI. Ed.Bd.
—BLDSC shelfmark: 9049.590500.
Description: Attempts to keep the researcher and the clinician informed of advances across the field of endocrinology, with emphasis on research. Features include endocrine rounds, journal club, and emergency techniques.
Refereed Serial

616   BU   ISSN 0506-2772
                                   CODEN: VTBLAU
VATRECHNI BOLESTI. (Text in Bulgarian; summaries in English, Russian) bi-m. 24 lv. (Ministerstvo na Narodnoto Zdrave) Izdatelstvo Meditsina i Fizkultura, 11 Pl. Slaveikov, Sofia, Bulgaria. (Dist. by: Hemus, 6 Rouski Blvd., 1000 Sofia, Bulgaria) (Co-sponsor: Nauchno Druzhestvo po Vatresni Bolesti) Ed. N. Belovezdov. circ. 2,584. **Indexed:** Abstr.Bulg.Sci.Med.Lit.
—BLDSC shelfmark: 0046.730000.

616.4058   US   ISSN 0084-3741
RC648
YEAR BOOK OF ENDOCRINOLOGY. 1950. a. $54.95. Mosby - Year Book, Inc., Continuity Division, 200 N. LaSalle, Chicago, IL 60601. TEL 312-726-9733. FAX 312-726-6075. TELEX 206155. Ed. John D. Bagdade, M.D. (reprint service avail.) **Indexed:** Anim.Breed.Abstr., Curr.Adv.Ecol.Sci.
—BLDSC shelfmark: 9411.690000.

616.4   CC   ISSN 1000-6699
ZHONGHUA NEIFENMI DAIXIE ZAZHI/CHINESE JOURNAL OF ENDOCRINOLOGY AND METABOLISM. (Text in Chinese; summaries in Chinese and English) 1985. q. Y12 (foreign $10). Shanghai Institute of Endocrinology - Shanghai-shi Neifenmi Yanjiusuo, 197 Ruijin Lu Sec. 2, Shanghai, People's Republic of China. TEL 4315587. (Co-sponsor: Chinese Medical Association - Zhonghua Yixue Hui) Eds. Chen Jialun, Zhang Daqing. adv.; circ. 10,000. (back issues avail.)
—BLDSC shelfmark: 3180.317200.

MEDICAL SCIENCES — Experimental Medicine, Laboratory Technique

616   US
A A B BULLETIN. 1965. bi-m. membership. American Association of Bioanalysts, 818 Olive St., Ste. 918, St. Louis, MO 63101. TEL 314-241-1445. Ed. Mark S. Birenbaum. circ. 1,700 (controlled). (tabloid format)

A A M I NEWS. (Association for the Advancement of Medical Instrumentation) see *INSTRUMENTS*

A I CH E EQUIPMENT TESTING PROCEDURES. (American Institute of Chemical Engineers) see *ENGINEERING — Chemical Engineering*

A I M S NEWSLETTER. (Australian Institute of Medical Scientists) see *MEDICAL SCIENCES*

616.15   AT
A I M S SELF ASSESSMENT PROGRAMMES SERIES. 1988. s-a. Aus.$25. Australian Institute of Medical Scientists, P.O. Box 450, Toowong, Qld. 4066, Australia. TEL 07-371-3370. FAX 07-870-4857. circ. 400. (back issues avail.)
Formerly: A I M L S Self Assessment Programmes Series (ISSN 1031-7074)

616   II
A M T CHRONICLE. q. Association of Medical Technologists, 55 Harish Mukherjee, Calcutta 25, India.

619   US
A S M T TODAY. bi-m. American Society of Medical Technology, Inc., 2021 L St., N.W., Ste. 400, Washington, DC 20036-4909. TEL 202-785-3311. Ed. Ronald Sanchez. circ. 21,000.

ABSTRACTS: CELLULAR PATHOLOGY. see *MEDICAL SCIENCES — Abstracting, Bibliographies, Statistics*

ACTA MEDICA CROATICA. see *MEDICAL SCIENCES*

ACTA TOXICOLOGICA ET THERAPEUTICA; international journal of toxicology, pharmacology and therapy. see *ENVIRONMENTAL STUDIES — Toxicology And Environmental Safety*

616   US   ISSN 1053-4261
GV1587   CODEN: ADLAEE
ADVANCED LABANOTATION. 8/yr. (in 2 vols., 4 nos/vol.). $63. Harwood Academic Publishers, 270 Eighth Ave., New York, NY 10011. TEL 212-206-8900. FAX 212-645-2459. TELEX 236735 GOPUB UR. (Subscr. to: Box 786, Cooper Sta., New York, NY 10276. TEL 800-545-8398; UK subscr. to: Box 90, Reading, Berkshire RG1 8JL, England. TEL 0734-560-080) Ed. Ann Hutchinson Guest. (also avail. in microform)
Description: Examines the symbols, rules and current usage of the movement notation system which has been in popular use since the 1920s.
Refereed Serial

MEDICAL SCIENCES — EXPERIMENTAL MEDICINE, LABORATORY TECHNIQUE

619 016 UK ISSN 0261-1929
QH301 CODEN: AALADQ
ALTERNATIVES TO LABORATORY ANIMALS: A T L A.
(Supplement avail.: Animal Experimentation. Improvements and Alternatives) 1973. 4/yr. £40($70) Fund for the Replacement of Animals in Medical Experiments, Eastgate House, 34 Stoney St., Nottingham NG1 1NB, England. TEL 0602-584740. FAX 0602-503570. Ed. Dr. Gilly Griffin. adv.; bk.rev.; bibl.; circ. 1,500. (back issues avail.) **Indexed:** Abstr.Hyg., Biol.Abstr., Curr.Adv.Ecol.Sci., Ind.Vet., Vet.Bull.
—BLDSC shelfmark: 1765.890900.
Formerly (until 1983): A T L A Abstracts (ISSN 0306-2465)
Description: Covers all aspects of the development, validation, introduction and implementation of alternatives to the use of laboratory animals in biomedical research and toxicity testing.

616 US
AMERICAN ASSOCIATION OF BIOANALYSTS. PROFICIENCY TESTING SERVICE. TEST OF THE MONTH. 1970. irreg. membership. American Association of Bioanalysts, 205 W. Levee, Brownsville, TX 78520. TEL 512-546-5313. Ed. Nicholas T. Serafy. charts; illus.; circ. 4,500 (controlled). (tabloid format)

AMERICAN BIOTECHNOLOGY LABORATORY. see BIOLOGY — Biotechnology

619 US ISSN 8750-9490
AMERICAN CLINICAL LABORATORY. (Includes annual Buyers' Guide) 1982. 10/yr. $190 (foreign $235). International Scientific Communications, Inc., 30 Controls Dr., Box 870, Shelton, CT 06484-0870. TEL 203-926-9300. FAX 203-926-9310. TELEX 964292. Ed. Brian Howard. adv.; bk.rev.; charts; illus.; stat.; tr.lit.; circ. 70,436 (controlled).
Formerly: American Clinical Products Review.

619 US
AMERICAN COLLEGE OF LABORATORY ANIMAL MEDICINE SERIES. 1974. irreg. Academic Press, Inc., 1250 Sixth Ave., San Diego, CA 92101. TEL 619-231-6616. FAX 619-699-6715. (back issues avail.)
Refereed Serial

619 US
AMERICAN CRYONICS. 1984. s-a. $25. American Cryonics Society, Box 761, Cupertino, CA 95015-0761. TEL 408-446-4425. FAX 408-725-0385. Ed. Peter Christiansen. adv.; bk.rev.; circ. 500.
Former titles: A C S Notebook; A C S Journal.
Description: Reports on cryonics, cryobiology, and life extension; articles speculating on future medicine, and life; how current discoveries may change lifestyles.

AMERICAN JOURNAL OF EMERGENCY MEDICINE. see MEDICAL SCIENCES — Orthopedics And Traumatology

AMERICAN POLYGRAPH ASSOCIATION NEWSLETTER. see CRIMINOLOGY AND LAW ENFORCEMENT

616 NE ISSN 0166-7688
ANALYSE. Bound with: International Association of Medical Laboratory Technologists. Newsletter. 1946. m. fl.125. Vereniging van Medische Analisten - Association of Medical Laboratory Technologists, Wilhelminapark 52, 3581 NM Utrecht, Netherlands. TEL 030-522881. (Co-sponsor: International Association of Medical Technologists) Ed. W.M.H.M. van den Eertwegh. adv.; bk.rev.; illus.; index; circ. 4,000. **Indexed:** INIS Atomind.
Formerly: Tijdschrift voor Medische Analisten.

ANALYTICAL INSTRUMENTATION; applications and design for chemical, biomedical and environmental science. see CHEMISTRY — Analytical Chemistry

ANLEITUNG FUER DIE CHEMISCHE LABORATORIUMSPRAXIS - CHEMICAL LABORATORY PRACTICE. see CHEMISTRY

616 CN ISSN 0709-8502
CODEN: ABCQD2
ANNALES DE BIOCHIMIE CLINIQUE DU QUEBEC. (Text in French) 1980. q. free. Societe Quebecoise de Biochimie Clinique, c/o Mary-Ann Kallai Sanfacon, Ed., Hopital Jean Talon, 1385 rue Jean Talon est, Montreal, Que. H2E 1S6, Canada. TEL 819-563-2366. FAX 514-495-6734. (Subscr. to: Bernard Billon, Service de Biochimie, C.H. Saint-Vincent de Paul, 300, King Est, Sherbrooke, Que. J1G 1B1, Canada) adv.; bk.rev.; abstr.; index; circ. 1,000. (back issues avail.) **Indexed:** Biol.Abstr., Chem.Abstr., Curr.Adv.Ecol.Sci.
—BLDSC shelfmark: 0967.590000.
Description: Studies clinical biochemistry.

616 US ISSN 0091-7370
RB37.A1 CODEN: ACLSCP
ANNALS OF CLINICAL AND LABORATORY SCIENCE. 1971. bi-m. $65 to individuals (foreign $100); institutions $100 (foreign $110). (Association of Clinical Scientists) Institute for Clinical Science, 1833 Delancey Place, Philadelphia, PA 19103. TEL 215-829-7068. FAX 215-829-3094. Ed. Dr. F. William Sunderman. adv.; bk.rev.; abstr.; charts; illus.; index; circ. 2,000. **Indexed:** Biol.Abstr., Chem.Abstr., Curr.Adv.Cancer Res., Curr.Adv.Ecol.Sci., Curr.Cont., Dent.Ind., Dok.Arbeitsmed., Excerp.Med., Ind.Med., Ind.Sci.Rev., INIS Atomind., Nutr.Abstr.
—BLDSC shelfmark: 1040.228000.

616 FI
ANNALS OF MEDICINE. 1969. bi-m. $240. Finnish Medical Society Duodecim, Kalevankatu 11 A, 00100 Helsinki, Finland. Ed. Leena Peltonen. adv.; bk.rev.; charts; illus.; index; circ. 1,670. (also avail. in microform from UMI) **Indexed:** Abstr.Hyg., Biol.Abstr., Chem.Abstr., Child Devel.Abstr., Curr.Adv.Ecol.Sci., Curr.Cont., Dairy Sci.Abstr., Excerp.Med., Helminthol.Abstr., Ind.Med., Ind.Sci.Rev., NRN, Nutr.Abstr., Psychol.Abstr., Risk Abstr., Sci.Cit.Ind., Trop.Dis.Bull.
Formerly (until vol.21, 1989): Annals of Clinical Research (ISSN 0003-4762); Incorporates: Annals of Clinical Research. Supplement (ISSN 0066-2291); Supersedes: Annales Paediatriae Fenniae; Annales Medicinae Internae Fenniae.

616 FR
ANNUAIRE DES LABORATOIRES D'ANALYSES DE BIOLOGIE MEDICALE DE FRANCE. a. Labo-France, 7 rue Godot de Mauroy, 75009 Paris, France. adv.
Formerly: Annuaire des Laboratoires d'Analyses de France.

ANNUAIRE FOURNI-LABO RECHERCHE (YEAR); fondamentale et appliquee. see BUSINESS AND ECONOMICS — Trade And Industrial Directories

ARCHIVES OF PATHOLOGY & LABORATORY MEDICINE. see MEDICAL SCIENCES

ARCHIVOS DE BIOLOGIA Y MEDICINA EXPERIMENTALES. see BIOLOGY

ARQUIVOS DE CIRURGIA CLINICA E EXPERIMENTAL. see MEDICAL SCIENCES — Surgery

619 US ISSN 0160-564X
RD130 CODEN: ARORD7
ARTIFICIAL ORGANS. 1977. bi-m. $320 (effective 1992). (International Society for Artificial Organs) Blackwell Scientific Publications Inc., Three Cambridge Center, Ste. 208, Cambridge, MA 02142-1413. TEL 617-225-0401. FAX 617-225-0412. Ed. Dr. Yukihiko Nose. adv.; bk.rev.; charts; illus.; index; circ. 2,000. (back issues avail.) **Indexed:** Biol.Abstr., Chem.Abstr., Curr.Cont., Dent.Ind., Excerp.Med, Ind.Med, Ind.Sci.Rev., Sci.Cit.Ind.
—BLDSC shelfmark: 1735.052000.
Description: Multidisciplinary journal publishing reports on the design, performance and evaluation of biomaterials and devices used in artificial organs for the medical, scientific and engineering communities; includes relevant coverage of biomechanics, bioelectronics, hemodynamics, and plasmapheresis.
Refereed Serial

ASSOCIATION OF TALENT AGENTS. NEWSLETTER. see THEATER

619 530 AT ISSN 0158-9938
CODEN: AUPMDI
AUSTRALASIAN PHYSICAL & ENGINEERING SCIENCES IN MEDICINE. 1977. q. Aus.$65 to individuals; institutions and library Aus.$60. Australasian College of Physical Scientists and Engineers in Medicine, Dept. of Medical Physics, Royal Adelaide Hospital, North Terrace, Adelaide, S.A. 5000, Australia. TEL 08-224-5536. FAX 08-223-2071. Ed. Dr. A.H. Beddoe. adv.; bk.rev.; index; circ. 450. (back issues avail.) **Indexed:** Chem.Abstr., Excerp.Med., Ind.Med., INIS Atomind., Sci.Abstr.
—BLDSC shelfmark: 1796.030000.
Formerly: Australasian Physical Sciences in Medicine.
Description: Covers applications of the physical sciences and engineering on medicine and biology; papers, reviews, technical reports and letters.

AUSTRALIAN JOURNAL OF MEDICAL SCIENCE. see MEDICAL SCIENCES

AYURVEDA SAUKHYAM SERIES. see MEDICAL SCIENCES — Chiropractic, Homeopathy, Osteopathy

B B A - GENE STRUCTURE AND EXPRESSION. see BIOLOGY — Genetics

B B A - MOLECULAR CELL RESEARCH. see BIOLOGY — Biophysics

BASIC PATTERNS IN UNION CONTRACTS. see LAW — Corporate Law

BIOELECTRONICS AND BIOSENSORS. see BIOLOGY — Biophysics

616 RU
BIOLOGIYA LABORATORNYKH ZHIVOTNYKH. irreg. 2 Rub. Akademiya Meditsinskikh Nauk S.S.S.R., Nauchno-Issledovatel'skaya Laboratoriya Eksperimental'no-Biologicheskikh Modelei, Moskovskaya Oblast', G. Khimki, Pos. Svetlye Gory, Russia. bibl.

610.28 660 US ISSN 1055-7172
RC856.A1 CODEN: BACBEU
BIOMATERIALS, ARTIFICIAL CELLS AND IMMOBILIZATION BIOTECHNOLOGY. 1973. 5/yr. $495 per vol. Marcel Dekker Journals, 270 Madison Ave., New York, NY 10016. TEL 212-696-9000. FAX 212-685-4540. TELEX 421419. (Subscr. to: Box 10018, Church St. Sta., New York, NY 10249) Ed. T.M.S. Chang. illus. (also avail. in microform from RPI) **Indexed:** Bioeng.Abstr., Biol.Abstr., Chem.Abstr., Curr.Cont., Dent.Ind., Excerp.Med., Ind.Med., Ind.Sci.Rev., Met.Abstr., Sci.Abstr., Sci.Cit.Ind., World Alum.Abstr.
—BLDSC shelfmark: 2087.718500.
Former titles (until 1991): Biomaterials, Artificial Cells and Artificial Organs; (until 1987): Biomaterials, Medical Devices, and Artificial Organs (ISSN 0890-5533)
Description: Focuses on medical instrumentation.
Refereed Serial

619 UK ISSN 0269-3879
CODEN: BICHE2
BIOMEDICAL CHROMATOGRAPHY. 1986. bi-m. $375 (effective 1992). John Wiley & Sons Ltd., Journals, Baffins Lane, Chichester, Sussex PO19 1UD, England. TEL 0243-779777. FAX 0243-775878. TELEX 86290 WIBOOK G. Eds. E.F. Hounsell, C.K. Lim. (reprint service avail. from SWZ) **Indexed:** Chem.Abstr., Curr.Cont., Excerp.Med.
—BLDSC shelfmark: 2087.758000.
Description: Devoted to the publication of original papers on the applications of chromatography and allied techniques in the biological and medical sciences.

BIOMEDICAL PRODUCTS. see MEDICAL SCIENCES

619 US
BIONICS. 1988. q. $20. Bionics Industry Association, c/o Ben Campbell, Ed., 115 W. Allegan St., Ste. 220, Lansing, MI 48933. TEL 517-485-7800. adv.; film rev.; charts; illus.; pat.; tr.lit.; cum.index: 1989-1990; circ. 4,000. (also avail. in microfilm)
Description: Reports on bionics, bio-sensors, artificial organs, cybernetics, industrial and governmental research, investment news.

MEDICAL SCIENCES — EXPERIMENTAL MEDICINE, LABORATORY TECHNIQUE

616 US
BIOPSY INTERPRETATION SERIES. irreg. price varies. Raven Press, 1185 Ave. of the Americas, New York, NY 10036. TEL 212-930-9500. FAX 212-869-3495. TELEX 640073. Ed. Steven G. Silverberg. **Indexed:** Curr.Cont.
Refereed Serial

BIOTECHNOLOGY SOFTWARE; the interface between researchers and computers. see *BIOLOGY — Biotechnology*

619 UK ISSN 0268-3369
CODEN: BMTRE9
BONE MARROW TRANSPLANTATION. 1986. m. £158. Macmillan Press Ltd., Scientific & Medical Division, Houndmills, Basingstoke, Hampshire RG21 2XS, England. TEL 0256 29242. FAX 0256-810526. Eds. John Goldman, Robert Peter Gale. abstr.; illus.; index. **Indexed:** Curr.Adv.Cancer Res., Curr.Adv.Cell & Devel.Biol., Curr.Adv.Ecol.Sci., Curr.Adv.Genetics & Molec.Biol., Curr.Cont., Excerp.Med., Ind.Med., Protozool.Abstr.
—BLDSC shelfmark: 2247.358000.
Description: Clinical results of bone marrow transplantation in man and experimental results with animals.

542 681.2 US ISSN 0093-8076
RB36.2
C L R. (Clinical Laboratory Reference) 1974. a. $29 (foreign $35). (Medical Laboratory Observer) Medical Economics Company Inc., Five Paragon Dr., Montvale, NJ 07645. TEL 201-358-7200. FAX 201-573-1045. Ed. Robert J. Fitzgibbon. adv.; circ. 59,000 (controlled). (reprint service avail.)
Description: Includes product information on diagnostic reagents, test systems, instruments, and equipment for the medical laboratory.
Refereed Serial

619 CN ISSN 0045-4354
CANADIAN ASSOCIATION FOR LABORATORY ANIMAL SCIENCE NEWSLETTER. (Text and summaries in English and French) 1968. bi-m. membership. Canadian Association for Laboratory Animal Science (CALAS), c/o Dr. Donald G. McKay, Biosciences Animal Service, University of Alberta, Edmonton, Alta. T6G 2E9, Canada. Ed. M. Buckley. adv.; bk.rev.; bibl.; charts; illus.; circ. 1,000 (controlled).

616 CN ISSN 0712-6875
CANADIAN CLINICAL LABORATORY. 6/yr. Can.$15. Sentry Communications (Subsidiary of: Maclean Hunter), 245 Fairview Mall Dr., Willowdale, Ont. M2J 4T1, Canada. TEL 416-596-5000. FAX 416-596-5553.
Incorporates (1989-1991): Canadian Laboratory (ISSN 0848-8002)

CANADIAN JOURNAL OF CARDIOLOGY. see *MEDICAL SCIENCES — Cardiovascular Diseases*

616 CN ISSN 0008-4158
CODEN: CJMTAY
CANADIAN JOURNAL OF MEDICAL TECHNOLOGY. (Editions in English, French) 1938. 4/yr. Can.$20. Canadian Society of Laboratory Technologists, P.O. Box 2830, Hamilton, Ont. L8N 3N8, Canada. TEL 416-528-8642. FAX 416-528-4968. Ed. Nancy McBride. adv.; bk.rev.; bibl.; charts; illus.; index; circ. 24,000. **Indexed:** Biol.Abstr., Chem.Abstr., CINAHL, Curr.Adv.Ecol.Sci., Curr.Cont., Helminthol.Abstr., Ind.Med., Nutr.Abstr., Sci.Cit.Ind.
—BLDSC shelfmark: 3032.600000.
Description: Explores medical laboratory technology, management and education.

CANADIAN MEDICAL AND BIOLOGICAL ENGINEERING SOCIETY. NEWSLETTER/SOCIETE CANADIENNE DE GENIE BIOMEDICAL. BULLETIN. see *MEDICAL SCIENCES*

616 CN ISSN 0381-5838
CANADIAN SOCIETY OF LABORATORY TECHNOLOGISTS. BULLETIN/ASSOCIATION CANADIENNE DES TECHNOLOGISTES DE LABORATOIRE. BULLETIN. (Text in English, French) 1951. m. membership. Canadian Society of Laboratory Technologists, P.O. Box 2830, Hamilton, Ont. L8N 3N8, Canada. TEL 416-528-8642. Ed. K. Davis. circ. 23,500.
Description: Includes society information, job advertisements, continuing education opportunities, examination information and public relations data.

CHEMIE-INGENIEUR-TECHNIK; Zeitschrift fuer technische Chemie, Verfahrenstechnik, Apparatewesen und Biotechnologie. see *ENGINEERING — Chemical Engineering*

616 IT ISSN 0391-2035
CODEN: CLLADN
CLINICA E LABORATORIO. 1977. q. L.65000($120) to individuals; institutions L.100000. Pensiero Scientifico Editore s.r.l., Via Panama 48, 00198 Rome, Italy. TEL 06 855-36-33. Eds. G. Sprovieri, M. Rossi. adv.; bk.rev.; circ. 800. (reprint service avail. from ISI) **Indexed:** Chem.Abstr., Excerp.Med. (1992-).
—BLDSC shelfmark: 3286.202500.

619 636 US ISSN 0277-0393
CLINICAL ENGINEERING INFORMATION SERVICE. 1977. bi-m. $98 (typically set in July). Scientific Enterprises, Inc., 5104 Randolph Rd., N. Little Rock, AR 72116-6836. TEL 501-771-1775. Ed. Dr. David Simmons. bk.rev.; charts; illus.; stat.; index. (looseleaf format; back issues avail.)
Description: Covers technical topics and maintenance management for engineers and technicians.
Refereed Serial

616 US ISSN 0197-8454
CLINICAL LAB LETTER. 1980. s-m. (m. in Jan. & Aug.). $204 (foreign $242). Quest Publishing Co., 1351 Titan Way, Brea, CA 92621. TEL 714-738-6400. FAX 714-525-6258. Ed. Allan F. Pacela. bk.rev.; tr.lit.; index. (back issues avail.)
Description: Published for clinical lab personnel. Covers latest diagnostic technology, safety hazards, recalls, legislation, standards, products, legal issues and education.

619 BE
CLINICAL LABORATORY INTERNATIONAL. 1977. 9/yr. $70 (free to qualified personnel). Pan European Publishing Co., Rue Verte 216, B-1210 Brussels, Belgium. TEL 02-242-29-92. FAX 02-242-71-11. TELEX 25828. Ed. Thomas Clark. bk.rev.; circ. 30,012 (controlled).
Description: Reports exclusively on what is new in clinical laboratory instrumentation, equipment and reagents in the international market.

681 US
CLINICAL LABORATORY PRODUCT COMPARISON SYSTEM. m. $645 (foreign $775). (Emergency Care Research Institute) E C R I, 5200 Butler Pike, Plymouth Meeting, PA 19462. TEL 215-825-6000. FAX 215-834-1275. Ed. Garrett Hayner.
Refereed Serial

CLINICAL TRIALS AND META-ANALYSIS; an international publication of scientific and clinical investigations. see *MEDICAL SCIENCES*

CLINICALLY IMPORTANT ADVERSE DRUG INTERACTIONS. see *PHARMACY AND PHARMACOLOGY*

619 US ISSN 0272-2712
RB37.A1 CODEN: CLMED6
CLINICS IN LABORATORY MEDICINE. 1981. 4/yr. $64. W.B. Saunders Co., Curtis Center, Independence Square W., Philadelphia, PA 19106. TEL 215-238-7800. Ed. Susan Short. (also avail. in microform from UMI) **Indexed:** ASCA, Curr.Adv.Ecol.Sci., Dok.Arbeitsmed., Excerp.Med., Ind.Med.
—BLDSC shelfmark: 3286.575000.

619 US ISSN 1058-2401
▼**COMPARATIVE MEDICINE;** animal models in biomedical research. 1992. 2/yr. $72 (foreign $82). Academic Press, Inc., Journal Division, 1250 Sixth Ave., San Diego, CA 92101. TEL 619-230-1840. FAX 619-699-6800. TELEX 181-726. Ed. Henry Baker.
Description: Focuses on topics relevant to the use of animal models in biomedical science, particularly human and animal health research.
Refereed Serial

616 US ISSN 1056-1471
CONTEMPORARY TOPICS IN LABORATORY ANIMAL SCIENCE. 1961. 6/yr. $70 (foreign $100). American Association for Laboratory Animal Science, 70 Timber Creek Dr., Ste. 5, Cordova, TN 38018. Ed. Abigail Smith. circ. 4,500. (processed)
Formerly (until Dec. 1991): A A L A S Bulletin.

619 US ISSN 0197-2456
R850.A1 CODEN: CCLTDH
CONTROLLED CLINICAL TRIALS; design, methods, and analysis. 1979. 6/yr. $218 to institutions (foreign $246)(effective 1992). (Society for Clinical Trials) Elsevier Science Publishing Co., Inc. (New York), 655 Ave. of the Americas, New York, NY 10010. TEL 212-989-5800. FAX 212-633-3965. TELEX 420643 AEP UI. Ed. C.L. Meinert. (also avail. in microform from RPI) **Indexed:** Abstr.Hyg., Biol.Abstr., Biostat., Biotech.Abstr., Curr.Adv.Ecol.Sci., Curr.Cont., Excerp.Med., Ind.Med., Ind.Sci.Rev., Oper.Res.Manage.Sci., Qual.Contr.Appl.Stat., Sci.Cit.Ind.
—BLDSC shelfmark: 3463.060000.
Description: Provides current information on the design, methods, and operational aspects of controlled clinical trials and follow-up studies.
Refereed Serial

619 US ISSN 0892-5798
CURRENT COMMENTS; the newsletter of discovery and innovation. 1986. 10/yr. $145. Chocorua Group, Box 193, Woodstock, CT 06281. TEL 203-928-3692. Ed. Thompson E. Upham. **Indexed:** ABC.
Description: Emerging research and innovation in life sciences.

D N A PROBES. see *BIOLOGY — Genetics*

DECHEMA MONOGRAPHIEN. see *CHEMISTRY — Analytical Chemistry*

DENTAL LABORATORY NEWS. see *MEDICAL SCIENCES — Dentistry*

618 US
DENTAL LABORATORY REVIEW BUYER'S GUIDE. 1975. a. $6. Dental Survey Publications (Subsidiary of: Harcourt Brace Jovanovich, Inc.), 7500 Old Oak Blvd., Cleveland, OH 44130. TEL 216-243-8100. adv.; circ. 17,264.
Formerly: Dental Laboratory Buyer's Guide.

DEVICES & DIAGNOSTICS LETTER. see *MEDICAL SCIENCES*

DIABETOLOGIA CROATICA. see *MEDICAL SCIENCES — Endocrinology*

DIAGNOSTYKA LABORATORYJNA. see *MEDICAL SCIENCES*

619 US
DIRECTORY OF FEDERAL LABORATORY RESOURCES AND TECHNOLOGIES. biennial. $59.95 in N. America; elsewhere $110. U.S. National Technical Information Service, 5285 Port Royal Rd., Springfield, VA 22161. TEL 703-487-4630. FAX 703-321-8547. TELEX 64617. Ed. Ed Lehmann.
Description: Includes detailed summaries of over 1,100 resources and descriptions of over 90 technical information centers.

619 US
DRUG AND DEVICE PRODUCT APPROVAL LIST. m. $80 in US, Canada, Mexico; elsewhere $160. (Department of Health and Human Services, Food and Drug Administration) U.S. National Technical Information Service, 5825 Port Royal Rd., Springfield, VA 22161. TEL 703-487-4630.
Description: Lists the most recent new drug approvals, new animal and drug devices, and licenses issued for biological products.

DRUG TARGETING. see *PHARMACY AND PHARMACOLOGY*

619 UA ISSN 1012-5558
CODEN: EJBEDR
EGYPTIAN JOURNAL OF BIOMEDICAL ENGINEERING. (Text in English; summaries in Arabic and English) 1980. s-a. $30. (Egyptian Society of Biomedical Engineering, Research Department) National Information and Documentation Centre (NIDOC), Tahrir Street, Dokki, Awqaf P.O., Cairo, Egypt. Ed. M.Y. Saada. charts; illus.; circ. 1,000.

MEDICAL SCIENCES — EXPERIMENTAL MEDICINE, LABORATORY TECHNIQUE

619 616   BU   ISSN 0367-0643
CODEN: EKMMA8
EKSPERIMENTALNA MEDICINA I MORFOLOGIJA. (Text in Bulgarian; summaries in English, Russian) q. 10 lv. (Ministerstvo na Nordnoto Zdrave) Izdatelstvo Meditsina i Fizkultura, 11 Pl. Slaveikov, Sofia, Bulgaria. (Dist. by: Hemus, 6 Rouski Blvd., 1000 Sofia, Bulgaria) (Co-sponsor: Nauchno Druzhestvo po Fiziologija, Anatomija, Pharmacologija, Patologija) Ed. K. Itchev. circ. 384. **Indexed:** Abstr.Bulg.Sci.Med.Lit., BSL Biol., Curr.Adv.Ecol.Sci., Excerp.Med.
—BLDSC shelfmark: 0057.150000.

619   US   ISSN 0888-7128
EUROPEAN CLINICAL LABORATORY. (Includes annual Buyers' Guide) 1982. 6/yr. $155 (foreign $135). International Scientific Communications, Inc., 30 Controls Dr., Box 870, Shelton, CT 06484-0870. TEL 203-926-9300. FAX 203-926-9310. TELEX 964292. Ed. Brian Howard. adv.; bk.rev.; charts; illus.; stat.; tr.lit.; circ. 39,300 (controlled). **Indexed:** ABC, Anal.Abstr., Lab.Haz.Bull.
—BLDSC shelfmark: 3829.606800.
Formerly: International Clinical Products Review.

EXPERIMENTAL AND CLINICAL IMMUNOGENETICS. see *BIOLOGY — Genetics*

619   GW   ISSN 0940-2993
EXPERIMENTAL AND TOXICOLOGIC PATHOLOGY. (Text in English) 1967. irreg. (8-12/yr.) DM.598($384) (foreign DM.601). Gustav Fischer Verlag, Villengang 2, Postfach 176, 6900 Jena, Germany. TEL 03778-27332. TELEX 18069-588676. Ed. F. Bolck. adv.; bk.rev.; bibl.; charts; illus.; index. (reprint service avail. from ISI) **Indexed:** Biol.Abstr., Chem.Abstr., Curr.Adv.Cancer Res., Curr.Adv.Cell & Devel.Biol., Curr.Adv.Ecol.Sci., Curr.Cont., Dairy Sci.Abstr., Dent.Ind., Excerp.Med., Helminthol.Abstr., Ind.Med., Ind.Sci.Rev., INIS Atomind., Nutr.Abstr., Sci.Cit.Ind.
Former titles: Experimental Pathology (ISSN 0232-1513); Experimentelle Pathologie (ISSN 0014-4908)

619   JA   ISSN 0007-5124
CODEN: JIDOAA
EXPERIMENTAL ANIMALS/JIKKEN DOBUTSU. (Text in English and Japanese; summaries in English) 1952. q. $70. Japanese Association for Laboratory Animal Science - Nihon Jikken Dobutsu Gakkai, c/o Tokyo Daigaku Nogakubu, Juigaku-ka, 1-1-1 Yayoi, Bunkyo-ku, Tokyo 113, Japan. FAX 03-5800-6925. Ed. Shigeru Sugano. adv.; bk.rev.; charts; illus.; cum.index; circ. 2,300. **Indexed:** Anim.Breed.Abstr., Biol.Abstr., Chem.Abstr., Curr.Adv.Ecol.Sci., Dent.Ind., Excerp.Med., Ind.Med., Ind.Vet., Poult.Abstr., Small Anim.Abstr., Vet.Bull.
—BLDSC shelfmark: 3838.730000.
Formerly: Bulletin of the Experimental Animals.

619   GW   ISSN 0863-4645
EXPERIMENTELLE MEDIZIN. MITTEILUNGSBLATT. 1963. bi-m. DM.60. Idemed Info-Dienst, Hermann-Matern-Str. 54-55, Postfach 140, 1040 Berlin - Mitte, Germany. TEL 030-2863138. adv.; bk.rev.; illus.

FERTILITAET, STERILITAET, IN-VITRO FERTILISATION, SEXUALITAET, KONTRAZEPTION. see *MEDICAL SCIENCES — Obstetrics And Gynecology*

619   UK   ISSN 0268-9499
CODEN: FBRIE7
FIBRINOLYSIS. 1987. q. £116($250) Churchill Livingstone Medical Journals, Robert Stevenson House, 1-3 Baxter's Pl., Leith Walk, Ediburgh EH1 3AF, Scotland. TEL 031-556-2424. (Subscr. to: Longman Group, Journals Subscr. Dept., P.O. Box 77, Fourth Ave., Harlow, Essex CM19 5AA, England; U.S. subscr. to: Churchill Livingstone, 650 Ave. of the Americas, New York, NY 10011. TEL 212-206-5000) Eds. J.F. Davidson, I.D. Walker. circ. 800.
—BLDSC shelfmark: 3918.118000.
Formerly: Journal of Fibrinolysis.
Description: Molecular biology of fibrinolysis, clinical trials of thrombolytic agents.

619   US
FLOATING. 1987. q. $25. Floatation Tank Association, Box 1396, Grass Valley, CA 95945-1396. TEL 916-432-3794. Ed. Lee Perry. adv.; bk.rev.; abstr.; bibl.; illus.; stat.; circ. 1,000. (back issues avail.)
Description: Collects and disseminates information on floatation tanks and floating to professionals and the general public.

619   PO
FOLIA ANATOMICA UNIVERSITATIS CONIMBRICENSIS. (Text in English, French and Portuguese) 1926. a. free or exchange basis. Imprensa de Coimbra, Ltd., Largo de S. Salvador, Coimbra, Portugal. Ed. A. Simoes de Carvalho. bibl.; illus.; index. **Indexed:** Biol.Abstr.

FUJIAN ZHONGYI YAO/FUJIAN JOURNAL OF TRADITIONAL CHINESE MEDICINE. see *MEDICAL SCIENCES*

616   GW   ISSN 0016-3538
CODEN: GITEAR
G I T; Fachzeitschrift fuer das Laboratorium. (Summaries in English and German) 1957. m. DM.120. G I T Verlag GmbH, Roesslerstr. 90, Postfach 110564, 6100 Darmstadt 11, Germany. TEL 06151-8090-0. FAX 06151-809045. Ed. Ernst Giebeler. adv.; bk.rev.; charts; illus.; pat.; tr.lit.; index; circ. 25,000. **Indexed:** Chem.Abstr., Dok.Arbeitsmed., Excerp.Med., INIS Atomind.
—BLDSC shelfmark: 4179.652000.

GENE AMPLIFICATION AND ANALYSIS SERIES. see *BIOLOGY — Genetics*

GENERAL CLINICAL RESEARCH CENTERS; a research resources directory. see *MEDICAL SCIENCES — Abstracting, Bibliographies, Statistics*

GUIA DE MATERIAL DE LABORATORIO. see *INSTRUMENTS*

616   US
GUIDE FOR THE CARE AND USE OF LABORATORY ANIMALS. 1963. irreg. $2.50. U.S. National Institutes of Health, National Center for Research Resources, Westwood Bldg., Rm. 10A15, 5333 Westbard Ave., Bethesda, MD 20892. TEL 301-496-5545. (Subscr. to: Supt. of Documents, Washington, DC 20402)
Formerly (until 1972): Guide for Laboratory Animal Facilities and Care (ISSN 0072-8098)
Description: Guidelines articles on the care and proper use of laboratory research animals.

610   GY
GUYANA ASSOCIATION OF MEDICAL TECHNOLOGISTS. NEWSLETTER. s-a. Guyana Association of Medical Technologists, Central Medical Laboratory, Public Hospital, Middle Street, Georgetown, Guyana.

619   US   ISSN 0887-3712
H L B NEWSLETTER; reporting on heart, lung and blood disease research program, policy development. 1985. 24/yr. $196 (foreign $265). 821 Delaware Ave., S.W., Washington, DC 20024. TEL 202-488-7533. Ed. Nathaniel Polster. bk.rev.

619 614   US   ISSN 0046-7022
R856.A1
HEALTH DEVICES. 1971. m. $1995. (Emergency Care Research Institute) E C R I, 5200 Butler Pike, Plymouth Meeting, PA 19462. TEL 215-825-6000. FAX 215-834-1275. Ed. Pamela Bond. bk.rev.; illus.; index; circ. 2,600. (back issues avail.)
—BLDSC shelfmark: 4274.963000.
Description: Contains evaluation and ratings of medical devices used by hospitals. Reports on hazardous devices, inspection procedures, access to ECRI's online computer network, consulting services, and other device-related information.
Refereed Serial

616   UK   ISSN 0261-4707
HIGH PERFORMANCE LIQUID CHROMATOGRAPHY. 1982. s-m. £100. Sheffield University Biomedical Information Service (SUBIS), The University, Sheffield S10 2TN, England. TEL 0742-768555. FAX 0742-739826. TELEX 547216-UGSHEF-G.
Description: Current awareness service for researchers focusing on pharmacological substances.

HOOFDLIJNEN. see *MEDICAL SCIENCES — Psychiatry And Neurology*

HUMAN GENE MAPPING. see *BIOLOGY — Genetics*

619   US   ISSN 0885-0615
R853.H8
HUMAN RESEARCH REPORT; protecting researchers and research subjects. 1986. m. $167. Deem Corporation, Box 44069, Omaha, NE 68144-0069. TEL 402-895-5748. Ed. Dr. Dennis M. Maloney. (back issues avail.)
Description: Covers regulatory, legal, legislative and practical aspects of human experimentation ethics.

619   US
HUMANE INNOVATIONS AND ALTERNATIVES. 1987. a. $25 to institutions (members $15). Psychologists for the Ethical Treatment of Animals, Box 1297, Washington Grove, MD 20880-1297. TEL 301-963-4751. Ed. Emmanuel Bernstein. cum.index; circ. 1,000. (back issues avail.)
Formerly: Humane Innovations and Alternatives in Animal Experimentation: A Notebook (ISSN 0893-9535)
Description: Brief articles describing changes in care and procedures involving animals in research and educational settings that reduce reliance upon animals and diminish their suffering.

619 574 591   US   ISSN 0018-9960
QL55
I L A R NEWS. 1957. q. free to qualified personnel. (Institute of Laboratory Animal Resources) National Academy Press, National Academy of Sciences, 2101 Constitution Ave., N.W., Washington, DC 20418. TEL 202-334-2590. Ed. Dorothy D. Greenhouse. bk.rev.; bibl.; illus.; circ. 4,200. (back issues avail.) **Indexed:** Ind.Vet., Vet.Bull.
Formerly: Information on Laboratory Animals for Research.

619   US   ISSN 0193-7758
I R B: A REVIEW OF HUMAN SUBJECTS RESEARCH. (Institutional Review Board) 1979. bi-m. $38 to individuals; libraries $60; institutions $225. Hastings Center, 255 Elm Rd., Briarcliff Manor, NY 10510. TEL 914-762-8500. Ed. Robert J. Levine. bk.rev.; bibl.; circ. 5,000. (back issues avail.) **Indexed:** Psychol.Abstr.
—BLDSC shelfmark: 4567.631000.

619   US
THE IMMORTALIST. 1970. m. $25. Immortalist Society, 24443 Roanoke, Oak Park, MI 48237. TEL 313-548-9549. FAX 408-255-5433. (And: Box 761, Cupertino, CA 95015. TEL 408-446-4425) (Co-sponsor: American Cryonics Society)
Formerly: The Outlook.
Description: News, information, conjecture, and opinion related to cryonics and life extension.

619   UK   ISSN 0142-8128
IMMUNOASSAY. 1970. s-m. £160. Sheffield University Biomedical Information Service (SUBIS), The University, Sheffield S10 2TN, England. TEL 0742-768555. FAX 0742-739826. TELEX 547216-UGSHEF-G. abstr. (looseleaf format)
Description: Current awareness service for researchers. Covers radioimmunoassay, fluorescence immunoassay and enzyme immunoassay.

IMMUNOHISTOCHEMISTRY. see *BIOLOGY — Cytology And Histology*

619   GR   ISSN 0258-851X
IN VIVO; international journal of in vivo research. 1987. bi-m. $1200 to individuals; institutions $350. John D. Delinassios, Ed. & Pub., 5 Argyropoulou St., Kato Patissia, 111 45 Athens, Greece. TEL 8171209. FAX 2016380. adv.; index; circ. 420. (back issues avail.) **Indexed:** Excerp.Med.
—BLDSC shelfmark: 4372.507000.
Description: Multi-disciplinary approach to the study of biomedical research involving experimental systems. Covers oncology, chemotherapy, pharmacology, immunology, radiology, toxicology, genetics, cytology, endocrinology biotechnology and nutrition.

MEDICAL SCIENCES — EXPERIMENTAL MEDICINE, LABORATORY TECHNIQUE

619   NE
INFOMEDICA.* 1978. m. fl.77.50. Uitgeverij Adex, Postbus 328, 3760 AH Soest, Netherlands. Ed. G. Verburg. adv.; bk.rev.; illus.; circ. 7,300.
Formerly: Z T (Ziekenhuistechniek) (ISSN 0165-019X)
Description: Covers the latest information and new developments concerning medical technology and related fields. Includes announcements of events, new product information and new publications.

619 574   FR   ISSN 0989-8735
INFORMATION DU TECHNICIEN BIOLOGISTE. 4/yr. 318 F. (foreign 428 F.). Doin Editeurs, 8, Place de l'Odeon, 75006 Paris, France. TEL 43-25-34-02. TELEX 203640.

616   UK
INSTITUTE OF MEDICAL LABORATORY SCIENCES, LONDON. ANNUAL REPORT. 1943. a. free. Institute of Medical Laboratory Sciences, 12 Queen Anne St., London W1M OAU, England. TEL 01-636 8192. circ. 17,000.
Formerly: Institute of Medical Laboratory Technology. London. Annual Report (ISSN 0073-9448)

INSTITUTION OF CHEMISTS (INDIA). JOURNAL. see CHEMISTRY

INSTITUTION OF CHEMISTS (INDIA). PROCEEDINGS. see CHEMISTRY

INTERNATIONAL BIOTECHNOLOGY LABORATORY. see BIOLOGY — Biotechnology

INTERNATIONAL JOURNAL OF ARTIFICIAL ORGANS. see MEDICAL SCIENCES

INTERNATIONAL JOURNAL OF RADIATION APPLICATIONS AND INSTRUMENTATION. PART A: APPLIED RADIATION AND ISOTOPES. including data, instrumentation and methods for use in agriculture, industry and medicine. see PHYSICS — Nuclear Physics

619   UK   ISSN 0266-4623
R855
INTERNATIONAL JOURNAL OF TECHNOLOGY ASSESSMENT IN HEALTH CARE. 1985. q. $80 to individuals; institutions $105. (International Society for Technology Assessment in Health Care) Cambridge University Press, Edinburgh Bldg., Shaftesbury Rd., Cambridge CB2 2RU, England. TEL 0223-312393. FAX 0223-315052. TELEX 851817256. (North American orders to: Cambridge University Press, 40 W. 20th St., New York, NY 10011) Eds. Egon Jonsson, Stanley J. Reiser. (also avail. in microform from UMI) **Indexed:** Abstr.Health Care Manage.Stud., Excerp.Med.
—BLDSC shelfmark: 4542.693300.
Description: Forum for professionals interested in the assessment of medical technology, its consequences for patients and its impact on society.

616 542   UK   ISSN 0143-5140
INTERNATIONAL LABMATE. 1976. bi-m. £70. Labmate Ltd., Newgate, Sandpit Lane, St. Albans, Hets. AL4 OBS, England. TEL 0727-55574. Ed. M.H. Pattison. adv.; stat.; tr.lit.; circ. 45,000. (back issues avail.)
—BLDSC shelfmark: 4542.702850.

INTERNATIONAL PRESS CUTTING SERVICE: SCIENTIFIC INSTRUMENTS, LABORATORY EQUIPMENT & CHEMICALS. see INSTRUMENTS

619   IS
ISRAEL INSTITUTE OF ANIMAL SCIENCE. SCIENTIFIC ACTIVITIES. (Text in English and Hebrew) 1971. triennial. $10. Agricultural Research Organization, Israel Institute of Animal Science, Volcani Centre, P.O. Box 6, Bet Dagan 50250, Israel. TEL 03-9683111. FAX 03-993998. **Indexed:** Biol.Abstr.

J E O L NEWS: ANALYTICAL INSTRUMENTATION. see INSTRUMENTS

J E O L NEWS: ELECTRON OPTICS INSTRUMENTATION. see INSTRUMENTS

619   JA   ISSN 0021-4965
JAPANESE JOURNAL OF CLINICAL AND EXPERIMENTAL MEDICINE/RINSHO TO KENKYU. (Text in English and Japanese) 1924. m. 11760 Yen($40) Daido Gakkan Shuppan-bu, Kyushu University Medical School, 3576 Hako Zaki, Higashi-ku, Fukuoka 812, Japan. **Indexed:** Biol.Abstr.
—BLDSC shelfmark: 4651.370000.
Description: Covers clinical and experimental medicine.

619   US   ISSN 1045-4861
                             CODEN: JABIEW
▼**JOURNAL OF APPLIED BIOMATERIALS.** 1990. q. $125 (foreign $175). (Society for Biomaterials) John Wiley & Sons, Inc., Journals, 605 Third Ave., New York, NY 10158-0012. TEL 212-850-6000. FAX 212-850-6088. TELEX 12-7063. Ed. Harold Alexander.
—BLDSC shelfmark: 4940.650000.
Description: Covers medical device development; implant retrieval and analysis, government regulations, liability and legal issues.

JOURNAL OF CARDIOVASCULAR TECHNOLOGY. see MEDICAL SCIENCES — Cardiovascular Diseases

619   US   ISSN 0887-8013
                             CODEN: JCANEM
JOURNAL OF CLINICAL LABORATORY ANALYSIS. 1987. bi-m. $252 (foreign $327). John Wiley & Sons, Inc., Journals, 605 Third, New York, NY 10158. TEL 212-850-6000. FAX 212-850-6088. TELEX 12-7063. Eds. Dr. Robert M. Nakamura, Ralph A. Reisfeld. **Indexed:** Biol.Abstr., Curr.Cont.
—BLDSC shelfmark: 4958.520000.
Description: Includes articles about immunochemistry, toxicology, hematology, immunopathology, microbiology, genetic testing, immunohematology, and clinical chemistry.

619   GW   ISSN 0044-3697
                             CODEN: ZEVRAJ
JOURNAL OF EXPERIMENTAL ANIMAL SCIENCE/ZEITSCHRIFT FUER VERSUCHSTIERKUNDE. (Text in English) 1961. bi-m. DM.234. Gustav Fischer Verlag Jena, Villengang 2, Postfach 176, 6900 Jena, Germany. TEL 03778-27332. FAX 03778-22638. TELEX 18069-588676. Ed. J. Guettner. adv.; bk.rev.; abstr.; bibl.; charts; illus.; index, cum.index: vols.1-25. (reprint service avail. from ISI) **Indexed:** Anim.Breed.Abstr., Biol.Abstr., Biotech.Abstr., Chem.Abstr., Curr.Adv.Cancer Res., Curr.Adv.Ecol.Sci., Curr.Adv.Genetics & Molec.Biol., Curr.Cont., Dairy Sci.Abstr., Dent.Ind., Excerp.Med., Helminthol.Abstr., Ind.Med., Ind.Vet., Nutr.Abstr., Pig News & Info., Protozool.Abstr., Ref.Zh., Small Anim.Abstr., Vet.Bull.

610   US   ISSN 0022-1007
                             CODEN: JEMEAV
JOURNAL OF EXPERIMENTAL MEDICINE. 1896. m. (2 vols./yr, 6 nos./vol.). $200 (effective 1992). Rockefeller University Press, 222 E. 70th St., New York, NY 10021. TEL 212-570-8572. FAX 212-570-7944. (Subscr. to: Box 5108, Church Street Sta., New York, NY 10249) Ed.Bd. charts; illus.; circ. 3,883. (also avail. in microform from UMI; reprint service avail. from ISI,UMI) **Indexed:** Anim.Breed.Abstr., Biol.Abstr., Biotech.Abstr., Chem.Abstr., Curr.Adv.Cancer Res., Curr.Adv.Cell & Devel.Biol., Curr.Adv.Genetics & Molec.Biol., Curr.Cont., Dairy Sci.Abstr., Excerp.Med., Helminthol.Abstr., Ind.Med., Ind.Sci.Rev., Ind.Vet., INIS Atomind., Nutr.Abstr., Poult.Abstr., Protozool.Abstr., Sci.Cit.Ind, Trop.Dis.Bull., Vet.Bull.
—BLDSC shelfmark: 4982.000000.
Description: Provides significant research in immunology and experimental medicine.
Refereed Serial

610   US   ISSN 0022-2143
R11   CODEN: JLCMAK
JOURNAL OF LABORATORY AND CLINICAL MEDICINE. 1915. m. $89 to individuals (foreign $109); institutions $167 (foreign $187); students $42 (foreign $62). (Central Society for Clinical Research) Mosby - Year Book, Inc. (Subsidiary of: Times Mirror Company), 11830 Westline Industrial Dr., St. Louis, MO 63146. TEL 800-325-4117. FAX 314-432-1380. TELEX 44-2402. Ed. Dr. Harry S. Jacob. adv.; abstr.; bibl.; charts; illus.; s-a. index; circ. 3,932. (also avail. in microfilm from UMI; reprint service avail. from UMI) **Indexed:** Abstr.Hyg., ASCA, Biol.Abstr., Biotech.Abstr., Chem.Abstr., Curr.Adv.Biochem., Curr.Adv.Cancer Res., Curr.Adv.Ecol.Sci., Curr.Cont., Dairy Sci.Abstr., Excerp.Med., Helminthol.Abstr., Ind.Med., Ind.Sci.Rev., Ind.Vet., INIS Atomind., Nutr.Abstr., Rev.Plant Path., Sci.Cit.Ind., Telegen, Trop.Dis.Bull., Vet.Bull.
●Also available online. Vendor(s): BRS.
—BLDSC shelfmark: 5010.000000.
Description: Information on clinical investigation and research with advanced information on hematology, nephrology, organ transplantation, cardiology and immunology.
Refereed Serial

JOURNAL OF MICROSURGERY. see MEDICAL SCIENCES — Surgery

619   US   ISSN 0896-548X
                             CODEN: JTEMEM
THE JOURNAL OF TRACE ELEMENTS IN EXPERIMENTAL MEDICINE. 1988. q. $168 (foreign $218). (International Society for Trace Element Research in Humans) John Wiley & Sons, Inc., Journals, 605 Third Ave., New York, NY 10158. TEL 212-850-6000. FAX 212-850-6088. TELEX 12-7063. Ed. Ananda S. Prasad.
—BLDSC shelfmark: 5069.744300.
Description: Focuses on the role of trace elements in human health and disease; provides special attention to their clinical, nutritional, biochemical, immunological, and toxicological aspects.
Refereed Serial

619   JA   ISSN 0301-2611
                             CODEN: KTGIDU
KENSA TO GIJUTSU/MODERN MEDICAL LABORATORY. (Text in Japanese) 1973. m. 13020 Yen($100) Igaku-Shoin Ltd., 5-24-3 Hongo, Bunkyo-ku, Tokyo 113-91, Japan. TEL 03-817-5713. Ed.Bd. circ. 8,500.
—BLDSC shelfmark: 5889.730000.

610   HU   ISSN 0023-1878
R850   CODEN: KIORAH
KISERLETES ORVOSTUDOMANY. 1949. bi-m. $43.50. Magyar Elettani Tarsasag, Puskin u. 9, Budapest 8, Hungary. (Subscr. to: Kultura, P.O. Box 149, H-1389 Budapest, Hungary) Ed. Peter Balint. adv.; bk.rev.; charts; illus. **Indexed:** Biol.Abstr., Chem.Abstr., Excerp.Med., Ind.Med., INIS Atomind.

616   GW   ISSN 0941-2131
                             CODEN: AELAAH
KLINISCHES LABOR. (Text and summaries in English and German) 1955. m. DM.120. Verlag Klinisches Labor, Im Breitspiel 15, 6900 Heidelberg, Germany. TEL 06221-343233. FAX 06221-343210. Ed. H. Schmidt-Gayk. adv.; bk.rev.; bibl.; charts; illus.; cum.index; circ. 5,000. **Indexed:** Biol.Abstr., Chem.Abstr., Curr.Adv.Ecol.Sci., Curr.Cont., Excerp.Med., Ind.Med., INIS Atomind.
Formerly: Aerztliche Laboratorium (ISSN 0001-9526)
Description: Publication for physicians concerning the latest research and findings in medical laboratories. Covers all fields of medicine and includes announcements of events and list of suppliers.

542   SA
L M S - LABORATORY EQUIPMENT BUYERS GUIDE. (Laboratory Marketing Spectrum) (Text in English) 1989. a. R.110. George Warman Publications (Pty.) Ltd., 77 Hout St., P.O. Box 704, Cape Town 8001, South Africa. TEL 021-245320. FAX 021-261332. Ed. Desmond Varley.
Description: Guide for buyers of laboratory equipment.

MEDICAL SCIENCES — EXPERIMENTAL MEDICINE, LABORATORY TECHNIQUE

619　　　　　SA　　ISSN 1013-1205
L M S - LABORATORY MARKETING SPECTRUM; new developments in laboratory equipment. (Text in English) 1982. bi-m. R.58. George Warman Publications (Pty.) Ltd., 77 Hout St., P.O. Box 704, 8000 Cape Town, South Africa. TEL 021-24-5320. FAX 021-26-1332. TELEX 5-21849 GWP CT SA. Ed. Debbie Welsh. adv.; bk.rev.; index; circ. 5,700 (controlled). (back issues avail.)
 Description: Provides product data on laboratory equipment and materials.

619　　　　　US　　ISSN 0093-7355
LAB ANIMAL. 1972. 10/yr. $49 (foreign $70)(effective 1992). Nature Publishing Co. (Subsidiary of: Macmillan Magazines, Ltd.), 65 Bleecker St., New York, NY 10012. TEL 212-477-9600. (Subscr. to: Lab Animal Subscription Fulfillment, Box 1710, Riverton, NJ 08077-7310) Ed. Julia Schuloff. adv.; bk.rev.; charts; illus.; tr.lit.; circ. 10,500.
 —BLDSC shelfmark: 5137.700000.
 Refereed Serial

542　　　　　GW
LAB-COMPACT SERVICE; Direktinformation Labortechnik. 1971. 4/yr. free to qualified personnel. G I T Verlag GmbH, Roesslerstr. 90, Postfach 110564, 6100 Darmstadt 11, Germany. TEL 06151-8090-0. FAX 06151-809045. Ed. Ernst Giebeler. adv.; illus.; tr.lit.; circ. 14,000.
 Description: Consists of requests-for-information postcards.

619　　　　　US
LAB HOTLINE. 1965. m. free. University of Iowa, University Hygienic Laboratory, Oakdale Campus, Iowa City, IA 52242. TEL 319-335-4500. FAX 319-335-4555. Ed. Tex Heald. charts; stat.; circ. 600.

619　　　　　NE　　ISSN 0368-7368
LAB INSTRUMENTEN; maandblad voor het wetenschappelijk en industriele laboratorium. 1964. m. fl.100. Uitgeverij Adex, Postbus 328, 3760 AH Soest, Netherlands. TEL 02155-10034. FAX 02155-25576. Ed. K.H.P. Broer. adv.; bk.rev.; illus.; circ. 2,500.
 Description: Covers new technological research and development in laboratory instruments. Includes new product listings.

619　　　　　BE
LAB PRODUCTS INTERNATIONAL. 1987. 8/yr. $70 (free to qualified personnel). Pan European Publishing Co. (Subsidiary of: Elsevier Librico N.V.), Rue Verte 216, B-1210 Brussels, Belgium. TEL 02-242-29-92. FAX 02-242-71-11. TELEX 25828 B. Ed. Thomas Clark. adv.; bk.rev.; circ. 50,000 (controlled).
 Description: Informs its readers about the latest laboratory products being introduced into the European market from around the world.

616　　　　　US　　ISSN 1054-0970
LABMEDICA. (Text in English; summaries in French, German, Japanese, Spanish) 1982. 6/yr. $120. Globetech Publishing, 30 Cannon Rd., Wilton, CT 06897. TEL 203-762-3432. FAX 203-762-8640. TELEX 4972075 TECHCOM. Ed. Jill Quigley Roberge. adv.; bk.rev.; index; circ. 26,000. (back issues avail.)
 Formerly (until 1984): Medilab.
 Description: Covers the latest developments in laboratory technology, including: microbiology, clinical chemistry, hematology and immunology.
 Refereed Serial

542　　　　　GW　　ISSN 0344-5208
LABO; Kennziffer-Zeitschrift fuer Labortechnik. 1970. 13/yr. free. Verlag Hoppenstedt und Co., Havelstr. 9, Postfach 4006, 6100 Darmstadt, Germany. TEL 06151-380-0. FAX 06151-380-360. Ed. Rainer Jupe. adv.; bk.rev.; circ. 16,000 (controlled).

619　　　　　GW
LABOR-MEDIZIN. 10/yr. DM.110. G I T Verlag, Roesslerstr. 90, Postfach 110564, 6100 Darmstadt 11, Germany. TEL 06151-8090-0. FAX 06151-809045. circ. 11,000. **Indexed:** INIS Atomind.

542　　　　　MX
LABORATORIOS DE ESPECIALIDADES Y CONTROL. 1963. a. Mex.$100000($50) Informatica Cosmos, S.A. de C.V., Fernandez Annieta 5-101, Col. Los Cipreses, 04830 Mexico D.F., Mexico. TEL 677-48-68. FAX 679-35-75. Ed. Cesar Macazaga. adv.

616 681　　　　　NE
LABORATORIUM PRAKTIJK/LABORATORY MAGAZINE. m. fl.99.50 (foreign fl.310). Stam Tijdshcriften B.V., Postbus 235, 2280 AE Rijswijk, Netherlands. TEL 070-3988100. FAX 070-3988276. TELEX 33702 STAM NL. adv.; circ. 5,895.

616.07　　　　　GW　　ISSN 0342-3026
　　　　　　　　　　CODEN: LABOD3
LABORATORIUMS MEDIZIN. m. DM.139.70. Kirchheim und Co. GmbH, Kaiserstr. 41, Postfach 2524, 6500 Mainz, Germany. TEL 06131-671081. Ed.Bd. adv.; charts; illus. **Indexed:** Chem.Abstr.
 —BLDSC shelfmark: 5137.974000.

LABORATORNOE DELO/LABORATORY TECHNIQUE. see *MEDICAL SCIENCES*

619　　　　　US　　ISSN 0023-6764
　　　　　　　　　　CODEN: LBASAE
LABORATORY ANIMAL SCIENCE. 1950. bi-m. $70 (foreign $100). American Association for Laboratory Animal Science, 70 Timber Creek Dr., Ste. 5, Cordova, TN 38018. bk.rev.; charts; illus.; index; circ. 4,500. **Indexed:** Anim.Breed.Abstr., Biol.Abstr., Biotech.Abstr., Chem.Abstr., Curr.Adv.Ecol.Sci., Curr.Cont., Dairy Sci.Abstr., Dent.Ind., Excerp.Med., Helminthol.Abstr., Ind.Med., Ind.Sci.Rev., Ind.Vet., INIS Atomind., Nutr.Abstr., Pig News & Info., Protozool.Abstr., Rev.Plant Path., Small Anim.Abstr., Vet.Bull.
 —BLDSC shelfmark: 5138.540000.
 Formerly: Laboratory Animal Care.
 Refereed Serial

619　　　　　UK　　ISSN 0023-6772
SF405.5　　　　　CODEN: LBANAX
LABORATORY ANIMALS. 1966. q. £70($139) (Laboratory Animal Science Association) Royal Society of Medicine Services Ltd., 1 Wimpole St., London W1M 8AE, England. TEL 071-408-2119. FAX 071-355-3198. adv.; bk.rev.; charts; illus.; index; circ. 1,700. **Indexed:** Anim.Breed.Abstr., Biol.Abstr., Chem.Abstr., Curr.Adv.Cell & Devel.Biol., Curr.Adv.Ecol.Sci., Curr.Cont., Dairy Sci.Abstr., Excerp.Med., Helminthol.Abstr., Ind.Med., Ind.Sci.Rev., Ind.Vet., Nutr.Abstr., Poult.Abstr., Rev.Plant Path., Vet.Bull.
 —BLDSC shelfmark: 5138.600000.
 Description: Provides an international forum for the publication of research carried out by scientists primarily concerned with the care, welfare and science of laboratory animals.

619　　　　　UK
LABORATORY ANIMALS. BUYERS GUIDE. 1977. irreg. Laboratory Animals Ltd., c/o Royal Society of Medicine Services, 1 Wimpole St., London W1M 8AE, England. TEL 071-408-2119. FAX 071-355-3198.

619　　　　　CN
LABORATORY BUYERS GUIDE. a. Can.$53.50 (foreign $50). Southam Business Communications Inc. (Subsidiary of: Southam Inc.), 1450 Don Mills Rd., Don Mills, Ont. M3B 2X9, Canada. TEL 416-445-6641. FAX 416-442-2261. TELEX 06-966612. adv.

542　　　　　US　　ISSN 0023-6810
LABORATORY EQUIPMENT. 1964. m. $12. Gordon Publications, Inc., 301 Gibraltar Dr., Morris Plains, NJ 07950. TEL 201-292-5100. FAX 201-898-9281. Ed. Helen Robinson. adv.; illus.; circ. 120,000. (tabloid format; also avail. in microform from UMI) **Indexed:** Curr.Pack.Abstr., Graph.Arts Lit.Abstr., World Text.Abstr.

542　　　　　UK　　ISSN 0023-6829
Q185　　　　　CODEN: LEQDA2
LABORATORY EQUIPMENT DIGEST. 1963. m. $120. Morgan-Grampian (Process Press) Ltd., 30 Calderwood St., Woolwich, London SE18 6QH, England. TEL 01-855-7777. FAX 01-854-7476. Ed. Mike Spear. adv.; bk.rev.; charts; illus.; tr.lit.; circ. 17,009. **Indexed:** Art & Archaeol.Tech.Abstr., Excerp.Med., Met.Abstr., Sci.Abstr., World Surf.Coat.

619　　　　　NE　　ISSN 0925-5281
▼**LABORATORY INFORMATION MANAGEMENT**. (Section of: Chemometrics and Intelligent Laboratory Systems (ISSN 0169-7439)) 1991. 3/yr. fl.406 (effective 1992). Elsevier Science Publishers B.V., P.O. Box 211, 1000 AE Amsterdam, Netherlands. TEL 020-5803911. FAX 020-5803598. TELEX 18582 ESPA NL. (Subscr. in U.S. and Canada to: Elsevier Science Publishing Co., Inc., Box 882, Madison Sq. Sta., New York, NY 10159. TEL 212-989-5800) Ed. R.D. McDowall. **Indexed:** Excerp.Med. (1992-).
 Description: Covers all aspects of information management in a laboratory environment, such as information technology, storage processing and flow of data.
 Refereed Serial

616　　　　　US　　ISSN 0023-6837
RB1　　　　　CODEN: LAINAW
LABORATORY INVESTIGATION; a journal of experimental methods and pathology. 1952. m. $105 to individuals; institutions $175. (United States and Canadian Academy of Pathology) Williams & Wilkins, 428 E. Preston St., Baltimore, MD 21202. TEL 301-528-4000. FAX 301-528-4312. TELEX 87669. Ed. Dr. Emanuel Rubin. adv.; abstr.; bibl.; charts; illus.; circ. 3,600. (also avail. in microform) **Indexed:** Biol.Abstr., Chem.Abstr., Curr.Adv.Cancer Res., Curr.Adv.Cell & Devel.Biol., Curr.Adv.Ecol.Sci., Curr.Adv.Genetics & Molec.Biol., Curr.Cont., Dairy Sci.Abstr., Dent.Ind., Excerp.Med., Helminthol.Abstr., Ind.Med., Ind.Sci.Rev., Ind.Vet., INIS Atomind., Nutr.Abstr., Pig News & Info., Protozool.Abstr., Small Anim.Abstr., Vet.Bull.
 —BLDSC shelfmark: 5140.000000.
 Description: Experimental, anatomical and comparative pathology, cytologic and histologic methods, tissue culturing for pathologists and laboratory technicians.
 Refereed Serial

LABORATORY MEDICINE. see *MEDICAL SCIENCES*

LABORATORY MEDICINE ABSTRACT AND COMMENT. see *MEDICAL SCIENCES — Abstracting, Bibliographies, Statistics*

619　　　　　AT
LABORATORY NEWS. m. free to qualified personnel. Business Press International Pty. Ltd., 162 Goulburn Pty. Ltd., Darlinghurst, N.S.W. 2010, Australia. Ed. John Collett. adv.; illus.; circ. 7,200. (tabloid format) **Indexed:** Br.Ceram.Abstr., Curr.Biotech.Abstr., Lab.Haz.Bull., Mass Spectr.Bull., World Surf.Coat.

619　　　　　UK　　ISSN 0266-7169
LABORATORY NEWS. 1971. fortn. £125. E M A P Maclaren Ltd., P.O. Box 109, Maclaren House, Scarbrook Rd., Croydon CR9 1QH, England. TEL 081-688-7788. FAX 081-688-9300. Ed. Alex Crawford. adv.; bk.rev.; circ. 16,000. **Indexed:** ABC, Curr.Biotech.Abstr.
 —BLDSC shelfmark: 5140.570000.
 Description: News of experimental medicine and laboratory technique.

616 542　　　　　UK　　ISSN 0023-6853
Q183　　　　　CODEN: LABPA3
LABORATORY PRACTICE; research techniques and equipment. (Text in English; summaries in French, German) 1952. m. £39($170) United Trade Press Ltd., U.T.P. House, 33-35 Bowling Green Ln., London EC1R 0DA, England. TEL 01-837 1212. Ed. Richard Davies. adv.; bk.rev.; abstr.; charts; illus.; index, cum.index; circ. 15,669. **Indexed:** Abstr.Hyg., Anal.Abstr., Biol.Abstr., Br.Ceram.Abstr., Br.Tech.Ind., Chem.Abstr., Curr.Adv.Ecol.Sci., Dairy Sci.Abstr., Excerp.Med., Field Crop Abstr., Fluidex, Food Sci.& Tech.Abstr., Herb.Abstr., Hort.Abstr., Ind.Vet., INIS Atomind., Lab.Haz.Bull., Mass Spectr.Bull., Met.Abstr., RAPRA, Sci.Abstr., Soils & Fert., Trop.Dis.Bull., Vet.Bull., W.R.C.Inf., World Surf.Coat.
 —BLDSC shelfmark: 5141.000000.

616　　　　　CN　　ISSN 0047-3855
LABORATORY PRODUCT NEWS. 1971. 7/yr. Can.$27.82($46) (foreign $74). Southam Business Communications Inc. (Subsidiary of: Southam Inc.), 1450 Don Mills Rd., Don Mills, Ont. M3B 2X7, Canada. TEL 416-445-6641. FAX 416-442-2261. Ed. Rita Tate. adv.; circ. 18,677 (controlled).

MEDICAL SCIENCES — EXPERIMENTAL MEDICINE, LABORATORY TECHNIQUE

619 US
LABORATORY REGULATION MANUAL. 1976. q. $585. Aspen Publishers, Inc., 200 Orchard Ridge Dr., Gaithersburg, MD 20878. TEL 301-417-7500. FAX 301-417-7550.

619 340 US ISSN 1048-0706
CODEN: LRENEX
▼**LABORATORY REGULATION NEWS**; biweekly news for testing and standards professionals. 1990. s-m. $492 (foreign $514). Buraff Publications (Subsidiary of: Millin Publications, Inc.), 1350 Connecticut Ave., N.W., Ste. 1000, Washington, DC 20036. TEL 202-862-0990. FAX 202-862-0999. Ed. George Kimmerling. index. (back issues avail.)
Description: For laboratory and standards professionals. Covers new state and federal requirements in the field.

LABORATORY TECHNIQUES IN BIOCHEMISTRY AND MOLECULAR BIOLOGY. see *BIOLOGY — Biological Chemistry*

619 CN
LABORATORY TIMES. 6/yr. Can.$15. Maclean Hunter Ltd., Maclean-Hunter Bldg., 777 Bay St., Toronto, Ont. M5W 1A7, Canada.

LABORATORY YELLOW PAGES. see *BUSINESS AND ECONOMICS — Trade And Industrial Directories*

619 GW ISSN 0344-1733
CODEN: LAPRDE
LABORPRAXIS. 1977. 10/yr. DM.180. Vogel-Verlag und Druck KG, Max-Planck-Str. 7-9, Postfach 67 40, 8700 Wuerzburg 1, Germany. Ed. Dieter Kneucker. adv.; bk.rev.; circ. 16,000 (controlled). **Indexed:** INIS Atomind.
—BLDSC shelfmark: 5141.942000.

542 SZ
LABORSCOPE; labortechnik-verfahrenstechnik-biotechnologie. 1974. 8/yr. free in Switzerland (foreign 47 Fr.). Verlag Binkert AG, CH-4335 Laufenburg, Switzerland. TEL 064-697272. FAX 064-697333. bk.rev.; illus.; circ. 6,250.

619 621.329 IT ISSN 1121-0656
▼**LASER AND TECHNOLOGY;** clinical and experimental. (Text in Italian; abstracts in English) 1991. 3/yr. L.80000($80) (effective 1992). Wichtig Editore s.r.l., Via Friuli, 72-73, 20135 Milan, Italy. TEL 02-5452306. FAX 02-5451843.

681 GW ISSN 0938-765X
LASERMEDIZIN. 1985. 4/yr. DM.196 (foreign DM.198). Gustav Fischer Verlag, Wollgrasweg 49, Postfach 720143, 7000 Stuttgart 70, Germany. TEL 0711-458030. FAX 0711-4580334. TELEX 7111488-FIBUCH-D.
—BLDSC shelfmark: 5156.597000.

LASERS IN MEDICINE. see *MEDICAL SCIENCES — Abstracting, Bibliographies, Statistics*

616 US ISSN 0580-7247
RB36 CODEN: MLOBAC
M L O. (Medical Laboratory Observer) 1969. m. $59 (foreign $75). Medical Economics Publishing Co., Five Paragon Dr., Montvale, NJ 07645. TEL 201-358-7200. FAX 201-573-1040. Ed. Robert J. Fitzgibbon. adv.; charts; illus.; stat.; index; circ. 58,000. **Indexed:** Bus.Ind., CINAHL, Tr.& Indus.Ind.
Description: Improves the management skills of clinical lab supervisors.

M T A - FACHZEITSCHRIFT FUER TECHNISCHE ASSISTENTEN DER MEDIZIN; Monatszeitschrift fuer MTA's, Labormediziner, Fachleute Radio-Diagnostik, Lehrer und Studenten. (Medizinisch-Technische Assistenten) see *MEDICAL SCIENCES*

619 US
▼**M T TODAY.** (Medical Technologist) 1991. w. free. Valley Forge Home, 1288 Valley Forge Rd., Box 1135, Valley Forge, PA 19481. TEL 215-935-1296. FAX 215-935-3072. Ed. Eileen Moran. bk.rev.; charts; illus.; circ. 60,000 (controlled).
Description: Items of general interest to medical laboratory professionals, managers and educators.

MADE IN EUROPE - MEDICAL EQUIPMENT AND SUPPLY GUIDE. see *MEDICAL SCIENCES*

MEDICAL AND RADIOLOGICAL DEVICES GUIDANCE MANUAL. see *PUBLIC HEALTH AND SAFETY*

619 681 US ISSN 1060-8338
MEDICAL DEVICE APPROVAL LETTER. 1992. m. $418. Washington Information Source, 5335 Wisconsin Ave. N.W., Ste. 440, Washington, DC 20015-2003. TEL 202-686-2887. Ed. Henneth Reid.

MEDICAL DEVICE ESTABLISHMENT REGISTRATION MASTER FILE. see *PUBLIC HEALTH AND SAFETY*

MEDICAL DEVICE PROBLEMS REPORT FROM THE D E N: REPORTS FROM MEDICAL DEVICE USERS. see *PUBLIC HEALTH AND SAFETY*

MEDICAL DEVICE REPORTING FROM THE D E N: REPORTS FROM MEDICAL DEVICE MANUFACTURERS. see *PUBLIC HEALTH AND SAFETY*

616 380.1 US
MEDICAL LABORATORY DIRECTORY. irreg., latest ed. 1987-88. $75. U S Directory Service, 655 N.W., 128th St., Box 68-1700, Miami, FL 33168. TEL 305-769-1700. FAX 305-769-0548.
Description: Lists 4,000 medicare approved and state licensed medical laboratories.

619 US
MEDICAL LABORATORY PRODUCTS. 1986. m. Medical Economics Company Inc., 680 Kinderkamack Rd., Oradell, NJ 07649. TEL 201-262-3030. Ed. Deborah Kaplan. circ. 53,000.

616 UK ISSN 0308-3616
CODEN: MLASDU
MEDICAL LABORATORY SCIENCES. 1951. q. £76 (foreign £85). (Institute of Medical Laboratory Sciences) Blackwell Scientific Publications Ltd., Osney Mead, Oxford OX2 0EL, England. TEL 0865-240201. FAX 0865-721205. TELEX 83355-MEDBOK-G. Ed. A.D. Farr. adv.; bk.rev.; abstr.; bibl.; charts; illus.; index; circ. 16,500. **Indexed:** Abstr.Hyg., Biol.Abstr., Chem.Abstr., CINAHL, Curr.Adv.Cancer Res., Curr.Adv.Ecol.Sci., Curr.Cont., Excerp.Med., Helminthol.Abstr., Ind.Med., Ind.Sci.Rev., Ind.Vet., INIS Atomind., Nutr.Abstr., Rev.Plant Path., Telegen, Trop.Dis.Bull., Vet.Bull.
—BLDSC shelfmark: 5529.393000.
Former titles: Medical Laboratory Technology (ISSN 0022-2607); Journal of Medical Laboratory Technology.

610 UK ISSN 0140-3028
CODEN: MLWODQ
MEDICAL LABORATORY WORLD. 1977. m. £33($131) United Trade Press Ltd., U.T.P. House, 33-35 Bowling Green Ln., London EC1R 0DA, England. TEL 01-387 1212. Ed. Julian Page. circ. 9,974. **Indexed:** ABC, Br.Tech.Ind., Chem.Abstr.
—BLDSC shelfmark: 5529.420000.

619 SA ISSN 1011-5528
MEDICAL TECHNOLOGY S A. 1987. q. R.45 (foreign R.50). (Society of Medical Laboratory Technologists of South Africa) Medical Technology News, P.O. Box 253, Rondebosch 7700, South Africa. TEL 021-4610054. Ed. G.W. Wikeley. charts; illus.; tr.lit.; circ. 2,100. (back issues avail.)
Refereed Serial

619 IT ISSN 0393-7623
LA MEDICINA DI LABORATORIO. 1985. q. L.130000($160) Piccin Editore, Via Altinate 107, 35100 Padua, Italy. TEL 049-655566. TELEX 432074 PICCIN I. circ. 3,000.

MICROSURGERY. see *MEDICAL SCIENCES — Surgery*

619 540 UK ISSN 0890-8508
RB43.7
MOLECULAR AND CELLULAR PROBES; the location, diagnosis, and montoring of disease by nucleic acid techniques. 1987. 6/yr. $191. Academic Press Ltd., 24-28 Oval Rd., London NW1 7DX, England. TEL 071-267-4466. FAX 071-482-2293. TELEX 25775 ACPRES G. Ed. R.H. Yolken. index. (back issues avail.) **Indexed:** Anim.Breed.Abstr., Ind.Vet.
—BLDSC shelfmark: 5900.761000.
Description: Examines location, diagnosis, and monitoring of both infectious and inherited diseases.

619 574.88 UK ISSN 0735-1313
CODEN: MBIMDG
MOLECULAR BIOLOGY AND MEDICINE. 1983. bi-m. £80($148) Academic Press Ltd., 24-28 Oval Rd., London NW1 7DX, England. TEL 071-267-4466. FAX 071-482-2293. Ed. J. Sambrook. (back issues avail.) **Indexed:** Abstr.Hyg., Chem.Abstr., Curr.Adv.Ecol.Sci., Curr.Biotech.Abstr., Ind.Med., Protozool.Abstr.

MONOCLONAL ANTIBODIES. see *MEDICAL SCIENCES — Allergology And Immunology*

619 US
MONOGRAPHS ON PATHOLOGY OF LABORATORY ANIMALS. 1983. irreg. price varies. (International Life Sciences Institute) Springer-Verlag, 175 Fifth Ave., New York, NY 10010. (Also Berlin, Heidelberg, Tokyo and Vienna) Ed. T.C. Jones.

NATIONAL ASSOCIATION OF PERFORMING ARTS MANAGERS AND AGENTS. NEWSLETTER. see *THEATER*

619 NE
NEDERLANDSE VERENIGING VOOR KLINISCHE CHEMIE. ALMANAK. a. membership. Speciaal Uitgeverij van Verenigings-Almanakken, Elandweide 52, 3437 CS Nieuwegein, Netherlands. adv.; circ. 650.

616 NZ ISSN 1171-0195
CODEN: NZJMAR
NEW ZEALAND JOURNAL OF MEDICAL LABORATORY SCIENCE. 1946. 4/yr. NZ.$40. New Zealand Institute of Medical Laboratory Technology, P.O. Box 9095, Newmarket, Auckland, New Zealand. Ed. Maree L. Gillies. adv.; bk.rev.; abstr.; charts; illus.; index; circ. 1,600. **Indexed:** Biol.Abstr., Chem.Abstr., Curr.Adv.Ecol.Sci., Excerp.Med., Hosp.Abstr., Ref.Zh.
Formerly (until Mar. 1991): New Zealand Journal of Medical Laboratory Technology (ISSN 0028-8349)

616 NR
NIGERIAN JOURNAL OF MEDICAL LABORATORY TECHNOLOGY. 1973. q. £N2.10. Institute of Medical Laboratory Technology of Nigeria, Lagos University Teaching Hospital, Department of Microbiology, P.M.B. 12003, Lagos, Nigeria. Ed. J.O. Isaacs. adv.; bk.rev.
Formerly: Association of Medical and Veterinary Technologists of Nigeria. Newsletter.

616 US ISSN 0048-069X
NORTH DAKOTA SOCIETY OF MEDICAL TECHNOLOGISTS. NEWSLETTER. vol.24, 1972. q. $6 to non-members. (North Dakota Society for Medical Technology) University of North Dakota, Department of Pathology, Grand Forks, ND 58201. TEL 701-777-2563. FAX 701-772-9636. Eds. Eileen Nelson, Linda Larson. adv.; bk.rev.; film rev.; bibl.; charts; illus.; circ. 400. (tabloid format) **Indexed:** Ind.Med.

542 CN ISSN 0832-5332
O S M T UPDATE. 1985. 6/yr. Ontario Society of Medical Technologists, 234 Eglinton Ave. E., Ste. 600, Toronto, Ont. M4P 1K5, Canada. Ed. Richard C. Lafferty. adv.; bk.rev.; circ. 5,180 (controlled).

PERITONEAL DIALYSIS INTERNATIONAL. see *MEDICAL SCIENCES*

610 IT ISSN 0033-9555
CODEN: RMSPAY
RASSEGNA DI MEDICINA SPERIMENTALE. (Text in English and Italian) 1954. m. L.60000($100) (effective 1992). Casa Editrice Idelson, Via A. de Gasperi 55, 80133 Naples, Italy. TEL 081-5524733. FAX 081-5518295. Ed. Giovanni de Franciscis. bk.rev.; charts; illus.; stat. **Indexed:** Biol.Abstr., Chem.Abstr., Curr.Adv.Ecol.Sci., Excerp.Med.
—BLDSC shelfmark: 7294.440000.
Description: Features research papers covering a wide variety of topics in experimental medicine.

619 IT
RASSEGNA SULLA SPERIMENTAZIONE ORGANIZZATIVA E DIDATTICA NELLE UNIVERSITA. bi-m. L.50000($80) Edizioni Minerva Medica, Corso Bramante 83, 10126 Turin, Italy. TEL (011) 67 82 82.

RAVEN PRESS SERIES IN PHYSIOLOGY. see *BIOLOGY — Physiology*

MEDICAL SCIENCES — FORENSIC SCIENCES

619   DK   ISSN 0105-9173
REGISTER OVER AUTORISEREDE LABORATORIER/REGISTER OF AUTHORIZED LABORATORIES. 1978. a. free. Teknologistyrelsen - Danish National Agency of Technology, Tagensvej 135, 2200 Copenhagen N, Denmark. illus.; circ. 3,000.
Formerly: Autorisationsregister.

RESEARCH IN CLINIC AND LABORATORY. see *MEDICAL SCIENCES*

610   GW   ISSN 0300-9130
R850.A1   CODEN: REXMAS
RESEARCH IN EXPERIMENTAL MEDICINE. (Text and summaries in English and German) vol.155, 1971. 6/yr. DM.680($364) Springer-Verlag, Heidelberger Platz 3, D-1000 Berlin 33, Germany. TEL 030-8207-1. (Also Heidelberg, Tokyo, Vienna, and New York) Ed. F.D. Goebel. (also avail. in microform from UMI; back issues avail.; reprint service avail. from ISI) **Indexed:** Biol.Abstr., Biotech.Abstr., Chem.Abstr., Curr.Adv.Cancer Res., Curr.Adv.Ecol.Sci., Curr.Cont., Dairy Sci.Abstr., Dent.Ind., Excerp.Med., Helminthol.Abstr., Ind.Med., Ind.Vet., Nutr.Abstr., Vet.Bull.
—BLDSC shelfmark: 7740.200000.
Continues: Zeitschrift fuer die Gesamte Experimentelle Medizin Einschliesslich Experimenteller Chirurgie (ISSN 0044-2534)
Description: Original papers and research reports cover experimental medicine and surgery, internal medicine, surgery, endocrinology, pathology, anesthesiology, biochemistry, physiology, and pharmacology.
Refereed Serial

RESOURCES FOR COMPARATIVE BIOMEDICAL RESEARCH ; a research resources directory. see *MEDICAL SCIENCES — Abstracting, Bibliographies, Statistics*

619   SP   ISSN 0214-3429
REVISTA ESPANOLA DE QUIMIOTERAPIA/SPANISH JOURNAL OF CHEMOTHERAPY. (Text in English and Spanish) 1988. q. 5300 ptas.($60) (typically set in Sep.). (Sociedad Espanola de Quimioterapia) J.R. Prous, S.A. International Publishers, Apdo. de Correos, 540, 08080 Barcelona, Spain. TEL 343-459-2220. FAX 343-258-1535. TELEX 98270 PROU E. Ed. M. Gobernado. adv.; circ. 3,000. (back issues avail.)
—BLDSC shelfmark: 7854.230000.

619   JA   ISSN 0485-1420
RINSHO KENSA/JOURNAL OF MEDICAL TECHNOLOGY. (Text in Japanese) 1957. m. 17700 Yen($136) Jgaku-Shoin Ltd., 5-24-3 Hongo, Bunkyo-ku, Tokyo 113-91, Japan. TEL 03-817-5712. Ed.Bd. circ. 12,000.
—BLDSC shelfmark: 5017.090000.

S E R B OFFICIAL REPORTER. (State Employment Relations Board) see *LAW*

616   FR   ISSN 0339-722X
    CODEN: STALDT
S T A L. (Sciences et Techniques de l'Animal de Laboratoire) (Text in English, French) 1976. q. 350 F. Societe Francaise d'Experimentation Animale (SFEA), Centre d'Experimentation Animale et de Recherches Chirurgicales, 6 rue du General-Sarrail, 94000 Creteil, France. TEL 31-47-02-00. (Subscr. to: C. Bugiani, Laboratoire Roussel-Uclaf, 102, route de Noisy, 93230 Romainville, France. TEL 1-48-91-51-90) Ed. J. Duteil. adv.; bk.rev.; circ. 1,000. **Indexed:** ASCA, Biol.Abstr., Curr.Adv.Ecol.Sci., Curr.Cont., Helminthol.Abstr., Ind.Vet., Int.Aerosp.Abstr., Met.Abstr., Vet.Bull.
—BLDSC shelfmark: 8430.120000.
Formerly: Association des Techniciens d'Animaux de Laboratoire. Bulletin Trimestriel (ISSN 0339-7238)

616   UK   ISSN 0036-5513
RB1   CODEN: SJCLAY
SCANDINAVIAN JOURNAL OF CLINICAL & LABORATORY INVESTIGATION. (Text in English) 1949. 8/yr. £105($190) (includes supplement). (Scandinavian Society for Clinical Chemistry) Blackwell Scientific Publications Ltd., Osney Mead, Oxford OX2 OEL, England. TEL 0865-240201. FAX 0865-721205. TELEX 83355-MEDBOK-G. Ed. O. Stokke. adv.; bibl.; charts; illus.; index; circ. 1,600. (back issues avail.; reprint service avail. from SWZ) **Indexed:** Abstr.Hyg., ASCA, Biol.Abstr., Biotech.Abstr., C.I.S.Abstr., Chem.Abstr., Curr.Adv.Cancer Res., Curr.Adv.Ecol.Sci., Curr.Cont., Dairy Sci.Abstr., Excerp.Med., Helminthol.Abstr., Ind.Med., Ind.Vet., Nutr.Abstr., Pig News & Info., Sci.Cit.Ind., Trop.Dis.Bull., Vet.Bull.
—BLDSC shelfmark: 8087.500000.

616   UK   ISSN 0085-591X
SCANDINAVIAN JOURNAL OF CLINICAL AND LABORATORY INVESTIGATION. SUPPLEMENT. (Text in English) 1951. irreg. (Scandinavian Society for Clinical Chemistry and Clinical Physiology) Blackwell Scientific Publications Ltd., Osney Mead, Oxford OX2 OEL, England. TEL 0865-240201. FAX 0865-721205. TELEX 83355-MEDBOK-G. Ed. O. Stokke. adv.; circ. 1,600. (back issues avail.; reprint service avail. from ISI) **Indexed:** Biol.Abstr., Chem.Abstr., Curr.Adv.Biochem., Curr.Adv.Cell & Devel.Biol., Curr.Adv.Ecol.Sci., Curr.Cont., Ind.Med., Nutr.Abstr.
—BLDSC shelfmark: 8087.505000.

SCANNING MICROSCOPY; an international journal of scanning electron microscopy, related techniques, and applications. see *BIOLOGY — Microscopy*

SCHWEIZERISCHE GESELLSCHAFT FUER KLINISCHE CHEMIE. BULLETIN. see *BIOLOGY — Biological Chemistry*

542   US
SCIENCE SUPPLY NEWS.* 1972. q. free. Markson Science Inc., 10201 S. 51st. St., Phoenix, AZ 85044. Ed. Alec Trode. adv.; illus.; circ. 500,000.

SCRIPTA SCIENTIFICA MEDICA. see *MEDICAL SCIENCES — Cancer*

SEMINARS IN NUCLEAR MEDICINE. see *MEDICAL SCIENCES — Radiology And Nuclear Medicine*

616 542   UK   ISSN 0950-7140
SEPARATION. 1987. bi-m. £85($150) Labmate Ltd., 12 Alban Park, Hatfield Rd., St. Albans AL4 0JJ, England. Ed. M.H. Pattison. circ. 2,000.

619
SERONO SYMPOSIA SERIES: ADVANCES IN EXPERIMENTAL MEDICINE. 1989. irreg., latest vol.3. price varies. Raven Press, 1185 Ave. of the Americas, New York, NY 10036. TEL 212-930-9500. FAX 212-869-3495. Eds. Luigi Frati, Stuart A. Aaronson.

619   IT   ISSN 0390-8283
SOCIETA MEDICO CHIRURGICA DE PAVIA. BOLLETTINO. 1886. q. Casa del Giovane, Via Lomonaco 43, I-27100 Pavia, Italy. TEL 0382-422932. Ed. Vittorio Malamavi. circ. 300.

SOCIETY FOR CRYOBIOLOGY. NEWS NOTES. see *BIOLOGY — Biophysics*

SOCIETY FOR EXPERIMENTAL BIOLOGY AND MEDICINE. PROCEEDINGS. see *BIOLOGY*

SOUTHERN CALIFORNIA DENTAL LABORATORY ASSOCIATION. BULLETIN. see *MEDICAL SCIENCES — Dentistry*

616   FR   ISSN 0766-5725
    CODEN: TEBIEY
TECHNIQUE ET BIOLOGIE; revue de documentation scientifique et d'information professionnelle. 1975. bi-m. 300 F. (foreign 450 F.). Societe Francaise d'Editions Medicales, 22-24 rue du Chateau des Rentiers, 75013 Paris, France. TEL 45-83-50-54. Ed. Colette Gallula. adv.; charts; illus. **Indexed:** C.I.S. Abstr., Chem.Abstr.
—BLDSC shelfmark: 8739.250000.
Formerly: Technicien Biologiste (ISSN 0337-9965)

TECHNIQUES OF CHEMISTRY. see *CHEMISTRY*

619   UK
TECHNIQUES OF MEASUREMENT IN MEDICINE SERIES. 1978. irreg., no.7, 1982. price varies. Cambridge University Press, Edinburgh Bldg., Shaftesbury Rd., Cambridge CB2 2RU, England. TEL 0223-312393. FAX 0223-315052. TELEX 851817256. (North American orders to: Cambridge University Press, Journal Fulfillment Dept., 110 Midland Avenue, Port Chester, NY 10573) **Indexed:** Biol.Abstr.

616   SP   ISSN 0371-5728
TECNICAS DE LABORATORIO. 1969. 10/yr. 7700 ptas.($85) (effective 1992). Publica, S.A., Ecuador, 75, entlo., 08029 Barcelona, Spain. TEL 93-321-50-46. FAX 93-439-10-27. Ed. Carlos Romagosa. adv.; bk.rev.; bibl.; charts; illus.; circ. 3,000. **Indexed:** Chem.Abstr., Ind.Med.Esp., Ind.SST.
—BLDSC shelfmark: 8762.710000.

616   SW   ISSN 0345-696X
TIDSKRIFTEN LABORATORIET. Short title: Laboratoriet. 1955. 8/yr. SEK 100. Svenska Laboratorieassistentfoereningen, Ostermalmsgatan 19, S-114 26 Stockholm, Sweden. Ed. Barbro Soederberg. adv.; bk.rev.; circ. 12,418.

TISSUE CULTURE. see *BIOLOGY — Cytology And Histology*

610   JA   ISSN 0040-8727
    CODEN: TJEMAO
TOHOKU JOURNAL OF EXPERIMENTAL MEDICINE. (Text in English, French and German) 1920. m. (3 vols./yr.) $233. Tohoku University Medical Press, 2-1 Seiryo-machi, Sendai-shi, Miyagi-ken 980, Japan. Ed. Dr. Toshi Yuki Yamamoto. abstr.; bibl.; charts; illus.; circ. 800. (also avail. in microform from UMI; reprint service avail. from UMI) **Indexed:** Abstr.Hyg., ASCA, Biol.Abstr., C.I.S.Abstr., Chem.Abstr., Curr.Adv.Ecol.Sci., Curr.Cont., Dairy Sci.Abstr., Dent.Ind., Excerp.Med., Helminthol.Abstr., Ind.Med., Nutr.Abstr., Risk Abstr., Sci.Cit.Ind., Trop.Dis.Bull.
—BLDSC shelfmark: 8861.000000.

610   JA   ISSN 0040-8875
    CODEN: TJXMAH
TOKUSHIMA JOURNAL OF EXPERIMENTAL MEDICINE. (Text in English and European languages) 1954. s-a. exchange basis. Tokushima Daigaku, Igakubu - Tokushima University, School of Medicine, 18-15 Kuramoto-cho 3-chome, Tokushima-shi, Tokushima-ken 770, Japan. FAX 0886-33-0771. Ed. S. Daikoku. charts; illus. **Indexed:** Abstr.Hyg., Biol.Abstr., Chem.Abstr., Curr.Adv.Ecol.Sci., Excerp.Med., Ind.Med., Nutr.Abstr., Trop.Dis.Bull.
—BLDSC shelfmark: 8862.900000.

TRANSPLANTATION PROCEEDINGS. see *MEDICAL SCIENCES — Surgery*

ULTRASTRUCTURAL PATHOLOGY. see *BIOLOGY — Cytology And Histology*

U.S. NATIONAL INSTITUTES OF HEALTH. NATIONAL CENTER FOR RESEARCH RESOURCES. PROGRAM HIGHLIGHTS. see *MEDICAL SCIENCES — Abstracting, Bibliographies, Statistics*

610 591   GW   ISSN 0300-1016
VERSUCHSTIERKUNDE. (Text in English, German) 1972. irreg. price varies. Verlag Paul Parey (Berlin), Seelbuschring 9-17, 1000 Berlin 42, Germany. TEL 030-70784-0. FAX 030-70784199. Eds. M. Merkenschlager, K. Gaertner. bibl.; illus.; index. (back issues avail.)

ZAVODSKAYA LABORATORIYA; zhurnal po analiticheskoi khimii, fizicheskim, matematicheskim i mekhanicheskim metodam issledovaniya materialov. see *CHEMISTRY — Analytical Chemistry*

ZHURNAL EKSPERIMENTAL'NOI I KLINICHESKOI MEDITSINY. see *MEDICAL SCIENCES*

MEDICAL SCIENCES — Forensic Sciences

614.19   US   ISSN 0883-1203
RB10
A B M S DIRECTORY OF CERTIFIED PATHOLOGISTS. 1985. biennial. $34.95. American Board of Medical Specialties, One Rotary Center, Ste. 805, Evanston, IL 60201. TEL 708-491-9091. FAX 708-328-3596. Ed. Dr. J. Lee Dockery.

MEDICAL SCIENCES — FORENSIC SCIENCES

ACCIDENT RECONSTRUCTION JOURNAL. see *LAW*

ACTA CRIMINOLOGIAE ET MEDICAE LEGALIS JAPONICA/HANZAIGAKU ZASSHI. see *CRIMINOLOGY AND LAW ENFORCEMENT*

340.6   BE   ISSN 0065-1397
ACTA MEDICINAE LEGALIS ET SOCIALIS. (Represents proceedings of its triennial world congress and its interim international meetings; not published 1969-1971) (Text in English, French) 1948. a. 1800 BEF. International Academy of Legal Medicine and Social Medicine, Elizabeth Francson, Treasurer, Avenue Nicolai, 49A/8, B-4802 Verviers, Belgium. TEL 32-87-229821. Ed. George Brahy. bk.rev.; circ. 450. Indexed: Biol.Abstr., Chem.Abstr., Ind.Med.
—BLDSC shelfmark: 0635.800000.

ALCOHOL, DRUGS AND DRIVING. see *DRUG ABUSE AND ALCOHOLISM*

614.19   US   ISSN 0195-7910
RA1001
AMERICAN JOURNAL OF FORENSIC MEDICINE AND PATHOLOGY. 1980. q. $116 to individuals; institutions $160. (National Association of Medical Examiners) Raven Press, 1185 Ave. of the Americas, New York, NY 10036. TEL 212-930-9500. FAX 212-869-3495. TELEX 640073. Ed. Dr. Vincent J.M. DiMaio. adv.; bk.rev.; charts; illus.; stat.; index; circ. 2,000. (also avail. in microform from MIM; back issues avail.) Indexed: Abstr.Anthropol., C.L.I., Curr.Cont., Dent.Ind., Excerp.Med., Ind.Med., INIS Atomind., Leg.Per.
—BLDSC shelfmark: 0824.630000.
Description: Features original articles on new examination and documentation procedures, case reports, new devices, and medico-legal aspects.
Refereed Serial

616.8 340   US   ISSN 0163-1942
RA1151
AMERICAN JOURNAL OF FORENSIC PSYCHIATRY. 1978. q. $50 to individuals (foreign $65); institutions $55 (foreign $70). (American College of Forensic Psychiatry) Edward Miller, Ed. & Pub., 26701 Quail Creek, No. 295, Laguna Hills, CA 92656. TEL 714-831-0236. bk.rev.; circ. 1,000. (also avail. in microfilm from WSH,PMC; microfiche; reprint service avail. from WSH) Indexed: Abstr.Bk.Rev.Curr.Leg.Per., Psychol.Abstr.
—BLDSC shelfmark: 0824.640000.
Description: For psychiatrists used as expert witnesses in civil and criminal court cases.
Refereed Serial

614.19   GW   ISSN 0570-5886
ARBEITSMETHODEN DER MEDIZINISCHEN UND NATURWISSENSCHAFTLICHEN KRIMINALISTIK. 1962. irreg., vol.18, 1988. price varies. Schmidt-Roemhild Verlag, Mengstr. 16, 2400 Luebeck 1, Germany. TEL 0451-1605-0. FAX 0451-1605253. TELEX 26536-MSRD.

ARCHIVUM IMMUNOLOGIAE ET THERAPIAE EXPERIMENTALIS. see *MEDICAL SCIENCES*

ARGUMENTATION & ADVOCACY. see *EDUCATION — Special Education And Rehabilitation*

614.19   AT   ISSN 0045-0618
K1   CODEN: AJFSB9
AUSTRALIAN JOURNAL OF FORENSIC SCIENCES. 1968. biennial. Aus.$65. Australian Academy of Forensic Sciences, c/o McGraw-Hill Book Company Australia, 4 Barcoo St., Roseville, N.S.W. 2069, Australia. TEL 02-417-4288. FAX 02-417-5687. TELEX 120849. Ed. Dr. O.R. Schmalzbach. adv.; bk.rev.; circ. 400. Indexed: Aus.P.A.I.S., C.L.I., Chem.Abstr., Excerp.Med., L.R.I.
—BLDSC shelfmark: 1808.100000.

340.6   AU   ISSN 0067-5016
RA1001   CODEN: BEGMA5
BEITRAEGE ZUR GERICHTLICHEN MEDIZIN. 1911. a., vol.69, 1986. price varies. Franz Deuticke, Helferstorfer Strasse 4, A-1010 Vienna, Austria. Ed. Werner Boltz. cum.index (vols. 1-20 in vol. 20; vols. 21-30 in vol. 31); circ. 250. (back issues avail.) Indexed: Chem.Abstr., Dent.Ind., Excerp.Med., Ind.Med.
—BLDSC shelfmark: 1883.700000.

340.6   US   ISSN 0009-7446
KF3821.A59
CITATION; current legal developments relating to medicine and allied professions. 1958. s-m. $80 (non-members $120). American Medical Association, Health Law Division, 515 N. State St., Chicago, IL 60610. TEL 312-464-4607. FAX 312-464-5846. Ed. Nancy Roemer Watson. index every 6 mos.; circ. 2,000. (looseleaf format) Indexed: I.P.A.
—BLDSC shelfmark: 3267.755000.

614.19   US   ISSN 0743-1872
HV8073
CRIME LABORATORY DIGEST. vol.11, 1984. q. free. U.S. Federal Bureau of Investigation Laboratory, FSRTC, F B I Academy, Quantico, VA 22135. (Co-sponsor: American Society of Crime Laboratory Directors (ASCLD)) Ed. Barry L. Brown. circ. 3,000.
Description: Covers all aspects of forensic science.

CRIMINALIST'S SOURCE BOOK. see *CRIMINOLOGY AND LAW ENFORCEMENT — Abstracting, Bibliographies, Statistics*

614.19 364   NE
ELSEVIER SERIES IN FORENSIC AND POLICE SCIENCE. 1981. irreg., vol.7, 1992. price varies. Elsevier Science Publishers B.V., Books Division, P.O. Box 211, 1000 AE Amsterdam, Netherlands. TEL 020-5803911. FAX 020-5803705. TELEX 18582 ESPA NL. (Subscr. in U.S. and Canada to: Elsevier Science Publishing Co., Inc., Box 882, Madison Sq. Sta., New York, NY 10159. TEL 212-989-5800)
Refereed Serial

614.19 364   NE
ELSEVIER SERIES IN PRACTICAL ASPECTS OF CRIMINAL & FORENSIC INVESTIGATION. (Text in English) 1983. irreg., latest 1992. price varies. Elsevier Science Publishers B.V., Books Division, P.O. Box 211, 1000 AE Amsterdam, Netherlands. TEL 020-5803911. FAX 020-5803705. TELEX 18582 ESPA NL. (Subscr. in U.S. and Canada to: Elsevier Science Publishing Co., Inc., Box 882, Madison Sq. Sta., New York, NY 10159. TEL 212-989-5800) (back issues avail.)
Refereed Serial

614.19   CC
FAYIXUE ZAZHI/JOURNAL OF FORENSIC SCIENCES. (Text in Chinese) q. Sifa Bu, Sifa Jianding Kexue Jishu Yanjiusuo - Ministry of Justice, Institute of Evidence Technology, 1347 Guangfu Xilu, Shanghai 200063, People's Republic of China. TEL 2572720. Ed. Zheng Zhongxuan.

FINGERPRINT WORLD. see *CRIMINOLOGY AND LAW ENFORCEMENT*

614.19   US   ISSN 0724-844X
FORENSIA; interdisziplinaeres Jahrbuch fuer Psychiatrie, Psychologie, Kriminologie und Recht. vol.4, 1983. a. price varies. (Gesellschaft Oesterreichischer Nervenaerzte und Psychiater) Springer-Verlag, Journals, 175 Fifth Ave., New York, NY 10010. Ed. G. Harrer. (also avail. in microfiche from UMI; reprint service avail from ISI) Indexed: Excerp.Med.
—BLDSC shelfmark: 3987.725000.

614.19   US
FORENSIC QUARTERLY. 1928. q. $20. National Federation of State High School Associations, 11724 N.W. Plaza Circle, Box 20626, Kansas City, MO 64195-6026. TEL 816-464-5400. FAX 816-464-5571. Ed. Richard G. Fawcett.

614.19   US   ISSN 0888-692X
K6   CODEN: FOREEI
FORENSIC REPORTS. 1987. q. $105. Hemisphere Publishing Corporation (Subsidiary of: Taylor & Francis Group), 1900 Frost Rd., Ste. 101, Bristol, PA 19007-1598. TEL 215-785-5800. FAX 215-785-5515. Ed. Martin I. Kurke. (also avail. in microform from UMI; reprint service avail. from UMI)
—BLDSC shelfmark: 3987.740000.
Description: Covers trial law and product liability consulting. Includes assessments of eyewitness testimony, jury selection method studies, human factors engineering and industrial design.
Refereed Serial

340.6   IE   ISSN 0379-0738
RA1001   CODEN: FSINDR
FORENSIC SCIENCE INTERNATIONAL; an international journal dedicated to the applications of science to the administration of justice. 1972. 12/yr.(in 6 vols.; 2 nos./vol.). $724 (effective 1992). Elsevier Scientific Publishers Ireland Ltd., P.O. Box 85, Limerick, Ireland. TEL 061-61944. FAX 061-62144. TELEX 72191 ENH EI. (Subscr. in U.S. and Canada to: Elsevier Science Publishing Co., Inc., Box 882, Madison Sq. Sta., New York, NY 10159. TEL 212-989-5800) Ed. B. Knight. charts; illus. (also avail. in microform from RPI) Indexed: Abstr.Anthropol., Biol.Abstr., Bull.Signal., C.L.I., Chem.Abstr., Crim.Just.Abstr., Curr.Cont., Dent.Ind., Excerp.Med., Hlth.Ind., HRIS, Ind.Med., L.R.I., Leg.Per., Sci.Cit.Ind., SSCI.
—BLDSC shelfmark: 3987.764000.
Former titles (until vol.13, no.1, 1979): Forensic Science (ISSN 0300-9432); Journal of Forensic Medicine (ISSN 0022-1171)
Description: Publishes original contributions in the many different scientific disciplines pertaining to the forensic sciences.
Refereed Serial

614.19   US   ISSN 0930-1461
HV8073   CODEN: FSPRE7
FORENSIC SCIENCE PROGRESS. 1986. irreg. price varies. Springer-Verlag, 175 Fifth Ave., New York, NY 10010. TEL 212-460-1550. (Also Berlin, Heidelberg, Tokyo, Vienna) (reprint service avail. form ISI)

340.6 614.19   UK   ISSN 0015-7368
     CODEN: FSSJAS
FORENSIC SCIENCE SOCIETY. JOURNAL. 1960. 4/yr. £54($135) Forensic Science Society, 18-A Mount Parade, Harrogate, North Yorkshire HG1 1BX, England. Ed. R.J. Davis. adv.; bk.rev.; charts; illus.; index; circ. 2,500. Indexed: Biol.Abstr., C.L.I., Chem.Abstr., Curr.Adv.Ecol.Sci., Curr.Adv.Genetics & Molec.Biol., Curr.Cont., Excerp.Med., Hlth.Ind., Ind.Med., Ind.Vet., L.R.I., Mass Spectr.Bull., Vet.Bull.
—BLDSC shelfmark: 4754.550000.

340.6   CN   ISSN 0226-8841
KE3646.A13
HEALTH LAW IN CANADA. 1980. q. Can.$95. Butterworths Canada Ltd., 75 Clegg Rd., Markham, Ont. L6G 1A1, Canada. TEL 416-479-2665. FAX 416-479-2826. Ed. Gilbert Sharpe. Indexed: C.L.I., Hlth.Ind., Ind.Can.L.P.L., L.R.I.
Description: Covers all major aspects of Canadian health law.

614.19   JA   ISSN 0289-0755
HOIGAKU NO JISSAI TO KENKYU/RESEARCH AND PRACTICE IN FORENSIC MEDICINE. (Text in Japanese, English; summaries in English) 1954. a. 5000 Yen. Tohoku Daigaku, Igakubu Hoigaku Danwakai - Tohoku University, School of Medicine, Department of Forensic Medicine, Sendai-shi, Miyagi-ken 980, Japan. TEL 022-274-1111. FAX 022-272-7273. Ed. Kaoru Sagisaka. circ. 1,000. (back issues avail.)

614.19   II   ISSN 0970-1982
RA1001
INDIAN JOURNAL OF FORENSIC SCIENCES. 1985. q. Rs.120($24) (free to members). Forensic Science Society of India, Forensic House, Kamarajar Salai, Madras 600 004, India. TEL 845085. Ed. P. Chandra Sekharan. adv.; circ. 1,000.
—BLDSC shelfmark: 4412.650000.
Formerly (until 1987): Forensic Science Society of India. Journal.
Description: Information geared to scientists, pathologists, police surgeons and members of the legal profession interested in forensic sciences.

340.6   US
INFORM QUARTERLY NEWSLETTER. 1969. q. $25. International Reference Organization in Forensic Medicine & Sciences, c/o Dr. William E. Eckert, Ed., Box 8282, Wichita, KS 67208. TEL 316-685-7612. bibl.; circ. 1,500. (looseleaf format) Indexed: Excerp.Med.
Formerly: Inform - Letter (ISSN 0019-9702)

INFORMATION EXCHANGE; newsletter of the National Sudden Infant Death Syndrome Clearinghouse. see *MEDICAL SCIENCES — Pediatrics*

MEDICAL SCIENCES — FORENSIC SCIENCES

614.19 340   CK
INSTITUTO NACIONAL DE MEDICINA LEGAL DE COLOMBIA. REVISTA. 1975. s-a. Instituto Nacional de Medicina Legal de Colombia, Carrera 13 no. 7-46, Bogota, Colombia. Ed. Guillermo Restrepo Isaza. **Indexed:** Excerp.Med.

340.6   IT   ISSN 0074-1248
INTERNATIONAL ACADEMY OF LEGAL MEDICINE AND OF SOCIAL MEDICINE. (CONGRESS REPORTS).* triennial, 9th, 1973, Rome. International Academy of Legal Medicine and Social Medicine, c/o Ferdinando Antoniotti, Viale Regina Elena 336, 00161 Rome, Italy.

614.19   GW   ISSN 0937-9827
RA1001   CODEN: IJLME
INTERNATIONAL JOURNAL OF LEGAL MEDICINE. 1922. 6/yr. DM.798($471.50) (effective 1992). (Deutsche Gesellschaft fuer Rechtsmedizin) Springer-Verlag, Heidelberger Platz 3, D-1000 Berlin 33, Germany. TEL 030-8207-1. (Also Heidelberg, Tokyo, Vienna and New York) Ed. G. Adebahr. adv.; illus.; index. (also avail. in microform from UMI; back issues avail.; reprint service avail. from ISI) **Indexed:** Biol.Abstr., C.L.I., Chem.Abstr., Curr.Cont., Excerp.Med., Ind.Med., L.R.I., Leg.Per.
—BLDSC shelfmark: 4542.315500.
Former titles (until 1992): Zeitschrift fuer Rechtsmedizin - Journal of Legal Medicine (ISSN 0044-3433); Deutsche Zeitschrift fuer die Gesamte Gerichtliche Medizin.

614.19   SW
INTERNATIONAL SYMPOSIUM ON WOUND BALLISTICS. PROCEEDINGS. (Supplement to: Acta Chirurgica Scandinavica) 3rd, 1978. irreg. $42. Almqvist & Wiksell International, P.O. Box 638, S-101 28 Stockholm, Sweden. Ed. T. Seeman. illus.

614.19   JA   ISSN 0047-1887
    CODEN: NHOZAX
JAPANESE JOURNAL OF LEGAL MEDICINE/NIPPON HOIGAKU ZASSHI. (Supplements accompany some numbers) (Table of contents and summaries in English) 1944. bi-m. $49.50. Medico-Legal Society of Japan - Nihon Hoi Gakkai, Faculty of Medicine, University of Tokyo, 7-3-1 Hongo, Bunkyo-ku, Tokyo 13, Japan. (Subscr. to: Japan Publications Trading Co., Box 5030, Tokyo International, Tokyo 100-31, Japan) illus. **Indexed:** Chem.Abstr., Dent.Ind., Excerp.Med., Ind.Med.
—BLDSC shelfmark: 4655.850000.

340.6 615.9   FR   ISSN 0249-6208
RA1001   CODEN: JMLMD7
JOURNAL DE MEDECINE LEGALE DROIT MEDICAL; expertise medicale, deontologie, urgence medicale. 1957. 8/yr. 180 ECU($210) (typically set in Jan.). Masson, 120 bd. Saint-Germain, 75280 Paris Cedex 06, France. TEL 1-46-34-21-60. FAX 1-45-87-29-99. TELEX 202 671 F. (Co-sponsors: Association Lyonnaise de Medecine Legale; Association Lyonnaise d'Economie Medicale) Ed. L. Roche. adv.; bk.rev.; index; circ. 1,900. (reprint service avail. from ISI) **Indexed:** Biol.Abstr., C.I.S. Abstr., Chem.Abstr., Curr.Cont., Excerp.Med., I.P.A.
●Also available online.
Former titles: Journal de Medecine Legale; Medecine Legale, Toxicologie, Urgence Medicale, Centre Anti-Poisons; Bulletin de Medecine Legale, Toxicologie, Urgence Medicale, Centre-Anti-Poisons; Bulletin de Medecine Legale, Urgence Medicale, Centre Anti-Poisons (ISSN 0395-4374); (until 1976): Bulletin de Medecine Legale et de Toxicologie Medicale (ISSN 0007-4365).

JOURNAL OF EVIDENCE PHOTOGRAPHY. see *PHOTOGRAPHY*

340.6 614.19   US   ISSN 0022-1198
RA1001   CODEN: JFSCAS
JOURNAL OF FORENSIC SCIENCES. 1956. bi-m. $100 to non-members; members $90. (American Academy of Forensic Sciences) American Society for Testing and Materials, 1916 Race St., Philadelphia, PA 19103. TEL 215-299-5400. FAX 215-977-9679. Ed. Abel M. Dominguez. adv.; bk.rev.; charts; illus.; index; circ. 4,200. (also avail. in microform from UMI; reprint service avail. from UMI) **Indexed:** Abstr.Bk.Rev.Curr.Leg.Per., Abstr.Bull.Inst.Pap.Chem., Art & Archaeol.Tech.Abstr., Biol.Abstr., C.L.I., Chem.Abstr., CJPI, Crim.Just.Abstr., Curr.Cont., Dent.Ind., Excerp.Med., Hlth.Ind., HRIS, Ind.Med., INIS Atomind., L.R.I., Leg.Per., Mass Spectr.Bull., W.R.C.Inf.
—BLDSC shelfmark: 4984.600000.
Supersedes: What's New in Forensic Sciences (ISSN 0511-8662)
Refereed Serial

614.19   JA   ISSN 0285-7960
KAGAKU KEISATSU KENKYUJO HOKOKU HOKAGAKU HEN/NATIONAL RESEARCH INSTITUTE OF POLICE SCIENCE. REPORT. RESEARCH OF FORENSIC SCIENCE. (Text in Japanese; summaries in English) 1948. q. Kagaku Keisatsu Kenkyujo - National Research Institute of Police Science, 6 Sanban-cho, Chiyoda-ku, Tokyo 102, Japan. Ed. Shoichi Yada. circ. 1,000. **Indexed:** Crim.Just.Abstr., INIS Atomind., Psychol.Abstr.
—BLDSC shelfmark: 7570.222600.
Formerly: National Research Institute of Police Science. Report (ISSN 0451-1980)

614.19 340   US   ISSN 0277-8459
KF3821.A15
LAW, MEDICINE & HEALTH CARE. 1973. q. $70 (foreign $100). American Society of Law & Medicine, Inc., 765 Commonwealth Ave., Ste. 1634, Boston, MA 02215. TEL 617-262-4990. FAX 617-437-7596. Ed. Larry Gostin. adv.; bk.rev.; circ. 7,500 (controlled). (also avail. in microfiche from UMI; back issues avail.; reprint service avail. from WSH) **Indexed:** Abstr.Bk.Rev.Curr.Leg.Per., Acad.Ind., C.L.I., CINAHL, Hlth.Ind., Hosp.Lit.Ind., I.P.A., Int.Nurs.Ind., L.R.I., Leg.Cont., Leg.Per., Psychol.Abstr., Sociol.Abstr., Telegen.
—BLDSC shelfmark: 5161.406500.
Formed by the merger of: Medicolegal News (ISSN 0097-0085); Nursing Law and Ethics (ISSN 0270-6636)
Description: Scholarly examination of policy and ethical issues at the intersection of law and medicine.

LEBENSMITTELCHEMIE. see *FOOD AND FOOD INDUSTRIES*

340.6   US   ISSN 0197-9981
RA1001
LEGAL MEDICINE. 1969-1987; resumed 1989. a. Butterworth Legal Publishers (Salem) (Subsidiary of: Reed International PLC), 90 Stiles Rd., Salem, NH 03079. TEL 800-548-4001. FAX 603-898-9858. Ed. Cyril H. Wecht. **Indexed:** C.L.I., Excerp.Med., Hlth.Ind., Ind.Med., L.R.I.
Formerly: Legal Medicine Annual (ISSN 0075-8590)
Description: Contains a collection of articles which addresses a variety of subjects in the fields of legal medicine and the forensic sciences.

LEGAL MEDICINE: LEGAL DYNAMICS OF MEDICAL ENCOUNTERS. see *MEDICAL SCIENCES*

340.6 614.19   II   ISSN 0047-6536
MEDICAL NEWS, MEDICINE AND LAW. (Text in English) 1970. m. Rs.15($7.50) Joshi Hospital, 778 Shivajinagar, Poona 411004, Maharashtra, India. Ed. Dr. L.B. Joshi. bk.rev.; circ. 2,500. (also avail. in microfilm from UMI)

614.19   UK   ISSN 0025-8172
LAW
MEDICO-LEGAL JOURNAL. 1933. q. £21. (Medico-Legal Society) Dramrite Printers Ltd., 15 Old Sq., Lincoln's Inn, London WC2A 3UH, England. TEL 071-831-0801. FAX 071-405-1387. Ed. Diana Brahams. adv.; bk.rev.; abstr.; index; circ. 1,200. **Indexed:** Abstr.Bk.Rev.Curr.Leg.Per., ASSIA, Br.Hum.Ind., C.L.I., Chem.Abstr., CINAHL, Excerp.Med., Ind.Med., L.R.I., Leg.Per.
—BLDSC shelfmark: 5534.200000.

340.6   CE
MEDICO-LEGAL SOCIETY OF SRI LANKA. PROCEEDINGS. irreg. Medico-Legal Society of Sri Lanka, 111 Francis Rd., Colombo 10, Sri Lanka.

614   US
MEDICOLEGAL-GRAM.* 1980. m. Board of Medicolegal Investigations, Office of the Chief Medical Examiner, Box 26901, 800 Northeast 13th St., Oklahoma City, OK 73190. TEL 405-848-6841. Ed. Dr. Fred B. Jordan. illus.; circ. 1,000.
Supersedes (1972-1979): Oklahoma Journal of Forensic Medicine (ISSN 0363-2679)

614.19   GW   ISSN 0723-8886
KK6206.A13
MEDIZINRECHT. 1983. 6/yr. DM.338. (Deutsche Gesellschaft fuer Medizinrecht) Springer-Verlag, Heidelberger Platz 3, 1000 Berlin 33, Germany. TEL 030-8207-1. (Also Heidelberg, Tokyo, Vienna, and New York)
—BLDSC shelfmark: 5535.586000.
Formerly: Med R-Medizinrecht.

MICROSCOPE. see *BIOLOGY — Microscopy*

340.6   IT   ISSN 0026-4849
HV6004
MINERVA MEDICOLEGALE; archivio di antropologia criminale. (Text in Italian; summaries in English) 1880. q. L.60000($70) Edizioni Minerva Medica, Corso Bramante 83-85, Turin, Italy. Ed. P.L. Baima-Bollone. bk.rev.; bibl.; charts; illus.; index. **Indexed:** C.I.S.Abstr., Chem.Abstr., Excerp.Med., Ind.Med.
—BLDSC shelfmark: 5794.260000.

RECHT & PSYCHIATRIE. see *PSYCHOLOGY*

615 340.6   US   ISSN 0273-2300
RA1190   CODEN: RTOPDW
REGULATORY TOXICOLOGY AND PHARMACOLOGY. 1981. bi-m. $152 (foreign $200). Academic Press, Inc., Journal Division, 1250 Sixth Ave., San Diego, CA 92101. TEL 619-230-1840. FAX 619-699-6800. TELEX 181726. Eds. Frederick Coulston, Albert C. Kolbye, Jr. adv.; index. (back issues avail.) **Indexed:** Chem.Abstr., Curr.Adv.Cancer Res., Curr.Adv.Ecol.Sci., Dok.Arbeitsmed., Energy Ind., Energy Info.Abstr., Excerp.Med., Ind.Med., Lab.Haz.Bull., Risk Abstr., Risk Abstr., Sel.Water Res.Abstr.
—BLDSC shelfmark: 7350.040000.
Description: Reports the concepts and problems involved with the generation, evaluation, and interpretation of experimental animal and human data in the large perspective of the societal considerations of protecting human health and the environment.
Refereed Serial

340.6   SP
REVISTA ESPANOLA DE MEDICINA LEGAL. 1974. bi-m. 1000 ptas. Asociacion Nacional de Medicos Forenses, Goya 99, Madrid 9, Spain. bk.rev.; circ. 1,000. **Indexed:** Ind.Med.Esp.

614.19   FR
REVUE FRANCAISE DU DOMMAGE CORPOREL. 1975. q. 360 F. (Federation Francaise des Associations de Medecins-Conseils de Societes d'Assurances) J. B. Bailliere et Fils, 10 rue Thenard, 75005 Paris, France. Ed. C. Rousseau. bibl.; charts; illus.; stat.; index.

614.19   IT
RIVISTA ITALIANA DI MEDICINA LEGALE. 1979. q. L.100000 (foreign L.150000). Casa Editrice Dott. A. Giuffre, Via Busto Arsizio 40, 20151 Milan, Italy. TEL 02-38000905. FAX 02-38009582. Ed. Francesco Introna. adv.; bk.rev.; index; circ. 2,200. (back issues avail.) **Indexed:** Excerp.Med.

SCIENTIFIC SLEUTHING REVIEW; forensic science in criminal law. see *LAW — Criminal Law*

614.19 368   IT
SOCIETA LOMBARDA DI MEDICINA LEGALE E DELLE ASSICURAZIONI. ARCHIVIO. 1965. q. L.15000. Universita degli Studi di Milano, Istituto di Medicina Legale, Via Mangiagalli 37, Milan, Italy. Dir. A. Fornari.

MEDICAL SCIENCES — GASTROENTEROLOGY

610   RU   ISSN 0039-4521
CODEN: SMEZA5
SUDEBNOMEDITSINSKAYA EKSPERTIZA/MEDICO-LEGAL EXPERT TESTIMONY. (Text in Russian; contents page and summaries in English) 1958. q. 8.80 Rub.($6.60) (Vsesoyuznoe Nauchnoe Obshchestvo Sudebnykh Medikov) Izdatel'stvo Meditsina, Petroverigskii pereulok 6-8, 101838 Moscow, Russia. (Co-sponsor: Ministerstvo Zdravookhraneniya S.S.S.R.) Ed. V.V. Tomilin. adv.; bk.rev.; abstr.; charts; illus.; circ. 18,800. **Indexed:** Biol.Abstr., Chem.Abstr., Dent.Ind., Excerp.Med., Ind.Med.
—BLDSC shelfmark: 0174.500000.
Description: Concerned with the theory and practice of forensic medicine. Examines the problems of thanatology, traumatology, toxicology, serology, forensic obstetrics, stomatology, psychiatry, chemistry, history of forensic medicine and certain problems of criminology and legal laws as they relate to forensic medicine.

SYNOPSIS (COLUMBIA). see *MEDICAL SCIENCES — Pediatrics*

614.1   CC   ISSN 1001-5728
ZHONGGUO FAYIXUE ZAZHI/CHINESE JOURNAL OF FORENSIC SCIENCES. (Text in Chinese) q. Zhongguo Fayi Xuehui - China Forensic Science Society, No. 14, Chang'an Jie, Beijing 100741, People's Republic of China. TEL 542831. Ed. Wu Jiayi.

MEDICAL SCIENCES — Gastroenterology

617   US   ISSN 0884-1470
RD10.U6
A B M S DIRECTORY OF CERTIFIED COLON & RECTAL SURGEONS. 1985. biennial. $19.95. American Board of Medical Specialties, One Rotary Center, Ste. 805, Evanston, IL 60201. TEL 708-491-9091. FAX 708-328-3596. Ed. Dr. J. Lee Dockery.

616.4 616.3   FR   ISSN 0240-642X
CODEN: AENDD5
ACTA ENDOSCOPICA. (Text in English, French) 1970. bi-m. 860 F. (foreign 900 F.). Endoscopica, 127 rue St. Dizier, 54000 Nancy, France. TEL 83-37-44-38. FAX 83-35-34-53. (Co-sponsors: Societe Medicale Internationale d'Endoscopie; Interamerican Society for Digestive Endoscopy) Ed. F. Vicari. adv.; bk.rev.; circ. 4,500. **Indexed:** Excerp.Med.
—BLDSC shelfmark: 0614.620000.

616.3   BE   ISSN 0001-5644
ACTA GASTRO-ENTEROLOGICA BELGICA. (Supplements avail.) (Text usually in French; occasionally in English or German) 1933. q. 2400 Fr. (foreign 2750 Fr.). Association des Societes Scientifiques Medicales Belges - Vereiniging van de Belgische Medische Wetenschappelijke Genootschappen, Av. Circulaire 138A, B-1180 Brussels, Belgium. TEL 02-374-5158. adv.; bk.rev.; abstr.; bibl.; charts; illus.; index; circ. 1,000. **Indexed:** ASCA, Biol.Abstr., Chem.Abstr., Curr.Adv.Cancer Res., Curr.Cont., Excerp.Med., Helminthol.Abstr., Ind.Med., Nutr.Abstr.
—BLDSC shelfmark: 0616.700000.

616.3   AG   ISSN 0300-9033
CODEN: AGLTBL
ACTA GASTROENTEROLOGICA LATINOAMERICANA. 1969. q. $50 (effective 1992). Juncal 2134, Planta Baja B 1125, Buenos Aires, Argentina. TEL 832139-8250050. Eds. Pablo Mazure, Mauricio Schraler. adv.; bk.rev.; circ. 3,500. **Indexed:** Biol.Abstr., Chem.Abstr., Excerp.Med., Ind.Med
—BLDSC shelfmark: 0616.730000.
Description: Original research papers in gastroenterology.

616.3   FR
ACTUALITES DIGESTIVES. 1978. bi-m. 230 F. (foreign 275 F.). 36 Bd. Gambetta, 29200 Brest, France. Ed. H. Gouerou. adv.; circ. 4,000.

ADVANCES IN GASTROINTESTINAL RADIOLOGY. see *MEDICAL SCIENCES — Radiology And Nuclear Medicine*

616.3   UK   ISSN 0269-2813
CODEN: APTHEN
ALIMENTARY PHARMACOLOGY AND THERAPEUTICS. (Supplement avail. (ISSN 0953-0673)) 1987. bi-m. £89.50 (foreign £99.50). Blackwell Scientific Publications Ltd., Osney Mead, Oxford OX2 0EL, England. TEL 0865-240201. FAX 0865-721205. TELEX 833355-MEDBOK-G. Eds. R.E. Pounder, M.J. Langman. adv.; bk.rev.; illus.; index. (back issues avail.) **Indexed:** Excerp.Med.
—BLDSC shelfmark: 0787.886000.

617.5   US   ISSN 0065-7204
AMERICAN ASSOCIATION OF GENITO-URINARY SURGEONS. TRANSACTIONS. a. American Association of Genito-Urinary Surgeons, 22 W. Greene St., Baltimore, MD 21201. (also avail. in microform from UMI) **Indexed:** Ind.Med.

616.3   US   ISSN 0002-9270
RC799   CODEN: AJGAAR
AMERICAN JOURNAL OF GASTROENTEROLOGY. 1934. m. $93 to individuals; institutions $137. (American College of Gastroenterology, Inc.) Williams & Wilkins, 428 E. Preston St., Baltimore, MD 21202. TEL 301-528-4000. FAX 301-528-4312. Ed. Dr. Martin H. Floch. adv.; bk.rev.; abstr.; bibl.; illus.; stat.; index; circ. 5,900. (also avail. in microform; microfilm from WWS) **Indexed:** Biol.Abstr., Biotech.Abstr., Chem.Abstr., Curr.Adv.Cancer Res., Curr.Adv.Ecol.Sci., Curr.Cont., Dent.Ind., Excerp.Med., Helminthol.Abstr., Ind.Med., Ind.Sci.Rev., INIS Atomind., Nutr.Abstr., Protozool.Abstr., Rev.Plant Path., Sci.Cit.Ind., Triticale Abstr.
—BLDSC shelfmark: 0824.650000.
Description: Articles and reviews of current topics for gastroenterologists and internists.
Refereed Serial

616.35   US   ISSN 0162-6566
RC864.A1
AMERICAN JOURNAL OF PROCTOLOGY, GASTROENTEROLOGY & COLON & RECTAL SURGERY.* 1950. bi-m. $14. (International Academy of Proctology) McMahon Publishing Co., 83 Peaceable St., West Redding, CT 06896. TEL 203-544-9343. Ed. Dr. Alfred J. Cantor. adv.; bk.rev.; bibl.; illus.; index; circ. 8,000. (also avail. in microform from UMI) **Indexed:** Biol.Abstr., Curr.Cont., Excerp.Med., Ind.Med.
—BLDSC shelfmark: 4089.025000.
Formerly: American Journal of Proctology (ISSN 0002-9521)
Refereed Serial

616.3   FR   ISSN 0066-2070
CODEN: AGHPBN
ANNALES DE GASTROENTEROLOGIE ET D'HEPATOLOGIE. 1963. 7/yr. 930 F. to individuals (foreign 1300 F.); students 465 F. (foreign 660 F.). Expansion Scientifique, 15 rue Saint Benoit, 75278 Paris Cedex 06, France. TEL 1-45-48-42-60. FAX 1-45-55-81-55. Ed. Guy Albot. adv.; bk.rev.; circ. 3,500. **Indexed:** Biol.Abstr., Curr.Cont., Excerp.Med., Helminthol.Abstr., INIS Atomind., Rev.Med.& Vet.Mycol.
—BLDSC shelfmark: 0974.500000.
Incorporates: Actualites Hepato-Gastro-Enterologiques de l'Hotel Dieu.

ANNUAL OF GASTROINTESTINAL ENDOSCOPY. see *MEDICAL SCIENCES — Abstracting, Bibliographies, Statistics*

616.3   AG   ISSN 0004-0517
ARCHIVOS ARGENTINOS ENFERMEDADES DEL APARATO DIGESTIVO. vol. 46, 1971. bi-m. $25. Sociedad Argentina de Gastroenterologia, Jeronimo Salguero 88 A, 1177 Buenos Aires, Argentina. TEL 983-0863. FAX 981-4936. Ed. Dr. Leonardo Pinchuck. adv.; bk.rev.; circ. 1,350.

ARCHIVOS DE ODONTOESTOMATOLOGIA. see *MEDICAL SCIENCES — Dentistry*

616.3   IT
ARGOMENTI DI GASTROENTEROLOGIA CLINICA. 1988. 6/yr. L.8000($44) (effective 1991). Masson Italia Periodici, Via Statuto 2-4, 20121 Milan, Italy. TEL 02-6367-1. FAX 02-6367-211. Ed. Gabriele Bianchi Porro. circ. 15,000.

616.3   BL   ISSN 0004-2803
CODEN: ARQGAF
ARQUIVOS DE GASTROENTEROLOGIA. (Text in Portuguese; summaries in English, French, Portuguese and Spanish) 1964. q. $35 (typically set in Jan.). Instituto Brasileiro de Estudos e Pesquisas de Gastroenterologia - Brazilian Institute for Studies and Research in Gastroenterology, Rua Dr. Seng 320, C.P. 6209-01331, Sao Paulo, Brazil. (Co-sponsor: Sociedade Latino-Americana de Gastroenterologia Pediatrica e Nutricao - Latin-American Society of Pediatric Gastroenterology and Nutrition) Eds. Joel Carlos Cunha, Nelson Henrique Michelsohn. adv.; bk.rev.; charts; illus.; index; circ. 5,000. (also avail. in microfilm from UMI; reprint service avail. from UMI) **Indexed:** Abstr.Hyg., Biol.Abstr., Chem.Abstr., Dairy Sci.Abstr., Excerp.Med., Gastroenterol.Abstr.& Cit., Ind.Med., Nutr.Abstr., Protozool.Abstr., Soyabean Abstr., Trop.Dis.Bull.
—BLDSC shelfmark: 1695.430000.
Description: Publishes original papers, review articles, and case reports concerning all aspects of the digestive tract, including the liver.

616.3   BL
ARS CVRANDI GASTRO. 1978. bi-m. Elea Ciencia Editorial Ltda., Rua Barao de Uba 48, CEP 20260 Rio de Janeiro RJ, Brazil. TEL 293-2112. Ed. J.G. Alves. circ. 4,500.

616.3   US   ISSN 0892-9386
AUDIO-DIGEST GASTROENTEROLOGY. 1987. m. $84. Audio-Digest Foundation (Subsidiary of: California Medical Association), 1577 E. Chevy Chase Dr., Glendale, CA 91206. TEL 213-245-8505. FAX 818-240-7379. Ed. Claron L. Oakley. circ. controlled. (audio cassette)
Refereed Serial

616.3   US
C C F A COMMUNIQUE. m. membership. Crohn's and Colitis Foundation of America, Inc., Philadelphia - Delaware Valley Chapter, 7718 Castor Ave., Philadelphia, PA 19152. TEL 215-742-1800. FAX 215-742-3501. Ed. Rosalyn C. Richman.

616.3   US   ISSN 0897-6759
C C F A FOUNDATION FOCUS. 1977. 3/yr. $25 membership. Crohn's & Colitis Foundation of America, Inc., 444 Park Ave. South, New York, NY 10016-7374. TEL 212-685-3440. FAX 212-779-4098. Ed. Barbara Rosenstein. adv.; bk.rev.; circ. 35,000. (back issues avail.)
Description: Features stories about coping with Crohn's disease (ileitis) and ulcerative colitis; articles on NFIC-sponsored research and education programs; medical news and profiles of individuals.

616.3   CN   ISSN 0835-7900
CANADIAN JOURNAL OF GASTROENTEROLOGY. 1987. 6/yr. Can.$67($58) (foreign $90) to individuals; institutions Can.$80 ($70)(foreign $117). Pulsus Group Inc., 2902 S. Sheridan Way, Oakville, Ont. L6J 7L6, Canada. TEL 416-829-4770. FAX 416-829-4799. Eds. Dr. C.N. Williams, A.B.R. Thomson. adv.; bk.rev.; circ. 18,000 (controlled). **Indexed:** Excerp.Med.
—BLDSC shelfmark: 3031.550000.
Description: Original papers, case reports and reviews pertaining to gastroenterology and hepatology.
Refereed Serial

616.3   CS   ISSN 0009-0565
CODEN: CKGAAM
CESKOSLOVENSKA GASTROENTEROLOGIE A VYZIVA. (Text in Czech and Slovak; summaries in English and Russian) 1947. 8/yr. $65.30. (Ceskoslovenska Spolecnost pro Gastroenterologii a Vyzivu) Avicenum, Czechoslovak Medical Press, Malostranske nam. 28, 118 02 Prague 1, Czechoslovakia. (Dist. by: Artia, Ve Smeckach 30, 111 27 Prague 1, Czechoslovakia) (Co-sponsor: Ceskoslovenska Lekarska Spolecnost J. Ev. Purkyne) Ed. Z. Maratka. adv.; bk.rev.; abstr.; charts; illus.; index; circ. 900. **Indexed:** Biol.Abstr., C.I.S. Abstr., Chem.Abstr., Curr.Adv.Ecol.Sci., Excerp.Med., Food Sci.& Tech.Abstr., Ind.Med., Nutr.Abstr.
—BLDSC shelfmark: 3122.200000.

MEDICAL SCIENCES — GASTROENTEROLOGY

616.3   IT   ISSN 0009-4765
CHIRURGIA GASTROENTEROLOGICA (ITALIAN EDITION); rassegna trimestrale di chirurgia dell'apparato digerente e degli organi addominali. (Text in Italian; summaries in English and Italian) 1967. q. L.80000($80) (effective Jan. 1992). Giovanni Battista Grassi, Cesare Correnti 6, 00179 Rome, Italy. FAX 06-7883156. **Indexed:** Excerp.Med.
—BLDSC shelfmark: 3181.186000.

616.3   US
CONTEMPORARY GASTROENTEROLOGY. 1988. 8/yr. $45 (foreign $59). Medical Economics Publishing Co., Five Paragon Dr., Montvale, NJ 07645. TEL 800-526-4870. FAX 201-573-1045. Ed. James E. Swan. adv.; circ. 40,000 (controlled). (also avail. in microfilm; reprint service avail. from RPI)
Description: Practical advice for office and hospital-based gastroenterologists and internists on clinical problems in gastroenterology.
Refereed Serial

CORE JOURNALS IN GASTROENTEROLOGY. see *MEDICAL SCIENCES — Abstracting, Bibliographies, Statistics*

616.3   US
CROHN'S & COLITIS FOUNDATION OF AMERICA. GREATER NEW JERSEY CHAPTER. NEWSLETTER. (Former name of issuing body: National Foundation for Ileitis & Colitis) q. Crohn's & Colitis Foundation of America, Inc., Greater New Jersey Chapter, 444 Park Ave. South, New York, NY 10016-7374. TEL 212-685-3440. FAX 212-779-4098. Dir. Margo L. Asay.
Formerly: National Foundation for Ileitis and Colitis. Greater New Jersey Chapter. Newsletter.

616.3   US
CROHN'S & COLITIS FOUNDATION OF AMERICA. GREATER NEW YORK CHAPTER. UPDATE. (Former name of issuing body: National Foundation for Ileitis & Colitis) 1975. q. membership. Crohn's & Colitis Foundation of America, Inc., Greater New York Chapter, 444 Park Ave. South, New York, NY 10016-7374. TEL 212-685-3440. FAX 212-779-4098. Ed. Celia Sorkin. circ. 3,500.
Formerly: National Foundation for Ileitis and Colitis. Greater New York Chapter. Update.

616.3   US   ISSN 0198-8085
RC799   CODEN: CUGADR
CURRENT GASTROENTEROLOGY. 1980. a. $69.95. Mosby - Year Book, Inc. (Chicago) (Subsidiary of: Times Mirror Company), 200 N. LaSalle St., Chicago, IL 60601-1080. TEL 312-726-9733. FAX 312-726-6075. TELEX 206155. (Subscr. to: 11830 Westline Industrial Dr., St. Louis, MO 63146. TEL 800-325-4177) Ed. Gary Gitnick, MD. illus.
—BLDSC shelfmark: 3496.920000.
Description: Surveys developments in gastroenterology and provides synopses of the past twelve months of medical literature.

CURRENT OPINION IN GASTROENTEROLOGY. see *MEDICAL SCIENCES — Abstracting, Bibliographies, Statistics*

DIABETIC MEDICINE. see *MEDICAL SCIENCES — Endocrinology*

DIARRHOEAL DISEASES/MALADIES DIARRHEIQUES. see *MEDICAL SCIENCES — Abstracting, Bibliographies, Statistics*

616.3   SZ   ISSN 0012-2823
QP141.A1   CODEN: DIGEBW
DIGESTION; international journal of gastroenterology. (Text in English) 1968. 12/yr. (3 vols./yr.). 256 Fr.($171) per vol. S. Karger AG, Allschwilerstr. 10, P.O. Box, CH-4009 Basel, Switzerland. TEL 061-3061111. FAX 061-3061234. TELEX CH 962652. Ed. W. Creutzfeldt. adv.; bibl.; illus.; circ. 1,250. (also avail. in microform from RPI) **Indexed:** Biol.Abstr., Chem.Abstr., Curr.Adv.Ecol.Sci., Curr.Cont., Dairy Sci.Abstr., Dent.Ind., Excerp.Med., Helminthol.Abstr., Ind.Med., Ind.Sci.Rev., NRN, Nutr.Abstr., Protozool.Abstr., Sci.Cit.Ind.
—BLDSC shelfmark: 3588.345000.
Formerly: Gastroenterologia.

616.3   SZ   ISSN 0257-2753
     CODEN: DIDIEW
DIGESTIVE DISEASES; current concepts in research and practice. (Text in English) 1983. bi-m. 453 Fr.($302) S. Karger AG, Allschwilerstr. 10, P.O. Box, CH-4009 Basel, Switzerland. TEL 061-3061111. FAX 061-3061234. TELEX CH 962652. Eds. T.S.N. Chen, R.K. Zetterman. adv.; illus.; index; circ. 800. (also avail. in microform) **Indexed:** Chem.Abstr, Curr.Cont., NRN.
—BLDSC shelfmark: 3588.346000.
Formerly: Survey of Digestive Diseases (ISSN 0253-4398)

616.3   US   ISSN 0163-2116
RC799   CODEN: DDSCDJ
DIGESTIVE DISEASES AND SCIENCES. 1934. m. $295 (foreign $345)(effective 1992). Plenum Publishing Corp., 233 Spring St., New York, NY 10013-1578. TEL 212-620-8000. FAX 212-463-0742. TELEX 23-421139. Ed. Richard L. Wechsler. adv.; bk.rev. (also avail. in microfilm from JSC; back issues avail.) **Indexed:** Abstr.Inter.Med., Biol.Abstr., Chem.Abstr., Curr.Adv.Cancer Res., Curr.Adv.Ecol.Sci., Curr.Adv.Genetics & Molec.Biol., Curr.Cont., Dairy Sci.Abstr., Dent.Ind., Excerp.Med., Fababean Abstr., Helminthol.Abstr., Ind.Med., Ind.Sci.Rev., Ind.Vet., INIS Atomind., Maize Abstr., NRN, Nutr.Abstr., Ref.Zh., Sci.Cit.Ind., Small.Anim.Abstr., Triticale Abstr., Vet.Bull.
—BLDSC shelfmark: 3588.346100.
Formerly (until vol.24, no.1, 1979): American Journal of Digestive Diseases (ISSN 0002-9211)
Refereed Serial

616.3   GW   ISSN 0013-726X
     CODEN: ENDCAM
ENDOSCOPY. (Text in English, German; summaries in English) 1969. bi-m. DM.260. (European Society of Gastrointestinal Endoscopy) Georg Thieme Verlag, Ruedigerstr. 14, Postfach 104853, 7000 Stuttgart 10, Germany. TEL 0711-8931-0. (Subscr. to: Thieme Medical Publishers, Inc., 381 Park Ave. S., New York, NY 10016) Ed.Bd. adv.; bk.rev.; abstr.; bibl.; charts; illus.; stat.; index; circ. 2,900. (also avail. in microform from UMI; reprint service avail. from UMI) **Indexed:** Biol.Abstr., Curr.Cont., Dent.Ind., Excerp.Med., Helminthol.Abstr., Ind.Med., Ind.Sci.Rev., INIS Atomind., Nutr.Abstr., Sci.Cit.Ind.
—BLDSC shelfmark: 3743.600000.

616.3   GW   ISSN 0933-811X
ENDOSKOPIE HEUTE; forum bildgebener verfahren. 1988. q. DM.60. Demeter Verlag, Wuermstr. 13, 8032 Graefelfing, Germany. TEL 089-852033. FAX 089-8543347. Eds. Drs. R. Ottenjann, J.F. Riemann. circ. 4,000.
—BLDSC shelfmark: 3743.630000.

EUROPEAN JOURNAL OF GASTROENTEROLOGY AND HEPATOLOGY. see *MEDICAL SCIENCES — Abstracting, Bibliographies, Statistics*

616.3   UK   ISSN 0353-9245
     CODEN: ECGAEQ
▼**EXPERIMENTAL AND CLINICAL GASTROENTEROLOGY.** 1991. q. £125 (effective 1992). Pergamon Press plc, Headington Hill Hall, Oxford OX3 0BW, England. TEL 0865-794141. FAX 0865-743911. TELEX 83177 PERGAP. (And: 660 White Plains Rd., Tarrytown, NY 10591-5153. TEL 914-524-9200) Ed. Predrag Sikiric. (also avail. in microform; back issues avail.)
—BLDSC shelfmark: 3838.634000.
Description: Systematic presentations of experimental and clinical studies in gastroenterology.
Refereed Serial

616.3   SZ
FRONTIERS OF GASTROINTESTINAL RESEARCH. (Text in English) 1960. irreg. price varies. S. Karger AG, Allschwilerstr. 10, P.O. Box, CH-4009 Basel, Switzerland. TEL 061-3061111. FAX 061-3061234. TELEX CH 962652. Ed. P. Rozen. (reprint service avail. from ISI) **Indexed:** Biol.Abstr., Chem.Abstr., Curr.Cont., Ind.Med.
Formerly: Bibliotheca Gastroenterologica (ISSN 0302-0665)

616.3   VE   ISSN 0016-3503
G E N. (Text in English, Portuguese, Spanish; summaries in English, Spanish) 1946. q. Bs.800($50) Sociedad Venezolana de Gastroenterologia - Venezuelan Society of Gastroenterology, Torre del Colegio, Piso 2, Av. Jose Maria Vargas, Santa Fe Norte, Caracas 1080, Venezuela. TEL 9799380. (Or: Apdo. 51890, Sabana Grande, Caracas 1050 A, Venezuela) Ed. Dr. Miguel A. Garassini S. adv.; bk.rev.; abstr.; bibl.; charts; illus.; circ. 1,500. **Indexed:** Abstr.Hyg., Biol.Abstr., Excerp.Med., Helminthol.Abstr., Ind.Med., Trop.Dis.Bull.
—BLDSC shelfmark: 4096.385000.

G I G NEWSLETTER. (Gluten Intolerance Group of North America) see *NUTRITION AND DIETETICS*

GASTRIC SECRETION. see *BIOLOGY — Physiology*

616.3   FR   ISSN 0399-8320
     CODEN: GCBIDC
GASTRO-ENTEROLOGIE CLINIQUE ET BIOLOGIQUE. (Text in French; summaries in English) 1907. 10/yr. 190 ECU($233) (typically set in Jan.). (Societe Nationale Francaise de Gastro-Enterologie) Masson, 120 bd. Saint-Germain, 75280 Paris Cedex 06, France. TEL 1-46-34-21-60. FAX 1-45-87-29-99. TELEX 202 761 F. Ed. J.L. Dupas. adv.; bk.rev.; illus.; index; circ. 4,300. (reprint service avail. from ISI) **Indexed:** Biol.Abstr., Chem.Abstr., Curr.Adv.Biochem., Curr.Adv.Cancer Res., Curr.Adv.Ecol.Sci., Curr.Adv.Genetics & Molec.Biol., Curr.Cont., Dairy Sci.Abstr., Dent.Ind., Excerp.Med., Helminthol.Abstr., Ind.Med., Nutr.Abstr., Protozool.Abstr., Risk Abstr.
—BLDSC shelfmark: 4088.973000.
Former titles: Archives Francaises des Maladies de l'Appareil Digestif (ISSN 0003-9772); Biologie et Gastro-Enterologie (ISSN 0006-3258); Archives Francaises des Maladies de l'Appareil Digestif et des Maladies de la Nutrition.

616.3   FR   ISSN 0016-5077
GASTRO-ENTEROLOGIE QUOTIDIENNE. 1967. 3/yr. free. Laboratoires Beaufour, 18 Place Doguereau, 28100 Dreux, France. Ed. P. Bernades. adv.; illus.; tr.mk.; circ. 30,000.

616.3   GW
GASTRO-VERDAUUNGS- UND STOFFWECHSELERKRANKUNGEN. 1983. 12/yr. DM.150. P M I Verlag GmbH, August-Schanz-Str. 21, 6000 Frankfurt a.M. 50, Germany. TEL 069-5480000. FAX 069-548000-77. TELEX 412952-PMID. Ed. Peter Hoffmann. adv.; bk.rev.; circ. 20,000.
Formerly: Gastro-Entero-Hepatologie (ISSN 0724-9179)

616.3   YU   ISSN 0352-082X
GASTROENTEROHEPATOLOSKI ARHIV/ARCHIVES OF GASTROENTEROHEPATOLOGY. (Text and summaries in English and Serbo-Croatian) 1982. a. 1200 din.($28) Srpsko Lekarsko Drustvo, Dzordza Vasingtona 19, 11000 Belgrade, Yugoslavia. TEL 011-346-090. Ed. Obren Popovic. adv.; abstr.; bibl.; charts; illus.; pat.; stat.; circ. 800.
Description: Basic and clinical studies of the digestive tract and liver.

616.3   IT
GASTROENTEROLOGIA CLINICA. Italian translation of: Clinics in Gastroenterology. 1972. q. L.75000 to individuals; institutions L.100000. Pensiero Scientifico Editore s.r.l., Via Panama 48, 00198 Rome, Italy. TEL 06 855-36-33. Eds. G. Rossi, G. Pippa. circ. 800.

616.3   JA   ISSN 0435-1339
     CODEN: GAJABC
GASTROENTEROLOGIA JAPONICA. (Text in English) 1966. bi-m. 6000 Yen($36) Japanese Society of Gastroenterology - Nihon Shokakibyo Gakkai, 8-9-13 Ginza, Chuo-ku, Tokyo 104, Japan. Ed. Keiichi Kawai. adv.; abstr.; circ. 1,500. **Indexed:** Biol.Abstr., Chem.Abstr., Excerp.Med., Ind.Med., INIS Atomind.
—BLDSC shelfmark: 4088.960000.

616.3   IT   ISSN 1120-3641
▼**GASTROENTEROLOGIA OGGI.** 1990. q. L.20000. E S I Stampa Medica s.r.l., Casella Postale 42, Lgo. Volontari del Sangue 10, 20097 S. Donato, Milan, Italy. TEL 02-5274241. FAX 02-5274775. TELEX 324-894. Ed. Bruno Pieroni. adv.; bk.rev.; circ. 8,000.

MEDICAL SCIENCES — GASTROENTEROLOGY

616.3   SP   ISSN 0210-5705
CODEN: GHEPDF
GASTROENTEROLOGIA Y HEPATOLOGIA. (Text in Spanish; summaries in English) 1978. m. (11/yr.). 5000 ptas.($57) (free to qualified personnel). Ediciones Doyma S.A., Travesera de Gracia 17-21, 08021 Barcelona, Spain. TEL 200 07 11. FAX 209-11-36. TELEX 51964 INK-E. Ed. Dr. J. Rodes Teixidor. adv.: page 145000 ptas.; trim 210 x 280; adv. contact: Cristina Garrote. circ. 4,000. (reprint service avail. from UMI) Indexed: Excerp.Med., Ind.Med.Esp.
—BLDSC shelfmark: 4088.955000.
Description: Covers gastroenterology, hepatology and pathology of the digestive tract, liver, pancreas and biliary paths.

616.3   JA   ISSN 0387-1207
GASTROENTEROLOGICAL ENDOSCOPY. (Text in Japanese) 1958. m. 10000 Yen($75) Nihon Shokaki Naishikyo Gakkai - Japan Gastroenterological Endoscopy Society, Taimei Bldg., 3-22, Kanda Ogawa-machi, Chiyoda-ku, Tokyo 101, Japan. FAX 03-3291-5568. Ed. Saburo Oshiba. adv.; charts; illus.; circ. 20,700. Indexed: Excerp.Med.
—BLDSC shelfmark: 4088.965000.
Description: Reports investigations relating to endoscopic diagnosis and treatment of digestive diseases.

616.3   JA   ISSN 0387-2645
GASTROENTEROLOGICAL SURGERY. (Text in Japanese; table of contents in English) m. Herusu Publishing Co. Inc., 2-3, Nakano 2-chome, Nakano-ku, Tokyo 164, Japan. Eds. Keizo Shogenji, Aki Ishibashi.
—BLDSC shelfmark: 4088.966000.

616.3   IT   ISSN 0391-8939
IL GASTROENTEROLOGO. bi-m. L.15000($15) C I C Edizioni Internazionali s.r.l., Via L. Spallanzani 11, 00161 Rome, Italy. TEL 06-8412673. FAX 06-8443365. TELEX 622099 CIC.
—BLDSC shelfmark: 4088.995000.

616.3
GASTROENTEROLOGY AND ENDOSCOPY NEWS. 1950. m. free to qualified personnel. McMahon Group, 148 W. 24th St., New York, NY 10011. TEL 212-620-4600. FAX 212-620-5928. Ed. Cornelia Kean. adv.; circ. 7,396.

616.3   US   ISSN 0889-8553
RC799   CODEN: GCNAEF
GASTROENTEROLOGY CLINICS. 1972. q. $84. W.B. Saunders Co., Curtis Center, Independence Square W., Philadelphia, PA 19106. TEL 215-238-7800. Ed. Kelly Thomas. Indexed: Biol.Abstr., Chem.Abstr., Curr.Adv.Ecol.Sci., Dent.Ind., Excerp.Med., Helminthol.Abstr., Ind.Med., Ind.Sci.Rev., INIS Atomind., Sci.Cit.Ind.
—BLDSC shelfmark: 4089.031500.
Formerly: Clinics in Gastroenterology (ISSN 0300-5089)

616.3   UK
GASTROENTEROLOGY IN PRACTICE. Abbreviated title: G I P. 1983. bi-m. £24 (foreign £34). Hayward Medical Publications, Hayward House, 1 Threshers Yard, Kingham, Oxon OX7 6YF, London WC2E 7LS, England. TEL 0608-659595. FAX 071-379-6737. Ed.Bd. adv.; bk.rev.; circ. 21,000.
Supersedes (in 1990): Gastroenterology and Rheumatology in Practice (ISSN 0959-3314); **Formerly:** Gastroenterology in Practice (ISSN 0264-7478); Which incorporated: Rheumatology in Practice (ISSN 0262-5512)

616.3   IT   ISSN 0950-5911
GASTROENTEROLOGY INTERNATIONAL. 1988. q. $50 to individuals; institutions $90. International University Press, Via Monte delle Gioie 22, 00199 Rome, Italy. TEL 06-8380067. FAX 06-8380064. Ed. Sydney F. Phillips. adv.: B&W page $1875, color page $4000; adv. contact: Isabella Leonardo. circ. 5,000.
—BLDSC shelfmark: 4089.032000.

616.3   US
GASTROENTEROLOGY JOURNAL. m. W.B. Saunders Company, 200 First St., S.W., Rochester, MN 02215-5491. TEL 507-284-9155. Ed. Nicholas LaRusso. circ. 16,000.
●Also available online. Vendor(s): BRS.

616.3   US   ISSN 1042-895X
RC804.E6   CODEN: GANUER
GASTROENTEROLOGY NURSING. 1977. q. $43 to individuals; institutions $70. (Society of Gastroenterology Nurses and Associates) Williams & Wilkins, 428 E. Preston St., Baltimore, MD 21202. TEL 301-528-4000. FAX 301-528-4312. Ed. Susan Trivits, C.G.C. adv.; bk.rev.; circ. 4,600. (also avail. in microform; back issues avail.) Indexed: CINAHL.
—BLDSC shelfmark: 4089.032300.
Formerly: S G A Journal (ISSN 0149-6212)
Description: Describes new procedures, techniques and equipment for gastroenterology nurses and associates.

616.3   US
GASTROENTEROLOGY SERIES. 1983. irreg., vol.2, 1986. Marcel Dekker, Inc., 270 Madison Ave., New York, NY 10016. TEL 212-696-9000. FAX 212-685-4540. TELEX 421419.
Refereed Serial

616.3   US   ISSN 0016-5107
RC804.E6   CODEN: GAENBQ
GASTROINTESTINAL ENDOSCOPY. 1953. bi-m. $70 to individuals; institutions $92. Williams & Wilkins, 428 E. Preston St., Baltimore, MD 21202. TEL 301-528-4000. FAX 301-528-4312. Ed. Charles J. Lightdale, M.D. adv.; bk.rev.; abstr.; index; circ. 8,600. (also avail. in microfilm; reprint service avail.) Indexed: Biol.Abstr., Curr.Adv.Cancer Res., Curr.Cont., Excerp.Med., Helminthol.Abstr., Ind.Med., Ind.Sci.Rev., INIS Atomind., Protozool.Abstr., Sci.Cit.Ind.
—BLDSC shelfmark: 4089.050000.
Formerly: Bulletin of Gastrointestinal Endoscopy.
Description: Current papers in fiberoptic endoscopy, for gastroenterologists and general surgeons.
Refereed Serial

616.3   UK   ISSN 0142-8101
GASTROINTESTINAL HORMONES. 1977. s-m. £95. Sheffield University Biomedical Information Service (SUBIS), The University, Sheffield S10 2TN, England. TEL 0742-768555. FAX 0742-739826. TELEX 547216-UGSHEF-G.
Description: Current awareness service for researchers. Studies gastrin, bombesin, G-I-polypeptide, secretin, motilin, VIP, pancreatic polypeptide and other hormones.

616.3   IT
GIORNALE ITALIANO DI ENDOSCOPIA DIGESTIVA. (Text in Italian; summaries in English) 1978. q. L.64500($87) (effective 1991). (Societa Italiana di Endoscopia Digestiva) Maason Italia Periodici, Via Statuto 2-4, 20121 Milan, Italy. Ed. Antonio Russo. circ. 1,500. (reprint service avail. from UMI) Indexed: Excerp.Med.
Formerly: Giornale di Gastroenterologia ed Endoscopia.

616.3   UK   ISSN 0017-5749
CODEN: GUTTAK
GUT. 1960. m. £157. (British Society of Gastroenterology) B M J Publishing Group, B.M.A. House, Tavistock Sq., London WC1H 9JR, England. TEL 071-387-4499. Ed. R.N. Allan. adv.; bk.rev.; charts; illus.; index. (also avail. in microform from UMI; reprint service avail. from UMI) Indexed: Biol.Abstr., Biotech.Abstr., Chem.Abstr., Curr.Adv.Ecol.Sci., Dent.Ind., Excerp.Med., Helminthol.Abstr., I.P.A., Ind.Med., Ind.Sci.Rev., Ind.Vet., INIS Atomind., NRN, Nutr.Abstr., Sci.Cit.Ind., Triticale Abstr., Vet.Bull.
●Also available online. Vendor(s): BRS.
—BLDSC shelfmark: 4232.400000.

616.3   GW   ISSN 0172-6390
CODEN: HEGAD4
HEPATO-GASTROENTEROLOGY. (Text in English; summaries in English and German) 1954. bi-m. DM.240($199) Georg Thieme Verlag, Ruedigerstr. 14, Postfach 104853, 7000 Stuttgart 10, Germany. TEL 0711-8931-0. FAX 0711-8931298. Ed.Bd. adv.; bk.rev.; abstr.; bibl.; charts; illus.; stat.; index; circ. 2,500. (also avail. in microform from UMI; back issues avail.; reprint service avail. from UMI) Indexed: Biol.Abstr., Chem.Abstr., Curr.Adv.Ecol.Sci., Dent.Ind., Excerp.Med., Helminthol.Abstr., Ind.Med., Ind.Sci.Rev., INIS Atomind., Nutr.Abstr., Sci.Cit.Ind.
—BLDSC shelfmark: 4295.835000.
Former titles: Acta Hepato-Gastroenterologica (ISSN 0300-970X); Acta Hepato- Splenologica (ISSN 0001-5822)

I C R D B CANCERGRAM: UPPER GASTROINTESTINAL TUMORS - DIAGNOSIS, TREATMENT. see *MEDICAL SCIENCES — Abstracting, Bibliographies, Statistics*

616.3   US   ISSN 0273-6608
R11   CODEN: IMSPE7
▼**I M - INTERNAL MEDICINE FOR THE SPECIALIST.** 1990. 14/yr. $60 (foreign $110); medical students $50. Med Publishing, Inc., Office Center at Princeton Meadows, Bldg. 1000, Plainsboro, NJ 08536. TEL 609-275-1900. FAX 609-275-1909. Ed. Susan A. Thomas. circ. 92,770.
—BLDSC shelfmark: 4368.580000.
Description: Articles on internal medicine for internists as well as physicians in other specialties.

616.3   JA   ISSN 0536-2180
I TO CHO/STOMACH AND INTESTINE. (Text in Japanese; captions and summaries in English) 1966. m. 22710 Yen($175) Igaku-Shoin Ltd., 5-24-3 Hongo, Bunkyo-ku, Tokyo 113-91, Japan. TEL 03-817-5714. Ed.Bd. circ. 15,000. Indexed: INIS Atomind.
●Also available online. Vendor(s): JICST.
—BLDSC shelfmark: 8465.870000.

616.3   II   ISSN 0970-0935
INDIAN JOURNAL OF COLO-PROCTOLOGY. (Text in English) 1986. s-a. Rs.60($20) Association of Colon and Rectal Surgeons of India, 30 Circus Ave., Calcutta 700 017, India. TEL 33-449776. Ed. Dr. Syed Abdul Momen. adv.; bk.rev.; index; circ. 500.

616.3   II   ISSN 0254-8860
INDIAN JOURNAL OF GASTROENTEROLOGY. (Supplement avail.: Proceedings of Annual Conference) (Text in English) 1982. q. Rs.250 (foreign $50). Indian Society of Gastroenterology, 23, Bombay Mutual Terrace, 534 Sandhurst Bridge, Bombay 400 007, India. TEL 3613344. Ed. Subhash R. Naik. adv.; bk.rev.; abstr.; bibl.; circ. 1,000. (back issues avail.) Indexed: Abstr.Hyg., Excerp.Med., Ind.Med.
—BLDSC shelfmark: 4412.760000.

616.3   II
INDIAN SOCIETY OF GASTROENTEROLOGY. PROCEEDINGS OF THE ANNUAL CONFERENCE. (Supplement to: Indian Journal of Gastroenterology) 1962. a. $20. Indian Society of Gastroenterology, 23, Bombay Mutual Terrace, 534 Sandhurst Bridge, Bombay 400 007, India. TEL 8113344. Ed. Dr. S.R. Naik. adv.; bk.rev.; circ. 500. Indexed: Excerp.Med., Ind.Med.

INTERNATIONAL JOURNAL OF PANCREATOLOGY. see *MEDICAL SCIENCES — Endocrinology*

616.3   UK   ISSN 0261-4995
INTESTINAL FUNCTION. 1965. s-m. £105. Sheffield University Biomedical Information Service (SUBIS), The University, Sheffield S10 2TN, England. TEL 0742-768555. FAX 0742-739826. TELEX 547216-UGSHEF-G.
Former titles (until 1981): Intestinal Absorption (ISSN 0306-3003); Intestinal Absorption and Related Topics.
Description: Current awareness service for researchers. Covers intestinal transport, structure, physiology, motility and biochemistry.

MEDICAL SCIENCES — GASTROENTEROLOGY

616.3   IT   ISSN 0392-0623
ITALIAN JOURNAL OF GASTROENTEROLOGY. (Text in English; summaries in English and Italian) 1969. m. (10/yr.). $120 to individuals; institutions $160. (Italian Society of Gastroenterology) International University Press, Via Monte delle Gioie 22, 00199 Rome, Italy. TEL 06-8380067. FAX 06-8380064. Ed. Romano Carratu. adv.: B&W page $1600, color page $2567; adv. contact: Isabella Leonardo. bk.rev.; index, cum.index; circ. 5,000. (also avail. in microform from UMI; reprint service avail. **Indexed:** Excerp.Med., Ind.Med, Nutr.Abstr.
—BLDSC shelfmark: 4588.340400.
Former titles: Rendiconti di Gastroenterologia (ISSN 0300-0877); (until 1971): Rendiconti Romani di Gastro-Enterologia (ISSN 0300-0524); (until 1970): Rendiconti delle Romane di Gastro-Enterology.

616.3   US   ISSN 0192-0790
RC799
JOURNAL OF CLINICAL GASTROENTEROLOGY. 1979. 8/yr. $106 to individuals; institutions $170. Raven Press, 1185 Ave. of the Americas, New York, NY 10036. TEL 212-930-9500. FAX 212-869-3495. TELEX 640073. Ed. Dr. Howard M. Spiro. adv.; bk.rev.; charts; illus.; stat.; index; circ. 2,500. (back issues avail.) **Indexed:** Curr.Adv.Cancer Res., Curr.Cont., Excerp.Med., Helminthol.Abstr., Ind.Med., Ind.Sci.Rev., NRN, Sci.Cit.Ind.
—BLDSC shelfmark: 4958.470000.
Description: Focuses on essential advances in the field of digestive diseases that relate directly to clinical practice and patient care problems.
Refereed Serial

616.3 613.2   SP
JOURNAL OF CLINICAL NUTRITION AND GASTROENTEROLOGY. (Text in English; summaries in Spanish) 1986. q. 4000 ptas. (Spanish Society of Parenteral and Enteral Nutrition) Salvat Publicaciones Cientificas, S.A., Muntaner, 262, 6o, 08021 Barcelona, Spain. TEL 2010911. FAX 2015911. (Subscr. to: Cempro, Plaza Conde Valle Suchil 20, 28015 Madrid, Spain) adv.; bk.rev.; index; circ. 2,000. (back issues avail.)

616.3   AT   ISSN 0815-9319
CODEN: JGHEEO
JOURNAL OF GASTROENTEROLOGY AND HEPATOLOGY. 1986. bi-m. Aus.$255($199) Blackwell Scientific Publications (Australia) Pty. Ltd., P.O. Box 378, Carlton, Vic. 3053, Australia. TEL 03-347-0300. FAX 03-347-5001. TELEX 10716421. Ed.Bd. illus.; index; circ. 1,300. (also avail. in microform from UMI; back issues avail.; reprint service avail. from UMI) **Indexed:** Chem.Abstr., Curr.Adv.Cancer Res., Curr.Cont., Excerp.Med., Ind.Med., Sci.Cit.Ind.
—BLDSC shelfmark: 4987.615000.
Description: Covers original contributions concerned with clinical practice and research in the fields of gastroenterology and hepatology.

616.3   NE   ISSN 0168-8278
CODEN: JOHEEC
JOURNAL OF HEPATOLOGY. (Text and summaries in English) 1985. 6/yr.(in 2 vols.; 3 nos./vol.) fl.1118 (effective 1992). (European Association for the Study of the Liver) Elsevier Science Publishers B.V., P.O. Box 211, 1000 AE Amsterdam, Netherlands. TEL 020-5803911. FAX 020-5803598. TELEX 18582 ESPA NL. (N. America dist. addr.: Elsevier Science Publishing Co., Inc., Box 882, Madison Sq. Sta., New York, NY 10159. TEL 212-989-5800) Ed. Jean-Pierre Benhamou. adv.; bk.rev.; illus.; index. (back issues avail.; reprint service avail. from ISI,SWZ) **Indexed:** Curr.Adv.Cell & Devel.Biol., Curr.Adv.Ecol.Sci., Excerp.Med., INIS Atomind., Sci.Cit.Ind.
—BLDSC shelfmark: 4997.700000.
Description: Publishes original papers and reviews concerned with practice and research in the field of hepatology.

616.3 612.3   US   ISSN 0277-2116
CODEN: JPGND6
JOURNAL OF PEDIATRIC GASTROENTEROLOGY AND NUTRITION. 1982. 8/yr. $158 to individuals; institutions $253. Raven Press, 1185 Ave. of the Americas, New York, NY 10036. TEL 212-930-9500. FAX 212-869-3495. TELEX 640073. (Co-sponsors: North American Society for Pediatric Gastroenterology and Nutrition; European Society for Pediatric Gastroenterology and Nutrition) Eds. William F. Balistreri, Michael Lentze. adv.; bk.rev.; charts; illus.; index; circ. 2,000. (back issues avail.) **Indexed:** Chem.Abstr., Curr.Adv.Ecol.Sci., Dairy Sci.Abstr., Dent.Ind., Ind.Sci.Rev., Ind.Vet., Maize Abstr., Pig News & Info., Protozool.Abstr., Soyabean Abstr., Triticale Abstr.
—BLDSC shelfmark: 5030.175000.
Description: Reports of studies on nutrition, normal and abnormal functions of the alimentary tract and associated organs, with emphasis on development and its relation to infant and childhood nutrition.
Refereed Serial

616.3   GW   ISSN 0006-3304
▼**KONTINENZ**; Zeitschrift fuer Funktionsstoerungen von Blase und Darm. 1992. bi-m. DM.98. Hippokrates Verlag, Ruedigerstr. 14, Postfach 102263, 7000 Stuttgart 10, Germany. TEL 0711-8931-0. FAX 0711-8931453. Ed. W. Jost.

616.3   GW   ISSN 0300-8622
CODEN: LBMDAT
LEBER MAGEN DARM; zeitschrift fuer angewandte gastroenterologie und stoffwechsel. 1971. 6/yr. DM.113.40 (foreign DM.117.60). Richard Pflaum Verlag GmbH und Co. KG, Lazarettstr. 4, Postfach 201920, 8000 Munich 19, Germany. TEL 089-12607-0. FAX 089-12607-281. Ed. P. Fruehmorgen. adv.; bk.rev.; circ. 18,000. **Indexed:** Curr.Cont., Excerp.Med., Helminthol.Abstr., Ind.Med., Ind.Sci.Rev., Nutr.Abstr.
—BLDSC shelfmark: 5179.660000.

616.3   DK   ISSN 0106-9543
CODEN: LIVEDR
LIVER; an international journal. (Text in English) 1981. bi-m. DKK 1030. Munksgaard International Publishers Ltd., 35 Noerre Soegade, P.O. Box 2148, DK-1016 Copenhagen K, Denmark. TEL 33-127030. FAX 33-129387. TELEX 19431-MUNKS-DK. Ed. Dr. Valeer Desmet. adv.; bk.rev.; illus.; stat.; index; circ. 800. (reprint service avail. from ISI) **Indexed:** Biol.Abstr., Curr.Adv.Biochem., Curr.Adv.Cell & Devel.Biol., Curr.Cont., Excerp.Med., Ind.Med.
—BLDSC shelfmark: 5280.400000.

616.3 574   US
LIVING HEALTHY;* learning to live with digestive disease. 1979. bi-m. $30. American Digestive Disease Society, 60 E 42nd St., Ste. 411, New York, NY 10165-0015. Ed. Martin I. Hassner. bibl.; charts; illus.; circ. 14,000. (back issues avail.)

616.3   FR   ISSN 0047-6412
CODEN: MCDGBC
MEDECINE ET CHIRURGIE DIGESTIVES. (Supplements avail.: Hepato-Gastro-Enterologie; Actualites sur la Pancreatite Chronique) (Text in English, French; summaries in English, French, German, Spanish) 1972. bi-m. 530 F. (foreign 580 F.). (Hopital Saint Antoine, Centre d'Enseignement d'Hepatologie) B.C. Diffusion, 116 Av. des Champs-Elysees, 75008 Paris, France. Eds. J. Caroli, B. Chevrel. adv.; bk.rev.; abstr.; bibl.; illus.; index; circ. 3,500. **Indexed:** Biol.Abstr., Bull.Signal., C.I.S. Abstr., Curr.Cont., Excerp.Med., Helminthol.Abstr., Ind.Med., Nutr.Abstr.
—BLDSC shelfmark: 5487.729000.
Description: Scientific journal covering research articles, statistics, treatments and medication available with respect to gastrointestinal ailments.

616.3   US
MEDICAL ESSENTIALS DIRECTORY - GASTROENTEROLOGY. 1984. a. $49 (foreign $149). Island Publishing Group, Inc., Box 598, Lawrence, NY 11559. TEL 516-295-3188. FAX 516-295-0648. Ed. Dr. Harold Jacob. adv.; circ. 10,221.
Description: For members of GI societies and others with a strong interest in gastroenterology. Covers colorectal surgery and pharmaceuticals used in the prevention and treatment of GI distress and disease.

616.3   BL
MEDISOM: GASTROENTEROLOGY. 1979. bi-m. $90. Grupo Editorial Q B D Ltda, Rua Caravelas 326, Caixa Postal 30329, 01051 Sao Paulo, Brazil. FAX 55-11-572-5957. Ed. Dr. Philip Querido. adv. (audio cassette)

616.3   IT   ISSN 0391-1993
RC799   CODEN: MDGADI
MINERVA DIETOLOGICA E GASTROENTEROLOGICA. (Text in Italian; summaries in English) 1960. q. L.60000($80) Edizioni Minerva Medica, Corso Bramante 83-85, 10126 Turin, Italy. Ed. A. Oliaro. adv.; bk.rev.; bibl.; charts; illus.; index; circ. 3,000. **Indexed:** Biol.Abstr., Chem.Abstr., Dent.Ind., Excerp.Med., Ind.Med., Nutr.Abstr.
Formed by the merger of: Minerva Dietologica (ISSN 0026-475X) & Minerva Gastroenterologica (ISSN 0026-4776)

616.3   UK
▼**N A C C NEWS.** 1990. 2/yr. National Association for Colitis and Crohn's Disease, 98A London Rd., St. Albans, Herts AL1 1NX, England. Ed. Maureen Lakeman. adv.; bk.rev.

616.3   UK   ISSN 0144-6967
N A C C NEWSLETTER. 1980. 4/yr. membership. National Association for Colitis and Crohn's Disease, 98A London Rd., St. Albans, Herts AL1 1NX, England. adv.; bk.rev.; circ. 15,000.
Description: Includes reports of inflammatory bowel disease lectures, activities of over 50 area groups in Great Britain, research progress, fundraising and members' letters.

NIHON KIKAN SHOKUDOKA GAKKAI KAIHO/JAPAN BRONCHO-ESOPHAGOLOGICAL SOCIETY. JOURNAL. see *MEDICAL SCIENCES — Respiratory Diseases*

PANCREAS. see *MEDICAL SCIENCES — Endocrinology*

616.3   US   ISSN 0277-4208
CODEN: PRGAEE
PRACTICAL GASTROENTEROLOGY; for the busy internist. 1977. 10/yr. $115 (foreign $160)(effective Jan. 1991). Shugar Publishing, 32 Mill Rd., Westhampton Beach, NY 11978. TEL 516-288-4404. FAX 516-288-4435. Ed. William Kitay. adv.; bk.rev.; film rev.; charts; illus.; index; circ. 65,000 (controlled). (also avail. in microfilm from UMI; back issues avail.; reprint service avail. from ISI,UMI) **Indexed:** Curr.Cont., Excerp.Med.
Former titles: Primary Care Physician's Guide to Practical Gastroenterology (ISSN 0163-7894); Physician's Guide to Practical Gastroenterology (ISSN 0149-9912)
Description: For the gastroenterologist, rheumatologist, and busy internist on the diagnosis, therapy and management of digestive disorders. Includes articles on topics that the practitioner encounters in daily practice.

616.3   SP   ISSN 1130-4588
CODEN: READBN
REVISTA ESPANOLA DE LAS ENFERMEDADES DIGESTIVAS. (Text in Spanish; summaries in English and Spanish) 1918. m. 8500 ptas.($143) (Sociedad Espanola de Patologia Digestiva) Editorial Garsi, S.A., Londres, 17, 28028 Madrid, Spain. TEL 256-08-00. FAX 361-10-07. Ed. Dr. F. Vilardell. adv.; bk.rev.; abstr.; bibl.; charts; illus.; stat.; circ. 3,500. (also avail. in microform from UMI; reprint service avail. from UMI) **Indexed:** Biol.Abstr., Chem.Abstr., Curr.Cont., Excerp.Med., Helminthol.Abstr., Ind.Med., Nutr.Abstr., Protozool.Abstr.
Former titles (until 1989): Revista Espanola de las Enfermedades del Aparato Digestivo (ISSN 0034-9437); (until 1967): Revista Espanola de las Enfermedades del Aparato Digestivo y de la Nutricion (ISSN 0370-4343) And (until 1934): Archivos Espanoles de las Enfermedades del Aparato Digestivo y de la Nutricion (ISSN 0210-1556).

616.3   FR   ISSN 0035-2888
REVUE FRANCAISE DE GASTRO ENTEROLOGIE. m. (10/yr.). 210 F. to individuals (foreign 295 F.); students 195 F. (students 280 F.). Galliena Promotion, 58 A, Rue du Dessous des Berges, 75013 Paris, France. TEL 45-84-97-66. FAX 45-84-92-56.
—BLDSC shelfmark: 7904.140000.

MEDICAL SCIENCES — HEMATOLOGY

616.3   IT   ISSN 0035-6255
RIVISTA DI GASTROENTEROLOGIA. (Text in Italian; summaries in English) 1949. s-a. L.60000 (foreign L.120000)(effective 1992). Casa Editrice Maccari, Via Trento 53, 43100 Parma, Italy. FAX 039-521-771268. Ed.Bd. adv.; bk.rev.; circ. 1,200. **Indexed:** Chem.Abstr., Excerp.Med.

616.3   NO   ISSN 0036-5521
                CODEN: SJGRA4
SCANDINAVIAN JOURNAL OF GASTROENTEROLOGY. (Editions in Chinese, English and Spanish) 1966. 12/yr. $414 includes supplements. Universitetsforlaget, P.O. Box 2959-Toeyen, N-0608 Oslo 1, Norway. (U.S. addr.: Publications Expediting Inc., 200 Meacham Ave., Elmont, NY 11003) Ed. E. Gjone. adv.; bk.rev.; charts; illus.; index; circ. 1,700. (also avail. in microform from UMI) **Indexed:** Biol.Abstr., Biotech.Abstr., Chem.Abstr, Curr.Adv.Cancer Res., Curr.Adv.Ecol.Sci., Curr.Adv.Genetics & Molec.Biol., Curr.Cont., Dairy Sci.Abstr., Dent.Ind., Excerp.Med., Helminthol.Abstr., Ind.Med., Nutr.Abstr., Protozool.Abstr.
—BLDSC shelfmark: 8087.507000.

616.3   NO   ISSN 0085-5928
                CODEN: SJGSB8
SCANDINAVIAN JOURNAL OF GASTROENTEROLOGY. SUPPLEMENT. (Text in English) 1968. irreg. $414 (includes Scandinavian Journal of Gastroenterology). Universitetsforlaget, P.O. Box 2959-Toeyen, N-0608 Oslo 1, Norway. (U.S. addr.: Publications Expediting Inc., 200 Meacham Ave., Elmont, NY 11003) Ed. E. Gjone. circ. 1,700. (also avail. in microform from UMI; back issues avail.; reprint service avail. from ISI) **Indexed:** Biol.Abstr., Chem.Abstr., Curr.Adv.Ecol.Sci., Dent.Ind., Excerp.Med., Ind.Med., Nutr.Abstr.
—BLDSC shelfmark: 8087.508000.

616.3   US   ISSN 0272-8087
                CODEN: SLDIEE
SEMINARS IN LIVER DISEASES. 1981. q. $75 to individuals; institutions $99. Thieme Medical Publishers, Inc., 381 Park Ave., So., Ste. 1501, New York, NY 10016. TEL 212-683-5088. Ed. Pual Berk, M.D. adv.; abstr. (also avail. in microform from UMI; reprint service avail. from UMI) **Indexed:** Abstr.Hyg., Curr.Adv.Genetics & Molec.Biol., Ind.Med.
—BLDSC shelfmark: 8239.454000.

616.3 610   CN
SEMINARS IN PEDIATRIC GASTROENTEROLOGY AND NUTRITION. q. Decker Periodicals, One James St. S., P.O. Box 620, LCD 1, Hamilton, Ont. L8N 3K7, Canada. TEL 416-522-7017. FAX 416-522-7839. Eds. W. Allan Walker, Kristy M. Hendricks.
    Description: Offers a review of current investigation and clinical practice in the nutritional management of children.

616.3   JA   ISSN 0389-9403
SHOKAKI NAISHIKYO NO SHINPO/PROGRESS OF DIGESTIVE ENDOSCOPY. (Text in Japanese; summaries in English) 1972. s-a. 18.000 Yen. Kyowa Kikaku Tsushin K.K., 2-20 Shinbashi, Minato-ku, Tokyo 105, Japan. charts; illus.; circ. 2,000. (back issues avail.)

SLIDE ATLAS OF GASTROINTESTINAL ENDOSCOPY (YEAR). see *MEDICAL SCIENCES — Abstracting, Bibliographies, Statistics*

SMOOTH MUSCLE. see *BIOLOGY — Physiology*

SURGICAL LAPAROSCOPY AND ENDOSCOPY. see *MEDICAL SCIENCES — Surgery*

616.3   GW   ISSN 0303-6294
TIPS FUER DIE GASTROENTEROLOGISCHE PRAXIS. 1974. s-a. (Gesellschaft fuer Gastroenterologie in Bayern e.V.) Demeter Verlag, Wuermstr. 13, 8032 Graefelfing, Germany. TEL 089-852033. FAX 089-8543347. circ. 2,500.

616.3   US
TOPICS IN GASTROENTEROLOGY. 1979. irreg., latest 1989. price varies. Plenum Publishing Corp., 233 Spring St., New York, NY 10013-1578. TEL 212-620-8000. FAX 212-463-0742. TELEX 23-421139. Ed. Howard M. Spiro. **Indexed:** Biol.Abstr.
    Refereed Serial

VATRECHNI BOLESTI. see *MEDICAL SCIENCES — Endocrinology*

616.3   AT   ISSN 0819-4610
WORLD COUNCIL OF ENTEROSTOMAL THERAPISTS JOURNAL. 1986. q. $48. (World Council of Enterostomal Therapists) Ink Press International, P.O. Box 910, Nedlands, W.A. 6009, Australia. TEL 389-8422. FAX 09-389-8458. Ed. Pat Blackley. adv.; bk.rev.; circ. 6,000. (back issues avail.)
    Description: Specializes in the care of patients who have had their bowel or bladder removed and are given an alternative method of elimination. Covers draining wounds and fistulae.

616.3   US   ISSN 0739-5930
RC799
YEAR BOOK OF DIGESTIVE DISEASES. a. $57.95. Mosby - Year Book, Inc., Continuity Division, 200 N. LaSalle, Chicago, IL 60601. TEL 312-726-9746. FAX 312-726-6933. TELEX 206155. Eds. Drs. Norton J. Greenberger, Frank G. Moody. illus.
 ●Also available online. Vendor(s): BRS.
—BLDSC shelfmark: 9411.629700.

616   GW   ISSN 0044-2771
                CODEN: ZGASAX
ZEITSCHRIFT FUER GASTROENTEROLOGIE. 1963. m. DM.136. (Deutsche Gesellschaft fuer Verdauungs- und Stoffwechselkrankheiten) Demeter Verlag, Wuermstr. 13, 8032 Graefelfing, Germany. TEL 089-852033. FAX 089-8543347. (Co-sponsors: Deutsche Gesellschaft fuer Gastroenterologische Endoskopie; Oesterreichische Gesellschaft fuer Gastroenterologie) Ed. Dr. N. Henning. adv.; bk.rev.; abstr.; charts; illus.; stat.; tr.lit.; circ. 2,000. **Indexed:** Biol.Abstr., Chem.Abstr., Curr.Cont., Excerp.Med., Helminthol.Abstr., Ind.Med., Nutr.Abstr.
—BLDSC shelfmark: 9462.350000.

616.3   CC   ISSN 1000-1174
ZHONGGUO GANGCHANGBING ZAZHI. (Text in Chinese) q. Zhonghua Quanguo Zhongyi Xuehui, Gangchang Xuehui, No. 42, Wenhua Xilu, Jinan, Shandong 250011, People's Republic of China. TEL 20414. Ed. Huang Naijian.

616.3   CC   ISSN 0254-1432
ZHONGHUA XIAOHUA ZAZHI/CHINESE JOURNAL OF GASTROENTEROLOGY. (Text in Chinese) bi-m. Zhonghua Yixuehui, Shanghai Fenhui - Chinese Society of Medical Sciences, Shanghai Branch, 1623 Beijing Xilu, Shanghai 200040, People's Republic of China. TEL 2531885. Ed. Jiang Shaoji.
—BLDSC shelfmark: 3180.317000.

MEDICAL SCIENCES — Hematology

616.15   SZ   ISSN 0001-5792
                CODEN: ACHAAH
ACTA HAEMATOLOGICA. (Text in English) 1948. 8/yr. (2 vols. per yr.) 360 Fr.($240) per vol. S. Karger AG, Allschwilerstr. 10, P.O. Box, CH-4009 Basel, Switzerland. TEL 061-3061111. FAX 061-3061234. TELEX CH 962652. Ed. B. Ramot. adv.; bk.rev.; abstr.; illus.; index; circ. 1,600. (also avail. in microform from RPI) **Indexed:** ASCA, Biol.Abstr., Chem.Abstr., Curr.Adv.Cancer Res., Curr.Adv.Ecol.Sci., Curr.Cont., Excerp.Med., Ind.Med., Ind.Sci.Rev., Ind.Vet., Nutr.Abstr., Sci.Cit.Ind., Telegen, Vet.Bull.
—BLDSC shelfmark: 0623.000000.

616.15   PL   ISSN 0001-5814
                CODEN: AHPLBO
ACTA HAEMATOLOGICA POLONICA. (Text and summaries in various languages) 1970. 2/yr. $60. (Polskie Towarzystwo Hematologiczne) Panstwowy Zaklad Wydawnictw Lekarskich, Ul. Dluga 38-40, Warsaw, Poland. TEL 31-42-81. (Dist. by: Ars Polona- Ruch, Krakowskie Przedmiescie 7, 00-068 Warsaw, Poland) (Co-sponsor: Instytut Hematologii) Ed. Stanislaw Maj. adv.; bk.rev.; index. (processed; also avail. in cards) **Indexed:** Biol.Abstr., Chem.Abstr., Excerp.Med., Ind.Med., INIS Atomind.
    Description: Features case reports on hematology, transfusion and immunology.

616.1   US   ISSN 0361-8609
QP91   CODEN: AJHEDD
AMERICAN JOURNAL OF HEMATOLOGY. 1976. m. $573 (foreign $723). John Wiley & Sons, Inc., Journals, 605 Third Ave., New York, NY 10158. TEL 212-850-6000. FAX 212-850-6-88. TELEX 12-7063. Ed. Ananda S. Prasad. adv.; bibl.; illus. (back issues avail.; reprint service avail. from ISI) **Indexed:** Abstr.Hyg., Abstr.Inter.Med., Biol.Abstr., Chem.Abstr., Curr.Adv.Ecol.Sci., Curr.Adv.Genetics & Molec.Biol., Curr.Cont., Dent.Ind., Excerp.Med., Helminthol.Abstr., Ind.Med., Ind.Sci.Rev., INIS Atomind., Nutr.Abstr., Protozool.Abstr., Sci.Cit.Ind., Trop.Dis.Bull.
—BLDSC shelfmark: 0824.800000.
    Description: Provides broad coverage of both human and animal hematologic topics and publishes original contributions from investigators and clinicians in hematology, and related areas such as immunology, blood banking, genetics, chemotherapy, and cell biology.
    Refereed Serial

AMERICAN JOURNAL OF KIDNEY DISEASES. see *MEDICAL SCIENCES — Urology And Nephrology*

AMERICAN JOURNAL OF PEDIATRIC HEMATOLOGY - ONCOLOGY. see *MEDICAL SCIENCES — Pediatrics*

616.15   GW   ISSN 0721-9318
ANGIO; Gefaesschirurgie - Angiologie - Angioradiologie. (Text in German; summaries in English) 1979. bi-m. DM.110. Demeter Verlag, Wuermstr. 13, 8032 Graefelfing, Germany. TEL 089-852033. FAX 089-8543347. Ed. Dr. P.C. Maurer. circ. 1,500.

616.15   GW   ISSN 0939-5555
ANNALS OF HEMATOLOGY. (Supplement avail: Haematolgie und Bluttransfusion (ISSN 0440-0607)) (Text in English and German) 1950. 12/yr. DM.996 (effective 1992). Springer-Verlag, Heidelberger Platz 3, D-1000 Berlin 33, Germany. TEL 030-8207-1. (Also Heidelberg, Tokyo, Vienna, and New York) (Co-sponsors: Deutsche Gesellschaft fuer Haematologie und Onkologie; Deutsche Haematologische Gesellschaft) Ed.Bd. adv.; bk.rev.; abstr.; bibl.; charts; illus.; index. (also avail. in microform from UMI; reprint service avail. from ISI) **Indexed:** Biol.Abstr., Chem.Abstr., Curr.Adv.Cancer Res., Curr.Adv.Ecol.Sci., Curr.Cont., Excerp.Med., Helminthol.Abstr., Ind.Med., Ind.Sci.Rev., Ind.Vet., INIS Atomind., Nutr.Abstr., Protozool.Abstr., Sci.Cit.Ind., Vet.Bull.
—BLDSC shelfmark: 1040.855000.
    Formerly (until 1991): Blut (ISSN 0006-5242)

616.15   US
APLASTIC ANEMIA FOUNDATION OF AMERICA. NEWSLETTER. 1987. q. free. Aplastic Anemia Foundation of America, Box 22689, Baltimore, MD 21203. FAX 301-955-0247. Ed. Lynn Rauch. circ. 4,500. (back issues avail.)

616.15   CN
ARTERIAL BLOOD GAS ANALYSIS. (Avail. on floppy disk only.) s-a. $149 to individuals; institutions $200. (American Association of Critical-Care Nurses) Decker Periodicals, One James St. S., P.O. Box 620, LCD 1, Hamilton, Ont. L8N 3K7, Canada. TEL 416-522-7017. FAX 416-522-7839. (U.S. addr.: Box 785, Lewiston, NY 14092-0785) Ed. Mary E. Mancini.
    Description: Step-by-step approach to interpretation and management techniques for new nurses and respiratory therapists.

616.15   YU   ISSN 0523-6150
BILTEN ZA HEMATOLOGIJU I TRANSFUZIJU. 1973. a. 200 din. Zavod za Transfuziju Krvi, Belgrade, Svetosavska 39, Belgrade, Yugoslavia. (Co-sponsor: Udruzenje Hematologa i Transfuziologa Jugoslavije) Ed. Budimir Dinic. adv.; circ. 500. **Indexed:** Ind.Med.

MEDICAL SCIENCES — HEMATOLOGY 3271

616.5 574.192 US ISSN 0006-4971
RB145 CODEN: BLOOAW
BLOOD. 1946. m. $210 to individuals; institutions $321; foreign $311. (American Society of Hematology) W.B. Saunders Co. (Subsidiary of: Harcourt Brace Jovanovich, Inc.), Curtis Center, Independence Square W., Philadelphia, PA 19106. TEL 215-238-7800. (Subscr. to: 6277 Sea Harbor Dr., 4th Fl., Orlando FL 32891) Ed. Dr. Arthur Nienhuis. adv.; bk.rev.; abstr.; bibl.; charts; illus.; index. Indexed: Abstr.Hyg., Abstr.Inter.Med., Anim.Breed.Abstr., Biol.Abstr., Biotech.Abstr., Chem.Abstr., Curr.Adv.Cancer Res., Curr.Adv.Ecol.Sci., Curr.Cont., Dairy Sci.Abstr., Dent.Ind., Excerp.Med., Helminthol.Abstr., Ind.Med., Ind.Sci.Rev., Ind.Vet., INIS Atomind., Nutr.Abstr., Protozool.Abstr., Risk Abstr., Sci.Cit.Ind., Small Anim.Abstr., Telegen, Trop.Dis.Bull.
●Also available online. Vendor(s): BRS, Mead Data Central.
—BLDSC shelfmark: 2112.000000.
Formerly: Blood: The Journal of Hematology.
Refereed Serial

616.1 US ISSN 0340-4684
CODEN: BLCEDD
BLOOD CELLS. 1975. 3/yr. $139. Springer-Verlag, Journals, 175 Fifth Ave., New York, NY 10010. TEL 212-460-1500. (Also Berlin, Heidelberg, Tokyo and Vienna) Ed. B.S. Bull. adv. (also avail. in microfrom from UMI; reprint service avail. from ISI) Indexed: Anim.Breed.Abstr., Chem.Abstr., Curr.Adv.Cell & Devel.Biol., Curr.Adv.Ecol.Sci., Curr.Adv.Genetics & Molec.Biol., Curr.Cont., Excerp.Med., Ind.Med., Ind.Sci.Rev., INIS Atomind., Sci.Cit.Ind.
—BLDSC shelfmark: 2112.200000.

616.15 UK ISSN 0957-5235
CODEN: BLFIE7
▼**BLOOD COAGULATION AND FIBRINOLYSIS**; international journal of haemostasis and thrombosis. 1990. bi-m. £220($395) Rapid Communications of Oxford Ltd., The Old Malthouse, Paradise St., Oxford OX1 1LD, England. TEL 0865-790447. FAX 0865-244012. Ed. John Francis. bk.rev. Indexed: Ind.Med.
—BLDSC shelfmark: 2112.650000.

616.15 UK ISSN 0266-6294
BLOOD COAGULATION FACTORS; current awareness service for researchers in life sciences. 1985. s-m. £110. Sheffield University Biomedical Information Service (SUBIS), The University, Sheffield S10 2TN, England. TEL 0742-768555. FAX 0742-739826. TELEX 547216-UGSHEF-G.
Description: Studies fibrinogen, thrombin, plasminogen activators and other coagulation factors.

616.15 SZ ISSN 0253-5068
CODEN: BLPUDO
BLOOD PURIFICATION. (Text and summaries in English) 1983. bi-m. Sfr.($266) per vol. S. Karger AG, Allschwilerstr. 10, P.O. Box, CH-4009 Basel, Switzerland. TEL 061-3061111. FAX 061-3061234. TELEX CH 962652. Ed. L.W. Henderson. adv.; illus.; index; circ. 950. (also avail. in microform from RPI; back issues avail.) Indexed: Curr.Cont., Excerp.Med.
—BLDSC shelfmark: 2113.037000.

616.15 UK ISSN 0268-960X
CODEN: BLOREB
BLOOD REVIEWS. 1987. q. £89($170) Churchill Livingstone Medical Journals, Robert Stevenson House, 1-3 Baxter's Pl., Leith Walk, Edinburgh EH1 3AF, Scotland. TEL 031-556-2424. FAX 031-558-1278. TELEX 727511. (Subscr. to: Longman Group, Journals Subscr. Dept., P.O. Box 77, Fourth Ave., Harlow, Essex CM19 5AA, England; U.S. subscr. to: Churchill Livingstone, 650 Ave. of the Americas, New York, NY 10011. TEL 212-206-5000) Eds. David Linch, David Golde. circ. 1,100.
—BLDSC shelfmark: 2113.038000.
Description: Covers all aspects of haematology - current ideas in clinical and laboratory practice.

616.15 II
BLOOD THERAPY JOURNAL INTERNATIONAL; committed to the cause of eradication of blood diseases & cancer. (Text in English and Hindi; summaries in English) 1965. bi-m. Rs.120($50) Institute of Haematology, 36, Vijay Block, Laxmi Nagar, New Delhi 110 092, India. TEL 2246228. Ed. Dr. V.B. Lal. adv.; bk.rev.; abstr.; bibl.; charts; illus.; circ. 3,000.
Supersedes (in 1980): Blood Therapy Journal (ISSN 0006-5005)

616.15 617 UK ISSN 0261-4596
BLOOD TRANSFUSION. m. £70. Sheffield University Biomedical Information Service (SUBIS), The University, Sheffield S10 2TN, England. TEL 0742-768555. FAX 0742-739826. TELEX 547216 UGSHEF G. (looseleaf format; back issues avail.)
Description: Current awareness service for researchers in clinical and life sciences.

616.15 UK ISSN 0007-1048
CODEN: BJHEAL
BRITISH JOURNAL OF HAEMATOLOGY. 1955. m. £152 (foreign £168). Blackwell Scientific Publications Ltd., Osney Mead, Oxford OX2 0EL, England. TEL 0865-240201. FAX 0865-721205. TELEX 83355-MEDBOK-G. Ed. E.C. Gordon-Smith. adv.; bk.rev.; bibl.; charts; illus.; index; circ. 3,690. (also avail. in microfilm from PMC; back issues avail.; reprint service avail. from ISI) Indexed: Abstr.Hyg., ASCA, Biol.Abstr., Chem.Abstr., Curr.Adv.Biochem., Curr.Adv.Cancer Res., Curr.Adv.Cell & Devel.Biol., Curr.Adv.Ecol.Sci., Curr.Adv.Genetics & Molec.Biol., Curr.Cont., Dairy Sci.Abstr., Dent.Ind., Excerp.Med., Helminthol.Abstr., Ind.Med., Ind.Sci.Rev., Ind.Vet., INIS Atomind., Nutr.Abstr., Protozool.Abstr., Sci.Cit.Ind., Telegen, Trop.Dis.Bull., Vet.Bull.
—BLDSC shelfmark: 2309.000000.

613.7 616.15 US
C C B C NEWSLETTER. 1978. w. $192 (foreign $240). Council of Community Blood Centers, 725 15th St., N.W., Ste. 700, Washington, DC 20005-2109. TEL 202-393-5725. FAX 202-393-1282. Ed. Jane M. Starkey. bk.rev.; index; circ. 400. (back issues avail.)
Description: Current events and trends in community blood services and transfusion medicine.

C C S S. FEDERAZIONE DELLE SOCIETA MEDICO-SCIENTIFICHE. ITALIANE BOLLETTINO CONGRESSI (YEAR). (Comitato per la Collaborazione tra Societa Medico-Scientifiche Italiane) see *MEDICAL SCIENCES*

616.15 CN
CANADIAN RED CROSS BLOOD TRANSFUSION SERVICE. ANNUAL REPORT. (Text in English and French) 1946. a. free. Canadian Red Cross Society, National Headquarters, 5700 Cancross Court, Mississauga, Ont. L5R 3E9, Canada. TEL 416-890-1000. circ. 6,000.

CEREBROVASCULAR DISEASES. see *MEDICAL SCIENCES — Psychiatry And Neurology*

616.15 UK ISSN 0141-9854
CODEN: CLHAD3
CLINICAL AND LABORATORY HAEMATOLOGY. 1979. q. £112.50 (foreign £126). Blackwell Scientific Publications Ltd., Osney Mead, Oxford OX2 0EL, England. TEL 0865-240201. FAX 0865-721205. TELEX 83355-MEDBOK-G. Ed. Dr. J.M. England. adv.; bk.rev.; abstr.; bibl.; charts; illus.; index; circ. 650. (back issues avail; reprint service avail. from ISI) Indexed: ASCA, Curr.Adv.Ecol.Sci., Curr.Cont., Excerp.Med., Ind.Med., Ind.Sci.Rev., Sci.Cit.Ind.
—BLDSC shelfmark: 3286.253200.

616.15 US ISSN 0271-5198
QP105 CODEN: CLHEDF
CLINICAL HEMORHEOLOGY. (Companion journal to: Biorheology) 1981. bi-m. £245 (effective 1992). (International Society of Biorheology) Pergamon Press, Inc., Journals Division, 660 White Plains Rd., Tarrytown, NY 10591-5153. TEL 914-524-9200. FAX 914-333-2444. (And: Headington Hill Hall, Oxford OX3 0BW, England. TEL 0865-794141) Eds. S. Witte, J.F. Stoltz. adv. (also avail. in microform) Indexed: Chem.Abstr., Curr.Adv.Ecol.Sci., Curr.Cont., Excerp.Med., Helminthol.Abstr.
—BLDSC shelfmark: 3286.290000.
Description: Topics covered include pathogenesis, symptomatology, and diagnostic, prophylactic and therapeutic methods.
Refereed Serial

616.15 IT ISSN 0393-487X
CLOT AND HEMATOLOGIC MALIGNANCIES; journal of blood coagulation, hemostasis, thrombosis, hemorheology, and malignant hemopathies. (Text in Italian) 1981. bi-m. L.27($27) Via le Unita d'Italia 743, 74029 Talsano, Italy. Ed. Teodoro Ripa. adv.; bk.rev.; index; circ. 2,500.
Formerly: Clot.

COMPLEMENTARY MEDICAL RESEARCH. see *MEDICAL SCIENCES — Chiropractic, Homeopathy, Osteopathy*

616.15 US ISSN 0197-3649
RB145 CODEN: CHONDF
CONTEMPORARY HEMATOLOGY - ONCOLOGY. 1977. irreg., vol.3, 1984. Plenum Publishing Corp., 233 Spring St., New York, NY 10013-1578. TEL 212-620-8000. FAX 212-463-0742611. Ed.Bd. Indexed: Biol.Abstr.
Formerly: Year in Hematology (ISSN 0160-7014)
Refereed Serial

CRITICAL REVIEWS IN ONCOLOGY - HEMATOLOGY. see *MEDICAL SCIENCES — Cancer*

616.1 SZ ISSN 0258-0330
CODEN: CSHTE8
CURRENT STUDIES IN HEMATOLOGY AND BLOOD TRANSFUSION. (Text in English) 1955. irreg. (approx. 1/yr.). price varies. (European Society of Hematology) S. Karger AG, Allschwilerstr. 10, P.O. Box, CH-4009 Basel, Switzerland. TEL 061-3061111. FAX 061-3061234. TELEX CH 962652. Eds. A. Haessig, P. Lundsgaard-Hansen. (reprint service avail. from ISI) Indexed: Biol.Abstr., Chem.Abstr., Curr.Cont., Excerp.Med., Ind.Med.
Formerly: Bibliotheca Heamatologica.

616.15 GW ISSN 0931-5551
DEUTSCHE GESELLSCHAFT FUER ANGIOLOGIE. MITTEILUNGEN. q. DM.36. Demeter Verlag, Wuermstr. 13, 8032 Graefelfing, Germany. TEL 089-852033. FAX 089-8543347. circ. 1,000.

610 UK
ERYTHROCYTES. 1979. s-m. £100. Sheffield University Biomedical Information Service (SUBIS), The University, Sheffield S10 2TN, England. TEL 0742-768555. FAX 0742-739826. TELEX 547216-UGSHEF-G. bk.rev.
Description: Current awareness service for researchers in clinical and life sciences.

616.15 DK ISSN 0902-4441
CODEN: EJHAEC
EUROPEAN JOURNAL OF HAEMATOLOGY. (Text in English) 1964. 10/yr. DKK 2200 includes supplements. Munksgaard International Publishers Ltd., 35 Noerre Soegade, P.O. Box 2148, DK-1016 Copenhagen K, Denmark. TEL 33-127030. FAX 33-129387. TELEX 19431-MUNKS-DK. Ed. Inge Olsson. adv.; bk.rev.; bibl.; charts; illus.; circ. 1,400. (reprint service avail. from ISI) Indexed: ASCA, Biol.Abstr., Chem.Abstr., Curr.Adv.Ecol.Sci., Curr.Cont., Dairy Sci.Abstr., Dent.Ind., Excerp.Med., Helminthol.Abstr., Ind.Med., Nutr.Abstr.
—BLDSC shelfmark: 3829.729700.
Formerly: Scandinavian Journal of Haematology (ISSN 0036-553X)

M

MEDICAL SCIENCES — HEMATOLOGY

616.15 DK ISSN 0902-4506
EUROPEAN JOURNAL OF HAEMATOLOGY. SUPPLEMENTUM. (Text in English) 1964. irreg. free with subscription to European Journal of Haematology. Munksgaard International Publishers Ltd., P.O. Box 2148, DK-1016 Copenhagen K, Denmark. TEL 33-127030. FAX 33-129387. TELEX 19431-MUNKS-DK. Ed. Inge Olsson. adv. (reprint service avail. from ISI) **Indexed:** Biol.Abstr., Chem.Abstr., Curr.Cont., Ind.Med., Nutr.Abstr.
—BLDSC shelfmark: 3829.729800.
Formerly: Scandinavian Journal of Haematology. Supplementum (ISSN 0080-6722)

616.15 US ISSN 0301-472X
CODEN: EXHMA6
EXPERIMENTAL HEMATOLOGY. (Includes supplements of Meeting Proceedings, published irreg.) 1973. 11/yr. $274. (International Society for Experimental Hematology) Springer-Verlag, Journals, 175 Fifth Ave., New York, NY 10010. Ed. Eugene P. Cronkite. adv.; circ. 1,100. (reprint service avail. from ISI) **Indexed:** Biol.Abstr., Chem.Abstr., Curr.Adv.Cell & Devel.Biol., Curr.Adv.Ecol.Sci., Curr.Cont., Dent.Ind., Excerp.Med., Ind.Med., Ind.Sci.Rev., INIS Atomind., Sci.Cit.Ind.
—BLDSC shelfmark: 3839.360000.

616.15 RU ISSN 0234-5730
GEMATOLOGIYA I TRANSFUSIOLOGIYA/HEMATOLOGY AND TRANSFUSIOLOGY. 1956. m. 25.20 Rub. (Vsesoyuznoe Nauchnoe Obshchestvo Gematologov i Transfuziologov) Izdatel'stvo Meditsina, Petroverigskii pereulok 6-8, 101838 Moscow, Russia. (Subscr. to: Mezhdunarodnaya Kniga, Moscow, G-200, Russia) (Co-sponsor: Ministerstvo Zdravookhraneniya S.S.S.R.) Ed. Yu.N. Tokarev. **Indexed:** Biol.Abstr., Chem.Abstr., Excerp.Med., Ind.Med., INIS Atomind., Nutr.Abstr.
—BLDSC shelfmark: 0047.072000.
Formerly (until 1983): Problemy Gematologii i Perelivaniya Krovi (ISSN 0552-2080)
Description: Publishes original theoretical and clinical investigations, reviews and clinical notes concerning different problems of hematology and blood transfusion.

616.15 CC
GUOWAI YIXUE (SHUXUE YU XUEYEXUE FENCE)/FOREIGN MEDICAL SCIENCE (BLOOD TRANSFUSION AND BLOOD). (Text in Chinese) bi-m. Chinese Academy of Medical Sciences, Blood Transfusion Research Institute, San Xiang, Xiaojiacun, Renmin Beilu, Chengdu, Sichuan 610081, People's Republic of China. TEL 331031-43.

H L B NEWSLETTER; reporting on heart, lung and blood disease research program, policy development. see *MEDICAL SCIENCES — Experimental Medicine, Laboratory Technique*

616.15 HU ISSN 0017-6559
CODEN: HAEMBY
HAEMATOLOGIA; international quarterly of haematology. (Text in English, French, German, Russian) 1967. q. DM.330. (Magyar Tudomanyos Akademia) Akademiai Kiado, Publishing House of the Hungarian Academy of Sciences, P.O. Box 24, H-1363 Budapest, Hungary. (Co-publisher: V S P, P.O. Box 346, 3700 AH Zeist, Netherlands) TEL 03404-25790) Eds. S.R. Hollan, I. Bernat. adv.; bk.rev. **Indexed:** Biol.Abstr., Chem.Abstr., Curr.Adv.Ecol.Sci., Curr.Adv.Genetics & Molec.Biol., Curr.Cont., Excerp.Med., Ind.Med., Ind.Sci.Rev
—BLDSC shelfmark: 4237.800000.

616.1 IT ISSN 0390-6078
CODEN: HAEMAX
HAEMATOLOGICA. (Text and summaries in English) 1914. bi-m. L.100000 to individuals; institutions L.130000($190). (Societa Italiana di Ematologia) Pensiero Scientifico Editore s.r.l., Via Panama 48, 00198 Rome, Italy. TEL 06 855-36-33. Ed. Edoardo Ascari. adv.; bk.rev.; abstr.; bibl.; charts; illus.; index; circ. 2,000. (back issues avail.; reprint service avail. from ISI) **Indexed:** Biol.Abstr., Chem.Abstr., Curr.Adv.Cell & Devel.Biol., Curr.Adv.Ecol.Sci., Curr.Adv.Genetics & Molec.Biol., Curr.Cont., Excerp.Med., Ind.Med., INIS Atomind., Sci.Cit.Ind.
—BLDSC shelfmark: 4238.000000.

616.15 US ISSN 0440-0607
CODEN: HABLAF
HAEMATOLOGIE UND BLUTTRANSFUSION. (Supplement to: Annals of Hematology (ISSN 0939-5555)) (Text in English or German) 1962. irreg. price varies. Springer-Verlag, 175 Fifth Ave., New York, NY 10010. TEL 212-460-1500. (Also Berlin, Heidelberg, Tokyo and Vienna) Eds. W. Stich, G. Ruhenstroth-Bauer. (also avail. in microform from UMI; reprint service avail. from ISI) **Indexed:** Chem.Abstr.
Formerly: Haematology and Blood Transfusion (ISSN 0171-7111)

616.15 AT
HAEMOPHILIA SOCIETY OF VICTORIA. NEWSLETTER. 1955. q. Aus.$10. Haemophilia Society of Victoria Inc., 1216 Toorak Rd., Hartwell, Vic. 3125, Australia. TEL 03 889-0200. FAX 03-889-6120. Ed. B. Spence. bk.rev.; circ. 400. (looseleaf format; back issues avail.)
Description: Information for parents and people with haemophilia.

616.15 GW ISSN 0720-9355
CODEN: HAEMD2
HAEMOSTASEOLOGIE; Zeitschrift fuer interdisziplinaere Fortbildung. 1981. q. DM.153.60($96) F.K. Schattauer Verlagsgesellschaft mbH, Lenzhalde 3, Postfach 104545, 7000 Stuttgart 10, Germany. TEL 0711-22987-0. FAX 0711-22987-50. Ed.Bd. circ. 6,200.

660 US ISSN 0886-0238
CODEN: HEPAEG
HEMATOLOGIC PATHOLOGY. 4/yr. $147.50 to individuals; institutions $295. Marcel Dekker Journals, 270 Madison Ave., New York, NY 10016. TEL 212-696-9000. FAX 212-685-4540. TELEX 421419 MARDEEK. (Subscr. to: Box 10018, Church St. Sta., New York, NY 10249) Ed. Sanford A. Stass. (microform) **Indexed:** Curr.Adv.Genetics & Molec.Biol., Excerp.Med.
—BLDSC shelfmark: 4291.300000.
Refereed Serial

616.15 UK ISSN 0278-0232
CODEN: HAONDL
HEMATOLOGICAL ONCOLOGY. 1983. bi-m. $295 (effective 1992). John Wiley & Sons Ltd., Journals, Baffins Lane, Chichester, Sussex PO19 1UD, England. TEL 0243-779777. FAX 0243-775878. Ed.Bd. adv.; bk.rev.; charts; illus.; index. (reprint service avail. from BLH,SWZ,UMI) **Indexed:** Chem.Abstr., Curr.Adv.Ecol.Sci., Curr.Adv.Genetics & Molec.Biol., Curr.Cont., Excerp.Med., Ind.Med., Telegen.
—BLDSC shelfmark: 4291.550000.
Description: Presents a variety of clinical and scientific specialites concerned with neoplastic disease of the hemopoietic system, and any neoplastic or related process which may directly or indirectly involve the hemopoietic system.

616.15 US ISSN 0882-8083
CODEN: HRCOEG
HEMATOLOGY REVIEWS AND COMMUNICATIONS; an international journal. 1985. 4/yr. (in 1 vol., 4 nos./vol.). $122. Harwood Academic Publishers, 270 Eighth Ave., New York, NY 10011. TEL 212-206-8900. FAX 212-645-2459. TELEX 236735 GOPUB UR. (Subscr. to: Box 786, Cooper Sta., New York, NY 10276. TEL 800-545-8398; UK subscr. to: P.O. Box 90, Reading, Berkshire RG1 8JL, England. TEL 0734-560-080) Ed. Stuart Roath. (also avail. in microform) **Indexed:** Excerp.Med.
—BLDSC shelfmark: 4291.620000.
Refereed Serial

616.15 US
HEMATOLOGY SERIES. irreg., vol.15, 1992. Marcel Dekker, Inc., 270 Madison Ave., New York, NY 10016. TEL 212-696-9000. FAX 212-658-4540. TELEX 421419. Ed. Kenneth M. Brinkhous.
Refereed Serial

616.15 US ISSN 0363-0269
RC641.7.H35 CODEN: HEMOD8
HEMOGLOBIN; international journal for hemoglobin research. 1977. 6/yr. $499. Marcel Dekker Journals, 270 Madison Ave., New York, NY 10016. TEL 212-696-9000. FAX 212-685-4540. TELEX 421419. (Subscr. to: Box 10018, Church St. Sta., New York, NY 10249) Ed. T.H.J. Huisman. (also avail. in microform from RPI) **Indexed:** Chem.Abstr., Curr.Adv.Ecol.Sci., Curr.Cont., Excerp.Med., Ind.Med., Ind.Sci.Rev., Sci.Cit.Ind.
—BLDSC shelfmark: 4295.040000.
Refereed Serial

616.15 CN ISSN 0046-7251
HEMOPHILIA TODAY. (Editions in English, French) 1964. q. free. Canadian Hemophilia Society, 1450 City Councillors, Suite 840, Montreal, Que. H3A 2E6, Canada. TEL 514-848-9661. FAX 514-848-0337. Ed. D. Rutherford. circ. 6,000.

I C R D B CANCERGRAM: LEUKEMIA AND MULTIPLE MYELOMA - DIAGNOSIS, TREATMENT. see *MEDICAL SCIENCES — Abstracting, Bibliographies, Statistics*

616.15 BL ISSN 0103-3263
INSTITUTO ESTADUAL DE HEMATOLOGIA ARTHUR DE SIQUEIRA CAVALCANTI. REVISTA. (Text in Portuguese; summaries in English) 1971. s-a. exchange basis. Instituto Estadual de Hematologia Arthur de Siqueira Cavalcanti, Biblioteca, Rua Frei Caneca, 08, Centro - CEP 20211, RJ, Brazil. TEL 021-242-6080. FAX 021-252-3739. Ed. Jose Moreira Pereira. bk.rev.; bibl.; charts; circ. 1,000. **Indexed:** Excerp.Med.
Formerly (until vol.4, no.2, 1976): Instituto Estadual de Hematologia Arthur de Siqueira Cavalcanti. Boletim (ISSN 0046-9963)

616.15 IT ISSN 0392-9590
CODEN: INANEK
INTERNATIONAL ANGIOLOGY. (Text in English) q. L.60000($70) (International Union of Angiology) Edizioni Minerva Medica, Corso Bramante 83-85, 10126 Turin, Italy. (Subscr. to: Martinus Nijhoff, P.O.B. 269, 2501 AX. The Hague, Netherlands) **Indexed:** ASCA, Excerp.Med.
—BLDSC shelfmark: 4535.770000.
Description: Addresses latest news concerning the vascular system.

612.1 US ISSN 0074-3682
INTERNATIONAL CONGRESS OF HEMATOLOGY. PROCEEDINGS. 1958. biennial, 23rd Boston, USA. International Society of Hematology, c/o Dr. Robert Kyle, Mayo Clinic, Rochester, MN 55905. circ. 2,000.
Description: Proceedings published in host country.

616.15 NE ISSN 0925-5710
CODEN: IJHEEY
INTERNATIONAL JOURNAL OF HEMATOLOGY. (Text in English) 1938. 6/yr. fl.542 (effective 1992). (Japanese Society of Hematology, JA) Elsevier Science Publishers B.V., P.O. Box 211, 1000 AE Amsterdam, Netherlands. TEL 020-5803911. FAX 020-5803598. TELEX 18582 ESPA NL. (Subscr. in U.S. and Canada to: Elsevier Science Publishing Co., Inc., Box 882, Madison Sq. Sta., New York, NY 10159. TEL 212-989-5800) Eds. H. Uchino, E. Yoshida. adv.; bk.rev.; circ. 5,000. **Indexed:** ASCA, Biol.Abstr., Curr.Adv.Biochem., Curr.Adv.Cancer Res., Curr.Adv.Cell & Devel.Biol., Curr.Adv.Ecol.Sci., Curr.Cont., Dent.Ind., Excerp.Med., Ind.Med., Nutr.Abstr.
—BLDSC shelfmark: 4542.280400.
Formerly (until 1991): Acta Haematologica Japonica (ISSN 0001-5806)
Description: Publishes original papers and reviews of international origin in basic and clinical hematology.
Refereed Serial

616.5 612.1 FR ISSN 0074-8528
INTERNATIONAL SOCIETY OF BLOOD TRANSFUSION. PROCEEDINGS OF THE CONGRESS. biennial. Societe Internationale de Transfusion Sanguine - International Society of Blood Transfusion, c/o C N T S, B.P. 100, 91943 Les Ulis Cedex, France. TEL 69-07-20-40. FAX 69-07-41-85. TELEX 603218. **Indexed:** Biol.Abstr.

IRON METABOLISM. see *BIOLOGY — Biological Chemistry*

MEDICAL SCIENCES — HEMATOLOGY

616.15   US   ISSN 0895-7762
IRONIC BLOOD; information on iron overload. 1981. bi-m. free. Iron Overload Diseases Association, Inc., International Consortium, 433 Westwind Dr., N. Palm Beach, FL 33408. TEL 407-840-8512. FAX 407-842-9881. Ed. Roberta Crawford. circ. 7,000. (back issues avail.)
   Description: Contains the latest information about hemochromatosis and other iron overload diseases for doctors, patients,and the public.

616.15   CN   ISSN 0715-8602
JOURNAL: NEWS OF THE BLOOD PROGRAMME IN CANADA. (Text in English and French) 1983. q. free. Canadian Red Cross Society, National Headquarters, 5700 Cancross Court, Mississauga, Ont. L5R 3E9, Canada. TEL 416-890-1000. circ. 4,000.

616.15   US   ISSN 0029-4810
   CODEN: NRFHA4
JOURNAL OF EXPERIMENTAL AND CLINICAL HEMATOLOGY; nouvelle revue francaise d'hematologie. (Text in English; summaries in English and French) 1946. bi-m. DM.428($240) (Societe Francaise d'Hematologie) Springer-Verlag, Journals, 175 Fifth Ave., New York, NY 10010. TEL 212-460-1500. (Also Berlin, Heidelberg, Tokyo and Vienna) Eds. J.L Binet, J.P. Cazenave. adv.; bk.rev.; illus.; index. (also avail. in microform from UMI; reprint service avail. from ISI) **Indexed:** Biol.Abstr., Chem.Abstr., Curr.Adv.Cancer Res., Curr.Adv.Ecol.Sci., Curr.Cont., Dent.Ind., Excerp.Med., Ind.Med., Ind.Sci.Rev., Nutr.Abstr.
   —BLDSC shelfmark: 6176.800000.
   Description: Provides editorials, original articles, and congress reports on the clinical, genetic, and experimental aspects of hematology. For physiologists, pathologists, oncologists, and physicians.

616.15   JA   ISSN 0451-1611
KYUSHU HEMATOLOGICAL SOCIETY. JOURNAL/KYUSHU KETSUEKI KENKYU DOKOKAI-SHI. (Text in English, Japanese; summaries in English) 1952. s-a. 5000 Yen($39) Kyushu University, Faculty of Dentistry, Department of Oral Pathology, 3-1-1 Maidashi, Higashi-ku, Fukuoka 812, Japan. Ed. Norizo Hashimoto. adv.; circ. 640. (back issues avail.) **Indexed:** Biol.Abstr., Excerp.Med., INIS Atomind.
   Description: Publishes histological and pathological research on the hematopoietic organs and clinical studies on the hematological diseases.

616.15   US   ISSN 1042-8194
   CODEN: LELYEA
LEUKEMIA AND LYMPHOMA. 12/yr. (in 2 vols., 6 nos./vol.) $74. Harwood Academic Publishers, 270 Eighth Ave., New York, NY 10011. TEL 212-206-8900. FAX 212-645-2459. TELEX 236735 GOPUB UR. (Subscr. to: Box 786, Cooper Sta., New York, NY 10276. TEL 800-545-8398; UK subscr. to: P.O. Box 90, Cooper Sta., New York, NY 10276. TEL 0734-560-080) Ed. Aaron Polliak. (also avail. in microform)
   —BLDSC shelfmark: 5185.251500.
   Description: Offers clinical-pathologic correlation and brings together clinical and laboratory data on lymphomas, leukemias, and allied disorders, including myeloma and myelodysplastic syndromes.
   Refereed Serial

616   US   ISSN 0145-2126
   CODEN: LEREDD
LEUKEMIA RESEARCH. 1977. 12/yr. £485 (effective 1992). Pergamon Press, Inc., Journals Division, 660 White Plains Rd., Tarrytown, NY 10591-5153. TEL 914-524-9200. FAX 914-333-2444. (And: Headington Hill Hall, Oxford OX3 0BW, England. TEL 0865-794141) Eds. Peter Reizenstein, Terry Hamblin. adv.; bk.rev.; abstr.; bibl.; charts; illus.; index; circ. 1,100. (also avail. in microform from MIM,UMI; back issues avail.) **Indexed:** Biol.Abstr., Chem.Abstr., Curr.Adv.Ecol.Sci., Curr.Cont., Excerp.Med., Ind.Med., Ind.Sci.Rev., INIS Atomind., Risk Abstr., Telegen, Vet.Bull.
   —BLDSC shelfmark: 5185.270000.
   Description: Integrates basic research in leukemia with recent reports of clinical applications.
   Refereed Serial

616.15   US
   CODEN: LYREDH
LYMPHOKINE AND CYTOKINE RESEARCH. 1982. bi-m. $140 (foreign $180). Mary Ann Liebert, Inc., 1651 Third Ave., New York, NY 10128. TEL 212-289-2300. FAX 212-289-4697. Ed. Lawrence B. Lachman. adv. **Indexed:** ASCA, Chem.Abstr., Curr.Adv.Ecol.Sci., Ind.Med., Ind.Sci.Rev., Telegen.
   Formerly: Lymphokine Research (ISSN 0277-6766)
   Description: Covers recent advances in lymphokine and monokine research, and provides information on laboratory findings, as well as on application of lymphokines as immunotherapeutic agents.
   Refereed Serial

M T TODAY. (Medical Technologist) see *MEDICAL SCIENCES — Experimental Medicine, Laboratory Technique*

616.15 574.192   US   ISSN 0740-9451
QP106.6   CODEN: MELYEL
MICROCIRCULATION, ENDOTHELIUM AND LYMPHATICS. 1984. bi-m. $230 (foreign $288). c/o B.M. Altura, Ed., Department of Physiology, Box 31, State University of New York, Downstate Medical Center, 450 Clarkson Ave., Brooklyn, NY 11203. adv.; abstr.; illus.; index. (also avail. in microform from UMI; back issues avail.) **Indexed:** Chem.Abstr., Curr.Cont.
   —BLDSC shelfmark: 5758.470000.
   Refereed Serial

PEDIATRIC HEMATOLOGY & ONCOLOGY. see *MEDICAL SCIENCES — Pediatrics*

PEDIATRIC HEMATOLOGY - ONCOLOGY SERIES. see *MEDICAL SCIENCES — Pediatrics*

PLATELETS (EDINBURGH). see *BIOLOGY — Biological Chemistry*

574 610   UK   ISSN 0142-8268
PLATELETS (SHEFFIELD). 1976. s-m. £100. Sheffield University Biomedical Information Service (SUBIS), The University, Sheffield S10 2TN, England. TEL 0742-768555. FAX 0742-739826. TELEX 547216-UGSHEF-G.
   Description: Current awareness service for researchers. Covers thrombocytopoiesis, pharmacology, aggregation, structure, biochemistry and functions of platelets.

PROGRESS IN CARDIOVASCULAR DISEASES. see *MEDICAL SCIENCES — Cardiovascular Diseases*

616.1508   US   ISSN 0079-6301
RB145   CODEN: PRHMAH
PROGRESS IN HEMATOLOGY. 1956. q. price varies. W.B. Saunders Co. (Subsidiary of: Harcourt Brace Jovanovich, Inc.), Curtis Center, Independence Square W., Philadelphia, PA 19106. TEL 215-238-7800. Ed. Dr. Elmer B. Brown. **Indexed:** Biol.Abstr., Chem.Abstr, Curr.Adv.Ecol.Sci., Ind.Med., Ind.Sci.Rev., Trop.Dis.Bull.
   Refereed Serial

616.15   US
PSYCHOSOCIAL NEWS. s-a. free to qualified personnel. National Hemophilia Foundation, Mental Health Committee, Soho Bldg., Ste. 303, 110 Greene St., New York, NY 10012. FAX 212-966-9247. Eds. Regina Bussing, Mike Lammer. circ. 600.

616.15   US
REVIEWS OF HEMATOLOGY. 1980. irreg. $69.95. P J D Publications Ltd., Box 966, Westbury, NY 11590. TEL 516-626-0650. Ed. Dr. Julian L. Ambrus. (back issues avail.) **Indexed:** Biol.Abstr., Chem.Abstr, Curr.Cont.
   Description: Information of value to hematologists, biochemists and other medical scientists.
   Refereed Serial

616.15   CU   ISSN 0864-0289
REVISTA CUBANA DE HEMATOLOGIA, INMUNOLOGIA Y HEMATERAPIA. (Text in Spanish; summaries in English, French, Spanish) s-a. C.$4,00($10) in N. America; S. America $12; Europe $14. Ministerio de Salud Publica, Centro Nacional de Informacion de Ciencias Medicas, Calle E No. 452, e-19 y 21, Plaza de la Revolucion, Apdo. 6520, Havana, Cuba. TEL 809-32-5338. (Dist. by: Ediciones Cubanas, Obispo No. 527, Apdo. 605, Havana, Cuba) Dir. Jose M. Ballester Santovenia. adv.; charts; illus.; stat.; index; circ. 1,200.
   Description: Covers anemia - antibody formation, sickle cell, and AIDS.

REVISTA IBEROAMERICANA DE TROMBOSIS Y HEMOSTASIA. see *MEDICAL SCIENCES — Cardiovascular Diseases*

616.1   FR   ISSN 0338-4535
   CODEN: RFTID6
REVUE FRANCAISE DE TRANSFUSION ET IMMUNO-HEMATOLOGIE. 1958. 6/yr. 635 F. (foreign 800 F.). (Societe Nationale de Transfusion) Librairie Arnette, 2 rue Casimir Delavigne, 75006 Paris, France. Ed.Bd. bk.rev.; index; circ. 1,000. (also avail. in microform from UMI; reprint service avail. from UMI) **Indexed:** Biol.Abstr., Chem.Abstr., Curr.Cont., Dent.Ind., Excerp.Med., Ind.Med.
   Former titles: Revue Francaise de Transfusion (ISSN 0035-2977) & Transfusion.

616.15   FR   ISSN 0999-7385
SANG THROMBOSE VAISSEAUX. 10/yr. 400 F. to individuals; institutions 700 F.; students 250 F. John Libbey Eurotext, 6 rue Blanche, 92120 Montrouge, France. TEL 1-47-35-85-52. FAX 1-46-57-10-09. (Dist. by: Gauthier-Villars, Centrales des Revues, 11 rue Gossin, 92543 Montrouge Cedex, France. TEL 1-46-56-52-66)
   —BLDSC shelfmark: 8073.160000.
   Description: Studies fundamental and practical aspects of blood and vascular problems.

616.1   SP   ISSN 0036-4355
RC633.A1   CODEN: SNGRAW
SANGRE; trabajos de hematologia y hemoterapia. (Text mainly in Spanish; summaries in English and Spanish) 1956. bi-m. 5300 ptas.($70) Revista Sangre, S.A., General Sueiro, 35, 50008 Zaragoza, Spain. TEL (976) 22 26 38. FAX 34-76-222638. Ed. M. Giralt. adv.; bk.rev.; index; circ. 2,200. (back issues avail.) **Indexed:** Biol.Abstr., Chem.Abstr., Curr.Adv.Genetics & Molec.Biol., Curr.Cont., Dent.Ind., Excerp.Med., Ind.Med.Esp., Ind.Med., Nutr.Abstr.
   —BLDSC shelfmark: 8073.200000.

616.15   US   ISSN 0037-1963
RC633.A1   CODEN: SEHEA3
SEMINARS IN HEMATOLOGY. 1964. q. $76 to individuals; institutions $102; foreign $121. W.B. Saunders Co. (Subsidiary of: Harcourt Brace Jovanovich, Inc.), Curtis Center, Independence Square W., Philadelphia, PA 19106. TEL 215-238-7800. (Subscr. to: 6277 Sea Harbor Dr., 4th Fl., Orlando FL 32891) Eds. Drs. Peter A. Miescher, Ernst R. Jaffe. adv.; bibl.; charts; illus.; index. (also avail. in microform from SWZ) **Indexed:** Biol.Abstr., Chem.Abstr., Curr.Adv.Cancer Res., Curr.Adv.Ecol.Sci., Curr.Cont., Excerp.Med., Ind.Med., Nutr.Abstr.
   ●Also available online. Vendor(s): Mead Data Central.
   —BLDSC shelfmark: 8239.450000.

SEMINARS IN NEPHROLOGY. see *MEDICAL SCIENCES — Urology And Nephrology*

616.15   US   ISSN 0094-6176
   CODEN: STHMBV
SEMINARS IN THROMBOSIS AND HEMOSTASIS. q. $77 to individuals; institutions $99. Thieme Medical Publishers, Inc., 381 Park Ave., So., Ste. 1501, New York, NY 10016. TEL 212-683-5088. Ed. Dr. Eberhard F. Mammen. (also avail. in microform from UMI; reprint service avail. from UMI) **Indexed:** ASCA, Biol.Abstr., Chem.Abstr., Curr.Adv.Ecol.Sci., Ind.Med.
   —BLDSC shelfmark: 8239.480000.

MEDICAL SCIENCES — HYPNOSIS

616.15   US   ISSN 0888-3920
RC633.A1   CODEN: SMCRE9
SOVIET MEDICAL REVIEWS. SECTION C: HEMATOLOGY REVIEWS. 2/yr. $118. Harwood Academic Publishers, 270 Eighth Ave., New York, NY 10011. TEL 212-206-8900. FAX 212-645-2459. TELEX 236735 GOPUB UR. (Subscr. to: Box 786, Cooper Sta., New York, NY 10276. TEL 800-545-8398; UK subscr. to: P.O. Box 90, Reading, Berkshire RG1 8JL, England. TEL 0734-560-080) Ed. O.K. Gavrilov. (also avail. in microform)
Refereed Serial

LA STILLA; organo di stampa dell'A.V.I.S. provinciale di Montova. see *SOCIAL SERVICES AND WELFARE*

616.15   UK   ISSN 0958-7578
▼**TRANSFUSION MEDICINE.** 1991. q. £55 (foreign £62). (British Blood Transfusion Society) Blackwell Scientific Publications Ltd., Osney Mead, Oxford OX2 0EL, England. TEL 0865-240201. FAX 0865-721205. TELEX 833355-MEDBOK-G. Ed. A.H. Waters. adv.; bk.rev.; illus.; index. (back issues avail.)

616.15   US   ISSN 0887-7963
                 CODEN: TMEREU
TRANSFUSION MEDICINE REVIEWS. 1987. q. $60 to individuals; institutions $83; foreign $100. W.B. Saunders Co. (Subsidiary of: Harcourt Brace Jovanovich, Inc.), Curtis Center, Independence Square W., Philadelphia, PA 19106. TEL 215-238-7800. Ed. Dr. Morris A. Blajchman. adv.; abstr.; bibl.; charts; illus.; index.
—BLDSC shelfmark: 9020.707000.

616.15   US   ISSN 0955-3886
                 CODEN: TRASEE
TRANSFUSION SCIENCE. 4/yr. £140 (effective 1992). (European Society for Haemapheresis) Pergamon Press, Inc., Journals Division, 660 White Plains Rd., Tarrytown, NY 10591-5153. TEL 914-524-9200. FAX 914-333-2444. (And: Headington Hill Hall, Oxford OX3 0BW, England. TEL 0865-794141) Ed. Dr. Gail Rock. circ. 2,000.
—BLDSC shelfmark: 9020.710000.
  Formerly: Plasma Therapy and Transfusion Technology; Incorporates: Apheresis Bulletin.
  Description: Presents scientific and clinical studies in the areas of immunohematology, transfusion practice and apheresis.
Refereed Serial

616.15   FR   ISSN 1015-3276
TRANSFUSION TODAY. French edition (ISSN 1015-3284); Spanish edition (ISSN 1015-3292) (Text in English) 1989. q. membership. Societe Internationale de Tranfusion Sanguine - International Society of Blood Transfusion, c/o C N T S, B.P. 100, 91943 Les Ulis Cedex, France. TEL 69-07-20-40. FAX 69-07-41-85. Ed. Bahman Habibi. adv.; bk.rev.; circ. 7,000.
  Description: Articles on blood transfusion and related topics.

616.15   IT   ISSN 0041-1787
                 CODEN: TRSABD
LA TRASFUSIONE DEL SANGUE. (Text in Italian; summaries in English, Italian) 1956. bi-m. L.75000 to individuals; institutions L.90000($147). Societa Italiana di Immunoematologia e Associazione Italiana Centri Trasfusionali, c/o Ospedale Galliera, Centro Trasfusionale, Genova, Italy. Ed. Giorgio Reali. adv.; bk.rev.; abstr.; bibl.; charts; illus.; index; circ. 700. **Indexed:** Biol.Abstr., Excerp.Med.
—BLDSC shelfmark: 9026.710000.

VATRECHNI BOLESTI. see *MEDICAL SCIENCES — Endocrinology*

616.15   US   ISSN 0882-5998
RB145   CODEN: YBHEEI
YEAR BOOK OF HEMATOLOGY. a. $57.95. Mosby - Year Book, Inc., Continuity Division, 200 N. LaSalle, Chicago, IL 60601. TEL 312-726-9733. FAX 312-726-6075. TELEX 206155. Ed. Dr. Jerry L. Spivak. illus. (reprint service avail.)
  ●Also available online. Vendor(s): BRS.
—BLDSC shelfmark: 9413.050000.

616.15   CC   ISSN 0253-2727
ZHONGHUA XUEYEXUE ZAZHI/CHINESE JOURNAL OF HEMATOLOGY. (Text in Chinese) m. Zhongguo Yixue Kexueyuan, Xueye Yanjiusuo - Chinese Academy of Medical Sciences, Institute of Hematoloy, 288 Nanjing Lu, Tianjin 300020, People's Republic of China. TEL 707938. Ed. Chen Wenjie.
—BLDSC shelfmark: 3180.350000.

MEDICAL SCIENCES — Hypnosis

154.7 616.891   US   ISSN 0002-9157
RC490   CODEN: AJHNA3
AMERICAN JOURNAL OF CLINICAL HYPNOSIS. 1958. q. $30 to individuals (foreign $37.60); institutions $45 (foreign $52.60). American Society of Clinical Hypnosis, 2200 E. Devon Ave., Ste. 291, Des Plaines, IL 60018-4501. TEL 708-297-3317. FAX 708-297-7309. Ed. Dr. Thurman Mott, Jr. bk.rev.; index, cum.index; circ. 5,000. (also avail. in microform from MIM,UMI; back issues avail.; reprint service avail. from UMI) **Indexed:** Adol.Ment.Hlth.Abstr., Bibl.Ind., Biol.Abstr., Curr.Cont., Excerp.Med., Ind.Med., Mid.East: Abstr.& Ind., Psychol.Abstr., SSCI.
—BLDSC shelfmark: 0822.800000.

159.7 616.891   US   ISSN 0517-5178
AMERICAN SOCIETY OF CLINICAL HYPNOSIS. DIRECTORY. q. price varies. American Society of Clinical Hypnosis, 2200 E. Devon Ave., Ste. 291, Des Plaines, IL 60018-4501. TEL 708-297-3317. FAX 708-297-7309.

616.891   AT   ISSN 0156-0417
                 CODEN: AJCHDV
AUSTRALIAN JOURNAL OF CLINICAL AND EXPERIMENTAL HYPNOSIS. 1977. s-a. Aus.$25 to individuals; institutions Aus.$40. Australian Society of Hypnosis, 14 Hammond Ave., Croydon, N.S.W. 2132, Australia. FAX 02-7166980. Ed. Wendy-Louise Walker. bk.rev.; circ. 1,100. (back issues avail.) **Indexed:** Excerp.Med., Ind.Med., Psychol.Abstr., Sci.Cit.Ind.
—BLDSC shelfmark: 1806.200000.
  Former titles: Australian Society of Hypnosis. Journal; Australian Society of Clinical and Experimental Hypnosis. Journal.

616.891   AT   ISSN 0810-0713
AUSTRALIAN JOURNAL OF CLINICAL HYPNOTHERAPY AND HYPNOSIS. 1980. s-a. Aus.$22 to individuals; institutions and libraries Aus.$25; foreign Aus.$30. Australian Academic Press Pty. Ltd., P.O. Box 18, Aspley, Qld. 4034, Australia. TEL 07-257-1176. FAX 07-252-5908. Ed. Zoltan A. Kelemen. bk.rev.; circ. 450. (back issues avail.) **Indexed:** Excerp.Med., Psychol.Abstr.
—BLDSC shelfmark: 1806.353000.
  Description: An interdisciplinary journal advancing the science and practice of hypnosis.

COMPREHENSIVE PSYCHIATRY. see *MEDICAL SCIENCES — Psychiatry And Neurology*

616.891 370.15   US   ISSN 0882-8652
HYPNOTHERAPY TODAY. 1980. q. membership. American Association of Professional Hypnotherapists, Box 731, McLean, VA 22101. Ed. William S. Brink. bk.rev.; circ. 2,000.
  Description: Studies the therapeutic uses of hypnosis for the body, mind and spiritual needs.

154.7 616.891   US   ISSN 0020-7144
RC490   CODEN: IJEHAO
INTERNATIONAL JOURNAL OF CLINICAL AND EXPERIMENTAL HYPNOSIS. (Text in English; summaries in French, German and Spanish) 1953. q. $52 to individuals; institutions $95. Society for Clinical and Experimental Hypnosis, 128A Kings Park Dr., Liverpool, NY 13090. TEL 215-748-2140. (Subscr. to: 111 N. 49th St., Philadelphia, PA 19139) Ed. Dr. Martin T. Orne. cum.index; circ. 2,278. (also avail. in microfilm from UMI; back issues avail.; reprint service avail. from UMI) **Indexed:** Adol.Ment.Hlth.Abstr., Biol.Abstr., Curr.Cont., Excerp.Med., Ind.Med., Ind.Sci.Rev., Mid.East: Abstr.& Ind., Psychol.Abstr., Sci.Cit.Ind., Soc.Work Res.& Abstr., SSCI.
—BLDSC shelfmark: 4542.170000.
  Formerly: Clinical and Experimental Hypnosis.

KWARTAALSCHRIFT VOOR DIRECTIEVE THERAPIE EN HYPNOSE. see *PSYCHOLOGY*

154.7 616.8 614.58   US
MEDICAL HYPNOANALYSIS JOURNAL. 1980. q. $24. (American Academy of Medical Hypnoanalysts) A A M H, c/o Dr. Daniel A. Zelling, 80 N. Miller Rd., Akron, OH 44313. TEL 216-867-6677. circ. 500. (back issues avail.) **Indexed:** Psychol.Abstr.

154.7 616.891   US   ISSN 0583-8975
S C E H NEWSLETTER. 1955. q. $8. Society for Clinical and Experimental Hypnosis, 128-A Kings Park Dr., Liverpool, NY 13090. TEL 315-652-7299. Ed. Marion Kenn. bk.rev.; circ. 1,200.

SEMINARS IN ANESTHESIA. see *MEDICAL SCIENCES — Anaesthesiology*

MEDICAL SCIENCES — Nurses And Nursing

see also Gerontology and Geriatrics; Hospitals

A A C N NURSING SCAN IN CRITICAL CARE. (American Association of Critical Care Nurses) see *MEDICAL SCIENCES — Abstracting, Bibliographies, Statistics*

610.73   US   ISSN 0094-6354
                 CODEN: ANJOEE
A A N A JOURNAL. 1933. bi-m. $24. (American Association of Nurse Anesthetists) A A N A Publishing, Inc., 216 Higgins Rd., Park Ridge, IL 60068. TEL 708-692-7050. FAX 708-692-6968. Ed. Betty Colitti-Stuffers. adv.; bk.rev.; circ. 24,000. (also avail. in microform from MIM,PMC,UMI) **Indexed:** CINAHL, Excerp.Med., Hosp.Lit.Ind., Int.Nurs.Ind.
—BLDSC shelfmark: 0537.340000.
  Formerly: American Association of Nurse Anesthetists. Journal (ISSN 0002-7448)

610.73   US
A A N N SYNAPSE. bi-m. membership only. American Association of Neuroscience Nurses, 224 N. Des Plaines, Ste. 601, Chicago, IL 60661. TEL 312-993-0043. Ed. Claudia Appeldorn. circ. 3,400.

610.73   CN   ISSN 0001-0197
A.A.R.N. NEWSLETTER. 1948. 11/yr. Can.$30 (foreign Can.$35). Alberta Association of Registered Nurses, 11620-168 St., Edmonton, Alta. T5M 4A6, Canada. TEL 403-451-0043. FAX 403-452-3276. Ed. Evelyn Henderson. adv.; bk.rev.; illus.; stat.; circ. 24,400 (controlled). **Indexed:** CINAHL, Int.Nurs.Ind.
—BLDSC shelfmark: 0537.537700.

A C O R N JOURNAL. (Australian Confederation of Operating Room Nurses) see *HOSPITALS*

613.7 615.53   US
A F H H A INSIDER. 1984. m. free to members. American Federation of Home Health Agencies, 1320 Fenwick Lane, Ste. 100, Silver Spring, MD 20910. TEL 301-588-1454. FAX 301-588-4732. Ed. Ann Howard. adv.; bk.rev.; circ. 500. (looseleaf format; back issues avail.)
  Description: Explores home health care industry issues.

610.73   US   ISSN 0898-4646
A J N GUIDE; to nursing career opportunities. 1982. a. free. American Journal of Nursing Company, 555 W. 57th St., New York, NY 10019. TEL 212-582-8820. FAX 212-586-5462. adv.; circ. 150,000.

610.73   CK   ISSN 0044-930X
A N E C. 1966. irreg. $7. Asociacion Nacional de Enfermeras de Colombia, Apdo. Aereo No. 059871, Bogota, D.E., Colombia. Ed.Bd. adv.; bk.rev.; illus.; circ. 1,500,811. **Indexed:** Int.Nurs.Ind.
  Formerly: Asociacion Nacional de Enfermeras de Colombia. A N E C. Revista.

610.73 616.1   US   ISSN 8750-0779
A N N A JOURNAL. 1974. 6/yr. $21 to individuals; institutions $27. (American Nephrology Nurses' Association) Anthony J. Jannetti, Inc., N. Woodbury Rd., Box 56, Pitman, NJ 08071. TEL 609-589-2319. FAX 609-589-7463. Ed. Sally Downs McCulloch. adv.; bk.rev.; circ. 5,743. **Indexed:** Int.Nurs.Ind., Nurs.Abstr.
—BLDSC shelfmark: 0905.346600.
  Formerly (until 1984): American Association of Nephrology Nurses and Technicians. Journal.

MEDICAL SCIENCES — NURSES AND NURSING

610.73   PH   ISSN 0065-0676
A N P H I PAPERS. (Text in English) 1966. s-a. P.30($10) Academy of Nursing of the Philippines, College of Nursing, University of the Philippines, Padre Faura, Manila, Philippines. Ed. Cecilia M. Laurente. bk.rev.; circ. 1,000. (also avail. in microfilm from UMI) **Indexed:** CINAHL, Int.Nurs.Ind.
—BLDSC shelfmark: 1541.822000.

610.73   UK   ISSN 0960-8508
A N S A JOURNAL. 3/yr. Association of Nurses in Substance Abuse, 18 St. Johns St., Bury St. Edmunds, Suffolk IP33 1SJ, England. TEL 0284-762377. FAX 0284-766656. Ed. Alan Staff.
—BLDSC shelfmark: 1541.844700.

610.73   US   ISSN 0001-2092
RD99.A1
A O R N JOURNAL. 1963. m. $50 to non-members; members $20; foreign $50. Association of Operating Room Nurses, Inc., c/o JoAnn Sansen, 10170 E. Mississippi Ave., Denver, CO 80231. TEL 303-755-6300. FAX 303-755-4511. TELEX 910-320-2273. Ed. Pat Niessner Palmer. adv.; bk.rev.; abstr.; bibl.; charts; illus.; stat.; index, cum.index; circ. 50,389. (also avail. in microfilm from UMI) **Indexed:** Abstr.Health Care Manage.Stud., CINAHL, Hosp.Lit.Ind., I.P.A., Ind.Med., Int.Nurs.Ind., Nurs.Abstr.
—BLDSC shelfmark: 1567.727000.
Supersedes: O R Nursing.
Description: Features items on nursing and health care.

610.73   CN
A R N N ACCESS. 1981. q. $10. Association of Registered Nurses of Newfoundland, 55 Military Road, P.O. Box 6116, St. John's, N.F. A1C 5X8, Canada. FAX 709-753-4940. adv.; circ. 5,500.
Formerly: A R N N News News News.

610.73   US
A R N NEWS. 1976. 6/yr. $40. Association of Rehabilitation Nurses, 5700 Old Orchard Rd., 1st Fl., Skokie, IL 60077-1024. TEL 708-966-3433. FAX 708-966-9418. adv.; circ. 7,500.
Description: Focuses on association news, upcoming educational events, committee functions, and new items of interest to those in the field of nursing and the specialty of rehabilitation nursing.

610.73   IS   ISSN 0048-1165
HA-ACHOTE BE-YISRAEL/NURSE IN ISRAEL. (Text in Hebrew) 1948. q. $3. National Association of Nurses in Israel, Box 303, Tel-Aviv, Israel. Ed.Bd. adv.; illus.; circ. 10,000. **Indexed:** Ind.Heb.Per., Ind.Med.

ACTA MEDICA AUXOLOGICA. see *MEDICAL SCIENCES — Endocrinology*

610.73   US   ISSN 0899-9112
ADDICTIONS NURSING NETWORK. q. $85 (foreign $125). Mary Ann Liebert, Inc., 1651 Third Ave., New York, NY 10128. TEL 212-289-2300. FAX 212-289-4697. Ed. Madeline A. Naegle.
—BLDSC shelfmark: 0678.730000.
Description: Recognizes the major role of nurses in identifying and intervening with drug and alcohol abuse. Provides current information on serious major health problems, as well as specialties of addictions nursing.

610.73   US   ISSN 0161-9268
RT1
ADVANCES IN NURSING SCIENCE. 1978. q. $57. Aspen Publishers, Inc., 200 Orchard Ridge Dr., Gaithersburg, MD 20878. TEL 301-417-7500. FAX 301-417-7550. **Indexed:** CINAHL, Ind.Med., Nurs.Abstr., Psychol.Abstr.
—BLDSC shelfmark: 0709.508000.
Refereed Serial

610.73   US   ISSN 0002-4546
ALASKA NURSE. 1951. q. $7 to non-members. Alaska Nurses Association, 237 E. Third Ave., Anchorage, AK 99501. TEL 907-274-0827. FAX 907-272-0292. Ed. Kathy North. adv.; bk.rev.; illus.; circ. 500. **Indexed:** CINAHL, Int.Nurs.Ind.

610.73   GW   ISSN 0002-6573
ALTENHEIM; Organ der gemeinnuetzigen und privaten Alten- und Altenpflegeheime. 1961. m. DM.108.30. Curt R. Vincentz Verlag, Schiffgraben 41-43, Postfach 6247, 3000 Hannover, Germany. TEL 0511-990980. FAX 0511-9909899. Ed. Reinhard Hein. adv.; bk.rev.; charts; illus.; stat.; index; circ. 7,637. (tabloid format) **Indexed:** Dok.Arbeitsmed.

610.73   GW   ISSN 0341-0455
ALTENPFLEGE. 1976. m. DM.67. (Fachkraefte in Ambulanter und Stationaerer Altenhilfe) Curt R. Vincentz Verlag, Schiffgraben 41-43, Postfach 6247, 3000 Hannover, Germany. TEL 0511-990980. FAX 0511-9909899. Ed. E. Gerster. adv.; bk.rev.; charts; illus.; stat.; index; circ. 25,000. (tabloid format)

610.73   US   ISSN 1041-2972
RT82.8   CODEN: JANPEB
AMERICAN ACADEMY OF NURSE PRACTITIONERS. JOURNAL. 1988. q. $30 to individuals (foreign $40); institutions $45 (foreign $55). J.B. Lippincott Co., E. Washington Sq., Philadelphia, PA 19105. TEL 215-238-4200. (Subscr. to: Downsville Pike, Rte. 3, Box 20-B, Hagerstown, MD 21740)
—BLDSC shelfmark: 4683.731500.
Description: Captures what's happening in clinical practice, management, education, research and legislation.
Refereed Serial

610.73   US   ISSN 0891-0162
RC966
AMERICAN ASSOCIATION OF OCCUPATIONAL HEALTH NURSES JOURNAL. Abbreviated title: A A O H N Journal. 1953. m. $40 to individuals; institutions $53. (American Association of Occupational Health Nurses, Inc.) Slack, Inc., 6900 Grove Rd., Thorofare, NJ 08086. TEL 609-848-1000. FAX 609-853-5991. adv.; bk.rev.; charts; illus.; index; circ. 14,000. (also avail. in microfilm) **Indexed:** C.I.S. Abstr., CINAHL, Excerp.Med., Int.Nurs.Ind., Noise Pollut.Publ.Abstr., Nurs.Abstr.
Former titles: Occupational Health Nursing (ISSN 0029-7933); (1953-1968): American Association of Industrial Nurses Journal (ISSN 0098-6097)
Refereed Serial

610   US   ISSN 0196-6553
RA969
AMERICAN JOURNAL OF INFECTION CONTROL. 1973. bi-m. $34 to individuals (foreign $43); institutions $97 (foreign $106): students $20 (foreign $29). (Association for Practitioners in Infection Control) Mosby - Year Book, Inc. (Subsidiary of: Times Mirror Company), 11830 Westline Industrial Dr., St. Louis, MO 63146. TEL 800-325-4117. FAX 314-432-1380. TELEX 44-2402. Ed. Mary Castle White. adv.; bk.rev.; film rev.; abstr.; bibl.; charts; illus.; stat.; index; circ. 9,850. (also avail. in microfilm from UMI; back issues avail.; reprint service avail. from UMI) **Indexed:** ASCA, Biol.Abstr., CINAHL, Curr.Adv.Ecol.Sci., Curr.Cont., Dok.Arbeitsmed., Excerp.Med., Helminthol.Abstr., Ind.Med., INIS Atomind., Int.Nurs.Ind, Nurs.Abstr., Rev.Med.& Vet.Mycol.
—BLDSC shelfmark: 0826.761000.
Former titles: A P I C Bulletin; A P I C Journal (ISSN 0161-6005); A P I C Newsletter.
Description: Serves infection control practitioners and hospital epidemiologists concerned with the control of infection associated with hospitals and extended-care facilities.

610.73   US   ISSN 0002-936X
RT1
AMERICAN JOURNAL OF NURSING. 1900. m. $35 to individuals; institutions $45. (American Nurses' Association) American Journal of Nursing Co., 555 W. 57th St., New York, NY 10019. TEL 212-582-8820. FAX 212-586-5462. Ed. Mary B. Mallison. adv.; bk.rev.; bibl.; charts; illus.; tr.lit.; index, cum.index: 1961-65, 1966-70, 1971-75; circ. 233,000. (also avail. in microform from PMC,UMI; reprint service avail. from UMI) **Indexed:** Abstr.Health Care Manage.Stud., Acad.Ind., Adol.Ment.Hlth.Abstr., ASSIA, Chem.Abstr., CINAHL, CLOA, Curr.Cont., Curr.Lit.Fam.Plan., Dent.Ind., Dok.Arbeitsmed., Except.Child.Educ.Abstr., Gen.Sci.Ind., Hlth.Ind., Hosp.Lit.Ind., I.P.A., Ind.Med., Ind.Sci.Rev., Int.Nurs.Ind., Med.Care Rev., Nurs.Abstr., Nutr.Abstr., P.A.I.S., Psychol.Abstr., Risk Abstr., Sci.Cit.Ind., Soc.Sci.Ind., Soc.Work Res.& Abstr., SSCI, Tr.& Indus.Ind.
●Also available online.
—BLDSC shelfmark: 0828.500000.
Description: Emphasizes the latest technological advances affecting nursing care for registered nurses.
Refereed Serial

610.73   US   ISSN 0098-1486
THE AMERICAN NURSE. 1969. 10/yr. $15. American Nurses Association, 2420 Pershing Rd., Kansas City, MO 64108. TEL 816-474-5720. Ed. Patricia McCarty. adv.; circ. 200,000. (also avail. in microform from UMI; reprint service avail. from UMI) **Indexed:** CINAHL, Hosp.Lit.Ind., Int.Nurs.Ind., Nurs.Abstr.
Formerly (until 1974): A N A in Action (ISSN 0587-3053)

610.73   US   ISSN 0739-6686
RT81.5
ANNUAL REVIEW OF NURSING RESEARCH. 1984. a. price varies. Springer Publishing Company, 536 Broadway, New York, NY 10012. TEL 212-431-4370. FAX 212-941-7842. Ed.Bd. circ. 1,212. **Indexed:** Int.Nurs.Ind.
—BLDSC shelfmark: 1524.200000.

610.73   US   ISSN 0897-1897
   CODEN: ANUREA
APPLIED NURSING RESEARCH. 1988. q. $38. W.B. Saunders Co. (Subsidiary of: Harcourt Brace Jovanovich, Inc.), Curtis Center, Independence Sq. W., Philadelphia, PA 19106. TEL 215-238-7800. Ed. Joyce J. Fitzpatrick.
—BLDSC shelfmark: 1576.236000.
Description: Devoted to advancing nursing as a research-based profession and bridging the gap between research and practice in nursing.

610.73 616.8   US   ISSN 0883-9417
ARCHIVES OF PSYCHIATRIC NURSING. 1987. bi-m. $38 to individuals; institutions $50; foreign $63. W.B. Saunders Co. (Subsidiary of: Harcourt Brace Jovanovich, Inc.), Curtis Center, Independence Square W., Philadelphia, PA 19106. TEL 215-238-7800. (Subscr. to: 6277 Sea Harbor Dr., 4th Fl., Orlando FL 32891) Ed. Judith B. Krauss. adv.; bk.rev.; abstr.; bibl.; charts; illus.; index. **Indexed:** Nurs.Abstr.
—BLDSC shelfmark: 1640.410000.
Refereed Serial

610.73   US   ISSN 0004-1599
ARIZONA NURSE. vol.23, 1970. 4/yr. $30. Arizona Nurses Association, 1850 E. Southern Ave., Ste. 1, Tempe, AZ 85282. FAX 602-839-4780. Ed. Chery May. adv.; bk.rev.; illus.; circ. 2,000. (also avail. in microfilm from UMI; reprint service avail. from UMI) **Indexed:** CINAHL, Int.Nurs.Ind.

ARTHRITIS CARE AND RESEARCH. see *MEDICAL SCIENCES — Rheumatology*

610.73   GW
DIE ARZTHELFERIN. 1963. m. Friedrich Kiehl Verlag GmbH, Pjaustr. 13, 6700 Ludwigshafen, Germany. adv.; bk.rev.; index; circ. 6,000.
Incorporates (in 1989): Helferin des Artzes (ISSN 0017-9949)

ARZTHELFERIN AKTUELL. see *MEDICAL SCIENCES — Surgery*

MEDICAL SCIENCES — NURSES AND NURSING

610.73   US
ASPEN'S ADVISOR FOR NURSING EXECUTIVES. 1985. m. $135. Aspen Publishers, Inc., 200 Orchard Ridge Dr., Gaithersburg, MD 20878. TEL 301-417-7500. FAX 301-417-7550.

610.73   IT   ISSN 0393-7550
ASSISTENZA INFERMIERISTICA DEL NORD AMERICA. q. L.90000($110) Piccin Editore, Via Altinate 107, 35100 Padua, Italy. TEL 049-655566. TELEX 432074 PICCIN I. (reprint service avail. from UMI)

610.73 378   US
ASSOCIATE DEGREE EDUCATION FOR NURSING. 1972. a. $5.95. National League for Nursing, 350 Hudson St., New York, NY 10014. TEL 212-989-9393.
  Formerly: National League for Nursing. Associate Degree Education for Nursing (ISSN 0077-5118)

ASSOCIATION OF MEDICAL WOMEN IN INDIA. JOURNAL. see WOMEN'S HEALTH

ASSOCIATION OF NURSES IN A I D S CARE. JOURNAL. see MEDICAL SCIENCES — Communicable Diseases

610.73   AT   ISSN 0813-0531
AUSTRALIAN JOURNAL OF ADVANCED NURSING. 1983. q. Aus.$55 to non-members; members Aus.$35; libraries Aus.$60; foreign Aus.$65. Australian Nursing Federation, 373-375 St. Georges Rd., North Fitzroy, Vic. 3068, Australia. TEL 03-482-2722. FAX 03-482-2330. Eds. Natalie Newman, Maxine Fine. circ. 1,600. **Indexed:** Int.Nurs.Ind.
  —BLDSC shelfmark: 1801.830000.
  Description: Covers nursing research and allied philosophical study.

610.73   AT   ISSN 0045-0758
AUSTRALIAN NURSES' JOURNAL. 1962. 11/yr. Aus.$33 to non-members; members Aus.$15.40; foreign Aus.$50. Australian Nursing Federation, 373-375 St. Georges Rd., North Fitzroy, Vic. 3068, Australia. TEL 03-482-2722. FAX 03-482-2330. Eds. Natalie Newman, Maxine Fine. adv.; bk.rev.; circ. 46,000. (also avail. in microfiche from UMI; reprint service avail. from UMI) **Indexed:** CINAHL, Int.Nurs.Ind., NRN.
  —BLDSC shelfmark: 1815.800000.
  Description: Multi-purpose professional and trade union nursing journal.

610.73   FR   ISSN 0240-6411
AVENIR ET SANTE. 1971. m. (10/yr.). 1000 F. Federation Nationale des Infirmiers et Infirmieres, 7 rue Godot de Mauroy, 75009 Paris, France. Ed. Michel Guennerin. adv.; circ. 12,916.

610.73 378   US   ISSN 0069-5602
BACCALAUREATE EDUCATION IN NURSING: KEY TO A PROFESSIONAL CAREER IN NURSING. 1964. a. $5.95. National League for Nursing, 350 Hudson St., New York, NY 10014. TEL 212-989-9393.

610.73   UK
BAILLIERE'S NURSES' DICTIONARY. 1912. irreg., vol.20, 1984. £2.50. Bailliere Tindall, 24-28 Oval Rd., London NW1 7DX, England.

610.73   UK
BAILLIERE'S POCKET BOOK OF WARD INFORMATION. 1933. irreg., vol.14, 1984. £2.95. Bailliere Tindall, 24-28 Oval Rd., London NW1 7DX, England.

610.73   BB   ISSN 0572-6042
BARBADOS NURSING JOURNAL. a. membership. Barbados Registered Nurses Association, Gibson House, Spry Street, Bridgetown, Barbados, W.I.

610.73 310.412   US
BEGINNINGS (RALEIGH). 1981. 10/yr. $16. American Holistic Nurses' Association, 4101 Lake Boone Trail, Ste. 210, Raleigh, NC 27607. TEL 919-787-5181. FAX 919-787-4916. Ed. Noreen Frish, RN. adv.; bk.rev.; circ. 1,800. (back issues avail.)

BETHLEM AND MAUDSLEY GAZETTE. see MEDICAL SCIENCES — Psychiatry And Neurology

BIRTH; issues in perinatal care and education. see MEDICAL SCIENCES — Obstetrics And Gynecology

BLAETTER AUS DEM HENRIETTENSTIFT. see HOSPITALS

BREATHLINE. see MEDICAL SCIENCES — Anaesthesiology

610.73   NE
C F O - MAGAZINE; league issue for nurses and other people working the health and social welfare field. 1948. fortn. fl.76.20. Nederlandse Christelijke Bond van Overheidspersoneel, Postbus 84500, 2508 The Hague, Netherlands. adv.; bk.rev.; circ. 18,000.
  Former titles: Welzijn (ISSN 0165-8379); Volksgezondheid.

610.73   CN   ISSN 0706-2192
C H C G PULSE. (Text in English) 1976. 5/yr. Can.$16 to non-members. Canadian Health Care Guild - Guilde Canadienne de la Sante, 17410-107 Ave., No. 200, Edmonton, Alta. T5S 1E9, Canada. TEL 403-483-8126. FAX 403-484-3341. Ed. Moira Mahl. adv.; circ. 5,000.
  Former titles: A A R N A Pulse & Alberta Association of Registered Nursing Assistants. Bulletin; Alberta Certified Nursing Aide Association. Newsletter (ISSN 0044-7102)
  Description: News of interest to members of CHCG and others in the health care professions.

610.73   BE   ISSN 0007-8417
C I C I A M S NEWS - NOUVELLES - NACHRICHTEN. (Text in English, French and German) 1964. 3/yr. International Catholic Committee of Nurses and Medico Social Assistants - C I C I A M S - Comite International Catholique des Infirmieres et des Assistantes Medico-Sociales, 43, Sq. Vergote, 1040 Brussels, Belgium. TEL 02-7321050. FAX 02-7348460. adv.; bk.rev.; bibl.; illus.; circ. 700.
  —BLDSC shelfmark: 3192.450000.

610.73   CN
C I N A. 1975. q. membership. (Canadian Intravenous Nurses Association) Pappin Communications, 73 Pembroke St. W., Pembroke, Ont. K8A 5M5, Canada. TEL 613-735-0952. Ed. Dianne Lopponen. adv. contact: Bruce Pappin. **Indexed:** CINAHL.

C O H S E JOURNAL. (Confederation of Health Service Employees) see PUBLIC HEALTH AND SAFETY

C O N A JOURNAL. (Canadian Orthopaedic Nurses Association) see MEDICAL SCIENCES — Orthopedics And Traumatology

C R N A: THE CLINICAL FORUM FOR NURSE ANESTHETISTS. see MEDICAL SCIENCES — Anaesthesiology

610.73   US   ISSN 0008-1310
CALIFORNIA NURSE. 1904. m. $30. California Nurses' Association, 1855 Folsom St., Ste. 670, San Francisco, CA 94103. TEL 415-864-4141. FAX 415-431-1011. Ed. Catherine M. Direen. adv.; circ. 27,000. (tabloid format; also avail. in microfilm from UMI; reprint service avail. from UMI, ISI) **Indexed:** Cal.Per.Ind. (1978-), CINAHL, Int.Nurs.Ind.
  —BLDSC shelfmark: 3015.085000.
  Formerly: C N A Bulletin.

610.73   US
CALIFORNIA SCHOOL NURSE. 3/yr. Health Information Publishers, 92 S. Highland Ave., Ossining, NY 10562. TEL 914-762-6498. Ed. Barbara Bradstock. circ. 1,888.

610.73   CN
CANADIAN CHILDBIRTH EDUCATOR. 1987. q. Professional Publishing Associates, 269 Richmond St. W., Toronto, Ont. M5V 1X1, Canada. TEL 416-596-8680. FAX 416-596-1991. adv.; circ. 6,821.

610.73   CN   ISSN 0843-6096
CANADIAN JOURNAL OF CARDIOVASCULAR NURSING. (Text in English or French) 1973. q. Can.$28 to individuals; institutions $42; students $20. Canadian Council of Cardiovascular Nurses, 160 George St., Ste. 200, Ottawa, Ont. K1N 9M2, Canada. TEL 613-237-4361. FAX 416-521-0048. Ed. Joanne Runions. adv.; bk.rev.; circ. 1,200.
  —BLDSC shelfmark: 3030.600000.
  Supersedes (in Apr. 1989): Canadian Bulletin of Cardiovascular Nursing (ISSN 0831-4462)
  Description: Concerned with health care issues related to cardiovascular diseases.
  Refereed Serial

610.73   CN   ISSN 0838-2948
CANADIAN JOURNAL OF NURSING ADMINISTRATION. 1988. q. Can.$28. Health Media Inc., 14453 29A Ave., White Rock, B.C. V4A 9K8, Canada. TEL 604-535-7933. Ed. Jan Dick. **Indexed:** Nurs.Abstr.
  —BLDSC shelfmark: 3033.350000.
  Description: For Canadian nurse administrators, managers and educators.
  Refereed Serial

610.73   CN
CANADIAN JOURNAL OF NURSING RESEARCH/REVUE CANADIENNE DE RECHERCHE EN SCIENCES INFIRMIERES. (Text in English and French) 1969. q. Can.$34 to individuals; institutions Can.$48; students Can.$20. McGill University, School of Nursing, 3506 University St., Montreal, Que. H3A 2A7, Canada. TEL 514-392-4160. FAX 514-398-8455. Ed. Mary Ellen Jeans. adv.; bk.rev.; circ. 1,200. **Indexed:** Abstr.Health Care Manage.Stud., CINAHL, Hosp.Abstr., Int.Nurs.Ind., Nurs.Abstr., Pt.de Rep. (1988-).
  Formerly: Nursing Papers - Perspectives en Nursing (ISSN 0318-1006)
  Description: Covers research and current issues in nursing.
  Refereed Serial

610.73   CN
CANADIAN NURSE - L'INFIRMIERE CANADIENNE. 1905. 11/yr. Can.$30($40) Canadian Nurses Association - Association des Infirmieres et Infirmiers du Canada, 50 The Driveway, Ottawa, Ont. K2P 1E2, Canada. TEL 613-237-2133. FAX 613-237-3520. Ed. Judith A. Banning. adv.; bk.rev.; film rev.; bibl.; charts; illus.; stat.; tr.lit.; index; circ. 104,000. (also avail. in microfilm from UMI,PMC; reprint service avail. from UMI) **Indexed:** Can.Per.Ind., CMI, Hosp.Abstr., Int.Nurs.Ind., Nurs.Abstr., Pt.de Rep. (1979-).
  Formed by the merger of: Infirmiere Canadienne (ISSN 0019-9605) & Canadian Nurse (ISSN 0008-4581)

610.73   CN   ISSN 1180-4920
CANADIAN NURSES ASSOCIATION. NURSING PROGRAMS AND ENTRANCE REQUIREMENTS AT CANADIAN UNIVERSITIES.. a. Can.$20. Canadian Nurses Association - Association des Infirmieres et Infirmiers du Canada, 50 the Driveway, Ottawa, Ont. K2P 1E2, Canada. TEL 613-237-2133. FAX 613-237-3520.
  Formed by the 1989 merger of: Canadian Nurses Association. Nursing Programs and Entrance Requirements at Canadian Universities (ISSN 0229-7345) & Canadian Nurses Association. Entrance Requirements for Diploma Schools of Nursing and Schools of Practical Nursing (ISSN 0319-4787)

610.73   CN
CANADIAN NURSING MANAGEMENT. 1987. 10/yr. Can.$109. M P L Communications Inc., 700-133 Richmond St., W., Toronto, Ont. M5H 2M8, Canada. TEL 416-869-1177. FAX 416-869-0456. Ed. Sheila Brawn. circ. 800. (looseleaf format)

610.73 616.99   CN
▼**CANADIAN ONCOLOGY NURSING JOURNAL/REVUE CANADIENNE DE NURSING ONCOLOGIQUE.** 1991. 4/yr. Can.$42 (foreign Can.$70). Pappin Communications, 73 Pembroke St. W., 3rd Fl., Pembroke, Ont. K8A 5M5, Canada. TEL 613-735-0952. FAX 613-735-7983. adv.; circ. 998.

610.73   CN   ISSN 0712-6778
CANADIAN OPERATING ROOM NURSING JOURNAL. 1983. 4/yr. Can.$16($22) (Operating Room Nurses Association of Canada) Health Media Inc., 14453 29A Ave., White Rock, B.C. V4A 9K8, Canada. TEL 604-535-7933. Ed. Agnes Forster. circ. 4,020.
  —BLDSC shelfmark: 3043.177000.

MEDICAL SCIENCES — NURSES AND NURSING

610.73 616.99 US ISSN 0162-220X
RC266
CANCER NURSING; an international journal for cancer care. 1978. bi-m. $40 to individuals; institutions $63. Raven Press, 1185 Ave. of the Americas, New York, NY 10036. TEL 212-930-9500. FAX 212-869-3495. TELEX 640073. Ed. Carol Reed-Ash. adv.; bk.rev.; charts; illus.; stat.; tr.lit.; circ. 7,300. (also avail. in microform from MIM; back issues avail.) **Indexed:** CINAHL, Dent.Ind., Int.Nurs.Ind., Nurs.Abstr.
—BLDSC shelfmark: 3046.491000.
Description: Covers problems arising in the care of cancer patients.
Refereed Serial

610.73 616.99 US
CANCER NURSING NEWS. 1982. q. free. American Cancer Society, Inc., 1599 Clifton Rd., N.E., Atlanta, GA 30329. TEL 404-329-7617. Ed. Patricia Greene. circ. 90,000.
Description: Provides information and educational resources on the care of cancer patients.

610.736 US ISSN 0008-6355
CARDIOVASCULAR NURSING. 1965. bi-m. $6 to individuals (foreign $15); institutions $11 (foreign $20). American Heart Association, 7272 Greenville Ave., Dallas, TX 75231-4596. TEL 214-706-1310. FAX 214-691-6342. (Subscr. to: Box 843543, Dallas, TX 75284-3543) Ed. Kathleen King, RN. charts; illus.; circ. 54,000. (also avail. in microform from UMI,MIM; reprint service avail. from UMI; back issues avail.) **Indexed:** CINAHL, Int.Nurs.Ind., Nurs.Abstr.
—BLDSC shelfmark: 3051.470000.
Description: Discusses new developments in care for patients with heart disease.
Refereed Serial

610.73 CN ISSN 0843-9966
CARE CONNECTION. 1985. q. Can.$22. Ontario Association of Registered Nursing Assistants, 5025 Orbitor Dr., Ste. 200, Bldg. 4, Mississauga, Ont. L4W 4X5, Canada. TEL 416-602-4664. FAX 416-602-4666. Ed. Linda Humphreys. adv.; bk.rev.; illus.; tr.lit.; circ. 5,000. (back issues avail.)
Former tites: Bedside Specialist (ISSN 0835-6203): Green Band.
Description: Contains educational articles and health care issue updates.

610.73 VI
CARIBBEAN CHRONICLE.* bi-m. Caribbean Nurses Organization, P.O. Box 583, Christiansted, St. Croix, VI 00820.

610.73 US
CARIBBEAN NURSES ORGANIZATION. NEWSLETTER.* q. Caribbean Nurses Organization, P.O. Box 583, Christiansted, St. Croix 00820, Virgin Islands, USA.

610.73 CN
CARING. bi-m. membership. Manitoba Association of Licensed Practical Nurses, P.O. Box 249, Transcona, 615 Kernaghan Ave., Winnipeg, Man. R2C 2Z9, Canada. TEL 204-222-6743. FAX 204-224-0166.
Formerly (until Dec.1990): Nurses News.

658 610 US ISSN 0738-467X
CODEN: CARGET
CARING (WASHINGTON). 1982. m. $45. National Association for Home Care, 519 C St., N.E., Washington, DC 20002-5809. TEL 202-547-7424. FAX 202-547-3540. Ed. Rebecca Staebler. adv.; bk.rev.; charts; stat.; index; circ. 5,361. (back issues avail.) **Indexed:** Abstr.Health Care Manage.Stud., CINAHL, Hosp.Lit.Ind.
—BLDSC shelfmark: 3053.222000.
Supersedes: Home Health Review (ISSN 0193-2683)
Description: Contains articles, special sections and departments covering national and international aspects of the home care field.

613 GW
CARITAS-GEMEINSCHAFT. PUBLICATION. bi-m. DM.18. Caritas-Gemeinschaft fuer Pflege- und Sozialberufe e.V., Maria Theresiastr. 10, 7800 Freiburg, Germany. TEL 0761-72272. FAX 0761-7086116. adv.; circ. 4,500.
Formerly: Caritasschwester.

CASSANDRA; radical feminist nurses newsjournal. see *WOMEN'S INTERESTS*

610.73 UK
CATHOLIC NURSE JOURNAL. 1933. q. membership. 167 Whalley New Rd., Seven Trees, Blackburn BB1 9TL, England. Ed. M. Proctor. adv.

610.73 US ISSN 0069-2778
CHART. 1904. m. (10/yr.). $25 to institutions. Illinois Nurses Association, 20 N. Wacker Dr., Chicago, IL 60606. TEL 312-236-9708. FAX 312-236-6228. Ed. Pamela Towne. adv.; circ. 9,100. **Indexed:** CINAHL, Int.Nurs.Ind.
—BLDSC shelfmark: 3129.960000.
Description: Covers health care and professional issues of importance to all nurses.

610.73 US ISSN 0199-2066
CHICAGO NURSE. 1946. 6/yr. $10. Chicago Nurses' Association, 180 N. Michigan Ave., Ste. 1510, Chicago, IL 60601. TEL 312-263-2708. Ed.Bd. adv.; bk.rev.; circ. 1,400.
Former titles (until 1979): Chicago District; First (ISSN 0015-2749)

610.73 II ISSN 0009-5540
CHRISTIAN NURSE.* (Text in English) 1930. bi-m. $10 for non-members. (Christian Medical Association of India, Nurses League) Christian Literature Society, Park Town, Madras 600 003, India. Ed. Manohari Sigamoni. adv.; bk.rev.; circ. 17,500. **Indexed:** CINAHL, Hum.Ind., Soc.Sci.Ind.

610.73 US ISSN 0887-6274
CLINICAL NURSE SPECIALIST. 1987. q. $42 to individuals; institutions $55. Williams & Wilkins, 428 E. Preston St., Baltimore, MD 21202. TEL 301-528-4000. FAX 301-528-4312. Ed. Pauline C. Beecroft. adv.; circ. 3,300. (also avail. in microform) **Indexed:** Nurs.Abstr.
—BLDSC shelfmark: 3286.314100.
Description: Information for the clinician, consultant, executive, peer, and patient educator.
Refereed Serial

610.73 US ISSN 1054-7738
▼**CLINICAL NURSING RESEARCH.** 1992. q. $35 to individuals; institutions $88. (University of Alberta, CN) Sage Publications, Inc., 2455 Teller Rd., Newbury Park, CA 91320. TEL 805-499-0721. FAX 805-499-0871. TELEX 516-1000799. Ed.Bd.
Description: Provides an international forum for scholarly research focusing on clinical nursing practice, including the clinical application of research findings.

610.73 SP
COLECCION LIBROS DE ENFERMERIA. 1975. irreg., no.12, 1988. price varies. (Universidad de Navarra, Escuela de Enfermeras) Ediciones Universidad de Navarra, S.A., Apdo. 396, 31080 Pamplona, Spain. TEL 94 825 6850.

610.73 MX ISSN 0045-7329
COLEGIO NACIONAL DE ENFERMERAS. REVISTA. 1967. 3/yr. $21 (effective Jan. 1992). Colegio Nacional de Enfermeras, Obrero Mundial 229, Mexico, D.F., Mexico. TEL 5-43-66-37. illus. **Indexed:** Int.Nurs.Ind.
Formerly: Asociacion Mexicana de Enfermeras. Revista.

610.73 SA
COLIMPEX PAEDIATRIC EXECUPED. (Text in Afrikaans and English) a. free to qualified personnel. Colimpex Africa (Pty) Ltd., P.O. Box 5838, Johannesburg 2000, South Africa. adv.

610.73 US ISSN 0010-1680
COLORADO NURSE. vol.73, 1973. m. $20 (foreign $27). Colorado Nurses Association, 5453 E. Evans Place, Denver, CO 80222. TEL 303-757-7483. Ed. Alison Biggs. adv.; bk.rev.; illus.; circ. 4,400. **Indexed:** CINAHL, Int.Nurs.Ind.

610.73 US ISSN 0069-634X
COLUMBIA UNIVERSITY - PRESBYTERIAN HOSPITAL SCHOOL OF NURSING. ALUMNAE ASSOCIATION. MAGAZINE.* 1906. 3/yr. $1 to non-members. Columbia University, School of Nursing, 617 W. 168th St., New York, NY 10032. TEL 212-854-1754. Ed. Ria Hawks. circ. 2,700.

COMMUNITY OUTLOOK. see *MEDICAL SCIENCES*

COMMUNITY PSYCHIATRIC NURSING JOURNAL. see *MEDICAL SCIENCES — Psychiatry And Neurology*

610.73 CN
CONCERN. 1968. 6/yr. ProWest Publications, No. 208, 438 Victoria Ave. E., Regina, Sask. S4N 0N7, Canada. TEL 306-352-3400. FAX 306-525-0960. adv.; circ. 9,700.

610.73 US ISSN 0278-4092
CONNECTICUT NURSING NEWS. 1921. m. $20 (effective Jan. 1991). Connecticut Nurses Association, 377 Research Pkwy., Ste. 2D, Meriden, CT 06450. TEL 203-238-1207. Ed. Sally E. Fogg. adv.; illus.; circ. 2,000. (also avail. in microform from UMI; reprint service avail. from UMI) **Indexed:** CINAHL, Int.Nurs.Ind.
Formerly: Nursing News (ISSN 0029-652X)

610.73 US ISSN 0279-5442
CODEN: CCNUEV
CRITICAL CARE NURSE. 1980. 10/yr. $27 (Canada and Mexico $31; elsewhere $37). American Association of Critical Care Nurses, 101 Columbia, Aliso Viejo, CA 92656. TEL 714-362-2000. (Subscr. to: Box 611, Holmes, PA 19043. TEL 800-345-8112) Ed. Joann Grif Alspach. adv.; bk.rev.; circ. 110,000. (reprint service avail. from UMI) **Indexed:** CINAHL, Int.Nurs.Ind., Nurs.Abstr.
—BLDSC shelfmark: 3487.451100.
Description: Provides current information and perspectives on a wide range of topics in critical care nursing.
Refereed Serial

610 US
CRITICAL CARE NURSING QUARTERLY. 1978. q. $56. Aspen Publishers, Inc., 200 Orchard Ridge Dr., Gaithersburg, MD 20878. TEL 301-417-7500. FAX 301-417-7550. (also avail. in microform from UMI; reprint service avail. from UMI) **Indexed:** Biol.Abstr., Excerp.Med., Nurs.Abstr., Psychol.Abstr.
Formerly: Critical Care Quarterly (ISSN 0160-2551)

610.73 US
DELAWARE NURSES' ASSOCIATION REPORTER. 1968. 10/yr. $15 (foreign $25). Delaware Nurses Association, 2634 Capitol Trail, Ste. C, Newark, DE 19711. TEL 302-368-2333. Ed. Patrina Smith. adv.: B&W page $150; trim 9 1/2 x 7 1/4. bk.rev.; circ. 1,000. **Indexed:** CINAHL.
Supersedes: Delaware Nurse (ISSN 0070-3281)

610.73 GW ISSN 0012-074X
DEUTSCHE KRANKENPFLEGE-ZEITSCHRIFT. 1948. m. DM.88. (Verbaende fuer die Deutschen Schwestern und Pfleger im In- und Ausland) W. Kohlhammer GmbH, Hessbruehlstr. 69, Postfach 800430, 7000 Stuttgart 80, Germany. TEL 0711-7863-1. Eds. Paul-Werner Schreiner, Brigitte Zuckschwerdt. bk.rev.; circ. 21,400. **Indexed:** Dok.Arbeitsmed.
—BLDSC shelfmark: 3570.280000.
Formerly: Deutsche Schwesternzeitung.

DIABETIC MEDICINE. see *MEDICAL SCIENCES — Endocrinology*

610.73 US ISSN 0730-4625
DIMENSIONS OF CRITICAL CARE NURSING. Abbreviated title: D C C N. 1982. bi-m. $45 to individuals; institutions $78. Hall Johnson Communications, Inc., 9737 W. Ohio Ave., Lakewood, CO 80226. TEL 303-988-0056. Ed. Suzanne Hall Johnson. adv.; illus.; index; circ. 3,504. **Indexed:** CINAHL, Int.Nurs.Ind., Nurs.Abstr.
—BLDSC shelfmark: 3588.471200.
Refereed Serial

DIRECTORY OF LONG-TERM CARE CENTRES IN CANADA/REPERTOIRE DES CENTRES DE SOINS DE LONGUE DUREE AU CANADA. see *GERONTOLOGY AND GERIATRICS*

610.73 DQ
DOMINICA NURSES ASSOCIATION. NEWSLETTER. q. membership. Dominica Nurses Association, Roseau, Dominica, West Indies.

DRUGS AND DEVICE RECALL BULLETIN. see *PHARMACY AND PHARMACOLOGY*

E N A NURSING SCAN IN EMERGENCY CARE. (Emergency Nurses Association) see *MEDICAL SCIENCES — Abstracting, Bibliographies, Statistics*

MEDICAL SCIENCES — NURSES AND NURSING

610.73 378 US ISSN 0070-9166
RT79
EDUCATION FOR NURSING: THE DIPLOMA WAY. 1966. a. $6.95. National League for Nursing, 350 Hudson St., New York, NY 10014. TEL 212-989-9393.

610 340 US ISSN 0098-1516
KF2915.N8
EMERGENCY NURSE LEGAL BULLETIN. Abbreviated title: E N L B. 1975. q. $20. Med-Law Publishers, Inc., Box 293, Westville, NJ 08093. Ed. Dr. James E. George. **Indexed:** CINAHL, Int.Nurs.Ind.

610.73 BL
ENFERMAGEM; o jornal brasileiro de enfermagem. 1977. bi-m. $50. (Associacao Brasileira de Enfermagem) Cidade - Editora Cientifica Ltda., Rua Mexico, 90-2 andar, 20031 Rio de Janeiro RJ, Brazil. TEL 021 240 4578. Ed. Fernardo Moyses. adv.; circ. 31,000.

610.73 MX ISSN 0185-0970
ENFERMERA AL DIA. 1976. m. Mex.$75000($50) Intersistemas S.A. de C.V., Fernando Alencastre No. 110 Lomas de Virreyes, 11000 Mexico D.F., Mexico. Ed. Elvia Espino B. adv.; charts; circ. 15,000.

610.73 MX
ENFERMERAS.* 1953. q. Mex.$20 per no. Colegio Nacional de Enfermeras, Obrero Mundial 229, Mexico, D.F., Mexico. Ed. Margarita Navarro Salazar. adv.

610.73 SP
▼**ENFERMERIA CLINICA.** 1990. bi-m. 4200 ptas.($43) Ediciones Doyma S.A., Travesera de Gracia 17-21, 08021 Barcelona, Spain. TEL 200-07-11. FAX 209-11-36. TELEX 51964 INK E. Ed. P. Vilagrasa. adv.: page 155000 ptas.; trim 210 x 280; adv. contact: Ana Ma. Alfonso. circ. 5,000.
Description: Studies clinical nursing to promote a solution to the health problems of individuals, families and communities. Contributes to the theoretical and practical development of the profession in Spain.

610.73 SP ISSN 1130-2399
▼**ENFERMERIA INTENSIVA.** 1990. q. 4000 ptas. (Sociedad Espanola de Enfermeria Intensiva y Unidades Coronarias) Salvat Publicaciones Cientificas, S.A., Muntaner, 262, 6o, 08021 Barcelona, Spain. TEL 2010911. FAX 2015911. (Subscr. to: Cempro, Plaza Conde Valle Suchil 20, 28015 Madrid, Spain) adv.; bk.rev.; index. (back issues avail.)

610.73 BE ISSN 0301-0813
F.N.I.B. - INFO/N.V.B.V. - INFO. (Text in Dutch, French) vol.48, 1970. bi-m. 1200 F. Federation Nationale des Infirmieres Belges - Nationaal Verbond van Belgische Verpleegsters, 18 rue de la Source, 1060 Brussels, Belgium. Ed.Bd. adv.; illus. (tabloid format)
Former titles: F.N.I.B; Infirmiere (ISSN 0019-9591)

610.73 US ISSN 0172-5238
FACHSCHWESTER - FACHPFLEGER. 1975. irreg. price varies. Springer-Verlag, 175 Fifth Ave., New York, NY 10010. TEL 212-460-1500. (Also Berlin, Heidelberg, Tokyo and Vienna) (reprint service avail. from ISI)

610.73 NO
FAGTIDSSKRIFTET SYKEPLEIEN. (Includes Journalen Sykepleien) 6/yr. DKK 520. Norsk Sykepleierforbund, Postboks 2633, St. Hanshaugen, 0131 Oslo 1, Norway. FAX 02-353663. Ed. Hanne Mai Svaboe. adv.; bk.rev.; circ. 45,000 (controlled).
Supersedes in part (in 1990): Sykepleien (ISSN 0039-7628)

610.73 SP ISSN 0211-5638
FISIOTERAPIA. (Text in Spanish; summaries in English) 1979. q. 3700 ptas. (Asociacion Espanola de Fisioterapeutas) Salvat Publicaciones Cientificas, S.A., Muntaner, 262, 2o, 08021 Barcelona, Spain. TEL 2010911. FAX 2015911. (Subscr. to: Cempro, Plaza Conde Valle Suchil 20, 28015 Madrid, Spain) adv.; bk.rev.; index.

610.73 US ISSN 0015-4199
FLORIDA NURSE. 1952. m. $15 (foreign $20). Florida Nurses Association, 1235 E. Concord St., Box 536985, Orlando, FL 32853-6985. TEL 407-896-3261. FAX 407-896-9042. Eds. Paula Massey, Karen Rogers. adv.; bk.rev.; illus.; circ. 8,500. (reprint service avail. from UMI) **Indexed:** CINAHL, Int.Nurs.Ind.
—BLDSC shelfmark: 3956.080000.
Description: Covers legislative, health policy, regulatory, labor, educational, and administrative issues that affect the registered nursing profession throughout the state.

610.73 US
FLORIDA NURSING NEWS.* (In 2 editions: South Florida and Gulf/Central) 1981. fortn. $9.95. Nursing News, Inc., 2750 S.W. 140th Terrace, Ft. Lauderdale, FL 33330-1175. FAX 305-748-3663. Ed. Steven Ricci. adv.; circ. 55,000.

610.73 US ISSN 0016-2116
FRONTIER NURSING SERVICE QUARTERLY BULLETIN. 1925. q. $5. Frontier Nursing Service, Inc., Wendover, KY 41775. TEL 606-672-2317. FAX 606-672-3022. Ed. Barb Gibson. illus.; circ. 6,000. (tabloid format; also avail. in microform from UMI; back issues avail.) **Indexed:** CINAHL, Int.Nurs.Ind.
—BLDSC shelfmark: 4041.200000.
Description: Overview of the Frontier Nursing Service of Eastern Kentucky.

610.73 US ISSN 0016-8335
GEORGIA NURSING. 1945. bi-m. $15. (Georgia Nurses Association) Commercial Publications, 1362 W. Peachtree St., Atlanta, GA 30309. TEL 404-876-4624. Ed. Susan Williamson. adv.; bk.rev.; circ. 3,000. **Indexed:** CINAHL, Int.Nurs.Ind.
—BLDSC shelfmark: 4158.457000.

GERIATRIC CARE NEWS. see *GERONTOLOGY AND GERIATRICS*

GERIATRIC NURSING; American journal of care for the aging. see *GERONTOLOGY AND GERIATRICS*

610.73 BE
GEST HOME; la revue des gestionnaires et du personnel soignant des maisons de repos, centres hopitaliers, c.p.a.s., centre de sante et de soins. (Text in Dutch, French) 1986. q. 450 Fr. Socorema s.c.r.l, Rue du Merlo, 28, 1180 Brussels, Belgium. TEL 02-376-62-28. FAX 02-376-12-80. Ed. J. Laffineur-Brouhon. adv.; bk.rev.; circ. 5,000.
Description: Intended to serve those involved and working in the health care profession, nursing homes, rehabilitation centers, and hospitals.

610.73 US
GRADUATE EDUCATION IN NURSING. 1989. a. $12.95. National League for Nursing, 350 Hudson St., New York, NY 10014. TEL 212-989-9393.

GRIEVANCE BULLETIN. see *BUSINESS AND ECONOMICS — Labor And Industrial Relations*

610.73 UK ISSN 0262-172X
H V A CURRENT AWARENESS BULLETIN. 1981. q. £16 to non-members; members £12. Health Visitors' Association, 50 Southwark St., London SE1 1UN, England. Ed. E. Burke. circ. 850.

610.73 CN
HAND IN HAND. 4/yr. membership. Saskatchewan Association of Certified Nursing Assistants, 2310 Smith, Regina, Sask. S4P 2P6, Canada. TEL 306-525-1436. FAX 306-347-7784.
Formerly: S N A A Newsletter.

610.73 US ISSN 0731-3381
RA971
HEALTH CARE SUPERVISOR. 1982. 4/yr. $82. Aspen Publishers, Inc., 200 Orchard Ridge Dr., Gaithersburg, MD 20878. TEL 301-417-7500. FAX 301-417-7550. Ed. Charles R. McConnell. **Indexed:** ABI Inform, CINAHL.
—BLDSC shelfmark: 4274.949500.
Formerly: Health Care Supervisors Journal.

HEALTH CAREER POST. see *HOSPITALS*

HEALTH MANPOWER MANAGEMENT. see *BUSINESS AND ECONOMICS — Management*

610.73 UK ISSN 0017-9140
HEALTH VISITOR. 1927. m. £47. (Health Visitors' Association) Professional & Scientific Publications, B.M.A. House, Tavistock Sq., London WC1H 9JR, England. Ed. N. Robin. adv.; bk.rev.; film rev.; illus.; index; circ. 18,000. (also avail. in microfilm from UMI; reprint service avail. from UMI) **Indexed:** Abstr.Hyg., ASSIA, CINAHL, Curr.Adv.Ecol.Sci., Dent.Ind., Int.Nurs.Ind., Sp.Ed.Needs Abstr., Trop.Dis.Bull.
—BLDSC shelfmark: 4275.245000.

610.73 US
HEALTHWIRE. 1980. q. membership. (American Federation of Teachers) Federation of Nurses and Health Professionals (Subsidiary of: American Federation of Teachers), 555 New Jersey Ave., N.W., Washington, DC 20001. TEL 202-879-4430. Ed. Trish Gorman. circ. 63,000.

610.73 US ISSN 0147-9563
RC681.A1 CODEN: HELUAI
HEART AND LUNG; the journal of critical care. 1972. bi-m. $36 to individuals (foreign $48); institutions $94 (foreign $106); students $19 (foreign $31). Mosby - Year Book, Inc. (Subsidiary of: Times Mirror Company), 11830 Westline Industrial Dr., St. Louis, MO 63146. TEL 800-325-4117. FAX 314-432-1380. TELEX 44-2402. Ed. Kathleen A. Stone. adv.; bk.rev.; charts; illus.; index; circ. 71,986. (also avail. in microform from UMI; reprint service avail. from UMI) **Indexed:** Abstr.Health Care Manage.Stud., ASCA, Biol.Abstr., Chem.Abstr, CINAHL, Curr.Adv.Ecol.Sci., Curr.Cont., Excerp.Med., Hosp.Lit.Ind., Ind.Med., Ind.Sci.Rev., INIS Atomind., Int.Nurs.Ind., Nurs.Abstr.
●Also available online. Vendor(s): BRS, BRS/Saunders Colleague.
—BLDSC shelfmark: 4275.295000.
Description: Scientific nursing journal with practical articles on critical care.
Refereed Serial

610.73 UK ISSN 0960-2348
HISTORY OF NURSING JOURNAL. 1983. 3/yr. £8.50 to individuals; institutions £10. Royal College of Nursing, 20 Cavendish Sq., London W1M 0AB, England. TEL 071-409-3333. FAX 071-408-0190. Ed. Dr. M.E. Baly. bk.rev.; circ. 200. (back issues avail.)
—BLDSC shelfmark: 4318.388100.
Formerly: History of Nursing Bulletin (ISSN 0265-3834)

610.73 NO ISSN 0332-7841
HJELPEPLEIEREN. 1967. 16/yr. NOK 315. Norsk Hjelpepleierforbund, P.O. Box 151, Brun, 0611 Oslo 1, Norway. FAX 645602. Ed. Randi Mollan Boelset. adv.; bk.rev.; circ. 38,000 (controlled).

610.73 IC ISSN 0250-4731
HJUKRUN. 1925. q. $30. Hjukrunarfelag Islands - Icelandic Nurses' Association, Sudurlandsbraut 22, 108 Reykjavik, Iceland. FAX 680-727. Eds. Stefania Sigurjonsdottir, Lilja Oskarsdottir. adv.; bk.rev.; illus.; circ. 2,200. **Indexed:** Int.Nurs.Ind.
—BLDSC shelfmark: 4319.111000.
Former titles (until Jan. 1978): Hjukrunarfelag Islands. Timarit (ISSN 0046-7634); Hjukrunarkvennabladid.

610.73 JA ISSN 0018-3369
HOKENFU NO KEKKAKU TENBO/REVIEW OF TUBERCULOSIS FOR PUBLIC HEALTH NURSE. (Text in Japanese) 1963. s-a. 3090 Yen. Japan Anti-Tuberculosis Association - Kekkaku Yobokai, 3-12 Misaki-cho 1-chome, Chiyoda-ku, Tokyo 101, Japan. TEL FAX 03-3292-9208. Ed. Dr. Masakazu Aoki. adv.; bk.rev.; charts; illus.; stat.; circ. 1,500.

610.73 JA ISSN 0047-1844
HOKENFU ZASSHI/JAPANESE JOURNAL FOR PUBLIC HEALTH NURSE. (Text in Japanese) 1951. m. 12090 Yen($93) Igaku-Shoin Ltd., 5-24-3 Hongo, Bunkyo-ku, Tokyo 113-91, Japan. TEL 03-817-5776. Ed.Bd. circ. 8,500.
—BLDSC shelfmark: 4658.420000.

610.73 US
HOLISTIC NURSING PRACTICE. 1979. q. $63. Aspen Publishers, Inc., 200 Orchard Ridge Dr., Gaithersburg, MD 20878. TEL 301-417-7500. FAX 301-417-7550. **Indexed:** CINAHL, Int.Nurs.Ind., Nurs.Abstr.
Formerly: Topics in Clinical Nursing (ISSN 0164-0534)

MEDICAL SCIENCES — NURSES AND NURSING

610.73 US
HOMECARE. 1978. m. $48 (free to qualified personnel). Miramar Publishing Co., Box 3640, Culver City, CA 90231-3640. TEL 213-337-9717. Ed. Denise Novoselski. adv.; circ. 16,000.
Formerly: Homecare Rental-Sales.

610.73 US
HOMECARE NEWS. m. National Association for Home Care, 519 C St., N.E., Washington, DC 20002-5809. TEL 202-547-7424. FAX 202-547-3540. Ed. Val Halamandaris. circ. 6,500.

610.73 HK ISSN 0073-3253
HONG KONG NURSING JOURNAL/HSIANG KANG HU LI TSA CHIH. (Text in Chinese and English) 1965. s-a. membership. Hong Kong Nurses Association, Hong Kong, Hong Kong. TEL 5-729255. adv.; bk.rev.; circ. 4,500. Indexed: CINAHL. Key Title: Xianggang Huli Zazhi.

HOSPITAL NEWS DELAWARE VALLEY. see HOSPITALS

HOSPITAL PHARMACY DIRECTOR'S MONTHLY MANAGEMENT SERIES. see PHARMACY AND PHARMACOLOGY

610.73 US
I N S NEWSLINE. 1973. bi-m. membership. Intravenous Nurses Society, Two Brighton St., Belmont, MA 02178. TEL 617-489-5205. FAX 617-489-0656. Ed. Gregory Brown. adv.; stat.; circ. 6,500.
Former titles: I N S Update; N I T A Update.

610.73 378 US ISSN 0743-5150
CODEN: IMNSEP
IMAGE: JOURNAL OF NURSING SCHOLARSHIP. 1967. 4/yr. $25 (foreign $35). Sigma Theta Tau International Honor Society of Nursing, 550 W. North St., Indianapolis, IN 46202. TEL 317-634-8171. FAX 317-634-8188. Ed. Donna Diers. adv.; circ. 95,000. (also avail. in microfiche) Indexed: CINAHL, Int.Nurs.Ind., Nurs.Abstr., Psychol.Abstr.
Formerly: Image (ISSN 0363-2792)

610.73 US ISSN 0019-3062
IMPRINT (NEW YORK). 1968. 5/yr. $15. National Student Nurses' Association, 555 W. 57 St., New York, NY 10019. TEL 212-581-2211. Ed. Caroline Jaffe. adv.; illus.; index; circ. 35,000. Indexed: CINAHL, Int.Nurs.Ind.
—BLDSC shelfmark: 4371.486500.
Formerly: N S N A Newsletter.
Description: Provides organization news.

INDUSTRIAL HEALTH FOUNDATION. NURSING SERIES. BULLETINS. see OCCUPATIONAL HEALTH AND SAFETY

610 UK
INFECTION CONTROL YEARBOOK. a. £25. (Infection Control Nurses Association) C M A Medical Data Ltd., Cambridge Research Laboratories, 181A Huntingdon Rd., Cambridge CB3 ODJ, England.
Description: Contains a complete listing of full time infection control nurses and other members of staff who have control of infection as one of their responsibilities. Members are listed alphabetically by both name and hospital.

610.73 CN ISSN 0822-8558
L'INFIRMIERE AUXILIAIRE. (Text in French) 1928. 3/yr. Can.$10. Corporation Professionnelle de Infirmieres et Infirmiers, Auxiliaires du Quebec, 531 Sherbrooke E., Montreal, Que. H2L 1K2, Canada. TEL 514-282-9511. FAX 514-282-0631. adv.; bk.rev.; charts; illus.; index; circ. 21,000.
Former titles: Auxiliaire (ISSN 0703-9484); Revue des Infirmieres et Infirmiers du Quebec; Cahiers du Nursing (ISSN 0008-0179)

610.73 BE
INFO-NURSING. bi-m. Association Nationale Catholique du Nursing, Av. Hippocrate 91, B-1200 Brussels, Belgium. TEL 02-7625618.

INFORMATIONSDIENST KRANKENHAUSWESEN/HEALTH CARE INFORMATION SERVICE. see HOSPITALS

610.73 US
INSIGHT. 1977. q. $35 (foreign $45). American Society of Ophthalmic Registered Nurses, Inc., Box 193030, San Francisco, CA 94119. TEL 415-561-8513. Ed. Kay McCoy. adv.

610.73 UK ISSN 0266-612X
INTENSIVE CARE NURSING. 1985. 4/yr. £45($868) (B A C C N) Churchill Livingstone Medical Journals, Robert Stevenson House, 1-3 Baxter's Pl., Leith Walk, Edinburgh EH1 3AF, Scotland. TEL 031-556-2424. FAX 031-558-1278. TELEX 727511. (Subscr. to: Longman Group, P.O. Box 77, Fourth Ave., Harlow, Essex CM19 5AA, England; U.S. subscr. to: Churchill Livingstone, 650 Ave. of the Americas, New York, NY 10011. TEL 212-206-5000) Ed. Pat Ashworth. circ. 4,500.

INTENSIVE CARING UNLIMITED. see CHILDREN AND YOUTH — About

610.73 FR ISSN 0242-3960
INTERBLOC; la revue des infirmiers et infirmieres de salles d'operations. q. 20 ECU($23) (typically set in Jan.). Masson, 120 bd. St. Germain, 75280 Paris Cedex 06, France. TEL 1-46-34-21-60. FAX 1-45-87-29-99. TELEX 202 671 F. Ed. Dr. J. Zucman. circ. 2,500.
Formerly: Journal of Operating Theatre Male and Female Nurses.
Description: Fields covered include hygiene, surgical technique, legal aspects, and epidemiology.

610.730 RT1 US ISSN 0020-7489
CODEN: IJNUA6
INTERNATIONAL JOURNAL OF NURSING STUDIES. 1965. q. £140 (effective 1992). Pergamon Press, Inc., Journals Division, 665 White Plains Rd., Tarrytown, NY 10591-5153. TEL 914-524-9200. FAX 914-333-2444. (And: Headington Hill Hall, Oxford OX3 0BW, England. TEL 0865-794141) Ed. Rosemary Crow. adv.; bk.rev.; charts; illus.; index; circ. 1,150. (also avail. in microform from MIM,UMI; reprint service avail. from UMI) Indexed: Abstr.Health Care Manage.Stud., CINAHL, Curr.Cont., Ind.Med., Int.Nurs.Ind., Psychol.Abstr., SSCI.
—BLDSC shelfmark: 4542.407000.
Description: Covers worldwide changes and developments in nursing.
Refereed Serial

610.73 RT1 SZ ISSN 0020-8132
INTERNATIONAL NURSING REVIEW. 1926. 6/yr. 50 Fr.($35) (International Council of Nurses) Imprimerie Sprint, 6, rue de la Colline, 1211 Geneve 9, Switzerland. FAX 22-7381036. Ed. Constance Holleran. adv.; bk.rev.; illus.; index; circ. 3,500. (also avail. in microform from UMI; reprint service avail. from UMI) Indexed: Abstr.Health Care Manage.Stud., ASSIA, CINAHL, Ind.Med., Int.Nurs.Ind.

610.73 CK ISSN 0120-5307
INVESTIGACION Y EDUCACION EN ENFERMERIA. 1983. a. Col.3000($15) (typically set in Sept.). Universidad de Antioquia, Facultad de Enfermeria, Apdo. Aereo 1226, Carrera 53, no. 62-65, Medellin, Colombia. TEL 5742-110058. FAX 5742-638282. Ed. Martha Lucia Palacio C. adv.; bk.rev.; bibl.; circ. 1,000 (controlled).
Description: Publishes works of importance from Latin American institutions.

610.73 US ISSN 0146-0862
CODEN: ICNUDS
ISSUES IN COMPREHENSIVE PEDIATRIC NURSING. 1976. bi-m. $83. Hemisphere Publishing Corporation (Subsidiary of: Taylor & Francis Group), 1900 Frost Rd., Ste. 101, Bristol, PA 19007-1598. TEL 215-785-5800. FAX 215-785-5515. Eds. Gladys M. Scipien, Martha Underwood Barnard. adv.; bk.rev.; bibl.; charts; illus.; index; circ. 1,200. (back issues avail.; reprint service avail. from UMI) Indexed: CINAHL, Int.Nurs.Ind., J.of Abstr.Int.Educ., Nurs.Abstr., Psychol.Abstr., Sage Fam.Stud.Abstr., Sociol.Abstr.
—BLDSC shelfmark: 4584.160000.
Description: Articles pertinent to the critical aspects of pediatric nursing.
Refereed Serial

616.8 US ISSN 0161-2840
CODEN: IHNUDT
ISSUES IN MENTAL HEALTH NURSING. 1978. q. $84. Hemisphere Publishing Corporation (Subsidiary of: Taylor & Francis Group), 1900 Frost Rd., Ste. 101, Bristol, PA 19007-1598. TEL 215-785-5800. FAX 215-785-5515. adv.; bk.rev.; film rev.; bibl.; charts; illus.; index; circ. 600. (back issues avail.; reprint service avail. from UMI) Indexed: CINAHL, Int.Nurs.Ind., J.of Abstr.Int.Educ., Nurs.Abstr., Psychol.Abstr., Sage Fam.Stud.Abstr., Sociol.Abstr.
—BLDSC shelfmark: 4584.305000.
Description: Presents practical information about psycho-social and mental health issues in nursing.
Refereed Serial

610.73 RT120.E4 US ISSN 0099-1767
J E N. (Journal of Emergency Nursing) 1975. bi-m. $35 to individuals (foreign $44); institutions $98 (foreign $107); students $20 (foreign $29). (Emergency Nurses Association) Mosby - Year Book, Inc. (Subsidiary of: Times Mirror Company), 11830 Westline Industrial Dr., St. Louis, MO 63146. TEL 800-325-4117. FAX 314-432-1380. TELEX 44-2402. Ed. Gail Pisarcik Lenehan. adv.; bk.rev.; illus.; index; circ. 24,475. (also avail. in microfilm from UMI; reprint service avail. from UMI) Indexed: CINAHL, Int.Nurs.Ind., Nurs.Abstr. Key Title: JEN, Journal of Emergency Nursing.
—BLDSC shelfmark: 4977.300000.
Description: Information on emergency care with articles written and reviewed by emergency nurses.

610.73 JA ISSN 0912-3741
J J N SUPESHARU/J J N SPECIAL. (Text in Japanese) 1986. irreg. 1545 Yen($12) per no. Igaku-Shoin Ltd., 5-24-3 Hongo, Bunkyo-ku, Tokyo 113-91, Japan. TEL 03-817-5771. Ed.Bd. circ. 30,000.

618 RG951 US ISSN 0884-2175
CODEN: JOGNEY
J O G N N. (Journal of Obstetric, Gynecologic and Neonatal Nursing) 1972. bi-m. $35 to individuals (foreign $45); institutions $65 (foreign $75). (N A A C O G: The Organization for Obstetric, Gynecologic, and Neonatal Nurses) J.B. Lippincott Co., E. Washington Sq., Philadelphia, PA 19105. TEL 215-238-4200. Ed. Diane E. Harpar. adv.; circ. 28,000. (also avail. in microform from UMI) Indexed: CINAHL, Ind.Med., Int.Nurs.Ind., Nurs.Abstr.
—BLDSC shelfmark: 4670.352000.
Former titles: J O G N Nursing (ISSN 0090-0311); Nurses Association of the American College of Obstetricians and Gynecologists. Bulletin News (ISSN 0044-7641); Nurses Association of A.C.O.G. Bulletin (ISSN 0095-2982)

610.73 JM ISSN 0021-4140
JAMAICAN NURSE. 1961. 3/yr. $15. Nurses Association of Jamaica, 4 Trevennion Park Road, P.O. Box 277, Kingston 5, Jamaica, W.I. Ed. Syringa Marshall Burnett. adv.; bk.rev.; charts; illus.; cum.index; circ. 2,500. Indexed: CINAHL, Int.Nurs.Ind.
—BLDSC shelfmark: 4645.150000.

610.73 JA ISSN 0389-8326
JAPANESE JOURNAL OF NURSING. (Text in Japanese) 1981. m. 9600 Yen. Gakken Co. Ltd., 40-5, 4-chome, Kamiikedai, Ohta-ku, Tokyo 145, Japan. Ed. Hisashi Nakamura. Indexed: Dent.Ind.

610.73 371.42 JA ISSN 0911-0844
JAPANESE NURSING ASSOCIATION RESEARCH REPORT. (Text in Japanese; summaries in English) 1975. irreg. 1300 Yen. Japanese Nursing Association, 8-2, 5-chome, Jingumae, Shibuya-ku, Tokyo 150, Japan. circ. 1,200.
Description: Official report on community health and nursing in Japan.

610.73 US ISSN 0002-6700
JOHNS HOPKINS HOSPITAL SCHOOL OF NURSING. ALUMNI MAGAZINE.* vol.70, 1971. q. $6. Johns Hopkins School of Nursing, c/o Allie Saularn, 515 N. Washington, Baltimore, MD 21205. Ed. Mary Kuntz. adv.; illus. (tabloid format) Indexed: CINAHL.

JOSANPU ZASSHI/JAPANESE JOURNAL FOR MIDWIVES. see MEDICAL SCIENCES — Obstetrics And Gynecology

M

MEDICAL SCIENCES — NURSES AND NURSING

610.73   UK   ISSN 0309-2402
JOURNAL OF ADVANCED NURSING. 1976. bi-m. £130 (foreign £145). Blackwell Scientific Publications Ltd., Osney Mead, Oxford OX2 OEL, England. TEL 0865-240201. FAX 0865-721205. TELEX 83355-MEDBOK-G. Ed. J.P. Smith. adv.; bk.rev.; bibl.; illus.; index; circ. 1,900. (back issues avail; reprint service avail. from ISI) **Indexed:** Abstr.Health Care Manage.Stud., ASCA, ASSIA, CINAHL, Curr.Cont., Excerp.Med., Ind.Med., Int.Nurs.Ind., Res.High.Educ.Abstr., Risk Abstr., SSCI.
—BLDSC shelfmark: 4918.947000.

JOURNAL OF AIR MEDICAL TRANSPORT. see TRANSPORTATION — Air Transport

JOURNAL OF CARDIOVASCULAR NURSING. see MEDICAL SCIENCES — Cardiovascular Diseases

616.89 155.4   US   ISSN 0897-9685
JOURNAL OF CHILD AND ADOLESCENT PSYCHIATRIC AND MENTAL HEALTH NURSING. 1988. q. $35 to individuals (foreign $40); institutions $70 (foreign $80). J.B. Lippincott Co., E. Washington Sq., Philadelphia, PA 19105. TEL 215-238-4200. (Subscr. to: Downville Pike, Rte. 3, Box 20-B, Hagerstown, MD 21740)
—BLDSC shelfmark: 4957.423000.
Description: Forum for nurses involved in promoting the mental health of children and adolescents and caring for emotionally disturbed youth and their families.

610.73   US   ISSN 0743-2550
JOURNAL OF CHRISTIAN NURSING. 1951. q. $17.95. Inter-Varsity Christian Fellowship, Nurses Christian Fellowship, 6400 Schroeder Rd., Box 7895, Madison, WI 53707. TEL 608-274-9001. (Subscr. to: Box 1650, Downers Grove, IL 60515; Alt. addr.: 5206 Main St., Box 1650, Downers Grove, IL 60515) Ed. Judy Shelly. adv.; bk.rev.; abstr.; cum.index; circ. 12,000. (also avail. in microform from UMI) **Indexed:** CINAHL, Int.Nurs.Ind., Nurs.Abstr.
—BLDSC shelfmark: 4958.275000.
Formerly (until 1984): Nurses Lamp.

610.73   US   ISSN 0737-0016
JOURNAL OF COMMUNITY HEALTH NURSING. 1984. q. $29.50 to individuals (foreign $54.50); institutions $120 (foreign $145). Lawrence Erlbaum Associates, Inc., 365 Broadway, Hillsdale, NJ 07642. TEL 201-666-4110. FAX 201-666-2394. Eds. Arlene Cairns, Alice Schroeder. adv.; bk.rev.; abstr.; charts; illus. **Indexed:** Excerp.Med., Int.Nurs.Ind.
—BLDSC shelfmark: 4961.722000.
Description: Focuses on health care issues relevant to all aspects of community practice - schools, homes, visiting nursing services, clinics, hospices, education, and public health administration.
Refereed Serial

610.73   US   ISSN 0022-0124
RT90
JOURNAL OF CONTINUING EDUCATION IN NURSING. 1970. bi-m. $42 to individuals; institutions $52. Slack, Inc., 6900 Grove Rd., Thorofare, NJ 08086. TEL 609-848-1000. FAX 609-853-5991. Ed. Patricia S. Yoder Wide. adv.; bk.rev.; circ. 3,800. (also avail. in microform from UMI; reprint service avail. from UMI) **Indexed:** C.I.J.E., CINAHL, Cont.Pg.Educ., Educ.Ind., Int.Nurs.Ind., Nurs.Abstr.

610.73   UK   ISSN 0263-4465
JOURNAL OF DISTRICT NURSING. 1977. m. £55. P T M Publishers Ltd., 282 High Street, Sutton, Surrey SM1 1PQ, England. TEL 081-642 0162. Ed. Sian Dulfer. adv.; bk.rev.; circ. 24,800.
Formerly: Journal of Community Nursing.

JOURNAL OF GERONTOLOGICAL NURSING. see GERONTOLOGY AND GERIATRICS

610.73   US
JOURNAL OF HOLISTIC NURSING. 1983. q. $32 to individuals; institutions $60. (American Holistic Nurses' Association) Sage Publications, Inc., 2455 Teller Rd., Newbury Park, CA 91320. TEL 919-787-5181. FAX 919-787-4916. Ed. Imelda Clements, R.N. index; circ. 3,000. (back issues avail.)

658   US   ISSN 0896-5846
JOURNAL OF INTRAVENOUS NURSING. 1978. bi-m. $50 to individuals (foreign $60); institutions $75 (foreign $90). (Intravenous Nurses Society) J.B. Lippincott Co., E. Washington Sq., Philadelphia, PA 19105. TEL 800-638-3030. (Subscr. to: Downville Pike, Rt. 3, Box 20-B, Hagerstown, MD 21740) Ed. Mary Larkin. adv.; abstr.; bibl.; charts; illus.; index; circ. 7,000. (also avail. in microform from UMI; back issues avail.) **Indexed:** CINAHL, Excerp.Med., Int.Nurs.Ind., Nurs.Abstr.
—BLDSC shelfmark: 5007.698000.
Formerly (until 1988): N I T A (ISSN 0160-3930)
Description: News of Society activities and clinical developments affecting intravenous therapy practice.
Refereed Serial

610.73   US   ISSN 0194-1658
JOURNAL OF INTRAVENOUS THERAPY. 1976. bi-m. $24 (foreign $38). (I.V. Therapy Association of the USA) Medical Education Consultants, Box 67159, Los Angeles, CA 90067. TEL 213-475-5141. Ed. William J. Kurdi. adv.; bk.rev.; circ. 1,000.
—BLDSC shelfmark: 5007.700000.

610.73   US   ISSN 0888-0395
RC350.5
JOURNAL OF NEUROSCIENCE NURSING. 1969. bi-m. $36 to individuals (foreign $46); institutions $49 (foreign $59). American Association of Neuroscience Nurses, 224 N. Des Plaines, Ste. 601, Chicago, IL 60661. TEL 312-993-0043. Ed. Christina Stewart-Amidi. adv.; bk.rev.; illus.; circ. 4,500. (also avail. in microform from UMI; reprint service avail. from UMI) **Indexed:** CINAHL, Hosp.Lit.Ind., Ind.Med., INIS Atomind., Int.Nurs.Ind., Nurs.Abstr.
Formerly (until 1986): Journal of Neurosurgical Nursing (ISSN 0047-2603)
Refereed Serial

JOURNAL OF NURSE-MIDWIFERY. see MEDICAL SCIENCES — Obstetrics And Gynecology

610.73   CH   ISSN 0047-262X
JOURNAL OF NURSING/HU LI TSA CHIH. (Text in Chinese; titles and table of contents in English) 1954. q. $35. Nurses' Association of the Republic of China, 12th Fl., No.315, Hsinyi Rd. Sec. 4, Taipei, Taiwan 10657, Republic of China. FAX 02-701-9817. Ed. Chuan-Min Lee. adv.; bk.rev.; illus.; circ. 15,000. **Indexed:** Int.Nurs.Ind.

610.73   US   ISSN 0002-0443
RT89   CODEN: JNUAA
JOURNAL OF NURSING ADMINISTRATION. Abbreviated title: J O N A. 1971. 11/yr. $45 to individuals (foreign $55); institutions $90 (foreign $110). J.B. Lippincott Co., E. Washington Sq., Philadelphia, PA 19105. TEL 215-238-4200. Ed. Suzanne Smith Blancett. adv.; index; circ. 13,309. (also avail. in microform from UMI) **Indexed:** Abstr.Health Care Manage.Stud., C.I.J.E., CINAHL, Hosp.Lit.Ind., Ind.Med., Int.Nurs.Ind., Nurs.Abstr.
—BLDSC shelfmark: 5023.700000.

610.73   US   ISSN 0022-3158
JOURNAL OF NURSING EDUCATION. 1962. 9/yr. $42 to individuals; institutions $52. Slack, Inc., 6900 Grove Rd., Thorofare, NJ 08086. TEL 609-848-1000. FAX 609-853-5991. Ed. Reba de Tornyay. adv.; illus.; index; circ. 4,300. (also avail. in microform from UMI; reprint service avail. from UMI) **Indexed:** CINAHL, Educ.Ind., Hosp.Lit.Ind., Ind.Med., Ind.Sci.Rev., Int.Nurs.Ind., Nurs.Abstr.
Formerly (until 1983): J N E: Journal of Nursing Education (ISSN 0148-4834)
Description: Presents study and teaching methods.

610.73   US   ISSN 0889-4647
JOURNAL OF NURSING QUALITY ASSURANCE. 1986. q. $69. Aspen Publishers, Inc., 200 Orchard Ridge Dr., Gaithersburg, MD 20878. TEL 301-417-7500. FAX 301-417-7550. (Subscr. to: 7201 McKinney Circle, Frederick, MD 21701) circ. 6,000. (also avail. in microfiche; back issues avail.) **Indexed:** Curr.Cont., Int.Nurs.Ind., Nurs.Abstr.
Description: Nursing QA programs, especially in the application of QA principles and concepts in the practice setting.

658   US   ISSN 0882-0627
JOURNAL OF NURSING STAFF DEVELOPMENT. 1985. bi-m. $40 to individuals (foreign $50); institutions $80 (foreign $90). J.B. Lippincott Co., E. Washington Sq., Philadelphia, PA 19105. TEL 215-238-4200. Ed. Belinda E. Puetz. adv.; illus.; index; circ. 4,000. (also avail. in microform from UMI)
—BLDSC shelfmark: 5023.900000.

610.73   US   ISSN 0744-7132
JOURNAL OF OPHTHALMIC NURSING & TECHNOLOGY. 1982. bi-m. $32 to individuals; institutions $44. Slack, Inc., 6900 Grove Rd., Thorofare, NJ 08086. TEL 609-848-1000. FAX 609-853-5991. Ed. Heather Boyd-Monk. adv.; circ. 3,000. **Indexed:** Int.Nurs.Ind., Nurs.Abstr.
—BLDSC shelfmark: 5026.344000.

JOURNAL OF PAIN AND SYMPTOM MANAGEMENT. see MEDICAL SCIENCES — Anaesthesiology

610.73   US   ISSN 0882-5963
         CODEN: JI.PNEO
JOURNAL OF PEDIATRIC NURSING; nursing care of children and families. 1986. bi-m. $38 to individuals; institutions $59; foreign $73. W.B. Saunders Co., Journals Department (Subsidiary of: Harcourt Brace Jovanovich, Inc.), Curtis Center, Independence Sq. W., Philadelphia, PA 19106. TEL 215-238-7800. (Subscr. to: Box 6209, Duluth, MN 55806) Ed. Cecily Lynn Betz. adv.; bk.rev.; bibl.; charts; illus.; index.
—BLDSC shelfmark: 5030.190000.
Refereed Serial

610.73   US   ISSN 0893-2190
         CODEN: JPNNE8
JOURNAL OF PERINATAL AND NEONATAL NURSING. 1987. q. $57. Aspen Publishers, Inc., 200 Orchard Ridge Dr., Gaithersburg, MD 20878. TEL 301-417-7500. FAX 301-417-7550. **Indexed:** Nurs.Abstr.
—BLDSC shelfmark: 5030.548000.

610.73 617.96   US   ISSN 0883-9433
JOURNAL OF POST ANESTHESIA NURSING. 1986. bi-m. $51 to individuals; institutions $79; foreign $97. (American Society of Post Anesthesia Nurses) W.B. Saunders Co. (Subsidiary of: Harcourt Brace Jovanovich, Inc.), Curtis Center, Independence Square W., Philadelphia, PA 19106. TEL 215-238-7800. (Subscr. to: 6277 Sea Harbor Dr., 4th Fl. Orlando FL 32891) Ed. Denise O'Brien, R.N. adv.; bibl.; charts; illus.; cum.index.
—BLDSC shelfmark: 5041.148400.
Refereed Serial

610.73   US   ISSN 0022-3867
JOURNAL OF PRACTICAL NURSING. 1951. q. $15. National Association for Practical Nurse Education and Service, Inc., 1400 Spring St., Ste. 310, Silver Spring, MD 20910. FAX 301-588-2839. Ed. Mary Beth Ryan. adv.; bk.rev.; abstr.; bibl.; charts; illus.; stat.; index. cum.index; circ. 13,000. (also avail. in microform from UMI; reprint service avail. from UMI) **Indexed:** CINAHL, Dent.Ind., Hosp.Lit.Ind., Int.Nurs.Ind., Rehabil.Lit.
—BLDSC shelfmark: 5041.600000.
Refereed Serial

610.73   US   ISSN 8755-7223
RT1   CODEN: JPNUET
JOURNAL OF PROFESSIONAL NURSING. 1985. bi-m. $59 to individuals; institutions $99; students $39; foreign $112. (American Association of Colleges of Nursing) W.B. Saunders Co., Curtis Center, Independence Sq. W., Philadelphia, PA 19106-3399. TEL 215-238-7800. Ed. Laurel Archer Copp. adv.; bk.rev.; circ. 1,800. (back issues avail.) **Indexed:** Nurs.Abstr.
—BLDSC shelfmark: 5042.697000.

MEDICAL SCIENCES — NURSES AND NURSING

610.736   US   ISSN 0279-3695
RC440
JOURNAL OF PSYCHOSOCIAL NURSING AND MENTAL HEALTH SERVICES. 1962. m. $44 to individuals; institutions $54. Slack, Inc., 6900 Grove Rd., Thorofare, NJ 08086. TEL 609-848-1000. FAX 609-853-5991. Ed. Shirley Smoyak. adv.; bk.rev.; charts; illus.; index; circ. 12,800. (also avail. in microform from UMI; reprint service avail. from UMI) **Indexed:** Adol.Ment.Hlth.Abstr., C.I.N.L., Chic.Per.Ind., Ind.Med., Int.Nurs.Ind., Mid.East: Abstr.& Ind., Nurs.Abstr., Psychol.Abstr.
—BLDSC shelfmark: 5043.475000.
Former titles: Journal of Psychiatric Nursing and Mental Health Services (ISSN 0360-5973); Journal of Psychiatric Nursing (ISSN 0022-3948)

610.73   US   ISSN 1043-6596
JOURNAL OF TRANSCULTURAL NURSING. 1989. s-a. $48. (Transcultural Nursing Society) University of Tennessee, Memphis College of Nursing, c/o Dr. Michael Carter, 877 Madison, Memphis, TN 38163. FAX 901-528-6100. Ed. Madeleine Leininger.
—BLDSC shelfmark: 5069.795000.
Description: Serves as an international forum for researchers who desire to share their ideas regarding transcultural nursing.

610.73   NO   ISSN 0802-9776
JOURNALEN SYKEPLEIEN. (Includes Fagtidsskriftet Sykepleien) 1912. 21/yr. NOK 520. Norsk Sykepleierforbund, Postboks 2633, St. Hanshaugen, 0131 Oslo 1, Norway. FAX 02-353663. Ed. Morten E. Mathiesen. adv.; bk.rev.; circ. 45,000 (controlled). **Indexed:** Dent.Ind., Int.Nurs.Ind.
—BLDSC shelfmark: 5072.823000.
Supersedes in part (in 1990): Sykepleien (ISSN 0039-7628)

610.73   JA   ISSN 0022-8362
KANGO/NURSING. (Text in Japanese; summaries in English) 1949. m. 8400 Yen($30) Japanese Nursing Association - Nihon Kango Kyokai Shuppanka, 8-11, 5-chome, Jingumae, Shibuya-ku, Tokyo 150, Japan. Ed. Yaeko Inada. adv.; bk.rev.; abstr.; bibl.; charts; film rev.; illus.; play rev.; stat.; index, cum.index; circ. 50,000. **Indexed:** Int.Nurs.Ind.
—BLDSC shelfmark: 5085.356000.

610.73   JA   ISSN 0385-5988
KANGO GAKUSEI/NURSE STUDENT. 1951. m.(plus suppl.). 10100 Yen. Medical Friend Co. Ltd. - Mejikaru Furendo-Sha, 2-4, 3-chome, Kudan-Kita, Chiyoda-ku, Tokyo 102, Japan. FAX 033261-6602. Ed. Kazuhazu Ogura. circ. 30,000. (also avail. in microfiche; back issues avail.)
Description: Learning guide and drills for student nurses.

610.7   JA   ISSN 0449-752X
KANGO GIJUTSU/JAPANESE JOURNAL OF NURSING ARTS. (Text in Japanese) 1950. m.(plus 4 supplements). 17600 Yen($133) Medical Friend Co., Ltd. - Mejikaru Furendo-Sha, 2-4, 3-chome, Kudan-Kita, Chiyoda-ku, Tokyo 102, Japan. FAX 03-3261-6602. Ed.Bd. adv.; bk.rev.; illus.; index; circ. 100,000. (also avail. in microfiche) **Indexed:** Dent.Ind., Int.Nurs.Ind.
—BLDSC shelfmark: 4656.740500.
Description: Case analyses and literature in clinical nursing.

610.73   JA   ISSN 0022-8370
KANGO KENKYU/JAPANESE JOURNAL OF NURSING RESEARCH. (Text in Japanese) 1968. q. 7760 Yen($60) Igaku-Shoin Ltd., 5-24-3 Hongo, Bunkyo-ku, Tokyo 113-91, Japan. TEL 03-817-5775. Ed.Bd. circ. 8,000. **Indexed:** Int.Nurs.Ind.

610.73   JA   ISSN 0047-1895
KANGO KYOIKU/JAPANESE JOURNAL OF NURSING EDUCATION. (Text in Japanese) 1960. m. 12630 Yen($97) Igaku-Shoin Ltd., 5-24-3 Hongo, Bunkyo-ku, Tokyo 113-91, Japan. TEL 03-817-5775. illus.; circ. 10,000. **Indexed:** Int.Nurs.Ind.
—BLDSC shelfmark: 4656.741000.

610.73   JA   ISSN 0385-549X
KANGO TENBO/JAPANESE JOURNAL OF NURSING SCIENCE. (Text in Japanese) 1976. m.(plus suppl.). 16500 Yen. Medical Friend Co. Ltd. - Mejikaru Furendo-Sha, 2-4, 3-chome, Kudan-Kita, Chiyoda-ku, Tokyo 102, Japan. FAX 03-3261-6602. Ed. Kazuhazu Ogura. index; circ. 30,000. (also avail. in microfiche; back issues avail.) **Indexed:** Int.Nurs.Ind.
—BLDSC shelfmark: 4656.746000.
Description: Administrative issues of nursing and various discussions on nursing education.

610.73   JA   ISSN 0387-351X
KANGOGAKU ZASSHI/NURSING MAGAZINE. (Text in Japanese) 1946. m. 9960 Yen($77) Igaku-Shoin Ltd., 5-24-3 Hongo, Bunkyo-ku, Tokyo 113-91, Japan. TEL 03-817-5771. Ed.Bd. circ. 50,000.
—BLDSC shelfmark: 6187.034900.

610.73   US   ISSN 0022-8710
KANSAS NURSE. vol.48, 1973. 12/yr. $24. Kansas State Nurses Association, 700 S.W. Jackson, Ste. 601, Topeka, KS 66603-3731. TEL 913-233-8638. adv.; bk.rev.; illus.; circ. 2,360. (also avail. in microform from UMI; reprint service avail. from UMI) **Indexed:** CINAHL, Int.Nurs.Ind.
—BLDSC shelfmark: 5085.648000.

610.73   US
KENTUCKY NURSE.* 1952? bi-m. $18. Kentucky Nurses Association, Box 2616, Louisville, KY 40201. TEL 502-637-2546. Ed. Jean P. Duncan. adv.; bk.rev.; circ. 2,000. (also avail. in microform from UMI) **Indexed:** CINAHL.
Formerly: Kentucky Nurse Association Newsletter (ISSN 0023-0316)

610.73   KE   ISSN 0301-0333
KENYA NURSING JOURNAL. 1972. s-a. EAs.7.50($1) per no. National Nurses Association of Kenya, P.O. Box 49422, Nairobi, Kenya. Ed. J. B. Khachina. adv.; bk.rev.; circ. 2,750. (back issues avail.) **Indexed:** Int.Nurs.Ind.

610.73 618.92   GW
KINDERKRANKENSCHWESTER. 1982. m. DM.35. Schmidt-Roemhild Verlag, Mengstr.16, Postfach 20 51, 2400 Luebeck, Germany. TEL 0451-1605-0. FAX 0451-1605224. TELEX 26536-MSRD. adv.; bk.rev.; circ. 17,000. (back issues avail.)

610.73   KO   ISSN 0047-3618
RT1
KOREAN NURSE/TAEHAN KANHO. 1961. bi-m. $1.49. Korean Nurses' Association, 88-7 Sanglim-Dong, Choong Ku, Seoul, S. Korea. Ed. San-Cho Chun. adv.; bk.rev.; illus. **Indexed:** Int.Nurs.Ind.

KRANKENDIENST; Zeitschrift fuer kath. Krankenhaeuser, Sozialstationen und Pflegeberufe. see HOSPITALS

610.73   SZ
KRANKENPFLEGE/SOINS INFIRMIERS. (Text in French and German) 1907. m. 72 Fr. (Swiss Association of Graduate Nurses) Vogt-Schild AG, Zuchwilerstr. 21, CH-4501 Solothurn 1, Switzerland. TEL 065-247247. FAX 065-247335. TELEX 934646. Eds. Nelly Haldi, Brigitte Kocher. adv.; bk.rev.; charts; illus.; stat.; index; circ. 18,000. **Indexed:** Int.Nurs.Ind.
Formerly: Zeitschrift fuer Krankenpflege - Revue Suisse des Infirmieres (ISSN 0044-2941)

610.73   GW   ISSN 0002-1008
KRANKENPFLEGE. 1946. m. DM.63. Deutscher Berufsverband fuer Pflegeberufe, Hauptstr. 392, 6236 Eschborn 2, Germany. FAX 06173-640913. Ed. Helga Veitel. adv.; bk.rev.; illus.; index; circ. 33,000. **Indexed:** Dok.Arbeitsmed., Int.Nurs.Ind.
—BLDSC shelfmark: 5118.146500.

610.73   JA   ISSN 0388-5585
KURINIKARU SUTADI/CLINICAL STUDY. (Text in Japanese) 1980. m. (plus 2 supplements). 12700 Yen. Medical Friend Co. Ltd. - Mejikaru Furendo-Sha, 2-4, 3-chome, Kudan-Kita, Chiyoda-ku, Tokyo 102, Japan. TEL 03-3261-6602. Ed. Kazuhazu Ogura. index; circ. 60,000. (also avail. in microfiche; back issues avail.) **Indexed:** Int.Nurs.Ind.
Description: Case studies in nursing process and miscellanies for novice nurses and student nurses.

610.73   CN
L P N ASSOCIATION OF BRITISH COLUMBIA NEWSLETTER. 1957. q. free to members. Licensed Practical Nurses of British Columbia, 448 Watfield Ave., Nanaimo, B.C. V9R 3P7, Canada. TEL 604-754-3428. Ed. Agnes Magnone.

610.7   AT   ISSN 0047-3936
LAMP. 1943. m. Aus.$55. New South Wales Nurses Association, 43 Australia St., Camperdown, N.S.W. 2050, Australia. TEL 02-550-3244. FAX 02-550-3667. Ed. Patricia Staunton. adv.; bk.rev.; circ. 39,500. (also avail. in microfiche) **Indexed:** CINAHL, Int.Nurs.Ind.
—BLDSC shelfmark: 5145.050000.
Description: Items of interest of nurses, industrial and professional.

610.73   US   ISSN 0888-6075
LASER NURSING. q. $70 (foreign $104). Mary Ann Liebert, Inc., 1651 Third Ave., New York, NY 10128. TEL 212-289-2300. FAX 212-289-4697. Ed. Carolyn Mackety.
—BLDSC shelfmark: 5156.603000.
Description: For nurses who work with patients receiving laser therapy. Covers safety, administration, diagnostic and therapeutic applications, and responsibilities pertaining to preoperative and postoperative patient care.

610.73 340   US
LEGISLATIVE NETWORK FOR NURSES. 1984. fortn. $192.96 (effective Sep. 1992). Business Publishers, Inc., 951 Pershing Dr., Silver Spring, MD 20910-4464. TEL 301-587-6300. FAX 301-585-9075. Ed. B.K. Morris. (looseleaf format)
●Also available online. Vendor(s): NewsNet.
Description: Regulations and how they impact the nursing profession - salaries, training, recruiting and unionizing.

610.73   US
LICENSED PRACTICAL NURSE.* 1968-1982 (July); resumed 1984. m. $12 to individuals; institutions $18. McClain Publishing Co., Box 10619, Charlotte, NC 28212-5677. Ed. Debbie Egan. adv.; bk.rev.; charts; illus.; index. cum.index; circ. 65,000. (processed; also avail. in microform from UMI; reprint service avail. from UMI) **Indexed:** C.I.N.L., Hosp.Lit.Ind., I.P.A., Int.Nurs.Ind.
●Also available online.
Former titles: Journal of Nursing Care (ISSN 0162-7155); Nursing Care (ISSN 0091-2379); Bedside Nurse (ISSN 0005-7665)

LIFT; the magazine for young ASBAH. see MEDICAL SCIENCES

LINK (LONDON, 1966); the magazine for people with spina bifida and/or hydrocephalus. see MEDICAL SCIENCES

LINK (WOODLAND HILLS). see MEDICAL SCIENCES — Psychiatry And Neurology

610.73   US
LONG TERM CARE MANAGEMENT. 1972. fortn. $365. Faulkner & Gray, Healthcare Information Center (Subsidiary of: J P T Publishing Group), 1133 15th St., N.W., Ste. 450, Washington, DC 20005. TEL 202-828-4150. FAX 202-828-2352. Ed. Karen Migadale. (looseleaf format)
Former titles: Long Term Care; Washington Report on Long Term Care (ISSN 0091-7311)
Description: Covers legal, medical, economic, and ethical issues in long term patient management.

610.73   US
LOUISIANA. STATE BOARD OF NURSING. REPORT (CALENDAR YEAR). 1973. a. $15. State Board of Nursing, 912 Pere Marquette Bldg., New Orleans, LA 70112. TEL 504-568-5464. FAX 504-568-5467. Dir. Barbara L. Morvant. circ. 150.
Formerly (until 1976): Louisiana. State Board of Nurse Examiners. Report (ISSN 0095-5884)

MEDICAL SCIENCES — NURSES AND NURSING

610.73 US ISSN 0361-929X
RG951 CODEN: MCNNEI
M C N: AMERICAN JOURNAL OF MATERNAL CHILD NURSING. 1976. bi-m. $23 to individuals; institutions $30. American Journal of Nursing Co., 555 W. 57th St., New York, NY 10019. TEL 212-582-8820. Ed. Barbara E. Bishop, R.N. adv.; bk.rev.; bibl.; charts; illus.; index; circ. 37,500. (also avail. in microfilm from UMI; reprint service avail. from UMI) Indexed: CINAHL, Ind.Med., Int.Nurs.Ind., Nurs.Abstr.
●Also available online.
—BLDSC shelfmark: 5413.499800.

610.73 US
M L N NEW DIRECTIONS. 1975. 2-4/yr. $30. Minnesota League for Nursing, 1711 W. County Rd. B., Ste. 300N, St. Paul, MN 55113. Ed. Marie Manthey. adv.; circ. 400.
Formerly: M L N Bulletin - Newsletter; Which superseded (1953-1975): M L N Bulletin (ISSN 0047-7508)

610.73 US ISSN 0047-6080
MARYLAND NURSE. 1970. 10/yr. $10. Maryland Nurses Association, 5820 Southwestern Blvd., Baltimore, MD 21227. TEL 410-242-7300. FAX 410-242-7307. Ed.Bd. adv.; bk.rev.; circ. 5,000. (also avail. in microfilm from UMI) Indexed: CINAHL, Int.Nurs.Ind.
Supersedes: Maryland Nurses News.

610.73 US ISSN 0163-0784
MASSACHUSETTS NURSE. 1932. m. $12. Massachusetts Nurses Association, 340 Turnpike St., 2nd Fl., Canton, MA 02021-2700. FAX 617-821-4445. Ed. Lynette Aznavourian. adv.; bk.rev.; charts; illus.; circ. 18,000. Indexed: CINAHL, Int.Nurs.Ind.
Formerly (until vol. 44, 1975): Massachusetts Nurses Association. Bulletin (ISSN 0025-4843)

610.73 US ISSN 0090-0702
RJ245 CODEN: MCNJA2
MATERNAL - CHILD NURSING JOURNAL. 1972. q. $21 (Canada $25; elsewhere $30). University of Pittsburgh, School of Nursing, Parent-Child Nursing, 437 Victoria Bldg., 3500 Victoria St., Pittsburgh, PA 15261. TEL 412-624-3847. FAX 412-624-2401. Eds. Corinne Barnes, Olive Rich. bk.rev.; circ. 1,500. (also avail. in microfilm from UMI, WSH) Indexed: CINAHL, Excerp.Med., Ind.Med., Nurs.Abstr., Psychol.Abstr.
—BLDSC shelfmark: 5399.275000.
Description: Focuses on clinically based research reports, including one monograph on the nursing care of mothers, fathers and children.

610.73 CN
MATERNAL HEALTH NEWS. 1975. q. Can.$12. Maternal Health Society, Box 46563, Sta. "G", Vancouver, B.C. V6R 4G8, Canada. Ed. Faye Ryder. adv.; bk.rev.; film rev.; cum.index; circ. 8,000. (tabloid format; back issues avail.)

MEDIA PROFILES: HEALTH SCIENCES EDITION. see *MEDICAL SCIENCES*

610.73 RU ISSN 0025-8342
CODEN: MESEAQ
MEDITSINSKAYA SESTRA/NURSE. 1942. m. 6 Rub.($5.40) (Ministerstvo Zdravookhraneniya R.S.F.S.R.) Izdatel'stvo Meditsina, Petroverigskii pereulok 6-8, 101838 Moscow, Russia. Ed. O.V. Aleksandrov. bk.rev.; index. Indexed: Biol.Abstr., Chem.Abstr., Dent.Ind., Int.Nurs.Ind.
—BLDSC shelfmark: 0106.050000.
Description: Publishes articles on the care of patients, medical technique, sanitary education.

610.73 US ISSN 0026-2366
MICHIGAN NURSE.* 1924. 11/yr. $33 (foreign $50). Michigan Nurses Association, 2310 Jolly Oak Rd., Okemos, MI 48864-3546. TEL 517-349-5640. FAX 517-349-5818. Ed. Andrea Shea Ralph. adv.; illus.; index; circ. 10,000. (also avail. in microform from UMI) Indexed: CINAHL, Int.Nurs.Ind., Mich.Mag.Ind.
—BLDSC shelfmark: 5755.540000.

614 UK ISSN 0306-9699
MIDWIFE, HEALTH VISITOR AND COMMUNITY NURSE. 1965. m. £17. (Newbourne Group) Home & Law Publishing Ltd., Greater London House, Hampstead Rd., London NW1 7QQ, England. Ed. N. Morris. adv.; bk.rev.; index; circ. 24,110. Indexed: ASSIA, CINAHL, Dent.Ind., Int.Nurs.Ind.
Formerly: Midwife and Health Visitor (ISSN 0026-3516)

610.73 618 UK ISSN 0266-6138
MIDWIFERY. (Text in English) 1984. 4/yr. £45($86) to individuals; institutions £79(£153). Churchill Livingstone Medical Journals, Robert Stevenson House, 1-3 Baxter's Pl., Leith Walk, Edinburgh EH1 3AF, Scotland. TEL 031-556-2424. FAX 031-558-1278. TELEX 727511. (Subscr. to: Longman Group, Journals Subscr. Dept., P.O. Box 77, Fourth Ave., Harlow, Essex CM19 5AA, England; U.S. subscr. to: Churchill Livingstone, 650 Ave. of the Americas, New York, NY 10011. TEL 212-206-5000) Ed. Ann Thomson. adv.; bk.rev. (back issues avail.) Indexed: Curr.Adv.Ecol.Sci.
—BLDSC shelfmark: 5761.449220.

610.73 TS
MINBAR AL-TAMRID/NURSING FORUM. (Text in Arabic, English) 1987. 5/yr. free. Ministry of Health, School of Nursing - Wizarat al-Sihhah, Madrasat al-Tamrid, P.O. Box 3798, Abu Dhabi, United Arab Emirates. TEL 665472. TELEX 22678 MEDAD EM. Ed. Nabil Kronfol. circ. 1,000 (controlled).
Description: Scientific articles in the field of nursing, and news of interest to the nursing profession.

610.73 GW ISSN 0179-3799
MINDENER KLINIKSCHRIFTEN. 1986. irreg., vol.3, 1990. price varies. Verlag Dr. Dieter Winkler, Katharinaster. 37, 4630 Bochum 1, Germany. TEL 0234-17508. Ed. Dr. Justus Meyer. (back issues avail.)
Description: Focuses on the education of medical personnel, particularly nurses.

610.73 US ISSN 0026-5586
MINNESOTA NURSING ACCENT. Variant title: M N A Accent. 1927. 10/yr. $25 to non-members. Minnesota Nurses Association, 1295 Bandana Blvd., Ste. 140, St. Paul, MN 55108. FAX 612-646-4807. Ed. Marilyn Cunningham. adv.; illus.; circ. 14,000. Indexed: CINAHL, Int.Nurs.Ind.

610.73 US ISSN 0026-6388
MISSISSIPPI R N. 1939. bi-m. $18. Mississippi Nurses' Association, 135 Bounds St., Jackson, MS 39206. TEL 601-982-9182. Ed. Patricia O'Bannon Muse. adv.; bk.rev.; illus.; circ. 2,500. Indexed: CINAHL, Int.Nurs.Ind.

610.73 US ISSN 0026-6655
MISSOURI NURSE. 1932. 6/yr. membership. Missouri Nurses Association, Box 325, Jefferson City, MO 65102. Dir. Belinda Heimericks. adv.; illus.; circ. 3,000. Indexed: CINAHL, Int.Nurs.Ind.
—BLDSC shelfmark: 5829.085000.

610.73 618 US ISSN 0889-0579
N A A C O G NEWSLETTER. 1974. m. $30. N A A C O G: The Organization for Obstetric, Gynecologic, & Neonatal Nurses, 409 12th St., S.W., Washington, DC 20024. TEL 202-638-0026. Ed. Connie S. Helminger. adv.; index; circ. 27,000. (back issues avail.)
—BLDSC shelfmark: 6001.733200.
Description: For nurses and others interested in obstetric, gynecologic, and neonatal healthcare.

N A A C O G'S WOMEN'S HEALTH NURSING SCAN. (Organization for Obstetric, Gynecologic and Neonatal Nurses) see *MEDICAL SCIENCES — Abstracting, Bibliographies, Statistics*

619.73 US ISSN 1047-4757
N A S NEWSLETTER. 1986. 5/yr. (National Association of School Nurses, Inc.) Health Information Publications, Inc., 92 S. Highland Ave., Ossining, NY 10562. TEL 914-762-6498. FAX 914-762-0239. (Subscr. to: Box 1300, Scarborough, ME 04074. TEL 207-883-2117) Ed. Beverly Farquhar. adv.; circ. 7,100.

610.73 UK ISSN 0027-6049
N A T NEWS; the British journal of theatre nursing. 1965. m. £19 (foreign £27). (National Association of Theatre Nurses) Newton Mann Ltd., Sherwood House, Matlock, Derbyshire DE4 3LY, England. TEL 0629 583941. FAX 0629-580479. adv.; bk.rev.; circ. 5,500 (controlled). Indexed: CINAHL, Int.Nurs.Ind.
—BLDSC shelfmark: 2325.700000.
Description: News and research articles on the technological, administrative, and procedural aspects of providing care and services to patients in the operating room, with announcements of the activities and membership of the association.

610.73 US
N L N NURSING DATA REVIEW. a. $29.95. National League for Nursing, 350 Hudson St., New York, NY 10014. TEL 212-989-9393.
Former titles: N L N Nursing Data Book; (until 1980): N L N Nursing Data Book: Statistical Information on Nursing Education and Newly Licensed Nurses; Some Statistics on Baccalaureate and Higher Degree Programs in Nursing (ISSN 0081-203X)

610.73 US ISSN 0028-1921
NEBRASKA NURSE. 1947. q. $10. Nebraska Nurses' Association, 941 O St., Ste. 707-711, Lincoln, NE 68508. TEL 402-475-3859. Ed. Donna R. Baker. adv.; charts; illus.; circ. 24,000. Indexed: CINAHL, Int.Nurs.Ind.

610.73 US ISSN 0730-0832
CODEN: NEONEE
NEONATAL NETWORK. 1982. 8/yr. $32 to individuals; institutions $44 (foreign $50)(effective 1992). Neonatal Network, 1304 Southpoint Blvd., Ste. 280, Petaluma, CA 94954-6859. TEL 707-762-2646. FAX 707-762-0401. Ed. Charles Rait. adv.; bk.rev.; index; circ. 14,500. (back issues avail.) Indexed: CINAHL, Ind.Med., Int.Nurs.Ind.
—BLDSC shelfmark: 6075.624000.

610.73 US
NEVADA R NFORMATION. 1931. q. $15. Nevada Nurses Association, 3660 Baker Ln., Reno, NV 89509-5409. FAX 702-825-3555. Ed. Linda Roide. adv.; circ. 11,000. (back issues avail.) Indexed: CINAHL, Int.Nurs.Ind.

610.73 US
NEW JERSEY NURSE. vol.26, 1970. bi-m. $15. New Jersey State Nurses' Association, 320 W. State St., Trenton, NJ 08618. TEL 609-392-4884. FAX 609-396-2330. Ed. Dorothy Flemming. adv.; bk.rev.; circ. 6,000. Indexed: CINAHL, Int.Nurs.Ind.
Formerly: N J S N A Newsletter (ISSN 0028-5870)

610.73 US ISSN 0028-7644
CODEN: JNYNA
NEW YORK STATE NURSES ASSOCIATION. JOURNAL. 1970. q. $15. New York State Nurses Association, 2113 Western Ave., Guilderland, NY 12084. TEL 518-456-5371. FAX 518-456-0697. Ed. Martha Orr. adv.; bk.rev.; abstr.; bibl.; charts; illus.; stat.; circ. 32,000. (also avail. in microform from UMI; back issues avail.) Indexed: CINAHL, Int.Nurs.Ind., Soc.Work Res.& Abstr.
—BLDSC shelfmark: 4832.940000.
Formerly: New York State Nurse.
Description: Publishes research reports and scholarly articles on nurses and nursing.
Refereed Serial

610.73 US ISSN 0028-7652
NEW YORK STATE NURSES ASSOCIATION. REPORT. 1969. 10/yr. $15. New York State Nurses Association, 2113 Western Ave., Guilderland, NY 12084. TEL 518-456-5371. FAX 518-456-0697. Ed. Martha Orr. adv.; charts; illus.; stat.; circ. 32,000. (tabloid format; back issues avail.)
Incorporates (in 1978): N Y S N A Legislative Bulletin.
Description: Covers news of interest to nurses, and reports activities of the Association.

610.73 NZ ISSN 0110-0890
NEW ZEALAND NURSING FORUM. 1973. q. NZ.$29.50. Nurses Society of New Zealand., P.O. Box 3195, Auckland 1, New Zealand. TEL 64-9-8178412. FAX 64-9-366-1914. Ed. David Wills. adv.; bk.rev.; abstr.; bibl.; charts; illus.; stat.; circ. 12,500. Indexed: C.I.N.L., Int.Nurs.Ind.
Description: Original papers, abstracts and reviews on nursing.

MEDICAL SCIENCES — NURSES AND NURSING

610.73   NZ   ISSN 0028-8535
NEW ZEALAND NURSING JOURNAL; Kai Tiaki. 1909. m. NZ.$50. New Zealand Nurses Association, P.O. Box 2128, Wellington, New Zealand. TEL 04-385-0847. FAX 04-382-9993. Eds. Claire O'Brien, Kathy Stodart. adv.; bk.rev.; charts; illus.; stat.; circ. 22,000. (tabloid format) **Indexed:** CINAHL, Int.Nurs.Ind.
—BLDSC shelfmark: 6096.350000.

610.73   NR   ISSN 0331-4448
NIGERIAN NURSE. 1973. bi-m. $13.50. (National Association of Nigeria Nurses and Midwives) Literamed Publications Nigeria, Ltd., Oregun Village, Private Mail Bag 1068, Ikeja, Nigeria. Ed. Anu Adegoroye. bibl.; illus.; circ. 10,000. **Indexed:** CINAHL.

610.73   US   ISSN 0894-5780
NIGHTINGALE. 1973. m. $15 or membership. National Association of Executive Secretaries, 900 S. Washington St., Ste. G-13, Falls Church, VA 22046. TEL 703-237-8616. stat.; tr.lit. (back issues avail.)

610.73   SP   ISSN 1130-734X
▼**NOTAS DE ENFERMERIA.** 1990. m. 4400 ptas. Salvat Publicaciones Cientificas, S.A., Muntaner, 262, 6o, 08021 Barcelona, Spain. TEL 2010911. FAX 2015911. (Subscr. to: Cempro, Plaza Conde Valle Suchil 20, 28015 Madrid, Spain) Ed.Bd. adv.; bk.rev.; index. (back issues avail.)

610.73   CN   ISSN 0382-8476
NURSCENE. 1967. 10/yr. Can.$20. Manitoba Association of Registered Nurses, 647 Broadway, Winnipeg, Man. R3C 0X2, Canada. TEL 204-774-3477. FAX 204-775-6052. Ed. Joan Lawless. adv.; bk.rev.; circ. 11,000 (controlled).
Formerly: Marnews.

610.73   US   ISSN 0897-7437
▼**NURSE ANESTHESIA.** 1990. q. $42 to individuals (foreign $55); institutions $62 (foreign $79); students $32 (foreign $44). Appleton & Lange, Journal Division (Subsidiary of: Simon & Schuster Company), 25 Van Zant St., Box 5630, Norwalk, CT 06856. TEL 203-838-4400. (Subscr. to: Dept. NA, Box 3000, Denville, NJ 07834) Ed. Dr. Wynne Waugaman. adv.; bk.rev.; index; circ. 1,000. (back issues avail.; reprint service avail.) **Indexed:** Int.Nurs.Ind., Nurs.Abstr.
●Also available online.
—BLDSC shelfmark: 6187.028330.
Description: Presents original and review articles, as well as research notes regarding CRNA practice and research.
Refereed Serial

610.73 070.4   US   ISSN 1054-2353
▼**NURSE AUTHOR AND EDITOR.** 1991. q. $38. Hall Johnson Communications, Inc., 9737 W. Ohio Ave., Lakewood, CO 80226. TEL 303-988-0056. FAX 303-988-0056. Ed. Suzanne Hall Johnson.
Description: Offers advice on writing and editing articles and books for nursing publications.

610.73   UK   ISSN 0260-6917
NURSE EDUCATION TODAY. 1981. bi-m. £69($134) to individuals; institutions £122.50($236.50). Churchill Livingstone Medical Journals, Robert Stevenson House, 1-3 Baxter's Place, Leith Walk, Edinburgh EH3 3AF, Scotland. TEL 031-556-2424. FAX 031-558-1278. TELEX 727511. (Subscr. to: Longman Group Ltd., Journals Subscr. Dept., Fourth Ave., Harlow, Essex CM19 5AA, England; U.S. subscr. to: Churchill Livingstone, 650 Ave. of the Americas, New York, NY 10011. TEL 212-206-5000) Ed. Jean Walker. adv.; bk.rev.; illus.; circ. 1,200. (also avail. in microform from UMI; back issues avail.)
—BLDSC shelfmark: 6187.028400.

610.73   US   ISSN 0363-3624
RT71   CODEN: NUEDEC
NURSE EDUCATOR. 1976. bi-m. $35 to individuals (foreign $40); institutions $60 (foreign $70). J.B. Lippincott Co., E. Washington Sq., Philadelphia, PA 19105. TEL 215-238-4200. Ed. Suzanne Smith Blancett. adv.; bk.rev.; index; circ. 4,000. (also avail. in microform from UMI) **Indexed:** C.I.J.E., CINAHL, Int.Nurs.Ind., Nurs.Abstr.
—BLDSC shelfmark: 6187.028500.

610.73   US   ISSN 1045-5485
▼**NURSE PRACTITIONER FORUM.** 1990. q. $39 to individuals; institutions $49; foreign $65. W.B. Saunders Co. (Subsidiary of: Harcourt Brace Jovanovich), Independent Sq. W., Philadelphia, PA 19106. TEL 215-238-7800. adv.; circ. 2,000.
—BLDSC shelfmark: 6187.028720.
Description: Each issue covers a single clinical topic, emphasizing diagnostic and therapeutic measures performed by the nurse practitioner.

610.73   US   ISSN 0361-1817
RT1
THE NURSE PRACTITIONER: THE AMERICAN JOURNAL OF PRIMARY HEALTH CARE. 1975. m. $36. Vernon Publications Inc., 3000 Northup Way, Ste. 200, Bellevue, WA 98004. TEL 206-827-9900. FAX 206-822-9372. Ed. Linda J. Pearson. adv.; charts; illus.; stat.; index; circ. 13,500. (also avail. in microfiche from UMI; reprint service avail. from UMI) **Indexed:** CINAHL, Curr.Lit.Fam.Plan., FAMLI, Hosp.Lit.Ind., I.P.A., Ind.Med., Int.Nurs.Ind., Nurs.Abstr.
●Also available online.

610.73 340   US   ISSN 0196-6790
KFC615.A15
THE NURSE, THE PATIENT AND THE LAW; the journal of nursing law & risk management. 1977-1983; resumed 1984. bi-m. $65 to individuals; institutions $100. Cox Publications, Box 20316, Billings, MT 59104-0316. TEL 406-256-8822. Ed. Meridith B. Cox. index; circ. 1,046. **Indexed:** CINAHL.
Description: Discusses nursing negligence cases from a risk management perspective; keeps readers current on new standards of care, new methods to reduce or eliminate risks and new laws affecting patient care and nursing practice.

610.73   CN   ISSN 0849-3383
NURSE TO NURSE. 1961. bi-m. membership. Registered Nurses Association of Nova Scotia, 6035 Coburg Rd., Halifax, N.S. B3H 1Y8, Canada. TEL 902-423-6156. FAX 902-423-8214. Ed. Shelley Zwicker. adv.; bk.rev.; circ. 9,600.
Formerly (until 1990): R N A N S Bulletin (ISSN 0319-4604)

610.73 615   US   ISSN 0191-2291
NURSES' DRUG ALERT. 1976. m. $22. Michael J. Powers and Co., 374 Millburn Ave., Millburn, NJ 07041. Ed. Rhoda M. Michaels. index; circ. 50,000. (looseleaf format; back issues avail.) **Indexed:** CINAHL, Nurs.Abstr.
—BLDSC shelfmark: 6187.034000.

610.73 615.53
NURSES IN TRANSITION.* 4/yr. $5. c/o Marta Johnson, Box 104, Glencoe, CA 95232. Ed. Claudia Deyton.

610.73
NURSEWEEK. 1986. bi-m. $40 (free to qualified personnel). 1156 Aster Ave., Ste. C, Sunnyvale, CA 94086-6801. TEL 408-249-5877. FAX 408-249-8204. Ed. Clarice Hutchison. adv.; circ. 190,000.
Formerly: California Nursing Review.
Description: For experienced, career-oriented nurses in hospitals and other California health care facilities.

NURSING (YEAR) CAREER DIRECTORY. see *BUSINESS AND ECONOMICS — Trade And Industrial Directories*

610.73   US   ISSN 0273-320X
RM301.12
NURSING (YEAR) DRUG HANDBOOK. a. Springhouse Corporation, 1111 Bethlehem Pike, Springhouse, PA 19477. TEL 215-646-8700. Ed. Helen Klusek Hamilton.

610.73   SP   ISSN 0212-5382
NURSING (YEAR) (EDICION ESPANOLA). 1983. m. (10/yr.). 5300 ptas.($55) (free to qualified personnel). Ediciones Doyma, S.A., Travesera de Gracia, 17-21, 08021 Barcelona, Spain. TEL 200-07-11. FAX 209-11-36. TELEX 51694 INK-E. (U.S. publisher: Springhouse Corporation, 1111 Bethlehem Pike, Springhouse, PA 19477) Dir. Margarita Peya. adv.: page 240000 ptas.; trim 200 x 273; adv. contact: Jordi Grau. circ. 26,500. (reprint service avail. from UMI)
Description: Covers nursing within and outside of the hospital environment. Serves the continuing education needs of nurses on a scientific and technical level.

610.73   US   ISSN 0360-4039
RT1
NURSING (YEAR) (SPRINGHOUSE). 1971. m. $38 (effective 1992). Springhouse Corporation (Subsidiary of: Elsevier Communications), 1111 Bethlehem Pike, Springhouse, PA 19477. TEL 215-646-8700. (Subscr. to: Box 2021, Marion, OH 43305-9974) Ed. Maryanne Wagner. adv.; bibl.; charts; illus.; index; circ. 466,459. (also avail. in microform from UMI,MIM; back issues avail.) **Indexed:** CINAHL, Curr.Lit.Fam.Plan., Gen.Sci.Ind., Hosp.Lit.Ind., Int.Nurs.Ind., Nurs.Abstr., Tr.& Indus.Ind.
—BLDSC shelfmark: 6187.037500.
Description: Presents news of developments in nursing, with emphasis on clinical techniques and procedures.

NURSING ABSTRACTS. see *MEDICAL SCIENCES — Abstracting, Bibliographies, Statistics*

610.73   US   ISSN 0363-9568
RT89
NURSING ADMINISTRATION QUARTERLY. 1976. q. $82. Aspen Publishers, Inc., 200 Orchard Ridge Dr., Gaithersburg, MD 20878. TEL 301-417-7500. FAX 301-417-7550. Ed.Bd. (also avail. in microform from UMI; reprint service avail. from UMI) **Indexed:** Abstr.Health Care Manage.Stud., CINAHL, Int.Nurs.Ind., Nurs.Abstr.

610.73   US   ISSN 0276-5284
RT1
NURSING AND HEALTH CARE. 1952 (except Jul.-Aug.). m. $30 to individuals; institutions $50. National League for Nursing, 350 Hudson St., New York, NY 10014. TEL 212-989-9393. Ed. Laura Clark. illus.; circ. 20,000. (also avail. in microform from UMI; reprint service avail. from UMI) **Indexed:** CINAHL, Int.Nurs.Ind., Med. Care Rev., Nurs.Abstr., SRI.
—BLDSC shelfmark: 6187.038800.
Supersedes (1952-1980): N L N News (ISSN 0027-6804)
Description: Contains organization news.

610.73   AT   ISSN 1033-6303
▼**NURSING AND HEALTH SCIENCE EDUCATION.** 1990. s-a. $95. James Nicholas Publishers, P.O. Box 244, Albert Park, Vic. 3206, Australia. TEL 03-696-5545. FAX 613-699-2040. Ed. Rea Zajda. adv.; bk.rev.; index.
Description: To provide nursing practitioners, nursing educators, hospital administrators and health science educators with current and innovative theory and practice in various major areas of nursing and health science education.

610.73   CN   ISSN 1185-3638
NURSING B C. 1968. 5/yr. Can.$18 to non-members. Registered Nurses Association of British Columbia, 2855 Arbutus St, Vancouver, B.C. V6J 3Y8, Canada. TEL 604-736-7331. FAX 604-738-2272. Ed. Bruce Wells. adv.; bk.rev.; illus.; circ. 33,600. (also avail. in microform from UMI; reprint service avail. from UMI) **Indexed:** CINAHL, Int.Nurs.Ind.
Formerly: R N A B C News (ISSN 0048-7104)
Description: News about nurses and nursing in Canada. Covers health issues.

610.73   US   ISSN 0029-6465
RT1   CODEN: NCNAAK
NURSING CLINICS OF NORTH AMERICA. 1966. q. $48. W.B. Saunders Co., Curtis Center, Independence Sq. W., Philadelphia, PA 19106. TEL 215-238-7800. Ed. Sandy Masse. index. (also avail. in microform from UMI,MIM; reprint service avail. from UMI,ISI) **Indexed:** Abstr.Health Care Manage.Stud., Chem.Abstr., CINAHL, Curr.Cont., Excerp.Med., Hosp.Lit.Ind., Ind.Med., Int.Nurs.Ind., Nurs.Abstr.
—BLDSC shelfmark: 6187.040000.
Description: Aimed at students and graduate nurses.

610.73   US   ISSN 0895-2809
NURSING CONNECTIONS; a forum for collaboration among nurses in pratice, education, research & administration. 1988. q. $49.95 to individuals (foreign $80); libraries $65 (foreign $110). Washington Hospital Center, Division of Nursing, 110 Irving St., N.W., Washington, DC 20010. TEL 202-877-3048. FAX 202-877-3078. Ed. Molly Billingsley. adv.; circ. 1,500. **Indexed:** Nurs.Abstr.
—BLDSC shelfmark: 6187.042000.

MEDICAL SCIENCES — NURSES AND NURSING

610.73 US ISSN 1046-7459
NURSING DIAGNOSIS. 1974. q. $39 to individuals (foreign $44); insitutions $75 (foreign $80). (North American Nursing Diagnosis Association) J.B. Lippincott Co., E. Washington Sq., Philadelphia, PA 19105. TEL 215-238-4200. (Subscr. to: Box 350, Hagerstown, MD 21741-9901) Ed. Dorothy Jones.
—BLDSC shelfmark: 6187.043000.

610.73 US ISSN 0746-1739
NURSING ECONOMICS. bi-m. $30 to individuals; institutions $45. Anthony J. Jannetti, Inc., North Woodbury Rd., Box 56, Pitman, NJ 08071. TEL 609-589-2319. FAX 609-589-7463. **Indexed:** Nurs.Abstr.
—BLDSC shelfmark: 6187.046800.

610.73 US
NURSING FACULTY CENSUS. 1988. biennial. $19.95. National League for Nursing, 350 Hudson St., New York, NY 10014. TEL 212-989-9393.

610.73 US ISSN 0029-6473
RT1 CODEN: NUFOA
NURSING FORUM. 1961. q. $35 to individuals; institutions $55. Nursecom Inc., 1211 Locust St., Philadelphia, PA 19107. TEL 215-545-7222. Ed. Dr. Phyllis Kritek. adv.; bk.rev.; charts; illus.; index; circ. 5,000. (also avail. in microform from UMI; reprint service avail. from UMI) **Indexed:** CINAHL, Excerp.Med., Hosp.Lit.Ind., Ind.Med., Int.Nurs.Ind.
—BLDSC shelfmark: 6187.050000.

610.73 US ISSN 0896-6915
RA997.A1
NURSING HOMES AND SENIOR CITIZEN CARE. 1950. bi-m. $33 (Canada and Mexico $48; elsewhere $53). International Publishing Group, 4959 Commerce Pkwy., Cleveland, OH 44128. TEL 216-464-1210. FAX 216-464-1835. Ed. Richard Peck. adv.; illus.; stat.; circ. 900. (also avail. in microform from UMI; back issues avail.; reprint service avail. from UMI) **Indexed:** Account.Ind. (1974-), B.P.I., Bus.Ind., CINAHL, Hosp.Lit.Ind., I.P.A., Int.Nurs.Ind., Rehabil.Lit., Tr.& Indus.Ind.
●Also available online. Vendor(s): DIALOG.
Formerly (until 1986): Nursing Homes (ISSN 0029-649X)
Description: For professionals in planning, directing, organizing and delivering long-term care in the proprietary nursing home field.

610.73 CN
NURSING INFO (FREDERICTON). (Text in English, French) 1967. 4/yr. Can.$20 (foreign $25). Nurses Association of New Brunswick - Association des Infirmieres et Infirmiers du Nouveau-Brunswick, 165 Regent St., Fredericton, N.B. E3B 3W5, Canada. TEL 506-458-8731. FAX 506-459-2857. Ed. George Bergeron. adv.; bk.rev.; illus.; circ. 8,100.
Former titles: Info (ISSN 0382-5574); N B A R N News (ISSN 0382-5566)

610.73 CE
NURSING JOURNAL. a. Sri Lanka Nurses Association, Post Basic School of Nursing, Regent St., Colombo 10, Sri Lanka. **Indexed:** CINAHL.

610.73 II ISSN 0029-6503
RT13
NURSING JOURNAL OF INDIA. (Text in English and Hindi) 1910. m. Rs.100($40) Trained Nurses Association of India, L-17 Green Park, New Delhi 110016, India. Ed. N. Nagpal. adv.; bk.rev.; charts; illus.; index; circ. 31,000. (also avail. in microform from UMI; reprint service avail. from UMI) **Indexed:** CINAHL, Int.Nurs.Ind.
—BLDSC shelfmark: 6187.080000.

610.73 SI ISSN 0067-5814
NURSING JOURNAL OF SINGAPORE/BERITA JURURAWAT. 1959. bi-m. Singapore Trained Nurses' Association, Manhattan House, Ste. 913, 9th Fl., 151 Chin Swee Rd., Singapore 0316, Singapore. TEL 7333984. Ed. Ranjit Singh. adv. **Indexed:** CINAHL, Int.Nurs.Ind.
—BLDSC shelfmark: 6187.090000.

610.73 US ISSN 0744-6314
NURSING MANAGEMENT. 1970. m. $25 (free to qualified personnel; $32 to Canada; elsewhere $45). S - N Publications, Inc., 103 N. Second St., Ste. 200, W. Dundee, IL 60118. TEL 708-426-6100. FAX 708-426-6146. Ed. Leah Curtin. adv.; bk.rev.; index; circ. 135,000 (controlled). (also avail. in microform from UMI; reprint service avail. from UMI) **Indexed:** ABI Inform, CINAHL, Hosp.Lit.Ind., Int.Nurs.Ind., Nurs.Abstr.
—BLDSC shelfmark: 6187.094000.
Formerly (until 1981): Supervisor Nurse (ISSN 0039-5870)
Description: Covers all aspects of nursing management and related medical, legal, personnel and ethical issues.
Refereed Serial

610.73 SA
NURSING NEWS/VERPLEEGNUUS. 1978. m. R.24 (effective 1992). South African Nursing Association, Box 1280, Pretoria 0001, South Africa. TEL 012-3432315. FAX 012-3440750. Ed. Thailia Kruger. adv.; illus.; circ. 120,000. **Indexed:** CINAHL.
Supersedes (1935-1978): South African Nursing Journal (ISSN 0038-2507)

610.73 US ISSN 0029 6546
NURSING NEWS (BROOKLYN). 1944. 5/yr. membership. Nurses Association of the Counties of Long Island, 1 Hanson Place, Brooklyn, NY 11243. TEL 718-783-4433. Ed. Barbara J. Malon. adv.; illus.; circ. 5,000.

610.73 US ISSN 0029-6538
NURSING NEWS (CONCORD). 1949. 6/yr. $20. New Hampshire Nurses' Association, 48 West St., Concord, NH 03301. TEL 603-225-3783. Ed. Theresa M. Bonanno. adv.; circ. 1,000. **Indexed:** Int.Nurs.Ind.
—BLDSC shelfmark: 6187.104000.

610.73 US
NURSING OPPORTUNITIES. (Supplement to: R N Magazine) 1970. a. $7.95 (foreign $10). (R N Magazine) Medical Economics Publishing Co., Five Paragon Dr., Montvale, NJ 07645. TEL 201-358-7200. FAX 201-573-1045. adv.; bk.rev.; circ. 130,000.
Description: Features comprehensive profiles of hundreds of hospitals emphasizing specific employment opportunities for nurses, and related information.

610.73 US ISSN 0029-6554
RT1
NURSING OUTLOOK. 1953. bi-m. $25 to individuals; institutions $35. (American Academy of Nursing) Mosby Year - Book, Inc. (Littleton) (Subsidiary of: Times Mirror Company), 545 Great Rd., Littleton, MA 01460. TEL 800-225-5020. FAX 508-486-9423. (Subscr. to: Journal Subscription Service, 11830 Westline Industrial Dr., St. Louis, MO 63146. TEL 800-325-4177) Ed. Lucie S. Kelly. adv.; bk.rev.; charts; illus.; tr.lit.; index; circ. 21,116. (also avail. in microform from UMI; reprint service avail. from UMI) **Indexed:** Abstr.Hosp.Manage.Stud., ASSIA, C.I.J.E., C.I.S. Abstr., CINAHL, Curr.Lit.Fam.Plan., Except.Child Educ.Abstr., Hosp.Lit.Ind., I.P.A., Ind.Med., Int.Nurs.Ind., Med.Care Rev., Nurs.Abstr., Psychol.Abstr., Rehabil.Lit., Soc.Sci.Ind., Soc.Work Res.& Abstr., SSCI.
●Also available online.

610.73 US
NURSING PHOTOBOOK. a. $16.95. Springhouse corporation, 1111 Bethlehem Pike, Springhouse, PA 19477. TEL 215-646-8700.

610.73 US
NURSING PULSE OF NEW ENGLAND. fortn. $7.50. 104 Charles St., Box 682, Boston, MA 02114. TEL 617-523-5123.
Description: News magazine for nurses.

610.73 CN ISSN 0381-6419
NURSING QUEBEC. (Text in English and French) 1976. 6/yr. Can.$22 to individuals; institutions Can.$33; students Can.$12. Order of Nurses of Quebec - Ordre des Infirmieres et Infirmiers du Quebec, 4200 Dorchester Blvd. W., Montreal, Que. H3Z 1V4, Canada. TEL 514-935-2501. FAX 514-935-1799. Ed. Guylaine Chabot. adv.; bk.rev.; illus.; circ. 61,803 (controlled). **Indexed:** Can.Per.Ind., Int.Nurs.Ind., Pt.de Rep. (1982-).
Formerly (until 1980): Order of Nurses of Quebec. News and Notes (ISSN 0319-2636)

610.73 SA ISSN 0258-1647
NURSING R S A VERPLEGING; magazine for today's nurse - die moderne verpleegkunidge se tydskrif. (Text and summaries in Afrikaans, English) 1986. m. R.59.95($30) (South African Nursing Association) Nursing R S A Verpleging, 18 Grotto Road, Rondebosch 7700, Capetown, South Africa. TEL 021-685-6037. FAX 021-531-4126. (Subscr. to: Subscription Manager, Private Bag X1, Pinelands 7430, Capetown, South Africa. TEL 021-531-3081) Ed. Lilian Medlen. adv.; bk.rev.; abstr.; bibl.; charts; illus.; circ. 13,000. **Indexed:** CINAHL, Ind.S.A.Per., Int.Nurs.Ind.
—BLDSC shelfmark: 6187.116310.
Incorporates: Curationis (ISSN 0379-8577)
Description: Covers a broad spectrum of issues of interest to nursing professionals, including practical, technical, historical and theoretical topics.

610.73 US ISSN 0029-6562
RT1 CODEN: NURNA
NURSING RESEARCH. 1952. bi-m. $35 to individuals; institutions $70. American Journal of Nursing Co., 555 W. 57th St., New York, NY 10019. TEL 212-582-8820. Ed. Florence S. Downs, R.N. adv.; bk.rev.; abstr.; charts; stat.; index. cum.index: 1952-1963; circ. 11,000. (also avail. in microform from UMI; reprint service avail. from UMI) **Indexed:** Abstr.Health Care Manage.Stud., ASSIA, Child Devel.Abstr., CINAHL, Curr.Cont., Dent.Ind., Excerp.Med., Hosp.Lit.Ind., I.P.A., Ind.Med., Ind.Sci.Rev., Int.Nurs.Ind., Med.Care Rev., MEDSOC, Ment.Retard.Abstr., Mid.East: Abstr.& Ind., Nucl.Sci.Abstr., Nurs.Abstr., Psychol.Abstr., Risk Abstr., Soc.Work Res.& Abstr., Sp.Ed.Needs Abstr., SSCI, Stud.Wom.Abstr.
●Also available online.
—BLDSC shelfmark: 6187.110000.

NURSING RESEARCH ABSTRACTS. see *MEDICAL SCIENCES — Abstracting, Bibliographies, Statistics*

NURSING SCAN IN ADMINISTRATION. see *MEDICAL SCIENCES — Abstracting, Bibliographies, Statistics*

NURSING SCAN IN RESEARCH: APPLICATION FOR CLINICAL PRACTICE. see *MEDICAL SCIENCES — Abstracting, Bibliographies, Statistics*

610.73 UK ISSN 0029-6570
CODEN: NSTAEU
NURSING STANDARD. 1968. w. £42($120) to non-members; members £38. (Royal College of Nursing) Scutari Projects Ltd., 17-19 Peterborough Rd., Harrow-on-the-Hill, Middlesex HA1 2AX. TEL 081-423-1066. FAX 081-423-3867. Ed. Norah Casey. adv.; bk.rev.; illus.; circ. 70,000. **Indexed:** Int.Nurs.Ind.
—BLDSC shelfmark: 6187.116700.
Incorporates: Lampada (ISSN 0266-8769) & Tradimus (ISSN 0269-0977)

610.73 US
NURSING STUDENT CENSUS. 1987. a. $19.95. National League for Nursing, 350 Hudson St., New York, NY 10014. TEL 212-989-9393.

610.73 II
▼**NURSING TECHNOLOGY.** 1991. bi-m. Rs.640($45) K.K. Roy (Private) Ltd., 55 Gariahat Road, P.O. Box 10210, Calcutta 700 019, India. Ed. K.K. Roy. adv.; abstr.; bibl.; index; circ. 2,240.

MEDICAL SCIENCES — NURSES AND NURSING

610.73 UK
NURSING TIMES. 1905. w. £51($140) Macmillan Magazines Ltd., 4 Little Essex St., London WC2R 3LF, England. TEL 01-836-6633.
FAX 01-379-4204. Ed. Linda Davidson. adv.; bk.rev.; illus.; index; circ. 90,045. (also avail. in microform from BLH,UMI; reprint service avail. from UMI) **Indexed:** Abstr.Health Care Manage.Stud., ASSIA, C.I.S. Abstr., CINAHL, Curr.Adv.Ecol.Sci., Dent.Ind., Hosp.Abstr., Hosp.Lit.Ind., Ind.Med., Int.Nurs.Ind., Sp.Ed.Needs Abstr.
Formed by the merger of: Nursing Times (ISSN 0029-6589); Nursing Mirror (ISSN 0029-6511)

610.73 US
NURSING YEARBOOK. a. $21.95. Springhouse Corporation, 1111 Bethlehem Pike, Springhouse, PA 19477. TEL 215-646-8700.

610.73 US
NURSINGWORLD JOURNAL. 1975. m. $22. Prime National Publishing Corp., 470 Boston Post Rd., Weston, MA 02193. TEL 617-899-2702. Ed. Eileen DeVito. adv.; bk.rev.; circ. 35,000. (tabloid format)
Formed by the merger of: Nursingworld Digest & Nursing Job News (ISSN 0163-223X); New England Nursing News.

610.73 US
NURSINGWORLD JOURNAL NURSING JOB GUIDE. 1979. a. $75. Prime National Publishing Corp., 470 Boston Post Rd., Weston, MA 02193. TEL 617-899-2702. Ed. Eileen F. DeVito. adv.; charts; illus.; stat.; circ. 3,000. (back issues avail.)
Former titles: Nursingworld Journal Annual Hospital Directory; Nursing Job News: Annual Hospital Directory; Nursing Job News: Nursing Job Guide to Over 7000 Hospitals (ISSN 0162-9069)

O R L - HEAD AND NECK NURSING. see *MEDICAL SCIENCES — Otorhinolaryngology*

610.73 AU ISSN 0303-4461
OESTERREICHISCHE KRANKENPFLEGEZEITSCHRIFT. 1948. 10/yr. S.330 (foreign S.360). Oesterreichischer Krankenpflegeverband, Mollgasse 3a, A-1180 Vienna, Austria. TEL 0222-346397. Ed. Ulrike Sokol. adv.; bk.rev.; abstr.; illus.; circ. 8,000. **Indexed:** Int.Nurs.Ind.
—BLDSC shelfmark: 6307.810000.

610.7 AU
OESTERREICHISCHER KRANKENPFLEGERVERBAND. FORTBILDUNGSPROGRAMM. 1969. a. free. Oesterreichischer Krankenpflegeverband, Mollgasse 3a, A-1180 Vienna, Austria. TEL 0222-346397. Ed. Marianne Kriegl. circ. 10,000.

OFFICIEL DE LA SAGE-FEMME. see *MEDICAL SCIENCES — Obstetrics And Gynecology*

610.73 US ISSN 0030-0993
OHIO NURSES REVIEW. 1926. m. $20. Ohio Nurses Association, 4000 E. Main St., Columbus, OH 43213-2950. TEL 614-237-5414. Ed. Carol A. Jenkins. index; circ. 8,500 (controlled). **Indexed:** CINAHL, Int.Nurs.Ind.
—BLDSC shelfmark: 6247.150000.

610.73 US ISSN 0030-1787
OKLAHOMA NURSE.* 1926. 5/yr. $10. Oklahoma Nurses Association, 6414 N. Santa Fe, Oklahoma City, OK 73118. Ed. Marjorie Wilhelm. adv.; illus.; circ. 2,000. **Indexed:** CINAHL, Int.Nurs.Ind.

610.73 616.99 US ISSN 0190-535X
ONCOLOGY NURSING FORUM. 1974. 10/yr. $35 to individuals; institutions $50. (Oncology Nursing Society, Inc.) Oncology Nursing Press, 501 Holiday Dr., Pittsburgh, PA 15220-2749.
FAX 412-921-6565. Ed. Rose Mary Carroll-Johnson. adv.; bk.rev.; index; circ. 21,000. (also avail. in microform; back issues avail.; reprint service avail. from UMI) **Indexed:** CINAHL, Int.Nurs.Ind., Nurs.Abstr.
—BLDSC shelfmark: 6256.980000.
Description: Contains news related to developments in oncology practice, technology, and research. Focuses on promoting a positive image of professional specialized nursing.

610.73 616.8 362.2 UK ISSN 0265-511X
OPEN MIND; the mental health magazine. 1983. bi-m. £10 to individuals; institutions £13. Mind, National Association for Mental Health, 22 Harley St., London W1N 2ED, England. TEL 071-637-0741.
FAX 071-323-0061. Ed. Helen Imam. adv.; bk.rev.; film rev.; play rev.; illus.; tr.lit.; index; circ. 5,000. (back issues avail.)
—BLDSC shelfmark: 6266.325000.

610.73 US ISSN 0030-4751
RT1
OREGON NURSE. 1932. 4/yr. $12. Oregon Nurses Association, 9600 S.W. Oak St., Ste. 550, Portland, OR 97223-6599. FAX 503-293-0013. Ed. Sandy Marron. adv.; bk.rev.; illus.; circ. 5,200. **Indexed:** CINAHL, Int.Nurs.Ind.

610.73 617.3 US ISSN 0744-6020
ORTHOPAEDIC NURSING JOURNAL; national association of orthopaedic nurses. 1981. bi-m. $21 to individuals; institutions $28. (National Association of Orthopaedic Nurses) Anthony J. Jannetti, Inc., North Woodbury Rd., Box 56, Pitman, NJ 08071.
TEL 609-589-2319. FAX 609-589-7463. Ed. Ann Maher. adv.; bk.rev.; circ. 10,000. **Indexed:** Nurs.Abstr.
—BLDSC shelfmark: 6296.125300.

610 US ISSN 0889-5899
OSTOMY - WOUND MANAGEMENT; the journal of extended patient care management. 1980. q. $36 (foreign $49.50). Health Management Publications, Inc., 550 American Ave., King of Prussia, PA 19406-1441. TEL 215-337-4466.
FAX 215-337-0890. Ed. Denise Wilson. adv.; charts; illus.; stat.
—BLDSC shelfmark: 6312.377000.
Formerly: Ostomy Management.

610.73 US
P M A. (Professional Medical Assistant) bi-m. American Association of Medical Assistants, Inc., 20 N. Wacker, No. 1575, Chicago, IL 60606-2903. TEL 312-899-1500. FAX 312-899-1259. Ed. Stacey J. Roseen. circ. 12,000.

610.73 UK ISSN 0269-9079
PAEDIATRIC NURSING. 1988. 10/yr. £30 (foreign £45). Scutari Projects Ltd., Viking House, 17-19 Peterborough Rd., Harrow-on-the-Hill, Middlesex HA1 2AX, England. TEL 081-423-1066.
FAX 081-423-3867. (Subscr. to: Subscription House, Robjohn's Farm, Vicarage Rd., Finchingfield, Essex CM7 4LF, England) Ed. Rosemary Rogers. circ. 3,500.
—BLDSC shelfmark: 6333.399760.
Refereed Serial

610.73 PK ISSN 0078-8376
PAKISTAN NURSING AND HEALTH REVIEW. 1951. q. Pakistan Nurses Federation, c/o College of Nursing, Jinnah Postgraduate Medical Centre, Karachi 35, Pakistan. Ed. Mushtaq Ahmad. circ. 2,000. **Indexed:** Int.Nurs.Ind.

610.73 US
PEDIATRIC NURSE PRACTITIONER. bi-m. National Association of Pediatric Nurse Associates and Practitioners, 1101 Kings Hwy. N., No. 206, Cherry Hill, NJ 08034. (Co-sponsor: Proctor & Gamble, CN) Ed. Timothy W. Gordon. circ. 3,100.

610.73 US ISSN 0097-9805
RJ245
PEDIATRIC NURSING. 1975. bi-m. $21 to individuals; institutions $28. Anthony J. Jannetti, Inc., North Woodbury Rd., Box 56, Pitman, NJ 08071.
TEL 609-589-2319. FAX 609-589-7463. Ed. Veronica Feeg. adv.; bk.rev.; illus.; circ. 8,763. (also avail. in microfilm from UMI; reprint service avail. from UMI) **Indexed:** CINAHL, Dent.Ind., Int.Nurs.Ind., Nurs.Abstr.

610.73 US ISSN 0031-4617
PENNSYLVANIA NURSE. 1946. 11/yr. (Nov./Dec. combined). $15. Pennsylvania Nurses Association, Editorial Board, Box 8525, Harrisburg, PA 17105-8525. TEL 717-657-1222.
FAX 717-657-3796. Ed. Janet L. Wall. adv.; bk.rev.; illus.; circ. 9,000. (tabloid format) **Indexed:** CINAHL, Int.Nurs.Ind.

PERSPECTIVES (TORONTO). see *GERONTOLOGY AND GERIATRICS*

610.736 US ISSN 0031-5990
RC475 CODEN: PEPYA
PERSPECTIVES IN PSYCHIATRIC CARE. 1963. q. $35 to individuals; institutions $55. Nursecom Inc., 1211 Locust St., Philadelphia, PA 19107.
TEL 215-545-7222. Ed. Norine Kerr. adv.; bk.rev.; index; circ. 6,000. (also avail. in microfilm from UMI; reprint service avail. from UMI) **Indexed:** CINAHL, Excerp.Med., Hosp.Lit.Ind., Ind.Med., Int.Nurs.ind., Nurs.Abstr., Psychol.Abstr.
—BLDSC shelfmark: 6428.160000.
Description: Focuses on research, clinical practice, trends and innovations in psychiatric and mental-health nursing.

PHARMACY HEALTH-LINE. see *PHARMACY AND PHARMACOLOGY*

610.73 PH ISSN 0048-3818
PHILIPPINE JOURNAL OF NURSING. 1953. q. P.25($15) Philippine Nurses Association, 1663 F. Tirena Benitez St., Malate, Manila 2801, Philippines. TEL 583092. Ed. Cecilia M. Laurente. adv.; bk.rev.; illus.; circ. 13,000. **Indexed:** CINAHL, Int.Nurs.Ind.
—BLDSC shelfmark: 6455.629000.
Formerly: Filipino Nurse.

610.73 618 PL ISSN 0048-4148
PIELEGNIARKA I POLOZNA. 1958. m. $6. (Zwiazek Zawodowy Pracownikow Sluzby Zdrowia) Wydawnictwo Wspolczesne R S W "Prasa-Ksiazka-Ruch", Ul. Wiejska 12, 00-420 Warsaw, Poland. TEL 48-22-285330. (Dist. by: Ars Polona-Ruch, Krakowskie Przedmiescie 7, Warsaw, Poland) Ed. Irena Kosobudzka. adv.; bk.rev.; illus.; circ. 35,000. **Indexed:** Int.Nurs.Ind.
—BLDSC shelfmark: 6498.830000.
Formed by the merger of: Pielegniarka Polska & Polozna.

610.73 617.95 US ISSN 0741-5206
CODEN: PSNUEE
PLASTIC SURGICAL NURSING. q. $20 to individuals; institutions $25. (American Society of Plastic and Reconstructive Surgical Nurses) Anthony J. Jannetti, Inc., North Woodbury Rd., Box 56, Pitman, NJ 08071. TEL 609-589-2319. **Indexed:** Nurs.Abstr.
—BLDSC shelfmark: 6528.938100.

610.73 UK ISSN 0953-6612
PRACTICE NURSE. 1988. 11/yr. £30. Reed Business Publishing Group, Reed Healthcare Communications (Subsidiary of: Reed International PLC), Quadrant House, The Quadrant, Sutton, Surrey SM2 5AS, England. TEL 081-661-3500. FAX 081-661-8946. Ed. Caley Montgomery. adv.; index; circ. 6,500.
—BLDSC shelfmark: 6597.170000.
Description: Information on patient care and management in general practice.

610.73 US ISSN 0032-6666
PRAIRIE ROSE. 1931. q. $10. (North Dakota Nurses Association) Arthur Davis Agency, 517 Washington St., Box 216, Cedar Falls, IA 50613.
FAX 319-277-4055. (Subscr. to: 212 N. 4th St., Bismarck, ND 58501. TEL 701-223-1385) Ed. Ida H. Rigley. adv.; bk.rev.; circ. 12,000. **Indexed:** CINAHL, Int.Nurs.Ind.

610.73 US
PRO RE NATA. 1975. q. $12 to non-members. (Utah Nurses Association) Art Davis Associates, Box 216, Cedar Falls, IA 50613. TEL 801-322-3439. Ed. Pam Gurrell. adv.; circ. 15,000 (controlled).
Former titles (until 1987): One on One; U N A Communique; Utah Nurse.
Description: Preofeesional journal for nurses in Utah.

610.73 UK
PROFESSIONAL NURSE. 1985. m. £30 to individuals; institutions £45. Austen Cornish Publishers Ltd., Brooke House, 2-16 Torrington Pl., London WC1E 7LT, England. TEL 071-636-4622.
FAX 071-637-3021. (Subscr. to: Stonehart Subscriptions Service, Hainault Rd., Little Heath, Romford RM6 5NP, England. TEL 081-597-7335) Ed. Ann Shuttleworth. adv.; bk.rev.; index; circ. 50,000. (back issues avail.)
Formerly: Professional Nursing (ISSN 0266-8130)
Description: Primarily clinical magazine with the aim of keeping nurses up-to-date on practice issues and improving their effectiveness.

MEDICAL SCIENCES — NURSES AND NURSING

610.73 — US — ISSN 0734-1431
PROGRAM PLANS: NURSING BASIC SERIES. 1979. m. $76. (Educational Planning Services Corp.) E P S C O, Box 930, E. Sandwich, MA 02537. TEL 508-888-3257. Ed. Jessica D. Terrill. bk.rev.; bibl.; charts; illus.; stat.; index; circ. 3,000. (looseleaf format; back issues avail.)
Description: For training non-professional staff in health service facilities.

PROGRESS IN CARDIOVASCULAR NURSING. see *MEDICAL SCIENCES — Cardiovascular Diseases*

610.73 574.16 — SZ — ISSN 0254-105X
CODEN: PRRMFP
PROGRESS IN REPRODUCTIVE BIOLOGY AND MEDICINE. (Text in English) 1976. irreg. (approx. 1/yr.). price varies. S. Karger AG, Allschwilerstr. 10, P.O. Box, CH-4009 Basel, Switzerland. TEL 061-3061111. FAX 061-3061234. TELEX CH 962652. Ed. M. L'Hermite. (reprint service avail. from ISI) **Indexed:** Biol.Abstr., Chem.Abstr., Curr.Cont., Dairy Sci.Abstr.
—BLDSC shelfmark: 6924.518500.
Formerly: Progress in Reproductive Biology (ISSN 0304-4262)

610.73 — US — ISSN 0737-1209
PUBLIC HEALTH NURSING. q. $42 to individuals; institutions $75. Blackwell Scientific Publications Inc., Three Cambridge Center, Ste. 208, Cambridge, MA 02142-1413. TEL 617-225-0401. FAX 617-225-0412. **Indexed:** Nurs.Abstr.
—BLDSC shelfmark: 6964.760000.

QUALITY OF CARE. see *MEDICAL SCIENCES — Psychiatry And Neurology*

610.73 — US
QUICKENING. bi-m. membership only. American College of Nurse-Midwives, 1522 K St., N.W., Ste. 1000, Washington, DC 20005. TEL 202-289-0171. FAX 202-289-4395. circ. 3,200.

610.73 — US — ISSN 0033-7021
RT1
R N. 1937. m. $35 (foreign $50). Medical Economics Publishing Co., Five Paragon Dr., Montvale, NJ 07645. TEL 201-358-7200. FAX 201-573-1045. (Subscr. to: Box 2119, Marion, OH 43305-2119) Ed. Marianne Mattera. adv.; bk.rev.; index; circ. 280,000. (also avail. in microform from RPI; reprint service avail.) **Indexed:** Acad.Ind., Bus.Ind., CINAHL, Curr.Lit.Fam.Plan., Gen.Sci.Ind., Hlth.Ind., Hosp.Lit.Ind., Int.Nurs.Ind., Nurs.Abstr., Tr.& Indus.Ind.
●Also available online. Vendor(s): DIALOG.
—BLDSC shelfmark: 7993.980000.
Description: Articles of interest to registered nurses particularly in the hospital environment.

610.73 — US — ISSN 0192-298X
R.N. IDAHO. 1942. 4/yr. $25 to non-members; foreign $30. Idaho Nurses Association, 200 N. 4th St., Ste. 20, Boise, ID 83702-6001. TEL 208-345-0500. Ed. Kathy Stockton. adv.; circ. 600.
Former titles: Gem State R.N. Newsletter; Gem State R.N. (ISSN 0072-0569); Idaho State Bulletin.

610.73 — US — ISSN 1044-0666
RECRUITMENT & RETENTION REPORT. 1988. m. $128. Hall Johnson Communications, Inc., 9737 W. Ohio Ave., Lakewood, CO 80226. TEL 303-988-0056. FAX 303-988-0056. Ed. Suzanne Hall Johnson. adv.; bk.rev.; abstr.; bibl.; charts.
—BLDSC shelfmark: 7326.922500.
Description: Offers marketing strategies for nursing recruitment and retention.

REGAN REPORT ON NURSING LAW. see *LAW*

610.73 — CN
REGISTERED NURSE. q. Can.$19.50($26) (foreign $39). B C S Communications Ltd., 101 Thorncliffe Park Dr., Toronto, Ont. M4H 1M2, Canada. TEL 416-421-7944. FAX 416-421-0966. adv.; circ. 70,231.

610.73 — US — ISSN 0278-4807
RT120.R4
REHABILITATION NURSING. 1975. bi-m. $40 to individuals; institutions $50. Association of Rehabilitation Nurses, 5700 Old Orchard Rd., 1st Fl., Skokie, IL 60077-1057. TEL 708-966-3433. FAX 708-966-9418. Ed. Belinda Puetz. adv.; bk.rev.; charts; illus.; index; circ. 8,000. (also avail. in microform from UMI; back issues avail.; reprint service avail. from UMI) **Indexed:** CINAHL, Int.Nurs.Ind., Nurs.Abstr.
—BLDSC shelfmark: 7350.285000.
Formerly: A R N Journal.

610.73 — US — ISSN 0160-6891
RT81.5
RESEARCH IN NURSING & HEALTH. 1978. bi-m. $185 to institutions (foreign $260). John Wiley & Sons, Inc., Journals, 605 Third Ave., New York, NY 10158-0012. TEL 212-850-6000. FAX 212-850-6088. TELEX 12-7063. Ed. Marilyn T. Oberst. circ. 1,650. (also avail. in microform from RPI; back issues avail.; reprint service avail. from RPI) **Indexed:** CINAHL, Curr.Cont., Ind.Med., Int.Nurs.Ind., Nurs.Abstr., Psychol.Abstr., Sociol.Abstr., SSCI.
—BLDSC shelfmark: 7750.150000.
Description: Covers nursing practice, education and administration.
Refereed Serial

610.73 — US — ISSN 1040-3957
RESPONSE (LEBANON).* 1988. m. $19.95. c/o D.J. Russell, Pub., 22 E. Cumberland St., Lebanon, PA 17042-5788. Ed. Terrilynn M. Quillen. adv.; bk.rev.; charts; illus.; pat.; circ. 600. (back issues avail.)
Description: Potpourri of clinical data, personal insights and humor. For all nurses: active, retired, students, or those with advanced degrees.

610.73 — BL — ISSN 0034-7167
REVISTA BRASILEIRA DE ENFERMAGEM. (Abstract in English) 1938. q. $30. Brazilian Nursing Association, Av. L2 Norte Q. 603, Modulo B, Brasilia, DF, Brazil. Ed. Maria Helia de Almeidago. circ. 2,400. **Indexed:** Int.Nurs.Ind.

610.73 — CU — ISSN 0864-0319
REVISTA CUBANA DE ENFERMERIA. (Text in Spanish; summaries in English, French, Spanish) 1985. s-a. $10 in N. America; S. America $12; Europe $14. Ministerio de Salud Publica, Centro Nacional de Informacion de Ciencias Medicas, Calle E No. 452, e-19 y 21, Plaza de la Revolucion, Apdo. 6520, Havana, Cuba. TEL 809-32-5338. (Dist. by: Ediciones Cubanas, Obispo No. 527, Apdo. 605, Havana, Cuba) Dir. Onelia Espinosa Ramos. bibl.; charts; illus.; index; circ. 2,500.
—BLDSC shelfmark: 7852.104000.

610.73 — US
▼**REVOLUTION: THE JOURNAL OF NURSE EMPOWERMENT.** 1991. q. $19.95. A.D. Von Publishers, Inc., 56 McArthur Ave., Staten Island, NY 10312. TEL 800-331-6534. Ed. Jaon Swirsky. adv.: B&W page $2000. circ. 10,000.
Description: Focuses on contemporary nursing issues, such as the roles of care, education, research and advocacy for AIDS patients; the relationship between nursing and feminism; media neglect of nurses; legislative matters; entrepreneurship; and sexism on the job.

610.73 — FR — ISSN 0987-8947
REVUE DE L'AIDE-SOIGNANTE. 10/yr. 200 F. (foreign 230 F.). Expansion Scientifique, 15 rue Saint Benoit, 75278 Paris Cedex 06, France. TEL 1-45-48-42-60. FAX 1-45-44-81-55.

610.73 — FR — ISSN 0397-7900
REVUE DE L'INFIRMIERE. 1951. 20/yr. 350 F. to individuals (foreign 545 F.); students 280 F. (foreign 450 F.). Expansion Scientifique, 15 rue Saint-Benoit, 75278 Paris Cedex 06, France. Ed. Nadine Wehrlin. adv.; bk.rev.; charts; illus.; index; circ. 60,000. **Indexed:** Dent.Ind., Int.Nurs.Ind., Pt.de Rep. (1979-).
—BLDSC shelfmark: 7924.170000.
Formerly: Revue de l'Infirmiere et de l'Assistante Sociale (ISSN 0035-144X)

610.73 — LU
REVUE DE L'INFIRMIERE LUXEMBOURGEOISE. (Text in French, German) 1989. 4/yr. 260 Fr. (Societe Pour Promouvoir la Distribution d'Articles Culturels) Promoculture, S.a.r.l., 14 rue Duchscher, B.P. 1142, L-1142 Luxembourg, Luxembourg. TEL 352-48-06-91. FAX 352-40-09-50. TELEX 3112. adv.; bk.rev.

610.73 — IT
RIVISTA DELL'INFERMIERE. q. L.40000($90) to individuals; students L.30000; institutions L.50000. Pensiero Scientifico Editore s.r.l., Via Panama 48, 00198 Rome, Italy. TEL 06 855-36-33. circ. 4,000. **Indexed:** Int.Nurs.Ind.

610.73 — PH — ISSN 0048-9123
SANTO TOMAS NURSING JOURNAL; devoted to the collegiate programmes of nursing in the Philippines. 1962-1976; resumed 1978. s-a. $8. University of Santo Tomas, College of Nursing, Espana St., Manila, Philippines. Ed. Conchita Torres-Maceda. adv.; bk.rev.; illus.; circ. 2,000. **Indexed:** CINAHL, Int.Nurs.Ind.

610.73 — CN
SASKATCHEWAN CONCE R N. 1948. bi-m. Can.$15 (foreign $25). Saskatchewan Registered Nurses' Association, 2066 Retallack St., Regina, Sask. S4T 2K2, Canada. TEL 306-527-4643. FAX 306-525-0849. Ed. Joy Johnson. adv.; bk.rev.; circ. 10,000.
Formerly (until 1987): Saskatchewan Registered Nurses' Association. Bulletin (ISSN 0319-8499)
Description: Information about the association's activities in nursing education.

610.73 — CN
SASKATCHEWAN PSYCHIATRIC NURSES' ASSOCIATION. NEWSLETTER.* q. Saskatchewan Psychiatric Nurses' Association, 1854 Portage Ave., Winnipeg, Man. R3J 0G9, Canada. TEL 306-586-4617. FAX 306-586-6000. Ed. Barbara Wright.

610.73 — US — ISSN 0889-7182
SCHOLARLY INQUIRY FOR NURSING PRACTICE: AN INTERNATIONAL JOURNAL. 1986. 3/yr. $28 to individuals; institutions $48. Springer Publishing Company, 536 Broadway, New York, NY 10012. TEL 212-431-4370. FAX 212-941-7842. Ed. Harriet Feldman. adv. (back issues avail.) **Indexed:** CINAHL, Int.Nurs.Ind., Psychol.Abstr.
—BLDSC shelfmark: 8092.540300.

610.73 — US — ISSN 1048-3896
SCHOOL HOUSE ALERT. 1984. m. (10/yr.). $25. Box 28008, San Antonio, TX 78228. TEL 512-433-7327.

610.73 — GW — ISSN 0340-5303
DIE SCHWESTER - DER PFLEGER. 1962. m. DM.63. Bibliomed - Medizinische Verlagsgesellschaft mbH, Postfach 150, Nuernbergerstr. 10, 3508 Melsungen, Germany. FAX 05661-8360. Ed.Bd. adv.; bk.rev.; charts; illus.; circ. 53,000. **Indexed:** Dok.Arbeitsmed.

610.73 — GW — ISSN 0048-9549
SCHWESTERN REVUE; das Journal fuer die Krankenpflege. 1963. m. DM.14. Die Schwesternrevue GmbH, Am Schwarzenberg 28, 8700 Wuerzburg, Germany. Ed. Susi Kirchner-Enders. adv.; illus. **Indexed:** Int.Nurs.Ind.

610.736 616.992 — US — ISSN 0749-2081
SEMINARS IN ONCOLOGY NURSING. 1985. q. $48 to individuals; institutions $82; foreign $96. W.B. Saunders Co. (Subsidiary of: Harcourt Brace Jovanovich, Inc.), Curtis Center, Independence Square W., Philadelphia, PA 19106. TEL 215-238-7800. (Subscr. to: 6277 Sea Harbor Dr., 4th Fl, Orlando Fl 32891) Ed. Connie H. Yarbro. adv.; bibl.; charts; illus.; index. **Indexed:** CINAHL, Nurs.Abstr.
—BLDSC shelfmark: 8239.456600.

610.73 — US
▼**SEMINARS IN PERIOPERATIVE NURSING.** 1992. q. W.B. Saunders Co., Journals Department (Subsidiary of: Harcourt Brace Jovanovich Inc.), Independence Sq. W., Philadelphia, PA 19106. TEL 215-238-7800. adv.; circ. 2,000.
Description: Reviews a clinical topic of operating room nursing in each issue.

MEDICAL SCIENCES — NURSES AND NURSING 3287

610.73 UK ISSN 0265-9999
SENIOR NURSE (HARROW). 1986. bi-m. £30 (foreign £45). Scutari Projects Ltd., Viking House, 17-19 Peterborough Rd., Harrow-on-the-Hill, Middlesex HA1 2AX, England. TEL 081-423-1066. FAX 081-423-3867. (Subscr. to: Subscription House, Robjohn's Farm, Vicarage Rd., Finchingfield, Essex CM7 4L, England) Ed. Phyllis Holbrook. **Indexed:** ASSIA, Curr.Cont.
—BLDSC shelfmark: 8241.478000.
Description: For senior clinical nurses and administrative nurse managers.
Refereed Serial

610.73 UK
SENIOR NURSE (LONDON). 1979. m. £17. (Newbourne Group) Home & Law Publishing Ltd., Greater London House, Hampstead Rd., London NW1 7QQ, England. Ed. Barbara Sim Rogers. bk.rev.; illus. **Indexed:** Abstr.Health Care Manage.Stud., CINAHL, Int.Nurs.Ind.
Supersedes (1979-1984): Nursing Focus.

610.73 CN
SERVO. (Text in English, French) 1967. 3/yr. Can.$5. Association of Hospital Auxiliaries of the Province of Quebec, 505 Maisonneuve W., Ste. 400, Montreal, Que. H3A 3C2, Canada. TEL 514-842-4861. FAX 514-873-5415. circ. 300. (back issues avail.)
Description: For hospital auxiliary volunteers.

610.73 JA ISSN 0038-0660
SOGO KANGO; comprehensive nursing quarterly. (Text in Japanese) 1966. q. 3200 Yen. Gendaisha Publishing Co. Ltd., 514 Waseda, Tsurumaki-cho, Shinjukuku, Tokyo 162, Japan. Ed. Yoshio Takeuchi. adv.; bk.rev.; circ. 12,000. **Indexed:** Int.Nurs.Ind.
—BLDSC shelfmark: 3366.385000.

610.73 FR ISSN 0038-0814
SOINS;* pathologie tropicale. 1956. 6/yr. 259 F. (students 223 F.). Centre d'Affaires Integral, 82 rue de Paris, 93804 Epinay-sur-Seine Cedex, France. Ed. Pascal Perrin. adv.; bk.rev.; circ. 2,500. **Indexed:** Int.Nurs.Ind., Pt.de Rep. (1979-).
—BLDSC shelfmark: 8327.117000.

610.73 US ISSN 0038-9986
STAT (MADISON). 1941. bi-m. membership. Wisconsin Nurses Association, 6117 Monona Dr., Madison, WI 53716-3932. FAX 608-221-2788. Ed. Susan Carter. adv.; illus.; circ. 2,700. **Indexed:** C.I.N.L., Int.Nurs.Ind.

610.73 US ISSN 0081-4423
RT74
STATE-APPROVED SCHOOLS OF NURSING - L.P.N. - L.V.N.. 1958. a. $21.95. National League for Nursing, 350 Hudson St., New York, NY 10014. TEL 212-989-9393. **Indexed:** SRI.
Formerly (1959-1966): State-Approved Schools of Practical and Vocational Nursing (ISSN 0095-6570)

610.73 US ISSN 0081-4431
STATE-APPROVED SCHOOLS OF NURSING - R.N.. a. $15.95. National League for Nursing, 350 Hudson St., New York, NY 10014. TEL 212-989-9393. **Indexed:** SRI.

610.73 UK ISSN 0302-1440
STUDY OF NURSING CARE: RESEARCH PROJECT SERIES. 1973. irreg. price varies. Royal College of Nursing, 20 Cavendish Sq., London W1M 0AB, England. TEL 071-409-3333. FAX 071-408-0190. bibl.

610.73 DK ISSN 0049-3856
SYGEPLEJERSKEN. 1901. w. DKK 772($30) Dansk Sygeplejeraad - Danish Nurses' Organization, Vimmelskaftet 38, Postbox 1084, DK-1008 Copenhagen K, Denmark. Ed. Peter Hjorth. adv.; bk.rev.; illus.; circ. 62,000. **Indexed:** Dent.Ind., Ind.Med., Int.Nurs.Ind.
—BLDSC shelfmark: 8579.400000.

610.73 US ISSN 0039-9620
TAR HEEL NURSE. 1939. bi-m. $25 (foreign $50). North Carolina Nurses Association, Box 12025, Raleigh, NC 27605. TEL 919-821-4250. FAX 919-829-5807. Ed. Hazel Browning Moore. adv.; charts; illus.; circ. 3,500. (also avail. in microform from UMI; reprint service avail. from UMI) **Indexed:** CINAHL, Int.Nurs.Ind.

610.73 US ISSN 1055-9620
TECHNOLOGY FOR CRITICAL CARE NURSES. 1986. bi-m. $85 to non-members; members $39.50. (Emergency Care Research Institute) E C R I, 5200 Butler Pike, Plymouth Meeting, PA 19462. TEL 215-825-6000. FAX 215-834-1274. Ed. Robert Hochschild.
Formerly (until 1990): Technology for Nursing (ISSN 0890-9059)
Refereed Serial

610.73 US
TECHNOLOGY FOR EMERGENCY CARE NURSES. bi-m. $39.50 to members. (Emergency Care Research Institute) E C R I, 5200 Butler Pike, Plymouth Meeting, PA 19462. TEL 215-825-6000. FAX 215-834-1275. Ed. Robert Hochschild.
Former titles: Technology for Emergency Medicine (ISSN 8756-8594); Health Devices Update: Emergency Medicine.
Refereed Serial

610.73 FI ISSN 0358-4038
TEHY. (Text in Finnish, Swedish) 1925. s-m. Fmk.370. Union of Health Professionals - Terveydenhuoltoalan Ammattijaresto Tehy, Asemamiehenkatu 4, 00520 Helsinki, Finland. TEL 90-1551. FAX 90-1483038. TELEX 122505. Ed. Sinikka Pitko. adv.; bk.rev.; film rev.; bibl.; charts; illus.; circ. 73,000.
Former titles (until 1981): Laboratoriohoitaja; Lastenhoitajalehti (ISSN 0355-5089); Sairaanhoitaja - Sjukskoterskan (ISSN 0036-3278); Sairaanhoitajalehti.

610.73 US ISSN 0040-3342
TENNESSEE NURSES ASSOCIATION. BULLETIN. 1934. bi-m. $20. Tennessee Nurses Association, 545 Mainstream Dr., Ste. 405, Nashville, TN 37228-1201. TEL 615-254-0350. Ed. Matt Little. adv.; illus.; circ. 3,000. (also avail. in microform from UMI) **Indexed:** CINAHL, Int.Nurs.Ind.

610.73 US ISSN 0095-036X
TEXAS NURSING. 1925. m. $30. Texas Nurses Association, 300 Highland Mall Blvd., Ste. 300, Austin, TX 78752. TEL 512-452-0645. FAX 512-452-0648. Ed. John Levis Brown. adv.; bk.rev.; circ. 6,000. (also avail. in microform; back issues avail.) **Indexed:** CINAHL, Int.Nurs.Ind.
—BLDSC shelfmark: 8799.560000.

610.73 DK ISSN 0900-3002
TIDSKRIFT FOR SYGEPLEJEFORSKNING. 1985. s-a. DKK 125 (typically set in Jan.). Dansk Selskab for Sygeplejeforskning - Danish Nursing Research Society, Postboks 37, 2930 Klampenborg, Denmark. Ed. Bente Kristensen. adv.; bk.rev.; circ. 400.

610.73 NE
TIJDSCHRIFT VOOR VERZORGENDEN. 1968. m. fl.47,50. Uitgeversmaatschappij De Tijdstroom b.v, Postbus 14, 7240 BA Lochem, Netherlands. TEL 05730-53651. FAX 05730-56724. adv.; bk.rev.; tr.lit.; index; circ. 10,050. **Indexed:** Int.Nurs.Ind.
Formerly: Tijdschrift voor Bejaarden-, Kraam- en Ziekenverzorging (ISSN 0049-3880)

610.73 NE
TIJDSCHRIFT VOOR ZIEKENVERPLEGING. Short title: T v Z. 1890. fortn. fl.99.50. (Stichting Redactie Tijdschriften voor Verpleegkundigen en Verzorgenden - National Nurses Association of the Netherlands) Uitgeversmaatschappij De Tijdstroom b.v., Postbus 14, 7240 BA Lochem, Netherlands. TEL 05730-53651. FAX 05730-56724. adv.; bk.rev.; charts; illus.; index; circ. 23,000. **Indexed:** C.I.S. Abstr., Dent.Ind., Int.Nurs.Ind.
Formerly: Stichting Tijdschriften voor Verpleegkundigen en Verzorgenden. Jaarboekje.

610.73 US ISSN 0194-5181
TODAY'S O R NURSE. 1979. m. $30 to individuals; institutions $40. Slack, Inc., 6900 Grove Rd., Thorofare, NJ 08086. TEL 609-848-1000. FAX 609-853-5991. Ed. Rose Marie McWilliams. adv.; bk.rev.; circ. 8,000. (back issues avail.) **Indexed:** CINAHL, Dent.Ind., Int.Nurs.Ind., Nurs.Abstr.
—BLDSC shelfmark: 8859.764000.

610.73 BL ISSN 0080-6234
UNIVERSIDADE DE SAO PAULO. ESCOLA DE ENFERMAGEM. REVISTA. 1967. q. $70. Universidade de Sao Paulo, Escola de Enfermagem, Av. Dr. Eneas de Carvalho Aguiar, 419, SP, Caixa Postal 5751, 05403 Sao Paolo, Brazil. FAX 011-280-8213. index. cum.index; circ. 1,000 (controlled). **Indexed:** Ind.Med., Int.Nurs.Ind.
—BLDSC shelfmark: 7805.530000.

610.73 375 AT ISSN 1036-0700
▼**UNIVERSITY OF TECHNOLOGY, SYDNEY. FACULTY OF NURSING HANDBOOK**. 1990. a. Aus.$5 (foreign Aus.$10). University of Technology, Sdyney, P.O. Box 123, City Campus, Broadway, N.S.W. 2007, Australia. TEL 02-330-1990. FAX 02-330-1551. circ. 3,000.
Description: Contains details about the faculty, schools, staff, courses, and other information pertaining to nursing students.

UROLOGIC NURSING. see *MEDICAL SCIENCES — Urology And Nephrology*

610.73 VI ISSN 0049-6464
V I N A QUARTERLY.* 1964. q. Virgin Islands Nurses Association, Box 2866, Charlotte Amalie, St. Thomas, Virgin Islands. illus. **Indexed:** Int.Nurs.Ind.

610.73 US
V N A NEWSLETTER. 1970. 4/yr. free. Visiting Nurse Association of Brooklyn, Department of Development and Public Relations, 138 South Oxford St., Brooklyn, NY 11217. TEL 718-636-7570. FAX 718-636-7572. Ed. Alan Grossman. charts; illus.; circ. 5,000.
Former titles: V N A Newsletter; In Step with the Visiting Nurse Association of Brooklyn (ISSN 0046-8770)
Description: Covers news and services of the Visiting Nurse Association of Brooklyn.

610.73 CN
V O N CANADA ANNUAL REPORT (YEAR). a. Victorian Order of Nurses for Canada, 5 Blackburn Ave., Ottawa, Ont. K1N 8A2, Canada. TEL 613-233-5694.

610.73 CN
V O N CANADA REPORT. s-a. Victorian Order of Nurses for Canada, 5 Blackburn Ave., Ottawa, Ont. K1N 8A2, Canada. TEL 613-233-5694.
Description: Reports on VON's commitment to innovative community based nursing and other health care and support services.

610.73 NO ISSN 0107-4083
VAARD I NORDEN; sygeplejevidenskab, omvaardnadsforskning og udvikling. (Text in Danish, English, Norwegian, Swedish; abstracts in English) 1981. q. NOK 150 (students NOK 75). Sygeplegerskernes Samarbejde i Norden - Northern Nurses Federation, P.O. Box 2681, St. Hanshaugen, N-131 Oslo 1, Norway. TEL 47-2 38 20 00. FAX 47-2-38-54-47. Ed. Randi Annikki Mortensen. bk.rev.; circ. 2,500.
●Also available online. Vendor(s): BRS, Data-Star, DIALOG.
Also available on CD-ROM. Producer(s): SilverPlatter.
Description: Focuses on development and research in nursing in the Nordic countries.
Refereed Serial

610.73 US
VERMONT REGISTERED NURSE. 1934. 4/yr. $18 (typically set in Dec.). Vermont State Nurses' Association, 500 Dorset St., S. Burlington, VT 05403. Ed. Bonnie Stiles. adv.; circ. 500. **Indexed:** Int.Nurs.Ind.
Description: Association news for members.

610.73 373.246 NE ISSN 0920-3273
VERPLEEGKUNDE; nederlandse-vlaams tijdschrift voor verpleegkundigen. 1986. q. fl.59.50 to individuals; institutions fl.92.50; students fl.39.50. Uitgeversmaatschappij De Tijdstroom b.v., Postbus 14, 7240 BA Lochem, Netherlands. TEL 05730-53651. FAX 05370-56724. adv.; bk.rev.; circ. 2,200.
Description: Covers case studies, research and items of interest to nursing leaders and teachers.

MEDICAL SCIENCES — OBSTETRICS AND GYNECOLOGY

610.73 NE ISSN 0168-9924
VERPLEEGKUNDIG HISTORISCHE CAHIERS. (Text in Dutch) 1983. irreg. price varies. Editions Rodopi B.V., Keizersgracht 302-304, 1016 EX Amsterdam, Netherlands. TEL 020-6227507. FAX 020-6380948. (US and Canada subscr. to: 233 Peachtree St. N.E., Ste. 404, Atlanta GA 30303-1504. TEL 800-225-3998) Ed. M.J. van Lieburg.
  Description: Discusses historical aspects of nursing.

610.73 NE ISSN 0168-9975
VERPLEEGKUNDIG HISTORISCHE MONOGRAFIEEN. 1983. irreg. price varies. Editions Rodopi B.V., Keizersgracht 302-304, 1016 EX Amsterdam, Netherlands. TFI 020-6227507. FAX 020-6380948. (US and Canada subscr. to: 233 Peachtree St. N.E., Ste. 404, Atlanta GA 30303-1504. TEL 800-225-3998) Ed. M.J. van Lieburg. circ. 800.

610.73 RM
VIATA MEDICALA - CADRE MEDII. (Text in Rumanian; summaries in English, French, German, Russian) 1953. 12/yr. $20. Uniunea Societatilor de Stiinte Medicale din Republica Socialista Rumania, Str. Progresului No. 8, Bucharest, Rumania. (Subscr. to: ILEXIM, Str. 13 Decembrie Nr. 3, P.O. Box 136-137, Bucharest, Rumania) Ed.Bd. adv.; bk.rev.; abstr. **Indexed:** Biol.Abstr., C.I.S. Abstr., Dent.Ind., Excerp.Med., Int.Nurs.Ind.
  Formerly: Munca Sanitaria (ISSN 0027-318X)

610.73 US ISSN 0270-7780
VIRGINIA NURSE. vol.34, 1966. q. $20 to non-members. Virginia Nurses Association, 1311 High Point Ave., Richmond, VA 23230. TEL 804-353-7311. FAX 804-353-4328. Ed. Marya Olgas, R.N. adv.; bk.rev.; charts; illus.; circ. 4,000. **Indexed:** CINAHL, Int.Nurs.Ind.
  Formerly: Virginia Nurse Quarterly (ISSN 0042-6695)

VITAL SIGNS PHARMACY SERVICES NEWSLETTER. see *PHARMACY AND PHARMACOLOGY*

616.86 610.73 CI ISSN 0352-3721
VJESNIK MEDICINSKIH SESTARA I MEDICINSKIH TEHNICARA HRVATSKE. (Text in Croatian) 1933. 6/yr. 60 din.($10) Savez Drustava Medicinskih Sestara SR Hrvatske, Butkoviceva 4, 51000 Rijeka, Croatia. Ed. Mirjana Longhino. adv.; bk.rev.; charts; illus.; pat.; index; circ. 13,500.
  Former titles (until 1982): Vjesnik Drustava Medicinskih Sestara i Medicinskih Tehnicara SR Hrvatske (ISSN 0351-6687); (until 1969): Vjesnik Drustva Diplomiranih Sestara NR Hrvatske; Sestrinska Rijec.

610.73 RU ISSN 0042-8825
CODEN: VOMDAQ
VOPROSY OKHRANY MATERINSTVA I DETSTVA/PROBLEMS OF MOTHERHOOD AND CHILDHOOD PROTECTION. 1956. m. 21 Rub.($18.60) (Ministerstvo Zdravookhraneniya R.S.F.S.R.) Izdatel'stvo Meditsina, Petroverigskii pereulok 6-8, 101838 Moscow, Russia. (Subscr. to: Mezhdunarodnaya Kniga, Moscow, G-200, Russia) Ed. N.I. Nisevich. bk.rev.; bibl.; index. **Indexed:** Bibl.Dev.Med.& Child Neur., Biol.Abstr., Chem.Abstr., Excerp.Med., Ind.Med., Nutr.Abstr., World Bibl.Soc.Sec.
  —BLDSC shelfmark: 0043.730000.
  Description: For pediatricians, obstetricians and gynecologists, working in different fields of maternal and child health at maternity and pediatric health centers, hospitals, nurseries and kindergarten, schools, rural medical centers.

610.73 US
WASHINGTON NURSE. 1977. 8/yr. $20 (Canada and Mexico $28; elswhere $35). Washington State Nurses Association, 2505 Second Ave., Ste. 500, Seattle, WA 98121-1460. TEL 206-433-9762. FAX 206-728-2074. Ed. Dennis Burnside. adv.; bk.rev.; circ. 7,000. **Indexed:** CINAHL, Int.Nurs.Ind.
  Supersedes (1929-1977): W S N A Mini Journal.

610.73 US ISSN 0043-1664
WEATHER VANE. 1927. q. $12. West Virginia Nurses Association, Box 1946, Charleston, WV 25327-1946. Ed. Carol S. Fulks. adv.; illus.; circ. 2,200. **Indexed:** CINAHL, Int.Nurs.Ind.
  —BLDSC shelfmark: 9283.850000.

WERKSTATTSCHRIFTEN ZUR SOZIALPSYCHIATRIE. see *PSYCHOLOGY*

610.73 US ISSN 0193-9459
WESTERN JOURNAL OF NURSING RESEARCH. 1979. bi-m. $56 to individuals; institutions $132. Sage Publications, Inc., 2455 Teller Rd., Newbury Park, CA 91320. TEL 805-499-0721. FAX 805-499-0871. Ed. Pamela Brink. adv.; bk.rev.; film rev.; cum.index; circ. 1,600. (back issues avail.) **Indexed:** CINAHL, Ind.Med., Int.Nurs.Ind.
  —BLDSC shelfmark: 9300.835000.

610.73 UK
WESTMINSTER HOSPITAL NURSES' LEAGUE. PUBLICATION. a. membership. Westminster Hospital Nurses' League, Queen Mary Nurses' Home, Page St., Westminster, London SW1, England.

610.73 IE
WORLD OF IRISH NURSING. 8/m. £15. (Irish Nurses' Organization) Maxwell Publicity, 49 Wainsfort Park, Dublin 6, Ireland. TEL 353-1-904168. FAX 351-1-900834. TELEX 01247 IMILEI. Ed. P.J. Modden. circ. 14,000. (processed) **Indexed:** ASSIA, CINAHL, Int.Nurs.Ind.
  Incorporates: Irish Nurses' Journal (ISSN 0021-1338); **Formerly:** Irish Nursing and Hospital World.

610.73 US
WYOMING NURSE. 1926. 4/yr. $15. Wyoming Nurses Association, 1603 Capitol Ave., No. 305, Cheyenne, WY 82001. TEL 307-635-3955. Ed. Peggy Pouppirt. adv.; bk.rev.; circ. 6,000. (processed)
  Formerly: Wyoming Nurses Newsletter (ISSN 0084-3164)

610.73 ZA
ZAMBIA NURSE. 1965. 3/yr. K.5. (Zambia Nurses Association) Mission Press, Ndola, Box 2104, Kitwe, Zambia. Eds. N. Booth, P.S. Chibuye. adv.; bk.rev.; circ. 1,000. **Indexed:** CINAHL, Int.Nurs.Ind.

610.73 XV ISSN 0350-9516
ZDRAVSTVENI OBZORNIK. (Text in Slovenian; summaries in English, Slovenian) 1966. q. 3000 din. Zveza Drustev Medicinskih Sester Slovenije, Vidovdanska 9, 61000 Ljublana, Slovenia. TEL 061 316-055. Ed. Dunja Kalcic. adv.; bk.rev.; index; circ. 5,000. (back issues avail.)

MEDICAL SCIENCES — Obstetrics And Gynecology

see also Women's Health

618 US ISSN 0884-1535
RG33.U6
A B M S DIRECTORY OF CERTIFIED OBSTETRICIANS & GYNECOLOGISTS. 1985. biennial. $44.95. American Board of Medical Specialties, One Rotary Center, Ste. 805, Evanston, IL 60201. TEL 708-491-9091. FAX 708-328-3596. Ed. Dr. J. Lee Dockery.

A C O G CURRENT JOURNAL REVIEW. (American College of Obstetricians and Gynecologists) see *MEDICAL SCIENCES — Abstracting, Bibliographies, Statistics*

618 CN
A C O G INTERACTIONS: PROGRAMS IN CLINICAL DECISION MAKING. (Avail. on floppy disk only) 1988. bi-m. $275 to non-fellows; fellows $325; jr. fellows $175. (American College of Obstetricians and Gynecologists) Decker Periodicals, One James St. S., P.O. Box 620, LCD 1, Hamilton, Ont. L8N 3K7, Canada. TEL 416-522-7017. FAX 416-522-7839. (U.S. addr.: Box 785, Lewiston, NY 14092-0785) Ed. Dr. Honor M. Wolfe. abstr.
  Description: Focuses on a challenging clinical topic in OB-GYN and combines case studies, animated color graphics, management options and references.

618 US
A C O G NEWSLETTER. 1952. m. membership. American College of Obstetricians and Gynecologists, 409 12th St., S.W., Washington, DC 20024. TEL 202-638-5577. FAX 202-484-5107. Ed. Martha S. Taggart. charts; illus.; circ. 31,000 (controlled).

ACTA CHIRURGICA MEDITERRANEA. see *MEDICAL SCIENCES — Surgery*

618 SP
ACTA GINECOLOGICA. Spanish edition of: Journal of Gynaecology and Obstetrics. 1958. 10/yr. 7500 ptas. Editores Medicos, S.A., Paseo de la Castellana, 53, 28046 Madrid, Spain. TEL 442-86-56. FAX 442-80-43. circ. 2,000.

ACTA MEDICA AUXOLOGICA. see *MEDICAL SCIENCES — Endocrinology*

618 SW ISSN 0001-6349
CODEN: AOGSAE
ACTA OBSTETRICA ET GYNECOLOGICA SCANDINAVICA. (Text in English) 1921. 8/yr. SEK 1080($185) incl. supplements. Scandinavian Association of Obstetricians and Gynecologists, Box 443, S-901 09 Umeaa, Sweden. Ed. Ingemar Joelsson. adv.; bk.rev.; bibl.; charts; illus.; cum.index: 1922-1952; 1953-1962; circ. 2,500. (also avail. in microfiche; back issues avail.) **Indexed:** Biol.Abstr., Biotech.Abstr., Chem.Abstr., Curr.Adv.Ecol.Sci., Curr.Cont., Curr.Lit.Fam.Plan., Dairy Sci.Abstr., Excerp.Med., Ind.Med., NRN, Nutr.Abstr., Risk Abstr., Sci.Cit.Ind.
  —BLDSC shelfmark: 0641.600000.
  Formerly: Acta Gynecologica Scandinavica.

618 SW ISSN 0300-8835
CODEN: AGSSAI
ACTA OBSTETRICA ET GYNECOLOGICA SCANDINAVICA. SUPPLEMENT. (Text in English) 10/yr. SEK 80($15) per no.; free to subscribers of Acta Obstetrica et Gynecologica Scandinavica. Scandinavian Association of Obstetricians and Gynecologists, Box 443, S-901 09 Umeaa, Sweden. Ed. Ingemar Joelsson. **Indexed:** Biol.Abstr., Chem.Abstr., Curr.Adv.Ecol.Sci., Dairy Sci.Abstr., Helminthol.Abstr., Ind.Med., Ind.Sci.Rev., Nutr.Abstr.
  —BLDSC shelfmark: 0641.605000.

618 TU
ACTA REPRODUCTIVA TURCICA. (Text and summaries in English) 1979-19??; resumed vol.14, no.1, 1992. q. TL.110000 (effective 1992). Hacettepe University, Department of Gynecology and Obstetrics, Ankara, Turkey. (Co-sponsor: Hacettepe University, Department of Public Health) Ed. Dr. Husnu A. Kisnisci. adv.; charts; illus.; circ. 1,000. **Indexed:** Bibl.Repro., Biol.Abstr.
  Description: Publishing original research studies in obstetrics and gynecology, reproductive biology, public health, and related fields, including endocrinology, pediatrics, surgery and population studies.
  Refereed Serial

ADOLESCENT AND PEDIATRIC GYNECOLOGY. see *MEDICAL SCIENCES — Pediatrics*

618.2 GW
AERZTLICHER RATGEBER FUER WERDENDE UND JUNGE MUETTER; die Schwangerschaft und das wichtige 1. Lebensjahr des Kindes. 1964. 3/yr. free. Wort und Bild Verlag Konradshoehe GmbH, Konradshoehe, 8021 Baierbrunn, Germany. TEL 089-7270-0. FAX 089-7934393. Ed. Rolf Becker. adv.; circ. 240,000 (controlled).

618 BU ISSN 0324-0959
CODEN: AKGIBP
AKUSERSTVO I GINEKOLOGIJA. (Text in Bulgarian; summaries in English, Russian) bi-m. 16 lv. (Ministerstvo na Narodnoto Zdrave) Izdatelstvo Meditsina i Fizkultura, 11 Pl. Slaveikov, Sofia, Bulgaria. (Dist. by: Hemus, 6 Rouski Blvd., 1000 Sofia, Bulgaria) (Co-sponsor: Nauchno Druzestvo po Akuserstvo i Ginekologija) Ed. K. Mirkov. circ. 2,213. **Indexed:** Abstr.Bulg.Sci.Med.Lit., Excerp.Med.
  —BLDSC shelfmark: 0006.300000.

MEDICAL SCIENCES — OBSTETRICS AND GYNECOLOGY

618   RU   ISSN 0300-9092
AKUSHERSTVO I GINEKOLOGIYA/OBSTETRICS AND GYNECOLOGY. (Text in Russian; summaries in English) 1922. m. 20.40 Rub. (Vsesoyuznoe Nauchnoe Obshchestvo Akusherov-Ginekologov) Izdatel'stvo Meditsina, Petroverigskii pereulok 6-8, 101838 Moscow, Russia. (Co-sponsor: Ministerstvo Zdravookhraneniya S.S.S.R.) Ed. A.P. Kirushenkov. bk.rev.; illus.; index. **Indexed:** Abstr.Bulg.Sci.Med.Lit., Biol.Abstr., Chem.Abstr., Dairy Sci.Abstr., Excerp.Med., Ind.Med., INIS Atomind., Nutr.Abstr.
—BLDSC shelfmark: 0006.200000.
    Description: Publishes original and survey papers dealing with modern scientific achievements in the field of obstetrics and gynecology. Covers physiology and pathology of the fetus and the newborn, scientific and practical problems of diagnosis, treatment of complications in pregnancy, labor and gynecologic diseases.

618.1 350   ISSN 0739-4179
ALAN GUTTMACHER INSTITUTE. WASHINGTON MEMO. 1966. bi-w. $54. Alan Guttmacher Institute, 111 Fifth Ave., New York, NY 10003. TEL 212-254-5656. Ed. Terry Sollom. bibl.; index; circ. 2,800. (back issues avail.; reprint service avail. from UMI)
    Formerly: Planned Parenthood - World Population. Washington Memo.

AMERICAN ASSOCIATION OF GENITO-URINARY SURGEONS. TRANSACTIONS. see *MEDICAL SCIENCES — Gastroenterology*

618.1 618.2   US   ISSN 0065-728X
AMERICAN ASSOCIATION OF OBSTETRICIANS AND GYNECOLOGISTS. TRANSACTIONS. 1888. a. (American Association of Obstetricians and Gynecologists) Mosby - Year Book, Inc. (Subsidiary of: Times Mirror Company), 11830 Westline Industrial Dr., St. Louis, MO 63146. TEL 800-325-4117. FAX 314-432-1380. Ed. Dr. James R. Scott. circ. 250.

618.1 618.2   US
AMERICAN GYNECOLOGICAL AND OBSTETRICAL SOCIETY. TRANSACTIONS OF THE A G O S. 1878. a. $55 (foreign $58.50). Mosby - Year Book, Inc. (Subsidiary of: Times Mirror Company), 11830 Westline Industrial Dr., St. Louis, MO 63146. TEL 800-325-4117. FAX 314-432-1380. TELEX 44-2402. circ. 300.
    Formerly: American Gynecological Society. Transactions of the A G S (ISSN 0065-8480)

618.1   US
AMERICAN JOURNAL OF GYNECOLOGIC HEALTH. bi-m. Macor Publishing Co., 116 W. 32nd St., 8th Fl., New York, NY 10001-3212. TEL 212-736-6688. FAX 212-564-1763. Ed. Michael Spence. circ. 32,868.

618   US   ISSN 0002-9378
RG1   CODEN: AJOGAH
AMERICAN JOURNAL OF OBSTETRICS AND GYNECOLOGY. 1920. m. $96 to individuals (foreign $128); institutions $169 (foreign $201); students $42 (foreign $74). (American Gynecological and Obstetrical Society) Mosby - Year Book, Inc. (Subsidiary of: Times Mirror Company), 11830 Westline Industrial Dr., St. Louis, MO 63146. TEL 800-325-4117. FAX 314-432-1380. TELEX 44-2402. (Co-sponsor: American Board of Obstetrics and Gynecology) Ed.Bd. adv.; illus.; s-a. index; circ. 19,843. (also avail. in microform from UMI,PMC; reprint service avail. from UMI) **Indexed:** Anim.Abstr., ASCA, Behav.Med.Abstr., Bibl.Dev.Med.& Child Neur., Biol.Abstr., Biol.Dig., Biotech.Abstr., Chem.Abstr., Curr.Adv.Biochem., Curr.Adv.Cancer Res., Curr.Adv.Cell & Devel.Biol., Curr.Adv.Ecol.Sci., Curr.Adv.Genetics & Molec.Biol., Curr.Cont., Curr.Lit.Fam.Plan., Dairy Sci.Abstr., Dok.Arbeitsmed., Excerp.Med., FAMLI, Helminthol.Abstr., I.P.A., Ind.Med., Ind.Sci.Rev., Ind.Vet., INIS Atomind., Int.Nurs.Ind., NRN, Nutr.Abstr., Rev.Med.& Vet.Mycol., Rev.Plant Path., Risk Abstr., Sage Fam.Stud.Abstr., Sci.Cit.Ind, Vet.Bull.
• Also available online. Vendor(s): BRS.
—BLDSC shelfmark: 0828.700000.
    Description: Articles devoted to obstetrics, gynecology, fetuses, the placenta and the newborn.
Refereed Serial

618.2   US   ISSN 0735-1631
RG600
AMERICAN JOURNAL OF PERINATOLOGY. 1983. bi-m. $75 to individuals; institutions $99. Thieme Medical Publishers, Inc., 381 Park Ave., So., Ste. 1501, New York, NY 10016. TEL 212-683-5088. FAX 212-779-9020. Ed. Peter A.M. Auld, M.D. bk.rev. **Indexed:** Bibl.Dev.Med.& Child Neur., Excerp.Med.
—BLDSC shelfmark: 0829.900000.
Refereed Serial

AMERICAN JOURNAL OF REPRODUCTIVE IMMUNOLOGY AND MICROBIOLOGY. see *MEDICAL SCIENCES — Allergology And Immunology*

616.13   FI   ISSN 0355-9521
          CODEN: ACGYDJ
ANNALES CHIRURGIAE ET GYNAECOLOGIAE. (Supplements avail.) (Text in English) 1946. q. FIM 380($200) (includes irreg. suppl.). Finnish Surgical Society, Maekelaenkatu 2 A, SF-00500 Helsinki, Finland. TEL 358-0-393-0768. FAX 358-0-393-0801. Ed. J. Niinikoski. adv.; bibl.; charts; illus.; circ. 2,000. (also avail. in microform from UMI; back issues avail.) **Indexed:** Biol.Abstr., Chem.Abstr., Curr.Adv.Ecol.Sci., Curr.Cont., Excerp.Med., Ind.Med., INIS Atomind.
—BLDSC shelfmark: 0970.510000.
    Formerly (until vol.65, no.1): Annales Chirurgiae et Gynaecologiae Fenniae (ISSN 0003-3855)

618   IT   ISSN 0300-0087
          CODEN: AOGMAU
ANNALI DI OSTETRICIA GINECOLOGIA MEDICINA PERINATALE. (Summaries in English, Italian) 1879. bi-m. L.70000 (foreign L.100000). (Universita degli Studi di Milano, Clinica Ostetrica e Ginecologica) Istituti Clinici di Perfezionamento, Via Daverio 6, 20122 Milan, Italy. Ed. Prof. G.B. Candiani. adv.; bibl.; charts; illus.; index. **Indexed:** Biol.Abstr., Chem.Abstr., Excerp.Med., Ind.Med.
    Formerly (until 1971): Annali di Ostetricia e Ginecologia (ISSN 0003-4657)

618.1   GW   ISSN 0932-0067
          CODEN: AGOBEJ
ARCHIVES OF GYNECOLOGY AND OBSTETRICS. 1870. 8/yr. (in 2 vols., 4 nos./vol.) DM.718($419) (Deutsche Gesellschaft fuer Gynaekologie) Springer-Verlag, Heidelberger Platz 3, D-1000 Berlin 33, Germany. TEL 030-8207-1. (Also Heidelberg, Tokyo, Vienna, and New York) Ed. H.A. Hirsch. adv.; bibl.; charts; illus.; index. (also avail. in microform from MIM,UMI; back issues avail.; reprint service avail. from ISI) **Indexed:** Anim.Breed.Abstr., Biol.Abstr., Chem.Abstr., Curr.Adv.Cancer Res., Curr.Adv.Cell & Devel.Biol., Curr.Adv.Ecol.Sci., Curr.Cont., Dairy Sci.Abstr., Excerp.Med., Ind.Med., Ind.Sci.Rev., INIS Atomind., NRN, Nutr.Abstr., Sci.Cit.Ind.
—BLDSC shelfmark: 1634.404000.
    Former titles: Archives of Gynecology (ISSN 0170-9925); Archiv fuer Gynaekologie (ISSN 0003-9128)
Refereed Serial

618   IT   ISSN 0004-0126
          CODEN: AOGNAX
ARCHIVIO DI OSTETRICIA E GINECOLOGIA. vol.80, 1975. bi-m. $90. Universita di Napoli, Clinica Ostetrica e Ginecologica, Via S. Andrea delle Dame 2, 80138 Naples, Italy. Ed. Enzo Martella. **Indexed:** Biol.Abstr., Chem.Abstr., Excerp.Med., Ind.Med.

ARHIV ZA ZASTITU MAJKE I DJETETA/ARCHIVES FOR MOTHER AND CHILD HEALTH. see *MEDICAL SCIENCES — Pediatrics*

ASIAN AND PACIFIC WOMEN'S RESOURCE AND ACTION SERIES. see *WOMEN'S INTERESTS*

618   US   ISSN 1051-2446
▼**ASSISTED REPRODUCTION REVIEWS.** 1991. q. $70 to individuals; institutions $95. Williams & Wilkins, 428 E. Preston St., Baltimore, MD 21202. TEL 301-528-4000. FAX 301-528-4321. Ed. Dr. Alan H. DeCherney.
    Description: Publishes reviews covering advances in reproductive medicine directed to obstetricians and gynecologists.

618.2   FR
ASSOCIATION DES SAGES-FEMMES DE LA MATERNITE DE NANCY. BULLETIN. 1946. q. 75 F. Association des Sages-Femmes de l'Ecole d'Accouchement de la Maternite de Nancy, Rue de Docteur-Heydendreich, 54000 Nancy, France. Dir. Mme Poutas. adv.; circ. 1,400.

618   IT   ISSN 0004-7317
ATTUALITA DI OSTETRICIA E GINECOLOGIA. (Text in Italian; summaries in English, French, German, Italian) 1955. bi-m. L.20000. (Universita degli Studi di Padova, Facolta di Medicina e Chirurgia) Societa Editrice Universo, Via G.B. Morgagni 1, 00161 Rome, Italy. Ed. Giuseppe Vecchietti. **Indexed:** Biol.Abstr.

618   US   ISSN 0271-129X
AUDIO-DIGEST OBSTETRICS - GYNECOLOGY. 1954. s-m. $168. Audio-Digest Foundation (Subsidiary of: California Medical Association), 1577 E. Chevy Chase Dr., Glendale, CA 91206. TEL 213-245-8505. FAX 818-240-7379. Ed. Claron L. Oakley. circ. controlled. (audio cassette)
Refereed Serial

618   AT   ISSN 0004-8666
          CODEN: AZOGBS
AUSTRALIAN AND NEW ZEALAND JOURNAL OF OBSTETRICS AND GYNAECOLOGY. 1961. q. Aus.$55 (foreign Aus.$60). Royal Australian College of Obstetricians & Gynecologists, 254 Albert St., Melbourne, Vic. 3002, Australia. TEL 03-471-1699. FAX 03-419-0672. (Co-sponsor: Arthur Wilson Memorial Foundation) Ed. Norman A. Beischer. adv.; bk.rev.; charts; illus.; index; circ. 4,500. (back issues avail.) **Indexed:** Bibl.Dev.Med.& Child Neur., Biol.Abstr., Curr.Adv.Ecol.Sci., Curr.Cont., Excerp.Med., Helminthol.Abstr., Ind.Med., NRN, Nutr.Abstr., So.Pac.Per.Ind.
—BLDSC shelfmark: 1796.890000.

649   US
▼**BABY ON THE WAY.** 1990. a. Time Venture Publishing Inc., Baby Talk, 636 Ave. of the Americas, New York, NY 10011. TEL 212-989-8181. adv. contact: Kevin Walsh. circ. 1,700,000.
    Description: Guide to a healthy pregnancy, labor and delivery, and taking care of a newborn.

618.2   UK
BAILLIERE'S MIDWIVES' DICTIONARY. 1951. irreg., vol.7, 1983. £2.95. Bailliere Tindall, 24-28 Oval Rd., London MW1 7DX, England.

574.33 618   SZ   ISSN 0006-3126
RJ251   CODEN: BNEOBV
BIOLOGY OF THE NEONATE; fetal and neonatal research. (Text in English) 1959. m. (2 vols./yr.). 439 Fr.($293) per vol. S. Karger AG, Allschwilerstr. 10, P.O. Box, CH-4009 Basel, Switzerland. TEL 061-3061111. FAX 061-3061234. TELEX CH 962652. Ed. J.P. Relier. adv.; bibl.; charts; illus.; circ. 1,150. (also avail. in microfilm from RPI) **Indexed:** Anim.Breed.Abstr., Bibl.Dev.Med.& Child Neur., Biol.Abstr., Chem.Abstr., Curr.Adv.Ecol.Sci., Curr.Cont., Dairy Sci.Abstr., Dent.Ind., Excerp.Med., Ind.Med., Ind.Sci.Rev., Ind.Vet., Nutr.Abstr., Pig News & Info., Sci.Cit.Ind, Vet.Bull.
—BLDSC shelfmark: 2087.100000.
    Formerly: Biologia Neonatorum.
    Description: Highlights aspects of embryology.

301.4 618   US   ISSN 0730-7659
RG651
BIRTH; issues in perinatal care and education. 1973. 4/yr. $30 to individuals; institutions $65. Blackwell Scientific Publications Inc., Three Cambridge Center, Ste. 208, Cambridge, MA 02142-1413. TEL 617-225-0401. FAX 617-225-0412. Ed. Donny Young. adv.; bk.rev.; circ. 3,500. (also avail. in microform from UMI; back issues avail.; reprint services avail. from UMI, ISI) **Indexed:** CINAHL, Curr.Cont., Dok.Arbeitsmed., Ind.Med., Int.Nurs.Ind., NRN, Psychol.Abstr.
—BLDSC shelfmark: 2094.081000.
    Formerly (until 1981): Birth and the Family Journal (ISSN 0098-860X)
    Description: Covers education and technology regarding childbirth for childbirth educators, midwives and physicians.

MEDICAL SCIENCES — OBSTETRICS AND GYNECOLOGY

618 AT ISSN 1032-9625
BIRTH. 1989. a. Aus.$5.95. Magazine House Pty. Ltd., P.O. Box 1067, Crows Nest, N.S.W. 2065, Australia. TEL 02-438-2399. FAX 02-436-3014. Ed. Carol Fallows. adv.; bk.rev.; circ. 40,000.
Description: Offers important information for expectant mothers.

618 US ISSN 0890-3255
BIRTH GAZETTE. 1977. q. $30. Practicing Midwife Foundation, 41, The Farm, Summertown, TN 38483. TEL 615-964-2519. Ed. Ina May Gaskin. adv.; bk.rev.; illus.; stat.; circ. 2,000.
Formerly (until vol.11, no.4, 1985): Practicing Midwife (ISSN 0733-8317)
Description: Covers midwifery, childbirth issues and access to maternity care.

618 US
BIRTH NOTES. 1976-1984; resumed 1985. q. $20. Association for Childbirth at Home, International (A C H I), 166 S. Louise, Glendale, CA 91205. TEL 213-667-0839. Ed. Tonya Brooks. adv.; bk.rev.; circ. 10,000 (controlled).

618 US ISSN 0734-3124
RG658
BIRTH PSYCHOLOGY BULLETIN. 1979. s-a. $9. Association for Birth Psychology, 444 E. 82nd St., New York, NY 10028. TEL 212-988-6617. Ed. Leslie Feher. bk.rev.; circ. 500. (back issues avail.) *Indexed:* ERIC, Psychol.Abstr.
—BLDSC shelfmark: 2094.092800.
Description: Clinical, theoretical, and empirical articles on pregnancy, birth, and the neonatal period.

618 CN
▼**BOUNTY PREGNANCY GUIDE.** French edition: Guide Bounty de la Grossesse. 1990. s-a. Bounty Family Publications Ltd., 746 Warden Ave., No. 2, Scarborough, Ont. M1L 4A2, Canada. TEL 416-750-1165. FAX 416-752-4137. Ed. Gerri Cansick. adv.; circ. 240,000 (180,000 Eng.ed., 60,000 Fr.ed.).

618.1 UK ISSN 0960-9776
▼**THE BREAST.** 1992. q. £119($219) Churchill Livingstone Medical Journals, Robert Stevenson House, 1-3 Baxter's Pl., Leith Walk, Edinburgh EA1 3AF, Scotland. TEL 031-556-2424. FAX 031-558-1278. TELEX 727511. (Subscr. to: Longman Group, Journals Subscr. Dept., P.O. Box 77, Fourth Ave., Harlow, Essex CM19 5AA, England; U.S. subscr. to: Churchill Livingstone, 650 Ave. of the Americas, New York, NY 10011. TEL 212-206-5000) Ed. J. Michael Dixon. abstr.; bibl.
—BLDSC shelfmark: 2277.492700.
Description: Covers the physiology of the normal breast and the aetiology, biology, investigation, medical and surgical treatment and management of benign and malignant breast diseases.

618 016 UK ISSN 0306-5456
CODEN: BJOGAS
BRITISH JOURNAL OF OBSTETRICS & GYNAECOLOGY. 1902. m. £80 (foreign £88.50). (Royal College of Obstetricians and Gynaecologists) Blackwell Scientific Publications Ltd., Osney Mead, Oxford OX2 0EL, England. TEL 0865-240201. FAX 0865-721205. TELEX 83355-MEDBOK-G. Ed. D.B. Paintin. adv.; bk.rev.; abstr.; bibl.; charts; illus.; index; circ. 4,800. (also avail. in microform from UMI,PMC; back issues avail., reprint service avail. from UMI) *Indexed:* ASCA, Bibl.Dev.Med.& Child Neur., Biol.Abstr., Biotech.Abstr., Chem.Abstr., Curr.Adv.Cancer Res., Curr.Adv.Ecol.Sci., Curr.Cont., Curr.Lit.Fam.Plan., Dairy Sci.Abstr., Dent.Ind., Excerp.Med., Helminthol.Abstr., I.P.A., Ind.Med., Ind.Sci.Rev., Ind.Vet., NRN, Nutr.Abstr, Risk Abstr., Sci.Cit.Ind, Vet.Bull.
●Also available online. Vendor(s): BRS.
—BLDSC shelfmark: 2312.300000.
Formerly: Journal of Obstetrics and Gynaecology of the British Commonwealth (ISSN 0022-3204)

618.1 GW ISSN 0068-337X
BUECHEREI DES FRAUENARZTES. (Beginning 1972, supplements Zeitschrift fuer Geburtshilfe und Perinatologie) 1956. irreg., vol.38, 1991. price varies. Ferdinand Enke Verlag, Postfach 101254, 7000 Stuttgart 10, Germany. TEL 0711-8931-0. FAX 0711-8931-419. TELEX 07252275-GTV-D. Ed. G. Martius. *Indexed:* Chem.Abstr.

618 CN ISSN 1183-2517
CANADIAN JOURNAL OF OB-GYN & WOMEN'S HEALTH CARE; for physicians dealing with today's issues. 1984. 6/yr. $60. Rodar Publishing Inc., 19180 Trans Canada Hwy., Baie d'Urfe, Que. H9X 3T9, Canada. TEL 514-457-2673. FAX 514-457-2679. adv.; circ. 17,000 (controlled). *Indexed:* CMI.
Former titles (until Jun. 1991): Canadian Journal of Ob-Gyn (ISSN 0843-4255) & Contemporary Ob-Gyn.
Description: Covers all areas of reproductive medicine, childbirth, sexually transmitted diseases, menopause, PMS, and ovarian cancer.

618 CS ISSN 0374-6852
CESKOSLOVENSKA GYNEKOLOGIE. (Text in Czech or Slovak; summaries in English and Russian) 1936. 10/yr. $62.60. (Ceskoslovenska Spolecnost Gynekologicka a Porodnicka) Avicenum, Czechoslovak Medical Press, Malostranske nam. 28, 118 02 Prague 1, Czechoslovakia. (Dist. by: Artia, Ve Smeckach 30, 111 27 Prague 1, Czechoslovakia) (Co-sponsor: Ceskoslovenska Lekarska Spolecnost J. Ev. Purkyne) Ed. Dr. K. Balak. bk.rev. *Indexed:* Biol.Abstr., Excerp.Med., Ind.Med.
—BLDSC shelfmark: 3122.220000.

618 CE
CEYLON COLLEGE OF OBSTETRICIANS AND GYNAECOLOGISTS. JOURNAL. (Text in English) q. Rs.25. Ceylon College of Obstetricians and Gynaecologists, C.M.A. House, 6 Wijerama Mawatha, Colombo 7, Sri Lanka.

CHATELAINE'S NEW MOTHER; including new father news. see *CHILDREN AND YOUTH — About*

618 US
CHILDBIRTH (YEAR). 1984. a. Cahners Publishing Company (New York), Childcare Group (Subsidiary of: Reed International PLC), Division of Reed Publishing (USA) Inc., 475 Park Ave. S., New York, NY 10016-6901. TEL 212-779-1999. FAX 212-545-5337. (Dist. by: Neodata Services, Box 2971, Boulder, CO 80329) Ed. Marsha Rehns. adv.; circ. 2,000,000.
Description: Answers the questions of couples approaching the birth of their child. The magazine's four sections include: the last three months of pregnancy, getting ready for baby, labor and birth, and life with baby.

618.2 375 US
▼**CHILDBIRTH INSTRUCTOR.** 1990. q. $14.97. Cradle Publishing, Inc., 145 E. 27th St. 4G, New York, NY 10016. TEL 212-447-6746. FAX 212-509-9805. adv.; circ. 15,000.
Description: Contains information, ideas and advice on teaching techniques for professionals who educate parents for the childbirth and-or new parent experience.

618.45 US
CHILDBIRTH WITHOUT PAIN EDUCATION ASSOCIATION. MEMO. 1960. bi-m. membership. Childbirth Without Pain Education Association, 20134 Snowden, Detroit, MI 48235. TEL 313-345-9850. Dir. Flora Hommel. adv.; bk.rev.; tr.mk.; circ. 3,000. (processed)
Formerly: Childbirth Without Pain Education Association. Newsletter (ISSN 0009-4048)

618 SP ISSN 0210-573X
CODEN: CIGODJ
CLINICA E INVESTIGACION EN GINECOLOGIA Y OBSTETRICIA. (Text in Spanish; summaries in English) 1974. m. (10/yr.) 5500 ptas.($57) (free to qualified personnel). Ediciones Doyma S.A., Travesera de Gracia 17-21, 08021 Barcelona, Spain. TEL 200 07 11. FAX 209-11-36. TELEX 51964 INK-E. Ed. J. Esteban-Altirriba. adv.: page 135000 ptas.; trim 210 x 280; adv. contact: Cristina Garrote. circ. 3,500. (reprint service avail. from UMI) *Indexed:* Excerp.Med., Ind.Med.Esp.
—BLDSC shelfmark: 3286.202000.
Description: Covers the early detection of gynecological diseases, the improvement of family planning methods, the treatment of sterility and infertility, and the mother-child relationship during pregnancy.

618 IT ISSN 0393-7607
CLINICA OSTETRICA E GINECOLOGICA. q. L.150000($160) Piccin Editore, Via Altinate 107, 35100 Padua, Italy. TEL 049-655566. TELEX 432074 PICCIN I. (reprint service avail. from UMI)

CLINICAL AND EXPERIMENTAL HYPERTENSION. PART B: HYPERTENSION IN PREGNANCY. see *MEDICAL SCIENCES*

618 IT ISSN 0390-6663
CODEN: CEOGA4
CLINICAL AND EXPERIMENTAL OBSTETRICS AND GYNECOLOGY. (Includes: Journal of Gynaecological Endocrinology and Journal of Foetal Medicine) (Text and summaries in English) 1974. q. $150 to individuals; institutions $250. Studi Ostetrico Ginecologici s.r.l., Galleria Storione 2-A, 35128 Padua, Italy. TEL 049-8758644. Ed. Prof. Antonio Onnis. (back issues avail.) *Indexed:* Biol.Abstr., Chem.Abstr, Excerp.Med., Ind.Med.
—BLDSC shelfmark: 3286.251900.

618 US ISSN 1043-0660
CLINICAL CONSULTATIONS IN OBSTETRICS AND GYNECOLOGY. 1989. q. W.B. Saunders Co., Curtis Center, Independence Square W., Philadelphia, PA 19106. TEL 215-238-7800. Ed. Ronald A. Chez, M.D.
—BLDSC shelfmark: 3286.269200.
Description: Aimed at obstetrics and gynecology practitioners. Each issue reviews a single topic in the care of patients.

CLINICAL CYTOGENETICS. see *BIOLOGY — Genetics*

618 UK ISSN 0962-8827
▼**CLINICAL DYSMORPHOLOGY.** 1992. q. £95 for EC (US & Canada $170). Chapman & Hall, 2-6 Boundary Row, London SE1 8HN, England. TEL 071-865-0066. FAX 071-522-9623. (Dist. by: International Thomson Publishing Services, Ltd., N. Way, Andover, Hampshire SP10 5BE, England. TEL 0264-33-2424; US addr.: Chapman & Hall, 29 W. 35th St., New York, NY 1001-2291. TEL 212-244-3336) Ed.Bd. bk.rev.; illus.
—BLDSC shelfmark: 3286.273700.
Description: Devoted to publishing reports of multiple congenital anomaly syndromes, original studies and review articles on aetiology, clinical delineation, genetic mapping and molecular embryology of birth defects.

618 US ISSN 0009-9201
RG101 CODEN: COGYAK
CLINICAL OBSTETRICS AND GYNECOLOGY. 1958. q. $80 to individuals (foreign $95); institutions $120 (foreign $140). J.B. Lippincott Co., E. Washington Sq., Philadelphia, PA 19105. TEL 215-238-4200. Ed. Roy Pitkin, M.D. circ. 11,526. (also avail. in microform from UMI) *Indexed:* Bibl.Dev.Med.& Child Neur., Biol.Abstr., Chem.Abstr, Curr.Adv.Cancer Res., Curr.Adv.Ecol.Sci., Curr.Cont., Dok.Arbeitsmed., Excerp.Med., Hosp.Lit.Ind., Ind.Med., Ind.Sci.Rev., INIS Atomind.
—BLDSC shelfmark: 3286.316000.
Refereed Serial

618 US
CLINICAL PERSPECTIVES IN OBSTETRICS AND GYNECOLOGY. 1983. irreg. price varies. Springer-Verlag, 175 Fifth Ave., New York, NY 10010. TEL 212-460-1500. (Also Berlin, Heidelberg, Tokyo and Vienna)

618. US ISSN 1043-3198
CODEN: CPGYEV
▼**CLINICAL PRACTICE OF GYNECOLOGY.** 1991. 3/yr. Elsevier Science Publishing Co., Inc. (New York), 655 Ave. of Americas, New York, NY 10010. Ed. Michael S. Baggish.
—BLDSC shelfmark: 3286.333650.
Description: Focusing exclusively on gynecology and covering everything from diagnosis to treatment.
Refereed Serial

618 AT ISSN 0725-556X
CODEN: CRFEDD
CLINICAL REPRODUCTION AND FERTILITY. 1982. bi-m. 160. (Fertility Society of Australia) C.S.I.R.O., 314 Albert St., E. Melbourne, Vic. 3002, Australia. Ed. W. Jones. adv.; index; circ. 500. *Indexed:* Bibl.Repro., Biol.Abstr, Chem.Abstr, Excerp.Med., Ind.Med.

618 SP ISSN 0009-9333
CLINICAS OBSTETRICAS Y GINECOLOGICAS DE NORTEAMERICA. Spanish translation of: Clinical Obstetrics and Gynecology. 1964. 4/yr. 17596 ptas.($129) (effective 1990). Interamericana de Espana, S.A., Division de Ciencias de la Salud de McGraw-Hill, Calle Manuel Ferrero, 13, 28036 Madrid, Spain. TEL 315-0340. FAX 733-6627. charts; illus.; cum.index.

MEDICAL SCIENCES — OBSTETRICS AND GYNECOLOGY

618 US ISSN 0095-5108
CODEN: CLPEDL
CLINICS IN PERINATOLOGY. 1974. q. $69. W.B. Saunders Co., Curtis Center, Independence Square W., Philadelphia, PA 19106. TEL 215-238-7800. Ed. Barton Dudlick. (reprint service avail. from UMI, ISI) **Indexed:** Bibl.Dev.Med.& Child Neur., Biol.Abstr., Chem.Abstr, Curr.Adv.Ecol.Sci., Dent.Ind., Excerp.Med., Helminthol.Abstr., Ind.Med., Ind.Sci.Rev., INIS Atomind., Sci.Cit.Ind.
—BLDSC shelfmark: 3286.585000.

CLIO; eine feministische Zeitschrift zur gesundheitlichen Selbsthilfe. see WOMEN'S HEALTH

COMBINED CUMULATIVE INDEX TO OBSTETRICS AND GYNECOLOGY. see MEDICAL SCIENCES — Abstracting, Bibliographies, Statistics

618 649 US ISSN 0829-8564
COMPLEAT MOTHER; the magazine of pregnancy, birth and breastfeeding. 1985. q. Can.$12. P.O. Box 209, Minot, ND 58702. TEL 701-852-2822. Ed. Jody McLaughlin. adv.; bk.rev.; circ. 20,000.
Description: Supports home birth, midwifery, cloth diapers, breastfeeding and the nurturing of self and family.

618 US ISSN 1050-9615
▼**CONTEMPORARY MANAGEMENT IN OBSTETRICS AND GYNECOLOGY.** 1992. q. $65 to individuals (foreign $85); institutions $85 (foreign $105). Churchill Livingstone Medical Journals, 650 Ave. of the Americas, New York, NY 10011.
TEL 212-206-5040. FAX 212-727-7808. TELEX 662266. (Dist. by: Transaction Publishers, Department 3091, Rutgers University, New Brunswick, NJ 08903. TEL 909-932-2280) Ed. Dr. Joe Leigh Simpson.

618 US ISSN 0090-3159
RG1
CONTEMPORARY OB-GYN. 1973. m. (plus 3 special issues). $65 (foreign $80). Medical Economics Company Inc., 680 Kinderkamack Rd., Oradell, NJ 07649. TEL 800-526-4870. FAX 201-262-2760. Ed. James E. Swan. adv.; charts; illus.; stat.; index; circ. 39,255. (also avail. in microfilm) **Indexed:** Curr.Cont., Curr.Lit.Fam.Plan.
—BLDSC shelfmark: 3425.196000.
Description: Includes practical advice by leading authorities in the ob-gyn field emphasizing solutions to common clinical problems.
Refereed Serial

618.1 UK ISSN 0953-9182
CODEN: CROGEV
CONTEMPORARY REVIEWS IN OBSTETRICS AND GYNAECOLOGY. 4/yr. £95 in UK and Europe; elsewhere £105. Butterworth - Heinemann Ltd. (Subsidiary of: Reed International PLC), Linacre House, Jordan Hill, Oxford OX2 8DP, England. TEL 0865-310366. FAX 0865-310898. TELEX 83111 BHPOXF G. (Subscr. to: Turpin Transactions Ltd., Distribution Centre, Blackhorse Rd., Letchworth, Herts SG6 1HN, England. TEL 0462-672555) Eds. Geoffrey V.P. Chamberlain, James Owen Drife. adv.; bk.rev. (also avail. in microform from UMI; back issues avail.)
—BLDSC shelfmark: 3425.300100.
Description: Aims to provide an up-to-date source on the latest trends and developments in obstetrics and gynaecology.
Refereed Serial

CONTRACEPTION. see BIRTH CONTROL

618.1 618.2 SZ ISSN 0304-4246
CODEN: CGOBD6
CONTRIBUTIONS TO GYNECOLOGY AND OBSTETRICS. (Text in English) 1950. irreg. (approx. a.). price varies. S. Karger AG, Allschwilerstr. 10, P.O. Box, CH-4009 Basel, Switzerland. TEL 061-3061111. FAX 061-3061234. TELEX CH 962652. Ed. P.J. Keller. (reprint service avail. from ISI; back issues avail.) **Indexed:** Biol.Abstr., Chem.Abstr., Curr.Adv.Ecol.Sci., Curr.Cont., Excerp.Med., Ind.Med.
—BLDSC shelfmark: 3458.610000.
Formerly: Advances in Obstetrics and Gynaecology (ISSN 0065-2997)

618 US ISSN 1051-077X
▼**CURRENT OBSTETRIC MEDICINE.** 1991. biennial. $65.95. Mosby - Year Book, Inc. (Chicago) (Subsidiary of: Times Mirror Company), 200 N. LaSalle St., Chicago, IL 60601-1080.
TEL 312-726-9733. FAX 312-726-6075. TELEX 206155. (Subscr. to: 11830 Westline Industrial Dr., St. Louis, MO 63146) Ed. Dr. Richard Lee.
Description: Geared toward the general physician. Surveys developments in obstetric medicine through a synopsis of the past twelve months of medical literature.

618 UK ISSN 0957-5847
▼**CURRENT OBSTETRICS AND GYNAECOLOGY.** 1991. q. £39($79) to individuals; institutions £89($180). Churchill Livingstone Medical Journals, Robert Stevenson House, 1-3 Baxter's Pl., Leith Walk, Edinburgh EH1 3AF, Scotland. TEL 031-556-2424. FAX 031-558-1278. (Subscr. to: Longman Publishing Group, Journals Subscr. Dept., P.O. Box 77, Harlow, Essex CM19 5AA, England. TEL 0279-623760; U.S. subscr. to: Churchill Livingstone, 650 Ave. of the Americas, New York, NY 10011. TEL 212-206-5000) Ed. E.M. Symonds.
—BLDSC shelfmark: 3500.715000.
Description: Provides reviews on themes of current interest and educational values for both practicing clinicians and training grade staff; includes self-evaluation sections for the examination candidate.

CURRENT OPINION IN OBSTETRICS & GYNECOLOGY. see MEDICAL SCIENCES — Abstracting, Bibliographies, Statistics

618 US ISSN 8756-0410
CODEN: CPOIEN
CURRENT PROBLEMS IN OBSTETRICS AND GYNECOLOGY AND FERTILITY. 1977. bi-m. $65 to individuals (foreign $85); institutions $90 (foreign $110); students $39 (foreign $59) (effective Jan. 1992). Mosby - Year Book, Inc. (Subsidiary of: Times Mirror Company), 11830 Westline Industrial Dr., St. Louis, MO 63146. TEL 800-325-4177. Ed. Robert L. Barbieri. cum.index; circ. 1,600. (also avail. in microform from UMI; reprint service avail. from UMI) **Indexed:** Excerp.Med., Ind.Med.
Formerly: Current Problems in Obstetrics and Gynecology (ISSN 0147-1988)
Description: Provides clinical monographic reviews in obstetrics, gynecology and fertility.

618 GW ISSN 0723-8029
DEUTSCHE GESELLSCHAFT FUER GYNAEKOLOGIE UND GEBURTSHILFE. MITTEILUNGEN. 1977. q. DM.48. Demeter Verlag, Wuermstr. 13, 8032 Graefelfing, Germany. TEL 089-852033. FAX 089-8543347. circ. 3,000.

618 GW ISSN 0012-026X
DEUTSCHE HEBAMMEN-ZEITSCHRIFT; Fachblatt fuer Hebammen und Entbindungspfleger. 1886. m. DM.63. (Bund Deutscher Hebammen) Elwin Staude Verlag GmbH, Fuchsrain 18A, 3000 Hannover 51, Germany. Ed. Dr. H. W. Vasterling. adv.; bk.rev.; charts; illus.; stat.; index; circ. 9,200.
—BLDSC shelfmark: 3568.700000.

618.2 IE ISSN 0378-3782
RG600 CODEN: EHDEDN
EARLY HUMAN DEVELOPMENT; an international, scientifically innovative journal concerned with the continuity of foetal and postnatal life. 1977. 12/yr.(in 4 vols.; 3 nos./vol.). $630 (effective 1992). Elsevier Scientific Publishers Ireland Ltd., P.O. Box 85, Limerick, Ireland. TEL 061-61944. FAX 061-62144. TELEX 72191 ENH EI. (Subscr. in U.S. and Canada to: Elsevier Science Publishing Co., Inc., Box 882, Madison Sq. Sta., New York, NY 10159. TEL 212-989-5800) Ed. David R. Harvey. adv.; bk.rev. (also avail. in microform from RPI)
Indexed: Abstr.Hyg., Bibl.Dev.Med.& Child Neur., Biol.Abstr., Chem.Abstr, CINAHL, Curr.Adv.Cell & Devel.Biol., Curr.Adv.Ecol.Sci., Curr.Cont., Dairy Sci.Abstr., Excerp.Med, Ind.Med., Ind.Sci.Rev., Nutr.Abstr., Psychol.Abstr., Sci.Cit.Ind, Trop.Dis.Bull.
—BLDSC shelfmark: 3642.983000.
Description: Publishes original research papers with particular emphasis on the continuum between foetal life and the perinatal period; aspects of postnatal growth influenced by early events; and the safeguarding of the quality of human survival.
Refereed Serial

618 US
▼**EMBARAZO/PREGNANCY.** (Text in Spanish) 1990. s-a. Gruner & Jahr U.S.A. Publishing, 685 Third Ave., New York, NY 10017. TEL 212-878-8700. Ed. Mirta Rodriguez.
Description: Provides information for expectant Hispanic mothers.

ENDOCRINOLOGIA IUGOSLAVICA. see MEDICAL SCIENCES — Endocrinology

618.1 US ISSN 0897-1870
ENDOMETRIOSIS ASSOCIATION NEWSLETTER. 1980. bi-m. $25. Endometriosis Association, Inc., 8585 N. 76th Pl., Milwaukee, WI 53223.
TEL 414-355-2200. FAX 414-355-6065. Ed. Mary Lou Ballweg. bk.rev.; circ. 10,000. (reprint service avail.)
Formerly: Endometriosis Association International Newsletter.
Description: Discusses endometriosis, a disease affecting women in their reproductive years.

EUROPEAN JOURNAL OF GYNECOLOGICAL ONCOLOGY. see MEDICAL SCIENCES — Cancer

618 NE ISSN 0301-2115
CODEN: EOGRAL
EUROPEAN JOURNAL OF OBSTETRICS, GYNECOLOGY AND REPRODUCTIVE BIOLOGY. (Supplement avail. (ISSN 0921-8750)) 1971. 15/yr.(in 5 vols.; 3 nos./vol.). fl.1810 (effective 1992). (European Association of Gynaecologists and Obstetricians) Elsevier Science Publishers B.V., P.O. Box 211, 1000 AE Amsterdam, Netherlands.
TEL 020-5803911. FAX 020-5803598. TELEX 18582 ESPA NL. (Subscr. in U.S. and Canada to: Elsevier Science Publishing Co., Inc., Box 882, Madison Sq. Sta., New York, NY 10159. TEL 212-989-5800) Ed. Dr. T.K.A.B. Eskes. adv.; bk.rev.; bibl.; charts; illus. (also avail. in microform from RPI) **Indexed:** Biol.Abstr., Chem.Abstr., Curr.Adv.Cancer Res., Curr.Adv.Ecol.Sci., Curr.Cont., Dairy Sci.Abstr., Dent.Ind., Excerp.Med., Ind.Med., Ind.Sci.Rev., NRN, Nutr.Abstr., Sci.Cit.Ind.
Formerly: European Journal of Obstetrics and Gynecology (ISSN 0028-2243)
Description: Serves both the clinical practitioner and researcher by publishing studies, case reports and reviews of developments, as well as basic biochemical, physiological, embryological and genetic research related to human reproduction.
Refereed Serial

618 US ISSN 0014-472X
EXPECTING. 1967. q. free. Gruner & Jahr U.S.A. Publishing, 685 Third Ave., New York, NY 10017. TEL 212-878-8700. Ed. Evelyn A. Podsiadlo. adv.; bk.rev.; illus.; circ. 1,300,000 (controlled). (also avail. in microform from UMI; reprint service avail. from UMI)

FAMILY PLANNING ASSOCIATION OF FIJI. NEWS. see BIRTH CONTROL

FAMILY PLANNING PERSPECTIVES. see BIRTH CONTROL

618 RU ISSN 0014-9772
FEL'DSHER I AKUSHERKA/FELDSCHER AND MIDWIFE. 1936. m. 10.20 Rub.($7.20) (Ministerstvo Zdravookhraneniya R.S.F.R.) Izdatel'stvo Meditsina, Petroverigskii pereulok 6-8, 101838 Moscow, Russia. Ed. V.K. Kuznetsov. illus.; index. (reprint service avail. from UMI) **Indexed:** Biol.Abstr., Chem.Abstr., Curr.Dig.Sov.Press, Dent.Ind., Int.Nurs.Ind.
—BLDSC shelfmark: 0389.300000.
Description: Publishes material on sanitary education, on exchange of experience of paramedical personnel of therapeutic-prophylactic and sanitary-antiepidemic institutions.

618.1 US ISSN 0364-1198
RG1 CODEN: FEPADR
FEMALE PATIENT; practical advice for better care. 1976. m. $50 to individuals; institutions $60 (effective 1992). Excerpta Medica, Inc., Core Publishing Division (Subsidiary of: Elsevier Science Publishers B.V.), 105 Raider Blvd., Belle Mead, NJ 08503. TEL 908-874-8550. FAX 908-874-0700. illus.; circ. 87,000. (also avail. in microform from UMI; reprint service avail. from UMI) **Indexed:** Curr.Lit.Fam.Plan., FAMLI.

MEDICAL SCIENCES — OBSTETRICS AND GYNECOLOGY

618 BL
FEMINA. 1972. bi-m. Elea Cientia Editorial Ltda., Rua Barao de Uba 48, CEP 20260 Rio de Janiero RJ, Brazil. TEL 293-2112. Ed. J.C. Nahoum. circ. 8,000.

618 619 GW ISSN 0179-1796
CODEN: FSIKEJ
FERTILITAET, STERILITAET, IN-VITRO FERTILISATION, SEXUALITAET, KONTRAZEPTION. 1985. 4/yr. DM.140($89) Springer-Verlag, Heidelberger Platz 3, D-1000 Berlin 33, Germany. TEL 030-2807-1. (Subscr. to: 44 Hartz Way, Secaucus, NJ 07094) Eds. L. Mettler, H.W. Michelmann. (also avail. in microform from UMI; back issues avail.; reprint service avail. from ISI) **Indexed:** Biotech.Abstr.
—BLDSC shelfmark: 3909.690000.

618.178 US ISSN 0015-0282
RC889 CODEN: FESTAS
FERTILITY AND STERILITY. 1949. m. $140. American Fertility Society, 2140 11th Ave., Ste. 200, Birmingham, AL 35205-2800. TEL 205-933-8494. FAX 205-930-9904. Ed. Dr. Roger D. Kempers. adv.; bk.rev.; bibl.; charts; illus.; index, cum.index: vols.1-50; circ. 14,000. (also avail. in microform from MIM,AFS) **Indexed:** Anim.Breed.Abstr., Biol.Abstr., Chem.Abstr., Curr.Adv.Cancer Res., Curr.Adv.Cell & Devel.Biol., Curr.Adv.Ecol.Sci., Curr.Cont., Curr.Lit.Fam.Plan., Dairy Sci.Abstr., Dent.Ind., Excerp.Med., Helminthol.Abstr., I.P.A., Ind.Med., Ind.Sci.Rev., Ind.Vet., INIS Atomind., Nutr.Abstr., Risk Abstr., Sci.Cit.Ind, Vet.Bull.
—BLDSC shelfmark: 3909.750000.

618 SZ ISSN 1015-3837
CODEN: FDTHES
FETAL DIAGNOSIS AND THERAPY; clinical advances and basic research. 1986. 4/yr. 360 Fr.($240) S. Karger AG, Allschwilerstr. 10, P.O. Box, CH-4009 Basel, Switzerland. TEL 061-3061111. FAX 061-3061234. TELEX CH 962652. (U.S. and Canada subscr. to: S. Karger Publishers, Inc., 79 Fifth Ave., New York, NY, 10003, U.S.A.) Eds. M. Michejda, S. Uzan. circ. 800. (also avail. in microform from RPI) **Indexed:** Excerp.Med.
—BLDSC shelfmark: 3910.848000.
Formerly: Fetal Therapy (ISSN 0257-2788)

618 UK ISSN 0953-8267
FETAL MEDICINE REVIEW. 1989. s-a. £44($70) to individuals; institutions £63($100). Edward Arnold (Subsidiary of: Hodder & Stoughton), Mill Rd., Dunton Green, Sevenoaks, Kent TN13 2YA, England. TEL 0732-450111. FAX 0732-461321. (Dist. in U.S. and Canada by: Cambridge University Press, 40 W. 20th St., New York, NY 10011, USA) Ed. W. Dunlop. adv.; bk.rev
—BLDSC shelfmark: 3910.856000.
Description: Aims to bring together all multidisciplinary interests and approaches appropriate to the advancement of knowledge and clinical practice in obstetrics.

FIRST YEAR OF LIFE; a guide to your baby's growth and development month by month. see *CHILDREN AND YOUTH — About*

618 376 618.92 US
FOCAL POINT.* 1972. bi-m. $10. National Association of Childbirth Education, 2931 Tennessee, Riverside, CA 92506. Ed. Gretchen Wetzel. adv.; bk.rev.; circ. 350. (looseleaf format; back issues avail.)

618.1 GW ISSN 0016-0237
DER FRAUENARZT. 1951. 9/yr. DM.136. (Berufsverband der Frauenaerzte e.V.) Demeter Verlag, Wuermstr. 13, 8032 Graefelfing, Germany. TEL 089-852033. FAX 089-8543347. Ed. Hans Kosdade. adv.; bk.rev.; bibl.; illus.; circ. 5,300.

A FRIEND INDEED. see *WOMEN'S INTERESTS*

618 GW ISSN 0016-5751
CODEN: GEFRA2
GEBURTSHILFE UND FRAUENHEILKUNDE; Ergebnisse der Forschung fuer die Praxis. (Text in German; summaries in English and German) 1940. m. DM.279. Georg Thieme Verlag, Ruedigerstr. 14, Postfach 104853, 7000 Stuttgart 10, Germany. TEL 0711-8931-0. Ed.Bd. adv.; bk.rev.; abstr.; bibl.; stat.; index; circ. 6,500. (reprint service avail. from UMI) **Indexed:** Biol.Abstr., Biotech.Abstr., Chem.Abstr., Curr.Adv.Cancer Res., Curr.Cont., Excerp.Med., Ind.Med., Ind.Sci.Rev., INIS Atomind., Sci.Cit.Ind.
—BLDSC shelfmark: 4095.650000.

618 US
GENESIS (WASHINGTON). 1966. bi-m. $30 to non-member institutions. American Society for Psychoprophylaxis in Obstetrics, Inc. (ASPO Lamaze), 1101 Connecticut Ave., N.W., Ste. 300, Washington, DC 20036. Ed. Sherry Jimenez. adv.; bk.rev.; circ. 6,200.
Former titles: A.S.P.O. Genesis; (until 1978): Conceptions; A.S.P.O. Newsletter.

618.1 SP ISSN 0211-6901
GINE DIPS; revista mensual hispano-americana de obstetricia y ginecologia. (Text mainly in Spanish; summaries in English and Spanish) 1970. m. 4000 ptas.($75) (Facultad de Medicina de Barcelona, Departamento de Ostetricia y Ginecologia) Editorial Rocas, Calaf. 29, 2-3, 08021 Barcelona, Spain. TEL 200 13 89. FAX 202-19-58. Dir. M. Carreras Roca. adv.; abstr.; bibl.; charts; illus.; stat. **Indexed:** Ind.Med.Esp.
—BLDSC shelfmark: 4176.280000.

618 IT ISSN 0392-2944
CODEN: GICLDY
GINECOLOGIA CLINICA. (Text in Italian; summaries in English) 1980. q. L.80000($90) Studi Ostetrico Ginecologici s.r.l., Galleria Storione 2A, 35123 Padua, Italy. TEL 049-8758644. Ed. A. Onnis. adv. (back issues avail.) **Indexed:** Biol.Abstr.
—BLDSC shelfmark: 4176.330000.

618 IT ISSN 0393-5337
GINECOLOGIA DELL'INFANZIA E DELL'ADOLESCENZA. (Text in Italian; summaries in English) 1985. q. L.50000($50) (Societa Italiana di Ginecologia dell'Infanzia e dell'Adolescenza) C I C Edizioni Internazionale s.r.l., Via L. Spallanzani, 11, 00161 Rome, Italy. TEL 06-8412673. FAX 06-8443365. TELEX 622099 CIC I.

618.1 IT ISSN 1120-365X
▼**GINECOLOGIA OGGI.** 1990. q. L.20000. E S I Stampa Medica s.r.l., Casella Postale 42, Lgo. Volontari del Sangue 10, 20097 S. Donato, Milan, Italy. TEL 02-5274241. FAX 02-5274775. TELEX 324894. Ed. Bruno Pieroni. adv.; bk.rev.; circ. 8,000.

618 SP
GINECOLOGIA Y OBSTETRICIA TEMAS ACTUALES. Spanish translation of: Clinics in Obstetrics and Gynecology. (Supplements: Clinicas Obstetricas y Ginecologicas) 1974. 4/yr. 17384 ptas.($128) (effective 1990). Interamericana de Espana, S.A., Division de Ciencias de la Salud de McGraw-Hill, Calle Manuel Ferrero, 13, 28036 Madrid, Spain. TEL 315-0340. FAX 733-6627. charts; illus.; index. **Indexed:** Excerp.Med.

618.1 IT ISSN 0391-8920
GINECORAMA. bi-m. L.15000($15) C I C Edizioni Internazionali s.r.l., Via L. Spallanzani 11, 00161 Rome, Italy. TEL 06-8412673. FAX 06-8443365. TELEX 622099 CIC.

618 IT ISSN 0391-9013
GIORNALE ITALIANO DI OSTETRICIA E GINECOLOGIA. (Text in Italian; summaries in English) m. L.80000($80) C I C Edizioni Internazionali s.r.l., Via L. Spallanzani 11, 00161 Rome, Italy. TEL 06-8412673. FAX 06-8443365. TELEX 622099 CIC. **Indexed:** Excerp.Med.
—BLDSC shelfmark: 4178.237000.

618 301.412 CN ISSN 0823-9266
GREAT EXPECTATIONS. 1972. q. Can.$12($18) Professional Publishing Associates, 269 Richmond St. W., Toronto, Ont. M5V 1X1, Canada. TEL 416-596-8680. FAX 416-596-1991. Ed. Fran Fearnley. adv.; bk.rev.; circ. 150,000.

618 US
GUIDE FOR EXPECTANT PARENTS. 1979. s-a. free. Educational Programs, Inc., 8003 Old York Rd., Elkins Park, PA 19117-1410. TEL 215-635-1700. FAX 215-635-6455. Ed. Deana C. Jamroz. adv.; circ. 850,000. (back issues avail.)
Description: For pregnant women in prenatal education classes.

618 US
GUIDELINES FOR PERINATAL CARE. 1983. irreg., 3rd ed., 1992. $40. American Academy of Pediatrics, 141 Northwest Point Blvd., Box 927, Elk Grove Village, IL 60009-0927. TEL 708-228-5005.
Description: Guidelines for care of pregnant women, fetuses, and neonates including discussion of preconceptional and antenatal screening, adoption, perinatal infections, and fetal monitoring.

618 CC
GUOWAI YIXUE (FUCHAN KEXUE FENCE)/FOREIGN MEDICAL SCIENCES (GYNECOLOGY & OBSTETRICS). (Text in Chinese) Tianjin Yixue Keji Qingbao Yanjiusuo - Tianjin Institute of Medical Science Information, 131, Chengdu Dao, Heping-qu, Tianjin 300050, People's Republic of China. TEL 302570. Ed. Yu Aifeng.

618.1 GW ISSN 0017-5994
CODEN: GYNKAP
DER GYNAEKOLOGE. (Text in German) 1968. 6/yr. DM.536($139) Springer-Verlag, Heidelberger Platz 3, D-1000 Berlin 33, Germany. TEL 030-8207-1. (Also Heidelberg, Tokyo, Vienna, and New York) Ed. L. Beck. adv. (also avail. in microform from UMI; back issues avail.; reprint service avail. from ISI) **Indexed:** Biol.Abstr., Curr.Adv.Ecol.Sci., Curr.Cont., Excerp.Med., Ind.Med., INIS Atomind.
—BLDSC shelfmark: 4233.550000.

618 GW ISSN 0341-8677
GYNAEKOLOGISCHE PRAXIS. 4/yr. DM.268. Hans Marseille Verlag, Buerkleinstr. 12, 8000 Munich 22, Germany. TEL 089-227988.
—BLDSC shelfmark: 4233.570000.

618.1 SZ ISSN 0017-6001
CODEN: GYRUA7
GYNAEKOLOGISCHE RUNDSCHAU. (Supplements avail.) (Text in English, French and German) 1964. q. 321 Fr.($214) (Oesterreichische Gesellschaft fuer Gynaekologie und Geburtshilfe) S. Karger AG, Allschwilerstr. 10, P.O. Box, CH-4009 Basel, Switzerland. TEL 061-3061111. FAX 061-3061234. TELEX CH 962652. Eds. E. Reinold, U. Haller. adv.; illus.; circ. 1,500. (reprint service avail. from ISI; back issues avail.) **Indexed:** Biol.Abstr., Ind.Med.
—BLDSC shelfmark: 4233.600000.

618 GW ISSN 0938-6467
▼**GYNCOMP.** 1991. q. DM.98. Georg Thieme Verlag, Ruedigerstr. 14, Postfach 104853, 7000 Stuttgart 10, Germany. TEL 0711-89310. FAX 0711-8931298. TELEX 07252275-GTV-D. Ed. Klaus Goeschen.
—BLDSC shelfmark: 4233.615000.

618 SZ ISSN 0378-7346
CODEN: GOBIDS
GYNECOLOGIC AND OBSTETRIC INVESTIGATION. (Text in English) 1895. 8/yr. (2 vols./yr.) 360 Fr.($240) S. Karger AG, Allschwilerstr. 10, P.O. Box, CH-4009 Basel, Switzerland. TEL 061-3061111. FAX 061-3061234. TELEX CH 962652. Ed. G. Zador. adv.; bibl.; illus.; index; circ. 950. (also avail. in microform from RPI; back issues avail.) **Indexed:** Anim.Breed.Abstr., Biol.Abstr., Chem.Abstr., Curr.Adv.Ecol.Sci., Curr.Cont., Dairy Sci.Abstr., Excerp.Med., Ind.Med., Ind.Sci.Rev., NRN, Sci.Cit.Ind.
—BLDSC shelfmark: 4233.650000.
Former titles: Gynecologic Investigation (ISSN 0017-5986); Gynaecologia.

618.1 US ISSN 0090-8258
RC280.G5 CODEN: GYNOA3
GYNECOLOGIC ONCOLOGY; an international journal. 1972. m. $568 (foreign $676). Academic Press, Inc., Journal Division, 1250 Sixth Ave., San Diego, CA 92101. TEL 619-230-1840. FAX 619-699-6800. TELEX 181726. Ed. David Gershenson. adv.; index. (back issues avail.) **Indexed:** Biol.Abstr., Chem.Abstr, Curr.Adv.Ecol.Sci., Curr.Cont., Excerp.Med., Ind.Med., Ind.Sci.Rev., INIS Atomind., NRN, Sci.Cit.Ind.
—BLDSC shelfmark: 4233.710000.
Description: Serves as an archive devoted to the publication of clinical and investigative articles that concern tumors of the female reproductive tract.
Refereed Serial

MEDICAL SCIENCES — OBSTETRICS AND GYNECOLOGY

618.1　　　　FR　　ISSN 0301-2204
GYNECOLOGIE; revue internationale de gynecologie. (Summaries in English, French) 1950. bi-m. 123 ECU($150) (Societe Francaise de Gynecologie) Masson, 120 bd. Saint Germain, 75280 Paris Cedex 06, France. TEL 1-46-34-21-60. FAX 1-45-87-29-99. TELEX 202 671 F. (Co-sponsor: Federation Internationale de Gynecologie Infantile et Juvenile) Ed. Hoang Ngoc Minh. adv.; bk.rev.; abstr.; bibl.; charts; illus.; stat.; index; circ. 2,150. (reprint service avail. from ISI) **Indexed:** Biol.Abstr., Excerp.Med., Ind.Med.
　—BLDSC shelfmark: 4233.740000.
　Formerly: Gynecologie Pratique (ISSN 0017-6028)

HEALTH CARE FOR WOMEN, INTERNATIONAL. see *WOMEN'S HEALTH*

618.202　　　GW　　ISSN 0932-8122
DIE HEBAMME; Fortbildungszeitschrift fuer Hebammen und Entbildungspfleger. 1988. q. DM.52. Ferdinand Enke Verlag, Postfach 101254, 7000 Stuttgart 10, Germany. TEL 0711-8931-0. FAX 0711-8931-419. TELEX 07252275-GTV-D. Eds. G. Martius, J.W. Dudenhausen.
　—BLDSC shelfmark: 4282.176000.

618　　　　　　UK
HUMAN CONCERN NEWSPAPER. 1968. q. membership. Society for the Protection of Unborn Children, 7 Tufton St., Westminster, London SW1P 3QN, England. TEL 071-222-5845. FAX 071-222-0630. Ed. Phyllis Bowman. adv.; bk.rev.; stat.; circ. 30,000. (tabloid format)
　Formerly: Society for the Protection of Unborn Children. Bulletin.

HUMAN DEVELOPMENT. see *PSYCHOLOGY*

618 616.4　　　UK　　ISSN 0268-1161
　　　　　　　　　　　CODEN: HUREEE
HUMAN REPRODUCTION. 1986. 8/yr. £185($295) (European Society of Human Reproduction and Embryology, EI) I R L Press Ltd. (Subsidiary of: Oxford University Press), Pinkmill House, Southfield Rd., Eymsham, Oxford OX8 1JJ, England. TEL 0865-882283. FAX 0865-882890. TELEX 837330-OXPRES-G. (U.S. subscr. addr.: I R L Press, Box Q, McLean, VA 22101) Ed. R.G. Edwards. adv.; bk.rev.; illus.; index. (back issues avail.; reprint service avail. from SWZ) **Indexed:** Bibl.Repro., Biol.Abstr., Chem.Abstr., Curr.Adv.Ecol.Sci., Curr.Cont., Excerp.Med., Ind.Med., Sci.Cit.Ind.
　—BLDSC shelfmark: 4336.431000.
　Description: For scientists and clinicians working in international human reproduction research and practice.

I C R D B CANCERGRAM: GYNECOLOGICAL TUMORS - DIAGNOSIS, TREATMENT. see *MEDICAL SCIENCES — Abstracting, Bibliographies, Statistics*

618　　　　US　　ISSN 0160-7626
RC889　　　　　　　　CODEN: INFEDH
INFERTILITY; an interdisciplinary journal devoted to the rapid communication of clinical aspects of human infertility. 1978. q. $137. Hemisphere Publishing Corporation (Subsidiary of: Taylor & Francis Group), 1900 Frost Rd., Ste. 101, Bristol, PA 19007-1598. TEL 215-785-5800. FAX 215-785-5515. Ed. Dr. Wayne Decker. adv.; charts; illus.; index. (back issues avail.; reprint service avail. from UMI) **Indexed:** Biol.Abstr., Chem.Abstr., Curr.Adv.Ecol.Sci., Curr.Cont., Excerp.Med., I.P.A.
　●Also available online.
　—BLDSC shelfmark: 4478.790000.
　Description: Female infertility, andrology, endocrinology, genetics, extra-corporeal fertilization and other aspects of human fertility.
　Refereed Serial

618　　　　US　　ISSN 0443-9058
INTERNATIONAL CORRESPONDENCE SOCIETY OF OBSTETRICS AND GYNECOLOGY. COLLECTED LETTERS. 1959. m. $89 (foreign $109). (International Correspondence Society of Obstetrics and Gynecology) Laux Company, Inc., 63 Great Rd., Maynard, MA 01754. TEL 617-897-5552. FAX 508-897-6824. Ed. Richard E. Hunter, M.D. circ. 2,000. (looseleaf format; back issues avail.)
　Formerly: Ob-Gyn Collected Letters (ISSN 0472-397X)

INTERNATIONAL FAMILY PLANNING PERSPECTIVES. see *BIRTH CONTROL*

618　　　　US　　ISSN 0887-8625
INTERNATIONAL JOURNAL OF CHILDBIRTH EDUCATION. 1961. q. $25. International Childbirth Education Association, Box 20048, Minneapolis, MN 55420-0048. TEL 612-854-8660. Ed. Connie Livingston. adv.; bk.rev.; bibl.; circ. 12,000. **Indexed:** Curr.Lit.Fam.Plan.
　Formerly (until 1986): I C E A News (ISSN 0445-0485)
　Description: Covers maternity and infant care.

618　　　　IE　　ISSN 0020-7292
RG1　　　　　　　　CODEN: IJGOAL
INTERNATIONAL JOURNAL OF GYNAECOLOGY AND OBSTETRICS. (Text in English) 1963. 12/yr.(in 3 vols.; 4 nos./vol.). $508 (effective 1992). (International Federation of Gynaecology and Obstetrics) Elsevier Scientific Publishers Ireland Ltd., P.O. Box 85, Limerick, Ireland. TEL 061-61944. FAX 061-62144. TELEX 72191 ENH EI. (Subscr. in U.S. and Canada to: Elsevier Science Publishing Co., Inc., Box 882, Madison Sq. Sta., New York, NY 10159. TEL 212-989-5800) (Co-sponsor: Family Health International) Ed. J.J. Sciarra. adv.; bibl.; illus.; index; circ. 4,000. (also avail. in microform from RPI) **Indexed:** Biol.Abstr., Chem.Abstr., Curr.Adv.Ecol.Sci., Curr.Cont., Curr.Lit.Fam.Plan., Dent.Ind., Excerp.Med., Ind.Med., Ind.Sci.Rev., INIS Atomind., NRN, Sci.Cit.Ind.
　—BLDSC shelfmark: 4542.273000.
　Supersedes: International Federation of Gynaecology and Obstetrics. Journal (ISSN 0020-6695)
　Refereed Serial

618 616.99　　　US　　ISSN 1048-891X
▼**INTERNATIONAL JOURNAL OF GYNECOLOGICAL CANCER.** 1991. bi-m. $195. (International Gynecological Cancer Society) Blackwell Scientific Publications Inc., Three Cambridge Center, Ste. 208, Cambridge, MA 02142-1413. TEL 617-225-0401. FAX 617-225-0412. Ed. Harold Fox.
　—BLDSC shelfmark: 4542.273000.
　Description: Interdisciplinary journal covering synecology, oncology, radiation therapy and pathology.

618.1　　　　US
INTERNATIONAL JOURNAL OF GYNECOLOGICAL PATHOLOGY. 1982. q. $135 to individuals; institutions $190. (International Society of Gynecological Pathologists) Raven Press, 1185 Ave. of the Americas, New York, NY 10036. TEL 212-930-9500. FAX 212-869-3495. TELEX 640073. Ed. Dr. Henry J. Norris. adv.; index; circ. 1,500. **Indexed:** Curr.Adv.Cancer Res., Excerp.Med., Ind.Med., Ind.Sci.Rev., Sci.Cit.Ind.
　Description: Reports on advances in the understanding and management of gynecological disease.
　Refereed Serial

618　　　　IS　　ISSN 0792-4569
▼**ISRAEL JOURNAL OF OBSTETRICS & GYNECOLOGY.** (Text in English) 1990. q. $80. (Israel Society of Obstetrics & Gynecology) Menachem Horowitz Publishing, 22 Shlomzion Hamalca St., Tel Aviv 62276, Israel. TEL 03-448676. FAX 03-449422. Ed. Dr. M. Lancet. adv.; bk.rev.; circ. 2,000. (back issues avail.)
　—BLDSC shelfmark: 4583.812500.
　Refereed Serial

J O G N N. (Journal of Obstetric, Gynecologic and Neonatal Nursing) see *MEDICAL SCIENCES — Nurses And Nursing*

618.202　　　JM
JAMAICA MIDWIVES ASSOCIATION. NEWSLETTER. bi-m. membership. Jamaica Midwives Association, c/o Victoria Jubilee Hospital, Kingston, Jamaica, W.I.

618　　　　GW　　ISSN 0177-9109
JATROS GYNAEKOLOGIE. 1985. 12/yr. DM.150. P M I Verlag GmbH, August-Schanz-Str. 21, 6000 Frankfurt a.M. 50, Germany. TEL 069-5480000. FAX 069-548000-77. Ed. Peter Hoffman. circ. 7,850. (back issues avail.)
　Description: Seminar paper journal with summaries of original articles, interviews and Congress reports.

618.2　　　　SW　　ISSN 0021-7468
JORDEMODERN. 1888. m. SEK 190. Svenska Barnmorskefoerbundet - Swedish Association of Midwives, Ostermalmsg. 19, 11426 Stockholm, Sweden. FAX 08-21-21-06. Ed. Anita Karlsson. adv.; bk.rev.; illus.; circ. 6,200. **Indexed:** Int.Nurs.Ind.
　—BLDSC shelfmark: 4673.940000.

618.1　　　　BL　　ISSN 0368-1416
　　　　　　　　　　　CODEN: JBGCA8
JORNAL BRASILEIRO DE GINECOLOGIA. (Text and summaries in English and Portuguese) 1935. m. $180. (Universidade Federal do Rio de Janeiro, Centro de Estudos da Maternidade) Cidade - Editora Cientifica Ltda., Rua Mexico 90, 2 and., 20031 Rio de Janeiro, RJ, Brazil. Ed. Fernando Moyses. adv.; bk.rev.; bibl.; charts; illus.; circ. 12,000. **Indexed:** Biol.Abstr., Excerp.Med., Ind.Med.
　—BLDSC shelfmark: 4674.637000.

618.202 610.73　　　JA　　ISSN 0047-1836
JOSANPU ZASSHI/JAPANESE JOURNAL FOR MIDWIVES. (Text in Japanese) 1952. m. 11160 Yen($86) Igaku-Shoin Ltd., 5-24-3 Hongo, Bunkyo-ku, Tokyo 113-91, Japan. TEL 03-817-5775. adv.; illus.; circ. 12,000. **Indexed:** Int.Nurs.Ind.
　—BLDSC shelfmark: 4656.510000.

618　　　　FR　　ISSN 0368-2315
　　　　　　　　　　　CODEN: JGOBAC
JOURNAL DE GYNECOLOGIE OBSTETRIQUE ET BIOLOGIE DE LA REPRODUCTION. (Summaries in English) 1920. 8/yr. 145 ECU($175) (typically set in Jan.). Masson, 120 bd. Saint-Germain, 75280 Paris Cedex 06, France. TEL 1-46-34-21-60. FAX 1-45-87-29-99. TELEX 202 671 F. Ed. Jacques Barrat. adv.; bk.rev.; abstr.; illus.; index; circ. 5,000. (also avail. in microform from UMI; reprint service avail. from ISI) **Indexed:** Biol.Abstr., Chem.Abstr., Excerp.Med., Ind.Med., Nutr.Abstr.
　—BLDSC shelfmark: 4996.600000.
　Formerly: Gynecologie et Obstetrique et Federation des Societes de Gynecologie et d'Obstetrique. Bulletin (ISSN 0017-601X)

618　　　　US
RG135
JOURNAL OF ASSISTED REPRODUCTION AND GENETICS. 1984. bi-m. $265 (foreign $310)(effective 1992). Plenum Publishing Corp., 233 Spring St., New York, NY 10013-1578. TEL 212-620-8000. FAX 212-463-0742. TELEX 23-421139. Ed. Norbert Gleicher. adv. (also avail. in microfilm from JSC; back issues avail.) **Indexed:** Excerp.Med., INIS Atomind.
　Formerly (until 1992): Journal of In Vitro Fertilization and Embryo Transfer (ISSN 0740-7769)
　Description: Covers research in the reproductive sciences, including assisted reproduction technologies, genetics of early gestation, relevant contributions from laboratory sciences affecting diagnosis and treatment of infertility, preimplantation genetics, and controversies in assisted reproduction.
　Refereed Serial

618 612　　　UK　　ISSN 0141-9846
　　　　　　　　　　　CODEN: JDPHDH
JOURNAL OF DEVELOPMENTAL PHYSIOLOGY. 1979. m. £172($320) Oxford University Press, Oxford Journals, Pinkhill House, Southfield Rd., Eynsham, Oxford OX1 1JJ, England. TEL 0865-882283. FAX 0865-882890. TELEX 837330 OXPRES G. (U.S. addr.: 200 Madison Ave., New York, NY 10016, USA) Ed. Colin T. Jones. adv.; bk.rev.; index; circ. 200. (also avail. in microform from UMI) **Indexed:** Biol.Abstr., Chem.Abstr., Curr.Cont., Dent.Ind., Excerp.Med., Ind.Med., Ind.Sci.Rev., Ind.Vet., Sci.Cit.Ind., Vet.Bull.
　—BLDSC shelfmark: 4969.300000.
　Description: Papers describing the results of pregnancy, the fetus, or the neonate of humans or experimental animals.

JOURNAL OF DIAGNOSTIC MEDICAL SONOGRAPHY. see *MEDICAL SCIENCES*

618　　　　IT　　ISSN 0392-9507
　　　　　　　　　　　CODEN: JFMED7
JOURNAL OF FOETAL MEDICINE. (Included in: Clinical and Experimental Obstetrics and Gynecology) (Text and summaries in English) 1981. q. Studi Ostetrico Ginecologici s.r.l., Galleria Storione 2A, 35123 Padua, Italy. TEL 049-8758644. (back issues avail.) **Indexed:** Excerp.Med.
　—BLDSC shelfmark: 4984.535000.

MEDICAL SCIENCES — OBSTETRICS AND GYNECOLOGY

JOURNAL OF GYNAECOLOGICAL ENDOCRINOLOGY. see *MEDICAL SCIENCES — Endocrinology*

618   US   ISSN 1042-4067
CODEN: JGYSEF
JOURNAL OF GYNECOLOGIC SURGERY. 1984. q. $135 (foreign $175). (Gynecologic Laser Society) Mary Ann Liebert, Inc., 1651 Third Ave., New York, NY 10128. TEL 212-289-2300. FAX 212-289-4697. (Co-sponsors: International Society for Gynecological Endocrinology; British Society for Cervical Pathology) Ed. Michael S. Baggish. adv.; bk.rev.; abstr. **Indexed:** Curr.Adv.Cancer Res., Excerp.Med.
—BLDSC shelfmark: 4996.595000.
Formerly (until 1989): Colposcopy and Gynecologic Laser Surgery (ISSN 0741-6113)
Description: Deals with all aspects of operative and office gynecology, including colposcopy, endoscopy (hysteroscopy and laparoscopy), laser and conventional surgery, female urology, microsurgery, and in vitro fertilization.
Refereed Serial

610.73 618   US   ISSN 0890-3344
CODEN: JHLAE5
JOURNAL OF HUMAN LACTATION. 1984. q. $110 (foreign $130). (International Lactation Consultants Association) Human Sciences Press, Inc. (Subsidiary of: Plenum Publishing Corp.), 233 Spring St., New York, NY 10013. TEL 212-620-8000. FAX 212-463-0742. TELEX 23-421139. Ed. Kathleen G. Auerbach. adv.; bk.rev.; film rev.; bibl.; index; circ. 2,000. (back issues avail.)
—BLDSC shelfmark: 5003.417000.
Formerly (until 1985): Consultants' Corner.
Description: Publishes scientific articles and commentaries on human lactation and breastfeeding, and discussions of clinical case reports relevant to practicing lactation consultants.
Refereed Serial

618.2   US
JOURNAL OF MATERNAL - FETAL INVESTIGATION. q. Springer-Verlag, 175 Fifth Ave., New York, NY 10010. TEL 212-460-1500. FAX 212-473-6272. Ed. Dev Maulik. circ. 1,500.

610.73 618   US   ISSN 0091-2182
CODEN: JNUMEQ
JOURNAL OF NURSE-MIDWIFERY. 1955. 6/yr. (plus suppl.). $110 to institutions (foreign $140)(effective 1992). (American College of Nurse-Midwives) Elsevier Science Publishing Co., Inc. (New York), 655 Ave. of the Americas, New York, NY 10010. TEL 212-989-5800. FAX 212-633-3965. TELEX 420643 AEP UI. Ed. Mary Ann Shah. adv.; bk.rev.; bibl.; charts; illus.; cum.index. (also avail. in microform from RPI) **Indexed:** ASSIA, C.I.N.L., Curr.Cont., Excerp.Med., Ind.Med., Int.Nurs.Ind., Nurs.Abstr., SSCI.
—BLDSC shelfmark: 5023.650000.
Former titles: American College of Nurse-Midwives. Bulletin (ISSN 0002-8002); (until 1969): American College of Nurse-Midwifery. Bulletin (ISSN 0098-3721)
Description: Includes the presentation of current knowledge in the fields of nurse-midwifery, parent-child health, obstetric, well-woman gynecology, family planning and neonatology.
Refereed Serial

618   II   ISSN 0022-3190
CODEN: JOBYA4
JOURNAL OF OBSTETRICS AND GYNAECOLOGY OF INDIA. 1950. bi-m. Rs.600($35) Federation of Obstetric & Gynaecological Societies of India, Purandare Griha, 31 C, Dr. N.A. Purandare Marg, Bombay 400 007, India. TEL 811-04-46. Ed. Dr. V.N. Purandare. adv.; bk.rev.; charts; illus.; stat.; circ. 8,600. **Indexed:** Biol.Abstr., Chem.Abstr.

618   CH
JOURNAL OF OBSTETRICS AND GYNAECOLOGY OF THE REPUBLIC OF CHINA. (Text and summaries in Chinese and English) 1962. q. NT.$320. Association of Obstetrics and Gynaecology of the Republic of China, No.1 Chang-Te St., Taipei, Taiwan, Republic of China. Ed. Pei-Chuan Ouyang. adv.; circ. 1,600. (also avail. in microform from UMI; reprint service avail. from UMI)

618 618.92   HK
JOURNAL OF PAEDIATRICS, OBSTETRICS AND GYNAECOLOGY. 1975. bi-m. $21 (students $10.50). Medpro Pacific Ltd., 19F Tung Sun Commercial Centre, 200 Lockhart Rd., Wanchai, Hong Kong. TEL 5-8920638. FAX 5-8345330. Ed. Rennie C. Heel. adv.; illus. **Indexed:** Abstr.Hyg.
Formerly: Mother and Child.

JOURNAL OF PEDIATRIC & PERINATAL NUTRITION. see *MEDICAL SCIENCES — Pediatrics*

JOURNAL OF PEDIATRIC SURGERY. see *MEDICAL SCIENCES — Surgery*

618   GW   ISSN 0300-5577
CODEN: JPEMAO
JOURNAL OF PERINATAL MEDICINE. 1973. 6/yr. $241. Walter de Gruyter und Co., Genthiner Str. 13, 1000 Berlin 30, Germany. TEL 030-26005-0. FAX 030-26005251. TELEX 184027. (U.S. addr.: Walter de Gruyter, Inc., 200 Saw Mill Rd., Hawthorne, NY 10532) Ed.Bd. adv. **Indexed:** Bibl.Dev.Med.& Child Neur., Biol.Abstr., Chem.Abstr., Curr.Adv.Biochem., Curr.Adv.Ecol.Sci., Curr.Cont., Dairy Sci.Abstr., Excerp.Med., Ind.Med., Ind.Sci.Rev., INIS Atomind., Nutr.Abstr.
—BLDSC shelfmark: 5030.550000.

618   US   ISSN 0743-8346
CODEN: JOPEEI
JOURNAL OF PERINATOLOGY. 1982. q. $70 to individuals (foreign $85); institutions $90 (foreign $105); students $55 (foreign $70). (National Perinatal Association) Appleton & Lange, Journal Division (Subsidiary of: Simon & Schuster Company), 25 Van Zant St., Box 5630, Norwalk, CT 06855. TEL 203-838-4400. (Subscr. to: Dept. JP, Box 3000, Denville, NJ 07834) Ed. Dr. Gilbert I. Martin. adv.; bk.rev.; charts; illus.; index; circ. 3,000. (also avail. in microform from UMI; back issues avail.) **Indexed:** Ind.Med.
—BLDSC shelfmark: 5030.570000.
Description: Contains original articles, commentaries, current concepts, case reports, editorials, and letters on all aspects of perinatal medicine from pregnancy through neonatal period.
Refereed Serial

618   UK   ISSN 0167-482X
CODEN: JPOGD
JOURNAL OF PSYCHOSOMATIC OBSTETRICS AND GYNAECOLOGY. (Text in English) 1982. q. Parthenon Publishing Group, Casterton Hall, Casterton, Carnforth, Lancs LA6 2LA, England. TEL 05242-72084. FAX 05242-71587. Ed.Bd. bk.rev.; charts; illus. (reprint service avail. from SWZ) **Indexed:** Dok.Arbeitsmed., Excerp.Med., Psychol.Abstr.
—BLDSC shelfmark: 5043.479000.

JOURNAL OF REPRODUCTIVE IMMUNOLOGY. see *MEDICAL SCIENCES — Allergology And Immunology*

618.05   US   ISSN 0024-7758
RG1   CODEN: JRPMAP
JOURNAL OF REPRODUCTIVE MEDICINE; for the obstetrician and gynecologist. 1968. m. $82 to individuals; institutions $113. Journal of Reproductive Medicine, Inc., 8342 Olive Blvd., St. Louis, MO 63132. TEL 314-991-4440. FAX 314-991-4654. adv.; bk.rev.; illus.; index; circ. 29,686. (also avail. in microform from UMI; back issues avail.; reprint service avail. from ISI) **Indexed:** Anim.Breed.Abstr., Biol.Abstr., Chem.Abstr., Curr.Adv.Ecol.Sci., Curr.Cont., Curr.Lit.Fam.Plan., Excerp.Med., Ind.Med., Ind.Sci.Rev., INIS Atomind., Nutr.Abstr.
—BLDSC shelfmark: 5049.700000.
Continues: Lying-in (ISSN 0096-7033)
Refereed Serial

618   CN
JOURNAL S O G C. (Text in English, French) 10/yr. Can.$40. (Society of Obstetricians and Gynecologists of Canada) Ribosome Communications, 55 Charles St., W., Ste. 3104, Toronto, Ont. M5S 2W9, Canada. TEL 416-925-7715. FAX 416-323-3064. Ed. Dr. P.J. Taylor. adv.; circ. 500 (paid); 30,000 (controlled).

618.2   FI   ISSN 0022-9415
KATILOLEHTI/TIDSKRIFT FOER BARNMORSKOR. (Text in Finnish, Swedish; summaries in English) 1896. m. FIM 170($37.75) (foreign Fmk.220). Suomen Katiloliitto - Federation of Finnish Midwives, Nervanderik 12-B-26, 00100 Helsinki 10, Finland. Ed. Arja Laiho. adv.; bk.rev.; charts; illus.; stat. **Indexed:** Int.Nurs.Ind.
—BLDSC shelfmark: 5087.773000.

KEY OBSTETRICS AND GYNECOLOGY. see *MEDICAL SCIENCES — Abstracting, Bibliographies, Statistics*

618   US
LAMAZE PARENTS' MAGAZINE. 1983. s-a. free to qualified personnel. (American Society for Psychoprophylaxis in Obstetrics, Inc.) Lamaze Publishing Co., 30 Old Kings Highway, Darien, CT 06820. TEL 203-656-1127. FAX 203-655-8960. Ed. Julia Kagan. adv.; circ. 2,000,000 (controlled).
Description: Offers prenatal and postpartum information to expectant couples who are preparing for birth through Lamaze classes.

618   IT
LUCINA. 1934. m. free. Federazione Nazionale dei Collegi delle Ostetriche, Piazza Tarquinia 5-D, 00183 Rome, Italy. Ed. Lino Businco. adv.; circ. 20,000.

618   US
M I D S NEWSLETTER. (Miscarriage, Infant Death, and Stillbirth) 1983. m. $25. M I D S Inc., 16 Crescent Dr., Parsippany, NJ 07054.
Description: Newsletter of announcements for families suffering miscarriages, infant deaths, and stillbirths.

M O M MAGAZINE. (Mothers and Others for Midwives) see *WOMEN'S INTERESTS*

610   HU   ISSN 0025-021X
CODEN: MNLAA8
MAGYAR NOORVOSOK LAPJA. (Summaries in English, German and Russian) bi-m. $42. Ifjusagi Lap-es Konyvkiado Vallalat, Revay u. 16, 1374 Budapest 6, Hungary. (Subscr. to: Kultura, Box 149, H-1389 Budapest, Hungary) Ed. Dr. Istvan Gati. bibl.; charts; illus. **Indexed:** Chem.Abstr., Excerp.Med., Ind.Med., INIS Atomind.
—BLDSC shelfmark: 5345.010000.

618 617   IO   ISSN 0216-4027
MANTAP: MAJALAH ILMAIH P K M I/INDONESIAN ASSOCIATION FOR SECURE CONTRACEPTION. JOURNAL. (Text mainly in Indonesian; occasionally in English) 1981. q. $120. Perkumpulan Kontrasepsi Mantap Indonesia (PKMI) - Indonesian Association for Secure Contraception, Jalan Kramat Sentiong 49A, Jakarta 10450, Indonesia. TEL 3804617. FAX 62-21-3800814. Ed. Azrul Azwar. circ. 1,000. (Reprint service avail.)

MATERNAL & CHILD HEALTH; the journal of family medicine. see *MEDICAL SCIENCES — Pediatrics*

MEDICAL MALPRACTICE: HANDLING OBSTETRIC AND NEONATAL CASES. see *LAW — Civil Law*

618.1   BL
MEDISOM: GYNECOLOGY. 1975. bi-m. $90. Grupo Editorial Q B D Ltda, Rua Caravelas 326, Caixa Postal 30329, 01051 Sao Paulo, Brazil. FAX 55-11-572-5957. Ed. Dr. Philip Querido. adv. (audio cassette)

MIDWIFE, HEALTH VISITOR AND COMMUNITY NURSE. see *MEDICAL SCIENCES — Nurses And Nursing*

MIDWIFERY. see *MEDICAL SCIENCES — Nurses And Nursing*

618.202 301.412   US
MIDWIFERY TODAY AND CHILDBIRTH EDUCATION. 1987. q. $30 (effective Jan. 1991). Box 2672, Eugene, OR 97402. TEL 503-344-7438. FAX 503-344-9919. Ed. Jan Tritten. adv.; bk.rev.; film rev.; abstr.; charts; illus.; stat.; tr.lit.; circ. 2,500.
Formerly: Midwifery Today (ISSN 0891-7701)
Description: Directed to professionals and non-professionals alike; balances technical articles with personal accounts and photography to present a wide range of options and perspectives on current birth care issues.

MEDICAL SCIENCES — OBSTETRICS AND GYNECOLOGY

618.202   UK   ISSN 0026-3524
MIDWIVES CHRONICLE. 1887. m. £10($24) (foreign £12). (Royal College of Midwives) Nursing Notes Ltd., 120 High Rd., East Finchley, London N2 8AG, England. TEL 081-442-0801. FAX 081-442-0623. Ed. A. Graveley. adv.; bk.rev.; index; circ. 35,000. (also avail. in microform from UMI; reprint service avail. from UMI) **Indexed:** ASSIA, CINAHL, Curr.Adv.Ecol.Sci., Int.Nurs.Ind.
—BLDSC shelfmark: 5761.449500.

618   IT   ISSN 0026-4784
MINERVA GINECOLOGICA. (Text in Italian; summaries in English and Italian) 1949. m. L.70000($100) Edizioni Minerva Medica, Corso Bramante 83-85, 10126 Turin, Italy. Ed. M. Pimoli. adv.; bk.rev.; bibl.; charts; illus.; index; circ. 4,000. **Indexed:** Biol.Abstr., Chem.Abstr., Excerp.Med., Helminthol.Abstr., Ind.Med.
—BLDSC shelfmark: 5794.185000.
Incorporates: Folia Gynaecologica; Ginecologia; Aggiornamenti di Ostetricia e Ginecologia (ISSN 0002-0931)

618 362.7   US   ISSN 0733-3013
MOTHERING. 1976. q. $22. Mothering Magazine, Box 1690, Santa Fe, NM 87504. FAX 505-986-8335. Ed. Peggy O'Mara. adv.; bk.rev.; circ. 60,000. (also avail. in microfiche; back issues avail.) **Indexed:** Alt.Press Ind., Hlth.Ind.
Description: Articles and departments pertaining to co-parental childrearing in the areas of health, learning, and emotional and personal development.

N A A C O G NEWSLETTER. (N A A C O G: The Organization for Obstetric, Gynecologic, & Neonatal Nurses) see *MEDICAL SCIENCES — Nurses And Nursing*

618   US   ISSN 0192-1223
N A P S A C NEWS. 1976. q. $20. National Association of Parents and Professionals for Safe Alternatives in Childbirth, International, Rt. 1, Box 646, Marble Hill, MO 63764. TEL 314-238-2010. Eds. David & Lee Stewart. adv.; bk.rev.; circ. 1,500.
Description: Information on parenting, breastfeeding, pregnancy, family health and the dangers of traditional medicine.

618 618.92   US
NEONATAL INTENSIVE CARE; the journal of perinatalogy/neonatology. 1988. 6/yr. Goldstein and Associates, 1150 Yale St., Ste. 12, Santa Monica, CA 90403-4738. TEL 213-828-1309. Ed. Les Plesko. adv.
Description: Covers diagnostic techniques, case studies and research findings in perinatology and neonatology.
Refereed Serial

NETWORK (DURHAM). see *BIRTH CONTROL*

618 613.9   AT   ISSN 1030-3987
NEW PARENT. 1968. q. Aus.$20. Parents Centers Australia, 71 Grand Ave., Westmead, N.S.W. 2150, Australia. TEL 02-633 5899. Ed. Beth Mitchell. adv.; bk.rev.; circ. 2,000.
Description: Provides information to general public about birthing and parenting options and practices.

618   US
▼**NUEVA VIDA/A NEW LIFE.** (Text in Spanish) 1990. a. Gruner & Jahr U.S.A. Publishing, 685 Third Ave., New York, NY 10017. TEL 212-878-8700. Ed. Mirta Rodriguez. circ. 450,000.
Description: Provides information on newborn baby care for Hispanic mothers.

618 658   US   ISSN 1044-307X
OB G MANAGEMENT. (Obstetrics and Gynecology) 1989. m. $65. Dowden Publishing Company, 110 Summit Ave., Montvale, NJ 07645. TEL 201-391-9100. FAX 201-391-2778. Ed. Carroll V. Dowden. adv.; circ. 31,000 (controlled).
Description: Provides information on how to run an ob-gyn medical practice better.

618   US   ISSN 0743-8354
OB-GYN CLINICAL ALERT. 1982. m. $95. American Health Consultants, Inc., Six Piedmont Center, Ste. 400, 3525 Piedmont Rd., N.E., Atlanta, GA 30305. TEL 404-262-7436. FAX 800-284-3291. (Subscr. to: Box 740056, Atlanta, GA 30374-9822. TEL 800-688-2421) Ed. Dr. Leon Speroff. index; circ. 2,100. (also avail. in audio cassette; reprint service avail.)

618   US   ISSN 0029-7437
RG1
OB-GYN NEWS. 1966. s-m. $96. International Medical News Group, 12230 Wilkins Ave., Rockville, MD 20852. TEL 301-770-6170. Ed. William Rubin. adv.; bk.rev.; circ. 30,450 (controlled). (tabloid format; also avail. in microform from UMI) **Indexed:** Curr.Lit.Fam.Plan.

618   US
▼**OB-GYN RESIDENT.** 1992. bi-m. $40. Slack, Inc., 6900 Grove Rd., Thorofare, NJ 08086. TEL 609-848-1000. Ed. Laura Ronge. adv.; circ. 5,189.
Description: Guide to career, lifestyle and business issues facing residents.

OBSTETRIC ANESTHESIA DIGEST. see *MEDICAL SCIENCES — Anaesthesiology*

618   US   ISSN 0029-7828
RG1   CODEN: OGSUA8
OBSTETRICAL & GYNECOLOGICAL SURVEY. 1946. m. $77 to individuals; institutions $105. Williams & Wilkins, 428 E. Preston St., Baltimore, MD 21202. TEL 301-528-4000. FAX 301-528-4312. TELEX 87669. Ed.Bd. adv.; bk.rev.; bibl.; charts; illus.; circ. 10,700. (also avail. in microform) **Indexed:** Biol.Abstr., Chem.Abstr., Curr.Adv.Cancer Res., Curr.Adv.Ecol.Sci., Curr.Lit.Fam.Plan., Excerp.Med., Ind.Med.
●Also available online. Vendor(s): BRS.
—BLDSC shelfmark: 6208.172000.
Description: Review articles and in-depth condensations of important obstetrical and gynecological articles from nearly 100 U.S. and international journals.

618   US   ISSN 0029-7844
RG1   CODEN: OBGNAS
OBSTETRICS AND GYNECOLOGY. 1952. 15/yr.(in 2 vols.). $170 to institutions (foreign $235)(effective 1992). (American College of Obstetricians and Gynecologists) Elsevier Science Publishing Co., Inc. (New York), 655 Ave. of the Americas, New York, NY 10010. TEL 212-989-5800. FAX 212-633-3965. TELEX 420643 AEP UI. Ed. Dr. Roy M. Pitkin. adv.; bk.rev.; bibl.; charts; illus.; s-a. index. (also avail. in microform from UMI; reprint service avail. from UMI) **Indexed:** Behav.Med.Abstr., Bibl.Dev.Med.& Child Neur., Biol.Abstr., Biotech.Abstr., Chem.Abstr., Curr.Adv.Cancer Res., Curr.Adv.Ecol.Sci., Curr.Adv.Genetics & Molec.Biol., Curr.Cont., Curr.Lit.Fam.Plan., Dairy Sci.Abstr., Dent.Ind., Excerp.Med., Helminthol.Abstr., I.P.A., Ind.Med., Int.Nurs.Ind., Nutr.Abstr., Risk Abstr., Sci.Cit.Ind.
●Also available online. Vendor(s): BRS.
—BLDSC shelfmark: 6208.200000.
Description: Provides information on current developments in women's health care.
Refereed Serial

618   US   ISSN 0889-8545
CODEN: OGCAE8
OBSTETRICS AND GYNECOLOGY CLINICS. 1974. q. $79 to individuals; institutions $100; foreign $105. W.B. Saunders Co., Curtis Center, Independence Sq. W., Philadelphia, PA 19106. TEL 215-238-7800. Ed. Naina Chohan. **Indexed:** Bibl.Dev.Med.& Child Neur., Biol.Abstr., Curr.Adv.Ecol.Sci., Curr.Lit.Fam.Plan., Dok.Arbeitsmed., Excerp.Med., Ind.Med., Ind.Sci.Rev., Sci.Cit.Ind.
—BLDSC shelfmark: 6208.206300.
Formerly: Clinics in Obstetrics and Gynaecology (ISSN 0306-3356)
Description: Each issue addresses a single topic in obstetric and gynecological care.
Refereed Serial

618   US
OBSTETRICS - GYNECOLOGY REPORT. 1988. 4/yr. $52.50 (foreign $58.50). Mosby - Year Book, Inc. (Subsidiary of: Times Mirror Company), 11830 Westline Industrial Dr., St. Louis, MO 63146. TEL 800-325-4117. FAX 314-432-1380. TELEX 44-2402. Ed. Dr. Frederick P. Zuspan. illus.

618   FR
OFFICIEL DE LA SAGE-FEMME.* 1953. 10/yr. 330 F. (Organisation Nationale des Syndicats de Sages Femmes (ONSSF)) Gamma, 77 rue de Vaugirard, 75006 Paris, France. adv.; circ. 2,500.

618.1   US
P M S ACCESS NEWSLETTER. (Premenstrual Syndrome) 1985. bi-m. $15. Madison Pharmacy Associates, Inc., 429 Gammon Pl., Madison, WI 53719. TEL 608-833-7046. FAX 608-833-7412. (Subscr. to: Box 9326, Madison, WI 53715) Ed. Tracy Colbert. bk.rev.; circ. 3,600.
Description: Information for women and professionals about the options in PMS education and treatment.

618.1 618.2   US   ISSN 0078-7442
RG1
PACIFIC COAST OBSTETRICAL AND GYNECOLOGICAL SOCIETY. TRANSACTIONS. 1944. a. $49 (foreign $52). (Pacific Coast Obstetrical and Gynecological Society) Mosby - Year Book, Inc. (Subsidiary of: Times Mirror Company), 11830 Westline Industrial Dr., St. Louis, MO 63146. TEL 314-872-8370. FAX 314-432-1380. TELEX 44-2402. circ. 250. **Indexed:** Ind.Med.
—BLDSC shelfmark: 8993.435000.
Formerly: Pacific Coast Society of Obstetrics and Gynecology. Transactions.
Description: Annual meetings of the Pacific Coast Obstetrical and Gynecological Society.

618   IT   ISSN 0304-0313
PATOLOGIA E CLINICA OSTETRICA E GINECOLOGICA. (Text in Italian; summaries in English) 1898. bi-m. $90. Edizioni Luigi Pozzi s.r.l., Via Panama 68, 00198 Rome, Italy. TEL 06-8553548. FAX 06-8554105. Ed.Bd. adv.; bk.rev.; abstr.; bibl.; charts; illus.; index; circ. 2,750. **Indexed:** Biol.Abstr., Chem.Abstr., Excerp.Med., Ind.Med.
—BLDSC shelfmark: 6412.890000.
Formerly: Clinica Ostetrica e Ginecologica (ISSN 0009-9031)

PEDI KAI NEI GONIS. see *MEDICAL SCIENCES — Pediatrics*

PEDIATRIYA, AKUSHERSTVO TA GINEKOLOGIYA. see *MEDICAL SCIENCES — Pediatrics*

618   US   ISSN 0160-7219
PERINATAL PRESS; for persons dedicated to improving the health care of the pregnant woman, fetus and newborn. 1977. 6/yr. $20. Perinatal Press, Inc., Box 710698, San Diego, CA 92171-0698. Ed. Dr. J.M. Schneider. bk.rev.; abstr.; charts; illus.; stat.; index; circ. 6,000. (looseleaf format; also avail. in microfilm from UMI; back issues avail.) **Indexed:** CINAHL.
—BLDSC shelfmark: 6425.126000.

618.9   GW   ISSN 0936-7160
CODEN: PEMDEU
PERINATALMEDIZIN. 1989. q. DM.96. (Deutschen Gesellschaft fuer Perinatale Medizin) Springer-Verlag, Heidelberger Platz 3, 1000 Berlin 33, Germany. TEL 030-8207-0. FAX 030-8207300. Ed. J.W. Dudenhausen. adv. contact: adv. contact: E. Lueckermann.
—BLDSC shelfmark: 6425.121500.

PERSPECTIVAS INTERNACIONALES EN PLANIFICACION FAMILIAR. see *BIRTH CONTROL*

PERSPECTIVES INTERNATIONALES SUR LE PLANNING FAMILIAL. see *BIRTH CONTROL*

PIELEGNIARKA I POLOZNA. see *MEDICAL SCIENCES — Nurses And Nursing*

618.2 613.9   US   ISSN 0883-3095
RG635
PRE- AND PERI-NATAL PSYCHOLOGY JOURNAL. 1986. q. $145 (foreign $170). (Pre- and Peri-Natal Psychology Association of North America) Human Sciences Press, Inc. (Subsidiary of: Plenum Publishing Corp.), 233 Spring St., New York, NY 10013-1578. TEL 212-620-8000. FAX 212-463-0742. Ed. Charles D. Laughlin. adv. (reprint service avail. from UMI) **Indexed:** Psychol.Abstr.
—BLDSC shelfmark: 6603.620000.
Description: Explores the psychological dimensions of human reproduction and pregnancy and the mental and emotional development of the unborn and newborn child.
Refereed Serial

MEDICAL SCIENCES — OBSTETRICS AND GYNECOLOGY

618 AT ISSN 1035-5448
PREGNANCY. 1986. s-a. Aus.$5.95 (foreign Aus.$6.15). Magazine House Pty. Ltd., P.O. Box 1067, Crows Nest, N.S.W. 2065, Australia. TEL 61-2-438-2399. FAX 61-2-436-3014. Ed. Carol Fallows. adv.; bk.rev.; circ. 45,000.
Formerly: Pregnancy, Birth and the Next 6 Months (ISSN 0817-2420)
Description: Covers birth process, moods of pregnancy, exercises, beauty, breastfeeding, and choosing a birth place.

618 UK ISSN 0197-3851
CODEN: PRDIDM
PRENATAL DIAGNOSIS. 1981. m. $495 (effective 1992). John Wiley & Sons Ltd., Journals, Baffins Lane, Chichester, Sussex PO19 1UD, England. TEL 0243-779777. FAX 0243-775878. TELEX 86290 WIBOOK G. Ed. M.A. Ferguson-Smith. adv. (reprint service avail. from ISI,SWZ,UMI) Indexed: Bibl.Dev.Med.& Child Neur., Biol.Abstr., Chem.Abstr, Curr.Adv.Ecol.Sci., Curr.Adv.Genetics & Molec.Biol., Curr.Cont., Dent.Ind., Excerp.Med., Ind.Med.
—BLDSC shelfmark: 6607.646000.
Description: Communicates the results of original research in a variety of clinical and scientific specialties concerned with "in-utero" diagnosis of fetal abnormality in man resulting from genetic and environmental factors.

618 SP ISSN 0304-5013
PROGRESOS DE OBSTETRICIA Y GINECOLOGIA. (Text in Spanish; summaries in English) 1958. m. 7300 ptas. (Sociedad Espanola de Ginecologia e Obstetricia) Salvat Publicaciones Cientificas, S.A., Muntaner, 262, 6o, 08021 Barcelona, Spain. TEL 2010911. FAX 2015911. TELEX 53132 SAEDI E. (Subscr. to: Cempro, Plaza Conde Valle Suchil 20, 28015 Madrid, Spain) Eds. Santiago Dexeus, Jesus Gonzalez-Merlo. adv.; bk.rev.; index; circ. 3,000. (back issues avail.) Indexed: Excerp.Med., Ind.Med.Esp.

618 SP ISSN 1130-0523
PROGRESOS EN DIAGNOSTICO PRENATAL. (Text in Spanish; summaries in English) 1989. q. 3250 ptas. (Asociacion Espanola de Diagnostico Prenatal) Salvat Publicaciones Cientificas, S.A., Muntaner, 262, 6o, 08021 Barcelona, Spain. TEL 2010911. FAX 2015911. TELEX 53132 SAEDI E. (Subscr. to: Cempro, Plaza Conde Valle Suchil 20, 28015 Madrid, Spain) adv.; bk.rev.; index; circ. 2,000. (back issues avail.)

PROLIFE NEWS. see *PUBLIC HEALTH AND SAFETY*

618 IT ISSN 0033-491X
QUADERNI DI CLINICA OSTETRICA E GINECOLOGICA. (Text in Italian; summaries in English) 1946. bi-m. L.60000 (foreign L.120000)(effective 1992). Casa Editrice Maccari, Via Trento 53, 43100 Parma, Italy. FAX 039-521-771268. Eds. Giuseppe Dellepiane, Eugenio Maurizio. circ. 1,600. Indexed: Chem.Abstr., Excerp.Med., Ind.Med.
—BLDSC shelfmark: 7165.900000.

618.2 GW
RATGEBER FUER SCHWANGERE UND JUNGE MUETTER. 1973. a. Informedia Verlags GmbH, Eupenerstr. 165, Postfach 450569, 5000 Cologne 41, Germany. TEL 0221-49810. FAX 0221-4981258. TELEX 8882071. Ed. Hildegard Schuster. charts; illus.

REPRODUCTIVE TOXICOLOGY. see *ENVIRONMENTAL STUDIES — Toxicology And Environmental Safety*

618.3 US ISSN 0362-5699
RG600 CODEN: PPMED7
REVIEWS IN PERINATAL MEDICINE. 1976. a. price varies. Raven Press, 1185 Ave. of the Americas, New York, NY 10036. TEL 212-930-9500. FAX 212-869-3495. TELEX 640073. Eds. Emile M. Scarpelli, Ermelando V. Cosmi. Indexed: Biol.Abstr. *Refereed Serial*

618 CL ISSN 0048-766X
REVISTA CHILENA DE OBSTETRICIA Y GINECOLOGIA.*
1961. bi-m. Sociedad Chilena de Obstetricia y Ginecologia, Mac - Iver 721 Of. 8, Casilla 639, Santiago, Chile. illus. Indexed: Chem.Abstr., Excerp.Med., Ind.Med.
—BLDSC shelfmark: 7848.930000.
Supersedes: Sociedad Chilena de Obstetricia y Ginecologia. Boletin.

618 CK ISSN 0034-7434
REVISTA COLOMBIANA DE OBSTETRICIA Y GINECOLOGIA. 1950. bi-m. Col.2000($50) Sociedad Colombiana de Obstetricia y Ginecologia, Carrera 23 No.39-82, Apdo. Aereo 14961 y 34188, Bogota, Colombia. (Co-sponsor: Federacion Colombiana de Sociedades de Obstetricia y Ginecologia) Eds. Jose Gabriel Acuna, Enrique Archila. adv.; bk.rev.; bibl.; charts; illus.; index; circ. 2,000. Indexed: Biol.Abstr., Excerp.Med., Ind.Med.
—BLDSC shelfmark: 7851.405000.

618 CU ISSN 0138-600X
REVISTA CUBANA DE OBSTETRICIA Y GINECOLOGIA. (Text in Spanish; summaries in English, French, Spanish) 1975. s-a. $10 in N. America; S. America $12; Europe $14. Ministerio de Salud Publica, Centro Nacional de Informacion de Ciencias Medicas, Calle E No. 452, e-19 y 21, Plaza de al Revolucion, Apdo. 6520, Havana, Cuba. TEL 809-32-5338. (Dist. by: Ediciones Cubanas, Obispo No. 527, Apdo. 605, Havana, Cuba) Dir. Dr. Felix A. Robaina Jorge. bibl.; charts; illus.; index; circ. 1,500.

618 VE ISSN 0048-7732
REVISTA DE OBSTETRICIA Y GINECOLOGIA DE VENEZUELA. 1941. q. $30. Sociedad de Obstetricia y Ginecologia de Venezuela, Biblioteca, Apartado 20081, Avenida San Martin, Caracas, Venezuela. Ed. Dr. Oscar Aguero. adv.; bk.rev.; circ. 2,000. Indexed: Biol.Abstr., Chem.Abstr., Excerp.Med., Ind.Med.
—BLDSC shelfmark: 7869.020000.

618 RM ISSN 0029-781X
REVISTA DE PEDIATRIE, OBSTETRICA, GINECOLOGIE. OBSTETRICA SI GINECOLOGIE. (Text in Rumanian; summaries in English, French, German, Russian) 1953. 4/yr. $20. Uniunea Societatilor de Stiinte Medicale din Republica Socialista Rumania, Str. Progresului No. 8, Bucharest, Rumania. (Subscr. to: ILEXIM, Str. 13 Decembrie Nr. 3, P.O. Box 136-137, Bucharest, Rumania) Ed.Bd. adv.; bk.rev.; bibl.; charts; illus. Indexed: Biol.Abstr., Chem.Abstr., Dent.Ind.

618 SP ISSN 0214-1582
REVISTA DE SENOLOGIA Y PATOLOGIA MAMARIA. q. 6500 ptas.($85) Editorial Garsi, S.A., Londres, 17, 28028 Madrid, Spain. TEL 256-08-00. FAX 361-10-07. Ed.Bd. circ. 1,000.

618 FR ISSN 1141-5886
REVUE DU GYNECOLOGUE OBSTETRICIEN. 1989. 8/yr. 100 ECU($120) (typically set in Jan.). Masson, 5 et 7, rue Laromiguiere, 75005 Paris, France. TEL 1-46-34-21-60. FAX 1-45-87-29-99. TELEX 202 671 F. Ed. Max Favier. adv.; bibl.; circ. 6,000.

618 FR ISSN 0035-290X
CODEN: RFGOAO
REVUE FRANCAISE DE GYNECOLOGIE ET D'OBSTETRIQUE. (Text in French; summaries in English, French and German) 1906. 10/yr. 880 F. to individuals (foreign 1130 F.); students 440 F. (foreign 620 F.). Expansion Scientifique, 15 rue Saint-Benoit, 75278 Paris Cedex 06, France. Eds. Y. Malinas, J. Seneze. adv.; bk.rev.; abstr.; charts; illus.; stat.; tr.lit.; circ. 5,000. (also avail. in microform from UMI; reprint service avail. from UMI) Indexed: Biol.Abstr., Chem.Abstr., Curr.Cont., Excerp.Med., Ind.Med., Rev.Plant Path.
—BLDSC shelfmark: 7904.170000.

618 JA ISSN 0386-9865
CODEN: RFUSA4
RINSHO FUJINKA SANKA/CLINICAL OBSTETRICS AND GYNECOLOGY. (Text in Japanese) 1946. m. 24720 Yen($190) Igaku-Shoin Ltd., 5-24-3 Hongo, Bunkyo-ku, Tokyo 113-91, Japan. TEL 03-817-5709. Ed.Bd. circ. 3,000.
—BLDSC shelfmark: 3286.289000.

618 IT
RISVEGLIO OSTETRICO.* 1922. m. L.8000. Editoriale Fenarete, Via Beruto 7, Milan, Italy. adv.; circ. 13,000.

ROYAL COLLEGE OF MIDWIVES. CURRENT AWARENESS SERVICE; recent literature on midwifery. see *MEDICAL SCIENCES — Abstracting, Bibliographies, Statistics*

618.1 FR ISSN 1163-1961
SEIN. (Summaries in French) q. 103 ECU($120) (typically set in Jan.). Masson, 120 bd. Saint-Germain, 75280 Paris Cedex 06, France. TEL 1-46-34-21-60. FAX 1-45-87-29-99. TELEX 202 671 F. Ed. J-L Lamarque. adv.; bk.rev.; circ. 5,000.

SEMINARS IN PERINATOLOGY. see *MEDICAL SCIENCES — Pediatrics*

SHARE NEWSLETTER. see *PSYCHOLOGY*

618 CC ISSN 1001-0858
SHIYONG FUKE YU CHANKE ZAZHI/JOURNAL OF PRACTICAL GYNECOLOGY AND OBSTETRICS. (Text in Chinese) 1986. bi-m. $7.50. Shiyong Yixue Zazhishe, 44-1, Jixian Jie, Heping Qu, Shenyang, Liaoning 110005, People's Republic of China. TEL 364398. Ed. Wang Dezhi.

618 SI ISSN 0129-3273
CODEN: SJOGDE
SINGAPORE JOURNAL OF OBSTETRICS & GYNAECOLOGY. vol.6, 1967. 3/yr. $25 to individuals; medical students $6. Obstetrical and Gynaecological Society of Singapore, c/o National University Hospital, Dept. of O & G, Lower Kent Ridge Road, Singapore 0511, Singapore. TEL 7724267. FAX 779-4753. Ed. Dilip K. Sen. adv.; bk.rev.; charts; illus.; circ. 1,000. (reprint service avail. from ISI) Indexed: ASCA, Biol.Abstr., Chem.Abstr., Curr.Cont.
Formerly: Kandang Kerbau Hospital Bulletin (ISSN 0022-8346)
Description: Original and review articles on all aspects of obstetrics and gynaecology.

618.1 618.2 BL
SINOPSE DE GINECOLOGIA E OBSTETRICIA. (Text in English and Portuguese) vol.5, 1973. bi-m. Moreira Jr. Editora Ltda., Rua Henrique Martins, 493, 04504 Sao Paulo, Brazil. Ed.Bd. adv.

618.2 FR
SOCIETE FRANCAISE DE PSYCHO-PROPHYLAXIE OBSTETRICALE. BULLETIN OFFICIEL. 1959. q. 350 F. Societe Internationale de Psycho-Prophylaxie Obstetricale, 31 rue Saint-Guillaume, 75007 Paris, France. Ed. Daniel Lipszyc. adv.; bk.rev.
Formerly: Societe Internationale de Psycho-Prophylaxie Obstetricale. Bulletin Officiel (ISSN 0037-9468)

618 BE ISSN 0037-9522
SOCIETE ROYALE BELGE DE GYNECOLOGIE ET D'OBSTETRIQUE. BULLETIN.* vol.36, 1966. bi-m. Societe Royale Belge de Gynecologie et d'Obstetrique, 309 Ave. Moliere, Brussels 6, Belgium. adv. Indexed: Biol.Abstr.

618.202 US
SPECIAL DELIVERY. 1977. q. $15. Informed Homebirth, Informed Birth and Parenting, Box 3675, Ann Arbor, MI 48106-3675. TEL 313-662-6857. Ed. Rahima Baldwin. adv.; bk.rev.; illus.; circ. 2,000. (back issues avail.) Indexed: Hlth.Ind.
Description: Discusses midwifery alternatives in birth, parenting, early childhood education.

SURGICAL LAPAROSCOPY AND ENDOSCOPY. see *MEDICAL SCIENCES — Surgery*

618 GW ISSN 0935-3208
T W GYNAEKOLOGIE. 1988. bi-m. DM.69. Verlag G. Braun GmbH, Karl-Friedrich-Str. 14, Postfach 1709, 7500 Karlsruhe 1, Germany. TEL 0721-165-0. FAX 0721-165-227.
—BLDSC shelfmark: 9076.749200.

618.1 SP ISSN 0040-8867
TOKO-GINECOLOGIA PRACTICA. 1936. m. (10/yr.) 4300 ptas.($72) Editorial Garsi, S.A., Londres, 17, 28028 Madrid, Spain. TEL 256-08-00. FAX 361-10-07. Ed. J. Cruz Hermida. adv.; bk.rev.; charts; stat.; circ. 3,000. Indexed: Biol.Abstr., Excerp.Med., Ind.Med.Esp., Nutr.Abstr.
—BLDSC shelfmark: 8862.885000.

618   US   ISSN 0891-9925
CODEN: TRREEN
TROPHOBLAST RESEARCH. 1984. irreg., vol.4, 1990. price varies. Plenum Publishing Corp., 233 Spring St., New York, NY 10013-1578. TEL 212-620-8000. FAX 212-463-0742. TELEX 23-421139. Eds. Richard K. Miller, Henry A. Thiede. (back issues avail.) **Indexed:** Chem.Abstr. (1984-).
—BLDSC shelfmark: 9051.930000.
Refereed Serial

618 610   NR   ISSN 0189-5117
TROPICAL JOURNAL OF OBSTETRICS AND GYNAECOLOGY. (Text in English) 1981. s-a. $10. (Society of Gynaecology and Obstetrics of Nigeria) Literamed Nigeria Ltd., Plot 45, Alausa, Oregun Village, P.M.B. 21068, Ikeja, Lagos, Nigeria. Ed. V.E. Aimaku. circ. 1,000.

618   IT   ISSN 0393-7801
ULTRASONICA. (Text in Italian; summaries in English) 1986. q. L.50000($50) (Societa Italiana di Ecografia Ostetrica e Ginecologica) C I C Edizioni Internazionale s.r.l., Via L. Spallanzani, 11, 00161 Rome, Italy. TEL 06-8412673. FAX 06-8443365. TELEX 622099 CIC I. (Co-sponsor: Societa Italian di Ecografia Pediatrica)
—BLDSC shelfmark: 9082.792000.

618   UK   ISSN 0960-7692
▼**ULTRASOUND IN OBSTETRICS & GYNECOLOGY.** 1991. bi-m. £85 to individuals; institutions £125. (International Society of Ultrasound in Obstetrics and Gynecology) Parthenon Publishing Group, Casterton Hall, Casterton, Carnforth, Lancashire LA6 2LA, England. TEL 05242-72084. FAX 05242-71587. bk.rev.
—BLDSC shelfmark: 9082.815300.

618.1   SA
UNIVERSITY OF CAPE TOWN. DEPARTMENT OF OBSTETRICS AND GYNAECOLOGY. ANNUAL REPORT. (Text in English) 1952. a. free. University of Cape Town, Department of Obstetrics and Gynaecology, Medical School, Anzio Rd., Observatory, Cape Town 7925, South Africa. TEL 021-471250. (Co-sponsor: Cape Provincial Administration) Ed. Herman A. van Coeverden de Groot. circ. 100.
Formerly: University of Cape Town. Department of Gynaecology. Annual Report (ISSN 0069-0228)
Description: Lists personnel, research in progress, publications and programs available in the department.

VIDEO JOURNAL OF COLOR FLOW IMAGING. see *MEDICAL SCIENCES — Radiology And Nuclear Medicine*

WOMENWISE. see *WOMEN'S HEALTH*

618.1 618.2   US   ISSN 0084-3911
RG26   CODEN: YOBGAD
YEAR BOOK OF OBSTETRICS AND GYNECOLOGY. 1933. a. $57.95. Mosby - Year Book, Inc., Continuity Division, 200 N. LaSalle, Chicago, IL 60601. TEL 312-726-9733. FAX 312-726-6075. TELEX 206155. Ed. Daniel R. Mishell, Jr., M.D. illus. (reprint service avail.) **Indexed:** Curr.Adv.Ecol.Sci.
●Also available online. Vendor(s): BRS.
—BLDSC shelfmark: 9414.650000.

618   CI   ISSN 0352-5562
YUGOSLAV GYNECOLOGY AND PERINATOLOGY. (Text in Serbo-Croatian; summaries in English) 1960. bi-m. 5000 din.($30) Udruzenje Ginekologa-Opstetricara Jugoslavije, Petrova 13, 41000 Zagreb, Croatia. TEL 041 444-270. Ed. Dr. Zdravko Pavlic. adv.; bk.rev.; bibl.; charts; illus.; index; circ. 1,700. **Indexed:** Biol.Abstr., Dent.Ind., Excerp.Med., Ind.Med.
—BLDSC shelfmark: 5073.838620.
Former titles: Jugoslavenska Ginekologija i Opstetricija (ISSN 0017-002X); Ginekologija i Opstetricija.

618   GW   ISSN 0300-967X
RG1   CODEN: ZGPRA3
ZEITSCHRIFT FUER GEBURTSHILFE UND PERINATOLOGIE. (Text in German; summaries in English and German) 1876. bi-m. DM.327. Ferdinand Enke Verlag, Postfach 101254, 7000 Stuttgart 10, Germany. TEL 0711-8931-0. FAX 0711-8931-419. TELEX 07252275-GTV-D. Ed.Bd. adv.; bk.rev.; charts; illus.; index per vol. (also avail. in microfiche from BHP) **Indexed:** Bibl.Dev.Med.& Child Neur., Biol.Abstr., Chem.Abstr., Curr.Cont., Dent.Ind., Excerp.Med., Ind.Med., Nutr.Abstr., Sci.Cit.Ind.
—BLDSC shelfmark: 9462.453000.
Formerly: Zeitschrift fuer Geburtshilfe und Gynaekologie (ISSN 0044-278X)

618.1   GW   ISSN 0044-4197
CODEN: ZEGYAX
ZENTRALBLATT FUER GYNAEKOLOGIE. Title varies: Zentralblatt fuer Gynaekologie und Geburtshilfe. 1877. s-m. DM.288. Johann Ambrosius Barth Verlag, Leipzig - Heidelberg, Salomonstr. 18b, 7010 Leipzig, Germany. TEL 70131. Ed. Prof. H. Wilken. adv.; bk.rev.; charts; illus.; index; circ. 3,500. (also avail. in microfiche from BHP) **Indexed:** Biol.Abstr., Chem.Abstr., Curr.Adv.Cancer Res., Curr.Adv.Ecol.Sci., Curr.Cont., Dent.Ind., Ind.Med., Nutr.Abstr.
—BLDSC shelfmark: 9508.400000.

618 614   CC
ZHONGGUO FUNU JIANKANG/CHINA WOMEN'S HEALTH. (Text in Chinese) bi-m. Liaoning Sheng Weisheng Ting, No.6, Heping Dajie 6 Duan 18 Li, Shenyang, Liaoning 110005, People's Republic of China. TEL 365444. Ed. Qin Xinhua.

618   CC
ZHONGGUO FUYOU BAOJIAN/CHINESE WOMEN AND CHILDREN'S HEALTH. (Text in Chinese) bi-m. Jilin Sheng Weisheng Ting - Jilin Provincial Bureau of Health, Fu 2, Dong Minzhu Dajie, Changchun, Jilin 130061, People's Republic of China. TEL 825027. Ed. He Jiesheng.

ZHONGGUO YIXUE WENZHAI (JIHUA SHENGYU, FUCHAN KEXUE)/CHINA MEDICAL ABSTRACTS (BIRTH CONTROL AND GYNECOLOGY). see *MEDICAL SCIENCES — Abstracting, Bibliographies, Statistics*

618   CC
ZHONGHUA FU-CHANKE ZAZHI/CHINESE JOURNAL OF OBSTETRICS AND GYNECOLOGY. (Text in Chinese) q. $3 per no. Guoji Shudian, Qikan Bu, Chegongzhuang Xilu 21, P.O. Box 399, Beijing 100044, People's Republic of China. **Indexed:** Chem.Abstr, Ind.Med.

ZHONGHUA NEIFENMI DAIXIE ZAZHI/CHINESE JOURNAL OF ENDOCRINOLOGY AND METABOLISM. see *MEDICAL SCIENCES — Endocrinology*

MEDICAL SCIENCES — Ophthalmology And Optometry

617.7   US   ISSN 8756-9175
RE22
A B M S DIRECTORY OF CERTIFIED OPHTHALMOLOGISTS. 1983. biennial. $29.95. American Board of Medical Specialties, One Rotary Center, Ste. 805, Evanston, IL 60201. TEL 708-491-9091. FAX 708-328-3596. Ed. Dr. J. Lee Dockery.

617.7   NE   ISSN 0065-115X
ACTA CONCILIUM OPHTHALMOLOGICUM.* (Represents: International Congress of Ophthalmology) (Text in English, French, German and Spanish) quadrennial, 1990, 26th, Singapore. International Federation of Ophthalmological Societies, c/o Prof. A. Deutman, Sec., Dept. of Ophthalmology, Univ. of Nijmegen, P. van Leijdenlaan 15, 6525 EX Nijmegen, Netherlands. TEL 080-573138. FAX 080-540522. circ. 8,500 (controlled). (reprint service avail. from ISI) **Indexed:** Curr.Cont., Excerp.Med.
Refereed Serial

617.7   DK   ISSN 0001-639X
CODEN: ACOPAT
ACTA OPHTHALMOLOGICA. (Supplement avail.) (Text in English) 1923. bi-m. DKK 1100 in Europe; elsewhere DKK 1150. Scriptor Publisher ApS, Gasvaerksvej 15, DK-1656 Copenhagen V, Denmark. Ed. Niels Ehlers. adv.; bibl.; charts; illus.; index, cum.index: vols.1-25; circ. 1,700. **Indexed:** ASCA, Biol.Abstr., Chem.Abstr., Curr.Adv.Cancer Res., Curr.Adv.Ecol.Sci., Curr.Cont., Dok.Arbeitsmed., Excerp.Med., Helminthol.Abstr., Ind.Med., Ind.Sci.Rev., INIS Atomind., Psychol.Abstr., Rev.Med.& Vet.Mycol., Sci.Cit.Ind.
—BLDSC shelfmark: 0641.750000.

617.7   DK   ISSN 0065-1451
CODEN: AOPSAP
ACTA OPHTHALMOLOGICA. SUPPLEMENTUM. (Text in English) 1923. irreg. free to subscribers to Acta Ophthalmologica. Scriptor Publisher ApS, Gasvaerksvej 15, 1656 Copenhagen V, Denmark. adv. **Indexed:** Biol.Abstr., Curr.Cont., Dent.Ind., Dok.Arbeitsmed., Ind.Med., INIS Atomind.

617.7   CI   ISSN 0001-6403
CODEN: AOPIBU
ACTA OPHTHALMOLOGICA IUGOSLAVICA. (Text in Serbo-Croatian; summaries in English, French, German) 1963. s-a. 1000 din. Zbor Lijecnika Hrvatske, Oftalmoloska Sekcija, Subiceva 12, 41000 Zagreb, Croatia. Ed. Dr. Kresimir Cupak. adv.; bk.rev.; abstr.; index; circ. 1,200. **Indexed:** Biol.Abstr., C.I.S. Abstr.
—BLDSC shelfmark: 0641.770000.

617.7   UK   ISSN 0276-3508
ADVANCES IN OPHTHALMIC PLASTIC & RECONSTRUCTIVE SURGERY. 1982. irreg. price varies. Pergamon Press plc, Headington Hill Hall, Oxford OX3 0BW, England. TEL 0865-794141. FAX 0865-743911. TELEX 83177 PERGAP. (And: 660 White Plains Rd., Tarrytown, NY 10591-5153. TEL 914-524-9200) Ed. Dr. Stephen Bosniak. (also avail. in microform) **Indexed:** Curr.Adv.Ecol.Sci., Curr.Cont.
—BLDSC shelfmark: 0709.540000.
Refereed Serial

617.7   IT   ISSN 0002-0915
AGGIORNAMENTI DI TERAPIA OFTALMOLOGICA. 1949. a. Via Carmignani, 2, 56121 Pisa, Italy. abstr.; circ. 5,500. (tabloid format)

617   II
ALL INDIA OPHTHALMOLOGICAL SOCIETY. PROCEEDINGS. (Text in English) a. All India Ophthalmological Society, 13, Cathedral Rd., Madras 600 086, India.

617.7   US   ISSN 0002-9394
RE1   CODEN: AJOPAA
AMERICAN JOURNAL OF OPHTHALMOLOGY. 1884. m. $55. Ophthalmic Publishing Co., 435 N. Michigan Ave., Ste. 1415, Chicago, IL 60611. TEL 312-787-3853. FAX 312-787-5186. Ed. Dr. Frank W. Newell. adv.; bk.rev.; abstr.; bibl.; illus.; index; circ. 18,000. (also avail. in microform from UMI; reprint service avail. from UMI) **Indexed:** Biodet.Abstr., Biol.Abstr., Biotech.Abstr., Chem.Abstr., Curr.Adv.Cancer Res., Curr.Adv.Ecol.Sci., Curr.Cont., Dent.Ind., Dok.Arbeitsmed., Excerp.Med., Helminthol.Abstr., Ind.Med., Ind.Sci.Rev., Ind.Vet., INIS Atomind., Lab.Haz.Bull., Nutr.Abstr., Protozool.Abstr., Psychol.Abstr., Rev.Med.& Vet.Mycol., Risk Abstr., Sci.Cit.Ind, Vet.Bull.
—BLDSC shelfmark: 0828.900000.
Refereed Serial

617.7   US   ISSN 0065-9533
RE1   CODEN: TAOSAT
AMERICAN OPHTHALMOLOGICAL SOCIETY. TRANSACTIONS. 1864. a. $50. American Ophthalmological Society, c/o Banks Anderson, M.D., Sec.-Treas., Duke University Eye Center, Durham, NC 27710. FAX 919-684-2230. Ed. Dr. William Tasman. index; circ. 600. (back issues avail.) **Indexed:** Biol.Abstr., Dent.Ind., Excerp.Med., Ind.Med.
—BLDSC shelfmark: 8893.650000.

MEDICAL SCIENCES — OPHTHALMOLOGY AND OPTOMETRY

617.75   US   ISSN 0003-0244
RE1   CODEN: JAOPBD
AMERICAN OPTOMETRIC ASSOCIATION. JOURNAL.
1928. m. $50 to non-members (foreign $75). American Optometric Association, 243 N. Lindbergh Blvd., St. Louis, MO 63141. TEL 314-991-4100. FAX 314-991-4101. Ed. John Potter. adv.; bk.rev.; abstr.; charts; illus.; stat.; tr.lit.; index, cum.index: 1925-1972; circ. 30,142. **Indexed:** Biol.Abstr., Curr.Cont., Dok.Arbeitsmed., Excerp.Med., Ind.Med., INIS Atomind., Psychol.Abstr.
—BLDSC shelfmark: 4689.370000.
Refereed Serial

617.7   US   ISSN 0094-9620
AMERICAN OPTOMETRIC ASSOCIATION NEWS. 1961. s-m. $35 (foreign $45). American Optometric Association, 243 N. Lindbergh Blvd., St. Louis, MO 63141. TEL 314-991-4100. FAX 314-991-4101. Ed. Bridget McDonald. adv.; circ. 30,325. (tabloid format)
Description: Covers news of the association for doctors of optometry.

617.7   US   ISSN 0065-955X
CODEN: AOJTAW
AMERICAN ORTHOPTIC JOURNAL. 1950. a. $22 to individuals; institutions $50. (American Association of Certified Othoptists) University of Wisconsin Press, Journal Division, 114 N. Murray St., Madison, WI 53715. TEL 608-262-4952. FAX 608-262-7560. Ed. Dr. Thomas France. adv.; cum.index: 1950-1960, 1971-1980; circ. 993. (also avail. in microform from UMI; back issues avail.; reprint service avail. from UMI) **Indexed:** Biol.Abstr., Excerp.Med.
—BLDSC shelfmark: 0847.750000.
Refereed Serial

617.7   IT   ISSN 0003-4665
CODEN: AOCOAG
ANNALI DI OTTAMOLOGIA E CLINICA OCULISTICA. (Text in Italian; summaries in English, French, German) 1874. m. L.120000 (foreign L. 240000)(effective 1992). Casa Editrice Maccari, Via Trento 53, 43100 Parma, Italy. FAX 039-521-771268. adv.; bk.rev.; charts; illus.; index; circ. 2,000. **Indexed:** Chem.Abstr., Excerp.Med., Ind.Med., INIS Atomind.
—BLDSC shelfmark: 1016.200000.

617.7   US   ISSN 0003-4886
RE1   CODEN: ANOPB5
ANNALS OF OPHTHALMOLOGY. 1969. m. $60 to individuals (foreign $80); libraries and institutions $75 (foreign $90). (American Society of Contemporary Ophthalmology) Altier & Maynard Communications, Inc., 6 Farmingville Rd., Ridgefield, CT 06877. Ed. Dr. John Bellows. adv.; bk.rev.; bibl.; illus.; index; circ. controlled. **Indexed:** Biol.Abstr., Chem.Abstr., Dent.Ind., Dok.Arbeitsmed., Excerp.Med., Helminthol.Abstr., Ind.Med., INIS Atomind.
—BLDSC shelfmark: 1043.350000.
Supersedes: Journal of Experimental and Clinical Ophthalmology.
Refereed Serial

617.7   FR   ISSN 0301-4495
ANNEE THERAPEUTIQUE ET CLINIQUE EN OPHTALMOLOGIE. 1950. a. 375 F. Fueri-Lamy, 21 rue Paradis, 13001 Marseille, France. FAX 91-54-87-88. TELEX 430627. Ed. Pierre Berard Vital. adv. **Indexed:** Ind.Med.
—BLDSC shelfmark: 1049.600000.
Formerly: Annee Therapeutique en Ophtalmologie (ISSN 0066-2402)

ANNUARIO OTTICO ITALIANO. see *BUSINESS AND ECONOMICS — Trade And Industrial Directories*

617.7   US   ISSN 0003-9950
CODEN: AROPAW
ARCHIVES OF OPHTHALMOLOGY. Spanish translation: Archives of Ophthalmology (Edicion Espanola) (SP ISSN 1130-5134) 1869. m. $65. American Medical Association, 515 N. State St., Chicago, IL 60610. TEL 312-464-0183. FAX 312-464-5834. Ed. Dr. Morton F. Goldberg. adv.; bk.rev.; charts; illus.; index; circ. 21,500. (also avail. in microform from UMI,PMC) **Indexed:** Abstr.Inter.Med., Biol.Abstr., Biotech.Abstr., C.I.S. Abstr., Chem.Abstr., Curr.Adv.Cancer Res., Curr.Adv.Ecol.Sci., Curr.Cont., Dent.Ind., Dok.Arbeitsmed., Excerp.Med., Helminthol.Abstr., HRIS, Ind.Med., Ind.Sci.Rev., Ind.Vet., INIS Atomind., Nutr.Abstr., Protozool.Abstr., Psychol.Abstr., Rev.Med.& Vet.Mycol., Rev.Plant Path., Sci.Cit.Ind., Small Anim.Abstr., Vet.Bull.
●Also available online. Vendor(s): Mead Data Central.
—BLDSC shelfmark: 1638.450000.
Refereed Serial

617.7   SP   ISSN 1130-5134
ARCHIVES OF OPHTHALMOLOGY (EDICION ESPANOLA). Spanish translation of: Archives of Ophthalmology (US ISSN 0003-9950) bi-m. (American Medical Association, US) Ediciones Doyma S.A., Travesera de Gracia, 17-21, 08021 Barcelona, Spain. TEL 200-07-11. FAX 209-11-36. TELEX 51964 INK E. Ed. J. Murube del Castillo. adv.: page 135000 ptas.; trim 210 x 280; adv. contact: Cristina Garrote. circ. 3,500.
Description: Contains translations of articles from the American edition including editorials, clinical cases, laboratory technique and investigative work.

617.7   AG   ISSN 0066-6777
ARCHIVOS DE OFTALMOLOGIA DE BUENOS AIRES. 1925. q. $30. Sociedad Argentina de Oftalmologia, Viamonte 1464-1 DTO. 2, Buenos Aires, Argentina. adv.; circ. 1,500. **Indexed:** Biol.Abstr., Excerp.Med.
—BLDSC shelfmark: 1655.480000.

617.7   US
ARGUS (SAN FRANCISCO). 1978. m. $36. American Academy of Ophthalmology, Box 7424, San Francisco, CA 94120-7424. TEL 415-561-8500. FAX 415-561-8567. Ed. Bruce E. Spivey. adv.; bk.rev.; circ. 16,000.

617.7   BL   ISSN 0004-2749
CODEN: AQBOAP
ARQUIVOS BRASILEIROS DE OFTALMOLOGIA. 1938. bi-m. $100. Belfort Editora, Rua Barao de Itapetininga 297, Caixa 4086, Sao Paulo, Brazil. Ed. Rubens Belfort Mattos. adv.; bk.rev.; abstr.; illus.; circ. 1,500. **Indexed:** Biol.Abstr., Excerp.Med., Ind.Med.
—BLDSC shelfmark: 1695.240000.

617.7 016   US   ISSN 0271-1281
AUDIO-DIGEST OPHTHALMOLOGY. 1963. s-m. $168. Audio-Digest Foundation (Subsidiary of: California Medical Association), 1577 E. Chevy Chase Dr., Glendale, CA 91206. TEL 213-245-8505. FAX 818-240-7379. Ed. Claron L. Oakley. circ. controlled. (audio cassette)
Refereed Serial

AUDIOPTICA. see *PHARMACY AND PHARMACOLOGY*

617.7   GW   ISSN 0341-1486
AUGENAERZTLICHE FORTBILDUNG; Jahreskurse fuer die praktische Augenheilkunde. 1977. q. DM.180 (foreign DM.198). Urban und Vogel, Postfach 152209, 8000 Munich 15, Germany. TEL 089-53292-0. FAX 089-53292-100. Ed. H.J. Merte. index; circ. 2,000. (back issues avail.)

617.7   GW   ISSN 0004-7902
DER AUGENARZT. 1967. 6/yr. (Berufsverband der Augenaerzte Deutschlands e.V.) Dr. R. Kaden Verlag, Poststr. 24-26, 6900 Heidelberg, Germany. TEL 06221-10313. FAX 06221-29910. adv.: B&W page DM.5020; trim 230 x 178. bk.rev.; abstr.; illus.; circ. 6,800.

617.7   GW   ISSN 0004-7929
DER AUGENOPTIKER. 1946. m. DM.83.40 (foreign DM.99). Konradin Verlag Robert Kohlhammer GmbH, Ernst-Mey-Str. 8, 7022 Leinfelden-Echterdingen, Germany. TEL 0711-7594-0. FAX 0711-7594-390. TELEX 7255421. Ed. Martin Graf. adv.; bk.rev.; bibl.; charts; illus.; stat.; circ. 11,170.
—BLDSC shelfmark: 1791.300000.

617.7   GW   ISSN 0004-7937
DER AUGENSPIEGEL; Forum der Augenaerzte. 1955. m. DM.182. Augenspiegel Verlags GmbH, Lintorfer Str. 7-9, D-4030 Ratingen 1, Germany. TEL 02102-23062. FAX 02102-25488. TELEX 8589002-FOC-D. Ed. Dr. Berthold Schwab. adv.; bk.rev.; charts; illus.; mkt.; stat.; tr.lit.; circ. 4,000.
—BLDSC shelfmark: 1791.400000.

617.7   AT   ISSN 0814-9763
CODEN: ANZOEQ
AUSTRALIAN AND NEW ZEALAND JOURNAL OF OPHTHALMOLOGY. q. Aus.$80. Royal Australian College of Ophthalmologists, 27 Commonwealth St., Sydney, N.S.W. 2010, Australia. TFI 61-2-267-7006. FAX 61-2-267-6534. Ed. A. McNab. circ. 1,200. (reprint service avail. from ISI) **Indexed:** Biol.Abstr., Curr.Cont., Dent.Ind., Excerp.Med., Ind.Med., Ind.Sci.Rev., Rev.Plant Path., Sci.Cit.Ind.
—BLDSC shelfmark: 1796.891000.
Formerly: Australian Journal of Ophthalmology; Incorporates: Australian College of Ophthalmologists Transactions. (ISSN 0067-1789)

617.3   US   ISSN 0067-9283
BLUE BOOK OF OPTOMETRISTS. 1912. biennial. $95. Butterworth - Heinemann Ltd. (Subsidiary of: Reed International PLC), 80 Montvale Ave., Stoneham, MA 02180. TEL 800-366-2665. FAX 617-438-1479. TELEX 880052. index.

617.7   IT   ISSN 0006-677X
CODEN: BOOCAH
BOLLETTINO D'OCULISTICA. (Text in Italian; summaries in English, French and German) 1930. bi-m. L.60000($60) Nuova Casa Editrice Licinio Cappelli S.p.a., Via Farini, 14, 40124 Bologna, Italy. TEL 051-239060. Ed. F. D'Ermo. adv.; bk.rev.; circ. 2,500. (back issues avail.) **Indexed:** Chem.Abstr., Excerp.Med., Ind.Med.
—BLDSC shelfmark: 2239.800000.

617.752   GW   ISSN 0933-9264
BRILLEN SPECIAL; Zeitschrift fuer gutes Sehen und besseres Aussehen. 1987. s-a. DM.15. Ivy Stoll Verlag, Ridlerstr. 36, 8000 Munich 2, Germany. TEL 089-509545. FAX 089-503189. adv.; bk.rev.; circ. 300,000.

617.7   UK   ISSN 0007-1161
CODEN: BJOPAL
BRITISH JOURNAL OF OPHTHALMOLOGY. 1917. m. £153. B M J Publishing Group, B.M.A. House, Tavistock Sq., London WC1H 9JR, England. TEL 071-387-4499. Ed. J.V. Forester. adv.; bk.rev.; abstr.; bibl.; charts; illus.; index. (also avail. in microform from UMI; reprint service avail. from UMI) **Indexed:** Biol.Abstr., Chem.Abstr., Curr.Adv.Cancer Res., Curr.Adv.Ecol.Sci., Curr.Cont., Dok.Arbeitsmed., Excerp.Med., Helminthol.Abstr., Ind.Med., Ind.Sci.Rev., INIS Atomind., Nutr.Abstr., Protozool.Abstr., Rev.Plant Path., Sci.Cit.Ind.
—BLDSC shelfmark: 2313.000000.

617.7   UK   ISSN 0068-2314
BRITISH ORTHOPTIC JOURNAL. 1939. a. £21. British Orthoptic Society, Tavistock House N., Tavistock Sq., London WC1H 9HX, England. Ed. A. Horwood. adv.; bk.rev.; cum.index every 5 yrs; circ. 1,800. **Indexed:** Biol.Abstr., Excerp.Med.
—BLDSC shelfmark: 2332.500000.
Description: Subjects covered include orthoptics, binocular vision, ocular motility, paediatric ophthalmology, neuro-ophthalmology, etc.

617.7   GW   ISSN 0068-3361
BUECHEREI DES AUGENARZTES. (Supplement to Klinische Monatsblaetter fuer Augenheilkunde) 1938. irreg., no.127, 1991. price varies. Ferdinand Enke Verlag, Postfach 101254, 7000 Stuttgart 10, Germany. TEL 0711-8931-0. FAX 0711-8931-419. TELEX 07252275-GTV-D. Ed.Bd. **Indexed:** Ind.Med.
—BLDSC shelfmark: 2354.900000.

617.7   UK   ISSN 0260-0145
BUTTERWORTHS INTERNATIONAL MEDICAL REVIEWS: OPHTHALMOLOGY. 1983. a. price varies. Butterworth & Co. (Publishers) Ltd. (Subsidiary of: Reed International PLC), 88 Kingsway, London WC2B 6AB, England. TEL 71-405-6900. FAX 71-405-1332. (US addr.: Butterworth Legal Publishers, 90 Stiles Rd., Salem, NH 03079. TEL 800-548-4001) (also avail. in microform from UMI; back issues avail.) **Indexed:** Biol.Abstr.

MEDICAL SCIENCES — OPHTHALMOLOGY AND OPTOMETRY

617.7   US   ISSN 0733-8902
RE977.C6   CODEN: CLAJEU
C L A O JOURNAL. 1975. q. $72. (Contact Lens Association of Ophthalmologists) Kellner-McCaffery Associates, Inc., 150 Fifth Ave., New York, NY 10011. TEL 212-741-0280. FAX 212-929-2174. Ed. Elisabeth J. Cohen, M.D. adv.; bk.rev.; circ. 3,300. (also avail. in microform from UMI) **Indexed:** Biol.Abstr., Chem.Abstr, Excerp.Med., Ind.Med., Protozool.Abstr.
Former titles: Contact and Intraocular Lens Medical Journal (ISSN 0360-1358); Contact Lens Medical Bulletin (ISSN 0010-728X)
Description: Research and review articles on contact lenses, and cornea and anterior segment of the eye for vision care professionals.
Refereed Serial

617.75   US   ISSN 0273-804X
CALIFORNIA OPTOMETRY. 1933. s-m. $35 to non-members. California Optometric Association, 801 12th St., Ste. 2020, Sacramento, CA 95814-2930. TEL 916-441-3990. Ed. Margaret Clausen. adv.; bk.rev.; illus.; circ. 3,500.
Former titles (until 1979): California Optometrist (ISSN 0361-7025); California Optometrist Association. Journal (ISSN 0008-1337)

617.7   CN   ISSN 0008-4182
   CODEN: CAJOBA
CANADIAN JOURNAL OF OPHTHALMOLOGY/JOURNAL CANADIEN D'OPTALMOLOGIE. (Text in English, French) 1966. 7/yr. Can.$70($80) (foreign $90). Canadian Ophthalmological Society, 1525 Carling Ave., No. 610, Ottawa, Ont. K1Z 8R9, Canada. TEL 613-729-6779. FAX 613-729-7209. Ed. D.J. Addison. adv.; bk.rev.; illus.; circ. 1,300. (also avail. in microform from UMI; reprint service avail. from UMI) **Indexed:** Biol.Abstr., Chem.Abstr., Curr.Cont., Excerp.Med., Ind.Med., Ind.Sci.Rev., Ophthal.Lit., Rev.Plant Path.
—BLDSC shelfmark: 3033.700000.
Description: Contains scientific papers presented at annual meetings, and contributions from within and outside Canada.
Refereed Serial

617.7   CN   ISSN 0045-5075
CANADIAN JOURNAL OF OPTOMETRY/REVUE CANADIENNE D'OPTOMETRIE. 1939. q. Can.$40 (foreign Can.$50). Canadian Association of Optometrists, 1785 Alta Vista Dr., Ste. 301, Ottawa, Ont. K1G 3Y6, Canada. TEL 613-738-4412. FAX 613-738-7161. Ed. Dr. M.J. Samek. adv.; bk.rev.; circ. 3,500.

617.7   US
CELL AND DEVELOPMENTAL BIOLOGY OF THE EYE. 1984. irreg. price varies. Springer-Verlag, 175 Fifth Ave., New York, NY 10010. TEL 212-460-1500. (Also Berlin, Heidelberg, Tokyo and Vienna) Eds. J.B. Sheffield, S.R. Hilfer.

617.7   CS   ISSN 0009-059X
CESKOSLOVENSKA OFTALMOLOGIE. (Text in Czech or Slovak; summaries in English and Russian) 1943. 6/yr. $48.60. (Ceskoslovenska Oftalmologicka Spolecnost) Avicenum, Czechoslovak Medical Press, Malostranske nam. 28, 118 02 Prague 1, Czechoslovakia. (Dist. by: Artia, Ve Smeckach 30, 111 27 Prague 1, Czechoslovakia) (Co-sponsor: Ceskoslovenska Lekarska Spolecnost J. Ev. Purkyne) Ed. Dr. H. Kraus. adv.; bk.rev.; abstr.; bibl.; illus.; index. **Indexed:** Chem.Abstr., Dent.Ind., Dok.Arbeitsmed., Excerp.Med., Ind.Med., INIS Atomind.

617.75   US   ISSN 0147-7633
RE1
CHILTON'S REVIEW OF OPTOMETRY. Variant title: Review of Optometry. 1891. m. $36. Chilton Co., Chilton Way, Radnor, PA 19089. TEL 215-964-4370. Ed. Rich Kirkner. adv.; bk.rev.; illus.; index; circ. 30,308. (also avail. in microform from UMI; microfiche from UMI; reprint service avail. from UMI)
—BLDSC shelfmark: 3172.996000.
Formerly (until Apr. 1977): Optical Journal and Review of Optometry (ISSN 0030-3925)
Refereed Serial

617.7   IT   ISSN 0391-8998
CLINICA OCULISTICA E PATOLOGIA OCULARE. (Summaries in English) bi-m. L.60000($60) C I C Edizioni Internazionali s.r.l., Via. L. Spallanzani 11, 00161 Rome, Italy. TEL 06-8412673. FAX 06-8443365. TELEX 622099 CIC. (Co-sponsors: Societa Oftalmologica Meridionale, Societa Oftalmologica Siciliana) Dir. G. Scuderi. **Indexed:** Excerp.Med.
—BLDSC shelfmark: 3286.215700.

617.75   AT   ISSN 0816-4622
CLINICAL AND EXPERIMENTAL OPTOMETRY. 1913. bi-m. Aus.$72 (foreign Aus.$85). Australian Optometrical Association, 204 Drummond St., Carlton, Vic. 3053, Australia. FAX 03-663-7478. Ed. Dr. Peter Swann. adv.; bk.rev.; abstr.; charts; illus.; stat.; index; circ. 2,150. (back issues avail.) **Indexed:** Excerp.Med.
—BLDSC shelfmark: 3286.251940.
Incorporates (1934-19??): New South Wales Journal of Optometry (ISSN 0047-9918); Formerly (until 1986): Australian Journal of Optometry (ISSN 0045-0642)

617.7   US   ISSN 0953-4431
   CODEN: CEVCEV
CLINICAL EYE AND VISION CARE. 1988. q. $105 (foreign $130). Butterworth - Heinemann Ltd. (Subsidiary of: Reed International PLC), 80 Montvale Ave., Stoneham, MA 02180. TEL 617-438-8464. FAX 617-438-1479. TELEX 880052. Ed. Anthony A. Cavallerano, O.D. adv.; bk.rev.; abstr.; charts; illus. (also avail. in microform from UMI; back issues avail.)
—BLDSC shelfmark: 3286.286300.
Description: Explains the various modalities of diagnosis and treatment and the management of clinical situations. Features case reports, new advances in disease detection, case presentations and reports, photo-abstracts, ophthalmic pharmaceuticals, instrumentation, and contact lenses.
Refereed Serial

617.7   UK   ISSN 0887-6169
CLINICAL VISION SCIENCES. 1986. 6/yr. £260 (effective 1992). Pergamon Press PLC, Headington Hill Hall, Oxford OX3 0BW, England. TEL 0865-794141. FAX 0865-743911. TELEX 83177 PERGAP. (And: 660 White Plains Rd., Tarrytown, NY 10591-5153. TEL 914-524-9200) Eds. R. Hess, I. Bodis-Wollner. adv.; charts; illus.; stat.; index. (also avail. in microform; back issues avail.) **Indexed:** Curr.Cont., Excerp.Med.
—BLDSC shelfmark: 3286.422000.
Description: Promotes communication among basic and clinical researchers on topics of vision research affecting clinical practice.
Refereed Serial

617.7   FR   ISSN 0009-9368
LA CLINIQUE, OPHTALMOLOGIQUE. 1935. q. 450 F. Laboratoires Martinet, 222 bd. Pereire, 75848 Paris Cedex 17, France. FAX 45-74-20-63. TELEX 644 265F. Ed. M.C. Vincent. adv.; bk.rev.; charts; illus.; circ. 5,000. **Indexed:** Biol.Abstr.
—BLDSC shelfmark: 3286.630000.

617.7   UK   ISSN 0953-6833
COMMUNITY EYE HEALTH; an international bulletin to promote eye health worldwide. 1988. s-a. free. International Centre for Eye Health, Institute of Ophthalmology, 27-29 Cayton St., London EC1V 9EJ, England. TEL 071-387-9621.
FAX 071-250-3207. TELEX 926606-ICEHG. Ed. Dr. Murray McGavin. bk.rev.; circ. 14,000.
—BLDSC shelfmark: 3363.624400.

617.7   GW
CONTACT. 1975. 3/yr. Median Verlag, Hauptstr. 64, Postfach 103964, 6900 Heidelberg 1, Germany. TEL 06221-25731. FAX 06221-25020. Ed. Hans-Juergen von Killisch-Horn. circ. 80,000.

617.75   UK   ISSN 0306-9575
CONTACT LENS JOURNAL. 1966. m. £3($75) Libra Publishing Ltd., 14 Fairfield Ave., Datchet, Berks SL3 9NQ, England. Ed. Annette Whibley. adv.; bk.rev.; abstr.; bibl.; charts; illus.; index; circ. 2,000. **Indexed:** Curr.Adv.Ecol.Sci., Excerp.Med.
—BLDSC shelfmark: 3424.974000.
Formerly: Contact Lens (ISSN 0010-7271)

617.752   US
RE977.C6
CONTACT LENS SPECTRUM. 1986. m. $38. Viscom Publications, Inc., 50 Washington St., Norwalk, CT 06854. TEL 203-838-9100. FAX 203-838-2550. Ed. Joe Barr. adv.; circ. 20,792.
Incorporates (1976-1991): Contact Lens Forum (ISSN 0363-1621)

CONTACT LENS UPDATE. see *MEDICAL SCIENCES — Abstracting, Bibliographies, Statistics*

CONTACTO. see *MEDICAL SCIENCES — Abstracting, Bibliographies, Statistics*

617.752   GW   ISSN 0171-9599
   CODEN: CNTCDF
CONTACTOLOGIA. French edition (ISSN 0171-9602); English edition (ISSN 0936-1235) (Supplement avail.: Contactolgia-Bucherei) 1979. q. DM.122. Ferdinand Enke Verlag, Postfach 101254, 7000 Stuttgart 10, Germany. TEL 0711-8931-0. FAX 0711-8931-419. TELEX 07252275-GTV-D. Ed.Bd. **Indexed:** Excerp.Med.

617.752   GW   ISSN 0724-6226
CONTACTOLOGIA-BUCHEREI. (Supplement to: Contactologia) 1983. irreg., no.4, 1991. price varies. Ferdinand Enke Verlag, Postfach 101254, 7000 Stuttgart 10, Germany. TEL 0711-8931-0. FAX 0711-8931-419. TELEX 07252275-GTV-D. Eds. W. Ehrich, R. Heitz.

617.75   US
CONTEMPORARY OPTOMETRY. 1982. s-a. free to qualified personnel. (Pilkington Visioncare Inc., Sola - Barnes-Hind) Academy Professional Information Services, Inc., 116 W. 32nd St., New York, NY 10001. TEL 212-736-6688. FAX 212-564-1763. Ed. Dr. Garold Edwards. circ. 25,000.
Description: Covers contact lenses.

617.7   US   ISSN 0277-3740
   CODEN: CORNDB
CORNEA. 1982. bi-m. $132 to individuals; institutions $174. (Castroviejo Society) Raven Press, 1185 Ave. of the Americas, New York, NY 10036.
TEL 212-930-9500. FAX 212-869-3495. TELEX 640073. Ed. Dr. H. Dwight Cavanagh. adv.; bk.rev.; abstr.; charts; illus.; index; circ. 1,500. (also avail. in microform from UMI) **Indexed:** Chem.Abstr, Excerp.Med.
—BLDSC shelfmark: 3470.927500.

617.7   US   ISSN 0090-1164
CURRENT CITATIONS ON STRABISMUS, AMBLYOPIA, AND OTHER DISEASES OF OCULAR MOTILITY. 1970. q. $10 to non-members. Wills Eye Hospital, Walnut St. & 9th, Philadelphia, PA 19107.
TEL 215-928-3003. FAX 215-928-3853. Ed. R.D. Reinecke, M.D. circ. 600. (processed)

617.7   UK   ISSN 0271-3683
QP476   CODEN: CEYRDM
CURRENT EYE RESEARCH. 1981. m. $350. I R L Press Ltd., Pinkhill House, Southfield Rd., Eynsham, Oxford OX8 1JJ, England. TEL 0865-882283.
FAX 0865-882890. TELEX 837330-OXPRES-G. (U.S. addr.: I R L Press, Box Q, McLean, VA 22101) adv.; illus.; index. (back issues avail.; reprint service avail. from SWZ) **Indexed:** Curr.Adv.Biochem., Curr.Adv.Cell & Devel.Biol., Curr.Adv.Ecol.Sci., Curr.Cont., Excerp.Med, Ind.Med, Ind.Vet., INIS Atomind., Ophthal.Lit., Sci.Cit.Ind, Vet.Bull.
—BLDSC shelfmark: 3496.570000.
Description: Rapidly publishes clinical and basic research on anatomy, physiology, biophysics, biochemistry, developmental biology, microbiology, pharmacology and immunology of the eye.

617.7   US   ISSN 0893-0147
RE725
CURRENT NEURO-OPHTHALMOLOGY. 1988. biennial. $88.95. Mosby - Year Book, Inc. (Chicago) (Subsidiary of: Times Mirror Company), 200 N. LaSalle St., Chicago, IL 60601-1080.
TEL 312-726-9733. FAX 312-726-6075. TELEX 206155. (Subscr. to: 11830 Westline Industrial Dr., St. Louis, MO 63146. TEL 800-325-4177) Eds. Simmons Lessell, M.D., J.T.W. van Dalen, M.D. illus.
—BLDSC shelfmark: 3500.635000.
Description: Presents a comprehensive collection of state-of-the-art articles from leading authorities in the growing fields of neuro-ophthalmology.

CURRENT OPINION IN OPHTHALMOLOGY. see *MEDICAL SCIENCES — Abstracting, Bibliographies, Statistics*

MEDICAL SCIENCES — OPHTHALMOLOGY AND OPTOMETRY

618   DK
DANISH OPHTHALMOLOGICAL SOCIETY. TRANSACTIONS. Issued with: Acta Ophthalmologica (ISSN 0001-639X) (Text in English) a. Scriptor Publisher ApS, Gasvaerksvej 15, DK-1656 Copenhagen V, Denmark. TEL 31 22 92 01. FAX 31-22-36-61.

617.752   GW   ISSN 0344-7103
RE1   CODEN: DDOPD4
DEUTSCHE OPTIKERZEITUNG. 1945. m. DM.74 (foreign DM.87). Optische Fachveroeffentlichung GmbH, Rohrbacher Str. 57, Postfach 104443, D-6900 Heidelberg 1, Germany. TEL 06221-14081. FAX 06221-13996. adv.; bk.rev.; circ. 7,700. (back issues avail.)
—BLDSC shelfmark: 3573.180000.

617.7   SZ   ISSN 0250-3751
CODEN: DEOPDB
DEVELOPMENTS IN OPHTHALMOLOGY. (Text in English and German) 1980. irreg. price varies. S. Karger AG, Allschwilerstr. 10, P.O. Box, CH-4009 Basel, Switzerland. TEL 061-3061111. FAX 061-3061234. TELEX CH 962652. Ed. W. Straub. (reprint service avail. from ISI, back issues avail.) **Indexed:** Biol.Abstr., Chem.Abstr., Curr.Cont., Ind.Med.
Formed by the merger of: Advances in Ophthalmology (ISSN 0065-3004); Bibliotheca Ophthalmologica (ISSN 0067-8090); Modern Problems in Ophthalmology (ISSN 0077-0078)

617.7   MX
▼**DICCIONARIO DE ESPECIALIDADES OFTAMOLOGICAS.** 1991. a. Ediciones P L M, S.A. de C.V., San Bernadino 17, Col. del Valle, 03100 Mexico, D.F., Mexico. TEL 687-1766. FAX 536-5027. Ed. Dr. Emilio Rosenstein. circ. 3,000.

617.7   US
DIRECTORY OF CERTIFIED OPHTHALMIC MEDICAL ASSISTANTS. 1984. a. $23 (free to qualified personnel). Joint Commission on Allied Health Personnel in Ophthalmology, 2025 Woodlane Dr., St. Paul, MN 55125-2995. TEL 800-284-3937. FAX 612-731-0410. Ed. Beverly Fanning. circ. 11,000.
Description: Lists every person holding certification with the Commission.

617.7   NE   ISSN 0012-4486
RE14   CODEN: DOOPAA
DOCUMENTA OPHTHALMOLOGICA. (Text in English) 1938. m. fl.1074($610.50) (International Society for Clinical Electrophysiology of Vision) Kluwer Academic Publishers, Postbus 17, 3300 AA Dordrecht, Netherlands. TEL 078-334911. FAX 078-334254. TELEX 29245. (Dist. by: Kluwer Academic Publishers Group, P.O. Box 322, 3300 AH Dordrecht, Netherlands; N. America dist. addr.: Box 358, Accord Sta., Hingham, MA 02018-0358. TEL 617-871-6600) Ed. Prof. L. Missotten. adv.; bk.rev.; circ. 800. (reprint service avail. from SWZ) **Indexed:** Biol.Abstr., Chem.Abstr., Curr.Cont., Excerp.Med., Ind.Med., Ind.Sci.Rev., Nutr.Abstr., Sci.Cit.Ind.
—BLDSC shelfmark: 3609.560000.

617.7   NE
DOCUMENTA OPHTHALMOLOGICA PROCEEDINGS SERIES. (Text in English) 1973. irreg. price varies. Kluwer Academic Publishers, Box 17, 3300 AA Dordrecht, Netherlands. (Dist. by: Kluwer Academic Publishers Group, P.O. Box 322, 3300 AH Dordrecht, Netherlands; U.S. addr.: Kluwer Academic Publishers, Box 358, Accord Sta., Hingham, MA 02018-0358) **Indexed:** Biol.Abstr., Curr.Adv.Ecol.Sci., Nutr.Abstr., Psychol.Abstr.

617.7   GW   ISSN 0936-1928
EURO-FOCUS; Pan-Europaeisches Magazin fuer Optik. (Text in English, French, German, Italian and Spanish) 1989. 4/yr. DM.120 (foreign DM.240). Spangemacher Verlags GmbH und Co. KG, Lintorfer Str. 7-9, D-4030 Ratingen 1, Germany. TEL 02102-23051. FAX 02102-25488. Ed. Heinz Juergen Hoeninger. circ. 25,000.
Description: For optometrists and dispensing opticians in Europe.

617.7   UK   ISSN 0955-3681
EUROPEAN JOURNAL OF IMPLANT AND REFRACTIVE SURGERY. 1989. q. $133. (European Society of Cataract and Refractive Surgeons (ESCRS)) Bailliere Tindall, 24-28 Oval Rd., London NW1 7DX, England. TEL 071-267-4466. FAX 019-482-2293. TELEX 25775-ACPRES-G. Ed. E. Rosen.
Description: Provides a forum for original full papers and rapid communications dealing with all aspects of ocular implants, refractive surgery, and topics of related interest.

617.7   IT   ISSN 1120-6721
▼**EUROPEAN JOURNAL OF OPHTHALMOLOGY.** 1991. q. L.140000($140) (effective 1992). Wichtig Editore s.r.l., Via Friuli 72-74, 20135 Milan, Italy. TEL 02-5452306. FAX 02-5451843.
—BLDSC shelfmark: 3829.733230.
Description: Covers clinical and basic research in ophthalmology.

617.7   FR   ISSN 0301-326X
EUROPEAN OPHTHALMOLOGICAL SOCIETY. CONGRESS ACTA. (Text in English, French and German) 1960. quadrennial, 9th, 1992, Brussels. (Royal Society of Medicine, London, UK) European Ophthalmological Society, c/o H. Saraux, Service d'Opthalmologie, Hopital St. Antoine, 184, rue du Faubourg St. Antoine, 75012 Paris, France. Ed. P.D. Trevor-Roper. circ. 1,500.

617.7   UK   ISSN 0014-4835
QP474   CODEN: EXERA6
EXPERIMENTAL EYE RESEARCH; an international journal devoted to scientific research on the eye. 1961. m. (2 vols./yr.). $814. Academic Press Ltd., 24-28 Oval Rd., London, NW1 7DX, England. TEL 071-267-4466. FAX 071-482-2293. TELEX 25775 ACPRES G. Ed. J.G. Hollyfield. adv.; charts; illus.; stat.; index. **Indexed:** Biol.Abstr., Chem.Abstr., Curr.Adv.Biochem., Curr.Adv.Ecol.Sci., Curr.Adv.Genetics & Molec.Biol., Curr.Cont., Dent.Ind., Excerp.Med., Ind.Med., Ind.Sci.Rev., INIS Atomind., Nutr.Abstr., Sci.Cit.Ind.
—BLDSC shelfmark: 3839.150000.
Description: Publishes original research papers on all aspects of the anatomy, physiology, biochemistry, biophysics, molecular biology, pharmacology, developmental biology, microbiology, and immunology of the eye.

617.7   II   ISSN 0255-4062
EYE CARE. (Text in English) 1979. a. Rs.400($40) (Update in Optics and Contact Lens) Dr. Narendra Kumar, Ed. & Pub., P.O. Box 2812, New Delhi 110 060, India. TEL 5599839. adv.; bk.rev.; circ. 1,200.
Description: Annual ocular health guidebook.

617.7   CC   ISSN 1000-4432
EYE SCIENCE/YANKE XUEBAO; a view of Chinese ophthalmology. (Text in Chinese, English) q. Sun Yat-sen University of Medical Sciences, Zhongshan Ophthalmic Center, Xianlie Road, Guangzhou, Guangdong 510060, People's Republic of China.
—BLDSC shelfmark: 3854.635000.
Refereed Serial

617.7   US
EYE TO EYE. 1971. q. free. International Eye Foundation, 7801 Norfolk Ave., Bethesda, MD 20814. TEL 301-986-1830. TELEX 271588 IEF UR. Ed. Jane D.N. Lewis. circ. 1,200. (tabloid format)
Former titles: International Eye Foundation - Society of Eye Surgeons. Newsletter; Eyelights.

617.7   US
EYECARE BUSINESS. m. Viscom Publications, Inc., 50 Washington St., Norwalk, CT 06854. TEL 203-838-9100. FAX 203-838-2550. Ed. Leo Robert. circ. 38,479.

617.7 362   US   ISSN 0899-7756
FIGHTING BLINDNESS NEWS. 1973. s-a. free. R P Foundation Fighting Blindness, 1401 Mt. Royal Ave., Baltimore, MD 21217. TEL 410-225-9400. FAX 410-225-3936. Ed. Kate McLane. circ. 65,000. (back issues avail.)
Description: Articles on retinitis pigmentosa and other inherited retinal degenerations. Includes information on research, human services and volunteer activities.

617.7   GW   ISSN 0721-1600
FOCUS; Magazin fuer den erfolgreichen Augenoptiker. 1981. m. DM.111. Spangemacher Verlags GmbH und Co. KG, Lintorfer Str. 7-9, D-4030 Ratingen 1, Germany. TEL 02102-23u51. FAX 02102-25488. Ed. Joerg Spangemacher. bk.rev.; charts; illus.; circ. 7,500.
Description: For optometrists and dispensing opticians: practice management, education and trade relations in political matters.

617.7   GW   ISSN 0323-4932
CODEN: FOOPDZ
FOLIA OPHTHALMOLOGICA. (Text and summaries in English and German) 1976. bi-m. DM.117. Georg Thieme Verlag, Ruedigerstr. 14, Postfach 104853, 7000 Stuttgart 10, Germany. TEL 0711-8931-0. FAX 0711-8931298. **Indexed:** Biol.Abstr., C.I.S. Abstr., Excerp.Med., INIS Atomind.
—BLDSC shelfmark: 3971.822000.

617.7   JA   ISSN 0015-5667
CODEN: NGKYA3
FOLIA OPHTHALMOLOGICA JAPONICA/NIHON GANKA KIYO. (Text in Japanese; summaries in English) 1950. m. 23000 Yen (effective 1991). Osaka University Medical School, Department of Ophthalmology, 1-1-50 Fukushima, Fukushima-ku, Osaka 553, Japan. FAX 81-6-458-2669. Ed. Yasuo Tano. adv.; bk.rev.; circ. 2,700. (also avail. in microform) **Indexed:** Excerp.Med., Ind.Med.
—BLDSC shelfmark: 3971.824000.
Refereed Serial

617.7   US   ISSN 1040-8495
FOREFRONT; the newsletter for optometric staff. 1988. bi-m. $36 (Canada and Mexico $46; elsewhere $51). Anadem Publishing, Inc., 3620 N. High St., Columbus, OH 43214. TEL 800-633-0055.

617.7   US
FORESIGHT (WASHINGTON, 1961). 1961. q. free. Eye Bank Association of America, 1001 Connecticut Ave. N.W., Ste601, Washington, DC 20036. TEL 202-775-4999. FAX 202-429-6036. stat.; circ. 5,000. (back issues avail.)
Description: Covers latest issues in eye banking and corneal transplantation.

617.7   GW   ISSN 0723-8045
CODEN: FORODD
FORTSCHRITTE DER OPHTHALMOLOGIE. 1982. 6/yr. DM.278($171) Springer-Verlag, Heidelberger Platz 3, D-1000 Berlin 33, Germany. TEL 030-8207-1. (Also Heidelberg, Tokyo, Vienna, and New York) Ed. H.E. Voelcker. (also avail. in microform from UMI; reprint service avail. from ISI) **Indexed:** Chem.Abstr., Dent.Ind., Dok.Arbeitsmed., Excerp.Med., Ind.Med.
—BLDSC shelfmark: 4022.650000.

617.752   US
FRAMES. q. Carmel Communications, Inc., 2 Park Plaza, Ste.900, Irvine, CA 92714-5904. TEL 714-756-2218. FAX 714-756-5322. Ed. Cindy Thomas. circ. 20,395.

617.7   US   ISSN 0164-4645
RE871   CODEN: GLAUD4
GLAUCOMA. 1979. bi-m. $55 to individuals (foreign $70); libraries and institutions $65 (foreign $90). (American Society of Contemporary Ophthalmology) Altier & Maynard Communications, Inc., 6 Farmingville Rd., Ridgefield, CT 06877. (Co-sponsor: International Glucoma Congress) Ed. John G. Bellows, M.D. adv.; bk.rev.; circ. 15,000. **Indexed:** Biol.Abstr.
—BLDSC shelfmark: 4194.240000.

GLEAMS. see *HANDICAPPED — Visually Impaired*

MEDICAL SCIENCES — OPHTHALMOLOGY AND OPTOMETRY

617.7   GW   ISSN 0721-832X
CODEN: GACODL
GRAEFE'S ARCHIVE FOR CLINICAL AND EXPERIMENTAL OPHTHALMOLOGY/V. GRAEFES ARCHIV FUER KLINISCHE UND EXPERIMENTELLE OPHTHALMOLOGIE. (Text in English) 1854. 6/yr. DM.536($279) Springer-Verlag, Heidelberger Platz 3, D-1000 Berlin 33, Germany. TEL 030-8207-1. (Also Heidelberg, Tokyo, Vienna, and New York) Ed. S.M. Drance. adv.; bibl.; charts; illus.; index, cum.index: vols.1-138. (also avail. in microform from UMI; back issues avail.; reprint service avail. from ISI) **Indexed:** Biol.Abstr., Chem.Abstr., Curr.Adv.Cell & Devel.Biol., Curr.Cont., Excerp.Med., Ind.Med., INIS Atomind., Nutr.Abstr.
—BLDSC shelfmark: 4207.850000.
Formerly: Albrecht von Graefes Archiv fuer Klinische und Experimentelle Ophthalmologie (ISSN 0065-6100)
Description: Articles by leading ophthalmologists and vision research scientists provide rapid dissemination of clinical and clinically related experimental information.

617.7   GR
GREEK ANNALS OF OPHTHALMOLOGY. (Text in Greek; summaries in English) 1964. q. $30. H. Leontiades Publishing Co., 32 Paraschou St., Athens, Greece. Ed. Dr. S. Liaricos. adv.; bk.rev.; film rev.; abstr.; bibl.; charts; illus.; stat.; tr.lit.; index; circ. 600. **Indexed:** Excerp.Med., Ophthal.Lit.
Formerly: Ofthalmologika Chronika (ISSN 0030-0683)

617.75   US   ISSN 0894-5810
HIGH PERFORMANCE OPTOMETRY. 1987. bi-m. $76 to individuals (foreign $91); institutions $86 (foreign $101). Anadem Publishing, Inc., 3620 N. High St., Columbus, OH 43214. TEL 614-262-2539. index.
Description: Summaries of medical and optometry journal articles about diagnosing and treating ocular disease and vision disorders.

617.7   SI   ISSN 0218-0367
IMPLANTS IN OPHTHALMOLOGY. 1987. q. $46 in Asia-Pacific; elsewhere $52. National University Hospital, Department of Ophthalmology, 5 Lower Kent Ridge Rd., Singapore 0511, Singapore. TEL 065-772-5319. FAX 065-733-3360. TELEX RS 39967 PGPUB. Ed. Arthur S.M. Lim. adv.; circ. 10,000.
Incorporates (in 1990): Asia Pacific Journal of Ophthalmology.
Description: Disseminates the latest research and developments in surgical techniques, complications, management. Includes geographical and historical notes, and information on new implants and instruments.

617.7   II   ISSN 0301-4738
CODEN: IJOMBM
INDIAN JOURNAL OF OPHTHALMOLOGY. (Text in English) 1953. 4/yr. Rs.200($60) All India Ophthalmological Society, 13, Cathedral Society, Madras 600 086, India. TEL 476233. illus.; cum.index: vols. 1-5 (1953-58); vols. 11-15 (1963-67). **Indexed:** Dent.Ind., Excerp.Med., Ind.Med.
Supersedes (in Sept. 1971): All India Ophthalmological Society. Journal (ISSN 0044-7307)

617.7   SP   ISSN 0020-3645
INSTITUTO BARRAQUER. ANALES. (Summaries in English, French and Spanish) 1959. q. $50. Instituto Barraquer, Laforja 88, Barcelona, Spain. FAX 93-200-24-69. TELEX 9948-1 COFBA-E. charts; illus.; circ. 2,000. **Indexed:** Ophthal.Lit.

617.752   US   ISSN 0892-8967
RE977.C6   CODEN: ICCLEF
INTERNATIONAL CONTACT LENS CLINIC. Short title: I C L C. 1973? bi-m. $100 (foreign $120). Butterworth - Heinemann Ltd. (Subsidiary of: Reed International PLC), 80 Montvale Ave., Stoneham, MA 02180. TEL 617-438-8464. FAX 617-438-1479. Eds. Gerald E. Lowther, N. Rex Ghormley. (also avail. in microform from UMI; back issues avail.)
—BLDSC shelfmark: 4539.435000.
Description: Provides the contact lens practitioner and researcher with clinical and research information relating to the contact lens field.
Refereed Serial

617.7   NE   ISSN 0165-5701
CODEN: INOPDR
INTERNATIONAL OPHTHALMOLOGY. (Text in English) 1978. 6/yr. fl.546($310) Kluwer Academic Publishers, Postbus 17, 3300 AA Dordrecht, Netherlands. TEL 078-334911. FAX 078-334254. TELEX 29245. (Dist. by: Kluwer Academic Publishers Group, P.O. Box 322, 3300 AH Dordrecht, Netherlands; N. America dist. addr.: Box 358, Accord Station, Hingham, MA 02018-0358. TEL 617-871-6600) Ed.Bd. adv.; bk.rev.; illus. (reprint service avail. from SWZ) **Indexed:** Biol.Abstr., Chem.Abstr., Curr.Cont., Excerp.Med., Ind.Med., Ind.Sci.Rev., Sci.Cit.Ind.
—BLDSC shelfmark: 4544.804000.

617.7   US   ISSN 0020-8167
CODEN: IOPCAV
INTERNATIONAL OPHTHALMOLOGY CLINICS. 1961. q. $86 to individuals (foreign $111); institutions $105 (foreign $137); residents $58 (foreign $80)(effective Nov. 1991). Little, Brown and Company, Medical Journals, 34 Beacon St., Boston, MA 02108. TEL 617-589-5500. FAX 617-589-0629. Eds. Drs. Gilbert L. Smolin, Mitchell H. Friedlaender. charts; illus.; stat.; index; circ. 2,500. (also avail. in microform from UMI; reprint service avail. from UMI; back issues avail.) **Indexed:** ASCA, Biol.Abstr., Curr.Cont., Dent.Ind., Excerp.Med., Ind.Med., INIS Atomind.
—BLDSC shelfmark: 4544.805000.
Description: Covers a single, current topic in ophthalmology with a focus on diagnosis and therapy in each issue.

617.7   UK
INTERNATIONAL OPTICAL YEAR BOOK. 1903. a. £28. Reed Business Publishing Group, Carew Division (Subsidiary of: Reed International PLC), Quadrant House, The Quadrant, Sutton, Surrey SM2 5AS, England. TEL 081-661-3500. Ed. Philip Mullins. adv.; bibl.; stat.

617.7   US   ISSN 0146-0404
RE1   CODEN: IOVSDA
INVESTIGATIVE OPHTHALMOLOGY & VISUAL SCIENCE. 1962. m. $118 to individuals (foreign $159); institutions $157 (foreign $198). (Association for Research in Vision and Ophthalmology) J.B. Lippincott Co., E. Washington Sq., Philadelphia, PA 19105. TEL 215-238-4200. Ed. J. Terry Ernest, M.D. adv.; illus.; index.; circ. 5,623. (also avail. in microform from UMI) **Indexed:** Biol.Abstr., Chem.Abstr., Curr.Adv.Biochem., Curr.Cont., Dent.Ind., Excerp Med., Helminthol.Abstr., Ind.Med., Ind.Sci.Rev., INIS Atomind., Sci.Cit.Ind., Small Anim.Abstr., SSCI.
—BLDSC shelfmark: 4560.220000.
Formerly (until 1977): Investigative Ophthalmology (ISSN 0020-9988)
Refereed Serial

617.75   US
IOWA JOURNAL OF OPTOMETRY. q. Iowa Optometric Association, 5721 Merle Hay Rd., Rm.14A, Box 64, Johnston, IA 50131-1216. TEL 515-278-1697. FAX 515-278-0016. Ed. Virgil Deering. circ. 600.

617.7 371.42   US
J C A H P O OUTLOOK. 1980. bi-m. $15 (free to qualified institutions). Joint Commission on Allied Health Personnel in Ophthalmology, 2025 Woodlane Dr., St. Paul, MN 55125-2995. TEL 800-284-3937. FAX 612-731-0410. Ed. Beverly Fanning. circ. 29,000.
Description: News related to the Commission including a list of continuing education courses in ophthalmology.

JAHRBUCH FUER BLINDENFREUNDE. see
HANDICAPPED — Visually Impaired

617.7   JA
JAPAN OPTICS. (Text in English) 1983. q. 8500 Yen($40) Kindai Kogaku Shuppan-Sha Ltd., Narita Bldg., 1-13-2 Higashi Veno, Taito-ku, Tokyo 110, Japan. TEL 03-832-0416. Ed. James Rickman. adv.; circ. 2,500. (back issues avail.)

617.7   JA   ISSN 0370-5579
CODEN: RIGAA3
JAPANESE JOURNAL OF CLINICAL OPHTHALMOLOGY. (Text in Japanese; summaries in English) 1947. m. 29420 Yen($226) Igaku-Shoin Ltd., 5-24-3 Hongo, Bunkyo-ku, Tokyo 113-91, Japan. TEL 03-817-5706. Ed. Koichi Shimizu. circ. 5,000. **Indexed:** Biol.Abstr.
—BLDSC shelfmark: 4651.380000.

617.7   JA   ISSN 0021-5155
CODEN: JJOPA7
JAPANESE JOURNAL OF OPHTHALMOLOGY. (Text in English) 1957. q. $90. (University of Tokyo, School of Medicine, Department of Ophthalmology) Japan Scientific Societies Press, 6-2-10 Hongo, Bunkyo-ku, Tokyo 113, Japan. TEL 3814-2001. FAX 3814-2002. TELEX 2722268 BCJSP J. (Dist. by: Business Center for Academic Societies Japan, Koshin Bldg., 6-16-3 Hongo, Bunkyo-ku, Tokyo 113, Japan; Dist. in U.S. by: International Specialized Book Services, Inc., 5602 N.E. Hassalo St., Portland, OR 97213; in Asia by: Toppan Company Pvt. Ltd., 38 Liu Fang Rd., Box 22 Jurong Town, Jurong, Singapore 2262) adv.; bk.rev.; charts; illus.; circ. 1,000. (also avail. in microform from UMI; reprint service avail. from UMI) **Indexed:** Biol.Abstr., Chem.Abstr., Curr.Adv.Cell & Devel.Biol., Curr.Cont., Dent.Ind., Excerp.Med., Ind.Med., Ind.Sci.Rev., INIS Atomind., Sci.Cit.Ind.
—BLDSC shelfmark: 4656.770000.
Description: Carries papers on new developments in ophthalmology reported by authors of all nationalities.

617.7   US
JOINT COMMISSION ON ALLIED HEALTH PERSONNEL IN OPHTHALMOLOGY. ANNUAL REPORT. 1983. a. Joint Commission on Allied Health Personnel in Ophthalmology, 2025 Woodlane Dr., St. Paul, MN 55125-2995. TEL 800-284-3837. FAX 612-731-0410. Ed. Beverly Fanning.
Description: Activities of the Commission.

617.7   FR   ISSN 0181-5512
JOURNAL FRANCAIS D'OPHTALMOLOGIE. 1978. 10/yr. 195 ECU($235) (typically set in Jan.). Masson, 120 bd. Saint-Germain, 75280 Paris Cedex 06, France. TEL 1-46-34-21-60. FAX 1-45-87-29-99. TELEX 202 671 F. Ed. H. Saraux. adv.; bk.rev.; abstr.; bibl.; illus.; index; circ. 3,400. (also avail. in microform from UMI; reprint service avail. from ISI) **Indexed:** Biol.Abstr., Chem.Abstr., Dent.Ind., Excerp.Med., Ind.Med.
—BLDSC shelfmark: 4986.410000.
Formed by the merger of (with vol.210, 1977): Annales d'Oculistique (ISSN 0003-4371); Archives d'Ophtalmologie (ISSN 0003-973X)

617.7   FR   ISSN 0240-7914
JOURNAL FRANCAIS D'ORTHOPTIQUE. 1969. a. 100 Fr. Association Francaise des Orthoptistes, Les Roussieres, 01390 St. Andre de Corcy, France. Ed. A.P. Ravault. circ. 2,000.
—BLDSC shelfmark: 4986.420000.

617.7   US   ISSN 0886-3350
CODEN: JCSUEV
JOURNAL OF CATARACT AND REFRACTIVE SURGERY. 1974. bi-m. $40 (foreign $60). American Society of Cataract and Refractive Surgery, 3702 Pender Dr., No. 250, Fairfax, VA 22030-6039. TEL 703-591-2220. FAX 703-591-0614. (Dist. by: Williams & Wilkins Co., Box 64025, Baltimore, MD 21264) Ed. Stephen A. Obstbaum, M.D. adv.; circ. 7,000. **Indexed:** Chem.Abstr., Curr.Cont., Excerp.Med., Ind.Med., INIS Atomind.
—BLDSC shelfmark: 4954.900000.
Formerly (until 1986): American Intra-Ocular Implant Society Journal.
Refereed Serial

617.7   US   ISSN 0272-846X
JOURNAL OF CLINICAL NEURO-OPHTHALMOLOGY. 1981. q. $104 to individuals; institutions $145. Raven Press, 1185 Ave. of the Americas, New York, NY 10036. TEL 212-930-9500. FAX 212-869-3495. TELEX 640073. Ed. J. Lawton Smith, M.D. adv.; bk.rev.; charts; illus.; stat.; index; circ. 1,200. (back issues avail.) **Indexed:** Dent.Ind., Excerp.Med., Ind.Med.
—BLDSC shelfmark: 4958.575000.
Description: Reports on recent developments in diagnosing and treating ophthalmic, neurologic, endocrine, inflammatory, and neoplastic conditions affecting the motor and visual systems.
Refereed Serial

MEDICAL SCIENCES — OPHTHALMOLOGY AND OPTOMETRY

617.741   US   ISSN 1057-0829
▼**JOURNAL OF GLAUCOMA.** 1992. q. $85 to individuals; institutions $105. Raven Press, 1185 Ave. of the Americas, New York, NY 10036. TEL 212-930-9500. FAX 212-869-3495. Ed. Dr. E. Michael van Buskirk. adv.; bk.rev.; illus.; circ. 1,000.
   Description: Publishes original articles on new approaches to diagnosis, innovations in pharmacological therapy and surgical technique, and basic science advances that affect clinical practice in the treatment of glaucomas.

617.7 615.7   US   ISSN 8756-3320
                              CODEN: JOPHER
JOURNAL OF OCULAR PHARMACOLOGY. 1985. q. $125 (foreign $165). Mary Ann Liebert, Inc., 1651 Third Ave., New York, NY 10128. TEL 212-289-2300. FAX 212-289-4697. Ed. George C.Y. Chiou. adv.; bk.rev.
   —BLDSC shelfmark: 5026.155000.
   Description: Contains research on all aspects of drug activity pertinent to preventing or controlling diseases of the eye.

JOURNAL OF OPHTHALMIC NURSING & TECHNOLOGY. see *MEDICAL SCIENCES — Nurses And Nursing*

617.75   US   ISSN 0149-886X
JOURNAL OF OPTOMETRIC VISION DEVELOPMENT. 1970. q. $45 to non-members; members $25. College of Optometrists in Vision Development, Box 285, Chula Vista, CA 91912. TEL 619-425-6191. Ed. Dr. Sidney Groffman. adv.; bk.rev.; abstr.; charts; illus.; bibl.; index; circ. 1,500.
   —BLDSC shelfmark: 5026.380000.

617.7   US   ISSN 0191-3913
                              CODEN: JPOSDR
JOURNAL OF PEDIATRIC OPHTHALMOLOGY AND STRABISMUS. 1964. bi-m. $85 to individuals; institutions $95. Slack, Inc., 6900 Grove Rd, Thorofare, NJ 08086. TEL 609-848-1000. FAX 609-853-5991. Ed. Dr. Marilyn Miller. adv.; bk.rev.; film rev.; abstr.; bibl.; charts; illus.; stat.; index; circ. 1,500. (also avail. in microform from UMI; reprint service avail. from UMI) **Indexed:** Biol.Abstr., Curr.Cont., Dent.Ind., Excerp.Med., Ind.Med., INIS Atomind.
   Formerly: Journal of Pediatric Ophthalmology (ISSN 0022-345X)
   Refereed Serial

JOURNAL OF TOXICOLOGY: CUTANEOUS AND OCULAR TOXICOLOGY. see *PHARMACY AND PHARMACOLOGY*

617.7   US
JOURNAL OF VISION REHABILITATION. 1985. q. $50. Media Periodicals (Subsidiary of: Westport Publishers, inc.), 2444 O St., Ste. 202, Lincoln, NE 68510-1185. TEL 402-474-2676. Ed. Richard Mettler. adv.; bk.rev.; index; circ. 750. (back issues avail.; reprint service avail. from UMI)
   Description: Forum providing information on the evaluation and instrumentation of low-vision, as well as the rehabilitation of low-vision people.

617.75   US
KANSAS OPTOMETRIC JOURNAL.* 1929. q. $3. Kansas Optometric Association, 1266 S.W. Topeka Blvd., Topeka, KS 66612. Ed. David R. Reynolds. adv.; bk.rev.; circ. 550.

617.7   US   ISSN 0886-8026
KEY OPHTHALMOLOGY. 1986. q. $69 to individuals (foreign $83); institutions $89 (foreign $103); students $45 (foreign $59). Mosby - Year Book, Inc. (Subsidiary of: Times Mirror Company), 11830 Westline Industrial Dr., St. Louis, MO 63146. TEL 800-325-4177. FAX 314-432-1380. TELEX 44-2402. Ed. Peter R. Laibson, M.D.
   Description: Surveys and abstracts of key medical literature in ophthalmology with expert commentary.

617.7   PL   ISSN 0023-2157
                              CODEN: KOAOAE
KLINIKA OCZNA. (Text in Polish; summaries in English) 1923. m. $174. Panstwowy Zaklad Wydawnictw Lekarskich, Ul. Dluga 38-40, Warsaw, Poland. TEL 31-42-81. Ed. Josef Kaluzny. adv.; bk.rev.; abstr.; illus.; index. **Indexed:** Biol.Abstr., Chem.Abstr., Dent.Ind., Dok.Arbeitsmed., Excerp.Med., Ind.Med., INIS Atomind.
   —BLDSC shelfmark: 5099.300000.

617.7   GW   ISSN 0023-2165
                              CODEN: KMAUAI
KLINISCHE MONATSBLAETTER FUER AUGENHEILKUNDE UND AUGENARZTLICHE FORTBILDUNG. (Supplements avail.) (Text in German; summaries in English and German) 1863. m. (2 vols. per yr.). DM.456. Ferdinand Enke Verlag, Postfach 101254, 7000 Stuttgart 10, Germany. TEL 0711-8931-0. FAX 0711-8931-419. TELEX 07252275-GTV-D. Ed.Bd. adv.; bk.rev.; abstr.; charts; illus.; index; circ. 3,000. **Indexed:** Biol.Abstr., Chem.Abstr., Curr.Cont., Dent.Ind., Excerp.Med., Helminthol.Abstr., Ind.Med., Ind.Sci.Rev., INIS Atomind., Sci.Cit.Ind.
   —BLDSC shelfmark: 5099.450000.

617.75   GW   ISSN 0721-5096
DIE KONTAKTLINSE. 1966. 10/yr. DM.140.50 (foreign DM.154). (Vereinigung Deutscher Contactlinsen-Spezialisten e.V.) Konradin Verlag Robert Kohlhammer GmbH, Ernst-Mey-Str. 8, 7022 Leinfelden-Echterdingen, Germany. TEL 0711-7594-249. FAX 0711-7594-390. TELEX 7255421. Eds. Wolfgang Cagnolati, Hilmar Bussacker. adv.; bk.rev.; circ. 2,970.
   —BLDSC shelfmark: 5112.560000.
   Description: Publication for specialists devoted to contact lens technology featuring clinical articles, the latest in research and new products.

617.7   NE   ISSN 0922-5307
LASERS AND LIGHT IN OPHTHALMOLOGY. (Text in English) 1986. q. 220 SFr.($160) Kugler Publications B.V., P.O. Box 516, 1180 AM Amstelveen, Netherlands. TEL 3120-6278070. FAX 3120-6380524. (back issues avail.)
   —BLDSC shelfmark: 5156.667500.
   Formerly: Lasers in Opthalmology (ISSN 0920-3265)
   Description: Forum covering uses of lasers and light in ophthalmology.

617.7   US   ISSN 1042-6922
RE401   CODEN: LETRET
LENS AND EYE TOXICITY RESEARCH. 1983. 4/yr. $162.50 to individuals; institutions $325. (International Society of Ocular Toxicology) Marcel Dekker Journals, 270 Madison Ave., New York, NY 10016. TEL 212-696-9000. FAX 212-685-4540. TELEX 421419 MARDEEK. (Subscr. to: Box 10018, Church St. Sta., New York, NY 10249) Ed. Sidney Lerman.
   —BLDSC shelfmark: 5182.431200.
   Refereed Serial

LIGHT (WHEATON). see *HANDICAPPED — Visually Impaired*

617.7   CC   ISSN 1000-0348
MEIGUO YIXUEHUI YANKE ZAZHI. (Text in Chinese) q. Beijing University of Medical Sciences, Affiliated No. 3 Hospital, Beijing 100083, People's Republic of China. TEL 2017691. (Co-sponsor: Zhonghua Yixuehui - China Medical Science Association) Ed. Li Fengming.

617.7   US   ISSN 0882-889X
                              CODEN: MPSODY
METABOLIC, PEDIATRIC AND SYSTEMIC OPHTHALMOLOGY; international journal of basic research and clinical applications. 1977. q. $60 to individuals (foreign $70); institutions $150 (foreign $175)(effective 1992). (International Society on Metabolic Eye Disease) Opto Ed Inc., 105 E. 90th St., New York, NY 10128. TEL 212-289-8024. (Co-sponsor: International Society of Pediatric Ophthalmology) Ed. H. M. Haddad. adv.; bk.rev.; charts; illus.; stat.; index; circ. 1,000. (also avail. in microform from MIM,UMI) **Indexed:** Biol.Abstr., Chem.Abstr., Curr.Adv.Ecol.Sci., Curr.Cont., Dent.Ind., Excerp.Med., Ind.Med., Ind.Sci.Rev., Nutr.Abstr. Key Title: Metabolic, Pediatric and Systemic Ophthalmology (1985).
   Former titles (until 1985): Metabolic Ophthalmology, Pediatric and Systemic (ISSN 0883-9522); (Until 1984): Metabolic, Pediatric, and Systemic Ophthalmology (ISSN 0277-9382); (Until 1982): Metabolic and Pediatric Ophthalmology (ISSN 0191-2771); Metabolic Ophthalmology (ISSN 0361-3674)

617.75   US
MICHIGAN OPTOMETRIST. 1921. m. $13. Michigan Optometric Association, 530 W. Ionia St., Ste. A, Lansing, MI 48933. FAX 517-482-1611. Ed. William D. Dansby. adv.; bk.rev.; charts; stat.; illus.; circ. 850.

617.7   IT   ISSN 0026-4903
MINERVA OFTALMOLOGICA. (Text in Italian; summaries in English and Italian) 1958. q. L.60000($70) Edizioni Minerva Medica, Corso Bramante 83-85, Turin, Italy. Ed.Bd. adv.; bk.rev.; bibl.; charts; illus.; index; circ. 3,000. **Indexed:** Excerp.Med., Ind.Med.

617.7   NE   ISSN 0167-8612
                              CODEN: MPTHDI
MONOGRAPHS IN OPHTHALMOLOGY. (Text in English) 1981. irreg., vol.13. price varies. Kluwer Academic Publishers, Postbus 17, 3300 AA Dordrecht, Netherlands. TEL 78-334622. FAX 78-334254. TELEX 29245. (Dist. by: Kluwer Academic Publishers Group, P.O. Box 322, 3300 AH Dordrecht, Netherlands; N. America dist. addr.: Box 358, Accord Sta., Hingham, MA 02018-0358. TEL 617-871-6600) **Indexed:** Biol.Abstr.

NATIONAL SOCIETY TO PREVENT BLINDNESS. MEMBER NEWS. see *HANDICAPPED — Visually Impaired*

617.7   NE   ISSN 0165-8107
NEURO-OPHTHALMOLOGY. (Text in English) 1979. bi-m. fl.413($212) Aeolus Press, Postbus 740, 4116 ZJ Buren, Netherlands. TEL 03447-2055. Ed.Bd. adv.; bk.rev.; index; circ. 800. (also avail. in microform from UMI; back issues avail; reprint service avail. from UMI) **Indexed:** Curr.Cont., Excerp.Med., Ind.Sci.Rev.
   —BLDSC shelfmark: 6081.509000.
   Description: Contains review articles, research papers and short communications on diagnostic methods in neuro-ophthalmology, the visual and occulo-motor systems, the pupil, neuro-opthalmic aspects of the orbit, migraine, and ocular manifestations of neurological diseases.

617.75   US   ISSN 0028-4807
NEW ENGLAND JOURNAL OF OPTOMETRY. 1949. m. (except Sep.-Jun.). $10 for members. New England Council of Optometrists, 101 Tremont St., Boston, MA 02108. TEL 617-542-1233. Ed. Virginia McGee. adv.; bk.rev.; index; circ. 1,360. (also avail. in microform from UMI; reprint service avail. from UMI) **Indexed:** PMR.
   Refereed Serial

617.7   US   ISSN 0077-8605
                              CODEN: TNOOA6
NEW ORLEANS ACADEMY OF OPHTHALMOLOGY. TRANSACTIONS. Variant Title--Symposia. a. price varies. New Orleans Academy of Ophthalmology, 2626 Napoleon Ave., New Orleans, LA 70115. TEL 504-899-9955. Ed.Bd. **Indexed:** Dent.Ind., Ind.Med.

617.7   JA   ISSN 0374-9851
NIHON CONTACT LENS GAKKAISHI. (Text in Japanese; summaries in English) 1959. q. 8000 Yen (effective 1991). (Japan Contact Lens Society) Nihon Kontakuto Renzu Gakkaishi Henshubu, Osaka University Medical School, Department of Ophthalmology, 1-1-50 Fukushima, Fukushima-ku, Osaka 553, Japan. FAX 81-6-458-2669. Ed. Yasuo Tano. adv.; bk.rev.; circ. 1,650. (also avail. in microform)
   —BLDSC shelfmark: 4804.740000.
   Refereed Serial

617.7   US
O A A NEWS. 7/yr. Opticians Association of America, Box 10110, Fairfax, VA 22030-8010. TEL 703-691-8355. FAX 703-691-3929. Ed. Jacqueline Fairbarns. circ. 7,500.

617.75   US
THE OBSERVER. m. Iowa Optometric Association, 5721 Merle Hay Rd., Rm.14A, Box 64, Johnston, IA 50131. TEL 515-278-1697. FAX 515-278-0016. Ed. Virgil Deering.

OCULAR SURGERY NEWS. see *MEDICAL SCIENCES — Surgery*

OCULAR SURGERY NEWS INTERNATIONAL EDITION. see *MEDICAL SCIENCES — Surgery*

617.7   US
OCULAR THERAPEUTICS AND PHARMACOLOGY. 4th ed., 1973. irreg., 7th ed., 1985. $51.95. Mosby - Year Book, Inc. (Subsidiary of: Times Mirror Company), 11830 Westline Industrial Dr., St. Louis, MO 63146. TEL 314-872-8370. FAX 314-432-1380. TELEX 44-2402. Ed. Philip P. Ellis.
   Formerly: Handbook of Ocular Therapeutics and Pharmacology (ISSN 0072-985X)

MEDICAL SCIENCES — OPHTHALMOLOGY AND OPTOMETRY

617.75   NE   ISSN 0029-8328
OCULUS. 1939. m. (11/yr.) fl.75 (foreign fl. 125). Nederlandse Unie van Optiekbedrijven, Honthorststraat 12, 1071 DE Amsterdam, Netherlands. TEL 020-6765804. FAX 020-6752791. Ed. A. van Hoof. adv.; bk.rev.; illus.; circ. 1,850. **Indexed:** Avery Ind.Archit.Per.

617.7   FR
OEIL ET LUMIERE. a. (Societes d'Ophtalmologie de France) Lamy S.A. (Marseille), 150 rue Paradis, 13006 Marseille, France. (Subscr. to: Diffusion Litteraire et Scientifique, 11 rue Moliere, 13001 Marseille, France. TEL 91-33-57-91) Ed. Dr. Korobelnik. circ. 2,200.

617.7   DK   ISSN 0108-5344
OFTALMOLOG. 1981. q. DKK 195 (free to members). (Nordiske Oftalmologiske Foreninger) Scriptor Publisher ApS, Gasvaerksvej 15, DK-1656 Copenhagen V, Denmark. (Co-sponsor: Acta Opthalmologica)

617.7   KR   ISSN 0030-0675
             CODEN: OFZHAV
OFTAL'MOLOGICHESKII ZHURNAL. (Text in Russian; summaries in English) 1946. 8/yr. 17 Rub. Ministerstvo Zdravookhraneniya Ukrainskoi S.S.R., Kiev, Ukraine. bk.rev.; bibl.; index. (tabloid format) **Indexed:** Biol.Abstr., Chem.Abstr., Excerp.Med., Ind.Med., Int.Aerosp.Abstr.
—BLDSC shelfmark: 0128.620000.

617.7   FR   ISSN 0989-3105
OPHTALMOLOGIE. bi-m. 94 ECU($110) (typically set in Jan.) Masson, 120 bd. Saint Germain, 75280 Paris Cedex 06, France. TEL 1-46-34-21-60. FAX 1-45-87-29-99. TELEX 202 671 F.

617.7   FR
OPHTALMOLOGISTE PRATICIEN. 1972. q. 15 F. (Association Francaise des Ophtalmologistes Praticiens) Societe Confraternelle d'Editions Medicale, 6 Chemin du Val, 78740 Vaux sur Seine, France. Ed. R. Bideau. adv.; bk.rev.; circ. 3,500.

617.75   UK   ISSN 0275-5408
RE939.2   CODEN: OPOPD5
OPHTHALMIC AND PHYSIOLOGICAL OPTICS. 1980. q. £180 in U.K. & Europe; elsewhere £190. (British College of Optometrists) Butterworth - Heinemann Ltd. (Subsidiary of: Reed International PLC), Linacre House, Jordan Hill, Oxford OX2 8DP, England. TEL 0865-310366. FAX 0865-310898. TELEX 83111 BHPOXF G. (Subscr. to: Turpin Transactions Ltd., Distribution Centre, Blackhorse Rd., Letchworth, Herts SG6 1HN, England. TEL 0462-672555) Ed. B. Gilmartin. adv.; bk.rev.; charts; illus.; index. (also avail. in microform from UMI; back issues avail.; reprint service avail. from SWZ) **Indexed:** Biol.Abstr., Curr.Adv.Ecol.Sci., Curr.Cont., Dent.Ind., Excerp.Med., Ind.Med., Psychol.Abstr., Sci.Abstr.
—BLDSC shelfmark: 6270.870000.
Supersedes: British Journal of Physiological Optics (ISSN 0007-1218)
Description: International and interdisciplinary original research in aspects of pure and applied vision science.
Refereed Serial

617.7   US
OPHTHALMIC FORUM. 1982. q. $25. Silver Press, Inc., 456 Clinic Dr., Columbus, OH 43210. TEL 614-421-4960. Ed. Dr. Frederick H. Davidorf. adv.; circ. 13,600.

617.7 618.92   NE   ISSN 0167-6784
OPHTHALMIC PAEDIATRICS AND GENETICS. (Text in English) 1981. q. fl.321($165) (International Society for Genetic Eye Disease, US) Aeolus Press, Postbus 740, 4116 ZJ Buren, Netherlands. TEL 03447-2055. (Co-sponsors: Ophthalmic Genetics Study Club, International Society of Paediatric Ophthalmology) Ed. M. Warburg. adv.; bk.rev.; circ. 500. (also avail. in microform from UMI; back issues avail.) **Indexed:** Curr.Cont., Excerp.Med.
—BLDSC shelfmark: 6271.420000.
Description: Contains review articles, research papers, and short communications on genetic ophthalmological problems of the newborn and of children, as well as adults.

617.7 617   US   ISSN 0740-9303
OPHTHALMIC PLASTIC AND RECONSTRUCTIVE SURGERY. 1985. q. $104 to individuals; institutions $150. (American Society of Ophthalmic Plastic and Reconstructive Surgery) Raven Press, 1185 Ave. of the Americas, New York, NY 10036. TEL 212-930-9500. FAX 212-869-3495. TELEX 640073. Eds.Bernice Brown, Richard K. Dortzbach. adv.; bk.rev.; illus.; index; circ. 1,200.
—BLDSC shelfmark: 6271.430000.
Description: Presents original articles and reviews on diagnostic techniques, surgical instruments and procedures, medical therapies, research findings, and clinical applications.

617.7   CN   ISSN 0832-9869
OPHTHALMIC PRACTICE. 1983. bi-m. Can.$40($60) Medicopea International Inc., 8200 Decarie Blvd., Ste. 212, Montreal, Que. H4P 2P5, Canada. TEL 514-340-9157. FAX 514-342-5783. TELEX 055-62171. Ed. Inara Gailis. adv.; bk.rev.; index; circ. 1,200.
Formerly: Current Canadian Ophthalmic Practice (ISSN 0823-4744)
Description: Studies ophthalmic surgery, ocular infection, intra-ocular lens implants, pediatric problems, technological advances.

617.7   SZ   ISSN 0030-3747
RE58   CODEN: OPRSAQ
OPHTHALMIC RESEARCH; journal for research in experimental and clinical ophthalmology. (Text in English) 1970. bi-m. 519 Fr.($346) S. Karger AG, Allschwilerstr. 10, P.O. Box, CH-4009 Basel, Switzerland. TEL 061-3061111. FAX 061-3061234. TELEX CH 962652. Ed. O. Hockwin. adv.; charts; illus.; stat.; index; circ. 850. (also avail. in microform from RPI) **Indexed:** Biol.Abstr., Chem.Abstr., Chem.Abstr., Curr.Adv.Ecol.Sci., Curr.Cont., Dent.Ind., Excerp.Med., Ind.Med.
—BLDSC shelfmark: 6271.450000.

OPHTHALMIC SURGERY. see *MEDICAL SCIENCES — Surgery*

617.7   GW   ISSN 0936-2517
OPHTHALMO CHIRURGIE. 1989. q. DM.108. Dr. R. Kaden Verlag, Poststr. 24-26, 6900 Heidelberg 1, Germany. TEL 6221-10313. FAX 6221-29910. adv.: B&W page DM.2315; trim 230 x 178. bk.rev.; circ. 1,200. (back issues avail.)
—BLDSC shelfmark: 6271.560000.

617.7   BU   ISSN 0374-2105
             CODEN: OPTMAI
OPHTHALMOLOGIA. (Text in Bulgarian; summaries in English, Russian) q. 8 lv. (Ministerstvo na Narodnoto Zdrave) Izdatelstvo Meditsina i Fizkultura, 11 Pl. Slaveikov, Sofia, Bulgaria. (Distr. by: Hemus, 6 Rouski Blvd., 1000 Sofia, Bulgaria) (Co-sponsor: Nauchno Druzhestvo po Ophthalmologia) Ed. S. Dabov. circ. 766.
—BLDSC shelfmark: 0128.630000.

617.7   SZ   ISSN 0030-3755
RE1   CODEN: OPHTAD
OPHTHALMOLOGICA; international journal of ophthalmology. (Supplement avail: Bibliotheca Ophthalmologica) (Text and summaries in English, French, German) 1899. 8/yr. (2 vols. per yr.) 280 Fr.($187) per vol. S. Karger AG, Allschwilerstr. 10, P.O. Box, CH-4009 Basel, Switzerland. TEL 061-3061111. FAX 061-3061234. TELEX CH 962652. Ed. W. Straub. adv.; bk.rev.; bibl.; illus.; index, cum.index vols.96-138; circ. 1,250. (also avail. in microform from RPI) **Indexed:** Biol.Abstr., Chem.Abstr., Curr.Cont., Excerp.Med., Helminthol.Abstr., Ind.Med., Nutr.Abstr., Protozool.Abstr., Psychol.Abstr., Rev.Plant Path.
—BLDSC shelfmark: 6271.600000.

617.7   UA   ISSN 0078-5342
OPHTHALMOLOGICAL SOCIETY OF EGYPT. BULLETIN. (Text in Arabic, English and French) 1902. a. $10. Ophthalmological Society of Egypt, Dar el Hekma, 42 Kasr el-Aini St., Cairo, Egypt. **Indexed:** Excerp.Med., Ind.Med., Ophthal.Lit.

617.7   JA   ISSN 0016-4488
OPHTHALMOLOGY/GANKA. (Text in Japanese) 1959. m. 1800 Yen per no. Kanehara & Co., Ltd., 2-31-14 Yushima, Bunkyo-ku, Tokyo 113, Japan. Ed. Dr. Matsuo. bk.rev.; cum.index; circ. 5,100. **Indexed:** INIS Atomind., Protozool.Abstr.
—BLDSC shelfmark: 6271.807000.

617.7 616.21   US   ISSN 0161-6420
OPHTHALMOLOGY. 1907. m. $81 to individuals (foreign $108); institutions $114 (foreign $141). (American Academy of Ophthalmology) J.B. Lippincott Co., E. Washington Sq., Philadelphia, PA 19105. TEL 215-238-4200. Ed. Paul Lichter, M.D. adv.; illus.; index.; circ. 20,200. (also avail. in microform from UMI) **Indexed:** Biol.Abstr., C.I.S. Abstr., Chem.Abstr., Curr.Adv.Cancer Res., Curr.Adv.Ecol.Sci., Curr.Cont., Dent.Ind., Dok.Arbeitsmed., Excerp.Med, Helminthol.Abstr., Hosp.Lit.Ind., Ind.Med., Int.Nurs.Ind., Protozool.Abstr., Sci.Cit.Ind., SSCI.
—BLDSC shelfmark: 6271.805000.
Formerly (until vol.85, 1978): American Academy of Ophthalmology and Otolaryngology. Transactions-Ophthalmology; Which superseded in part (as of 1975): American Academy of Ophthalmology and Otolaryngology. Transactions (ISSN 0002-7154)
Refereed Serial

617.7   US
▼**OPHTHALMOLOGY REPORT.** 1991. q. $54.50 to individuals and institutions (foreign $62); students $27.25 (foreign $34.75). Mosby - Year Book, Inc. (Subsidiary of: Times Mirror Company), 11830 Westline Industrial Dr., St. Louis, MO 63146. TEL 800-325-4177. FAX 314-432-1380. TELEX 44-2402. Ed. Dr. Andrew P. Schachat.
Description: Addresses different clinical topics in each issue.

617.7   US   ISSN 0193-032X
OPHTHALMOLOGY TIMES. 1976. s-m. $100 to individuals; institutions $130. Avanstar Communications, Inc., 7500 Old Oak Blvd., Cleveland, OH 44130. TEL 216-243-8100. FAX 216-891-2726. (Subscr. to: 1 E. First St., Duluth, MN 55802) Ed. Dean Celia. circ. 15,321. (tabloid format) **Indexed:** Biol.Dig.
Description: Features meeting announcements and industry news.

617.7   CN   ISSN 0824-3441
OPTICAL PRISM; Canada's optical goods and services magazine. 1983. 9/yr. Can.$30 (effective Oct. 1991). VezCom Inc., 31 Hastings Dr., Unionville, Ont. L3R 4Y5, Canada. FAX 416-477-2821. Ed. Allan K. Vezina. adv.; bk.rev.; circ. 7,964 (controlled). (back issues avail.)
Description: Independent national optical magazine which deals with all aspects of the practitioner's life. Presents a variety of optical information and articles, as well as a forum in which readers may express their views.

617.7   UK   ISSN 0266-9390
OPTICAL RECEPTIONIST. 1980. q. £2($20.80) Reed Business Publishing Ltd., Carew, Quadrant House, The Quadrant, Sutton, Surrey SM2 5AS, England. TEL 081-652-3198. (Subscr. to: Oakfield House, Perrymount Rd., Haywards Heath, W. Sussex RH16 3DH, England) Ed. Philip Mullins. adv.; circ. 7,000. (back issues avail.)

617.7   UK
OPTICAL WORLD. 1972. 10/yr. £48($105) Optical World Ltd., 200 London Rd., Southend-on-Sea, Essex SS1 1PJ, England. TEL 0702-345443. FAX 0702-431806. TELEX 995701-9-INTCOM-G. Ed. Gerald Ward. adv.; bk.rev.; charts; illus.; circ. 4,000.
Description: International publication of interest to manufacturers, distributors and users of optical machinery and equipment.

617.7   UK   ISSN 0030-3968
OPTICIAN. 1891. w. £66($188.50) Reed Business Publishing Ltd., Carew, Quadrant House, The Quadrant, Sutton, Surrey SM2 5AS, England. TEL 081-652-3198. (Subscr. to: Oakfield House, Perrymount Rd., Haywards Heath, W. Sussex RH16 3DH, England) Ed. Philip Mullins. adv.; bk.rev.; circ. 6,930. (back issues avail.) **Indexed:** High.Educ.Curr.Aware.Bull.
—BLDSC shelfmark: 6273.400000.

617.75   FR   ISSN 0030-3984
OPTICIEN-LUNETIER; l'optique francaise. 1952. m. 472 F.($50) Societe d'Editions Lancry, 45 rue de Lancry, 75010 Paris, France. TEL 42 00 90 55. FAX 42-45-76-40. Ed. Alain Brovillard. adv.; bk.rev.; bibl.; stat.; index; circ. 4,500.
Description: Informs readers of the latest technical developments in the field of optometry.

MEDICAL SCIENCES — OPHTHALMOLOGY AND OPTOMETRY

617.7   FI   ISSN 0048-2021
OPTIKKO. 1958. 6/yr. Fmk.200 in Scandinavia; elsewhere Fmk.300. Suomen Silmaoptikkojen Liitto - Association of Ophthalmic Opticians in Finland, Mannerheimintie 76 A, 00250 Helsinki, Finland. FAX 90-492147. Ed. Eero Lang. adv.; bk.rev.; circ. 1,450.

617.75   FR   ISSN 0988-3525
OPTO. 1954. 11/yr. 591 F. Mediacom Vision, 134 route de Chartres, 91440 Bures sur Yvette, France. FAX 69-28-78-06. (U.S. subscr. to: 21 Oak Rise, Irvington on Hudson, NY 10533) Ed. J.P. Roosen. adv.; bk.rev.; charts; illus.; circ. 3,650. **Indexed:** Vis.Ind.
Formerly: Optometrie (ISSN 0030-4115)

617.75 535   BE
OPTO MAGAZINE. (Supplement avail.) (Editions in Dutch, French) 6/yr. Algemene Professionele Opticiensbond van Belgie - Association Professionnelle des Opticiens de Belgique, 26 rue Capitaine Crespel, B-1050 Brussels, Belgium. TEL 02-5125526. FAX 02-5023402. Ed. Ph. Carlier. adv.; circ. 2,500.
Formerly: Association Professionelle des Opticiens de Belgique. Bulletin d'Information Mensuel.

617.7   US   ISSN 1052-7346
RE959.3
▼**OPTOMETRIC ECONOMICS.** 1991. m. $24 to non-members (foreign $60). American Optometric Association, 243 N. Lindbergh Blvd., St. Louis, MO 63141. TEL 314-991-4100. FAX 314-991-4101. Ed. Jack Runninger. circ. 30,095.
Description: Non-clinical journal for optometrists in private practice that covers how to manage an optometric practice.

617.7   US
RE956
OPTOMETRIC EDUCATION. 1975. q. $15 (foreign $20). Association of Schools and Colleges of Optometry, 6110 Executive Blvd., Ste. 690, Rockville, MD 20852. TEL 301-231-5944. FAX 301-770-1828. Ed. Patricia C. O'Rourke. adv.; bk.rev.; circ. 3,000.
Indexed: C.I.J.E.
Formerly: (until Fall 1991): Journal of Optometric Education (ISSN 0098-6917)

617.75   US   ISSN 0030-4085
OPTOMETRIC MANAGEMENT; the business and marketing magazine for optometry. 1964. m. $28. Viscom Enterprises, 656 E. Swedesford Rd., Ste. 218, Wayne, PA 19087. TEL 215-964-8801. FAX 215-964-8664. Ed. Stan Herrin. adv.; charts; illus.; tr.lit.; index; circ. 25,934. (also avail. in microform from UMI; reprint service avail. from UMI) **Indexed:** Account.Ind. (1987-).

617.75   US   ISSN 0030-4107
OPTOMETRIC WORLD.* 1912. m. $3. Occidental Publishing Co., Box 955, Palm Springs, CA 92263. Ed. L.D. Bronson. adv.; abstr.; illus. (also avail. in microform from UMI; reprint service avail. from UMI)

OPTOMETRY; current literature in perspective. see MEDICAL SCIENCES — Abstracting, Bibliographies, Statistics

617.75   US   ISSN 1040-5488
RE1   CODEN: OVSCET
OPTOMETRY AND VISION SCIENCE. 1924. m. $75 to individuals; institutions $98. (American Academy of Optometry) Williams & Wilkins, 428 E. Preston St., Baltimore, MD 21202. TEL 301-528-4000. FAX 301-528-4312. TELEX 87669. Ed. William M. Lyle, O.D. adv.; bk.rev.; abstr.; bibl.; charts; illus.; stat.; index; circ. 4,500. (also avail. in microform; microfilm from WWS) **Indexed:** Biol.Abstr., C.I.S. Abstr., Curr.Adv.Ecol.Sci., Curr.Cont., Excerp.Med., Helminthol.Abstr., Ind.Med., INIS Atomind., Psychol.Abstr, Sci.Abstr.
—BLDSC shelfmark: 6276.450000.
Former titles: American Journal of Optometry and Physiological Optics (ISSN 0093-7002); (until 1974): American Journal of Optometry and Archives of American Academy of Optometry.
Description: Research and clinical findings in optometry, plus case reports and instrument and technique reviews.
Refereed Serial

617.7   US   ISSN 1050-6918
RE1
▼**OPTOMETRY CLINICS.** 1991. q. $70 to individuals (foreign $90); institutions $90 (foreign $110); students $55 (foreign $80). (Prentice Society) Appleton & Lange, Journal Division (Subsidiary of: Simon & Schuster Company), 25 Van Zant St., Box 5630, Norwalk, CT 06856. TEL 203-838-4400. (Subscr. to: Dept. OP, Box 3000, Denville, NJ 07834) Ed. Dr. John Classe. illus.; index; circ. 1,600. (back issues avail.)
●Also available online.
—BLDSC shelfmark: 6276.460000.
Description: Each issue devoted to a single topic with articles written on methods of diagnosis and management as well as practical information on the latest techniques and pertinent legal issues.
Refereed Serial

617.7   II   ISSN 0048-203X
OPTOMETRY TODAY. (Text in English) 1970. q. Rs.1000($100) Dr. Narendra Kumar, Ed. & Pub., P.O. Box 2812, New Delhi 110 060, India. TEL 5599839. Ed. Dr. Narendra Kumar. adv.; bk.rev.; abstr.; bibl.; tr.lit.; circ. 1,200. (also avail. in microform from UMI; reprint service avail. from UMI) **Indexed:** Vis.Ind.
Incorporating: Indian Optometric Association. Journal.
Description: Ophthalmic medicine quarterly journal.

617.7   UK   ISSN 0268-5485
OPTOMETRY TODAY. 1961. fortn. £50 (foreign £70). Association of Optometrists, Bridge House, 233-234 Blackfriars Rd., London SE1 8NW, England. TEL 041-331-2161. FAX 041-332-3785. Ed. M. Callender. adv.; bk.rev.; circ. 12,000. **Indexed:** C.I.S. Abstr., High.Educ.Curr.Aware.Bull.
Formerly: Ophthalmic Optician (ISSN 0030-3739)

617.7 616.21   NE   ISSN 0167-6830
ORBIT; an international journal on orbital disorders, oculoplastic and lacrimal surgery. (Text in English) 1981. q. fl.290($149) Aeolus Press, Postbus 740, 4116 ZJ Buren, Netherlands. TEL 03447-2055. Ed. M.Ph. Mourits. adv.; bk.rev.; index, cum.index; circ. 600. (also avail. in microform from UMI; back issues avail.) **Indexed:** Curr.Cont., Excerp.Med.
—BLDSC shelfmark: 6277.869600.
Description: Contains review articles, research papers, and short communications on orbital disorders, ophthalmology, otolaryngology, reconstructive and maxillofacial surgery, endocrinology, radiology, radiotherapy, oncology, neurology, neuro-opthalmology, neurosurgery, pathology, immunology, and hematology.

617.75   US   ISSN 0274-6549
OREGON OPTOMETRY.* 1934. q. $9 (foreign $24). Oregon Optometric Association, 6901 S.E. Lake Rd., Ste. 26, Portland, OR 97267-2195. TEL 503-639-5036. (Co-sponsor: Pacific University Optometric Alumni Association) Ed. Wanda Laukkanea. adv.; bk.rev.; circ. 2,000. (processed)
Formerly: Oregon Optometrist (ISSN 0030-476X)

617.7   IT   ISSN 0394-0314
L'OROPTERO; rivista di scienze della visione. (Text in Italian; abstract in English) 1986. q. L.40000 (foreign L.60000)(free to qualified personnel) Istituto Regionale Studi Ottici e Optometrici, Piazza della Liberta 17, 50059 Vinci (Fi), Italy. TEL 0571-567923. FAX 0571-56520. Ed. Luigi Tafi. adv.; bk.rev.; circ. 4,000.
Supersedes (after vol.2, 1983): Visione.

PERCEPTION. see PSYCHOLOGY

617.7   PH   ISSN 0031-7659
PHILIPPINE JOURNAL OF OPHTHALMOLOGY. 1969. q. P.300($20) Philippine Society of Ophthalmology, Philippine General Hospital, Taft Ave., Manila 1000, Philippines. Ed. Dr. Romeo V. Fajardo. adv.; bk.rev.; abstr.; index; circ. 1,000. (also avail. in microform from UMI; reprint service avail. from UMI) **Indexed:** Biol.Abstr., Chem.Abstr., Excerp.Med., Ophthal.Lit.
—BLDSC shelfmark: 6455.640000.

617.7   US
PHYSICIANS' DESK REFERENCE FOR OPHTHALMOLOGY. irreg., 18th ed., 1990. $39.95 (foreign $47.95). Medical Economics Company Inc., 680 Kinderkamack Rd., Oradell, NJ 07649. TEL 201-262-3030. FAX 201-262-5461.
●Also available online.
Description: Contains product information relating to optometry and ophthalmology.

PHYSIOTHERAPISTS' QUARTERLY. see HANDICAPPED — Visually Impaired

617.75   CN   ISSN 1181-6058
PRACTICAL OPTOMETRY. q. Can.$40. Medicopea International Inc., 212 - 8200 Decarie Blvd., Montreal, Que. H4P 2P5, Canada. TEL 514-340-9157. FAX 514-342-5783. TELEX 055-62171.

617.7   US   ISSN 0278-4327
QP479
PROGRESS IN RETINAL RESEARCH. 1982. a. £140 (effective 1992). Pergamon Press, Inc., Journals Division, 660 White Plains Rd., Tarrytown, NY 10591-5153. TEL 914-524-9200. FAX 914-333-2444. (And: Headington Hill Hall, Oxford OX3 0BW, England. TEL 0865-794141) Eds. Neville Osborne, G.J. Chader. (also avail. in microform) **Indexed:** Chem.Abstr, Curr.Adv.Ecol.Sci.
—BLDSC shelfmark: 6924.525610.
Description: Reviews relevant developments and current advances in retinal science for clinicians and scientists.
Refereed Serial

PROGRESS IN VETERINARY & COMPARATIVE OPHTHALMOLOGY; an international journal of clinical and investigational ophthalmology. see VETERINARY SCIENCE

617.7   US   ISSN 0146-4582
RE22
RED BOOK OF OPHTHALMOLOGY. biennial. $85. Butterworth - Heinemann Ltd. (Subsidiary of: Reed International PLC), 80 Montvale Ave., Stoneham, MA 02180. TEL 800-366-2665. FAX 617-438-1479. TELEX 880052. adv.
Formerly: Red Book of Eye, Ear, Nose and Throat Specialists.

617.7   US   ISSN 0275-004X
     CODEN: RETIDX
RETINA; the journal of retinal and vitreous diseases. 1981. q. $75 to individuals (foreign $90); institutions $110 (foreign $130). J.B. Lippincott Co., E. Washington Sq., Philadelphia, PA 19105. TEL 215-238-4200. Ed. Alexander J. Brucker, M.D. adv.; illus.; index.; circ. 2,500. (also avail. in microform from UMI) **Indexed:** Curr.Adv.Ecol.Sci., Curr.Cont., Dent.Ind., Excerp.Med., Ind.Med.
—BLDSC shelfmark: 7785.510300.
Refereed Serial

617.7   BL   ISSN 0034-7280
     CODEN: RBOFA9
REVISTA BRASILEIRA DE OFTALMOLOGIA. (Text in Portuguese; summaries in English) 1942. q. $40. Sociedade Brasileira de Oftalmologia, Rua Sao Salvador, 107, Rio de Janeiro ZC 01, Brazil. Ed.Bd. adv.; bk.rev.; abstr.; bibl.; index; circ. 1,000. **Indexed:** Biol.Abstr., Chem.Abstr., Excerp.Med., Ind.Med.
—BLDSC shelfmark: 7845.400000.

617.7   RM
REVISTA DE CHIRURGIE, ONCOLOGIE, RADIOLOGIE, O.R.L., OFTALMOLOGIE, STOMATOLOGIE. OFTALMOLOGIE. (Text in Rumanian; summaries in English, French, German, Russian) 1957. 4/yr. $20. Uniunea Societatilor de Stiinte Medicale din Republica Socialista Rumania, Str. Progresului No. 8-10, Sectorul 1, Bucharest 70754, Rumania. (Subscr. to: ILEXIM, Str. 13 Decembrie Nr. 3, P.O. Box 136-137, Bucharest, Rumania) Ed.Bd. adv.; bk.rev.; bibl.; charts; index. **Indexed:** Chem.Abstr., Dent.Ind., Excerp.Med. (until 1992), Ind.Med.
Supersedes: Oftalmologia (ISSN 0030-0667)

617.7   MX   ISSN 0187-4519
     CODEN: RMOFEM
REVISTA MEXICANA DE OFTALMOLOGIA. (Text in Spanish; abstracts in English and Spanish) 1890. q. Mex.$50000($50) Sociedad Mexicana de Oftalmologia, Boston, No. 99, Col. Noche Buena, 03720 Mexico D.F., Mexico. TEL 563-93-93. Ed. Dr. Jaime Villasenor. index; circ. 1,000. (back issues avail.) **Indexed:** Biol.Abstr.

MEDICAL SCIENCES — OPHTHALMOLOGY AND OPTOMETRY 3305

617.7   FR   ISSN 0301-5017
REVUE INTERNATIONALE DU TRACHOME ET DE PATHOLOGIE TROPICALE ET SUBTROPICALE. 1923. q. free. Laboratoires H. Faure, B.P. 131, 07104 Annonay Cedex, France. FAX 75-67-01-74. TELEX 345023. adv.; bibl.; illus. **Indexed:** Abstr.Hyg., Biol.Abstr., Chem.Abstr., Excerp.Med., Ind.Med., Trop.Dis.Bull.
     Former titles: Revue Internationale du Trachome; Revue Internationale du Trachome et des Maladies Oculaires des Pays Tropicaux et Sub Tropicaux (ISSN 0035-3531)

617.7   IT   ISSN 0048-8410
RIVISTA OTO-NEURO-OFTALMOLOGICA.* (Text in Italian; summaries in English, French, German) Clinica Oculistica, Policlinico S. Orsola, Bologna, Italy. illus. **Indexed:** Ind.Med.

617.7   UK
SCOTTISH OPTOMETRIST. 1976. m. £28. Scottish Committee of Optometrist, c/o 24 Tweed Crescent, Pean Park, Renfred, Scotland. Ed. Maureen A. Callender. adv.; bk.rev.; charts; illus.; circ. controlled. (tabloid format)
     Formerly (until Jan. 1988): Scottish Ophthalmic Practitioner (ISSN 0308-7670); Supersedes: Optics (ISSN 0048-2013)

617.7   US   ISSN 0882-0538
     CODEN: SEOPE7
SEMINARS IN OPHTHALMOLOGY. 1986. q. $78 to individuals; institutions $99; foreign $121. W.B. Saunders Co. (Subsidiary of: Harcourt Brace Jovanovich, Inc.), Curtis Center, Independence Square W., Philadelphia, PA 19106. TEL 215-238-7800. (Subscr. to: 6277 Sea Harbor Dr., 4th Fl., Orlando FL 32891) Ed.Bd. adv.; bibl.; charts; illus.; index.
     —BLDSC shelfmark: 8239.456650.

SIGHT AND SOUND NEWS. see *HOSPITALS*

SKULL BASE SURGERY. see *MEDICAL SCIENCES — Surgery*

SLIDE ATLAS OF CURRENT OPTOMOLOGY (YEAR). see *MEDICAL SCIENCES — Abstracting, Bibliographies, Statistics*

117.7   CK   ISSN 0037-8364
SOCIEDAD AMERICANA DE OFTALMOLOGIA Y OPTOMETRIA. ARCHIVOS/AMERICAN SOCIETY FOR OPHTHALMOLOGY AND OPTOMETRY. ARCHIVES. 1958. q. Col.$4,000($40) Sociedad Americana de Oftalmologia y Optometria, Apdo. Aereo 091019, Bogota, D.E. 8, Colombia. Ed. Dr. Carmen Barraquer Coll. adv.; bk.rev.; illus.; stat.; index, cum.index every 10 yrs.; circ. 750. **Indexed:** Biol.Abstr., Excerp.Med.
     —BLDSC shelfmark: 1653.950000.

617.7   BE   ISSN 0081-0746
SOCIETE BELGE D'OPHTALMOLOGIE. BULLETIN. 1896. q. 3500 Fr. Societe Belge d'Ophtamologie, c/o Mme. Gillis, 24 Ave. des Jardins, 1030 Brussels, Belgium. adv.; circ. 900. **Indexed:** Biol.Abstr., Dent.Ind., Excerp.Med., Ind.Med.
     —BLDSC shelfmark: 2727.220000.

617.7   US
SOCIETY OF GERIATRIC OPHTHALMOLOGY. NEWSLETTER. 1979. irreg., latest 1988. Society of Geriatric Ophthalmology, c/o Frank J. Weinstock, M.D., 2912 W. Rusc, Canton, OH 44708. FAX 216-497-8990.

617.752   SA   ISSN 0038-2612
SOUTH AFRICAN REFRACTIONIST/SUID-AFRIKAANSE GESIGKUNDIGE. (Text in Afrikaans and English) 1953. q. free to qualified personnel. Society of Opticians (S.A.), 342 Giovanetti St., Pretoria, South Africa. Ed. A.S. Konya. adv.; bk.rev.; abstr.; charts; illus.; stat.; circ. 1,000.

617.75   US   ISSN 0038-4275
SOUTHERN JOURNAL OF OPTOMETRY. 1959. q. $12. Southern Council of Optometrists, 4661 N. Shallowford Rd., Atlanta, GA 30338. TEL 404-451-8206. Ed. Dr. Lyman Norden. adv.; bk.rev.; illus.; circ. 5,500.
     —BLDSC shelfmark: 8354.270000.

617.7   US   ISSN 0930-4282
SPEKTRUM DER AUGENHEILKUNDE. (Text mainly in German) 1987. 6/yr. DM.120($84) (Oesterreichische Ophthalmologische Gesellschaft) Springer-Verlag, Journals, 175 Fifth Ave., New York, NY 10010. TEL 212-460-1500. (Also Berlin, Heidelberg, Tokyo, and Vienna) Ed. P. Drobec.
     —BLDSC shelfmark: 8411.400150.

617.7   US
▼**SPORTSVISION QUARTERLY.** 1991. q. Miller Freeman Inc. (New York) (Subsidiary of: United Newspapers Group), 1515 Broadway, New York, NY 10036. TEL 212-869-1300. FAX 212-302-6273. Ed. Jody Stone. circ. 57,000 (controlled).
     Description: For vision care professionals; covers how to build a sports vision practice.

SUNGLASS ASSOCIATION OF AMERICA. NEWSLETTER. see *CLOTHING TRADE*

617.7   HU   ISSN 0039-8101
SZEMESZET/OPHTHALMOLOGICA HUNGARICA. (Summaries in English, German and Russian) 1864. q. $35.50. (Orvos- es Egeszsegugyi Dolgozok Szakszervezete) Ifjusagi Lap-es Konyvkiado Vallalat, Revay u.16, 1374 Budapest 6, Hungary. (Subscr. to: Kultura, Box 149, H-1389 Budapest, Hungary) Ed. Laszlo Remenar. illus. **Indexed:** Chem.Abstr., Excerp.Med., Ind.Med.

617.7   US   ISSN 0738-7644
TEXAS OPTOMETRY. 1945. 3/yr. $12. Texas Optometric Association, 1016 La Posada, Ste. 174, Austin, TX 78752. TEL 512-451-8476. Ed. Beverly Wiatrek. adv.; bk.rev.; charts; illus.; circ. 1,600.
     Formerly: Texas Optometric Association. Journal.

TID OG SYN. see *JEWELRY, CLOCKS AND WATCHES*

617.752   IT   ISSN 0392-0453
VEDERE CONTACT INTERNATIONAL. (Text in English and Italian) 1977. bi-m. (plus 1 special issue). L.45000($38) Edizioni Ariminum, Via Negroli 51, 20133 Milan, Italy. TEL 02-70102026. FAX 02-717346. Ed. Isabella Morpurgo. adv.; circ. 5,500.
     Description: International journal on contactology.

617.7   IT   ISSN 0302-6256
VEDERE-INTERNATIONAL; international journal on optics frame industry and optical instruments. (Text in English, French, Spanish and Italian) 1953. bi-m. (plus 2 special issues). L.95000($85) Edizioni Ariminum, Via Negroli 51, 20133 Milan, Italy. TEL 02-70123727. FAX 02-717346. Ed. Isabella Morpurgo. adv.; circ. 8,500.
     Formerly: Vedere.
     Description: Covers the optical industry.

617.7   RU   ISSN 0042-465X
     CODEN: VEOFA6
VESTNIK OFTAL'MOLOGII/ANNALS OF OPHTHALMOLOGY. (Text in Russian; summaries in English) 1884. bi-m. 12.90 Rub.($10.20) (Vsesoyuznoe Nauchnoe Obshchestvo Oftal'mologov) Izdatel'stvo Meditsina, Petroverigskii pereulok 6-8, 101838 Moscow, Russia. (Co-sponsor: Ministerstvo Zdravookhraneniya S.S.S.R.) Ed. M.M. Krasnov. bk.rev.; illus.; index. **Indexed:** Biol.Abstr., Chem.Abstr., Curr.Cont., Dent.Ind., Dok.Arbeitsmed., Excerp.Med., Helminthol.Abstr., Ind.Med., Int.Aerosp.Abstr.
     —BLDSC shelfmark: 0033.600000.
     Description: Publishes materials on the diagnosis and treatment of eye diseases, hygiene of vision, prevention of ophthalmic infections, history of Russian ophthalmology, organization of ophthalmological aid to the population, as well as the problems of technology.

617.7   UK   ISSN 0142-8543
VISION (SHEFFIELD). 1981. s-m. £105. Sheffield University Biomedical Information Service (SUBIS), The University, Sheffield S10 2TN, England. TEL 0742-768555. FAX 0742-739826. TELEX 547216-UGSHEF-G.
     Description: Current awareness service for researchers in clinical and life sciences. Studies the structure, function, and pharmacology of the eye and its transmitters.

617.7   US
VISION CARE ASSISTANT. 1988. bi-m. Jobson Publishing Corp., 352 Park Ave, S., New York, NY 10010. TEL 212-685-4848. Ed. Lynn Faught. circ. 2,500.

617.7 658.8   US   ISSN 0891-1770
VISION MONDAY. 1987. fortn. $43. Jobson Publishing Corp., 352 Park Ave. S., New York, NY 10010. TEL 212-685-4848. FAX 212-696-5318. (Subscr. to: Box 2092 Mahopal NY 10541) Ed. Marge Axelrad. adv.; circ. 25,000. (tabloid format)
     Description: Covers news and information about the world-wide optical industry.

617.7   US
VISION QUARTERLY. q. $45 to individuals; institutions $60. Society of Manufacturing Engineers, One SME Dr., Box 930, Dearborn, MI 48121-0930. TEL 313-271-1500. FAX 313-271-2861. TELEX 297742 SME UR (VIA RCA).

535   US   ISSN 0042-6989
QP474   CODEN: VISRAM
VISION RESEARCH; an international journal. (Text in English, French, German, Russian) 1961. m. £585 (effective 1992). (Association for Research in Vision and Ophthalmology) Pergamon Press, Inc., Journals Division, 660 White Plains Rd., Tarrytown, NY 10591-5153. TEL 914-524-9200. FAX 914-333-2444. (And: Headington Hill Hall, Oxford OX3 0BW, England. TEL 0865-794141) Eds. G. Westheimer, H. Speikreijse. adv.; bk.rev.; charts; illus.; index; circ. 2,500. (also avail. in microform from MIM,UMI; back issues avail.) **Indexed:** Appl.Mech.Rev., Biol.Abstr., Chem.Abstr., Curr.Adv.Ecol.Sci., Curr.Cont., Ergon.Abstr., Excerp.Med., Ind.Med., Int.Aerosp.Abstr., Int.Build.Serv.Abstr., Nutr.Abstr., Phys.Ber., Psychol.Abstr., Sci.Abstr.
     —BLDSC shelfmark: 9240.925000.
     Refereed Serial

610 617.7 613.7   US
VISIONARY. 1962. 3/yr. free. Illinois Society for the Prevention of Blindness, 407 S. Dearborn St., Ste. 1000, Chicago, IL 60605-1117. TEL 312-922-8710. FAX 312-922-8713. Ed. Jeanne Zasadil. bk.rev.; charts; illus.; stat.; circ. 10,000. (looseleaf format; back issues avail.)

617.7   US
VISIONS (CHULA VISTA). bi-m. membership only. College of Optometrists in Vision Development, Box 285, Chula Vista, CA 91912. TEL 619-425-6191. Ed. Robert M. Greenburg. circ. 1,200.

VISUAL NEUROSCIENCE. see *MEDICAL SCIENCES — Psychiatry And Neurology*

VOICE OF THE DIABETIC; a support and information network. see *HANDICAPPED — Visually Impaired*

617.7   US
WISCONSIN OPTOMETRIC ASSOCIATION. JOURNAL. 1956. q. $10. Wisconsin Optometric Association, 5721 Odana Rd., Madison, WI 53719. TEL 608-272-4322. (Affiliate: American Optometric Association) Ed. Dr. Peter Bergenske. adv.; bk.rev.; circ. 1,100.

617.7   GW
WISSENSCHAFTLICHE VEREINIGUNG FUER AUGENOPTIK UND OPTOMETRIE. FACHVORTRAEGE DES W V A O JAHRESKONGRESSES. 1952. a. price varies. Wissenschaftliche Vereinigung fuer Augenoptik und Optometrie e.V., Adam-Karrillon-Str. 32, 6500 Mainz, Germany. Ed. Hartmut Glaser. adv.
     Formerly: Wissenschaftliche Vereinigung der Augenoptiker. Fachvortraege der Jahrestagungen (ISSN 0084-1005)

617.7   CC   ISSN 1001-4071
YANDI BING/OCULAR FUNDUS. (Text in Chinese and English) 1985. q. Y4.8 (foreign $30). West China University of Medical Sciences, Ist Teaching Hospital, No. 37, Guo-Xie-Xiong, Chengdu, Sichuan 610041, People's Republic of China. TEL 551255. FAX 028-582-944. (Dist. outside China by: Guoji Shudian - China International Book Trading Corporation, P.O. Box 399, Beijing, P.R.C.) Ed. Cheng Ren Luo. abstr.; bibl.; charts; illus.; stat.; index; circ. 5,000. (back issues avail.)
     Description: Clinical reports and research works on ocular fundus diseases relating to the infections of the interior eye and systemic involvements.
     Refereed Serial

617.705 US ISSN 0084-392X
RE6
YEAR BOOK OF OPHTHALMOLOGY. 1901. a. $51.95.
Mosby - Year Book, Inc., Continuity Division, 200 N.
LaSalle, Chicago, IL 60601. TEL 312-726-9733.
FAX 312-726-6075. TELEX 206155. Ed. Peter R.
Laibson, M.D. (reprint service avail.)
●Also available online. Vendor(s): BRS.
—BLDSC shelfmark: 9414.670000.

617.7 GW ISSN 0173-2595
Z P A. (Zeitschrift fuer Praktische Augenheilkunde)
1980. 12/yr. DM.108. Dr. R. Kaden Verlag, Poststr.
24-26, 6900 Heidelberg 1, Germany.
TEL 06221-10313. FAX 06221-29910. adv.: B&W
page DM.3620; trim 230 x 178. bk.rev.; circ.
5,300. (back issues avail.)
—BLDSC shelfmark: 9484.670000.

617.752 GW
ZEISS MARKT - MODE - MEINUNGEN; Informationen fuer
Augenoptiker. 1977. 3/yr. Carl Zeiss
Geschaeftsbereich Augenoptik, Postfach 1865,
7080 Aalen, Germany. TEL 07361-591365. Ed.Bd.
circ. 7,500. (back issues avail.)

617.7 CC
ZHONGXIYI JIEHE YANKE ZAZHI. (Text in Chinese) q.
Wenzhou Yixueyuan - Wenzhou Institute of Medical
Sciences, Wenzhou, Zhejiang 325003, People's
Republic of China. TEL 34941. Ed. Yao Fangwei.
  Description: Covers the combined application of
Western and traditional Chinese medicine in
ophthalmology.

617.7 US ISSN 0192-1304
20-20. 1974. m. $85 free to qualified personnel.
Jobson Publishing Corp., 352 Park Ave. S., New
York, NY 10010. TEL 212-685-4848.
FAX 212-696-5318. Ed.Bd. adv.; illus.

617.7 US
20-20 EUROPE. m. Jobson Publishing Corp., 352 Park
Ave. S., New York, NY 10010. TEL 212-685-4848.
FAX 212-696-5318.

MEDICAL SCIENCES — Orthopedics And Traumatology

617.3 US ISSN 0883-1211
RD724
**A B M S DIRECTORY OF CERTIFIED ORTHOPAEDIC
SURGEONS.** 1985. biennial. $39.95. American
Board of Medical Specialties, One Rotary Center, Ste.
805, Evanston, IL 60201. TEL 708-491-9091.
FAX 708-328-3596. Ed. Dr. J. Lee Dockery.

617 CS ISSN 0001-5415
**ACTA CHIRURGIAE ORTHOPAEDICAE ET
TRAUMATOLOGIAE CECHOSLOVACA.** (Text in Czech
or Slovak; summaries in English and Russian) 1934.
6/yr. 66 Kcs.($50) (Ceskoslovenska Spolecnost pro
Ortopedickou Chirurgii a Traumatologii) Avicenum,
Czechoslovak Medical Press, Malostranske nam. 28,
118 02 Prague 1, Czechoslovakia. (Dist. by: Artia,
Ve Smeckach 30, 111 27 Prague 1,
Czechoslovakia) (Co-sponsor: Ceskoslovenska
Lekarska Spolecnost J. Ev. Purkyne) Ed. Dr. R.
Pavlansky. bk.rev. Indexed: Biol.Abstr., C.I.S. Abstr.,
Dent.Ind., Excerp.Med., Ind.Med.
—BLDSC shelfmark: 0611.050000.

617.3 BE ISSN 0001-6462
ACTA ORTHOPAEDICA BELGICA. (Supplements avail.)
(Text in English and French) 1945. 4/yr. 3000 Fr.
(foreign 3500Fr.). Association des Societes
Scientifiques Medicales Belges - Vereiniging van de
Belgische Medische Wetenschappelijke
Genootschappen, Av. Circulaire 138A, B-1180
Brussels, Belgium. TEL 02-374-5158. Eds. C.
Coutelier, H. Kinzinger. bk.rev.; abstr.; bibl.; index.
Indexed: Bibl.Dev.Med.& Child Neur., Biol.Abstr.,
Excerp.Med., Ind.Med.
—BLDSC shelfmark: 0642.060000.

617.3 DK ISSN 0001-6470
CODEN: AOSAAK
ACTA ORTHOPAEDICA SCANDINAVICA. (Text in English)
1930. bi-m. DKK 920 includes supplements.
(Scandinavian Orthopaedic Association) Munksgaard
International Publishers Ltd., Journals Division, 35
Noerre Soegade, P.O. Box 2148, DK-1016
Copenhagen K, Denmark. TEL 33-127030.
FAX 33-129387. TELEX 19431-MUNKS-DK. Ed.
Goeran H.C. Bauer. adv.; bk.rev.; bibl.; charts; illus.;
index; circ. 4,700. (reprint service avail. from
ISI,SWZ) Indexed: ASCA, Bibl.Dev.Med.& Child Neur.,
Biol.Abstr., Chem.Abstr., Curr.Adv.Ecol.Sci.,
Curr.Cont., Dent.Ind., Excerp.Med., Ind.Med., INIS
Atomind., Rev.Med.& Vet.Mycol., Sci.Cit.Ind.
—BLDSC shelfmark: 0642.100000.

617.3 DK ISSN 0300-8827
CODEN: AOSUAC
ACTA ORTHOPAEDICA SCANDINAVICA. SUPPLEMENTUM.
irreg. free to subscribers of Acta Orthopaedica
Scandinavica. (Scandinavian Orthopaedic
Association) Munksgaard International Publishers
Ltd., 35 Noerre Soegade, P.O. Box 2148, DK-1016
Copenhagen K, Denmark. TEL 33-127030.
FAX 33-129387. TELEX 19431-MUNKS-DK.
(reprint service avail. from ISI) Indexed: Biol.Abstr.,
Curr.Cont., Excerp.Med., Ind.Med.
—BLDSC shelfmark: 0642.105000.

617.3 US ISSN 0738-2278
RD701 CODEN: AOSUEG
ADVANCES IN ORTHOPAEDIC SURGERY. 1977. bi-m.
$58 to individuals, residents $25, institutions $115
(effective 1992; typically set in Dec.). Data Trace
Medical Publishers, Inc., 606 Baltimore Ave.,
Ste.322, Baltimore, MD 21204.
TEL 301-494-4994. FAX 301-494-0515. Ed.
William Cooney. adv.; circ. 2,800. (also avail. in
microform; microfilm from WWS; back issues avail.)
Indexed: Excerp.Med.
  Formerly: Orthopaedic Survey (ISSN 0147-6793)
  Description: Each issue contains 20-25
condensations of important recent literature
accompanied by expert commentaries from
prominent editorial board members.
Refereed Serial

617.1 US
ADVANCES IN TRAUMA AND CRITICAL CARE. 1986. a.
$69.95. Mosby - Year Book, Inc. (Chicago)
(Subsidiary of: Times Mirror Company), 200 N.
LaSalle St., Chicago, IL 60601-1080.
TEL 312-726-9733. FAX 312-726-6075. TELEX
206155. (Subscr. to: 11830 Westline Industrial Dr.,
St. Louis, MO 63146. TEL 800-325-4177) Ed. Dr.
Kimball I. Maull. illus.
  Formerly: Advances in Trauma (ISSN 0886-7755)
  Description: Presents a collection of original,
fully-referenced review articles on selected clinical
topics in the fields of trauma and critical care.

617.1 GW ISSN 0044-6173
AKTUELLE TRAUMATOLOGIE. (Text in German;
summaries in English) 1971. bi-m. DM.243. Georg
Thieme Verlag, Ruedigerstr. 14, Postfach 104853,
7000 Stuttgart 10, Germany. Ed.Bd. bk.rev.; index;
circ. 2,300. (reprint service avail. from UMI) Indexed:
Biol.Abstr., Curr.Cont., Dok.Arbeitsmed., Excerp.Med.,
Ind.Med., Sci.Cit.Ind.
—BLDSC shelfmark: 0785.885000.

617.3 US ISSN 0516-8856
**AMERICAN ACADEMY OF ORTHOPAEDIC SURGEONS.
DIRECTORY.** 1933. a. membership only. American
Academy of Orthopaedic Surgeons, 222 S. Prospect
St., Park Ridge, IL 60068. TEL 312-823-7186. Ed.
Pamela Winkler. circ. 12,000.

617.11 US
**AMERICAN BURN ASSOCIATION. ANNUAL MEETING.
PROCEEDING.** 1967. a. $12.50. American Burn
Association, c/o Glenn D. Warden, M.D., Sec., 202
Goodman St., Cincinnati, OH 45219.
TEL 513-751-3900. Ed.Bd. circ. 4,000. (tabloid
format; back issues avail.)

617.3 US ISSN 0002-7987
**AMERICAN COLLEGE OF FOOT ORTHOPEDISTS
NEWSLETTER.** 1964. q. $5 to non-members.
American College of Foot Orthopedists, 108 Orange
St., Ste. 6, Redlands, CA 92373.
TEL 714-798-8910. Dr. Richard H. Baerg. bk.rev.;
abstr.; charts; illus.; circ. 400 (controlled). (looseleaf
format)

**AMERICAN COLLEGE OF FOOT SPECIALISTS. ANNUAL
YEARBOOK.** see *MEDICAL SCIENCES — Surgery*

617 619 US ISSN 0735-6757
CODEN: AJEMEN
AMERICAN JOURNAL OF EMERGENCY MEDICINE. 1983.
bi-m. $79 to individuals; institutions $105; foreign
$135. W.B. Saunders Co., Curtis Center,
Independence Square W., Philadelphia, PA 19106.
TEL 215-238-7800. (Subscr. to: Journals Fulfillment
Dept., 6277 Sea Harbor Dr., Orlando, FL 32891)
Ed. J. Douglas White. adv.; bk.rev.; abstr.; bibl.;
charts; illus.; index; circ. 2,429. (also avail. in
microform from UMI) Indexed: ASCA, Excerp.Med.
—BLDSC shelfmark: 0824.480000.
Refereed Serial

617.3 US
**AMERICAN ORTHOTIC AND PROSTHETIC ASSOCIATION.
ALMANAC;** the magazine for the orthotics &
prosthetics profession. vol.36, 1987. m. $24.
American Orthotic & Prosthetic Association, National
Office, 1650 King St., Ste. 500, Alexandria, VA
22314. TEL 703-836-7114. FAX 703-836-0838.
Ed. Stacey Bell. adv.; circ. 4,500. (back issues avail.)

617.3 MX ISSN 0044-8184
ANALES DE ORTOPEDIA Y TRAUMATOLOGIA.* (Text in
Spanish; summaries in English and Spanish) vol.5,
1969. q. Mex.$100($10.) Sociedad Mexicana de
Ortopedia, Ejercito Nacional 475, Primer Piso,
Mexico 17, D.F., Mexico. Ed. Dr. Carlos Hernandez
Esquivel. adv.; bibl.; charts; illus.

617.1 FR ISSN 0003-4126
**ANNALES DE MEDECINE DES ACCIDENTS ET DU TRAFIC
TRAUMATOLOGIE.** 1964. bi-m. Institut National de
Medecine du Trafic, 21 rue l'Ecole de Medecine,
75006 Paris, France. (Co-sponsor: Societe Francaise
de Medecine du Trafic) adv.

610 US ISSN 0196-0644
RC86 CODEN: AEMED3
ANNALS OF EMERGENCY MEDICINE. 1972. m. $55.
(Society for Academic Emergency Medicine)
American College of Emergency Physicians, Box
619911, Dallas, TX 75261-9911.
TEL 214-550-0911. FAX 214-580-2816. Ed. Dr.
Joseph F. Waeckerle. adv.; bk.rev.; circ. 17,000.
(also avail. in microfilm from UMI; reprint service
avail. from UMI) Indexed: Abstr.Health Care
Manage.Stud., CINAHL, Curr.Cont., Dent.Ind.,
Excerp.Med., FAMLI, I.P.A., Ind.Med., INIS Atomind.,
Lab.Haz.Bull., Rev.Med.& Vet.Mycol.
—BLDSC shelfmark: 1040.425000.
  Formerly: J A C E P (ISSN 0361-1124)
Refereed Serial

APARATO LOCOMOTOR. see *MEDICAL SCIENCES —
Rheumatology*

APUNTS; medicina de l'esport. see *MEDICAL
SCIENCES — Sports Medicine*

617.3 GW ISSN 0344-8444
CODEN: AOTSDE
ARCHIVES OF ORTHOPAEDIC AND TRAUMATIC SURGERY.
1903. 6/yr. DM.596($345) (Deutsche Gesellschaft
fuer Unfallheilkunde, Versicherungs-, Versorgungs-
und Verkehrsmedizin) Springer-Verlag, Heidelberger
Platz 3, D-1000 Berlin 33, Germany.
TEL 030-8207-1. (Also Heidelberg, Tokyo, Vienna,
and New York) Ed. H. Wagner. adv.; bk.rev.; bibl.;
charts; illus.; index. (also avail. in microform from
UMI; back issues avail.; reprint service avail. from
ISI) Indexed: Biol.Abstr., Chem.Abstr., Curr.Cont.,
Dent.Ind., Excerp.Med., Ind.Med., Ind.Sci.Rev., INIS
Atomind., Sci.Cit.Ind.
  Formerly (until 1978): Archiv fuer Orthopaedische
und Unfallchirurgie (ISSN 0003-9330)

617.3 616.742 IT ISSN 0390-7368
ARCHIVIO DI ORTOPEDIA E REUMATOLOGIA.
(Summaries in English) 1884. q. L.200000.
(Istituto Ortopedico "Gaetano Pini") Editrice Grafiche
Zanini S.r.l., Via Emilia, 41 E, 40011 Anzola
dell'Emilia (BO), Italy. TEL 3951-765562.
FAX 3951-766060. Ed. Luigi Parrini. adv.; bk.rev.;
abstr.; bibl.; illus.; index; circ. 500. Indexed:
Biol.Abstr., Chem.Abstr., Ind.Med.
—BLDSC shelfmark: 1647.822000.
  Formerly: Archivio di Ortopedia (ISSN
0004-0118)

**ARQUIVOS DE REUMATOLOGIA E DOENCAS OSTED
ARTICULARES.** see *MEDICAL SCIENCES —
Rheumatology*

MEDICAL SCIENCES — ORTHOPEDICS AND TRAUMATOLOGY   3307

617 US ISSN 0749-8063
CODEN: ARTHE3
ARTHROSCOPY; journal of arthroscopic and related surgery. 1985. q. $118 to individuals; institutions $160. Raven Press, 1185 Ave. of the Americas, New York, NY 10036. TEL 212-930-9500. FAX 212-869-3495. TELEX 640073. Ed. Dr. Gary G. Poehling. adv.; bk.rev.; charts; illus.; index; circ. 4,500. (back issues avail.) **Indexed:** Excerp.Med.
—BLDSC shelfmark: 1733.940000.
Description: Explores current trends and innovations in both diagnostic and operative arthroscopy.
Refereed Serial

617.1 616.7 JA ISSN 0910-223X
ARTHROSCOPY. (Text in Japanese; summaries in English) 1976. a. 5000 Yen($35) Japan Arthroscopy Association, c/o Teikyo University School of Medicine, Kaga 2-11-1, Itabashi-Ku, Tokyo 173, Japan. TEL 03-3964-1211. FAX 03-5375-0154. Ed. J. Sakakibara. adv.; circ. 1,500. (back issues avail.)
Description: Publishes proceedings of the annual meeting and original papers.

617.3 US ISSN 0271-132X
AUDIO-DIGEST ORTHOPAEDICS. 1978. m. $84. Audio-Digest Foundation (Subsidiary of: California Medical Association), 1577 E. Chevy Chase Dr., Glendale, CA 91206. TEL 213-245-8505. FAX 818-240-7379. Ed. Claron L. Oakley. circ. controlled. (audio cassette)
Refereed Serial

617.533 GW ISSN 0931-6779
BERUFSVERBAND AERZTE FUER ORTHOPAEDIE. INFORMATIONEN. bi-m. Demeter Verlag, Wuermstr. 13, 8032 Graefelfing, Germany. TEL 089-852033. FAX 089-8543347. Ed. Dr. G. Holfelder. circ. 4,000.

BLOOD TRANSFUSION. see *MEDICAL SCIENCES — Hematology*

617.3 CN
BODY CAST. 1986. q. Can.$30($35) (outside N. America Can.$35). Pappin Communications, 73 Pembroke St. W. 3rd fl., Pembroke, Ont. K8A 5M5, Canada. (Subscr. to: 4433 Sheppard Ave. E. No. 200, Agincourt, Ont. M1S 1V3, Canada) Ed. Martin McPolin. adv.; circ. 1,200. (back issues avail.)

BONE. see *MEDICAL SCIENCES — Dentistry*

617.533 NE
BONE AND MINERAL RESEARCH ANNUAL. 1983. irreg., vol.7, 1990. price varies. Elsevier Science Publishers B.V., Books Division, P.O. Box 211, 1000 AE Amsterdam, Netherlands. TEL 020-5803911. FAX 020-5803705. TELEX 18582 ESPA NL. (Subscr. in U.S. and Canada to: Elsevier Science Publishing Co., Inc., Box 882, Madison Sq. Sta., New York, NY 10159. TEL 212-989-5800)
Formerly: Annual Advances in Bone and Mineral Research.
Refereed Serial

617.3 US
BRISTOL-MYERS - ZIMMER ORTHOPAEDIC SYMPOSIUM SERIES. 1988. irreg., latest 1992. price varies. Raven Press, 1185 Ave. of the Americas, New York, NY 10036. TEL 212-930-9500. FAX 212-869-3495.

617.3 UK ISSN 0267-3258
BRITISH ASSOCIATION FOR IMMEDIATE CARE. JOURNAL. 1977. 3/yr. £18. British Association for Immediate Care, 7 Black Horse Lane, Ipswich, Suffolk IP1 2EF, England. TEL 0473-218407. FAX 0473-280585. Ed. B. Robertson. adv.; bk.rev.; film rev.; abstr.; illus.; cum.index; circ. 2,100. (back issues avail.)
—BLDSC shelfmark: 4712.850000.

617.3 GW ISSN 0068-3388
BUECHEREI DES ORTHOPAEDEN. (Supplement to Zeitschrift fuer Orthopaedie und ihre Grenzgebiete) 1969. irreg., no.57, 1991. price varies. Ferdinand Enke Verlag, Postfach 101254, 7000 Stuttgart 10, Germany. TEL 0711-8931-0. FAX 0711-8931-419. TELEX 07252275-GTV-D. Eds. J. Kraemer, K.F. Schlegel.

617.11 US
BURN RESOURCES IN NORTH AMERICA. 1984. biennial. $5. American Burn Association, c/o Glenn D. Warden, M.D., Sec., 202 Goodman St., Cincinnati, OH 45219. TEL 513-751-3900. Ed.Bd. circ. 4,500.
Description: Lists burn care facilities, skin banks and available fellowships in U.S. and Canada.

617.95 UK ISSN 0305-4179
CODEN: BURND8
BURNS; including thermal injury. 1974. bi-m. £108 in UK and Europe; elsewhere £115. (International Society for Burn Injuries) Butterworth - Heinemann Ltd. (Subsidiary of: Reed International PLC), Linacre House, Jordan Hill, Oxford OX2 8DP, England. TEL 0865-310366. FAX 0865-310898. TELEX 83111 BHPOXF G. (Dist. by: Turpin Transactions Ltd., Distribution Centre, Blackhorse Rd., Letchworth, Herts SG6 1HN, England) Ed. J.W.L. Davies. adv.; bk.rev.; index; circ. 850. (also avail. in microform from UMI; back issues avail.) **Indexed:** Biol.Abstr., Curr.Adv.Cancer Res., Curr.Adv.Ecol.Sci., Curr.Cont., Dent.Ind., Excerp.Med., Ind.Med., Nutr.Abstr.
—BLDSC shelfmark: 2931.728000.
Description: Focuses on the scientific, clinical and social aspects of burns. Includes clinical and scientific papers, and case reports.
Refereed Serial

617 610.73 CN ISSN 0708-6474
C O N A JOURNAL. 1978. q. Can.$45. Canadian Orthopaedic Nurses Association, 43 Wellesley St. E., Toronto, Ont. M4Y 1H1, Canada. Ed. Jim Rankin. adv.; bk.rev.; index; circ. 600. (back issues avail.) **Indexed:** CINAHL.

617.3 JA ISSN 0008-9443
CODEN: CORTBR
CENTRAL JAPAN JOURNAL OF ORTHOPAEDIC & TRAUMATIC SURGERY/CHUBU NIPPON SEIKEI GEKA SAIGAI GEKA GAKKAI ZASSHI.* (Contents page in English) 1958. bi-m. 10000 Yen or exchange basis. Kyoto University, Faculty of Medicine, Department of Orthopaedic Surgery - Kyoto Daigaku Igakubu Seikei Geka Kyoshitsu, 53 Shogoin Kawara-cho, Sakyo-ku, Kyoto 606, Japan. (Co-sponsor: Central Japan Association of Orthopaedic and Traumatic Surgery) Ed. Takao Yamamuro. adv.; circ. 3,600. **Indexed:** INIS Atomind.
—BLDSC shelfmark: 3106.144100.

CLINICAL JOURNAL OF SPORT MEDICINE. see *MEDICAL SCIENCES — Sports Medicine*

617.3 US ISSN 0009-921X
RD701 CODEN: CORTBR
CLINICAL ORTHOPAEDICS AND RELATED RESEARCH. 1952. m. $225 to individuals (foreign $275); institutions $325 (foreign $375). J.B. Lippincott Co., E. Washington Sq., Philadelphia, PA 19105. TEL 215-238-4200. Ed. Dr. Marshall R. Urist. illus.; index.; circ. 14,371. (also avail. in microform from UMI) **Indexed:** Bibl.Dev.Med.& Child Neur., Biol.Abstr., Chem.Abstr., Curr.Adv.Cell & Devel.Biol., Curr.Adv.Ecol.Sci., Curr.Cont., Dent.Ind., Dok.Arbeitsmed., Excerp.Med., Hosp.Lit.Ind., Ind.Med., Ind.Sci.Rev., INIS Atomind., Risk Abstr., Sci.Cit.Ind., SSCI.
●Also available online. Vendor(s): BRS, BRS/Saunders Colleague, Mead Data Central.
—BLDSC shelfmark: 3286.323000.
Refereed Serial

617 US
CONTEMPORARY ORTHOPAEDICS. 1979. m. $53 (Canada $64; elsewhere $80). Bobit Publishing Company, 2512 Artesia Blvd., Redondo Beach, CA 90278. TEL 310-376-8788. FAX 310-376-9043. Ed. Judi Prow. circ. 30,000 (controlled). **Indexed:** Biol.Abstr.
Description: Practical "how-to" clinical information for the teaching and practicing orthopaedic surgeon.
Refereed Serial

CURRENT OPINION IN ORTHOPAEDICS. see *MEDICAL SCIENCES — Abstracting, Bibliographies, Statistics*

617.2 UK ISSN 0268-0890
CODEN: BLOREB
CURRENT ORTHOPAEDICS. 1986. q. £55($109) to individuals; institutions £102($197). Churchill Livingstone Medical Journals, Robert Stevenson House, 1-3 Baxter's Pl., Leith Walk, Edinburgh EH1 3AF, Scotland. TEL 031-556-2424. FAX 031-558-1278. TELEX 727511. (Subscr. to: Longman Group Ltd., Journals, Subscr. Dept., Fourth Ave. Harlow, Essex CM19 5AA, England; U.S. subscr. to: Churchill Livingstone, 650 Ave. of the Americas, New York, NY 10011. TEL 212-206-5000) Ed. R.A. Dickson. illus. (also avail. in microfilm; back issues avail.; reprint service avail. from UMI) **Indexed:** Excerp.Med.
—BLDSC shelfmark: 3500.840000.
Description: Reviews topics in orthopaedics for qualified and trainee orthopaedic surgeons.

D.C. TRACTS. see *MEDICAL SCIENCES — Chiropractic, Homeopathy, Osteopathy*

617.3 US
DANCE MEDICINE-HEALTH NEWSLETTER. 1983. q. $15. International Center for Dance Orthopaedics and Dance Therapy, 7922 Oceanus Drive, Hollywood, CA 90048. TEL 213-261-0326. Ed. Ernest L. Washington, M.D. adv.; bk.rev.; circ. 200. (looseleaf format)

617.533 GW ISSN 0723-8002
DEUTSCHE GESELLSCHAFT FUER ORTHOPAEDIE UND TRAUMATOLOGIE. MITTEILUNGSBLATT. 1971. q. DM.60. Demeter Verlag, Wuermstr. 13, 8032 Graefelfing, Germany. TEL 089-852033. FAX 089-8543347. Ed. Dr. K.F. Schlegel. circ. 2,200.

617.3 UA ISSN 1110-1148
EGYPTIAN ORTHOPAEDIC JOURNAL/AL-MAJALLAH AL-MISRIYYAH LI-JIRAHAT AL-'ITHAM. (Text in Arabic, English, French) 1966. q. $50. Egyptian Orthopaedic Association, 19 Midan Saad Zaghloul, P.O. Box 4, Alexandria 21111, Egypt. TEL 03-4225626. Ed. Amin M. Rida. adv.; bk.rev.; abstr.; bibl.; charts; illus.; circ. 4,000. **Indexed:** Biol.Abstr., Excerp.Med.
Formerly: Egyptian Orthopaedic Journal (ISSN 0013-242X)
Description: Publishes original research articles, news, and proceedings.

610 US ISSN 0162-5942
RA995.A1
EMERGENCY; the journal of emergency services. 1969. m. $21.95 (foreign $33.95) effective 1991. Hare Publications, 6300 Yarrow Dr., Carlsbad, CA 92009-1597. TEL 619-438-2511. FAX 619-931-5809. (Subscr. to: Box 159, Carlsbad, CA 92008) Ed. Rhonda Foster. adv.; bk.rev.; charts; illus.; circ. 26,500. (also avail. in microform from UMI,MIM; back issues avail.; reprint service avail. from UMI) **Indexed:** CINAHL.
—BLDSC shelfmark: 3733.168000.
Formerly (until 1978): Emergency Product News (ISSN 0098-2180)
Description: Trade journal for paramedics and EMTs covering topics and trends in EMS.

610 US ISSN 0094-6575
EMERGENCY MEDICAL SERVICES; the journal of emergency care and transportation. 1972. 12/yr. $18.95. Creative Age Publications, 7628 Densmore Ave., Van Nuys, CA 91406-2088. TEL 818-782-7328. Ed. Barbara Feiner. adv.; bk.rev.; circ. 45,228. **Indexed:** Curr.Cont., Ind.Med.
—BLDSC shelfmark: 3733.187000.

610 US ISSN 0013-6654
RC86
EMERGENCY MEDICINE; acute medicine for the primary care physician. 1969. 16/yr. $45 to individuals (foreign $75); physicians $45; students $37. Cahners Publishing Company (New York), Medical-Health Care Group (Subsidiary of: Reed International PLC), Division of Reed Publishing (USA) Inc., 249 W. 17th St., New York, NY 10011. TEL 212-645-0067. FAX 212-242-6987. (Subscr. to: 44 Cook St., Denver, CO 80206. TEL 800-662-7776) Ed. Harry A. Atkins. adv.; bk.rev.; charts; illus.; index; circ. 129,450. (also avail. in microform from RPI; reprint service avail. from UMI) **Indexed:** C.I.N.L., Curr.Cont., Helminthol.Abstr., Hosp.Lit.Ind.
—BLDSC shelfmark: 3733.190000.
Description: Emphasizes acute care medicine for primary care physicians.

M

MEDICAL SCIENCES — ORTHOPEDICS AND TRAUMATOLOGY

617.1 US ISSN 0733-8627
CODEN: EMCAD7
EMERGENCY MEDICINE CLINICS OF NORTH AMERICA.
1983. q. $78. W.B. Saunders Co., Curtis Center, Independence Sq. W., Philadelphia, PA 19106. TEL 215-238-7800. Ed. Mary Mulroy. (also avail. in microform from UMI) **Indexed:** Dok.Arbeitsmed., Excerp.Med.
●Also available online. Vendor(s): BRS, BRS/Saunders Colleague.
—BLDSC shelfmark: 3733.190400.

617.3 616.8 FR ISSN 0223-4696
FLASH-INFORMATIONS. 1978. 3/w. 550 Fr. Centre Technique National d'Etudes et de Recherches sur les Handicaps et les Inadaptations, 2 rue Auguste Comte, B.P. 47, 92173 Vanves, France. TEL 47-36-74-10. bk.rev.

617.3 DK
FODTERAPEUTEN. 1932. m. (10/yr.). DKK 145. Landsforeningen af Statsautoriserede Fodterapeuter, Bjelkes Alle 43, 2200 Copenhagen, Denmark. Ed. Anita Ellekjaer Hansen. adv.; bk.rev.; circ. 1,600.

617.1 UK ISSN 0958-2592
▼**THE FOOT**; international journal of foot surgery. 1991. q. £60($119) to individuals; institutions £120($250). (International College of Foot Medicine and Surgery (CIP)) Churchill Livingstone Medical Journals, Robert Stevenson House, 1-3 Baxter's Pl., Leith Walk, Edinburgh EH1 3AF, Scotland. TEL 031-556-2424. FAX 031-558-1278. (Subscr. to: Longman Group, Journals Subscr. Dept., P.O. Box 77, Fourth Ave., Harlow, Essex CM19 5AA, England; U.S. subscr. to: Churchill Livingstone, 650 Ave. of the Americas, New York, NY, 10011. TEL 212-206-5000) Eds. T. Duckworth, T. Smith.
—BLDSC shelfmark: 3984.840000.
Description: Primary articles and commissioned reviews on disorders of the foot and their medical or surgical treatment.
Refereed Serial

617.3 US ISSN 0198-0211
RD781 CODEN: FANKDJ
FOOT & ANKLE. 1980. bi-m. $60 to individuals; institutions $70. (American Orthopaedic Foot and Ankle Society Inc.) Williams & Wilkins, 428 E. Preston St., Baltimore, MD 21202. TEL 301-528-4000. FAX 301-528-4312. Ed. Kenneth A. Johnson, M.D. adv.; bk.rev.; circ. 3,700. (also avail. in microform; back issues avail.) **Indexed:** Curr.Cont., Excerp.Med., Ind.Med., Sportsearch (1981-).
—BLDSC shelfmark: 3984.850000.
Description: Focuses on new approaches to foot and ankle disorders and surgical treatment for orthopedic surgeons and podiatrists.
Refereed Serial

617.3 GW ISSN 0015-816X
FORTSCHRITTE DER KIEFERORTHOPAEDIE. 1931. bi-m. DM.188. (Deutsche Gesellschaft fuer Kieferorthopaedie) Urban und Vogel, Lindwurmstr. 95, Postfach 152309, 8000 Munich 15, Germany. TEL 089-53292-0. FAX 089-53292-100. Eds. Dr. H.G. Sergl, Dr. Eva Holtgrave. adv.; bk.rev.; bibl.; charts; illus.; index; circ. 2,500. **Indexed:** Biol.Abstr., Curr.Adv.Ecol.Sci., Curr.Tit.Dent., Dent.Ind., Excerp.Med., Ind.Med.
—BLDSC shelfmark: 4021.730000.

DIE FUNKTIONSKRANKHEITEN DES BEWEGUNGSAPPARATES; Zeitschrift fuer interdisziplinaere Diagnostik und Therapie. see *MEDICAL SCIENCES — Chiropractic, Homeopathy, Osteopathy*

617.3 IT ISSN 0390-0134
GIORNALE ITALIANO DI ORTOPEDIA E TRAUMATOLOGIA. English edition: Italian Journal of Orthopaedics and Traumatology (ISSN 0390-5489) (Supplement avail.) 1975. 4/yr. $80. Aulo Gaggi Editore, Via Andrea Costa 131-5, 40134 Bologna, Italy. TEL 0222-5339614. FAX 0222-638158. TELEX 114506. Eds. G. Monticelli, E.A. Nicoll. adv.; bk.rev.; circ. 4,750. **Indexed:** Biol.Abstr., Dent.Ind., Excerp.Med., Ind.Med.
Description: Covers current thought, practice and research in the science of orthopedics and traumatology.

617.1 FR ISSN 0992-6739
GUIDE ANNUEL DES S A M U ET S M U R DE FRANCE. (Services d'Aide Medicale Urgente) a. 250 F. per no. Societe Francaise d'Editions Medicales, 22-24 rue du Chateau des Rentiers, 75013 Paris, France.

617 US ISSN 0749-0712
HAND CLINICS. 1985. q. $99 to individuals; institutions $114. W.B. Saunders Co., Curtis Center, Independence Sq. W., Philadelphia, PA 19106. TEL 215-238-7800. (Subscr. to: Journals 6277 Sea Harbor Dr., 4th Fl., Orlando FL 32891) Ed. Melissa Mitchell. circ. 2,350. (also avail. in microfilm; back issues avail.) **Indexed:** Excerp.Med.
—BLDSC shelfmark: 4241.558000.
Description: Each issue addresses a single topic in the surgical therapy of patients with disorders of the hand.

HEAT SHOCK PROTEINS. see *BIOLOGY — Biological Chemistry*

610 US ISSN 0085-1469
CODEN: HUFHAR
HEFTE ZUR UNFALLHEILKUNDE. irreg. price varies. Springer-Verlag, 175 Fifth Ave., New York, NY 10010. TEL 212-460-1500. (Also Berlin, Heidelberg, Tokyo and Vienna) (also avail. in microform from UMI; reprint service avail. from ISI) **Indexed:** Biol.Abstr., Excerp.Med., Ind.Med.
—BLDSC shelfmark: 4283.700000.

617.3 JA ISSN 0018-3377
HOKKAIDO JOURNAL OF ORTHOPEDIC & TRAUMATIC SURGERY/HOKKAIDO SEIKEI SAIGAI GEKA ZASSHI. (Text in Japanese; summaries in English) 1954. s-a. 5000 Yen($7) (Hokkaido Orthopedic and Traumatic Surgery Society - Hokkaido Seikei Saigai Geka Gakkai) Santou Publishing Co. Ltd., c/o Hokkaido Daigaku Igakubu Seikei Geka Kyoshitsu, Nishi-5-chome, Kita-14-jo, Kita-ku, Sapporo 060, Japan. Ed.Bd. circ. 750. **Indexed:** Excerp.Med., INIS Atomind.

617.3 US ISSN 0018-5647
HOSPITAL FOR JOINT DISEASES ORTHOPAEDIC INSTITUTE. BULLETIN. 1940. s-a. $25. Hospital for Joint Diseases Orthopaedic Institute, Bernard Aronson Plaza, 301 E. 17th St., New York, NY 10003. TEL 212-460-0121. Ed. June Mintz. bk.rev.; charts; illus.; cum.index: 1965-81; 1982-85; 1986-89; circ. 2,500. (also avail. in microform from UMI,ISI) **Indexed:** Bioeng.Abstr., Biol.Abstr., Curr.Cont., Eng.Ind., Excerp.Med., Ind.Med., INIS Atomind.
—BLDSC shelfmark: 2555.330000.
Formerly: Hospital for Joint Diseases. Bulletin.

617.3 II ISSN 0019-5413
CODEN: INJOAU
INDIAN JOURNAL OF ORTHOPAEDICS. (Text in English) 1967. s-a. Rs.125($30) (Indian Orthopaedic Association) Banaras Hindu University, Institute of Medical Sciences, Varanasi 221005, India. Eds. Dr. S.M. Tuli, Dr. T.P. Srivastava. adv.; bk.rev.; bibl.; charts; illus.; index; circ. 1,600. **Indexed:** Excerp.Med., Indian Sci.Abstr.
—BLDSC shelfmark: 4417.750000.

617 UK ISSN 0020-1383
CODEN: INJUBF
INJURY; British journal of accident surgery. 1969. 8/yr. £120 (foreign £132). (Institute of Accident Surgery) Butterworth - Heinemann Ltd. (Subsidiary of: Reed International PLC), Linacre House, Jordan Hill, Oxford OX2 8DP, England. TEL 0865-310366. FAX 0865-310898. TELEX 83111 BHPOXF G. (Dist. by: Turpin Transactions Ltd., Distribution Centre, Blackhorse Rd., Letchworth, Herts SG6 1HN, England) Ed. O.N. Tubbs. adv.; bk.rev.; abstr.; bibl.; illus.; index. (also avail. in microform from UMI; back issues avail.) **Indexed:** Biol.Abstr., Curr.Adv.Ecol.Sci., Curr.Cont., Dent.Ind., Dok.Arbeitsmed., Excerp.Med., Ind.Med.
—BLDSC shelfmark: 4514.400000.
Description: Deals with all aspects of trauma, including fractures and soft-tissue injuries, and covers problems in the accident unit.
Refereed Serial

617.3 GW ISSN 0341-2695
INTERNATIONAL ORTHOPAEDICS. 1977. 4/yr. DM.328($184) (Societe Internationale de Chirurugie Orthopedique et de Traumatologie, BE - International Society of Orthopaedic Surgery and Traumatology) Springer-Verlag, Heidelberger Platz 3, D-1000 Berlin 33, Germany. TEL 030-8207-1. (Also Heidelberg, Tokyo, Vienna, and New York) Ed. P. Masse. adv.; illus.; index. (also avail. in microform from UMI; reprint service avail. from ISI) **Indexed:** Curr.Adv.Cancer Res., Curr.Cont., Excerp.Med., Ind.Med., Ind.Sci.Rev., INIS Atomind., Sci.Cit.Ind.
—BLDSC shelfmark: 4544.856000.
Supersedes (1929-1972): International Society of Orthopaedic Surgery and Traumatology. Proceedings of Congresses (ISSN 0074-8552)

ISOKINETICS AND EXERCISE SCIENCE. see *MEDICAL SCIENCES — Sports Medicine*

617.3 IT ISSN 0390-5489
ITALIAN JOURNAL OF ORTHOPAEDICS AND TRAUMATOLOGY. Italian Edition: Giornale Italiano di Ortopedia e Traumatologia (ISSN 0390-0134) (Text in English) 1975. 4/yr. Aulo Gaggi Editore, Via Andrea Costa, 131-5, 40134 Bologna, Italy. TEL 0222-5339614. FAX 114506. TELEX 0222-638158. (Co-publisher: Springer-Verlag) Eds. S.G. Monticelli, E.A. Nicoll.
—BLDSC shelfmark: 4588.341000.
Description: Covers current thought, practice and research in the science of orthopedics and traumatology.

J M P T: JOURNAL OF MANIPULATIVE AND PHYSIOLOGICAL THERAPEUTICS. see *MEDICAL SCIENCES — Chiropractic, Homeopathy, Osteopathy*

617.3 JA ISSN 0021-5325
CODEN: NSGZA2
JAPANESE ORTHOPAEDIC ASSOCIATION. JOURNAL/NIPPON SEIKEI GEKA GAKKAI ZASSHI. (Text in English and Japanese) 1926. m. 10000 Yen. Japanese Orthopaedic Association - Nippon Seikei Geka Gakkai, 30-10, Hongo 3-chome, Bunkyo-ku, Tokyo 113, Japan. FAX 03-818-2337. Ed. Takahide Kurokawa. adv.; circ. 16,000. **Indexed:** Biol.Abstr., Chem.Abstr., Dent.Ind., Excerp.Med., Ind.Med.
—BLDSC shelfmark: 4809.370000.

617.3 GW ISSN 0930-8326
JATROS ORTHOPAEDIE. 1986. 12/yr. DM.150. P M I Verlag GmbH, August-Schanz-Str. 21, 6000 Frankfurt a.M. 50, Germany. TEL 069-5480000. FAX 069-548000-77. Ed. Peter Hoffmann. circ. 3,300. (back issues avail.)
Description: Seminar paper journal containing summaries of orthopaedic articles, interviews and Congress reports.

JOURNAL OF AIR MEDICAL TRANSPORT. see *TRANSPORTATION — Air Transport*

617 US ISSN 0886-9723
RA645.5 •
JOURNAL OF AMBULATORY CARE MARKETING. 1980. s-a. $32 to individuals; institutions $48; libraries $75. Haworth Press, Inc., 10 Alice St., Binghamton, NY 13904. TEL 800-342-9678. Ed. Robert Sweeney. circ. 124. (also avail. in microfiche from HAW; reprint service avail. from HAW,ISI) **Indexed:** Abstr.Health Care Manage.Stud., Bull.Signal., Excerp.Med., Hosp.Abstr., Hosp.Lit.Ind., Med.Care Rev., Ref.Zh., Saf.Sci.Abstr., Soc.Work Res.& Abstr.
—BLDSC shelfmark: 4927.230000.
Former titles (until 1987): Emergency Health Services Review (ISSN 0738-6192); Emergency Health Services Quarterly; Emergency Medical Services Quarterly (ISSN 0163-9358)
Description: Focuses on the marketing of traditional emergency health care, urgent and convenient care services, surgicenters, group practices providing emergency ambulatory care, and new sectors of health care, such as HMOs, IPAs, and PPOs that are involved in the provision of ambulatory health care services.
Refereed Serial

MEDICAL SCIENCES — ORTHOPEDICS AND TRAUMATOLOGY

617.3 　　　US　ISSN 0883-5403
**　　　　　　　　　CODEN: JOAREG**
JOURNAL OF ARTHROPLASTY. 1986. q. $95 to individuals (foreign $118); institutions $120 (foreign $143). Churchill Livingstone Medical Journals, 650 Ave. of the America, New York, NY 10011. TEL 212-206-4050. FAX 212-727-7808. TELEX 662266. (Dist. by: Transaction Publishers, Department 3091, Rutgers University, New Brunswick, NJ 08903. TEL 908-932-2280) Ed. David Hungerford. adv.; charts; illus.; tr.lit.; index; circ. 6,864. (also avail. in microfilm; back issues avail.) Indexed: Excerp.Med., Ind.Med.
—BLDSC shelfmark: 4947.211500.
Description: Basic scientific and clinical information on joint replacement surgery. Covers surgical techniques, prosthetic design, biomechanics, biomaterials, metallurgy, and the biologic response to arthroplasty materials in vivo and in vitro.
Refereed Serial

617.3　　　US　ISSN 1053-8127
▼**JOURNAL OF BACK AND MUSCULOSKELETAL REHABILITATION.** 1991. q. $58 to individuals (foreign $70); institutions $82 (foreign $94). Andover Medical Publishers Inc., 125 Main St., Reading, MA 01867. TEL 617-438-8464. FAX 617-438-1479. TELEX 880052. (Dist. by: Butterworth - Heinemann Ltd., 80 Montvale Ave., Stoneham, MA 02180. TEL 800-366-2665) Ed. Dr. Karen Rucker. (back issues avail.)
—BLDSC shelfmark: 4950.900000.
Description: Provides clinicians with a current guide to the assessment, diagnosis, and management of back and musculoskeletal disorders.

617.3　　　US　ISSN 0021-9355
**　　　　　　　　　CODEN: JBJSA3**
JOURNAL OF BONE AND JOINT SURGERY: AMERICAN VOLUME. 1903. 10/yr. $50. Journal of Bone and Joint Surgery, Inc., 10 Shattuck St., Boston, MA 02115. TEL 617-734-2835. Ed. Henry R. Cowell. adv.; bk.rev.; bibl.; charts; illus.; index; cum.index every 5 yrs; circ. 38,036. (also avail. in microfilm from UMI; reprint service avail. from UMI) Indexed: Abstr.Health Care Manage.Stud., Bibl.Dev.Med.& Child Neur., Biol.Abstr., Chem.Abstr., CINAHL, Curr.Cont., Dent.Ind., Excerp.Med., Ind.Med., Ind.Sci.Rev., INIS Atomind., Nutr.Abstr., Sci.Cit.Ind, Vet.Bull.
●Also available online. Vendor(s): BRS, BRS/Saunders Colleague.
—BLDSC shelfmark: 4954.250000.
Supersedes in part: Journal of Bone and Joint Surgery (ISSN 0375-9229)
Refereed Serial

617.3　　　UK　ISSN 0301-620X
**　　　　　　　　　CODEN: JBSUAK**
JOURNAL OF BONE AND JOINT SURGERY: BRITISH VOLUME. 1948. 6/yr. £31($45.50) British Editorial Society of Bone and Joint Surgery, 35-43 Lincolns Inn Fields, London WC2A 3PN, England. TEL 071-405-7227. FAX 071-405-8865. Ed. John Goodfellow. adv.; bk.rev.; bibl.; charts; illus.; index; cum.index every 5 yrs; circ. 31,600. (also avail. in microform from UMI; reprint service avail. from UMI) Indexed: Bibl.Dev.Med.& Child Neur., Biol.Abstr., Chem.Abstr., Curr.Adv.Cancer Res., Dent.Ind., Excerp.Med., Ind.Med., Ind.Sci.Rev., Ind.Vet., Nutr.Abstr., Sci.Cit.Ind, Vet.Bull.
—BLDSC shelfmark: 4954.255000.
Description: Devoted to traumatic and orthopaedic surgery and rheumatology.

611.71　　　US　ISSN 0884-0431
**　　　　　　　　　CODEN: JBMREJ**
JOURNAL OF BONE AND MINERAL RESEARCH. m. $260 (foreign $310). (American Society for Bone and Mineral Research) Mary Ann Liebert, Inc., 1651 Third Ave., New York, NY 10128. TEL 212-289-2300. FAX 212-289-4697. (Co-sponsor: National Osteoporosis Foundation) Ed. Dr. Lawrence G. Raisz. Indexed: Dairy Sci.Abstr.
—BLDSC shelfmark: 4954.255530.
Description: Publishes papers on all areas of calcium regulation, skeletal physiology, and metabolic bone diseases.

JOURNAL OF BURN CARE AND REHABILITATION. see *MEDICAL SCIENCES*

JOURNAL OF CRITICAL CARE. see *MEDICAL SCIENCES*

617　　　US　ISSN 0885-9701
JOURNAL OF HEAD TRAUMA REHABILITATION. 1986. q. $70. Aspen Publishers, Inc., 200 Orchard Ridge Dr., Gaithersburg, MD 20878. TEL 301-417-7500. FAX 301-417-7550. Indexed: Excerp.Med., Psychol.Abstr.
—BLDSC shelfmark: 4996.672000.
Refereed Serial

617.3　　　US　ISSN 0899-2517
JOURNAL OF MUSCULOSKELETAL MEDICINE. 1983. m. $65. Cliggott Publishing Co., 55 Holly Hill Lane, Box 4010, Greenwich, CT 06830. TEL 203-661-0600. Ed. Leo Cristofar. adv.; circ. 92,843. (reprint service avail.)
—BLDSC shelfmark: 5021.125000.
Description: Provides practical information on diagnosis and management of a wide variety of common musculoskeletal disorders.
Refereed Serial

617　　　US　ISSN 1058-2452
▼**JOURNAL OF MUSCULOSKELETAL PAIN.** 1992. q. $18 to individuals; institutions $32; libraries $48. Haworth Press, Inc., 10 Alice St., Binghamton, NY 13904. TEL 800-342-9678. FAX 607-722-1424. TELEX 4932599. Ed. I. Jon Russel. adv.; bk.rev. (also avail. in microfiche from HAW; reprint service avail. from HAW)
Description: Publishes articles by the vast array of professionals who must deal with acute and chronic musculoskeletal pain.
Refereed Serial

JOURNAL OF NEUROLOGICAL AND ORTHOPAEDIC MEDICINE & SURGERY. see *MEDICAL SCIENCES — Surgery*

617　　　US　ISSN 0897-7151
**　　　　　　　　　CODEN: JNEUE4**
JOURNAL OF NEUROTRAUMA. 1984. q. $125 (foreign $165). (Neurotrauma Society) Mary Ann Liebert, Inc., 1651 Third Ave., New York, NY 10128. TEL 212-289-2300. FAX 212-289-4697. Ed. Dr. Wise Young. adv.; bk.rev. (back issues avail.)
—BLDSC shelfmark: 5022.270000.
Formerly: Central Nervous System Trauma (ISSN 0737-5999)
Description: Covers advances in the mechanisms and treatments of neurotrauma of the central and peripheral nervous system. Focuses on neurochemical, neurophysiological, and neuropathological research on spinal cord injury, head trauma, neural injury, and stroke.

JOURNAL OF ORTHOPAEDIC AND SPORTS PHYSICAL THERAPY. see *MEDICAL SCIENCES — Sports Medicine*

617.3　　　US　ISSN 0736-0266
**　　　　　　　　　CODEN: JOREDR**
JOURNAL OF ORTHOPAEDIC RESEARCH; a journal for musculoskeletal investigations. 1983. bi-m. $164 to individuals; institutions $231. (Orthopaedic Research Society) Raven Press, 1185 Ave. of the Americas, New York, NY 10036. TEL 212-930-9500. FAX 212-869-3495. TELEX 640073. Eds. Dr. Wayne H. Akeson, Wilson C. Hayes. adv.; illus.; index; circ. 2,500. (back issues avail.) Indexed: Curr.Adv.Ecol.Sci., Dok.Arbeitsmed., Ind.Med., INIS Atomind.
—BLDSC shelfmark: 5027.665000.
Description: Covers experimental, theoretical and clinical aspects of orthopaedics.
Refereed Serial

JOURNAL OF ORTHOPAEDIC RHEUMATOLOGY. see *MEDICAL SCIENCES — Rheumatology*

617.3　　　FR
JOURNAL OF ORTHOPAEDIC SURGERY. French edition: Revue de Chirurgie Orthopedique. 1987. q. 105 ECU($131) (typically set in Jan.). Masson, 120 bd. St. Germain, 75280 Paris Cedex 06, France. TEL 1-46-34-21-60. FAX 1-45-87-29-99. TELEX 202 671 F.
Formerly: French Journal of Orthopaedic Surgery (ISSN 0981-1974)
Description: Information on orthopaedic surgery, anatomy and reconstructive surgery.

617.3　　　US　ISSN 0890-5339
**　　　　　　　　　CODEN: JORTE5**
JOURNAL OF ORTHOPAEDIC TRAUMA. 1987. q. $94 to individuals; institutions $110. Raven Press, 1185 Ave. of the Americas, New York, NY 10036. TEL 212-930-9500. FAX 212-869-3495. TELEX 640073. Ed. Dr. Philip G. Spiegel. adv.; bk.rev.; charts;illus.; index; circ. 2,000. (back issues avail.)
—BLDSC shelfmark: 5027.675000.
Description: Publishes original articles on the diagnosis and management of hard and soft tissue trauma.

JOURNAL OF ORTHOPEDIC SURGICAL TECHNIQUES. see *MEDICAL SCIENCES — Surgery*

617.533　　　US
JOURNAL OF OSTEOPATHIC MEDICINE. 1987. m. (except Apr.-May, Nov.-Dec. combined). membership only. (American College of General Practitioners of Osteopathic Medicine and Surgery) Professional Marketing Systems, Inc., 10 E. 21st St., New York, NY 10010. TEL 212-505-2423. adv.; circ. 33,000 (controlled).

617.3　　　US　ISSN 0271-6798
**　　　　　　　　　CODEN: JPORDO**
JOURNAL OF PEDIATRIC ORTHOPEDICS. 1981. bi-m. $118 to individuals; institutions $196. Raven Press, 1185 Ave. of the Americas, New York, NY 10036. TEL 212-930-9500. FAX 212-869-3495. TELEX 640073. Eds. Dr. Lynn T. Staheli, Dr. Robert N. Hensinger. adv.; bk.rev.; illus.; index; circ. 3,500. (back issues avail.) Indexed: Bibl.Dev.Med.& Child Neur., Biol.Abstr., Excerp.Med., Ind.Med., Psychol.Abstr.
—BLDSC shelfmark: 5030.225000.
Description: Provides answers to pediatric orthopaedic problems.
Refereed Serial

617.3　　　US　ISSN 0748-7711
RD130　　　　　CODEN: JRRDDB
JOURNAL OF REHABILITATION RESEARCH AND DEVELOPMENT. 1964. q. free to qualified personnel. Department of Veterans Affairs, Office of Technology Transfer, 103 S. Gay St., Baltimore, MD 21202. TEL 202-745-8480. FAX 410-962-9670. (Subscr. to: Supt. of Documents, U.S. Gov't Printing Office, Washington, D.C. 20402) bk.rev.; abstr.; bibl.; charts; illus.; pat.; stat.; circ. 36,000. (also avail. in microform from UMI; reprint service avail. from UMI) Indexed: Appl.Mech.Rev., Bioeng.Abstr., Biol.Abstr., Except.Child.Educ.Abstr., Excerp.Med., HRIS, Ind.Med., Rehabil.Lit.
Former titles: Journal of Rehabilitation R and D; Bulletin of Prosthetics Research (ISSN 0007-506X)

617.3　　　US　ISSN 0895-0385
**　　　　　　　　　CODEN: JSDIEW**
JOURNAL OF SPINAL DISORDERS. 1985. q. $89 to individuals; institutions $106. Raven Press, 1185 Ave. of the Americas, New York, NY 10036. TEL 212-930-9500. FAX 212-869-3495. TELEX 640073. Ed. Dan M. Spengler. adv.; charts; illus.; circ. 2,000.
—BLDSC shelfmark: 5066.182000.
Description: Features research and clinical articles on diagnosis, management, and treatment of lumbar spine disorders.
Refereed Serial

JOURNAL OF SPORTS TRAUMATOLOGY AND RELATED RESEARCH. see *MEDICAL SCIENCES — Sports Medicine*

617.1 614.49　　SW　ISSN 0345-5564
JOURNAL OF TRAFFIC MEDICINE; an international journal of traffic safety. (Text in English) 1973. q. 75 SFr. (effective Jan. 1991). International Association for Accident and Traffic Medicine, c/o K. Roos, IAATM Headquarters, P.O. Box 1644, S-75146 Uppsala, Sweden. TEL 4618-175-158. FAX 44-382-22094. Ed. James A. Dunbar. adv.; bk.rev.; illus.; stat.; circ. 1,000. Indexed: Excerp.Med., HRIS.
—BLDSC shelfmark: 5069.755000.

MEDICAL SCIENCES — ORTHOPEDICS AND TRAUMATOLOGY

610   JA   ISSN 0022-5274
CODEN: KOIGAU
JOURNAL OF TRANSPORTATION MEDICINE; kotsu igaku. (Text in English, Japanese) 1947. bi-m. 7000 Yen (membership). Japanese Association of Transportation Medicine - Nihon Kotsu Igakkai, c/o Nihon Gakkai Jimu Center, Yayoi 2-4-16, Bunkyo-ku, Tokyo 112, Japan. TEL 03-3817-5801. FAX 03-3817-5815. Ed. Takashi Murayama. adv.; circ. 600 (controlled). **Indexed:** C.I.S. Abstr., Excerp.Med., Ind.Med., INIS Atomind.
—BLDSC shelfmark: 5070.400000.

617   US   ISSN 0022-5282
RD92   CODEN: JOTRA5
JOURNAL OF TRAUMA. 1961. m. $89 to individuals; institutions $123. (American Association for the Surgery of Trauma) Williams & Wilkins, 428 E. Preston St., Baltimore, MD 21202. TEL 301-528-4000. FAX 301-528-4312. Ed. John H. Davis, M.D. adv.; abstr.; charts; illus.; stat.; tr.lit.; index; circ. 6,300. (also avail. in microform) **Indexed:** Biol.Abstr., C.I.S. Abstr., C.L.I., Chem.Abstr., CINAHL, Curr.Adv.Ecol.Sci., Curr.Cont., Dent.Ind., Excerp.Med., HRIS, Ind.Med., Ind.Sci.Rev., Ind.Vet., INIS Atomind., Int.Nurs.Ind., L.R.I., Sci.Cit.Ind.
●Also available on CD-ROM.
—BLDSC shelfmark: 5070.500000.
Description: Diagnosis, management and recommendations for surgical approaches to traumatic injury for orthopedic, plastic and general surgeons.
Refereed Serial

JOURNAL OF VETERINARY EMERGENCY AND CRITICAL CARE. see *VETERINARY SCIENCE*

617.3 617.95   HU   ISSN 0025-0317
MAGYAR TRAUMATOLOGIA, ORTHOPEDIA ES HELYREALLITO-SEBESZET/HUNGARIAN TRAUMATOLOGY, ORTHOPAEDY AND RESTORATIVE SURGERY. (Summaries in English, German and Russian) 1958. q. 38.50 Ft. Ifjusagi Lap-es Konyvkiado Vallalat, Revay u. 16, 1374 Budapest 6, Hungary. Ed. Dr. Jeno Manninger. adv.; bk.rev.; charts; illus.; pat.; index; circ. 1,000. **Indexed:** Biol.Abstr., Excerp.Med., Ind.Med., INIS Atomind.
—BLDSC shelfmark: 5345.800000.

MEDICINE AND SPORT SCIENCE. see *MEDICAL SCIENCES — Sports Medicine*

617.3   BL
MEDISOM: ORTHOPEDICS. 1981. bi-m. $90. Grupo Editorial Q B D Ltda, Rua Caravelas 326, Caixa Postal 30329, 01051 Sao Paulo, Brazil. FAX 55-11-572-5957. Ed. R. Philip Querido. adv. (audio cassette)

617.3   GW   ISSN 0340-5508
MEDIZINISCH-ORTHOPAEDISCHE TECHNIK. 1880. bi-m. DM.109.20 (foreign DM.128.40). A.W. Gentner Verlag, Forststr. 131, Postfach 101742, 7000 Stuttgart 10, Germany. TEL 0711-63672-0. FAX 0711-6367211. Ed. R. Baumgartner. adv.; bk.rev.; charts; illus.; pat.; index; circ. 3,343.
—BLDSC shelfmark: 5535.073800.

617.3   IT
CODEN: MIORA5
MINERVA ORTOPEDICA E TRAUMATOLOGICA. (Text in Italian; summaries in English) 1950. m. L.70000($90) (Societa Piemontese-Ligure-Lombarda di Ortopedia e Traumatologia) Edizioni Minerva Medica, Corso Bramante 83-85, Turin, Italy. Ed. C. Re. adv.; bk.rev.; bibl.; charts; illus.; index; circ. 3,000. **Indexed:** Chem.Abstr., Excerp.Med., Ind.Med.
Formerly: Minerva Ortopedica (ISSN 0026-4911)

628   US
N H I F NEWSLETTER. 1982. q. $35 membership (free to persons with head injuries). National Head Injury Foundation, 1140 Connecticut Ave., N.W., Ste. 812, Washington, DC 20036. TEL 202-296-6443. FAX 202-296-8850. Ed. Silvana Guerci-Lena. circ. 30,000. (back issues avail.)
Description: Covers topics related to rehabilitation, prevention and legislation as they pertain to the needs and rights of persons with head injuries and their families.

628   US
NATIONAL DIRECTORY OF HEAD INJURY REHABILITATION SERVICES. 1985. a. $70. National Head Injury Foundation, 1140 Connecticut Ave., N.W., Ste. 812, Washington, DC 20036. TEL 202-296-6443. FAX 202-296-8850.

370   US
NATIONAL HEAD INJURY FOUNDATION. CATALOGUE OF EDUCATIONAL MATERIALS. 1987. a. National Head Injury Foundation, 1140 Connecticut Ave., N.W., Ste. 812, Washington, DC 20036. TEL 202-296-6443. FAX 202-296-8850.

617.3 617   US   ISSN 0177-7955
NEURO-ORTHOPEDICS. 1986. 4/yr. (in 2 vols., 2 nos./vol.). DM.246($147) Springer-Verlag, Journals, 175 Fifth Ave., New York, NY 10010. TEL 212-460-1500. (Also Berlin, Heidelberg, Tokyo, Vienna) Ed. H. Verbiest.
—BLDSC shelfmark: 6081.512000.

617.1   US
NEUROORTHOPAEDIE. (Represents material presented at annual Erlangen Workshops) 1983. irreg. price varies. Springer-Verlag, 175 Fifth Ave., New York, NY 10010. TEL 212-460-1500.

610   GW   ISSN 0341-2903
NOTFALLMEDIZIN. 1975. m. DM.96. Perimed Verlag Dr. D. Straube, Weinstr. 70, Postfach 3740, 8520 Erlangen, Germany. TEL 09131-609-1. FAX 09131-609217. TELEX 629851-PEMEDD. Ed.Bd. bk.rev.; abstr.; index; circ. 40,000. **Indexed:** Excerp.Med.
—BLDSC shelfmark: 6170.050000.

617.3   US
O & P ALMANAC; magazine for the orthotics and prosthetics profession. 1951. m. $35. American Orthotics and Prosthetics Association, 1650 King St., Ste. 500, Alexandria, VA 22314. TEL 703-836-7114. FAX 703-836-0838. adv.: B&W & color; trim 8 1/2 x 11. circ. 5,210.
Description: Covers professional, business and government activities affecting the field.

617.3   GW   ISSN 0934-6694
OPERATIVE ORTHOPAEDIE UND TRAUMATOLOGIE; Standardeingriffe und neue Verfahren. 1989. q. DM.298. Urban und Vogel GmbH, Lindwurmstr. 95, Postfach 152209, 8000 Munich 2, Germany. TEL 089-53292-0. FAX 089-53292-100. Ed. W. Blauth. adv.; bk.rev.; circ. 2,800.

617   US
OPERATIVE TECHNIQUES IN ORTHOPAEDICS. q. W.B. Saunders, Curtis Center, Independence Square W., West Philadelphia, PA 19106-3399. TEL 215-238-7862. Ed. Richard Balderston. circ. 2,000.

617.3   GW   ISSN 0085-4530
CODEN: ORHPBG
DER ORTHOPAEDE. (Text in German) 1972. 6/yr. DM.292($178) Springer-Verlag, Heidelberger Platz 3, D-1000 Berlin 33, Germany. TEL 030-8207-1. (Also Heidelberg, Tokyo, Vienna, and New York) Ed. R. Bauer. (also avail. in microform from UMI; reprint service avail. from ISI) **Indexed:** Curr.Cont., Excerp.Med., Ind.Med.
—BLDSC shelfmark: 6296.114000.

610   JA   ISSN 0387-4095
ORTHOPAEDIC AND TRAUMATIC SURGERY/SEKEISAI GAIGEKA. (Text in English and Japanese) 1958. m. 1750 Yen per no. Kanehara & Co., Ltd., 2-31-14 Yushima, Bunkyo-ku, Tokyo 113, Japan. Ed. Dr. Yoshio Yamauchi. bk.rev.; index; circ. 7,100. **Indexed:** C.I.S. Abstr.
—BLDSC shelfmark: 6296.126200.
Formerly (until 1979): Journal of Accidental Medicine (ISSN 0036-2689)

ORTHOPAEDIC NURSING JOURNAL; national association of orthopaedic nurses. see *MEDICAL SCIENCES — Nurses And Nursing*

617.3   US
ORTHOPAEDIC PHYSICAL THERAPY PRACTICE. q. Orthopaedic Section A P T A, 505 King St., La Crosse, WI 54601. TEL 608-784-0910. Ed. John Medeiros. circ. 11,083.

617.3   US   ISSN 0094-6591
RD701   CODEN: ORTRDG
ORTHOPAEDIC REVIEW. 1972. m. $55 (foreign $82). Excerpta Medica, Inc., Core Publishing Division (Subsidiary of: Elsevier Science Publishers B.V.), 105 Raider Blvd., Belle Mead, NJ 08052. TEL 908-874-8550. FAX 908-874-0700. adv.; bk.rev.; charts; illus.; stat.; index; circ. 25,000. (back issues avail.) **Indexed:** Excerp. Med., Ind.Med.
—BLDSC shelfmark: 6296.126000.
Refereed Serial

617.3   US   ISSN 0162-9379
CODEN: ORTTDM
ORTHOPAEDIC TRANSACTIONS. 1977. 3/yr. $22. Journal of Bone and Joint Surgery, Inc., 10 Shattuck St., Boston, MA 02115. TEL 617-734-2835. illus. **Indexed:** Biol.Abstr.

617.3   GW   ISSN 0030-588X
CODEN: OPBAAS
ORTHOPAEDISCHE PRAXIS; mit Traumatologie, Rheumatologie, physikalischer, physiotherapeutischer und balneologischer Therapie des Bewegungsapparates. 1965. m. DM.182 (students DM.137). (Vereinigung Sueddeutscher Orthopaeden e.V.) Medizinisch-Literarische Verlagsgesellschaft mbH, Postfach 1161-1162, 3110 Uelzen 1, Germany. TEL 0581-808-151. FAX 0581-808158. TELEX 91326-AZ-D. Ed. Dr. Hermann G. Bauer. adv.; bk.rev.; charts; illus.; index, cum.index; circ. 5,000. (back issues avail.) **Indexed:** Excerp.Med.
—BLDSC shelfmark: 6296.120000.

617.3   US   ISSN 0030-5898
CODEN: OCLNAQ
ORTHOPEDIC CLINICS OF NORTH AMERICA. 1970. 4/yr. $84. W.B. Saunders Co., Curtis Center, Independence Square W., Philadelphia, PA 19106. TEL 215-238-7800. Ed. Melissa Mitchell. charts; illus.; index. (also avail. in microform from MIM,UMI; reprint service avail. from UMI, ISI) **Indexed:** Bibl.Dev.Med.& Child Neur., Biol.Abstr., Curr.Adv.Ecol.Sci., Curr.Cont., Excerp.Med., Ind.Med.
—BLDSC shelfmark: 6296.135000.
Refereed Serial

617.3   US
▼**ORTHOPEDIC RESIDENT.** 1991. bi-m. $40. Slack, Inc., 6900 Grove Rd., Thorofare, NJ 08086. TEL 609-848-1000. FAX 609-853-5991. Ed. Dr. G. Dean MacEwen. adv.; circ. 3,000.
Description: Guide to career, lifestyle and business issues facing residents. Covers preparing for boards, choosing fellowships, establishing a practice and decision-making.

617.3   JA   ISSN 0030-5901
ORTHOPEDIC SURGERY/SEIKEI GEKA. (Text in Japanese; title and captions in English) 1950. m. 41,300 Yen (foreign 49,323 Yen). Nankodo Co., Ltd., 42-6, Hongo 3-chome, Bunkyo-ku, Tokyo 113, Japan. TEL 03-3811-7239. FAX 03-3811-7230. Ed. Makoto Yamamoto. adv.; charts; illus.; index; circ. 8,500. **Indexed:** Biol.Abstr., Ind.Med.
—BLDSC shelfmark: 6296.140000.

617.3   US   ISSN 0147-7447
RD701
ORTHOPEDICS (THOROFARE). 1978. m. $95 to individuals; institutions $105. Slack, Inc., 6900 Grove Rd., Thorofare, NJ 08086. TEL 609-848-1000. FAX 609-853-5991. Ed. Robert D'Ambrosia, M.D. adv.; circ. 28,000. (back issues avail.) **Indexed:** Bibl.Dev.Med.& Child Neur., Curr.Cont., Excerp.Med.
—BLDSC shelfmark: 6296.146000.
Refereed Serial

617.3   US   ISSN 0279-5647
ORTHOPEDICS TODAY. 1981. m. $110 to individuals; institutions $120. Slack, Inc., 6900 Grove Rd., Thorofare, NJ 08086. TEL 609-848-1000. FAX 609-853-5991. Ed. Dr. Robert P. Nirschl. adv.; illus.; circ. 23,800.
●Also available online.
—BLDSC shelfmark: 6296.163000.

685.31 617.3   NE
ORTHOPEDISCHE SCHOENTECHNIEK. 1981. q. fl.67. Stichting Voorlichting Orthopedische Schoentechniek, Postbus 25, 3430 AA Nieuwegein, Netherlands. FAX 03402-51558. Ed. J.W.M. Lazet. adv.; bk.rev.; circ. 600.
Description: Discusses orthopedic shoes and boots, foot diseases, and orthopedic surgery.

MEDICAL SCIENCES — ORTHOPEDICS AND TRAUMATOLOGY 3311

617.3   IT   ISSN 0392-1417
ORTOPEDIA E TRAUMATOLOGIA OGGI. (Text in Italian; summaries in English) bi-m. L.60000($60) C I C Edizioni Internazionali s.r.l., Via L. Spallanzani 11, 00161 Rome, Italy. TEL 06-8412673. FAX 06-8443365. TELEX 622099 CIC. Dir. V. Pietrogrande.
—BLDSC shelfmark: 6296.258000.

617.3   BU   ISSN 0473-4378
ORTOPEDIA I TRAUMATOLOGIA. (Text in Bulgarian; summaries in English, Russian) q. 15 lv. (Ministerstvo na Narodnoto Zdrave) Izdatelstvo Meditsina i Fizkultura, 11 Pl. Slaveikov, Sofia, Bulgaria. (Distr. by: Hemus, 6 Rouski Blvd., 1000 Sofia, Bulgaria) (Co-sponsor: Nauchno Druzhestvo po Ortopedija i Traumatologija) Ed. D. Djerov. circ. 815. Indexed: Abstr.Bulg.Sci.Med.Lit.
—BLDSC shelfmark: 0128.280000.

617.3   IT   ISSN 0030-5979
ORTOPEDICI E SANITARI. 1964. m. free. Editgraf s.r.l., Via L. del Maino 2, 20146 Milan, Italy. FAX 02-4984625. Ed. Marcella Boneschi. adv.; illus.; pat.; circ. 14,000.

617.3   RU   ISSN 0030-5987
                                      CODEN: ORTPA7
ORTOPEDIYA, TRAVMATOLOGIYA I PROTEZIROVANIE/ORTHOPEDICS, TRAUMATOLOGY AND PROSTHETICS. (Text in Russian; summaries in English) 1927. m. 27 Rub.($22.20) (Vsesoyuznoe Nauchnoe Obshchestvo Travmatologov i Ortopedov) Izdatel'stvo Meditsina, Petroverigskii pereulok 6-8, 101838 Moscow, Russia. (Dist. by: Mezhdunarodnaya Kniga, Moscow, G-200, Russia) (Co-sponsor: Ministerstvo Zdravookhraneniya S.S.S.R.) Ed. A.A. Korzh. bk.rev.; bibl. (tabloid format) Indexed: Biol.Abstr., Dent.Ind., Excerp.Med., Ind.Med.
—BLDSC shelfmark: 0128.300000.
     Description: Discusses basic theoretical and practical problems of orthopedics, traumatology and prosthetics.

OUTREACH (CHICAGO). see *HOSPITALS*

617.13   US   ISSN 0890-3972
PODIATRIC PRODUCTS. 1984. 6/yr. $14 (free to qualified personnel). Novicom, Inc., 3510 Torrance Blvd., No.315, Torrance, CA 90503. TEL 310-316-8112. FAX 310-316-8422. Ed. Nancy Pauley. adv.; bk.rev.; charts; illus.; circ. 12,116.
     Formerly (until 1986): Podiatry Products Report.
     Description: Product news releases and articles related to the profession.

617.3   US
PODIATRY TODAY. m. Staff Publications Inc., Box 507, Fayetteville, NY 13066-0507. TEL 315-449-0295. FAX 315-449-3113. Ed. Edwin Black. circ. 16,995.

617.3   US   ISSN 0894-6116
▼**PODIATRY TRACTS.** 1988. bi-m. $225 to individuals; residents $95; institutions $325 (effective 1992; typically set in Dec.). Data Trace Medical Publishers, Inc., 606 Baltimore Ave., Ste. 322, Baltimore, MD 21204. TEL 301-494-4994. FAX 301-494-0515. Ed. Charles Gudas.
     Description: Provides condensations of current podiatric literature accompanied by in-depth commentaries written by experts on editorial board. Each issue also includes one 90-minute audio tape lecture.

PREHOSPITAL AND DISASTER MEDICINE; an international journal. see *MEDICAL SCIENCES*

RECONSTRUCTION SURGERY AND TRAUMATOLOGY. see *MEDICAL SCIENCES — Surgery*

617.3   US
REHABILITATION TODAY. 9/yr. Sportscape, Inc., 492 Old Connecticut Path, Framingham, MA 01701. TEL 508-872-2021. FAX 508-872-2114. Ed. Michelle Deakin. circ. 25,000.

617.3   CU
REVISTA CUBANA DE ORTOPEDIA Y TRAUMATOLOGIA. 1987. q. $24. (Centro Nacional de Informacion de Ciencias Medicas) Ediciones Cubanas, Obispo No. 527, Apdo. 605, Havana, Cuba.

617.3   SP   ISSN 0482-5985
REVISTA DE ORTOPEDIA Y TRAUMATOLOGIA. bi-m. 8400 ptas.($130) (Sociedad Espanola de Cirugia Ortopedica y Traumatologia) Editorial Garsi, S.A., Londres, 17, 28028 Madrid, Spain. TEL 256-08-00. FAX 361-10-07. Ed. F. Gomez Castresana Bachiller. circ. 4,000.

617.3   FR   ISSN 0337-9736
REVUE D'ORTHOPEDIE DENTO-FACIALE. 1967. q. 660 F. (foreign 770 F.); students 415 F. (Association de la Revue d'Orthopedie Dento-Faciale) Societe d'Information et de Diffusion, Librairie international, 49, bvd. du Lycee, 92170 Vanves, France. TEL 33-1-645-53-11. Ed. Y. Barat. adv.; bk.rev.; circ. 2,500. **Indexed:** Dent.Ind.
—BLDSC shelfmark: 7940.070000.

617.3   FR   ISSN 0035-1040
REVUE DE CHIRURGIE ORTHOPEDIQUE ET REPARATRICE DE L'APPAREIL MOTEUR. (Text in French; summaries in English) 1890. 9/yr. 135 ECU($163) (typically set in Jan.). Editions Masson, 120 bd. Saint-Germain, 75280 Paris Cedex 06, France. TEL 1-46-34-21-60. FAX 1-45-87-29-99. TELEX 202 671 F Ed. J. Zucman. bk.rev.; illus.; index.; circ. 6,100. (also avail. in microform from UMI; reprint service avail. from ISI) **Indexed:** Bibl.Dev.Med.& Child Neur., Dent.Ind., Excerp.Med., Ind.Med.
—BLDSC shelfmark: 7897.150000.

RIHABIRITESHON IGAKU/JAPANESE JOURNAL OF REHABILITATION MEDICINE. see *MEDICAL SCIENCES*

617.3   JA
RINSHO SEIKEI GEKA/CLINICAL ORTHOPAEDIC SURGERY. (Text in Japanese) 1966. m. 24180 Yen($186) Igaku-Shoin Ltd., 5-24-3 Hongo, Bunkyo-ku, Tokyo 113-91, Japan. TEL 03-817-5704. Ed.Bd. circ. 9,000.

617.3   IT
RIVISTA ITALIANA DI ORTOPEDIA E TRAUMATOLOGIA. 1961. L.60000 (foreign L.120000)(effective 1992). Casa Editrice Maccari, Via Trento, 53, 43100 Parma, Italy. FAX 039-521-771268. circ. 1,400.

617.3   IT   ISSN 0393-5221
RIVISTA ITALIANA DI ORTOPEDIA E TRAUMATOLOGIA PEDIATRICA. 1975. 2/yr. $60. (Italian Society of Paediatric Orthopaedics and Traumatology) Aulo Gaggi Editore, Via Andrea Costa, 131-5, 40134 Bologna, Italy. Ed. A. Dal Monte.
—BLDSC shelfmark: 7987.465000.

SCHMERZDIAGNOSTIK UND THERAPIE. see *MEDICAL SCIENCES — Anaesthesiology*

617.3   JA   ISSN 0037-1033
SEIKEI GEKA TO SAIGAI GEKA/ORTHOPEDICS AND TRAUMATOLOGY. (Text in English and Japanese) 1952. s-a. 6000 Yen($3) Nishi Nihon Seikei Saigai Geka Gakkai - West Japan Society of Orthopedics and Traumatology, c/o Dept. of Orthopedic Surgery, Kyushu Daigaku, 1276 Katakasu, Fukuoka 812, Japan. Ed. Atsuto Nishio. adv.; circ. 1,000.

SEMINARS IN ARTHRITIS & RHEUMATISM. see *MEDICAL SCIENCES — Rheumatology*

617.3   US   ISSN 1045-4527
▼**SEMINARS IN ARTHROPLASTY.** 1990. q. $74 to individuals; institutions $96. W.B. Saunders Company (Subsidiary of: Harcourt Brace Jovanovich), Curtis Center, Independence Square W., Philadelphia, PA 19106-3399. TEL 215-238-7800. (Subscr. to: Box 6209, Duluth, MN 55806) Ed. Dr. Richard Rothman.
—BLDSC shelfmark: 8239.448100.

617.3   US   ISSN 0882-052X
                                        CODEN: SEORED
SEMINARS IN ORTHOPAEDICS. 1986. q. $83 to individuals; institutions $105; foreign $123. W.B. Saunders Co. (Subsidiary of: Harcourt Brace Jovanovich, Inc.), Curtis Center, Independence Square W., Philadelphia, PA 19106. TEL 215-238-7800. Ed. Sean P.F. Hughes. adv.; bibl.; charts; illus.; index.
—BLDSC shelfmark: 8239.456700.

SEMINARS IN ROENTGENOLOGY. see *MEDICAL SCIENCES — Radiology And Nuclear Medicine*

SEMINARS IN ULTRASOUND, C T AND M R. see *MEDICAL SCIENCES — Radiology And Nuclear Medicine*

617.1   FR   ISSN 0399-0265
SERVICES D'AIDE MEDICALE URGENTE. REVUE. Cover title: Revue des S A M U. 1978. 6/yr. 320 F. (foreign 550 F.). (Services d'Aide Medicale Urgente) Societe Francaise d'Editions Medicales, 22-24 rue du Chateau des Rentiers, 75013 Paris, France. TEL 45-83-50-54. Ed. Colette Gallula. adv.; bibl.; charts; illus.

SHINKEI GAISHO/NEUROTRAUMATOLOGY. see *MEDICAL SCIENCES — Psychiatry And Neurology*

SLIDE ATLAS OF CURRENT ORTHOPAEDICS (YEAR). see *MEDICAL SCIENCES — Abstracting, Bibliographies, Statistics*

617.2   SP   ISSN 0212-0771
SOCIEDAD ANDALUZA DE ORTOPEDIA Y TRAUMATOLOGIA. REVISTA. 1981. q. 3100 ptas.($48) Editorial Garsi, S.A., Londres, 17, 28028 Madrid, Spain. TEL 256-08-00. FAX 361-10-07. Ed. E. Queipo de Llano Gimenez. circ. 1,000.

617.3   IT   ISSN 0394-0713
SOCIETA DI ORTOPEDIA E TRAUMATOLOGIA DELL' ITALIA MERIDIONALE ED INSULARE. ATTI E MEMORIE. s-a. L.40000($55) (effective 1992). Casa Editrice Idelson, Via A. DeGasperi, 55, 80133 Naples, Italy. TEL 081-5524733. FAX 081-5518295. Ed. Nicola Misasi.

617.3   IT
SOCIETA EMILIANA ROMAGNOLA TRIVENETA DI ORTOPEDIA E TRAUMATOLOGIA. ATTI. (Text in Italian; summaries in English) s-a. L.39000. Societa Emiliana Romagnola Triveneta di Ortopedia e Traumatologia, Viale Dei Mille 140, 43100 Parma, Italy. TEL 0521-290191. FAX 0521-291314. TELEX 530476 EMMEVI I. adv. (back issues avail.)

617.3   FR   ISSN 0081-1033
SOCIETE FRANCAISE DE CHIRURGIE ORTHOPEDIQUE ET TRAUMATOLOGIQUE. CONFERENCES D'ENSEIGNEMENT. 1967. irreg., latest 1973. price varies. Expansion Scientifique, 15 rue Saint-Benoit, 75278 Paris Cedex 06, France. TEL 1-45-48-42-60. FAX 1-45-44-81-55. Ed. J. Duparc.

610.73 618.92   US
SPINAL CONNECTION. 1984. s-a. $15. National Scoliosis Foundation, 72 Mt. Auburn St., Watertown, MA 02172. TEL 617-926-0397. FAX 617-926-0398. Ed. Kalo Clarke. adv.; bk.rev.; circ. 22,000. (back issues avail.)
     Description: Provides medical information on scoliosis, including an overview of the Foundation's activities and services.

617.375   US   ISSN 0362-2436
RD768   CODEN: SPINDD
SPINE (PHILADELPHIA, 1976). 1976. 11/yr. $150 to individuals (foreign $190); institutions $210 (foreign $270). J.B. Lippincott Co., E. Washington Sq., Philadelphia, PA 19105. TEL 215-238-4200. (Subscr. to: Downville Pike, Rte. 3, Box 20-B, Hagerstown, MD 21740) Ed. Henry LaRocca, M.D. adv.; illus.; index.; circ. 8,500. (also avail. in microform from UMI) **Indexed:** Bibl.Dev.Med.& Child Neur., Biol.Abstr., Chem.Abstr., Curr.Adv.Ecol.Sci., Curr.Cont., Dent.Ind., Dok.Arbeitsmed., Excerp.Med., Hosp.Lit.Ind., Ind.Med., Ind.Vet.
—BLDSC shelfmark: 8413.903000.

617.375   US   ISSN 0887-9869
RD768
SPINE (PHILADELPHIA, 1986); state of the art reviews. 1986. 3/yr. $82 (foreign $92). Hanley & Belfus, Inc., 210 S. 13th St., Philadelphia, PA 19107. TEL 215-546-7293. FAX 215-790-9330.
—BLDSC shelfmark: 8413.902980.
     Refereed Serial

617.3   US   ISSN 0885-9698
TECHNIQUES IN ORTHOPEDICS. 1986. q. $124. Aspen Publishers, Inc., 200 Orchard Ridge Dr., Gaithersburg, MD 20878. TEL 301-417-7500. FAX 301-417-7550. Ed. Dr. Lawrence Dorr. circ. 2,500.
—BLDSC shelfmark: 8745.278000.

MEDICAL SCIENCES — OTORHINOLARYNGOLOGY

617.1   FR   ISSN 0397-3999
TECHNIQUES ORTHOPEDIQUES. 1976. irreg., latest 1981. 875 F. Expansion Scientifique, 15 rue Saint Benoit, 75278 Paris Cedex 06, France. TEL 1-45-48-42-60. FAX 1-45-44-81-55. Eds. J. Casaing, L. Descamps.

617.3   JA
TOHOKU ARCHIVES OF ORTHOPAEDIC SURGERY AND TRAUMATOLOGY. (Text in Japanese) 1957. s-a. membership. Tohoku Society of Orthopaedic Surgery and Traumatology - Tohoku Seikei Saigai Geka Gakkai, c/o Dept. of Orthopaedic Surgery, Tohoku University School of Medicine, 1-1 Seiryo-machi, Aoba-ku, Sendai 980, Japan. Ed.Bd. bk.rev.; abstr.; bibl.; charts; illus.; index, curr.index, circ. 650 (controlled).
    Formerly (until vol. 20, 1977): Tohoku Archivo por Orthopedia Kej Akcidenta Hirurgio (ISSN 0040-8751)

617.1   SA
TRAUMA & EMERGENCY MEDICINE. vol.8, 1991. 6/yr. R.50. Helm Publishing Co. (Pty.) Ltd., P.O. Box 41706, Craighall 2024, South Africa. TEL 011-788-0612.

617.3   US   ISSN 0743-6637
    CODEN: TRAUEK
TRAUMA QUARTERLY. 1984. q. $89. Aspen Publishers, Inc., 200 Orchard Ridge Dr., Gaithersburg, MD 20878. TEL 301-417-7500. FAX 301-417-7550. **Indexed:** Hlth.Ind.

617.1   GW   ISSN 0177-5537
R51   CODEN: UNFAE2
DER UNFALLCHIRURG; gesamte Unfallchirurgie Einschliesslich Sporttraumatologie. 1894. 12/yr. DM.354($231) (Deutsche Gesellschaft fuer Unfallheilkunde, Versicherungs-, Versorgungs- und Verkehrsmedizin) Springer-Verlag, Heidelberger Platz 3, D-1000 Berlin 33, Germany. TEL 030-8207-1. (Also: Heidelberg, Tokyo, Vienna, and New York) Ed.Bd. (also avail. in microform from UMI; back issues avail.; reprint service avail. from ISI) **Indexed:** Biol.Abstr., Curr.Cont., Excerp.Med., Ind.Med.
—BLDSC shelfmark: 9090.235280.
    Former titles: Unfallheilkunde (ISSN 0341-5694); Monatsschrift fuer Unfallheilkunde (ISSN 0340-1669); Monatsschrift fuer Unfallheilkunde, Versicherungs-, Versorgungs- und Verkehrsmedizin (ISSN 0026-9336)

617.1   GW   ISSN 0340-2649
UNFALLCHIRURGIE. (Text in English and German; summaries in English) 1975. 6/yr. DM.256. Urban und Vogel, Lindwurmstr. 95, Postfach 152209, 8000 Munich 15, Germany. TEL 089-53292-0. FAX 089-53292-100. circ. 1,900. **Indexed:** Ind.Med.
—BLDSC shelfmark: 9090.235300.

VETERINARY AND COMPARATIVE ORTHOPAEDICS AND TRAUMATOLOGY. see *VETERINARY SCIENCE*

617.3   HK   ISSN 0043-4019
WESTERN PACIFIC ORTHOPAEDIC ASSOCIATION. JOURNAL. (Text in English) 1962. s-a. $30. Hong Kong University Press, 139 Pokfulam Rd., Hong Kong. TEL 8170018. FAX 8557350. (Subscr. addr.: c/o MacLehose Medical Rehabilitation Centre, 7 Sha Wan Dr., Sandy Bay, Rokfulam Rd., Hong Kong) Ed. Dr. S.F. Lam. adv.; bk.rev.; charts; illus.; circ. 2,000 (controlled). (also avail. in microform from UMI; reprint service avail. from UMI) **Indexed:** Excerp.Med.

617   US   ISSN 0271-7964
RC86
YEAR BOOK OF EMERGENCY MEDICINE. 1981. a. $57.95. Mosby - Year Book, Inc., Continuity Division, 200 N. LaSalle, Chicago, IL 60601. TEL 312-726-9733. FAX 312-726-6075. TELEX 206155. Ed. Dr. David K. Wagner. (reprint service avail.)
●Also available online. Vendor(s): BRS.

YEAR BOOK OF HAND SURGERY. see *MEDICAL SCIENCES — Surgery*

617.305   US   ISSN 0276-1092
RD711
YEAR BOOK OF ORTHOPEDICS. 1940. a. $57.95. Mosby - Year Book, Inc., Continuity Division, 200 N. LaSalle, Chicago, IL 60601. TEL 312-726-9733. FAX 312-726-6075. TELEX 206155. Ed. Clement B. Sledge, M.D. illus. (reprint service avail.)
●Also available online. Vendor(s): BRS.
—BLDSC shelfmark: 9414.677000.
    Former titles: Year Book of Orthopedics, Traumatic and Plastic Surgery; Year Book of Orthopedics and Traumatic Surgery (ISSN 0084-3938)

617.3   US   ISSN 0742-194X
RD563
YEAR BOOK OF PODIATRIC MEDICINE AND SURGERY. a. $57.95. Mosby - Year Book, Inc., Continuity Division, 200 N. LaSalle, Chicago, IL 60601. TEL 312-726-9733. FAX 312-726-6075. TELEX 206155. illus. (reprint service avail.)
—BLDSC shelfmark: 9415.550000.

617.3   GW   ISSN 0044-3220
    CODEN: ZOIGAP
ZEITSCHRIFT FUER ORTHOPAEDIE UND IHRE GRENZGEBIETE. (Supplement avail.: Bucherei des Orthopaeden) (Text in English and German) 1891. bi-m. DM.456. (Deutsche Gesellschaft fuer Orthopaedie und Traumatologie) Ferdinand Enke Verlag, Postfach 101254, 7000 Stuttgart 10, Germany. TEL 0711-8931-0. FAX 0711-8931-419. TELEX 07252275-GTV-D. Ed.Bd. adv.; bk.rev.; bibl.; charts; illus.; index; circ. 1,600. **Indexed:** Biol.Abstr., C.I.S. Abstr., Curr.Adv.Cancer Res., Curr.Cont., Dent.Ind., Excerp.Med., Ind.Med., Sci.Cit.Ind.
—BLDSC shelfmark: 9475.670000.
    Incorporates: Deutsche Gesellschaft fuer Orthopaedie und ihre Grenzgebiete. Verhandlungen (ISSN 0070-4091)

617.3   CC
ZHONGHUA GUKE ZAZHI/CHINESE JOURNAL OF ORTHOPEDICS. (Text in Chinese) bi-m. $1.50 per no. Guoji Shudian, Qikan Bu, Chegongzhuang Xilu 21, P.O. Box 399, Beijing 100044, People's Republic of China.

617.3   CC
ZHONGYI ZHENGGU. (Text in Chinese) q. Luoyang Zhenggu Yanjiusuo, No. 1, Qiming Nanlu, Luoyang, Henan 471002, People's Republic of China. TEL 51838. Ed. Guo Weizhun.

MEDICAL SCIENCES — Otorhinolaryngology

A A O A NEWS. (American Academy of Otolaryngic Allergy) see *MEDICAL SCIENCES — Allergology And Immunology*

616.21   US   ISSN 0883-3001
RF28
A B M S DIRECTORY OF CERTIFIED OTOLARYNGOLOGISTS. 1985. biennial. $39.95. American Board of Medical Specialties, One Rotary Center, Ste. 805, Evanston, IL 60201. TEL 708-491-9091. FAX 708-328-3596. Ed. Dr. J. Lee Dockery.

616.21   US   ISSN 0149-8886
RF297
ACADEMY OF REHABILITATIVE AUDIOLOGY. JOURNAL. Short title: J A R A. 1969. a. $15. Academy of Rehabilitative Audiology, c/o H.L. Beykirch, Ph.D., CAC 229, University of Northern Iowa, Cedar Falls, IA 50614. TEL 319-273-2542. FAX 319-273-3509. Ed. Donald Sims. circ. 500. **Indexed:** ERIC, Lang.& Lang.Behav.Abstr., Psychol.Abstr., Sociol.Abstr.
    Description: Forum for the exchange of ideas on, knowledge of, and experience with habilitative and rehabilitative aspects of audiology.

616.31 617   US
ACOUSTIC NEUROMA ASSOCIATION NOTES. 1981. q. membership. Acoustic Neuroma Association, Box 398, Carlisle, PA 17013. TEL 717-249-4783. FAX 717-249-0353. Ed. Virginia Fickel. circ. 4,000.
    Description: Provides support and information for patients who have had acoustic neuromas or other cranial nerve tumors.

616.21   SW   ISSN 0001-6489
    CODEN: AOLAAJ
ACTA OTO-LARYNGOLOGICA. (Supplements avail.) (Text in English) 1918. m. SEK 800 incl. supplements. (Scandinavian Oto-Laryngological Society) Almqvist & Wiksell Periodical Company, P.O. Box 638, S-101 28 Stockholm, Sweden. Ed. Borje Drettner. adv.; charts; illus.; index; circ. 2,100. **Indexed:** ASCA, Biol.Abstr., Biotech.Abstr., C.I.S. Abstr., Chem.Abstr., Curr.Adv.Ecol.Sci., Curr.Cont., Dent.Ind., Dok.Arbeitsmed., Excerp.Med., Helminthol.Abstr., Hort.Abstr., Ind.Med., Ind.Sci.Rev., Ind.Vet., Lang.& Lang.Behav.Abstr., Noise Pollut.Publ.Abstr., Psychol.Abstr., Sci.Cit.Ind.
—BLDSC shelfmark: 0642.250000.

616.21   DK   ISSN 0365-5237
    CODEN: AOLSA5
ACTA OTO-LARYNGOLOGICA. SUPPLEMENT. a. SEK 142. (Scandinavian Oto-Laryngological Society) Almqvist & Wiksell Periodicals Company, P.O. Box 638, S-101 28 Stockholm, Sweden. **Indexed:** Excerp.Med., Ind.Vet.
—BLDSC shelfmark: 0642.255000.

616.21   BE   ISSN 0001-6497
    CODEN: AORLAE
ACTA OTO-RHINO-LARYNGOLOGICA BELGICA. (Supplements avail.) vol.21,1967. 4/yr. 3000 Fr. (foreign 3200 Fr.). Association des Societes Scientifiques Medicales Belges - Vereiniging van de Belgische Medische Wetenschappelijke Genootschappen, Av. Circulaire 138A, B-1180 Brussels, Belgium. TEL 02-374-5158. Ed. Dr. P. Hennebert. **Indexed:** Biol.Abstr., Chem.Abstr., Dent.Ind., Excerp.Med., Ind.Med., Lang.& Lang.Behav.Abstr., Rev.Med.& Vet.Mycol.
—BLDSC shelfmark: 0642.270000.

616.21   IT   ISSN 0392-100X
    CODEN: AOITDU
ACTA OTORHINOLARYNGOLOGICA ITALICA. 1980? bi-m. L.70000 (foreign L.90000)(effective 1992). Pacini Editore s.r.l., Via della Gherardesca 1, 56014 Ospedaletto (Pisa), Italy. TEL 050-982439. FAX 050-983906. TELEX 501628 PACINI I. Ed. C. Calearo. **Indexed:** Excerp.Med., Ind.Med.
—BLDSC shelfmark: 0642.280000.

616.21   SP   ISSN 0001-6519
ACTA OTORRINOLARINGOLOGICA ESPANOLA. 1949. bi-m. 6100 ptas.($99) (Sociedad Espanola de Otorrinolaringologia) Editorial Garsi, S.A., Londres, 17, 28028 Madrid, Spain. TEL 256-08-00. FAX 361-10-07. Ed. Teodoro Sacristan Alonso. adv.; bk.rev.; bibl.; charts; illus.; circ. 2,500. **Indexed:** Biol.Abstr., Excerp.Med., Ind.Med.Esp.
—BLDSC shelfmark: 0642.300000.

617.89   SZ   ISSN 0254-8747
ADVANCES IN AUDIOLOGY. (Text in English) 1983. irreg. price varies. S. Karger AG, Allschwilerstr. 10, P.O. Box, CH-4009 Basel, Switzerland. TEL 061-3061111. FAX 061-3061234. TELEX CH 962652. Ed. M. Hoke.
—BLDSC shelfmark: 0699.830000.

616.21   SZ   ISSN 0065-3071
RF16   CODEN: ADORB9
ADVANCES IN OTO-RHINO-LARYNGOLOGY. (Text in English) 1953. irreg. price varies. S. Karger AG, Allschwilerstr. 10, P.O. Box, CH-4009 Basel, Switzerland. TEL 061-3061111. FAX 061-3061234. TELEX CH 962652. Ed. C.R. Pfaltz. (reprint service avail. from ISI) **Indexed:** Biol.Abstr., Chem.Abstr., Curr.Cont., Dent.Ind., Ind.Med.
—BLDSC shelfmark: 0709.570000.

616.21   US   ISSN 0887-6916
RF1
ADVANCES IN OTOLARYNGOLOGY - HEAD AND NECK SURGERY. 1987. a. $69.95. Mosby - Year Book, Inc. (Chicago) (Subsidiary of: Times Mirror Company), 200 N. LaSalle St., Chicago, IL 60601-1080. TEL 312-726-9733. FAX 312-726-6075. TELEX 206155. (Subscr. to: 11830 Westline Industrial Dr., St. Louis, MO 63146. TEL 800-325-4177) Ed. Eugene N. Myers, M.D.
—BLDSC shelfmark: 0709.569000.
    Description: Presents a collection of original fully referenced clinical reviews from the experts in the field.

MEDICAL SCIENCES — OTORHINOLARYNGOLOGY

617.89   CN
AMERICAN ACADEMY OF AUDIOLOGY. JOURNAL. bi-m. $90 to individuals; institutions $120. Decker Periodicals, One James St. S., P.O. Box 620, LCD 1, Hamilton, Ont. L8N 3K7, Canada. TEL 416-522-7017. FAX 416-522-7839. (U.S. addr.: Box 785, Lewiston, NY 14092-0785) Ed. James Jerger. abstr.
Description: Features original contributions, abstracts, research reports, case studies and a clinical forum.

616.21   US   ISSN 0731-8359
AMERICAN ACADEMY OF OTOLARYNGOLOGY - HEAD AND NECK SURGERY. BULLETIN. 1982. m. $40. American Academy of Otolaryngology - Head and Neck Surgery, Inc., One Prince St., Alexandria, VA 22314. TEL 703-836-4444. FAX 703-683-5100. Ed. Jerome C. Goldstein, M.D. adv.; charts; stat.; index; circ. 9,300.
Description: Provides information about academy meetings, publications, policies and activities and news of interest to members. Contains employment listings and a calendar of courses, meetings and workshops.

616.21   US   ISSN 0065-7603
AMERICAN BRONCHO-ESOPHAGOLOGICAL ASSOCIATION. TRANSACTIONS. 1921. a. $40. American Broncho-Esophagological Association, c/o Stanley M. Sharpshay, M.D., Ed., Lahey Clinic Medical Center, 41 Mall Rd., Burlington, MA 01805. TEL 617-273-8854. FAX 617-273-5209. circ. 150.
—BLDSC shelfmark: 8886.150000.
Description: Publishes all papers presented at the annual spring meeting.

617.89   US
▼**AMERICAN JOURNAL OF AUDIOLOGY**; a journal of clinical practice. 1991. 3/yr. $20 to individuals (foreign $32); institutions $32 (foreign $44). American Speech - Language - Hearing Association, 10801 Rockville Pike, Rockville, MD 20852. TEL 301-897-5700. FAX 301-571-0457.
Description: Addresses all aspects of clinical practice in audiology.

616.21   US   ISSN 0196-0709
RF1   CODEN: AJOTDP
AMERICAN JOURNAL OF OTOLARYNGOLOGY; head and neck medicine and surgery. 1979. q. $73 to individuals; institutions $94; foreign $130. W.B. Saunders Co., Curtis Center, Independence Square W., Philadelphia, PA 19106. TEL 215-574-4874. (Subscr. to: Journals Dept., 6277 Sea Harbor Dr., 4th Fl., Orlando, FL 32891) Ed. John M. Frederickson, M.D. circ. 1,258. (reprint service avail. from UMI) **Indexed:** Chem.Abstr., CINAHL, Dent.Ind., Excerp.Med., Ind.Med.
—BLDSC shelfmark: 0829.300000.
Refereed Serial

616.21   CN   ISSN 0192-9763
                           CODEN: AJOTBN
AMERICAN JOURNAL OF OTOLOGY. (Text in English) 1979. bi-m. $80 to physicians; institutions $110; residents $60. Decker Periodicals, One James St. S., P.O. Box 620, LCD 1, Hamilton, Ont. L8N 3K7, Canada. TEL 416-522-7017. FAX 416-522-7839. (US addr.: Box 785, Lewiston, NY 14092) Ed. Dr. Gary Jackson. adv.; bk.rev.; bibl.; illus.; circ. 1,700. (also avail. in microform from UMI; back issues avail.) **Indexed:** Biol.Abstr., Dent.Ind., Excerp.Med., Ind.Med., Noise Pollut.Publ.Abstr.
—BLDSC shelfmark: 0829.400000.
Description: Original articles and reviews in otology, neurology and audiology.

616.21   US
AMERICAN JOURNAL OF RHINOLOGY. 1987. bi-m. $68. Ocean Side Publications, Inc., 95 Pitman St., Providence, RI 02906. TEL 401-331-2510. FAX 401-331-5138. Ed. David Kennedy. adv.; circ. 7,500.
Description: Clinical discussions regarding rhinology.

616.21 616.8   US
▼**AMERICAN JOURNAL OF SPEECH - LANGUAGE PATHOLOGY**; a journal of clinical practice. 1991. 3/yr. $20 to individuals (foreign $32); institutions $32 (foreign $44). American Speech - Language - Hearing Association, 10801 Rockville Pike, Rockville, MD 20852. TEL 301-897-5700. FAX 301-571-0457. adv.; circ. 70,865.
Description: For speech - language professionals who see clients, prescribe rehabilitation, and are trained to handle a broad range of communication disorders.

617.8   US
AMERICAN OTOLOGICAL SOCIETY. TRANSACTIONS. 1868. a. price varies. Annals Publishing Co., 4507 Laclede Ave., St. Louis, MO 63108. TEL 314-367-4987. FAX 314-367-4988. Ed. Dr. Mansfield F.W. Smith. circ. 300.
Description: Papers presented at the meeting of the society.

616.855 612.85   US
AMERICAN SPEECH - LANGUAGE - HEARING ASSOCIATION. DIRECTORY. biennial. price varies. American Speech - Language - Hearing Association, 10801 Rockville Pike, Rockville, MD 20852. TEL 301-897-5700. FAX 301-571-0457.
Formerly: A S H A Directory (ISSN 0569-8561)

371.9 617.8 612.85   US
AMERICAN SPEECH - LANGUAGE - HEARING ASSOCIATION REPORTS. 1972. irreg., no.20, 1990. American Speech - Language - Hearing Association, 10801 Rockville Pike, Rockville, MD 20852. TEL 301-897-5700. FAX 301-571-0457. Ed. David P. Kuehn. **Indexed:** Biol.Abstr., Educ.Ind., Psychol.Abstr.
Formerly: A S H A Reports (ISSN 0569-8553)

616.21   SP   ISSN 0303-8874
                           CODEN: AOIAA4
ANALES OTORRINOLARINGOLOGICOS IBERO-AMERICANOS. (Text in Spanish; summaries in English, French, German) 1950. bi-m. 12249 ptas. ($119 in Latin America; elsewhere $146)(effective 1992). Provenza 319, 08037 Barcelona, Spain. Ed. E. Perello Scherdel. adv.; bk.rev.; cum.index: 1950-1973, 1974-1983; circ. 1,000. (reprint service avail.) **Indexed:** Biol.Abstr., Dent.Ind., Excerp.Med., Ind.Med.
—BLDSC shelfmark: 0890.130000.
Formerly (until 1973): Acta Oto-Rino-Laringologica Ibero-Americana (ISSN 0001-6500)

616.21   FR   ISSN 0003-438X
ANNALES D'OTO-LARYNGOLOGIE ET DE CHIRURGIE CERVICO FACIALE. (Text in French; summaries in English) 1875. 8/yr. 175 ECU($215) Masson, 120 bd. Saint Germain, 75280 Paris Cedex 06, France. Ed.Bd. adv.; bk.rev.; bibl.; illus.; index; circ. 2,000. (also avail. in microform from UMI; reprint service avail. from ISI) **Indexed:** Chem.Abstr., Dent.Ind., Excerp.Med., Ind.Med., Lang.& Lang.Behav.Abstr.
—BLDSC shelfmark: 0990.700000.
Formerly: Annales d'Oto-Laryngologie.

616.21   US   ISSN 0003-4894
RF1   CODEN: AORHA2
ANNALS OF OTOLOGY, RHINOLOGY AND LARYNGOLOGY; annals of head and neck medicine and surgery. 1892. m. $92. Annals Publishing Co., 4507 Laclede Ave., St. Louis, MO 63108. TEL 314-367-4987. FAX 314-367-4988. Ed. Dr. Brian F. McCabe. adv.; bk.rev.; charts; index; circ. 5,900. (also avail. in microfiche; reprint service avail. from UMI) **Indexed:** Abstr.Anthropol., Biol.Abstr., Chem.Abstr., Curr.Adv.Ecol.Sci., Curr.Cont., Dent.Ind., Dok.Arbeitsmed., Excerp.Med., Ind.Med., Ind.Sci.Rev., INIS Atomind., Lang.& Lang.Behav.Abstr., Noise Pollut.Publ.Abstr., Nutr.Abstr., Psychol.Abstr., Sci.Cit.Ind.
—BLDSC shelfmark: 1043.400000.
Description: Publishes original manuscripts of clinical and research importance in otolaryngology - head and neck medicine and surgery, broncho-esophagology, maxillofacial surgery, audiology, speech pathology, and related specialties.
Refereed Serial

616.21   GW   ISSN 0302-9530
                           CODEN: AORLCG
ARCHIVES OF OTO-RHINO-LARYNGOLOGY/ARCHIV FUER OHREN-, NASEN- UND KEHLKOPFHEILKUNDE. (Text in English or German) 1864. 6/yr. DM.758($434) (Deutsche Gesellschaft fuer Hals-, Nasen-, Ohrenheilkunde, Kopf- und Halschirurgie - German Society of Oto-Rhino-Laryngology-Head and Neck Surgery) Springer-Verlag, Heidelberger Platz 3, D-1000 Berlin 33, Germany. TEL 030-8207-1. (Also Heidelberg, Tokyo, Vienna, and New York) Ed. C. Beck. adv.; bibl.; charts; illus.; index. (also avail. in microform from UMI; back issues avail.; reprint service avail. from ISI) **Indexed:** Biol.Abstr., Curr.Adv.Ecol.Sci., Curr.Cont., Dent.Ind., Excerp.Med., Ind.Med., Ind.Sci.Rev., INIS Atomind., Sci.Cit.Ind.
Formerly: Archiv fuer Klinische und Experimentelle Ohren-, Nasen- und Kehlkopfheilkunde (ISSN 0003-9195)

616.21 016   US   ISSN 0886-4470
RF1   CODEN: AONSEJ
ARCHIVES OF OTOLARYNGOLOGY - HEAD & NECK SURGERY. 1925. m. $74. American Medical Association, 515 N. State St., Chicago, IL 60610. TEL 312-464-0183. FAX 312-464-5834. Ed. Dr. Byron J. Bailey. adv.; bk.rev.; bibl.; charts; illus.; index; circ. 13,000. (also avail. in microform from UMI) **Indexed:** Biol.Abstr., C.I.S. Abstr., Chem.Abstr., Curr.Cont., Dent.Ind., Except.Child.Educ.Abstr., Excerp.Med., Ind.Med., Ind.Sci.Rev., INIS Atomind., Noise Pollut.Publ.Abstr., Rev.Med.& Vet.Mycol., Rev.Plant Path., Sci.Cit.Ind.
●Also available online. Vendor(s): Mead Data Central.
—BLDSC shelfmark: 1638.510000.
Former titles: Archives of Otolaryngology (ISSN 0003-9977); A.M.A. Archives of Otolaryngology (ISSN 0096-6894)
Refereed Serial

616.2   IT   ISSN 0066-9865
ASSOCIAZIONE ITALIANA LARINGECTOMIZZATI. ATTI (DEL) CONVEGNO NAZIONALE. 1957. q. Associazione Italiana Laringectomizzati, Via Friuli 28, Milan, Italy. TEL 02-86-45-29-92.
Description: Addresses all laringectomees and their families with news about Association life and medical advice.

616.21   US   ISSN 0271-1354
AUDIO-DIGEST OTOLARYNGOLOGY - HEAD AND NECK SURGERY. 1968. s-m. $168. Audio-Digest Foundation (Subsidiary of: California Medical Association), 1577 E. Chevy Chase Dr., Glendale, CA 91206. TEL 213-245-8505. FAX 818-240-7379. (audio cassette)
Former titles: Audio-Digest Otorhinolaryngology - Head and Neck Surgery; Audio-Digest Otorhinolaryngology (ISSN 0030-6673)
Refereed Serial

617.89   IT   ISSN 0393-3393
AUDIOLOGIA ITALIANA. (Text in English and Italian; summaries in English) q. $90. (Italian Society of Audiology) Edizioni Luigi Pozzi s.r.l., Via Panama 68, 00198 Rome, Italy. TEL 06-8553548. FAX 06-8554105. Ed. G. Rossi. adv.; bk.rev.; circ. 900.
Former titles: Bollettino Italiano di Audiologia e Foniatria; Giornale Italiano di Audiologia.

617.8   SZ   ISSN 0020-6091
RF290   CODEN: AUDLAK
AUDIOLOGY; journal of auditory communication. (Text in English and French; summaries in French) 1962. bi-m. 360 Fr.($240) per vol. (International Society of Audiology) S. Karger AG, Allschwilerstr. 10, P.O. Box, CH-4009 Basel, Switzerland. TEL 061-3061111. FAX 061-3061234. TELEX CH 962652. (US addr.: 26 W. Avon Rd., Box 529, Farmington, CT 06085. TEL 203-675-7834) Ed. J. M. Aran. adv.; abstr.; bibl.; illus.; index, cum.index; circ. 1,650. (also avail. in microfilm) **Indexed:** Bibl.Dev.Med.& Child Neur., Biol.Abstr., Curr.Adv.Ecol.Sci., Curr.Cont., Dok.Arbeitsmed., Excerp.Med., Ind.Med., Ind.Sci.Rev., Lang.& Lang.Behav.Abstr., Noise Pollut.Publ.Abstr., Psychol.Abstr., Sci.Cit.Ind.
—BLDSC shelfmark: 1789.080000.
Formerly: International Audiology (ISSN 0538-4915)

MEDICAL SCIENCES — OTORHINOLARYNGOLOGY

617.89   JA   ISSN 0303-8106
CODEN: AUJADK
AUDIOLOGY JAPAN. (Text in Japanese; summaries in English) 1958. bi-m. 8000 Yen. Japan Audiological Society - Nihon Chokaku Igakkai, c/o Chateau Takanawa 703, 3-23-14 Takanawa, Minato-ku, Tokyo 108, Japan. FAX 03-3445-5834. TELEX 03-3445-5834. Ed. T. Tsuiki. adv. (reprint service avail.) **Indexed:** Biol.Abstr., Excerp.Med.
•Also available online. Vendor(s): JICST.
—BLDSC shelfmark: 1789.083000.
Formerly: Audiology (ISSN 0571-8724)

617.89 420   SP
AUDIOLOGY PROTESICA. q. 2000 ptas. (foreign 3600 ptas.). (Asociacion Nacional de Audio Protesistas) Reclamo Tecnico, S.A., Casanova 212, 1-2, 08036 Barcelona, Spain. TEL 3212149. FAX 3223812. circ. 2,500.

617.89   CN
AUDIOLOGY TODAY. bi-m. $40 to individuals; institutions $80. (American Academy of Audiology) Decker Periodicals, One James St. S., P.O. Box 620, LCD 1, Hamilton, Ont. L8N 3K7, Canada. TEL 416-522-7017. FAX 416-522-7839. (US addr.: P.O. Box 785, Lewiston, NY 14092-0785) Ed. John T. Jacobson.
Description: Covers academy affairs and clinic practice which offers a series of pragmatic applications in evaluative, diagnostic and rehabilitative services.

616.21   JA
AURIS. NASUS. LARYNX. (Text in English, French or German; summaries in English) 1973. s-a. $15. Society for the Promotion of International Otorhinolaryngology - Kokusai Jibi Inkokagaku Shinkokai, Japan Academic Societies Centre, 2-4-16 Yayoi, Bunkyo-ku, Tokyo 113, Japan. Ed. Dr. Ichiro Kirikae. adv.; charts; illus. **Indexed:** Biol.Abstr., Dent.Ind., Excerp.Med., Ind.Med.

616.21   UK   ISSN 0260-0102
CODEN: BIRODT
BUTTERWORTHS INTERNATIONAL MEDICAL REVIEWS: OTOLARYNGOLOGY. 1983. a. price varies. Butterworth & Co. (Publishers) Ltd. (Subsidiary of: Reed International PLC), 88 Kingsway, London WC2B 6AB, England. TEL 71-405-6900. FAX 71-405-1332. (US addr.: Butterworth Legal Publishers, 90 Stiles Rd., Salem NH 03079. TEL 800-548-4001) (also avail. in microform from UMI; back issues avail.) **Indexed:** Biol.Abstr.

616.21   FR
CAHIERS D'O R L ET DE CHIRURGIE CERVICO-FACIALE. 1966. 10/yr. 370 F. (foreign 400 F.)(effective 1991). Editions la Simarre, Z.I. No. 2 - rue Joseph-Cugnot, 37300 Joue-les-Tours, France. TEL 47-53-53-66. FAX 47-67-45-05.
Formerly: Cahiers d'Oto-Rhinolaryngologie.
Description: Focuses of cervico-facial pathology and anatomy, laryngology, and otology.

CAPTION. see COMMUNICATIONS — Television And Cable

616.21   CS   ISSN 0009-0603
CODEN: CEOTA9
CESKOSLOVENSKA OTOLARYNGOLOGIE. (Text in Czech or Slovak; summaries in English and Russian) 1952. 6/yr. $48.60. (Ceskoslovenska Otolaryngologicka Spolecnost) Avicenum, Czechoslovak Medical Press, Malostranske nam. 28, 118 02 Prague 1, Czechoslovakia. (Dist. by: Artia, Ve Smeckach 30, 111 27 Prague 1, Czechoslovakia) (Co-sponsor: Ceskoslovenska Lekarska Spolecnost J. Ev. Purkyne) Ed. Josef Kiml. bk.rev.; abstr.; index. **Indexed:** C.I.S. Abstr., Dent.Ind., Excerp.Med., Ind.Med.
—BLDSC shelfmark: 3122.460000.

616.21   UK   ISSN 0307-7772
CODEN: COTSD2
CLINICAL OTOLARYNGOLOGY AND ALLIED SCIENCES. 1976. bi-m. £155 (foreign £170). Blackwell Scientific Publications Ltd., Osney Mead, Oxford OX2 0EL, England. TEL 0865-240201. FAX 0865-721205. TELEX 83355-MEDBOK-G. Ed. J. Hibbert. adv.; bk.rev.; charts; illus.; index; circ. 920. (back issues avail; reprint service avail. from ISI) **Indexed:** ASCA, Biol.Abstr., Curr.Adv.Ecol.Sci., Curr.Cont., Excerp.Med., Ind.Med., Sci.Cit.Ind.
—BLDSC shelfmark: 3286.324000.

616.21   SP
CLINICAS OTORRINOLARINGOLOGICAS DE NORTEAMERICA. Spanish translation of: Otolaryngologic Clinics of North America. 1986. 6/yr. 19716 ptas.($120) (effective 1990). Interamericana de Espana, S.A., Division de Ciencias de la Salud de McGraw-Hill, Calle Manuel Ferrero, 13, 28036 Madrid, Spain. TEL 315-0340. FAX 733-6627.

CORRIERE DEI LARINGECTOMIZZATI. see SOCIAL SERVICES AND WELFARE

617.89   US   ISSN 0196-0202
RF286   CODEN: EAHEDS
EAR AND HEARING. 1975. bi-m. $44 to individuals; institutions $77. (American Auditory Society) Williams & Wilkins, 428 E. Preston St., Baltimore, MD 21202. TEL 301-528-4000. FAX 301-528-4312. Ed. Robert W. Keith. adv.; illus.; index; circ. 4,400. (also avail. in microform; back issues avail.) **Indexed:** Chic.Per.Ind., Excerp.Med., Ind.Med., Ind.Sci.Rev., Noise Pollut.Publ.Abstr., Sci.Cit.Ind.
—BLDSC shelfmark: 3642.866000.
Former titles: American Auditory Society. Journal (ISSN 0164-5080); American Audiology Society. Journal (ISSN 0360-9294)
Description: Covers assessment, diagnosis and management of auditory disorders.
Refereed Serial

616.21   US   ISSN 0145-5613
EAR, NOSE AND THROAT JOURNAL. 1922. m. $50 to individuals (foreign $80); institutions $70 (foreign $110); residents $38 (foreign $53). International Publishing Group, 4959 Commerce Pkwy., Cleveland, OH 44128. TEL 800-342-6237. FAX 216-464-1835. Eds. Drs. Serge Martinez, Ian M. Windmill. adv.; bk.rev.; charts; illus.; index; circ. 11,000. (also avail. in microfilm from UMI; reprint service avail.) **Indexed:** Biol.Abstr., Chem.Abstr., Dent.Ind., Excerp.Med., Ind.Med.
—BLDSC shelfmark: 3642.867000.
Formerly: Eye, Ear, Nose and Throat Monthly (ISSN 0014-5491)
Description: Presents original articles and case studies for all otorhinolaryngologists in private and hospital practice, including residents and full-time staff.
Refereed Serial

617.8   SZ   ISSN 0015-5705
RC423   CODEN: FOPHAD
FOLIA PHONIATRICA; international journal of phoniatrics, speech therapy and communication pathology. (Text in English, French, German; summaries in English) 1947. bi-m. 280 Fr.($187) (International Association of Logopedics and Phoniatrics) S. Karger AG, Allschwilerstr. 10, P.O. Box, CH-4009 Basel, Switzerland. TEL 061-3061111. FAX 061-3061234. TELEX CH 962652. Ed.Bd. adv.; bk.rev.; bibl.; charts; illus.; index; circ. 1,600. (also avail. in microform from RPI) **Indexed:** Bibl.Dev.Med.& Child Neur., Biol.Abstr., Chem.Abstr., Curr.Cont., Dent.Ind., Excerp.Med., Ind.Med., Lang.& Lang.Behav.Abstr., M.L.A., Mid.East: Abstr.& Ind., Psychol.Abstr., SSCI.
—BLDSC shelfmark: 3973.550000.
Description: Covers speech disorders.

616.21   HU   ISSN 0016-237X
CODEN: FOGGAX
FUL-, ORR-, GEGEGYOGYASZAT. (Text in Hungarian; summaries in English, German and Russian) 1955. q. $36. Ifjusagi Lap-es Konyvkiado Vallalat, Revay u. 16, 1374 Budapest 6, Hungary. (Subscr. to: Kultura, Box 149, H-1389 Budapest, Hungary) Ed. Dr. Tamas Szekely. illus. **Indexed:** Excerp.Med., Ind.Med., INIS Atomind.

616.21   GW   ISSN 0017-6192
CODEN: HBZHAS
H N O (BERLIN). (Hals-, Nasen-, Ohren-Heilkunde) (Text in German; summaries in English and German) 1947. 12/yr. DM.312($167) (Deutsche Gesellschaft fuer Hals-Nasen-Ohrenheilkunde, Kopf- und Hals-chirurgie) Springer-Verlag, Heidelberger Platz 3, D-1000 Berlin 33, Germany. TEL 030-8207-1. (Also Heidelberg, Tokyo, Vienna, and New York) Ed. E. Lehnhardt. adv.; bk.rev.; bibl.; charts; illus.; index. (also avail. in microform from UMI; reprint service avail. from ISI) **Indexed:** Biol.Abstr., Curr.Adv.Ecol.Sci., Curr.Cont., Excerp.Med., Ind.Med., INIS Atomind.
—BLDSC shelfmark: 4319.500000.
Formerly: H N O: Wegweiser fuer Die Fachaerztliche Praxis.

616.21   GW   ISSN 0341-9746
H N O (COLOGNE); Mitteilungsblatt. 1950. bi-m. DM.21. (Deutsche Berufsverband der Hals-, Nasen-, Ohrenaerzte e.V.) Deutscher Aerzte-Verlag GmbH, Dieselstr. 2, PF 40 02 65, 5000 Cologne 40, Germany. TEL 02234-7011-0. FAX 02234-7011444. adv.; circ. 3,300. **Indexed:** Dent.Ind., Excerp.Med.

616.21   GW
H N O - NACHRICHTEN. 1971. bi-m. DM.30. Verlag A. Fruehmorgen, Schwindstr. 5, 8000 Munich 40, Germany. TEL 089-526083. circ. 3,200.

616.21   GW   ISSN 0323-5033
H N O - PRAXIS. (Hals, Nasen, Ohren); mit Folia-broncho oesphagologica. (Text in English and German) 1976. q. DM.130. Georg Thieme Verlag, Ruedigerstr. 14, Postfach 104853, 7000 Stuttgart 10, Germany. TEL 0711-8931-0. FAX 0711-8931298. **Indexed:** Biol.Abstr., Excerp.Med.

616.21   NE   ISSN 0378-5955
CODEN: HERED3
HEARING RESEARCH. (Text in English) 1978. 16/yr.(in 8 vols.; 2 nos./vol.). fl.2696 (effective 1992). Elsevier Science Publishers B.V., P.O. Box 211, 1000 AE Amsterdam, Netherlands. TEL 020-5803911. FAX 020-5803598. TELEX 18582 ESPA NL. (Subscr. in U.S. and Canada to: Elsevier Science Publishing Co., Inc., Box 882, Madison Sq. Sta., New York, NY 10159. TEL 212-989-5800) Ed. A.R. Moeller. adv.; bk.rev. (also avail. in microform from RPI; back issues avail.; reprint service avail.) **Indexed:** Biol.Abstr., Chem.Abstr., Curr.Adv.Ecol.Sci., Curr.Cont., Dent.Ind., Excerp.Med., Ind.Med., Ind.Sci.Rev., Noise Pollut.Publ.Abstr., Sci.Abstr., Sci.Cit.Ind.
—BLDSC shelfmark: 4275.286700.
Description: Publishes papers concerned with basic auditory mechanisms.
Refereed Serial

617.89   UK   ISSN 0262-6853
I A P A BULLETIN. 1981. irreg. $5 per issue. International Association of Physicians in Audiology, c/o D. Stephens, Welsh Hearing Institute, University Hospital of Wales, Cardiff CF4 4XW, Wales. adv.; bk.rev.; charts; illus.; circ. 200.

I F H O H JOURNAL. (International Federation of the Hard of Hearing) see HANDICAPPED — Hearing Impaired

616.21   II   ISSN 0019-5421
RF1   CODEN: IJOLBJ
INDIAN JOURNAL OF OTOLARYNGOLOGY. (Text in English) 1948. q. Rs.80($20) Association of Otolaryngologists of India, 61 Lenin Saranee, Calcutta 13, India. Ed. S.D. Mukhopadhyay. adv.; bk.rev.; abstr.; index; circ. 1,200. **Indexed:** Biol.Abstr., Excerp.Med.
—BLDSC shelfmark: 4417.800000.

MEDICAL SCIENCES — OTORHINOLARYNGOLOGY

616.21 618.92   NE   ISSN 0165-5876
CODEN: IPOTDJ
INTERNATIONAL JOURNAL OF PEDIATRIC OTORHINOLARYNGOLOGY. 1979. 6/yr.(in 2 vols.; 3 nos./vol.). fl.782 (effective 1992). Elsevier Science Publishers B.V., P.O. Box 211, 1000 AE Amsterdam, Netherlands. TEL 020-5803911. FAX 020-5803598. TELEX 18582 ESPA NL. (Subscr. in U.S. and Canada to: Elsevier Science Publishing Co., Inc., Box 882, Madison Sq. Sta., New York, NY 10159. TEL 212-989-5800) Ed. R.J. Ruben. bk.rev. (also avail. in microform from RPI) **Indexed:** Biol.Abstr., Curr.Adv.Cancer Res., Curr.Cont., Dent.Ind., Excerp.Med., Ind.Med., Ind.Sci.Rev., Sci.Cit.Ind.
— BLDSC shelfmark: 4542.451000.
Description: Provides a medium for clinical and basic contributions in all of the areas of pediatric otorhinolaryngology.
Refereed Serial

616.21   GW   ISSN 0930-8318
JATROS H N O. 1986. 12/yr. DM.150. P M I Verlag GmbH, August-Schanz-Str. 21, 6000 Frankfurt a.M. 50, Germany. TEL 069-5480000.
FAX 069-548000-77. Ed. Peter Hoffmann. circ. 2,90C. (back issues avail.)
Description: Seminar papers with brief summaries of original articles, interviews and congress reports.

616.21   JA   ISSN 0914-3491
JIBI INKOKA, TOKEIBU GEKA/OTOLARYNGOLOGY - HEAD AND NECK SURGERY. (Text in Japanese; summaries in English) 1946. m. 28,830 Yen($222) Igaku-Shoin Ltd., 5-24-3 Hongo, Bunkyo-ku, Tokyo 113-91, Japan. TEL 03-817-5710. Ed.Bd. circ. 4,000.
●Also available online. Vendor(s): JICST.
— BLDSC shelfmark: 6313.524000.

616.21   FR
JOURNAL FRANCAIS D'OTO-RHINO-LARYNGOLOGIE - AUDIOPHONOLOGIE - CHIRURGIE MAXILLO-FACIALE.
10/yr. $156. S.P.P.I.F. (Subsidiary of: Masson), 120 bd. Saint-Germain, 75280 Paris Cedex 06, France. Ed. Dr. C. Dubreuil. **Indexed:** Biol.Abstr., Dent.Ind., Ind.Med.
Former titles (until 1990): Journal Francais d'Oto-Rhino-Laryngologie (ISSN 0398-9771); Journal Francais d'Oto-Rhino-Laryngologie et Chirurgie Maxillo-Faciale (ISSN 0021-8332)

JOURNAL OF CARDIOTHORACIC AND VASCULAR ANESTHESIA. see *MEDICAL SCIENCES — Anaesthesiology*

616.21   UK   ISSN 0022-2151
CODEN: JLOTAX
JOURNAL OF LARYNGOLOGY AND OTOLOGY. 1887. m. £90($225) individuals; institutions £80($200). Headley Bros. Ltd., Invicta Press, Ashford, Kent TN24 8HH, England. Ed. B. Booth. adv.; bibl.; illus.; index, cum.index every 10 yrs.; circ. 2,500. (also avail. in microform from UMI) **Indexed:** Biol.Abstr., Chem.Abstr., Curr.Adv.Cancer Res., Curr.Adv.Cell & Devel.Biol., Curr.Adv.Ecol.Sci., Curr.Cont., Dent.Ind., Excerp.Med., Helminthol.Abstr., Ind.Med., Ind.Sci.Rev., INIS Atomind., Lang.& Lang.Behav.Abstr., Nutr.Abstr., Rev.Plant Path., Sci.Cit.Ind.

616.21   CN   ISSN 0381-6605
CODEN: JOTODX
JOURNAL OF OTOLARYNGOLOGY. (Text in English, French) 1972. bi-m. Can.$75 (foreign $90). (Canadian Society of Otolaryngology) Keith Health Care Communications, Sunnybrook Medical Centre, 4953 Dundas St. W., Toronto, Ont. H9A 1B6, Canada. TEL 416-239-1233. Ed. Dr. Derek Birt. adv.; bk.rev.; index; circ. 1,000. (tabloid format; also avail. in microfilm from UMI; reprint service avail. from UMI) **Indexed:** Biol.Abstr., Curr.Adv.Cancer Res., Curr.Adv.Cell & Devel.Biol., Curr.Cont., Dok.Arbeitsmed., Excerp.Med, Ind.Med.
— BLDSC shelfmark: 5027.710000.
Formerly: Canadian Journal of Otolaryngology (ISSN 0045-5083)

616.21   AT
JOURNAL OF OTOLARYNGOLOGY. 1962. a. Aus.$50. Australian Society of Otolaryngology Head & Neck Surgery Ltd., 33-35 Atchison St., St. Leonards, N.S.W. 2065, Australia. TEL 02-438-5141. FAX 02-906-7103. Ed. Dr. G.D. Beaumont. adv.; bk.rev.; circ. 1,000. (also avail. in microform from UMI; reprint service avail. from UMI) **Indexed:** DSH Abstr, Excerp.Med.
Former titles: Australian Society of Otolaryngology Head and Neck Surgery. Journal; Oto-Laryngological Society of Australia. Journal (ISSN 0030-6614)

616.21   JA   ISSN 0030-6622
JOURNAL OF OTOLARYNGOLOGY OF JAPAN/NIHON JIBI INKOKA GAKKAI KAIHO. (Text in Japanese; summaries in English) 1890. m. 12000 Yen($85) Oto-Rhino-Laryngological Society of Japan - Nihon Jibi Inkoka Gakkai, c/o Chateau Takanawa, 23-14, 3-chome, Minato-ku, Tokyo 108, Japan. TEL 03-3443-3085. FAX 03-3443-3037. Ed. Dr. Toyoji Soda. adv.; circ. 9,700. **Indexed:** Excerp.Med., Ind.Med., Lang.& Lang.Behav.Abstr.
— BLDSC shelfmark: 5027.720000.

JOURNAL OF SPEECH AND HEARING RESEARCH. see *MEDICAL SCIENCES — Psychiatry And Neurology*

616.21   US   ISSN 0892-1997
QP306   CODEN: JOVOEA
JOURNAL OF VOICE. 1987. q. $84 to individuals; institutions $120. (Voice Foundation) Raven Press, 1185 Ave. of the Americas, New York, NY 10036. TEL 212-930-9500. FAX 212-869-3495. TELEX 640073. Ed. Robert T. Sataloff. adv.; charts; illus.; circ. 3,000. (back issues avail.)
— BLDSC shelfmark: 5072.512700.
Supersedes (1978-1985): Annual Symposium on Care of the Professional Voice. Transcripts.
Description: Publishes articles on the development and care of the professional voice.
Refereed Serial

616.21   KO
KOREAN OTOLARYNGOLOGICAL SOCIETY. JOURNAL.
(Text in Korean; summaries in English) 1958. q. Korean Otolaryngological Society, c/o Seoul National University Hospital, Chongno-gu, Seoul, S. Korea. Ed. Kim Hong Ki. adv.; abstr.; charts; illus.; pat.; stat.; circ. 600 (controlled).

616.21   GW   ISSN 0935-8943
CODEN: LROTEX
LARYNGO- RHINO- OTOLOGIE; Zeitschrift fuer Hals-Nasen-Ohrenheilkunde. (Text in German; summaries in English and German) 1921. m. DM.276 to non-members; members DM.234. (Deutsche Gesellschaft fuer Hals-, Nasen-, Ohrenheilkunde, Kopf- und Halschirurgie) Georg Thieme Verlag, Ruedigerstr. 14, Postfach 104853, 7000 Stuttgart 10, Germany. TEL 0711-8931-0. FAX 0711-8931298. (Co-sponsor: Oesterreichische Gesellschaft fuer Hals-Nasen-Ohrenheilkunde, Kopf- und Halschirurgie) Ed.Bd. adv.; bk.rev.; abstr.; bibl.; charts; illus.; stat.; index; circ. 2,800. (reprint service avail. from UMI) **Indexed:** Biol.Abstr., C.I.S. Abstr., Curr.Adv.Cancer Res., Curr.Adv.Cell & Devel.Biol., Curr.Cont., Dent.Ind., Excerp.Med., Ind.Med., INIS Atomind., Lang.& Lang.Behav.Abstr., Sci.Cit.Ind.
— BLDSC shelfmark: 5156.150000.
Former titles: Laryngologie, Rhinologie, Otologie und ihre Grenzgebiete Vereinigt mit Monatsschrift fuer Ohrenheilkunde (ISSN 0340-1588); Laryngologie, Rhinologie, Otologie und ihre Grenzgebiete (ISSN 0302-9379); Zeitschrift fuer Laryngologie, Rhinologie, Otologie und ihre Grenzgebiete (ISSN 0044-3018); Incorporates (in 1974): Monatsschrift fuer Ohrenheilkunde und Laryngo-Rhinologie (ISSN 0026-9328)

616.21   US   ISSN 0023-852X
CODEN: LARYA8
LARYNGOSCOPE. 1896. m. $100 to individuals (foreign $120); institutions $125 (foreign $150). (American Laryngological, Rhinological and Otological Society) Triological Foundation, Inc., 10 S. Broadway, Ste. 1401, St. Louis, MO 63102-1714. TEL 314-621-6550. FAX 314-621-6688. Ed. Gershon J. Spector. adv.; bk.rev.; bibl.; illus.; index; circ. 8,288. (also avail. in microform from UMI; reprint service avail. from UMI) **Indexed:** Biol.Abstr., Chem.Abstr., Curr.Adv.Ecol.Sci., Curr.Cont., Dairy Sci.Abstr., Dent.Ind., Dok.Arbeitsmed., Excerp.Med., Ind.Med., Ind.Sci.Rev., INIS Atomind., Noise Pollut.Publ.Abstr., Rev.Plant Path., Risk Abstr.
— BLDSC shelfmark: 5156.200000.
Description: Journal comprising medical, clinical and research contributions in otolaryngology, broncho-esophagology, communicative disorders, maxillofacial surgery, head and neck surgery, facial plastic and reconstructive surgery, speech and hearing defects.
Refereed Serial

616.21   BL
MEDISOM: OTORHINOLARYNGOLOGY. 1980. bi-m. $90. Grupo Editoria Q B D Ltda, Rua Caravelas 326, Caixa Postal 30329, 01051 Sao Paulo, Brazil. FAX 55-11-572-5957. Ed. Dr. Philip Querido. adv. (audio cassette)

616.21 371.9   US
MINNESOTA SPEECH - LANGUAGE - HEARING ASSOCIATION. NEWSLETTER. 1955. s-a. $25. Minnesota Speech - Language - Hearing Association, Box 26115, St. Louis Park, MN 55426. TEL 612-935-5057. Ed. Maxine Slobof. adv.; circ. 650.
Former titles: Minnesota Speech and Hearing Association. Newsletter; (until 1976): Minnesota Speech and Hearing Association Journal.

617.89   US   ISSN 0736-0312
RC423.A1
N S S L H A JOURNAL. 1973. a. $8 (free to members). National Student Speech Language Hearing Association, 10801 Rockville Pike, Rockville, MD 20852. TEL 301-967-5700. FAX 301-571-0457.
Description: Features articles and reports on a variety of current speech-language-hearing topics of special interest to students and practicing clinicians.

610   NZ   ISSN 0110-571X
NEW ZEALAND SPEECH-LANGUAGE THERAPISTS JOURNAL. 1946. a. NZ.$7. New Zealand Speech-Language Therapists Association, Christchurch East School, Gloucester St., Christchurch 1, New Zealand. Ed. D. Murray Gordon. adv.; bk.rev.; circ. 320. (also avail. in microfilm from UMI; reprint service avail. from UMI) **Indexed:** DSH Abstr, Rehabil.Lit.
— BLDSC shelfmark: 6097.499000.
Formerly (until May 1983): New Zealand Speech Therapists Journal (ISSN 0028-8713)
Description: Covers speech pathology.

616.21 016   IT   ISSN 0392-3711
NOTIZARIO BIBLIOGRAFICO DI AUDIOLOGIA. 1967. s-a. free. Centro Ricerche e Studi Amplifon, Via Ripamonti, 129, 20141 Milan, Italy. TEL 53591. Ed. F. Grandori. adv.; bk.rev.; circ. 2,000. (back issues avail)

616.21   IT
NUOVA, CLINICA OTORINOLARINGOIATRICA. (Text in Italian; summaries in English, French and German) bi-m. L.40000. Universita degli Studi di Catania, Universita Ospedale Garibaldi, Otorinolaringoiatrica, Catania, Italy. FAX 095-316207. circ. 350. **Indexed:** Biol.Abstr., Dent.Ind., Excerp.Med., Ind.Med.
Formerly: Clinica Otorinolaringoiatrica (ISSN 0009-904X)

616.2   SZ   ISSN 0301-1569
CODEN: ORLJAH
O R L; journal for oto-rhino-laryngology and its related specialties. (Text in English) 1938. bi-m. 519 Fr.($348) S. Karger AG, Allschwilerstr. 10, P.O. Box, CH-4009 Basel, Switzerland.
TEL 061-3061111. FAX 061-3061234. TELEX CH 962652. Ed. W. Arnold. bk.rev.; circ. 850. (also avail. in microform) **Indexed:** Biol.Abstr., Chem.Abstr., Curr.Cont., Dent.Ind., Excerp.Med., Ind.Med., Noise Pollut.Publ.Abstr.
— BLDSC shelfmark: 6291.378000.
Formerly: Practica Oto-Rhino-Laryngologica (ISSN 0032-6305)

MEDICAL SCIENCES — OTORHINOLARYNGOLOGY

616.21 SP ISSN 0210-7309
O.R.L. DIPS; revista internacional de otorrinolaringologia. (Text in Spanish; summaries in English, Spanish) bi-m. 3750 ptas.($75) Editorial Rocas, Calaf. 29, 2-3, 08021 Barcelona, Spain. TEL 3-200-13-89. FAX 202-19-58. Dir. Dr. P. Quesada Marin. adv.; bibl.; charts; illus.; stat.; index; circ. 2,800. **Indexed:** Ind.Med.Esp.
Description: Original research articles in the science of otorhinolaryngology.

616.21 610.73 US
O R L - HEAD AND NECK NURSING. 1982. q. (Society of Otorhinolaryngology and Head - Neck Nurses) Health Information Publications, Inc., 92 S. Highland Ave., Ossining, NY 10562. TEL 914-762-6498. FAX 914-762-0239. adv.: B&W page $750; trim 8 1/4 x 11. circ. 970.
Description: Covers the practice of ORL nursing, pertinent research projects and legal issues.
Refereed Serial

O S L A NEWSLETTER. (Ontario Association of Speech - Language Pathologists and Audiologists) see HANDICAPPED — Hearing Impaired

617.8 JA ISSN 0030-2813
ONSEI GENGO IGAKU/JAPAN JOURNAL OF LOGOPEDICS AND PHONIATRICS. (Text in Japanese; titles and summaries in English) 1960. 4/yr. membership. Nihon Onsei Gengo Igakkai - Japan Society of Logopedics and Phoniatrics, c/o Research Institute of Logopedics and Phoniatrics, Faculty of Medicine, University of Tokyo, 7-3-1 Hongo, Bunkyo-ku, Tokyo 113, Japan. FAX 03-813-2739. Ed. Yoshisato Tanaka. adv.; bk.rev.; circ. 1,507 (controlled). **Indexed:** Excerp.Med.
—BLDSC shelfmark: 4648.329000.

616.21 US
OPERATIVE TECHNIQUES IN OTOLARYNGOLOGY. q. W.B. Saunders, Curtis Center, Independence Square West, Philadelphia, PA 19106-3399. TEL 215-238-7800. Ed. Michael Friedman. circ. 1,680.

OPHTHALMOLOGY. see MEDICAL SCIENCES — Ophthalmology And Optometry

ORBIT; an international journal on orbital disorders, oculoplastic and lacrimal surgery. see MEDICAL SCIENCES — Ophthalmology And Optometry

616.21 610 BE ISSN 0773-4409
OTICA; cahier des gradues en audiologie. (Text in French; summaries in English) 1977. 2/yr. 600 Fr.($40) Groupe Otica, Ave. Edouard Benes 195-15, B-1080 Brussels, Belgium. TEL 425.57.45. (Subscr. to: Otica, Woluweveld 59, B-1940 Sint-Stevens-Woluwe, Belgium) Ed. Gaston Warton Madeira. adv.; bk.rev.; abstr.; bibl.; circ. 200. (back issues avail.)

616.21 US
OTO REVIEW. 1966. 3/yr. $5. House Ear Institute, 2100 W. Third St., 5th Fl., Los Angeles, CA 90057. TEL 213-483-4431. Ed. Susan Hubler. circ. 22,000.

616.21 RM ISSN 0030-6649
OTO-RINO LARINGOLOGIE. (Text in Rumanian; summaries in English, French, German and Russian) 1956. 4/yr. $20. Uniunea Societatilor de Stiinte Medicale din Republica Socialista Rumania, Str. Progresului, No. 8, Bucharest, Rumania. Ed.Bd. adv.; bk.rev.; bibl.; charts; illus. **Indexed:** Biol.Abstr., Chem.Abstr., Excerp.Med., Ind.Med.

616.21 PL ISSN 0030-6657
CODEN: OTPOAW
OTOLARYNGOLOGIA POLSKA. (Text in Polish; summaries in English and Russian) vol.24, 1970. bi-m. $87. (Polskie Towarzystwo Otolaryngologiczne) Panstwowy Zaklad Wydawnictw Lekarskich, Ul. Dluga 38-40, Warsaw, Poland. TEL 31-42-81. (Dist. by: Ars Polona-Ruch, Krakowskie Przedmiescie 7, Warsaw, Poland) Ed. Zygmunt Szmeja. adv.; bk.rev.; index. **Indexed:** Biol.Abstr., Chem.Abstr., Dent.Ind., Excerp.Med., Ind.Med.
Description: Focuses on diseases of the ear, larynx and throat.

616.21 US ISSN 0030-6665
RF1 CODEN: OCNAB
OTOLARYNGOLOGIC CLINICS OF NORTH AMERICA. 1968. 4/yr. $99. W.B. Saunders Co., Curtis Center, Independence Square W., Philadelphia, PA 19106. TEL 215-238-7800. Ed. Susan Short. (also avail. in microform from MIM,UMI; reprint service avail. from UMI,ISI) **Indexed:** Biol.Abstr., Curr.Adv.Cancer Res., Curr.Adv.Ecol.Sci., Curr.Cont., Dent.Ind., Excerp.Med., Ind.Med.
—BLDSC shelfmark: 6313.510000.

616.21 US ISSN 0194-5998
CODEN: OHNSDL
OTOLARYNGOLOGY - HEAD AND NECK SURGERY. 1896. m. $93 to individuals (foreign $117); institutions $158 (foreign $182); students $48 (foreign $72). (American Academy of Otolaryngology, Head and Neck Surgery Foundation) Mosby - Year Book, Inc., 11830 Westline Industrial Dr., St. Louis, MO 63146. TEL 800-325-4117. FAX 314-432-1380. TELEX 44-2402. Ed. Dr. J. Gail Neely. adv.; bk.rev.; s-a index; circ. 9,268. (also avail. in microfilm from UMI; reprints avail. from UMI) **Indexed:** ASCA, Biol.Abstr., Chem.Abstr., Curr.Adv.Cell & Devel.Biol., Curr.Cont., Excerp.Med., Ind.Med., Rev.Plant Path., Sci.Cit.Ind.
—BLDSC shelfmark: 6313.523000.
Former titles: Otolaryngology; Journal of Otolaryngology and Head and Neck Surgery (ISSN 0161-6439); (until Vol.86, 1978): American Academy of Ophthalmology and Otolaryngology. Transactions-Otolaryngology; Which supersedes in part: American Academy of Ophthalmology and Otolaryngology. Transactions.
Description: Scientific articles to meet the clinical and continuing educational needs of all specialists in head and neck surgery.
Refereed Serial

616.21 JA
OTOLOGIA FUKUOKA - JIBI TO RINSHO. (Text in Japanese; summaries in English, German) 1955. bi-m. 6000 Yen. Otologia Fukuoka Co., Department of Otorhinolaryngology, Kyushu University, Fukuoka 812, Japan. TEL 092-641-1151. FAX 092-651-0975. Ed. Dr. Takuya Uemura. adv.; bk.rev.; circ. 1,500. (back issues avail.) **Indexed:** Excerp.Med., INIS Atomind., Lang.& Lang.Behav.Abstr.
Formerly: Jibi to Rinsho (ISSN 0447-7227)

616.21 618.92 IT ISSN 1120-3455
OTORINOLARINGOLOGIA PEDIATRICA. (Text in Italian; summaries in English) 1989. q. L.50000($50) (Societa Italiana di Otorinolaringologia Pediatrica) C I C Edizioni Internazionale s.r.l., Via L. Spallanzani, 11, 00161 Rome, Italy. TEL 06-8412673. FAX 06-8443365. TELEX 622099 CIC I. Dir. G. Motta.
—BLDSC shelfmark: 6313.650000.

616.21 IT
OTORINOLARINGOLOGICA. (Text in Italian; summaries in English and Italian) 1951. bi-m. L.65000($80) Edizioni Minerva Medica, Corso Bramante 83-85, 10126 Turin, Italy. TEL 011 6782-82603. Eds. G. Rossi, M. Arslan. adv.; bk.rev.; bibl.; charts; illus.; index; circ. 3,000. (also avail. in microform) **Indexed:** Biol.Abstr., Chem.Abstr., Excerp.Med., Ind.Med., INIS Atomind.
Incorporates (in 1981): Minerva Otorinolaringologica (ISSN 0026-4938); Bollettino delle Malattie dell'Orecchio, della Gola, del Naso (ISSN 0006-6567); Otorinolaringologia Italiana; Nuovo Archivio Italiano di Otologia, Rinologia e Laringologia (ISSN 0301-3693); Which was formerly: Archivio Italiano di Otologia, Rinologia e Laringologia (ISSN 0004-0258)

616.21 BU ISSN 0473-5609
OTORINOLARINGOLOGIJA. (Text in Bulgarian; summaries in English, Russian) q. 8 lv. (Ministerstvo na Narodnoto Zdrave) Izdatelstvo Meditsina i Fizkultura, 11 Pl. Slaveikov, Sofia, Bulgaria. (Distr. by: Hemus, 6 Rouski Blvd., 1000 Sofia, Bulgaria) (Co-sponsor: Nauchno Druzhestvo po Otorinolaringologia) Ed. V. Pavlov. circ. 765. **Indexed:** Abstr.Bulg.Sci.Med.Lit.
—BLDSC shelfmark: 0128.440000.

616.21 CN
P M P : PATIENT OF THE MONTH PROGRAM. (Avail. on floppy disk or latent-image print version) 1982. 8/yr. $280 to members; non-members $375. (American Academy of Otolaryngology, Head and Neck Surgery) Decker Periodicals, One James St. S., P.O. Box 620, LCD 1, Hamilton, Ont. L8N 3K7, Canada. TEL 416-522-7017. FAX 416-522-7839. Ed. Dr. William Shockley. abstr.; charts.
Description: Aims to perfect clinical decision-making skills by simulating clinical situations with a personal computer.

616.21 PK ISSN 0257-4985
PAKISTAN JOURNAL OF OTOLARYNGOLOGY. 1985. q. Rs.200($35) Pakistan Society of Otolaryngology, Anklesaria Nursing Home, Garden Road, Karachi, Pakistan. TEL 7731107. FAX 2412480. Ed. M.H.A. Beg. adv.; bk.rev.; circ. 2,000. **Indexed:** Excerp.Med.
—BLDSC shelfmark: 6341.675000.
Description: Publishes scientific research and articles.

616.21 JA ISSN 0032-6313
CODEN: JIBIAG
PRACTICA OTOLOGICA KYOTO/JIBI INKOKA RINSHO. (Text in Japanese; summaries in English) 1908. m. 10000 Yen. Kyoto University, Faculty of Medicine, Department of Otolaryngology - Kyoto Daigaku Igakubu Jibi Inkoka Kyushitsu, 54 Shogoin Kawara-cho, Sakyo-ku, Kyoto 606, Japan. TEL 095-771-2301. Ed. Iwao Houjo. adv.; abstr.; bibl.; charts; illus.; index; circ. 1,500. **Indexed:** Biol.Abstr., Excerp.Med., INIS Atomind.
—BLDSC shelfmark: 6593.810000.

616.21 CL ISSN 0716-4084
REVISTA DE OTORRINOLARINGOLOGIA Y CIRUGIA DE CABEZA Y CUELLO. (Text in Spanish; summaries in English) 1941. 3/yr. $30 (foreign $33)(typically set in Oct.). Sociedad Chilena de Otorrinolaringologia, Medicina y Cirugia de Cabeza y Cuello, Casilla 124 Torres de Tajamar, Santiago 9, Chile. Ed. Dr. Juan Viada Lozano. adv.; bk.rev.; bibl.; charts; illus.; stat.; index; circ. 400. **Indexed:** Biol.Abstr., Chem.Abstr., Excerp.Med.
Formerly: Revista de Otorrinolaringologia (ISSN 0034-8643)

616.2 VE
REVISTA OTORRINOLARINGOLOGICA. (Text in Spanish; summaries in English) 1965. q. Bs.30($9) Instituto Celis Perez, Apartado Postal 163, Valencia, Venezuela. (Subscr. to: Medicina Libros, Edif. Pax Cruce, Av. Avila y Caracas, Caracas, Venezuela) Ed. Dr. A. Celis Perez. bibl.; index; circ. 500.

616.21 610 FR ISSN 0035-1334
REVUE DE LARYNGOLOGIE - OTOLOGIE - RHINOLOGIE. (Text and summaries in English and French) 1880. 5/yr. 670 F. Revue de Laryngologie, 114 av. d'Ares, 33074 Bordeaux Cedex, France. TEL 56-24-30-15. FAX 56-98-02-15. Ed. Michel Portmann. adv.; bk.rev.; abstr.; bibl.; charts; illus.; stat.; index; circ. 2,200. **Indexed:** Biol.Abstr., Dent.Ind., Excerp.Med., Ind.Med., Lang.& Lang.Behav.Abstr.
—BLDSC shelfmark: 7926.450000.

616.21 NE ISSN 0300-0729
CODEN: RNGYA8
RHINOLOGY. (Text in English) 1963. q. fl.150. International Rhinologic Society, c/o Department of Otorhinolaryngology, University Hospital Utrecht, Postbus 85500, 3508 GA Utrecht, Netherlands. FAX 01736-93499. Ed. Dr. E.H. Huizing. adv.; bk.rev.; index; circ. 1,200. (back issues avail.) **Indexed:** Biol.Abstr., Dent.Ind., Excerp.Med., Ind.Med.
—BLDSC shelfmark: 7960.743000.
Description: Contains papers dealing with physiology, diagnostics, pathology, medical therapy and surgery of the mose and paranasal sinuses, including allergology.

616.21 617.89 IT ISSN 0392-1360
RIVISTA ITALIANA DI OTORINOLARINGOLOGIA, AUDIOLOGIA E FONIATRIA. (Text in Italian; summaries in English) q. L.50000($50) C I C Edizioni Internazionali s.r.l., Via L. Spallanzani 11, 00161 Rome, Italy. TEL 06-8412673. FAX 06-8443365. TELEX 622099 CIC. Dir. T. Marullo. **Indexed:** Excerp.Med.
—BLDSC shelfmark: 7987.470000.

616 US ISSN 0734-0451
SEMINARS IN HEARING. 1980. q. $53 to individuals; institutions $82. Thieme Medical Publishers, Inc., 381 Park Ave., So., Ste. 1501, New York, NY 10016. TEL 212-683-5088. Ed. Jerry L. Northern. adv. (also avail. in microfilm; reprint service avail. from UMI)
—BLDSC shelfmark: 8239.449800.
Supersedes in part: Seminars in Speech, Language and Hearing (ISSN 0196-108X)

617.89 US ISSN 0734-0478
RC423.A1 CODEN: SSLAEB
SEMINARS IN SPEECH AND LANGUAGE. 1980. q. Thieme Medical Publishers, Inc., 381 Park Ave., So., Ste. 1501, New York, NY 10016. TEL 212-683-5088. Ed. Richard Curlee. adv.; abstr.; bibl.; illus.; circ. 1,000. (also avail. in microfilm; reprint service avail. from UMI)
—BLDSC shelfmark: 8239.462000.
Supersedes in part: Seminars in Speech, Language and Hearing (ISSN 0196-108X)

SIGHT AND SOUND NEWS. see *HOSPITALS*

616.21 SA
SOUTH AFRICAN JOURNAL OF COMMUNICATION DISORDERS/SUID-AFRIKAANSE TYDSKRIF VIR KOMMUNIKASIEAFWYKINGS. (Text mainly in English) 1948. a. R.10. South African Speech - Language - Hearing Association, P.O. Box 31782, Braamfontein 2017, South Africa. TEL 011-716-2374. FAX 011-403-1926. Ed. G. Jager. adv.; bk.rev.; circ. 1,000. **Indexed:** Biol.Abstr., DSH Abstr., Ind.Med., Ind.S.A.Per.
Former titles: South African Speech and Hearing Association. Journal (ISSN 0081-2471); South African Logopedic Society. Journal.

SPEECH AND HEARING ASSOCIATION OF VIRGINIA. JOURNAL. see *HANDICAPPED — Hearing Impaired*

371 616 GW ISSN 0342-0477
SPRACHE - STIMME - GEHOER; Zeitschrift fuer Kommunikationsstoerungen. 1977. q. DM.67. Georg Thieme Verlag, Ruedigerstr. 14, Postfach 104853, 7000 Stuttgart 10, Germany. TEL 0711-8931-0. FAX 0711-8931298. Ed.Bd. index; circ. 3,900. (reprint service avail. from UMI) **Indexed:** Curr.Cont., Excerp.Med.
—BLDSC shelfmark: 8419.867000.

616.21 CI ISSN 0586-9145
SYMPOSIA OTORHINOLARYNGOLOGICA IUGOSLAVICA. (Text in Croatian; summaries in English) 1966. 3/yr. 4000 din.($30) (Klinicka Bolnica "Dr. M. Stojanovic" u Zagrebu, Klinika za Otorinolaringologiju i Cervikofacijalnu Kirurgiju) Zavod za Proucavanje i Zastitu Uha i Disnih Organa, Vinogradska 29, 41000 Zagreb, Croatia. Ed. Ivo Padovan. adv.; bk.rev.; circ. 600. **Indexed:** Excerp.Med., Ind.Med.
—BLDSC shelfmark: 8585.630000.

616.21 362.42 US ISSN 0897-6368
TINNITUS TODAY. 1975. q. $15 (foreign $25). American Tinnitus Association, Box 5, Portland, OR 97207. TEL 503-248-9985. FAX 503-241-5905. Ed. Gloria Reich. adv.; bk.rev.; circ. 170,000.
Formerly (until 1988): A T A Newsletter.
Description: Serves professionals and laypeople with scientific and anecdotal articles.

616.21 IT ISSN 0042-2371
VALSALVA. (Text in Italian; summaries in English) 1923. q. $90. Edizioni Luigi Pozzi s.r.l., Via Panama 68, Rome, Italy. TEL 06-8553548. FAX 06-8554105. Eds. I. de Vincentiis, T. Marullo. adv.; bk.rev.; circ. 2,200. **Indexed:** Chem.Abstr., Dent.Ind., Excerp.Med., Ind.Med.
—BLDSC shelfmark: 9141.800000.
Description: Covers all aspects of otorhinolaryngology.

616.21 RU ISSN 0042-4668
  CODEN: VORLA7
VESTNIK OTORINOLARINGOLOGII/ANNALS OF OTORHINOLARYNGOLOGY. (Text in Russian; summaries in English) 1936. bi-m. 13.50 Rub.($11.40) (Vsesoyuznoe Nauchnoe Obshchestvo Otorinolaringologov) Izdatel'stvo Meditsina, Petroverigskii pereulok 6-8, 101838 Moscow, Russia. (Co-sponsor: Ministerstvo Zdravookhraneniya S.S.S.R.) Ed. V.T. Pal'chun. bk.rev.; bibl.; index. **Indexed:** Biol.Abstr., Chem.Abstr., Dent.Ind., Dok.Arbeitsmed., Excerp.Med., Ind.Med., Int.Aerosp.Abstr.
—BLDSC shelfmark: 0033.550000.
Description: Publishes original papers of clinical, laboratory, experimental and theoretical nature dedicated to problems of etiology, pathogenesis, diagnosis of different otorhinolaryngological diseases, their relation to other infections.

616.21 US ISSN 1041-892X
RF11
YEAR BOOK OF OTOLARYNGOLOGY - HEAD AND NECK SURGERY. 1900. a. $57.95. Mosby - Year Book, Inc., Continuity Division, 200 N. LaSalle, Chicago, IL 60601. TEL 312-726-9733. Eds. Michael M. Paparella, M.D., Bryon J. Bailey, M.D. illus. (reprint service avail.) **Indexed:** Curr.Adv.Ecol.Sci.
Supersedes (in 1985): Year Book of Otolaryngology (ISSN 0146-7247); *Formerly (1958-1975):* Year Book of the Ear, Nose and Throat (ISSN 0084-4055); *Supersedes in part:* Yearbook of the Eye, Ear, Nose and Throat.

616.21 RU ISSN 0044-4650
  CODEN: ZUNBA9
ZHURNAL USHNYKH, NOSOVYKH I GORLOVYKH BOLEZNEI. 1924. bi-m. $13.20. Petroverigskii Per. 6-8, Moscow K-142, Russia. charts; illus.; index. **Indexed:** Biol.Abstr., Chem.Abstr., Ind.Med., Int.Aerosp.Abstr.
—BLDSC shelfmark: 0066.500000.

MEDICAL SCIENCES — Pediatrics

618.92 US
A A P NEWS. 1984. m. American Academy of Pediatrics, 141 Northwest Point Blvd., Elk Grove Village, IL 60009-0927. Ed. Elizabeth Oplatka. adv.: B&W page $2500, color page $3895; trim 11 x 17. circ. 44,345.
Description: Contains news reports, clinical policy statements, legislation news, and practice management tips.

618.92 US
A A P POLICY REFERENCE GUIDE. irreg., 5th ed., 1992. $59. American Academy of Pediatrics, 141 Northwest Point Blvd., Box 927, Elk Grove Village, IL 60009-0927. TEL 708-228-5005.

618.92 US ISSN 0884-1497
RJ29
A B M S DIRECTORY OF CERTIFIED PEDIATRICIANS. 1984. biennial. $39.95. American Board of Medical Specialties, One Rotary Center, Ste. 805, Evanston, IL 60201. TEL 708-491-9091. FAX 708-328-3596. Ed. Dr. J. Lee Dockery.

618.92 371.9 US
A C C H NETWORK; family centered care for children with special health care needs. 1983. q. Association for the Care of Children's Health, 7910 Woodmont Ave., Ste. 300, Bethesda, MD 20814-3015. TEL 301-654-6549. Ed. Josie Thomas. adv.; bk.rev.; circ. 1,700.
Description: Reports on innovative programs and current research of interest to parents and professionals concerned about children with special health care needs.

618.92 016 US ISSN 0002-922X
RJ1 CODEN: AJDCAI
A J D C: AMERICAN JOURNAL OF DISEASES OF CHILDREN. French edition: Journal de Pediatrie (ISSN 0750-6252) 1911. m. $58. American Medical Association, 515 N. State St., Chicago, IL 60610. TEL 312-464-0183. FAX 312-464-5834. Ed. Dr. Vincent A. Fulginiti. adv.; bk.rev.; abstr.; bibl.; charts; illus.; index; circ. 41,000. (also avail. in microform from UMI) **Indexed:** Abstr.Anthropol., Abstr.Hyg., Abstr.Inter.Med., Adol.Ment.Hlth.Abstr., Bibl.Dev.Med.& Child Neur., Biol.Abstr., Biotech.Abstr., Chem.Abstr., Curr.Adv.Ecol.Sci., Curr.Cont., Dairy Sci.Abstr., Dok.Arbeitsmed., Except.Child.Educ.Abstr., Excerp.Med., FAMLI, Helminthol.Abstr., HRIS, I.P.A., Ind.Med., Ind.Sci.Rev., INIS Atomind., NRN, Nutr.Abstr., Psychol.Abstr., Rev.Plant Path., Risk Abstr., Sci.Cit.Ind., Soyabean Abstr.
●Also available online. Vendor(s): Mead Data Central.
—BLDSC shelfmark: 0824.300000.
Formerly: A M A American Journal of Diseases of Children (ISSN 0096-8994)
Refereed Serial

ACTA DE ODONTOLOGIA PEDIATRICA. see *MEDICAL SCIENCES — Dentistry*

618.92 HU ISSN 0231-441X
  CODEN: APHUDZ
ACTA PAEDIATRICA HUNGARICA. (Text in English, French, German, Russian) 1960. q. $56. (Magyar Tudomanyos Akademia) Akademiai Kiado, Publishing House of the Hungarian Academy of Sciences, P.O. Box 24, H-1363 Budapest, Hungary. Ed. M. Miltenyi. adv.; bk.rev.; bibl.; charts; illus.; index. **Indexed:** Biol.Abstr., Chem.Abstr., Curr.Cont., Excerp.Med., Helminthol.Abstr., Ind.Med., INIS Atomind., Nutr.Abstr.
Formerly: Academia Scientiarum Hungarica. Acta Paediatrica (ISSN 0001-6527)

618.92 NO ISSN 0803-5253
  CODEN: APAEEL
ACTA PAEDIATRICA, INTERNATIONAL JOURNAL OF PAEDIATRICS. (Supplement avail. (ISSN 0803-5326)) (Text in English) 1921. 6/yr. Scandinavian University Press, P.O. Box 2959 Toeyen, N-0608 Oslo, Norway. TEL 47-2-677600. FAX 47-2-677575. Ed. Rolf Zetterstrom. adv.; bk.rev.; charts; illus.; index, cum.index: vols.1-30, 1921-19 43; circ. 2,200. **Indexed:** ASCA, Bibl.Dev.Med.& Child Neur., Biol.Abstr., C.I.S. Abstr., Chem.Abstr., Curr.Adv.Ecol.Sci., Curr.Adv.Genetics & Molec.Biol., Curr.Cont., Dairy Sci.Abstr., Dent.Ind., Dok.Arbeitsmed., Excerp.Med., Helminthol.Abstr., Ind.Med., Ind.Sci.Rev., NRN, Nutr.Abstr., Protozool.Abstr., Risk Abstr., Sci.Cit.Ind.
Former titles (until 1991): Acta Paediatrica Scandinavica (ISSN 0001-656X); Acta Paediatrica.

618.92 NO ISSN 0803-5326
ACTA PAEDIATRICA, INTERNATIONAL JOURNAL OF PAEDIATRICS, SUPPLEMENT. (Text in English) irreg. Scandinavian University Press, P.O. Box 2959 Toeyen, N-0608 Oslo, Norway. TEL 47-2-677600. FAX 47-2-677575. **Indexed:** Excerp.Med.
Formerly (until 1991): Acta Paediatrica Scandinavica, Supplement (ISSN 0300-8843)

618.92 IT ISSN 0001-6551
ACTA PAEDIATRICA LATINA. (Text and summaries in English, Italian) 1948. q. L.40000($16) (foreign L.50000)(effective 1992). (Universita degli Studi di Padova, Clinica Pediatrica) Artigianato Grafico Editoriale s.n.c., Via Casorati, 29, 42100 Reggio Emilia, Italy. FAX 0522-921276. Ed. Ernesto Sartori. adv.; bk.rev.; charts; illus.; circ. 3,000. (back issues avail.) **Indexed:** Biol.Abstr., Chem.Abstr, Excerp.Med., Nutr.Abstr.
—BLDSC shelfmark: 0642.424000.

618.92 CH ISSN 0001-6578
  CODEN: CHEKAL
ACTA PAEDIATRICA SINICA. (Text in Chinese and English) 1960. bi-m. $60. Chinese Taipei Pediatric Association, No. 11, Ching-tao West Road, 4F-4, Taipei, Taiwan 10022, Republic of China. TEL 02-331-4917. FAX 02-314-2184. Ed. Chin-Yun Lee. adv.; abstr.; stat.; index; circ. 2,200. **Indexed:** Biol.Abstr., Chem.Abstr., Excerp.Med., Ind.Med., Trop.Dis.Bull. Key Title: Zhonghua Minguo Xiao'erke Yixuehui Zazhi.
—BLDSC shelfmark: 0642.435000.

M

MEDICAL SCIENCES — PEDIATRICS

618.92 IT ISSN 0393-6392
ACTA PEDIATRICA MEDITERRANEA. (Text in English, Italian) 1960. 3/yr. L.35000($38) Carbone Editore, Via G. Daita, 29, 90139 Palermo, Italy.
TEL 091-321273. FAX 091-321782. adv.; abstr.; bibl.; illus.; stat.; index; circ. 3,000.
—BLDSC shelfmark: 0644.350000.
Formerly: Archivio Siciliano di Medicina e Chirurgia (Sezione Pediatrica).
Description: Clinical cases of pediatrics and newborns are reviewed and discussed.

618.92 US ISSN 0932-8610
RJ478
ADOLESCENT AND PEDIATRIC GYNECOLOGY. 1988. 4/yr. $135. (North American Society for Pediatric and Adolescent Gynecology) Springer-Verlag, Journals, 175 Fifth Ave., New York, NY 10010. TEL 212-460-1612. Ed. Joseph S. Sanfilippo.
—BLDSC shelfmark: 0696.584000.
Description: Presents papers, case reports, reviews of literature and trends in this medical specialty.
Refereed Serial

618.92 US ISSN 1041-3499
RJ550 CODEN: AMSRER
▼**ADOLESCENT MEDICINE (PHILADELPHIA).** 1990. 3/yr. $63 (foreign $73). Hanley & Belfus, Inc., 210 S. 13th St., Philadelphia, PA 19107.
TEL 215-546-7293. FAX 215-790-9330.
—BLDSC shelfmark: 0696.588000.
Refereed Serial

ADVANCES IN CHILD DEVELOPMENT AND BEHAVIOR. see *PSYCHOLOGY*

618.92 UK
ADVANCES IN DEVELOPMENTAL AND BEHAVIORAL PEDIATRICS. 1980. a? $88. Jessica Kingsley Publishers, 118 Pentonville Rd., London N1 9JN, England. TEL 071-883-2307. FAX 071-837-2917. (Dist. in U.S. by: Taylor & Francis, 1900 Frost Rd., Ste. 101, Bristol PA 19007-1598. TEL 215-785-5800) Eds. Mark Wolraich, Donald K. Routh. **Indexed:** Psychol.Abstr.
Formerly: Advances in Behavioral Pediatrics (ISSN 0198-7089)
Description: Directed to those concerned with behavioural aspects of pediatric medicine and the clinical applications of child and adolescent psychology.
Refereed Serial

618.92 US ISSN 0732-9598
BF719
ADVANCES IN INFANCY RESEARCH. 1981. a. $37.50 to individuals; institutions $65. Ablex Publishing Corporation, 355 Chestnut St., Norwood, NJ 07648. TEL 201-767-8450. FAX 201-767-6717. TELEX 135-393. Eds. Carolyn Rovee-Collier, Lewis P. Lipsitt. (reprint service avail. from ISI) **Indexed:** Psychol.Abstr.
—BLDSC shelfmark: 0709.120000.
Refereed Serial

ADVANCES IN PEDIATRIC INFECTIOUS DISEASES. see *MEDICAL SCIENCES — Communicable Diseases*

618.92 US ISSN 0065-3101
RJ23
ADVANCES IN PEDIATRICS. 1942. a. $59.95. Mosby - Year Book, Inc. (Chicago) (Subsidiary of: Times Mirror Company), 200 N. LaSalle St., Chicago, IL 60601-1080. TEL 312-726-9733.
FAX 312-726-6075. TELEX 206155. (Subscr. to: 11830 Westline Industrial Dr., St. Louis, MO 63146. TEL 800-325-4177) Ed. Dr. L.A. Barness. illus. (also avail. in microfilm from UMI; reprint service avail. from UMI) **Indexed:** CINAHL, Curr.Adv.Ecol.Sci., Dent.Ind., Ind.Med., INIS Atomind.
—BLDSC shelfmark: 0709.590000.
Description: Presents a collection of original, fully-referenced clinical review articles in pediatrics.

618.92 GW ISSN 0001-9518
AERZTLICHE JUGENDKUNDE. 1888. 5/yr. DM.60. Johann Ambrosius Barth Verlag, Leipzig - Heidelberg, Salomonstr. 18b, 7010 Leipzig, Germany. TEL 70131. Ed. K. Jaehrig. adv.; bk.rev.; charts; illus.; stat.; index. **Indexed:** Biol.Abstr., Dent.Ind., Excerp.Med., Ind.Med.
—BLDSC shelfmark: 1738.503000.
Supersedes: Zeitschrift fuer Schulgesundheitspflege.

AERZTLICHER RATGEBER FUER WERDENDE UND JUNGE MUETTER; die Schwangerschaft und das wichtige 1. Lebensjahr des Kindes. see *MEDICAL SCIENCES — Obstetrics And Gynecology*

618.92 IT ISSN 0002-0958
CODEN: AGPEAT
AGGIORNAMENTO PEDIATRICO; rivista mensile di pediatria. (Text in Italian; summaries in English, French and German) vol.21, 1970. m. L.34000. Viale Gorizia 24-A, 00198 Rome, Italy. Ed. Dr. V. Genoese. adv.; bk.rev.; abstr.; bibl.; index; circ. 2,500. **Indexed:** Biol.Abstr., Chem.Abstr., Curr.Adv.Ecol.Sci., Excerp.Med.
—BLDSC shelfmark: 0736.280700.

618.92 US ISSN 0002-7006
AMBULATORY PEDIATRIC ASSOCIATION NEWSLETTER. 1964. 3/yr. membership. Ambulatory Pediatric Association, Department of Pediatrics, c/o Dr. John P. Pascoe, 600 Highland Ave., Madison, WI 53792. TEL 608-263-9405. FAX 608-263-0440. adv.; bk.rev.; film rev.; circ. 1,500 (controlled). (processed)

618.92 US ISSN 0065-6909
AMERICAN ACADEMY OF PEDIATRICS. COMMITTEE ON INFECTIOUS DISEASES. REPORT (YEAR). 1938. irreg., 22nd ed., 1991. $50. American Academy of Pediatrics, 141 Northwest Point Blvd., Box 927, Elk Grove Village, IL 60009-0927. TEL 708-228-5005.
●Also available on CD-ROM.
—BLDSC shelfmark: 7405.555000.

AMERICAN JOURNAL OF ASTHMA & ALLERGY FOR PEDIATRICIANS. see *MEDICAL SCIENCES — Allergology And Immunology*

618.92 616.99 US ISSN 0192-8562
RJ411 CODEN: APHODH
AMERICAN JOURNAL OF PEDIATRIC HEMATOLOGY - ONCOLOGY. 1979. q. $116 to individuals; institutions $160. (American Society of Pediatric Hematology, Oncology) Raven Press, 1185 Ave. of the Americas, New York, NY 10036.
TEL 212-930-9500. FAX 212-869-3495. TELEX 640073. Ed. Dr. Carl Pochedly. adv.; bk.rev.; abstr.; bibl.; charts; illus.; stat.; tr.lit.; index; circ. 1,200. (also avail. in microform from MIM; back issues avail.) **Indexed:** Curr.Cont., Dent.Ind., Excerp.Med., Ind.Med., Ind.Sci.Rev., INIS Atomind., Sci.Cit.Ind.
—BLDSC shelfmark: 0829.800000.
Description: Reports on advances in the diagnosis and treatment of cancer and blood diseases in children.
Refereed Serial

618.92 SP ISSN 0302-4342
CODEN: AEPEDI
ANALES ESPANOLES DE PEDIATRIA. (Supplement avail.: (ISSN 0213-9146)) 1968. m. 9400 ptas.($136) to doctors; institutions and hospitals 10900 ptas.($166). Editorial Garsi, S.A., Londres, 17, 28028 Madrid, Spain. TEL 256-08-00.
FAX 361-10-07. Ed. M. Sanchez Bueno. circ. 5,000. **Indexed:** Chem.Abstr., Dent.Ind., Excerp.Med., Helminthol.Abstr., Ind.Med., Ind.Med.Esp., Nutr.Abstr.
—BLDSC shelfmark: 0889.045000.

ANNA FREUD CENTRE. BULLETIN. see *MEDICAL SCIENCES — Psychiatry And Neurology*

618.92 FR ISSN 0037-1769
ANNALES DE PEDIATRIE. (Text in French; summaries in English) 1954. 10/yr. 930 F. to individuals (foreign 1290); students 465 F. (foreign 710 F.). (Semaine des Hopitaux) Expansion Scientifique, 15 rue Saint-Benoit, 75278 Paris Cedex 06, France. Ed. Prof. Mozziconacci. circ. 17,500. **Indexed:** Bibl.Dev.Med.& Child Neur., Biol.Abstr., Chem.Abstr., Curr.Adv.Genetics & Molec.Biol., Curr.Cont., Dent.Ind., Excerp.Med., Helminthol.Abstr., Ind.Med., INIS Atomind., Nutr.Abstr., Protozool.Abstr., Rev.Med.& Vet.Mycol.
—BLDSC shelfmark: 0991.400000.

618.92 JA ISSN 0003-4495
CODEN: SHKIAH
ANNALES PAEDIATRICI JAPONICI/SHONIKA KIYO. (Text in Japanese and European languages) 1955. q. 5000 Yen or exchange basis. Kyoto University, Faculty of Medicine, Department of Pediatrics - Kyoto Daigaku Igakubu Shonika Kyushitsu, 54 Shogoin Kawara-cho, Sakyo-ku, Kyoto 606, Japan. Ed. Haruki Mikawa. adv.; bk.rev.; charts; circ. 1,000. **Indexed:** Excerp.Med., Nutr.Abstr.
—BLDSC shelfmark: 0990.900000.

618.92 UK ISSN 0272-4936
CODEN: ATPAD9
ANNALS OF TROPICAL PAEDIATRICS. 1981. q. $88 to individuals; institutions $220. Carfax Publishing Co., P.O. Box 25, Abingdon, Oxfordshire OX14 3UE, England. TEL 0235-555335. FAX 0235-553559. (U.S. subscr. to: Carfax Publishing Co., Box 2025, Dunnellon, FL 32630) Ed. R.G. Hendrickse. adv.; bk.rev. (back issues avail.) **Indexed:** Abstr.Hyg., Curr.Adv.Ecol.Sci., Dairy Sci.Abstr., Dent.Ind., Excerp.Med., Helminthol.Abstr., Ind.Med., NRN, Protozool.Abstr., Rev.Med.& Vet.Mycol.
—BLDSC shelfmark: 1045.100000.
Description: International forum for problems and achievements in child health and paediatrics in the tropics and sub-tropics.

618.92 FR ISSN 0066-3514
ANNUAIRE NATIONAL DES SPECIALISTES QUALIFIES EXCLUSIFS EN PEDIATRIE. 1962. a. 50 F. (Revue de Pediatrie) Societe Internationale d'Edition Medicale, 62 rue Ivan Tourgueniev, 78380 Bougival, France. Ed. Jeanine Guillin. adv.

618.92 FR ISSN 0003-9764
CODEN: AFPEAM
ARCHIVES FRANCAISES DE PEDIATRIE. (Text in French; summaries in English) 1942. 10/yr. 820 F. (foreign 995 F.). Doin Editeurs, 8 Place de l'Odeon, 75006 Paris, France. TEL 43-25-34-02. FAX 43-29-05-88. TELEX 203640. Ed. M. Odievre. adv.; bk.rev.; charts; illus.; index; circ. 3,200. **Indexed:** Bibl.Dev.Med.& Child Neur., Biol.Abstr., Chem.Abstr., Curr.Adv.Cancer Res., Curr.Adv.Ecol.Sci., Curr.Cont., Dent.Ind., Excerp.Med., Helminthol.Abstr., Ind.Med., Ind.Sci.Rev., Nutr.Abstr., Sci.Cit.Ind.
—BLDSC shelfmark: 1634.300000.

618.92 II ISSN 0044-8710
CODEN: ACHHA4
ARCHIVES OF CHILD HEALTH. 1959. bi-m. Rs.25. Archives of Child Health, 144 Ashutosh Mukherji Rd., Calcutta 25, India. Ed.Bd. adv.; bk.rev.; bibl.; charts; index. **Indexed:** Abstr.Hyg., Biol.Abstr., Excerp.Med., Trop.Dis.Bull.

618.92 UK ISSN 0003-9888
RJ1 CODEN: ADCHAK
ARCHIVES OF DISEASES IN CHILDHOOD. 1926. m. £148 (plus four Fetal and Neonatal editions). B M J Publishing Group, B.M.A. House, Tavistock Sq., London WC1H 9JR, England. Eds. Malcolm Chiswick, Bernard Valman. adv.; bk.rev.; charts; illus.; index. (also avail. in microfilm; reprint service avail. from UMI) **Indexed:** Abstr.Health Care Manage.Stud., Abstr.Hyg., Biol.Abstr., Chem.Abstr., Curr.Adv.Biochem., Curr.Adv.Ecol.Sci., Curr.Cont., Curr.Lit.Fam.Plan., Dairy Sci.Abstr., Dent.Ind., Dok.Arbeitsmed., Excerp.Med., Helminthol.Abstr., Ind.Med., Ind.Sci.Rev., NRN, Nutr.Abstr., Psychol.Abstr., Rev.Plant Path., Risk Abstr., Sci.Cit.Ind, Triticale Abstr., Trop.Dis.Bull.
●Also available online. Vendor(s): BRS, BRS/Saunders Colleague.
—BLDSC shelfmark: 1634.200000.

618.9 SP ISSN 0402-9054
ARCHIVOS DE PEDIATRIA; revista de formacion medica continuada. (Text in Spanish; summaries in English) 1950. bi-m. 3200 ptas.($30) (Universidad de Barcelona, Departamento de Pediatria) Salvat Publicaciones Cientificas, S.A., Muntaner, 262, 6o, 08021 Barcelona, Spain. TEL 2010911.
FAX 2015911. (Subscr. to: Cempro, Plaza Conde Valle Suchil 20, 28015 Madrid, Spain) Eds. Dr. M. Cruz, Dr. R. Jimenez. adv.; bk.rev.; bibl.; illus.; index; circ. 2,500. (back issues avail.) **Indexed:** Ind.Med.Esp., Nutr.Abstr.
—BLDSC shelfmark: 1655.490000.

618.92 UY ISSN 0004-0584
ARCHIVOS DE PEDIATRIA DEL URUGUAY. (Text in Spanish; summaries in English and French) 1929. q. $12. Sociedad Uruguaya de Pediatria, Av.Libert.Brig.Gral. Antonio Lavalleja 1414, Piso 13, Montevideo, Uruguay. Ed. Carlos A. Bauza. adv.; bk.rev.; abstr.; bibl.; charts; illus.; index; circ. 1,000. **Indexed:** Biol.Abstr., Excerp.Med., Ind.Med., Nutr.Abstr.
—BLDSC shelfmark: 1655.500000.

MEDICAL SCIENCES — PEDIATRICS

618.92   DR   ISSN 0004-0606
ARCHIVOS DOMINICANOS DE PEDIATRIA. (Text in Spanish; summaries in English) 1965. 3/yr. $15. Sociedad Dominicana de Investigaciones Pediatricas, Fernando Valerio 7, Bella Vista, Santo Domingo, Dominican Republic. TEL 809-532-7663. (Co-sponsors: Academia Americana de Pediatria (Capitulo Dominicano); Hospital de Ninos de Santo Domingo) Dir. Emilio Mena Castro. adv.; bk.rev.; charts; illus.; bibl.; index, cum.index every 10 yrs.; circ. 1,500. **Indexed:** Abstr.Hyg., Ind.Med., Trop.Dis.Bull.

618.92   VE   ISSN 0004-0649
ARCHIVOS VENEZOLANOS DE PUERICULTURA Y PEDIATRIA. (Summaries in English) 1939. q. Bs.30. Sociedad Venezolana de Puericultura y Pediatria, Av. Libertador-Edf. La Linca, 9 piso, Ofc. 93a, Caracas 105, Venezuelaq. Ed. Dr. Eduardo Urdoneta. adv.; bk.rev.; bibl.; charts; illus.; index; circ. 2,000. **Indexed:** Biol.Abstr., Chem.Abstr., Excerp.Med., Nutr.Abstr.
—BLDSC shelfmark: 1657.200000.

618.92   CI   ISSN 0004-1289
CODEN: AZMD8
ARHIV ZA ZASTITU MAJKE I DJETETA/ARCHIVES FOR MOTHER AND CHILD HEALTH. (Text in Croatian) 1957. q. 200 din.($20) Institut za Zastitu Majki i Djece - Institute for Mother and Child Health, Klaiceva 16, 41000 Zagreb, Croatia. TEL 440-455. FAX 041-451-308. Ed. Vladimir Kolbas. adv.; bk.rev.; circ. 850. **Indexed:** Excerp.Med.

618.92   US   ISSN 0271-1346
AUDIO-DIGEST PEDIATRICS. 1955. s-m. $168. Audio-Digest Foundation (Subsidiary of: California Medical Association), 1577 E. Chevy Chase Dr., Glendale, CA 91206. TEL 213-245-8505. FAX 818-240-7379. (audio cassette)
Refereed Serial

618.92 310.412   US
BEGINNINGS (NEW YORK);* pediatrics edition. 1989. q. $14.95. HealthTeam Interactive Communications, Inc., 274 Madison Ave., No. PH, New York, NY 10016-0701. TEL 212-689-1520. FAX 212-779-2094.

616.8 367   GW   ISSN 0067-5105
BEITRAEGE ZUR KINDERPSYCHOTHERAPIE. 1965. irreg., no.30, 1985. price varies. Ernst Reinhardt, GmbH und Co., Verlag, Kemnatenstr. 46, 8000 Munich 19, Germany. TEL 089-1783005. Ed. Gerd Biermann. index.

618.92   PL
BIBLIOTEKA PEDIATRY. 1974. irreg. Panstwowy Zaklad Wydawnictw Lekarskich, Ul. Dluga 38-40, Warsaw, Poland. TEL 31-42-81. Ed. Krystyna Bozkowa.

618.92 649   CN
▼**BOUNTY INFANT CARE GUIDE.** French edition: Guide Bounty des Soins au Nourisson. 1990. s-a. Bounty Family Publications Ltd., 746 Warden Ave., No. 2, Scarborough, Ont. M1L 4A2, Canada. TEL 416-750-1165. Ed. Gerri Cansick. adv.; circ. 395,000 (285,000 Eng.ed., 110,000 Fr.ed.).

BRAIN AND DEVELOPMENT. see *MEDICAL SCIENCES — Psychiatry And Neurology*

618.92   UK
BREAST FEEDING.* 1983. a. $2 free in U.K. B. Edsall & Co. Ltd., Greater London House, Hampstead Rd., London NW1 7QP, England. Ed. Patricia Scowen. adv.; circ. 650,000.

618.92   GW   ISSN 0373-3165
BUECHEREI DES PAEDIATERS. 1972. irreg., no.95, 1991. price varies. Ferdinand Enke Verlag, Postfach 101254, 7000 Stuttgart 10, Germany. TEL 0711-8931-0. FAX 0711-8931-419. TELEX 07252275-GTV-D. Ed.Bd. **Indexed:** Nutr.Abstr.
Formerly: Archiv fuer Kinderheilkunde. Beihefte (ISSN 0066-6378)

C O N A JOURNAL. (Canadian Orthopaedic Nurses Association) see *MEDICAL SCIENCES — Orthopedics And Traumatology*

618.92   CN   ISSN 0843-4263
CANADIAN JOURNAL OF PEDIATRICS. 1985. 6/yr. Can.$60($67) Rodar Publishing Inc., 19180 Trans Canada Hwy., Baie d'Urfe, Que. H9X 3T9, Canada. TEL 514-457-2673. FAX 514-457-2679. Ed. Sonia Osorio. adv.; charts; illus.; circ. 14,500 (controlled). (also avail. in microfilm; back issues avail.) **Indexed:** CMI.
Formerly: Contemporary Pediatrics.
Description: Covers issues in neonatology, child psychology, infant nutrition for the general practioner and the specialists.
Refereed Serial

618.92   CN   ISSN 0831-7682
CANADIAN PAEDIATRIC SOCIETY. NEWS BULLETIN. French edition (ISSN 0831-7674) 1954. bi-m. Can.$50($60) (effective 1991). Canadian Paediatric Society, 401 Smyth Rd., Ottawa, Ont. K1H 8L1, Canada. TEL 613-737-2728. FAX 613-737-2794. Ed. Dr. Sidney Kardash. adv.; bk.rev.; circ. 2,500.
Description: Promotes the advancement of knowledge of the sciences pertaining to infancy, childhood and adolescence.

CANDLELIGHTERS CHILDHOOD CANCER FOUNDATION QUARTERLY NEWSLETTER. see *MEDICAL SCIENCES — Cancer*

618.92   CS   ISSN 0069-2328
CODEN: CEPEA3
CESKOSLOVENSKA PEDIATRIE. (Text in Czech or Slovak; summaries in English and Russian) 1945. 12/yr. $83.30. (Ceskoslovenska Pediatricka Spolecnost) Avicenum, Czechoslovak Medical Press, Malostranske nam. 28, 118 02 Prague 1, Czechoslovakia. (Dist. by: Artia, Ve Smeckach 30, 111 27 Prague 1, Czechoslovakia) (Co-sponsor: Ceskoslovenska Lekarska Spolecnost J. Ev. Purkyne) Ed. Dr. K. Kubat. bk.rev.; abstr. **Indexed:** Chem.Abstr., Child Devel.Abstr., Curr.Adv.Ecol.Sci., Dairy Sci.Abstr., Dent.Ind., Excerp.Med., Ind.Med., INIS Atomind., Nutr.Abstr., Protozool.Abstr.
—BLDSC shelfmark: 3122.480000.
Formerly: Pediatricke Listy.

618.92 155.4
616.89   US   ISSN 0193-7421
CHILD BEHAVIOR AND DEVELOPMENT.* 1975. irreg. S P Medical & Scientific Books, Inc. (Subsidiary of: Spectrum Publications Inc.), c/o Fisher, 200 Park Ave.S., New York, NY 10003-1503.

618.92   UK   ISSN 0305-1862
CODEN: CCHDDH
CHILD: CARE, HEALTH AND DEVELOPMENT. 1975. bi-m. £72 (foreign £79). Blackwell Scientific Publications Ltd., Osney Mead, Oxford OX2 0EL, England. TEL 0865-240201. FAX 0865-721205. TELEX 83355-MEDBOK-G. Ed. R.B. Jones. adv.; bk.rev.; bibl.; charts; illus.; index; circ. 710. (back issues avail.; reprint service avail. from ISI) **Indexed:** Abstr.Hyg., ASCA, ASSIA, Bibl.Dev.Med.& Child Neur., Child Devel.Abstr., CINAHL, Curr.Adv.Ecol.Sci., Curr.Cont., Excerp.Med., Ind.Med., Nutr.Abstr., Psychol.Abstr., Psyscan D.P., Sp.Ed.Needs Abstr., SSCI, Yrbk.Assoc.Educ.& Rehab.Blind.
—BLDSC shelfmark: 3172.925000.

CHILD NEPHROLOGY AND UROLOGY. see *MEDICAL SCIENCES — Urology And Nephrology*

CHILD PSYCHIATRY AND HUMAN DEVELOPMENT. see *MEDICAL SCIENCES — Psychiatry And Neurology*

CHILDREN & SOCIETY. see *CHILDREN AND YOUTH — About*

618.92   US
CHILDREN'S HOSPICE INTERNATIONAL NEWSLETTER. q. $35. Children's Hospice International, 901 N. Wathington St., Ste. 700, Alexandria, VA 22314-1535. TEL 703-684-0330. FAX 703-684-0226. circ. 5,000. (back issues avail.)
Description: Pediatric hospice care issues.

618.92   US   ISSN 0899-5869
CODEN: CHQUED
CHILDREN'S HOSPITAL QUARTERLY; a journal for practicing pediatricians and those who care for the health of children. 1989. q. $125 (foreign $145). Human Sciences Press, Inc. (Subsidiary of: Plenum Publishing Corp.), 233 Spring St., New York, NY 10013. TEL 212-620-8000. FAX 212-463-0742. TELEX 23-421139. Ed. Philip Lankowsky. adv.
—BLDSC shelfmark: 3172.990210.
Description: Features the latest information available in the various pediatric subspecialties.
Refereed Serial

CHILD'S NERVOUS SYSTEM. see *MEDICAL SCIENCES — Psychiatry And Neurology*

CHILD'S PLAY. see *CHILDREN AND YOUTH — About*

618.92   SP   ISSN 0211-3465
CODEN: PEDTDW
CIENCIA PEDIATRIKA. 1981. 10/yr. 7000 ptas. (Hospital Nino Jesus) Alpe Editores, S.A., Pedro Rico, 27, 28029 Madrid, Spain. TEL 733 88 11. FAX 315-96-52. Dir. Dr. D. Juan Casado Flores. adv.; bibl.; charts; illus. **Indexed:** Chem.Abstr., Excerp.Med., Ind.Med.Esp.
—BLDSC shelfmark: 6417.694000.
Formerly: Pediatrika.

CIRUGIA PEDIATRICA. see *MEDICAL SCIENCES — Surgery*

618.92   IT   ISSN 0009-9058
CLINICA PEDIATRICA. (Text in Italian; summaries in English, French, German and Spanish) 1930. m. $12. Via Massarenti 11, Bologna, Italy. Ed. G. Salvioli. adv.; bk.rev.; abstr.; illus.; index. **Indexed:** Biol.Abstr., Chem.Abstr., Dent.Ind., Excerp.Med.
—BLDSC shelfmark: 3286.220000.

618.92   IT
CLINICA PEDIATRICA DEL NORD AMERICA. bi-m. L.150000($160) Piccin Editore, Via Altinate 107, 35100 Padua, Italy. TEL 049-655566. TELEX 432074 PICCIN I. (reprint service avail. from UMI)

616.8   US
CLINICAL INFANT REPORTS. MONOGRAPH. irreg., no.5. price varies. (National Center for Clinical Infant Programs) International Universities Press, Inc., 59 Boston Post Rd., Box 1524, Madison, CT 06443-1524. TEL 203-245-4000. **Indexed:** Psychol.Abstr.
Refereed Serial

618.92   US   ISSN 0009-9228
RJ1 CODEN: CPEDAM
CLINICAL PEDIATRICS. 1962. m. $58 to individuals (foreign $70); institutions $78 (foreign $90); students $28 (foreign $40). Cortlandt Group, Inc., 500 Executive Blvd., Ste. 302, Ossining, NY 10562. TEL 914-762-0647. FAX 914-762-8820. Ed. Dr. Ben H. Brouhard. adv.; illus.; index.; circ. 31,481. (also avail. in microform from UMI; back issues avail.) **Indexed:** Bibl.Dev.Med.& Child Neur., Biol.Abstr., Chem.Abstr., Child Devel.Abstr., Curr.Adv.Ecol.Sci., Curr.Cont., Dent.Ind., Excerp.Med., Hosp.Lit.Ind., Ind.Med., Ind.Sci.Rev., INIS Atomind., Int.Nurs.Ind., NRN, Psychol.Abstr., Sci.Cit.Ind., SSCI.
●Also available online. Vendor(s): BRS, BRS/Saunders Colleague, Mead Data Central.
—BLDSC shelfmark: 3286.325000.
Description: For practitioners in all areas of child care. Contains articles on pediatric practice, clinical research, behavioral and educational problems, community health and subspecialty or affiliated specialty applications.
Refereed Serial

618.92   US
CLINICAL PEDIATRICS SERIES. 1984. irreg., vol.7, 1990. price varies. Marcel Dekker, Inc., 270 Madison Ave., New York, NY 10016. TEL 212-696-9000. FAX 212-685-4540. TELEX 421419.
Refereed Serial

MEDICAL SCIENCES — PEDIATRICS

618.92   SP
CLINICAS DE ATENCION PRIMARIA DE NORTEAMERICA. Spanish translation of: Primary Care - Clinics in Office Practice. 1988. 4/yr. 13144 ptas.($87) (effective 1990). Interamericana de Espana, S.A., Division de Ciencias de la Salud de McGraw-Hill, Calle Manuel Ferrero, 13, 28036 Madrid, Spain. TEL 315-0340. FAX 733-6627. Ed. Jose Antonio Tapia Granados. charts; illus.; cum.index.
   Formerly: Temas Actuales en Medicina General.

618.92   SP
CLINICAS PEDIATRICAS DE NORTEAMERICA. Spanish translation of: Pediatrics Clinics of North America (US ISSN 0031-3955) 1964. 4/yr. $111. Interamericana de Espana, S.A., Division de Ciencias de la Salud de McGraw-Hill, Calle Manuel Ferrero, 13, 28036 Madrid, Spain. TEL 1-315-03-40. charts; illus.; index.

612   UK   ISSN 0069-4835
               CODEN: CDVMAG
CLINICS IN DEVELOPMENTAL MEDICINE. 1959. q. £60($110) Mac Keith Press, 5A Netherhall Gardens, London NW3 5RN, England. TEL 071-794-9859. FAX 071-431-5183. (Dist. in U.S. by: Cambridge University Press, 100 Midland Ave. Port Chester NY, 10573-9864) Ed. Martin C.O. Bax.
   —BLDSC shelfmark: 3286.550000.
   Description: Covers a wide range of circumstances affecting child development. Each thematic volume provides a comprehensive study of the theoretical and clinical aspects of a specific childhood condition or disorder.

618.92   TU   ISSN 0010-0161
               CODEN: CSHDAO
COCUK SAGLIGI VE HASTALIKLARI DERGISI. (Text in Turkish; summaries in English) 1958. q. $50. Turkish and International Children's Center - Turkiye ve Uluslararasi Cocuk Sagligi Merkezi, P.O. Box 66, Samanpazari, 06240 Ankara, Turkey. TEL 4-324-2326. FAX 4-311-2253. TELEX 42999 TCSM TR. (Co-sponsor: Turkish National Pediatric Society) Ed. Dr. Ihsan Dogramaci. bk.rev.; abstr.; bibl.; charts; illus.; index; circ. 1,500. **Indexed:** Biol.Abstr., Excerp.Med. (1992-).
   —BLDSC shelfmark: 3292.760800.
   Refereed Serial

COMBINED CUMULATIVE INDEX TO PEDIATRICS. see *MEDICAL SCIENCES — Abstracting, Bibliographies, Statistics*

COMPREHENSIVE MANUALS IN PEDIATRICS. see *MEDICAL SCIENCES — Abstracting, Bibliographies, Statistics*

CONCEPTS IN PEDIATRIC NEUROSURGERY. see *MEDICAL SCIENCES — Psychiatry And Neurology*

618.92   US   ISSN 8750-0507
CONTEMPORARY PEDIATRICS. 1984. m. plus 1 special issue. $65 (foreign $76). Medical Economics Publishing Co., Five Paragon Dr., Montvale, NJ 07645. TEL 201-358-7200. FAX 201-573-1045. (Subscr. to: Box 430, Montvale, NJ 07645) Ed. Jeffrey H. Forster. adv.; charts;illus.stat.; index; circ. 36,500. (also avail. in microform from RPI; reprint service avail. from RPI)
   —BLDSC shelfmark: 3425.197900.
   Description: Clinical articles on diagnosis and treatment of illnesses from infancy through young adulthood; trends in pediatrics and infectious diseases, dermatology, child development and behavior.
   Refereed Serial

CRITICAL ISSUES IN DEVELOPMENTAL & BEHAVIORAL PEDIATRICS. see *PSYCHOLOGY*

618.92   US   ISSN 0172-1232
CURRENT DIAGNOSTIC PEDIATRICS. 1977. irreg. price varies. Springer-Verlag, 175 Fifth Ave., New York, NY 10010. TEL 212-460-1500. (Also Berlin, Heidelberg, Tokyo and Vienna) Ed. A. Chrispin. (reprint service avail. from ISI)
   —BLDSC shelfmark: 3496.320000.

CURRENT OPINION IN PEDIATRICS. see *MEDICAL SCIENCES — Abstracting, Bibliographies, Statistics*

618.92   UK   ISSN 0957-5839
▼**CURRENT PAEDIATRICS.** 1991. q. £35($70) to individuals; institutions £89($180). Churchill Livingstone Medical Journals, Robert Stevenson House, 1-3 Baxter's Pl., Leith Walk, Edinburgh EH1 3AF, Scotland. TEL 031-556-2424. FAX 031-558-1278. (Subscr. to: Longman Group, Journals Subscr. Dept., P.O. Box 77, Fourth Ave., Harlow, Essex CM19 5AA, England; U.S. subscr. to: Churchill Livingstone, 650 Ave. of the Americas, New York, NY 10011. TEL 212-206-5000) Ed. R.G. Wilson.
   —BLDSC shelfmark: 3500.900000.
   Description: Provides concise updates on clinical practice, delivery of care, technical procedures, innovations, legal matters and basic science.

618.92   US   ISSN 0045-9380
CURRENT PROBLEMS IN PEDIATRICS. Short title: C P P. 1970. 10/yr. $65 to individuals (foreign $90); institutions $90 (foreign $115); students $39 (foreign $64) (effective Jan. 1992). Mosby - Year Book, Inc. (Subsidiary of: Times Mirror Company), 11830 Westline Industrial Dr., St. Louis, MO 63146. TEL 800-325-4177. Ed. James A. Stockman, III. illus.; cum.index; circ. 2,200. (also avail. in microform from UMI; back issues avail.; reprint service avail. from UMI) **Indexed:** Adol.Ment.Hlth.Abstr., Excerp.Med., Ind.Med.
   —BLDSC shelfmark: 3501.390000.
   Description: Provides monthly monographic clinical reviews from authorities in the field, intended for practitioners.

DEUTSCHE BEHINDERTENZEITSCHRIFT. see *MEDICAL SCIENCES*

618.92 616.8   UK   ISSN 0012-1622
RJ1   CODEN: DMCNAW
DEVELOPMENTAL MEDICINE AND CHILD NEUROLOGY. (Text in English; summaries in French, German, Spanish) 1958. m. £70($95) to individuals; institutions $120. (American Academy for Cerebral Palsy and Developmental Medicine, US) Mac Keith Press, 5A Netherhall Gardens, London NW3 5RN, England. TEL 071-794-9859. FAX 071-431-5183. (Dist. in U.S. by: Cambridge University Press, 110 Midland Ave. Port Chester, NY 10573-9864) (Co-sponsor: British Paediatric Neurology Association) Ed. Dr. Martin C.O. Bax. adv.; bk.rev.; abstr.; circ. 5,200. (also avail. in microfilm from UMI; reprint service avail. from UMI) **Indexed:** Abstr.Hyg., Behav.Med.Abstr., Bibl.Dev.Med.& Child Neur., Biol.Abstr., Cadscan, Child Devel.Abstr., Curr.Adv.Ecol.Sci., Curr.Cont., Dent.Ind., Dok.Arbeitsmed., DSH Abstr., Except.Child.Educ.Abstr., Excerp.Med., Helminthol.Abstr., Ind.Med., Ind.Sci.Rev., Lead Abstr., Ment.Retard.Abstr., NRN, Nutr.Abstr., Psychol.Abstr., Rehabil.Lit., Sci.Cit.Ind., Sp.Ed.Needs Abstr., Trop.Dis.Bull., Zincscan.
   —BLDSC shelfmark: 3579.055000.
   Description: Covers a wide range of clinical topics involving diseases or disabilities of children.

DEVELOPMENTAL PHARMACOLOGY AND THERAPEUTICS; international journal of perinatal-pediatric pharmacology and drug therapy. see *PHARMACY AND PHARMACOLOGY*

618.92 616.6   US   ISSN 0164-9507
DIALOGUES IN PEDIATRIC UROLOGY. 1977. m. $52 (foreign $54). William J. Miller Associates, Inc., 45 Villa Rd., Pearl River, NY 10965. TEL 914-735-7853. FAX 914-735-6628. Ed. Dr. Richard M. Ehrlich. index; circ. 560. (back issues avail.)
   —BLDSC shelfmark: 3579.775850.

EARLY CHILD DEVELOPMENT AND CARE. see *CHILDREN AND YOUTH — About*

EARLY HUMAN DEVELOPMENT; an international, scientifically innovative journal concerned with the continuity of foetal and postnatal life. see *MEDICAL SCIENCES — Obstetrics And Gynecology*

EARLY INTERVENTION. see *EDUCATION — Special Education And Rehabilitation*

618.92   US   ISSN 1044-3797
EMERGENCY PEDIATRICS. bi-m. $70 (foreign $100). Mary Ann Liebert, Inc., 1651 Third Ave., New York, NY 10128. TEL 212-289-2300. FAX 212-289-4697. Ed.Bd. abstr.
   Description: For physicians and nurses who deliver acute and urgent care to children's emergency rooms and other settings. Includes original articles on medical and surgical problems, questions and answers, tips, and commentary.

ENDOCRINOLOGIA IUGOSLAVICA. see *MEDICAL SCIENCES — Endocrinology*

ENFANCE; psychologie, pedagogie, neuro-psychiatrie, sociologie. see *CHILDREN AND YOUTH — About*

EPIDEMIOLOGIA CIENTIFICA: TEORIA Y PRACTICA. see *MEDICAL SCIENCES*

ERGEBNISSE DER INNEREN MEDIZIN UND KINDERHEILKUNDE. NEW SERIES/ADVANCES IN INTERNAL MEDICINE AND PEDIATRICS. see *MEDICAL SCIENCES*

618.92   GW   ISSN 0340-6199
               CODEN: EJPEDT
EUROPEAN JOURNAL OF PEDIATRICS. (Text and summaries in English and German) 1910. 12/yr. DM.1532($763) Springer-Verlag, Heidelberger Platz 3, D-1000 Berlin 33, Germany. TEL 030-8207-1. (Also Heidelberg, Tokyo, Vienna, and New York) Eds. J. Spranger, L. Corbeel. adv.; charts; illus. (also avail. in microform from UMI; back issues avail.; reprint service avail. from ISI) **Indexed:** Bibl.Dev.Med.& Child Neur., Biol.Abstr., Biotech.Abstr., Chem.Abstr., Curr.Adv.Biochem., Curr.Adv.Ecol.Sci., Curr.Adv.Genetics & Molec.Biol., Curr.Cont., Dairy Sci.Abstr., Dent.Ind., Excerp.Med., Helminthol.Abstr., Ind.Med., Ind.Sci.Rev., Ind.Vet., INIS Atomind., NRN, Nutr.Abstr., Protozool.Abstr., Risk Abstr., Sci.Cit.Ind.
   —BLDSC shelfmark: 3829.733500.
   Incorporates: Acta Paediatrica Belgica (ISSN 0001-6535) & Helvetica Paediatrica Acta (ISSN 0018-022X); Zeitschrift fuer Kinderheilkunde.
   Description: Covers the whole broad field of pediatrics in all its aspects.

FETAL MEDICINE REVIEW. see *MEDICAL SCIENCES — Obstetrics And Gynecology*

FOCAL POINT. see *MEDICAL SCIENCES — Obstetrics And Gynecology*

FRUEHFOERDERUNG INTERDISZIPLINAER; Zeitschrift fuer Praxis und Theorie der fruehen Hilfe fuer behinderte und Entwicklungsauffaellige Kinder. see *EDUCATION — Special Education And Rehabilitation*

GIORNALE INTERNAZIONALE DI DERMATOLOGIA PEDIATRICA. see *MEDICAL SCIENCES — Dermatology And Venereology*

GROWTH PROMOTING HORMONES. see *BIOLOGY — Biological Chemistry*

618.92   GT   ISSN 0017-5064
GUATEMALA PEDIATRICA.* 1960. q. Q.2.($2.) (Asociacion Pediatrica de Guatemala) Imprenta Fray Payo, Ciudad 7, Guatemala. Ed. Dr. Victor A. Argueta von Kaenel. illus.; circ. 600.

618.92   CC
GUOWAI YIXUE (ERKEXUE FENCE)/FOREIGN MEDICAL SCIENCES (PEDIATRICS). (Text in Chinese) bi-m. Zhongguo Yike Daxue - Chinese University of Medical Sciences, 6, Sanhao Jie 1 Duan, Heping-qu, Shenyang, Liaoning 393501, People's Republic of China. TEL 393501. Ed. Li Yongxu.

618.92   HU   ISSN 0017-5900
GYERMEKGYOGYASZAT. (Text in Hungarian; summaries in German and Russian) 1950. q. $38.50. Ifjusagi Lap-es Konyvkiado Vallalat, Revay u. 6, 1374 Budapest 6, Hungary. (Subscr. to: Kultura, PO Box 149, H-1389 Budapest, Hungary) Ed. Dr. Antal Brantner. adv.; index; circ. 1,750. **Indexed:** Chem.Abstr., Ind.Med.
   —BLDSC shelfmark: 4233.400000.

618.92   US
HEALTH IN DAY CARE: A MANUAL FOR HEALTH PROFESSIONALS. 1987. irreg. $35. American Academy of Pediatrics, 141 Northwest Point Blvd., Box 927, Elk Grove Village, IL 60009-0927. TEL 708-228-5005.

MEDICAL SCIENCES — PEDIATRICS

618.92   HO   ISSN 0018-4535
HONDURAS PEDIATRICIA. (Text in Spanish; summaries in English) 1963. q. free to qualified personnel. Asociacion Pediatrica Hondurena, PO Box 105-C, Tegucigalpa D.C., Honduras. Eds. Dr. Oscar Gonzalez Ardon, Dra. Argentina Alas de Chavez. adv.; abstr.; bibl.; charts; illus.; index; circ. 750.

618.92   UK   ISSN 0959-1362
HORIZONS; continuing education in primary care. 1987. m. £50. Medicom (UK) Ltd., 118 London Rd., Kingston Upon Thames, Surrey KT2 6QJ, England. TEL 01-541-5666. FAX 01-541-4746. adv. contact: George Gunn. bk.rev.; circ. 10,500.
—BLDSC shelfmark: 4326.794040.

618.92   AG   ISSN 0521-517X
HOSPITAL DE NINOS. REVISTA. 1959. 5/yr. $40. Asociacion Medica del Hospital de Ninos, Gallo 1330, 1425-Buenos Aires, Argentina. Ed. Jose A. Bodino, M.D. adv.; bk.rev.; circ. 2,000.
—BLDSC shelfmark: 7815.870000.

HOSPITAL FOR SICK CHILDREN, TORONTO. RESEARCH INSTITUTE. ANNUAL REPORT. see *MEDICAL SCIENCES*

HOSPITAL INFANTIL DE MEXICO. BOLETIN MEDICO. see *HOSPITALS*

HUMAN DEVELOPMENT. see *PSYCHOLOGY*

I C R D B CANCERGRAM: PEDIATRIC ONCOLOGY. see *MEDICAL SCIENCES — Abstracting, Bibliographies, Statistics*

618.92   II   ISSN 0019-5456
                   CODEN: IJPEA2
INDIAN JOURNAL OF PEDIATRICS. (Text in English) 1933. bi-m. Rs.300($60) to individuals; institutions Rs.600($100); students Rs.250($50). All India Institute of Medical Sciences, Department of Pediatrics, Old Operation Theatre Bldg., D II-45 Ansari Nagar, New Delhi 110 029, India. TELEX 31-730-42-AIMS-IN. Ed. Dr. I.C. Verma. adv.; bk.rev.; abstr.; charts; index; circ. 3,000. (also avail. in microfilm from UMI; reprint service avail. from UMI) **Indexed:** Biol.Abstr., Chem.Abstr., Child Devel.Abstr., Dairy Sci.Abstr., Dent.Ind., DSH Abstr., Excerp.Med., Ind.Med., Nutr.Abstr., Rural Ext.Educ.& Tr.Abstr.
—BLDSC shelfmark: 4418.000000.
Description: Features discussions on pediatric emergencies, current issues, clinical and technological techniques, and neonatology. Includes pharmacology and nutrition.

618.92   II   ISSN 0019-6061
RJ1   CODEN: INPDAR
INDIAN PEDIATRICS. (Text in English) 1964. m. Rs.250($100) Indian Academy of Pediatrics, PO Box 4509, New Delhi-110016, India. TEL (0291)22567. Ed. Dr. R.N. Srivastava. adv.; bk.rev.; charts; illus.; circ. 4,800. **Indexed:** Biol.Abstr., Chem.Abstr., Curr.Adv.Ecol.Sci., Dairy Sci.Abstr., Dent.Ind., Excerp.Med., Helminthol.Abstr., Ind.Med., Indian Sci.Abstr., Maize Abstr., Nutr.Abstr., Triticale Abstr.
—BLDSC shelfmark: 4425.280000.

INFANT BEHAVIOR AND DEVELOPMENT; an international & interdisciplinary journal. see *PSYCHOLOGY*

618.92   US   ISSN 0163-9641
RJ502.5   CODEN: IMHJDZ
INFANT MENTAL HEALTH JOURNAL. 1980. q. $48 to individuals; institutions $90. (Michigan Association for Infant Mental Health) Clinical Psychology Publishing Co., Inc., 4 Conant Sq., Brandon, VT 05733. TEL 802-247-6871. FAX 802-247-6853. Ed. Dr. Joy D. Osofsky. adv.; circ. 1,050. (back issues avail.; reprint service avail. from ISI,UMI) **Indexed:** Child Devel.Abstr., Excerp.Med., Lang.& Lang.Behav.Abstr., Psychol.Abstr., Sociol.Abstr.
—BLDSC shelfmark: 4478.274000.
Refereed Serial

618.92 616.8   US   ISSN 0886-1315
INFANT SCREENING. 1979. 4/yr. $15 (foreign $18). 3907 Galacia Dr., Austin, TX 78759. TEL 512-345-5685. Ed. Dr. Brad Therrell.

618.92   US   ISSN 1053-5586
▼**INFANT - TODDLER INTERVENTION;** the transdisciplinary journal. 1991. q. $48. Singular Publishing Group, 4284 41st St., San Diego, CA 92105. Ed. Louis M. Rossetti.
Description: Provides all members of the early intervention team with information that will enhance the clinical service they provide to infants and toddlers who are at risk or have disabilities, and to their families.

618.92 649   US   ISSN 0896-3746
RJ102   CODEN: IYCHEL
INFANTS AND YOUNG CHILDREN; an interdisciplinary journal of special care practices. 1988. q. $55. Aspen Publishers, Inc., 200 Orchard Ridge Dr., Gaithersburg, MD 20878. TEL 301-417-7500. FAX 301-417-7550. **Indexed:** Nurs.Abstr.
—BLDSC shelfmark: 4478.283000.

618.92   US   ISSN 1044-9779
INFECTIOUS DISEASES IN CHILDREN. 1988. m. $110 to individuals; institutions $120. Slack, Inc., 6900 Grove Rd., Thorofare, NJ 08086-9447. TEL 609-848-1000. FAX 609-853-5991. Ed. Philip A. Brunell. circ. 33,000. (tabloid format)

614.19   US
INFORMATION EXCHANGE; newsletter of the National Sudden Infant Death Syndrome Clearinghouse. 1983. q. National Sudden Infant Death Syndrome Clearinghouse, 8201 Greensboro Dr., Ste. 600, McLean, VA 22102. TEL 703-821-8955. FAX 703-506-0384. circ. 2,600.
Description: National forum for exchange of information and resources on SIDS, death investigation, apnea, grief of parents and the role of professionals.

618.92   US
INJURY CONTROL FOR CHILDREN AND YOUTH. 1987. irreg. $35. American Academy of Pediatrics, 141 Northwest Point Blvd., Box 927, Elk Grove Village, IL 60009-0927. TEL 708-228-5005.

618.92   FR   ISSN 1016-8699
INTERNATIONAL CHILD HEALTH: A DIGEST OF CURRENT INFORMATION. (Text in English) 1990. 4/yr. $48. International Pediatric Association, Chateau de Longchamp, Bois de Boulogne, Paris, France. TEL 33-1-45271590. FAX 33-1-45257367. (Co-sponsors: UNICEF; World Health Organization) Ed.Bd. circ. 6,500.

610   US
INTERNATIONAL GUILD FOR INFANT SURVIVAL NEWSLETTER.* (Former name of organization: International Guild for Infant Survival) 1965. bi-m. $1. International Council for Infant Survival, c/o Council of Guilds, 9178 Nadne River Circle, Fountain Valley, CA 92708. TEL 319-322-4870. Ed. Mrs. William Reuling. stat.; research synopsis.; circ. 500.

618.92   UK   ISSN 0334-0139
                   CODEN: IJAHE8
INTERNATIONAL JOURNAL OF ADOLESCENT MEDICINE AND HEALTH. 1985. q. $140. Freund Publishing House, Ltd., Suite 500, Chesham House, 150 Regent St., London W1R 5FA, England. (Alt. addr.: P.O. Box 35010, Tel Aviv, Israel. TEL 972-3-61533) Ed. E. Chigier. adv.; bk.rev.; circ. 1,000. (back issues avail.) **Indexed:** Curr.Adv.Ecol.Sci., Excerp.Med., Psychol.Abstr.
—BLDSC shelfmark: 4541.565000.

INTERNATIONAL JOURNAL OF CHILDBIRTH EDUCATION. see *MEDICAL SCIENCES — Obstetrics And Gynecology*

INTERNATIONAL JOURNAL OF PEDIATRIC OTORHINOLARYNGOLOGY. see *MEDICAL SCIENCES — Otorhinolaryngology*

618.92   FR   ISSN 0074-7300
INTERNATIONAL PEDIATRIC ASSOCIATION. PROCEEDINGS OF CONGRESS. triennial, 1989, 20th. International Pediatric Association - Association Internationale de Pediatrie, Chateau de Longchamp, Bois de Boulogne, 75016 Paris, France. TEL 33-1-45271590. FAX 33-1-45257367. TELEX 648 379.

INTERNATIONAL REVIEW OF CHILD NEUROLOGY SERIES. see *MEDICAL SCIENCES — Psychiatry And Neurology*

ISSUES IN COMPREHENSIVE PEDIATRIC NURSING. see *MEDICAL SCIENCES — Nurses And Nursing*

618.92   GW   ISSN 0177-9095
JATROS PAEDIATRIE. 1985. 12/yr. DM.150. P M I Verlag GmbH, August-Schanz-Str. 21, 6000 Frankfurt a.M. 50, Germany. TEL 069-5480000. FAX 069-548000-77. Ed. Peter Hoffmann. circ. 5,000. (back issues avail.)
Description: Seminar paper journal with summaries of pediatric articles, interviews and congress reports.

JOURNAL OF CHILD AND ADOLESCENT GROUP THERAPY. see *MEDICAL SCIENCES — Psychiatry And Neurology*

JOURNAL OF CHILD AND ADOLESCENT PSYCHOPHARMACOLOGY. see *MEDICAL SCIENCES — Psychiatry And Neurology*

JOURNAL OF CLINICAL PEDIATRIC DENTISTRY. see *MEDICAL SCIENCES — Dentistry*

618.92   JA   ISSN 0035-550X
                   CODEN: RSHIAY
JOURNAL OF CLINICAL PEDIATRICS/RINSHO SHONI IGAKU. (Text in Japanese; summaries in English) 1953. bi-m. 2000 Yen($6.60) Association for the Care of the Child - Shoni Aiiku Kyokai, c/o Hokkaido University School of Medicine, Kita-14-jo, Nishi-5-chome, Kita-ku, Sapporo 060, Japan. Ed. Naomichi Yamada. adv.; bk.rev.; abstr.; bibl.; charts; illus.; stat.; index; circ. 575. **Indexed:** Chem.Abstr., Excerp.Med.
—BLDSC shelfmark: 4958.670000.

JOURNAL OF DENTISTRY FOR CHILDREN. see *MEDICAL SCIENCES — Dentistry*

618.92   US
JOURNAL OF DEVELOPMENTAL AND BEHAVIORAL PEDIATRICS. 1980. bi-m. $83 to individuals; institutions $115. (Society for Behavioral Pediatrics) Williams & Wilkins, 428 E. Preston St., Baltimore, MD 21202. TEL 301-528-4000. FAX 301-528-4312. Ed. Stanford B. Friedman, M.D. adv.; bk.rev.; circ. 1,500. (also avail. in microfilm) **Indexed:** ASSIA, Bibl.Dev.Med.& Child Neur., Curr.Cont., Excerp.Med., HRIS, Ind.Med., Psychol.Abstr., Psycscan D.P., SSCI, Yrbk.Assoc.Educ.& Rehab.Blind.
Former titles: J D B P: Journal of Development and Behavioral Pediatrics; Journal of Development and Behavioral Pediatrics (ISSN 0196-206X)
Description: Covers learning disabilities, behavioral reactions of children, and family dynamics. For pediatricians, child psychiatrists and special educators.
Refereed Serial

618.92   NE   ISSN 0141-8955
                   CODEN: JIMDDP
JOURNAL OF INHERITED METABOLIC DISEASE. 1978. 6/yr. fl.448($254.50) (Society for the Study of Inborn Errors of Metabolism) Kluwer Academic Publishers, Postbus 17, 3300 AA Dordrecht, Netherlands. TEL 078-334911. FAX 078-334254. TELEX 29245. (Dist. by: Kluwer Academic Publishers Group, P.O. Box 322, 3300 AH Dordrecht, Netherlands; N. America dist. addr.: Box 358, Accord Station, Hingham, MA 02018-0358. TEL 617-871-6600) Ed.Bd. adv.; bk.rev.; charts; illus.; index; circ. 850. (reprint service avail. from ISI,SWZ) **Indexed:** Bibl.Dev.Med.& Child Neur., Biol.Abstr., Bull.Signal., Chem.Abstr., Curr.Adv.Ecol.Sci., Curr.Cont, Excerp.Med., Genet.Abstr., Ind.Med., Ind.Sci.Rev., Sci.Cit.Ind.
—BLDSC shelfmark: 5006.950000.

MEDICAL SCIENCES — PEDIATRICS

618.92   AT   ISSN 1034-4810
CODEN: JPCHE3
JOURNAL OF PAEDIATRICS AND CHILD HEALTH. 1965. bi-m. Aus.$139($195) (Australian College of Paediatrics) Blackwell Scientific Publications (Australia) Pty. Ltd., P.O. Box 378, Carlton, Vic. 3053, Australia. TEL 03-347-0300. FAX 03-3475001. TELEX 10716421. Ed.Bd. adv.; bk.rev.; charts; illus.; index; circ. 1,300. (also avail. in microfiche from UMI; back issues avail.; reprint service avail. from UMI) Indexed: Adol.Ment.Hlth.Abstr., Bibl.Dev.Med.& Child Neur., Biol.Abstr., Chem.Abstr., Curr.Adv.Ecol.Sci., Curr.Cont., Excerp.Med., Helminthol.Abstr., Ind.Med., Ind.Sci.Rev., NRN, Nutr.Abstr., Rev.Med.& Vet.Mycol., Sci.Cit.Ind.
—BLDSC shelfmark: 5027.778000.
Formerly: Australian Paediatric Journal (ISSN 0004-993X)
Description: Covers original contributions concerned with both the formal aspects of paediatric medicine and the broader filds of child health.
Refereed Serial

JOURNAL OF PAEDIATRICS, OBSTETRICS AND GYNAECOLOGY. see *MEDICAL SCIENCES — Obstetrics And Gynecology*

618.92   US   ISSN 8756-6206
JOURNAL OF PEDIATRIC & PERINATAL NUTRITION. 1987. s-a. $24 to individuals; institutions $32; libraries $45. Haworth Press, Inc., 10 Alice St., Binghamton, NY 13904. TEL 800-342-9678. FAX 607-722-1424. TELEX 4932599. Ed. Christine Trahms. adv.; bk.rev.; circ. 207. (also avail. in microfiche from HAW; reprint service avail. from HAW) Indexed: Excerp.Med., Human Resour.Abstr., Int.Nurs.Ind., Ref.Zh., Sage Fam.Stud.Abstr., Soc.Work Res.& Abstr.
—BLDSC shelfmark: 5030.158000.
Description: Focuses on the nutrition needs of patients in pediatrics and perinatal care; deals with both normal and therapeutic needs, and will assist the practitioner in anticipating conditions that require nutritional management.
Refereed Serial

JOURNAL OF PEDIATRIC ENDOCRINOLOGY. see *MEDICAL SCIENCES — Endocrinology*

JOURNAL OF PEDIATRIC ENDOCRINOLOGY. see *MEDICAL SCIENCES — Endocrinology*

JOURNAL OF PEDIATRIC GASTROENTEROLOGY AND NUTRITION. see *MEDICAL SCIENCES — Gastroenterology*

618.92   US
JOURNAL OF PEDIATRIC HEALTH CARE (PHILADELPHIA). q. W.B. Saunders, Curtis Center, Independence Square W., Philadelphia, PA 19106-3399. TEL 800-654-2452. Ed. Dianne Fochtman. circ. 1,783.

618.92   US   ISSN 0891-5245
CODEN: JPHCED
JOURNAL OF PEDIATRIC HEALTH CARE (ST. LOUIS). 1987. bi-m. $32 to individuals (foreign $42); institutions $62 (foreign $72); students $19 (foreign $29). (National Association of Pediatric Nurse Associates and Practitioners) Mosby - Year Book, Inc. (Subsidiary of: Times Mirror Company), 11830 Westline Industrial Dr., St. Louis, MO 63146. TEL 800-325-4117. FAX 314-432-1380. TELEX 44-2402. Ed. Bobbie Crew Nelms. adv.; abstr.; charts; illus.; index; circ. 4,723. (also avail. in microform from UMI; back issues avail.; reprint service avail. from UMI) Indexed: CINAHL, Nurs.Abstr.
—BLDSC shelfmark: 5030.180000.
Description: Provides information on examination and developmental assessments, treatment, and coordination of care for various childhood illnesses.
Refereed Serial

JOURNAL OF PEDIATRIC NURSING; nursing care of children and families. see *MEDICAL SCIENCES — Nurses And Nursing*

JOURNAL OF PEDIATRIC ORTHOPEDICS. see *MEDICAL SCIENCES — Orthopedics And Traumatology*

JOURNAL OF PEDIATRIC SURGERY. see *MEDICAL SCIENCES — Surgery*

618.92   US   ISSN 0022-3476
RJ1   CODEN: JOPDAB
JOURNAL OF PEDIATRICS; devoted to the problems and diseases of infancy and childhood. 1932. m. $80 to individuals (foreign $105); institutions $162 (foreign $187); students $38 (foreign $63). Mosby - Year Book, Inc. (Subsidiary of: Times Mirror Company), 11830 Westline Industrial Dr., St. Louis, MO 63146. TEL 800-325-4117.
FAX 314-432-1380. TELEX 44-2402. Ed. Dr. Joseph M. Garfunkel. adv.; bk.rev.; abstr.; bibl.; charts; illus.; s-a index; circ. 22,102. (also avail. in microfilm from UMI; reprint service avail. from UMI) Indexed: Abstr.Hyg., ASCA, ASSIA, Behav.Med.Abstr., Bibl.Dev.Med.& Child Neur., Biol.Abstr., Biotech.Abstr., Chem.Abstr, Child Devel.Abstr., Curr.Adv.Cancer Res., Curr.Adv.Ecol.Sci., Curr.Cont., Dairy Sci.Abstr., Dok.Arbeitsmed., Except.Child.Educ.Abstr., Excerp.Med., Food Sci.& Tech.Abstr., Helminthol.Abstr., Hosp.Lit.Ind., I.P.A., Ind.Med., Ind.Sci.Rev., INIS Atomind., Nutr.Abstr., Potato Abstr., Protozool.Abstr., Rev.Plant Path., Risk Abstr., Sci.Cit.Ind., Soyabean Abstr., Trop.Dis.Bull.
●Also available online. Vendor(s): BRS.
—BLDSC shelfmark: 5030.300000.
Description: Practical guide for physicians who diagnose and treat disorders in infants and children.
Refereed Serial

JOURNAL OF PERINATOLOGY. see *MEDICAL SCIENCES — Obstetrics And Gynecology*

618.92   UK   ISSN 0142-6338
CODEN: JTRPAO
JOURNAL OF TROPICAL PEDIATRICS. 1954. 6/yr. £72($145) Oxford University Press, Oxford Journals, Pinkhill House, Southfield Road, Eynsham, Oxford OX8 1JJ, England. TEL 0865-882283. FAX 0865-882890. TELEX 837330 OXPRES G. Eds. G. Ebrahim, D. Jelliffe. adv.; bk.rev.; charts; illus.; index. Indexed: Abstr.Hyg., Curr.Adv.Ecol.Sci., Curr.Cont., Dairy Sci.Abstr., Dent.Ind., Excerp.Med., Helminthol.Abstr., Ind.Med., Ind.Sci.Rev., Nutr.Abstr., Protozool.Abstr., Rice Abstr., Rural Devel.Abstr., Rural Ext.Educ.& Tr.Abstr., So.Pac.Per.Ind., Trop.Dis.Bull.
—BLDSC shelfmark: 5071.090000.
Formerly: Journal of Tropical Pediatrics and Environmental Child Health (ISSN 0300-9920)
Description: Covers all aspects of child health nutrition, including locality and quality of environment.

618.92   FR   ISSN 0399-029X
JOURNEES PARISIENNES DE PEDIATRIE. 1966. a. price varies. (Hopital des Enfants Malades, Centre d'Etudes sur les Maladies du Metabolisme chez l'Enfant) Flammarion Medecine-Sciences, 4 rue Casimir Delavigne, 75006 Paris, France. (U.S. subscr. addr.: S.F.P.A., c/o M. Benech, 14 E. 60th St., New York, NY 10022) Ed. P. Royer.

618.92 688.72   GW
JUNGE FAMILIE. 1969. bi-m. DM.18. Junior-Verlag GmbH & Co. KG, Fehlandstr. 41, 2000 Hamburg 36, Germany. TEL 040-344434. FAX 040-352540.

618.92   CN
KALEIDOSCOPE. (Text in English) 1984. q. Hospital for Sick Children, 555 University Ave., Toronto, Ont. M5G 1X8, Canada. TEL 416-598-6377. Ed. Claudia Anderson. circ. 10,000.

618.92   NE
KIND EN ZIEKENHUIS. 1977. q. fl.7.50 per no. (Vereniging Kind en Ziekenhuis) Landelijke Vereniging Kind en Ziekenhuis, Appelmarkt 3, 3311 BA Dordrecht, Netherlands. TEL 078-146361. Ed. Tom Graat. adv.; bk.rev.; circ. 1,700.

KINDER; das Journal des Kindergartens. see *CHILDREN AND YOUTH — About*

618.92   GW   ISSN 0023-1495
KINDERAERZTLICHE PRAXIS. (Text in German; summaries in English and German) 1930. m. DM.144. Georg Thieme Verlag, Ruedigerstr. 14, Postfach 104853, 7000 Stuttgart 10, Germany. TEL 0711-8931-0. FAX 0711-8931298. Ed.Bd. adv.; bk.rev.; abstr.; charts; illus.; index; circ. 3,000. Indexed: Biol.Abstr., Chem.Abstr., Dent.Ind., Excerp.Med., Ind.Med., INIS Atomind., Nutr.Abstr.
—BLDSC shelfmark: 5095.600000.

KINDERGESUNDHEIT. see *CHILDREN AND YOUTH — About*

KINDERKRANKENSCHWESTER. see *MEDICAL SCIENCES — Nurses And Nursing*

618.92   GW   ISSN 0300-8630
CODEN: KLPDB2
KLINISCHE PAEDIATRIE; Zeitschrift fuer Klinik und Praxis. (Text in German; summaries in English and German) 1880. bi-m. DM.312. Ferdinand Enke Verlag, Postfach 101254, 7000 Stuttgart 10, Germany. TEL 0711-8931-0. FAX 0711-8931-419. TELEX 07252275-GTV-D. Ed.Bd. adv.; bk.rev.; abstr.; charts; illus.; circ. 800. (also avail. in microfiche from BHP) Indexed: Bibl.Dev.Med.& Child Neur., Biol.Abstr., Biotech.Abstr., Chem.Abstr., Curr.Adv.Ecol.Sci., Curr.Cont., Dairy Sci.Abstr., Excerp.Med., Helminthol.Abstr., Ind.Med., Ind.Sci.Rev., INIS Atomind., Nutr.Abstr., Sci.Cit.Ind., Soyabean Abstr.
—BLDSC shelfmark: 5099.460000.
Formerly: Archiv fuer Kinderheilkunde (ISSN 0003-9179)

LYSOSOMES. see *BIOLOGY — Biological Chemistry*

618.92   SP   ISSN 0210-8135
M T A PEDIATRIA. (Metodos Terapeutico-diagnosticos de Actualidad) 1980. m. 6890 ptas.($50) J.R. Prous, S.A. International Publishers, Apdo. Postal 540, 08080 Barcelona, Spain. TEL 343-258-5250. Ed. Dr. F. Prandi. adv. (back issues avail.)

618.92   UK   ISSN 0262-0200
MATERNAL & CHILD HEALTH; the journal of family medicine. 1976. 12/yr. £40 (foreign £70). Barker Publications Ltd., Barker House, 539 London Rd., Isleworth, Middlesex TW7 4DA, England. TEL 081-847-1774. Ed. Dr. David Harvey. adv.; bk.rev.; charts; illus.; circ. 17,000 (controlled). (back issues avail.) Indexed: Curr.Adv.Ecol.Sci.
—BLDSC shelfmark: 5399.272000.
Formerly: Journal of Maternal and Child Health (ISSN 0308-4426)

618.92   FR   ISSN 0025-6773
CODEN: MINFAW
MEDECINE INFANTILE; revue de clinique, de therapeutique et d'hygiene sociale de l'enfance. 1894. 8/yr. 460 F. (Comite National de l'Enfance) Editions Maloine, 27 rue de l'Ecole-De-Medecine, 75006 Paris, France. TEL 1-43-25-60-45. TELEX 203 215 F. Ed. R. Perelman. adv.; bk.rev.; abstr.; bibl.; charts; illus.; circ. 6,000. Indexed: Biol.Abstr., Chem.Abstr., Excerp.Med., Ind.Med., Nutr.Abstr.
—BLDSC shelfmark: 5487.735000.

MEDICAL AND PEDIATRIC ONCOLOGY. see *MEDICAL SCIENCES — Cancer*

618.92   IT
MEDICO E BAMBINO. 10/yr. (Associazione Culturale Pediatri) Edifarm S.p.A., Viale Sabotino 19-2, 20135 Milan, Italy. adv.; circ. 80,000.

MIDWIFERY. see *MEDICAL SCIENCES — Nurses And Nursing*

618.92   IT   ISSN 0026-4946
CODEN: MIPEA5
MINERVA PEDIATRICA; review of pediatrics, child psychology and puericulture. (Text in Italian; summaries in English) 1949. m. L.70000($100) Edizioni Minerva Medica, Corso Bramante 83-85, 10126 Turin, Italy. Eds. R. Bulgarelli, N. Nigro. bk.rev.; abstr.; bibl.; illus.; index; circ. 5,000. Indexed: Biol.Abstr., Chem.Abstr., Curr.Adv.Ecol.Sci., Curr.Cont., Dent.Ind., Excerp.Med., Helminthol.Abstr., Ind.Med., Nutr.Abstr.
—BLDSC shelfmark: 5794.400000.
Incorporates: Policlinico Infantile; Pediatria del Medico Pratico; Medicina Italiana; Lattante; Rivista di Clinica Pediatrica (ISSN 0035-6077)

MEDICAL SCIENCES — PEDIATRICS

618.92   GW   ISSN 0026-9298
CODEN: MOKIAY
MONATSSCHRIFT KINDERHEILKUNDE. (Summaries in English and German) 1903. 12/yr. DM.328($179) (Deutsche Gesellschaft fuer Kinderheilkunde) Springer-Verlag, Heidelberger Platz 3, D-1000 Berlin 33, Germany. TEL 030-8207-1. (Also Heidelberg, Tokyo, Vienna, and New York) Eds. F. Blaeker, W. Schroeter. adv.; bk.rev.; bibl.; charts, (also avail. in microform from UMI; back issues avail.; reprint service avail. from ISI) **Indexed:** Bibl.Dev.Med.& Child Neur., Biol.Abstr., Chem.Abstr., Curr.Adv.Ecol.Sci., Curr.Cont., Dairy Sci.Abstr., Excerp.Med., Helminthol.Abstr., Ind.Med., Ind.Sci.Rev., Nutr.Abstr., Triticale Abstr.
—BLDSC shelfmark: 5906.400000.

618.92   US
MONOGRAPHS ON INFANCY. 1981. irreg. price varies. Ablex Publishing Corporation, 355 Chestnut St., Norwood, NJ 07648. TEL 201-767-8450. FAX 201-767-6717. TELEX 135-393. Ed. Lewis P. Lipsitt. **Indexed:** Psychol.Abstr.

NEONATAL INTENSIVE CARE; the journal of perinatalogy/neonatology. see *MEDICAL SCIENCES — Obstetrics And Gynecology*

NEONATAL NETWORK. see *MEDICAL SCIENCES — Nurses And Nursing*

616.8   GW   ISSN 0174-304X
CODEN: NRPDDB
NEUROPEDIATRICS; journal of pediatric neurobiology, neurology and neurosurgery. (Text in English) 1970. q. DM.236 per vol. Hippokrates Verlag GmbH, Ruedigerstr. 14, Postfach 10 22 63, D-7000 Stuttgart 30, Germany. Ed.Bd. adv.; circ. 1,200. **Indexed:** Bibl.Dev.Med.& Child Neur., Biol.Abstr., Chem.Abstr., Child Devel.Abstr., Curr.Adv.Ecol.Sci., Curr.Cont., Excerp.Med., Helminthol.Abstr., Ind.Med., Ind.Sci.Rev., Nutr.Abstr.
—BLDSC shelfmark: 6081.515500.
Formerly: Neuropaediatrie (ISSN 0028-3797)

616.8   FR   ISSN 0222-9617
NEUROPSYCHIATRIE DE L'ENFANCE ET DE L'ADOLESCENCE. 1953. 8/yr. 760 F. to individuals (foreign 1015 F.); students 380 F. (foreign 555 F.). (Societe Francaise de Psychiatrie de l'Enfant et de l'Adolescent) Expansion Scientifique, 15 rue Saint-Benoit, 75278 Paris Cedex 06, France. Eds. D. J. Duche, N. Moor. adv.; bk.rev.; bibl.; charts; illus.; circ. 5,000. (also avail. in microform) **Indexed:** Biol.Abstr., Curr.Cont., Excerp.Med., Ind.Med., Psychol.Abstr., SSCI.
—BLDSC shelfmark: 6081.536000.
Formerly: Revue de Neuropsychiatrie Infantile et d'Hygiene Mentale de l'Enfance (ISSN 0035-1628)

618.92   US
NEW YORK PEDIATRICIAN; a forum on issues affecting pediatric practice in New York State. 1983. s-a. membership. American Academy of Pediatrics, District II, Queens Hospital Center, 82-68 164th St., Jamaica, NY 11432. Ed. Dr. Philip W.H. Eskes. adv.; bk.rev.; charts; illus.; circ. 3,500. (also avail. in microform)
Formerly: Long Island Pediatrician.

618.92   NR
NIGERIAN JOURNAL OF PAEDIATRICS. 1974. q. £N16($6) (Paediatric Association of Nigeria) Ibadan University Press, University of Ibadan, Dept. of Pediatrics, Ibadan, Nigeria. (Orders to: University College Hospital, c/o Department of Paediatrics, Ibadan, Nigeria) Ed.Bd. adv.; charts; illus.; circ. 500. (back issues avail.) **Indexed:** Abstr.Hyg., Biol.Abstr., Excerp.Med., Trop.Dis.Bull.

618.92 610   JA   ISSN 0029-0386
NIHON SHINSEIJI GAKKAI ZASSHI/ACTA NEONATOLOGICA JAPONICA. (Text in Japanese; summaries in English and Japanese) 1965. q. 1000 Yen($2.80) Nihon Shinseiji Gakkai - Japan Society of Neonatology, c/o Nihon University, School of Medicine, Department of Pediatrics, 30-1 Oyaguchi-Kami-machi, Itabashi-ku, Tokyo 173, Japan. Ed. Dr. Kazuo Baba. adv.; bk.rev.; bibl.; cum.index; circ. 4,000. (controlled). **Indexed:** Excerp.Med.
—BLDSC shelfmark: 0639.757000.

618.92   US
NO CIRC NEWSLETTER. 1986. s-a. $15. National Organization of Circumcision Information Resource Centers, Box 2512, San Anselmo, CA 94979. TEL 415-488-9883. Ed. Marilyn Fayre Milos. circ. 18,000.
Description: Provides parents, health-care professionals, and other concerned individuals with the most current medical and legal facts on routine neonatal circumcision, and focuses on efforts to reduce the frequency of the practice.

OPHTHALMIC PAEDIATRICS AND GENETICS. see *MEDICAL SCIENCES — Ophthalmology And Optometry*

618.92   IT   ISSN 0030-6274
OSPEDALI ITALIANI-PEDIATRIA; e specialita chirurgiche. 1966. bi-m. plus supplements. L.50000($40) (L.40000 without supplements). Giuseppe Caracciolo, Ed. & Pub., Via Cimarosa 180-A, 80127 Naples, Italy. bk.rev.; charts; illus.; stat.; index, cum.index; circ. 1,000. **Indexed:** Biol.Abstr., Excerp.Med.
—BLDSC shelfmark: 6301.770000.
Description: Features research papers on the science of pediatrics and specialized surgery.

OTORINOLARINGOLOGIA PEDIATRICA. see *MEDICAL SCIENCES — Otorhinolaryngology*

618.92   UK   ISSN 0269-5022
PAEDIATRIC & PERINATAL EPIDEMIOLOGY. 1988. q. £94 (foreign £102.50). (Society for Paediatric Epidemiological Research) Blackwell Scientific Publications Ltd., Osney Mead, Oxford OX2 0EL, England. TEL 0865-240201. FAX 0865-721205. TELEX 833355-MEDBOK-G. Ed.Bd. adv.; bk.rev.; illus.; index. (back issues avail.)
—BLDSC shelfmark: 6333.399710.

618.92   IO   ISSN 0030-9311
CODEN: PIDOA8
PAEDIATRICA INDONESIANA. (Text and summaries in English) 1961. bi-m. $15. Indonesian Pediatric Association, c/o Department of Child Health, University of Indonesia Medical School, 6 Salemba, Jakarta, Indonesia. Ed. Dr. Sunoto. adv.; abstr.; bibl.; charts; illus.; stat.; circ. 2,000. (also avail. in microfilm from UMI; microfiche; reprint service avail. from UMI) **Indexed:** Abstr.Hyg., Biol.Abstr., Excerp.Med., Ind.Med., Nutr.Abstr., Trop.Dis.Bull.

618.92   GW   ISSN 0030-932X
PAEDIATRIE UND GRENZGEBIETE/PEDIATRICS AND RELATED TOPICS. (Text and summaries in English, German) 1962. bi-m. DM.190.20. Akademie-Verlag Berlin, Leipziger Str. 3-4, 1086 Berlin, Germany. TELEX 114420-AVERL-DD. Eds. B. Schneeweiss, H.W. Ocklitz. bk.rev.; charts; illus.; stat.; index. **Indexed:** Curr.Adv.Ecol.Sci., Excerp.Med., Ind.Med., Nutr.Abstr.
—BLDSC shelfmark: 6333.200000.

618.92   US   ISSN 0030-9338
CODEN: PAPAB5
PAEDIATRIE UND PAEDOLOGIE. (Text in English, French and German) 1965. q. DM.210($118) Springer-Verlag, Journals, 175 Fifth Ave., New York, NY 10010. TEL 212-460-1500. (Also Berlin, Heidelberg, Tokyo and Vienna) Ed. G. Weippl. bk.rev.; charts; illus.; index. (also avail. in microform from UMI; reprint service avail. from ISI) **Indexed:** Bibl.Dev.Med.& Child Neur., Biol.Abstr., Chem.Abstr., Curr.Adv.Cancer Res., Curr.Cont., Excerp.Med., Ind.Med., Nutr.Abstr.
—BLDSC shelfmark: 6333.230000.

618.92   US   ISSN 0300-9556
PAEDIATRIE UND PAEDOLOGIE. SUPPLEMENT. 1972. irreg. price varies. Springer-Verlag, 175 Fifth Ave., New York, NY 10010. TEL 212-460-1500. (Also Berlin, Heidelberg, Vienna) (reprint service avail. from ISI) **Indexed:** Ind.Med.

618.92   US
PAEDIATRIE: WEITER- UND FORTBILDUNG. (Text in German) 1980. irreg. price varies. Springer-Verlag, 175 Fifth Ave., New York, NY 10010. TEL 212-460-1500. (Also Berlin, Heidelberg, Tokyo and Vienna) Ed. H. Ewerbeck. (reprint service avail. from ISI)

618.92   GW   ISSN 0030-9346
PAEDIATRISCHE PRAXIS; Zeitschrift fuer Kinder- und Jugendmedizin. 1962. 7/yr. DM.268. Hans Marseille Verlag, Buerkleinstr. 12, 8000 Munich 22, Germany. TEL 089-227988. Ed. W. Stoegmann, G.F. Wuendisch. bk.rev.; abstr.; bibl.; charts; illus.; index, cum.index every 5 yrs.; circ. 4,500. (also avail. in microfilm from UMI; reprint service avail. from UMI) **Indexed:** Excerp.Med.
—BLDSC shelfmark: 6333.300000.
Description: Practical information of interest to specialists in pediatrics. Features current research, questions and answers, and photographs.

618.92   PK   ISSN 0048-2722
PAKISTAN PEDIATRIC JOURNAL.* (Text in English) 1971. q. Rs.10. Association of Pediatricians of Pakistan, 111-D 27-7 Nazimabad, Karachi 18, Pakistan. Dr. Abdul Jamil Khan. adv.; bk.rev.; bibl.; charts; illus.

618.92   GR
PEDI KAI NEI GONIS. 1984. m. Dr.4,500($29) International Publications S.A., 14th klm Marathon Ave., Pallini 15344, Greece. TEL 6667312. Ed. Katerina Boura. adv.; circ. 30,000. (back issues avail)

618.92   FR   ISSN 0397-9180
PEDIATRE (PARIS). 1963. bi-m. 500 F. Pediatre Parisien, s.a.r.l., B.P. 132, 75821 Paris Cedex 17, France. TEL 42-67-27-13. FAX 1-47-54-00-08. (Co-sponsors: SNPF, Groupement des Pediatres; Cercle d'Etudes Pediatriques) Ed. Dr. Feigelson. adv.; bk.rev.; circ. 2,000. (reprint service avail. from ISI) **Indexed:** Excerp.Med.
—BLDSC shelfmark: 6417.447000.

618.92   IT   ISSN 0031-3890
PEDIATRIA; rivista d'igiene, medicina e chirurgia dell'infanzia. (Text in Italian; summaries in English, French, German, Italian and Spanish) 1893. q. L.6000.($14.) Universita degli Studi di Napoli, Clinica Pediatrica, S. Andrea delle Dame 4, Naples, Italy. Ed. Prof. Giulio Murano. adv.; bk.rev.; abstr.; illus.; index. **Indexed:** Chem.Abstr., Dent.Ind., Ind.Med., Nutr.Abstr.

618.92   BU   ISSN 0479-7876
CODEN: PDTAAB
PEDIATRIA. (Text in Bulgarian; summaries in English and Russian) 1962. bi-m. 24 lv.($7) (Ministerstvo na Narodnoto Zdrave) Izdatelstvo Meditsina i Fizkultura, 11, Pl. Slaveikov, Sofia, Bulgaria. (Dist. by: Hemus, 6, Rouski Blvd., 1000 Sofia, Bulgaria) (Co-sponsor: Nauchno Druzhestvo po Pediatria) Ed. Sh. Ninjo. circ. 1,950. **Indexed:** Abstr.Bulg.Sci.Med.Lit., Dent.Ind., Excerp.Med., Ind.Med.
—BLDSC shelfmark: 0129.240000.

618.92   SP
PEDIATRIA. BOLETIN. (Text in Spanish; summaries in English and Spanish) 1960. q. 350 ptas.($7) Sociedad de Pediatria de Asturias, Cantabria, Castilla y Leon, Facultad de Medicina, C. Ramon y Cajal, 47005 Valladolid, Spain. Ed. Alfredo Blanco. adv.; bk.rev.; abstr.; charts; illus.; index; circ. 3,000.
Formerly: Sociedad Castellano-Astur-Leonosa de Pediatria. Boletin (ISSN 0037-8429)

618.92   BL   ISSN 0031-3912
PEDIATRIA E PUERICULTURA.* (Text in Portuguese; summaries in English and French) 1930. 4/yr. Liga Alvaro Bahia Contra a Mortalidade Infantil, Avenida Joana Angelica 75, Salvador, Bahia, Brazil. bibl.; charts; illus.; stat.; circ. 600.

618.92   BL   ISSN 0031-3920
PEDIATRIA MODERNA. (Text in Portuguese; summaries in English, Portuguese, and Spanish) 1966. m. Cr.$56000($250) (free to qualified personnel). Grupo Editorial Moreira Jr., Rua Henrique Martins 493, Sao Paulo, Brazil. FAX 884-9993. Ed. Friederich T. Simon. adv.; bk.rev.; abstr.; bibl.; charts; illus.; stat.; cum.index; circ. 12,000 (controlled). **Indexed:** Biol.Abstr.

M

MEDICAL SCIENCES — PEDIATRICS

618.92 617.3   IT   ISSN 0391-898X
PEDIATRIA OGGI MEDICA E CHIRURGICA. (Text in Italian; summaries in English) 10/yr. L.60000($60) (Societa Italiana de Pediatria, Gruppo di Lavoro di Pediatria Ospedaliera) C I C Edizioni Internazionali s.r.l., Via L. Spallanzani 11, 00161 Rome, Italy. TEL 06-8412673. FAX 06-8443365. TELEX 622099 CIC. Dirs. M. Calvani, R. DiToro. **Indexed:** Excerp.Med.
—BLDSC shelfmark: 6417.488000.

618.92   BL   ISSN 0031-3947
CODEN: PEPAAW
PEDIATRIA PRATICA; revista de puericultura e clinica infantil. (Text in Portuguese; summaries in English and Spanish) 1930. fortn. Cr.$200($20.) (Sociedade de Pediatria de Sao Paulo) Centro de Estudos da Clinica Infantil do Ipiranga, Avda Nazare 1361, Sao Paulo, Brazil. Ed. A.G. de Mattos. adv.; bk.rev.; abstr.; charts; index, cum.index; circ. 3,000. **Indexed:** Biol.Abstr., Chem.Abstr., Excerp.Med., Ind.Med, Nutr.Abstr.

PEDIATRIC A I D S AND H I V INFECTION: FETUS TO ADOLESCENT. see *MEDICAL SCIENCES — Communicable Diseases*

618.92   US   ISSN 0160-0184
PEDIATRIC ALERT. 1976. bi-w. $59 to individuals; institutions $75; students $39. Medical Alert, Inc., Box 338, Newton Highlands, MA 02161. Ed. Dr. Allen A. Mitchell.

618.92   SZ   ISSN 1017-5989
CODEN: PEAMEV
PEDIATRIC AND ADOLESCENT MEDICINE. (Text in English) 1954. irreg. price varies. S. Karger AG, Allschwilerstr. 10, P.O. Box, CH-4009 Basel, Switzerland. TEL 061-3061111. FAX 061-3061234. TELEX CH 962652. Ed. D. Branski. (reprint service avail. from ISI) **Indexed:** Biol.Abstr., Chem.Abstr., Curr.Cont., Ind.Med.
  Incorporates (1954-1989): Modern Problems in Paediatrics (ISSN 0077-0086); (1971-1989): Monographs in Paediatrics (ISSN 0077-0914); Which was formerly (1924-1971): Bibliotheca Paediatrica.

618.92   US   ISSN 0090-4481
RJ1
PEDIATRIC ANNALS; a journal of continuing pediatric education. 1972. m. $85 to individuals; institutions $95. Slack, Inc., 6900 Grove Rd., Thorofare, NJ 08086. TEL 609-848-1000. FAX 609-853-5991. Ed. Dr. Robert A. Hoekelman. adv.; bk.rev.; bibl.; illus.; stat.; index; circ. 33,140. (also avail. in microfilm from UMI; reprint service avail. from UMI,ISI) **Indexed:** Bibl.Dev.Med.& Child Neur., Biol.Abstr., CINAHL, Curr.Cont., Excerp.Med., Helminthol.Abstr., Ind.Med.
—BLDSC shelfmark: 6417.530000.

618.92   US   ISSN 0883-1874
CODEN: PAAIEP
PEDIATRIC ASTHMA, ALLERGY & IMMUNOLOGY. 1987. q. $130 (foreign $170). Mary Ann Liebert, Inc., 1651 Third Ave., New York, NY 10128. TEL 212-289-2300. FAX 212-289-4697. Ed. Dr. Herbert C. Mansmann, Jr. adv.
—BLDSC shelfmark: 6417.532000.
  Description: Emphasizes the developmental implications of the morphologic, physiologic, and sociologic components of these problems in infants, children, and adolescents, as well as the impact of the disease processes on their families.

PEDIATRIC CARDIOLOGY. see *MEDICAL SCIENCES — Cardiovascular Diseases*

618.92   II   ISSN 0048-3133
PEDIATRIC CLINICS OF INDIA. (Text in English) vol.12, 1977. q. Rs.100. LTMG Hospital, Sion, Bombay 400022, India. Ed. V.B. Athavale. adv.; charts; illus.; circ. 500. (also avail. in microform from UMI; reprint service avail. from UMI) **Indexed:** Nutr.Abstr.
—BLDSC shelfmark: 6417.540000.

618.92   US   ISSN 0031-3955
RJ23   CODEN: PCNAA8
PEDIATRIC CLINICS OF NORTH AMERICA. Spanish translation: Clinicas Pediatricas de Norteamerica. 1954. bi-m. $65. W.B. Saunders Co., Curtis Center, Independence Square W., Philadelphia, PA 19106. TEL 215-238-7800. Ed. Sandy Masse. (also avail. in microform from MIM,UMI; reprint service avail. from UMI,ISI) **Indexed:** Adol.Ment.Hlth.Abstr., Bibl.Dev.Med.& Child Neur., Biol.Abstr., Chem.Abstr., Curr.Adv.Cancer Res., Curr.Adv.Ecol.Sci., Curr.Cont., Dairy Sci.Abstr., Except.Child.Educ.Abstr., Excerp.Med., Helminthol.Abstr., I.P.A., Ind.Med., Int.Nurs.Ind., Nutr.Abstr.
●Also available online. Vendor(s): BRS, BRS/Saunders Colleague.
—BLDSC shelfmark: 6417.550000.

PEDIATRIC DERMATOLOGY. see *MEDICAL SCIENCES — Dermatology And Venereology*

PEDIATRIC EMERGENCY & CRITICAL CARE; a clinical update for those who care for infants and children. see *MEDICAL SCIENCES — Abstracting, Bibliographies, Statistics*

618.92   US   ISSN 0749-5161
CODEN: PECAE5
PEDIATRIC EMERGENCY CARE. 1985. q. $65 to individuals; institutions $99. Williams & Wilkins, 428 E. Preston St., Baltimore, MD 21202. TEL 301-528-4000. FAX 301-528-4312. TELEX 87669. Eds. Drs. Stephen Ludwig, Gary Fleisher. adv.; circ. 2,300. (also avail. in microfilm; back issues avail.)
—BLDSC shelfmark: 6417.586000.
  Description: Clinical information for emergency physicians and pediatricians who care for acutely ill or injured children and adolescents.
  Refereed Serial

618.92   US   ISSN 0899-8493
PEDIATRIC EXERCISE SCIENCE. Short title: P E S. 1989. q. $40 to individuals (foreign $44); institutions $90 (foreign $94); students $24 (foreign $28). Human Kinetics Publishers, Inc., Box 5076, Champaign, IL 61825-5076. TEL 217-351-5076. FAX 217-351-2674. Ed. Dr. Thomas Rowland. adv.; bk.rev.; charts; circ. 380. **Indexed:** Sportsearch (1990-).
—BLDSC shelfmark: 6417.590000.
  Description: Addresses the importance of exercise during childhood and adolescence.
  Refereed Serial

618.92   US
PEDIATRIC HABILITATION SERIES. 1980. irreg., vol.7, 1991. price varies. Marcel Dekker, Inc., 270 Madison Ave., New York, NY 10016. TEL 212-696-9000. FAX 212-685-4540. TELEX 421419.
  Refereed Serial

618.92   US   ISSN 0888-0018
CODEN: PHONEN
PEDIATRIC HEMATOLOGY & ONCOLOGY. 1984. q. $157. Hemisphere Publishing Corporation (Subsidiary of: Taylor & Francis Group), 1900 Frost Rd., Ste. 101, Bristol, PA 19007-1598. TEL 215-785-5800. FAX 215-785-5515. Ed. Jorgen Cohn. adv.; bk.rev.; circ. 600. (also avail. in microform from UMI; back issues avail.; reprint service avail. from UMI) **Indexed:** Curr.Cont., Excerp.Med.
—BLDSC shelfmark: 6417.599500.
  Formerly (until 1986): European Paediatric Haematology and Oncology (ISSN 0800-2789)
  Description: Experimental, biochemical and clinical articles covering immunology, pathology and pharmacology.
  Refereed Serial

618.92 616   US
PEDIATRIC HEMATOLOGY - ONCOLOGY SERIES. 1988. irreg., latest 1990. price varies. Raven Press, 1185 Ave. of the Americas, New York, NY 10036. TEL 212-930-9500. FAX 212-869-3495.

618.92 616.9   US   ISSN 0891-3668
CODEN: PIDJEV
THE PEDIATRIC INFECTIOUS DISEASE JOURNAL. m. $57.50 to individuals; institutions $95. Williams & Wilkins, 428 E. Preston St., Baltimore, MD 21202. TEL 301-528-4000. FAX 301-528-4312. TELEX 87669. Eds. John D. Nelson, M.D., George H. McCracken, M.D. bk.rev.; circ. 16,600. (also avail. in microform) **Indexed:** Abstr.Hyg., Bibl.Dev.Med.& Child Neur., Dent.Ind., Dok.Arbeitsmed., Ind.Med., Ind.Vet., Protozool.Abstr., Small Anim.Abstr.
—BLDSC shelfmark: 6417.601600.
  Description: Covers the treatment of viral and bacterial illness in children.
  Refereed Serial

618.92 658   US
▼**PEDIATRIC MANAGEMENT.** 1990. m. $65. Dowden Publishing Company, 110 Summit Ave., Montvale, NJ 07645. TEL 201-391-9100. FAX 201-391-2778. Ed. Carroll V. Dowden. adv.; circ. 33,000 (controlled).
  Description: Contains information and advice to help pediatricians manage their practices. Covers third-party reimbursement, malpractice, fees, patient relations, referrals, managed care, medicaid and personal finance.

PEDIATRIC MENTAL HEALTH. see *PSYCHOLOGY*

618.92   US   ISSN 0031-398X
RJ1
PEDIATRIC NEWS. 1967. m. $60. International Medical News Group, 12230 Wilkins Ave., Rockville, MD 20852. TEL 301-770-6170. Ed. William Rubin. adv.; bk.rev.; charts; illus.; circ. 33,500. (tabloid format; also avail. in microform from UMI)
—BLDSC shelfmark: 6417.605000.

618.92   US
PEDIATRIC NUTRITION HANDBOOK. 1979. irreg., 2nd ed., 1985. $30. American Academy of Pediatrics, 141 Northwest Point Blvd., Box 927, Elk Grove Village, IL 60009-0927. TEL 708-228-5005.

618.92   US   ISSN 0277-0938
CODEN: PPATDQ
PEDIATRIC PATHOLOGY. 1983. bi-m. $355. (International Paediatric Pathology Association) Hemisphere Publishing Corporation (Subsidiary of: Taylor & Francis Group), 1900 Frost Rd., Ste. 101, Bristol, PA 19007-1598. TEL 215-785-5800. FAX 215-785-5515. (Co-sponsor: Society for Pediatric Pathology) Ed. Ronald Jaffe. adv.; bk.rev.; bibl.; charts; illus.; index; circ. 350. (also avail. in microform from UMI; back issues avail.; reprint service avail. from UMI) **Indexed:** Curr.Adv.Cancer Res., Curr.Adv.Ecol.Sci., Ind.Med.
—BLDSC shelfmark: 6417.605500.
  Refereed Serial

615.8 618.92   US   ISSN 0898-5669
CODEN: PPTHEI
PEDIATRIC PHYSICAL THERAPY. 1989. q. $37 to individuals; institutions $63. (American Physical Therapy Association, Section on Pediatrics) Williams & Wilkins, 428 Preston St., Baltimore, MD 21202. TEL 301-528-4000. FAX 301-528-4312. Ed. Toby Long. circ. 5,100.
—BLDSC shelfmark: 6417.605700.
  Description: Delivers practical information on the full range of pediatric conditions, including developmental, orthopedic and respiratory concerns.
  Refereed Serial

618.92 616.2   US   ISSN 8755-6863
CODEN: PEPUES
PEDIATRIC PULMONOLOGY. 1985. m. $270 (foreign $ 420). John Wiley & Sons, Inc., Journals, 605 Third Ave., New York, NY 10158. TEL 212-850-6000. FAX 212-850-6088. TELEX 12-7063. Ed. George Polgar. adv.; bk.rev. **Indexed:** Biol.Abstr., Curr.Cont., Ind.Med.
—BLDSC shelfmark: 6417.605800.
  Description: Covers various aspects of respiratory system disorders in infants and children.
  Refereed Serial

MEDICAL SCIENCES — PEDIATRICS

618.92 615.842 GW ISSN 0301-0449
CODEN: PDRYA5
PEDIATRIC RADIOLOGY; roentgenology, nuclear medicine, ultrasonics, CT, MRI. (Text in English) 1973. 8/yr. DM.534($263) Springer-Verlag, Heidelberger Platz 3, D-1000 Berlin 33, Germany. TEL 030-8207-1. (Also Heidelberg, Tokyo, Vienna, and New York) Eds. W.E. Berdon, A.R. Chrispin. adv. (also avail. in microform from UMI; reprint service avail. from ISI) **Indexed**: Bibl.Dev.Med.& Child Neur., Chem.Abstr., Curr.Adv.Cancer Res., Curr.Cont., Dent.Ind., Excerp.Med., Ind.Med., Nutr.Abstr.
—BLDSC shelfmark: 6417.606000.

618.92 US ISSN 0031-3998
RJ1 CODEN: PEREBL
PEDIATRIC RESEARCH; international journal of human developmental biology. 1967. m. $105 to individuals; institutions $180. (International Pediatric Research Foundation Inc.) Williams & Wilkins, 428 E. Preston St., Baltimore, MD 21202. TEL 301-528-4000. FAX 301-528-4312. TELEX 87669. (Co-sponsors: American Pediatric Society; European Society for Pediatric Research; Society for Pediatric Research) Ed. Dennis M. Bier, M.D. adv.; charts; illus.; circ. 3,800. (also avail. in microform) **Indexed**: Bibl.Dev.Med.& Child Neur., Biol.Abstr., Chem.Abstr., Chic.Per.Ind., Child Devel.Abstr., Curr.Adv.Biochem., Curr.Adv.Cell & Devel.Biol., Curr.Adv.Ecol.Sci., Curr.Cont., Dairy Sci.Abstr., Dent.Ind., Excerp.Med., Helminthol.Abstr., Ind.Med., Lang.& Lang.Behav.Abstr., Nutr.Abstr., Pig News & Info., Soyabean Abstr.
—BLDSC shelfmark: 6417.620000.
Description: Covers advances in the understanding and management of pediatric pulmonary, endocrinological, gastroenterological, and nutritional disorders.
Refereed Serial

618.92 US ISSN 0882-9225
CODEN: PRECEA
PEDIATRIC REVIEWS AND COMMUNICATIONS. 4/yr. (in 1 vol; 4 nos./vol.). $96. Harwood Academic Publishers, 270 Eighth Ave., New York, NY 10011. TEL 212-206-8900. FAX 212-645-2459. TELEX 236735 GOPUB UR. (Subscr. to: Box 786, Cooper Sta., New York, NY 10276. TEL 800-545-8398; UK subscr. to: P.O. Box 90, Reading, Berkshire RG1 8JL, England. TEL 0734-560-080) Eds. David Burman, Philip Lanzowsky. (also avail. in microform)
—BLDSC shelfmark: 6417.620400.
Refereed Serial

PEDIATRIC SURGERY INTERNATIONAL. see *MEDICAL SCIENCES — Surgery*

PEDIATRIC THERAPEUTICS & TOXICOLOGY; practical pediatrics for the pediatric practitioner. see *MEDICAL SCIENCES — Abstracting, Bibliographies, Statistics*

618.92 US
PEDIATRICIAN. 1984. q. free to qualified personnel. E P I Inc., 8003 Old York Rd., Elkins Park, PA 19117. TEL 215-635-1700. Ed. Deana Jamroz. adv.; tr.lit.; circ. 10,565.
Description: For pediatricians and their patient families with pre-school children. Covers advances in neonatal and pediatric medicine, psychology, and dentistry, plus relevant consumer product information.

618.92 US ISSN 0031-4005
RJ1 CODEN: PEDIAU
PEDIATRICS. Spanish edition (ISSN 0210-5721) 1948. m. $70 to individuals; institutions $115. American Academy of Pediatrics, 141 Northwest Point Blvd., Box 927, Elk Grove Village, IL 60009-0927. TEL 708-228-5005. Ed. Jerold F. Lucey, M.D. adv.; bk.rev.; illus.; index every 6 mos; circ. 50,000. (also avail. in microfiche from AAP; back issues avail.; reprint service avail. from UMI) **Indexed**: Abstr.Health Care Manage.Stud., Abstr.Hyg., Bibl.Dev.Med.& Child Neur., Biol.Abstr., Biotech.Abstr., Chem.Abstr., Curr.Adv.Ecol.Sci., Dairy Sci.Abstr., Dent.Ind., Dok.Arbeitsmed., Except.Child.Educ.Abstr., Excerp.Med., FAMLI, Food Sci.& Tech.Abstr., Helminthol.Abstr., Hlth.Ind., I.P.A., Ind.Med., Ind.Vet., Int.Nurs.Ind., Nutr.Abstr., Poult.Abstr., Rev.Plant Path., Risk Abstr., Trop.Dis.Bull., Vet.Bull.
●Also available online. Vendor(s): BRS, BRS/Saunders Colleague, Mead Data Central.
Also available on CD-ROM.
—BLDSC shelfmark: 6417.650000.

618.9 SP ISSN 0210-5721
PEDIATRICS (EDICION ESPANOLA). English edition (ISSN 0031-4005) 1976. m. 6400 ptas.($67) (free to qualified personnel). (American Academy of Pediatrics, US) Ediciones Doyma S.A., Travesera de Gracia 17-21, 08021 Barcelona, Spain. TEL 200-07-11. FAX 209-11-36. TELEX 51964 INK-E. Ed. A. Ballabriga Aguado. adv.: page 165000 ptas., trim 210 x 280; adv. contact: Cristina Garrote. circ. 7,000. (reprint service avail. from UMI) **Indexed**: Dok.Arbeitsmed., Vet.Bull.
Description: Covers infectious illnesses, immunity, nutrition, comunity medicine, premature and newborn babies, neurology, psychiatry, cardiology, endocrinology and toxicology.

618.92 649 US ISSN 0730-6725
PEDIATRICS FOR PARENTS; the monthly newsletter for caring adults. 1980. m. $15. Pediatrics for Parents, Inc., Box 1069, Bangor, ME 04402-1069. TEL 207-942-6212. Ed. Dr. Richard J. Sagall. bk.rev.; circ. 1,500. (looseleaf format; back issues avail.) **Indexed**: Hlth.Ind.

618.92 US ISSN 0191-9601
PEDIATRICS IN REVIEW. 1979. 12/yr. $115 to non-members. American Academy of Pediatrics, 141 Northwest Point Blvd., Box 927, Elk Grove Village, IL 60009-0927. TEL 708-228-5005. Ed. Robert J. Haggerty, M.D. abstr.; charts; illus.; cum.index; circ. 27,000. (back issues avail.)
—BLDSC shelfmark: 6417.657000.
Refereed Serial

618.92 FR ISSN 0031-4021
CODEN: PEDRAN
PEDIATRIE. (Text in French; summaries in English, French) 1945. 12/yr. 800 F.($150) (foreign 860 F.)(effective 1992). (Reunion Rhone Alpes de Pediatrie) Editions Scientifiques Elsevier, 29, rue Buffon, 75005 Paris, France. TEL 47-07-11-22. FAX 43-36-80-93. TELEX 202 400 F. (Subscr. in U.S. and Canada to: Elsevier Science Publishing Co., Inc., Box 882, Madison Sq. Sta., New York, NY 10159. TEL 212-989-5800) Ed.Bd. adv.; bk.rev.; charts; illus.; stat.; circ. 3,000. (also avail. in microfilm from UMI; reprint service avail. from UMI) **Indexed**: Bibl.Dev.Med.& Child Neur., Biol.Abstr., Chem.Abstr., Curr.Adv.Ecol.Sci., Excerp.Med., Helminthol.Abstr., Ind.Med., Nutr.Abstr.
—BLDSC shelfmark: 6417.670000.
Description: Publishes original articles, short communications, special editorials and interviews which provide a forum for specialists in pediatric research, teaching and practice.

618.92 RU ISSN 0031-403X
CODEN: PEDTAT
PEDIATRIYA/PEDIATRICS. (Text in Russian; summaries in English) 1922. m. $17.40. (Vsesoyuznoe Nauchnoe Obshchestvo Detskikh Vrachei) Izdatel'stvo Meditsina, Petroverigskii pereulok 6-8, 101838 Moscow, Russia. (Co-sponsor: Ministerstvo Zdravookhraneniya S.S.S.R.) Ed. N.S. Kislyak. bk.rev.; bibl.; index. **Indexed**: Bibl.Dev.Med.& Child Neur., Biol.Abstr., Chem.Abstr., Dairy Sci.Abstr., Excerp.Med., Ind.Med., Nutr.Abstr., Poult.Abstr.
—BLDSC shelfmark: 0129.220000.
Description: Covers major problems of modern pediatrics in the Soviet Union and other countries. Includes articles and reviews devoted to the etiology, pathogenesis, clinical picture, prophylaxis and treatment of childhood diseases, surgery, neuropathology, psychiatry and other branches of pediatrics.

618 KR ISSN 0031-4048
CODEN: PDAGA2
PEDIATRIYA, AKUSHERSTVO TA GINEKOLOGIYA. 1936. bi-m. $11.20. Ministerstvo Zdravookhraneniya Ukrainskoi S.S.R., Kiev, Ukraine. bk.rev.; index. (tabloid format) **Indexed**: Biol.Abstr., Chem.Abstr., Ind.Med.
—BLDSC shelfmark: 0129.260000.

618.92 616.07 SZ ISSN 0091-2921
RJ49 CODEN: PPEPDY
PERSPECTIVES IN PEDIATRIC PATHOLOGY. (Text in English) 1976. irreg. price varies. S. Karger AG, Allschwilerstr. 10, P.O. Box, CH-4009 Basel, Switzerland. TEL 061-3061111. FAX 061-3061234. TELEX CH 962652. Eds. S. Rosenberg, Dr. Jay Bernstein. **Indexed**: ASCA, Ind.Med.

618.92 PH ISSN 0031-7667
PHILIPPINE JOURNAL OF PEDIATRICS. (Text in English) 1950. bi-m. P.70($20) Philippine Pediatric Society, PO Box 3527, Manila, Philippines. Ed. Dr. Felix A. Estrada. adv.; bk.rev.; abstr.; index; circ. 2,000. **Indexed**: Biol.Abstr., Excerp.Med.

618.92 US ISSN 0194-2638
RJ53.P5 CODEN: POTPDY
PHYSICAL & OCCUPATIONAL THERAPY IN PEDIATRICS; the quarterly journal of developmental therapy. 1980. q. $32 to individuals; institutions $95; libraries $175. Haworth Press, Inc., 10 Alice St., Binghamton, NY 13904. TEL 800-342-9678. FAX 607-722-1424. TELEX 4932599. Eds. Suzann Campbell, Irma Wilhelm. adv.; bk.rev.; circ. 1,365. (also avail. in microfiche from HAW; back issues avail.; reprint service avail. from HAW) **Indexed**: Biol.Abstr., CINAHL, Excerp.Med., Psychol.Abstr., Rehabil.Lit., Sage Fam.Stud.Abstr., Yrbk.Assoc.Educ.& Rehab.Blind.
—BLDSC shelfmark: 6475.280000.
Description: Brings information to all therapists involved in developmental and physical rehabilitation of infants and children. Covers current clinical research and practical applications.
Refereed Serial

618.92 PL ISSN 0079-4279
POSTEPY PEDIATRII. (Text in Polish; summaries in English, Polish, and Russian) 1955. a. Panstwowy Zaklad Wydawnictw Lekarskich, Dluga 38-40, Warsaw, Poland. TEL 31-42-81. Ed. Jana Raszka, M.D.

618.92 US
PRENATAL EDUCATOR. q. free to qualified personnel. E P I Inc., 8003 Old York Rd., Elkins Park, PA 19117. TEL 215-635-1700. Ed. Deana Jamroz. adv.; tr.lit.; circ. 8,540.
Description: For health care professionals who instruct prenatal education classes, as well as couples expecting the birth of a child. Covers advances in medicine, classroom techniques, and relevant consumer product information.

618.92 IS ISSN 0334-7524
PREVENTIVE PEDIATRICS. (Text in English) q. Freund Publishing House, P.O. Box 35010, 61 Nachmani St., Tel Aviv 61 350, Israel. Ed D. Tamir.
—BLDSC shelfmark: 6612.793000.

618.92 US ISSN 0893-9837
PRIMARY CARE REPORTS. 1989. m. $169. American Health Consultants, Inc., Six Piedmont Center, Ste. 400, 3525 Piedmont Rd., N.E., Atlanta, GA 30305. TEL 404-262-7436. FAX 800-284-3291. (Subscr. to: Box 740056, Atlanta, GA 30374-9822. TEL 800-688-2421) Ed. Dr. Shiranand S. Karkal. circ. 400.

618.92 617 US
PRINCIPLES OF PEDIATRIC NEUROSURGERY. 1986. irreg. price varies. Springer-Verlag, 175 Fifth Ave., New York, NY 10010. TEL 212-460-1500. (Also Berlin, Heidelberg, Tokyo, Vienna) (reprint service avail. from ISI)

PROGRESS IN PEDIATRIC CARDIOLOGY. see *MEDICAL SCIENCES — Cardiovascular Diseases*

618.92 US ISSN 0079-6654
CODEN: PPDSAZ
PROGRESS IN PEDIATRIC SURGERY. (Text in German; summaries in French) 1971. a. price varies. Springer-Verlag, 175 Fifth Ave., New York, NY 10010. **Indexed**: Biol.Abstr., Ind.Med.
—BLDSC shelfmark: 6872.600000.

618.92 136.7 FR ISSN 0079-726X
CODEN: PSYEAH
PSYCHIATRIE DE L'ENFANT. 1958. s-a. 330 F. (foreign 420 F.). Presses Universitaires de France, Departement des Revues, 14 Avenue du Bois-de-l'Epine, B.P.90, 91003 Evry Cedex, France. TEL 1-60-77-82-05. FAX 1-60-79-20-45. TELEX PUF 600 474 F. Ed.Bd. cum.index. (reprint service avail. from KTO) **Indexed**: Excerp.Med., Ind.Med., Psychol.Abstr., SSCI.
—BLDSC shelfmark: 6946.243000.
Description: Original works in the clinical, technical and social psychological areas.

MEDICAL SCIENCES — PEDIATRICS

618.92   US   ISSN 1050-964X
▼**THE REPORT OF PEDIATRIC INFECTIOUS DISEASES.**
1991. 10/yr. $32 to individuals (foreign $55); institutions $52 (foreign $75). (Pediatric Infectious Diseases Society) Churchill Livingstone Medical Journals, 650 Ave. of the Americas, New York, NY 10011. TEL 212-206-5040. FAX 212-727-7808. TELEX 332266. (Dist. by: Transaction Publishers, Department 3091, Rutgers University, New Brunswick, NJ 08903) Eds. Dr. Jerome Klein, Dr. Georges Peter.
— BLDSC shelfmark: 7661.924500.
Description: Includes articles on issues of importance to practicing physicians responsible for the care of infants and children.

618.92   CK   ISSN 0034-7442
REVISTA COLOMBIANA DE PEDIATRIA Y PUERICULTURA. (Text in Spanish; summaries in English) 1941. 4/yr. $12. Apdo. 606, Bogota, Colombia. Ed. Jorge Gamacho Gamba. adv.; bk.rev.; abstr.; bibl.; charts; illus.; index, cum.index; circ. 2,000. (also avail. in microform from UMI; reprint service avail. from UMI) **Indexed:** Excerp.Med.
— BLDSC shelfmark: 7851.410000.

618.92   CU   ISSN 0034-7531
REVISTA CUBANA DE PEDIATRIA. (Text in Spanish; summaries in English, French, Spanish) 1928. 3/yr. $21 in N. America; S. America $23; Europe $28. Ministerio de Salud Publica, Centro Nacional de Informacion de Ciencias Medicas, Calle E No. 452, 3-19 y 21, Plaza de la Revolucion, Apdo. 6520, Havana, Cuba. TEL 809-32-5338. (Dist. by: Ediciones Cubanas, Obispo No. 527, Apdo. 605, Havana, Cuba) Dir. Manuel Amador. bibl.; charts; illus.; circ. 2,500. **Indexed:** Abstr.Hyg., Biol.Abstr., Chem.Abstr., Excerp.Med., Ind.Med., Nutr.Abstr., Trop.Dis.Bull.
— BLDSC shelfmark: 7852.130000.
Description: Covers child development including infant/newborn diseases, child nutrition, respiratory tract diseases, infant mortality, airway obstruction, low birth weight, heart and congenital defects.

618.92   RM   ISSN 0031-3904
REVISTA DE PEDIATRIE, OBSTETRICA, GINECOLOGIE. PEDIATRIE. (Text in Rumanian; summaries in English, French, German, Russian) 1952. 4/yr. $15. Uniunea Societatilor de Stiinte Medicale din Republica Socialista Rumania, Str. Progresului 8, Bucharest, Rumania. (Subscr. to: ILEXIM, Str. 13 Decembrie Nr. 3, P.O. Box 136-137, Bucharest, Rumania) Ed.Bd. adv.; bk.rev.; abstr.; charts; illus. **Indexed:** Biol.Abstr., Chem.Abstr., Ind.Med.

618.92   SP   ISSN 0034-947X
                                CODEN: REPEAW
REVISTA ESPANOLA DE PEDIATRIA. 1946. bi-m. 4300 ptas.($65) Editorial Garsi, S.A., Londres, 17, 28028 Madrid, Spain. TEL 256-08-00. FAX 361-10-07. Ed. Dr. Manuel Hernandez. bk.rev.; abstr.; bibl.; illus.; circ. 4,000. **Indexed:** Biol.Abstr., Chem.Abstr., Dairy Sci.Abstr., Excerp.Med., Ind.Med.Esp., Nutr.Abstr.
— BLDSC shelfmark: 7854.200000.

618.92   CK   ISSN 0120-6311
REVISTA INTERNACIONAL DE PEDIATRIA. 1984. irreg. (4-6/yr.). (Miami Children's Hospital) Ediciones Lerner Ltda., Calle 8A No.68A-41, Bogota, Colombia. circ. 35,000.
— BLDSC shelfmark: 7861.695000.
Formerly (until Dec. 1984): Miami Children's Hospital Journal.

618.92   PO   ISSN 0048-7880
REVISTA PORTUGUESA DE PEDIATRIA E PUERICULTURA. m. Clinica Pediatrica Universitaria de Lisboa, Hospital de Santa Maria, Lisbon, Portugal. illus. **Indexed:** Ind.Med.

618.92   FR   ISSN 0035-1644
                                CODEN: REVPBS
REVUE DE PEDIATRIE. (Text in French; summaries in English, French) 1965. 10/yr. 440 F. (Europe 500 F.; elsewhere 660 F.). Societe Internationale d'Edition Medicale, B.P. 98-41, ave. du Bac, 94210 La Varenne-Saint-Hilaire, France.
TEL 16-1-49-76-08-56. FAX 49-76-04-81. Ed. Francois Carruzzo. adv.; bk.rev.; bibl.; charts; illus.; stat.; circ. 6,000. **Indexed:** Biol.Abstr., Curr.Cont., Excerp.Med., Nutr.Abstr.
— BLDSC shelfmark: 7942.100000.

618.92   FR   ISSN 0995-1180
REVUE DU PEDIATRE. 1988. 8/yr. 100 ECU($120) (typically set in Jan.). Masson, 5 et 7, rue Laromiguiere, 75005 Paris, France.
TEL 1-46-34-21-60. FAX 1-45-87-29-99. TELEX 202 671 F. Ed. Bernard Grenier. adv.; circ. 6,000.

618.92   FR
REVUE INTERNATIONALE DE PEDIATRIE. (Text in French; summaries in English and French) 1969. m. 210 F. to individuals (foreign 295 F.); students 195 F. (foreign 280 F.). Galliena Promotion, 58 A, Rue du Dessous des Berges, 75013 Paris, France.
TEL 45-84-97-66. **Indexed:** Excerp.Med.

618.92   IT   ISSN 0392 4416
RIVISTA DI PEDIATRIA PREVENTIVA E SOCIALE-NIPIOLOGIA. (Text in Italian; summaries in English and Italian) 1951. bi-m. L.60000($70) (Societa Italiana di Pediatria Preventiva e Sociale-Nipiologia) Edizioni Minerva Medica, Corso Bramante 83-85, 10126 Turin, Italy. Ed. E. Mensi. adv.; bk.rev.; bibl.; charts; illus.; index; circ. 3,000. **Indexed:** Biol.Abstr., Chem.Abstr., Ind.Med.
— BLDSC shelfmark: 7992.540000.
Formerly: Minerva Nipiologica (ISSN 0026-489X)

RIVISTA ITALIANA DI ODONTOIATRIA INFANTILE. see MEDICAL SCIENCES — Dentistry

618.92   IT
RIVISTA ITALIANA DI PEDIATRIA. 1975. bi-m. L.65000($90) Edizioni Minerva Medica, Corso Bramante 83, 10126 Turin, Italy. Ed. G. Giovannelli. **Indexed:** Excerp.Med.

618.92   US
SCHOOL HEALTH: A GUIDE FOR HEALTH PROFESSIONALS. 1972. irreg., 4th ed., 1987. $30. American Academy of Pediatrics, 141 Northwest Point Blvd., Box 927, Elk Grove Village, IL 60009-0927. TEL 708-228-5005.

618.92   NE   ISSN 0925-6164
SCREENING. (Text in English) 1992. 4/yr. fl.305($150) (effective 1992). (International Society of Neonatal Screening) Elsevier Science Publishers B.V., P.O. Box 211, 1000 AE Amsterdam, Netherlands. TEL 020-5803911. FAX 020-5803598. TELEX 18582 ESPA NL. (Subscr. in U.S. and Canada to: Elsevier Science Publishing Co., Inc., Box 882, Madison Sq. Sta., New York, NY 10159. TEL 212-989-5800) Eds. H. Naruse, H. Levy. adv.; abstr.; illus.; stat.
— BLDSC shelfmark: 8211.815570.
Previously announced as: International Journal of Neonatal and Later Screening.
Description: Provides scientific, technical and medical information about newborn screening and all other population based screening, including all types of mass screening for genetic and non-genetic diseases.
Refereed Serial

SEMINARS IN ORTHOPAEDICS. see MEDICAL SCIENCES — Orthopedics And Traumatology

618.92   US   ISSN 0146-0005
                                CODEN: SEMPDU
SEMINARS IN PERINATOLOGY. 1977. bi-m. $82 to individuals; institutions $121; foreign $144. W.B. Saunders Co. (Subsidiary of: Harcourt Brace Jovanovich, Inc.), Curtis Center, Independence Square W., Philadelphia, PA 19106.
TEL 215-238-7800. Eds. Drs. Robert K. Creasy, Joseph B. Warshaw. adv.; bk.rev.; bibl.; charts; illus.; index. **Indexed:** ASCA, Bibl.Dev.Med.& Child Neur., Biol.Abstr., Curr.Cont., Excerp.Med., Ind.Med., Ind.Sci.Rev., Sci.Cit.Ind.
●Also available online.
— BLDSC shelfmark: 8239.456800.

SEMINARS IN UROLOGY. see MEDICAL SCIENCES — Urology And Nephrology

618.92   CC   ISSN 1001-0866
SHIYONG ERKE ZAZHI/JOURNAL OF PRACTICAL PEDIATRICS. (Text in Chinese) 1986. bi-m. $7.50. Shiyong Yixue Zazhishe, 44-1, Jixian Jie, Heping Qu, Shenyang, Liaoning 110005, People's Republic of China. TEL 364398. Ed. Xiang Quanshen.

618.92   JA   ISSN 0583-1180
                                CODEN: SHOIB4
SHONI IGAKU/PEDIATRIC REVIEW. (Text in Japanese; summaries in English) 1968. bi-m. 26460 Yen($204) Igaku-Shoin Ltd., 5-24-3 Hongo, Bunkyo-ku, Tokyo 113-91, Japan.
TEL 03-817-5707. Ed.Bd. circ. 3,000.

618.92   JA   ISSN 0385-6305
SHONI NAIKA/JAPANESE JOURNAL OF PEDIATRIC MEDICINE. (Text in Japanese) 1969. m. 31,600 Yen($248) Tokyo Igaku-sha, 35-4, 3-chome, Hongo, Bunkyo-ku, Tokyo 113, Japan. Ed.Bd. circ. 6,000.
— BLDSC shelfmark: 4656.940000.

618.92   JA   ISSN 0037-4121
SHONIKA/CLINICAL PEDIATRICS. (Text in Japanese) 1960. m. 1600 Yen per no. Kanehara & Co., Ltd., 31-14 Yushima 2-chome, Bunkyo-ku, Tokyo 113, Japan. Ed. Dr. Teruji Shinozuka. bk.rev.; index; circ. 6,200. **Indexed:** CINAHL, Curr.Cont., Helminthol.Abstr., Nutr.Abstr.
●Also available online. Vendor(s): BRS.
— BLDSC shelfmark: 6417.656000.

618.92   SP   ISSN 0037-8658
SOCIEDAD VASCO-NAVARRA DE PEDIATRIA. BOLETIN. vol.5, 1970. q. 2000 ptas.($35) Editorial Garsi, S.A., Londres, 17, 28028 Madrid, Spain.
TEL 256-08-00. FAX 361-10-07. Dir. A. Blanco Quiros. adv.; charts; illus.; stat.; circ. 1,500. **Indexed:** Excerp.Med.

618.92   SA   ISSN 1017-1711
SOUTH AFRICAN PAEDIATRICS MAGAZINE. Short title: Pedmed. (Text in English) 1986. bi-m. R.92. George Warman Publications (Pty.) Ltd., 77 Hout St., P.O. Box 704, Cape Town 8000, South Africa.
TEL 021-245320. FAX 021-261332. TELEX 521849. Ed. Anthea Barker. adv.; circ. 3,300.

618.92   GW   ISSN 0171-9327
                                CODEN: SPKLEI
SOZIAL PAEDIATRIE; in praxis und klinik. 1979. m. DM.120. Verlag Kirchheim und Co. GmbH, Kaiserstr. 41, Postfach 2524, 6500 Mainz, Germany.
TEL 06131-671081. FAX 06131-638843. Ed.Bd. circ. 7,100.
— BLDSC shelfmark: 8361.008000.

SPINAL CONNECTION. see MEDICAL SCIENCES — Orthopedics And Traumatology

618.92 617.1   US
SPORTS MEDICINE: HEALTH CARE FOR YOUNG ATHLETES. 1983. irreg., 2nd ed., 1991. $40. American Academy of Pediatrics, 141 Northwest Point Blvd., Box 927, Elk Grove Village, IL 60009-0927. TEL 708-228-5005.

614.19   US
▼**SYNOPSIS (COLUMBIA).** 1990. q. membership. Sudden Infant Death Syndrome Alliance (SIDS), 10500 Little Patuxent Pkwy., Ste. 420, Columbia, MD 21044. TEL 301-964-8000, 800-221-7437. FAX 301-964-8009. Ed. Phipps Cohe. circ. 40,000.
Description: Unites families and professionals concerned about SIDS; provides up-to-date information about the syndrome to the general public, particularly to new and expectant parents. Hotline number included.

618.92   GW   ISSN 0935-3216
T W PAEDIATRIE. 1988. bi-m. DM.65 (foreign DM.87). Verlag G. Braun GmbH, Karl-Friedrich-Str. 14, Postfach 1709, 7500 Karlsruhe 1, Germany.
TEL 0721-165-0. FAX 0721-165227.

THEIR WORLD. see CHILDREN AND YOUTH — About

THEORY AND RESEARCH IN BEHAVIORAL PEDIATRICS. see PSYCHOLOGY

618.92   NE
TIJDSCHRIFT VOOR KINDERGENEESKUNDE. (Text in Dutch and English) 1932. m. fl.105. Bohn Stafleu Van Loghum B.V., P.O. Box 246, 3990 GA Houten, Netherlands. TEL 03403-95711.
FAX 03403-50903. Ed. Dr. T.D. Stahlie. adv.; bk.rev.; charts; illus.; stat.; index; circ. 850. **Indexed:** Biol.Abstr., Chem.Abstr., Dent.Ind., Excerp.Med., Ind.Med.
Formerly: Maandschrift voor Kindergeneeskunde (ISSN 0024-869X)

MEDICAL SCIENCES — PSYCHIATRY AND NEUROLOGY

618.92 US
TOPICS IN PEDIATRICS. 1982. 3/yr. free. Minneapolis Children's Medical Center, 2525 Chicago Ave., S., Minneapolis, MN 55404. TEL 612-863-6222. FAX 612-863-6674. Ed. Dr. John MacDonald. circ. 10,000.
Description: For physicians, nurses and psycho-social professionals who care for children.

575.1 618.92 US ISSN 0737-5174
TRISOMY 21; an international, multidisciplinary journal of Downs Syndrome. 1984. q. Eterna International, Inc., 27 W. 560 Warrenville Rd., Warrenville, IL 60555. TEL 708-393-2930. Ed. Dr. Siegfried M. Pueschel. abstr.; charts; illus.; index.
Refereed Serial

618.92 TU ISSN 0041-4301
TURKISH JOURNAL OF PEDIATRICS. (Text in English) 1958. q. $50. Turkish and International Children's Center - Turkiye ve Uluslararasi Cocuk Sagligi Merkezi, P.O. Box 66, Samanpazari, 06240 Ankara, Turkey. FAX 4-311-2253. TELEX 42999 TCSM TR. (Co-sponsor: Turkish National Pediatric Society) Ed. Dr. Ihsan Dogramaci. bk.rev.; abstr.; bibl.; charts; illus.; index; circ. 1,500. **Indexed:** Biol.Abstr., Curr.Adv.Ecol.Sci., Dent.Ind., Excerp.Med., Ind.Med., Nutr.Abstr.
—BLDSC shelfmark: 9072.480000.
Refereed Serial

WOMAN'S DAY MOTHER - CHILD. see *CHILDREN AND YOUTH — About*

618.92 CC
XINSHENG ERKE ZAZHI/JOURNAL OF PEDIATRICS FOR THE NEW-BORN. (Text in Chinese) bi-m. Beijing University of Medical Sciences, Affiliated No. 1 Hospital, Beijing 100034, People's Republic of China. TEL 656631. Ed. Huang Demin.

618.92 US ISSN 0084-3954
RJ16
YEAR BOOK OF PEDIATRICS. 1933. a. $51.95. Mosby - Year Book, Inc., Continuity Division, 200 N. LaSalle, Chicago, IL 60601. TEL 312-726-9733. FAX 312-726-6075. TELEX 206155. Ed. Dr. James A. Stockman, III. (reprint service avail.) **Indexed:** Curr.Adv.Ecol.Sci.
●Also available online. Vendor(s): BRS.
—BLDSC shelfmark: 9414.800000.

618.92 US ISSN 1044-4890
RG631
YEAR BOOK OF PERINATAL - NEONATAL MEDICINE. 1987. a. $54.95. Mosby - Year Book, Inc., Continuity Division, 200 N. LaSalle, Chicago, IL 60601. TEL 312-726-9746. FAX 312-726-6075. TELEX 206155. Eds. Drs. Marshall H. Klaus, Avroy Fanaroff. illus. (reprint service avail.)
●Also available online. Vendor(s): BRS.
—BLDSC shelfmark: 9414.624000.

YOUR FIRST BABY. see *CHILDREN AND YOUTH — About*

618.92 GW ISSN 0174-3082
CODEN: ZEKID8
ZEITSCHRIFT FUER KINDERCHIRURGIE/SURGERY IN INFANCY AND CHILDHOOD. 1964. bi-m. DM.372. (Deutsche, Schweizerische und Oesterreichischen Gesellschaft fuer Kinderchirurgie) Hippokrates Verlag GmbH, Ruedigerstr. 14, Postfach 10 22 63, D-7000 Stuttgart 1, Germany. adv.; bk.rev.; abstr.; charts; illus.; index; circ. 1,300. **Indexed:** Bibl.Dev.Med.& Child Neur., Biol.Abstr., Curr.Adv.Cell & Devel.Biol., Curr.Adv.Ecol.Sci., Curr.Cont., Excerp.Med., Helminthol.Abstr., Ind.Med., Nutr.Abstr.
Formerly: Zeitschrift fuer Kinderchirurgie und Grenzgebiete (ISSN 0044-2909)

ZHONGGUO YIXUE WENZHAI (ERKEXUE)/CHINA MEDICAL ABSTRACTS (PEDIATRICS). see *MEDICAL SCIENCES — Abstracting, Bibliographies, Statistics*

618.2 CC
ZHONGHUA ERKE ZAZHI/CHINESE JOURNAL OF PEDIATRICS. (Text in Chinese) bi-m. $3 per no. Guoji Shudian, Qikan Bu, Chegongzhuang Xilu 21, P.O. Box 399, Beijing, People's Republic of China.

MEDICAL SCIENCES — Psychiatry And Neurology

616.8 617 US ISSN 0882-2832
RD592.5
A B M S DIRECTORY OF CERTIFIED NEUROLOGICAL SURGEONS. 1983. biennial. $24.95. American Board of Medical Specialties, One Rotary Center, Ste. 805, Evanston, IL 60201. TEL 708-491-9091. FAX 708-328-3596. Ed. Dr. J. Lee Dockery.

616.8 US ISSN 0884-1500
RC335
A B M S DIRECTORY OF CERTIFIED NEUROLOGISTS. 1985. biennial. $29.95. American Board of Medical Specialties, One Rotary Center, Ste. 805, Evanston, IL 60201. TEL 708-491-9091. FAX 708-328-3596. Ed. Dr. J. Lee Dockery.

616.89 US ISSN 0884-1519
RC335
A B M S DIRECTORY OF CERTIFIED PSYCHIATRISTS. 1985. biennial. $39.95. American Board of Medical Specialties, One Rotary Center, Ste. 805, Evanston, IL 60201. TEL 708-491-9091. FAX 708-328-3596. Ed. Dr. J. Lee Dockery.

362.1 616.8 BE ISSN 0001-0553
A B P - ASSOCIATION BELGE DES PARALYSES. BULLETIN/B V V - BELGISCHE VERENIGING VOOR VERLAMDEN. BULLETIN. (Text in Flemish, French) 1938. q. 250 Fr. Association Belge des Paralyses, 61-63 rue des Champs Elysees, B-1050 Brussels, Belgium. TEL 02-648-64-33. FAX 02-647-56-70. adv.; bk.rev.; illus.; circ. 4,000.
Description: Articles concerning activities of the association and information for disabled persons.

616.8 US
A C O NEWSLETTER. 1968. s-a. $12.50. American College of Orgonomy, Box 490, Princeton, NJ 08542. TEL 908-821-1144. FAX 908-821-0174. Ed. Barbara Koopman. circ. 1,000. (also avail. in microform from UMI)

362.2 US ISSN 0001-1436
A H R C CHRONICLE. 1949. irreg. (3-4/yr.). membership. Association for the Help of Retarded Children, New York City Chapter, 200 Park Ave. S., New York, NY 10003. TEL 212-254-8203. FAX 212-473-2225. Eds. John Wykert, Belle Press. adv.; bk.rev.; illus.; circ. 10,000.
Description: Covers work being done by the agency with the mentally handicapped.

A I D S CARE; psychological and socio-medical aspects of AIDS-HIV. see *MEDICAL SCIENCES — Communicable Diseases*

616.8 616.2 US ISSN 0897-9375
A P S S NEWSLETTER.* (Former name of issuing body: American Association of Sleep Disorders Centers) 1978. q. $50 includes membership. Association of Professional Sleep Societies, 1610 14th St., N.W., Rochester, MN 55901-0246. TEL 507-287-6006. FAX 507-287-6008. Ed. Ralph Lydic. adv.; circ. 2,700.
Fomerly (until 1986): A S D C Newsletter.
Description: Current information on sleep disorders medicine.

A R C. (Association for Retarded Citizens) see *SOCIAL SERVICES AND WELFARE*

616.8 US ISSN 0886-5620
A S E T NEWSLETTER. 1976. q. membership only. American Society of Electroneurodiagnostic Technologists, Inc., Executive Office, 204 W. Seventh, Carroll, IA 51401. TEL 712-792-2978. Ed. M. Fran Pedelty. circ. 2,300. (looseleaf format)
Description: Contains news of the society, educational articles, and calendar of events.

616.8 378 US ISSN 1042-9670
RC336 CODEN: JPSEDS
ACADEMIC PSYCHIATRY. 1977. q. $85 to individuals (foreign $100); institutions $135 (foreign $150). (American Association of Directors of Psychiatric Residency Training) American Psychiatric Press, Inc., Journals Division, 1400 K St., N.W., Ste. 1101, Washington, DC 20005. TEL 202-682-6272. FAX 202-789-2648. (UK addr.: 17 Belgrave Sq., London SW1X 8PG, England) (Co-sponsor: Association for Academic Psychiatry) Ed. Dr. Jonathan F. Borus. adv.; bk.rev.; bibl.; charts; illus.; circ. 1,000. (also avail. in microform from UMI; back issues avail.; reprint service avail. from ISI,UMI)
Indexed: Chicago Psychoanal.Lit.Ind., Cont.Pg.Educ., Curr.Cont., Excerp.Med., Mid.East: Abstr.& Ind., Psychol.Abstr., Risk Abstr., Sp.Ed.Needs Abstr., SSCI.
—BLDSC shelfmark: 0570.514150.
Formerly: Journal of Psychiatric Education (ISSN 0363-1907)
Description: Provides a forum for work which furthers knowledge in psychiatric education and stimulates improvements in academic psychiatry.
Refereed Serial

616.8 IT ISSN 0393-6384
ACTA MEDICA MEDITERRANEA. (Text in English, French and Italian) 1960. 3/yr. L.35000($35) Carbone Editore, Via G. Daita, 29, 90139 Palmero, Italy. TEL (091) 321 273. FAX 091-321782. abstr.; bibl.; illus.; stat.; index; circ. 3,000.
—BLDSC shelfmark: 0635.140000.
Formerly: Archivio Siciliano di Medicina e Chirurgia (Sezione Medica).
Description: Clinical cases are reviewed and discussed.

ACTA NEUROCHIRURGICA. see *MEDICAL SCIENCES — Surgery*

616.8 US ISSN 0001-6268
ACTA NEUROCHIRURGICA. SUPPLEMENTA. 1950. irreg., vol.34, 1984. price varies. Springer-Verlag, Journals, 175 Fifth Ave., New York, NY 10010. TEL 212-460-1500. (Also Berlin, Heidelberg, Tokyo and Vienna) Ed. F. Loew. (also avail. in microform from UMI; reprint service avail. from ISI) **Indexed:** Biol.Abstr., Ind.Med., INIS Atomind.
—BLDSC shelfmark: 0639.850000.
Formerly: Acta Neurochirurgica. Supplement (ISSN 0065-1419)

616.8 IT ISSN 0001-6276
CODEN: ACNLAC
ACTA NEUROLOGICA. (Text in English) 1946. bi-m. L.180000. Universita degli Studi di Napoli, Seconda Facolta di Medicina e Chirurgia, Clinica Neurologica, Nuovo Policlinico, Via S. Pansini 5, 80100 Naples, Italy. FAX 081-7463738. Ed. G.A. Buscaino. adv.; bk.rev.; charts; illus.; stat.; index; circ. 1,400.
Indexed: Biol.Abstr., Chem.Abstr., Curr.Adv.Ecol.Sci., Dent.Ind., Excerp.Med., Ind.Med., Int.Z.Bibelwiss., Psychol.Abstr.
—BLDSC shelfmark: 0639.900000.

616.8 BE ISSN 0300-9009
RC321 CODEN: ANUBBR
ACTA NEUROLOGICA BELGICA. (Supplements avail.) (Text in English and French) 1900. 5/yr. 2200 Fr. (foreign 2500 Fr.). Association des Societes Scientifiques Medicales Belges - Vereiniging van de Belgische Medische Wetenschappelijke Genootschappen, Av. Circulaire 138A, B-1180 Brussels, Belgium. TEL 02-374-5158. Ed. Dr. Andre Capon. **Indexed:** ASCA, Bibl.& Ind.Geol., Bibl.Dev.Med.& Child Neur., Biol.Abstr., Chem.Abstr., Curr.Cont., Excerp.Med., Ind.Med., Psychol.Abstr.
—BLDSC shelfmark: 0639.902000.
Supersedes in part: Acta Neurologica et Psychiatrica Belgica (ISSN 0001-6284)

MEDICAL SCIENCES — PSYCHIATRY AND NEUROLOGY

616.8   DK   ISSN 0001-6314
RC321   CODEN: ANRSAS
ACTA NEUROLOGICA SCANDINAVICA. (Text in English) 1961. m. DKK 2000 includes supplements. Munksgaard International Publishers Ltd., 35 Noerre Soegade, P.O. Box 1248, DK-1016 Copenhagen K, Denmark. TEL 33-127030. FAX 33-129387. TELEX 19431-MUNKS-DK. Eds. Mogens Dam, Ronald F. Polinsky. adv.; bk.rev.; bibl.; charts; illus.; index; circ. 1,400. (reprint service avail. from ISI) **Indexed:** ASCA, Bibl.Dev.Med.& Child Neur., Biol.Abstr., Biotech.Abstr., Chem.Abstr., Curr.Adv.Ecol.Sci., Curr.Cont., Dent.Ind., Dok.Arbeitsmed., Excerp.Med., Ind.Med., Ind.Sci.Rev., INIS Atomind., Nutr.Abstr., Psychol.Abstr., Sci.Cit.Ind.
—BLDSC shelfmark: 0639.910000.
Supersedes in part: Acta Psychiatrica et Neurologica Scandinavica.

616.8   DK   ISSN 0065-1427
CODEN: ANSLAC
ACTA NEUROLOGICA SCANDINAVICA. SUPPLEMENTUM. (Text in English) 1932. irreg. free to subscribers of Acta Neurologica Scandinavica. Munksgaard International Publishers Ltd., 35 Noerre Soegade, P.O. Box 2148, DK-1016 Copenhagen K, Denmark. TEL 33-127030. FAX 33-129387. TELEX 19431-MUNKS-DK. Eds. Mogens Dam, Ronald F. Polinsky. adv. (reprint service avail. from ISI) **Indexed:** Biol.Abstr., Chem.Abstr., Curr.Adv.Ecol.Sci., Curr.Cont., Excerp.Med., Ind.Med., INIS Atomind.
—BLDSC shelfmark: 0639.912000.

616.8   GW   ISSN 0001-6322
CODEN: ANPTAL
ACTA NEUROPATHOLOGICA. 1961. 12/yr. (in 2 vols., 6 nos./vol.). DM.2,352($1,218) (World Federation of Neurology) Springer-Verlag, Heidelberger Platz 3, D-1000 Berlin 33, Germany. TEL 030-8207-1. (Also Heidelberg, Tokyo, Vienna, and New York) Ed. K. Jellinger. adv.; bibl.; charts; illus.; index. (also avail. in microform from UMI; reprint service avail. from ISI) **Indexed:** ASCA, Biol.Abstr., Chem.Abstr., Curr.Adv.Ecol.Sci., Curr.Cont., Dent.Ind., Excerp.Med., Helminthol.Abstr., Ind.Med., Ind.Sci.Rev., Ind.Vet., INIS Atomind., Nutr.Abstr., Pig News & Info., Poult.Abstr., Protozool.Abstr., Rev.Med.& Vet.Mycol., Sci.Cit.Ind., Small Anim.Abstr., Vet.Bull.
—BLDSC shelfmark: 0639.920000.
Description: Provides information on subjects related to nerve tissue research based on modern investigative techniques, including histochemistry, electron microscopy, immunology, tissue culture, biophysics, neurochemistry, and experimental neuropathology.

616.8   GW   ISSN 0065-1435
CODEN: ANLSBX
ACTA NEUROPATHOLOGICA. SUPPLEMENT. 1962. irreg., no.9, 1983. price varies. Springer-Verlag, Heidelberger Platz 3, D-1000 Berlin 33, Germany. TEL 030-8207-1. (Also Heidelberg, Tokyo, Vienna, and New York) (also avail. in microform from UMI; reprint service avail. from ISI) **Indexed:** Biol.Abstr., Chem.Abstr., Ind.Med., Vet.Bull.
—BLDSC shelfmark: 0639.921000.

616.89   AG   ISSN 0001-6896
CODEN: APQPAS
ACTA PSIQUIATRICA Y PSICOLOGICA DE AMERICA LATINA. 1954. q. $50. Fundacion Acta Fondo para la Salud Mental, Malabia 2274 13 A, 1425 Buenos Aires, Argentina. FAX 541-7856935. Dir. Guillermo Vidal. adv.; bk.rev.; abstr.; charts; illus.; index; circ. 5,000. (reprint service avail. from ISI, UMI) **Indexed:** ASCA, Biol.Abstr., Chem.Abstr., Curr.Cont., Excerp.Med., Ind.Med., Psychol.Abstr., SSCI.
●Also available on CD-ROM.
—BLDSC shelfmark: 0661.399000.

616.89   DK   ISSN 0001-690X
CODEN: APYSA9
ACTA PSYCHIATRICA SCANDINAVICA. (Text in English) 1926. 12/yr. DKK 2045 includes supplements. Munksgaard International Publishers Ltd., 35 Noerre Soegade, P.O. Box 2148, DK-1016 Copenhagen K. TEL 33-127030. FAX 33-129387. TELEX 19431-MUNKS-DK. Ed. Jan-Otto Ottosson. adv.; bk.rev.; charts; illus.; index; circ. 1,900. (reprint service avail. from ISI) **Indexed:** Abstr.Health Care Manage.Stud., Adol.Ment.Hlth.Abstr., ASCA, Bibl.Dev.Med.& Child Neur., Biol.Abstr., Biotech.Abstr., Chem.Abstr., Curr.Adv.Ecol.Sci., Curr.Cont., Dent.Ind., Dok.Arbeitsmed., Excerp.Med., Ind.Med., Ind.Sci.Rev., INIS Atomind., Mid.East: Abstr.& Ind., Psychol.Abstr., Risk Abstr., Sci.Cit.Ind, SSCI.
—BLDSC shelfmark: 0661.470000.
Supersedes in part: Acta Psychiatrica et Neurologica Scandinavica.

616.8   DK   ISSN 0065-1591
CODEN: ASSUA6
ACTA PSYCHIATRICA SCANDINAVICA. SUPPLEMENTUM. (Text in English) 1932. irreg. free to subscribers of Acta Psychiatrica Scandinavica. Munksgaard International Publishers Ltd., P.O. Box 2148, DK-1016 Copenhagen K, Denmark. TEL 33-127030. FAX 33-129387. TELEX 19431-MUNKS-DK. Ed. Jan-Otto Ottosson. adv. (reprint service avail. from ISI) **Indexed:** Biol.Abstr., Chem.Abstr., Curr.Adv.Ecol.Sci., Curr.Cont., Excerp.Med., Ind.Med., INIS Atomind., Mid.East: Abstr.& Ind.
—BLDSC shelfmark: 0661.472000.

616.8   SP   ISSN 0300-5062
CODEN: ALNPAJ
ACTAS LUSO ESPANOLAS DE NEUROLOGIA PSIQUIATRIA Y CIENCIAS AFINES. 1940. bi-m. 4300 ptas.($80) Editorial Garsi, S.A., Londres, 17, 28028 Madrid, Spain. TEL 256-08-00. FAX 361-10-07. Ed. J.J. Lopez Ibor. circ. 2,000. **Indexed:** Biol.Abstr., Excerp.Med., Ind.Med.Esp., Ind.Med., Psychol.Abstr.
—BLDSC shelfmark: 0629.700000.
Former titles (until 1971): Actas Luso Espanolas de Neurologia y Psiquiatria (ISSN 0001-7329); (until 1946): Actas Espanolas de Neurologia y Psiquiatria (ISSN 0300-5054)

ACTING OUT. see SOCIAL SERVICES AND WELFARE

616.8   FR   ISSN 0300-8274
ACTUALITES PSYCHIATRIQUES. 1971. 8/yr. 200 F. (Europe and North Africa 350 F.). 27 av. Leon-Blum, 92350 Le Plessis-Robinson, France. TEL 46-30-09-61. Dir. H. Richou. adv.; bk.rev.; circ. 3,000.
—BLDSC shelfmark: 0677.329500.

616.8   US   ISSN 0065-2008
RJ499.A1
ADOLESCENT PSYCHIATRY; development and clinical studies. Represents: American Society for Adolescent Psychiatry. Annals. 1971. a. price varies. (American Society for Adolescent Psychiatry) University of Chicago Press, Journals Division, 5720 S. Woodlawn Ave., Chicago, IL 60637. TEL 312-702-7600. FAX 312-702-0694. TELEX 25-4603. (Orders to: Box 37005, Chicago, IL 60637) Ed. Sherman C. Feinstein. (also avail. in microfilm from PMC; reprint service avail. from UMI) **Indexed:** ASCA, Biol.Abstr., CINAHL, Psychol.Abstr., SSCI.
—BLDSC shelfmark: 0696.589000.
Description: Reports on specific clinical and theoretical issues, as well as considerations of social, cultural, and political themes. Contains scholarly articles from contributors in a variety of disciplines.
Refereed Serial

616.8   SI
ADVANCED SERIES IN NEUROSCIENCE. (Text in English) 1988. irreg., vol. 2, 1990. price varies. World Scientific Publishing Co. Pte. Ltd., Farrer Rd., P.O. Box 128, Singapore 9128, Singapore. TEL 3825663. FAX 3825919. TELEX RS 28561 WSPC. (UK addr.: 73 Lynton Mead, Totteridge, London N20 8DH, England. TEL 44-81-4463356; US addr.: 1060 Main St., Ste. 1B, River Edge, NJ 07661. TEL 800-227-7562)

616.8   US   ISSN 0095-4829
ADVANCES AND TECHNICAL STANDARDS IN NEUROSURGERY. 1974. irreg., no.17, 1990. price varies. Springer-Verlag, 175 Fifth Ave., New York, NY 10010. TEL 212-460-1500. (Also Berlin, Heidelberg, Tokyo and Vienna) Ed.Bd. (reprint service avail. from ISI)
—BLDSC shelfmark: 0698.820000.

ADVANCES IN BIOCHEMICAL PSYCHOPHARMACOLOGY. see PHARMACY AND PHARMACOLOGY

616.8   SZ   ISSN 0378-7354
CODEN: ABPSD5
ADVANCES IN BIOLOGICAL PSYCHIATRY. 1978. irreg. (approx. 2/yr.). price varies. S. Karger AG, Allschwilerstr. 10, P.O. Box, CH-4009 Basel, Switzerland. TEL 061-3061111. FAX 061-3061234. TELEX CH 962652. Eds. J. Mendlewicz, H.M. van Praag. (reprint service avail. from ISI) **Indexed:** Biol.Abstr., Chem.Abstr., Curr.Cont., Psychol.Abstr.
—BLDSC shelfmark: 0700.070000.

ADVANCES IN CONNECTIONIST AND NEURAL COMPUTATION THEORY. see COMPUTERS — Artificial Intelligence

ADVANCES IN CONTROL NETWORKS AND LARGE SCALE PARALLEL DISTRIBUTED PROCESSING MODELS. see COMPUTERS — Artificial Intelligence

616.853   US
ADVANCES IN EPILEPTOLOGY. 1980. irreg., vol.17, 1991. price varies. Raven Press, 1185 Ave. of the Americas, New York, NY 10036. TEL 212-930-9500. FAX 212-869-3495.

ADVANCES IN HUMAN FACTORS - ERGONOMICS. see PSYCHOLOGY

ADVANCES IN HUMAN PSYCHOPHARMACOLOGY; a research annual. see PHARMACY AND PHARMACOLOGY

ADVANCES IN NEUROCHEMISTRY. see BIOLOGY — Biological Chemistry

616.8   US   ISSN 0091-3952
RC321   CODEN: ADNRA3
ADVANCES IN NEUROLOGY. 1973. irreg., latest vol.57. price varies. Raven Press, 1185 Ave. of the Americas, New York, NY 10036. TEL 212-930-9500. FAX 212-869-3495. TELEX 640073. **Indexed:** Biol.Abstr., Chem.Abstr., Curr.Cont., Dent.Ind., Ind.Med.
—BLDSC shelfmark: 0709.482000.
Refereed Serial

615.75 616.8   US
▼**ADVANCES IN NEUROPSYCHIATRY AND PSYCHOPHARMACOLOGY.** 1991. irreg., vol.2, 1991. price varies. Raven Press, 1185 Ave. of the Americas, New York, NY 10036. TEL 212-930-9500. FAX 212-869-3495.

616.8   US
▼**ADVANCES IN NEUROSCIENCES.** 1991. irreg. price varies. Raven Press, 1185 Ave. of the Americas, New York, NY 10036. TEL 212-930-9500. FAX 212-869-3495.

616.8   US   ISSN 0302-2366
CODEN: AVNSBV
ADVANCES IN NEUROSURGERY. (Includes Gesellschaft fuer Neurochirurgie. Proceedings) 1973. irreg., vol.17, 1989. price varies. Springer-Verlag, 175 Fifth Ave., New York, NY 10010. TEL 212-460-1500. (And Berlin, Heidelberg, Tokyo and Vienna) (reprint service avail. from ISI) **Indexed:** Biol.Abstr., Chem.Abstr.
—BLDSC shelfmark: 0709.483000.

616.8   US   ISSN 0146-0722
CODEN: APRTDE
ADVANCES IN PAIN RESEARCH AND THERAPY. 1976. irreg., latest vol.20. price varies. Raven Press, 1185 Ave. of the Americas, New York, NY 10036. TEL 212-930-9500. FAX 212-869-3495. TELEX 640073. Ed. John J. Bonica. index. **Indexed:** Biol.Abstr., Chem.Abstr., Curr.Cont., Ind.Sci.Rev., Sci.Cit.Ind.
—BLDSC shelfmark: 0709.576000.
Refereed Serial

ADVANCES IN PERSONALITY ASSESSMENT. see PSYCHOLOGY

MEDICAL SCIENCES — PSYCHIATRY AND NEUROLOGY

616.8 SZ ISSN 0065-3268
ADVANCES IN PSYCHOSOMATIC MEDICINE. (Text in English) 1960. irreg. (approx. 1/yr.). price varies. S. Karger AG, Allschwilerstr. 10, P.O. Box, CH-4009 Basel, Switzerland. TEL 061-3061111. FAX 061-3061234. TELEX CH 962652. Ed. T.N. Wise. (reprint service avail. from ISI, back issues avail.) **Indexed:** Biol.Abstr., Chem.Abstr., Curr.Cont., Ind.Med., SSCI.
—BLDSC shelfmark: 0711.100000.

616.85 NE ISSN 0922-3061
ADVANCES IN SUICIDOLOGY. 1989. irreg. price varies. E.J. Brill, P.O. Box 9000, 2300 PA Leiden, Netherlands. TEL 071-312624. FAX 071-317532. TELEX 39296 BRILL NL. (In N. America: E.J. Brill, 24 Hudson St., Kinderhook, NY 12106. TEL 800-962-4406)
Description: Scholarly treatment of issues pertaining to the prevention of suicide.

AFTERWORDS; suicide: the busy professionals newsletter. see PSYCHOLOGY

616.8 GW ISSN 0302-4350
W1 AK995GN
AKTUELLE NEUROLOGIE. 1974. bi-m. DM.216. Georg Thieme Verlag, Ruedigerstr. 14, Postfach 104853, 7000 Stuttgart 10, Germany. Ed.Bd. adv.; index; circ. 2,000. (reprint service avail. from UMI) **Indexed:** Biol.Abstr., Curr.Adv.Genetics & Molec.Biol., Curr.Cont., Excerp.Med., INIS Atomind.
—BLDSC shelfmark: 0785.775000.

ALZHEIMER DISEASE AND ASSOCIATED DISORDERS. see GERONTOLOGY AND GERIATRICS

616.89 US ISSN 0890-8567
RJ499.A1 CODEN: JAAPEE
AMERICAN ACADEMY OF CHILD AND ADOLESCENT PSYCHIATRY. JOURNAL. 1962. bi-m. $80 to individuals; institutions $135. Williams & Wilkins, 428 E. Preston St., Baltimore, MD 21202. TEL 301-528-4000. FAX 301-528-4312. Ed. Dr. John F. McDermott, Jr. adv.; bk.rev.; abstr.; bibl.; charts; illus.; index; circ. 7,450. (also avail. in microform from WWS) **Indexed:** Adol.Ment.Hlth.Abstr., ASSIA, Bibl.Dev.Med.& Child Neur., Child Devel.Abstr., Dent.Ind., Dok.Arbeitsmed., Educ.Ind., Excerp.Med., Ind.Med., Mid:East: Abstr.& Ind., NRN, Psychol.Abstr., Risk Abstr., Soc.Work Res.& Abstr.
—BLDSC shelfmark: 4683.690000.
Formerly: American Academy of Child Psychiatry. Journal (ISSN 0002-7138)
Description: Original papers in psychiatric research and treatment of the child and adolescent.
Refereed Serial

616.89 340 US ISSN 0091-634X
RA1151
AMERICAN ACADEMY OF PSYCHIATRY AND THE LAW. BULLETIN. 1973. q. $45 to individuals; institutions $65. American Academy of Psychiatry and the Law, 819 Park Ave., Baltimore, MD 21201. TEL 301-539-0379. FAX 301-385-0154. Ed. Dr. Seymour Halleck. bk.rev.; bibl.; circ. 1,750. (also avail. in microform from UMI,WSH; reprint service avail. from UMI,WSH) **Indexed:** Abstr.Bk.Rev.Curr.Leg.Per., Adol.Ment.Hlth.Abstr., C.L.I., Crim.Just.Abstr., Dok.Arbeitsmed., Excerp.Med., Hlth.Ind., Med.Ind., L.R.I., Leg.Cont., Leg.Per., Psychol.Abstr. Key Title: Bulletin of the American Academy of Psychiatry and the Law.

AMERICAN ACADEMY OF PSYCHIATRY AND THE LAW. NEWSLETTER. see LAW

616.8 US ISSN 0895-8033
AMERICAN ASSOCIATION ON MENTAL RETARDATION. NEWS AND NOTES. 1988. bi-m. $35. American Association on Mental Retardation, 1719 Kalorama Rd., N.W., Washington, DC 20009-2683. TEL 202-387-1968. FAX 202-387-2193. Ed. Margaret Seiter. adv.; circ. 8,247. (tabloid format; back issues avail.)
Description: For individuals with special needs in the field of mental retardation.

616.89 150 US ISSN 0065-860X
BF173.A2 CODEN: AMIAAO
AMERICAN IMAGO; a psychoanalytic journal for culture, science and the arts. 1939. q. $28 to individuals; institutions $58. (Association for Applied Psychoanalysis) Johns Hopkins University Press, Journals Publishing Division, 701 W. 40th St., Ste. 275, Baltimore, MD 21211. TEL 401-516-6980. FAX 410-516-6998. Eds. Martin J. Gliserman. bk.rev.; bibl.; charts; illus.; index; circ. 872. (also avail. in microform from UMI,MIM,PMC; back issues avail.: from Kraus-Thompson Org. Ltd., Rte. 100, Millwood, NY 10546 (vols. 1-22) and WSU Press (vols. 23-43); reprint service avail. from KTO) **Indexed:** Abstr.Engl.Stud., Arts & Hum.Cit.Ind., Biog.Ind., Chem.Abstr., Curr.Cont., Film Lit.Ind. (1974-), Ind.Med, M.L.A., Mag.Ind., Mid.East: Abstr.& Ind., Psychoanal.Abstr., Psychol.Abstr., R.G., SSCI.
Description: Contributors investigate culture, science, and the arts, religion, philosophy, history and education from a psychoanalytic perspective.
Refereed Serial

AMERICAN JOURNAL OF ART THERAPY; art in psychotherapy, education, and rehabilitation. see EDUCATION — Special Education And Rehabilitation

616.804 US ISSN 0002-9238
RC386.5 CODEN: AJETA6
AMERICAN JOURNAL OF E E G TECHNOLOGY. 1960. q. $35 (foreign $45). American Society of Electroneurodiagnostic Technologists, Inc., Executive Office, 204 W. Seventh, Carroll, IA 51401. TEL 712-792-2978. Ed. Janet Ghigo. adv.; bk.rev.; charts; illus.; index, cum.index; circ. 3,500. (back issues avail.) **Indexed:** Biol.Abstr., Excerp.Med., Psychol.Abstr., Sci.Abstr.
—BLDSC shelfmark: 0824.400000.
Refereed Serial

AMERICAN JOURNAL OF FORENSIC PSYCHIATRY. see MEDICAL SCIENCES — Forensic Sciences

616.89 US ISSN 0002-953X
RC321 CODEN: AJPSAO
AMERICAN JOURNAL OF PSYCHIATRY. 1844. m. $56 (foreign $86). (American Psychiatric Association) American Psychiatric Press, Inc., Journals Division, 1400 K St., N.W., Washington, DC 20005. TEL 202-682-6020. FAX 202-682-6016. (UK addr.: 17 Belgrave Sq., London SW1X 8PG, England) Ed. Dr. John C. Nemiah. adv.; bk.rev.; bibl.; charts; illus.; index; circ. 45,000. (also avail. in microform from UMI,PMC) **Indexed:** Abstr.Health Care Manage.Stud., ASSIA, Bibl.Dev.Med.& Child Neur., Biol.Abstr., Biotech.Abstr., C.I.S. Abstr., Chem.Abstr., Crim.Just.Abstr., Curr.Adv.Ecol.Sci., Curr.Cont., Dairy Sci.Abstr., Dent.Ind., Excerp.Med., FAMLI, Hosp.Lit.Ind., HRIS, Ind.Med., Ind.Sci.Rev., Int.Nurs.Ind., Lang.& Lang.Behav.Abstr., Med.Care Rev., Mid.East: Abstr.& Ind., NRN, Nutr.Abstr., Past.Care & Couns.Abstr., Psychol.Abstr., Psycscan C.P., Risk Abstr., Soc.Sci.Ind., Soc.Work Res.& Abstr., SSCI.
●Also available online. Vendor(s): BRS, BRS/Saunders Colleague.
—BLDSC shelfmark: 0835.000000.
Description: Presents clinical research and discussion on current psychiatric issues for psychiatrists and other mental health professionals.
Refereed Serial

616.8 US ISSN 0002-9564
RC321 CODEN: AJPTAR
AMERICAN JOURNAL OF PSYCHOTHERAPY. 1946. q. $50. Association for the Advancement of Psychotherapy, 114 E. 78th St., New York, NY 10021. TEL 212-529-1087. Ed. Stanley Lesse. adv.; bk.rev.; abstr.; bibl.; index, cum.index: 1941-1965; circ. 5,000. (also avail. in microform from RPI) **Indexed:** Adol.Ment.Hlth.Abstr., Biol.Abstr., Chem.Abstr., CINAHL, Curr.Adv.Ecol.Sci., Curr.Cont., Excerp.Med., Ind.Med., Ind.Sci.Rev., Lang.& Lang.Behav.Abstr., Mid.East: Abstr.& Ind., Psychol.Abstr., Psycscan C.P., Sci.Cit.Ind, SSCI.
—BLDSC shelfmark: 0835.600000.
Refereed Serial

AMERICAN JOURNAL OF SPEECH - LANGUAGE PATHOLOGY; a journal of clinical practice. see MEDICAL SCIENCES — Otorhinolaryngology

616.8 US ISSN 1055-0496
▼**AMERICAN JOURNAL ON ADDICTIONS.** 1992. q. $85 to individuals (foreign $100); institutions $135 (foreign $150). (American Academy of Psychiatrists in Alcoholism and Addictions) American Psychiatric Press, Inc., Journals Division, 1400 K St., N.W., Ste. 1101, Washington, DC 20005. TEL 202-682-6130. FAX 202-789-2648. (UK addr.: 17 Belgrave Sq., London SW1X 8PG, England) Ed. Dr. Sheldon Miller. bk.rev.; abstr.; bibl.; charts; illus.; stat.; index.
Description: Presents original research related to the assessment and treatment of addictive disorders.

616.858 US ISSN 0895-8017
RC326 CODEN: AJMREA
AMERICAN JOURNAL ON MENTAL RETARDATION. 1876. bi-m. $95. American Association on Mental Retardation, 1719 Kalorama Rd., N.W., Washington, DC 20009-2683. TEL 202-387-1968. FAX 202-387-2193. Ed. Earl C. Butterfield. adv.; bk.rev.; bibl.; charts; illus.; stat.; index; circ. 11,600. (also avail. in microform from UMI; back issues avail.) **Indexed:** Adol.Ment.Hlth.Abstr., Bibl.Dev.Med.& Child Neur., Bibl.Ind, Biol.Abstr., Bk.Rev.Ind. (1980-), C.I.J.E., Chem.Abstr., Chic.Per.Ind., Child.Bk.Rev.Ind. (1980-), Child Devel.Abstr., Curr.Adv.Ecol.Sci., Curr.Cont., Dent.Ind., Educ.Admin.Abstr., Educ.Ind., Except.Child.Educ.Abstr., Excerpt.Med., Ind.Med., Ind.Sci.Rev., Lang.& Lang.Behav.Abstr., Mid.East: Abstr.& Ind., NRN, Psychol.Abstr., Psyscan D.P., Rehabil.Lit., Sci.Cit.Ind., Soc.Work Res.& Abstr., Sp.Ed.Needs Abstr., SSCI.
—BLDSC shelfmark: 0828.280000.
Formerly (until 1987): American Journal of Mental Deficiency (ISSN 0002-9351)
Description: Current research on biological, behavioral and educational sciences in mental retardation and related developmental disabilities.

616.89 US ISSN 0090-1881
AMERICAN PSYCHIATRIC ASSOCIATION. SCIENTIFIC PROCEEDINGS IN SUMMARY FORM. a. $15. (American Psychiatric Association) American Psychiatric Press, Inc., Journals Division, 1400 K St., N.W., Washington, DC 20005. TEL 202-682-6000. FAX 202-789-2648. (UK addr.: 17 Belgrave Sq., London SW1X 8PG, England)

616.89 US
AMERICAN PSYCHIATRIC ASSOCIATION. TASK FORCE REPORTS. 1970. irreg., no.21, 1982. price varies. (American Psychiatric Association) American Psychiatric Press, Inc., Journals Division, 1400 K St., N.W., Washington, DC 20005. TEL 202-682-6268. FAX 202-789-2648. (UK addr.: 17 Belgrave Sq., London SW1X 8PG, England)

AMERICAN PSYCHOANALYTIC ASSOCIATION. JOURNAL. see PSYCHOLOGY

616.89 US ISSN 0091-7389
AMERICAN PSYCHOPATHOLOGICAL ASSOCIATION. PROCEEDINGS OF THE ANNUAL MEETING. 1945. a. price varies. Guilford Publications, Inc., 72 Spring St., 4th Fl., New York, NY 10012. TEL 212-431-9800. FAX 212-966-6708. (reprint service avail. from UMI)

616.8 US
AMERICAN PSYCHOPATHOLOGICAL ASSOCIATION SERIES. 1978. a. price varies. Raven Press, 1185 Ave. of the Americas, New York, NY 10036. TEL 212-930-9500. FAX 212-869-3495.

616.8 US
AMERICAN SOCIETY FOR ADOLESCENT PSYCHIATRY. NEWSLETTER. 1967. 4/yr. $10 or membership. American Society for Adolescent Psychiatry, 4330 East-West Hwy., Ste. 1117, Bethesda, MD 20814. FAX 301-656-0989. Ed. Dr. Leonard Henschel. adv.; bk.rev.; stat.; circ. 2,700.

MEDICAL SCIENCES — PSYCHIATRY AND NEUROLOGY

616.8 US ISSN 0066-0132
QP356.3
AMERICAN SOCIETY FOR NEUROCHEMISTRY. TRANSACTIONS. 1970. a. $15 (foreign $20). American Society for Neurochemistry, c/o Lawrence F. Eng, Sec., Dept. of Pathology Research, Rm. 151B, Veterans Administration Medical Center, 3801 Miranda Ave., Palo Alto, CA 94304. FAX 415-725-7023. adv.; circ. 1,500. (back issues avail.)
—BLDSC shelfmark: 8898.050000.
Description: Annual meeting of investigators in the American hemisphere in neurochemistry, neurobiology, and molecular biology.

616.8 SZ ISSN 1011-6982
CODEN: AMPDE4
ANIMAL MODELS OF PSYCHIATRIC DISORDERS. (Text in English) 1988. irreg. price varies. S. Karger AG, Allschwilerstr. 10, P.O. Box, CH-4009 Basel, Switzerland. TEL 061-3061111. FAX 021-3061234. TELEX CH 962652. Ed.Bd.
—BLDSC shelfmark: 0905.008000.

618.2 616.8 UK ISSN 0267-3061
ANNA FREUD CENTRE. BULLETIN. 1978. q. $50. Anna Freud Centre, 21 Maresfield Gardens, London NW3 5SH, England. FAX 071-794-6506. Ed. George Moran. bk.rev.; circ. 400. **Indexed:** Psychol.Abstr.
—BLDSC shelfmark: 2393.986000.
Formerly (until 1985): Hampstead Clinic. Bulletin (ISSN 0263-9688)
Description: For diagnosticians, therapists and social workers. Contains research and clinical papers from the center's psychoanalytic study and treatment of children.

616.8 FR ISSN 0768-7559
ANNALES DE PSYCHIATRIE. 8/yr. 490 F. (foreign 705 F.). Expansion Scientifique Francaise, 15 rue Saint Benoit, 75221 Paris Cedex 06, France. TEL 1-45-48-42-60. FAX 1-45-44-81-55.
—BLDSC shelfmark: 0994.800000.

616.8 US ISSN 1040-1237
RC321 CODEN: APSYEZ
ANNALS OF CLINICAL PSYCHIATRY. 1989. q. $150 (foreign $172)(effective 1992). (American Academy of Clinical Psychiatrists) Elsevier Science Publishing Co., Inc. (New York), 655 Ave. of the Americas, New York, NY 10010. TEL 212-989-5800. FAX 212-633-3965. TELEX 420643 AEP UI. Ed. Dr. Charles L. Rich. **Indexed:** Excerp.Med., Psychol.Abstr., Sociol.Abstr.
—BLDSC shelfmark: 1040.245000.
Description: Provides clinical practitioners with the results of current research into the phenomenology and treatment of psychiatric disorders.
Refereed Serial

616.8 US ISSN 0364-5134
RC321 CODEN: ANNED3
ANNALS OF NEUROLOGY. 1977. m. $110 to individuals (foreign $170); institutions $150 (foreign $205); residents $80 (foreign $122)(effective Nov. 1991. (American Neurological Association) Little, Brown and Company, Medical Journals, 34 Beacon St., Boston, MA 02108. TEL 617-859-5500. FAX 617-859-0629. (Co-sponsor: Child Neurology Society) Ed. Dr. Arthur K. Asbury. adv.; bk.rev.; abstr.; charts; illus.; stat.; index; circ. 9,313. (also avail. in microform from UMI; back issues avail.; reprint service avail. from UMI) **Indexed:** Abstr.Inter.Med., Behav.Med.Abstr., Bibl.Dev.Med.& Child Neur., Biol.Abstr., Chem.Abstr., Curr.Adv.Ecol.Sci., Curr.Cont., Dent.Ind., Dok.Arbeitsmed., Excerp.Med., Ind.Med., Ind.Sci.Rev., INIS Atomind., Nutr.Abstr., Rev.Plant Path., Risk Abstr., Sci.Cit.Ind.
●Also available online. Vendor(s): BRS, Mead Data Central.
—BLDSC shelfmark: 1043.140000.
Description: Contains original articles on research and clinical advances, brief communications, neurological progress, and editorials.
Refereed Serial

618.928 US ISSN 0066-4030
RJ499.A1
ANNUAL PROGRESS IN CHILD PSYCHIATRY AND CHILD DEVELOPMENT. 1968. a. price varies. Brunner-Mazel Publishing Co., 19 Union Sq. W., New York, NY 10003. TEL 212-924-3344. Eds. S. Chess, A. Thomas. bk.rev. (reprint service avail. from UMI) **Indexed:** Biol.Abstr., Psychol.Abstr.
—BLDSC shelfmark: 1091.400000.
Description: New developments and trends in child psychiatry and development for professionals working with normal and disturbed children.
Refereed Serial

ANNUAL REVIEW OF ADDICTIONS RESEARCH AND TREATMENT. see *DRUG ABUSE AND ALCOHOLISM*

616.8 US ISSN 0147-006X
QP351 CODEN: ARNSD5
ANNUAL REVIEW OF NEUROSCIENCE. 1977. a. $44 (foreign $49)(effective Jan. 1992). Annual Reviews Inc., 4139 El Camino Way, Box 10139, Palo Alto, CA 94303-0897. TEL 415-493-4400. FAX 415-855-9815. TELEX 910-290-0275. Ed. W. Maxwell Cowan. bibl.; index, cum.index. (back issues avail.; reprint service avail. from ISI) **Indexed:** Biol.Abstr., Chem.Abstr., Curr.Adv.Ecol.Sci., Curr.Cont., Excerp.Med., Ind.Med., Ind.Sci.Rev., Psychol.Abstr., Sci.Cit.Ind.
—BLDSC shelfmark: 1523.350000.
Description: Original reviews of critical literature and current developments in neuroscience.
Refereed Serial

616.8 UK ISSN 0268-7038
RC425
APHASIOLOGY. 1987. bi-m. £28.23($49.50) to individuals; institutions £154($270). Taylor & Francis Ltd., Rankine Rd., Basingstoke, Hants RG24 0PR, England. TEL 0256-840366. FAX 0256-479438. TELEX 858540. (U.S. subscr. to: Taylor & Francis Inc., 1900 Frost Rd., Ste. 101, Bristol, PA 19007-1598) Eds. Dave Muller, Chris Code. bk.rev.; bibl.; charts; illus. (back issues avail.) **Indexed:** Excerp.Med., Lang.& Lang.Behav.Abstr. (1987-).
—BLDSC shelfmark: 1567.923000.
Description: Information on all aspects of brain damage-related language problems for neurologists, speech therapists, psychologists in universities, hospitals and clinics.
Refereed Serial

APPLIED PSYCHOLINGUISTICS; psychological studies of language processes. see *LINGUISTICS*

616.8 GW ISSN 0172-7311
ARBEITSGEMEINSCHAFT FUER KLINISCHE NEPHROLOGIE. MITTEILUNGEN. a. DM.32. (Arbeitsgemeinschaft fuer Klinische Nephrologie e.V.) Vandenhoeck und Ruprecht, Postfach 3753, Theaterstr. 13, 3400 Goettingen, Germany. TEL 0551-6959-22. FAX 0551-695917. Ed. E. Quellhorst.

616.8 574.1 IT ISSN 0003-9829
CODEN: AIBLAS
ARCHIVES ITALIENNES DE BIOLOGIE; a journal of neuroscience. (Text in English or French) 1882. q. L.170000($105) (effective 1992). Universita degli Studi di Pisa, Rettorato, Lungarno A. Pacinotti 43, Pisa, Italy. FAX 39-50552183. Ed. O. Pompeiano. bk.rev.; abstr.; bibl.; charts; illus.; index; circ. 400. (also avail. in microfiche from BHP; back issues avail.) **Indexed:** Biol.Abstr., Chem.Abstr., Curr.Adv.Ecol.Sci., Curr.Cont., Excerp.Med., Helminthol.Abstr., Ind.Med., Ind.Sci.Rev., Nutr.Abstr., Phys.Ber., Psychol.Abstr., Sci.Cit.Ind.
—BLDSC shelfmark: 1637.200000.

616.8 150 US ISSN 0887-6177
ARCHIVES OF CLINICAL NEUROPSYCHOLOGY. 1986. 6/yr. $185 (effective 1992). Pergamon Press, Inc., Journals Division, 660 White Plains Rd., Tarrytown, NY 10591-5153. TEL 914-524-9200. FAX 914-333-2444. (And: Headington Hill Hall, Oxford OX3 0BW, England. TEL 0865-794141) Ed. Cecil Reynolds. (also avail. in microform; back issues avail.) **Indexed:** Excerp.Med., Psychol.Abstr.
—BLDSC shelfmark: 1634.090000.
Refereed Serial

616.89 US ISSN 0003-990X
RC321 CODEN: ARGPAQ
ARCHIVES OF GENERAL PSYCHIATRY. 1959. m. $58. American Medical Association, 515 N. State St., Chicago, IL 60610. TEL 312-464-0183. FAX 312-464-5834. Ed. Dr. Daniel X. Freedman. adv.; bk.rev.; bibl.; charts; illus.; index; circ. 38,500. (also avail. in microform from MIM,UMI) **Indexed:** Abstr.Health Care Manage.Stud., Adol.Ment.Hlth.Abstr., Bibl.Dev.Med.& Child Neur., Biol.Abstr., Biotech.Abstr., Chem.Abstr., Child Devel.Abstr., Curr.Adv.Ecol.Sci., Curr.Cont., Dent.Ind., Excerp.Med., I.P.A., Ind.Med., Ind.Sci.Rev., Mid.East: Abstr.& Ind., NRN, Nutr.Abstr., Psychol.Abstr., Psycscan C.P., Risk Abstr., Sci.Cit.Ind, SSCI.
●Also available online. Vendor(s): Mead Data Central.
—BLDSC shelfmark: 1634.350000.
Refereed Serial

616.8 016 US ISSN 0003-9942
RC321 CODEN: ARNEAS
ARCHIVES OF NEUROLOGY. 1959. m. $74. American Medical Association, 515 N. State St., Chicago, IL 60610. TEL 312-464-0183. FAX 312-464-5834. Ed. Dr. Robert J. Joynt. adv.; bk.rev.; charts; illus.; index; circ. 17,500. (also avail. in microform from PMC,UMI) **Indexed:** Abstr.Inter.Med., Bibl.Dev.Med.& Child Neur., Biol.Abstr., Biotech.Abstr., Chem.Abstr., Curr.Adv.Cancer Res., Curr.Adv.Ecol.Sci., Curr.Adv.Genetics & Molec.Biol., Curr.Cont., Dent.Ind., Dok.Arbeitsmed., Excerp.Med., Ind.Med., Ind.Sci.Rev., INIS Atomind., Nutr.Abstr., Psychol.Abstr., Rev.Med.& Vet.Mycol., Sci.Cit.Ind, So.Pac.Per.Ind.
●Also available online. Vendor(s): Mead Data Central.
—BLDSC shelfmark: 1638.400000.
Refereed Serial

ARCHIVES OF PSYCHIATRIC NURSING. see *MEDICAL SCIENCES — Nurses And Nursing*

616.89 IT
ARCHIVIO DI PSICHIATRIA GENERALE. q. L.90000($150) (effective 1992). Casa Editrice Idelson, Via A. De Gasperi 55, 80133 Naples, Italy. TEL 081-5524733. FAX 081-5518295. Ed. Ernesto Catena.

616.8 IT ISSN 0004-0150
CODEN: APNPAD
ARCHIVIO DI PSICOLOGIA, NEUROLOGIA E PSICHIATRIA. (Text in English, French and Italian; summaries in English, French and German) 1940. q. L.118000($90) (effective 1992). (Universita Cattolica del Sacro Cuore, Istituto di Psicologia) Vita e Pensiero, Largo Gemelli 1, 20123 Milan, Italy. TEL 02-8856310. FAX 02-8856260. TELEX 321033 UCATMI 1. Ed. Leonardo Ancona. adv.; bk.rev.; abstr.; bibl.; charts; illus.; stat.; index. **Indexed:** Biol.Abstr., Ind.Med., Lang.& Lang.Behav.Abstr., Psychol.Abstr.
—BLDSC shelfmark: 1647.880000.
Description: Covers psychology and neurology.

616.8 364 EC ISSN 0004-0541
ARCHIVOS DE CRIMINOLOGIA, NEURO-PSIQUIATRIA Y DISCIPLINAS CONEXAS. (Second Series) vol.12, 1964. q. S/3000($5) per no. Universidad Central del Ecuador, Instituto de Criminologia, Apdo. 3663, Quito, Ecuador. TEL 542-971. Dr. Hernando Rosero Cueva. bk.rev.; abstr.; bibl.; charts; illus.; stat.; index; circ. 1,200. (also avail. in microfilm) **Indexed:** Biol.Abstr.

616.8 SP ISSN 0004-0576
CODEN: ARNBBK
ARCHIVOS DE NEUROBIOLOGIA. (Text in Spanish; summaries in English) 1920. bi-m. 4500 ptas.($80) Editorial Garsi, S.A., Londres, 17, 28028 Madrid, Spain. TEL 256-08-00. FAX 361-10-07. Ed. V. Rodriguez Lafora. circ. 1,000. **Indexed:** Biol.Abstr., Dent.Ind., Excerp.Med., Ind.Med.Esp., Ind.Med., Psychol.Abstr., Yrbk.Assoc.Educ.& Rehab.Blind.
—BLDSC shelfmark: 1655.450000.

616.8 IT
▼**ARGOMENTI DI NEUROLOGIA.** 1991. q. Masson Italia Periodici, Via Statuto 2-4, 20121 Milan, Italy. TEL 02-6367-1. FAX 02-6367-211. Ed. Nicola Canal.

MEDICAL SCIENCES — PSYCHIATRY AND NEUROLOGY

616.89   BL   ISSN 0004-282X
CODEN: ANPIAM
ARQUIVOS DE NEURO-PSIQUIATRIA. (Text in Portuguese; summaries in English) 1943. q. $80 (typically set in Oct.). (Academia Brasileira de Neurologia - Brazilian Academy of Neurology) Associacao Arquivos Neuro-Psiquiatria Dr. Oswaldo Lange, Caixa Postal 8877, Sao Paulo 01065, SP, Brazil.
TEL 5511-2879726. FAX 5511-2898879. Ed. Dr. Antonio Spina-Franca. adv.; bk.rev.; abstr.; bibl.; charts; index, cum.index: 1943-1982; circ. 1,400. (also avail. in microfilm from UMI) **Indexed:** Biol.Abstr., Dent.Ind., Excerp.Med., Ind.Med., Psychol.Abstr.
●Also available on CD-ROM.
—BLDSC shelfmark: 1695.630000.
Description: Covers the medical sciences of psychiatry, neurology, and applied neuroscience.

616.8   BL   ISSN 0103-0809
RA790.7.S25
ARQUIVOS DE SAUDE MENTAL DO ESTADO DE SAO PAULO. (Supplement avail.) (Text in Portuguese; summaries in English) 1924. a. exchange basis. Biblioteca do Hospital de Juqueri, Franco da Rocha E.F.S.J., CEP 07780 Sao Paulo, Brazil.
FAX 432-54-44. TELEX 11-79736. Ed.Bd. bk.rev.; charts; illus.; circ. 1,000.
Formerly: Sao Paulo. Coordenadoria de Saude Mental. Arquivos (ISSN 0080-6404)

616.89   BL   ISSN 0102-7646
ASSOCIACAO BRASILEIRA DE PSIQUIATRIA E ASOCIACION PSIQUIATRICA DE LA AMERICA LATINA. REVISTA. Abbreviated title: Revista A B P - A P A L. (Text in Portuguese; summaries in English, Spanish) 1979. q. Cr.$20000($100) (Associacao Brasileira de Psiquiatria) Ponto Cardeal Publicacoes, Ltda., Rua Borges Lagoa, 394, CEP 04038 Sao Paulo, Brazil.
TEL 011-549-6699. (Co-sponsor: Asociacion Psiquiatrica de la America Latina) Ed. Dr. Helena M. Calil. adv.; bk.rev.; bibl.; charts; stat.; circ. 3,500. **Indexed:** Biol.Abstr., Excerp.Med., Ind.Med., Psychol.Abstr.
Formerly: Revista Brasileira de Psiquiatria.
Description: Papers on psychiatry and correlated disciplines of general interest to mental health professionals from Brazil and other Latin American countries.

ASSOCIATION FOR APPLIED PSYCHOPHYSIOLOGY AND BIOFEEDBACK. PROCEEDINGS OF THE ANNUAL MEETING. see *PSYCHOLOGY*

ASSOCIATION FOR CHILD PSYCHOANALYSIS. NEWSLETTER. see *CHILDREN AND YOUTH — About*

610   US   ISSN 0091-7443
CODEN: RPARA5
ASSOCIATION FOR RESEARCH IN NERVOUS AND MENTAL DISEASE. RESEARCH PUBLICATIONS. a., latest vol.70. price varies. Raven Press, 1185 Ave. of the Americas, New York, NY 10036.
TEL 212-930-9500. FAX 212-869-3495. TELEX 640073. **Indexed:** Biol.Abstr., Chem.Abstr., Curr.Cont., Dent.Ind., Ind.Med.
Refereed Serial

610 016   US   ISSN 0271-1311
AUDIO-DIGEST PSYCHIATRY. 1971. s-m. $168.
Audio-Digest Foundation (Subsidiary of: California Medical Association), 1577 E. Chevy Chase Dr., Glendale, CA 91206. TEL 213-245-8505.
FAX 818-240-7379. Ed. Claron L. Oakley. (audio cassette)
Refereed Serial

616.858 371.9   AT   ISSN 0726-3864
CODEN: ANZDDQ
AUSTRALIA AND NEW ZEALAND JOURNAL OF DEVELOPMENTAL DISABILITIES. 1970. q. Aus.$55 to individuals; institutions Aus.$90. Australian Society for the Study of Intellectual Disability, Unit for Rehabilitation Studies, Special Education Centre, University of Newcastle, N.S.W. 2308, Australia.
TEL 02-805-8706. Ed. P.J. Foreman. adv.; bk.rev.; charts; illus.; index; circ. 1,400. (tabloid format; also avail. in microfilm from UMI; reprint service avail. from UMI) **Indexed:** Aus.P.A.I.S., Biol.Abstr., Child Devel.Abstr., Except.Child Educ.Abstr., Excerp.Med., Ind.Med., Ment.Retard.Abstr., Psychol.Abstr., Rehabil.Lit., Sp.Ed.Needs Abstr.
—BLDSC shelfmark: 1796.550000.
Former titles (until vol.7, 1981): Australian Journal of Developmental Disabilities (ISSN 0159-9011); (Until vol.6, Mar.1980): Australian Journal of Mental Retardation (ISSN 0045-0634)
Description: Reports of research in the area of mental retardation and related disabilities.

616.89   AT   ISSN 0004-8674
RC321   CODEN: ANZPBQ
AUSTRALIAN & NEW ZEALAND JOURNAL OF PSYCHIATRY. 1967. q. Aus.$60 to individuals; institutions Aus.$90. Royal Australian and New Zealand College of Psychiatrists, P.O. Box 126, Karrinyup, W.A. 6018, Australia. TEL 09-401-1799. Ed. Sidney Bloch. adv.; bk.rev.; abstr.; charts; illus.; index; circ. 3,100. **Indexed:** Adol.Ment.Hlth.Abstr., Aus.Sci.Ind., Biol.Abstr., Curr.Cont., Dok.Arbeitsmed., Excerp.Med., Ind.Med., Mid.East: Abstr.& Ind., Nutr.Abstr., Psychol.Abstr., So.Pac.Per.Ind., Sp.Ed.Needs Abstr., SSCI.
—BLDSC shelfmark: 1796.893000.

AUSTRALIAN JOURNAL OF PSYCHOTHERAPY. see *PSYCHOLOGY*

616.8 360   US   ISSN 0740-5197
B A S H MAGAZINE. (Bulimia Anorexia Self-Help) 1982. m. $25. B A S H, Inc., Box 39903, St. Louis, MO 63139. TEL 800-227-4785. FAX 314-768-3794. Ed. Felix E.F. Larocca, M.D. bk.rev.; index; circ. 1,000. (back issues avail.)
Formerly: B A S H Monthly Newsletter.
Description: Information on eating and mood disorders.

616.8 910.03   US
B P A QUARTERLY.* 1969. q. $20 to individuals; institutions $45. Black Psychiatrists of America, c/o Dr. Thelissa Harris, 664 Prospect Ave., CT 06015. Ed. Dr. William Lawson. adv.; bk.rev.; circ. 600.
Former titles: Bottom Line (New York, 1969); Black Psychiatrists of America Newsletter.

BEHAVIORAL AND BRAIN SCIENCES; an international journal of current research and theory with open peer commentary. see *PSYCHOLOGY*

616.8   NE   ISSN 0166-4328
CODEN: BBREDI
BEHAVIORAL BRAIN RESEARCH; an international journal. (Text in English) 1980. 12/yr.(in 6 vols.; 2 nos./vol.). fl.2316 (effective 1992). Elsevier Science Publishers B.V., P.O. Box 211, 1000 AE Amsterdam, Netherlands. TEL 020-5803911.
FAX 020-5803598. TELEX 18582 ESPA NL.
(Subscr.in U.S. and Canada to: Elsevier Science Publishing Co., Inc., Box 882, Madison Sq. Sta., New York, NY 10159. TEL 212-989-5800) Ed. I. Steele Russell. charts; illus. (reprint service avail. from ISI) **Indexed:** Anim.Behav.Abstr., Biol.Abstr., Chem.Abstr., Curr.Cont., Dent.Ind., Excerp.Med., Ind.Med., Psychol.Abstr., Yrbk.Assoc.Educ.& Rehab.Blind.
—BLDSC shelfmark: 1877.320000.
Description: Publishes articles in the neurosciences, with special emphasis on neural mechanisms of behaviour.
Refereed Serial

BEHAVIORAL MEDICINE; investigations of environmental influences on health and behavior. see *PSYCHOLOGY*

616.8   UK   ISSN 0953-4180
BEHAVIORAL NEUROLOGY. 1988. q. £64 to individuals; institutions £115. Rapid Communications of Oxford Ltd., The Old Malthouse, Paradise St., Oxford OX1 1LD, England. TEL 0865-790447.
FAX 0865-793533. Ed. Andrew J. Lees. adv.; bk.rev.
—BLDSC shelfmark: 1877.590000.
Description: Original and review papers of a predominantly clinical nature, with emphasis on the meaning of expression of disordered human behavior.

616.8   US   ISSN 0005-7932
RC321   CODEN: BENPBG
BEHAVIORAL NEUROPSYCHIATRY. 1969. bi-m. $48.50. Behavioral Neuropsychiatry Medical Publishers, Inc., 61 East 86th St., New York, NY 10028. Ed. Dr. Albert A. LaVerne. adv.; bk.rev.; charts; illus.; index, cum.index; circ. 25,000 (controlled). **Indexed:** Biol.Abstr., Chem.Abstr., Excerp.Med., Ind.Med., Psychol.Abstr.
Supsedes: International Journal of Neuropsychiatry.
Refereed Serial

BEHAVIORAL NEUROSCIENCE. see *PSYCHOLOGY*

616.8   UK   ISSN 0884-5581
RJ505.B4.
BEHAVIORAL RESIDENTIAL TREATMENT; an interdisciplinary journal. 1986. 4/yr. (plus special issue). $185 (effective 1992). John Wiley & Sons Ltd., Journals, Baffins Lane, Chichester, Sussex PO19 1UD, England. TEL 0243-779777.
FAX 0243-775878. TELEX 8620 WIBOOK G. Ed. Fredrick J. Fuoco. **Indexed:** Psychol.Abstr.
—BLDSC shelfmark: 1877.840000.
Description: Deals specifically with the application of behavioral techniques in residential treatment settings.

619.8   NE   ISSN 0376-6357
QL750   CODEN: BPRODA
BEHAVIOURAL PROCESSES; an international journal of comparative and physiological ethology. (Text in English, French, German) 1976. 6/yr.(in 2 vols.; 3 nos./vol.). fl.698 (effective 1992). Elsevier Science Publishers B.V., P.O. Box 211, 1000 AE Amsterdam, Netherlands. TEL 020-5803911.
FAX 020-5803598. TELEX 18582 ESPA NL.
(Subscr. in U.S. and Canada to: Elsevier Science Publishing Co., Inc., Box 882, Madison Sq. Sta., New York, NY 10159. TEL 212-989-5800) Eds. R. Zayan, J.E.R. Staddon. adv.; bk.rev.; bibl.; illus.; index. (also avail. in microform from RPI; reprint service avail. from ISI) **Indexed:** Anim.Behav.Abstr., Biol.Abstr., Curr.Adv.Ecol.Sci., Curr.Cont., Dairy Sci.Abstr., Deep Sea Res.& Oceanogr.Abstr., Excerp.Med., Ind.Sci.Rev., Psychol.Abstr., Sci.Cit.Ind, SSCI.
—BLDSC shelfmark: 1877.700000.
Incorporates (1981-1983): Behaviour Analysis Letters.
Description: Covers comparative ethology, behavioural ecology, theoretical and quantitative ethology, neuroethology, experimental analysis and operant conditioning.
Refereed Serial

616.8   UK   ISSN 0263-9963
BETHLEM AND MAUDSLEY GAZETTE. 1953. q. Bethlem and Maudsley Health Authority, Maudsley Hospital, Denmark Hill, London SE5 8AZ, England.
TEL 01-703-6333. Ed. K.R. Lloyd. bk.rev.; circ. 3,000.
—BLDSC shelfmark: 1942.640000.

BIBLIOGRAPHIES IN THE HISTORY OF PSYCHOLOGY AND PSYCHIATRY. see *PSYCHOLOGY — Abstracting, Bibliographies, Statistics*

616.8   SZ   ISSN 0067-8147
CODEN: BIBPBI
BIBLIOTHECA PSYCHIATRICA. (Text in English and German) 1917. irreg. (approx. 1/yr.). price varies. S. Karger AG, Allschwilerstr. 10, P.O. Box, CH-4009 Basel, Switzerland. TEL 061-3061111.
FAX 061-3061234. TELEX CH962652. Ed. B. Saletu. (reprint service avail. from ISI, back issues avail.) **Indexed:** Biol.Abstr., Chem.Abstr., Curr.Cont., Ind.Med., SSCI.
—BLDSC shelfmark: 2019.390000.

BIOFEEDBACK. see *PSYCHOLOGY*

MEDICAL SCIENCES — PSYCHIATRY AND NEUROLOGY

616.89 574 US ISSN 0006-3223
RC321 CODEN: BIPCBF
BIOLOGICAL PSYCHIATRY; a journal of psychiatric research. 1969. 24/yr. plus supplement. $730 to institutions (foreign $810)(effective 1992). (Society of Biological Psychiatry) Elsevier Science Publishing Co., Inc. (New York), 655 Ave. of the Americas, New York, NY 10010. TEL 212-989-5800.
FAX 212-633-3965. TELEX 420643 AEP UI. Ed. Dr. Joseph Wortis. bk.rev.; charts; illus.; index. (also avail. in microfilm from JSC) **Indexed:** Adol.Ment.Hlth.Abstr., Bibl.Dev.Med.& Child Neur., Biol.Abstr., Chem.Abstr., Curr.Adv.Biochem., Curr.Adv.Ecol.Sci., Curr.Cont., Dairy Sci.Abstr., Dent.Ind., Excerp.Med., Ind.Med., Ind.Sci.Rev., Psychol.Abstr., Sci.Cit.Ind.
—BLDSC shelfmark: 2077.550000.
Supersedes: Recent Advances in Biological Psychiatry.
Description: Covers the whole range of psychiatric research interest.
Refereed Serial

616.89 US ISSN 1044-422X
BIOLOGICAL THERAPIES IN PSYCHIATRY NEWSLETTER. 1978. m. $52 to individuals (foreign $72); institutions $70 (foreign $90); students $37 (foreign $57). Mosby - Year Book, Inc. (Subsidiary of: Times Mirror Company), 11830 Westline Industrial Dr., St. Louis, MO 63146. Ed. Dr. Alan J. Gelenberg. circ. 6,000.
Former titles: Biological Therapies in Psychiatry (ISSN 0895-8262); Massachusetts General Hospital Biological Therapies in Psychiatry Newsletter (ISSN 0199-2716)
Description: Provides updates on the clinical use of psychotropic drugs to practicing psychiatrists, psychiatric house staff, residents, and students.

616.89 574 IT ISSN 0393-4853
BOLLETTINO DI PSICHIATRIA BIOLOGICA/PSYCHIATRIC NEWS. 1985. q. L.40000($55) (effective 1992). (Societa Italiana di Psichiatria Biologica) Casa Editrice Idelson, Via A. De Gasperi, 55, 80133 Naples, Italy. TEL 081-5524733.
FAX 081-5518295. Ed. Mario Maj. (back issues avail.)
—BLDSC shelfmark: 7981.800000.

616.8 UK ISSN 0006-8950
RC321 CODEN: BRAIAK
BRAIN; journal of neurology. 1878. 6/yr. £99($195) Oxford University Press, Oxford Journals, Pinkhill House, Southfield Road, Eynsham, Oxford OX8 1JJ, England. TEL 0865-882283. FAX 0865-882890.
TELEX 8373300-OXPRES-G. Ed. P.K. Thomas. adv.; bk.rev.; bibl.; illus.; index; circ. 4,250. (also avail. in microform from SWZ,UMI;PMC; reprint service avail. from SWZ,UMI) **Indexed:** Bibl.Dev.Med.& Child Neur., Biol.Abstr., Biotech.Abstr., Chem.Abstr., Curr.Adv.Ecol.Sci., Curr.Cont., Ergon.Abstr., Excerp.Med., Helminthol.Abstr., Ind.Med., Ind.Sci.Rev., Ind.Vet., Nutr.Abstr., Psychol.Abstr., Sci.Cit.Ind., So.Pac.Per.Ind., Vet.Bull.
—BLDSC shelfmark: 2268.000000.
Description: Original papers in clinical neurology and related disciplines.

616.8 618.92 JA ISSN 0387-7604
BRAIN AND DEVELOPMENT. Japanese edition: No to Hattatsu. (Text in English) 1969. bi-m. $110.
Japanese Society of Child Neurology - Nihon Shoni Shinkei Gakkai, Kobayashi Bldg. 2F, 10-1 Wakamatsu-cho, Shinjuku-ku, Tokyo 162, Japan.
Indexed: Bibl.Dev.Med.& Child Neur., Curr.Cont., Excerp.Med., Ind.Med., INIS Atomind., Int.Abstr.Biol.Sci., Sci.Cit.Ind.
—BLDSC shelfmark: 2268.032900.
Supersedes in part (in 1979): Brain and Development - No to Hattatsu (ISSN 0029-0831)
Description: Contains both clinical and basic studies in the field of child neurology.

616.8 JA ISSN 0006-8969
CODEN: BRNED8
BRAIN AND NERVE/NO TO SHINKEI. (Text in Japanese; summaries in English) 1948. m.
23,520 Yen($181) Igaku-Shoin Ltd., 5-24-3 Hongo, Bunkyo-ku, Tokyo 113-91, Japan.
TEL 03-817-5701. Ed.Bd. adv.; bk.rev.; abstr.; cum.index; circ. 4,500. **Indexed:** Biol.Abstr., C.I.S. Abstr., Chem.Abstr., Dent.Ind., Excerp.Med., Ind.Med. ●Also available online. Vendor(s): JICST.
—BLDSC shelfmark: 2268.050000.

616.8 SZ ISSN 0006-8977
QL750 CODEN: BRBEBE
BRAIN, BEHAVIOR AND EVOLUTION. (Text in English) 1968. m. (in 2 vol.). 663 Fr.($442) per vol. S. Karger AG, Allschwilerstr. 10, P.O. Box, CH-4009 Basel, Switzerland. TEL 061-3061111.
FAX 061-3061234. TELEX CH 962652. Ed. G. Glenn Northcutt. adv.; bibl.; illus.; index; circ. 1,000. (also avail. in microform from RPI) **Indexed:** Abstr.Anthropol., Biol.Abstr., Curr.Adv.Ecol.Sci., Dent.Ind., Excerp.Med., Ind.Med., Ind.Sci.Rev., Psychol.Abstr., Sci.Cit.Ind.
—BLDSC shelfmark: 2268.100000.

616.8 SZ ISSN 0259-1278
CODEN: BRDYEJ
BRAIN DYSFUNCTION. (Text in English) 1988. 6/yr. 373 Fr.($249) to institutions; individuals 261.40 Fr.($174.30). S. Karger AG, Allschwilerstr. 10, P.O. Box, CH-4009 Basel, Switzerland.
TEL 061-3061111. FAX 061-3061234. TELEX CH 962652. Ed. U. Scapagnini. (also avail. in microfiche; microfilm) **Indexed:** Excerp.Med.
—BLDSC shelfmark: 2268.113000.

616.8 UK ISSN 0269-9052
RC387.5 CODEN: BRAIEO
BRAIN INJURY. 1987. bi-m. £25.85($44.73) to individuals; institutions £141($244). Taylor & Francis Ltd., Rankine Rd., Basingstoke, Hants RG24 0PR, England. TEL 0256-840366.
FAX 0256-479438. TELEX 858540. Ed. Henry H. Stonnington. **Indexed:** Excerp.Med.
—BLDSC shelfmark: 2268.132000.
Description: Covers all aspects of brain injury, ranging from basic scientific research to epidemiology, neuropathology, neurosurgical and other medical procedures, assessment methods, rehabilitation and outcome.
Refereed Serial

616.8 II ISSN 0006-8985
BRAIN NEWS.* (Text in English) 1964. s-a.
Rs.30.($10.) Indian Brain Research Association, Dept. of Biochemistry, 35 Ballygunge Circular Rd., Calcutta 19, India. Ed. Dr. J.J. Ghosh. adv.; bk.rev.; circ. 500. **Indexed:** Biol.Abstr.

616.8 NE ISSN 0921-8246
QP376 CODEN: BRREAP
BRAIN RESEARCH; international multidisciplinary journal devoted to fundamental research in the brain sciences. (Text in English) 1966. w. fl.13635 includes subscr. to Brain Research Reviews, Cognitive Brain Research, Developmental Brain Research, and Molecular Brain Research (effective 1992). Elsevier Science Publishers B.V., P.O. Box 211, 1000 AE Amsterdam, Netherlands.
TEL 020-5803911. FAX 020-5803598. TELEX 18582 ESPA NL. (N. America dist. addr.: Elsevier Science Publishing Co., Inc., Box 882, Madison Sq. Sta., New York, NY 10159. TEL 212-989-5800) Ed. D. Purpura. adv.; bk.rev.; abstr.; bibl.; illus.; index, cum.index: 1966-1977. (also avail. in microform from RPI) **Indexed:** Biol.Abstr., Biotech.Abstr., Chem.Abstr., Curr.Adv.Biochem., Curr.Adv.Cell & Devel.Biol., Curr.Adv.Ecol.Sci., Curr.Cont., Dairy Sci.Abstr., Dent.Ind., Excerp.Med., Helminthol.Abstr., Ind.Med., Ind.Sci.Rev., Ind.Vet., INIS Atomind., Int.Abstr.Biol.Sci., Int.Aerosp.Abstr., Nutr.Abstr., Psychol.Abstr., Sci.Cit.Ind, Vet.Bull.
Description: Covers neuroanatomy, neurochemistry, neurophysiology, neyroendocrinology, neuropharmacology, neurotoxicology, neurocommunications, behavioural sciences, neurology and biocybernetics.

618 US ISSN 0361-9230
QP376 CODEN: BRBUDU
BRAIN RESEARCH BULLETIN. 1976. m. £620 (effective 1992). Pergamon Press, Inc., Journals Division, 660 White Plains Rd., Tarrytown, NY 10591-5153.
TEL 914-524-9200. FAX 914-333-2444. (And: Headington Hill Hall, Oxford OX3 0BW, England. TEL 0865-794141) Ed. Matthew J. Wayner. adv.; bk.rev.; illus.; index. (also avail. in microform from UMI; reprint service avail. from ISI,UMI) **Indexed:** Anim.Behav.Abstr., Biol.Abstr., Chem.Abstr., Curr.Adv.Biochem., Curr.Adv.Cancer Res., Curr.Adv.Ecol.Sci., Curr.Cont., Dent.Ind., Excerp.Med., Helminthol.Abstr., Ind.Med., Ind.Sci.Rev., INIS Atomind., Nutr.Abstr., Psychol.Abstr., Sci.Cit.Ind.
—BLDSC shelfmark: 2268.201000.
Incorporating: Journal of Electrophysiological Techniques (ISSN 0361-0209)
Description: Broad spectrum of articles in the neurosciences, emphasizing rapid communication of comprehensive articles, meeting reports and special issues.
Refereed Serial

616.8 US
BRAIN RESEARCH FOUNDATION ANNUAL REPORT. 1983. a. Brain Research Foundation, 208 S. LaSalle St., Ste. 1426, Chicago, IL 60604.
TEL 312-782-4311. FAX 312-782-6437. Ed. Nancy W. Hohfeler. circ. 1,300.
Description: Presents financial statement, year's activities, list of the foundation's grants to scientists at University of Chicago's Brain Research Institute, donors lists, and scientific articles highlighting a specific area of research at the institute.

616.8 NE ISSN 0165-0173
CODEN: BRERD2
BRAIN RESEARCH REVIEWS. Issued with: Brain Research (ISSN 0921-8246) (Text and summaries in English) 1980. 3/yr. fl.351 (effective 1992). Elsevier Science Publishers B.V., P.O. Box 211, 1000 AE Amsterdam, Netherlands. TEL 020-5803911.
FAX 020-5803598. TELEX 18582 ESPA NL. (N. America dist. addr.: Elsevier Science Publishing Co., Inc., Box 882, Madison Sq. Sta., New York, NY 10159. TEL 212-989-5800) Ed. Dr. Dominick P. Purpura. adv. (back issues avail.; reprint service avail. from ISI) **Indexed:** Biol.Abstr., Biotech.Abstr., Chem.Abstr., Curr.Adv.Cell & Devel.Biol., Curr.Adv.Ecol.Sci., Curr.Cont., Excerp.Med., Ind.Med., Psychol.Abstr.
—BLDSC shelfmark: 2268.205000.
Description: Publishes articles and research papers which give analytical surveys that define heuristic hypotheses and provide new insights into brain mechanisms.

616.8 US ISSN 0896-0267
CODEN: BRTOEZ
BRAIN TOPOGRAPHY; journal of functional neurophysiology. 1988. q. $225 (foreign $265). Human Sciences Press, Inc. (Subsidiary of: Plenum Publishing Corp.), 233 Spring St., New York, NY 10013-1578. TEL 212-620-8000.
FAX 212-463-0742. adv. (also avail. in microform from UMI) **Indexed:** Psychol.Abstr.
—BLDSC shelfmark: 2268.221200.
Description: Reviews new research in the areas of EEG, MEG, pshchiatry, and neuropsychology, and explores new methodology and techniques of data analysis and manipulation.
Refereed Serial

616.8 UK
BREAKTHROUGH.* 1965. bi-m. £1. (National Society for Mentally Handicapped Children, Northwest Region) Europress, 17 Ridgemont Rd., Bramhall, Cheshire, England.

BRILL'S STUDIES IN EPISTEMOLOGY, PSYCHOLOGY AND PSYCHIATRY. see *PHILOSOPHY*

BRITISH JOURNAL OF MEDICAL PSYCHOLOGY. see *PSYCHOLOGY*

BRITISH JOURNAL OF PROJECTIVE PSYCHOLOGY. see *PSYCHOLOGY*

MEDICAL SCIENCES — PSYCHIATRY AND NEUROLOGY

616.89   UK   ISSN 0007-1250
RC321   CODEN: BJPYAJ
BRITISH JOURNAL OF PSYCHIATRY. 1853. 12/yr. £105($185) to individuals; institutions £130($285). Royal College of Psychiatrists, 17 Belgrave Sq., London SW1X 8PG, England. TEL 071-235-8857. FAX 071-245-1231. (Subscr. to: Royal Society of Medicine, 1 Wimpole St., London W1M 8AE, England) Ed. Hugh Freeman. adv.; bk.rev.; bibl.; charts; illus.; index; circ. 12,500. **Indexed:** Abstr.Health Care Manage.Stud., Abstr.Hyg., Adol.Ment.Hlth.Abstr., Bibl.Dev.Med.& Child Neur., Biol.Abstr., Biotech.Abstr., Chem.Abstr., Curr.Adv.Ecol.Sci., Curr.Cont., Dok.Arbeitsmed., Excerp.Med., Helminthol.Abstr., I.P.A., Ind.Med., Ind.Sci.Rev., Int.Nurs.Ind., Mid.East: Abstr.& Ind., Nutr.Abstr., Psychol.Abstr., Risk Abstr., Sci.Cit.Ind., SSCI, Trop.Dis.Bull.
—BLDSC shelfmark: 2320.800000.
    Description: Covers all branches of psychiatry, with emphasis on the clinical aspects of various topics in field.

616.891   UK   ISSN 0265-9883
BRITISH JOURNAL OF PSYCHOTHERAPY. 1984. 4/yr. £25 to individuals; institutions £45. Artesian Books Ltd., 18 Artesian Rd., London W2, England. Ed. Dr. R.D. Hinshelwood. adv.; bk.rev.; circ. 1,400. **Indexed:** Psychol.Abstr.
—BLDSC shelfmark: 2321.200000.

362.4 616.835   UK   ISSN 0007-1633
BRITISH POLIO FELLOWSHIP. BULLETIN. 1939. bi-m. £0.20 per no. British Polio Fellowship, 126 Radnor Ave., Bexleyheath, Kent DA16 2BY, England. TEL 081-304-3166. FAX 081-304-3166. Ed. Kathleen M. Dibley. adv.; bk.rev.; illus.; circ. 8,000. (tabloid format)

616.8   SZ   ISSN 1016-9229
CAHIERS PSYCHIATRIQUES GENEVOIS. 1987. s-a. 50 SFr. (foreign 60 SFr.). Editions Medecine et Hygiene, Case Postale 456, CH-1211 Geneva 4, Switzerland. TEL 022-469355. FAX 022-475610.

616.8   CN   ISSN 0317-1671
RC321   CODEN: CJNSA2
CANADIAN JOURNAL OF NEUROLOGICAL SCIENCES. 1974. q. Can.$70 (students Can.$35; foreign Can.$80). (Canadian Congress of Neurological Sciences) Canadian Journal of Neurological Sciences, P.O. Box 4220, Station "C", Calgary, Alta. T2T 5N1, Canada. TEL 403-229-9575. FAX 403-229-1661. Ed. Dr. J.A. Sharpe. adv.; bk.rev.; index; circ. 1,600. (also avail. in microform from UMI; reprint service avail. from UMI,ISI) **Indexed:** Biol.Abstr., Chem.Abstr., Curr.Adv.Ecol.Sci., Curr.Cont., Dent.Ind., Excerp.Med., Ind.Med., Ind.Sci.Rev., INIS Atomind., Nutr.Abstr., Sci.Cit.Ind., Weed Abstr.
—BLDSC shelfmark: 3033.300000.
    Description: Original work in the clinical and basic neurosciences.

616.89   CN   ISSN 0706-7437
RC321   CODEN: CPAJAK
CANADIAN JOURNAL OF PSYCHIATRY/REVUE CANADIENNE DE PSYCHIATRIE. (Text in English, French) 1956. 10/yr. Can.$75($95) Canadian Psychiatric Association, 237 Argyle Ave., Ste. 200, Ottawa, Ont. K2P 1B8, Canada. TEL 613-234-2815. FAX 613-234-9857. Ed. Dr. E. Kingstone. adv.; bk.rev.; bibl.; charts; illus.; index; circ. 3,300. (also avail. in microform from UMI; reprint service avail. from UMI) **Indexed:** Adol.Ment.Hlth.Abstr., ASSIA, Bibl.Dev.Med.& Child Neur., Chem.Abstr., Child Devel.Abstr., CINAHL, Curr.Adv.Ecol.Sci., Curr.Cont., Dok.Arbeitsmed., Excerp.Med., Ind.Med., Lang.& Lang.Behav.Abstr., Mid.East: Abstr.& Ind., NRN, Psychol.Abstr., Sage Fam.Stud.Abstr., Sage Urb.Stud.Abstr., So.Pac.Per.Ind., Sp.Ed.Needs Abstr., SSCI, Yrbk.Assoc.Educ.& Rehab.Blind.
—BLDSC shelfmark: 3034.800000.
    Formerly: Canadian Psychiatric Association Journal (ISSN 0008-4824)

616.8   US   ISSN 0272-4340
QP351   CODEN: CMNEDI
CELLULAR & MOLECULAR NEUROBIOLOGY. 1981. q. $275 (foreign $320)(effective 1992). Plenum Publishing Corp., 233 Spring St., New York, NY 10013-1578. TEL 212-620-8000. FAX 212-463-0742. TELEX 23-4211139. Ed. Juan M. Saavedra. adv.; bk.rev. (also avail. in microfilm from JSC; back issues avail.) **Indexed:** Biol.Abstr., Chem.Abstr., Curr.Adv.Ecol.Sci., Curr.Cont., Excerp.Med., Ind.Med., INIS Atomind.
—BLDSC shelfmark: 3097.925000.
    Refereed Serial

CELLULAR NEUROBIOLOGY. see *BIOLOGY*

616.8   NO   ISSN 0333-1024
                 CODEN: CEPHDF
CEPHALAGIA. (Text in English) 1981. q. $95 to individuals; institutions $190. (International Headache Society) Universitetsforlaget, P.O. Box 2959-Toeyen, N-0608 Oslo 1, Norway. (U.S. address: Publications Expediting Inc., 200 Meacham Ave., Elmont, NY 11003) Ed. Marcia Wilkinson. adv.; index; circ. 800. (also avail. in microform from UMI) **Indexed:** Biol.Abstr., Curr.Adv.Ecol.Sci., Dent.Ind., Excerp.Med., Ind.Med., INIS Atomind., NRN.
—BLDSC shelfmark: 3113.691000.

616.8   FR   ISSN 0264-6900
                 CODEN: CMCEEW
CEREBRAL CIRCULATION AND METABOLISM/CIRCULATION ET METABOLISME DU CERVEAU. 1983. q. 380 F. to individuals (foreign 480 F.); institutions 480 F. (foreign 580 F.). (Societe Francaise de Circulation et Metabolisme du Cerveau) John Libbey Eurotext, 6 rue Blanche, 92120 Montrouge, France. TEL 1-47-35-85-52. FAX 1-46-57-10-09. (Dist. by: Gauthier-Villars, Centrale des Revues, 11 rue Gossin, 95543 Montrouge Cedex, France. TEL 1-46-56-52-66) Ed. J.C. Depresseux. circ. 500. (back issues avail.) **Indexed:** Curr.Adv.Biochem., Curr.Adv.Cell & Devel.Biol.
—BLDSC shelfmark: 3265.280000.
    Description: Explores the circulation and metabolism of the brain from clinical, physiological, physiopathological and pharmacological approaches.

CEREBRO; Zerebrale und periphere Gefaesskrankheiten. see *MEDICAL SCIENCES — Cardiovascular Diseases*

616.8   US   ISSN 1040-8827
RC386   CODEN: CEMREV
CEREBROVASCULAR AND BRAIN METABOLISM REVIEWS. 1989. q. $98 to individuals; institutions $120. Raven Press, 1185 Ave. of the Americas, New York, NY 10036. TEL 212-930-9500. FAX 212-869-3495. TELEX 640073. Ed. A. Murray Harper. adv.; charts, illus.; circ. 1,000.
—BLDSC shelfmark: 3120.037500.
    Description: Provides current reviews of topics of interest to neurologists, neurosurgeons, neuroscientists, physiologists, pharmacologists, and general practitioners.
    Refereed Serial

616.8 616.15   SZ   ISSN 1015-9770
                 CODEN: CDISE7
▼**CEREBROVASCULAR DISEASES.** (Text in English) 1991. 6/yr. 139.80 Fr.($93.30) to individuals; institutions 466 Fr.($311). S. Karger AG, Allschwilerstr. 10, P.O. Box, CH-4009 Basel, Switzerland. TEL 061-3061111. FAX 061-3061234. Eds. J. Bogousslavsky, M. Hennerici.
—BLDSC shelfmark: 3120.037790.

616.8 617.48   CS   ISSN 0301-0597
CESKOSLOVENSKA NEUROLOGIE A NEUROCHIRURGIE. (Text in Czech or Slovak; summaries in Czech, English, Russian) 1937. 6/yr. $48.60. (Ceskoslovenska Neurologicka Spolecnost) Avicenum, Czechoslovak Medical Press, Malostranske nam. 28, 118 02 Prague 1, Czechoslovakia. (Dist. by: Artia, Ve Smeckach 30, 111 27 Prague 1, Czechoslovakia) (Co-sponsor: Ceskoslovenska Lekarska Spolecnost J. Ev. Purkyne) Ed. Dr. D. Bartko. bk.rev.; abstr.; bibl.; charts; illus.; index. **Indexed:** C.I.S. Abstr., Chem.Abstr., Curr.Adv.Ecol.Sci., Dent.Ind., Excerp.Med., Ind.Med., INIS Atomind.
    Former titles: Ceskoslovenska Neurologie (ISSN 0009-0581) & Neurologie a Psychiatrie Ceskoslovenska.

616.89   CS   ISSN 0069-2336
CESKOSLOVENSKA PSYCHIATRIE. (Text in Czech; summaries in Czech, English, Russian) 1904. 6/yr. $48.60. (Ceskoslovenska Psychiatricka Spolecnost) Avicenum, Czechoslovak Medical Press, Malostranske nam. 28, 118 02 Prague 1, Czechoslovakia. (Dist. by: Artia, Ve Smeckach 30, 111 27 Prague 1, Czechoslovakia) (Co-sponsor: Ceskoslovenska Lekarska Spolecnost J. Ev. Purkyne) Ed. Dr. M. Zapletalek. bk.rev.; abstr. **Indexed:** C.I.S. Abstr., Excerp.Med., Ind.Med., Psychol.Abstr.
—BLDSC shelfmark: 3122.490000.

CHILD BEHAVIOR AND DEVELOPMENT. see *MEDICAL SCIENCES — Pediatrics*

616.89   US   ISSN 0009-398X
RJ499.A1   CODEN: CPHDA3
CHILD PSYCHIATRY AND HUMAN DEVELOPMENT. 1970. q. $175 (foreign $205). (American Association of Psychiatric Services for Children) Human Sciences Press, Inc. (Subsidiary of: Plenum Publishing Corp.), 233 Spring St., New York, NY 10013-1578. TEL 212-620-8000. FAX 212-463-0742. Ed. Dr. Jack C. Westman. adv.; bibl.; index. (also avail. in microform from UMI; back issues avail.; reprint service avail. from ISI,UMI) **Indexed:** Adol.Ment.Hlth.Abstr., Bibl.Dev.Med.& Child Neur., Biol.Abstr., C.I.J.E., Child Devel.Abstr., Curr.Cont., Educ.Ind., Except.Child.Educ.Abstr., Excerp.Med., Ind.Med., Nutr.Abstr., Psychol.Abstr., Psycscan D.P., Risk Abstr., Soc.Work Res.& Abstr., SSCI, Wom.Stud.Abstr.
—BLDSC shelfmark: 3172.945000.
    Description: Serves allied professional groups of specialists in child psychiatry, social science, pediatrics, psychology, and human development.
    Refereed Serial

618.92 612   GW   ISSN 0256-7040
                 CODEN: CNSYE9
CHILD'S NERVOUS SYSTEM. (Text in English) 1972. 8/yr. DM.648($396) (effective 1992). (International Society for Paediatric Neurosurgery) Springer-Verlag, Heidelberger Platz 3, D-1000 Berlin 33, Germany. TEL 030-8207-1. (U.S. subscr. to: Box 2485, Secaucus, NJ 07096-2491. TEL 201-348-4033) Ed. Anthony J. Raimondi. adv.; bibl.; charts; illus.; circ. 1,125. (also avail. in microform from RPI; reprint service avail. from ISI) **Indexed:** Bibl.Dev.Med.& Child Neur., Biol.Abstr., Curr.Adv.Ecol.Sci., Curr.Cont., Dent.Ind., Excerp.Med., Helminthol.Abstr., Ind.Med., Nutr.Abstr., Protozool.Abstr., Sci.Cit.Ind.
—BLDSC shelfmark: 3172.993080.
    Supersedes in part (in 1985): Child's Brain (ISSN 0302-2803)
    Refereed Serial

616.8   IT
CLINICA NEUROPSICHIATRICA. (Text in Italian; summaries in English, French, German, Italian) 1965. irreg. Ospedale Neuropsichiatrico, Teramo, Italy.

616.8   AT   ISSN 0158-1597
CLINICAL AND EXPERIMENTAL NEUROLOGY. 1963. a. Aus.$100. Australian Association of Neurologists, c/o Dr. J. King, Dept of Neurology, Royal Melbourne Hospital, Parville, Melbourne, Vic. 3050, Australia. TEL 03-429004. FAX 03-4285375. Ed. M.J. Eadie. circ. 300. (also avail. in microform from UMI) **Indexed:** Chem.Abstr., Excerp.Med., Ind.Med.
    Formerly: Australian Association of Neurologists Proceedings (ISSN 0084-7224)

616.804   US   ISSN 0009-9155
                 CODEN: CEEGA
CLINICAL ELECTROENCEPHALOGRAPHY. 1970. q. $39. American Medical Electroencephalographic Association, 850 Elm Grove Rd., Ste. 11, Elm Grove, WI 53122. TEL 414-797-7800. adv.; bk.rev.; charts; illus.; circ. 2,424. (also avail. in microform from UMI; reprint service avail. from ISI,ISI) **Indexed:** Bibl.Dev.Med.& Child Neur., Biol.Abstr., Curr.Cont., Excerp.Med., Ind.Med., Ind.Sci.Rev., Sci.Cit.Ind.
—BLDSC shelfmark: 3286.274000.
    Refereed Serial

MEDICAL SCIENCES — PSYCHIATRY AND NEUROLOGY

616.8 US ISSN 0749-8047
CLINICAL JOURNAL OF PAIN. 1985. q. $84 to individuals; institutions $125. (American Academy of Pain Medicine) Raven Press, 1185 Ave. of the Americas, New York, NY 10036. TEL 212-930-9500. FAX 212-869-3495. TELEX 640073. Ed. Peter R. Wilson. adv.; bk.rev.; charts; illus.; index; circ. 2,500. (back issues avail.) **Indexed:** Excerp.Med.
Description: Explores all aspects of pain and pain management, including diagnostic procedures, therapeutic modalities, psychosocial dimensions, and ethical problems.
Refereed Serial

420 616.8 UK ISSN 0269-9206
RC423.A1
CLINICAL LINGUISTICS & PHONETICS. 1987. q. £20.90($36.30) to individuals; institutions £76($132). Taylor & Francis Ltd., Rankine Rd., Basingstoke, Hants RG24 0PR, England. TEL 0256-840366. FAX 0256-479438. TELEX 858540. Ed. Martin J. Ball. bk.rev. **Indexed:** Excerp.Med., Lang.& Lang.Behav.Abstr. (1987-).
—BLDSC shelfmark: 3286.297800.
Description: Articles range from theoretical discussions to extremely practical "tutorial" reviews. Language development and other psycho- or neurolinguistic areas are included where they shed light on normative behavior against which to judge the non-normal.
Refereed Serial

616.8 617 NE ISSN 0303-8467
CODEN: CNNSBV
CLINICAL NEUROLOGY AND NEUROSURGERY. 1975. q. $85. Van Gorcum en Co. B.V., P.O. Box 43, 9400 AA Assen, Netherlands. TEL 05920-46846. FAX 05920-72064. adv.; bk.rev. **Indexed:** Bibl.Dev.Med.& Child Neur., Biol.Abstr., Curr.Adv.Cancer Res., Curr.Cont., Excerp.Med., Ind.Med.
—BLDSC shelfmark: 3286.310100.

616.8 GW ISSN 0722-5091
CODEN: CLNPDA
CLINICAL NEUROPATHOLOGY. (Text in English) 1982. bi-m. DM.230($124) Dustri-Verlag Dr. Karl Feistle, Bahnhofstr. 9, 8024 Deisenhofen, Germany. TEL 089-613861-0. FAX 089-6135412. Eds. Dr. W. Schlote, Dr. F. St. Vogel. **Indexed:** Curr.Adv.Ecol.Sci., Dent.Ind., Excerp.Med., Ind.Med., Ind.Sci.Rev., Sci.Cit.Ind.
—BLDSC shelfmark: 3286.310400.

CLINICAL NEUROPHARMACOLOGY. see *PHARMACY AND PHARMACOLOGY*

616.8 NE ISSN 0920-1637
CODEN: CLNEEC
CLINICAL NEUROPSYCHOLOGIST. (Text in English) 1987. 4/yr. $75 for individuals; institutions $125. Swets Publishing Service (Subsidiary of: Swets en Zeitlinger B.V.), Heereweg 347, 2126 CA Lisse, Netherlands. TEL 31-2521-35111. FAX 31-2521-15888. TELEX 41325. (Dist in N. America by: Swets & Zeitlinger, Box 517, Berwyn, PA 19312. TEL 215-644-4944) Eds. Byron P. Rourke, Kenneth M. Adams. circ. 3,000. (reprint service avail. from SWZ) **Indexed:** Excerp.Med., Psychol.Abstr.
—BLDSC shelfmark: 3286.310680.

617.48 US ISSN 0069-4827
RD593.A1 CODEN: CLNEA8
CLINICAL NEUROSURGERY: PROCEEDINGS. 1953. a. price varies. (Congress of Neurological Surgeons) Williams & Wilkins, 428 E. Preston St., Baltimore, MD 21202. TEL 301-528-4000. FAX 301-528-4312. **Indexed:** Ind.Med., INIS Atomind.
—BLDSC shelfmark: 3286.311000.

616.89 US ISSN 0270-6644
CLINICAL PSYCHIATRY NEWS. 1973. m. $60. International Medical News Group (Subsidiary of: Capital Cities- ABC Inc.), 12230 Wilkins Ave., Rockville, MD 20852. TEL 301-770-6170. Ed. William Rubin. adv.; bk.rev.; circ. 30,800. (tabloid format; also avail. in microform from UMI)

CLINICS IN DEVELOPMENTAL MEDICINE. see *MEDICAL SCIENCES — Pediatrics*

616.8 NE ISSN 0926-6410
▼**COGNITIVE BRAIN RESEARCH.** (Section of: Brain Research (ISSN 0921-8246)) (Text in English) 1992. 4/yr. fl.350($174) (effective 1992). Elsevier Science Publishers B.V., P.O. Box 211, 1000 AE Amsterdam, Netherlands. TEL 020-5803911. FAX 020-5803598. TELEX 18582 ESPA NL. (Subscr. in U.S. and Canada to: Elsevier Science Publishing Co., Inc., Box 882, Madison Sq. Sta., New York, NY 10159. TEL 212-989-5800) Ed. D.P. Purpura. adv.; bk.rev
Description: Publishes original reports of research in computational neuroscience, including neural networks, brain mechanisms subserving cognition, and applications of chaos theory to the analysis of brain functions and aberrant neurobehavioral processes.
Refereed Serial

616.8 US ISSN 0896-5099
QP363.5 CODEN: CDNEEO
▼**COMMENTS ON DEVELOPMENTAL NEUROBIOLOGY.** 1990. 6/yr. $131. Gordon and Breach Science Publishers, 270 Eighth Ave., New York, NY 10011. TEL 212-206-8900. FAX 212-645-2459. TELEX 236735 GOPUB UR. (Subscr. to: Box 786, Cooper Sta., New York, NY 10276. TEL 800-545-8398; UK subscr. to: P.O. Box 90, Reading, Berkshire RG1 8JL, England. TEL 0734-560-080) Eds. Alain Prochiantz, Jean Lauder. (also avail. in microform)
—BLDSC shelfmark: 3336.027800.

616.8 CN
COMMUNIQUE (VANCOUVER). 1986. q. free. Amyotrophic Lateral Sclerosis Society of B.C., 411 Dunsmuir St., 2nd Fl., Vancouver, B.C. V6B 1X4, Canada. TEL 604-685-0737. FAX 604-685-0725. Ed. Rhelda Evans. bk.rev.; circ. 875. (looseleaf format; also avail. on diskette; back issues avail.)
Description: Studies ALS research, fundraising and coping mechanisms and services for families with the disease.

COMMUNITY MENTAL HEALTH JOURNAL. see *SOCIAL SERVICES AND WELFARE*

616.8 UK ISSN 0265-7007
COMMUNITY PSYCHIATRIC NURSING JOURNAL. 6/yr. L.35 to non-members. Community Psychiatric Nurses Association, 44 Dartford Rd., Sevenoaks, Kent TN13 3TQ, England. TEL 0732 455244. FAX 0732-450151. TELEX 727422 UNIVED G. Eds. Susan Sladden, Geoff Allcock. adv.; bk.rev.; video rev.; circ. 1,500.
—BLDSC shelfmark: 3363.648900.
Former titles (until 1984): C P N A Journal (ISSN 0264-5483); (until 1978): C P N A Newsletter.
Description: Contains news of interest to CPNs, feature articles, research papers, conference reports, events listings and news of the Association.

616.8 II
COMMUNITY PSYCHIATRY JOURNAL. Institute of Community Psychiatry and Mental Health, Department of Psychiatry, J. J. Group of Hospitals, Byculla, Bombay 400008, India.

616.89 US ISSN 0010-440X
RC321 CODEN: COPYAV
COMPREHENSIVE PSYCHIATRY. 1960. bi-m. $105 to individuals; institutions $141; foreign $156. (American Psychopathological Association) W.B. Saunders Co. (Subsidiary of: Harcourt Brace Jovanovich, Inc.), Curtis Center, Independence Square W., Philadelphia, PA 19106. TEL 215-238-7800. (Subscr. to: Box 6209, Duluth, MN 55806) Ed. Dr. Ralph A. O'Connell. adv.; bk.rev.; abstr.; bibl.; charts; illus.; index. **Indexed:** Adol.Ment.Hlth.Abstr., Biol.Abstr., Chem.Abstr., Curr.Cont., Dent.Ind., Excerp.Med., Ind.Med., Ind.Sci.Rev., Mid.East: Abstr.& Ind., NRN, Psychol.Abstr., Sci.Cit.Ind., SSCI.
●Also available online.
—BLDSC shelfmark: 3366.390000.
Refereed Serial

616.8 SZ ISSN 0251-2068
CODEN: COPNDZ
CONCEPTS IN PEDIATRIC NEUROSURGERY. (Text in English) 1981. irreg. price varies. (American Society for Pediatric Neurosurgery) S. Karger AG, Allschwilerstr. 10, P.O. Box, CH-4009 Basel, Switzerland. TEL 061-3061111. FAX 061-3061234. TELEX CH 962652. **Indexed:** Biol.Abstr.
—BLDSC shelfmark: 3399.413700.

616.8 US ISSN 0069-9446
CODEN: CNRSAG
CONTEMPORARY NEUROLOGY SERIES. 1966. irreg., vol.39, 1992. price varies. F.A. Davis Company, 1915 Arch St., Philadelphia, PA 19103. TEL 800-523-4049. TELEX 83-4837. Ed. Fred Plum, M.D. **Indexed:** Chem.Abstr, Ind.Med.
—BLDSC shelfmark: 3425.193000.
Refereed Serial

CONTRIBUICOES EM PSICOLOGIA, PSIQUIATRIA E PSICANALISE. see *PSYCHOLOGY*

616.8 US ISSN 0749-8055
CODEN: COTHE4
CONVULSIVE THERAPY. 1985. q. $99 to individuals; institutions $145. Raven Press, 1185 Ave. of the Americas, New York, NY 10036. TEL 212-930-9500. FAX 212-869-3495. TELEX 640073. Ed. Dr. Max E. Fink. adv.; bk.rev.; charts; illus.; index; circ. 1,000. (back issues avail.) **Indexed:** Excerp.Med.
—BLDSC shelfmark: 3463.679300.
Description: Reports on major clinical and research advances worldwide on the the effects of electroconvulsive therapy, mode of seizure induction, and ethical issues.
Refereed Serial

CORRECTIVE AND SOCIAL PSYCHIATRY AND JOURNAL OF BEHAVIORAL TECHNOLOGY METHODS AND THERAPY. see *PSYCHOLOGY*

616.8 IT ISSN 0010-9452
CORTEX; journal devoted to study of the nervous system and behavior. (Text in English) 1964. q. L.105000($123) to individuals; institutions L.210000($243)(effective 1992). (Associazione per lo Sviluppo delle Recerche Neuropsicologiche) Masson Italia Periodici, Via Statuto 2-4, 20121 Milan, Italy. TEL 02-6367-1. FAX 02-6367211. Ed. Ennio De Renzi. adv.; bk.rev.; charts; index; circ. 1,800. (also avail. in microform from SWZ,UMI; reprint service avail. from SWZ) **Indexed:** Bibl.Dev.Med.& Child Neur., Biol.Abstr., Curr.Adv.Ecol.Sci., Curr.Cont., Dent.Ind., Ergon.Abstr., Excerp.Med., Ind.Med., Ind.Sci.Rev., Psychol.Abstr., Sci.Cit.Ind., Yrbk.Assoc.Educ.& Rehab.Blind.
—BLDSC shelfmark: 3477.150000.

COUNSELLING PSYCHOLOGY QUARTERLY. see *PSYCHOLOGY*

616.8 US ISSN 0892-0915
RC321 CODEN: CCNBE8
CRITICAL REVIEWS IN NEUROBIOLOGY. 1985. q. $79.95 to individuals; institutions $225. C R C Press, Inc., 2000 Corporate Blvd., N.W., Boca Raton, FL 33431. TEL 407-994-0555. FAX 407-998-9784. Ed. James S. Nelson.
—BLDSC shelfmark: 3487.478500.
Formerly: Critical Reviews in Clinical Neurobiology.

CULTURE, MEDICINE AND PSYCHIATRY; an international journal of comparative cross-cultural research. see *ANTHROPOLOGY*

CURRENT ADVANCES IN NEUROSCIENCE. see *MEDICAL SCIENCES — Abstracting, Bibliographies, Statistics*

616.8 US ISSN 0161-780X
RC321 CODEN: CNEUDS
CURRENT NEUROLOGY. 1980. a. $69.95. Mosby - Year Book, Inc. (Chicago) (Subsidiary of: Times Mirror Company), 200 N. LaSalle St., Chicago, IL 60601-1080. TEL 312-726-9733. FAX 312-726-6075. TELEX 206155. (Subscr. to: 11830 Westline Industrial Dr., St. Louis, MO 63146. TEL 800-325-4177) Ed. Stanley H. Appel, M.D. illus. **Indexed:** Chem.Abstr.
—BLDSC shelfmark: 3500.630000.
Description: Presents reviews of the pertinent literature combined with original papers in neurology.

CURRENT OPINION IN NEUROBIOLOGY. see *BIOLOGY — Abstracting, Bibliographies, Statistics*

CURRENT OPINION IN NEUROLOGY & NEUROSURGERY. see *MEDICAL SCIENCES — Abstracting, Bibliographies, Statistics*

CURRENT OPINION IN PSYCHIATRY. see *MEDICAL SCIENCES — Abstracting, Bibliographies, Statistics*

MEDICAL SCIENCES — PSYCHIATRY AND NEUROLOGY

616.4   US
CURRENT TOPICS IN NEUROENDOCRINOLOGY. 1982. irreg. price varies. Springer-Verlag, 175 Fifth Ave., New York, NY 10010. TEL 212-460-1500. (Also Berlin, Heidelberg, Tokyo and Vienna) **Indexed:** Chem.Abstr.

616.8   GW
D G S P RUNDBRIEF. 1977. q. DM.40. Deutsche Gesellschaft fuer Soziale Psychiatrie e.V., Stuppstr. 14, D-5000 Cologne 30, Germany. TEL 221-511002. adv.; bk.rev.; circ. 3,000. (back issues avail.)

616.89   SZ   ISSN 0254-6221
    CODEN: DABAD9
DASEINSANALYSE; phaenomenologische Antropologie und Psychiatrie. 1984. 4/yr. 108 Fr.($72) S. Karger AG, Allschwilerstr. 10, P.O. Box, CH-4009 Basel, Switzerland. TEL 061-3061111. FAX 061-3061234. TELEX CH 962652. Eds. G. Condrau, A. Hicklin. adv.; bk.rev.; illus.; index; circ. 1,150. (back issues avail.)
—BLDSC shelfmark: 3533.920000.

616.8   SZ   ISSN 1013-7424
    CODEN: DEMNEU
▼**DEMENTIA.** (Text in English) 1990. bi-m. 141 Fr.($94) to individuals; institutions 637 Fr.($425). S. Karger AG, Allschwilerstr. 10, P.O. Box, CH-4009 Basel, Switzerland. TEL 061-3061111. FAX 061-3061234. TELEX CH 962652. (US and Canada subscr. to: S. Karger Publishers, Inc., 26 W. Avon Rd., Farmington, CT 06085) Ed. V. Chan-Palay. bibl.; charts; stat.
—BLDSC shelfmark: 3550.524000.
    Description: Examines the neural bases of cognitive dysfunction. Concentrates on neuro-degenerative diseases such as Alzheimer's and Parkinson's diseases, as well as Huntington's chorea. Covers topics of interest to professional in neurobiology, pharmacology, genetics, gerontology, and psychiatry.

DEVELOPMENT AND PSYCHOPATHOLOGY. see *PSYCHOLOGY*

616.858   CN   ISSN 1184-0412
DEVELOPMENT DISABILITY BULLETIN. 1972. s-a. Can.$19.25 to individuals (foreign $15); institutions Can.$32.10 (foreign $25). University of Alberta, Developmental Disabilities Centre, 6-123D Education North, Edmonton, Alta. T6G 2G5, Canada. TEL 403-432-4505. FAX 403-492-1318. adv.; bk.rev.; circ. 250. **Indexed:** Psychol.Abstr., Yrbk.Assoc.Educ.& Rehab.Blind.
—BLDSC shelfmark: 3579.054450.
    Formerly: Mental Retardation and Learning Disability Bulletin (ISSN 0822-4277)
    Description: Articles with both research and direct application to the education of, and provision of services for persons with mental retardation, learning disability and multiple handicaps.

616.8   NE   ISSN 0165-3806
QP376   CODEN: DBRRDB
DEVELOPMENTAL BRAIN RESEARCH. Issued with: Brain Research (ISSN 0921-8246) 1981. 12/yr.(in 6 vols.; 2 nos./vol.) fl.1986 (effective 1992). Elsevier Science Publishers B.V., P.O. Box 211, 1000 AE Amsterdam, Netherlands. TEL 020-5803911. FAX 020-5803598. TELEX 18582 ESPA NL. (N. America dist. addr.: Elsevier Science Publishing Co., Inc., Box 882, Madison Sq. Sta., New York, NY 10159. TEL 212-989-5800) Ed. D.P. Purpura. (reprint service avail. from ISI) **Indexed:** Bibl.Dev.Med.& Child Neur., Biol.Abstr., Chem.Abstr., Curr.Adv.Biochem., Curr.Adv.Ecol.Sci., Curr.Cont., Excerp.Med., Ind.Sci.Rev., Psychol.Abstr., Sci.Cit.Ind.
—BLDSC shelfmark: 3579.054200.
    Description: Provides a medium for prompt publication of vitro and in vivo developmental studies concerned with the mechanism of neurogenesis, neuro migration, cell death, neuronal differentiation, synaptogenesis, myelination, the establishment of neuroglia relations and the development of various brain-barrier mechnisms.

DEVELOPMENTAL MEDICINE AND CHILD NEUROLOGY. see *MEDICAL SCIENCES — Pediatrics*

616.8   SZ   ISSN 0378-5866
    CODEN: DENED7
DEVELOPMENTAL NEUROSCIENCE; international journal of experimental and clinical neuroscience. 1979. bi-m. 663 Fr.($442) S. Karger AG, Allschwilerstr. 10, P.O. Box, CH-4009 Basel, Switzerland. TEL 061-3061111. FAX 061-3061234. TELEX CH 962652. Eds. N. Baumann, A.T. Campagnoni. adv.; illus.; index; circ. 800. (also avail. in microform from RPI) **Indexed:** ASCA, Biol.Abstr., Chem.Abstr., Curr.Adv.Biochem., Curr.Adv.Cell & Devel.Biol., Curr.Adv.Ecol.Sci., Curr.Cont., Excerp.Med., Helminthol.Abstr., Ind.Med., Ind.Sci.Rev, Sci.Cit.Ind.
—BLDSC shelfmark: 3579.057500.

616.8   NE
DEVELOPMENTS IN NEUROSCIENCE. 1977. irreg., vol.18, 1984. price varies. Elsevier Science Publishers B.V., Books Division, P.O. Box 211, 1000 AE Amsterdam, Netherlands. TEL 020-5803911. FAX 020-5803705. TELEX 18582 ESPA NL. (Subscr. in U.S. and Canada to: Elsevier Science Publishing Co., Inc., Box 882, Madison Sq. Sta., New York, NY 10159. TEL 212-989-5800) **Indexed:** Chem.Abstr., Ind.Sci.Rev., Sci.Cit.Ind.
    Refereed Serial

616.8   NE   ISSN 0166-2481
    CODEN: DPSYDX
DEVELOPMENTS IN PSYCHIATRY. 1979. irreg., vol,8, 1987. Elsevier Science Publishers B.V., Books Division, P.O. Box 211, 1000 AE Amsterdam, Netherlands. TEL 020-5803911. FAX 020-5803705. TELEX 18582 ESPA NL. (Subscr. in U.S. and Canada to: Elsevier Science Publishing Co., Inc., Box 882, Madison Sq. Sta., New York, NY 10159. TEL 212-989-5800) illus. (back issues avail.) **Indexed:** Chem.Abstr.
    Refereed Serial

616.891 615.1   US
DI CYAN BULLETIN. 1950. m. Erwin Di Cyan, Ed. & Pub., 1486 E. 33rd St., Brooklyn, NY 11234. TEL 718-252-8844. bk.rev.
    Formerly: Di Cyan and Brown Bulletin (ISSN 0012-1754)

DIALECT. see *SOCIAL SERVICES AND WELFARE*

DIRECTORY OF GRADUATE TRAINING IN BEHAVIOR THERAPY. see *EDUCATION — Guides To Schools And Colleges*

DIRECTORY OF SUICIDE PREVENTION AND CRISIS INTERVENTION CENTERS. see *PSYCHOLOGY*

616.8   NE   ISSN 0254-8852
QP351   CODEN: DISNEK
DISCUSSIONS IN NEUROSCIENCE. (Text and summaries in English) 1984. q. fl.69 (effective 1992). (Fondation pour l'Etude du Systeme Nerveux Central et Peripherique) Elsevier Science Publishers B.V., P.O. Box 211, 1000 AE Amsterdam, Netherlands. TEL 020-5803911. FAX 020-5803598. TELEX 18582 ESPA NL. (Subscr. in U.S. and Canada to: Elsevier Science Publishing Co., Inc., Box 882, Madison Sq. Sta., New York, NY 10159. TEL 212-989-5800) Ed. P.J. Magistretti. adv.; bk.rev. (reprint service avail. from ISI)
—BLDSC shelfmark: 3597.053700.
    Description: Publishes monographs and proceedings on various areas in neurosience.
    Refereed Serial

616.8   US
DORMANT BRAIN SELF-RELEASE RESEARCH REPORTS. 1957. m. $12. Dormant Brain Research and Development Laboratory, Laughing Coyote Mountain, Box 10, Black Hawk, CO 80422. Ed. T.D. Lingo. bk.rev.; circ. 2,000. (looseleaf format; back issues avail.)

DREAMING. see *BIOLOGY — Physiology*

621.3   GW   ISSN 0012-7590
    CODEN: EEGEAG
E E G-E M G; Zeitschrift fuer Elektroenzephalographie, Elektromyographie und verwandte Gebiete. 1970. q. DM.232. Georg Thieme Verlag, Ruedigerstr. 14, Postfach 104853, 7000 Stuttgart 10, Germany. TEL 0711-8931-0. Ed.Bd. adv.; bk.rev.; abstr.; bibl.; charts; illus.; stat.; index; circ. 1,200. (also avail. in microform from UMI; reprint service avail. from UMI) **Indexed:** Curr.Cont., Excerp.Med., Ind.Med.
—BLDSC shelfmark: 3663.394000.

616.8   IE   ISSN 0921-884X
RC321   CODEN: ECNEAZ
ELECTROENCEPHALOGRAPHY AND CLINICAL NEUROPHYSIOLOGY INCLUDING EVOKED POTENTIALS AND ELECTROMYOGRAPHY AND MOTOR CONTROL. Variant title: E E G Journal. (Text in English and French) 1949. s-m. $376 (effective 1992). (International Federation of Societies for Electroencephalography and Clinical Neurophysiology) Elsevier Scientific Publishers Ireland Ltd., P.O. Box 85, Limerick, Ireland. TEL 061-61944. FAX 061-62144. TELEX 72191 ENH EI. (Subscr. in U.S. and Canada to: Elsevier Science Publishing Co., Inc., Box 882, Madison Sq. Sta., New York, NY 10159. TEL 212-989-5800) Ed.Bd. adv.; bk.rev.; abstr.; charts; illus.; index. (also avail. in microform from RPI) **Indexed:** Bibl.Dev.Med.& Child Neur., Biol.Abstr., C.I.S. Abstr., Chem.Abstr., Curr.Adv.Ecol.Sci., Curr.Cont., Dent.Ind., Ergon.Abstr., Excerp.Med., Ind.Med., Ind.Sci.Rev., Int.Abstr.Biol.Sci., Psychol.Abstr., Sci.Abstr.
    Supersedes: Electroencephalography and Clinical Neurophysiology (ISSN 0013-4694); Which incorporates: Index to Current E E G Literature (ISSN 0019-3976)
    Description: Provides comprehensive coverage of research into the electrical activity in the central nervous system.
    Refereed Serial

616.8   IE   ISSN 0924-980X
ELECTROMYOGRAPHY AND MOTOR CONTROL. 1991. 6/yr. $112 (effective 1992). (International Federation of Societies for Electroencephalography and Clinical Neurophysiology) Elsevier Scientific Publishers Ireland Ltd., P.O. Box 85, Limerick, Ireland. TEL 061-61944. FAX 061-62144. TELEX 72191 ENH EI. (Subscr. in U.S. and Canada to: Elsevier Science Publishing Co., Inc., Box 882, Madison Sq. Sta., New York, NY 10159. TEL 212-989-5800) Eds. F. Maugiere, G.G. Celesis. **Indexed:** Excerp.Med. (1992-).
    Description: Covers all clinical applications of EMG, reflexology, premotor evoked potentials and brain stimulation as well as experimental studies of human motor physiology.
    Refereed Serial

616.8   US   ISSN 0734-9890
    CODEN: EBMOEN
EMOTIONS AND BEHAVIOR. MONOGRAPH. irreg. price varies. (Chicago Institute for Psychoanalysis) International Universities Press, Inc., 59 Boston Post Rd., Box 1524, Madison, CT 06443-1524. TEL 203-245-4000. Ed. George H. Pollock. **Indexed:** Psychol.Abstr.
—BLDSC shelfmark: 3733.569500.
    Refereed Serial

616.89   FR   ISSN 0013-7006
    CODEN: ENCEAN
ENCEPHALE; revue de psychiatrie biologique et therapeutique. (Text in French; summaries in English, French) 1906; N.S. 1973. 6/yr. 630 F. (foreign 740 F.). Doin Editeurs, 8 place de l'Odeon, 75006 Paris, France. Ed. Prof. P. Deniker. adv.; bk.rev.; charts; tr.lit.; index; circ. 1,200. (also avail. in microform from UMI; reprint service avail. from UMI) **Indexed:** Biol.Abstr., Chem.Abstr., Curr.Cont., Excerp.Med., Ind.Med., Psychol.Abstr.
—BLDSC shelfmark: 3738.390000.

ENCOUNTERER. see *PSYCHOLOGY*

616.8 574.192   YU   ISSN 0351-2665
ENGRAMI. (Text in Serbo-Croatian; summaries in English and Russian) 1979. q. 4000 din. Institut za Psihijatriju, University Clinical Center, Pasterova br. 2, 11000 Belgrade, Yugoslavia. (Co-sponsor: Yugoslav Psychiatric Association) Ed. Dimitrije Milovanovic. circ. 500.

M

MEDICAL SCIENCES — PSYCHIATRY AND NEUROLOGY

616.858 300   CN   ISSN 0829-8815
ENTOURAGE. (Text in English, French) 1958. q. Can.$18. (Canadian Association for the Community Living) G. Allan Roeher Institute, Kinsmen Bldg., York University, 4700 Keele St., Toronto, Ont. M3J 1P3, Canada. TEL 416-661-9611. FAX 416-661-5701. Ed. Laura Code. adv.; bk.rev.; circ. 6,000. **Indexed:** C.I.J.E., Can.Educ.Ind, Can.Per.Ind., Except.Child.Educ.Abstr., Psychol.Abstr., Sp.Ed.Needs Abstr.
—BLDSC shelfmark: 3790.527000.
   Incorporates (in Jun. 1988): Information Exchange Bulletin; **Former titles (until 1986):** Revue Canadienne de la Deficience Mentale - Canadian Journal on Mental Retardation; Deficience Mentale - Mental Retardation (ISSN 0011-7668)
   Description: Explores the issues affecting people who have been labelled mentally handicapped, their families and the advocates working for them. Keeps readers up-to-date on new developments in the disability movement across Canada and around the world.

616.853   DK   ISSN 0107-2668
EPILEPSI. 1980. q. DKK 65. Dansk Epilepsiforening, Korsgade 16,1, 2200 Copenhagen N, Denmark. TEL 31-39-41-00. Ed. Knud K. Brander. adv.; bk.rev.; illus.; circ. 8,000.
   Formerly: Tidsskrift for Epilepsi.

616.853   US   ISSN 0013-9580
RC395   CODEN: EPILAK
EPILEPSIA. (Text mainly in English with occasional articles in French and German; summaries in English, French, Spanish and German) 1959. bi-m. $180 to individuals; institutions $290. (International League against Epilepsy) Raven Press, 1185 Ave. of the Americas, New York, NY 10036. TEL 212-930-9500. FAX 212-869-3495. TELEX 640073. Ed. James J. Cereghino. adv.; bk.rev.; charts; illus.; circ. 4,000. (reprint service avail. from KTO) **Indexed:** Bibl.Dev.Med.& Child Neur., Biol.Abstr., Chem.Abstr., Curr.Adv.Ecol.Sci., Curr.Cont., Dent.Ind., Excerp.Med., Helminthol.Abstr., Ind.Med., Ind.Sci.Rev., Psychol.Abstr., Sci.Cit.Ind.
—BLDSC shelfmark: 3793.700000.
   Description: Provides current clinical and research results on all aspects of epilepsy.
   Refereed Serial

616.853   SZ
EPILEPSIE. (Text and summaries in French, German and Italian) 1983. 2/yr. 25 Fr. Schweizerische Liga gegen Epilepsie, c/o Pro Infirmis, Feldeggstr. 71, Postfach 129, CH-8032 Zurich, Switzerland. Ed.Bd. bk.rev.; circ. 800.
   Description: Covers medical and social aspects, featuring research in treatment, diagnosis, therapy, and heredity, as well as social and educational problems of different age groups. Includes list of events.

616.853   FR
EPILEPSIE. 4/yr. 260 F. to individuals; institutions 370 F. (Ligue Francaise Contre l'Epilepsie) John Libbey Eurotext, 6 rue Blanche, 92120 Montrouge, France. TEL 1-47-35-85-52. FAX 1-46-57-10-09.

616.8   NE   ISSN 0920-1211
CODEN: EPIRE8
EPILEPSY RESEARCH. (Supplement avail.) (Text in English) 1987. 9/yr.(in 3 vols.; 3 nos./vol.) fl.1281 (effective 1992). Elsevier Science Publishers B.V., P.O. Box 211, 1000 AE Amsterdam, Netherlands. TEL 020-5803911. FAX 020-5803598. TELEX 18582 ESPA NL. (Subscr. in U.S. and Canada to: Elsevier Science Publishing Co., Inc., Box 882, Madison Sq. Sta., New York, NY 10159. TEL 212-989-5800) Ed.Bd. adv.; bk.rev.; index; circ. 850. (back issues avail.; reprint service avail. from ISI) **Indexed:** Excerp.Med.
—BLDSC shelfmark: 3793.805000.
   Description: Provides for rapid publication of high quality articles in both experimental and clinical epileptology, where the principal emphasis of the research is concerned with brain mechanisms in epilepsy.
   Refereed Serial

616.853   UK
EPILEPSY TODAY. 1976. q. £6 membership (foreign £10). British Epilepsy Association, Anstey House, 40 Hanover Sq., Leeds, W. Yorks, England. TEL 01-636-1544. FAX 0532-428804. Ed. Maggie Heaton. adv.; bk.rev.; circ. 12,000. **Indexed:** Sp.Ed.Needs Abstr.
   Former titles (until 1987): Epilepsy Now! (ISSN 0262-5474); (until 1981): Epilepsy News (ISSN 0308-9703); Candle (ISSN 0008-5502)

EPILETTER. see *SOCIAL SERVICES AND WELFARE*

616.8   CN   ISSN 0708-1987
ETAPE.* (Text in French) 1978. q. membership. Association de Paralysie Cerebrale du Quebec, 525 Boul. Hamel Est., Sous-Sol, Aila A, no.50, Quebec, Que. G1M 2S8, Canada. TEL 418-529-5371. illus.

616.8   GW   ISSN 0175-758X
EUROPEAN ARCHIVES OF PSYCHIATRY AND
NEUROLOGICAL SCIENCES. (Vereinigt mit Zeitschrift fuer die Gesamte Neurologie und Psychiatrie) 1868. 6/yr. DM.668($258) (Gesamtverband Deutscher Nervenaerzte) Springer-Verlag, Heidelberger Platz 3, D-1000 Berlin 33, Germany. TEL 030-8207-1. (Also Heidelberg, Tokyo, Vienna, and New York) Ed. R. Goldsmith. adv.; bibl.; charts; illus. (also avail. in microform from UMI; microfiche from BHP; back issues avail.; reprint service avail. from ISI) **Indexed:** ASCA, Biol.Abstr., Chem.Abstr., Curr.Adv.Ecol.Sci., Curr.Adv.Genetics & Molec.Biol., Curr.Cont., Excerp.Med., Ger.J.Psych., Ind.Med., Ind.Sci.Rev., Psychol.Abstr., Risk Abstr., Sci.Cit.Ind.
   Formerly (until 1984): Archiv fuer Psychiatrie und Nervenkrankheiten (ISSN 0003-9373)
   Description: Covers clinical psychiatry, psychopathology, and epidemiology, as well as neuropathological, neurophysiological, and neurochemical studies of psychiatric disorders.

616.8   UK   ISSN 0953-816X
CODEN: EJONEI
EUROPEAN JOURNAL OF NEUROSCIENCE. 1989. m. £215($395) Oxford University Press, Oxford Journals, Pinkhill House, Southfield Road, Eynsham, Oxford OX8 1JJ, England. TEL 0865-882283. FAX 0865-882890. TELEX 837330 OXPRES G. Ed. R.W. Guillery. adv.; circ. 3,000.
—BLDSC shelfmark: 3829.731700.
   Description: Presents a broad scope of neuroscience, ranging from the behavioral to the molecular, with a European focus and a worldwide orientation.

616.8   SZ   ISSN 0014-3022
CODEN: EUNEAP
EUROPEAN NEUROLOGY. (Text in English) 1968. bi-m. 584 Fr.($390) S. Karger AG, Allschwilerstr. 10, P.O. Box, CH-4009 Basel, Switzerland. TEL 061-3061111. FAX 061-3061234. TELEX CH 962652. Ed. H.E. Kaeser. index; circ. 1,050. (also avail. in microform from RPI) **Indexed:** Bibl.Dev.Med.& Child Neur., Biol.Abstr., Chem.Abstr., Curr.Adv.Ecol.Sci., Curr.Cont., Dent.Ind., Excerp.Med., Helminthol.Abstr., Ind.Med., Ind.Sci.Rev., Nutr.Abstr., Protozool.Abstr., Sci.Cit.Ind.
—BLDSC shelfmark: 3829.765000.
   Formerly (until 1968): Psychiatria et Neurologia.

616.8 615.1   NE   ISSN 0924-977X
CODEN: EURNE8
▼**EUROPEAN NEUROPSYCHOPHARMACOLOGY.** (Text in English) 1990. 4/yr. fl.421 (effective 1992). (European College of Neuropsychopharmacology) Elsevier Science Publishers B.V., P.O. Box 211, 1000 AE Amsterdam, Netherlands. TEL 020-5803911. FAX 020-5803598. TELEX 18582 ESPA NL. (Subscr. in U.S. and Canada to: Elsevier Science Publishing Co., Inc., Box 882, Madison Sq. Sta., New York, NY 10159. TEL 212-989-5800) Eds. J.M. van Ree, S.A. Montgomery. adv.; bk.rev. (back issues avail.)
—BLDSC shelfmark: 3829.765350.
   Description: Publishes clinical and basic research articles in the field of neuropsychopharmacology, with particular focus on the effects of centrally acting agents.
   Refereed Serial

616.8   FR   ISSN 0924-9338
CODEN: PPSYEU
EUROPEAN PSYCHIATRY. (Text in English; summaries in English, French) 1986. bi-m. 890 F. (foreign 1020 F.)(effective 1992). (Association of European Psychiatrists) Editions Scientifiques Elsevier, 29, rue Buffon, 75005 Paris, France. TEL 47-07-11-22. (Subscr. in U.S. and Canada to: Elsevier Science Publishing Co., Inc., Box 882, Madison Sq. Sta., New York, NY 10159. TEL 212-989-5800) Ed.Bd. adv.; bk.rev.; circ. 3,000. (also avail. in microform; back issues avail.) **Indexed:** Biol.Abstr., Excerp.Med.
   Formerly: Psychiatry and Psychobiology (ISSN 0767-399X)
   Description: Presents original research in psychopathology, nosography, chemotherapy, psychotherapy, clinical methodology, biological disorders and mental pathology, psychophysiology, neurophychology, and animal behavior.
   Refereed Serial

616.8   IE   ISSN 0168-5597
EVOKED POTENTIALS. 1984. 6/yr. $136 (effective 1992). (International Federation of Societies for Electroencephalography and Clinical Neurophysiology) Elsevier Scientific Publishers Ireland Ltd., P.O. Box 85, Limerick, Ireland. TEL 061-61944. FAX 061-62144. TELEX 72191 ENH EI. (Subscr. in U.S. and Canada to: Elsevier Science Publishing Co., Inc., Box 882, Madison Sq. Sta., New York, NY 10159. TEL 212-989-5800) Eds. F. Mauguiere, G.G. Celesia. **Indexed:** Biol.Abstr., Curr.Cont., Excerp.Med.
   Description: Covers anaesthesiology, clinical medicine, neurology, neuro-physiology, neurosurgery, psychiatry, psychology.
   Refereed Serial

616.89   FR   ISSN 0014-3855
CODEN: EVPSAG
EVOLUTION PSYCHIATRIQUE. 1925. q. 620 F. Dunod, 15 rue Gossin, 92543 Montrouge Cedex, France. TEL 33-1-40-92-65-00. FAX 33-1-40-92-65-97. TELEX 270 004. (Subscr. to: Centrale des Revues, 11 rue Gossin, 92543 Montrouge Cedex, France. TEL 33-1-46-56-52-66) Ed. Y. Thoret. adv.; bibl. **Indexed:** Biol.Abstr., Excerp.Med., Ind.Med., Lang.& Lang.Behav.Abstr., Psychol.Abstr.
—BLDSC shelfmark: 3834.320000.
   Description: Exposes psychiatry to the different currents in scientific and philosophical thought, and in clinical research and critical reflection, as they develop both in this field and in related areas.

616.8   US
EXPERIMENTAL AND CLINICAL PSYCHIATRY. 1979. irreg., vol.8, 1983. price varies. Marcel Dekker, Inc., 270 Madison Ave., New York, NY 10016. TEL 212-696-9000. FAX 212-685-4540. TELEX 421419. Ed. Van Praag. **Indexed:** Psychol.Abstr.
   Refereed Serial

616.8   GW   ISSN 0014-4819
CODEN: EXBRAP
EXPERIMENTAL BRAIN RESEARCH. (Supplements avail.) (Text in English, French or German) 1965. 15/yr. DM.3490. (International Brain Research Organization) Springer-Verlag, Heidelberger Platz 3, D-1000 Berlin 33, Germany. TEL 030-8207-1. (Also Heidelberg, Tokyo, Vienna, and New York) Ed. O. Creutzfeldt. adv.; bibl.; charts; illus.; index. (also avail. in microform from UMI; back issues avail.; reprint service avail. from ISI) **Indexed:** Bibl.Dev.Med.& Child Neur., Biol.Abstr., Chem.Abstr., Curr.Adv.Ecol.Sci., Curr.Cont., Dairy Sci.Abstr., Dent.Ind., Excerp.Med., Ind.Med., INIS Atomind., Nutr.Abstr., Psychol.Abstr., Sci.Cit.Ind.
—BLDSC shelfmark: 3838.800000.
   Description: Interdisciplinary approach to the study of the central and peripheral nervous systems. Covers the fields of morphology, physiology, behavior, neurochemistry, developmental neurobiology, and experimental pathology relevant to general problems of brain function.

616.8   US   ISSN 0172-9039
CODEN: EBRSDP
EXPERIMENTAL BRAIN RESEARCH. SUPPLEMENTA. 1976. irreg. price varies. Springer-Verlag, 175 Fifth Ave., New York, NY 10010. TEL 212-460-1500. (reprint service avail. from ISI) **Indexed:** Chem.Abstr., Ind.Sci.Rev.

MEDICAL SCIENCES — PSYCHIATRY AND NEUROLOGY   3337

616.8　　　　US　ISSN 0014-4886
RC321　　　　　　CODEN: EXNEAC
EXPERIMENTAL NEUROLOGY. 1959. m. $592 (foreign $745). Academic Press, Inc., Journal Division, 1250 Sixth Ave., San Diego, CA 92101. TEL 619-230-1840. FAX 619-699-6800. TELEX 181726. Ed. John R. Sladek, Jr. index. (back issues avail.) **Indexed:** Bibl.Dev.Med.& Child Neur., Biol.Abstr., Chem.Abstr., Curr.Adv.Biochem., Curr.Adv.Cell & Devel.Biol., Curr.Adv.Ecol.Sci., Curr.Cont., Dairy Sci.Abstr., Dent.Ind., Excerp.Med., Helminthol.Abstr., Ind.Med., Ind.Sci.Rev., INIS Atomind., Int.Aerosp.Abstr., Nutr.Abstr., Psychol.Abstr., Sci.Cit.Ind.
—BLDSC shelfmark: 3839.850000.
Description: Publishes the results and conclusions of original research in neuroscience with emphasis on novel findings in neural development, regeneration, plasticity, and transplantation.
Refereed Serial

616.8　　　　US
EYE OPENER. 1976. q. $25 includes membership. American Narcolepsy Association, Box 26230, San Francisco, CA 94126-6230. TEL 415-788-4793. Ed. Stephen B. Texeira. circ. 5,000.
Description: Directed to people with narcolepsy, their friends and family members. Provides research updates, information on coping strategies and the advocacy efforts of the association in job discrimination, social security help and insurance problems.

616.8　　　　SP　ISSN 0213-7429
FACULTAD DE MEDICINA DE BARCELONA. REVISTA DE PSIQUIATRIA. (Supplement avail.) (Text in Spanish; summaries in English and Spanish) 1973. bi-m. 4000 ptas.($73) (Departamento de Psiquiatria y Psicologia Medica del Hospital Clinico y Provincial de Barcelona) Editorial Rocas, Calaf. 29, 2-3, 08021 Barcelona, Spain. TEL 200-13-89. FAX 202-19-58. Dir. Carlos Ballus Pascual. adv.; bk.rev.; illus.; charts; stat.; index; circ. 2,000. (back issues avail.) **Indexed:** Excerp.Med., Psychol.Abstr.
Formerly: Facultad de Medicina de Barcelona. Departamento de Psiquiatria. Revista (ISSN 0210-1793)
Description: Original research articles on various topics in psychiatry, medicine and psychology.

FAMILY SUPPORT BULLETIN. see *HANDICAPPED — Physically Impaired*

616.8　　　　US　ISSN 0091-6544
RC488.5.A1　　　　CODEN: FATHD6
FAMILY THERAPY. 1972. 3/yr. $44 to individuals; institutions $50. (California Graduate School of Family Psychology) Libra Publishers, Inc., 3089C Clairemont Dr., Ste. 383, San Diego, CA 92117. TEL 619-581-9449. Ed. Dr. Martin G. Blinder. adv.; index, cum.index. (also avail. in microform from UMI; back issues avail.; reprint service avail. from ISI,UMI) **Indexed:** Adol.Ment.Hlth.Abstr., ASSIA, Mid.East: Abstr.& Ind., Psychol.Abstr., Psyscan D.P., Sage Fam.Stud.Abstr., Sage Urb.Stud.Abstr., Soc.Work Res.& Abstr., Sp.Ed.Needs Abstr.
—BLDSC shelfmark: 3865.576350.

FLASH-INFORMATIONS. see *MEDICAL SCIENCES — Orthopedics And Traumatology*

616.891 360　　　NO　ISSN 0332-5415
FOKUS PAA FAMILIEN; Norwegian journal on family therapy. 1972. q. $39 to individuals; institutions $56. Universitetsforlaget, P.O. Box 2959-Toeyen, N-0608 Oslo 1, Norway. (U.S. addr.: Publications Expediting Inc., 200 Meacham Ave., Elmont, NY 11003) Ed. Sissel Gran. circ. 2,200.

616.8　　　　SP
FOLIA NEUROPSIQUIATRICA DEL SUR DE ESPANA. 1966. 3/yr. 2115 ptas. Universidad de Granada, Servicio de Publicaciones, Antiguo Colegio Maximo, Campus de Cartuja, 18071 Granada, Spain. TEL 281356. Ed. M. Soler Vinolo. **Indexed:** Biol.Abstr., Excerp.Med., Ind.Med.Esp.

FOLIA PHONIATRICA; international journal of phoniatrics, speech therapy and communication pathology. see *MEDICAL SCIENCES — Otorhinolaryngology*

616.8　　　　GW
FORTSCHRITTE DER NEUROLOGIE, PSYCHIATRIE. (Supplement avail.: Neurochirurgia) 1931. m. DM.240. Georg Thieme Verlag, Ruedigerstr. 14, Postfach 104853, 7000 Stuttgart 10, Germany. TEL 0711-8931-0. Ed.Bd. adv.; bk.rev.; bibl.; charts; illus.; stat.; index; circ. 2,200. (reprint service avail. from UMI) **Indexed:** Biol.Abstr., Chem.Abstr., Curr.Cont., Dent.Ind., Excerp.Med., Ger.J.Psych., Ind.Med., Ind.Sci.Rev., INIS Atomind., Psychol.Abstr., Sci.Cit.Ind.
Former titles: Fortschritte der Neurologie, Psychiatrie und ihrer Grenzgebiete; Fortschritte der Neurologie - Psychiatrie (ISSN 0720-4299); (until 1980): Fortschritte der Neurologie, Psychiatrie und Ihrer Grenzgebiete (ISSN 0015-8194)

616.8　　　　GW　ISSN 0071-8025
FORUM DER PSYCHIATRIE. 1961; N.S. 1977. irreg., vol.32, 1990. price varies. Ferdinand Enke Verlag, Postfach 101254, 7000 Stuttgart 10, Germany. TEL 0711-8931-0. FAX 0711-8931-419. TELEX 07252275-GTV-D. Ed.Bd.

616.8　　　　US
FROM THE COUCH.... 1983. q. $25. American Health Information Management Association, Mental Health Record Section, 919 N. Michigan Ave., Ste. 1400, Chicago, IL 60611-1601. TEL 312-787-2672. FAX 312-787-9793. Ed. Laura Feste. adv.; circ. 1,200. (back issues avail.)
Description: Medical recordkeeping and documentation in the mental health care facilities.

616.8　　　　NE
FUNCTIONS OF THE NERVOUS SYSTEM. vol.4, 1983. irreg. price varies. Elsevier Science Publishers B.V., Books Division, P.O. Box 211, 1000 AE Amsterdam, Netherlands. TEL 020-5803911. FAX 020-5803705. TELEX 18582 ESPA NL. (Subscr. in U.S. and Canada to: Elsevier Science Publishing Co., Inc., Box 882, Madison Sq. Sta., New York, NY 10159. TEL 212-989-5800) Ed. M. Monier.
Refereed Serial

616.8　　　　GW　ISSN 0931-0428
FUNDAMENTA PSYCHIATRICA; Psychiatrie in Theorie und Praxis. 1987. 4/yr. DM.153.60($96) F.K. Schattauer Verlagsgesellschaft mbH, Lenzhalde 3, Postfach 104545, 7000 Stuttgart 10, Germany. TEL 0711-22987-0. FAX 0711-22987-50. Ed. E. Lungershausen. adv.; index; circ. 2,200.

GEISTIGE BEHINDERUNG; Fachzeitschrift der Lebenshilfe fuer geistig Behinderte. see *EDUCATION — Special Education And Rehabilitation*

616.8　　　　US　ISSN 0163-8343
　　　　　　　　　　　　CODEN: GHPSDB
GENERAL HOSPITAL PSYCHIATRY; psychiatry, medicine and primary care. 1979. 7/yr. $216 to institutions (foreign $244)(effective 1992). Elsevier Science Publishing Co., Inc. (New York), 655 Ave. of the Americas, New York, NY 10010. TEL 212-989-5800. FAX 212-633-3965. TELEX 420643 AEP UI. Ed. Don R. Lipsitt. (also avail. in microform from RPI) **Indexed:** Abstr.Health Care Manage.Stud., Biol.Abstr., CINAHL, Curr.Cont., Excerp.Med., Ind.Med., INIS Atomind., Psychol.Abstr., Soc.Work Res.& Abstr., SSCI.
—BLDSC shelfmark: 4104.344000.
Description: Emphasizes a biopsychosocial approach to illness and health, and provides a forum for communication among professionals with clinical, academic, and research interests in psychiatry.
Refereed Serial

616.8　　　　US
GENERATIONS (WAYZATA). 1957. s-a. $15. National Ataxia Foundation, 750 Twelve Oaks Center, 15500 Wayzata Blvd., Wayzata, MN 55391. TEL 612-473-7666. FAX 612-473-9289..Ed. Donna Gruetzmacher. bk.rev.; circ. 7,000. (back issues avail.) **Indexed:** Hlth.Ind.
Description: Covers meetings, current research, events and activities and other Foundation news.

155
GENESIS OF BEHAVIOR. 1978. irreg., vol.6, 1990. price varies. Plenum Publishing Corp., 233 Spring St., New York, NY 10013-1578. TEL 212-620-8000. FAX 212-463-0742. TELEX 23-421139. Eds. Michael Lewis, Leonard A. Rosenblum. (back issues avail.)
Refereed Serial

GESTALT JOURNAL. see *PSYCHOLOGY*

616.8　　　　IT　ISSN 0392-4483
GIORNALE DI NEUROPSICHIATRIA DELL'ETA EVOLUTIVA. 1980. q. L.74400($102) (effective 1992). (Societa Italiana di Neuropsichiatria Infantile) Masson Italia Periodici, Via Statuto 2-4, 20121 Milan, Italy. TEL 02-6367-1. FAX 02-6367211. Ed. Fabio Canziani. circ. 2,000. **Indexed:** Excerp.Med.
—BLDSC shelfmark: 4178.470000.

616　　　　　IT　ISSN 0391-9048
GIORNALE DI NEUROPSICOFARMACOLOGIA. bi-m. L.50000($50) C I C Edizioni Internazionali s.r.l., Via Lazzaro Spallanzani, 11, 00161 Rome, Italy. TEL 06-8412673. FAX 06-8443365. TELEX 622099 CIC. Dir. A. Agnoli.
—BLDSC shelfmark: 4178.475000.

616.834　　　YU　ISSN 0353-5746
GLASILO M S. (Text in Serbo-Croatian) 1974. q. 1000 din.($20) (typically set in January). Savez Drustava Multiple Skleroze S F R J - Yugoslav Multiple Sclerosis Society, Bulevar AVNOJ-a 104, 11000 Belgrade, Yugoslavia. TEL 199-292. FAX 195-244. (Co-sponsor: Federal Executive Council of SFRJ) Ed. Dr. Miso Tiganjevic. adv.; bk.rev.; circ. 50,000. (back issues avail.)

616.8　　　　US　ISSN 0894-1491
QP363.2　　　　　CODEN: GLIAEJ
GLIA. 1988. 8/yr. $350 (foreign $ 450). John Wiley & Sons, Inc., Journals, 605 Third Ave, New York, NY 10158. TEL 212-850-6000. FAX 212-850-6088. TELEX 12-7063. Eds. Bruce R. Ransom, Helmut Hettenmann.
—BLDSC shelfmark: 4195.208000.
Description: Devoted to the study of the form and fucntion of neuroglial cells in health and disease.

616.89　　　　US
GROUP FOR THE ADVANCEMENT OF PSYCHIATRY. PUBLICATION. 1947. irreg., approx. 10 in 3 yrs. price varies. American Psychiatric Press, Inc., 1400 K St., N.W., Ste. 1101, Washington, DC 20005. TEL 202-682-6130. FAX 202-789-2648. (UK addr.: 17 Belgrave Sq., London SW1X 8PG, England) cum.index. **Indexed:** Ind.Med., Psychol.Abstr.
Supersedes (as of vol.9, 1977): Group for the Advancement of Psychiatry. Report (ISSN 0072-775X); Group for the Advancement of Psychiatry. Symposium.
Description: Reports from the Group for the Advancement of Psychiatry representing the latest thinking of the field on diverse and socially relevant topics.

616.89　　　　GW　ISSN 0017-4947
GRUPPENPSYCHOTHERAPIE UND GRUPPENDYNAMIK. (Text in German; summaries in English and German) 1968. irreg. (4 nos. per vol.) DM.96. Vandenhoeck und Ruprecht, Theaterstr 13., Postfach 3753, 3400 Goettingen, Germany. TEL 0551-6959-22. FAX 0551-695917. Ed. Dr. Anneliese Heigl-Evers. circ. 1,050. **Indexed:** Curr.Cont., Excerp.Med., Ger.J.Psych., SSCI.
—BLDSC shelfmark: 4223.460000.

616.858 371.9　　US　ISSN 1057-3291
HABILITATIVE MENTAL HEALTHCARE NEWSLETTER. 1982. m. $44 to individuals (foreign $60); institutions $57 (foreign $79). Psych-Media, Inc., Box 57, Bear Creek, NC 27207-0057. TEL 919-581-3700. FAX 919-581-3766. Eds. Dr. Robert Sovner, Anne DesNoyers Hurely. adv.; bibl.; index; circ. 2,000. (tabloid format; back issues avail.) **Indexed:** Psychol.Abstr.
Former titles (until vol.8, 1989): Psychiatric Aspects of Mental Retardation Reviews; (until 1983): Psychiatric Aspects of Mental Retardation Newsletter (ISSN 0278-9493)

616.834　　　SW　ISSN 0348-8071
HANDIKAPP - REFLEX. 1954. bi-m. SEK 75. Neurologiskt Handikappades Riksfoerbund - Swedish Association of Neurologically Disabled, Kungsgatan 32, S-111 35 Stockholm, Sweden. Ed. Ulla Richter. adv.; bk.rev.; illus.; stat.; circ. 11,500.
Formerly: M S-Brevet (ISSN 0345-8199)
Description: Discusses Multiple Sclerosis research.

M

MEDICAL SCIENCES — PSYCHIATRY AND NEUROLOGY

616.857 US ISSN 0017-8748
RC392 CODEN: HEADAE
HEADACHE; the journal of head and face pain. 1961. 10/yr. $60 (foreign $80). American Association for the Study of Headache, 875 Kings Hwy., Ste. 200, W. Depford, NJ 08096. TEL 609-845-0322. FAX 609-384-5811. Ed. Dr. John Edmeads. adv.; bk.rev.; abstr.; charts; illus.; stat.; cum.index; circ. 5,000. (also avail. in microform from UMI; reprint service avail. from UMI) **Indexed:** Bibl.Dev.Med.& Child Neur., Biol.Abstr., Chem.Abstr., Curr.Adv.Ecol.Sci., Curr.Cont., Curr.Tit.Dent., Dent.Ind., Excerp.Med., Ind.Med., Ind.Sci.Rev., NRN, Psychol.Abstr., Sci.Cit.Ind.
—BLDSC shelfmark: 4274.640000.

616.89 CN ISSN 0831-8530
HEALTH AND NUTRITION UPDATE. 1974. q. $30 (foreign $35)(effective 1992). Canadian Schizophrenia Foundation, 7375 Kingsway, Burnaby, B.C. V3N 3B5, Canada. TEL 604-521-1728. (Co-sponsor: Huxley Institute for Biosocial Research) Ed. Lorna Vander Haeghe. bk.rev.; circ. 3,500. (reprint service avail. from UMI) **Indexed:** Excerp.Med.
Formerly: Huxley Institute - C S F Newsletter (ISSN 0318-8272); Incorporates: Schizophrenics Anonymous International. Bulletin (ISSN 0048-9360)

616.858 US
HILL TOPIC. 1954. 3/yr. free. Glenwood State Hospital-School, 711 Vine, Glenwood, IA 51534. TEL 712-527-4811. Ed. Paul P. Brodigan. circ. 1,750.
Description: Highlights work with the mentally retarded.

616.8 UK ISSN 0957-154X
▼**HISTORY OF PSYCHIATRY.** 1990. q. £63($126) Alpha Academic (Subsidiary of: Richard Sadler Ltd.), Halfpenny Furze, Mill Lane, Chalfont St. Giles, Bucks HP8 4NR, England. TEL 02407-2509. (back issues avail.)
—BLDSC shelfmark: 4318.408000.
Description: Aims to publish research articles, analysis, information and reviews across the entire field of the history of mental illness and the forms of medicine, cultural response and social policy which have evolved to understand and treat it.

616.8 US ISSN 0960-7560
QP351.S65 CODEN: HOMOEB
HOMEOSTASIS IN HEALTH & DISEASE. (Text in English) 1959. 6/yr. £105($190) (effective 1992). (International Association for Integrative Nervous Functions) Pergamon Press, Inc., Journals Division, 660 White Plains Rd., Tarrytown, NY 10591-5153. TEL 914-524-9200. FAX 914-333-2444. (And: Headington Hill Hall, Oxford OX3 0BW, England. TEL 0865-794141) (Co-sponsors: Ceskoslovenska Spolecnost pro Studium Vyssi Nervove Cinnosti; Ceskoslovenska Lekarska Spolecnost J. Ev. Purkyne) Ed. M. Horvath. adv.; bk.rev.; illus.; index. **Indexed:** ASCA, Biol.Abstr., C.I.S. Abstr., Chem.Abstr., Curr.Adv.Ecol.Sci., Curr.Cont., Excerp.Med., Ind.Med., Ind.Sci.Rev., Nutr.Abstr., Psychol.Abstr., Psychopharmacol.Abstr., Sci.Cit.Ind.
—BLDSC shelfmark: 4326.176430.
Formerly (until vol.33, 1991): Activitas Nervosa Superior (ISSN 0001-7604)
Description: Devoted to understanding regulatory mechanisms ranging from molecular to systemic processes in health and disease, with emphasis on integrative functions in homeostatic control and their adaptation to environmental conditions and behavioral needs.
Refereed Serial

616.8 NE ISSN 0018-4705
HOOFDLIJNEN. 1965. 4/yr. fl.70 (effective 1992). (Nederlandse Vereniging van Laboranten Klinische Neurofysiologie - Dutch Association of Electro-Encephalographic Technicians) M. Dekker, Ed. & Pub., Graan voor Visch 15917, 2132 ET Hoofddorp, Netherlands. adv.; bk.rev.; charts; illus.; circ. 550.

616.89 US ISSN 0022-1597
RC443.A1 CODEN: HSCPAM
HOSPITAL AND COMMUNITY PSYCHIATRY. 1950. m. $37 to individuals (foreign $57); institutions $55 (foreign $75). (American Psychiatric Association) American Psychiatric Press, Inc., Journals Division, 1400 K St., N.W., Washington, DC 20005. TEL 202-682-6240. FAX 202-789-2648. (UK addr.: 17 Belgrave Sq., London SW1X 8PG, England) Ed. Dr. John A. Talbott. adv.; bk.rev.; film rev.; charts; illus.; stat.; index; circ. 23,000. (also avail. in microform from MIM,UMI; reprint service avail. from UMI) **Indexed:** Abstr.Health Care Manage.Stud., Biol.Abstr., C.I.N.L., Chic.Per.Ind., Crim.Just.Abstr., Curr.Cont., Curr.Lit.Fam.Plan., Excerp.Med., Hosp.Lit.Ind., Ind.Med., Int.Nurs.Ind., Media Rev.Dig., Past.Care & Couns.Abstr., Psychol.Abstr., Risk Abstr., Soc.Work Res.& Abstr., SSCI.
—BLDSC shelfmark: 4333.116000.
Formerly: Mental Hospitals (ISSN 0096-5502)
Description: Interdisciplinary approach to issues related to the delivery of mental health services in organized settings.
Refereed Serial

616.89 CU ISSN 0138-7103
HOSPITAL PSIQUIATRICO DE LA HABANA. REVISTA. (Text in Spanish; summaries in English) 1959. s-a. $20 in America; elsewhere $26. Hospital Psiquiatrico de la Habana, Avenida de la Independencia No. 26520, Mazorra, Havana, Cuba. TEL 5-683-4574. (Dist. by: Ediciones Cubanas, Obispo No. 527, Apdo. 605, Havana, Cuba) Ed. Dr. Edmundo Gutierrez Agramonte. adv.; abstr.; bibl.; illus.; stat.; circ. 8,000. (back issues avail.) **Indexed:** Psychol.Abstr.
—BLDSC shelfmark: 7815.900000.

616.8 615 UK ISSN 0885-6222
CODEN: HUPSEC
HUMAN PSYCHOPHARMACOLOGY: CLINICAL AND EXPERIMENTAL. 1986. bi-m. $275 (effective 1992). John Wiley & Sons Ltd., Journals, Baffins Lane, Chichester, Sussex PO19 1UD, England. TEL 0243 779777. FAX 0243-775878. TELEX 86290 WIBOOK G. Ed. Guy Edwards. adv. (reprint service avail. from SWZ) **Indexed:** Chem.Abstr., Curr.Cont., Excerp.Med., Psychol.Abstr.
—BLDSC shelfmark: 4336.380000.
Description: Communicates the results of clinical and experimental studies relevant to the understanding of new and established psychtropic drugs.

I A S T E D. INTERNATIONAL CONFERENCE PROCEEDINGS. (International Association of Science and Technology for Development) see *COMPUTERS — Artificial Intelligence*

616.8 AU ISSN 0539-0230
I E S A INFORMATION. (Editions in English) 1967. irreg. (3-4/yr.). membership. International Society for Electrosleep and Electroanaesthesia, Chirurgische Universitaetsklinik, A-8036 Graz, Austria. Ed.Bd. adv.; bk.rev.; abstr.; bibl.; charts; illus.; circ. 300. (processed)

I L S M H NEWS. (International League of Societies for Persons with Mental Handicap see *PSYCHOLOGY*

616.8 US
I T F NEWSLETTER. 1988. q. $25. International Tremor Foundation, 360 W. Superior St., Chicago, IL 60610. TEL 312-664-2344. Ed. Judy Rosner. circ. 6,500. (back issues avail.)
Description: Reports recent advances in research in layman's terms for patient and family education.

616.891 US
I U P STRESS AND HEALTH SERIES. irreg. price varies. International Universities Press, Inc., 59 Boston Post Rd., Box 1524, Madison, CT 06443-1524. TEL 203-245-4000. Ed. Leo Goldberger.
Refereed Serial

616.8 HU ISSN 0019-1442
CODEN: IDSZA4
IDEGGYOGYASZATI SZEMLE. (Summaries in German and Russian) 1948. 12/yr. $46. (Magyar Neurologiai es Pszichiatriai Tarsasag) Ifjusagi Lap-es Konyvkiado Vallalat, Revay u. 16, 1374 Budapest 6, Hungary. (Subscr. to: Kultura, Box 149, H-1389 Budapest, Hungary) Ed. Dr. Istvan Tariska. adv.; bk.rev.; illus. **Indexed:** Chem.Abstr., Excerp.Med., Ind.Med., INIS Atomind.

616.89 150.19 AG
IMAGO; revista de psicoanalisis, psiquiatria y psicologia. 1974. q. Letra Viva, Coronel Diaz 1837, Buenos Aires, Argentina.

616.8 614.58 US
IMPACT (AUSTIN). 1971. bi-m. free. Department of Mental Health and Mental Retardation, Public Information Office, Box 12668, Austin, TX 78711. TEL 512-465-4540. FAX 512-465-4711. Ed. Laurie Lentz. bk.rev.; charts; illus.; pat.; stat.; circ. 30,000.

INDEPENDENT LIVING. see *SOCIAL SERVICES AND WELFARE*

362.3 II ISSN 0019-5375
HV3004
INDIAN JOURNAL OF MENTAL RETARDATION. 1968. s-a. Rs.50($10) All India Association of Mental Retardation, c/o Dr. K. G. Agrawal, Ed., National Labour Institute, AB-6 Safdarjang Enclave, New Delhi 110029, India. adv.; bk.rev.; abstr. **Indexed:** Psychol.Abstr.

616.89 II ISSN 0019-5545
CODEN: IJRPAB
INDIAN JOURNAL OF PSYCHIATRY. (Text in English) 1959. q. $50. Indian Psychiatric Society, K.G.'s Medical College, B 104-2 Niralanagar, Lucknow 226 020, India. TEL 74044. Ed. A.K. Agarwal. adv.; bk.rev.; charts; illus.; stat.; index; circ. 1,500. **Indexed:** Chem.Abstr., Excerp.Med., Psychol.Abstr.
—BLDSC shelfmark: 4420.280000.

616.8 II ISSN 0253-7176
CODEN: IJPMEU
INDIAN JOURNAL OF PSYCHOLOGICAL MEDICINE. (Text in English) 1956. s-a. $15. Indian Psychiatric Society, South Zone, c/o Dr. Palaniappun M.D., Ed., D.P.M., Mnams 4A, V.P. Extension, Ayanavaran, Madras 23, India. TEL 5340. adv.; bk.rev.; bibl.; charts; illus.; stat.; circ. 600. (reprint service avail.) **Indexed:** Biol.Abstr., Curr.Adv.Ecol.Sci., Indian Psychol.Abstr., Indian Sci.Abstr., Lang.& Lang.Behav.Abstr.
Formerly (until 1978): Indian Journal of Psychology (ISSN 0019-5553)
Description: Research and review articles, and conference papers in various areas of psychiatry and related subjects.

INDIVIDUAL PSYCHOLOGY REPORTER. see *PSYCHOLOGY*

INFANT SCREENING. see *MEDICAL SCIENCES — Pediatrics*

616.8 CN
INFO A L S. 1980. a. Amyotrophic Lateral Sclerosis Society of Canada, B101 - 90 Adelaide St. E., Toronto, Ont. M5C 2R4, Canada. TEL 416-362-0269. FAX 416-362-0414. Ed. Dr. Michael Sribney. abstr.
Description: Conveys latest research discoveries on the cause and cure of the A L S disease.

616.8 BL ISSN 0101-4331
INFORMACAO PSIQUIATRICA. (Text in Portuguese; summaries in English) 1980-1983 (vol.4, no.4); resumed 198? q. Cr.$3500($60) Editora Cientifica Nacional Ltda., Avenida Almirante Barroso, No. 97 s.701-703, 20031 Rio de Janeiro RJ, Brazil. Eds. Malvine Zalcberg; Maria Thereza Costa de Aquino. adv.; bk.rev.; index, cum.index; circ. 3,000. (back issues avail.)

616.8 FR
INFORMATION PSYCHIATRIQUE. 1947. m. 570 F. (students 380 F.) P D G Communications, 11 rue Denis Poisson, 75015 Paris, France. Ed. Patrick de Gavre. **Indexed:** Excerp.Med., Psychol.Abstr.

616.834 301 US
INSIDE M S; the magazine of the National Multiple Sclerosis Society. 1983. q. $20 membership. National Multiple Sclerosis Society, 205 E. 42nd St., New York, NY 10017. TEL 212-986-3240. FAX 212-986-7981. Ed. Shirley Silverberg. adv.; bk.rev.; illus.; circ. 400,000. (also avail. in audio cassette) **Indexed:** Hlth.Ind., Rehabil.Lit.
Incorporating (in 1983): Focus on Research; M S Messenger; National Multiple Sclerosis Society. Annual Report; Patient Service News.
Description: For people with MS and their families, with items of interest to health professionals and counselors.

MEDICAL SCIENCES — PSYCHIATRY AND NEUROLOGY 3339

INSTITUTE FOR ORGONOMIC SCIENCE. ANNALS. see *BIOLOGY — Physiology*

616.8   US   ISSN 0735-3847
RC321   CODEN: IPSYDK
INTEGRATIVE PSYCHIATRY; an international journal for the synthesis of medicine and psychiatry. 1983. 4/yr. $52 to individuals (foreign $104); institutions $104. (Academia Medicina Psychiatria) International Universities Press, Inc., 59 Boston Post Rd., Box 1523, CT 06443-1524. TEL 203-245-4000. FAX 203-245-0775. Eds. Drs. Alfred M. Freedman, Turan M. Itil. abstr.; bibl. **Indexed:** Excerp.Med., Psychol.Abstr.
—BLDSC shelfmark: 4531.816600.
Description: Covers psychiatry, neurology, medicine, biology, and relevant advances in the behavioral and social sciences.
Refereed Serial

616.8   US
INTERNATIONAL ANNALS OF ADOLESCENT PSYCHIATRY. 1988. irreg. (approx. a.). $45. (International Society for Adolescent Psychiatry) University of Chicago Press, Journals Division, 5720 S. Woodlawn Ave., Chicago, IL 60637. TEL 312-702-7600. (Orders to: Box 37005, Chicago, IL 60637) Eds. Allan Z. Schwartzberg.
Description: Explores the issues and problems concerning adolescents and the professionals who serve them. Provides a forum for international and interdisciplinary research in adolescent psychiatry.
Refereed Serial

616.89   UK   ISSN 0085-2007
INTERNATIONAL ASSOCIATION FOR SCIENTIFIC STUDY OF MENTAL DEFICIENCY. PROCEEDINGS OF INTERNATIONAL CONGRESS.* 1967. triennial, 8th, 1988, Dublin. £40. (International Association for Scientific Study of Mental Deficiency) Methuen Educational, Micheline House, 81 Fulham Rd., London SW3 6RB, England. Ed. J. Berg. circ. 4,000.

616.855   SZ   ISSN 0074-1655
INTERNATIONAL ASSOCIATION OF LOGOPEDICS AND PHONIATRICS. REPORTS OF CONGRESS. 1947. triennial, 21st, 1989, Prague. $30. International Association of Logopedics and Phoniatrics, c/o Dr. A. Muller, Pres., Av. de la Gare 6, CH-1003 Lausanne, Switzerland. FAX 021-3112025. adv.; bk.rev.

616.8   US   ISSN 1046-5448
INTERNATIONAL BRAIN DOMINANCE REVIEW. 1984. s-a. $15 (foreign $30). Brain Dominance Institute, 2075 Buffalo Creek Rd., Lake Lure, NC 28746. TEL 704-625-9153. FAX 704-625-2198. Ed. Laura Herrmann. bk.rev.; circ. 500.
Description: Reports the latest advances in brain dominance technology. Provides an international forum for the exchange of new ideas and applications on the subject of brain dominance.

610   US   ISSN 0361-0462
CODEN: IBRSDZ
INTERNATIONAL BRAIN RESEARCH ORGANIZATION MONOGRAPH SERIES. Short title: I B R O Monograph Series. 1975. irreg., latest vol.11. price varies. Raven Press, 1185 Ave. of the Americas, New York, NY 10036. TEL 212-930-9500. FAX 212-869-3495. TELEX 640073. **Indexed:** Biol.Abstr., Chem.Abstr., Curr.Cont., Sci.Cit.Ind.

616.8   SZ   ISSN 0074-5847
INTERNATIONAL FEDERATION FOR MEDICAL PSYCHOTHERAPY. CONGRESS REPORTS.* 1972. triennial, 8th, 1970, Milan; 10th, 1976, Paris. International Federation for Medical Psychotherapy, c/o Dr. Edgar Heim, Murtenstr. 21, CH-3010 Bern, Switzerland. (Order 8th report from: S. Karger AG, Arnold-Boecklin-Str. 25, CH-4011 Basel, Switzerland)

616.8 150   US   ISSN 0197-3681
INTERNATIONAL JOURNAL OF CLINICAL NEUROPSYCHOLOGY. 1979. q. $75 to individuals; libraries $110; students $35. Melnic Press, Inc., Box 6216, Madison, WI 53716-0216. TEL 608-222-6611. (Dist. in Europe by: Karger Libri AG, Petersgraben 31, CH-4009 Basel, Switzerland) Ed. Charles J. Golden. adv.; bk.rev.; illus.; stat.; circ. 1,500. (also avail. in microform from UMI; back issues avail.; reprint service avail. from UMI) **Indexed:** ASCA, Bibl.Dev.Med.& Child Neur., Biol.Abstr., Child Devel.Abstr., Curr.Cont., Excerp.Med., Psychol.Abstr., SSCI.
Formerly (until 1984): Clinical Neuropsychology.

616.8   US   ISSN 0736-5748
QP363.5   CODEN: IJDND6
INTERNATIONAL JOURNAL OF DEVELOPMENTAL NEUROSCIENCE. 1983. bi-m. £310 (effective 1992). (International Society for Developmental Neuroscience) Pergamon Press, Inc., Journals Division, 660 White Plains Rd., Tarrytown, NY 10591-5153. TEL 914-524-9200. FAX 914-333-2444. (And: Headington Hill Hall, Oxford OX3 0BW, England. TEL 0865-794141) Ed. J. Regino Perez-Polo. (also avail. in microform from UMI,MIM) **Indexed:** ASCA, Curr.Adv.Biochem., Curr.Adv.Ecol.Sci., Curr.Adv.Genetics & Molec.Biol., Excerp.Med., Ind.Sci.Rev., Psychol.Abstr., Sci.Cit.Ind.
—BLDSC shelfmark: 4542.185100.
Description: Publishes research on basic and clinical aspects of the developing nervous system.
Refereed Serial

INTERNATIONAL JOURNAL OF GERIATRIC PSYCHIATRY. see *GERONTOLOGY AND GERIATRICS*

INTERNATIONAL JOURNAL OF GROUP PSYCHOTHERAPY. see *PSYCHOLOGY*

INTERNATIONAL JOURNAL OF LAW AND PSYCHIATRY. see *LAW*

616.8   UK   ISSN 1049-8931
RC337   CODEN: IPSREY
▼**INTERNATIONAL JOURNAL OF METHODS IN PSYCHIATRIC RESEARCH.** 1991. q. $150. John Wiley & Sons Ltd., Journals, Baffins Lane, Chichester, Sussex PO19 1UD, England. TEL 0243-779777. FAX 0243-775878. TELEX 86290-WIBOOK-G. Ed. Chris Thompson.
—BLDSC shelfmark: 4542.352300.
Description: Contains articles pertaining to important issues in the methods of psychiatric research, the measurement of psychiatric phenomena and related biological variables.

616.8   UY   ISSN 0020-7446
CODEN: IJONAO
INTERNATIONAL JOURNAL OF NEUROLOGY. (Editions in English, French, German and Spanish) 1960. q. $240 to individuals; institutions $300. Fulton Society, Calle Buenos Aires 363, Montevideo, Uruguay. TEL 95-61-07. Ed. Victor Soriano. adv.; bk.rev.; bibl.; charts; illus. **Indexed:** Biol.Abstr., Chem.Abstr., Curr.Adv.Ecol.Sci., Excerp.Med., Ind.Med.
—BLDSC shelfmark: 4542.374000.
Description: Focuses on specific topics in neurology, with additional sections on teaching neurology and the history of medicine.

616.8   US   ISSN 0020-7454
QP351   CODEN: IJNUB7
INTERNATIONAL JOURNAL OF NEUROSCIENCE. 1970. 24/yr. (in 6 vols., 4 nos./vol.). $250. Gordon and Breach Science Publishers, 270 Eighth Ave., New York, NY 10011. TEL 212-206-8900. FAX 212-645-2459. TELEX 236735 GOPUB UR. (Subscr. to: Box 786, Cooper Sta., New York, NY 10276. TEL 800-545-8398; UK subscr. to: P.O. Box 90, Reading, Berkshire RG1 8JL, England. TEL 0734-560-080) Ed. Dr. Sidney Weinstein. adv.; bk.rev.; index. (also avail. in microform from MIM) **Indexed:** Biol.Abstr., Chem.Abstr., Curr.Adv.Ecol.Sci., Curr.Cont., Dent.Ind., Excerp.Med., Ind.Med., Ind.Sci.Rev., Psychol.Abstr.
—BLDSC shelfmark: 4542.386000.
Refereed Serial

INTERNATIONAL JOURNAL OF OFFENDER THERAPY AND COMPARATIVE CRIMINOLOGY. see *CRIMINOLOGY AND LAW ENFORCEMENT*

616.89   US   ISSN 0091-2174
RC321   CODEN: IJMEDO
INTERNATIONAL JOURNAL OF PSYCHIATRY IN MEDICINE; an international journal of medical psychology and psychiatry in the general hospital. 1970. q. $36 to individuals; institutions $102. Baywood Publishing Co., Inc., 26 Austin Ave., Box 337, Amityville, NY 11701. TEL 516-691-1270. FAX 516-691-1770. Ed. Dr. Daniel S.P. Schubert. bk.rev.; bibl.; charts; illus.; stat.; index. (back issues avail.) **Indexed:** Abstr.Health Care Manage.Stud., Biol.Abstr., Curr.Cont., Excerp.Med., Ind.Med., Mid.East: Abstr.& Ind., Nutr.Abstr., Psychol.Abstr., Soc.Work Res.& Abstr., SSCI.
—BLDSC shelfmark: 4542.495000.
Formerly: Psychiatry in Medicine (ISSN 0033-278X)
Description: Contains articles which apply the methods of psychiatry and psychology to the further understanding of disorders which are primarily psychiatric in nature.
Refereed Serial

616.89   UK   ISSN 0020-7640
RC321
INTERNATIONAL JOURNAL OF SOCIAL PSYCHIATRY. 1955. q. £20($70) to individuals; institutions £40($110). Avenue Publishing Co., 55 Woodstock Ave., London NW11 9RG, England. TEL 081-455 2940. Ed. Frank Holloway. adv.; bk.rev.; illus.; stat.; index; circ. 2,000. **Indexed:** Abstr.Health Care Manage.Stud., Adol.Ment.Hlth.Abstr., ASSIA, Curr.Cont., Excerp.Med., Ind.Med., Lang.& Lang.Behav.Abstr., Mid.East: Abstr.& Ind., Psychol.Abstr., Soc.Sci.Ind., SSCI.
—BLDSC shelfmark: 4542.560000.
Description: Publishes articles on psychiatric problems, strategies for survival, drug abuse, psychiatry, social psychiatry, and psychotherapy.

616.8   UK   ISSN 0196-1365
RC489.T67   CODEN: IJTCDJ
INTERNATIONAL JOURNAL OF THERAPEUTIC COMMUNITIES. 1980. q. £28 to individuals; institutions £45 (typically set in Jan.). Association of Therapeutic Communities, c/o Mr. K. Beach, Business Editor, P.O. Box 109, Dorking, Surrey, England. Ed. D.W. Millard. adv.; bk.rev.; circ. 500. **Indexed:** ASSIA, Excerp.Med.
—BLDSC shelfmark: 4542.695100.
Description: Aimed at professionals and students in residential and day care, and related disciplines.

616.8 618.92   US
INTERNATIONAL REVIEW OF CHILD NEUROLOGY SERIES. 1982. irreg., latest 1990. price varies. Raven Press, 1185 Ave. of the Americas, New York, NY 10036. TEL 212-930-9500. FAX 212-869-3495.

616.8   US   ISSN 0074-7742
RC341   CODEN: IRNEAE
INTERNATIONAL REVIEW OF NEUROBIOLOGY. 1959. irreg., vol.31, 1989. Academic Press, Inc., 1250 Sixth Ave., San Diego, CA 92101. TEL 619-231-0926. FAX 619-699-6715. Eds. Carl C. Pfeiffer, John R. Smythies. index. (back issues avail. from ISI) **Indexed:** Biol.Abstr., Chem.Abstr., Dent.Ind., Excerp.Med., Ind.Med., Ind.Sci.Rev., Sci.Cit.Ind.
Refereed Serial

616.8   UK   ISSN 0954-0261
CODEN: IRPSE2
INTERNATIONAL REVIEW OF PSYCHIATRY. 1989. $108 to individuals; institutions $264. Carfax Publishing Co., P.O. Box 25, Abindon, Oxfordshire OX14 3UE, England. TEL 0235-555335. FAX 0235-553559. (U.S. subscr. to: Carfax Publishing Co., Box 2025, Dunnellon, FL 32630) Ed. Paul Bebbington. adv.; bk.rev. (also avail. in microfiche) **Indexed:** Excerp.Med. (1992-), Sp.Ed.Needs Abstr.
—BLDSC shelfmark: 4547.515000.
Description: Undergraduate-level reviews of topics in psychiatry.

157 616.858   US   ISSN 0074-7750
RC570
INTERNATIONAL REVIEW OF RESEARCH IN MENTAL RETARDATION. 1966. irreg., vol.16, 1991. Academic Press, Inc., 1250 Sixth Ave., San Diego, CA 92101. TEL 619-231-0926. FAX 619-699-6715. Eds. Norman R. Ellis, Norman W. Bray. (back issues avail. from ISI) **Indexed:** SSCI.
Refereed Serial

MEDICAL SCIENCES — PSYCHIATRY AND NEUROLOGY

616.8   IE   ISSN 0790-1186
IRISH JOURNAL OF PSYCHIATRY. s-a. £2. Irish Institute of Psychiatry, 73 Lower Baggot St., Dublin 2, Ireland. Ed. Dermot Walsh. **Indexed:** Psychol.Abstr.
—BLDSC shelfmark: 4572.170000.

616.89   IE   ISSN 0790-9667
CODEN: IPMEEX
IRISH JOURNAL OF PSYCHOLOGICAL MEDICINE. 1982. s-a. £42($84) Irish Institute of Psychological Medicine, c/o Dr. Mark Hartman, Ed., St. Brendan's Hospital, Rathdown Rd., Dublin 7, Ireland. TEL 35388-578406. FAX 3531-2800504. adv.; bk.rev.; circ. 3,500. **Indexed:** Biol.Abstr., CINAHL, Excerp.Med., Lang.& Lang.Behav.Abstr., Nutr.Abstr., Psychol.Abstr., Rcf.Zh., Sociol.Abstr., SOPODA.
—BLDSC shelfmark: 4572.180000.
Former titles: Irish Journal of Psychotherapy and Psychosomatic Medicine (ISSN 0790-0848); Irish Journal of Psychotherapy.
Description: Publishes original scientific contributions in psychiatry, psychological medicine, and related basic sciences (neurosciences, biological, psychological and social sciences).
Refereed Serial

616.8   IS   ISSN 0333-7308
RC321   CODEN: IPRDAH
ISRAEL JOURNAL OF PSYCHIATRY AND RELATED SCIENCES. 1963. q. $55 to individuals (foreign $65); institutions $75 (effective 1992). (Israel Psychiatric Association) International Universities Press, Inc., 59 Boston Post Rd., Box 1524, Madison, CT 06443. TEL 203-245-4000. FAX 203-245-0775. TELEX 282986 IUP BK. Ed. E.L. Edelstein. adv.; bk.rev.; charts; illus.; index; circ. 950. (also avail. in microform from UMI; back issues avail.; reprint service avail. from UMI) **Indexed:** Biol.Abstr., Chem.Abstr., Child Devel.Abstr., Curr.Cont., Excerp.Med., Ind.Med., Psychol.Abstr., SSCI.
—BLDSC shelfmark: 4583.813000.
Supersedes: Israel Annals of Psychiatry and Related Disciplines.
Description: Articles dealing with the bio-psycho-social aspects of mobility, relocation, acculturation, ethnicity, stress situations in war and peace, victimology and mental health in developing countries.

ISSUES IN EGO PSYCHOLOGY. see *PSYCHOLOGY*

ISSUES IN MENTAL HEALTH NURSING. see *MEDICAL SCIENCES — Nurses And Nursing*

610   IT
ITALIAN JOURNAL OF NEUROLOGICAL SCIENCES. (Text in English) 1980. bi-m. L.96000($129) (effective 1991). (Societa Italiana di Neurologia) Masson Italia Periodici, Via Statuto 2-4, 20121 Milan, Italy. TEL 02-6367-1. FAX 02-6367-211. Ed. Renato Boeri. circ. 1,500. **Indexed:** Curr.Cont., Excerp.Med.

616.8   IT
ITALIAN JOURNAL OF PSYCHIATRY AND BEHAVIOURAL SCIENCES. q. L.90000($150) (effective 1992). (Societa Italiana di Psichiatria) Casa Editrice Idelson, Via A. De Gasperi 55, 80133 Naples, Italy. TEL 081-5524733. FAX 081-5518295. Ed. Carlo Lorenzo Cazzullo.

JAMES ARTHUR LECTURE ON THE EVOLUTION OF THE HUMAN BRAIN. see *BIOLOGY — Genetics*

616.89   JA   ISSN 0289-0968
JAPANESE JOURNAL OF CHILD & ADOLESCENT PSYCHIATRY/JIDO SEINEN SEISHIN IGAKU TO SONO KINSETSU RYOIKI. (Text in Japanese; summaries in English) 1960. 5/yr. $30. Japanese Society of Child and Adolescent Psychiatry, c/o Department of Neuropsychiatry, School of Medicine, Kyoto University, Sakyo-ku, Kyoto 606, Japan. (Subscr. to: Maruzen Co. Ltd., Export Dept., Box 605, Tokyo Central, Tokyo, Japan) Ed. Dr. Kiyoyuki Koike. adv.; bk.rev.; abstr.; charts; index; circ. 2,000. (back issues avail.) **Indexed:** Child Devel.Abstr., Curr.Cont., Psychol.Abstr., SSCI.
—BLDSC shelfmark: 4651.358000.
Formerly: Japanese Journal of Child Psychiatry (ISSN 0021-4957)
Description: Addresses problems, issues, treatments, trends, and syndromes unique to child and adolescent psychology.

616.8   JA   ISSN 0912-2036
CODEN: JJPNEA
JAPANESE JOURNAL OF PSYCHIATRY AND NEUROLOGY. (Text in English) 1933. q. $115. (Folia Publishing Society) Japan Scientific Societies Press, 6-2-10 Hongo, Bunkyo-ku, Tokyo 113, Japan. TEL 3814-2001. FAX 38147-20021. (Dist. by: Business Center for Academic Societies Japan, Koshin Bldg., 6-16-3 Hongo, Bunkyo-ku, Tokyo 113, Japan; Dist. in U.S. by: International Specialized Book Services, Inc., 5602 N.E. Hassalo St., Portland, OR 97213; in Asia by: Toppan Company Pvt. Ltd., 38, Liu Fang Rd., Box 22 Jurong Town, Jurong, Singapore 2262) Ed. Teruo Okuma. adv.; abstr. **Indexed:** Biol.Abstr., Chem.Abstr., Curr.Cont., Excerp.Med., Ind.Med., INIS Atomind., Psychol.Abstr.
—BLDSC shelfmark: 4658.250000.
Formerly: Folia Psychiatrica et Neurologica Japonica (ISSN 0015-5721)

616.8   GW   ISSN 0178-7535
JATROS NEUROLOGIE - PSYCHIATRIE. 1985. 12/yr. DM.150. P M I Verlag GmbH, August-Schanz-Str. 21, 6000 Frankfurt a.M. 50, Germany. TEL 069-5480000. FAX 069-548000-77. Ed. Peter Hoffmann. circ. 4,500. (back issues avail.)
Description: Seminar papers containing brief summaries of original articles, interviews and congress reports.

616.89   BL   ISSN 0047-2085
CODEN: JBPSAX
JORNAL BRASILEIRO DE PSIQUIATRIA. (Text in Portuguese; summaries in English and Portuguese) 1942. m. from Feb.-Nov. Cr.$3500($80) or exchange basis. (Universidade Federal do Rio de Janeiro, Instituto de Psiquiatria) Editora Cientifica Nacional Ltda., Av. Almirante Barroso 97-1.205-1210, CEP 20031 Rio de Janeiro, RJ, Brazil. TEL 262-2825. (Subscr. to: ECN-Editora Cientifica Nacional Ltda., Caixa Postal 590, 20001 Rio de Janeiro, Brazil) Ed. Jeremias Ferraz Lima. adv.; bk.rev.; bibl.; charts; illus.; stat.; index, cum.index; circ. 3,000. (also avail. in microform from UMI; back issues avail.) **Indexed:** Biol.Abstr., Chem.Abstr., Excerp.Med., Ind.Med., Psychol.Abstr.
—BLDSC shelfmark: 4674.680000.
Description: Studies in clinical psychiatry.

616.89   FR   ISSN 1155-1704
JOURNAL DE THERAPIE COMPORTAMENTALE ET COGNITIVE. (Text in English, French) q. 94 ECU($110) (typically set in Jan.). (Association Francaise de Therapie Comportementale et Cognitive) Masson, 120 bd. Saint-Germain, 75280 Paris Cedex 06, France. TEL 1-46-34-21-60. FAX 1-45-87-29-99. TELEX 202 671 F. Ed. J. Cottraux. adv.; bk.rev.; circ. 1,000.

616.8 574   GW   ISSN 0021-8359
JOURNAL FUER HIRNFORSCHUNG; international journal of brain research and neurobiology. (Text in English, French and German) 1961. 6/yr. DM.358.80. Akademie-Verlag Berlin, Leipziger-Str. 3-4, 1086 Berlin, Germany. TELEX 114420-AVERL-DD. Ed. W. Kirsche. abstr.; charts; illus.; mkt.; index. **Indexed:** Curr.Cont., Excerp.Med., Ind.Med., Ind.Vet., INIS Atomind., Sci.Cit.Ind., Vet.Bull.
—BLDSC shelfmark: 4999.000000.

616.8   NE   ISSN 0165-0327
CODEN: JADID7
JOURNAL OF AFFECTIVE DISORDERS. 1979. 12/yr.(in 3 vols.; 4 nos./vol.). fl.1101 (effective 1992). Elsevier Science Publishers B.V., P.O. Box 211, 1000 AE Amsterdam, Netherlands. TEL 020-5803911. FAX 020-5803598. TELEX 18582 ESPA NL. (Subscr. in U.S. and Canada to: Elsevier Science Publishing Co., Inc., Box 882, Madison Sq. Sta., New York, NY 10159. TEL 212-989-5800) Eds. E.S. Paykel, G. Winokur. illus. (also avail. in microform from RPI; reprint service avail. ISI) **Indexed:** Adol.Ment.Hlth.Abstr., Biol.Abstr., Chem.Abstr., Curr.Cont., Excerp.Med., Ind.Med., Ind.Sci.Rev., Psychol.Abstr., Sci.Cit.Ind.
—BLDSC shelfmark: 4919.986000.
Description: Publishes papers concerned with affective disorders in the widest sense: depression, mania and anxiety.
Refereed Serial

JOURNAL OF ANXIETY DISORDERS. see *PSYCHOLOGY*

616.89   US   ISSN 0162-3257
RJ499   CODEN: JADDDQ
JOURNAL OF AUTISM AND DEVELOPMENTAL DISORDERS. 1971. q. $230 (foreign $270)(effective 1992). Plenum Publishing Corp., 233 Spring St., New York, NY 10013-1578. TEL 212-620-8000. FAX 212-463-0742. TELEX 23-421139. Ed. Eric Schopler. adv.; bk.rev.; abstr.; charts; illus.; stat.; index. (also avail. in microform from JSC; back issues avail.) **Indexed:** ASSIA, Bibl.Dev.Med.& Child Neur., Biol.Abstr., C.I.J.E., Chem.Abstr., Child Devel.Abstr., Curr.Cont., Educ.Ind., Except.Child.Educ.Abstr., Excerp.Med., Ind.Med., INIS Atomind., Mid.East: Abstr.& Ind., Psychol.Abstr., Psycscan D.P., Risk Abstr., Soc.Work Res.& Abstr., SSCI.
—BLDSC shelfmark: 4949.552000.
Formerly (until 1979): Journal of Autism and Childhood Schizophrenia (ISSN 0021-9185)
Refereed Serial

616.89   US   ISSN 0005-7916
RC489.B4   CODEN: JBTEAB
JOURNAL OF BEHAVIOR THERAPY AND EXPERIMENTAL PSYCHIATRY; an interdisciplinary journal. 1970. 4/yr. £160 (effective 1992). (Behavior Therapy and Research Society) Pergamon Press, Inc., Journals Division, 660 White Plains Rd., Tarrytown, NY 10591-5153. TEL 914-524-9200. FAX 914-333-2444. (And: Headington Hill Hall, Oxford OX3 0BW, England. TEL 0865-794141) Ed. Joseph Wolpe. adv.; bk.rev.; index; circ. 3,100. (also avail. in microform from MIM,UMI; back issues avail.) **Indexed:** Adol.Ment.Hlth.Abstr., ASCA, ASSIA, Biol.Abstr., Child Devel.Abstr., CINAHL, Curr.Cont., Excerp.Med., Ind.Med., Mid.East: Abstr.& Ind., Psychol.Abstr., SSCI.
—BLDSC shelfmark: 4951.250000.
Description: Covers all aspects of behavior therapy and its applications in clinical psychiatry.
Refereed Serial

616.8   US   ISSN 0160-7715
R726.5   CODEN: JBMEDD
JOURNAL OF BEHAVIORAL MEDICINE. 1978. bi-m. $240 (foreign $280)(effective 1992). Plenum Publishing Corp., 233 Spring St., New York, NY 10013-1578. TEL 212-620-8000. FAX 212-463-0742. TELEX 23-421139. Ed. W. Doyle Gentry. adv.; bk.rev. (also avail. in microform from JSC; back issues avail.) **Indexed:** Adol.Ment.Hlth.Abstr., Behav.Med.Abstr., Biol.Abstr., CINAHL, Curr.Cont., Dent.Ind., Excerp.Med., Ind.Med., Lang.& Lang.Behav.Abstr., NRN, Psychol.Abstr., Psycscan C.P., Ref.Zh., Soc.Work Res.& Abstr., Sociol.Abstr., SSCI.
—BLDSC shelfmark: 4951.262000.
Refereed Serial

616.8   US   ISSN 0748-7304
QH527   CODEN: JBRHEE
JOURNAL OF BIOLOGICAL RHYTHMS. 1985. 4/yr. $60 to individuals; institutions $125. (Society for Research in Biological Rhythms) Guilford Publications, Inc., 72 Spring St., 4th Fl., New York, NY 10012. TEL 212-431-9800. FAX 212-966-6708. Ed. Benjamin Rusak. adv.; index. (back issues avail.; reprint service avail.) **Indexed:** Biol.Abstr., Psychol.Abstr.
—BLDSC shelfmark: 4953.260000.
Description: Reports on nature and functions of biological rhythms using genetic, biochemical, physiological behavioral, and modeling approaches.
Refereed Serial

616.8 612.015   US   ISSN 0271-678X
QP108.5.C4   CODEN: JCBMDN
JOURNAL OF CEREBRAL BLOOD FLOW AND METABOLISM. 1981. bi-m. $271 to individuals; institutions $424. (International Society of Cerebral Blood Flow and Metabolism) Raven Press, 1185 Ave. of the Americas, New York, NY 10036. TEL 212-930-9500. FAX 212-869-3495. TELEX 640073. Ed. Dr. Myron Ginsberg. adv.; bk.rev.; charts; illus.; index; circ. 2,000. (back issues avail.) **Indexed:** Biol.Abstr., Chem.Abstr., Curr.Cont., Excerp.Med., Ind.Med., Ind.Sci.Rev., INIS Atomind., Sci.Cit.Ind.
Description: Gathers experimental, theoretical, and clinical information on brain circulation and metabolism.
Refereed Serial

MEDICAL SCIENCES — PSYCHIATRY AND NEUROLOGY 3341

616.8 UK ISSN 0891-0618
CODEN: JCNAEE
JOURNAL OF CHEMICAL NEUROANATOMY. 1988. bi-m. $395 (effective 1992). John Wiley & Sons Ltd., Baffins Lane, Chichester, Sussex PO19 1UD, England. TEL 0243-779777. FAX 0243-775878. TELEX 86290 WIBOOK G. Eds. H.W.M. Steinbusch, A. Claudio Cuello. **Indexed:** Chem.Abstr., Curr.Adv.Cell & Devel.Biol.
—BLDSC shelfmark: 4956.850000.

616.8 618.92 US ISSN 1053-0800
CODEN: JAGTEM
▼**JOURNAL OF CHILD AND ADOLESCENT GROUP THERAPY.** 1991. q. $85 (foreign $100). Human Sciences Press, Inc. (Subsidiary of: Plenum Publishing Corp.), 233 Spring St., New York, NY 10013. TEL 212-620-8000. FAX 212-463-0742. TELEX 23-421139. Ed. Edward S. Soo. adv.
—BLDSC shelfmark: 4957.421000.
Description: Covers issues in child, adolescent and parent group therapy. Includes clinical reports, articles on new developments, theoretical issues, applications of group therapy and different group methods, and the group process.
Refereed Serial

JOURNAL OF CHILD AND ADOLESCENT PSYCHIATRIC AND MENTAL HEALTH NURSING. see *MEDICAL SCIENCES — Nurses And Nursing*

616.8 US ISSN 1044-5463
▼**JOURNAL OF CHILD AND ADOLESCENT PSYCHOPHARMACOLOGY.** 1990. q. $99 (foreign $132). Mary Ann Liebert, Inc., 1651 Third Ave., New York, NY 10128. TEL 212-289-2300. FAX 212-289-4697. Eds. Drs. Charles W. Popper, Shervert H. Frazier.
—BLDSC shelfmark: 4957.424000.
Description: Emphasizes the clinical aspects of psychotropic therapy. Includes depression, hyperactivity, attention deficit disorder, bulimia and anorexia, obsessive-compulsive disorder, phobias, retardation, and psychotic disorders.

616.8 610 US ISSN 0883-0738
CODEN: JOCNEE
JOURNAL OF CHILD NEUROLOGY. 1986. q. $90 to individuals (foreign $110); institutions $115 (foreign $135); students $49 (foreign $69). Mosby - Year Book, Inc. (Subsidiary of: Times Mirror Company), 11830 Westline Industrial Dr., St. Louis, MO 63146. TEL 800-325-4177. Ed. Roger A. Brumback. circ. 900. **Indexed:** Excerp.Med., INIS Atomind., Psychol.Abstr.
—BLDSC shelfmark: 4957.625000.
Description: Covers all aspects of nervous system disorders in children, including medical, surgical, pathological and psychological perspectives.
Refereed Serial

JOURNAL OF CHILD PSYCHOLOGY & PSYCHIATRY & ALLIED DISCIPLINES. see *PSYCHOLOGY*

616.8 NE ISSN 0168-8634
CODEN: JCENE8
JOURNAL OF CLINICAL AND EXPERIMENTAL NEUROPSYCHOLOGY. 1979. bi-m. $232 to individuals; institutions $367. Swets Publishing Service (Subsidiary of: Swets en Zeitlinger B.V.), Heereweg 347, 2161 CA Lisse, Netherlands. TEL 31-2521-35111. FAX 31-2521-15888. TELEX 41325. (Dist. in N. America by: Swets & Zeitlinger, Box 517, Berwyn, PA 19312. TEL 215-644-4944) Eds. L. Costa, B.P. Rourke. (reprint service avail. from SWZ) **Indexed:** Biol.Abstr., Child Devel.Abstr., Excerp.Med., Ind.Med., Psychol.Abstr., Psycscan C.P.
—BLDSC shelfmark: 4958.375000.
@**Formerly:** Journal of Clinical Neuropsychology (ISSN 0165-0475)

616.8 US ISSN 0736-0258
JOURNAL OF CLINICAL NEUROPHYSIOLOGY. 1984. q. $115 to individuals; institutions $190. (American Electroencephalographic Society) Raven Press, 1185 Ave. of the Americas, New York, NY 10036. TEL 212-930-9500. FAX 212-869-3495. TELEX 640073. Ed. Han Lueders. adv.; bk.rev.; charts; illus.; index; circ. 2,500. **Indexed:** ASCA, Bibl.Dev.Med.& Child Neur., Excerp.Med., Ind.Sci.Rev., Psychol.Abstr., Sci.Cit.Ind.
—BLDSC shelfmark: 4958.578000.
Description: Covers clinical neurology, neurosurgery, psychiatry, electroencephalography and evoked potentials, and experimental research of the central nervous system.
Refereed Serial

616.8 US ISSN 0160-6689
RC321 CODEN: JCLPDE
JOURNAL OF CLINICAL PSYCHIATRY. (Supplement avail.: Proceedings from Scientific Symposia.) 1940. m. $54 (foreign $94). Physicians Postgraduate Press, Inc., Box 240008, Memphis, TN 38124. TEL 901-682-1001. FAX 901-682-6992. (Street addr.: Bldg. B, Ste. 209, 785 Crossover Lane, Memphis, TN 38117) Ed. Alan Gelenberg, M.D. adv.; bk.rev.; charts; illus.; stat.; index; circ. 32,000. (also avail. in microfilm from UMI; back issues avail.; reprint service avail. from UMI) **Indexed:** Adol.Ment.Hlth.Abstr., ASSIA, Behav.Med.Abstr., Biol.Abstr., Biotech.Abstr., C.I.J.E., Chem.Abstr., CINAHL, Curr.Cont., Curr.Lit.Fam.Plan., Dent.Ind., Excerp.Med., HRIS, Ind.Med., Ind.Sci.Rev., Int.Nurs.Ind., Lang.& Lang.Behav.Abstr., Nutr.Abstr., Psychol.Abstr., Risk Abstr., Sci.Cit.Ind, SSCI.
—BLDSC shelfmark: 4958.688000.
Formerly (until 1978): Diseases of the Nervous System (ISSN 0012-3714)
Description: Presents original material in the psychiatric, behavioral, and neural sciences, with special emphasis on papers dealing with practical and clinical subjects.
Refereed Serial

616.8 US ISSN 0898-929X
QP360 CODEN: JCONEO
JOURNAL OF COGNITIVE NEUROSCIENCE. 1989. q. $58 to individuals (foreign $72); institutions $130 (foreign $144); students $40 (foreign $54). (Cognitive Neuroscience Institute) M I T Press, 55 Hayward St., Cambridge, MA 02142. TEL 617-253-2889. FAX 617-258-6779. TELEX 921473. (Editorial addr.: Box 1204, Norwich, VT 05055) Ed. Michael S. Gazzaniga. circ. 900. (back issues avail.; reprint service avail. from UMI)
—BLDSC shelfmark: 4958.798500.
Description: Provides a forum for research involving the interaction of brain and behavior. Devoted to the field of cognitive neuroscience.
Refereed Serial

JOURNAL OF COMMUNICATION DISORDERS. see *PSYCHOLOGY*

616.8 US ISSN 0021-9967
QL1 CODEN: JCNEAM
THE JOURNAL OF COMPARATIVE NEUROLOGY. 1891. 48/yr. $4,910 (foreign $5,510). John Wiley & Sons, Inc., Journals, 605 Third Ave., New York, NY 10158. TEL 212-850-6000. FAX 212-850-6088. TELEX 12-7063. Ed. Sanford L. Palay. adv.; abstr.; bibl.; charts; illus.; index. (also avail. in microfiche from BHP,SWZ; reprint service avail. from SWZ) **Indexed:** Biol.Abstr., Chem.Abstr., Curr.Adv.Cell & Devel.Biol., Curr.Cont., Dent.Ind., Excerp.Med., Helminthol.Abstr., Ind.Med., Ind.Sci.Rev., Ind.Vet., INIS Atomind., Poult.Abstr., Sci.Cit.Ind., Small Anim.Abstr., Vet.Bull.
—BLDSC shelfmark: 4962.000000.
Description: Presents original articles about the anatomy and physiology of the nervous system, especially with regard to its structure, growth and function.
Refereed Serial

JOURNAL OF CONSULTING AND CLINICAL PSYCHOLOGY. see *PSYCHOLOGY*

JOURNAL OF CONTEMPORARY PSYCHOTHERAPY. see *PSYCHOLOGY*

616.8 US ISSN 0896-6974
CODEN: JOEPEU
JOURNAL OF EPILEPSY. 1988. q. $95 to individuals (foreign $120); institutions $130 (foreign $165). Butterworth - Heinemann Ltd. (Subsidiary of: Reed International PLC), 80 Montvale Ave., Stoneham, MA 02180. TEL 617-438-8464. FAX 617-279-4851. TELEX 880052. Ed. Allen R. Wyler.
—BLDSC shelfmark: 4979.477000.

JOURNAL OF ESTHETIC DENTISTRY. see *MEDICAL SCIENCES — Dentistry*

JOURNAL OF FAMILY PSYCHOTHERAPY; the quarterly journal of case studies, treatment reports, and strategies in clinical practice. see *PSYCHOLOGY*

616.8 150 301.1 UK ISSN 0163-4445
RC488.5
JOURNAL OF FAMILY THERAPY. 1979. q. £61.50($112) (Association of Family Therapy) Basil Blackwell Ltd., 108 Cowley Rd., Oxford OX4 1JF, England. TEL 0865-791100. (Subscr. addr.: c/o Marston Book Services, P.O. Box 87, Oxford OX2 0DT, England) Eds. John Carpenter, Bebe Speed. adv.; bk.rev.; index; circ. 2,500. (back issues avail.) **Indexed:** ASSIA, C.I.J.E., Curr.Cont., Lang.& Lang.Behav.Abstr., Psychol.Abstr., SSCI.
—BLDSC shelfmark: 4983.740000.

616.8 US ISSN 1050-5350
RC569.5.G35 CODEN: JGSTEM
JOURNAL OF GAMBLING STUDIES. 1985. q. $150 (foreign $175). (National Council on Problem Gambling) Human Sciences Press, Inc. (Subsidiary of: Plenum Publishing Corp.), 233 Spring St., New York, NY 10013-1578. TEL 212-620-8000. FAX 212-463-0742. Ed. Henry R. Lesieur. adv. (reprint service avail. from UMI) **Indexed:** Psychol.Abstr., Soc.Work Res.& Abstr.
—BLDSC shelfmark: 4987.180000.
Formerly: Journal of Gambling Behavior (ISSN 0742-0714)
Description: Covers social and pathological gambling research by professionals in all disciplines, including law, psychiatry, sociology, history, and counseling.
Refereed Serial

JOURNAL OF GAY & LESBIAN PSYCHOTHERAPY. see *HOMOSEXUALITY*

616.89 US ISSN 0022-1414
RC451.4.A5 CODEN: JGPSBZ
JOURNAL OF GERIATRIC PSYCHIATRY. 1967. s-a. $47.50 to individuals (foreign $60); institutions $70 (foreign $80). (Boston Society for Gerontologic Psychiatry, Inc.) International Universities Press, Inc., Journal Department, 59 Boston Post Rd., Box 1524, Madison, CT 06443-1524. TEL 203-245-4000. FAX 203-245-0775. Eds. Drs. David Blau, Ralph J. Kahana. bk.rev. (back issues avail.) **Indexed:** Biol.Abstr., CINAHL, CLOA, Curr.Cont., Excerp.Med., Ind.Med., Mid.East: Abstr.& Ind., Psychol.Abstr., Sage Fam.Stud.Abstr., SSCI.
—BLDSC shelfmark: 4995.080000.
Description: Presents current ideas and recent findings in the field of geriatric psychiatry. Also contains articles on Alzheimer's Disease.
Refereed Serial

JOURNAL OF GERIATRIC PSYCHIATRY AND NEUROLOGY; an interdisciplinary forum for clinicians and scientists. see *GERONTOLOGY AND GERIATRICS*

JOURNAL OF INTEGRATIVE AND ECLECTIC PSYCHOTHERAPY. see *PSYCHOLOGY*

157.8 616.8 UK
RC321
JOURNAL OF INTELLECTUAL DISABILITY RESEARCH. 1957. q. £72.50 (foreign £82). (Royal Society for Mentally Handicapped Children & Adults) Blackwell Scientific Publications Ltd., Osney Mead, Oxford OX2 0EL, England. TEL 0865-240201. FAX 0865-721205. TELEX 83355-MEDBOK-G. Ed. Dr. W.I. Fraser. adv.; bk.rev.; bibl.; charts; illus.; index; circ. 1,100. (also avail. in microfilm from UMI; reprint service avail. from SWZ,UMI) **Indexed:** Adol.Ment.Hlth.Abstr., ASCA, ASSIA, Bibl.Dev.Med.& Child Neur., Biol.Abstr., Br.Educ.Ind., C.I.J.E., Chem.Abstr., Child Devel.Abstr., Curr.Adv.Ecol.Sci., Curr.Cont., Dent.Ind., Except.Child.Educ.Abstr., Excerp.Med., Ind.Med., Ind.Sci.Rev., Lang.& Lang.Behav.Abstr., Mid.East: Abstr.& Ind., Nutr.Abstr., Psychol.Abstr., Sci.Cit.Ind., Sp.Ed.Needs Abstr., SSCI.
Formerly (until 1991): Journal of Mental Deficiency Research (ISSN 0022-264X)
Description: Focuses on the defective and delinquent classes.

JOURNAL OF INTERPROFESSIONAL CARE. see *MEDICAL SCIENCES — Chiropractic, Homeopathy, Osteopathy*

616.8 UK ISSN 0963-8237
▼**JOURNAL OF MENTAL HEALTH.** 1992. 4/yr. $74 to individuals; institutions $220. Carfax Publishing Co., P.O. Box 25, Abingdon, Oxfordshire OX14 3UE, England. TEL 0235-555335. FAX 0235-553559. (U.S. subscr. addr.: Carfax Publishing Co., Box 2025, Dunnellon, FL 32360) Ed. Ian Hughes. (also avail. in microfiche; back issues avail.)

MEDICAL SCIENCES — PSYCHIATRY AND NEUROLOGY

616.8 US ISSN 0895-8696
QP356.2 CODEN: JMNEES
JOURNAL OF MOLECULAR NEUROSCIENCE. 1989. 4/yr. $120 (foreign $130). Birkhaeuser Boston, Inc., 675 Massachusetts Ave., Cambridge, MA 02139-3309. FAX 201-348-4505. (Dist. by: Springer-Verlag New York, Inc., Journal Fulfillment Services, Box 2485, Secaucus, NJ 07096-2491. TEL 201-348-4033)
—BLDSC shelfmark: 5020.717000.

616.8 US ISSN 0022-3018
RC321 CODEN: JNMDAN
JOURNAL OF NERVOUS AND MENTAL DISEASE; an educational journal of neuropsychiatry. 1874. m. $85 to individuals; institutions $134. Williams & Wilkins, 428 E. Preston St., Baltimore, MD 21202. TEL 301-528-4000. FAX 301-528-4312. Ed. Eugene B. Brody. adv.; bk.rev.; bibl.; illus.; index; circ. 2,400. (also avail. in microform) **Indexed:** Abstr.Health Care Manage.Stud., ASSIA, Biol.Abstr., Biotech.Abstr., Chem.Abstr., Chic.Per.Ind., Child Devel.Abstr., Curr.Adv.Ecol.Sci., Curr.Cont., Curr.Lit.Fam.Plan., Dent.Ind., Dok.Arbeitsmed., Except.Child.Educ.Abstr., Excerp.Med., I.P.A., Ind.Med., Ind.Sci.Rev., INIS Atomind., Int.Nurs.Ind., M.L.A., Nutr.Abstr., Psychol.Abstr., Psycscan C.P., Risk Abstr., SSCI.
●Also available online. Vendor(s): Mead Data Central.
—BLDSC shelfmark: 5021.400000.
Description: Studies in the social, behavioral and neurological sciences relevant to clinical psychiatry.
Refereed Serial

616.8 US ISSN 0300-9564
QP364.5 CODEN: JNTMAH
JOURNAL OF NEURAL TRANSMISSION. (Text in English, French and German) 1950. 4/yr. $192. Springer-Verlag, Journals, 175 Fifth Ave., New York, NY 10010. TEL 212-460-1500. (Also Berlin, Heidelberg, Tokyo and Vienna) Ed. A. Carlsson. adv.; charts; illus.; index. (also avail. in microform from UMI; reprint service avail. from ISI) **Indexed:** Biol.Abstr., Biotech.Abstr., Chem.Abstr., Curr.Adv.Ecol.Sci., Curr.Cont., Dairy Sci.Abstr., Excerp.Med., Ind.Med., Ind.Sci.Rev., INIS Atomind.
—BLDSC shelfmark: 5021.421000.
Formerly: Journal of Neuro-Visceral Relations (ISSN 0022-3026)

616.8 US ISSN 0303-6995
CODEN: JNTSD4
JOURNAL OF NEURAL TRANSMISSION. SUPPLEMENT. no.11, 1974. irreg., no.33, 1991. Springer-Verlag, Journals, 175 Fifth Ave., New York, NY 10010. TEL 212-460-1500. (Also Berlin, Heidelberg, Tokyo and Vienna) (also avail. in microform from UMI; reprint service avail. from ISI) **Indexed:** Chem.Abstr., Excerp.Med. (1992-), Ind.Med.
Formerly: Journal of Neuro-Visceral Relations. Supplement (ISSN 0075-4323); Continues: Acta Neurovegetativa. Supplement.

JOURNAL OF NEUROBIOLOGY; an international journal. see *BIOLOGY — Physiology*

JOURNAL OF NEUROCHEMISTRY. see *BIOLOGY — Biological Chemistry*

616.8 616.4 UK ISSN 0953-8194
CODEN: JOUNE2
JOURNAL OF NEUROENDOCRINOLOGY. 1989. 6/yr. £140($273) Oxford University Press, Oxford Journals, Pinkhill House, Southfield Road, Eynsham, Oxford OX8 1JJ, England. TEL 0865-882283. FAX 0865-882890. TELEX 837330 OXPRES G. Ed. Stafford Lightman. adv.; bk.rev.; circ. 2,000.
—BLDSC shelfmark: 5021.543000.
Description: Integrates the fields of endocrinology and neuroscience. Covers non-vertebrate, vertebrate and clinical endocrinology.

616.8 US ISSN 0167-7063
QP356.22 CODEN: JLNEDK
JOURNAL OF NEUROGENETICS. 1983-1987. 8/yr. (in 2 vols., 4 nos./vol.). $111. Harwood Academic Publishers, 270 Eighth Ave., New York, NY 10011. TEL 212-206-8900. FAX 212-645-2459. TELEX 236735 GOPUB UR. (Subscr. to: Box 786, Cooper Sta., New York, NY 10276. TEL 800-545-8398; UK subscr. to: P.O. Box 90, Reading, Berkshire RG1 8JL, England. TEL 0734-560-080) Ed. Jeffrey C. Hall. (also avail. in microform) **Indexed:** Chem.Abstr., Curr.Adv.Cell & Devel.Biol., Curr.Adv.Ecol.Sci., Curr.Adv.Genetics & Molec.Biol., Excerp.Med.
—BLDSC shelfmark: 5021.545000.
Refereed Serial

616.8 615.842 US ISSN 1051-2284
CODEN: JNERET
▼**JOURNAL OF NEUROIMAGING.** 1991. q. $95 to individuals (foreign $122); institutions $145 (foreign $175); residents $50 (foreign $75)(effective Nov. 1991). (American Society of Neuroimaging) Little, Brown and Company, Medical Journals, 34 Beacon St., Boston, MA 02108. TEL 617-859-5500. FAX 617-859-0629. Ed. Dr. Leon Prockop. adv.; bk.rev.; abstr.; charts; illus.; stat.; index; circ. 1,819. (also avail. in microform from UMI; reprint service avail. from UMI; back issues avail.) **Indexed:** Excerp.Med. (1992-).
—BLDSC shelfmark: 5021.548000.
Description: Includes coverage of MRI, CT, SPECT, PET, neurosonology, transcranial doppler, and carotid ultrasound, for specialists who rely on neuroimaging.
Refereed Serial

616.8 616.97 NE ISSN 0165-5728
CODEN: JNRIDW
JOURNAL OF NEUROIMMUNOLOGY. (Text in English) 1981. 18/yr.(in 6 vols.; 3 nos./vol.). fl.2250 (effective 1992). (International Society for Neuroimmunology) Elsevier Science Publishers B.V., P.O. Box 211, 1000 AE Amsterdam, Netherlands. Ed. Cedric S. Raine. adv.; charts; illus. (also avail. in microform from RPI; back issues avail.; reprint service avail. from ISI,SWZ) **Indexed:** Biol.Abstr., Chem.Abstr., Curr.Adv.Cell & Devel.Biol., Curr.Adv.Ecol.Sci., Curr.Adv.Genetics & Molec.Biol., Curr.Cont., Excerp.Med., Ind.Med., Ind.Sci.Rev., Protozool.Abstr., Psychol.Abstr.
—BLDSC shelfmark: 5021.550000.
Description: Publishes both basic research and clinical problems in neuroimmunology and related neuroscientific disciplines.
Refereed Serial

616.8 US ISSN 0911-6044
JOURNAL OF NEUROLINGUISTICS. 1985. 4/yr. £135 (effective 1992). Pergamon Press, Inc., Journals Division, 660 White Plains Rd., Tarrytown, NY 10591-5153. TEL 914-524-9200. FAX 914-333-2444. (And: Headington Hill Hall, Oxford OX3 0BW, England. TEL 0865-794141) Ed. Fred C.C. Peng. (also avail. in microform; back issues avail.) **Indexed:** Lang.& Lang.Behav.Abstr. (1985-).
—BLDSC shelfmark: 5021.553000.
Refereed Serial

616.8 US ISSN 0888-4390
JOURNAL OF NEUROLOGIC REHABILITATION. vol.2, 1988. q. $95 to individuals (foreign $115); institutions and libraries $135 (foreign $155). Demos Publications, Inc., 386 Park Ave. S., 201, New York, NY 10016-8804. TEL 212-683-0072. FAX 212-683-0118. Ed. Labe Scheinberg.
—BLDSC shelfmark: 5021.553500.

616.8 GW ISSN 0340-5354
CODEN: JNRYA9
JOURNAL OF NEUROLOGY/ZEITSCHRIFT FUER NEUROLOGIE. (Supplement avail. (ISSN 0939-1517) (Text in English or German) 1891. 8/yr. DM.928($521) (Deutsche Gesellschaft fuer Neurologie) Springer-Verlag, Heidelberger Platz 3, D-1000 Berlin 33, Germany. TEL 030-8207-1. (Also Heidelberg, Tokyo, Vienna, and New York) (Co-sponsor: Deutsche Gesellschaft fuer Neurochirurgie) Eds. R.A.C. Hughes, A. Compston. adv.; bibl.; charts; illus.; index. (also avail. in microform from UMI; back issues avail.; reprint service avail. from ISI) **Indexed:** ASCA, Biol.Abstr., Chem.Abstr., Curr.Adv.Cancer Res., Curr.Cont., Dent.Ind., Excerp.Med., Ind.Med., INIS Atomind.
—BLDSC shelfmark: 5021.584000.
Former titles: Zeitschrift fuer Neurologie (ISSN 0012-1037); Deutsche Zeitschrift fuer Nervenheilkunde.
Description: Original investigations in clinical neurology, and related basic research.

616.8 UK ISSN 0022-3050
RC321 CODEN: JNNPAU
JOURNAL OF NEUROLOGY, NEUROSURGERY AND PSYCHIATRY. 1926. m. £153. B M J Publishing Group, B.M.A. House, Tavistock Sq., London WC1H 9JR, England. TEL 071-387-4499. Ed. R.A.C. Hughes. adv.; bk.rev.; abstr.; bibl.; illus.; index. (also avail. in microform from UMI; reprint service avail. from UMI) **Indexed:** ASCA, Behav.Med.Abstr., Bibl.Dev.Med.& Child Neur., Biol.Abstr., Chem.Abstr., Curr.Adv.Ecol.Sci., Curr.Cont., Dent.Ind., Dok.Arbeitsmed., Excerp.Med., Ind.Med., Ind.Sci.Rev., INIS Atomind., Nutr.Abstr., Protozool.Abstr., Psychol.Abstr., Risk Abstr.
●Also available online. Vendor(s): BRS.
—BLDSC shelfmark: 5021.600000.

616.8 US ISSN 0022-3069
RC321 CODEN: JNENAD
JOURNAL OF NEUROPATHOLOGY AND EXPERIMENTAL NEUROLOGY. 1942. bi-m. $60 to individuals (foreign $72); institutions $80 (foreign $92). American Association of Neuropathologists, Inc., c/o Dr. Michael N. Hart, Ed., Division of Neuropathology, University of Iowa, College of Medicine, Rm. 147A ML, Iowa City, IA 52242-1009.
TEL 319-335-8273. FAX 319-335-6510. adv.; bk.rev.; abstr.; bibl.; charts; illus.; index, cum.index: vol. 1-15 (1942-1956); vol. 16-25 (1957-1966); circ. 1,800. (also avail. in microform from UMI; reprint service avail. from UMI) **Indexed:** Bibl.Dev.Med.& Child Neur., Biol.Abstr., Chem.Abstr., Curr.Adv.Cell & Devel.Biol., Curr.Adv.Ecol.Sci., Curr.Cont., Excerp.Med., Ind.Med., Ind.Sci.Rev., Ind.Vet., INIS Atomind., Nutr.Abstr., Poult.Abstr., Protozool.Abstr., Vet.Bull.
—BLDSC shelfmark: 5021.700000.
Refereed Serial

JOURNAL OF NEUROPHYSIOLOGY. see *BIOLOGY — Physiology*

616.8 US ISSN 0895-0172
RC321 CODEN: JNCNE7
JOURNAL OF NEUROPSYCHIATRY AND CLINICAL NEUROSCIENCES. 1989. q. $85 to individuals (foreign $100); institutions $135 (foreign $150). (American Psychiatric Association) American Psychiatric Press, Inc., Journals Division, 1400 K St. N.W., Ste., 1101, Washington, DC 20005. TEL 202-682-6272. FAX 202-789-2648. (UK addr.: 17 Belgrave Sq., London SW1X 8PG, England) Ed. Dr. Stuart Yudofsky. adv.; bk.rev.; abstr.; bibl.; charts; illus.; stat.; index; circ. 1,500. (also avail. in microform from UMI) **Indexed:** Soc.Work Res.& Abstr.
—BLDSC shelfmark: 5022.040000.
Description: Devoted to the relationships between the original research in psychiatry and neurology.
Refereed Serial

616.8 US ISSN 0270-6474
QP351 CODEN: JNRSDS
JOURNAL OF NEUROSCIENCE. 1981. m. $675 (foreign $785). (Society for Neuroscience) Oxford University Press, Journals, 200 Madison Ave., New York, NY 10016. TEL 212-679-7300. FAX 212-725-2972. TELEX 6859654. (Subscr. to: Journals Fulfillment, 2001 Evans Rd., Cary, NC 27513. TEL 919-677-0977) Ed. Dale Purves. circ. 3,000. (also avail. in microfilm; microfiche; back issues avail.) **Indexed:** Chem.Abstr., Curr.Adv.Biochem., Curr.Adv.Cell & Devel.Biol., Curr.Adv.Ecol.Sci., Curr.Adv.Genetics & Molec.Biol., Curr.Cont., Dent.Ind., Excerp.Med., Ind.Med., Ind.Sci.Rev.
—BLDSC shelfmark: 5022.075000.
Refereed Serial

MEDICAL SCIENCES — PSYCHIATRY AND NEUROLOGY

616.8 NE ISSN 0165-0270
CODEN: JNMEDT
JOURNAL OF NEUROSCIENCE METHODS. (Text in English) 1979. 15/yr.(in 5 vols.; 3 nos./vol.) fl.1835 (effective 1992). Elsevier Science Publishers B.V., P.O. Box 211, 1000 AE Amsterdam, Netherlands. TEL 020-5803911. FAX 020-5803598. TELEX 18582 ESPA NL. (Subscr. in U.S. and Canada to: Elsevier Science Publishing Co., Inc., Box 882, Madison Sq. Sta., New York, NY 10159. TEL 212-989-5800) Ed. J.S. Kelly. adv.; charts; abstr.; bibl.; illus. (also avail. in microform from RPI; back issues avail.; reprint service avail. from ISI) **Indexed:** Biol.Abstr., Chem.Abstr., Curr.Adv.Cell & Devel.Biol., Curr.Adv.Ecol.Sci., Curr.Cont., Excerp.Med., Ind.Med., Ind.Sci.Rev., Mass Spectr.Bull., Sci.Abstr.
—BLDSC shelfmark: 5022.080000.
  Description: Publishes research papers and critical reviews addressing new methods or significant developments of recognized methods.
  Refereed Serial

616.8 US ISSN 0360-4012
QP351 CODEN: JNREDK
JOURNAL OF NEUROSCIENCE RESEARCH. 1975. m. $1,242 (foreign $ 1,392). John Wiley & Sons, Inc., Journals, 605 Third Ave., New York, NY 10158. TEL 212-850-6000. FAX 212-850-6088. TELEX 12-7063. Ed. Bernard Haber. adv.; bk.rev.; charts; illus.; index. (reprint service avail. from ISI) **Indexed:** Biol.Abstr., Chem.Abstr., Curr.Adv.Ecol.Sci., Curr.Cont., Excerp.Med., Ind.Med., Ind.Sci.Rev., INIS Atomind.
—BLDSC shelfmark: 5022.090000.
  Description: Concerned with basic research reports on molecular, cellular, and subcellular aspects of the neurosciences.
  Refereed Serial

616.8 US ISSN 0022-3085
RD1 CODEN: JONSAC
JOURNAL OF NEUROSURGERY. 1944. m. $100. American Association of Neurological Surgeons, Dartmouth Medical School, Hanover, NH 03756. TEL 603-643-4163. FAX 603-643-4166. Ed. Dr. Thoralf M. Sundt, Jr. adv.; bk.rev.; bibl.; charts; illus.; cum.index covering 50 vols.; circ. 11,500. (also avail. in microform from MIM,UMI) **Indexed:** Biol.Abstr., Chem.Abstr., Curr.Adv.Cancer Res., Curr.Cont., Dent.Ind., Excerp.Med., Helminthol.Abstr., Ind.Med., Ind.Sci.Rev., INIS Atomind., Rev.Plant Path.
—BLDSC shelfmark: 5022.100000.
  Description: Presents medical articles relating to neurosurgery and allied specialties.
  Refereed Serial

JOURNAL OF NEUROSURGICAL SCIENCES. see *MEDICAL SCIENCES — Surgery*

JOURNAL OF NEUROTRAUMA. see *MEDICAL SCIENCES — Orthopedics And Traumatology*

616.8 US ISSN 0022-3298
RZ460
JOURNAL OF ORGONOMY. 1967. s-a. $40. American College of Orgonomy, Box 490, Princeton, NJ 08542. TEL 908-821-1144. FAX 908-821-0174. Ed. Dr. Richard A. Blasband. bk.rev.; bibl.; charts; illus.; stat.; index, cum.index: 1967-1986; circ. 2,000. (also avail. in microfilm from UMI; back issues avail.; reprint service avail. from UMI)
—BLDSC shelfmark: 5027.150000.
  Description: Devoted to the study of orgone energy functions in living and nonliving nature, based on the discoveries of Wilhelm Reich.
  Refereed Serial

616.89 CN
JOURNAL OF ORTHOMOLECULAR MEDICINE. 1967. q. $75 to individuals (foreign $90); institutions $85 (foreign $100)(effective 1992). Canadian Schizophrenia Foundation, 7375 Kingsway, Burnaby, B.C. V3W 3B5, Canada. TEL 604-521-1728. Ed. A. Hoffer. adv.; bk.rev.; bibl.; charts; illus.; circ. 1,400. (also avail. in microform from UMI; back issues avail.; reprint service avail. from UMI) **Indexed:** Biol.Abstr., Chem.Abstr., Curr.Adv.Biochem., Curr.Cont., Excerp.Med., Mid.East: Abstr.& Ind., Nutr.Abstr., Psychol.Abstr., SSCI.
  Former titles: Journal of Orthomolecular Psychiatry (ISSN 0317-0209); (until 1973): Orthomolecular Psychiatry; (until 1972): Schizophrenia (ISSN 0036-6129); (until 1969): Journal of Schizophrenia (ISSN 0449-3109)

616.8 DK ISSN 0742-3098
QP188.P55 CODEN: JPRSE9
JOURNAL OF PINEAL RESEARCH. (Text in English) 8/yr. $622. Munksgaard International Publishers Ltd., P.O. Box 2148, DK-1016 Copenhagen K, Denmark. TEL 45-33-12-70-30. FAX 45-33-12-70-30. TELEX 19431 MUNKS DK. Ed. Russel J. Reiter. circ. 300. **Indexed:** Anim.Breed.Abstr., Biol.Abstr., Chem.Abstr., Curr.Adv.Cancer Res., Curr.Adv.Ecol.Sci., Curr.Cont., Excerp.Med., Ind.Med., Pig News & Info., Poult.Abstr.
●Also available online.
—BLDSC shelfmark: 5040.329000.
  Refereed Serial

JOURNAL OF POLYMORPHOUS PERVERSITY. see *PSYCHOLOGY*

616.89 US ISSN 0022-3956
RC321 CODEN: JPYRA3
JOURNAL OF PSYCHIATRIC RESEARCH. 1961. 4/yr. £165 (effective 1992). Pergamon Press, Inc., Journals Division, 660 White Plains Rd., Tarrytown, NY 10591-5153. TEL 914-524-9200. FAX 914-333-2444. (And: Headington Hill Hall, Oxford OX3 0BW, England. TEL 0865-794141) Eds. Merton Sandler, Joseph J. Schildkraut. adv.; bk.rev.; charts; illus.; index; circ. 1,250. (also avail. in microform from MIM,UMI; back issues avail.) **Indexed:** Biol.Abstr., Chem.Abstr., Curr.Adv.Ecol.Sci., Curr.Cont., Dent.Ind., Excerp.Med., Hosp.Lit.Ind., Ind.Med., Ind.Sci.Rev., Lang.& Lang.Behav.Abstr., Mid.East: Abstr.& Ind., Psychol.Abstr., Sci.Cit.Ind., SSCI.
—BLDSC shelfmark: 5043.250000.
  Description: Covers the latest developments in psychiatry and cognate disciplines.
  Refereed Serial

JOURNAL OF PSYCHIATRY AND LAW. see *LAW*

616.8 CN ISSN 1180-4882
RC321 CODEN: JPNEEF
JOURNAL OF PSYCHIATRY AND NEUROSCIENCE. (Text in English, French) 1976. 5/yr. Can.$65. University of Ottawa, Journal Management Committee, c/o Margaret Pivik, 501 Smyth Road, Rm. 4417, Ottawa, Ont. K1H 8L6, Canada. TEL 613-526-1690. FAX 613-737-8470. Ed. Dr. Y.D. Lapierre. adv.; bk.rev.; index; circ. 5,500. **Indexed:** Biol.Abstr., Child Devel.Abstr., Curr.Cont., Excerp.Med., Ind.Med., Psychol.Abstr., Sociol.Abstr.
—BLDSC shelfmark: 5043.261000.
  Formerly: Psychiatric Journal of the University of Ottawa (ISSN 0702-8466)

JOURNAL OF PSYCHOACTIVE DRUGS; a multidisciplinary forum. see *DRUG ABUSE AND ALCOHOLISM*

JOURNAL OF PSYCHOPHYSIOLOGY. see *PSYCHOLOGY*

616.08 US ISSN 0022-3999
RC52 CODEN: JPCRAT
JOURNAL OF PSYCHOSOMATIC RESEARCH. 1956. 8/yr. £280 (effective 1992). Pergamon Press, Inc., Journals Division, 660 White Plains Rd., Tarrytown, NY 10591-5153. TEL 914-524-9200. FAX 914-333-2444. (And: Headington Hill Hall, Oxford OX3 0BW, England. TEL 0865-794141) Ed. Geoffrey Lloyd. adv.; bk.rev.; bibl.; charts; index; circ. 1,600. (also avail. in microform from MIM,UMI) **Indexed:** Adol.Ment.Hlth.Abstr., ASSIA, Bibl.Dev.Med.& Child Neur., Biol.Abstr., Chem.Abstr., Curr.Adv.Ecol.Sci., Curr.Cont., Dent.Ind., Dok.Arbeitsmed., Excerp.Med., Ind.Med., Ind.Sci.Rev., Mid.East: Abstr.& Ind., Nutr.Abstr., Psychol.Abstr., Risk Abstr., SSCI, Stud.Wom.Abstr.
—BLDSC shelfmark: 5043.480000.
  Description: Reflects current research in the psychosomatic approach from both clinical and experimental perspectives, including scientific examination of theoretical topics.
  Refereed Serial

616.891 US ISSN 1053-0479
RC475 CODEN: JPINEH
▼**JOURNAL OF PSYCHOTHERAPY INTEGRATION.** 1991. q. $75 (foreign $90)(effective 1992). Plenum Publishing Corp., 233 Spring St., New York, NY 10013-1578. TEL 212-620-8000. FAX 212-463-0742. TELEX 23-421139. Ed. Hal Arkowitz. (back issues avail.)
—BLDSC shelfmark: 5043.483300.
  Refereed Serial

616.8 US ISSN 1055-050X
RC475
▼**JOURNAL OF PSYCHOTHERAPY PRACTICE AND RESEARCH.** 1992. q. $85 to individuals (foreign $100); institutions $135 (foreign $150). American Psychiatric Press, Inc., Journals Division, 1400 K St., N.W., Ste. 1101, Washington, DC 20005. TEL 202-682-6130. FAX 202-789-2648. (UK addr.: 17 Belgrave Sq., London SW1X 8PG, England) Ed. Dr. Jerald Kay. adv.; bk.rev.; abstr.; bibl.; charts; illus.; stat.; index.
  Description: Aims to advance the professional understanding of human behavior and to enhance the psychotherapeutic treatment of mental disorders.

616.8 US
RC321
JOURNAL OF RUSSIAN AND EAST EUROPEAN PSYCHIATRY. 1968. q. $287 to institutions. M.E. Sharpe, Inc., 80 Business Park Dr., Armonk, NY 10504. TEL 914-273-1800. FAX 914-273-2106. Ed. Gordon Mangan. adv.; charts; stat. **Indexed:** Biol.Abstr., Curr.Cont., Excerp.Med., Psychol.Abstr.
  Formerly: Soviet Neurology and Psychiatry (ISSN 0038-559X); Which superseded: Soviet Psychology and Psychiatry.
  Description: Contains translations of the pertinent articles that appear in Soviet publications.
  Refereed Serial

616.8 612.3 US ISSN 0887-8250
TX546 CODEN: JSSDEO
JOURNAL OF SENSORY STUDIES. 1986. q. $104. Food & Nutrition Press, Inc., 2 Corporate Dr., Box 374, Trumbull, CT 06611. TEL 203-261-8587. Ed. M.C. Gacula, Jr. **Indexed:** Dairy Sci.Abstr.
—BLDSC shelfmark: 5063.600000.
  Description: Promotes the technical and practical advancement of sensory science, publishing a broad spectrum of papers, including observational and experimental studies in the application of sensory evaluation to the food, medical, agricultural, biological, pharmaceutical, cosmetic, consumer, and materials industries.

617.8 US ISSN 0022-4685
RC423 CODEN: JSPHAH
JOURNAL OF SPEECH AND HEARING RESEARCH. 1958. bi-m. $60 to individuals (foreign $70); institutions $114 (foreign $126). American Speech - Language - Hearing Association, 10801 Rockville Pike, Rockville, MD 20852. TEL 301-897-5700. FAX 301-571-0457. Ed. Dianne J. Van Tasell. bibl.; charts; illus.; circ. 73,000. (also avail. in microform from UMI; reprint service avail. from UMI) **Indexed:** ASSIA, Bibl.Dev.Med.& Child Neur., Biol.Abstr., C.I.J.E., Chem.Abstr., Curr.Cont., Dent.Ind., Educ.Ind., Except.Child.Educ.Abstr., Excerp.Med., Ind.Med., Lang.& Lang.Behav.Abstr., M.L.A., Noise Pollut.Publ.Abstr., Psychol.Abstr., Rehabil.Lit., Sci.Abstr, Sp.Ed.Needs Abstr., SSCI.
—BLDSC shelfmark: 5066.150000.
  Description: Relates findings on speech and hearing disorders.

JOURNAL OF STRATEGIC AND SYSTEMIC THERAPIES. see *PSYCHOLOGY*

616.8 NE ISSN 0165-1838
CODEN: JASYDS
JOURNAL OF THE AUTONOMIC NERVOUS SYSTEM. (Text in English) 1979. 12/yr.(in 4 vols.; 3 nos./vol.). fl.1444 (effective 1992). Elsevier Science Publishers B.V., P.O. Box 211, 1000 AE Amsterdam, Netherlands. TEL 020-5803911. FAX 020-5803598. TELEX 18582 ESPA NL. (Subscr. in U.S. and Canada to: Elsevier Science Publishing Co., Inc., Box 882, Madison Sq. Sta., New York, NY 10159. TEL 212-989-5800) Ed. G. Burnstock. adv.; bk.rev.; charts; illus. (also avail. in microform from RPI; back issues avail.; reprint service avail. from ISI,SWZ) **Indexed:** Biol.Abstr., Chem.Abstr., Curr.Cont., Dent.Ind., Excerp.Med., Ind.Med., Ind.Sci.Rev.
—BLDSC shelfmark: 4949.750000.
  Description: Presents papers that deal with any aspect of the autonomic nervous system, including structure, physiology, pharmacology, biochemistry, development, evoluation, ageing, behavioural aspects, integrative role and influence on emotional and physical states of the body.
  Refereed Serial

M

MEDICAL SCIENCES — PSYCHIATRY AND NEUROLOGY

616.8   NE   ISSN 0022-510X
RC321   CODEN: JNSCAG
JOURNAL OF THE NEUROLOGICAL SCIENCES. (Text and summaries in English, French, German, Spanish) 1964. 14/yr.(in 7 vols.; 2 nos./vol.). fl.2233 (effective 1992). (World Federation of Neurology) Elsevier Science Publishers B.V., P.O. Box 211, 1000 AE Amsterdam, Netherlands. TEL 020-5803911. FAX 020-5803598. TELEX 18582 ESPA NL. (Subscr. in U.S. and Canada to: Elsevier Science Publishing Co., Inc., Box 882, Madison Sq. Sta., New York, NY 10159. TEL 212-989-5800) Ed. J.F. Toole. adv.; bk.rev.; bibl.; charts; illus.; index. (reprint service avail. from ISI,SWZ) **Indexed:** Bibl.Dev.Med.& Child Neur., Biol.Abstr., Chem.Abstr., Curr.Adv.Ecol.Sci., Curr.Cont., Excerp.Med., Helminthol.Abstr., Ind.Med., Ind.Sci.Rev., Ind.Vet., Nutr.Abstr., Psychol.Abstr., Vet.Bull.
—BLDSC shelfmark: 5021.560000.
Description: Provides a medium for the publication of studies on the interface between clinical neurology and the basic sciences.
Refereed Serial

616.8   JA   ISSN 0288-9617
KANAGAWA-KEN SEISHIN IGAKKAISHI/KANAGAWA ASSOCIATION OF PSYCHIATRY. JOURNAL. (Text in Japanese) 1959. a. 2000 Yen. Kanagawa Association of Psychiatry, c/o Department of Neurology and Psychiatry, Yokohama City University School of Medicine, 3-46, Urafune-Cho, Minami-Ku, Yoakohama 232, Japan. Ed. Masaaki Matsushita. adv.; circ. 2,000. (back issues avail.)

616.8 617   US   ISSN 0886-8018
KEY NEUROLOGY AND NEUROSURGERY. 1986. q. $69 to individuals (foreign $83); institutions $89 (foreign $103); students $45 (foreign $59). Mosby - Year Book, Inc. (Subsidiary of: Times Mirror Company), 11830 Westline Industrial Dr., St. Louis, MO 63146. TEL 800-325-4177.
FAX 314-432-1380. TELEX 44-2402. Ed.Bd.
Description: Provides surveys, with commentary, of key medical literature in neurology and neurosurgery.

KLINISCHE NEURORADIOLOGIE. see *MEDICAL SCIENCES — Radiology And Nuclear Medicine*

616.853   SZ
KONTAKTE; Epilepsie Selbsthilfe Zeitung. 1986. s-a. Schweizerische Liga gegen Epilepsie, Feldeggstr. 71, Postfach 129, CH-8032 Zurich, Switzerland. TEL 01-3830531. Ed.Bd. bk.rev.; circ. 900.

616.8   KO   ISSN 1015-4817
KOREAN NEUROPSYCHIATRIC ASSOCIATION. JOURNAL. (Text in Korean; summaries in English) 1962. bi-m. free. Korean Neuropsychiatric Association, RN.1005 Shinmoonro Bd.238, 1-ga Shinmoonro, Chongro-gu, Seoul 110-061, S. Korea. TEL 02-736-7043. Ed. Dr. Kwang-Iel Kim. adv. Key Title: Taehan Sin'gyong Chongsin Uihak Hoeji.
—BLDSC shelfmark: 4812.340900.
Formerly: Neuro-Psychiatry.

616.89   JA   ISSN 0023-6144
CODEN: KSSIAC
KYUSHU NEURO-PSYCHIATRY/KYUSHU SHINKEI SEISHIN IGAKU. (Text in Japanese; summaries in English) 1954. q. 5000 Yen. Kyushu Association of Neuro-Psychiatry - Kyushu Shinkei Seishin Igaku, c/o Department of Neuro-Psychiatry, Faculty of Medicine, Kyushu University 60, Maidashi, Higashi-ku, Fukuoka 812, Japan. FAX 092-632-3558. Ed. N. Tashiro. adv.; bk.rev.; bibl.; charts; stat.; index; circ. 690 (controlled; processed; also avail. in microfilm from UMI) **Indexed:** Chem.Abstr., Psychol.Abstr.
—BLDSC shelfmark: 5136.200000.

616.8   IT   ISSN 0023-9097
LAVORO NEUROPSICHIATRICO. (Supplement avail.) (Text in Italian; summaries in French, German and Italian) 1947. bi-m. L.8000. Amministrazione Provinciale, Piazza S. Maria della Pieta 5, 00135 Rome, Italy. Ed. Giovanni Bonfiglio. bk.rev.; bibl.; charts; illus.; index; circ. 1,200. **Indexed:** Chem.Abstr., Excerp.Med., Psychol.Abstr.

616.8 155.67   UK   ISSN 0143-7534
LEARNING AND MEMORY. m. £70. Sheffield University Biomedical Information Service (SUBIS), The University, Sheffield S10 2TN, England.
TEL 0742-768555. FAX 0742-739826. TELEX 547216 UGSHEF G. (looseleaf format; back issues avail.)
Description: Current awareness service for researchers in clinical and life sciences.

616.89 340   US
LEGAL RESOURCES FOR THE MENTALLY DISABLED: A DIRECTORY OF LAWYERS AND OTHER SPECIALISTS. 1982. a. American Bar Association, 1800 M St., N.W., Washington, DC 20036. TEL 202-331-2258. Ed. John Parry.
Formerly: Mental and Developmental Disabilities Directory of Legal Advocates.

616.8   FR   ISSN 0223-9434
LETTRE DU PSYCHIATRE; psychiatrie et medicaments. 1979. 10/yr. 55 ECU($72) (typically set in Jan.). Masson, 120 bd. Saint-Germain, 75280 Paris Cedex 06, France. TEL 1-46-34-21-60.
FAX 1-45-87-29-99. TELEX 202 671 F. Ed. H. Ollat. circ. 800. (also avail. in microform from UMI)

616.8 371.4   US   ISSN 1059-6593
LIFE-LINE. 1982. q. $10. National Hydrocephalus Foundation, 400 N. Michigan Ave., Ste. 1102, Chicago, IL 60611-4102. TEL 312-645-0701. FAX 312-427-9311. Ed. Warren Barshers. bk.rev.; tr.lit.; circ. 275. (looseleaf format; back issues avail.) **Formerly:** National Hydro Cephalus Foundation Newsletter.
Description: Information relating to hydrocephalus and associated problems of a medical and educational nature.

616.8 610.73   US
LINK (WOODLAND HILLS). 1987. bi-m. free. Amyotrophic Lateral Sclerosis Association, 21021 Ventura Blvd., Ste. 321, Woodland Hills, CA 91364. TEL 818-340-7500. FAX 818-340-2060. Ed.Bd. bk.rev.; circ. 80,000. (tabloid format; back issues avail.)

616.8   UK   ISSN 0954-1381
▼**LITHIUM.** 1990. 4/yr. £116($223) to individuals; institutions £142($276). Churchill Livingstone Medical Journals, Robert Stevenson House, 1-3 Baxter's Pl., Leith Walk, Edinburgh EH1 3AF, Scotland. TEL 031-556-2424. FAX 031-558-1278. TELEX 727511. (Subscr. to: Longman Group, Journals Subscr. Dept., P.O. Box 77, Fourth Ave., Harlow, Essex CM19 5AA, England; U.S. subscr. to: Churchill Livingstone, 650 Ave. of the Americas, New York, NY 10011. TEL 212-206-5000) Ed. F.N. Johnson. adv.; bk.rev.
—BLDSC shelfmark: 5276.875480.
Description: Publishes original research, review articles, discussion papers, short communications and letters, on all biomedical aspects of lithium: biochemical, physiological, pharmacological, psychopharmacological and clinical.
Refereed Serial

616.89   NE
M G V. (Maandblad Geestelijke Volksgezondheid) 1946. 11/yr. fl.73.50. Nederlands Centrum Geestelijke Volksgezondheid, Postbus 5103, 3502 JC Utrecht, Netherlands. TEL 02154-82211. Ed.Bd. adv.; bk.rev.; index; circ. 9,000.

616.834   UK   ISSN 0047-5270
M S NEWS. 1954. 3/yr. membership. Multiple Sclerosis Society, 25 Effie Rd., London SW6 1EE, England. Ed. John Walford. bk.rev.; illus.; stat.; circ. 60,000.

616.8   II
MADRAS INSTITUTE OF NEUROLOGY. PROCEEDINGS. (Text in English) vol. 2, 1972. 3/yr. $4. Wardha Press, 541 Swami Naichen St., Madras 600002, India. Ed. B. Ramamurthi. bk.rev.; bibl.; index; circ. 1,000. **Indexed:** Excerp.Med.

MANAB MON; a journal depicting the modern trends in psychology, biology, and sociology. see *PSYCHOLOGY*

616.8   US
MARKER. 1967. q. free. Huntington's Disease Society of America, 140 W. 22nd St., 6th Fl., New York, NY 10011. TEL 212-242-1968. FAX 212-243-2443. Ed. Andrew J. McInnes. bk.rev.; circ. 40,000. (back issues avail.)
Formerly: Committee to Combat Huntington's Disease Newsletter.
Description: Covers national and local news and events relevant to Huntington's Disease patients and their families. Includes medical and scientific research updates.

MEDICAL HYPNOANALYSIS JOURNAL. see *MEDICAL SCIENCES — Hypnosis*

MEDICAL MALPRACTICE: PSYCHIATRIC CARE. see *LAW — Civil Law*

616.8 150.5   IT   ISSN 0394-1531
MEDICINA E PSYCHE/MEDICINE AND MIND; semestrale di psicologia medica e di filosofia della medicina - semi-annual journal of philosophy of medicine and medical psychology. 1983. s-a. L.50000($70) Centro Italiano Studi di Psicologia Medica, Viale Romagna 51, 20133 Milan, Italy.
FAX 02-2361226. (Subscriptions to: Swets Subscription Service, LACP Dept., Helen deJongh, PO Box 849, 2160 SZ Lisse, Netherlands) Ed. Giuseppe R. Brera. adv.; bk.rev.; circ. 1,000.

616.89   IT   ISSN 0025-7893
CODEN: MDPSAC
MEDICINA PSICOSOMATICA; rivista di medicina psicosomatica, psicologia clinica e psicoterapia. (Text in Italian; summaries in English, French, Italian) 1956. q. L.18000. Societa Editrice Universo, Via G. B. Morgagni 1, 00161 Rome, Italy. Ed. Ferruccio Antonelli. adv.; bk.rev.; abstr.; bibl.; charts; index. **Indexed:** Biol.Abstr., Curr.Adv.Ecol.Sci., Excerp.Med., Psychol.Abstr.
—BLDSC shelfmark: 5533.650000.

616.8   CI   ISSN 0351-4501
MEDITERRANEAN JOURNAL OF SOCIAL PSYCHIATRY. (Text in English and French; summaries in Arabic) 1980. s-a. $15. Mediterranean Sociopsychiatric Association, Vinogradska 29, 41000 Zagreb, Croatia. (Co-sponsor: Association for Mental Health Protection and Promotion of the SR of Croatia) Ed. Vladimir Hudolin. adv.; bk.rev.; charts; illus.; stat.; circ. 1,000. **Indexed:** Excerp.Med.
—BLDSC shelfmark: 5534.736000.

616.89 616.89   US   ISSN 0025-9284
RC321   CODEN: BMCLA4
MENNINGER CLINIC. BULLETIN; a journal for the mental health professions. 1936. q. $40 to individuals (foreign $45); institutions $55 (foreign $60); students $20. Menninger Foundation, Box 829, Topeka, KS 66601-0829. TEL 913-273-7500. FAX 913-273-8625. Ed. Dr. Jon G. Allen. adv.; bk.rev.; bibl.; charts; illus.; index, cum.index.; circ. 2,200. (also avail. in microform from UMI; reprint service avail. from UMI) **Indexed:** Biol.Abstr., Chicago Psychoanal.Lit.Ind., Curr.Cont., Excerp.Med., Hosp.Lit.Ind., Ind.Med., Int.Nurs.Ind., Lang.& Lang.Behav.Abstr., Mid.East: Abstr.& Ind., Psychoanal.abstr., Psychol.Abstr., Soc.Work Res.& Abstr., SSCI.
—BLDSC shelfmark: 2612.200000.
Description: Contains articles on psychiatry, psychology, psychoanalysis, child psychiatry, neuropsychology and cliinical research.
Refereed Serial

616.89 616.89   US   ISSN 0025-9292
RC321   CODEN: MNPVB
MENNINGER PERSPECTIVE. 1970. q. Menninger Foundation, Box 829, Topeka, KS 66601-0829. TEL 913-273-7500. Eds. Judith Craig, Emlin E. North, Jr. circ. 26,000. (also avail. in microform from UMI; reprint service avail. from UMI) **Indexed:** Intl.Mgmt.Info, Psychol.Abstr.
Formerly: Menninger Quarterly.

MENTAL AND PHYSICAL DISABILITY LAW REPORTER; covers all aspects of handicapped law. see *LAW — Civil Law*

MEDICAL SCIENCES — PSYCHIATRY AND NEUROLOGY 3345

616.8   UK   ISSN 0261-9997
MENTAL HANDICAP. 1973. q. £15.50 to individuals; institutions £17.50. (British Institute of Mental Handicap) B I M H Publications, Stourport House, Stourport Rd., Kidderminster, Worcs. DY11 7QG, England. TEL 0562-824933. Ed. S.J. Newbould. adv.; circ. 3,500. **Indexed:** Curr.Adv.Ecol.Sci., Rehabil.Lit., Sp.Ed.Needs Abstr.
—BLDSC shelfmark: 5678.562000.
Formerly (until March 1982): Apex.
Description: Original articles with multidisciplinary appeal covering all aspects of mental handicap.

616.858   UK   ISSN 0260-1222
MENTAL HANDICAP BULLETIN. q. £16.50 to individuals; institutions £18.50. (British Institute of Mental Handicap) B I M H Publications, Stourport House, Stourport Rd., Kidderminster, Worcs. DY11 7QG, England. TEL 0562-824933. Ed. S.J. Newbould. adv.; circ. 1,000.

616.858   UK   ISSN 0952-9608
MENTAL HANDICAP RESEARCH. 1987. s-a. £21 to individuals; institutions £27. B I M H Publications, Stourport House, Stourport Rd., Kidderminster, Worcs. DY11 7QG, England. TEL 0562-824933. Ed. S.J. Newbould. circ. 2,000. **Indexed:** Sp.Ed.Needs Abstr.
—BLDSC shelfmark: 5678.567000.
Description: Applied research in mental handicap undertaken in the UK and overseas from all professional disciplines.

616.8   AT   ISSN 0025-9667
MENTAL HEALTH IN AUSTRALIA. 1964. s-a. Aus.$10. Australian National Association for Mental Health, 168 Hoddle St., Abbotsford, Vic. 3067, Australia. TEL 011-61-3-4176655. FAX 011-61-3-4197463. Ed. G.D. Burrows. adv.; bk.rev.; circ. 1,000. (back issues avail.) **Indexed:** Aus.P.A.I.S., Psychol.Abstr.
Description: Contains articles for debate and learned papers covering advocacy, disrcimination, illness prevention, health promotion and social justice issues.

MENTAL HEALTH IN CHILDREN. see *PSYCHOLOGY*

MENTAL HEALTH REPORT. see *SOCIAL SERVICES AND WELFARE*

MENTAL RETARDATION (WASHINGTON). see *EDUCATION — Special Education And Rehabilitation*

618.9   US   ISSN 0091-6315
RC570   CODEN: MRDDD8
MENTAL RETARDATION AND DEVELOPMENTAL DISABILITIES. 1970. a. Plenum Publishing Corp., 233 Spring St., New York, NY 10013-1578. TEL 212-620-8000. FAX 212-463-0742. TELEX 23-421139. Ed. J. Wortis. **Indexed:** Adol.Ment.Hlth.Abstr., Biol.Abstr., Except.Child.Educ.Abstr., Mid.East: Abstr.& Ind., Rehabil.Lit., Soc.Work Res.& Abstr., SSCI.
Supersedes: Mental Retardation.
Refereed Serial

616.834   UK
MESSENGER (LONDON). 1974. 6/yr. membership. Multiple Sclerosis Society, 25 Effie Rd., London SW6 1EE, England. Ed. John Walford.
Formerly: M S S Bulletin.

616.857   UK   ISSN 0544-1153
MIGRAINE NEWS. 1967. 4/yr. £10 membership. Migraine Trust, 45 Great Ormond St., London WC1N 3HZ, England. TEL 071-278-2676.
FAX 071-831-5174. adv.; bk.rev.; circ. 17,500. (tabloid format)

616.8   IT
MINERVA PSICHIATRICA. (Text in Italian; summaries in English and Italian) 1960. q. L.60000($70) Edizioni Minerva Medica, Corso Bramante 83-85, 10126 Turin, Italy. Ed. G. Campailla. adv.; bk.rev.; bibl.; charts; illus.; index; circ. 2,000. **Indexed:** Biol.Abstr., Excerp.Med., Ind.Med., Lang.& Lang.Behav.Abstr.
Formerly (until 1972): Minerva Psichiatrica e Psicologica.

616.8   SZ   ISSN 0077-0094
RC483   CODEN: MPPPBK
MODERN PROBLEMS OF PHARMACOPSYCHIATRY. (Text in English) 1968. irreg. price varies. S. Karger AG, Allschwilerstr. 10, P.O. Box, CH-4009 Basel, Switzerland. TEL 061-3061111.
FAX 061-3061234. TELEX CH 962652. Ed.Bd. (reprint service avail. from ISI) **Indexed:** Biol.Abstr., Chem.Abstr., Curr.Cont., Ind.Med., Psychol.Abstr.
—BLDSC shelfmark: 5894.400000.

MODERN TECHNICS IN SURGERY. NEUROSURGERY. see *MEDICAL SCIENCES — Surgery*

616.8   US   ISSN 1044-7431
QP356.2   CODEN: MOCNED
▼**MOLECULAR AND CELLULAR NEUROSCIENCES.** 1990. bi-m. $195 (foreign $216). Academic Press, Inc., Journal Division, 1250 Sixth Ave., San Diego, CA 92101. TEL 619-230-1840. FAX 619-699-6800. TELEX 181726. Ed. P. Michael Conn. (back issues avail.) **Indexed:** Excerp.Med. (1992-).
Description: Describes novel and original results in the areas of neurobiology, neuropharmacology, neuroendocrinology, neurochemistry, and neuroanatomy at the molecular, cellular, and tissue levels.
Refereed Serial

616.8   US   ISSN 1044-7393
   CODEN: MCHNEM
MOLECULAR AND CHEMICAL NEUROPATHOLOGY. 1983. bi-m. $200. Humana Press Inc., Box 2148, Clifton, NJ 07015. TEL 201-256-1699.
FAX 201-256-8341. Ed. Lloyd A. Horrocks. bk.rev.; abstr.; bibl.; charts; illus. **Indexed:** Biol.Abstr., Chem.Abstr., Curr.Adv.Ecol.Sci., Curr.Cont., Excerp.Med., Ind.Med.
—BLDSC shelfmark: 5900.762000.
Formerly (until 1989): Neurochemical Pathology (ISSN 0734-600X)
Refereed Serial

616.8 547.88   NE   ISSN 0169-328X
   CODEN: MBREE4
MOLECULAR BRAIN RESEARCH. Issued with: Brain Research (ISSN 0921-8246) (Text in English) 1986. 16/yr.(in 4 vols., 4 nos./vol.). fl.1404 (effective 1992). Elsevier Science Publishers B.V., P.O. Box 211, 1000 AE Amsterdam, Netherlands. TEL 020-5803911. FAX 020-5803598. TELEX 18582 ESPA NL. (N. America dist. addr.: Elsevier Science Publishing Co., Inc., Box 882, Madison Sq. Sta., New York, NY 10159. TEL 212-989-5800) Ed. D.P. Purpura. bibl.; index. (microfiche; back issues avail.; reprint service avail. from ISI) **Indexed:** Anim.Breed.Abstr., Biol.Abstr., Chem.Abstr., Curr.Adv.Biochem., Curr.Adv.Cell & Devel.Biol., Curr.Adv.Genetics & Molec.Biol., Curr.Cont., Excerp.Med., Ind.Med.
—BLDSC shelfmark: 5900.799000.
Description: Provides a medium for the prompt publications of studies of molecular mechanisms of neuronal synaptic and related processes that underline the structure and funcion of the brain.

616.8 573.21   US   ISSN 0893-7648
QP365.2   CODEN: MONBEW
MOLECULAR NEUROBIOLOGY; a review journal. 1987. q. $150. Humana Press Inc., Crescent Manor, Box 2148, Clifton, NJ 07015. TEL 201-256-1699.
FAX 201-256-8341. Eds. Nicolas Bazan, David U'Prichard. adv.; bk.rev.; abstr.; bibl.; charts; illus.; index. (back issues avail.) **Indexed:** Biol.Abstr., Chem.Abstr., Curr.Cont., Excerp.Med., Ind.Med., Sci.Cit.Ind.
—BLDSC shelfmark: 5900.817980.
Description: For neuroscientists needing to keep abreast of current molecular brain research.
Refereed Serial

616.894   US   ISSN 0077-0620
MONOGRAPH SERIES ON SCHIZOPHRENIA. 1950. irreg., no.8, 1969. price varies. International Universities Press, Inc., 59 Boston Post Rd., Box 1524, Madison, CT 06443-1524. TEL 203-245-4000.
Refereed Serial

616.8   US   ISSN 0077-0671
   CODEN: MGGPBE
MONOGRAPHIEN AUS DEM GESAMTGEBIETE DER PSYCHIATRIE - PSYCHIATRY SERIES. (Text in English and German) 1970. irreg. price varies. Springer-Verlag, 175 Fifth Ave., New York, NY 10010. TEL 212-460-1500. (Also Berlin, Heidelberg, Tokyo and Vienna) (reprint service avail. from ISI) **Indexed:** Ind.Med., Psychol.Abstr.
Supersedes in part: Monographien aus dem Gesamtgebiete der Neurologie und Psychiatrie.

616.8   SZ   ISSN 0300-5186
   CODEN: MNUSB6
MONOGRAPHS IN NEURAL SCIENCES. (Text in English) 1972. irreg. price varies. S. Karger AG, Allschwilerstr. 10, P.O. Box, CH-4009 Basel, Switzerland. TEL 061-3061111.
FAX 061-3061234. TELEX CH 962652. Ed. A. Korczyn. (reprint service avail. from ISI) **Indexed:** Biol.Abstr., Chem.Abstr., Curr.Cont., Ind.Med.
—BLDSC shelfmark: 5915.590000.
Formerly: Monographs in Basic Neurology.

616.8   US   ISSN 0737-3953
MONOGRAPHS IN NEUROSCIENCE. 1984. irreg., vol.3, 1988. Gordon & Breach Science Publishers, 270 Eighth Ave., New York, NY 10011.
TEL 212-206-8900. FAX 212-645-2459. TELEX 236735 GOPUB UR. (Subscr. to: Box 786, Cooper Sta., New York, NY 10276. TEL 800-545-8398; UK subscr. to: P.O. Box 90, Reading, Berkshire RG1 8JL, England. TEL 0734-560-080) Ed. S. Weinstein.
—BLDSC shelfmark: 5915.593000.
Refereed Serial

616.8   FR   ISSN 0245-5919
MOTRICITE CEREBRALE: READAPTATION NEUROLOGIE DU DEVELOPPEMENT.. 1980. q. 63 ECU($77) Masson, 120 bd. Saint-Germain, 75280 Paris Cedex 06, France. TEL 1-46-34-21-60.
FAX 1-45-87-29-99. TELEX 202 671 F. Ed. M. le Metayer. circ. 1,200. (also avail. in microform from UMI) **Indexed:** Excerp.Med.
—BLDSC shelfmark: 5978.710000.

616.8   US   ISSN 0885-3185
MOVEMENT DISORDERS. 1986. q. $177 to individuals; institutions $223. Raven Press, 1185 Ave. of the Americas, New York, NY 10036.
TEL 212-930-9500. FAX 212-869-3495. TELEX 640073. Eds. Dr. Stanley Fahn, Dr. David Marsden. adv.; bk.rev.; video rev.; charts; illus.; index; circ. 1,500. (back issues avail.) **Indexed:** Excerp.Med.
—BLDSC shelfmark: 5980.317200.
Description: Publishes articles on all aspects of movement disorders, their etiology, and management.
Refereed Serial

MUSIK-, TANZ- UND KUNSTTHERAPIE. see *MEDICAL SCIENCES*

616.858   US
N A M I ADVOCATE. 1979. bi-m. $25. National Alliance for the Mentally Ill, 2101 Wilson Blvd. no. 302, Arlington, VA 22201-3008. TEL 703-524-9094. Ed. James A. Buie. adv.; bk.rev.; circ. 85,000.
Formerly: N A M I News.

616.8   II   ISSN 0254-0886
N I M H A N S JOURNAL. 1983. s-a. Rs.50($20) National Institute of Mental Health & Neuro Sciences, Bangalore 560 029, India.
FAX 009-1812-641256. TELEX 845-2186 NIMH IN. Ed. S.M. Channabasavanna. adv.; bk.rev.; circ. 1,000. **Indexed:** Excerp.Med., Psychol.Abstr.

616.8   US   ISSN 1040-3671
N S T A NEWSLETTER. 1984. q. $20. National Spasmodic Torticollis Association, Box 873, Royal Oak, MI 48068-0873. TEL 313-647-2280. Ed. Phyllis Jones. circ. 800.
Formerly (until 1986): National Spasmodic Torticollis Association Newsletter.
Description: Provides information for patients on the treatment of spasmodic torticollis, a neurological condition.

MEDICAL SCIENCES — PSYCHIATRY AND NEUROLOGY

616.8 362.2   US   ISSN 0738-9159
NATIONAL COUNCIL NEWS. 1977. m. $21. National Council of Community Mental Health Centers, 12300 Twinbrook Parkway, Ste. 320, Rockville, MD 20852. TEL 301-984-6200. Ed. Joanne Petro. adv.; bk.rev.; circ. 2,600. (tabloid format)
Description: Covers issues of interest to mental health care professionals and reports Council activities.

616.857   US
NATIONAL HEADACHE FOUNDATION NEWSLETTER. 1970. q. $15. National Headache Foundation, 5252 N. Western Ave., Chicago, IL 60625. TEL 312-878-7715. FAX 312-878-2782. circ. 45,000. (tabloid format; back issues avail.)
Formerly: National Migraine Foundation Newsletter.
Description: Research and information on headache causes and treatments.

616.853   US   ISSN 0091-2387
NATIONAL SPOKESMAN; medical, legal, and legislative news and features for people with epilepsy. vol.5, 1972. 10/yr. $10. Epilepsy Foundation of America, 4351 Garden City Dr., Ste. 406, Landover, MD 20785. TEL 301-459-3700. FAX 301-577-2684. Ed. Ed Costello. bk.rev.; circ. 30,000. (tabloid format) **Indexed:** Rehabil.Lit.

NEIROFIZIOLOGIYA/NEUROPHYSIOLOGY; nauchno-teoreticheskii zhurnal. see BIOLOGY — Physiology

616.8   GW   ISSN 0028-2804
           CODEN: NERVAF
DER NERVENARZT; Monatsschrift fuer alle Gebiete nervenaerztlicher Forschung und Praxis. (Includes: Deutsche Gesellschaft fuer Neurologie. Mitteilungsblatt und Gesellschaft Oesterreichischer Nervenaertze und Psychiater) 1928. 12/yr. DM.344($184) (Deutsche Gesellschaft fuer Psychiatrie und Nervenheilkunde) Springer-Verlag, Heidelberger Platz 3, D-1000 Berlin 33, Germany. TEL 030-8207-1. (Also Heidelberg, Tokyo, Vienna, and New York) Ed. T. Brandt. adv.; bk.rev.; charts; illus.; index. (also avail. in microform from UMI; back issues avail.; reprint service avail. from ISI) **Indexed:** Biol.Abstr., Biotech.Abstr., Chem.Abstr., Curr.Adv.Ecol.Sci., Curr.Cont., Excerp.Med., Ger.J.Psych., Ind.Med., Nutr.Abstr., Psychol.Abstr.
—BLDSC shelfmark: 6076.500000.
Description: Covers neurology, psychiatry, neurosurgery, and psychotherapy.

616.8   GW   ISSN 0722-1541
NERVENHEILKUNDE; Zeitschrift fuer interdisziplinaere Fortbildung. 1982. 7/yr. DM.136.50($91) F.K. Schattauer Verlagsgesellschaft mbH, Lenzhalde 3, Postfach 104545, 7000 Stuttgart 10, Germany. TEL 0711-22987-0. FAX 0711-22987-50. Eds. D. Soyka, E. Lungershausen. circ. 41,000.
—BLDSC shelfmark: 6076.520000.

NEURAL COMPUTATION. see COMPUTERS — Artificial Intelligence

NEURAL NETWORKS. see COMPUTERS — Artificial Intelligence

NEURO-CHIRURGIE. see MEDICAL SCIENCES — Surgery

NEURO-FIBROMA-TOSIS. see BIOLOGY — Genetics

NEURO-FIBROMA-TOSIS RESEARCH NEWSLETTER. see BIOLOGY — Genetics

NEURO-ORTHOPEDICS. see MEDICAL SCIENCES — Orthopedics And Traumatology

616.8   BL   ISSN 0028-3800
RC321   CODEN: NURBAX
NEUROBIOLOGIA; revista de neurologia psiquiatria e neurocirurgia. (Text and summaries in English and Portuguese) 1938. q. $45 (effective 1992). (Sociedade de Neurologia, Psiquiatria e Higiene Mental do Brasil, Hospital das Clinicas Pedro II) Sociedade Editora da Revista Neurobiologia, Caixa Postal 651, 50000 Recife PE, Brazil. TEL 81-268-5495. (Affiliate: Sociedade de Medicina de Pernambuco. Departamento de Neurologia e Neurocirurgia) Ed. A. Codeceira Jr. adv.; bk.rev.; abstr.; bibl.; charts; illus.; index; circ. 1,000. (also avail. in talking book; back issues avail.) **Indexed:** Biol.Abstr., Excerp. Med., Psychol.Abstr.
—BLDSC shelfmark: 6081.300000.

NEUROBIOLOGY OF AGING; experimental and clinical research. see BIOLOGY — Physiology

619   US   ISSN 0364-3190
QP356.3   CODEN: NEREDZ
NEUROCHEMICAL RESEARCH. 1976. m. $595 (foreign $695)(effective 1992). Plenum Publishing Corp., 233 Spring St., New York, NY 10013-1578. TEL 212-620-8000. FAX 212-463-0742. TELEX 23-421139. Ed. Abel Lathja. adv. (also avail. in microfilm from JSC; back issues avail.) **Indexed:** Biol.Abstr., Chem.Abstr., Curr.Adv.Biochem., Curr.Adv.Cell & Devel.Biol., Curr.Adv.Ecol.Sci., Curr.Cont., Dent.Ind., Excerp.Med., Ind.Med., Ind.Sci.Rev.
—BLDSC shelfmark: 6081.312000.
Refereed Serial

NEUROCHEMISTRY. see BIOLOGY — Biological Chemistry

616.8 540   US   ISSN 0197-0186
QP356.3   CODEN: NEUIDS
NEUROCHEMISTRY INTERNATIONAL; the international journal for the rapid publication of critical reviews, original and rapid research communications in neurochemistry. 1980. 8/yr. £300 (effective 1992). Pergamon Press, Inc., Journals Division, 660 White Plains Rd., Tarrytown, NY 10591-5153. TEL 914-524-9200. FAX 914-333-2444. (And: Headington Hill Hall, Oxford OX3 0BW, England. TEL 0865-794141) Eds. N. Osborne, W. Lovenberg. (also avail. in microform from MIM,UMI) **Indexed:** Biol.Abstr., Chem.Abstr., Curr.Adv.Ecol.Sci., Curr.Cont., Excerp.Med., Ind.Sci.Rev., Int.Aerosp.Abstr., Psychol.Abstr.
—BLDSC shelfmark: 6081.317000.
Description: Publishes papers concerned with the metabolism and function of the nervous system.
Refereed Serial

616.8   GW   ISSN 0028-3819
           CODEN: NURABV
NEUROCHIRURGIA. (Suppl. to: Fortschritte der Neurologie und Psychiatrie) (Text in German; summaries in English, French, German and Spanish) 1958. bi-m. DM.231. (German Society of Neurosurgery) Georg Thieme Verlag, Ruedigerstr. 14, Postfach 104853, 7000 Stuttgart 10, Germany. TEL 0711-8931-0. FAX 0711-8931298. Ed.Bd. adv.; bk.rev.; charts; illus.; circ. 1,000. (also avail. in microform from UMI; reprint service avail. from UMI) **Indexed:** Bibl.Dev.Med.& Child Neur., Biol.Abstr., Curr.Cont., Dent.Ind., Excerp.Med., Helminthol.Abstr., Ind.Med., Ind.Sci.Rev., Sci.Cit.Ind.
—BLDSC shelfmark: 6081.320000.

616.8   US   ISSN 0047-942X
NEUROELECTRIC NEWS. 1970. 3/yr. $25. Neuroelectric Society, Inc., c/o Anthony Sances, Jr., Ed., Medical College of Wisconsin, 8700 W. Wisconsin Ave., Milwaukee, WI 53226. bk.rev.; abstr.; bibl.; circ. 200. (also avail. in microform from UMI; reprint service avail. from UMI)
Description: Emphasizes theory and clinical applications of electroneurophysiology.

616.8   US   ISSN 0168-0617
QP365.4   CODEN: NEPEEQ
NEUROENDOCRINE PERSPECTIVES. 1982. irreg., vol.9, 1991. price varies. Springer-Verlag, 175 Fifth Ave., New York, NY 10010. TEL 212-460-1500. Eds. E.E. Mueller, R.M. Macleod. **Indexed:** Biol.Abstr., Chem.Abstr.
Refereed Serial

NEUROENDOCRINOLOGY; international journal for basic and clinical studies on neuroendocrine relationships. see MEDICAL SCIENCES — Endocrinology

616.8   GW   ISSN 0172-780X
           CODEN: NLETDU
NEUROENDOCRINOLOGY LETTERS.* 1979. bi-m. $120 to individuals; institutions $216. V C H Verlagsgesellschaft mbH, Postfach 10116, 6940 Weinheim, Germany. (And: Pappelalle 3, Postfach 1260, 69 Weinheim, W. Germany (B.R.D.)) adv.; bk.rev.; illus. (reprint service avail. from ISI) **Indexed:** Chem.Abstr., Curr.Adv.Biochem., Curr.Adv.Ecol.Sci., Dairy Sci.Abstr., Excerp.Med., Ind.Sci.Rev.
—BLDSC shelfmark: 6081.371000.

616.8   SZ   ISSN 0251-5350
           CODEN: NEEPD3
NEUROEPIDEMIOLOGY. (Text in English) 1982. bi-m. 398 Fr.($266) S. Karger AG, Allschwilerstr. 10, P.O. Box, CH-4009 Basel, Switzerland. TEL 061-3061111. FAX 061-3061234. TELEX CH 962652. (Or: S. Karger Publishers, Inc., 79 Fifth Ave., New York, NY 10011 U.S.A.) Ed. M. Alter. adv.; illus.; index; circ. 800. (also avail. in microform from RPI) **Indexed:** Biol.Abstr., Excerp.Med.
—BLDSC shelfmark: 6081.371200.

616.8   US   ISSN 1053-8119
▼**NEUROIMAGE.** 1992. 4/yr. $235 (foreign $261). Academic Press, Inc., Journal Division, 1250 Sixth Ave., San Diego, CA 92101. TEL 619-230-1840. FAX 619-699-6800. TELEX 181726. Ed. Arthur W. Toga.
Description: Focuses on the visualization of all neuroscientific data.
Refereed Serial

616.8   SP   ISSN 0213-4853
           CODEN: NERLEN
NEUROLOGIA. (Text in Spanish; summaries in English) 1986. m. (10/yr). 5500 ptas.($57) to non-members. (Sociedad Espanola de Neurologia) Ediciones Doyma, S.A., Travesera de Gracia, 17-21, 08021 Barcelona, Spain. TEL 200-07-11. FAX 209-11-36. TELEX 51695 INK-E. Ed. Jose Grau Veciana. adv.; page 135000 ptas.; trim 210 x 280; adv. contact: Marta Cisa. circ. 3,200. (reprint service avail. from UMI) **Indexed:** Ind.Med.Esp.
—BLDSC shelfmark: 6081.374900.
Description: Covers the investigative research of the Society and accredited clinics throughout the country.

616.8   CK   ISSN 0120-1034
NEUROLOGIA COLOMBIA. (Text and summaries in English and Spanish) 1977. 3/yr. Col.$1000($25) Fundacion Instituto Neurologico de Colombia, Apdo. Aereo 90303, Bogota 8, Colombia. Ed. Edwin Ruiz-Alarcon, M.D. adv.; bk.rev.; bibl.; charts; illus.; stat.; index; circ. 3,000. **Indexed:** Ind.Med.

616.89   CI   ISSN 0353-8842
NEUROLOGIA CROATICA; journal of neurology and its related fields. (Text in English; summaries in Croatian) 1953. q. $25. Department of Neurology, Kspaticeva 12, 41000 Zagreb, Croatia. TEL 041-222-706. (Co-sponsor: Department of Neuropathology) Ed. Dubravka Jadro-Santel. adv.; bk.rev.; illus.; circ. 1,000. (also avail. in microform from UMI; reprint service avail. from UMI) **Indexed:** Biol.Abstr., Dent.Ind., Excerp.Med., Ind.Med., Psychol.Abstr.
—BLDSC shelfmark: 6081.377000.
Supersedes (in 1991): Neurologija (ISSN 0350-9559); (in 1977): Neuropsihijatrija (ISSN 0047-9438)

616.8   JA   ISSN 0387-2572
NEUROLOGIA MEDICO-CHIRURGICA. Japanese edition: Shinkei Geka (ISSN 0470-8105) (Text in English) m. $178. (Japan Neurosurgical Society) Japan Scientific Societies Press, 6-2-10 Hongo, Bunkyo-ku, Tokyo 113, Japan. TEL 3814-2001. FAX 3814-2002. TELEX 2722268 BCJSP J. (Dist. by: Business Center for Academic Societies Japan, Koshin Bldg., 6-16-3 Hongo, Bunkyo-ku, Tokyo 113, Japan; Dist. in U.S. by: International Specialized Book Services, Inc., 5602 N.E. Hassalo St., Portland, OR 97213)
—BLDSC shelfmark: 6081.390000.

616.8   US   ISSN 0733-8619
RC321
NEUROLOGIC CLINICS. 1983. q. $82. W.B. Saunders Co., Curtis Center, Independence Square W., Philadelphia, PA 19106. TEL 215-238-7800. Ed. Leslie Kramer. (also avail. in microform from UMI) **Indexed:** Ind.Med., Psychol.Abstr.
—BLDSC shelfmark: 6081.441000.

MEDICAL SCIENCES — PSYCHIATRY AND NEUROLOGY

616.8 US ISSN 0161-6412
RC321 CODEN: NRESDZ
NEUROLOGICAL RESEARCH; a journal of progress in neurosurgery, neurology and neurosciences. 1979. q. $60 to individuals; institutions $310 (effective 1992). Forefront Publishing Group, c/o Dr. G. Austin, 2320 Bath St., Ste. 301, Santa Barbara, CA 93105. FAX 508-443-0221. Ed.Bd. adv.; bk.rev.; abstr.; illus.; index. (also avail. in microfilm from UMI; back issues avail.) **Indexed:** Chem.Abstr., Curr.Adv.Ecol.Sci., Excerp.Med., Ind.Med., Ref.Zh., Telegen.
—BLDSC shelfmark: 6081.442000.
Description: Covers clinical neurosurgery, neuroanatomy, neuroradiology and other aspects of neurological research.
Refereed Serial

618 617 JA ISSN 0301-2603
CODEN: NOKGB6
NEUROLOGICAL SURGERY/SHINKEI GEKA. (Text in Japanese; summaries in English) 1973. m. 23520 Yen($181) Igaku-Shoin Ltd., 5-24-3 Hongo, Bunkyo-ku, Tokyo 113-91, Japan. TEL 03-817-5702. adv.; bk.rev.; circ. 6,000. **Indexed:** Biol.Abstr., Chem.Abstr., Dent.Ind., Excerp.Med., Ind.Med.
●Also available online. Vendor(s): JICST.
—BLDSC shelfmark: 6081.445000.

616.8 US ISSN 0028-3878
RC321 CODEN: NEURAI
NEUROLOGY. 1977. m. $170 (foreign $195). Avanstar Communications, Inc., 7500 Old Oak Blvd., Cleveland, OH 44130. TEL 216-826-2839. FAX 216-891-2726. (Subscr. to: 1 E. First St., Duluth, MN 55802) Ed. Peter G. Studer. adv.; bk.rev.; bibl.; charts; illus.; index; circ. 14,496. (also avail. in microform) **Indexed:** Bibl.Dev.Med.& Child Neur., Biol.Abstr., Chem.Abstr., Curr.Adv.Cancer Res., Curr.Adv.Ecol.Sci., Curr.Cont., Dent.Ind., Excerp.Med., Helminthol.Abstr., Ind.Med., Ind.Sci.Rev., Lang.& Lang.Behav.Abstr., Nutr.Abstr., Psychol.Abstr., Yrbk.Assoc.Educ.& Rehab.Blind.
●Also available online. Vendor(s): BRS.
—BLDSC shelfmark: 6081.500000.
Description: Reports, discussions, case findings and clinical findings on current research and developments in neurology. Covers neurological symptoms of diseases, diagnostic methods and treatments.
Refereed Serial

616.8 US ISSN 0741-4234
NEUROLOGY ALERT. 1982. m. $108. American Health Consultants, Inc., Six Piedmont Center, Ste. 400, 3525 Piedmont Rd., N.E., Atlanta, GA 30305. TEL 404-262-7436. FAX 800-284-3291. (Subscr. to: Box 740056, Atlanta, GA 30374-9822. TEL 800-688-2421) Ed. Dr. Fred Plum. index; circ. 2,300. (also avail. in audio cassette; reprint service avail.)

616.8 US
NEUROLOGY AND NEUROBIOLOGY. 1982. irreg., vol.37, 1990. price varies. Wiley-Liss, Inc., 41 E. 11th St., New York, NY 10003. TEL 212-475-7700. **Indexed:** Biol.Abstr., Chem.Abstr.

616.8 II ISSN 0028-3886
NEUROLOGY INDIA. (Text in English) 1952. q. Rs.550($110) Neurological Society of India, Dept. of Neurology, Post-graduate Institute of Medical Education & Research, Chandigarh 160 012, India. TEL 0172-541004. Ed. J.S. Chopra. adv.; bk.rev.; cum.index; circ. 1,200. **Indexed:** Biol.Abstr., Chem.Abstr., Curr.Cont., Excerp.Med., Ind.Med.

616.8 UK
NEUROMUSCULAR DISEASES. m. £70. Sheffield University Biomedical Information Service (SUBIS), The University, Sheffield S10 2TN, England. TEL 0742-768555. FAX 0742-739826. TELEX 547216-UGSHEF-G.
Description: Current awareness service for researchers in clinical and life sciences.

616.8 UK ISSN 0960-8966
CODEN: NEDIEC
▼**NEUROMUSCULAR DISORDERS.** 1991. 6/yr. £170 (effective 1992). Pergamon Press plc, Headington Hill Hall, Oxford OX3 0BW, England. TEL 0865-794141. FAX 0865-60285. (And: 660 White Plains Rd., Tarrytown, NY 10591-5153. TEL 914-524-9200) Ed. Victor Dubowitz. index. (also avail. in microform; back issues avail.) **Indexed:** Excerp.Med. (1992-).
—BLDSC shelfmark: 6081.504850.
Description: Covers all aspects of neuromuscular disorders in childhood and adult life.
Refereed Serial

616.8 US ISSN 0896-6273
QP356.2 CODEN: NERNET
NEURON. 1988. m. $99 to individuals (foreign $160); institutions $275 (foreign $335). Cell Press, 50 Church St., Cambridge, MA 02138. TEL 617-661-7060. FAX 617-661-7061. adv.; bk.rev.
—BLDSC shelfmark: 6081.504900.

NEUROORTHOPAEDIE. see *MEDICAL SCIENCES — Orthopedics And Traumatology*

616.8 UK ISSN 0305-1846
CODEN: NANEDL
NEUROPATHOLOGY AND APPLIED NEUROBIOLOGY. 1975. bi-m. £230 (foreign £260). (British Neuropathological Society) Blackwell Scientific Publications Ltd., Osney Mead, Oxford OX2 0EL, England. TEL 0865-240201. FAX 0865-721205. TELEX 83355-MEDBOK-G. Ed. J.B. Cavanagh. adv.; bk.rev.; bibl.; charts; illus.; index; circ. 480. (back issues avail.; reprint service avail. from ISI) **Indexed:** ASCA, Biol.Abstr., Chem.Abstr., Curr.Adv.Cell & Devel.Biol., Curr.Adv.Ecol.Sci., Curr.Cont., Excerp.Med., Ind.Med., Ind.Sci.Rev., Ind.Vet., Sci.Cit.Ind., Small Anim.Abstr., Vet.Bull.
—BLDSC shelfmark: 6081.514000.

616.8 PL ISSN 0028-3894
CODEN: NUPOBT
NEUROPATOLOGIA POLSKA. (Text and summaries in English, Polish and Russian) 1963. q. $40. Ossolineum, Publishing House of the Polish Academy of Sciences, Rynek 1-9, 106 Wroclaw, Poland. TELEX 0712771 OSS PL. (Dist. by: Ars Polona-Ruch, Krakowskie Przedmiescie 7, Warsaw, Poland) Ed. M.J. Mossakowski. bk.rev.; illus.; index, cum.index. **Indexed:** Biol.Abstr., Chem.Abstr., Excerp.Med., Ind.Med.
—BLDSC shelfmark: 6081.515000.
Description: Papers devoted to achievements in experimental and clinical neuropathology.

NEUROPEDIATRICS; journal of pediatric neurobiology, neurology and neurosurgery. see *MEDICAL SCIENCES — Pediatrics*

NEUROPHARMACOLOGY. see *PHARMACY AND PHARMACOLOGY*

616.8 FR ISSN 0987-7053
CODEN: NCLIE4
NEUROPHYSIOLOGIE CLINIQUE/CLINICAL NEUROPHYSIOLOGY; exploration fonctionnelle du systeme nerveux. (Text in French; summaries in English, French) 1970. 6/yr. 995 F.($201) (foreign 1150 F.)(effective 1992). (Societe d'E E G et de Neurophysiologie Clinique de Langue Francaise) Editions Scientifiques Elsevier, 29, rue Buffon, 75005 Paris, France. TEL 47-07-11-22. FAX 43-36-80-93. TELEX 202 400 F. (Subscr. in U.S. and Canada to: Elsevier Science Publishing Co., Inc., Box 882, Madison Sq. Sta., New York, NY 10159. TEL 212-989-5800) Ed. A. Autret. adv.; bk.rev.; illus.; index; circ. 3,000. (also avail. in microform from RPI; reprint service avail. from ISI) **Indexed:** Bibl.Dev.Med.& Child Neur., Biol.Abstr., Bull.Signal., Curr.Cont., Excerp.Med., Ind.Med.
—BLDSC shelfmark: 6081.517800.
Formerly: Revue d'Electroencephalographie et de Neurophysiologie Clinique (ISSN 0370-4475)
Description: Covers the field of neurophysiology, electroencephalography, electromyography, evoked potentials and other investigative approaches in neurology and psychiatry.
Refereed Serial

NEUROPHYSIOLOGY. see *BIOLOGY — Physiology*

616.8 US ISSN 0090-2977
CODEN: NPHYBI
NEUROPHYSIOLOGY. English translation of: Neirofiziologiya. 1969. bi-m. $955 (foreign $1115)(effective 1992). Plenum Publishing Corp., Consultants Bureau, 233 Spring St., New York, NY 10013-1578. TEL 212-620-8468. FAX 212-463-0742. TELEX 23-421139. Ed. V.I. Skok. (back issues avail.) **Indexed:** Biol.Abstr., Excerp.Med., Ind.Med., Int.Abstr.Biol.Sci., Psychol.Abstr.
—BLDSC shelfmark: 0416.260000.
Refereed Serial

616.8 US ISSN 1058-6741
▼**NEUROPROTOCOLS.** 1992. 3/yr. $66 (foreign $85). Academic Press, Inc., Journal Division, 1250 Sixth Ave., San Diego, CA 92101. TEL 619-230-1840. FAX 619-699-6800. TELEX 181726. Ed. P. Michael Conn.
Refereed Serial

616.8 615 IT ISSN 0394-9540
NEUROPSICOFARMACOLOGIA DEL COMPORTAMENTO. (Text in Italian; summaries in English) 1988. q. L.30000($30) (Club Internazionale di Neuropsicofarmacologia del Comportamento) C I C Edizioni Internazionali s.r.l., Via L. Spallanzani, 11, 00161 Rome, Italy. TEL 06-8412673. FAX 06-8443365. TELEX 622099 CIC I. Dir. P. Pancheri.

616.8 GW
NEUROPSYCHIATRIE. 1985. irreg. DM.125($69.50) per vol. Dustri-Verlag Dr. Karl Feistle, Bahnhofstr. 9, 8024 Deisenhofen, Germany. TEL 089-613861-0. FAX 089-6135412. Ed. Dr. F. Gerstenbrand.

NEUROPSYCHIATRIE DE L'ENFANCE ET DE L'ADOLESCENCE. see *MEDICAL SCIENCES — Pediatrics*

616.8 US ISSN 0894-878X
CODEN: NNNEEB
NEUROPSYCHIATRY, NEUROPSYCHOLOGY AND BEHAVIORAL NEUROLOGY. 1989. q. $89 to individuals; institutions $119. Raven Press, 1185 Ave. of the Americas, New York, NY 10036. TEL 212-930-9500. FAX 212-869-3495. TELEX 640073. Ed. Michael Alan Taylor. adv.; charts; illus.; circ. 1,000.
—BLDSC shelfmark: 6081.543000.
Description: Presents original research articles on basic brain processes; includes critical review articles, case reports, and brief reports on preliminary studies and pertinent clinical issues.
Refereed Serial

616.8 612 SZ ISSN 0302-282X
CODEN: NPBYAL
NEUROPSYCHOBIOLOGY; international journal of experimental and clinical research in biological psychiatry, pharmacopsychiatry, biological psychology, pharmacopsychology and pharmacoelectroencephalography. (Text in English) 8/yr. (in 2 vols.). 347 Fr.($232) per vol. (International Pharmaco-EEG Group) S. Karger AG, Allschwilerstr. 10, P.O. Box, CH-4009 Basel, Switzerland. TEL 061-3061111. FAX 061-3061234. TELEX CH 962652. Ed.Bd. bk.rev.; adv.; index; circ. 1,000. (also avail. in microform from RPI) **Indexed:** Biol.Abstr., Biotech.Abstr., Chem.Abstr., Curr.Adv.Ecol.Sci., Curr.Cont., Dent.Ind., Excerp.Med., Ind.Med., Ind.Sci.Rev., Nutr.Abstr., Psychol.Abstr.
—BLDSC shelfmark: 6081.545000.
Incorporates: International Pharmacopsychiatry (ISSN 0020-8272)

MEDICAL SCIENCES — PSYCHIATRY AND NEUROLOGY

616.8 US ISSN 0028-3932
RC321 CODEN: NUPSA6
NEUROPSYCHOLOGIA; an international journal in behavioural neuroscience. (Text in English, French or German; summaries in French, German) 1963. 12/yr. £500 (effective 1992). Pergamon Press, Inc., Journals Division, 660 White Plains Rd., Tarrytown, NY 10591-5153. TEL 914-524-9200. FAX 914-333-2444. (And: Headington Hill Hall, Oxford OX3 0BW, England. TEL 0865-794141) Ed. M. Jeeves. adv.; bk.rev.; charts; illus.; upd. 27 92127; circ. 1,950. (also avail. in microform from MIM,UMI; reprint service avail. from UMI) **Indexed:** Behav.Med.Abstr., Bibl.Dev.Med.& Child Neur., Biol.Abstr., Curr.Adv.Ecol.Sci., Curr.Cont., Dent.Ind., Excerp.Med., Ind.Med., Ind.Sci.Rev., Psychol.Abstr., Yrbk.Assoc.Educ.& Rehab.Blind.
—BLDSC shelfmark: 6081.550000.
Description: Promotes the study of human behavior from a neurological point of view, and integrates clinical, general, and experimental contributions to the field.
Refereed Serial

616.8 UK ISSN 0960-2011
CODEN: NREHE3
▼**NEUROPSYCHOLOGICAL REHABILITATION;** an international journal. 1991. q. £25($47.50) to individuals; institutions £50($95). Lawrence Erlbaum Associates Ltd., 27 Palmeira Mansions, Church Rd., Hove, E. Sussex, BN3 2FA, England. TEL 0273-207411. FAX 0273-205612. Ed. Barbara A. Wilson.
—BLDSC shelfmark: 6081.551000.
Description: Provides an international forum for the publication of well-designed and properly evaluated intervention strategies, surveys and observational procedures which are clinically relevent and may also back up theoretical arguments or models.

616.8 150 US ISSN 0894-4105
CODEN: NEUPEG
NEUROPSYCHOLOGY. 1987. q. $88. Taylor & Francis, 1900 Frost Rd., Ste. 101, Bristol, PA 19007-1598. TEL 215-785-5800. FAX 215-785-5515. Ed. B.P. Uzzell.
—BLDSC shelfmark: 6081.553000.
Description: Features interdisciplinary contributions on assessment, treatment, and rehabilitation in clinical neuropsychology, focusing on neuropsychological measurement techniques and psychosocial adjustment of the impaired patient.
Refereed Serial

616.8 US ISSN 1040-7308
QP360 CODEN: NERVEJ
NEUROPSYCHOLOGY REVIEW. 1989. 4/yr. $95 (foreign $110)(effective 1992). Plenum Publishing Corp., 233 Spring St., New York, NY 10013-1578. TEL 212-620-8000. FAX 212-463-0742. TELEX 23-421139. Ed. Gerald Goldstein. adv. (also avail. in microfilm from JSC; back issues avail.) **Indexed:** Soc.Work Res.& Abstr.
—BLDSC shelfmark: 6081.553600.
Description: Integrates and interprets topics of interest to clinical or research neuropsychologists and behavioral neurologists.
Refereed Serial

616.8 US ISSN 0893-133X
CODEN: NEROEW
NEUROPSYCHOPHARMACOLOGY. 1987. 8/yr.(in 2 vols.; 4 nos./vol.). $286 to institutions (foreign $320)(effective 1992). (American College of Neuropsychopharmacology) Elsevier Science Publishing Co., Inc. (New York), 655 Ave. of the Americas, New York, NY 10010. TEL 212-989-5800. FAX 212-633-3965. TELEX 420643 AEP UI. Ed. Dr. J. Christian Gillin. **Indexed:** Chem.Abstr., Curr.Cont., Excerp.Med., Psychol.Abstr., Sci.Cit.Ind.
—BLDSC shelfmark: 6081.554000.
Description: Focuses on clinical and basic science contributions to the field of neuropsychopharmacology.
Refereed Serial

616.8 US ISSN 1053-8135
▼**NEUROREHABILITATION;** an interdisciplinary journal. 1991. q. $55 to individuals (foreign $72); institutions $75 (foreign $92). Andover Medical Publishers Inc., 125 Main St., Reading, MA 01867. TEL 617-438-8464. FAX 617-438-1479. TELEX 880052. (Dist. by: Butterworth - Heinemann Ltd., 80 Montvale Ave., Stoneham, MA 02180. TEL 800-366-2665) Eds. Jeffrey Kreutzer, Nathan Zasler. bk.rev. (back issues avail.)
—BLDSC shelfmark: 6081.558400.
Description: Provides multidisciplinary rehabilitation teams with current clinical information for treating patients who are cognitively or physically challenged due to acquired or congenital neurologic disability.

616.8 UK ISSN 0959-4965
CODEN: NERPE
▼**NEUROREPORT.** 1990. m. £380. Rapid Communications of Oxford Ltd., The Old Malthouse, Paradise St., Oxford OX1 1LD, England. TEL 0865-790447. FAX 0865-244012. Ed. David Ottoson. **Indexed:** Curr.Cont., Excerp.Med. (1992-), Ind.Med., Sci.Cit.Ind.
—BLDSC shelfmark: 6081.558500.

616.8 US ISSN 0306-4522
QP351 CODEN: NRSCDN
NEUROSCIENCE; an international journal. 1976. 24/yr. £1595 (effective 1992). (International Brain Research Organization) Pergamon Press, Inc., Journals Division, 660 White Plains Rd., Tarrytown, NY 10591-5153. TEL 914-524-9200. FAX 914-333-2444. (And: Headington Hill Hall, Oxford OX3 0BW, England. TEL 0865-794141) Ed.Bd. adv.; bk.rev.; illus.; stat.; index; circ. 1,500. (also avail. in microform from MIM,UMI) **Indexed:** Biol.Abstr., Curr.Adv.Ecol.Sci., Curr.Cont., Dairy Sci.Abstr., Dent.Ind., Excerp.Med., Ind.Med., Ind.Sci.Rev., Telegen.
—BLDSC shelfmark: 6081.559000.
Description: Original research on any aspect of the scientific study of the nervous system.
Refereed Serial

616.8 US ISSN 0097-0549
RC331 CODEN: NBHPBT
NEUROSCIENCE AND BEHAVIORAL PHYSIOLOGY. 1967. bi-m. $495 (foreign $580)(effective 1992). (Federation of American Societies for Experimental Biology) Plenum Publishing Corp., Consultants Bureau, 233 Spring St., New York, NY 10013-1578. TEL 212-620-8468. FAX 212-463-0742. TELEX 23-421139. Ed. Charles D. Woody. (also avail. in microform from UMI; microfilm from JSC; reprint service avail. from UMI) **Indexed:** Biol.Abstr., Chem.Abstr., Curr.Cont., Excerp.Med., Psychol.Abstr.
—BLDSC shelfmark: 6081.560000.
Formerly (until 1972, vol.5): Neuroscience Translations (ISSN 0028-3959)
Description: Translation of selected articles from Soviet neurology journals.
Refereed Serial

616.8 US ISSN 0149-7634
QP360 CODEN: NBREDE
NEUROSCIENCE AND BIOBEHAVIORAL REVIEWS. 1977. 4/yr. £255 (effective 1992). Pergamon Press, Inc., Journals Division, 660 White Plains Rd., Tarrytown, NY 10591-5153. TEL 914-524-9200. FAX 914-333-2444. (And: Headington Hill Hall, Oxford OX3 0BW, England. TEL 0865-794141) Ed. Matthew J. Wayner. bk.rev.; index. (also avail. in microform from UMI; reprint service avail. from UMI,ISI) **Indexed:** Biol.Abstr., Chem.Abstr., Curr.Adv.Ecol.Sci., Curr.Cont., Dent.Ind., Excerp.Med., Ind.Med., Ind.Sci.Rev., Psychol.Abstr., Sci.Cit.Ind.
—BLDSC shelfmark: 6081.561000.
Formerly: Biobehavioral Reviews.
Description: Articles on anatomy, biochemistry, embryology, endocrinology, genetics, pharmacology, physiology and all aspects of biological sciences related to the problems of the nervous system.
Refereed Serial

616.8 IE ISSN 0304-3940
QP351 CODEN: NELED5
NEUROSCIENCE LETTERS; international multidisciplinary journal devoted to the rapid publication of basic research in neurosciences. 1975. 32/yr.(in 16 vols.; 2 nos./vol.). $2448 (effective 1992). Elsevier Scientific Publishers Ireland Ltd., P.O. Box 85, Limerick, Ireland. TEL 061-69144. FAX 061-62144. TELEX 72191 ENH El. (Subscr. in U.S. and Canada to: Elsevier Science Publishing Co., Inc., Box 882, Madison Sq. Sta., New York, NY 10159. TEL 212-989-5800) Ed. M. Zimmermann. bibl.; charts; illus. (also avail. in microform from RPI; reprint service avail. from SWZ) **Indexed:** Biol.Abstr., Chem.Abstr., Curr.Adv.Biochem., Curr.Adv.Cell & Devel.Biol., Curr.Adv.Ecol.Sci., Curr.Cont., Dairy Sci.Abstr., Dent.Ind., Excerp.Med., Ind.Med., Ind.Sci.Rev., Ind.Vet., Sci.Cit.Ind., Vet.Bull.
—BLDSC shelfmark: 6081.562000.
Refereed Serial

616.8 US ISSN 0278-3738
NEUROSCIENCE NEWSLETTER. 1970. bi-m. $50. Society for Neuroscience, 11 Dupont Circle, N.W., Ste. 500, Washington, DC 20036. TEL 202-462-6688. Ed. Susan Frensili. adv.; circ. 18,500. (back issues avail.)

616.8 IE ISSN 0168-0102
RC337 CODEN: NERADN
NEUROSCIENCE RESEARCH. (Text and summaries in English) 1984. 12/yr.(in 3 vols.; 4 nos./vol.). $555 (effective 1992). (Japan Neuroscience Society, JA) Elsevier Scientific Publishers Ireland Ltd., P.O. Box 85, Limerick, Ireland. TEL 061-61944. FAX 016-62144. TELEX 72191 ENH El. (Subscr. in U.S. and Canada to: Elsevier Science Publishing Co., Inc., Box 882, Madison Sq. Sta., New York, NY 10159. TEL 212-989-5800) Ed. Masao Ito. index. (back issues avail.; reprint service avail. from SWZ) **Indexed:** Biol.Abstr., Chem.Abstr., Curr.Cont., Excerp.Med., Psychol.Abstr.
—BLDSC shelfmark: 6081.563600.
Description: Covers all fields of neuroscience, from the molecular to behavioral levels.
Refereed Serial

616.8 UK ISSN 0893-6609
RC346 CODEN: NRCOEE
NEUROSCIENCE RESEARCH COMMUNICATONS. vol.10-11, 1992. bi-m. $295 (effective 1992). John Wiley & Sons Ltd., Journals, Baffins Lane, Chichester, Sussex PO19 1UD, England. TEL 0243-779777. FAX 0243-775878. TELEX 86290 WIBOOK G. Ed. W.H. Gispen. (reprint service avail. from SWZ) **Indexed:** A.I.Abstr., Chem.Abstr., Curr.Cont., Excerp.Med., Telegen.
—BLDSC shelfmark: 6081.563800.
Description: Contains international and multidisciplinary original contributions to the neurosciences.

616.8 JA ISSN 0388-7448
CODEN: NUOCDO
NEUROSCIENCES. Variant title: No Kenkyukai Kaishi. (Text in English and Japanese) 1975. q. 10000 Yen. (Japan Neurosciences Research Association - No Kenkyukai) Kinokuniya Shoten - Kinokuniya Co., Ltd., Yokohama Office, Ryoko Shin-Takashimadai Bldg., 7th Fl., 102 Sawatari, Kanagawa-ku, Yokohama-shi 221, Japan. FAX 0862-23-3569. (Editorial and subscr. addr.: Dept. of Neurochemistry, Institute for Neurobiology, Okayama University Medical School, 5-1, Shikata-cho 2-chome, Okayama 700, Japan) Ed. Akitane Mori. adv.; circ. 800. (back issues avail.) **Indexed:** Biol.Abstr.
Formerly: Joken Hansha (ISSN 0368-2803)
Description: Promotes integrated, interdisciplinary studies of the interaction between the neural system and the behavior and homeostasis of the living body, as well as the mental activity of the human being.

MEDICAL SCIENCES — PSYCHIATRY AND NEUROLOGY

616.8 US ISSN 0148-396X
RD593
NEUROSURGERY (BALTIMORE). 1977. m. $100 to individuals; institutions $145. (Congress of Neurological Surgeons) Williams & Wilkins, 428 E. Preston St., Baltimore, MD 21202. TEL 301-528-4000. FAX 301-528-4312. Ed. Edward R. Laws, Jr., M.D. adv.; bk.rev.; abstr.; bibl.; charts; illus.; index; circ. 7,600. (also avail. in microform; back issues avail.) **Indexed:** Bibl.Dev.Med.& Child Neur., Curr.Adv.Cancer Res., Curr.Cont., Dent.Ind., Excerp.Med., Ind.Med., Ind.Sci.Rev.
—BLDSC shelfmark: 6081.582000.
Description: Explains techniques and devices, plus pertinent research in neuroscience.
Refereed Serial

NEUROSURGERY CLINICS. see *MEDICAL SCIENCES — Surgery*

NEUROSURGICAL REVIEW. see *MEDICAL SCIENCES — Surgery*

616.8 US ISSN 0892-0362
CODEN: NETEEC
NEUROTOXICOLOGY AND TERATOLOGY. 1979. 6/yr. £295 (effective 1992). (Behavioral Toxicology Society) Pergamon Press, Inc., Journals Division, 660 White Plains Rd., Tarrytown, NY 10591-5153. TEL 914-524-9200. FAX 914-333-2444. (And: Headington Hill Hall, Oxford OX3 0BW, England. TEL 0865-794141) (Co-sponsor: Neurobehavioral Teratology Society) Ed. Donald E. Hutchings. adv.; illus.; index. (also avail. in microform from UMI; reprint service avail. from ISI,UMI) **Indexed:** Biol.Abstr., Chem.Abstr., Curr.Adv.Ecol.Sci., Curr.Cont., Dairy Sci.Abstr., Dent.Ind., Excerp.Med., Ind.Med., Ind.Sci.Rev., Psychol.Abstr., Sci.Cit.Ind.
—BLDSC shelfmark: 6081.586500.
Former titles: Neurobehavioral Toxicology and Teratology (ISSN 0275-1380); Neurobehavioral Toxicology (ISSN 0191-3581)
Refereed Serial

616.8 BU ISSN 0548-3794
CODEN: NPNMAB
NEVROLOGIA, PSIHIATRIJA I NEVROHIRURGIJA. (Text in Bulgarian; summaries in Russian and English) 1962. bi-m. 16 lv.($7) (Ministerstvo na Narodnoto Zdrave) Izdatelstvo Meditsina i Fizkultura, 11, Pl. Slaveikov, Sofia, Bulgaria. (Dist. by: Hemus, 6, Rouski Blvd., 1000 Sofia, Bulgaria) (Co-sponsor: Nauchno Druzhestvo po Nevrologija, Psihiatrija i Nevrohirurgija) Ed. V. Ivanov. circ. 1,360. **Indexed:** Abstr.Bulg.Sci.Med.Lit., Chem.Abstr., Excerp.Med.

188 US ISSN 0193-9416
RA790.A1
NEW DIRECTIONS FOR MENTAL HEALTH SERVICES. 1979. q. $52 to individuals; institutions $70. Jossey-Bass Inc., Publishers, 350 Sansome St., 5th Fl., San Francisco, CA 94104. TEL 415-433-1767. FAX 415-433-0499. Ed. H. Richard Lamb. circ. 1,350. (back issues avail.) **Indexed:** Educ.Ind., Ind.Med., PSI, Psychol.Abstr.
—BLDSC shelfmark: 6083.396000.
Description: Gives practical descriptions of new treatment techniques, models and approaches. Also presents guidelines for planning and implementing effective services.

616.8 GW ISSN 1012-9871
NEW ISSUES IN NEUROSCIENCES. 1988. 3/yr. DM.175. Georg Thieme Verlag, Ruedigerstr. 14, Postfach 104853, 7000 Stuttgart 10, Germany. TEL 0711-89310. FAX 0711-8931298. TELEX 07252275-GTV-D. Ed.Bd.
—BLDSC shelfmark: 6113.235560.
Description: Provides new perspectives on particular neurological diseases and related topics.

616.8 US
NEW SENSE BULLETIN; news from the leading edge. 1976. m. $45 (foreign $55). Interface Press, 4717 N. Figueroa St., Box 42211, Los Angeles, CA 90042. TEL 800-553-6463. FAX 213-223-2519. Ed. Marilyn Ferguson. bk.rev.; illus.; circ. 8,000. (also avail. in microform from UMI; back issues avail.) **Indexed:** New.Per.Ind.
Incorporates: Brain - Mind Bulletin (ISSN 0273-8546)
Description: Ground-breaking news from the clinical, social, educational, creative and spiritual sciences.

NEW YORK (STATE). COMMISSION ON QUALITY OF CARE FOR THE MENTALLY DISABLED. ANNUAL REPORT. see *HOSPITALS*

NEWSLINK (DENVER). see *PSYCHOLOGY*

616.8 JA
NO TO HATTATSU. English edition: Brain and Development (ISSN 0387-7604) (Text in Japanese; summaries in English) 1969. bi-m. 8000 Yen($60) Japanese Society of Child Neurology - Nihon Shoni Shinkei Gakkai, Kobayashi Bldg. 2F, 10-1 Wakamatsu-cho, Shinjuku-ku, Tokyo 162, Japan. Ed. Dr. Masataka Arima. adv.; bk.rev.; abstr.; index; circ. 3,000. **Indexed:** Adol.Ment.Hlth.Abstr., Bibl.Dev.Med.& Child Neur., Biol.Abstr., Chem.Abstr., Curr.Adv.Ecol.Sci., Dent.Ind., Excerp.Med., Ind.Med., Ind.Sci.Rev., Nutr.Abstr., Risk Abstr., Sci.Cit.Ind.
Supersedes in part (in 1979): Brain and Development - No to Hattatsu (ISSN 0029-0831)

616.89 NO ISSN 0029-1455
NORDISK PSYKIATRISK TIDSSKRIFT/NORDIC JOURNAL OF PSYCHIATRY. (Text in English and Scandinavian languages; summaries in English) 1946. bi-m. $63 to individuals; institutions $103. Universitetsforlaget, P.O. Box 2959-Toeyen, N-0608 Oslo 1, Norway. (U.S. addr.: Publications Expediting Inc., 200 Meacham Ave., Elmont, NY 11003) Ed. Truls-Eirik Mogstad. adv.; bk.rev.; index; circ. 4,000. **Indexed:** Biol.Abstr., Curr.Adv.Ecol.Sci., Psychol.Abstr.
—BLDSC shelfmark: 6122.730000.

616.8 301.15 FR ISSN 0762-6819
NOUVELLE REVUE D'ETHNOPSYCHIATRIE. (Text in French; summaries in English) 1978. 2/yr. 260 F. to individuals; institutions 380 F. Pensee Sauvage Editions, B.P. 141, 38002 Grenoble, France. TEL 76-87-13-03. Ed. Marie Rose Noro.
Formerly: Ethnopsychiatrica (ISSN 0151-9808)

616.8 IT
NUOVA RIVISTA DI NEUROLOGIA. (Text in English and Italian) 1931. bi-m. L.70000($130) to individuals; institutions L.100000. Pensiero Scientifico Editore s.r.l., Via Panama 48, Rome, Italy. TEL 06 855-36-33. Ed. Vincenzo Floris. adv.; bk.rev.; bibl.; charts; illus.; circ. 900. **Indexed:** Biol.Abstr., Chem.Abstr., Dent.Ind., Excerp.Med., Ind.Med.
Formerly: Rivista di Neurologia (ISSN 0035-6344)

616.858 AT
▼**O C D - THE HIDDEN DISORDER.** 1992. q. Obsessive Compulsive Disorder Support Groups of New South Wales, 60 Victoria Rd., Gladesville, N.S.W. 2111, Australia. TEL 02-816-5688. (Co-sponsor: New South Wales Association for Mental Health) circ. 500.

150 361.3 610 US ISSN 0164-212X
RC487 CODEN: OTMHDX
OCCUPATIONAL THERAPY IN MENTAL HEALTH; a journal of psychosocial practice and research. 1980. q. $36 to individuals; institutions $90; libraries $165. Haworth Press, Inc., 10 Alice St., Binghamton, NY 13904. TEL 800-342-9678. FAX 607-722-1424. TELEX 4932599. Ed. Diane Gibson. adv.; bk.rev.; bibl.; circ. 760. (also avail. in microfiche from HAW; back issues avail.; reprint service avail. from HAW) **Indexed:** Abstr.Health Care Manage.Stud., Adol.Ment.Hlth.Abstr., Behav.Abstr, Biol.Abstr., Bull.Signal., Chicago Psychoanal.Lit.Ind., Child Devel.Abstr., CINAHL, Excerp.Med., Past.Care & Couns.Abstr., Psychol.Abstr., Rehabil.Lit., Soc.Work Res.& Abstr.
—BLDSC shelfmark: 6231.260000.
Description: Provides current material specifically for occupational therapists in mental health clinics, psychiatric hospitals, mental health programs, hospitals, and other settings.
Refereed Serial

616.89 150 DK ISSN 0105-0621
ODENSE UNIVERSITY STUDIES IN PSYCHIATRY AND MEDICAL PSYCHOLOGY. (Text in Danish and English) 1973. irreg. price varies. Odense University Press, Campusvej 55, DK-5230 Odense M, Denmark. TEL 66-157999. (back issues avail.) **Indexed:** Excerp.Med.
Description: Biographies of important historical figures and how they influenced psychiatric medical history.

OPEN MIND; the mental health magazine. see *MEDICAL SCIENCES — Nurses And Nursing*

150.198 615.856 US
▼**ORGONOMIC FUNCTIONALISM.** 1990. s-a. Wilhelm Reich Infant Trust Fund, Orgonon, Box 687, Rangley, ME 04970.
Description: Covers the work of Wilhelm Reich.

616.835 IT ISSN 0030-5618
ORIZZONTI APERTI; la voce dei poliomielitici. vol.4, 1970. irreg. (3-5/yr.) free. Associazione Nazionale Invalidi Esiti Poliomielite, Via Coltelli 7-D, 40124 Bologna, Italy. Ed. Gianni Selleri. circ. 16,000.
Description: Concerns poliomyelitis.

ORTHOMOLEKULAR; Fachzeitschrift fuer Ernaehrung, Gesundheit und Umwelt. see *NUTRITION AND DIETETICS*

616.8 US
OXFORD NEUROLOGICAL MONOGRAPHS. irreg. price varies. Oxford University Press, 200 Madison Ave., New York, NY 10016. TEL 212-679-7300. Ed. W. Ritchie Russell.
Refereed Serial

616.8 US
P.M. NEWS. 1972. bi-m. $12. White Plains Hospital Center, Phobia Clinic, Davis Ave. at Post Rd., White Plains, NY 10601. TEL 914-681-1038. Ed. Judy Chessa. circ. 1,000.

616.835 DK
P T U NYT; tidsskrift for polioforeningen. 1985. q. DKK 50. Polioforeningen, Arresoevej 11, DK-8240 Risskov, Denmark. TEL 8617-7122. FAX 4586-176043. Ed. Hanne Birgitte Pedersen. adv.; circ. 10,500.
Formerly: Polio-Nyt (ISSN 0900-5587)

616.8 NE ISSN 0304-3959
RB127 CODEN: PAINDB
PAIN. 1975. 12/yr.(in 4 vols; 3 nos./vol.) fl.1172 (effective 1992). (International Association for the Study of Pain) Elsevier Science Publishers B.V., P.O. Box 211, 1000 AE Amsterdam, Netherlands. TEL 020-5803911. FAX 020-5803598. TELEX 18582 ESPA NL. (Subscr. in U.S. and Canada to: Elsevier Science Publishing Co., Inc., Box 882, Madison Sq. Sta., New York, NY 10159. TEL 212-989-5800) Eds. P.D. Wall, R. Dubner. adv.; bk.rev.; abstr.; circ. 5,000. (also avail. in microform from RPI; reprint service avail. from ISI,SWZ) **Indexed:** Behav.Med.Abstr., Biol.Abstr., Biotech.Abstr., Chem.Abstr., CINAHL, Curr.Adv.Cancer Res., Curr.Adv.Ecol.Sci., Curr.Cont., Dent.Ind., Excerp.Med., Ind.Med., Psychol.Abstr.
—BLDSC shelfmark: 6333.795000.
Description: Provides a forum for information about the nature, mechanism and treatment of pain.
Refereed Serial

616.8 SZ ISSN 0255-3910
PAIN AND HEADACHE. (Text in English) 1967. irreg. price varies. S. Karger AG, Allschwilerstr. 10, P.O. Box, CH-4009 Basel, Switzerland. TEL 061-3061111. FAX 061-3061234. TELEX CH 962652. Ed. P.L. Gildenberg. (reprint service avail. from ISI) **Indexed:** Biol.Abstr., Chem.Abstr., Curr.Cont., Ind.Med.
—BLDSC shelfmark: 6333.798500.
Formerly: Research and Clinical Studies in Headache (ISSN 0080-1453)

THE PAIN CLINIC. see *MEDICAL SCIENCES — Anaesthesiology*

PARAGRAPHIC. see *EDUCATION — Special Education And Rehabilitation*

PARAPLEGIA NEWS. see *EDUCATION — Special Education And Rehabilitation*

616.8 US
PARKINSON REPORT. 1957. q. membership. National Parkinson Foundation, Inc., 1501 N.W. 9th Ave. - Bob Hope Rd., Miami, FL 33136-9990. TEL 305-547-6666. FAX 305-548-4403. Ed. Lazarus M. Orkin, M.D. charts; illus. (tabloid format)
Formerly: National Parkinson Foundation. Newsletter.
Description: Written for people affected by Parkinson's disease and explores various areas of the research.

MEDICAL SCIENCES — PSYCHIATRY AND NEUROLOGY

616.8   IT
PEDAGOGIA MEDICA. 1987. q. L.36500($54) (effective 1992). (Societa Italiana di Pedagogia Medica) Masson Italia Periodici, Via Statuto 2-4, 20212 Milan, Italy. TEL 02-6367-1. FAX 02-6367211. Ed. Ottavio Albano. circ. 3,300.

616.8   SZ   ISSN 1016-2291
CODEN: PDNEEV
PEDIATRIC NEUROSURGERY. (Text in English) 6/yr. 213 SFr.($142) to individuals; institutions 426 SFr.($284). (International Society for Paediatric Neurosurgery) S. Karger AG, Allschwilerstr. 10, P.O. Box, CH-4009 Basel, Switzerland. TEL 061-3061111. FAX 061-3061234. Ed. F. Epstein. Indexed: Excerp.Med.
—BLDSC shelfmark: 6417.604700.
Formerly (until 1991): Pediatric Neuroscience (ISSN 0255-7975); Which supersedes in part (in 1985): Child's Brain (ISSN 0302-2803)

PENNSYLVANIA MESSAGE. see EDUCATION — Special Education And Rehabilitation

616.8 410   US
PERSPECTIVES IN NEUROLINGUISTICS, NEUROPSYCHOLOGY, AND PSYCHOLINGUISTICS; a series of monographs and treatises. 1976. irreg. Academic Press, Inc., 1250 Sixth Ave., San Diego, CA 92101. TEL 619-231-6616. FAX 619-699-6715. Ed. Harry A. Whitaker.
Refereed Serial

PERSPECTIVES IN PSYCHIATRIC CARE. see MEDICAL SCIENCES — Nurses And Nursing

616.89   FR   ISSN 0031-6032
PERSPECTIVES PSYCHIATRIQUES. 1963. 5/yr. 315 F. to individuals (foreign 390 F.); students 245 F. (foreign 315 F.). (Groupe d'Etudes de Psychiatrie Psychologie et Sciences Sociales) Galliena Promotion, 58 A, Rue du Dessous des Berges, 75013 Paris, France. TEL 45-84-97-66. FAX 45-84-92-56. Ed. Dr. Bernard Gibello. adv.; bk.rev.; circ. 2,500. Indexed: Psychol.Abstr.
—BLDSC shelfmark: 6428.161000.

616.89   GW   ISSN 0176-3679
RM315   CODEN: PHRMEZ
PHARMACOPSYCHIATRY; clinical pharmacology, psychiatry, psychology, neurophysiology advances in theoretical and clinical research. (Text and summaries in English and German) 1968. bi-m. DM.228 (members of the Arbeitsgemeinschaft fuer Neuropsychopharmakologie DM.165). Georg Thieme Verlag, Rudeigerstr. 14, Postfach 104853, 7000 Stuttgart 10, Germany. TEL 0711-8931-0. FAX 0711-8931298. Ed. B. Muller-Oerlinghausen. adv.; bibl.; charts; illus.; stat.; index; circ. 1,000. (also avail. in microfilm from UMI; microfiche; reprint service avail. from UMI) Indexed: Biol.Abstr., Biotech.Abstr., Chem.Abstr., Curr.Adv.Ecol.Sci., Curr.Cont., Dent.Ind., Excerp.Med., Ger.J.Psych., Ind.Med., Sci.Cit.Ind.
—BLDSC shelfmark: 6447.087950.
Former titles: Pharmacopsychiatria (ISSN 0720-4280); (until 1980): Pharmakopsychiatrie - Neuro-Psychopharmakologie (ISSN 0031-7098)

616.8 248.86   US
PILGRIMAGE: THE JOURNAL OF PSYCHOTHERAPY AND PERSONAL EXPLORATION. 1972. 5/yr. $39. Pilgrimage Press, Inc., 427 Lakeshore Dr., Atlanta, GA 30307. Ed. David Barstow. bk.rev.; circ. 1,000. (also avail. in microform from UMI; back issues avail.)
Formerly: Pilgrimage: The Journal of Pastoral Psychotherapy (ISSN 0361-0802)

362.3   US   ISSN 0031-9856
PINE CONE. 1966. q. free. Pinecrest State School, Box 191, Pineville, LA 71360. TEL 318-640-0754. illus.; circ. 1,600. (processed)
Description: Articles related to mental retardation.

616.835   FR   ISSN 0032-2741
POLIO-FRANCE. 1952. bi-m. 1000 F. Association Nationale des Polios de France, 23 rue de la Cerisaie, 75004 Paris, France. Ed. Georges Creteur. adv.; bk.rev.; index; circ. 50,000.

616.89 150   GW   ISSN 0032-7034
CODEN: PKIKAZ
PRAXIS DER KINDERPSYCHOLOGIE UND KINDERPSYCHIATRIE. (Text in German; summaries in English and German) 1952. 10/yr. DM.78. Vandenhoeck und Ruprecht, Theaterstr. 13, Postfach 3753, 3400 Goettingen, Germany. TEL 0551-6959-22. FAX 0551-695917. Eds. Annemarie Duehrssen, Rudolf Adam. adv.; bk.rev.; abstr.; illus.; stat.; index; circ. 2,900. (reprint service avail. from SWZ) Indexed: Biol.Abstr., Curr.Cont., Excerp.Med., Ger.J.Psych., Ind.Med., Psychol.Abstr., SSCI.
—BLDSC shelfmark: 6603.171400.

PRAXIS DER KINDERPSYCHOLOGIE UND KINDERPSYCHIATRIE. BEIHEFTE. see PSYCHOLOGY

616.89   GW   ISSN 0171-791X
CODEN: PRPPDZ
PRAXIS DER PSYCHOTHERAPIE UND PSYCHOSOMATIK; Zeitschrift fuer Fort- und Weiterbildung. (Text in German) 1956. 6/yr. DM.134($72) (Deutsche Kollegiums fuer Psychosomatische Medizin) Springer-Verlag, Heidelberger Platz 3, D-1000 Berlin 33, Germany. TEL 030-8207-1. (Subscr. to: 44 Hartz Way, Secaucus, NJ 07094) (Co-sponsor: Deutsche Gesellschaft fuer psychosomatische Geburtshilfe und Gynaekologie) Ed. J. Bastiaans. adv.; bk.rev.; bibl.; charts; illus. (tabloid format; also avail. in microform from UMI; back issues avail.; reprint service avail. from ISI) Indexed: Biol.Abstr., Chem.Abstr., Curr.Cont., Excerp.Med., Psychol.Abstr., SSCI.
—BLDSC shelfmark: 6603.183000.
Formerly: Praxis der Psychotherapie (ISSN 0032-7077)

616.858   CI   ISSN 0032-7298
PREGLED PROBLEMA MENTALNO RETARDIRANIH OSOBA. (Text in Serbo-Croatian) 1965. bi-m. 100 din. Savjet Organizacija za Pomoc Mentalno Retardiranim Osobama u SFRJ, Prilaz JNA 43-III, Zagreb, Croatia. Ed. Sulejman Masovic. adv.; bk.rev. Indexed: Biol.Abstr.
Description: Concerns mental retardation.

PROBLEMS OF INDUSTRIAL PSYCHIATRIC MEDICINE SERIES. see PSYCHOLOGY

616.8 612.821   NE   ISSN 0079-6123
CODEN: PBRRA4
PROGRESS IN BRAIN RESEARCH. 1963. irreg., vol. 89, 1991. price varies. Elsevier Science Publishers B.V., Books Division, P.O. Box 211, 1000 AE Amsterdam, Netherlands. TEL 020-5803911. FAX 020-5803705. TELEX 18582 ESPA NL. (Subscr. in U.S. and Canada to: Elsevier Science Publishing Co., Inc., Box 882, Madison Sq. Sta., New York, NY 10159. TEL 212-989-5800) (back issues avail.) Indexed: Biol.Abstr., Chem.Abstr., Dent.Ind., Excerp.Med., Ind.Med., Ind.Sci.Rev.
Refereed Serial

PROGRESS IN NEURAL NETWORKS. see COMPUTERS — Artificial Intelligence

617.48   SZ   ISSN 0079-6492
PROGRESS IN NEUROLOGICAL SURGERY. (Text in English) 1966. irreg. (approx. a.). price varies. S. Karger AG, Allschwilerstr. 10, P.O. Box, CH-4009 Basel, Switzerland. TEL 061-3061111. FAX 061-3061234. TELEX CH 962652. Ed. A.M. Landolt. (reprint service avail. from ISI) Indexed: Biol.Abstr., Chem.Abstr., Curr.Cont., Ind.Med.
—BLDSC shelfmark: 6870.340000.

616.8   US
PROGRESS IN NEUROPATHOLOGY. 1971. irreg., latest vol.7. price varies. Raven Press, 1185 Ave. of the Americas, New York, NY 10036. TEL 212-930-9500. FAX 212-869-3495. TELEX 640073. Ed. H.M. Zimmerman, M.D. Indexed: Biol.Abstr.
Refereed Serial

616.8   IT
PROSPETTIVE PSICOANALITICHE NEL LAVORO ISTITUZIONALE. 1983. s-a. L.40000 to individuals; institutions L.70000($100). Pensiero Scientifico Editore s.r.l., Via Panama 48, 00198 Rome, Italy. TEL 06 855-36-33. Ed. Massimo Ammaniti. bibl.; index; circ. 1,000.

616.89   IT   ISSN 0393-361X
PSICHIATRIA DELL'INFANZIA E DELL'ADOLESCENZA. (Text in Italian; summaries in English) 1907. bi-m. $54 to individuals (foreign $100); institutions $70 (foreign $120). Universita di Roma, Istituto di Neuropsichiatria Infantile, Via dei Sabelli 108, 00185 Rome, Italy. TEL 4952233. Ed. Giovanni Bollea. adv.; bk.rev.; charts; illus.; stat.; tr.lit.; index, cum.index; circ. 3,000. Indexed: Biol.Abstr., Bull.Signal., Excerp.Med., Lang.& Lang.Behav.Abstr.
—BLDSC shelfmark: 6945.843000.
Former titles (until 1983): Neuropsichiatria Infantile (ISSN 0028-3924); (until 1969): Infanzia Anormale.
Description: Encompasses all branches of psychiatry, from neonatal age to late adolescence. Comprises original research, synthetic reviews, case histories, field research, magazine reviews and more.

616.8 150.19   IT   ISSN 0393-9774
PSICHIATRIA E PSICOTERAPIA ANALITICA/ANALYTIC PSYCHOTHERAPY AND PSYCHOPATHOLOGY. (Text in English, Italian) 1984. q. L.50000($70) to individuals; institutions L.60000(effective Jan. 1992). (Universita degli Studi di Roma II, Cattedra di Clinica Psychiatrica) Giovanni Fioriti, Via Trionfale 11224, 00135 Rome, Italy. TEL 06-3098097. Ed. Maria Ilena Marozza. adv.; bk.rev.; charts; illus.; stat.; circ. 6,000. Indexed: Excerp.Med., Psychol.Abstr., Ref.Zh.
—BLDSC shelfmark: 6945.841000.
Description: Features research papers by doctors worldwide in the field of analytical psychotherapy and psychopathology. Includes articles on mental health and psychopathology of infants, group psychotherapy and biological psychotherapy.

616.8   IT   ISSN 0555-5299
PSICHIATRIA GENERALE E DELL'ETA EVOLUTIVA. q. L.120000 includes supplement. Tipografia Editrice la Garangola, Via Montona, 4, 35137 Padua, Italy. FAX 049-8751743. Indexed: Psychol.Abstr.

616.8 150.5   AG   ISSN 0325-0695
PSICOLOGIA MEDICA; revista argentina de psicologia medica, psicoterapia y ciencias afines. 1973. s-a. (Fundacion Argentina para la Salud Mental (FASAM)) Carril Impresores, Avda. Salvado Maria del Caril 2639-41, Buenos Aires, Argentina. TEL 821-6887. Ed. Andres Magaz. Indexed: Psychol.Abstr.

616.891 001.3   IT
PSICOTERAPIA E SCIENZE UMANE. 1967. q. L.68000 (foreign L.85000)(effective 1992). Franco Angeli Editore, Viale Monza, 106, Casella Postale 17175, 20100 Milan, Italy. TEL 02-2895762. Ed.Bd.

131.3   YU   ISSN 0350-2538
CODEN: AZMZB7
PSIHIJATRIJA DANAS/PSYCHIATRY TODAY. (Text in Serbo-Croatian; summaries in English) 1969. q. 250 din.($50) to individuals; institutions 500 din.($100). Institut za Mentalno Zdravlje - Institute for Mental Health, Palmoticeva 37, 11000 Belgrade, Yugoslavia. FAX 331-333. Ed. Predrag Kalicanin. adv.; bk.rev.; circ. 700. Indexed: Excerp.Med., Psychol.Abstr., Yrbk.Assoc.Educ.& Rehab.Blind.
—BLDSC shelfmark: 6945.873000.
Formerly: Zavod za Mentalno Zdravlje. Anali (ISSN 0350-1442)

616.8 614.58   SP   ISSN 0210-8348
PSIQUIS; revista de psiquiatria, psicologia y psicosomatica. 1979. 10/yr. 7000 ptas. Alpe Editores, S.A., Pedro Rico, 27, 28029 Madrid, Spain. TEL 733 88 11. FAX 315-96-52. Dir. Dr. J.L. Gonzalez de Rivera. adv.; charts. Indexed: Curr.Cont., Excerp.Med., Ind.Med.Esp., Psychol.Abstr., SSCI.
—BLDSC shelfmark: 6945.935500.

616.8   GW   ISSN 0721-0949
PSYCHE UND SOMA. 1978. q. (Schuerholz Arzneimittel GmbH) P M I Verlag GmbH, August-Schanz-Str. 21, 6000 Frankfurt a.M. 50, Germany. TEL 069-5480000. FAX 069-548000-77. circ. 20,000. (tabloid format)

MEDICAL SCIENCES — PSYCHIATRY AND NEUROLOGY

616.8 JA ISSN 0033-2658
CODEN: SSHZAS
PSYCHIATRIA ET NEUROLOGIA JAPONICA (TOKYO, 1899)/SEISHIN SHINKEIGAKU ZASSHI.* (Text in Japanese; title, contents page and summaries in English) 1899. m. $96.75. Japan Publications Trading Co. Ltd., Box 5030, Tokyo International, Tokyo 100-31, Japan. Ed. Haruo Akimoto. adv.; bibl.; charts; illus.; index. **Indexed:** Biol.Abstr., Chem.Abstr., Ind.Med.
—BLDSC shelfmark: 6946.130000.

616.8 FI ISSN 0079-7227
RC321 CODEN: PSFNBI
PSYCHIATRIA FENNICA. (Text mainly in English) 1970. a. Fmk.165. (Foundation for Psychiatric Research in Finland) Psychiatrica Fennica, Arkadiankatu 35 B 37, 00100 Helsinki 10, Finland. FAX 358-0-409663. adv.; bk.rev.; circ. 2,000. **Indexed:** Biol.Abstr., CINAHL, Excerp.Med., Psychol.Abstr.
—BLDSC shelfmark: 6946.160000.

616.8 FI ISSN 0355-7707
CODEN: MPFEE8
PSYCHIATRIA FENNICA. MONOGRAFIASARJA/PSYCHIATRIA FENNICA. MONOGRAPHS. (Text in English and Finnish) 1970. irreg. price varies. Psychiatria Fennica, Arkadiankatu 35 B 37, 00100 Helsinki 10, Finland. FAX 358-0-409663. circ. 900. **Indexed:** Excerp.Med., Psychol.Abstr.

616.8 FI
PSYCHIATRIA FENNICA. REPORTS. (Text mainly in English and Finnish) 1970. irreg. price varies. (Foundation for Psychiatric Research in Finland) Psychiatria Fennica, Arkadiankatu 35 B 37, 00100 Helsinki 10, Finland. FAX 358-0-409663. Ed. K.A. Achte. circ. 150-300. **Indexed:** Excerp.Med., Psychol.Abstr.
Former titles: Psychiatria Fennica. Julkaisusarja (ISSN 0355-7693); Helsingin Yliopisto Keskussairaala. Psykiatrian Kliinikka. Julkaisusarja (ISSN 0073-1730).

616.89 US ISSN 0048-5713
RC321 CODEN: PSANCS
PSYCHIATRIC ANNALS. 1971. m. $85 to individuals; institutions $95. Slack, Inc., 6900 Grove Rd., Thorofare, NJ 08086. TEL 609-848-1000. FAX 609-853-5991. Ed. Dr. Howard P. Rome. adv.; bk.rev.; illus.; index; circ. 30,035. (also avail. in microform from UMI; reprint service avail. from UMI,ISI) **Indexed:** Adol.Ment.Hlth.Abstr., Biol.Abstr., Curr.Cont., Excerp.Med., Mid.East: Abstr.& Ind., Psychol.Abstr., Soc.Sci.Ind., SSCI.

616.8 UK
PSYCHIATRIC BULLETIN. (Supplement avail.) 1971. m. £15($30) Royal College of Psychiatrists, 17 Belgrave Square, London SW1X 8P, England. TEL 071-235-8857. FAX 071-245-1231. Eds. Alan Kerr, Greg Wilkinson. bk.rev.; circ. 7,000.
Formerly: Royal College of Psychiatrists. Bulletin (ISSN 0140-0789)

616.89 US ISSN 0193-953X
RC321
PSYCHIATRIC CLINICS OF NORTH AMERICA. 1978. 4/yr. $79. W.B. Saunders Co., Curtis Center, Independence Square W., Philadelphia, PA 19106. TEL 215-238-7800. Ed. Lesley Kramer. bibl.; illus.; index, cum.index. (reprint service avail. from UMI) **Indexed:** Adol.Ment.Hlth.Abstr., Curr.Adv.Ecol.Sci., Curr.Cont., Ind.Med., Psychol.Abstr., SSCI.
—BLDSC shelfmark: 6946.212500.

616.89 US ISSN 0033-2690
RC321 CODEN: PSYFAK
PSYCHIATRIC FORUM. 1969. s-a. free. Department of Mental Health, William S. Hall Psychiatric Institute, Box 202, Columbia, SC 29202. TEL 803-734-7154. FAX 803-734-0791. Ed. Dr. Lucius C. Pressley. bk.rev.; circ. 4,000 (controlled). **Indexed:** Adol.Ment.Hlth.Abstr., Chicago Psychoanal.Lit.Ind., CINAHL, Curr.Cont., Psychol.Abstr., SSCI.
Description: Original articles related to mental health.

PSYCHIATRIC GENETICS. see *BIOLOGY — Genetics*

616.89 US
PSYCHIATRIC HOSPITAL. 1969. q. $25. National Association of Private Psychiatric Hospitals, 1319 F St. N.W., Ste. 1000, Washington, DC 20004-1154. TEL 202-393-6700. FAX 202-783-6041. Ed. Frieda Eastman. adv.; bk.rev.; bibl.; circ. 9,000. **Indexed:** Abstr.Health Care Manage.Stud., Hosp.Lit.Ind., Psychol.Abstr.
Formerly: National Association of Private Psychiatric Hospitals. Journal (ISSN 0027-8629)

616.8 US
PSYCHIATRIC LENGTH OF STAY SERIES. (Editions avail.: United States Northcentral Region, Northeastern Region, Southern Region, Western Region) 1985. a. Healthcare Knowledge Resources, 3853 Research Park Dr., Box 303, Ann Arbor, MI 48106-0303. TEL 800-521-6210. FAX 313-930-7611.

616.8 US ISSN 0732-0868
CODEN: PSMDEQ
PSYCHIATRIC MEDICINE.* 1983. q. $55 to individuals; institutions $75. S P Medical & Scientific Books, Inc. (Subsidiary of: Spectrum Publications, Inc.), c/o Fisher, 200 Park Ave. S., New York, NY 10003-1503. Ed. Richard C.W. Hall, M.D. circ. 500. (back issues avail.) **Indexed:** Chem.Abstr., Psychol.Abstr.
—BLDSC shelfmark: 6946.214450.

616.89 US ISSN 0033-2704
RC321
PSYCHIATRIC NEWS. 1966. fortn. $40 to individuals (foreign $60); institutions $60 (foreign $80). (American Psychiatric Association) American Psychiatric Press, Inc., Journals Division, 1400 K St., N.W., Washington, DC 20005. TEL 202-682-6240. FAX 202-789-2648. (UK addr.: 17 Belgrave Sq., London SW1X 8PG, England) Ed. Robert Campbell, M.D. adv.; bk.rev.; stat.; circ. 35,700. (also avail. in microform from UMI; reprint service avail. from UMI) **Indexed:** Soc.Work Res.& Abstr.
—BLDSC shelfmark: 6946.215000.
Formerly: American Psychiatric Association. Newsletter.
Description: Delivers current information on everything from legislative activities to the latest developments in the drug and therapy fields.

616.89 US ISSN 0033-2720
CODEN: PSQUAP
PSYCHIATRIC QUARTERLY. 1927. q. $175 (foreign $205). (New York School of Psychiatry) Human Sciences Press, Inc. (Subsidiary of: Plenum Publishing Corp.), 233 Spring St., New York, NY 10013-1578. TEL 212-620-8000. FAX 212-463-0742. Ed. Dr. Stephen Rachlin. adv. (also avail. in microform from UMI; reprint service avail. from ISI,UMI) **Indexed:** Abstr.Hosp.Manage.Stud., Adol.Ment.Hlth.Abstr., ASCA, Biol.Abstr., CINAHL, Community Ment.Health Rev., Curr.Cont., Excerp.Med., Hosp.Lit.Ind., Ind.Med., Psychol.Abstr., Sociol.Abstr., SSCI.
—BLDSC shelfmark: 6946.240000.
Description: Includes articles on the social, clinical, administrative, legal, political, and ethical aspects of mental illness care. Presents pertinent scientific and delivery system data.
Refereed Serial

616.8 US
▼**PSYCHIATRIC RESIDENT.** 1992. bi-m. Slack, Inc., 6900 Grove Rd., Thorofare, NJ 08086. TEL 609-848-1000. FAX 609-853-5991. Ed. Laura Ronge. adv.; circ. 6,323.
Description: Covers career, lifestyle and business issues facing residents.

616.89 US ISSN 0893-2905
PSYCHIATRIC TIMES. 1985. m. $108 (foreign $200)(effective 1992). C M E Inc., 1924 E. Deere Ave., Santa Ana, CA 92705-5723. TEL 800-447-4474. FAX 714-250-0445. Ed. John L. Schwartz, M.D. adv.; bk.rev.; circ. 39,545 (controlled).

PSYCHIATRIE DE L'ENFANT. see *MEDICAL SCIENCES — Pediatrics*

157 616.8 GW ISSN 0303-4259
PSYCHIATRISCHE PRAXIS. 1974. bi-m. DM.141. Georg Thieme Verlag, Ruedigerstr. 14, Postfach 104853, 7000 Stuttgart 10, Germany. TEL 0711-8931-0. FAX 0711-8931298. Ed.Bd. adv.; bk.rev.; bibl.; charts; illus.; index; circ. 1,600. (reprint service avail. from UMI) **Indexed:** Biol.Abstr., Curr.Cont., Excerp.Med., Ger.J.Psych., Ind.Med., Risk Abstr., SSCI.
—BLDSC shelfmark: 6946.258000.

616.89 US ISSN 0033-2747
RC321 CODEN: PSYCAB
PSYCHIATRY; interpersonal and biological processes. 1937. q. $32 to individuals; institutions $88. (Washington School of Psychiatry) Guilford Publications, Inc., 72 Spring St., 4th Fl., New York, NY 10012. TEL 212-431-9800. FAX 212-966-6708. Ed. Dr. David Reiss. adv.; bk.rev.; index, cum.index: 1938-1967, 1968-1977; circ. 2,000. (also avail. in microform from MIM,UMI; back issues avail.; reprint service avail. from ISI,UMI) **Indexed:** Abstr.Anthropol., Adol.Ment.Hlth.Abstr., ASSIA, Biol.Abstr., Child Devel.Abstr., Curr.Cont., Excerp.Med., Hist.Abstr., Hosp.Lit.Ind., Ind.Med., Int.Nurs.Ind., Mid.East: Abstr.& Ind., Psychol.Abstr., Sage Fam.Stud.Abstr., Sage Urb.Stud.Abstr., Soc.Sci.Ind., SSCI.
—BLDSC shelfmark: 6946.260000.
Description: New and controversial issues in psychiatry and related social and biological science disciplines.
Refereed Serial

616.8 CN
PSYCHIATRY. 1987. 4/yr. M P I Publishing Inc., 14 Ronan Ave., Toronto, Ont. M4N 2X9, Canada. TEL 416-481-6384. Ed. Dr. Vivian Rakoff. circ. 14,123.

616.8 UK ISSN 0262-5377
PSYCHIATRY IN PRACTICE. Abbreviated title: P I P. 1981-198?? suspended; N.S. 1990. q. £24. Hayward Medical Communications, Hayward House, 1 Threshers Yard, Kingham, OX7 6YF, England. TEL 0608-659595. Ed. Dr. George Beaumont. adv.; bk.rev.; circ. 21,000.
—BLDSC shelfmark: 6946.263600.

616.8 JO
PSYCHIATRY JOURNAL/MAJALLAT AL-SIHHAH AL-NAFSIYYAH.* (Text in Arabic) 1972. bi-m. Psychiatry Association, Box 1317, Amman, Jordan. Ed. Samir Liddawi.

616.8 IE ISSN 0165-1781
CODEN: PSRSDR
PSYCHIATRY RESEARCH; an international journal for rapid communication. (Text in English) 1979. 16/yr. $865 (includes Neuroimaging Section)(effective 1991). Elsevier Scientific Publishers Ireland Ltd., P.O. Box 85, Limerick, Ireland. TEL 061-61944. FAX 061-62144. TELEX 72191 ENH EI. (Subscr. in U.S. and Canada to: Elsevier Science Publishing Co., Inc., Box 882, Madison Sq. Sta., New York, NY 10159. TEL 212-989-5800) Eds. Monte S. Buchsbaum, Frederick K. Goodwin. illus. (also avail. in microform from RPI; back issues avail.; reprint service avail. from SWZ) **Indexed:** Biol.Abstr., Biotech.Abstr., Chem.Abstr., Curr.Cont., Excerp.Med., Ind.Med., Psychol.Abstr.
—BLDSC shelfmark: 6946.263700.
Refereed Serial

616.8 IE ISSN 0925-4927
▼**PSYCHIATRY RESEARCH: NEUROIMAGING SECTION.** 1990. 4/yr. $144 (effective 1992). Elsevier Science Publishers Ireland Ltd., P.O. Box 85, Limerick, Ireland. TEL 061-61944. FAX 061-62144. TELEX 72191 ENH EI. (Subscr. in U.S. and Canada to: Elsevier Science Publishing Co., Inc., Box 882, Madison Sq. Sta., New York, NY 10159. TEL 212-989-5800) (back issues avail.)
Refereed Serial

616.8 GW ISSN 0340-7845
PSYCHO; Psychiatrie, Neurologie und Psychotherapie. 1975. m. DM.48. Perimed Verlag Dr. D. Straube, Weinstr. 70, Postfach 3740, 8520 Erlangen, Germany. TEL 09131-609-1. FAX 09131-609217. TELEX 629851-PEMEDD. adv.; bk.rev.; abstr.; circ. 5,800. **Indexed:** Excerp.Med.
—BLDSC shelfmark: 6946.264150.

M

MEDICAL SCIENCES — PSYCHIATRY AND NEUROLOGY

616.9 US
PSYCHOANALYSIS AND CONTEMPORARY THOUGHT; a quarterly of integrative and interdisciplinary studies. 1978. q. $60 to individuals (foreign $80); institutions $105. (Psychoanalysis and Contemporary Science, Inc.) International Universities Press, Inc., Journal Department, 59 Boston Post Rd., Box 1524, Madison, CT 06443-1524. TEL 203-245-4000. FAX 203-245-0775. Ed. Dr. Leo Goldberger. bk.rev.; index. (back issues avail.) Indexed: Biol.Abstr., Excerp.Med., Lang.& Lang.Behav.Abstr., Psychoanal.Abstr., Psychol.Abstr.
 Incorporating (after vol.5): Psychoanalysis and Contemporary Science.
 Description: Aimed at broadening the scientific and intellectual horizon of psychoanalysis. Includes original clinical, theoretical and experimental contributions intergrating psychoanalysis with social, biological and behaviorial sciences.
 Refereed Serial

616.891 US
PSYCHOANALYSIS AND PSYCHOTHERAPY. 1983. s-a. $24 to individuals (foreign $28); institutions $50 (foreign $54). (Postgraduate Center for Mental Health) Brunner-Mazel Publishing Co., 19 Union Sq. W., New York, NY 10003. TEL 212-924-3344. Eds. Harry Sands, Bernard F. Riess. bk.rev.; index; circ. 1,000. Indexed: Psychoanal.Abstr., Psychol.Abstr.
 Formerly (until 1989): Dynamic Psychotherapy (ISSN 0736-508X)
 Description: Represents contemporary thinking, application and recent advances in the art and techniques of dynamic psychotherapy-psychoanalyses.

616.89 A2 US ISSN 1044-2103
BF173.A2
▼**PSYCHOANALYTIC BOOKS**; a quarterly journal of reviews. 1990. q. $50 to individuals (foreign $60); institutions $90 (foreign $100). Psychoanalytic Books, Inc., 211 E. 70th St., New York, NY 10021. TEL 212-628-8792. FAX 212-628-8792. Ed. Joseph Reppen. adv.; bk.rev.; index; circ. 1,000. (back issues avail.)
 Description: Reviews of books in psychoanalysis including Freud studies, history of psychoanalysis, psychobiology, psychohistory, and psychoanalytic study of literature and the arts.

PSYCHOANALYTIC PSYCHOLOGY. see *PSYCHOLOGY*

616.8 GW ISSN 0478-6866
PSYCHOBIOLOGIE. 1952. s-a. DM.16. Psychobiologische Gesellschaft, Freundhofweg 5, 4330 Muelheim, Germany.

616.89 UK ISSN 0033-2917
CODEN: PSMDCO
PSYCHOLOGICAL MEDICINE. 1970. q. plus irreg. suppl. $119 to individuals; institutions $242. Cambridge University Press, Edinburgh Bldg., Shaftesbury Rd., Cambridge CB2 2RU, England. TEL 0223-312393. FAX 0223-315052. TELEX 851817256. (North American addr.: Cambridge University Press, 40 W. 20th St., New York, NY 10011) Ed. M. Shepherd. bk.rev.; charts; illus.; index. (also avail. in microfilm from UMI; reprint service avail. from SWZ) Indexed: Abstr.Health Care Manage.Stud., Adol.Ment.Hlth.Abstr., ASSIA, Chem.Abstr., CINAHL, Curr.Adv.Ecol.Sci., Curr.Cont., Dok.Arbeitsmed., Excerp.Med., Ind.Med., Mid.East: Abstr.& Ind., Nutr.Abstr., Psychol.Abstr., Res.High.Educ.Abstr., Risk Abstr., SSCI.
 —BLDSC shelfmark: 6946.450000.
 Description: Original research in clinical psychiatry and the basic sciences related to it.

616.89 FR ISSN 0048-5756
PSYCHOLOGIE MEDICALE. (Text in French, summaries in English, French) 1969. 14/yr. 400 F. (foreign 500 F.)(effective 1991). Service de Presse, Edition et Information (SPEI), Dept. des Editions Medicales, 14 rue Drouot, 75009 Paris, France. TEL 48-14-96-93. FAX 47-70-02-73. TELEX OTRASPE 660484 F. Ed. E.J. Caille. adv.; bk.rev.; index; circ. 7,500. Indexed: Biol.Abstr., Excerp.Med., Psychol.Abstr.
 —BLDSC shelfmark: 6946.532300.
 Description: Covers a number of case studies in psychiatry and psychological medicine coming out of France, Switzerland, Canada and Argentina.

616.8 616.4 US ISSN 0306-4530
CODEN: PSYCDE
PSYCHONEUROENDOCRINOLOGY. 1976. 6/yr. £240 (effective 1992). (International Society of Psychoneuroendocrinology) Pergamon Press, Inc., Journals Division, 660 White Plains Rd., Tarrytown, NY 10591-5153. TEL 914-524-9200. FAX 914-333-2444. (And: Headington Hill Hall, Oxford OX3 0BW, England. TEL 0865-794141) Ed. Robert T. Rubin. adv.; bk.rev.; charts; illus.; stat.; index; circ. 1,000. (also avail. in microform from MIM,UMI) Indexed: Biol.Abstr., Biotech.Abstr., Curr.Adv.Ecol.Sci., Curr.Cont., Dairy Sci.Abstr., Excerp.Med., Ind.Med., Nutr.Abstr., Psychol.Abstr.
 —BLDSC shelfmark: 6946.540300.
 Description: Multidisciplinary journal addressing issues in psychiatry, psychology, neurology and endocrinology.
 Refereed Serial

616.89 SG ISSN 0033-314X
CODEN: PSAFB3
PSYCHOPATHOLOGIE AFRICAINE; sciences sociales et psychiatrie en Afrique. (Text and summaries in English and French) 1965. 3/yr. 7500 Fr.CFA to individuals; institutions 12000 Fr.CFA. Societe de Psychopathologie et d'Hygiene Mentale de Dakar, B.P. 5097, Dakar-Fann, Senegal. Dir. Babacar Diop. adv.; bk.rev.; charts; index; circ. 11,250. (also avail. in microfiche) Indexed: Biol.Abstr., Curr.Cont., Psychol.Abstr., SSCI.
 Description: Seeks to collect and make known works related to psychiatry, psychopathology and mental health in sub-Saharan Africa.

616.89 SZ ISSN 0254-4962
CODEN: PSYHEU
PSYCHOPATHOLOGY. (Text in English) 1968. 6/yr. 360 Fr.($240) S. Karger AG, Allschwilerstr. 10, P.O. Box, CH-4009 Basel, Switzerland. TEL 061-3061111. FAX 061-3061234. TELEX CH 962652. Ed. P. Berner, E. Gabriel. adv.; bk.rev.; index; circ. 800. (also avail. in microform from RPI) Indexed: ASCA, Biol.Abstr., Curr.Cont., Dent.Ind., Excerp.Med., Ind.Med., Psychol.Abstr., SSCI.
 —BLDSC shelfmark: 6946.543700.
 Formerly (until vol.17, 1984): Psychiatria Clinica (ISSN 0033-264X)

PSYCHOPHARMACOLOGY BULLETIN. see *PHARMACY AND PHARMACOLOGY*

616.89 US ISSN 0033-3174
RC49 CODEN: PSMEAP
PSYCHOSOMATIC MEDICINE. 1939. bi-m. $110 to individuals; institutions $220. (American Psychosomatic Society) Williams & Wilkins, 428 E. Preston St., Baltimore, MD 21202. TEL 301-528-4000. FAX 301-528-4312. Ed. Donald Oken, M.D. adv.; bk.rev.; index; circ. 2,500. (also avail. in microform from RPI; reprint service avail. from KTO) Indexed: Biol.Abstr., Chem.Abstr., Curr.Cont., Excerp.Med., Ind.Med., Psychol.Abstr., Sociol.Abstr., SSCI.
 —BLDSC shelfmark: 6946.555000.
 Description: Presents research and clinical studies concerning psychosomatic disorders. Examines many disciplines including psychiatry, psychology, and social sciences.
 Refereed Serial

616.89 US ISSN 0033-3182
RC49 CODEN: PSYCBC
PSYCHOSOMATICS; the journal of consultation and liaison psychiatry. 1960. q. $85 to individuals (foreign $100); institutions $135 (foreign $150). (Academy of Psychosomatic Medicine) American Psychiatric Press, Inc., Journals Division, 1400 K St., N.W., Ste. 1101, Washington, DC 20005. TEL 202-682-6130. FAX 202-789-2648. (UK addr.: 17 Belgrave Sq., London SW1X 8PG, England) Ed. Dr. Thomas Wise. adv.; bk.rev.; abstr.; bibl.; charts; illus.; stat.; index; circ. 2,500. (also avail. in microform from UMI; reprint service avail. from UMI) Indexed: Adol.Ment.Hlth.Abstr., Biol.Abstr., Chem.Abstr., CINAHL, Curr.Cont., Excerp.Med., Ind.Med., Nutr.Abstr., Psychol.Abstr., Soc.Work Res.& Abstr., SSCI.
 —BLDSC shelfmark: 6946.557000.
 Description: Devoted to the relationship between medical and psychiatric phenomena.
 Refereed Serial

616.8 360 GW ISSN 0930-4177
PSYCHOSOZIALE UMSCHAU.* 1985. q. DM.27 (foreign DM.30). (Dachverband fuer Psychosoziale Hilfsvereinigungen) Psychiatrie-Verlag, Celsiusstr. 112, 5300 Bonn 1, Germany.

616.89 GW ISSN 0173-7937
PSYCHOTHERAPIE - PSYCHOSOMATIK - MEDIZINISCHE PSYCHOLOGIE. Short title: P P M P. (Text in German; summaries in English) 1951. m. DM.189. (Allgemeine Aerztliche Gesellschaft fuer Psychotherapie) Georg Thieme Verlag, Ruedigerstr. 14, Postfach 104853, 7000 Stuttgart 10, Germany. TEL 0711-8931-0. FAX 0711-8931298. (Co-sponsor: Oesterreichische Aerzte-Gesellschaft fuer Psychotherapie) Ed.Bd. adv.; bk.rev.; abstr.; bibl.; charts; illus.; index; circ. 1,900. (also avail. in microform from UMI; reprint service avail. from UMI) Indexed: Biol.Abstr., Curr.Cont., Excerp.Med., Ger.J.Psych., Ind.Med., Psychol.Abstr., Risk Abstr., SSCI.
 —BLDSC shelfmark: 6946.558250.
 Former titles (until 1980): Psychotherapie Medizinische Psychologie; Psychotherapie und Medizinische Psychologie (ISSN 0302-8984); Zeitschrift fuer Psychotherapie und Medizinische Psychologie (ISSN 0044-3417)

616.89 SZ ISSN 0033-3190
RC49 CODEN: PSPSBF
PSYCHOTHERAPY AND PSYCHOSOMATICS. (Text in English) 1953. 8/yr. (2 vols.). 256 Fr.($171) per vol. (International Federation for Medical Psychotherapy) S. Karger AG, Allschwilerstr. 10, P.O. Box, CH-4009 Basel, Switzerland. TEL 061-3061111. FAX 061-3061234. TELEX CH 962652. Ed. G. Fava. adv.; bk.rev.; charts; illus.; bibl.; index; circ. 1,000. (also avail. in microform from RPI; back issues avail.) Indexed: Adol.Ment.Hlth.Abstr., Biol.Abstr., Chem.Abstr., Curr.Cont., Dent.Ind., Excerp.Med., Ind.Med., Nutr.Abstr., Psychol.Abstr., SSCI, Stud.Wom.Abstr.
 —BLDSC shelfmark: 6946.559000.

PSYCHOTROPES; un journal d'information sur les drogues et leurs usages. see *PHARMACY AND PHARMACOLOGY*

616.8 AT
PSYCHOTROPIC GUIDELINES. 1989. biennial. Aus.$12. Victorian Medical Postgraduate Foundation Inc., Therapeutics Commiittee, Chelsea House, Level 3, 55 Flemington Rd., N. Melbourne, Vic. 3051, Australia. TEL 03-329-1566. FAX 03-326-5632. (Co-sponsor: Victorian Drug Usage Advisory Committee) bk.rev.; circ. 5,000.
 Description: Treatment compliance in psychiatric illnesses for doctors, nurses and pharmacists.

PSYKISK HAELSA/MENTAL HEALTH. see *PSYCHOLOGY*

616.8 664.06 US
PURE FACTS. 1978. 10/yr. $15. Feingold Association of the United States, Box 6550, Alexandria, VA 22306. TEL 703-768-3287. Ed. Jane Hersey. circ. 6,000. (back issues avail.)
 Description: Non-profit support group helping children with learning or behavior problems and chemically-sensitive adults.

616.8 IT ISSN 0393-0645
QUADERNI ITALIANI DI PSICHIATRIA. 1981. bi-m. L.92000($129) (effective 1992). Masson Italia Periodici, Via Statuto 2-4, 20121 Milan, Italy. TEL 02-6367-1. FAX 02-6367211. Eds. Vittorino Andreoli, Giovanni B. Cassano. circ. 1,000.

QUADRANT; the journal of contemporary Jungian thought. see *PSYCHOLOGY*

616.8 610.73 371.9 US
QUALITY OF CARE. 1980. bi-m. Commission on Quality of Care for the Mentally Disabled, 99 Washington Ave., Ste. 1002, Albany, NY 12210. TEL 518-473-8683. FAX 518-473-6296. Ed. Marcus A. Gigliotti. bk.rev.; circ. 11,000.

READING AND WRITING; an interdisciplinary journal. see *LINGUISTICS*

MEDICAL SCIENCES — PSYCHIATRY AND NEUROLOGY

150 028   US   ISSN 0886-3784
READINGS; a journal of reviews and commentary in mental health. 1986. q. $20 to individuals; institutions $30. American Orthopsychiatric Association, Inc., 19 W. 44th St., Ste. 1616, New York, NY 10036. TEL 212-354-5770. FAX 212-302-9463. (Subscr. to: 49 Sheridan Ave., Albany, NY 12201-1413) Ed. Ernest Herman. adv.; bk.rev.; circ. 11,000. (also avail. in microfiche; back issues avail.) **Indexed:** Bk.Rev.Ind. (1990-), Child.Bk.Rev.Ind. (1990-).
   Description: 4-6 essay reviews and 30-40 brief reviews of books interesting to the mental health professional.

616.8   SZ   ISSN 1013-7467
RECENT ACHIEVEMENTS IN RESTORATIVE NEUROLOGY. (Text in English) 1985. irreg., vol.3, 1990. price varies. S. Karger AG, Allschwilerstr. 10, P.O. Box, CH-4009 Basel, Switzerland. TEL 061-3061111. FAX 061-3061234. TELEX CH 962652. Ed. M.R. Dimitrijevic. **Indexed:** Biol.Abstr., Curr.Cont., Ind.Med.

616.853   UK
RECENT ADVANCES IN EPILEPSY. 1983. irreg. price varies. Churchill Livingstone Medical Journals, Robert Stevenson House, 1-3 Baxter's Pl., Leith Walk, Edinburgh EH1 3AF, Scotland. (Subscr. to: Longman Group, Journals Subscr. Dept., P.O. Box 77, Fourth Ave., Harlow, Essex CM19 5AA, England; U.S. subscr. to: Churchill Livingstone, 650 Ave. of the Americas, New York, NY 10011. TEL 212-206-5000) Eds. Timothy A. Pedley, Brian S. Meldrum.

RECHT & PSYCHIATRIE. see *PSYCHOLOGY*

REHABILITATION COUNSELING BULLETIN. see *HANDICAPPED*

RESEARCH COMMUNICATIONS IN PSYCHOLOGY, PSYCHIATRY AND BEHAVIOR. see *PSYCHOLOGY*

RESEARCH METHODS IN NEUROCHEMISTRY. see *BIOLOGY — Biological Chemistry*

616.8   NE   ISSN 0922-6028
RESTORATIVE NEUROLOGY AND NEUROSCIENCE. (Text in English) 1989. 6/yr. fl.462 (effective 1992). Elsevier Science Publishers B.V., P.O. Box 1527, 1000 BM Amsterdam, Netherlands. TEL 020-5803911. FAX 020-5803598. TELEX 18582 ESPA NL. (Subscr. in U.S. and Canada to: Elsevier Science Publishing Co., Inc., Box 882, Madison Sq. Sta., New York, NY 10159. TEL 212-989-5800) Ed. D.G. Stein. bk.rev. (back issues avail.) **Indexed:** Curr.Cont., Excerp.Med.
—BLDSC shelfmark: 7777.865000.
   Description: Interdisciplinary journal; contains papers on plasticity and response of the nervous system to accidental or experimental injuries, or transplantation.
Refereed Serial

616.8   UK   ISSN 0334-1763
                        CODEN: RNEUEO
REVIEWS IN THE NEUROSCIENCES. (Text in English) 1986. q. $160. Freund Publishing House, Ltd., Suite 500, Chesham House, 150 Regent St., London W1R 5FA, England. (Alt. addr.: P.O. Box 35010, Tel Aviv, Israel. TEL 972-3-615335) Ed. J.P. Huston. adv.; circ. 1,000. (back issues avail.) **Indexed:** Curr.Adv.Ecol.Sci.
—BLDSC shelfmark: 7793.571000.

616.8   BL   ISSN 0101-8469
REVISTA BRASILEIRO DE NEUROLOGIA. (Text in Portuguese; summaries in English and Portuguese) 1949. bi-m. Cr.$3500($60) (Universidade Federal do Rio de Janeiro, Instituto de Neurologia) Editora Cientifica Nacional Ltda., Av. Almirante Barroso 97-1.205-1210, CEP 20031 Rio de Janeiro, RJ, Brazil. Ed. Clovis de Oliveira. charts; illus. **Indexed:** Chem.Abstr., Ind.Med.
   Formerly: Jornal Brasileiro de Neurologia (ISSN 0021-7514)

616.8   CL   ISSN 0034-7388
REVISTA CHILENA DE NEUROPSIQUIATRIA. vol.16, 1978. q. $30. Sociedad Chilena de Neurologia, Psiquiatria y Neurocirugia, Av. Presidente Riesco 6007, Las Condes Clasificados, Correo, 27, Santiago, Chile. FAX 56-2-212-1521. Ed. Dr. Otto Dorr Zegers. adv.; bk.rev.; abstr.; bibl.; charts; illus.; stat.; circ. 1,000. (reprint service avail.) **Indexed:** Chem.Abstr., Excerp.Med., Ind.Med., Psychol.Abstr.
—BLDSC shelfmark: 7848.900000.

616.89   CK   ISSN 0034-7450
                        CODEN: RCPSBR
REVISTA COLOMBIANA DE PSIQUIATRIA. 1964. q. $40. Sociedad Colombiana de Psiquiatria, Carrera 18, No. 8487, Apdo. 203, Bogota, Colombia. TEL 57-1-2561148. Ed. R. Chaskel. adv.; bk.rev.; abstr.; charts; illus.; index; circ. 1,500. **Indexed:** Excerp.Med., Psychol.Abstr.

616.8 616.5   RM   ISSN 0028-386X
REVISTA DE MEDICINA INTERNA, NEUROLOGIE, PSIHIATRIE, NEURO-CHIRURGIE, DERMATO-VENEROLOGIE. (Text in Rumanian; summaries in English, French, German and Russian) 1956. 4/yr. $25. Uniunea Societatilor de Stiinte Medicale din Republica Socialista Rumania, Str. Progresului No. 8, Bucharest, Rumania. (Subscr. to: ILEXIM, Str. 13 Decembrie Nr. 3, P.O. Box 136-137, Bucharest, Rumania) Ed.Bd. adv.; bk.rev.; abstr.; charts; illus. **Indexed:** Biol.Abstr., Chem.Abstr., Ind.Med.
   Formerly: Dermato-Venerologie (ISSN 0011-9024)

616.8   PE   ISSN 0034-8597
REVISTA DE NEURO-PSIQUIATRIA. (Text in Spanish; summaries in English, French and German) 1938. q. $50. Talleres Graficos P.L. Villanueva S.A., Casilla 1589, Lima 100, Peru. Eds. Javier Mariategui, Luis Trelles. adv.; bk.rev.; abstr.; charts; illus.; index; circ. 1,000. **Indexed:** Biol.Abstr., Excerp.Med., Ind.Med., Psychol.Abstr.

616.89   FR   ISSN 0035-1547
REVUE DE MEDECINE PSYCHOSOMATIQUE. (Text in French; summaries in English) 1959. q. 320 F. to individuals; institutions 400 F. (Societe Francaise de Medecine Psychosomatique) Pensee Sauvage Editions, B.P. 141, 38002 Grenoble, France. TEL 76-47-96-85. Eds. Dr. L. Chertok, Dr. M. Sapir. **Indexed:** Excerp.Med., Ind.Med., Psychol.Abstr.
—BLDSC shelfmark: 7931.300000.

616.8   FR   ISSN 0035-161X
REVUE DE NEUROPSYCHIATRIE DE L'OUEST. 1963. q. 130 Fr. Societe de Neuro-Psychiatrie de l'Ouest, B.P. 226, Rennes, France.
—BLDSC shelfmark: 7937.800000.

REVUE EUROPEENE DE PSYCHOLOGIE APPLIQUEE/EUROPEAN REVIEW OF APPLIED PSYCHOLOGY. see *PSYCHOLOGY*

616.89   FR
▼**REVUE INTERNATIONALE DE PYSCHOPATHOLOGIE.** 1990. s-a. 450 F. (foreign 510 F.). Presses Universitaires de France, Departement des Revues, 14 av. du Bois-de-l'Epine, B.P. 90, 91003 Evry Cedex, France. TEL 1-60-77-82-05. FAX 1-60-79-20-45. TELEX PUF 600 474 F. Eds. Daniel Widlocher, Pierre Fedida.

616.8   FR   ISSN 0035-3787
                        CODEN: RENEAM
REVUE NEUROLOGIQUE. (Text in French; summaries in English) 1893. 10/yr. 185 ECU($230) (typically set in Jan.). (Societe Francaise de Neurologie) Masson, 120 bd. Saint-Germain, 75280 Paris Cedex 06, France. TEL 1-46-34-21-60. FAX 1-45-87-29-99. TELEX 202 671 F. Ed. J.C. Gautier. adv.; bk.rev.; abstr.; illus.; index; circ. 2,600. (also avail. in microform from UMI,BHP; reprint service avail. from ISI) **Indexed:** Bibl.Dev.Med.& Child Neur., Biol.Abstr., C.I.S. Abstr., Chem.Abstr., Curr.Adv.Biochem., Curr.Adv.Cancer Res., Curr.Adv.Cell & Devel.Biol., Curr.Adv.Ecol.Sci., Curr.Cont., Excerp.Med., Helminthol.Abstr., Ind.Med., Protozool.Abstr.
—BLDSC shelfmark: 7937.750000.

616.8   RM
REVUE ROUMAINE DE NEUROLOGIE ET PSYCHIATRIE/ROMANIAN JOURNAL OF NEUROLOGY AND PSYCHIATRY. (Text in English, French, German and Russian; summaries in English) 1964. 4/yr. 200 lei($55) (Academia de Stiinte Medicale) Editura Academiei Romane, Calea Victoriei 125, 79717 Bucharest, Rumania. (Dist. by: Rompresfilatelia, Calea Grivitei 64-66, P.O. Box 12-201, 78104 Bucharest, Rumania) Ed. Vlad Voiculescu. bk.rev.; charts; illus.; index; circ. 700. **Indexed:** Biol.Abstr., Excerp.Med., Ind.Med., Psychol.Abstr.
   Former titles: Revue Roumaine de Medecine. Serie Neurologie et Psychiatrie (ISSN 0301-7303) & Revue Roumaine de Neurologie; (until 1974): Revue Roumaine de Neurologie et Psychiatrie (ISSN 0035-3981)

616.8   JA   ISSN 0009-918X
RINSHO SHINKEIGAKU/CLINICAL NEUROLOGY. (Text in Japanese; summaries in English) 1960. m. 13000 Yen. Japanese Society of Neurology - Nihon Shinkei Gakkai, Ichimaru Bldg., 2-31-21 Yushima, Bunkyo-ku, Tokyo 113, Japan. TEL 03-815-1080. FAX 03-815-1931. Ed. Toru Mannen. adv.; charts; illus.; index; circ. 6,216. **Indexed:** Biol.Abstr., Dent.Ind., Excerp.Med., Ind.Med.
—BLDSC shelfmark: 3286.309000.

616.8   IT   ISSN 0035-6336
                        CODEN: RNBLAC
RIVISTA DI NEUROBIOLOGIA. (Text in Italian; summaries in English) 1955. q. Ospedale Neuropsichiatrico Provinciale, 52100 Arezzo, Italy. Ed. Marino Benvenuti. adv.; bibl.; charts; illus.; index; circ. 300. **Indexed:** Biol.Abstr., Chem.Abstr., Dent.Ind., Excerp.Med., Ind.Med.

616.8   ISSN 0035-6352
RIVISTA DI NEUROPSICHIATRIA E SCIENZE AFFINI. (Text in Italian; summaries in English) 1955. q. L.60000 (foreign L.120000)(effective 1992). Casa Editrice Maccari, Via Trento 53, 43100 Parma, Italy. FAX 039-521-771268. Ed.Bd. adv.; bk.rev.; circ. 1,600. **Indexed:** Chem.Abstr., Excerp.Med.
—BLDSC shelfmark: 7991.420000.

RIVISTA DI NEURORADIOLOGIA; periodico quadrimestrale scientifico indipendente. see *MEDICAL SCIENCES — Radiology And Nuclear Medicine*

616.89   IT   ISSN 0035-6484
                        CODEN: RPSID3
RIVISTA DI PSICHIATRIA. (Text in Italian; abstracts in English) 1966. q. L.70000($130) to individuals; institutions L.100000. Pensiero Scientifico Editore s.r.l., Via Panama 48, 00198 Rome, Italy. TEL 06 855-36-33. Eds. G.C. Reda, P. Pancheri. adv.; bk.rev.; charts; illus.; index; circ. 1,000. **Indexed:** Excerp.Med., Psychol.Abstr.
—BLDSC shelfmark: 7992.731000.

616.8   IT
RIVISTA DI RIABILITAZIONE PSICHIATRICA E PSICOSOCIALE. q. L.60000($85) (effective 1992). Casa Editrice Idelson, Via A. De Gasperi 55, 80133 Naples, Italy. TEL 081-5524733. FAX 081-5518295. Ed. Massimo Casacchia.

616.8   IT   ISSN 0035-7057
RIVISTA SPERIMENTALE DI FRENIATRIA; medicina legale delle alienazioni mentali. (Text in Italian; summaries in English and French) 1875. bi-m. L.60000 (foreign L.80000)(effective 1992). (Istituti Ospedalieri Neuropsichiatrici di San Lazzaro) Artigianato Grafico Editoriale s.n.c., Via Casorati, 29, 42100 Reggio Emilia, Italy. Ed. Piero Benassi. adv.; bk.rev. **Indexed:** Biol.Abstr., Chem.Abstr., Ind.Med., Psychol.Abstr.

S A M I K S A. see *PSYCHOLOGY*

616.8 371.9   IT   ISSN 0390-5179
SAGGI; neuropsicologia infantile psicopedagogia riabilitazione. (Supplements avail.) (Text in Italian; summaries in English) 1975. s-a. L.40000 (foreign L.50000)(typically set in Jan.). (Scientific Institute "Eugenio Medea" - Bosisio Parini) Edizioni La Nostra Famiglia, Via Don Luigi Monza, 1, 22037 Ponte Lambro, Italy. TEL 031-625111. FAX 031-625275. Ed. Giaele Spreafico. adv.; bk.rev.; cum.index: 1975-1991; circ. 800 (controlled).
   Description: Covers infant neuropsychology and psychopedagogic rehabilitation.
Refereed Serial

616.89   MX   ISSN 0185-3325
SALUD MENTAL. (Text in Spanish; summaries in English) 1978. q. Mex.$100000($40) to individuals; institutions $56. Instituto Mexicana de Psiquiatria, Calz. Mexico-Xochimilco, No. 101, Col. San Lorenzo Huipulco, Delegacion Tlalpan, 14370 Mexico, D.F., Mexico. TEL 655-28-11. FAX 655-0411. Ed. Hector Perez-Rincon. adv.; bk.rev.; charts; illus.; stat.; cum.index; circ. 3,000. (back issues avail.) **Indexed:** Curr.Cont., Ind.Med., Psychol.Abstr., SSCI.
—BLDSC shelfmark: 8071.770000.
   Description: Covers research in neurosciences, clinical psychiatry, epidemiology, mental health psychopharmacology, history of psychiatry and problems of ethics.

MEDICAL SCIENCES — PSYCHIATRY AND NEUROLOGY

616.891   DK   ISSN 0106-2301
RC500
SCANDINAVIAN PSYCHOANALYTIC REVIEW. (Text in English) 1978. s-a. DKK 380. (Psycho-Analytical Societies in Denmark, Finland, Norway and Sweden) Munksgaard International Publishers Ltd., 35 Noerre Soegade, P.O. Box 2148, DK-1016 Copenhagen K, Denmark. TEL 33-127030. FAX 33-129387. TELEX 19431-MUNKS-DK. Ed. Lis Lind. bk.rev.; circ. 900. (reprint service avail. from ISI) **Indexed:** ASCA, Curr.Cont., Psychoanal.Abstr., Psychol.Abstr., SSCI.
—BLDSC shelfmark: 8087.572800.

618 150   US   ISSN 0586-7614
RC514   CODEN: SCZBB3
SCHIZOPHRENIA BULLETIN.* 1969. q. $10. U.S. Public Health Service, Alcohol, Drug Abuse & Mental Health Administration, Center for Studies of Schizophrenia, 5600 Fishers Lane, Rockville, MD 20857. TEL 301-496-4000. (Orders to: Supt. of Documents, Washington, DC 20402) Ed. Dr. Loren R. Mosher. abstr.; bibl.; circ. 4,700. (also avail. in microform from MCA,MIM,UMI; reprint service avail. from UMI) **Indexed:** Adol.Ment.Hlth.Abstr., ASCA, Biol.Abstr., CINAHL, Curr.Adv.Ecol.Sci., Curr.Cont., Except.Child.Educ.Abstr., Excerp.Med., Ind.Med., Ind.U.S.Gov.Per., MEDOC, Psychol.Abstr., SSCI.
—BLDSC shelfmark: 8089.400000.

616.8   NE   ISSN 0920-9964
CODEN: SCRSEH
SCHIZOPHRENIA RESEARCH; an international multidisciplinary journal. (Text in English) 1988. 6/yr.(in 2 vols.; 3 nos./vol.) fl.858 (effective 1992). Elsevier Science Publishers B.V., P.O. Box 211, 1000 AE Amsterdam, Netherlands. TEL 020-5803911. FAX 020-5803598. TELEX 18582 ESPA NL. (Subscr. in U.S. and Canada to: Elsevier Science Publishing Co., Inc., Box 882, Madison Sq. Sta., New York, NY 10159. TEL 212-989-5800) Eds. H.A. Nasrallah, L.E. DeLisi. circ. 800. (reprint service avail. from ISI) **Indexed:** Curr.Cont., Excerp.Med., Psychol.Abstr.
—BLDSC shelfmark: 8089.440000.
Description: Presents new international research that contributes to the understanding of schizophrenic disorders.
Refereed Serial

SCHMERZDIAGNOSTIK UND THERAPIE. see *MEDICAL SCIENCES — Anaesthesiology*

616.8   US   ISSN 0080-715X
SCHRIFTENREIHE NEUROLOGIE - NEUROLOGY SERIES. (Text in German; occasionally in English) 1959. irreg. price varies. Springer-Verlag, 175 Fifth Ave., New York, NY 10010. TEL 212-460-1500. (Also Berlin, Heidelberg, Tokyo and Vienna) (reprint service avail. from ISI) **Indexed:** Biol.Abstr., Ind.Med.
—BLDSC shelfmark: 8104.375000.
Supersedes in part: Monographien aus dem Gesamtgebiete der Neurologie und Psychiatrie.

616.89   SZ   ISSN 0036-7273
CODEN: SANNAW
SCHWEIZER ARCHIV FUER NEUROLOGIE, NEUROCHIRURGIE UND PSYCHIATRIE. (Text and title in English, French, German and Italian) 1917. 6/yr. 198 SFr. (foreign 219 SFr.). (Schweizerische Neurologische Gesellschaft) Orell Fuessli Graphische Betriebe AG, Dietzingerstr. 3, CH-8036 Zurich, Switzerland. (Co-sponsor: Schweizerische Gesellschaft fuer Psychiatrie) Ed.Bd. adv.; bk.rev.; charts; illus.; index per vol.; circ. 750. (also avail. in microform from UMI; reprint service avail. from UMI) **Indexed:** Biol.Abstr., Chem.Abstr., Curr.Cont., Excerp.Med., Ind.Med., Ind.Vet., Nutr.Abstr., Psychol.Abstr., Vet.Bull.

616.8   JA   ISSN 0488-1281
SEISHIN IGAKU/CLINICAL PSYCHIATRY. (Text in Japanese; summaries in English) 1959. m. 22320 Yen($172) Igaku-Shoin Ltd., 5-24-3 Hongo, Bunkyo-ku, Tokyo 113-91, Japan. TEL 03-817-5711. Ed.Bd. circ. 6,000.
●Also available online. Vendor(s): JICST.
—BLDSC shelfmark: 3286.340000.

616.8   JA   ISSN 0080-8547
SEISHIN IGAKU KENKYUJO, TOKYO. GYOSEKISHU/SEISHIN IGAKU INSTITUTE OF PSYCHIATRY, TOKYO. BULLETIN. (Text in Japanese; table of contents and summaries in English) 1954. a. free. Seishin Igaku Institute of Psychiatry - Seishin Igaku Kenkyujo, 11-11 Komone 4-chome, Itabashi-ku, Tokyo 173, Japan. FAX 03-956-9644. (reprint service avail.) **Indexed:** Biol.Abstr., Excerp.Med.

616.8   UK   ISSN 1059-1311
▼**SEIZURE.** 1992. 4/yr. $160. Academic Press Ltd., 24-28 Oval Rd., London NW1 7DX, England. TEL 071-267-4466. FAX 071-482-2293. TELEX 25775-ACPRES-G. Eds. T. Betts, D. Chadwick.

SEMINARS IN NEUROLOGICAL SURGERY. see *MEDICAL SCIENCES — Surgery*

616.8   US   ISSN 0271-8235
CODEN: SEMNEP
SEMINARS IN NEUROLOGY. 1980. q. $75 to individuals; institutions $99. Thieme Medical Publishers, Inc., 381 Park Ave. So., Ste. 1501, New York, NY 10016. TEL 212-683-5088. Ed. David Goldblatt, M.D. adv.; abstr.; bibl.; charts; illus.; stat.; index. (also avail. in microform from UMI) **Indexed:** Curr.Adv.Ecol.Sci., Curr.Cont.
●Also available online. Vendor(s): BRS.
—BLDSC shelfmark: 8239.455550.

616.8   UK   ISSN 1044-5765
CODEN: SNEUEZ
SEMINARS IN NEUROSCIENCES SERIES. m. $75. Harcourt Brace Jovanovich, 24-28 Oval Rd., London NW1 7DX, England.
—BLDSC shelfmark: 8239.455580.
Description: For scientists in the neurological sciences, as well as the life sciences.

616.89   CC
SHANGHAI JINGSHEN YIXUE/SHANGHAI PSYCHIATRY. (Text in Chinese) q. Shanghai Shi Jingshen Weisheng Zhongxin - Shanghai Municipal Psychiatic Hygiene Center, 600 Wanping Nanlu, Shanghai 200030, People's Republic of China. TEL ND from CPFC, p.170 91345.

616.8 617.7   JA   ISSN 0389-5610
SHINKEI GAISHO/NEUROTRAUMATOLOGY. Variant title: Nihon Shinkei Gaisho Kenkyukai Koenshu. (Text in Japanese; summaries in English) 1979. a. 5000 Yen. Japanese Society of Neurotraumatology - Nihon Shinkei Gaisho Kenkyukai, Tokyo Jikei University School of Medicine, Department of Neurosurgery, 3-25-8, Nishi-Shinbashi, Minato-ku, Tokyo 105, Japan. circ. 1,000. (back issues avail.)

618   JA   ISSN 0470-8105
CODEN: NMCHBN
SHINKEI GEKA. English edition: Neurologia Medico-Chirurgica (ISSN 0387-2572) (Text in Japanese; summaries in English) 1959. m. Japan Neurosurgical Society - Nihon Noshinkei Geka Gakkai, Department of Neurosurgery, Faculty of Medicine, University of Tokyo, 7-3-1 Hongo, Bunkyo-ku, Tokyo 113, Japan. **Indexed:** Biol.Abstr., Dent.Ind., Excerp.Med., Ind.Med.

616.8   JA   ISSN 0037-3796
SHINKEI KAGAKU/JAPANESE NEUROCHEMICAL SOCIETY. BULLETIN. (Text in Japanese) 1962. a. price varies. Japanese Neurochemical Society - Nihon Shinkei Kagakkai, c/o Business Center for Academic Studies, 4-16, Yayoi 2-chome, Bunkyo-ku, Tokyo 113, Japan. Ed. Yasuo Kakimoto. adv.; bk.rev.; bibl.; circ. 1,500. (processed) **Indexed:** Biol.Abstr., Chem.Abstr.
—BLDSC shelfmark: 2593.910000.
Formerly: Nerve Chemistry.

616.8   JA   ISSN 0001-8724
CODEN: SKNSAF
SHINKEI KENKYU NO SHINPO/ADVANCES IN NEUROLOGICAL SCIENCES. (Text in Japanese; summaries in European languages) 1966. bi-m. 29,100 Yen($224) Igaku-Shoin Ltd., 5-24-3 Hongo, Bunkyo-ku, Tokyo 113-91, Japan. TEL 03-817-5702. Ed.Bd. circ. 3,000. **Indexed:** Biol.Abstr., Chem.Abstr., Excerp.Med., Ind.Med.
—BLDSC shelfmark: 0709.480000.

616.8   JA   ISSN 0385-0307
CODEN: SHIGD4
SHINSHIN-IGAKU/JAPANESE JOURNAL OF PSYCHOSOMATIC MEDICINE. (Text in Japanese; summaries in English) 1976. 7/yr. 10990 Yen($85) (Japanese Society of Psychosomatic Medicine) Igaku-Shoin Ltd., 5-24-3 Hongo, Bunkyo-ku, Tokyo 113-91, Japan. TEL 03-817-5711. Ed.Bd. circ. 4,500.
●Also available online. Vendor(s): JICST.
—BLDSC shelfmark: 4658.340000.

SIGNAL'NAYA INFORMATSIYA. NEIROPEPTIDY. see *MEDICAL SCIENCES — Abstracting, Bibliographies, Statistics*

616.8   US   ISSN 0161-8105
QP425   CODEN: SLEED6
SLEEP. 1978. bi-m. $129 to individuals; institutions $180. (American Sleep Disorders Association) American Sleep Disorders Association, c/o Allen Press, 1041 New Hampshire St., Box 368, Lawrence, KS 66044. TEL 913-843-1234. FAX 913-843-1244. (Co-publisher: Sleep Research Society) (Co-sponsors: European Sleep Research Society, Latin American Sleep Research Society, Japanese Sleep Research Society) Ed. Christian Guilleminault. adv.; bk.rev.; index; circ. 3,000. (back issues avail.) **Indexed:** ASCA, Bibl.Dev.Med.& Child Neur., Dent.Ind., Excerp.Med., Ind.Med., Psychol.Abstr., Risk Abstr.
—BLDSC shelfmark: 8309.440000.
Description: Focuses on sleep and circadian rhythms.

616.8   US   ISSN 0093-0407
SLEEP RESEARCH. 1972. a. $85. Brain Research Institute, Brain Information Service, University of California, Los Angeles, No. 43-367 CHS, Los Angeles, CA 90024-1746. TEL 213-825-3417. Ed.Bd. bk.rev.; abstr.; bibl.; circ. 2,000. (back issues avail.)
—BLDSC shelfmark: 8309.460000.
Description: Current claims and abstracts from the annual meeting of the Association of Professional Sleep Societies.

616.89   GW   ISSN 0933-7954
RC321   CODEN: SPPEEM
SOCIAL PSYCHIATRY AND PSYCHIATRIC EPIDEMIOLOGY/SOZIALPSYCHIATRIE/PSYCHIATRIE SOCIALE. (Text mainly in English; also French and German) 1966. 6/yr. DM.478($211) Springer-Verlag, Heidelberger Platz 3, D-1000 Berlin 33, Germany. TEL 030-8207-1. (Also: Heidelberg, Tokyo, Vienna, and New York) Ed. R.S. Daniels. adv.; charts; illus.; index. (also avail. in microform from UMI; reprint service avail. from ISI) **Indexed:** Biol.Abstr., Curr.Cont., Excerp.Med., Psychol.Abstr., SSCI, Trop.Dis.Bull.
Formerly: Social Psychiatry (ISSN 0037-7813)
Description: Concerned with the effects of social conditions on behavior, and the relationship between psychiatric disorders and the social environment.

SOCIOLOGY OF HEALTH AND ILLNESS. see *SOCIOLOGY*

616.836   SA   ISSN 0036-0600
SOUTH AFRICAN CEREBRAL PALSY JOURNAL/SUID-AFRIKAANSE TYDSKRIF VIR SEREBRAALVERLAMMING. 1956. 3/yr. R.8. National Council for the Physically Disabled in South Africa, P.O. Box 426, Melville 2109, South Africa. adv.; bk.rev.; illus.; circ. 1,200. **Indexed:** Excerp.Med, Ind.S.A.Per., Sp.Ed.Needs Abstr.

606.89   US   ISSN 1047-6334
SOUTHERN CALIFORNIA PSYCHIATRIST. 1955. 11/yr. $25. Southern California Psychiatric Society, 2425 Colorado Ave., Ste. 314, Santa Monica, CA 90404-3540. TEL 213-450-4610. FAX 213-392-2505. Ed. Dr. Elizabeth Galton. adv.; bk.rev.; film rev.; play rev.; circ. 1,900.
Formerly (until Aug. 1988): Southern California Psychiatric Society. Newsletter.

SOVIET MEDICAL REVIEWS. SECTION G: NEUROPHARMACOLOGY REVIEWS. see *PHARMACY AND PHARMACOLOGY*

SOZIALPSYCHIATRISCHE INFORMATIONEN. see *PSYCHOLOGY*

MEDICAL SCIENCES — PSYCHIATRY AND NEUROLOGY

616.8   GW   ISSN 0341-9738
SPEKTRUM DER PSYCHIATRIE UND NERVENHEILKUNDE.
1971. bi-m. DM.33. Deutscher Aerzte-Verlag GmbH, Dieselstr. 2, Postfach 400265, 5000 Cologne 40, Germany. TEL 02234-7011-0.
FAX 02234-7011444. adv.; circ. 6,000.
Description: Clinical and scientific information for psychiatrists and neurologists.

616.8   SZ   ISSN 1011-6125
CODEN: SFUNE4
STEREOTACTIC AND FUNCTIONAL NEUROSURGERY.
(Text in English) 1938. 8/yr (in 2 vols.).
216 Fr.($144) per vol. (World Society for Stereotactic and Functional Neurosurgery) S. Karger AG, Allschwilerstr. 10, P.O. Box, CH-4009 Basel, Switzerland. TEL 061-3061111.
FAX 061-3061234. TELEX CH 962652. Ed. P.L. Gildenberg. adv.; bibl.; illus.; charts; index; circ. 1,000. (also avail. in microform from RPI; back issues avail.) **Indexed:** Bibl.Dev.Med.& Child Neur., Biol.Abstr., Chem.Abstr., Curr.Adv.Ecol.Sci., Curr.Cont., Dent.Ind., Excerp.Med., Helminthol.Abstr., Ind.Med., Ind.Sci.Rev., Psychol.Abstr., Sci.Cit.Ind.
—BLDSC shelfmark: 8464.368000.
Former titles: Applied Neurophysiology (ISSN 0302-2773); Confinia Neurologia (ISSN 0010-5678)

616.8   UK   ISSN 0748-8386
CODEN: STMEEZ
STRESS MEDICINE. 1985. q. $395 (effective 1992). John Wiley & Sons Ltd., Journals, Baffins Lane, Chichester, Sussex PO19 1UD, England.
TEL 0243-779777. FAX 0243-775878. TELEX 86290 WIBOOK G. Ed. David Wheatley. adv.; bk.rev. (back issues avail.; reprint service avail. from SWZ) **Indexed:** Curr.Adv.Ecol.Sci., Curr.Cont., Excerp.Med., Psychol.Abstr., Risk Abstr.
—BLDSC shelfmark: 8474.129500.
Description: Provides a forum for the discussion of all aspects of stress which affect the individual in both health and disease.

STRESSFORSKNINGSRAPPORTER. see *PSYCHOLOGY*

STUDIES IN NEUROSCIENCE. see *MEDICAL SCIENCES — Surgery*

616.8   US   ISSN 0172-5742
STUDIES OF BRAIN FUNCTION. 1977. irreg. price varies. Springer-Verlag, 175 Fifth Ave., New York, NY 10010. TEL 212-460-1500. (Also Berlin, Heidelberg, Tokyo and Vienna) Ed.Bd. (reprint service avail. from ISI) **Indexed:** Biol.Abstr.

SUICIDE AND LIFE-THREATENING BEHAVIOR. see *PSYCHOLOGY*

616.8 360   GW   ISSN 0173-458X
SUIZIDPROPHYLAXE. 1973. q. DM.64. (German Association of Suicide Prevention) S. Roderer Verlag, Postfach 110506, 8400 Regensburg, Germany. TEL 0941-72281. FAX 0941-709648. Eds. Michel Heinrich, Hans Wedler. adv.; bk.rev.; circ. 1,000. (back issues avail.)
—BLDSC shelfmark: 8515.760000.

SURGICAL NEUROLOGY. see *MEDICAL SCIENCES — Surgery*

616.8   US
SYNAPSE (NEW YORK). m. $558 (foreign $708). John Wiley & Sons, Inc., Journals, 605 Third Ave., New York, NY 10158. TEL 212-850-6000.
FAX 212-850-6088. TELEX 12-7063. Ed. John E. Johnson, Jr. adv.; circ. 166.
Description: Embraces new basic and clinical research pertaining to all aspects of synaptic structure and function, including attention to practical clinical consideration.

616.8   GW   ISSN 0933-3053
SYSTEM FAMILIE; Forschung und Therapie. 4/yr. DM.98($66) Springer-Verlag, Heidelberger Platz 3, D-1000 Berlin 33, Germany. TEL 030-8207-1.
—BLDSC shelfmark: 8589.151500.

616.8   GW   ISSN 0935-3224
T W NEUROLOGIE - PSYCHIATRIE. 1987. bi-m. DM.125. Verlag G. Braun GmbH, Karl-Friedrich-Str. 14, Postfach 1709, 7500 Karlsruhe 1, Germany. TEL 0721-165-0. FAX 0721-165-227.
—BLDSC shelfmark: 9076.749500.

616.8   SZ   ISSN 1013-2791
TANIGUCHI SYMPOSIA ON BRAIN SCIENCES. no.11, 1988. irreg. (approx. a). price varies. (Taniguchi Foundation, Division of Brain Science) S. Karger AG, Allschwilerstr. 10, P.O. Box, CH-4009 Basel, Switzerland. TEL 061-3061111.
FAX 061-3061234. TELEX CH 962652. Ed. O. Hayaishi.
Description: Contains original in vitro and in vivo studies in numerous physiological aspects of the brain. Caters to fields of genetics and pathology.

616.8   SZ   ISSN 0250-4952
THERAPIE FAMILIALE. (Text in French) 1980. q. 64 SFr.($46) Editions Medecine et Hygiene, Case Postale 456, CH-1211 Geneva 4, Switzerland.
TEL 022-469355. FAX 022-475610. Ed.Bd.
—BLDSC shelfmark: 8814.754000.

THERMOLOGY. see *BIOLOGY — Physiology*

616.89   NE   ISSN 0303-7339
CODEN: TPSYB3
TIJDSCHRIFT VOOR PSYCHIATRIE. (Summaries in English) vol.15, 1973. 10/yr. fl.83.25 (students fl.41.50)(effective 1992). (Nederlandse Vereniging voor Psychiaters in Dienstverband) Uitgeverij Boom, P.O. Box 1058, 7940 KB Meppel, Netherlands.
TEL 05220-66111. FAX 05220-66198. Ed. Dr. P.J. Jongerius. adv.; bk.rev.; illus.; index; circ. 3,600. **Indexed:** Excerp.Med., Nutr.Abstr., Psychol.Abstr.
—BLDSC shelfmark: 8844.180000.
Formerly: Nederlands Tijdschrift voor Psychiatrie (ISSN 0028-2197)

616.8   JA
TOKYO-TO SHINKEI KAGAKU SOGO KENKYUJO NENPO/TOKYO METROPOLITAN INSTITUTE OF NEUROSCIENCES. ANNUAL REPORT. (Text in Japanese) 1972. a. Tokyo-to Shinkei Kagaku Sogo Kenkyujo - Tokyo Metropolitan Institute of Neurosciences, 2-6 Musashidai, Fuchu-shi, Tokyo 183, Japan.

616.89   FR   ISSN 0040-9375
BF173.A2
TOPIQUE - REVUE FREUDIENNE. 1969. 2/yr. 290 F. Dunod, 15 rue Gossin, 92543 Montrouge Cedex, France. TEL 33-1-40-92-65-00.
FAX 33-1-40-92-65-97. TELEX 270 004. (Subscr. to: Centrale des Revues, 11 rue Gossin, 92543 Montrouge Cedex, France. TEL 33-1-46-56-52-66) Ed. S. De Mijolla-Mellor. **Indexed:** Psychoanal.Abstr., Psychol.Abstr.
Description: Scope is to offer a place where theoretical reflection and clinical experience in psychoanalysis may enrich each other and confront their conflictual borders.

TRANSACTIONAL ANALYSIS JOURNAL. see *PSYCHOLOGY*

616.89   CN   ISSN 0041-1108
TRANSCULTURAL PSYCHIATRIC RESEARCH REVIEW. (Text in English) 1956. q. Can.$30 to individuals; institutions Can.$46. McGill University, Psychiatry Department, 1033 Pine Ave. W., Montreal, Que. H3A 1A1, Canada. TEL 514-398-7302.
FAX 514-398-4370. Ed. L. J. Kirmayer. adv.; bk.rev.; charts; index,cum.index: 1956-1972; circ. 600. (also avail. in microfilm from UMI; reprint service avail. from UMI) **Indexed:** Excerp.Med., Ind.Med., Psychol.Abstr.
—BLDSC shelfmark: 9020.580500.
Formerly: Transcultural Psychiatric Research Review and Newsletter.
Description: Publishes critical reviews and peer commentary on current research in culture and psychiatry.

TRANSMITTERS, RECEPTORS & SYNAPSES. see *PHARMACY AND PHARMACOLOGY*

TRAVEL MEDICINE INTERNATIONAL. see *TRAVEL AND TOURISM*

616.8   UK   ISSN 0166-2236
CODEN: TNSCDR
TRENDS IN NEUROSCIENCES. (Published in 2 editions: Library ed. and Personal ed. (ISSN 0378-5912)) (Text in English) 1978. m. £239 (effective 1992). Elsevier Science Publishers Ltd., Crown House, Linton Rd., Barking, Essex IG11 8JU, England.
TEL 081-594-7272. FAX 081-594-5942. TELEX 896950 APPSCI G. (N. America dist. addr.: Elsevier Science Publishing Co., Inc., Box 882, Madison Sq. Sta., New York, NY 10159. TEL 212-989-5800) Ed. Gavin Swanson. adv.; bk.rev.; illus.; index; circ. 6,000. (also avail. in microform from RPI; back issues avail.) **Indexed:** ASCA, Biol.Abstr., Chem.Abstr., Curr.Adv.Biochem., Curr.Adv.Cell & Devel.Biol., Curr.Adv.Ecol.Sci., Curr.Adv.Genetics & Molec.Biol., Curr.Cont., Excerp.Med., Ind.Sci.Rev., Psychol.Abstr., Sci.Cit.Ind., Telegen.
Description: For research workers, teachers and students concerned with the structure and function of the brain and with the biological substrates of behavior.
Refereed Serial

616.8   US
U P F NEWSLETTER. 1968. q. $25. United Parkinson Foundation, 360 W. Superior St., Chicago, IL 60610. TEL 312-664-2344. Ed. Judy Rosner. bk.rev.; circ. 38,000.

UNDERSTANDING PEOPLE. see *PSYCHOLOGY*

616.835   US
U.S. CENTERS FOR DISEASE CONTROL. NEUROTROPIC VIRAL DISEASES SURVEILLANCE: POLIOMYELITIS. a. free. U.S. Centers for Disease Control, 1600 Clifton Rd., Atlanta, GA 30333. TEL 404-329-3311.

616.858   US
U.S. CONGRESS: MENTAL HEALTH; legal updates, children & youth updates, federal agencies, state reports, studies on state mental health systems. vol.11, 1972. irreg. (several times a month). $350. National Association of State Mental Health Program Directors, 1101 King St., No. 160, Alexandria, VA 22314. Ed. Harry Schnibbe. circ. 135.
Formerly: U.S. Congress: Mental Health, Mental Retardation.

616.89 301.364   US
URBAN PSYCHIATRY. JOURNAL.* s-a. $9 to individuals; institutions $18. Creedmoor Psychiatric Center, 80-45 Winchester Blvd., Queens Village, NY 11427. TEL 718-464-7500. **Indexed:** Psychol.Abstr.

616.8   CN   ISSN 0083-5196
VANCOUVER NEUROLOGICAL CENTRE. ANNUAL REPORTS. a. free. Vancouver Neurological Centre, 1195 W. 8th Ave., Vancouver, B.C. V6H 1C5, Canada. TEL 604-734-2221.

616.8   SZ   ISSN 1016-6262
▼**VERHALTENSTHERAPIE.** 1991. q. 109 Fr.($73) S. Karger AG, Allschwilerstr. 10, P.O. Box, CH-4009 Basel, Switzerland. TEL 061-3061111.
FAX 061-3061234. Eds. I. Hand, H.-U. Wittchen.
—BLDSC shelfmark: 9156.600000.

616.8   UK   ISSN 0952-5238
QP474   CODEN: VNEUEY
VISUAL NEUROSCIENCE. 1988. m. $120 to individuals; institutions $295. Cambridge University Press, Edinburgh House, Shaftesbury Rd., Cambridge CB2 2RU, England. TEL 0223-312393.
FAX 0223-315052. TELEX 851817256. (North American addr.: Cambridge University Press, 40 W. 20th St., New York, NY 10011) Ed. Katherine V. Fite. **Indexed:** Curr.Cont., Sci.Cit.Ind.
—BLDSC shelfmark: 9241.296000.
Description: Theoretical and research-based articles on visual neuroscience, with primary emphasis on retinal and brain mechanisms underlying visually-guided behavior and visual perception.

VOPROSY NEIROKHIRURGII/JOURNAL OF NEUROSURGICAL PROBLEMS. see *MEDICAL SCIENCES — Surgery*

WERKSTATTSCHRIFTEN ZUR SOZIALPSYCHIATRIE. see *PSYCHOLOGY*

MEDICAL SCIENCES — RADIOLOGY AND NUCLEAR MEDICINE

616.89 AU ISSN 0084-1609
WORLD CONGRESS OF PSYCHIATRY. PROCEEDINGS. 1950. irreg., 5th, 1971, Mexico. $100. World Psychiatric Association, c/o Prof. P. Berner, Psychiatrische Universitaetsklinik, Lazarettg. 14, A-1097 Vienna, Austria. (Proceedings of 5th, 1971 avail. from: Excerpta Medica, Box 211, Amsterdam, Netherlands) Ed.Bd.

616.89 US ISSN 0043-860X
RC475
WORLD JOURNAL OF PSYCHOSYNTHESIS. 1969. biennial. $20. (Michigan Institute of Psychosynthesis) World Journal Press, Box 859, E. Lansing, MI 48823. TEL 517-372-4660. FAX 517-372-9959. Ed. Dr. H.C. Tien. adv.; bk.rev.; bibl.; charts; illus.; stat.; index; circ. 1,000. (also avail. in microfilm from UMI; reprint service avail. from UMI)
Refereed Serial

616.8 617 US ISSN 0513-5117
RC329
YEAR BOOK OF NEUROLOGY & NEUROSURGERY. 1902. a. $54.95. Mosby - Year Book, Inc., Continuity Division, 200 N. LaSalle, Chicago, IL 60601. TEL 312-726-9733. FAX 312-726-6075. TELEX 206155. Eds. Drs. Robert D. Currier, Robert M. Crowell. (reprint service avail.) **Indexed:** Curr.Adv.Ecol.Sci.
●Also available online. Vendor(s): BRS.

YEAR BOOK OF NEURORADIOLOGY. see *MEDICAL SCIENCES — Radiology And Nuclear Medicine*

616.89 US ISSN 0084-3970
RC329
YEAR BOOK OF PSYCHIATRY AND APPLIED MENTAL HEALTH. 1970. a. $54.95. Mosby - Year Book, Inc., Continuity Division, 200 N. LaSalle, Chicago, IL 60601. TEL 312-726-9733. FAX 312-726-6075. TELEX 206155. Ed. Dr. John A. Talbott. (reprint service avail.)
●Also available online. Vendor(s): BRS.
—BLDSC shelfmark: 9415.700000.

ZEITSCHRIFT FUER GERONTOPSYCHOLOGIE UND PSYCHIATRIE. see *GERONTOLOGY AND GERIATRICS*

616.89 SZ ISSN 0301-6811
ZEITSCHRIFT FUER KINDER- UND JUGENDPSYCHIATRIE. 1973. q. 88 Fr. Verlag Hans Huber, Laenggassstr. 76, Postfach, CH-3000 Berne 9, Switzerland. TEL 031-24-25-33. FAX 031-24-33-80. TELEX 911886-HAHU. Ed.Bd. circ. 1,300. **Indexed:** Biol.Abstr., Curr.Cont., Excerp.Med., Psychol.Abstr., SSCI.
—BLDSC shelfmark: 9467.480000.

616.8 GW ISSN 0300-869X
CODEN: ZKPPAP
ZEITSCHRIFT FUER KLINISCHE PSYCHOLOGIE UND PSYCHOTHERAPIE. 1951. q. DM.58. (Goerres-Gesellschaft) Karl Alber GmbH, Hermann-Herder-Str. 4, 7800 Freiburg, Germany. Ed.Bd. adv.; bk.rev.; index; circ. 1,000. **Indexed:** Biol.Abstr., Excerp.Med., Ger.J.Psych., Ind.Med., Lang.& Lang.Behav.Abstr., Psychol.Abstr.
Formerly: Jahrbuch fuer Psychologie, Psychotherapie, und Medizinische Anthropologie (ISSN 0021-4000)

616.89 GW ISSN 0340-5613
CODEN: ZPPSB2
ZEITSCHRIFT FUER PSYCHOSOMATISCHE MEDIZIN UND PSYCHOANALYSE. (Text in German; summaries in English and German) 1954. q. DM.116. Vandenhoeck und Ruprecht, Theaterstr. 13, Postfach 3753, 3400 Goettingen, Germany. TEL 0551-6959-22. FAX 0551-695917. Eds. Annemarie Duehrssen, Rudolf Adam. adv.; bk.rev.; abstr.; index; circ. 1,100. **Indexed:** Biol.Abstr., CERDIC, Curr.Cont., Ger.J.Psych., Ind.Med., Nutr.Abstr., Psychoanal.Abstr., Psychol.Abstr., Risk Abstr., SSCI.
—BLDSC shelfmark: 9485.270000.
Formerly: Zeitschrift fuer Psycho-Somatische Medizin (ISSN 0044-3395)

150 616.89 GW ISSN 0085-8412
ZEITSCHRIFT FUER PSYCHOSOMATISCHE MEDIZIN UND PSYCHOANALYSE. BEIHEFTE. 1970. irreg., no.13, 1990. price varies. Vandenhoeck und Ruprecht, Theaterstr. 13, Postfach 3753, 3400 Goettingen, Germany. TEL 0551-6959-22. FAX 0551-695917. **Indexed:** Psychol.Abstr., SSCI.

616.8 GW ISSN 0044-4251
ZENTRALBLATT FUER NEUROCHIRURGIE. (Text and summaries in English and German) 1936. 4/yr. DM.88. Johann Ambrosius Barth Verlag, Leipzig - Heidelberg, Salomonstr. 18b, 7010 Leipzig, Germany. TEL 70131. Ed. W. Bock. adv.; bk.rev.; abstr.; illus.; index per vol. **Indexed:** Biol.Abstr., Dent.Ind., Ind.Med.
—BLDSC shelfmark: 9511.300000.

616.8 CC
ZHONGHUA SHENJING-JINGSHENKE ZAZHI/CHINESE JOURNAL OF NEUROLOGY AND PSYCHOLOGY. (Text in Chinese) bi-m. $3 per no. Guoji Shudian, Qikan Bu, Chegongzhuang Xilu 21, P.O. Box 399, Beijing 100044, People's Republic of China. **Indexed:** Ind.Med.

616.8 CC ISSN 1001-2346
ZHONGHUA SHENJING WAIKE ZAZHI/CHINESE JOURNAL OF NEUROSURGERY. (Text in Chinese; summaries in English) 1985. q. Y11($2) per no. Beijing Neurosurgical Institute, No.6, Tiantan Xili, Beijing, People's Republic of China. (Co-sponsor: Chinese Medical Association) Ed. Jia Zengfu. adv.; bk.rev.; index; circ. 7,000. (back issues avail.)

616.8 RU ISSN 0044-4588
CODEN: ZNPIAP
ZHURNAL NEVROPATOLOGII I PSIKHIATRII IM. S.S. KORSAKOVA/JOURNAL OF NEUROPATHOLOGY AND PSYCHIATRY. S.S. KORSAKOV. (Text in Russian; summaries in English) 1901. m. 31.80 Rub.($27.60) (Vsesoyuznoe Nauchnoe Obshchestvo Nevropatologov i Psikhiatrov) Izdatel'stvo Meditsina, Petroverigskii pereulok 6-8, 101838 Moscow, Russia. (Co-sponsor: Ministerstvo Zdravookhraneniya S.S.S.R.) Ed. L.O. Badalyan. bk.rev.; bibl.; index. **Indexed:** Bibl.Dev.Med.& Child Neur., Biol.Abstr., Biotech.Abstr., Chem.Abstr., Curr.Cont., Dent.Ind., Ind.Med., Int.Aerosp.Abstr., Nutr.Abstr., Psychol.Abstr.
—BLDSC shelfmark: 0061.500000.
Description: Disseminates medical aid to patients by publishing original scientific investigations in etiology and pathogenesis, including the prevention and treatment of neurological and mental diseases.

ZHURNAL VYSSHEI NERVNOI DEYATEL'NOSTI. see *BIOLOGY — Physiology*

MEDICAL SCIENCES — Radiology And Nuclear Medicine

615.842 CN
A A M R T JOURNAL. vol.18, 1982. 3/yr. Can.$7. Alberta Association of Medical Radiation Technologists, Red Deer Regional Hospital Centre, P.O. Bag 5030, Red Deer, Alta. T4N 6N2, Canada. Ed. Pat Kehoe. adv.; circ. 1,500.

615.842 US ISSN 0884-1454
R895.A4
A B M S DIRECTORY OF CERTIFIED NUCLEAR MEDICINE SPECIALISTS. 1984. biennial. $24.95. American Board of Medical Specialties, One Rotary Center, Ste. 805, Evanston, IL 60201. TEL 708-491-9091. FAX 708-328-3596. Ed. Dr. J. Lee Dockery.

615.842 US ISSN 0883-1238
R895.A4
A B M S DIRECTORY OF CERTIFIED RADIOLOGISTS. 1985. biennial. $39.95. American Board of Medical Specialties, One Rotary Center, Ste. 805, Evanston, IL 60201. TEL 708-491-9091. FAX 708-328-3596. Ed. Dr. J. Lee Dockery.

615.842 US ISSN 0098-6070
A C R BULLETIN. 1942. m. $40. American College of Radiology, 1891 Preston White Dr., Reston, VA 22091. FAX 703-648-9176. Ed. Marion Dinitz. illus.; circ. 24,200. **Indexed:** Med.Care Rev.
Former titles (until 1968): American College of Radiology. Bulletin (ISSN 0002-8037); (until 1958): American College of Radiology. Monthly Newsletter.
Description: Provides organization news and member information, and examines current issues in radiology.

615.842 US
A H R A ANNOUNCEMENT. 1982. m. membership. American Healthcare Radiology Administrators, 111 Boston Post Rd., Box 334, Sudbury, MA 01776. TEL 508-443-7591. Ed. Teresa V. Cryan. circ. 3,500. (back issues avail.)

615.842 US ISSN 0195-6108
RC349.R3
A J N R. (American Journal of Neuroradiology) 1980. bi-m. $133 to individuals; institutions $160. (American Society of Neuroradiology) Williams & Wilkins, 428 E. Preston St., Baltimore, MD 21202. TEL 301-528-4000. FAX 301-528-4312. Ed. Michael I. Huckman. adv.; bk.rev.; circ. 5,460. (also avail. in microfilm from WWS; back issues avail.) **Indexed:** Curr.Cont., Dent.Ind., Excerp.Med., Helminthol.Abstr., Ind.Med., Ind.Sci.Rev., INIS Atomind., Rev.Med.& Vet.Mycol., Sci.Cit.Ind.
—BLDSC shelfmark: 0828.400000.
Description: Original clinical articles on imaging diagnosis of the CNS, including the spine, for radiologists, neuroradiologists, neurosurgeons and neurologists.
Refereed Serial

615.842 US ISSN 0361-803X
RM845 CODEN: AJROAM
A J R. (American Journal of Roentgenology) 1906. m. $125 to individuals; institutions $135. (American Roentgen Ray Society) Williams & Wilkins, 428 E. Preston St., Baltimore, MD 21202. TEL 301-528-4000. FAX 301-528-4312. (Co-sponsor: American Radium Society) Ed. Robert N. Berk, M.D. adv.; bk.rev.; abstr.; bibl.; illus.; index; cum.index every 5 yrs.; circ. 22,500. (also avail. in microform; microfilm from WWS) **Indexed:** Bibl.Dev.Med.& Child Neur., Biol.Abstr., Biotech.Abstr., C.I.S. Abstr., Chem.Abstr., Curr.Adv.Cancer Res., Curr.Adv.Ecol.Sci., Curr.Cont, Dent.Ind., Excerp.Med., Helminthol.Abstr., I.P.A., Ind.Med., Ind.Sci.Rev., INIS Atomind., Nutr.Abstr., Rev.Plant Path., Risk Abstr., Sci.Cit.Ind.
●Also available online.
—BLDSC shelfmark: 0836.980000.
Former titles (1952-1976): American Journal of Roentgenology, Radium Therapy and Nuclear Medicine (ISSN 0002-9580); (1923-1951): American Journal of Roentgenology and Radium Therapy (ISSN 0092-5632)
Description: Original articles on all aspects of general and diagnostic radiology, covering all current modalities, including MRI.
Refereed Serial

615.842 DK
CODEN: ACRDA8
ACTA RADIOLOGICA. (Text in English) 1921. bi-m. DKK 980 in Europe; elsewhere DKK 1060. (Acta Radiologica, SW) Munksgaard International Publishers Ltd., 35 Noerre Soegade, P.O. Box 2148, DK-1016 Copenhagen K, Denmark. TEL 33-127030. FAX 33-129387. TELEX 19431-MUNKS-DK. Ed. Erik Boijsen, M.D. adv.; bk.rev.; bibl.; illus.; index; cum.index; circ. 3,500. **Indexed:** ASCA, Biol.Abstr., Biotech.Abstr., Chem.Abstr., Curr.Adv.Cell & Devel.Biol., Curr.Adv.Ecol.Sci., Curr.Cont., Dent.Ind., Excerp.Med., Helminthol.Abstr., Ind.Med., Ind.Sci.Rev., Met.Abstr., Nutr.Abstr., Sci.Abstr., Sci.Cit.Ind.
Formerly: Acta Radiologica. Series 1: Diagnosis (ISSN 0567-8056)

615.842 658 US ISSN 0738-6974
ADMINISTRATIVE RADIOLOGY; the journal of medical imaging administration & management. 1981. m. $42 (Canada $72; elsewhere $96)(effective Dec. 1990). Glendale Publishing Corp., 1305 Glenoaks Blvd., Glendale, CA 91201. TEL 818-500-1872. Ed. Darla Haight. adv.; bk.rev.; index. cum.index; circ. 11,412. (also avail. in microform; back issues avail.; reprint service avail. from UMI)
—BLDSC shelfmark: 1583.209500.
Description: Healthcare management publication serving healthcare executives in people, business and administrative management relative to medical imaging and radiation sciences.
Refereed Serial

615.842 US
ADVANCE FOR RADIOLOGIC SCIENCE PROFESSIONALS. w. Merion Publications, 650 Park Ave. W., King of Prussia, PA 19406. TEL 215-265-7812. Ed. Jeff Cope.

ADVANCES IN ECHO-CONTRAST. see *MEDICAL SCIENCES*

MEDICAL SCIENCES — RADIOLOGY AND NUCLEAR MEDICINE

615.842 616.3 US ISSN 1055-808X
▼**ADVANCES IN GASTROINTESTINAL RADIOLOGY**.
1991. a. $69.95. Mosby - Year Book, Inc. (Chicago) (Subsidiary of: Times Mirror Company), 200 N. LeSalle St., Chicago, IL 60601-1080. TEL 312-726-9733. FAX 312-726-6075. TELEX 206155. (Subscr. to: Journal Subscription Services, 11830 Westline Industrial Dr., St. Louis, MO 63146) Eds. Dr. Hans Herlinger, Dr. Alec J. Megivow.
Description: Presents a collection of original review articles by experts in the field, covering the most current trends.

ADVANCES IN X-RAY ANALYSIS. see *TECHNOLOGY: COMPREHENSIVE WORKS*

619 GW ISSN 0939-267X
RC78 CODEN: AKRAE
AKTUELLE RADIOLOGIE. 1948. bi-m. DM.150. Georg Thieme Verlag, Ruedigerstr. 14, Postfach 104853, 7000 Stuttgart 10, Germany. TEL 0711-8931-0. FAX 0711-8931298. Ed.Bd. adv.; index; circ. 2,200. (also avail. in microfilm from UMI; reprint service avail. from UMI) **Indexed:** Biol.Abstr., Dent.Ind., Excerp.Med., Ind.Med.
—BLDSC shelfmark: 0785.865000.
Formed by the 1991 merger of: Roentgen Blaetter (ISSN 0300-8592) & Digitale Bilddiagnostik (ISSN 0724-7591)

615.842 US
AMERICAN BOARD OF NUCLEAR MEDICINE. INFORMATION POLICIES AND PROCEDURES. 1975. a. American Board of Nuclear Medicine, 900 Veteran Ave., Los Angeles, CA 90024. TEL 213-825-6787. FAX 213-825-9433. circ. 1,500.
Description: Information on requirements for certifying examination in nuclear medicine.

AMERICAN JOURNAL OF CARDIAC IMAGING. see *MEDICAL SCIENCES — Cardiovascular Diseases*

615.842 UN
ANIMAL PRODUCTION AND HEALTH NEWSLETTER. (Text in English) 1976. irreg. free. International Atomic Energy Agency, Wagramer Str. 5, Box 100, A-1400 Vienna, Austria. (Co-sponsor: Food and Agriculture Organization) circ. 230. **Indexed:** Nutr.Abstr.

615.842 FR ISSN 0003-4185
CODEN: ANLRAT
ANNALES DE RADIOLOGIE; radiologie clinique, radiobiologie. (Text in English and French) 1958. 8/yr. 1300 F. to individuals (foreign 1795 F.); students 650 F. (foreign 970 F.). (Semaine des Hopitaux) Expansion Scientifique, 15 rue Saint Benoit, 75278 Paris Cedex 06, France. TEL 1-45-48-42-60. FAX 1-45-44-81-55. adv.; bk.rev.; abstr.; charts; illus.; index. **Indexed:** Biol.Abstr., C.I.S. Abstr., Chem.Abstr., Curr.Cont., Excerp.Med., Helminthol.Abstr., Ind.Med., Ind.Sci.Rev., INIS Atomind., Sci.Cit.Ind.
—BLDSC shelfmark: 0995.100000.

615.842 US ISSN 0160-9963
RM845
APPLIED RADIOLOGY; the journal of practical medical imaging and management. 1972. m. $55. Anderson Publishing, Inc., 80 Shore Rd., Port Washington, NY 11050. TEL 516-883-0164. Ed. John McCormack. adv.; bk.rev.; charts; illus.; tr.lit.; cum.index; circ. 31,982. **Indexed:** Biol.Abstr., CINAHL, Excerp.Med., Hosp.Lit.Ind.
—BLDSC shelfmark: 1576.570000.
Former titles: Applied Radiology and Nuclear Medicine (ISSN 0099-2364); Applied Radiology (ISSN 0044-8451)

ARQUIVOS DE REUMATOLOGIA E DOENCAS OSTED ARTICULARES. see *MEDICAL SCIENCES — Rheumatology*

615.842 AT ISSN 0004-8461
CODEN: AURDAW
AUSTRALASIAN RADIOLOGY. 1957. 4/yr. Aus.$75. Royal Australasian College of Radiologists, 37 Lower Fort St., Millers Point, N.S.W. 2000, Australia. TEL 02-247-7797. FAX 02-251-4629. Ed. F.J. Palmer. adv.; bk.rev.; charts; illus.; index, cum.index; circ. 1,900. **Indexed:** Biol.Abstr., Chem.Abstr., Curr.Cont., Dent.Ind., Excerp.Med., Ind.Med., INIS Atomind.
—BLDSC shelfmark: 1796.300000.

615.842 SZ ISSN 1012-5655
CODEN: BILDEZ
BILDGEBUNG/IMAGING. (Text in English, German) 1933. q. 148 Fr.($98) S. Karger AG, Allschwilerstr. 10, P.O. Box, CH-4009 Basel, Switzerland. TEL 061-3061111. FAX 061-3061234. TELEX CH 962652.
—BLDSC shelfmark: 2058.988000.

BIOELECTROMAGNETICS. see *MEDICAL SCIENCES*

615.842 UK ISSN 0007-1285
QC1 CODEN: BJRAAP
BRITISH JOURNAL OF RADIOLOGY. (Supplements avail.) 1896. m. £125 (foreign £140). (British Institute of Radiology) Allen Wells International, Member Line House, Farndon Rd., Market Harborough, Links, England. Eds. J.T. Patton, N.J. McNally. adv.; bk.rev.; abstr.; charts; illus.; stat.; index; circ. 4,600. (back issues avail.) **Indexed:** Biol.Abstr., Biotech.Abstr., C.I.S. Abstr., Chem.Abstr., Curr.Adv.Cancer Res., Curr.Adv.Ecol.Sci., Curr.Cont., Dairy Sci.Abstr., Dent.Ind., Dok.Arbeitsmed., Excerp.Med., Helminthol.Abstr., Ind.Med., Ind.Sci.Rev., INIS Atomind., Nutr.Abstr., Protozool.Abstr., Risk Abstr., Sci.Abstr., Sci.Cit.Ind.
—BLDSC shelfmark: 2323.000000.
Description: Presents research covering the spectrum of radiological disciplines, including radio-diagnosis and therapy, nuclear medicine, ultrasound, NMR, radiobiology, radiation protection, and hyperthermia.

BULLETIN DU CANCER - RADIOTHERAPIE. see *MEDICAL SCIENCES — Cancer*

615.842 CN ISSN 0008-2902
CANADIAN ASSOCIATION OF RADIOLOGISTS. JOURNAL/ASSOCIATION CANADIENNE DES RADIOLOGISTES. JOURNAL. (Text and title in English, French) 1950. bi-m. Can.$105($105) Canadian Medical Association, P.O. Box 8650, Ottawa, Ont. K1G 0G8, Canada. TEL 613-731-9331. FAX 613-523-0937. Ed. Dr. Michel Azouz. adv.; bk.rev.; illus.; index; circ. 2,200. (also avail. in microfilm from UMI; reprint service avail. from UMI) **Indexed:** Biol.Abstr., Chem.Abstr., Curr.Adv.Cancer Res., Curr.Cont., Excerp.Med., Ind.Med., INIS Atomind.
—BLDSC shelfmark: 4722.500000.
Description: Contains original articles, case reports, editorials, technical notes, letters, book reviews, announcements, obituaries.
Refereed Serial

615.842 CN ISSN 0820-5930
CANADIAN JOURNAL OF MEDICAL RADIATION TECHNOLOGY/JOURNAL CANADIEN DES TECHNIQUES EN RADIATION MEDICALE. (Text in English, French) 1943. q. Can.$25($30) Canadian Association of Medical Radiation Technologists - Association Canadienne des Techniciens en Radiation Medicale, Ste. 601, 294 Albert St., Ottawa, Ont. K1P 6E6, Canada. TEL 613-234-0012. FAX 613-234-1097. Ed. S. Besner. adv.; bk.rev.; charts; illus.; stat.; index. cum.index; circ. 9,892. (also avail. in microform from UMI; reprint service avail. from UMI) **Indexed:** Biol.Abstr., CINAHL.
Former titles: Canadian Journal of Radiography, Radiation Therapy, Nuclear Medicine (ISSN 0382-6333); (until 1987): Canadian Journal of Radiography, Radiotherapy, Nuclear Medicine (ISSN 0319-4434); Canadian Journal of Radiography, Radiotherapy, Nucleography (ISSN 0015-4938); (until 1970): Focal Spot.

615.84 CS ISSN 0069-2344
CESKOSLOVENSKA RADIOLOGIE. (Text in Czech or Slovak; summaries in English and Russian) 1946. 6/yr. $48.60. (Ceskoslovenska Radiologicka Spolecnost) Avicenum, Czechoslovak Medical Press, Malostranske nam. 28, 118 02 Prague 1, Czechoslovakia. (Dist. by: Artia, Ve Smeckach 30, 111 27 Prague 1, Czechoslovakia) (Co-sponsor: Ceskoslovenska Lekarska Spolecnost J. Ev. Purkyne) Ed. Dr. J. Kolar. bk.rev.; circ. 1,000. **Indexed:** Curr.Adv.Ecol.Sci., Dent.Ind., Excerp.Med., Ind.Med., INIS Atomind.
—BLDSC shelfmark: 3122.550000.
Formerly: Ceskoslovenska Roentgenologie.

615.8 US ISSN 0899-7071
RC78.7.T6 CODEN: CLIMEB
CLINICAL IMAGING. 1977. q. $176 to institutions (foreign $198)(effective 1992). Elsevier Science Publishing Co., Inc. (New York), 655 Ave. of the Americas, New York, NY 10010. TEL 212-989-5800. FAX 212-633-3965. TELEX 420643 AEP UI. Ed. Dr. Joseph P. Whalen. adv.; bk.rev.; abstr.; charts; illus.; index; circ. 2,200. (also avail. in microform from RPI; back issues avail.; reprint service avail. from ISI) **Indexed:** Biol.Abstr., Comput.Cont., Curr.Cont., Excerp.Med., Ind.Med., INIS Atomind., Sci.Cit.Ind.
—BLDSC shelfmark: 3286.290600.
Former titles: C T: The Journal of Computed Tomography (ISSN 0149-936X); Journal of Computed Tomography; Computed Axial Tomography (ISSN 0145-7616)
Description: Provides information for radiologists, radiology residents, and radiologic technologists. Covers new technology, new applications, and important issues concerning all diagnostic imaging methods.
Refereed Serial

615.842 US ISSN 0363-9762
R895.A1 CODEN: CNMEDK
CLINICAL NUCLEAR MEDICINE. 1976. m. $70 to individuals (foreign $90); institutions $105 (foreign $135). J.B. Lippincott Co., E. Washington Sq., Philadelphia, PA 19105. TEL 215-238-4200. Ed. Dr. Sheldon Baum. adv.; illus.; index.; circ. 3,072. (also avail. in microform from UMI) **Indexed:** Biol.Abstr., Curr.Adv.Cancer Res., Curr.Cont., Dent.Ind., Excerp.Med., Ind.Med., Ind.Sci.Rev., INIS Atomind., Protozool.Abstr., Sci.Cit.Ind., SSCI.
—BLDSC shelfmark: 3286.314000.
Refereed Serial

615.842 616.99 UK ISSN 0009-9260
CODEN: CLRAAG
CLINICAL RADIOLOGY. 1949. m. £95 (foreign £109). (Royal College of Radiologists) Blackwell Scientific Publications Ltd., Osney Mead, Oxford OX2 0EL, England. TEL 0865-240201. FAX 0865-721205. TELEX 833355-MEDBOK-G. Ed. P. Armstrong. adv.; bk.rev.; index. cum.index: 1970-1979. (also avail. in microfilm) **Indexed:** Biol.Abstr., C.I.S. Abstr., Curr.Adv.Cancer Res., Curr.Adv.Ecol.Sci., Curr.Cont., Dent.Ind., Excerp.Med., Helminthol.Abstr., Ind.Med., INIS Atomind., Sci.Cit.Ind.
—BLDSC shelfmark: 3286.350000.

615.842 US ISSN 0172-4843
COMPREHENSIVE MANUALS IN RADIOLOGY. 1978. irreg. price varies. Springer-Verlag, 175 Fifth Ave., New York, NY 10010. TEL 212-460-1500. (Also Berlin, Heidelberg, Tokyo, Vienna) (reprint service avail. from ISI)

COMPUTERIZED MEDICAL IMAGING AND GRAPHICS; the international journal on imaging and image archiving in all medical specialties. see *MEDICAL SCIENCES — Computer Applications*

616.842 US
CONTEMPORARY NEUROIMAGING. 1990. irreg. price varies. Raven Press, 1185 Ave. of the Americas, New York, NY 10036. TEL 212-930-9500. FAX 212-869-3495.

615.842 US ISSN 1040-8371
RC78.A1 CODEN: CRDIDF
CRITICAL REVIEWS IN DIAGNOSTIC IMAGING. 1970. bi-m. $79.95 to individuals; institutions $325. C R C Press, Inc., 2000 Corporate Blvd., N.W., Boca Raton, FL 33431. TEL 407-994-0555. FAX 407-998-9784. Ed. Yen Wang. bibl.; charts; illus.; circ. 340. (back issues avail.) **Indexed:** Biol.Abstr., Ind.Med., Ind.Sci.Rev., Sci.Cit.Ind.
—BLDSC shelfmark: 3487.474000.
Former titles: C R C Critical Reviews in Diagnostic Imaging (ISSN 0147-6750); C R C Critical Reviews in Clinical Radiology and Nuclear Medicine (ISSN 0091-6536); C R C Critical Reviews in Radiological Sciences and Nuclear Medicine (ISSN 0007-9014)
Refereed Serial

CURRENT OPINION IN RADIOLOGY. see *MEDICAL SCIENCES — Abstracting, Bibliographies, Statistics*

MEDICAL SCIENCES — RADIOLOGY AND NUCLEAR MEDICINE

615.842   US   ISSN 0363-0188
CODEN: CPDRDS
CURRENT PROBLEMS IN DIAGNOSTIC RADIOLOGY. Short title: C P D R. 1972. bi-m. $65 to individuals; institutions $90; students $39; (foreign $85; $110; $59) (effective Jan. 1992). Mosby - Year Book, Inc. (Subsidiary of: Times Mirror Company), 11830 Westline Industrial Dr., St. Louis, MO 63146. TEL 800-325-4177. Ed. Theodore E. Keats. bibl.; illus.; cum.index; circ. 3,000. (also avail. in microform from UMI) **Indexed:** Biol.Abstr., Excerp.Med., Ind.Med.
—BLDSC shelfmark: 3501.380000.
Formerly: Current Problems in Radiology (ISSN 0045-9399)
Description: Provides monographic clinical reviews written by and intended for practitioners.

615.842   UK   ISSN 0250-832X
DENTO MAXILLO FACIAL RADIOLOGY. 1971. 4/yr. £80 in UK and Europe; elsewhere £90. (International Association of Dento Maxillo Facial Radiology) Butterworth - Heinemann Ltd. (Subsidiary of: Reed International PLC), Linacre House, Jordan Hill, Oxford OX2 8DP, England. TEL 0865-310366. FAX 0865-310898. TELEX 83111 BHPOXF G. (Subscr. to: Turpin Transactions Ltd., Distribution Center, Blackhorse Rd., Letchworth, Herts SG6 1HN, England. TEL 0462-672555) Ed. P.N. Hirschmann. adv. (also avail. in microform from UMI; back issues avail.)
—BLDSC shelfmark: 3553.561000.
Description: Contains research papers on radiology of the "lower third" together with clinical reports that illustrate specific uses of diagnostic imaging.
Refereed Serial

615.842   GW   ISSN 0998-433X
DIAGNOSTIC & INTERVENTIONAL RADIOLOGY. (Text in English) 1989. s-a. $175. (French Society of Radiology) Springer-Verlag, Heidelberger Platz 3, 1000 Berlin 33, Germany. TEL 030-8207-0. FAX 030-8214091.

615.842   US   ISSN 0194-2514
DIAGNOSTIC IMAGING. 1979. m. $90 (free to qualified personnel). Miller Freeman, Inc. (Subsidiary of: United Newspapers), 600 Harrison St., San Francisco, CA 94107. TEL 415-905-2200. FAX 415-905-2232. TELEX 278273. Ed. Peter Ogle. adv.; bk.rev.; circ. 28,000. (also avail. in microform from UMI; back issues avail.; reprint service avail. from UMI) **Indexed:** Dent.Ind., Ind.Sci.Rev.
—BLDSC shelfmark: 3579.658050.

615.842   US
DIAGNOSTIC IMAGING & RADIOLOGY PRODUCT COMPARISON SYSTEM. m. $695 (foreign $835). (Emergency Care Research Institute) E C R I, 5200 Butler Pike, Plymouth Meeting, PA 19462. TEL 215-825-6000. FAX 215-834-1275. Ed. Garrett Hayner.
Refereed Serial

615.842   US
DIAGNOSTIC IMAGING INTERNATIONAL. 1985. 7/yr. $65. Miller Freeman, Inc. (Subsidiary of: United Newspapers), 600 Harrison St., San Francisco, CA 94107. TEL 415-905-2200. FAX 415-905-2232. TELEX 278273. Ed. Peter Ogle. circ. 10,000.

615.842   US
DIAGNOSTIC RADIOLOGY SERIES. 1982. irreg., vol.2, 1983. price varies. Marcel Dekker, Inc., 270 Madison Ave., New York, NY 10016. TEL 212-696-9000. FAX 212-685-4540. TELEX 421419. **Indexed:** Biol.Abstr.
Refereed Serial

ENDOCRINOLOGIA IUGOSLAVICA. see *MEDICAL SCIENCES — Endocrinology*

618 619   GW   ISSN 0340-6997
CODEN: EJNMD9
EUROPEAN JOURNAL OF NUCLEAR MEDICINE. 1976. 12/yr. DM.576($324) (European Nuclear Medicine Society) Springer-Verlag, Heidelberger Platz 3, D-1000 Berlin 33, Germany. TEL 030-8207-1. (Also Heidelberg, Tokyo, Vienna, and New York) Ed. P.J. Ell. (also avail. in microfiche from UMI; reprint service avail. from ISI) **Indexed:** Chem.Abstr., Curr.Adv.Cancer Res., Curr.Adv.Ecol.Sci., Curr.Cont., Excerp.Med., Ind.Med., Ind.Sci.Rev., INIS Atomind., Sci.Abstr., Sci.Cit.Ind.
—BLDSC shelfmark: 3829.731800.

615.842   NE   ISSN 0720-048X
CODEN: EJRADR
EUROPEAN JOURNAL OF RADIOLOGY. (Text in English) 1980. 6/yr. (in 2 vols., 3 nos./vol.) fl.752 (effective 1992). (European Association of Radiology) Elsevier Science Publishers B.V., P.O. Box 211, 1000 AE Amsterdam, Netherlands. TEL 020-5803911. FAX 020-5803598. TELEX 18582 ESPA NL. (Subscr. in U.S. and Canada to: Elsevier Science Publishing Co., Inc., Box 882, Madison Sq. Sta., New York, NY 10159. TEL 212-989-5800) Ed. J.H. Goethlin. adv.; bk.rev.; charts; illus.; index; circ. 800. (reprint service avail. from UMI) **Indexed:** Chem.Abstr., Curr.Cont., Dent.Ind., Excerp.Med., Ind.Med., INIS Atomind.
—BLDSC shelfmark: 3829.738050.
Incorporates (1987-1989): Journal of Medical Imaging (ISSN 0920-5497)
Description: Provides information on the use of radiological and allied medical imaging techniques in clinical diagnosis and practice and of interventional techniques.
Refereed Serial

615.842   GW   ISSN 0938-7994
▼**EUROPEAN RADIOLOGY.** (Text in English) 1991. 6/yr. DM.360. (European Association of Radiology) Springer-Verlag, Heidelberger Platz 3, 1000 Berlin 33, Germany. TEL 030-8207-1. Ed.Bd.
—BLDSC shelfmark: 3829.847300.

615.8   FR   ISSN 0181-9801
FEUILLETS DE RADIOLOGIE. 1961. bi-m. 125 ECU($155) (typically set in Jan.). Masson, 120 bd. Saint-Germain, 75280 Paris Cedex 6, France. TEL 1-46-34-21-60. FAX 1-45-87-29-99. TELEX 202 671 F. Eds. V. Bismuth, M. Blery. circ. 3,800. (also avail. in microform from UMI; reprint service avail. from UMI) **Indexed:** Excerp.Med., INIS Atomind.

615.842   US
FRONTIERS IN EUROPEAN RADIOLOGY. 1982. irreg. price varies. Springer-Verlag, 175 Fifth Ave., New York, NY 10010. TEL 212-460-1500. (Also Berlin, Heidelberg, Tokyo, Vienna) (reprint service avail. from ISI)

615 616.9   SZ   ISSN 0071-9676
CODEN: FRTOA7
FRONTIERS OF RADIATION THERAPY AND ONCOLOGY. (Text in English) 1967. irreg. (approx. 1/yr.). price varies. S. Karger AG, Allschwilerstr. 10, P.O. Box, CH-4009 Basel, Switzerland. TEL 061-3061111. FAX 061-3061234. TELEX CH 962652. Ed. J.L. Meyer. (reprint service avail. from ISI) **Indexed:** Biol.Abstr., Chem.Abstr., Curr.Cont., Dent.Ind., Ind.Med.
—BLDSC shelfmark: 4042.060000.
Description: Covers developments in the treatment of cancer with radiation therapy.

615.842   NE   ISSN 0016-4380
CODEN: GAMMDV
GAMMA. 1950. m. membership. Nederlandse Vereniging van Radiologisch Laboranten, Catharijnesingel 73, 3511 GM Utrecht, Netherlands. Ed. G.J.R. Bos. adv.; bk.rev.; circ. 3,000. **Indexed:** Chem.Abstr.

618   US   ISSN 0364-2356
CODEN: GARADK
GASTROINTESTINAL RADIOLOGY; a journal of diagnostic imaging. 1976. q. $145. Springer-Verlag, Journals, 175 Fifth Ave., New York, NY 10010. TEL 212-460-1500. (And Berlin, Heidelberg, Tokyo and Vienna) Eds. Morton A. Meyers, Gary G. Ghahremani. (also avail. in microform from UMI; reprint service avail. from ISI) **Indexed:** Curr.Cont., Excerp.Med., Helminthol.Abstr., Ind.Med., Ind.Sci.Rev., INIS Atomind., Sci.Cit.Ind.
—BLDSC shelfmark: 4089.070000.

615.842   CC
GUOWAI YIXUE (LINCHUANG FANGSHEXUE FENCE)/FOREIGN MEDICAL SCIENCES (CLINICAL RADIOLOGY). (Text in Chinese) bi-m. Tianjin Fangshe Zhenliao Yanjiu Peixun Zhongxin, 123, Anshan Dao, Tianjin 300052, People's Republic of China. TEL 705960. Ed. Wu Enhui.

612.014   US   ISSN 0073-1498
HEALTH PHYSICS SOCIETY. NEWSLETTER. 1959. m. membership. Health Physics Society, 8000 Westpark Dr., No.400, McLean, VA 22102-3101. Ed. O.L. Cordes. circ. 6,600.

612.014   JA   ISSN 0073-232X
HIROSHIMA UNIVERSITY. RESEARCH INSTITUTE FOR NUCLEAR MEDICINE AND BIOLOGY. PROCEEDINGS/HIROSHIMA DAIGAKU GENBAKU HOSHANO IGAKU KENKYUJO NENPO. (Text in English and Japanese) 1960. a. Hiroshima University, Research Institute for Nuclear Medicine and Biology - Hiroshima Daigaku Genbaku Hoshano Kenkyujo, Kasumi, Hiroshima 734, Japan. Ed.Bd. circ. 450 (controlled). **Indexed:** INIS Atomind.
—BLDSC shelfmark: 6789.310000.

615.842   NO   ISSN 0332-9410
HOLD PUSTEN. 1974. 11/yr. NOK 180. Norsk Radiografforbund, FAX 2-175204. Ed. Per Zaring. adv.; circ. 1,200 (controlled).

I C R D B CANCERGRAM: CANCER DETECTION AND MANAGEMENT - DIAGNOSTIC RADIOLOGY. see *MEDICAL SCIENCES — Abstracting, Bibliographies, Statistics*

I C R D B CANCERGRAM: CANCER DETECTION AND MANAGEMENT - NUCLEAR MEDICINE. see *MEDICAL SCIENCES — Abstracting, Bibliographies, Statistics*

I C R D B CANCERGRAM: CLINICAL TREATMENT OF CANCER - RADIATION THERAPY. see *MEDICAL SCIENCES — Abstracting, Bibliographies, Statistics*

615.842   II   ISSN 0019-560X
CODEN: IJRAAY
INDIAN JOURNAL OF RADIOLOGY. (Text in English) vol.30, 1976. q. Rs.88($13) Indian Radiological Association, 13 Bheemanna Mudali Garden St., Madras 600018, India. Eds. Dr. M.G. Varadarajan, Dr. R. Ganapathi. adv.; bk.rev.; abstr.; bibl.; charts; illus.; stat.; index; circ. 1,500. **Indexed:** Biol.Abstr., Excerp.Med.

615.842   UN
INFORMATION CIRCULAR ON RADIATION TECHNIQUES AND THEIR APPLICATIONS TO INSECT PESTS. (Text in English) 1963. irreg. free. International Atomic Energy Agency, Wagramer Str. 5, Box 100, A-1400 Vienna, Austria. (Co-sponsor: Food and Agriculture Organization) circ. 600. **Indexed:** Rev.Appl.Entomol.

574.191   PL   ISSN 0074-0640
INSTYTUT BADAN JADROWYCH. ZAKLAD RADIOBIOLOGII I OCHRONY ZDROWIA. PRACE DOSWIADCZALNE. (Text in English, French, German or Polish; summaries in English) 1960. irreg., vol.4, 1973. free. Osrodek Informacji o Energii Jadrowej, Palac Kultury i Nauki, Warsaw, Poland. Ed. Maria Kopec. author index.

612   US   ISSN 0146-6453
RA1231.R2   CODEN: ANICD6
INTERNATIONAL COMMISSION ON RADIOLOGICAL PROTECTION. ANNALS. 1960. 4/yr. £105 (effective 1992). Pergamon Press, Inc., Journals Division, 660 White Plains Rd., Tarrytown, NY 10591-5153. TEL 914-524-9200. FAX 914-333-2444. (And: Headington Hill Hall, Oxford OX3 0BW, England. TEL 0865-794141) Ed. H. Smith. (also avail. in microform from MIM,UMI) **Indexed:** Abstr.Hyg., AESIS, Biol.Abstr., C.I.S. Abstr., Curr.Adv.Ecol.Sci., Energy Ind., Energy Info.Abstr., Excerp.Med., Ind.Med., Trop.Dis.Bull. Key Title: Annals of the I C R P.
Formerly: Advances in Radiological Protection.
Description: Covers topics in the field of radiation protection for members of the medical professions and other interested groups.
Refereed Serial

615.84 612.014   FI   ISSN 0074-3933
INTERNATIONAL CONGRESS OF RADIOLOGY. (REPORTS). quadrennial; 17th, 1989, Paris; 18th, 1994, Singapore. International Society of Radiology, c/o Prof. Dr. C.G. Standertskjoeld, Department of Radiology, Helsinki University Central Hospital, 00290 Helsinki, Finland. FAX 0471-4404. Ed. Gomez Lopez Bonmati. circ. 10,000. **Indexed:** Excerp.Med.

INTERNATIONAL JOURNAL OF RADIATION APPLICATIONS AND INSTRUMENTATION. PART A: APPLIED RADIATION AND ISOTOPES; including data, instrumentation and methods for use in agriculture, industry and medicine. see *PHYSICS — Nuclear Physics*

612.014 US ISSN 0883-2897
R895.A1 CODEN: NMBIEO
INTERNATIONAL JOURNAL OF RADIATION APPLICATIONS AND INSTRUMENTATION. PART B: NUCLEAR MEDICINE AND BIOLOGY. 1973. 8/yr. £255 (effective 1992). Pergamon Press, Inc., Journals Division, 660 White Plains Rd., Tarrytown, NY 10591-5153. TEL 914-524-9200. FAX 914-333-2444. (And: Headington Hill Hall, Oxford OX3 0BW, England. TEL 0865-794141) Ed. W.C. Eckelman. adv.; circ. 1,200. (also avail. in microform from MIM,UMI; reprint service avail. from UMI) **Indexed:** Biol.Abstr., Chem.Abstr., Curr.Adv.Ecol.Sci., Curr.Cont., Excerp.Med., Ind.Med., Ind.Sci.Rev., Nutr.Abstr., Sci.Abstr., Sci.Cit.Ind.
—BLDSC shelfmark: 6180.920500.
Formerly (until 1985): International Journal of Nuclear Medicine and Biology (ISSN 0047-0740)
Refereed Serial

INTERNATIONAL JOURNAL OF RADIATION: ONCOLOGY - BIOLOGY - PHYSICS. see *PHYSICS — Nuclear Physics*

615.842 US ISSN 0020-9996
RC78 CODEN: INVRAV
INVESTIGATIVE RADIOLOGY. 1966. m. $110 to individuals (foreign $140); institutions $160 (foreign $200). (Association of University Radiologists) J.B. Lippincott Co., E. Washington Sq., Philadelphia, PA 19105. TEL 215-238-4200. (Co-sponsor: Society of Chairmen of Academic Radiology Depts.) Ed: Dr. Charles E. Putman. adv.; illus.; index; circ. 2,593. (also avail. in microform from UMI; reprint service avail. from UMI) **Indexed:** Biol.Abstr., Biotech.Abstr., Chem.Abstr., Curr.Adv.Cancer Res., Curr.Cont., Excerp.Med., Hosp.Lit.Ind., Ind.Med., Ind.Sci.Rev., INIS Atomind., Sci.Cit.Ind., SSCI.
—BLDSC shelfmark: 4560.350000.
Refereed Serial

615.842 UA ISSN 0021-1907
 CODEN: ISRRAC
ISOTOPE AND RADIATION RESEARCH. (Text in English; summaries in Arabic) 1968. s-a. $20. Middle Eastern Regional Radioisotope Centre for the Arab Countries, Sh. Malaeb el Gamaa, Dokki 11321, Cairo, Egypt. TELEX 2098-94381 PBDKIUN. Ed.Bd. adv.; circ. 500. **Indexed:** Chem.Abstr., Excerp.Med., Soils & Fert.
—BLDSC shelfmark: 4583.325000.

615.842 574 HU ISSN 0865-0497
 CODEN: IZTTA9
IZOTOPTECHNIKA, DIAGNOSZTIKA/ISOTOPE TECHNICS, DIAGNOSTICS. Short title: I T D. (Text in Hungarian; summaries in English) 1958. 4/yr. $25. Magyar Tudomanyos Akademia, Izotopkutato Intezet, P.O. Box 77, 1525 Budapest, Hungary. FAX 1-156-5045. TELEX 225360. (Subscr. to: Kultura, Box 149, 1389 Budapest, Hungary) Ed. Arpad Veres. adv.; bk.rev.; circ. 350. **Indexed:** Biol.Abstr., Chem.Abstr., INIS Atomind., Sci.Abstr.
—BLDSC shelfmark: 4588.535000.
Former titles (until 1989): Izotoptechnika (ISSN 0004-7201); Atomtechnikai Tajekoztato.

615.842 JA
JAPANESE JOURNAL OF CLINICAL RADIOLOGY/RINSHO HOSHASEN. (Text in Japanese; captions and headings in English) 1956. m. 1800 Yen per no. Kanehara & Co., Ltd., 2-31-14 Yushima, Bunkyo-ku, Tokyo 113, Japan. Ed. Dr. Katsutoshi Yoshimura. abstr.; charts; illus.; index; circ. 4,700. **Indexed:** Dent.Ind., Excerp.Med., Ind.Med., Ind.Sci.Rev.
Formerly (until Apr. 1977): Clinical Radiology (ISSN 0009-9252)

574.191 615.842 FR ISSN 0992-3039
 CODEN: JMNBEJ
JOURNAL DE MEDECINE NUCLEAIRE ET BIOPHYSIQUE. (Text and summaries in English and French) 1976. 6/yr. 935 F. (Societe Francaise de Boiphysique et Medecine Nucleaire) Gauthier-Villars, 15 rue Gossin, 92543 Montrouge Cedex, France. TEL 33-1-40-92-65-00. FAX 33-1-40-92-65-97. TELEX 270 004. (Subscr. to: Centrale des Revues, 11 rue Gossin, 92543 Montrouge Cedex, France. TEL 33-1-46-56-52-66) Ed. A. Desgrez. adv.; circ. 700. (also avail. in microform from MIM,UMI; reprint service avail. from UMI) **Indexed:** Chem.Abstr., Curr.Cont., Excerp.Med., Ind.Sci.Rev., Sci.Abstr., Sci.Cit.Ind.
—BLDSC shelfmark: 5017.023000.
Former titles: Journal Francais de Biophysique et Medecine Nucleaire (ISSN 0399-0435); Annales de Physique Biologique and Medicale (ISSN 0029-0793)
Description: Emphasizes current nuclear medicine practices in vivo as well as in vitro.

615.842 FR ISSN 0227-9363
JOURNAL DE RADIOLOGIE. (Text in French; summaries in English) 1914. 10/yr. 235 ECU($285) (typically set in Jan.). (Societe Francaise d'Electroradiologie Medicale et Filiales) Masson, 120 bd. Saint-Germain, 75280 Paris Cedex 06, France. TEL 1-46-34-21-60. FAX 1-45-87-29-99. TELEX 202 671 F. Ed. J.F. Moreau. adv.; bk.rev.; abstr.; illus.; index; circ. 3,400. (also avail. in microform from UMI; reprint service avail. from ISI) **Indexed:** Biol.Abstr., Chem.Abstr., Dent.Ind., Excerp.Med., Helminthol.Abstr., Ind.Med., INIS Atomind.
—BLDSC shelfmark: 5043.972000.
Formerly: Journal de Radiologie d'Electrologie et de Medecine Nucleaire (ISSN 0021-7964)

615.842 US ISSN 1044-5471
 CODEN: JCLSEO
JOURNAL OF CLINICAL LASER MEDICINE & SURGERY. 1983. bi-m. $125 (foreign $165). (International Society for Laser Surgery and Medicine) Mary Ann Liebert, Inc., 1651 Third Ave., New York, NY 10128. TEL 212-289-2300. FAX 212-289-4697. Ed. Dr. Eugene W. Friedman. adv.
—BLDSC shelfmark: 4958.540000.
Former titles: Laser Medicine and Surgery News and Advances; Laser Medicine and Surgery News (ISSN 0736-9417)
Description: Covers advances and expanded applications and procedures, significant clinical and basic research, safety programs, and new instrumentation. Includes profiles of laser institutes, companies, and physicians.

JOURNAL OF CLINICAL ONCOLOGY. see *MEDICAL SCIENCES — Cancer*

615.842 US ISSN 0363-8715
RC78.7.T6 CODEN: JCATD5
JOURNAL OF COMPUTER ASSISTED TOMOGRAPHY; a radiological journal dedicated to the basic and clinical aspects of reconstructive tomography. 1977. bi-m. $116 to individuals; institutions $248. Raven Press, 1185 Ave. of the Americas, New York, NY 10036. TEL 212-930-9500. FAX 212-869-3495. TELEX 640073. Ed. Dr. Giovanni Di Chiro. adv.; bk.rev.; index; circ. 6,000. (back issues avail.) **Indexed:** Bibl.Dev.Med.& Child Neur., Biol.Abstr., Curr.Cont., Chem.Abstr., Excerp.Med., Helminthol.Abstr., Ind.Med., Ind.Sci.Rev., INIS Atomind., Nutr.Abstr., Sci.Abstr., Sci.Cit.Ind.
—BLDSC shelfmark: 4963.650000.
Description: Articles and reports on technological advances in radiology.
Refereed Serial

615.842 UK ISSN 0268-0882
JOURNAL OF INTERVENTIONAL RADIOLOGY. q. £77($149) to individuals; institutions £102.50($197). (B S I R) Churchill Livingstone Medical Journals, Robert Stevenson House, 1-3 Baxter's Pl., Leith Walk, Edinburgh EH1 3AF, Scotland. TEL 031-556-2424. FAX 031-558-1278. (Subscr. to: Longman Group, Journals Subscr. Dept., P.O. Box 77, Fourth Ave., Harlow, Essex CM19 5AA, England; U.S. subscr. to: Churchill Livingstone, 650 Ave. of the Americas, New York, NY 10011. TEL 212-206-5000)
—BLDSC shelfmark: 5007.697000.

615.842 US ISSN 1040-9564
JOURNAL OF J A S T R O. (Text in English, Japanese; summaries in English) 1989. 4/yr. $225 (effective 1992). (Japanese Society for Therapeutic Radiation and Oncology, JA) Pergamon Press, Inc., Journals Division, 660 White Plains Rd., Tarrytown, NY 10591-5153. TEL 914-524-9200. FAX 914-333-2444. (And: Headington Hill Hall, Oxford OX3 0BW, England. TEL 0865-794141) Ed. H. Tsunemoto. abstr. (also avail. in microform; back issues avail.)
—BLDSC shelfmark: 4809.575000.
Description: Reports research focusing on clinical radiation therapy, combined with surgery, chemotherapy and hyperthermia, and on radiation physics and radiation biology.
Refereed Serial

615.842 530 US
▼**JOURNAL OF MAGNETIC RESONANCE IMAGING.** 1991. bi-m. $100. (Society of Magnetic Resonance Imaging) Radiological Society of North America, Inc., 2021 Spring Rd., Ste. 600, Oak Brook, IL 60521. TEL 708-571-7819. FAX 708-571-7837. Ed. Dr. Gary D. Fullerton. adv.; circ. 1,587.
Description: Focuses on research technique, equipment, and clinical applications of the non-invasive diagnostic procedure.

JOURNAL OF NEUROIMAGING. see *MEDICAL SCIENCES — Psychiatry And Neurology*

615.842 FR ISSN 0150-9861
 CODEN: JNEUD3
JOURNAL OF NEURORADIOLOGY - JOURNAL DE NEURORADIOLOGIE. (Text in English, French) q. 175 ECU($213) (typically set in Jan.). (Societe Francaise de Neuroradiologie) Masson, 120 bd. Saint-Germain, 75280 Paris Cedex 06, France. TEL 1-46-34-21-60. FAX 1-45-87-29-99. TELEX 202 671 F. Ed. L. Picard. adv.; bk.rev.; illus.; circ. 1,100. (also avail. in microform from UMI; reprint service avail. from ISI) **Indexed:** Bibl.Dev.Med.& Child Neur., Biol.Abstr., Curr.Cont., Excerp.Med., Ind.Med.
—BLDSC shelfmark: 5022.072000.
Formerly (until Mar. 1978): Journal de Neuroradiologie.

612.014 IT
R61 CODEN: JNBMA
JOURNAL OF NUCLEAR BIOLOGY AND MEDICINE. (Text and summaries in English) 1957. q. L.60000($70) (Italian Association of Biology and Nuclear Medicine) Edizioni Minerva Medica, Corso Bramante 83-85, 10126 Turin, Italy. TEL 11-678282. Ed.Bd. adv.; bk.rev.; bibl.; charts; illus.; index; circ. 2,000. (also avail. in microform from UMI; reprint service avail. from UMI) **Indexed:** C.I.S. Abstr., Chem.Abstr., Curr.Adv.Ecol.Sci., Curr.Cont., Dairy Sci.Abstr., Excerp.Med., Ind.Med., Ind.Sci.Rev., INIS Atomind., Nutr.Abstr., Sci.Abstr.
Former titles (until 1991): Journal of Nuclear Medicine and Allied Sciences (ISSN 0392-0208); Minerva Mediconucleare (ISSN 0026-4857); Minerva Nuclear Medical Section.

615.842 US ISSN 0161-5505
RM845 CODEN: JNMEAQ
JOURNAL OF NUCLEAR MEDICINE. 1960. m. $120 to individuals; institutions $170; students $70. Society of Nuclear Medicine, 136 Madison Ave., New York, NY 10016. TEL 212-889-0717. FAX 212-545-0221. Ed. Dr. H. William Strauss. adv.; bk.rev.; abstr.; bibl.; charts; illus.; index; circ. 13,700. (also avail. in microform from UMI; back issues avail.; reprint service avail. from UMI) **Indexed:** Biol.Abstr., Chem.Abstr., Curr.Adv.Biochem., Curr.Adv.Cancer Res., Curr.Adv.Ecol.Sci., Curr.Cont., Dairy Sci.Abstr., Dent.Ind., Excerp.Med., Helminthol.Abstr., I.P.A., Ind.Med., Ind.Sci.Rev., Ind.Vet., INIS Atomind., Nutr.Abstr., Sci.Abstr., Vet.Bull.
●Also available online.
—BLDSC shelfmark: 5023.300000.
Incorporates: S N M Newsline; **Former titles:** J N M (ISSN 0097-9031); Journal of Nuclear Medicine (ISSN 0022-3123)
Refereed Serial

MEDICAL SCIENCES — RADIOLOGY AND NUCLEAR MEDICINE

615.8   US   ISSN 0091-4916
R895.A1   CODEN: JNMTB4
JOURNAL OF NUCLEAR MEDICINE TECHNOLOGY. 1973. q. $60 (foreign $70). Society of Nuclear Medicine, 136 Madison Ave., New York, NY 10016. TEL 212-889-0717. FAX 212-545-0221. Ed. Susan C. Weiss. adv.; bk.rev.; charts; illus.; index; circ. 5,500. (also avail. in microform from UMI; back issues avail.; reprint service avail. from UMI) **Indexed:** Biol.Abstr., Chem.Abstr., Excerp.Med., I.P.A., INIS Atomind., Sci.Abstr.
● Also available online.
—BLDSC shelfmark: 5023.340000.
Refereed Serial

615   JA
JOURNAL OF RADIATION RESEARCH. (Text in English) 1960. q. $72. (Japan Radiation Research Society) Japan Scientific Societies Press, 6-2-10 Hongo, Bunkyo-ku, Tokyo 113, Japan. TEL 3814-2001. FAX 3814-2002. TELEX 2722268 BCJSP J. (Dist. by: Business Center for Academic Societies Japan; Dist. in U.S. by: International Specialized Book Services, Inc., 5602 N.E. Hassalo St., Portland, OR 97213; in Asia by: Toppan Company Pvt. Ltd., 38 Liu Fang Rd., Box 22 Jurong Town, Jurong, Singapore 2622) adv.; bk.rev.; circ. 1,500. **Indexed:** Biol.Abstr., Biwk.Pap.Rad.Chem.& Photochem., Chem.Abstr., Curr.Adv.Ecol.Sci., Curr.Cont., Dairy Sci.Abstr., Deep Sea Res.& Oceanogr.Abstr., Dent.Ind., Excerp.Med., Ind.Med., Ind.Sci.Rev., INIS Atomind., Pollut.Abstr., Sci.Abstr.
Formerly: Japan Radiation Research Society. Journal (ISSN 0449-3060)

JOURNAL OF RADIOLOGICAL PROTECTION. see
ENERGY — Nuclear Energy

615.842   US
▼**JOURNAL OF VASCULAR AND INTERVENTIONAL RADIOLOGY.** 1990. q. $125. Radiological Society of North America, Inc., 2021 Spring Rd., Ste. 600, Oak Brook, IL 60521. TEL 708-571-7819. FAX 708-571-7837. adv.; circ. 1,691.
Description: Covers clinical and laboratory studies in the field of radiology.
Refereed Serial

615.842   CN   ISSN 0022-7439
K V P NEWS. 1964. q. membership. Manitoba Association of Medical Radiation Technologists Inc., 215-819 Sargent Ave., Winnipeg, Man. R3E 0B9, Canada. TEL 204-774-5346. Ed. E. Kirk. adv.; charts; illus.; circ. 800. (processed)

615.8   JA   ISSN 0022-7854
   CODEN: KAIGBZ
KAKU IGAKU/JAPANESE JOURNAL OF NUCLEAR MEDICINE. Variant title: Nihon Kaku Igakkai Kikanshi. (Text and summaries in English and Japanese) 1964. 12/yr. $150. Japanese Society of Nuclear Medicine - Nihon Kaku Igakkai, c/o Japan Radioisotope Association, 2-28-45 Honkomagome, Bunkyo-ku, Tokyo 113, Japan. Ed. Dr. S. Hashimoto. adv.; abstr.; charts; illus.; index. **Indexed:** Biol.Abstr., Chem.Abstr., Excerp.Med., Ind.Med., INIS Atomind., JTA.
—BLDSC shelfmark: 4656.650000.

615.8   KZ   ISSN 0075-529X
KAZAKHSKII NAUCHNO-ISSLEDOVATEL'SKII INSTITUT ONKOLOGII I RADIOLOGII. TRUDY. (Text in Russian; summaries in English) 1965. a. price varies. Kazakhskii Nauchno-Issledovatel'skii Institut Onkologii i Radiologii, Alma-Ata, Kazakhstan. (Co-sponsor: Ministerstvo Zdravokhraneniya Kazakhskoi S.S.R.) Eds. O.K. Kabiev, S.B. Balmukhanov. circ. 400. **Indexed:** Biol.Abstr.

615.842   GW   ISSN 0939-7116
▼**KLINISCHE NEURORADIOLOGIE.** 1991. q. DM.200.80. Georg Thieme Verlag, Ruedigerstr. 14, Postfach 104853, 7000 Stuttgart 10, Germany. TEL 0711-8931-0. FAX 0711-8931-298. TELEX 7252275-GTV-D. Ed. Dr. M. Nadjmi.
—BLDSC shelfmark: 5099.455000.

615.842   US   ISSN 0730-725X
RC78.7.N83   CODEN: MRIMDQ
MAGNETIC RESONANCE IMAGING; an international journal of basic research & clinical applications. 1982. 6/yr. £235 (effective 1992). (Society for Magnetic Resonance Imaging) Pergamon Press, Inc., Journals Division, 660 White Plains Rd., Tarrytown, NY 10591-5153. TEL 914-524-9200. FAX 914-333-2444. (And: Headington Hill Hall, Oxford OX3 0BW, England. TEL 0865-794141) Eds. John Gore, Francis W. Smith. adv.; bk.rev.; circ. 2,000. (also avail. in microform; back issues avail.) **Indexed:** Biol.Abstr., Chem.Abstr., Curr.Adv.Cancer Res., Curr.Adv.Ecol.Sci., Curr.Cont., INIS Atomind., Sci.Abstr.
—BLDSC shelfmark: 5337.795000.
Refereed Serial

615.842   US   ISSN 0740-3194
RC78.7.N83   CODEN: MRMEEN
MAGNETIC RESONANCE IN MEDICINE. 1984. m. $426 (foreign $503). Academic Press, Inc., Journal Division, 1250 Sixth Ave., San Diego, CA 92101. TEL 619-230-1840. FAX 619-699-6800. TELEX 181726. Ed. Felix W. Wehrli. adv.; index; circ. 1,189. (back issues avail.) **Indexed:** Curr.Adv.Cancer Res.
—BLDSC shelfmark: 5337.798000.
Description: Publishes original investigations concerned with all aspects of the development and use of nuclear magnetic resonance and electron paramagnetic resonance techniques for medical applications.
Refereed Serial

615   US   ISSN 0899-9422
RC78.7.N83   CODEN: MRQUEN
MAGNETIC RESONANCE QUARTERLY. 1989. q. $94 to individuals; institutions $118. Raven Press, 1185 Ave. of the Americas, New York, NY 10036. TEL 212-930-9500. FAX 212-869-3495. TELEX 640073. Ed. Herbert Y. Kressel. adv.; illus.; index; circ. 1,900. (back issues avail.)
—BLDSC shelfmark: 5337.799000.
Formerly (until 1988): Magnetic Resonance Annual.
Description: Presents international advances in MRI that affect daily practice.

615.842   HU   ISSN 0025-0287
RM845   CODEN: MARAAF
MAGYAR RADIOLOGIA. (Text in Hungarian; summaries in English, German and Russian) 1949. 6/yr. $52. (Magyar Radiologiai Tarsasag) Ifjusagi Lap-es Konyvkiado Vallalat, Revay u. 16, 1374 Budapest 6, Hungary. (Subscr. to: Kultura, Box 149, H-1389 Budapest, Hungary) Ed. Dr. Gyula Vargha. adv.; bk.rev.; bibl.; index; circ. 700. **Indexed:** Chem.Abstr., Excerp.Med., Ind.Med., INIS Atomind.
—BLDSC shelfmark: 5345.300000.

615.84   FR
MEDECIN ELECTRO-RADIOLOGISTE QUALIFIE DE FRANCE. 1947. bi-m. Federation Nationale des Medecins Electroradiologistes Qualifies, 60 bd. de Latour Maubourg 60, 75007 Paris, France.
Formerly: Electro-Radiologiste Qualifie de France. Annuaire (ISSN 0076-5813)

MEDICAL AND RADIOLOGICAL DEVICES GUIDANCE MANUAL. see PUBLIC HEALTH AND SAFETY

615   US   ISSN 0739-0211
   CODEN: JAADEC
MEDICAL DOSIMETRY. 4/yr. $165 (effective 1992). (American Association of Medical Dosimetrists) Pergamon Press, Inc., Journals Division, 660 White Plains Rd., Tarrytown, NY 10591-5153. TEL 914-524-9200. FAX 914-333-2444. (And: Headington Hill Hall, Oxford OX3 0BW, England. TEL 0865-794141) Ed. Ray Garcia. (also avail. in microform; back issues avail.) **Indexed:** Curr.Adv.Cancer Res.
—BLDSC shelfmark: 5527.130000.
Refereed Serial

615.842   US
MEDICAL RADIOLOGY. 1985. irreg. price varies. Springer-Verlag, 175 Fifth Ave., New York, NY 10010. TEL 212-460-1500. (Also Berlin, Heidelberg, Tokyo, Vienna) (reprint service avail. from ISI)

615.842   NE   ISSN 0025-7664
   CODEN: MEMUAA
MEDICAMUNDI. (Text in English; summaries in French, German, Spanish) 1955. q. free to qualified personnel. Philips Medical Systems International, P.O. Box 10000, 5680 DA Best, Netherlands. FAX 40-762317. (U.S. addr.: c/o Janet Collins, Advertising Manager, Philips Medical Systems, Inc., 710 Bridgeport Ave., Shelton, CT 06484) Ed. Dr. L.C.J. Baghuis. adv.; charts; illus.; stat.; index; circ. 14,000 (paid); 14,000 (controlled). **Indexed:** Biol.Abstr., Chem.Abstr., Excerp.Med., Ind.Med., Sci.Abstr.

615.842   RU   ISSN 0025-8334
RM845   CODEN: MERAA9
MEDITSINSKAYA RADIOLOGIYA/MEDICAL RADIOLOGY. (Text in Russian; summaries in English) 1956. m. 51 Rub.($16.20) (Akademiya Meditsinskikh Nauk S.S.S.R.) Izdatel'stvo Meditsina, Petroverigskii pereulok 6-8, 101838 Moscow, Russia. (Co-sponsor: Vsesoyuznoe Nauchnoe Obshchestvo Rentgenologov i Radiologov) Ed. G.A. Zedgenidze. bk.rev.; index. **Indexed:** Biol.Abstr., Chem.Abstr., Dent.Ind., Excerp.Med., Ind.Med., INIS Atomind., Nutr.Abstr., Sci.Abstr.
—BLDSC shelfmark: 0106.000000.
Description: Publishes papers devoted to pathogenesis, clinical picture, prevention and treatment of radiation injuries in man. Includes information on radiological conferences and congresses held in the USSR and abroad.

615.842   US
MODERN NEURORADIOLOGY SERIES. 1983. irreg., latest vol.4. price varies. Raven Press, 1185 Ave. of the Americas, New York, NY 10036. TEL 212-930-9500. FAX 212-869-3495. Ed. Thomas H. Newton.

615.842   US   ISSN 0098-2997
RB112   CODEN: MAMED5
MOLECULAR ASPECTS OF MEDICINE; an interdisciplinary review journal. 1975. 6/yr. £230 (effective 1992). Pergamon Press, Inc., Journals Division, 660 White Plains Rd., Tarrytown, NY 10591-5153. TEL 914-524-9200. FAX 914-333-2444. (And: Headington Hill Hall, Oxford OX3 0BW, England. TEL 0865-794141) Ed.Bd. adv.; bk.rev.; illus.; stat.; index. (also avail. in microform from MIM,UMI) **Indexed:** Biol.Abstr., Chem.Abstr, Curr.Adv.Biochem., Curr.Adv.Cell & Devel.Biol., Curr.Adv.Ecol.Sci., Curr.Cont., Excerp.Med., Ind.Med., Ind.Sci.Rev.
—BLDSC shelfmark: 5900.768000.
Description: Integrates molecular biochemistry and clinical medicine, focusing on the application of molecular insights to medical problems.
Refereed Serial

615.842   SP
MONOGRAFIAS DE DIAGNOSTICO POR IMAGEN. Short title: M.D.I. 3/yr. 13197 ptas. (effective 1990). Interamericana de Espana, S.A., Manuel Ferrero, 13, 28036 Madrid, Spain. TEL 315-0340. FAX 733-6627. Ed. R. Casanova.

615.842   US
N C R P STATEMENTS. 1954. irreg. free. National Council on Radiation Protection and Measurements, 7910 Woodmont Ave., Ste. 800, Bethesda, MD 20814. TEL 301-657-2652. Ed. W. Roger Ney.

615.842   UK   ISSN 0952-3480
   CODEN: NMRBEF
N M R IN BIOMEDICINE. (Nuclear Magnetic Resonance) 1988. bi-m. $365 (effective 1992). John Wiley & Sons Ltd., Journals, Baffins Lane, Chichester, Sussex PO19 1UD, England. TEL 0243-779777. FAX 0243-775878. TELEX 86290 WIBOOK G. Ed. John R. Griffiths. adv.
—BLDSC shelfmark: 6113.931000.
Description: Presents original papers in which nuclear magnetic resonance spectroscopy is used for investigating basic biochemical and clinical problems.

615.842   JA   ISSN 0439-5956
R895.A1   CODEN: HISKBI
NATIONAL INSTITUTE OF RADIOLOGICAL SCIENCES. ANNUAL REPORT. a. Kagaku Gijutsu-cho, National Institute of Radiological Science - Science and Technology Agency, 9-1 Anagawa 4-chome, Chiba-shi, Chiba-ken 260, Japan. TEL 0472-51-2111. FAX 0472-56-9616. TELEX 03722205-NIRS-J. Ed. T. Iwakura. circ. 1,400.
—BLDSC shelfmark: 1364.740000.

MEDICAL SCIENCES — RADIOLOGY AND NUCLEAR MEDICINE

615.842   GW   ISSN 0028-3940
RC349.R3
NEURORADIOLOGY; a journal devoted to neuroimaging and interventional neuroradiology. (Text in English) 1970. 6/yr. DM.522($280) (European Society of Neuroradiology) Springer-Verlag, Heidelberger Platz 3, D-1000 Berlin 33, Germany. TEL 030-8207-1. (Also Heidelberg, Tokyo, Vienna, and New York) (Co-sponsor: Japanese Neuroradiological Society) Ed. G. DuBoulay. adv.; charts. (also avail. in microform from UMI; back issues avail.; reprint service avail. from ISI) **Indexed:** Bibl.Dev.Med.& Child Neur., Curr.Adv.Cancer Res., Curr.Adv.Ecol.Sci., Curr.Cont., Dent.Ind., Excerp.Med., Helminthol.Abstr., Ind.Med., Ind.Sci.Rev.
—BLDSC shelfmark: 6081.558000.

615.8   JA   ISSN 0048-0428
CODEN: NHGZAR
NIPPON ACTA RADIOLOGICA/NIPPON IGAKU HOSHASEN GAKKAI ZASSHI. (Text in Japanese; table of contents and summaries in English) 1940. m. 12000 Yen. Nippon Societas Radiologica - Japan Radiological Society, Rm. 301 Akamon Habitation, 5-29-13 Hongo, Bunkyo-ku, Tokyo 113, Japan. FAX 03-5684-4075. Ed. Takahiro Kozuka. adv.; bk.rev.; illus.; circ. 5,000. **Indexed:** Biol.Abstr., Chem.Abstr., Excerp.Med., Ind.Med., JTA.
—BLDSC shelfmark: 6113.254000.

615.842   US   ISSN 0896-0607
NUCLEAR MEDICINE. 1985. a. Gordon & Breach Science Publishers, 270 Eighth Ave., New York, NY 10011. TEL 212-206-8900. FAX 212-645-2459. TELEX 236735 GOPUB UR. (Subscr. to: Box 786, Cooper Sta., New York, NY 10276. TEL 800-545-8398; UK subscr. to: P.O. Box 90, Reading, Berkshire RG1 8JL, England. TEL 0734-560-080) Ed. P. Cox.
Formerly: Monographs in Nuclear Medicine (ISSN 0882-6455)
Refereed Serial

615.842   US   ISSN 0272-0108
R895.A1   CODEN: NMANDX
NUCLEAR MEDICINE ANNUAL. a. Raven Press, 1185 Ave. of the Americas, New York, NY 10036. TEL 212-930-9500. FAX 212-869-3495. TELEX 640073. Ed. Leonard M. Freeman. **Indexed:** Biol.Abstr., Chem.Abstr.
Refereed Serial

615.8   UK   ISSN 0143-3636
CODEN: NMCODC
NUCLEAR MEDICINE COMMUNICATIONS. 1980. m. £140 to individuals (US & Canada $250); institutions £295 (US & Canada $495). Chapman & Hall, 2-6 Boundary Row, London SE1 8HN, England. TEL 071-865-0066. FAX 071-522-9623. TELEX 290164-CHAPMAG. (Dist. by: International Thomson Publishing Services, Ltd., N. Way, Andover, Hampshire SP10 5BE. TEL 0264-33-2424; US addr.: Chapman & Hall, 29 W. 35th St., New York, NY 10001-2291. TEL 212-244-3336) Ed.Bd. bk.rev.; index. (reprint service avail. from UMI) **Indexed:** Biol.Abstr., Chem.Abstr., Curr.Adv.Cancer Res., Curr.Adv.Ecol.Sci., Excerp.Med.
—BLDSC shelfmark: 6180.923000.
Description: Describes research and clinical work in nuclear medicine, worldwide.
Refereed Serial

NUCLEUS. see *ENERGY* — *Nuclear Energy*

615.8   GW   ISSN 0029-5566
R895.A1   CODEN: NMIMAX
NUKLEARMEDIZIN. (Text in English and German) 1959. 6/yr. DM.210($138) to individuals; institutions DM.288($178.20). (German Society of Nuclear Medicine) F. K. Schattauer Verlagsgesellschaft mbH, Lenzhalde 3, Postfach 104545, 7000 Stuttgart 10, Germany. TEL 0711-22987-0. FAX 0711-22987-50. adv.; bk.rev.; abstr.; bibl.; charts; illus.; index; circ. 2,300. **Indexed:** Biol.Abstr., Chem.Abstr., Curr.Cont., Excerp.Med., Ind.Med., Risk Abstr.
—BLDSC shelfmark: 6184.453000.
Description: Original material covering experimental and clinical research with radionucleides, radionucleide imaging, new concepts of functional imaging, case reports.

615.842   GW   ISSN 0723-7065
CODEN: NKLZD8
DER NUKLEARMEDIZINER. (Text in German; summaries in English) 1977. 5/yr. DM.150. (Berufsverband Deutscher Nuklearmediziner) Demeter Verlag, Wuermstr. 13, 8032 Graefelfing, Germany. TEL 089-852033. FAX 089-8543347. Ed. Dr. D.W. Nitz. circ. 1,800.
—BLDSC shelfmark: 6184.485000.

PEDIATRIC RADIOLOGY; roentgenology, nuclear medicine, ultrasonics, CT, MRI. see *MEDICAL SCIENCES — Pediatrics*

615.842   US   ISSN 0273-0278
CODEN: PORADD
POSTGRADUATE RADIOLOGY; a journal of continuing education. 1981. q. $80 to individuals(foreign $100); institutions $105(foreign $125); students $49(foreign $69). Mosby - Year Book, Inc. (Subsidiary of: Times Mirror Company), 11830 Westline Industrial Dr., St. Louis, MO 63146. TEL 800-325-4177. TELEX 44-2402. Ed. Dr. Herbert L. Abrams. adv.; bk.rev.; abstr.; index; circ. 1,500. (back issues avail.) **Indexed:** Excerp.Med.
Description: Provides timely review articles and abstracts of current literature.

615.842   US
R B M A BULLETIN; progress through sharing. vol.23, no.11, 1988. m. $100 to non-members (foreign $110). Radiology Business Management Association, 27241 La Paz Rd., No. 120, Laguna Niguel, CA 92656-3602. TEL 714-833-1651. Ed. Sharon Urch. adv.; bk.rev.

615.842   US
▼**R S WAVELENGTH.** (Radiologic Science) 1990. 12/yr. free. American Society of Radiologic Technologists, 15000 Central Ave. S.E., Albuquerque, NM 87123. TEL 508-298-4500. FAX 508-298-5063. Ed. Paul Young. adv.; circ. 50,000 (controlled).
Description: Covers radiologic sciences and medical imaging.

615.842   US   ISSN 1041-2182
R T IMAGE. (Radiologic Technology) 1988. w. free. Valley Forge Press, 1288 Valley Forge Rd., Box 1135, Valley Forge, PA 19481. TEL 215-935-1296. FAX 215-935-3072. Ed. Brian Keefer. bk.rev.; charts; illus.; circ. 144,000 (controlled).
Description: Items of interest to radiologic technologists and therapists in all modalities and in hospitals, free-standing centers, and schools.

615.842   UK   ISSN 0264-6412
RAD FOR RADIOGRAPHERS, RADIOLOGISTS AND RADIOTHERAPISTS. 1975. m. £39.60. Kingsmoor Publications Ltd., P.O. Box 3, Harlow, Essex CM19 4RF, England. FAX 0279-441038. Eds. D.G. Messer, D.J. Roberts. adv.; bk.rev.; circ. 15,000.
Incorporates: Consultant Radiologist and Radiotherapist.

615   UN
RADIATION DOSIMETRY DATA: CATALOGUE. 1964. irreg. free. International Atomic Energy Agency, Wagramer Str. 5, Box 100, A-1400 Vienna, Austria. circ. 3,000.
Formerly (until 1969): International Atomic Energy Agency. Radiation Data for Medical Use; Catalogue (ISSN 0538-4850)

615.842 616.99   JA   ISSN 0288-2043
CODEN: RAMEER
RADIATION MEDICINE; medical imaging and radiation oncology. 1983. bi-m. 12000 Yen($80) Radiation Medicine Association, University of Tokyo, Faculty of Medicine, Department of Radiology, 7-3-1 Hongo, Bunkyo-ku, Tokyo 113, Japan. (Subscr. to: Igaku-Shoin Medical Publishers Inc., 1140 Ave. of the Americas, New York, N.Y. 10036, U.S.A.. TEL 212-944-7540) Ed. Masahiro Iio. adv.; circ. 1,500. **Indexed:** Excerp.Med., Ind.Med.
—BLDSC shelfmark: 7227.975000.

615.842   US
RADIATION ONCOLOGY NEWS. 1986. 4/yr. $50 (foreign $60). Society for Radiation Oncology Administrators, 2021 Spring Rd., Ste. 600, Oak Brook, IL 60521. FAX 708-571-7837. Ed. Rita Cipollo. bibl.; tr.lit.; circ. 275. (back issues avail.)
Formerly (until vol.4, 1990): S R O A Newsletter.

615.832   RU   ISSN 0033-8192
CODEN: RADOA8
RADIOBIOLOGIYA. 1961. bi-m. 33.30 Rub. (Akademiya Nauk S.S.S.R.) Izdatel'stvo Nauka, 90 Profsoyuznaya ul., 117864 Moscow, Russia. Ed. A.M. Kuzin. bk.rev.; index. (tabloid format) **Indexed:** Biol.Abstr., Chem.Abstr., Excerp.Med., Ind.Med., Int.Aerosp.Abstr., Sci.Abstr.
—BLDSC shelfmark: 0137.700000.

615.842   AT   ISSN 0033-8273
CODEN: RDGRAJ
RADIOGRAPHER. 1948. 4/yr. Aus.$30. Australian Institute of Radiography, Attn: E.M. Hughes, Sec., P.O. Box 1169, Collingwood, Vic. 3066, Australia. FAX 03-416-0783. Ed. E.M. Hughes. adv.; bk.rev.; illus.; index; circ. 2,900. **Indexed:** Chem.Abstr., Sci.Abstr.
—BLDSC shelfmark: 7236.850000.

615.842   US   ISSN 0271-5333
RC78.A1
RADIOGRAPHICS. 1981. bi-m. $80 (foreign $90). Radiological Society of North America, Inc., 2021 Spring Rd., Ste. 600, Oak Brook, IL 60521-1860. TEL 708-571-2670. FAX 708-574-3037. (Subscr. to: 1991 Northampton St., Easton, PA 18042. TEL 215-250-7277) Ed. William W. Olmsted. adv.; circ. 22,530. **Indexed:** Ind.Med.
—BLDSC shelfmark: 7236.900000.

615.842   UK   ISSN 0033-8281
RADIOGRAPHY. 1935. 6/yr. £42. (Society of Radiographers) College of Radiographers, 14 Upper Wimpole St., London W1M 8BN, England. Ed. Gwyneth Stokes. adv.; bk.rev.; charts; illus.; index; circ. 14,000. **Indexed:** Biol.Abstr., CINAHL, Curr.Adv.Ecol.Sci., Ind.Med.

615.842   RU   ISSN 0033-8311
CODEN: RADKAU
RADIOKHIMIYA. 1959. bi-m. 40.20 Rub. (Akademiya Nauk S.S.S.R.) Izdatel'stvo Nauka, 90 Profsoyuznaya ul., 117864 Moscow, Russia. Ed. V.M. Vdovenko. index. (tabloid format) **Indexed:** Chem.Abstr., Fuel & Energy Abstr., Ocean.Abstr.
—BLDSC shelfmark: 0139.500000.

616.842   GW
▼**RADIOLIT;** radiologische Literatur mit Abstracts. 1992. s-a. DM.99. Georg Thieme Verlag, Ruedigerstr. 14, Postfach 104853, 7000 Stuttgart 10, Germany. TEL 0711-8931-0. FAX 0711-8931298. (also avail. on diskette)

615.842   US   ISSN 0033-832X
CODEN: RDLGBC
DER RADIOLOGE; die Fachzeitschrift fuer bildgebende Verfahren, Radioonkologie und Nuklearmedizin. (Text in German; summaries in English) 1961. m. DM.398($219) Springer-Verlag, Journals, 175 Fifth Ave., New York, NY 10010. TEL 212-460-1500. (Also Berlin, Heidelberg, and Tokyo) Ed.Bd. adv.; bk.rev.; charts; illus.; index. (also avail. in microform from UMI; back issues avail.; reprint service avail. from ISI) **Indexed:** Biol.Abstr., Curr.Cont., Dent.Ind., Excerp.Med., Helminthol.Abstr., Ind.Med., INIS Atomind.
—BLDSC shelfmark: 7237.700000.

615.842   SP   ISSN 0033-8338
RADIOLOGIA. 1958. m. (9/yr.). 7300 ptas.($100) (Sociedad Espanola de Radiologia y Electrologia Medicas y de Medicina Nuclear) Editorial Garsi, S.A., Londres, 17, 28028 Madrid, Spain. TEL 256-08-00. FAX 361-10-07. Dir. Dr. L. Ramos Gonzalez. adv.; bk.rev.; abstr.; bibl.; charts; illus.; stat.; index; circ. 3,000. **Indexed:** Biol.Abstr., Curr.Cont., Excerp.Med., Helminthol.Abstr., Ind.Med.Esp.
—BLDSC shelfmark: 7237.730000.

615.842   BL   ISSN 0100-3984
RADIOLOGIA BRASILEIRA. 1958. 4/yr. $40. Colegio Brasileiro de Radiologia, Departamento da Associacao Medica Brasileira, Av. Paulista, 491, C.P. 5984, CEP 01311 Sao Paulo, Brazil. Ed. Adilson Prando. circ. 3,500.

MEDICAL SCIENCES — RADIOLOGY AND NUCLEAR MEDICINE

615.842   XV   ISSN 0485-893X
CODEN: RDIUA4
RADIOLOGIA IUGOSLAVICA. (Text in English, French, German, Macedonian, Serbo-Croatian, Slovene) 1964. q. 120000 din. Onkoloski Institut, Zaloska 2, 61105 Ljubljana, Slovenia. TEL 061 327-955. (Co-sponsor: Assembly of the Research Community of Slovenia) Ed. Dr. Tomaz Benulic. adv.; bk.rev.; abstr.; illus.; circ. 1,500. **Indexed:** Chem.Abstr., Excerp.Med.
—BLDSC shelfmark: 7237.794000.
    Description: Covers radiology, radiotherapy, oncology, nuclear medicine, radiophysics, radiobiology and radiation protection.

615.842   IT   ISSN 0033-8362
RADIOLOGIA MEDICA. (Text in Italian; summaries in English, Italian) 1914. m. L.80000($120) (Societa Italiana di Radiologia Medica e Medicina Nucleare) Edizioni Minerva Medica, Corso Bramante 83-85, 10126 Turin, Italy. Ed. Di Guglielmo. adv.; bk.rev.; bibl.; charts; illus.; index; circ. 6,000. (also avail. in microform from UMI; reprint service avail. from UMI) **Indexed:** Biol.Abstr., Chem.Abstr., Dent.Ind., Excerp.Med., Ind.Med.
—BLDSC shelfmark: 7237.800000.
    Formerly: Minerva Radiologica (ISSN 0026-4962)

615.842   US   ISSN 0033-8389
RM846   CODEN: RCNAAU
RADIOLOGIC CLINICS OF NORTH AMERICA. 1963. 6/yr. $89. W.B. Saunders Co., Curtis Center, Independence Square W., Philadelphia, PA 19106. TEL 215-238-7800. Ed. Mary Mulroy. illus. (also avail. in microform from MIM,UMI; reprint service avail. from UMI) **Indexed:** Biol.Abstr., Curr.Adv.Ecol.Sci., Curr.Cont., Dent.Ind., Excerp.Med., Ind.Med.
● Also available online. Vendor(s): BRS.
—BLDSC shelfmark: 7237.830000.

615.842   GW   ISSN 0720-3322
RADIOLOGIE. (Text in French) 1981. 6/yr. DM.408($242) (C E P U R - College d'Enseignement Post-Universitaire de Radiologie) Springer-Verlag, Heidelberger Platz 3, D-1000 Berlin 33, Germany. TEL 030-8207-1. (Also Heidelberg, Tokyo, Vienna, and New York) Ed. A. Wackenheim. charts; illus.; index. (also avail. in microfiche from UMI; reprint service avail. from ISI) **Indexed:** Excerp.Med.
—BLDSC shelfmark: 7237.990000.

615.842   US
RADIOLOGISCHE KLINIK. 1983. irreg. price varies. Springer-Verlag, 175 Fifth Ave., New York, NY 10010. TEL 212-460-1500.

615.842   US   ISSN 0033-8419
RC78   CODEN: RADLAX
RADIOLOGY; a monthly journal devoted to clinical radiology and allied sciences. 1915. m. $185 (foreign $225). Radiological Society of North America, Inc., 2021 Spring Rd., Ste. 600, Oak Brook, IL 60521-1860. TEL 708-571-2670. FAX 708-574-3037. (Subscr. to: 1991 Northampton St., Easton, PA 18042. TEL 215-250-7277) Ed. Dr. Stanley S. Siegelman. adv.; bk.rev.; abstr.; charts; illus.; index. cum.index every 3 yrs.; circ. 32,374. (also avail. in microform from UMI; reprint service avail. from UMI) **Indexed:** Bibl.Dev.Med.& Child Med., Biol.Abstr., Biotech.Abstr., C.I.S. Abstr., Cadscan, Chem.Abstr., Curr.Adv.Cancer Res., Curr.Adv.Ecol.Sci., Curr.Adv.Genetics & Molec.Biol., Curr.Cont., Dairy Sci.Abstr., Dent.Ind., Excerp.Med., Helminthol.Abstr., I.P.A., Ind.Med., Int.Nurs.Ind., Lead Abstr., Rev.Plant Path., Sci.Abstr., Zincscan.
● Also available online.
—BLDSC shelfmark: 7238.000000.

615.842   US   ISSN 0741-160X
RADIOLOGY AND IMAGING LETTER. 1981. s-m. (m. in Jan. & Aug.) $204 (foreign $242). Quest Publishing Co., 1351 Titan Way, Brea, CA 92621. Ed. Allan F. Pacela. bk.rev.; charts; illus.; tr.lit.; index. (looseleaf format; back issues avail.)
    Formerly (until 1984): Radiology Letter (ISSN 0273-4958)
    Description: For clinical professionals. Covers latest advances in all areas of diagnostic imaging, radiation therapy and nuclear medicine, as well as safety hazards, recalls, legislation, products, legal issues and education.

RADIOLOGY MANAGEMENT. see *HOSPITALS*

615.842   US
RADIOLOGY OF IATROGENIC DISORDERS. 1981. irreg. price varies. Springer-Verlag, 175 Fifth Ave., New York, NY 10010. TEL 212-460-1500. (Also Berlin, Heidelberg, Tokyo, Vienna) (reprint service avail. from ISI)

615.842   US
RADIOLOGY TODAY (NEW YORK). 1981. irreg. price varies. Springer-Verlag, 175 Fifth Ave., New York, NY 10010. TEL 212-460-1500. (Also Berlin, Heidelberg, Tokyo and Vienna) (reprint service avail. from ISI)

615.842   US   ISSN 0893-1054
RADIOLOGY TODAY (THOROFARE). 1983. m. $110 to individuals; institutions $120. Slack, Inc., 6900 Grove Rd., Thorofare, NJ 08086.
TEL 609-848-1000. FAX 609-853-5991. Ed. Dr. Jack G. Rabinowitz. adv.; circ. 27,000. (reprint service avail.)

615.842   NE   ISSN 0167-8140
CODEN: RAONDT
RADIOTHERAPY & ONCOLOGY. (Text in English) 12/yr.(in 3 vols.; 4 nos./vol.). fl.1371 (effective 1992). (European Society for Therapeutic Radiology and Oncology) Elsevier Science Publishers B.V., P.O. Box 211, 1000 AE Amsterdam, Netherlands. TEL 020-5803911. FAX 020-5803598. TELEX 18582 FSPA NL. (Subscr. in U.S. and Canada to: Elsevier Science Publishing Co., Inc., Box 882, Madison Sq. Sta., New York, NY 10159. TEL 212-989-5800) Eds. H. Bartelink, J. Overgaard. adv.; index. (also avail. in microform from RPI; back issues avail.; reprint service avail. from SWZ) **Indexed:** ASCA, Chem.Abstr., Curr.Adv.Cancer Res., Curr.Adv.Ecol.Sci., Curr.Cont., Excerp.Med., Ind.Med.
—BLDSC shelfmark: 7240.790000.
    Description: Covers areas of interest relating to radiation oncology.
    Refereed Serial

615.8   IT   ISSN 0390-7740
CODEN: RAYSDQ
RAYS; international journal of radiological sciences. (Text in English; summaries in Italian) 1976. 3/yr. L.39000($54) (effective 1991). (Universita Cattolica del Sacro Cuore, Istituto di Radiologia) Masson Italia Periodici, Via Statuto 2-4, 20121 Milan, Italy. TEL 02-6367-1. FAX 02-6367-211. Ed. Pasquale Marano. adv.; abstr.; charts; illus.; stat.; circ. 1,000. **Indexed:** Biol.Abstr., Chem.Abstr., Excerp.Med.
—BLDSC shelfmark: 7298.087000.
    Description: Provides an internation forum for the discussion of physical, biological, clinical, and technical problems involved in the use of radiation in medicine.

616.9   US   ISSN 0163-6170
R895.A1
RECENT ADVANCES IN NUCLEAR MEDICINE. 1965. irreg., vol.6, 1983. price varies. W.B. Saunders Co. (Subsidiary of: Harcourt Brace Jovanovich, Inc.), Curtis Center, Independence Square W., Philadelphia, PA 19106. TEL 215-238-7800. Eds. Drs. John H. Lawrence, Thomas Budinger.
    Former titles: Progress in Nuclear Medicine (ISSN 0079-6581); Progress in Atomic Medicine (ISSN 0085-5189)
    Refereed Serial

616 615   BU   ISSN 0486-400X
CODEN: RENRAR
RENTGENOLOGIJA I RADIOLOGIJA. (Text in Bulgarian; summaries in Russian and English) 1962. q. 16 lv.($5) (Ministerstvo na Narodnoto Zdrave) Izdatelstvo Meditsina i Fizkultura, 11, Pl. Slaveikov, Sofia, Bulgaria. (Dist. by: Hemus, 6, Rouski Blvd., 1000 Sofia, Bulgaria) (Co-sponsor: Nauchno Druzhestvo po Rentgenologija i Radiologija) Ed. J.V. Nikolov. circ. 620. **Indexed:** Abstr.Bulg.Sci.Med.Lit., Chem.Abstr., Excerp.Med.
—BLDSC shelfmark: 0140.770000.

615.842   US   ISSN 0883-8291
REVIEWS OF MAGNETIC RESONANCE IN MEDICINE. 1986. 2/yr. £85 (effective 1992). Pergamon Press, Inc., Journals Division, 660 White Plains Rd., Tarrytown, NY 10591-5153. TEL 914-524-9200. FAX 914-333-2444. (And: Headington Hill Hall, Oxford OX3 0BW, England. TEL 0865-794141) Ed. John C. Gore. (also avail. in microform; back issues avail.)
—BLDSC shelfmark: 7791.250000.
    Refereed Serial

615.842   RM   ISSN 0481-6684
CODEN: ROORD
REVISTA DE CHIRURGIE, ONCOLOGIE, RADIOLOGIE, O.R.L., OFTALMOLOGIE, STOMATOLOGIE. RADIOLOGIE. (Text in Rumanian; summaries in English, French, German, Russian) 1956. 4/yr. $20. Uniunea Societatilor de Stiinte Medicale din Republica Socialista Rumania, Str. Progresului No. 8-10, Sectorul 1, Bucharest 70754, Rumania. (Subscr. to: ILEXIM, Str. 13 Decembrie Nr. 3, P.O. Box 136-137, Bucharest, Rumania) Ed.Bd. adv.; bk.rev. **Indexed:** Excerp.Med.
    Supersedes in part: Oncologia si Radiologia (ISSN 0030-2406)

615.842   SP   ISSN 0212-6982
REVISTA ESPANOLA DE MEDICINA NUCLEAR. (Supplement avail. (ISSN 0213-814X)) 1982. 3/yr. 4900 ptas.($80) (Sociedad Espanola de Medicina Nuclear) Editorial Garsi, S.A., Londres, 17, 28028 Madrid, Spain. TEL 256-08-00. FAX 361-10-07. Ed. A. Gomez Embuena. circ. 1,000. **Indexed:** Excerp.Med. (1992-).

615.842 616.8   IT
RIVISTA DI NEURORADIOLOGIA; periodico quadrimestrale scientifico indipendente. vol.4, 1991. q. Lit.100000. Edizioni del Centauro, Via Casattini 32, 33100 Udine, Italy. Ed. Marco Leonardi. **Indexed:** Excerp.Med., Ref.Zh.

615.842   IT
RIVISTA DI RADIOLOGIA. q. L.18000. Societa Editrice Universo, Via G.B. Morgagni 1, 00161 Rome, Italy. Ed. Adamo Grilli. **Indexed:** Biol.Abstr., Excerp.Med.

615.842   GW   ISSN 0936-6652
CODEN: RFGVEF
ROEFO. FORTSCHRITTE AUF DEM GEBIETE DER ROENTGENSTRAHLEN UND DER NEUEN BILDGEBENDEN VERFAHREN. (Summaries in English, French, German and Spanish) 1897. m. DM.558. (Deutsche Roentgengesellschaft) Georg Thieme Verlag, Ruedigerstr. 14, Postfach 104853, 7000 Stuttgart 10, Germany. TEL 0711-8931-0. FAX 0711-8931298. (Co-sponsor: Oesterreichische Roentgengesellschaft) Eds. W. Frommhold, P. Thurn. adv.; bk.rev.; abstr.; bibl.; charts; illus.; stat.; index; circ. 3,100. (also avail. in microform from UMI; reprint service avail. from UMI) **Indexed:** Biol.Abstr., C.I.S. Abstr., Chem.Abstr., Curr.Cont., Dairy Sci.Abstr., Dent.Ind., Excerp.Med., Helminthol.Abstr., Ind.Med., Ind.Sci.Rev., Sci.Cit.Ind.
    Former titles: RoeFo. Fortschritte auf dem Gebiete der Roentgenstrahlen und der Nuklearmedizin (ISSN 0340-1618); Fortschritte auf dem Gebiete der Roentgenstrahlen und der Nuklearmedizin (ISSN 0015-8151)

615.842   II   ISSN 0303-2590
ROENTGEN TECHNOLOGY. (Text in English) 1974. s-a. Rs.10($3) Indian Association of Radiological Technologists, Postgraduate Institute of Medical Education and Research, Dept. of Radiology, Chandigarh, India.

615.842   GW   ISSN 0035-7820
CODEN: RGPXB2
ROENTGENPRAXIS; Bildgebende Diagnostik, Strahlentherapie, Nuklearmedizin. 1947. m. DM.198. S. Hirzel Verlag, Postfach 102237, 7000 Stuttgart 10, Germany. TEL 0711-2582-0. FAX 0711-2582290. TELEX 723636-DAZ-D. Ed. Dr. Paul Gerhardt. adv.; bk.rev.; charts; illus.; index; circ. 3,000. **Indexed:** Chem.Abstr., Dent.Ind., Excerp.Med., Ind.Med.
—BLDSC shelfmark: 8021.700000.
    Description: Examines the various aspects of radiology and nuclear medicine.

612   US   ISSN 0739-9529
CODEN: SIRAE5
SEMINARS IN INTERVENTIONAL RADIOLOGY. 1984. q. $76 to individuals; institutions $105. Thieme Medical Publishers, Inc., 381 Park Ave. So., Ste. 1501, New York, NY 10016. TEL 212-683-5088. Ed. Peter Mueller. adv.; abstr.; bibl.; illus.; circ. 1,000.
—BLDSC shelfmark: 8239.453000.

MEDICAL SCIENCES — RADIOLOGY AND NUCLEAR MEDICINE   3363

615.842　　　　US　ISSN 0001-2998
　　　　　　　　　CODEN: SMNMAB
SEMINARS IN NUCLEAR MEDICINE. 1981. q. $84 to individuals; institutions $121; foreign $138. W.B. Saunders Co. (Subsidiary of: Harcourt Brace Jovanovich, Inc.), Curtis Center, Independence Square W., Philadelphia, PA 19106. TEL 215-238-7800. (Subscr. to: Journals 6277 Sea Harbor Dr., 4th Fl., Orlando FL 32891) Eds. Drs. Leonard Freeman, M. Donald Blaufox. adv.; abstr.; bibl.; charts; illus. **Indexed:** ASCA, Biol.Abstr., Chem.Abstr., Curr.Adv.Ecol.Sci., Curr.Cont., Excerp.Med., Ind.Med., Sci.Abstr., Sci.Cit.Ind.
●Also available online.
—BLDSC shelfmark: 8239.456000.

SEMINARS IN ONCOLOGY NURSING. see *MEDICAL SCIENCES — Nurses And Nursing*

SEMINARS IN RESPIRATORY INFECTIONS. see *MEDICAL SCIENCES — Respiratory Diseases*

615.842　　　　US　ISSN 0037-198X
RC78　　　　　　CODEN: SEROAF
SEMINARS IN ROENTGENOLOGY. 1966. q. $79 to individuals; institutions $111; foreign $130. W.B. Saunders Co., Journals Department (Subsidiary of: Harcourt Brace Jovanovich, Inc.), Curtis Center, Independence Square W., Philadelphia, PA 19106. TEL 215-238-7800. (Subscr. to: Box 6209, Duluth, MN 55806) Ed. Dr. Wallace T. Miller. adv.; bibl.; charts; illus. **Indexed:** ASCA, Bibl.Dev.Med.& Child Neur., Biol.Abstr., Curr.Cont., Dent.Ind., Excerp.Med., Ind.Med., Sci.Cit.Ind.
●Also available online.
—BLDSC shelfmark: 8239.460000.

615.842　　　　US　ISSN 0887-2171
SEMINARS IN ULTRASOUND, C T AND M R. 1980. bi-m. $79 to individuals; institutions $105; foreign $129. W.B. Saunders Co., Journals Department (Subsidiary of: Harcourt Brace Jovanovich, Inc.), Curtis Center, Independence Square W., Philadelphia, PA 19106. TEL 215-238-7800. (Subscr. to: Box 6209, Duluth, MN 55806) Ed.Bd. adv.; bibl.; charts; illus.; index. (back issues avail.) **Indexed:** ASCA, Biol.Abstr.
●Also available online.
Formerly: Seminars in Ultrasound (ISSN 0194-1720)

615.842　　　　NZ　ISSN 1170-9758
SHADOWS; journal of the New Zealand Institute of Medical Radiation Technology. 1958. q. NZ.$60. New Zealand Institute of Medical Radiation Technology, Radiology Dept., Princess Margaret Hospital, Christchurch 2, New Zealand. TEL 03-337-7200. FAX 03-337-7214. Ed. Jan Palmer. adv.; bk.rev.; circ. 800.

618　　　　GW　ISSN 0364-2348
SKELETAL RADIOLOGY. 1976. 8/yr. DM.539($336) (International Skeletal Society) Springer-Verlag, Heidelberger Platz 3, D-1000 Berlin 33, Germany. TEL-030-8207-1. (Also Heidelberg, Tokyo, Vienna, and New York) Ed. H.G. Jacobson. adv.; bk.rev.; charts, illus.; index. (also avail. in microfilm from UMI; reprint service avail. from ISI) **Indexed:** ASCA, Bibl.Dev.Med.& Child Neur., Curr.Adv.Cancer Res., Curr.Cont., Dent.Ind., Excerp.Med., Ind.Med.
—BLDSC shelfmark: 8295.200000.

SLIDE ATLAS OF CURRENT RADIOLOGY (YEAR). see *MEDICAL SCIENCES — Abstracting, Bibliographies, Statistics*

SOLID STATE NUCLEAR MAGNETIC RESONANCE. see *CHEMISTRY — Analytical Chemistry*

615.842　　　　GW　ISSN 0179-7158
　　　　　　　　　CODEN: STONE4
STRAHLENTHERAPIE UND ONKOLOGIE; Zeitschrift fuer Radiologie, Strahlenbiologie, Strahlenphysik. (Text and summaries in English and German) 1912. m. DM.648 (foreign DM.672). (Deutsche Roentgengesellschaft) Urban und Vogel, Lindwurmstr. 95, Postfach 15 22 09, 8000 Munich 15, Germany. TEL 089-53292-0. FAX 089-53292-0. (Co-sponsors: Gesellschaft fuer Medizinische Radiologie, Strahlenbiologie und Nuklearmedizin; Deutsche Gesellschaft fuer Medizinische Physik; Deutsche Krebsgesellschaft; Arbeitsgemeinschaft Radioonkologie (ARO)) Eds. E. Scherer, J. Lissner. adv.; bk.rev.; bibl.; charts; illus.; index; cum.index: vols.1-125 (in 5 vols.); circ. 1,600. **Indexed:** ASCA, Biol.Abstr., Chem.Abstr., Curr.Adv.Cancer Res., Curr.Cont., Dent.Ind., Excerp.Med., Ind.Med., Nutr.Abstr.
—BLDSC shelfmark: 8470.010000.
Formerly: Strahlentherapie; Zeitschrift fuer Radiologie und Onkologie (ISSN 0039-2073)

SURGICAL AND RADIOLOGIC ANATOMY. see *BIOLOGY — Physiology*

615.842　　　　US　ISSN 0892-7340
TECHNOLOGY FOR IMAGING & RADIOLOGY. 1987. m. $90 (Canada $100; elsewhere $120). (Emergency Care Research Institute) E C R I, 5200 Butler Pike, Plymouth Meeting, PA 19462. TEL 215-825-6000. FAX 215-834-1275. Ed. Robert Hochschild.
Refereed Serial

THERMOLOGY. see *BIOLOGY — Physiology*

615.842　　　　US
TRACERS. 1985. a. American Board of Nuclear Medicine, 900 Veteran Ave., Los Angeles, CA 90024. TEL 213-825-6787. FAX 213-825-9433. Ed. J.F. Ross. circ. 3,700. (back issues avail.)
Description: Information regarding specialty of nuclear medicine and certification.

615.842　　　　US　ISSN 0888-8264
ULTRASOUND ANNUAL. 1984? a. price varies. Raven Press, 1185 Ave. of the Americas, New York, NY 10036. TEL 212-930-9500. FAX 212-869-3495. TELEX 640073. Ed. Roger C. Sanders. (back issues avail.)
Refereed Serial

615.842　　　　US　ISSN 0894-8771
RC78.7.U4　　　　CODEN: ULQUEZ
ULTRASOUND QUARTERLY. 1983. q. $98 to individuals; institutions $118. Raven Press, 1185 Ave. of the Americas, New York, NY 10036. TEL 212-930-9500. FAX 212-869-3495. TELEX 640073. Ed. Roger C. Sanders. adv.; charts; illus.; circ. 2,000.
—BLDSC shelfmark: 9082.815550.
Description: Publishes original articles on diagnostic information obtained by recent technological advances, and discussions of fundamental or controversial subjects.
Refereed Serial

UROLOGIC RADIOLOGY; a journal of diagnostic imaging and interventional uroradiology. see *MEDICAL SCIENCES — Urology And Nephrology*

615.8　　　　NE　ISSN 0921-2574
VANGNET. 1978. bi-m. fl.90. Vereniging voor Medisch Nucleair Werkers, c/o V.A.N.G., P.J., Graan voor Visch 14509, 2132 VE Hoofddorp, Netherlands. adv.; bk.rev.; circ. 350.

615.842　　　　RU　ISSN 0042-4676
　　　　　　　　　CODEN: VRRAAT
VESTNIK RENTGENOLOGII I RADIOLOGII/ANNALS OF ROENTGENOLOGY AND RADIOLOGY. (Text in Russian; summaries in English) 1920. bi-m. 21 Rub.($11.40) (Vsesoyuznoe Nauchnoe Obshchestvo Rentgenologov i Radiologov) Izdatel'stvo Meditsina, Petroverigskii pereulok 6-8, 101838 Moscow, Russia. (Co-sponsor: Ministerstvo Zdravookhraneniya S.S.S.R.) Ed. A.P. Savchenko. bk.rev.; bibl.; index. **Indexed:** Biol.Abstr., Chem.Abstr., Dent.Ind., Excerp.Med., Ind.Med.
—BLDSC shelfmark: 0033.700000.
Description: Publishes original papers devoted to elaboration on new methods of X-ray examination and updating the existing ones, their clinical use, problems of computer diagnosis in roentgenology, and more.

615.842 618　　　　US　ISSN 1052-2182
VIDEO JOURNAL OF COLOR FLOW IMAGING. (Includes 4 video cassettes.) 1987. q. $225 (effective 1991). Dynamedia, Inc., 2 Fulham Court, Silver Spring, MD 20902-3016. TEL 301-649-6886. FAX 301-579-3447. Ed. C.R.B. Merritt. adv.; circ. 1,000. (back issues avail.)
Description: Covers ultrasound imaging. Consists of tutorials, reviews, case reports and original research.
Refereed Serial

615.84 612.014　　　　US
VIEWBOX. 4/yr. American Osteopathic College of Radiology, 1402 Cottage Lane, Kirksville, MO 63501. TEL 816-626-2121. circ. 400.
Formerly: American Osteopathic College of Radiology. Newsletter. (ISSN 0065-9576)

618 574　　　　RU
VOPROSY RADIOBIOLOGII I BIOLOGICHESKOGO DEISTVIYA TSITOSTATICHESKIKH PREPARATOV. 1969. irreg. (Tomskii Meditsinskii Institut, Tsentral'naya Nauchno-Issledovatel'skaya Laboratoriya) Izdatel'svo Tomskii Universitet, Prospekt Lenina, 36, Tomsk-10, Russia. bibl.; illus.

615.84　　　　US　ISSN 0098-1672
RC78　　　　　　CODEN: YBDRE3
YEAR BOOK OF DIAGNOSTIC RADIOLOGY. 1932. a. $57.95. Mosby - Year Book, Inc., Continuity Division, 200 N. LaSalle, Chicago, IL 60601. TEL 312-726-9733. FAX 312-726-6075. TELEX 206155. Ed. Dr. Michael P. Federle. (reprint service avail.) **Indexed:** Curr.Adv.Ecol.Sci.
●Also available online. Vendor(s): BRS.
—BLDSC shelfmark: 9411.629000.
Formerly (until 1975): Year Book of Radiology (ISSN 0084-3989)

615.842 616.8　　　　US
▼**YEAR BOOK OF NEURORADIOLOGY.** 1992. a. $79.95. Mosby - Year Book, Inc. (Chicago) (Subsidiary of: Times Mirror Company), 200 N. LaSalle St., Chicago, IL 60601. TEL 312-726-9733. Ed. Dr. Anne Osborn.
●Also available online. Vendor(s): BRS.

615.8　　　　US　ISSN 0084-3903
RC93.A1　　　　CODEN: YNUMAH
YEAR BOOK OF NUCLEAR MEDICINE. 1966. a. $57.95. Mosby - Year Book, Inc., Continuity Division, 200 N. LaSalle, Chicago, IL 60601. TEL 312-726-9733. FAX 312-726-6075. TELEX 206155. Ed. Dr. Paul Hoffer. illus. (reprint service avail.) **Indexed:** Curr.Adv.Ecol.Sci.
●Also available online. Vendor(s): BRS.
—BLDSC shelfmark: 9414.645000.

615.842 610　　　　US　ISSN 1050-4443
RC78.7.U4
▼**YEAR BOOK OF ULTRASOUND.** 1991. a. $75. Mosby - Year Book, Inc. (Chicago) (Subsidiary of: Times Mirror Company), 200 N. LaSalle St., Chicago, IL 60601-1080. TEL 312-726-9733. FAX 312-726-6075. TELEX 206155. Ed. Dr. Christopher R.B. Merritt. illus.
●Also available online. Vendor(s): BRS.

615.842　　　　CC　ISSN 1001-6384
YINGXIANG YIXUE/MEDICAL IMAGING. (Text in Chinese) 1988. s-a. $10. Tianjin Di'er Yixueyuan - Tianjin No. 2 Medical Academy, 1 Guangdong Lu, Tianjin 300203, People's Republic of China. TEL 395086. (Co-sponsor: Japan Association of Radiological Technologists) Ed. Wu Enhui. adv.; bk.rev.

615.842　　　　GW　ISSN 0722-5067
ZEITSCHRIFT FUER CHEMOTHERAPIE. 1980. 6/yr. DM.48. c/o Prof. Lode, Eichenallee 36a, 1000 Berlin 19, Germany. TEL 030-3125059. Ed. Dr. R. Stahlmann. (back issues avail.)

615.842　　　　CC
ZHONGGUO YIXUE YINGXIANG JISHU/CHINESE MEDICAL PHOTOGRAPHY TECHNOLOGY. (Text in Chinese) q. Zhongguo Kexueyuan, Kejian Gongsi, A-1 Xi'erhuan Lu, Beijing 100037, People's Republic of China. TEL 8316302. Ed. Zhang Xingfu.

MEDICAL SCIENCES — Respiratory Diseases

616.2   US   ISSN 0893-8520
CODEN: AATIEN
A A R C TIMES. 1977. m. $50. (American Association for Respiratory Care) Daedalus Enterprises, Inc., 11030 Ables Ln., Dallas, TX 75229. TEL 214-243-2272. FAX 214-484-2720. Ed. Marsha Cathcart. adv.; circ. 31,000. (also avail. in microfilm; reprint service avail. from UMI) **Indexed:** CINAHL.
     Formerly: A A R Times (ISSN 0195-1777)
     Description: Presents news and features for the cardiorespiratory care profession.

A P S S NEWSLETTER. (Association of Professional Sleep Societies) see MEDICAL SCIENCES — Psychiatry And Neurology

616.2   US
A T S NEWS. 1975. bi-m. membership. American Thoracic Society, 1740 Broadway, New York, NY 10019-4374. TEL 212-315-8808. FAX 265-5642. Ed. Graham M. Nelan. cum.index; circ. 10,500.

616.2   US
ADVANCE FOR RESPIRATORY CARE PRACTITIONERS. w. Merion Publications, 650 Park Ave. W., King of Prussia, PA 19406. TEL 215-265-7812. FAX 215-265-8971. Ed. Vern Enge. circ. 49,732.

616.2   CN
AIRWAVE. 3/yr. free. (Manitoba Lung Association) Idea Marketing Group, 207 - 110 Osborne St. S., Winnipeg, Man. R3L 1Y5, Canada. TEL 204-479-5267. FAX 204-477-4339. (Subscr. to: M.L.A., 629 McDermott Ave., Winnipeg, Man. R3A 1P6, Canada. TEL 204-744-5501) Ed. Catherine Rudick. adv.; stat.; circ. 5,000. (back issues avail.)
     Description: Keeps MLA program users, donors and volunteers up-to-date regarding organization activities.

AMERICAN JOURNAL OF ASTHMA & ALLERGY FOR PEDIATRICIANS. see MEDICAL SCIENCES — Allergology And Immunology

616.2   US   ISSN 1044-1549
QP121.A1   CODEN: AJRBEL
AMERICAN JOURNAL OF RESPIRATORY CELL AND MOLECULAR BIOLOGY. 1989. m. $95 (foreign $115). (American Thoracic Society) American Lung Association, 1740 Broadway, New York, NY 10019-4374. TEL 212-315-8700.
     —BLDSC shelfmark: 0836.600000.

616.2   US   ISSN 0003-0805
RC306   CODEN: ARDSBL
AMERICAN REVIEW OF RESPIRATORY DISEASE; clinical and laboratory studies of tuberculosis and respiratory diseases. 1917. m. $130 to individuals (foreign $170); institutions $185 (foreign $225)(effective Jan.1991). (American Thoracic Society) American Lung Association, 1740 Broadway, New York, NY 10019-4374. TEL 212-315-8700. Ed. Robert A. Klocke. adv.; bk.rev.; abstr.; bibl.; charts; illus.; stat.; index; cum.index; circ. 14,500. (also avail. in microform from UMI,PMC; reprint service avail. from UMI) **Indexed:** Abstr.Hyg., Abstr.Inter.Med., Biol.Abstr., Biol.Dig., Biotech.Abstr., C.I.S. Abstr., Chem.Abstr., Curr.Adv.Cell & Devel.Biol., Curr.Adv.Ecol.Sci., Curr.Adv.Genetics & Molec.Biol., Curr.Cont., Dairy Sci.Abstr., Dent.Ind., Energy Ind., Energy Info.Abstr., Excerp.Med., Helminthol.Abstr., Hosp.Lit.Ind., Ind.Med., Ind.Sci.Rev., Ind.Vet., INIS Atomind., Lab.Haz.Bull., Ocean.Abstr., Pollut.Abstr., Protozool.Abstr., Rev.Med.& Vet.Mycol., Rev.Plant Path., Risk Abstr., Sci.Cit.Ind., Trop.Dis.Bull., Vet.Bull.
     —BLDSC shelfmark: 0853.860000.
     Former titles (1955-1959): American Review of Tuberculosis and Pulmonary Diseases (ISSN 0096-039X); American Review of Tuberculosis (ISSN 0096-0381)
     Refereed Serial

616.2   IT
CODEN: AMTIC3
ARCHIVIO MONALDI PER LE MALATTIE DEL TORACE. 1946. bi-m. L.70000($100) (effective 1992). Casa Editrice Idelson, Via A. De Gasperi 55, 80133 Naples, Italy. TEL 081-5524733. FAX 018-5518295. Ed. Ernesto Catena. adv. **Indexed:** Biol.Abstr., Chem.Abstr., Dent.Ind., Excerp.Med., Ind.Med.
     Formerly: Archivio di Tisiologia e delle Malattie dell'Aparato Respiratorio (ISSN 0004-0185)

616.2   AG   ISSN 0004-0509
ARCHIVOS ARGENTINOS DE TISIOLOGIA Y NEUMONOLOGIA. 1924. q. Hospital Municipal Dr. Enrique Tornu, Sociedad de Tisiologia y Neumologia, Hospital Tornu, Buenos Aires, Argentina. **Indexed:** Biol.Abstr., Chem.Abstr.
     Formerly: Archivos de Tisiologia.

616.2   SP   ISSN 0300-2896
CODEN: ARBRDA
ARCHIVOS DE BRONCONEUMOLOGIA. (Text in Spanish; summaries in English) m. (9/yr.). 5200 ptas.($53) to non-members. (Sociedad Espanola de Neumologia y Cirugia Toracica) Ediciones Doyma, S.A., Travesera de Gracia 17-21, 08021 Barcelona, Spain. TEL 200 07 11. FAX 209-11-36. TELEX 51964 INK-E. Ed. Dr. F. Manresa Presas. adv.: page 135000 ptas.; trim 210 x 280; adv. contact: Marta Cisa. bk.rev.; circ. 3,000. (reprint service avail. from UMI) **Indexed:** Excerp.Med., Ind.Med.Esp.
     Description: Covers broncho-pneumology, respiratory immunology, biochemical studies of secretions, and pulmonary surgery.

ARERUGIA. see MEDICAL SCIENCES — Allergology And Immunology

616.246   BL   ISSN 0004-2765
ARQUIVOS BRASILEIROS DE TUBERCULOSE E DOENCAS DO TORAX. (Summaries in English) 1938-1982; resumed 1987. q. gift or exchange basis. Instituto Brasileiro para Investigacao do Torax, Caixa Postal 635, Salvador, Bahia, Brazil. Ed. Jose Silveira. adv.; bk.rev.; bibl.; charts; illus.; circ. 1,000. **Indexed:** Biol.Abstr., Chem.Abstr.
     Formerly: I B I T Arquivos.

ASTHMA AND ALLERGY ADVOCATE. see MEDICAL SCIENCES — Allergology And Immunology

616.2   GW   ISSN 0724-5238
ASTHMA BRONCHITIS EMPHYSEM; Erkrankungen von Lunge und Atemwegen. 1982. 12/yr. DM.150. P M I Verlag GmbH, August-Schanz-Str. 21, 6000 Frankfurt a.M. 50, Germany. TEL 069-548000-0. FAX 069-548000-77. TELEX 412952-PMID. Ed. Peter Hoffmann. adv.; bk.rev.; circ. 20,000. (back issues avail.)
     Description: Summarizes seminar papers and articles for pulmonary specialists.

616.23   US   ISSN 1050-5253
▼**ASTHMA MANAGEMENT.** 1991. bi-m. $120 (foreign $170). Mary Ann Liebert, Inc., 1651 Third Ave., New York, NY 10128. TEL 212-289-2300. FAX 212-289-4697.
     Description: Covers current management techniques for clinicians and other health care professionals who treat patients with asthma. Includes current therapies, new treatment modalities, and sources for information.

616.23   AT   ISSN 0044-9776
ASTHMA WELFARER.* 1964. 2-3/yr. Aus.$10. Asthma Foundation of New South Wales, 1-82-86 Pacific Hwy., St. Leonards, N.S.W 2065, Australia. TEL 02 235-1293. Ed. Clair Isbister. adv.; bk.rev.; circ. 5,000.
     Description: Journal of the Asthma Foundation of N.S.W., a voluntary organisation involved in research, welfare and education to assist asthma sufferers.

616.2   GW   ISSN 0341-3055
CODEN: ATLUDF
ATEMWEGS- UND LUNGENKRANKHEITEN. 1975. m. DM.210($140) Dustri-Verlag Dr. Karl Feistle, Bahnhofstr. 9, 8024 Deisenhofen, Germany. TEL 089-613861-0. FAX 089-6135412. Ed. Dr. E. Krieger. **Indexed:** Biol.Abstr., Chem.Abstr., Curr.Adv.Ecol.Sci., Curr.Cont., Dok.Arbeitsmed., Excerp.Med., Ind.Sci.Rev., Sci.Cit.Ind.
     —BLDSC shelfmark: 1765.856000.

616.2   US   ISSN 0005-6367
BATTING THE BREEZE. 1965. bi-m. $15. Emphysema Anonymous, Inc., 12405-91st Terr. No., Box 3224, Seminole, FL 34642. TEL 813-391-9977. Ed. William E. Jaeckle. adv.; circ. 3,500.
     Description: Educational articles for patients with emphysema and other respiratory diseases.

616.2   US
BRONCHIAL MUCOLOGY SERIES. 1988. irreg., latest 1990. price varies. Raven Press, 1185 Ave. of the Americas, New York, NY 10036. TEL 212-930-9500. FAX 212-869-3495.

616.2   US
BUYER'S GUIDE OF CARDIO-RESPIRATORY EQUIPMENT AND SUPPLIES. 1983. a. $10. (American Association for Respiratory Care) Daedalus Enterprises, Inc., 11030 Ables Lane, Dallas, TX 75229. TEL 214-243-2272. FAX 214-484-2720. Ed. Dale L. Griffiths. adv.; circ. 25,000.

616.2   PE   ISSN 0069-2166
CENTRO DE SALUD "MAX ARIAS SCHREIBER", LIMA. CONGRESO NACIONAL DE TUBERCULOSIS Y ENFERMEDADES RESPIRATORIAS.* irreg., 1970, 9th. Dispensario Antituberculoso "Max Arias Schreiber", Raymondi 2da Cuadra (La Victoria), Lima, Peru.

616.246   PK
THE CHALLENGE. (Text in English) 1959. q. Rs.60($16) Pakistan Anti-Tuberculosis Association, Block No. 55, Rm. 8, Pakistan Secretariat, Karachi, Pakistan. TEL 21-510856. Ed. Dr. Al-Haj Syed Amjed Ali Jafri. adv.; bk.rev.; charts; stat.; bibl.; illus.; circ. 2,000. **Indexed:** Acad.Ind., Ind.Med.

616.2 616.12   US   ISSN 0012-3692
RC705   CODEN: CHETBF
CHEST; the journal of circulation, respiration and related systems. 1935. m. $84 to individuals; institutions $96. American College of Chest Physicians, 3300 Dundee Rd., Northbrook, IL 60062. FAX 708-498-5460. Ed. Dr. Alfred Soffer. adv.; bk.rev.; bibl.; illus.; index every 6 mos.; circ. 22,300. (also avail. in microfiche; reprint service avail. from UMI) **Indexed:** Abstr.Inter.Med., Biol.Abstr., C.I.S. Abstr., Chem.Abstr., CINAHL, Curr.Adv.Ecol.Sci., Curr.Cont., Dent.Ind., Dok.Arbeitsmed., Excerp.Med., Helminthol.Abstr., Ind.Med., Ind.Sci.Rev., Ind.Vet., INIS Atomind., Int.Nurs.Ind., Nutr.Abstr., Protozool.Abstr., Rev.Plant Path., Risk Abstr., Sci.Cit.Ind., Small Anim.Abstr.
     ●Also available online.
     —BLDSC shelfmark: 3172.530000.
     Formerly: Diseases of the Chest.
     Refereed Serial

616.2   US   ISSN 0272-5231
RC941
CLINICS IN CHEST MEDICINE. 1980. 4/yr. $84. W.B. Saunders Co., Curtis Center, Independence Square W., Philadelphia, PA 19106. TEL 215-238-7800. Ed. Susan Short. **Indexed:** Dok.Arbeitsmed., Excerp.Med., Ind.Med., Ind.Sci.Rev., Sci.Cit.Ind.
     —BLDSC shelfmark: 3286.545000.

616.2   US   ISSN 0163-7800
RC756
CURRENT PULMONOLOGY. 1977. a. $69.95. Mosby - Year Book, Inc. (Chicago) (Subsidiary of: Times Mirror Company), 200 N. LaSalle St., Chicago, IL 60601-1080. TEL 312-726-4177. FAX 312-726-6075. TELEX 206155. (Subscr. to: 11830 Westline Industrial Dr., St. Louis, MO 63146. TEL 800-325-1380) Eds. Dr. Daniel H. Simmons, Dr. Donald F. Tierney. illus.
     —BLDSC shelfmark: 3501.850000.
     Description: Survey developments in the field through a synopsis of the past twelve months of medical literature.

MEDICAL SCIENCES — RESPIRATORY DISEASES 3365

616.2   DK   ISSN 0903-1936
CODEN: ERJOEI
EUROPEAN RESPIRATORY JOURNAL. (Supplement avail. (ISSN 0904-1850)) (Text in English; summaries in French) 1924. 10/yr. DKK 1646 includes supplements. (European Respiratory Society) Munksgaard International Publishers Ltd., 35 Noerre Soegade, P.O. Box 2148, DK-1016 Copenhagen K, Denmark. TEL 33-127030. FAX 33-129387. TELEX 19431-MUNKS-DK. Ed. P. Vermiere. adv.; bk.rev.; illus.; index; circ. 4,500. (reprint service avail. from ISI) **Indexed:** Abstr.Hyg., Agri.Eng.Abstr., Biol.Abstr., Biotech.Abstr., C.I.S. Abstr., Chem.Abstr., CINAHL, Curr.Adv.Ecol.Sci., Curr.Cont., Dent.Ind., Dok.Arbeitsmed., Excerp.Med., Helminthol.Abstr., Ind.Med., Ind.Vet., Pig News & Info., Rev.Plant Path., Sci.Cit.Ind., Triticale Abstr., Trop.Dis.Bull., Vet.Bull.
—BLDSC shelfmark: 3829.924200.
Formed by the merger of: European Journal of Respiratory Diseases (ISSN 0106-4339); Which was formerly: Acta Tuberculosa et Pneumologica Belgica (ISSN 0001-7078) & Clinical Respiratory Physiology (ISSN 0271-9983); Which was formerly: Bulletin Europeen de Physiopathologie Respiratoire (ISSN 0395-3890)

616.2   US   ISSN 0190-2148
QP121.A1   CODEN: EXLRDA
EXPERIMENTAL LUNG RESEARCH. 1979. bi-m. $370. Hemisphere Publishing Corporation (Subsidiary of: Taylor & Francis Group), 1900 Frost Rd., Ste. 101, Bristol, PA 19007-1598. TEL 215-785-5800. FAX 215-785-5515. Ed. Paul Nettesheim. adv.; circ. 400. (back issues avail.; reprint service avail. from UMI) **Indexed:** Biol.Abstr., Chem.Abstr., Curr.Adv.Cell & Devel.Biol., Curr.Adv.Ecol.Sci., Curr.Cont., Excerp.Med., Ind.Med., Ind.Sci.Rev., Ind.Vet., INIS Atomind., Sci.Cit.Ind., Vet.Bull.
—BLDSC shelfmark: 3839.440000.
Description: Mechanisms of pulmonary biology and pathobiology, investigated at biochemical, subcellular, cellular and tissue levels.
Refereed Serial

G AND B. see *MEDICAL SCIENCES — Cardiovascular Diseases*

616.2   CC
GUOWAI YIXUE (HUXI XITONG FENCE)/FOREIGN MEDICAL SCIENCES (RESPIRATORY DISEASES). (Text in Chinese) q. Hebei Yixueyuan - Hebei Medical Institute, 5, Chang'an Xilu, Shijiazhuang, Hebei 050017, People's Republic of China. TEL 44121. Ed. Sun Yiyu.

H L B NEWSLETTER; reporting on heart, lung and blood disease research program, policy development. see *MEDICAL SCIENCES — Experimental Medicine, Laboratory Technique*

616.2   SW
HJAERT-LUNGFONDEN; Kvartalsskrift. 1906. q. $3.50. National-foereningen mot Hjaert-och Lungssjukdomar, Kungsgatan 54, S-111 35 Stockholm, Sweden. TEL 08-110173. FAX 08-7231725. Ed. Bjoern Lilliehoeoek. circ. 2,500. (back issues avail.)
Formerly: Hjaerta Kaerl Lungor (ISSN 0280-4638)

616.2   JA
HOKKAIDO UNIVERSITY. INSTITUTE OF IMMUNOLOGICAL SCIENCE. BULLETIN. (Text in Japanese; summaries in English and Japanese) 1953. a. exchange basis. Hokkaido University, Institute of Immunological Science, North 15, West 7, Sapporo 060, Japan. Ed. Ken-Ichi Yamamoto. circ. 300. **Indexed:** Biol.Abstr.
Formerly (until 1975): Kekkaku No Kenkyu (ISSN 0075-5354)

I C R D B CANCERGRAM: LUNG CANCER - DIAGNOSIS, TREATMENT. see *MEDICAL SCIENCES — Abstracting, Bibliographies, Statistics*

616.2   US   ISSN 0046-8762
IN-SHORT. 1971. m. free. American Lung Association of Brooklyn, 165 Cadman Plaza E., Brooklyn, NY 11201-1484. TEL 718-624-8531. Ed.Bd. bk.rev.; charts; illus.; circ. 2,300.
Formerly: Life and Breath of Brooklyn - Fresh Air News.

616.2   II   ISSN 0019-5707
CODEN: IJTBAD
INDIAN JOURNAL OF TUBERCULOSIS. (Text in English) 1953. q. Rs.60($20) Tuberculosis Association of India, c/o V.N. Swamy, 3 Red Cross Rd., New Delhi 1, India. TEL 381303. Ed. V.N. Swamy. adv.; bk.rev.; abstr.; bibl.; charts; illus.; stat.; index; cum.index; circ. 3,000. **Indexed:** Abstr.Hyg., Biol.Abstr., Chem.Abstr., Excerp.Med., Trop.Dis.Bull.
Description: Covers all aspects of tuberculosis and other chest diseases.

616.246   FR
INTERNATIONAL UNION AGAINST TUBERCULOSIS. CONFERENCE PROCEEDINGS. (Format varies; some reports also issued in Union's Bulletin) biennial, 23th, Tokyo. International Union against Tuberculosis, 199 rue des Pyrenees, F-85020 Paris, France.

616.2   BL   ISSN 0102-3586
JORNAL DE PNEUMOLOGIA. (Text in English, Portuguese, Spanish; summaries in English, Portuguese) 1974. q. Esc.1700($30) (Sociedade Brasileira de Pneumologia e Tisiologia) Ponto Cardeal Publicacoes Ltda., Rua Sete de Abril, 261 cj 512, 01043 Sao Paulo, Brazil. TEL 255-7340. Ed. Dr. Miguel Bogossian. circ. 2,200.

JOURNAL FOR ETHNOMUSICOLOGY. see *MUSIC*

616.2   US   ISSN 0894-2684
JOURNAL OF AEROSOL MEDICINE; deposition, clearance, and effects in the lung. q. $126 (foreign $166). Mary Ann Liebert, Inc., 1651 Third Ave., New York, NY 10128. TEL 212-289-2300. FAX 212-289-4697. Ed. Dr. Gerald C. Smaldone.
—BLDSC shelfmark: 4919.054000.
Description: Contains original articles and reviews that apply aerosols to the delivery of medication and the investigation for physiologic, pharmacologic, and toxicologic phenomena in the lung.

616.97   US   ISSN 0277-0903
RC591   CODEN: JOUADU
JOURNAL OF ASTHMA (NEW YORK). 1963. 6/yr. $65 to individuals; institutions $375. (Association for the Care of Asthma) Marcel Dekker Journals, 270 Madison Ave., New York, NY 10016. FAX 212-685-4540. TELEX 421419. (Subscr. to: Box 10018, Church St. Sta., New York, NY 10249) Ed. David Tinkelman. adv.; bk.rev.; bibl.; charts; illus.; stat.; index; cum. index: 1963-1965. (also avail. in microfilm; reprint service avail.) **Indexed:** Biol.Abstr., Chem.Abstr., Curr.Cont., Dent.Ind., Excerp.Med., Ind.Med., INIS Atomind., NRN, Psychol.Abstr., Ref.Zh.
—BLDSC shelfmark: 4947.295000.
Formerly (until vol.18, 1981): Journal of Asthma Research (ISSN 0021-9134)
Refereed Serial

616.2   US   ISSN 0194-259X
RC705
JOURNAL OF RESPIRATORY DISEASES. 1979. m. $65. Cliggott Publishing Co., 55 Holly Hill Ln., Box 4010, Greenwich, CT 06830. TEL 203-661-0600. Ed. Craig R. Borders. adv.; circ. 85,762. (reprint service avail.)
—BLDSC shelfmark: 5052.038200.
Description: Provides practical information about diagnosis and treatment pertaining to the respiratory system, both as the site of primary disease and as a complication of other clinical problems.
Refereed Serial

616.246   JA   ISSN 0022-9776
CODEN: KEKKAG
KEKKAKU/TUBERCULOSIS. (Text in Japanese; summaries in English) 1923. m. 15000 Yen (effective Jan. 1992). Japanese Society for Tuberculosis, c/o Research Institute of Tuberculosis, Matsuyama 3-chome, Kiyose-shi, Tokyo 204, Japan. FAX 0424-91-8315. Ed. Toru Katayama. adv.; abstr.; bibl.; charts; illus.; index; circ. 3,000. **Indexed:** Biol.Abstr., Chem.Abstr., Excerp.Med., Ind.Med., INIS Atomind.
—BLDSC shelfmark: 5089.250000.

616.2   JA   ISSN 0452-3458
CODEN: KOJUA9
KOKYO TO JUNKAN. (Text in Japanese; summaries in English) 1953. m. 24720 Yen($190) Igaku-Shoin Ltd., 5-24-3 Hongo, Bunkyo-ku, Tokyo 113-91, Japan. TEL 03-817-5703. Ed.Bd. circ. 4,500. **Indexed:** INIS Atomind.
●Also available online. Vendor(s): JICST.
—BLDSC shelfmark: 7777.630000.

616.2   JA   ISSN 0009-3378
CODEN: KDKBBH
KYOTO UNIVERSITY. CHEST DISEASE RESEARCH INSTITUTE. BULLETIN/KYOTO DAIGAKU KEKKAKU KYOBU SHIKKAN KENKYUJO KIYO. (Text and summaries in English and Japanese) 1968. s-a. free or exchange basis. Kyoto University, Chest Disease Research Institute - Kyoto Daigaku Kekkaku Kyobu Shikkan Kenkyujo, 53 Shogoin, Kawara-machi, Sakyo-ku, Kyoto 606, Japan. Ed.Bd. **Indexed:** Abstr.Hyg., Biol.Abstr., Excerp.Med., Ind.Med., INIS Atomind.
Formed by the merger of: Acta Tuberculosea Japonica; Keken Kiyo.

LIVEWELL. see *PHYSICAL FITNESS AND HYGIENE*

616.2   IT
LOTTA CONTRO LA TUBERCOLOSI E LE MALATTIE POLMONARI SOCIALI. (Text in Italian) 1930. q. L.45000($15.50) Federazione Italiana Contro la Tubercolosi e le Malattie Polmonari Sociali, Via Ezio 24, 00192 Rome, Italy. adv.; bk.rev.; bibl.; charts; illus.; stat.; index. cum.index: 1943-1944; circ. 3,000. **Indexed:** Abstr.Hyg., Biol.Abstr., C.I.S. Abstr., Chem.Abstr., Excerp.Med., Ind.Med., Trop.Dis.Bull.
Formerly: Lotta Contro la Tubercolosi (ISSN 0024-6638)
Description: Covers the study and research of tuberculosis and respiratory diseases.

616.2   US   ISSN 0341-2040
CODEN: LUNGD9
LUNG; an international journal on lungs, airways and breathing. (Text in English or German) 1903. 6/yr. $173.50. (Deutsche Gesellschaft fuer Lungen- und Atmungsforschung, GW) Springer-Verlag, Journals, 175 Fifth Ave., New York, NY 10010. TEL 212-460-1500. (Also Berlin, Heidelberg, Tokyo and Vienna) Ed. T. Higenbottam. adv.; bibl.; illus. (also avail. in microform from UMI; back issues avail.; reprint service avail. from ISI) **Indexed:** Biol.Abstr., Biotech.Abstr., C.I.S. Abstr., Chem.Abstr., Curr.Adv.Ecol.Sci., Curr.Cont., Excerp.Med., Ind.Med., Ind.Sci.Rev., Ind.Vet., INIS Atomind., Vet.Bull.
—BLDSC shelfmark: 5307.160000.
Former titles: Pneumonologie - Pneumonology (ISSN 0033-4073); Beitraege zur Klinik and Erforschung der Tuberkulose und der Lungenkrankheiten.
Description: Original articles on all aspects of basic and clinical research dealing with the lungs, airways, and breathing, including developmental, environmental, and genetic aspects.

616.2   GW   ISSN 0176-1749
LUNG AND RESPIRATION; diseases of lung and respiratory tract. 1984. q. P M I Verlag GmbH, August-Schanz-Str. 21, 6000 Frankfurt a.M. 50, Germany. TEL 069-548000-0. FAX 069-548000-77. TELEX 412952-PMI-D. Ed. Peter Hoffmann. circ. 5,000. (back issues avail.)

616.2   US
LUNG BIOLOGY IN HEALTH AND DISEASE. 1976. irreg., vol.57, 1992. price varies. Marcel Dekker, Inc., 270 Madison Ave., New York, NY 10016. TEL 212-696-9000. FAX 212-685-4540. TELEX 421419. **Indexed:** Biol.Abstr., Chem.Abstr.
Refereed Serial

616.2   GW   ISSN 0720-0706
LUNGE UND ATMUNG. 1975. bi-m. DM.40. P M I Verlag GmbH, August-Schanz-Str. 21, 6000 Frankfurt a.M. 50, Germany. TEL 069-548000-0. FAX 069-548000-77. TELEX 412952-PMI-D. (Co-sponsor: Dr. Karl Thomae GmbH) Ed. Peter Hoffmann. circ. 24,500. (back issues avail.)
Description: Seminar paper journal containing summaries of pneumologic articles and interviews.

616.2   JA
MEDICAL CONFERENCE SERIES. 1961. a. Japan Anti-Tuberculosis Association - Kekkaku Yobokai, 3-12, Misakicho 1-chome, Chiyoda-ku, Tokyo 101, Japan. FAX 03-3292-9208. Ed. Masakazu Aoki. circ. 20,000.

MEDICAL SCIENCES — RESPIRATORY DISEASES

616.2   IT
MEDICINA TORACICA; rassegna di fisiopatologia, clinica e riabilitazione cardiorespiratoria. 1978. q. L.72500($89) (Societa Italiana di Fisiopatologia Respiratoria) Masson Italia Periodici, Via Statuto 2-4, 20121 Milan, Italy. TEL 02-6367-1. FAX 02-6367211. (Co-sponsor: Fondazione Pro Clinica del Lavoro di Pavia) Ed. Carlo Grassi. circ. 1,000.
Refereed Serial

616.2   US   ISSN 0047-7060
MICHIGAN SOCIETY FOR RESPIRATORY THERAPY. JOURNAL. 1965. s-a. membership. Michigan Society for Respiratory Therapy, Box 950, 120 W. Saginaw St., East Lansing, MI 48823. Ed. John Darin. adv.; bk.rev.; abstr.; circ. 2,000. (tabloid format) **Indexed:** CINAHL.
—BLDSC shelfmark: 5980.871300.
Formerly (until spring 1975): Michigan Airway.

616.2   IT   ISSN 0026-4954
MINERVA PNEUMOLOGICA. (Text in Italian; summaries in English and Italian) 1962. q. L.60000($70) (Societa Italiana di Pneumologia) Edizioni Minerva Medica, Corso Bramante 83-85, 10126 Turin, Italy. Ed. O. Orlandi. adv.; bibl.; charts; illus.; index; circ. 2,000. **Indexed:** Biol.Abstr., Excerp.Med.
—BLDSC shelfmark: 5794.450000.

616.246 614   II   ISSN 0047-9136
N T I NEWSLETTER. (Text in English) 1964. q. free. National Tuberculosis Institute, No. 8 Bellary Rd., Bangalore 560003, India. Ed.Bd. bk.rev.; bibl.; illus.; circ. 800.

NATIONAL CENTRE FOR OCCUPATIONAL HEALTH. ANNUAL REPORT. see *OCCUPATIONAL HEALTH AND SAFETY*

616.2   NE   ISSN 0925-1944
NEDERLANDSE CYSTIC FIBROSIS STICHTING. C F NIEUWS. 1969. q. fl.1.75. Nederlandse Cystic Fibrosis Stichting, Lt. Gen. van Heutszlaan 6, 3743 JN Baarn, Netherlands. circ. 1,800.
Formerly: Nederlandse Cystic Fibrosis Stichting. Bericht.

616.2   JA   ISSN 0029-0645
NIHON KIKAN SHOKUDOKA GAKKAI KAIHO/JAPAN BRONCHO-ESOPHAGOLOGICAL SOCIETY. JOURNAL. (Text in Japanese; summaries in English) 1949. bi-m. 10000 Yen. Nihon Kikan Shokudoka Gakkai - Japan Broncho-Esophagological Society, Uno Bldg., 2-3-11 Koraku, Bunkyo-ku, Tokyo 112, Japan. FAX 03-3815-2810. Ed. Dr. Kiyoshi Togawa. adv.; bk.rev.; abstr.; cum.index; circ. 3,700. **Indexed:** Biol.Abstr., Excerp.Med.
—BLDSC shelfmark: 4804.700000.

613   US
NOVA REPORT ON LUNG HEALTH AND WELLNESS. 1964. bi-m. free. American Lung Association of Northern Virginia, 9735 Main St., Fairfax, VA 22031. TEL 703-591-4131. Ed. Kurt Gregory Erickson. film rev.; stat.; circ. 6,000. (processed)
Former titles (until 1983): Potomac View on Lung Health; Potomac View (ISSN 0032-5643)

PEDIATRIC PULMONOLOGY. see *MEDICAL SCIENCES — Pediatrics*

616.2   US
PNEUMOGRAM.* 1980. q. free. California Society of Respiratory Care, c/o Equicor Health Plan, Box 25789, Anaheim, CA 92825-5789. TEL 818-995-7338. FAX 818-995-0878. Ed. Chuck Swanson. adv.; circ. 2,623.

616.2   BU   ISSN 0324-1491
                 CODEN: PNFTD3
PNEUMOLOGIA I FTIZIATRIA. (Text in Bulgarian; summaries in English, Russian) 1964. q. 10 lv. (Ministerstvo na Narodnoto Zdrave) Izdatelstvo Meditsina i Fizkultura, 11, Pl. Slaveikov, Sofia, Bulgaria. (Co-sponsor: Nauchno Druzhestvo po Pneumologia i Ftiziatria) Ed. P. Dobrev. circ. 603. **Indexed:** Abstr.Bulg.Sci.Med.Lit., C.I.S. Abstr.
—BLDSC shelfmark: 0129.694000.
Formerly: Ftiziatria.

616.2   GW   ISSN 0934-8387
                 CODEN: PNEMEC
PNEUMOLOGIE. (Text in German; summaries in English, French, German, Spanish) 1945. m. DM.246. (Deutsches Zentralkommittee zur Bekaempfung der Tuberkulose) Georg Thieme Verlag, Ruedigerstr. 14, Postfach 104853, 7000 Stuttgart 10, Germany. TEL 0711-8931-0. FAX 0711-8931298. (Co-sponsor: Deutsche Gesellschaft fuer Lungenkrankheiten und Tuberkulose) Ed. R. Ferlinz. adv.; bk.rev.; charts; illus.; stat.; index; circ. 2,100. (also avail. in microfilm from UMI; reprint service avail. from UMI) **Indexed:** Biol.Abstr., C.I.S. Abstr., Chem.Abstr., Curr.Cont., Dent.Ind., Ind.Med., Ind.Vet., Sci.Cit.Ind., Vet.Bull.
—BLDSC shelfmark: 6541.113200.
Former titles: Praxis und Klinik der Pneumologie (ISSN 0342-7498); Praxis der Pneumologie (ISSN 0032-7069); Incorporates: Tuberkulosearzt.

616.246   HU
PNEUMONOLOGIA HUNGARICA. (Text in Hungarian; summaries in English, German and Russian) 1945. m. 180 Ft.($18) Ifjusagi Lap-es Konyvkiado Vallalat, Revay u. 16, 1374 Budapest 6, Hungary. (Subscr. to: Kultura, Box 149, H-1389 Budapest, Hungary) Ed. Dr. Laszlo Mihoczy. adv.; bk.rev.; charts; illus.; index; circ. 1,200. **Indexed:** Ind.Med.
Formerly: Tuberkulozis es Tudobetegsegek (ISSN 0041-3887)

616.2   PL
                 CODEN: PNPOD4
PNEUMONOLOGIA I ALERGOLOGIA POLSKA. (Text and abstracts in English and Polish) 1926. bi-m. $168. Institute of Tuberculosis and Pulmonary Deseases, Ul. Plocka 26, Warsaw, Poland. TEL 48-22-324451. (Co-sponsors: Polish Society of Allergology; Polish Society of Phtysiopneumomology) Ed. Tadeusz Plusa. adv.; bk.rev.; abstr.; illus.; stat.; circ. 1,500. **Indexed:** Chem.Abstr., Dok.Arbeitsmed., Excerp.Med., Ind.Med.
Former titles (until 1991): Pneumonologia Polska (ISSN 0376-4761); Gruzlica i Choroby Pluc (ISSN 0017-4955)
Description: Discusses diseases of the lungs, epidemiology, physiology of respiration and clinical pneumonology.

616.2   US   ISSN 0897-9677
RC731
PROBLEMS IN RESPIRATORY CARE. q. $60 to individuals (foreign $80); institutions $85 (foreign $100). J.B. Lippincott Co., E. Washington Sq., Philadelphia, PA 19105. TEL 215-238-4295. (Subscr. to: Downville, Rte. 3, Box 20-B, Hagerstown, MD 21740) Eds. Richard D. Branson, RRT, Neil MacIntyre, M.D. (also avail. in microform from UMI)
—BLDSC shelfmark: 6617.926300.
Description: For problems encountered in daily practice with patients with acute or chronic respiratory problems.

616.246   RU   ISSN 0032-9533
                 CODEN: PRTUAX
PROBLEMY TUBERKULEZA/PROBLEMS OF TUBERCULOSIS. (Text in Russian; summaries in English) 1923. m. 20.40 Rub.($17.40) (Vsesoyuznoe Nauchnoe Obshchestvo Ftiziatrov) Izdatel'stvo Meditsina, Petroverigskii pereulok 6-8, 101838 Moscow, Russia. (Co-sponsor: Ministerstvo Zdravookhraneniya S.S.S.R.) Ed. A.G. Khomenko. bk.rev.; index. **Indexed:** Biol.Abstr., Chem.Abstr., Dent.Ind., Dok.Arbeitsmed., Excerp.Med., Ind.Med., Ind.Vet., Vet.Bull.
—BLDSC shelfmark: 0133.840000.
Description: Deals with problems of epidemiology and organization of tuberculosis control, as well as prophylaxis, clinical diagnosis and treatment of tuberculosis. Includes data on the theoretical and practical achievements in phthisis and pulmonology.

616.2   SZ   ISSN 0079-6751
QP121.A1   CODEN: PGRRB6
PROGRESS IN RESPIRATION RESEARCH. (Text in English) 1963. irreg. (approx. 1/yr.). price varies. S. Karger AG, Allschwilerstr. 10, P.O. Box, CH-4009 Basel, Switzerland. TEL 061-3061111. FAX 061-3061234. TELEX CH 962652. Ed. H. Herzog. (reprint service avail. from ISI) **Indexed:** Biol.Abstr., Chem.Abstr., Curr.Adv.Ecol.Sci., Curr.Cont., Ind.Med.
—BLDSC shelfmark: 6924.525500.

615.64   CN   ISSN 0831-2478
R R T: THE CANADIAN JOURNAL OF RESPIRATORY THERAPY. 1965. q. (plus suppl.). Can.$30($30) Canadian Medical Association, P.O. Box 8650, Ottawa, Ont. K1G 0G8, Canada. TEL 613-731-9331. FAX 613-523-0937. Eds. Les Mattews, Cliff Seville. adv.; bk.rev.; charts; illus.; stat.; bibl.; circ. 2,600. **Indexed:** C.I.N.L.
—BLDSC shelfmark: 8036.660000.
Former titles: Respiratory Technology; Canadian Inhalation Therapy (ISSN 0008-3852)
Description: Official publication of Canadian Society of Respiratory Therapists. Contains feature articles, new product news, history, editorials and abstracts.
Refereed Serial

616.2   US
R T: JOURNAL OF RESPIRATORY CARE PROFESSIONALS. bi-m. Allied Healthcare Publications, 1849 Sawtelle Blvd., Los Angeles, CA 90025-7012. TEL 213-479-1769. FAX 213-479-6275. Ed. Amy Allen. circ. 20,000.

616.2   US
R T MAGAZINE. (Respiratory Therapy) 1988. bi-m. Curant Communications, Inc., 4676 Admiralty Way., Ste. 202, Marina Del Rey, CA 90292-6603. TEL 213-479-1769. FAX 213-301-3329. Ed. Sandra Todd.

616.2   IT   ISSN 0033-9563
RASSEGNA DI PATOLOGIA DELL'APPARATO RESPIRATORIO. 1951. q. L.100000 (foreign L.130000)(effective 1992). (Federazione Italiana Lotta Contro la Tubercolosi) Pacini Editore s.r.l., Via Gherardesca 1, 56014 Ospedaletto (Pisa), Italy. TEL 050-982439. FAX 050-983906. Ed. Benito Leoncini. adv.; bk.rev.; bibl.; charts; illus.; index; circ. 1,000. **Indexed:** Chem.Abstr., Excerp.Med.

616.2   JA   ISSN 0016-2531
RED DOUBLE-BARRED CROSS/FUKUJUJI. (Text in Japanese) 1955. bi-m. free. Japan Anti-Tuberculosis Association - Kekkaku Yobokai, 1-3-12 Misaki-cho, Chiyoda-ku, Tokyo 101, Japan. FAX 03-3292-9208. Ed. Tetsuo Kawakami. adv.; bk.rev.; charts; illus.; stat.; circ. 20,000.

617.54 616.995   SZ   ISSN 0025-7931
RC705   CODEN: RESPBD
RESPIRATION; international review of thoracic diseases. (Text in English, French and German; summaries in English) 1944. bi-m. 545 Fr.($364) S. Karger AG, Allschwilerstr. 10, P.O. Box, CH-4009 Basel, Switzerland. TEL 061-3061111. FAX 061-3061234. TELEX CH 962652. Ed. H. Herzog. adv.; charts; illus.; circ. 1,200. (also avail. in microform from RPI) **Indexed:** Biol.Abstr., C.I.S. Abstr., Chem.Abstr., Curr.Adv.Ecol.Sci., Curr.Cont., Dok.Arbeitsmed., Excerp.Med., Helminthol.Abstr., Ind.Med., Rev.Plant Path.
—BLDSC shelfmark: 7777.620000.
Formerly: Medicina Thoracalis.

615.64   US   ISSN 0730-8418
RESPIRATORY CARE; a monthly science journal. 1956. m. $50. (American Association for Respiratory Care) Daedalus Enterprises, Inc., 11030 Ables Lane, Dallas, TX 75229. TEL 214-243-2272. FAX 214-484-2720. Ed. Pat Brougher. adv.; bk.rev.; abstr.; charts; illus.; index; circ. 32,000. (also avail. in microform from UMI; reprint service avail. from UMI) **Indexed:** Biol.Abstr., C.I.N.L., CINAHL, Excerp.Med., Hosp.Lit.Ind., Nurs.Abstr.
—BLDSC shelfmark: 7777.660000.
Former titles (until 1979): R C Respiratory Care (ISSN 0098-9142); (until 1973): Respiratory Care (ISSN 0020-1324); (until 1970): Inhalation Therapy.

616.2   UK   ISSN 0262-7043
RESPIRATORY DISEASE IN PRACTICE. Abbreveiated title: R D I P. 1982. bi-m. £18. Hayward Medical Communications, Hayward House, 1 Threshers Yard, Kingham, Oxon OX7 6YF, England. TEL 0608-659595. Ed. Dr. Martyn Partridge. adv.; bk.rev.; circ. 21,000.
—BLDSC shelfmark: 7777.661000.

616.2   NE
RESPIRATORY DISEASES DIGEST. 8/yr. fl.60.50. Uitgeverij Promedia B.V., De Steiger 180, 1351 AT Almere, Netherlands. Ed. Hans Weill. adv.; circ. 400.

MEDICAL SCIENCES — RESPIRATORY DISEASES

616.246 KE
RESPIRATORY DISEASES RESEARCH CENTRE. ANNUAL REPORT. (Text in English) 1974. a. free. Kenya Medical Research Institute, Kenya Tuberculosis & Respiratory Diseases Research Centre, Box 47855, Nairobi, Kenya. circ. 200. (back issues avail.) Indexed: Biol.Abstr.
Former titles: Kenya Tuberculosis and Respiratory Diseases Research Center. Annual Report; Kenya Tuberculosis Investigation Centre. Annual Report; **Supersedes in part:** East African Tuberculosis Investigation Centre. Annual Report.

615.64 US ISSN 0892-9289
RESPIRATORY MANAGEMENT. suspended 1988 (vol.18, no.4); resumed 1989 (vol.19, no.1). bi-m. $48. Choices Publishing Group, 129 Washington St., Hoboken, NJ 07030. TEL 201-792-1900. FAX 201-792-3955. Ed. Thomas C. Holland. adv.; bk.rev.; charts; illus.; cum.index; circ. 39,500. Indexed: CINAHL, Hosp.Lit.Ind.
Formerly: Respiratory Therapy (ISSN 0048-7392)

616.2 UK ISSN 0954-6111
CODEN: RMEDEY
RESPIRATORY MEDICINE. 1907. bi-m. $146. Bailliere Tindall, 24-28 Oval Rd., London NW1 7DX, England. TEL 071-267-4466. FAX 071-482-2293. Ed. R. Davies. adv.; bk.rev.; charts; illus.; stat.; index. (also avail. in microform from UMI; back issues avail.) Indexed: Abstr.Hyg., Biol.Abstr., Biotech.Abstr., C.I.S. Abstr., Chem.Abstr., Curr.Adv.Ecol.Sci., Curr.Cont., Excerp.Med., Helminthol.Abstr., Ind.Med., Ind.Sci.Rev., Protozool.Abstr., Rev.Plant Path., Trop.Dis.Bull.
●Also available online. Vendor(s): BRS.
—BLDSC shelfmark: 7777.661900.
Formerly: British Journal of Diseases of the Chest (ISSN 0007-0971)
Description: Provides an international forum for people who are involved in the various disciplines concerned with all aspects of respiratory diseases.

616.2 US
RESPIRATORY PRACTITIONER.* 1986. q. $25. Reliable Multi-Media Productions, 5705 Sepulveda Blvd., Culver City, CA 90230-6405. Eds. James B. Fink, Stephan W. Ruesh. adv.; circ. 20,000.
Description: For individuals and institutions involved in the services and technologies of respiratory care and its associated diseases.

RESPIRATORY SYSTEM. see BIOLOGY — Physiology

616.2 615.8 IE ISSN 0300-9572
CODEN: RSUSBS
RESUSCITATION; an exciting journal for the dissemination of clinical and basic science research relating to critical care and emergency medicine. 1972. 6/yr.(in 2 vols./3 nos./vol.) $357 (effective 1992). Elsevier Scientific Publishers Ireland Ltd., P.O. Box 85, Limerick, Ireland. TEL 061-61944. FAX 061-62144. TELEX 72191 ENH EI. (Subscr. in U.S. and Canada to: Elsevier Science Publishing Co., Inc., Box 882, Madison Sq. Sta., New York, NY 10159. TEL 212-989-5800) Ed. J.B. McCabe. adv.; bk.rev.; charts; illus.; index. (also avail. in microform from RPI) Indexed: Biol.Abstr., Chem.Abstr., Curr.Adv.Ecol.Sci., Curr.Cont., Excerp.Med., Ind.Med.
—BLDSC shelfmark: 7785.420000.
Description: Covers etiology, pathophysiology, diagnosis and treatment of acute diseases.
Refereed Serial

616.995 616.2 RM
REVISTA DE IGIENA, BACTERIOLOGIE, VIRUSOLOGIE, PARAZITOLOGIE, PNEUMOFTIZIOLOGIE. (Text in Rumanian; summaries in English, French, German, Russian) 1952. 4/yr. $20. Uniunea Societatilor de Stiinte Medicale din Republica Socialista Rumania, Str. Progresului No. 8, Bucharest, Rumania. (Subscr. to: ILEXIM, Str. 13 Decembrie Nr. 3, P.O. Box 136-137, Bucharest, Rumania) Ed.Bd. adv.; bk.rev.; abstr.; charts; illus. Indexed: Biol.Abstr., Chem.Abstr., Ind.Med.
Formerly: Ftiziologia (ISSN 0016-2329)

616.2 616.1 FR ISSN 0761-8417
CODEN: RPCLEZ
REVUE DE PNEUMOLOGIE CLINIQUE; le poumon et le coeur. (Text in French; summaries in English) 1945. bi-m. 133 ECU($161) (typically set in Jan.). Masson, 120 bd. Saint Germain, 75280 Paris Cedex 06, France. TEL 1-46-34-21-60. FAX 1-45-87-29-99. TELEX 202 671 F. Ed. C. Mayaud. adv.; bk.rev.; abstr.; bibl.; charts; illus.; stat.; index; circ. 1,350. (also avail. in microform from UMI; reprint service avail. from ISI,UMI) Indexed: Biol.Abstr., C.I.S. Abstr., Chem.Abstr., Dent.Ind., Dok.Arbeitsmed., Excerp.Med., Ind.Med., Rev.Plant Path.
Formerly: Poumon et le Coeur (ISSN 0032-5821)

616.2 FR ISSN 0761-8425
CODEN: RFMRAT
REVUE DES MALADIES RESPIRATOIRES. 1893. bi-m. 145 ECU($185) (typically set in Jan.). (Societe Francaise de Tuberculose) Masson, 120 bd. Saint-Germain, 75280 Paris Cedex 06, France. TEL 1-46-34-21-60. FAX 1-45-87-29-99. TELEX 202 671 F. (Co-sponsor: Comite National de Defense Contre la Tuberculose) Ed. J.L. Racineux. adv.; bk.rev.; abstr.; illus.; index; circ. 2,800. (also avail. in microfilm; reprint service avail. from ISI) Indexed: ASCA, Biol.Abstr., C.I.S. Abstr., Chem.Abstr., Curr.Adv.Ecol.Sci., Curr.Cont., Dok.Arbeitsmed., Excerp.Med., Helminthol.Abstr., Ind.Med., Rev.Plant Path.
—BLDSC shelfmark: 7926.824000.
Former titles (until 1983): Revue Francaise des Maladies Respiratoires (ISSN 0301-0279); (until 1973): Revue de Tuberculose et de Pneumologie (ISSN 0035-1792)
Description: Information on pneumonia, tuberculosis and respiratory diseases.

616.2 IT ISSN 0302-4717
RIVISTA DI PATOLOGIA E CLINICA DELLA TUBERCOLOSI E DI PNEUMOLOGIA. (Text in Italian; summaries in English, French) 1927. bi-m. L.40000($70) Associazione Emilia Romagna Contro la Tubercolosi e le Malatie Polmonari Sociali, Via Brugnoli 5, 40122 Bologna, Italy. Ed. Enrico Fasano. adv.; bk.rev.; abstr.; index. cum.index; circ. 1,000. Indexed: Biol.Abstr., Excerp.Med.
—BLDSC shelfmark: 7992.335000.
Formerly: Rivista di Patologia e Clinica della Tubercolosi (ISSN 0035-6425)

616.246 SA ISSN 0036-0872
S A N T A. T B NEWS/S A N T A. T B NUUS. (Text in Afrikaans, English) 1953. m. donation. South African National Tuberculosis Association - Suid-Afrikaanse Nasionale Tuberkulose Vereniging, P.O. Box 10501, Johannesburg 2000, South Africa. TEL 011-29-9636. FAX 011-333-9057. Ed. Heather Basson. adv.; illus.; stat.; circ. 9,000.
Description: Informs readers of news and events involving the association.

616.246 SA ISSN 0081-2501
S A N T A ANNUAL REPORT/S A N T A JAARLIKSE VERSLAG. (Text in Afrikaans, English) 1949. a. free. South African National Tuberculosis Association - Suid-Afrikaanse Nasionale Tuberkulose Vereniging, P.O. Box 10501, Johannesburg 2000, South Africa. TEL 011-29-9636. FAX 011-333-9057. Ed. Heather Basson. circ. 2,000.
Description: Features SANTA's financial statements, review of the year's activities, history of investments made, as well as the present status of TB containment.

616.246 SA
S A N T A HEALTH MAGAZINE. (Text in English) 1953. q. free. South African National Tuberculosis Association, P.O. Box 10501, Johannesburg 2000, South Africa. TEL 011-29-9636. FAX 011-333-9057. Ed. Heather Basson. abstr.; illus.; circ. 20,000.
Formerly: S A N T A Bantu (ISSN 0036-0880)
Description: Purpose is to provide information conducive to a healthier informed community.

616.2 US ISSN 0882-0546
CODEN: SRINES
SEMINARS IN RESPIRATORY INFECTIONS. (Translated into Spanish) 1986. q. $87 to individuals; institutions $116; foreign $119. W.B. Saunders Co., Curtis Center, Independence Square W., Philadelphia, PA 19106. TEL 215-238-7800. Ed. Dr. George A. Sarosi. adv.; abstr.; bibl.; charts; illus.; index.
—BLDSC shelfmark: 8239.457500.

616.2 US ISSN 0192-9755
CODEN: SRMEDK
SEMINARS IN RESPIRATORY MEDICINE. 1979. q. $68 to individuals; institutions $90. Thieme Medical Publishers, Inc., 381 Park Avenue South, New York, NY 10016. Eds. T.L. Petty, R.M. Cherniack. adv.; index; circ. 1,700. (also avail. in microform from UMI; reprint service avail. from UMI) Indexed: ASCA, Curr.Adv.Ecol.Sci., Excerp.Med.
●Also available online. Vendor(s): BRS, BRS/Saunders Colleague.
—BLDSC shelfmark: 8239.458000.
Description: Clinical articles written by pulmonary clinicians providing an overview of principles and practice of modern respiratory care.

616.2 CS ISSN 0371-2222
CODEN: SPPCAC
STUDIA PNEUMOLOGICA ET PHTISEOLOGICA CECHOSLOVACA. (Text in Czech or Slovak; summaries in Czech, English, Russian) 1940. 10/yr. $48.60. (Ceskoslovenska Pneumologicka a Ftizeologicka Spolecnost) Avicenum, Czechoslovak Medical Press, Malostranske nam. 28, 118 02 Prague 1, Czechoslovakia. (Dist. by: Artia, Ve Smeckach 30, 111 27 Prague 1, Czechoslovakia) (Co-sponsor: Ceskoslovenska Lekarska Spolecnost J. Ev. Purkyne) Ed. Dr. L. Sula. bk.rev. Indexed: Abstr.Hyg., Biol.Abstr., C.I.S. Abstr., Chem.Abstr., Trop.Dis.Bull.
Formerly: Rozhledy v Tuberkuloze a Nemocech Plicnich.

TASK FORCE ON ENVIRONMENTAL CANCER AND HEART AND LUNG DISEASE. ANNUAL REPORT TO CONGRESS. see ENVIRONMENTAL STUDIES — Toxicology And Environmental Safety

616.2 US ISSN 8756-8616
TECHNOLOGY FOR RESPIRATORY THERAPY. m. $90 (Canada $100; elsewhere $120). (Emergency Care Research Institute) E C R I, 5200 Butler Pike, Plymouth Meeting, PA 19462. TEL 215-825-6000. FAX 215-834-1275. Ed. Robert Hochschild.
Formerly: Health Devices Update: Respiratory Therapy.
Refereed Serial

616.2 NE ISSN 0040-2125
TEGEN DE TUBERCULOSE. 1904. q. fl.7.50($4.) Koninklijke Nederlandse Centrale Vereniging tot Bestrijding der Tuberculose, Box 146, 2501 CC The Hague, Netherlands. Ed.Bd. adv.; bk.rev.; illus.; circ. 3,500. (also avail. in microfilm)
—BLDSC shelfmark: 8763.510000.

616.2 UY ISSN 0049-4143
TORAX. (Text in Spanish; summaries in English) 1952. q. Urg.$15($20) Sociedad de Tisiologia y Enfermedades del Torax de Uruguay, Avda. 18 de Julio 2175, Casilla de Correo 10724, Montevideo, Uruguay. (Co-sponsor: Sociedad de Cardiologia) Ed. Dante Tomalino. adv.; bibl.; charts; illus.; index. Indexed: Biol.Abstr., Excerp.Med., Ind.Med.
Supersedes: Revista de Tuberculosis del Uruguay.

616.246 UK ISSN 0962-8479
CODEN: TUBEAS
TUBERCLE AND LUNG DISEASE. 1992. 4/yr. £125($232) (International Union against Tuberculosis and Lung Disease) Churchill Livingstone Medical Journals, Robert Stevenson House, 1-3 Baxter's Pl., Leith Walk, Edinburgh EH1 3AF, Scotland. TEL 031-556-2424. FAX 031-558-1278. TELEX 727511. (Subscr. to: Longman Group, Journals Subscr. Dept, P.O. Box 77, Fourth Ave., Harlow, Essex CM19 5AA, England; U.S. subscr. to: Churchill Livingstone, 650 Ave. of the Americas, New York, NY 10011. TEL 212-206-5000) Ed. Jaques Cretien. bk.rev.; adv.; bibl.; illus.; index; circ. 2,300. Indexed: Abstr.Hyg., Biol.Abstr., Biotech.Abstr., Chem.Abstr., Curr.Adv.Ecol.Sci., Curr.Cont., Excerp.Med., Ind.Med., Ind.Vet., Trop.Dis.Bull., Vet.Bull.
—BLDSC shelfmark: 9068.105000.
Formed by the merger of (1919-1992): Tubercle (ISSN 0041-3879); (1924-1992): International Union against Tuberculosis and Lung Disease. Bulletin (ISSN 0074-9249)
Description: Publishes primary articles and commissioned reviews on both research and clinical work in tuberculosis and other lung diseases, with particular emphasis on community health.

TUBERCULOSIS, LEPROSY AND CANCER. see MEDICAL SCIENCES — Communicable Diseases

MEDICAL SCIENCES — RHEUMATOLOGY

616.246 614   US
RC313
U.S. CENTERS FOR DISEASE CONTROL. TUBERCULOSIS STATISTICS IN THE UNITED STATES. 1974. a. free. U.S. Centers for Disease Control, Tuberculosis Control Division, 1600 Clifton Rd. N.E., Atlanta, GA 30333. TEL 404-329-2501. charts; illus.; stat.; circ. 7,000.
   Formed by the merger of: U.S. Centers for Disease Control. Tuberculosis in the United States (ISSN 0149-2616); U.S. Centers for Disease Control. Tuberculosis Statistics: States and Cities; Which was formerly: U.S. Centers for Disease Control. Tuberculosis: States and Cities. Tuberculosis Statistics: States and Cities was formed by the merger of: U.S. Centers for Disease Control. Reported Tuberculosis Data; U.S. Centers for Disease Control. Tuberculosis Program Reports.

616.995   AG
UNIVERSIDAD DE BUENOS AIRES. CATEDRA DE PATOLOGIA Y CLINICA DE LA TUBERCULOSIS. ANALES. vol.29, 1970. irreg. Universidad de Buenos Aires, Catedra de Patologia y Clinica de la Tuberculosis, Avda. Velez Sarsfield 405, Buenos Aires, Argentina. **Indexed:** Biol.Abstr.

616.2
VOICE FOUNDATION. NEWSLETTER.* q. Voice Foundation, 40 W. 57th St., New York, NY 10019.

616.2   US   ISSN 8756-3452
RC705
YEAR BOOK OF PULMONARY DISEASE. 1986. a. $57.95. Mosby - Year Book, Inc., Continuity Division, 200 N. LaSalle, Chicago, IL 60601. TEL 312-726-9746. FAX 312-726-6075. TELEX 206155. Ed. Dr. Gareth M. Green. illus. (reprint service avail.)
  ●Also available online. Vendor(s): BRS.
  —BLDSC shelfmark: 9415.850000.

616.2   CN   ISSN 0044-104X
YOUR HEALTH. 1918. biennial. free. British Columbia Lung Association, 906 W. Broadway, Vancouver, B.C. V5Z 1K7, Canada. TEL 604-731-4961. FAX 604-731-5810. Ed. Jerry Miller. charts; illus.; circ. 18,500.

616.2   ZA   ISSN 0084-5000
ZAMBIA. PNEUMOCONIOSIS MEDICAL AND RESEARCH BUREAU AND PNEUMOCONIOSIS COMPENSATION BOARD. ANNUAL REPORTS. 1964. a. 25 n. Government Printer, P.O. Box 136, Lusaka, Zambia.

MEDICAL SCIENCES — Rheumatology

616.7   US
A H A P PERSPECTIVE. 1965. q. membership. (Arthritis Health Professions Association) Arthritis Foundation, 1314 Spring St., N.W., Atlanta, GA 30309. TEL 404-872-7100. FAX 404-872-8694. Ed. Dr. Gail Davis.

ACTA MEDICA MEDITERRANEA. see *MEDICAL SCIENCES — Psychiatry And Neurology*

616.742   PO
ACTA REUMATOLOGICA PORTUGUESA. (Text in Portuguese; summaries in Portuguese, English, French) 1973. q. free. Sociedade Portuguesa de Reumatologia, Rua de Dona Estefania, 187-189, Lisbon-1, Portugal. adv.; bk.rev.; abstr.; bibl.; charts; illus.; stat.; circ. 1,000. **Indexed:** Excerp.Med.

616.742   FR   ISSN 0065-1818
ACTUALITE RHUMATOLOGIQUE PRESENTEE AU PRATICIEN; cahier annuel d'informations et de renseignements. a. price varies. Expansion Scientifique, 15 rue Saint Benoit, 75278 Paris Cedex 06, France. TEL 1-45-48-42-60. FAX 1-45-44-81-55.

616.7   US
RC933
ADVISORY BOARD FOR ARTHRITIS AND MUSCULOSKELETAL AND SKIN DISEASES. ANNUAL REPORT. 1977. a. free. Advisory Board for Arthritis and Musculoskeletal and Skin Diseases, National Institute of Arthritis and Musculoskeletal and Skin Diseases, 1801 Rockville Pike, Ste. 500, Rockville, MD 20852. circ. 1,000.
  Formerly: U.S. National Arthritis Advisory Board. Annual Report (ISSN 0190-5422)

616.72   GW   ISSN 0341-051X
CODEN: AKRHDB
AKTUELLE RHEUMATOLOGIE. 1976. bi-m. DM.165. Georg Thieme Verlag, Ruedigerstr. 14, Postfach 104853, 7000 Stuttgart 10, Germany. Ed.Bd. index; circ. 4,200. (reprint service avail. from UMI) **Indexed:** Curr.Adv.Ecol.Sci., Curr.Cont., Excerp.Med., INIS Atomind.
  —BLDSC shelfmark: 0785.873000.

616.742   UK   ISSN 0003-4967
CODEN: ARDIAO
ANNALS OF THE RHEUMATIC DISEASES. 1939. m. £198. B M J Publishing Group, B.M.A. House, Tavistock Sq., London WC1H 9JR, England. TEL 071-387-4499. FAX 071-383-6402. Ed. A.K. Thould. adv.; bk.rev.; charts; illus.; index. (also avail. in microform from UMI; reprint service avail. from UMI) **Indexed:** Abstr.Inter.Med., Biol.Abstr., C.I.S. Abstr., Chem.Abstr., CINAHL, Curr.Cont., Dent.Ind., Excerp.Med., Helminthol.Abstr., Ind.Med., Ind.Sci.Rev., INIS Atomind., Nutr.Abstr., Sci.Cit.Ind.
  ●Also available online. Vendor(s): BRS.
  —BLDSC shelfmark: 1043.800000.

616.7   SP
APARATO LOCOMOTOR. Spanish edition of: Rheumatology and Traumatology. 1984. q. 4500 ptas. Editores Medicos, S.A., Paseo de la Castellana, 53, 28046 Madrid, Spain. TEL 442-86-56. FAX 442-80-43. circ. 10,000.

ARCHIVIO DI ORTOPEDIA E REUMATOLOGIA. see *MEDICAL SCIENCES — Orthopedics And Traumatology*

617.3   PO   ISSN 0871-4304
ARQUIVOS DE REUMATOLOGIA E DOENCAS OSTED ARTICULARES. (Text in English, French and Portuguese) 1980. m. Esc.2500($40) Mediedicoes-Soc. Com. Editora, Lda., Avenida Almirante Reis, 89-F 4 Dto., 1100 Lisbon, Portugal. Ed. Manuel Martins. bk.rev.; circ. 3,000. (back issues avail.) **Indexed:** Excerp.Med.
  —BLDSC shelfmark: 1695.835000.

616.7   AT
ARTHRITIS ACTION. 1983. bi-m. membership. Arthritis Foundation of Australia - South Australia, 99 Anzac Hwy., Ashford, S.A. 5035, Australia. TEL 08-294-2488. Ed. Paul Howard. circ. 8,000. (back issues avail.)
  Formerly: Arthritis News.
  Description: News of foundation activities and information on self-help courses. Includes branch news articles on arthritis.

616.742   US   ISSN 0004-3591
RC927.A1   CODEN: ARHEAW
ARTHRITIS AND RHEUMATISM. 1958. m. $90 to individuals (foreign $100); institutions $115 (foreign $130). (American College of Rheumatology) J.B. Lippincott Co., E. Washington Sq., Philadelphia, PA 19105. TEL 215-238-4200. FAX 215-238-4227. Ed. Dr. William J. Koopman. adv.; bk.rev.; bibl.charts; illus.; circ. 9,000. (also avail. in microform from UMI; back issues avail.) **Indexed:** Behav.Med.Abstr., Biol.Abstr., Biotech.Abstr., C.I.S. Abstr., Chem.Abstr., Curr.Adv.Ecol.Sci., Curr.Cont., Dent.Ind., Excerp.Med., Helminthol.Abstr., I.P.A., Ind.Med., Ind.Sci.Rev., INIS Atomind., Sci.Cit.Ind.
  ●Also available online. Vendor(s): BRS, Mead Data Central.
  Refereed Serial

616.742   UK
ARTHRITIS AND RHEUMATISM COUNCIL. MAGAZINE. 1965. 3/yr. £8. Arthritis and Rheumatism Council, Copen House, St. Mary's Ct., Chesterfield S41 7TD, England. TEL 0742-5580332. charts; illus.; circ. 150,000.
  Description: Contains reviews of ARC-funded research and its progress plus advice for coping with the arthritis affliction every day.

616.7   US   ISSN 0893-7524
RC933.A1   CODEN: ARCREG
ARTHRITIS CARE AND RESEARCH. 1988. 4/yr. $98 to institutions (foreign $120)(effective 1992). (Arthritis Foundation, Arthritis Health Professions Association) Elsevier Science Publishing Co., Inc. (New York), 655 Ave. of the Americas, New York, NY 10010. TEL 212-989-5800. FAX 212-633-3965. TELEX 420643 AEP UI. Ed. Donna J. Hawley, RN.
  —BLDSC shelfmark: 1733.840000.
  Description: Offers papers on rheumatology and rheumatology-related issues.
  Refereed Serial

616.7   US   ISSN 0191-2836
ARTHRITIS FOUNDATION ANNUAL REPORT. 1948. a. Arthritis Foundation, 1314 Spring St., N.W., Atlanta, GA 30309. TEL 404-872-7100. FAX 404-872-0457.

616.7   UK   ISSN 0144-6339
ARTHRITIS NEWS; the quarterly paper for people with arthritis. 1950. 4/yr. £3 (free to qualified personnel). Arthritis Care, 5 Grosvenor Crescent, London SW1X 7ER, England. FAX 071-259-5330. Ed. James Pollard. adv.; bk.rev.; illus.; circ. 100,000. (tabloid format) **Indexed:** Rehabil.Lit.
  Formerly (until Jan-Feb 1980): B R A Review (ISSN 0005-3279)
  Description: A paper for people with arthritis and how it affects their lives; both professional and private.

616.742   CN   ISSN 0820-9006
ARTHRITIS NEWS. 1979. 4/yr. membership. Arthritis Society, No. 401, 250 Bloor St. E., Toronto, Ont. M4W 3P2, Canada. TEL 416-967-1414. Ed. Dennis Jeanes. bk.rev.; circ. 35,000.
  Formerly: C.A.R. Scope (ISSN 0068-8258)

616.7   US
ARTHRITIS TODAY; the magazine for help and hope. 1987. bi-m. $20. Arthritis Foundation, 1314 Spring St., N.W., Atlanta, GA 30309. TEL 404-872-7100. FAX 404-872-8694. Ed. Ann Rossetti. circ. 500,000. **Indexed:** Hlth.Ind.
  Formerly: National Arthritis News.

ARTHROSCOPY. see *MEDICAL SCIENCES — Orthopedics And Traumatology*

AUTOIMMUNE DISEASES. see *MEDICAL SCIENCES — Allergology And Immunology*

616.7   UK   ISSN 0950-3579
RC925.A1
BAILLIERE'S CLINICAL RHEUMATOLOGY. 1975. 3/yr. $57. Grune & Stratton Ltd., Harcourt Brace Jovanovich, Publishers, 24-28 Oval Rd., London NW1, 7DX, England. **Indexed:** Biol.Abstr., Curr.Adv.Ecol.Sci., Excerp.Med., Ind.Med., Ind.Sci.Rev., Sci.Cit.Ind.
  —BLDSC shelfmark: 1856.727000.
  Former titles: Rheumatic Diseases Clinics (ISSN 0889-857X); (until 1986): Clinics in Rheumatic Diseases (ISSN 0307-742X)
  Refereed Serial

616.7   SW
BERTINE KOPERBERG CONFERENCE (PROCEEDINGS). (Supplement to: Scandinavian Journal of Rheumatology) 2nd, 1978. irreg. $28.50. Almqvist & Wiksell International, Box 638, S-101 28 Stockholm, Sweden. Ed. T.W. Feltkamp. illus.

BRITISH JOURNAL OF RHEUMATOLOGY. see *MEDICAL SCIENCES*

616.742   US   ISSN 0007-5248
RC927   CODEN: BRDIAZ
BULLETIN ON THE RHEUMATIC DISEASES. 1950. bi-m. $15 (free in US). Arthritis Foundation, 1314 Spring St., N.W., Atlanta, GA 30309. TEL 404-872-7100. FAX 404-872-0457. Ed. Dr. John S. Sergent. bibl.; cum.index.every 4 yrs.; circ. 45,000. (also avail. in microform from UMI; reprint service avail. from UMI) **Indexed:** Biol.Abstr., Chem.Abstr., Curr.Cont., Excerp.Med., Ind.Med., Ind.Sci.Rev., Sci.Cit.Ind.
  ●Also available online. Vendor(s): Mead Data Central.
  —BLDSC shelfmark: 2885.200000.

MEDICAL SCIENCES — RHEUMATOLOGY

616.742   BE
CLINICAL RHEUMATOLOGY. (Supplements avail.) 1946. 4/yr. 3200 Fr. (foreign 3300 Fr.). Association des Societes Scientifiques Medicales Belges - Vereiniging van de Belgische Medische Wetenschappelijke Genootschappen, Av. Circulaire 138A, B-1180 Brussels, Belgium. TEL 02-374-5158. Ed. J. Dequeker. adv.; abstr.; illus. **Indexed:** Biol.Abstr., Chem.Abstr., Excerp.Med., Ind.Med.
Formerly: Journal Belge de Rhumatologie et de Medecine Physique (ISSN 0021-7654)

616.7   IT
CONNECTIVE TISSUE DISEASES/MALATTIE DEL TESSUTO CONNETTIVO. s-a. L.50000($70) (effective 1992). Casa Editrice Idelson, Via A. De Gasperi 55, 80133 Naples, Italy. TEL 081-5524733. FAX 081-5518295. Ed. Giuseppe Tirri. stat.
Description: Presents research papers on the study of connective tissue diseases.

CURRENT OPINION IN RHEUMATOLOGY. see *MEDICAL SCIENCES — Abstracting, Bibliographies, Statistics*

616.7   SZ   ISSN 0379-1041
E U L A R BULLETIN; journal for education and information in rheumatology. German edition (ISSN 0379-0789); French edition (ISSN 0379-105X) 1972. q. 117 Fr. (European League Against Rheumatism) E U L A R Publishers, P.O. Box, CH-4012 Basel, Switzerland. TEL 061-2611317. FAX 061-2616213. TELEX 963755-REIN-CH. Ed. Dr. K. Chlud. adv.; bk.rev.; circ. 19,000.
—BLDSC shelfmark: 3827.520000.

616.742   SZ   ISSN 0071-7851
FORTBILDUNGSKURSE FUER RHEUMATOLOGIE. (Text in German) 1971. irreg. price varies. S. Karger AG, Allschwilerstr. 10, P.O. Box, CH-4009 Basel, Switzerland. TEL 061-3061111. FAX 061-3061234. TELEX CH 962652. Ed.Bd. (reprint service avail. from ISI) **Indexed:** Biol.Abstr., Chem.Abstr., Curr.Cont., Ind.Med.

FORTSCHRITTE IN DER ARTHROSKOPIE. see *MEDICAL SCIENCES*

DIE FUNKTIONSKRANKHEITEN DES BEWEGUNGSAPPARATES; Zeitschrift fuer interdisziplinaere Diagnostik und Therapie. see *MEDICAL SCIENCES — Chiropractic, Homeopathy, Osteopathy*

616.742   CS   ISSN 0072-0038
CODEN: FYRVAX
FYSIATRICKY A REUMATOLOGICKY VESTNIK. (Text in Czech; summaries in Czech, English, Russian) vol.51, 1973. 6/yr. $48.60. (Ceskoslovenska Fysiatricka Spolecnost) Avicenum, Czechoslovak Medical Press, Malostranske nam. 28, 118 02 Prague 1, Czechoslovakia. (Dist. by: Artia, Ve Smeckach 30, 111 27 Prague 1, Czechoslovakia) (Co-sponsor: Ceskoslovenska Lekarska Spolecnost J. Ev. Purkyne) Ed. Dr. V. Rauser. bk.rev. **Indexed:** Biol.Abstr., Excerp.Med., Ind.Med.
—BLDSC shelfmark: 4061.800000.
Supersedes: Fysiatricky Vestnik.

GASTROENTEROLOGY IN PRACTICE. see *MEDICAL SCIENCES — Gastroenterology*

616.7   US   ISSN 0887-168X
HELIOGRAM (BRIDGEPORT). 1986. 4/yr. $10. Lupus Network, Inc., 230 Ranch Dr., Bridgeport, CT 06606. TEL 203-372-5795. Ed. Linda Rosinsky. bk.rev.
Description: Educational information on lupus for patients and professionals.

616.7   NE   ISSN 0169-1163
JAPANESE JOURNAL OF RHEUMATOLOGY. (Text in English) 1986. q. DM.237. V S P, P.O. Box 346, 3700 AH Zeist, Netherlands. TEL 03404-25790. FAX 03404-32081. TELEX 40217 VSP NL. Ed. T. Azuma. adv. (back issues avail.)
—BLDSC shelfmark: 4658.680000.
Description: Current Japanese research in rheumatology and associated areas (pathology, physiology, clinical immunology). Main source is Ryumachi, organ of Japan Rheumatism Association.

JOURNAL OF MUSCULOSKELETAL MEDICINE. see *MEDICAL SCIENCES — Orthopedics And Traumatology*

JOURNAL OF MUSCULOSKELETAL PAIN. see *MEDICAL SCIENCES — Orthopedics And Traumatology*

616.7   617.3   UK   ISSN 0951-9580
CODEN: JORHE3
JOURNAL OF ORTHOPAEDIC RHEUMATOLOGY. 1988. q. £45 to individuals (US & Canada $80); institutions £110 (US & Canada $195). Chapman & Hall, 2-6 Boundary Row, London SE1 8HN, England. TEL 071-865-0066. FAX 071-522-9623. TELEX 290164-CHAPMAG. (Dist. by: International Thomson Publishing Services, Ltd., N. Way, Andover, Hampshire SP10 5BE, England. TEL 0264-33-2424; US addr.: Chapman & Hall, 29 W. 35th St., New York, NY 10001-2291. TEL 212-244-3336) Ed.Bd. (reprint service avail. from UMI)
—BLDSC shelfmark: 5027.664000.
Description: Covers techniques and evaluation of reconstructive surgery in arthritis patients; investigation and treatment of spinal problems; soft tissues disorders, and sports injuries.

616.742   CN   ISSN 0315-162X
CODEN: JRHUA9
JOURNAL OF RHEUMATOLOGY. 1974. m. $130. Journal of Rheumatology Publishing Co. Ltd., 920 Yonge St., Ste. 115, Toronto, Ont. M4W 3C7, Canada. TEL 416-967-5155. FAX 416-967-7556. Ed. D.A. Gordon. adv.; bk.rev.; index; circ. 3,300. (also avail. in microform from UMI; reprint service avail. from UMI) **Indexed:** Biol.Abstr., Chem.Abstr., Chic.Per.Ind., Curr.Adv.Cancer Res., Curr.Adv.Ecol.Sci., Curr.Adv.Genetics & Molec.Biol., Curr.Cont., Dent.Ind., Dok.Arbeitsmed., Excerp.Med., Ind.Med., Ind.Sci.Rev., INIS Atomind., Nutr.Abstr., Protozool.Abstr.
—BLDSC shelfmark: 5052.070000.

616.7   US
L.E. BEACON. (Lupus Erythematosus) 1984. bi-m. $16 in U.S.: Mexico and Canada $18. L. E. Support Group, 8039 Nova Court, N. Charleston, SC 29420. TEL 803-764-1769. Ed. Harriet B. Mesic. bk.rev.; circ. 1,000. (back issues avail.)
Description: Educational and medical news for patients with systemic Lupus Erythematosus.

616.742   UK
MATHILDA AND TERENCE KENNEDY INSTITUTE OF RHEUMATOLOGY. ANNUAL REPORT. 1967. a. free. Mathilda and Terence Kennedy Institute of Rheumatology, 6 Bute Gardens, Hammersmith, London W6 7DW, England. TEL 01-748-9966. FAX 01-748-5090. circ. 1,000 (controlled).

616.7   BL
MEDISOM: RHEUMATOLOGY. 1981. bi-m. $90. Grupo Editorial Q B D Ltda, Rua Caravelas 326, Caixa Postal 30329, 01051 Sao Paulo, Brazil. FAX 55-11-572-5957. Ed. Dr. Philip Querido. adv. (audio cassette)

616.7   GW   ISSN 0939-219X
▼**MIT RHEUMA LEBEN.** 1991. q. DM.20. Verlag fuer Medizin Dr. Ewald Fischer GmbH, Fritz-Frey-Str. 21, Postfach 105767, 6900 Heidelberg 1, Germany. TEL 06221-4062-0. FAX 06221-400727. TELEX 461683-HVVFM. Ed. Arndt Kroedel. adv.; bk.rev.; illus.

PRACTICAL GASTROENTEROLOGY; for the busy internist. see *MEDICAL SCIENCES — Gastroenterology*

616.742   US
PRIMARY CARE RHEUMATOLOGY. 1989. bi-m. free. American College of Rheumatology, 60 Executive Park S., Ste. 150, Atlanta, GA 30329. TEL 404-633-3777. FAX 404-633-1870. Ed. Robert F. Willkens. adv.; circ. 30,000 (controlled).
Formerly: Arthritis and Rheumatism Primary Care Review (ISSN 1044-2626)
Description: For the primary care physician treating patients with rheumatic disease.
Refereed Serial

616.742   FR
"R" (RHUMATOLOGIE). (Text in English, French and Spanish) 1928. 6/yr. 350 F. "R" Rhumatologie, 15 rue Turgot, 78100 St. Germain en Laye, France. adv.; bk.rev.; circ. 4,000. **Indexed:** Curr.Cont.

616.742   UK   ISSN 0048-7279
REPORTS ON RHEUMATIC DISEASES; practical problems. 1959; N.S. 1983. 3/yr. free. Arthritis and Rheumatism Council, Copen House, St. Mary's Ct., Chesterfield S41 7TD, England. TEL 0742-558033. circ. 40,000. **Indexed:** Biol.Abstr., Ind.Med.
Description: Gives advice on diagnosis and treatment of common problems, topical research findings and theories.

616.742   SW   ISSN 0034-6209
REUMA. 1947. 6/yr. SEK 90. Riksfoerbundet mot Reumatism - Swedish National Association Against Rheumatism, P.O. Box 12 851, Alstrimergatan 39, S-112 98 Stockholm, Sweden. TEL 46-8-653-21-00. FAX 46-8-650-64-15. Ed. Elsemarie Bjellqvist. adv.; circ. 53,000.

616.742   NE   ISSN 0034-6217
REUMA BULLETIN. q. fl.10. Nationaal Reumafonds, Statenlaan 128, 2582 GW The Hague, Netherlands.

616.7   IT   ISSN 0048-7449
REUMATISMO. (Supplements avail.) 1949. 4/yr. $75 to non-members (effective 1992). Societa Italiana di Reumatologia (S.I.R.), C.so Plebisciti 9, 20129 Milano, Italy. TEL 02-7387945. FAX 02-7385763. TELEX 33215 BOFFIS I. Ed. Bruno Colombo. adv.; bk.rev.; illus. (back issues avail.) **Indexed:** Biol.Abstr., Chem.Abstr., Ind.Med.

616.7   CI   ISSN 0374-1338
REUMATIZAM. (Text in Croatian; summaries in English) 1954. bi-m. 500 din. Croatian League Against Rheumatism, Lovcenska 100, 41000 Zagreb, Croatia. TEL 041-572-440. (Subscr. to: Jurjevska 25-I, 41000 Zagreb, Croatia) Ed. Ivo Jajic. adv.; bk.rev.; index; circ. 1,000. (back issues avail.) **Indexed:** Biol.Abstr., Ind.Med.

616.742   PL   ISSN 0034-6233
CODEN: RMTOA2
REUMATOLOGIA. (Text in Polish; summaries in English) 1963. q. $124. Instytut Reumatologiczny, Spartanska 1, 02-637 Warsaw, Poland. TEL 48-22-444241. TELEX 816458 REUM. (Co-sponsor: Polskie Towarzystwo Reumatologiczne) Ed. Stanislaw Luft. adv.; bk.rev.; bibl.; illus.; index. **Indexed:** Biol.Abstr., Chem.Abstr., Dent.Ind., Excerp.Med., Ind.Med., Ind.Rheum.
—BLDSC shelfmark: 7785.548000.

616.7   IT   ISSN 0391-8963
REUMATOLOGO. (Text in Italian; summaries in English) 1980. bi-m. L.15000($15) C I C Edizioni Internazionale s.r.l., Via L. Spallanzani, 11, 00161 Rome, Italy. TEL 06-8412673. FAX 06-8443365. TELEX 622099 CIC I. Dir. C. Cervini.

616.7   SP   ISSN 0048-7791
REVISTA ESPANOLA DE REUMATISMO Y ENFERMEDADES OSTEOARTICULARES. 1945. q. 9000 ptas.($13) Editorial ECO, S.A., Calle de la Cruz 44, Barcelona 34, Spain. Ed. Dr. P. Barcelo. adv.; charts; illus.; stat.; index; circ. 4,000. **Indexed:** Biol.Abstr., C.I.S. Abstr., Excerp.Med.

616.7   SP   ISSN 0304-4815
REVISTA ESPANOLA DE REUMATOLOGIA. (Text in Spanish; summaries in English, Spanish) 1974. 10/yr. 5500 ptas.($57) to non-members. (Sociedad Espanola de Reumatologia) Ediciones Doyma, S.A., Travesera de Gracia, 17-21, 08021 Barcelona, Spain. TEL 200-07-11. FAX 209-11-36. TELEX 51964 INK-E. Ed. A. Rodriquez de la Serna. adv.: page 135000 ptas.; trim 210 x 280; adv. contact: Marta Cisa. charts; illus.; stat.; index; circ. 3,000. (reprint service avail. from UMI) **Indexed:** Excerp.Med., Ind.Med.Esp.
—BLDSC shelfmark: 7854.310000.
Description: Contains investigative work in the field of rheumatology done in Spain. Serves to continue the education of internists and physicians.

616.742   NO
REVMATIKEREN. q. (Norsk Revmatike Forbund) E.K.B. Boktrykkeri, Platousgate 9, Oslo 1, Norway.

MEDICAL SCIENCES — SPORTS MEDICINE

616.742   RU   ISSN 0233-7029
CODEN: REVMD
REVMATOLOGIYA/RHEUMATOLOGY. 1961. q. 8.40 Rub.($7.80) (Vsesoyuznoe Nauchnoe Obshchestvo Revmatologov) Izdatel'stvo Meditsina, Petroverigskii pereulok 6-8, 101838 Moscow, Russia. TEL 095-1204033. (Co-sponsor: Ministerstvo Zdravookhraneniya S.S.S.R.) Ed. V.N. Anokhin. bk.rev.; index. **Indexed:** Biol.Abstr., Chem.Abstr., Dent.Ind., Excerp.Med., Ind.Med.
—BLDSC shelfmark: 0140.585770.
Formerly (until 1982): Voprosy Revmatizma (ISSN 0042-885X)
Description: Publishes works treating problems relative to the etiology, pathogenesis, clinical picture, prophylaxis and treatment of rheumatism and other collagenoses and diseases of the joints.

616.742   FR   ISSN 0035-2659
CODEN: RRMOA2
REVUE DU RHUMATISME ET DES MALADIES OSTEOARTICULAIRES. (Text in French; summaries in English, German and Spanish) 1933. 10/yr. 940 F. to individuals (foreign 1230 F.); students 470 F. (foreign 670 F.). (Societe Francaise de Rhumatologie) Expansion Scientifique, 15 rue St. Benoit, 75278 Paris Cedex 06, France. Ed. Stanislas De Seze. adv.; bk.rev.; abstr.; bibl.; charts; illus.; index; circ. 4,000. (also avail. in microform from UMI; reprint service avail. from UMI) **Indexed:** Biol.Abstr., C.I.S. Abstr., Chem.Abstr., Curr.Cont., Excerp.Med., Helminthol.Abstr., Ind.Med., Nutr.Abstr.
—BLDSC shelfmark: 7945.600000.

616.7   GW   ISSN 0721-8222
RHEUMA SCHMERZ UND ENTZUENDUNG. 1981. 12/yr. DM.150. P M I Verlag GmbH, August-Schanz-Str. 21, 6000 Frankfurt a.M. 50, Germany. TEL 069-548000-0. FAX 069-548000-77. TELEX 412952-PMI-D. Ed. Peter Hoffmann. circ. 14,000. (tabloid format; back issues avail.)

616.742   II   ISSN 0035-4546
RHEUMATISM. (Text and summaries in English and Hindi) 1965. q. Rs.32($12) (£10). M M L Centre for Rheumatic Diseases, Sanskriti Bhawan, Jhandewalan, New Delhi 110055, India. TEL 011-3313306. Ed. Kaviraj A. Majumdar. adv.; bk.rev.; abstr.; charts; illus.; index; circ. 200. **Indexed:** Biol.Abstr.

616.742 616.97   HU   ISSN 0035-4554
RHEUMATOLOGIA, BALNEOLOGIA, ALLERGOLOGIA. (Text in Hungarian; summaries in English, German and Russian) 1960. q. $18. (Reumatologiai Tarsasag) Ifjusagi Lap-es Konyvkiado Vallalat, Revay u.16, 1374 Budapest 6, Hungary. (Subscr. to: Kultura, Box 149, H-1389 Budapest, Hungary) Ed. Dr. Geza Balint. adv.; bk.rev. **Indexed:** Biol.Abstr., Chem.Abstr., Excerp.Med.

616.742   SZ   ISSN 0080-2727
RC927.A1   CODEN: RHEUBD
RHEUMATOLOGY. (Text in English) 1966. irreg. (approx. 1/yr.). price varies. S. Karger AG, Allschwilerstr. 10, P.O. Box, CH-4009 Basel, Switzerland. TEL 061-3061111. FAX 061-3061234. TELEX CH 962652. Eds. M. Schattenkirchner, F.W. Hagena. (reprint service avail. from ISI) **Indexed:** Biol.Abstr., Chem.Abstr., Curr.Cont., Ind.Med.
—BLDSC shelfmark: 7960.730000.

616.7   GW   ISSN 0172-8172
CODEN: RHINDE
RHEUMATOLOGY INTERNATIONAL; clinical and experimental investigations. 1981. 6/yr. DM.298($182) Springer-Verlag, Heidelberger Platz 3, D-1000 Berlin 33, Germany. TEL 030-8207-1. (Also Heidelberg, Tokyo, Vienna, and New York) Ed. B. Bresnihan. adv. (also avail. in microform from UMI; reprint service avail. from ISI) **Indexed:** Chem.Abstr, Curr.Adv.Ecol.Sci., Curr.Cont., Dent.Ind., Excerp.Med., Ind.Med.
—BLDSC shelfmark: 7960.738300.

616.7   UK   ISSN 0958-2584
▼**RHEUMATOLOGY REVIEW.** 1991. q. £49($99) to individuals; institutions £99($200). Churchill Livingstone Medical Journals, Robert Stevenson House, 1-3 Baxter's Pl., Leith Walk, Edinburgh EH1 3AF, Scotland. TEL 031-556-2424. FAX 031-558-1278. (Subscr. to: Longman Group, Journals Subscr. Dept., P.O. Box 77, Fourth Ave., Harlow, Essex CM19 5AA, England; U.S. subscr. to: Churchill Livingstone, 650 Ave. of the Americas, New York, NY 10011. TEL 212-206-5000) Eds. R.D. Sturrock, M. Liang.
—BLDSC shelfmark: 7960.738550.
Description: Provides educational and updated reviews in rheumatological medicine and research.

616.7   FR
RHUMATOLOGIE.* m. 320 Fr. Editions du Trevoux, 91 Rte. de Vienne, 69007 Lyon, France. adv.; bk.rev. **Indexed:** Biol.Abstr.

616.742   SW   ISSN 0300-9742
RC927   CODEN: SJRHAT
SCANDINAVIAN JOURNAL OF RHEUMATOLOGY. (Supplements avail.) 6/yr. SEK 640($88) incl. supplements. (Scandinavian Society of Rheumatologists) Almqvist & Wiksell Periodical Company, Box 638, S-101 28 Stockholm, Sweden. Ed. Eimar Munthe. adv.; circ. 1,800. **Indexed:** ASCA, Biol.Abstr., Biotech.Abstr., Chem.Abstr., Curr.Adv.Ecol.Sci., Curr.Cont., Dent.Ind., Excerp.Med., Ind.Med.
—BLDSC shelfmark: 8087.546000.
Formerly: Acta Rheumatologica Scandinavica (ISSN 0001-6934)

616.7 574.192   US   ISSN 0049-0172
RC933.A1   CODEN: SAHRBF
SEMINARS IN ARTHRITIS & RHEUMATISM. 1971. 6/yr. $94 to individuals; institutions $143; foreign $168. W.B. Saunders Co. (Subsidiary of: Harcourt Brace Jovanovich, Inc.), Curtis Center, Independence Square W., Philadelphia, PA 19106. TEL 215-238-7800. (Subscr. to: 6277 Sea Harbor Dr., 4th Fl., Orlando FL 32891) Ed.Bd. adv.; bibl.; charts; illus.; index. **Indexed:** ASCA, Biol.Abstr., Chem.Abstr., Curr.Adv.Ecol.Sci., Curr.Cont., Dent.Ind., Excerp.Med., Ind.Med., Nutr.Abstr., Protozool.Abstr., Sci.Cit.Ind.
●Also available online. Vendor(s): Mead Data Central.
—BLDSC shelfmark: 8239.448000.
Refereed Serial

616.742   PO
SOCIEDADE PORTUGUESA DE REUMATOLOGIA. BOLETIM INFORMATIVO. 1972. q. free. Sociedade Portuguesa de Reumatologia, Rua de Dona Estefania 187-189, Lisbon 1, Portugal. Dir. Joao Figueirinhas. adv.; bibl.; illus.; stat.; circ. 1,000.

VATRECHNI BOLESTI. see *MEDICAL SCIENCES — Endocrinology*

616.742   GW   ISSN 0340-1855
CODEN: ZRHMBQ
ZEITSCHRIFT FUER RHEUMATOLOGIE. (Text and summaries in English, German) 1938. bi-m. DM.296. Dr. Dietrich Steinkopff Verlag, Saalbaustr. 12, Postfach 111442, 6100 Darmstadt 11, Germany. TEL 06151-26538. FAX 06151-20849. (Co-sponsors: Deutsche Gesellschaft fuer Rheumatologie; Oesterreichische Rheumaliga; Schweizerische Gesellschaft fuer Rheumatologie; Berufsverband Deutscher Rheumatologen) Ed.Bd. adv.; bk.rev.; abstr.; bibl.; charts; illus.; pat.; circ. 1,500. **Indexed:** Biol.Abstr., Biotech.Abstr., Chem.Abstr., Curr.Adv.Ecol.Sci., Curr.Cont., Dent.Ind., Ind.Med.
—BLDSC shelfmark: 9485.455000.
Formerly: Zeitschrift fuer Rheumaforschung (ISSN 0044-345X)

MEDICAL SCIENCES — Sports Medicine

617.1   US
AMERICAN ACADEMY OF PODIATRIC SPORTS MEDICINE NEWSLETTER. 1982. q. $15. American Academy of Podiatric Sports Medicine, 1729 Glastonberry Rd., Potomac, MD 20854. TEL 301-424-7440. Ed. Larry Shane. adv.; circ. 8,000. **Indexed:** Sportsearch (1988-).
Formerly: American Academy of Podiatric Sports Medicine Journal.

617.1   US
AMERICAN COLLEGE OF SPORTS MEDICINE. CAREER SERVICES BULLETIN. m. $20 to non-members; members $10. American College of Sports Medicine, Box 1440, Indianapolis, IN 46206-1440. TEL 317-637-9200. (Street addr.: 401 W. Michigan St., Indianapolis, IN 46202-3233) Ed. Juli Knutson. circ. 1,000. (looseleaf format)
Description: Lists current positions available in a variety of fields across the nation for both members and non-members of the American College of Sports Medicine.

AMERICAN JOURNAL OF KNEE SURGERY. see *MEDICAL SCIENCES — Surgery*

AMERICAN JOURNAL OF PHYSICAL MEDICINE AND REHABILITATION. see *MEDICAL SCIENCES*

617   US   ISSN 0363-5465
RC1200   CODEN: AJSMDO
AMERICAN JOURNAL OF SPORTS MEDICINE. 1972. bi-m. $70 (foreign $85). American Orthopaedic Society for Sports Medicine, 230 Calvary St., Waltham, MA 02154. TEL 617-736-0707. FAX 617-736-0607. Ed. Dr. Robert E. Leach. adv.; illus.; circ. 11,000. (also avail. in microform; microfilm from WWS) **Indexed:** Abstr.Anthropol., CINAHL, Curr.Cont., Educ.Ind., Excerp.Med., Hlth.Ind., Ind.Med., NRN, Phys.Ed.Ind., Sportsearch (1976-).
—BLDSC shelfmark: 0838.400000.
Formerly (until 1976): Journal of Sports Medicine (ISSN 0090-4201)

ANNALES DE KINESITHERAPIE. see *MEDICAL SCIENCES*

617.3   SP   ISSN 0212-4009
APUNTS; medicina de l'esport. (Text in Catalan, Spanish) 1963. q. Centro d'Estudis de l'Alt Rendiment Esportiu, Direccio General de l'Esport, Av. Paisos Catalan, 12, 08950 Esplugas de Llobregat, Barcelona, Spain. TEL 371-90-11. FAX 372-01-84. TELEX 54845 GCDE. (Dist. by: Les Punxes, Calle Escornalbou, 12, Barcelona, Spain) Ed.Bd. adv.; bibl.; illus.; index; circ. 2,000. (back issues avail.) **Indexed:** Ind.Med.Esp.
Formerly: Apuntes de Medicina Deportiva.

617.1   SP   ISSN 0212-8799
ARCHIVOS DE MEDICINA DEL DEPORTE. (Text in Spanish; summaries in English, French, Spanish) 1984. q. 4000 ptas.($50) (Federacion Espanola de Medicina del Deporte) Graficas San Juan, Calle Zubiarte, 27, 31620 Huarte (Pamplona), Spain. TEL 948-3307-64. (Subscr. to: c/o FEMEDE, Calle Iturrama 43 bis E, 31007 Pamplona, Spain) Ed. Jon Ajuria Blanco. adv.; bk.rev.; index; circ. 2,000. (back issues avail.) **Indexed:** Ind.Med.

610   AT   ISSN 0813-6289
AUSTRALIAN JOURNAL OF SCIENCE AND MEDICINE IN SPORT. 1961. q. Aus.$20 (foreign Aus.$31). Australian Sports Medicine Federation, Box 897, Belconnen, A.C.T. 2616, Australia. TEL 06-2516944. FAX 06-2531489. TELEX AUSIS 62400. Ed. Bruce Abernethy. adv.; bk.rev.; charts; illus.; stat.; circ. 3,500. (back issues avail.) **Indexed:** Ergon.Abstr., Excerp.Med., Geotech.Abstr., Phys.Ed.Ind., Sportsearch (1984-).
Formerly: Australian Journal of Sports Medicine (ISSN 0045-0650)

BALTIMORE SPORTS FOCUS. see *SPORTS AND GAMES*

BARIATRICIAN. see *NUTRITION AND DIETETICS*

617.1   SZ
BEHINDERTENSPORT/SPORT-HANDICAP. (Text and summaries in French, German) m. 36 Fr. Schweizerischer Verband fuer Behindertensport, Chriesbaumstr. 6, CH-8604 Volketswil, Switzerland. TEL 1-9460860. FAX 1-9460870. Ed. Martin Bucher. adv.; bk.rev.; circ. 8,500.
Formerly: Invalidensport (ISSN 0020-9880)

MEDICAL SCIENCES — SPORTS MEDICINE

617   UK   ISSN 0306-3674
CODEN: BJSMDZ
BRITISH JOURNAL OF SPORTS MEDICINE. 1968. q. £77 in UK and Europe; elsewhere £84. (British Association of Sport and Medicine) Butterworth - Heinemann Ltd. (Subsidiary of: Reed International PLC), Linacre House, Jordan Hill, Oxford OX2 8DP, England. TEL 0865-310366. FAX 0865-310898. TELEX 83111 BHPOXF G. (Subscr. to: Turpin Transactions Ltd., Distribution Centre, Blackhorse Rd., Letchworth, Kent TN15 8PL, England. TEL 0462-672555) Eds. Drs. Adrianne Hardman, Wendy Dodds. adv.; bk.rev.; illus.; stat. (also avail. in microform from UMI; back issues avail.) Indexed: CINAHL, Curr.Adv.Ecol.Sci., Ergon.Abstr., Ind.Med., NRN, Phys.Ed.Ind., Sportsearch (1975-).
—BLDSC shelfmark: 2324.900000.
    Incorporates: British Association of Sport and Medicine. Bulletin.
    Description: Covers management of injuries and physio-therapy, physiological evaluations of sports performance, psychology, nutrition, and the role of medical personnel.

617.1 615.53   FR   ISSN 0007-9782
CAHIERS DE KINESITHERAPIE; revue d'enseignement post-scolaire et de documentation technique. 1962. bi-m. 92 ECU($111) (typically set in Jan.). Masson, 120 bd. Saint-Germain, 75280 Paris Cedex 06, France. TEL 1-46-34-21-60. FAX 1-45-87-29-99. TELEX 202 671 F. Ed. J. Barthe. adv.; bk.rev.; circ. 2,900. (also avail. in microform from UMI) Indexed: Biol.Abstr., Chem.Abstr., Excerp.Med.
—BLDSC shelfmark: 2949.560000.

CANADIAN JOURNAL OF SPORT SCIENCES/REVUE CANADIENNE DES SCIENCES DU SPORT. see *SPORTS AND GAMES*

CAPITAL SPORTS FOCUS. see *SPORTS AND GAMES*

CARDIOVASCULAR PHYSIOLOGY. see *BIOLOGY — Physiology*

CHIROPRACTIC SPORTS MEDICINE. see *MEDICAL SCIENCES — Chiropractic, Homeopathy, Osteopathy*

610   FR   ISSN 0009-7209
CINESIOLOGIE; la revue internationale des medecins du sport. 1962. 6/yr. 300 F. (foreign 400 F.). Syndicat National des Medecins du Sport, 1, rue d'Alsace, 49100 Angers, France. TEL 41-88-35-35. FAX 33-41-88-13-55. Ed. A. Monroche. adv.; bk.rev. Indexed: Sportsearch (1975-).
—BLDSC shelfmark: 3198.645000.

617.1 613.7   US   ISSN 1050-642X
RC1200
CLINICAL JOURNAL OF SPORT MEDICINE. 1975. q. $87.25 to individuals; institutions $112.25 (effective 1992). (Canadian Academy of Sport Medicine, CN) Raven Press, 1185 Ave. of the Americas, New York, NY 10036. TEL 212-930-9500. FAX 212-869-3495. (Academy membership addr.: 1600 James Naismith Dr., Ste. 502, Gloucester, Ont. K1B 5N4, Canada. TEL 613-748-5671) Ed. Dr. Gordon Matheson. adv.; bk.rev.; circ. 575. Indexed: Sportsearch (1991-).
—BLDSC shelfmark: 3286.294300.
    Former titles (until 1990): Canadian Academy of Sport Medicine Review (ISSN 0831-2893); Canadian Academy of Sport Medicine Newsletter.
    Description: Features original research articles, clinical reviews, editorials, case reports, new techniques and procedures in physical examination, exercise testing, and diagnostic imaging.
    Refereed Serial

617.1 371.9   US
CLINICAL KINESIOLOGY. 1947. q. $20 to individuals; institutions $35. American Kinesiotherapy Association, Box 890665, Houston, TX 77289-0665. Ed. Dr. Evelyn Scott. adv.; bk.rev.; bibl.; charts; illus.; index; circ. 1,064. (also avail. in microform from UMI; reprint service avail. from KTO) Indexed: Adol.Ment.Hlth.Abstr., Biol.Abstr., CINAHL, Excerp.Med., Hosp.Lit.Ind., HRIS, Ind.Med., Phys.Ed.Ind., Psychol.Abstr., Rehabil.Lit., Sportsearch (1988-), Yrbk.Assoc.Educ.& Rehab.Blind.
    Former titles (until 1987): American Corrective Therapy Journal (ISSN 0002-8088); (until 1967): Association for Physical and Mental Rehabilitation. Journal (ISSN 0098-8448)
    Refereed Serial

617.102   UK   ISSN 0953-9875
CLINICAL SPORTS MEDICINE. 1989. q. £35($60) to individuals; institutions £75. (International Association of Olympic Medical Officers) Chapman & Hall, 2-6 Boundary Row, London SE1 8HN, England. TEL 071-865-0066. FAX 071-522-9623. (Dist. by: International Thomson Publishing Services, Ltd., N. Way, Andover, Hampshire SP10 5BE, England. TEL 0264-33-2424; US addr.: Chapman & Hall, 29 W. 35th St., New York, NY 10001-2291. TEL 212-244-3336) Eds. Mark Harries, Robert Voy.
    Description: Emphasizes the practical aspect of medicine versus theoretical; provides a forum for doctors handling sportsmen and for sports physicians in clinical medicine.

617   US   ISSN 0278-5919
CLINICS IN SPORTS MEDICINE. 1982. q. $80. W.B. Saunders Co., Curtis Center, Independence Square W., Philadelphia, PA 19106. TEL 215-238-7800. Ed. Barton Dudlick. (also avail. in microform from UMI) Indexed: ASCA, Dent.Ind., Excerp.Med., Ind.Med., Sportsearch (1982-).
—BLDSC shelfmark: 3286.595500.

DANCE MEDICINE-HEALTH NEWSLETTER. see *MEDICAL SCIENCES — Orthopedics And Traumatology*

617.102   GW   ISSN 0344-5925
CODEN: DZSPD8
DEUTSCHE ZEITSCHRIFT FUER SPORTMEDIZIN. 1949. m. DM.72. Deutscher Aerzte-Verlag GmbH, Dieselstr. 2, PF 40 02 65, 5000 Cologne 40, Germany. TEL 02234-7011-0. FAX 02234-7011444. TELEX 889168-DAEV-D. Ed. Dr. Urte Kuenstlinger. adv.; circ. 14,500. Indexed: Chem.Abstr., Nutr.Abstr., Sportsearch (1978-).
    Formerly: Sportarzt und Sportmedizin.

617.11   AT   ISSN 0817-4792
EXCEL. 1985. q. Aus.$107($107) (Australia Institute of Sport) Blackwell Scientific Publications (Australia) Pty. Ltd., P.O. Box 378, Carlton, Vic. 2053, Australia. TEL 03-347-0300. FAX 03-347-5001. TELEX 10716421. Eds. P. Fricker, R. Telford. adv.; bk.rev.; illus.; index; circ. 2,000. Indexed: Sportsearch (1986-).
—BLDSC shelfmark: 3835.143000.
    Formerly: Sports Science and Medicine Quarterly.
    Description: A multidisciplinary journal concerning all aspects of sports medicine, physiology and science.

613.7   US   ISSN 0091-6331
RC1200   CODEN: ESSRB8
EXERCISE AND SPORT SCIENCES REVIEWS. 1973. a. price varies. (American College of Sports Medicine) Collamore Press, c/o D.C. Heath & Co., Distribution Center, 2700 Richardt Ave., Indianapolis, IA 46219. TEL 212-702-9549. Ed. Kent B. Pandolf. charts; illus.; circ. 1,000. (back issues avail.) Indexed: Biol.Abstr., Ind.Med., Ind.Sci.Rev., Sportsearch (1973-).
—BLDSC shelfmark: 3836.233000.

EXERCISE STANDARDS AND MALPRACTICE REPORTER. see *LAW*

FOOT & ANKLE. see *MEDICAL SCIENCES — Orthopedics And Traumatology*

FUJIAN TIYU KEJI/FUJIAN SPORTS SCIENCE AND TECHNOLOGY. see *SPORTS AND GAMES*

610 613   NE   ISSN 0016-6448
CODEN: GESPBS
GENEESKUNDE EN SPORT. 1968. 6/yr. fl.57,50 (foreign fl.70)(effective 1992). (Vereniging voor Sportgeneeskunde) Uitgeversmaatschappij De Tijdstroom b.v., Postbus 14, 7240 BA Lochem, Netherlands. TEL 05730-53651. FAX 05730-56724. adv.; bk.rev.; illus.; stat.; circ. 4,000. Indexed: Biol.Abstr.

INTERNATIONAL JOURNAL OF SPORT NUTRITION. see *NUTRITION AND DIETETICS*

INTERNATIONAL JOURNAL OF SPORT PSYCHOLOGY. see *SPORTS AND GAMES*

610   GW   ISSN 0172-4622
CODEN: IJSMDA
INTERNATIONAL JOURNAL OF SPORTS MEDICINE. (Text in English) 1980. bi-m. DM.298. (German Society of Sports Medicine) Georg Thieme Verlag, Ruedigerstr. 14, Postfach 104853, 7000 Stuttgart 10, Germany. TEL 0711-8931-0. FAX 0711-8931298. (US addr.: Thieme-Stratton Inc., 381 Park Ave., S., New York, NY 10016) Eds. H. Cotill, H. Weicker. adv.; bk.rev.; abstr.; bibl.; charts; illus.; circ. 1,500. Indexed: Chem.Abstr., Dok.Arbeitsmed., Excerp.Med., Ind.Med., Ind.Sci.Rev., NRN, Sci.Cit.Ind., Sportsearch (1980-).
—BLDSC shelfmark: 4542.681300.

617 613   US   ISSN 0959-3020
CODEN: IESCEE
▼**ISOKINETICS AND EXERCISE SCIENCE.** 1991. q. $105 (foreign $125). Butterworth - Heinemann Ltd. (Subsidiary of: Reed International PLC), 80 Montvale Ave., Stoneham, MA 02180. TEL 617-438-8464. FAX 617-438-1479. TELEX 880052. Ed.Bd. illus.
—BLDSC shelfmark: 4583.269000.
    Description: Meets the needs of the contemporary exercise scientist and medical practitioner through a consolidated focus on the field of isokinetics.

JAPANESE JOURNAL OF PHYSICAL FITNESS AND SPORTS MEDICINE. see *PHYSICAL FITNESS AND HYGIENE*

617.1   FR   ISSN 0762-915X
JOURNAL DE TRAUMATOLOGIE DU SPORT. 1983. q. 85 ECU($104) (typically set in Jan.). Masson, 120 bd. St. Germain, 75280 Paris Cedex 06, France. TEL 1-46-34-21-60. FAX 1-45-87-29-99. TELEX 202 671 F. Eds. J. Rodineau, G. Saillant. circ. 2,100.
—BLDSC shelfmark: 5070.525100.
    Description: Concerns practitioners, physicians, physiotherapists, rehabilitation doctors and surgeons involved with accidents associated with the practice of sports. Fields covered include aetiology, diagnosis, therapeutics.

617.1   US   ISSN 1041-3200
GV706.4
JOURNAL OF APPLIED SPORT PSYCHOLOGY. 1989. s-a. $50 (foreign $60). Association for the Advancement of Applied Sport Psychology, University of North Carolina, 203 Fetzer-8700, Chapel Hill, NC 27599. Ed. John M. Silva. adv.; circ. 1,000.
—BLDSC shelfmark: 4947.105000.
    Description: Promotes quality research in the field of sport psychology.
    Refereed Serial

617.1   US
JOURNAL OF APPLIED SPORTS SCIENCE RESEARCH. 1987. q. membership. National Strength and Conditioning Association, Box 81410, Lincoln, NE 68501-8410. Eds. Ken Kontor, Dr. William Kraemer. circ. 5,500. Indexed: Sportsearch (1987-).
    Description: Publishes research pertinent to sports conditioning, emphasizing practical application.

796   US
RC1200   CODEN: ATHTA
JOURNAL OF ATHLETIC TRAINING. 1956. q. $28. National Athletic Trainers Association, Inc., 2952 N. Stemmons Fwy., Dallas, TX 75247-6117. TEL 800-879-6282. FAX 214-637-2206. Ed. Steve Yates. adv.; bk.rev.; bibl.; illus.; index, cum.index; circ. 15,000 (controlled). (also avail. in microform from UMI; avail. on records; reprint service avail. from UMI) Indexed: Excerp.Med., Phys.Ed.Ind., Sports Per.Ind., Sportsearch (1974-).
    Former titles (until 1992): Athletic Training (ISSN 0160-8320); National Athletic Trainers Association. Journal (ISSN 0027-8718).

MEDICAL SCIENCES — SPORTS MEDICINE

JOURNAL OF BACK AND MUSCULOSKELETAL REHABILITATION. see *MEDICAL SCIENCES — Orthopedics And Traumatology*

617.1   US   ISSN 1053-2137
QP321
▼**JOURNAL OF HUMAN MUSCLE PERFORMANCE.** 1991. q. $75. Aspen Publishers, Inc., 200 Orchard Ridge Dr., Gaithersburg, MD 20878. TEL 301-417-7500. FAX 301-417-7550.
—BLDSC shelfmark: 5003.418500.

JOURNAL OF MUSCLE RESEARCH AND CELL MOTILITY. see *MEDICAL SCIENCES*

JOURNAL OF MUSCULOSKELETAL MEDICINE. see *MEDICAL SCIENCES — Orthopedics And Traumatology*

615.8   US   ISSN 0190-6011
RD701   CODEN: JOSPDV
JOURNAL OF ORTHOPAEDIC AND SPORTS PHYSICAL THERAPY. 1979. m. $60 to individuals; institutions $85. (American Physical Therapy Association, Orthopaedic and Sports Physical Therapy Sections) Williams & Wilkins, 428 E. Preston St., Baltimore, MD 21202. TEL 301-528-4000. FAX 301-528-4312. Ed. Gary L. Schmidt. circ. 17,300. (also avail. in microform) Indexed: CINAHL, Excerp.Med., Phys.Ed.Ind., Rehabil.Lit., Sportsearch (1980-).
—BLDSC shelfmark: 5027.660000.
Description: Clinical developments in sports medicine for practicing PT's, athletic trainers and orthopedic surgeons.
Refereed Serial

617.1   US   ISSN 0893-3871
JOURNAL OF OSTEOPATHIC SPORTS MEDICINE. 5/yr. American Osteopathic Academy of Sports Medicine, 7611 Elmwood Ave., Middleton, WI 53562-3161. TEL 608-831-4400. Ed. Allen Jacobs. circ. 12,500. Indexed: Sportsearch (1987-).
—BLDSC shelfmark: 5027.679000.

JOURNAL OF SMOOTH MUSCLE RESEARCH. see *MEDICAL SCIENCES*

JOURNAL OF SPORT AND EXERCISE PSYCHOLOGY. see *PSYCHOLOGY*

617.1   US   ISSN 1056-6716
▼**JOURNAL OF SPORT REHABILITATION.** Short title: J S R. 1992. q. $36 to individuals (foreign $40); institutions $72 (foreign $76); students $22 (foreign $26). Human Kinetics Publishers, Inc., Box 5076, Champaign, IL 61825. TEL 217-351-5076. FAX 217-351-2674. Ed. Dr. David H. Perrin. adv.; bk.rev.; abstr.; bibl.; charts; stat.; index.
—BLDSC shelfmark: 5066.189000.
Description: Investigates the process of rehabilitation of sport and exercise injuries regardless of age, gender, athletic ability, level of fitness or health status of the participant.
Refereed Serial

610 613.7   IT   ISSN 0022-4707
                            CODEN: JMPFA3
JOURNAL OF SPORTS MEDICINE AND PHYSICAL FITNESS. (Text in English) 1961. q. L.60000($70) (International Federation of Sportive Medicine - Federation Internationale de Medecine Sportive) Edizioni Minerva Medica, Corso Bramante 83-85, 10126 Turin, Italy. (Dist. in U.S. by: J.B. Lippincott Company, E. Washington Square, Philadelphia, PA 19105) Ed. A. Venerando. adv.; bk.rev.; bibl.; charts; illus.; index; circ. 4,000. (also avail. in microform from SWZ; back issues avail. from SWZ) Indexed: Chem.Abstr., CINAHL, Curr.Cont., Excerp.Med., Ind.Med., Mid.East: Abstr.& Ind., Nutr.Abstr., Phys.Ed.Ind., Sportsearch (1975-).
—BLDSC shelfmark: 5066.200000.

JOURNAL OF SPORTS SCIENCES. see *SPORTS AND GAMES*

617   IT   ISSN 1120-3137
JOURNAL OF SPORTS TRAUMATOLOGY AND RELATED RESEARCH. (Text and summaries in English, Italian) 1979. q. L.80000($80) Editrice Kurtis s.r.l., Via L. Zoja, 30, 20153 Milan, Italy. TEL 02-48202740. FAX 02-48201219. Ed. Lamberto Perugia. adv.; bk.rev.; circ. 5,000. Indexed: Excerp.Med., Sportsearch (1989-).
Formerly: Italian Journal of Sports Traumatology (ISSN 0391-4089)
Description: Contains original studies on experimental and clinical research. Includes case reports, short communications, interviews and conferences.

617.1 796.552   UK   ISSN 0953-9859
                            CODEN: JWMEEP
▼**JOURNAL OF WILDERNESS MEDICINE.** 1990. q. £95 for EC (US & Canada $170). (Wilderness Medical Society) Chapman & Hall, 2-6 Boundary Row, London SE1 8HN, England. TEL 071-865-0066. FAX 071-522-9623. (Dist. by: International Thomson Publishing Services, Ltd., N. Way, Andover, Hampshire SP10 5BE, England. TEL 0264-33-2424; US addr.: Chapman & Hall, 29 W. 35th St., New York, NY 10001-2291. TEL 212-244-3336) Eds. Paul S. Auerback, Oswald Oelz. Indexed: Energy Rev., Environ.Per.Bibl.
—BLDSC shelfmark: 5072.615000.
Description: Publishes research on all aspects of medicine in hostile, natural environments.
Refereed Serial

617.1   AT   ISSN 1035-5715
▼**M I M S DRUGS AND SPORT.** 1990. a. Aus.$20. M I M S Australia, 100 Alexander St., Crows Nest, N.S.W. 2065, Australia. Ed. Linda H. Badewitz-Dodd. circ. 18,000.
Description: Listing of banned and permitted prescription and non-prescription drugs available in Australia.

617.1   US
MAIN EVENT; monthly sports journal for physicians. 1985. m. $36. Thomas S. Boron, Inc., 17-17 Rte. 208 N., Fair Lawn, NJ 07410. TEL 201-791-4111. adv.; circ. 106,976.
Description: Features include profiles of prominent sports figures and physicians involved in sports, analysis of current issues in sports and medicine and previews of current sports events.

MASSAGE THERAPY JOURNAL. see *PHYSICAL FITNESS AND HYGIENE*

610 613.7   FR   ISSN 0025-6722
                            CODEN: MNSPBL
MEDECINE DU SPORT. (Text in French; summaries in English, German) 1925. bi-m. 500 F. Medispor Co., 17 rue du 8 Mai 1945, 75010 Paris, France. Ed. Dr. Robert J. Lederer. adv.; bk.rev.; abstr.; bibl.; charts; illus.; stat.; index; circ. 1,500. Indexed: Biol.Abstr., Sportsearch (1971-).
Formerly: Medecine Education Physique et Sport.

617.102   IT   ISSN 0025-7826
MEDICINA DELLO SPORT. (Text in Italian; summaries in English) 1947. bi-m. L.65000($80) (Federazione Medico-Sportiva Italiana) Edizioni Minerva Medica, Corso Bramante 83-85, 10126 Turin, Italy. Eds. M. Montanaro, A. Venerando. bk.rev.; bibl.; charts; illus.; index; circ. 6,000. Indexed: Biol.Abstr., Chem.Abstr., Excerp.Med., Ind.Med, Sportsearch (1974-).
—BLDSC shelfmark: 5533.700000.

617.102 796   BL
MEDICINA DO ESPORTE. (Text in Portuguese; summaries in English, French, Spanish) 1973. q. Cr.$160($10) Federacao Brasileira de Medicina Desportiva, Centro de Documentacao e Informacao Em Ciencias do Esporte, Av. Sen. Salgado Filho, 135 - 6, 90000 Porto Alegre, R.S., Brazil. abstr.; bibl.; illus.; index, cum.index; circ. 1,000 (controlled). Indexed: Biol.Abstr., Excerp.Med.

617.1   SP
MEDICINA Y DEPORTE. 1986. q. (Asociacion Asturiana de Medicina de la Educacion Fisica y el Deporte) Universidad de Oviedo, Calle Catedratico Gimeno, Oviedo, Spain. bibl.; illus.

617.102   US   ISSN 0195-9131
RC1200   CODEN: MSPEDA
MEDICINE AND SCIENCE IN SPORTS AND EXERCISE. 1969. m. $70 to individuals; institutions $125. (American College of Sports Medicine) Williams & Wilkins, 428 E. Preston St., Baltimore, MD 21202. TEL 301-528-4000. FAX 301-528-4312. Ed. Peter B. Raven. adv.; bk.rev.; abstr.; bibl.; charts; illus.; index; circ. 14,500. (also avail. in microform from UMI; back issues avail.) Indexed: Abstr.Anthropol., Biol.Abstr., Chem.Abstr., CINAHL, Curr.Adv.Biochem., Curr.Adv.Ecol.Sci., Curr.Cont., Excerp.Med., Ind.Med., Ind.Sci.Rev., INIS Atomind., Int.Aerosp.Abstr., Nucl.Sci.Abstr., Phys.Ed.Ind., Psychol.Abstr., Sci.Cit.Ind., Sportsearch (1980-), Wom.Stud.Abstr.
—BLDSC shelfmark: 5534.006700.
Formerly: Medicine and Science in Sports (ISSN 0025-7990)
Description: Research in sports medicine topics for exercise physiologists, physiatrists, physical therpists and athletic trainers.
Refereed Serial

617.102   SZ   ISSN 0254-5020
MEDICINE AND SPORT SCIENCE. (Text in English) 1966. irreg. price varies. S. Karger AG, Allschwilerstr. 10, P.O. Box, CH-4009 Basel, Switzerland. TEL 061-3061111. FAX 061-3061234. TELEX CH 962652. Eds. M. Hebbelinck, R.J. Shephard. (reprint service avail. from ISI; back issues avail.) Indexed: Biol.Abstr., Chem.Abstr., Curr.Cont., Ind.Med.
—BLDSC shelfmark: 5534.007300.
Formerly: Medicine and Sport (ISSN 0076-6070)

ORTHOPAEDIC AND TRAUMATIC SURGERY/SEKEISAI GAIGEKA. see *MEDICAL SCIENCES — Orthopedics And Traumatology*

617.1   US
ORTHOPEDIC AND SPORTS MEDICINE NEWS. 1988. m. $50. McMahon Group, 148 W. 24th St., New York, NY 10011. TEL 212-620-4600. FAX 212-620-5928. Ed. James Prudden. adv.; circ. 20,384.
Formerly: Sports Medicine News.
Description: For orthopedic surgeons and rheumatologists. Covers arthroscopy, arthroplasty, pain management, braces, rheumatic disease, and orthopedic technology.

PEDIATRIC EXERCISE SCIENCE. see *MEDICAL SCIENCES — Pediatrics*

PERSONAL FITNESS. see *PHYSICAL FITNESS AND HYGIENE*

PHILADELPHIA SPORTS FOCUS. see *SPORTS AND GAMES*

PHYSICAL FITNESS - SPORTS MEDICINE; a bibliographic service encompassing exercise physiology, sports injuries, physical conditioning and the medical aspects of exercise. see *MEDICAL SCIENCES — Abstracting, Bibliographies, Statistics*

610 617.102   US   ISSN 0091-3847
RC1200
PHYSICIAN AND SPORTSMEDICINE. 1973. m. $46 (free to qualified personnel) in U.S.; in Canada $61; elsewhere $100. McGraw-Hill, Inc., 1221 Avenue of the Americas, New York, NY 10020. TEL 212-512-2000. (Subscr. to: 4530 W. 77th St., Minneapolis, MN 55435) Ed. Glenn Griffin. adv.; bk.rev.; cum.index: 1973-1986; circ. 102,844. (also avail. in microform from UMI; reprint service avail. from UMI) Indexed: Bus.Ind., C.I.J.E, Excerp.Med., Gen.Sci.Ind., Hlth.Ind., Phys.Ed.Ind., Sportsearch (1974-), Tr.& Indus.Ind.
●Also available online. Vendor(s): DIALOG, Dow Jones/News Retrieval, Mead Data Central.
—BLDSC shelfmark: 6476.357000.
Description: Serves healthcare professionals' interests in the medical aspects of sports, exercise and fitness.

PSYCHOLOGY AND SOCIOLOGY OF SPORT: CURRENT SELECTED RESEARCH. see *PSYCHOLOGY*

QUEST (CHAMPAIGN). see *EDUCATION — Teaching Methods And Curriculum*

REFERATOVY VYBER ZE SPORTOVNI MEDICINY A LECEBNE REHABILITACE/ABSTRACTS OF SPORTS MEDICINE AND REHABILITATION. see *MEDICAL SCIENCES — Abstracting, Bibliographies, Statistics*

617.1   DK   ISSN 0905-7188
RC1200   CODEN: SMSSEO
SCANDINAVIAN JOURNAL OF MEDICINE & SCIENCE IN SPORTS. (Text in English) 1979. 4/yr. DKK 740. Munksgaard International Publishers Ltd., P.O. Box 2148, DK-1016 Copenhagen K, Denmark. (U.S. addr.: Three Cambridge Center, Ste. 208, Cambridge, MA 02142) Ed. Bengt Saltin. circ. 3,000. **Indexed:** Sportsearch (1979-).
—BLDSC shelfmark: 8087.517400.
   Formerly (until 1990): Scandinavian Journal of Sports Sciences (ISSN 0357-5632)
   Description: Publishes original articles in the fields of traumatology and orthopedics, physiology, biomechanics, and cardiology, as well as sociological, pedagogic, historical and philosophical contributions to the study of sports.
   Refereed Serial

617.102   SZ   ISSN 0036-7885
RC1200
SCHWEIZERISCHE ZEITSCHRIFT FUER SPORTMEDIZIN/REVUE SUISSE DE MEDECINE DES SPORTS/REVISTA SVIZZERA DI MEDICINA DELLO SPORT. (Title in French, German and Italian; summaries in English and French) 1963. 4/yr. 30 Fr. (Schweizerische Gesellschaft fuer Sportmedizin) Paul Haupt AG, Falkenplatz 11, 3001 Berne, Switzerland. TEL 031-232434. Ed. H. Howald. adv.; bk.rev.; bibl.; charts; illus.; index. **Indexed:** Biol.Abstr., Chem.Abstr., Excerp.Med., Ind.Med., Sportsearch.
—BLDSC shelfmark: 8123.480000.

617.1   FR   ISSN 0765-1597
                       CODEN: SCSPED
SCIENCE ET SPORTS; journal de la medecine, des sciences et des techniques. (Text in French; summaries in English, French) 1986. 4/yr. 560 F.($109) (foreign 620 F.)(effective 1992). (Societe Francaise de Medecine du Sport) Editions Scientifiques Elsevier, 29, rue Buffon, 75005 Paris, France. (Subscr. in U.S. and Canada to: Elsevier Science Publishing Co., Inc., Box 882, Madison Sq. Sta., New York, NY 10159. TEL 212-989-5800) Ed. Pierre Pesquies. circ. 2,000. (back issues avail.) **Indexed:** Biol.Abstr., Excerp.Med.
—BLDSC shelfmark: 8142.998000.
   Description: Covers central topics related to sports medicine, connected with internal medicine, traumatology, psychology, physiology, biochemistry, biomechanics or technology. Includes original articles, letters to the editor and technical notes.
   Refereed Serial

SOCIOLOGY OF SPORT JOURNAL. see *SOCIOLOGY*

SOMATICS; magazine-journal of the bodily arts and sciences. see *PHYSICAL FITNESS AND HYGIENE*

613.707   US   ISSN 0275-598X
GV201
SOVIET SPORTS REVIEW; specializing in track and field, weightlifting (weight training) and sports medicine. 1966. q. $33.50 (foreign $40)(effective Feb. 1992). Sports Training Inc., Box 2878, Escondido, CA 92033. TEL 619-480-0558. FAX 619-480-1277. Ed. Michael Yessis. bk.rev.; illus.; circ. 900. (back issues avail.) **Indexed:** Educ.Ind., Phys.Ed.Ind., R.G., Sportsearch (1979-).
—BLDSC shelfmark: 8359.919100.
   Formerly: Yessis Review of Soviet Physical Education and Sports (ISSN 0513-5389)

617.1   IT   ISSN 0392-9647
SPORT & MEDICINA. 1984. bi-m. L.30000 (foreign L.60000). Edi. Ermes, Via Timavo 12, 20124 Milan, Italy. TEL 02-66984715. FAX 02-66800773. Ed. Raffaele Grandi. adv.; bk.rev.; cum.index; circ. 18,000. (back issues avail.)
   Description: Features articles in fields of sports and medicine. Includes articles on pharmaceutical aids and physical fitness.

617.1   AT   ISSN 1032-5662
SPORT HEALTH. 1983. q. Aus.$31($30) Australian Sports Medicine Federation, P.O. Box 897, Belconnen, A.C.T 2616, Australia. TEL 062-516944. FAX 06-2531489. TELEX AUSUS 62400. Ed. Peter Brukner. bk.rev.; video rev.; charts; illus.; stat.; index. (back issues avail.) **Indexed:** Sportsearch (1983-).
   Description: Education and news in sports medicine and science.

617.1   US   ISSN 1056-6724
▼**SPORT SCIENCE REVIEW.** Short title: S S R. 1992. s-a. $24 to individuals (foreign $26); institutions $48 (foreign $50). Human Kinetics Publishers, Inc., Box 5076, Champaign, IL 61825-5076. TEL 217-351-5076. FAX 217-351-3674. Eds. Drs. Roy Shephard, Guido Schilling. adv.; abstr.; bibl.; charts; stat.
   Description: Provides an international review of new developments in areas of sport science.
   Refereed Serial

617.1   US   ISSN 0899-3815
SPORTCARE & FITNESS.* 1988. bi-m. $36. 1941 Limestone Rd., Ste. 209, Wilmington, DE 19808-5407. TEL 302-984-2600. Ed. Dr. Ali Kalamchi. adv.; circ. 35,000.
   Description: Deals with the "front-line" of athletics, including: injury prevention and management; training and conditioning; sports nutrition, psychology, equipment evaluation, and strategies.

617.102   GW   ISSN 0075-8655
SPORTMEDIZINISCHE SCHRIFTENREIHE. 1967. irreg. price varies. Johann Ambrosius Barth Verlag, Leipzig - Heidelberg, Salomonstr. 18b, 7010 Leipzig, Germany. TEL 70131. Ed.Bd. (back issues avail.)

SPORTS AND RECREATIONAL INJURIES. see *LAW*

610   US   ISSN 0112-1642
                       CODEN: SPMEE7
SPORTS MEDICINE; an international review of applied medicine and science in sport and exercise. 1984. bi-m. $195. Adis International Ltd., 401 S. State St., Newtown, PA 18940. TEL 479-8100. Ed. Jeremy N. Shanahan. abstr.; bibl.; illus. **Indexed:** Curr.Adv.Ecol.Sci., Ind.Med., Sportsearch (1984-).
—BLDSC shelfmark: 8419.837340.

617.1 613.7   US   ISSN 0746-9306
SPORTS MEDICINE BULLETIN. 1966. q. membership only. American College of Sports Medicine, Box 1440, Indianapolis, IN 46206-1440. TEL 317-637-9200. (Street addr.: 401 W. Michigan St., Indianapolis, IN 46202-3233) Ed. Juli Knutson. bk.rev.; circ. 12,000.
   Description: Newsmagazine to inform members about ACSM issues, upcoming events, future plans and member news.

617.102   US   ISSN 0731-9770
RC1200
SPORTS MEDICINE DIGEST. 1978. m. $49. P.M. Inc., Box 10172, Van Nuys, CA 91410. TEL 213-873-4399. Eds. G. Mckee, Dr. L. Yokum. bk.rev.; circ. 2,500. (back issues avail.) **Indexed:** Sportsearch (1980-).
—BLDSC shelfmark: 8419.837530.

SPORTS MEDICINE: HEALTH CARE FOR YOUNG ATHLETES. see *MEDICAL SCIENCES — Pediatrics*

SPORTS MEDICINE STANDARDS & MALPRACTICE REPORTER. see *LAW*

617.1   US   ISSN 1057-8315
SPORTS MEDICINE, TRAINING AND REHABILITATION; an international journal. 4/yr. (in 1 vol., 4 nos./vol.). $107. Harwood Academic Publishers, 270 Eighth Ave., New York, NY 10011. TEL 212-206-8900. FAX 212-645-2459. TELEX 236735 GOPUB UR. (Subscr. to: Box 786, Cooper Sta., New York, NY 10276. TEL 800-545-8398; UK subscr. to: P.O. Box 90, Reading, Berkshire RG1 8JL, England. TEL 0734-560-080) Ed. Eric Banister. (also avail. in microform)
   Formerly: Sports Training, Medicine and Rehabilitation (ISSN 0893-102X)
   Refereed Serial

617.102   US
SPORTS MEDISCOPE. q. United States Olympic Committee, Sports Medicine Division, 1750 E. Boulder St., Colorado Springs, CO 80909. TEL 719-632-5551. FAX 719-578-4677. **Indexed:** Sportsearch (1982-).

SPORTS - NUTRITION NEWS; incorporating the latest in health and fitness. see *NUTRITION AND DIETETICS*

SPORTSVISION QUARTERLY. see *MEDICAL SCIENCES — Ophthalmology And Optometry*

STRATEGIES (RESTON); a journal for physical and sport educators. see *EDUCATION — Teaching Methods And Curriculum*

SUID-AFRIKAANSE TYDSKRIF VIR NAVORSING IN SPORT, LIGGAAMLIKE OPVOEDKUNDE EN ONTSPANNING/SOUTH AFRICAN JOURNAL FOR RESEARCH IN SPORT, PHYSICAL EDUCATION AND RECREATION. see *PHYSICAL FITNESS AND HYGIENE*

TENNISPRO. see *SPORTS AND GAMES — Ball Games*

DER UNFALLCHIRURG; gesamte Unfallchirurgie Einschliesslich Sporttraumatologie. see *MEDICAL SCIENCES — Orthopedics And Traumatology*

617.1   US   ISSN 0162-0908
RC1200
YEAR BOOK OF SPORTS MEDICINE. 1979. a. $57.95. Mosby - Year Book, Inc., Continuity Division, 200 N. LaSalle, Chicago, IL 60601. TEL 312-726-9733. FAX 312-726-6075. TELEX 206155. Ed. Dr. Roy J. Shephard. illus. (reprint service avail.)
—BLDSC shelfmark: 9416.417000.

617.1   CC   ISSN 1000-6710
ZHONGGUO YUNDONG YIXUE ZAZHI/CHINESE JOURNAL OF SPORTS MEDICAL SCIENCE. (Text in Chinese) q. (Zhongguo Tiyu Kexue Xuehui - China Sports Science Society) Renmin Tiyu Chubanshe, 8 Tiyuguan Lu, Chongwen Qu, Beijing 100061, People's Republic of China. TEL 757161. (Co-sponsor: Yundong Yixue Xuehui - Sports Medical Science Association) Ed. Qu Jincheng.

MEDICAL SCIENCES — Surgery

A B M S DIRECTORY OF CERTIFIED NEUROLOGICAL SURGEONS. see *MEDICAL SCIENCES — Psychiatry And Neurology*

617   US   ISSN 0749-839X
RD10.U6
A B M S DIRECTORY OF CERTIFIED PLASTIC SURGEONS. 1983. biennial. $24.95. American Board of Medical Specialties, One Rotary Center, Ste. 805, Evanston, IL 60201. TEL 708-491-9091. FAX 708-328-3596. Ed. Dr. J. Lee Dockery.

617   US   ISSN 0884-1527
RD10.U6
A B M S DIRECTORY OF CERTIFIED SURGEONS. 1985. biennial. $44.95. American Board of Medical Specialties, One Rotary Center, Ste. 805, Evanston, IL 60201. TEL 708-491-9091. FAX 708-328-3596. Ed. Dr. J. Lee Dockery.

A B M S DIRECTORY OF CERTIFIED THORACIC SURGEONS. see *MEDICAL SCIENCES*

617   US   ISSN 0001-0790
A C O S NEWS. 1962. m. (American College of Osteopathic Surgeons) Business Service Network, 5031 Mussetter Rd., Ijamsville, MD 21754. TEL 301-663-0103. Ed. Susan Hill Rozynek. adv.; abstr.; circ. 1,450.

617   PE   ISSN 0001-3854
ACADEMIA PERUANA DE CIRUGIA REVISTA.* (Text in English and Spanish) 1948. q. S.400($9.) Academia Peruana de Cirugia, Camana 773, Lima, Peru. adv.; illus.; index; circ. 800. **Indexed:** Ind.Med.

ACOUSTIC NEUROMA ASSOCIATION NOTES. see *MEDICAL SCIENCES — Otorhinolaryngology*

617.95   CS   ISSN 0001-5423
ACTA CHIRURGIAE PLASTICAE; international journal of plastic surgery. (Editions in English and Russian; English edition has summaries in English, French, German, Spanish) 1959. q. 109 Fr.($40) (Association of Czechoslovak Plastic Surgeons) Avicenum, Czechoslovak Medical Press, Malostranske nam. 28, 11802 Prague 1, Czechoslovakia. (Dist. in Western countries by: Karger Libri A G, Petersgraben 31, 4001 Basel, Switzerland) Ed. Dr. H. Peskova. adv.; bk.rev.; charts; illus.; index; circ. 200. **Indexed:** Biol.Abstr., Dent.Ind., Excerp.Med., Ind.Med.

617   AU   ISSN 0001-544X
ACTA CHIRURGICA AUSTRIACA. (Text in German or English; summaries in English) 1968. 6/yr. S.1100. (Oesterreichische Gesellschaft fuer Chirurgie) Blackwell Medizinische Zeitschriftenverlagsgesellschaft mbH, Feldgasse 13, A-1238 Vienna, Austria. TEL 0222-8893646. FAX 0222-889364724. Ed. Dr. B. Niederle. circ. 1,500. (reprint service avail. from ISI) **Indexed:** ASCA, Biol.Abstr., Curr.Cont., Excerp.Med.
—BLDSC shelfmark: 0611.128000.

MEDICAL SCIENCES — SURGERY

617   BE   ISSN 0001-5458
CODEN: ACBEAX
ACTA CHIRURGICA BELGICA. (Supplements avail.) (Text in French; summaries in English) 1901. 6/yr. 1950 Fr. (foreign 2200 Fr.). Association des Societes Scientifiques Medicales Belges - Vereiniging van de Belgische Medische Wetenschappelijke Genootschappen, Av. Circulaire 138A, B-1180 Brussels, Belgium. TEL 02-374-5158. adv.; bk.rev.; charts; illus.; index. **Indexed:** ASCA, Biol.Abstr., C.I.S. Abstr., Chem.Abstr., Curr.Cont., Dent.Ind., Excerp.Med., Ind.Med.
—BLDSC shelfmark: 0611.130000.

617   HU   ISSN 0231-4614
ACTA CHIRURGICA HUNGARICA. (Text in English, French, German, Russian) 1960. q. $56. (Magyar Tudomanyos Akademia) Akademiai Kiado, Publishing House of the Hungarian Academy of Sciences, P.O. Box 24, H-1363 Budapest, Hungary. Eds. A. Babics, S. Csata. adv.; bk.rev.; bibl.; charts; illus.; index. **Indexed:** Biol.Abstr., Chem.Abstr., Curr.Adv.Ecol.Sci., Curr.Cont., Excerp.Med., Ind.Med., INIS Atomind.
—BLDSC shelfmark: 0611.138000.
Formerly: Academia Scientiarum Hungarica. Acta Chirurgica (ISSN 0001-5431)

617   IT   ISSN 0001-5466
CODEN: ACHIA7
ACTA CHIRURGICA ITALICA. (Text in Italian; summaries in English) 1944. bi-m. L.120000 includes supplements. Tipografia Editrice la Garangola, Via Montona 4, 35137 Padua, Italy.
FAX 049-8751743. Ed. R. Vecchioni. bk.rev.; index. (back issues avail.) **Indexed:** Biol.Abstr., Chem.Abstr., Dent.Ind., Excerp.Med., Ind.Med.
—BLDSC shelfmark: 0611.140000.

617   YU   ISSN 0001-5474
ACTA CHIRURGICA JUGOSLAVICA. (Text in English, German, Serbo-Croatian) 1954. q. $50. Udruzenje Hirurga Jugoslavije - Association of Yugoslav Surgeons, Univerzitetski Klinicki Centar, Institut za Bolesti Digestivnog Sistema, Ul. Koste Todorivica 6, 11000 Belgrade, Yugoslavia. TEL 011-643-070. FAX 011-646-988. TELEX 011-12099 CLI CTRYU. Ed. Dr. Zoran Gerzic. adv.; bk.rev.; circ. 2,000. **Indexed:** Ind.Med.
—BLDSC shelfmark: 0611.150000.

617   IT   ISSN 0393-6376
ACTA CHIRURGICA MEDITERRANEA. (Text in English, Italian) 1960. bi-m. L.35000($35) Carbone Editore, Via G. Daita, 29, 90139 Palermo, Italy. TEL (091) 321 273. FAX 091-321782. adv.; abstr.; bibl.; illus.; stat.; index; circ. 6,000.
—BLDSC shelfmark: 0611.170000.
Formerly: Archivio Siciliano di Medicina e Chirurgia (Sezione Chirurgica).
Description: Clinical cases in the surgical field are reviewed and discussed.

617   NO   ISSN 1102-1101
CODEN: ACHIEB
ACTA CHIRURGICA SCANDINAVICA - EUROPEAN JOURNAL OF SURGERY. (Supplement avail.) (Text in English) 1869. 10/yr. NOK 1300. Scandinavian University Press, P.O. Box 2959 Toeyen, N-0608 Oslo, Norway. TEL 47-2-677600.
FAX 47-2-677575. Ed. Lars Thoren. adv.; index. cum.index every 10-15 yrs.; circ. 2,400. **Indexed:** ASCA, Biol.Abstr., Chem.Abstr., Curr.Adv.Ecol.Sci., Curr.Cont., Excerp.Med., Helminthol.Abstr., Ind.Med., Ind.Sci.Rev., Nutr.Abstr., Sci.Cit.Ind.
—BLDSC shelfmark: 3829.745300.
Formerly (until 1991): Acta Chirurgica Scandinavica (ISSN 0001-5482)

616   US   ISSN 0001-6268
CODEN: ACNUA5
ACTA NEUROCHIRURGICA. 1950. 24/yr. (in 6 vols., 4 nos./vol.). DM.1494($880) (European Association of Neurosurgical Societies) Springer-Verlag, Journals, 175 Fifth Ave., New York, NY 10010.
TEL 212-460-1500. Ed. F. Loew. adv. (also avail. in microfilm from UMI; reprint service avail. from ISI) **Indexed:** ASCA, Bibl.Dev.Med.& Child Neur., Curr.Adv.Cancer Res., Curr.Adv.Ecol.Sci., Curr.Cont., Excerp.Med., Ind.Med., Ind.Sci.Rev., INIS Atomind., Sci.Cit.Ind.

ACTA NEUROCHIRURGICA. SUPPLEMENTA. see *MEDICAL SCIENCES — Psychiatry And Neurology*

617   IT   ISSN 0392-3088
ACTA PHONIATRICA LATINA. 1978. q. L.120000 includes supplements. Tipografia Editrice la Garangola, Via Montona 4, 35137 Padua, Italy. FAX 049-8751743. (back issues avail.) **Indexed:** Excerp.Med.
—BLDSC shelfmark: 0648.600000.

ADVANCES AND TECHNICAL STANDARDS IN NEUROSURGERY. see *MEDICAL SCIENCES — Psychiatry And Neurology*

ADVANCES IN CARDIAC SURGERY. see *MEDICAL SCIENCES — Cardiovascular Diseases*

ADVANCES IN NEUROSURGERY. see *MEDICAL SCIENCES — Psychiatry And Neurology*

ADVANCES IN OTOLARYNGOLOGY - HEAD AND NECK SURGERY. see *MEDICAL SCIENCES — Otorhinolaryngology*

617.95   US   ISSN 0748-5212
RD118.A1
ADVANCES IN PLASTIC AND RECONSTRUCTIVE SURGERY. 1984. a. $69.95. Mosby - Year Book, Inc. (Chicago) (Subsidiary of: Times Mirror Company), 200 N. LaSalle St., Chicago, IL 60601-1080. TEL 312-726-9733. FAX 312-726-6075. TELEX 206155. (Subscr. to: 11830 Westline Industrial Dr., St. Louis, MO 63146. TEL 800-325-4177) Eds. Drs. Mutaz B. Habal, William D. Morain. illus.
—BLDSC shelfmark: 0710.235000.
Description: Presents a collection of original, fully-referenced review articles written by experts in plastic and reconstructive surgery.

617.082   US   ISSN 0065-3411
RD1
ADVANCES IN SURGERY. 1966. a. $59.95. Mosby - Year Book, Inc. (Chicago) (Subsidiary of: Times Mirror Company), 200 N. LaSalle St., Chicago, IL 60601-1080. TEL 312-726-9733.
FAX 312-726-6075. TELEX 206155. (Subscr. to: 11830 Westline Dr., St. Louis, MO 63146. TEL 800-325-4177) Ed. Dr. John L. Cameron. illus. (also avail. in microfilm from UMI; reprint service avail. from UMI) **Indexed:** Ind.Med.
—BLDSC shelfmark: 0711.595000.
Description: Presents a collection of original, fully-referenced review articles in selected clinical topics important in the field of surgery.

617.95   US   ISSN 0364-216X
RD119
AESTHETIC PLASTIC SURGERY. 1976. 4/yr. $145. (International Society of Aesthetic Plastic Surgery) Springer-Verlag, Journals, 175 Fifth Ave., New York, NY 10010. TEL 212-460-1500. (Also Berlin, Heidelberg, Tokyo and Vienna) Ed. Blair O. Rogers. adv. (also avail. in microfilm from UMI; reprint service avail. from ISI) **Indexed:** Curr.Cont., Dent.Ind., Excerp.Med., Ind.Med., INIS Atomind.
—BLDSC shelfmark: 0730.380000.

617   GW   ISSN 0001-785X
AKTUELLE CHIRURGIE. 1966. bi-m. DM.264. Georg Thieme Verlag, Ruedigerstr. 14, Postfach 104853, 7000 Stuttgart 10, Germany. Ed.Bd. adv.; bibl.; charts; illus.; stat.; index; circ. 2,000. (reprint service avail. from UMI) **Indexed:** Excerp.Med.
—BLDSC shelfmark: 0785.729500.

617.585 378   US
ALUMNUS. 1975. q. New York College of Podiatric Medicine, 52 E. 124th St., New York, NY 10035. Ed. Judy Eisenkraft. bk.rev.; illus.; circ. 3,000.

617.585   US
AMERICAN ACADEMY OF PODIATRY ADMINISTRATION NEWS-LETTER.* vol. 3, 1973. q. $15. American Academy of Podiatry Administration, c/o John V. Cicero, D.P.M., Sec., Ten Meadow Lane, Bloomfield, NJ 07003. (Subscr. to: Dr. Leonard Light, 614 Central Ave., Dunkirk, NY 14048)
Formerly: American Academy of Practice Management in Podiatry. News-Letter.

617.585   US
AMERICAN COLLEGE OF FOOT SPECIALISTS. ANNUAL YEARBOOK. 1958. a. American College of Foot Specialists, 1801 Vauxhall Rd., Box 54, Union, NJ 02083. circ. 2,000.
Formerly (until 1980): American Association of Foot Specialists. Program Journal (ISSN 0065-7190)

617   US   ISSN 0002-8045
RD1
AMERICAN COLLEGE OF SURGEONS. BULLETIN. 1916. m. American College of Surgeons, 55 E. Erie St., Chicago, IL 60611-2797. TEL 312-664-4050.
FAX 312-440-7014. Ed. Stephen J. Regnier. charts; illus.; index; circ. 65,000 (controlled). (also avail. in microform from UMI; reprint service avail. from UMI) **Indexed:** Chem.Abstr., Med.Care Rev.
—BLDSC shelfmark: 2386.540000.

617.95   US   ISSN 0748-8068
AMERICAN JOURNAL OF COSMETIC SURGERY. 1984. q. $60 (foreign $70). American Academy of Cosmetic Surgery, Inc., 159 E. Live Oak St., Ste. 204, Arcadia, CA 91006. TEL 818-447-7880.
FAX 818-447-7880. Ed. Richard B. Aronsohn, M.D. adv.; bk.rev.; circ. 7,000. (reprint service avail.)
Description: Covers thought, experience, opinion, technique, research, legal aspects, patient relations, office protocol and any other subject relating to cosmetic surgery.

617   US   ISSN 0899-7403
AMERICAN JOURNAL OF KNEE SURGERY. Abbreviated title: A J K S. 1988. q. $85 to individuals; institutions $100; foreign $124. Slack, Inc., 6900 Grove Rd., Thorofare, NJ 08086-9447.
TEL 609-848-1000. FAX 609-853-5991. TELEX 517108. Ed. Kelly Vince, M.D. adv.; circ. 1,500. (also avail. in microform from UMI)
—BLDSC shelfmark: 0826.870000.
Description: Geared towards knee specialists and sports trainers, including articles on surgery and rehabilitation.
Refereed Serial

617   US   ISSN 0002-9610
RD1   CODEN: AJSUAB
AMERICAN JOURNAL OF SURGERY. 1891. m. $76 to individuals (foreign $125); institutions $95 (foreign $150)(effective Mar. 1992). Cahners Publishing Company (New York), Medical-Health Care Group, Yorke Medical Journals (Subsidiary of: Reed International PLC), Division of Reed Publishing (USA) Inc., 249 W. 17th St., New York, NY 10011-5301. TEL 212-463-6441. FAX 212-463-6470. (Subscr. to: Box 173306, Denver, CO 80217-3306. TEL 800-662-7776) Eds. Dr. Hiram C. Polk, Monica Schmidt. adv.; bk.rev.; bibl.; charts; illus.; circ. 15,500. (also avail. in microform from RPI,PMC; reprint service avail. from UMI) **Indexed:** Abstr.Inter.Med., Biol.Abstr., C.I.S. Abstr., Chem.Abstr., Curr.Adv.Cancer Res., Curr.Adv.Ecol.Sci., Curr.Cont., Dairy Sci.Abstr., Dent.Ind., Excerp.Med., Helminthol.Abstr., I.P.A., Ind.Med., Ind.Sci.Rev., INIS Atomind., Nutr.Abstr., Rev.Med.& Vet.Mycol., Rev.Plant Path., Risk Abstr., Sci.Cit.Ind.
●Also available online. Vendor(s): BRS, Mead Data Central.
—BLDSC shelfmark: 0838.500000.
Description: Specializes in clinical papers on general surgery, including latest operative techniques and procedures. The official publication of record of eight major surgical associations in the US.
Refereed Serial

616 616.07   US   ISSN 0147-5185
RD57   CODEN: AJSPDX
AMERICAN JOURNAL OF SURGICAL PATHOLOGY. 1977. m. $132 to individuals; institutions $206. (Arthur Purdy Stout Society of Surgical Pathologists) Raven Press, 1185 Ave. of the Americas, New York, NY 10036. TEL 212-930-9500. FAX 212-869-3495. TELEX 640073. Ed. Dr. Stephen S. Sternberg. adv.; bk.rev.; charts; illus.; stat.; index; circ. 6,800. (also avail. in microform from MIM; back issues avail.)
Indexed: Biol.Abstr., Curr.Adv.Cancer Res., Curr.Adv.Ecol.Sci., Curr.Cont., Dent.Ind., Excerp.Med., Ind.Med., Ind.Sci.Rev., INIS Atomind., Protozool.Abstr., Rev.Med.& Vet.Mycol., Sci.Cit.Ind.
—BLDSC shelfmark: 0838.520000.
Description: Covers diagnostic and prognostic technical advances.
Refereed Serial

MEDICAL SCIENCES — SURGERY

617.585 US ISSN 8750-7315
RD563.A2 CODEN: JAPAEA
AMERICAN PODIATRIC MEDICAL ASSOCIATION. JOURNAL. 1907. m. $55. American Podiatric Medical Association, 9312 Old Georgetown Rd., Bethesda, MD 20814-1621. TEL 301-571-9200. FAX 301-530-2752. Ed. Glenn B. Gastwirth. adv.; bk.rev.; bibl.; illus.; index, cum.index: 1973-1984; circ. 13,000. (also avail. in microfilm) **Indexed:** Biol.Abstr., Curr.Adv.Ecol.Sci., Curr.Cont., Dent.Ind., Excerp.Med., Hosp.Lit.Ind., Ind.Med., INIS Atomind., Int.Nurs.Ind., Nutr.Abstr.
•Also available online. Vendor(s): National Library of Medicine.
Incorporates: Podiatric Medicine and Surgery; Former titles (until 1984): American Podiatry Association. Journal (ISSN 0003-0538); (until 1957): National Association of Chiropodists. Journal (ISSN 0360-1684); (until 1921): Pedic Items.
Refereed Serial

AMERICAN PODIATRIC MEDICAL WRITERS ASSOCIATION. NEWSLETTER. see *JOURNALISM*

617 US ISSN 0003-1348
RD1 CODEN: AMSUAW
AMERICAN SURGEON. 1935. m. $70 to individuals (foreign $85); institutions $90 (foreign $110). (Southeastern Surgical Congress) J.B. Lippincott Co., E. Washington Sq., Philadelphia, PA 19105. TEL 215-238-4273. (Co-sponsors: Midwest Surgical Association; Association of Clinical Anatomists; Society of American Gastrointestinal and Endoscopic Surgeons) Ed. P. William Currieri, M.D. adv.; illus.; index; circ. 4,259. (also avail. in microform from UMI; reprint service avail. from UMI) **Indexed:** Biol.Abstr., Chem.Abstr., Curr.Cont., Excerp.Med., Hosp.Lit.Ind., Ind.Med., Ind.Sci.Rev., Ind.Vet., INIS Atomind., Rev.Myd.& Vet.Mycol., Sci.Cit.Ind., Small Anim.Abstr., SSCI.
—BLDSC shelfmark: 0857.750000.
Refereed Serial

617 617 BL ISSN 0003-245X
ANAIS PAULISTAS DE MEDICINA E CIRURGIA. 1913. q. Cr.$5000($30) Real e Benerita Sociedade Portuguesa de Sao Paulo, Rua Maestro Cardim, 769, 01323 Sao Paulo, Brazil. Ed. Abrahao Kerzner. adv.; bk.rev.; bibl.; illus.; index; circ. 2,000. **Indexed:** Biol.Abstr., Chem.Abstr., Excerp.Med., Ind.Med.
—BLDSC shelfmark: 0869.130000.

617 AG ISSN 0066-1465
ANALES DE CIRUGIA. 1935. irreg. Calle Paraguay 40, Rosario, Prov. de Santa Fe, Argentina. **Indexed:** Biol.Abstr., Excerp.Med.

ANESTEZIOLOGIYA I REANIMATOLOGIYA/ANESTHESIOLOGY AND REANIMATOLOGY. see *MEDICAL SCIENCES — Anaesthesiology*

617 FR ISSN 0003-3944
ANNALES DE CHIRURGIE. 1947. 10/yr. 945 F. (foreign 1340 F.). (Semaine des Hopitaux) Expansion Scientifique, 15 rue Saint-Benoit, 75278 Paris Cedex 06, France. Ed. M. Edelmann. **Indexed:** Biol.Abstr., Chem.Abstr., Curr.Adv.Cancer Res., Curr.Cont., Excerp.Med., Ind.Med.

617 FR ISSN 1153-2424
CODEN: AMSPEL
ANNALES DE CHIRURGIE DE LA MAIN ET DU MEMBRE SUPERIEUR. (Text in English and French) 5/yr. 1000 F. to individuals (foreign 1225 F.); institutions 1385 F. (foreign 1725 F.); students 685 F. (foreign 960 F.). (Societes de Chirurgie de la Main) Expansion Scientifique, 15 rue Saint-Benoit, 75278 Paris Cedex 06, France. TEL 1-45-48-42-60. FAX 1-45-44-81-55. (Co-sponsors: Societe Belge de Chirurgie de la Main; Groupe d'Etude de la Main; Societe Francaise de Chirurgie de la Main) **Indexed:** Biol.Abstr., Excerp.Med.
Formerly: Annales de Chirurgie de la Main (ISSN 0753-9053)

617.95 FR ISSN 0294-1260
CODEN: ACESE
ANNALES DE CHIRURGIE PLASTIQUE ET ESTHETIQUE. (Text in French; summaries in English) 1956. 6/yr. 1140 F. to individuals (foreign 1450 F.); students 570 F. (foreign 725 F.). (Semaine des Hopitaux) Expansion Scientifique, 15 rue Saint-Benoit, 75278 Paris Cedex 06, France. TEL 1-45-48-42-60. FAX 1-45-44-81-55. Ed. J.T. Lalardrie. adv.; abstr.; charts; illus. **Indexed:** Biol.Abstr., Chem.Abstr., Curr.Cont., Excerp.Med., Ind.Med.
Formerly: Annales de Chirurgie Plastique (ISSN 0003-3960)

ANNALES DE CHIRURGIE THORACIQUE ET CARDIO-VASCULAIRE. see *MEDICAL SCIENCES — Cardiovascular Diseases*

617 IT ISSN 0003-469X
CODEN: AICHAL
ANNALI ITALIANI DI CHIRURGIA. 1922. 6/yr. L.80000($100) Nuova Casa Editrice Licinio Cappelli. S.p.a., Via Farini, 14, 40124 Bologna, Italy. Ed. N. Picardi. adv.; bk.rev.; abstr.; charts; illus.; circ. 3,000. **Indexed:** Biol.Abstr., Chem.Abstr., Dent.Ind., Excerp.Med., Ind.Med.
—BLDSC shelfmark: 1014.300000.

ANNALS DE MEDICINA. see *MEDICAL SCIENCES*

617.95 US ISSN 0148-7043
RD118.A1 CODEN: APCSD4
ANNALS OF PLASTIC SURGERY. 1978. m. $121 to individuals (foreign $185); institutions $160 (foreign $225); residents $75 (foreign $115)(effective Nov. 1991). Little, Brown and Company, Medical Journals, 34 Beacon St., Boston, MA 02108. TEL 617-859-5500. FAX 617-859-0629. Ed. Dr. Lars M. Vistnes. adv.; bk.rev.; abstr.; charts; illus.; stat.; index; circ. 4,427. (also avail. in microform from UMI; reprint service avail. from UMI; back issues avail.) **Indexed:** Biol.Abstr., CINAHL, Curr.Cont., Dent.Ind., Excerp.Med., Ind.Med., Ind.Sci.Rev., INIS Atomind., Sci.Cit.Ind.
•Also available online. Vendor(s): Mead Data Central.
—BLDSC shelfmark: 1043.525000.
Description: Forum for the latest in surgical techniques, interesting cases, and practical briefs on surgical devices. Includes articles, case reports, hypotheses, and letters to the editor.
Refereed Serial

617 US ISSN 0003-4932
RD1 CODEN: ANSUA5
ANNALS OF SURGERY. 1885. m. $65 to individuals (foreign $95); institutions $100 (foreign $135). J.B. Lippincott Co., E. Washington Sq., Philadelphia, PA 19105. TEL 215-238-4200. (Co-sponsors: Southern Surgical Association; Philadelphia Academy of Surgery; New York Surgical Society; American Surgical Association) Ed. David C. Sabiston, Jr., M.D. adv.; illus.; index.; circ. 19,066. (also avail. in microform from UMI,PMC; reprint service avail. from UMI) **Indexed:** Abstr.Health Care Manage.Stud., Abstr.Inter.Med., Biol.Abstr., Chem.Abstr., Curr.Adv.Cancer Res., Curr.Adv.Ecol.Sci., Curr.Cont., Excerp.Med., Helminthol.Abstr., Hosp.Lit.Ind., Ind.Med., Ind.Sci.Rev., INIS Atomind., Risk Abstr., Sci.Cit.Ind., SSCI.
•Also available online. Vendor(s): BRS, BRS/Saunders Colleague, Mead Data Central.
—BLDSC shelfmark: 1044.500000.
Refereed Serial

617.54 US ISSN 0003-4975
RD536 CODEN: ATHSAK
ANNALS OF THORACIC SURGERY. 1965. m. $165 (foreign $200)(effective 1992). (Society of Thoracic Surgeons) Elsevier Science Publishing Co., Inc. (New York), 655 Ave. of the Americas, New York, NY 10010. TEL 212-989-5800. FAX 212-633-3965. TELEX 420643 AEP UI. (Co-sponsor: Southern Thoracic Surgical Association) Ed. Dr. Thomas Ferguson. adv.; bk.rev.; charts; illus.; index; circ. 8,100. (also avail. in microform from UMI; back issues avail.) **Indexed:** Abstr.Inter.Med., Biol.Abstr., CINAHL, Curr.Adv.Cancer Res., Curr.Cont., Excerp.Med., Helminthol.Abstr., Ind.Med., Ind.Sci.Rev., INIS Atomind., Nutr.Abstr., Rev.Med.& Vet.Mycol., Sci.Cit.Ind.
•Also available online. Vendor(s): Mead Data Central.
—BLDSC shelfmark: 1044.750000.
Description: Presents original papers on topics in thoracic and cardiovascular surgery, featuring case reports, "how-to-do-it" articles, classics in thoracic surgery, collective and current reviews, and correspondence.
Refereed Serial

617 616.1 US ISSN 0890-5096
CODEN: AVSUEV
ANNALS OF VASCULAR SURGERY. 1986. bi-m. Blackwell Scientific Publications Inc., Three Cambridge Center, Ste. 208, Cambridge, MA 02142-1413. TEL 617-225-0401. FAX 617-225-0412. Ed. R. Berguer.
—BLDSC shelfmark: 1045.350000.
Description: Worldwide coverage of all clinical or research-oreinted work going on today in vascular surgery.

ANNUAL OF CARDIAC SURGERY. see *MEDICAL SCIENCES — Abstracting, Bibliographies, Statistics*

617 FR ISSN 0003-5394
ANTENNE MEDICALE. (Includes supplements) 1964. m. 150 F. Service de Radiologie Adulte, c/o Docteur G. Pelissier, 439 rue Paradise, 13008 Marseille, France. Ed.Bd. adv.; bk.rev.; bibl, illus.

617 II ISSN 0003-5998
R97
THE ANTISEPTIC; monthly journal of medicine and surgery. (Text in English) 1904. m. Rs.150 (foreign Rs.900)(effective 1992). Professional Publications Ltd., P.O. Box 2, Satya Sai Nagar, Madurai 625 003, Tamil Nadu, India. TEL 35000. Ed.Bd. adv.; bk.rev.; abstr.; bibl.; illus.; index; circ. 22,563. (reprint service avail. from UMI) **Indexed:** Chem.Abstr., Excerp.Med., Ind.Med.
—BLDSC shelfmark: 1552.000000.

617 JA ISSN 0003-9152
ARCHIV FUER JAPANISCHE CHIRURGIE/NIHON GEKA HOKAN. (Text in various languages) 1924. bi-m. 6000 Yen or exchange basis. Kyoto University, Faculty of Medicine, Department of Surgery, 53 Shogoin Kawara-cho, Sakyo-ku, Kyoto 606, Japan. Ed. Kazae Ozawa. abstr.; charts; illus.; index; circ. 1,000. **Indexed:** Biol.Abstr., Chem.Abstr., Curr.Cont., Excerp.Med., Ind.Med.
—BLDSC shelfmark: 1615.400000.

617 UK ISSN 0264-4924
ARCHIVES OF EMERGENCY MEDICINE. 1984. q. £95($173) (British Association for Accident and Emergency Medicine) Blackwell Scientific Publications Ltd., Osney Mead, Oxford OX2 OEL, England. TEL 0865-240201. FAX 0865-721205. TELEX 83355-MEDBOK-G. (Co-sponsor: Australian College of Emergency Physicians) Ed. A.D. Redmond. adv.; bk.rev.; abstr.; bibl.; illus.; index. **Indexed:** ASCA, Excerp.Med.
—BLDSC shelfmark: 1634.235000.

MEDICAL SCIENCES — SURGERY

617   US   ISSN 0004-0010
CODEN: ARSUAX
ARCHIVES OF SURGERY. 1920. m. $62. American Medical Association, 515 N. State St., Chicago, IL 60610. TEL 312-464-0183. FAX 312-464-5834. Ed. Dr. Claude H. Organ. adv.; bk.rev.; charts; illus.; index; circ. 39,000. (also avail. in microform from UMI,PMC) **Indexed:** Abstr.Inter.Med., Biol.Abstr., C.I.S.Abstr., Chem.Abstr., CINAHL, Curr.Adv.Cancer Res., Curr.Adv.Cell & Devel.Biol., Curr.Adv.Ecol.Sci., Dairy Sci.Abstr., Dent.Ind., Excerp.Med., Helminthol.Abstr., Ind.Med., Ind.Sci.Rev., INIS Atomind., Int.Nurs.Ind., Nutr.Abstr., Protozool.Abstr., Rev.Med.& Vet.Mycol., Risk Abstr., Sci.Cit.Ind.
●Also available online. Vendor(s): Mead Data Central.
—BLDSC shelfmark: 1643.200000.
Refereed Serial

617.54 616.1   IT   ISSN 0391-7029
ARCHIVIO DI CHIRURGIA TORACICA E CARDIOVASCOLARE. (Text in English and Italian) 1979. bi-m. $100. (Italian Society of Cardiovascular Surgery) Edizioni Luigi Pozzi s.r.l., Via Panama 68, 00198 Rome, Italy. TEL 06-8553548. FAX 06-8554105. Ed. L. Provenzale. adv.; bk.rev.; circ. 1,200.
Description: Articles on thoracic and cardiovascular surgery.

617   IT   ISSN 0066-670X
ARCHIVIO PUTTI DI CHIRURGIA DEGLI ORGANI DI MOVIMENTO. (Text in Italian; summaries in English, Italian) 1951. a. $70. Aulo Gaggi Editore, Via Andrea Costa 131-5, 40134 Bologna, Italy. FAX 51-436119. Ed. O. Scaglietti. bk.rev.; circ. 1,500. **Indexed:** Dent.Ind., Excerp.Med., Ind.Med.
—BLDSC shelfmark: 1647.900000.

617   BL   ISSN 0066-7846
ARQUIVOS DE CIRURGIA CLINICA E EXPERIMENTAL.* (Supplements accompany some issues) (Some summaries in English) 1937. irreg. $35. Universidade de Sao Paulo, Hospital das Clinicas, Caixa Postal 8091, Sao Paulo, Brazil. Ed. Ruy G. Bevilacqua. index, cum.index; circ. 10,000. **Indexed:** Biol.Abstr.

ARTHROSCOPY; journal of arthroscopic and related surgery. see *MEDICAL SCIENCES — Orthopedics And Traumatology*

ARTHROSCOPY. see *MEDICAL SCIENCES — Orthopedics And Traumatology*

617   GW   ISSN 0176-1897
ARZTHELFERIN AKTUELL. 1970. m. DM.86. (Berufsverband der Arzthelferinnen) Verlag Johann August Koch, Postfach 1829, 3550 Marburg, Germany. circ. 19,100. (back issues avail.)

617 370   ZA
ASSOCIATION OF SURGEONS OF EAST AFRICA. PROCEEDINGS. (Text and summaries in English) 1978. a. 15 n.($20) Association of Surgeons of East Africa, Box 320159, Woodlands, Lusaka, Zambia. Ed. John E. Jellis. adv.; bk.rev.; cum.index; circ. 800. (back issues avail.)
Description: Publishes the seventy best papers read at the meetings of the Association of Surgeons of East Africa during the previous year.

617   IT   ISSN 0390-5527
ATTUALITA IN CHIRURGIA. 3/yr. $60. Edizioni Luigi Pozzi s.r.l., Via Panama 68, 00198 Rome, Italy. TEL 06-8553548. FAX 06-8554105. Ed. G. F. Fegiz.
Description: Monographs on surgery.

616.21   US
AUDIO-DIGEST GENERAL SURGERY. 1954. s-m. $168. Audio-Digest Foundation (Subsidiary of: California Medical Association), 1577 E. Chevy Chase Dr., Glendale, CA 91206. TEL 213-245-8505. FAX 818-240-7379. Ed. Claron L. Oakley. (audio cassette)
Formerly: Audio-Digest Surgery (ISSN 0271-1273)
Refereed Serial

617   AT   ISSN 0004-8682
CODEN: ANZJA7
AUSTRALIAN AND NEW ZEALAND JOURNAL OF SURGERY. 1931. m. Aus.$195($299) (Royal Australasian College of Surgeons) Blackwell Scientific Publications (Australia) Pty. Ltd., P.O. Box 378, Carlton, Vic. 3053, Australia. TEL 03-347-0300. FAX 03-347-5001. TELEX 10716421. Ed. G.J.A. Clunie. adv.; bk.rev.; bibl.; illus.; index; circ. 5,400. (also avail. in microform from UMI; back issues avail.; reprint service avail. from UMI) **Indexed:** Biol.Abstr., Curr.Adv.Cancer Res., Curr.Cont., Dent.Ind., Excerp.Med., Ind.Med., Nutr.Abstr., Rev.Med.& Vet.Mycol., Sci.Cit.Ind.
—BLDSC shelfmark: 1796.900000.
Description: Covers original contributions related to clinical practice and research in all fields of surgery and related disciplines.

616   AT
AUSTRALIAN SURGEON. 1977. bi-m. Aus.$60. Australian Association of Surgeons, 795 Pacific Highway, Gordon, N.S.W. 2072, Australia. FAX 02-499-2695. Ed. Christopher Thomas. adv.; circ. 2,000.

617   SZ   ISSN 1013-7459
CODEN: BBCHEL
BASELER BEITRAEGE ZUR CHIRURGIE; Aktuelle Entwicklungen und neue Verfahren aus der chirurgischen Praxis kompakt vermittelt. (Text in German) 1989. irreg. varies. (University of Basel, Department of Surgery) S. Karger AG, Allschwilerstr. 10, P.O. Box, CH-4009 Basel, Switzerland. TEL 061-3061111. FAX 061-3061234. TELEX CH 962652. Eds. U. Laffer, M. Duerig. abstr.; bibl.; charts.
Description: Discusses developments in surgery and its techniques.

BLOOD TRANSFUSION. see *MEDICAL SCIENCES — Hematology*

BRITISH DENTAL SURGERY ASSISTANT. see *MEDICAL SCIENCES — Dentistry*

617   UK   ISSN 0268-8697
CODEN: BJNEEL
BRITISH JOURNAL OF NEUROSURGERY. 1987. 6/yr. $116 to individuals; institutions $272. Carfax Publishing Co., P.O. Box 25, Abingdon, Oxfordshire OX14 3UE, England. TEL 0235-555335. FAX 0235-553559. (U.S. subscr. addr.: Carfax Publishing Co., Box 2025, Dunnellon, FL 32630) Ed. Robert Maurice-Williams. adv.; bk.rev.; index. (also avail. in microfiche; back issues avail.) **Indexed:** Excerp.Med.
—BLDSC shelfmark: 2311.940000.

BRITISH JOURNAL OF ORAL AND MAXILLOFACIAL SURGERY. see *MEDICAL SCIENCES — Dentistry*

617.95   UK   ISSN 0007-1226
CODEN: BJPSAZ
BRITISH JOURNAL OF PLASTIC SURGERY. 1948. 8/yr. £79($159) (British Association of Plastic Surgeons) Churchill Livingstone Medical Journals, Robert Stevenson House, 1-3 Baxter's Pl., Leith Walk, Edinburgh EH1 3AF, Scotland. TEL 031-556-2424. FAX 031-558-1278. TELEX 727511. (Subscr. to: Longman Group, Journals Subscr. Dept., P.O. Box 77, Fourth Ave., Harlow, Essex CM19 5AA, England; U.S. subscr. to: Churchill Livingstone, 650 Ave. of the Americas, New York, NY 10011. TEL 212-206-5000) Ed. M.D. Poole. adv.; bk.rev.; abstr.; illus.; index. (also avail. in microform from UMI; back issues avail.; reprint service avail. from SWZ) **Indexed:** Biol.Abstr., Chem.Abstr., Curr.Adv.Ecol.Sci., Curr.Cont., Dent.Ind., Excerp.Med., Ind.Med., Ind.Sci.Rev., Sci.Cit.Ind.
—BLDSC shelfmark: 2319.500000.

617   UK   ISSN 0007-1323
CODEN: BJSUAM
BRITISH JOURNAL OF SURGERY. 1913. m. £99 in UK and Europe; elsewhere £112. (Surgery Society Ltd.) Butterworth - Heinemann Ltd. (Subsidiary of: Reed International PLC), Linacre House, Jordan Hill, Oxford OX2 8DP, England. TEL 0865-310366. FAX 0865-310898. TELEX 83111 BHPOXF G. (Subscr. to: Turpin Transactions Ltd., Distribution Centre, Blackhorse Rd., Letchworth, Herts SG6 1HN, England. TEL 0462-672555) Eds. R.C.G. Russell, D.C. Carter. adv.; bk.rev.; abstr.; illus.; index; circ. 6,877. (also avail. in microform from UMI; back issues avail.) **Indexed:** Abstr.Inter.Med., Biol.Abstr., Biotech.Abstr., Chem.Abstr., Curr.Adv.Ecol.Sci., Curr.Cont., Dent.Ind., Dok.Arbeitsmed., Excerp.Med., Helminthol.Abstr., Ind.Med., Ind.Sci.Rev., Ind.Vet., INIS Atomind., Int.Nurs.Ind., Nutr.Abstr., Pig News & Info., Protozool.Abstr., Risk Abstr., Sci.Cit.Ind., Small Anim.Abstr., Vet.Bull.
●Also available online. Vendor(s): BRS, Mead Data Central.
—BLDSC shelfmark: 2325.000000.
Description: Original papers and reviews covering the latest techniques, treatment, and advances in surgery. Includes abstracts of the Surgical Research and the Vascular Societies.
Refereed Serial

617   SP   ISSN 0214-2376
BRITISH JOURNAL OF SURGERY (EDICION ESPANOLA). 1974. m. (10/yr.). 11200 ptas.($112) (free to qualified personnel). Ediciones Doyma S.A., Travesera de Gracia 17-21, 08021 Barcelona, Spain. TEL 200 07 11. FAX 209-11-36. TELEX 51694 INK-E. (Co-sponsors: Association of Surgeons of Great Britain and Ireland, Surgical Research Society, UK) Ed. C. Pera Blanco-Morales. adv.: page 140000 ptas.; trim 210 x 280; adv. contact: Jordi Grau. circ. 2,500. **Indexed:** Ind.Med.Esp.
Supersedes (Jan. 1989): Revista Quirurgica Espanola (ISSN 0210-2196)
Description: Covers all areas of surgery as translated from the English edition.

CANADIAN JOURNAL OF CARDIOLOGY. see *MEDICAL SCIENCES — Cardiovascular Diseases*

617   CN   ISSN 0008-428X
CODEN: CJSUAX
CANADIAN JOURNAL OF SURGERY/JOURNAL CANADIEN DE CHIRURGIE. (Text in English and French) 1957. bi-m. Can.$54($59) (Royal College of Physicians and Surgeons of Canada) Canadian Medical Association, 1867 Alta Vista Dr., Box 8650, Ottawa, Ont. K1G 0G8, Canada. TEL 613-731-9331. FAX 613-523-0937. adv.; bk.rev.; bibl.; charts; illus.; index; circ. 9,000. (also avail. in microform from UMI; reprint service avail. from UMI) **Indexed:** Biol.Abstr., Chem.Abstr., Curr.Cont., Dent.Ind., Excerp.Med., Helminthol.Abstr., Ind.Med., Ind.Sci.Rev., NRN, Nutr.Abstr., Sci.Cit.Ind.
—BLDSC shelfmark: 3035.800000.

CANADIAN OPERATING ROOM NURSING JOURNAL. see *MEDICAL SCIENCES — Nurses And Nursing*

CARDIAC SURGERY; state of the art reviews. see *MEDICAL SCIENCES — Cardiovascular Diseases*

CARDIOTHORACIC SURGERY SERIES. see *MEDICAL SCIENCES — Cardiovascular Diseases*

CARDIOVASCULAR SURGERY. see *MEDICAL SCIENCES — Cardiovascular Diseases*

CESKOSLOVENSKA NEUROLOGIE A NEUROCHIRURGIE. see *MEDICAL SCIENCES — Psychiatry And Neurology*

615.534   UK   ISSN 0009-4714
CHIROPODY REVIEW. 1939. bi-m. £10 (foreign £13.50). Institute of Chiropodists, 1 Lushington Rd., Eastbourne, E. Sussex BN21 4LG, England. FAX 0323-28886. Ed. Philip G.F. Basham. adv.; bk.rev.; circ. 1,500.
—BLDSC shelfmark: 3181.140000.
Description: Features innovations in the field of podiatry.

MEDICAL SCIENCES — SURGERY

617   BU   ISSN 0450-2167
CODEN: KHIGAF
CHIRURGIA. (Text in Bulgarian; summaries in English, Russian) 1948. bi-m. 24 Iv.($11) (Ministerstvo na Narodnoto Zdrave) Izdatelstvo Meditsina i Fizkultura, 11, Pl. Slaveikov, Sofia, Bulgaria. (Co-sponsor: Nauchno Druzhestvo po Chirurgia) Ed. N. Vasilev. circ. 1,200. **Indexed:** Chem.Abstr., Dent.Ind., Excerp.Med., Helminthol.Abstr., Ind.Med.
—BLDSC shelfmark: 0394.790000.

617   IT
CHIRURGIA. (Text in Italian; summaries in English) 1988. m. $90. (Societa Italiana di Chirurgia) Edizioni Minerva Medica, Corso Bramante 83-85, 10126 Turin, Italy. TEL 011-678282. FAX 011-674502. Ed. Alberto Oliaro. adv.; bk.rev.; bibl.; charts; illus.; circ. 7,000. (back issues avail.)
Description: Original articles on scientific and medical experiments and research.

617   IT   ISSN 0009-4749
CODEN: CHOMA9
CHIRURGIA DEGLI ORGANI DI MOVIMENTO. (Text in Italian, English) 1917. q. L.80000($100) Nuova Casa Editrice Licinio Cappelli S.p.a., Via Farini, 14, 40124 Bologna, Italy. TEL 051-239060. Ed. M. Campanacci. adv.; bk.rev.; abstr.; bibl.; illus.; circ. 3,000. **Indexed:** Biol.Abstr., Chem.Abstr., Dent.Ind., Excerp.Med., Ind.Med.
—BLDSC shelfmark: 3181.300000.

616   IT
CHIRURGIA DEL PIEDE/FOOT SURGERY. (Text and summaries in English, French, Italian) 1977. bi-m. L.65000($80) Edizioni Minerva Medica, Corso Bramante 83-85, Box 491, Turin 10126, Italy. **Indexed:** Excerp.Med.
Formerly: Rivista di Chirurgia del Piede.

617   IT   ISSN 0394-9079
CHIRURGIA DELLA TESTA E DEL COLLO. 1984? s-a. L.60000 includes supplement. Tipografia Editrice la Garangola, Via Montona, 4, 35137 Padua, Italy. FAX 049-8751743.

617   IT   ISSN 0009-4757
CHIRURGIA E PATOLOGIA SPERIMENTALE. vol. 18, 1970. q. L.47000($59) Universita Cattolica del Sacro Cuore, Clinica Chirurgica, Via della Pineta Sacchetti N. 526, 00168 Rome, Italy. Dir. Gian Carlo Castiglioni. adv.; circ. 500. **Indexed:** Biol.Abstr., Chem.Abstr., Dent.Ind., Excerp.Med., Ind.Med.
—BLDSC shelfmark: 3181.185000.

617   IT   ISSN 0393-1471
CHIRURGIA EPATOBILIARE. 1982. q. L.40000. (Istituto di Patologia Chirurgia) Casa Editrice Fratelli Palombi, Via dei Gracchi 181-185, 00192 Rome, Italy. illus.; index.
Description: Forum covers hepatic, biliary and pancreatic surgery.

CHIRURGIA GASTROENTEROLOGICA (ITALIAN EDITION); rassegna trimestrale di chirurgia dell'apparato digerente e degli organi addominali. see *MEDICAL SCIENCES — Gastroenterology*

617   IT   ISSN 0009-4773
CHIRURGIA ITALIANA. (Text in English, Italian) 1948. bi-m. L.30000. c/o Clinica Chirurgica dell'Universita, Policlinico di Borgo Roma, 37100 Verona, Italy. Ed.Bd. adv.; bk.rev.; index, cum.index. **Indexed:** Biol.Abstr., Chem.Abstr., Excerp.Med., Ind.Med.
—BLDSC shelfmark: 3181.187000.

617.95   CI   ISSN 0009-4781
CODEN: CMXPAU
CHIRURGIA MAXILLOFACIALIS ET PLASTICA/MAXILLOFACIAL AND PLASTIC SURGERY. (Text in Croatian or English; abstracts in English) 1957. 3/yr. $30. Zbor Lijecnika Hrvatske, Sekcija za Maksilofacijalnu i Plasticnu Kirurgiju - Medical Association of Croatia, Section for Maxillofacial and Plastic Surgery, Subiceva 9, Zagreb. TEL 041-276 313. FAX 041-420-470. Ed. Dr. Miso Virag. adv.; bk.rev.; circ. 500. **Indexed:** Dent.Ind., Excerp.Med., Ind.Med., Ref.Zh.
●Also available online.
—BLDSC shelfmark: 3181.190000.
Description: Publishes articles on maxillofacial, plastic and reconstructive surgery, as well as related disciplines.

617   IT   ISSN 0009-4811
CHIRURGIA TRIVENETA. (Text in Italian; summaries in English, French and German) 1960. q. L.50000. Ospedale Civile Maggiore, Divisione Chirurgica, II, Piazzale Stefani 1, 37126 Verona, Italy. Ed. G. Fattovich. adv.; bk.rev.; charts; illus.; circ. 900.
—BLDSC shelfmark: 3181.450000.

617   FR   ISSN 0001-4001
CHIRURGIE. 1851. 10/yr. 205 ECU($245) (typically set in Jan.). (Academie de Chirurgie) Masson, 120 bd. Saint-Germain, 75280 Paris Cedex 06, France. TEL 1-46-34-21-60. FAX 1-45-87-29-99. TELEX 202 671 F. Ed. Cerbonnet. adv.; bk.rev.; illus.; index; circ. 2,600. (also avail. in microform from UMI; reprint service avail. from ISI) **Indexed:** Chem.Abstr., Curr.Cont., Dent.Ind., Excerp.Med., Ind.Med., Ind.Sci.Rev., Sci.Cit.Ind.
—BLDSC shelfmark: 3181.462000.

617   GW   ISSN 0009-4846
CODEN: CHPXBE
CHIRURGISCHE PRAXIS; taegliche Praxis der gesamten Chirurgie. 1957. bi-m. DM.268. Hans Marseille Verlag, Buerkleinstr. 12, 8000 Munich 22, Germany. TEL 089-227988. Ed.Bd. bk.rev.; abstr.; charts; illus.; index, cum.index every 5 yrs.; circ. 5,000. (also avail. in microfilm from UMI) **Indexed:** Biol.Abstr., Excerp.Med.
Description: Articles about orthopedic, internal and plastic surgery, featuring new techniques. Includes questions and answers, detailed photographs.

617   UY   ISSN 0009-7381
CODEN: CRGUAT
CIRUGIA DEL URUGUAY. Abbreviated title: C U. (Table of contents in English, Spanish) 1920. bi-m. (with supplements). Urg.$50000($25) to non-members. Sociedad de Cirugia del Uruguay, Hospital de Clinicas "Dr. Manuel Quintela", C.C. 10.972, Piso 4, Montevideo, Uruguay. (Co-sponsor: Congresos Uruguayos de Cirugia) Ed. Dr. Gustavo Bogliaccini. adv.; abstr.; bibl.; illus.; index; circ. 1,000 (controlled). **Indexed:** Biol.Abstr., Excerp.Med.
—BLDSC shelfmark: 3267.623000.
Formerly (1965-1969): Revista de Cirugia del Uruguay; **Supersedes (1930-1964):** Sociedad de Cirugia del Uruguay. Boletines.

617   SP   ISSN 0009-739X
CODEN: CRESAD
CIRUGIA ESPANOLA. (Text in English, French and Spanish; abstracts in English) 1946. m. 7300 ptas.($75) (Asociacion Espanola de Cirujanos) Ediciones Doyma S.A., Traversa de Gracia, 17-21, 08021 Barcelona, Spain. TEL 200-07-11. FAX 209-11-36. TELEX 51964 INK E. Ed. A. Gomez Alonso. adv.; bk.rev.; abstr.; bibl.; illus.; charts; index; circ. 2,500. **Indexed:** Biol.Abstr., Chem.Abstr., Excerp.Med., Helminthol.Abstr., Ind.Med.Esp.
—BLDSC shelfmark: 3267.550000.
Formerly (until 1969): Cirugia, Ginecologia y Urologia (ISSN 0412-5878)

617 618.92   SP   ISSN 0214-1221
CIRUGIA PEDIATRICA. q. 10000 ptas.($120) Editorial Garsi, S.A., Londres, 17, 28028 Madrid, Spain. TEL 256-08-00. FAX 361-10-07. Dir. A. Marques Gubern. circ. 1,000.

617.95   UY   ISSN 0009-7403
CIRUGIA PLASTICA URUGUAYA.* (Text in Spanish; summaries in English and Spanish) 1960. q. (Sociedad de Cirugia Plastica del Uruguay) Hospital de Clinicas "Dr. Manuel Quintela", Piso 4, Montevideo, Uruguay.
Formerly: Cirugia Plastica del Uruguay.

617   MX   ISSN 0009-7411
CIRUGIA Y CIRUJANOS. 1933. bi-m. $50. Academia Mexicana de Cirugia, Col. Centro. Deleg. Cuauhtemoc, Apdo. Postal 7994, 06080 Mexico, D.F., Mexico. Ed. Humberto Hurtado. abstr.; bibl.; illus. **Indexed:** Biol.Abstr., Chem.Abstr., Excerp.Med., Ind.Med.

617.522   CN   ISSN 1055-6656
RD525   CODEN: CPJOEG
CLEFT PALATE - CRANIOFACIAL JOURNAL; an international journal of craniofacial anomalies. 1964. bi-m. $100 to individuals; institutions $135. (American Cleft Palate-Craniofacial Association) Decker Periodicals, One James St. S., P.O. Box 620, LCD 1, Hamilton, Ont. L8N 3K7, Canada. TEL 416-522-7017. FAX 416-522-7839. (U.S. addr.: Box 785, Lewiston, NY 14092) Ed. Stewart R. Rood. adv.; bk.rev.; abstr.; charts; illus.; stat.; cum.index: 1964-1988; circ. 3,500. (also avail. in microform from MIM; back issues avail.; reprint service avail. from UMI) **Indexed:** Chic.Per.Ind., Child Devel.Abstr., Curr.Adv.Ecol.Sci., Curr.Cont., Dent.Ind., Excerp.Med., Ind.Med., Ind.Sci.Rev., Rehabil.Lit., Sci.Cit.Ind.
—BLDSC shelfmark: 3278.559800.
Formerly: Cleft Palate Journal (ISSN 0009-8701)
Description: International interdisciplinary professional journal on clinical and research activities in cleft palate and other craniofacial anomalies.
Refereed Serial

616   IT   ISSN 0393-7577
CLINICA CHIRURGICA DEL NORD AMERICA. bi-m. L.130000($160) Piccin Editore, Via Altinate 107, 35100 Padua, Italy. TEL 049-655566. TELEX 432074 PICCIN I. (reprint service avail. from UMI)

617   US   ISSN 0746-469X
CLINICAL LASER MONTHLY. 1983. m. $259. American Health Consultants, Inc., Six Piedmont Center, Ste. 400, 3525 Piedmont Rd., N.E., Atlanta, GA 30305. TEL 404-262-7436. FAX 800-284-3291. (Subscr. to: Department L100, Box 740056, Atlanta, GA 30374-9822. TEL 800-688-2421) Ed. Carol Willey. circ. 1,700. (back issues avail.; reprint service avail.)
●Also available online. Vendor(s): Mead Data Central.
—BLDSC shelfmark: 3286.295900.

CLINICAL NEUROLOGY AND NEUROSURGERY. see *MEDICAL SCIENCES — Psychiatry And Neurology*

CLINICAL NEUROSURGERY: PROCEEDINGS. see *MEDICAL SCIENCES — Psychiatry And Neurology*

617   DK   ISSN 0902-0063
CODEN: CLTRED
CLINICAL TRANSPLANTATION. (Text in English) 1987. 6/yr. DKK 1055 includes supplements. Munksgaard International Publishers Ltd., 35 Noerre Soegade, P.O. Box 2148, DK-1016 Copenhagen K, Denmark. TEL 33-12-70-30. FAX 33-12-93-87. TELEX 19431 MUNKS DK. Eds. John S. Najarian, R.L. Simmons. bk.rev.; circ. 1,000.

617   SP
CLINICAS QUIRURGICAS DE NORTEAMERICA. Spanish translation of: Surgical Clinics of North America. 1961. 6/yr. 20670 ptas.($150) (effective 1990). Interamericana de Espana, S.A., Division de Ciencias de la Salud de McGraw-Hill, Calle Manuel Ferrero, 13, 28036 Madrid, Spain. TEL 315-0340. FAX 733-6627. charts; illus.; index.

617   US   ISSN 0094-1298
CLINICS IN PLASTIC SURGERY. 1974. q. $110. W.B. Saunders Co., Curtis Center, Independence Square W., Philadelphia, PA 19106. TEL 215-238-7800. Ed. Susan Short. (also avail. in microform from MIM; reprint service avail. from ISI,UMI) **Indexed:** Dent.Ind., Excerp.Med., Ind.Med., Ind.Sci.Rev., INIS Atomind., Sci.Cit.Ind.
—BLDSC shelfmark: 3286.590000.

617   BL
COLEGIO BRASILEIRO DE CIRURGIOES. REVISTA. 1944. bi-m. Cr.$600($40) Colegio Brasileiro de Cirurgioes, R. Visconde de Silva, 52, 22281 Rio de Janeiro, RJ, Brazil. TEL 286-3795. Ed. Marcos Moraes. adv.; bk.rev.; circ. 7,000. (back issues avail.)

617   US   ISSN 1053-749X
CODEN: CSURE
COMPLICATIONS IN SURGERY. 1982. m. $50 to individuals; residents and students $30. S C P Communications, Inc., 134 W. 29th St., New York, NY 10001-5304. TEL 212-714-1740. Ed. Katherine Rice. adv. **Indexed:** Excerp.Med.
—BLDSC shelfmark: 3364.588000.
Formerly (until 1991): Infections in Surgery (ISSN 0277-7746)

MEDICAL SCIENCES — SURGERY

617 US ISSN 0172-4827
COMPREHENSIVE MANUALS OF SURGICAL SPECIALITIES. 1975. irreg. price varies. Springer-Verlag, 175 Fifth Ave., New York, NY 10010. TEL 212-460-1500. (Also Berlin, Heidelberg, Tokyo and Vienna) Ed. R.H. Egdahl. (reprint service avail. from ISI)

617 US
CONTEMPORARY SURGERY. 1972. m. $25 (Canada $64; elsewhere $80). Bobit Publishing Company, 2512 Artesia Blvd., Redondo Beach, CA 90278. TEL 310-376-8788. FAX 310-376-9043. Ed. Seymour Schwartz. bk.rev.; bibl.; charts; illus.; index; circ. 51,000 (controlled). (also avail. in microform from UMI; reprint service avail. from UMI) **Indexed:** Biol.Abstr., Excerp.Med.
Description: Original clinical information covering the latest developments and techniques in surgery.
Refereed Serial

617 US ISSN 0162-6477
CORRESPONDENCE SOCIETY OF SURGEONS. COLLECTED LETTERS. m. $89 (foreign $109). Laux Company, Inc., 63 Great Rd., Maynard, MA 01754. TEL 617-897-5552. FAX 508-897-6824. index; circ. 500. (looseleaf format)

617 UK ISSN 0952-0627
CODEN: CRPSE4
CURRENT PRACTICE IN SURGERY. q. £39($75) to individuals; institutions £89($170). Churchill Livingstone Medical Journals, Robert Stevenson House, 1-3 Baxter's Pl., Leith Walk, Edinburgh EH1 3AF, Scotland. TEL 031-556-2424. FAX 031-558-1278. (Subscr. to: Longman Group, Journals Subscr. Dept., P.O. Box 77, Fourth Ave., Harlow, Essex CM19 5AA, England; U.S. subscr. to: Churchill Livingstone, 650 Ave. of the Americas, New York, NY 10011. TEL 212-206-5000) Ed. W.E.G. Thomas.
—BLDSC shelfmark: 3501.315500.
Description: International review journal which covers all the disciplines of general surgery.

617 US ISSN 0011-3840
RD1 CODEN: CPSUA
CURRENT PROBLEMS IN SURGERY. Short title: C P S. 1964. m. $78 to individuals (foreign $103); institutions $100 (foreign $125); students $49 (foreign $70)(effective Jan. 1992). Mosby - Year Book, Inc. (Subsidiary of: Times Mirror Company), 11830 Westline Industrial Dr., St. Louis, MO 63146. TEL 800-325-4177. Ed. Dr. Samuel A. Wells. charts; illus.; cum.index; circ. 6,600. (also avail. in microform from UMI; back issues avail.; reprint service avail. from UMI) **Indexed:** Curr.Cont., Dent.Ind., Excerp.Med., Ind.Med., Ind.Sci.Rev.
—BLDSC shelfmark: 3501.450000.
Description: Written by recognized surgical experts. CPS is a monographic journal which provides current fully referenced information to practicing surgeons.

617 US ISSN 0149-7944
RD1 CODEN: CUSUDB
CURRENT SURGERY. 1933. bi-m. $45 to individuals (foreign $60); institutions $65 (foreign $80). (Association of Program Directors in Surgery) J.B. Lippincott Co., E. Washington Sq., Philadelphia, PA 19105. TEL 215-238-4200. Ed. Lloyd M. Nyhus, M.D. adv.; illus.; index; circ. 2,153. (also avail. in microform from UMI) **Indexed:** Biol.Abstr., Chem.Abstr., Dent.Ind., Ind.Med.
—BLDSC shelfmark: 3504.047000.
Formerly: Review of Surgery (ISSN 0034-6780)
Refereed Serial

617 US ISSN 0894-2277
CURRENT SURGICAL DIAGNOSIS & TREATMENT. 1980. irreg., 9th ed., 1990. $39.95. Appleton & Lange (Subsidiary of: Simon & Schuster Company), 25 Van Zant St., Box 5630, Norwalk, CT 06856. TEL 203-838-4400. Ed. Lawrence W. Way.
●Also available online. Vendor(s): Mead Data Central.

617 DK ISSN 0900-4041
DANSK KIRURGISK SELSKAB. NYHEDSBREV. 1982. q. Dansk Kirurgisk Selskab, Hoersholm Hospital, Kirurgisk Afdeling, 2970 Hoerscholm, Denmark. TEL 02-861600. Ed. Dr. Anders Fischer. adv.; bk.rev.

DENTO MAXILLO FACIAL RADIOLOGY. see *MEDICAL SCIENCES — Radiology And Nuclear Medicine*

617 SZ ISSN 0253-4886
DIGESTIVE SURGERY. (Text in English) 1984. bi-m. 584 Fr.($390) per vol. S. Karger AG, Allschwilerstr. 10, P.O. Box, CH-4009 Basel, Switzerland. TEL 061-3061111. FAX 061-3061234. TELEX CH 962652. Ed.Bd. adv.; illus.; index; circ. 1,000. (also avail. in microform from RPI) **Indexed:** Curr.Cont., Excerp.Med.
—BLDSC shelfmark: 3588.346900.
Incorporates: Surgical Gastroenterology.

617 UK
DIRECTORY OF OPERATING THEATRES AND DEPARTMENTS OF SURGERY (YEAR). a? £40. C M A Medical Data Ltd., Cambridge Research Laboratories, 181A Huntingdon Rd., Cambridge CB3 0DJ, England. TEL 0223-277709. FAX 0223-276444.
Description: Contains detailed information on operating theatres and Departments of Surgery in NHS and independent hospitals throughout the U.K.

617 US ISSN 0012-3706
CODEN: DICRAG
DISEASES OF THE COLON AND RECTUM. 1958. m. $95 to individuals (foreign $120); institutions $130 (foreign $155). (American Society of Colon and Rectal Surgeons) Williams & Wilkins, 428 E. Preston St., Baltimore, MD 21202. TEL 301-528-4000. FAX 301-528-4321. Ed. Dr. Robert W. Beart, Jr. adv.; illus.; index.; circ. 4,804. (also avail. in microform from UMI) **Indexed:** Biol.Abstr., Chem.Abstr., Curr.Adv.Cancer Res., Curr.Adv.Ecol.Sci., Curr.Cont., Dent.Ind., Excerp.Med., Hosp.Lit.Ind., Ind.Med., Ind.Sci.Rev., INIS Atomind., NRN, Protozool.Abstr., Sci.Cit.Ind., SSCI.
●Also available online. Vendor(s): Mead Data Central.
—BLDSC shelfmark: 3598.200000.
Description: Contains original articles on the surgical management of lower gastrointestinal tract disorders.
Refereed Serial

DISEASES OF THE ESOPHAGUS. see *MEDICAL SCIENCES*

617 UA ISSN 0013-2454
EGYPTIAN SURGICAL SOCIETY QUARTERLY REVIEW. (Text in English) 1966. q. £E1. Egyptian Surgical Society, Dar el Hekma, 42 Kasr el-Aini St., Cairo, Egypt. Ed. Ahmed Abu-Zikry. adv.; bk.rev.; bibl.; charts; illus.

617 CN ISSN 0836-7272
EMERGENCY PREHOSPITAL MEDICINE. 1986. 6/yr. $35 (foreign Can.$45). C M E Communications, Inc., 20854 Dalton Rd., P.O. Box 507, Sutton West, Ont. L0E 1L0, Canada. TEL 416-722-9839. FAX 416-722-9687. Ed. Alastair Dempster. adv.; bk.rev.; abstr.; charts; illus.; stat.; tr.lit.; circ. 6,200. (back issues avail.)
Description: Provides a source of continuing medical, business education and professional news for ambulance officers, paramedics, emergency physicians and nurses, and EMS management and training officers in Canada.
Refereed Serial

EUROPEAN JOURNAL OF EPIDEMIOLOGY. see *MEDICAL SCIENCES*

617 FR ISSN 0939-7248
EUROPEAN JOURNAL OF PEDIATRIC SURGERY. 1960. bi-m. 200 ECU($268) (Societe Francaise de Chirurgie Infantile) Masson, 120 bd. Saint-Germain, 75280 Paris Cedex 06, France. TEL 1-46-34-21-60. FAX 1-45-87-29-99. TELEX 202 671 F. (Co-publisher: Hippokrates Verlag) Ed. S. Juskiewenski. adv.; bk.rev.; illus.; index; circ. 1,100. (also avail. in microform from UMI; reprint service avail. from ISI) **Indexed:** Bibl.Dev.Med.& Child Neur., Biol.Abstr., Curr.Cont., Dent.Ind., Excerp.Med., Helminthol.Abstr., Ind.Med.
Former titles: Chirurgie Pediatrique (ISSN 0180-5738); (until vol. 18, 1977): Annales de Chirurgie Infantile (ISSN 0003-3952)

617.95 GW ISSN 0930-343X
EUROPEAN JOURNAL OF PLASTIC SURGERY. (Text in English) 1971. 6/yr. DM.1532($151) Springer-Verlag, Heidelberger Platz 3, D-1000 Berlin 33, Germany. TEL 030-8207-1. (Also Heidelberg, Tokyo, Vienna, and New York) Ed. I.T. Jackson. (also avail. in microform from UMI; reprint service avail. from ISI) **Indexed:** Biol.Abstr., Curr.Adv.Cancer Res., Excerp.Med., Sci.Cit.Ind.
—BLDSC shelfmark: 3829.736300.
Formerly: Chirurgia Plastica (ISSN 0340-5664)
Description: Covers developments in microsurgery, tissue expansion, craniofacial surgery, and the spin-offs of these techniques into the areas of trauma, the treatment of malignancy, and aesthetic surgery.

EUROPEAN JOURNAL OF VASCULAR SURGERY. see *MEDICAL SCIENCES — Cardiovascular Diseases*

617 SZ ISSN 0014-312X
CODEN: EUSRBM
EUROPEAN SURGICAL RESEARCH; clinical and experimental surgery. (Text in English) 1969. bi-m. 453 Fr.($302) S. Karger AG, Allschwilerstr. 10, P.O. Box, CH-4009 Basel, Switzerland. TEL 061-3061111. FAX 061-3061234. TELEX CH 962652. Ed. K. Messmer. adv.; circ. 800. (also avail. in microform from RPI; back issues avail.) **Indexed:** Biol.Abstr., Chem.Abstr., Curr.Adv.Ecol.Sci., Curr.Cont., Excerp.Med., Ind.Med., Ind.Sci.Rev., Ind.Vet., Sci.Cit.Ind., Vet.Bull.
—BLDSC shelfmark: 3830.235000.

617 IT
EUROSURGERY. q. Casa Editrice Idelson, Via A. DeGasperi, 55, 80133 Naples, Italy. TEL 081-5524733. FAX 5518295. Ed. Marco DeFazio.

617.95 US ISSN 0736-6825
CODEN: FPSUEA
FACIAL PLASTIC SURGERY. 1983. q. $89 (foreign $115). Thieme Medical Publishers, Inc., 381 Park Ave., So., Ste. 1501, New York, NY 10016. TEL 212-683-5088. (also avail. in microfilm) **Indexed:** Excerp.Med.
—BLDSC shelfmark: 3863.421000.
Formerly: Seminars in Facial Plastic Surgery.

617 US ISSN 0071-8041
CODEN: SUFOAX
FORUM ON FUNDAMENTAL SURGICAL PROBLEMS. Variant title: Surgical Forum. 1950. a. $20. American College of Surgeons, 55 E. Erie St., Chicago, IL 60611-2797. TEL 312-664-4050. FAX 312-440-7014. Ed. Kevin Oliver. circ. 3,500. (also avail. in microform from UMI; reprint service avail. from UMI) **Indexed:** ASCA, Biol.Abstr., Curr.Adv.Ecol.Sci., Curr.Cont., Excerp.Med.

617.585 GW ISSN 0427-7783
DER FUSS. 1948. m. DM.72 (foreign DM.80). (Zentralverband der Fusspfleger Deutschlands e.V.) Verlag Neuer Merkur GmbH, Ingolstaedter Str. 63a, 8000 Munich 46, Germany. TEL 089-318905-0. FAX 089-31890538. TELEX 5215-520. adv.; bk.rev.; charts; illus.; index; circ. 6,633.

617 IT ISSN 0016-5662
GAZZETTA INTERNAZIONALE DI MEDICINA E CHIRURGIA.* vol.76, 1971. s-m. L.12320. Edizioni Mediche e Scientifiche, Largo A.Ravizza 17, Rome, Italy. Eds. C. Bazzicalupo, G. Marcozzi. **Indexed:** Chem.Abstr.

617 US
GENERAL SURGERY NEWS. m. McMahon Group, 148 W. 24th St., 8th Fl., New York, NY 10011-1916. TEL 212-620-4600. FAX 212-620-5928. Ed. Cornelia Kean. circ. 36,862.

616 IT
IL GIORNALE DI CHIRURGIA. (Text in Italian; summaries in English) 1980. 10/yr. L.80000($80) (Societa Italiana di Ricerche in Chirurgia) C I C Edizioni Internazionali s.r.l., Via L. Spallanzani 11, 00161 Rome, Italy. TEL 06-8412673. FAX 06-8443365. TELEX 622099 CIC. Dir. G. Di Matteo. adv. **Indexed:** Excerp.Med.

617.95 IT ISSN 1120-0405
GIORNALE DI CHIRURGIA PLASTICA RICOSTRUTTIVA ED ESTETICA. 3/yr. L.70000($85) (effective 1992). Casa Editrice Idelson, Via A. DeGasperi, 55, 80133 Naples, Italy. TEL 081-5524733. FAX 081-5518295. Ed. Nicolo Scuderi.

MEDICAL SCIENCES — SURGERY

617   IT   ISSN 0017-0453
GIORNALE ITALIANO DI CHIRURGIA. (Text in Italian; summaries in English) 1945. w. L.80000. Casa Editrice l' Antologia, Via E. Suarez 5, 80129 Naples, Italy. Ed. Roberto Ruggiero. adv.; charts; illus.
Indexed: Chem.Abstr., Excerp.Med., Ind.Med.
—BLDSC shelfmark: 4178.203000.

617   RU   ISSN 0017-4866
CODEN: GRKHAK
GRUDNAYA KHIRURGIYA/CHEST SURGERY. (Text in Russian; summaries in English) 1959. bi-m. 27.30 Rub. (Vsesoyuznoe Nauchnoe Obshchestvo Khirurgov) Izdatel'stvo Meditsina, Petroverigskii pereulok 6-8, 101838 Moscow, Russia. (Dist. by: Mezhdunarodnaya Kniga, Moscow, G-200, Russia) (Co-sponsor: Ministerstvo Zdravookhraneniya S.S.S.R.) Ed. V.S. Savel'ev. bk.rev.; bibl.; index.
Indexed: Biol.Abstr., Excerp.Med., Ind.Med.
Description: Deals with theoretical and organization problems of chest surgery and with problems of allied fields.

617   US   ISSN 0894-8569
CODEN: HPBSE9
H P B SURGERY; a world journal of hepatic, pancreatic, and biliary surgery. 8/yr. (in 2 vols., 4 nos./vol.) $98. Harwood Academic Publishers, 270 Eighth Ave., New York, NY 10011. TEL 212-206-8900. FAX 212-645-2459. TELEX 236735 GOPUB UR. (Subscr. to: Box 786, Cooper Sta., New York, NY 10276. TEL 800-545-8398; UK subscr. to: P.O. Box 90, Reading, Berkshire RG1 8JL, England. TEL 0734-560-080) Ed. Stig Bengmark. (also avail. in microform)
—BLDSC shelfmark: 4335.262350.
Refereed Serial

617   TU
HACETTEPE MEDICAL JOURNAL/HACETTEPE TIP DERGISI. (Editions in English, Turkish) 1968. q. $30. (University of Hacettepe - Hacettepe Universitesi) Hacettepe University Press, Ankara, Turkey. TELEX 42-237 HKT TR. Ed. Dr. Dogan Taner. adv.; bibl.; charts; illus.; index; circ. 980.
Indexed: Biol.Abstr., Excerp.Med.
Formerly: Hacettepe Bulletin of Medicine-Surgery - Hacettepe Tip Cerrahi Bulteni (ISSN 0017-6451)
Description: Contains papers on original research, case reports, reviews, short communications for practical applications, letters, editorials, and announcements concerning the medical sciences.

617   GW   ISSN 0046-6794
HANDCHIRURGIE. 1969. q. DM.75. (Deutschsprachige Arbeitsgemeinschaft fuer Handchirurgie) V L E Verlags-GmbH, Wasserturmstr. 8, 8520 Erlangen, Germany. Ed.Bd. bk.rev.; illus.; circ. 1,600. **Indexed:** Excerp.Med., Ind.Med.

617.95   GW   ISSN 0722-1819
CODEN: HMPCD9
HANDCHIRURGIE - MIKROCHIRURGIE - PLASTISCHE CHIRURGIE. 1969. bi-m. DM.252. Hippokrates Verlag GmbH, Ruedigerstr. 14, Postfach 10 22 63, 7000 Stuttgart 10, Germany. (Co-sponsors: Deutschsprachige Arbeitsgemeinschaft fuer Handchirurgie; Deutschsprachige Arbeitsgemeinschaft fuer Mikrochirurgie der Peripheren Nerven; Verein der Deutschen Plastischen Chirurgie) Ed.Bd. circ. 1,300. **Indexed:** Biol.Abstr., Dent.Ind., Excerp.Med., Ind.Med.
—BLDSC shelfmark: 4254.577000.
Formerly: Zeitschrift fuer Plastische Chirurgie (ISSN 0342-7978)

617   US   ISSN 1043-3074
RD523   CODEN: HEANEE
HEAD & NECK. 1978. bi-m. $215 to individuals; institutions $290. John Wiley & Sons, Inc., Journals, 605 Third Ave., New York, NY 10158-0012. TEL 212-692-6000. Ed. Dr. Helmuth Goepfert. adv.; bk.rev.; abstr.; charts; illus.; stat.; index; circ. 2,500. (also avail. in microform from RPI; reprint service avail. from UMI) **Indexed:** Curr.Cont., Excerp.Med., Ind.Med., Ind.Sci.Rev., Sci.Cit.Ind.
—BLDSC shelfmark: 4274.608500.
Formerly: Head and Neck Surgery (ISSN 0148-6403)
Description: Examines the management and prevention of all diseases in the head and neck area, including benign and malignant tumors, congenital deformities, and trauma.
Refereed Serial

617   SZ   ISSN 0018-0181
CODEN: HCATAE
HELVETICA CHIRURGICA ACTA. (Text in French and German; summaries in original language and English) 1945. m. 194 Fr. (Schweizerische Gesellschaft fuer Chirurgie) Schwabe und Co. AG, Steinentorstr. 13, CH-4010 Basel, Switzerland. TEL 061-2725523. FAX 061-2725573. Eds. M. Rossetti, G. Chapuis. adv.; bibl.; charts; illus.; index; circ. 1,150. **Indexed:** Biol.Abstr., Chem.Abstr., Curr.Cont., Dent.Ind., Excerp.Med., Helminthol.Abstr., Ind.Med.
—BLDSC shelfmark: 4287.050000.
Description: Also covers annual meetings of the Swiss Societies for urology and throat, heart, and vessel surgery.

617.3   US
HOSPITAL PODIATRIST. 1976. s-a. $10. American Association of Hospital Podiatrists, c/o Earl L. Cherniak, D.P.M., Ed., 3940 S. Figueroa St., Los Angeles, CA 90037. TEL 213-747-7272. bk.rev.; circ. 2,000. (back issues avail.)

INDIAN JOURNAL OF COLO-PROCTOLOGY. see *MEDICAL SCIENCES — Gastroenterology*

617.95   II   ISSN 0970-0358
INDIAN JOURNAL OF PLASTIC SURGERY. 1968. s-a. Rs.150($20) Association of Plastic Surgeons of India, c/o Postgraduate Dept. of Plastic Surgery, K.G.'s Medical College, A-15 Nirala Nagar, Lucknow 226 007, India. TEL 71080. Ed. Ramesh Chandra. adv.; bk.rev.; circ. 450.
—BLDSC shelfmark: 4420.160000.

617   II   ISSN 0019-5650
RD1   CODEN: IJSUAV
INDIAN JOURNAL OF SURGERY. (Text in English) vol. 32, 1970. bi-m. Rs.50.($15.) (Association of Surgeons in India) Popular Prakashan Pvt. Ltd., 35-C Tardeo Rd., Bombay 400034, India. Ed. Dr. R.K. Gandhi. adv.; bk.rev.; charts; illus.; circ. 2,400.
Indexed: Biol.Abstr., Chem.Abstr., Excerp.Med., INIS Atomind.

617   II   ISSN 0019-5863
CODEN: IMGAAY
INDIAN MEDICAL GAZETTE.* (Text in English) 1961. m. Rs.150. Martin & Harris Private Ltd., Savory Chambers, Wallace St., Bombay 400001, India. Ed. L.K. Pandeya. bk.rev.; abstr.; bibl.; illus.; circ. 27,689. **Indexed:** Chem.Abstr., Excerp.Med., Nutr.Abstr.
Description: Promotes the development of modern medicine and surgery in India.

INTERNATIONAL JOURNAL OF ADULT ORTHODONTICS AND ORTHOGNATHIC SURGERY. see *MEDICAL SCIENCES — Dentistry*

617   GW   ISSN 0179-1958
CODEN: IJCDE6
INTERNATIONAL JOURNAL OF COLORECTAL DISEASE. 1986. 4/yr. DM.224($135) Springer-Verlag, Heildelberger Platz 3, D-1000 Berlin 33, Germany. TEL 030-8207-1. (Also Heidelberg, Tokyo, Vienna, and New York) Ed. R.J. Nicholls. **Indexed:** Excerp.Med.
—BLDSC shelfmark: 4542.172400.

INTERNATIONAL JOURNAL OF ORAL & MAXILLOFACIAL SURGERY. see *MEDICAL SCIENCES — Dentistry*

INTERNATIONAL JOURNAL OF PERIODONTICS & RESTORATIVE DENTISTRY. see *MEDICAL SCIENCES — Dentistry*

617   IT   ISSN 0020-8868
CODEN: INTSAO
INTERNATIONAL SURGERY. (Text in English) 1937. q. $70. (International College of Surgeons) Edizioni Minerva Medica, Corso Bramante 83-85, 10126 Turin, Italy. Ed. Dr. Giuseppe Pezzuoli. adv.; bk.rev.; abstr.; illus.; index; circ. 12,000. (also avail. in microform from JAI,UMI; reprint service avail. from UMI) **Indexed:** Biol.Abstr., Chem.Abstr., Curr.Cont., Excerp.Med., Hosp.Lit.Ind., Ind.Med., INIS Atomind.
—BLDSC shelfmark: 4550.020000.
Formerly: International College of Surgeons. Journal.
Description: Publishes original scientific articles covering important clinical observations, surgical techniques, experimental surgery and research.

617.54   US
INTERNATIONAL TRENDS IN GENERAL THORACIC SURGERY. vol.5, 1989. irreg., vol.7, 1990. $95. Mosby - Year Book, Inc. (Subsidiary of: Times Mirror Company), 11830 Westline Industrial Dr., St. Louis, MO 63146. TEL 800-325-4117. FAX 314-432-1380. TELEX 44-2402. Eds. N.C. Delarue, H. Eschapasse.

617.95   JA   ISSN 0021-5228
JAPANESE JOURNAL OF PLASTIC & RECONSTRUCTIVE SURGERY/KEISEI GEKA. (Text mainly in Japanese; headings and occasional articles in English) vol.22, 1979. q. $65. Kokuseido Publishing Co., Ltd., 3-23-5, 202 Hongo, Bunkyo-ku, Tokyo 113, Japan. Ed.Bd. adv.; charts; illus.; index. **Indexed:** Biol.Abstr., Excerp.Med., INIS Atomind.
—BLDSC shelfmark: 4658.100000.

617.54   JA   ISSN 0021-5252
JAPANESE JOURNAL OF THORACIC SURGERY/KYOBU GEKA. (Text in Japanese; contents page and summaries in English) 1948. m. 29100 Yen (foreign 33383 Yen). Nankodo Co., Ltd., 42-6, Hongo 3-chome, Bunkyo-ku, Tokyo 113, Japan. TEL 03-3811-7239. FAX 03-3811-7230. Eds. Ken-ichi Asano, Tsuneo Ishihara. adv.; charts; illus.; index; circ. 3,000. **Indexed:** Curr.Cont., Excerp.Med., Ind.Med., INIS Atomind.
—BLDSC shelfmark: 4658.900000.

617   FR   ISSN 0021-7697
CODEN: JOCHAQ
JOURNAL DE CHIRURGIE. 1908. 10/yr. 1085 ECU($225) (typically set in Jan.). Masson, 120 bd. Saint-Germain, 75280 Paris Cedex 06, France. TEL 1-46-34-21-60. FAX 1-45-87-29-99. TELEX 202 671 F. Ed. Ph. Detrie. adv.; bk.rev.; abstr.; bibl.; illus.; index; circ. 3,500. (also avail. in microform from UMI; reprint service avail. from UMI) **Indexed:** Biol.Abstr., C.I.S. Abstr., Excerp.Med., Helminthol.Abstr., Ind.Med., Ind.Sci.Rev., Sci.Cit.Ind.
—BLDSC shelfmark: 4958.200000.

617   FR   ISSN 0021-7913
JOURNAL DE MEDECINE ET DE CHIRURGIE PRATIQUES. 1830. s-m. 250 F. Association des Amis de Just Lucas Championniere, 67 rue St. Dominique, 75007 Paris, France. (Subscr. to: Expansion Scientifique, 15 rue St-Benoit, 75278 Paris Cedex 06) **Indexed:** Excerp.Med.
—BLDSC shelfmark: 5017.005000.

617   US   ISSN 0021-8421
JOURNAL OF ABDOMINAL SURGERY. Variant title: Abdominal Surgery. 1959. m. $15. American Society of Abdominal Surgeons, 675 Main St., Melrose, MA 02176. TEL 617-665-6102. Eds. John M. Langone, Dr. Meyer O. Cantor. adv.; bk.rev.; abstr.; charts; illus.; stat.; index; circ. 13,900.
Indexed: Biol.Abstr., Excerp.Med.
Refereed Serial

615.534   UK
JOURNAL OF BRITISH PODIATRIC MEDICINE; Chiropodist. 1914. m. £36. Society of Chiropodists, 53 Welbeck St., London W1M 7HE, England. TEL 071-486-3381. FAX 071-935-6359. Ed. B.L. Berry. adv.; bk.rev.; illus.; index; circ. 7,500. (also avail. in microfilm from UMI) **Indexed:** Curr.Adv.Ecol.Sci.
Formerly (until 1991): Chiropodist (ISSN 0009-4706)
Description: Journal of British podiatric medicine.

JOURNAL OF CARDIOVASCULAR SURGERY. see *MEDICAL SCIENCES — Cardiovascular Diseases*

JOURNAL OF CLINICAL LASER MEDICINE & SURGERY. see *MEDICAL SCIENCES — Radiology And Nuclear Medicine*

MEDICAL SCIENCES — SURGERY

617   UK   ISSN 1010-5182
CODEN: JCMSET
JOURNAL OF CRANIO-MAXILLO-FACIAL SURGERY. 1973. 8/yr. £70($140) elsewhere £80. (European Association for Maxillo-Facial Surgery) Churchill Livingstone Medical Journals, Robert Stevenson House, 1-3 Baxter's Pl., Leith Walk, Edinburgh EH1 3AF, Scotland. TEL 031-556-2424. FAX 031-558-1278. TELEX 727511. (Subscr. to: Longman Group, Journals Subscr. Dept., P.O. Box 77, Fourth Ave., Harlow, Essex CM19 5AA, England; U.S. subscr. to: Churchill Livingstone, 650 Ave. of the Americas, New York, NY 10011. TEL 212-206-5000) Ed. Karsten Gundlach. illus.; index; circ. 2,200. (also avail. in microform from UMI; reprint service avail. from SWZ,UMI) **Indexed:** Biol.Abstr., Curr.Adv.Cancer Res., Curr.Cont., Curr.Tit.Dent., Dent.Ind., Excerp.Med., Ind.Med., Ind.Sci.Rev., Sci.Cit.Ind.
Former titles: Journal of Cranio and Maxillofacial Surgery; Journal of Maxillofacial Surgery (ISSN 0301-0503)

617.95   US   ISSN 1049-2275
▼**JOURNAL OF CRANIOFACIAL SURGERY.** 1990. q. $150 to individuals (foreign $175); institutions $200 (foreign $225); residents $75 (foreign $100)(effective Nov. 1991). (American Association of Pediatric Plastic Surgeons) Little, Brown and Company, Medical Journals, 34 Beacon St., Boston, MA 02108. TEL 617-859-5500. FAX 617-859-0629. (Co-sponsor: International Society of Craniofacial Surgery) Ed. Dr. Mutaz B. Habal. adv.; bk.rev.; abstr.; charts; illus.; stat.; index; circ. 600. (also avail. in microform from UMI; reprint service avail. from UMI; back issues avail.) **Indexed:** Curr.Tit.Dent.
—BLDSC shelfmark: 4965.476000.
Description: Covers all areas of craniofacial surgery, including treatment of congenital malformation, repair of post-traumatic deformation, treatment of oncological deformities, and resection of tumors in the skull base.
Refereed Serial

617.585   US   ISSN 0893-2034
CODEN: JCPMEQ
JOURNAL OF CURRENT PODIATRIC MEDICINE.* a digest for the podiatrist. 1950. m. $45. Current Podiatry Publications, Inc., Box 141, Fall River, WI 53932-0141. TEL 914-679-5913. FAX 914-679-5359. Ed. Howard J. Dananberg. adv.; bk.rev.; illus.; index; circ. 12,000. (also avail. in microform from UMI; back issues avail., reprint service avail. from UMI) **Indexed:** Excerp.Med.
Formerly: Current Podiatry (ISSN 0011-3824)
Description: Promotes growth of the profession by serving as an open forum for information and ideas. Publishes original material of interest to the doctor of podiatric medicine.

617   US   ISSN 0148-0812
RD520
JOURNAL OF DERMATOLOGIC SURGERY AND ONCOLOGY. 1975. m. $105 to institutions (foreign $151)(effective 1992). (American Society for Dermatologic Surgery) Elsevier Science Publishing Co., Inc. (New York), 655 Ave. of the Americas, New York, NY 10010. TEL 212-989-5800. FAX 212-633-3965. TELEX 420643 AEP UI. (Co-sponsors: American College of Mohs Micrographic Surgery and Cutaneous Oncology; International Society for Dermatologic Surgery; North American Society of Phlebology) Ed. C. William Hanke. adv.; bk.rev.; index; circ. 13,015. (also avail. in microform from RPI) **Indexed:** Biol.Abstr., Curr.Adv.Cancer Res., Curr.Cont., Dent.Ind., Excerp.Med., Helminthol.Abstr., Ind.Med., Ind.Sci.Rev., INIS Atomind., Sci.Cit.Ind.
—BLDSC shelfmark: 4968.765000.
Formerly (until 1976): Journal of Dermatologic Surgery (ISSN 0097-9716)
Description: Publishes information on new research, methods and instruments used in performing all types of cutaneous surgery.
Refereed Serial

617   IT
JOURNAL OF EMERGENCY SURGERY AND INTENSIVE CARE. (Multilingual text) 1978. q. L.60000($80) (effective 1991). (Societa Italiana di Chirurgia d'Urgencia) Masson Italia Periodici, Via Statuto 2-4, 20121 Milan, Italy. TEL 02-6367-1. FAX 02-6367-211. Ed. Vittorio Staudacher. circ. 1,500.
Formerly: Urgentis Chirurgiae Commentaria.

617   US   ISSN 0270-1170
RD540.6 CODEN: JETHEB
JOURNAL OF ENTEROSTOMAL THERAPY. 1974. bi-m. $40 to individuals (foreign $50); institutions $98 (foreign $108); students $25 (foreign $35). (International Association for Enterostomal Therapy) Mosby - Year Book, Inc. (Subsidiary of: Times Mirror Company), 11830 Westline Industrial Dr., St. Louis, MO 63146. TEL 800-325-4117. FAX 314-432-1380. TELEX 44-2402. Ed. Dorothy B. Smith. adv.; charts; illus.; stat.; index; circ. 3,194. (also avail. in microform from UMI; reprint service avail. from UMI) **Indexed:** CINAHL, Int.Nurs.Ind., Nurs.Abstr.
Formerly: E T Journal (ISSN 0195-9883)
Description: Serves enterostomal therapy practitioners with data relating to the care of persons with stomas, draining wounds, fistulas, dermal ulcers and incontinence.
Refereed Serial

617   US   ISSN 0449-2544
CODEN: JFSUBF
JOURNAL OF FOOT SURGERY. bi-m. $73 to individuals; institutions $97. Williams & Wilkins, 428 E. Preston St., Baltimore, MD 21202. TEL 301-528-4000. FAX 301-528-4312. Ed. Dr. Richard Reinherz. circ. 6,200. (also avail. in microform from UMI) **Indexed:** Excerp.Med., Ind.Med., INIS Atomind.
—BLDSC shelfmark: 4984.573000.
Description: Clinical advances in foot surgery for podiatrists and orthopedic foot surgeons.
Refereed Serial

JOURNAL OF GYNECOLOGIC SURGERY. see *MEDICAL SCIENCES — Obstetrics And Gynecology*

616   US   ISSN 0363-5023
RD559 CODEN: JHSUDV
JOURNAL OF HAND SURGERY: AMERICAN VOLUME. 1976. bi-m. $65 to individuals (foreign $78); institutions $128 (foreign $141); students $32 (foreign $45). (American Society for Surgery of the Hand) Mosby - Year Book, Inc. (Subsidiary of: Times Mirror Company), 11830 Westline Industrial Dr., St. Louis, MO 63146. TEL 800-325-4117. FAX 314-432-1380. TELEX 44-2402. Ed. Dr. F. William Bora, Jr. adv.; bk.rev.; charts; illus.; index; circ. 7,738. (also avail. in microform from UMI; reprint service avail. from UMI) **Indexed:** ASCA, Bibl.Dev.Med.& Child Neur., Biol.Abstr., Curr.Adv.Ecol.Sci., Curr.Cont., Dok.Arbeitsmed., Excerp.Med., Ind.Med., INIS Atomind.
—BLDSC shelfmark: 4996.620000.
Description: Edited for hand, orthopedic, plastic and reconstructive, and general surgeons who seek to restore function to the hand and upper extremity.
Refereed Serial

617   UK   ISSN 0266-7681
JOURNAL OF HAND SURGERY: BRITISH VOLUME. 1969. 6/yr. £81($161) (British Society for Surgery of the Hand) Churchill Livingstone Medical Journals, Robert Stevenson House, 1-3 Baxter's Pl., Leith Walk, Edinburgh EH1 3AF, Scotland. TEL 031-556-2424. FAX 031-558-1278. TELEX 727511. (Subscr. to: Longman Group, Journals Subscr. Dept, P.O. Box 77, Fourth Ave., Harlow, Essex CM19 5AA, England; U.S. subscr. to: Churchill Livingstone, 650 Ave. of the Americas, New York, NY 10011. TEL 212-206-5000) Ed. N.S. Barton. (also avail. in microform from UMI; back issues avail.) **Indexed:** ASCA, Curr.Cont., Excerp.Med., Ind.Med.
Formerly: Hand (ISSN 0072-968X)

617   US   ISSN 1053-2498
RD598 CODEN: JHLTES
JOURNAL OF HEART AND LUNG TRANSPLANTATION. 1981. bi-m. $59 to individuals (foreign $83); institutions $91 (foreign $115); students $29 (foreign $53). (International Society for Heart Transplantation) Mosby - Year Book, Inc. (Subsidiary of: Times Mirror Company), 11830 Westline Industrial Dr., St. Louis, MO 63146. TEL 800-325-4117. FAX 314-432-1380. TELEX 44-2402. Ed. Dr. Michael P. Kaye. adv.; charts; illus.; index; circ. 2,387. (also avail. in microform from UMI; back issues avail.; reprint service avail. from UMI) **Indexed:** Curr.Cont., Excerp.Med., Ind.Med., INIS Atomind.
—BLDSC shelfmark: 4996.874000.
Former titles (until Jan.1991): Journal of Heart Transplantation (ISSN 0887-2570); Heart Transplantation.
Description: Latest information on heart and heart-lung transplantation.
Refereed Serial

617   US   ISSN 0894-1939
CODEN: JISUE5
JOURNAL OF INVESTIGATIVE SURGERY. 1988. q. $120. Taylor & Francis, 1900 Frost Rd., Ste. 101, Bristol, PA 19007. TEL 215-785-5800. FAX 215-785-5515. Ed. Philip Sawyer.
—BLDSC shelfmark: 5008.020000.
Description: Discusses development of novel surgical concepts, development of surgical models, device and instruments, etc.
Refereed Serial

627   US
JOURNAL OF MICROSURGERY.* 1979. q. $45. Le Jacq Communications, 47 Arch St., Greenwich, CT 06830. TEL 212-766-4300. Ed. Dr. R.M. Peardon Donaghy. adv.

617   US   ISSN 0890-6599
RD593
JOURNAL OF NEUROLOGICAL AND ORTHOPAEDIC MEDICINE & SURGERY. Short title: J O N O M A S. 1979. q. $35 to members; institutions $98. American Academy of Neurological and Orthopaedic Surgeons, 2320 Rancho Dr., Ste. 108, Las Vegas, NV 89102-4592. TEL 702-385-6886. Ed. Dr. Michael R. Rask. adv.; bk.rev.; bibl.; charts; illus.; stat.; index, cum.index; circ. 1,500. (also avail. in microform from UMI; talking book; back issues avail.) **Indexed:** Excerp.Med.
Formerly: Journal of Neurological and Orthopaedic Surgery (ISSN 0271-1575)

JOURNAL OF NEUROLOGY, NEUROSURGERY AND PSYCHIATRY. see *MEDICAL SCIENCES — Psychiatry And Neurology*

JOURNAL OF NEUROSURGERY. see *MEDICAL SCIENCES — Psychiatry And Neurology*

JOURNAL OF NEUROSURGICAL ANESTHESIOLOGY. see *MEDICAL SCIENCES — Anaesthesiology*

617 616.8   IT
JOURNAL OF NEUROSURGICAL SCIENCES. (Text in English) 1957. q. L.60000($70) (Italian Society of Neurosurgery) Edizioni Minerva Medica, Corso Bramante 83-85, 10126 Turin, Italy. Eds. C.A. Pagni, P. Paoletti. adv.; bk.rev.; bibl.; charts; illus.; index; circ. 1,000. (also avail. in microform from RPI) **Indexed:** Bibl.Dev.Med.& Child Neur., Biol.Abstr., Curr.Adv.Cancer Res., Curr.Adv.Genetics & Molec.Biol., Curr.Cont., Ind.Med., Ind.Vet., Nutr.Abstr.
Former titles: Journal of Neurological Sciences; Minerva Neurochirurgica (ISSN 0026-4881)

JOURNAL OF ORAL AND MAXILLOFACIAL SURGERY. see *MEDICAL SCIENCES — Dentistry*

617.3   UK   ISSN 0334-0236
CODEN: JOSTEA
JOURNAL OF ORTHOPEDIC SURGICAL TECHNIQUES. 1985. q. $60 to individuals; institutions $120. Med. Advanced Techniques Publishing House Ltd., 48 Aylestone Ave., London NW6 7AA, England. FAX 081-960-8901. Ed. Dan Herness. adv.; bk.rev.; circ. 1,000. **Indexed:** Curr.Adv.Ecol.Sci., Excerp.Med.

617   US   ISSN 0022-3468
RD137.A1 CODEN: JPDSA3
JOURNAL OF PEDIATRIC SURGERY. 1966. m. $151 to individuals; institutions $207; foreign $235. (American Academy of Pediatrics, Surgical Section) W.B. Saunders Co. (Subsidiary of: Harcourt Brace Jovanovich, Inc.), Curtis Center, Independence Square W., Philadelphia, PA 19106. TEL 215-238-7800. (Subscr. to: 6277 Sea Harbor Dr., 4th Fl., Orlando FL 32891) (Co-sponsors: British Association of Pediatric Surgeons; American Pediatric Surgical Association; Canadian Association of Pediatric Surgeons) Ed. Stephen L. Gans, M.D. adv.; bk.rev.; abstr.; bibl.; charts; illus.; index. **Indexed:** Bibl.Dev.Med.& Child Neur., Biol.Abstr., Curr.Adv.Cancer Res., Curr.Adv.Genetics & Molec.Biol., Curr.Cont., Dent.Ind., Excerp.Med., Ind.Med., Ind.Sci.Rev., INIS Atomind., Nutr.Abstr., Protozool.Abstr., Sci.Cit.Ind.
●Also available online. Vendor(s): Mead Data Central.
—BLDSC shelfmark: 5030.275000.
Refereed Serial

MEDICAL SCIENCES — SURGERY

616 US ISSN 0743-684X
CODEN: JRMIE2
JOURNAL OF RECONSTRUCTIVE MICROSURGERY. 1984. q. $89 to individuals; institutions $109. Thieme Medical Publishers, Inc., 381 Park Ave. So., Ste. 1501, New York, NY 10016. Ed. Berish Strauch. adv. (also avail. in microfilm)
—BLDSC shelfmark: 5048.157000.

617 US
▼**JOURNAL OF SHOULDER AND ELBOW SURGERY.** 1992. bi-m. $70. Mosby - Year Book, Inc. (Subsidiary of: Times Mirror Company), 11830 Westline Industrial Dr., St. Louis, MO 63146. TEL 314-872-8370. FAX 314-432-1380. Ed. Dr. Robert H. Cofield. adv.; circ. 2,000.
Description: For orthopaedic surgeons who seek to restore form and function of the shoulder girdle, arm, and elbow by medical and surgical means.
Refereed Serial

JOURNAL OF SPINAL DISORDERS. see *MEDICAL SCIENCES — Orthopedics And Traumatology*

617 616.994 US ISSN 0022-4790
RD651 CODEN: JSONAU
JOURNAL OF SURGICAL ONCOLOGY. 1969. m. $570 (foreign $720). John Wiley & Sons, Inc., Journals, 605 Third Ave., New York, NY 10158. TEL 212-850-6000. FAX 212-850-6088. TELEX 12-7063. Ed. Gerald P. Murphy. adv.; charts; illus.; stat.; index. (also avail. in microform from UMI; reprint service avail. from ISI) **Indexed:** Biol.Abstr., Chem.Abstr., Curr.Adv.Cancer Res., Curr.Adv.Ecol.Sci., Curr.Cont., Dent.Ind., Excerp.Med., Ind.Med., INIS Atomind.
●Also available online.
—BLDSC shelfmark: 5067.380000.
Description: Encompasses surgical approaches and presents studies of related topics such as radiotherapy, chemotherapy, and immunotherapy.
Refereed Serial

617 US ISSN 0161-9721
RD1
JOURNAL OF SURGICAL PRACTICE.* 1972. bi-m. McMahon Publishing Co., 8 Peaceable St., West Redding, CT 06896. Ed. Kenneth J. Zeserson. adv.; circ. 90,000.
Formerly: Surgical Team (ISSN 0091-6277)

617 US ISSN 0022-4804
RD1 CODEN: JSGRA2
JOURNAL OF SURGICAL RESEARCH; clinical and laboratory investigation. 1961. m. $328 (foreign $407). (Association for Academic Surgery) Academic Press, Inc., Journal Division, 1250 Sixth Ave., San Diego, CA 92101. TEL 619-230-1840. FAX 619-699-6800. TELEX 181726. Eds. Bruce L. Gewertz, Christopher K. Zarins. adv.; bk.rev.; charts; illus.; index. (back issues avail.) **Indexed:** Biol.Abstr., Chem.Abstr., Curr.Cont., Excerp.Med., Ind.Med., Ind.Sci.Rev., Ind.Vet., INIS Atomind., Nutr.Abstr., Vet.Bull.
—BLDSC shelfmark: 5067.400000.
Description: Publishes original articles concerned with clinical and laboratory investigations relevant to surgical practice and teaching.
Refereed Serial

617 US ISSN 0022-5223
RD536 CODEN: JTCSAQ
JOURNAL OF THORACIC AND CARDIOVASCULAR SURGERY. 1931. m. $102 to individuals (foreign $130); institutions $175 (foreign $203); students $49 (foreign $77). (American Association for Thoracic Surgery) Mosby - Year Book, Inc. (Subsidiary of: Times Mirror Company), 11830 Westline Industrial Dr., St. Louis, MO 63146. TEL 800-325-4117. FAX 314-432-1380. TELEX 44-2402. (Co-sponsor: Western Thoracic Surgical Association) Ed. Dr. John W. Kirklin. adv.; bibl.; illus.; s-a index; circ. 10,064. (also avail. in microfilm from UMI; reprint service avail. from UMI) **Indexed:** ASCA, Biol.Abstr., Chem.Abstr., Curr.Adv.Cancer Res., Curr.Cont., Excerp.Med., Helminthol.Abstr., Ind.Med., Ind.Sci.Rev., INIS Atomind., Nutr.Abstr., Rev.Plant Path., Sci.Cit.Ind.
—BLDSC shelfmark: 5069.100000.
Formerly: Journal of Thoracic Surgery.
Description: Devoted to conditions of the heart, lungs, chest and great vessels where surgical intervention is indicated.
Refereed Serial

650 616.1 US ISSN 0741-5214
RD598.5
JOURNAL OF VASCULAR SURGERY. 1984. m. $89 to individuals (foreign $113); institutions $164 (foreign $188); students $40 (foreign $64). (Society for Vascular Surgery) Mosby - Year Book, Inc. (Subsidiary of: Times Mirror Company), 11830 Westline Industrial Dr., St. Louis, MO 63146. TEL 800-325-4117. FAX 314-432-1380. TELEX 44-2402. (Co-sponsor: International Society for Cardiovascular Surgery (North American Chapter)) Eds. Drs. Calvin B. Ernst, James C. Stanley. adv.; bk.rev.; s-a index; circ. 7,711. (also avail. in microfilm from UMI; reprint service avail. from UMI) **Indexed:** ASCA, Curr.Adv.Cancer Res., Curr.Cont., Ind.Med., INIS Atomind., Sci.Cit.Ind.
—BLDSC shelfmark: 5072.270000.
Description: Presentation of the latest advances in the knowledge of the peripheral vascular system and vascular surgery.
Refereed Serial

KEY NEUROLOGY AND NEUROSURGERY. see *MEDICAL SCIENCES — Psychiatry And Neurology*

617 RU ISSN 0023-1207
CODEN: KHIRAE
KHIRURGIYA/SURGERY. (Text in Russian; summaries in English) 1925. m. 31.20 Rub.($25.20) (Vsesoyuznoe Nauchnoe Obshchestvo Khirurgov) Izdatel'stvo Meditsina, Petroverigskii pereulok 6-8, 101838 Moscow, Russia. (Co-sponsor: Ministerstvo Zdravookhraneniya S.S.S.R.) Ed. N.N. Malinovskii. bk.rev.; index. **Indexed:** Biol.Abstr., Chem.Abstr., Curr.Cont., Dent.Ind., Excerp.Med., Helminthol.Abstr., Ind.Med., Nutr.Abstr.
—BLDSC shelfmark: 0394.785000.
Description: Discusses general and abdominal surgery, oncology, traumatology, endocrinology, pediatric surgery, problems of chest surgery and anesthesiology.

617 GW ISSN 0023-8236
CODEN: LAACBS
LANGENBECKS ARCHIV FUER CHIRURGIE. (Text in German; summaries in English, German) 1860. 6/yr. DM.492($276) (Deutsche Gesellschaft fuer Chirurgie) Springer-Verlag, Heidelberger Platz 3, D-1000 Berlin 33, Germany. TEL 030-8207-1. (Also Heidelberg, Tokyo, Vienna, and New York) Ed. M. Allgoewer. (also avail. in microform from UMI; back issues avail.; reprint service avail. from ISI) **Indexed:** Biol.Abstr., Chem.Abstr., Curr.Cont., Dent.Ind., Excerp.Med., Ind.Med., Ind.Sci.Rev., INIS Atomind.
—BLDSC shelfmark: 5155.675000.
Incorporates (in 1975): Bruns' Beitraege fuer Klinische Chirurgie (ISSN 0007-2680)

617 535.58 US ISSN 0196-8092
CODEN: LSMEDI
LASERS IN SURGERY AND MEDICINE. 1980. bi-m (plus Supplement). $312 (foreign $399.50). John Wiley & Sons, Inc., Journals, 605 Third Ave., New York, NY 10158. TEL 212-850-6000. FAX 212-850-6088. TELEX 12-7063. Ed. Carmen A. Puliafito. adv.; abstr.; bibl.; charts; illus.; index. (reprint service avail. from ISI) **Indexed:** Curr.Cont., Dent.Ind., Excerp.Med., Ind.Med.
—BLDSC shelfmark: 5156.683000.
Description: Covers clinical and experimental applications of various types of lasers.
Refereed Serial

617 FR ISSN 0024-3493
CODEN: LICHA6
LILLE CHIRURGICAL.* 1945. q. 160 F. (Societe de Chirurgie de Lille) Editions Morel et Corduant, 11 Rue des Bouchers, 59000 Lille, France. adv.; bk.rev.; illus.; index; circ. 1,000. **Indexed:** Biol.Abstr., Excerp.Med., Ind.Med.

617 FR ISSN 0024-7782
LYON CHIRURGICAL. (Text in French; summaries in English) 1908. 6/yr. 450 F. (foreign 500 F.). Hotel Dieu, 69288 Lyon Cedex 02, France. TEL 78-92-20-81. FAX 78-37-03-64. Ed. Ph. Berard. adv.; bk.rev.; bibl.; charts; illus.; index; circ. 2,050. (also avail. in microform from UMI; reprint service avail. from ISI) **Indexed:** Biol.Abstr., Chem.Abstr., Curr.Cont., Excerp.Med., Helminthol.Abstr., Ind.Med., Nutr.Abstr.
—BLDSC shelfmark: 5311.900000.

617 HU ISSN 0025-0295
CODEN: MASEAW
MAGYAR SEBESZET. 1948. 6/yr. $38.50. Ifjusagi Lap-es Konyvkiado Vallalat, Revay u. 16, 1374 Budapest 6, Hungary. (Subscr. to: Kultura, Box 149, H-1389 Budapest, Hungary) Ed. Andor Szecsenyi. adv.; bk.rev.; bibl.; illus. **Indexed:** Chem.Abstr., Excerp.Med., Ind.Med., INIS Atomind.

MANTAP: MAJALAH ILMAIH P K M I/INDONESIAN ASSOCIATION FOR SECURE CONTRACEPTION. JOURNAL. (Perkumpulan Kontrasepsi Mantap Indonesia (PKMI)) see *MEDICAL SCIENCES — Obstetrics And Gynecology*

617 FR ISSN 0759-2280
MEDECINE ET CHIRURGIE DU PIED. 1984. 4/yr. 785 F. to individuals (foreign 975 F.); students 545 F. (foreign 700 F.). (Societe Francaise de Medecine et Chirurgie du Pied) Expansion Scientifique, 15 rue Saint Benoit, 75278 Paris Cedex 06, France. TEL 1-45-48-42-60. FAX 1-45-44-81-55.
—BLDSC shelfmark: 5487.729300.

617 US
MEDICAL ECONOMICS FOR SURGEONS. 1982. m. $59 (foreign $104). Medical Economics Publishing Co., Five Paragon Dr., Montvale, NJ 07645. TEL 201-358-7200. FAX 201-573-1045. Ed. Steve Murata. adv.; circ. 46,000. (also avail. in microform from RPI) **Indexed:** Ind.Med.
Description: Covers non-clinical aspects of a surgeon's practice, including investments, taxes, office management and family spending.

617 CR
MEDICINA Y CIRUGIA. (Text in Spanish; summaries in English, Spanish) 1974. Colegio de Medicos y Cirujanos, Apartado 4054, San Jose, Costa Rica. **Indexed:** Biol.Abstr.

617 II ISSN 0025-8008
MEDICINE & SURGERY. (Text in English) m. $30. Praveen Corp., Sayajiganj, Baroda 390005, India. **Indexed:** Biol.Abstr., Excerp.Med.

617 681 US ISSN 0738-1085
MICROSURGERY. 1979. bi-m. $220 (foreign $295). John Wiley & Sons, Inc., Journals, 605 Third Ave., New York, NY 10158. TEL 212-850-6000. FAX 212-850-6088. TELEX 12-7063. Ed. John S. Gould. adv.; bibl.; charts; illus.; index. (back issues avail.; reprint service avail. from ISI) **Indexed:** Biol.Abstr., Excerp.Med., Ind.Med.
—BLDSC shelfmark: 5760.770000.
Description: Acts as a multidisciplinary forum for original ideas regarding the use of the operating microscope in a variety of areas.
Refereed Serial

617 IT ISSN 0026-4733
MINERVA CHIRURGICA. (Text in Italian; summaries in English and Italian) 1946. s-m. L.80000($120) Edizioni Minerva Medica, Corso Bramante 83-85, 10126 Turin, Italy. Ed. P.A. Giudice. adv.; bk.rev.; bibl.; charts; illus.; index; circ. 5,000. **Indexed:** Biol.Abstr., Chem.Abstr., Dent.Ind., Excerp.Med., Ind.Med., Nutr.Abstr.
—BLDSC shelfmark: 5794.100000.

616 US
MODERN NEUROSURGERY. (Consists of selected papers from the Congress of the World Federation of Neurosurgical Societies) 1982. quadrennial. price varies. Springer-Verlag, 175 Fifth Ave., New York, NY 10010. TEL 212-460-1500. (And Berlin, Heidelberg) Ed. M. Brock.

617 US ISSN 0271-8219
MODERN TECHNICS IN SURGERY. HEAD AND NECK SURGERY. 1981. irreg. (approx. a.) price varies. Futura Publishing Company, Inc., 2 Bedford Ridge Rd., Box 330, Mount Kisco, NY 10549. TEL 800-877-8761. FAX 914-666-0993. Ed. Dr. Moses Nussbaum. index.

617 US ISSN 0163-7037
MODERN TECHNICS IN SURGERY. NEUROSURGERY. 1979. irreg. (approx. a.) price varies. Futura Publishing Company, Inc., 2 Bedford Ridge Rd., Box 330, Mount Kisco, NY 10549. TEL 800-877-8761. FAX 914-666-0993. Ed. Dr. Joseph Ransohoff. index.
Refereed Serial

MEDICAL SCIENCES — SURGERY

617 US ISSN 0193-8568
MODERN TECHNICS IN SURGERY. UROLOGIC SURGERY. 1980. irreg. (approx. a.). price varies. Futura Publishing Company, Inc., 2 Bedford Ridge Rd., Box 330, Mount Kisco, NY 10549. TEL 914-666-7528. FAX 914-666-0993. Ed. Dr. Richard M. Ehrlich.
Refereed Serial

617 616.8 FR ISSN 0028-3770
CODEN: NUREB9
NEURO-CHIRURGIE. 1955. 7/yr. 215 ECU($261) (typically set in Jan.). (Societe de Neuro-Chirurgie de Langue Francaise) Masson, 120 bd. Saint-Germain, 75280 Paris Cedex 06, France.
TEL 1-46-34-21-60. FAX 1-45-87-29-99. TELEX 202 671 F. Ed. P.M. Hurth. adv.; bk.rev.; illus.; index; circ. 1,500. (also avail. in microform from UMI; reprint service avail. from ISI) **Indexed:** Biol.Abstr., Excerp.Med., Ind.Med., Ind.Sci.Rev.
—BLDSC shelfmark: 6081.350000.

NEURO-ORTHOPEDICS. see *MEDICAL SCIENCES — Orthopedics And Traumatology*

NEUROBIOLOGIA; revista de neurologia psiquiatria e neurocirurgia. see *MEDICAL SCIENCES — Psychiatry And Neurology*

NEUROCHIRURGIA. see *MEDICAL SCIENCES — Psychiatry And Neurology*

NEUROLOGICAL SURGERY/SHINKEI GEKA. see *MEDICAL SCIENCES — Psychiatry And Neurology*

NEUROPEDIATRICS; journal of pediatric neurobiology, neurology and neurosurgery. see *MEDICAL SCIENCES — Pediatrics*

NEUROSURGERY (BALTIMORE). see *MEDICAL SCIENCES — Psychiatry And Neurology*

617 616.8 US
NEUROSURGERY CLINICS. 1989. q. $89. W.B. Saunders Co., Curtis Center, Independence Square W., Philadelphia, PA 19106. TEL 215-238-7800. Ed. Susan Short.
Description: Each issue addresses a single topic in the diagnosis and therapy of patients with neurological disorders.

617 US ISSN 1050-6438
CODEN: NEQUEB
▼**NEUROSURGERY QUARTERLY.** 1991. q. $89 to individuals; institutions $112. Raven Press, 1185 Ave. of the Americas, New York, NY 10036. TEL 212-930-9500. FAX 212-869-3495. TELEX 640073. Ed. Donlin M. Long. adv.; charts; illus.; circ. 1,000. **Indexed:** Excerp.Med. (1992-).
—BLDSC shelfmark: 6081.582800.
Description: Presents comprehensive reviews by international authorities on the surgical management and treatment of neurological disorders.
Refereed Serial

616 GW ISSN 0344-5607
CODEN: NSREDV
NEUROSURGICAL REVIEW. 1978. 4/yr. $215 to institutions. (German Society for Neurosurgery) Walter de Gruyter und Co., Genthinerstr. 13, 1000 Berlin 30, Germany. TEL 030-26005-0.
FAX 030-26005251. TELEX 184027. (U.S. addr.: Walter de Gruyter, Inc., 200 Saw Mill Rd., Hawthorne, NY 10532) **Indexed:** Curr.Adv.Ecol.Sci., Dent.Ind., Excerp.Med., Ind.Med.
—BLDSC shelfmark: 6081.585000.

NEVROLOGIA, PSIHIATRIJA I NEVROHIRURGIJA. see *MEDICAL SCIENCES — Psychiatry And Neurology*

617 US
NEWS & NOTES (CHICAGO). 1940. q. membership. International College of Surgeons, United States Section, 1516 N. Lake Shore Dr., Chicago, IL 60610-1694. TEL 312-787-6274.
FAX 312-787-1624. Ed. Philip Lesser. circ. 7,000. (tabloid format)
Formerly: U S News and Notes.

617 IT
NOTIZIARIO CHIRURGICO. q. Edizione Minerva Medica, Corso Bramante 83-85, 10126 Turin, Italy. **Indexed:** Excerp.Med.

617 GW ISSN 0178-1715
O P JOURNAL; wissenschaftlich - medizinische informationen fuer das O P personal. 1985. 3/yr. DM.60. Georg Thieme Verlag, Ruedigerstr. 14, Postfach 104853, 7000 Stuttgart 10, Germany. TEL 0711-8931-0. FAX 0711-8931-298. TELEX 7252275-GTV-D. Ed. K.G. Hug.

617 UK ISSN 0960-8923
▼**OBESITY SURGERY.** 1991. q. £70($125) Rapid Communications of Oxford Ltd., The Old Malthouse, Paradise St., Oxford OX1 1LD, England.
TEL 0865-790447. FAX 0865-244012.
(Co-sponsors: American Society for Bariatric Surgery, Obesity Surgery Society of Australia and New Zealand, Obesity Surgery Section of the British Surgical Stapling Group) Ed. Mervyn Deitel. (reprint service avail.) **Indexed:** Excerp.Med.
—BLDSC shelfmark: 6196.953000.

617.7 US ISSN 8750-3085
OCULAR SURGERY NEWS. s-m. $150 to individuals; institutions $160. Slack, Inc., 6900 Grove Rd., Thorofare, NJ 08086. TEL 609-848-1000.
FAX 609-853-5991. Ed. Dr. Donald R. Sanders. adv. (tabloid format)
—BLDSC shelfmark: 6235.154600.
Formerly: I O L and Ocular Surgery News.

617.7 US ISSN 1047-9120
▼**OCULAR SURGERY NEWS INTERNATIONAL EDITION.** Abbreviated title: O S N I E. 1990. m. $100 to individuals; institutions $115. Slack, Inc., 6900 Grove Rd., Thorofare, NJ 08086-9447.
TEL 609-848-1000. FAX 609-853-5991. Ed. Dr. Donald R. Sanders. circ. 17,000.

617 US
OPERATING ROOM RISK MANAGEMENT. bi-m. $295 (Canada $325; elsewhere $375). (Emergency Care Research Institute) E C R I, 5200 Butler Pike, Plymouth Meeting, PA 19462. TEL 215-825-6000. FAX 215-834-1275. Ed. Ronni Solomon.
Refereed Serial

OPHTHALMIC PLASTIC AND RECONSTRUCTIVE SURGERY. see *MEDICAL SCIENCES — Ophthalmology And Optometry*

617.7 US ISSN 0022-023X
RE80 CODEN: OPSGAT
OPHTHALMIC SURGERY. 1968. m. $47 to individuals; institutions $70. Slack, Inc., 6900 Grove Rd., Thorofare, NJ 08086. TEL 609-848-1000.
FAX 609-853-5991. Ed. Dr. George L. Spaeth. adv.; bk.rev.; charts; illus.; circ. 4,300. (also avail. in microform from UMI; back issues avail.; reprint service avail. from UMI) **Indexed:** Biol.Abstr., Curr.Cont., Dent.Ind., Excerp.Med., Ind.Med.
—BLDSC shelfmark: 6271.500000.
Supersedes: Journal of Cryosurgery.
Description: Articles of clinical interest for the opthalmic surgeon.

617.6 US ISSN 1042-3680
ORAL AND MAXILLOFACIAL SURGERY CLINICS. 1989. 4/yr. W.B. Saunders Co., Curtis Center, Independence Square W., Philadelphia, PA 19106. TEL 215-238-7800. Ed. Livia Berardi.
—BLDSC shelfmark: 6081.582500.
Description: Aimed at oral maxillofacial surgeons and discusses surgical procedures including orthroscopy, cosmetic oral, maxillofacial surgery, & surgery of cleft lip and palate.

ORBIT; an international journal on orbital disorders, oculoplastic and lacrimal surgery. see *MEDICAL SCIENCES — Ophthalmology And Optometry*

617 IT ISSN 0394-0756
ORIZZONTI DI CHIRURGIA; trimestrale di scienze chirurgiche e branche affini. q. L.50000($85) (effective 1992). (Societa Italiana di Chirurgia Oncologica) Casa Editrice Idelson, Via A. De Gasperi 55, 80133 Naples, Italy. TEL 081-5524733.
FAX 081-5518295. (Co-sponsor: Societa Italiana di Patologia dell'Apparato Digerente) Ed. Francesco Mazzeo.
Description: Presents research papers on the science of surgery focusing on oncology. Includes diagrams and statistical data.

ORTHOPAEDIC AND TRAUMATIC SURGERY/SEKEISAI GAIGEKA. see *MEDICAL SCIENCES — Orthopedics And Traumatology*

617 IT ISSN 0030-6266
OSPEDALI D'ITALIA-CHIRURGIA. (Summaries in English) 1959. bi-m. L.100000. Editrice Sedicesimo, Via Mannelli 29r, 50136 Florence, Italy.
TEL 055-2476781. FAX 055-2478568. Ed. Carlo Massimo. adv.; bk.rev.; abstr.; bibl.; charts; illus.; index; circ. 3,000. **Indexed:** Biol.Abstr., Ind.Med.
—BLDSC shelfmark: 6301.750000.

OSTOMY - WOUND MANAGEMENT; the journal of extended patient care management. see *MEDICAL SCIENCES — Nurses And Nursing*

OTOLARYNGOLOGY - HEAD AND NECK SURGERY. see *MEDICAL SCIENCES — Otorhinolaryngology*

PEDIATRIA OGGI MEDICA E CHIRURGICA. see *MEDICAL SCIENCES — Pediatrics*

PEDIATRIC CARDIOLOGY. see *MEDICAL SCIENCES — Cardiovascular Diseases*

617 618.92 US ISSN 0179-0358
CODEN: PSUIED
PEDIATRIC SURGERY INTERNATIONAL. 6/yr. DM.348($191) Springer-Verlag, Journals, 175 Fifth Ave., New York, NY 10010. TEL 212-640-1500.
—BLDSC shelfmark: 6417.628000.

617 PH ISSN 0031-7691
PHILIPPINE JOURNAL OF SURGICAL SPECIALTIES. vol.25, 1970. q. P.50($20) to non-members; members P.40. Philippine College of Surgeons, Box 513, Greenhills, San Juan, Metro Manila, Philippines. Ed. Enrique T. Ona. adv.; charts; illus.; stat.; circ. 1,000. **Indexed:** Biol.Abstr., Chem.Abstr., Ind.Med.
—BLDSC shelfmark: 6456.040000.
Formerly: Philippine Journal of Surgery and Surgery Specialties.

617.95 US ISSN 0032-1052
CODEN: PRSUAS
PLASTIC AND RECONSTRUCTIVE SURGERY. 1946. m. $125 to individuals; institutions $150. (American Society of Plastic & Reconstructive Surgeons) Williams & Wilkins, 428 E. Preston St., Baltimore, MD 21202. TEL 301-528-4000.
FAX 301-528-4312. Ed. Dr. Robert M. Goldwyn. adv.; bk.rev.; abstr.; charts; illus.; index, cum.index vols.59-72, 1985; circ. 13,100. (also avail. in microform) **Indexed:** Biol.Abstr., Chem.Abstr., Curr.Adv.Cancer Res., Curr.Adv.Cell & Devel.Biol., Curr.Cont., Dent.Ind., Excerp.Med., Ind.Med.
—BLDSC shelfmark: 6528.924000.
Description: Examines plastic and reconstructive surgery techniques.
Refereed Serial

617.95 US
PLASTIC SURGERY NEWS. m. American Society of Plastic and Reconstructive Surgeons, 444 E. Algonquin Rd., Arlington Heights, IL 60005-4664. TEL 708-228-9900. FAX 708-229-9131. Ed. Pam Rasmussen. circ. 5,200.

617.95 US
▼**PLASTIC SURGERY PRODUCTS.** 1991. bi-m. $12. Novicom, Inc., 3510 Torrance Blvd., Ste. 315, Torrance, CA 90503. TEL 310-316-8112.
FAX 310-316-8422. adv.: B&W page $1200, color page $1800; trim 8 3/8 x 10 7/8. circ. 18,000.
Description: Contains new product and services news and applications.

PLASTIC SURGICAL NURSING. see *MEDICAL SCIENCES — Nurses And Nursing*

617 IT ISSN 0032-2636
POLICLINICO. SEZIONE CHIRURGICA. (Summaries in English) 1897. bi-m. $100. (Societa di Ricerche in Chirurgia) Edizioni Luigi Pozzi s.r.l., Via Panama 68, 00198 Rome, Italy. TEL 06-8553548.
FAX 06-8554105. Eds. G.F. Fegiz, S. Stipa. adv.; charts; illus.; stat.; circ. 2,750. **Indexed:** Chem.Abstr., Excerp.Med., Ind.Med.
—BLDSC shelfmark: 6543.300000.

617.96 GW ISSN 0079-4899
PRAKTISCHE CHIRURGIE. 1936. irreg., no.103, 1991. price varies. Ferdinand Enke Verlag, Postfach 101254, 7000 Stuttgart 10, Germany.
TEL 0711-8931-0. FAX 0711-8931-419. TELEX 07252275-GTV-D. Eds. K. Kremer, A. Encke.
Supersedes: Vortraege aus der Praktischen Chirurgie (ISSN 0083-6931).

MEDICAL SCIENCES — SURGERY

616   US
PRAXIS DER CHIRURGIE. 1982. irreg. price varies. Springer-Verlag, 175 Fifth Ave., New York, NY 10010. TEL 212-460-1500. (Also Berlin, Heidelberg, Tokyo and Vienna)

PRINCIPLES OF PEDIATRIC NEUROSURGERY. see *MEDICAL SCIENCES — Pediatrics*

617   US   ISSN 0739-8328
RD98
PROBLEMS IN GENERAL SURGERY. 1984. q. $80 to individuals (foreign $100); institutions $110 (foreign $140). J.B. Lippincott Co., E. Washington Sq., Philadelphia, PA 19105. TEL 215-238-4200. illus.; circ. 4,000. (also avail. in microform from UMI)
—BLDSC shelfmark: 6617.885000.

617   US   ISSN 1050-0197
▼**PROBLEMS IN PLASTIC AND RECONSTRUCTIVE SURGERY.** 1991. 3/yr. $85 to individuals; institutions $99. J.J. Lippincott Co., 227 E. Washington Sq., Philadelphia, PA 19106. TEL 215-238-4200. FAX 215-238-4493. (Subscr. to: Subscriber Services Dept., Downville Pike, Rt. 3, Box 20-B, Hagerstown, MD 21740. TEL 800-638-3030) Ed. Dr. Donald Serafin.
Description: Focuses on trends, problems and techniques in all aspects of plastic and reconstructive surgery.
Refereed Serial

PROGRESS IN NEUROLOGICAL SURGERY. see *MEDICAL SCIENCES — Psychiatry And Neurology*

PROGRESS IN PEDIATRIC SURGERY. see *MEDICAL SCIENCES — Pediatrics*

617   SZ   ISSN 0079-6824
RD11   CODEN: PSURA2
PROGRESS IN SURGERY. (Text in English) 1961. irreg. (approx. 1/yr.). price varies. S. Karger AG, Allschwilerstr. 10, P.O. Box, CH-4009 Basel, Switzerland. TEL 061-3061111. FAX 061-3061234. TELEX CH 962652. Ed. E.H. Farthmann. (reprint service avail. from ISI) **Indexed:** Biol.Abstr., Chem.Abstr., Curr.Cont., Ind.Med.
—BLDSC shelfmark: 6924.580000.

617   IT   ISSN 0393-764X
PROGRESSI CLINICI: CHIRURGIA. 1985. bi-m. L.130000($160) Piccin Editore, Via Altinate 107, 35100 Padua, Italy. TEL 049-655566. TELEX 432074 PICCIN I. Eds. M. Lise, D. Nitti. circ. 3,000.

617   II   ISSN 0033-5657
QUARTERLY JOURNAL OF SURGICAL SCIENCES. (Text in English) 1965. q. Rs.40($10) Banaras Hindu University, Institute of Medical Sciences, Surgical Research Laboratory, Varanasi 221 005, India. Ed. K.N. Udupa. charts; illus.; stat.; circ. 1,200. (also avail. in microform from UMI; reprint service avail. from UMI) **Indexed:** Chem.Abstr., Ind.Med.

617   IT   ISSN 0033-9776
CODEN: RMSAAN
RASSEGNA MEDICA SARDA. (Text in Italian; summaries in English) 1882. bi-m. L.30000. Universita degli Studi di Cagliari, Facolta di Medicina Chirurgia, Casella Postale 287, 09100 Cagliari, Italy. Ed. A. Cabitza. adv.; bk.rev.; charts; illus.; index; cum.index; circ. 550. **Indexed:** Biol.Abstr., C.I.S.Abstr., Chem.Abstr., Excerp.Med., Rev.Plant Path.
—BLDSC shelfmark: 7294.410000.

617.95   SZ   ISSN 0080-0260
RECONSTRUCTION SURGERY AND TRAUMATOLOGY. (Text in English) 1953. irreg. (approx. 1/yr.). price varies. S. Karger AG, Allschwilerstr. 10, P.O. Box, CH-4009 Basel, Switzerland. TEL 061-3061111. FAX 061-3061234. TELEX CH 962652. Ed. H. Eberle. (reprint service avail. from ISI) **Indexed:** Biol.Abstr., Chem.Abstr., Curr.Cont., Ind.Med.
—BLDSC shelfmark: 7310.680000.

617   US   ISSN 0883-0444
CODEN: JRSUEY
REFRACTIVE & CORNEAL SURGERY. 1983. bi-m. $95 to individuals; institutions $105. (International Society of Refractive Keratoplasty) SLACK, Inc., 6900 Grove Rd., Thorofare, NJ 08068. TEL 609-848-1000. FAX 609-853-5991. (Co-sponsor: European Refractive Surgery Society) Ed. Dr. George O. Waring, III. adv.; bk.rev.; abstr.; charts; illus.; stat.; tr.lit.; index; circ. 2,000. (back issues avail.)
Formerly: Journal of Refractive Surgery.
Description: Contains original articles, new industry trends, and op-ed concerning corneal and refractive surgery.
Refereed Serial

RESPIRATION; international review of thoracic diseases. see *MEDICAL SCIENCES — Respiratory Diseases*

617   BL   ISSN 0034-7124
CODEN: RBCHAN
REVISTA BRASILEIRA DE CIRURGIA. (Text in Portuguese; summaries in English and Portuguese) 1932. bi-m. $180. Cidade - Editora Cientifica Ltda., Rua Mexico 90-2 Andar, 20031 Rio de Janeiro RJ, Brazil. Ed. Fernando Moyses. adv.; bk.rev.; charts; illus.; index; circ. 7,000. **Indexed:** Biol.Abstr., Chem.Abstr., Excerp.Med., Ind.Med.
—BLDSC shelfmark: 7844.150000.

617   CU   ISSN 0034-7493
REVISTA CUBANA DE CIRUGIA. (Summaries in English, French, Spanish) 1962. s-a. $10 in N. America; S. America $12; Europe $14. Ministerio de Salud Publica, Centro Nacional de Informacion de Ciencias Medicas, Calle E No. 452, e-19 y 21, Plaza de la Revolucion, Apdo. 6520, Havana, Cuba. TEL 809-32-5338. (Dist. by: Ediciones Cubanas, Obispo No. 527, Apdo. 605, Havana, Cuba) Dir. Gilberto Pardo Gomez. bibl.; charts; illus.; index; circ. 1,500. **Indexed:** Biol.Abstr., Chem.Abstr., Excerp.Med., Ind.Med.
—BLDSC shelfmark: 7852.100000.

617   RM
REVISTA DE CHIRURGIE, ONCOLOGIE, RADIOLOGIE, O.R.L, OFTALMOLOGIE, STOMATOLOGIE. CHIRURGIA. (Text in Rumanian; summaries in English, French, German, Russian) 1952. 6/yr. $25. Uniunea Societatilor de Stiinte Medicale din Republica Socialista Rumania, Str. Progresului No. 8-10, Sectorul 1, Bucharest 70754, Rumania. (Subscr. to: ILEXIM, Str. 13 Decembrie Nr. 3, P.O. Box 136-137, Bucharest, Rumania) Ed.Bd. adv.; bk.rev.; abstr.; charts; illus. **Indexed:** Biol.Abstr., Chem.Abstr., Excerp.Med., Ind.Med.
Formerly: Chirurgia (ISSN 0009-4730)

617.6   SP   ISSN 1130-0558
REVISTA ESPANOLA DE CIRUGIA ORAL Y MAXILOFACIAL. (Text in Spanish; summaries in English) 1979. 3/yr. 3000 ptas.($40) (Sociedad Espanola de Cirugia Oral y Maxilofacial) Ediciones Ergon, S.A., Muntaner, 262, 6o, 08021 Barcelona, Spain. TEL 2010911. FAX 2015911. (Subscr. to: Cempro, Plaza Conde Valle Suchil 20, 28015 Madrid, Spain)

REVISTA MEDICO-CHIRURGICALA. see *MEDICAL SCIENCES*

REVISTA PORTUGUESA DE ESTOMATOLOGIA E CIRURGIA MAXILO-FACIAL. see *MEDICAL SCIENCES — Dentistry*

REVUE DE STOMATOLOGIE ET DE CHIRURGIE MAXILLO-FACIALE. see *MEDICAL SCIENCES — Dentistry*

617   IT   ISSN 0080-3243
RIVISTA DI CHIRURGIA DELLA MANO. 1962. 3/yr. L.80000($110) (Societa Italiana di Chirurgia della Mano) Piccin Editore, Via Altinate 107, 35100 Padua, Italy. TEL 049-655566. TELEX 432074 PICCIN I. Ed. Renzo Mantero. illus.; index, cum.index; circ. 1,500. (also avail. in microform)

RIVISTA DI MEDICINA E CHIRURGIA. see *MEDICAL SCIENCES*

617   IT
RIVISTA DI MICROCHIRURGIA. q. L.40000($65) (effective 1992). Casa Editrice Idelson, Via A. DeGasperi, 55, 80133 Naples, Italy. TEL 081-5524733. FAX 5518295. Ed. Beniamino Tesauro.

617   IT   ISSN 0035-6689
RIVISTA GENERALE ITALIANA DI CHIRURGIA. (Text in Italian; summaries in English) 1950. bi-m. L.60000 (foreign L.120000)(effective 1992). Casa Editrice Maccari, Via Trento 53, 43100 Parma, Italy. FAX 039-521-771268. Ed. F. Morino. adv.; bk.rev.; circ. 1,400. **Indexed:** Excerp.Med., Psychol.Abstr.
—BLDSC shelfmark: 7986.400000.

617.95   IT   ISSN 0391-2221
RIVISTA ITALIANA DI CHIRURGIA PLASTICA. 1968. q. L.120000 includes supplement. (Societa Italiana di Chirurgia Plastica) Tipografia Editrice la Garangola, Via Montona 4, 35137 Padua, Italy. FAX 049-8751743. (back issues avail.) **Indexed:** Excerp.Med.

617   UK   ISSN 0035-8835
CODEN: JRCSAC
ROYAL COLLEGE OF SURGEONS OF EDINBURGH. JOURNAL. 1955. bi-m. £112 in U.K. & Europe; elsewhere £125. (Royal College of Surgeons of Edinburgh) Butterworth - Heinemann Ltd. (Subsidiary of: Reed International PLC), Linacre House, Jordan Hill, Oxford OX2 8DP, England. TEL 0865-310366. FAX 0865-310898. TELEX 83111 BHPOXF G. (Subscr. to: Turpin Transactions Ltd., Distribution Center, Blackhorse Rd., Letchworth, Herts SG6 1HN, England. TEL 0462-672555) Ed. A. Cuschieri. adv.; bk.rev.; charts; illus.; index, cum.index every 5 yrs.; circ. 8,500. (also avail. in microform from UMI; back issues avail.) **Indexed:** Biol.Abstr., CINAHL, Curr.Adv.Ecol.Sci., Dent.Ind., Excerp.Med., Helminthol.Abstr., Ind.Med., Nutr.Abstr.
—BLDSC shelfmark: 4856.200000.
Description: Papers of interest to practising surgeons.
Refereed Serial

617   UK   ISSN 0035-8843
CODEN: ARCSAF
ROYAL COLLEGE OF SURGEONS OF ENGLAND. ANNALS. 1947. bi-m. £82 (foreign £94). Royal College of Surgeons of England, 35-43 Lincolns Inn Fields, London WC2A 3PN, England. TEL 071-405-3474. FAX 071-831-9438. TELEX 936573-RCSENG. Ed. Barry Jackson. adv.; bk.rev.; charts; illus.; index, cum.index every 10 yrs. (also avail. in microform from UMI) **Indexed:** Biol.Abstr., Chem.Abstr., Curr.Adv.Ecol.Sci., Dent.Ind., Excerp.Med., Helminthol.Abstr., Ind.Med., Nutr.Abstr., Sci.Cit.Ind.
—BLDSC shelfmark: 1031.550000.
Description: Scientific journal covering aspects of surgery and dental surgery.

617   CS   ISSN 0035-9351
ROZHLEDY V CHIRURGII. (Text in Czech; summaries in Czech, English, Russian) vol. 44, 1965. 12/yr. $79.90. (Ceskoslovenska Chirurgicka Spolecnost) Avicenum, Czechoslovak Medical Press, Malostranske nam. 28, 118 02 Prague 1, Czechoslovakia. (Dist. by: Artia, Ve Smeckach 30, 111 27 Prague 1, Czechoslovakia) (Co-sponsor: Ceskoslovenska Lekarska Spolecnost J. Ev. Purkyne) Ed. B. Spacek. bk.rev. **Indexed:** Curr.Adv.Ecol.Sci., Ind.Med.

658   US   ISSN 0190-5066
SAME-DAY SURGERY. 1977. m. $279. American Health Consultants, Inc., Six Piedmont Center, Ste. 400, 3525 Piedmont Rd., N.E., Atlanta, GA 30305. TEL 404-262-7436. FAX 800-284-3291. (Subscr. to: Box 740056, Atlanta, GA 30374-9822. TEL 800-688-2421) Ed. Joy Daughtery. bk.rev.; circ. 2,400. (also avail. in microform from UMI; back issues avail.; reprint service avail.) **Indexed:** CINAHL.
●Also available online. Vendor(s): Mead Data Central.
—BLDSC shelfmark: 8071.966000.

617   BL   ISSN 0036-4258
SANATORIO SAO LUCAS. BOLETIM.* 1939. bi-m. free. Fundacao para o Progresso da Cirurgia, Rua Pirapitingui 80, Sao Paulo, Brazil. Ed. R. Ney Penteado De Castro. adv.; bk.rev.; illus.; index; circ. 2,000 (controlled). (also avail. in microfilm from UMI) **Indexed:** Excerp.Med., Ind.Med.

MEDICAL SCIENCES — SURGERY

617.95 SW ISSN 0036-5556
CODEN: SJPRBG
SCANDINAVIAN JOURNAL OF PLASTIC AND RECONSTRUCTIVE SURGERY. (Supplements avail.) (Text in English) 1967. 4/yr. SEK 650 incl. supplements. (Scandinavian Association of Plastic Surgeons) Almqvist & Wiksell Periodical Company, Box 638, S-101 28 Stockholm, Sweden. Ed. Bengt Johanson. **Indexed:** ASCA, Biol.Abstr., Curr.Adv.Cell & Devel.Biol., Curr.Cont., Dent.Ind., Excerp.Med., Ind.Med., Nutr.Abstr.
—BLDSC shelfmark: 8087.518500.

617.54 617.41 SW ISSN 0036-5580
RD536 CODEN: SJTCAO
SCANDINAVIAN JOURNAL OF THORACIC AND CARDIOVASCULAR SURGERY. (Supplements avail.) (Text in English) 1967. 3/yr. SEK 520 (free to subscribers of Acta Chirurgica Scandinavica). (Scandinavian Association for Thoracic and Cardiovascular Surgery) Almqvist & Wiksell Periodical Company, Box 638, S-101 28 Stockholm, Sweden. Ed. Axel Henze. adv.; circ. 2,600. **Indexed:** ASCA, Biol.Abstr., Curr.Cont., Excerp.Med., Ind.Med.
—BLDSC shelfmark: 8087.550000.

SCHWEIZER ARCHIV FUER NEUROLOGIE, NEUROCHIRURGIE UND PSYCHIATRIE. see *MEDICAL SCIENCES — Psychiatry And Neurology*

617 US
SCIENCE AND PRACTICE OF SURGERY SERIES. 1980. irreg., vol.15, 1988. price varies. Marcel Dekker, Inc., 270 Madison Ave., New York, NY 10016. TEL 212-696-9000. FAX 212-685-4540. TELEX 421419.
Refereed Serial

617 US
SELECTED READINGS IN GENERAL SURGERY. 1974. m (11/yr.). $169 (Canada and Mexico $218.50; elsewhere $229.50). University of Texas, Southwestern Medical School, Department of Surgery, P.O. Box 36483, Dallas, TX 75235-9031. TEL 800-631-0033. FAX 214-688-6700. Ed. Robert N. McClelland.

617.6 US ISSN 1044-7032
SELECTED READINGS IN ORAL AND MAXILLOFACIAL SURGERY. irreg. $185. Guild for Scientific Advancement in Oral and Maxillofacial Surgery, 124 Danvers St., San Francisco, CA 94114. TEL 415-665-9416. Ed. Dr. Felice O'Ryan.
—BLDSC shelfmark: 8234.855000.

617.95 US ISSN 0739-5523
SELECTED READINGS IN PLASTIC SURGERY. 1980. 20/yr. $190 (foreign $210) for print ed.; audio cassette $250 (foreign $290)(effective July 1991). Baylor Universtiy Medical Center, 411 N. Washington Ave., Ste. 6900, Dallas, TX 75246. TEL 214-824-0154. FAX 214-824-0463. Ed. Fritz E. Barton, Jr., M.D. circ. 1,800 (controlled). (also avail. in audio cassette)

SEMINARS IN ANESTHESIA. see *MEDICAL SCIENCES — Anaesthesiology*

617 US ISSN 1043-1489
SEMINARS IN COLON AND RECTAL SURGERY. 1989. q. W.B. Saunders Co. (Subsidiary of: Harcourt Brace Jovanovich, Inc.), Curtis Center, Independence Square W., Philadelphia, PA 19106. TEL 215-238-2800. Ed. Dr. Malcolm C. Veidenheimer.
—BLDSC shelfmark: 8239.448400.
Description: Each issue focuses on a single topic in the management of patients with colon and rectal disorders.

SEMINARS IN NEPHROLOGY. see *MEDICAL SCIENCES — Urology And Nephrology*

616 US ISSN 0160-2489
SEMINARS IN NEUROLOGICAL SURGERY. 1978. irreg., latest 1985. Raven Press, 1185 Ave. of the Americas, New York, NY 10036. TEL 212-930-9500. FAX 212-869-3495. TELEX 640073. **Indexed:** ASCA, Excerp.Med.

SEMINARS IN OPHTHALMOLOGY. see *MEDICAL SCIENCES — Ophthalmology And Optometry*

SEMINARS IN ORTHOPAEDICS. see *MEDICAL SCIENCES — Orthopedics And Traumatology*

SEMINARS IN PERINATOLOGY. see *MEDICAL SCIENCES — Pediatrics*

SEMINARS IN SURGICAL ONCOLOGY. see *MEDICAL SCIENCES — Cancer*

617.54 616.1 US
SEMINARS IN THORACIC AND CARDIOVASCULAR SURGERY. 1989. q. W.B. Saunders Co., Journals Department (Subsidiary of: Harcourt Brace Jovanovich, Inc.), Curtis Center, Independence Sq. W., Philadelphia, PA 19106. TEL 215-238-7800. Ed. Dr. Floyd D. Loop. adv.; circ. 1,371.
Description: Covers new instrumentation and techniques for practicing surgeons.

SEMINARS IN UROLOGY. see *MEDICAL SCIENCES — Urology And Nephrology*

616 US ISSN 0895-7967
SEMINARS IN VASCULAR SURGERY. q. $65 to individuals; institutions $85. W.B. Saunders Co., Curtis Center, Independence Square W., Philadelphia, PA 19106-3399. TEL 215-238-7880. Ed. Dr. Robert B. Rutherford. adv. (back issues avail.)
—BLDSC shelfmark: 8239.486500.

SHINKEI GEKA. see *MEDICAL SCIENCES — Psychiatry And Neurology*

617 CC ISSN 1001-0831
SHIYONG WAIKE ZAZHI/JOURNAL OF PRACTICAL SURGERY. (Text in Chinese) 1981. m. $15. Shiyong Yixue Zazhishe, 44-1, Jixian Jie, Heping Qu, Shenyang, Liaoning 110005, People's Republic of China. TEL 364398. Ed. He Sanguang.

617 JA ISSN 0037-4423
SHUJUTSU/OPERATION. (Text in Japanese) 1947. m. 1750 Yen per no. Kanehara & Co., Ltd., 2-31-14 Yushima, Bunkyo-ku, Tokyo 113, Japan. Ed. Dr. Tokuji Ichikawa. bk.rev.; cum.index; circ. 9,500. **Indexed:** Ind.Med.
—BLDSC shelfmark: 6267.900000.

617 US ISSN 1052-1453
CODEN: SBSUEL
▼**SKULL BASE SURGERY.** 1991. q. $95 to individuals; institutions $125. Thieme Medical Publishers, Inc., 381 Park Ave. So., Ste. 1501, New York, NY 10016. TEL 212-683-5088. FAX 212-779-9020. Eds. Douglas Mattox, Ugo Fisch.
—BLDSC shelfmark: 8308.850000.
Description: Multidisciplinary journal publishing original research articles.

617 VE
SOCIEDAD VENEZOLANA DE CIRUGIA BOLETIN.* vol. 29, 1975. Bs.13.50. Sociedad Venezolana de Cirugia, Torre del Colegio 150, Of. A, Avde. Jose Maria Vargas, Urb. Santa Fe, Caracas 1080, Venezuela.

617 BL
SOCIEDADE DE MEDICINA E CIRURGIA DE SAO JOSE DO RIO PRETO. REVISTA. (Text and summaries in English and Portuguese) 1968. q. Cr.$100($15) Sociedade de Medicina e Cirurgia de Sao Jose do Rio Preto, Rua Spinola s-n, Sao Jose da Rio Preto 15100, Brazil. Ed. Dr. Jorge Paulete. adv.; bk.rev.; illus.; index; circ. controlled. (also avail. in microform) **Indexed:** Biol.Abstr.

617 IT ISSN 0037-8852
SOCIETA MEDICA CHIRURGICA, CREMONA. BOLLETTINO.* (Summaries in English) 1946. q. L.4000.($6.50) Societa Medica Chirurgica, Cremona, Via Alle Tramvie N. 5, Cremona, Italy. Ed. Prof. Toscani. adv.; abstr.; bibl.; charts; illus.; index; circ. 400. **Indexed:** Biol.Abstr., Ind.Med.

616 IT
SOCIETA MEDICO-CHIRURGICA DI MODENA. BOLLETTINO. (Text in Italian; summaries in English) vol. 82, 1982. fortn. L.10000($7) Societa Medico-Chirurgica di Modena, Policlinico, Via del Pozzo, 41100 Modena, Italy. circ. 500. **Indexed:** Biol.Abstr.

617 FR ISSN 0037-9492
SOCIETE MEDICO-CHIRURGICALE DES HOPITAUX ET FORMATIONS SANITAIRES DES ARMEES. BULLETIN. 1969. 10/yr. 20 F. Societe Medico-Chirurgicale des Hopitaux et Formations Sanitaires des Armees, Val-De-Grace, 277 bis rue Saint Jacques, 75005 Paris, France. adv.; bibl.; charts; illus.; index. **Indexed:** Biol.Abstr.

617 SA ISSN 0038-2361
CODEN: SAJSBS
SOUTH AFRICAN JOURNAL OF SURGERY/SUID-AFRIKAANSE TYDSKRIF VIR CHIRURGIE. (Text in Afrikaans and English) 1963. q. R.46.42 (to U.S. and Canada R.75). (Association of Surgeons of South Africa) Medical Association of South Africa, Publications Division, Private Bag X1, Pinelands 7430, South Africa. TEL 5313081. FAX 5314126. Ed. Cedric Bremner. adv.; bk.rev.; bibl.; charts; illus.; index; circ. 1,200. (also avail. in microform from UMI; reprint service avail. from ISI,UMI) **Indexed:** Abstr.Hyg., ASCA, Biol.Abstr., Curr.Cont., Excerp.Med., Helminthol.Abstr., Ind.Med., Ind.S.A.Per., Trop.Dis.Bull.
—BLDSC shelfmark: 8340.300000.

617 US
▼**SOUTHERN SURGICAL ASSOCIATION. TRANSACTIONS.** 1991. a. J.B. Lippincott Co., E. Washington Sq., Philadelphia, PA 19105. TEL 215-238-4200. (also avail. in microform from UMI)

617.102 TU
SPOR HEKIMLIGI DERGISI/TURKISH JOURNAL OF SPORTS MEDICINE. q. (Institute of Sports Medicine) Ege University, Medical Faculty, Bornova, Izmir, Turkey. Ed. Necati Akgun. **Indexed:** Sportsearch (1979-).

616.8 UK
STUDIES IN NEUROSCIENCE. 1985. irreg. price varies. Pergamon Press plc, Headington Hill Hall, Oxford OX3 0BW, England. TEL 0865-794141. FAX 0865-743911. TELEX 83177 PERGAP. (And: 660 White Plains Rd., Tarrytown, NY 10591-5153. TEL 914-524-9200) Ed. W. Winlow.

617 JA ISSN 0016-593X
SURGERY/GEKA. (Text in Japanese) 1937. m. 29500 Yen (foreign 35713 Yen). Nankodo Co., Ltd., 42-6, Hongo 3-chome, Bunkyo-ku, Tokyo 113, Japan. TEL 03-3811-7239. FAX 03-3811-7230. Ed. Motokazu Hori. adv.; charts; illus.; index; circ. 6,000. **Indexed:** INIS Atomind.
—BLDSC shelfmark: 8548.130000.

617 US ISSN 0039-6060
RD1 CODEN: SURGAZ
SURGERY; devoted to the art and science of surgery. 1937. m. $81 to individuals (foreign $101); institutions $159 (foreign $179); students $38 (foreign $58). (Society of University Surgeons) Mosby - Year Book, Inc., 11830 Westline Industrial Dr., St. Louis, MO 63146. TEL 800-325-4117. FAX 314-432-1380. TELEX 44-2402. (Co-sponsors: American Association of Endocrine Surgeons; Central Surgical Association) Eds. Drs. Walter F. Ballinger, George D. Zuidema. adv.; illus.; s-a index; circ. 8,385. (also avail. in microfilm from UMI; reprint service avail. from UMI) **Indexed:** Abstr.Health Care Manage.Stud., ASCA, Biol.Abstr., Chem.Abstr., Curr.Adv.Cancer Res., Curr.Adv.Ecol.Sci., Curr.Adv.Genetics & Molec.Biol., Curr.Cont., Dairy Sci.Abstr., Excerp.Med., Helminthol.Abstr., Ind.Med., Nutr.Abstr, Risk Abstr., Sci.Cit.Ind.
—BLDSC shelfmark: 8548.125000.
Description: Developments in clinical and experimental surgery.
Refereed Serial

617 US ISSN 0748-1942
SURGERY ALERT. 1984. m. $93. American Health Consultants, Six Piedmont Center, Ste. 400, 3525 Piedmont Rd., N.E., Atlanta, GA 30305. TEL 404-262-7436. FAX 800-284-3291. (Subscr. to: Box 740056, Atlanta, GA 30374-9822. TEL 800-688-2421) Ed. Dr. Leonard Schultz. index; circ. 1,700. (also avail. in audio cassette; reprint service avail.)

617 IT ISSN 1120-4834
SURGERY AND IMMUNITY. s-a. L.40000($50) to non-members. (Societa Italiana di Chirugia ed Immunobiologia - Italian Society of Surgery and Immunobiology) Edizioni Minerva Medica, Corso Bramante 83-85, 10126 Turin, Italy. TEL 011-67-82-82. FAX 011-31-21-736. Ed. G. Balbo.
—BLDSC shelfmark: 8548.134000.

MEDICAL SCIENCES — SURGERY

616 US ISSN 0081-9638
RD9 CODEN: SURABI
SURGERY ANNUAL. 1969. s-a. $75 per vol. Appleton & Lange (Subsidiary of: Simon & Schuster Company), 25 Van Zant St., Box 5630, Norwalk, CT 06856. TEL 203-838-4400. Ed. Dr. Lloyd Nyhus. **Indexed:** Biol.Abstr., Dent.Ind., Excerp.Med., Ind.Med.
Description: Selection of original articles on latest surgical advances.

617 016 US ISSN 0039-6087
RD1 CODEN: SGOBA9
SURGERY, GYNECOLOGY & OBSTETRICS. (With: International Abstracts of Surgery) 1905. m. $60. (American College of Surgeons) Franklin H. Martin Memorial Foundation, 54 E. Erie St., Chicago, IL 60611. TEL 312-787-9282. FAX 312-440-7026. Ed. G. Tom Shires. adv.; bk.rev.; bibl.; charts; illus.; s-a. index; circ. 19,370. (also avail. in microform from UMI; reprint service avail. from UMI) **Indexed:** ASCA, Biol.Abstr., Chem.Abstr., Curr.Adv.Ecol.Sci., Curr.Cont., Dent.Ind., Excerp.Med., Helminthol.Abstr., Hosp.Lit.Ind., Ind.Med., Ind.Vet., Nutr.Abstr., Rev.Plant Path., Vet.Bull.
●Also available online. Vendor(s): Mead Data Central.
—BLDSC shelfmark: 8548.150000.
Description: General surgical journal edited by participating surgeons.

SURGICAL AND RADIOLOGIC ANATOMY. see BIOLOGY — Physiology

617 US ISSN 0039-6109
RD34 CODEN: SCNAA7
SURGICAL CLINICS OF NORTH AMERICA. 1912. bi-m. $84. W.B. Saunders Co., Curtis Center, Independence Square W., Philadelphia, PA 19106. TEL 215-238-7800. Ed. Livia Berardi. bibl.; illus.; index, cum.index every 3 yrs. (also avail. in microform from UMI; reprint service avail. from UMI, ISI) **Indexed:** ASCA, Biol.Abstr., Chem.Abstr., Curr.Adv.Ecol.Sci., Curr.Cont., Excerp.Med., Helminthol.Abstr., Ind.Med., Int.Nurs.Ind., Nutr.Abstr.
●Also available online. Vendor(s): BRS.
—BLDSC shelfmark: 8548.200000.

617 GW ISSN 0930-2794
CODEN: SUREEX
SURGICAL ENDOSCOPY, ULTRASOUND AND INTERVENTIONAL TECHNIQUES. 1987. 4/yr. DM.240($144) Springer-Verlag, Heidelberger Platz 3, D-1000 Berlin 33, Germany. TEL 030-8207-1. (Also Heidelberg, Tokyo, Vienna, and New York) Ed. J.P. Chevrel.
—BLDSC shelfmark: 8548.215000.

617 616.3 618 US ISSN 1051-7200
CODEN: SLENEY
▼**SURGICAL LAPAROSCOPY AND ENDOSCOPY.** 1991. q. $85 to individuals; institutions $116. Raven Press, 1185 Ave. of the Americas, New York, NY 10036. TEL 212-930-9500. FAX 212-869-3495. TELEX 640073. Ed. Karl A. Zucker. adv.; charts; illus.; circ. 2,000. **Indexed:** Excerp.Med. (1992-).
—BLDSC shelfmark: 8548.234000.
Description: Publishes reports on major developments in laparoscopic and endoscopic techniques and procedures, current clinical and basic science research, patient management, surgical complications, and new developments in instrumentation and technology.
Refereed Serial

617 616.8 US ISSN 0090-3019
RD593 CODEN: SGNRAI
SURGICAL NEUROLOGY. 1973. 12/yr.(in 2 vols.; 6 nos./vol.). $225 to institutions (foreign $271)(effective 1992). Elsevier Science Publishing Co., Inc. (New York), 655 Ave. of the Americas, New York, NY 10010. TEL 212-989-5800. FAX 212-633-3965. TELEX 420643 AEP UI. Ed. Eben Alexander, Jr. adv.; bk.rev.; index; circ. 4,300. (also avail. in microform from RPI; back issues avail.) **Indexed:** ASCA, Bibl.Dev.Med.& Child Neur., Biol.Abstr., Curr.Adv.Cancer Res., Curr.Adv.Ecol.Sci., Curr.Cont., Excerp.Med., Helminthol.Abstr., Ind.Med., Sci.Cit.Ind.
—BLDSC shelfmark: 8548.240000.
Description: Presents original papers on clinical and research advances in neurosurgery.
Refereed Serial

610 US ISSN 0273-7655
SURGICAL PRACTICE NEWS. 1981. m. $28. McMahon Publishing Co., 83 Peaceable St., West Redding, CT 06896. TEL 203-944-9343. (Subscr. to: 121 S. Gertrude Ave., Paramus, NJ 07652) Ed. Hank Rogers. (tabloid format; back issues avail.)
Refereed Serial

617 US
SURGICAL PRODUCT COMPARISON SYSTEM. m. (plus q. updates). $245 (foreign $295). (Emergency Care Research Institute) E C R I, 5200 Butler Pike, Plymouth Meeting, PA 19462. TEL 215-825-6000. FAX 215-834-1275. Ed. Garrett Hayner.

617 US ISSN 0882-9233
CODEN: SRCOEZ
SURGICAL RESEARCH COMMUNICATIONS. 1986. 4/yr. (in 1 vol., 4 nos./vol.). $93. Harwood Academic Publishers, 270 Eighth Ave., New York, NY 10011. TEL 212-206-8900. FAX 212-645-2459. TELEX 236735 GOPUB UR. (Subscr. to: Box 786, Cooper Sta., New York, NY 10276. TEL 800-545-8398; UK subscr. to: P.O. Box 90, Reading, Berkshire RG1 8JL, England. TEL 0734-560-080) Ed. D.J. Leaper. (also avail. in microform)
—BLDSC shelfmark: 8548.247000.
Refereed Serial

616 US ISSN 0161-1372
RD1
SURGICAL ROUNDS. 1978. m. $50 (foreign $92). Romaine Pierson Publishers, Inc., 80 Shore Rd., Port Washington, NY 11050. TEL 516-883-6350. FAX 516-883-6609. Ed. Dr. Bernard M. Jaffe. adv.; circ. 53,530. (also avail. in microform from UMI; back issues avail.) **Indexed:** CINAHL.
—BLDSC shelfmark: 8548.249000.

617 US ISSN 0164-4238
SURGICAL TECHNOLOGIST. 1972. bi-m. $18. Association of Surgical Technologists, Inc., 7108-C S. Alton Way, Englewood, CO 80112-2106. TEL 303-694-9130. FAX 303-694-9164. Ed. Michelle M. Armstrong. adv.; bk.rev.; illus.; circ. 12,500. **Indexed:** CINAHL, Hosp.Lit.Ind.
—BLDSC shelfmark: 8548.259000.
Formerly (until 1978): O R Tech.
Description: Emphasis is given to surgical procedures and equipment, legislative-regulatory issues, aseptic techniques and professional development.

617 UK ISSN 0039-6125
SURGO. 1933. 3/yr. £5. University of Glasgow, Medico-Chirurgical Society, University Union, 32 University Ave., Glasgow, G12 8LX, Scotland. Ed. Paul Jarrett. adv.; bk.rev.; bibl.; charts; illus.; circ. 1,000.
—BLDSC shelfmark: 8548.270000.

617 US
SUTURELINE. q. American Association of Surgeon Assistants, 1730 N. Lynn St., Ste. 502, Arlington, VA 22209. TEL 703-525-1191. circ. 500.

617 US ISSN 8756-8624
TECHNOLOGY FOR SURGERY. m. $90 (Canada $100; elsewhere $120). (Emergency Care Research Institute) E C R I, 5200 Butler Pike, Plymouth Meeting, PA 19462. TEL 215-825-6000. FAX 215-834-1275. Ed. Robert Hochschild.
Former titles: Health Devices Update: Surgery; Health Services Update: Surgery.
Refereed Serial

617 GW ISSN 0179-8669
CODEN: THSUE6
THEORETICAL SURGERY; a journal of decision making in surgery, anaesthesia and intensive care. 1986. 4/yr. DM.240($144) Springer-Verlag, Heidelberger Platz 3, D-1000 Berlin 33, Germany. TEL 030-8207-1. (Also Heidelberg, Tokyo, Vienna, and New York) Ed. G. Wenzel.
—BLDSC shelfmark: 8814.576000.

617 GW ISSN 0171-6425
CODEN: TCSUD4
THORACIC AND CARDIOVASCULAR SURGEON. (Text in English) 1952. bi-m. DM.282. (Deutsche Gesellschaft fuer Thorax-, Herz- und Gefaesschirurgie - German Society for Thorax and Cardiovascular Surgery) Georg Thieme Verlag, Ruedigerstr. 14, Postfach 104853, 7000 Stuttgart 10, Germany. TEL 0711-8931-0. FAX 0711-8931298. (Subscr. to: Thieme Medical Publishers, Inc., 381 Park Ave. S., New York, NY 10016, U.S.A.) Ed. H.G. Borst. adv.; bk.rev.; abstr.; bibl.; charts; illus.; stat.; index; circ. 1,400. (reprint service avail. from UMI) **Indexed:** ASCA, Chem.Abstr., Curr.Cont., Excerp.Med., Ind.Med., Sci.Cit.Ind.
—BLDSC shelfmark: 8820.240000.
Formerly (until 1979): Thoraxchirurgie - Vaskulaere Chirurgie (ISSN 0040-6384)

617 US ISSN 0041-1337
QP89 CODEN: TRPLAU
TRANSPLANTATION. 1963. m. $135 to individuals; institutions $215. (Transplantation Society) Williams & Wilkins, 428 E. Preston St., Baltimore, MD 21202. TEL 301-528-4000. FAX 301-528-4312. TELEX 87669. Ed. A.P. Monaco, M.D. adv.; bk.rev.; illus.; index; circ. 3,500. (also avail. in microform; back issues avail.) **Indexed:** Anim.Breed.Abstr., ASCA, Biol.Abstr., Chem.Abstr., Curr.Adv.Cancer Res., Curr.Adv.Ecol.Sci., Curr.Cont., Dairy Sci.Abstr., Excerp.Med., Ind.Med., Ind.Vet., Poult.Abstr., Protozool.Abstr., Risk Abstr., Telegen, Vet.Bull.
—BLDSC shelfmark: 9024.990000.
Description: Original papers and abstracts from pertinent specialties: immunology, hematology, endocrinology and embryology.
Refereed Serial

617 US ISSN 0041-1345
RD120.7 CODEN: TRPPA8
TRANSPLANTATION PROCEEDINGS. 1969. bi-m. $156 to individuals (foreign $217); institutions $205 (foreign $239); students $120 (foreign $156). (Transplantation Society) Appleton & Lange, Journal Division (Subsidiary of: Simon & Schuster Company), 25 Van Zant St., Box 5630, Norwalk, CT 06856. TEL 203-838-4400. (Subscr. to: Dept. TP, Box 3000, Denville, NJ 07834) Ed. Dr. Felix T. Rapaport. adv.; bibl.; charts; illus.; index; circ. 2,600. (also avail. in microform from UMI; back issues avail.; reprint service avail. from UMI) **Indexed:** Anim.Breed.Abstr., ASCA, Biol.Abstr., Chem.Abstr., Curr.Adv.Cancer Res., Curr.Adv.Ecol.Sci., Curr.Cont., Excerp.Med., Ind.Med., Ind.Vet., Sci.Cit.Ind.
●Also available online.
—BLDSC shelfmark: 9025.100000.
Description: Includes reviews and original reports in current problems in transplantation biology and medicine.
Refereed Serial

617 IT ISSN 0014-648X
UNIVERSITA DEGLI STUDI DI PERUGIA. FACOLTA DI MEDICINA E CHIRURGIA. ANNALI. (Includes: Accademia Anatomico Chirurgica. Atti) 1885. q. L.30000. Universita degli Studi di Perugia, Facolta di Medicina e Chirugia, Perugia, Italy. Ed. Giovanni Bolis. circ. 500. **Indexed:** Chem.Abstr., Excerp.Med.

616 US ISSN 0042-2835
VASCULAR SURGERY. 1967. 9/yr. $80. Westminster Publications, Inc., 1044 Northern Blvd., Ste. 103, Roslyn, NY 11576. TEL 516-484-6882. FAX 516-625-1174. adv.; circ. 4,249. **Indexed:** Biol.Abstr., Curr.Adv.Cancer Res., Excerp.Med.
—BLDSC shelfmark: 9148.900000.
Description: Original papers relating to any phase of vascular diseases, operative procedures, clinical or laboratory research and case reports.

617 RU ISSN 0042-4625
CODEN: VKHGAG
VESTNIK KHIRURGII IM. I.I. GREKOVA/I.I. GREKOV ANNALS OF SURGERY. (Text in Russian; summaries in English) 1885. m. 31.80 Rub.($27.60) (Khirurgicheskoe Obshchestvo im. Pirogova) Izdatel'stvo Meditsina, Petroverigskii pereulok 6-8, 101838 Moscow, Russia. (Co-sponsor: Ministerstvo Zdravookhraneniya S.S.S.R.) Ed. F.G. Uglov. bk.rev.; illus.; index. **Indexed:** Biol.Abstr., Chem.Abstr., Dent.Ind., Dok.Arbeitsmed., Excerp.Med., Ind.Med.
—BLDSC shelfmark: 0036.700000.
Description: Carries articles touching on various problems of clinical and experimental surgery, anesthesiology and reanimatology.

616.89 RU ISSN 0042-8817
CODEN: ZVNBDJ
VOPROSY NEIROKHIRURGII/JOURNAL OF NEUROSURGICAL PROBLEMS. Title varies slightly: Voprosy Neirokhirurgii. Zhurnal im. N.N. Burdenko. (Text in Russian; summaries in English) 1937. bi-m. 18.30 Rub.($8.40) (Vsesoyuznoe Nauchnoe Obshchestvo Neirokhirurgov) Izdatel'stvo Meditsina, Petroverigskii pereulok 6-8, 101838 Moscow, Russia. (Co-sponsor: Ministerstvo Zdravookhraneniya S.S.S.R.) Ed. A.N. Konovalov. bk.rev.; index. **Indexed:** Biol.Abstr., Chem.Abstr., Ind.Med., Int.Aerosp.Abstr.
—BLDSC shelfmark: 0060.630000.
Description: Discusses theoretical, practical and organization problems of modern neurosurgery. Informs of the advances in the treatment of neurosurgical diseases of the central, peripheral and vegetative nervous system.

617 US ISSN 0364-2313
CODEN: WJSUDI
WORLD JOURNAL OF SURGERY. 1936. 6/yr. $183.50. (Societe Internationale de Chirurgie, BE) Springer-Verlag, Journals, 175 Fifth Ave., New York, NY 10010. TEL 212-460-1500. (Also Berlin, Heidelberg, Tokyo and Vienna) (Co-sponsors: Collegium Internationale Chirurgie Digestivae; International Association of Endocrine Surgeons) Ed. Dr. Samuel A. Wells, Jr. adv.; bk.rev.; illus. (also avail. in microform from UMI; reprint service avail. from ISI) **Indexed:** Chem.Abstr., Curr.Cont., Excerp.Med., Ind.Med.
—BLDSC shelfmark: 9356.074300.
Supersedes (until 1976): Societe Internationale de Chirurgie. Bulletin (ISSN 0037-945X); **Continues:** Journal International de Chirurgie.

YEAR BOOK OF DERMATOLOGIC SURGERY. see *MEDICAL SCIENCES — Dermatology And Venereology*

617 617.3 US
YEAR BOOK OF HAND SURGERY. a. $57.95. Mosby - Year Book, Inc., Continuity Division, 200 N. LaSalle St., Chicago, IL 60601-1080. TEL 312-726-9733. FAX 312-726-6075. TELEX 206155. Ed. Dr. Peter C. Amadio. illus. (reprint service avail.)
●Also available online. Vendor(s): BRS.

YEAR BOOK OF NEUROLOGY & NEUROSURGERY. see *MEDICAL SCIENCES — Psychiatry And Neurology*

617.95 US ISSN 1040-175X
RD118.A1 CODEN: YPRSA
YEAR BOOK OF PLASTIC, RECONSTRUCTIVE, AND AESTHETIC SURGERY. 1970. a. $54.95. Mosby - Year Book, Inc., Continuity Division, 200 N. LaSalle, Chicago, IL 60601. TEL 312-726-9733. FAX 312-726-6075. TELEX 206155. Ed. Stephen Miller. illus. (reprint service avail.)
●Also available online. Vendor(s): BRS.
—BLDSC shelfmark: 9415.520000.
Formerly: Year Book of Plastic and Reconstructive Surgery (ISSN 0084-3962)

YEAR BOOK OF PODIATRIC MEDICINE AND SURGERY. see *MEDICAL SCIENCES — Orthopedics And Traumatology*

617.005 US ISSN 0090-3671
RD9
YEAR BOOK OF SURGERY. 1901. a. $54.95. Mosby - Year Book, Inc., Continuity Division, 200 N. LaSalle, Chicago, IL 60601. TEL 312-726-9733. FAX 312-726-6075. TELEX 206155. Ed. Seymour Schwartz. illus. (reprint service avail.)
●Also available online. Vendor(s): BRS.
—BLDSC shelfmark: 9416.450000.
Formerly: Year Book of General Surgery.

617
▼**YEAR BOOK OF TRANSPLANTATION.** 1992. a. $89. Mosby - Year Book, Inc. (Chicago) (Subsidiary of: Times Mirror Company), 200 LaSalle St., Chicago, IL 60601. TEL 312-726-9733. Ed. Dr. Nancy L. Ascher.
●Also available online. Vendor(s): BRS.

617 GW ISSN 0930-9225
ZEITSCHRIFT FUER HERZ, THORAX- UND GEFAESSCHIRURGIE. (Summaries in English) 1987. 4/yr. DM.170. Dr. Dietrich Steinkopff Verlag, Saalbaustr. 12, Postfach 111442, 6100 Darmstadt 11, Germany. TEL 06151-26538. FAX 06151-20849. Ed.Bd.
—BLDSC shelfmark: 9464.530000.

ZEITSCHRIFT FUER KINDERCHIRURGIE/SURGERY IN INFANCY AND CHILDHOOD. see *MEDICAL SCIENCES — Pediatrics*

617 GW ISSN 0935-1965
ZEITSCHRIFT FUER TRANSPLANTATIONSMEDIZIN. (Text in English or German) 1989. q. DM.64($50) Wolfgang Pabst Verlag, Am Eichengrund 28, 4540 Lengerich, Germany. TEL 05484-308. FAX 05481-7587. Ed. A.-E. Lison. adv.; bk.rev.; circ. 1,600.
Description: Review articles and case reports on transplantation in surgery, immunology, internal medicine, urology, nephrology.

617 GW ISSN 0044-409X
CODEN: ZECHAU
ZENTRALBLATT FUER CHIRURGIE. 1874. s-m. DM.216. Johann Ambrosius Barth Verlag, Leipzig - Heidelberg, Salomonstr. 18b, 7010 Leipzig, Germany. TEL 70131. Ed. Dr. H. Wolff. adv.; bk.rev.; abstr.; charts; illus.; index; circ. 4,600. (also avail. in microfiche from BHP) **Indexed:** Curr.Cont., Dent.Ind., Ind.Med., Nutr.Abstr.
—BLDSC shelfmark: 9504.700000.

ZENTRALBLATT FUER NEUROCHIRURGIE. see *MEDICAL SCIENCES — Psychiatry And Neurology*

ZHONGHUA SHENJING WAIKE ZAZHI/CHINESE JOURNAL OF NEUROSURGERY. see *MEDICAL SCIENCES — Psychiatry And Neurology*

313 CC
ZHONGHUA WAIKE ZAZHI/CHINESE JOURNAL OF SURGERY. (Text in Chinese) m. $3 per no. Guoji Shudian, Qikan Bu, Chegongzhuang Xilu 21, P.O. Box 399, Beijing 100044, People's Republic of China. **Indexed:** Ind.Med.

617.95 CC ISSN 1000-7806
ZHONGHUA ZHENGXING SHAOSHANG WAIKE ZAZHI/CHINESE JOURNAL OF PLASTIC SURGERY AND BURNS. (Text in Chinese; summaries in English) 1985. q. Y10($35) Chinese Academy of Medical Sciences (CAMS), Plastic Surgery Hospital, Institute of Plastic Surgery - Zhongguo Yixue Kexueyuan Zhengxing Waike Yiyuan, Ba-Da-Chu, Beijing 100041, People's Republic of China. TEL 86-1-874826. FAX 86-1-8204137. (Dist. overseas by: China International Book Trading Corporation, P.O. Box 399, Beijing 100044, P.R.C.) (Co-sponsor: Chinese Medical Association of Plastic Surgeons) Ed. Xu Xiang-min. adv.; bk.rev.; circ. 5,000. (back issues avail.)
—BLDSC shelfmark: 3180.558000.

MEDICAL SCIENCES — Urology And Nephrology

616.6 US ISSN 0742-0374
RC870
A B M S DIRECTORY OF CERTIFIED UROLOGISTS. 1983. biennial. $29.95. American Board of Medical Specialties, One Rotary Center, Ste. 805, Evanston, IL 60201. TEL 708-491-9091. FAX 708-328-3596. Ed. Dr. J. Lee Dockery.

616.6 US
A K F NEPHROLOGY LETTER. 1984. q. free. American Kidney Fund, 6110 Executive Blvd., Ste. 1010, Rockville, MD 20852-3903. TEL 800-638-8299. FAX 301-881-0898. Eds. Drs. Serafino Garella, William D. Mattern. circ. 10,000. (back issues avail.)
Description: Each issue contains a review of a clinical topic emphasizing recent scientific advances, descriptions of new technology, notices of upcoming meetings, and legislative developments of interest to the nephrology community.

616.6 US
A K F NEWSLETTER; for health professionals. 1984. 4/yr. free. American Kidney Fund, 6110 Executive Blvd., Ste. 1010, Rockville, MD 20852-3903. TEL 800-638-8299. FAX 301-881-0898. index; circ. 12,000. (back issues avail.)
Description: Offers current information to health professionals in the renal community. Reports on developments in the renal field as well as the AKF services and programs.

A N N A JOURNAL. (American Nephrology Nurses' Association) see *MEDICAL SCIENCES — Nurses And Nursing*

616.6 CN
A U A DECISION MAKING. (Avail. on floppy disk only.) 1986. bi-m. $320. (American Urological Association) Decker Periodicals, One James St. S., P.O. Box 620, LCD 1, Hamilton, Ont. L8N 3K7, Canada. TEL 416-522-7017. FAX 416-522-7839. (U.S. addr.: Box 785, Lewiston, NY 14092-0785) Ed. Martin I. Resnich.
Description: Each diskette focuses on a challenging clinical topic in urology, and uses an interactive format to review intricacies of the decision making process involved with that particular clinical problem.

616.6 US
A U A TODAY; urology's clinical, research, and socioeconomic newsletter. 1987. m. $80. (American Urological Association) Williams & Wilkins, 428 E. Preston St., Baltimore, MD 21202. TEL 301-528-4000. FAX 301-528-4321. Ed. Dr. Abraham T.K. Cockett. circ. 5,700.
Description: Issues news and developments in urology, including clinical information, case studies, and reports on economic policies and legislation.

616.6 BE ISSN 0001-7183
CODEN: AUBEAN
ACTA UROLOGICA BELGICA. (Text in English, French) 1927. 4/yr. 2800 Fr. (foreign 3800 Fr.). Association des Societes Scientifiques Medicales Belges - Vereiniging van de Belgische Medische Wetenschappelijke Genootschappen, Av. Circulaire 138A, B-1180 Brussels, Belgium. TEL 02-374-5158. Ed. Ch. Bouffioux. adv.; bk.rev.; abstr.; bibl.; charts; illus.; index. **Indexed:** Biol.Abstr., Chem.Abstr., Excerp.Med., Ind.Med.
—BLDSC shelfmark: 0670.415000.

616.6 JA ISSN 0001-7191
ACTA UROLOGICA JAPONICA/HINYOKIKA KIYO. (Text in Japanese; summaries in English) 1955. m. 10000 Yen($50) Kyoto University, Faculty of Medicine, Department of Urology - Kyoto Daigaku Igakubu Hinyokikagaku Kyoshitsu, 53 Shogoin Kawara-cho, Sakyo-ku, Kyoto 606, Japan. TEL 075-751-3326. FAX 075-761-3441. Ed. Osamu Yoshida. adv.; index; circ. 2,500. **Indexed:** Biol.Abstr., Excerp.Med., Ind.Med., INIS Atomind.

616.6 FR ISSN 0073-3326
ACTUALITES NEPHROLOGIQUES. 1960. a. price varies. (Hopital Necker, Clinique Nephrologique) Flammarion Medecine Sciences, 4 rue Casimir Delavigne, 75006 Paris, France. (U.S. subscr. address: S.F.P.A, c/o Mr. Bench, 14 E. 60th St., New York, NY 10022) Ed. J.P. Grunfeld. cum.index: 1960-69. **Indexed:** Chem.Abstr., Excerp.Med.

616.6 US
ADVANCES IN NEPHROLOGY. 1971. a. $69.95. Mosby - Year Book, Inc. (Chicago) (Subsidiary of: Times Mirror Company), 200 N. LaSalle St., Chicago, IL 60601-1080. TEL 312-726-9733. FAX 312-726-6075. TELEX 206155. (Subscr. to: 11830 Westline Industrial Dr., St. Louis, MO 63146. TEL 800-325-4177) Ed. Dr. Jean-Pierre Grunfeld. (also avail. in microfilm from UMI; reprint service avail. from UMI) **Indexed:** Biol.Abstr., Chem.Abstr., Ind.Med.
Formerly: Advances in Nephrology from the Necker Hospital (ISSN 0084-5957)
Description: Presents original topical review articles of importance in nephrology.

616.6 US ISSN 0894-4385
RC870
ADVANCES IN UROLOGY. 1988. a. $69.95 to individuals; residents $40. Mosby - Year Book, Inc. (Chicago) (Subsidiary of: Times Mirror Company), 200 N. LaSalle St., Chicago, IL 60601-1080. TEL 312-726-9733. FAX 312-726-6075. TELEX 206155. (Subscr. to: 11830 Westline Industrial Dr., St. Louis, MO 63146) Ed. Bernard Lytton, M.D.
—BLDSC shelfmark: 0711.695000.
Description: Presents a collection of original, fully-referenced review articles on selected clinical topics in the field of urology.

MEDICAL SCIENCES — UROLOGY AND NEPHROLOGY

616.6   GW   ISSN 0001-7868
AKTUELLE UROLOGIE. (Text in German; summaries in English) 1970. bi-m. DM.264. Georg Thieme Verlag, Ruedigerstr. 14, Postfach 104853, 7000 Stuttgart 10, Germany. Ed.Bd. adv.; bk.rev.; abstr.; bibl.; charts; illus.; stat.; index; circ. 2,500. (reprint service avail. from UMI) **Indexed:** Biol.Abstr., Chem.Abstr., Curr.Adv.Cancer Res., Curr.Cont., Excerp.Med. (until 1992), Ind.Med., INIS Atomind., Sci.Cit.Ind.
—BLDSC shelfmark: 0785.887000.
Incorporates (1907-1991): Zeitschrift fuer Urologie und Nephrologie (ISSN 0044-3611)

616.6 574.8   US   ISSN 0272-6386
AMERICAN JOURNAL OF KIDNEY DISEASES. 1981. m. $164 to individuals; institutions $266 (foreign $297). (National Kidney Foundation) W.B. Saunders Co. (Subsidiary of: Harcourt Brace Jovanovich, Inc.), Curtis Center, Independence Square W., Philadelphia, PA 19106. TEL 215-238-7800. (Subscr. to: 6277 Sea Harbor Dr., 4th Fl., Orlando FL 32891) Ed. Saulo Klahr. adv.; bk.rev.; abstr.; bibl.; charts; illus.; index. **Indexed:** Abstr.Inter.Med., Curr.Adv.Ecol.Sci., Curr.Cont., Excerp.Med., Ind.Med., Rev.Med.& Vet.Mycol., Sci.Cit.Ind.
●Also available online.
—BLDSC shelfmark: 0826.860000.
Refereed Serial

616.6   SZ   ISSN 0250-8095
                         CODEN: AJNED9
AMERICAN JOURNAL OF NEPHROLOGY. (Text in English) 1981. 6/yr. 584 Fr.($390) per vol. S. Karger AG, Allschwilerstr. 10, P.O. Box, Ch-4009 Basel, Switzerland. TEL 061-3061111. FAX 061-3061234. TELEX CH 962652. Ed. S.G. Massry. adv.; illus.; index; circ. 2,900. (also avail. in microform from RPI) **Indexed:** Biol.Abstr., Chem.Abstr., Curr.Adv.Ecol.Sci., Curr.Cont., Dent.Ind., Excerp.Med., Ind.Med., Protozool.Abstr.
—BLDSC shelfmark: 0828.370000.

616.6   US
AMERICAN KIDNEY FUND. ANNUAL REPORT. 1971. a. free. American Kidney Fund, 6110 Executive Blvd., Ste. 1010, Rockville, MD 20852-3903. TEL 301-881-3052. FAX 301-881-0898. circ. 1,000.

616.6   US   ISSN 1046-6673
                         CODEN: JASNEU
▼**AMERICAN SOCIETY OF NEPHROLOGY. JOURNAL.** 1990. m. $110 to individuals; institutions $160. Williams & Wilkins, 428 E. Preston St., Baltimore, MD 21202. TEL 301-528-4000. FAX 301-528-4321. Ed. Dr. Jared J. Grantham. circ. 5,100.
—BLDSC shelfmark: 4693.005000.
Description: Contains original articles for nephrologists and other specialists who study kidney function and renal diseases.
Refereed Serial

616.6   FR   ISSN 0003-4401
                         CODEN: AUROAV
ANNALES D'UROLOGIE. (Text in French; summaries in English) 1967. 7/yr. 1200 F. to individuals (foreign 1690 F.); students 600 F. (foreign 845 F.). (Semaine des Hopitaux) Expansion Scientifique, 15 rue Saint-Benoit, 75278 Paris Cedex 06, France. TEL 1-45-48-42-60. FAX 1-45-44-81-55. Ed. A. Steg. bk.rev. **Indexed:** Biol.Abstr., Curr.Cont., Excerp.Med., Helminthol.Abstr., Ind.Med., Ind.Sci.Rev., Sci.Cit.Ind.
—BLDSC shelfmark: 1003.500000.

616.6   IT
ARCHIVIO ITALIANO DI UROLOGIA E NEFROLOGIA, ANDROLOGIA. (Text in Italian; summaries in English, French) 1924. 6/yr. L.69500($92) (effective 1992). (University of Milan, Istituto di Urologia) Masson Italia Periodici, Via Statuto 2-4, 20121 Milan, Italy. TEL 02-6367-1. FAX 02-6367211. TELEX 335447 ETM1 I. Ed. E. Pisani. adv.; bk.rev.; charts; illus.; circ. 2,000. (back issues avail.) **Indexed:** Biol.Abstr., Excerp.Med., Ind.Med.
Former titles: Archivio Italiano di Dermatologia, Sifilografia, Venereologia e Sessuologia; Archivio Italiano di Urologia e Nefrologia (ISSN 0004-0460)

616.6   US   ISSN 0271-1338
AUDIO-DIGEST UROLOGY. 1978. m. $84. Audio-Digest Foundation (Subsidiary of: California Medical Association), 1577 E. Chevy Chase Dr., Glendale, CA 91206. TEL 213-245-8505. FAX 818-240-7379. Ed. Claron L. Oakley. circ. controlled. (audio cassette)
Refereed Serial

616.602   SZ   ISSN 0250-3212
                         CODEN: BEURDP
BEITRAEGE ZUR UROLOGIE. (Text in German) 1979. irreg. varies. S. Karger AG, Allschwilerstr. 10, P.O. Box, CH-4009 Basel, Switzerland. TEL 061-390880. FAX 061-385383. TELEX CH-962652. Ed. H. Melchior. charts; illus. (back issues avail.) **Indexed:** Biol.Abstr., Curr.Cont.

616.6   UK   ISSN 0007-1331
                         CODEN: BJURAN
BRITISH JOURNAL OF UROLOGY. 1929. 12/yr. £90($160) (British Association of Urological Surgeons) Churchill Livingstone Medical Journals, Robert Stevenson House, 1-3 Baxter's Pl., Leith Walk, Edinburgh EH1 3AF, Scotland. TEL 031-556-2424. FAX 031-558-1278. TELEX 727511. (Subscr. to: Longman Group, Journals Dept., P.O. Box 77, Fourth Ave., Harlow, Essex CM19 5AA, England; U.S. subscr. to: Churchill Livingstone, 650 Ave. of the Americas, New York, NY 10011. TEL 212-206-5000) Ed. G.D. Chisholm. adv.; bk.rev.; abstr.; bibl.; illus.; index, cum.index; circ. 6,000. (also avail. in microform from UMI; back issues avail.) **Indexed:** Biol.Abstr., Chem.Abstr., Curr.Adv.Cancer Res., Curr.Adv.Ecol.Sci., Curr.Cont., Excerp.Med., Helminthol.Abstr., Ind.Med., Ind.Sci.Rev., Ind.Vet., INIS Atomind., NRN, Nutr.Abstr., Rev.Plant Path., Sci.Cit.Ind., Small Anim.Abstr.
●Also available online. Vendor(s): BRS.
—BLDSC shelfmark: 2326.100000.

616.6 618.92   SZ   ISSN 1012-6694
                         CODEN: CNUREW
CHILD NEPHROLOGY AND UROLOGY. (Text in English) 1980. q. 334 Fr.($223) S. Karger AG, Allschwilerstr. 10, P.O. Box, CH-4009 Basel, Switzerland. TEL 061-3061111. FAX 061-3061234. TELEX CH 962652. Ed. Carmelo Giordano. adv.; bk.rev.; index, cum.index; circ. 800. (back issues avail.) **Indexed:** Chem.Abstr, Curr.Cont., Excerp.Med., Ind.Med., Ind.Sci.Rev., Sci.Cit.Ind.
—BLDSC shelfmark: 3172.944790.
Formerly (until 1988): International Journal of Pediatric Nephrology (ISSN 0391-6510)

616.6   GW   ISSN 0301-0430
                         CODEN: CLNHBI
CLINICAL NEPHROLOGY. (Text in English) 1973. m. DM.324($162) Dustri-Verlag Dr. Karl Feistle, Bahnhofstr. 9, 8024 Deisenhofen, Germany. TEL 089-613861-0. FAX 089-613-5412. Ed. Dr. K.M. Koch. (reprint service avail. from SWZ) **Indexed:** Biol.Abstr., Chem.Abstr., Curr.Adv.Ecol.Sci., Curr.Cont., Excerp.Med., Ind.Med., Ind.Sci.Rev., INIS Atomind., Nutr.Abstr., Rev.Plant Path., Sci.Cit.Ind.
—BLDSC shelfmark: 3286.307100.

616.1   US
CLINICAL PRACTICE IN UROLOGY. 1982. irreg. price varies. Springer-Verlag, 175 Fifth Ave., New York, NY 10010. TEL 212-460-1500. (And Berlin, Heidelberg, Tokyo and Vienna) Ed. G.D. Chisholm.

616.6   US   ISSN 0899-837X
CONTEMPORARY DIALYSIS & NEPHROLOGY; the news and issues journal of the renal care field. 1980. m. $40. Contemporary Dialysis, Inc., 20335 Ventura Blvd., Ste. 400, Woodland Hills, CA 91364. TEL 818-704-5555. FAX 818-704-6500. TELEX 181545 CDLA. Ed. Rick Shively. adv.; bk.rev.; charts; illus.; stat.; index; circ. 18,339. (back issues avail.) **Indexed:** Chem.Abstr.
Formerly: Contemporary Dialysis (ISSN 0273-6535)

616.6   US
CONTEMPORARY NEPHROLOGY. 1981. biennial. price varies. Plenum Publishing Corp., 233 Spring St., New York, NY 10013-1578. TEL 212-620-8000. FAX 212-463-0742. TELEX 23-421139. Eds. Saulo Klahr, Shaul G. Massry. (back issues avail.)
Refereed Serial

616.6   US
CONTEMPORARY UROLOGY. 1989. m. $89 (foreign $105). Medical Economics Publishing Co., Five Paragon Dr., Montvale, NJ 07645. TEL 201-358-7200. FAX 201-573-1045. Ed. Deborah Kaplan. adv.; charts; illus.; index; circ. 9,075. (also avail. in microfilm; reprint service avail. from RPI)
Description: For office and hospital-based urologists. Includes news and features on solving clinical problems.
Refereed Serial

616.6   SZ   ISSN 0302-5144
                         CODEN: CNEPDD
CONTRIBUTIONS TO NEPHROLOGY. (Text in English) 1975. irreg. varies. S. Karger AG, Allschwilerstr. 10, P.O. Box, CH-4009 Basel, Switzerland. TEL 061-3061111. FAX 061-3061234. TELEX CH 962652. Eds. G.M. Benlyne, S. Giovannetti. (reprint service avail. from ISI) **Indexed:** Biol.Abstr., Chem.Abstr., CINAHL, Curr.Cont., Ind.Med.
—BLDSC shelfmark: 3461.035000.

616.6   US   ISSN 0148-4265
RC902.A1   CODEN: CUNED6
CURRENT NEPHROLOGY. 1977. a. $79.95. Mosby - Year Book, Inc. (Chicago) (Subsidiary of: Times Mirror Company), 200 N. LaSalle St., Chicago, IL 60601-1080. TEL 312-726-9733. FAX 312-726-6075. TELEX 206155. (Subscr. to: 11830 Westline Industrial Dr., St. Louis, MO 63146. TEL 800-325-4177) Ed. Harvey C. Gonick, M.D. illus. **Indexed:** Biol.Abstr., Chem.Abstr.
—BLDSC shelfmark: 3500.620000.
Description: Surveys developments in the field through a synopsis of the medical literature from the past twelve months.

616.6   US   ISSN 1052-4010
▼**CURRENT PROBLEMS IN UROLOGY.** 1991. bi-m. $65 to individuals (foreign $85); institutions $90 (foreign $110); students $39 (foreign $59). Mosby - Year Book, Inc. (Subsidiary of: Times Mirror Company), 11830 Westline Industrial Dr., St. Louis, MO 63146. TEL 800-325-4177. FAX 508-486-9423. Ed. Dr. Larry I. Lipshultz.
—BLDSC shelfmark: 3501.451500.
Description: Covers diseases and disorders seen in urologic practice.

616.6   GW   ISSN 0178-4625
DEUTSCHE GESELLSCHAFT FUER UROLOGIE. MITTEILUNGEN. 1985. q. DM.60. Demeter Verlag, Wuermstr. 13, 8032 Graefelfing, Germany. TEL 089-852033. FAX 089-8543347. circ. 4,400.
—BLDSC shelfmark: 3567.990000.

616.6   US
DEUTSCHE GESELLSCHAFT FUER UROLOGIE. VERHANDLUNGEN. 19th Session, 1962. irreg. price varies. Springer-Verlag, 175 Fifth Ave., New York, NY 10010. TEL 212-460-1500. (Also Berlin, Heidelberg, Tokyo and Vienna) (reprint service avail. from ISI)
Formerly: Deutsche Gesellschaft fuer Urologie. Verhandlungsbericht (ISSN 0070-413X)

DIALOGUES IN PEDIATRIC UROLOGY. see *MEDICAL SCIENCES — Pediatrics*

616.6   GW   ISSN 0724-0252
DER DIALYSEPATIENT; Zeitschrift fuer chronisch Nierenkranke. 1976. q. DM.35. (Dialysepatienten Deutschlands e.V.) Verlag Kirchheim und Co., Kaiserstr. 41, 6500 Mainz 1, Germany. TEL 06131-671081. FAX 06131-638843. adv.; bk.rev.; circ. 19,000.
Description: Covers nephrology in the areas of medicine, law and social services and welfare: for doctors, patients and medical personnel.

616.61   US   ISSN 0090-2934
                         CODEN: DITRD2
DIALYSIS & TRANSPLANTATION. 1972. m. $35. Creative Age Publications, 7628 Densmore Ave., Van Nuys, CA 91406-2088. TEL 818-782-7328. Ed. Marie Nordberg. adv.; charts; illus.; circ. 17,000. **Indexed:** Biol.Abstr., Curr.Adv.Ecol.Sci., Curr.Cont., Excerp.Med., Nutr.Abstr.
—BLDSC shelfmark: 3579.785000.
Refereed Serial

MEDICAL SCIENCES — UROLOGY AND NEPHROLOGY

616.6 SW
EUROPEAN COLLOQUIUM ON RENAL PHYSIOLOGY (PROCEEDINGS). (Supplement to: Uppsala Journal of Medical Sciences) 3rd, 1979. irreg. price varies. Almqvist & Wiksell International, Box 638, S-101 28 Stockholm, Sweden. Ed. Hans R. Ulfendahl.

616.6 SZ ISSN 0302-2838
CODEN: EUURAV
EUROPEAN UROLOGY. (Text in English) 8/yr. (in 2 vols.). 413 Fr.($276) per vol. (European Association of Urology) S. Karger AG, Allschwilerstr. 10, P.O. Box, CH-4009 Basel, Switzerland. TEL 061-3061111. FAX 061-3061234. TELEX CH 962652. Ed. C.C. Schulman. abstr.; index; circ. 1,400. (also avail. in microform from RPI) **Indexed:** Biol.Abstr., Chem.Abstr., Curr.Adv.Cell & Devel.Biol., Curr.Adv.Ecol.Sci., Curr.Cont., Excerp.Med., Helminthol.Abstr., Ind.Med., Ind.Sci.Rev., NRN, Sci.Cit.Ind.
—BLDSC shelfmark: 3830.370500.

616.6 US
FOR PATIENTS ONLY. 1988. bi-m. $17. Contemporary Dialysis, Inc., 20335 Ventura Blvd., Ste. 400, Woodland, CA 91364. TEL 818-704-6500. FAX 818-704-6500. adv.: B&W page $1715, color page $2540; trim 8 1/4 x 11 1/8. circ. 11,106.
Description: Brings professional understanding to patients living with chronic kidney disease. Covers patient-caregiver relationships, psychological issues, homecare and rehabilitation.

616.6 NE ISSN 0924-8455
CODEN: GNURE8
▼**GERIATRIC NEPHROLOGY AND UROLOGY.** (Text in English) 1991. 6/yr. fl.376($214) Kluwer Academic Publishers, Postbus 17, 3300 AA Dordrecht, Netherlands. TEL 078-334911. FAX 078-334254. TELEX 29245. (Dist. by: Kluwer Academic Publishers, P.O. Box 322, 3300 AH Dordrecht, Netherlands; N. America dist. addr.: Box 358, Accord Station, Hingham, MA 02018-0358. TEL 617-871-6600) Ed. Dimitros G. Oreopoulos.
—BLDSC shelfmark: 4161.697000.

616.6 IT ISSN 0394-9362
GIORNALE DI TECHNICHE NEFROLOGICHE E DIALITICHE. q. L.90000($90) (effective 1992). Wichtig Editore s.r.l., Via Friuli, 72-74, 20135 Milan, Italy. TEL 02-5452306. FAX 02-5451843.

616.6 IT ISSN 0393-5590
GIORNALE ITALIANO DI NEFROLOGIA. (Text in Italian; summaries in English) q. L.140000($140) (effective 1992). Wichtig Editore s.r.l., Via Friuli, 72-74, 20135 Milan, Italy. TEL 02-5452306. FAX 02-5451843.
—BLDSC shelfmark: 4178.233000.

616.6 GW ISSN 0935-8234
HAEUSLICHE PFLEGE; mit Kontinenztraining. q. DM.28. Verlag fuer Medizin Dr. Ewald Fischer, Fritz-Frey-Str. 21, Postfach 105767, 6900 Heidelberg 1, Germany. TEL 06221-4062-0. FAX 06221-400727. Ed. Peter Mand.

616.6 360 AT
HARICOT; newsletter for the renal patients of Australia. 1983. q. free. P.O. Box 3, Diamond Creek, Vic. 3089, Australia. Eds. J. Coleman, S. Evans. bk.rev.; circ. 1,500. (back issues avail.)

I C R D B CANCERGRAM: GENITOURINARY CANCERS - DIAGNOSIS, TREATMENT. see *MEDICAL SCIENCES — Abstracting, Bibliographies, Statistics*

616.6 GR ISSN 0074-3771
INTERNATIONAL CONGRESS OF NEPHROLOGY. ABSTRACTS OF REPORTS AND COMMUNICATIONS.* 1960. irreg., 4th, 1969, Stockholm. International Society of Nephrology, c/o Prof. Papadimitriou, Hopital Sainte Sophia, Thessalolinki, Greece. **Indexed:** Chem.Abstr.

616.65 UK ISSN 0105-6263
CODEN: IJANDP
INTERNATIONAL JOURNAL OF ANDROLOGY. (Text in English) bi-m. £87.50($159.50) Blackwell Scientific Publications Ltd., Osney Mead, Oxford OX2 OEL, England. TEL 0865-240201. FAX 0865-721205. TELEX 83355-MEDBOK-G. Ed. N.E. Skakkebaek. illus.; index. **Indexed:** Anim.Breed.Abstr., Biol.Abstr., Chem.Abstr., Curr.Adv.Ecol.Sci., Dent.Ind., Excerp.Med., Ind.Med., Ind.Vet., Protozool.Abstr., Sci.Cit.Ind., Small Anim.Abstr., Vet.Bull.
—BLDSC shelfmark: 4542.080000.

616.65 UK ISSN 0106-1607
CODEN: IJSPDJ
INTERNATIONAL JOURNAL OF ANDROLOGY. SUPPLEMENT. 1978. irreg. price varies. Blackwell Scientific Publications Ltd., Osney Mead, Oxford OX2 OEL, England. illus. **Indexed:** Biol.Abstr., Chem.Abstr.

616.6 FR ISSN 0074-8579
INTERNATIONAL SOCIETY OF UROLOGY. REPORTS OF CONGRESS. (Reports published in host country) irreg., 17th, 1975, Madrid. International Society of Urology, c/o Prof. Rene Kuess, 63 Ave. Niel, 75017 Paris, France.

616.6 HU ISSN 0301-1623
CODEN: IURNAE
INTERNATIONAL UROLOGY AND NEPHROLOGY. (Text in English) 1969. bi-m. DM.458. (Magyar Tudomanyos Akademia) Akademiai Kiado, Publishing House of the Hungarian Academy of Sciences, P.O. Box 24, H-1363 Budapest, Hungary. (Co-publisher: V S P, P.O. Box 346, 3700 AH Zeist, Netherlands. TEL 03404-25790) Eds. A. Babics, Z. Szendroi. adv.; bk.rev. **Indexed:** Biol.Abstr., Chem.Abstr., Curr.Cont., Excerp.Med., Ind.Med., INIS Atomind.
—BLDSC shelfmark: 4551.568000.
Formerly: Urology and Nephrology (ISSN 0042-1162)

616.6 JA ISSN 0021-5287
CODEN: NGKZA6
JAPANESE JOURNAL OF UROLOGY/NIHON HINYOKIKA GAKKAI ZASSHI. (Text in Japanese; summaries in English) 1911. m. $130. Japanese Urological Association, Faculty of Medicine - Nihon Hinyokika Gakkai, Taisei Bldg., 3-14-10 Hongo, Bunkyo-ku, Tokyo 113, Japan. FAX 03-3814-4117. Ed. Y. Aso. adv.; circ. 5,500. (also avail. in microform from UMI; reprint service avail. from UMI) **Indexed:** C.I.S. Abstr., Curr.Cont., Excerp.Med., Ind.Med.
—BLDSC shelfmark: 4659.050000.

616.6 GW ISSN 0178-7527
JATROS UROLOGIE. 1986. 12/yr. DM.150. P M I Verlag GmbH, August-Schanz-Str. 21, 6000 Frankfurt a.M. 50, Germany. TEL 069-5480000. FAX 069-548000-77. Ed. Peter Hoffmann. circ. 2,500. (back issues avail.)
Description: A seminar paper journal with summaries of original articles, interviews and congress reports.

JIN TO TOSEKI. see *MEDICAL SCIENCES*

616.6 FR ISSN 0248-0018
CODEN: JOURDD
JOURNAL D'UROLOGIE. 1912. 8/yr. 205 ECU($253) (typically set in Jan.). (Association Francaise d'Urologie) Masson, 120 bd. Saint-Germain, 75280 Paris Cedex 06, France. TEL 1-46-34-21-60. FAX 1-45-87-29-99. TELEX 202 671 F. Ed. D. Burton. adv.; bk.rev.; abstr.; illus.; index; circ. 2,100. (also avail. in microform from UMI; reprint service avail. from ISI) **Indexed:** Chem.Abstr., Curr.Adv.Cancer Res., Excerp.Med., Helminthol.Abstr., Ind.Med., Ind.Sci.Rev., Nutr.Abstr., Sci.Cit.Ind.
—BLDSC shelfmark: 5071.799950.
Formerly: Journal d'Urologie et de Nephrologie (ISSN 0021-8200)

616.1 US ISSN 0733-2459
CODEN: JCAPES
JOURNAL OF CLINICAL APHERESIS. 1982. q. $124 (foreign $174). (American Society for Apheresis) John Wiley & Sons, Inc., Journals, 605 Third Ave., New York, NY 10158. TEL 212-850-6000. FAX 212-850-6088. TELEX 12-7063. Ed.Bd. (also avail. in microfilm) **Indexed:** Excerp.Med., Ind.Med.
—BLDSC shelfmark: 4958.381500.
Description: Examines research articles on all topics relating to apheresis: plasmapheresis, lymphoplasmapheresis, and cytapheresis, including experimental and technical developments.
Refereed Serial

616.6 US ISSN 0892-7790
CODEN: JENDE3
JOURNAL OF ENDOUROLOGY. q. $140 (foreign $180). (Endourological Society) Mary Ann Liebert, Inc., 1651 Third Ave., New York, NY 10128. TEL 212-289-2300. FAX 212-289-4697. Eds. Drs. Ralph V. Clayman, Arthur D. Smith.
—BLDSC shelfmark: 4978.210000.
Description: Covers topics including percutaneous renal and ureteral procedures, ureteroscopy for diagnostic and therapeutic indications, endoscopic use of lasers, and extracorporeal lithotripsy of renal and ureteral stones.
Refereed Serial

JOURNAL OF RENAL NUTRITION. see *NUTRITION AND DIETETICS*

616.6 US ISSN 0022-5347
RC870 CODEN: JOURAA
JOURNAL OF UROLOGY. 1917. m. $150 to individuals; institutions $170. (American Urological Association) Williams & Wilkins, 428 E. Preston St., Baltimore, MD 21202. TEL 301-528-4000. FAX 301-528-4312. TELEX 87669. Ed. Dr. John T. Grayhack. adv.; bibl.; illus.; index; circ. 17,300. (also avail. in microform) **Indexed:** Biol.Abstr., Biotech.Abstr., C.I.S.Abstr., Chem.Abstr., Curr.Adv.Cancer Res., Curr.Adv.Cell & Devel.Biol., Curr.Adv.Ecol.Sci., Curr.Adv.Genetics & Molec.Biol., Curr.Cont., Excerp.Med., Helminthol.Abstr., Ind.Med., Ind.Sci.Rev., INIS Atomind., Int.Nurs.Ind., Nutr.Abstr., Rev.Plant Path.
—BLDSC shelfmark: 5071.900000.
Incorporates (in Jan. 1982): Investigation Urology (ISSN 0021-0005); Urological Survey (ISSN 0042-1146)
Description: Clinical papers, abstracts, commentary, research and new techniques for the urologist.
Refereed Serial

616.6 US ISSN 0023-1304
CODEN: KIDNA
KIDNEY. 1968. bi-m. $25. National Kidney Foundation, 30 East 33rd St., New York, NY 10016. TEL 212-889-2210. Ed. Dr. Thomas Ferris. charts; illus.; circ. 8,000. (looseleaf format) **Indexed:** Biol.Abstr., Excerp.Med.
—BLDSC shelfmark: 5094.200000.
Refereed Serial

616.6 US
▼**KIDNEY (NEW YORK, 1992)**; a current survey of world literature. 1992. bi-m. Springer-Verlag, 175 Fifth Ave., New York, NY 10010. TEL 212-460-1500. FAX 212-473-6272. (Also Berlin, Heidelberg, Tokyo and Vienna) adv.: B&W page $650, color page $1525; trim 8 1/4 x 11. circ. 3,000.
Description: For clinicians and specialists in nephrology and related fields.

616.6 US
KIDNEY DISEASES. 1979. irreg., vol.9, 1991. price varies. Marcel Dekker, Inc., 270 Madison Ave., New York, NY 10016. TEL 212-696-9000. FAX 212-685-4540. TELEX 421419. **Indexed:** Chem.Abstr.
Refereed Serial

616.6 US ISSN 0085-2538
RC902.A1 CODEN: KDYIA5
KIDNEY INTERNATIONAL. 1972. 12/yr. (in 2 vols., 6 nos./vol.). $460 (effective 1992). (International Society of Nephrology) Blackwell Scientific Publications Inc., Three Cambridge Center, Ste. 208, Cambridge, MA 02142-1413. TEL 617-225-0401. FAX 617-225-0412. Ed. Dr. Thomas E. Andreoli. adv.; circ. 7,250. (also avail. in microform from UMI; reprint service avail. from ISI) **Indexed:** Biol.Abstr., Chem.Abstr., Curr.Adv.Ecol.Sci., Curr.Cont., Dairy Sci.Abstr., Excerp.Med., Ind.Med., Ind.Sci.Rev., Nutr.Abstr.
—BLDSC shelfmark: 5094.300000.
Description: Provides current information on renal physiology, biochemistry, pathology, immunology and morphology.

616.6 US ISSN 0098-6577
KIDNEY INTERNATIONAL. SUPPLEMENT. 1974. irreg., vol.14, 1983. price varies (free to subscribers of Kidney International). Springer-Verlag, Journals, 175 Fifth Ave., New York, NY 10010. TEL 212-460-1500. (Also Berlin, Heidelberg, Vienna) (reprint service avail. from ISI) **Indexed:** Biol.Abstr., Chem.Abstr., Ind.Med., Nutr.Abstr.

MEDICAL SCIENCES — UROLOGY AND NEPHROLOGY

616.6 UK
KIDNEY RESEARCH NEWS. 1974. s-a. free. National Kidney Research Fund, 184b Station Rd., Harrow, London HA1 2RH, England. Ed. John F. Ringrose. circ. 9,000.
Formerly: Kidney Research Fund Newsletter.

616.6 GW ISSN 0174-2752
CODEN: KEURDM
KLINISCHE UND EXPERIMENTELLE UROLOGIE. (Each edition has distinctive title) 1980. irreg., vol.21, 1989. DM.58. W. Zuckschwerdt Verlag GmbH, Kronwinklerstr. 24, 8000 Munich 60, Germany. TEL 089-864949-0. FAX 089-86494950. Ed. G. Kleinhans. circ. 1,000. (back issues avail.)
—BLDSC shelfmark: 5099.490000.

616.6 IT
MINERVA UROLOGICA E NEFROLOGICA. (Text in Italian; summaries in English) 1949. q. L.60000($70) Edizioni Minerva Medica, Corso Bramante 83-85, 10126 Turin, Italy. Eds. R. Marten-Perolino, G. Sesia. adv.; bk.rev.; bibl.; charts; illus.; index; circ. 3,000. **Indexed:** Biol.Abstr., Chem.Abstr., Excerp.Med., Ind.Med.
Formed by the merger of: Minerva Urologica (ISSN 0026-4989) & Minerva Nefrologica (ISSN 0026-4873)

MODERN TECHNICS IN SURGERY. UROLOGIC SURGERY.
see MEDICAL SCIENCES — Surgery

616.6 US
▼**N N & I - E S R D PRODUCT AND SERVICE DIRECTORY.** 1991. a. Nephrology News and Issues, Inc., 13901 N. 73rd St., Ste. 214, Scottsdale, AZ 85260. TEL 602-443-4638. FAX 602-443-4528. Ed. Mark E. Newmann. adv.; circ. 3,000.

616.6 US ISSN 0077-5096
NATIONAL KIDNEY FOUNDATION. ANNUAL REPORT. 1957. a. free. National Kidney Foundation, 30 E. 33rd St., New York, NY 10016. TEL 212-889-2210.

616.6 SZ ISSN 0250-4960
CODEN: NEPHDY
NEPHROLOGIE. (Text in French) 1980. q. 80 SFr.($58) Editions Medecine et Hygiene, Case Postale 456, CH-1211 Geneva 4, Switzerland. TEL 022-469355. FAX 022-475610. adv.; bk.rev.; circ. 1,100. **Indexed:** Biol.Abstr., Excerp.Med., Ind.Med.
—BLDSC shelfmark: 6075.677000.

616.6 GW ISSN 0931-0509
CODEN: NDTREA
NEPHROLOGY, DIALYSIS AND TRANSPLANTATION. 1986. 12/yr. DM.362($235) (European Dialysis and Transplant Association) Springer-Verlag, Heidelberger Platz 3, D-1000 Berlin 33, Germany. TEL 030-8207-1. (Also Heidelberg, Tokyo, Vienna, and New York) (Co-sponsor: European Renal Association) Ed. A.M. Davison.

616.6 US ISSN 0896-1263
CODEN: NNISES
NEPHROLOGY NEWS & ISSUES. 1987. m. $45. Nephrology News & Issues, Inc., 13901 N. 73rd St., Ste. 214, Scottsdale, AR 85260. TEL 602-443-4635. FAX 602-443-4528. Ed. Mark E. Neumann. circ. 13,000.
—BLDSC shelfmark: 6075.685600.

616.6 SZ ISSN 0028-2766
CODEN: NPRNAY
NEPHRON. (Text in English) 1964. m. (3 vols./yr.). 334 Fr.($223) per vol. S. Karger AG, Allschwilerstr. 10, P.O. Box, CH-4009 Basel, Switzerland. TEL 061-3061111. FAX 061-3061234. TELEX CH 962652. Eds. G. M. Berlyne, S. Giovannetti. adv.; charts; illus.; index; circ. 3,000. (also avail. in microform from RPI) **Indexed:** Biol.Abstr., Chem.Abstr., Curr.Adv.Cancer Res., Curr.Adv.Ecol.Sci., Curr.Cont., Dent.Ind., Excerp.Med., Helminthol.Abstr., Ind.Med., Ind.Sci.Rev., Nutr.Abstr.
—BLDSC shelfmark: 6075.690000.

616.6 US ISSN 0733-2467
NEUROUROLOGY AND URODYNAMICS. 1982. bi-m. $258 (foreign $333). Journals, New York, NY 10158. TEL 212-850-6000. FAX 212-850-6088. TELEX 12-7063. Ed. Jerry G. Blaivas. bk.rev. (also avail. in microfilm) **Indexed:** Biol.Abstr., Chem.Abstr., Curr.Adv.Ecol.Sci., Curr.Cont., Excerp.Med.
—BLDSC shelfmark: 6081.589000.
Description: Provides multidisciplinary coverage of recent developments in the study of the urinary tract function.
Refereed Serial

616.6 GW ISSN 0176-5183
NIERENPATIENT; Journal fuer das nephrologische Team. (Text in German; summaries in English and German) 1983. q. DM.20($15) Wolfgang Pabst Verlag, Am Eichengrund 28, 4540 Lengerich, Germany. TEL 05484-308. FAX 05481-7587. Ed. Wolfgang Pabst. adv.; bk.rev.; circ. 11,600. (back issues avail.)
Description: Original articles and case reports on nephrology and dialysis.

616.6 JA ISSN 0029-0726
NISHINIHON JOURNAL OF UROLOGY/NISHI NIHON HINYOKIKA. (Text in Japanese; summaries in English) 1969. bi-m. 3000 Yen. Kyushu University, Faculty of Medicine, Department of Urology, Maidashi 3-1-1, Higashi-ku, Fukuoka 812, Japan. Ed. Shunro Momose. adv.; bk.rev.; circ. 1,300. **Indexed:** Biol.Abstr.
—BLDSC shelfmark: 6113.604000.

616.6 DK ISSN 0108-2388
NYRENYT; medlemsblad. 1981. 6/yr. DKK 75. Nyreforeningen, Valbyvej 20, 2630 Taastrup, Denmark. TEL 4252 4252. FAX 43-71-00-96. Ed. Poul Joergensen. adv.; bk.rev.; illus.
Formerly: Dialyse og Transplantation (ISSN 0108-2779)

616.6 GW ISSN 0931-041X
CODEN: PEDNEF
PEDIATRIC NEPHROLOGY. 1987. 6/yr. DM.478($281) (International Pediatric Nephrology Association) Springer-Verlag, Heidelberger Platz 3, D-1000 Berlin 33, Germany. TEL 030-8207-1. (Also Heidelberg, Tokyo, Vienna, and New York) Ed. A.M. Robson.
—BLDSC shelfmark: 6417.603000.
Description: Laboratory and clinical research of acute and chronic diseases that affect renal function in children.

PERITONEAL DIALYSIS INTERNATIONAL. see MEDICAL SCIENCES

616.6 US ISSN 0889-471X
RC870 CODEN: PRUREX
PROBLEMS IN UROLOGY. 1987. q. $70 to individuals (foreign $90); institutions $95 (foreign $110). J.B. Lippincott Co., E. Washington Sq., Philadelphia, PA 19105. TEL 215-238-4200. Ed. David F. Paulson. circ. 1,500. (also avail. in microform from UMI)
—BLDSC shelfmark: 6617.941500.
Refereed Serial

616.6 US ISSN 0886-022X
CODEN: REFAE8
RENAL FAILURE. 1977. 4/yr. $130 to individuals; institutions $260. Marcel Dekker Journals, 270 Madison Ave., New York, NY 10016. TEL 212-696-9000. FAX 212-685-4540. TELEX 421419 MARDEEK. (Subscr. to: Box 10018, Church St. Sta., New York, NY 10249) Ed. William F. Finn. (also avail. in microform from RPI) **Indexed:** Biol.Abstr., Chem.Abstr., Curr.Cont., Excerp.Med., Ind.Med., Ind.Sci.Rev., INIS Atomind., Sci.Cit.Ind.
—BLDSC shelfmark: 7356.869800.
Former titles: Uremia Investigation; Clinical and Experimental Dialysis and Apheresis (ISSN 0276-5497); (until 1981): Journal of Dialysis (ISSN 0362-8558)
Refereed Serial

612 UK ISSN 0300-3434
RENAL PHYSIOLOGY. 1970. s-m. £100. Sheffield University Biomedical Information Service (SUBIS), The University, Sheffield S10 2TN, England. TEL 0742-768555. FAX 0742-739826. TELEX 547216-UGSHEF-G. **Indexed:** Biol.Abstr., Chem.Abstr., Ind.Med.
Description: Current awareness service for researchers. Covers the structure and function of kidneys, immunology, toxicology, pharmacology.

616.6 SZ ISSN 1011-6524
CODEN: RPBIEL
RENAL PHYSIOLOGY AND BIOCHEMISTRY; international journal of experimental renal physiology, pathophysiology, biochemistry and pharmacology. 1979. bi-m. 398 Fr.($266) S. Karger AG, Allschwilerstr. 10, P.O. Box, CH-4009 Basel, Switzerland. TEL 061-3061111. FAX 061-3061234. TELEX CH 962652. Eds. G.M. Berlyne, F. Lang. adv.; illus.; index; circ. 800. (also avail. in microfilm; back issues avail.) **Indexed:** Biol.Abstr., Curr.Adv.Ecol.Sci., Curr.Cont., Excerp.Med.
—BLDSC shelfmark: 7356.880500.
Formerly (until 1989): Renal Physiology (ISSN 0378-5858)

616.6 UK ISSN 0142-8357
RENAL TRANSPLANTATION AND DIALYSIS. 1971. m. £65. Sheffield University Biomedical Information Service (SUBIS), The University, Sheffield S10 2TN, England. TEL 0742-768555. FAX 0742-739826. TELEX 547216-UGSHEF-G.
Description: Current awareness service for researchers. Studies dialysis, artificial kidneys and peritoneal dialysis.

616.6 BO ISSN 1018-5321
▼**REVISTA BOLIVIANA DE NEFROLOGIA.** 1990. s-a. free. Sociedad Boliviana de Nefrologia, Casilla Correo 6, Sucre, Bolivia. TEL 591-064-23282. FAX 591-064-25559. Ed. Antonio Dubravcic L. adv.; charts; illus.; stat.; circ. 500.

616.6 JA ISSN 0385-2393
RINSHO HINYOKIKA/JAPANESE JOURNAL OF CLINICAL UROLOGY. (Text in Japanese; summaries in English) 1967. m. 24720 Yen($190) Igaku-Shoin Ltd., 5-25-3 Hongo, Bunkyo-ku, Tokyo 113-91, Japan. TEL 03-817-5709. Ed. Bd. circ. 4,000.
—BLDSC shelfmark: 4651.450000.

616.6 SW ISSN 0036-5599
CODEN: SJUNAS
SCANDINAVIAN JOURNAL OF UROLOGY AND NEPHROLOGY. (Supplements avail.) (Text in English) 1967. 4/yr. SEK 600 (free to subscribers of Acta Chirurgica Scandinavica). (Scandinavian Association of Urology) Almqvist & Wiksell Periodical Company, Box 638, S-101 28 Stockholm, Sweden. Ed. A. Fritjofsson. adv.; charts; illus.; circ. 2,600. **Indexed:** ASCA, Biol.Abstr., Biotech.Abstr., Chem.Abstr., Curr.Adv.Ecol.Sci., Curr.Cont., Excerp.Med., Ind.Med., Nutr.Abstr.
—BLDSC shelfmark: 8087.560000.

616.6 US
SEMINARS IN DIALYSIS. q. Williams & Wilkins, 428 E. Preston St., Baltimore, MD 21202. TEL 301-528-4000. FAX 301-528-4452. Ed. Richard Sherman. circ. 3,000.

616.6 US ISSN 0270-9295
CODEN: SNEPDJ
SEMINARS IN NEPHROLOGY. 1981. q. $101 to individuals; institutions $140; foreign $159. W.B. Saunders Co. (Subsidiary of: Harcourt Brace Jovanovich, Inc.), Curtis Center, Independence Square W., Philadelphia, PA 19106. TEL 215-238-7800. (Subscr. to: 6277 Sea Harbor Dr., 4th Fl., Orlando FL 32891) Ed. Neil Kurtzman, M.D. adv.; bibl.; charts; illus.; index. **Indexed:** ASCA, Chem.Abstr., Curr.Cont., Sci.Cit.Ind.
●Also available online.
—BLDSC shelfmark: 8239.455200.

616.6 US ISSN 0730-9147
SEMINARS IN UROLOGY. 1983. q. $68 to individuals; institutions $89; foreign $106. W.B. Saunders Co. (Subsidiary of: Harcourt Brace Jovanovich, Inc.), Curtis Center, Independence Square W., Philadelphia, PA 19106. TEL 215-238-7800. Ed. E. Darracott Vaughan, Jr., M.D. adv.; bibl.; charts; illus.; index. **Indexed:** Ind.Med.
—BLDSC shelfmark: 8239.486000.

616.6 US
TORCHBEARER. 1973. s-a. free. American Kidney Fund, 6110 Executive Blvd., Ste. 1010, Rockville, MD 20852-3903. TEL 301-881-3052. FAX 301-881-0898. Eds. Anna E. Monsef, Kathleen Richmond. illus.; circ. 40,000.
Description: Features articles on patients who have benefited from AKF programs. Provides the general public with information on AKF activities as well as kidney disease and its treatment.

3390 MEETINGS AND CONGRESSES

616.6 US
URO-GRAM. 1976. bi-m. membership. American Urological Association Allied, 11512 Allecingie Pkwy., Richmond, VA 23235. TEL 804-379-1306. FAX 804-379-1386. Ed. Paula M. Smith. circ. 2,500.
Description: Urology health care workers update providing information, news and events of the Association.

616.6 GW ISSN 0938-8184
▼**URO-IMAGING;** Zeitschrift fuer Bildgebende Systeme in der Urologie. 1991. q. DM.198. Urban und Vogel, Lindwurmstr. 95, Postfach 152209, 8000 Munich 2, Germany. TEL 089-53292-0. FAX 089-53292-100. circ. 1,500.

616.6 IT ISSN 1120-5989
▼**URODINAMICA, NEUROUROLOGY, URODYNAMICS AND CONTINENCE.** (Text in English) 1991. q. L.80000($80) Editrice Kurtis s.r.l., Via L. Zoja, 30, 20153 Milan, Italy. TEL 02-48202740. FAX 02-48201219. Ed. W. Artibani.
Description: Publishes original articles on urodynamics and related research.

616.6 GW ISSN 0340-2592
CODEN: URGABW
DER UROLOGE. SECTION A; Zeitschrift fuer klinische und praktische Urologie. (Text in German; summaries in English, German) 1962. 6/yr. DM.328($184) (Deutsche Gesellschaft fuer Urologie) Springer-Verlag, Heidelberger Platz 3, D-1000 Berlin 33, Germany. TEL 030-8207-1. (Also Heidelberg, Tokyo, Vienna, and New York) Ed. R. Hautmann. adv.; bk.rev.; abstr.; charts; illus.; index, cum.index: 1962-1969. (Also avail. in microform from UMI; back issues avail.; reprint service avail. from ISI) **Indexed:** Curr.Cont., Excerp.Med., Helminthol.Abstr., Ind.Med.
—BLDSC shelfmark: 9124.410000.
Formerly: Urologe-Ausgabe A (ISSN 0042-1103)

616.6 GW
DER UROLOGE. SECTION B. 1961. 6/yr. DM.348($196) (Berufsverband der Deutschen Urologen) Springer-Verlag, Heidelberger Platz 3, D-1000 Berlin 33, Germany. TEL 030-8207-1. (Also Heidelberg, Tokyo, Vienna, and New York) Ed. W. Knipper. adv.; charts; illus.; index. (also avail. in microform from UMI; back issues avail.; reprint service avail. from ISI) **Indexed:** Curr.Cont., Excerp.Med., Helminthol.Abstr.
Former titles: Urologe-Ausgabe B (ISSN 0042-1111); Urologische Facharzt.

616.6 IT ISSN 0042-112X
UROLOGIA. (Supplements avail.) (Text in English, French, German, Italian, Spanish) 1934. bi-m. L.110000($100) Libreria Editrice Canova, Viale della Liberazione 40, 31030 Dosso di Casier (Treviso), Italy. Ed. Vittorio Scrufari. adv.; bk.rev.; charts; illus.; index; circ. 1,300. **Indexed:** Biol.Abstr., Chem.Abstr., Excerp.Med.

616.6 SZ ISSN 0042-1138
CODEN: URINAC
UROLOGIA INTERNATIONALIS. (Text in English) 1955. 8/yr (in 2 vols.). 439 Fr.($293) per vol. S. Karger AG, Allschwilerstr. 10, P.O. Box, CH-4009 Basel, Switzerland. TEL 061-3061111. FAX 061-3061234. TELEX CH 962652. Ed. D. Hauri. adv.; bk.rev.; bibl.; charts; illus.; index; circ. 1,000. (also avail. in microform from RPI) **Indexed:** Biol.Abstr., Chem.Abstr., Curr.Cont., Excerp.Med., Helminthol.Abstr., Ind.Med.
—BLDSC shelfmark: 9124.480000.

616.6 US ISSN 0094-0143
CODEN: UCNADW
UROLOGIC CLINICS OF NORTH AMERICA. 1974. q. $86. W.B. Saunders Co., Curtis Center, Independence Square W., Philadelphia, PA 19106. TEL 215-238-7800. Ed. Livia Berardi. (also avail. in microform from MIM,UMI; reprint service avail. from UMI, ISI) **Indexed:** Biol.Abstr., Curr.Cont., Dent.Ind., Excerp.Med., Ind.Med.
—BLDSC shelfmark: 9124.620000.

616.6 610.73 US
UROLOGIC NURSING. 1980. q. $30. Mosby - Year Book, Inc. (Subsidiary of: Times Mirror Company), 11830 Westline Industrial Dr., St. Louis, MO 63146. TEL 314-872-8370. FAX 314-431-1380. Ed. Patricia Bates. adv.; circ. 2,610.
Description: For nurses, technicians, and allied health care professionals.

616.6 615.8 US ISSN 0171-1091
UROLOGIC RADIOLOGY; a journal of diagnostic imaging and interventional uroradiology. 1979. 4/yr. $119. Springer-Verlag, Journals, 175 Fifth Ave., New York, NY 10010. TEL 212-460-1500. (Also Berlin, Heidelberg, Tokyo, Vienna) Ed. J. Becker. circ. 799. (also avail. in microform from UMI; reprint service avail. from ISI) **Indexed:** Curr.Cont., Excerp.Med., Ind.Med.
—BLDSC shelfmark: 9124.630000.

616.6 GW ISSN 0300-5623
CODEN: URLRA5
UROLOGICAL RESEARCH; journal of clinical and laboratory investigation. (Text and summaries in English) 1973. 6/yr. DM.428($218) Springer-Verlag, Heidelberger Platz 3, D-1000 Berlin 33, Germany. TEL 030-8207-1. (Also Heidelberg, Tokyo, Vienna, and New York) Ed. R. Ackermann. adv.; charts; index. (also avail. in microform from UMI; reprint service avail. from ISI) **Indexed:** Chem.Abstr., Curr.Adv.Cancer Res., Curr.Cont., Excerp.Med., Ind.Med.
—BLDSC shelfmark: 9124.650000.

616.6 GW ISSN 0936-9732
UROLOGIE POSTER; Fortschritte in Wissenschaft und Praxis. 1989. q. DM.96. Demeter Verlag, Wuermstr. 13, 8032 Graefelfing, Germany. TEL 089-852033. FAX 089-8543347. TELEX 524068-DELTA-D. Ed.Bd. adv. contact: Hermann Krieger.
—BLDSC shelfmark: 9124.701000.

616.6 GW
UROLOGISCHE ONKOLOGIE. (Text in German; summaries in English) 1980. irreg. DM.58. W. Zuckschwerdt Verlag GmbH, Kronwinklerstr. 24, 8000 Munich 60, Germany. TEL 089-864949-0. FAX 089-86494950. Ed.Bd. circ. 2,500. (back issues avail.)
Description: Articles on chemotherapy and radiotherapy, hormonal therapy, immunotherapy, genito-urinary carcinoma.

616.6 RU ISSN 0042-1154
CODEN: URNEAA
UROLOGIYA I NEFROLOGIYA/UROLOGY AND NEPHROLOGY. (Text in Russian; summaries in English) 1923. bi-m. 13.80 Rub.($10.20) (Vsesoyuznoe Nauchnoe Obshchestvo Urologov) Izdatel'stvo Meditsina, Petroverigskii pereulok 6-8, 101838 Moscow, Russia. (Co-sponsor: Ministerstvo Zdravookhraneniya S.S.S.R.) Ed. N.A. Lopatkin. bk.rev.; bibl. **Indexed:** Biol.Abstr., Chem.Abstr., Excerp.Med., Ind.Med.
—BLDSC shelfmark: 0385.120000.
Description: Reports on the advances of Soviet and foreign medicine in the domain of urology and nephrology.

616.6 US ISSN 0090-4295
RC870 CODEN: URGYA
UROLOGY. 1973. m. $75 to individuals (foreign $120); institutions $110 (foreign $140). Cahners Publishing Company (New York), Medical-Health Care Group (Subsidiary of: Reed International PLC), Division of Reed Publishing (USA) Inc., 249 W. 17th St., New York, NY 10011. TEL 212-645-0067. FAX 212-463-6700. (Subscr. to: Box 633, Holmes, PA 19043) Eds. Dr. Pablo A. Morales, Mary Politano. adv.; bk.rev.; abstr.; bibl.; charts; stat.; circ. 7,500. (also avail. in microform; reprint service avail. from UMI, ISI) **Indexed:** Biol.Abstr., Curr.Adv.Cancer Res., Curr.Adv.Ecol.Sci., Curr.Cont., Dent.Ind., Excerp.Med., Ind.Med., Nutr.Abstr., Rev.Plant Path.
—BLDSC shelfmark: 9124.703000.
Description: For hospital based and private practice physicians. Contains original scientific reports, case reports and review updates.
Refereed Serial

616.6 IT ISSN 0391-5603
UROLOGY. (Text in English, French, German, Italian; summaries in English, Italian) 1934. bi-m. L.130,000. Urologia, Viale della Liberazione 40, 31030 Dosson di Casier (Treviso), Italy. Ed. Vittorio Scrufari. adv.; bk.rev.; circ. 700. (back issues avail.)
—BLDSC shelfmark: 9124.460000.

616.6 US ISSN 0889-6283
RC870
UROLOGY ANNUAL. 1987. a. $75. Appleton & Lange (Subsidiary of: Simon & Schuster Company), 25 Van Zant St., Box 5630, Norwalk, CT 06856. TEL 203-838-4400. Ed. Stephen N. Rous, M.D.
—BLDSC shelfmark: 9124.706000.

616.6 US ISSN 0093-9722
UROLOGY TIMES. 1973. m. $60. Avanstar Communications, Inc., 7500 Old Oak Blvd., Cleveland, OH 44130. TEL 216-243-8100. FAX 216-891-2726. (Subscr. to: 1 E. First St., Duluth, MN 55802) Ed. Dean Celia. circ. 8,957.
Description: News for office-based urologists and osteopathic urologists.

616.6 US ISSN 0724-4983
WORLD JOURNAL OF UROLOGY. 1983. q. DM.158($87) Springer-Verlag, Journals, 175 Fifth Ave., New York, NY 10010. TEL 212-460-1500. (And Berlin, Heidelberg, Tokyo and Vienna) Eds. U. Jonas, R.J. Krane. adv.; bk.rev.; charts; illus. (reprint service avail. from ISI) **Indexed:** Curr.Adv.Ecol.Sci., Curr.Cont.
—BLDSC shelfmark: 9356.074500.

616.6 US
▼**YEAR BOOK OF NEPHROLOGY.** 1991. a. $69.95. Mosby - Year Book, Inc. (Chicago) (Subsidiary of: Times Mirror Company), 200 N. LaSalle St., Chicago, IL 60601-1080. TEL 312-726-9733. FAX 312-726-6075. TELEX 206155. Ed. Dr. Fredric L. Coe. illus.
●Also available online. Vendor(s): BRS.

616.6 US ISSN 0084-4071
YEAR BOOK OF UROLOGY. 1933. a. $57.95. Mosby - Year Book, Inc., Continuity Division, 200 N. LaSalle, Chicago, IL 60601. TEL 312-726-9733. FAX 312-726-6075. Eds. Drs. Jay Y. Gillenwater, Stuart S. Howards. illus. (reprint service avail.) **Indexed:** Curr.Adv.Ecol.Sci.
●Also available online. Vendor(s): BRS.
—BLDSC shelfmark: 9417.500000.

MEETINGS AND CONGRESSES

578 011 US ISSN 0569-2628
SF97 CODEN: OPFMAG
A A F M PROCEEDINGS OF ANNUAL MEETING. 1952. a. $25. American Association of Feed Microscopists, c/o Patricia Ramsey, Secy.-Treas., 3292 Meadowview Rd., Sacramento, CA 95832. TEL 916-427-4997. Ed. Janet Windsor. circ. 300.

A P S A NEWSLETTER. (Australasian Political Studies Association) see *POLITICAL SCIENCE*

A P S S NEWSLETTER. (Association of Professional Sleep Societies) see *MEDICAL SCIENCES — Psychiatry And Neurology*

A U M A HANDBOOK INTERNATIONAL. see *BUSINESS AND ECONOMICS — Marketing And Purchasing*

A U M A HANDBOOK REGIONAL. see *BUSINESS AND ECONOMICS — Marketing And Purchasing*

ADVANCE BAND MAGAZINE; the international voice of adult bands. see *MUSIC*

AERZTE ZEITUNG; die Tagesinformation fuer den Aerzt. see *MEDICAL SCIENCES*

ALLESTIRE; politica-tecnica-economia per mostre fiere congressi vetrine negozi stand. see *BUSINESS AND ECONOMICS*

AMERICAN LIBRARY ASSOCIATION. ANNUAL CONFERENCE PROGRAM. see *LIBRARY AND INFORMATION SCIENCES*

011 HK ISSN 1015-3128
ASIAN MEETINGS AND INCENTIVES. Short title: A M I. (Text in English) 1988. m. free to qualified personnel. (Convention and Visitors Bureaus) Travel & Trade Publishing (Asia) Ltd., 16-F, Capitol Centre, 5-19 Jardine's Bazaar, Causeway Bay, Hong Kong. TEL 890-3067. FAX 895-2378. TELEX 76591-TPAL-HX. Ed. Sue Girdwood. adv.; circ. 12,000 (controlled).
Formerly: (until Jan. 1989): M I C E Asia.
Description: For meetings and exhibitions industry executives around the world.

MEETINGS AND CONGRESSES 3391

011 US ISSN 1042-3141
AS6
ASSOCIATION MEETINGS; conventions, conferences, and exhibitions. 1916. bi-m. $42. Laux Company, Inc., 63 Great Rd., Maynard, MA 01754. TEL 508-897-5552. FAX 508-897-6824. Ed. John Halbrook. adv.; charts; illus.; circ. 21,000.
Formerly (until 1989): Convention World; Incorporates: Health Care Conferences; Which was formerly: World Convention News; World Convention Dates (ISSN 0043-8383)

ASSOCIATION OF HUMAN RESOURCE SYSTEMS PROFESSIONALS. CONFERENCE HIGHLIGHTS. see BUSINESS AND ECONOMICS — Office Equipment And Services

ASSOCIATIONS REPORT. see BUSINESS AND ECONOMICS — Management

011 US
▼**AWARDS ALMANAC**; an international guide to career, research and education funds. 1990. a. $89.95. St. James Press, 845 Penobscot Bldg., 645 Griswold St., Detroit, MI 48226-4232. TEL 800-345-0392. Ed. George W. Schmidt.

011 US
B O M A INTERNATIONAL CONVENTION DIRECTORY. 1908. a. Building Owners and Managers Association International, 1201 New York Ave., N.W., Ste. 300, Washington, DC 20005. TEL 202-408-2662. FAX 202-321-0181. Ed. Patricia Areno. adv.; circ. 5,000.

011 GW ISSN 0940-533X
▼**BERLINER KONGRESSKALENDER**. 1991. m. DM.60. Infoexpert Verlag GmbH, Koepenickerstr. 80-82, 1020 Berlin, Germany. TEL 030-2344282. FAX 030-2793996.

011 910.09 UK ISSN 0958-2010
▼**BUSINESS TRAVEL INTERNATIONAL**; quarterly review of international business travel, conferencing and incentive. 1990. q. £150. Contract Communications Limited, Refuge House, 9-10 River Front, Enfield, Middlesex EN1 3SZ, England. TEL 081-367-3939. FAX 081-366-9091. TELEX 927826-CONTCO-G. Ed. Peter Hardy. circ. 20,000. (back issues avail.)

C C S S. FEDERAZIONE DELLE SOCIETA MEDICO-SCIENTIFICHE. ITALIANE BOLLETTINO CONGRESSI (YEAR). (Comitato per la Collaborazione tra Societa Medico-Scientifiche Italiane) see MEDICAL SCIENCES

029.7 500 SA
CALENDAR OF CONFERENCES, MEETINGS AND EXHIBITIONS TO BE HELD IN SOUTH AFRICA. (Text in Afrikaans and English) s-a. price varies. Council for Scientific and Industrial Research, Division of Information Services, P.O. Box 395, Pretoria 0001, South Africa. Ed. Ingrid de Bont. circ. 3,200 (controlled). (back issues avail.)
Formerly (until 1984): Calendar of Scientific and Technical Meetings in South Africa (ISSN 0378-4053)

610 011 SZ ISSN 0301-2891
CALENDAR OF CONGRESSES OF MEDICAL SCIENCES. (Text in English and French) 1949. a. 10 Fr.($5.50) Council for International Organizations of Medical Sciences - Conseil des Organisations Internationales des Sciences Medicales, c/o World Health Organization, 20 Ave. Appia, CH-1211 Geneva 27, Switzerland. FAX 22-7910746. TELEX 415416. Ed. Dr. Zbigniew Bankowski. adv.; circ. 2,000.
Formed by the merger of, and assuming the numbering of: Calendar of International Congresses of Medical Sciences (ISSN 0589-915X); Calendar of Regional Congresses of Medical Sciences (ISSN 0574-248X)

500 600 011 IS ISSN 0333-6131
AS8
CALENDAR OF SCIENTIFIC AND TECHNOLOGICAL MEETINGS IN ISRAEL. (Text in English) 1968. s-a. $30. National Center of Scientific and Technological Information, ATIDIM Scientific Park, Devorah Haneviah St., Israel. TEL 03-492040. FAX 03-492033. TELEX 03-2332-IL. Ed. H. Mena. circ. 250.
Formerly: Calendar of Forthcoming Scientific and Technological Meetings to Be Held in Israel (ISSN 0008-0764)
Description: Covers conferences and professional meetings in the fields of science, medicine, engineering, technology and social sciences.

340 US
CALENDARS OF THE UNITED STATES HOUSE OF REPRESENTATIVES AND HISTORY OF LEGISLATION. 1986. w. $210. (House of Representatives) Superintendent of Documents, Government Printing Office, Washington, DC 20402. FAX 202-512-2250.

011 338 CN ISSN 0068-8967
CANADIAN INDUSTRY SHOWS AND EXHIBITIONS. 1964. a. (plus 3 updates). Can.$59. Maclean-Hunter Ltd., Business Publication Division, Maclean-Hunter Bldg., 777 Bay St., Toronto, Ont. M5W 1A7, Canada. TEL 416-596-5891. FAX 416-596-1240. Ed. Irvine Brace.
Description: Describes major shows and exhibitions held each year in Canada along with selected American shows, in addition to major European and Asian exhibitions. Complete listings of location, dates, products displayed, personnel, exhibition rates etc.

323.4 US
CIVIL LIBERTIES ALERT. vol.8, no.1, 1985. 2/yr. free. (Center for National Securities Studies, Washington Legislative Office) American Civil Liberties Union (Washington, D.C.), 122 Maryland Ave., N.E., Washington, DC 20002. TEL 202-544-1681. FAX 202-546-0738. (National Headquarters addr.: 132 W. 43rd St., New York, NY 10036) Ed. Rachel A. Fischer. circ. 5,000.

011 001.6 HK
COMPUTER EXPO (YEAR): EXHIBITION GUIDE. 1985. a. $25. Business & International Trade Fairs, 18-F First Pacific Bank Centre, 51 Gloucester Rd., Wanchai, Hong Kong. TEL 852-865-2633. FAX 852-866-1770. adv.
Formerly: Hong Kong Computer Expo (Year).
Description: Directory of exhibitors with address and brief description.

011 UK ISSN 0260-2431
THE CONFERENCE BLUE BOOK; your guaranteed guide to conference venues in the British Isles. 1978. a. £55 (foreign £75) including Green Book. Benn Business Information Services Ltd., P.O. Box 20, Sovereign Way, Tonbridge, Kent TN9 1RQ, England. TEL 0732-362666. FAX 0732-770483. TELEX 95162-BENTON-G. Ed. Julia Allen. adv.; illus.; charts; circ. 8,000.
—BLDSC shelfmark: 3409.030000.
Description: For all meeting organisers - from 3,000 delegates conferences to small training seminars. Provides a regionalised listing of over 4,000 UK venues indexed alphabetically detailing contact names and numbers; address details; delegate rates; details on meeting room dimension; lighting, sound, power and telephone facilities. Bars, restaurants, sports and conference facilities are also listed. Concentrates on technical information (the companion volume "Green Book" concentrates on special interest and leisure facilities).

011 US
CONFERENCE CHRONICLES. s-a. General Merchandise Distributors Council, 1275 Lake Ave., Colorado Springs, CO 80906. TEL 303-576-4260.

011 UK ISSN 0260-2199
THE CONFERENCE GREEN BOOK; guide to conference venues in the British Isles offering sports, leisure, and "special interest" facilities. 1980. £50 (foreign £70) including Blue Book. Benn Business Information Services Ltd., P.O. Box 20, Sovereign Way, Tonbridge, Kent TN9 1RQ, England. TEL 0732-362666. FAX 0732-770483. TELEX 95162-BENTON-G. Ed. Sally Greenhill. adv.; charts; illus.; circ. 8,000.
—BLDSC shelfmark: 3409.538000.
Description: For all meeting organisers - from 3,000 delegates conferences to small training seminars. Fully regionalized listing of over 4,000 UK venues indexed alphabetically detailing contact names and numbers; address details; delegate rates; details on meeting room dimension; lighting, sound, power and telephone facilities. Bars, restaurants, sports and conference facilities are also listed. The "Green" book concentrates on special interest and leisure facilities (the companion volume "Blue Book" concentrates on technical information).

CONFERENCE PAPERS ANNUAL INDEX. see MEETINGS AND CONGRESSES — Abstracting, Bibliographies, Statistics

CONFERENCE PAPERS INDEX. see MEETINGS AND CONGRESSES — Abstracting, Bibliographies, Statistics

011 UK ISSN 0143-7895
CONFERENCE WORLD. 1972. bi-m. £12 to non-members. Association of Conference Executives, Riverside House, High St., Huntingdon, Cambs. PE18 6SG, England. adv.; bk.rev.; circ. 4,500. **Indexed**: Build.Manage.Abstr., Fluidex.
Formerly (until Dec.-Jan. 1978): A C E News.

011 CN
CONGRES MENSUEL. English edition: Meetings Monthly. 1988. m. $40 (effective Jan. 1991). Publicom Inc., 1055 Beaver Hall, Ste. 200, Montreal, Que. H2Z 1S5, Canada. TEL 514-874-0874. FAX.514-878-9779. TELEX 055-61866. Ed. Guy Jonkman. adv.; circ. 5,583.
Description: A trade publication for meeting planners.

711 UK
CONGRESS IN PARK AND RECREATION ADMINISTRATION. PROGRAMME. triennial. International Federation of Park and Recreation Administration, General Secretary, The Grotto, Lower Basildon, Reading, Berks. RG8 9NE, England. TEL 0491-874222. FAX 0491-874059.
Formerly: World Congress in Public Park Administration. Programme (ISSN 0510-8233)

060 BE ISSN 0573-5661
CONGRESS OF INTERNATIONAL CONGRESS ORGANIZERS AND TECHNICIANS. PROCEEDINGS. (Subseries of International Congress Sciences Series) irreg., 6th, 1977. Kyoto. 600 Fr. Union of International Associations, Rue Washington 40, 1050 Brussels, Belgium.

CONTROLLED RELEASE NEWSLETTER. see CHEMISTRY — Organic Chemistry

CONVENE. see BUSINESS AND ECONOMICS — Management

011 AT ISSN 0156-0166
CONVENTION ROSTRUM. 1976. s-a. Aus.$60. Rank Publishing Company, 66 Chandos St., St. Leonards, N.S.W. 2065, Australia. TEL 02-438-2300. FAX 02-438-5962. Ed. Sandra Yeomans. adv.; bk.rev.; stat.; circ. 9,000. (back issues avail.)
Description: Covers Australasian Pacific venues and services register.

CONVENTIONS AND EXPOSITIONS. see BUSINESS AND ECONOMICS — Management

011 CN ISSN 0226-8922
CONVENTIONS & MEETINGS CANADA. 1971. a. Can.$39. Effective Communications Ltd., 5762 Highway 7, Ste. 207, Markham, Ont. L3P 1A8, Canada. TEL 416-471-1550. FAX 416-471-1552. Ed. James Nuttall. adv.; circ. 10,688 (controlled). (back issues avail.)
Description: Includes information on hotels, motor inns, convention centers and other meeting facilities across Canada.

M

MEETINGS AND CONGRESSES

011 US
CONVENTIONSOUTH. 1982. m. $15. Covey Communications Corp., Box 2267, Gulf Shores, AL 36547. TEL 205-968-5300. FAX 205-968-4532. Ed. J. Talty O'Connor. adv.; circ. 7,500 (controlled).
Description: For people who plan meetings, conferences and conventions that are held in the Southeast. Covers 11 southeastern states. Articles include how-to features, meeting site profiles, and related news items.

D W J - INFO; Mitteilungen des Bundesverbandes. (Deutsche Waldjugend) see *FORESTS AND FORESTRY*

DAWSONS VENUE DIRECTORY. see *TRAVEL AND TOURISM*

011 UK
DELEGATES. 1986. 12/yr. £59.50. British Association of Conference Towns, Premier House, 10 Greycoat Place, London SW1P 1SB, England. TEL 01-2228866. FAX 01-222-5689. adv.; circ. 22,230.
Description: Covers conferences, ventures, incentives, meetings, exhibitions and seminars.

011 GW ISSN 0933-9760
DEMETER KONGRESS KALENDER MEDIZIN. 1961. a. DM.36. Demeter Verlag, Wuermstr. 133, 8032 Graefelfing, Germany. TEL 089-852033.

011 617.6 GW
DEUTSCHER KONGRESS KALENDER ZAHNMEDIZINER. 1980. a. DM.18. Demeter Verlag, Wuermstr. 13, 8032 Graefelfing, Germany. TEL 089-852033. FAX 089-8543347.

610 011 SP ISSN 0210-5578
DIARIO DE CONGRESOS MEDICOS. 1972. irreg. (40/yr.). free to qualified personnel. Ediciones Doyma S.A., Travesera de Gracia 17-21, 80821 Barcelona, Spain. TEL 200 07 11. FAX 209-11-36. TELEX 51964 INK-E. Ed. Pedro Espinosa Bravo. adv.: page 200000 ptas.; trim 305 x 420; adv. contact: Roberto Garcia. circ. 2,900. (reprint service avail. from UMI).
Description: Publishes the best and most interesting papers from national and international medical conferences.

011 US ISSN 0417-5751
AS8
DIRECTORY OF CONVENTIONS. 1952. a. (plus mid-year supplement). $140. Successful Meetings Data Bank, 633 Third Ave., New York, NY 10017. TEL 212-986-4800. FAX 212-973-4890. TELEX 9102404217-SUCCESS-UQ. Ed. Jean L. Jaworek. circ. 800.
—BLDSC shelfmark: 3593.351000.

DOMOVA POKLADNICA. see *LITERATURE*

011 GW
DORTMUNDER MESSEBRIEF. s-a. Westfalenhallen Dortmund GmbH, Postfach 104444, 4600 Dortmund 1, Germany. TEL 0231-1204521. FAX 0231-1204678. Ed. Peter Weber. adv.; bk.rev.; illus.

011 BL
EMPRESA BRASILEIRA DE TURISMO. CALENDARIO DE CONGRESOS NACIONAIS Y INTERNACIONAIS/INTERNATIONAL AND NATIONAL MEETING EVENTS. a. free. Empresa Brasileira de Turismo, Rua Mariz e Barros 13, Rio de Janeiro 20270, Brazil. TEL 55-21-273-2212. FAX 55-21-273-9290. TELEX 38-21-21066 ETUR.

011 EI
EUROPEAN PARLIAMENT. COMMITTEE REPORT. 1967. irreg. Office for Official Publications of the European Communities, L-2985 Luxembourg, Luxembourg. (Dist. in the U.S. by: Unipub, 4611-F Assembly Dr., Lanham, MD 20706-4391) Ed.Bd. charts. (microfiche)
Formerly: European Parliament. Selected Documents.

EXECUTIVE UPDATE. see *BUSINESS AND ECONOMICS — Management*

011 UK ISSN 0014-4649
EXHIBITION BULLETIN. 1948. m. £56. London Bureau, 266-272 Kirkdale, London SE26 4RZ, England. FAX 01-659-8495. Ed. P.B.H. Cole. adv.; charts; illus.; index; circ. 4,950. **Indexed**: Key to Econ.Sci.
—BLDSC shelfmark: 3836.250000.
Description: Advance listings of fairs and shows throughout the world.

011 UK ISSN 0307-6601
EXHIBITIONS & CONFERENCES. 1972. q. £52($98) York Publishing Co., 70 Abingdon Rd., London W8 6AP, England. TEL 071-937-6636. FAX 071-937-5948. Ed. Jane Nightingale. adv.; circ. 8,000.
—BLDSC shelfmark: 3836.318000.
Description: Exhibition calendars in the UK and Europe, conference venues in the UK.

011 PH ISSN 0116-9688
▼**EXHIBITS ASIA**. 1990. 6/yr. Asian Exhibitors & Publishers, Philippines International Convention Centre S331, Manila, Philippines. TEL 8320309. FAX 8340536. Ed. M. Jane Thesessa Stangl-Alvero.
Description: Focuses mainly on exhibits in the Philippines. Some articles on development and travel aspects of the Philippines.

011 NE ISSN 0014-5254
EXPOVISIE; maandblad voor tentoonstellingen, congressen en hotellerie. 1950. m. fl.34. Euro Fair B.V., Gerrit van der Veenstraat 94, Amsterdam-Z, Netherlands. Ed. J. Van Rijswijk. adv.; illus.; circ. 5,000. **Indexed**: Key to Econ.Sci.
Formerly: Beursklanken.
Description: Lists fairs and exhibitions.

F I A B C I - U S A NEWS. see *BUSINESS AND ECONOMICS — International Commerce*

011 US ISSN 1043-3740
FAIR NEWS. 1968. bi-m. $15 (foreign $25). World's Fair Collectors Society, Inc., Box 20806, Sarasota, FL 34276-3806. TEL 813-923-2590. Ed. Michael R. Pender. adv.; bk.rev.; circ. 500. (looseleaf format; back issues avail.)

011 IT
IN FIERA. (Text in English, Italian) 1989. m. Ente Autonomo Fiera Milano, Largo Domodossola, 1, 20145 Milan, Italy. TEL 02-49971. FAX 4813072. TELEX 331360 EAFM 1. Ed. Vittorio Reali. adv.; charts; illus.

FIERA DEL LIBRO. see *PUBLISHING AND BOOK TRADE*

500 600 011 UK ISSN 0046-4686
FORTHCOMING INTERNATIONAL SCIENTIFIC AND TECHNICAL CONFERENCES. no.48, 1971. q. £75 to non-members; members £60. Aslib, Association for Information Management, Publications Department, Information House, 20-24 Old St., London EC1V 9AP, England. TEL 071-253-4488.
FAX 071-430-0514. (Dist. in N. America by: Learned Information, Inc., 143 Old Marlton Pike, Medford, NJ 08055-8750. TEL 609-654-6266) Ed. Caroline Gulliver. adv. **Indexed**: Fluidex.
—BLDSC shelfmark: 4018.000000.
Description: Covers forthcoming international conferences in science, technology and medicine.

FRANCE. INSTITUT NATIONAL DE LA SANTE ET DE LA RECHERCHE MEDICALE. COLLOQUES. see *MEDICAL SCIENCES*

011 US
GENERAL MERCHANDISE DISTRIBUTORS COUNCIL. MARKETING CONFERENCE TRANSCRIPTS. s-a. General Merchandise Distributors Council, 1275 Lake Ave., Colorado Springs, CO 80906. TEL 303-576-4260.

GENETICS SOCIETY OF CANADA BULLETIN. see *BIOLOGY — Genetics*

GERMANY. BUNDESINSTITUT FUER SPORTWISSENSCHAFT. BIENNIAL REPORTS. see *SPORTS AND GAMES*

011 610 IT
GIORNALE DEI CONGRESSI MEDICI. (Text in English, French, German, Italian and Spanish) m. L.40000($40) C I C Edizioni Internazionali s.r.l., Via L. Spallanzani, 11, 00161 Rome, Italy. TEL 06-862-289. FAX 06-844-3365. TELEX 622-099-CIC I.

011 AG ISSN 0301-7567
Q101
GUIA DE REUNIONES CIENTIFICAS Y TECNICAS EN LA ARGENTINA. 1959. a. free. (Secretaria de Estado de Ciencia y Tecnologia, Ministerio de Cultura y Educacion) Fundacion para la Educacion la Ciencia y la Cultura, Moreno 431 (Guia de Reuniones) 1091, Buenos Aires, Argentina. adv.; circ. 4,000.
—BLDSC shelfmark: 4224.836020.

011 CN
▼**GUIDE ANNUEL (YEAR) SALONS EXPOSITIONS CONGRES**. 1990. a. Can.$39. Editions Guide Annuel, 5144 bvd. St-Laurent, Ste. 200, Montreal, Que. H2T 1R8, Canada. TEL 514-278-7788. FAX 514-272-0672. adv.; circ. 10,000.

610 011 US
H C E A EXHIBITORS ADVISORY COUNCIL'S ACTION MEMO. s-a. free to members. Healthcare Convention & Exhibitors Association, 5775 Peachtree-Dunwoody Rd., Ste. 500 G, Atlanta, GA 30342. TEL 404-252-3663. FAX 404-252-0774. Ed.Bd. circ. 1,800. (back issues avail.)
Description: Promotes the use of exhibitors advisory councils in the healthcare convention and exhibition industry.

I E NEWS: AEROSPACE. (Institute of Industrial Engineers) see *AERONAUTICS AND SPACE FLIGHT*

011 SZ
IDEA MAGAZIN. (Text in German) 1975. s-m. 85 Fr. (Informationsdienst der Schweizerischen Evangelischen Allianz) Idea Schweiz, Postfach 3320, CH-6002 Lucerne, Switzerland. TEL 236779. FAX 041-232904. TELEX 817-585-146-COM-CH. Ed. Fritz Imhof. adv.; bk.rev.; illus.; tr.lit.; circ. 4,500.
Former titles: Idea Schweiz; Schweizerische Arbeitsgemeinschaft fuer Evangelisation.

INCENTIVE JOURNAL; magazine for motivation and sales promotion. see *BUSINESS AND ECONOMICS — Marketing And Purchasing*

INNOVATION AND TECHNOLOGY TRANSFER. see *LIBRARY AND INFORMATION SCIENCES*

610 011 US
INSIGHT (ATLANTA). 3/yr. free to members. Healthcare Convention & Exhibitors Association, 5775 Peachtree-Dunwoody Rd., Ste. 500 G, Atlanta, GA 30342. TEL 404-252-3663. FAX 404-252-0774. Ed.Bd. circ. 1,000. (back issues avail.)

011 US ISSN 0193-0516
INSURANCE CONFERENCE PLANNER. 1965. bi-m. $29. Laux Company, Inc., 63 Great Rd., Maynard, MA 01754. TEL 508-897-5552. FAX 508-897-6824. Ed. Susan Hatch. adv.; circ. 6,000.
Formerly: Insurance Magazine's Green Book of Convention Planning.

011 GW ISSN 0538-6349
INTERNATIONAL CONGRESS CALENDAR. (Text in English) 1961. q. 900 Fr.($345) (Union of International Associations, BE) K.G. Saur Verlag KG, Ortlerstr. 8, Postfach 701620, 8000 Munich 70, Germany. TEL 089-76902-0. FAX 089-76902150. (N. America subscr. to: K.G. Saur, A Reed Reference Publishing Company, 121 Chanlon Rd., New Providence, NJ 07974. TEL 908-665-3576) Ed. G. de Coninck. adv.; index, cum.index.
—BLDSC shelfmark: 4539.057000.
Description: Provides current information on over 7,000 international events scheduled for the next 12 to 15 months.

011 BE ISSN 0538-6772
INTERNATIONAL CONGRESS SCIENCE SERIES. 1961. irreg. price varies. Union of International Associations, Rue Washington 40, 1050 Brussels, Belgium.

011 500 NE ISSN 0531-5131
CODEN: EXMDA4
INTERNATIONAL CONGRESS SERIES. irreg.(approx. 40/yr.), vol.999, 1992. price varies. Elsevier Science Publishers B.V., Books Division, P.O. Box 211, 1000 AE Amsterdam, Netherlands. TEL 020-5803911. FAX 020-5803705. TELEX 18582 ESPA NL. (Subscr. in U.S. and Canada to: Elsevier Science Publishing Co., Inc., Box 882, Madison Sq. Sta., New York, NY 10159. TEL 212-989-5800) (back issues avail.) **Indexed:** Anim.Breed.Abstr., Biol.Abstr., Chem.Abstr.
—BLDSC shelfmark: 3835.850000.
Refereed Serial

011 PH ISSN 0074-588X
INTERNATIONAL FEDERATION OF ASIAN AND WESTERN PACIFIC CONTRACTORS' ASSOCIATIONS. PROCEEDINGS OF THE ANNUAL CONVENTION. (Proceedings published by organizing committee) irreg. International Federation of Asian and Western Pacific Contractors Associations, Padilla Building, 3rd Fl., Ortigas Commercial Center, Emerald Ave., Pasig, Metro Manila, Philippines. FAX 632-631-2789. TELEX 29083 IFAWPCA PH.

INTERNATIONAL SOCIETY OF CITRICULTURE. PROCEEDINGS. see *AGRICULTURE*

INTERNATIONAL THIRD WORLD STUDIES - JOURNAL AND REVIEW. see *POLITICAL SCIENCE — International Relations*

INTERNATIONAL TRADESHOW DIRECTORY. see *BUSINESS AND ECONOMICS — Trade And Industrial Directories*

011 323.4 GW
JULI-MAGAZIN. 1984. q. DM.24. Junge Liberale NRW e.V., Luisenstr. 7, D-4000 Dusseldorf 1, Germany. TEL 0211-378085. Ed. Oliver Kroehl. adv.; bk.rev.; bibl.; stat.; circ. 3,000. (back issues avail.)

KALENDAR ODBORARA. see *LABOR UNIONS*

910.09 GW
KOELNER KONGRESS REPORT. English edition: Cologne Convention. 1970. s-a. free. Cologne Tourist Office, Convention Department, Unter Fettenhennen 19, 5000 Cologne 1, Germany. FAX 0221-2213320. Eds. Erhard Schlieter, Elke Reiff. circ. 6,000.

011 GW
KONCIZE. (Text in Esperanto) 1975. bi-m. DM.10. European Esperanto Youth, Deutsche Esperanto-Jugend, Rheinweg 15, 5300 Bonn 1, Germany. TEL 0228-235898. FAX 0228-232764. Ed. Ulrich Matthias. adv.; bk.rev.; circ. 2,000.
Description: Information on Esperanto meetings, travel.

011 NE ISSN 0083-3851
KONGRESA LIBRO. (Text in Esperanto) 1905. a. fl.12($6) Universala Esperanto-Asocio, Nieuwe Binnenweg 176, 3015 BJ Rotterdam, Netherlands. TEL 010-4361044. FAX 010-4361751. TELEX 23721 UEA NL. Ed. Nikola Rasic. adv.; circ. 2,500.
Description: Contains program information, background articles and lists of participants.

057.87 CS
KULTURNOPOLITICKY KALENDAR. a. 30 Kcs. Obzor, Ceskoslovenskej Armady 35, 815 85 Bratislava, Czechoslovakia. illus.

L I N K LINE. (Library and Information Network) see *BIRTH CONTROL*

LEADER IN ACTION. see *EDUCATION*

L5 SPACE DEVELOPMENT CONFERENCE. PROCEEDINGS. see *AERONAUTICS AND SPACE FLIGHT*

011 IT
M & C. (Meeting & Congressi) 1973. 10/yr. L.210000. Ediman Srl, C.so S. Gottardo 39, 20136 Milan, Italy. FAX 039-2-58103791. adv.; circ. 19,000.

M UND A - MESSEPLANER INTERNATIONAL; schedule for fairs and exhibitions worldwide. see *BUSINESS AND ECONOMICS — Trade And Industrial Directories*

MADISON AREA'S GAY - LESBIAN CALENDAR. see *HOMOSEXUALITY*

011 US ISSN 0093-1314
MEDICAL MEETINGS. 1973. 8/yr. $42 (foreign $56). 63 Great Rd., Maynard, MA 01754. TEL 508-897-5552. FAX 508-897-6824. Ed. Elizabeth W. Milner. adv.; circ. 15,600. **Indexed:** Rehabil.Lit.
—BLDSC shelfmark: 5529.972000.

011 GW ISSN 0175-3053
MEDIZINISCHE KONGRESSE; National - International. 1957. a. DM.30($25) M K und K Verlagsgesellschaft, W E F R A Haus, 6078 Neu-Isenburg 4, Germany. TEL 069-69500845. FAX 069-69500850. adv.; circ. 40,000. (back issues avail.)

011 910 CN
▼**MEETING COMMUNICATIONS.** (Text in French) 1991. 4/yr. Can.$3.95 per no. Editions Guide Annuel, 5144 bvd. St-Laurent, Ste. 200, Montreal, Que. H2T 1R8, Canada. TEL 514-278-7788. FAX 514-272-0672. adv.; circ. 10,000.

011 US
MEETING MANAGER. 1981. m. $35. Meeting Planners International, 1950 Stemmons Freeway, Ste. 5018, Dallas, TX 75207-3109. TEL 214-746-5233. TELEX 535109 MPI. Ed. Tina Berres Filipski. circ. 10,636. (back issues avail.)
Formerly (until 1984): Meeting Place.
Description: Focuses on educating readers on all aspects of meeting planning, including site selection and negotiation, food and beverage tips, special event ideas, budgeting, and general meeting management.

011 US
MEETING NEWS; news, information & ideas for better meetings. (Supplement avail.: V I P) 1977-1992. m. $65. Miller Freeman Inc. (New York) (Subsidiary of: United Newspapers Group), 1515 Broadway, New York, NY 10036. TEL 212-869-1300. FAX 212-302-6273. Ed. Anthony Rutigliano. adv.; circ. 75,000 (controlled).
Description: Methods and ideas for meeting planners and convention managers.

350 US ISSN 0743-3832
MEETING PLANNERS ALERT. (Supplement included: Tradeshow Marketing Journal) 1984. m. $89 (elsewhere $99). M P A Communications Inc., Box 404, Derry, NH 03038. TEL 603-432-0084. Ed. Joan Hough. bk.rev.; index; circ. 1,000. (looseleaf format; back issues avail.)

350 US
MEETING PLANNERS GUIDEBOOK. 1982. a. $12.95. M P G Productions, 6 Morton Court, Ste. C, Mill Valley, CA 94941. TEL 415-388-1140. FAX 415-388-0804. adv.; circ. 50,000.
Description: Lists information on sites and services in western US.

011 US ISSN 0025-8652
AS6
MEETINGS AND CONVENTIONS. 1966. m. $65 (Canada $101.65; Mexico $95; elsewhere $95). Reed Travel Group (Subsidiary of: Reed Publishing (USA) Inc.), 500 Plaza Dr., Secaucus, NJ 07096. TEL 201-902-2000. FAX 201-319-1796. (Subscr. to: 44 Cook St., Denver, CO 80206. TEL 800-662-7776) Ed. Kate Rounds. adv.; bk.rev.; illus.; tr.lit.; circ. 80,141. (also avail. in microform from UMI) **Indexed:** Bus.Ind., Tr.& Indus.Ind.
●Also available online. Vendor(s): DIALOG.
Incorporates: Incentive World.

011 US
MEETINGS AND CONVENTIONS GAVEL; international guide to facilities and services. 1966. a. Reed Travel Group (Subsidiary of: Reed Publishing (USA) Inc.), 500 Plaza Dr., Secaucus, NJ 07096. TEL 201-902-1700. FAX 201-319-1796. (Subscr. to: 44 Cook St., Denver, CO 80206. TEL 800-662-7776) adv.: B&W page $10700, color $13825; trim 8 x 10 7/8. circ. 80,513.

011 CN ISSN 0318-1049
MEETINGS & INCENTIVE TRAVEL. 1972. 7/yr. Can.$36. Maclean-Hunter Ltd., Maclean-Hunter Bldg., 777 Bay St., Toronto, Ont. M5W 1A7, Canada. TEL 416-596-2697. FAX 416-596-5810. Ed. Ms. Tommi Lloyd. adv.; circ. 12,300. **Indexed:** Can.B.P.I.
Formerly: Canadian Sales Meetings and Conventions.
Description: News, trends and technologies for corporate and association meeting, convention and incentive travel planners.

011 CN
MEETINGS MONTHLY; for Canadian meeting planners. French edition: Congres Mensuel. 1988. m. $40. (Association of Meeting Organizers) Publicom Inc., 1055 Beaver Hall Hill, Ste. 200, Montreal, Que. H2Z 1S5, Canada. TEL 514-874-0874. FAX 514-878-9779. TELEX 055-61866. Ed. Guy Jonkman. adv.; bk.rev.; circ. 12,168 (controlled). (back issues avail.)

539.7 UN ISSN 0047-6641
QC770
MEETINGS ON ATOMIC ENERGY. (Text in English) 1969. 4/yr. S.400($29) International Atomic Energy Agency, Wagramer Str. 5, Box 100, A-1400 Vienna, Austria. (Dist. in U.S. by: Unipub, 4611-F Assembly Dr., Lanham, MD 20706-4391) index; circ. 2,150.

011 GW
MESSE- UND KONGRESS-VORSCHAU/FAIRS AND CONVENTIONS PREVIEW. 1923. m. DM.27.50. Verlag Horst Deike KG, Robert-Bosch-Str. 18, Postfach 100452, 7750 Konstanz, Germany. TEL 07531-65061. FAX 07531-65063. adv.; bk.rev.; circ. 5,400.
Former titles: Vorschau-Monats-Tabelle (ISSN 0723-5259) & Vorschau-Tabelle (ISSN 0042-8914)

011 II
N A S S D O C RESEARCH INFORMATION SERIES. CONFERENCE ALERT; quarterly calendar. (Text in English) q. Rs.40. Indian Council of Social Science Research, National Social Science Documentation Centre, 35 Ferozshah Rd., New Delhi 110 001, India. TEL 385959. TELEX 31-61083 ISSR IN. Eds. Mrs. O.K. Choudhary, K.G. Tyagi. circ. 100.
Description: Quarterly list of conferences, seminars and training courses in social sciences, and library and information sciences.

011 020 US
NATIONAL ONLINE MEETING. PROCEEDINGS. 1980. a. $55. Learned Information, Inc., 143 Old Marlton Pike, Medford, NJ 08055-8750. TEL 609-654-6266. FAX 609-654-4309. Eds. Martha Williams, Thomas H. Hogan. (back issues avail.)
Formerly (until 1980): National Online Information Meeting. Proceedings.
Description: Examines changes and challenges that will face the online industry as it reaches the 21st century.

011 US
NATIONWIDE DIRECTORY OF ASSOCIATION MEETING PLANNERS & CONFERENCE - CONVENTION DIRECTORS. a. (plus s-a. supplement). $207. Salesman's Guide, Inc., A Reed Reference Publishing Company, Division of Reed Publishing (USA) Inc., 121 Chanlon Rd., New Providence, NJ 07974. TEL 800-521-8110. FAX 908-665-6688. TELEX 138 755. (Subscr. to: R.R. Bowker, Order Dept., Box 31, New Providence, NJ 07974)
Description: Lists 14,025 convention planners for 8,823 national associations that have off-site meetings and, or conventions. Includes separate information on conventions and meetings.

MEETINGS AND CONGRESSES

011   US
NATIONWIDE DIRECTORY OF CORPORATE MEETING PLANNERS. a. (plus s-a. supplement). $257. Salesman's Guide, Inc., A Reed Reference Publishing Company, Division of Reed Publishing (USA) Inc., 121 Chanlon Rd., New Providence, NJ 07974. TEL 800-521-8110. FAX 908-665-6688. TELEX 138 755. (Subscr. to: R.R. Bowker, Order Dept., Box 31, New Providence, NJ 07974)
  Description: Lists over 18,400 corporate meeting planners who plan off-site meetings for over 12,000 corporations. Arranged alphabetically by state and city, information includes: type of business, addresses and telephone numbers, FAX numbers, number of meetings per year, number of attendees, basic geographic destination (including outside USA), and months meetings are held.

011   YU   ISSN 0350-011X
NAUCNI I STRUCNI SKUPOVI U JUGOSLAVII I U INOSTRANSTVU/SCIENTIFIC AND PROFESSIONAL MEETINGS IN YUGOSLAVIA AND FOREIGN COUNTRIES. (Text in English and Serbo-Croatian) 1975. s-a. $102. Jugoslovenski Centar za Tehnicku i Naucnu Dokumentaciju - Yugoslav Center for Technical and Scientific Documentation (YCTSD), Slobodana Penezica-Krcuna 29-31, Belgrade, Yugoslavia. Ed. Ljiljana Kojic-Bogdanovic.
  Formerly: Nauncni Skupovi u SFRJ i u Inostranstvu (ISSN 0028-1220)

NEWSMETER. see *ADVERTISING AND PUBLIC RELATIONS*

011   JA
NIKKEI EVENTS. (Text in Japanese) 1987. m. 17800 Yen. Nikkei Business Publications, Inc., 3-3-23, Misakicho, Chiyoda-ku, Tokyo 101, Japan. TEL 03-5210-8502. FAX 03-5210-8119. Ed. Junro Sato. adv.; circ. 17,223.
  Description: For planners of events, meetings, and conventions. Provides news on exhibitions, conventions, conferences and seminars, including guidelines for the planning of corporate events.

O S A ANNUAL MEETING DIGEST. (Optical Society of America, Inc.) see *PHYSICS — Optics*

647   US   ISSN 0094-5242
TX907   CODEN: OMFGDE
OFFICIAL MEETING FACILITIES GUIDE. 1974. s-a. $38. Reed Travel Group (Subsidiary of: Reed Publishing USA), 500 Plaza Dr., Secaucus, NJ 07096. TEL 202-902-2000. Ed. Virginia Nonnenman. illus.; circ. 19,285.

647   US
OFFICIAL MEETING FACILITIES GUIDE - EUROPEAN EDITION. s-a. Reed Travel Group (Subsidiary of: Reed Publishing USA), 500 Plaza Dr., Secaucus, NJ 07096. TEL 201-902-2000.

PEN IN HAND. see *JOURNALISM*

PHILATELIC EXHIBITOR. see *PHILATELY*

POLITICA MERIDIONALISTA; rivista mensile di cultura, economia e attualita. see *BUSINESS AND ECONOMICS — Economic Situation And Conditions*

011   AT   ISSN 0811-594X
QUORUM. 1982. bi-m. Aus.$35 (foreign Aus.$45). Braynart Group Pty.Ltd., 64 Talavera Rd., North Ryde, N.S.W. 2113, Australia. TEL 02-878-1011. FAX 02-878-8016. TELEX AA 73746. Ed. David Latta. circ. 8,500.

RESOURCES IN AGING; an international newsletter featuring new developments in aging. see *GERONTOLOGY AND GERIATRICS*

S C A L A C S. (American Chemical Society) see *CHEMISTRY*

S R D S TRADESHOW CATALOG. see *BUSINESS AND ECONOMICS — Marketing And Purchasing*

011   US
SCIENCE FICTION CONVENTION REGISTER. 1974. q. $10. Erwin S. "Filthy Pierre" Strauss, Ed. & Pub., Box 3343, Fairfax, VA 22038-3343. circ. 300.

500 011   US   ISSN 0487-8965
Q101
SCIENTIFIC MEETINGS. 1957. q. $60. Scientific Meetings Publications, Box 81662, San Diego, CA 92138. Ed. Mrs. W. Roy Holleman. circ. 1,200. (also avail. in microform from UMI; reprint service avail. from UMI) **Indexed:** Fluidex.
  —BLDSC shelfmark: 8183.290000.
  Description: Directory of forthcoming scientific, technical, medical, engineering and management meetings and international conferences.

011   UK
SCOTLAND: CONFERENCE AND INCENTIVE BROCHURE. irreg. free. Scottish Tourist Board, 23 Ravelston Terrace, Edinburgh EH4 3EU, Scotland. TEL 031-332-2433. FAX 031-343-1513. TELEX 72272.
  Formerly: Scotland: Conferences, Meetings, Seminars.

SHOW MEETING. see *COMMUNICATIONS*

011 616.07   SA
SOUTH AFRICAN SOCIETY OF PATHOLOGISTS. CONGRESS BROCHURE. (Text in Afrikaans and English) a. South Africa Society of Pathologists, Beatrix St., Pretoria, South Africa. adv.

SUCCESSFUL MEETINGS; the authority on meetings and incentive travel management. see *BUSINESS AND ECONOMICS — Marketing And Purchasing*

011   GW   ISSN 0342-7951
T W/CONVENTION INDUSTRY. (Tagungs-Wirtschaft); international magazine for fair, meetings and incentives. (Text in English, German) 1977. 8/yr. DM.70($42) M und A Verlag fuer Messen, Ausstellungen und Kongresse GmbH, Postfach 101528, 6000 Frankfurt a.M. 1, Germany. TEL 069-759502. FAX 069-75951900. TELEX 411-699-MUA-D. Ed. Klaus Goschmann. adv.; tr.lit.; circ. 16,000. (back issues avail.)
  Description: International trade magazine for fairs, meetings and incentives.

011   GW
T W VERANSTALTUNGSPLANER. 1983. a. DM.47.50. M und A Verlag fuer Messen, Ausstellungen und Kongresse GmbH, Mainzer Landstr. 251, 6000 Frankfurt a.M. 1, Germany. TEL 069-759502. FAX 069-75951900. TELEX 4-11699-MUAD. adv.; circ. 9,175.
  Former titles: M und A Tagungsplaner; M und A Tagungsplaner Europa (ISSN 0343-0545)

TOURISPRESS ITALIA; giornale d'informazione turistica. see *TRAVEL AND TOURISM*

011   JA
▼**TRADE FAIRS IN JAPAN (YEAR);** a guide to trade fairs designed for specific products and industries. 1990. a. 6000 Yen. Japan External Trade Organization, Publications Department, 2-5 Toranomon 2-chome, Minato-ku, Tokyo 105, Japan. TEL 03-5823518. FAX 03-5872485.
  Description: Basic source for information on trade exhibition centers and overseas representatives of exhibitions.

TRADE SHOWS & EXHIBITS SCHEDULE. see *BUSINESS AND ECONOMICS*

TRADESHOW DIRECTORY. see *BUSINESS AND ECONOMICS — Trade And Industrial Directories*

TRAVEL PLANNER. see *TRAVEL AND TOURISM*

616.994 011   SZ
U I C C INTERNATIONAL CALENDAR OF MEETINGS ON CANCER. a. free. International Union Against Cancer, 3 rue de Conseil-General, 1205 Geneva, Switzerland.
  Formerly: U I C C Calendar of International Meetings on Cancer.

U N CHRONICLE. see *POLITICAL SCIENCE — International Relations*

UNITY: UNITED NEWSLETTER. see *HOMOSEXUALITY*

011 658   AT
UNIVERSAL DIRECTORY - CONFERENCES - EXHIBITIONS - FUNCTIONS. 1988. a. Aus.$50. Universal Press Pty. Ltd., 64 Talavera Rd., Macquarie Park, N.S.W. 2113, Australia. TEL 02-8881877. FAX 02-8889850. adv.; circ. 20,000.
  Description: Contains information on venues, guest speakers, conference organizers and all the support companies you might need to organize a meeting in N.S.W. and A.C.T.

011 613.7   GW
V D S M - INFORMATIONSDIENST. m. Internationaler Verband der Stadt-, Sport- und Mehrzwerkhallen, Albersloher Weg 32, 4400 Munster, Germany. TEL 60021. TELEX 892681.

VIRGATS. see *ETHNIC INTERESTS*

WELLA AKTIENGESELLSCHAFT. REPORT; Informationen fuer Mitarbeiter und Pensionaere der weltweiten Wella-Unternehmen. see *BUSINESS AND ECONOMICS*

WOLFENBUETTELER BIBLIOTHEKS - INFORMATIONEN. see *HISTORY*

669 011   US   ISSN 0263-7987
WORLD CALENDAR; comprehensive international coverage of forthcoming events in metallurgy and materials science. 1965. q. £80($135) (Institute of Metals, UK) A S M International, Materials Information, Materials Park, OH 44073. TEL 216-338-5151. FAX 216-338-4634. TELEX 980-619. (UK addr.: Institute of Metals, Materials Information, 1 Carlton House Terr., London SW1Y 5DB, England. TEL 071-839-4071) Ed. G. Moody.
  —BLDSC shelfmark: 9352.973500.
  Formerly (until 1976): World Calendar of Forthcoming Meetings: Metallurgical and Related Fields (ISSN 0043-8294)
  Description: Lists forthcoming meetings in metals and materials.

011 610   US   ISSN 0161-2875
   CODEN: WMMEDT
WORLD MEETINGS: MEDICINE. 1978. q. $155. Macmillan Publishing Company, Macmillan Reference, 866 Third Ave., New York, NY 10022. TEL 212-702-4301. FAX 212-605-9368. Ed. Peter J. Jaskowiak.
  —BLDSC shelfmark: 9356.655750.

011   US   ISSN 0043-8677
Q101   CODEN: WMUCBR
WORLD MEETINGS: OUTSIDE UNITED STATES AND CANADA. 1968. q. $175. Macmillan Publishing Company, Macmillan Reference, 866 Third Ave., New York, NY 10022. TEL 212-702-4301. FAX 212-605-9368. Ed. Peter J. Jaskowiak. **Indexed:** BMT, Fluidex.
  —BLDSC shelfmark: 9356.655900.

300 650 011   US   ISSN 0194-6161
WORLD MEETINGS: SOCIAL & BEHAVIORAL SCIENCES, HUMAN SERVICES AND MANAGEMENT. 1971. q. $160. Macmillan Publishing Company, Macmillan Reference, 866 Third Ave., New York, NY 10022. TEL 212-702-4301. FAX 212-605-9368. Ed. Peter J. Jaskowiak.
  —BLDSC shelfmark: 9356.655840.
  Formerly: World Meetings: Social and Behavioral Sciences, Education and Management (ISSN 0043-8685)

011   US   ISSN 0043-8693
Q11   CODEN: WMUCAQ
WORLD MEETINGS: UNITED STATES AND CANADA. 1963. q. $175. Macmillan Publishing Company, Macmillan Reference, 866 Third Ave., New York, NY 10022. TEL 212-702-4301. FAX 212-605-9368. Ed. Peter J. Jaskowiak. **Indexed:** BMT.
  —BLDSC shelfmark: 9356.657000.

1 X 1 IHR PARTNER. see *AGRICULTURE*

MEETINGS AND CONGRESSES — Abstracting, Bibliographies, Statistics

020 015   UK   ISSN 0959-4906
Z7403
BRITISH LIBRARY. DOCUMENT SUPPLY CENTRE. INDEX OF CONFERENCE PROCEEDINGS. 1964. m. (annual, 25 year cumulation 1964-1988). £89 (foreign £94). British Library, Document Supply Centre, Boston Spa, Wetherby, W. Yorkshire LS23 7BQ, England. TEL 0937-843434. FAX 0937-546333. TELEX 557381. (back issues avail.) Indexed: AESIS, Dairy Sci.Abstr., Rev.Appl.Entomol., Rev.Plant Path. ● Also available online.
—BLDSC shelfmark: 4377.416600.
   Formerly: British Library. Lending Division. Index of Conference Proceedings Received (ISSN 0305-5183)

011 600 500   US   ISSN 0194-0546
Z7403
CONFERENCE PAPERS ANNUAL INDEX. a. $455 (foreign $535). Cambridge Scientific Abstracts, 7200 Wisconsin Ave., 6th Fl., Bethesda, MD 20814. TEL 301-961-6750. FAX 301-961-6720. TELEX 910 2507547 CAMB MD. Ed. E. Reid.
● Also available online. Vendor(s): DIALOG (File no. 77), European Space Agency (File no. 36).
   Formerly: Current Programs Annual Index.

600 500 011   US   ISSN 0162-704X
Z7403
CONFERENCE PAPERS INDEX. 1973. bi-m. $865 (foreign $945); with annual index $975 (foreign $995); annual index only $455 (foreign $535). Cambridge Scientific Abstracts, 7200 Wisconsin Ave., 6th Fl., Bethesda, MD 20814. TEL 301-961-6750. FAX 301-961-6720. TELEX 910 2507547 CAMB MD. index. (also avail. in magnetic tape; back issues avail.) Indexed: Cal.Tiss.Abstr., Chemorec.Abstr., Comput.& Info.Sys., Oncol.Abstr., Pollut.Abstr.
● Also available online. Vendor(s): DIALOG (File no.77), European Space Agency (File no.36/CONFERENCE PAPERS INDEX).
   Formerly: Current Programs (ISSN 0300-6956)
   Description: Lists authors and titles of papers presented at scientific conferences worldwide.

614.7 011   US   ISSN 0093-5816
Z7916
DIRECTORY OF PUBLISHED PROCEEDINGS. SERIES P C E : POLLUTION CONTROL & ECOLOGY. 1974. a. $150. Interdok Corp., 173 Halstead Ave., Box 326, Harrison, NY 10528. TEL 914-835-3506. FAX 914-835-6757. index, cum.index.
—BLDSC shelfmark: 3594.925000.
   Description: Index of conferences and their published proceedings in the pollution control-ecology fields.

500 600 016   US   ISSN 0012-3293
Z7409
DIRECTORY OF PUBLISHED PROCEEDINGS. SERIES S E M T - SCIENCE, ENGINEERING, MEDICINE AND TECHNOLOGY. 1965. 10/yr. $495. Interdok Corp., 173 Halstead Ave., Box 326, Harrison, NY 10528. TEL 914-835-3506. FAX 914-835-6757. bibl.; index, cum.index.
—BLDSC shelfmark: 3594.930000.
   Description: Index of conferences and the published proceedings in the fields of science, engineering, medicine and technology. Domestic and foreign conferences are cited.

300 016   US   ISSN 0012-3307
Z7161
DIRECTORY OF PUBLISHED PROCEEDINGS. SERIES S S H - SOCIAL SCIENCES - HUMANITIES. 1968. q. $325. Interdok Corp., 173 Halstead Ave., Box 326, Harrison, NY 10528. TEL 914-835-3506. FAX 914-835-6757. bibl.; index, cum.index.
—BLDSC shelfmark: 3594.950000.
   Description: Index of conferences and the published proceedings in the fields of the social sciences and the humanities.

011   MY   ISSN 0127-4880
INDEX TO MALAYSIAN CONFERENCES/INDEKS PERSIDANGAN MALAYSIA. (Text in Bahasa Malaysia, Chinese, English, Tamil) 1976. a. M.$35 (foreign M.$53). National Library of Malaysia, Bibliography and Indexing Division, 3rd Fl., Wisma Sachdev, Jalan Raja Laut, 50572 Kuala Lumpur, Malaysia. TEL 2923144. TELEX MA 30092. (Orders to: University of Malaya Co-operative Bookshop Ltd., Library Bldg., University of Malaya, 59100 Kuala Lumpur, Malaysia) Ed. Siti Rodziah Othman. circ. 120.
—BLDSC shelfmark: 4382.310000.

011   GW   ISSN 0933-1905
INTERNATIONALE JAHRESBIBLIOGRAPHIE DER KONGRESSBERICHTE/INTERNATIONAL ANNUAL BIBLIOGRAPHY OF CONGRESS PROCEEDINGS. Short title: I J B K. 1987. a. DM.1200. Felix Dietrich Verlag, Jahnstr. 15, Postfach 1949, 4500 Osnabrueck, Germany. FAX 0541-41255.

011 330   PE
JUNINDEX; resumenes de documentos. 1984. irreg., vol.6, 1987. free. Junta del Acuerdo de Cartagena, Casilla de Correo 18-1177, Lima 18, Peru. TEL 14-41-4212. FAX 14-420911. TELEX JUNAC-20104-PE. abstr.; cum.index.
   Description: Provides abstracts of all documents existent at the Junta since the organization's founding in 1969. Abstracts are listed by type of document, with indexes to personal authors, corporate authors, conferences, titles, subjects, and geographic places and codes. Aimed at member countries of the Cartagena Agreement and other organizations for Latin American integration.

011   US   ISSN 0032-9568
Z5063.A2   CODEN: PPRNA
PROCEEDINGS IN PRINT. 1964. bi-m. $610 (cum.index $295). Proceedings in Print, Inc., Box 369, Halifax, MA 02338-0369. Ed. Barbara A. Spence. index. (back issues avail.)
—BLDSC shelfmark: 6848.850000.
   Description: Lists and indexes of proceedings of conferences, symposia in all subject areas, and in all languages.

MEN'S HEALTH

BACK TO HEALTH MAGAZINE; your guide to relief recovery and well-being. see *PHYSICAL FITNESS AND HYGIENE*

EXERCISE FOR MEN ONLY. see *PHYSICAL FITNESS AND HYGIENE*

HEALTH & FITNESS; magazine for healthy, sound living. see *PHYSICAL FITNESS AND HYGIENE*

HEALTH EDUCATION JOURNAL. see *PHYSICAL FITNESS AND HYGIENE*

HEALTH NOW. see *NUTRITION AND DIETETICS*

MAENNER AKTUELL. see *HOMOSEXUALITY*

MASSAGE THERAPY JOURNAL. see *PHYSICAL FITNESS AND HYGIENE*

610   US
MEN'S HEALTH. 1986. q. $11.97. Rodale Press, Inc., 33 E. Minor St., Emmaus, PA 18098. TEL 215-967-5171. TELEX 847338. Indexed: Hlth.Ind.
   Description: Tells you how to look good, live better - and longer.

613.7   US
MEN'S HEALTH NEWSLETTER. m. $24. Rodale Press, Inc., 33 E. Minor St., Emmaus, PA 18098. TEL 215-967-5171. TELEX 847338.
   Description: Delivers current medical advice on health subjects unique to men with ways to improve health, "slow down" the aging process, reduce stress, plus information on nutrition.

OUTLOOK (SEATTLE); drug regulation and reproductive health. see *PUBLIC HEALTH AND SAFETY*

MEN'S INTERESTS

051   US
A A G INTERNATIONAL. (Adult Action Guide) 9/yr. $4.95 per no. Eton Publishing, 475 Park Ave. S., New York, NY 10016. TEL 212-213-8620. FAX 212-532-1309.

054.1   FR
ABSOUS. 1978. m. 140 F. Societe Francaise des Revues, 9 rue Diderot, 93100 Montreuil, France. Ed. Michel Buh. adv.; circ. 110,000.
   Formerly: Nouvel Absolu.

051   US   ISSN 0001-8007
HQ450
ADAM; the man's home companion. 1956. m. $4.95 per no. Knight Publishing Corp., 8060 Melrose Ave., Los Angeles, CA 90046. TEL 213-653-8060. Ed. Jared Rutter. adv.; bk.rev.; circ. 200,000.

305.3   HU   ISSN 0230-1911
ADAM. 1980. m. $48 (effective 1992). Hirlapkiado Vallalat, Blaha Lujza ter. 3, 1959 Budapest 8, Hungary. (Subscr. to: Kultura, P.O.B. 149, 1389 Budapest 62, Hungary) Ed. Bacskai Laszlo.
   Description: About Hungarian men and artists.

051   US
ADAM EROTOMIC. q. $5.95 per no. Knight Publishing Corp., 8060 Melrose Ave., Los Angeles, CA 90046. TEL 213-653-8060. FAX 213-655-9452.

051   US
ADAM GIRLS INTERNATIONAL. bi-m. $5.95. Knight Publishing Corp., 8060 Melrose Ave., Los Angeles, CA 90046. TEL 213-653-8060. FAX 213-655-9452.

051   US
ADULT CINEMA REVIEW. 9/yr. $4.95 per no. Adult Movie Review, Inc., 300 W. 43rd St., New York, NY 10036. TEL 212-397-5200.

051   US
ADVOCATE MEN. m. $5.95 per no. Liberation Publications, Inc., Box 4371, Los Angeles, CA 90078. TEL 800-669-6565. FAX 213-467-6805.

051   US
ALL-AMERICAN MAN. bi-m. $4.95 per no. Liberation Publications, Inc., Box 4371, Los Angeles, CA 90078. TEL 800-669-6565. FAX 213-467-6805.

051   US
ALL MALE. vol.2, no.2, 1988. bi-m. $24.95. Bruce Publications, Ltd. (Subsidiary of: Mavety Media Group Ltd.), 462 Broadway, Ste. 4000, New York, NY 10013. TEL 212-966-8400. (Dist. by: Flynt Distributing Co., 9171 Wilshire Blvd., Ste. 300, Beverly Hills, CA 90210) Ed. Jason Fairchild. illus.

ANDERSCHUME - KONTIKI; das Schweizer Magazin fuer den schwulen Mann. see *HOMOSEXUALITY*

070.4834 917.306   US
AQUI (RIVER EDGE). (Text in Spanish) 1988. m. $33. Aqui Publications Inc., 63 Grand Ave., Ste. 115, River Edge, NJ 07661. TEL 201-487-3255. Ed. Fernando Moreno. circ. 100,000.
   Description: Includes articles on lifestyle, sports, humor and pictorials of nude women geared towards Spanish men between the ages of 18-49.

052   AT   ISSN 0158-0655
AUSTRALIAN PENTHOUSE; Australian men's magazine. 1979. m. Aus.$74. P H Editorial Services Pty. Ltd., P.O. Box 42, Cammeray, N.S.W. 2062, Australia. Ed. Phil Abraham. circ. 132,000. (back issues avail.)

052   AT
AUSTRALIAN PLAYBOY. 1979. m. Aus.$34.98. Mason Stewart Publishing Pty. Ltd., P.O. Box 747, Darlinghust, N.S.W. 2010, Australia. FAX 02-360-5367. Ed. Andrew Cowell. circ. 43,000.

051 301.4157   US
BEAU. 1989. 8/yr. $17.97. Medi-Media Publications, Inc., Box 470, Port Chester, NY 10573. TEL 914-939-2362. Ed. Dan Maxwell. adv.; film rev.; circ. 75,000. (back issues avail.)
   Description: Covers safe sexual relations between gay men.

MEN'S INTERESTS

051   US
BEELINE BOOKS. m. Carlyle Communications, Ltd. (Subsidiary of: Mavety Media Group Ltd.), 462 Broadway, Ste. 4000, New York, NY 10013. TEL 212-966-8400. (Dist. by: Kable News Co., 11 W. 42nd St,m 28th Fl., New York, NY 10036. TEL 212-768-1000)

051   US
BEST OF CLUB. bi-m. $4.95 per no. Fiona Press, Inc., Box 1379, South Norwalk, CT 06856. TEL 203-838-5484. FAX 203-775-1931.

051   US
BEST OF CLUB INTERNATIONAL. bi-m. $4.95 per no. Fiona Press, Inc., Box 1379, South Norwalk, CT 06856. TEL 203-838-5484. FAX 203-775-1931.

051   US
BEST OF GENESIS. 10/yr. $4.95 per no. Jakel Corp., 1776 Broadway, 20th Fl., New York, NY 10019-2002. TEL 212-265-3500. FAX 212-265-8087.

051   US
BEST OF OUI. m. $4.95 per no. Laurant Publishing, Ltd., 300 W. 43rd St., New York, NY 10136. TEL 212-967-6262. FAX 212-967-6288.

051   US
BEST OF REAL LETTERS. s-a. $3.50 per no. Vanity Publications, 475 Park Ave. S., New York, NY 10016. TEL 212-213-8620. FAX 212-532-1302.

051   US
BEST OF SENSUOUS LETTERS. s-a. $3.50 per no. Vanity Publications, 475 Park Ave. S., New York, NY 10016. TEL 212-213-8620. FAX 212-532-1302.

051   US
BI-LIFESTYLE; devoted to the interests of bisexual swingers. a. $11. Continental Spectator, Box 278, Canal St. Sta., New York, NY 10013. TEL 718-625-6309. Ed. Linda Lee. adv.

BIG APPLE PARENTS' PAPER. see *CHILDREN AND YOUTH — About*

051   US
BIG BUTT. q. Heat Wave Publications, Inc. (Subsidiary of: Mavety Media Group Ltd.), 462 Broadway, Ste. 4000, New York, NY 10013. TEL 212-966-8400. (Dist. by: Flynt Distributing Co., 9171 Wilshire Blvd., Ste. 300, Beverly Hills, CA 90210)

BIRTH OF TRAGEDY MAGAZINE; the fear issue, the God issue, the power issue, the love issue, the sex issue. see *LITERARY AND POLITICAL REVIEWS*

051   US
▼**BLACK TAIL.** 1989. q. $4.95 per no. Leisure Plus Publications, Inc. (Subsidiary of: Mavety Media Group Ltd.), 462 Broadway, Ste. 4000, New York, NY 10013. TEL 212-966-8400. (Dist. by: Flynt Distributing Co., 9171 Wilshire Blvd., Ste. 300, Beverly Hills, CA 90210) illus.
    Formerly (until 1991): Mocha.

BOLD GAY LIFE STYLE. see *HOMOSEXUALITY*

055.1   IT   ISSN 0006-775X
AP37
BORGHESE. 1950. w. L.20000. Viale Regina Margherita 7, 20122 Milan, Italy. TEL 02-592966. Ed. Mario Tedeschi. adv.; bk.rev.; illus.; index; circ. 100,000.

BRAUT UND BRAEUTIGAM; wissenswertes ueber heiraten und wohnen. see *WOMEN'S INTERESTS*

BRIDE AND GROOM. see *MATRIMONY*

BRITISH G Q. see *CLOTHING TRADE — Fashions*

070.48346   JA
BRUTUS. (Text in Japanese) 1980. bi-w. Magazine House, 3-13-10, Ginza, Chuo-ku, Tokyo 104, Japan. TEL 03-3545-7100. FAX 03-3546-0034. Ed. Giichiro Hata. circ. 200,000.

051   US
BUXOM. q. $4.95 per no. Drake Publishers, 801 Second Ave., New York, NY 10017. TEL 212-661-7878. FAX 212-883-1244.

CADET. see *CONSUMER EDUCATION AND PROTECTION*

070.48   US
CAVALIER. m. Dungent Publishing Company, 2600 Douglas Rd., Ste. 600, Coral Gables, FL 33134-6125. TEL 305-443-2378. Ed. Nye Willden. circ. 125,000.

051   US
CELEBRITY CONFIDENTIAL. bi-m. Fast Lane Publishing, Inc., 462 Broadway, Ste. 4000, New York, NY 10013. TEL 212-966-8400. (Dist. by: Flynt Distributing Co., 9171 Wilshire Blvd., Ste. 300, Beverly Hills, CA 90210)

051   US
CELEBRITY SKIN. bi-m. $4.95 per no. Drake Publishers, 801 Second Ave., New York, NY 10017. TEL 212-986-5100.

051   US
CELEBRITY SLEUTH. vol.2, no.4, 1989. bi-m. $4.95 per no. Broadcast Communications, Inc. (Subsidiary of: Mavety Media Group Ltd.), 462 Broadway, Ste. 4000, New York, NY 10013. TEL 212-966-8400. (Dist. by: Flynt Distributing Co., 9171 Wilshire Blvd., Ste. 300, Beverly Hills, CA 90210) illus.

CHALLENGE (CONVENT STATION). see *HOMOSEXUALITY*

070.48   JA
CHECKMATE. (Text in Japanese) 1974. m. Kodansha Ltd., International Division, 12-21, Otowa 2-chome, Bunkyo-ku, Tokyo 112, Japan. TEL 03-3945-1111. FAX 03-3943-7815. TELEX J34509 KODANSHA. Ed. Minoru Takeuchi. circ. 300,000.
    Description: Fashion magazine for young men.

051   US
CHERI; the all-true sex news magazine. m. Drake Publishers, 801 Second Ave., New York, NY 10017. TEL 212-661-7878. Ed. Jim Russell.

051   US
CHERI BOOK OF LINGERIE. q. $4.95 per no. Drake Publishers, 801 Second Ave., New York, NY 10017. TEL 212-661-7878.

051   US
CHERI LETTERS. q. $4.50 per no. Drake Publishers, 801 Second Ave., New York, NY 10017. TEL 212-661-7878.

051   US
CHERI PILLOW TALK. bi-m. $2.95 per no. Drake Publishers, 801 Second Ave., New York, NY 10017. TEL 212-661-7878. FAX 212-883-1244.

070.48346   808.87   US
CHERRY. 2/yr. $5 per no. Last Gasp of San Francisco, 2180 Bryant St., San Francisco, CA 94110. TEL 415-824-6636. FAX 415-824-1836. Ed. Larry Welz. circ. 40,000. (back issues avail.)
    Description: Adult cartoon satire.

051   US
CHIC LETTERS. 9/yr. $2.95 per no. Larry Flynt Publications, Inc., 9171 Wilshire Blvd., Ste.300, Beverly Hills, CA 90210. TEL 213-858-7100. FAX 213-275-3857.

646.32   US   ISSN 0194-648X
CHIC MAGAZINE. 1976. m. $39.95. Larry Flynt Publications, Inc., 9171 Wilshire Blvd., Ste. 300, Beverly Hills, CA 90210-5530. TEL 310-858-7100. FAX 310-275-3857. Ed. Doug Oliver. adv.

CHILD CARE ACTION NEWS. see *CHILDREN AND YOUTH — About*

CHILD, YOUTH, AND FAMILY FUTURES CLEARINGHOUSE. see *SOCIAL SERVICES AND WELFARE*

051   US
CINEMA BLUE. vol.6, no.4, 1989. 9/yr. $32.95. Hudson Communications, Inc. (Subsidiary of: Mavety Media Group Ltd.), 462 Broadway, Ste. 4000, New York, NY 10013. TEL 212-966-8400. (Dist. by: Flynt Distributing Co., 9171 Wilshire Blvd., Ste. 300, Beverly Hills, CA 90210) Ed. Felicia Freedom.
    Description: Reviews of x-rated video cassettes.

051   US
CINEMA BLUE PRESENTS EROTIC STARS. 1989. bi-m. $4.95 per no. Hudson Communications, Inc. (Subsidiary of: Mavety Media Group Ltd.), 462 Broadway, Ste. 4000, New York, NY 10013. TEL 212-966-8400. (Dist. by: Flynt Distributing Co., 9171 Wilshire Blvd., Ste. 300, Beverly Hills, CA 90210) illus.

051   US
CINEMA BLUE PRESENTS RED-HOT COUPLES. 1989. bi-m. $4.95 per no. Hudson Communications, Inc. (Subsidiary of: Mavety Media Group Ltd.), 462 Broadway, Ste. 4000, New York, NY 10013. TEL 212-966-8400. (Dist. by: Flynt Distributing Co., 9171 Wilshire Blvd., Ste. 300, Beverly Hills, CA 90210) illus.

051   US
CLOSE SHAVE. 1989. 9/yr. $4.95 per no. Leisure Plus Publications, Inc. (Subsidiary of: Mavety Media Group Ltd.), 462 Broadway, Ste. 4000, New York, NY 10013. TEL 212-966-8400. (Dist. by: Flynt Distributing Co., 9171 Wilshire Blvd., Ste. 300, Beverly Hills, CA 90210) illus.

051   US
CLUB INTERNATIONAL. 13/yr. $4.50 per no. Fiona Press, Inc., Box 1379, South Norwalk, CT 06856. TEL 203-838-5484. FAX 203-775-1931.

051   US   ISSN 0747-0827
CLUB MAGAZINE. 1954. m. $39. Fiona Press, Inc., Box 1379, South Norwalk, CT 06856. TEL 203-838-5484. FAX 203-775-1931. Ed. Nigel Franks. adv.; circ. 805,000. (back issues avail.)
    Description: Contains erotically entertaining articles and cartoons and pictorials featuring popular models.

051   US
COLT STUDIO PUBLICATIONS. m. $12.50 per no. Colt Studio, Box 4371, Los Angeles, CA 90078. TEL 213-871-1225. FAX 213-467-6805.

COLUMBUS BRIDE AND GROOM. see *MATRIMONY*

COMPETITION ANGLER. see *SPORTS AND GAMES — Outdoor Life*

CONNECTICUT PARENT. see *WOMEN'S INTERESTS*

CONTINENTAL SPECTATOR. see *SINGLES' INTERESTS AND LIFESTYLES*

070.483   GW
COUPE. 1985. m. DM.66. Heinrich Bauer Verlag, Burchardstr. 11, 2000 Hamburg 1, Germany. TEL 040-3019-0. FAX 040-326589. Ed. Karl Knecht. circ. 627,114.

051   US
COUPLES ONLY. bi-m. $2.95 per no. Vanity Publications, 475 Park Ave. S., New York, NY 10016. TEL 212-213-8620. FAX 212-532-1302.

D N R MONDAY. (Daily News Record) see *CLOTHING TRADE — Fashions*

051   US
▼**DAD.** 1990. bi-m. $13.50. Creative Publishing Group, Inc., 30 Moran St., Newton, NJ 07860. TEL 201-579-5900. Ed. Wendi R. Blanchard.
    Description: Includes information on family life, single fatherhood, finance, law, sports and health.

DETAILS. see *GENERAL INTEREST PERIODICALS — United States*

051   US
DIVERSIONS. bi-m. $3.95 per no. Vanity Publications, 475 Park Ave. S., New York, NY 10016. TEL 212-213-8620. FAX 212-532-1302.

DO-IT-YOURSELF (HAMPTON). see *HOW-TO AND DO-IT-YOURSELF*

051   US
DOMINATRIX CROSS ROADS. no.119, 1991. 12/yr. R S Connections, Box 97077-DM, Las Vegas, NV 89193.

051   US
E F G HIGHLIGHTS. bi-m. $4.95 per no. Eton Publishing, 475 Park Ave. S., New York, NY 10016. TEL 212-213-8620. FAX 212-532-1302.

MEN'S INTERESTS

056.1 MX
EL.* 1971. m. Mex.$400($43) Corporacion Editorial, S.A., Lucio Blanco 435, Col. San Juan Tlihuaca, 02400 Mexico D.F., Mexico. Ed. Javier Ortiz Camorlinga. adv.; circ. 120,000.

ELE E ELA; uma revista para ler a dois. see *WOMEN'S INTERESTS*

L'ELEGANTE UOMO SUD. see *CLOTHING TRADE — Fashions*

305.3 301.412 US
EMERGE PLAYCOUPLE. 1970. bi-m. $15. Lifestyles Press, Box 7128, Buena Park, CA 90622. TEL 714-821-9953. FAX 714-821-1465. (Subscr. to: Box 5366, Buena Park, CA 90622) Ed. Robert L. McGinley. adv.; bk.rev.; circ. 3,000.
   Description: For those unique couples who have romance and adventure in their hearts and seek excitement and freedom in their sexual and intimate life and erotic relationship.

EROTIC WRITER'S AND COLLECTOR'S MARKET. see *PUBLISHING AND BOOK TRADE*

051 US
EROTIC X-FILM GUIDE. m. $4.95 per no. Eton Publishing, 475 Park Ave. S., New York, NY 10016. TEL 212-213-8620. FAX 212-532-1309.

051 US ISSN 0194-9535
AP2
ESQUIRE (1979); the magazine for men. 1933. m. $15.94. Hearst Corporation, Esquire, 1790 Broadway, New York, NY 10019. TEL 212-459-7500. Ed. Terry McDonell. adv.; bk.rev.; film rev.; record rev.; illus.; circ. 702,611. (also avail. in microform from UMI; reprint service avail. from UMI) **Indexed:** Abstr.Engl.Stud., Acad.Ind., Bk.Rev.Ind. (1965-), Child.Bk.Rev.Ind. (1965-), Curr.Lit.Fam.Plan., Film Lit.Ind. (1973-), Hlth.Ind., Mag.Ind., PMR, R.G.
   —BLDSC shelfmark: 3811.662500.
   Former titles: Esquire Fortnightly; (until 1978): Esquire (ISSN 0014-0791)
   Description: Features interviews and the latest in contemporary fiction and non-fiction writer; also includes, information about popular culture with takes on fashion, travel, and more.

EXERCISE FOR MEN ONLY. see *PHYSICAL FITNESS AND HYGIENE*

EXPRESSMALE. see *OCCUPATIONS AND CAREERS*

EZERMESTER. see *HOW-TO AND DO-IT-YOURSELF*

790.13 910.09 LE
AL-FAEZ/WINNER. (Text in Arabic; summaries in Arabic, English) 1985. m. $40. Barson Publications, Ltd., P.O. Box 113-5358, Beirut, Lebanon. TEL 361580. TELEX 23388 BARSON LE. Ed. Sadri Barrage. adv. (back issues avail.)

808 US
FAMILY AFFAIRS. 1980. m. $48. J L J Communications, 310 Cedar Lane, Teaneck, NJ 07666. TEL 201-836-9177. FAX 201-836-5055. Ed. Jackie Lewis. adv.; circ. 80,000. (back issues avail.)
   Description: Erotic literature.

051 US
FAMILY HEAT. bi-m. Mountainside Press, Inc. (Subsidiary of: Mavety Media Group Ltd.), 462 Broadway, Ste. 4000, New York, NY 10013. TEL 212-966-8400. (Dist. by: Flynt Distributing Co., 9171 Wilshire Blvd., Ste. 300, Beverly Hills, CA 90210)

051 US
FAMILY LETTERS. m. $4.50 per no. J L J Communications, 310 Cedar Lane, Teaneck, NJ 07666. TEL 201-836-9177. FAX 201-836-5055.

056.1 US
FASCINACION.* (Avail. in editions for Central America, Colombia, Mexico, Puerto Rico, Venezuela) (Text in Spanish) 1974. m. De Armas Publications, 535 Fifth Ave., No. 903, New York, NY 10017-3610. adv.; circ. 70,000.

070.48346 US
FATHERS. 1988. bi-m. Fathers, Inc., 643 E. Capitol St., S.E., Washington, DC 20003. TEL 202-544-4220. Ed. Duncan Spencer. adv.; circ. 500,000.

051 US
FATHERS' JOURNAL. m. membership. Fathers for Equal Rights of America, Box 2272, Southfield, MI 48037. TEL 313-354-3080.
   Description: Dedicated to preserving the rights of fathers.

DER FEMINIST; beitraege zur theorie und praxis. see *WOMEN'S INTERESTS*

FERRARI ITALIAN STYLE; periodico internazionale d'immagine, automobilismo e cultura. see *TRANSPORTATION — Automobiles*

051 US
FETISH LETTERS. bi-m. Domino Press, Inc. (Subsidiary of: Mavety Media Group Ltd.), 462 Broadway, Ste. 4000, New York, NY 10013. TEL 212-966-8400. (Dist. by: Flynt Distributing Co., 9171 Wilshire Blvd., Ste. 300, Beverly Hills, CA 90210)

052 UK ISSN 0265-1270
FIESTA. 1965. m. £19. Galaxy Publications Ltd., P.O. Box 312, Witham, Essex CM8 3SZ, England. FAX 0376-510680. TELEX 98431. Ed. Douglas Heard. adv.; bk.rev.; circ. 327,998.

051 US
FIRST HAND. m. $4.50 per no. J L J Communications, 310 Cedar Lane, Teaneck, NJ 07666. TEL 201-836-9177. FAX 201-836-5055.

070.48 UK ISSN 0958-0980
FOR HIM; style, grooming and fitness. 1985. bi-m. £12($50) Tayvale Ltd., 9-11 Curtain Rd., London EC2A 3LT, England. TEL 071-247-5447. FAX 071-247-5892. Ed. Geoffrey Aquilina Ross. adv.; bk.rev.; circ. 51,000.
   Description: For image conscious men.

051 US
FORBIDDEN CONNECTIONS; the kinkiest magazine from coast to coast. bi-m. $19. Forbidden Connection Publication, Box 97077, Las Vegas, NV 89193. Ed. B.J. Crystal.

051 US
FORBIDDEN LETTERS. bi-m. $4.50 per no. Vanity Publications, 475 Park Ave. S., New York, NY 10016. TEL 212-213-8620. FAX 212-532-1302.

FORMALWORDS. see *CLOTHING TRADE — Fashions*

051 US
FORUM (NEW YORK, 1974). m. $3.95 per no. General Media, 1965 Broadway, New York, NY 10023. TEL 800-227-1346. FAX 212-873-4071.

051 US ISSN 0160-2195
HQ1
FORUM (NEW YORK, 1976); the international journal of human relations. 1976. m. $23. Penthouse International Ltd., 1965 Broadway, New York, NY 10023. TEL 212-496-6100. (Subscr. to: Box 3225, Harlan, IA 51593) Ed. Don Myrus. bk.rev.; index; circ. 500,000. (back issues avail.)
   Formerly: Penthouse Forum.

051 US
FORUM SPECIALS. q. $4.95 per no. General Media, 1965 Broadway, New York, NY 10023. TEL 800-227-1346. FAX 212-873-4071.

051 US
FOX MAGAZINE. 1984. m. $35. Montcalm Publishing Corp., 401 Park Ave. S., New York, NY 10016-8802. TEL 212-779-8900. Ed. Marc Lichter. adv.; bk.rev.; film rev.; illus.; circ. 150,000.

053.1 GW
FREITAG; die Monatszeitschrift fuer freie Tage. 1975. s-m. DM.4 per no. Sonnenverlag GmbH, Bismarckstr. 4, Postfach 720, 7570 Baden-Baden, Germany. Ed. Helmut Eilers. adv.

051 US
FRESHMEN. m. $5.95 per no. Liberation Publications, Inc., Box 4371, Los Angeles, CA 90078. TEL 800-669-6565. FAX 213-467-6805.

051 US
FRICTION. m. $36. Momentum Publishing, Inc. (Subsidiary of: Mavety Media Group Ltd.), 462 Broadway, Ste. 4000, New York, NY 10013. TEL 212-966-8400. (Dist. by: Flynt Distributing Co., 9171 Wilshire Blvd., Ste. 300, Beverly Hills, CA 90210)

G Q. (Gentlemen's Quarterly) see *CLOTHING TRADE — Fashions*

051 US ISSN 0195-072X
GALLERY. 1972. m. $25. Montcalm Publishing Corp., 401 Park Ave. S., New York, NY 10016-8802. TEL 212-779-8900. Ed. Barry Janoff. adv.; bk.rev.; film rev.; illus.; circ. 386,549.

051 US
GALLERY SPECIALS. q. $4.95 per no. Montcalm Publishing Corp., 401 Park Ave. S., New York, NY 10016-8802. TEL 212-779-8900.

051 US ISSN 1052-8555
GENESIS (NEW YORK). 1973. m. $41 in Canada $47; elsewhere $51. Jakel Corp., 1776 Broadway, 20th fl., New York, NY 10019-2002. TEL 212-265-3500. FAX 212-265-8087. Ed. Michael Banka. adv.; bk.rev.; illus.; circ. 212,910.

051 US
▼**GENRE (NEW YORK).** 1991. bi-m. $11.95. Don Tuthill, Ed.& Pub, 60 E. 42nd St., Ste. 1166, New York, NY 10017. TEL 212-714-8160. circ. 100,000 (controlled).

070.38 US
GENT; home of the D-cups. 1959. m. $30. Dugent Publishing Corp., 2600 Douglas Rd., Ste. 600, Coral Gables, FL 33134. TEL 305-443-2378. (Subscr. to: Box 141, Mt. Morris, IL 61054) Ed. Bruce Arthur. film rev.; illus.; circ. 100,000.

051 US
GIRLS - GIRLS. 10/yr. $4.95 per no. Jakel Corp., 1776 Broadway, 20th Fl., New York, NY 10019. TEL 212-265-3500. FAX 212-265-8087.

051 US ISSN 0031-4935
GIRLS OF PENTHOUSE. 1969. m. $36. Penthouse International Ltd., 1965 Broadway, New York, NY 10023-4965. TEL 212-496-6100. Ed. Don Myrus. adv.; illus.; circ. 3,172,898. (back issues avail.) **Indexed:** Access, Film Lit.Ind., Mag.Ind., PMR.
   Description: Erotic literature.

616.858 UK ISSN 0265-8143
HQ77.9
GLAD RAG. 1982. bi-m. $60. Transvestite - Transsexual Support Group (UK), 2 French Place, London E1 6JB, England. TEL 081-908-1573. FAX 081-908-0460. Ed. Christine-Jane Wilson. adv.; bk.rev.; circ. 1,000. (back issues avail.)
   Description: Articles, fiction and humor for transvestites, transsexuals, their partners, families and friends.

051 MX ISSN 0187-8999
GOLDEN PENTHOUSE; para el hombre internacional. 1987. m. Mex.$12000 per issue. Corporacion Editorial, S.A. de C.V., Lucio Blanco 435, Col. San Juan Tlihuaca, 02400 Mexico D.F., Mexico. TEL 352-6056. Ed. Javier Ortiz. adv.; bk.rev.; circ. 40,000. (back issues avail.)

GREATER CINCINNATI - NORTHERN KENTUCKY BRIDE & GROOM MAGAZINE. see *MATRIMONY*

GUIDE MAGAZINE (SEATTLE). see *HOMOSEXUALITY*

H A C TECHLINE. (Historical Aircraft Corporation) see *AERONAUTICS AND SPACE FLIGHT*

305.2 US
HARVEY FOR LOVING PEOPLE. 1979. m. $34.95. Harvey Shapiro, Ed. & Pub. (New York), 450 Seventh Ave., Ste. 2305, New York, NY 10001. TEL 212-564-0112. adv.; circ. 200,000.

051 US
▼**HAWK.** 1991. 13/yr. $36. Killer Joe Productions, Inc., 801 Second Ave., New York, NY 10017. TEL 212-986-5100. Ed. Bob Johnson. adv.: B&W page $2000. circ. 250,000.
   Description: Targets men in their 20s and 30s, with editorial on fashion, fitness, and music.

305.3 301.412 US
HE - SHE DIRECTORY. a. $11. Continental Spectator, Box 278, Canal St. Sta., New York, NY 10013. TEL 718-625-6309. Ed. Linda Lee.
   Description: Devoted to the interest of transvestites, transsexuals, cross-dressers, female impersonators, and people who want to contact these people.

3398 MEN'S INTERESTS

070.48 US
HEARTLAND U.S.A. q. U S T Publishing, 418 N. River St., Box 925, Hailey, ID 83333.
TEL 208-788-4500. Ed. Brad Pearson. circ. 800,000.

051 US
HEAT. vol.2, 1989. 9/yr. $35.95 (foreign $39.95). Heat Publications, Inc. (Subsidiary of: Mavety Media Group Ltd.), 462 Broadway, Ste. 4000, New York, NY 10013. TEL 212-966-8400.
FAX 212-966-9366. (Dist. by: Flynt Distributing Co., 9171 Wilshire Blvd., Ste. 300, Beverly Hills, CA 90210) Ed. Chuck Love. illus.

070.48346 US
HIGH SOCIETY. 1976. m. (13/yr.). $39. Drake Publishers, 801 Second Ave., New York, NY 10017. TEL 212-986-5100. Ed. Stephen Loshiavo. adv.; illus.; circ. 294,952.

051 US
HIGH SOCIETY BOOK OF LINGERIE. q. $4.95 per no. Drake Publishers, 801 Second Ave., New York, NY 10017. TEL 212-661-7878. FAX 212-883-1244.

301.412 US
HIGH SOCIETY'S PRIVATE LETTERS. bi-m. $2.95 per no. Drake Publishers, 801 Second Ave., New York, NY 10017. TEL 212 661-7878.

305.3 056.1
HOMBRE DE MUNDO. (Editions avail. for Central America, Chile, Columbia, Ecuador, Mexico, Peru, Puerto Rico, U.S., Venezuela) (Text in Spanish) 1976. m. $22.50. Editorial America, S.A., Vanidades Continental Bldg., 6355 N.W. 36th St., Virginia Gardens, FL 33166. TEL 305-871-6400. FAX 305-871-8769. Ed. Frank Calderon. adv.; circ. 95,418.

051 US
HOMESTYLE AFFAIRS. bi-m $2.95 per no. Vanity Publications, 475 Park Ave. S., New York, NY 10016. TEL 212-213-8620. FAX 212-532-1302.

051 US
HONCHO. vol.12, no.5, 1989. m. $39.95 (foreign $59.95). Modernismo Publications, Inc. (Subsidiary of: Mavety Media Group Ltd.), 462 Broadway, Ste. 4000, New York, NY 10013. TEL 212-966-8400. (Dist. by: Flynt Distributing Co., 9171 Wilshire Blvd., Ste. 300, Beverly Hills, CA 90210) Ed. Stan Leventhal.
  Description: Contains male erotica, stories, and nonfiction articles.

051 US
HONCHO OVERLOAD; two handed man to man action. vol.4, no.3, 1989. 9/yr. $19.95 (foreign $34). Overload Company, Ltd. (Subsidiary of: Mavety Media Group Ltd.), 462 Broadway, Ste. 4000, New York, NY 10013. TEL 212-966-8400. (Dist. by: Flynt Distributing Co., 9171 Wilshire Blvd., Ste. 300, Beverly Hills, CA 90210) Ed. Jake Savage. illus.

051 US
HOOTERS. q. Leisure Plus Publications, Inc. (Subsidiary of: Mavety Media Group Ltd.), 462 Broadway, Ste. 4000, New York, NY 10013. TEL 212-966-8400. (Dist. by: Flynt Distributing Co., 9171 Wilshire Blvd., Ste. 300, Beverly Hills, CA 90210)

070.48 JA
HOT DOG PRESS. (Text in Japanese) 1979. s-m. Kodansha Ltd., International Division, 12-21 Otowa 2-chome, Bunkyo-ku, Tokyo 112, Japan.
TEL 03-3945-1111. FAX 03-3943-7815. TELEX J34509 KODANSHA. Ed. Atsuhide Kokubo. circ. 650,000.
  Description: Variety magazine for young men.

808 US
HOT LETTERS. 1980. bi-m. $18. J L J Communications, 310 Cedar Lane, Teaneck, NJ 07666. TEL 201-836-9177. FAX 201-836-5055. Ed. Jackie Lewis. adv.; circ. 65,900. (back issues avail.)
  Description: Erotic literature.

051 US
HOT TALK. bi-m. $4.95 per no. General Media, 1965 Broadway, New York, NY 10023.
TEL 800-227-1346. FAX 212-873-4071.

301.412 US ISSN 0149-4635
AP2
HUSTLER. 1974. 13/yr. $39.95. Larry Flynt Publications, Inc., 9171 Wilshire Blvd., Ste. 300, Beverly Hills, CA 90210. TEL 310-858-7100.
FAX 310-275-3857. Ed. Allan McDonell. adv.; bk.rev.; film rev.; play rev.; circ. 1,500,000. (back issues avail.)

051 US
HUSTLER BUSTY BEAUTIES. 1988. m. $39.95. H G Publications, Inc., 9171 Wilshire Blvd., Ste. 300, Beverly Hills, CA 90210. TEL 213-858-7100. Ed. N. Morgen Hagen. circ. 180,000. (back issues avail.)

051 US
HUSTLER EROTIC VIDEO GUIDE. 1985. m. $39.95. Larry Flynt Publications, Inc., 9171 Wilshire, Ste. 300, Beverly Hills, CA 90210. TEL 310-858-7100. FAX 310-275-3857. (Subscr. to: Box 16507, N. Hollywood, CA 91615) Ed. Mal O'Ree. film rev. (back issues avail.)
  Description: Reviews of and behind-the-scene looks at erotic video, the performers and producers, plus interviews.

301.412 US
HUSTLER FANTASIES. m. $27.95. Larry Flynt Publications, Inc., 9171 Wilshire Blvd., Ste. 300, Beverly Hills, CA 90210. TEL 310-858-7100. FAX 310-275-3857.

301.412 US ISSN 0199-5405
HUSTLER HUMOR. m. $33.95. Larry Flynt Publications, Inc., 9171 Wilshire Blvd., Ste. 300, Beverly Hills, CA 90210. TEL 310-858-7100. FAX 310-275-3857. Ed. Minette Watkins.

305.3 FR
IL; magazine de l'homme cosmopolite. m. 150 Fr. 30 bis rue Spontini, 75016 Paris, France. Ed. S. Slama.

IMPETUS. see ART

051 US
INCHES. vol.5, no.4, 1989. m. $39.95 (foreign $59.95). Inches, Inc. (Subsidiary of: Mavety Media Group Ltd.), 462 Broadway, Ste. 4000, New York, NY 10013. TEL 212-966-8400. (Dist. by: Flynt Distributing Co., 9171 Wilshire Blvd., Ste. 300, Beverly Hills, CA 90210) Ed. John W. Rowberrgy. illus.

JIATING/FAMILY. see HOME ECONOMICS

JOURNAL OF COUPLES THERAPY. see PSYCHOLOGY

305.3 US
▼**JOURNEYMEN.** 1991. q. $18 (Canada $24). 513 Chester Turnpike, Candia, NH 03034. Ed. Paul S. Boynton. adv.: B&W page $155; trim 7 1/2 x 10. illus.
  Description: Presents a wide variety of subject matter, as it relates to the male experience.

051 US ISSN 0734-4309
JUGGS. vol.8, no.8, 1989. m. $39.95 (foreign $55.95). M M Publications, Ltd. (Subsidiary of: Mavety Media Group Ltd.), 462 Broadway, Ste. 4000, New York, NY 10013. TEL 212-966-8400. (Dist. by: Flynt Distributing Co., 9171 Wilshire Blvd., Ste. 300, Beverly Hills, CA 90210) Ed. Dian Hanson. illus.

KING. see CLOTHING TRADE — Fashions

052 UK ISSN 0265-1289
KNAVE. 1968. m. £40. Galaxy Publications Ltd., P.O. Box 312, Witham, Essex CM8 3SZ, England. Ed. David Rider. adv.; bk.rev.; circ. 154,735.

051 US
LATIN MEN. q. Heat Publications, Inc. (Subsidiary of: Mavety Media Group Ltd.), 462 Broadway, Ste. 4000, New York, NY 10013. TEL 212-966-8400. (Dist. by: Flynt Distributing Co., 9171 Wilshire Blvd., Ste. 300, Beverly Hills, CA 90210)

051 US
LATIN WOMEN. q. Leisure Plus Publications, Inc. (Subsidiary of: Mavety Media Group Ltd.), 462 Broadway, Ste. 4000, New York, NY 10013. TEL 212-966-8400. (Dist. by: Flynt Distributing Co., 9171 Wilshire Blvd., Ste. 300, Beverly Hills, CA 90210

051 US ISSN 0734-4295
LEG SHOW. vol.7, no.2, 1989. m. $39.95 (foreign $55.95). Leg Glamour, Inc. (Subsidiary of: Mavety Media Group Ltd.), 462 Broadway, Ste. 4000, New York, NY 10013. TEL 212-966-8400. (Dist. by: Flynt Distributing Co., 9171 Wilshire Blvd., Ste. 300, Beverly Hills, CA 90210) Ed. Dian Hanson. illus.

051 US
LEG SHOW PRESENTS HIGH-HEELED WOMEN. vol.2, no.2, 1989. q. $4.95 per no. Leg Glamour, Inc. (Subsidiary of: Mavety Media Group Ltd.), 462 Broadway, Ste. 4000, New York, NY 10013.
TEL 212-966-8400. (Dist. by: Flynt Distributing Co., 2029 Century Park E., Ste. 3800, Los Angeles, CA 90067) illus.

LEGEND OF JENNIE LEE. see CLUBS

808 US ISSN 0279-1250
LETTERS MAGAZINE (TEANECK). 1979. m. $32. J L J Communications, 310 Cedar Lane, Box 1314, Teaneck, NJ 07666. TEL 201-836-9177.
FAX 201-836-5055. Ed. Jackie Lewis. adv.; circ. 97,535. (back issues avail.)
  Description: Erotic literature.

305.3 340 US ISSN 1040-3760
LIBERATOR; male call. 1968. m. $20. Men's Rights Association, 17854 Lyons St., Forest Lake, MN 55025. TEL 612-464-7663. Ed. Richard F. Doyle. adv.; bk.rev.; circ. 2,000. (back issues avail.)
  Formerly: Legal Beagle.
  Description: Supports equal treatment for men in gender issues, divorce, employment, crime and punishment, and image.

051 US
LIPS (NEW YORK). 1989. m. $32.95. Leisure Plus Publications, Inc. (Subsidiary of: Mavety Media Group Ltd.), 462 Broadway, Ste. 4000, New York, NY 10013. TEL 212-966-8400. (Dist. by: Flynt Distributing Co., 9171 Wilshire Blvd., Ste. 300, Beverly Hills, CA 90210) illus.

051 US
LIVERPOOL LIBRARY - CLASSIC. m. Liverpool International, Ltd. (Subsidiary of: Mavety Media Group Ltd.), 462 Broadway, Ste. 4000, New York, NY 10013. TEL 212-966-8400. (Dist. by: Kable News Co., 11 W. 42nd St., 28th Fl., New York, NY 10036. TEL 212-768-1000)

LONG ISLAND PARENTING NEWS. see CHILDREN AND YOUTH — About

LOVING MORE. see SOCIOLOGY

054.1 FR
LUI; magazine de l'homme moderne. 1963. m. 220 F. (foreign 355 F.). Publications Filipacchi, 63-65 Champs Elysees, 75008 Paris, France.
TEL 42-56-72-72. TELEX 290294. (Subscr. to: 99 rue d'Amsterdam, 75008 Paris, France) adv.; illus.; circ. 507,530.

070.48346 GW
LUI. 1977. m. DM.99. RedMag Gesellschaft fuer Redaktionelle Dienstleistungen, Buttermelcherstr. 16, D-8000 Munich 5, Germany. TEL 089-2025200. (Subscr. to: I P V Presse Vertrieb GmbH, Wendenstr. 27-29, D-2000 Hamburg 1, Germany) Ed. Heinz van Nouhuys. circ. 303,200. (back issues avail.)

M. see CLOTHING TRADE — Fashions

M G F. (Mens's Guide to Fashion) see CLOTHING TRADE — Fashions

M R. (Menswear Retailing) see CLOTHING TRADE

MAENNER VOGUE. see CLOTHING TRADE — Fashions

051 US
MALE INSIDER. Short title: M I. vol.3, no.6, 1989. q. $14.95 (foreign $34.95). Macho Publications, Inc. (Subsidiary of: Mavety Media Group Ltd.), 462 Broadway, Ste. 4000, New York, NY 10013. TEL 212-966-8400. (Dist. by: Flynt Distributing Co., 9171 Wilshire Blvd., Ste. 300, Beverly Hills, CA 90210) Ed. Joe Mauro. illus.

MEN'S INTERESTS

070.48346 US ISSN 1056-5175
▼**MAN!**. 1990. q. $12 (Canada $17; elsewhere $27). 1611 W. Sixth St., Austin, TX 78703. Ed. Lyman Grant. circ. 10,000. (also avail. in microfilm from KTO)
Description: Addresses issues of men in modern society, and recovery from unhealthy life patterns. Includes essays, articles and poetry.

301 NE
MAN. 1972. m. fl.72. B.V. Uitgeversmaatschappij Bonaventura, Hoogoorddreef 60, 1101 BE Amsterdam, Netherlands. TEL 20-5674911. FAX 20-56749629. TELEX 14013 BONAV NL. Ed. Rupert V. Woerkom. adv.; illus.

070.48346 SI
MAN - LIFE & STYLE. (Text in English) 1986. bi-m. 322A Jalan Besar, SLS Bldg., Singapore 0820, Singapore. TEL 2968178. FAX 2968319. TELEX 24200. Ed. Michael Chiang. circ. 20,000.

070.483 059.992 IO
MATRA. 1986. m. Jalan H.R. Rasuna Said, Lav. 62, Jakarta, Indonesia. TEL 021-515952. TELEX 46777. Ed. Fikri Jufri. circ. 100,000.

051 US ISSN 8756-7644
MAX. vol.4, no.3, 1989. 9/yr. $37.95 (foreign $47.95). Max Magazine, Inc. (Subsidiary of: Mavety Media Group Ltd.), 462 Broadway, Ste. 4000, New York, NY 10013. TEL 212-966-8400. (Dist. by: Kable News Co., 11 W. 42nd St., 28th Fl., New York, NY 10036. TEL 212-768-1000) Ed. Dian Hanson. illus.

070.48346 UK ISSN 0025-6161
MAYFAIR. 1966. m. £20. Paul Raymond Organisation, Ed. Kenneth Bound. adv.; bk.rev.; circ. 354,000.

051 US
▼**MEN.*** 1990. bi-m. $14.95. Norris Publishing, Inc., 7 Worcester Sq., Boston, MA 02118-2701. TEL 203-259-7015. Ed. Peter Kaplan. circ. 140,000.
Description: For men in their early thirties who are starting to make major lifestyle decisions. Covers clothing, food, travel, sports, health, money, home repair and women.

052 UK ISSN 0025-9217
MEN ONLY. m. 50s.($9) Paul Raymond Publications Ltd., 2 Archer St., London W1, England. Ed. Tony Power. bk.rev.; film rev.; circ. 150,000.

305.3 GW
MEN'S FASHION. (Text in English, French and German) 1983. s-a. DM.31 (foreign DM.32). Deutscher Fachverlag GmbH, Mainzer Landstr. 251, Postfach 100606, 6000 Frankfurt 1, Germany. TEL 069-7595-01. Ed. Peter Alex Pohl. circ. 10,000.

051 US
▼**MEN'S JOURNAL.** 1992. 2/yr. Straight Arrow Publishers, Inc., 1290 Ave. of the Americas, New York, NY 10104. TEL 212-484-1616. (Subscr. to: Box 57055, Boulder, CO 80322-7055) Ed. John Rasmus. circ. 100,000.
Description: Active men's journal with articles featuring travel and adventure.

MISS MOM - MISTER MOM. see *CHILDREN AND YOUTH — About*

305.3 CN
MOMENTUM. 3/yr. $10. Alberta Men's Resource Centre, 4342 - 97 St., Edmonton, Alta. T6E 5R9, Canada. TEL 403-430-0418.

054.1 FR
MR. q. 12 F. per copy. Publications Mandel, 3, rue de l'Arrivee, 75749 Paris, France. Ed. Charles Mandel. adv.

056.1 808 CU
MUJERES Y MUCHACHA. m. $48. (Federacion de Mujeres Cubanas) Ediciones Cubanas, Departamento de Exportacion, Obispo No. 461, Apdo. 605, Havana, Cuba. illus.
Formerly: Romances.

070.483 US
NANZI HAN/MANLINESS. (Text in Chinese) bi-m. $20.70. China Books & Periodicals, Inc., 2929 24th St., San Francisco, CA 94110. TEL 415-282-2994. FAX 415-282-0994.

051 US
NASTY LETTERS. bi-m. Starlight Press, Inc. (Subsidiary of: Mavety Media Group Ltd.), 462 Broadway, Ste. 4000, New York, NY 10013. TEL 212-966-8400. (Dist. by: Flynt Distributing Co., 9171 Wilshire Blvd., Ste. 300, Beverly Hills, CA 90210)

051 US
NASTY PHOTOS. q. Leisure Plus Publications, Inc. (Subsidiary of: Mavety Media Group Ltd.), 462 Broadway, Ste. 4000, New York, NY 10013. TEL 212-966-8400. (Dist. by: Flynt Distributing Co., 9171 Wilshire Blvd., Ste. 300, Beverly Hills, CA 90210)

NATURAL PHYSIQUE. see *PHYSICAL FITNESS AND HYGIENE*

NORTH COAST BRIDE AND GROOM. see *MATRIMONY*

051 US
OFF-BEAT LETTERS. bi-m. Opal Press, Inc. (Subsidiary of: Mavety Media Group Ltd.), 462 Broadway, Ste. 4000, New York, NY 10013. TEL 212-966-8400. (Dist. by: Flynt Distributing Co., 9171 Wilshire Blvd., Ste. 300, Beverly Hills, CA 90210)

ONTARIO WRESTLER MAGAZINE. see *SPORTS AND GAMES*

051 US
OPTIONS (PORT CHESTER). 1981. 10/yr. $19.90. A J A Publishing Corp., Box 470, Port Chester, NY 10573. Ed. Don Stone. adv.; film rev.; circ. 75,000. (back issues avail.)
Description: Emphasizes safe, loving relationships. Covers sexual interactions between homosexuals, bisexuals, and lesbians.

051 US
ORALRAMA!. 1989. q. $4.95 per no. Leisure Plus Publications, Inc. (Subsidiary of: Mavety Media Group Ltd.), 462 Broadway, Ste. 4000, New York, NY 10013. TEL 212-966-8400. (Dist. by: Flynt Distributing Co., 9171 Wilshire Blvd., Ste. 300, Beverly Hills, CA 90210) illus.

051 US
ORIENTAL DOLLS. q. Leisure Plus Publications, Inc. (Subsidiary of: Mavety Media Group Ltd.), 462 Broadway, Ste. 4000, New York, NY 10013. TEL 212-966-8400. (Dist. by: Flynt Distributing Co., 9171 Wilshire Blvd., Ste. 300, Beverly Hills, CA 90210)

OSTENTATIOUS MIND. see *LITERARY AND POLITICAL REVIEWS*

051 US ISSN 0090-2047
AP2
OUI; for the man of the world. 1972. m. $59.40. Laurant Publishing, Ltd., 300 W. 43rd St., New York, NY 10136. FAX 212-247-3367. Ed.Bd. adv.; bk.rev.; circ. 350,000. **Indexed:** Access, Mag.Ind.

OUT. see *HOMOSEXUALITY*

070.48346 US
OUTRAGEOUS LETTERS. bi-m. $18. Vanity Publications, 475 Park Ave. S., New York, NY 10016. Ed. Sybil Norfolk.
Description: Contains erotica.

051 US
OVER 40. vol.2, no.2, 1989. bi-m. $39.95. Leisure Plus Publications, Inc. (Subsidiary of: Mavety Media Group Ltd.), 462 Broadway, Ste. 4000, New York, NY 10013. TEL 212-966-8400. (Dist. by: Flynt Distributing Co., 2029 Century Park E., Ste. 3800, Los Angeles, CA 90067) illus.

051 US
OVER 50. q. Leisure Plus Publications, Inc. (Subsidiary of: Mavety Media Group Ltd.), 462 Broadway, Ste. 4000, New York, NY 10013. TEL 212-966-8400. (Dist. by: Flynt Distributing Co., 9171 Wilshire Blvd., Ste. 300, Beverly Hills, CA 90210)

070.48346 UK
PAUL RAYMOND'S MODEL DIRECTORY. 1980. q. Paul Raymond Publications Ltd., 2 Archer St., London W1V 7HE, England. TEL 01 734 9191. (back issues avail.)

363.47 HK
PENTHOUSE. (Text in Chinese) 1985. m. Yongder Hall Ltd., G-F, Cheung Kong Bldg., 661 Kings Road, Quarry Bay, Hong Kong, Hong Kong. TEL 565-1313. FAX 565-8217. Eds. Alan Zie Yongder, Andrew Ho. adv.; film rev.; circ. 51,684.

051 US ISSN 0090-2020
AP2
PENTHOUSE; international magazine for men. 1969. m. $36. Penthouse International Ltd., 1965 Broadway, New York, NY 10023-5965. TEL 212-496-6100. Ed. Bob Guccione. adv.; circ. 2,000,000. **Indexed:** Access (1975-).

052 UK
PENTHOUSE (UK). 1964. m. £31. Infonet Ltd., 5 River Park Ind. Area, Billet Lane, Berkhamsted, Herts HP4 1HL, England. TEL 04427 76661. circ. 114,191.

051 US ISSN 0883-8798
PENTHOUSE LETTERS. 1979. m. $28. Penthouse International Ltd., 1965 Broadway, New York, NY 10023-4965. TEL 212-496-6100. Ed. Don Myrus. adv.; bk.rev.; circ. 550,000.

051 US
PERSUASION. bi-m. Domino Press, Inc., 462 Broadway, Ste. 4000, New York, NY 10013. TEL 212-966-8400. (Dist. by: Flynt Distributing Co., 9171 Wilshire Blvd., Ste. 300, Beverly Hills, CA 90210)

051 US
PILLOW TALK; the journal of sexual fulfillment. 1977. m. $12. Carla Publishing, 801 Second Ave., New York, NY 10017. Ed. I. Catherine Duff.

051 US ISSN 0032-1478
AP2
PLAYBOY. 1953. m. $29.97 (foreign $45; Canada $47.48)(effective 1992). Playboy Enterprises, Inc., 1680 N. Lake Shore Dr., Chicago, IL 60611. TEL 312-751-8000. FAX 312-751-2818. TELEX 190166. (Subscr. to: Box 2007, Harlan, IA 51537. TEL 800-999-4438) Ed. Hugh Hefner. adv.; bk.rev.; film rev.; illus.; record rev.; index, cum.index: 1953-68, 1969-73, 1974-78, 1979-83, 1984-88; circ. 3,555,663. (also avail. in microform from UMI,BHP; reprint service avail. from UMI)
Indexed: Access (1975-), Film Lit.Ind. (1973-), Mag.Ind., Media Rev.Dig., PMR.

056.9 BL
PLAYBOY. 1975. m. $120. Editora Abril, S.A., R. Geraldo Flausino Gomes, 61, 04575 Sao Paulo, Brazil. TEL 011-8239222. FAX 011-86437964. TELEX 011-80360 EDAB BR. (Subscr. to: Rua do Curtume, 769 CEP 05065 Lapa, Sao Paulo, Brazil) adv.; film rev.; illus.; circ. 289,728.
Formerly: Homen.
Description: Presents the most beautiful and famous women of Brazil and the world.

055.1 UK
PLAYBOY.* m. Publicitas Ltd., 525-527 Fulham Rd., London SW6 1HF, England. adv.

054.1 FR
PLAYBOY. m. 150 F. Publications Filipacchi, 63-65 Champs Elysees, 75008 Paris, France. (Subscr. to: 99 rue d'Amsterdam, 75008 Paris, France)

070.48346 NE
PLAYBOY.* 1983. m. fl.7.50. Uitgeverij Spaarnestad B.V., Europalaan 93, 3526 KP Utrecht, Netherlands. FAX 023-304213. TELEX 41371. Ed. Jan Heemskerk. adv.; bk.rev.; circ. 164,000.

070.48346 GW
PLAYBOY. 1972. m. $80. Heinrich Bauer Verlag (Munich), Charles-de-Gaulle-Str. 8, 8000 Munich 83, Germany. TEL 089-6786-400. FAX 089-672981. (Distr. by: German Language Publications Inc., 560 Sylvan Ave., Englewood Cliffs, NJ 07632. TEL 201-871-1010) Ed. W. Maier. circ. 281,023.

PLAYBOY ENTERPRISES. ANNUAL REPORT. see *BUSINESS AND ECONOMICS — Abstracting, Bibliographies, Statistics*

3400 MEN'S STUDIES

051   US   ISSN 0733-5695
PLAYGUY. vol.13, 1989. m. $39.95. Playguy Publications, Ltd. (Subsidiary of: Mavety Media Group Ltd.), 462 Broadway, Ste. 4000, New York, NY 10013. TEL 212-966-8400. (Dist. by: Flynt Distributing Co., 9171 Wilshire Blvd., Ste. 300, Beverly Hills, CA 90210) Ed. Stan Leventhal. adv.; bk.rev.; film rev.; play rev.; illus.; circ. 75,000. (back issues avail.)

070.4834   IT   ISSN 0032-1532
PLAYMEN; mensile di cultura, attualita, politica e costume. 1967. m. L.66000. Periodici Tattilo s.r.l., Via del Casale Piombino N. 30, 00135 Rome, Italy. Ed. Giuseppe Catalano. adv.; bk.rev.; illus.; circ. 300,000.

PRIMAVERA (CHICAGO). see *WOMEN'S INTERESTS*

051   US
PRIVATE MOMENTS. bi-m. Mountainside Press, Inc., 462 Broadway, Ste. 4000, New York, NY 10013. TEL 212-966-8400. (Dist. by: Flynt Distributing Co., 9171 Wilshire Blvd., Ste. 300, Beverly Hills, CA 90210).

Q W. (Queer World) see *HOMOSEXUALITY*

RELATIONSHIPS TODAY. see *WOMEN'S INTERESTS*

305.3 301.412   US
SANDMUTOPIA GUARDIAN & DUNGEON JOURNAL.* 1988. q. $24. Desmodus Inc., Box 410390, San Francisco, CA 94141-0390. TEL 415-252-1195. Ed. Carol Truscott. adv.; bk.rev.; film rev.; play rev.; illus.; circ. 5,000. (back issues avail.)

305.3   SA   ISSN 0036-9012
SCOPE. 1966. fortn. R.80.60. Republican Press (Pty) Ltd., Box 32083, Mobeni 4060, Natal, South Africa. Ed. David Mullany. bk.rev.; film rev.; circ. 120,000.
Description: Features glamour, sensationalism, adventure, humour, and escapism.

SCREW. see *LITERARY AND POLITICAL REVIEWS*

SENSATIONS. see *LITERATURE*

070.48346   US
SENSUOUS LETTERS. bi-m. $18. Vanity Publications, 475 Park Ave. S., New York, NY 10016.

SER PADRES/BEING PARENTS. see *WOMEN'S INTERESTS*

SINGLE SOURCE NEWSLETTER. see *SINGLES' INTERESTS AND LIFESTYLES*

SINGLE'S LIFE. see *SINGLES' INTERESTS AND LIFESTYLES*

SKIP MAGAZINE; the community service magazine for schools, kids, involved parents. see *EDUCATION — Teaching Methods And Curriculum*

051   US
SPECIAL EDITION; personal letters; red-hot letters; confidential letters. 1981. bi-m. A J A Publishing Corp., Box 470, Port Chester, NY 10573. Ed. Josh Piano. adv.; circ. 75,000.
Description: Letters from readers on a variety of sexual topics.

SPOSA 2000; the bilingual wedding planner. see *MATRIMONY*

051   US   ISSN 0745-3639
STALLION; the new breed of rugged male. vol.2, no.3, 1989. 9/yr. $32.95 (foreign $59.95). Stallion Publications, Inc. (Subsidiary of: Mavety Media Group Ltd.), 462 Broadway, Ste. 4000, New York, NY 10013. TEL 212-966-8400. (Dist. by: Flynt Distributing Co., 9171 Wilshire Blvd., Ste. 300, Beverly Hills, CA 90210) Ed. Joe Mauro. illus.

STEPFAMILIES & BEYOND; America's first independent newsletter about remarriage for stepparents and professionals. see *CHILDREN AND YOUTH — About*

051   US
SWANK. 1956. m. $52. G C R Publishing Group, Inc., 1700 Broadway, 34th Fl., New York, NY 10019. TEL 212-541-7100. Ed. Michael Wilde. adv.; circ. 200,000.

051   US
SWINGERS UPDATE. 1980. bi-m. $29.95. Contact Advertising, 2010 St. Lucie Blvd., Ft. Pierce, FL 34946. (Subscr. to: Box 3431, Ft. Pierce, FL 34948) Ed. Holly Adams. film rev.; circ. 9,000 (controlled).
Description: Provides news to couples interested in sexual experimentation.

051   US
SWINGING TIMES. 1982. m. $19.95. Contact Advertising, 2010 St. Lucie Blvd., Ft. Pierce, FL 34946. TEL 407-464-5447. (Subscr. to: Box 3431, Ft. Pierce, FL 34948) Ed. Holly Adams. film rev.; circ. 12,500. (tabloid format)
Description: Introductory lifestyles publication intended to educate singles interested in sexual experimentation.

051   US
TAIL ENDS. 1989. m. $39.95. Leisure Plus Publications, Inc. (Subsidiary of: Mavety Media Group Ltd.), 462 Broadway, Ste. 4000, New York, NY 10013. TEL 212-966-8400. (Dist. by: Flynt Distributing Co., 9171 Wilshire Blvd., Ste. 300, Beverly Hills, CA 90210) illus.

TO US. see *WOMEN'S INTERESTS*

TORCH RUNNER. see *RELIGIONS AND THEOLOGY — Protestant*

TORCHLIGHT. see *RELIGIONS AND THEOLOGY — Judaic*

051   US   ISSN 0733-5865
TORSO; the new era in all-male erotica. 1981. m. $39.95. Varsity Communications, Ltd. (Subsidiary of: Mavety Media Group Ltd.), 462 Broadway, Ste. 4000, New York, NY 10013. TEL 212-966-8400. (Dist. by: Flynt Distributing Co., 9171 Wilshire Blvd., Ste. 300, Beverly Hills, CA 90210) Ed. Stan Leventhal. adv.; bk.rev.; circ. 150,000. (back issues avail.)

051   US
TURN-ON LETTERS. 1981. 10/yr. $18.75. A J A Publishing Corp., Box 470, Port Chester, NY 10573. Ed. Julie Silver. adv.; circ. 75,000.
Description: Letters from readers on a variety of sexual subjects.

051   US
TURN-ONS. 1980. 5/yr. A J A Publishing Corp., Box 470, Port Chester, NY 10573. Ed. John Velvel. adv.; circ. 75,000.
Description: Letters from readers on a variety of sexual topics.

TWIN CITIES GAZE; the news weekly for the gay and lesbian community. see *HOMOSEXUALITY*

051 301.412   US
UNCENSORED SWINGER. a. $11. Continental Spectator, Box 278, Canal St. Sta., New York, NY 10013. TEL 718-625-6309. Ed. Linda Lee.

051   US
UNCUT; the magazine of the natural man. vol.3, no.6, 1989. bi-m. $19.95 (foreign $34.95). Crete International, Inc. (Subsidiary of: Mavety Media Group Ltd.), 462 Broadway, Ste. 4000, New York, NY 10013. TEL 212-966-8400. (Dist. by: Flynt Distributing Co., 2029 Century Park E., Ste. 3800, Los Angeles, CA 90067) Ed. John W. Rowberry. illus.

058.82   NO   ISSN 0042-4951
VI MENN. 1951. w. NOK 1196. Ernst G. Mortensens Forlag AS, Soerkedalsveien 10 A, 0369 Oslo, Norway. TEL 02-603090. FAX 02-692542. TELEX 77626. Ed. Putte Oederud. illus.; circ. 118,912.

VIDEO RESERVED COLLECTION. see *COMMUNICATIONS — Video*

VIVE LA DIFFERENCE. see *SOCIOLOGY*

051   US
WANTED. bi-m. Metal Hammer Communications, Inc., 462 Broadway, Ste. 4000, New York, NY 10013. TEL 212-966-8400. (Dist. by: Flynt Distributing Co., 9171 Wilshire Blvd., Ste. 300, Beverly Hills, CA 90210)

051   US
WILD WEST. bi-m. $16.95 (foreign $22.95). Empire Press, 602 S. King St. Ste. 300, Leesburg, VA 22075. TEL 703-771-9400. FAX 703-777-4627. (Subscr. to: Box 385, Mt. Morris, IL 61054-7943. TEL 815-734-1115)
Description: Explains the struggle to settle America's frontier.

WILDFOWL; the magazine for duck & goose hunters. see *SPORTS AND GAMES — Outdoor Life*

808   US
X LETTERS. 1980. bi-m. $18. J L J Communications, 310 Cedar Lane, Teaneck, NJ 07666. TEL 201-836-9177. FAX 201-836-5055. Ed. Jackie Lewis. adv.; circ. 66,000. (back issues avail.)
Description: Erotic literature.

051   US
YELLOW PAGE MODEL DIRECTORY. a. $11. Continental Spectator, Box 278, Canal St. Sta., New York, NY 10013. TEL 718-625-6309. Ed. Linda Lee.
Description: Photo lay-outs and personal ads of nude models nationwide.

051   US
▼**YOUNG EXECUTIVE.** 1992. q. $2.95 per no. Rodale Press, Inc., 33 Minor St., Emmaus, PA 18098. TEL 215-967-5171. Ed. Mark Bricklin. adv.; illus.; circ. 200,000.
Description: Covers lifestyle and career advancement issues for career oriented men 25-40.

070.48346   UK
ZIPPER. 1977. every 6 weeks. £35($70) Millivres Ltd., 283 Camden High St., London NW1 7BX, England. TEL 01-267 7665. Ed. Alex McKenna. circ. 40,000. (back issues avail.)

MEN'S STUDIES

301   US   ISSN 0889-7174
HQ1090.3
CHANGING MEN; issues in gender, sex and politics. 1979. 2/yr. $40 to individuals; institutions $40 for 4 nos. Feminist Men's Publications, 306 N. Brooks St., Madison, WI 53715. Eds. Michael Biernbaum, Rick Cote. adv.; bk.rev.; illus.; circ. 4,000. **Indexed:** Alt.Press Ind.
Formerly (until Apr. 1985): M: Gentle Men for Gender Justice.
Description: Covers men's psychology, health, relationships, the men's movement, ending violence, rape, fathering and sexuality.

GENDER AND EDUCATION. see *EDUCATION*

GENDER AND HISTORY. see *HISTORY*

GENDER AND SOCIETY. see *SOCIOLOGY*

MALE - FEMALE ROLES; opposing viewpoints sources. see *ANTHROPOLOGY*

MAN!. see *MEN'S INTERESTS*

MEN'S JOURNAL. see *MEN'S INTERESTS*

STUDIES IN GENDER AND CULTURE. see *SOCIOLOGY*

TODAY'S DADS. see *LAW — Family And Matrimonial Law*

155.362 305.3   US
WINGSPAN: JOURNAL OF THE MALE SPIRIT. 1986. q. donation. Box 23550, Brightmoor Sta., Detroit, MI 48223. TEL 617-876-1999. Ed. Christopher Harding. circ. 150,000 (controlled).
Description: Covers issues pertaining to male psychology and spirituality, with think pieces from leaders of the men's movement, workshop profiles and extensive listings of nationwide men's events.

METALLURGY

see also Metallurgy–Welding

669   BL
TN4   CODEN: MABMA5
A B M METALURGIA E MATERIAIS. 1965. m. $45 (foreign $90). Associacao Brasileira de Metalurgia e Materiais, Rua Antonio Comparato 218, C.P. 42081, 04605 Sao Paulo, Brazil. FAX 2404273. TELEX 2404273. Ed. Vicente Chiaverini. adv.; bk.rev.; abstr.; charts; illus.; stat.; index, cum.index every 10 yrs.; circ. 8,000. (also avail. in microform from UMI) Indexed: Chem.Abstr., Met.Abstr.
   Formerly: Metalurgia A B M (ISSN 0026-0983); Formed by the merger of: A B M Boletim; A B M Noticiario.

669   US
A E S NEWSLETTER. m. Abrasive Engineering Society, 108 Elliot Dr., Butler, PA 16001-1118. TEL 412-282-6210. Ed. Ted Giese. circ. 1,000.

A F P - AUTO; bulletin quotidien d'informations. (Agence France-Presse) see *TRANSPORTATION — Automobiles*

A I M M SYMPOSIA SERIES. (Australasian Institute of Mining and Metallurgy) see *MINES AND MINING INDUSTRY*

669   US
A I S E YEARBOOK. 1907. a. $60 to non-members; members $45. Association of Iron and Steel Engineers, Three Gateway Center, Ste. 2350, Pittsburgh, PA 15222. TEL 412-281-6323. Ed. Charles J. Labee. index; circ. 600.
   Formerly: Association of Iron and Steel Engineers. A I S E Proceedings.

A M C JOURNAL. (American Mining Congress) see *MINES AND MINING INDUSTRY*

669   US   ISSN 0044-7889
A S M NEWS (MATERIALS PARK). 1929. m. membership only. (American Society for Metals) A S M International, Materials Park, OH 44073-0002. TEL 216-338-5151. FAX 216-338-4634. TELEX 98-0619 ASMINT. Ed. Sarina Pastoric. adv.; illus.; stat.; circ. 52,000.
   Description: Covers materials technology with news from professional, political, industrial and public sectors.

669.1   IT   ISSN 0001-4567
L'ACCIAIO INOSSIDABILE. 1933. q. free. Edizioni Avesta S.P.A. Acciai Inossidabili, Viale Lancetti 36, 20158 Milan, Italy. TEL FAX 6965325. TELEX 330398 ASPA I. Ed. Alessandro Amoroso. bk.rev.; bibl.; charts; illus.; stat.; index; circ. 2,000. (also avail. in microform from UMI) Indexed: Chem.Abstr., Met.Abstr., World Alum.Abstr.
   Description: Features technical articles on the different uses of stainless steel, both in engineering and in art.

ACIER DANS LE MONDE. see *BUILDING AND CONSTRUCTION*

669   US   ISSN 0956-7151
CODEN: AMATEB
ACTA METALLURGICA ET MATERIALIA; an international journal for the science of materials. (Text in English, French, German) 1953. m. $625 (effective 1992.) Pergamon Press, Inc., Journals Division, 660 White Plains Rd., Tarrytown, NY 10591-5153. TEL 914-524-9200. FAX 914-333-2444. (And: Headington Hill Hall, Oxford OX3 0BW, England. TEL 0865-794141) Ed. M.F. Ashby. adv.; bk.rev.; charts; illus.; index; circ. 2,300. (also avail. in microform from MIM,UMI) Indexed: Appl.Mech.Rev., ASCA, Bibl.& Ind.Geol., Cadscan, Chem.Abstr., Curr.Cont., Eng.Ind., Fuel & Energy Abstr., Ind.Sci.Rev., INIS Atomindx., Int.Aerosp.Abstr., Lead Abstr., Met.Abstr., Phys.Ber., Sci.Abstr., Sci.Cit.Ind, World Alum.Abstr., Zincscan.
   —BLDSC shelfmark: 0637.100000.
   Formerly (until 1990): Acta Metallurgica (ISSN 0001-6160)
   Description: Publishes papers on the structure of solids and their properties, on the thermodynamics, kinetics and mechanics of solids, and recent advances in engineering materials.
   Refereed Serial

669   CC   ISSN 1000-9442
TN689   CODEN: AMMSEY
ACTA METALLURGICA SINICA. SERIES A: PHYSICAL METALLURGY & MATERIALS SCIENCE. (Publication interrupted twice and resumed in 1974) (Editions in Chinese and English) 1956. bi-m. $290. Chinese Society of Metals, 46 Dongsi Xidajie, Beijing 100711, People's Republic of China. TEL 557431. (Dist. by: Allerton Press, Inc., 150 Fifth Ave., New York, NY 10011. TEL 212-924-3950) Eds. Shi Changxu, Tan Bingyu. circ. 400. (back issues avail.) Indexed: Chem.Abstr., Corros.Abstr., Eng.Ind., Met.Abstr.
   —BLDSC shelfmark: 0637.520000.
   Description: Covers research on physical metallurgy and materials science. Includes original research papers, critical reviews, notes, letters, discussions and academic activities.

669   CC   ISSN 1000-9450
TN600   CODEN: ASBME3
ACTA METALLURGICA SINICA. SERIES B: PROCESS METALLURGY & MISCELLANEOUS. (Publication interrupted twice and resumed in 1974) (Editions in Chinese and English) 1956. bi-m. $310. Chinese Society of Metals, 46 Dongsi Xidajie, Beijing 100711, People's Republic of China. TEL 557431. (Dist. by: Allerton Press, Inc., 150 Fifth Ave., New York, NY 10011. TEL 212-924-3950) Eds. Shi Changxu, Tan Bingyu. (back issues avail.) Indexed: Chem.Abstr., Corros.Abstr., Eng.Ind., Met.Abstr.
   —BLDSC shelfmark: 0637.530000.
   Description: Covers metallurgical research in China, including mining and ore dressing, production metallurgy, oxidation and corrosion, foundry, metal working, joining and welding, powder metallurgy, testing methods, and refractories. Includes original research papers, critical reviews, notes, letters, discussions, and academic activities.

ACTA POLYTECHNICA SCANDINAVICA. CHEMICAL TECHNOLOGY AND METALLURGY SERIES. see *CHEMISTRY*

669   FR   ISSN 0044-6165
ACTUALITES INDUSTRIELLES LORRAINES. 1949. bi-m. 85 F. Maisonneuve S.A., 386 Route de Verdun a Sainte Ruffine, 57160 Moulin-les-Mets, France. Ed. Louis Labbez. adv.; bk.rev.; charts; illus.; circ. 29,000.

669   KR   ISSN 0136-1732
TA401   CODEN: ARPMDV
ADGEZIYA RASPLAVOV I PAIKA MATERIALOV; respublikanskii mezhvedomstvennyi sbornik nauchnykh trudov. (Text in Russian) 1976. s-a. (Akademiya Nauk Ukrainskoi S.S.R., Institut Problem Materialovedeniya) Izdatel'stvo Naukova Dumka, c/o Yu.A. Khramov, Dir, Ul. Repina, 3, Kiev 252 601, Ukraine. TEL 224-40-68. (Subscr. to: Mezhdunarodnaya Kniga, Moscow, G-200, Russia) Ed. Yu.V. Naidich. Indexed: Chem.Abstr.
   —BLDSC shelfmark: 0005.278000.

ADVANCED COMPOSITES BULLETIN; an international newsletter. see *PLASTICS*

669   UK   ISSN 0957-9729
▼**ADVANCED METALS TECHNOLOGY.** 1990. 12/yr. £219 (effective 1992). Elsevier Science Publishers Ltd., Crown House, Linton Rd., Barking, Essex IG11 8JU, England. TEL 081-594-7272. FAX 081-594-5942. TELEX 896950 APPSCI G. (Subscr. in U.S. and Canada to: Elsevier Science Publishing Co., Inc., Box 882, Madison Sq. Sta., New York, NY 10159. TEL 212-989-5800) Eds. D. Grant, N. Brooks. adv. contact: Tamar Baldwin.
   Description: Covers developments in materials technologies and applications in the field of advanced metals.

671.732   UK   ISSN 0267-4009
TN681
ADVANCES IN SPECIAL ELECTROMETALLURGY. English translation of: Problemy Spetsial'noi Elektrometallurgii (UR ISSN 0131-1611) 1985. q. £75($124) Riecansky Science Publishing Co., 7 Meadow Walk, Great Abington, Cambridge CB1 6AZ, England. TEL 0223 893295. FAX 0223-893295. Ed. V.E. Riecansky.
   —BLDSC shelfmark: 0404.613000.

ADVANCES IN X-RAY ANALYSIS. see *TECHNOLOGY: COMPREHENSIVE WORKS*

669   PL   ISSN 0372-9443
TN4
AKADEMIA GORNICZO-HUTNICZA IM. STANISLAWA STASZICA. ZESZYTY NAUKOWE. METALURGIA I ODLEWNICTWO. (Text in English or Polish; summaries in English, Polish) 1954. irregr., no.140, 1991. price varies. Wydawnictwo A G H, Al. Mickiewicza 30, paw. B-5, 30-059 Krakow, Poland. (Dist. by: Ars Polona, Krakowskie Przedmiescie 7, 00-068 Warsaw, Poland) Ed. Z. Kleczek. illus.; circ. 300.

669   PL   ISSN 0137-6535
TN4   CODEN: ZNAOD5
AKADEMIA GORNICZO-HUTNICZA IM. STANISLAWA STASZICA. ZESZYTY NAUKOWE. METALURGIA I ODLEWNICTWO. KWARTALNIK. (Text in English, Polish; summaries in Polish, Russian) 1975. q. 5,000 Zl. per issue (effective 1992). Wydawnictwo A G H, Al. Mickiewicza 30, paw. B-5, 30-059 Krakow, Poland. (Dist. by: Ars Polona, Krakowskie Przedmiescie 7, 00-068 Warsaw, Poland) Ed. E. Wosiek. bibl.; charts; circ. 600. Indexed: Chem.Abstr., Met.Abstr., World Alum.Abstr.

669   RU
AKADEMIYA NAUK KAZAKHSKOI S.S.R. INSTITUT METALLURGII I OBOGASHCHENIYA. TRUDY. vol.52, 1977. irregr. 1.80 Rub. per no. Izdatel'stvo Nauka, 90 Profsoyuznaya ul., 117864 Moscow, Russia. TEL 234-05-84. Ed. A. Kunaev. abstr.; bibl.; illus.; circ. 1,000. Indexed: Chem.Abstr.

ALAMBRE; revista tecnica para la produccion y manufacturacion de alambres, barras y derivados y todos los sectores marginales. see *ENGINEERING — Electrical Engineering*

620   GW
ALCAN INFORMIERT. 1970. q. free. Alcan Deutschland GmbH, Geisseestr. 13, 8500 Nuernberg 1, Germany. Ed. R. Wypior. illus.; circ. 10,000. (back issues avail.)

669   US   ISSN 0002-614X
ALLOY DIGEST. 1952. m. $115. Alloy Digest, Inc., 27 Canfield St., Orange, NJ 07050. TEL 201-677-9161. Ed. Dr. Robert J. Raudebough. abstr.; charts; index, cum.index: 1952-1986; circ. 1,000. (looseleaf format; back issues avail.) Indexed: Met.Abstr., World Alum.Abstr.

669.722   IT   ISSN 0365-3927
CODEN: ALLUAO
ALLUMINIO. 1932. m. L.50000. Edital s.r.l., P.zza G. Marconi, 25, Box 10359, 00144 Rome, Italy. Ed. Giancarlo Viotti. adv.; bk.rev.; abstr.; bibl.; charts; illus.; mkt.; stat.; index; circ. 6,200. Indexed: Chem.Abstr., Eng.Ind., Met.Abstr., World Alum.Abstr.
   Formerly: Alluminio e Nuova Metallurgia (ISSN 0002-6212)

669.722   JA
ALUMI-AGE. (Text in Japanese) 1964. q. free. Japan Aluminum Federation, Nihonbashi Asahiseimei Bldg., 1-3 Nihonbashi, 2-chome, Chuo-ku, Tokyo 103, Japan. TEL 03-274-4551. FAX 03-274-3179. TELEX 02223074-JALF-J. Ed.Bd. adv.; circ. 10,000.
   Description: Aims to educate the public about aluminum.

ALUMINIUM INDUSTRY. see *ENGINEERING*

669.722   GW   ISSN 0934-3938
ALUMINIUM INTERN: ALUMINIUM UND AUTOMOBIL. irreg. (approx. 3/yr.). DM.75. (Aluminium-Zentrale e.V.) Aluminium-Verlag GmbH, Koenigsallee 30, Postfach 101262, 4000 Duesseldorf 1, Germany. Indexed: Int.Packag.Abstr.

669.722   UK
ALUMINIUM TODAY; the international journal of aluminium production and processing. 1989. q. £105.60 (foreign £110.25). F M J International Publications Ltd., Queensway House, 2 Queensway, Redhill, Surrey RH1 1QS, England. TEL 0737-768611. FAX 0737-761685. TELEX 948669-TOPJNL-G. Ed. Jonathan Mitchell.

METALLURGY

669.722   GW   ISSN 0002-6689
CODEN: ALUMAB
ALUMINUM. (Text in English and German) 1919. m. DM.386($276) (Aluminum-Zentrale e.V.) Aluminium-Verlag GmbH, Koenigsallee 30, Postfach 101262, 4000 Duesseldorf 1, Germany. TEL 0211-320821. adv.; bk.rev.; abstr.; bibl.; charts; illus.; stat.; index; circ. 3,300. **Indexed:** Chem.Abstr., Eng.Ind., Excerp.Med., INIS Atomind., Int.Packag.Abstr., Met.Abstr., Packag.Sci.Tech., PROMT, World Alum.Abstr.
—BLDSC shelfmark: 0804.050000.

669.722   US
ALUMINUM SITUATION. m. free. Aluminum Association, Inc., 900 19th St., N.W., Ste. 300, Washington, DC 20006. TEL 202-862-5100. **Indexed:** SRI.

673   US   ISSN 0065-6658
ALUMINUM STANDARDS AND DATA. 1968. biennial. $25. Aluminum Association, Inc., 900 19th St., N.W., Ste. 300, Washington, DC 20006. TEL 202-862-5100. circ. 40,000.

673   US
ALUMINUM STANDARDS AND DATA-METRIC. biennial. $12. Aluminum Association, Inc., 900 19th St., N.W., Ste. 300, Washington, DC 20006. TEL 202-862-5100. circ. 40,000.

673 338.4   US   ISSN 0065-6666
ALUMINUM STATISTICAL REVIEW. (Title varies: Aluminum Industry Annual Statistical Review) 1962. a. $50. Aluminum Association, Inc., 900 19th St., N.W., Ste. 300, Washington, DC 20006. TEL 202-862-5100. circ. 15,000. **Indexed:** SRI.

669.722   NE
ALURAMA. (Text in Dutch) 1987. q. fl.55. C. Misset B.V., Postbus 4, 7000 BA Doetinchem, Netherlands. TEL 08340-49502. FAX 08340-43839. TELEX 45481-MISSET-DTC. Ed. Th. Evers. adv.; B&W page fl.2145; unit 187 x 257; adv. contact: Cor van Nek. circ. 6,020.
Description: Covers aluminum metallurgy.

669.028 671.2   US   ISSN 0065-8375
TS200   CODEN: TAFOA6
AMERICAN FOUNDRYMEN'S SOCIETY. TRANSACTIONS. 1896. a. $200 to non-members. American Foundrymen's Society, Inc., 505 State St., Des Plaines, IL 60016. TEL 708-824-0181. cum.index every 10 yrs. (also avail. in microform from PMC,UMI; reprint service avail. from UMI) **Indexed:** B.C.I.R.A., Chem.Abstr.
—BLDSC shelfmark: 8887.000000.

AMERICAN GOLD NEWS AND WESTERN PROSPECTOR. see *MINES AND MINING INDUSTRY*

669   US   ISSN 0002-9998
HD9506.U6   CODEN: AMMKA6
AMERICAN METAL MARKET. 1882. d. (Mon.-Fri.). $495 in US; Canada, Mexico $580; Americas, Europe $910; elsewhere $1090. Capital Cities - A B C, Inc., 825 Seventh Ave., New York, NY 10019. TEL 212-887-8532. FAX 212-887-8358. TELEX 125308-NYK. (Subscr. to: Box 1086, Southeastern, PA 19398-1085) Ed. Michael G. Botta. adv.; bk.rev.; charts; illus.; mkt.; stat.; circ. 13,000. (tabloid format; also avail. in microform from MIM; back issues avail.) **Indexed:** Bus.Ind., CAD CAM Abstr., Chem.Abstr., Met.Abstr., Robomat, Tr.& Indus.Ind., World Alum.Abstr.
●Also available online. Vendor(s): DIALOG.
—BLDSC shelfmark: 0842.600000.
Description: Covers all aspects of metals business, including production, trade, activity on commodities markets, supply and demand; covers nonferrous, ferrous, precious metals, scrap and competing materials.

ANNUAL BOOK OF A S T M STANDARDS. VOLUME 01.01. STEEL-PIPING, TUBING, FITTINGS. (American Society for Testing and Materials) see *ENGINEERING — Engineering Mechanics And Materials*

ANNUAL BOOK OF A S T M STANDARDS. VOLUME 01.02. FERROUS CASTINGS, FERRO ALLOYS. see *ENGINEERING — Engineering Mechanics And Materials*

ANNUAL BOOK OF A S T M STANDARDS. VOLUME 01.03. STEEL PLATE, SHEET, STRIP WIRE. see *ENGINEERING — Engineering Mechanics And Materials*

ANNUAL BOOK OF A S T M STANDARDS. VOLUME 01.04. STEEL-STRUCTURAL, REINFORCING, PRESSURE VESSEL; RAILWAY. see *ENGINEERING — Engineering Mechanics And Materials*

ANNUAL BOOK OF A S T M STANDARDS. VOLUME 01.05. STEEL-BARS, BEARINGS, FORGINGS, CHAIN, SPRINGS. see *ENGINEERING — Engineering Mechanics And Materials*

ANNUAL BOOK OF A S T M STANDARDS. VOLUME 01.06. COATED STEEL PRODUCTS. see *ENGINEERING — Engineering Mechanics And Materials*

ANNUAL BOOK OF A S T M STANDARDS. VOLUME 01.07. SHIPBUILDING. see *ENGINEERING — Engineering Mechanics And Materials*

ANNUAL BOOK OF A S T M STANDARDS. VOLUME 02.01. COPPER AND COPPER ALLOYS. see *ENGINEERING — Engineering Mechanics And Materials*

ANNUAL BOOK OF A S T M STANDARDS. VOLUME 02.02. DIE-CAST METALS; ALUMINUM AND MAGNESIUM ALLOYS. see *ENGINEERING — Engineering Mechanics And Materials*

ANNUAL BOOK OF A S T M STANDARDS. VOLUME 02.04. NONFERROUS METALS-NICKEL, LEAD, TIN ALLOYS, PRECIOUS, PRIMARY, REACTIVE METALS. see *ENGINEERING — Engineering Mechanics And Materials*

ANNUAL BOOK OF A S T M STANDARDS. VOLUME 02.05. METALLIC AND INORGANIC COATINGS; METAL POWDERS, SINTERED P-M STRUCTURAL PARTS. see *ENGINEERING — Engineering Mechanics And Materials*

ANNUAL BOOK OF A S T M STANDARDS. VOLUME 03.01. METALS - MECHANICAL TESTING; ELEVATED AND LOW-TEMPERATURE TESTS METALLOGRAPHY. see *ENGINEERING — Engineering Mechanics And Materials*

ANNUAL BOOK OF A S T M STANDARDS. VOLUME 03.02. WEAR AND EROSION; METAL CORROSION. see *ENGINEERING — Engineering Mechanics And Materials*

ANNUAL BOOK OF A S T M STANDARDS. VOLUME 03.03. NONDESTRUCTIVE TESTS. see *ENGINEERING — Engineering Mechanics And Materials*

ANNUAL BOOK OF A S T M STANDARDS. VOLUME 03.05. CHEMICAL ANALYSIS OF METALS; METAL BEARING ORES. see *ENGINEERING — Engineering Mechanics And Materials*

669   UK
ANTI-CORROSION HANDBOOK & DIRECTORY. a. free with Anti-Corrosion Methods and Materials. Sawell Publications Ltd., 127 Stanstead Rd., London SE23 1JE, England. Ed. J.E. Bean. circ. 2,880.

620.162   UK   ISSN 0003-5599
TA462   CODEN: ACMEBL
ANTI-CORROSION METHODS AND MATERIALS; the first British journal of corrosion control, prevention, engineering and research. 1954. m. $94. Sawell Publications Ltd., 127 Stanstead Rd., London SE23 1JE, England. Ed. T.R. Savage. adv.; bk.rev.; abstr.; bibl.; charts; illus.; tr.lit.; index; circ. 2,880. **Indexed:** AESIS, API Abstr., API Catal., API Hlth.& Environ., API Oil., API Pet.Ref., API Pet.Subst., API Transport., BMT, Br.Tech.Ind., Cadscan, Chem.Abstr., Chem.Eng.Abstr., Eng.Ind., Fluidex, Fuel & Energy Abstr., Gas Abstr., HRIS, INIS Atomind., Lead Abstr., Met.Abstr., Petrol.Abstr., RAPRA, W.R.C.Inf., World Surf.Coat., Zincscan.
—BLDSC shelfmark: 1547.450000.
Formerly: Corrosion Technology.

669   US   ISSN 0890-2534
ANVIL. 1975. m. $40 (Canada $46; elsewhere $60). Rob Edwards, Ed. & Pub., 2776 Sourdough Flat, Box 1810, Georgetown, CA 95634-1810. TEL 916-333-2142. FAX 916-333-2906. adv.; bk.rev.; circ. 5,000. (back issues avail.)
Description: Trade magazine for farriers and blacksmiths.

669 541.37   NE   ISSN 0169-4332
TA418.7   CODEN: ASUSEE
APPLIED SURFACE SCIENCE; a journal devoted to the properties of interfaces in relation to the synthesis and behaviour of materials. (Text in English) 1978. 32/yr.(in 8 vols.; 4 nos./vol.). fl.2768 (combined subscr. with Surface Science; Surface Science Letters; Surface Science Reports fl.10287)(effective 1992). North-Holland (Subsidiary of: Elsevier Science Publishers B.V.), P.O. Box 211, 1000 AE Amsterdam, Netherlands. TEL 020-5803911. FAX 020-5803598. TELEX 18582 ESPA NL. (Subscr. in U.S. and Canada to: Elsevier Science Publishing Co., Inc., Box 882, Madison Sq. Sta., New York, NY 10159. TEL 212-989-5800) Eds. L.C. Feldman, W.F. van der Weg. cum.index: vols.11-20, 1986. (also avail. in microform from RPI; back issues avail.) **Indexed:** Cadscan, Chem.Abstr., Ind.Sci.Rev., INIS Atomind., Lead Abstr., Mass Spectr.Bull., Met.Abstr., Sci.Abstr., Sci.Cit.Ind, Soils & Fert., World Alum.Abstr., Zincscan.
—BLDSC shelfmark: 1580.082000.
Formerly: Applications of Surface Science (ISSN 0378-5963)
Description: Concerned with the microscopic understanding of the synthesis and behaviour of surfaces and interfaces.
Refereed Serial

669 913   US   ISSN 0891-2920
CODEN: ARCMEZ
ARCHEOMATERIALS. 1986. s-a. $50 to individuals; institutions $65. University of Pennsylvania, University Museum, Philadelphia, PA 19104. TEL 215-898-2281. FAX 215-898-0657. Ed. Tamara Stech. adv.; bk.rev.; circ. 250. (back issues avail.) **Indexed:** Chem.Abstr., Eng.Mat.Abstr., Met.Abstr.
—BLDSC shelfmark: 1595.753000.
Description: Pre- and non-industrial manipulation of materials, using scientific methods for humanistic ends.

669   PL
TN4.P57   CODEN: AHUTA4
ARCHIVES OF METALLURGY. (Text in various languages; summaries in Polish, Russian) q. $33. (Polska Akademia Nauk, Komitet Metalurgii) Panstwowe Wydawnictwo Naukowe, Miodowa 10, 00-251 Warsaw, Poland. (Dist. by: Ars Polona, Krakowskie Przedmiescie 7, 00-068 Warsaw, Poland) Ed. W. Ptak. charts; illus.; circ. 510. **Indexed:** Chem.Abstr., Copper Abstr., Eng.Ind., INIS Atomind., Met.Abstr., Sci.Abstr., World Alum.Abstr.
Formerly: Archiwum Hutnictwa (ISSN 0004-0770)

ARCHIWUM NAUKI O MATERIALACH. see *ENGINEERING — Engineering Mechanics And Materials*

671.2   FR
ASSOCIATION TECHNIQUE DE FONDERIE. ANNUAIRE; ingenieurs et techniciens. 1911. biennial. Agence de Diffusion et de Publicite, 24 Place du General Catroux, 75017 Paris, France. adv.

B H M. BERG- UND HUETTENMAENNISCHE MONATSHEFTE.. see *MINES AND MINING INDUSTRY*

669.1   II   ISSN 0005-3325
B S P MAGAZINE/ISPAT VIHANGAM. (Editions in English and Hindi) 1959. q. free. Steel Authority of India Ltd., Bhilai Steel Plant, Bhilai 490001 (M.P.), India. Ed. Pradip Singh. circ. 20,000 (combined circ.).

669   GW   ISSN 0005-3848
CODEN: BBROAB
BAENDER, BLECHE, ROHRE; Fachzeitschrift fuer Walzwerkstechnik, Blechbearbeitung, gezogene und geschweisste Rohre. 1959. m. DM.180. Vogel-Verlag und Druck KG, Max-Planck-Str. 7-9, Postfach 67 40, 8700 Wuerzburg 1, Germany. TEL 0931-418-0. Ed. Hasso Reschenberg. adv.; bk.rev.; charts; illus.; index; circ. 8,536 (controlled). **Indexed:** C.I.S. Abstr., Cadscan, Chem.Abstr., INIS Atomind., Lead Abstr., Met.Abstr., World Alum.Abstr., Zincscan.
—BLDSC shelfmark: 1861.580000.

669   II
BANARAS METALLURGIST. (Text in English and Hindi) 1968. a. free. Banaras Hindu University, Institute of Technology, Department of Metallurgical Engineering, Varanasi 221 005, Uttar Pradesh, India. TELEX 0545-208. Ed. J.S. Kachhawaha. adv.; bk.rev.; circ. 500. **Indexed:** Met.Abstr.

METALLURGY 3403

669 HU ISSN 0005-5670
TN4 CODEN: BKLKBX
BANYASZATI ES KOHASZATI LAPOK - KOHASZAT.
(Summaries in English, German and Russian) 1868.
m. $52. (Orszagos Magyar Banyaszati es Kohaszati
Egyesulet) Lapkiado Vallalat, Lenin korut 9-11,
1073 Budapest 7, Hungary. TEL 222-408. (Subscr.
to: Kultura, Box 149, H-1389 Budapest, Hungary)
Ed. Antal Ovari. adv.; bk.rev.; charts; illus.; pat.;
tr.mk.; index; circ. 3,450. **Indexed:** Appl.Mech.Rev.,
Bibl.& Ind.Geol., Chem.Abstr., INIS Atomind.,
Met.Abstr., Petrol.Abstr., World Alum.Abstr.
 —BLDSC shelfmark: 1862.860000.
 Formerly: Kohaszati Lapok.

669 HU ISSN 0375-9504
BANYASZATI ES KOHASZATI LAPOK - ONTODE.
(Summaries in English, German and Russian) 1950.
m. $25. (Orszagos Magyar Banyaszati es Kohaszati
Egyesulet) Lapkiado Vallalat, Lenin korut 9-11,
1073 Budapest 7, Hungary. TEL 222-408. (Subscr.
to: Kultura, Box 149, H-1389 Budapest, Hungary)
Ed. Dr. Lajos Pilissy. adv.; bk.rev.; charts; pat.; index;
circ. 500. **Indexed:** B.C.I.R.A., Chem.Abstr.,
Met.Abstr., World Alum.Abstr.
 —BLDSC shelfmark: 1862.890000.
 Continues: Ontode (ISSN 0030-3143)

BAYERN METALL. see *ENGINEERING — Mechanical Engineering*

669.1 CC ISSN 0476-0255
BEIJING UNIVERSITY OF IRON AND STEEL TECHNOLOGY. JOURNAL/BEIJING GANGTIE JISHU DAXUE XUEBAO.
1955. q. $25. Beijing Gangtie Jishu Daxue - Beijing
University of Iron and Steel Technology, 30 Xueyuan
Lu, Haidian Qu, Beijing, People's Republic of China.
(reprint service avail.)

BERGSMANNEN. see *MINES AND MINING INDUSTRY*

BERGVERKS-NYTT; the Scandinavian journal of mining
and quarrying. see *MINES AND MINING INDUSTRY*

669 375 GW
BETRIEBLICHE AUSBILDUNGSPRAXIS; Merkblaetter fuer
Ausbilder in der Eisen- und Metallindustrie. 1955.
bi-m. DM.14. (Wirtschaftsvereinigung Eisen- und
Stahlindustrie) Verlag und Vertriebsgesellschaft
mbH, Breite Str. 69, Postfach 8232, 4000
Duesseldorf 1, Germany. (Co-sponsors:
Arbeitgeberverband Eisen- und Stahlindustrie e.V.;
Verband der Metallindustrie Nordrhein-Westfalens
e.V.) Ed.Bd. adv.; bk.rev.; charts; illus.; stat.; tr.lit.;
circ. 1,800 (controlled). (also avail. in microform;
back issues avail.)

669 US ISSN 0933-5854
QP532 CODEN: BMETE8
BIOLOGY OF METALS. 1989. 4/yr. DM.248.
Springer-Verlag, Journals, 175 Fifth Ave., New York,
NY 10010. TEL 212-460-1500. **Indexed:**
Biodet.Abstr.

660 UK ISSN 0269-7572
CODEN: BRECEQ
BIORECOVERY; an international journal of biotechnology
applied to materials recovery and handling. 4/yr.
£89($179) free. A B Academic Publishers, P.O. Box 42,
Bicester, Oxon OX6 7NW, England.
TEL 0869-320949. Ed. Robert Edyvean. adv.;
bk.rev. (back issues avail.) **Indexed:** Biodet.Abstr.,
Energy Info.Abstr., Environ.Abstr., Environ.Per.Bibl.
 —BLDSC shelfmark: 2089.477000.
 Description: Use of living organisms and their
products in extraction recovery of minerals, oils and
other materials.

669 537.5 BE ISSN 0379-0401
BISMUTH INSTITUTE. BULLETIN. (Text in English) 1973.
irreg. (3-4/yr.) free. Bismuth Institute - Information
Centre, 301 Borgstraat, B-1850 Grimbergen,
Belgium. TEL 322-252-4747. FAX 322-252-2775.
TELEX 27000 MAIL B, BISMUTH. Ed. Yves Palmieri.
bk.rev.; pat.; tr.lit.; cum.index: 1973-1988; circ.
2,000. (back issues avail.) **Indexed:** Energy
Info.Abstr.
 —BLDSC shelfmark: 2411.710000.
 Description: Technical publication reporting
advances of permanent interest in metallurgy,
electronics, chemistry, medicine, and cosmetics.

669 GW ISSN 0006-4688
CODEN: BRPFBJ
BLECH-ROHRE-PROFILE; Fachzeitschrift fuer die
Herstellung, Verarbeitung und Veredelung von Band,
Blech, Rohren und Profilen einschliesslich aller
Randgebiete. 1953. m. DM.149 (foreign DM.164).
Meisenbach Verlag, Hainstr. 18, Postfach 2069,
8600 Bamberg, Germany. TEL 0951-861-134.
FAX 0951-861-161. TELEX 662844-MEIBA-D. Ed.
K. Dengler. adv.; bk.rev.; charts; illus.; mkt.; pat.;
tr.lit.; circ. 8,055. (also avail. in microfilm from UMI)
Indexed: Appl.Mech.Rev., Chem.Abstr., Eng.Ind.,
Excerp.Med., INIS Atomind., Met.Abstr., World
Alum.Abstr.
 —BLDSC shelfmark: 2110.630000.
 Formerly: Blech.

620.162 UK ISSN 0007-0599
TA462 CODEN: BCRJA3
BRITISH CORROSION JOURNAL. 1965. q. £114($247)
to non-members; members £67($128). Institute of
Materials, 1 Carlton House Terrace, London SW1Y
5DB, England. TEL 071-839-4071.
FAX 071-839-2078. TELEX 8814813-METSOC-G.
Ed. A.D. Mercer. adv.; bk.rev.; charts; illus.; index;
circ. 950. (back issues avail.) **Indexed:** ABTICS,
AESIS, API Abstr., API Catal., API Hlth.& Environ., API
Oil., API Pet.Ref., API Pet.Subst., API Transport., Art
& Archaeol.Tech.Abstr., B.C.I.R.A., Br.Tech.Ind.,
Cadscan, Chem.Abstr., Chem.Eng.Abstr.,
Corros.Abstr., Curr.Cont., Eng.Ind., Excerp.Med.,
Fluidex, Ind.Sci.Rev., INIS Atomind., ISMEC, Lead
Abstr., Met.Abstr., Petrol.Abstr., Sci.Abstr., Sci.Cit.Ind,
T.C.E.A., W.R.C.Inf., World Alum.Abstr., World
Surf.Coat., Zincscan.
 —BLDSC shelfmark: 2298.400000.
 Description: Covers all aspects of the theory and
practice of corrosion processes and control.

669 UK
BRITISH INDEPENDENT STEEL COMPANIES AND THEIR PRODUCTS. 1969. irreg. free. British Independent
Steel Producers Association (B.I.S.P.A.), c/o B.D.
Orchard, Ed., 5 Cromwell Rd., London SW7 2HX,
England. circ. 5,000.

620.112 UK ISSN 0007-1137
TA417.2 CODEN: BJNTAS
BRITISH JOURNAL OF NON-DESTRUCTIVE TESTING.
1959. m. £77($135) British Institute of
Non-Destructive Testing, 1 Spencer Parade,
Northampton NN1 5AA, England. TEL 0604 30124.
FAX 0604-231489. Ed. Jackie Percival. adv.;
bk.rev.; bibl.; charts; illus.; index; circ. 2,750. (also
avail. in microform from UMI; reprint service avail.
from UMI) **Indexed:** Appl.Mech.Rev., B.C.I.R.A.,
Br.Tech.Ind., Chem.Abstr., Eng.Ind., Fuel & Energy
Abstr., INIS Atomind., INSPEC, ISMEC, Met.Abstr.,
Sci.Abstr., World Alum.Abstr.
 —BLDSC shelfmark: 2311.950000.

669 UK
BRITISH STEEL PLC. ANNUAL REPORT AND ACCOUNTS.
1967. a. £1. British Steel Plc., 9 Albert
Embankment, London SE1 7SN, England.
FAX 071-587-1142. TELEX 916061. illus.
 Formerly: British Steel Corporation. Annual Report
and Accounts (ISSN 0068-2586)

669.1 US
C B I NEWS. 1914. s-m. free. C B I Industries, Inc.,
Public Relations Department, 800 Jorie Blvd., Oak
Brook, IL 60521. TEL 312-654-7305. Ed. Jerry
Patterson. circ. 22,000. **Indexed:** Acid Rain Abstr.,
Acid Rain Ind.
 Former titles: Water Tower; C B I Water Tower
News.

669.3 US
C B S A CAPSULES. 1951. m. $25. Copper & Brass
Servicenter Association, Adams Bldg., Ste. 109, 251
W. Dekalb Pike, King of Prussia, PA 19406.
TEL 215-265-6658. FAX 215-265-3419. Ed. R.
Franklin Brown, Jr. charts; illus.; stat.; tr.lit.; circ.
165. (back issues avail.)
 Description: Includes legislative and regulatory
news related to metal industry, management and
business news, and news about members.

C I M DIRECTORY. (Canadian Institute of Mining,
Metallurgy & Petroleum) see *MINES AND MINING
INDUSTRY*

669 GW ISSN 0177-1469
C P & T. (Casting Plant and Technology) 1985. q.
DM.115. (Verein Deutscher Giessereifachleute)
Giesserei-Verlag GmbH, Sohnstr. 65, Postfach
102532, 4000 Duesseldorf 1, Germany.
TEL 0211-6707-0. circ. 7,500.

671.2 GW ISSN 0935-7262
C P & T INTERNATIONAL. (Casting Plant & Technology)
(Text in English) 1985. q. DM.115. (German
Foundrymen's Association (VDG)) Giesserei Verlag
GmbH, Sohnstr. 65, Postfach 102532, 4000
Duesseldorf 1, Germany. TEL 0211-67070. circ.
7,205.
 —BLDSC shelfmark: 3486.144000.

669 CC ISSN 1000-8500
CAILIAO KEXUE JINZHAN/ADVANCES IN MATERIAL SCIENCE. (Text in Chinese) bi-m. Zhongguo
Kexueyuan, Jinshu Yanjiusuo - Chinese Academy of
Sciences, Institute of Metallurgy, 72, Wenhua Lu,
Shenyang, Liaoning 110015, People's Republic of
China. TEL 483125. Ed. Li De.

669.1 MX
CAMARA NACIONAL DE LA INDUSTRIA DEL HIERRO Y DEL ACERO. INFORME DEL PRESIDENTE. a. $5.
Camara Nacional de la Industria del Hierro y del
Acero, Amores 338, Apdo. Postal 12783, Mexico
12, D.F., Mexico.

669 CN ISSN 0835-0116
HD9539.A3
CANADA. STATISTICS CANADA. PRIMARY METAL INDUSTRIES. (Catalogue 41-250) (Text in English
and French) 1927. a. Can.$20($42) (foreign $49).
Statistics Canada, Publications Sales and Services,
Ottawa, Ont. K1A 0T6, Canada.
TEL 613-951-7277. FAX 613-951-1584. (also
avail. in microform from MML)
 Supersedes (in 1985): Canada. Statistics Canada.
Smelting and Refining (ISSN 0384-4935)
 Description: Annual census of manufactures.

669.3 CN ISSN 0008-3291
CANADIAN COPPER/CUIVRE CANADIEN. (Text in English,
French) 1960. q. free. Canadian Copper and Brass
Development Association, 10 Gateway Blvd., Ste.
375, Don Mills, Ont. M3C 3A1, Canada.
TEL 416-421-0788. FAX 416-421-8092. Ed.Bd.
illus.; circ. 14,000. **Indexed:** Copper Abstr.,
Met.Abstr.
 —BLDSC shelfmark: 3019.495000.
 Formerly: Canadian Coppermetals.
 Description: Articles promoting and developing the
uses of copper, its alloys and compounds.

CANADIAN MACHINERY & METALWORKING. see
MACHINERY

669 US ISSN 0008-4433
CODEN: CAMQAU
CANADIAN METALLURGICAL QUARTERLY. 1977. 4/yr.
$315 (effective 1992). (Canadian Institute of
Mining & Metallurgy, Metallurgical Society, CN)
Pergamon Press, Inc., Journals Division, 660 White
Plains Rd., Tarrytown, NY 10591-5153.
TEL 914-524-9200. FAX 914-333-2444. (And:
Headington Hill Hall, Oxford OX3 0BW, England. TEL
0865-794141) Ed. W.M. Williams. adv.; circ. 1,200.
(also avail. in microform from MIM,UMI; back issues
avail.; reprint service avail. from UMI) **Indexed:** AESIS,
B.C.I.R.A., Cadscan, Chem.Abstr., Curr.Cont.,
Ind.Sci.Rev., INIS Atomind., Lead Abstr., Met.Abstr.,
Sci.Cit.Ind, World Alum.Abstr., Zincscan.
 —BLDSC shelfmark: 3038.800000.
 Description: Devoted to the science, practice and
technology of metallurgy, including mineral
processing, extractive metallurgy, alloy development
and metal working.
 Refereed Serial

671.2 UK
CAST METALS. q. £200. F M J International
Publications Ltd., Queensway House, 2 Queensway,
Redhill, Surrey RH1 1QS, England.
TEL 0737-768611. FAX 0737-761685. TELEX
948669-TOPJNL-G.
 Description: Covers the science and technology of
metal casting and cast products.

METALLURGY

669 US
CASTING DESIGN & APPLICATION; the magazine for designers and buyers of castings. q. $20 (free to qualified personnel). Penton Publishing (Subsidiary of: Pittway Company), 1100 Superior Ave., Cleveland, OH 44114. TEL 216-696-7000. Ed. Bob Rodgers. circ. 22,000 (controlled).
Description: Devoted to the interests of OEM designers and buyers of engineered cast parts. Covers casting design, including the sourcing of qualified producers of all types of castings.

671.2 JA ISSN 0019-2813
CASTING DIGEST/IMONO DAIJESUTO. (Text in Japanese) 1949. m. 1200 Yen. Nihon Cast Iron Foundry Association - Nihon Imono Kogyokai, 501 Kikai Shinko Kaikan, 3-5-8 Shiba Koen, Minato-ku, Tokyo 105, Japan. Ed. G. Kunitomo.

669 US
CASTING DIGEST. 1976. m. $145 to non-members (foreign $155); members $120 (foreign $130). A S M International, Materials Information, Materials Park, OH 44073. TEL 216-338-5151. FAX 216-338-4634. TELEX 980-619. (UK addr.: Institute of Metals, Materials Information, 1 Carlton House Terr., London SW1Y 5DB, England. TEL 071-839-4071) **Indexed:** Met.Abstr.

CASTING SOURCE DIRECTORY, see BUSINESS AND ECONOMICS — Trade And Industrial Directories

671.2 US ISSN 0887-9060
TS200
CASTING WORLD. 1969. q. $20. Continental Communications Inc., Box 1919, Bridgeport, CT 06601-1919. Ed. W. Troland. adv.; bk.rev.; illus.; circ. 76,000. **Indexed:** B.C.I.R.A., Cadscan, Lead Abstr., Met.Abstr., World Alum.Abstr., Zincscan.
Formerly: Casting Engineering and Foundry World (ISSN 0273-9607); Formed by the merger of: Casting Engineering (ISSN 0008-7513) & Foundry World (ISSN 0191-1767)

669 UK
CASTINGS BUYER. 1987. 3/yr. $42. F M J International Publications, 2 Queensway, Redhill, Surrey RH1 1QS, England. TEL 44-737-768611. FAX 44-737-761685. adv.; B&W page £1690, color page £2265; trim 280 x 405; adv. contact: Colin Robinson. circ. 20,000.

669.1 SP
CATALOGO EXPOFERRO. 1986. a. 3500 ptas. Tecnipublicaciones, S.A., Fernando VI, 27, 28004 Madrid, Spain. TEL 91-319-7889. FAX 91-319-7089. TELEX 43905 YEBE E. Ed. Juan M. Fernandez. adv.; circ. 5,000.

669.1 SP
CATALOGO SIDERURGICO. 1987. a. 4000 ptas. Tecnipublicaciones, S.A., Fernando VI, 27, 28004 Madrid, Spain. TEL 91-319-7889. FAX 91-319-7089. TELEX 43905 YEBE E.

CHEMPRESS; economic and technical newsmagazine for Benelux chemical and metal industries and trades. see ENGINEERING — Chemical Engineering

669.142 CH ISSN 1015-6070
CHINA STEEL TECHNICAL REPORT/CHUNG KANG CHI PAO. (Text in English) 1987. a. China Steel Corporation, R & D Department, No. 1 Chungkang Rd., Lin Hai Industrial District, Hsiaokang, Kaohsiung, Taiwan, Republic of China. TEL 07-8021111. TELEX 71108-KAOHSIUNG. Ed. Jo-Chi Tsou. Key Title: C S C China Steel Technical Report - Zhonggang Jibao.
—BLDSC shelfmark: 3180.234639.
Description: Covers steelmaking, new materials and technology. Highlights current technical activities at China Steel, and serves to exchange information with foreign and domestic steelmakers.

669 CH ISSN 0379-6906
CODEN: TLKHAJ
CHINESE JOURNAL OF MATERIALS SCIENCE. Variant title: Materials Science Quarterly. (Text in Chinese and English) 1969. q. $22 (foreign $36). Chinese Society for Materials Science, 195-5 Chung-Hsing Rd. Sec. 4, Chutung, Hsinchu, Taiwan 31015, Republic of China. TEL 035-976836. FAX 036-945517. TELEX 34684-MRL. Ed. Sing-Tien Wu. circ. 1,500. (reprint service avail. from NTIS) Key Title: Cailiao Kexue.
—BLDSC shelfmark: 3180.370000.

669 CC ISSN 1000-3029
CODEN: CJMTE4
CHINESE JOURNAL OF METAL SCIENCE & TECHNOLOGY; an invaluable overview of the metallurgy field in China. (Text in English) 1985. bi-m. $270. Chinese Society of Metals, Dongsi Xidajie 46, Beijing 100711, People's Republic of China. (Editorial addr.: Wenhua Lu 72, Shenyang, Liaoning, P.R.C.; Dist. by: Allerton Press, Inc., 150 Fifth Ave., New York, NY 10011. TEL 212-924-3950) Ed. Shi Changxu. abstr.
Description: Includes ferrous and non-ferrous metallurgy, ore beneficiation and exploration, hydro-, pyro-, and electrometallurgy, physical chemistry and mass transport, metallurgical plant engineering, corrosion science and technology.
Refereed Serial

669 CC
CHINESE JOURNAL OF METALLURGY/ZHONGGUO JINSHU KEXUE JISHU ZAZHI. (Text in English) bi-m. Zhongguo Kexueyuan, Jinshu Yanjiusuo - Chinese Academy of Sciences, Institute of Metallurgy, 72, Wenhua Lu, Shenyang, Liaoning 110015, People's Republic of China. TEL 483125. Ed. Shi Changxu.

669 CH ISSN 1011-6761
CHUKUNG. (Text in Chinese) 1969. q. NT.$600($70) Chinese Foundrymen's Association, 1001 Kaonan Highway, Kaohsiung, Taiwan, Republic of China. TEL 07-351-3121. FAX 07-352-4989. Ed. Han Chung Wu. adv.; bk.rev.; circ. 1,000. Key Title: Zhugong (Gaoxiong).
—BLDSC shelfmark: 3189.654500.

671.2 JA
CHUTANZO, NETSUSHORI/CASTING, FORGING & HEAT TREATMENTS. (Text in Japanese) 1947. m. 8500 Yen($49.25) Nihon Chutanzo Kyokai - Japan Casting & Forging Society, 3-13 Urashima Bldg., Kyobashi, Higashi-ku, Osaka-shi, Osaka-fu 540, Japan. Ed. Jun Dodo. adv.; bk.rev.; abstr.; bibl.; charts; illus.; mkt.; pat.; stat.; index; circ. 20,000. **Indexed:** Chem.Abstr.
Formerly (until Aug. 1978): Casting and Forging (ISSN 0009-6652)

669 US
CLEANING-FINISHING-COATING DIGEST. 1974. m. $145 to non-members (foreign $155); members $120 (foreign $130). A S M International, Materials Information, Materials Park, OH 44073. TEL 216-338-5151. FAX 216-338-4634. TELEX 980-619. (UK addr.: Institute of Metals, Materials Information, 1 Carlton House Terr., London SW1Y 5DB, England. TEL 071-839-4071) **Indexed:** Met.Abstr.

COKE OVEN MANAGERS' ASSOCIATION. YEAR BOOK. see MINES AND MINING INDUSTRY

671.2 SP ISSN 0010-0544
CODEN: CLDADH
COLADA.* (Text in Spanish; summaries in English) vol.5, 1973. m. 1200 ptas. Asociacion Tecnica y de Investigacion de Fundicion, Rosano Pino 6, 28020 Madrid, Spain. Ed. J. Fernandez. adv.; bk.rev.; abstr.; bibl.; charts; illus.; stat.; index; circ. 3,500. **Indexed:** Art & Archaeol.Tech.Abstr., B.C.I.R.A., Met.Abstr., World Alum.Abstr.

669.1 FR
COMPTOIR FRANCAIS DES PRODUITS SIDERURGIQUES. BULLETIN STATISTIQUE. SERIE BLEUE. COMMERCE EXTERIEUR. a. 470 F. (includes Serie Rouge - Production). Comptoir Francais des Produits Siderurgiques, 1, Rue Paul Cezanne, B.P. 710-08, 75360 Paris Cedex, France. TEL 45-63-17-10. FAX 45-61-02-91. TELEX FRASIA 280172F.
Formerly: Chambre Syndicale de la Siderurgie Francaise. Bulletin Statistique. Serie Bleue. Commerce Exterieur.

669.1 FR
COMPTOIR FRANCAIS DES PRODUITS SIDERURGIQUES. BULLETIN STATISTIQUE. SERIE ROUGE. PRODUCTION. a. 470 F. (includes Serie Bleue - Commerce Exterieur). Comptoir Francais des Produits Siderurgiques, 1, Rue Paul Cezanne, B.P. 710-08, 75360 Paris Cedex 08, France. TEL 45-63-17-10. FAX 45-61-02-91. TELEX FRASIA 280172F.
Formerly: Chambre Syndicale de la Siderurgie Francaise. Bulletin Statistique. Serie Rouge. Production (ISSN 0755-2025)

669 CL ISSN 0589-2813
HD9524.L3 CODEN: CLSMBO
CONGRESO LATINAMERICANO DE SIDERURGIA. MEMORIA TECNICA.* 1961. irreg. Instituto Latinoamericano del Fierro y el Acero, Secretaria General, Moneda 1140, Casilla Postal 13810, Santiago, Chile. **Indexed:** Chem.Abstr.

CONSTRUCT IN STEEL. see BUILDING AND CONSTRUCTION

669.3 621 US
COPPER TOPICS. 1968. q. free. Copper Development Association Inc., Box 1840, Greenwich, CT 06836. TEL 203-625-8210. FAX 203-625-0174. Ed. Estes Jones. circ. 25,000 (controlled). (back issues avail.)
Description: Cites newsworthy applications of copper, brass and bronze products in the USA.

CORROSION; journal of science and engineering. see ENGINEERING — Mechanical Engineering

CORROSION AND COATINGS. see PAINTS AND PROTECTIVE COATINGS

669 541.37 US ISSN 0892-4228
TA418.74
CORROSION ENGINEERING. English translation of: Zairyo to Kankyo (JA ISSN 0917-0480) 1987. m. $515. (Japan Society of Corrosion Engineering, JA) Allerton Press, Inc., 150 Fifth Ave., New York, NY 10011. TEL 212-924-3950.
—BLDSC shelfmark: 3473.585000.

620.112 UK ISSN 0010-9371
TA462 CODEN: CRPCAK
CORROSION PREVENTION AND CONTROL. 1954. bi-m. $119. Scientific Surveys Ltd., Box 21, Beaconsfield, Bucks. HP9 1NS, England. TEL 0494-675139. FAX 0494-670155. TELEX 94016686-SSSP-G. Ed. J. Tiratsoo. adv.; bk.rev.; illus.; pat.; tr.lit.; index. **Indexed:** Abstr.Bull.Inst.Pap.Chem., Agri.Eng.Abstr., API Abstr., API Catal., API Hlth.& Environ., API Oil., API Pet.Ref., API Pet.Subst., API Transport., BMT, Br.Tech.Ind., Cadscan, Chem.Abstr., Copper Abstr., Corros.Abstr., Eng.Ind., Fluidex, INIS Atomind., Lead Abstr., Met.Abstr., Petrol.Abstr., W.R.C.Inf., World Alum.Abstr., World Surf.Coat., Zincscan.
—BLDSC shelfmark: 3475.000000.
Description: Technical journal concerning corrosion prevention research.

620.112 US ISSN 0364-3301
TA462
CORROSION PREVENTION - INHIBITION DIGEST. 1976. m. $145 to non-members (foreign $155); members $120 (foreign $130). A S M International, Materials Information, Materials Park, OH 44073. TEL 216-338-5151. FAX 216-338-4634. TELEX 980-619. (UK addr.: Institute of Metals, Materials Information, 1 Carlton House Terr., London SW1Y 5DB, England. TEL 071-839-4071) **Indexed:** Abstr.Bull.Inst.Pap.Chem., Met.Abstr.

669 016 UK
CORROSION REVIEWS. 1972. q. $140. Freund Publishing House Ltd., Suite 500, Chesham House, 150 Regent St., London W1R 5FA, England. (Alt. addr.: P.O. BOx 35010, Tel Aviv, Israel. TEL 972-3-615335) Ed. M. Schorr. adv.; bk.rev.; index; circ. 1,000. (back issues avail.) **Indexed:** Chem.Abstr., Corros.Abstr., Excerp.Med., Met.Abstr., World Alum.Abstr.
Formerly: Reviews on Coatings and Corrosion (ISSN 0048-7538)

METALLURGY

620.112 US ISSN 0010-938X
TA462 CODEN: CRRSAA
CORROSION SCIENCE; journal on environmental degradation of materials and its control. 1961. m. £620 (effective 1992). (Institute of Corrosion) Pergamon Press, Inc., Journals Division, 660 White Plains Rd., Tarrytown, NY 10591-5153. TEL 914-524-9200. FAX 914-333-2444. (And: Headington Hill Hall, Oxford OX3 0BW, England. TEL 0865-794141) Ed. J.C. Scully. adv.; charts; illus.; index; circ. 1,800. (also avail. in microform from MIM,UMI) **Indexed:** A.S.& T.Ind., Abstr.Bull.Inst.Pap.Chem., API Abstr., API Catal., API Hlth.& Environ., API Oil., API Pet.Ref., API Pet.Subst., API Transport., Appl.Mech.Rev., Art & Archaeol.Tech.Abstr., BMT, Br.Tech.Ind., Cadscan, Chem.Abstr., Chem.Eng.Abstr., Chem.Infd., Copper Abstr., Corros.Abstr., Curr.Cont., Deep Sea Res.& Oceanogr.Abstr., Energy Rev., Eng.Ind., Environ.Per.Bibl., Excerp.Med., Fuel & Energy Abstr., Ind.Sci.Rev., INIS Atomind., Int.Aerosp.Abstr., ISMEC, Lead Abstr., Mass Spectr.Bull., Met.Abstr., Pet rol.Abstr., Sci.Abstr., Sci.Cit.Ind., T.C.E.A., W.R.C.Inf., World Alum.Abstr., World Surf.Coat., Zincscan.
—BLDSC shelfmark: 3476.500000.
Description: Covers topics including high temperature oxidation, passivity, anodic oxidation, biochemical corrosion, stress corrosion cracking, and corrosion control.
Refereed Serial

COULEE CONTINUE. see *OCCUPATIONAL HEALTH AND SAFETY*

CURRENT BIBLIOGRAPHIES ON SCIENCE AND TECHNOLOGY: METALLURGY, NATURAL RESOURCES & ENERGY. see *METALLURGY — Abstracting, Bibliographies, Statistics*

669.142 US
D R I - MCGRAW-HILL STEEL INDUSTRY REVIEW. 1978. q. D R I - McGraw-Hill, 24 Hartwell Ave., Lexington, MA 02173. TEL 617-863-5100. FAX 617-860-6332. TELEX 200 284. illus.
Formerly: Data Resources Steel Industry Review (ISSN 0163-206X)

669 SP ISSN 0210-685X
DEFORMACION METALICA; revista de las tecnicas de fabricacion, acabado y transformacion del fleje, de la chapa, de tubos, perfiles y alambre. 1974. 16/yr. 14500 ptas.($150) Prensa XXI, S.A., Avda Paral.lel, 180, Apdo. No. 350 F.D., 08015 Barcelona, Spain. TEL 93-325-53-50. FAX 93-425-28-80. Ed. Pere Molera Sola. adv.; charts; illus.; circ. 7,500. **Indexed:** Art & Archaeol.Tech.Abstr., Ind.SST, Met.Abstr., World Alum.Abstr.
—BLDSC shelfmark: 3546.292230.

669 943.7 CS
Z DEJINI HUTNICTVI. (Text in Czech; summaries in English and German) 1972. irreg. exchange basis. Narodni Technicke Muzeum, Kostelni 42, 170 78 Prague 7, Czechoslovakia. illus.; bibl.

DENNITSA. see *COLLEGE AND ALUMNI*

DIE CASTING BUYERS GUIDE. see *MACHINERY*

DIE CASTING ENGINEER. see *ENGINEERING — Engineering Mechanics And Materials*

669 US ISSN 0745-449X
TS239
DIE CASTING MANAGEMENT. 1983. bi-m. $35 (foreign $84). C-K Publishing, Inc., Box 247, Wonder Lake, IL 60097-0247. TEL 815-728-0912. adv.; circ. 4,200. **Indexed:** Cadscan, Lead Abstr., Met.Abstr., World Alum.Abstr., Zincscan.
—BLDSC shelfmark: 3580.483000.

669 LH ISSN 0377-6883
QD543 CODEN: DDDAD6
DIFFUSION AND DEFECT DATA; reviews and original contributions in solid state data. 1967. 12/yr. $864. Sci-Tech Publications, P.O. Box 8383, Haus Gafadura, FL-9490 Vaduz, Liechtenstein. Ed. G. E. Murch. bk.rev.; index, cum.index; circ. 700. **Indexed:** Chem.Abstr., Met.Abstr., Nucl.Sci.Abstr., Phys.Abstr.
—BLDSC shelfmark: 3584.254000.
Formerly: Diffusion Data (ISSN 0012-267X)

671 US
DIRECT FROM MIDREX. 1974. 4/yr. free. (Midrex International B.V.) Midrex Corporation, Charlotte Plaza, Charlotte, NC 28244. TEL 704-373-1600. FAX 704-373-1611. TELEX 6827031 MIDRX UW. Ed. Frank N. Griscom. charts; illus.; circ. 2,000. **Indexed:** Met.Abstr., World Alum.Abstr.
Description: News, features, and announcements pertaining to direct reduction in the iron and steel industries.

669 ISSN 0070-5039
DIRECTORY IRON AND STEEL PLANTS. 1917. a. $45. Association of Iron and Steel Engineers, Three Gateway Center, Ste. 2350, Pittsburgh, PA 15222. TEL 412-281-6323. Ed. Dorothy Sukits. adv.; circ. 5,000.

DIRECTORY OF METALLURGICAL CONSULTANTS & TRANSLATORS. see *BUSINESS AND ECONOMICS — Trade And Industrial Directories*

DIRECTORY OF STEEL FOUNDRIES IN THE UNITED STATES, CANADA AND MEXICO. see *BUSINESS AND ECONOMICS — Trade And Industrial Directories*

669.142 CN
DOFASCO ILLUSTRATED NEWS. 1937. 6/yr. free. Dofasco Inc., 1330 Burlington St. E., P.O. Box 2460, Hamilton, Ont. L8N 3J5, Canada. TEL 416-544-3761. FAX 416-545-3236. Ed. Debby Belding. circ. 30,000.

671.84 GW ISSN 0012-5911
CODEN: DRAHA5
DRAHT; Fachzeitschrift fuer alle Bereiche der Herstellung und Verarbeitung von Draehten und Stangen einschliesslich aller Randgebiete. English edition: Wire (ISSN 0043-5996); French edition: Trefile (ISSN 0374-2261); Italian edition: Filo Metallico (ISSN 0430-4578); Spanish edition: Alambre (ISSN 0002-4406) 1950. m. DM.149.50 (foreign DM.164). Meisenbach GmbH, Hainstr. 18, Postfach 2069, 8600 Bamberg, Germany. TEL 0951-861-134. TELEX 662844-MEIBA-D. Ed. K. Dengler. adv.; bk.rev.; illus.; pat.; circ. 7,500. (also avail. in microfilm from UMI) **Indexed:** Cadscan, Chem.Abstr., Eng.Ind., Excerp.Med., INIS Atomind., Lead Abstr., Met.Abstr., Zincscan.

669 GW ISSN 0940-2691
DRAHT UND KABEL PANORAMA; internationale Fachzeitschrift fuer alle Gebiete in der Draht-, Kabel- und verwandten Industrie. English edition: Wire and Cable Panorama. French edition: Panorama de Fils et Cables. 1984. 4/yr. DM.80($50) D K S Fachverlag GmbH, Im Wiesengrund 21, Postfach 41, 5489 Kelberg, Germany. TEL 02692-1071. FAX 02692-1073. Ed. Juergen Hendricks. adv.; bk.rev.; bibl.; illus.; tr.lit.; circ. 7,100. (back issues avail.)

671.84 GW ISSN 0012-592X
DRAHTWELT; Fachorgan fuer die Erzeugung, Bearbeitung und Verarbeitung von Draehten und Stangen. English edition: Wireworld. 1907. m. DM.105. Vogel-Verlag und Druck KG, Max-Planck-Str. 7-9, Postfach 6740, 8700 Wuerzburg 1, Germany. TEL 0931-418-0. Ed. Dietmar Kuhn. adv.; bk.rev.; abstr.; bibl.; charts; illus.; index; circ. 7,216 (controlled). **Indexed:** Chem.Abstr., Eng.Ind., Excerp.Med., INIS Atomind., Met.Abstr., World Alum.Abstr.

669.1 US
DUCTILE IRON NEWS. 1976. 3/yr. (Ductile Iron Society) Charnas, Inc., 76 Eastern Blvd., Glastonbury, CT 06033-1201. TEL 203-657-8600. FAX 203-657-8753. Ed. Arthur Avedisian. adv.; circ. 2,800 (controlled).
Description: For producers, metallurgists, suppliers, researchers and those in the ductile iron industry.

669 380 US ISSN 0278-8799
TS203
DUN'S INDUSTRIAL GUIDE - THE METALWORKING DIRECTORY. 1961. a. $795 to commercial institutions; libraries $465. Dun and Bradstreet Information Services (Subsidiary of: Dun & Bradstreet, Inc.), 3 Sylvan Way, Parsippany, NJ 07054-3896. TEL 201-605-6000. (also avail. in magnetic tape)
Formerly: Dun and Bradstreet Metalworking Directory (ISSN 0070-7597)
Description: Data on over 71,000 equipment manufacturers and metal distributors.

669 US
E & M J MINING ACTIVITY DIGEST. (Engineering & Mining Journal) 1974. m. $110. Maclean Hunter Publishing Company, 29 N. Wacker Dr., Chicago, IL 60606. TEL 312-726-2802. FAX 312-726-2574. TELEX 270258 EXP. Ed. Charles Richardson. circ. 162. (back issues avail.)
●Also available online. Vendor(s): Mead Data Central.
Incorporates (in Sept. 1975): Metals Sourcebook.

669.6 UK
E E C - TIN IN TINPLATE. (European Economic Community) 1981. irreg. £15. International Tin Council, 1 Oxendon St., London SW1Y 4EQ, England.
Description: Surveys tinplate manufacturing, can making and canning in the EEC.

E M S A BULLETIN. (Electron Microscopy Society of America, Inc.) see *BIOLOGY — Microscopy*

E R A TECHNOLOGY NEWS. (Electrical Research Association) see *BUSINESS AND ECONOMICS — Marketing And Purchasing*

EDELMETAAL. see *JEWELRY, CLOCKS AND WATCHES*

669.1 US
ELECTRIC FURNACE CONFERENCE PROCEEDINGS. 1943. a., latest 49th ed. $80 to non-members; members $40. Iron & Steel Society, 410 Commonwealth Dr., Warrendale, PA 15086. TEL 412-776-1535. FAX 412-776-0430. (also avail. in microfilm from UMI; back issues avail.)
Description: For iron and steelmakers.

669.142 JA ISSN 0011-8389
CODEN: DESEAT
ELECTRIC FURNACE STEEL/DENKI SEIKO. (Text in Japanese; summaries in English) 1925. q. 600 Yen($3.20) (Electric Furnace Steel Research Association - Denki Seiko Kenkyukai) Daido Steel Co., Ltd., 2-30 Daido-cho, Minami-ku, Nagoya 457, Japan. Ed. Isao Sekio. bk.rev.; charts; illus. (processed) **Indexed:** Chem.Abstr., Met.Abstr., World Alum.Abstr.

ELEKTROWAERME INTERNATIONAL. PART B: INDUSTRIELLE ELEKTROWAERME. see *HEATING, PLUMBING AND REFRIGERATION*

ENGINEERED MATERIALS DIRECTORY OF CONSULTANTS & TRANSLATORS. see *BUSINESS AND ECONOMICS — Trade And Industrial Directories*

669 620 II
ENGINEERING & METALS REVIEW. 1975. m. Rs.120. Association of Indian Engineering Industry, Calcutta, 6, Netaji Subhas Rd., Calcutta 700001, India. Ed. Tarun Das. adv.; bk.rev.; abstr.; bibl.; charts; illus.; mkt.; circ. 8,000. **Indexed:** Chem.Abstr.
Incorporates (1949-1975): Eastern Metals Review (ISSN 0012-8856); Metal Market Review; Engineering News; Which incorporated: Indian Engineering Association. News Bulletin; Engineering News of India (ISSN 0046-2055)

669 622 GW ISSN 0044-2658
TN3 CODEN: ERZMAK
ERZMETALL; journal for exploration, mining and metallurgy. (Text in German; summaries in English) 1912. m. DM.507. (Gesellschaft Deutscher Metallhuetten und Bergleute e.V) V C H Verlagsgesellschaft mbH, Postfach 101161, 6940 Weinheim, Germany. TEL 06201-602-0. FAX 06201-602328. TELEX 465516-VCHWH-D. (US addr.: V C H Publishers Inc., 220 E. 23rd St., New York, NY 10010-4606. TEL 212-683-8333) Ed. H. Aly. adv.; bk.rev.; charts; illus.; mkt.; pat.; stat.; index; circ. 2,985. (reprint service avail. from ISI) **Indexed:** C.I.S. Abstr., Cadscan, Chem.Abstr., Copper Abstr., Eng.Ind., Excerp.Med., Fuel & Energy Abstr., GeoRef, INIS Atomind., Lead Abstr., Met.Abstr., World Alum.Abstr., Zincscan.
—BLDSC shelfmark: 3810.920000.
Formerly (until 1945): Metall und Erz.

669.6 546 BE ISSN 0014-1631
L'ETAIN ET SES USAGES. English edition: Tin and Its Uses (ISSN 0040-7941) 1953. q. free to qualified personnel. (International Tin Research Institute) Centre d'Information de l'Etain, 44 rue d'Arenberg, Bte. 33, B-1000 Brussels, Belgium. FAX 02-5145518. Ed. N. Andre. bk.rev.; circ. 2,500.

METALLURGY

669   UK
EUROPEAN ADHESIVES AND SEALANTS. 1983. q. £64.90 (foreign £72.45). F M J International Publications Ltd., Queensway House, 2 Queensway, Redhill, Surrey RH1 1QS, England. TEL 0737-768611. FAX 0737-761685. TELEX 948669-TOPJNL-G. Ed. John Ward. **Indexed:** World Surf.Coat.

671.732 621.9   GW
F B M - FERTIGUNGSTECHNOLOGIE. (Summaries in English) 1963. bi-m. DM.360. Sprechsaal Publishing Group, Mauer 2, Postfach 2962, 8630 Coburg, Germany. TEL 09561-76773. FAX 09561-90009. TELEX 663226. Ed. Christoph Mueller. adv.; bk.rev.; abstr.; bibl.; charts; illus.; tr.lit.; index; circ. 12,000. **Indexed:** Chem.Abstr., INIS Atomind.
Former titles: Fachberichte fuer Metallbearbeitung (ISSN 0014-6323); Fachberichte fuer Oberflaechentechnik.

669   GW   ISSN 0937-2733
FABRIK 2000. 1983. 5/yr. DM.100. Vogel Verlag und Druck KG, Max-Planck-Str. 7-9, Postfach 6740, 8700 Wuerzburg 1, Germany. TEL 0931-418-0. Ed. Helmut Groessl. adv.; circ. 29,913 (controlled).

669   GW   ISSN 0014-6854
DER FAHRZEUG- UND METALL-LACKIERER; das Lackiererhandwerk. 1956. m. DM.80 (foreign DM.88). Verlag Neuer Merkur GmbH, Ingolstaedter Str. 63a, Postfach 460805, 8000 Munich 46, Germany. TEL 089-318905-0. FAX 089-31890538. TELEX 5215-520. Ed. Wolfgang Auer. adv.; bk.rev.; abstr.; charts; illus.; mkt.; pat.; stat.; tr.lit.; index; circ. 4,500. **Indexed:** World Surf.Coat.

674.84   US
FASTENER INDUSTRY NEWS. 1979. s-m. $180 (foreign $225). Business Information Services, Inc., 7 Hampden Rd., Stafford Springs, CT 06076. TEL 203-684-5877. FAX 203-684-9158. Ed. Ricard Callahan. (back issues avail.)
Description: Focuses on management, mergers, buyouts, current events in manufacturing and distribution segments of the industry.

FEDERATIE GOUD EN ZILVER. VADEMECUM. see *JEWELRY, CLOCKS AND WATCHES*

669   BE
FEDERATION DES ENTREPRISES DE L'INDUSTRIE DES FABRICATIONS METALLIQUES, MECANIQUES, ELECTRIQUES ET DE LA TRANSFORMATION DES MATIERES PLASTIQUES. REVUE MENSUELLE. (Editions in Flemish and French) 1946. m. 800 Fr. Federation des Entreprises de l'Industrie des Fabrications Metalliques, Mecaniques, Electriques et de la Transformation des Matieres Plastiques, 21 rue des Drapiers, 1050 Brussels, Belgium. Ed. J. Melange. adv.; bk.rev.; charts; illus.; mkt.; index; circ. 7,000 (3,000 Flemish ed.; 4,000 French ed.).
Formerly: Federation des Entreprises de l'Industrie des Fabrications Metalliques, Mecaniques, Electriques et de la Transformation des Matieres Plastiques. Bulletin d'Information Mensuel (ISSN 0014-9330).

671.2   BE
FEDERATION DES ENTREPRISES DE L'INDUSTRIE DES FABRICATIONS METALLIQUES, MECANIQUES, ELECTRIQUES ET DE LA TRANSFORMATION DES MATIERES PLASTIQUES. CENTRE DE RECHERCHES SCIENTIFIQUES ET TECHNIQUES. SECTION: FONDERIE (FD). RESEARCH REPORTS. 1965. irreg. Federation des Entreprises de l'Industrie des Fabrications Metalliques, Mecaniques, Electriques et de la Transformation des Matieres Plastiques, 21 rue des Drapiers, 1050 Brussels, Belgium.

669   GW   ISSN 0940-2675
FEDERN - KETTEN - BIEGETEILE; internationale Fachzeitschrift fuer die Herstellung, Behandlung und Pruefung von Federn, Ketten sowie Biege- und Stanzteilen aus Draht und Bandmaterial. English edition: Springs - Chains - Formed Parts. 1988. 2/yr. DM.40($25) D K S Fachverlag GmbH, Im Wiesengrund 21, Postfach 41, 5489 Kelberg, Germany. TEL 02692-1071. FAX 02692-1073. Ed. Juergen Hendricks. adv.; bk.rev.; bibl.; illus.; tr.lit.; circ. 3,500. (back issues avail.)

669.6   FR   ISSN 0085-0519
FER-BLANC EN FRANCE ET DANS LE MONDE. 1956. a. free. (Chambre Syndicale des Producteurs de Fer-Blanc et de Fer-Noir) C P S Publications, 5 rue Paul Cezanne, 75008 Paris, France. FAX 45-63-74-80. TELEX A280-172F. charts; stat.; circ. 800.

669   VE
FERRETARIA. 1973. m. Camara Ferreteria Nacional, Av. Este 2, Edif. Camara de Comercio, Piso 5, Los Caobos, Caracas, Venezuela. Ed. Candido Marcano Rios.

669   MX
FERRETECNIC - F Y T; la revista de la industria ferretera. 1963. m. free. Publitecnic S.A., Calle 4, no. 188, Apdo. Postal 74-290, C.P. 09070, Mexico 13, D.F., Mexico. TEL 685-28-19. FAX 6706318. Ed. Fernando Ulacia Esteve. adv.; bk.rev.; circ. 10,000 (controlled). (back issues avail.)

669   US   ISSN 0953-721X
FERRO ALLOY DIRECTORY AND DATABOOK. 1984. irreg., 2nd ed., 1988. $139. Metal Bulletin Inc., 220 Fifth Ave., New York, NY 10001. TEL 212-213-6202. adv.
Supersedes: Ferro Alloy Directory (ISSN 0266-3198).
Description: Lists ferro alloy producers and traders with product guides.

669.1   SZ
FERRUM; Nachrichten aus der Eisenbibliothek. 1954. irreg. (1-2/yr.). free. Eisenbibliothek, Klostergut Paradies, CH-8246 Langwiesen, Switzerland. TEL 053-293810. FAX 053-291666. Ed. Annette Bouheiry. bk.rev. (back issues avail.)
Description: Examines iron and the history of technology.

669   FR   ISSN 0249-6704
FILS, TUBES, BANDES ET PROFILES. 1967. 6/yr. 305 F. (foreign 400 F.). Editions Ampere, Groupe C.E.P.P, 25, rue Dagorno, 75012 Paris, France. TEL 43-47-30-20. Ed. Claude Chapelon. adv.; circ. 4,500. **Indexed:** Met.Abstr.

671.732   US   ISSN 0015-2358
FINISHERS' MANAGEMENT. 1957. m. (10/yr.). $28 to non-members; members $14. (National Association of Metal Finishers) Publications Management, Inc., 4350 DiPaolo Center, Deerlove Rd., Glenview, IL 60025. TEL 708-699-1700. FAX 708-699-1703. Ed. Hugh Morgan. adv.; bk.rev.; charts; illus.; mkt.; circ. 9,200. (also avail. in microfilm from UMI; reprint service avail. from UMI) **Indexed:** Met.Abstr., World Alum.Abstr.
—BLDSC shelfmark: 3928.170000.
Formerly: Plating Management and Metal Finishers Management.

671   UK   ISSN 0071-5182
FINISHING HANDBOOK AND DIRECTORY. 1950. a. free to subscribers to Product Finishing. Sawell Publications Ltd., 127 Stanstead Rd., London SE23 1JE, England. Ed. J.E. Bean. adv.; circ. 4,500.

669   RU   ISSN 0015-3230
TN690   CODEN: FMMTAK
FIZIKA METALLOV I METALLOVEDENIE. 1955. m. 77.40 Rub. (Akademiya Nauk S.S.S.R.) Izdatel'stvo Nauka, Fizmatlit, Leninskii prospekt, 15, 117971 Moscow, V-71, Russia. Ed. S.V. Vonsovski. index. (tabloid format) **Indexed:** Cadscan, Chem.Abstr., Copper Abstr., Curr.Cont., Eng.Ind., Ind.Sci.Rev., INIS Atomind., Int.Aerosp.Abstr., Lead Abstr., Met.Abstr., Phys.Ber., Sci.Abstr., Sci.Cit.Ind., World Alum.Abstr., Zincscan.
—BLDSC shelfmark: 0389.800000.

671.2   IT   ISSN 0015-6078
TS200   CODEN: FNDAAR
FONDERIA. 1951. bi-m. L.75000. E T M, S.r.l., Via Roncaglia 14, 20146 Milan, Italy. TEL 02-48010095. FAX 02-48010011. Dir. Antonio Urti. adv.; bk.rev.; charts; illus.; tr.lit.; index; circ. 3,500. **Indexed:** B.C.I.R.A., Chem.Abstr., Met.Abstr., World Alum.Abstr.
Description: Technical review of Italian foundry industry. Metals, metallurgy, casting processes, treatments, foundry items and equipment.

671.2   FR   ISSN 0249-3136
TS200   CODEN: FFAUDJ
FONDERIE, FONDEUR D'AUJOURD'HUI. (Summaries in English, French, German) 1981. m. 587 F. (foreign 910 F.)(effective Jan. 1992). Editions Techniques des Industries de la Fonderie, 44 Av. de la Division Leclerc, 92310 Sevres, France. FAX 45-34-14-34. TELEX 270953 CTIFSE. Dir. P. Grandier Vazeille. adv.; bk.rev.; abstr.; bibl.; charts; illus.; index; cum.index; circ. 2,700. **Indexed:** B.C.I.R.A., Cadscan, Chem.Abstr., Eng.Ind., Lead Abstr., Met.Abstr., Sci.Abstr., Zincscan.
—BLDSC shelfmark: 3976.050000.
Incorporates (in 1981): Fondeur d'Aujourd'hui (ISSN 0015-6116)
Description: Publishes results of studies of CTIF. Features original works of French as well as foreign engineers, practical advice, industrial projects, information on the professional life of engineers, etc.

671.2   UK
FORGE (YEAR). 1908. bi-m. £2.50($40) (National Association Farriers, Blacksmiths and Agricultural Engineers) Farriers' Journal Publishing Co. Ltd., Ave. R., 7th St., N.A.C. Stoneleigh, Warks. CV8 2LG, England. TEL 0203-696595. FAX 0203-696708. Ed. J.A. Webb. adv.; bk.rev.; bibl.; stat.; tr.lit.; circ. 1,200.
Formerly: Farriers Journal.
Description: News about farriery and blacksmithing.

671.2   US   ISSN 1054-1756
▼**FORGING.** 1990. q. $20 (free to qualified personnel). Penton Publishing (Subsidiary of: Pittway Company), 1100 Superior Ave., Cleveland, OH 44114-2534. TEL 216-696-7000. FAX 216-696-7658. Ed. Wallace D. Huskonen. adv.; illus.; tr.lit.; circ. 5,000 (controlled).

699   US
FOUNDRY DATABOOK & CATALOG FILE. 1970. a. $10 (free to qualified personnel). Penton Publishing (Subsidiary of: Pittway Company), 1100 Superior Ave., Cleveland, OH 44114-2543. TEL 216-696-7000. FAX 216-696-8765. (Subscr. to: Box 95759, Cleveland, OH 44101) adv.; circ. 24,000 (controlled). (reprint service avail. from UMI)
Formerly: Foundry Catalog File (ISSN 0533-005X)

669   US   ISSN 0071-8130
FOUNDRY DIRECTORY AND REGISTER OF FORGES. 1959. biennial. $110. Metal Bulletin Inc., 220 Fifth Avenue, New York, NY 10001. TEL 212-213-6202.
Description: List of iron founders in Europe.

671.2   US   ISSN 0360-8999
TS200   CODEN: FNMTBS
FOUNDRY MANAGEMENT & TECHNOLOGY. 1892. m. $45 (free to qualified personnel). Penton Publishing (Subsidiary of: Pittway Company), 1100 Superior Ave., Cleveland, OH 44114-2543. TEL 216-696-7000. FAX 216-696-8765. (Subscr. to: Box 95759, Cleveland, OH 44101) Ed. Robert C. Rodgers. adv.; bk.rev.; illus.; stat.; tr.lit.; circ. 22,000 (controlled). (also avail. in microfilm from UMI; reprint service avail. from UMI) **Indexed:** A.S.& T.Ind., B.C.I.R.A., Bus.Ind., Ceram.Abstr., Ergon.Abstr., Excerp.Med., ISMEC, Met.Abstr., PROMT, SRI, Tr.& Indus.Ind., World Alum.Abstr.
●Also available online. Vendor(s): DIALOG.
—BLDSC shelfmark: 4026.600000.
Formerly: Foundry (ISSN 0015-9034)
Description: Includes technical developments, foundry management problems and operating practices.

671.2   UK   ISSN 0015-9042
TS200   CODEN: FUTJAD
FOUNDRY TRADE JOURNAL. 1902. fortn. (m. in Jan., Aug., Dec.). £100.50 (foreign £131.25). (National Society of Master Patternmakers) F M J International Publications Ltd., Queensway House, 2 Queensway, Redhill, Surrey RH1 1QS, England. TEL 0737-768611. FAX 0737-761685. TELEX 948669-TOPJNL-G. (Co-sponsors: Diecasting Society, B.I.C.T.A., L.M.F.A.) Ed. J. Mitchell. adv.; bk.rev.; film rev.; abstr.; charts; illus.; mkt.; pat.; stat.; tr.lit.; s-a. index. (also avail. in microfilm from UMI; reprint service avail. from UMI) **Indexed:** Art & Archaeol.Tech.Abstr., B.C.I.R.A., Br.Tech.Ind., C.I.S. Abstr., Cadscan, Chem.Abstr., Copper Abstr., Eng.Ind., Ergon.Abstr., Excerp.Med., Fuel & Energy Abstr., ISMEC, Lead Abstr., Met.Abstr., World Alum.Abstr., Zincscan.
—BLDSC shelfmark: 4028.000000.

METALLURGY 3407

671.2 UK
FOUNDRY TRADE JOURNAL INTERNATIONAL. (Text in English; summaries in French, German, Italian and Spanish) 1978. q. £72.60 (foreign £85.05). F M J International Publications Ltd., Queensway House, 2 Queensway, Redhill, Surrey RH1 1QS, England. TEL 0737-768611. FAX 0737-761685. TELEX 948669-TOPJNL-G. Ed. C. McCombe. **Indexed:** Art & Archaeol.Tech.Abstr., B.C.I.R.A., Met.Abstr., World Alum.Abstr.

671.2 UK ISSN 0306-4212
FOUNDRY YEARBOOK. 1972. a. £75.50. F M J International Publications Ltd., Queensway House, 2 Queensway, Redhill, Surrey RH1 1QS, England. TEL 0737-768611. FAX 0737-761685. TELEX 948669-TOPJNL-G. Ed. K. Tolley. adv.; charts; tr.lit.; circ. 3,000. **Indexed:** Copper Abstr.

671.2 UK ISSN 0953-6035
FOUNDRYMAN. 1956. 12/yr. £60 (foreign £77). (Institute of British Foundrymen) I B F Publications, 3rd Fl., Bridge House, 121 Smallbrook Queensway, Birmingham B5 4JP, England. TEL 0732-884023. FAX 021-631-2872. (Subscr. to: 6 Bourne Enterprise Centre, Wrotham Rd., Borough Green, Kent TN15 8DG, England) Ed. L.M. Postle. adv.; bk.rev.; abstr.; bibl.; charts; illus.; index; circ. 3,000. (also avail. in microform from UMI; reprint service avail. from UMI) **Indexed:** Art & Archaeol.Tech.Abstr., B.C.I.R.A., Br.Tech.Ind., C.I.S. Abstr., Chem.Abstr., Eng.Ind., Ergon.Abstr., Excerp.Med., ISMEC, Met.Abstr., World Alum.Abstr.
—BLDSC shelfmark: 4028.024000.
Formerly: British Foundryman (ISSN 0007-0718)

669 GW
FREIBERGER FORSCHUNGSHEFTE. MONTANWISSENSCHAFTEN: REIHE B. METALLURGIE UND WERSTOFFTECHNIK. 1951. irreg. price varies. (Bergakademie Freiberg) Deutscher Verlag fuer Grundstoffindustrie, Karl-Heine-Str. 27, 7031 Leipzig, Germany. TEL 4081011. FAX 4012571. TELEX 51451-FACHB-DD. **Indexed:** INIS Atomind., Met.Abstr., World Alum.Abstr.
Formerly: Freiberger Forschungshefte. Montanwissenschaften: Reihe B. Metallurgie (ISSN 0071-9420)

671.2 PO
FUNDICAO. (Text in Portuguese; summaries in English, French and Portuguese) 1964. 4/yr. Esc.12000($80) Associacao Portuguesa de Fundicao, Rua do Campo Alegre 672, Porto, Portugal. FAX 6000764. TELEX 27180 APFP. Ed.Bd. adv.; bk.rev.; film rev.; stat.; tr.lit.; index; circ. 1,000. (tabloid format) **Indexed:** Met.Abstr., World Alum.Abstr.

669 BL
▼**FUNDICAO E SERVICOS.** 1990. bi-m. $80. Aranda Editora Ltda., Rua Dona Elisa 167, 01155 Sao Paulo SP, Brazil. TEL 11-826-4511. FAX 11-66-9585. Ed. Maria C. Bottura. circ. 12,000. (back issues avail.)

669 AG ISSN 0429-8950
FUNDIDOR. 3/yr. free. Camara de Industriales Fundidores, Alsina 1607, 1088 Capital Federal, Buenos Aires, Argentina. adv.; bk.rev.; circ. 1,700. **Indexed:** B.C.I.R.A., Chem.Abstr., Met.Abstr., World Alum.Abstr.
Formerly: Fundidas.

669 AT
GALVANIZE. 1981. q. free. Galvanizers Association of Australia, 124 Exhibition St., Melbourne, Vic. 3000, Australia. TEL 613-654-1611. FAX 613-654-1136. TELEX AA28806. Ed. M.J. Dennett. bk.rev.; circ. 8,500.
Formerly (until 1981): Galvanizing Report.
Description: Data sheet on uses and performance of hot-dip galvanizing.

671.732 IT
GALVANOTECNICA E NUOVE FINITURE. 1950. bi-m. L.100000. Associazione Italiana Finiture dei Metalli, Via Campigli 16, 21100 Varese, Italy. TEL 0332-312707. Ed. Eugenio Bertorelle. adv.; bk.rev.; abstr.; bibl.; illus.; index, cum.index: 1953-1987; circ. 25,000. **Indexed:** Chem.Abstr., Met.Abstr., World Alum.Abstr.
Former titles: Galvanotecnica e Processi al Plasma and Galvanotecnica; Galvanotecnica (ISSN 0016-4240)
Description: Electroplating, ion plating and new finishing.

669 CC ISSN 0449-749X
GANGTIE/IRON AND STEEL. (Text in Chinese) m. Yejin Gongye Chubanshe - Metallurgical Industry Publishers, 39 Songzhuyuan Beixiang, Shatan, Beijing 100009, People's Republic of China. TEL 4015782. Ed. Lu Da.
—BLDSC shelfmark: 4577.900000.

GENERAL COMMISSION ON SAFETY AND HEALTH IN THE IRON AND STEEL INDUSTRY. REPORT. see *OCCUPATIONAL HEALTH AND SAFETY*

GEOLOGICAL, MINING AND METALLURGICAL SOCIETY OF INDIA. BULLETIN. see *EARTH SCIENCES — Geology*

GEOLOGY AND WORLD DEPOSITS. see *EARTH SCIENCES — Geology*

671.2 GW ISSN 0016-9765
CODEN: GIESAS
GIESSEREI; Zeitschrift fuer das gesamte Giessereiwesen. (Contents page in English and French) 1914. s-m. DM.267. (Verein Deutscher Giessereifachleute e.V.) Giesserei-Verlag GmbH, Sohnstr. 65, Postfach 102532, 4000 Duesseldorf 1, Germany. adv.; bk.rev.; bibl.; charts; illus.; mkt.; pat.; index; circ. 5,000. **Indexed:** B.C.I.R.A., C.I.S. Abstr., Chem.Abstr., Excerp.Med., INIS Atomind., ISMEC, Met.Abstr., Numis.Lit., PROMT, World Alum.Abstr.
—BLDSC shelfmark: 4174.000000.

671.2 GW ISSN 0016-9773
GIESSEREI-ERFAHRUNGSAUSTAUSCH. 1957. m. DM.26. Fachverlag Giesserei-Erfahrungsaustausch, Kleistr. 10, 6805 Heddesheim, Germany. Ed. Max Schied. adv.; bk.rev. **Indexed:** Met.Abstr., World Alum.Abstr.
—BLDSC shelfmark: 4174.300000.

669 GW ISSN 0340-8175
GIESSEREI-KALENDER. 1954. a. (Verein Deutscher Giessereifachleute) Giesserei-Verlag GmbH, Sohnstr. 65, Postfach 102532, 4000 Duesseldorf 1, Germany. TEL 0211-6707-0.

671.2 GW ISSN 0016-9781
CODEN: GIPXAU
GIESSEREI-PRAXIS. 1950. s-m. DM.165.60. Fachverlag Schiele und Schoen GmbH, Markgrafenstr. 11, 1000 Berlin 61, Germany. TEL 030-251-6029. FAX 030-2517248. TELEX 181470-SUNDS-D. Ed. E. Brunhuber. adv.; bk.rev.; abstr.; charts; illus.; mkt.; tr.lit.; index; circ. 4,000. **Indexed:** B.C.I.R.A., C.I.S. Abstr., Cadscan, Chem.Abstr., Eng.Ind., INIS Atomind., Lead Abstr., Met.Abstr., World Alum.Abstr., Zincscan.

671.2 AU ISSN 0016-979X
CODEN: GIERBQ
GIESSEREI RUNDSCHAU. 1954. 6/yr. S.552 incl. news-letters annually. (Verein Oesterreichischer Giessereifachleute) Verlag Lorenz, Ebendorferstr. 10, A-1010 Vienna, Austria. TEL 0222-426695. FAX 0222-438693. (Co-sponsor: Fachverband der Giessereiindustrie und des Oesterreichischen Giesserei Institutes) Ed. G. Kosicek. adv.; bk.rev.; bibl.; illus.; pat.; stat.; tr.lit.; circ. 1,000. (tabloid format) **Indexed:** B.C.I.R.A., Chem.Abstr.
—BLDSC shelfmark: 4175.050000.

671.2 GW ISSN 0046-5933
CODEN: GSFGBY
GIESSEREIFORSCHUNG. (Text in German; contents page in English, French, and German) 1949. q. DM.282. (Verein Deutscher Giessereifachleute e.V.) Giesserei-Verlag GmbH, Sohnstr. 65, Postfach 102532, 4000 Duesseldorf 1, Germany. TEL 0211-6707-0. adv. **Indexed:** B.C.I.R.A., Chem.Abstr., Eng.Ind., INIS Atomind., Met.Abstr.
—BLDSC shelfmark: 4175.090000.

669 NE
GIETWERK PERSPEKTIEF. bi-m. (Nederlandse Vereniging van Gieterijtechnici) Technische Uitgeverij de Vey Mestdagh BV, Markt 51, 4331 LK Middelburg, Netherlands. TEL 01180-81240. FAX 01180-81215. Ed. H. Nieswaag. adv.; bk.rev.; circ. 1,000. **Indexed:** B.C.I.R.A.

669 IT
GIORNALE DELLA LAMIERA. bi-m. L.30000 (foreign L.80000)(effective 1992). Tecniche Nuove s.p.a., Via C. Menotti, 14, 20129 Milan, Italy. TEL 02-75701. FAX 02-7570205.

669 IT ISSN 0392-3622
IL GIORNALE DELLA SUBFORNITURA. 1980. m. L.65000($113) (foreign L.130000). Stammer S.P.A., Centro Commerciale Milano San Felice, 20090 Segrate, Milan, Italy. TEL 02-7530651. FAX 02-7530587. TELEX 321083 STAMMER. Ed. Girolamo Bellina. circ. 30,000.

669 SW ISSN 0017-0682
CODEN: GJUTAG
GJUTERIET. 1910. m. SEK 300. Sveriges Gjuteritekniska Foerening, Bransch Information, Torstenssonsgatan 12, 114 56 Stockholm, Sweden. FAX 8-6669825. Ed. Lars Cyrus. adv.; charts; illus.; circ. 1,700. **Indexed:** B.C.I.R.A., Chem.Abstr., Eng.Ind., Met.Abstr., World Alum.Abstr.

GOLD NEWS/NOUVELLES DE L'OR. see *MINES AND MINING INDUSTRY*

669 US
GUIDE TO PRODUCTS AND SERVICES OF MEMBER COMPANIES. 1985. a. Titanium Development Association, Box 2307, Dayton, OH 45401. TEL 513-223-8432. FAX 513-223-6307. Ed. Georgiana M. Hockaday. adv.; circ. 1,500.
Formerly: Titanium Development Association. (Year) Buyer's Guide.
Description: Covers titanium companies, products, services.

669 CC ISSN 1000-7563
GUOWAI NAIHUO CAILIAO. (Text in Chinese) m. Anshan Jiaohua Nanhuo Cailiao Sheji Yanjiuyuan, Qingbao Shi, 27, Shengli Lu, Anshan, Liaoning 114002, People's Republic of China. TEL 29738. Ed. Wang Jing'er.

669 GW ISSN 0341-101X
HAERTEREI-TECHNISCHE MITTEILUNGEN; Zeitschrift fuer Waermebehandlung und Werkstofftechnik. Short title: H T M. 1941. bi-m. DM.343.80. (Arbeitsgemeinschaft Waermebehandlung und Werkstoff-Technik e.V.) Carl Hanser Verlag, Kolbergerstr. 22, Postfach 860420, 8000 Munich 80, Germany. TEL 089-926940. Eds. Johann Grosch, Rudi Jonck. adv.; bibl.; charts; illus.; index; circ. 1,600. **Indexed:** Chem.Abstr., Eng.Ind., Met.Abstr., World Alum.Abstr.
—BLDSC shelfmark: 4265.000000.

669.1 530 NE
HANDBOOK ON FERROMAGNETIC MATERIALS. 1980. irreg., vol.5, 1990. price varies. Elsevier Science Publishers B.V., Books Division, P.O. Box 211, 1000 AE Amsterdam, Netherlands. TEL 020-5803911. FAX 020-5803705. TELEX 18582 ESPA NL. (Subscr. in U.S. and Canada to: Elsevier Science Publishing Co., Inc., Box 882, Madison Sq. Sta., New York, NY 10159. TEL 212-989-5800) Ed. E.P. Wohlfarth.
Refereed Serial

669 US
HEAT PROCESSING DIGEST. 1974. m. $145 to non-members (foreign $155); members $120 (foreign $130). A S M International, Materials Information, Materials Park, OH 44073. TEL 216-338-5151. FAX 216-338-4634. TELEX 980-619. (UK addr.: Institute of Metals, Materials Information, 1 Carlton House Terrace, London SW1Y 5DB, England. TEL 071-839-4071) Ed. H. David Chafe. (reprint service avail. from UMI) **Indexed:** Met.Abstr.
Description: Digest of materials information for heat processing.

671 US ISSN 0017-9345
TN672 CODEN: HETRDI
HEAT TREATING. 1969. m. $55 (free to qualified personnel). Hitchcock Publishing, Heat Treating (Subsidiary of: Capital Cities - A B C, Inc.), 191 S. Gary Ave., Carol Stream, IL 60188. TEL 708-462-2286. FAX 708-462-2225. Ed. Anne Armel. adv.; bk.rev.; circ. 21,426 (controlled). (also avail. in microform from UMI; reprint service avail. from UMI) **Indexed:** Met.Abstr., World Alum.Abstr.

METALLURGY

669   UK   ISSN 0305-4829
TN672   CODEN: HTRMBS
HEAT TREATMENT OF METALS. 1974. q. £64($130) to individuals; educational institutions £54.50($109). Wolfson Heat Treatment Centre, Aston University, Aston Triangle, Birmingham B4 7ET, England. TEL 021-359-3611. FAX 021-359-8910. TELEX 336997 UNIAST G. Ed. A.J. Hick. adv.; bk.rev.; index; circ. 1,000. (back issues avail.) **Indexed:** B.C.I.R.A., Cadscan, Chem.Abstr., Curr.Cont., Lead Abstr., Met.Abstr., Risk Abstr., Sci.Abstr., World Alum.Abstr., Zincscan.
—BLDSC shelfmark: 4276.370000.
Description: Devoted to industrial heat treatment practice and innovation.

HIGH - TC UPDATE. see *PHYSICS*

669   UK   ISSN 0142-3304
                          CODEN: HIMED6
HISTORICAL METALLURGY. 1963. 2/yr. £15 (effective Jan. 1992). Historical Metallurgy Society Ltd., Rock House, Bowens Hill, Coleford, Glos. GL16 8DH, England. TEL 0594-33778. Eds. Justine Bayley, David Crossley. adv.; bk.rev.; cum.index: vols.1-7, vols.8-18; circ. 700. **Indexed:** Art & Archaeol.Tech.Abstr., B.C.I.R.A., Br.Archaeol.Abstr., Chem.Abstr., Met.Abstr., Numis.Lit., World Alum.Abstr.
—BLDSC shelfmark: 4758.360000.
Formerly: Historical Metallurgy Group. Bulletin.
Description: Covers metallurgy from prehistoric times to the present.

671.2   FR   ISSN 0018-4357
                          CODEN: HFONDM
HOMMES ET FONDERIE. 1970. m. 380 F. (foreign 505 F.). (Association Technique de Fonderie) P Y C Edition, B.P. 105, 5, av. de Verdun, 94208 Ivry sur Seine Cedex, France. TEL 1-49-60-86-36. FAX 1-46-72-41-85. TELEX 263 424. Ed. Regis Foques-Duparc. adv.; illus.; circ. 3,139. **Indexed:** B.C.I.R.A., Met.Abstr., World Alum.Abstr.
—BLDSC shelfmark: 4326.265000.
Formed by the merger of: Technicien de Fonderie & Association Technique de Fonderie. Bulletin Mensuel d'Information.

HOOGOVENS GROEP BULLETIN. see *ENGINEERING*

HUAGONG YEJIN/JOURNAL OF ENGINEERING CHEMISTRY AND METALLURGY. see
ENGINEERING — Chemical Engineering

669   CS   ISSN 0018-8069
TN4   CODEN: HUTLA7
HUTNICKE LISTY. English translation: Metallurgical Journal (UK ISSN 0951-0869) (Text in Czech; summaries in English, French, German, Russian) 1945. m. $65.70. (Federalni Ministerstvo Hutnictvi a Tezkeho Strojirenstvi) Nakladatelstvi Technicke Literatury, Spalena 51, 113 02 Prague 1, Czechoslovakia. (Dist. by: Artia, Ve Smeckach 30, 111 27 Prague 1, Czechoslovakia) Ed. Jaroslav Kucera. adv.; bk.rev.; charts; illus.; pat.; tr.lit.; index; circ. 2,900. **Indexed:** Anal.Abstr., Art & Archaeol.Tech.Abstr., C.I.S. Abstr., Cadscan, Chem.Abstr., Eng.Ind., INIS Atomind., Lead Abstr., Met.Abstr., World Alum.Abstr., Zincscan.

669   CS
HUTNIK. 1951. m. $24.90. Nakladatelstvi Technicke Literatury, Spalena 51, 113 02 Prague 1, Czechoslovakia. (Dist. by: Artia, Ve Smeckach 30, 111 27 Prague 1, Czechoslovakia) Ed. Alexader Michl. illus.; circ. 3,700. **Indexed:** C.I.S. Abstr., Ceram.Abstr., INIS Atomind., Met.Abstr., World Alum.Abstr.

671.2   PL
TS200
HUTNIK - WIADOMOSCI HUTNICZE. (Text in Polish; summaries in English, German, Russian) 1929. m. $82. Wydawnictwo Naczelnej Organizacji Technicznej "Sigma", Ul. Dabrowskiego 23, 40-032 Katowice, Poland. TELEX SIGMA PL 814-877. (Dist. by: Ars Polona - Ruch, Krakowskie Przedmiescie 7, Warsaw, Poland) Ed. Wladyslaw Sabela. adv.: B&W page $750. bk.rev.; circ. 500. **Indexed:** Ceram.Abstr., Chem.Abstr., Eng.Ind., Met.Abstr., World Alum.Abstr.
Formerly (until 1992): Hutnik (ISSN 0018-8077)
Description: Covers steel production.

669   NE   ISSN 0304-386X
TN688   CODEN: HYDRDA
HYDROMETALLURGY; international journal devoted to all aspects of the aqueous processing of metals. (Text in English) 1975. 9/yr.(in 3 vols.; 3 nos./vol.). fl.1098 (effective 1992). Elsevier Science Publishers B.V., P.O. Box 211, 1000 AE Amsterdam, Netherlands. TEL 020-5803911.
FAX 020-5803598. TELEX 18582 ESPA NL. (Subscr. in U.S. and Canada to: Elsevier Science Publishing Co., Inc., Box 882, Madison Sq. Sta., New York, NY 11059. TEL 212-989-5800) Eds. G.M. Ritcey, M.J. Slater. adv.; bk.rev.; charts; illus.; index. (also avail. in microform from RPI) **Indexed:** AESIS, Cadscan, Chem.Abstr., Chem.Eng.Abstr., Copper Abstr., Curr.Cont., Eng.Ind., Ind.Sci.Rev., Lead Abstr., Met.Abstr., Sci.Cit.Ind., Soils & Fert., T.C.E.A., World Alum.Abstr., Zincscan.
—BLDSC shelfmark: 4352.153000.
Description: Brings together studies on novel processes, process design, chemistry, modelling, control, economics and interfaces between unit operations, and provides a forum for discussions on case histories and operational difficulties.
Refereed Serial

671.3   SZ
I M F NEWS. 1972. fortn. free. International Metalworkers Federation, 54 bis, Rte. des Acacias, CH-1227 Geneva, Switzerland. FAX 022-3431510. TELEX 423298-METL-CH.

669.1   JA   ISSN 0915-1559
TS300.   CODEN: IINTEY
I S I J INTERNATIONAL. (Text in English) 1961. m. 42000 Yen to non-members (effective 1991). Iron and Steel Institute of Japan - Nippon Tekko Kyokai, Keidanren Kaikan, 3rd Fl., 9-4, Otemachi 1-chome, Chiyoda-ku, Tokyo 100, Japan. TEL 03-3279-6021. FAX 03-3245-1355. TELEX 02228153-ISIJTK-J. Ed. Jin Shimada. adv.; abstr.; bibl.; charts; illus.; stat.; index, cum.index; circ. 5,000. (also avail. in microfilm; back issues avail.) **Indexed:** Chem.Abstr., Corros.Abstr., Curr.Cont., Eng.Ind., JCT, JTA, Met.Abstr., World Alum.Abstr.
—BLDSC shelfmark: 4582.963000.
Formerly: Iron and Steel Institute of Japan. Transactions (ISSN 0021-1583); **Supersedes:** Tetsu-To-Hagane Overseas.
Description: Provides the core subject matter of iron and steel worldwide. Intended for those concerned with the processing, structure, property, and application of engineering materials.

669.142 690   UK
I S T C PHOENIX. Short title: Phoenix. 1980. 4/yr. free. Iron and Steel Trades Confederation, Swinton House, 324 Gray's Inn Rd., London WC1 8DD, England. FAX 01-278-8378. Ed. Len Powell. adv.; illus.; circ. 40,000.
Former titles: I S T C Banner (ISSN 0260-0625); Steelworker's Banner.

671.2   II   ISSN 0379-5446
                          CODEN: IFOJAI
INDIAN FOUNDRY JOURNAL. (Text in English) 1956. m. $100. Institute of Indian Foundrymen, Middleton Court, 1st Floor, 4-2 Middleton St., Calcutta 700071, W. Bengal, India. TEL 29-2110. TELEX 021-5166-IIF-IN. Ed. P.N. Chakraborty. adv.; film rev.; abstr.; bibl.; charts; illus.; pat.; stat.; circ. 1,300. **Indexed:** B.C.I.R.A., Cadscan, Chem.Abstr., Lead Abstr., Met.Abstr., World Alum.Abstr., Zincscan.
—BLDSC shelfmark: 4409.300000.

669   II
INDIAN INSTITUTE OF METALS. PROCEEDINGS. irreg. Indian Institute of Metals, 2 Sambhunath Pandit St., Calcutta 700020, India. **Indexed:** Chem.Abstr.

669   II   ISSN 0019-493X
TN4   CODEN: TIIMA3
INDIAN INSTITUTE OF METALS. TRANSACTIONS. (Text in English) 1946. bi-m. Rs.225. Indian Institute of Metals, 2 Sambhunath Pandit St., Calcutta 700020, India. Ed. P. Rama Rao. adv.; bk.rev.; charts; illus.; index, cum.index covering 5 yrs.; circ. 4,000. **Indexed:** Art & Archaeol.Tech.Abstr., Curr.Cont., Energy Ind., Energy Info.Abstr., Eng.Ind., Fuel & Energy Abstr., Met.Abstr., World Alum.Abstr.

INDIAN JOURNAL OF GEOLOGY. see *EARTH SCIENCES — Geology*

669.1   II   ISSN 0019-641X
INDIAN STEEL AGE;* a journal on iron, steel and engineering. (Indo-German Supplement) (Text in English) 1961. m. Rs.20. S.K. Bhanot, Ed. & Pub., 640 Double Storey, New Rajinder Nagar, New Delhi 5, India. adv.; illus.; stat.

669.1   MX
INDUSTRIA SIDERURGICA EN MEXICO. 1981. a. Mex.$5000($11) Instituto Nacional de Estadistica, Geografia e Informatica, Secretaria de Programacion y Presupuesto, Prol. Heroe de Nacozari, 2301, Acceso 10, C.P. 20290, Aguascalientes, Ags., Mexico. TEL 91-491-81968. FAX 91-491-80739. (Subscr. to: Rio Rhin No. 56, Col. Cuauhtemoc, 06500 Mexico, D.F., Mexico) circ. 2,000.

INDUSTRIAL CORROSION. see *ENGINEERING — Engineering Mechanics And Materials*

INDUSTRIAL PRODUCT IDEAS. see *BUSINESS AND ECONOMICS — Production Of Goods And Services*

669   US
INDUSTRIAL WORLD'S METALWORKING EDITION. (Supplement to: Industrial World) (Editions in English and Spanish) 1983. 6/yr. Johnston International Publishing (Subsidiary of: Hunter Publishing Limited Partnership), 950 Lee St., Des Plaines, IL 60016. TEL 708-296-0770. FAX 708-803-3328. Ed. Jose Fuentecilla. circ. 42,100 (23,070 English ed.; 19,030 Spanish ed.).

669   US
INFOMET. (Supplement to: World Industrial Reporter) (Editions in English and Spanish) 6/yr. Keller International Publishing Corporation, 150 Great Neck Rd., Great Neck, NY 11021.
TEL 516-829-9210. FAX 516-829-5414. TELEX 221547 KELLE. circ. 60,061 (30,041 English ed.; 30,020 Spanish ed.).

669.722   CN   ISSN 0707-8013
INGOT. (Text in French) 1936. fortn. free. Alcan Smelters and Chemicals Ltd., Box 1370, Jonquiere, Que. G7S 4K9, Canada. TEL 418-548-1121. Ed. Raymond Arcand. circ. 15,000. (tabloid format) **Indexed:** Met.Abstr., World Alum.Abstr.
Formerly: Kitimat-Kemano Ingot.

INORGANIC MATERIALS. see *CHEMISTRY — Inorganic Chemistry*

669   UK   ISSN 0020-2967
                          CODEN: TIMFA2
INSTITUTE OF METAL FINISHING. TRANSACTIONS. 1951. q. £88. Institute of Metal Finishing, Exeter House, 48 Holloway Head, Birmingham B1 1NQ, England. TEL 021-622-7387. FAX 021-666-6316. Ed. C. Larson. adv.; bk.rev.; charts; illus.; upd 27 92099; circ. 2,250. **Indexed:** C.I.S. Abstr., Chem.Abstr., Copper Abstr., Excerp.Med., Met.Abstr., Sci.Abstr., World Alum.Abstr., World Surf.Coat.
—BLDSC shelfmark: 8941.000000.

669   AT
INSTITUTE OF METALS AND MATERIALS AUSTRALASIA. PROCEEDINGS. 1947. a. price varies. Institute of Metals and Materials Australasia Ltd., 191 Royal Parade, Parkville, Vic. 3052, Australia.
TEL 03-347-2544. FAX 03-348-1208. Ed. R. Nethercott. bibl.; charts; illus.; circ. 300. **Indexed:** Met.Abstr.
Former titles: Australasian Institute of Metals. Proceedings of the Annual Conference & Australian Institute of Metals. Proceedings of the Annual Conference.

669   SW   ISSN 0015-7953
INSTITUTET FOER METALLFORSKNING. FORSKNINGSVERKSAMHETEN. 1952. a. free. Institutet foer Metallforskning - Swedish Institute for Metals Research, Drottning Kristinas Vaeg 48, S-114 28 Stockholm, Sweden.
FAX 46-8-723-0423. Ed. Rune Lagneborg. bibl.; illus.; circ. 2,400.

669   II   ISSN 0257-4411
CODEN: JIMDEQ
INSTITUTION OF ENGINEERS (INDIA). METALLURGY & MATERIAL SCIENCE DIVISION. JOURNAL. (Text in English) 1983. s-a. Rs.40($5) Institution of Engineers (India), Metallurgy & Material Science Division, 8 Gokhale Rd., Calcutta 700 020, India. TEL 033-288334. FAX 033-288345. TELEX 0217885 IEIC IN. Ed. K.N. Majumdar. adv.; charts; illus.; index; circ. 3,000.
—BLDSC shelfmark: 4794.039500.

INSTITUTION OF ENGINEERS (INDIA). MINING ENGINEERING DIVISION. JOURNAL. see *MINES AND MINING INDUSTRY*

INSTITUTION OF MINING AND METALLURGY. TRANSACTIONS. SECTION A: MINING INDUSTRY. see *MINES AND MINING INDUSTRY*

INSTITUTION OF MINING AND METALLURGY. TRANSACTIONS. SECTION B: APPLIED EARTH SCIENCES. see *MINES AND MINING INDUSTRY*

INSTITUTION OF MINING AND METALLURGY. TRANSACTIONS. SECTION C: MINERAL PROCESSING & EXTRACTIVE METALLURGY. see *MINES AND MINING INDUSTRY*

669   US   ISSN 0361-3070
TN153   CODEN: IMIDBK
INSTRUMENTATION IN THE MINING AND METALLURGY INDUSTRIES. 1975. irreg. price varies. Instrument Society of America, 67 Alexander Dr., Box 12277, Research Triangle Park, NC 27709. TEL 919-549-8411. FAX 919-549-8288. TELEX 802540 ISA DURM. (reprint service avail. from ISI,UMI) **Indexed:** Chem.Abstr., INIS Atomind.
Formerly: I S A Mining and Metallurgy Instrumentation Symposium. Proceedings.
Refereed Serial

669   PL   ISSN 0137-9941
TN4   CODEN: PIMZDL
INSTYTUT METALURGII ZELAZA. PRACE/INSTITUTE OF FERROUS METALLURGY. TRANSACTIONS. (Text in Polish; summaries in English and Russian) 1949. q. $120. Instytut Metalurgii Zelaza, Ul. K. Miarki 12, 44-100 Gliwice, Poland. TEL 31 35 94. TELEX 036363 IMZ PL. Ed. Edward Barszcz. circ. 400. **Indexed:** Chem.Abstr., Met.Abstr., Ref.Zh.
Description: Covers production of iron and steel and further processing of steel.

INTERGOVERNMENTAL COUNCIL OF COPPER EXPORTING COUNTRIES. QUARTERLY REVIEW. see *BUSINESS AND ECONOMICS — International Commerce*

669.4   UK   ISSN 0074-316X
TA480.L4   CODEN: ICLPAY
INTERNATIONAL CONFERENCE ON LEAD. PROCEEDINGS. 1962. triennial, 9th, 1986, Goslar. Lead Development Association, 42 Weymouth St., London W1N 3LQ, England. Ed. D.N. Wilson. circ. 1,000.

620.112   CN   ISSN 0074-4123
INTERNATIONAL CONGRESS ON METALLIC CORROSION. (PROCEEDINGS).* (Proceedings published by host country) 1961. triennial, 10th, 1987. DM.250. (International Corrosion Council) National Research Council of Canada, Publication Sales and Distribution, Ottawa, Ontario K1A 0R6, Canada.

669 692.1   US   ISSN 0074-6118
INTERNATIONAL FOUNDRY CONGRESS. PAPERS AND COMMUNICATIONS. (Papers published in host countries) a. price varies. c/o American Foundrymen's Society, 505 State St., Des Plaines, IL 60016. TEL 708-824-0181. FAX 708-824-7848. **Indexed:** Chem.Abstr.
Formerly: World Foundry Congress.

338.2 672   BE   ISSN 0074-6630
INTERNATIONAL IRON AND STEEL INSTITUTE. REPORT OF CONFERENCE PROCEEDINGS. 1967. a. 1500 Fr. International Iron and Steel Institute, Rue Colonel Bourg 120, B-1140 Brussels, Belgium. TEL 02-735-90-75. FAX 02-7358012. TELEX 22639. charts; illus.; stat.
Description: Includes a verbatim record of the proceedings as well as the question and answer periods of the annual conference.

INTERNATIONAL JOURNAL OF MINERAL PROCESSING. see *MINES AND MINING INDUSTRY*

669   US   ISSN 0888-7462
TN695   CODEN: IPMTEA
INTERNATIONAL JOURNAL OF POWDER METALLURGY. 1965. q. $70 to individuals; institutions $135. American Powder Metallurgy Institute, 105 College Rd. E., Princeton, NJ 08540. TEL 609-452-7700. FAX 609-987-8523. TELEX 510-685-2516. Ed. Dr. Alan Lawley. adv.; bk.rev.; abstr.; charts; stat.; index; circ. 3,300. (also avail. in microform from UMI; reprint service avail. from UMI) **Indexed:** A.S.& T.Ind., Cadscan, Chem.Abstr., Copper Abstr., Curr.Cont., Ind.Sci.Rev., Int.Aerosp.Abstr., Lead Abstr., Met.Abstr., Sci.Cit.Ind., World Alum.Abstr., Zincscan.
Former titles: International Journal of Powder Metallurgy and Powder Technology (ISSN 0361-3488); International Journal of Powder Metallurgy (ISSN 0020-7535)

669 621   UK   ISSN 0265-0916
CODEN: IJRSEO
INTERNATIONAL JOURNAL OF RAPID SOLIDIFICATION. 1984. 4/yr. £99($198) A B Academic Publishers, P.O. Box 42, Bicester, Oxon OX6 7NW, England. TEL 0869-320949. Ed. Howard Jones.
—BLDSC shelfmark: 4542.525200.
Description: Covers science and technology of rapid solidification and allied processes and the formation, structure, properties and application of its products.

669   UK   ISSN 0958-0611
CODEN: IJRMD5
INTERNATIONAL JOURNAL OF REFRACTORY METALS & HARD MATERIALS. 1982. 6/yr. £120 (effective 1992). (International Plansee Society for Powder Metallurgy) Elsevier Science Publishers Ltd., Crown House, Linton Rd., Barking, Essex IG11 8JU, England. TEL 081-594-7272. FAX 081-594-5942. TELEX 896950 APPSCI G. (Subscr. in U.S. and Canada to: Elsevier Science Publishing Co., Inc., Box 882, Madison Sq. Sta., New York, NY 10159. TEL 212-989-5800) Ed. B. Lux. adv. contact: Claire Coakley. **Indexed:** Chem.Abstr., Int.Aerosp.Abstr., Met.Abstr., Sci.Abstr., World Alum.Abstr.
—BLDSC shelfmark: 4542.525420.
Formerly (until 1988): International Journal of Refractory and Hard Metals (ISSN 0263-4368)
Refereed Serial

INTERNATIONAL JOURNAL OF SURFACE MINING AND RECLAMATION. see *MINES AND MINING INDUSTRY*

669   UK   ISSN 0950-6608
TN1   CODEN: INMREO
INTERNATIONAL MATERIALS REVIEW. 1956. 6/yr. £158($345) to non-members; members £83($152). Institute of Materials, 1 Carlton House Terrace, London SW1 5DB, England. TEL 071-839-4071. FAX 071-839-2078. TELEX 8814813-METSCO-G. (And: A S M International, Materials Information, Materials Park, OH 44073) Ed. Mary Chim. bk.rev.; charts; illus.; cum.index: 1976-1986; circ. 1,200. (back issues avail.) **Indexed:** ABTICS, B.C.I.R.A., Deep Sea Res.& Oceanogr.Abstr., Excerp.Med., Ind.Sci.Rev., Int.Aerosp.Abstr., Met.Abstr., Sci.Abstr., World Alum.Abstr.
—BLDSC shelfmark: 4543.995000.
Former titles (until 1987): International Metals Review (ISSN 0308-4590); International Metallurgical Reviews; Metallurgical Reviews (ISSN 0076-6690)
Description: Critical reviews on specific topics covering all aspects of metals and alloys.

671.3   SZ   ISSN 0074-6983
INTERNATIONAL METALWORKERS' CONGRESS. REPORTS. quadrennial, 27th, 1989, Copenhagen, Denmark. $10. International Metalworkers' Federation, 54 bis, Rte. des Acacias, 1227 Geneva, Switzerland. FAX 022-3431510. TELEX 423298-METL-CH.

INTERNATIONAL PRESS CUTTING SERVICE: MACHINE TOOL AND IRON STEEL INDUSTRY. see *MACHINERY*

669.722   II   ISSN 0047-1011
INTERNATIONAL PRESS CUTTING SERVICE: NON-FERROUS METALS - ALUMINIUM. 1967. w. $65. International Press Cutting Service, Box 63, Allahabad 211001, India. Ed. N. Khanna. bk.rev.; index; circ. 1,200. (processed)

669   US
INTERNATIONAL SCRAP DIRECTORY. 1976. irreg. $153. Metal Bulletin Inc., 220 Fifth Ave., New York, NY 10001. TEL 212-213-6202. Ed.Bd.
Supersedes: European and North American Scrap Directory (ISSN 0261-426X); Formerly: European Scrap Directory (ISSN 0308-7786)
Description: International directory of companies engaged in trading and physical processing of iron and steel and non-ferrous scrap metals.

669.6   UK
INTERNATIONAL TIN COUNCIL. MONTHLY STATISTICAL SUMMARY. m. £4 per no. International Tin Council, 1 Oxendon St., London SW1Y 4EQ, England.
Description: Covers the production and consumption of tin.

669.6   UK
INTERNATIONAL TIN RESEARCH INSTITUTE. ANNUAL REPORT. 1938. a. free. International Tin Research Institute, Kingston Lane, Uxbridge, Middlesex UB8 3PJ, England. TEL 0895-272406. (Subscr. in U.S.: Tin Information Center of North America, 1353 Perry St., Columbus, OH 43201) circ. 5,000. **Indexed:** IIS, Met.Abstr., World Alum.Abstr.
Formerly: International Tin Research Council. Annual Report (ISSN 0074-9125)

699.1   US   ISSN 0897-4365
HD9506.U6
IRON AGE; the management magazine for metal producers. 1865. m. $55. Hitchcock Publishing (Subsidiary of: Capital Cities - A B C, Inc.), 191 S. Gary Ave., Carol Stream, IL 60188. TEL 708-462-2286. FAX 708-462-2225. (Subscr. to: Box 3038, Southeastern, PA 19398-9862) Ed. Anne Armel. adv.; circ. 24,000 (controlled). (reprint service avail. from UMI) **Indexed:** A.S.& T.Ind., ABI Inform., Met.Abstr., SRI, Tr.& Indus.Ind.
●Also available online. Vendor(s): DIALOG.
—BLDSC shelfmark: 4576.002000.
Formerly: Iron Age: Metal Producer; Supersedes in part and continues numbering of: Chilton's Iron Age (ISSN 0164-5137)

669.1   US   ISSN 0021-1559
TS300   CODEN: IRSEA5
IRON AND STEEL ENGINEER. 1924. m. $42. Association of Iron and Steel Engineers, Three Gateway Center, Ste. 2350, Pittsburgh, PA 15222. TEL 412-281-6323. Ed. Charles J. Labee. adv.; bk.rev.; charts; illus.; tr.lit.; index; circ. 12,000. (also avail. in microform from UMI; reprint service avail. from UMI) **Indexed:** A.S.& T.Ind., Appl.Mech.Rev., Br.Ceram.Abstr., Cadscan, Chem.Abstr., Eng.Ind., Excerp.Med., Fuel & Energy Abstr., Ind.Sci.Rev., ISMEC, Lead Abstr., Met.Abstr., Sci.Abstr., World Alum.Abstr., Zincscan.
—BLDSC shelfmark: 4580.000000.

669.1   II   ISSN 0021-1613
TS304.I4
IRON & STEEL JOURNAL OF INDIA. (Text in English) 1957. m. $50. Wadhera Publications, General Assurance Bldg., 232 Dr. D.N. Rd., Bombay 400 001, India. Ed. Roshanlal Wadhera. adv.; bk.rev.; illus.; pat.; stat.; tr.lit.; circ. 7,800.
Former titles: Iron, Steel; Hardware Journal of India.

669.1   US
IRON & STEEL SOCIETY. IRONMAKING PROCEEDINGS. 1943. a. $80 to non-members; members $40. Iron & Steel Society, 410 Commonwealth Dr., Warrendale, PA 15086. TEL 412-776-1535. FAX 412-776-0430. (also avail. in microfilm from UMI; back issues avail.)
Description: For iron and steelmakers.

669.1   US
IRON & STEEL SOCIETY. MECHANICAL WORKING AND STEEL PROCESSING CONFERENCE PROCEEDINGS. 1964. a. $80 to non-members; members $40. Iron & Steel Society, 410 Commonwealth Dr., Warrendale, PA 15086. TEL 412-776-1535. FAX 412-776-0430. (also avail. in microfilm from UMI; back issues avail.)

669.1   US
IRON & STEEL SOCIETY. PROCESS TECHNOLOGY CONFERENCE PROCEEDINGS. 1981. a. $80 to non-members; members $40. Iron & Steel Society, 410 Commonwealth Dr., Warrendale, PA 15086. TEL 412-776-1535. FAX 412-776-0430. (also avail. in microfilm from UMI; back issues avail.)
Description: For iron and steel makers.

METALLURGY

669.1   US
IRON & STEEL SOCIETY. TRANSACTIONS. 1982. a. $52 to non-members; members $27. Iron and Steel Society, 410 Commonwealth Dr., Warrendale, PA 15086. TEL 412-776-9460. FAX 412-776-0430. (back issues avail.)
Description: For iron and steel workers.

669.1   US   ISSN 0075-0875
IRON AND STEEL WORKS OF THE WORLD. 1952. quadrennial, 10th ed., 1991. $322. Metal Bulletin Inc., 220 Fifth Ave., New York, NY 10001. TEL 212-213-6202. Ed.Bd. adv.
Description: Information on major iron and steel producers.

672 622   US
IRON & STEELMAKER. 1974. m. $45. Iron and Steel Society, 410 Commonwealth Dr., Warrendale, PA 15086. TEL 412-776-1535. FAX 412-776-0430. Ed. Thomas P. McAloon. adv.: B&W page $1348, color page $1994; adv. contact: Peg Simanaitis. bk.rev.; charts; illus.; tr.lit.; index; circ. 7,500. Indexed: Cadscan, Chem.Abstr., Lead Abstr., Met.Abstr., World Alum.Abstr., Zincscan.
Formerly: I and S M (ISSN 0097-8388)
Description: Professional journal for the iron and steel industry.

669.1   US   ISSN 0950-2548
IRON ORE DATABOOK. 1986. irreg. $100.80. Metal Bulletin Inc., 220 Fifth Ave., New York, NY 10001. TEL 212-213-6202. Eds. Henry Cooke, John Bailey.
Description: Worldwide production statistics and analysis of iron ore mines.

669.1   UK   ISSN 0301-9233
TS300   CODEN: IMKSB7
IRONMAKING AND STEELMAKING. 1974. bi-m. £137($308) to non-members; members £69($132). Institute of Materials, 1 Carlton House Terrace, London SW1Y 5DB, England. TEL 071-839-4071. FAX 071-839-2078. TELEX 8814813-METSOC-G. Ed. Mary Chim. adv.; bk.rev.; charts; illus.; circ. 1,220. (back issues avail.) Indexed: ABTICS, Br.Tech.Ind., Cadscan, Chem.Abstr., Ergon.Abstr., Fuel & Energy Abstr., Ind.Sci.Rev., INIS Atomind., Lead Abstr., Met.Abstr., Sci.Cit.Ind., World Alum.Abstr., Zincscan.
—BLDSC shelfmark: 4580.440000.
Description: Covers all aspects of the ironmaking and steelmaking industry, including the rolling and application of ferrous products.

IRONWORKER. see *LABOR UNIONS*

669.1   SA   ISSN 0019-0594
ISCOR NEWS/YSKORNUUS. (Text and summaries in Afrikaans, English) 1936. bi-m. free. Iscor Limited - Yscor Beperk, H.Q. Bldg., Roger Dyason Rd., Box 450, Pretoria 0001, South Africa. TEL 012-298-1111. FAX 021-26-4721. TELEX 32-2007 SA. Ed.Bd. illus.; circ. 28,000. Indexed: Ind.S.A.Per., Met.Abstr., World Alum.abstr.
Description: Covers the latest techniques, productivity improvements and developments in metallurgy, as well as other corporate activities.

669.142   BG
ISPAT (CHITTAGONG). (Text in Bengali or English) 1973. a. free. Chittagong Steel Mills Ltd., Box 429, Chittagong, Bangladesh. Ed.Bd. adv.; circ. 2,500.

620.112   RU   ISSN 0202-7976
ITOGI NAUKI I TEKHNIKI: KORROZIYA I ZASHCHITA OT KORROZII. irreg., vol.15, 1989. 8 Rub. Vsesoyuznyi Institut Nauchno-Tekhnicheskoi Informatsii (VINITI), Ul. Baltiiskaya 14, Moscow A-219, Russia. (Subscr. to: Mezhdunarodnaya Kniga, Dimitrova ul. 39, 113095 Moscow, Russia) Indexed: Chem.Abstr.
—BLDSC shelfmark: 0092.460000.

669   RU   ISSN 0202-7739
ITOGI NAUKI I TEKHNIKI: METALLOVEDENIE I TERMICHESKAYA OBRABOTKA. irreg., vol.23, 1989. 6.60 Rub. Vsesoyuznyi Institut Nauchno-Tekhnicheskoi Informatsii (VINITI), Ul. Baltiiskaya 14, Moscow A-219, Russia. (Subscr. to: Mezhdunarodnaya Kniga, Dimitrova ul. 39, 113095 Moscow, Russia) Indexed: Chem.Abstr.
—BLDSC shelfmark: 0108.190000.

669   RU   ISSN 0202-7755
TN4   CODEN: IMTKAR
ITOGI NAUKI I TEKHNIKI: METALLURGICHESKAYA TEPLOTEKHNIKA; oborudovanie, izmerenie, kontrol' i avtomatizatsiya v metallurgicheskom proizvodstve. irreg., vol.8, 1989. price varies. Vsesoyuznyi Institut Nauchno-Tekhnicheskoi Informatsii (VINITI), Ul. Baltiiskaya 14, Moscow A-219, Russia. (Subscr. to: Mezhdunarodnaya Kniga, Dimitrova ul. 39, 113095 Moscow, Russia) Indexed: Chem.Abstr.
—BLDSC shelfmark: 0109.071500.

669   RU   ISSN 0202-7747
TN758   CODEN: ITMRAS
ITOGI NAUKI I TEKHNIKI: METALLURGIYA TSVETNYKH METALLOV. irreg., vol.19, 1989. 4.20 Rub. Vsesoyuznyi Institut Nauchno-Tekhnicheskoi Informatsii (VINITI), Ul. Baltiiskaya 14, Moscow A-219, Russia. (Subscr. to: Mezhdunarodnaya Kniga, Dimitrova ul. 39, 113095 Moscow, Russia) Indexed: Chem.Abstr.
—BLDSC shelfmark: 0109.160000.

669   US   ISSN 1047-4838
TN1   CODEN: JOMMER
J O M. 1949. m. $50 to non-members; institutions $90. Minerals, Metals and Materials Society, 420 Commonwealth Dr., Warrendale, PA 15086. TEL 412-776-9080. adv.; bk.rcv.; charts; illus.; index; circ. 14,000. (also avail. in microform from UMI; reprint service avail. from UMI) Indexed: A.S.& T.Ind., AESIS, B.C.I.R.A., Cadscan, Chem.Abstr., Corros.Abstr., Curr.Cont., Eng.Ind., Fuel & Energy Abstr., GeoRef., Ind.Sci.Rev., Int.Aerosp.Abstr., Lead Abstr., Met.Abstr., PROMT, Sci.Abstr., World Alum.Abstr., Zincscan.
—BLDSC shelfmark: 4673.254500.
Former titles (until 1989): Journal of Metals (ISSN 0148-6608); (until 1977): JOM (ISSN 0098-4558)

J O T. (Journal fuer Oberflaechentechnik) see *MACHINERY*

669   GW   ISSN 0075-2819
TS670   CODEN: JBOFAN
JAHRBUCH OBERFLAECHENTECHNIK (YEAR). a. DM.128. Metall-Verlag GmbH, Hubertusallee 18, 1000 Berlin 33, Germany. Ed.Bd. adv.; circ. 4,200. Indexed: Cadscan, Chem.Abstr., Lead Abstr., Zincscan.

JAHRBUCH SCHWEISSTECHNIK. see *TECHNOLOGY: COMPREHENSIVE WORKS*

672   GW   ISSN 0724-8482
HD9523.1
JAHRBUCH STAHL. 1951. a. DM.36. (Verein Deutscher Eisenhuettenleute) Verlag Stahleisen mbH, Sohnstr. 65, Postfach 105164, 4000 Duesseldorf 1, Germany. TEL 0211-6707-0.
—BLDSC shelfmark: 4632.355000.
Former titles: Stahleisen Kalender (ISSN 0081-4180); Taschenbuch fuer die Stahlindustrie.

671.2   JA   ISSN 0021-4396
**   CODEN: IMNOA9**
JAPAN FOUNDRYMEN'S SOCIETY. JOURNAL/IMONO. (Text in Japanese; titles in English and Japanese) 1929. m. 15400 Yen. Japan Foundrymen's Society - Nippon Imono Kyokai, 8-12-13 Ginza, Chuo-ku, Tokyo 104, Japan. Ed. Kisao Abe. adv.; bk.rev. Indexed: B.C.I.R.A., Chem.Abstr., INIS Atomind., Met.Abstr., World Alum.Abstr.
—BLDSC shelfmark: 4804.950000.

669   JA   ISSN 0021-4426
**   CODEN: NKZKAU**
JAPAN INSTITUTE OF METALS. BULLETIN/NIHON KINZOKU GAKKAI KAIHO. (Text in Japanese) 1962. m. 14400 Yen. Japan Institute of Metals - Nihon Kinzoku Gakkai, Aoba Aramaki, Aoba-ku, Sendai 980, Japan. TEL 022-223-3685. FAX 022-223-6312. TELEX 852250-JIM-J. Ed. Hiroyasu Fujimori. adv.; charts; circ. 10,000. Indexed: JTA, Met.Abstr., World Alum.Abstr.
—BLDSC shelfmark: 5699.210000.

669   JA   ISSN 0021-4876
**   CODEN: NIKGAV**
JAPAN INSTITUTE OF METALS. JOURNAL/NIPPON KINZOKU GAKKAISHI. (Text in Japanese; title, contents page and summaries in English) 1937. m. 14400 Yen. Japan Institute of Metals - Nihon Kinzoku Gakkai, Aoba Aramaki, Aoba-ku, Sendai 980, Japan. TEL 022-223-3685. FAX 02-223-6312. TELEX 852250-JIM-J. Ed. Koji Sumino. adv.; index; circ. 5,000. Indexed: Cadscan, Chem.Abstr., Curr.Cont., Int.Aerosp.Abstr., JCT, JTA, Lead Abstr., Met.Abstr., Phys.Ber., Sci.Abstr., World Alum.Abstr., Zincscan.
—BLDSC shelfmark: 4805.250000.

669   JA   ISSN 0021-4523
JAPAN METAL BULLETIN. (Text in English) 1953. 3/w. $386 in Asia and Oceania; N. America $396; elsewhere $406. Sangyo Press Ltd., Toei Bldg., 4-4-3, Muro-machi, Nihonbashi, Chuo-ku, Tokyo 103, Japan. FAX 03-3246-1925. Ed. Kinji Fujisawa. adv.; bk.rev.; mkt.; stat.; circ. 10,000. (looseleaf format)

669   JA
JAPAN STEEL WORKS TECHNICAL NEWS. (Text in European languages) 1961. irreg. exchange basis. Nihon Seikosho - Japan Steel Works, Ltd., 1-12 Yuraku-cho, Chiyoda-ku, Tokyo 100, Japan.

669.6   UK
JAPAN - TIN IN TINPLATE. 1984. irreg. £15. International Tin Council, 1 Oxendon St., London SW1Y 4EQ, England.
Description: Surveys tinplate manufacturing, can making and canning in Japan.

669   JA   ISSN 0385-9282
**   CODEN: TJWSAU**
JAPAN WELDING SOCIETY. TRANSACTIONS. (Text in English) 1970. s-a. 5200 Yen. Japan Welding Society, 1-11 Kanda Sakuma-cho, Chiyoda-ku, Tokyo 101, Japan. FAX 03-3253-3059. Indexed: Chem.Abstr., JCT, JTA, Met.Abstr., World Alum.Abstr.
—BLDSC shelfmark: 8975.110000.

669.2   JA   ISSN 0075-3475
HD9526.J3
JAPAN'S IRON AND STEEL INDUSTRY. (Text in English) 1951. a. $60. Kawata Publicity Inc. - Kawata Paburishiti K.K., 5-6, 5-chome, Koishikawa, Bunkyo-ku, Tokyo 112, Japan. Ed. Sukeyuki Kawata. adv.; circ. 6,000.

669   CC   ISSN 1001-0181
JINSHU KEXUE YU GONGYI/METALLURGICAL SCIENCE AND TECHNIQUES. (Text in Chinese) q. Harbin Gongye Daxue - Harbin University of Industry, 166, Dazhi Jie, Harbin, Heilongjiang 150006, People's Republic of China. TEL 228383. Ed. Jia Jun.

JINSHU RECHULI/HEAT TREATMENT OF METALS. see *ENGINEERING — Engineering Mechanics And Materials*

669   CC   ISSN 0412-1961
JINSHU XUEBAO. English edition: Journal of Metallurgy, Part A & B. (Text in Chinese) m. (Chinese Academy of Sciences, Institute of Metallurgy) Science Press, 16 Donghuangchenggen Beijie, Beijing 100707, People's Republic of China. TEL 4010642. FAX 4012180. TELEX 210247 SPBJ CN. Ed. Shi Changxu.
—BLDSC shelfmark: 0637.500000.

669   CC   ISSN 1001-4446
JINSHU ZAISHENG. (Text in Chinese) bi-m. Wuzi Bu, Jinshu Huishou-ju, Huanghe Nanlu Xiduan, Xuzhou, Jiangsu 211006, People's Republic of China. TEL 56600. Ed. Chen Lizhu.

| 669 | SZ | ISSN 0925-8388 |
TN1 | | CODEN: JALCEU
JOURNAL OF ALLOYS AND COMPOUNDS; an interdisciplinary journal of materials science and solid-state chemistry and physics. (Text in English, French and German) 1959. 24/yr.(in 12 vols.; 2 nos./vol.). 4200 SFr. Elsevier Sequoia S.A., P.O. Box 564, CH-1001 Lausanne, Switzerland. TEL 021-207381. FAX 021-235444. TELEX 450620-ELSA-CH. (Subscr. in U.S. and Canada to: Elsevier Science Publishing Co., Inc., Box 882, Madison Sq. Sta., New York, NY 10159. TEL 212-989-5800) Ed.Bd. adv.; bk.rev.; bibl.; illus.; index. (also avail. in microform from UMI; back issues avail.) **Indexed:** Br.Ceram.Abstr., Cadscan, Chem.Abstr., Chem.Infd., Curr.Cont., Eng.Ind., GeoRef., Ind.Sci.Rev., INIS Atomind., Lead Abstr., Mass Spectr.Bull., Met.Abstr., Phys.Ber., Sci.Abstr., Sci.Cit.Ind., Soils & Fert., World Alum.Abstr., Zincscan.
—BLDSC shelfmark: 4927.180000.
Formerly (until 1991): Journal of the Less-Common Metals (ISSN 0022-5088)
Description: Provides an international forum where materials scientists, chemists and physicists can present their results both to workers in their own fields and to others active in related areas.
Refereed Serial

671 | US | ISSN 0190-9177
TN672 | | CODEN: JHTRDR
JOURNAL OF HEAT TREATING. 1979. 2/yr. $59.50. (A S M International, Heat Treating Division Council) Springer-Verlag, Journals, 175 Fifth Ave., New York, NY 10010. TEL 212-460-1583. Ed. Jon L. Dossett. bk.rev.; circ. 1,200. (also avail. in microform from UMI; reprint service avail. from UMI) **Indexed:** B.C.I.R.A., Chem.Abstr., Met.Abstr., Petrol.Abstr., World Alum.Abstr.
—BLDSC shelfmark: 4996.905000.
Description: Information on day-to-day heat treating operations.
Refereed Serial

669 | US | ISSN 0931-7058
TA401 | | CODEN: JMAEEV
JOURNAL OF MATERIALS ENGINEERING. 1979. 4/yr. $114. (A S M International, Energy Division) Springer-Verlag, Journals, 175 Fifth Ave., New York, NY 10010. TEL 212-460-1583. Ed. Dr. John R. Ogren. circ. 500. (also avail. in microform from UMI; back issues avail.; reprint service avail. from UMI) **Indexed:** Abstr.Bull.Inst.Pap.Chem., Ceram.Abstr., Chem.Abstr., Fluidex, Gas Abstr., Met.Abstr., World Alum.Abstr.
Formerly: Journal of Materials for Energy Systems (ISSN 0162-9719)
Description: Focuses on the engineering response of well-characterized materials to a well-characterized test environment.
Refereed Serial

669 | US | ISSN 0931-704X
TS200
JOURNAL OF MATERIALS SHAPING TECHNOLOGY. 1979. 4/yr. $114. (A S M International, Mechanical Working and Forming Division) Springer-Verlag, Journals, 175 Fifth Ave., New York, NY 10010. TEL 212-460-1583. Ed. Harold L. Gegel. adv.; bk.rev.; abstr.; illus.; stat; cum.index; circ. 886. (also avail. in microform from UMI; reprint service avail. from UMI; back issues avail.) **Indexed:** Chem.Abstr., Met.Abstr., World Alum.Abstr.
—BLDSC shelfmark: 5012.260000.
Formerly: Journal of Applied Metalworking (ISSN 0162-9700)
Description: Applied technology in shaping and forming all materials toward end-product manufacture.
Refereed Serial

JOURNAL OF MINES, METALS AND FUELS. see *MINES AND MINING INDUSTRY*

669 | US | ISSN 1054-9714
TN689 | | CODEN: JPEQE6
JOURNAL OF PHASE EQUILIBRIA. 1979. bi-m. $410 to non-members; members $80. A S M International, Materials Park, OH 44073-0002. TEL 216-338-5151. FAX 216-338-4634. TELEX 98-0619 ASMINT. Ed. Jack F. Smith. adv.; bk.rev.; circ. 450. (also avail. in microform from UMI; reprint service avail.) **Indexed:** Chem.Abstr., Copper Abstr., Met.Abstr., World Alum.Abstr.
—BLDSC shelfmark: 5034.060000.
Formerly: Bulletin of Alloy Phase Diagrams (ISSN 0197-0216)
Description: Features articles using evaluated alloy phase diagram data in applications.
Refereed Serial

669 | II | ISSN 0257-4993
JOURNAL OF POTASSIUM RESEARCH. (Text in English) q. Rs.15($10) per no. Rotash Research Institute of India, Sector 19, Dundabera, Gurgaon 122 001 (Haryana), India. Ed. G.S. Sekhon.
—BLDSC shelfmark: 5041.170000.
Refereed Serial

669 | CC | ISSN 1002-0721
JOURNAL OF RARE EARTHS. Chinese edition: Zhongguo Xitu Xuebao (ISSN 1000-4343) (Text in English) q. $140. (Zhongguo Xitu Xuehui - Chinese Society of Rare Earths) International Academic Publishers, Beijing Zhanlanguan, Xizhimenwai Dajie, Beijing 100044, People's Republic of China. TEL 8316677. FAX 0086-1-4015664. TELEX 22313 CPC CN. Ed. Xu Guangxian. circ. 400. **Indexed:** Chem.Abstr., Eng.Ind.
—BLDSC shelfmark: 5046.600000.
Formerly (until 1991): Chinese Rare Earth Society. Journal.
Description: International journal that introduces development in the rare earth science and technology and its wide range of applications.
Refereed Serial

669 016 | UK | ISSN 0334-8938
TA417.6 | | CODEN: RDBMDG
JOURNAL OF THE MECHANICAL BEHAVIOR OF MATERIALS. 1972. q. $140. Freund Publishing House Ltd., Suite 500, Chesham House, 150 Regent St., London W1R 5FA, England. (Alt. addr.: P.O. Box 35010, Tel Aviv, Israel. TEL 972-3-615335) Ed. B-Z Weiss. adv.; bk.rev.; circ. 1,000. (back issues avail.) **Indexed:** Met.Abstr.
—BLDSC shelfmark: 5015.810000.
Formerly: Reviews on Deformation Behaviour of Materials (ISSN 0048-7589)

671 | GW |
DER JUNGE METALL-FACHARBEITER. 1955. m. DM.64.80. Frankfurter Fachverlag, Emil-Sulzbach-Str. 12, 6000 Frankfurt a.M. 97, Germany. Ed. Heinz Kirsch. bk.rev.; illus.; index; circ. 35,000. (also avail. in microform from UMI; reprint service avail. from UMI)
Formerly: Junge Metallhandwerker (ISSN 0022-6335)

669 | JA | ISSN 0916-6211
KAWASAKI STEEL BULLETIN. (Text in English) 1979. bi-m. free. Kawasaki Steel Corporation, Public Relations Section, Hibiya Kokusai Bldg., 2-2-3 Uchisaiwai-cho, Chiyoda-ku, Tokyo 100, Japan. FAX 03-3597-3160.
Description: Publishes economic and technical reports of Kawasaki Steel Corporation.

669 | JA | ISSN 0388-9475
TS300 | | CODEN: KSTRDD
KAWASAKI STEEL TECHNICAL REPORT. (Text in English) 1980. s-a. free. Kawasaki Steel Corporation, Public Relations Section, Hibiya Kokusai Bldg., 2-2-3 Uchisaiwai-cho, Chiyoda-ku, Tokyo 100, Japan. FAX 03-3597-4868. illus.; circ. 1,600. **Indexed:** Chem.Abstr., Corros.Abstr., Met.Abstr.
—BLDSC shelfmark: 5088.103500.
Description: Technical reports on the latest developments of Kawasaki Steel.

METALLURGY 3411

669 666 | SZ |
KEY ENGINEERING MATERIALS. 1975. 12/yr. 1185 Fr. Trans Tech Publications, Hardstr. 13, P.O. Box 10, CH-4714 Aedermannsdorf, Switzerland. FAX 62-741058. Ed. F.H. Wohlbier. bk.rev.; abstr.; bibl.; charts; illus.; cum.index. **Indexed:** Int.Aerosp.Abstr., Met.Abstr., World Alum.Abstr.
Formerly: Mechanical and Corrosion Properties. Series A. Key Engineering Materials (ISSN 0252-1059); Supersedes in part: Mechanical and Corrosion Properties (ISSN 0250-9784); Which was formerly (until Jan. 1979): Mechanical Properties (ISSN 0361-2821)

KJEMI. see *CHEMISTRY*

669.142 621 | GW | ISSN 0937-6186
KLOECKNER WERKE HEUTE; Stahl, Maschinenbau, Kunststoff. 1952. q. (Kloeckner-Werke AG) Kloeckner Presse und Information GmbH, Kloecknerstr. 29, 4100 Duisburg 1, Germany. TEL 0203-396-1. FAX 0203-343695. bk.rev.; circ. 40,000.
Formerly: K W Heute.
Description: Staff magazine of Kloeckner-Werke.

671 | FI | ISSN 0023-3277
TJ4
KONEPAJAMIES; Finnish journal of metalworking production. (Text in Finnish; summaries in English, Finnish, Swedish) 1947. 11/yr. FIM 520. (Suomen Metalliteollisuusyhdistys - Federation of Finnish Metal and Engineering Industries) Oy Talentum Ab, Ratavartijvankatu 2, 00520 Helsinki, Finland. FAX 358-0-148801. Ed. Jorma Collin. adv.; bk.rev.; abstr.; bibl.; charts; illus.; circ. 6,946. **Indexed:** B.C.I.R.A.
Description: For metallurgy professionals in Finland.

669 | KO |
KOREAN INSTITUTE OF METALS. JOURNAL. (Text in English and Korean) 1963. m. membership. Korean Institute of Metals, Rm.301, Keoyang Bldg., 51-8 Susong-dong, Chongruku, Seoul 110-140, S. Korea. TEL 02-734-0595. Ed.Bd. adv.; circ. 2,500. **Indexed:** Corros.Abstr., INIS Atomind., Soils & Fert.
Description: Original papers covering metallurgy and materials science.

669 | CS | ISSN 0023-432X
| | CODEN: KOMAAW
KOVOVE MATERIALY/METAL MATERIALS. (Text in Slovak; summaries in English, German and Russian) 1952. bi-m. 156 Kcs.($34) (Slovenska Akademia Vied) Veda, Publishing House of the Slovak Academy of Sciences, Klemensova 19, 814 30 Bratislava, Czechoslovakia. (Dist. by: Slovart, Nam. Slobody 6, 817 64 Bratislava, Czechoslovakia) Ed. Premysl Rys. bk.rev.; charts; illus.; index; circ. 900. **Indexed:** Cadscan, Chem.Abstr., Curr.Cont., Eng.Ind., INIS Atomind., Int.Aerosp.Abstr., Lead Abstr., Met.Abstr., Sci.Abstr., World Alum.Abstr., Zincscan.
—BLDSC shelfmark: 5115.120000.
Description: Publishes original works from research of metal structure and structure of metal alloys as well as the results of basic research in physical metallurgy and metallurgical processes of iron and non-iron metals.

669 | UK | ISSN 0208-9386
TS228.9 | | CODEN: KMSTD6
KRZEPNIECIE METALI I STOPOW. (Text in Polish; summaries in English, Russian) irreg., vol.11, 1987. price varies. (Polish Academy of Sciences, Katowice Section, Commission on Founding) Ossolineum, Publishing House of the Polish Academy of Sciences, Rynek 9, 50-106 Wroclaw, Poland. TEL 386-25. (Dist. by: Ars Polona, Krakowskie Przedmiescie 7, 00-068 Warsaw, Poland) Ed. Waclaw Sakwa.
Description: Original papers on different questions of iron and non-iron metallurgy.

669 551 | CC | ISSN 1001-5663
KUANGCHAN YU DIZHI/MINERALS AND GEOLOGY. (Text in Chinese) q. Zhongguo Youse Jinshu Gongye Zonggongsi, Kuangshan Dizhi Yanjiuyuan, Sanlidian, Guilin, Guangxi 541004, People's Republic of China. TEL 443865. Ed. Li Jiazhen.

METALLURGY

671   RU   ISSN 0023-5806
KUZNECHNO-SHTAMPOVOCHNOE PROIZVODSTVO.
English translation: Soviet Forging and Sheet Metal Stamping Technology (US ISSN 0891-334X) 1959. m. $22.20. Izdatel'stvo Mashinostroenie, 4, Stromynsky Lane, Moscow, 107076, Russia. Ed. E.P. Unksov. index. **Indexed:** Chem.Abstr., INIS Atomind., Met.Abstr., World Alum.Abstr.

669   IT   ISSN 0391-5891
                               CODEN: LAMID6
LAMIERA. 1964. 11/yr. L.80000 (foreign L.200000)(effective 1992). Tecniche Nuove s.p.a., Via C. Menotti 14, 20129 Milan, Italy. TEL 02-75701. FAX 02-7570205. Ed. G. Nardella. adv.; illus.; circ. 6,000. **Indexed:** Chem.Abstr.
—BLDSC shelfmark: 5144.200000.
     Description: Information on the pressing, deformation, cut finishing and assembling of cut metal.

669   FR   ISSN 0181-1223
LETTRE D'INFORMATION METAUX. (Text in French) 1959. w. 960 F. Societe d' Information et Documentation, Bureau d'Informations Professionnelles, 142 rue Montmartre, 75002 Paris, France. FAX 42-33-28-42. TELEX 220 528 F. Ed. Philippe Dommanget.

669   US   ISSN 0024-3345
TN1   CODEN: LMAGAL
LIGHT METAL AGE. 1943. bi-m. $35. Fellom Publishing, 170 S. Spruce Ave., Ste. 120, S. San Francisco, CA 94080. TEL 415-588-8832. Ed. Roy Fellom. adv.; bk.rev.; abstr.; bibl.; illus.; pat.; index; circ. 5,132. **Indexed:** A.S.& T.Ind., B.C.I.R.A., Chem.Abstr., Eng.Ind., Ind.Sci.Rev., Met.Abstr., PROMT, World Alum.Abstr.
—BLDSC shelfmark: 5210.500000.

671.2   RU   ISSN 0024-449X
T4   CODEN: LIPRAX
LITEINOE PROIZVODSTVO. English translation: Soviet Casting Technology (US ISSN 0891-0316) (Contents page in English) 1930. m. 22.20 Rub. (Ministerstvo Avtomobil'noi Promyshlennosti) Izdatel'stvo Mashinostroenie, 4, Stromynsky Lane, Moscow, 107076, Russia. Ed. D.P. Ivanov. adv.; bk.rev.; abstr.; bibl.; charts; illus.; stat.; index; circ. 13,287. **Indexed:** B.C.I.R.A., Chem.Abstr., INIS Atomind., Met.Abstr., World Alum.Abstr.
—BLDSC shelfmark: 0098.000000.

669   RU   ISSN 0302-9069
TS200
LITEINOE PROIZVODSTVO, METALLOVEDENIE I OBRABOTKA METALLOV DAVLENIEM. irreg. 0.47 Rub. (Krasnoyarskii Institut Tsvetnykh Metallov) Krasnoyarskoe Knizhnoe Izdatel'stvo, Prospekt Mira, 89, Krasnoyarsk, Russia. illus. **Indexed:** Chem.Abstr.

669   GW   ISSN 0933-8934
LITERATURSCHAU "STAHL UND EISEN". s-m. DM.2140. (Fachinformationszentrum Technik e.V.) Verlag Stahleisen mbH, Sohnstr. 65, Postfach 105164, 4000 Duesseldorf 1, Germany.
     Formerly: Zeitschriften- und Buecherschau "Stahl und Eisen" (ISSN 0340-4951)

671.2   BX   ISSN 0024-5135
TS200   CODEN: LIVVA7
LIVARSKI VESTNIK. (Text in Slovenian; summaries in English) 1953. bi-m. 600 SLT($12) Drustvo Livarjev Slovenije, Lepi Pot 6, Ljubljana, Slovenia. TEL 061 222-488. Ed. Milan Trbizan. adv.; bk.rev.; abstr.; bibl.; charts; illus.; index; circ. 2,500. **Indexed:** Chem.Abstr.

671.2   YU   ISSN 0352-8936
TS228.99
LIVARSTVO. 1986. q. 45000 din.($20) Savez Organizacija Livaca Jugoslavije, Bulevar Avnoja 86, 11000 Belgrade, Yugoslavia. TEL 011 141-092. (Subscr. to: Savez Gevaca Hrvatske, Forudeova 9, 41020 Novi Zagreb, Yugoslavia) Eds. Miroslav Vranesic, Mile Galic. circ. 2,250.
     Description: For theory and application in foundry.

M & T - METALLHANDWERK & TECHNIK. see *BUILDING AND CONSTRUCTION*

M I T E. (Manufacturing Ideas for Today's Engineers) see *ENGINEERING — Mechanical Engineering*

669   GW   ISSN 0933-8810
M - MODERNE METALLTECHNIK; das Magazin fuer Ausbildung und Beruf. 1987. m. Verlag Moderne Metalltechnik GmbH, Am Spargelhof 2, D-2400 Luebeck 1, Germany. TEL 0451-478311. Ed. Jean-Herbert Wahl.

669   GW   ISSN 0171-4511
TN600   CODEN: MMPTDD
M P T - METALLURGICAL PLANT AND TECHNOLOGY. (Text and summaries in English) 1978. bi-m. DM.184. Verlag Stahleisen mbH, Postfach 105164, 4000 Duesseldorf 1, Germany. TEL 0211-6707-0. FAX 0211-6707-517. Ed.Bd. circ. 11,000. **Indexed:** Met.Abstr.

M T I A INPUT. (Metal Trades Industry Association of Australia) see *BUSINESS AND ECONOMICS — Labor And Industrial Relations*

M T I A METAL & ENGINEERING INDUSTRY YEARBOOK. (Metal Trades Industry Association of Australia) see *BUSINESS AND ECONOMICS — Labor And Industrial Relations*

671 382   AT
M T I A'S ENGINEERING EXPORTER. 1969. fortn. Aus.$150. Metal Trades Industry Association, National Export Council, National Office, 214 Northbourne Ave., Canberra, A.C.T. 2600, Australia. Ed. B.H. Trevanion. adv.; circ. 1,000.
     Former titles: M T I A N E G's Export Note Pad; Australian Metal Trades Export Group's Export Note Pad.

669   SA
MACHINE TOOL BUYERS GUIDE FOR SOUTHERN AFRICA. (Text in English) 1988. a. R.110. George Warman Publications (Pty.) Ltd., 77 Hout St., P.O. Box 704, Cape Town 8001, South Africa. TEL 021-24-5320. FAX 021-261-332. TELEX 521849. Ed. Desmond Varley.
     Description: Intended for users of metalworking machinery.

MACHINERY AND STEEL. see *MACHINERY*

669   US   ISSN 0047-5491
MAGNESIUM MONTHLY REVIEW. 1971. m. $45. 106 Spring Forest Rd., Greenville, SC 29615-2241. Ed. David C. Brown. bk.rev.; index; circ. 416. **Indexed:** Met.Abstr., World Alum.Abstr.
     Description: Updates on and predictions for this structural metal industry, covering production, markets, techniques, and foreign developments.

669   US   ISSN 0891-6942
MAGNESIUM NEWSLETTER. 1944. 9/yr. $90. International Magnesium Association, 2010 Corporate Ridge, Ste. 700, McLean, VA 22102. TEL 703-442-8888. FAX 703-821-1824. Ed. Felicia Garber. circ. 300. (looseleaf format)

669.722   HU   ISSN 0025-0058
HD9539.A63   CODEN: MAGABT
MAGYAR ALUMINIUM/HUNGARIAN ALUMINUM. (Text in Hungarian; table of contents in English, German and Russian; summaries in English) 1964. m. $41.50. Lapkiado Vallalat, Lenin korut 9-11, 1073 Budapest 7, Hungary. TEL 222-408. (Subscr. to: Kultura, Box 149, H-1389 Budapest, Hungary) Ed. Dr. Andras Domony. adv.; bk.rev.; illus. **Indexed:** Chem.Abstr., Hung.Build.Bull., INIS Atomind., Met.Abstr., World Alum.Abstr.
—BLDSC shelfmark: 5340.302500.

669 540   UK   ISSN 0334-7575
QD1   CODEN: SGTLEY
MAIN GROUP METAL CHEMISTRY. 1972. 6/yr. $180. Freund Publishing House Ltd., Chesham House, 150 Regent St., Ste. 500, London W1R 5FA, England. (Alt. addr.: P.O. Box 35010, Tel Aviv, Israel. TEL 972-3-615335) Ed. M. Gielen. adv.; bk.rev.; index; circ. 1,000. (back issues avail.) **Indexed:** Chem.Abstr., Met.Abstr., World Alum.Abstr.
     Formerly (until 1987): Reviews on Silicon, Germanium, Tin and Lead Compounds (ISSN 0048-7570)

669   US
MANUFACTURING & MANAGEMENT MAGAZINE. Short title: M & M Magazine. 1965. 6/yr. $20 (foreign $60); free to qualfied personnel. Rimol Associates, Inc., RR3, Box 820, Lafayette, NJ 07848-9536. TEL 201-383-7080. FAX 201-383-8090. Ed. Andrew J. Rimol. adv.; bk.rev.; circ. 11,410.
     Formerly (until 1991): Tool and Die Magazine.
     Description: Covers all aspects of tool, die and manufacturing operations.

MAQUINAS & METAIS. see *MACHINERY*

669   DK
MASKIN - AKTUELT. 1950. 15/yr. DKK 310. Teknisk Forlag A-S, Skelbaekgade 4, DK-1717 Copenhagen V, Denmark. TEL 45-31-21-68-01. FAX 45-31-21-23-96. Ed. Ralf Pedersen. adv.; bk.rev.; bibl.; illus.; circ. 24,923. (tabloid format) **Indexed:** ASCA.
     Former titles (until 1989): S M E A; S M E A Maskin - Industrien (ISSN 0036-164X)
     Description: Focuses on people and companies in the iron, metal and engineering industry. Provides information on the products and services which form the basis of production, as well as on the political and economic conditions in the industry.

MATERIALS AND MANUFACTURE. see *ENGINEERING — Mechanical Engineering*

669   US   ISSN 0887-1949
MATERIALS AND PROCESSING REPORT; the leading edge of technology worldwide. 1986. m. $395 (foreign $430)(effective 1992). Elsevier Science Publishing Co., inc. (New York), 655 Ave. of the Americas, New York, NY 10010. TEL 212-989-5800. FAX 212-633-3965. TELEX 420643 AEP Ul. Ed. Renee G. Ford. index; circ. 350. (also avail. in microform from UMI; back issues avail.; reprint service avail. from UMI) **Indexed:** Met.Abstr.
—BLDSC shelfmark: 5394.102400.
     Description: Publishes news, articles, and announcements pertaining to technological advancements and research in the fields of metallurgy, ceramics, polymers, fibers, and composites.
     Refereed Serial

MATERIALS AT HIGH TEMPERATURE; materials generation applications. see *ENGINEERING — Engineering Mechanics And Materials*

669   AT   ISSN 0818-3597
                              CODEN: MATAET
MATERIALS AUSTRALASIA. 1969. 10/yr. Aus.$75 (foreign Aus.$115). Institute of Metals and Materials Australasia Ltd., 191 Royal Parade, Parkville, Vic. 3052, Australia. TEL 61-3-347-2544. FAX 61-3-348-1208. Ed.Bd. adv.; bk.rev.; circ. 1,700. **Indexed:** Chem.Abstr., INIS Atomind., Met.Abstr., World Alum.Abstr.
     Former titles (until 1986): Metals Australasia (ISSN 0156-174X); (until 1977): Metals Australia (ISSN 0047-6897)

669.95   US   ISSN 1044-5803
TN690   CODEN: MACHEX
MATERIALS CHARACTERIZATION; an international journal on materials structure and behavior. 1968. 8/yr.(in 2 vols.; 4 nos./vol.). $338 (foreign $372)(effective 1992). (International Metallographic Society Inc.) Elsevier Science Publishing Co., Inc. (New York), 655 Ave. of the Americas, New York, NY 10010. TEL 212-989-5800. FAX 212-633-3965. TELEX 420643 AEP Ul. Ed. Chris Bagnall. adv.; bk.rev.; bibl.; charts; illus.; index. (also avail. in microform from RPI) **Indexed:** Appl.Mech.Rev., Cadscan, Chem.Abstr., Curr.Cont., Eng.Ind., INIS Atomind., INSPEC, Lead Abstr., Met.Abstr., Nucl.Sci.Abstr., Phys.Ber., Ref.Zh., Sci.Abstr., Sci.Cit.Ind., Zincscan.
—BLDSC shelfmark: 5394.106500.
     Formerly: Metallography (ISSN 0026-0800)
     Description: Covers technical knowledge, advances in materials structure and behavior.
     Refereed Serial

METALLURGY

669 AT
TN1 CODEN: MEFODS
MATERIALS FORUM. 1955. q. Aus.$275($259) Institute of Metals and Materials Australasia, 314 Albert St., E. Melbourne, Vic. 3002, Australia. TEL 61-3-418-7333. FAX 61-3-419-4096. Ed. B.C. Muddle. adv.; bk.rev.; bibl.; charts; illus.; index; circ. 1,800. (also avail. in microform from MIM,UMI) **Indexed:** B.C.I.R.A., Cadscan, Chem.Abstr., Curr.Cont., Eng.Ind., Eng.Mat.Abstr., Ind.Sci.Rev., INIS Atomind., ISMEC, Lead Abstr., Met.Abstr., Sci.Abstr., World Alum.Abstr., Zincscan.
Formerly (until 1985): Metals Forum (ISSN 0160-7952); Supersedes (in 1977): Australasian Institute of Metals. Journal; Which was formerly: Australian Institute of Metals. Journal (ISSN 0004-9352)
Description: Structure and properties of engineering materials: metals, ceramics, polymers, composites.

669 671.52 UK
MATERIALS INFORMATION DIGEST SERIES. 1975. m. £90($145) to non-members; members £75($120). Institute of Materials, 1 Carlton House Terrace, London SW1Y 5DB, England. TEL 071-839-4071. FAX 071-839-2078. Ed. H.D. Chafe. **Indexed:** Met.Abstr.
Formerly: Metals Society. Digest Series.

669 UK
MATERIALS INFORMATION TRANSLATIONS SERVICE.
Short title: M I T S. 1957. m. £20($20) Institute of Materials, 1 Carlton House Terrace, London SW1Y 5DB, England. TEL 071-839-4071. FAX 071-839-2289. (also avail. in microfiche) **Indexed:** Cadscan, Corros.Abstr., Lead Abstr., Zincscan.
●Also available online. Vendor(s): DIALOG.
Formerly: British Industrial and Scientific International Translations Service.
Description: Contains articles about metals and materials translated into English.

669 628.44 UK ISSN 0025-5386
MATERIALS RECLAMATION WEEKLY. 1912. w. £49.50. E M A P Maclaren Ltd., 19 Scarbrook Rd., Croydon, Surrey CR9 1QH, England. TEL 081-688 7788. FAX 081-760-0473. Ed. Ian Martin. adv.; bk.rev.; charts; illus.; mkt.; tr.lit.; circ. 5,100. (also avail. in microform from UMI) **Indexed:** Excerp.Med., Int.Packag.Abstr., Key to Econ.Sci., Paper & Bd.Abstr.
—BLDSC shelfmark: 5396.300000.
Formerly: Waste Trade World and Iron and Steel Scrap Review.
Description: Information for the metallurgy industry.

669 US
MATERIALS RESEARCH AND ENGINEERING/REINE UND ANGEWANDTE METALLKUNDE. 1980. irreg. price varies. Springer-Verlag, 175 Fifth Ave., New York, NY 10010. TEL 212-460-1500. (Also: Berlin, Heidelberg, Tokyo and Vienna) Ed. B. Ilschner. (reprint service avail. from ISI)
Supersedes (1948-1976): Reine und Angewandte Metallkunde in Einzeldarstellungen (ISSN 0080-0791)

669 UK ISSN 0267-0836
TA401 CODEN: MSCTEP
MATERIALS SCIENCE AND TECHNOLOGY. 1985. m. £348($626) to non-members; members £143($260). Institute of Materials, 1 Carlton House Terrace, London SW1Y 5DB, England. TEL 071-839-4071. FAX 071-839-2078. TELEX 8814813-METSOC-G. Ed. Mary Chim. bk.rev.; charts; illus.; circ. 1,600. (back issues avail.) **Indexed:** A.S.& T.Ind., B.C.I.R.A., Br.Tech.Ind., Cadscan, Lead Abstr., Met.Abstr., Zincscan.
—BLDSC shelfmark: 5396.434400.
Incorporates: Metals Science & Metals Technology.
Description: Covers metals alloys and non-metallic materials: engineering ceramics, cements and concrete, polymers, adhesives, composites and electronic materials.

669 JA ISSN 0916-1821
TN4 CODEN: MTJIEY
MATERIALS TRANSACTIONS, J I M. (Text in English) 1960. m. 24000 Yen. Japan Institute of Metals - Nihon Kinzoku Gakkai, Aoba Aramaki, Aoba-ku, Sendai 980, Japan. TEL 022-223-3685. FAX 022-223-6312. TELEX 852250-JIM-J. Ed. Masanori Tokuda. circ. 2,000. **Indexed:** Chem.Abstr., Corros.Abstr., Curr.Cont., Eng.Ind., GeoRef., Int.Aerosp.Abstr., JCT, JTA, Met.Abstr., Sci.Abstr., World Alum.Abstr.
—BLDSC shelfmark: 5396.520000.
Formerly (until 1989): Japan Institute of Metals. Transactions (ISSN 0021-4434)

669 GW ISSN 0933-5137
TA401 CODEN: MATWER
MATERIALWISSENSCHAFT UND WERKSTOFFTECHNIK. (Text in English, German) 1970. m. DM.737. V C H Verlagsgesellschaft mbH, Postfach 101161, 6940 Weinheim, Germany. TEL 06201-602-0. FAX 06201-60-23-28. TELEX 465516-VCHWH-D. (U.S. addr.: V C H Publishers Inc., 220 E. 23rd St., New York, NY 10010-4606) (Co-sponsors: Verein Deutscher Eisenhuettenleute; Deutsche Gesellschaft fuer Chemisches Apparatewesen (DECHEMA); Deutsche Gesellschaft fur Materialkunde) Eds. E. Broszeit, H. Speckhardt. adv.; bk.rev.; index; circ. 780. (also avail. in microfilm from VCI; reprint service avail. from ISI) **Indexed:** B.C.I.R.A., Chem.Abstr., Copper Abstr., Int.Aerosp.Abstr., Met.Abstr., Sci.Abstr., World Alum.Abstr.
—BLDSC shelfmark: 5396.640000.
Formerly: Zeitschrift fuer Werkstofftechnik (ISSN 0049-8688)

669 GW
MAX-PLANCK-INSTITUT FUER METALLFORSCHUNG. MITTEILUNGEN. (Text in English and German) 1966. 3/yr. Max-Planck-Institut fuer Metallforschung, Seestr. 92, 7000 Stuttgart 1, Germany. TEL 0711-2095-1. FAX 0711-225722. (back issues avail.)

669 IT ISSN 0025-9829
MERCATO METALSIDERURGICO. 1954. s-m. L.50000. Assofermet, Corso Venezia 47-49, 20121 Milan, Italy. TEL 76008824. FAX 02-781027. TELEX 333420 ASFER I. Ed. Eugenio Turchetti. adv.; bk.rev.; circ. 1,800. (tabloid format)

671 NE ISSN 0026-0479
METAAL & TECHNIEK; vakblad voor de metaalnijverheid. Short title: M & T. 1955. m. fl.127.50. Audet Tijdschriften bv, Postbus 16, 6500 AA Nijmegen, Netherlands. TEL 080-228316. FAX 080-239561. TELEX 48633. (Co-sponsor: Metaalunie) Ed. F.A. Wolters. adv.; B&W page fl.2336; trim 215 x 285; adv. contact: Cor van Nek. stat.; circ. 8,380. **Indexed:** Key to Econ.Sci., Met.Abstr., World Alum.Abstr.
Description: Follows the latest developments in methods of production and new products. Also discusses organizational, marketing and economic aspects of the metallurgical industry.

METAL. see *LABOR UNIONS*

METAL ARCHITECTURE. see *ARCHITECTURE*

METAL BUILDING REVIEW. see *BUILDING AND CONSTRUCTION*

669 US ISSN 0026-0533
TN1 CODEN: MTBLAX
METAL BULLETIN. 1913. s-w. $849. Metal Bulletin Inc., 220 Fifth Ave., 10th Fl., New York, NY 10001. TEL 800-638-2525. FAX 212-213-6273. Eds. H. Cooke, A-M. Moreno. adv.; mkt.; stat.; tr.lit.; index; circ. 11,000. **Indexed:** AESIS, Art & Archaeol.Tech.Abstr., Cadscan, Chem.Abstr, Copper Abstr., Key to Econ.Sci., Lead Abstr., PROMT, World Alum.Abstr., Zincscan.

669 US ISSN 0373-4064
METAL BULLETIN MONTHLY. 1972. m. $376. Metal Bulletin Inc., 220 Fifth Ave., 10th Fl., New York. TEL 800-638-2525. FAX 212-213-6273. Ed. P. Millbank. adv.; bk.rev.; tr.lit.; index; circ. 10,000. **Indexed:** AESIS, Art & Archaeol.Tech.Abstr., Cadscan, Copper Abstr., Key to Econ.Sci., Lead Abstr., Met.Abstr., PROMT, World Alum.Abstr., Zincscan.
—BLDSC shelfmark: 5683.770000.

669 338.2 US ISSN 0269-1698
METAL BULLETIN PRICES & DATA BOOK. 1968. a. $94. Metal Bulletin Inc., 220 Fifth Ave., New York, NY 10001. TEL 212-213-6202. Ed. R. Serjeantson. adv. (back issues avail.)
—BLDSC shelfmark: 5683.777000.
Formerly (until 1986): Metal Bulletin Handbook (ISSN 0262-6454); Supersedes: Quin's Metal Handbook.
Description: National and international prices, key international statistical information and data for the steel and non-ferrous metals and minerals industries.

671.2 AT
TS200
METAL CASTING AND SURFACE FINISHING; a journal for the foundryman metal finishers, diecasters and general metals industry. 1955. bi-m. Aus.$66 (Asia Aus.$84). (Australian Foundry Institute) Rala Publications, 203-205 Darling St., Balmain, N.S.W. 2041, Australia. TEL 02-555-1944. FAX 02-555-1496. Ed. Shane Rochfort. adv.; bk.rev.; illus.; pat.; stat.; index; circ. 1,250. (also avail. in microform from UMI; back issues avail.) **Indexed:** AESIS, B.C.I.R.A., C.I.S.Abstr., Chem.Abstr., Met.Abstr., World Alum.Abstr.
Former titles: Metals and Castings Australasia; Castings (ISSN 0008-7521)

669 US
METAL CENTER NEWS. 1961. m. $55. Hitchcock Publishing (Subsidiary of: Capital Cities - A B C, Inc.), 191 S. Gary Ave., Carol Stream, IL 60188. TEL 708-665-1000. FAX 708-462-2225. TELEX 72-0404. Ed. Joseph C. Marino. adv.; bk.rev.; charts; illus.; stat.; circ. 12,600 (controlled).

METAL CONSTRUCTION NEWS. see *BUILDING AND CONSTRUCTION*

381 US ISSN 0098-2210
HD9506.U6
METAL DISTRIBUTION. 1975. a. $15. Hitchcock Publishing (Subsidiary of: Capital Cities - A B C, Inc.), 191 S. Gary Ave., Carol Stream, IL 60188. TEL 708-665-1000. FAX 708-462-2225. Ed. Joseph C. Marino. adv.; illus.; circ. 11,800.

669 US ISSN 0026-055X
METAL FABRICATING NEWS. vol.8, 1970. bi-m. $1.50. Metal Fabricating Institute Inc., Box 1178, Rockford, IL 61105. TEL 815-965-4031. Ed. Ronald L. Fowler. adv.; bk.rev.; charts; illus.; tr.lit.; circ. 40,000. **Indexed:** Met.Abstr., World Alum.Abstr.

669 US ISSN 0026-0576
TS550 CODEN: MEFIA7
METAL FINISHING; devoted exclusively to metallic surface treatments. (Includes the annual: Metal Finishing Guidebook & Directory) 1903. m. $97 (foreign $183)(effective 1992). Elsevier Science Publishing Co., Inc. (New York), 655 Ave of the Americas, New York, NY 10010. TEL 212-989-5800. FAX 212-633-3965. TELEX 420643 AEP UI. adv.; bk.rev.; abstr.; illus.; mkt.; pat.; tr.lit.; index; circ. 11,293. (also avail. in microfilm from UMI; reprint service avail. from UMI) **Indexed:** A.S.& T.Ind., Cadscan, Chem.Abstr., Eng.Ind., Excerp.Med., Ind.Sci.Rev., Int.Packag.Abstr., Lead Abstr., Met.Abstr., PROMT, Sci.Abstr., W.R.C.Inf., World Alum.Abstr., World Surf.Coat., Zincscan.
—BLDSC shelfmark: 5684.000000.
Former titles: Metal Industry (New York) (ISSN 0360-5159) Aluminum World and Brass and Copper Industries; Brass Founder and Finisher and Electro-Platers' Review; Copper and Brass; Platers' Guide.
Description: Covers technical and practical aspects of finishing metal and plastic products, including waste treatment and pollution control.
Refereed Serial

671 US ISSN 1040-967X
METAL FORMING. 1967. m. $25 (free to qualified personnel). Precision Metal Forming Association, 27027 Chardon Rd., Richmond Hts., OH 44143. TEL 216-585-8800. Ed. R. Green. adv.; circ. 52,000 (controlled). **Indexed:** Excerp.Med., Met.Abstr., World Alum.Abstr.
Formerly: Metal Stamping (ISSN 0026-069X)

METAL MARKETING CORPORATION OF ZAMBIA. ANNUAL REPORT. see *BUSINESS AND ECONOMICS — Marketing And Purchasing*

METALLURGY

669   II
METAL NEWS. q. Indian Institute of Metals, 2 Sambhunath Pandit St., Calcutta 700 020, India. **Indexed:** Met.Abstr.

671   US   ISSN 0026-0673
TN4   CODEN: MHTRAN
METAL SCIENCE AND HEAT TREATMENT. English translation of: Metallovedenie i Termicheskaya Obrabotka Metallov. 1959. m. $1075 (foreign $1260)(effective 1992). (Ministerstvo Moshinostroeniya i Aiborostroeniya S.S.S.R., Tsentral'nyi Sovet Nauchno-Tekhnicheskogo Obshchestva po Mashinostroeniyi, UR) Plenum Publishing Corp., Consultants Bureau, 233 Spring St., New York, NY 10013-1578. TEL 212-620-8468. FAX 212-463-0742. TELEX 23-421139. Ed. A.P. Gulyaev. (also avail. in microfilm from JSC; back issues avail.) **Indexed:** Cadscan, Chem.Titles, Curr.Cont., Energy Res.Abstr., Eng.Ind., Ind.Sci.Rev., INIS Atomind., INSPEC, ISMEC, Lead Abstr., Solid St.Abstr., Zincscan.
—BLDSC shelfmark: 0415.895000.
Refereed Serial

669 671   US   ISSN 0076-6658
HD9506.U6
METAL STATISTICS. 1904. a. $88 (softcover $53). Capital Cities - A B C, Inc., 825 Seventh Ave., New York, NY 10019. TEL 212-887-8532. FAX 212-887-8358. adv.; circ. 13,000. **Indexed:** AESIS.

669   US   ISSN 0143-7607
METAL TRADERS OF THE WORLD. 1980. irreg., 4th ed., 1990. $188.40. Metal Bulletin Inc., 220 Fifth Ave., New York, NY 10001. TEL 212-213-6202. Ed. R. Serjeantson. adv.
Description: Directory of metal traders worldwide; includes trading personnel, ownership, products handled and an ore classification guide.

METALCASTER. see *BUSINESS AND ECONOMICS — Management*

669 621.9   SP
METALES Y METALURGIA. 1959. w. 26000 ptas.($210) (foreign 3600 ptas.). Tecnipublicaciones, S.A., Fernando VI, 27, 28004 Madrid, Spain. TEL 91-419 90 66. TELEX 43905 YEBE E. Ed. Jesus Heras. adv.; bk.rev.; illus.; stat.; circ. 5,000 (controlled).
Formerly: Metales y Maquinas (ISSN 0210-055X)

METALETTER. see *LABOR UNIONS*

669   US
METALFORMING DIGEST. m. $145 to non-members (foreign $155); members $120 (foreign $130). A S M International, Materials Information, Materials Park, OH 44073. TEL 216-338-5151. FAX 216-338-4634. TELEX 980-619. (UK addr.: Institute of Metals, Materials Information, 1 Carlton House Terr., London SW1Y 5DB, England. TEL 071-839-4071) (Co-sponsor: Institute of Metals) (reprint service avail. from UMI)
Description: For metalforming professionals.

669   GW   ISSN 0026-0746
TN3   CODEN: MTLLAF
METALL; internationale Zeitschrift fuer Technik und Wirtschaft. (Text in German; summaries in English) 1946. m. DM.414. Metall-Verlag GmbH, Postfach 102869, 6900 Heidelberg 1, Germany. Ed.Bd. adv.; bk.rev.; abstr.; charts; illus.; mkt.; pat.; tr.lit.; index, cum.index; circ. 5,771. **Indexed:** Art & Archaeol.Tech.Abstr., Chem.Abstr., Copper Abstr., Eng.Ind., Excerp.Med., INIS Atomind., Int.Aerosp.Abstr., Key to Econ.Sci., Met.Abstr., PROMT, World Alum.Abstr.
—BLDSC shelfmark: 5692.000000.

669   AU
METALL; Fachblatt fuer die Metallverarbeitende Wirtschaft. m. S.596. (Wiener Innung der Schlosser) Oesterreichischer Wirtschaftsverlag, Nikolsdorfer Gasse 7-11, A-1051 Vienna, Austria. TEL 0222-555585. TELEX 1-11669. Ed. Wolfgang Biedermann. adv.; bk.rev.; illus.; circ. 8,600. **Indexed:** Met.Abstr., PROMT, World Alum.Abstr.

669 331.8   SW   ISSN 0026-0754
METALLARBETAREN. 1890. w. SEK 125. Svenska Metallindustriarbetarefoerbundet, S-10552 Stockholm, Sweden. Ed. Per Aahlstroem. adv.; bk.rev.; charts; stat.; index; circ. 450,192. (also avail. in microfilm)

669   AU   ISSN 0026-0762
METALLE. 1950. 5/w. S.1150 per month. Austria Presse Agentur (APA), Gunoldstrasse 14, A-1199 Vienna, Austria. Ed. H. Jaros. (processed) **Indexed:** Cadscan, Lead Abstr., Zincscan.

669   GW   ISSN 0369-2345
METALLGESELLSCHAFT AKTIENGESELLSCHAFT. REVIEW OF THE ACTIVITIES. (Text in English and German) 1929; N.S. 1959. a. free. Metallgesellschaft AG, Reuterweg 14, 6000 Frankfurt a.M., Germany. TEL 069-159-2131. FAX 069-159-2107. TELEX 412250-MGF-D. Eds. Hans Schreiber, Sylvia Noske. bk.rev.; bibl.; charts; illus.; circ. 7,000. **Indexed:** Chem.Abstr., Eng.Ind., Met.Abstr.

METALLIC MATERIALS. see *ENGINEERING — Engineering Mechanics And Materials*

669 600   GW   ISSN 0026-0797
TS200   CODEN: MOFEAV
METALLOBERFLAECHE; Zeitschrift fuer Oberflaechenbearbeitung metallischer und nichtmetallischer Werkstoffe. 1946. m. DM.120. Carl Hanser Verlag, Kolbergerstr. 22, Postfach 860420, 8000 Munich 80, Germany. TEL 089-926940. Ed. W. Jantsch. adv.; bk.rev.; abstr.; illus.; circ. 3,500. **Indexed:** Art & Archaeol.Tech.Abstr., Cadscan, Chem.Abstr., Corros.Abstr., Eng.Ind., Excerp.Med., INIS Atomind., Lead Abstr., Met.Abstr., Packag.Sci.Tech., World Alum.Abstr., World Surf.Coat., Zincscan.
—BLDSC shelfmark: 5693.000000.

669   KR   ISSN 0204-3580
TN689   CODEN: MANFDD
METALLOFIZIKA; nauchno-teoreticheskii zhurnal. English translation: Physics of Metals (UK ISSN 0275-9144) 1979. bi-m. 7.80 Rub. (Akademiya Nauk Ukrainskoi S.S.R., Otdelenie Fiziki i Astronomii) Izdatel'stvo Naukova Dumka, c/o Yu.A. Khramov, Dir, Ul. Repina, 3, Kiev 252 601, Ukraine. TEL 444-12-21. (Subscr. to: Mezhdunarodnaya Kniga, Moscow, G-200, Russia) Ed. V.G. Bariyakhtar. **Indexed:** Chem.Abstr., INIS Atomind., Int.Aerosp.Abstr., Met.Abstr., Phys.Ber., Sci.Abstr., World Alum.Abstr.
—BLDSC shelfmark: 0108.650000.

669   US
METALLOGRAPHY & TESTING DIGEST. 1976. m. $145 to non-members (foreign $155); members $120 (foreign $130). A S M International, Materials Information, Materials Park, OH 44073. TEL 216-338-5151. FAX 216-338-4634. TELEX 980-619. (UK addr.: Institute of Metals, Materials Information, 1 Carlton House Terr., London SW1Y 5DB, England. TEL 071-839-4071) **Indexed:** Met.Abstr.
Formerly: Testing and Control Digest.

669   RU   ISSN 0026-0819
    CODEN: MTOBD3
METALLOVEDENIE I TERMICHESKAYA OBRABOTKA METALLOV. 1955. m. 25.80 Rub. Izdatel'stvo Metallurgiya, 2-i Obydenskii Per., 14, Moscow G-34, Russia. bk.rev.; bibl.; index. **Indexed:** Chem.Abstr., Eng.Ind., INIS Atomind., ISMEC, Met.Abstr., Sci.Abstr., World Alum.Abstr.
—BLDSC shelfmark: 0108.300000.

671.2   RU   ISSN 0026-0827
TS300   CODEN: METGA3
METALLURG. English translation: Metallurgist (US ISSN 0026-0894) 1956. m. 16.80 Rub. (Profsoyuz Rabochikh Metallurgicheskoi Promyshlennosti) Izdatel'stvo Metallurgiya, 2-i Obydenskii Per., 14, Moscow G-34, Russia. (Subscr. to: Mezhdunarodnaya Kniga, Moscow, G-200, Russia) (Co-sponsor: Ministerstvo Chernoi Metallurgii) Ed. M.A. Pertsev. bk.rev.; bibl.; charts; illus.; stat.; index; circ. 24,000. **Indexed:** Chem.Abstr., Eng.Ind., INIS Atomind., ISMEC, Met.Abstr., World Alum.Abstr.
—BLDSC shelfmark: 0109.000000.

669   IT   ISSN 0026-0843
TN4   CODEN: MITLAC
LA METALLURGIA ITALIANA. 1909. m. L.100000 (foreign L.140000)(effective 1992). (Associazione Italiana di Metallurgia) Franco Angeli Editore, Viale Monza, 106, 20127 Milan, Italy. TEL 02-2895762. Dir. Aurelio Molaroni. adv.; bk.rev.; illus.; index; circ. 3,500. **Indexed:** Anal.Abstr., Appl.Mech.Rev., Cadscan, Chem.Abstr., Copper Abstr., Eng.Ind., INIS Atomind., Met.Abstr., World Alum.Abstr., Zincscan.
—BLDSC shelfmark: 5697.000000.

669   UK   ISSN 0141-8602
TN1   CODEN: MEMFAX
METALLURGIA: THE JOURNAL OF METALS TECHNOLOGY, METAL FORMING AND THERMAL PROCESSING. 1929. m. £81.95 (foreign £93). (British Forging Industry Association) F M J International Publications Ltd., Queensway House, 2 Queensway, Redhill, Surrey RH1 1QS, England. TEL 0737-768611. FAX 0737-761-685. TELEX 948669-TOPJNL-G. (Co-sponsors: British Industrial Furnace Constructors Association; British Cold Forging Group) Ed. K. Stanford. adv.; bk.rev.; charts; illus.; tr.lit.; s-a. index. (also avail. in microform from UMI) **Indexed:** A.S.& T.Ind., Anal.Abstr., Appl.Mech.Rev., BMT, Br.Ceram.Abstr., Br.Tech.Ind., Cadscan, Chem.Abstr., Copper Abstr., Curr.Cont., Eng.Ind., Excerp.Med., ISMEC, Lead Abstr., Met.Abstr., PROMT, Zincscan.
—BLDSC shelfmark: 5695.000000.
Former titles: Metallurgia and Metal Forming (ISSN 0368-945X); Metallurgia (ISSN 0026-0835); Metal Forming (ISSN 0026-0622)

669   UK   ISSN 0951-0869
METALLURGICAL JOURNAL. English translation of: Hutnicke Listy (CS ISSN 0018-8069) 1987. m. £120($200) Riecansky Science Publishing Co., 7 Meadow Walk, Great Abingdon, Cambridge CB1 6AZ, England. TEL 0223 893295. FAX 0223-893295. **Indexed:** Eng.Ind., Met.Abstr.

669   US   ISSN 0308-7794
METALLURGICAL PLANTMAKERS OF THE WORLD. 1973. irreg., latest 1988. $167. Metal Bulletin Inc., 220 Fifth Ave., New York, NY 10001. TEL 212-213-6202. Ed. R. Serjeantson. adv.
Description: International guide to ferrous and non-ferrous plant and equipment designers.

669   US   ISSN 0360-2133
    CODEN: MTTABN
METALLURGICAL TRANSACTIONS A - PHYSICAL METALLURGY AND MATERIALS SCIENCE. 1970. m. $480 to non-members; members $50. A S M International, Materials Park, OH 44073-0002. TEL 216-338-5151. FAX 216-338-4634. TELEX 98-0619 ASMINT. (Co-sponsor: Minerals, Metals, and Materials Society) Ed. David E. Laughlin. charts; illus.; stat.; index; circ. 3,425. (also avail. in microform from UMI; reprint service avail. from UMI) **Indexed:** AESIS, Agri.Eng.Abstr., B.C.I.R.A., Br.Ceram.Abstr., Cadscan, Chem.Abstr., Deep Sea Res.& Oceanogr.Abstr., Eng.Ind., Ind.Sci.Rev., INIS Atomind., Int.Aerosp.Abstr., Lead Abstr., Mass Spectr.Bull., Met.Abstr., Phys.Ber., Sci.Abstr., World Alum.Abstr., Zincscan.
Supersedes in part: Metallurgical Transactions (ISSN 0026-086X); Which was formed by the merger of: American Society for Metals. Transactions Quarterly; T M S Transactions.
Description: Written to transfer basic research in physical metallurgy and materials science from the laboratory into the shop.
Refereed Serial

669   US   ISSN 0360-2141
    CODEN: MTTBCR
METALLURGICAL TRANSACTIONS B - PROCESS METALLURGY. 1975. bi-m. $345 to non-members; members $36. A S M International, Materials Park, OH 44073-0002. TEL 216-338-5151. FAX 216-338-4634. TELEX 98-0619 ASMINT. (Co-sponsor: The Minerals, Metals, and Materials Society, Metallurgical) Ed. David E. Laughlin. bk.rev.; charts; illus.; stat.; index; circ. 1,570. (also avail. in microform from UMI; reprint service avail.) **Indexed:** AESIS, Agri.Eng.Abstr., Cadscan, Chem.Abstr., Deep Sea Res.& Oceanogr.Abstr., Eng.Ind., INIS Atomind., Lead Abstr., Mass Spectr.Bull., Met.Abstr., Phys.Ber., Sci.Abstr., Soils & Fert., Zincscan.
Supersedes in part: Metallurgy Transactions.
Description: Articles on extractive and process metallurgy.
Refereed Serial

669 671.52   FR
METALLURGIE. LEXIQUE. (Text in English, French and German) 1978. a. 465 F. Centre National de la Recherche Scientifique, Institut de l'Information Scientifique et Technique, B.P. 54, 54514 Vandoevre-Les-Nancy Cedex, France.

669   US   ISSN 0026-0894
TS300   CODEN: MTLUA8
METALLURGIST. English translation of: Metallurg (UR ISSN 0026-0827) 1959. m. $1075 (foreign $1260)(effective 1992). (Ministerstvo Chernoi Metallurgii S.S.S.R., UR) Plenum Publishing Corp., Consultants Bureau, 233 Spring St., New York, NY 10013-1578. TEL 212-620-8468. FAX 212-463-0742. TELEX 23-421139. Ed. A.G. Belikov. (also avail. in microfilm from JSC; back issues avail.) **Indexed:** Cadscan, Curr.Cont., Eng.Ind., INIS Atomind., ISMEC, Lead Abstr., Met.Abstr., Solid St.Abstr., Zincscan.
—BLDSC shelfmark: 0416.000000.
Refereed Serial

669   US   ISSN 0094-5447
TN675.3
METALLURGY - MATERIALS EDUCATION YEARBOOK. 1961. a. $35 to non-members; members $15. A S M International, Student Outreach, Materials Park, OH 44073-0002. TEL 216-338-5151. FAX 216-338-4634. TELEX 98-0619 ASMINT.
Description: Reference source of metallurgy-materials science and engineering for four-year and graduate college programs. Lists faculty members in those departments.

669   GW   ISSN 0026-0908
               CODEN: MLVBAD
METALLVERARBEITUNG; Fachzeitschrift fuer alle Gebiete der Metallbe- und -verarbeitund sowie fuer Lehrkraefte und Lehrlinge. 1947. bi-m. DM.15 (foreign DM.22.20). Verlag Metallverabeitung, Franzoesche Str. 13-14, Postfach 1220, 1080 Berlin, Germany. Ed. Joerg Dombrowski. adv.; bk.rev.; bibl.; charts; illus.; pat.; index, cum.index; circ. 14,100. **Indexed:** Art & Archaeol.Tech.Abstr., Chem.Abstr., Excerp.Med., Met.Abstr., Numis.Lit., World Alum.Abstr.
Description: Technical journal dealing with traditional production methods; aimed at skilled workers from all branches of metals processing.

669   US
METALMECHANICS: LATIN AMERICAN INDUSTRIAL REPORT. (Avail. for each of 22 Latin American countries) 1985. a. $435 per country report. Aquino Productions, Box 15760, Stamford, CT 06901. TEL 203-325-3138. Ed. Andres C. Aquino.

METALS ALERT. see *MINES AND MINING INDUSTRY*

669   UK   ISSN 0266-7185
               CODEN: MEMTA7
METALS AND MATERIALS. 1967-1981 (Dec.); resumed 1985. m. £110($225) to non-members. Institute of Materials, 1 Carlton House Terrace, London SW1Y 5DB, England. TEL 071-839-4071. FAX 071-839-2078. TELEX 8814813-METSOC-G. Ed. Nuna Staniaszek. adv.; bk.rev.; charts; illus.; tr.lit.; index; circ. 13,000. **Indexed:** ABTICS, Art & Archaeol.Tech.Abstr., B.C.I.R.A., Br.Ceram.Abstr., Br.Tech.Ind., Cadscan, Chem.Abstr., Copper Abstr., Eng.Ind., Excerp.Med., Lead Abstr., Met.Abstr., Zincscan.
—BLDSC shelfmark: 5699.315000.
Supersedes: Metallurgist and Materials Technologist (ISSN 0306-526X) & Metals Society World (ISSN 0265-2722)
Description: Covers the science, manufacturing technology and use of metals and other engineering materials.

METALS AND MINERALS REVIEW. see *MINES AND MINING INDUSTRY*

669   UK
METALS INDUSTRY NEWS. 1984. q. $48. F M J International Publications, Queensway House, 2 Queensway, Redhill, Surrey RH1 1QS, England. TEL 44-737-768611. FAX 44-737-761685. adv.: B&W page £2060, color page £3095; trim 280 x 405. circ. 40,000.
Description: Features reports on various aspects of the metal industry worldwide.

669   II   ISSN 0970-423X
METALS MATERIALS AND PROCESSES. (Text in English) 1989. q. Rs.1500($125) Meshap Science Publishers, 75, 4th Floor, Lakshmi Building, Sir P.M. Road, Fort, Bombay 400 001, India. (Subscr. to: Meshap Science Publishers, Circulation Department, P.O. Box 8319, T.F. Deonar, Bombay 400 088, India) Ed. C.V. Sundaram. bk.rev.
—BLDSC shelfmark: 5699.388000.
Description: Covers the broad spectrum of materials systems including alloys, amorphous materials, ceramics, composites, metals, and polymers.

METALS MONITOR. see *BUSINESS AND ECONOMICS — Labor And Industrial Relations*

669.142   US
METALS PRICE REPORT - ALLOY STEEL. w. $450. McGraw-Hill, Inc., 1221 Ave. of the Americas, New York, NY 10020. TEL 212-512-2000.

669   US
METALS PRICE REPORT - BASE METALS. w. $450. McGraw-Hill, Inc., 1221 Ave. of the Americas, New York, NY 10020. TEL 212-512-2000.

METALS WEEK. see *MINES AND MINING INDUSTRY*

METALS WEEK INSIDER REPORT. see *MINES AND MINING INDUSTRY*

METALS WEEK PRICE NOTIFICATION SERVICE. see *MINES AND MINING INDUSTRY*

METALSMITH. see *ARTS AND HANDICRAFTS*

669   AG
METALURGIA.* Asociacion de Industriales Metalurgicos, Alsina 1607 1 Piso, Buenos Aires, Argentina. **Indexed:** Chem.Abstr.

669   AG   ISSN 0325-0202
METALURGIA MODERNA. (Text in Spanish; summaries in English and Spanish) 1959. biennial. Sociedad Argentina de Metales, Santa Fe 1145, 1059 Buenos Aires, Argentina. adv.; circ. 1,000.
Description: Covers the structure and behavior of metals.

669 643   CI   ISSN 0543-5846
METALURGIJA. 1962. q. 32000 din. Faculty of Metallurgy, Aleja Narodnih Heroja 3, 44103 Sisak, Croatia. TEL 044 35226. FAX 044-30284. TELEX 23617. Ed. Ilija Mamuzic. adv.; circ. 600. **Indexed:** Chem.Abstr., Met.Abstr., Ref.Zh.
—BLDSC shelfmark: 5700.120000.
Description: Presents scientific and professional papers.

671.3   US   ISSN 0026-1009
METALWORKING DIGEST. 1968. 12/yr. $12. Gordon Publications, Inc., 301 Gibraltar Dr., Morris Plains, NJ 07950. TEL 201-292-5100. FAX 201-898-9281. Ed. Richard Stevancsez. adv.; illus.; circ. 115,000. (tabloid format)

671.3   US
METALWORKING DIGEST LITERATURE REVIEW. 1989. 3/yr. Gordon Publications, Inc., 301 Gibraltar Dr., Morris Plains, NJ 07950. TEL 201-292-5100. adv.; circ. 100,000.

669   US
METALWORKING INTERFACES;* bimonthly international report on lubrication and roles of interfaces in metalworking. 1976. bi-m. $55. Mk Infotech Company, 98 Schiller Ln., Lake Zurich, IL 60047. Ed. Mark Mrozek. abstr.; pat.; circ. 1,000. **Indexed:** Chem.Abstr., Met.Abstr.

669   UK   ISSN 0026-1033
METALWORKING PRODUCTION. 1900. m. £40. Morgan-Grampian (Publishers) Ltd., 30 Calderwood St., Woolwich, London SE18 6QH, England. TEL 081-855-7777. FAX 071-316-3034. Ed. Ted Holland. adv.; charts; illus.; tr.lit.; index; circ. 17,025. (also avail. in microform from UMI) **Indexed:** BMT, Br.Tech.Ind., ISMEC, Key to Econ.Sci., Met.Abstr., Sci.Abstr., World Alum.Abstr., World Text.Abstr.
—BLDSC shelfmark: 5700.250000.
Description: For production executives and engineers responsible for purchase of production machine tools and auxilliary equipment.

METALLURGY 3415

669   CN   ISSN 0383-090X
METALWORKING PRODUCTION & PURCHASING; Canadian publication for production, purchasing & management in metalworking. 1974. 6/yr. Can.$30. Action Communications Inc., 135 Spy Court, Markham, Ont. L3R 5H6, Canada. TEL 416-477-3222. FAX 416-477-4320. Ed. M. Holtham. adv.; circ. 21,558.

620.112   FR   ISSN 0026-1084
TA462   CODEN: MTUXAS
METAUX; corrosion-industries. 1925. m. 1700 F. Editions Metaux, 32 rue du Marechal-Joffre, 78100 Saint-Germain-en-Laye, France. Ed. Dir. Jose Delville. adv.; bk.rev.; bibl.; charts; illus.; index; circ. 3,500. **Indexed:** Chem.Abstr., Eng.Ind., Met.Abstr.
—BLDSC shelfmark: 5702.000000.

669   US   ISSN 0026-1297
METLFAX. 1956. m. $45 (foreign $85; Canada $65). Huebcore Communications, Inc., 29100 Aurora Rd., Ste. 200, Solon, OH 44139. TEL 216-248-1125. FAX 612-686-0214. (Subscr. to: Box 21640, Eagan, MN 55121-0640. TEL 612-686-0303) Ed. James A. Masar. adv.; bk.rev.; charts; illus.; tr.lit.; circ. 102,000.

MINERACAO METALURGIA. see *MINES AND MINING INDUSTRY*

669 531.64   US   ISSN 0882-7508
TN496   CODEN: MPERE8
MINERAL PROCESSING AND EXTRACTIVE METALLURGY REVIEW. 1982. 16/yr. (in 4 vols., 4 nos./vol.) $228. Gordon and Breach Science Publishers, 270 Eighth Ave., New York, NY 10011. TEL 212-206-8900. FAX 212-645-2459. TELEX 236735 GOPUB UR. (Subscr. to: Box 786, Cooper Sta., New York, NY 10276. TEL 800-545-8398; UK subscr. to: P.O. Box 90, Reading, Berkshire RG1 8JL, England. TEL 0734-560-080) Eds. Fiona Doyle, Kenneth N. Han. (also avail. in microform)
—BLDSC shelfmark: 5779.681500.
Former titles: Mineral Processing and Technology Review; Extractive and Process Metallurgy (ISSN 0273-3706)
Refereed Serial

MINERALES. see *MINES AND MINING INDUSTRY*

MINERALS INDUSTRY INTERNATIONAL. see *MINES AND MINING INDUSTRY*

MINERIA CHILENA. see *MINES AND MINING INDUSTRY*

669   JA   ISSN 0289-6214
MINING AND MATERIALS PROCESSING INSTITUTE OF JAPAN. METALLURGICAL REVIEW. (Text in English) s-a. $20. Mining and Materials Processing Institute of Japan - Shigen, Sozai Gakkai, Nogizaka Bldg., 9-6-41 Akasaka, Minato-ku, Tokyo 107, Japan. TEL 03-3402-0541. FAX 03-3402-1776.
—BLDSC shelfmark: 5698.497000.

MINING, GEOLOGICAL AND METALLURGICAL INSTITUTE OF INDIA. TRANSACTIONS. see *MINES AND MINING INDUSTRY*

671   US   ISSN 0277-9951
MODERN APPLICATIONS NEWS; the metalworking idea magazine. Short title: M A N. 1967. 10/yr. $59 (foreign $70). Nelson Publishing Co., 2504 N. Tamiami Trail, Nokomis, FL 34275-3476. TEL 813-966-9521. FAX 813-966-2590. Ed. A. Verner Nelson. adv.; illus.; tr.lit.; circ. 71,101. (reprint service avail. from UMI)
—BLDSC shelfmark: 5358.026500.
Former titles: Modern Applications News for Design and Manufacturing (ISSN 0026-7473); Materials Application News for Design and Manufacturing.

671.2   US   ISSN 0026-7562
TS200   CODEN: MOCAB5
MODERN CASTING. 1938. m. $35 (foreign $45). American Foundrymen's Society, Inc., 505 State St., Des Plaines, IL 60016. TEL 708-824-0181. Ed. David P. Kanicki. adv.; bk.rev.; charts; illus.; tr.lit.; circ. 24,000. (also avail. in microform; reprint service avail. from UMI) **Indexed:** A.S.& T.Ind., AESIS, B.C.I.R.A., Chem.Abstr., Eng.Ind., Excerp.Med., Ind.Sci.Rev., Met.Abstr., PROMT, World Alum.Abstr.
—BLDSC shelfmark: 5884.800000.

METALLURGY

671 US ISSN 0026-8127
TS200 CODEN: MOMLAJ
MODERN METALS. 1945. m. $50. Delta Communications, Inc. (Chicago) (Subsidiary of: Elsevier Business Press, Inc. (New York)), 400 N. Michigan Ave., Ste. 1200, Chicago, IL 60611. FAX 312-222-2026. Ed. Victor Cassidy. adv.; charts; illus.; mkt.; tr.lit.; circ. 32,170. **Indexed:** A.S.& T.Ind., Chem.Abstr., Copper Abstr., Eng.Ind., Excerp.Med., Ind.Sci.Rev., Met.Abstr., Packag.Sci.Tech., World Alum.Abstr.
—BLDSC shelfmark: 5890.000000.

MODERN STEEL CONSTRUCTION. see *BUILDING AND CONSTRUCTION*

669 US ISSN 0730-9163
MOLYSULFIDE NEWSLETTER. 1956. irreg. free. Climax Molybdenum Co., Box 407, Ypsilanti, MI 48197. TEL 313-481-3000. FAX 313-481-3005. Ed. Deborah Edwards Hallada. bk.rev.; circ. 10,000.

672 RU
MOSKOVSKII INSTITUT STALI I SPLAVOV. NAUCHNYE TRUDY.. 1972. irreg. 0.85 Rub. Izdatel'stvo Metallurgiya, 2-i Obydenskii Per., 14, Moscow G-34, Russia. illus. **Indexed:** Chem.Abstr.

N A D C A INTERNATIONAL DIE CASTING CONGRESS. TRANSACTIONS. (North American Die Casting Association) see *ENGINEERING — Engineering Mechanics And Materials*

669 658.5 US ISSN 0077-3379
N A M F MANAGEMENT MANUAL. 1960. irreg., latest 1990. $100 to non-members; members $50. National Association of Metal Finishers, 401 N. Michigan Ave., Chicago, IL 60611-4267. TEL 312-644-6610. Ed. Brad Parcells. index.

669 658.5 US
N A M F REGULATORY COMPLIANCE MANUAL. irreg., updates approx. 3/yr. $250 to non-members; members $50. National Association of Metal Finishers, 401 N. Michigan Ave., Chicago, IL 60611-4267. TEL 312-644-6610. (looseleaf format)

669 GW
N C FERTIGUNG; Fachmagazin fuer Metallbearbeitung und Automation. 1980. 8/yr. DM.120. N C Technologie Verlags GmbH, Katernbergerstr. 55, Postfach 101169, 5600 Wuppertal 1, Germany. TEL 0202-389050. Ed. Juergen Kromberg.

669 II ISSN 0027-6839
TN1 CODEN: NLMJA3
N M L TECHNICAL JOURNAL. (Text in English) 1959. q. Rs.18.($9) (effective 1990). National Metallurgical Laboratory, P.O. Burmamines, Jamshedpur 831 007, Bihar, India. TEL 26091. FAX 0657-27356. TELEX 0626-210. (Affiliate: Council of Scientific and Industrial Research) Ed. O.N. Mohanty. bk.rev.; charts; illus.; mkt.; pat.; circ. 1,000. **Indexed:** Chem.Abstr., Eng.Ind., Met.Abstr., World Alum.Abstr.
—BLDSC shelfmark: 6113.900000.

669 CC ISSN 1001-1935
NAIHUO CAILIAO. (Text in Chinese) bi-m. Yejin Bu, Luoyang Naihuo Cailiao Yanjiusuo, No. 43, Xiyuan Lu, Jianxi-qu, Luoyang, Henan 471039, People's Republic of China. TEL 23501. Ed. Fang Zhengguo.

669.2 JA ISSN 0027-772X
NAMARI TO AEN/LEAD AND ZINC. (Text in Japanese) 1964. bi-m. free. Japan Lead Zinc Development Association - Nihon Namari Aen Juyo Kenkyukai, New Hibiya Bldg., 1-3-6 Uchisaiwai-cho, Chiyoda-ku, Tokyo 100, Japan. FAX 03-591-9841. Ed. Hiroshi Tokunaga. adv.; bk.rev.; abstr.; charts; illus.; stat.; cum.index; circ. 1,900. **Indexed:** JTA, Met.Abstr., World Alum.Abstr.

669 JA ISSN 0453-9222
TN4 CODEN: TNRMAF
NATIONAL RESEARCH INSTITUTE FOR METALS. TRANSACTIONS/KINZOKU ZAIRYO GIJUTSU KENKYUJO OBUN KENKYU HOKOKU. (Text in European languages) 1959. q. exchange basis. National Research Institute for Metals - Kagaku Gijutsu-cho Kinzoku Zairyo Gijutsu Kenkyujo, 2-3-12 Nakameguro, Meguro-ku, Tokyo 153, Japan. circ. 660. **Indexed:** Curr.Cont., INSPEC, Met.Abstr., Sci.Abstr., World Alum.Abstr.

669 600 JA ISSN 0288-0490
CODEN: NESHDF
NETSU SHORI/JAPAN SOCIETY FOR HEAT TREATMENT. JOURNAL. 1960. bi-m. 6600 Yen. Japan Society for Heat Treatment, Shinsen Bldg., 8-2, Shinsen-cho, Shibuya-ku, Tokyo 150, Japan. TEL 03-461-7116. FAX 03-461-0750. Ed. Suzuki Tomoo. adv.; bk.rev.; circ. 5,000. **Indexed:** Chem.Abstr.
—BLDSC shelfmark: 4807.500000.

671 GW ISSN 0028-3207
TN3 CODEN: NEUHAM
NEUE HUETTE; Metallurgisch-Metallkundliche Fachzeitschrift fuer Forschung und Praxis. 1955. m. DM.240. (Verein Deutscher Eisenhuettenleute) Deutscher Verlag fuer Grundstoffindustrie, Karl-Heine-Str. 27, 7031 Leipzig, Germany. TEL 4081011. FAX 4012571. TELEX 51451-FACHB-DD. adv.; bk.rev.; charts; illus.; index. **Indexed:** C.I.S. Abstr., Cadscan, Ceram.Abstr., Chem.Abstr., Copper Abstr., Curr.Cont., Eng.Ind., Lead Abstr., Met.Abstr., World Alum.Abstr., Zincscan.
—BLDSC shelfmark: 6077.500000.
Description: Publication on the technical aspects of metallurgy and metal processing. Covers the development, production, processing, and testing of metals. Includes reports of events.

671.37 US ISSN 0146-9711
CODEN: NPPMDO
NEW PERSPECTIVES IN POWDER METALLURGY. 1966. irreg., vol.8, 1988. price varies. Metal Powder Industries Federation, 105 College Rd. E., Princeton, NJ 08540. TEL 609-452-7700. FAX 609-987-8523. circ. 1,000.
Formerly: Perspectives in Powder Metallurgy (ISSN 0079-1032)
Description: Collection of papers on one specific topic from various sources.

669.1 JA ISSN 0911-8764
NEWS FROM NISSHIN STEEL. (Text in English) m. Nisshin Steel Co., Ltd., 4-1 Marunouchi 3-chome, Chiyoda-ku, Tokyo 100, Japan. TEL 03-216-5511. FAX 03-214-1895. TELEX 222-2788. illus.
Description: Contains news and articles about the company.

669 CS ISSN 0322-7189
NEZELEZNE KOVY; technickoekonomicky zpravodaj. 1959. m. free. Vyzkumny Ustav Kovu - Research Institute for Metals, Oborove Informacni Stredisko, 250 70 Panenske Brezany. TEL 896041. circ. 290.
Description: Production, treatment and application of non-ferrous metals.

669 CN ISSN 0829-8351
NICKEL. 1985. q. free. Nickel Development Institute (NiDI), 15 Toronto St., Suite 402, Toronto, Ont. M5C 2E3, Canada. TEL 416-362-8850. FAX 416-362-6346. TELEX 06-218656. Ed. Desmond M. Chorley. circ. 30,000.
Description: Devoted to nickel and its applications.

669 JA ISSN 0546-126X
NIHON SEIKOSHO GIHO/JAPAN STEEL WORKS TECHNICAL REVIEW. (Text in English and Japanese) 1959. s-a. Nihon Seikosho - Japan Steel Works, Ltd., 1-12 Yuraku-cho, Chiyoda-ku, Tokyo 100, Japan. **Indexed:** Met.Abstr., World Alum.Abstr.

669.1 JA
NIPPON STEEL FORUM. s-a. free. Nippon Steel Corporation, Public Relations Dept., Corporate Secretariat Div., 6-3 Ote-machi 2-chome, Chiyoda-ku, Tokyo 100-71, Japan. TEL 03-242-4111. (US addr.: 345 Park Ave. S., 41st Fl., New York, NY 10154. TEL 212-486-7150) charts; illus.
Description: Aims to survey the company's full range of activities in the context of the economic environment in which it operates. Also attempts to present the current trends in Japan's industry and economy. Cultural factors affecting the economy are examined.

669.1 JA ISSN 0048-0452
NIPPON STEEL NEWS. (Text in English) 1970. m. free. Nippon Steel Corporation, 6-3 Ote-machi 2-chome, Chiyoda-ku, Tokyo 100-71, Japan. TEL 03-242-4111. FAX 03-275-5607. TELEX J-22291. (US addr.: 345 Park Ave., 41st Fl., New York, NY 10154. TEL 212-486-7150) illus. **Indexed:** Br.Ceram.Abstr., Met.Abstr., World Alum.Abstr.
Description: Focuses on technological innovations, new companies and mergers.

669.1 JA
NIPPON STEEL REPORT. a. Nippon Steel Corporation, 6-3 Ote-machi 2-chome, Chiyoda-ku, Tokyo 100-71, Japan. TEL 03-242-4111. FAX 03-275-5607. TELEX J-22291. (US addr.: 345 Park Ave., 41st Fl., New York, NY 10154. TEL 212-486-7150)
Description: Presents financial information on the company. Explores business developments, electronics information, new materials, sales, revenue and future management risks.

672.05 JA ISSN 0300-306X
TS300
NIPPON STEEL TECHNICAL REPORT. English translation of: Seitetsu Kenkyu. 1972. s-a. free. Nippon Steel Corporation, 2-6-3 Otemachi, Chiyoda-ku, Tokyo 100, Japan. TEL 03-242-4111. (U.S. addr.: 345 Park Ave, 41st Fl., New York, NY 10154. TEL 212-486-7150) illus. **Indexed:** Br.Ceram.Abstr., Corros.Abstr., JCT, JTA, Met.Abstr., World Alum.Abstr.
—BLDSC shelfmark: 6113.557000.
Formerly: Nippon Steel Technical Report. Overseas.

669.1 JA
NISSHIN. (Text in Japanese) no.434, Apr. 1990. m. Nisshin Steel Co., Inc., 4-1 Marunouchi 3-chome, Chiyoda-ku, Tokyo 100, Japan. TEL 03-216-5511. FAX 03-214-1895. TELEX 222-2788.
Description: In-house magazine for company employees.

669.1 JA
NISSHIN STEEL. ANNUAL REPORT. (Text in English) a. Nisshin Steel Co., Ltd., General Administration Department, Public Relations Section, 4-1 Marunouchi 3-chome, Chiyoda-ku, Tokyo 100, Japan. TEL 03-216-5511. FAX 03-214-1895. TELEX 222-2788. (Or: 16 Raffles Quay, No.20-01, Hong Leong Bldg., Singapore 0104, Singapore; Nisshin USA, Inc., 375 Park Ave., New York, NY 10152; Immermannstr. 45, D-4000 Dusseldorf 1, Germany; Changfugong Center Office Bldg., 5F, Jianguomenwai Dajie 26, Chaoyang Qu, Beijing, People's Republic of China) charts; illus.; stat.

NON-DESTRUCTIVE TESTING - AUSTRALIA; a journal of measurement control & testing. see *ENGINEERING — Engineering Mechanics And Materials*

669 US ISSN 0360-9553
HD9506.U6
NON-FERROUS METAL DATA. 1920. a. $350. American Bureau of Metal Statistics Inc., Box 1405, Plaza Sta., 400 Plaza Dr., Secaucus, NJ 07094-0405. TEL 201-863-6900. FAX 201-863-6050. Ed. William J. Lambert. cum.index; circ. 3,000. **Indexed:** SRI.
Formerly (until 1974): American Bureau of Metal Statistics. Year Book (ISSN 0065-7611)
Refereed Serial

673 US ISSN 0078-0987
HD9539.A1
NON-FERROUS METAL WORKS OF THE WORLD. 1967. irreg., latest 1989. $167. Metal Bulletin Inc., 220 Fifth Ave., NY 10001. TEL 212-213-6202. (Dist. in U.S. by: Metal Bulletin Inc., 220 Fifth Ave., New York, NY 10001) Ed. R. Serjeantson. adv.
Description: Definitive guide to the world's nonferrous metal smelters, refiners, semi-fabricators and secondary ingot makers.

669 SW
NORDISK AATERVINNING; organ foer skrotindustrii de Nordiska laenderna. (Text in Swedish; summaries in English and Finnish) 1952. 4/yr. Skrothandelns Branchkommite (SBK), P.O. Box 3560, S-103 69 Stockholm, Sweden. circ. 3,000.

NORTH CAROLINA METALWORKING DIRECTORY. see *BUSINESS AND ECONOMICS — Trade And Industrial Directories*

669.6 UK ISSN 0029-4098
NOTES ON TIN. 1956. m. £24. International Tin Council, Haymarket House, 1 Oxendon St., London SW1Y 4EQ, England. stat.; circ. 500. (processed)
Description: World press digest on tin prospecting, mining, smelting, recycling, tin-using industry, trade, prices, market, government legislation and taxes.

METALLURGY

669   RU
NOVYE ISSLEDOVANIYA V KHIMII, METALLURGII I OBOGASHCHENII. (Subseries of: Gornyi Institut, Leningrad. Nauchnye Trudy) irreg. 0.75 Rub. Leningradskii Gornyi Institut, St. Petersburg, Russia. illus.

338.47 672   FR   ISSN 0474-5973
O E C D. IRON AND STEEL INDUSTRY. (Text in English, French) 1953. a. price varies. Organization for Economic Cooperation and Development, 2 rue Andre-Pascal, 75775 Paris Cedex 16, France. TEL 45-24-82-00. FAX 45-24-85-00. (U.S. orders to: O.E.C.D. Publications and Information Center, 2001 L St., N.W., Ste. 700, Washington, D.C. 20036-4910. TEL 202-785-6323) (also avail. in microfiche from OEC)

669   PL   ISSN 0867-2628
OBROBKA PLASTYCZNA METALI/METAL FORMING. 4/yr. 30000 Zl. Instytut Obrobki Plastycznej, Ul. Zamenholfa 4, 61-120 Poznan, Poland. TEL 77-10-81. Ed. Zbigniew Lukomski.
Formerly: Obrobka Plastyczna (ISSN 0472-4313)

671   RU
OCHISTKA VODNOGO I VOZDUSHNOGO BASSEINOV NA PREDPRIYATIYAKH CHERNOI METALLURGII. irreg. 1.12 Rub.($18.60) Izdatel'stvo Metallurgiya, 2-i Obydenskii Per., 14, Moscow G-34, Russia. (Co-sponsor: Ministerstvo Chernoi Metallurgii) illus. Indexed: Chem.Abstr.

669   PL
OCHRONA POWIETRZA. 1967. bi-m. $20. (Stowarzyszenie Inzynierow i Technikow Przemyslu Hutniczego) Wydawnictwo Czasopism i Ksiazek Technicznych SIGMA - NOT, Ul. Biala 4, 00-950 Warsaw, Poland. (Dist. by: SIGMA NOT Ltd., Ul. Bartycka 20, 00-716 Warsaw, Poland) circ. 2,150. Indexed: Met.Abstr., World Alum.Abstr.

669   GW   ISSN 0078-3420
OERLIKON SCHWEISSMITTEILUNGEN. 1955. irreg. free. Oerlikon Elektrodenfabrik Eisenberg GmbH, 6719 Eisenberg-Pfalz, Germany. FAX 06351-76335. TELEX 451242. (Co-sponsor: Schweissindustrie Oerlikon Buehrle AG, Zurich) Ed. K. Weigel. circ. 5,000. Indexed: BMT, Chem.Abstr.
Description: Technical and scientific information on welding and related fields.

669   US
ORGANOMETALLIC SYNTHESES. 1965. irreg., vol.2, 1982. Academic Press, Inc., 1250 Sixth Ave., San Diego, CA 92101. TEL 619-231-0926. FAX 619-699-6715. Eds. John J. Eisch, R. Bruce King. (reprint service avail. from ISI)
Refereed Serial

669   US
ORNAMENTAL - MISCELLANEOUS METAL FABRICATOR. 1959. bi-m. $15. National Ornamental & Miscellaneous Metals Association, 804-10 Main St., Ste. E, Forest Park, GA 30050. TEL 404-237-5334. FAX 404-366-1852. Ed. Elizabeth Rawlins. adv.; bk.rev.; circ. 10,000.
Formerly (until 1977): Ornamental Metal Fabricator.

OXIDATION OF METALS; an international journal of the science of gas-solid reactions. see CHEMISTRY — Physical Chemistry

671   GW   ISSN 0048-5012
                          CODEN: PWMIBW
P M I - POWDER METALLURGY INTERNATIONAL. (Text in English) 1968. bi-m. DM.260. Verlag Schmid GmbH (Freiburg), Hofackerstr. 92, Postfach 6609, 7800 Freiburg, Germany. TEL 0761-82051. FAX 0761-84863. adv.; circ. 6,000. Indexed: Br.Ceram.Abstr., Cadscan, Ceram.Abstr., Chem.Abstr., Copper Abstr., Curr.Cont., Eng.Ind., Excerp.Med., Int.Aerosp.Abstr., ISMEC, Lead Abstr., Met.Abstr., Sci.Abstr., World Alum.Abstr., Zincscan.
—BLDSC shelfmark: 6572.150000.
Description: Provides information about the whole area of powder metallurgy, composite materials and advanced ceramics.

671   US
P - M TECHNOLOGY NEWSLETTER. (Powder Metallurgy) 1960. m. $70 to individuals; institutions $135. American Powder Metallurgy Institute, 105 College Rd. E., Princeton, NJ 08540. TEL 609-452-7700. FAX 609-987-8523. TELEX 510-685-2516. Ed. Peter K. Johnson. bk.rev.; charts; illus.; stat.; tr.lit.; circ. 3,000. (reprint service avail. from UMI)

PARTICULATE SCIENCE AND TECHNOLOGY; an international journal. see ENGINEERING — Chemical Engineering

PHOENIX: VOICE OF THE SCRAP RECYCLING INDUSTRIES. see CONSERVATION

669 530   US   ISSN 0275-9144
TN689   CODEN: PMTSDT
PHYSICS OF METALS. English translation of: Metallofizika (UR ISSN 0204-3580) vol.3, 1982. 6/yr. (in 1 vol.; 6 nos./vol.). $393. Gordon and Breach Science Publishers, 270 Eighth Ave., New York, NY 10011. TEL 212-206-8900. FAX 212-645-2459. TELEX 236735 GOPUB UR. (Subscr. to: Box 786, Cooper Sta., New York, NY 10276. TEL 800-574-8398; UK subscr. to: P.O. Box 90, Reading, Berkshire RG1 8JL, England. TEL 0734-560-080) Ed. V. Baryakhtar. adv. (also avail. in microform; back issues avail.) Indexed: Met.Abstr., Sci.Abstr., World Alum.Abstr.
—BLDSC shelfmark: 0416.855000.
Refereed Serial

620.1 669   US   ISSN 0031-918X
TN690   CODEN: PHMMA6
PHYSICS OF METALS AND METALLOGRAPHY. English translation of: Fizika Metallov i Metallovedenie (UR ISSN 0015-3230) 1957. 12/yr. (in 2 vols., 6 nos./vol.). £820 (effective 1992). Pergamon Press, Inc., Journals Division, 660 White Plains Rd., Tarrytown, NY 10591-5153. TEL 914-524-9200. FAX 914-333-2444. (And: Headington Hill Hall, Oxford OX3 0BW, England. TEL 0865-794141) Ed. Brian Ralph. adv.; bk.rev.; bibl.; charts; illus.; circ. 900. (also avail. in microform from MIM,UMI; back issues avail.) Indexed: Eng.Ind., Met.Abstr., Phys.Ber., Sci.Abstr., World Alum.Abstr.
—BLDSC shelfmark: 0416.860000.
Description: Contains investigations of the physical properties of metals and alloys, and studies of phenomena occuring during all phases of manufacture.
Refereed Serial

671.732   US   ISSN 0360-3164
TS670   CODEN: PSFMDH
PLATING AND SURFACE FINISHING; electroplating, finishing of metals, organic finishing. 1909. m. $35 (foreign $45). American Electroplaters and Surface Finishers Society, Inc. (AESF), 12644 Research Pkwy., Orlando, FL 32826-3298. TEL 407-281-6441. FAX 407-281-6446. TELEX 510-601-6246. Ed. Sylvia L. Baxley. adv.; bk.rev.; abstr.; bibl.; charts; illus.; pat.; tr.lit.; index; circ. 10,975. (also avail. in microform from UMI; reprint service avail. from UMI) Indexed: A.S.& T.Ind., Cadscan, Chem.Abstr., Copper Abstr., Curr.Cont., Eng.Ind., Excerp.Med., Lead Abstr., Met.Abstr., Risk Abstr., Sci.Abstr., World Alum.Abstr., Zincscan.
—BLDSC shelfmark: 6538.050000.
Supersedes: Plating (ISSN 0032-1397)

669.2   UK   ISSN 0032-1400
TN799.P7   CODEN: PTMRA3
PLATINUM METALS REVIEW. 1957. q. free. Johnson Matthey PLC, 78 Hatton Garden, London EC1N 8JP, England. TEL 071-269-8000. FAX 071-269-8133. Ed. I.E. Cottington. bk.rev.; abstr.; illus.; pat.; index; circ. 10,000. Indexed: AESIS, Art & Archaeol.Tech.Abstr., Br.Ceram.Abstr., Chem.Abstr., Energy Info.Abstr., Eng.Ind., Environ.Abstr., Excerp.Med., Met.Abstr., Soils & Fert., World Alum.Abstr., World Text.Abstr.
Description: Survey of research on the platinum metals (platinum, palladium, rhodium, iridium, osmium, rutherium) and developments in their application in industry.

669   PL   ISSN 0372-9699
POLITECHNIKA CZESTOCHOWSKA. ZESZYTY NAUKOWE. NAUKI TECHNICZNE. HUTNICTWO. (Text in Polish; summaries in English and Russian) 1969. irreg., no.17, 1985. (Politechnika Czestochowska) Wydawnictwo Politechniki Czestochowskiej, Ul. Deglera 31, 42-200 Czestochowa, Poland. (Dist. by: Ars Polona-Ruch, Krakowskie Przedmiescie 7, Warsaw, Poland) Ed. Wladyslaw Sabela. Indexed: Chem.Abstr., Met.Abstr.
Description: The subject matter connected with problems of metallurgy, metal physical chemistry, physical metallurgy, foundry engineering, metallurgical power engineering, and plastic working of metals.

669   PL   ISSN 0324-802X
TN600   CODEN: ZNPHBN
POLITECHNIKA SLASKA. ZESZYTY NAUKOWE. HUTNICTWO. (Text in Polish; summaries in English and Russian) 1971. irreg. price varies. Politechnika Slaska, Katowicka 7, 44-100 Gliwice, Poland. FAX 371655. TELEX 036304. (Dist. by: Ars Polona, Krakowskie Przedmiescie 7, 00-068 Warsaw, Poland) Ed. Stanislaw Serkowski. circ. 205. Indexed: Chem.Abstr., Met.Abstr.

669   PL   ISSN 0079-3345
TN607
POLSKA AKADEMIA NAUK. ODDZIAL W KRAKOWIE. KOMISJA METALURGICZNO-ODLEWNICZA. PRACE: METALURGIA. (Text in English and Polish; summaries in English and Russian) 1965. irreg., no.36, 1988. price varies. Ossolineum, Publishing House of the Polish Academy of Sciences, Rynek 9, Wroclaw, Poland. TELEX 0712771 OSS PL. (Dist. by: Ars Polona-Ruch, Krakowskie Przedmiescie 7, Warsaw, Poland) Ed. Czeslaw Podrzucki. circ. 500. Indexed: Chem.Abstr., Eng.Ind.
—BLDSC shelfmark: 6588.010000.
Formerly: Polska Akademia Nauk. Komisja Metalurgii i Odlewnictwa. Metalurgia.

POLYTECHNISCH TIJDSCHRIFT: WERKTUIGBOUW/MECHANICAL ENGINEERING. see ENGINEERING — Mechanical Engineering

666   KR   ISSN 0032-4795
TN695   CODEN: PMANAI
POROSHKOVAYA METALLURGIYA; vsesoyznyi nauchno-tekhnicheskii zhurnal. (Text in Russian; summaries in English and Russian) 1961. m. 12 Rub.($32) (Akademiya Nauk Ukrainskoi S.S.R., Institut Problem Materialovedeniya) Izdatel'stvo Naukova Dumka, c/o Yu.A. Khramov, Dir, Ul. Repina, 3, Kiev 252 601, Ukraine. TEL 444-14-01. Ed. V.I. Trefilov. bk.rev.; illus.; circ. 1,300. Indexed: Chem.Abstr., Copper Abstr., Eng.Ind., Int.Aerosp.Abstr., ISMEC, Met.Abstr., Sci.Abstr., World Alum.Abstr.
—BLDSC shelfmark: 0130.280000.

671   UK   ISSN 0032-5899
TN695   CODEN: PWMTAU
POWDER METALLURGY. 1958. q. £114($247) to non-members; members £67($128). Institute of Materials, 1 Carlton House Terrace, London SW1Y 5DB, England. TEL 071-839-4071. FAX 071-839-2078. TELEX 8814813-METSOC-G. Ed. Mary Chim. adv.; index; circ. 850. Indexed: ABTICS, Br.Ceram.Abstr., Br.Tech.Ind., Cadscan, Chem.Abstr., Copper Abstr., Curr.Cont., Eng.Ind., Int.Aerosp.Abstr., Lead Abstr., Met.Abstr., Sci.Abstr., World Alum.Abstr., Zincscan.
—BLDSC shelfmark: 6571.950000.
Description: International coverage of the science and practice of powder metallurgy.

669   GW   ISSN 0032-678X
TN690   CODEN: PMTLA5
PRAKTISCHE METALLOGRAPHIE. (Text in English and German) 1964. m. DM.169. Carl Hanser Verlag, Kolbergerstr. 22, 8000 Munich 80, Germany. Ed. G. Petzow. adv.; bk.rev.; abstr.; charts; illus.; mkt.; index; circ. 2,000. Indexed: Ceram.Abstr., Chem.Abstr., Eng.Ind., Met.Abstr., World Alum.Abstr.
—BLDSC shelfmark: 6595.060000.

669   UK   ISSN 0264-4703
PRECISION TOOLMAKER. 1983. bi-m. £49. International Business & Technical Magazines Ltd., Queensway House, 2 Queensway, Redhill, Surrey RH1 1QS, England. TEL 0737-768611. FAX 0737-761939. Ed. K. Murrell. adv. circ. 5,000.
—BLDSC shelfmark: 6604.015000.
Incorporates (in vol.3, 1985): Tooling and Machining.

METALLURGY

PREVISIONS GLISSANTES DETAILLEES EN PERSPECTIVES SECTORIELLES (VOL.8): FONDERIE ET TRANSFORMATION DES METAUX. see *BUSINESS AND ECONOMICS — Economic Situation And Conditions*

PREVISIONS GLISSANTES DETAILLEES EN PERSPECTIVES SECTORIELLES (VOL.15): SIDERUGIE ET PREMIERE TRANSFORMATION DE L'ACIER. see *BUSINESS AND ECONOMICS — Economic Situation And Conditions*

PREVISIONS GLISSANTES DETAILLEES EN PERSPECTIVES SECTORIELLES (VOL.16): INDUSTRIE DES NON-FERREUX. see *BUSINESS AND ECONOMICS — Economic Situation And Conditions*

660 546   PL
PROBLEMY PROJEKTOWE PRZEMYSLU I BUDOWNICTWA. 1953. q. 200000 Zl. Biuro Projektow Przemyslu Hutniczego - Biprohut, Ul. Dubois 16, 44-100 Gliwice, Poland. TEL 31-60-11. TELEX 036227 PL. Ed. Ryszard Gorczynski. adv.; bk.rev.; index; circ. 1,800. (back issues avail.)
Formerly: Problemy Projektowe (ISSN 0239-7404)
Description: For engineers, technicians, designers and constructors.

669   NE
PROCESS METALLURGY. 1978. irreg., vol.7, 1992. price varies. Elsevier Science Publishers B.V., Books Division, P.O. Box 211, 1000 AE Amsterdam, Netherlands. TEL 020-5803911. FAX 020-5803705. TELEX 18582 ESPA NL. (Subscr. in U.S. and Canada to: Elsevier Science Publishing Co., Inc., Box 882, Madison Sq. Sta., New York, NY 10159. TEL 212-989-5800) Eds. G.M. Ritcey, A.W. Ashbrook.
Refereed Serial

PRODUKTIONS NYTS LEVERANDOERREGISTER. see *MACHINERY*

669   US   ISSN 0033-1732
TA462   CODEN: PTNMAR
PROTECTION OF METALS. English translation of: Zashchita Metallov. 1964. bi-m. $1075 (foreign $1260)(effective 1992). (Russian Academy of Sciences, RU) Plenum Publishing Corp., Consultants Bureau, 233 Spring St., New York, NY 10013-1578. TEL 212-620-8468. FAX 212-463-0742. TELEX 23-421139. Ed. Ya.M. Kolotyrkin. (also avail. in microfilm from JSC; back issues avail.) **Indexed:** Chem.Titles, Corros.Abstr., Energy Res.Abstr., Eng.Ind., ISMEC.
—BLDSC shelfmark: 0420.520000.
Refereed Serial

669   PL   ISSN 0209-3413
PRZEGLAD DOKUMENTACYJNY OBROBKI PLASTYCZNEJ. 1965. 6/yr. 50000 Zl. (typically set in Jan.). Instytut Obrobki Plastycznej, Branzowy Osrodek Informacji Naukowej, Technicznej i Ekonomicznej, Ul. Zamenhofa 4, 61-120 Poznan, Poland. TEL 77-10-81. FAX 79-16-82. TELEX 0413480 INOP PL. bk.rev.

671.2   PL   ISSN 0033-2275
TS200   CODEN: PRZOAB
PRZEGLAD ODLEWNICTWA. (Text in Polish; summaries in English, German and Russian) 1951. m. $26. Wydawnictwo Czasopism i Ksiazek Technicznych SIGMA - NOT, Ul. Biala 4, P.O. Box 1004, 00-950 Warsaw, Poland. (Dist. by: Zaklad Kolportazu SIGMA-NOT, ul. Bartycka 20, P.O. Box 1004, 00-950 Warsaw, Poland) adv.; bk.rev.; abstr.; charts; illus.; pat.; index; circ. 1,000. **Indexed:** B.C.I.R.A., C.I.S. Abstr., Chem.Abstr., Met.Abstr., World Alum.Abstr.

669   HU   ISSN 0324-4679
TN600   CODEN: PTUBDW
PUBLICATIONS OF THE TECHNICAL UNIVERSITY FOR HEAVY INDUSTRY. SERIES B, METALLURGY. (Text in English, German, Russian) irreg., vol.37, no.3, 1989. Nehezipari Muszaki Egyetem, Miskolc, Hungary. TEL 46-65111. FAX 46-69554. TELEX 62223-NMEMIS. Ed.Bd. bibl.; index; circ. 300. **Indexed:** Met.Abstr.
—BLDSC shelfmark: 7113.412000.

669   FR
R F M. (Revue Francaise des Metallurgistes) 1965. 10/yr. 435 F. 46 rue St. Anne, 75002 Paris, France. Ed. A. Willemetz. adv.; bk.rev.; circ. 2,650. **Indexed:** Chem.Abstr., Met.Abstr., World Alum.Abstr.
Incorporates: Metaux Deformations.

669 622   US
R I C INSIGHT. 1988. m. $300. Rare-earth Information Center, Institute for Physical Research and Technology, Iowa State University, 255 Spedding Hall, Ames, IA 50011-3020. TEL 515-294-2272. FAX 515-294-3709. TELEX 269 266. Ed. Karl A. Gscheidner, Jr. circ. 250.
Description: Covers current developments and trends in the science and technology of rare earth minerals, with emphasis on applications and commercialization of these materials.

669 622   US
R I C NEWS. 1966. q. free. Rare-earth Information Center, Institute for Physical Research and Technology, Iowa State University, 255 Spedding Hall, Ames, IA 50011-3020. TEL 515-294-2272. FAX 515-294-3709. TELEX 269 266. Ed. Karl A. Gscheidner, Jr. bk.rev.; bibl.; illus.; circ. 10,200.
●Also available online.
Description: Emphasizes research and business news in the areas of metallurgy and physics of rare earth metals, alloy, and compounds.

669   UK   ISSN 0143-4861
R L J: ROSKILL'S LETTER FROM JAPAN. 1976. m. £140($250) Roskill Information Services Ltd., 2 Clapham Rd., London SW9 0JA, England. TEL 071-582-5155. FAX 071-793-0008. index; circ. 75. (back issues avail.)

669   UK   ISSN 0307-8531
QD172.R2
RARE EARTH BULLETIN. 1973. bi-m. £141 (foreign £152). Multi-Science Publishing Co. Ltd., 107 High St., Brentwood, Essex CM14 4RX, England. TEL 0277-224632. FAX 0277-224632. Ed. Carolyn Kirby. index. (back issues avail.)
Description: Covers work on the lanthanides, yttrium and scandium.

669   JA
RARE METAL NEWS. (Text in Japanese) 1955. w. 50000 Yen($350) Arumu Shuppansha, 5-6, 2-chome, Hongo, Bunkyo-ku, Tokyo 113, Japan. TEL 03-814-1009. Ed. Megumi Hiramatsu. circ. 5,000.

669   CC   ISSN 1001-0521
TN758
RARE METALS. Chinese edition: Xiyou Jinshu (ISSN 0258-7076) (Text in English) 1982. q. $60. Zhongguo Youse Jinshu Xuehui - Chinese Society of Nonferrous Metal, 2 Xinjiekouwai Dajie, Room 603, Beijing 100088, People's Republic of China. TEL 2014488. FAX 2015019. Ed. Yang Yinghui. adv.
Description: Devoted to experimental and theoretical developments in metallurgy, characterization and applications of rare metals and alloys, with particular emphasis on semiconductor applications.

669   US   ISSN 0950-8198
RAW MATERIALS FOR THE REFACTORIES INDUSTRY. irreg. (every 4-5 yrs.). $53. Metal Bulletin Inc., 220 Fifth Ave., 10th Fl., New York, NY 10001. TEL 800-638-2525. FAX 212-213-6273. Eds. B.M. Coope, E.M. Dickson.
Description: Comprised of twenty-one review articles on the world's metallurgy industries and the major minerals used.

REACTIVE POLYMERS. see *ENGINEERING — Chemical Engineering*

RECYCLING TODAY (SCRAP MARKET EDITION). see *ENVIRONMENTAL STUDIES — Waste Management*

669.6   GW
REFLEXIONEN; Verpackung und Umwelt. 1981. q. Informations-Zentrum Weissblech e.V., Kasernenstr. 36, 4000 Duesseldorf 1, Germany. FAX 0211-326217. TELEX 8581811-WAV-D. Ed. Max Wild. adv.; circ. 5,000. (back issues avail.)
Formerly: Weissblech Reflexionen.
Description: Covers tin, steel packaging, tinplate.

669   UK   ISSN 0379-0002
    CODEN: RMPCDH
REVIEWS ON POWDER METALLURGY & PHYSICAL CERAMICS. 1979. 4/yr. £105 (effective 1992). Elsevier Science Publishers Ltd., Crown House, Linton Rd., Barking, Essex IG11 8JU, England. TEL 081-594-7272. FAX 081-594-5942. TELEX 896950 APPSCI G. (Subscr. in U.S. and Canada to: Elsevier Science Publishing Co., Inc., Box 882, Madison Sq. Sta., New York, NY 10159. TEL 212-989-5800) Ed. C.A. Brookes. adv.: B&W page £345; 192 x 258; adv. contact: Claire Coakley. bk.rev.; index. (back issues avail.) **Indexed:** Br.Ceram.Abstr., Chem.Abstr., Met.Abstr., World Alum.Abstr.
—BLDSC shelfmark: 7794.134000.
Formerly: Reviews on Powder Metallurgy (ISSN 0334-2344)
Description: Reviews current research and development in powder metallurgy and physical ceramics, for scientists, engineers and researchers in this field.
Refereed Serial

669   SP   ISSN 0034-8570
TN600   CODEN: RMTGAC
REVISTA DE METALURGIA. (Text in Spanish; summaries in English) 1965. bi-m. 10000 ptas. (effective 1992). Centro Nacional de Investigaciones Metalurgicas, Avda. Gregorio del Amo, 8, 28040 Madrid, Spain. FAX 341-5347425. Ed. J. Fernandez. adv.; bk.rev.; abstr.; index; circ. 2,500. (also avail. in microfilm; back issues avail.) **Indexed:** Anal.Abstr., Cadscan, Chem.Abstr., Chem.Eng.Abstr., Ind.SST, Int.Aerosp.Abstr., Lead Abstr., Met.Abstr., T.C.E.A., World Alum.Abstr., Zincscan.
—BLDSC shelfmark: 7865.800000.

620.112   SP   ISSN 0210-6604
    CODEN: RCPRDQ
REVISTA IBEROAMERICANA DE CORROSION Y PROTECCION. (Text in English, Portuguese, Spanish) 1970. bi-m. 900 ptas.($69) per no. Instituto de Corrosion y Proteccion, Claudio Coello, 20-5-D, 28001 Madrid, Spain. FAX 91-4313291. Ed. Miguel A. Guillen Rodrigo. adv.; bk.rev.; bibl.; charts; illus.; circ. 8,000. **Indexed:** Met.Abstr., World Alum.Abstr.
—BLDSC shelfmark: 7858.815000.
Formerly: Corrosion y Proteccion (ISSN 0045-8678)

669   CU
REVISTA TECNOLOGIA: MINERIA Y METALURGIA. s-a. $12. (Ministerio de la Industria Basica) Ediciones Cubanas, Obispo No. 461, Apdo. 605, Havana, Cuba. TEL 32-5556-60.

669   FR
TN2   CODEN: CITMDA
REVUE DE METALLURGIE. CAHIERS D'INFORMATION TECHNIQUES. (Text in French; summaries in English) 1904. m. Revue de Metallurgie, Elysees la Defense, 19 le Parvis Cedex 35, 92072 Paris La Defense, France. TEL 47-67-87-11. FAX 47-67-85-77. TELEX 611672 SISYNDL. adv.; bk.rev.; abstr.; bibl.; charts; pat.; index; circ. 5,245. **Indexed:** Appl.Mech.Rev., Cadscan, Chem.Abstr., Curr.Cont., Eng.Ind., Ergon.Abstr., Excerp.Med., Fuel & Energy Abstr., INIS Atomind., Lead Abstr., Met.Abstr., World Alum.Abstr., Zincscan.
Formerly: Revue de Metallurgie (ISSN 0035-1563); Incorporates: Centre de Documentation Siderurgique. Circulaire d'Informations (ISSN 0008-963X)

669   FR   ISSN 0245-8292
TN2   CODEN: MESMDJ
REVUE DE METALLURGIE. MEMOIRES ET ETUDES SCIENTIFIQUES. Title varies: Memoires et Etudes Scientifiques de la Revue de Metallurgie. (Text in French; summaries in English, French, German, Spanish) 1904. m. Revue de Metallurgie, 5 rue Paul Cezanne, 75008 Paris, France. adv.; bk.rev.; abstr.; bibl.; charts; illus.; index. **Indexed:** Appl.Mech.Rev., Art & Archaeol.Tech.Abstr., Cadscan, Chem.Abstr., Eng.Ind., Ind.Sci.Rev., Int.Aerosp.Abstr., Lead Abstr., Met.Abstr., Sci.Abstr., World Alum.Abstr., Zincscan.
Formerly: Revue de Metallurgie. Memoires Scientifiques (ISSN 0025-9128)

051   US   ISSN 0192-9569
REYNOLDS REVIEW. q. Reynolds Metals Company, 6601 W. Broad St., Richmond, VA 23230. TEL 804-281-2660. Ed. Frances A. Schools. circ. 30,750. (back issues avail.)

669   DK   ISSN 0108-8599
RISOE INTERNATIONAL SYMPOSIUM ON METALLURGY AND MATERIALS SCIENCE. PROCEEDINGS. 1980. a. DKK 400. Risoe National Laboratory, P.O. Box 49, DK-4000 Roskilde, Denmark.
—BLDSC shelfmark: 6848.967000.

671.3   IT   ISSN 0391-4631
RIVISTA DI MECCANICA INTERNATIONAL EDITION. (Text in English) bi-m. L.62000 (foreign L.95000). Etas s.r.l., Via Mecenate 91, 20138 Milan, Italy. TEL 02-580841. FAX 02-5064867. Ed. Sergio Oltolini.
 Formerly: I.M.E.
 Description: Italian suppliers to the metalworking industry in the world.

RUDARSKO-METALURSKI ZBORNIK/MINING AND METALLURGY QUARTERLY. see *MINES AND MINING INDUSTRY*

669 622   YU   ISSN 0350-2627
RUDARSTVO - GEOLOGIJA - METALURGIJA. (Supplement to: Tehnika) (Text in Serbo-Croatian; summaries in English, Russian) vol.27, 1976. m. $50. Savez Inzenjera i Tehnicara Jugoslavije, Kneza Milosa 9, Box 187, 11000 Belgrade, Yugoslavia. Ed. Dejan Milovanovic. **Indexed:** Met.Abstr.

669   PL   ISSN 0035-9696
       CODEN: RMNZA5
RUDY I METALE NIEZELAZNE. (Text in Polish; summaries in English, French, German, Russian) 1956. m. $162. (Polish Nonferrous Metals Institute) Wydawnictwo Naczelnej Organizacji Technicznej "Sigma", Ul. Dabrowskiego 23, 40-032 Katowice, Poland. (Dist. by: Ars Polona- Ruch, Krakowskie Przedmiescie 7, Warsaw, Poland) Ed. Marian Zatcher. adv.; bk.rev.; abstr.; charts; illus.; mkt.; index; circ. 1,100. **Indexed:** Ceram.Abstr., Chem.Abstr., Copper Abstr., Met.Abstr., World Alum.Abstr.
 Description: Explores mining, ore geology and dressing, metallurgy of nonferrous metals (mainly Zn, Pb, Cu, Ag, Al) and roll mills.

669   US   ISSN 0036-0295
       CODEN: RMLYAQ
RUSSIAN METALLURGY. English translation of: Akademiya Nauk S.S.S.R. Metally. 1962. bi-m. $875. Allerton Press, Inc., 150 Fifth Ave., New York, NY 10011. TEL 212-924-3950. Ed. A.F. Belov. charts; illus.; index. **Indexed:** Cadscan, Curr.Cont., Excerp.Med., Lead Abstr., Met.Abstr., Sci.Abstr., World Alum.Abstr., Zincscan.
—BLDSC shelfmark: 0420.769000.
 Former titles: Russian Metallurgy and Fuels; Russian Metallurgy and Mining.

671 669   UK   ISSN 0080-505X
RYLAND'S DIRECTORY. a. £70. Guardian Communications Ltd., Albany House, Hurst St., Birmingham B5 4BD, England. TEL 021-622-4011. FAX 021-625-3564. TELEX 948669-TOPJNL-G. adv.
 Description: List of engineering companies, engineers' products and services, plus stockholders in the UK.

669.1   PH   ISSN 0129-5721
TS300   CODEN: SEQUDV
S E A I S I QUARTERLY JOURNAL. (Text in English) 1972. q. $50 in Asia, Pacific and the Middle East; elsewhere $55. South East Asia Iron and Steel Institute, Ortigas Bldg., 5th Fl., Ortigas Ave., Pasig, Metro Manila 1600, Philippines. TEL 02-6315782. FAX 02-6315781. TELEX 29084-SEAISI-PH. (Subscr. to: P.O. Box 7759, Airmail Distribution Center, NAIA, 1300 Pasay City, Philippines) Ed. Richard M. Johns. circ. 1,200. (back issues avail.) **Indexed:** B.C.I.R.A., Chem.Abstr., Corros.Abstr., Met.Abstr., World Alum.Abstr.
—BLDSC shelfmark: 8213.725000.

669   SZ
S M U V ZEITUNG. vol.72, 1973. w. 44 Fr. Schweizerischer Metall- und Uhrenarbeitnehmer-Verband - Federation Suisse des Travailleurs de la Metallurgie et de l'Horlogerie, Postfach 272, CH-3000 Bern 15, Switzerland. FAX 031-435501. TELEX 912411. adv.; bk.rev.; charts; illus.; circ. 60,002. (newspaper)

669   DK   ISSN 0371-0459
TN1   CODEN: SJMLAG
SCANDINAVIAN JOURNAL OF METALLURGY. (Text in English) 1971. 6/yr. DKK 1340. Munksgaard International Publishers Ltd., 35 Noerre Soegade, P.O. Box 2148, DK-1016 Copenhagen K, Denmark. TEL 33-127030. FAX 33-129387. TELEX 19431-MUNKS-DK. Ed. J.O. Edstroem. bk.rev.; circ. 600. **Indexed:** Soils & Fert.
—BLDSC shelfmark: 8087.517500.

669   GW   ISSN 0933-8330
SCHMIEDE JOURNAL. 1988. s-a. DM.30. Industrieverband Deutscher Schmieden e.V., Informationsstelle Schmiedestueck-Verwaltung, Goldene Pforte 1, 5800 Hagen 1, Germany. TEL 02331-958828. FAX 02331-51046. Ed. Werner Adlof. adv.; bk.rev.; circ. 6,000.

669 666   YU   ISSN 0350-820X
TN695   CODEN: SCSNB4
SCIENCE OF SINTERING. (Text in English; summaries in Russian, Serbo-Croatian) 1969. 3/yr. $83 (effective Jan. 1991). Committee for Etan, Kneza Milosa 9, 11000 Belgrade, Yugoslavia. TEL 637-239. FAX 182825. TELEX 72593 SANY JU. (Subscr. to: Jugoslovenska Knjiga, Export Dept., Trg Repulike 5-VIII, 11000 Belgrade, Yugoslavia) (Co-sponsor: Serbian Academy of Sciences and Arts) Ed. M.M. Ristic. adv.; bk.rev.; circ. 700. (back issues avail.) **Indexed:** Br.Ceram.Abstr., Chem.Abstr., Eng.Ind., Met.Abstr., Nucl.Sci.Abstr., Sci.Abstr., World Alum.Abstr.
—BLDSC shelfmark: 8164.278000.
 Formerly: Physics of Sintering (ISSN 0031-9198)
 Description: Provides a suitable medium for the publication of papers on theoretical and experimental studies.

SCRAP PROCESSING AND RECYCLING. see *CONSERVATION*

669   US   ISSN 0956-716X
TN1   CODEN: SCRMEX
SCRIPTA METALLURGICA ET MATERIALIA. 1967. 12/yr. $365. Pergamon Press, Inc., Journals Division, 660 White Plains Rd., Tarrytown, NY 10591-5153. TEL 914-524-9200. FAX 914-333-2444. (And: Headington Hill Hall, Oxford OX3 0BW, England. TEL 0865-794141) Ed. John P. Hirth. adv.; bk.rev.; bibl.; charts; illus.; stat.; circ. 1,600. (also avail. in microform from MIM,UMI; back issues avail.) **Indexed:** ASCA, Biol.Abstr., Cadscan, Chem.Abstr., Curr.Cont., Eng.Ind., Int.Aerosp.Abstr., Lead Abstr., Met.Abstr., Phys.Ber., Sci.Abstr., World Alum.Abstr., Zincscan.
—BLDSC shelfmark: 8213.151000.
 Formerly (until 1990): Scripta Metallurgica (ISSN 0036-9748)
 Description: Publishes papers advancing the understanding of the physical properties of materials, including metals, alloys, ceramics, polymers, and glasses.
 Refereed Serial

SEARCHER. see *LABOR UNIONS*

661.072   BE
SELENIUM - TELLURIUM DEVELOPMENT ASSOCIATION. BULLETIN. irreg. (3-4/yr.) free. Selenium - Tellurium Development Association, 301 Borgstraat, B-1850 Grimbergen, Belgium. TEL 322-252-1490. FAX 322-252-2775. Ed. Yves Palmieri. circ. 2,000.
 Description: Promote knowledge about applications of selenium and tellurium in metallurgy, pharmaceuticals, feed additives, pigments, chemicals and electronics.

669   CC   ISSN 0253-2344
SHANGHAI JINSHU. (Text in Chinese) bi-m. Shanghai Jinshu Xuehui - Shanghai Metal Association, 1114 Dingsi Lu, Shanghai 200050, People's Republic of China. TEL 2512527.

669   CC   ISSN 1001-2125
SHANGHAI JINSHU (YOUSE FENCE). (Text in Chinese) bi-m. Shanghai Youse Jinshu Xiehui - Shanghai Nonferrous Metal Society, P.O. Box 600-402, Shanghai 201600, People's Republic of China. TEL 7811812. Ed. Guan Dagao.

669   AT   ISSN 0818-1764
SHEET METAL AUSTRALIA. 1986. bi-m. Aus.$28. Thomson Publications Australia, 47 Chippen St., Chippendale, N.S.W. 2008, Australia. TEL 02-699-2411. FAX 02-698-3920. TELEX 122226. Ed. Kate O'Donnell. adv.; circ. 4,240.

METALLURGY   3419

669   UK   ISSN 0305-7798
TS250
SHEET METAL INDUSTRIES YEAR BOOK. a. £46. International Business & Technical Magazines Ltd., Queensways House, 2 Queensway, Redhill, Surrey RH1 1QS, England. TEL 0737-768611. FAX 0737-761989. Ed. G. Lloyd. adv.; bibl.; index.

SHIGEN SOZAI/MINING AND MATERIALS PROCESSING INSTITUTE OF JAPAN. JOURNAL. see *MINES AND MINING INDUSTRY*

669.142   BL
SIDERURGIA BRASILEIRA. RELATORIO DE DIRETORIA. (Text in English) 1973. a. free. Siderurgia Brasileira S.A., Setor de Autarquias sul, Quadra 2, Bloco E, 70070 Brazil. FAX 061-226-5844. TELEX 061-1542. stat.; circ. 5,000.

669   CL
SIDERURGIA LATINOAMERICANA. (Text in Portuguese and Spanish; summaries in English) 1960. m. $56. Instituto Latinoamericano del Fierro y el Acero, Casilla 16065, Santiago 9, Chile. Ed. Jorge Ramirez. adv.; bk.rev.; bibl.; charts; illus.; index; circ. 6,000. (also avail. in microform from UMI; reprint service avail. from UMI) **Indexed:** Chem.Abstr., Met.Abstr., World Alum.Abstr.
 Formerly: Revista Latinoamericana de Siderurgia (ISSN 0034-9798)

SILVER INSTITUTE LETTER; information on silver for industry. see *MINES AND MINING INDUSTRY*

669.23 336   US   ISSN 0066-4332
SILVER MARKET. 1916. a. free. Handy and Harman, 850 Third Ave., New York, NY 10022. TEL 212-752-3400. FAX 212-207-2614. Ed. Stephen Mudd. circ. 10,000. **Indexed:** SRI.

SINDACATO MODERNO. see *LABOR UNIONS*

669   CS   ISSN 0037-6825
       CODEN: SLEVAK
SLEVARENSTVI/FOUNDRY INDUSTRY; casopis pro slevarensky prumysl. (Text in Czech; summaries in English, French, German, Russian) 1953. m. $56.70. (Federalni Ministerstvo Hutnictvi, Strojirenstvi a Elektrotechniky) Nakladatelstvi Technicke Literatury, Spalena 51, 113 02 Prague 1, Czechoslovakia. (Dist. by: Artia, Ve Smeckach 30, 111 27 Prague 1, Czechoslovakia) Ed. O. Shromazdil. abstr.; bibl.; charts; illus.; circ. 2,900. **Indexed:** B.C.I.R.A., C.I.S. Abstr., Chem.Abstr., Met.Abstr., World Alum.Abstr.

669   US
SOURCE JOURNALS IN METALS AND MATERIALS. 1981. biennial. $70. (Institute of Metals, UK) A S M International, Materials Information, Materials Park, OH 44073. TEL 216-338-5151. FAX 216-338-4634. TELEX 980-619. (UK addr.: Institute of Metals, Materials Information, 1 Carlton House Terr., London SW1Y 5DB, England. TEL 071-839-4071)
 Formerly: Source Journals in Metallurgy.

669   US
SOURCES (RICHMOND HEIGHTS). 1962. a. $35. Precision Metal Forming Association, 27027 Chardon Rd., Richmond Heights, OH 44143. TEL 216-585-8800. adv.; circ. 12,000.
 Former titles: Sources for Stamping; (until 1979): Metal Stamping Buyer's Guide.

SOUTH AFRICAN INSTITUTE OF ASSAYERS AND ANALYSTS. JOURNAL. see *MINES AND MINING INDUSTRY*

METALLURGY

669 622   SA   ISSN 0038-223X
CODEN: JSAMAP
SOUTH AFRICAN INSTITUTE OF MINING AND METALLURGY. JOURNAL. 1894. m. R.120. South African Institute of Mining and Metallurgy - Suid-Afrikaanse Instituut vir Mynbou en Metallurgie, P.O. Box 61127, Marshalltown 2107, South Africa. TEL 011-834-1273. FAX 011-838-5923. TELEX 4-86431. Ed. H. Glen. adv.; bk.rev.; bibl.; charts; illus.; index, cum.index: vols. 35-54 (July 1935-June 1954); circ. 3,800. (also avail. in microform from UMI; reprint service avail. from UMI) **Indexed:** AESIS, Anal.Abstr., Appl.Mech.Rev., C.I.S. Abstr., Cadscan, Chem.Abstr., Chem.Eng.Abstr., Curr.Cont., Energy Info.Abstr., Eng.Ind., Ergon.Abstr., GeoRef., HRIS, Ind.S.A.Per., INIS Atomind., Lead Abstr., Met.Abstr., T.C.E.A., W.R.C.Inf., World Alum.Abstr., Zincscan.
—BLDSC shelfmark: 4901.500000.
Refereed Serial

669 622   SA
SOUTH AFRICAN INSTITUTE OF MINING AND METALLURGY. MONOGRAPH SERIES. 1978. irreg. price varies. South African Institute of Mining and Metallurgy - Suid-Afrikaanse Instituut vir Mynbou en Metallurgie, P.O. Box 61127, Marshallton 2107, South Africa. TEL 011-834-1273. FAX 011-838-5923. TELEX 4-86431. **Indexed:** GeoRef.

669   US   ISSN 0891-0316
TS200
SOVIET CASTINGS TECHNOLOGY. English translation of: Liteinoe Proizvodstvo (UR ISSN 0024-449X) 1986. m. $535. (Soviet Machine Tool Industry and Scientific-Technical Society for the Engineering Industry, UR) Allerton Press, Inc., 150 Fifth Ave., New York, NY 10011. TEL 212-924-3950.
—BLDSC shelfmark: 0421.390000.

669   US   ISSN 0038-5484
TN758
SOVIET JOURNAL OF NON-FERROUS METALS. English translation of: Tsvetnye Metally (UR ISSN 0041-4891) 1960. m. $398. (Ministerstvo Tsvetnoi Metallurgii, UR) Primary Sources, Box 472, Cooper Sta., New York, NY 10276. TEL 212-254-8748. Ed. R.L. Toby. charts; illus.; index. **Indexed:** Met.Abstr., World Alum.Abstr.

671.37   US   ISSN 0038-5735
CODEN: SPMCAV
SOVIET POWDER METALLURGY AND METAL CERAMICS. English translation of: Poroshkovaya Metallurgiya. 1962. m. $1075 (foreign $1260)(effective 1992). (Ukrainian Academy of Sciences, KR) Plenum Publishing Corp., Consultants Bureau, 233 Spring St., New York, NY 10013-1578. TEL 212-620-8468. FAX 212-463-0742. TELEX 23-421139. Ed. V.I. Trefilov. (also avail. in microfilm from JSC; back issues avail.) **Indexed:** Chem.Titles, Curr.Cont., Energy Res.Abstr., Eng.Ind., INSPEC, ISMEC, Met.Abstr., Solid St.Abstr.
—BLDSC shelfmark: 0425.620000.

669   II
SPOTLIGHT BHILAI. (Text in English) fortn. free. Steel Authority of India Ltd., Bhilai Steel Plant, Bhilai 490001 (M.P.), India. Ed. Pradip Singh. circ. 30,000.

669.1   DK
STAALET. 10/yr. Foreningen af Vaerkstedsfunktionaerer i Jernindusttrien i Danmark, Kronprinsessegade 20, 1306 Copenhagen K, Denmark. Ed. Poul Andersen. adv.; circ. 17,500.

669.1   GW   ISSN 0340-4803
STAHL UND EISEN; Zeitschrift fuer die Herstellung und Verarbeitung von Eisen und Stahl. (Text in German; contents page in English) 1881. 12/yr. DM.345. (Verein Deutscher Eisenhuettenleute) Verlag Stahleisen mbH, Sohnstr. 65, Postfach 105164, 4000 Duesseldorf 1, Germany. TEL 0211-6707-0. Ed. D. Springorum. adv.; bk.rev.; bibl.; charts; illus.; mkt.; pat.; stat.; tr.lit.; index; circ. 8,000. **Indexed:** Appl.Mech.Rev., ASCA, B.C.I.R.A., C.I.S. Abstr., Ceram.Abstr., Chem.Abstr., Corros.Abstr., Curr.Cont., Eng.Ind., Excerp.Med., ISMEC, Key to Econ.Sci., Met.Abstr., Phys.Abstr., Risk Abstr., World Alum.Abstr.
—BLDSC shelfmark: 8427.000000.

STAHLBAU - NACHRICHTEN. see *BUILDING AND CONSTRUCTION*

STAHLBAU - RUNDSCHAU - MITTEILUNGEN. see *BUILDING AND CONSTRUCTION*

669   GW
STAHLBERATUNG. 1976. 5/yr. DM.48. Ministerium fuer Erzbau, Metallurgie und Kali Stahlberatungsstelle, Agricolastr. 24, 9200 Freiberg, Germany. **Indexed:** Chem.Abstr.

669.142   GW
STAHLMARKT; Informationen ueber Erzeugnisse aus Stahl und anderen Werkstoffen. 1951. m. DM.132 (foreign DM.143). Montan- und Wirtschaftsverlag GmbH, Postfach 111253, 6000 Frankfurt a.M. 11, Germany. TEL 069-299070. FAX 02101-602541. Ed. Hans-Heinrich Eichler. adv.; bk.rev.; illus.; stat.; index; circ. 7,900. **Indexed:** Key to Econ.Sci., Met.Abstr., World Alum.Abstr.
Former titles: Contintentaler Stahlmarkt (ISSN 0010-7743); Contintentaler Eisenhandel.

669.1   SA   ISSN 0038-917X
STAINLESS STEEL. (Text in English) 1965. bi-m. free. Southern Africa Stainless Steel Development Association, P.O. Box 4479, Rivonia 2128, South Africa. TEL 011-803-5610. FAX 011-803-2011. Ed. Jan Lancaster. adv.; bk.rev.; charts; illus.; circ. 9,500 (controlled).
Description: Includes technical articles, association news, company profiles, new products.

669.1   SA
STAINLESS STEEL BUYER'S GUIDE (YEAR). (Text in English) a. free. Southern Africa Stainless Steel Development Association, P.O. Box 4479, Rivonia 2128, South Africa. TEL 011-803-5610. FAX 011-803-2011. Ed. Jan Lancaster. adv.; circ. 4,000 (controlled).
Description: Provides company and product profiles and technical data for the stainless steel industry.

669   US   ISSN 0953-7228
STAINLESS STEEL DATABOOK. 1957. irreg., latest 1991. $144. Metal Bulletin Inc., 220 Fifth Ave., 10th Fl., New York, NY 10001. TEL 800-638-2525. FAX 212-213-6273. Eds. Henry Cooke, Richard Serjeantson. adv.
Supersedes: Stainless Steel: An International Survey and Directory; Formerly: Stainless Steel: An International Directory (ISSN 0143-5442)
Description: Directory of international stainless steel producers, processors and traders with data on world refining plants.

669.142   UK
STAINLESS STEEL DIRECTORY. 1975. biennial. £15. Modern Metals Publications Ltd., 5 Pond St., Hampstead London NW3 2PN, England. Ed. F.W.S. Russell. adv.; circ. 700.
Formerly: Directory of the Stainless Steel Industry.

669.142   UK   ISSN 0306-2988
CODEN: SSTID6
STAINLESS STEEL INDUSTRY. 1973. bi-m. £24. Modern Metals Publications Ltd., 5 Pond St., Hampstead, London NW3 2PN, England. Ed. F.W.S. Russell. adv.; bk.rev.; circ. 4,000. (back issues avail.) **Indexed:** Chem.Abstr., Met.Abstr., World Alum.Abstr.
—BLDSC shelfmark: 8430.120000.

669   AT
STAINLESS STEEL SCOPE. 1971. 2/yr. free. Dickson and Johnson Pty. Ltd., 327-341 Chisholm Rd., Auburn, N.S.W. 2144, Australia. Ed. Wendy Huggard. illus.; tr.lit.; circ. 2,000 (controlled).

669.142   US
STAINLESS STEELS DIGEST. 1976. m. $145 to non-members (foreign $155); members $120 (foreign $130). A S M International, Materials Information, Materials Park, OH 44073. TEL 216-338-5151. FAX 216-338-4634. TELEX 980-619. (UK addr.: Institute of Metals, Materials Information, 1 Carlton House Terr., London SW1Y 5DB, England. TEL 071-839-4071) Ed. H. David Chafe. **Indexed:** Met.Abstr.
Description: Covers austenitic, martensitic and ferritic stainless steels.

669.1   RU   ISSN 0038-920X
TS300   CODEN: STALAQ
STAL'. 1931. m. 21.60 Rub. (Nauchno-Tekhnicheskoe Obshchestvo Chernoi Metallurgii) Izdatel'stvo Metallurgiya, 2-i Obydenskii Per., 14, Moscow G-34, Russia. (Dist. by: Mezhdunarodnaya Kniga, Moscow, G-200, Russia) (Co-sponsor: Ministerstvo Chernoi Metallurgii) Ed. S.V. Colpacov. adv.; bk.rev.; charts; illus.; index; circ. 10,020. **Indexed:** Chem.Abstr., Eng.Ind., Met.Abstr., Ref.Zh.
—BLDSC shelfmark: 0166.740000.

669 621   US   ISSN 1043-5093
STAMPING QUARTERLY. 1989. q. $15 (Canada $25; elsewhere $45); free to qualified personnel. Croydon Group, Ltd. (Subsidiary of: Fabricators & Manufacturers Association, International), 5411 E. State St., Rockford, IL 61108-2392. TEL 815-399-8700. FAX 815-399-7279. Ed. Kathy Velasco. adv.: B&W page $2070; trim 8 1/4 x 10 3/4; adv. contact: Dyan Larson. circ. 35,890.
Description: Disseminates news and information relating to the metal stamping industry. Contains articles and news releases designed to assist owners, managers, manufacturing engineers, supervisors and foremen in the evaluation of new methods and techniques.

669.1   II
STEEL BULLETIN. English edition added title: Panorama (Bhilai). Hindi edition added title: Bhilai Darshan. (English and Hindi editions alternate, each published once a month.) s-m. free. Steel Authority of India Ltd., Bhilai Steel Plant, Bhilai 490001 (M.P.), India. Ed. Pradip Singh.

STEEL CONSTRUCTION. see *BUILDING AND CONSTRUCTION*

STEEL CONSTRUCTION. see *BUILDING AND CONSTRUCTION*

669   US
STEEL DIGEST. 1983. bi-m. free. Intersteel Technology, Inc., 3041 Shallowood Lane, Charlotte, NC 28277. TEL 704-542-8210. FAX 704-542-5107. Ed. John A. Vallomy. circ. 700. (back issues avail.)
Description: Examines continuous steelmaking process; reports on development and new technologies in international steelmaking industry.

669.1   UK   ISSN 0038-9218
STEEL IN THE U S S R. (Includes articles from: "Izvestiya Vysshikh Uchebnykh Zavedenii. Chernaya Metallurgiya" & "Stal'") 1971. m. £357($839) to non-members; members £299($627). Institute of Materials, 1 Carlton House Terrace, London SW1 5DB, England. TEL 071-839-4071. FAX 071-839-2078. TELEX 8814813-METSOC-G. bibl.; charts; illus.; index; circ. 300. **Indexed:** ASCA, Ceram.Abstr., Chem.Abstr., Curr.Cont., Eng.Ind., Ergon.Abstr., Excerp.Med., Met.Abstr., World Alum.Abstr.
—BLDSC shelfmark: 0425.890100.
Supersedes (in 1971): Stal' in English (ISSN 0585-0282)
Description: Covers technical and scientific developments in ferrous metallurgy.

669   II   ISSN 0970-1311
CODEN: STINE8
STEEL INDIA. (Text in English) 1978. s-a. free. Steel Authority of India Ltd., R & D Centre for Iron & Steel, Ranchi 834 002, India. FAX 0651-300023. TELEX 0625-267. Ed. Sanak Mishra. abstr.; bibl.; charts; illus.; stat.; index; circ. 1,000.
Description: Technical journal covering the iron and steel industry in India. Provides a forum for exchange of knowledge between academicians and professionals.
Refereed Serial

669.142 613.62   EI
STEEL INDUSTRY SAFETY AND HEALTH COMMISSION. INFORMATION BULLETIN. irreg. free. Office for Official Publications of the European Communities, L-2985 Luxembourg, Luxembourg. (Dist. in the U.S. by: European Community Information Service, 2100 M St., Ste. 707, Washington, DC 20037)

METALLURGY 3421

669.1   UN   ISSN 0497-9478
JX1977
STEEL MARKET. French edition: Marche de l'Acier (ISSN 0497-9486); Russian edition: Rynok Produktsii Chernoi Metallurgii (ISSN 0255-5069) 1953. a. price varies. (Economic Commission for Europe (ECE)) United Nations Publications, Room DC2-0853, New York, NY 10017. TEL 212-963-8302, 212-963-3489. (Or: Distribution and Sales Section, Palais des Nations, 1211 Geneva 10, Switzerland) **Indexed:** IIS.
   Description: Provides trade information on iron and steel industry in Europe.

669.1   GW   ISSN 0177-4832
TS300   CODEN: STRSEY
STEEL RESEARCH - ARCHIV FUER DAS EISENHUETTENWESEN. 1927. m. DM.425. (Verein Deutscher Eisenhuettenleute) Verlag Stahleisen mbH, Sohnstr. 65, Postfach 105164, 4000 Duesseldorf 1, Germany. TEL 0211-6707-0. (Co-sponsor: Max-Planck-Institut fuer Eisenforschung) adv.; charts; illus.; index; circ. 1,150. (also avail. in microfilm from PMC) **Indexed:** Anal.Abstr., Appl.Mech.Rev., Chem.Abstr., Curr.Cont., Eng.Ind., Excerp.Med., GeoRef., Met.Abstr., Sci.Abstr., Sci.Cit.Ind., World Alum.Abstr.
   —BLDSC shelfmark: 8464.090400.
   Formerly: Archiv fuer das Eisenhuettenwesen (ISSN 0003-8962)

671   AT   ISSN 0310-7582
STEEL SPIEL. 1971. 5/yr. free. Dickson and Johnson Pty. Ltd., 327-341 Chisholm Rd., Auburn, N.S.W. 2144, Australia. Ed. Wendy Huggard. circ. 200 (controlled).

669.142   UK   ISSN 0953-2412
TS300
STEEL TECHNOLOGY INTERNATIONAL. a. Sterling Publications Ltd. (Subsidiary of: Sterling Publishing Group PLC), 86-88 Edgware Road, London W2 2YW, England. TEL 01-258-0066. Ed. Peter H. Scholes.
   —BLDSC shelfmark: 8464.103500.

669.1   UK   ISSN 0039-095X
TN1   CODEN: STLTA3
STEEL TIMES. 1866. m. £82.50 (foreign £109.20). F M J International Publications Ltd., Queensway House, 2 Queensway, Redhill, Surrey RH1 1QS, England. TEL 0737-768611. FAX 0737-761685. TELEX 948669-TOPJNL-G. Ed. Tim Smith. adv.; bk.rev.; abstr.; charts; mkt.; stat.; index. (also avail. in microform from UMI; reprint service avail. from UMI) **Indexed:** Br.Ceram.Abstr., Br.Tech.Ind., C.I.S. Abstr., Ceram.Abstr., Chem.Abstr., Eng.Ind., Excerp.Med., Fuel & Energy Abstr., Key to Econ.Sci., Met.Abstr., World Alum.Abstr.
   —BLDSC shelfmark: 8464.104000.

669.1 338.4   UK   ISSN 0143-7798
TN730   CODEN: STTIDD
STEEL TIMES INTERNATIONAL. 6/yr. £69.20 (foreign £86). F M J International Publications Ltd., Queensway House, 2 Queensway, Redhill, Surrey RH1 1QS, England. TEL 0737-768611. FAX 0737-761685. TELEX 948669-TOPJNL-G. Ed. B. Cooper. **Indexed:** C.I.S. Abstr., Cadscan, Chem.Abstr., ISMEC, Lead Abstr., Met.Abstr., World Alum.Abstr., Zincscan.
   —BLDSC shelfmark: 8464.105300.
   Incorporates: Iron and Steel International (ISSN 0308-9142); Which was formerly: Iron and Steel (ISSN 0021-1524)

669   JA
STEEL TODAY AND TOMORROW. (Text in English) 1973. 5/yr. free. Japan Iron and Steel Exporter's Association - Nihon Tekko Yushutsu Kumiai, c/o Tekko Kaikan, 3-2-10 Nihonbashi Kayaba-cho, Chuo-ku, Tokyo 103, Japan. Ed. Soichiro Yoshimura. **Indexed:** Met.Abstr., World Alum.Abstr.

669   US   ISSN 0308-8006
STEEL TRADERS OF THE WORLD. 1976. quadrennial, 5th ed., 1990. $188.40. Metal Bulletin Inc., 220 Fifth Ave., New York, NY 10001. TEL 212-213-6202. Ed. John Bailey. adv.
   Description: World listing of steel traders and products handled.

669.142   CN
STEEL WEST. q. Naylor Communications Ltd., 920 Yonge St., 6th fl., Toronto, Ont. M4W 3C7, Canada. (Subscr. to: 100 Sutherland Ave., Winnipeg, Man. R2W 3C7, Canada) circ. 10,000.

STEELABOR. see LABOR UNIONS

669.1 622 665.5   US
STEELMAKING CONFERENCE: PROCEEDINGS. 1928. a. $80 to non-members; members $40. Iron and Steel Society, 410 Commonwealth Dr., Warrendale, PA 15086. TEL 412-776-1535. FAX 412-776-0430. (back issues avail.) **Indexed:** Iron & Steel Indus.Pr.
   Former titles: Steelmaking Proceedings; American Institute of Mining, Metallurgical and Petroleum Engineers. National Open Hearth and Basic Oxygen Steel Division. Proceedings of the Conference.
   Description: For iron and steel makers.

671.2   NO   ISSN 0039-1824
          CODEN: STOEA7
STOPERITIDENDE. 1935. 6/yr. NOK 170. Norges Stoperitekniske Forening - Norwegian Foundry Technical Association, Box 7117 H, N-0307 Oslo 3, Norway. adv.; bk.rev.; abstr.; bibl.; charts; illus.; circ. 800. **Indexed:** B.C.I.R.A., Met.Abstr., World Alum.Abstr.
   —BLDSC shelfmark: 8466.310000.

STUDIES OF HIGH TEMPERATURE SUPERCONDUCTORS. see CHEMISTRY — Electrochemistry

669   JA   ISSN 0039-4963
          CODEN: SKEGA2
SUMITOMO KEIKINZOKU GIHO/SUMITOMO LIGHT METAL TECHNICAL REPORTS. (Text in English and Japanese) 1960. q. exchange basis. Sumitomo Light Metal Industries, Ltd., Technical Research Labratories - Sumitomo Keikinzoku Kogyo K. K., 3-1-12 Chitose, Minato-ku, Nagoya 455, Japan. Ed. Toshio Suzuki. adv.; charts; illus.; index; circ. 1,700. **Indexed:** Chem.Abstr., Copper Abstr., Curr.Cont., Eng.Ind., Met.Abstr., World Alum.Abstr.
   —BLDSC shelfmark: 8517.985000.

669   UK   ISSN 0267-0844
TA418.7   CODEN: SUENET
SURFACE ENGINEERING. 1985. q. £122($239) to non-members; members £70($134). Institute of Materials, 1 Carlton House Terrace, London SW1Y 5DB, England. TEL 071-839-4071. FAX 071-839-2078. TELEX 8144813-METSOC-G. Ed. Tom Bell. circ. 600. **Indexed:** B.C.I.R.A.
   —BLDSC shelfmark: 8547.850000.
   Incorporates: Surfacing Journal International (ISSN 0269-2848); Which superseded (1972-1986): Surfacing Journal (ISSN 0307-7365)
   Description: Developments in processes and techniques of surface engineering, and its industrial applications.

671.7   UK
SURFACE TREATMENT PLANT AND PROCESSES; bi-monthly international market service and product guide. 1965. bi-m. £145($285) Finishing Publications Ltd., 105 Whitney Drive, Stevenage, Hertfordshire SG1 4DF, England. TEL 0438-745115. FAX 0438-364536. Ed. A.T. Kuhn. adv.; bk.rev.; abstr.; illus.; pat.; tr.lit.; tr.mk.; index, cum.index; circ. 2,000. **Indexed:** World Surf.Coat.
   Former titles: Surface Treatment (ISSN 0950-5202); Metal Finishing Plant and Processes (ISSN 0026-0606); International Trade Literature Supplement of Metal Finishing Abstracts.
   Description: Provides a worldwide survey of new processes for finishing and surface treatment of metals and printed circuit production.

669.1   SW
SWEDISH STEEL MANUAL. (Text and summaries in English) 1962. irreg. SEK 130. Jernkontoret - Swedish Ironmasters' Association, Box 1721, S-111 87 Stockholm, Sweden. FAX 08-21-90-89. Ed. Hans von Delwig.

669.1   II   ISSN 0039-8411
T I S C O TECHNICAL JOURNAL. (Text in English) 1954. q. Rs.12($3) Tata Iron and Steel Co. Ltd., Jamshedpur 831001, Bihar, India. Ed. K. Banerjee. adv.; charts; illus.; index; circ. 1,500. **Indexed:** ABTICS, Chem.Abstr., Eng.Ind., Met.Abstr.

669 621   US   ISSN 1051-4120
TS280
▼**T P Q: THE TUBE & PIPE QUARTERLY.** 1990. q. $15 (Canada $25; elsewhere $45); free to qualified personnel. Croydon Group, Ltd. (Subsidiary of: Fabricators & Manufacturers Association, International), 5411 E. State St., Rockford, IL 61108-2392. TEL 815-399-8700. FAX 815-399-7279. Ed. Kathy Velasco. adv.: B&W page $2070; trim 8 1/4 x 10 3/4; adv. contact: Dyan Larson. circ. 31,381.
   Description: Contains news and information relating to the metal tube and pipe industry. Includes articles and news releases to assist owners, managers, manufacturing engineers, supervisors, and foremen in the evaluation of new methods and techniques.

669   JA   ISSN 0039-8993
          CODEN: TAKOAV
TAIKABUTSU/REFRACTORIES. (Text in Japanese) 1949. m. 15000 Yen. Technical Association of Refractories - Taikabutsu Gijutsu Kyokai, c/o New Ginza Bldg., 7-3-13 Ginza Chuo-ku, Tokyo 104, Japan. FAX 81-33572-0175. Ed. Tadashi Nishino. adv.; charts; illus.; stat.; circ. 2,500. **Indexed:** Br.Ceram.Abstr., Ceram.Abstr., Chem.Abstr., JTA.
   —BLDSC shelfmark: 8598.515000.

669   JA   ISSN 0285-0028
TAIKABUTSU OVERSEAS/REFRACTORIES OVERSEAS. (Text in English) 1981. q. 40000 Yen. Technical Association of Refractories - Taikabutsu Gijutsu Kyokai, c/o New Ginza Bldg., 7-3-13 Ginza Chuo-ku, Tokyo 104, Japan. FAX 81-33572-0175. Ed. Kazunori Kijima. adv.; illus.; charts; stat.; circ. 600.
   —BLDSC shelfmark: 8598.516000.

669   BE
TANTALUM-NIOBIUM INTERNATIONAL STUDY CENTER. QUARTERLY BULLETIN. 1974. q. free. Tantalum-Niobium International Study Center, 40 rue Washington, B-1050 Brussels, Belgium. TEL 02-649-5158. FAX 02-649-32-69. TELEX 65080 INAC B. circ. 1,000. (back issues avail.)

669   GW   ISSN 0082-1772
TASCHENBUCH DER GIESSEREI-PRAXIS. 1952. a. DM.52.80. Fachverlag Schiele und Schoen GmbH, Markgrafenstr. 11, 1000 Berlin 61, Germany. TEL 030-251-6029. FAX 030-3517248. TELEX 181470-SUNDS-D. Ed. E. Brunhuber. adv.; circ. 5,000.

669   GW
TASCHENBUCH DES METALLHANDELS. irreg. DM.182. Metall-Verlag GmbH, Postfach 102869, 6900 Heidelberg 1, Germany. TEL 030-8919055.

671.33   FR
TJ2
TECHNIQUES ET EQUIPMENTS DE PRODUCTION. 1907. 10/yr. 325 F. (foreign 413 F.)(effective Jan. 1992). Groupe Usine Nouvelle, 59 rue du Rocher, 75008 Paris, France. TEL 43-87-37-88. FAX 48-24-34-89. TELEX 650 485 F. Ed. Michel Defaux. adv.; bk.rev.; bibl.; charts; illus.; circ. 8,000. **Indexed:** Excerp.Med., INIS Atomind., Met.Abstr., World Alum.Abstr.
   Formerly: Machine Moderne (ISSN 0024-9130); Incorporates: Formage et Traitements des Metaux (ISSN 0015-7732); Estampage, Forge et Boulonnerie; Metaux en Feuilles.

669   GW   ISSN 0040-1439
          CODEN: TEMIAH
TECHNISCHE MITTEILUNGEN. 1907. 4/yr. DM.130. (Haus der Technik e.V., Essen) Vulkan-Verlag GmbH, Hollestr. 1G, Postfach 103962, 4300 Essen, Germany. TEL 0201-82002-0. FAX 0201-82002-40. Ed. E. Steinmetz. adv.; bk.rev.; charts; illus.; pat.; index; circ. 4,000. **Indexed:** Chem.Abstr., Eng.Ind., Excerp.Med., Geo.Abstr., Met.Abstr., World Alum.Abstr.
   —BLDSC shelfmark: 8750.500000.

TECHNISCHE MITTEILUNGEN KRUPP. see TECHNOLOGY: COMPREHENSIVE WORKS

TECNOLOGIA DELLA DEFORMAZIONE. see MACHINERY

669   IT   ISSN 0392-7954
TECNOLOGIE DEL FILO. 1983. bi-m. L.48000 (foreign L.135000)(effective 1992). Tecniche Nuove s.p.a., Via C. Menotti 14, 20129 Milan, Italy. TEL 02-75701. FAX 02-7570205. circ. 3,000.
   Description: Technical information on wire, steel wire and new ferrous wire work.

METALLURGY

669 621   IT   ISSN 0391-1683
TECNOLOGIE MECCANICHE. 1970. m. L.90000($157) (foreign L.180000). Stammer S.p.A., Centro Commerciale Milano San Felice, 20090 Segrate-Milan, Italy. TEL 02 7530651. FAX 027530587. TELEX 321083 STAMMER. Ed. Girolamo Bellina. adv.; circ. 14,000.

669   PO
TECNOMETAL; revista de informacao tecnica. 1979. bi-m. Esc.375. Associacao dos Industriais Metalurgicos e Metalomecanicos do Norte, Rua Guedes de Azevedo, 233-1, 4000 Porto, Portugal. TEL 313494. FAX 25019. TELEX 28178 AIMMNOR P. Ed. Miguel Bandeira Quaresma. adv.; circ. 2,500.

669.1   JA   ISSN 0040-2273
TEKKO RODO EISEI/JOURNAL OF LABOR HYGIENE IN IRON AND STEEL INDUSTRY. (Text in Japanese; table of contents in English) 1950. 2/yr. free. Japan Iron and Steel Federation, Hygiene Committee - Nihon Tekko Renmei, Eisei Iinkai, Keidanren Kaikan, 9-4, 1-chome, Ote-machi, Chiyoda-ku, Tokyo 100, Japan. TEL 03-3279-3611. FAX 03-3245-0144. TELEX 222-4210. bk.rev.; circ. 500. **Indexed:** C.I.S. Abstr.

669.1   JA   ISSN 0021-1575
                   CODEN: TEHAA2
TETSU-TO-HAGANE. (Text in Japanese; summaries in English) 1915. m. 47900 Yen to non-members (effective 1991). Iron and Steel Institute of Japan - Nippon Tekko Kyokai, Keidanren Kaikan, 3rd Fl., 9-4, Otemachi, 1-chome, Chiyoda-ku, Tokyo 100, Japan. TEL 03-3279-6011. FAX 03-3245-1355. TELEX 02228153-ISIJTK-J. Ed. Jin Shimada. adv.; index; circ. 11,000. **Indexed:** ASCA, Br.Ceram.Abstr., Ceram.Abstr., Chem.Abstr., JTA, Met.Abstr., World Alum.Abstr.
—BLDSC shelfmark: 4803.045000.

669   GW   ISSN 0724-7265
                   CODEN: TETBDY
THYSSEN EDELSTAHL TECHNISCHE BERICHTE. 1961. 4/yr. free. Thyssen Edelstahlwerke AG, Postfach 730, 4150 Krefeld, Germany. FAX 02151-832022. bk.rev.; bibl.; charts; illus.; index; circ. 5,500. **Indexed:** Chem.Abstr., Met.Abstr., World Alum.Abstr.
   Former titles: T E W Technische Berichte; D E W Technische Berichte (ISSN 0011-4898)

669   GW   ISSN 0340-5060
TN690   CODEN: TBTHDV
THYSSEN TECHNISCHE BERICHTE. (Text mainly in German, summaries in English and French) 1969. s-a. free. Thyssen Stahl AG, Postfach 110561, 4100 Duisburg 11, Germany. TEL 0203-52-24147. FAX 0203-52-25721. TELEX 855483 TST D. Ed. Alfred Altgeld. bibl.; charts; illus.; circ. 7,500. **Indexed:** Chem.Abstr., Eng.Ind., Excerp.Med., Met.Abstr., World Alum.Abstr.
—BLDSC shelfmark: 8820.387500.
   Formerly: Thyssenforschung (ISSN 0040-666X)
   Description: Trade magazine for the steel industry covering metallurgy and manufacturing.

669   NE   ISSN 0923-1722
TIJDSCHRIFT VOOR OPPERVLAKTETECHNIEKEN EN CORROSIEBESTRIJDING. 1957. m. fl.118.50. (Vereniging voor Oppervlaktetechnieken van Materialen) Tijl Tijdschriften B.V., P.B. 9943, 1006 AP Amsterdam, Netherlands. FAX 030-287674. Ed. R.I. de Jong. adv.; bk.rev.; circ. 2,200. **Indexed:** C.I.S. Abstr., Chem.Abstr., Excerp.Med.
—BLDSC shelfmark: 8843.850000.
   Former titles (until 1988): Belgisch-Nederlands Tijdschrift voor Oppervlaktetechnieken van Metalen (ISSN 0366-144X); Tijdschrift voor Oppervlaktetechnieken van Materialen (ISSN 0040-7569)

669.6   UK   ISSN 0040-7941
TN793.A1   CODEN: TIUSAD
TIN AND ITS USES. 1939. q. free. (Association of Tin Producing Countries (ATPC)) International Tin Research Institute, Kingston Lane, Uxbridge, Middlesex UB8 3PJ, England. TEL (0895) 272406. bk.rev.; abstr.; charts; illus.; stat.; circ. 30,000. **Indexed:** AESIS, BMT, Br.Ceram.Abstr., Br.Tech.Ind., Chem.Abstr., Corros.Abstr., Curr.Pack.Abstr., Dairy Sci.Abstr., Eng.Ind., Fluidex, Int.Packag.Abstr., Met.Abstr., RAPRA, World Alum.Abstr., World Surf.Coat.
—BLDSC shelfmark: 8856.000000.

669.6 688   UK   ISSN 0040-795X
TN793.A1
TIN INTERNATIONAL. 1928. m. £96. M I I D A Ltd., P.O. Box 2137, London NW10 6TN, England. TEL 081-961-7487. FAX 081-961-2137. Ed. R. Amlot. adv.; bk.rev.; charts; illus.; mkt.; stat.; index; circ. 7,200. (also avail. in microfilm from UMI; reprint service avail. from UMI) **Indexed:** Art & Archaeol.Tech.Abstr., Br.Tech.Ind., Curr.Pack.Abstr., Int.Packag.Abstr., Key to Econ.Sci., Met.Abstr., PROMT, World Alum.Abstr.
●Also available online. Vendor(s): DIALOG.
   Incorporates: Tin Printer and Box Maker (ISSN 0040-7976) & Canning and Packing (ISSN 0008-5588)

669.6   UK
TIN PRODUCTION AND INVESTMENT. 1979. irreg. £40. International Tin Council, 1 Oxendon St., London SW1Y 4EQ, England.
   Description: Designed to assess the economics of investment in new tin mining ventures.

669 664   UK   ISSN 1010-609X
TINPLATE WORLD. 1985. s-a. International Tin Research Institute, Kingston Lane, Uxbridge, Middlesex UB8 3PJ, England. TEL 0895-272406. Ed. Colin Evans. circ. 4,000.

669   US
TITANIUM DIGEST. 1976. m. $145 to non-members (foreign $155); members $120 (foreign $130). A S M International, Materials Information, Materials Park, OH 44073. TEL 216-338-5151. FAX 216-338-4634. TELEX 980-619. (UK addr.: Institute of Metals, Materials Information, 1 Carlton House Terr., London SW1Y 5DB, England. TEL 071-839-4071) **Indexed:** Met.Abstr.

669 622   JA   ISSN 0040-876X
                   CODEN: TDSSA2
TOHOKU DAIGAKU SENKO SEIREN KENKYUJO IHO/TOHOKU UNIVERSITY. RESEARCH INSTITUTE OF MINERAL DRESSING AND METALLURGY. BULLETIN. (Text in Japanese; summaries in English) 1942. 2/yr. exchange basis. Tohoku Daigaku, Senko Seiren Kenkyujo - Tohoku University, Research Institute of Mineral Dressing and Metallurgy, 1-1 Katahira 2-chome, Aoba-ku, Sendai 980, Japan. FAX 022-261-0938. Ed. Yoshio Waseda. charts; illus.; stat.; circ. controlled. **Indexed:** Chem.Abstr., JTA, Met.Abstr.
—BLDSC shelfmark: 2696.000000.
   Description: Covers the field of metallurgical, environmental and nuclear chemistry.

TOHOKU UNIVERSITY. SCIENCE REPORTS OF THE RESEARCH INSTITUTES. SERIES A: PHYSICS, CHEMISTRY, AND METALLURGY/TOHOKU DAIGAKU KENKYUJO HOKOKU. A-SHU: BUTSURIGAKU, KAGAKU, YAKINGAKU. see **PHYSICS**

669   II   ISSN 0377-9408
                   CODEN: TASTDL
TOOL AND ALLOY STEELS. 1967. m. Rs.350($75) Alloy Steel Producers Association of India, 332 Hind Rajasthan Bldg., D.S. Phalke Rd., Dadar, Bombay 400 014, India. TEL 4110364. Ed. K.S. Mathew. adv.; bk.rev.; tr.lit.; circ. 5,000. **Indexed:** Chem.Abstr., Met.Abstr., World Alum.Abstr.

671   FR   ISSN 0041-0950
TN672   CODEN: TRTHA4
TRAITEMENT THERMIQUE/HEAT TREATMENT. 1963. m. 650 F. (foreign 940 F.). P Y C Editions, 5 ave de Verdun, B.P. 105, 94280 Ivry sur Seine Cedex, France. TEL 1-49-60-86-36. FAX 1-46-72-41-85. TELEX 263 424. Ed. Rene Caule. adv.; bk.rev.; charts; illus.; index; circ. 2,700. **Indexed:** Chem.Abstr., Met.Abstr., World Alum.Abstr.
—BLDSC shelfmark: 8883.800000.
   Description: Technical review for engineers and technicians of heat treatment.

TRANSACTIONS OF THE MONUMENTAL BRASS SOCIETY. see **ARCHAEOLOGY**

669   UK   ISSN 0340-4285
                   CODEN: TMCHDN
TRANSITION METAL CHEMISTRY. bi-m. £360 for EC (US & Canada $590). Chapman & Hall, 2-6 Boundary Row, London SE1 8HN, England. TEL 071-865-0066. FAX 071-522-9623. (Dist. by: International Thomson Publishing Services, Ltd., N. Way, Andover, Hampshire SP10 5BE, England. TEL 0264-33-2424; US addr.: Chapman & Hall, 29 W. 35th St., New York, NY 10001-2291. TEL 212-244-3336) Ed. D.R.M. Walton. (also avail. in microfilm; reprint service avail. from ISI) **Indexed:** ASCA, Curr.Cont.
—BLDSC shelfmark: 9020.860000.
   Description: Designed to bring together from many sub-disciplines all aspects of the chemistry of this important group of metals, including the f-group elements.

TRATTAMENTI E FINITURE; rivista tecnica dei trattamenti, processi, finiture delle superfici. see **PAINTS AND PROTECTIVE COATINGS**

669   RU   ISSN 0041-4891
TSVETNYE METALLY. English translation: Soviet Journal of Non-Ferrous Metals (US ISSN 0038-5484) 1926. m. 37.20 Rub. Izdatel'stvo Metallurgiya, 2-i Obydenskii Per., 14, Moscow G-34, Russia. (Dist. by: Mezhdunarodnaya Kniga, Moscow, G-200, Russia) (Co-sponsor: Ministerstvo Chernoi Metallurgii) Ed. I.A. Strigin. bibl.; illus.; index; circ. 5,400. **Indexed:** Chem.Abstr., Eng.Ind., Met.Abstr., World Alum.Abstr.

671.8   UK   ISSN 0263-6794
TUBE INTERNATIONAL. 1982. bi-m. free. Publex International Ltd., 110-112 Station Rd. E., Oxted, Surrey RH8 0QA, England. TEL 0883-717755. FAX 0883-714554. Ed. Graham Bullock. circ. 7,242. **Indexed:** Met.Abstr., World Alum.Abstr.
—BLDSC shelfmark: 9068.070000.

671.2   ISSN 0041-8048
U S PIPER. 1928. q. free. United States Pipe and Foundry Company, Box 10406, Birmingham, AL 35202. TEL 205-254-7000. FAX 205-254-7170. Ed. George J. Bogs. illus.; circ. 8,500. **Indexed:** Met.Abstr.

U S S R REPORT: MACHINE TOOLS AND METAL - WORKING EQUIPMENT. see **MACHINERY**

671 621.9 668.4   GW   ISSN 0300-3167
UMFORMTECHNIK. 1967. bi-m. DM.104. Meisenbach GmbH, Hainstr. 18, Postfach 2069, 8600 Bamberg, Germany. TEL 0951-861-130. FAX 0951-861-161. TELEX 662844-MEIBA-D. Ed. Konrad Dengler. charts; illus.; index; circ. 6,000. **Indexed:** Excerp.Med., Met.Abstr., World Alum.Abstr.
   Description: Methods, machines and tooling for sheet-metal forming, forging and rolling processes, parting techniques as well as plastics processing.

669.6   UK
UNITED KINGDOM - TIN IN TINPLATE. 1981. irreg. £10. International Tin Council, 1 Oxendon St., London SW1Y 4EQ, England.
   Description: Surveys tinplate manufacturing, can making and canning in the UK.

669.6   UK
UNITED STATES OF AMERICA - TIN IN TINPLATE. 1983. irreg. £15. International Tin Council, 1 Oxendon St., London SW1Y 4EQ, England. **Indexed:** Refug.Abstr.
   Description: Surveys tinplate manufacturing, can making, and canning in the United States.

UNITED STEELWORKERS OF AMERICA. INFORMATION. see **LABOR UNIONS**

UNIVERSIDAD AUTONOMA DE SAN LUIS POTOSI. INSTITUTO DE GEOLOGIA. FOLLETO TECNICO. see **EARTH SCIENCES — Geology**

669   PL   ISSN 0208-578X
UNIWERSYTET SLASKI W KATOWiCACH. PRACE NAUKOWE. FIZYKA I CHEMIA METALI. (Text in Polish; summaries in English, Polish) 1976. irreg. price varies. Wydawnictwo Uniwersytetu Slaskiego, Ul. Bankowa 14, 40-007 Katowice, Poland. TEL 48-32-596-915. FAX 48-32-599-605. TELEX 0315584 USKPL. (Dist. by: CHZ Ars Polona, P.O. Box 1001, 00-950 Warsaw, Poland)
   Description: Covers metalselectrodeposition of alloys, texture, epitaxie, electrocrystallization of metals and alloys, structure investigation method, underpotential effects, electrooxidation processes, martensit transformation, sharp memory effect.

METALLURGY

669.2931 FR
URANIUM: RESOURCES, PRODUCTION AND DEMAND/URANIUM: RESSOURCES, PRODUCTION ET DEMANDE. 1965. biennial. price varies. Organization for Economic Cooperation and Development, Nuclear Energy Agency, 38 bd. Suchet, 75016 Paris, France. TEL 45-24-96-67. FAX 45-24-96-24. (U.S. subscr. to: O.E.C.D. Publications and Information Center, 2001 L St., N.W., Ste. 700, Washington, DC 20036-4095. TEL 202-785-6323) charts; illus.; circ. 2,030.
Description: Compares uranium supply data with the nuclear industry's requirements until the year 2030. Reviews exploration, resources and production.

669 GW ISSN 0170-9526
V D I INFORMATIONSDIENST. BLECHBEARBEITUNG. (Verein Deutscher Ingenieure) 1970. 6/yr. DM.270.30. (Fachinformation Zentrum Technik e.V.) V D I Verlag GmbH, Postfach 101054, 4000 Duesseldorf 1, Germany. TEL 0211-6214-468. TELEX 08586525. (Co-sponsor: Dokumentation Maschinenbau) Ed. G. Gentzsch. adv.; abstr.; bibl.; charts; illus. (back issues avail.)

669 621.3 GW ISSN 0170-9569
V D I INFORMATIONSDIENST. ELEKTRISCH ABTRAGENDE FERTIGUNGSVERFAHREN. (Verein Deutscher Ingenieure) 1971. q. DM.235.40. (Fachinformations Zentrum Technik e.V.) V D I Verlag GmbH, Heinrichstr. 24, Postfach 101054, 4000 Duesseldorf 1, Germany. TEL 0211-6214-468. FAX 0211-6188-112. TELEX 8587-743. adv.; abstr.; bibl.; charts; illus.

669 GW ISSN 0170-9550
V D I INFORMATIONSDIENST. KALTMASSIVUMFORMUNG. (Verein Deutscher Ingenieure) 1970. 6/yr. DM.270.30. (Fachinformation Zentrum Technik e.V.) V D I Verlag GmbH, Heinrichstr. 24, Postfach 101054, 4000 Duesseldorf 1, Germany. TEL 0211-6214-468. FAX 0211-6188-112. TELEX 8587-743. Ed. G. Gentzsch. adv.; abstr.; bibl.; charts; illus.

669 GW ISSN 0720-9878
V D I INFORMATIONSDIENST. NEUE FERTIGUNGSVERFAHREN. (Verein Deutscher Ingenieure) 1977. bi-m. DM.270.30. (Fachinformations Zentrum Technik e.V.) V D I Verlag GmbH, Heinrichstr. 24, Postfach 101054, 4000 Duesseldorf 1, Germany. TEL 0221-6214-468. FAX 0211-6188-112. TELEX 8587-743. Ed. G. Gentzsch. adv.; abstr.; bibl.; charts; illus.

669 GW ISSN 0171-3647
V D I INFORMATIONSDIENST. SCHMIEDEN UND PRESSEN. (Verein Deutscher Ingenieure) 1976. 6/yr. DM.270.30. (Fachinformations Zentrum Technik e.V.) V D I Verlag GmbH, Heinrichstr. 24, Postfach 101054, 4000 Duesseldorf 1, Germany. TEL 0211-6214468. FAX 0211-6188-112. TELEX 8587-743. Ed. G. Gentzsch. adv.; abstr.; bibl.; charts; illus.

669 GW ISSN 0721-7242
V D I INFORMATIONSDIENST. STRANGPRESSEN VON METALLEN. (Verein Deutscher Ingenieure) 1977. 3/yr. DM.177.80. (Fachinformations Zentrum Technik e.V.) V D I Verlag GmbH, Heinrichstr. 24, Postfach 101054, 4000 Duesseldorf 1, Germany. TEL 0211-6214-468. FAX 0211-6188-112. TELEX 8587-743. adv.; abstr.; bibl.; charts; illus.

V W D - NE-METALLE. (Vereinigte Wirtschaftsdienste GmbH) see *BUSINESS AND ECONOMICS — Investments*

V W D - STAHL. (Vereinigte Wirtschaftsdienste GmbH) see *BUSINESS AND ECONOMICS — Investments*

VUORITEOLLISUS/BERGSHANTERINGEN. see *MINES AND MINING INDUSTRY*

669 CS ISSN 0042-3726
VYSOKA SKOLA BANSKA. SBORNIK VEDECKYCH PRACI: RADA HUTNICKA/INSTITUTE OF MINING AND METALLURGY. TRANSACTIONS: METALLURGICAL SERIES. (Text in Czech; summaries in English, German, Russian) 1955. irreg. (2-8/yr.). 25 Kcs.($1) per issue. Statni Pedagogicke Nakladatelstvi, Ostrovni 30, 113 01 Prague 1, Czechoslovakia. bk.rev.; abstr.; bibl.; charts; illus.; stat.; index. **Indexed:** Copper Abstr., Fuel & Energy Abstr., Geo.Abstr., Met.Abstr., World Alum.Abstr.

671.2 JA
CODEN: RCRLAF
WASEDA UNIVERSITY. REPORT OF MATERIALS SCIENCE AND TECHNOLOGY. (Text in English) 1950. a. exchange basis. Waseda University, Kagami Memorials Laboratory for Materials Science and Technology, 2-8-26 Nishiwaseda Shinjuku-ku, Tokyo 169, Japan. TEL 03-3203-4782. FAX 03-3205-1353. **Indexed:** Chem.Abstr., Met.Abstr.
Formerly (until 1989): Waseda University. Report of Castings Research Laboratory (ISSN 0511-1927)

620.112 GW ISSN 0043-2822
TA401 CODEN: WSKRAT
WERKSTOFFE UND KORROSION/MATERIALS AND CORROSION; with international corrosion abstracts. (Text in English and German) 1949. m. DM.736. (Arbeitsgemeinschaft Korrosion od DECHEMA) V C H Verlagsgesellschaft mbH, Postfach 101161, 6940 Weinheim, Germany. TEL 06201-602-0. FAX 06201-602328. TELEX 465516-VCHWH-D. (U.S. addr.: V C H Publishers Inc., 220 E. 23rd St., New York, NY 10010-4606) Eds. H-J Engell, A. Rahmel. adv.; bk.rev.; abstr.; charts; illus.; pat.; tr.lit.; index; circ. 1,450. (also avail. in microfilm from VCI; reprint service avail. from ISI) **Indexed:** API Catal., API Hlth.& Environ., API Oil., API Pet.Ref., API Pet.Subst., API Transport., Appl.Mech.Rev., Art & Archaeol.Tech.Abstr., BMT, Chem.Abstr., Copper Abstr., Corros.Abstr., Curr.Cont., Dok.Arbeitsmed., Eng.Ind., Excerp.Med., Met.Abstr., Petrol.Abstr., World Alum.Abstr., World Surf.Coat.
—BLDSC shelfmark: 9298.000000.

669 PL ISSN 0043-5139
CODEN: WIHUAL
WIADOMOSCI HUTNICZE. 1945. m. $82. Wydawnictwo Czasopism i Ksiazek Technicznych SIGMA - NOT, Ul. Biala 4, 00-950 Warsaw, Poland. (Dist. by: Zaklad Kolportazu SIGMA-NOT, ul. Bartycka 20, 00-950 Warsaw, Poland) Ed. Janusz Czerminski. adv.; bk.rev.; abstr.; illus.; index; circ. 650. **Indexed:** Chem.Abstr., Met.Abstr., World Alum.Abstr.

671.84 GW ISSN 0043-5996
WIRE; technical journal covering all aspects of wire and bar production and treatment including all related subjects. French edition: Trefile (ISSN 0374-2261); German edition: Draht (ISSN 0012-5911); Italian edition: Filo Metallico (ISSN 0430-4578); Spanish edition: Alambre (ISSN 0002-4406). (Text in English) 1951. bi-m. DM.104. Meisenbach GmbH, Hainstr. 18, Postfach 2069, 8600 Bamberg, Germany. TEL 0951-861-134. FAX 0951-861-161. TELEX 662844-MEIBA-D. Ed. K. Dengler. adv.; bk.rev.; charts; illus.; circ. 8,045. (also avail. in microfilm from UMI) **Indexed:** Chem.Abstr., Copper Abstr., Eng.Ind., Met.Abstr.
—BLDSC shelfmark: 9320.350000.

671.84 UK ISSN 0043-6011
CODEN: WIRIAZ
WIRE INDUSTRY; international monthly journal. 1934. m. £72. Publex International Ltd., 110-112 Station Rd. E., Oxted, Surrey RH8 0QA, England. TEL 0883-717755. FAX 0883-714554. Ed. Graham Bullock. adv.; bk.rev.; bibl.; charts; illus.; pat.; index; circ. 8,500. **Indexed:** Br.Tech.Ind., Chem.Abstr., Copper Abstr., Eng.Ind., Excerp.Med., Met.Abstr., World Alum.Abstr.
—BLDSC shelfmark: 9321.000000.

674.84 US
WIRE INDUSTRY NEWS. 1973. bi-w. $250 (foreign $285). Business Information Services, Inc., 7 Hampden Rd., Stafford Springs, CT 06076-9310. TEL 203-684-5877. FAX 203-684-9158. Ed. Richard J. Callahan.
Description: Focuses on management, mergers, buy-outs, current events in the industry, promotions and business conditions.

671.8 UK ISSN 0084-0424
WIRE INDUSTRY YEARBOOK; international buyers guide. (Text in English, French, German, Italian and Spanish) 1951. a. £53. Publex International Ltd., 110-112 Station Rd. E., Oxted, Surrey RH8 0QA, England. TEL 0883-717755. FAX 0883-714554. Ed. B.J. Mitchell. adv.; circ. 8,500.

WIRE ROPE NEWS AND SLING TECHNOLOGY. see *PACKAGING*

671.84 GW ISSN 0934-5906
WIREWORLD. German edition: Drahtwelt. 1959. 6/yr. DM.126. Vogel-Verlag und Druck KG, Max-Planck-Str. 7-9, Postfach 6740, 8700 Wuerzburg 1, Germany. TEL 0931-418-2449. FAX 0931-418-2025. TELEX 680131. Ed. Dietmar Kuhn. adv.; bk.rev.; circ. 9,889. **Indexed:** Chem.Abstr., Eng.Ind., Excerp.Med., ISMEC, Met.Abstr., Sci.Abstr., World Alum.Abstr.
Formerly: Wire World International (ISSN 0043-6046); **Incorporates:** Wire Production.

669 658.8 US ISSN 0144-5960
WOLFF'S GUIDE TO THE LONDON METAL EXCHANGE. 1976. irreg., latest 1991. $91. Metal Bulletin Inc., 220 Fifth Ave., 10th Fl., New York, NY 10001. TEL 800-638-2525. FAX 212-213-6273. (Co-publisher: Rudolf Wolff and Co. Ltd.)
Description: Covers market operations together with historical background and individual chapters devoted to each product traded.

669 US ISSN 0951-2233
WORLD ALUMINIUM. 1954. irreg., latest 1990. $171.60. Metal Bulletin Inc., 220 Fifth Ave, 10th Fl., New York, NY 10001. TEL 800-638-2525. FAX 212-213-6273. Ed. Richard Serjeantson. adv. —BLDSC shelfmark: 9352.910500.
Formerly (until 1987): World Aluminium Databook.
Description: Divided into producers and products directories; lists alphabetically by country and product.

WORLD CALENDAR; comprehensive international coverage of forthcoming events in metallurgy and materials science. see *MEETINGS AND CONGRESSES*

669.6 UK
WORLD CONFERENCE ON TIN. PROCEEDINGS. irreg., 4th, 1974 Kuala Lumpur. £36. International Tin Council, Haymarket House, 1 Oxendon St., London SW1Y 4EQ, England.
Description: Papers on tin resources, prospecting and mining, processing and smelting, and marketing and consumption.

669 UK
WORLD METAL STATISTICS. YEARBOOK. 1984. a. $200. World Bureau of Metal Statistics, 27a High St., Ware, Herts SG12 9BA, England. TEL 0920-461274. **Indexed:** Copper Abstr.

669 US
WORLD PRECIOUS METALS DATABOOK. 1982. irreg. $144. Metal Bulletin Inc., 220 Fifth Ave., 10th Fl., New York, NY 10001. TEL 800-213-6273. FAX 212-213-6273. adv.
Formerly: World Precious Metals Survey (ISSN 0263-9661)

669.1 GW ISSN 0934-5965
WORLD STEEL & MATERIALS FACHBERICHTE. 1962. bi-m. DM.480. Sprechsaal Publishing Group, Mauer 2, Postbox 2962, 8630 Coburg, Germany. TEL 09561-76773. FAX 09561-90009. TELEX 663226-SPRECH-D. adv.; circ. 7,700. **Indexed:** Chem.Abstr., INIS Atomind., Met.Abstr., World Alum.Abstr.
Former titles: Fachberichte International Steel and Metals Magazine; Fachberichte Huettenpraxis Metallweiterverarbeitung (ISSN 0340-8043)

669.6 UK
WORLD - TIN IN TINPLATE. 1986. irreg. £25. International Tin Council, 1 Oxendon St., London SW1Y 4EQ, England.
Description: Survey of world tinplate manufacturing, can making and canning.

METALLURGY — ABSTRACTING, BIBLIOGRAPHIES, STATISTICS

669 UK
WORLD TIN MINING OPERATIONS, EXPLORATION AND DEVELOPMENTS. irreg. £20. International Tin Council, 1 Oxendon St., London SW1Y 4EQ, England.
  Description: Inventory of tin mining operations in 40 countries giving production details and planned developments.

669 CC ISSN 1001-1587
WUJIN KEJI. (Text in Chinese) bi-m. Shengyang Di 2 Qinggongye Yanjiusuo, 7, Ningshan Donglu, Huanggu-qu, Shenyang, Liaoning 110032, People's Republic of China. TEL 465196. (Co-sponsor: Quanguo Riyong Wujin Gongye Keji Qingbaozhan) Ed. Hou Zhiguang.

669 CC ISSN 1001-1617
YEJIN NENGYUAN. (Text in Chinese) bi-m. Yejin Bu, Anshan Reneng Yanjiusuo - Ministry of Metallurgy, Anshan Institute of Heat Energy, Luhua Jie, Tiedong-qu, Anshan, Liaoning 114004, People's Republic of China. TEL 539115. Ed. Huang Renxiang.

669 CC ISSN 1001-1269
YEJIN SHEBEI/METALLURGICAL EQUIPMENT. (Text in Chinese) bi-m. Beijing Yejin Shebei Yanjiusuo - Beijing Institute of Metallurgical Equipment, P.O. Box 2430, Beijing 100081, People's Republic of China. TEL 892531. Ed. Chen Zhongming.
  —BLDSC shelfmark: 5698.181000.

669 CC ISSN 1001-0211
      CODEN: YSCSAE
YOUSE JINSHU/CHINESE JOURNAL OF NONFERROUS METAL. (Text in Chinese) 1980. q. $19.18. Zhongguo Youse Jinshu Gongye Zonggongsi - China Nonferrous Metal Industrial Company, 1 Wenxingjie, Xiwai, Beijing 100044, People's Republic of China. TEL 8322211. FAX 861-8321362. TELEX 222589 GRIMM CN. (Co-sponsor: Nonferrous Metals Society of China) Ed. Huang Digong. adv.: B&W page $1200, color page $1800. bk.rev.; circ. 12,000.
  —BLDSC shelfmark: 6117.069000.
  Description: Covers the fields of geology, mining, mineral processing, metallurgy, materials science and engineering.

620.112 JA ISSN 0917-0480
TA418.74   CODEN: ZAKAEP
ZAIRYO TO KANKYO. English translation: Corrosion Engineering (US ISSN 0892-4228) (Text in Japanese, summaries in English) 1951. m. 27640 Yen (members 9000 Yen). Japan Society of Corrosion Engineering, 1-11, 4-chome, Hongo, Bunkyo-ku, Tokyo 113, Japan. FAX 03-5689-3390. Ed. Junichi Hashimoto. adv.; bk.rev.; charts; illus.; pat.; index; circ. 1,200. **Indexed:** Chem.Abstr., Corros.Abstr., INIS Atomind., JTA, Met.Abstr., World Alum.Abstr.
  Formerly (until vol.40, no.1, 1991): Boshoku Gijutsu (ISSN 0010-9355)

ZAMBIA CONSOLIDATED COPPER MINES LTD. ANNUAL REPORT AND ACCOUNTS. see *MINES AND MINING INDUSTRY*

620.1 RU ISSN 0044-1856
TA467   CODEN: ZAMEA9
ZASHCHITA METALLOV. 1965. bi-m. 27 Rub. (Akademiya Nauk S.S.S.R.) Izdatel'stvo Nauka, 90 Profsoyuznaya ul., 117864 Moscow, Russia. TEL 234-05-84. Ed. Ya.U. Kolotyrkin. index; circ. 3,175. (tabloid format) **Indexed:** Art & Archaeol.Tech.Abstr., Chem.Abstr., ISMEC, Met.Abstr., World Alum.Abstr., World Surf.Coat.
  —BLDSC shelfmark: 0070.930000.

663 KR ISSN 0130-1519
ZASHCHITNYE POKRYTIYA NA METALLAKH; respublikanskii mezhvedomstvennyi sbornik nauchnykh trudov. (Text in Russian) 1967. a. (Akademiya Nauk Ukrainskoi S.S.R., Institut Problem Materialovedeniya) Izdatel'stvo Naukova Dumka, c/o Yu.A. Khramov, Dir, Ul. Repina, 3, Kiev 252 601, Ukraine. (Subscr. to: Mezhdunarodnaya Kniga, Moscow, G-200, Russia) Ed. J.M. Fedorchenko. **Indexed:** Chem.Abstr.
  —BLDSC shelfmark: 0071.010000.

ZBORNIK RADOVA MUZEJA RUDARSTVA I METALURGIJE BOR. see *ARCHAEOLOGY*

669 GW ISSN 0044-3093
      CODEN: ZEMTAE
ZEITSCHRIFT FUER METALLKUNDE. (Summaries in English) 1911. m. DM.384. (Deutsche Gesellschaft fuer Materialkunde e.V.) Carl Hanser Verlag, Kolbergerstr. 22, 8000 Munich 80, Germany. adv.; bk.rev.; charts; illus.; pat.; index; circ. 2,000. **Indexed:** Appl.Mech.Rev., Chem.Abstr., Chem.Infd., Copper Abstr., Curr.Cont., Eng.Ind., GeoRef, Int.Aerosp.Abstr., Met.Abstr., Sci.Abstr., World Alum.Abstr.
  —BLDSC shelfmark: 9471.000000.

ZHONGNAN KUANGYE XUEYUAN XUEBAO/CENTRAL-SOUTH INSTITUTE OF MINING AND METALLURGY. JOURNAL. see *MINES AND MINING INDUSTRY*

669 AT ISSN 0158-7765
ZINC TODAY. 1969. q. free. Pasminco Metals Pty. Ltd., 114 William St., Melbourne, Vic. 3000, Australia. FAX 03-6071848. Ed. T.M. Perkins. bk.rev.; circ. 25,000. **Indexed:** AESIS.

669 US ISSN 0149-1210
TS300
33 METAL PRODUCING. 20000. 1963. m. $50 (free to qualified personnel). Penton Publishing (Subsidiary of: Pittway Company), 1100 Superior Ave., Cleveland, OH 44114. TEL 216-696-7000. FAX 216-696-8765. Ed. Wally Huskonen. adv.; charts; illus.; pat.; stat.; tr.lit.; circ. 22,000 (controlled). (also avail. in microform from UMI; back issues avail.) **Indexed:** Br.Ceram.Abstr., Met.Abstr.
  Former titles: 33 Magazine (ISSN 0563-4725); Magazine of Metals Producing (ISSN 0040-6155)
  Description: Covers metal smelting through processing and distribution of both ferrous and nonferrous metals.

METALLURGY — Abstracting, Bibliographies, Statistics

669 016 US ISSN 0094-8233
Z6679.A4
ALLOYS INDEX. (Auxiliary publication to Metals Abstracts and Metals Abstracts Index) 1974. m. $350 in US, Canada, Mexico; elsewhere $380. A S M International, Materials Information, Materials Park, OH 44073. TEL 216-338-5151. FAX 216-338-4634. TELEX 980-619. (UK addr.: Institute of Metals, Materials Information, 1 Carlton House Terr., London SW1Y 5DB, England. TEL 071-839-4071) (Co-sponsor: Institute of Metals, London) Ed. H.D. Chafe.
  ●Also available online. Vendor(s): CEDOCAR, CISTI, Data-Star (META), DIALOG (File no.32/METADEX), European Space Agency (File no.3), FIZ Technik (META), Orbit Information Technologies (METADEX), STN International.
  Also available on CD-ROM. Producer(s): Dialog Information Services.
  Description: Monthly information and updates on alloys.

669.142 310 UN ISSN 0250-9903
ANNUAL BULLETIN OF STEEL STATISTICS FOR EUROPE. (Text in English, French and Russian) 1974. a. price varies. Economic Commission for Europe (ECE), Palais des Nations, 1211 Geneva 10, Switzerland. TEL 734-6011. FAX 733-9879. TELEX 412962. (Or: United Nations Publications, Rm. DC2-853, New York, NY 10017) (also avail. in microfiche) **Indexed:** IIS, PROMT.

669 016 BE ISSN 0003-6412
APERCU TECHNIQUE - TECHNISCH OVERZICHT (A T O). (Text in Dutch, English, French and German) 1962. m. (11/yr.). 1000 Fr. Federation des Entreprises de l'Industrie des Fabrications Metalliques, Mecaniques, Electriques et de la Transformation des Matieres Plastiques, 21 rue des Drapiers, 1050 Brussels, Belgium. Ed. C. Franzen. bk.rev.; abstr.; circ. 1,500.

AVANCE DE INFORMACION ECONOMICA. INDUSTRIA MINEROMETALURGICA. see *MINES AND MINING INDUSTRY — Abstracting, Bibliographies, Statistics*

669 016 UK ISSN 0268-3393
Z7914.F7
B C I R A ABSTRACTS OF INTERNATIONAL LITERATURE ON METAL CASTINGS PRODUCTION. 1969. bi-m. £90. British Cast Iron Research Association, Alvechurch, Birmingham B48 7QB, England. TEL 0527 66414. FAX 0527-585070. TELEX 337125 BCIRA G. bk.rev.; abstr.; index; circ. 250.
  Former titles: B C I R A Abstracts of International Foundry Literature (ISSN 0141-2930); (until 1978): B C I R A Abstracts of Foundry Literature (ISSN 0005-2868)
  Description: Information on cast metals technology. Abstracts contain full bibliographical information, together with details of references, tables, figures.

669 016 YU ISSN 0006-2642
BILTEN DOKUMENTACIJE. METALURGIJA/BULLETIN OF DOCUMENTATION. METALLURGY. 1950. bi-m. $264. Jugoslovenski Centar za Tehnicku i Naucnu Dokumentaciju - Yugoslav Center for Technical and Scientific Documentation (YCTSD), Sl. Penezica-Krcuna 29-31, Box 724, 11000 Belgrade, Yugoslavia. Ed. Ljiljana Kojic-Bogdanovic. (also avail. in microfilm)

C A SELECTS. INORGANIC & ORGANOMETALLIC REACTION SYSTEMS. see *CHEMISTRY — Abstracting, Bibliographies, Statistics*

C A SELECTS. METALLO ENZYMES & METALLO COENZYMES. see *CHEMISTRY — Abstracting, Bibliographies, Statistics*

669.7 016 US ISSN 0749-7350
      CODEN: CSSCEC
C A SELECTS. SELENIUM & TELLURIUM CHEMISTRY. 1984. s-w. $195. Chemical Abstracts Service (Subsidiary of: American Chemical Society), 2540 Olentangy River Rd., Box 3012, Columbus, OH 43210. TEL 614-447-3600. FAX 614-447-3713. TELEX 6842086. abstr.; index; circ. 800. (looseleaf format)
  Incorporates: Selenium and Tellurium Abstracts (ISSN 0037-1467)
  Description: Covers all aspects of selenium and tellurium chemistry.

669 US ISSN 0148-2440
      CODEN: CSCMDT
C A SELECTS. SILVER CHEMISTRY. s-w. $195. Chemical Abstracts Service (Subsidiary of: American Chemical Society), 2540 Olentangy River Rd., Box 3012, Columbus, OH 43210. TEL 614-447-3600. FAX 614-447-3713. TELEX 6842086.
  Description: Covers the chemistry and chemical technology of silver and silver-containing compounds.

669 UK
CADSCAN. 1977. q. £50. Cadmium Association, 42 Weymouth St., London W1N 3LQ, England. Ed. C. Larson. adv.; bk.rev.; index; circ. 400. (back issues avail.) **Indexed:** AESIS, Br.Ceram.Abstr., Corros.Abstr., World Surf.Coat.
  Formerly (until Oct. 1986): Cadmium Abstracts (ISSN 0309-1139)

338.4 CN ISSN 0835-0124
HD9506.C2
CANADA. STATISTICS CANADA. FABRICATED METAL PRODUCTS INDUSTRIES. (Catalogue 41-251) (Text in English and French) 1960. a. Can.$20($42) (foreign $49). Statistics Canada, Publications Sales and Services, Ottawa, Ont. K1A 0T6, Canada. TEL 613-951-7277. FAX 613-951-1584. (also avail. in microform from MML)
  Supersedes: Canada. Statistics Canada. Wire and Wire Products Industries (ISSN 0828-9913); Canada. Statistics Canada. Ornamental and Architectural Metal Products Industry (ISSN 0828-9921); Which was formerly: Canada. Statistics Canada. Ornamental and Architectural Metal Industry (ISSN 0527-5997)

669.1 CN ISSN 0380-7851
HD9524.C2
CANADA. STATISTICS CANADA. PRIMARY IRON AND STEEL. (Catalogue 41-001) (Text in English and French) 1946. m. Can.$50($60) (foreign $70). Statistics Canada, Publications Sales and Services, Ottawa, Ont. K1A 0T6, Canada. TEL 613-951-7277. FAX 613-951-1584.
  Description: Provides current data on the Canadian iron and steel industry.

METALLURGY — ABSTRACTING, BIBLIOGRAPHIES, STATISTICS

669.1 016   FR   ISSN 0007-4063
CENTRE DE DOCUMENTATION SIDERURGIQUE. BULLETIN ANALYTIQUE. 1943. m. membership only. Centre de Documentation Siderurgique, 1 rue Paul Cezanne, 75008 Paris, France. TEL 1-45-63-17-10. FAX 1-45-61-02-91. TELEX FRASI 280 172 F. abstr.; circ. 500.

669   FR
CHAMBRE SYNDICALE DES ACIERS POUR EMBALLAGE. RAPPORT STATISTIQUES ANNUEL. a. Chambre Syndicale des Aciers Pour Emballage, 5 Rue Paul Cezanne, 75008 Paris, France. TEL 45-63-17-10.
 Formerly: Chambre Syndicale des Producteurs de Fer-blanc. Rapport Statistiques Annuel.

CHINESE JOURNAL OF METAL SCIENCE & TECHNOLOGY; an invaluable overview of the metallurgy field in China. see *METALLURGY*

CORROSION ABSTRACTS; abstracts of the world's literature on corrosion and corrosion mitigation. see *ENGINEERING — Abstracting, Bibliographies, Statistics*

620.112 016   UK   ISSN 0010-9347
CORROSION CONTROL ABSTRACTS. English translation of: Referativnyi Zhurnal. Korroziya i Zashchita ot Korrozii (UR ISSN 0131-3533) 1966. m. £720. Scientific Information Consultants Ltd., 661 Finchley Rd., London NW2 2HN, England. Ed. Eugene Gros. abstr.
 —BLDSC shelfmark: 0411.072000.

016 621.9 669   KO
CURRENT BIBLIOGRAPHIES ON SCIENCE AND TECHNOLOGY: MECHANICAL ENGINEERING & CONSTRUCTION ENGINEERING. 1962. m. $92. Korea Institute for Economics and Technology, P.O.Box 250, Seoul, S. Korea. circ. 300. (reprint service avail. from UMI)
 Formerly: Current Index to Journals in Science and Technology: Mechanical, Metallurgical, Natural Resources and Construction Engineering; Supersedes in part: Current Bibliography on Science and Technology.

011 669   KO
CURRENT BIBLIOGRAPHIES ON SCIENCE AND TECHNOLOGY: METALLURGY, NATURAL RESOURCES & ENERGY. m. $92. Institute for Economics and Technology, P.O. Box 205, Seoul, S. Korea. circ. 300.

CURRENT BIBLIOGRAPHY ON SCIENCE AND TECHNOLOGY: EARTH SCIENCE, MINING AND METALLURGY/KAGAKU GIJUTSU BUNKEN SOKUHO. KINZOKU KOGAKU, KOZAN KOGAKU, CHIKYU NO KAGAKU-HEN. see *EARTH SCIENCES — Abstracting, Bibliographies, Statistics*

669   US   ISSN 1049-1384
▼**C2C ABSTRACTS: JAPAN - METALS.** 1990. m. $200. Scan C2C, 500 E St. S.W., Ste. 800, Washington, DC 20024. TEL 800-525-3865. FAX 202-863-3855.
 ●Also available online. Vendor(s): Data-Star (JPTC), DIALOG (File no.582), European Space Agency (File no.241), Orbit Information Technologies (JTEC). Also available on CD-ROM. Producer(s): Dialog Information Services.
 Description: Contains abstracts of articles from Japanese scientific, business, and technical journals. Lists title, author, author affiliation, journal title, volume and number, date, page numbers, abstract, number of bibliographic references, and language.

669.1   GW
EISEN UND STAHL. 1958. m. DM.76.80. Statistisches Bundesamt, Postfach 104851, 4000 Duesseldorf 1, Germany. TEL 0211-384110. FAX 0211-3841128. TELEX 2114568-SBA-D. adv.; bk.rev.; circ. 350.

620.1 016   RU   ISSN 0131-0232
EKSPRESS-INFORMATSIYA. KORROZIYA I ZASHCHITA METALLOV. 1959. 48/yr. 52.80 Rub. Vsesoyuznyi Institut Nauchno-Tekhnicheskoi Informatsii (VINITI), Baltiiskaya ul., 14, Moscow A-219, Russia. (Subscr. to: Mezhdunarodnaya Kniga, Dimitrova ul. 39, 113095 Moscow, Russia)

EURO ABSTRACTS SECTION II. COAL AND STEEL. see *MINES AND MINING INDUSTRY — Abstracting, Bibliographies, Statistics*

669   FR
FRANCE. SERVICE D'ETUDE DES STRATEGIES ET DES STATISTIQUES INDUSTRIELLES. RESULTATS MENSUELS DES ENQUETES DE BRANCHE. TRAVAIL DES METAUX. m. 260 F. (foreign 310 F.)(effective 1991). Service d'Etude des Strategies et des Statistiques Industrielles (SESSI), 85 Bd. du Montparnasse, 75270 Paris Cedex 06, France. TEL 45-56-42-34. FAX 45-56-40-71. stat.
 Description: Follows developments in the metalworking industry through the performance of selected indicators.

669   FR
FRANCE. SERVICE D'ETUDE DES STRATEGIES ET DES STATISTIQUES INDUSTRIELLES. RESULTATS TRIMESTRIELS DES ENQUETES DE BRANCHE. TRAVAIL DES METAUX. q. 180 F. (foreign 210 F.)(effective 1991). Service d'Etude des Strategies et des Statistiques Industrielles (SESSI), 85 Bd. du Montparnasse, 75270 Paris Cedex 06, France. TEL 45-56-42-34. FAX 45-56-40-71. stat.
 Description: Provides detailed industry-wide performance statistics for comparative evaluations.

669 016   GW   ISSN 0721-9679
GIESSEREI-LITERATURSCHAU. 1982. m. DM.280 (members DM.252). Verein Deutscher Giessereifachleute, Sohnstr. 70, 4000 Duesseldorf 1, Germany. TEL 0211-6871-344. FAX 0211-6871333. TELEX 8586885-D. Ed.Bd. bk.rev.; circ. 200.
 Description: Comprehensive information about new publications in the field of foundry technology, including related issues such as environmental protection, energy industry, and industrial safety.

669.22 016   SZ   ISSN 0017-1557
 CODEN: GLDBBS
GOLD BULLETIN; research on gold and its applications in industry. 1968. q. free. World Gold Council, 1 rue de la Rotisserie, CH-1204 Geneva, Switzerland. TEL 022-219666. FAX 022-288160. TELEX 428471. Ed. Dr. P. Taimsula. bk.rev.; abstr.; illus.; circ. 5,500 (controlled). (tabloid format) **Indexed:** AESIS, Art & Archaeol.Tech.Abstr., Br.Archaeol.Abstr., Br.Ceram.Abstr., Bull.Signal., Chem.Abstr., Corros.Abstr., Eng.Ind., Ind.S.A.Per., INIS Atomind., Met.Abstr., World Alum.Abstr., World Text.Abstr.
 —BLDSC shelfmark: 4201.141700.
 Incorporates: Gold Patent Digest (ISSN 0258-7262)

669.142   UK
GUIDE TO THE CLASSIFICATION OF STEEL INDUSTRY PRODUCTS IN THE U K CUSTOMS TARIFF. a.? £25. U.K. Iron and Steel Statistics Bureau, Canterbury House, 2 Sydenham Rd., Croydon CR9 2LZ, England. TEL 081-686-9050. FAX 081-680-8616. TELEX 932575.

I M M ABSTRACTS AND INDEX; a survey of world literature on the economic geology and mining of all minerals (except coal), mineral processing and non-ferrous extraction metallurgy. (Institution of Mining and Metallurgy) see *MINES AND MINING INDUSTRY — Abstracting, Bibliographies, Statistics*

620.112   UK   ISSN 0955-7040
INDUSTRIAL CORROSION ABSTRACTS. 1989. q. $250 (foreign £140). S T I Ltd., 4 Kings Meadow, Ferry Hinksey Rd., Oxford OX2 0DU, England. TEL 0865-798898. FAX 0865-798788. (Dist. in U.S. by: Air Science Co., P.O. Box 143, Corning, NY 14830) Ed. Lindsay Gale. bk.rev.; abstr.; index. cum.index. **Indexed:** Corros.Abstr.
 ●Also available online. Vendor(s): DIALOG (File no. 96), European Space Agency (File no. 48).
 Description: Covers all aspects of corrosion in the industrial environment, specific problems, protection techniques, corrosion-resistant materials, testing equipment and remedial techniques.

INSTYTUT OBROBKI SKRAWANIEM. PRZEGLAD DOKUMENTACYJNY. see *ENGINEERING — Abstracting, Bibliographies, Statistics*

669.3   UK   ISSN 0309-2216
TN780
INTERNATIONAL COPPER INFORMATION BULLETIN; recent reports, publications and abstracts on copper, its alloys and compounds. 1976. 3/yr. free. Copper Development Association, Orchard House, Mutton Lane, Potters Bar, Herts. EN6 3AP, England. TEL 0707-50711. FAX 0707-42769. Ed. G. Greetham. adv.; bk.rev.; circ. 2,000. **Indexed:** AESIS, Cadscan, Copper Abstr., Lead Abstr., Met.Abstr., Zincscan.
 Supersedes: Copper Abstracts (ISSN 0010-8596); **Incorporates:** Kupfer-Mitteilungen (ISSN 0023-5628); Cuivre, Laitons, Alliages-Bibliographie; Rame-Schede Bibliographiche; Cobre-Resumes Bibliograficos.

669.1   UK   ISSN 0952-5831
INTERNATIONAL STEEL STATISTICS - AUSTRALIA. (Part of: International Steel Statistics Country Books Series) 1970. a. £75 (Complete Series of all 25 Country Books and the Summary Tables £1000). U.K. Iron & Steel Statistics Bureau, Canterbury House, 2 Sydenham Rd., Croydon CR9 2 LZ, England. TEL 081-686-9050. FAX 081-680-8616. TELEX 932575.
 Formerly: International Steel Statistics - Australia and New Zealand.
 Description: Covers the production, consumption, and import and export of iron and steel products by quality and market in Australia.

669.1   UK   ISSN 0952-584X
INTERNATIONAL STEEL STATISTICS - AUSTRIA. (Part of: International Steel Statistics Country Books Series) 1970. a. £75 (Complete Series of all 25 Country Books and Summary Tables £1000). U.K. Iron & Steel Statistics Bureau, Canterbury House, 2 Sydenham Rd., Croydon CR9 2LZ, England. TEL 081-686-9050. FAX 081-680-8616. TELEX 932575.
 Description: Provides information on the production, consumption, import and export of iron and steel products by quality and market in Austria.

669.1   UK   ISSN 0952-5858
INTERNATIONAL STEEL STATISTICS - BELGIUM, LUXEMBOURG. (Part of: International Steel Statistics Country Books Series) 1979. a. £75 (Complete Series of all 25 Country Books and Summary Tables £1000). U.K. Iron & Steel Statistics Bureau, Canterbury House, 2 Sydenham Rd., Croydon CR9 2LZ, England. TEL 081-686-9050. FAX 081-680-8616. TELEX 932575.
 Description: Provides information on the consumption, production, export and import of steel products by quality and market in Belgium and Luxemburg.

669.1   UK   ISSN 0952-5866
INTERNATIONAL STEEL STATISTICS - BRAZIL. (Part of: International Steel Statistics Country Books Series) 1970. a. £75 (Complete Series of all 25 Country Books and Summary Series £1000). U.K. Iron & Steel Statistics Bureau, Canterbury House, 2 Sydenham Rd., Croydon CR9 2LZ, England. TEL 081-686-9050. FAX 081-680-8616. TELEX 932575.
 Description: Covers the production, consumption, import and export of iron and steel products by quality and market in Brazil.

669.1   UK   ISSN 0952-5874
INTERNATIONAL STEEL STATISTICS - CANADA. (Part of: International Steel Statistics Country Books Series) 1970. a. £75 (Complete Series of all 25 Country Books and Summary Tables £1000). U.K. Iron & Steel Statistics Bureau, Canterbury House, 2 Sydenham Rd., Croydon CR9 2LZ, England. TEL 081-686-9050. FAX 081-680-8616. TELEX 932575.
 Description: Provides information on the production, consumption, import and export of iron and steel products by quality and market in Canada.

METALLURGY — ABSTRACTING, BIBLIOGRAPHIES, STATISTICS

669.1 UK ISSN 0960-2372
INTERNATIONAL STEEL STATISTICS - DENMARK. (Part of: International Steel Statistics Country Books Series) 1979. a. £75 (Complete Series of all 25 Country Books and Summary Tables £1000). U.K. Iron & Steel Statistics Bureau, Canterbury House, 2 Sydenham Rd., Croydon CR9 2LZ, England. TEL 081-686-9050. FAX 081-680-8616. TELEX 932575.
—BLDSC shelfmark: 4549.707400.
Formerly: International Steel Statistics - Denmark and Greece (ISSN 0952-5882)
Description: Provides information on the production, consumption, import and export of iron and steel products by quality and market in Denmark.

669.1 UK ISSN 0952-6056
INTERNATIONAL STEEL STATISTICS - EASTERN EUROPEAN COUNTRIES, TURKEY AND YUGOSLAVIA. (Part of: International Steel Statistics Country Books Series) 1970. a. £75 (Complete Series of all 25 Country Books and Summary Tables £1000). U.K. Iron & Steel Statistics Bureau, Canterbury House, 2 Sydenham Rd., Croydon CR9 2LZ, England. TEL 081-686-9050. FAX 081-680-8616. TELEX 932575.
—BLDSC shelfmark: 4549.705400.
Description: Covers the production, consumption, import and export of iron and steel products by quality and market.

669.1 UK ISSN 0952-5890
INTERNATIONAL STEEL STATISTICS - FINLAND. (Part of: International Steel Statistics Country Books) 1970. a. £75 (Complete Series of all 25 Country Books and Summary Tables £1000). U.K. Iron & Steel Statistics Bureau, Canterbury House, 2 Sydenham Rd., Croydon CR9 2LZ, England. TEL 081-686-9050. FAX 081-680-8616. TELEX 932575.
Description: Covers the production, consumption, import and export of iron and steel products by quality and market in Finland.

669.1 UK ISSN 0952-5904
INTERNATIONAL STEEL STATISTICS - FRANCE. (Part of: International Steel Statistics Country Books) 1970. a. £75 (Complete Series of 25 Country Books and Summary Tables £1000). U.K. Iron & Steel Statistics Bureau, Canterbury House, 2 Sydenham Rd., Croydon CR9 2LZ, England. TEL 081-686-9050. FAX 081-680-8616. TELEX 982575.
Description: Provides information on the production, consumption, import and export of iron and steel products by quality and market in France.

669.1 UK ISSN 0952-5912
INTERNATIONAL STEEL STATISTICS - GERMANY, FEDERAL REPUBLIC. (Part of: International Steel Statistics Country Books) 1970. a. £75 (Complete Series of all 25 Country Books and Summary Tables £1000). U.K. Iron & Steel Statistics Bureau, Canterbury House, 2 Sydenham Rd., Croydon CR9 2LZ, England. TEL 081-686-9050. FAX 081-680-8616. TELEX 932575.
Description: Provides information on the consumption, production, export and import of iron and steel products by quality and market in Germany.

669.1 UK ISSN 0960-2380
INTERNATIONAL STEEL STATISTICS - GREECE. (Part of: International Steel Statistics Country Book Series) a. £75 (Complete Series of all 25 Country Books and Summary Tables £1000). U.K. Iron & Steel Statistics Bureau, Canterbury House, 2 Sydenham Road, Croydon CR9 2LZ, England. TEL 081-686-9050. FAX 081-680-8616. TELEX 932575.
Description: Provides information on the consumption, production, export and import of iron and steel products by quality and markets in Greece.

669.1 UK ISSN 0952-5920
INTERNATIONAL STEEL STATISTICS - IRISH REPUBLIC. (Part of: International Steel Statistics Country Books Series) 1970. a. £75 (Complete Series of all 25 Country Books and Summary Tables £1000). U.K. Iron & Steel Statistics Bureau, Canterbury House, 2 Sydenham Rd., Croydon CR9 2LZ, England. TEL 081-686-9050. FAX 081-680-8616. TELEX 932575.
—BLDSC shelfmark: 4549.707700.
Description: Covers the production, consumption, import and export of iron and steel products by quality and market in Ireland.

669.1 UK ISSN 0952-5939
INTERNATIONAL STEEL STATISTICS - ITALY. (Part of: International Steel Statistics Country Books Series) 1970. a. £75 (Complete Series of all 25 Country Books and Summary Tables £1000). U.K. Iron & Steel Statistics Bureau, Canterbury House, 2 Sydenham Rd., Croydon CR9 2LZ, England. TEL 081-686-9050. FAX 081-680-8616. TELEX 932575.
Description: Provides information on the production, consumption, import and export of iron and steel products by quality and market in Italy.

669.1 UK ISSN 0952-5947
INTERNATIONAL STEEL STATISTICS - JAPAN. (Part of: International Steel Statistics Country Books) 1970. a. £75 (Complete Series of 25 Country Books and Summary Tables £1000). U.K. Iron & Steel Statistics Bureau, Canterbury House, 2 Sydenham Rd., England. TEL 081-686-9050. FAX 081-680-8616. TELEX 932575.
Description: Covers the production, consumption, import and export of iron and steel products by quality and market in Japan.

669.1 UK ISSN 0952-603X
INTERNATIONAL STEEL STATISTICS - KOREA (SOUTH). (Part of: International Steel Statistics Country Books Series) 1970. a. £75 (Complete Series of all 25 Country Books and Summary Tables £1000). U.K. Iron & Steel Statistics Bureau, Canterbury House, 2 Sydenham Rd., Croydon CR9 2LZ, England. TEL 081-686-9050. FAX 081-680-8616. TELEX 932575.
Description: Provides information on the production, consumption, import and export of iron and steel products by quality and market in South Korea.

669.1 UK ISSN 0952-6005
INTERNATIONAL STEEL STATISTICS - NETHERLANDS. (Part of: International Steel Statistics Country Books Series) 1970. a. £75 (Complete Series of 25 Country Books and Summary Tables £1000). U.K. Iron & Steel Statistics Bureau, Canterbury House, 2 Sydenham Rd., Croydon CR9 2LZ, England. TEL 081-686-9050. FAX 081-680-8616. TELEX 932575.
Description: Provides information on the consumption and production, import and export of iron and steel products by quality and market in the Netherlands.

669.1 UK ISSN 0952-6013
INTERNATIONAL STEEL STATISTICS - NORWAY. (Part of: International Steel Statistics Country Books Series) 1970. a. £75 (Complete Series of 25 Country Books and Summary Tables £1000). U.K. Iron & Steel Statistics Bureau, Canterbury House, 2 Sydenham Rd., Croydon CR9 2LZ, England. TEL 081-686-9050. FAX 081-680-8616. TELEX 932575.
Description: Covers the production, consumption and import and export of iron and steel products by quality and market in Norway.

669.1 UK ISSN 0958-4951
INTERNATIONAL STEEL STATISTICS - PORTUGAL. (Part of: International Steel Statistics Country Book Series) a. £75 (Complete Series of all 25 Country Books and Summary Tables £1000). U.K. Iron & Steel Statistics Bureau, Canterbury House, 2 Sydenham Rd., Croydon CR9 2LZ, England. TEL 081-686-9050. FAX 081-680-8616. TELEX 932575.
—BLDSC shelfmark: 4549.710900.
Description: Provides information on the consumption, production, export and import of iron and steel products by quality and markets in Portugal.

669.1 UK ISSN 0958-515X
INTERNATIONAL STEEL STATISTICS - SELECTED ASIAN AND AFRICAN COUNTRIES. (Part of: International Steel Statistics Country Books Series) 1970. a. £75 (Complete Series of all 25 Country Books and Summary Tables £1000). U.K. Iron & Steel Statistics Bureau, Canterbury House, 2 Sydenham Rd., Croydon CR9 2LZ, England. TEL 081-686-9050. FAX 081-680-8616. TELEX 932575.
Formerly: International Steel Statistics - Selected Asian Countries (ISSN 0952-6110)
Description: Provides information on the production, consumption, import and export of iron and steel products by quality and market in selected countries of Asia and Africa.

669.1 UK ISSN 0952-6102
INTERNATIONAL STEEL STATISTICS - SELECTED CENTRAL AND SOUTH AMERICAN COUNTRIES. (Part of: International Steel Statistics Country Books Series) 1970. a. £75 (Complete Series of all 25 Country Books and Summary Tables £1000). U.K. Iron & Steel Statistics Bureau, Canterbury House, 2 Sydenham Rd., Croydon CR9 2LZ, England. TEL 081-686-9050. FAX 081-680-8616.
Description: Covers the production, consumption, import and export of iron and steel products by quality and market.

669.1 UK ISSN 0958-4943
INTERNATIONAL STEEL STATISTICS - SPAIN. (Part of: International Steel Statistics Country Books Series) 1970. a. £75 (Complete Series of 25 Country Books and Summary Tables £1000). U.K. Iron & Steel Statistics Bureau, Canterbury House, 2 Sydenham Rd., Croydon CR9 2LZ, England. TEL 081-686-9050. FAX 081-680-8616. TELEX 932575.
—BLDSC shelfmark: 4549.713500.
Formerly: International Steel Statistics - Spain and Portugal (ISSN 0952-6129)
Description: Covers the production, consumption, import and export of iron and steel products by quality and market in Spain.

310 671 UK ISSN 0952-6803
INTERNATIONAL STEEL STATISTICS - SUMMARY TABLES. 1970. a. £100 (Complete Series of all 25 Country Books £1000). U.K. Iron & Steel Statistics Bureau, Canterbury House, 2 Sydenham Rd., Croydon CR9 2LZ, England. TEL 081-686-9050. FAX 081-680-8616. TELEX 932575.
Description: A publication setting out summary tables for the countries covered in the International Steel Statistics Country Books Series. The tables cover production of iron and crude steel, imports and exports of finished steel products.

669.1 UK ISSN 0952-6048
INTERNATIONAL STEEL STATISTICS - SWEDEN. (Part of: International Steel Statistics Country Books Series) 1970. a. £75 (Complete Series of all 25 Country Books and Summary Tables £1000). U.K. Iron & Steel Statistics Bureau, Canterbury House, 2 Sydenham Rd., Croydon CR9 2LZ, England. TEL 081-686-9050. FAX 081-680-8616. TELEX 932575.
Description: Provides information on the production, consumption, import and export of iron and steel products by quality and market in Sweden.

669.1 UK ISSN 0952-6099
INTERNATIONAL STEEL STATISTICS - SWITZERLAND. (Part of: International Steel Statistics Country Books Series) 1970. a. £75 (Complete Series of all 25 Country Books and Summary Tables £1000). U.K. Iron & Steel Statistics Bureau, Canterbury House, 2 Sydenham Rd., Croydon CR9 2LZ, England. TEL 081-686-9050. FAX 081-680-8616. TELEX 932575.
Description: Provides information on the consumption, production, export and import of iron and steel products by quality and markets in Switzerland.

METALLURGY — ABSTRACTING, BIBLIOGRAPHIES, STATISTICS

669.1   UK   ISSN 0952-6811
INTERNATIONAL STEEL STATISTICS - U S A. (Part of: International Steel Statistics Country Books Series) 1970. a. £75 (Complete Series of all 25 Country Books and Summary Tables £1000). U.K. Iron & Steel Statistics Bureau, Canterbury House, 2 Sydenham Rd., Croydon CR9 2LZ, England. TEL 081-686-9050. FAX 081-680-8616. TELEX 932575.
   Description: Provides information on the production, consumption and import and export of iron and steel products by quality and market in the U.S.

669.1   UK   ISSN 0307-7608
HD9521.4
INTERNATIONAL STEEL STATISTICS - UNITED KINGDOM. (Part of: International Steel Statistics Country Books Series) 1970. a. £75 (Complete Series of all 25 Country Books and Summary Tables £1000). U.K. Iron & Steel Statistics Bureau, Canterbury House, 2 Sydenham Rd., England. TEL 081-686-9050. FAX 081-680-8616. TELEX 932575.
   Description: Covers the production, consumption, import and export of iron and steel products by quality and market in the United Kingdom.

INTERNATIONAL TIN COUNCIL. MONTHLY STATISTICAL SUMMARY. see METALLURGY

669   UK
INTERNATIONAL TIN COUNCIL. QUARTERLY STATISTICAL BULLETIN. 1948. q. £60 (includes 8 monthly statistical summaries). International Tin Council, 1 Oxendon St., London SW1Y 4EQ, England. (also avail. in microform from UMI; reprint service avail. from UMI) **Indexed:** Cadscan, IIS, Lead Abstr., Zincscan.
   Formerly (1974-1983): International Tin Council. Monthly Statistical Bulletin.
   Description: Tables of data on mine and smelter production and tin metal consumption.

314 669   EI
IRON AND STEEL STATISTICAL YEARBOOK. (Text in English) 1977. a. $30. (Statistical Office of the European Communities) Office for Official Publications of the European Communities, L-2985 Luxembourg, Luxembourg. (Dist. in the U.S. by: Unipub, 4611-F Assembly Dr., Lanham, MD 20706-4391) Ed.Bd.
   Formerly: Statistical Office of the European Communities. Iron and Steel. Yearbook.

669   JA   ISSN 0451-6001
KEIKINZOKU KOGYO TOKEI NENPO/LIGHT METAL STATISTICS IN JAPAN. Variant title: Light Metal Statistics in Japan. Annual Report. (Text in English, Japanese) 1950. a. 15000 Yen. Japan Aluminium Federation, Nihonbashi Asahi Seimei Bldg., 1-3 Nihonbashi 2-chome, Chuo-ku, Tokyo 103, Japan. FAX 03-3274-3179. TELEX 02223074-JALF-J. Ed. K. Nagakubo. adv.; bk.rev.; stat.; circ. 1,200.

669 016   HU   ISSN 0231-0708
KOHASZATI ES ONTESZETI SZAKIRODALMI TAJEKOZTATO/METALLURGY AND FOUNDRY ABSTRACTS. 1949. m. 9700 Ft. Orszagos Muszaki Informacios Kozpont es Konyvtar (O.M.I.K.K.) - National Technical Information Centre and Library, Muzeum u. 17, Box 12, 1428 Budapest, Hungary. (Subscr. to: Kultura, Box 149, 1389 Budapest, Hungary) Ed. Gabor Libertiny. abstr.; index; circ. 330.
   Supersedes (in 1982): Muszaki Lapszemle. Kohaszat, Onteszet - Technical Abstracts. Metallurgy, Foundry (ISSN 0027-5034)

669.2   UK   ISSN 0023-9577
LEAD AND ZINC STATISTICS. (Text in English and French) 1961. m. £60($120) International Lead and Zinc Study Group, 58 St. James's St., London SW1A 1LD, England. TEL 071-499-9373. FAX 071-493-3725. TELEX 299819-ILZSG-G. mkt.; stat.; circ. 700. **Indexed:** IIS, P.A.I.S., PROMT.
   ●Also available online.
   Description: Provides long term historical coverage of world production and consumption of lead and zinc since 1960, combining detailed annual tables with quarterly and monthly series.

669 016   UK   ISSN 0950-1584
LEADSCAN;* a review of recent technical literature on the uses of lead and its products. 1958. 4/yr. £55. (Zinc-Lead Library and Abstracts Service) Lead Development Association, 42 Weymouth St., London W1X 3LQ, England. Ed. C. Larson. bk.rev.; abstr.; index; circ. 1,300. (also avail. in microform from UMI) **Indexed:** AESIS, Br.Ceram.Abstr., Corros.Abstr., Lead Abstr., World Surf.Coat.
   Formerly: Lead Abstracts (ISSN 0023-9569)

669   UK
MATERIALS BUSINESS INFORMATION. 1985. m. price avail. to applicable subscribers. Institute of Materials, 1 Carlton House Terrace, London SW1Y 5DB, England. TEL 071-839-4071. FAX 071-839-2078. TELEX 8814813-METSOC-G. (And: Materials Information, A S M International, Metals Park, OH 44073, U.S.A.)
   ●Also available online. Vendor(s): DIALOG (File no.269).
   Formerly: Materials Business Abstracts.
   Description: Discusses steel, non-ferrous metals, polymers, ceramics and composites.

MATERIALS INFORMATION ENGINEERED MATERIALS SEARCH-IN-PRINT SERIES. see ENGINEERING — Abstracting, Bibliographies, Statistics

669 016   US
MATERIALS INFORMATION METALLURGICAL SEARCH-IN-PRINT SERIES. (248 topics avail.) 1967. a. $95 per topic to non-members; members $85. A S M International, Materials Information, Materials Park, OH 44073. TEL 216-338-5151. FAX 216-338-4634. TELEX 980-619. (UK addr.: Institute of Metals, Materials Information, 1 Carlton House Terr., London SW1Y 5DB, England. TEL 071-839-4071)
   Former titles: Materials Information Metallurgical Published Search Series; Materials Information Metallurgical Bibliography Series; A S M Bibliography Series (ISSN 0001-2556)

669 016   UK   ISSN 0026-0657
TN695
METAL POWDER REPORT. 1946. 11/yr. £89 (effective 1992). Elsevier Science Publishers Ltd., Crown House, Linton Rd., Barking, Essex IG11 8JU, England. TEL 081-594-7272. FAX 081-594-5942. TELEX 896950 APPSCI G. (Subscr. in U.S. and Canada to: Elsevier Science Publishing Co., Inc., Box 882, Madison Sq. Sta., New York, NY 10159. TEL 212-989-5800) Ed. A. Weaver. adv. contact: Tamar Baldwin. bk.rev.; abstr.; charts; pat.; tr.lit.; index; circ. 1,200. **Indexed:** Br.Ceram.Abstr., Cadscan, Copper Abstr., Lead Abstr., Met.Abstr., World Alum.Abstr., Zincscan.
   —BLDSC shelfmark: 5687.825000.
   Description: Reports the latest developments in worldwide powder production, consolidation, sintering and new powder metallurgy products and their applications.

310 669   GW   ISSN 0170-9933
METAL STATISTICS (YEARS). (Text in English, German) 1889. a. DM.150($95) Metallgesellschaft AG, Reuterweg 14, 6000 Frankfurt a.M., Germany. TEL 069-1592390. FAX 069-1592125. TELEX 0412250-MGF-D. Ed. Michael Hergenhahn.
   —BLDSC shelfmark: 5694.800000.

880 016   US   ISSN 0026-0924
TN1
METALS ABSTRACTS. 1968. m. $1775 (foreign $1875). A S M International, Materials Information, Materials Park, OH 44073. TEL 216-338-5151. FAX 216-338-4634. TELEX 980-619. (UK addr.: Institute of Metals, Materials Information, 1 Carlton House Terr., London SW1Y 5DB, England. TEL 071-839-4071) (Co-sponsor: Institute of Metals, London) circ. 1,500. **Indexed:** AESIS, Br.Ceram.Abstr.
   ●Also available online. Vendor(s): CEDOCAR, CISTI, Data-Star (META), DIALOG (File no.32/METADEX), European Space Agency (File no.3/METADEX), FIZ Technik (META), Orbit Information Technologies (METADEX), STN International (METADEX). Also available on CD-ROM. Producer(s): Dialog Information Services.
   —BLDSC shelfmark: 5699.250000.
   Formed by the merger of: Review of Metal Literature; Metallurgical Abstracts.
   Description: Monitors international literature on all aspects of metallurgical science and technology.

669 016   US   ISSN 0026-0932
METALS ABSTRACTS INDEX. 1968. m. $775 (foreign $825). A S M International, Materials Information, Materials Park, OH 44073. TEL 216-338-5151. FAX 216-338-4634. TELEX 980-619. (UK addr.: Institute of Metals, Materials Information, 1 Carlton House Terr., London SW1Y 5DB, England. TEL 071-839-4071) (Co-sponsor: Institute of Metals, London) cum.index.
   ●Also available online. Vendor(s): CEDOCAR, CISTI, Data-Star (META), DIALOG (File no.32/METADEX), European Space Agency (File no.3/METADEX), FIZ Technik (META), Orbit Information Technologies (METADEX), STN International (METADEX). Also available on CD-ROM. Producer(s): Dialog Information Services.
   —BLDSC shelfmark: 5699.260000.
   Description: Companion publication of Metals Abstract containing subject, author and corporate author indexes.

669.23   US
MINE PRODUCTION OF SILVER. 1973. a. $40. Silver Institute, 1112 16th St., N.W., Ste. 240, Washington, DC 20036-4823. TEL 202-783-0500. TELEX 904233. Ed. John H. Lutley. (back issues avail.)
   Description: Covers silver production in 58 countries.

669.1   JA   ISSN 0497-1140
MONTHLY REPORT OF THE IRON AND STEEL STATISTICS. (Text in English and Japanese) vol.20, 1977. m. 6000 Yen. Japan Iron and Steel Federation, Economic Research and Statistics Department - Nihon Tekko Renmei, Keidanren Kaikan, 9-4, 1-chome, Ote-machi, Chiyoda-ku, Tokyo 100, Japan. TEL 03-279-3611. FAX 03-245-0144. TELEX 222-4210. charts; stat.

669.7 310   US   ISSN 0146-5678
HD9539.5.C383   CODEN: CINCDI
NONFERROUS CASTINGS. (Series MA33E) a. price varies. U.S. Bureau of the Census, Data User Services Division, Washington, DC 20233. TEL 301-763-4100. (Subscr. to: Supt. of Documents, Washington, DC 20402) (also avail. in microfiche) **Indexed:** Chem.Abstr.

669 338   US
NONFERROUS METALS ALERT. (Part of: Materials Business Information Series) 1985. m. $330 (foreign $340); Metal Abstracts subscribers $245 (foreign $255). A S M International, Materials Information, Materials Park, OH 44073. TEL 216-338-5151. FAX 216-338-4634. TELEX 980-619. (UK addr.: Institute of Metals, Materials Information, 1 Carlton House Terr., London SW1Y 5DB, England. TEL 071-839-4071) Ed.Bd.
   ●Also available online. Vendor(s): CEDOCAR, CISTI, Data-Star (MBUS), DIALOG (File no.269), European Space Agency (File no.111), Orbit Information Technologies (MATERIALS/B), STN International (MATBUS). Also available on CD-ROM. Producer(s): Dialog Information Services.
   Formerly: Nonferrous Alert.
   Description: International coverage of business developments for the nonferrous metals industry.

O E C D. STEEL MARKET IN (YEAR) AND OUTLOOK FOR (YEAR). (Organization for Economic Cooperation and Development) see BUSINESS AND ECONOMICS — Abstracting, Bibliographies, Statistics

669 016   FR   ISSN 0761-1684
P A S C A L THEMA. T 240: METAUX. METALLURGIE. 1985. 10/yr. 1575 F. Centre National de la Recherche Scientifique, Institut de l'Information Scientifique et Technique, B.P. 54, 54514 Vandoeuvre-Les-Nancy Cedex, France. TEL 83-50-46-00. abstr.; index. cum.index. (also avail. in microform from MIM) **Indexed:** World Alum.Abstr.
   ●Also available online. Vendor(s): European Space Agency, Telesystemes - Questel.
   Formerly: P A S C A L Thema. Part 240: Metaux. Metallurgie; Which superseded (1969-1984): Bulletin Signaletique. Part 740: Metaux. Metallurgie (ISSN 0007-5655)

METALLURGY — ABSTRACTING, BIBLIOGRAPHIES, STATISTICS

671.52 016   GW   ISSN 0340-4749
REFERATE: SCHWEISSEN UND VERWANDTE VERFAHREN/BULLETIN OF ABSTRACTS: WELDING AND ALLIED PROCESSES. 1956. 10/yr. DM.266.35. Bundesanstalt fuer Materialforschung und -pruefung, Unter den Eichen 87, 1000 Berlin 45, Germany. TEL 030-8104-6401. FAX 030-8112029. (Co-sponsor: Deutscher Verband fuer Schweisstechnik (DVS)) bk.rev.; abstr.; charts; illus.; cumulative author and keyword index; circ. 400. (back issues avail.)
●Also available online.
   Formerly: Selective Abstracting Service: Welding and Allied Processes (ISSN 0037-1432)
   Description: Features developments in welding, metallurgy, engineering weldability of materials, equipment, application, failures, testing, etc.

620.1 016   RU   ISSN 0131-3533
Z6679.C7   CODEN: RKZKA6
REFERATIVNYI ZHURNAL. KORROZIYA I ZASHCHITA OT KORROZII. English translation: Corrosion Control Abstracts (UK ISSN 0010-9347) 1968. m. 83.20 Rub. Vsesoyuznyi Institut Nauchno-Tekhnicheskoi Informatsii (VINITI), Baltiiskaya ul., 14, Moscow A-219, Russia. (Subscr. to: Mezhdunarodnaya Kniga, Dimitrova ul. 39, 113095 Moscow, Russia) **Indexed:** Chem.Abstr., Met.Abstr., World Alum.Abstr.

669 016   RU   ISSN 0034-2491
REFERATIVNYI ZHURNAL. METALLURGIYA. 1961. m. 256 Rub. (320 Rub. including index). Vsesoyuznyi Institut Nauchno-Tekhnicheskoi Informatsii (VINITI), Baltiiskaya ul., 14, Moscow A-219, Russia. (Subscr. to: Mezhdunarodnaya Kniga, Dimitrova ul. 39, 113095 Moscow, Russia) abstr.; bibl.; pat.; circ. 1,649. **Indexed:** Chem.Abstr., Met.Abstr., World Alum.Abstr.

671.52 316   RU   ISSN 0131-3525
REFERATIVNYI ZHURNAL. SVARKA. 1965. m. 76.20 Rub. Vsesoyuznyi Institut Nauchno-Tekhnicheskoi Informatsii (VINITI), Baltiiskaya ul., 14, Moscow A-219, Russia. (Subscr. to: Mezhdunarodnaya Kniga, Dimitrova ul. 39, 113095 Moscow, Russia)
—BLDSC shelfmark: 0148.460000.

669 016   RU   ISSN 0135-0935
SIGNAL'NAYA INFORMATSIYA. KOMPOZITSIONNYE MATERIALY. 1976. m. 8.40 Rub. Vsesoyuznyi Institut Nauchno-Tekhnicheskoi Informatsii (VINITI), Baltiiskaya ul. 14, Moscow A-219, Russia. (Subscr. to: Mezhdunarodnaya Kniga, Dimitrova ul. 39, 113095 Moscow, Russia)

620.112 016   RU   ISSN 0202-8670
SIGNAL'NAYA INFORMATSIYA. KORROZIYA I ZASHCHITA OT KORROZII. 1970. s-m. 30.40 Rub. Vsesoyuznyi Institut Nauchno-Tekhnicheskoi Informatsii (VINITI), Baltiiskaya ul. 14, Moscow A-219, Russia. (Subscr. to: Mezhdunarodnaya Kniga, Dimitrova ul. 39, 113095 Moscow, Russia)

SOURCE JOURNALS IN METALS AND MATERIALS. see *METALLURGY*

338 314   EI   ISSN 0378-7559
HD9525.A2
STATISTICAL OFFICE OF THE EUROPEAN COMMUNITIES. MONTHLY STATISTICS IRON AND STEEL. (Text in English, French, German) 1962. m. $62. Statistical Office of the European Communities, L-2985 Luxembourg, Luxembourg. (Dist. in the U.S. by: Unipub, 4611-F Assembly Dr., Lanham, MD 20706-4391)
—BLDSC shelfmark: 4578.050000.
   Formerly: Statistical Office of the European Communities. Iron and Steel (ISSN 0021-1532)

669.1 310   II   ISSN 0081-511X
HD9526.I6
STATISTICS FOR IRON AND STEEL INDUSTRY IN INDIA. (Text in English) 1964. s-a. price varies. Steel Authority of India Ltd., Ispat Bhavan, Lodi Rd., New Delhi 110003, India. FAX 694015. TELEX 031-62689. Eds. K. Viswanathan, M. Usman. index; circ. 1,000.

669.142 310   UN   ISSN 0501-3062
HD9510.4
STATISTICS OF WORLD TRADE IN STEEL. 1961. a. price varies. Economic Commission for Europe (ECE), Palais des Nations, 1211 Geneva 10, Switzerland. TEL 22-740-0921. TELEX 412962. (Or: United Nations Publications, Rm. DC2-853, New York, NY 10017) (also avail. in microfiche) **Indexed:** IIS.

310   UN   ISSN 0084-8174
STATISTICS ON WORLD TRADE IN ENGINEERING PRODUCTS. BULLETIN. (Text in English, French and Russian; tables in English) 1963. a. price varies. Economic Commission for Europe (ECE), Palais des Nations, 1211 Geneva 10, Switzerland. TEL 734-6011. FAX 733-9879. TELEX 412962. (Or: United Nations Publications, Rm. DC2-853, New York, NY 10017) (also avail. in microfiche)
—BLDSC shelfmark: 2909.535000.

669 310   GW   ISSN 0081-5365
STATISTISCHES JAHRBUCH DER EISEN- UND STAHLINDUSTRIE. 1929. a. DM.49. (Wirtschaftsvereinigung Eisen- und Stahlindustrie) Verlag Stahleisen mbH, Sohnstr. 65, Postfach 105164, 4000 Duesseldorf 1, Germany. TEL 0211-6707-0.

669.1   BE
STEEL STATISTICAL YEARBOOK (YEAR). (Text in English) a. 2200 Fr. (diskette 3000 Fr.). International Iron and Steel Institute, Rue Colonel Bourg 120, B-1040 Brussels, Belgium. TEL 02-7359075. FAX 02-7358012. TELEX 22639. charts; illus.; stat. (also avail. on diskette)
   Description: Presents statistics and information, by country, on crude steel production, casting development, trade figures, consumption, and raw materials.

669 338   US
STEELS ALERT. (Part of: Materials Business Information Series) 1983. m. $265 (foreign $275); Metals Abstracts subscribers $165 (foreign $175). A S M International, Materials Information, Materials Park, OH 44073. TEL 216-338-5151. FAX 216-338-4634. TELEX 980-619. (UK addr.: Institute of Metals, Materials Information, 1 Carlton House Terr., London SW1Y 5DB, England. TEL 071-839-4071) Ed.Bd. circ. 180.
●Also available online. Vendor(s): CISTI, CREDO, Data-Star (MBUS), DIALOG (File no.269), European Space Agency (File no.111), Orbit Information Technologies (MATERIALS/B), STN International (MATBUS).
Also available on CD-ROM. Producer(s): Dialog Information Services.
   Formerly (until 1985): Materials Business Abstracts: Steels Supplement to Metals Abstracts.
   Description: International coverage of business developments for the steel industry.

669 016   UK   ISSN 0950-5199
SURFACE TREATMENT TECHNOLOGY ABSTRACTS. 1959. bi-m. £360($750) Finishing Publications Ltd., 105 Whitney Drive, Stevenage, Hertfordshire SG1 4DF, England. TEL 0438-745115. FAX 0438-364536. Ed. R. Pinner. adv.; bk.rev.; abstr.; pat.; index; circ. 1,000. **Indexed:** Art & Archaeol.Tech.Abstr., Corros.Abstr., World Surf.Coat.
   Formerly: Metal Finishing Abstracts (ISSN 0026-0584)
   Description: Details, patents, reports, standards and translations from industrial countries of the world.

669 310   UK
TIN STATISTICS. 1973. a. £25. International Tin Council, Haymarket House, 1 Oxendon St., London SW1Y 4EQ, England. TEL 01 930 0451. **Indexed:** IIS.
   Supersedes in part: International Tin Council. Statistical Yearbook (ISSN 0074-9117); International Tin Council. Statistical Supplement. Tin, Tinplate Canning (ISSN 0074-9109)
   Description: Statistical profile of tin productions, consumption, trade, stocks, tin prices and price indices of non- ferrous metals.

669   US   ISSN 0278-4238
Z6678
TRANSLATIONS INDEX; a quarterly source and author index to the available translations into English of technical papers in metals and materials. 1977. q. $135. A S M International, Materials Information, Materials Park, OH 44073. TEL 216-338-5151. FAX 216-338-4634. TELEX 980-619. (UK addr.: Institute of Metals, Materials Information, 1 Carlton Terr., London SW1Y 5DB, England. TEL 071-839-4071)
   Formerly: A S M Translations Index (ISSN 0263-2659)

669 310   UN   ISSN 0049-4828
HD9539.T8
TUNGSTEN STATISTICS. 1967. q. $25 per no. (United Nations Conference on Trade and Development (UNCTAD)) United Nations Publications, Room DC2-853, New York, Switzerland, NY 10017. TEL 212-963-8302, 212-063-3489. (Or: Palais des Nations, CH-1211 Geneva 10, Switzerland) **Indexed:** IIS.
—BLDSC shelfmark: 9070.990000.

669.1 338.4   UK   ISSN 0952-5505
U K IRON AND STEEL INDUSTRY. ANNUAL STATISTICS. 1918. a. £60. U K Iron and Steel Statistics Bureau, Canterbury House, 2 Sydenham Rd., Croydon CR9 2LZ, England. TEL 081-686-9050. FAX 081-680-8616. TELEX 932575. stat.; circ. 600. (back issues avail.)
   Formerly: Iron and Steel. Annual Statistics for the United Kingdom (ISSN 0075-0867)
   Description: Provides UK iron and steel industry with historical comparisons and detailed trade information.

U S S R REPORT: MATERIALS SCIENCE. see *ENGINEERING — Abstracting, Bibliographies, Statistics*

669 016   NE
VERENIGING VOOR OPPERVLAKTETECHNIEKEN VAN MATERIALEN. DOCUMENTATIESERVICE. (Text in Dutch; summaries in various languages) 1957. m. $340. Vereniging voor Oppervlaktetechnieken van Materialen - Association for Surface Finishing Techniques, P.O. Box 120, 3720 AC Bilthoven, Netherlands. FAX 030-287674. Ed. T. van der Klis. abstr.; circ. 95.
   Formerly: Vereniging voor Oppervlaktetechnieken van Metalen. Documentatieservice (ISSN 0042-3882)

671.52 016   UK
WELDALERT; selective dissemination of information. 12/yr. £200 (effective 1992). (T W I - The Welding Institute) Pergamon Press plc, Headington Hill Hall, Oxford OX3 0BW, England. TEL 0865-794141. FAX 0865-743911. TELEX 83177 PERGAP. (And: 660 White Plains Rd., Tarrytown, NY 10591-5153. TEL 914-524-9200)
   Description: Provides selections according to a subscriber's specific information need of current abstracts from the Weldasearch database covering all aspects of welding technology.

671.52   US   ISSN 0952-0287
TS227.A1
WELDING ABSTRACTS. 1988. m. £340 (effective 1992). (T W I - The Welding Institute, UK) Pergamon Press, Inc., Journals Division, 660 White Plains Rd., Tarrytown, NY 10591-5153. TEL 914-524-9200. FAX 914-333-2444. (And: Headington Hill Hall, Oxford OX3 0BW, England. TEL 0865-794141) Ed. Peter Adams. abstr. (also avail. in microform; back issues avail.)
●Also available online. Vendor(s): Orbit Information Technologies.
   Description: Covers all aspects of research into joining and welding, including relevant developments in adhesives and automation.

669.722 016 US ISSN 0002-6697
Z6679.A47
WORLD ALUMINUM ABSTRACTS; a monthly review of the world's technical literature on aluminum. (Text in English) 1968. m. $325 to individuals; libraries $175. Aluminum Association, Inc., 900 19th St., N.W., Ste. 300, Washington, DC 20006. TEL 202-862-5100. (Co-sponsors: European Aluminum Association; Japan Light Metal Association; Aluminum Development Council) abstr.; index; circ. 1,100. (magnetic tape; also avail. in microfiche from UMI) **Indexed:** Chem.Abstr. ●Also available online. Vendor(s): DIALOG (File no.33), European Space Agency (File no.9/ALUMINUM).

669 UK
WORLD BUREAU OF METAL STATISTICS. ANNUAL REPORT. a. World Bureau of Metal Statistics, 27a High St., Ware, Herts SG12 9BA, England. TEL 0920-461274.

669 UK ISSN 0043-8758
HD9539.A1
WORLD METAL STATISTICS. 1948. m. $1850. World Bureau of Metal Statistics, 27a High St., Ware, Herts SG12 9BA, England. TEL 0920-461274. Ed. J.L.T. Davies. adv.; stat.; circ. 520. (also avail. in microfilm) **Indexed:** P.A.I.S.
—BLDSC shelfmark: 9356.670000.
Formerly: World Non-Ferrous Metal Statistics.

WORLD METAL STATISTICS. YEARBOOK. see *METALLURGY*

669.142 UK ISSN 0141-0806
WORLD STAINLESS STEEL STATISTICS. 1972. a. $400. World Bureau of Metal Statistics, 27a High St., Ware, Herts SG12 9BA, England. TEL 0920-461274. (Subscr. to: Metal Bulletin PLC., Park House, Park Terrace, Worcester Park, Surrey KT4 7HY, England) Ed. J.L.T. Davies.

669.1 BE
WORLD STEEL IN FIGURES (YEAR). (Text in English) a. free. International Iron and Steel Institute, Rue Colonel Bourg 120, B-1040 Brussels, Belgium. TEL 02-7359075. FAX 02-7358012. TELEX 22639. charts; illus.; stat.
Description: Contains facts on employment, capital investment expenditure, iron ore production, scrap consumption and the geographic distribution of production and consumption.

669.142 UK ISSN 0952-5742
WORLD TRADE - STAINLESS, HIGH SPEED & OTHER ALLOY STEEL. 1979. q.(quantities); a.(values). £250. U.K. Iron and Steel Statistics Bureau, Canterbury House, 2 Sydenham Rd., Croydon CR9 2LZ, England. TEL 081-686-9050. FAX 081-680-8616. TELEX 932575.
Description: Cumulative (quarterly) book detailing the export trade of major steel producing countries in selected alloy products.

669 UK ISSN 0952-5734
WORLD TRADE STEEL. 1970. q.(quantities); a.(values). £250. U.K. Iron and Steel Statistics Bureau, Canterbury House, 2 Sydenham Road, Croydon CR9 2LZ, England. TEL 081-686-9050. FAX 081-680-8616. TELEX 932575. circ. 200.
Description: Cumulative (quarterly) book detailing the export trade of 16 major steel producing countries collectively accounting for over 85% of world exports. Covers 28 product groups and 100 export markets.

669.142 UK ISSN 0266-7347
WORLD WROUGHT COPPER STATISTICS. 1985. a. $400. World Bureau of Metal Statistics, 27a High St., Ware, Herts SG12 9BA, England. TEL 0920-461274. Ed. J.L.T. Davies. **Indexed:** Copper Abstr.

669.5 016 UK ISSN 0950-1592
ZINCSCAN; a review of recent technical literature on the uses of zinc and its products. 1943. q. £50. C & C Associates, 4 Newmans Row, Lincolns Rd., High Wycombe, Bucks HP12 3RE, England. adv.; bk.rev.; abstr.; index; circ. 1,000. **Indexed:** AESIS, Br.Ceram.Abstr., Chem.Abstr., Corros.Abstr., World Surf.Coat.
Formerly: Zinc Abstracts (ISSN 0044-4731)

METALLURGY — Welding

671.52 SA ISSN 0002-0672
AFROX NEWS. (Text in Afrikaans or English) 1955. q. free. African Oxygen Ltd., Box 5404, Johannesburg 2000, South Africa. Ed. Christopher Fieldgate. adv.; charts; illus.; circ. 15,000.

671.52 US
AMERICAN WELDING SOCIETY ANNUAL MEETING. ABSTRACTS OF PAPERS. a. American Welding Society, Box 351040, Miami, FL 33135. TEL 305-443-9353.

669 KR ISSN 0005-2302
AVTOMATICHESKAYA SVARKA; vsesoyuznyi nauchno-tekhnicheskii i proizvodstvennyi zhurnal. 1948. m. 10.80 Rub.($39) (Akademiya Nauk Ukrainskoi S.S.R., Institut Elektrosvarki im. E.O. Patona) Izdatel'stvo Naukova Dumka, c/o Yu.A. Khramov, Dir, Ul. Repina, 3, Kiev 252 601, Ukraine. TEL 224-40-68. (Subscr. to: Mezhdunarodnaya Kniga, Moscow, G-200, Russia) Ed. B.E. Paton. adv.; bk.rev.; charts; illus.; index; circ. 6,000. **Indexed:** Chem.Abstr., INIS Atomind., Met.Abstr., Sci.Abstr.

671.52 FR
CAHIERS DE LA FONDERIE; bulletin economique mensual. 1963. m. 280 F. Groupement d'Achats des Fondeurs de France, 2 rue de Bassano, 75783 Paris Cedex 16, France. TELEX 620617. Ed. G. Cornet. bk.rev.; stat.; index; circ. 1,400.

671.52 SA
F W P MATERIALS ENGINEERING JOURNAL. 1961. m. $55 (effective 1992). (South African Institutes of Foundrymen, Welding and Production Engineers) Mattec Publishing, P.O. Box 31548, Braamfontein 2017, South Africa. TEL 011-403-3798. Ed. Susan Custers. adv.; bk.rev.; charts; illus.; tr.lit.; index. cum.index: 1961-1963; circ. 3,650. (also avail. in microform from UMI; reprint service avail. from UMI) **Indexed:** B.C.I.R.A., Br.Ceram.Abstr., Chem.Abstr., Eng.Ind., Excerp.Med., Ind.S.A.Per., INIS Atomind., ISMEC, Met.Abstr., World Alum.Abstr.
Former titles: Founding, Welding, Production Engineering Journal; (until vol.17, no.3, 1977): F.W.P. Journal (ISSN 0015-9026)

671.52 UK
FAB GUIDE; guide to the UK welding & welding fabrication industry. a. £35. International Business & Technical Magazines Ltd., Queensway House, 2, Queensway, Redhill, Surrey RH1 1QS, England. TEL 0737-768611. FAX 0737-761989. Ed. Richard Southgate.

671.52 CC ISSN 1001-1382
HANJIE/WELDING. (Text in Chinese) m. Jixie Dianzi Bu, Harbin Hanjie Yanjiusuo - Ministry of Mechanics and Electronics, Harbin Welding Research Institute, 65, Hexing Lu, Harbin, Heilongjiang 150080, People's Republic of China. TEL 36695. Ed. Ren Dacheng.

671.52 CC ISSN 0253-360X
HANJIE XUEBAO/JOURNAL OF WELDING. (Text in Chinese) q. Zhongguo Jixie Gongcheng Xuehui - Chinese Society of Mechanical Engineering, 65, Hexing Lu, Harbin, Heilongjiang 150080, People's Republic of China. TEL 36695. Ed. Li Shaoshan.
—BLDSC shelfmark: 8912.450000.

671.52 US
HAYNES ALLOYS DIGEST. 1950. q. Haynes International, Inc., 1020 W. Park Ave., Box 9013, Kokomo, IN 46904-9013. TEL 317-456-6000. FAX 317-456-6905. TEL 317-2280. Ed. Elaine Maddox. circ. 11,000. (back issues avail.)
Former titles: Haynes High Performance Alloys Digest; Cabot High Performance Alloys Digest.
Description: Solutions to problems caused by deterioration of equipment from heat and corrosion.

671.52 FI
HITSAUSTEKNIIKKA - SVETSTEKNIK. 1949. 5/yr. FIM 220 (outside Scandinavia FIM 250). Suomen Hitsausteknillinen Yhdistys - Welding Society of Finland, Makelankatu 36A, 00510 Helsinki, Finland. FAX 0-715093. Ed. Juha Lukkari. adv.; circ. 5,000 (paid); 5,500 (controlled). **Indexed:** Met.Abstr.

671.52 II ISSN 0046-9092
CODEN: IWLJAK
INDIAN WELDING JOURNAL. 1969. 4/yr. Rs.80. Indian Institute of Welding, 3A Loudon St., Calcutta 700 017, India. TEL 91-33-401350. Ed. A.K. Mitra. adv.; bk.rev.; abstr.; bibl.; charts; illus.; circ. 2,500.
Indexed: Chem.Abstr., Met.Abstr., World Alum.Abstr.
Description: Promotes knowledge and technology of joining materials.

671.52 II ISSN 0377-7391
TS227.A1
INDUSTRIAL WELDER. (Text in English) 1971. m. Rs.36. Industrial Welder Publications, Zita Villa, 212, Kalina, Santa Cruz E., Bombay 400029, India. Ed. Felix K. Soans. adv.; bk.rev.; illus.; circ. 3,700.

671.52 US
INTERNATIONAL THERMAL SPRAYING CONFERENCE. PREPRINT OF PAPERS. irreg., 9th, 1980. $25. American Welding Society, Box 351040, Miami, FL 33135. TEL 305-443-9353.

671.52 GW ISSN 0930-9241
INTERNATIONAL WELDING ENGINEERING. (Text in Chinese) 1987. a. free in the Peoples Republic of China. Deutscher Verlag fuer Schweisstechnik, Aachener Str. 172, 4000 Duesseldorf 1, Germany. TEL 0211-15759-0. FAX 0211-1575950. TELEX 8582583. circ. 7,000. (back issues avail.)

671.52 RU ISSN 0202-778X
ITOGI NAUKI I TEKHNIKI: SVARKA. (Text in Russian) 1967. irreg., vol.20, 1989. 5.40 Rub. Vsesoyuznyi Institut Nauchno-Tekhnicheskoi Informatsii (VINITI), Ul. Baltiiskaya 14, Moscow A-219, Russia. (Subscr. to: Mezhdunarodnaya Kniga, Dimitrova ul. 39, 113095 Moscow, Russia) **Indexed:** Chem.Abstr.
—BLDSC shelfmark: 0160.800000.

671.52 JA ISSN 0021-4787
TS227.A1 CODEN: YOGAAK
JAPAN WELDING SOCIETY. JOURNAL/YOSETSU GAKKAISHI. (Text in Japanese; summaries in English) 1926. q. 12000 Yen. Japan Welding Society - Yosetsu Gakkai, 1-11 Kanda Sakumo-cho, Chiyoda-ku, Tokyo 101, Japan. FAX 03-3253-3059. Ed. Keiji Tachiki. adv.; bk.rev.; bibl.; charts; illus. **Indexed:** Chem.Abstr., JTA, Met.Abstr., World Alum.Abstr.
—BLDSC shelfmark: 4808.480000.

671.52 NE ISSN 0023-8694
CODEN: LASTAW
LASTECHNIEK. 1934. m. fl.45. (Nederlands Instituut voor Lastechniek - Dutch Welding Institute) Wijt en Zn. B.V., Box 268, Rotterdam, Netherlands. adv.; index; circ. 3,000. **Indexed:** C.I.S. Abstr., Excerp.Med., Met.Abstr., World Alum.Abstr.
—BLDSC shelfmark: 5157.000000.

671.52 US
M E M C O NEWS. 1950. q. free to qualified personnel. Miller Electric Manufacturing Co., 1635 W. Spencer, Box 1079, Appleton, WI 54911. TEL 414-734-9821. FAX 414-735-4135. Ed. R.F. Metko. circ. 54,000 (controlled). **Indexed:** Met.Abstr., World Alum.Abstr.
Description: News, features, and photography on contemporary applications of arc welding equipment.

MATERIALS AND MANUFACTURE. see *ENGINEERING — Mechanical Engineering*

MATERIALS INFORMATION DIGEST SERIES. see *METALLURGY*

METALLIC MATERIALS. see *ENGINEERING — Engineering Mechanics And Materials*

METALLURGIE. LEXIQUE. see *METALLURGY*

671.52 CC ISSN 1001-4934
MO JU. (Text in Chinese) bi-m. Shanghai Moju Jishu Yanjiusuo, Jiaotong Daxue Nei, No. 1954, Huashan Lu, Shanghai 200030, People's Republic of China. TEL 4310310.

671.52 GW
DER PRAKTIKER; Schweissen und Schneiden. 1948. m. DM.117 (foreign DM.122). Deutscher Verlag fuer Schweisstechnik, Aachener Str. 172, Postfach 101965, 4000 Duesseldorf 1, Germany. TEL 0211-15759-0. FAX 0211-1575950. TELEX 8582583. Ed. D. Flemming. circ. 18,000. **Indexed:** Met.Abstr., World Alum.Abstr.

METALLURGY — WELDING

671.52   PL   ISSN 0033-2364
PRZEGLAD SPAWALNICTWA. 1949. m. $90. (Stowarzyszenie Inzynierow i Technikow Mechanikow Polskich - Association of Polish Mechanical Engineers and Technicians) Oficyna Wydawnicza SIMP Press, Ltd., Ul. Zurawia 22, 00-515 Warsaw, Poland. (Dist. by: Ars Polona-Ruch, Krakowskie Przedmiescie 7, Warsaw, Poland) adv.; bk.rev.; bibl.; charts; illus.; index; circ. 5,480. (also avail. in microfilm) **Indexed:** C.I.S. Abstr., Chem.Abstr., Met.Abstr., World Alum.Abstr.

671.52   US
R & D FOCUS. 1986. 3/yr. free. International Lead Zinc Research Organization, Inc., Box 12036, Research Triangle Park, NC 27709-2036. TEL 919-361-4647. FAX 919-361-1957. TELEX 261533. Ed. John A. Sharpe III. charts; illus.; circ. 1,100.
Description: Covers ongoing cooperative research and development in zinc and lead.

671.52   SP   ISSN 0048-7759
                               CODEN: RSLDB6
REVISTA DE SOLDADURA. 1971. q. 7100 ptas. (effective 1992). Centro Nacional de Investigaciones Metalurgicas, Avda. Gregorio De Amo, 8, 28040 Madrid, Spain. FAX 341-5347425. Ed. J. Fernandez. adv.; bk.rev.; bibl.; charts; illus.; circ. 1,800. **Indexed:** Chem.Abstr., Ind.SST, Met.Abstr., World Alum.Abstr.

671.52   BE   ISSN 0035-127X
TS227   CODEN: RSOUA3
REVUE DE LA SOUDURE/LASTIJDSCHRIFT. (Text in Dutch, English, French) 1945. q. 1875 BEF to non-members (foreign 2350 BEF); members 2500 BEF (foreign 1875 BEF)(effective 1992). Institut Belge de la Soudure - Belgisch Instituut voor Lastechniek, Rue des Drapiers 21, B-1050 Brussels, Belgium. adv.; bk.rev.; abstr.; charts; illus.; tr.lit.; index; circ. 800. **Indexed:** Chem.Abstr., Met.Abstr., World Alum.Abstr.
—BLDSC shelfmark: 7952.000000.
Incorporates (in 1976): Pratique du Soudage (ISSN 0032-6909)

671.52   IT   ISSN 0035-6794
TS227   CODEN: RISAAT
RIVISTA ITALIANA DELLA SALDATURA. 1949. bi-m. L.180000. Istituto Italiano della Saldatura, Lungobisagno Istria 15, 16141 Genoa, Italy. FAX 010-867780. TELEX 283054 SALDIS I. Ed. Sergio Giorgi. adv.; bk.rev.; bibl.; charts; illus.; pat.; index; circ. 3,200. **Indexed:** Bull.Signal., C.I.S. Abstr., Chem.Abstr., Met.Abstr., World Alum.Abstr.
—BLDSC shelfmark: 7987.600000.

671.52   GW   ISSN 0036-7184
TS227   CODEN: SCSCA4
SCHWEISSEN UND SCHNEIDEN. 1948. m. DM.228 (foreign DM.330). Deutscher Verlag fuer Schweisstechnik, Aachener Str. 172, Postfach 101965, 4000 Duesseldorf 1, Germany. TEL 0211-15759-0. FAX 0211-1575950. TELEX 8582583. Ed. D. Flemming. adv.; B&W page DM.4200; trim 253 x 176. bk.rev.; bibl.; charts; illus.; pat.; index; circ. 14,000. (also avail. in microform from UMI; reprint service avail. from UMI) **Indexed:** Appl.Mech.Rev., BMT, C.I.S. Abstr., Chem.Abstr., Copper Abstr., Dok.Arbeitsmed., Eng.Ind., Excerp.Med., Met.Abstr., World Alum.Abstr.
—BLDSC shelfmark: 8106.000000.
Incorporates: Schweisstechnik (ISSN 0036-7192)

671.52   SZ   ISSN 0036-7206
SCHWEISSTECHNIK/SOUDURE. (Supplement to: Technica) (Text in French and German) 1911. m. 95 Fr. to non-members. (Schweizerischer Verein fuer Schweisstechnik) Industrie-Verlag AG, Muehlebachstr. 43, CH-8032 Zurich, Switzerland. Ed.Bd. adv.; charts; illus.; pat.; circ. 3,330. **Indexed:** C.I.S. Abstr., Chem.Abstr., Eng.Ind., Excerp.Med., Met.Abstr.

671   UK   ISSN 0037-3435
TS250   CODEN: SHMIAR
SHEET METAL INDUSTRIES. 1927. m. £72. International Business & Technical Magazines Ltd., Queensway House, 2 Queensway, Redhill, Surrey RH1 1QS, England. TEL 0737-768611. FAX 0737-761989. Ed. R. Pendrous. adv.; bk.rev.; charts; illus.; tr.lit.; index. (also avail. in microfiche from UMI) **Indexed:** Br.Tech.Ind., C.I.S. Abstr., Chem.Abstr., Eng.Ind., Excerp.Med., Int.Packag.Abstr., ISMEC, Met.Abstr., World Alum.Abstr.
—BLDSC shelfmark: 8255.000000.

SHEET METAL INDUSTRIES YEAR BOOK. see METALLURGY

671.52   NE
SMITWELD REPORTAGE. (Editions in Dutch, English and German) 1962. bi-m. (Dutch ed.); 3/yr. (English and German eds.). free. Smitweld B.V., Box 253, Nieuwe Dukenburgseweg 20, Nijmegen, Netherlands. TEL 080-522204. FAX 080-522670. TELEX 48129. Ed. A. Schreuder. bk.rev.; charts; illus.; stat.; index; circ. 13,000.
Formerly: Smit-las (ISSN 0037-7287)

671.52   PO
SOLDADURA & CONSTRUCAO METALICA. 1981. q. membership. Instituto de Soldadura e Qualidade, Rua Tomas de Figueiredo 16-A, 1500 Lisbon, Portugal. Ed. F. Carvalheiro. adv.; bk.rev.; abstr.; bibl.; circ. 2,500. **Indexed:** Met.Abstr.

671.52   UK
SOLDERING & SURFACE MOUNT TECHNOLOGY. 1981. 3/yr. £38.50($77) (Surface Mount and Related Technologies (SMART) Group) Wela Publications Ltd., 8 Barns St., Ayr KA7 1XA, Scotland. TEL 0292-283186. FAX 0292-284719. Ed. William Goldie. charts; illus. **Indexed:** Cadscan, Chem.Abstr., Lead Abstr., Met.Abstr., World Alum.Abstr., Zincscan.
Formerly (until 1989): Brazing and Soldering (ISSN 0263-0060)

671.52   FR   ISSN 0038-173X
TS227   CODEN: SOTCAP
SOUDAGE ET TECHNIQUES CONNEXES. 1947. bi-m. 242 F. (Institut de Soudure) Publications de la Soudure Autogene, 32 bd. de la Chapelle, 75018 Paris, France. Ed. Daniele Schley. adv.; bk.rev.; charts; illus.; tr.lit.; index; circ. 4,200. **Indexed:** Chem.Abstr., Eng.Ind., Excerp.Med., Met.Abstr., World Alum.Abstr.

671.52   US
TS227.A1   CODEN: STCREO
SOVIET TECHNOLOGY REVIEWS. SECTION C: WELDING AND SURFACING REVIEWS. 1989. a. $118. Harwood Academic Publishers, 270 Eighth Ave., New York, NY 10011. TEL 212-206-8900. FAX 212-645-2459. TELEX 236735 GOPUB UR. (Subscr. to: Box 786, Cooper Sta., New York, NY 10276. TEL 800-545-8398; UK subscr. to: P.O. Box 90, Reading, Berkshire RG1 8JL, England. TEL 0734-560-080) Ed. B.E. Paton. (also avail. in microform)
Formerly: Soviet Technology Reviews. Section C: Welding Reviews (ISSN 1040-7073)
Refereed Serial

STROJNISKI VESTNIK/MECHANICAL ENGINEERING JOURNAL. see ENGINEERING — Mechanical Engineering

671   RU   ISSN 0491-6441
                             CODEN: SVAPAI
SVAROCHNOE PROIZVODSTVO. 1930. m. $18.60. Izdatel'stvo Mashinostroenie, 4, Stromynsky Lane, Moscow, 107076, Russia. Ed. V.M. Kudinov. adv.; bk.rev.; abstr.; bibl.; charts; illus.; index; circ. 22,500. **Indexed:** C.I.S. Abstr., Chem.Abstr., Met.Abstr., Sci.Abstr., World Alum.Abstr.
—BLDSC shelfmark: 0160.860000.

671.52   SW   ISSN 0039-7083
SVETSAREN; a welding review. (Text in English) 1936. 2/yr. free. Esab AB, P.O. Box 8004, S-40277 Goeteborg, Sweden. FAX 46-31509390. Ed. Lennart Lundberg. adv.; charts; illus.; circ. 25,000. **Indexed:** Appl.Mech.Rev., Chem.Abstr., Met.Abstr., World Alum.Abstr.
Formerly: Kjelberg och S A B Schriften (ISSN 0075-6261)

671.52   SW   ISSN 0039-7091
                             CODEN: SVTNA5
SVETSEN. (Text in Scandinavian languages) 1942. bi-m. SEK 230. Svetstekniska Foereningen, Box 5073, S-102 42 Stockholm 5, Sweden. TEL 791-29-00. FAX 611-56-23. Ed. Hans Wickstrom. adv.; bk.rev.; charts; illus.; circ. 3,800. **Indexed:** Chem.Abstr., Met.Abstr.

671.52   UK   ISSN 0963-6927
▼**T W I JOURNAL.** 1992. q. L.150 in Europe; America £250; elsewhere £160. (The Welding Institute) Abington Publishing, Abington Hall, Abington, Cambridge CB1 6AH, England. TEL 0223-891358. FAX 0223-893694.
—BLDSC shelfmark: 9076.953800.
Description: Contains research papers from the engineers and scientists at TWI.

671.52   UK
TECHNICAL DIAGNOSTICS AND NONDESTRUCTIVE TESTING. English translation of: Tekhnicheskaya Diagnostika i Nerazrushayushchii Kontrol' 1989. q. £79($130) (E.O. Paton Welding Institute, UR) Riecansky Science Publishing Co., 7 Meadow Walk, Great Abington, Cambridge CB1 6AZ, England. TEL 0223-893295. FAX 0223-893295. Ed. B.E. Paton.
Formerly: Technical Diagnostics and Nondestructive Testing in Welding (ISSN 0955-3835)
Description: Presents the latest achievements in the field of technical diagnostics and nondestructive testing in welding.

671.52   US
W R C PROGRESS REPORTS. 6/yr. $1,100 includes Welding Research Abroad, W R C Bulletins, W R C News and Welding Journal. Welding Research Council, United Engineering Center, 345 E. 47th St., New York, NY 10017. TEL 212-705-7956. **Indexed:** Met.Abstr., World Alum.Abstr.

671.52   II   ISSN 0970-4477
W R I JOURNAL. (Text in English) 1977. q. Rs.180($36) Bharat Heavy Electricals Ltd., Welding Research Institute, Tiruchirapalli 620 014, Tamil Nadu, India. TEL 0431-842311. TELEX 0455-211 BHTP IN. Ed. B. Pullat. adv.; circ. 300. (back issues avail.) **Indexed:** Eng.Ind.
—BLDSC shelfmark: 9364.598200.
Formerly (until 1989): W R I Keywords.

671.52   AT
W T I A TECHNICAL NOTES. irreg. Welding Technology Institute of Australia, P.O. Box 28, Lidcombe, N.S.W. 2141, Australia. TEL 02-748-4443. FAX 02-748-2858.
Description: Provides information on technical aspects of welding and cutting.

WELDALERT; selective dissemination of information. see METALLURGY — Abstracting, Bibliographies, Statistics

671.52   UK   ISSN 0043-2237
TK1
WELDER. 1929. q. free. Boc-Murex, Hertford Rd., Waltham Cross, Herts., England. Ed. A.S. Ailes. adv.; bk.rev.; charts; illus.; index every 3 yrs; circ. 15,500 (controlled). **Indexed:** Br.Tech.Ind., Chem.Abstr., Eng.Ind., Met.Abstr.

WELDING ABSTRACTS. see METALLURGY — Abstracting, Bibliographies, Statistics

671.52   CN
TT218
WELDING & FABRICATING CANADA. 1909. 6/yr. Can.$30. Sanford Evans Communications Ltd. (Downsview), 103 - 3500 Dufferin Ave., Downsview, Ont. M3K 1M2, Canada. TEL 416-633-2020. FAX 416-633-5725. Ed. Suzanne Lyons. adv.; charts; illus.; tr.lit.; circ. 7,500. **Indexed:** Met.Abstr., World Alum.Abstr.
Formerly: Canadian Welder and Fabricator (ISSN 0008-5324)

671.5   US   ISSN 0278-7067
TS227
WELDING AND FABRICATING DATA BOOK. 1958. biennial. $30. Penton Publishing, 1100 Superior Ave., Cleveland, OH 44114-2543. TEL 216-696-7000. FAX 216-696-8765. (Subscr. to: Box 95759, Cleveland, OH 44101) Ed. Rosalie Brosilow. adv.; charts; illus.; circ. 24,000. (reprint service avail. from UMI)
Formerly: Welding Data Book (ISSN 0511-4365)

671.52 UK ISSN 0043-2245
TS227 CODEN: WLMFAM
WELDING AND METAL FABRICATION. 1933. 10/yr. £77. International Business and Technical Magazines Ltd., Queensway House, 2 Queensway, Redhill, Surrey RH1 1QS, England. FAX 0737-761989. Ed. Roderick Robinson. adv.; bk.rev.; charts; illus.; index. (also avail. in microfiche; reprint service avail. from ISI) **Indexed:** BMT, Br.Tech.Ind., C.I.S. Abstr., Chem.Abstr., Eng.Ind., Fuel & Energy Abstr., ISMEC, Met.Abstr., Robomat, Sci.Abstr., World Alum.Abstr.
—BLDSC shelfmark: 3863.070000.
Description: For welding engineers, supervisors, distributors, sales and purchasing personnel as well as welders.

671.52 US
TS227.A1
WELDING - BRAZING - SOLDERING DIGEST. m. $145 to non-members (foreign $155); members $120 (foreign $130). A S M International, Materials Information, Materials Park, OH 44073. TEL 216-338-5151. FAX 216-338-4634. TELEX 980-619. (UK addr.: Institute of Metals, Materials Information, 1 Carlton House Terr., London SW1Y 5DB, England. TEL 071-839-4071) Ed. H. David Chafe. circ. 100. **Indexed:** Met.Abstr.
Formerly: Welding and Joining Digest (ISSN 0361-3747)
Description: Covers brazing, soldering, hard facing, adhesive-diffusion bonding, riveting and welding processes.

671.52 US ISSN 0043-2253
TS227 CODEN: WDEFAS
WELDING DESIGN AND FABRICATION. 1930. m. $50 (free to qualified personnel). Penton Publishing (Subsidiary of: Pittway Company), 1100 Superior Ave., Cleveland, OH 44114-2543. TEL 216-696-7000. FAX 216-696-8765. (Subscr. to: Box 95759, Cleveland, OH 44101) Ed. Rosalie Brosilow. adv.; bk.rev.; charts; illus.; index; circ. 40,000 (controlled). (also avail. in microform from UMI; reprint service avail. from UMI) **Indexed:** A.I.Abstr., A.S.& T.Ind., CAD CAM Abstr., Chem.Abstr., Eng.Ind., Excerp.Med., ISMEC, Met.Abstr., Robomat., World Alum.Abstr.
—BLDSC shelfmark: 9290.200000.
Incorporates (in 1975): Welding Engineer (ISSN 0043-227X)
Description: Welding processes and equipment, fabrication of weldments, structural projects and maintenance.

671.52 US ISSN 0192-7671
TS227
WELDING DISTRIBUTOR. 1921. bi-m. $30 (free to qualified personnel). Penton Publishing (Subsidiary of: Pittway Company), 1100 Superior Ave., Cleveland, OH 44114-2543. TEL 216-696-7000. FAX 216-696-8765. (Subscr. to: Box 95759, Cleveland, OH 44101) Ed. Michael Vasilakes. circ. 8,000 (controlled). (reprint service avail. from UMI)
Description: Informs on management, market statistics, selling techniques, merchandizing methods and case histories.

671.52 UK ISSN 0043-2288
TS227 CODEN: WDWRAI
WELDING IN THE WORLD/SOUDAGE DANS LE MONDE. (Text in English and French) 1963. 7/yr. £85 (effective 1992). (International Institute of Welding - Institut International de la Soudure) Pergamon Press plc, Headington Hill Hall, Oxford OX3 0BW, England. TEL 0865-794141. FAX 0865-743911. TELEX 83177 PERGAP. (And: 660 White Plains Rd., Tarrytown, NY 10593-5153. TEL 914-524-9200) Eds. P.D. Boyd, M. Bramat. adv.; abstr.; charts; illus.; circ. 900. (also avail. in microform from UMI; back issues avail.) **Indexed:** BMT, Br.Tech.Ind., C.I.S. Abstr., Chem.Abstr., Curr.Cont., Eng.Ind., ISMEC, Met.Abstr., World Alum.Abstr.
—BLDSC shelfmark: 9293.200000.
Description: Contains reports, recommendations, addresses and draft standards emanating from commissioned reports and surveys of the IIW, including coverage of processes, metallurgy, testing and inspection, health and safety issues.
Refereed Serial

671.52 US
WELDING INNOVATION QUARTERLY. q. James F. Lincoln Arc Welding Foundation, Box 17035, Cleveland, OH 44117-0035. TEL 216-481-4300. Ed. Richard Smith. circ. 60,000.

671.52 UK
WELDING INSTITUTE RESEARCH BULLETIN. 1968. m. membership only. Welding Institute, Abington Hall, Abington, Cambridge CB1 6AL, England. TEL 0223-891162.
Formerly: B W R A Bulletin.

671.52 UK ISSN 0950-7116
TS227.A1 CODEN: WEINEF
WELDING INTERNATIONAL. 1987. m. £625 in Europe; America £1050; elsewhere £650(effective 1992). (Welding Institute) Woodhead Publishing Ltd., Abington Hall, Abington, Cambridge CB1 6AH, England. TEL 0223-891358. FAX 0223-893694. bibl.; charts; illus.; index. **Indexed:** Excerp.Med.
—BLDSC shelfmark: 9290.670000.
Description: Provides translations of complete articles selected from major welding journals of the world.

671.52 US ISSN 0043-2296
TS227 CODEN: WEJUA3
WELDING JOURNAL. 1922. m. $30. American Welding Society, Box 351040, Miami, FL 33135. TEL 305-443-9353. Ed. Jeff Weber. adv.; bk.rev.; illus.; pat.; tr.lit.; index; circ. 40,000. (also avail. in microform from UMI) **Indexed:** A.S.& T.Ind., AESIS, Appl.Mech.Rev., BMT, CAD CAM Abstr., Chem.Abstr., Curr.Cont., Eng.Ind., Ergon.Abstr., Excerp.Med., Int.Aerosp.Abstr., ISMEC, Met.Abstr., Robomat, World Alum.Abstr.
—BLDSC shelfmark: 9291.000000.

671.52 US ISSN 0043-2318
TS227
WELDING RESEARCH ABROAD. 1954. 10/yr. $1,100 includes Progress Reports, W R C Bulletins, W R C News and Welding Journal. Welding Research Council, 345 E. 47th St., New York, NY 10017. TEL 212-705-7956. Ed. C.R. Felmley, Jr. charts; illus.; stat.; index; circ. 800 (controlled). **Indexed:** Met.Abstr., World Alum.Abstr.
—BLDSC shelfmark: 9291.500000.

671.52 US ISSN 0043-2326
TS227 CODEN: WRCBA2
WELDING RESEARCH COUNCIL BULLETIN. 1949. 10/yr. $1,100 includes Welding Research Abroad, Progress Reports, W R C News and Welding Journal. Welding Research Council, 345 E. 47th St., New York, NY 10017. TEL 212-705-7956. Ed. C.R. Felmley, Jr. charts; illus.; circ. 900 (controlled). **Indexed:** Chem.Abstr., Curr.Cont., Eng.Ind., Int.Aerosp.Abstr., Met.Abstr., World Alum.Abstr.
—BLDSC shelfmark: 9364.585000.

671.52 US
WELDING RESEARCH COUNCIL YEARBOOK. 1936. a. membership. Welding Research Council, United Engineering Center, 345 E. 47th St., New York, NY 10017. TEL 212-705-7956. circ. 700.

671.52 US
WELDING RESEARCH NEWS. 4/yr. $1,100 includes Welding Research Abroad, Progress Reports, W R C Bulletins and Welding Journal. Welding Research Council, 345 E. 47th St., New York, NY 10017. TEL 212-705-7956.
Description: Highlights articles and items on current developments in welding research.

671.52 UK
CODEN: WELRD7
WELDING REVIEW INTERNATIONAL. 1982. q. £52. International Business & Technical Magazines Ltd., Queensway House, 2 Queensway, Redhill, Surrey RH1 1QS, England. TEL 0737-768611. FAX 0737-761989. Ed. Richard Southgate. adv.; bk.rev.; circ. 5,000. **Indexed:** BMT, Chem.Abstr., Met.Abstr., World Alum.Abstr.
Formerly: Welding Review (ISSN 0262-642X)

671.5 AT
WELDING TECHNOLOGY INSTITUTE OF AUSTRALIA. BULLETIN. 1966. irreg. $1 per no. Welding Technology Institute of Australia, P.O. Box 28, Lidcombe, N.S.W. 2131, Australia. TEL 02-922-3711.
Formerly: Australian Welding Research Association. Bulletin (ISSN 0084-7631)

671.52 CN
WHAT'S NEW IN WELDING. 1988. 6/yr. Maclean-Hunter Ltd., Maclean-Hunter Bldg., 777 Bay St., Toronto, Ont. M5W 1A7, Canada. TEL 416-596-5713. FAX 416-593-3193. TELEX 06-219547.
Formerly: Welding Quarterly.

671.52 CI ISSN 0044-1902
CODEN: ZAVAA 8
ZAVARIVANJE. (Text in Croatian; summaries and content pages in English and German) 1958. bi-m. 1200 din.($70) (Jugoslavenski Savez za Zavarivanje) Drustvo za Tehniku Zavarivanja Hrvatske, Dure Salaja 1, 41000 Zagreb, Croatia. TELEX 22648 FSB YU. Ed. Goran Vrucimic. adv.; bk.rev.; index; circ. 2,000. **Indexed:** Bull.Signal., Chem.Abstr., Eng.Ind., Met.Abstr., Ref.Zh., World Alum.Abstr.

671.52 CS ISSN 0044-5525
CODEN: ZVARAX
ZVARANIE/WELDING. (Text in Czech or Slovak; summaries in English, German, Russian) 1952. m. 96 Kcs.($33) (Ministerstvo Hospodarstva Slovenskej Republiky - Ministry of Economy of the Slovak Republik) Alfa, Hurbanovo nam. 3, 815 89 Bratislava, Czechoslovakia. TEL 331-441. (Dist. by: Slovart, nam. Slobody 6, 817 64 Bratislava, Czechoslovakia) adv.; bk.rev.; charts; illus.; pat.; circ. 3,000. **Indexed:** C.I.S. Abstr., Chem.Abstr., Met.Abstr., World Alum.Abstr.
—BLDSC shelfmark: 9538.500000.

METEOROLOGY

551.5 US
A M S NEWSLETTER (BOSTON). 1980. m. $80 (foreign $100). American Meteorological Society, 45 Beacon St., Boston, MA 02108-3693. TEL 617-227-2425. FAX 617-742-8718. Ed. Roland D. Paine. circ. 595.
Description: Contains news briefs, dates, notes on people, information on grants, and contracts for meteorologists, oceanographers, and hydrologists.

551 US ISSN 0001-4338
ACADEMY OF SCIENCES OF THE U S S R. IZVESTIYA. ATMOSPHERIC AND OCEANIC PHYSICS. English translation of: Akademiya Nauk S.S.S.R. Izvestiya. Seriya Fizika Atmosfery i Okeana (UR ISSN 0002-3515) 1965. 12/yr. $550 to non-members (foreign $560); members $440 (foreign $450). American Geophysical Union, 2000 Florida Ave., N.W., Washington, DC 20009. TEL 202-462-6900. FAX 202-328-0566. TELEX 710-882-9300. (Germany addr.: Postfach 49, Max-Planck-Str. 1, 3411 Katlenburg-Lindau, Germany. TEL 49-5556-1440) (Co-publisher: American Meteorological Society) bibl.; charts; illus.; index; circ. 270. (reprint service avail. from ISI) **Indexed:** Math.R., Ocean.Abstr., Sci.Abstr.
—BLDSC shelfmark: 0412.735000.

551.5 CC ISSN 0894-0525
QC851 CODEN: AMTSEZ
ACTA METEOROLOGICA SINICA. Chinese edition: Qixiang Xuebao (ISSN 0577-6619) (Text in English) 1987. q. $590. (Zhongguo Qixiang Xuehui - Chinese Meteorological Society) China Meteorological Press, 46 Baishiqiao Road, West Suburb, Beijing 100081, People's Republic of China. (Dist. by: Pergamon Press plc, Headington Hill Hall, Oxford OX3 0BW, England. TEL 0865-794141) Ed. Zhou Shijian. **Indexed:** Cadscan, Chem.Abstr., Corros.Abstr., Environ.Per.Bibl., Int.Aerosp.Abstr., Lead Abstr., Met.Abstr., Phys.Ber., Sci.Abstr., Zincscan.
—BLDSC shelfmark: 0637.710000.
Refereed Serial

551.6 HU ISSN 0563-0614
ACTA UNIVERSITATIS DE ATTILA JOZSEF NOMINATAE. ACTA CLIMATOLOGICA. (Text in English) 1959. biennial. exchange basis. Attila Jozsef University, c/o E. Szabo, Exchange Librarian, Dugonics ter 13, P.O.B 393, Szeged H-6701, Hungary. (Subscr. to: Kultura, P.O. Box 149, H-1389 Budapest, Hungary) Ed. Gyorgy Koppany. charts; illus.; circ. 400.
Description: Focus on general climatology, bio- and agrometeorology.

METEOROLOGY

551.5   CC   ISSN 0256-1530
ADVANCES IN ATMOSPHERIC SCIENCES. Chinese Edition: Daqi Kexue Jinzhan. (Editions in Chinese, English) 1984. q. $249. (Chinese Committee of Meteorology and Atmospheric Physics) China Ocean Press, International Cooperation Department, Haimao Dalou, 1 Fuxingmenwai Dajie, Beijing 100860, People's Republic of China. TEL 868941. FAX 862209. TELEX NBO CN. (Dist. in US by: Science Press New York, Ltd., 63-117 Alderton St., Rego Park, NY 11374. TEL 718-459-4638) (Co-sponsor: Institute of Atmospheric Physics, Academia Sinica) Eds. Tao Shiyan, Ruan Zhongjia. circ. 1,000. (also avail. in microform from UMI; reprint service avail. from ISI)
—BLDSC shelfmark: 0699.600000.
Refereed Serial

551.65   JA   ISSN 0001-9216
AEROLOGICAL DATA OF JAPAN/JO-KOSO GEPPO. (Text in English) 1947. m. $107. Japan Weather Association, c/o Japan Meteorological Agency, 1-3-4 Otemachi, Chiyoda-ku, Tokyo 101, Japan. stat.; circ. controlled. (processed)

551.5   SG   ISSN 0065-4248
AGENCE POUR LA SECURITE DE LA NAVIGATION AERIENNE EN AFRIQUE ET A MADAGASCAR. DIRECTION DE L'EXPLOITATION METEOROLOGIQUE. PUBLICATIONS. SERIE 1. 1966. Irreg. price varies. Agence pour la Securite de la Navigation Aerienne en Afrique et a Madagascar, Direction de l'Exploitation Meteorologique, B.P. 3144, Dakar, Senegal.

551.5   SG   ISSN 0084-6015
AGENCE POUR LA SECURITE DE LA NAVIGATION AERIENNE EN AFRIQUE ET A MADAGASCAR. DIRECTION DE L'EXPLOITATION METEOROLOGIQUE. PUBLICATIONS. SERIE 2. 1965. irreg. price varies. Agence pour la Securite de la Navigation Aerienne en Afrique et a Madagascar, Direction de l'Exploitation Meteorologique, B.P. 3144, Dakar, Senegal.

AGRARMETEOROLOGISCHER WOCHENBERICHT FUER NORDRHEIN - WESTFALEN. see *AGRICULTURE*

AGRARMETEOROLOGISCHER WOCHENHINWEIS FUER DAS GEBIET BUNDESREPUBLIK DEUTSCHLAND. see *AGRICULTURE*

551.5 630   NE   ISSN 0168-1923
AGRICULTURAL AND FOREST METEOROLOGY; an international journal. (Text in English, French and German) 1964. 20/yr. (in 5 vols.; 4 nos./vol.). fl.1680 (effective 1992). Elsevier Science Publishers B.V., P.O. Box 211, 1000 AE Amsterdam, Netherlands. TEL 020-5803911. FAX 020-5803598. TELEX 18582 ESPA NL. (Subscr. in U.S. and Canada to: Elsevier Science Publishing Co., Inc., Box 882, Madison Sq. Sta., New York, NY 10159. TEL 212-989-5800) Ed. W.E. Reifsnyder. adv.; bk.rev.; abstr.; bibl.; charts; illus.; index. (also avail. in microform from RPI) Indexed: Agri.Eng.Abstr., Agroforest.Abstr., Anim.Breed.Abstr., ASCA, Biol.Abstr., Cott.& Trop.Fibr.Abstr., Crop Physiol.Abstr., Curr.Adv.Ecol.Sci., Curr.Cont., Dairy Sci.Abstr., Environ.Abstr., Environ.Per.Bibl., Excerp.Med., Field Crop Abstr., Forest.Abstr., Forest Prod.Abstr., Geo.Abstr., Helminthol.Abstr., Herb.Abstr., Hort.Abstr., Ind.Sci.Rev., Int.Abstr.Oper.Res., Irr.& Drain.Abstr., Maize Abstr., Meteor.& Geoastrophys.Abstr., Ornam.Hort., Rev.Plant Path., Rice Abstr., Sci.Cit.Ind., Seed Abstr., Sel.Water Res.Abstr., Soils & Fert., Sorghum & Millets Abstr., Soyabean Abstr., Triticale Abstr., Vet.Bull., VITIS, W.R.C.Inf., Weed Abstr.
—BLDSC shelfmark: 0742.890000.
Formerly (until 1984): Agricultural Meteorology (ISSN 0002-1571)
Description: Publishes articles and reviews in the interdisciplinary fields of meteorology and climatology applied to agriculture and forestry.
Refereed Serial

551.5   TH   ISSN 0857-2410
AGROMETEOROLOGICAL REPORT. (Text in Thai) 1968. m. free. Ministry of Transport and Communications, Meteorological Department, 612 Sukhumwit Road, Bangkok 10110, Thailand. TEL 258-0439. FAX 258-9212. TELEX 72002 DEPMETE TH. Ed.Bd. circ. 250.

551.5   XV   ISSN 0352-1818
AGROMETEOROLOSKO POROCILO. (ISSN 0352-180X for 3/m.) (Text in Slovenian) 1955. m. (Dec.-Feb.); 3/m. (Mar.-Nov.). $80 (effective 1992). Hidrometeoroloski Zavod SR Slovenije, Oddelek za Agrometeorologijo, Vojkova ul. 1-b, 61000 Ljubljana, Slovenia. TEL 3861 327 461. FAX 3861-320466. TELEX 31620. Ed. Janko Pristov. abstr.; circ. 120.
Description: Textual tabular, graphical and cartographical survey of climatological data, the influence of weather elements on crops and day to day operations of plant growing.

551.5   US   ISSN 0002-2616
AIR WEATHER SERVICE OBSERVER. Short title: A W S Observer. 1954. m. qualified personnel only. U.S. Air Force, Air Weather Service, Headquarters AWS-PA, Scott Air Force Base, IL 62225-5008. TEL 618-256-2065. Ed. Sgt. David L. Black. circ. 2,400. (tabloid format)

551.5   RU   ISSN 0002-3515
QC851   CODEN: IFAOAV
AKADEMIYA NAUK S.S.S.R. IZVESTIYA. SERIYA FIZIKA ATMOSFERY I OKEANA. English translation: Academy of Sciences of the U S S R. Izvestiya. Atmospheric and Oceanic Physics (US ISSN 0001-4338) (Text in Russian; summaries in English and Russian) 1965. m. 53.40 Rub. Izdatel'stvo Nauka, 90 Profsoyuznaya ul., 117864 Moscow, Russia. (Dist. by: Mezhdunarodnaya Kniga, ul. Dimitrova D.39, 113095, Moscow, Russia) Ed. A.M. Oboukhov. adv.; bk.rev.; charts; illus.; index; circ. 1,000. Indexed: Bibl.Cart., Chem.Abstr., INIS Atomind., Math.R., Phys.Ber., Sci.Abstr.
—BLDSC shelfmark: 0075.360000.

551   CN
ALBERTA RESEARCH COUNCIL. ATMOSPHERIC SCIENCES REPORTS. 1968. irreg. price varies. Alberta Research Council, Publications Department, P.O. Box 8330, Sta. F, Edmonton, Alta. T6H 5X2, Canada. TEL 403-450-5390. FAX 403-461-2651. TELEX 037-2147.
Formerly: Alberta Research Council. Hail Studies Reports (ISSN 0080-1542)
Description: Presents reports dealing primarily with hail studies.

551.5   US   ISSN 0003-0007
QC851   CODEN: BAMIAT
AMERICAN METEOROLOGICAL SOCIETY. BULLETIN. 1920. m. $60 (foreign $80). American Meteorological Society, 45 Beacon St., Boston, MA 02108-3693. TEL 617-227-2425. FAX 618-742-8718. Ed. Richard E. Hallgren. adv.; bk.rev.; abstr.; bibl.; charts; illus.; stat.; index; circ. 11,304. (also avail. in microfilm from PMC; back issues avail.) Indexed: A.S.& T.Ind., Acid Pre.Dig., Appl.Mech.Rev., Biol.Abstr., Chem.Abstr., Curr.Adv.Ecol.Sci., Curr.Cont., Deep Sea Res.& Oceanogr.Abstr., Environ.Abstr., Excerp.Med., Fluidex, Geo.Abstr., GeoRef, INIS Atomind., Meteor.& Geoastrophys.Abstr., Ocean.Abstr., Pollut.Abstr., Risk Abstr., Rural Recreat.Tour.Abstr., Sci.Abstr., Sci.Cit.Ind., Sel.Water Res.Abstr., World Agri.Econ.& Rural Sociol.Abstr.
—BLDSC shelfmark: 2388.000000.
Description: Contains survey articles, professional and membership news, announcements and society activities.
Refereed Serial

551.5   US   ISSN 0065-9401
CODEN: MMONAL
AMERICAN METEOROLOGICAL SOCIETY. METEOROLOGICAL MONOGRAPHS. 1947. irreg., latest vol.21, no.43. price varies. American Meteorological Society, 45 Beacon St., Boston, MA 02108-3693. TEL 617-227-2425. FAX 617-742-8718. Ed. Donald R. Johnson. Indexed: Biol.Abstr., Chem.Abstr., Meteor.& Geoastrophys.Abstr., Sci.Abstr.
Description: Collections of scientific papers devoted to individual research topics of concern to meteorologists, oceanographers, and hydrologists.
Refereed Serial

551.6   US
AMERICAN METEOROLOGICAL SOCIETY HISTORICAL MONOGRAPH SERIES. 1963. irreg., latest 1989. $55. American Meteorological Society, 45 Beacon St., Boston, MA 02108-3693. TEL 617-227-2425. FAX 617-742-8718. Ed. Ronald C. Taylor.
Description: Covers the history of weather, weather forecasting, and the science of meteorology from its inception through the present day, with special emphasis on US weather.
Refereed Serial

551.5   US   ISSN 8755-9552
AMERICAN WEATHER OBSERVER. 1984. m. $21 to non-members; members $15. Association of American Weather Observers, 401 Whitney Blvd., Box 455, Belvidere, IL 61008. TEL 815-544-5665. FAX 815-544-6334. Ed. Steven D. Steinke. index; circ. 2,100. (tabloid format; back issues avail.)
Description: For amateur or professional weather observers, weather enthusiasts, or school weather clubs.

555.1   PH   ISSN 0115-5032
ANG TAGAMASID. (Text in English) 1973. bi-m. free. Philippine Atmospheric, Geophysical and Astronomical Services Administration (PAGASA), Public Information and International Affairs Staff, PAGASA Central Office, 1424 Quezon Ave., Quezon City, Philippines. TELEX 42021-PAGASA-PM. Ed. Juanito E. Lucas. circ. 1,000.

551.5   GW   ISSN 0072-4122
QC851
ANNALEN DER METEOROLOGIE. NEUE FOLGE. 1948; N.S. 1963. irreg., no.26, 1986. Deutscher Wetterdienst, Frankfurter Str. 135, Postfach 10 04 65, 6050 Offenbach a.M. 1, Germany. Indexed: Deep Sea Res.& Oceanogr.Abstr.

551.6   BD
ANNUAIRE PLUVIOMETRIQUE. a. Institut Geographique du Burundi, Centre National d'Hydrometeorologie, B.P. 331, Bujumbura, Burundi.

ANTARKTIESE BULLETIN/ANTARCTIC BULLETIN. see *EARTH SCIENCES*

551.5   PO   ISSN 0870-2950
ANUARIO CLIMATOLOGICO. (Since 1977 issued in 3 parts: A: Continente (ISSN 0870-6360); B: Acores (ISSN 0870-6379); C: Madeira (ISSN 0870-6387)) 1947. a. (Part A, Esc.1800; Part B, Esc.900; Part C, Esc.900)(effective Jan. 1991). Instituto Nacional de Meteorologia e Geofisica, Rua C do Aeroporto, 1700 Lisbon, Portugal. TEL 8472880. FAX 802370. TELEX 12742 DIRMET P. stat.; circ. 500.

551.5   JA   ISSN 0003-6323
AOMORI-KEN NOGYO KISHO JUNPO.* (Text in Japanese) 1963. every 10 days. free to qualified personnel. Aomori Local Meteorological Observatory - Aomori Chiho Kishodai, 155-4 Tsukuda, Matsumori, Aomori 030, Japan. bk.rev.; charts; stat.; circ. 180 (controlled). (processed)

551.5   JA   ISSN 0029-7399
AOMORI PREFECTURE. MONTHLY REPORT OF METEOROLOGY/AOMORI-KEN KISHO GEPPO. (Text in Japanese) 1951. m. free. Aomori Local Meteorological Observatory - Aomori Chiho Kishodai, 155-4 Tsukuda, Matsumori, Aomori 030, Japan. bk.rev.; charts; stat.; circ. 340 (controlled).

551.6   FR   ISSN 0242-4002
ASSOCIATION NATIONALE D'ETUDE ET DE LUTTE CONTRE LES FLEAUX ATMOSPHERIQUES. RAPPORT DE CAMPAGNE. 1951. a. free. Association Nationale de Lutte Contre les Fleaux Atmospheriques, 52 rue Alfred-Dumeril, 31400 Toulouse, France. TEL 61-52-05-65. bk.rev.; charts; illus.; circ. 1,000. Indexed: Meteor.& Geoastrophys.Abstr.
Formerly: Association Nationale de Lutte Contre les Fleaux Atmospheriques. Rapport de Campagne (ISSN 0373-7349) Continues the Rapport sur la Campagne issued by the association under its earlier name: Association d' Etudes des Moyens de Lutte Contre les Fleaux Atmospheriques.
Description: Presents research conducted in the control and relief of natural disasters.

METEOROLOGY

551.5 LI ISSN 0135-1419
ATMOSFEROS FIZIKA/ATMOSPHERIC PHYSICS. (Text in English, Russian; summaries in English, Lithuanian, Russian) 1973. a. 3 Rub. Lithuanian Academy of Sciences, Institute of Physics, K. Pozelos g-ve 54, Vilnius 232600, Lithuania. TEL 61-26-10. TELEX 261135 FISU. Ed. R. Baltramiejunas. circ. 800.
—BLDSC shelfmark: 0389.680000.
Description: Treats problems of the atmosphere's and hydrosphere's pollution by radioactive and chemical substances.

551.5 CN ISSN 0705-5900
QC851 CODEN: ATOCDA
ATMOSPHERE - OCEAN. (Text in English and French) 1963. q. Can.$35 to individuals; institutions Can.$65. Canadian Meteorological and Oceanographic Society - Societe Canadienne de Meteorologie et d'Oceanographie, P.O. Box 334, Newmarket, Ont. L3Y 4X7, Canada.
TEL 416-898-1040. FAX 416-898-7937. Eds. R. Daley, W.R. Crawford. adv.; bk.rev.; charts; illus.; stat.; index; circ. 1,200. (processed) **Indexed:** Deep Sea Res.& Oceanogr.Abstr., Environ.Per.Bibl., Geo.Abstr., Meteor. & Geoastrophys.Abstr.
—BLDSC shelfmark: 1767.117000.
Supersedes (with vol. 16, 1978): Atmosphere (ISSN 0004-6973)
Description: Contains scientific articles on all aspects of meteorology and oceanography, and relevant notes, correspondence.

551.5 NE ISSN 0169-8095
CODEN: ATREEW
ATMOSPHERIC RESEARCH; clouds - precipitation - aerosols - radiation - weather modification. (Text in English and French) 1963. 8/yr. (in 2 vols., 4 nos./vol.). fl.612 (effective 1992). Elsevier Science Publishers B.V., P.O. Box 211, 1000 AE Amsterdam, Netherlands. TEL 020-5803911. FAX 020-5803598. TELEX 18582 ESPA NL. (Subscr. in U.S. and Canada to: Elsevier Science Publishing Co., Inc., Box 882, Madison Sq. Sta., New York, NY 10159. TEL 212-989-5800) Eds. J. Dessens, A.W. Hogan. bk.rev.; abstr.; bibl.; charts; illus.; index; circ. 350. **Indexed:** Bull.Signal., Chem.Abstr., Energy Rev., Environ.Per.Bibl., Geo.Abstr., GeoRef, INIS Atomind., Meteor.& Geoastrophys.Abstr., Ocean.Abstr., Phys.Ber., Pollut.Abstr., Sci.Abstr.
—BLDSC shelfmark: 1767.470000.
Formerly (until 1986): Journal de Recherches Atmospheriques (ISSN 0021-7972)
Description: Publishes scientific papers dealing with the part of the atmosphere where meteorological events occur.
Refereed Serial

551.5 AT ISSN 0067-1312
AUSTRALIA. BUREAU OF METEOROLOGY. BULLETIN. 1908. irreg., no.51, 1984. price varies. Australian Government Publishing Service, G.P.O. Box 84, Canberra, A.C.T., Australia. **Indexed:** Meteor.& Geoastrophys.Abstr.

551.5 AT ISSN 0067-1320
AUSTRALIA. BUREAU OF METEOROLOGY. METEOROLOGICAL STUDY. 1954. irreg., no.34, 1984. avail. on exchange. Australian Government Publishing Service, G.P.O. Box 84, Canberra, A.C.T., Australia. **Indexed:** Meteor.& Geoastrophys.Abstr.

551.5 AT ISSN 1035-6576
AUSTRALIAN METEOROLOGICAL AND OCEANOGRAPHIC SOCIETY. BULLETIN. 1988. bi-m. Aus.$90($75) (effective 1991). Australian Meteorological and Oceanographic Society, G.P.O. Box 654 E, Melbourne, Vic. 3001, Australia. TEL 03-669-4506. FAX 61-3-586-7600. Ed. Ian Smith. adv.; bk.rev.; circ. 400. (back issues avail.)
Formerly (until 1991): Australian Meteorological and Oceanographic Society. Newsletter.
Description: For all readers with an interest in the meteorology or the oceanography of the southern hemisphere.

551.5 AT ISSN 0004-9743
QC851
AUSTRALIAN METEOROLOGICAL MAGAZINE. 1952. q. Aus.$28. (Australian Bureau of Meteorology) Australian Government Publishing Service, G.P.O. Box 84, Canberra, A.C.T. 2601, Australia. (Co-sponsor: Royal Meteorological Society, Australian Branch) Ed. Mike Manton. abstr.; charts; illus.; index. **Indexed:** Chem.Abstr., Curr.Tit.Ocean, Deep Sea Res.& Oceanogr.Abstr., Geo.Abstr., Meteor.& Geoastrophys.Abstr., Ocean.Abstr., Phys.Abstr., Pollut.Abstr., Sel.Water Res.Abstr.
—BLDSC shelfmark: 1814.300000.

551.5 551 AU ISSN 0067-2351
AUSTRIA. ZENTRALANSTALT FUER METEOROLOGIE UND GEODYNAMIK. JAHRBUCH. 1864. irreg. price varies. Zentralanstalt fuer Meteorologie und Geodynamik, Hohe Warte 38, A-1190 Vienna, Austria. circ. 500. **Indexed:** GeoRef.

551.6 CN
AVALANCHE NEWS. 1979. 3/yr. free. Ministry of Transportation and Highways, 940 Blansherd St., Victoria, B.C. V8W 3E6, Canada.
TEL 604-387-6361. FAX 604-837-4624.
(Co-sponsor: Canadian Avalanche Association) circ. 900. (looseleaf format)
Description: Information about developments, equipment, publications, activities and events in the avalanche business.

AVALANCHE REVIEW. see *EARTH SCIENCES*

551.5 IO ISSN 0126-0561
QC925.8 .I5
BADAN METEOROLOGI DAN GEOFISIKA. LAPORAN EVALUASI HUJAN DAN PERKIRAAN HUJAN. 1976. m. Meteorological and Geophysical Institute, Jalan Arief Rakhman Hakim 3, Jakarta, Indonesia.
Formerly: Pusat Meteorologi dan Geofisika. Laporan Evaluasi Hujan dan Perkiraan Hujan.

538.7 BE ISSN 0524-7764
BELGIUM. INSTITUT ROYAL METEOROLOGIQUE. ANNUAIRE: MAGNETISME TERRESTRE/JAARBOEK: AARDMAGNETISME. (Text in Dutch, French) a. 500 Fr. Institut Royal Meteorologique, 3 av. Circulaire, 1180 Brussels, Belgium. circ. 150.

551.5271 BE ISSN 0524-7780
BELGIUM. INSTITUT ROYAL METEOROLOGIQUE. ANNUAIRE: RAYONNEMENT SOLAIRE/JAARBOEK: ZONNESTRALING. irreg., latest 1982. 500 Fr. Institut Royal Meteorologique, 3 av. Circulaire, 1180 Brussels, Belgium. circ. 182.

529 BE ISSN 0007-5280
BELGIUM. INSTITUT ROYAL METEOROLOGIQUE. BULLETIN QUOTIDIEN DU TEMPS. (Text in Dutch, French) d. 7500 Fr. Institut Royal Meteorologique, 3 av. Circulaire, 1180 Brussels, Belgium. charts; stat.; circ. 300.

551.6 BE ISSN 0029-7682
QC989.B8
BELGIUM. INSTITUT ROYAL METEOROLOGIQUE. OBSERVATIONS CLIMATOLOGIQUES. (Text in Dutch, French) 1928. m. 2000 Fr. Institut Royal Meteorologique, 3 av. Circulaire, 1180 Brussels, Belgium. charts; stat.; circ. 540.
—BLDSC shelfmark: 2870.980000.

551.514 BE ISSN 0029-7690
BELGIUM. INSTITUT ROYAL METEOROLOGIQUE. OBSERVATIONS D'OZONE. (Text in Dutch and French) 1965. q. 750 Fr. Institut Royal Meteorologique, 3 av. Circulaire, 1180 Brussels, Belgium. charts; circ. 190.

551.514 523.01 BE ISSN 0020-2533
BELGIUM. INSTITUT ROYAL METEOROLOGIQUE. OBSERVATIONS IONOSPHERIQUES ET DU RAYONNEMENT COSMIQUE. (Text in Dutch, French) 1961. m. 2000 Fr. Institut Royal Meteorologique, 3 av. Circulaire, 1180 Brussels, Belgium. charts; stat.; circ. 320. **Indexed:** Ocean.Abstr., Pollut.Abstr.

551.5 BE ISSN 0020-2541
BELGIUM. INSTITUT ROYAL METEOROLOGIQUE. OBSERVATIONS SYNOPTIQUES. (Text in Dutch, French) 1949. m. 2000 Fr. Institut Royal Meteorologique, 3 av. Circulaire, 1180 Brussels, Belgium. stat.; circ. 165.
—BLDSC shelfmark: 2871.200000.

551.5 551 BE ISSN 0020-255X
CODEN: PMBAAI
BELGIUM. INSTITUT ROYAL METEOROLOGIQUE. PUBLICATIONS. (Text in Dutch, English and French) 1952. irreg. Institut Royal Meteorologique, 3 av. Circulaire, 1180 Brussels, Belgium. circ. 290.

551.63 US ISSN 0749-3584
BIBLE OF WEATHER FORECASTING. 1984. bi-m. $18. Singer Press, 1540 Rollins Dr., Box 63302, Los Angeles, CA 90063. TEL 213-263-2640. Ed. Oscar Singer. bk.rev.; circ. 150.
Formerly: Lock.

551.5 GW ISSN 0067-8902
QH543 CODEN: BMTLAL
BIOMETEOROLOGY; PROCEEDINGS. Represents: International Biometeorological Congress. Proceedings. triennial, 10th, 1984, Tokyo, Japan. fl.160. (International Society of Biometeorology) Springer-Verlag, Postfach 105280, D-6900 Heidelberg, Germany. FAX 06221-43982. TELEX 461723. **Indexed:** Biol.Abstr., Chem.Abstr.

551.5 PL
BIULETYN METEOROLOGICZNY. (Subseries of its: Acta Universitatis Wratislaviensis) 1971. irreg. price varies. Wydawnictwo Uniwersytetu Wroclawskiego, Pl. Uniwersytecki 9-13, 50-137 Wroclaw, Poland. (Dist. by: Foreign Trade Office, Wroclaw University, ul. Kuznicza 34, 50-138 Wroclaw, Poland)

551.5 PO ISSN 0870-4740
BOLETIM ACTINOMETRICO DE PORTUGAL. 1955. m. Esc.1600 (effective Jan. 1991). Instituto Nacional de Meteorologia e Geofisica, Rua C do Aeroporto, 1700 Lisbon, Portugal. TEL 8472880.
FAX 802370. TELEX 12742 DIRMET P. stat.
Formerly: Boletim Actinometrico (ISSN 0477-7166)
Description: Information on global and diffuse radiation.

551.5 BL ISSN 0067-9585
BOLETIM CLIMATOLOGICO. 1960. irreg., no.5, 1984. price varies or avail. on exchange. Universidade de Sao Paulo, Instituto Oceanografico, Cidade Universitaria, Butanta, 05508 Sao Paulo, SP, Brazil. circ. 100.

551.5 PO ISSN 0870-4686
BOLETIM METEOROLOGICO. 1948. d. Esc.16000. Instituto Nacional de Meteorologia e Geofisica, Rua C do Aeroporto, 1700 Lisbon, Portugal.
TEL 8472880. FAX 802370. TELEX 12742 DIRMET P. charts; stat.
Description: Charts of isobaric surfaces.

551.5 630 PO ISSN 0870-4694
BOLETIM METEOROLOGICO PARA A AGRICULTURA. 1951-1958; resumed 19?? 3/m. Esc.3000. Instituto Nacional de Meteorologia e Geofisica, Rua C do Aeroporto, 1700 Lisbon, Portugal.
TEL 8472880. FAX 802370. TELEX 12742 DIRMET P. charts; illus.; stat.
Description: Meteorological information and its impact on agriculture.

551.5 GW ISSN 0006-7156
BONNER METEOROLOGISCHE ABHANDLUNGEN. (Text in English and German) 1962. irreg. price varies. (Universitaet Bonn, Meteorologisches Institut) Ferd. Duemmlers Verlag, Postfach 1480-Kaiserstr. 31-37, 5300 Bonn 1, Germany. Ed. Michael Hantel. abstr.; charts; illus. **Indexed:** Geo.Abstr., Meteor.& Geoastrophys.Abstr.

METEOROLOGY

551.5 574   NE   ISSN 0006-8314
QC880   CODEN: BLMEBR
BOUNDARY-LAYER METEOROLOGY; an international journal of physical and biological processes in the atmospheric boundary layer. 1970. 16/yr. $784. Kluwer Academic Publishers, Postbus 17, 3300 AA Dordrecht, Netherlands. TEL 078-334911. FAX 078-334254. TELEX 29245. (Dist. by: Kluwer Academic Publishers Group, P.O. Box 322, 3300 AH Dordrecht, Netherlands; N. America dist. addr.: Box 358, Accord Station, Hingham, MA 02018-0358. TEL 617-871-6600) Ed. R.E. Munn. adv.; bk.rev.; illus.; index. (reprint service avail. from SWZ) **Indexed:** Acid Pre.Dig., Appl.Mech.Rev., Biol.Abstr., Curr.Adv.Ecol.Sci., Curr.Cont., Curr.Tit.Ocean, Deep Sea Res.& Oceanogr.Abstr., Energy Rev., Environ.Per.Bibl., Excerp.Med., Fluidex, Forest.Abstr., Geo.Abstr., GeoRef, Herb.Abstr., Ind.Sci.Rev., Int.Aerosp.Abstr., Ocean.Abstr., Phys.Ber., Pollut.Abstr., Sci.Abstr., Sci.Cit.Ind., Soils & Fert.
—BLDSC shelfmark: 2264.270000.

551.579   CN   ISSN 0045-303X
QC929.S7
BRITISH COLUMBIA SNOW SURVEY BULLETIN. 1940. 6/yr. free. Ministry of the Environment, Water Investigation Branch, Parliament Bldgs., Victoria, B.C. V8V 1X5, Canada. TEL 604-387-5162. Ed. C.H. Coulson. circ. 1,200.

332.6   US
BROWNING NEWSLETTER. vol.5, 1981. m. $225. Fraser Management Associates, Inc., 309 S. Willard St., Box 494, Burlington, VT 05402. TEL 802-658-0322. FAX 802-658-0260. Ed. Evelyn Browning Garriss. charts; stat.
Description: Based on the proposition that the earth's climate has entered a period of sharp change and that this change in climate is the driving force behind human history. Extensive studies of physical data and phenomena (named for Dr. Iben Browning, a climatologist).

CALIFORNIA. AGRICULTURAL STATISTICS SERVICE. CROP WEATHER REPORT. see *AGRICULTURE — Abstracting, Bibliographies, Statistics*

551.5   CN
CANADIAN METEOROLOGICAL AND OCEANOGRAPHIC SOCIETY. ANNUAL CONGRESS. 1967. a. Can.$15 (typically set in Jun.). Canadian Meteorological and Oceanographic Society - Societe Canadienne de Meteorologie et d'Oceanographie, P.O. Box 334, Newmarket, Ont. L3Y 4X7, Canada. TEL 416-898-1040. FAX 416-898-7937. Ed. E. Truhlar. adv.; circ. 1,000 (controlled). **Indexed:** Meteor.& Geoastrophys.Abstr.
Formerly: Canadian Meteorological Society. Annual Congress (ISSN 0068-9254)
Description: Program for, and abstracts of, papers on all aspects of meteorology and oceanography, presented at yearly CMOS congresses.

551.6   CN   ISSN 0541-6256
CANADIAN METEOROLOGICAL AND OCEANOGRAPHIC SOCIETY. CLIMATOLOGICAL BULLETIN. 1967. 3/yr. Can.$20 to non-members; institutions Can.$25. Canadian Meteorological and Oceanographic Society - Societe Canadienne de Meteorologie et d'Oceanographie, P.O. Box 334, Newmarket, Ont. L3Y 4X7, Canada. TEL 416-898-1040. FAX 416-898-7937. Ed. A. Paul. bk.rev.; circ. 500.
—BLDSC shelfmark: 3279.800000.
Description: Scientific publication containing articles, notes, and correspondence of interest to workers in the field of climatology (including oceans).

551.5   US
QC851   CODEN: TKHSDX
CHINESE JOURNAL OF ATMOSPHERIC SCIENCES. English translation of: Daqi Kexue (CC ISSN 0254-0002) 1987. q. $345. (Academia Sinica (Chinese Academy of Sciences), Institute of Atmospheric Physics, CC - Zhongguo Kexueyuan Daqi Wuli Yanjiusuo) Allerton Press, Inc., 150 Fifth Ave., New York, NY 10011. TEL 212-924-3950. Ed. Zhou Xiaoping.
Description: Covers meteorological research in mainland China, including climate changes and prediction, and acid rain.
Refereed Serial

CIEL ET TERRE. see *ASTRONOMY*

551.6   GW   ISSN 0930-7575
QC981.7.D94   CODEN: CLDYEM
CLIMATE DYNAMICS; observational, theoretical and computational research on the climate system. 1986. 4/yr. DM.348($205) Springer-Verlag, Heidelberger Platz 3, 1000 Berlin 33, Germany. TEL 030-8207-1. (Also Heidelberg, Tokyo, Vienna, and New York) Eds. W.L. Gates, H. Oeschger.
—BLDSC shelfmark: 3279.108000.

551.6   UK   ISSN 0140-458X
CLIMATE MONITOR. vol.5, 1976. q. £14 to individuals; institutions £20. University of East Anglia, Climatic Research Unit, School of Environmental Sciences, Norwich NR4 7TJ, England. TEL 0603-56161. FAX 0603-507784. Ed. P.D. Jones. circ. 250. **Indexed:** Deep Sea Res.& Oceanogr.Abstr.
—BLDSC shelfmark: 3279.150000.
Description: Contains summaries of global climatic conditions and articles of general interest on climatology.

551.5   NE   ISSN 0165-0009
QC981.8.C5   CODEN: CLCHDX
CLIMATIC CHANGE; an interdisciplinary, international journal devoted to the description, causes and implications of climatic change. 1977. 6/yr. fl.576($327) Kluwer Academic Publishers, P.O. Box 17, 3300 AA Dordrecht, Netherlands. TEL 078-334911. FAX 078-334254. TELEX 29245. (Dist. by: Kluwer Academic Publishers Group, P.O. Box 322, 3300 AH Dordrecht, Netherlands; N. America dist. addr.: Box 358, Accord Station, Hingham, MA 02018-0358. TEL 617-871-6600) Ed. Stephen H. Schneider. adv.; bk.rev.; illus.; index. (reprint service avail. from SWZ) **Indexed:** Astron.& Astrophys.Abstr., Biol.Abstr., Chem.Abstr., Curr.Adv.Ecol.Sci., Curr.Cont., Deep Sea Res.& Oceanogr.Abstr., Energy Ind., Energy Info.Abstr., Energy Rev., Eng.Ind., Environ.Abstr., Environ.Abstr., Environ.Ind., Environ.Per.Bibl., Excerp.Med., Field Crop Abstr., Geo.Abstr., GeoRef, Herb.Abstr., Ind.Sci.Rev., Sci.Abstr., Sci.Cit.Ind., Soils & Fert.
—BLDSC shelfmark: 3279.250000.

551.6   JA
CLIMATIC TABLE OF JAPAN. (Text in Japanese) 1918. every 10 yrs. 5900 Yen. (Japan Meteorological Agency) Japan Weather Association, 2-9-2, Kanda-nishikicho, Chiyoda-ku, Tokyo 101, Japan. circ. 1,472.

551.5   US
CLIMATOLOGICAL DATA. (Issued separately for 42 states, 6 New England states, Maryland-Delaware, Puerto Rico, Virgin Islands and Pacific Islands) 1897. m. (plus an annual). $25. U.S. National Climatic Data Center, Federal Bldg., MC-02, Asheville, NC 28801-2696. TEL 704-259-0682. circ. 25,000. (also avail. in microfiche; magnetic tape) **Indexed:** Abstr.Bull.Inst.Pap.Chem.

551.5   IO   ISSN 0009-8957
CLIMATOLOGICAL DATA FOR JAKARTA OBSERVATORY. (Text in English) 1956. a. exchange basis. Meteorologi and Geophysical Institute - Badan Meteorologi dan Geofisika, Jalan Arief Rakhman Hakim 3, Jakarta, Indonesia.

551.5   US   ISSN 0067-0340
COLORADO STATE UNIVERSITY. ATMOSPHERIC SCIENCE PAPER. 1959. irreg. avail. on exchange. Colorado State University, Atmospheric Science Department, College of Engineering, Fort Collins, CO 80523. TEL 303-491-8360. FAX 303-491-8449. Ed. T.B. McKee. (also avail. in microfiche) **Indexed:** Meteor.& Geoastrophys.Abstr.
Supersedes: Atmospheric Science Technical Paper; Atmospheric Science Research Report.

551.51   AT   ISSN 0159-0219
QC869.4.A8
COMMONWEALTH SCIENTIFIC AND INDUSTRIAL RESEARCH ORGANIZATION. DIVISION OF ATMOSPHERIC RESEARCH. RESEARCH REPORT. biennial. Aus.$3 per no. C.S.I.R.O., Division of Atmospheric Research, Station St., Aspendale, Vic. 3195, Australia. TEL 03-586-7666. FAX 03-586-7600. TELEX AA 34463. illus.
Formerly: Commonwealth Scientific and Industrial Research Organization. Division of Atmospheric Physics. Annual Report (ISSN 0310-1908)

551.51   AT
COMMONWEALTH SCIENTIFIC AND INDUSTRIAL RESEARCH ORGANIZATION. DIVISION OF ATMOSPHERIC RESEARCH. TECHNICAL PAPER. 1983. irreg. (approx. 1-3/yr.). price varies. C.S.I.R.O., Division of Atmospheric Research, Station St., Aspendale, Vic. 3195, Australia. TEL 03-586-7666. FAX 03-586-7600. TELEX AA 344463. circ. 750. **Indexed:** Biol.Abstr., Deep Sea Res.& Oceanogr.Abstr.
Formerly: Commonwealth Scientific and Industrial Research Organization. Division of Atmospheric Physics. Technical Paper.

551.5   UN
COMPOSITION OF THE W M O. q. $110. World Meteorological Organization, 41 Av. Giuseppe Motta, CH-1211 Geneva 2, Switzerland. TEL 730-8011. (Dist. in U.S. by: American Meteorogical Society, 45 Beacon St., Boston, MA 02108. TEL 617-227-2425)
Description: Lists members of the WMO and the composition of WMO constituent bodies, panels, committees and working groups.

551.5   GW   ISSN 0005-8173
    CODEN: BPYAAY
CONTRIBUTIONS TO ATMOSPHERIC PHYSICS/BEITRAEGE ZUR PHYSIK DER ATMOSPHAERE. (Text in English; summaries in English, French and German) 1957. q. DM.268($179) Friedr. Vieweg und Sohn Verlagsgesellschaft mbH, Postfach 5829, 6200 Wiesbaden 1, Germany. TEL 0611-160230. FAX 0611-160229. TELEX 4186928-VWVD. Ed. D. Etling. bk.rev.; bibl.; charts; illus. **Indexed:** Chem.Abstr., Deep Sea Res.& Oceanogr.Abstr., INIS Atomind., Int.Aerosp.Abstr., Meteor.& Geoastrophys.Abstr., Phys.Ber., Sci.Abstr.
—BLDSC shelfmark: 3458.265000.

551.5 630   CU   ISSN 0138-6190
CUBA. MINISTERIO DE LA AGRICULTURA. CENTRO DE INFORMACION Y DOCUMENTACION AGROPECUARIO. NOTICIERO AGROPECUARIO. SUPLEMENTO AGROMETEOROLOGICO. irreg. Ministerio de la Agricultura, Centro de Informacion y Documentacion Agropecuario, Calle 11 No. 1057, Vedado, Havana, Cuba.

551.5 370   US
CURRICULA IN THE ATMOSPHERIC, OCEANIC AND RELATED SCIENCES. 1963. biennial. $30. American Meteorological Society, 45 Beacon St., Boston, MA 02108. TEL 617-227-2425. FAX 617-742-8718. (Co-sponsor: University Corporation for Atmospheric Research)
Formerly: Curricula in the Atmospheric and Oceanographic Sciences.
Description: Contains description of the curricula in atmospheric, oceanic and related sciences at the major colleges and universities in the U.S., Canada and Puerto Rico.

D M I NEWS. (Danish Maritime Institute) see *TRANSPORTATION — Ships And Shipping*

DAIKIKYU SHINPOJUMU. see *ASTRONOMY*

551.5   JA
DAILY WEATHER MAPS. 1940. m. 180,000 Yen. (Japan Meteorological Agency) Japan Weather Association, 2-9-2, Kanda-nishikicho, Chiyoda-ku, Tokyo 101, Japan. circ. 501.
Incorporates (in 1989): Taifu Keirozu.

551.5   CC   ISSN 0254-0002
QC851   CODEN: TKHSDX
DAQI KEXUE/SCIENTIA ATMOSPHERICA SINICA. English translation: Chinese Journal of Atmospheric Sciences. (Text in Chinese; summaries in English) 1976. q. Y16.80($7) per no. (Chinese Academy of Sciences, Institute of Atmospheric Physics) Science Press, Marketing and Sales Department, 16 Donghuangchenggen Beijie, Beijing 100707, People's Republic of China. TEL 4010642. FAX 4012180. TELEX 210247-SPBJ-CN. adv.; circ. 6,000. **Indexed:** Chem.Abstr., Math.R., Sci.Abstr.
—BLDSC shelfmark: 8169.600000.
Description: Covers meteorological research in mainland China, including weather modification and prediction, atmospheric turbulence and diffusion, climatology, and acid rain.
Refereed Serial

551.5   IO   ISSN 0303-1969
DATA-DATA IKLIM DI INDONESIA. (Text in English and Indonesian) 1971. a. Meteorological and Geophysical Institute - Badan Meteorologi dan Geofisika, Jalan Arif Rachman Hakim 3, Jakarta, Indonesia.

551.5   GW   ISSN 0072-4130
QC857.G3
DEUTSCHER WETTERDIENST. BERICHTE. 1953. irreg., no.180, 1990. price varies. Deutscher Wetterdienst, Frankfurter Str. 135, Postfach 10 04 65, 6050 Offenbach a.M. 1, Germany. **Indexed:** Deep Sea Res.& Oceanogr.Abstr.

551.5   GW   ISSN 0433-8251
QC989
DEUTSCHER WETTERDIENST. JAHRESBERICHT. 1953. a. DM.20. Deutscher Wetterdienst, Bibliothek, Frankfurterstr. 135, 6050 Offenbach a.M. 1, Germany. circ. 800.

551.65   GW   ISSN 0435-7965
DEUTSCHER WETTERDIENST. MONATLICHER WITTERUNGSBERICHT. (Includes "Jahresuebersicht") 1953. m. DM.55. Deutscher Wetterdienst, Frankfurter Str. 135, Postfach 10 04 65, 6050 Offenbach a.M. 1, Germany.

551.5   GW   ISSN 0072-1603
DEUTSCHER WETTERDIENST. SEEWETTERAMT. EINZELVEROEFFENTLICHUNGEN. 1953. irreg., no.117, 1990. price varies. Deutscher Wetterdienst, Seewetteramt, Bernhard Nocht-Str. 76, Postfach 301190, 2000 Hamburg 36, Germany. TELEX 211291. bk.rev.; circ. 250.
Description: Different meteorological topics, mainly on the marine climatological sector.

551.63   GW   ISSN 0724-7125
QC989.G3
DEUTSCHES METEOROLOGISCHES JAHRBUCH, BUNDESREPUBLIK DEUTSCHLAND. 1953. a. DM.150. Deutscher Wetterdienst, Bibliothek, Frankfurterstr. 135, 6050 Offenbach a.M. 1, Germany.

551.5   NE
DEVELOPMENTS IN ATMOSPHERIC SCIENCE. 1974. irreg., vol.19, 1991. price varies. Elsevier Science Publishers B.V., Books Division, P.O. Box 211, 1000 AE Amsterdam, Netherlands. TEL 020-5803911. FAX 020-5803705. TELEX 18582 ESPA NL. (Subscr. in U.S. and Canada to: Elsevier Science Publishers Co., Inc., Box 882, Madison Sq. Sta., New York, NY 10159. TEL 212-989-5800) (back issues avail.)
Refereed Serial

DISASTERS; the journal of disaster relief and management. see *EARTH SCIENCES — Geophysics*

551.5 551.46   NE   ISSN 0377-0265
GC190.2   CODEN: DAOCDC
DYNAMICS OF ATMOSPHERES AND OCEANS; planetary fluids, climatic and biogeochemical systems. (Text mainly in English; occasionally French and German) 1977. 6/yr. fl.536 (effective 1992). Elsevier Science Publishers B.V., P.O. Box 211, 1000 AE Amsterdam, Netherlands. TEL 020-5803911. FAX 020-5803705. TELEX 18582 ESPA NL. (Subscr. in U.S. and Canada to: Elsevier Science Publishing Co., Inc., Box 882, Madison Sq. Sta., New York, NY 10159. TEL 212-989-5800) Ed. A.R. Robinson. adv.; bk.rev. (also avail. in microform from RPI; reprint service avail. from SWZ) **Indexed:** Appl.Mech.Rev., Curr.Cont., Deep Sea Res.& Oceanogr.Abstr., Environ.Per.Bibl., Fluidex. Geo.Abstr., Ind.Sci.Rev., Mar.Sci.Cont.Tab., Meteor.& Geoastrophys.Abstr., Ocean.Abstr., Phys.Ber., Sci.Abstr., Sci.Cit.Ind.
—BLDSC shelfmark: 3637.143300.
Description: Deals with the process studies common to the air and the sea.
Refereed Serial

551.5   EC
ECUADOR. INSTITUTO NACIONAL DE METEOROLOGIA E HIDROLOGIA. ANUARIO METEOROLOGICO. 1959. a. exchange basis. Instituto Nacional de Meteorologia e Hidrologia, Daniel Hidalgo 132 y 10 de Agosto, Quito, Ecuador. index.
Supersedes: Ecuador. Servicio Nacional de Meteorologia e Hidrologia. Anuario Meteorologico (ISSN 0070-8941)

551.6   EC
ECUADOR. INSTITUTO NACIONAL DE METEOROLOGIA E HIDROLOGIA. BOLETIN CLIMATOLOGICO. 1962. m. Instituto Nacional de Meteorologia e Hidrologia, Daniel Hidalgo 132 y 10 de Agosto, Quito, Ecuador.
Supersedes: Ecuador. Servicio Nacional de Meteorologia e Hidrologia. Boletin Climatologico.

551.5   UA
EGYPT. METEOROLOGICAL AUTHORITY. ANNUAL METEOROLOGICAL REPORT. a. $1.50. Meteorological Authority, Kubri-el-Qubbeh, Cairo, Egypt.

551.5   UA
EGYPT. METEOROLOGICAL AUTHORITY. METEOROLOGICAL RESEARCH BULLETIN. (Text in English; summaries in Arabic) 1969. s-a. $4.50. Meteorological Authority, Koubri-el-Qubbeh, Cairo, Egypt. charts.

550   UA
EGYPT. METEOROLOGICAL AUTHORITY. MONTHLY WEATHER REPORT. (Text in English) 1909. m. $18. Meteorological Authority, Kubri-el-Qubbeh, Cairo, Egypt. charts; stat.

551.5 318   PN
ESTADISTICA PANAMENA. SITUACION FISICA. SECCION 121. METEOROLOGIA. 1952. a. Bl.0.75. Direccion de Estadistica y Censo, Contraloria General, Apartado 5213, Panama 5, Panama. FAX 63-9322. circ. 800.
Formerly: Estadistica Panamena. Situacion Fisica. Seccion 121-Clima. Meteorologia (ISSN 0378-6757)

551.65   GW   ISSN 0341-2970
EUROPAEISCHER WETTERBERICHT. 1976. d. DM.360. Deutscher Wetterdienst, Frankfurter Str. 135, Postfach 10 04 65, 6050 Offenbach a.M. 1, Germany. charts; stat.
Formerly (1876-1975): Taeglicher Wetterbericht (ISSN 0039-8926)

551.5   FI   ISSN 0782-6117
FINNISH METEOROLOGICAL INSTITUTE. CONTRIBUTIONS. (Text in English) 1925. irreg. price varies. Ilmatieteen Laitos - Finnish Meteorological Institute, P.O. Box 503, SF-00101 Helsinki, Finland. FAX 1929218. TELEX 124436 EFKL SF. (Dist. by: Government Printing Centre, P.O. Box 516, SF-00101 Helsinki, Finland)
Formerly (until 1988): Ilmatieteen Laitoksen Toimituksia - Finnish Meteorological Institute Contributions (ISSN 0071-5190)

550   KR   ISSN 0367-1631
QC882   CODEN: FADSAO
FIZIKA AERODISPERSNYKH SISTEM. (Text in Russian; summaries in English) 1969. irreg. Izdatel'stvo Kievskii Universitet, Bul'var Tarasa Shevchenko, 14, Kiev, Ukraine. TEL 23-62-93. (Dist. by: Mezhdunarodnaya Kniga, ul. Dimitrova D.39, 113095 Moscow, Russia) Ed. D.J. Polyschuk. illus. **Indexed:** Chem.Abstr.
—BLDSC shelfmark: 0389.705000.

550   RU
FIZIKA NIZHNEI ATMOSFERY. (Subseries of: Institut Eksperimental'noi Meteorologii. Trudy) 1972. irreg. (Institut Eksperimental'noi Meteorologii) Gidrometeoizdat, Vasil'evskii Ostrov, 3, St. Petersburg V-53, Russia. illus.

551.5   AT
FLINDERS INSTITUTE FOR ATMOSPHERIC AND MARINE SCIENCES. COMPUTING REPORTS. 1972. irreg., no.11, 1978. Flinders Institute for Atmospheric and Marine Sciences, Flinders University of South Austalia, Bedford Park, S.A. 5042, Australia. Ed. Peter Schwerdtfeger. circ. 150.

551.5   AT
FLINDERS INSTITUTE FOR ATMOSPHERIC AND MARINE SCIENCES. RESEARCH REPORTS. 1972. irreg., no.33, 1980. Flinders Institute for Atmospheric and Marine Sciences, Flinders University of South Australia, Bedford Park, S.A. 5042, Australia. Ed. Peter Schwerdtfeger. circ. 200.

551.5   AT
FLINDERS INSTITUTE FOR ATMOSPHERIC AND MARINE SCIENCES. TECHNICAL REPORTS. 1973. irreg., no.4, 1980. Aus.$20. Flinders Institute for Atmospheric and Marine Sciences, Flinders University of South Australia, Bedford Park, S.A. 5042, Australia. Ed. Peter Schwerdtfeger. circ. 150.

551.5   JA   ISSN 0016-2566
FUKUOKA DISTRICT METEOROLOGICAL OBSERVATORY. TECHNICAL TIMES/FUKUOKA KANKU KISHODAI GIJUTSU TSUSHIN. (Text in Japanese) 1955. m. free. Fukuoka District Meteorological Observatory - Fukuoka Kanku Kishodai, 1-2-36 Ohori, Chuo-ku, Fukuoka 810, Japan. bk.rev.; circ. 170.

551.5   JA   ISSN 0016-2558
FUKUOKA DISTRICT METEOROLOGICAL OBSERVATORY. UNUSUAL METEOROLOGICAL REPORT/FUKUOKA KANKU KISHODAI IJO KISHO HOKOKU. (Text in Japanese) 1961. q. free. Fukuoka District Meteorological Observatory - Fukuoka Kanku Kishodai, 1-2-36 Ohori, Chuo-ku, Fukuoka 810, Japan. circ. 200.

551.65   JA   ISSN 0016-2574
FUKUOKA PREFECTURE. MONTHLY REPORT OF METEOROLOGY/FUKUOKA-KEN KISHO GEPPO. (Text in Japanese) 1927. m. 1600 Yen. Fukuoka District Meteorological Observatory - Fukuoka Kanku Kishodai, 1-2-36 Ohori, Chuo-ku, Fukuoka 810, Japan. circ. 140.

551.5   PL   ISSN 0208-4325
GAZETA OBSERWATORA I M G W/JOURNAL OF I M W M OBSERVER. (Instytut Meteorologii i Gospodarki Wodnej) 1948. 6/yr. $12. Instytut Meteorologii i Gospodarki Wodnej - Institute of Meteorology and Water Management, 61 Podlesna St., 00-967 Warsaw, Poland. (Dist. by: Ars Polona - Ruch, Krakowskie Przedmiescie 7, Warsaw, Poland) Ed. Stefan Chojnowski. charts, illus.; cum.index; circ. 4,000.
Formerly: Gazeta Obserwatora P I H M.
Description: Articles on meteorology, hydrology, oceanology, water management, hydrotechnics, water quality, methodic, measurements, and instruments.

551.5   GW   ISSN 0138-5658
QC851
GERMANY (DEMOCRATIC REPUBLIC, 1949-). METEOROLOGISCHER DIENST. ABHANDLUNGEN.* 1964. irreg., no.143, 1989. price varies. Akademie-Verlag Berlin, Leipziger Strasse 3-4, 1086 Berlin, Germany. TELEX 114420-AVERL-DD.

551.5 630   GH
GHANA. METEOROLOGICAL DEPARTMENT. AGROMETEOROLOGICAL BULLETIN. 1965. m. Meteorological Department, Box 87, Legon, Accra, Ghana. stat.

551.5   GH
GHANA. METEOROLOGICAL DEPARTMENT. CLIMATOLOGICAL NOTES. irreg., latest no.5. price varies. Meteorological Department, Box 87, Legon, Accra, Ghana.

551.5   GH
GHANA. METEOROLOGICAL DEPARTMENT. MONTHLY SUMMARY OF EVAPORATION. 1961. m. NC.50. Meteorological Department, Box 87, Legon, Accra, Ghana.

551.5   GH   ISSN 0431-8315
GHANA. METEOROLOGICAL DEPARTMENT. MONTHLY SUMMARY OF RAINFALL. 1952. m. NC.60. Meteorological Department, Box 87, Legon, Accra, Ghana.

551.5   GH   ISSN 0431-8323
GHANA. METEOROLOGICAL DEPARTMENT. MONTHLY WEATHER REPORT. 1949. m. NC.60. Meteorological Department, Box 87, Legon, Accra, Ghana.

551.5   GH
GHANA. METEOROLOGICAL DEPARTMENT. PROFESSIONAL NOTES. irreg., latest no.23. price varies. Meteorological Department, Box 87, Legon, Accra, Ghana.

551.5   GH
GHANA. METEOROLOGICAL DEPARTMENT. SUN AND MOON TABLES FOR GHANA. Short title: Sun and Moon Tables for Ghana. 1954. a. NC.1. Meteorological Department, Box 87, Legon, Accra, Ghana.

551.5   UK   ISSN 0072-6605
GREAT BRITAIN. METEOROLOGICAL OFFICE. ANNUAL REPORT. a. price varies. H.M.S.O., P.O. Box 276, London SW8 5DT, England. (reprint service avail. from UMI)

METEOROLOGY

551.5 — UK — ISSN 0027-0636
GREAT BRITAIN. METEOROLOGICAL OFFICE. MONTHLY WEATHER REPORT. 1884. avail. from vol.87, 1970. m. £27. H.M.S.O., P.O. Box 276, London SW8 5DT, England. charts; circ. 1,250. (reprint service avail. from UMI)

551.65 — GW — ISSN 0017-4645
QC880.4.A8
GROSSWETTERLAGEN EUROPAS. 1962. m. DM.50. Deutscher Wetterdienst, Frankfurter Str. 135, Postfach 10 04 65, 6050 Offenbach a.M. 1, Germany. charts.
Formerly: Grosswetterlagen Mitteleuropas.

551.6 — GY
GUYANA. HYDROMETEOROLOGICAL SERVICE. ANNUAL CLIMATOLOGICAL DATA SUMMARY. (Subseries of: Guyana. Hydrometeorological Service) 1973. a. G.$1000 (typically set in Dec.). Ministry of Agriculture, Hydrometeorological Service, Homestretch Ave., Georgetown, Guyana. TEL 02-72463. Ed. G. Persaud. illus.; circ. 200.

551.5 — IT
HABITAT - CALABRIA. 1965. m. free. Habitat-Calabria s.r.l., Via Parco Fiamma, 8, I-89100 Reggio Calabria, Italy. TEL 0039 965 92183. Ed.Bd. circ. 400. (back issues avail.)

551.63 631 — US
HAWAII WEEKLY WEATHER & CROP BULLETIN. 1955. w. $15 (foreign $60). Agricultural Service, National Agricultural Statistics Service, Box 22159, Honolulu, HI 96823-2159. TEL 808-973-9588. stat.; circ. 500. (processed)

551.5 — HK
HONG KONG. ROYAL OBSERVATORY. DAILY WEATHER CHART. (Text in English) 1934. d. price varies. Royal Observatory, 134 A Nathan Road, Kowloon, Hong Kong. Ed.Bd. charts; stat.

551.5 — HK
HONG KONG. ROYAL OBSERVATORY. HISTORICAL PUBLICATIONS. (Text in English) 1884. irreg. price varies. Royal Observatory, 134A Nathan Rd., Kowloon, Hong Kong. Ed.Bd.

551.5 — HK
HONG KONG. ROYAL OBSERVATORY. METEOROLOGICAL RESULTS - PART III; tropical cyclone summaries. (Text in English) 1968. a. Royal Observatory, 134A Nathan Rd., Kowloon, Hong Kong. Ed.Bd.

551.5 — HK
HONG KONG. ROYAL OBSERVATORY. MONTHLY WEATHER SUMMARY. 1976. m. Royal Observatory, 134A Nathan Rd., Kowloon, Hong Kong.

551.5 — HK
HONG KONG. ROYAL OBSERVATORY. OCCASIONAL PAPER. 1950. irreg., no. 62, 1985. Royal Observatory, 134 A Nathan Rd., Kowloon, Hong Kong.

551.5 — HK
HONG KONG. ROYAL OBSERVATORY. RAINFALL CHART. (Text in English) 1952. a. price varies. Royal Observatory, 134A Nathan Rd., Kowloon, Hong Kong. Ed.Bd. charts; stat.

551.5 — HK
HONG KONG. ROYAL OBSERVATORY. TECHNICAL MEMOIRS. (Text in English) 1948. irreg., latest 1974. price varies. Royal Observatory, 134A Nathan Rd., Kowloon, Hong Kong. Ed.Bd.

551.5 — HK
HONG KONG. ROYAL OBSERVATORY. TECHNICAL NOTE. 1949. irreg., no.74, 1986. price varies. Royal Observatory, 134A Nathan Rd., Kowloon, Hong Kong.
Formerly: Hong Kong. Royal Observatory. Climatological Note.

551.5 — HK
HONG KONG. ROYAL OBSERVATORY. TECHNICAL NOTES (LOCAL). (Text in English) 1961. irreg., lastest 1986. price varies. Royal Observatory, 134A Nathan Rd., Kowloon, Hong Kong. Ed.Bd.

551.5 — US
HOURLY PRECIPITATION DATA. (Published separately for 41 states and 6 New England states, Maryland-Delaware, Puerto Rico, omitting Alaska) 1951. m. $38. U.S. National Climatic Data Center, Federal Bldg., MC-02, Asheville, NC 28801-2696. circ. 5,000. (also avail. in microfiche; magnetic tape)

551.5 — BU — ISSN 0018-1331
HYDROLOGY AND METEOROLOGY/HIDROLOGIJA I METEOROLOGIJA. (Summaries in various languages) 1964. irreg. price varies. Publishing House of the Bulgarian Academy of Sciences, Acad. G. Bonchev St., Bldg. 6, 1113 Sofia, Bulgaria. (Dist. by: Hemus, 6, Rouski Blvd., 1000 Sofia, Bulgaria) Ed. I. Marinov. circ. 500. Indexed: BSL Geo.
Formerly: Bulgarska Akademiia na Naukite. Institut po Khidrologiia i Meteorologiia. Izvestiia (ISSN 0068-3876)

551.5 — CS
HYDROMETEOROLOGICKY USTAV. VYROCNI ZPRAVA. a. price varies. Nakladatelstvi Technicke Literatury, Spalena 51, 113 02 Prague 1, Czechoslovakia.

551.57 — CS
HYDROMETEOROLOGICKY USTAV, BRATISLAVA. ZBORNIK PRAC. (Text in Russian; summaries in Czech or Slovak, and in German) 1972. irreg. (approx. biennial). 30 Kcs. Slovenske Pedagogicke Nakladatelstvo, Sasinkova 5, 815 60 Bratislava, Czechoslovakia. illus.

I C R R ANNUAL REPORT. (Institute for Cosmic Ray Research) see ASTRONOMY

551.5 — FI — ISSN 0782-6109
ILMATIETEEN LAITOS. METEOROLOGISIA JULKAISUJA/FINNISH METEOROLOGICAL INSTITUTE. PUBLICATIONS. irreg. Ilmatieteen Laitos - Finnish Meteorological Institute, P.O. Box 503, SF-00101 Helsinki, Finland. FAX 1929218. TELEX 124436 EFKL SF. (Dist. by: Government Printing Centre, P.O. Box 516, SF-00101 Helsinki, Finland)

551.5 — II
INDIA. METEOROLOGICAL DEPARTMENT. MEMOIRS. (Text in English) irreg. price varies. Meteorological Department, Lodi Rd., New Delhi 110003, India. (Dist. by: Controller of Publications, Government of India, Civil Lines, Delhi 110 054, India)

551.5 — II — ISSN 0250-6017
INDIAN INSTITUTE OF TROPICAL METEOROLOGY. ANNUAL REPORT. 1971. a. free. Indian Institute of Tropical Meteorology, Ramdurg House, University Rd., Poona 411 005, India. circ. controlled.

551.5 — II — ISSN 0252-1075
INDIAN INSTITUTE OF TROPICAL METEOROLOGY. CONTRIBUTIONS. 1980. irreg. Indian Institute of Tropical Meteorology, Ramdurg House, University Rd., Poona 411 005, India. circ. controlled. Key Title: Contributions from the Indian Institute of Tropical Meteorology.
Supersedes (1971-1980): Indian Institute of Tropical Meteorology. Research Report (ISSN 0250-6009)

INDIAN JOURNAL OF RADIO & SPACE PHYSICS. see ASTRONOMY

551.5 — AO
INSTITUTO DE INVESTIGACAO AGRONOMICA DE ANGOLA. DIVISAO DE METEOROLOGIA AGRICOLA. ANUARIO. 1972. a. free. Instituto de Investigacao Agronomica de Angola, C.P. 406, Nova Lisboa, Angola. Indexed: Trop.Abstr.

551.5 — PL — ISSN 0239-6262
INSTYTUT METEOROLOGII I GOSPODARKI WODNEJ. MATERIALY BADAWCZE. SERIA: METEOROLOGIA/INSTITUTE OF METEOROLOGY AND WATER MANAGEMENT. RESEARCH PAPERS SERIES: METEOROLOGY. (Text in Polish; summaries in English and Russian) 1974. irreg. $5. Instytut Meteorologii i Gospodarki Wodnej - Institute of Meteorology and Water Management, 61 Podlesna St., 01-673 Warsaw, Poland. circ. 300.
Description: Articles on meteorology, meteorological elements, observational data, forecastings, measurements, instruments, research works.

551.5 — PL — ISSN 0208-6263
QC869.4.P63 — CODEN: WIMWDL
INSTYTUT METEOROLOGII I GOSPODARKI WODNEJ. WIADOMOSCI/INSTITUTE OF METEOROLOGY AND WATER MANAGEMENT. REPORTS. Cover title: Wiadomosci Instytutu Meteorologii i Gospodarki Wodnej. (Text in Polish; summaries in English and Russian) 1947. q. $40. Instytut Meteorologii i Gospodarki Wodnej - Institute of Meteorology and Water Management, 61 Podlesna St., 01-673 Warsaw, Poland. (Dist. by: Ars Polona - Ruch, Krakowskie Przedmiescie 7, Warsaw, Poland) abstr.; bibl.; charts; illus.; stat.; cum.index; circ. 450.
Indexed: Deep Sea Res.& Oceanogr.Abstr., Meteor.& Geoastrophys.Abstr.
Formerly: Wiadomosci Sluzby Hydrologicznej i Meteorologicznej (ISSN 0043-5171)
Description: Articles on meteorology, hydrology, oceanology, water management, water quality, forecastings, methodics measurements.

551.5 — AU — ISSN 0074-1663
INTERNATIONAL ASSOCIATION OF METEOROLOGY AND ATMOSPHERIC PHYSICS. REPORT OF PROCEEDINGS OF GENERAL ASSEMBLY. 1924. biennial. $20. International Association of Meteorology and Atmospheric Physics, c/o Prof. M. Kuhn, Institut fuer Met. und Geophys., Univ. Innsbruck, Innrain 52, A-6020 Innsbruck, Austria. TEL 512-5072183. FAX 512-5072170. circ. controlled.

551.576 — CN — ISSN 0074-3011
INTERNATIONAL CONFERENCE ON CLOUD PHYSICS. PROCEEDINGS. (Proceedings published in host countries) 1968. irreg., 8th, 1982, Aubiere, France. Can.$20. (International Association of Meteorology and Atmospheric Physics) International Commission on Cloud Physics, c/o Prof. R. List, University of Toronto, Toronto, Ont. M5S 1A6, Canada. adv.; circ. 1,500.

551.5 574 — GW — ISSN 0020-7128
QH543 — CODEN: IJBMAO
INTERNATIONAL JOURNAL OF BIOMETEOROLOGY. (Text in English, French and German) 1957. 4/yr. fl.455. Springer-Verlag, Postfach 105280, 6900 Heidelberg, Germany. FAX 06221-43982. TELEX 461723. Ed. R.W. Gloyne. abstr.; bibl.; charts; illus.; index; circ. 1,300. (reprint service avail. from SWZ)
Indexed: Anim.Breed.Abstr., Biol.Abstr., Chem.Abstr., Curr.Adv.Ecol.Sci., Curr.Cont., Dairy Sci.Abstr., Excerp.Med., Field Crop Abstr., Geo.Abstr., Helminthol.Abstr., Herb.Abstr., Ind.Med., Ind.Sci.Rev., Ind.Vet., Meteor.& Geoastrophys.Abstr., Pig News & Info., Sci.Cit.Ind., Soils & Fert., Vet.Bull.
—BLDSC shelfmark: 2087.950000.

551.5 — UK — ISSN 0899-8418
QC980 — CODEN: IJCLEU
INTERNATIONAL JOURNAL OF CLIMATOLOGY. 1981. 8/yr. $425 (effective 1992). (Royal Meteorological Society) John Wiley & Sons Ltd., Journals, Baffins Lane, Chichester, Sussex PO19 1UD, England. TEL 0243-779777. FAX 0243-775878. TELEX 86290 WIBOOK G. Ed. B.D. Giles. adv.; bk.rev.; charts; illus.; maps; index. (back issues avail.; reprint service avail. from SWZ,UMI) Indexed: Acid Pre.Dig., Curr.Cont., Deep Sea Res.& Oceanogr.Abstr., Energy Rev., Environ.Per.Bibl., Geo.Abstr., Ind.Sci.Rev., Sci.Abstr., Sci.Cit.Ind., Sel.Water Res.Abstr.
—BLDSC shelfmark: 4542.168000.
Formerly: Journal of Climatology (ISSN 0196-1748)
Description: Spans the field of climatology, encompassing regional and global studies, local and microclimatological investigations, changes in climate, and applications.

551.5 — SW — ISSN 0349-0068
QC851.I53
INTERNATIONAL METEOROLOGICAL INSTITUTE IN STOCKHOLM. ANNUAL REPORT. (Report year ends June 30) 1973. a. free. International Meteorological Institute in Stockholm, Arrhenius Laboratory, S-106 91 Stockholm, Sweden. FAX 8-157185. TELEX 15950-MISU S. Ed. Marianne Skaarman. circ. 600.

550 — JA — ISSN 0389-8237
IONOSPHERIC DATA AT SHOWA STATION (ANTARCTICA). s-a. Ministry of Posts and Telecommunications, Communications Research Laboratory - Yusei-sho Tsushinsogo Kenkyujo, 2-1 4-chome Nukui-Kitamachi, Koganei-shi, Tokyo 184, Japan. TEL 0423-21-1211. TELEX 2832611-DEMPA-J. stat.

551.514   JA   ISSN 0021-0382
IONOSPHERIC DATA IN JAPAN/DENRISO GEPPO. (Text in English) 1950. m. free. Ministry of Posts and Telecommunications, Communications Research Laboratory, Ionospheric Observation Section - Yusei-sho Tsushinsogo Kenkyujo, 2-1, 4-chome, Nukui-Kita-machi, Koganei-shi, Tokyo 184, Japan. TEL 0423-21-1211. FAX 0423-27-7606. TELEX 2832611 DEMPA J. charts; stat.; circ. 250.

551.5   IS   ISSN 0333-7936
ISRAEL. METEOROLOGICAL SERVICE. MONTHLY AGROCLIMATOLOGICAL REPORT. (Headings in English and Hebrew) 1975. m. Meteorological Service, Box 25, Bet Dagan, Israel.
   Former titles: Israel. Meteorological Service. Monthly Agroclimatological Bulletin; Israel. Meteorological Service. Agro-Meteorological Bulletin (ISSN 0002-1806)

551.5 333.91   IS
ISRAEL. METEOROLOGICAL SERVICE. RAINFALL SEASON. (Text in English and Hebrew) a. Meteorological Service, P.O. Box 25, Beit Dagan 50 200, Israel. TEL 03-625231.

551.5   IS   ISSN 0075-126X
ISRAEL. METEOROLOGICAL SERVICE. SERIES B: OBSERVATIONAL DATA. ANNUAL RAINFALL SUMMARY. (Text in Hebrew, summaries in English and Hebrew) 1947. a. Meteorological Service, Box 25, Bet Dagan, Israel.

551.5   IS   ISSN 0075-1286
ISRAEL. METEOROLOGICAL SERVICE. SERIES B: OBSERVATIONAL DATA. ANNUAL WEATHER REPORT. (Text in Hebrew; summaries in English, Hebrew) 1948. a. Meteorological Service, Box 25, Bet Dagan, Israel.

551.5   IS   ISSN 0021-2261
ISRAEL. METEOROLOGICAL SERVICE. SERIES B: OBSERVATIONAL DATA. MONTHLY WEATHER REPORT. (Text and summaries in English, Hebrew) 1947. m. $0.20. Meteorological Service, Box 25, Bet Dagan, Israel.

551.5   IS
ISRAEL. METEOROLOGICAL SOCIETY. METEOROLOGIA BE-ISRAEL. (Text in Hebrew) 1963. irreg. $5. Meteorological Society, Box 25, Bet-Dagan, Israel. Ed.Bd. bk.rev.; charts; illus.; circ. 300. (processed) **Indexed:** Meteor. & Geoastrophys.Abstr.
   Formerly: Israel. Meteorologia Be-Israel. (ISSN 0026-1122)

551.51   IT   ISSN 0075-191X
ISTITUTO DI FISICA DELL'ATMOSFERA, ROME. CONTRIBUTI SCIENTIFICI: PUBBLICAZIONI DI FISICA DELL'ATMOSFERA E DI METEOROLOGIA. (Contributions in English, German and Italian) 1964. irreg. Istituto di Fisica dell'Atmosfera, Piazzale Luigi Sturzo 31, 00144 Rome, Italy. TEL 06-59-10-941. FAX 06-59-15-790. **Indexed:** Meteor.& Geoastrophys.Abstr.

551.51   IT   ISSN 0075-1928
ISTITUTO DI FISICA DELL'ATMOSFERA, ROME. PUBBLICAZIONI DIDATTICHE. 1962. irreg. $10. Istituto di Fisica dell'Atmosfera, Piazzale Luigi Sturzo 31, 00144 Rome, Italy. TEL 06-59-10-941. FAX 06-59-15-790. **Indexed:** Meteor.& Geoastrophys.Abstr.

551.51   IT   ISSN 0075-1936
ISTITUTO DI FISICA DELL'ATMOSFERA, ROME. PUBBLICAZIONI SCIENTIFICHE. (Contributions in English and Italian) 1962. irreg. Istituto di Fisica dell'Atmosfera, Piazzale Luigi Sturzo 31, 00144 Rome, Italy. TEL 06-59-10-941. FAX 06-59-15-790. **Indexed:** Meteor.& Geoastrophys.Abstr.

551.51   IT   ISSN 0075-1944
ISTITUTO DI FISICA DELL'ATMOSFERA, ROME. PUBBLICAZIONI VARIE.. (Contributions in English and Italian) 1962. irreg. Istituto di Fisica dell'Atmosfera, Piazzale Luigi Sturzo 31, 00144 Rome, Italy. TEL 06-59-10-941. FAX 06-59-15-790. **Indexed:** Meteor.& Geoastrophys.Abstr.

551.51   IT   ISSN 0075-1952
ISTITUTO DI FISICA DELL'ATMOSFERA, ROME. RAPPORTI INTERNI PROVVISORI ADIFFUSIONE LIMITATA. (Contributions in English and Italian) 1966. irreg. Istituto di Fisica dell'Atmosfera, Piazzale Luigi Sturzo 31, 00144 Rome, Italy. TEL 06-59-10-941. FAX 06-59-15-790. **Indexed:** Meteor.& Geoastrophys.Abstr.

551.51   IT   ISSN 0075-1960
ISTITUTO DI FISICA DELL'ATMOSFERA, ROME. RAPPORTI SCIENTIFICI. (Contributions in English and Italian) 1962. irreg. Istituto di Fisica dell'Atmosfera, Piazzale Luigi Sturzo 31, 00144 Rome, Italy. TEL 06-59-10-941. FAX 06-59-15-790. **Indexed:** Meteor.& Geoastrophys.Abstr.

551.51   IT   ISSN 0075-1979
ISTITUTO DI FISICA DELL'ATMOSFERA, ROME. RAPPORTI TECNICI. (Contributions in English, French and Italian) 1961. irreg. Istituto di Fisica dell'Atmosfera, Piazzale Luigi Sturzo 31, 00144 Rome, Italy. TEL 06-59-10-941. FAX 06-59-15-790. **Indexed:** Meteor.& Geoastrophys.Abstr.

551.5   US   ISSN 0148-0227
QC811   CODEN: JGREA2
J G R: JOURNAL OF GEOPHYSICAL RESEARCH. 1896. m. $2555 includes J G R: Space Physics; J G R: Solid Earth; J G R: Planets; J G R: Oceans; and J G R: Atmospheres. American Geophysical Union, 2000 Florida Ave., N.W., Washington, DC 20009. TEL 202-462-6900. FAX 202-328-0566. TELEX 710-882-9300. **Indexed:** Environ.Abstr., INIS Atomind.
   —BLDSC shelfmark: 4995.000000.
   Description: Current geophysical research in the earth sciences with emphasis on atmospheric science.
   Refereed Serial

551.5   US
J G R: JOURNAL OF GEOPHYSICAL RESEARCH: ATMOSPHERE. 1896. m. $90 to members (foreign $126); students $58 (foreign $94). American Geophysical Union, 2000 Florida Ave., N.W., Washington, DC 20009. TEL 202-462-6900. FAX 202-328-0566. TELEX 710-882-9300.
   Description: Covers the physics and chemistry of the atmosphere, as well as the atmospheric, biospheric, lithospheric, and hydrospheric interface.

551.65   JA   ISSN 0448-374X
JAPAN. METEOROLOGICAL AGENCY. MONTHLY REPORT/KISHO-CHO GEPPO ZENKOKU KISHCHYO. (Text in Japanese) 1892. m. $227. Japan Weather Association, c/o Japan Meteorological Agency, 1-3-4 Otemachi, Chiyoda-ku, Tokyo 100, Japan.

551.5 630   JA   ISSN 0368-5942
JAPAN METEOROLOGICAL AGENCY. AGRICULTURAL METEOROLOGY. ANNUAL REPORT. (Text in Japanese) 1950. a. membership. (Japan Meteorological Agency) Japan Weather Association, 2-9-2, Kanda-nishikicho, Chiyoda-ku, Tokyo 101, Japan. circ. 383.
   —BLDSC shelfmark: 5018.800000.

551.65   JA   ISSN 0448-3758
JAPAN METEOROLOGICAL AGENCY. ANNUAL REPORT/KISHO-CHO NENPO ZENKOKU KISHOHYO. (Issued in two parts) 1887. a. 2163 Yen. (Japan Meteorological Agency) Japan Weather Association, 2-9-2, Kanda-nishikicho, Chiyoda-ku, Tokyo 101, Japan. circ. 724.

551.636   JA
JAPAN METEOROLOGICAL AGENCY. MONTHLY REPORT ON CLIMATE SYSTEM. (Text in English) 1960. m. 13,390 Yen. (Japan Meteorological Agency) Japan Weather Association, 2-9-2, Kanda-nishikicho, Chiyoda-ku, Tokyo 101, Japan. stat.; circ. 624.
   Formerly (until 1987): Japan. Meteorological Agency. Mean Maps. Long Range Weather Forecasting.

551.5 630   JA   ISSN 0021-8588
JOURNAL OF AGRICULTURAL METEOROLOGY/NOGYO KISHO. (Text in English and Japanese; summaries in English) 1943. q. 8000 Yen($24) Society of Agricultural Meteorology of Japan - Nihon Nogyo Kisho Gakkai, c/o Division of Agro-Meteorology, National Institut of Agro-Environmental Sciences, 3-1-1 Kannondai, Yatabecho, Tsukuba-gun, Ibaraki 305, Japan. Ed. Zenbei Uchijima. adv.; bk.rev.; abstr.; charts; index; circ. 1,100. **Indexed:** Agri.Eng.Abstr., Biol.Abstr., Chem.Abstr., Excerp.Med., Field Crop Abstr., Fluidex, Herb.Abstr., Hort.Abstr., Meteor.& Geoastrophys.Abstr., Ornam.Hort., Plant Breed.Abstr., Rice Abstr.
   —BLDSC shelfmark: 4922.000000.

551.5   US   ISSN 0733-3021
QC851   CODEN: JCAMEJ
JOURNAL OF APPLIED METEOROLOGY. 1962. m. $165 (foreign $185). American Meteorological Society, 45 Beacon St., Boston, MA 02108-3693. TEL 617-227-2425. FAX 617-742-8718. Ed. Steven R. Hanna. abstr.; bibl.; charts; illus.; stat.; index; circ. 2,066. (back issues avail.; reprint service avail.) **Indexed:** A.S.& T.Ind., Acid Pre.Dig., Appl.Mech.Rev., Biol.Abstr., Biol.& Agr.Ind., Chem.Abstr., Curr.Cont., Deep Sea Res.& Oceanogr.Abstr., Eng.Ind., Environ.Per.Bibl., Excerp.Med., Field Crop Abstr., Fluidex, Forest.Abstr., Geo.Abstr., GeoRef, Herb.Abstr., Hort.Abstr., Ind.Sci.Rev., INIS Atomind., Int.Aerosp.Abstr., Meteor.& Geoastrophys.Abstr., Ocean.Abstr., Pollut.Abstr., Sci.Abstr., Sci.Cit.Ind., Sel.Water Res.Abstr., So.Pac.Per.Ind., Soils & Fert.
   Supersedes in part: Journal of Climate and Applied Meteorology; Formerly (until 1983): Journal of Applied Meteorology (ISSN 0021-8952)
   Description: Publishes applied research related to physical meteorology, weather modification, cloud physics, satellite meteorology, air pollution.
   Refereed Serial

551.5   US   ISSN 0739-0572
JOURNAL OF ATMOSPHERIC AND OCEANIC TECHNOLOGY. 1984. bi-m. $135 (foreign $150). American Meteorological Society, 45 Beacon St., Boston, MA 02108-3693. TEL 617-227-2425. FAX 617-742-8718. Eds. William A. Cooper, Thomas Sanford. abstr.; bibl.; charts; illus.; stat.; index; circ. 779. (back issues avail.; reprint service avail.) **Indexed:** Chem.Abstr., Deep Sea Res.& Oceanogr.Abstr., Meteor.& Geoastrophys.Abstr., Ocean.Abstr.
   —BLDSC shelfmark: 4947.900000.
   Description: Presents information related to the state-of-the-art development of technical support to the atmospheric and oceanic science.
   Refereed Serial

JOURNAL OF ATMOSPHERIC CHEMISTRY. see *CHEMISTRY*

551.5   US   ISSN 0894-8755
QC851   CODEN: JLCLEL
JOURNAL OF CLIMATE. 1986. m. $175 (foreign $195). American Meteorological Society, 45 Beacon St., Boston, MA 02108-3693. TEL 617-227-2425. FAX 617-742-8718. Ed. Peter J. Lamb. abstr.; bibl.; charts; illus.; stat.; index; circ. 1,591. (back issues avail.; reprint service avail.) **Indexed:** Environ.Per.Bibl., Meteor.& Geoastrophys. Abstr.
   —BLDSC shelfmark: 4958.369730.
   Supersedes in part (Dec. 1987): Journal of Climate and Applied Meteorology.
   Description: Provides a focus for articles on climate research and impact analysis.
   Refereed Serial

551.1   JA
JOURNAL OF METEOROLOGICAL RESEARCH. (Text in Japanese; summaries in English) 1891. bi-m. 7,200 Yen. (Japan Meteorological Agency) Japan Weather Association, 2-9-2, Kanda-nishikicho, Chiyoda-ku, Tokyo 101, Japan. circ. 879.

551.5   UK   ISSN 0307-5966
JOURNAL OF METEOROLOGY. 1975. 10/yr. $150. (Tornado & Storm Research Organisation) Artetech Publishing Co., 54 Frome Rd., Bradford-on-Avon, Wilts BA15 1LD, England. TEL 02216-2482. FAX 02216-5601. Ed. G.T. Meaden. adv.; bk.rev.; index. **Indexed:** Deep Sea Res.& Oceanogr.Abstr., Meteor.& Geoastrophys.Abstr., W.R.C.Inf.
   —BLDSC shelfmark: 5019.020000.

METEOROLOGY

551.5 US ISSN 0022-4928
QC851 CODEN: JAHSAK
JOURNAL OF THE ATMOSPHERIC SCIENCES. 1944. s-m. $320 (foreign $350). American Meteorological Society, 45 Beacon St., Boston, MA 02108-3693. TEL 617-227-2425. FAX 617-742-8718. Eds. Robert L. Gall, G. Brant Foote. abstr.; bibl.; charts; illus.; stat.; index; circ. 2,213. (back issues avail.; reprint service avail.) Indexed: A.S.& T.Ind., Acid Pre.Dig., Chem.Abstr., Excerp.Med., Gen.Sci.Ind., Geo.Abstr., GeoRef, Ind.Sci.Rev., INIS Atomind., Int.Aerosp.Abstr., Math.R., Meteor.& Geoastrophys.Abstr., Sci.Abstr., So.Pac.Per.Ind.
—BLDSC shelfmark: 4949.200000.
Description: Publishes basic research related to the physics and dynamics of the atmosphere of the earth and other planets, with emphasis on the quantitative and deductive aspects of the subject.
Refereed Serial

551.63 US ISSN 0739-1781
CODEN: JWMOEL
JOURNAL OF WEATHER MODIFICATION. 1969. a. $40. Weather Modification Association, Box 8116, Fresno, CA 93747. TEL 209-434-3486. FAX 209-291-5579. Ed. James A. Miller. adv.; cum.index: 1969-1991; circ. 500. (back issues avail.)

551.65 630 JA ISSN 0022-7706
KAGOSHIMA-KEN NOGYO KISHO GEPPO/MONTHLY REPORT OF AGRICULTURAL METEOROLOGY, KAGOSHIMA PREFECTURE. (Text in Japanese) 1923. m. Japan Weather Association, Kagoshima Local Meteorological Observatory - Kagoshima Chiho Kishodai, 24-13, 1-chome, Arata, Kagoshima-shi 890, Japan. charts; stat.

551.5 JA
KANSOKUJO KISHO NENPO/ANNUAL REPORT OF CLIMATOLOGICAL STATIONS. (Text in Japanese) 1968. a. 2100 Yen. (Japan Meteorological Agency) Japan Weather Association, 2-9-2, Kanda-nishikicho, Chiyoda-ku, Tokyo 101, Japan. circ. 542.

551.5 RU
KATALOG RADIATSIONNYKH DANNYKH/CATALOGUE OF SOLAR RADIATION DATA. 1987. a. $6 (effective Mar. 1991). Glavnaya Geofizicheskaya Observatoriya im. A.I. Voeikova, Ul. Karbysheva 7, St. Petersburg 194018, Russia.

551.656 KE
KENYA METEOROLOGICAL DEPARTMENT. ANNUAL REPORT. 1929. a. Meteorological Department, P.O. Box 30259, Dagoretti Corner, Ngong Rd., Nairobi, Kenya. circ. 1,200.
Supersedes in part: East African Community. East African Meteorological Department. Annual Report.

551.5 JA
KISHO-CHO KANSOKU GIJUTSU SHIRYO/TECHNICAL DATA SERIES. (Text in Japanese) 1956. a. 2000 Yen. (Japan Meteorological Agency) Japan Weather Association, 2-9-2, Kanda-nishikicho, Chiyoda-ku, Tokyo 101, Japan. circ. 461.

551.6 GW
KLIMA-EILINFORMATION. 1972. m. DM.15. Deutscher Wetterdienst, Frankfurter Str. 135, Postfach 10 04 65, D-6050 Offenbach, Germany. TEL 069-8062-839.
Description: Updates on the weather in Germany.

551.5 RU
KLIMAT I GIDROGRAFIYA ZABAIKAL'YA. 1972. irreg. 0.40 Rub. Geograficheskoe Obshchestvo S.S.S.R., Zabaikal'skii Filial, Chita, Russia. illus.

551.6 GW
KLIMATOLOGISCHE WERTE. 1968. m. DM.15. Deutscher Wetterdienst - German Weather Service, Frankfurter Str. 135, Postfach 10 04 65, D-6050 Offenbach, Germany. TEL 069-8062-839.

KOBE KAIYO KISHODAI IHO/KOBE MARINE OBSERVATORY. BULLETIN. see *EARTH SCIENCES — Oceanography*

KUKI SHAWA KENKYU. see *ASTRONOMY*

551.5 JA
KUMAMOTO PREFECTURE. MONTHLY REPORT. 1953. m. Kumamoto Prefecture, 12-20, Kyo-machi 2-chome, Kumamoto-shi, Kumamoto-ken 860, Japan. circ. 100.

551.5 FI ISSN 0303-2485
QC989.F3
KUUKAUSIKATSAUS SUOMEN ILMASTOON/MAANADSOEVERSIKT OEVER FINLANDS KLIMAT. (Text and summaries in Finnish and Swedish) 1907. m. Fmk.140. Ilmatieteen Laitos - Finnish Meteorological Institute, Box 503, SF-00101 Helsinki, Finland. (Dist. by: Government Printing Centre, P.O. Box 516 Helsinki, Finland) (back issues avail.)
Description: Examines climatological and meteorological data.

551.5 US
LOCAL CLIMATOLOGICAL DATA. (Published separately for 274 cities) 1897. m. (plus an annual). $17. U.S. National Climatic Data Center, Federal Bldg., MC-02, Asheville, NC 28801-2696. TEL 704-259-0682. circ. 40,000. (also avail. in microfiche)
Former titles (until 1951): Monthly Climatological Summary; (until 1947): Monthly Meteorological Summary.

551.6 CN ISSN 0076-1931
QC851
MCGILL UNIVERSITY, MONTREAL. DEPARTMENT OF GEOGRAPHY. CLIMATOLOGICAL RESEARCH SERIES. 1966. irreg. price varies. McGill University, Department of Geography, 805 Sherbrooke St. W., Montreal, Que. H3A 2R6, Canada. TEL 514-392-5700. Eds. T. Moore, J. Lewis.

551.5 MW
MALAWI. METEOROLOGICAL DEPARTMENT. MONTHLY SUMMARIES. (Text in English) 1969. m. free. Meteorological Department, Box 2, Chileka, Malawi. TELEX 44611. circ. 100.
Formerly: Malawi. Meteorological Services. Monthly Summaries.

551.5 MW
MALAWI. METEOROLOGICAL DEPARTMENT. TOTALS OF MONTHLY AND ANNUAL RAINFALL. (Text and summaries in English) 1969. a. K.1. Meteorological Department, Box 2, Chileka, Malawi. TELEX 44611. stat.
Formerly: Malawi. Meteorlogical Services. Totals of Monthly and Annual Rainfall.

551.5 MY
MALAYSIA. METEOROLOGICAL SERVICE. ANNUAL SUMMARY OF METEOROLOGICAL OBSERVATIONS. (Text and summaries in English) 1930. a. M.30. Malaysian Meteorological Service - Perkhidmatan Kajicuaca Malaysia, Jalan Sultan, Petaling Jaya 46667, Selangor, Malaysia. TELEX MA 37245. circ. 210.
Former titles: Malaysia. Meteorological Service. Summary of Observations for Malaysia (ISSN 0126-8864); Malaysia. Meterological Service. Summary of Observations for Malaya, Sabah and Sarawak.

551 UK ISSN 0025-3251
QC851
MARINE OBSERVER; a quarterly journal of maritime meteorology. 1924. q. £12. H.M.S.O., P.O. Box 276, London SW8 5DT, England. adv.; bk.rev.; charts; illus.; maps; index. (also avail. in microform from UMI; reprint service avail. from UMI) Indexed: Chem.Abstr., Deep Sea Res.& Oceanogr.Abstr., Geo.Abstr., Meteor.& Geoastrophys.Abstr., Ocean.Abstr., Pollut.Abstr.
—BLDSC shelfmark: 5377.000000.

551 US ISSN 0025-3367
QC994
MARINERS WEATHER LOG; a climatic review of North Atlantic and North Pacific Ocean and Great Lake areas. 1957. q. $8 (foreign $10). U.S. National Oceanographic Data Center, NOAA-NESDIS, E-OC2, Universal Bldg. 1, Rm. 415, 1825 Connecticut Ave. N.W., Washington, DC 20235. TEL 202-606-4561. Ed. Richard De Angelis. charts; illus.; stat.; index; circ. 4,500. (also avail. in microform from MIM,UMI) Indexed: Amer.Stat.Ind., Deep Sea Res.& Oceanogr.Abstr., Ind.U.S.Gov.Per., Meteor.& Geoastrophys.Abstr., Ocean.Abstr., Pollut.Abstr., So.Pac.Per.Ind.

551.5 MF ISSN 0076-5511
MAURITIUS. METEOROLOGICAL SERVICES. REPORT. a. price varies. Government Printing Office, Elizabeth II Ave., Port Louis, Mauritius.

551.5 II ISSN 0252-9416
QC851 CODEN: MAUSDJ
MAUSAM. (Text in English and Hindi) 1950. q. Rs.200($72) Meteorological Department, Lodi Rd., New Delhi 110 003, India. (Dist. by: Controller of Publications, Government of India, Civil Lines, Delhi 110 054, India) Ed. S.M. Kulshretha. adv.; bk.rev.; abstr.; charts; illus.; index; circ. 850. Indexed: Chem.Abstr., Deep Sea Res.& Oceanogr.Abstr., GeoRef, Meteor.& Geoastrophys.Abstr., Rice Abstr., Sci.Abstr., Sel.Water Res.Abstr.
—BLDSC shelfmark: 5413.279550.
Former titles: Indian Journal of Meteorology, Hydrology and Geophysics (ISSN 0376-4796); Indian Journal of Meteorology and Geophysics (ISSN 0019-5383)

551.5 UK ISSN 0026-1149
CODEN: MTMGA5
METEOROLOGICAL MAGAZINE. 1866. m. £28. H.M.S.O., P.O. Box 276, London SW8 5DT, England. Ed. R.P.W. Lewis. adv.; bk.rev.; abstr.; bibl.; charts; illus.; index; circ. 1,950. (also avail. in microfiche from BHP; reprint service avail. from UMI) Indexed: Chem.Abstr., Curr.Adv.Ecol.Sci., Curr.Cont., Deep Sea Res.& Oceanogr.Abstr., Geo.Abstr., Hort.Abstr., Meteor.& Geoastrophys.Abstr., Sci.Abstr., Sci.Cit.Ind., So.Pac.Per.Ind., Soils & Fert.
—BLDSC shelfmark: 5708.000000.

551.5 JA ISSN 0026-1165
QC851 CODEN: JMSJAU
METEOROLOGICAL SOCIETY OF JAPAN. JOURNAL/KISHO SHUSHI. (Text in English) 1882. bi-m. $65. Meteorological Society of Japan - Nihon Kisho Gakkai, c/o Japan Meteorological Agency, 1-3-4 Ote-machi, Chiyoda-ku, Tokyo 100, Japan. Ed. M. Murakami. circ. 2,000. Indexed: Chem.Abstr., Deep Sea Res.& Oceanogr.Abstr., INIS Atomind., JTA, Meteor.& Geoastrophys.Abstr., Sel.Water Res.Abstr.
—BLDSC shelfmark: 4825.000000.

551.5 FI ISSN 0076-6747
QC989.R5
METEOROLOGICAL YEARBOOK OF FINLAND. PART 1: CLIMATOLOGICAL DATA. Finnish edition: Suomen Meteorologinen Vuosikiria. Part 1. Ilmastohavainnot (ISSN 0782-0380) (Text in English, Finnish) 1981. a. price varies. Ilmatieteen Laitos - Finnish Meteorological Institute, P.O. Box 503, SF-00101 Helsinki, Finland. FAX 1929218. TELEX 124436 EFKL SF. (Dist. by: Government Printing Centre, P.O. Box 516, SF-00101 Helsinki, Finland)
Description: Review of climatological data in Finland.

551.5 FI ISSN 0076-6755
METEOROLOGICAL YEARBOOK OF FINLAND. PART 2: PRECIPITATION AND SNOW COVER DATA. (Text in English and Finnish) 1960. a. price varies. Ilmatieteen Laitos - Finnish Meteorological Institute, P.O. Box 503, SF-00101 Helsinki, Finland. FAX 1929218. TELEX 124436 EFKL SF. (Dist. by: Government Printing Centre, P.O. Box 516, SF-00101 Helsinki, Finland)

551.5 FI ISSN 0780-7295
METEOROLOGICAL YEARBOOK OF FINLAND. PART 3. STATISTICS OF RADIOSONDE OBSERVATIONS 1961-1980. (Text in English and Finnish) 1984. irreg. price varies. Ilmatieteen Laitos - Finnish Meteorological Institute, P.O. Box 503, SF-00101, Helsinki, Finland. FAX 1929218. TELEX 124436 EFKL SF. (Dist. by: Government Printing Centre, P.O. Box 516, SF-00101 Helsinki, Finland)

551.5 FI ISSN 0783-103X
METEOROLOGICAL YEARBOOK OF FINLAND. PART 4: 1 MEASUREMENTS OF SOLAR RADIATION. (Text in English and Finnish) 1982. a. price varies. Ilmatieteen Laitos - Finnish Meteorological Institute, P.O. Box 503, SF-00101 Helsinki, Finland. FAX 1929218. TELEX 124436 EFKL SF. (Dist. by: Government Printing Centre, P.O. Box 516, SF-00101 Helsinki, Finland)
Supersedes in part: Meteorological Yearbook of Finland. Part 4: Measurements of Radiation and Bright Sunshine (ISSN 0076-6763)

551.5 FI ISSN 0783-0556
METEOROLOGICAL YEARBOOK OF FINLAND. PART 4: 2 MEASUREMENTS OF SUNSHINE DURATION. (Text in English and Finnish) 1982. a. price varies. Ilmatieteen Laitos - Finnish Meteorological Institute, P.O. Box 503, SF-00101 Helsinki, Finland. FAX 1929218. TELEX 124436 EFKL SF. (Dist. by: Government Printing Centre, P.O. Box 516 Helsinki, Finland)
  Supersedes in part: Meteorological Yearbook of Finland. Part 4: Measurements of Radiation and Bright Sunshine (ISSN 0076-6763)

551.5 CS ISSN 0026-1173
QC851 CODEN: MEZPAQ
METEOROLOGICKE ZPRAVY. (Text in Czech or Slovak; summaries in English, German, Russian) 1948. bi-m. $27.70. Nakladatelstvi Technicke Literatury, Spalena 51, 113 02 Prague 1, Czechoslovakia. (Subscr. to: Artia, Ve Smeckach 30, 111 27 Prague 1, Czechoslovakia) Ed. O. Sebek. adv.; bk.rev.; bibl.; charts; illus.; maps; stat.; index. **Indexed:** Chem.Abstr., Field Crop Abstr., Herb.Abstr., Meteor.& Geoastrophys.Abstr., Ref.Zh.

551.5 FR ISSN 0026-1181
METEOROLOGIE. 1925. q. 260 F. Societe Meteorologique de France, Direction de la Meteorologie Nationale, 73-77 rue de Sevres, 92100 Boulogie-sur-Seine, France. Ed. A. Bougary. bk.rev.; illus.; circ. 1,800. **Indexed:** Chem.Abstr., Curr.Tit.Ocean, Int.Aerosp.Abstr., Math.R., Meteor.& Geoastrophys.Abstr.

551.5 GW ISSN 0026-1203
QC851
METEOROLOGISCHE ABHANDLUNGEN. (Text in English or German) 1950. price varies. (Freie Universitaet Berlin, Institut fuer Meteorologie) Fachbereichsverwaltung, Geowissenschaften, Podbielskiallee 61, D-1000 Berlin 33, Germany. TEL 030-831-4081. charts; illus.; index.

551.5 GW
QC851 CODEN: MERUAZ
METEOROLOGISCHE ZEITSCHRIFT. (Text and summaries in English and German) 1948. 6/yr. price varies. (Deutsche Meteorologische Gesellschaft) Gebrueder Borntraeger Verlagsbuchhandlung, Johannesstr. 3 A, 7000 Stuttgart 1, Germany. TEL 0711-625001. FAX 0711-625005. TELEX 723363-SCHB-D. Ed.Bd. adv.; bk.rev.; bibl.; charts; illus.; index. (back issues avail.) **Indexed:** Appl.Mech.Rev., Bibl.Cart., Chem.Abstr., Curr.Cont., Deep Sea Res.& Oceanogr.Abstr., Excerp.Med., Ind.Sci.Rev., Int.Aerosp.Abstr., Sci.Abstr.
  Formerly: Meteorologische Rundschau (ISSN 0026-1211)

551.5 GW ISSN 0138-1105
METEOROLOGISCHEN DIENSTES DER D D R. VEROEFFENTLICHUNGEN. (Text in German; summaries in English, German and Russian) 1949. irreg., vol.27, 1989. (Meteorologische Dienst der DDR) Akademie-Verlag Berlin, Leipziger Str. 3-4, 1086 Berlin, Germany. TELEX 114420-AVERL-DD.

551.5 NO
METEOROLOGISKE ANNALER. (Text in English) vol.6, 1974. m. Norske Meteorologiske Institutt, Blindern, Oslo 3, Norway. Ed. O. Haug. charts.

551.5 RU ISSN 0130-2906
METEOROLOGIYA I GIDROLOGIYA. English translation: Soviet Meteorology and Hydrology (US ISSN 0146-4108) 1935. m. 20.40 Rub. Gidrometeoizdat, Vasil'evskii Ostrov, 3, St. Petersburg V-53, Russia. (Subscr. to: Mezhdunarodnaya Kniga, Moscow G-200, Russia) Ed. E.I. Tolstikov. bk.rev.; charts; illus.; circ. 4,000. **Indexed:** Biol.Abstr., Chem.Abstr., Deep Sea Res.& Oceanogr.Abstr., Field Crop Abstr., GeoRef, Herb.Abstr., Int.Aerosp.Abstr., Meteor.& Geoastrophys.Abstr., Ocean.Abstr., Pollut.Abstr., Sci.Abstr.
  —BLDSC shelfmark: 0110.000000.

551.5 US ISSN 0177-7971
CODEN: MAPHEU
METEOROLOGY AND ATMOSPHERIC PHYSICS. (Text in English and German) 1949. 12/yr. DM.960($551) Springer-Verlag, Journals, 175 Fifth Ave., New York, NY 10010. Ed. E.R. Reiter. **Indexed:** Curr.Adv.Ecol.Sci., Curr.Cont., Deep Sea Res.& Oceanogr.Abstr., Environ.Per.Bibl., Geo.Abstr., Ind.Sci.Rev., INIS Atomind., Sci.Abstr., Sci.Cit.Ind.
  —BLDSC shelfmark: 5744.045000.
  Formerly (until 1986): Archives for Meteorology, Geophysics, and Bioclimatology. Series A: Meteorology and Geophysics - Archiv Fuer Meteorologie, Geophysik und Bioklimatologie. Series A. (ISSN 0066-6416)

551 RM
METEOROLOGY AND HYDROLOGY. (Text in English; summaries in Russian) 1971. s-a. exchange basis. Institutul de Meteorologie si Hidrologie, Soseaua Bucuresti-Ploiesti 97, Bucharest, Rumania. TEL 793240. TELEX 11514 R. (Co-sponsor: Consiliul National al Apelor) Ed. I. Draghici. bk.rev.; bibl.; circ. 250. **Indexed:** Curr.Tit.Ocean, Deep Sea Res.& Oceanogr.Abstr., GeoRef.
  ●Available only online.

551.65 US
MINNESOTA WEATHER GUIDE CALENDAR. Short title: Weatherguide. 1975. a. $11. Freshwater Foundation, 725 County Rd. 6, Waynata, MN 55391. TEL 612-449-0092. FAX 612-449-0592. Eds. Bruce Watson, Jim Gilbert. circ. 25,000.
  Former titles: Weather Guide Calendar (ISSN 0270-9031); Weather Guide Calendar Almanac; (until 1977): Minnesota and Environs Weather Almanac (ISSN 0095-7348)

551.5 US ISSN 0027-0296
QC982
MONTHLY CLIMATIC DATA FOR THE WORLD. 1948. m. $36. U.S. National Climatic Data Center, Federal Building, MC-02, Asheville, NC 28801-2696. TEL 704-259-0682. (Co-sponsor: World Meteorological Organization) charts; circ. 1,000. (also avail. in microfiche) **Indexed:** Amer.Stat.Ind.

551.5 AT
MONTHLY RAINFALL REVIEW - AUSTRALIA. 1966. m. price varies. Bureau of Meteorology, 150 Lonsdale St, Melbourne, Vic. 3000, Australia. FAX 03-669-4699. TELEX AA 30664. Ed. W. Rushton. (back issues avail.)

551.5 JA
MONTHLY REPORT ON CLIMATE SYSTEM. (Text in Japanese) 1974. m. 2100 Yen. (Japan Meteorological Agency) Japan Weather Association, 2-9-2, Kanda-nishikicho, Chiyoda-ku, Tokyo 101, Japan.
  Formerly (until 1987): Ijo Tennko Kanshi Hokoku.

551.5 US ISSN 0027-0644
QC983 CODEN: MWREAB
MONTHLY WEATHER REVIEW. 1872. m. $205 (foreign $225). American Meteorological Society, 45 Beacon St., Boston, MA 02108-3693. TEL 617-227-2425. FAX 617-742-8718. Eds. T.N. Krishamurti, Peter S. Rag. abstr.; bibl.; charts; illus.; stat.; index; circ. 2,300. (back issues avail.; reprint service avail.) **Indexed:** A.S.& T.Ind., Chem.Abstr., Curr.Cont., Excerp.Med., Fluidex, Geo.Abstr., GeoRef, Ind.Sci.Rev., Int.Aerosp.Abstr., Meteor.& Geoastrophys.Abstr., Ocean.Abstr., Pollut.Abstr., Sci.Abstr., Sel.Water Res.Abstr., So.Pac.Per.Ind.
  —BLDSC shelfmark: 5965.000000.
  Description: Publishes research related to weather analysis and forecasting, observed and modelled circulations including techniques development and verification studies.

551.5 US ISSN 0027-2523
QC875
MOUNT WASHINGTON OBSERVATORY NEWS BULLETIN. 1937. q. $15 to individuals; families $25. Mount Washington Observatory, Box 2310, Main St., North Conway, NH 03860. Ed. C. Francis Belcher. adv.; bk.rev.; charts; illus.; stat.; cum.index: 1937-1960; circ. 2,500.

551.5 MZ
MOZAMBIQUE. INSTITUTO NACIONAL DE GEOLOGIA. BOLETIM METEOROLOGICO PARA A AGRICULTURA. 1963. 3/m. free. Instituto Nacional de Geologia, C.P. 217, Maputo, Mozambique. stat. (processed)
  Formerly: Mozambique. Servico Meteorologico. Boletim Meteorologico para a Agricultura (ISSN 0006-6044)

551.636 US
N O A A NATIONAL WEATHER SERVICE. CLIMATE ANALYSIS CENTER. MONTHLY AND SEASONAL WEATHER OUTLOOK. 1947. bi-m. $32 (foreign $48). U.S. National Oceanic and Atmospheric Administration, National Weather Service, Climate Analysis Center, Washington, DC 20233. TEL 202-655-4000. FAX 301-763-8395. (Orders to: U.S. Government Printing Office. Supt. of Documents, Washington, DC 20402)) illus.; circ. 2,000. (also avail. in microfiche from NTI)
  Formerly: N O A A National Weather Service. Climate Analysis Center. Average Monthly Weather Outlook (ISSN 0090-0613)

551.51 JA
QC851 CODEN: PATUAG
NAGOYA UNIVERSITY. SOLAR-TERRESTRIAL ENVIRONMENT LABORATORY. PROCEEDINGS. (Text in English) 1953. a. Nagoya University, Solar-Terrestrial Environment Laboratory, 3-13 Honohara, Toyokawa-shi, Aichi-ken 442, Japan. FAX 533-86-0811. **Indexed:** Int.Aerosp.Abstr.
  Formerly (until vol.37, 1990): Nagoya University. Research Institute of Atmospherics. Proceedings - Nagoya Daigaku Kuden Kenkyujo Hokoku (ISSN 0077-264X)

551.5 JA ISSN 0386-5517
NATIONAL INSTITUTE OF POLAR RESEARCH. MEMOIRS. SERIES A: AERONOMY.. (Text and summaries in English) 1963. irreg., no.19, 1989. exchange basis. National Institute of Polar Research - Kokuritsu Kyokuchi Kenkyujo, Library 9-10, Kaga 1-chome, Itabashi-ku, Tokyo 173, Japan. Ed. Takao Hoshiai. circ. 1,000. **Indexed:** Int.Aerosp.Abstr.

551.65 JA ISSN 0386-5525
NATIONAL INSTITUTE OF POLAR RESEARCH. MEMOIRS. SERIES B: METEOROLOGY.. (Text and summaries in English) 1969. irreg., no.2, 1974. exchange basis. National Institute of Polar Research - Kokuritsu Kyokuchi Kenkyujo, Library 9-10, Kaga 1-chome, Itabashi-ku, Tokyo 173, Japan. Ed. Takao Hoshiai. circ. 1,000.
  Supersedes: Japanese Antarctic Research Expedition, 1956-1962. Scientific Reports. Series B: Meteorology (ISSN 0075-336X)

NATIONAL OCEANIC AND ATMOSPHERIC ADMINISTRATION. NATIONAL GEOPHYSICAL DATA CENTER. PALEOCLIMATE PUBLICATIONS SERIES. see *PALEONTOLOGY*

551.63 US ISSN 0271-1044
NATIONAL WEATHER ASSOCIATION NEWSLETTER. (Supplement to: National Weather Digest) 1976. m. $18. National Weather Association, 4400 Stamp Rd., Rm. 404, Temple Hills, MD 20748. TEL 301-899-3784. Ed. Thomas H. Grayson. circ. 2,000.
  Description: Details association news and provides meeting announcements for members. Also covers new equipment and techniques.

551.63 US ISSN 0271-1052
QC983
NATIONAL WEATHER DIGEST. 1976. q. $29. National Weather Association, 4400 Stamp Rd., Rm 404, Temple Hills, MD 20748. TEL 301-899-3784. Eds. Robert Maddox, Steve Weiss. adv.; bk.rev.; bibl.; circ. 2,100. (back issues avail.) **Indexed:** Meteor.& Geoastrophys.Abstr.
  —BLDSC shelfmark: 6033.330500.

551.6 NR ISSN 0545-9923
NIGERIA. METEOROLOGICAL SERVICE. AGROMETEOROLOGICAL BULLETIN. 1965. m. K.50 per no. Meteorological Service, Department Headquarters, Strachan St., Near Tafawa Balewa Square, Lagos, Nigeria. Ed. L.E. Akeh. stat.

METEOROLOGY

551.5 620   JA   ISSN 0389-1313
NIHON SEIKISHO GAKKAI ZASSHI/JAPANESE JOURNAL OF BIOMETEOROLOGY. (Text and summaries in English or Japanese) 1966. 3/yr. 5000 Yen($40) (Japanese Society of Biometeorology - Nihon Seikisho Gakkai) I P E C, Inc., 2-11-3 Sugamo, Tokyo 170, Japan. TEL 0552-73-6730. FAX 03-910-2830. (Subscr. to: Kanazawa University School of Medicine, Department of Physiology - Kanazawa Daigaku Igakubu Seirigaku Kyoshitsu, 13-1 Takara-machi, Kanazawa-shi, Ishikawa-ken 920, Japan) Ed. Masami Iriki. adv.; bk.rev.; circ. 600. (back issues avail.)
   Description: Covers the effects of climate, weather, season and temperature on homes, physiology, pathology of man, animals and plants.

NIHON SHASHIN SOKURYO GAKKAI. GAKUJUTSU KOENKAI HAPPYO RONBUNSHU. see *GEOGRAPHY*

551.5   GW
OESTERREICHISCHE BEITRAEGE ZU METEOROLOGIE UND GEOPHYSIK. (Text in English, German) 1989. irreg. Zentralanstalt fuer Meteorologie und Geodynamik, Hohe Warte 38, A-1191 Vienna, Austria. TEL 43-1-364453. FAX 43-1-3691233. TELEX 43-1-131837-METW. Ed. Peter Steinhauser. circ. 350.

551.5   JA
OITA PREFECTURE MONTHLY REPORT OF METEOROLOGY. (Text in Japanese) 1956. m. Oita Chiho Kishodai - Oita Regional Observatory, 1-38, 3-chome, Nagahama-machi, Oita-shi, Oita-ken, Japan. FAX 0975-36-0091. circ. 100.
   Description: Circulated only in the domestic government and municipal office.

551.5   PL
OPADY ATMOSFERYCZNE/PRECIPITATION. (Text in Polish; table and chart titles in English and Russian) 1945. a. $200. Instytut Meteorologii i Gospodarki Wodnej - Institute of Meteorology and Water Management, 61 Podlesna St., 01-673 Warsaw, Poland. (Dist. by: Ars Polona-Ruch, Krakowskie Przedmiescie 7, 00-068 Warsaw, Poland) charts; illus.; circ. 350.
   Description: Articles on meteorology, precipitations, measurements and observational data yearly.

551.65   JA   ISSN 0030-6088
OSAKA DISTRICT METEOROLOGICAL OBSERVATORY. MONTHLY REPORT/OSAKA-FU KISHO GEPPO. (Text in Japanese) 1965. m. Osaka District Meteorological Observatory - Osaka Kanku Kishodai, 6-25 Hoenzakacho, Higashi-ku, Osaka 540, Japan. stat.; circ. 120.

551.5   JA
OSHIMA-HIYAMA CHIHO NOGYO KISHO SOKUHO/MONTHLY REPORT OF AGRICULTURAL METEOROLOGY. (Text in Japanese) 1979. m. Hakodate Marine Observatory, 3-4-4 Mihar, Hakodate, Hokkaido, Japan. circ. 100.

551.5   US
OXFORD MONOGRAPHS ON METEOROLOGY AND PHYSICAL OCEANOGRAPHY. irreg. price varies. Oxford University Press, 200 Madison Ave., New York, NY 10016. TEL 212-679-7300. Ed. P.A. Sheppard.
   Formerly: Oxford Monographs on Meteorology.
   Refereed Serial

OZONE LAYER BULLETIN. see *ENVIRONMENTAL STUDIES — Pollution*

OZONE NEWS. see *ENVIRONMENTAL STUDIES — Pollution*

PALEOCLIMATE DATA RECORD. see *PALEONTOLOGY*

551.5 551   JA   ISSN 0031-126X
QC851   CODEN: PMGTAW
PAPERS IN METEOROLOGY AND GEOPHYSICS. (Text in English, Japanese) 1950. q. 4800 Yen (or on exchange basis). Meteorological Research Institute, Yoshitsugu Nagasawa, Office of Planning, 1-1 Nagamine, Tukuba-si, Ibaraki-ken 305, Japan. Ed. M. Katsumato. charts; illus. **Indexed:** Appl.Mech.Rev., Chem.Abstr., Curr.Cont., Deep Sea Res.& Oceanogr.Abstr., JTA, Sci.Cit.Ind.

551.5   PH
PHILIPPINE AGRICULTURAL METEOROLOGY BULLETIN. 1970. irreg. 42p.($3) Philippine Atmospheric, Geophysical and Astronomical Services Administration, Agricultural Meteorological Division, 424 Quezon Ave., Quezon City, Philippines. Ed.Bd. charts; stat.; circ. 130.

PHYSICAL GEOGRAPHY. see *EARTH SCIENCES*

PROBLEMY FIZIKI ATMOSFERY. see *PHYSICS*

610 551.5   NE
PROGRESS IN BIOMETEOROLOGY. (Text in English) 1972. irreg. price varies. S P B Academic Publishing b.v., P.O. Box 97747, 2509 GC the Hague, Netherlands. circ. 300. **Indexed:** Biol.Abstr., Chem.Abstr.

036   PO   ISSN 0870-4724
PROJECTO I2 DO PIDDAC. BOLETIM. 1978. q. Esc.1200 (effective Jan. 1991). Instituto Nacional de Meterologia e Geofisica, Rua C do Aeroporto, 1700 Lisbon, Portugal. TEL 8472880. FAX 802370. TELEX 12742 DIRMET P. stat.; circ. 150.

551.5   GW   ISSN 0340-4552
PROMET; meteorologische Fortbildung. 1971. q. DM.36. Deutscher Wetterdienst, Frankfurter Str. 135, Postfach 10 04 65, 6050 Offenbach (Main) 1, Germany.

551.6   US
PUBLICATIONS IN CLIMATOLOGY.* 1948. a. (3 or 4 nos./vol.). price varies. (Laboratory of Climatology, Centerton) C.W. Thornthwaite Associates, Rt. 1, Box 324, Elmer, NJ 08318. TEL 609-358-2350. Ed. John R. Mather. circ. 500. **Indexed:** GeoRef.

551.5   CC   ISSN 1000-0526
QIXIANG/METEOROLOGICAL MONTHLY. (Text in Chinese) 1975. m. Y21.60($54) (Guojia Qixiangju - State Meteorological Administration) Qixiang Chubanshe - China Meteorological Press, 46 Baishiqiao Road, West Suburb, Beijing 100081, People's Republic of China. TEL 8312277-2736. TELEX 22094 FD SMA CN. (Dist. by: China International Book Trading Corporation, P.O. Box 2820, Beijing, P.R.C.) Ed. Lu Tongwen. charts; stat.; index; circ. 6,000. (back issues avail.)
   Description: Middle-level journal for academic exchange. Covers all aspects of atmospheric science, especially synoptic meteorology, climatology, atmospheric physics, and atmospheric sounding.

551.5   CC   ISSN 0577-6619
QC851   CODEN: CHIHAW
QIXIANG XUEBAO. English edition: Acta Meteorologica Sinica (ISSN 0894-0525) (Text in Chinese) 1941. q. $2.30 per no. (Zhongguo Qixiang Xuehui - Chinese Meteorological Society) China Meteorological Press, 46 Baishiqiao Road, Xijiao (West Suburb), Beijing 100081, People's Republic of China. TEL 8312277. Ed. Yuan Xinxuan.
   —BLDSC shelfmark: 0637.700000.
   Refereed Serial

551.527   NO
RADIATION OBSERVATIONS IN BERGEN; radiation yearbook. 1965. a. free. Universitetet i Bergen - University of Bergen, Geophysical Institute, Bergen, Norway. FAX 47-5-960566. Ed. A. Skartveit. circ. 300.
   Description: Presentation of different radiation parameters: global radiation, diffuse radiation, solar and ultraviolet radiation and duration of sunshine.

551.6   CC   ISSN 1000-4068
REDAI QIXIANG/TROPICAL ATMOSPHERE. (Text in Chinese) q. Guangdong Redai Haiyang Qixiang Yanjiusuo, No. 6, Fujin Lu, Dongshan-qu, Guangzhou, Guangdong 510080, People's Republic of China. TEL 775231. Ed. Shi Jianian.

551.5   MH   ISSN 0460-3060
RESULTADOS DAS OBSERVACOES METEOROLOGICAS DE MACAU. (Text in English and Portuguese; summaries in Portuguese) 1952. m. (plus a. issue). free. Servicos Meteorologicos e Geofisicos de Macau, Caixa Postal 93, Macao. FAX 308601. TELEX 88523-METEO. Ed.Bd. charts; stat.; circ. 120.

551.5 551   BE   ISSN 0072-4440
RIJKSUNIVERSITEIT TE GENT. STERRENKUNDIG OBSERVATORIUM. MEDEDELINGEN: METEOROLOGIE EN GEOFYSICA. (Text and summaries in Dutch, English or French) 1961. irreg. free. Rijksuniversiteit te Gent, Sterrenkundig Observatorium, Krijgslaan 281, B-9000 Ghent, Belgium.

551.5   IT   ISSN 0035-6328
TL556
RIVISTA DI METEOROLOGIA AERONAUTICA. 1937. q. L.125000. Ispettorato Telecomunicazioni e Assitenza al Volo, Servizio Meteorologico Aeronautica, Palazzo della Civilta del Lavoro, Quadrato della Concordia 7, 00144 Rome, Italy. Ed.Bd. adv.; bk.rev.; abstr.; bibl.; charts; illus.; index; circ. 1,700. **Indexed:** Chem.Abstr., Curr.Cont., Deep Sea Res.& Oceanogr.Abstr., Int.Aerosp.Abstr., Meteor.& Geoastrophys.Abstr.

551.5   PL
ROCZNIK METEOROLOGICZNY/METEOROLOGICAL YEARBOOK. (Text in English, Polish, Russian) 1904. irreg. $150. Instytut Meteorologii i Gospodarki Wodnej - Institute of Meteorology and Water Management, Podlesna 61; 01-673 Warsaw, Poland. (Dist. by: Ars Polona-Ruch, Krakowskie Przedmiescie 7, 00-068 Warsaw, Poland) Ed. Krzysztof Lembowicz. charts; map.; circ. 50.

ROYAL ASTRONOMICAL SOCIETY. MONTHLY NOTICES. see *ASTRONOMY*

551.5   UK   ISSN 0035-9009
QC851   CODEN: QJRMAM
ROYAL METEOROLOGICAL SOCIETY. QUARTERLY JOURNAL. 1871. 6/yr. $250. Royal Meteorological Society, 104 Oxford Rd., Reading, Berks RG1 7LJ, England. TEL 0734-568500. FAX 0734-568571. Ed. P.W. White. adv.; bk.rev.; charts; index; circ. 1,600. **Indexed:** Biol.Abstr., Curr.Adv.Ecol.Sci., Curr.Cont., Curr.Tit.Ocean, Deep Sea Res.& Oceanogr.Abstr., Excerp.Med., Field Crop Abstr., Fluidex, Geo.Abstr., GeoRef., Herb.Abstr., Hort.Abstr., Int.Aerosp.Abstr., Meteor.& Geoastrophys.Abstr, Sci.Abstr., Soils & Fert.
   —BLDSC shelfmark: 7186.000000.
   Description: Includes some oceanographic aspects of meteorology.

551.527   FR
S B A R M O BULLETIN. (Text in English) vol.6, 1974. 4/yr. 130 F.($20) Scientific Ballooning and Radiations Monitoring Organization, Observatoire de Parc Saint-Marie, 4 av. Neptune, 94 Saint-Maur des Fosses, France. bibl.; charts.

551.5   JA
SAGA-KEN KISHO GEPPO/SAGA PREFECTURE. MONTHLY REPORT OF METEOROLOGY. (Text in Japanese) 1957. m. Japan Meteorological Agency, Saga Local Meteorological Observatory - Nihon Kisho-cho, Saga Chiho Kishodai, 8-14 Jonai 2-chome, Saga-shi, Saga-ken 840, Japan. circ. 100.

551.656   MG
SAISON CYCLONIQUE A MADAGASCAR. (Text in French) 1973. a. Service de la Meteorologie Nationale, B.P. 1254, Antananarivo, Malagasy Republic.
   Description: Presents meteorological readings in Madagascar for the year.

551.6   CN
SASKATCHEWAN RESEARCH COUNCIL. CLIMATOLOGICAL REFERENCE STATION. ANNUAL SUMMARY. 1975. a. Can.$15. Saskatchewan Research Council, Environment Division, 15 Innovation Blvd., Saskatoon, Sask. S7N 2X8, Canada. TEL 306-933-8179. FAX 306-933-7446. Ed. Elaine Wheaton. circ. 350.
   Former titles: Saskatoon S.R.C. Climatological Reference Station. Annual Summary; Saskatchewan Research Council. Physics Division. Annual Climatic Summary (ISSN 0706-9391)

551.6   CC
SHANXI QIXIANG/SHANXI METEOROLOGY. (Text in Chinese) q. Shanxi Sheng Qixiang Ju - Shanxi Provincial Bureau of Meteorology, 28, Xinjian Lu, Taiyuan, Shanxin 030002, People's Republic of China. TEL 220713. Ed. Zhou Yihe.

551.5　　　　　CS　ISSN 0231-9004
QC851　　　　　　　CODEN: CGIMD9
SLOVAK ACADEMY OF SCIENCES. GEOPHYSICAL INSTITUTE. CONTRIBUTIONS. SERIES OF METEOROLOGY. (Text in English, German, Russian) 1974. a. exchange basis. Veda, Publishing House of the Slovak Academy of Sciences, Klemensova 19, 814 67 Bratislava, Czechoslovakia. (Subscr. addr.: Slovak Academy of Sciences, Geophysical Institute, Dept. of Physics of the Atmosphere, Dubravska cesta 9, 842 28 Bratislava, Czechoslovakia) Ed. Eva Zavodska. circ. 600.
  Description: Presents new research results in the field of atmospheric sciences, applied meteorology, climatology and air pollution meteorology.

551.5　　　　　RU　ISSN 0235-4519
SOLNECHNAYA RADIATSIYA I RADIATSIONNYI BALANS. MIROVAYA SET/SOLAR RADIATION AND RADIATION BALANCE DATA. THE WORLD NETWORK. (Supplement avail.) (Text in English, Russian) 1964. m. (plus s-a. supplement). $92 (effective Mar. 1991). Glavnaya Geofizicheskaya Observatoriya im. A.I. Voeikova, Ul. Karbysheva, 7, St. Petersburg 194018, Russia. (Co-sponsor: World Meteorological Organization) stat.
  Description: Provides the users with data on solar radiation, radiation balance and sunshine duration.

551.65　　　　　SA　ISSN 0011-5517
SOUTH AFRICA. WEATHER BUREAU. DAILY WEATHER BULLETIN. (Text in Afrikaans, English) 1950. d. Weather Bureau, Department of Environment Affairs, Private Bag X97, Pretoria 0001, South Africa. bibl.; circ. 400.

551.65　　　　　SA　ISSN 0038-1942
SOUTH AFRICA. WEATHER BUREAU. MONTHLY WEATHER REPORT. (Text and summaries in Afrikaans, English) 1936. m. Weather Bureau, Department of Environment Affairs, Private Bag X97, Pretoria 0001, South Africa. stat.; circ. 400.

551.6　　　　　SA　ISSN 0032-7948
SOUTH AFRICA. WEATHER BUREAU. NEWSLETTER. (Text in Afrikaans, English) 1949. m. Weather Bureau, Department of Environment Affairs, Private Bag X97, Pretoria 0001, South Africa. charts; stat.; index; circ. 400.

551.6　　　　　SA　ISSN 0379-6736
SOUTH AFRICA. WEATHER BUREAU. TECHNICAL PAPER. 1974. irreg., no.19, 1988. Weather Bureau, Department of Environment Affairs, Private Bag X97, Pretoria 0001, South Africa.
—BLDSC shelfmark: 8700.240000.

551.578　　　　　SA
SOUTH AFRICA. WEATHER BUREAU. TEN DAILY RAINFALL REPORT.. 3/m. Weather Bureau, Department of Environment Affairs, Private Bag X97, Pretoria 0001, South Africa.

551.5　　　　　SA　ISSN 0081-2331
SOUTH AFRICA. WEATHER BUREAU. W.B. SERIES. 1971. irreg., no.40, 1986. Weather Bureau, Department of Environment Affairs, Private Bag X97, Pretoria 0001, South Africa. circ. 1,500.

551.5 551.4　　US　ISSN 0146-4108
QC851　　　　　　　CODEN: SMHYDK
SOVIET METEOROLOGY AND HYDROLOGY. English translation of: Meteorologiya i Gidrologiya (RU ISSN 0026-119X) 1976. m. $775. Allerton Press, Inc., 150 Fifth Ave., New York, NY 10011. TEL 212-924-3950. Ed. E.I. Tolstikov. bibl.; charts; illus.; stat.; index. **Indexed:** Agri.Eng.Abstr., Deep Sea Res.& Oceanogr.Abstr., Excerp.Med., Field Crop Abstr., Forest.Abstr., Herb.Abstr., Irr.& Drain.Abstr., Sci.Abstr., Seed Abstr., Soils & Fert., Triticale Abstr., W.R.C.Inf.
—BLDSC shelfmark: 0424.150000.

551.5　　　　　CE
SRI LANKA METEOROLOGICAL SOCIETY. JOURNAL. (Text in English) 1972. q. Sri Lanka Meteorological Society, 26 Clifford Place, Colombo 4, Sri Lanka. adv.; bibl.; charts; stat.; circ. 150-200.

551.6　　　　　PL
STACJA ARCTOWSKIEGO. ROCZNIK METEOROLOGICZNY. (Text in Polish or English) 1978. irreg. $200. Instytut Meteorologii i Gospodarki Wodnej, Oddzial Morski w Gdyni - Institute of Meteorology and Water Management, Maritime Branch in Gdynia, 42 Waszyngtona St., 81-342 Gdynia, Poland. TEL 4858-203532. FAX 4858-201641. TELEX 54216 PL. Eds. Danuta Wielbinska, Miroslaw Mietus. circ. 120. (tabloid format)
  Description: Covers meteorology and observation results at the subantarctic meteorological research station.

551.6　　　　　PL
STACJA HORNSUND. ROCZNIK METEOROLOGICZNY. (Text in Polish or English) 1979. irreg. $200. Instytut Meteorologii i Gospodarki Wodnej, Oddzial Morski w Gdyni - Institute of Meteorology and Water Management, Maritime Branch in Gdynia, 42 Waszyngtona St., 81-342 Gdynia, Poland. TEL 4858-203532. FAX 4858-201641. TELEX 54216 PL. Eds. Danuta Wielbinska, Miroslaw Mietus. circ. 120. (tabloid format)
  Description: Covers meteorology and observation results at the polar meteorological research station.

551.55　　　　　US　ISSN 0039-1972
QC943.5.U6
STORM DATA. 1922. m. $40. U.S. National Climatic Data Center, Federal Building, MC-02, Asheville, NC 28801-2696. TEL 704-259-0682. FAX 704-259-0876. circ. 2,000. (also avail. in microfiche) **Indexed:** Amer.Stat.Ind.
—BLDSC shelfmark: 8466.500000.

STUDIA GEOPHYSICA ET GEODAETICA; a journal of geophysics, geodesy, meteorology and climatology. see EARTH SCIENCES — Geophysics

551.5 620　　　　JA
SYMPOSIUM ON WIND ENGINEERING. PROCEEDINGS. (Text in Japanese; summaries in English) 1970. biennial. price varies. Nihon Gakujutsu Kaigi, Meteorological Society of Japan - Science Council of Japan, c/o Japan Meteorological Agency, 1-3 Ote-machi, Chiyoda-ku, Tokyo 100, Japan. adv.
  Former titles: Symposium on Wind Effects on Structures in Japan. Proceedings; National Symposium on Wind Engineering. Proceedings.

551.5　　　　　JA　ISSN 0546-0921
　　　　　　　　　　　CODEN: TENKBT
TENKI. (Text in Japanese) 12/yr. price varies. Meteorological Society of Japan - Nihon Kisho Gakkai, c/o Japan Meteorological Agency, 1-3-4 Ote-machi, Chiyoda-ku, Tokyo 100, Japan.

551.5　　　　　US　ISSN 0177-798X
　　　　　　　　　　　CODEN: TACLEK
THEORETICAL AND APPLIED CLIMATOLOGY. (Text in English and German) 1949. 8/yr. DM.736($430) (effective 1992). Springer-Verlag, Journals, 175 Fifth Ave., New York, NY 10010. Ed. I. Dirmhirn. **Indexed:** Curr.Adv.Ecol.Sci., Deep Sea Res.& Oceanogr.Abstr., Forest.Abstr., Geo.Abstr., Ind.Sci.Rev., Sci.Cit.Ind., Soils & Fert.
—BLDSC shelfmark: 8814.551500.
  Formerly (until 1985): Archives for Meteorology, Geophysics, and Bioclimatology. Series B: Climatology, Environmental Meteorology, Radiation Research - Archiv fuer Meteorologie, Geophysik und Bioklimatologie. Series B (ISSN 0066-6424)

551.5　　　　　TG
TOGO. DIRECTION DE LA METEOROLOGIE NATIONALE. RESUME ANNUEL DU TEMPS. a. Direction de la Meteorologie Nationale, B.P. 1505, Lome, Togo.

551.5　　　　　TG
TOGO. DIRECTION DE LA METEOROLOGIE NATIONALE. RESUME MENSUEL DU TEMPS. m. Direction de la Meteorologie Nationale, B.P. 1505, Lome, Togo.

TOPICS IN ATMOSPHERIC AND OCEANOGRAPHIC SCIENCES. see EARTH SCIENCES — Oceanography

551.5　　　　　UK
TORNADOES AND STORMS; Oxford conference proceedings. 1985. triennial. £7($15) (Tornado & Storm Research Organisation) Artetech Publishing Co., 54 Frome Rd., Bradford-on-Avon, Wilts BA15 1LD, England. TEL 02216-2482. FAX 02216-5601. Ed. G.T. Meaden. circ. 2,000. (back issues avail.)
  Description: Discusses tornadoes, waterspouts, whirlwinds, damaging hail, ball lightning and thunderstorms.

METEOROLOGY 3441

551.5　　　　　US
THE TRIPOD. 1988. 2/yr. University of Nebraska, Lincoln, High Plains Climate Center, 237 L.W. Chase Hall, Lincoln, NE 68583-0728. TEL 402-472-6704. FAX 402-472-6615. Ed. Deborah Wood. circ. 294.

551.5　　　　　PL　ISSN 0860-7222
TA357.5.T87
TURBULENCE. (Text and summaries in English) 1989. a. (Politechnika Czestochowska) Wydawnictwo Politechniki Czestochowskiej, Ul. Deglera 30, 42-200 Czestochowa, Poland. TEL 50-974. (Dist. by: Ars Polona-Ruch, Krakowskie Przedmiescie 7, Warsaw, Poland) Ed. Janusz Elsner. circ. 1,000.
  Description: Theoretical and experimental approach to the phenomena of turbulence.

TYDSKRIF VIR SKOONLUG/CLEAN AIR JOURNAL. see ENVIRONMENTAL STUDIES — Pollution

551.5　　　　　US
U C A R NEWSLETTER. 1977. 8/yr. free. University Corporation for Atmospheric Research, Box 3000, Boulder, CO 80307. TEL 303-497-8602. FAX 303-497-8610. Ed. Louise Carroll. index; circ. 2,500. (back issue avail.)
  Description: Covers meteorology, climate studies, earth sciences, oceanography, and "global change."

551.6　　　　　US
U.S. NATIONAL OCEANIC AND ATMOSPHERIC ADMINISTRATION. ANNUAL CLIMATE DIAGNOSTIC WORKSHOP. PROCEEDINGS. 1976. a. U.S. National Oceanic and Atmospheric Administration, 6010 Executive Blvd., Rockville, MD 20852. TEL 301-655-4000. (Orders to: N T I S, U.S. Dept. of Commerce, Sills Bldg., 5285 Port Royal Rd., Springfield, VA 22161)

551.552　　　　US　ISSN 0092-2056
QC851
U.S. NATIONAL OCEANIC AND ATMOSPHERIC ADMINISTRATION. INTERDEPARTMENTAL COMMITTEE FOR METEOROLOGICAL SERVICES AND SUPPORTING RESEARCH. NATIONAL HURRICANE OPERATIONS PLAN. (Formerly issued by: Office of Federal Coordinator for Meteorological Services and Supporting Research) 1962. irreg. U.S. National Oceanic and Atmospheric Administration, Interdepartmental Committee for Meteorological Services and Supporting Research, Rockville, MD 20852. TEL 301-655-4000. illus.; circ. 1,000. Key Title: National Hurricane Operations Plan.

UNIVERSIDAD DE GUADALAJARA. INSTITUTO DE ASTRONOMIA Y METEOROLOGIA. INFORMACION. see ASTRONOMY

UNIVERSITAET ZU KOELN. INSTITUT FUER GEOPHYSIK UND METEOROLOGIE. MITTEILUNGEN. see EARTH SCIENCES — Geophysics

UNIVERSITY OF ALASKA. GEOPHYSICAL INSTITUTE. REPORT SERIES. see EARTH SCIENCES — Geophysics

551.6　　　　　UK
UNIVERSITY OF EAST ANGLIA. CLIMATIC RESEARCH UNIT. RESEARCH PUBLICATION. 1973. irreg. price varies. University of East Anglia, Climatic Research Unit, School of Environmental Sciences, Norwich NR4 7TJ, England. TEL 0603-56161. FAX 0603-507784. TELEX 975197. **Indexed:** Geo.Abstr.

551.5271　　　　US　ISSN 0193-9629
TA1
UNIVERSITY OF WISCONSIN, MADISON. ENGINEERING EXPERIMENT STATION. ANNUAL REPORT. a. free. University of Wisconsin-Madison, Engineering Experiment Station, Informational Resources Office, 1500 Johnson Dr., Madison, WI 53706. TEL 605-263-1610. Ed. Ann Bitter. charts; illus. Key Title: Annual Report - Engineering Experiment Station (Madison).
  Refereed Serial

V Z L U ZPRAVODAJ. (Vyzkumny a Zkusebni Letecky Ustav) see AERONAUTICS AND SPACE FLIGHT

METEOROLOGY

551.5   **NO**
VAER OG KLIMA; popular science journal on climate and weather. 1977. q. $33. (Norwegian Institute of Meteorology) Universitetsforlaget, P.O. Box 2050-Toeyen, N-0608 Oslo, Norway. (U.S. addr.: Publications Expediting Inc., 200 Meacham Ave., Elmont, NY 11003) Ed. Alf Sunde. circ. 2,000.
     Formerly: Vaeret (ISSN 0332-5040)

551.5   **II**   **ISSN 0970-1397**
VAYU MANDAL; science journal on the human environment. (Text in English) 1971. s-a. Rs.24($10) Indian Meteorological Society, The Observatory, Lodi Rd., New Delhi 3, India. Ed. S.K. Das. adv.; bk.rev.; charts; illus.; circ. 1,000.

551.5   **UN**   **ISSN 0042-9767**
QC851   **CODEN: WMOBAR**
W M O BULLETIN. (Editions in English, French, Russian and Spanish) 1952. q. 48 SFr. World Meteorological Organization, 41 Av. Giuseppe Motta, Ch-1211 Geneva 2, Switzerland. TEL 730-8111. (Dist. in U.S. by: American Meteorological Society, 45 Beacon St., Boston, MA 02108. TEL 617-227-2425) Ed. R. Czelnai. adv.; bk.rev.; illus.; index; circ. 7,000. **Indexed:** Curr.Adv.Ecol.Sci., Field Crop Abstr., Geo.Abstr., Herb.Abstr., Meteor.& Geoastrophys.Abstr.
    —BLDSC shelfmark: 2819.520000
     Description: Provides a summary of the work and developments in international meteorology and hydrology.

551.65   **JA**
WAKAYAMA PREFECTURE. ANNUAL REPORT OF METEOROLOGY/WAKAYAMA-KEN KISHO NENPO. (Text in Japanese) a. Wakayama Local Meteorological Observatory - Wakayama Chiho Kishodai, 4 Onoshiba-cho, Wakayama 640, Japan. charts; stat.

551.65   **JA**   **ISSN 0043-0021**
WAKAYAMA PREFECTURE. MONTHLY REPORT OF METEOROLOGY/WAKAYAMA-KEN KISHO GEPPO. (Text in Japanese) 1917. m. Wakayama Local Meteorological Observatory - Wakayama Chiho Kishodai, 4 Onoshiba-cho, Wakayama 640, Japan. charts; illus.

551.6   **UK**   **ISSN 0043-1656**
QC851   **CODEN: WTHRAL**
WEATHER. 1946. m. $44. Royal Meteorological Society, 104 Oxford Rd., Reading, Berks RG1 7LJ, England. TEL 0734-568500. FAX 0734-568571. Ed. J. Turner. adv.; bk.rev.; illus.; index; circ. 4,800. **Indexed:** Agri.Eng.Abstr., Chem.Abstr., Curr.Adv.Ecol.Sci., Curr.Tit.Ocean, Deep Sea Res.& Oceanogr.Abstr., Forest.Abstr., Geo.Abstr., Hort.Abstr., Int.Aerosp.Abstr., Mid.East: Abstr.& Ind., Ocean.Abstr., Pollut.Abstr., Sci.Abstr., So.Pac.Per.Ind., Soils & Fert., W.R.C.Inf.
    —BLDSC shelfmark: 9282.000000.
     Description: Articles on the science, technology, informational aspects, and broadcasting of meteorology and climatology, with announcements of conferences, seminars and meetings.

551.6   **US**   **ISSN 0731-5627**
QC983
WEATHER ALMANAC. 1974. irreg., 6th ed., 1991. $120. Gale Research Inc., 835 Penobscot Bldg., Detroit, MI 48226. TEL 313-961-2242. FAX 313-961-6083. TELEX 810-221-7086. Eds. James A. Ruffner, Frank E. Bair.
     Description: Provides information on weather in the U.S.

551.6   **NZ**   **ISSN 0111-5499**
WEATHER AND CLIMATE. 1981. s-a. NZ.$60 to non-members; members NZ.$25. Meteorological Society of New Zealand, P.O. Box 6523, Te Aro, Wellington, New Zealand. Ed. Dr. S.J. Reid. adv.; bk.rev.; circ. 450.
    —BLDSC shelfmark: 9282.150000.

551.6   **US**
WEATHER & CLIMATE REPORT. 1977. m. $95 (foreign $100). Nautilus Press, Inc., 1201 National Press Bldg., Washington, DC 20045. TEL 202-347-6643. Ed. John R. Botzum, Jr.
     Description: Features federal actions impacting weather and climate research.

551.5 310   **US**   **ISSN 0882-8156**
QC994.95   **CODEN: WEFOE3**
WEATHER AND FORECASTING. 1986. q. $110 (foreign $125). American Meteorological Society, 45 Beacon St., Boston, MA 02108-3693. TEL 617-227-2427. FAX 617-742-8718. Eds. Paul J. Kocin, Louis J. Uccellini. abstr.; bibl.; charts; illus.; stat.; index; circ. 1,640. (back issues avail.; reprint service avail.)
Indexed: Meteor.& Geoastrophys.Abstr.
    —BLDSC shelfmark: 9282.600000.
     Description: Published operational forecasting techniques, applications of new analysis methods, forecasting verification studies, and meso-scale and synoptic-scale case studies that have direct applicability to forecasting.

551.5   **JA**
WEATHER SERVICE BULLETIN. 1930. bi-m. 7800 Yen. (Japan Meteorological Agency) Japan Weather Association, 2-9-2, Kanda-nishikicho, Chiyoda-ku, Tokyo 101, Japan. index; circ. 914.

551.6   **US**   **ISSN 0043-1672**
QC851   **CODEN: WTHWA2**
WEATHERWISE; popular weather magazine. 1948. bi-m. $28 to individuals; institutions $47. (Helen Dwight Reid Educational Foundation) Heldref Publications, 1319 Eighteenth St., N.W., Washington, DC 20036-1802. TEL 202-296-2627. FAX 202-296-5149. Ed. Patrick Hughes. adv.; bk.rev.; charts; illus.; index, cum.index: vols.1-31; circ. 10,000. (also avail. in microform; reprint service avail.) **Indexed:** Acid Rain Abstr., Acid Rain Ind., Chem.Abstr., Curr.Tit.Ocean, Deep Sea Res.& Oceanogr.Abstr., Environ.Abstr., Gen.Sci.Ind., Geo.Abstr., GeoRef., Int.Aerosp.Abstr., Mag.Ind., Meteor.& Geoastrophys.Abstr., PMR, R.G., Sel.Water Res.Abstr.
    —BLDSC shelfmark: 9283.900000.
Refereed Serial

551.5   **AU**   **ISSN 0043-4450**
QH543   **CODEN: WTLBAR**
WETTER UND LEBEN; Zeitschrift fuer angewandte Meteorologie. (Summaries in English) 1948. q. S.500. Oesterreichische Gesellschaft fuer Meteorologie, Hohe Warte 38, A-1190 Vienna, Austria. FAX 3691233. TELEX 131837-METW. Ed. Hartwig Dobesch. adv.; bk.rev.; abstr.; illus.; index; circ. 600. **Indexed:** Chem.Abstr., Meteor.& Geoastrophys.Abstr., Ocean.Abstr., Pollut.Abstr.
    —BLDSC shelfmark: 9308.000000.

551.654   **GW**   **ISSN 0936-5818**
WETTERKARTE; Amtsblatt des Deutschen Wetterdienstes. 1973. d. Deutschen Wetterdienstes, Frankfurterstr. 135, Postfach 100465, 6050 Offenbach a.M. TEL 069-8062225. FAX 069-3062339.

551.5   **GW**
DER WETTERLOTSE. 1949. m. DM.20. Deutscher Wetterdienst, Seewetteramt, Postfach 301190, 2000 Hamburg 36, Germany. index; circ. 1,000. (back issues avail.)
     Description: For weather observers on ships.

WHOLE EARTH FORECASTER. see *BUSINESS AND ECONOMICS — Investments*

551.65   **AU**   **ISSN 0043-7077**
WITTERUNG IN OESTERREICH. MONATSUEBERSICHT. 1946. m. price varies. Zentralanstalt fuer Meteorologie und Geodynamik, A-1190 Vienna, Austria. charts; stat.

551.6   **GW**   **ISSN 0043-7085**
WITTERUNG IN UEBERSEE. 1953. m. DM.60. Deutscher Wetterdienst, Seewetteramt, Postfach 301190, 2000 Hamburg 36, Germany. TELEX 211291. charts; circ. 300.
     Description: Monthly and annual global climate review of tropical storms, temperature, precipitation and sea level pressure (actual values and departures from normal).

551.3   **UN**   **ISSN 0251-8783**
WORLD METEORLOGICAL ORGANIZATION. COMMISSION FOR INSTRUMENTS AND METHODS OF OBSERVATION. ABRIDGED FINAL REPORT OF THE (NO.) SESSION. French edition: Organisation Meteorologique Mondiale. Commission des Instruments et des Methodes d'Observation. Rapport Final Abrege de la (No.) Session (ISSN 0251-8791); Russian edition: Vsemirnaya Meteorologicheskaya Organizatsiya. Komissiya po Priboram i Metodam Nablyudenii. Okonchatel'nyi Sokrashchennyi Otchet (No.) Sessii (ISSN 0251-8813); Spanish edition: Organizacion Meteorologica Mundial. Comision de Instrumentos y Metodos de Observacion. Informe Final Abreviado de la (No.) Reunion. 1953. quadrennial. World Meteorological Organization, Commission for Instruments and Methods of Observation, 41 Av. Giuseppe-Motta, CH-1211 Geneva 20, Switzerland.

551.5   **UN**   **ISSN 0084-1935**
WORLD METEOROLOGICAL CONGRESS. PROCEEDINGS. (Text in English and French) 1952. quadrennial. World Meteorological Organization, 41 Av. Giuseppe Motta, CH-1211 Geneva 2, Switzerland. TEL 730-8111. (Dist. in U.S. by: American Meteorological Society, 45 Beacon St., Boston, MA 02108. TEL 617-227-2425)

551.5   **UN**
WORLD METEOROLOGICAL ORGANIZATION. ABRIDGED FINAL REPORTS OF SESSIONS OF TECHNICAL COMMISSIONS. irreg. price varies. World Meteorological Organization, 41 Av. Giuseppe Motta, CH-1211 Geneva 2, Switzerland. TEL 730-8111. (Dist. in U.S. by: American Meteorological Society, 45 Beacon St., Boston, MA 02108. TEL 617-227-2425)
     Formerly: World Meteorological Association. Technical Commissions Abridged Final Reports (ISSN 0084-1919)

551.5   **UN**   **ISSN 0084-1994**
WORLD METEOROLOGICAL ORGANIZATION. ANNUAL REPORTS. 1953. a. price varies. World Meteorological Organization, 41 Av. Giuseppe Motta, CH-1211 Geneva 2, Switzerland. TEL 730-8111. (Dist. in U.S. by: American Meteorological Society, 45 Beacon St., Boston, MA 02108. TEL 617-227-2425) **Indexed:** IIS.
     Description: Reports on the activities.

551.5   **UN**
WORLD METEOROLOGICAL ORGANIZATION. BASIC DOCUMENTS. irreg. World Meteorological Organization, 41 Av. Giuseppe Motta, CH-1211 Geneva 2, Switzerland. TEL 730-8111. (Dist. in U.S. by: American Meteorological Society, 45 Beacon St., Boston, MA 02108. TEL 617-227-2425)
     Former titles: World Meteorological Organization. Basic Documents and Official Reports; World Meteorological Organization. Basic Documents, Records and Reports (ISSN 0084-1943)
     Description: Contains regulations of the WMO and agreements with the UN and the Swiss governments by which the WMO operates.

551.3 387.7   **UN**   **ISSN 0510-906X**
WORLD METEOROLOGICAL ORGANIZATION. COMMISSION FOR AERONAUTICAL METEOROLOGY. ABRIDGED FINAL REPORT OF THE (NO.) SESSION. French edition: Organisation Meteorologique Mondiale. Commission de Meteorologie Aeronautique. Rapport Final Abrege de la (No.) Session (ISSN 0251-8899); Russian edition: Vsemirnaya Meteorologicheskaya Organizatsiya. Komissiya po Aviatsionnoi Meteorologii. Okonchatel'nyi Sokrashchennyi Otchet (No.) Sessii (ISSN 0251-8880); Spanish edition: Organizacion Meteorologica Mundial. Comision de Meteorologia Aeronautica. Informe Final Abreviado de la (No.) Reunion (ISSN 0251-8902) 1954. irreg. World Meteorological Organization, Commission for Aeronautical Meteorology, 41 Av. Giuseppe-Motta, CH-1211 Geneva 20, Switzerland.

METEOROLOGY

551.3 630   UN   ISSN 0510-9078
WORLD METEOROLOGICAL ORGANIZATION. COMMISSION FOR AGRICULTURAL METEOROLOGY. ABRIDGED FINAL REPORT OF THE (NO.) SESSION. French edition: Organisation Meteorologique Mondiale. Commission de Meteorologie Agricole. Rapport Final Abrege de la (No.) Session (ISSN 0251-883X); Russian edition: Vsemirnaya Meteorologicheskaya Organizatsiya Komissiya po Sel'skokhozyaistvennoi Meteorologii. Okonchatel'nyi Sokrashchennyi Otchet (No.) Sessii (ISSN 0251-8848); Spanish edition: Organizacion Meteorologica Mundial. Comision de Meteorologia Agricola. Informe Final Abreviado de la (No.) Reunion (ISSN 0251-8821) 1953. irreg. World Meteorological Organization, Commission for Agricultural Meteorology, 41 Av. Giuseppe-Motta, CH-1211 Geneva 20, Switzerland.

551.3   UN   ISSN 0250-9172
WORLD METEOROLOGICAL ORGANIZATION. COMMISSION FOR ATMOSPHERIC SCIENCES. ABRIDGED FINAL REPORT OF THE (NO.) SESSION. French edition: Organisation Meteorologique Mondiale. Commission des Sciences de l'Atmosphere. Rapport Final Abrege de la (No.) Session (ISSN 0250-9156); Russian edition: Vsemirnaya Meteorologicheskaya Organizatsiya. Komissiya po Atmosfernym Naukam. Okonchatel'nyi Sokrashchennyi Otchet (No.) Sessii. (ISSN 0250-9164); Spanish edition: Organizacion Meteorologica Mundial. Comision de Ciencias Atmosfericas. Informe Final Abreviado de la (No.) Reunion (ISSN 0250-9180) 1953-1965; N.S. 1970. irreg. World Meteorological Organization, Commission for Atmospheric Sciences, 41 Av. Giuseppe-Motta, CH-1211 Geneva 20, Switzerland.
Formerly (until 1965): World Meteorological Organization. Commission of Aerology. Abridged Final Report of the (No.) Session (ISSN 1011-3223)

551.3   UN   ISSN 0251-8953
WORLD METEOROLOGICAL ORGANIZATION. COMMISSION FOR BASIC SYSTEMS. ABRIDGED FINAL REPORT OF THE (NO.) SESSION. French edition: Organisation Meteorologique Mondiale. Commission des Systems de Base. Rapport Final Abrege de la (No.) Session (ISSN 0251-8988); Russian edition: Vsemirnaya Meteorologicheskaya Organizatsiya. Komissya po Osnovnym Sistemam. Okonchatel'nyi Sokrashchennyi Otchet (No.) Sessii (ISSN 0251-8961); Spanish edition: Meteorologica Mundial. Comision de Sistemas Basicos. Informe Final Abreviado de la (No.) Reunion (ISSN 0251-897X) 1953-1970; N.S. 1974. irreg. World Meteorological Organization, Commission for Basic Systems, 41 Av. Giuseppe-Motta, CH-1211 Geneva 20, Switzerland.
Formerly (until 1970): World Meteorological Organization. Commission of Synoptic Meteorology. Abridged Final Report of the (No.) Session (ISSN 0510-9116)

551.3 551.46   UN   ISSN 0251-8775
WORLD METEOROLOGICAL ORGANIZATION. COMMISSION FOR HYDROLOGY. ABRIDGED FINAL REPORT OF THE (NO.) SESSION. French edition: Organisation Meteorologique Mondiale. Commission d'Hydrologie. Rapport Final Abrege de la (No.) Session (ISSN 0251-8740); Russian edition: Vsemirnaya Meteorologicheskaya Organizatsiya. Komissiya po Gidrologii. Okonchatel'nyi Sokrashchennyi Otchet (No.) Sessii (ISSN 0251-8767); Spanish edition: Organizacion Meteorologica Mundial. Comision de Hidrologia. Informe Final Abreviado de la (No.) Reunion (ISSN 0251-8759) 1972. irreg. World Meteorological Organization, Commission for Hydrology, 41 Av. Giuseppe-Motta, CH-1211 Geneva 20, Switzerland.

551.3 387   UN   ISSN 1011-3207
WORLD METEOROLOGICAL ORGANIZATION. COMMISSION FOR MARINE METEOROLOGY. ABRIDGED FINAL REPORT OF THE (NO.) SESSION. French edition: Organisation Meteorologique Mondiale. Commission de Meteorologie Maritime. Rapport Final Abrege de la (No.) Session (ISSN 0251-8872); Russian edition: Vsemirnaya Meteorologicheskaya Organizatsiya. Komissiya po Morskoi Meteorologii. Okonchatel'nyi Sokrashchennyi Otchet (No.) Sessii (ISSN 0251-8856); Spanish edition: Organizacion Meteorologica Mundial. Comision de Meteorologia Marina. Informe Final Abreviado de la (No.) Reunion (ISSN 0251-8864) 1952. quadrennial. World Meteorological Organization, Commission for Marine Meteorology, 41 Av. Giuseppe-Motta, CH-1211 Geneva 20, Switzerland.
Formerly (until 1968): World Meteorological Organization. Commission for Maritime Meteorology. Abridged Final Report of the (No.) Session (ISSN 0084-1951)

551.5   UN   ISSN 0084-1927
WORLD METEOROLOGICAL ORGANIZATION. CONGRESS. ABRIDGED REPORT WITH RESOLUTIONS. French edition: Organisation Meteorologique Mondiale. Congres. Rapport Abrege et Resolutions (ISSN 0250-9261); Spanish edition: Organizacion Meteorologica Mundial. Congreso. Informe Abreviado y Resoluciones (ISSN 0250-9253); Russian edition: Vsemirnaya Meteorologicheskaya Organizatsiya. Kongress. Sokrashchennyi Otchet s Rezolyutsiyami (ISSN 0250-9245) 1951. quadrennial. price varies. World Meteorological Organization, 41 Av. Giuseppe-Motta, CH-1211 Geneva 20, Switzerland. TEL 34 64 00. (Dist. in U.S. by: American Meteorological Society, 45 Beacon St., Boston, MA 02108. TEL 617-227-2425)

551.5   UN   ISSN 1011-3231
WORLD METEOROLOGICAL ORGANIZATION. EXECUTIVE COUNCIL SESSION. ABRIDGED FINAL REPORTS WITH RESOLUTIONS. French edition: Organisation Meteorologique Mondiale. Session du Conseil Executif. Rapport Abrege et Resolutions (ISSN 1011-3592); Spanish edition: Organizacion Meteorologica Mundial. Reunion del Consejo Ejecutivo. Informe Abreviado y Resoluciones (ISSN 1011-3576); Russian edition: Vsemirnaya Meteorologicheskaya Organizatsiya. Sessiya Ispolnitel'nogo Soveta. Sokrashchennyi Otchet s Rezolyutsiyami (ISSN 1011-3673) a. price varies. World Meteorological Organization, 41 Av. Giuseppe Motta, CH-1211 Geneva 2, Switzerland. TEL 730-8111. (Dist. in U.S. by: American Meteorological Society, 45 Beacon St., Boston, MA 02108. TEL 617-227-2425)
Former titles: World Meteorological Organization. Executive Committee Reports. Abridged Final Reports with Resolutions; World Meteorological Organization. Executive Committee Sessions: Abridged Reports with Resolutions (ISSN 0084-196X)

551.656   UN   ISSN 0510-9124
WORLD METEOROLOGICAL ORGANIZATION. REGIONAL ASSOCIATION I (AFRICA). ABRIDGED FINAL REPORT OF THE (NO.) SESSION. French edition: Organisation Meteorologique Mondiale. Association Regionale I (Afrique). Rapport Final Abrege de la (No.) Session (ISSN 0250-9059) irreg. price varies. World Meteorological Organization, 41 Av. Giuseppe Motta, CH-1211 Geneva 20, Switzerland. TEL 730-8111. (Dist. in U.S. by: American Meteorological Society, 45 Beacon St., Boston, MA 02108. TEL 617-227-2425)

551.655   UN   ISSN 0509-3007
WORLD METEOROLOGICAL ORGANIZATION. REGIONAL ASSOCIATION II (ASIA). ABRIDGED FINAL REPORT OF THE (NO.) SESSION. French edition: Organisation Meteorologique Mondiale. Association Regionale II (Asie). Rapport Final Abrege de la (No.) Session (ISSN 0250-9113); Russian edition: Vsemirnaya Meteorologicheskaya Organizatsiya. Regional'naya Assotsiatsiya II (Aziya). Okonchatel'nyi Sokrashchennyi Otchet (No.) Sessii (ISSN 0250-9105) 1955. irreg. World Meteorological Organization, 41 Av. Giuseppe-Motta, CH-1211 Geneva 20, Switzerland.

551.658   UN   ISSN 0510-9132
WORLD METEOROLOGICAL ORGANIZATION. REGIONAL ASSOCIATION III (SOUTH AMERICA). ABRIDGED FINAL REPORT OF THE (NO.) SESSION. Spanish edition: Organizacion Meteorologica Mundial. Asociacion Regional III (America del Sur). Informe Final Abreviado de la (No.) Reunion (ISSN 0250-9148) 1953. irreg. World Meteorological Organization, 41 Av. Giuseppe-Motta, CH-1211 Geneva 20, Switzerland.

551.657   UN   ISSN 0250-9121
WORLD METEOROLOGICAL ORGANIZATION. REGIONAL ASSOCIATION IV (NORTH AMERICA AND CENTRAL AMERICA). ABRIDGED FINAL REPORT OF THE (NO.) SESSION. Spanish edition: Organizacion Meteorologica Mundial. Asociacion Regional IV (America del Norte y America Central). Informe Final Abreviado de la (No.) Reunion (ISSN 0250-913X) 1953. irreg. World Meteorological Organization, 41 Av. Giuseppe-Motta, CH-1211 Geneva 20, Switzerland.

551.659   UN   ISSN 0250-9040
WORLD METEOROLOGICAL ORGANIZATION. REGIONAL ASSOCIATION V (SOUTH WEST PACIFIC). ABRIDGED FINAL REPORT OF THE (NO.) SESSION. French edition: Organisation Meteorologique Mondiale. Association Regionale V (Pacifique Sud-Ouest). Rapport Final Abrege de la (No.) Session (ISSN 0250-9032) 1954. quadrennial. World Meteorological Organization, 41 Av. Giuseppe-Motta, CH-1211 Geneva 20, Switzerland.

551.654   UN   ISSN 0509-3015
WORLD METEOROLOGICAL ORGANIZATION. REGIONAL ASSOCIATION VI (EUROPE). ABRIDGED FINAL REPORT OF THE (NO.) SESSION. French edition: Organisation Meteorologique Mondiale. Association Regionale VI (Europe). Rapport Final Abrege de la (No.) Session (ISSN 0250-9016); Russian edition: Vsemirnaya Meteorologicheskaya Organizatsiya. Regional'naya Assotsiatsiya VI (Evropa). Okonchatel'nyi Sokrashchennyi Otchet (No.) Sessii (ISSN 0250-9024) 1952. irreg. World Meteorological Organization, 41 Av. Giuseppe-Motta, CH-1211 Geneva 20, Switzerland.

WORLD METEOROLOGICAL ORGANIZATION. SPECIAL ENVIRONMENTAL REPORTS. see *ENVIRONMENTAL STUDIES*

551.5   UN   ISSN 0084-201X
QC851   CODEN: WMOTAD
WORLD METEOROLOGICAL ORGANIZATION. TECHNICAL NOTES. 1954. irreg. price varies. World Meteorological Organization, 41 Av. Giuseppe Motta, CH-1211 Geneva 2, Switzerland. TEL 730-8111. (Dist. in U.S. by: American Meteorological Society, 45 Beacon St., Boston, MA 02108) Indexed: Biol.Abstr., GeoRef., Rural Recreat.Tour.Abstr., World Agri.Econ.& Rural Sociol.Abstr.

551.632   UN   ISSN 0250-9393
WORLD METEOROLOGICAL ORGANIZATION. WEATHER REPORTING. VOLUME A: OBSERVING STATIONS. (Catalogue W M O No. 9) 1952. base vol. plus s-a updates. $154 for updates; base vol. $92. World Meteorological Organization, 41 Av. Giuseppe Motta, CH-1211 Geneva 2, Switzerland. TEL 617-227-2425. (Dist. in U.S. by: American Meteorological Society, 45 Beacon St., Boston, MA 02108) (looseleaf format)
Description: Contains information on stations providing synoptic meteorological reports.

551.632   UN   ISSN 0250-9407
WORLD METEOROLOGICAL ORGANIZATION. WEATHER REPORTING. VOLUME B: DATA PROCESSING. (Catalogue W M O No.9) 1974. base vol. plus irreg. updates. $30 for updates; base vol. $78. World Meteorological Organization, 41 Av. Giuseppe Motta, CH-1211 Geneva 2, Switzerland. TEL 617-227-2425. (Dist. in U.S. by: American Meteorological Society, 45 Beacon St., Boston, MA 02108) (looseleaf format)

METEOROLOGY — ABSTRACTING, BIBLIOGRAPHIES, STATISTICS

551.632   UN   ISSN 0250-9415
WORLD METEOROLOGICAL ORGANIZATION. WEATHER REPORTING. VOLUME C: TRANSMISSIONS. (Catalogue W M O No. 9) 1952. base vol. plus bi-m. updates. $164 for updates; base vol. $152. World Meteorological Organization, 41 Av. Giuseppe Motta, CH-1211 Geneva 2, Switzerland. TEL 617-227-2425. (Dist. in U.S. by: American Meteorological Society, 45 Beacon St., Boston, MA 02108) (looseleaf format)
Description: Contains schedules of broadcasts and point-to-point transmission of coded meteorological information.

551.632   UN   ISSN 0250-9423
WORLD METEOROLOGICAL ORGANIZATION. WEATHER REPORTING. VOLUME D: INFORMATION FOR SHIPPING. (Catalogue W M O No.9) 1952. base vol. plus bi-m. updates. $96 for updates; base vol. $183. World Meteorological Organization, 41 Av. Giuseppe Motta, CH-1211 Geneva 2, Switzerland. TEL 671-227-2425. (Dist. in U.S. by: American Meteorological Society, 45 Beacon St., Boston, MA 02108) (looseleaf format)
Description: Information about meteorological forecasts and warnings to shipping and on the collection of ships' weather reports.

551.63   UN   ISSN 0084-2451
WORLD WEATHER WATCH PLANNING REPORTS. 1966. irreg. price varies. World Meteorological Organization, 41 Av. Giuseppe Motta, CH-1211 Geneva 2, Switzerland. TEL 617-227-2425. (Dist. in U.S. by: American Meteorological Society, 45 Beacon St., Boston, MA 02108)

551.6   PL
WYNIKI POMIAROW PIONOWEGO ROZKLADU OZONU W ATMOSFERZE/VERTICAL DISTRIBUTION OF OZONE FROM OZONOSONDE OBSERVATION. (Text in English, until 1987 in Polish) 1981. irreg. $40. Instytut Meteorologii i Gospodarki Wodnej - Institute of Meteorology and Water Management, 61 Podlesna St., 10-673 Warsaw, Poland. Ed. Bogumila Jaworska. charts; circ. 100. (tabloid format)
Description: Covers meteorology, vertical distribution of atmospheric ozone, measurement of results.

551.6   CC   ISSN 1001-7313
YINGYONG QIXIANG XUETA. (Text in Chinese) q. Zhongguo Qixiang Kexueyuan - Chinese Academy of Meteorology, 46, Baishiqiao Lu, Beijing 100081, People's Republic of China. TEL 8312277. Ed. Zhou Xiuji.

551.5   ZA   ISSN 0302-5047
ZAMBIA. METEOROLOGICAL DEPARTMENT. TOTALS OF MONTHLY AND ANNUAL RAINFALL; for selected stations in Zambia. (Former name of issuing body: Department of Meteorology) irreg. K.1. Meteorological Department, P.O. Box 30200, Lusaka, Zambia. (Orders to: Government Printer, P.O. Box 30136, Lusaka, Zambia)

551.6   ZA
ZAMBIAN CLIMATOLOGICAL SUMMARY; SURFACE AND UPPER AIR DATA. (Former name of issuing body: Department of Meteorology) m. Meteorological Department, P.O. Box 30200, Lusaka, Zambia. (Orders to: Government Printer, P.O. Box 30136, Lusaka, Zambia)

551.5   GW   ISSN 0084-5361
QC851   CODEN: ZMETAU
ZEITSCHRIFT FUER METEOROLOGIE. (Text in English, German, Russian) 1957. bi-m. DM.232.20. (Meteorologische Gesellschaft der DDR) Akademie-Verlag Berlin, Leipziger Str. 3-4, 1086 Berlin, Germany. TELEX 114420-AVERL-DD. Ed.Bd. bk.rev.; charts; illus.; index. **Indexed:** Appl.Mech.Rev., Curr.Cont., Deep Sea Res.& Oceanogr.Abstr., Excerp.Med., Field Crop Abstr., Herb.Abstr., Int.Aerosp.Abstr., Sci.Abstr., Soils & Fert.
—BLDSC shelfmark: 9472.000000.

551.5   CC   ISSN 1000-6362
ZHONGGUO NONGYE QIXIANG/CHINESE AGRICULTURAL METEOROLOGY. (Text in Chinese) q. Zhongguo Nongye Kexueyuan - Chinese Academy of Agriculture, 30 Baishiqiao Lu, Beijing 100081, People's Republic of China. TEL 8314433. Ed. Min Jinru.
Refereed Serial

551.5   RH   ISSN 0085-5707
QC875.Z55
ZIMBABWE. DEPARTMENT OF METEOROLOGICAL SERVICES. REPORT OF THE DIRECTOR. a. Department of Meteorological Services, P.O. Box BE 150, Belvedere, Harare, Zimbabwe. TEL 704955. TELEX 4460 ZW. circ. 80. (back issues avail.)

METEOROLOGY — Abstracting, Bibliographies, Statistics

AGRARMETEOROLOGISCHE BIBLIOGRAPHIE. see *AGRICULTURE — Abstracting, Bibliographies, Statistics*

ALASKA WEEKLY CROP WEATHER. see *AGRICULTURE — Abstracting, Bibliographies, Statistics*

551.5   PL   ISSN 0239-958X
BIBLIOGRAFIA AGROMETEOROLOGII/BIBLIOGRAPHY OF AGROMETEOROLOGY. (Text in English, Polish, Russian) 1958. a. $10. Instytut Meteorologii i Gospodarki Wodnej - Institute of Meteorology and Water Management, 61 Podlesna St., 01-673 Warsaw, Poland. circ. 120.
Formerly: Bibliografia z Zakresu Meteorologii Rolniczej i Lesnej.
Description: Articles on agrometeorology. Covers agrohydrology, forecasts, meteorological conditions, atmospheric pollution, plant cultivation, plant diseases, regionization and meteorological elements.

551.5   PL   ISSN 0239-6270
BIBLIOGRAFIA METEOROLOGII/BIBLIOGRAPHY OF METEOROLOGY. (Text in English, French, German, Polish and Russian) 1963. irreg. $75. Instytut Meteorologii i Gospodarki Wodnej - Institute of Meteorology and Water Management, 61 Podlesna St., 01-673 Warsaw, Poland. circ. 150.
Description: Articles on meteorology, climatology, hydrometeorology, meteorological elements, meteorological instruments, biometeorology, agrometeorology, atmospheric phenomena, weather forecasting, and dynamical meteorology.

551.5 016   GW   ISSN 0072-4149
Z6681
DEUTSCHER WETTERDIENST. BIBLIOGRAPHIEN. 1955. irreg., no.46, 1989. price varies. Deutscher Wetterdienst, Frankfurter Str. 135, Postfach 10 04 65, 6050 Offenbach (Main) 1, Germany.

551.5 016   IT   ISSN 0075-1901
ISTITUTO DI FISICA DELL'ATMOSFERA, ROME. BIBLIOGRAFIA GENERALE. (Text in Italian; occasional English or French editions avail.) 1963. irreg. Istituto di Fisica dell'Atmosfera, Piazzale Luigi Sturzo 31, 00144 Rome, Italy. TEL 06-59-10-941. FAX 06-59-15-790. **Indexed:** Meteor.& Geoastrophys.Abstr.

551.65   IT
QC851
ITALY. ISTITUTO CENTRALE DI STATISTICA. STATISTICHE METEOROLOGICHE. 1959. a. L.15800. Istituto Centrale di Statistica, Via Cesare Balbo 16, 00100 Rome, Italy. circ. 1,200.
Formerly: Italy. Istituto Centrale di Statistica. Annuario di Statistiche Meteorologiche (ISSN 0075-1731)

551.5 523.01 016   US   ISSN 0026-1130
QC851   CODEN: MGEAAQ
METEOROLOGICAL AND GEOASTROPHYSICAL ABSTRACTS. 1950. m. $750 (foreign $770). American Meteorological Society, c/o Inforonics, Inc., 550 Newtown Rd., Box 458, Littleton, MA 01460. TEL 508-486-8976. FAX 508-486-0027. bk.rev.; abstr.; index; circ. 334. (back issues avail.; reprint service avail.) **Indexed:** Chem.Abstr., Sci.Abstr.
●Also available online. Vendor(s): DIALOG (File no.29).
—BLDSC shelfmark: 5705.200000.
Description: Presents current abstracts of books, reports, research papers, and miscellaneous literature published worldwide in the areas of environmental sciences, meteorology, astrophysics, hydrology, glaciology, and physical oceanography.
Refereed Serial

551.5   MY   ISSN 0126-8872
MONTHLY ABSTRACT OF METEOROLOGICAL OBSERVATIONS OF MALAYSIA. (Text and summaries in English) 1950. m. M.$12. Malaysian Meteorological Service - Perkhidmatan Kajicuaca Malaysia, Jalan Sultan, Petaling Jaya 46667, Selangor, Malaysia. FAX 6-03-7550964. TELEX MA37243. circ. 210.

551.5 011   FR   ISSN 0761-2117
P A S C A L EXPLORE. E 49: METEOROLOGIE. 1985. 10/yr. 675 F. Centre National de la Recherche Scientifique, Institut de l'Information Scientifique et Technique, B.P. 54, 54514 Vandoeuvre-Les-Nancy Cedex, France. TEL 83-50-46-00.
Formerly: P A S C A L Explore. Part 49: Meteorologie; Which superseded in part: Bulletin Signaletique. Part 120: Astronomie - Physique Spatiale - Geophysique (ISSN 0240-849X)

551.5   JA
REKISHO NENPYO. (Text in Japanese) 1946. a. University of Tokyo, Tokyo Astronomical Observatory - Tokyo Daigaku Tokyo Tenmondai, 21-1, Osawa 2-chome, Mitaka-shi, Tokyo 181, Japan. charts; stat.
Description: Publishes meteorological data.

551.5   JA   ISSN 0388-3515
SEIKEI KISHO KANSOKUJO HOKOKU. (Text in Japanese) 1958. a. (Seikei Kisho Kansokujo - Seikei Meteorological Observatory) Seikei Gakuen Integrated Educational Institute, 3-1, Kichijoji Kita-machi 3-chome, Musashino-shi, Tokyo 180, Japan. stat.

SOLAR TERRESTRIAL ACTIVITY CHART. see *ASTRONOMY — Abstracting, Bibliographies, Statistics*

TRANSLATED TABLES OF CONTENTS OF CURRENT FOREIGN FISHERIES, OCEANOGRAPHIC, AND ATMOSPHERIC PUBLICATIONS. see *BIOLOGY — Abstracting, Bibliographies, Statistics*

METROLOGY AND STANDARDIZATION

389   US
A M J - S I METRICPAC. 1973. bi-m. $48. (Polymetric Services Inc.) American Metric Journal Publishing Co., Box 3251, Camarillo, CA 93010-3251. Ed. R.A. Hopkins. adv.; bk.rev.; circ. 26,000. **Indexed:** A.S.& T.Ind., C.I.J.E.
Formerly (until 1976): American Metric Journal (ISSN 0094-3096)

620.1 389   US   ISSN 0038-9676
A N S I REPORTER. 1967. m. $100 includes Standards Action. American National Standards Institute, Inc., 11 W. 42nd St., 13th Fl., New York, NY 10036. TEL 212-642-4900. FAX 212-302-1286. circ. 8,000. (also avail. in microform from UMI; reprint service avail.)
Formerly: Standards Institute Reporter.

620.1 389   US   ISSN 0090-1210
TA368   CODEN: STDNA
A S T M STANDARDIZATION NEWS. 1973. m. $18. American Society for Testing and Materials, 1916 Race St., Philadelphia, PA 19103. TEL 215-299-5400. FAX 215-977-9679. Ed. K. Riley. charts; illus.; index; circ. 32,000. (also avail. in microform from MIM,UMI,PMC; reprint service avail. from UMI) **Indexed:** A.S.& T.Ind., Abstr.Bull.Inst.Pap.Chem., AESIS, Appl.Mech.Rev., BMT, Br.Ceram.Abstr., Cadscan, Chem.Abstr., Copper Abstr., Deep Sea Res.& Oceanogr.Abstr., Eng.Ind., Ergon.Abstr., Excerp.Med., GeoRef., INIS Atomind., Intl.Civil Eng.Abstr., J.of Ferroc., Lead Abstr., Met.Abstr., RAPRA, Sci.Abstr., Soft.Abstr.Eng., Text.Tech.Dig., W.R.C.Inf., World Alum.Abstr., World Surf.Coat., World Text.Abstr., Zincscan.
—BLDSC shelfmark: 1747.091000.
Supersedes: Materials Research and Standards - MIRS (ISSN 0025-5394)

A 2 L A (YEAR) DIRECTORY OF ACCREDITED LABORATORIES. see *BUSINESS AND ECONOMICS — Trade And Industrial Directories*

A 2 L A NEWS. (American Association for Laboratory Accreditation) see *BUSINESS AND ECONOMICS — Trade And Industrial Directories*

METROLOGY AND STANDARDIZATION

681 389   HU   ISSN 0237-028X
ACTA I M E K O. 1958. triennial. International Measurement Confederation, I M E K O Secretariat, P.O. Box 457, 1371 Budapest, Hungary. FAX 361-153-1406. TELEX 225792. Ed.Bd. circ. 500. Indexed: Chem.Abstr.
—BLDSC shelfmark: 0627.820000.
Formerly: International Measurement Conference. Proceedings. Acta IMEKO (ISSN 0074-6916)

AMERICAN ASSOCIATION FOR LABORATORY ACCREDITATION ANNUAL REPORT. see *BUSINESS AND ECONOMICS — Trade And Industrial Directories*

389 658.5   US   ISSN 0360-6929
TP149   CODEN: AQATAZ
AMERICAN SOCIETY FOR QUALITY CONTROL. ANNUAL TECHNICAL CONFERENCE TRANSACTIONS. 1946. a. American Society for Quality Control, 611 E. Wisconsin Ave., Milwaukee, WI 53202. TEL 414-272-8575. index by category, author and title; circ. 5,500. (also avail. in microfiche from UMI) **Indexed:** Eng.Ind.
Formerly: American Society for Quality Control. Transactions of Annual Technical Conferences (ISSN 0066-0159)

389   AT   ISSN 0158-3999
AUSTRALIAN STANDARD. 1980. m. membership. Standards Australia, Standards House, 80 Arthur St., N. Sydney, N.S.W. 2059, Australia. FAX 02-959-3896. TELEX 26514. Ed. J. Moncrieff. adv.; bibl.; circ. 10,700. Indexed: Dairy Sci.Abstr., Food Sci.& Tech.Abstr.
Supersedes (in Jan.1980): S A A Monthly Information Sheet.

389   AU
AUSTRIA. BUNDESAMT FUER EICH- UND VERMESSUNGSWESEN. AMTSBLATT FUER DAS EICHWESEN. 1952. 8/yr. S.690. Kommissionsverlag der Oesterreichischen Staatsdruckerei, Rennweg 12a, A-1037 Vienna, Austria. index; circ. 500.

389   UK
B S I CATALOGUE. a. £32 to non-members. British Standards Institution, Linford Wood, Milton Keynes MK14 6LE, England. circ. 34,000.
●Also available on CD-ROM.
Formerly: British Standards Year Book (ISSN 0068-2578)

620.1 389   UK   ISSN 0005-3309
T59   CODEN: BSINAE
B S I NEWS. 1956. m. British Standards Institution, Linford Wood, Milton Keynes MK14 6LE, England. TEL 0908-220022. FAX 0908-320856. TELEX 825777. Ed. C. Park. circ. 41,000. **Indexed:** Agri.Eng.Abstr., BMT, Br.Ceram.Abstr., Build.Manage.Abstr., Cadscan, Copper Abstr., Dairy Sci.Abstr., Ergon.Abstr., Fluidex, Int.Packag.Abstr., Lead Abstr., Met.Abstr., Paper & Bd.Abstr., Print.Abstr., World Alum.Abstr., World Surf.Coat., World Text.Abstr., Zincscan.
—BLDSC shelfmark: 2354.200000.

BENCHMARK. see *ENGINEERING*

640.73   CN   ISSN 0011-2313
C S A AND THE CONSUMER. (Editions in English and French) 1970. q. free. Canadian Standards Association, Public Affairs, 178 Rexdale Blvd., Toronto (Rexdale), Ont. M9W 1R3, Canada. TEL 416-747-4129. illus.; circ. 600,000 (500,000 English ed.; 100,000 French ed.). **Indexed:** Sportsearch.

389.6   GW   ISSN 1131-6047
▼**CALIDAD, GESTION Y TECNICA.** 1991. q. 4000 ptas.($63) (effective 1991). Carl Hanser Verlag, Kolbergerstr. 22, Postfach 860420, 8000 Munich 80, Germany. TEL 089-926940. (In Spain: Gran Via Corts Catalanes, 322-324, 08004 Barcelona, Spain. TEL 3-425-45-44) Ed. Daniel Crespo. adv.; bk.rev.; bibl.; charts; illus.; circ. 4,000.

389.6   CN
CANADIAN STANDARDS ASSOCIATION. ANNUAL REPORT. (Editions in English and French) 1919. a. free. Canadian Standards Association, Public Affairs, 178 Rexdale Blvd., Toronto (Rexdale), Ont. M9W 1R3, Canada. TEL 416-747-4129. Ed.Bd. circ. 10,000.

389.6   CN
CANADIAN STANDARDS ASSOCIATION. CATALOGUE. 1930. a. free. Canadian Standards Association, Standards Sales, 178 Rexdale Blvd., Toronto (Rexdale), Ont., M9W 1R3, Canada. TEL 416-747-4044. FAX 416-747-2475. Ed.Bd. circ. 50,000.
Supersedes: Canadian Standards Association. Standards Catalogue; Canadian Standards Association. List of Publications.

389.6   CN
CANADIAN STANDARDS ASSOCIATION. INFO UPDATE. 1981. 8/yr. Can.$38.50($51) Canadian Standards Association, 178 Rexdale Blvd., Toronto (Rexdale), Ont. M9W 1R3, Canada. TEL 416-747-4116. FAX 416-747-2473. Ed. Terri DeVriese. circ. 3,500.
Formerly: C S A Information Update (ISSN 0702-7583)

389   FR   ISSN 0750-7046
TA368
CATALOGUE AFNOR (NORMES FRANCAISES). vol.32, 1976. a. 249.06 F. Association Francaise de Normalisation, Tour Europe - Cedex 7, 92049 Paris La Defense, France. TEL 42-91-55-33. FAX 42-91-56-56. TELEX 611974F. Ed. Luc Lemiere. adv.; circ. 11,000.
●Also available online. Vendor(s): Telesystemes - Questel.
Also available on CD-ROM.
Formerly: Catalogue des Normes Francaises.

389.1   GW   ISSN 0174-3805
CATALOGUE: ENGLISH TRANSLATIONS OF GERMAN STANDARDS (YEAR). 1978. a. DM.52($16) per no. (Deutsches Institut fuer Normung e.V. (D I N)) Beuth Verlag GmbH, Postfach 1145, 1000 Berlin 30, Germany. FAX 030-2601231. TELEX 183622-BVB-D. (Dist in U.S. by: Global Engineering Documents, 2805 McGaw Ave., Box 19539, Irvine, CA 92714) circ. 10,000.
Formerly: English Translations of German Standards (ISSN 0071-0660)

389.6   GW   ISSN 0936-577X
QC851   CODEN: CLREEW
▼**CLIMATE RESEARCH.** 1990. irreg. (approx. 3/yr.). DM.285. Inter-Research, Box 1120, 2124 Amelinghausen, Germany. TEL 04132-727. FAX 04132-8883. **Indexed:** Environ.Abstr., Environ.Per.Bibl.
—BLDSC shelfmark: 3279.180000.

389.6   FR   ISSN 1016-3778
COMITE CONSULTATIF POUR LA MASSE ET LES GRANDEURS APPARENTEES. 1981. irreg., 3rd session, 1988. Bureau International des Poids et Mesures, Pavillon de Breteuil, 92312 Sevres, France. FAX 45-34-20-21. TELEX BIPM 631 351. circ. 500.

621.3   FR   ISSN 0069-6455
COMITE INTERNATIONAL DES POIDS ET MESURES. COMITE CONSULTATIF D'ELECTRICITE. (RAPPORT ET ANNEXES). (Travaux of sessions 1-8 (1928-57) issued in Proces-Verbaux du Comite International des Poids et Mesures) 1961, 9th. irreg., 18th session, 1988. Bureau International des Poids et Mesures, Pavillon de Breteuil, 92312 Sevres Cedex, France. FAX 45-34-20-21. TELEX BIPM 631 351.

535   FR
COMITE INTERNATIONAL DES POIDS ET MESURES. COMITE CONSULTATIF DE PHOTOMETRIE ET RADIOMETRIE. (RAPPORT ET ANNEXES). (Sessions 1-4, 1937-1957 issued in Proces-Verbaux du Comite International des Poids et Mesures)) irreg., 12th session, 1990. Bureau International des Poids et Mesures, Pavillon de Breteuil, 92312 Sevres, France. FAX 45-34-20-21. TELEX BIPM 631 351. charts; illus.
Formerly: Comite International des Poids et Mesures. Comite Consultatif de Photometrie. (Rapport et Annexes) (ISSN 0588-621X); **Supersedes:** Comite International des Poids et Mesures. Comite Consultatif de Photometrie. Travaux (ISSN 0069-6447)

536.5   FR   ISSN 0069-6463
COMITE INTERNATIONAL DES POIDS ET MESURES. COMITE CONSULTATIF DE THERMOMETRIE. RAPPORTS ET ANNEXES. (Sessions 1-5 (1939-1958) issued in Proces-Verbaux du Comite International des Poids et Mesures) (Editions in English, French) 1950. biennial, 17th session, 1989. Bureau International des Poids et Mesures, Pavillon de Breteuil, 92312 Sevres Cedex, France. FAX 45-34-20-21. TELEX BIPM 631 351. bibl.; charts; stat.

389   FR   ISSN 0373-3181
COMITE INTERNATIONAL DES POIDS ET MESURES. COMITE CONSULTATIF DES UNITES (RAPPORT ET ANNEXES). (Editions in English, French) 1967. irreg., 10th session, 1990. Bureau International des Poids et Mesures, Pavillon de Breteuil, 92312 Sevres Cedex, France. FAX 45-34-20-21. TELEX BIPM 631 351.

389   FR   ISSN 0588-6228
COMITE INTERNATIONAL DES POIDS ET MESURES. COMITE CONSULTATIF POUR LA DEFINITION DE LA SECONDE. (RAPPORT ET ANNEXES). (First session issued in Proces-Verbaux du Comite International des Poids et Mesures) 1957. irreg., 11th session, 1989. Bureau International des Poids et Mesures, Pavillon de Breteuil, 92310 Sevres Cedex, France. FAX 45-34-20-21. TELEX BIPM 631 351.

389   FR   ISSN 0253-2182
COMITE INTERNATIONAL DES POIDS ET MESURES. COMITE CONSULTATIF POUR LA DEFINITION DU METRE (RAPPORT ET ANNEXES). (Sessions 1-2 (1953-1957) Issued in Proces-Verbaux du Comite International des Poids et Mesures) (Editions in English and French) 3rd, 1962. irreg., 7th session, 1982. Bureau International des Poids et Mesures, Pavillon de Breteuil, 92312 Sevres Cedex, France. FAX 45-34-20-21. TELEX BIPM 631 351.

389   FR   ISSN 0255-3147
COMITE INTERNATIONAL DES POIDS ET MESURES. COMITE CONSULTATIF POUR LES ETALONS DES MESURE DES RAYONNEMENTS IONISANTS (RAPPORT ET ANNEXES). (First session issued in Proces-Verbaux du Comite International des Poids et Mesures) (Editions in English, French) 1959. irreg., latest 1988. Bureau International des Poids et Mesures, Pavillon de Breteuil, 92312 Sevres, France. FAX 45-34-20-21. TELEX BIPM 631 351.
Formerly: Comite International des Poids et Mesures. Comite Consultatif pour les Etalons des Mesure des Radiations Ionisantes (Rapport et Annexes) (ISSN 0588-6244)

389   FR   ISSN 0370-2596
                      CODEN: PVSPA7
COMITE INTERNATIONAL DES POIDS ET MESURES. PROCES-VERBAUX DES SEANCES. 1875. a., 79th session, 1990. Bureau International des Poids et Mesures - International Bureau of Weights and Measures, Pavillon de Breteuil, 92312 Sevres Cedex, France. FAX 45-34-20-21. TELEX BIPM 631 351. charts; illus.; stat.; index; circ. 650.

389   FR
COMITE INTERNATIONAL DES POIDS ET MESURES. SYSTEME INTERNATIONAL D'UNITES. 1970. irreg., 6th ed., 1991. Bureau International des Poids et Mesures, Pavillon de Breteuil, F-92312 Sevres, France. FAX 45-34-20-21. TELEX BIPM 631 351.

389.6   FR   ISSN 1016-5983
CONFERENCE GENERALE DES POIDS ET MESURES. COMPTES RENDUS DES SEANCES. 1889. irreg., 18th, 1987. Bureau International des Poids et Mesures, 92312 Sevres Cedex, France. FAX 45-34-20-21. TELEX BIPM 631 351.

389.6   MX
CONGRESO MEXICANO DE CONTROL DE CALIDAD. ANNUAL PROCEEDINGS. (In 2 vols.) 1973. a. $30. Instituto Mexicano de Control de Calidad, Thiers 251-Col. Anzures, 11590 Mexico, D.F., Mexico. Ed. Patricia Gonzalez Prado. adv.; bk.rev.; circ. 3,000.

389.6   CN   ISSN 0380-1314
CONSENSUS (OTTAWA). (Editions in English, French) 1974. q. free. Standards Council of Canada, 350 Sparks St., Ottawa, Ont. K1P 6N7, Canada. TEL 613-238-3222. FAX 613-995-4564. TELEX 053-4403. Ed. Steven Brasier. adv.; bk.rev.; circ. 10,000.

METROLOGY AND STANDARDIZATION

389.6   CS   ISSN 0042-4714
CZECHOSLOVAKIA. FEDERALNI URAD PRO NORMALIZACI A MERENI. VESTNIK. 1962. m. 42 Kcs. Federalni Urad pro Normalizaci a Mereni, Vaclavske nam. 19, 113 47 Prague 1, Czechoslovakia. (Dist. by: SEVT, Trziste 9, 118 16 Prague 1, Czechoslovakia) Ed. Marie Bartunkova. charts; circ. 13,400. (looseleaf format)

389.1   GW   ISSN 0722-7337
D I N - HANDBOOKS. 1982. irreg. price varies. (Deutsches Institut fuer Normung e.V. (D I N)) Beuth Verlag GmbH, Burggrafenstrasse 6, 1000 Berlin 30, Germany. FAX 030-2601-231. TELEX 183622-BVB-D. (Dist. in U.S. by: Global Engineering Documents, 2805 McGaw Ave., Box 19539, Irvine, CA 92714)

620.1 389   GW   ISSN 0722-2912
D I N MITTEILUNGEN & ELEKTRONORM. 1918. m. DM.504.67. (Deutsches Institut fuer Normung e.V.) Beuth Verlag GmbH, Burggrafenstr. 6, 1000 Berlin 30, Germany. FAX 030-2601231. TELEX 183633-BVB-D. (Dist. in U.S. by: Global Engineering Documents, 2805 McGaw Ave., Box 19539, Irvine, CA 92714) bk.rev.; charts; illus.; index; circ. 8,400. **Indexed:** C.I.S. Abstr., INIS Atomind.
Formed by the merger of: D I N Mitteilungen (ISSN 0011-4952); (1947-1977): Elektronorm (ISSN 0013-5747); Formerly (1961-198?): Schiffbau-Normung (ISSN 0036-6048)

389.1   GW   ISSN 0342-801X
D I N - TASCHENBUECHER. 1963. irreg. price varies. (Deutsches Institut fuer Normung e.V. (D I N)) Beuth Verlag GmbH, Burggrafenstr. 6, 1000 Berlin 30, Germany. FAX 030-2601231. TELEX 183622-BVB-D. (Dist. in U.S. by: Global Engineering Documents, 2805 McGaw Ave., Box 19539, Irvine, CA 92714)

620.1 389   DK   ISSN 0011-6505
DANSK TEKNISK TIDSSKRIFT/DANISH TECHNICAL MAGAZINE. 1876. 10/yr. DKK 480. Forlaget Beilin og Johansen ApS, Rosenborggade 1, DK-1130 Copenhagen K, Denmark. TEL 33 15 22 77. FAX 33-15-93-43. Ed. Stig Juul Hesselaa. circ. 6,188.
Description: Directed to engineers and individuals in the technological departments of industry.

621.38   US   ISSN 0900-5579
CODEN: DAINEG
DANTEC INFORMATION. (Text in English; summaries in English, French and German) 1965. a. free. Dantec Electronics, 777 Corporate Dr., Mahwah, NJ 07430. TEL 201-512-0037. FAX 201-512-0120. Ed. J.J. Ramskor. circ. 21,000. **Indexed:** BMT, Fluidex, Int.Aerosp.Abstr., Met.Abstr., Sci.Abstr., W.R.C.Inf., World Alum.Abstr.
—BLDSC shelfmark: 3533.151000.
Former titles: D I S A Information. Measurement and Analysis (ISSN 0070-6639); D I S A Information. Electronic Measurement of Mechanic Events.
Description: Measurement and analysis of fluid, surface, and particle dynamics research programs.

350.821   DK
DENMARK. DANTEST-NYT. AARSBERETNING. 1977. a. DKK 20. Dantest-National Institute for Testing and Verification, Amager Blvd. 115, 2300 Copenhagen S, Denmark. TEL 01-54 08 30.
Formerly (until 1979): Denmark. Justervaesenet. Aarsberetning.

389.6 574   SZ   ISSN 0301-5149
CODEN: DVBSA3
DEVELOPMENTS IN BIOLOGICAL STANDARDIZATION. (Text in English) 1964. a. price varies. (International Association of Biological Standardization) S. Karger AG, Allschwilerstr. 10, P.O. Box, CH-4009 Basel, Switzerland. TEL 061-3061111. FAX 061-3061234. TELEX CH 962652. (reprint service avail. from ISI; back issues avail.) **Indexed:** Biol.Abstr., Chem.Abstr., Curr.Cont., Dairy Sci.Abstr., Excerp.Med., Ind.Med., Ind.Sci.Rev., Ind.Vet., Rev.Plant Path., Sci.Cit.Ind., Vet.Bull.
—BLDSC shelfmark: 3579.067000.
Supersedes: Progress in Immunobiological Standardization (ISSN 0079-6344); Symposia Series in Immunobiological Standardization (ISSN 0082-0768)

ELEKTRICHESKIE STANTSII. see *ENGINEERING — Electrical Engineering*

620.1 389   FR   ISSN 0223-4866
ENJEUX. 1981. m. 720 F. Association Francaise de Normalisation, Tour Europe Cedex 7, 92049 Paris La Defense, France. TEL 42-91-55-57. FAX 42-91-56-56. TELEX 611 974F. Ed. J. Abecassis. adv.; bk.rev.; abstr.; bibl.; charts; illus.; stat.; circ. 10,300. **Indexed:** Biol.Abstr., C.I.S. Abstr., Chem.Abstr., Excerp.Med.
—BLDSC shelfmark: 3775.480000.
Supersedes: Bulletin Mensuel de la Normalisation Francaise (ISSN 0300-1164); Courrier de la Normalisation (ISSN 0011-0485)

F D C CONTROL NEWSLETTER. (Food, Drug, and Cosmetics) see *FOOD AND FOOD INDUSTRIES*

F UND M, FEINWERKTECHNIK UND MESSTECHNIK. see *ENGINEERING*

389   US
FEDERAL INFORMATION PROCESSING STANDARDS PUBLICATION. Abbreviated title: F I P S Publication. irreg. price varies. U.S. National Institute of Standards and Technology, Gaithersburg, MD 20899. TEL 301-975-3058. (Orders to: NTIS, Springfield, VA 22161)
Formerly: U.S. National Bureau of Standards. Federal Information Processing Standards (ISSN 0083-1816)
Refereed Serial

FLOW MEASUREMENT AND INSTRUMENTATION. see *INSTRUMENTS*

620.1 389   CN
FOCUS. (Editions in English and French) 1970. q. free. Canadian Standards Association, Public Affairs, 178 Rexdale Blvd., Toronto (Rexdale), Ont. M9W 1R3, Canada. TEL 416-747-4129. illus.; circ. 30,000. **Indexed:** Can.B.P.I.
Formerly: Standards - Canada (ISSN 0038-965X)

I E C BULLETIN. (International Electrotechnical Commission) see *ENGINEERING — Electrical Engineering*

I E E E INSTRUMENTATION AND MEASUREMENT TECHNOLOGY CONFERENCE. PROCEEDINGS.. see *INSTRUMENTS*

621.37   US   ISSN 0018-9456
CODEN: IEIMAO
I E E E TRANSACTIONS ON INSTRUMENTATION AND MEASUREMENT. 1952. bi-m. $135 to non-members. (I E E E, Instrumentation and Measurement Society) Institute of Electrical and Electronics Engineers, Inc., 345 E. 47th St., New York, NY 10017-2394. TEL 212-705-7366. FAX 212-705-7682. (Subscr. to: Box 1331, 445 Hoes Lane, Piscataway, NJ 08855-1331. TEL 908-562-3948) Ed. Ed Richter. bk.rev.; abstr.; illus.; index. (also avail. in microform from MIM,UMI,EEE) **Indexed:** A.S.& T.Ind., Appl.Mech.Rev., Chem.Abstr., Comput.Abstr., Comput.Cont., Curr.Cont., Deep Sea Res.& Oceanogr.Abstr., Eng.Ind., Excerp.Med., Ind.Sci.Rev., Int.Aerosp.Abstr., Math.R., Sci.Abstr., Sci.Cit.Ind., Sh.& Vib.Dig.
—BLDSC shelfmark: 4363.199100.

389.6   IR
I S I R I YEARBOOK. (Text in English) 1975. a. free. Institute of Standards and Industrial Research of Iran, PO Box 15875-4618, Teheran, Iran. Ed. F. Hazegh. circ. 1,000.

658.7   SZ   ISSN 0303-805X
T59.A1
I S O BULLETIN (ENGLISH EDITION). French edition (ISSN 0303-8009) 1970. m. International Organization for Standardization, 1 rue de Varembe, CH-1211 Geneva 20, Switzerland. TEL 4122-7490111. FAX 4122-7333430. TELEX 412205 ISO CH. (Dist. in the U.S. by: American National Standards Institute, 11 W. 42nd St., 13th Fl., New York, NY 10036) illus.; circ. 6,800. **Indexed:** Cadscan, Lead Abstr., Zincscan.
Description: Includes standardization news, calendar of ISO meetings, list of new draft standards and newly published standards.

389.6   SZ   ISSN 0303-3309
Z7914.A22
I S O CATALOGUE. (Text in English and French) a. plus q. supplements. International Organization for Standardization, 1 rue de Varembe, CH-1211 Geneva 20, Switzerland. TEL 4122-7490111. FAX 4122-7333430. TELEX 412205-ISO-CH. (Dist. in US by: American National Standards Institute, 11 W. 42nd Fl., New York, NY 10036)
—BLDSC shelfmark: 4583.261000.
Description: Lists all published ISO standards.

389   SZ
I S O INTERNATIONAL STANDARDS. 1954. irreg. price varies. International Organization for Standardization, 1 rue de Varembe, CH-1211 Geneva 20, Switzerland. TEL 4122-7490111. FAX 4122-7333430. TELEX 412205 ISO CH. (Dist. in the U.S. by: American National Standards Institute, 11 W. 42nd St., 13th Fl., New York, NY 10036) **Indexed:** HRIS.

389   SZ   ISSN 0536-2067
I S O MEMENTO. (Text in English and French) a. International Organization for Standardization, 1 rue de Varembe, CH-1211 Geneva 20, Switzerland. TEL 4122-7490111. FAX 4122-7333430. TELEX 412205 ISO CH. (Dist. in the U.S. by: American National Standards Institute, 11 W. 42nd St., 13th Fl., New York, NY 10036)
Description: Gives the scope of responsibility, organizational structure and secretariats for each technical committee.

389.6   US
IDENTIFIED SOURCES OF SUPPLY. 1960. q. $245 for print; microfiche $195. National Standards Association, Inc., 1200 Quince Orchard Blvd., Gaithersburg, MD 20878. TEL 301-590-2300. Ed. K. Stover. (also avail. in microfiche)
Formerly: Source (Washington).

389   US
INDEX AND DIRECTORY OF INDUSTRY STANDARDS. (In 7 vols.) 1983. a. price varies. Information Handling Services, 15 Inverness Way. E., Box 1154, Englewood, CO 80150. TEL 800-841-7179. FAX 303-799-4085. TELEX 4322083 IHS UI. (Subscr. to: Global Engineering, 2805 McGaw Ave., Irvine, CA 92714. TEL 714-261-1455) Ed. Liz Maynard Prigge. circ. 500.
Formerly: Index and Directory of U.S. Industry Standards.
Description: Provides access to subject and numeric international and domestic standards documents of professional societies.

389.6   US
JK1673
INDEX OF FEDERAL SPECIFICATIONS, STANDARDS AND COMMERCIAL ITEM DESCRIPTIONS. 1952. a. $27. U.S. Federal Supply Service, General Services Administration, 1941 Jefferson Davis Hwy., Washington, DC 20406. TEL 202-655-4000. (Orders to: Supt. of Documents, Washington, DC 20402. TEL 202-783-3238)
Former titles: Index of Federal Specifications, Standards, and Handbooks (ISSN 0364-1414); Index of Federal Specifications and Standards.
Description: Provides alphabetic, numeric and Federal Supply Classification listings of specifications, lists and descriptions in general use throughout the Federal Government.

389.6   NE   ISSN 0921-5956
QC81
▼**INDUSTRIAL METROLOGY;** the international journal of automated measurements & control. (Text in English) 1990. 6/yr. fl.290 (effective 1992). Elsevier Science Publishers B.V., P.O. Box 211, 1000 AE Amsterdam, Netherlands. TEL 020-5803911. FAX 020-5803598. TELEX 18582 ESPA NL. (Subscr. in U.S. and Canada to: Elsevier Science Publishing Co., Inc., Box 882, Madison Sq. Sta., New York, NY 10159. TEL 212-989-5800) Ed. A. Choudry. bk.rev.; charts; illus.; circ. 700. (back issues avail.) **Indexed:** Curr.Cont., INSPEC.
—BLDSC shelfmark: 4457.892000.
Description: Addresses issues related to the development and integration of metrologic techniques for the industrial environment. Seeks to improve communication between researchers and the industry.
Refereed Serial

METROLOGY AND STANDARDIZATION

INSTITUTE OF MEASUREMENT AND CONTROL. TRANSACTIONS. see *INSTRUMENTS*

389.6   UK
ISOTECH JOURNAL OF THERMOMETRY. 2/yr. £10($15) Isothermal Technology Inc., Southport PR9 9AG, England. (U.S. addr.: 2307 Whitley Dr., Durham, NC 27707)

JOURNAL OF DYNAMIC SYSTEMS, MEASUREMENT AND CONTROL. see *ENGINEERING — Engineering Mechanics And Materials*

350.821   US
LAB DATA. 1969. q. $6 (foreign $7.50). Underwriters Laboratories Inc., Corporate Communications, 333 Pfingsten Rd., Northbrook, IL 60062. TEL 708-272-8800. FAX 708-272-8129. TELEX 6502543343. Ed. Ward Wilson.
Description: Emphasizes the underlying philosophy of Underwriters Laboratories requirements and safety issues.

620.1 389   SW
MAANADENS STANDARD. (Supplements avail.) 1971. m. SEK 265. Standardiseringskommissionen; Sverige - Swedish Standards Institution, P.O. Box 3295, S-103 66 Stockholm 3, Sweden. Ed. Roine Lundin. adv.; bibl.; charts; illus.; circ. 3,100.
Formerly: Standard (ISSN 0037-5861)

389   CS
MAGAZIN C S N; odborny casopis pro jakost, technickou normalizaci, zkusebnictvi a metrologii. (Text in Czech or Slovak; summaries in English and Czech) 1976. m. $10 per issue. Federalni Urad pro Normalizaci a Mereni, Vaclavske nam. 19, 113 47 Prague 1, Czechoslovakia. (Dist. by: VN, Hornomechulopska 40, 102 04 prague 10, Czechoslovakia) Ed. Alena Tomanova. charts; illus.; circ. 5,200. **Indexed:** INIS Atomind.
Formerly: Ceskoslovenska Standardizace; Which was formed by the merger of: Merova Technika (ISSN 0026-0142) & Normalizace (ISSN 0029-1781)
Description: Deals with standardization, quality control, testing and metrology.

389.6   MW
MALAWI. MALAWI BUREAU OF STANDARDS. ANNUAL REPORT AND STATEMENT OF ACCOUNTS. (Text in English) a. Malawi Bureau of Standards, PO Box 946, Blantyre, Malawi.

620.1 389   IS   ISSN 0025-5912
TA368
MATI. (Text in Hebrew; summaries in English) 1968. q. free. Standards Institution of Israel, 42 Chaim Levanon St., Tel Aviv 69977, Israel. TEL 03-5454154. FAX 03-6419683. TELEX 35508-SIIT-IL. Ed. Adina Caspi. circ. 5,000. **Indexed:** Ind.Heb.Per.

350.821   MF
MAURITIUS STANDARDS BUREAU. ANNUAL REPORT. (Text in English) a., latest 1978. Government Printing Office, Elizabeth II Ave., Port Louis, Mauritius.

389.6 621 530   UK   ISSN 0263-2241
MEASUREMENT. 1983. q. £65($162) (foreign £80). (International Measurement Confederation) Institute of Measurement and Control, 87 Gower St., London WC1E 6AA, England. TEL 01-387 4949. (Subscr. to: c/o Carl Associates, 60 Thames St., Sunbury-on-Thames, Middlesex TW16 6AF, England) Ed. T.R. Warren. charts; illus.; circ. 200. (back issues avail.)
—BLDSC shelfmark: 5413.544700.
Description: Gives a worldwide report on the state and progress of the science and technology of measurement.

MEASUREMENT AND CONTROL. see *INSTRUMENTS*

389.6   US   ISSN 0543-1972
TJ1313   CODEN: MSTCAL
MEASUREMENT TECHNIQUES. English translation of: Izmeritel'naya Tekhnika. 1958. m. $1075 (foreign $1260)(effective 1992). (Komitet po Delam Standartov Mer i Izmeritel'noy Tekhniki Soveta Ministrov S.S.S.R., RU) Plenum Publishing Corp., Consultants Bureau, 233 Spring St., New York, NY 10013-1578. TEL 212-620-8468. FAX 212-463-0742. TELEX 23-421139. Ed. V.I. Pustovoit. (also avail. in microfilm from JSC; back issues avail.) **Indexed:** Appl.Mech.Rev., Curr.Cont., Electron.& Communic.Abstr.J., Energy Res.Abstr., Eng.Ind., Ind.Sci.Rev., INIS Atomind., INSPEC, ISMEC, Solid St.Abstr.
—BLDSC shelfmark: 0415.830000.
Refereed Serial

389   HU   ISSN 0025-9993
CODEN: MEAUAI
MERES ES AUTOMATIKA. (Summaries in English, German and Russian) 1952. m. $47. (Merestechnikai es Automatizalasi Tudomanyos Egyesulet) Lapkiado Vallalat, Lenin korut 9-11, 1073 Budapest 7, Hungary. TEL 222-408. (Subscr. to: Kultura, P.O. Box 149, H-1389 Budapest, Hungary) Ed. Telkes Bela. adv.; bk.rev.; charts; illus.; circ. 1,500. **Indexed:** Appl.Mech.Rev., Chem.Abstr., Eng.Ind., Fluidex, Met.Abstr., Sci.Abstr., World Alum.Abstr.
—BLDSC shelfmark: 5680.500000.
Description: Contains articles on all aspects of automation technology. Covers a broad range of pertinent topics - from semiconductor optoelectronic sensors to operation of and developments in automation devices and systems.

389   HU   ISSN 0026-0002
MERESUGYI KOZLEMENYEK. 1959. q. $24.50. (Orszagos Meresugyi Hivatal) Lapkiado Vallalat, Lenin korut 9-11, 1073 Budapest 7, Hungary. TEL 222-408. (Subscr. to: Kultura, P.O. Box 149, H-1389 Budapest, Hungary) charts. **Indexed:** INIS Atomind.

389.6   CN   ISSN 0383-9184
METRIC FACT SHEETS. 1973. irreg. $5. Canadian Metric Association, P.O. Box 35, Fonthill, Ont. L0S 1E0, Canada. TEL 416-358-0171. Ed. Albert J. Mettler. adv.; circ. 1,000.
Description: Presents various aspects of metrication and international standardization.

389   US
METRIC REPORTER.* 1973. m. $100 membership. American National Metric Council, 1735 N. Lynn St., Ste. 950, Arlington, VA 22209-2019. TEL 202-857-0474. FAX 202-659-5427. Ed. Deborah Odell Moss. bk.rev.; circ. 5,000.

389.6   US   ISSN 1050-5628
METRIC TODAY. 1966. bi-m. $20 membership. U S Metric Association, Inc., 10245 Andasol Ave., Northridge, CA 91325. TEL 818-368-7443. Ed. Louis F. Sokol. adv.; bk.rev.; cum.index; circ. 2,500. (processed)
Former titles (until Mar. 1990): U S M A Newsletter (ISSN 0271-2555); U S Metric Association Newsletter; Metric Association Newsletter (ISSN 0300-7308)
Description: Provides information on the progress of the U.S. government's congressionally directed changeover to use only metric system measurements in conducting its business by 1992 (except where inefficiencies can be proven).

389   GW   ISSN 0026-1394
QC81   CODEN: MTRGAU
METROLOGIA; international journal of scientific metrology. (Text in English, French or German) 1965. 4/yr. DM.348($190) (International Committee of Weights and Measures) Springer-Verlag, Heidelberger Platz 3, D-1000 Berlin 33, Germany. TEL 030-8207-1. (And: Heidelberg, Tokyo, Vienna, and New York) Ed. R.P. Hudson. adv.; charts; illus.; index. (also avail. in microform from UMI; back issues avail.; reprint service avail. from ISI) **Indexed:** Chem.Abstr., Curr.Cont., Eng.Ind., Phys.Ber., Sci.Abstr.
—BLDSC shelfmark: 5748.800000.
Description: Disseminates new and fundamental knowledge in all areas of scientific metrology.

389   US
N I S T HANDBOOK. irreg. price varies. U.S. National Institute of Standards and Technology, MD 20899. TEL 301-975-3058. (Dist. by: Supt. of Documents, Washington, D.C. 20402)
Formerly (until 1989): N B S Handbook (ISSN 0083-1824)
Refereed Serial

389   US
QC100   CODEN: NBSMA6
N I S T MONOGRAPH. 1959. irreg. price varies. U.S. National Institute of Standards and Technology, Gaithersburg, MD 20899. TEL 301-975-3058. (Orders to: Supt. of Documents, Washington, DC 20402) **Indexed:** GeoRef.
Formerly (until 1988): U.S. National Bureau of Standards. Monograph (ISSN 0083-1832)
Refereed Serial

389   US   ISSN 1048-776X
QC100   CODEN: NSPUE2
N I S T SPECIAL PUBLICATION. (Subseries avail.: Standards Activities of Organizations in the US; National Conference on Weights and Measures. Report (ISSN 0077-3964)) irreg. price varies. U.S. National Institute of Standards and Technology, Gaithersburg, MD 20899. TEL 301-975-3058. (Dist. by: Supt. of Documents, Washington, D.C. 20402)
Formerly (until 1988): N B S Special Publication (ISSN 0083-1883)
Refereed Serial

389   US   ISSN 1054-013X
QC100
N I S T TECHNICAL NOTE. 1959. irreg. price varies. U.S. National Institute of Standards and Technology, Gaithersburg, MD 20899. TEL 301-975-3058. (Orders to: Supt. of Documents, Washington, DC 20402) **Indexed:** Chem.Abstr.
—BLDSC shelfmark: 6113.655300.
Formerly (until 1988): U.S. National Bureau of Standards. Technical Notes (ISSN 0083-1913)
Refereed Serial

389   US   ISSN 0097-0395
CODEN: NSRDAP
N S R D S - N B S: NATIONAL STANDARD REFERENCE DATA SERIES. irreg. price varies. U.S. National Institute of Standards and Technology, Gaithersburg, MD 20899. TEL 301-975-3058. (Orders to: Supt. of Documents, Washington, DC 20402)
Formerly: U.S. National Bureau of Standards. National Standard Reference Data Series (ISSN 0083-1840)
Description: Quantitative data on physical and chemical properties of materials; compiled from world literature and critically evaluated.
Refereed Serial

389.6   US
NATIONAL CONFERENCE OF STANDARDS LABORATORIES. NEWSLETTER.. vol.12, 1972. q. $15. National Conference of Standards Laboratories, 1800 30th St., Ste. 305B, Boulder, CO 80301. TEL 303-440-3339. FAX 303-440-3384. Ed. John Minck. circ. 2,000. (processed)
Incorporating (1962-19??): National Conference of Standards Laboratories. Proceedings (ISSN 0081-4318)

389.1   US   ISSN 0077-3964
QC100
NATIONAL CONFERENCE ON WEIGHTS AND MEASURES. REPORT. (Subseries of: NIST Special Publication (ISSN 1048-776X)) 1905. a. price varies. U.S. National Institute of Standards and Technology, Gaitherburg, MD 20899. TEL 301-975-3058. cum.index: 1905-60.
Refereed Serial

M

METROLOGY AND STANDARDIZATION

500 600   US   ISSN 1044-677X
QC100.U6   CODEN: JRITEF
NATIONAL INSTITUTE OF STANDARDS AND TECHNOLOGY. JOURNAL OF RESEARCH. 1928. bi-m. $23. U.S. National Institute of Standards and Technology, U.S. Dept. of Commerce, Gaithersburg, MD 20899. TEL 301-975-3069. (Orders to: Supt. of Documents, Washington, DC 20402. TEL 301-975-3058) Ed. Barry Taylor. illus.; index; circ. 2,000. (also avail. in microform from UMI; reprint service avail. from UMI) **Indexed:** A.S.& T.Ind., Anal.Abstr., Appl.Mech.Rev., Biol.Abstr., Br.Ceram.Abstr., Chem.Abstr., Deep Sea Res.& Oceanogr.Abstr., Eng.Ind., Ind.U.S.Gov.Per., INIS Atomind., Mass Spectr.Bull., Math.R., Met.Abstr., RAPRA, Sci.Abstr., Sci.Cit.Ind., World Text.Abstr.
—BLDSC shelfmark: 5050.600000.
    Former titles (until 1988): U.S. National Bureau of Standards. Journal of Research (ISSN 0160-1741); Formed by the 1977 merger of: U.S. National Bureau of Standards. Journal of Research. Section A. Physics and Chemistry (ISSN 0022-4332); U.S. National Bureau of Standards. Journal of Research. Section B. Mathematical Sciences (ISSN 0098-8979) Which was formerly (until 1967): U.S. National Bureau of Standards. Journal of Research. Section B. Mathematics and Mathematical Physics (ISSN 0022-4340); Which superseded in part (in 1959): U.S. National Bureau of Standards. Journal of Research (ISSN 0091-0635).
    Description: Reports on research conducted in the fields of the physical and engineering sciences.
Refereed Serial

681   JA   ISSN 0451-6109
CODEN: BNLMAP
NATIONAL RESEARCH LABORATORY OF METROLOGY. BULLETIN. (Text in English, Japanese) 1955. s-a. exchange basis. National Research Laboratory of Metrology - Tsusho Sangyo-sho Kogyo Gijutsu-in Keiryo Kenkyujo, 1-1-4 Umezono, Tsukuba, Ibaraki-ken 305, Japan. FAX 0298-54-4135. TELEX 3652570-AIST-J. Ed. Toshio Sakurai. circ. 700. **Indexed:** Fluidex, JCT, Met.Abstr., Sci.Abstr., World Alum.Abstr.

389.6   NE   ISSN 0921-8211
NORMALISATIE MAGAZINE. 1924. m. fl.62. Nederlands Normalisatie-instituut, Kalfjeslaan 2, 2623 AA Delft, Netherlands. FAX 015-690190. TELEX 015-38144. Ed. P.W.V. Vos. adv.; bk.rev.; illus.; index; circ. 4,500. **Indexed:** C.I.S. Abstr., Excerp.Med., Key to Econ.Sci.

NORMALIZACJA. see *ENGINEERING*

NUCLEAR STANDARDS NEWS. see *ENERGY — Nuclear Energy*

530   GW
P T B - MITTEILUNGEN FORSCHEN UND PRUEFEN. 1890. bi-m. DM.199. (Physikalisch-Technische Bundesanstalt) Friedr. Vieweg und Sohn Verlagsgesellschaft mbH, Postfach 5829, 6200 Wiesbaden 1, Germany. TEL 0611-160230. FAX 0611-160229. TELEX 4186928-VWVD. Eds. W. Hauser, E. Seiler. adv.; bk.rev. **Indexed:** C.I.S. Abstr., Cadscan, Chem.Abstr., Curr.Cont., Excerp.Med., Lead Abstr., Phys.Ber., Zincscan.
    Formerly: P T B Mitteilungen (ISSN 0030-834X)

POLITECHNIKA WROCLAWSKA. INSTYTUT METROLOGII ELEKTRYCZNEJ. PRACE NAUKOWE. KONFERENCJE. see *ENGINEERING — Electrical Engineering*

POLITECHNIKA WROCLAWSKA. INSTYTUT METROLOGII ELEKTRYCZNEJ. PRACE NAUKOWE. MONOGRAFIE. see *ENGINEERING — Electrical Engineering*

POLITECHNIKA WROCLAWSKA. INSTYTUT METROLOGII ELEKTRYCZNEJ. PRACE NAUKOWE. STUDIA I MATERIALY. see *ENGINEERING — Electrical Engineering*

658   PL   ISSN 0137-8651
PROBLEMY JAKOSCI; dwumiesiecznik naukowo-techniczny. (Text in Polish; summaries in various languages) 1968. bi-m. $25. Wydawnictwo Czasopism i Ksiazek Technicznych SIGMA - NOT, Ul. Biala 4, P.O. Box 1004, 00-950 Warsaw, Poland. (Dist. by: SIGMA - NOT Ltd., Ul. Bartycka 20, 00-716 Warsaw, Poland) Ed. H. Chojecki. adv.; bk.rev.; circ. 1,600. (microform)

389.6   NE   ISSN 0924-3089
TJ212   CODEN: PCQUEJ
▼**PROCESS CONTROL AND QUALITY.** (Text in English) 1990. 8/yr. (in 2 vols., 4 nos./vol.). fl.822 (effective 1992). Elsevier Science Publishers B.V., P.O. Box 211, Amsterdam, Netherlands. TEL 020-5803911. FAX 020-5803598. TELEX 18582 ESPA NL. (Subscr. in U.S. and Canada to: Elsevier Science Publishign Co., Inc., Box 882, Madison Sq. Sta., New York, NY 10159. TEL 212-989-5800) Ed. K.J. Clevett. adv.; bk.rev.; cum.index. (back issues avail.) **Indexed:** Anal.Abstr., Chem.Abstr.
—BLDSC shelfmark: 6849.985020.
    Description: Covers the science and technology of process quality measurement systems, with emphasis on the practical application of in-process analyzer technology for process control and product quality measurement.
Refereed Serial

PROTECTION OF ATMOSPHERE AGAINST POLLUTION; determination of atmospheric background pollution in South Prebaltic. see *ENVIRONMENTAL STUDIES — Pollution*

620.1   US
Q A QUEST. 1981. m. membership. Quality Assurance Institute, 7575 Dr. Phillips Blvd., Ste. 350, Orlando, FL 32819. TEL 407-363-1111. FAX 407-363-1112. Ed. Martha Platt. bk.rev.; circ. 1,000. (back issues avail.)

620   IT
QUALITA. vol.4, 1974. q. L.50000. Associazione Italiana per la Qualita, Piazza Diaz 2, Milan, Italy. Ed. Sandro Doglio. adv.; bk.rev.; circ. 2,200.

658.5   GW
QUALITAET UND ZUVERLAESSIGKEIT (1980); Zeitschrift fuer industrielle Qualitaetssicherung. 1956. m. DM.135.60. (Deutsche Gesellschaft fuer Qualitaet) Carl Hanser Verlag, Kolbergerstr. 22, Postfach 860420, 8000 Munich 80, Germany. TEL 089-926940. adv.; bk.rev.; bibl.; charts; illus.; index; circ. 12,000. **Indexed:** Excerp.Med., Oper.Res.Manage.Sci., Qual.Contr.Appl.Stat., Sci.Abstr.
    Former titles: Q Z Qualitaet und Zuverlaessigkeit (ISSN 0720-1214); Qualitaet und Zuverlaessigkeit (1969) (ISSN 0033-5126); Qualitaetskontrolle.

620.1   FR
QUALITE EN MOUVEMENT. 1960. 5/yr. 630 F. Mouvement Francais pour la Qualite, 5 esplanade Charles de Gaulle, 92733 Nanterre Cedex, France. adv.; bk.rev.; bibl.; charts; illus.; circ. 1,500.
    Former titles: Qualite Magazine (ISSN 0768-858X); A F C I Q Bulletin (ISSN 0033-4782)

620.1 389.9   UK   ISSN 0959-3268
TS156.A1   CODEN: QUFOEF
QUALITY FORUM. 1935. q. £26. Institute of Quality Assurance, 10 Grosvenor Gardens, London SW1W 0DQ, England. Ed. T. Harris. charts; illus.; stat.; circ. 12,414. (reprint service avail. from UMI) **Indexed:** Account.& Data Proc.Abstr., BMT, Br.Tech.Ind., Eng.Ind., Ergon.Abstr., ISMEC, Oper.Res.Manage.Sci., Qual.Contr.Appl.Stat., Sci.Abstr.
—BLDSC shelfmark: 7168.152220.
    Former titles (until 1990): Quality Assurance (ISSN 0306-2856); Quality Engineer (ISSN 0033-5215)

620.1   UK   ISSN 0959-3756
QUALITY NEWS. 1973. m. membership. Institute of Quality Assurance, 10 Grosvenor Gardens, London SW1W 0DQ, England. TEL 071-730-7154. adv.; bk.rev.; circ. 11,682.
    Former titles (until 1990): Q A News; Quality Assurance News.

620.1 389   UK
QUALITY TODAY. 1969. 11/yr. £60.50 (foreign £72.50). Whitehall Press Ltd., Earl House, Maidstone, Kent ME14 1PE, England. TEL 0622-759841. FAX 0622-675734. Ed. Brendan Coyne. circ. 4,700. **Indexed:** B.C.I.R.A., BMT, Br.Ceram.Abstr., Br.Rail.Bd., Br.Tech.Ind., Fluidex, ISMEC, Met.Abstr., World Alum.Abstr.
    Former titles (until 1983): Measurement and Inspection Technology (ISSN 0143-4020); (until 1979): Metrology and Inspection (ISSN 0026-1408)

REVISTA DE NORMALIZACION. see *SCIENCES: COMPREHENSIVE WORKS*

620.1 389   FR   ISSN 1161-4951
REVUE DE METROLOGIE PRATIQUE ET LEGALE; poids et mesures. 1923. m. 770 F. (effective Jan. 1990). (Service des Instruments de Mesure) Editions de Genie Moderne S.a.r.l., 102 rue de la Tour, 75116 Paris, France. TEL 45-04-80-11. Ed. Paul Rey. adv.; charts; illus.; cum.index: 1957-1970; circ. 1,500. **Indexed:** C.I.S. Abstr.

389.6   FR   ISSN 0766-5210
REVUE PRATIQUE DE CONTROLE INDUSTRIEL. 1962. 8/yr. 350 F. (foreign 460 F.). Editions Ampere, Groupe C.E.P.P., 25, rue Dagorno, 75012 Paris, France. TEL 43-47-30-20. Ed. C. Guedes. adv.; bk.rev.; abstr.; bibl.; charts; illus.; stat.; index; cum.index; circ. 5,000. **Indexed:** C.I.S. Abstr., Met.Abstr., World Alum.Abstr.
    Formerly (until 1984): Qualite (ISSN 0033-5142); (until 1967): Revue Pratique de Controle Industriel (ISSN 0373-8809)
    Description: Quality control, material testing, NDT testing in industry.

389   SA   ISSN 1018-4295
TA368
S A B S CATALOGUE/S A B S KATALOGUS. (Text in Afrikaans, Enlish) 1963. a. price varies. South African Bureau of Standards, Information and Publications, Private Bag X191, Pretoria 0001, South Africa. TEL 012-428-7911. FAX 012-344-1568. TELEX 321308. Ed. E.M. Grobler. circ. 2,000.
    Supersedes: S A B S Katalogus (Afrikaans Edition) (ISSN 0259-3610); S A B S Catalogue (English Edition) (ISSN 0259-3602); **Formerly:** S A B S Yearbook (ISSN 0081-2137)

389.6 620   FI
S F S CATALOGUE; catalogue of Finnish national standards. (Supplement avail. (ISSN 0780-766X)) (Text and summaries in English and Finnish) 1924. a. plus s-a. updates. FIM 100 (FIM 160 with supplements). Suomen Standardisoimisliitto - Finnish Standards Association, P.O. Box 205, Bulevardi 5 A 7, SF-00121 Helsinki, Finland. TEL 358-0-645 601. FAX 358-0-643-147. circ. 2,000.

389.6   US
S M A WEIGHLOG. q. Scale Manufacturers Association, 932 Hungerford Dr., Ste. 36, Rockville, MD 20850. TEL 301-738-2448. FAX 301-738-0076. Ed. R.J. Lloyd.

658.5   SZ
SCHWEIZERISCHE ARBEITSGEMEINSCHAFT FUER QUALITAETSFOERDERUNG. BULLETIN. (Text in French and German) 1965. m. (10/yr.). 120 SFr. Schweizerische Arbeitsgemeinschaft fuer Qualitaetsfoerderung, Postfach, CH-4601 Olten, Switzerland. TEL 062-261616. FAX 062-267337. adv.; bk.rev.; circ. 2,500.

389.6   CS
SEZNAM PLATNYCH CESKOSLOVENSKYCH STATNICH A OBOROVYCH NOREM. 1953. a. $120. Federalni Urad pro Normalizaci a Mereni, Vaclavske nam. 19, 113 47 Prague 1, Czechoslovakia. circ. 25,000.

658   MX
SISTEMAS DE CALIDAD. 1973. bi-m. $15. Instituto Mexicano de Control de Calidad, Division de Divulgacion - Mexican Institute for Quality Control, Thiers No. 251-Penthouse, Mexico 5, D.F., Mexico. FAX 525-2547390. TELEX 1763190 IMECME. Ed. Patricia Gonzalez Prado. adv.; bk.rev.; index; circ. 5,000.

620.1 389   SA   ISSN 0038-2698
SOUTH AFRICAN BUREAU OF STANDARDS. BULLETIN. (Text in Afrikaans and English) 1947. m. free. South African Bureau of Standards, Private Bag X191, Pretoria 0001, South Africa. FAX 12-344-1568. TELEX 3-21308 SA. illus.; circ. 5,150. **Indexed:** Ind.S.A.Per.

620   US
STANDARD SPECIFICATIONS FOR TRANSPORTATION MATERIALS AND METHODS OF SAMPLING AND TESTING. (In 2 vols.) 1931. a. $115. American Association of State Highway and Transportation Officials, 444 N. Capital St., N.W., Ste. 225, Washington, DC 20001. TEL 202-624-5800.
    Formerly (until 1935): Tentative Specifications for Highway Materials and Methods of Sampling and Testing.

389　　　　　　　　NO　ISSN 0038-9625
STANDARDISERING. 1964. bi-m. NOK 230. Norges Standardiseringsforbund - Norwegian Standards Association, P.O. Box 7020, 0306 Oslo 3, Norway. TEL 02-46-60-94. FAX 02-46-44-57. TELEX 19050-NSF-N. Ed. J. Johan Bing. adv.; bk.rev.; charts; illus.; circ. 3,100.

389.6　　　　　　　DK　ISSN 0107-2870
STANDARDNYT. 1958. bi-m. DKK 250. Dansk Standardiseringsraad - Danish Standards Association, Baunegaardsvej 73, DK-2900 Hellerup, Denmark. TEL 45 39-77-01-01. FAX 45-39-77-02-02. TELEX 11-92-03 DS STAND. Ed. Jacob E. Holmblad. bk.rev.; circ. 1,000.

389　　　　　　　　US
STANDARDS ACTIVITIES OF ORGANIZATIONS IN THE U S. (Subseries of: NIST Special Publication (ISSN 1048-776X)) irreg. $31. U.S. National Institute of Standards and Technology, Gaithersburg, MD 20899. TEL 301-975-3058. (Orders to: Supt. of Documents, Washington, DC 20402)
   Formerly: Directory of United States Standardization Activities (ISSN 0070-6558)
   Refereed Serial

389.6 389　　　　　US　ISSN 0038-9641
STANDARDS AND SPECIFICATIONS INFORMATION BULLETIN. 1964. w. $70. National Standards Association, Inc., 1200 Quince Orchard Blvd., Gaithersburg, MD 20878. TEL 301-590-2300.

620.1　　　　　　　US　ISSN 0038-9668
T59
STANDARDS ENGINEERING. bi-m. $30 (foreign $40). Standards Engineering Society, Box 2307, Dayton, OH 45401. adv.; bk.rev.; bibl.; charts; illus.; stat.; circ. 1,000.

620.1 389　　　　　II　ISSN 0970-2628
T59.2.I4
STANDARDS INDIA. (Text in English) 1949. m. $70. Bureau of Indian Standards, Manak Bhavan, 9 Bahadur Shah Zafar Marg, New Delhi 110 002, India. Ed. R.B. Mathur. adv.; bk.rev.; charts; illus.; index; circ. 4,000. **Indexed:** Chem.Abstr., Food Sci.& Tech.Abstr., Sci.Abstr.
   Formerly (until 1987): Indian Standards Institution Bulletin (ISSN 0019-0632)

620.1 389　　　　　II　ISSN 0038-9684
STANDARDS: MONTHLY ADDITIONS. (Text in English) 1960. m. free. Bureau of Indian Standards, Manak Bhavan, 9 Bahadur Shah Zafar Marg, New Delhi 110 002, India. Ed. R.B. Mathur. circ. 2,000.
   Formerly (until 1987): I S I Standards: Monthly Additions (Indian Standards Institution).

350.821　　　　　　CE
STANDARDS NEWS. (Text in English) 1975. s-a. free. Bureau of Ceylon Standards, 53 Dharmapala Mawatha, Colombo 3, Sri Lanka. Ed. S.G. Weragoda. adv.; circ. 1,000. **Indexed:** Sri Lanka Sci.Ind.

620.1 389　　　　　RU　ISSN 0038-9692
　　　　　　　　　　　CODEN: STKABA
STANDARTY I KACHESTVO. 1927. m. 31.20 Rub. Izdatel'stvo Kniga, 125047 Moscow, Russia. **Indexed:** Chem.Abstr.
—BLDSC shelfmark: 0167.600000.

620.1　　　　　　　TZ　ISSN 0856-0374
TANZANIA. BUREAU OF STANDARDS. ANNOUNCER. 1979. q. Bureau of Standards, P.O. Box 9524, Dar es Salaam, Tanzania. TEL 255-51-48051. TELEX 41667 TBS TZ. Ed. N.N. Maingu. circ. 830. (back issues avail.)

620.1　　　　　　　TZ　ISSN 0856-2539
TANZANIA. BUREAU OF STANDARDS. DIRECTOR'S ANNUAL REPORT. 1976. a. Bureau of Standards, P.O. Box 9524, Dar es Salaam, Tanzania. TEL 255-51-48051. TELEX 416677 TBS TZ. Ed. N.N. Maingu. circ. controlled.

TEST & MEASUREMENT WORLD BUYER'S GUIDE. see *ENGINEERING — Electrical Engineering*

350.821　　　　　　US
UNDERWRITERS LABORATORIES. ANNUAL PRODUCT DIRECTORIES.. a. Underwriters Laboratories Inc., 333 Pfingsten Rd., Northbrook, Chicago, IL 60062. TEL 708-272-8800. FAX 708-272-8129. TELEX 6502543343.
   Formerly: Underwriters Laboratories. Annual Product Directories. Semi-Annual Supplement.
   Description: Lists the manufacturers who have demonstrated the ability to produce items, devices or systems that comply with UL safety requirements.

389.6　　　　　　　US　ISSN 0363-8464
UC263
U.S. DEPARTMENT OF DEFENSE. INDEX OF SPECIFICATIONS AND STANDARDS. (In 3 parts) 1952. bi-m. $40 for pts. 1 & 2; $60 for all 3 pts. U.S. Naval Publications and Forms Center, 5801 Tabor Ave., Philadelphia, PA 19111. TEL 215-697-2000. (Orders to Supt. of Documents, Washington, DC 20402) circ. 8,200. (also avail. in microfiche)

389.6　　　　　　　US　ISSN 0095-537X
TS410
WEIGHING & MEASUREMENT. 1914. bi-m. $10. Key Markets Publishing Co., Box 5867, Rockford, IL 61125-0867. TEL 815-229-1818. FAX 815-229-4086. Ed. David M. Mathieu. adv.; bk.rev.; charts; illus.; tr.lit.; circ. 14,500. **Indexed:** Br.Ceram.Abstr.
   Formerly: Scale Journal.

WEIGHING & MEASURING DIRECTORY; buyers guide. see *ENGINEERING*

389.6　　　　　　　ZA
ZABS REVIEW. (Text in English) 1988. q. $15. Bureau of Standards, P.O. Box RW 50259, Lusaka, Zambia. TEL 213918. Ed. George Simasiku. adv.; bk.rev.; circ. 500.
   Formerly: Zambian Standards Reporter.
   Description: Monitors quality control of products coming out of Zambia.

METROLOGY AND STANDARDIZATION — Abstracting, Bibliographies, Statistics

621.3 389.6 016　　UK　ISSN 0950-4818
QC39
KEY ABSTRACTS - MEASUREMENTS IN PHYSICS. 1976. m. £78. INSPEC, I.E.E., Michael Faraday House, Six Hills Way, Stevenage, Herts. SG1 2AY, England. TEL 0438-313311. FAX 0438-742840. TELEX 825578-IEESTV-G. (U.S. addr.: 445 Hoes Lane, Piscataway, NJ 08854. TEL 908-562-5549) index. **Indexed:** Agri.Eng.Abstr., Excerp.Med.
   Formerly (until 1987): Key Abstracts - Physical Measurements and Instrumentation (ISSN 0307-7969)
   Description: Radiation detectors and measurement, mass spectrometry, plasma diagnostics, measurements and instrumentation in mechanics, heat, optics, fluid dynamics and the environment.

389.6　　　　　　　MW
MALAWI. MALAWI BUREAU OF STANDARDS. LIBRARY. ADDITIONS TO THE LIBRARY. (Text in English) 1978. m. Malawi Bureau of Standards, Library, P.O. Box 946, Blantyre, Malawi.

389.6　　　　　　　FR　ISSN 0761-2044
P A S C A L EXPLORE. E 32: METROLOGIE ET APPAREILLAGE EN PHYSIQUE ET PHYSICOCHIMIE. 1984. 10/yr. 785 F. Centre National de la Recherche Scientifique, Institut de l'Information Scientifique et Technique, B.P. 54, 54514 Vandoevre-Les-Nancy Cedex, France. TEL 83-50-46-00.
   Formerly: P A S C A L Explore. Part 32: Metrologie et Appareillage en Physique et Physicochimie; Which superseded in part (1961-1984): Bulletin Signaletique. Part 130: Physique Mathematique, Optique, Acoustique, Mecanique, Chaleur (ISSN 0397-7757)

389 016　　　　　　RU　ISSN 0034-2505
REFERATIVNYI ZHURNAL. METROLOGIYA I IZMERITEL'NAYA TEKHNIKA. 1963. m. 121.80 Rub. (129.20 Rub. including index). Vsesoyuznyi Institut Nauchno-Tekhnicheskoi Informatsii (VINITI), Baltiiskaya ul., 14, Moscow A-219, Russia. (Dist. by: Mezhdunarodnaya Kniga, Dimitrova ul. 39, 113095 Moscow, Russia) **Indexed:** Chem.Abstr.

600 016　　　　　　US　ISSN 0038-9633
T59.A1
STANDARDS ACTION. 1970. fortn. $100 includes A N S I Reporter. American National Standards Institute, Inc., 11 W. 42nd St., 13th Fl., New York, NY 10036. TEL 212-642-4900. FAX 212-302-1286. circ. 8,000. (also avail. in microform from UMI)

MICROBIOLOGY

see *Biology–Microbiology*

MICROCOMPUTERS

see *Computers–Microcomputers*

MICROSCOPY

see *Biology–Microscopy*

MILITARY

see also *Civil Defense*

355 658　　　　　　US
A L A WORLDWIDE DIRECTORY AND FACT BOOK. 1982. a. $50. American Logistics Association, 1133 15th St., N.W., Ste. 640, Washington, DC 20005. TEL 202-466-2520. Ed. Paul Pierpoint. adv. **Indexed:** SRI.
   Description: Military resale directory.

A M S STUDIES IN THE EMBLEM. see *GENEALOGY AND HERALDRY*

355.155　　　　　　US　ISSN 0001-2874
A V C BULLETIN. 1946. irreg., approx. q. $5. American Veterans Committee, Inc., 6309 Bannockburn Dr., Bethesda, MD 20817-5403. TEL 301-320-6490. FAX 301-654-5508. Ed. June A. Willenz. adv.; bk.rev.; illus.; circ. 15,000.

355　　　　　　　　PE　ISSN 0001-3811
ACADEMIA MILITAR DE CHORRILLOS. REVISTA.* 1926. q. Academia Militar de Chorrillos, Chorrillos, Peru.

355 790.1　　　　　CN　ISSN 0705-0992
ADSUM. (Text in French) 1972. w. Can.$37.45. Fonds Non-Publics, Bldg. 513, Room 140, BFC Valcartier, PQ G0A 1R0, Canada. TEL 418-844-5598. Ed. Yvon Nick Thibeault. adv.; bk.rev.; index, cum.index; circ. 5,000. (tabloid format; back issues avail.)

358.4　　　　　　　UK
AEROMILITARIA; Air-Britain military aviation historical journal. 1975. q. £14. Air-Britain (Historians) Ltd., 1 East St., Tonbridge, Kent TN9 1HP, England. (Subscr. to: c/o 15 Mallory Close, St. Athan, S. Glamorgan CF6 9JJ, Wales)

AEROPHILE. see *HOBBIES*

623 629.1　　　　　US
AEROSPACE & DEFENSE SCIENCE. 1982. q. $24. Aerospace and Defense Science, Inc., Box 033619, Indialantic, FL 32903-3619. FAX 407-773-0286. Ed. Robert daCosta. adv.; bk.rev.; circ. 60,000. **Indexed:** Air Un.Lib.Ind., PROMT.
   Former titles: Defense Science & Defense Science and Electronics (ISSN 0744-6241)
   Description: Treats all aspects of US and international defense policy and technology, with an emphasis on electronics and computer science.

355 629.1　　　　　US　ISSN 1057-0950
AEROSPACE FINANCIAL NEWS. 1988. fortn. $595 (effective 1992). Phillips Publishing, Inc., Defense - Aviation Group, 1925 N. Lynn St., Ste. 1000, Arlington, VA 22209. TEL 703-522-8333. FAX 703-522-8334. Ed. Ed Hazelwood, Sr. (back issues avail.)
   ●Also available online. Vendor(s): Data-Star, DIALOG, NewsNet.
   Former titles (until June 1991): Defense - Aerospace Business Digest (ISSN 1051-2462); Aerospace Electronics Business (ISSN 1041-1631); Defense Industry Report.

MILITARY

355   AF
AFGHAN MILITARY REVIEW. (Text in Persian or Pushto) vol.56, 1976. m. $15. Military Press, Urdoo Moojella, Kabul 23208, Afghanistan.

355 940   UK   ISSN 0306-154X
AFTER THE BATTLE. 1973. q. $26. Battle of Britain Prints International Ltd., Church House, Church St., Stratford, London E15 3JA, England. (Dist. in U.S. by: Sky Books International Inc., 48 E. 50th St., New York, NY 10022) Ed. Winston G. Ramsey.
—BLDSC shelfmark: 0735.620000.
Description: Explores twentieth century British history.

355.31   FR
AGENDA DES ARMEES. 1977. a. 69 F. per no. Editions Charles Lavauzelle, Le Prouet, B.P. 8, 87350 Panazol, France. FAX 55-31-24-20. TELEX 580995 F.

AGENT ORANGE REVIEW; for veterans who served in Vietnam. see *LAW*

358.4   FR   ISSN 0002-2152
AIR ACTUALITES; le magazine de l'Armee de l'air. 1968. 10/yr. 140 F. (foreign 180 F.). (Service d'Information de Recruitement et de Presse de l'Armee de l'Air, Antenne "Air") Association pour le Developpement et la Diffusion de l'Information Militaire, 6 rue Saint Charles, 75015 Paris, France. TEL 45-77-03-76. FAX 45-73-53-73. TELEX 200795. Ed. Lcl Henry Guyot. adv.; bk.rev.; circ. 30,000.
Supersedes: France. Secretariat d'Etat aux Forces Armees "Air". Bulletin d'Information.
Description: Provides editorials, news, reviews of aircraft.

358.4   US
AIR COMBAT. m. Challenge Publications, Inc., 7950 Deering Ave., Canoga Park, CA 91304. TEL 818-887-0550. FAX 818-883-3019. Ed. Michael O'Leary.

358.4   FR   ISSN 0223-0038
AIR FAN; mensuel de l'aeronautique militaire. 1978. m. 330 F. (foreign 400 F.). Edimat, 48 bd. des Batignolles, 75017 Paris, France. TEL 42-93-67-24. FAX 42-94-25-40. Ed. Olivier Cabiac. adv.; bk.rev.; charts; illus.; circ. 28,000.

358.4   US   ISSN 0002-2365
UG633   CODEN: AFCTB3
AIR FORCE COMPTROLLER. 1967. q. $5 (foreign $6.25). U.S. Air Force, Office of the Comptroller, The Pentagon, Washington, DC 20330. TEL 202-275-3054. (Subscr. to: Supt. of Documents, Washington, D.C. 20402) Ed. Claire Claysmith. bk.rev.; charts; illus.; circ. 4,500. **Indexed:** Air Un.Lib.Ind., BPIA, Bus.Ind., Ind.U.S.Gov.Per., Tr.& Indus.Ind.

AIR FORCE ENGINEERING & SERVICES QUARTERLY. see *ENGINEERING — Civil Engineering*

358.4   US   ISSN 0270-403X
UG1123
AIR FORCE JOURNAL OF LOGISTICS. 1976. q. $5. U.S. Air Force, Logistics Management Center, Gunter AFB, AL 36114-6693. TEL 205-416-4087. FAX 205-596-4638. Ed. Lt. Col. Keith R. Ashby. bk.rev.; circ. 9,600. (also avail. in microfiche) **Indexed:** Air Un.Lib.Ind., Ind.U.S.Gov.Per., PROMT.
Formerly: Pipeline.
Description: Provides an open forum for the presentation of issues, ideas, research, and information of concern to logisticians who plan, acquire, maintain, supply, transport, and provide supporting engineering and services for military aerospace forces.

358.4   UK
AIR FORCE LIST. a. price varies. H.M.S.O., P.O. Box 276, London SW8 5DT, England. circ. 3,400.

358.4   US   ISSN 0730-6784
UG633
AIR FORCE MAGAZINE. 1942. m. $21 (foreign $25). Air Force Association, 1501 Lee Hwy., Arlington, VA 22209-1198. TEL 703-247-5800. FAX 703-247-5855. Ed. John T. Correll. adv.; bk.rev.; charts; illus.; tr.lit.; circ. 212,000. (also avail. in microform from UMI) **Indexed:** Abstr.Mil.Bibl., Air Un.Lib.Ind., Amer.Bibl.Slavic & E.Eur.Stud, Amer.Hist.& Life, DM & T, Hist.Abstr., Int.Aerosp.Abstr.
—BLDSC shelfmark: 0776.073000.
Formerly: Air Force and Space Digest (ISSN 0002-2349)

358.4   US   ISSN 0002-2403
AIR FORCE TIMES. (In three eds.: Domestic, European, Pacific) 1947. w. $48. Army Times Publishing Co., 6883 Commercial Dr., Springfield, VA 22159-0240. TEL 703-750-8646. FAX 703-750-8622. Ed. Lee Ewing. adv.; bk.rev.; charts; illus.; stat.; circ. 93,000. (tabloid format; also avail. in microform from UMI; reprint service avail. from UMI) **Indexed:** Air Un.Lib.Ind.

358.4   UK   ISSN 0955-7091
AIR FORCES MONTHLY. 1988. m. £21($49) (foreign £27). Key Publishing Ltd., P.O. Box 100, Stamford, Lincs. PE9 1XQ, England. TEL 0780-55131. FAX 0780-57261. TELEX 265871-MONREF-G. Ed. David Oliver. adv.; bk.rev.; bibl.; illus.; circ. 30,766. (back issues avail.)

358.4   US   ISSN 1059-7468
AIRBORNE STATIC LINE; your airborne lifeline. 1965. m. $25 (Canada and Mexico $30; elsewhere $35). Spearhead, Inc., Box 87518, College Park, GA 30337. TEL 404-478-5301. FAX 404-478-5301. Ed. Don Lassen. adv.; bk.rev.; illus.; circ. 20,000. (tabloid format)
Description: Directed to former military paratroopers; perpetuates the camaraderie of military service.

358.4   US   ISSN 0002-2756
UG 633.A1
AIRMAN. 1957. m. $17 (foreign $21.25). U.S. Air Force, Air Force News Agency, Kelly AFB, TX 78241-5000. TEL 512-925-7757. FAX 512-925-7750. (Orders to: Supt. of Documents, Gov't Printing Office, Washington, DC 20402) Ed. Michael B. Perini. illus.; circ. 1,000,000. (also avail. in microform from MIM,UMI; reprint service avail. from UMI) **Indexed:** Air Un.Lib.Ind., Ind.U.S.Gov.Per., Mid.East: Abstr.& Ind.

358.4   US   ISSN 0897-0823
UG633
AIRPOWER JOURNAL. (Semi-annual editions in Spanish and Portuguese) 1947. q. $9.50 (foreign $11.90). U.S. Air Force, Air University, Maxwell Air Force Base, AL 36112. TEL 205-953-5322. Ed. Lt. Col. Richard B. Clark. bk.rev.; charts; illus.; stat.; circ. 20,000. (also avail. in microform from UMI,MIM) **Indexed:** Abstr.Mil.Bibl., Air Un.Lib.Ind., Amer.Bibl.Slavic & E.Eur.Stud, Amer.Hist.& Life, DM& T, Eng.Ind., Hist.Abstr., Ind.U.S.Gov.Per., Mid.East: Abstr.& Ind., P.A.I.S., PROMT.
—BLDSC shelfmark: 0785.090000.
Formerly (until 1987): Air University Review (ISSN 0002-2594)

355   YU
AKADEMAC. 1969. m. free. Vojna Akademija Rodova Kopnene Vojske i Intendantske Sluzbe, Veljka Lukica-Kurjaka 33, Belgrade, Serbia, Yugoslavia. Ed. Djordje Zirojevic.

355   IT
ALERE FLAMMAM; bollettino d'informazione della Scuola di Guerra. 1952. bi-m. qualified personnel only. Comando Scuola di Guerra, 00053 Civitavecchia, Italy. bk.rev.; bibl.; illus.; circ. 900 (controlled).

359   US   ISSN 0002-5577
ALL HANDS. 1922. m. $17. U.S. Navy, Internal Relations Activity, 601 N. Fairfax St., Ste. 230, Alexandria, VA 22314-2007. FAX 703-274-4313. (Subscr. to: Supt. of Documents, Washington, D.C. 20402) Ed. M.G. Johnston. bk.rev.; illus.; circ. 87,000. **Indexed:** Abstr.Mil.Bibl., Air Un.Lib.Ind, Ind.U.S.Gov.Per.

359.96   NE   ISSN 0002-5674
VA530
ALLE HENS. 1947. m. fl.29.50. Koninklijke Marine, Directie Voorlichting Ministerie van Defensie, Postbus 20701, 2500 ES The Hague, Netherlands. FAX 070-3188426. adv.; bk.rev.; charts; illus.; circ. 28,000. **Indexed:** Abstr.Mil.Bibl.

355   SZ   ISSN 0002-5925
ALLGEMEINE SCHWEIZERISCHE MILITAERZEITSCHRIFT. Short title: A S M Z. 1855. m. 78 SFr. (Schweizerische Offiziersgesellschaft) Huber und Co. AG, Promenadenstr. 16, CH-8501 Frauenfeld, Switzerland. TEL 054-271111. Ed. Hans Bachofner. adv.; bk.rev.; abstr.; bibl.; charts; illus.; maps; index; circ. 33,806.
—BLDSC shelfmark: 0791.942000.
Description: Covers all aspects of the Swiss military, including training, equipment, information, international news, new publications and positions available.

359   US   ISSN 0736-3559
V1
ALMANAC OF SEAPOWER. (Special issue of: Sea Power) a. $14.95 to non-members (hardbound $24.95)(effective 1992). Navy League of the United States, 2300 Wilson Blvd., Arlington, VA 22201-3308. TEL 703-528-1775. FAX 703-528-2333. Ed. Vincent C. Thomas, Jr.

355.155   IT
ALPIN JO, MAME!. 1967. q. free. Alpino National Association (A.N.A.), Via S. Agostino 8-A, 33100 Udine, Italy. Ed. Claudio Cojutti. circ. 16,000. (tabloid format)

AMERICAN COUNCIL ON EDUCATION. CENTER FOR ADULT LEARNING AND EDUCATIONAL CREDENTIALS UPDATE. see *EDUCATION — Higher Education*

355   US
AMERICAN DEFENSE ANNUAL (YEAR). a. price varies. Lexington Books, 866 Third Ave., New York, NY 10022. TEL 212-702-2102. FAX 212-605-4872. Ed. Joseph J. Kruzel.

355 384.554   GW
AMERICAN FORCES NETWORK T V GUIDE. 1965. m. International Publications GmbH, 199 Landstr., 6000 Frankfurt a.M. 70, Germany. TEL 0611-681010. adv.; circ. 176,181.
Description: Provides radio and television program listings. Includes features on travel, shopping, military news, homemaking, health and beauty, sports and photography.

355   US   ISSN 0883-072X
AMERICAN INTELLIGENCE JOURNAL. 1977. q. $25 (foreign $55). National Military Intelligence Association, Pentagon Station, Box 46583, Washington, DC 20050-6583. TEL 301-840-6642. FAX 301-840-8502. Ed. Roy K. Jonkers. adv.; bk.rev.; circ. 1,800.
Description: Contains articles of professional and academic interest in the areas of intelligence and counter-intelligence.

AMERICAN LEGION MAGAZINE. see *CLUBS*

355   US
AMERICAN LEGION NEWS SERVICE. 1983. fortn. $7.50. American Legion, National Headquarters, Box 1055, Indianapolis, IN 46204. TEL 317-635-8411. Ed. Frank L. Megnin. circ. 17,000.
Description: Covers Veterans issues.

AMERICA'S CIVIL WAR. see *HISTORY — History Of North And South America*

366   FR
AMICALES REGIMENTAIRES. 1925. q. 15 F. Federation des Amicales Regimentaires et d'Anciens Combattants, 28 bd. de Strasbourg, 75010 Paris, France.

359.96   US
AMPHIBIOUS WARFARE REVIEW. q. Marine Corps League, Capital Marines, 25 S. Quaker Ln., No. 20, Alexandria, VA 22314. TEL 703-823-5208. FAX 703-823-2813. Ed. Cyril Kammeier. adv.; bk.rev.; circ. 25,000 (controlled).

MILITARY 3451

355.115 FR ISSN 0044-815X
AMPUTE DE GUERRE. 1932. m. 25 F. Federation des Amputes de Guerre de France, 74 bd. Haussmann, 75008 Paris, France. TEL 43-87-41-00. Ed. Maurice Desmier. adv.; bk.rev.; circ. 11,500.

359 975 US
ANCHOR WATCH. 1983. q. $10. (Historic Naval Ships Association of North America) U S Naval Institute, c/o US Naval Academy Museum, 118 Maryland Ave., Annapolis, MD 21402-5035. TEL 301-267-2108. Ed. James W. Cheevers. circ. 100. (looseleaf format; back issues avail.)
Description: Information on historic ships. Includes news clips, announcements, calendar of events, and member information.

355 PH ISSN 0115-5814
UA853.P6
ANG TALA. (Text in English) 1974. m. (Armed Forces of the Philippines) Civil Relations Service, AFP Camp General Emilio Aguinaldo, Quezon City, Philippines. Ed. E. Cadua-Nunez.

355 327 US
ANTI-DRAFT. 1979. irreg. $5 to individuals; institutions $10. Committee Against Registration and the Draft, Box 262, Madison, WI 53701-0262. TEL 608-257-7562. Ed. Gillam Kerley. adv.; bk.rev.; circ. 7,000. (back issues avail.)
Description: Articles covering draft registration and other military personnel issues.

320 GW ISSN 0342-5789
ANTIMILITARISMUS INFORMATION. 1971. m. DM.32.25. (Gesellschaft buergerlichen Rechts) A M I-Verlag G.b R., Elssholzstr. 11, 1000 Berlin 30, Germany. TEL 030-2151035. Ed.Bd. adv.; bk.rev.; circ. 3,800.

355 RM
APARAREA PATRIEI. 1945. w. Ministry of National Defense, Str. Izvor 137, Bucharest, Rumania. Ed. Col. Radu Olaru. circ. 75,000.

APPROACH; naval aviation safety review. see AERONAUTICS AND SPACE FLIGHT

355 JO
AL-AQSA. w. P.O. Box 1957, Amman, Jordan.

355 LE
ARAB DEFENCE. (Text in Arabic) 1976. m. $100. Dar Assayad S.A.L., P.O. Box 1038, Beirut, Lebanon. FAX 4529957. TELEX 44224 SAYYAD LE. (UK addr.: c/o Contact Public Relations, 3 Park Pl., 12 Lawn Ln., London SW8, England. TEL 071-582-2220) Ed. Elias Badawi. adv.; circ. 22,120. **Indexed:** PROMT.

355 BE
ARES. (Text in Dutch, French) 1935. q. 250 BEF. (Union Royale Nationale des Officiers de Reserve (URNOR) - National Association of Reserve Officers (NARO)) F. Lepeer, Ed. & Pub., 110 Ave. de Heyn, B-1090 Brussels, Belgium. bk.rev.; circ. 9,000.
Formerly: Officier de Reserve (ISSN 0030-0551)

359 AG ISSN 0066-703X
ARGENTINA. DEPARTAMENTO DE ESTUDIOS HISTORICOS NAVALES. SERIE A: CULTURA NAUTICA. 1961. irreg. Departamento de Estudios Historicos Navales, Instituto de Publicaciones Navales, Av. Cordoba 547, Buenos Aires, Argentina.

359 AG ISSN 0066-7048
ARGENTINA. DEPARTAMENTO DE ESTUDIOS HISTORICOS NAVALES. SERIE B: HISTORIA NAVAL ARGENTINA. 1960. irreg., no.18, 1975. price varies. Departamento de Estudios Historicos Navales, Instituto de Publicaciones Navales, Av. Cordoba 547, Buenos Aires, Argentina.

359 920 AG ISSN 0066-7056
ARGENTINA. DEPARTAMENTO DE ESTUDIOS HISTORICOS NAVALES. SERIE C: BIOGRAFIAS NAVALES ARGENTINAS. irreg. Departamento de Estudios Historicos Navales, Instituto de Publicaciones Navales, Av. Cordoba 547, Buenos Aires, Argentina.

359 980 AG
ARGENTINA. DEPARTAMENTO DE ESTUDIOS HISTORICOS NAVALES. SERIE E: DOCUMENTOS. 1977. irreg. Departamento de Estudios Historicos Navales, Instituto de Publicaciones Navales, Av. Cordoba 547, Buenos Aires, Argentina.

ARGENTINA. ESCUELA DE DEFENSA NACIONAL. REVISTA. see POLITICAL SCIENCE — International Relations

ARGENTINA. SECRETARIA DE GUERRA. DIRECCION DE ESTUDIOS HISTORICOS. BOLETIN BIBLIOGRAFICO. see HISTORY — History Of North And South America

ARMADA INTERNATIONAL. see AERONAUTICS AND SPACE FLIGHT

355 949.2 NE ISSN 0168-1672
ARMAMENTARIA. 1966. a. fl.25. Kon. Nederlands Leger- en Wapenmuseum "Generaal Hoefer", Korte Geer 1, 2611 CA Delft, Netherlands. circ. 1,500.
Description: Covers Dutch military history; history of arms and uniforms.

355 SA ISSN 0379-6477
U1
ARMED FORCES; a monthly journal devoted to defence matters. 1975. m. $25. Military Publications Pty. Ltd., PO Box 23022, Joubert Park 2044, Johannesburg, South Africa. TEL 011-725-2701. FAX 011-725-2703. Ed. S.J. McIntosh. adv.; bk.rev.; circ. 10,000. (back issues avail.) **Indexed:** Abstr.Mil.Bibl., Ind.S.A.Per., PROMT.

355 320 301 US ISSN 0095-327X
U21.5
ARMED FORCES AND SOCIETY; an interdisciplinary journal on military institutions, civil-military relations, arms control and peacekeeping, and conflict management. 1974. q. $35 to individuals (foreign $55); institutions $68 (foreign $88). (Inter-University Seminar on Armed Forces & Society) Transaction Publishers, Transaction Periodicals Consortium, Department 3092, Rutgers University, New Brunswick, NJ 08903. TEL 908-932-2280. FAX 908-932-3138. Ed. Claude E. Welch, Jr. adv.; bk.rev.; charts; illus.; index; circ. 2,200. (also avail. in microfilm from UMI; back issues avail.) **Indexed:** A.B.C.Pol.Sci., Abstr.Mil.Bibl., Air Un.Lib.Ind., Amer.Bibl.Slavic & E.Eur.Stud., Amer.Hist.& Life, Bk.Rev.Ind. (1991-), Chic.Per.Ind., Child.Bk.Rev.Ind. (1991-), Curr.Cont., Hist.Abstr., Mid.East: Abstr.& Ind., P.A.I.S., Psychol.Abstr., Soc.Sci.Ind., Sociol.Abstr., SSCI.
—BLDSC shelfmark: 1682.970000.
Description: Provides an international forum for a wide range of topics, including war, revolution, recruitment and conscription policies, arms control, peacekeeping, military history, economics of defense, and strategic issues.

355 US ISSN 0004-2188
UC20
ARMED FORCES COMPTROLLER.* 1956. q. $15 to non-members. American Society.of Military Comptrollers, 225 Reinekers Ln., Ste.250, Alexandria, VA 22314-2875. Ed. Col. E.W. Edmonds. adv.; bk.rev.; charts; circ. 20,000. (also avail. in microform from UMI) **Indexed:** Account.Ind. (1974-), Air Un.Lib.Ind., BPIA, Bus.Ind., Manage.Abstr., Manage.Cont., Tr.& Indus.Ind.
—BLDSC shelfmark: 1683.005000.

355 US ISSN 0196-3597
U1 CODEN: AFJIE8
ARMED FORCES JOURNAL INTERNATIONAL. 1863. m. $24. Armed Forces Journal International, Inc., 2000 L St., N.W., Ste. 520, Washington, DC 20036. TEL 202-296-0450. FAX 202-296-5727. Ed. B.F. Schemmer. adv.; bk.rev.; circ. 50,000. (also avail. in microform from UMI; reprint service avail. from UMI) **Indexed:** Abstr.Mil.Bibl., Air Un.Lib.Ind, DM & T, Mid.East: Abstr.& Ind., PROMT.
—BLDSC shelfmark: 1683.007200.
Formerly: Armed Forces Journal (ISSN 0004-220X)
Description: Defense news for career military officers and government officials involved in defense.

355 GH
ARMED FORCES NEWS. 1966. q. General Headquarters, Directorate of Public Relations, Burma Camp, Accra, Ghana. Ed. A. Hoffman. circ. 8,000.

355 UV
ARMEE DU PEUPLE. 1982. m. Ouagadougou, Burkina Faso. Ed. Seydou Niang.
Description: Presents armed forces and defense information.

355 SZ ISSN 0004-2269
ARMEE-MOTOR. (Text in French and German) 1956. m. 38 SFr. Graf und Neuhaus AG, Moehrlistr. 69, CH-8033 Zurich, Switzerland. FAX 01-3617715. Ed. Col. Furrer. adv.; circ. 4,300.

356 GW ISSN 0004-2277
ARMEE-RUNDSCHAU; Soldaten Magazin. 1956. m. DM.44.40. Militaerverlag der Deutschen Demokratischen Republik, Storkower Str. 158, 1055 Berlin, Germany. TEL 4300618. Ed. Karl-Heinz Freitag. adv.; bk.rev.; film rev.; play rev.; record rev.; illus. **Indexed:** DM & T.

355 FR
ARMEES D'AUJOURD'HUI. 1962. 10/yr. 150 F. (foreign 200 F.). Association pour le Developpement et la Diffusion de l'Information Militaire, 6 rue Saint-Charles, 75015 Paris, France. TEL 45-77-03-76. bk.rev.; index; circ. 100,000. **Indexed:** Abstr.Mil.Bibl., Hist.Abstr.
Supersedes: Forces Armees Francaises; Armee (ISSN 0004-2234)

356 BU ISSN 0004-2285
ARMEISKI PREGLED. 1954. 12/yr. 39 Fr. (Ministerstvo na Narodnata Otbrana) Foreign Trade Co. "Hemus", 7 Levsky St., Sofia, Bulgaria. TELEX 22267 HEMKIK. circ. 5,280.

355 FR
ARMEMENT. 5/yr. 300 F. (foreign 350 F.). Association pour le Developpement et la Diffusion de l'Information Militaire, 6 rue St. Charles, 75015 Paris, France. TEL 45-77-03-76. FAX 45-79-53-73.
Description: News of the Delegation Generale pour l'Armement for members and the public.

356 SW ISSN 0004-2404
ARMENYTT. 1949. 6/yr. SEK 20 (foreign SEK 40). Armestaben, 10782 Stockholm, Sweden. FAX 08-7888541. TELEX 19633. Ed. Anders Person. adv.; bk.rev.; illus.; circ. 140,000.

355 NE ISSN 0922-2979
ARMEX; defensiemagazine. 1919. m. fl.40($20) Koninklijke Nederlandse Vereniging "Ons Leger" - Royal Netherlands Army Association, Postbus 11586, 2502 AN The Hague, Netherlands. TEL 070-3186841. FAX 070-3659599. Ed. A.W. Schulte. adv.; bk.rev.; illus.; circ. 10,000.
Formerly (until Apr. 1988): Ons Leger (ISSN 0030-2724)
Description: Discusses peace, security, arms control, military technology and history, defense policies, and current developments affecting the Netherlands Armed Forces, independent from the Ministry of Defense.

355 US ISSN 0004-2420
UE1
ARMOR;* the magazine of mobile warfare. 1888. bi-m. $16 to members; non-members $20. U.S. Army Armor School, HHC 20 Brigade, 1st Armored Division, APO, NY 09066-5000. TEL 502-624-2249. FAX 502-942-6219. Ed. Maj. P.J. Cooney. bk.rev.; illus.; charts; index, cum.index: 1888-1968; circ. 20,500. (also avail. in microfilm) **Indexed:** Abstr.Mil.Bibl., Air Un.Lib.Ind., Amer.Bibl.Slavic & E.Eur.Stud, DM & T, Ind.U.S.Gov.Per., Mid.East: Abstr.& Ind.
—BLDSC shelfmark: 1683.040000.

ARMS CONTROL; the journal of arms control and disarmament. see POLITICAL SCIENCE

ARMS CONTROL REPORTER. see POLITICAL SCIENCE — International Relations

355 AT
ARMY; the soldiers newspaper. 1959. s-m. Aus.$20. Department of Defence, Army Newspaper Unit, P.O. Box E33, QVT, Canberra, A.C.T. 2600, Australia. FAX 06-266-5137. Ed. W.E. Pickering. adv.; B&W page Aus.$1000, color page Aus.$2000; trim 276 x 206. bk.rev.; circ. 42,000. (tabloid format)

355.31 US ISSN 0004-2455
ARMY. 1950. m. $25. Association of U.S. Army, 2425 Wilson Blvd., Arlington, VA 22201-3385. TEL 703-841-4300. FAX 703-525-9039. Ed. James Binder. adv.; bk.rev.; circ. 130,078. **Indexed:** Air Un.Lib.Ind.

MILITARY

355   UK   ISSN 0004-2463
ARMY, AIR FORCE & NAVAL AIR STATISTICAL RECORD.
6/yr. $615 (with Weekly Report $1300; with Weekly Profile $810). Aviation Studies International, Sussex House, Parkside, Wimbledon, London SW19 5NB, England. TEL 081-946-5082.
Description: Aircraft, helos, AFV's, nuclears, missiles, guns, ships, personnel, funds: AF, Navy, Army, Marine, Coast Guard, Customs, Police, DOT, CRAF/airline assets, for 200 territories.

358.4   US   ISSN 0004-248X
ARMY AVIATION. 1953. m. $25. Army Aviation Publications Inc., 49 Richmondville Ave., Westport, CT 06880. TEL 203-226-8184. FAX 203-222-9863. Ed. William R. Harris, Jr. adv.; circ. 16,100.

355.27 621.38   US   ISSN 0362-5745
UA943
ARMY COMMUNICATOR; voice of the Signal Corps. 1976. q. $6 (foreign $9). U.S. Army Signal Center, Ft. Gordon, GA 30905-5301. TEL 404-791-7204. (Co-sponsor: Ft. Gordon Signal Towers) Ed. Richard Davis, Jr. bk.rev.; circ. 10,000. (also avail. in microform from UMI) **Indexed:** Abstr.Mil.Bibl., Ind.U.S.Gov.Per.
—BLDSC shelfmark: 1683.151000.

358.4   US
ARMY FLIER. w. Box 1140, Enterprise, AL 36331. TEL 205-347-9533. adv.; circ. 8,000.

ARMY LAWYER. see *LAW*

355.31   UK
ARMY LIST. a. price varies. H.M.S.O., P.O. Box 276, London SW8 5DT, England.

355   US
ARMY LOGISTICIAN; the professional bulletin of United States Army logistics. 1969. bi-m. $6.50. U.S. Army Logistics Management College, Ft. Lee, VA 23801-6044. TEL 804-734-4342. FAX 804-734-3576. (Dist. by: Supt. of Documents, Washington, DC 20402) Ed. Terry R. Speights. bk.rev.; bibl.; charts; illus.; circ. 72,000 (controlled). (also avail. in microform from MIM,UMI) **Indexed:** Abstr.Mil.Bibl., Air Un.Lib.Ind., DM& T, Ind.U.S.Gov.Per., PROMT.
Former titles: Log Magazine; (until 1984): Army Logistician (ISSN 0004-2528)

355.31   US
ARMY MASTER DATA FILE: ARMY RETRIEVAL MICROFORM SYSTEMS AND INTERC. Short title: A M D F: A R M S and Interc. m. $900 per no. in N. America; elsewhere $1800. (Department of the Army) U.S. National Technical Information Service, 5825 Port Royal Rd., Springfield, VA 22161. TEL 703-487-4630. (magnetic tape)
Description: Provides commonly used supply management data required to perform logistics functions, relating them to their mission responsibilities.

610.6 610.6   UK
ARMY MEDICAL SERVICES MAGAZINE. 1927. 3/yr. £2.40. R A M C Historial Museum, Keogh Barracks, Ashv Vale, Aldershot, Hants. GU12 5RQ, England. Ed. Lt. Col. R. Eyeions. adv.; circ. 3,200.

ARMY MOTORS. see *HOBBIES*

355   UK   ISSN 0004-2552
U1
ARMY QUARTERLY AND DEFENCE JOURNAL. 1829. q. £44. AQ & DJ Publications, One West St., Tavistock, Devon PL19 8DS, England. TEL 0822-613577. FAX 0822-612785. Ed. T.D. Bridge. adv.; bk.rev.; charts; illus.; index; circ. 21,000. (also avail. in microform from RPI; reprint service avail.) **Indexed:** Air Un.Lib.Ind., Amer.Hist.& Life, Hist.Abstr., P.A.I.S., PROMT.
—BLDSC shelfmark: 1683.180000.
Description: Coverage of current and historical international defense subjects.

355   US   ISSN 0004-2579
UA23.A1
ARMY RESERVE MAGAZINE. 1954. 4/yr. $5. U.S. Army Reserve, Support Center, 1815 N. Ft. Myer Dr., Rm. 501, Arlington, VA 22209-1005. TEL 703-696-3962. FAX 703-696-5300. TELEX 703-696-3962. Ed. Lt. Col. Dick Devlin. bk.rev.; charts; illus.; index; circ. 600,000 (controlled). (also avail. in microform from MIM) **Indexed:** Air Un.Lib.Ind, Ind.U.S.Gov.Per.
Formerly: Army Reservist.

355   US   ISSN 0004-2595
ARMY TIMES. (In three eds.: Domestic, European, Pacific) 1940. w. $48. Army Times Publishing Co., 6883 Commercial Dr., Springfield, VA 22159-0240. TEL 703-750-8699. FAX 703-750-8622. Ed. Tom Donnelly. adv.; bk.rev.; charts; illus.; circ. 134,000. (tabloid format; also avail. in microform from UMI; reprint service avail. from UMI)

355   IT   ISSN 0004-3745
ARTIGLIERE; voce di tutti gli artiglieri. 1935. m. L.6500. Associazione Nazionale Artiglieri d'Italia, Via Aureliana 25, 00187 Rome, Italy. TEL 06/4814046. Ed. Alberto Raimondi. adv.; bk.rev.; bibl.; charts; illus.; stat.; circ. 2,000.

356   SW   ISSN 0004-3788
ARTILLERI-TIDSKRIFT. 1872. 4/yr. SEK 120. Artilleriklubben, c/o F M V, S-11588 Stockholm, Sweden. Ed. Jan Anshelm. adv.; bk.rev.; charts; illus.; index, cum.index every 4 yrs.; circ. 600.

356   SZ   ISSN 0004-3796
ARTILLERIE, ARMEE & TECHNIK.* m. Verband Schweizerischer Artillerie-Vereine, Berne, Switzerland.
Formerly: Schweizer Artillerist.

355   II   ISSN 0004-3826
ARTILLERY JOURNAL. 1948. a. Rs.20 (members Rs.14). Artillery Association, Nasik Road Camp, Deolali, India. Ed. Lt.Col. A.K. Sakhuja. adv.; bk.rev.; circ. 6,300.
Description: Articles on tactical and technical doctrines, primarily with a gunner military application.

355   US
ASIA - PACIFIC DEFENSE FORUM. 1976. q. free to qualified foreign personnel. United States Pacific Command (USCINCPAC), Box 13, Camp H.M. Smith, HI 96861. TEL 808-477-0760. FAX 808-477-6247. Ed. Paul R. Stankiewicz. circ. 34,200. (back issues avail.)
Description: International forum for military personnel of the Asian and Pacific areas.

355   MY   ISSN 0126-6403
UA830
ASIAN DEFENCE JOURNAL. (Text in English) 1971. m. $100. Syed Hussain Publications (Sdn) Bhd., 61A & B Jalan Dato, Haji Eusoff Damai Complex, Box 10836, 50726 Kuala Lumpur, Malaysia. TEL 442-0852. Eds. Syed Abdul Karim, Mohd Shuhud. adv.; bk.rev.; charts; illus.; circ. 16,500. (back issues avail.) **Indexed:** Abstr.Mil.Bibl., Air Un.Lib.Ind., PROMT.
—BLDSC shelfmark: 1742.407700.

ASSEMBLY. see *EDUCATION — Higher Education*

355   GU
ASSIGNMENT GUAM. 1976. a. free. Glimpses Guam, Inc., P.O. Box 3191, Agana, 96910, Guam. TEL 618-477-7606. Ed. Jonathan Needham.

ASSOCIAZIONE FRA MUTILATI E INVALIDI DI GUERRA. BOLLETTINO. see *SOCIAL SERVICES AND WELFARE*

355.15   IT   ISSN 0004-5993
ASSOCIAZIONE NAZIONALE MUTILATI E INVALIDI DI GUERRA. SEZIONE DI ROMA. NOTIZIARIO.* 1950. m. L.400. Associazione Nazionale Mutilati e Invalidi di Guerra, Sezione di Roma, Lungotevere Castello N.2, 00193 Rome, Italy.

358.4   IT   ISSN 0004-7279
ATTERRAGGIO FORZATO;* voce libera dei sottufficiali dell'aeronautica. vol.18, 1967. m. Largo Don Morosini 1a, 00195 Rome, Italy. Ed. Dr. Aldo Cini. illus. (newspaper)

335   AT
AUSTRALIAN DEFENCE EQUIPMENT CATALOGUE. 1974. biennial. Aus.$45. (Department of Defence Support) Peter Isaacson Publications Pty. Ltd., 45-50 Porter St., Prahran, Vic. 3181, Australia. TEL 03-520-5555. FAX 03-521-3647. adv.; illus.

355 900   AT
U1
AUSTRALIAN DEFENCE FORCE JOURNAL. 1976. bi-m. free. Department of Defence, Board of Management, Canberra A.C.T. 2600, Australia. FAX 06-2510991. Ed. Michael P. Tracey. adv.; bk.rev.; charts; illus.; index; circ. 17,500 (controlled). (back issues avail.) **Indexed:** Abstr.Mil.Bibl., DM & T, PROMT.
Former titles (until 1991): Defence Force Journal (ISSN 0314-1039); Army Journal (ISSN 0004-251X); Australian Army Journal.

355   AT   ISSN 0312-5807
AUSTRALIAN NAVAL INSTITUTE. JOURNAL. 1975. q. Aus.$27. Australian Naval Institute, P.O. Box 80, Campbell, ACT 2601, Australia. Ed. Don Agar. adv.; bk.rev.; charts; illus.; stat.; cum.index: 1975-1985; circ. 800. **Indexed:** Aus.P.A.I.S.

355 388   GW
AUTO MAGAZINE. (Text in English) 1982. bi-m. DM.60. International Publications GmbH, Waechtersbacher Str. 89, D-6000 Frankfurt-Main 61, Germany. TEL 011-49694209. FAX 011-49696042. TELEX 411500-INPUB-D. Ed. Mark Vaughn. adv.; bk.rev.; circ. 80,000.

355   US   ISSN 0888-1081
AVALON HILL GENERAL. 1964. bi-m. $15. Avalon Hill Game Co., (Subsidiary of: Monarch Avalon, Inc.), 4517 Harford Rd., Baltimore, MD 21214. TEL 301-254-5300. FAX 301-254-0991. Ed. Rex A. Martin. charts; illus.; circ. 15,000. (tabloid format)
Description: Devoted to the strategy and play of the company's line of simulation games, with emphasis on military, political and economic history.

355   CU
AVANTE. a. Ministerio de las Fuerzas Armadas Revolucionarias, Ave. del Puerto esq. a, Obrapia, Habana Vieja, Havana, Cuba.

358.4   PE   ISSN 0005-2078
AVIACION. 1936. m. Fuerza Aerea, Edificio Ministerio de Aeronautica, 28 de Julio, Campo de Marte, Lima, Peru.
Description: Discusses Peruvian Air Force.

355.37   FR
AZUR ET OR. q. Associations Nationales des Officiers et Sous-Officiers de Reserve de l'Armee de l'Air, 5 bis Av de la Porte de Sevres, 75731 Paris Cedex 15, France. adv.

B G S. (Bundesgrenzschutz) see *POLITICAL SCIENCE — International Relations*

355.115   US   ISSN 0005-3767
BADGER LEGIONNAIRE. vol.48, 1970. m. $1. Wisconsin American Legion, 812 E. State St., Milwaukee, WI 53202. TEL 414-271-1940. Ed. Rick Barnett. adv.; circ. 75,000. (tabloid format)
Description: Contains articles of interest to veterans.

355   IS
BAMACHANE. (Text in Hebrew) 1948. w. Defense Department, Military P.O. Box 01013, Israel. Ed. Avi Lavski. adv.; circ. 70,000.

355
BAMACHANE NACHAL. (Text in Hebrew) 10/yr. IS.15. Ministry of Defense Publishing House, Subscription Dept., 25 David Eleazer St., Hakirya, Tel Aviv 64 734, Israel. TEL 03-205516.

355   GW   ISSN 0930-7974
BARETT; internationales Militaermagazin. 1986. bi-m. DM.32 (foreign DM.36). Barett Verlag GmbH, Opladenerstr. 11, 4000 Duesseldorf 13, Germany. TEL 0211-764180. FAX 0211-764147. adv.; bk.rev.; circ. 22,000. (back issues avail.)

BAROMETER. see *POLITICAL SCIENCE — International Relations*

355 NE ISSN 0005-6146
BASIS. vol.17, 1975. s-m. fl.25. Stichting Geestelijke Weerbaarheid, Zomerstraat 1, Heerlen, Netherlands. Ed. M.G. Haringman. adv.; bk.rev.; illus.; circ. 4,000.
Indexed: E.I.

355 977 US
BATTLE CALL. 1963. m. $20. Army of Tennessee, C S A - U S A, Box 91, Rosedale, IN 47874. TEL 317-548-2594. Ed. Ruby I. Walker. adv.; bk.rev.; circ. 350.
Description: Presents articles on the Civil War, including military uniform and battle information.

355 GW
BERNARD UND GRAEFE AKTUELL.* 1967. irreg., no.18, 1976. price varies. (Arbeitskreis fuer Wehrforschung) Bernard und Graefe Verlag, Karl-Mand-Str. 2, Postfach 2060, 5400 Koblenz, Germany.
Incorporating: Wehrwissenschaftliche Berichte (ISSN 0083-7822); Wehrforschung Aktuell; Beitraege zur Wehrforschung.

355 UK
BIBLIOTHECA HISTORICO MILITARIS. (Text in German) 1976. irreg. £3.50. Carl Slienger, PO Box 4ST, London W1P 1AA, England.

BITAON HEYL HA-AVIR/ISRAEL AIR FORCE MAGAZINE. see *AERONAUTICS AND SPACE FLIGHT*

359.96 GW ISSN 0936-3971
BLAUE JUNGS; Magazin der Marine. m. DM.56. A. Bernecker Verlag, Unter dem Schoeneberg 1, 3508 Melsungen, Germany. TEL 05661-731-0. FAX 05661-73189. Ed. Holger Hoffmann. adv.; bk.rev.; circ. 9,800.

BOEI DAIGAKKO RIKOGAKU KENKYU HOKOKU/NATIONAL DEFENSE ACADEMY. SCIENTIFIC AND ENGINEERING REPORTS. see *ENGINEERING*

355.133 MX ISSN 0006-6419
BOLETIN JURIDICO MILITAR. 1935. bi-m. Secretaria de la Defensa Nacional y de la Procuraduria General de Justicia Militar, Mexico, D.F., Mexico.

359 PY ISSN 0006-646X
BOLETIN NAVAL.* 1944. bi-m. Armada Nacional, Asuncion, Paraguay.

355 GW
DER BOTE AUS DEM WEHRGESCHICHTLICHEN MUSEUM. 1977. s-a. DM.40($25) Vereinigung der Freunde des Wehrgeschichtlichen Museums Schloss Rastatt e.V., Postfach 1633, 7550 Rastatt, Germany. TEL 07222-34244. Ed. Sabina Hermes. cum.index every 15 nos.; circ. 1,000. (back issues avail.)

BRIGADIER. see *COLLEGE AND ALUMNI*

355 UK
BRITAIN'S TOP 500 DEFENCE COMPANIES. 1985. irreg., latest 1990. £150. Jordan & Sons Ltd., 21 St. Thomas St., Bristol BS1 6JS, England. TEL 0272-230600. FAX 0272-230063. TELEX 449119.
Formerly: Britain's Defence Service Industry.
Description: Contains financial data and company addresses of Britain's top 500 defence companies.

355 UK ISSN 0272-4782
UA647
BRITISH DEFENCE DIRECTORY.* 1982. q. $387. Brassey's, 50 Fetter Ln., London EC4A 1AA, England. TEL 071-3774881. FAX 071-377-4888. (Subscr. to: Turpin Transactions, Distribution Centre, Blackhorse Rd., Letchworth, Herts. SG6 1HN, England. TEL 0462-672555) Ed. D.H. Sutton. (also avail. in microform from MIM,UMI)
—BLDSC shelfmark: 2298.762000.
Incorporating: Defence Attache.

DER BUECHSENMACHER. see *HOBBIES*

355 BU
BULGARSKI VOENEN KNIGOPIS. 1955. bi-m. free. (Institut po Voena Istoriia) Durzhavno Voenno Izdatelstvo, 12, Ul. Ivan Vazov, Sofia, Bulgaria. Ed. L. Ilieva. bibl.; circ. 835.

355 GW ISSN 0007-5949
DIE BUNDESWEHR; groesste deutsche Soldatenzeitschrift-unabhaengig-ueberparteilich aktuell. 1956. m. DM.36. Deutscher Bundeswehr-Verband e.V, Suedstr. 123, Postfach 20 04 63, 5300 Bonn 2, Germany. TEL 0228-3823212. FAX 0228-3823219. Ed. Dr. Horst Rohde. adv.; bk.rev.; illus.; index; circ. 205,000. (tabloid format)

BUNDESWEHRVERWALTUNG; Fachzeitschrift fuer Administration. see *LAW*

358.4 976 US
C A F DISPATCH; American airpower a proud heritage. 1976. bi-m. $32. Confederate Air Force, 6919 Wright Dr., Box 62080, Midland, TX 77711-2000. TEL 915-563-1000. FAX 915-563-8046. adv.; charts; illus.; stat.; circ. 12,500.
Description: Covers W.W. II aviation history (1939-1945).

355 CN ISSN 0045-8872
C F B COLD LAKE COURIER. 1967. w. Can.$20. Canadian Forces Base, Cold Lake, PO Box 3190, Medley, Alta. T0A 2M0, Canada. TEL 403-594-5206. FAX 403-594-2139. Ed. Debbie Lawrence. adv.; bk.rev.; circ. 3,100.

355 CN ISSN 0713-391X
C F B GAGETOWN GAZETTE. 1960. w. Can.$1 per no. Canadian Forces Base Gagetown, Bldg. H-10, Oromocto, N.B. E0G 2P0, Canada. TEL 506-422-2136. FAX 506-422-3545. Ed. R.B. Wagstaff. adv.; circ. 6,000.

C H I DISPATCH. (Confederate Historical Institute) see *HISTORY — History Of North And South America*

355 US
C 3 I HANDBOOK. (Command, Control, Communications and Intelligence) 1986. a. $50. Cardiff Publishing Co., 6300 S. Syracuse Way, 650, Englewood, CO 80111-9912. TEL 303-220-0600. (back issues avail.; reprint service avail.)

355.27 US
C 3 I NEWS. 1984. m. $195. Washington Defense Reports, Inc., Box 34312, Bethesda, MD 20817. TEL 703-573-1600. Ed. Clay Wick. bk.rev. (back issues avail.)
Description: Confidential Washington report on new research, development, and marketing opportunities in the fields of command, control, communications and intelligence.

CAL - VET INSURANCE PLANS. ANNUAL REPORT. see *INSURANCE*

355.115 US
CALIFORNIA LEGIONNAIRE. 1930. m. $3. American Legion, Department of California, 117 War Memorial Bldg., San Francisco, CA 94102. TEL 415-431-2400. Ed. Norman H. Bowman. adv.; bk.rev.; tr.lit.; circ. 161,200. (tabloid format; back issues avail.)

355.115 US
CALIFORNIA VETERAN. 1954. m. Veterans of Foreign Wars of the United States, 7111 Governors Circle, Sacramento, CA 95823. TEL 916-424-1684. Ed. Oren D. Robinson. adv.; circ. 120,500.
Description: Provides news on legislation, benefits, rights, and other veteran-related information.

355 US
CAMP CHASE GAZETTE; the voice of Civil War reenacting. 1972. 10/yr. $24. Camp Chase Publishing Company, Inc., Box 707, Marietta, OH 45750. TEL 614-373-1865. FAX 614-374-5710. adv.
Description: Source of information for those individuals and organizations that participate in Civil War Reenacting. Each issue contains a complete national calendar of events, articles on topics of interest to Civil War Reenactors, event reports, and letters to the editor.

CAMPAIGN; journal of strategy gaming. see *HOBBIES*

359 US
CAMPUS; the Navy education and training monthly. m. $18. U.S. Office of Naval Operations, Department of the Navy, Washington, DC 20390. TEL 202-545-6200. (Dist. by: Supt. of Documents, Washington, DC 20402)

354 CN ISSN 0383-4638
UA600
CANADA. DEPARTMENT OF NATIONAL DEFENCE. DEFENCE (YEAR). (Catalog no. D3-6-1992) (Text in English and French) 1970. a. free. Canada Communication Group, Publishing Division, Ottawa, Ont. K1A 0S9, Canada. TEL 613-951-7277. illus.; circ. 25,000.

355 CN
CANADA. DEPARTMENT OF NATIONAL DEFENCE. DIRECTORATE OF HISTORY. MONOGRAPH SERIES. (Catalog D63-1-1992) 1976. irreg. price varies. Canada Communication Group, Publishing Division, Ottawa, Ont. K1A 0S9, Canada. TEL 613-951-7277.
Supersedes (as from 1983): Canada. Department of National Defence. Directorate of History. Occasional Paper.

359 CN
CANADA'S NAVY ANNUAL. 1986. a. Can.$15. Corvus Publishing Group Ltd., 158 1224 Aviation Park N.E., Calgary, Alta. T2E 7E2, Canada. TEL 403-275-9457. FAX 403-275-3925. Ed. Richard Donaldson. adv.; circ. 15,000. (back issues avail.)
Description: Covers Canadian naval and military subjects of the past, present and future.

355 CN ISSN 0315-3495
UA600
CANADIAN DEFENCE QUARTERLY/REVUE CANADIENNE DE DEFENSE. (Text in English, French) 1969. q. Can.$30. Baxter Publishing Co., 310 Dupont St., Toronto, Ont. M5R 1V9, Canada. TEL 416-968-7252. FAX 416-968-2377. TELEX 065-28085. Ed. David McClung. adv.; bk.rev.; circ. 11,019. **Indexed:** Abstr.Mil.Bibl., Air Un.Lib.Ind., DM & T, PROMT.
—BLDSC shelfmark: 3020.450000.
Description: Strategic and military studies and military history.

358 CN ISSN 0068-8843
CANADIAN GUNNER. 1965. a. Can.$15. (Royal Regiment of Canadian Artillery) Leech Printing Ltd., 18th and Park, Brandon, Man., Canada. TEL 204-728-3037. FAX 204-727-3338. (back issues avail.)

359 CN ISSN 0008-4972
CANADIAN SAILOR. (Text in English, French) 1950. m. Can.$15. Seafarers International Union of Canada, 1333 rue St-Jacques, Montreal, Que. H3C 4K2, Canada. FAX 514-931-3667. Ed. Andrew Boyle. circ. 5,000 (controlled).

355 CN ISSN 0701-0427
CANADIAN SOCIETY OF MILITARY MEDALS AND INSIGNIA. JOURNAL. 1965. q. Can.$15 (typically set in Jan.). Canadian Society of Military Medals and Insignia, 15 Greenhill Dr., Thorold, Ont. L2V 1W4, Canada. Ed. Jim Steel. circ. 550.

CENTRAL INTELLIGENCE AGENCY. MONOGRAPHS. see *POLITICAL SCIENCE*

CENTRAL INTELLIGENCE AGENCY. MONOGRAPHS. ALL COMMUNIST COUNTRIES REPORTS. see *POLITICAL SCIENCE*

CENTRAL INTELLIGENCE AGENCY. MONOGRAPHS. ALL COUNTRIES REPORTS. see *POLITICAL SCIENCE*

CENTRAL INTELLIGENCE AGENCY. MONOGRAPHS. ALL NON-COMMUNIST COUNTRY REPORTS. see *POLITICAL SCIENCE*

CENTRAL INTELLIGENCE AGENCY. MONOGRAPHS. CHINA REPORTS. see *POLITICAL SCIENCE*

CENTRAL INTELLIGENCE AGENCY. MONOGRAPHS. MAPS ONLY. see *POLITICAL SCIENCE*

CENTRAL INTELLIGENCE AGENCY. MONOGRAPHS. U.S.S.R. REPORTS. see *POLITICAL SCIENCE*

359 AG ISSN 0009-0123
CENTRO NAVAL. BOLETIN. (Abstracts in English, Spanish) 1882. q. $40. Centro Naval Argentina, Florida 826, 1St, 1005 Buenos Aires, Argentina. adv.; bk.rev.; bibl.; index; circ. 5,000. (also avail. in microform) **Indexed:** Abstr.Mil.Bibl., INIS Atomind.

MILITARY

355   CS   ISSN 0009-0506
CESKOSLOVENSKA ARMADA.* 1952. fortn. Federalni Ministerstvo Narodni Obrany, Hlavni Politicka Sprava, c/o Historicky Ustav CS Armady, U Pamatniku 2, Prague 3 - Zizkov, Czechoslovakia.

355   CS   ISSN 0009-0751
CESKOSLOVENSKY VOJAK.* vol.14, 1965. fortn. 65 Kcs.($40.50) Ceskoslovenska Lidova Armada, Hlavni Politicka Sprava, c/o Historicky Ustav CS Armady, U Pamatniku 2, Prague 3 - Zizkov, Czechoslovakia. (Subscr. to: Artia, Ve Smeckach 30, 111 27 Prague 1, Czechoslovakia) Ed. Jiri Prazak. illus.; circ. 60,000.

355   II   ISSN 0069-2654
CHANAKYA DEFENCE ANNUAL. (Text in English) 1969. a. $10. Chanakya Publishing House, 3 Thornhill Rd., Allahabad 1, India. Ed. Ravi Kaul. adv.; bk.rev.; circ. 5,200. (back issues avail.)

CHINA REPORT: POLITICAL, SOCIOLOGICAL, AND MILITARY AFFAIRS. see POLITICAL SCIENCE

CHINA'S MILITARY: P L A IN (YEAR). (Sun Yat-sen Center for Policy Studies) see HISTORY — History Of Asia

355 028.1
CIVIL AND MILITARY REVIEW. m. Rs.10. Deep & Deep Publications, D-1-24, Rajouri Garden, New Delhi 110 027, India. TEL 5435369. Ed. G.S. Bhatia.

355   US   ISSN 0897-6015
E461
CIVIL WAR. 1983. bi-m. $19.97. (Civil War Society) Cool Spring Associates, Inc., 24 N. Buckmarsh St., Box 770, Berryville, VA 22611-0770. TEL 703-955-1176. FAX 703-955-1297. Ed. William J. Miller. adv.; bk.rev.; circ. 16,000. (back issues avail.)
   Description: Covers the events, personalities and lessons of the American Civil War; features news about the society.

CIVIL WAR COLLECTORS' DEALER DIRECTORY. see ANTIQUES

355
▼**THE CIVIL WAR LADY**; women in reenacting, historical information, research, medical. 1991. 6/yr. $20 (foreign $30). 622 Third Ave., S.W., Dept. I, Pipestone, MN 56164. TEL 507-825-3182. adv.

CIVILIAN - BASED DEFENSE: NEWS AND OPINION. see POLITICAL SCIENCE — International Relations

CIVILIAN CONGRESS; includes a directory of persons holding executive branch-military office in Congress contrary to constitutional prohibition (Art.1, Sec.6, Cl.2) of concurrent office-holding. see LAW

355   BL   ISSN 0101-6547
CLUBE MILITAR. REVISTA. 1926. 6/yr. free. Clube Militar, Av. Rio Branco 251 9, CEP 20040, Rio de Janeiro, RJ, Brazil. TEL (021) 220-9076. TELEX (21) 38 848 TPPG. Ed. Luiz Paulo Macedo Carvalho. adv.; bk.rev.; circ. 40,000.
   Description: Covers the history, economics, politics, and strategy of soldiering.

359   BL   ISSN 0102-0382
CLUBE NAVAL REVISTA. 1888. 4/yr. free. Clube Naval, Departamento Cultural, Av. Rio Branco, 180, 5o andar, 20040 Rio de Janeiro, Brazil. TEL 021-282-1273-225. FAX 021-220-8681. adv.; bk.rev.; circ. 8,000.
   Supersedes (in 1975): Mar (ISSN 0025-2727); Which was formerly (until 1966): Clube Naval. Boletim.

COLLEGE ALUMNI AND MILITARY PUBLICATIONS. see COLLEGE AND ALUMNI

355   CK   ISSN 0010-1389
COLOMBIA. MINISTERIO DE DEFENSA. BOLETIN.* 1926. Ministerio de Defensa, Bogota D.E., Colombia.

355
COLORADO LEGIONNAIRE. 1967. m. $1 to non-members. (American Legion, Department of Colorado) Barnum Publishing Company, 3003 Tejon, Denver, CO 80211. TEL 303-234-2458. Ed. E. Dean Hunter. adv.; circ. 27,000. (tabloid format)

355   FR   ISSN 0010-1834
COLS BLEUS. 1945. w. 310 F. (foreign 440 F.). (Service d'Information et des Relations Publique des Armees) Association pour le Developpement et la Diffusion de l'Information Militaire, 6 rue Saint Charles, 75015 Paris, France. TEL 45-77-03-76. FAX 45-79-53-73. Ed. C.V. Croullebois. adv.; bk.rev.; play rev.; film rev.; charts; illus.; stat.; circ. 22,500. (tabloid format)

358.4   US   ISSN 0010-213X
UG633
COMBAT CREW. 1950. m. $30 (foreign $37.50). U.S. Air Force Strategic Air Command, c/o Superintendant of Documents, U.S. Govt. Printing Office, Washington, DC 20402. TEL 202-275-0186. FAX 202-512-2233. circ. controlled. **Indexed:** Air Un.Lib.Ind., DM & T, PROMT.
   Supersedes: Professional Pilot.
   Description: Articles for the purpose of promoting safety.

355   CU
COMBATIENTE. w. Ministerio de las Fuerzas Armadas Revolucionarias, Hermanos Villasana No. 70, Santiago de Cuba, Cuba.

355.115   BE
COMBATTANT 1940-1945; revue belge de documentation militaire sur la Seconde Guerre Mondiale. 1976. 6/yr. 325 BEF. La Vie Militaire a.s.b.l., 14 rue des Balkans, 1180 Brussels, Belgium. Ed. Henri de Pinchart. adv.; bk.rev.; circ. 150.

355   CU
CON LA GUARDIA EN ALTO. 1961. m. Ministerio de las Fuerzas Armadas Revolucionarias, Ave. Salvador Allende No. 601, La Habana 3, Havana, Cuba. TEL 7-79-4443. Dir. Omelia Guerra Perez. circ. 60,000.
   Description: For members of the Committees for the Defense of the Revolution.

355   HK   ISSN 1013-9214
CONMILIT. (Text in Chinese) 1976. m. HK.$440($56.80) Conmilit Press Ltd., Sing Pao Bldg., 22nd Fl., 101 King's Road, North Point, Hong Kong, Hong Kong. TEL 5-716039. FAX 5-8070219. TELEX 62489 CANID HX. Ed. Zhang Si Wei. adv.; charts; illus.; stat.; circ. 17,430.
   Description: Developments in international hi-tech defence-related fields, both hardware and software. Focus on Asia-Pacific region.

355   US
CONSTITUTION CHRONICLE. 1976. q. membership. U S S Constitution Museum Foundation, Box 1812, Boston, MA 02129. TEL 617-426-1812. FAX 617-242-0496. Ed. Jean Roberts. circ. 2,500 (controlled). (tabloid format; back issues avail.)
   Formerly (until 1981): U S S Constitution Museum. News and Notes.
   Description: For members of the USS Constitution Museum to keep them informed of museum activities and exhibits.

909   US   ISSN 0883-6884
CONTRIBUTIONS IN MILITARY STUDIES. 1969. irreg., no.128, 1992. price varies. Greenwood Press, Inc. (Subsidiary of: Greenwood Publishing Group Inc.), 88 Post Rd. W., Box 5007, Westport, CT 06881-5007. TEL 203-226-3571. FAX 203-222-1502. Eds. Thomas E. Griess, Jay Luvass.
—BLDSC shelfmark: 3460.805000.
   Formerly: Contributions in Military History (ISSN 0084-9251)

355   IE
AN COSANTOIR; Irish defence forces magazine. 1940. m. £13 (foreign £26). An Cosantoir Army Headquarters, Parkgate, Dublin 8, Ireland. TEL 01-771881. FAX 01-771726. Ed. Capt. D. Cunningham. adv.; bk.rev.; illus.; index; circ. 5,200. (also avail. in microform from UMI; back issues avail., reprint service avail. from UMI)
   Description: For troops; chronicles the Irish Defense Forces involvement with United Nations Peacekeeping Missions.

614.7 531.64   US
COUNCIL FOR A LIVABLE WORLD. NEWSLETTER. 12/yr. Council for a Livable World, 110 Maryland Ave., N.E., Washington, DC 20002. TEL 202-543-4100.

COUNCIL ON AMERICA'S MILITARY PAST. PERIODICAL. see HISTORY — History Of North And South America

327
COVERT INTELLIGENCE LETTER. 1974. bi-m. $14 for 12 nos. to individuals (foreign $18); institutions $20. Horizone, Box 67, St. Charles, MO 63302. TEL 314-731-0993. Ed. W. Waltzer. bk.rev.; circ. 300.

358.4   UK
CROSS & COCKADE INTERNATIONAL. 1970. q. £15($27) First World War Aviation Historical Society, Cragg Cottage, The Cragg, Bramham, Wetherby LS23 6QB, W. Yorkshire, England. Ed. Paul Stuart Leaman. adv.; bk.rev.; circ. 1,400. (back issues avail.)

CURRENT MILITARY AND POLITICAL LITERATURE. see POLITICAL SCIENCE — International Relations

355   CI   ISSN 0011-4200
CUVAR JADRANA. 1947. s-m. Saveznicka Obala 18, Split, Croatia. Ed. Dusan Vesic.

355   IS
CYCLONE; digest of military literature. (Supplement to: Maarachot) (Text in Hebrew) 1939. q. P.O. Box 7026, Tel Aviv 61070, Israel. (Subscr. to: 29 El' azar St., Tel Aviv, Israel) Eds. Rachel Rojansky, Uri Dromi. (back issues avail.) **Indexed:** Ind.Heb.Per.

355.115   US   ISSN 0011-474X
D A V MAGAZINE. 1960. m. $4 to non-members. Disabled American Veterans, 807 Maine Ave., S.W., Washington, DC 20024. TEL 202-554-3501. FAX 202-554-3581. Ed. Gary Logan. bk.rev.; circ. 1,100,000. (also avail. in audio cassette)
   Description: Covers issues affecting disabled veterans and their families.

355   GW
D I Z SCHRIFTEN. 1989. 2/yr. DM.22. (Dokumentations und Informations Zentrum Emslandlager) Edition Temmen, Hohenlohestr. 21, 2800 Bremen 1, Germany. TEL 0421-344280. FAX 0421-348094.

363.35 629.13   US
D M S MARKET INTELLIGENCE REPORTS: AEROSPACE COMPANIES. (Defense Market Services) m. updated suppl. $1200. Forecast International Inc. - D M S, 22 Commerce Rd., Newtown, CT 06470. TEL 203-426-0800. FAX 203-426-1964. TELEX 467615. (looseleaf format; back issues avail.)
   Description: Presents studies of forecast sales volume by division for major defense programs, including merger, acquisition, and divestiture news, and provides data on aerospace and defense teaming, competition, and joint ventures. More than 100 top U.S. aerospace defense contractors are analyzed.

355   US
D M S MARKET INTELLIGENCE REPORTS: "AN" EQUIPMENT. (Defense Market Services) m. updated suppl. $1200. Forecast International Inc. - D M S, 22 Commerce Rd., Newtown, CT 06470. TEL 203-426-0800. FAX 203-426-1964. TELEX 467615. (looseleaf format; back issues avail.)
   Description: Identifies 5,500 AN system with descriptions, applications, contractors, contract values, and major components. More than 260 major AN equipment programs procured by the Air Force, Navy, Army, and defense agencies are covered.

355 629.13   US
D M S MARKET INTELLIGENCE REPORTS: ANTI-SUBMARINE WARFARE. m. updated suppl. $1200. Forecast International Inc. - D M S, 22 Commerce Rd., Newtown, CT 06470. TEL 203-426-0800. FAX 203-426-1964. TELEX 467615. (looseleaf format; back issues avail.)
   Description: Presents a guide to more than 130 western ASW programs detailing status and outlook, development, funding and contract history, and program analysis. It includes information on sonobuoys, torpedoes and ASW missile-rocket systems, submarine and helicopter-borne sonars.

355 629.13 363.35   US
D M S MARKET INTELLIGENCE REPORTS: C 3 I.
(Command, Control, Communications & Intelligence)
m. updated suppl. $1200. Forecast International Inc.
- D M S, 22 Commerce Rd., Newtown, CT 06470.
TEL 203-426-0800. FAX 203-426-1964. TELEX
467615. (looseleaf format; back issues avail.)
  Description: Presents an analysis of 150 C3I
projects worldwide, in five mission areas: Strategic,
Theater and Tactical, Special Warfare, Intelligence
and Information, and Communications. Also
contained are marked overviews of RDT & E and
procurement budget trends.

**D M S MARKET INTELLIGENCE REPORTS: CIVIL
AIRCRAFT.** see *AERONAUTICS AND SPACE FLIGHT*

629.13 355 363.35   US
**D M S MARKET INTELLIGENCE REPORTS: DEFENSE
MARKET.** (Defense Market Services) m. updated
suppl. $1200. Forecast International Inc. - D M S,
22 Commerce Rd., Newtown, CT 06470.
TEL 203-426-0800. FAX 203-426-1964. TELEX
467615. (looseleaf format)
  Description: Current examination of the U.S.
congressional review of RDT & E and Procurement
portions of the Department of Defense budget.

629.13 355   US
**D M S MARKET INTELLIGENCE REPORTS: ELECTRONIC
SYSTEMS.** m. updated suppl. $1200. Forecast
International Inc. - D M S, 22 Commerce Rd.,
Newtown, CT 06470. TEL 203-426-0800.
FAX 203-426-1964. TELEX 467615. (looseleaf
format; back issues avail.)
  Description: Reviews of the major U.S. electronic
systems developed and procured by the Army, Navy,
Air Force, defense agencies, and the FAA. Emphasis
is placed on multifaceted electronics that can
incorporate C3I, EW, radar, and other technologies
into a comprehensive program.

355   US
**D M S MARKET INTELLIGENCE REPORTS: ELECTRONIC
WARFARE.** m. updated suppl. $1200. Forecast
International Inc. - D M S, 22 Commerce Rd.,
Newtown, CT 06470. TEL 203-426-0800.
FAX 203-426-1964. TELEX 467615. (looseleaf
format; back issues avail.)
  Description: Covers research and development,
procurement, and major production efforts. Over
125 EW programs (funded by the U.S. Department
of Defense) are examined in full detail, according to
sea-based, and airborne systems.

355   US
**D M S MARKET INTELLIGENCE REPORTS: LATIN
AMERICA & AUSTRALASIA.** m. updated suppl.
$1200. Forecast International Inc. - D M S, 22
Commerce Rd., Newtown, CT 06470.
TEL 203-426-0800. FAX 203-426-1964. TELEX
467615. (looseleaf format)
  Description: Analysis of the military requirements
and market opportunities in the South American and
Australasian regions. Details of each country's
military equipment inventories are discussed.

355   US
**D M S MARKET INTELLIGENCE REPORTS: MIDDLE EAST -
AFRICA.** m. updated suppl. $1200. Forecast
International Inc. - D M S, 22 Commerce Rd.,
Newtown, CT 06470. TEL 203-426-0800.
FAX 203-426-1964. TELEX 467615. (looseleaf
format)
  Description: Details the region's military budget,
military posture, manufacturing capability, and
future requirements. Detailed inventories of each
country's aircraft, warships, missiles, electronics,
ordnance, and vehicles are supplied.

355 629.13   US
**D M S MARKET INTELLIGENCE REPORTS: MILITARY
AIRCRAFT.** m. updated suppl. $1200. Forecast
International Inc. - D M S, 22 Commerce Rd.,
Newtown, CT 06470. TEL 203-426-0800.
FAX 203-426-1964. TELEX 467615. (looseleaf
format)
  Description: Over 100 military aircraft programs
are covered, from concept through retirement,
excluding Warsaw Pact nations. Contains information
on performance, historical data, milestones and
budget for U.S. platforms, price range, procurement,
and budget forecast.

255   US
**D M S MARKET INTELLIGENCE REPORTS: MILITARY
VEHICLES.** m. updated suppl. $1200. Forecast
International Inc. - D M S, 22 Commerce Rd.,
Newtown, CT 06470. TEL 203-426-0800.
FAX 203-426-1964. TELEX 467615. (looseleaf
format; back issues avail.)
  Description: Over 150 U.S. and international
military vehicle programs are examined, covering
tanks, self-propelled tactical vehicles, trucks, and
APCs.

355 629.13   US
D M S MARKET INTELLIGENCE REPORTS: MISSILES. m.
updated suppl. $1200. Forecast International Inc. -
D M S, 22 Commerce Rd., Newtown, CT 06470.
TEL 203-426-0800. FAX 203-426-1964. TELEX
467615. (looseleaf format; back issues avail.)
  Description: Covers the development and
manufacture of tactical and strategic missiles
worldwide. Includes an examination of the
characteristics, background, funding, current status,
and contracting activity of more than 100 U.S. and
international missile programs.

355 629.13   US
**D M S MARKET INTELLIGENCE REPORTS: NATO &
EUROPE.** m. updated suppl. $1200. Forecast
International Inc. - D M S, 22 Commerce Rd.,
Newtown, CT 06470. TEL 203-426-0800.
FAX 203-426-1964. TELEX 467615. (looseleaf
format; back issues avail.)
  Description: Country-by-country examination of the
military capabilities, equipment requirements, and
current inventories for 15 NATO and 6 other
European countries. Discusses manufacturing
capabilities, military budgets, recent transactions,
and future requirements.

355   US
D M S MARKET INTELLIGENCE REPORTS: ORDNANCE. m.
updated suppl. $1200. Forecast International Inc. -
D M S, 22 Commerce Rd., Newtown, CT 06470.
TEL 203-426-0800. FAX 203-426-1964. TELEX
467615. (looseleaf format; back issues avail.)
  Description: Examines U.S. and European ordnance
programs, provides information on project history,
funding, mission requirements, modification
programs, development and replacement plans.
Covers air defense guns, mine neutralization, tank
guns, howitzers, bombs, mortars, light and anti-tank
weapons, and ammunition.

355 629.13   US
D M S MARKET INTELLIGENCE REPORTS: RADAR. m.
updated suppl. $1200. Forecast International Inc. -
D M S, 22 Commerce Rd., Newtown, CT 06470.
TEL 203-426-0800. FAX 203-426-1964. TELEX
467615. (looseleaf format; back issues avail.)
  Description: Analysis of sea-based, airborne,
land-based, and space-based radar systems in the
U.S., NATO alliance, and other major western
military powers. Details over 160 radar programs in
R&D, modification, and procurement.

355 629.13   US
**D M S MARKET INTELLIGENCE REPORTS: SPACE
SYSTEMS.** m. updated suppl. $1200. Forecast
International Inc. - D M S, 22 Commerce Rd.,
Newtown, CT 06470. TEL 203-426-0800.
FAX 203-426-1964. TELEX 467615. (looseleaf
format)
  Description: Details business opportunities
associated with major spacecraft and satellite
programs worldwide. Every major R&D, modification,
and procurement effort is evaluated, with
information on missions, manufacturers, price range,
timetable, funding recent activity, and
characteristics.

355   US
D M S MARKET INTELLIGENCE REPORTS: WARSHIPS. m.
updated suppl. $1200. Forecast International Inc. -
D M S, 22 Commerce Rd., Newtown, CT 06470.
TEL 203-426-0800. FAX 203-426-1964. TELEX
467615. (looseleaf format; back issues avail.)
  Description: Guide to warships, weapons, and
subsystems worldwide, including aircraft carriers,
frigates, nuclear and conventional attack
submarines, naval radar, and naval EW systems.
Analyzes major warship development and overhaul.

DANKE FUER IHRE HILFE. see *FUNERALS*

355   DK   ISSN 0011-6203
DANSK ARTILLERI-TIDSSKRIFT. 1914. 6/yr. DKK 170.
Artilleriofficersforeningen - Artillery Officers
Association, Postbox 182, DK-6800 Varde,
Denmark. Ed. Lt.Col. K.D. Yttesen. adv.; bk.rev.;
abstr.; charts; illus.; index; circ. 700.

355   UK   ISSN 0142-6184
UF500
DEFENCE. 1970. m. £75($149) (foreign £83).
International Trade Publications Ltd., Queensway
House, 2 Queensway, Redhill, Surrey RH1 1QS,
England. TEL 0737-768611. FAX 0737-760564.
TELEX 948669-TOPJNL-G. Ed. George
Paloczi-Horvath. adv.; bk.rev.; charts; illus.; index;
circ. 25,000. (back issues avail.) **Indexed:**
Abstr.Mil.Bibl., Cadscan, DM & T, Lead Abstr.,
PROMT, Zincscan.
—BLDSC shelfmark: 3541.482500.
  Incorporates: Defence Africa and Middle East &
Defensa Latino Americana; Formerly: Defence Digest.
  Description: Covers defence issues worldwide on a
tri-service basis.

355 330   GR
▼**DEFENCE AND THE ECONOMY.** (Supplement to:
Epilogi) 1990. a. Dr.1000. Electra Press, 4 Stadiou
St., 10564 Athens, Greece. TEL 01-32-33-203.
FAX 01-32-35-160. TELEX 210564. Ed. Christos
Papaioannou. adv.; circ. 9,000.

623   UK
DEFENCE DOCUMENTS MICROFILE. Short title: DEFDOCS
Microfile. q. Technical Indexes Ltd., Willoughby Rd.,
Bracknell, Berkshire RG12 8DW, England.
TEL 0344-426311. FAX 0344-424971.

355   US   ISSN 1043-0717
HC79.D4   CODEN: DEECEP
▼**DEFENCE ECONOMICS**; the political economy of
defence, disarmament and peace. 1990. 4/yr. (in 1
vol.). $75. Harwood Academic Publishers, 270
Eighth Ave., New York, NY 10011.
TEL 212-206-8900. FAX 212-645-2459. TELEX
236735 GOPUB UR. (Subscr. to: Box 786, Cooper
Sta., New York, NY 10276. TEL 800-545-8398; UK
subscr. to: P.O. Box 90, Reading, Berkshire RG1
8JL, England. TEL 0734-560-080) Ed. Keith
Hartley. (also avail. in microform)
—BLDSC shelfmark: 3541.610100.

DEFENCE HELICOPTER. see *AERONAUTICS AND SPACE
FLIGHT*

DEFENCE INDUSTRY DIGEST. see *BUSINESS AND
ECONOMICS*

335   PK   ISSN 0257-2141
DEFENCE JOURNAL. (Text in English) 1975. m.
Rs.180($30) 16-B 7th Central St., Defence Housing
Society, Karachi 46, Pakistan. TEL 21-541911.
FAX 21-571710. TELEX 23625 EMMAY PK. Ed.
A.R. Siddiqi. adv.; bk.rev.; bibl.; circ. 10,000.
Indexed: Abstr.Mil.Bibl.

355   II
DEFENCE MANAGEMENT. (Text in English) s-a. Rs.20.
Institute of Defence Management, Bolarum P.O.,
Secunderabad 500010, India. Ed. R. Prabhakar.
bk.rev.; bibl.; charts.
  Formerly: Defence Manager.

356   PK
DEFENCE REVIEW. (Text in English) 1989. 2/yr. $8.
Inspector General Training & Evaluation Branch,
Training Publications & Information Directorate,
General Staff Branch, General Headquarters,
Rawalpindi, Pakistan. TELEX 32854 GHQ PK. Ed.
Syed Ishfaq Ali. circ. 3,500.

355   II   ISSN 0011-748X
U395.I5   CODEN: DSJOAA
DEFENCE SCIENCE JOURNAL. (Text in English)
1949-1986. q. Rs.500($18) to individuals;
institutions Rs.100 ($36). Ministry of Urban
Development, Department of Publication, Civil Lines,
New Delhi 110 054, India. TEL 11-2517409. Ed.
G.S. Sharma. charts; illus.; index; circ. 450. **Indexed:**
Appl.Mech.Rev., Biol.Abstr., Chem.Abstr.,
Corros.Abstr., Eng.Ind., INIS Atomind.,
Int.Abstr.Biol.Sci., Int.Aerosp.Abstr., Math.R.,
Nutr.Abstr., Phys.Abstr., Plast.Abstr., Sci.Abstr.
—BLDSC shelfmark: 3546.200000.

MILITARY

355   SP   ISSN 0211-3732
DEFENSA; revista internacional de ejercitos, armamento y tecnologia. 1978. m. 5990 ptas. (Europe 9790 ptas.; America 11590 ptas.). Defensa Edefa, S.A., Editorial de Publicaciones, Jorge Juan, 98-2, 28009 Madrid, Spain. TEL 577-49-57. FAX 577-46-70. Ed. Vicente Talon. adv.: B&W page 338000 ptas., color page 535000 ptas.; trim 186 x 275. bk.rev.; index; circ. 21,520. (back issues avail.)
  Description: Covers armies, weapons, and industries.

355   US   ISSN 0737-1217
UA23.A1
DEFENSE (YEAR). 1980. bi-m. $23. (U.S. Department of Defense) American Forces Information Service, 601 N. Fairfax St., No.310, Alexandria, VA 22314-2006. FAX 703-274-4865. (Subscr. to: Supt. of Documents, Washington, DC 20402) Ed. S. Hara. circ. 80,000. **Indexed:** Abstr.Mil.Bibl., Air Un.Lib.Ind., Ind.U.S.Gov.Per.

355 629.1   US
DEFENSE - AEROSPACE DIRECTORY. a. Phillips Publishing, Inc., Defense - Aviation Group, 1925 N. Lynn St., Ste. 1000, Arlington, VA 22209. TEL 703-522-8333. FAX 703-522-6448.

350   UK   ISSN 0743-0175
UA11
DEFENSE ANALYSIS.* 1985. q. $115. Brassey's, 50 Fetter Ln., London EC4A 1AA, England. TEL 071-377-4881. FAX 071-377-4888. (Subscr. to: Turpin Transactions, Distribution Centre, Blackhorse Rd., Letchworth, Herts SG6 1HN, England. TEL 0462-672555) Ed. Martin Edmonds. adv. (also avail. in microfilm from MIM,UMI) **Indexed:** Curr.Cont.
—BLDSC shelfmark: 3546.212600.

355 001.535   US   ISSN 1056-747X
DEFENSE & AEROSPACE ELECTRONICS. 1985. w. $497 (effective 1992). Pasha Publications Inc., 1401 Wilson Blvd., Ste. 900, Arlington, VA 22209-9970. TEL 703-528-1244. FAX 703-528-1253. Ed. Len Famiglietti. **Indexed:** A.I.Abstr., CAD CAM Abstr., Comput.Lit.Ind.
  ●Also available online. Vendor(s): BRS (TSAP), Data-Star (PTBN), DIALOG (File nos.636,648), NewsNet (DE03).
  Incorporates (in 1991): C 4 I Report; Former titles (until 1991): Training, Electronics, C 4 I; (until 1990): Advanced Military Computing (ISSN 0884-9471); (until 1985): Military Electronics (ISSN 8755-7215) Which was formerly: C 3 I Report; C I Report (ISSN 0889-4728).
  Description: Business opportunities and technological innovations of interest to government contractors.

629.22   US
▼**DEFENSE & AEROSPACE ELECTRONICS**. 1991. w. $497 (foreign $527). Pasha Publications Inc., 1401 Wilson Blvd., Ste. 900, Arlington, VA 22209-9970. TEL 703-528-1244. FAX 703-528-1253. Ed. Doug Rekenthaler.
  Description: Covers defense simulation and electronic research in industry and government laboratories, commercial applications of new technologies, and budgetary developments affecting defense contractors.

355 629.1   US
DEFENSE AND AEROSPACE MARKETS. a. $1495. Forecast International Inc. - D M S, 22 Commerce Rd., Newtown, CT 06470. TEL 203-426-0800. FAX 203-426-1964. TELEX 467615.
  Description: Worldwide business opportunities (excluding the U.S.) are identified and analyzed in the following markets: military aircraft, civil aircraft, missiles, warships, ordnance, space systems, SDI, C3I, electronic warfare, military laser and EO, military vehicles, radar, and ASW.

DEFENSE AND AEROSPACE NOTES. see *BUSINESS AND ECONOMICS*

350.71   US
DEFENSE & ECONOMY WORLD REPORT. 1969. w. $320. Government Business Worldwide Reports, Box 5997, Washington, DC 20016. TEL 202-244-7050. FAX 202-244-5410. Ed. J.H. Wagner. bk.rev.; bibl.; charts; illus.; stat.; index. (looseleaf format; back issues avail.)
  Former titles: Defense and Economy World Report and Survey; Defense Business (ISSN 0364-9008); International Defense Business (ISSN 0360-8417); Government Business Worldwide (ISSN 0017-2588); Government Equipment Reports (ISSN 0017-2618)
  Description: Presents information on international and military-economic affairs, with emphasis on defense plans and requirements, force changes, procurement, arms transfer, defense budget and industry.

DEFENSE & FOREIGN AFFAIRS; the international journal of national management and national security management. see *POLITICAL SCIENCE*

355 327   US
DEFENSE AND FOREIGN AFFAIRS STRATEGIC POLICY. m. International Media Corp., 110 N. Royal St., Ste. 307, VA 22314. TEL 703-684-8455. FAX 703-684-2207. **Indexed:** Air Un.Lib.Ind.
  ●Also available online. Vendor(s): Mead Data Central.

623 355   US
DEFENSE AND FOREIGN AFFAIRS WEEKLY; the weekly report on the Middle East, Africa, Asia, the Pacific and Latin America. 1976. w. $486. International Media Corporation, 110 N. Royal St., Ste. 307, Alexandria, VA 22314. TEL 703-684-8455. FAX 703-684-2207. Ed. Gregory R. Copley. adv.; circ. 1,000. **Indexed:** DM & T, PROMT.
  ●Also available online. Vendor(s): Mead Data Central.
  Incorporates (in 1982): Canadian Strategic Report; Former titles: Strategy Week; Strategic Report on Middle Eastern Affairs; Incorporates (as of 1980): Strategic Latin American Affairs; Strategic Asian Affairs. Strategic Mid-East and Africa.

DEFENSE DAILY. see *AERONAUTICS AND SPACE FLIGHT*

DEFENSE DES GRADES DE LA POLICE NATIONALE. see *LABOR UNIONS*

355   FR
DEFENSE ET ARMEMENT - HERACLES INTERNATIONAL. (Text in Arabic, English, French) 6/yr. 240 F. (foreign 300 F.). Editions Lariviere, 15-17 Quai de l'Oise, 75166 Paris Cedex 19, France. TEL 1-40-34-22-07. FAX 1-40-35-84-41. TELEX 211 678 F. Ed. Stephane Ferrard. adv.

355 327   US   ISSN 0160-5836
UA10
DEFENSE FOREIGN AFFAIRS HANDBOOK; political, economic & defense data on every country in the world. 1976. a. $192. International Media Corporation, 110 N. Royal St., Ste. 307, Alexandria, VA 22314. TEL 703-684-8455. FAX 703-684-2207. Ed. Gregory Copley. adv.; circ. 4,000. (back issues avail.)

355 352.7   US   ISSN 1047-6504
DEFENSE HOUSING. 1986. bi-m. $15. (Professional Housing Management Association) Stratton Publishing and Marketing Inc., 2800 Shirlington Rd., Ste. 706, Arlington, VA 22206. TEL 703-250-3218. FAX 703-379-4561. Ed. Sharon Bonar. adv.; circ. 3,000.
  Description: For military and civilian managers of on- and off-base military housing.

355   AT
DEFENSE INDUSTRY. fortn. Aus.$295. Co-operative Consulting, P.O. Box 250, Mawson, A.C.T. 2607, Australia. Ed. Treyor Thomas.

355 380.1   US
DEFENSE INDUSTRY SERVICE. base vol. (plus updates every 90 days). $700. Carroll Publishing Company, 1058 Thomas Jefferson St., N.W., Washington, DC 20007. TEL 202-333-8620. FAX 202-337-7020. (looseleaf format)
  Formerly: Defense Organization Service - Industry.
  Description: Organization charts for 120 of the major aerospace, electronics, and military Department of Defense contractors.

355   US
▼**DEFENSE MANUFACTURERS & SUPPLIERS ASSOCIATION OF AMERICA NEWSLETTER**; providing service and support to the defense community. 1991. m. $47. D M S A Corporation, 1000 Shelard Pky., Ste. 200, Saint Louis Park, MN 55426-4918. TEL 612-595-0244. bk.rev.; circ. 6,253.

355 658   US   ISSN 1044-3975
DEFENSE MARKETING INTERNATIONAL. 1989. fortn. $595 (effective 1992). Phillips Publishing, Inc., Defense - Aviation Group, 1925 N. Lynn St., Ste. 1000, Arlington, VA 22209. TEL 703-522-8333. FAX 703-522-6448.
  ●Also available online. Vendor(s): Data-Star, DIALOG, NewsNet.
  Incorporates: Pac-Rim Defense Marketing (ISSN 1051-2497)

355   US   ISSN 0893-0619
DEFENSE MEDIA REVIEW; a survey of the National Security Press with analysis and commentary. 1987. m. $48 (foreign $68). Boston University, Center for Defense Journalism, 640 Commonwealth Ave., Boston, MA 02215. TEL 617-353-6186. FAX 617-353-8707. Ed. H. Joachim Maitre. circ. 600.
  Description: Tracks media coverage of defense issues and policies.

355   US   ISSN 0195-6450
UA23.A1
DEFENSE MONITOR. 1972. 10/yr. $25. Center for Defense Information, 1500 Massachusetts Ave., N.W., Washington, DC 20005. FAX 202-862-0708. TELEX 904059 WSH (CDI). illus.; circ. 50,000. (reprint service avail.) **Indexed:** Air Un.Lib.Ind., DM & T, HR Rep.
—BLDSC shelfmark: 3546.225500.

355   FR   ISSN 0336-1489
D410
DEFENSE NATIONALE; problemes politiques, economiques, scientifiques, militaires. 1939. m. 390 F. (foreign 590 F.). Comite d'Etudes de Defense Nationale, c/o Dir.Gen. M. Paul-Marie de La Gorce, 1, place Joffre, 75700 Paris, France. TEL 45-55-31-92. FAX 45-55-31-89. Ed. J. Hugon. adv.: B&W page 5000 F., color page 8650 F.; trim 195 x 116; adv. contact: Gerard de la Rochere. bk.rev.; bibl.; circ. 9,000. (back issues avail.) **Indexed:** Abstr.Mil.Bibl., Amer.Hist.& Life, Hist.Abstr., INIS Atomind., P.A.I.S.For.Lang.Ind., PROMT.
—BLDSC shelfmark: 3546.226500.
  Formerly (until 1973): Revue de Defense Nationale (ISSN 0035-1075)
  Description: Discusses political, economical, scientific and military problems.

355   US   ISSN 0884-139X
DEFENSE NEWS. 1986. w. $89 (Canada $130; elsewhere $155). Army Times Publishing Co., 6883 Commercial Dr., Springfield, VA 22159. TEL 703-750-2000. Ed. Sharon Denny. adv.; charts; stat.; circ. 36,000. (tabloid format; also avail. in microform; reprint service avail. from UMI)
—BLDSC shelfmark: 3546.227000.

355   JA
DEFENSE OF JAPAN; the white paper on defense. 1989. a. 5150 Yen. (Defense Agency) Japan Times Ltd., 4-5-4 Shibaura, Minato-ku, Tokyo 108, Japan. TEL 03-3453-2013. FAX 03-3453-8023.
  Description: Gives a full account of Japan's defense policy and the current state of the Japanese "self-defense" forces. Includes reference material and statistical data related to Japan's defense.

355 350   US
DEFENSE ORGANIZATION SERVICE. base vol. (plus updates every 6 w.). $925. Carroll Publishing Company, 1058 Thomas Jefferson St., N.W., Washington, DC 20007. TEL 202-333-8620. FAX 202-337-7020. (looseleaf format)
  Formerly: Federal Organization Service - Military.
  Description: Organization charts covering key officials in more than 1,600 military departments and offices.

MILITARY

355   US
DEFENSE PROGRAMS SERVICE. 1989. base vol. (plus irreg. updates). $850. Carroll Publishing Company, 1058 Thomas Jefferson St., N.W., Washington, DC 20007. TEL 202-333-8620. FAX 202-337-7020. (looseleaf format)
    Incorporates (in 1990): Defense Programs Service - R D T and E (Research, Development, Test and Evaluation) & Defense Program Service - Procurement.
    Description: Details information about nearly 900 key programs in the procurement and research, development, test, and evaluation stages of the United States defense budget.

355   US   ISSN 0099-166X
UA10
DEFENSE REFERENCE REPORTS. 1974. m. $250. Government Business Worldwide Reports, Box 5997, Washington, DC 20016. TEL 202-244-7050. Ed. J.H. Wagner. charts; stat.
    Description: Information on defense establishments and armed forces around the world, military activities, and armament and procurement.

355 330   US   ISSN 1047-353X
DEFENSE TECHNOLOGY BUSINESS. 1989. fortn. $495 (effective 1992). Phillips Publishing, Inc., Defense - Aviation Group, 1925 N. Lynn St., Ste. 1000, Arlington, VA 22209. TEL 703-522-8333. FAX 703-522-6448.
●Also available online. Vendor(s): Data-Star, DIALOG, NewsNet.

355   IS   ISSN 0931-7317
DEFENSE UPDATE; international. Hebrew edition: Romach (ISSN 0334-8466) (Text in English) 1978. m. $42. Eshel-Drahmit Publishing, P.O.B. 115, Hod Hasharon, Israel. TEL 052-31357. FAX 972-3-285456. TELEX 35770-COIN-IL. (U.S. adress: 4350 DiPaulo Center-Dearlove Road, Glenview, IL 60025) Ed. Tamir Eshel. adv.; bk.rev.; index; circ. 50,000. **Indexed:** Air Un.Lib.Ind.
—BLDSC shelfmark: 3546.210380.
    Formerly: Born in Battle.

355   US   ISSN 0273-3188
DEFENSE WEEK. 1980. w. $897. King Publishing Group, Inc., 627 National Press Bldg., Washington, DC 20045. TEL 202-638-4260. FAX 202-662-9744. Ed. David J. Lynch. bk.rev.
●Also available online.
—BLDSC shelfmark: 3546.255000.

355   DK   ISSN 0109-5757
DENMARK. FORSVARSMINISTERIET. AARLIGE REDEGOERELSE. 1982. a. free. Forsvarsministeriet - Ministry of Defense, Slotsholmsgade 10, 1216 Copenhagen K, Denmark. TELEX DK-33-32-06-55. illus.; circ. 6,000.
    Formerly: Denmark. Forsvarsministeriet. Forsvarsministerens Aarlige Redegoerelse (ISSN 0108-7193)

DENTAL CORPS INTERNATIONAL. see *MEDICAL SCIENCES — Dentistry*

355   US
DESERT AIRMAN. 1942. w. $12 free to qualified miltary personnel. Territorial Newspapers, Box 35250, Tucson, AZ 85740. TEL 602-297-1107. Ed. Sgt. Cindy Beam. adv.; circ. 11,500. (tabloid format)

355   AT   ISSN 0046-0079
DESPATCH. 1966. bi-m. Aus.$30. New South Wales Military Historical Society, c/o Hon.Secr., Mrs. M. Taplin, 397 Willarong Rd., Caringbah, N.S.W. 2229, Australia. Ed. R. Sutton. adv.; bk.rev.; circ. 200.

355 364   US   ISSN 0744-2955
DETECTIVE (FALLS CHURCH); the journal of Army criminal investigation. 1969. s-a. $5 (foreign $6.25). U.S. Army Criminal Investigation Command (USACIDC), 5611 Columbia Pike, Falls Church, VA 22041-5015. FAX 703-756-1027. TELEX 703-756-1430. (Orders to: Supt. of Documents, Washington, DC 20402) Ed. Alice J. Russell. bk.rev.; circ. 3,200.

355   GW   ISSN 0417-3635
DEUTSCHES SOLDATENJAHRBUCH. 1953. a. Schild-Verlag GmbH, Federseestr. 1, 8000 Munich 60, Germany. TEL 089-8641189. Ed. Helmut Damerau. adv.; bk.rev.; bibl.; charts; illus.; stat.; circ. 7,000 (controlled).

DEUTSCHLAND-MAGAZIN. see *POLITICAL SCIENCE*

623.8   UK   ISSN 0046-0184
DEVONPORT NEWS; H.M. Naval Base newspaper. 1969. m. 60p. Ministry of Defence, Dockyard Department, Rm. 211, Carpenter House, Broad Quay, Bath, Avon BA1 5AB, England. Ed. Mrs. G.J. Harraway. adv.; bk.rev.; charts; illus.; circ. 3,500. (tabloid format)

355   IT   ISSN 1120-1657
DIFESA OGGI. 1977. 9/yr. $87. Publi & Consult S.P.A., Via Tagliamento 29, 00198 Rome, Italy. TEL 06-8543603. FAX 06-8440697. TELEX 622368. Ed. Paolo F. Bancale. adv.; illus.; circ. 17,400.

DIPLOMATIST; the review of the diplomatic and consular world. see *POLITICAL SCIENCE — International Relations*

355.115   US
DIRECTORY OF VETERANS ORGANIZATIONS. 1984. a. U.S. Veterans Administration, Office of the Administrator, 810 Vermont Ave., N.W., Rm. 1018, Washington, DC 20420.

DIR'U AL-ISLAM. see *RELIGIONS AND THEOLOGY — Islamic*

355   TS
DIR'U AL-WATAN. 1971. m. General Command for the Armed Forces, Public Relations Administration, P.O. Box 4224, Abu Dhabi, United Arab Emirates. TEL 447999. circ. 1,000.
    Description: Covers military issues.

327.174   UN   ISSN 0251-9518
JX1974
DISARMAMENT; a periodic review by the United Nations. Arabic edition: Naz' al-silah (ISSN 0251-950X); Chinese edition: Caijun (ISSN 0251-9496); French edition: Desarmement (ISSN 0251-9542); Russian edition: Razoruzhenie (ISSN 0251-9526); Spanish edition: Desarme (ISSN 0251-9534) 1978. irreg. (2-3/yr.) latest vol.13, no.3. $15 per no. United Nations Publications, Subscription Office, Box 361, Birmingham, AL 35201-0361. bibl.; charts. **Indexed:** Amer.Bibl.Slavic & E.Eur.Stud; P.A.I.S.

327.174   FI
DISARMAMENT FORUM. (Text in English, French, German, Spanish) 1982. bi-m. World Peace Council, Loennrotinkatu 25A-6K, 00180 Helsinki 18, Finland. FAX 0-6933703. bk.rev. (tabloid format; back issues avail.)

355 327   CN   ISSN 0711-3765
DISMANTLER. (Text in English) 1979. q. Can.$10. Operation Dismantle, Inc., P.O. Box 3887, Station C, Ottawa, Ont. K1Y 4M5, Canada. TEL 613-722-6001. Ed. T. James Stark. adv.; bk.rev.; circ. 10,000.

355.31 320   AE
AL-DJEICH; revue de l'Armee Nationale Populare. (Text in Arabic, French) 1963. m. Office de l'Armee Nationale Populaire, 3 Chemin de Gascogne, Algiers, Algeria. film rev.; illus.; circ. 10,000.

355   US
EAGLE (NEW YORK). 1981. bi-m. $3.95 per no. Command Publications, Inc., 1115 Broadway, New York, NY 10010. Ed. Harry Kane. adv.; bk.rev.; circ. 75,000.
    Formerly: Eagle: For the American Fighting Man.

355   GW
EICHENBLATT. 1954. q. Kameradschaftsbund Erste Panzerdivision, Ludwigsteinstr. 63, D-3430 Witzenhausen 6, Germany. TEL 05542-3028. circ. 850.

355   SP   ISSN 0013-2918
EJERCITO;* revista de las armas y servicios. 1940. m. 2835 ptas. Ministerio de Defensa, Estado Mayor del Ejercito, Servicio de Publicaciones, Alcala 18, p.4, 28014 Madrid, Spain. Ed. Juan Cano Hevia. adv.; bk.rev.; bibl.; charts; illus.; index; circ. 180,000. **Indexed:** Amer.Hist.& Life, Hist.Abstr.

355   CU
EJERCITO. w. Ministerio de las Fuerzas Armadas Revolucionarias, Calzada de Managua No. 1829, Claverio, Havana, Cuba.

355   US   ISSN 0884-4828
ELECTRONIC WARFARE DIGEST. 1977. m. $195. Washington National News Reports Inc., 3918 Prosperity Ave., Ste. 318, Fairfax, VA 22031-3334. TEL 703-573-1600. FAX 703-573-1604. Ed. David Sheehan. (looseleaf format; back issues avail.)

355   CU
EN GUARDIA.* m. (Ministerio de las Fuerzas Armadas Revolucionarias, Ejercito Central) Ediciones Cubanas, Obispo 527, Apdo. 605, Havana, Cuba.

355   UK   ISSN 0013-8401
ENGLISH WESTERNERS' BRAND BOOK. 1954. s-a. £9.75($15) English Westerners' Society, 90 Babbacombe Rd., Bromley, Kent, England. Ed. Francis B. Taunton. bk.rev.; bibl.; cum.index; circ. 350.

355   UK   ISSN 0013-841X
ENGLISH WESTERNERS' TALLY SHEET. 1958. 3/yr. $15. English Westerners Society, 90 Babbacombe Road, Bromley, Kent, England. Ed. Francis B. Taunton. bk.rev.; bibl.; cum.index; circ. 300. **Indexed:** A.I.C.P.

355   CN
ENSIGN. (Text in English, French) 1959. fortn. free. Canadian Forces Base Cornwallis, CFB Cornwallis, Cornwallis, N.S. BOS 1H0, Canada. TEL 902-638-8536. Ed. Anne M. Wanstall. adv.; bk.rev.; circ. 800 (controlled). (tabloid format; back issues avail.)

355   GR
EPITHEORISIS ETHNIKIS AMYNIS/NATIONAL DEFENSE REVUE. q. $8. Hellenic Army General Staff, 10 Pittakou St., Athens, Greece.

355   GW   ISSN 0421-3750
ERKENNUNGSBLAETTER. 1957. fortn. DM.25.20. Umschau Verlag Breidenstein GmbH, Stuttgarter Str. 18-24, 6000 Frankfurt a.M. 1, Germany. TEL 069-2600-0. circ. 25,000. (back issues avail.)

355   CN
ESQUIMALT LOOKOUT. 1955. s-m. Can.$20 (foreign Can.$25). Canadian Forces Base (CFB), Esquimalt F M O, Victoria, B.C. VOS 1B0, Canada. TEL 604-385-0313. Ed. R.R. Godden. adv.; circ. 5,000.

355 327   US   ISSN 1043-1667
THE ESTIMATE; political and security intelligence analysis of North Africa, the Middle East, South Asia, East Asia, & the Pacific. 1989. fortn. $295 (foreign $330). The International Estimate, Inc., 1514 17th St., N.W., No. 115, Washington, DC 20036. TEL 202-332-0849. Eds. Julia A. Ackerman, Michael C. Dunn. bk.rev.; index; circ. 100. (back issues avail.)
    Description: Political and security intelligence and risk analysis.

355   GW
EUROPAEISCHE SICHERHEIT. 1951. m. DM.86.80. (Clausewitz-Gesellschaft Arbeitskreis fuer Wehrforschung, Gesellschaft fuer Wehr- und Sicherheitspolitik e.V.) E.S. Mittler und Sohn GmbH, Postfach 2352, 4900 Herford, Germany. Ed. Wolfram von Raven. illus.; circ. 8,500.
    Former titles: Europaeische Wehrkunde - Wehrwissenschaftliche Rundschau (ISSN 0723-9432) & Wehrwissenschaftliche Rundschau.

355   GW
EUROPAEISCHE SICHERHEIT. AUSGABE "A"; Kampftruppen. 1959. m. DM.112.80. (Arbeitskreis der Kampftruppen) Verlag E.S. Mittler und Sohn GmbH, Postfach 2352, 4900 Herford, Germany. Ed. Egbert Thomer. adv.; bk.rev.; abstr.; bibl.; illus.; index; circ. 1,500.
    Former titles: Europaeische Wehrkunde. Ausgabe "A; Kampftruppen (ISSN 0022-8257)

355   GW
EUROPAEISCHE WEHRKUNDE. 1952. m. DM.45. (Gesellschaft fuer Wehrkunde e.V.) Verlag Europaeische Wehrkunde GmbH, Herzog-Rudolf-Str. 1, 8000 Munich 22, Germany. Ed. Ewald von Kleist. adv.; bk.rev.; circ. 11,000.
    Formerly: Wehrkunde.

MILITARY

355   US
▼**EVANS & NOVAK DEFENSE LETTER**. 1991. fortn. $175 (effective 1992). Phillips Publishing, Inc., Defense - Aviation Group, 1925 N. Lynn St., Ste. 1000, Arlington, VA 22209. TEL 703-522-8333. FAX 703-522-6448.

355.15   US   ISSN 0014-388X
D769.A15
EX - C B I ROUNDUP. (China - Burma - India Veterans Association) 1946. m. (except Aug.-Sep.). $12. Dwight O. King, Ed. & Pub., Box 2665, La Habra, CA 90631. TEL 310-947-2007. adv.; bk.rev.; circ. 6,185.

355   US   ISSN 0161-7451
EX - P O W BULLETIN. 1949. m. $13. American Ex-Prisoners of War, c/o Clydie J. Morgan, 3201 E. Pioneer Pkwy., Ste. 40, Arlington, TX 76010. TEL 817-649-2979. Ed. Susan Langseth. adv.; bk.rev.; circ. 23,000. (back issues avail.)

355   US   ISSN 0014-4452
EXCHANGE & COMMISSARY NEWS. 1962. m. $40. Executive Business Media, Inc., Box 1500, 825 Old Country Rd., Westbury, NY 11590. TEL 516-334-3030. Ed. Robert Moran. adv.; circ. 10,200. (tabloid format)

355   BL
EXPEDICIONARIO. m. (Associacao Nacional dos Veteranos da FEB) Editora Expedicionario, Rua Leandro Martins, 20, Grupos 504, 505, 506, Rio de Janeiro CEP 20080, Brazil. (Co-sponsor: Associacao dos Ex-Combatentes do Brazil)

355   SW   ISSN 0005-7797
F B U - BEFAEL. (Frivilliga Befaelsutbildningsroerelsen) 1917. 6/yr. SEK 30. Centralfoerbundet Foer Befaelsutbildning, P.O. Box 5034, 102 41 Stockholm, Sweden. Ed. Bertil Flodin. adv.; bk.rev.; circ. 37,000.
    Formerly: Befael.

355   SW   ISSN 0014-6013
F O A ORIENTERAR OM. 1964. irreg. Foersvarets Forskningsanstalt - Swedish Defense Research Establishment, S-172 90 Sundbyberg, Sweden. (Subscr. to: FOA Info, S-17290 Sundberg, Sweden) charts; illus.

F X O REPORT. see *ENGINEERING — Electrical Engineering*

F-5 TECHNICAL DIGEST. see *AERONAUTICS AND SPACE FLIGHT*

DIE FACKEL. see *SOCIAL SERVICES AND WELFARE*

355   UK   ISSN 0956-2400
FALLING LEAF. 1958. q. £8($15) Psywar Society, c/o R. Oakland, 21 Metchley Lane, Harborne, Birmingham B17 0HT, England. Ed. R.G. Auckland. adv.; bk.rev.; illus.; circ. 150.
    Description: Primarily concerns the dissemination and effects of aerial propaganda leaflets in wars and conflicts.

355   US
FAMILY (NEW YORK); the magazine for military wives. 1973. m. free. Military Family Communications, 169 Lexington Ave., New York, NY 10016-7305. TEL 212-545-9740. Ed. Barbara Ehlrich. adv.; illus.; circ. 500,000.
    Formerly: Stateside Family.

614.8 623.8   US   ISSN 0014-8822
V383
FATHOM; surface ship and submarine safety review. 1969. bi-m. $9 (foreign $11.25). U.S. Naval Safety Center, Naval Air Station, Norfolk, Norfolk, VA 23511. TEL 804-444-6970. FAX 804-444-7205. (Subscriptions to: Supt. of Documents, Washington, DC 20402) Ed. Thomas Parham. charts; illus.; circ. 22,000. **Indexed**: Abstr.Mil.Bibl., BMT, Ind.U.S.Gov.Per., Mid.East: Abstr.& Ind.

355.11 368.4   US
FEDERAL BENEFITS FOR VETERANS AND DEPENDENTS, IS-1 FACT SHEET. 1961. a. $2.25. U.S. Department of Veterans Affairs, 810 Vermont Ave., N.W., Washington, DC 20420. (Orders to: Supt. of Documents, Washington, DC 20402)
    Formerly: U.S. Veterans Administration. V A Fact Sheets (ISSN 0083-3576)

623.73   FR   ISSN 0024-1709
TK5101.A1
FEDERATION NATIONALE DES ANCIENS COMBATTANTS ET COALETS DES TRANSMISSIONS. LIAISON DES TRANSMISSIONS. 1946. bi-m. 35 F. Federation Nationale des Anciens Combattants et Coalets des Transmissions, 60 Quai Michelet, Levallois 92, France. Ed. Colonel Lorant.
    —BLDSC shelfmark: 5186.240000.
    Formerly: Revue des Transmissions.

355   SZ   ISSN 0014-9780
FELDWEBEL/SERGENT-MAJOR/SERGENTE MAGGIORE. (Text in French and German) vol.12, 1970. m. 45 SFr. (Schweizerischer Feldwebelverband) Huber und Co. AG, Promenadenstr. 16, CH-8501 Frauenfeld, Switzerland. TEL 054-271111. Ed. P. Roethlin. adv.; charts; illus.
    Description: Covers association news and information, training, technical information. Includes reports and calendar of events.

355   US   ISSN 0899-2525
UF1
FIELD ARTILLERY; the journal of fire support. 1911. bi-m. $16. U.S. Army Field Artillery School, Box 33311, Fort Sill, OK 73503. TEL 405-351-5121. FAX 405-351-6205. Ed. Major Colin K Dunn. bk.rev.; illus.; circ. 15,000. (also avail. in microform from UMI; reprint service avail. from UMI) **Indexed**: Abstr.Mil.Bibl., Air Un.Lib.Ind., Amer.Bibl.Slavic & E.Eur.Stud, Amer.Hist.& Life, DM & T, Hist.Abstr., Mid.East: Abstr.& Ind., PROMT.
    —BLDSC shelfmark: 3919.340000.
    Formerly: Field Artillery Journal (ISSN 0191-975X); Supersedes (in 1953): Army (ISSN 0004-2455)

FISSION CHIPS. see *ENERGY*

359   SW   ISSN 0015-4431
FLOTTANS MAEN. 1935. q. SEK 26. Foereningen Flottans Maen, Teatergatan 3, 111 48 Stockholm, Sweden. Eds. Christer Hammarberg, Emanuel Fornander. adv.; bk.rev.; illus.; circ. 3,000. **Indexed**: Abstr.Mil.Bibl.

FLYING M. see *AERONAUTICS AND SPACE FLIGHT*

FLYING SAFETY. see *AERONAUTICS AND SPACE FLIGHT*

355   SW   ISSN 0015-5225
FOERBUNDET SVENSKA FINLANDSFRIVILLIGA. TIDNING. 1940. q. SEK 60($8) Foerbundet Svenska Finlandsfrivilliga - Association of Swedish Volunteers in the Finnish Wars, PO Box 4043, 181 04 Lidingoe, Sweden. Ed. Mascoll Silfverstolpe. adv.; bk.rev.; circ. 2,000. (processed)

355   SW   ISSN 0046-4643
FOERSVAR I NUTID. 1965. bi-m. SEK 140. Centralfoerbundet Folk och Foersvar, Sibyllegatan 9, S-114 42 Stockholm, Sweden. Ed.Bd. bk.rev.; charts; illus.; stat.; circ. 1,200.

355   US   ISSN 0738-4203
FOR YOUR EYES ONLY; an open intelligence summary of current military affairs. Short title: F.Y.E.O. 1980. fortn. $60 in U.S. and Canada (typically set in Oct.). Tiger Publications, Box 8759, Amarillo, TX 79114-8759. TEL 806-655-2009. Ed. Stephen V. Cole. bk.rev.; charts; illus.; stat.; circ. 1,000. (back issues avail.)
    ●Also available online. Vendor(s): NewsNet.

355   UK
FORCES WEEKLY ECHO. 1980. w. £55. Combined Service Publications, P.O. Box 4, Farnborough, Hants GU14 7LR, England. TEL 0252-515891. FAX 0252-517918. Ed. D.D. Crossley. adv.; circ. 25,000. (tabloid format)

FOREIGN INTELLIGENCE LITERARY SCENE. see *LITERATURE*

355   NO   ISSN 0332-9062
FORSVARETS FORUM. 1945. fortn. (25/yr.). NOK 50($10) Forsvarets Rekrutterings- og Opplysningstjeneste, Oslo MIL-Akershus, Oslo 1, Norway. Ed. Rolv Hoeiland. adv.; bk.rev.; illus.; circ. 90,000. (tabloid format)
    Supersedes: Mannskapsavisa (ISSN 0025-2352); Militaer Orienterung.

355 900   UK   ISSN 0261-586X
FORT; the international journal of fortification and military architecture. 1976. a. $34. Fortress Study Group, c/o D.W. Quarmby, Blackwater Forge House, Blackwater, Newport, Isle of Wight PO30 3BJ, England. TEL 0983-526207. bk.rev.; circ. 570. (also avail. in microfiche) **Indexed**: Avery Ind.Archit.Per., Br.Archaeol.Abstr., RILA.
    —BLDSC shelfmark: 4014.820000.

FORT CONCHO MEMBERS DISPATCH. see *MUSEUMS AND ART GALLERIES*

355 974   US   ISSN 0015-8070
E199
FORT TICONDEROGA MUSEUM. BULLETIN. 1927. s-a. $7 per no.(effective 1989). Fort Ticonderoga Association Inc., Fort Ticonderoga Museum, Ticonderoga, NY 12883. TEL 518-585-2821. FAX 518-585-2210. Ed.Bd. bk.rev.; illus.; index; circ. 750. **Indexed**: Amer.Hist.& Life, Hist.Abstr.
    Description: Covers military history from 1609 to 1781.

359.96   US   ISSN 0362-9910
VE23.A1
FORTITUDINE; newsletter of the Marine Corps historical program. 1970. 4/yr. free. U.S. Marine Corps, History and Museums Division, Director of Marine Corps History and Museums, Headquarters, Washington, DC 20380. TEL 202-433-3840. Ed. V. Keith Fleming, Jr. bibl.; charts; illus.; circ. 18,000. **Indexed**: Ind.U.S.Gov.Per.
    Formerly: Harumfrodite.

FORTRESS. see *ARCHITECTURE*

355   CN   ISSN 0843-5995
FORUM. 1985. q. $72 (foreign $80). Synergistic Enterprises, 132 Adrian Cres., Markham, Ont. L3P 7B3, Canada. TEL 416-472-2801. FAX 416-472-3091. Ed. Peter A. Kitchen. adv.; circ. 12,000. (back issues avail.)
    Description: Independent publication whose mandate is to write about issues and events concerning Canada's defense community.

355   BE   ISSN 0015-8488
FORUM DE LA FORCE TERRESTRE. Dutch edition: Forum Landmacht. (Text in French) 1970. bi-m. 250 BEF. Forum A.S.B.L., Rue d'Evere Quartier Reine Elisabeth, 1140 Brussels, Belgium. FAX 3222433550. Ed. Jacobs Marcel. adv.; bk.rev.; charts; illus.; circ. 20,000.

355   SZ   ISSN 0015-914X
FOURIER. 1928. m. 28 SFr.($23) (Schweizerischer Fourierverband) Buchdruckerei Robert Mueller AG, Postfach 2840, CH-6002 Luzern, Switzerland. FAX 041-237122. Ed. Schuler Meinrad. adv.; bk.rev.; circ. 10,736.

355   FR   ISSN 0015-9719
FRANCE. MINISTERE DE LA DEFENSE NATIONALE. BULLETIN D'INFORMATION TECHNIQUE ET SCIENTIFIQUE. 12/yr. 220 F. (foreign 240 F.). Ministere de la Defense Nationale, 14 rue Saint Dominique, 75007 Paris, France.

355   FR   ISSN 0015-9727
FRANCE. MINISTERE DE LA DEFENSE NATIONALE. BULLETIN OFFICIEL. 1947. w. Ministere de la Defense Nationale, 14 rue Saint Dominique, 75007 Paris, France.

351.06   FR
FRANCE. MINISTERE DES ARMEES. BULLETIN OFFICIEL DES ARMEES. (Supplement to: Armee Francaise. Journal Officiel) w. 3673 F. Editions Charles Lavauzelle, Le Prouet, B.P. 8, 87350 Panazol, France. FAX 55-30-66-67. TELEX 580995 F.

355   GW   ISSN 0016-092X
DER FREIWILLIGE. 1955. m. DM.54. (Bundesverband der Soldaten der ehemaligen Waffen-SS e.V.) Munin-Verlag Gmbh, Postfach 3023, 4500 Osnabrueck, Germany. adv.; bk.rev.; circ. 9,000.

355   FR   ISSN 0016-1144
FRERES D'ARMES; organe de Liaison des Forces Armees Francaises, Africaines et Malgaches. 1963. bi-m. 75 F. (foreign 120 F.). Association pour le Developpement et la Diffusion de l'Information Militaire, 6, rue Saint-Charles, 75015 Paris, France. TEL 45-77-03-76. bk.rev.; bibl.; illus.; circ. 7,000.

MILITARY 3459

FRIEDENSFORSCHUNG AKTUELL. see *POLITICAL SCIENCE*

355 973 US ISSN 0071-9641
FRONTIER MILITARY SERIES. 1951. irreg. price varies. Arthur H. Clark Co., Box 230, Glendale, CA 91209-0230. index.

358.4 CL ISSN 0716-4866
FUERZA AEREA. 1941. q. $60. Editorial Fuerza Aerea, Av. B. O'Higgins 1316 of 63, Santiago, Chile. adv.; circ. 15,000.
Formerly: Revista de la Fuerza Aerea.

G M V. (Government and Military Video) see *COMMUNICATIONS — Video*

DAS GELTENDE SEEVOELKERRECHT IN EINZELDARSTELLUNGEN. see *LAW — International Law*

355 CN ISSN 0707-0403
GENERAL SAFETY DIGEST/DIGEST DE SECURITE GENERALE. (Text in English, French) 1973. 6/yr. Can.$11($13.40) Department of National Defence, Directorate of General Safety, National Defense Headquarters, Major - General George Pearkes Bldg., 101 Colonel By Drive, Ottawa, Ont. K1A 0K2, Canada. (Dist. by: Canada Communication Group, Publishing Division, Ottawa, Ont. K1A 0S9, Canada) Ed. Andy Seguin. illus.; circ. 13,000.

GEORGE C. MARSHALL FOUNDATION. TOPICS. see *HISTORY — History Of North And South America*

355 IT
GIORNALE DEI MILITARI. 1952. w. L.8500. Giormil s.r.l., Piazza Manfredo Fanti 10, 00185 Rome, Italy. adv.; circ. 60,000.

GLADIUS; etudes sur les armes anciennes, l'armement, l'art militaire et la vie culturelle en Orient et Occident. see *ANTIQUES*

359.96 UK ISSN 0017-1204
GLOBE AND LAUREL. 1892. 6/yr. £7.20. Royal Marines, HMS Nelson (WI), Whale Island, Portsmouth, Hants PO2 8ER, England. TEL 0705-651305. FAX 0705-822351. Ed. Captain A.G. Newing. adv.; bk.rev.; charts; illus.; index; circ. 12,000.

369.11 US
GOPHER OVERSEA'R. 1929. 6/yr. $2 to non-members. Veterans of Foreign Wars of the United States, Department of Minnesota, Veterans Service Bldg., St. Paul, MN 55155. TEL 612-291-1757. FAX 612-291-2753. Ed. Jim Hesselgrave. adv.; bk.rev.; circ. 85,000 (controlled). (tabloid format; back issues avail.)

GOVERNMENT BUSINESS WORLDWIDE REPORT. see *BUSINESS AND ECONOMICS — International Commerce*

GOVERNMENT LIFE INSURANCE PROGRAMS FOR VETERANS AND MEMBERS OF THE SERVICES. ANNUAL REPORT. see *INSURANCE*

355.115 FR
GRAND INVALIDE. 1924. bi-m. 140 F. Federation Nationale des Plus Grands Invalides de Guerre, 13 av. de La Motte-Picquet, 75007 Paris, France. Ed. Jean-Claude Gouellain. adv.; circ. 5,000.

355.347 UK
GREAT BRITAIN. ROYAL ARMY CHAPLAINS' DEPARTMENT. JOURNAL. 1922. 2/yr. £5. Ministry of Defense (Army), Royal Army Chaplains' Department Centre, Bagshot Park, Bagshot, Surrey GU19 5PL, England. adv.; bk.rev.; circ. 800.
Formerly: Royal Army Chaplains Department. Quarterly Journal (ISSN 0035-8657)

359 US ISSN 0891-124X
GRENADE. 1979. bi-m. $2 per no. Scipio Society of Naval and Military History, Inc., 15 Ridge Rd., Cold Spring Harbor, New York, NY 11724. Ed. Robert S. Robe, Jr. bk.rev.; circ. 53. (back issues avail.)

355 UK ISSN 0017-503X
GUARDS MAGAZINE. 1862. q. £12. B P C C Paulton Books Ltd., H Q Household Division, Horse Guards, Whitehall, London SW1A 2AX, England. Ed. Maj. H.W. Schofield. adv.; bk.rev.; illus.; circ. 4,000.
Formerly: Household Brigade Magazine.

GUIDE TO GOVERNMENT-LOAN FILMS. see *MOTION PICTURES*

355 SP ISSN 0017-5455
GUION; * revista ilustrada de los mandos subalternos. 1942. m. 1500 ptas. Ministerio de Defensa, Estado Mayor del Ejercito, Servicio de Publicaciones, Alcala 18, p.4, 28014 Madrid, Spain. Ed. Enrique Jarnes Bergua. adv.; circ. 168,000. **Indexed:** Amer.Hist.& Life, Hist.Abstr.

355 330 US ISSN 1055-744X
▼**GULF RECONSTRUCTION REPORT.** 1991. fortn. $396 (foreign $426). Pasha Publications Inc., 1401 Wilson Blvd., Ste. 900, Arlington, VA 22209-9970. TEL 703-528-1244. FAX 703-528-1253. Ed. David Gump.
Description: Covers the campaign to rebuild Kuwait and Iraq, presenting information on new contract requests from Kuwaiti agencies, the U.S. Army Corps of Engineers, and private companies seeking subcontracts for work assigned; also follows developments in the private sector and in privatized agencies.

H B S A NEWSLETTER. (Historical Breechloading Smallarms Association) see *ANTIQUES*

H V W P IN ACTION. (Hospitalized Veterans Writing Project, Inc.) see *LITERATURE*

355 HU ISSN 0017-6540
DB925.5
HADTORTENELMI KOZLEMENYEK. 1954. q. $24.50. Kultura, P.O. Box 149, 1389 Budapest 62, Hungary. **Indexed:** Amer.Hist.& Life, Hist.Abstr.

623 FI ISSN 0017-6796
HAKKU; Pioneerien lehti. 1923. q. FIM 50. Pioneeriaselajin Liitto r.y., PL 919, SF-00101 Helsinki 10, Finland. Ed. Kari Melleri. adv.; bk.rev.; charts; illus.; circ. 3,500.

355 US
HARRISON POST. 1965. w. 7962 Pendleton Park, Lawrence, KS 46226. TEL 317-542-8149. circ. 10,000.

HAUL DOWN AND EASE OFF. see *AERONAUTICS AND SPACE FLIGHT*

358.4 UK
HAWK; the independent journal of the Royal Air Force Staff College. a. Royal Air Force Staff College, Bracknell, Berkshire RG12 3DD, England. **Indexed:** Air Un.Lib.Ind.

HEADQUARTERS HELIOGRAM; military history - historic preservation. see *HISTORY — History Of North And South America*

355.31 GW ISSN 0342-3867
HEER. m. DM.56. A. Bernecker Verlag, Unter dem Schoeneberg 1, 3508 Melsungen, Germany. TEL 05661-731-0. FAX 05661-73189. adv.; bk.rev.; circ. 81,000.

355 NO ISSN 0017-985X
HEIMEVERNSBLADET. 1946. 8/yr. NOK 50 free to members of the Home Guard. (Norwegian Armed Forces) AS Naper, P.O. Box 53, 3771 Krageroe, Norway. TEL 008 25 91053. FAX 02-49-83-12. Ed. Lars Reiermark. bk.rev.; index; circ. 87,500.

HELICOPTER INTERNATIONAL MAGAZINE. see *AERONAUTICS AND SPACE FLIGHT*

363.35 SW ISSN 0018-0351
HEMVAERNET. 1940. 6/yr. SEK 125. Hemvaernets Centrala Foertroendenaemnd, P.O. Box 5345, 102 46 Stockholm, Sweden. FAX 08-667-6011. Ed. Stig Wallin. adv.; bk.rev.; illus.; circ. 130,000.

HIGH FLIGHT. see *AERONAUTICS AND SPACE FLIGHT*

623 US ISSN 0899-8531
HIGH RELIABILITY & MILITARY COMPONENTS GUIDE; microcircuits and semiconductors. (Subseries of : D.A.T.A. Digest Electronic Information Series) q. $184. D.A.T.A. Business Publishing (Subsidiary of: Information Handling Services), 15 Inverness Way E., Box 6510, Englewood, CO 80155-6510. TEL 800-447-4666. FAX 303-799-4082. TELEX 4322083 IHS UI.
Formerly: Military Electronic Devices Guide D.A.T.A. Book.

355 944 FR ISSN 0765-0531
HISTOIRE ET DEFENSE. * 1986. 2/yr. Universite de Montpellier III (Universite Paul Valery), Centre d'Histoire Militaire et d'Etudes de Defense Nationale, Montpellier, France. TEL 67-14-20-00.
Formerly (until 1986): Cahiers de Montpellier (ISSN 0298-7996)

HISTOIRE ET MAQUETTISME. see *HOBBIES*

HISTORIA MILITAR DEL PARAGUAY. see *HISTORY — History Of North And South America*

335 909 FR
HISTORICA. 6/yr. 470 F. Editions Heimdal, Chateau de Damigny, 14400 Bayeux, France.

355 UK ISSN 0305-0440
HISTORICAL BREECHLOADING SMALLARMS ASSOCIATION. JOURNAL. 1973. a. £5. Historical Breechloading Smallarms Association, c/o Imperial War Museum, Lambeth Road, London SE1 6HZ, England. Ed. J.B. Bell. bk.rev.; bibl.; charts; illus.; circ. 2,000.
—BLDSC shelfmark: 4758.350000.
Description: Gives a history of both military & civilian firearms & ammunition from 1800-1945.

355 900 CS ISSN 0018-2583
DB2070
HISTORIE A VOJENSTVI. (Text in Czech; summaries in English) 1953. bi-m. $26.40. (Ceskoslovenska Armada, Historicky Ustav) Vydavatelstvi Magnet-Press, s.p., Vladislavova 26, Prague 1, Czechoslovakia. (Subscr. to: Artia, Ve Smeckach 30, 111 27 Prague 1) **Indexed:** Amer.Hist.& Life, Hist.Abstr.

355 DK
HJEMMEVAERNSBLADET. 1945. m. (10/yr.). free. Generalstok, 2100 Kastellet OE, Denmark. Ed. Knud Damgaard. adv.; charts; illus.; circ. 97,000.

355 US
HOBBY BOOKWATCH; military, gun and hobby book review. 1986. m. $12.50. Box 52033, Tulsa, OK 74152. FAX 918-743-4616. Ed. Jack Britton. adv.; bk.rev.; circ. 9,000.

355.115 SA
HOME FRONT. (Text in English) m. R.10 (free to war veterans). (Memorable Order of Tin Hats) Home Front - M O T H, P.O. Box 2549, Durban 4000, South Africa. TEL 031-3054148. Ed. Reg Sweet. bibl.; illus.; stat. (back issues avail.)
Description: Contains articles and news relevant to war veterans.

355 CM ISSN 0046-7855
HONNEUR ET FIDELITE; bulletin de liaison des forces armees. 1953. 6/yr. free. Bureau Information Presse de Forces Armees de la Republique, B.P. 1191, Yaounde, Cameroon. Ed. Lt. Mpeck Marius. adv.; film rev.; charts; illus.; circ. 2,000.

355 UK ISSN 0046-7863
HONOURABLE ARTILLERY COMPANY JOURNAL. 1923. q. £1.00($5) membership. Honourable Artillery Company, Armoury House, London, EC1Y 2BQ, England. Ed. Capt. G.C. Lloyd. adv.; bk.rev.; circ. 2,800 (controlled).

355 US ISSN 0736-9220
THE HOOK. 1977. q. $25 (effective Jan. 1991). Tailhook Association, Box 40, Bonita, CA 91908-0040. TEL 619-689-9227. FAX 619-578-8839. Ed. Stephen T. Millikin. adv.; bk.rev.; circ. 16,300. (back issues avail.)
Description: Covers US Naval Carrier Aviation, past and present.

355.15 US ISSN 0018-4772
HOOSIER LEGIONNAIRE. 1926. bi-m. $3. American Legion, Department of Indiana, 777 N. Meridian St., Indianapolis, IN 46204. TEL 317-635-8411. FAX 317-237-9891. Ed. Tina Gilbert Siefert. adv.; bk.rev.; illus.; circ. 167,000. (tabloid format)
Description: Contains news, features and issues of interest to Indiana war time veterans and their families.

M

MILITARY

355 658   US   ISSN 0273-7485
I S. (Interservice) 1980. q. $20. American Logistics Association, 1133 15th St., N.W., Ste 600, Washington, DC 20005. TEL 202-466-2520. Ed. Paul Pierpoint. adv.; illus.; circ. 10,000. (back issues avail.) **Indexed:** Abstr.Mil.Bibl., Air Un.Lib.Ind.
    Supersedes (1921-1980): American Logistics Association Review (ISSN 0034-6322); Which was formerly: Quartermaster Review.

355   CU
I T C N. INFORMACION TECNICO CIENTIFICO NAVAL. 3/yr. Ministerio de las Fuerzas Armadas Revolucionarias, Ave. del Puerto No. 53, Habana Vieja, Havana, Cuba.

355.351   US
ILLINOIS GUARD CHRONICLE. 1985. 4/yr. membership. Illinois National Guard, Public Affairs Office, 1301 N. MacArthur Blvd., Springfield, IL 62702-2399. TEL 217-789-3569. FAX 217-785-3527. Ed. Capt. Brian E. DeLoche. circ. 16,000.
    Description: Informs Guard members on training and events.

IMPERIAL WAR MUSEUM REVIEW. see *MUSEUMS AND ART GALLERIES*

355   II   ISSN 0970-2512
INDIAN DEFENCE REVIEW. 1986. s-a. Rs.300($50) Lancer Publishers Pvt. Ltd., P.O. Box 3802, New Delhi 110 049, India. TEL 664933. FAX 6862077. Ed. Lt.Gen. Mathew Thomas. adv.; circ. 2,000.
    Description: Examines a wide range of military-related matters concerning the Indian sub-continent.

355   IO   ISSN 0303-4992
UA853.I5
INDONESIA. LEMBAGA PERTAHANAN NASIONAL. KETAHANAN NASIONAL. 1965. bi-m. Rps.3500. Lembaga Pertahanan Nasional, Jalan Kebon Sirih 26, Jakarta, Indonesia. adv.; circ. 10,000.

355   IO   ISSN 0216-3217
INDONESIA. LEMBAGA PERTAHANAN NASIONAL. NATIONAL RESILIENCE. q. Lembaga Pertahanan Nasional, Jalan Kebon Sirih 26, Jakarta, Indonesia.

356.1   PE   ISSN 0019-9524
INFANTERIA.* 1950. q. Ministerio de Guerra, Avda. Boulevar s-n, Lima, Peru.

356.1   US   ISSN 0019-9532
UD1
INFANTRY; a professional journal for the combined arms team. 1921. bi-m. $12 (typically set in Oct.). U.S. Army Infantry School, Box 2005, Fort Benning, GA 31905-0605. TEL 404-545-2350. Ed. Albert N. Garland. bk.rev.; circ. 16,000. (also avail. in microform from UMI; reprint service avail. from UMI) **Indexed:** Abstr.Mil.Bibl., Air Un.Lib.Ind., DM & T, Ind.U.S.Gov.Per., PROMT.
    —BLDSC shelfmark: 4478.280000.
    Formerly: U.S. Army Infantry School Quarterly.

355   II   ISSN 0019-9540
UD1
INFANTRY JOURNAL. 1949. s-a. Rs.20. Infantry School, Mhow, India. Ed. B.D. Dogra. bk.rev.; circ. 3,500. (also avail. in microfilm from UMI; reprint service avail. from UMI)

355   FR
INFO D G A. (Delegation Generale pour l'Armement) m. 250 F. (foreign 350 F.). Association pour le Developpement et la Diffusion de l'Information Militaire, 6 rue St. Charles, 75015 Paris, France. TEL 45-77-03-76. FAX 45-79-53-73.

355   GW
INFOPOST. 1977. q. free. Bundesministerium der Verteidigung, Informations- und Pressestab 3, Postfach 1328, 5300 Bonn 1, Germany. circ. 200,000.
    Description: Discusses life in the Armed Forces; directed at teenagers.

355   GW   ISSN 0443-1243
INFORMATION FUER DIE TRUPPE; innere Fuehrung. 1956. m. free. Bundesministerium der Verteidigung, Fue SI 3, Postfach 1328, 5300 Bonn 1, Germany. bk.rev.; circ. controlled.
    Description: Covers defense policy in the NATO troops.

621.38 355.31   US
INSIDE DEFENSE ELECTRONICS. w. $485 (foreign $535). Inside Washington Publishers, Box 7167, Benjamin Franklin Sta., Washington, DC 20044. TEL 703-892-8500. FAX 703-685-2606.
    Former titles: Electronics Report & Electronic Combat Report.

355   US
INSIDE THE ARMY. w. $425 (foreign $475). Inside Washington Publishers, Box 7167, Benjamin Franklin Sta., Washington, DC 20044. TEL 703-892-8500. FAX 703-685-2606.

359   US
INSIDE THE NAVY. w. $435 (foreign $485). Inside Washington Publishers, Box 7167, Benjamin Franklin Sta., Washington, DC 20044. TEL 703-892-8500. FAX 703-685-2606.

359   US
INSIDE THE PENTAGON. w. $595 (foreign $645). Inside Washington Publishers, Box 7167, Benjamin Franklin Sta., Washington, DC 20044. TEL 703-892-8500. FAX 703-685-2606.

355   US
INSPECTOR GENERAL BRIEF. bi-m. T.I.G. Brief Editor, HQ AFISC/SCM, Norton AFB, CA 92409-7001. **Indexed:** Air Un.Lib.Ind.

INSTITUTE FOR DEFENCE STUDIES AND ANALYSES. JOURNAL. see *CIVIL DEFENSE*

INSTITUTE FOR DEFENCE STUDIES AND ANALYSES. STRATEGIC ANALYSES. see *CIVIL DEFENSE*

INSTITUTE FOR DEFENCE STUDIES AND ANALYSES. STRATEGIC DIGEST. see *CIVIL DEFENSE*

INSTITUTO DE GEOGRAFIA E HISTORIA MILITAR DO BRASIL. REVISTA. see *HISTORY — History Of North And South America*

INTELLIGENCE AND NATIONAL SECURITY. see *POLITICAL SCIENCE*

355 364   FR   ISSN 0762-8374
INTELLIGENCE NEWSLETTER. French edition: Monde du Renseignement (ISSN 0765-9776) 1980. 23/yr. 2700 F.($500) Indigo Publications, 10, rue du Sentier, 75002 Paris, France. TEL 45-08-14-80. FAX 45-08-59-83. TELEX LOI 215405F. Ed. Olivier Schmidt.

355   IT
INTERARMA MILITARY NEWS. (Text in Italian; summaries in English) 1969. s-m. L.205000 (foreign L.340000). Editoriale Aeronautica s.r.l., Via Nicolo Paganini 7, 00198 Rome, Italy. TEL 8414691. FAX 8443154. Ed. Oscar Dariz. adv.; circ. 1,350.

INTERNATIONAL ASSOCIATION OF MUSEUMS OF ARMS AND MILITARY HISTORY. CONGRESS REPORTS. see *MUSEUMS AND ART GALLERIES*

355   US   ISSN 0145-2584
UG485
INTERNATIONAL COUNTERMEASURES HANDBOOK. 1975. a. $78 (foreign $93). Cardiff Publishing Co., 6300 S. Syracuse Way, Ste. 650, Englewood, CO 80111-9912. TEL 303-220-0600. FAX 303-773-9716. adv.; bibl.; charts; illus.; stat.; circ. 4,000. (back issues avail.; reprint service avail.)
    —BLDSC shelfmark: 4539.493000.
    Description: Explores electronic warfare, technology and Soviet weapons systems.

355   UK   ISSN 0256-7822
UC260
INTERNATIONAL DEFENSE DIRECTORY. a. £250($395) Jane's Information Group, Sentinel House, 163 Brighton Rd., Coulsdon, Surrey CR5 2NH, England. TEL 081-763-1030. FAX 081-763-1005. TELEX 916907-JANES-G. adv.
    —BLDSC shelfmark: 4539.509600.
    Description: Lists defense companies, organisations worldwide. Includes company name, key personnel and product, service description.

355   UK   ISSN 0020-6512
U1   CODEN: IDRVAL
INTERNATIONAL DEFENSE REVIEW. (Text in English) 1968. m. £70($120) Jane's Information Group, Sentinel House, 163 Brighton Rd., Coulsdon, Surrey CR3 2NX, England. TEL 081-763-1030. FAX 081-763-1005. TELEX 916907 JANES G. Ed. Gowri Sundaram. adv.; bk.rev.; abstr.; charts; illus.; stat.; index. (also avail. in microform from UMI; reprint service avail. from UMI) **Indexed:** Abstr.Mil.Bibl., Air Un.Lib.Ind., DM & T, PROMT. ●Also available online. Vendor(s): DIALOG, Mead Data Central.
    —BLDSC shelfmark: 4539.510000.
    Description: Coverage on all aspects of defense affairs.

355.15   BE
INVALIDE BELGE. Dutch edition: Belgische Verminkte. (Text in French) 1917. m. 350 BEF (foreign 450 BEF). Place E. Flagey 7-4, B-1050 Brussels, Belgium. TEL 02-647-07-78. Ed. Roger Thysebaert. adv.; bk.rev.; circ. 16,000 (6,000 Dutch ed.; 10,000 French ed.).

355   IE   ISSN 0021-1389
IRISH SWORD. 1949. 2/yr. £20. Military History Society of Ireland, c/o University College Dublin, Newman House, 86 St. Stephen's Green, Dublin 2, Ireland. Ed. Harman Murtagh. bk.rev.; charts; illus.; index; circ. 1,200. **Indexed:** Amer.Hist.& Life, Br.Archaeol.Abstr., Hist.Abstr.
    —BLDSC shelfmark: 4574.840000.

623   IT   ISSN 0021-2555
ISTITUTO STORICO E DI CULTURA DELL'ARMA DEL GENIO. BOLLETTINO. 1935. s-a. L.5000($6.) Istituto Storico e di Cultura dell'Arma del Genio, Lungotevere della Vittoria 31, 00195 Rome, Italy. Dir. Roberto Scorza. adv.; bk.rev.; abstr.; charts; illus.; index; circ. 650. **Indexed:** Amer.Hist.& Life, Hist.Abstr.

ITALY. SCUOLA DI GUERRA. BIBLIOTECA. BOLLETTINO. see *LIBRARY AND INFORMATION SCIENCES*

358 623   GW   ISSN 0075-2428
UF530
JAHRBUCH DER WEHRTECHNIK. 1966. a. DM.39.80. Bernard & Graefe Verlag, Karl-Mand-Strasse 2, 5400 Koblenz, Germany. TEL 0261-80706-0. FAX 0228-6483109. TELEX 862662-SPS-D. Ed. Wolfgang Flume. adv.; circ. 5,000.

358.4   UK
JANE'S A F V RETROFIT SYSTEMS. (Armoured Fighting Vehicle) 1988. a. £135($225) Jane's Information Group, Sentinel House, 163 Brighton Rd., Coulsdon, Surrey CR5 2NH, England. TEL 081-763-1030. FAX 081-763-1005. TELEX 916907 JANES G. (Orders in U.S. and Canada to: Dept. DSM, 1340 Braddock Pl., Ste. 300, Box 1436, Alexandria, VA 22314-1651) Ed. Christopher F. Foss. illus.
    ●Also available on CD-ROM.
    Formerly: Jane's A F V Systems.
    Description: Covers the key armoured fighting vehicle sub-systems available for installation in new and rebuilt vehicles, with development histories, descriptions, specifications, photographs, and supplier contact information for manufacturers worldwide.

355   UK   ISSN 0143-9952
UG446.5
JANE'S ARMOUR AND ARTILLERY. 1979. a. £135($210) Jane's Information Group, Sentinel House, 163 Brighton Rd., Coulsdon, Surrey CR5 2NH, England. TEL 081-763-1030. FAX 081-763-1005. TELEX 916907 JANES G. (Orders in U.S. and Canada to: Dept. DSM, 1340 Braddock Pl., Ste. 300, Box 1436, Alexandria, VA 22314-1651) Ed. Christopher F. Foss. adv.; index.
    ●Also available on CD-ROM.
    Description: Covers development histories, detailed descriptions, lists of variants and modifications, full specifications, lists of user countries and manufacturer contact details for armoured fighting vehicles and artillery worldwide.

355 629.13 UK
JANE'S BATTLEFIELD SURVEILLANCE. a. £135($210) Jane's Information Group, Sentinel House, 163 Brighton Rd., Coulsdon, Surrey CR5 2NH, England. TEL 081-763-1030. FAX 081-763-1005. TELEX 916907 JANES G. (Orders in U.S. and Canada to: Dept. DSM, 1340 Braddock Pl., Ste. 300, Box 1436, Alexandria, VA 22314-1651) Eds. T. Hooton, K. Munson.
●Also available on CD-ROM.
   Supersedes in part: Jane's Weapon Systems (ISSN 0075-3068)
   Description: Analysis of airborne ground-based reconnaisance and surveillance systems used in the modern battle field.

355 629.13 UK
JANE'S C 3 I SYSTEMS. (Command, Control, Communications & Intelligence) a. £135($210) Jane's Information Group, Sentinel House, 163 Brighton Rd., Coulsdon, Surrey CR5 2NH, England. TEL 081-763-1030. FAX 081-763-1005. TELEX 916907 JANES G. (Subscr. in U.S. and Canada to: Dept. DSM, 1340 Braddock Pl., Ste. 300, Box 1436, Alexandria, VA 22314-1651) Ed. Peter Rackman.
●Also available on CD-ROM.
   Formerly: Jane's C 3 I; Which supersedes in part: Jane's Weapon Systems (ISSN 0075-3068)
   Description: Guide to all "C3I" systems around the world, including command information systems, communications networks, and intelligence gathering sytems.

355 UK ISSN 0265-3818
UF530
JANE'S DEFENCE WEEKLY. 1980. w. £95($145) Jane's Information Group, Sentinel House, 163 Brighton Rd., Coulsdon, Surrey CR5 2NH, England. TEL 081-763-1030. FAX 081-763-1005. TELEX 916907 JANE G. Ed. Peter Howard. Indexed: Abstr.Mil.Bibl., Air Un.Lib.Ind, DM & T.
●Also available online. Vendor(s): DIALOG.
—BLDSC shelfmark: 4646.840000.
   Formerly (until 1984): Jane's Defence Review (ISSN 0144-0470)

359 UK ISSN 0075-3025
VA40
JANE'S FIGHTING SHIPS. 1898. a. £135($210) Jane's Information Group, Sentinel House, 163 Brighton Rd., Coulsdon, Surrey CR5 2NH, England. TEL 081-763-1030. FAX 081-763-1005. TELEX 916907 JANES G. (Orders in U.S. and Canada to: Dept. DSM, 1430 Braddock Pl., Ste. 300, Box 1436, Alexandria, VA 22314-1651) Ed. Capt. Richard Sharpe. adv.; index.
●Also available on CD-ROM.
   Description: Survey of the fleets, equipment, structures, and personnel of the world's navy.

355 UK ISSN 0306-3410
JANE'S INFANTRY WEAPONS. 1975. a. £135($210) Jane's Information Group, Sentinel House, 163 Brighton Rd., Coulsdon, Surrey CR5 2NH, England. TEL 081-763-1030. FAX 081-763-1005. TELEX 916907 JANES G. (Orders in U.S. and Canada to: Dept. DSM, 1340 Braddock Pl., Ste. 300, Box 1436, Alexandria, VA 22314-1651) Ed. Ian V. Hogg. adv.; index.
●Also available on CD-ROM.
   Description: Describes and analyzes over 1500 weapons from every manufacturing country in the world. Also details national inventories.

355 UK
UA770
JANE'S INTELLIGENCE REVIEW. 1989. 12/yr. £110($185) Jane's Information Group, Sentinel House, 163 Brighton Rd, Couldsdon, Surrey CR3 2NH, England. TEL 081-763-1030. FAX 081-763-1007. TELEX 916907. (Subscr. in U.S. and Canada to: Dept. DSM, 1340 Braddock Pl., Ste. 300, Box 1436, Alexandria, VA 22313-2036) bk.rev.; circ. 3,000. Indexed: Air Un.Lib.Ind.
●Also available online. Vendor(s): DIALOG.
   Formerly: Jane's Soviet Intelligence Review (ISSN 0955-1247)
   Description: Intelligence briefing reports.

355 UK
JANE'S LAND-BASED AIR DEFENCE. a. £135($210) Jane's Information Group, Sentinel House, 163 Brighton Rd., Coulsdon, Surrey CR5 2NH, England. TEL 081-763-1030. FAX 081-763-1005. TELEX 916907 JANES G. (Orders in U.S. and Canada to: Dept. DSM, 1340 Braddock Pl., Ste. 300, Box 1436, Alexandria, VA 22314-1651) Eds. C. Foss, T. Cullen.
●Also available on CD-ROM.
   Formerly (until 1988): Jane's Battlefield Air Defence.
   Description: Presents data on land-based air defence weapons, covering all types of static and mobile anti-aircraft, anti-helicopter and anti-missile systems in service or under development all over the world.

355 UK ISSN 0144-0004
UG590
JANE'S MILITARY COMMUNICATIONS. 1979. a. £135($210) Jane's Information Group, Sentinel House, 163 Brighton Rd., Coulsdon, Surrey CR5 2NH, England. TEL 081-763-1030. FAX 081-763-1005. TELEX 916907 JANE G. (Orders in U.S. and Canada to: Dept. DSM, 1340 Braddock Pl., Ste. 300, Box 1436, Alexandria, VA 22314-1651) Ed. John Williamson. adv.; index.
●Also available on CD-ROM.
   Description: Devoted to communication systems, equipment and ancillaries designed for, and used by, the world's armed forces. Includes sections devoted to test and maintenance, security, surveillance and signal analysis, direction finding and jamming.

355 UK
JANE'S MILITARY TRAINING SYSTEMS. a. £135($210) Jane's Information Group, Sentinel House, 163 Brighton Rd., Coulsdon, Surrey CR5 2NH, England. TEL 081-763-1030. FAX 081-763-1005. TELEX 916907 JANES G. (Orders in U.S. and Canada to: Dept. DSM, 1340 Braddock Pl., Ste. 300, Box 1436, Alexandria, VA 22314-1651) Ed. Terry Gander.
●Also available on CD-ROM.
   Description: Incorporates technical profiles of more than 400 items of land, sea, and air military training equipment from small arms ranges to full-scale aviation and ship-building simulators.

355 UK
JANE'S MILITARY VEHICLES AND LOGISTICS. 1978. a. £135($210) Jane's Information Group, Sentinel House, 163 Brighton Rd., Coulsdon, Surrey CR5 2NH, England. TEL 081-763-1030. FAX 081-763-1005. TELEX 916907 JANES G. (Orders in U.S. and Canada to: Dept. DSM, 1340 Braddock Pl., Ste. 300, Box 1436, Alexandria, VA 22314-1651) Ed. Terry Gander. illus.; index.
●Also available on CD-ROM.
   Former titles: Jane's Military Logistics; Jane's Military Vehicles and Ground Support Equipment; Jane's Combat Support Equipment.
   Description: Worldwide survey using text, photographs, drawings and diagrams of logistic vehicles and associated equipment including materials handling equipment, personnel transport, bridging, land and mine warfare plus fuel and water supplies.

355 UK
JANE'S N B C PROTECTION EQUIPMENT. a. £135($210) Jane's Information Group, Sentinel House, 163 Brighton Rd., Coulsdon, Surrey CR5 2NH, England. TEL 081-763-1030. FAX 081-763-1005. TELEX 916907 JANES G. (Orders in U.S. and Canada to: Dept. DSM, 1340 Braddock Pl., Ste. 300, Box 1436, Alexandria, VA 22314-1651) Ed. Terry Gander.
   Description: Covers all types of NBC protection from respirators and clothing to new medical and life support equipment.

355 UK ISSN 0958-126X
UA646.3
JANE'S NATO HANDBOOK. a. £135($210) Jane's Information Group, Sentinel House, 163 Brighton Rd., Coulsdon, Surrey CR5 2NH, England. TEL 081-763-1030. FAX 081-763-1005. TELEX 916907 JANES G. (Orders in U.S. and Canada to: Dept. DSM, 1340 Braddock Pl., Ste. 300, Box 1436, Alexandria, VA 22314-1651) Ed. Bruce George.
—BLDSC shelfmark: 4647.087300.
   Description: Gives detailed and current overview of the North Atlantic Treaty Organization, its civilian and military institutions and machinery, and its 16 member countries.

359 UK
JANE'S NAVAL WEAPON SYSTEM. 1988. q. £225. Jane's Information Group, Sentinel House, 163 Brighton Rd., Coulsdon, Surrey CR5 2NH, England. TEL 081-763-1030. FAX 081-763-1005. TELEX 916907. Ed. Edward Robert Hooton. (looseleaf format; back issues avail.)
●Also available on CD-ROM.
   Description: Examines naval weapon systems and associated equipment.

621.38 355 UK
JANE'S RADAR AND E-W SYSTEMS. (Electronic Warfare) 1989. a. £135($210) Jane's Information Group, Sentinel House, 163 Brighton Rd., Coulsdon, Surrey CR5 2NH, England. TEL 081-763-1030. FAX 081-763-1005. TELEX 916907 JANES G. (Subscr. in U.S. and Canada to: Dept. DSM, 1340 Braddock Pl., Ste. 300, Box 1436, Alexandria, VA 22314-1651) Ed. Bernard Blake.
●Also available on CD-ROM.
   Description: Covers international air-defence systems, land-based air defence radars, land, sea, space, and air-based surveillance radars, naval and airborne fire control radars, ATC systems and land, sea and air based COMINT, ELINT AND ECM systems.

355 UK
JANE'S RADAR AND ELECTRONIC WARFARE. a. £125($225) Jane's Information Group, Sentinel House, 163 Brighton Rd., Coulsdon, Surrey CR5 2NH, England. TEL 081-763-1030. FAX 081-763-1005. TELEX 916907-JANES-G. Indexed: PROMT.
   Formerly: Electronic Warfare.

355 UK
JANE'S SECURITY & CO-IN EQUIPMENT. a. £135($210) Jane's Information Group, Sentinel House, 163 Brighton Rd., Coulsdon, Surrey CR5 2NH, England. TEL 081-763-1030. FAX 081-763-1005. TELEX 916907 JANES G. (Orders in U.S. and Canada to: Dept. DSM, 1340 Braddock Pl., Ste. 300, Box 1436, Alexandria, VA 22314-1651) Ed. Ian Hogg.
   Description: Over 2,000 items of security equipment for police, military, and security organisaitons.

355 UK
JANE'S UNDERWATER WARFARE SYSTEMS. a. £135($210) Jane's Information Group, Sentinel House, 163 Brighton Rd., Coulsdon, Surrey CR5 2NH, England. TEL 081-763-1030. FAX 081-763-1005. TELEX 916907 JANES G. (Orders in U.S. and Canada to: Dept. DSM, 1340 Braddock Pl., Ste. 300, Box 1436, Alexandria, VA 22314-1651) Ed. T. Watts.
●Also available on CD-ROM.
   Description: Covers all aspects of the underwater warfare scene, including underwater weapons and their fire control systems, sonar, sonobuoys, MAD, underwater commmunications ranges and targets.

355.15 296 US ISSN 0047-2018
DS101
JEWISH VETERAN; the patriotic voice of American Jewry. 1933. 6/yr. $5 to non-members; members $2.50. Jewish War Veterans of the U.S.A., 1811 R St., N.W., Washington, DC 20009. TEL 202-265-6280. FAX 202-234-5662. Ed. Howard Metzer. adv.; bk.rev.; charts; illus.; circ. 100,000. (also avail. in microfilm from AJP)

JIANCHUAN ZHISHI. see *TRANSPORTATION — Ships And Shipping*

MILITARY

355 US
JIEFANGJUN BAO/LIBERATION ARMY DAILY. (Text in Chinese) d. $329.80. (Zhongguo Renmin Jiefangjun, CC - Chinese People's Liberation Army) China Books & Periodicals, Inc., 2929 24th St., San Francisco, CA 94110. TEL 415-282-2994. FAX 415-282-0994.

355.1 CC ISSN 0009-3823
JIEFANGJUN HUABAO/P L A PICTORIAL. (Text in Chinese) 1951. m. Y43.20($108) (Zhongguo Renmin Jiefangjun, Zong Zhengzhibu - Chinese People's Liberation Army) Jiefangjun Huabao She, 40 Sanlihe Lu, Ganjiakou, Beijing 100037, People's Republic of China. TEL 831-1525. (Dist. outside China by: China International Book Trading Corp., P.O. Box 399, Beijing, P.R.C.; Dist. in US by: China Books & Periodicals, Inc., 2929 24th St., San Francisco, CA 94110. TEL 415-282-2994) Ed. Liu Tiesheng. illus. (tabloid format)

355.1 US
JIEFANGJUN SHENGHUO/LIFE OF P L A SOLDIERS. (Text in Chinese) m. $39.50. (Zhongguo Renmin Jiefangjun, CC - Chinese People's Liberation Army) China Books & Periodicals, Inc., 2929 24th St., San Francisco, CA 94110. TEL 415-282-2994. FAX 415-282-0994.

JIEFANGJUN WENYI/LITERATURE AND ART OF PEOPLE'S LIBERATION ARMY. see *LITERATURE*

355 US
JING BAO JOURNAL. 1948. bi-m. membership only. Flying Tigers of the 14th Air Force Association, Inc., Box 285, Selden, NY 11784. TEL 516-698-1782. Ed. Milt Miller. bk.rev.; film rev.; play rev.; circ. 4,070.
— *Description:* Covers association activities and tales of members during World War II in China.

355 II
JODESA. (Text in English) 1978. q. Rs.5. Defence Scientists Association, Metcalfe House, Delhi 110 054, India. FAX 11-2919151. TELEX 031-78030.

355 PO ISSN 0447-8819
JORNAL DO EXERCITO. 1960. m. Esc.950. Estado Maior do Exercito, Largo da Graca 94, 1100 Lisbon, Portugal. Ed. Maj. Jose Machado Diniz. adv.; bk.rev.; charts; illus.; index; circ. 8,000.

355 FR ISSN 0021-8014
JOURNAL DES COMBATTANTS. 1916. w. 180 F. 80 rue des Prairies, 75020 Paris, France. Ed. Mrs. Daniel. adv.; bk.rev.; bibl.; illus.; stat.; circ. 30,000.

355 US ISSN 0897-0475
E487
JOURNAL OF CONFEDERATE HISTORY. 1988. q. $43.95. Southern Heritage Press, Box 1615, Murfreesboro, TN 37133-1615. TEL 615-890-9795. Ed. John McGlone. adv.; bk.rev.
— *Description:* Scholarly articles on the Civil War.

355 US ISSN 0192-429X
UG485 CODEN: JELDER
JOURNAL OF ELECTRONIC DEFENSE. 1978. m. $60 to non-members; foreign $75. (Association of Old Crows) Horizon - House - Publications, Inc., 685 Canton St., Norwood, MA 02062. TEL 617-769-9884. FAX 617-762-9230. TELEX 951 659. Ed. Hal Gershanoff. adv.; circ. 25,000. (reprint service avail.) Indexed: Abstr.Mil.Bibl., Air Un.Lib.Ind., DM & T, PROMT.
—BLDSC shelfmark: 4974.920000.
— *Description:* Planning and procurement, technology and application of EW equipment and subsystems, EW system integration, performance and operations.

355 US ISSN 0899-3718
E181
JOURNAL OF MILITARY HISTORY. 1937. q. $25 to individuals; institutions $45. Society for Military History, c/o Virginia Military Institute, Lexington, VA 24450. TEL 703-464-7468. FAX 703-464-7169. (Co-sponsors: George C. Marshall Foundation, Virginia Military Institute) Ed. Henry S. Bausum. adv.; bk.rev.; bibl.; charts; index, cum.index: 1937-1969; circ. 2,400. Indexed: Abstr.Mil.Bibl., Air Un.Lib.Ind., Amer.Bibl.Slavic & E.Eur.Stud, Amer.Hist.& Life, Arts & Hum.Cit.Ind., Curr.Cont., Hist.Abstr, Mid.East: Abstr.& Ind., So.Pac.Per.Ind.
—BLDSC shelfmark: 5019.945000.
Formerly (until vol.52): Military Affairs (ISSN 0026-3931)
— *Description:* Scholarly articles and reviews on all aspects of military history.

355 UK ISSN 0954-254X
UA770 CODEN: JSMSE5
JOURNAL OF SOVIET MILITARY STUDIES. 1988. 4/yr. £35($45) to individuals; institutions £85($130). Frank Cass & Co. Ltd., Gainsborough House, 11 Gainsborough Rd., London E11 IRS, England. TEL 081-530-4226. FAX 081-530-7795. Eds. Christopher Donnelly, David Glantz. adv.; bk.rev.; index. (back issues avail.) Indexed: Air Un.Lib.Ind, Polit.Sci.Abstr.
—BLDSC shelfmark: 5066.081000.
— *Description:* Covers all aspects of the evolution and practice of Soviet military art.

355 UK ISSN 0140-2390
U162
JOURNAL OF STRATEGIC STUDIES. 1978. 4/yr. £35($45) to individuals; institutions £90($140). Frank Cass & Co. Ltd., Gainsborough House, 11 Gainsborough Rd., London E11 1RS, England. TEL 081-530-4226. FAX 081-530-7795. Eds. Amos Perlmutter, John Gooch. adv.; bk.rev.; index. (also avail. in microfilm from UMI; back issues avail.) Indexed: Abstr.Mil.Bibl., Amer.Hist.& Life, Curr.Cont., Hist.Abstr., Psychol.Abstr., SSCI.
—BLDSC shelfmark: 5066.873000.

355 990 900 AT ISSN 0729-6274
JOURNAL OF THE AUSTRALIAN WAR MEMORIAL. 1982. 2/yr. Aus.$12. Australian War Memorial, G.P.O. Box 345, Canberra, A.C.T. 2601, Australia. TEL 06-243-4345. FAX 06-243-4325. Ed. P. Macpheron. adv.; bk.rev.; illus.; circ. 1,200. (back issues avail.) Indexed: Aus.P.A.I.S.
— *Description:* Articles on all aspects of Australian military history, notes on the memorial's collection, and reviews of latest publications in the field.

355 UK ISSN 0022-5134
JOURNAL OF THE ROYAL ARTILLERY. 1858. s-a. £4. Royal Artillery Institution, Woolwich, London SE18 4DN, England. TEL 01-854-2242. FAX 01-856-3659. Ed. P.J.F. Painter. adv.; bk.rev.; illus.; maps; index every 10 yrs.; circ. 4,500. Indexed: Air Un.Lib.Ind, DM & T.
—BLDSC shelfmark: 4853.100000.

355.15 SA ISSN 0022-5770
JUDEAN. (Text in Afrikaans and English) 1946. s-a. South African Jewish Ex-Service League, P.O. Box 7309, Johannesburg, South Africa. Ed. L.L. Spilg. adv.; bk.rev.; abstr.; bibl.; illus.; circ. 3,000. (tabloid format)

355 MK
JUND OMAN. m. Ministry of Defence, P.O. Box 113, Muscat, Sultanate of Oman. TEL 613615. TELEX 5228. illus.

355 TS
AL-JUNDI. 1973. m. $82 (effective 1992). Ministry of Defence - Wizarat al-Difa'a, P.O. Box 2838, Dubai, United Arab Emirates. TEL 04-451515. FAX 04-45503. TELEX 45554 MOD EM. Ed. Ismail Khamis Mubarak. adv.: color page $4000; adv. contact: Khalid M. Al-Shaibah. circ. 4,000 (controlled).
— *Description:* Covers military affairs in the U.A.E., the region and worldwide, including recent developments in weapons technology and cultural topics.

JUNDUI ZHUANYE GANBU. see *BUSINESS AND ECONOMICS — Personnel Management*

KAISERZEIT. see *HISTORY — History Of Europe*

355 AU ISSN 0029-974X
KAMERADSCHAFT DER WIENER PANZER-DIVISION. MITTEILUNGSBLATT. 1961. q. Kameradschaft der Wiener Panzer-Division, Postfach 159, A-1061 Vienna, Austria. Ed. Franz Steinzer. adv.; bk.rev.; illus.; circ. 4,000.

355.115 GW
KAMERADSCHAFTSBUND SECHSTE PANZERDIVISION. NACHRICHTENBLATT. 1955. q. DM.18. Kameradschaftsbund Sechste Panzerdivision e.V., Postfach 160126, 4600 Dortmund 16, Germany. TEL 0231-854058.

355.15 US ISSN 0022-9199
U4
KARYS; monthly for American-Lithuanian veterans. (Text in Lithuanian) 1950. m. $10. L.V.A. "Ramove" Inc., 341 Highland Blvd., Brooklyn, NY 11207. Ed. Z.A. Raulinaitis. bk.rev.; circ. 1,300. (tabloid format)

970.04 US
KENTUCKY. ADJUTANT-GENERAL'S OFFICE. REPORT. Variant Title--Annual Report. a. Adjutant-General's Office, Frankfort, KY 40601. TEL 502-564-8558.

355 FR
KEPI BLANC. 1947. m. 110 F. Service du moral et du foyer d'entraide de la Legion Etrangere, B.P. 78, 13673 Aubagne, France. Ed. Jean-Baptiste Chiaroni. adv.; bk.rev.; circ. 12,000.

KESHER ELEKTRONIKA MACHSHAVIM. see *COMMUNICATIONS*

356 UK ISSN 0140-0991
KINGSMAN. vol.6, 1970. s-a. 75p. Kings Regiment, T and AVR Center, Townsend Ave., Liverpool L11 5AF, England. Ed. B.W.R. Baker. adv.; charts; illus.; circ. 1,500.
Formerly: White Horse and Fleur de Lys (ISSN 0043-4930)

355 IR
KITAB-I MUQAVAMAT. 1989. q. Rs.720 per no. Hawzah-i Hunari Sazman-i Tablighat-i Islami, 213 Summaiyah St., P.O. Box 1677-15815, Teheran, Iran. illus.

KOEHLERS FLOTTENKALENDER. JAHRBUCH FUER SCHIFFAHRT UND HAEFEN. see *TRANSPORTATION — Ships And Shipping*

355 GW ISSN 0023-4648
KRIEGSGRAEBERFUERSORGE; Stimme und Weg. 1921. q. membership. Volksbund Deutsche Kriegsgraeberfuersorge e.V., Werner-Hilpert-Str. 2, 3500 Kassel 1, Germany. Ed. Willi Kammerer. illus.; stat.; index; circ. 396,000.
— *Description:* For members of the German war graves commission.

358.4 YU ISSN 0023-4672
KRILA ARMIJE. 1948. fortn. 50 din. per no. Ratno Vozduhoplovstvo i Protivvazdusne Odbrane, Marsala Tita 1, Zemun, Belgrade, Serbia, Yugoslavia. Ed. Predrag Pejcic.

KUN LUN/ARMY LITERATURE. see *LITERATURE*

355 SW ISSN 0023-5369
U43.D4
KUNGLIGA KRIGSVETENSKAPSAKADEMIEN. HANDLINGAR OCH TIDSKRIFT. 1796. 7/yr. SEK 50. Kungliga Krigsvetenskapsakademien - Royal Swedish Academy of Military Sciences, 100 45 Stockholm, Sweden. Ed. Brig. Carl Herlitz. adv.; bk.rev.; charts; maps; index; circ. 1,500. Indexed: Amer.Hist.& Life, Hist.Abstr.
—BLDSC shelfmark: 5125.500000.

355 US ISSN 1044-8756
KF337.5.A7
L A M P LIGHTER. 1970. q. free. American Bar Association, Standing Committee on Legal Assistance for Military Personnel, 750 N. Lake Shore Dr., Chicago, IL 60611. TEL 312-988-5760. FAX 312-988-5664. bk.rev.; charts; circ. 4,000. (back issues avail.)
Former titles: Legal Assistance Newsletter; L A M P Occasional Newsletter (ISSN 0163-1373); American Bar Association. Standing Committee on Legal Assistance for Servicemen. Occasional Newsletter (ISSN 0065-7522)
— *Description:* Information for legal assistance officers of the armed forces.

MILITARY 3463

355 US ISSN 1050-7310
▼LANGUAGE OF DEFENSE. 1990. biennial. $85. Carroll Publishing Company, 1058 Thomas Jefferson St., N.W., Washington, DC 20007. TEL 202-333-8620. FAX 202-337-7020.
 Description: Handbook of acronyms and terminologies. Identifies and defines over 5,000 key current US and international defense acronyms, code names, abbreviations, nomenclatures, and concepts.

051 US ISSN 0742-7972
LAPIDUS LETTER. 1957. m. $40. Lapidus Advisory Service, 2339 N. Quantico St., Arlington VA 22205. TEL 703-534-4738. Ed. Herbert M. Lapidus.
 Description: Keeps readers abreast of government-military packaging developments as reflected by federal-military specifications standards, handbooks, reports and qualified products lists.

359.96 US ISSN 0023-981X
D501
LEATHERNECK; magazine of the Marines. 1917. m. $15. Marine Corps Association, Box 1775, MCB, Quantico, VA 22134. TEL 800-336-0291. FAX 703-640-0823. Ed. Col. William White. adv.; bk.rev.; illus.; index; circ. 106,742. (also avail. in microfilm from UMI; reprint service avail. from UMI)
 Description: Information on what Marines do throughout the world.

356 NE ISSN 0024-0389
LEGERKOERIER. 1951. m. fl.31. M.O.D.-Directorate of Information, Kalvermarkt 38, 2500 ES The Hague, Netherlands. Ed. Lt. Col. J.Th.I.M. de Waart. adv.; bk.rev.; film rev.; record rev.; circ. 65,000.

355.115 CN ISSN 0024-0435
LEGION. 1926. 10/yr. Can.$10($15) Canvet Publications Ltd., Legion House, 359 Kent St., Ste. 504, Ottawa, Ont. K2P 0R6, Canada. TEL 613-235-8741. Ed. Mac Johnston. adv.; bk.rev.; charts; illus.; tr.lit.; circ. 521,585. (also avail. in microfilm from UMI)
 Description: Of particular interest to veterans, serving and ex-serving personnel and their families.

354 LB
LIBERIA. MINISTRY OF NATIONAL DEFENSE. ANNUAL REPORT.* a. Ministry of National Defense, Monrovia, Liberia.

LINCOLN MEMORIAL ASSOCIATION NEWSLETTER. see HISTORY — History Of North And South America

355 DK ISSN 0024-3973
LINIEOFFICEREN. 1968. m. $4. Hovedorganisationen af Officerer i Forsvaret (AC), Rosenvaengets Alle 33, 2100 Copenhagen OE, Denmark. FAX 35-430220. Ed. K.A. Thomsen. adv.; bk.rev.; circ. 3,600.
 Supersedes: Vor Haer.

355.31 CY
LION. w. includes Services Sound & Vision Corp. Guide. British Sovereign Base, British Forces Post Office 53, Nicosia, Cyprus. TEL 02-263926. Ed. Maj. M.P. Beaumont. circ. 3,600.

355 UK
LIONESS. 1945. 2/yr. £1.50 per issue to non-members. Women's Royal Army Corps Association, W R A C Centre, Queen Elizabeth Park, Guildford, Surrey GU2 6QM, England. Ed. Capt. (Retd.) M.B.S. Purkis. adv.; bk.rev.; illus.; circ. 12,000.

355 IS
LITANI. (Text in English) m. P.O. Box 75, Nahariya 22 100, Israel. Ed. Lt.Col. F.E.A. Quayson.

355.115 IS ISSN 0334-357X
HALOCHAME. 1950. q. Organization of Disabled Veterans, Beit Halochame, P.O. Box 39262, Tel Aviv 61 392, Israel. FAX 03-421316. Ed. Gil Yudelevich. adv.; bk.rev.; circ. 35,000.

LOGISTICS AND TRANSPORTATION REVIEW. see TRANSPORTATION

355 322 UK
▼LONDON DEFENCE STUDIES.* 1991. 10/yr. $117. (Centre for Defence Studies) Brassey's, 50 Fetter Ln., London EC4A 1AA, England. TEL 071-377-4881. FAX 071-377-4888. (Subscr. to: Turpin Transactions, Distribution Centre, Blackhorse Rd., Letchworth, Herts SG1 1HN, England. TEL 0462-672555) (also avail. in microform)

355.351 NO
LOTTEBLADET. 1928. 6/yr. NOK 200 (membership). Norges Lotteforbund - Norwegian Women's Voluntary Defense League, Oslo Mil-Akershus, Oslo 1, Norway. Ed. Astrid Thon. adv.; bk.rev.; illus.; circ. 4,000.

355.37 GW ISSN 0343-0103
LOYAL; das Deutsche Wehrmagazin. 1960. m. DM.36. (Verband der Reservisten der Deutschen Bundeswehr e.V.) Moench Verlagsgesellschaft mbH, Postfach 140261, 5300 Bonn 1, Germany. TEL 0261-80706-0. (Susbcr. to: Special Publication Service, Karl-Mand-Str. 2, 5400 Koblenz, Germany) adv.; illus.; circ. 120,000. (back issues avail.)
 Formerly: Reserve.

LUCIANO MANARA. see HISTORY — History Of Europe

358.4 GW
LUFTWAFFEN-FORUM. 1987. q. DM.20($30) (German Air Force) Verlag Dr. Neufang KG, Nordring 10, Postfach 200254, 4650 Gelsenkirchen-Buer, Germany. TEL 0209-37431. FAX 0209-395398. Ed. Rolf Dorpinghaus. circ. 22,780.
 Description: News, events and features concerning military aviation for the German Armed Forces as well as their NATO partners.

355 RM
LUPTA INTREGULUI POPOR. (Supplement to: Viata Militara) 1984. q.(Rumanian ed.); s-a.(English, French, German, Russian and Spanish eds.). 32 lei($20) Rumanian Commission of Military History, 5-7 Drumul Taberei Str., Bucharest, Rumania. TEL 313044. TELEX 10376. (Subscr. to: Rompresfilatelia, Sector Export-Import Presa, Calea Grivitei, P.O. Box 12-201, nr.64-66, sector 1, Bucharest, Rumania) Ed. Ilie Ceausescu. bk.rev.; illus.

355 US ISSN 0024-788X
UC333
M A C FLYER.* (Military Airlift Command) 1954. m. $19. U.S. Air Force, Military Airlift Command, Headquarters MAC-IGFE, Scott Air Force Base, IL 62225-5101. TEL 618-256-3534. (Orders to: Supt. of Documents, Washington, DC 20402) Ed. Maj. James M. Lee. bk.rev.; stat.; circ. 12,000. (also avail. in microform from MIM,UMI; reprint service avail. from UMI) Indexed: Air Un.Lib.Ind., Ind.U.S.Gov.Per.

355 974 US ISSN 1040-5992
D25
M H Q: THE QUARTERLY JOURNAL OF MILITARY HISTORY. 1988. q. $60 (foreign $70). M H Q, Inc., 29 W. 38th St., New York, NY 10018. TEL 212-398-1550. FAX 212-840-6790. (Subscr. to: Box 1954, Marion, OH 43306-4054. TEL 800-347-6969) Ed. Robert Cowley. bk.rev.; illus.
 Description: Examines all aspects of military history from the past to the present.

M O D CONTRACTS BULLETIN. (Ministry of Defence) see BUSINESS AND ECONOMICS

M O D NEWS. (Ministry of Defence) see BUSINESS AND ECONOMICS

355 NO ISSN 0024-8517
M T T.* bi-m. Forsvarets Bygningstekniske Korps, Oslo, Norway. (Co-sponsors: Ingenioervaapenet; Haerens Samband) adv.; bk.rev.; abstr.; charts; illus.; index.
 Description: Military technical journal for the Armed Forces technical construction corps, engineers, and communications troops.

355 IS ISSN 0464-2147
MA'ARACHOT. (Text and summaries in Hebrew) 1939. bi-m. Ministry of Defense Publishing House, 29 Elaazar St., P.O. Box 7026, Hakirya, Tel Aviv 61070, Israel. Eds. U. Dromi, R. Rojanski. bk.rev. (back issues avail.) Indexed: Ind.Heb.Per.

355 IS
MAARACHOT CHEIMUSH. bi-m. IS.12. Ministry of Defense Publishing House, Subscription Department, 25 David Eleazer St., Hakirya, Tel Aviv 64 273, Israel. TEL 03-205516.

MANUAL OF AIR FORCE LAW - AMENDMENTS. see LAW — Military Law

MANUAL OF MILITARY LAW - AMENDMENTS. see LAW — Military Law

355 IO
MARI JO. 1970. q. Marine Corps - Korps Marinir, Jalan Prapatan No. 40, Jakarta, Indonesia. Ed. Masril Madjid. adv.; charts; illus.
 Formerly: Korps Komando (ISSN 0047-3626)

359.96 FR
MARINE. 1951. q. 130 F. Association Centrale des Officiers de Reserve de l'Armee de Mer, 15 rue de LaBorde, B.P. 12, 00312 Paris, France. Eds. Alain Dannery, H. Nguyen Tan. adv.; bk.rev.; circ. 10,600.

359.96 US ISSN 0025-3170
VE7
MARINE CORPS GAZETTE; the professional magazine for United States Marines. 1916. m. $15. Marine Corps Association, Box 1775, MCB, Quantico, VA 22134. TEL 800-336-0291. FAX 703-640-0823. Ed. Col. John E. Greenwood. adv.; bk.rev.; illus.; index; circ. 37,660. (also avail. in microfilm from UMI; reprint service avail. from UMI) Indexed: Abstr.Mil.Bibl., Air Un.Lib.Ind., Amer.Hist.& Life, DM & T, Hist.Abstr., PROMT, So.Pac.Per.Ind.
 —BLDSC shelfmark: 5373.765000.
 Description: Professional Marines journal.

MARINE-RUNDSCHAU. see TRANSPORTATION — Ships And Shipping

359 NE ISSN 0025-3340
V5
MARINEBLAD. 1887. m. (11/yr.) fl.62.50. (Vereniging van Marine-Officieren - Netherlands Society of Royal Navy Officers) C. de Boer Jr. N.V., Postbus 507, 1200 AM Hilversum, Netherlands. FAX 035-231939. Ed.Bd. adv.; bk.rev.; charts; illus.; circ. 4,000. Indexed: Excerp.Med.
 —BLDSC shelfmark: 5379.000000.

MARINEHISTORISK TIDSSKRIFT. see HISTORY — History Of Europe

359.96 US
MARINES. 1983. m. U.S. Marine Corps, Public Affairs, HQMC, Washington, DC 20380. TEL 202-694-1494.

358.4 CN ISSN 0025-3413
MARITIME COMMAND TRIDENT. (Text in English and French) 1966. s-m. Can.$20 (foreign Can.$25). Trident Military Newspaper Ltd., P.O. Box 3308 S., Halifax, N.S. B3J 3J1, Canada. TEL 902-427-2347. FAX 902-427-6066. Ed. S. Mander. adv.; bk.rev.; circ. 14,000. (tabloid format)

359 UK
MARITIME DEFENCE; the journal of international naval technology. 1976. m. $70. Eldon Publications Ltd., 292-294 Walton Rd., E. Molesey, Surrey KT8 OHY, England. TEL 081-941-7510. FAX 081-941-7449. Ed. Geoffrey Wood. adv.; illus.; stat.; circ. 4,069. (also avail. in microform from UMI; back issues avail) Indexed: Abstr.Mil.Bibl., DM & T, PROMT.
 Formerly: Maritime Defence International (ISSN 0308-5201)

355 FR ISSN 0025-3480
MARJOLAINE; bulletin trimestriel. 1920. q. membership. Association Amicale des Anciens Combattants du 27e et 32e Dragons, 34 Avenue Franklin Roosevelt, 94300 Vincennes, France. Dir. Col. de Montille. bk.rev.; circ. 850.

355 BE
MARS ET MERCURE/MARS EN MERCURIUS. 1928. 10/yr. 500 BEF. F. Lepeer, Ed. & Pub., 110 Ave. de Heyn, B-1090 Brussels, Belgium. adv.; bk.rev.; circ. 1,500.

355 NE ISSN 0025-4029
MARS IN CATHEDRA. (Supplement to: Militaire Spectator) 1865. q. fl.40. Koninklijke Vereniging ter Beoefening van de Krijgswetenschap - Royal Society for Military Science, Karel Doormanlaan 274, 2283 BB Rijswijk, Netherlands. Ed. T. de Kruyf.

359 US ISSN 0025-6471
VG93
MECH; naval aviation maintenance safety review. 1968. bi-m. $9 (foreign $11.25). U.S. Naval Safety Center, Norfolk, VA 23511. TEL 804-444-6970. FAX 804-444-7205. (Subscr. to: Supt. of Documents, Washington, DC 20402) Ed. Joe Casto. charts; illus.; circ. 13,000. Indexed: Ind.U.S.Gov.Per.

MEDDELANDE ARMEMUSEUM. YEARBOOK. see MUSEUMS AND ART GALLERIES

M

MILITARY

MEDIATUS; Zeitschrift fuer handlungsrientierte Friedensforschung. see POLITICAL SCIENCE — International Relations

MEDICINE AND WAR. see MEDICAL SCIENCES

355   FR   ISSN 0025-9160
UF1
MEMORIAL DE L'ARTILLERIE FRANCAISE; sciences et techniques de l'armement. 1862. q. Imprimerie Nationale, Service des Ventes, 59128 Flers en Escrebieux, France. adv.; charts; illus.; index. **Indexed:** Appl.Mech.Rev., Chem.Abstr.

355   IS
MIDDLE EAST MILITARY BALANCE (YEAR). (Text in English) 1983. a. IS.99($69.50) (Tel Aviv University, Jaffee Center for Stategic Studies) Jerusalem Post, P.O. Box 81, Jerusalem 91000, Israel. TEL 02-551616. FAX 02-537527. (U.S. subscr. to: 221 E. 43rd St., Ste. 601, New York, NY 10017) circ. 2,000. (back issues avail.)

355   UK   ISSN 0954-1136
MIDDLE EAST STRATEGIC STUDIES QUARTERLY.* 1989. q. £129. (Gulf Centre for Strategic Studies) Brassey's, 50 Fetter Ln., London EC4A 1AA, England. TEL 071-377-4881. FAX 071-377-4888. Ed. Omar Al-Hassan.

MIKROWELLEN AND H F - MAGAZIN; Telecommunications. see ENGINEERING — Electrical Engineering

355   SZ   ISSN 0026-3907
MILITAER-KUECHENCHEF. vol.15, 1971. bi-m. (Verband Schweizerischer Militaerkuechenchefs) Schoch und Co., Schermenweg 190, 3072 Ostermundigen BE, Switzerland. Ed. Major Qm Stampfli Pius. adv.; charts; illus.

355   SW   ISSN 0047-7354
MILITAER TEKNISK TIDSKRIFT. 1931. q. SEK 100 (typically set in Oct.). (Militaer Tekniska Foereningen) Dordius HB, Djurgaardsslaetten 92, S-115 21 Stockholm, Sweden. Ed. Walter Wicklund. adv.; bk.rev.; circ. 1,153.
—BLDSC shelfmark: 5767.961000.

355   GW   ISSN 0323-5254
D25
MILITAERGESCHICHTE. 1962. 6/yr. DM.49.20($13.86) (Militaergeschichtliches Institut der D D R) Militaerverlag der Deutschen Demokratischen Republik, Storkower Str. 158, 1055 Berlin, Germany. TEL 4300618. bk.rev.; bibl.; charts; illus.; index; circ. 4,000. **Indexed:** Amer.Hist.& Life, Hist.Abstr.
Formerly: Zeitschrift fuer Militaergeschichte (ISSN 0044-3115)

355   GW   ISSN 0026-3826
DD101
MILITAERGESCHICHTLICHE MITTEILUNGEN. (Supplement: War and Society. Newsletter.) 1967. s-a. DM.43. (Militaergeschichtliches Forschungsamt) R. Oldenbourg, Postfach 801360, 8000 Munich 80, Germany. FAX 089-4112207. Ed.Bd. adv.; bk.rev.; charts; illus.; stat.; cum.index: 1967-1971. (reprint service avail. from SCH) **Indexed:** Amer.Hist.& Life, Arts & Hum.Cit.Ind., Curr.Cont., Hist.Abstr.

MILITAERHISTORISK TIDSKRIFT. see HISTORY — History Of Europe

355   NO   ISSN 0026-3842
MILITAERPSYKOLOGISKE MEDDELELSER. 1955. irreg. free. Norwegian Armed Forces Psychological and Educational Centre, Oslo Mil, Akerhus, 0015 Oslo 1, Norway.

355.347   GW   ISSN 0047-7362
MILITAERSEELSORGE. (Supplements avail.) 1958. q. free. Katholisches Militaerbischofsamt, Postfach 19 01 99, 5300 Bonn, Germany. FAX 0228-221015. Ed. Werner Koester. bk.rev.; circ. 3,000.
Description: Catholic publication with articles devoted to the spiritual care of people in the military.

355   DK   ISSN 0026-3850
MILITAERT TIDSSKRIFT. 1871. m. (8/yr.). DKK 97.50. Krigsvidenskabelige Selskab, Forsvarsakademiet, Oesterbrogades Kaserne, P.B. 2715, 2100 Copenhagen OE, Denmark. Ed. K.V. Nielsen. adv.; bk.rev.; index; circ. 1,900. **Indexed:** Hist.Abstr. (until 1990).

355   GW   ISSN 0047-7346
MILITAERTECHNIK; Theorie - Praxis - Informationen: Fachzeitschrift fuer technische Fragen der Land-, Luft- und Seestreitkraefte. 1961. 6/yr. DM.52.80. Militaerverlag der Deutschen Demokratischen Republik, Storkowerstr. 158, 1055 Berlin, Germany. TEL 4300618.

355   NE   ISSN 0026-3869
MILITAIRE SPECTATOR. 1832. m. fl.30 (foreign fl.40). (Ministerie van Defensie - Royal Society for Military Science) Koninklijke Vereniging ter Beoefening van de Krijgswetenschap, Karel Doormanlaan 274, 2283 BB Rijswijk, Netherlands. adv.; bk.rev.; charts; illus.; index, cum.index; circ. 7,800. (back issues avail.)
—BLDSC shelfmark: 5767.900000.

355   IT
MILITALY. q. L.40000($32) Dragan & Bush S.r.l., Via Luigi Anelli, 4, 20122 Milan, Italy. TEL 02-5465615.

355   GW   ISSN 0724-3529
MILITARIA; Wissenschaftliches Organ fur Orden, Uniformen, Militar- und Zeitgeschicht. 1971. bi-m. DM.54 (foreign DM.60). Verlag Patzwall, Tangstedter Weg 52, 2000 Norderstedt, Germany. TEL 040-524-92-97. Ed. K.D. Patzwall.

355   BE
MILITARIA BELGICA; revue d'uniformologie et d'histoire militaire Belge. (Text in Dutch and French) 1977. q. 700 BEF includes Revue Belge d'Histoire Militaire. Societe Royale des Amis du Musee Royal de l'Armee et d'Histoire Militaire, Parc du Cinquantenaire 3, 1040 Brussels, Belgium. Ed. E.-A. Jacobs. circ. 1,000. (back issues avail.)
Description: Highlights arms and armor.

355   US   ISSN 1046-2511
MILITARY. 1985. 12/yr. $14. M H R Publishing Corp., 2122 28 St., Sacramento, CA 95818. TEL 916-457-8990. Ed. LTC Mike Mark. adv.; bk.rev.; circ. 14,280.
Formerly: Military History Review.
Description: Covers World War II, Korea, Vietnam, and present military actions worldwide.

MILITARY AIRCRAFT AND MISSILE DATA SHEETS. see AERONAUTICS AND SPACE FLIGHT

358.4 629.13   UK
MILITARY AIRCRAFT MARKINGS. 1980. a. Ian Allan Ltd., Terminal House, Station Approach, Shepperton, Surrey TW17 8AS, England. TEL 0932-228950. Ed. Peter R. March. circ. 15,000. (reprint service avail. from UMI)
Description: Annual listing of military aircraft markings.

MILITARY & AEROSPACE ELECTRONICS. see AERONAUTICS AND SPACE FLIGHT

358 629.132   US   ISSN 0887-2465
MILITARY & COMMERCIAL FIBER BUSINESS. 1987. fortn. $445 (foreign $480)(effective 1992). Phillips Publishing, Inc., Defense - Aviation Group, 1925 N. Lynn St., Ste. 1000, Arlington, VA 22209. TEL 703-522-8333. FAX 703-522-6448. Ed. Eric DeRitis.
●Also available online. Vendor(s): Data-Star, DIALOG, NewsNet.
Former titles: Military Fiber Optics News; Military Avionics (ISSN 0895-9242); Inside Military Aviation.
Description: Covers all navigation, communications and weapons electronics systems aircraft.

355   UK   ISSN 0459-7222
MILITARY BALANCE. 1959. a. $52.50. (International Institute for Strategic Studies) Brassey's, 50 Fetter Ln., London EC4A 1AA, England. TEL 071-377-4881. FAX 071-377-4888. (Subscr. to: Turpin Transactions, Distribution Centre, Blackhorse Rd., Letchworth, Herts. SG6 1HN, England. TEL 0462-672555) charts; stat.; circ. 22,000.
—BLDSC shelfmark: 5767.990000.
Description: Quantitative assessment of military strength and defense spending of every country with armed forces.

262 355   US   ISSN 0026-3958
MILITARY CHAPLAIN. 1931. bi-m. $10 for non-members. Military Chaplains Association of the United States of America, Box 42660, Washington, DC 20015-0660. FAX 717-642-6792. Ed. G. William Dando. adv.; bk.rev.; illus.; circ. 1,700. **Indexed:** Air Un.Lib.Ind.

355.347   US   ISSN 0360-9693
UH23
MILITARY CHAPLAINS' REVIEW. 1972. q. free to reserve and active-duty military chaplains and theological school libraries. U.S. Army Chaplaincy Services Support Agency, 1730 K St., N.W., Ste. 401, Washington, DC 20006-3868. TEL 202-653-1461. FAX 202-653-0768. Ed. Chaplain (Maj.) Granville E. Tyson. bk.rev.; circ. 6,000. **Indexed:** Ind.U.S.Gov.Per.

MILITARY CLUB & HOSPITALITY. see FOOD AND FOOD INDUSTRIES

647   US   ISSN 0192-2718
MILITARY CLUBS & RECREATION. 1961. m. $10. Club Executive, Inc., Box 7088, Alexandria, VA 22307. Ed. Paul E. Reece. adv.; illus.; index; circ. 7,000.
Former titles: Club Executive (ISSN 0009-9554); Clubs and Recreation.

MILITARY COLLECTOR & HISTORIAN. see ANTIQUES

MILITARY COLLECTORS NEWS. see HOBBIES

355   II   ISSN 0462-4874
MILITARY DIGEST. 1973. q. Director of Military Training, General Staff Branch MT4, Army Headquarters, DHQ P.O., New Delhi 110 011, India. bk.rev.; charts; illus.

MILITARY EDUCATORS & COUNSELORS ASSOCIATION NEWS. see EDUCATION — Higher Education

MILITARY ENGINEER. see ENGINEERING

355   US
MILITARY FUZES. a. $1495. Forecast International Inc. - D M S, 22 Commerce Rd., Newtown, CT 06470. TEL 203-426-0800. FAX 203-426-1964. TELEX 467615.
Description: Features market overviews of major fuze market segments: artillery, missiles, bombs, mines, rockets, small arms, and submunitions. Reports on more than 350 U.S., European, and international fuze programs with 10-year production forecasts.

355   UK   ISSN 0026-4008
DA49
MILITARY HISTORICAL SOCIETY. BULLETIN. 1951. q. £10 (foreign £15). Military Historical Society, National Army Museum, Royal Hospital Rd., London SW3 4HT, England. adv.; bk.rev.; charts; illus.; cum.index every 5 yrs.; circ. 1,400. **Indexed:** Amer.Hist.& Life, Hist.Abstr.
Description: Covers all aspects of British and Commonwealth Military History.

MILITARY HISTORY. see HISTORY — History Of North And South America

MILITARY HISTORY. see HISTORY — History Of North And South America

355   SA   ISSN 0026-4016
DT769
MILITARY HISTORY JOURNAL/KRYGSHISTORIESE TYDSKRIF. (Text and summaries in Afrikaans, English) 1967. s-a. R.35 (overseas R.50)(effective 1992). South African National Museum of Military History, P.O. Box 52090, Saxonwold 2132, South Africa. TEL 011-646-5513. FAX 011-646-5256. (Co-sponsor: South African Military History Society) Ed.Bd. bk.rev.; charts; illus.; cum.index; circ. 750. (back issues avail.) **Indexed:** Ind.S.A.Per.
—BLDSC shelfmark: 5768.080000.
Incorporates (1985-1991): South African National Museum of Military History. Review (ISSN 1016-2550)

MILITARY HISTORY OF THE SOUTHWEST. see HISTORY — History Of North And South America

MILITARY HISTORY PRESENTS GREAT BATTLES. see HISTORY — History Of North And South America

MILITARY

355 US ISSN 1040-4961
MILITARY IMAGES. 1979. bi-m. $20 (foreign $24). Harry Roach, Ed. & Pub., RD 1, Box 99A, Henryville, PA 18332. TEL 717-629-9152. adv.; bk.rev.; cum.index every 5 yrs.; circ. 3,000. (also avail. in microform from UMI; microfiche; back issues avail.; reprint service avail. from UMI)
 Formerly: Military Images Magazine (ISSN 0193-9866)
 Description: Covers U.S. photographic history from 1839 to 1900 and celebrates the American soldier of the 19th century.

355 UK
MILITARY INTELLIGENCE CRITICAL ATTRIBUTES. 1981. irreg. $605. Aviation Studies International, Sussex House, Parkside, Wimbledon, London SW19 5NB, England. TEL 081-946-5082.
 Description: For military intelligence planners and leaders. Covers organization, roles, missions, costs, manpower, NIE planning, and kinds of intelligence.

355 JO
MILITARY JOURNAL/MAJALLAH AL-ASKARIYYAH.* (Text in Arabic) 1955. q. Armed Forces, Army Headquarters, Amman, Jordan.

355 376 US
MILITARY LIFESTYLE. 1969. 10/yr. $40. Downey Communications, Inc., 4800 Montgomery Ln., 7th Fl., Bethesda, MD 20814-5341. TEL 301-718-7600. FAX 301-718-7652. Ed. Hope M. Daniels. adv.; bk.rev.; circ. 520,000 (controlled). (also avail. in microform from UMI; back issues avail.)
 Former titles: Military Lifestyle - Your Ladycom Magazine; (until 1985): Ladycom - The Military Lifestyle Magazine (ISSN 0023-7183)
 Description: Publishes articles on parenting, health, travel, fashion and food for America's active-duty military families.

640.73 US ISSN 0740-5065
MILITARY LIVING. 1969. m. $7. Military Living Publications, Box 2347, Falls Church, VA 22042-0347. TEL 703-237-0203.
 Description: Military benefits, facilities, rest and recreation.

355 US ISSN 0740-5073
MILITARY LIVING'S R & R REPORT; the voice of the military traveler. 1971. bi-m. $13. Military Living Publications, Box 2347, Falls Church, VA 22042-0347. TEL 703-237-0203. Ed. Ann Crawford. adv. (tabloid format; back issues avail.)
 Description: Military rest and recreation and travel.

355.621 US ISSN 0026-4067
MILITARY MARKET; magazine for the military retail system. 1954. m. $60 (Special numbers: Buyers Guide; Almanac and Directory Number $10 ea.). Army Times Publishing Co., 6883 Commercial Dr., Springfield, VA 22159. TEL 703-750-8676. Ed. Nancy Tucker. adv.; charts; illus.; tr.lit.; circ. 8,400. (also avail. in microform from UMI; reprint service avail. from UMI) **Indexed:** SRI.
 Description: Aimed at military officials and key civilians who buy for and operate base stores.

MILITARY MEDAL SOCIETY OF SOUTH AFRICA. JOURNAL. see NUMISMATICS

355 US ISSN 0095-635X
UH805
MILITARY MEDIA REVIEW. 1974. q. free to qualified government offices. Defense Information School, Fort Benjamin Harrison, IN 46216. Ed. Connie McKean. bk.rev.; bibl.; charts; illus.; circ. 6,000. **Indexed:** Ind.U.S.Gov.Per.
 Former titles: Military Journalist (ISSN 0026-4032); Journalist.

355 621.3 UK
MILITARY MICROWAVES (YEAR). PROCEEDINGS OF CONFERENCE. 1978. biennial. price varies. Microwave Exhibitions & Publishers Ltd., 90 Calverley Rd., Tunbridge Wells, Kent TN1 2UN, England. TEL 0892-544027. FAX 0892-541023. TELEX 95604-MEPNCL-G. circ. 1,500. (back issues avail.)

355 US
MILITARY MODELER. 1974. m. $27.95. Challenge Publications, Inc., 7950 Deering Ave., Canoga Park, CA 91304. TEL 213-887-0550. Ed. Sydney P. Chivers. adv.; circ. 20,039.

MILITARY MODELLING. see HOBBIES

355 US ISSN 0275-5823
MILITARY OPERATIONS RESEARCH. 1981. irreg., vol.2, 1982. Gordon & Breach Science Publishers, 270 Eighth Ave., New York, NY 10011. TEL 212-206-8900. FAX 212-645-2459. TELEX 236735 GOPUB UR. (Subscr. to: Box 786, Cooper Sta., New York, NY 10276. TEL 800-545-8398; UK subscr. to: P.O. Box 90, Reading, Berkshire RG1 8JL, England. TEL 0734-560-080) Ed. Stephen W. Leibholz.
 Refereed Serial

343.01 US ISSN 0895-4208
UB825.U54
MILITARY POLICE. 1951. s-a. $5 (foreign $6.25). U.S. Army Military Police School, Fort McClellan, AL 36205. TEL 205-238-5405. Ed. Lois C. Perry. bk.rev.; illus.; index; circ. 11,000. **Indexed:** Air Un.Lib.Ind.
 —BLDSC shelfmark: 5768.166000.
 Former titles (until 1987): Military Police Journal (ISSN 0884-0024); Military Police Law Enforcement Journal (ISSN 0199-7211)

MILITARY PSYCHOLOGY. see PSYCHOLOGY

355 US ISSN 0026-413X
MILITARY RESEARCH LETTER. 1958. s-m. $175. Callahan Publications, Box 3751, Washington, DC 20007. TEL 703-356-1925. FAX 703-356-9614. Ed. Vincent F. Callahan, Jr. bk.rev.; charts; stat. (processed)

355 US ISSN 0026-4148
Z6723
MILITARY REVIEW. Portuguese edition (ISSN 0193-2985); Spanish edition (ISSN 0193-2977) 1922. m. (Portuguese ed. bi-m.). $22 (foreign $29)(Portuguese and Spanish eds. $14)(typically set in July). U.S. Army Command and General Staff College, Funston Hall, Fort Leavenworth, KS 66027-6910. TEL 913-684-5642. FAX 913-684-4647. Ed. Lt. Col. Steven F. Rausch. bk.rev.; abstr.; charts; illus.; maps; index; circ. 27,000. (also avail. in microfilm from UMI; back issues avail.) **Indexed:** Abstr.Mil.Bibl., Air Un.Lib.Ind., Amer.Bibl.Slavic & E.Eur.Stud, Amer.Hist.& Life, DM & T, Hist.Abstr., Ind.U.S.Gov.Per., P.A.I.S., PROMT.
 —BLDSC shelfmark: 5768.170000.

MILITARY ROBOTICS NEWSLETTER; covering government and defense applications of robotics. see COMPUTERS — Artificial Intelligence

MILITARY ROBOTICS SOURCEBOOK. see COMPUTERS — Artificial Intelligence

355 UK
▼**MILITARY SIMULATION AND TRAINING.** 1985. bi-m. £24. Moench (UK) Ltd., 84 Alexandra Road, Farnborough, Hants GU14 6DD, England. TEL 0252-517974. FAX 0252-512714. Ed. David Saw. adv.; circ. 21,630.
 Description: Provides reports and descriptions on training armed forces throughout the world, with an emphasis on targeting DODs, serving officers and training establishments.

621.3 629 US ISSN 0743-7897
MILITARY SPACE. 1984. fortn. $496 (foreign $511). Pasha Publications Inc., 1401 Wilson Blvd., Ste. 900, Arlington, VA 22209-9970. TEL 703-528-1244. FAX 703-528-1253. Ed. Richard Buehnneke.
 ●Also available online. Vendor(s): NewsNet (DE04).
 Description: Reports on political issues, technological and international developments and opportunities in military space programs.

623 US
MILITARY SPECIFICATIONS AND STANDARDS SERVICES NUMERIC INDEX. (In 2 vols.) 1963. bi-m. $200. Information Handling Services, 15 Inverness Way East, Englewood, CO 80150. TEL 303-790-0600. FAX 303-799-4085. TELEX 4322083 IHS UI. Ed. Liz Maynard Prigge. adv.; circ. 2,715.
 ●Also available online. Vendor(s): DIALOG. Also available on CD-ROM.
 Formerly: Military Specifications and Standard Services Index.
 Description: Provides numeric access to military specifications and standards documents.

623 US
MILITARY TECHNOLOGY. m. $80. N & A Military Publishing Service Inc., 101 W. Read St., Ste. 314, Baltimore, MD 21201. **Indexed:** Air Un.Lib.Ind.

355 GW
MILITARY TECHNOLOGY: MILTECH. (Text in English) 1977. m. DM.110($80) Wehr und Wissen Verlag, Postfach 140261, 5300 Bonn 1, Germany. TEL 0228-6483-0. FAX 0228-6483-200. TELEX 8869429 MVBD. Ed. Ezio Bonsignore. adv.; bk.rev.; circ. 28,500. **Indexed:** DM & T, PROMT.
 Formerly: Military Technology (ISSN 0722-3226)
 Description: Journal of defense technology and economics.

MILITARY TRAVEL GUIDE. see TRAVEL AND TOURISM

MILITARY TRAVEL NEWS. see TRAVEL AND TOURISM

355 388.3 US ISSN 0893-3863
MILITARY VEHICLES. 1987. bi-m. $15. Eagle Press, Box 1748, Union, NJ 07083. TEL 908-688-6015. FAX 908-686-0358. (And: Box 1913, Bloomfield, NJ 07003) Eds. R.G. Ivory, D.R. Spence. adv.; bk.rev.; circ. 8,000. (back issues avail.)

355 II ISSN 0076-8782
U10.I5
MILITARY YEAR BOOK. (Text in English) 1965. a. Rs.425($99.50) (£55.05). Guide Publications, P.O. Box 2525, New Delhi 110 005, India. TEL 11-572-5793. TELEX 031-77174 GPUB IN. (Dist. in U.S. by: Taylor & Francis Inc, 242 Cherry St., Philadelphia, PA 19106) Ed. S.P. Baranwal. adv.; illus.; stat.; circ. 5,800.
 Description: Covers organizational and technological aspects, global events affecting the security environment, and a complete equipment catalogue of army, navy, air force of India.

355 UK ISSN 0144-5243
CODEN: MLTREL
MILTRONICS. vol.4, 1983. bi-m. $115. International Trade Publications Ltd., 2, Queensway, Redhill, Surrey RH1 1QS, England. TEL 0737-768611. FAX 0737-761989. TELEX 948669-TOPJNL-G. Ed. Anthony Farrar. adv.; illus.; circ. 10,000. **Indexed:** Abstr.Mil.Bibl., DM & T, PROMT.
 —BLDSC shelfmark: 5774.572000.

301 US ISSN 0736-718X
UB418.W65
MINERVA; quarterly report on women and the military. 1983. q. $40 to individuals; institutions $60; students $20. (Minerva Center) Linda Grant DePauw, Ed. & Pub., 1101 S. Arlington Ridge Rd., Rm. 210, Arlington, VA 22202. TEL 703-892-4388. bk.rev.; film rev.; play rev.; bibl.; charts; illus.; cum.index: 1983-1984; circ. 800. (back issues avail.) **Indexed:** Amer.Hist.& Life, Hist.Abstr.
 Description: Contains articles relating to service women, military wives, and women veterans (both military and civilian) from all nations and all eras.

301 US ISSN 0897-6104
UB418.W65
MINERVA'S BULLETIN BOARD. 1988. q. $20 to individuals; institutions $40; students $10. (Minerva Center) Linda Grant DePauw, Ed. & Pub., 1101 S. Arlington Ridge Rd., Rm. 210, Arlington, VA 22202. TEL 703-892-4388. adv.
 Description: Focuses on women and the military. Includes news briefs, short announcements and letters to the editors.

355 900 UK ISSN 0266-3228
MINIATURE WARGAMES. m. £18. Prieme Publishing, 34 Chatsworth Rd., Charminster, Bournemouth BM8 8SW, England. Ed. Ian Dickie. circ. 15,000. (back issues avail.)

355 US
MINNESOTA LEGIONNAIRE. 1922. m. $5. American Legion, Department of Minnesota, Veterans Service Bldg., St. Paul, MN 55155. TEL 612-291-1800. FAX 612-291-1057. Ed. Ron D. Johnson. adv.; bk.rev.; circ. 137,000. (back issues avail.)

MILITARY

355 US ISSN 0026-5993
MISSILE - ORDINANCE LETTER. 1957. s-m. $175. Callahan Publications, Box 3751, Washington, DC 20007. TEL 703-356-1925. FAX 703-356-9614. Ed. Vincent F. Callahan, Jr. bk.rev.; charts;stat. (processed)
Description: Contract opportunities in the field of military missiles and related equipment.

355.347 200 UK
MISSION TO MILITARY GARRISONS QUARTERLY RECORD. 1971. 4/yr. free to supporters. Mission to Military Garrisons Inc., 23 Royal Exchange Square, Glasgow G1 3AJ, Scotland. TEL 041-221-3575.
Formerly: Mission to Mediterranean Garrisons Quarterly Record.
Description: Covers the activities at each of the centers operated by the Mission. Includes prayer topics.

MISSISSIPPI LEGION-AIRE. see *CLUBS*

MONTANA LEGIONNAIRE. see *CLUBS*

MONTHLY WINGS. see *AERONAUTICS AND SPACE FLIGHT*

359 YU ISSN 0027-1136
MORNARICKI GLASNIK/NAVY JOURNAL. 1951. bi-m. $20. (Ratna Mornarica) Vojnoizdavacki Zavod, Svetozara Markovica 70, 11002 Belgrade, Serbia, Yugoslavia. Ed. Malin Malivuk.

355 US
MOUNTAINEER (COLORADO SPRINGS). 1949. w. $50 (effective Dec. 1990). Fort Carson, Public Affairs Office, Bldg. 1544, Fort Carson, CO 80913-5000. TEL 719-579-4144. FAX 719-632-0762. Ed. Sam Sears. circ. 15,000.

335.115 AT
MUFTI. 1934. q. Aus.$2. (Returned Services League of Australia, Victorian Branch) Newsprinters Pty. Ltd. Shepparton, Anzac House, 4 Collins St., Melbourne, Vic. 3000, Australia. Ed. P. O'Neil. adv.; bk.rev.; circ. 65,000.

355 UK ISSN 0027-5662
N A A F I NEWS. 1945. m. Navy, Army & Air Force Institutes, Kennington, London SE11, England. Ed. Patrick Breen. illus.; circ. 11,000 (controlled).

N A T O'S SIXTEEN NATIONS. (North Atlantic Treaty Organization) see *POLITICAL SCIENCE — International Relations*

355.115 US
N C O A JOURNAL. m. membership. Non-Commissioned Officers Association, Box 33610, San Antonio, TX 78265. TEL 512-653-6161. FAX 512-656-6225. Ed. Bill Noonan. adv.; circ. 160,000. (newspaper)
Description: Covers news items of interest to current and former members of the armed forces.

355 US ISSN 0882-9667
N S I ADVISORY. 1985. m. $275. National Security Institute, 161 Worcester Rd., Framingham, MA 02171. TEL 508-872-8001. FAX 508-872-6153. Ed. David A. Marston.
Description: Provides news, analysis, and commentary on national security issues of concern to cleared U.S. defense and intelligence contractors.

356 YU ISSN 0027-7908
U4
NARODNA ARMIJA; list jugoslavenske narodne armije. 1945. w. ($10.85) Narodna Armija, Proletarskih Brigada 13, Belgrade, Serbia, Yugoslavia. Ed. Ivo Tominic.

355 YU ISSN 0027-7916
NARODNA ODBRANA. 1948. w. Korpus Narodne Odbrane, Kommanda, Belgrade, Yugoslavia.

356 BN ISSN 0027-7959
NARODNI BORAC; list Sarajevske armijske oblasti. 1948. fortn. 24 din. per no. Sarajevska Armijska Oblast, Box 01-25, Sarajevo, Bosnia Hercegovina. Ed. Petar Jankovic.

355 FR
NATION ARMEE.* irreg., vol.2, 1977. Editions Copernic, 21 rue Cassette, 75006 Paris, France. Dir. Philippe Conrad.

355.15 US ISSN 0027-853X
NATIONAL AMVET. 1947. q. $10. American Veterans of World War II, Korea and Viet Nam (AMVETS), 4647 Forbes Blvd., Lanham, MD 20706. TEL 301-459-9600. FAX 301-459-7924. Ed. Richard W. Flanagan. adv.; bk.rev.; charts; illus.; stat.; circ. 153,000.

355 US ISSN 0092-1491
UF1 CODEN: NTDFA2
NATIONAL DEFENSE. 1920. 10/yr. $30 to non-members. American Defense Preparedness Association, 2101 Wilson Blvd., Ste. 400, Arlington, VA 22201-3061. TEL 703-522-1820. FAX 703-522-1885. Ed. F.C. Berry. adv.; bk.rev.; charts; illus.; stat.; index; circ. 35,000. (also avail. in microform from UMI; reprint service avail. from UMI) Indexed: Abstr.Mil.Bibl., Air Un.Lib.Ind., Chem.Abstr., DM & T, Eng.Ind., PROMT.
—BLDSC shelfmark: 6021.869000.
Formerly: Ordnance (ISSN 0030-4557); Incorporates: American Defense Preparedness Association. Annual Directory. (ISSN 0092-7422); Defense Manager (ISSN 0011-7609); Which was formerly titled: Armed Forces Management Association. A.F.M.A. Bulletin.
Description: Covers the issues influencing US defense policy and the defense industrial base.

355 US ISSN 0163-3945
UA42
NATIONAL GUARD. 1947. m. $10 for non-members. National Guard Association of the United States, 1 Massachusetts Ave., N.W., Washington, DC 20001. TEL 202-789-0031. FAX 202-543-5692. Ed. Col. Reid K. Beveridge. adv.; bk.rev.; illus.; circ. 70,000. (also avail. in microform from UMI; reprint service avail. from UMI) Indexed: Air Un.Lib.Ind.
Formerly (until 1979): National Guardsman (ISSN 0027-9412)

355 US ISSN 0363-8618
U9
NATIONAL GUARD ALMANAC. 1975. a. $6. Uniformed Services Almanac, Inc., Box 4144, Falls Church, VA 22044. TEL 703-532-1631. Ed. Lt. Col. Sol Gordon, USAF-Ret.
Formerly: Uniformed Services Almanac. National Guard Edition (ISSN 0363-8588)
Description: Annual guide to pay, benefits, entitlements and subjects of interest to guardsmen and other military personnel.

355 CN ISSN 0316-1919
F1028
NATIONAL MUSEUM OF MAN. MERCURY SERIES. CANADIAN WAR MUSEUM. PAPERS/MUSEE NATIONAL DE L'HOMME. COLLECTION MERCURE. MUSEE CANADIEN DE LA GUERRE. DOSSIERS. (Text in English or French) 1972. irreg., no.9, 1978. free. (National Museum of Man) National Museums of Canada, Ottawa, Ont. K1A 0M8, Canada. TEL 613-992-3497.

NATIONAL SECURITY REVIEW. see *POLITICAL SCIENCE*

355 947 BU ISSN 0324-0835
NATSIONALEN VOENNOISTORICHESKI MUZEI, SOFIA. IZVESTIYA. 1973. a. Durzhavno Voenno Izdatelstvo, c/o Hemus Foreign Trade Co., 6 Ruski Blvd., 1000 Sofia, Bulgaria. illus.

359 US ISSN 0028-1409
VA49
NAVAL AFFAIRS; in the interest of the enlisted active duty, fleet reserve and retired personnel of the U.S. Navy, Marine Corps and Coast Guard. 1922. m. $7 to non-members. Fleet Reserve Association, 125 N. West St., Alexandria, VA 22314-2754. TEL 703-683-1400. Ed. James T. McClung. adv.; bk.rev.; illus.; circ. 160,000.

359 551.46 JA
NAVAL ARCHITECTURE AND OCEAN ENGINEERING. (Text in English) a. 4000 Yen. Society of Naval Architects of Japan, 15-16 Toranomon 1-chome, Minato-ku, Tokyo 105, Japan.

355 UK
NAVAL BASE NEWSPAPERS. m. Ministry of Defense (Navy), Carpenter House, Broad Quay, Bath, Avon, England. Ed. M. Howitt. adv.; circ. 27,000.

NAVAL ENGINEERS JOURNAL. see *ENGINEERING*

359 UK
NAVAL FORCES. 1980. bi-m. £40. Moench (UK) Ltd., 84 Alexandra Rd., Farnborough, Hants. GU14 6DD, England. TEL 0252 517974. FAX 0252-512714. Ed. Antony Preston. adv.; bk.rev.; circ. 17,050. (back issues avail.) Indexed: Abstr.Mil.Bibl., Air Un.Lib.Ind., BMT, DM & T, PROMT.
Description: Provides specialist naval reports and features.

359 975 US
NAVAL HISTORY. 1987. q. $20 to non-members; members $12. U S Naval Institute, 118 Maryland Ave., Annapolis, MD 21402-5035. TEL 410-268-6110. Ed. Paul Stillwell. bk.rev.; illus.; circ. 28,000.
Description: Covers naval history including various areas, subjects and countries, and services - U.S. Coast Guard, Marine Corps, Merchant Marine and Navy.

359 US
VA40
NAVAL INSTITUTE GUIDE TO COMBAT FLEETS OF THE WORLD. (Editions in English and French) 1897. biennial. $120. (U.S. Naval Institute) Naval Institute Press, Annapolis, MD 21402. TEL 301-268-6110. FAX 301-269-7940. TELEX 187-114-AIR COURS PHX. Eds. Bernard Prezelin (French ed.), A.D. Baker (English ed.). (reprint service avail.)
Formerly: Combat Fleets of the World (ISSN 0364-3263)

NAVAL LAW REVIEW. see *LAW*

359 US
NAVAL RESERVIST NEWS; news of the total force Navy for the Naval Reserve community. vol.11, 1987. m. free to qualified personnel. Commander, Naval Reserve Force, Public Affairs Office (Code 004), 4400 Dauphine St., New Orleans, LA 70146-5000. TEL 504-942-6058. FAX 504-942-5049. Ed. Nat Chesnut. illus.; circ. 210,000. (tabloid format)

359 US ISSN 0077-6238
V10
NAVAL REVIEW; annual review of world seapower. (May issue of: U S Naval Institute, Proceedings) 1962. a. $10 paperback; hardbound $20. U S Naval Institute, 118 Maryland Ave., Anaapolis, MD 21402-5035. TEL 410-268-6110. Ed. Fred H. Rainbow. adv.; circ. 119,790. (back issues avail.)
Description: Covers the previous year's events in the naval-maritime field.

359 UK
NAVAL REVIEW. 1912. q. £15. 32 West St., Chichester, W. Sussex PO19 1QS, England. Ed. Richard Hill. adv.; bk.rev.; circ. 3,000.

359 US ISSN 0028-1484
V1
NAVAL WAR COLLEGE REVIEW. 1948. q. free to qualified personnel. U.S. Naval War College, Naval War College Press, Newport, RI 02841. TEL 401-841-4552. Ed. Frank Uhlig, Jr. bk.rev.; index; circ. controlled. (also avail. in microform from MIM,UMI,BHP; reprint service avail. from UMI) Indexed: Abstr.Mil.Bibl., Air Un.Lib.Ind., Amer.Bibl.Slavic & E.Eur.Stud, Amer.Hist.& Life, DM & T, Hist.Abstr., Ind.U.S.Gov.Per., Mid.East: Abstr.& Ind., Ocean.Abstr., Peace Res.Abstr, PROMT.

355.347 US ISSN 0028-1654
VG23
NAVY CHAPLAINS BULLETIN. 1955. q. free to qualified personnel. U.S. Navy, Bureau of Naval Personnel, Office of the Navy Chief of Chaplains, Washington, DC 20370. TEL 202-545-6700. circ. 2,400. Indexed: CERDIC.

355 624 US ISSN 0096-9419
VG593
NAVY CIVIL ENGINEER. 1946. q. $5.50. U.S. Naval Facilities Engineering Command, c/o Supt. of Documents, Washington, DC 20402. FAX 202-512-2233. (Subscr. to: Supt. of Documents, Box 371594, Pittsburgh, PA 15250-7954) (Co-sponsor: U.S. Naval School, Civil Engineer Corps Officers) Ed. Les Helsdon. bk.rev.; abstr.; charts; illus.; stat.; index, cum.index; circ. 15,400. (also avail. in microform from UMI) Indexed: Geotech.Abstr., Ind.U.S.Gov.Per.

MILITARY

359 UK ISSN 0144-3194
V1
NAVY INTERNATIONAL. 1895. 11/yr. £51($102) Maritime World Ltd., 114 South St., Dorking, Surrey RH4 2EZ, England. FAX 0306-77226. Ed. Anthony Watts. adv.; bk.rev.; illus.; circ. 3,000. **Indexed:** Abstr.Mil.Bibl., BMT, DM & T, PROMT.
—BLDSC shelfmark: 6067.580000.
Incorporates: Combat Craft (ISSN 0264-4649); Which was formerly: Navy (ISSN 0028-1646)

359 UK
NAVY LIST OF RETIRED OFFICERS. a. price varies. H.M.S.O., P.O. Box 276, London SW8 5DT, England.

359 UK ISSN 0028-1670
NAVY NEWS. 1954. m. £9.25 (foreign £10.25). Navy News, H.M.S. Nelson, Portsmouth, Hants, England. TEL 0705-826040. FAX 0705-830149. Ed. R. J. Tucker. adv.; illus.; circ. 101,000.
Description: Directed to the navy and to naval enthusiasts.

359 US ISSN 0028-1662
NAVY NEWS. 1927. w. $29.95. Scope Enterprises, Inc., Navy News, Inc., 2429 Bowland Pkwy., Ste.118, Virginia Beach, VA 23454-5230.
TEL 804-486-8000. FAX 804-486-8017. Ed. Robert N. Sandler. adv.; bk.rev.; charts; illus.; circ. 46,000. (tabloid format)

359 US
NAVY NEWS (VIRGINIA BEACH). 1927. w. $29.95. Orkand Communications, Inc., Box 8918, Virginia Beach, VA 23450-0918. TEL 804-486-8000. Ed. Patrick Finneran. adv.; bk.rev.; circ. 41,000. (tabloid format)

359 551.46 US ISSN 8756-1700
NAVY NEWS & UNDERSEA TECHNOLOGY. 1984. w. $495 (foreign $525). Pasha Publications Inc., 1401 Wilson Blvd., Ste. 900, Arlington, VA 22209-9970. TEL 703-528-1244.
FAX 703-528-1253. Ed. Stan Zimmerman. index.
●Also available online. Vendor(s): Data-Star, DIALOG, NewsNet.
—BLDSC shelfmark: 6067.595900.
Description: Tracks naval aircraft, computers, electronics, shipbuilding and weapons programs as well as domestic and foreign policy.

359 US ISSN 0360-716X
VC35
NAVY SUPPLY CORPS NEWSLETTER. 1937. bi-m. U.S. Department of the Navy, Supply Systems Command, Navy Supply Corps, Washington, DC 20374.
TEL 703-607-1301. FAX 703-607-2221. Ed. Nancy Dimond. circ. 15,000 (controlled).

359 US ISSN 0028-1697
V1
NAVY TIMES; Marine Corps, Navy, Coast Guard. (In 3 editions: Domestic, European, Pacific) 1951. w. $48. Army Times Publishing Co., 6883 Commercial Dr., Springfield, VA 22159. TEL 703-750-2000. Ed. Tom Philpott. adv.; bk.rev.; charts; illus.; mkt.; stat.; circ. 90,000. (tabloid format; also avail. in microform from UMI; reprint service avail. from UMI)

355 US
NEW BREED. 1982. bi-m. $17. New Breed Publications, Inc., Box 428, Nanuet, NY 10954. Ed. Harry Belil. adv.; bk.rev.; circ. 68,000.
Description: Covers all areas of the military: history, law enforcement, weapons and intelligence.

353.9 US ISSN 0094-7326
UB358.N6
NEW MEXICO. VETERANS' SERVICE COMMISSION. REPORT. a. free. Veterans' Service Commission, Bataan Memorial Building, 408 Galisteo St., Box 2324, Santa Fe, NM 87503. TEL 505-827-6300. FAX 505-827-6300. charts; stat.; circ. 100. Key Title: Report of the New Mexico Veteran's Service Commission.

355.45 US
NEW YORK (STATE). ASSEMBLY. STANDING COMMITTEE ON VETERANS' AFFAIRS. ANNUAL REPORT. a. State Assembly, Room 524, State Capitol, Albany, NY 12248. TEL 518-455-4178.

NEW ZEALAND R S A REVIEW. see *SOCIAL SERVICES AND WELFARE*

359 US
NEWPORT NAVALOG. 1901. w. free. Edward A. Sherman Publishing Co., 101 Malbone Rd., Box 420, Newport, RI 02840. FAX 401-849-3300. adv.; circ. 7,200 (controlled).
Description: Civilian enterprise newspaper published for the naval eduction and training center, Newport, Rhode Island.

355 NO ISSN 0029-1692
NORGES FORSVAR. (Includes annual report) 1951. 10/yr. NOK 110. Norges Forsvarsforening - Norwegian Defence Association, Sporveisgaten 29, 0354-Oslo 3, Norway. TEL 02-696500.
FAX 02-4608. Ed. Bjoern Hoelseth. adv.; bk.rev.; illus.; index; circ. 11,500.

355 NO ISSN 0029-1854
NORSK ARTILLERI-TIDSSKRIFT. 1900. 3/yr. NOK 90. Artilleriets Offisersforening, FO-HST-ARTINSP, Oslo Mil-Huseby, N-0016 Oslo 1, Norway.
TEL 2-498603. FAX 2-498312. Ed. E. Davidsen. adv.; bk.rev.; charts; illus.; index; circ. 600.

359 NO ISSN 0029-2222
V5
NORSK TIDSSKRIFT FOR SJOVESEN. 1882. 6/yr. NOK 90. Sjomilitaere Samfund, P.O. Box 105, 5078 Haakonsven, Norway. Ed. Svein C. Sivertsen. adv.; bk.rev.; illus.; index; circ. 2,300.

NORTHERN IRELAND NEWS SERVICE; NINS NewsBreak. see *POLITICAL SCIENCE*

355 US
NOUNCEMENTS. 1967. q. $4.50. (Women Marine Association) Marine Corps Association, Box 1775, MCB Quantico, VA 22134-0387.
TEL 703-640-6161. (Subscr. to: Assistant Secretary, Box 387, MCB Quantico, VA 22134-0387) Ed. Mary Bennett. circ. 3,500.
Description: Includes items of interest, and Marine Corps and Veterans information for all WMA members.

NUCLEAR ARMS; opposing viewpoints sources. see *POLITICAL SCIENCE — International Relations*

NUCLEAR TIMES; issues & activism for global survival. see *POLITICAL SCIENCE*

355 UK
NUCLEAR WEAPONS DATA FILE. 1979. q. $590. Aviation Studies International, Sussex House, Parkside, Wimbledon, London SW19 5NB, England. TEL 081-946-5082.

355 IT ISSN 0048-1122
NUOVA TRADOTTA. vol.15, 1971. m. Associazione Nazionale Combattenti e Reduci Federazione Provinciale di Milano, Via Bagutta 12, Milan, Italy. Ed. Franco Mattavelli. bibl.; illus.

355 629.4 US
O & M INTELLIGENCE. (Operation & Maintenance) w. $300. Forecast International Inc. - D M S, 22 Commerce Rd., Newtown, CT 06470.
TEL 203-426-0800. FAX 203-426-1964. TELEX 467615. (back issues avail.)
●Also available online. Vendor(s): DIALOG (File no.587/DMS DEFENSE NEWSLETTERS).
Description: Provides information on developments and trends in defense and aerospace O & M, including budget actions, congressional directives on contracting, major competition announcements and contract awards.

355 976 US
O I W COMMUNIQUE. 1979. m. $20. Order of the Indian Wars, Box 7401, Little Rock, AR 72217. TEL 501-225-3996. Ed. Jerry L. Russell. circ. 550.
Description: Devoted to the study and historic preservation of Indian Wars sites.

359 US ISSN 0029-7356
OAK LEAF. vol.30, 1974. bi-m. free. Naval Surface Weapons Center, Public Affairs Office, Silver Spring, MD 20910. TEL 301-394-1796. Ed. Karen L. Pelham. charts; illus.; circ. 4,500.

355 GW ISSN 0029-7402
DIE OASE. 1951. m. DM.36. (Deutsches Afrika-Korps e.V.) Heinrich Poeppinghaus GmbH, Alte Bahnhofstr. 148a, 4630 Bochum-Langendreer, Germany.
TEL 0234-287254. Ed. Paul-Peter Jagnow. bk.rev.; illus.
Description: Publication of the German Africa Corps. Includes reports of events and activities, history, personal stories, travel stories and announcements of events.

358.4 YU ISSN 0029-8336
ODBRANA. 1949. bi-m. Savez Rezervnih Vojnih Staresina Beograda, Trg Bratstva i Jedinstva 9, Belgrade, Serbia, Yugoslavia.

ODBRANA I ZASTITA. see *CIVIL DEFENSE*

355 AU ISSN 0048-1440
U3
OESTERREICHISCHE MILITAERISCHE ZEITSCHRIFT. 1963. bi-m. S.160 (foreign S.200). (Ministry of Defense) Carl Ueberreuter, Alserstr. 24, A-1090 Vienna, Austria. TEL 0222-40444. Ed. Franz Freistetter. adv.; bk.rev.; charts; illus.; index; circ. 5,000. **Indexed:** Abstr.Mil.Bibl.
—BLDSC shelfmark: 6307.955000.

355.12 US
OFF DUTY AMERICA. 1974. bi-m. $12. Off Duty Enterprises, 3303 Harbor Blvd., Ste. C-2, Costa Mesa, CA 92626. TEL 714-549-7172. Ed. Gary Burch. adv.; bk.rev.; film rev.; tr.lit.; index; circ. 525,000.
Formerly: Off Duty West.
Description: Written for service personnel in the U.S. and the Caribbean.

355 US
OFF DUTY - EUROPE. 1970. m. $10 (free to U.S. military personnel). Off Duty Enterprises, 3303 Harbor Blvd., Ste. C-2, Costa Mesa, CA 92626. TEL 714-549-7172. Ed. James Shaw. adv.; bk.rev.; film rev.; tr.lit.; index; circ. 95,000.
Description: Information on U.S. military personnel and their families in Europe and the Middle East.

355.12 HK
OFF DUTY - PACIFIC. (Text in English) 1971. m. $18. Off Duty Publications Ltd., 14-F Park Commercial Centre, 8 Shelter St., Causeway Bay, Hong Kong. FAX 852-5-8901761. (U.S. addr.: Off Duty Enterprises, 303 Harbor Blvd., Ste. C-2, Costa Mesa, CA 92626. TEL 714-549-7172) Ed. James Shaw. adv.; bk.rev.; film rev.; tr.lit.; index; circ. 80,000.
Description: For U.S. military personnel and their families.

355 US ISSN 0030-0268
UA23.A1
OFFICER. 1924. m. $12. Reserve Officers Association of the United States, 1 Constitution Ave. N.E., Washington, DC 20002. TEL 202-479-2200. Ed. Norman S. Burzynski. adv.; bk.rev.; illus.; circ. 124,000. (also avail. in microform from UMI; reprint service avail. from UMI) **Indexed:** Air Un.Lib.Ind.
Description: Covers active and reserve force activities of the Army, Navy, Air Force, Coast Guard, Public Health Service and National Oceanic and Atmospheric Administration, as well as congressional and administrative actions affecting the nation's uniformed services.

355 US ISSN 0736-7317
OFFICER REVIEW. vol.14, 1976. 10/yr. $7.50. Military Order of the World Wars, 435 N. Lee St., Alexandria, VA 22314. TEL 703-683-4911.
FAX 703-683-4501. Ed. R. Remler. adv.; bk.rev.; charts; illus.; circ. 17,000.

355 US ISSN 1040-029X
OFFICERS CALL. 1981. q. membership. National Officers Association, 1304 Vincent Pl., McLean, VA 22101. TEL 703-821-0557. FAX 703-821-0008. Ed. Carolyn Jones. adv.; bk.rev.; circ. 17,000. (looseleaf format; back issues avail.)
Description: Focuses on benefits and entitlement programs from a military perspective.

355 CU
EL OFICIAL. m. Ministerio de las Fuerzas Armadas Revolucionarias, Ave. 47, No. 1414th, 14 y 18 Playa, Marianao, Cuba.

MILITARY

355 US
OKINAWA TODAY. 1982. fortn. 825 Old Country Rd., Westbury, NY 11590. TEL 516-334-3030. Ed. Kari Valtaoja. adv.; circ. 15,000.
Description: Military consumer magazine.

355 323.4 US
ON GUARD. 1986. q. $10. Citizen Soldier, 175 Fifth Ave., No.808, New York, NY 10010. Eds. Tod Ensign, Tricia Critchfield. bk.rev.; circ. 15,000. (also avail. in microform from UMI; back issues avail.)
Indexed: Alt.Press Ind.

359 US
ON WATCH. q. Fleet Reserve Association, 125 N. West St., Alexandria, VA 22314-2754. TEL 703-683-1400. FAX 703-549-6610. Ed. Patricia Williamson. circ. 200,000.

355.133 NE ISSN 0030-2783
ONS WAPEN. 1954. bi-m. fl.10. Stichting Tijdschrift Ons Wapen, Raamweg 4, The Hague, Netherlands. adv.; bk.rev.; illus.; circ. 5,000.

358.4 NE ISSN 0030-3208
ONZE LUCHTMACHT/OUR AIR FORCE. 1948. bi-m. fl.35($23) Koninklijke Nederlandse Vereniging "Onze Luchtmacht" - Royal Dutch Airforce Association, Potgieterlaan 1, 1215 AH Hilversum, Netherlands. TEL 035-47335 Fd. W.F. Helfferich. adv.; bk.rev.; illus.; index; circ. 10,000.

355 NE
OORLOGSDOCUMENTATIE '40-'45. 1989. a. fl.39.50. (Rijksinstituut voor Oorlogsdocumentatie) Walberg Pers BV, P.O. Box 222, 7200 AE Zutphen, Netherlands. TEL 05750-10522. FAX 05750-41025.

ORDERS AND MEDALS SOCIETY OF AMERICA. OFFICIAL JOURNAL. see *HOBBIES*

355 GU
ORDERS GUAM. 1976. a. free to qualified personnel. Glimpses of Guam, Inc., P.O. Box 3191, Agana, Guam 96910. circ. 10,000.

360 IT
ORDRE SOUVERAIN MILITAIRE DE MALTA. REVUE INTERNATIONAL. (Editions in English, French and Italian) 1969. 3/yr. L.2500($3) Ordre Souverain Militaire de Malta, Palazzo Malta, 68 via Condotti, Rome, Italy. charts; illus.; circ. 4,000.

355 US
OVERSEAS!. m. Military Consumer Today, Inc., Box 1500, 825 Old Country Rd., Westbury, NY 11590. TEL 516-334-3030. FAX 516-334-3059. adv.; circ. 82,300.
Description: Concerns leisure time for military men serving in Europe.

355 FR ISSN 0154-7313
P G - C A T M. vol.26, 1971. 11/yr. 4350 F. Federation Nationale des Combattants Prisonniers de Guerre Combattants d'Algerie, Tunise et Maroc, 46 rue Copernic, 75782 Paris Cedex 16, France. Ed. Jacques Goujat. bk.rev.; bibl.; charts; illus.; circ. 3,300,000.
Former titles: C A T M; P G - Prisonniers de Guerre (ISSN 0048-2595)

355 NE
P M T - NIEUWS. vol.82, 1971. 4/yr. free. Koninklijke Nederlandse Militaire Bond pro Rege, Nieuwe Gracht 90, 3512 LW Utrecht, Netherlands. FAX 030-316578. adv.; bk.rev.; charts; illus.; circ. 100,000.
Formerly: Nederlandse Krijgsman.

358.4 US
PACESETTER. w. $25. East Central Communications, Inc., 1332 E. Harmon Dr., Rantoul, IL 61866. TEL 217-892-9613. Ed. Francis G. McLoughlin. circ. 8,250. (tabloid format)
Description: Military tabloid serving Chanute Air Force.

355 AT
PACIFIC DEFENCE REPORTER. 1974. bi-m. Aus.$60. Peter Isaacson Publications Pty. Ltd., 45-50 Porter St., Prahran, Vic. 3181, Australia. TEL 03-520-5555. FAX 03-521-3647. **Indexed:** Abstr.Mil.Bibl., Air Un.Lib.Ind., Aus.P.A.I.S., DM & T, PROMT.

PACIFIC RESEARCH. see *POLITICAL SCIENCE — International Relations*

356 PK ISSN 0030-9656
PAKISTAN ARMY JOURNAL. 1956. q. Rs.90($8) Inspector General Training & Evaluation Branch, Training Publications & Information Directorate, General Staff Branch, General Headquarters, Rawalpindi, Pakistan. Ed. Lt. Col. Syed Ishia Ali. bk.rev.; circ. 3,500.

355 IT ISSN 0394-3429
PANORAMA DIFESA. 1982. m. (11/yr.). L.65000 (foreign L.80000). Ed.A.I. s.r.l. (Edizioni Aeronautiche Italiane), V. Guinicelli 4, 50133 Florence, Italy. TEL 055-574774. FAX 055-570103. TELEX 580217 EDAI I. Ed. Ruggero Stanglini. adv.; circ. 31,600.
Description: Features a broad view of novelties in the following sectors: Air Force, Navy, space and civil defense.

355 US ISSN 0031-1723
U1
PARAMETERS (CARLISLE BARRACKS); United States Army War College. 1971. q. $7 (foreign $8.75). U.S. Army War College, Carlisle Barracks, PA 17013. TEL 717-245-4943. FAX 717-245-3603. TELEX AUTOVON 242-4943. (Dist by: Supt. of Documents, Washington, DC 20402) Ed. Lloyd J. Matthews. bk.rev.; charts; illus.; circ. 11,000. (also avail. in microfilm from UMI; microfiche from UMI)
Indexed: A.B.C.Pol.Sci., Abstr.Mil.Bibl., Air Un.Lib.Ind., Bk.Rev.Ind. (1989-), Child.Bk.Rev.Ind. (1989-), Hist.Abstr., Ind.U.S.Gov.Per., Mid.East: Abstr.& Ind., P.A.I.S., PROMT, R.G.
—BLDSC shelfmark: 6404.837000.
Description: Provides a forum for the expression of mature, professional thought on the art and science of land warfare; national and international security affairs, military strategy, military leadership and management, military history; ethics and other topics of significant and current interest to the U.S. Army, and the Department of Defense.

355 CN ISSN 0384-0417
PARAPET. (Text in English, French) 1971. m. free. Canadian Forces Base Montreal, St. Hubert, Que. J3Y 5T4, Canada. TEL 514-462-7409. FAX 514-462-7045. Ed. Maj. J.A. Rioux. adv.; bk.rev.; illus.; circ. 3,000.

355 SA ISSN 0031-1839
PARATUS. (Text in Afrikaans, English) 1949. m. R.14. South African Defence Force, Private Bag X158, Pretoria 0001, South Africa. TEL 012-3220610. Ed. J.H. Moody. adv.; bk.rev.; circ. 45,000.
Indexed: Abstr.Mil.Bibl., Ind.S.A.Per.
Formerly: Commando (ISSN 0010-2504)

PEACE MAGAZINE. see *POLITICAL SCIENCE — International Relations*

358.4 UK ISSN 0031-4080
PEGASUS JOURNAL. (Includes 3 supplements) 1946. 3/yr. £7 (foreign £9). Royal British Legion, Parachute Regiment and Airborne Forces, Browning Barracks, Aldershot, Hampshire GU11 2BU, England. TEL 0252-349624. FAX 0252-349203. Ed. Maj. Donald Cuthbertson-Smith. adv.; bk.rev.; circ. 6,000 (controlled).

355.115 UK ISSN 0048-3192
THE PENNANT. 1946. s-a. membership. Officers' Pensions Society Ltd., 15 Buckingham Gate, London SW1E 6NS, England. TEL 071-834-0853. Ed. Maj. Gen. Sir Laurence New. adv.; bk.rev.; circ. 37,000.

PERISCOPE; Chatham Naval Base newspaper. see *TRANSPORTATION — Ships And Shipping*

355 US ISSN 0195-1920
PHALANX; bulletin of military operations research and related sciences. 1965. q. $20 for 2 yrs. Military Operations Research Society, Inc., Landmark Towers, 101 S. Whiting St., Ste. 202, Alexandria, VA 22304. TEL 703-751-7290. FAX 703-751-7290. (Co-sponsor: Operations Research Society of America) Ed. John K. Walker, Jr. bk.rev.; circ. 9,100. (back issues avail.)

PHYLLIS SCHLAFLY REPORT. see *WOMEN'S INTERESTS*

PILOT UND FLUGZEUG. see *TRANSPORTATION — Air Transport*

355 SI ISSN 0048-4199
PIONEER; Singapore armed forces news. 1969. m. S.$0.50 per no. Ministry of Defense, Public Affairs Department, Tanglin Rd., Singapore 1024, Singapore. Ed. Francis Gomes. adv.; bk.rev.; charts; illus.; circ. 120,000. **Indexed:** Abstr.Mil.Bibl.

355 SZ
PIONIER. m. Redaktion Pionier, H & W Wiesner, Stutzweg 23, 4434 Hoelstein, Switzerland.

POLITICA E ESTRATEGIA. see *POLITICAL SCIENCE — International Relations*

POLITICS OF LIBERATION SERIES. see *HISTORY — History Of Europe*

POPULAR SCIENCE AND TECHNOLOGY. see *SCIENCES: COMPREHENSIVE WORKS*

355 PO
PORTUGAL. SERVICO DE ADMINISTRACAO MILITAR. REVISTA BIMESTRAL. bi-m. Esc.150. Servico de Administracao Militar, Rua Rodrigo da Fonseca, No. 180, Lisbon, Portugal. illus.
Supersedes: Portugal. Servico de Administracao Militar. Revista Mensal (ISSN 0037-2714)

355 949.7 YU ISSN 0351-3912
UA18.Y8
POZADINA. 1947. b-m. Savezni Sekretarijat za Narodnu Odbranu, 11002 Belgrade, Serbia, Yugoslavia. (Dist. by: Vojnoizdavacki i Novinski Centar, Svetozara Markovica 70, 11002 Belgrade, Serbia, Yugoslavia) Ed. Borisav Nedic. bk.rev.
Formerly (until 1980): Vojnoekonomski Pregled (ISSN 0350-0578)

355 US
PRECISION GUIDED MUNITIONS. a. $1495. Forecast International Inc. - D M S, 22 Commerce Rd., Newtown, CT 06470. TEL 203-426-0800. FAX 203-426-1964. TELEX 467615.
Description: Presents comprehensive study of more than 125 U.S. and international PGM programs, covering a broad range of new anti-armor weapons such as short-range, direct-fire systems and indirect fire PGMs.

355 NO ISSN 0032-910X
PRO PATRIA. 1922. 6/yr. NOK 80. Norske Reserveoffiserers Forbund - Norwegian Reserve Officers Federation, Oslo Mil, Oslo 1, Norway. Ed. K. Jorgensen. adv.; bk.rev.; bibl.; illus.; circ. 11,000.

335 US ISSN 0145-112X
UA23.A1
PROFILE (NORFOLK). 1956. 6/yr. free. (U.S. Department of the Navy, Office of Information) U.S. Department of Defense, High School News Service, Building X-18, Naval Station, Norfolk, VA 23511. TEL 804-444-2828. Ed. Clark M. Gammell. circ. 30,000. **Indexed:** Ind.Free Per., Ind.U.S.Gov.Per.
Formerly: High School News Service Report.

PROGRAM MANAGER. see *COMPUTERS — Computer Systems*

PROPEL; tidsskrift for flyvning og rumfart. see *AERONAUTICS AND SPACE FLIGHT*

355.133 UK ISSN 0033-1945
PROVOST PARADE. 1947. s-a. £1.20. (R.A.F. Provost Branch) Royal Air Force Police School, RAF Newton, Nottingham NG13 8HR, England. Ed. B. Hicks. adv.; bk.rev.; charts; illus.; stat.; circ. 2,000. (back issues avail.)

PRZYSPOSOBIENIE OBRONNE W SZKOLE. see *EDUCATION*

PUBLI AND CONSULT NEWS. see *AERONAUTICS AND SPACE FLIGHT*

355 US
PUPUKAHI/HARMONIOUSLY UNITED. 1950. q. Department of Defense, 3949 Diamond Head Rd., Honolulu, HI 96816-4495. FAX 808-737-6787. circ. 7,500.
Formerly (until 1973): Hawaii Guardsman (ISSN 0017-8578)

MILITARY

355.115 US
PURPLE HEART MAGAZINE. vol.43, 1980. bi-m. $5 to non-members. Military Order of the Purple Heart of the U.S.A., 5413-B Backlick Rd., Springfield, VA 22151. TEL 703-642-5360. FAX 817-767-5201. Ed. Carroll Wilson. bk.rev.; circ. 20,000.

355 IT
QUADRANTE; rivista per le forze armate Italiane. 1966. s-m. Ministero della Difesa, Rome, Italy.

355.1 UK
QUEEN'S REGULATIONS FOR THE ARMY AMENDMENTS. irreg. price varies. H.M.S.O., P.O. Box 276, London SW8 5DT, England.

358.4 343.01 UK
QUEEN'S REGULATIONS FOR THE R.A.F. AMENDMENTS. irreg. price varies. H.M.S.O., P.O. Box 276, London SW8 5DT, England.

355 BA
AL-QUWWA. m. Bahrain Defence Forces, P.O. Box 245, Manama, Bahrain. Ed. Maj. Ahmad Muhammad as-Suwaidi.

358.4 TS
AL-QUWWAT AL-JAWWIYYAH/U A E AIR FORCE MAGAZINE. (Text in Arabic) 1984. bi-m. 120DH. (Europe 380DH.; N. America 460DH.). General Command for the Armed Forces, Air Force and Air Defence Command, P.O. Box 3231, Abu Dhabi, United Arab Emirates. TEL 2-478128. FAX 2-479585. TELEX 24345 AIRFORM EM. Ed. Ahmad Khamis al-Hamili. adv.; circ. 22,000.
Description: Covers military aviation and air force and air defence matters.

R & D CONTRACTS MONTHLY; a continuously up-dated sales and R & D tool for all research organizations and manufacturers. (Research & Development) see *SCIENCES: COMPREHENSIVE WORKS*

355 US
R & R ENTERTAINMENT DIGEST. (Rest & Relaxation) 1982. m. 825 Old Country Rd., Westbury, NY 11590. TEL 516-334-3030. Ed. Tory Billard. adv.; circ. 182,500.
Description: Military consumer magazine.

R & R SHOPPERS NEWS. (Rest & Relaxation) see *COMMUNICATIONS — Television And Cable*

356 US ISSN 0162-7082
U393
R, D & A. (Research, Development and Acquisition) 1960. bi-m. $5.25. U.S. Department of the Army, Office of Chief, Research and Development, Washington, DC 20310-1508. TEL 202-545-6700. (Orders to: Supt. of Documents, Washington, DC 20402) (Published in coordination with DARCOM Information Office, Office of Chief of Engineers, Office of Surgeon General's Medical R & D Command, and Office of Deputy Chief of Staff for Research, Development and Acquisition. HQ. Dept. of the Army) circ. 42,000. (also avail. in microform from MIM,UMI) Indexed: Ind.U.S.Gov.Per.
Former titles: Army R D and A; (until 1978): Army Research and Development (ISSN 0004-2560)

355.058 UK ISSN 0305-6155
V10
R U S I AND BRASSEY'S DEFENCE YEARBOOK. 1890. a. $20. Royal United Services Institute for Defence Studies, Whitehall, London SW1A 2ET, England. TEL 071-930-5854. FAX 071-321-0943.
Formerly: Brassey's Annual - the Armed Forces Year-Book (ISSN 0068-0702)

355 UK ISSN 0307-1847
U1
R U S I JOURNAL. 1858. q. £35($65) Royal United Services Institute for Defence Studies, Whitehall, London SW1A 2ET, England. TEL 071-930-5854. FAX 071-231-0943. Ed. Jane Alford. adv.; bk.rev.; bibl.; illus.; index; circ. 4,000. (also avail. in microform from UMI; reprint service avail. from UMI) Indexed: Abstr.Mil.Bibl., Air Un.Lib.Ind., Amer.Hist.& Life, Br.Hum.Ind., DM & T, Hist.Abstr., P.A.I.S.
—BLDSC shelfmark: 8052.647530.
Formerly: Royal United Service Institution. Journal (ISSN 0035-9289)

355 UK ISSN 0268-2656
R U S I NEWSBRIEF. 1981. m. Royal United Services Institute for Defence Studies, Whitehall, London SW1A 2ET, England. TEL 071-930-5854. FAX 071-321-0943. Ed. Jonathan Eyal. circ. 1,000. (back issues avail.)
—BLDSC shelfmark: 6106.244600.

355.347 UK
READY. 1912. 2/yr. £2. Soldiers' & Airmen's Scripture Readers Association, Havelock House, Barrack Rd., Aldershot, Hants. GU11 3NP, England. TEL 0252-310033. Ed. M. Hitchcott. circ. 17,000.
Description: Presents claims of Jesus Christ to members of Her Majesty's Armed Forces and their families.

355 US ISSN 0093-5336
U1
RECON. 1973. q. $15. Recon Publications, Box 14602, Philadelphia, PA 19134. Ed. Chris Robinson. adv.; bk.rev.; illus.; index; circ. 2,000.
Description: Exposes undercover military activities worldwide originating from the Pentagon.

356 US
RECRUITER JOURNAL. 1919. m. free. U.S. Army Recruiting Command, Public Affairs Office, USARCAPA-PA, Ft. Sheridan, IL 60037. TEL 708-926-3918. FAX 708-926-7001. (Subscr. to: Supt. of Documents., Washington, DC 20402) Ed. Kathleen Welker. bk.rev.; charts; illus.; circ. 12,000.
Supersedes (in 1984): All Volunteer (ISSN 0192-6071); Which was formerly: U.S. Army Recruiting and Re-Enlisting Journal (ISSN 0162-3141); (Until vol.31, no.4, 1978): U.S. Army Recruiting and Career Counseling Journal (ISSN 0041-7513)
Description: Provides professional development and command information to members.

355 US
▼**REENACTOR'S JOURNAL**; for Civil War military and civilian reenactors. 1990. 12/yr. $20. Box 1864, Dept. N, Varna, IL 61375. adv.; bk.rev.

REGULAR. see *BUSINESS AND ECONOMICS — Labor And Industrial Relations*

358.4 US
REPORTER (WASHINGTON). 1977. q. $9. U.S. Air Force, Judge Advocate General School, AUCPD-JAR, Maxwell AFB, AL 36112-5712. TEL 202-545-6700. (Subscr. to: Supt. of Documents, Washington, D.C. 20402) Ed. Capt. Amy J. McDonough, USAF. index; circ. 3,000. (back issues avail.) Indexed: Ind.U.S.Gov.Per.
Description: Legal forum for articles of interest to Air Force judge advocates, civilian attorneys and other military lawyers.

355.81 US ISSN 0099-6335
CODEN: RMFABR
RESEARCH & DEVELOPMENT ASSOCIATES FOR MILITARY FOOD AND PACKAGING SYSTEMS. ACTIVITIES REPORT. 1947. s-a. $50 to non-members; members $20; foreign $85. Research and Development Associates for Military Food & Packaging Systems, Inc., 16607 Blanco Rd., Ste. 305, San Antonio, TX 78232. TEL 512-493-8024. FAX 512-493-8036. Ed. Anna May Schenck. circ. 800. (back issues avail.) Indexed: Biol.Abstr.
Formerly: U.S. Army Natick Laboratories. Activities Report (ISSN 0041-7505)

355 US ISSN 0899-0166
RESEARCH GUIDES IN MILITARY STUDIES. 1988. irreg. price varies. Greenwood Press, Inc. (Subsidiary of: Greenwood Publishing Group Inc.), 88 Post Rd. W., Box 5007, Westport, CT 06881-5007. TEL 203-226-3571. FAX 203-222-1502.

355.3 US ISSN 0363-860X
U9
RESERVE FORCES ALMANAC. 1975. a. $6. Uniformed Services Almanac, Inc., Box 4144, Falls Church, VA 22044. TEL 703-532-1631. Ed. Lt.Col. Sol Gordon, USAF-Ret.
Formerly: Uniformed Services Almanac. Special Reserve Forces Edition (ISSN 0360-554X)
Description: Annual guide to pay, benefits, entitlements and subjects of interest to Reservists and other military personnel.

355.37 US
RESERVIST.* 1971. q. free to qualified personnel. Reserve Enlisted Association, 1020 St. Paul St., Baltimore, MD 21202. Ed. Donald Kohr. adv.; bk.rev.; charts; illus.; circ. 100,000.

355.37 SI
RESERVIST. (Text in English) 1973. bi-m. 5200 Jalan Bukit Merah, Singapore 0315, Singapore. TEL 2786011. FAX 2737441. TELEX 28837. Ed. Paul Jansen. circ. 95,000.

RESISTANCE NEWS. see *POLITICAL SCIENCE — Civil Rights*

355 US ISSN 0149-7197
UB357
RETIRED MILITARY ALMANAC. 1978. a. $6. Uniformed Services Almanac, Inc., Box 4144, Falls Church, VA 22044. TEL 703-532-1631. Ed. Lt. Col. Sol Gordon, USAF-Retired. circ. 50,000.
Description: Annual guide to retired pay, benefits, entitlements and other important subjects for active and retired military personnel.

355.5 US ISSN 0034-6160
UB413
THE RETIRED OFFICER. 1945. m. $20. Retired Officers' Association, 201 N. Washington St., Alexandria, VA 22314-2529. TEL 703-549-2311. FAX 703-838-8173. Ed. Col. Charles D. Cooper. adv.; bk.rev.; circ. 380,000 (controlled). (also avail. in microfilm from UMI; reprint service avail. from UMI)
Description: For men and women who are or have been commissioned or warrant officers in any component of the seven uniformed services of the United States.

355.115 AT ISSN 0034-6306
REVEILLE; the voice of more than 126,000 ex-servicemen and women. 1927. bi-m. Aus.$6. Returned and Services League of Australia, New South Wales State Branch, Anzac House, 365 Kent St., Sydney, N.S.W. 2000, Australia. TEL 02-299-2671. FAX 02-290-2046. Ed. Tom Jackson. adv.; bk.rev.; circ. 110,000.

355 RM ISSN 1220-5710
REVISTA DE ISTORIE MILITARA. English edition (annual): Review of Military History. bi-m. $21 (effective Jan. 1990). Ministerul Apararii Nationale - Ministry of National Defense, Str. Cobalcescu Nr. 28A, Sector 1 Bucharest, Rumania. TEL 15-78-27. FAX 400-15-94-56. (Subscr. to: Orion, C. Grivitei Nr. 64-66, Sector 1, P.O. Box 12-201, Bucharest, Rumania) Ed. Ilie Manole. adv.
Description: Covers archaeology, numismatics, heraldics, philately, and uniforms.

355 CK ISSN 0120-0631
REVISTA DE LAS FUERZAS ARMADAS. 1976. 6/yr. Escuela Superior de Guerra, Fuerzas Militares de Colombia, Avenida 81, No. 45a-40, Apdo. Aereo 4403, Bogota, D.E., Colombia. Dir. Miguel Rodriguez Casas. adv.; bibl.; charts; illus.; circ. 6,800.

355 VE ISSN 0034-8473
REVISTA DE LAS FUERZAS ARMADAS.* 1946. m. Ministerio de la Defenza, La Planicie, Caracas, Venezuela.

359 CL ISSN 0034-8511
V5
REVISTA DE MARINA. 1885. bi-m. $70 (effective 1992). Armada de Chile, Correo Naval, Valparaiso, Chile. Dir. Claudio Collados. bk.rev.; index; circ. 3,000. Indexed: Hist.Abstr.
—BLDSC shelfmark: 7863.750000.

359 EC ISSN 0034-852X
REVISTA DE MARINA.* vol.13, 1970. Comandancia General de Marina, Apdo. 2095, Quito, Ecuador. charts; illus.

359 PE ISSN 0034-8538
REVISTA DE MARINA DEL PERU.* 1916. m. Escuela Naval del Peru, Callao, Peru.

REVISTA DE MEDICINA MILITARA. see *MEDICAL SCIENCES*

359 MX ISSN 0034-9046
REVISTA DEL EJERCITO. 1906. m. Mex.$35,000. Secretaria de la Defensa Nacional, Estado Mayor del Ejercito, Mexico, D.F., Mexico. circ. 4,000.

MILITARY

355   PY   ISSN 0034-9054
REVISTA DEL EJERCITO Y ARMADA.* 1937. m. Centro Militar y Naval, Asuncion, Paraguay.

355   AG   ISSN 0034-9119
REVISTA DEL SUBOFICIAL.* bi-m. Ministerio del Ejercito, Buenos Aires, Argentina.
   Description: Non-commissioned officer's review.

355   BL   ISSN 0101-7284
U4
REVISTA DO EXERCITO BRASILEIRO. 1882. q. $50. Diretoria de Assuntos Culturais, Educacao Fisica e Desportos, Biblioteca do Exercito, Palacio Duque De Caxais, 25, Ala Marcilio Dias, 3 andar, Rio de Janeiro, RJ - 20455, Brazil. TEL (021) 233-1338. Ed. Davis Ribeiro de Sena. adv.; circ. 2,000.
   Formerly (until vol.119, 1982): Revista Militar Brasileira (ISSN 0035-0125) From 1920-1923: Boletim do Estado Major do Exercito.

REVISTA ESPANOLA DE DERECHO MILITAR. see *LAW*

359   SP   ISSN 0034-9569
REVISTA GENERAL DE MARINA. 1877. m. (except Aug.-Sep.). 2400 ptas. Estado Mayor de la Armada, Montalban, 2, 28014 Madrid, Spain. Dir. Juan Genova. adv.; bk.rev.; circ. 3,000. **Indexed:** Abstr.Mil.Bibl, Hist.Abstr., Ind.SST.
   —BLDSC shelfmark: 7856.675000.

359   BL   ISSN 0034-9860
V5
REVISTA MARITIMA BRASILEIRA. 1851. q. $12.20. Ministerio da Marinha, Servico de Documentacao Geral da Marinha., Rua Dom Manuel 15, 20010 Rio de Janeiro RJ, Brazil. Ed. Max Justo Guedes. adv.; bibl.; charts; illus.; index; circ. 3,000.

REVISTA MEDICA DA AERONAUTICA DO BRASIL. see *MEDICAL SCIENCES*

355   DR   ISSN 0035-0117
REVISTA MILITAR.* 1934. Ejercito Nacional, Ciudad Trujillo, Dominican Republic.

355   PE   ISSN 0035-0141
REVISTA MILITAR DEL PERU.* 1904. m. Ministerio de Guerra, Avda. Boulevar s-n, Lima, Peru.

355   CU
REVISTA TECNICA MILITAR. m. Ministerio de las Fuerzas Armadas Revolucionarias, Avda. 47 No. 1414th, 14 y 18, Playa, Havana, Cuba.

355   BE   ISSN 0035-0877
REVUE BELGE D'HISTOIRE MILITAIRE/BELGISCH TIJDSCHRIFT VOOR MILITAIRE GESCHIEDENIS. (Text in Dutch and French) 1924. q. 700 BEF includes Militaria Belgica. Societe Royale des Amis du Musee Royal de l'Armee et d'Histoire Militaire, Parc du Cinquantenaire 3, 1040 Brussels, Belgium. Ed. J. Lorette. bk.rev.; circ. 1,000. (back issues avail.) **Indexed:** Numis.Lit.
   —BLDSC shelfmark: 7891.920000.

355   FR   ISSN 0035-2306
REVUE D'ETUDES MILITAIRES, AERIENNES ET NAVALES. 1912. m. 270 F. Societe d'Etudes, 5 bd. Beaumarchais, 75180 Paris Cedex 04, France. TEL 42-72-23-39.

355.15   FR   ISSN 0035-1210
REVUE DE LA FRANCE LIBRE. 1945. q. 20 Fr. per issue. Association des Francais Libres, 59 rue Vergniaud, 75013 Paris, France. TEL 45-88-72-52. adv.; bk.rev.; illus.; circ. 9,500.

909   FR   ISSN 0035-3299
UA700
REVUE HISTORIQUE DES ARMEES. q. 280 F. (foreign 500 F.). Association pour le Developpement et la Diffusion de l'Information Militaire, 6 rue Saint Charles, 75015 Paris, France. TEL 45-77-03-76. FAX 45-79-53-73. **Indexed:** Hist.Abstr.
   —BLDSC shelfmark: 7920.730500.

355   BE   ISSN 0254-8186
D25
REVUE INTERNATIONALE D'HISTOIRE MILITAIRE. (Text in English, French, German, Italian, Russian and Spanish) 1939. irreg. price varies. Commission Internationale d'Histoire Militaire, c/o Secretary-General Dr. P. Lefeure, Musee Royal de l'Armee et d'Histoire Militaire, Parc du Cinquantenaire 3, 1040 Brussels, Belgium. FAX 02-734-54-21. Ed.Bd. circ. 1,500. **Indexed:** Hist.Abstr.
   Description: Each volume devoted to the military history of a single country.

359   FR
REVUE MARITIME. 1861. m. 180 F. (foreign 250 F.). Institut Francais de la Mer, 9 av. du Dr. Gley, 75020 Paris, France. TEL 40-31-04-00. Ed. Claude Benoit. adv.; circ. 7,000.
   Former titles: Nouvelle Revue Maritime; (until 1974): Institut de la Mer. Revue Maritime.

355   SZ   ISSN 0035-368X
REVUE MILITAIRE SUISSE. 1856. m. 60 SFr. Association de la Revue Militaire Suisse, 39 av. de la Gare, Ch-1000 Lausanne, Switzerland. adv.; bk.rev.; abstr.; bibl.; charts; illus.; circ. 3,105 (controlled). **Indexed:** Abstr.Mil.Bibl.
   —BLDSC shelfmark: 7933.620000.

RIVER CURRENTS. see *TRANSPORTATION — Ships And Shipping*

355   IT
RIVISTA ITALIANA DIFESA. 1982. m. L.65000 (foreign L.90000). Cooperativa Giornalistica Riviera s.r.l., Via Martiri Liberazione 79-3, 16043 Chiavari (Genoa), Italy. TEL 185-308606. FAX 0185-309063. Ed. Giovanni Lazzari. adv.; bk.rev.; index; circ. 30,500. (back issues avail.)

359   IT   ISSN 0035-6964
V4
RIVISTA MARITTIMA. 1868. m. L.45000. Stato Maggiore della Marina, Via Romeo Romei 5, 00136 Rome, Italy. FAX 3251408. TELEX 312825. Ed. Vincenzo Pellegrino. bk.rev.; abstr.; charts; illus.; index; cum.index; circ. 5,500. (tabloid format) **Indexed:** Abstr.Mil.Bibl., Hist.Abstr.
   —BLDSC shelfmark: 7989.000000.

355   IT   ISSN 0035-6980
U4
RIVISTA MILITARE. (Text in English and Italian) 1856. bi-m. L.22000 (foreign L.30000). Stato Maggiore Esercito, Via di San Marco 8, Rome 00186, Italy. Ed. Pier G. Franzosi. adv.; bk.rev.; bibl.; charts; illus.; index; circ. 30,000. **Indexed:** Abstr.Mil.Bibl., Hist.Abstr.

355   SZ   ISSN 0035-6999
RIVISTA MILITARE DELLA SVIZZERA ITALIANA.* 1927. bi-m. 30 SFr. Via Rodari 10a, 6900 Lugano, Switzerland. adv.; charts; illus.

355   IS   ISSN 0334-8466
U1
ROMACH. English edition: Defense Update (ISSN 0931-7317) 1986. 9/yr. $57. Eshel-Drahmit Publishing, P.O. Box 115, Hod Hasharon 45 100, Israel. TEL 052-31357. FAX 972-3-285456. TELEX 35770-COIN-IL. Ed. Tamir Eshel. adv.; bk.rev.; circ. 6,500.

358.4   UK   ISSN 0035-8606
ROYAL AIR FORCE COLLEGE JOURNAL.* 1920. a. £1($5) Ministry of Defence, PR11 - RAF, Turnstile House, 98 High Holborn, London WC1V 6LL, England. Ed. Sgr. Ldr. Parker. adv.; bk.rev.; circ. 1,800.

358.4   UK
ROYAL AIR FORCE EDUCATION BULLETIN. 1964. a. free. Royal Air Force School of Education & Training Support, Educational and Training Technology Development Unit, RAF Newton, Nottingham NG13 8HL, England. (Co-sponsor: Ministry of Defence) circ. 1,500 (controlled). (back issues avail.) **Indexed:** Cont.Pg.Educ., Educ.Tech.Abstr., Res.High.Educ.Abstr.

358.4   UK   ISSN 0035-8614
ROYAL AIR FORCE NEWS. 1961. fortn. £12. Royal Air Force, Turnstile House, 97-99 High Holborn, London WC1V 6LL, England. Ed. P.H. Burden. adv.; bk.rev.; illus.; circ. 30,000. (tabloid format)

358.4   UK   ISSN 0954-092X
ROYAL AIR FORCE YEARBOOK. 1975. a. £4. Royal Air Force Benevolent Fund, International Air Tattoo, Building 1108, RAF Fairford, Glos GL7 4DL, England. TEL 0285-713300. FAX 0285-713268. TELEX 45311-IATFFD-G. Ed. Peter R. March. adv.; circ. 130,000.

355   UK
ROYAL BRITISH LEGION ANNUAL REPORT AND ACCOUNTS. 1921. a. free. Royal British Legion, National Executive Council, 48 Pall Mall, London SW1Y 5JY, England. circ. 8,000.

623   UK   ISSN 0035-8878
UG1
ROYAL ENGINEERS JOURNAL. 1870. q. £12. Institution of Royal Engineers, Brompton Barracks, Chatham, Kent ME4 4UG, England. Ed. Lt.Col. F.R. Beringer. adv.; bk.rev.; illus.; index; circ. 4,400. **Indexed:** Chem.Abstr., Eng.Ind., GeoRef.
   —BLDSC shelfmark: 8030.000000.

355.133   UK   ISSN 0035-9025
ROYAL MILITARY POLICE JOURNAL. 1950. q. £5.50. Royal Military Police, R M P Corps Committee, Ed. Lt.Col. P. Squier, Roussillon Barracks, Chichester, W. Sussex, England. adv.; bk.rev.; illus.; circ. 3,000.

355   UK   ISSN 0035-9076
ROYAL PIONEER. 1942. 2/yr. £4. Royal Pioneer Corps, Simpson Barracks, Wootton, Northampton NN4 0HX, England. Ed. C.D. Spears. adv.; bk.rev.; charts; illus.; circ. 1,600.

355 327   AT   ISSN 0728-1188
ROYAL UNITED SERVICES INSTITUTE OF AUSTRALIA. JOURNAL. 1977. s-a. Aus.$20 (foreign Aus.$30)(typically set Feb.). Royal United Services Institute of Australia Inc., G.P.O. Box 590, Canberra, A.C.T. 2601, Australia. FAX 06-265-3105. Ed. W. Crews. adv.; bk.rev.; circ. 6,000. (back issues avail.)

355   RW
RWANDA. MINISTERE DE LA DEFENSE NATIONALE. FORCES DE SECURITE AU SERVICE DE LA NATION. bi-m. Ministere de la Defense Nationale, B.P. 85, Kigali, Rwanda.

355   US
S D I INTELLIGENCE REPORT; monitoring Strategic Defense Initiative Procurement. 1985. fortn. $475.50. Business Publishers, Inc., 951 Pershing Dr., Silver Spring, MD 20910-4464. TEL 301-587-6300. FAX 301-587-1081. Ed. David Ritchie. (back issues avail.)
   ●Also available online. Vendor(s): NewsNet (DE09).
   Formerly: Star Wars Intelligence Report (ISSN 0884-3260); Incorporates (as of 1985): Independent Report on Martin Marietta (ISSN 0882-617X)

621.3   US   ISSN 0886-7607
S D I MONITOR. (Strategic Defense Initiative) 1986. fortn. $685 (foreign $700). Pasha Publications Inc., 1401 Wilson Blvd., Ste. 900, Arlington, VA 22209-9970. TEL 703-528-1244. FAX 703-528-1253. Ed. Jeff W. Schomisch. **Indexed:** CAD CAM Abstr.
   ●Also available online. Vendor(s): NewsNet (DE05).
   Description: Follows technical, political and policy aspects of the SDI program.

355   US
S S A M.* (Soldier, Sailor, Airman, Marine) 1978. m. $13. U.S. Department of Defense, The Pentagon, Washington, DC 20301. (Dist. by: Supt. of Documents, Washington, DC 20402)

355   AT   ISSN 0048-8933
SABRETACHE. 1958. q. Aus.$26. Military Historical Society of Australia, P.O. Box 30, Garran, A.C.T. 2605, Australia. Ed. Elizabeth Topperwien. adv.; bk.rev.; index; circ. 440. **Indexed:** Aus.P.A.I.S.

355   US   ISSN 0080-5335
UF526.3
SAGAMORE ARMY MATERIALS RESEARCH CONFERENCE. PROCEEDINGS. 1954. irreg., vol.31, 1986. price varies. Plenum Publishing Corp., 233 Spring St., New York, NY 10013-1578. TEL 212-620-8000. FAX 212-463-0742. TELEX 23-421139. **Indexed:** Chem.Abstr.
   Refereed Serial

MILITARY 3471

355   II   ISSN 0036-2743
U4
SAINIK SAMACHAR; pictorial weekly of India's armed forces. (Editions in 12 languages) 1909. w. Rs.20 (foreign Rs. 90). Ministry of Defence, Directorate of Public Relations, Block L-1, Church Rd., New Delhi 110 011, India. TEL 3019668. Ed. Bibekananda Ray. adv.; bk.rev.; charts; illus.; circ. 18,000.
   Incorporates: Fauji Akhbar.
   Description: Provides news and entertainment as well as education to those enrolled in Indian Armed Forces.

SALVO. see HISTORY — *History Of North And South America*

SANE - FREEZE NEWS; campaign for global security. see POLITICAL SCIENCE — *International Relations*

355 629.1   TU
SAVUNMA VE HAVACILIK; defence and aerospace. (Text in Turkish; summaries in English) 1987. bi-m. TL.50000($16.50) Monch Media Ltd., Ahmet Mithat Efendi Sk. 20-2, 06550 Cankaya Ankara, Turkey. TEL 4-139-1937. FAX 4-139-5724. Ed. Hakki Aris. adv.; circ. 20,000. (back issues avail.)
   Description: Covers technical issues in the defense and civilian sectors of the aviation and aerospace industries.

355   US   ISSN 0036-5408
SCABBARD AND BLADE JOURNAL. 1913. 3/yr. $3. National Society of Scabbard and Blade, 205 Thatcher Hall, Oklahoma State University, Stillwater, OK 74078. TEL 405-624-5000. Ed. Max Rodgers. bk.rev.; illus.; circ. 2,000.

SCHWEIZER KAVALLERIST; Zeitschrift fuer Pferdesport und Pferdezucht. see SPORTS AND GAMES — *Horses And Horsemanship*

355   SZ
SCHWEIZER SOLDAT UND M F D; Die Monatszeitschrift fuer Armee und Kader mit MFD-Zeitung. 1925. m. 59 SFr. Huber und Co. AG, Promenadestr. 16, CH-8501 Frauenfeld, Switzerland. TEL 054-271111. Ed. Edwin Hofstetter. adv.; bk.rev.; circ. 12,500.
   Incorporates: M F D-Zeitung (ISSN 0014-584X)
   Description: Covers current issues, news, information and new developments concerning the national and foreign military. Includes list of events, new publications and positions available.

355.15   UK
SCOTTISH LEGION NEWS. 1950. 6/yr. free to Legion clubs and branches in Scotland. Royal British Legion Scotland, New Haig House, Logie Green Rd., Edinburgh EH7 4HR, Scotland. TEL 031-447-2782. Ed. Charles Nicholas. adv.; bk.rev.; illus.; circ. 13,000.
   Incorporates (as of 1987): Claymore (ISSN 0009-8590)

335   US
SCREAMING EAGLE. 1945. bi-m. $20. 101st Airborne Division Association, 101 E. Morris St., Box 586, Sweetwater, TN 37874. TEL 615-337-4103. Ed. Ivan G. Worrell. adv.; bk.rev.; circ. 5,500.
   Description: News and features for veterans of the 101st Airborne Division.

359   US   ISSN 0199-1337
VA49
SEA POWER. (Includes annual: Almanac of Seapower) 1958. m. $25 to non-members (effective 1992). Navy League of the United States, 2300 Wilson Blvd., Arlington, VA 22201-3308.
TEL 703-528-1775. FAX 703-528-2333. Ed. James D. Hessman. adv.; bk.rev.; charts; illus.; index; circ. 74,000. (also avail. in microform from UMI) Indexed: Abstr.Mil.Bibl, Air Un.Lib.Ind., Amer.Bibl.Slavic & E.Eur.Stud, DM & T, Ocean.Abstr., Pollut.Abstr., PROMT.
   Formerly: Navy: the Magazine of Sea Power (ISSN 0028-1689)

355   CN   ISSN 0048-9883
SEALANDAIR. 1969. fortn. Can.$10($20) Canadian Forces Base Edmonton, Lancaster Park, Edmonton, Alta. T0A 2H0, Canada. TEL 403-457-8481. adv.; charts; illus.; circ. 3,000.

SECURITY INTELLIGENCE REPORT. see POLITICAL SCIENCE

355   UK   ISSN 0963-6412
▼**SECURITY STUDIES.** 1991. q. £28($45) to individuals; institutions £70($115). Frank Cass & Co. Ltd., Gainsborough House, 11 Gainsborough Rd., London E11 1RS, England. TEL 081-530-4226. FAX 081-530-7795. Eds. Amos Perlmutter, Benjamin Frankel. adv.; bk.rev.; index. (back issues avail.)
—BLDSC shelfmark: 8217.219900.
   Description: Covers international security and the role of force in international politics.

355   VE
SEGURIDAD Y DEFENSA; revista plural sobre temas militares y geopolitica. q. Miraciellos a Hospital, Edif. Sur 2, piso 8, Of. 812, Caracas 1010, Venezuela. TEL 4835853. Ed. Manuel Molina Penaloza.

355   CN   ISSN 0037-2315
SENTINEL (OTTAWA); magazine of the Canadian Forces. French edition: Sentinelle. (ISSN 0037-2358) 1965. 6/yr. Can.$15.50($18.60) Directorate Public Affairs, National Defence Headquarters, Ottawa, Ont. K1A 0K2, Canada. TEL 613-992-7012. FAX 613-992-6468. (Subscr. to: Supply and Services Canada, Ottawa, Ont. K1A 0S9, Canada. TEL 819-997-1658) Eds. Marsha Dorge, Denise LaViolette. bk.rev.; charts; illus.; index; circ. 54,000 (40,000 English ed., 14,000 French ed.).
   Description: International information magazine of the Canadian Forces providing a wide view of its functions, objectives, accomplishments and activities.

355   CN   ISSN 0037-3729
SHILO STAG. vol.9, 1970. s-m. Can.$12.50. Leech Printing Ltd., 18th and Park, Brandon, Man., Canada. TEL 204-728-3037. FAX 204-727-3338. adv.; bibl.; charts; illus.; tr.lit.

355   JA   ISSN 0286-9241
SHIN BOEI RONSHU/JOURNAL OF NATIONAL DEFENSE. (Text in Japanese; abstract in English) 1973. 4/yr. 3172 Yen (effective since 1989). (Boei Gakkai - National Defense Society) Boei Kosaikai, 2F Nichijukin-roppongi Bldg., 4-12-8, Roppongi, Minato-ku, Tokyo 106, Japan.
TEL 81-3-3403-6716. FAX 81-3-3713-6149. Ed. Kuniko Miyauchi. bk.rev.; circ. 2,200.
   Description: Promotes society members' theoretical study on the defense problem.

SHIPMATE. see COLLEGE AND ALUMNI

359   US   ISSN 0080-9292
VA61
SHIPS AND AIRCRAFT OF THE UNITED STATES FLEET. 1939. irreg., 14th ed., 1987. $38.95. (U.S. Naval Institute) Naval Institute Press, Annapolis, MD 21402. TEL 301-268-6110. FAX 301-269-7940. TELEX 187-114-AIR COURS PHX. Ed. Norman Polmar. index. (reprint service avail.)

355 387   US
SHIPYARD LOG. Cover title: Pearl Harbor Shipyard Log. 1946. s-m. free. Pearl Harbor Naval Shipyard, Box 400, Pearl Harbor, HI 96860-5350.
TEL 808-474-7108. FAX 808-471-1514. adv.; illus.; circ. 6,300 (controlled). (tabloid format)

355   GW
SHOPPERS BI-WEEKLY NEWS. 1974. Shoppers Bi-Weekly News, Kolpingstrasse 1, 6906 Leimen, Germany. TEL 49-6224-7060.
FAX 49-6224-70616. adv.; circ. 60,000.
   Description: Focuses on shopping, personal and leisure-time information for military personnel in Europe.

355.115   US   ISSN 0276-8135
DS557
SHORT-TIMER'S JOURNAL;* soldiering in Vietnam. 1981. 5/yr. $3 to veterans; non-veterans $15. Winter Soldier Archive, 2315 Oak St., Berkeley, CA 94708-1628. Ed. Clark C. Smith. circ. 1,000. (back issues avail.)

355   US   ISSN 0733-0367
DD253.65
SIEGRUNEN;* the Waffen-SS in historical perspective. 1975. q. $20. Merriam Press, Box 6718, Brookings, OR 97415. Ed. Richard Landwehr. adv.; bk.rev.; circ. 375. (back issues avail.)
   Description: Covers history of Waffen-SS and biographies of personalities, units, and battles.

355   CU
SIEMPRE ALERTA. w. Ministerio de las Fuerzas Armadas Revolucionarias, 84 No. 8401 esq. 19, Playa, Havana, Cuba.

355   CS   ISSN 0037-492X
SIGNAL; ilustrovany tydenik. w. 62.40 Kcs.($35.20) Jungmannova 24, Prague 1, Czechoslovakia. (Subscr. to: Artia, Ve Smeckach 30, 111 27 Prague 1, Czechoslavkia) Ed. Vlado Kaspar. illus. **Indexed:** Abstr.Engl.Stud.

355   BU   ISSN 0861-7333
SIGNAL A. 1893. m. 84 lv.($4) (Glavno Politichesko Upravlenie na Narodnata Armiia) Area Pte, 46B Galitchiza Str., Sofia, Bulgaria. TEL 359-2-688-001. FAX 359-2-627-444. (Dist. by: Hemus, 6, Rouski Blvd., 1000 Sofia, Bulgaria) adv.; bk.rev.; illus.; circ. 20,000.
   Former titles (until 1990): Bulgarski Voin (ISSN 0007-4004); (until 1922): Voinishka Sbirka.
   Description: Covers technical information and military comments.

351.06   GW
SISTRA. 1986. irreg. DM.11 per issue. Sistra Verlag, Postfach 160163, 5300 Bonn 1, Germany. TEL 0228-281852. FAX 0228-285798. Ed. Michael Forster. circ. 300. (looseleaf format)

SMALL WARS AND INSURGENCIES. see POLITICAL SCIENCE

355 900   UK   ISSN 0037-9700
DA49
SOCIETY FOR ARMY HISTORICAL RESEARCH. JOURNAL. 1921. q. £12. Society for Army Historical Research, National Army Museum, Royal Hospital Rd., London SW3 4HT, England. Ed. M.A. Cane. adv.; bk.rev.; illus.; maps; cum.index; circ. 1,200. **Indexed:** Amer.Hist.& Life, Br.Hum.Ind., Hist.Abstr.
—BLDSC shelfmark: 4880.790000.

SOCIETY OF COLONIAL WARS. BULLETIN. see HISTORY — *History Of North And South America*

355   AG   ISSN 0038-0954
SOLDADO ARGENTINO. m. Ministerio del Ejercito, Rio Bamba 707, Buenos Aires, Argentina.

355   AU   ISSN 0038-0962
DER SOLDAT; Oesterreichische Soldaten-zeitung. 1956. s-m. S.260. Der Soldat Zeitungs- und Zeitschriftenverlags-Gesellschaft MbH, Seidengasse 11, A-1070 Vienna, Austria. TEL 0222-934713. adv.; charts; illus.; circ. 15,000. (tabloid format)

355   GW   ISSN 0038-0989
U3
SOLDAT UND TECHNIK. 1958. m. DM.109.20. (Bundesministerium der Verteidigung) Umschau Verlag Breidenstein GmbH, Stuttgarter Str. 18-24, 6000 Frankfurt a.M. 1, Germany. TEL 069-2600-0. FAX 069-2600-609. TELEX 411964. Ed. Gerhard Hubatschek. adv.; bk.rev.; charts; illus.; stat.; index; circ. 31,000. **Indexed:** Bibl.Cart., DM & T, PROMT.
—BLDSC shelfmark: 8327.240000.

355   UK
SOLDIER. 1945. fortn. £18.55. Ministry of Defence, Ordnance Rd., Aldershot, Hants GU11 2DU, England. FAX 0252-24431. Ed. Roland Thick. adv.; bk.rev.; circ. 25,000. (back issues avail.)
   Description: Official magazine of the British Army.

355.115   II
SOLDIER IN NATIONAL SERVICE. 1982. q. All India Congress Committee, 24 Akbar Rd., New Delhi 110 011, India. Ed. Proash Shyan.

355   US   ISSN 0145-6784
SOLDIER OF FORTUNE; the journal of professional adventurers. 1975. m. $24.95 ($24.95 to Canada; elsewhere $45.95). Omega Group Ltd., Box 693, Boulder, CO 80306. TEL 303-449-3750. Ed. Robert K. Brown. adv.; bk.rev.; tr.lit.; circ. 104,593. (back issues avail.) **Indexed:** PMR.
   Description: Reports on combat from front lines around the world.

SOLDIER SHOP ANNUAL. see HOBBIES

MILITARY

355   US   ISSN 0093-8440
UA23.A1
SOLDIERS. 1946. m. $14. U.S. Department of the Army, Cameron Sta., Alexandria, VA 22304-5050. TEL 703-274-6671. FAX 703-274-1896. (Subscr. to: Supt. of Documents, Washington D.C. 20402) Ed. Robert V. Bryant. illus.; index; circ. 250,000 (controlled). (also avail. in microform from MIM,UMI; reprint service avail. from UMI) Indexed: Air Un.Lib.Ind., Ind.U.S.Gov.Per., P.A.I.S.
   Formerly: Army Digest (ISSN 0004-2498)
   Description: Operation and technical developments of the Army and its reserve components.

948 355   FI   ISSN 0357-816X
SOTAHISTORIALLINEN AIKAKAUSKIRJA. (Text in Finnish, Swedish; summaries in English) 1948. a. FIM 60. Sotahistoriallinen Seura - Society for Military History, Maurinkatu 1, 00170 Helsinki 17, Finland. TEL 90-7616211. (Co-sponsor: Sotatieteen Laitos) Ed.Bd. circ. 1,000.

355   FI   ISSN 0038-1675
SOTILASAIKAKAUSLEHTI. (Text in Finnish; contents page in English and Finnish) 1921. m. Fmk.265. Upseeriliitto, Luotsik 7 A 2, 00160 Helsinki, Finland. TEL 90-294-1648. FAX 90-294-1842. Ed. Esko Nieminen. adv.; bk.rev.; charts; illus.; maps, stat.; index, cum.index; circ. 6,700.

355.03   SA
SOUTH AFRICA. DEPARTMENT OF DEFENSE. WHITE PAPER ON DEFENSE AND ARMAMENT PRODUCTION. (Text in Afrikaans and English) irreg. Department of Defense, Cape Town, South Africa.

355.133 350   RU   ISSN 0320-2259
HV8224   CODEN: SOMIEC
SOVETSKAYA MILITSIYA. 1922. m. 1 Rub. per issue. Ministerstvo Vnutrennikh Del S.S.S.R., c/o A.G. Chernenko, Ed., Ul. Ivanovskaya 24, 127434 Moscow, Russia. TEL 216-87-19. circ. 923,928.

355 310   US
SOVIET ARMED FORCES REVIEW ANNUAL. Abbreviated title: S A F R A. 1977. a. 71. Academic International Press, Box 1111, Gulf Breeze, FL 32562-1111. Ed. David R. Jones. bibl.; charts; illus.; stat. (back issues avail.) Indexed: Amer.Bibl.Slavic & E.Eur.Stud.

355   RU   ISSN 0038-5220
U1
SOVIET MILITARY REVIEW/SOVETSKOE VOENNOE OBOZRENIE. (Editions in Arabic, English, French and Spanish) m. $8. Voenizdat, Bol'shoi Kisel'nyi Per., 14, Moscow, Russia. (Subscr. to: Mezhdunarodnaya Kniga, Moscow, G-200, Russia) illus. (also avail. in microform from MIM) Indexed: Abstr.Mil.Bibl., Air Un.Lib.Ind., DM & T, PROMT.

SOZIALRECHT & PRAXIS; Fachzeitschrift des VdK Deutschland fuer Vertrauensleute der Behinderten und fuer Sozialpolitiker. see *SOCIAL SERVICES AND WELFARE*

355   US
SPEARHEAD (OAKTON). 1945. q. membership only. First Special Service Force Association, 11815 Quarter Horse Ct., Oakton, VA 22124. TEL 703-620-5990. Ed. Bill Story. circ. 1,500.

355   US
SPECIAL WARFARE. q. $5. Special Warfare Editor, USAJFKSWCS, Fort Bragg, NC 28307-5000. Indexed: Air Un.Lib.Ind.

SPORT - OVERSEAS MILITARY EDITION. see *SPORTS AND GAMES*

385   UK   ISSN 0049-2000
SPOTLIGHT (BATH). 1969. m. 60p. Ministry of Defence, Dockyard Department, Rm. 211, Carpenter House, Broad Quay, Bath, Avon BA1 5AB, England. Ed. P. Connor. adv.; bk.rev.; charts; illus.; circ. 4,000. (tabloid format)

355   SA
SPRINGBOK. (Text in Afrikaans and English) 1922. bi-m. R.5. South African Legion, P.O. Box 8751, Johannesburg 2000, South Africa. Ed. Les Stewart. adv.; bk.rev.; charts; illus.; circ. 4,750.

SPUREN UND MOTIVE; Informationsdienst fuer innere Sicherheit. see *CRIMINOLOGY AND LAW ENFORCEMENT*

STAND TO!. see *HISTORY — History Of Europe*

STAR AND GARTER MAGAZINE. see *HOSPITALS*

355.15   CN   ISSN 0038-9889
STAR SERVICEMAN.* 1946. m. Can.$3. Media Public Relations Ltd., P.O. Box 2929, Vancouver 3, B.C., Canada. Ed. George S. Hobson. adv.; bk.rev.; charts; illus.; index; circ. 2,410.
   Supersedes: New Veteran.

355.115   US   ISSN 0894-8542
STARS AND STRIPES - THE NATIONAL TRIBUNE. 1877. w. $19. National Tribune Corporation, Box 1803, Washington, DC 20013. TEL 202-829-3225. FAX 202-829-5657. Ed. John H. Carroll. adv.; bk.rev. (tabloid format; also avail. in microfilm from BHP,KTO)
   Description: News and information concerning veterans and veterans affairs.

341.1   AU   ISSN 0039-1085
STEIRISCHE KRIEGSOPFER ZEITUNG. 1947. q. membership. Kriegsopferverband Steiermark, Burggasse 4, A-8011 Graz, Austria. FAX 0316-832853-85. Ed. Johann Pocsics. adv.; bk.rev.; bibl.; illus.; stat.; index; circ. 22,000. (tabloid format)

355   IT
STRATEGIA GLOBALE. q. L.60000 (foreign L.80000). Editore Selm, Via Donati 1, Turin, Italy. TEL 011-534061. Ed. Edgardo Sogno.

STRATEGIC AND DEFENCE STUDIES CENTRE NEWSLETTER. see *POLITICAL SCIENCE*

355   US   ISSN 0091-6846
U162
STRATEGIC REVIEW. 1973. q. $25 (foreign $35). United States Strategic Institute, Box 15618 Kenmore Sta., Boston, MA 02215. TEL 617-890-5030. FAX 617-353-7330. Ed. Mackubin T. Owens. bk.rev.; circ. 3,500. (back issues avail.) Indexed: A.B.C.Pol.Sci., Abstr.Mil.Bibl, Air Un.Lib.Ind., Amer.Bibl.Slavic & E.Eur.Stud, Chic.Per.Ind., Mid.East: Abstr.& Ind., P.A.I.S., PROMT, Soc.Sci.Ind.
   —BLDSC shelfmark: 8474.031700.
   Description: Provides a forum for the discussion of matters of current significance in the politico-military field.

STRATEGIC REVIEW FOR SOUTHERN AFRICA. see *CIVIL DEFENSE*

355   PK
STRATEGIC STUDIES. (Text in English) 1977. q. Rs.50($10) to individuals; students Rs. 30 per no. Institute of Strategic Studies, P.O. Box 1173, Islamabad, Pakistan. TEL 824658. Ed. Ross Masood Husain. adv.; bk.rev.; circ. 1,000. Indexed: Abstr.Mil.Bibl.

355 320   FR   ISSN 0224-0424
U162
STRATEGIQUE. 1979. q. 295 F. (Fondation pour les Etudes de Defense Nationale (F.E.D.N.)) Documentation Francaise, 29-31 Quai Voltaire, 75340 Paris cedex 07, France. TEL 1-40-15-70-00. circ. 1,500. (back issues avail.)
   —BLDSC shelfmark: 8474.034500.

355   US   ISSN 0736-6531
U310
STRATEGY AND TACTICS; the magazine of conflict simulation. 1967. 8/yr. $50. World Wide Wargames, Inc., Box F, Cambria, CA 93428. TEL 805-927-5439. FAX 805-927-1852. Ed. Jim Dunnigan. adv.; bk.rev.; charts; illus.; stat.; circ. 13,500. (tabloid format) Indexed: Abstr.Mil.Bibl., Hist.Abstr.
   Description: Each issue contains a complete war game.

355   GR
STRATIOTIKI EPITHEORISIS/MILITARY REVUE. m. $25. Hellenic Army General Staff, 10 Pittakou St., Athens, Greece. Indexed: Abstr.Mil.Bibl.

355 069   PL   ISSN 0137-5733
STUDIA DO DZIEJOW DAWNEGO UZBROJENIA I UBIORU WOJSKOWEGO. (Text in Polish; summaries in English) 1963. irreg., nos.9-10, 1990. price varies. Muzeum Narodowe w Krakowie - National Museum in Crakow, Ul. J. Pilsudskiego 12, 31-109 Krakow, Poland. (Co-sponsor: Association of Old Arms and Uniforms Amateurs) Ed. Katarzyna Onderka. circ. 1,000. (also avail. in microfilm)

355 943.8   PL   ISSN 0562-2786
STUDIA I MATERIALY DO HISTORII WOJSKOWOSCI. vol.27, 1984. irreg., vol.29, 1987. price varies. (Polska Akademia Nauk, Komitet Nauk Historycznych) Ossolineum, Publishing House of the Polish Academy of Sciences, Rynek 9, Wroclaw, Poland. TELEX 0712771 OSS PL. (Dist by: Ars Polona-Ruch, Krakowskie Przedmiescie 7, Warsaw, Poland) Ed. Benon Miskiewicz.
   Description: History of Polish military science and arms.

355 320   US
STUDIES IN DEFENSE POLICY. 1971. irreg. price varies. Brookings Institution, 1775 Massachusetts Ave., N.W., Washington, DC 20036-2188. TEL 202-797-6255. FAX 202-797-6004.

355   NE
STUDIES IN U S NATIONAL SECURITY. 1977. irreg. (U.S. Army War College, Strategic Studies Institute, US) Kluwer Academic Publishers, P.O. Box 17, 3300 AA Dordrecht, Netherlands. TEL 078-334911. FAX 078-334254. TELEX 29245. (Dist. by: Kluwer Academic Publishers Group, P.O. Box 322, 3300 AH Dordrecht) Ed. James A. Kuhlman.

359   US   ISSN 0145-1073
V1
SURFACE WARFARE. 1976. bi-m. $6. U.S. Navy, Chief of Naval Operations, 601 N. Fairfax St., Rm. 270, Alexandria, VA 22314. TEL 703-274-4535. FAX 703-274-4535. (Dist. by: Supt. of Documents, Washington, DC 20402) bk.rev.; circ. 45,000. Indexed: DM & T.

355.155   UK   ISSN 0491-6204
SURMACH. (Text in Ukrainian) 1955. a. £3 (effective Jan. 1991). Association of Ukranian Former Combatants in Great Britain, 49 Linden Gardens, London W2 4HG, England. Ed. S.M. Fostun. adv.; bk.rev.; circ. 1,000.
   Description: Covers historical events of Ukraine and other nations with news of the activities of the Association of Ukrainian Former Combatants in Great Britain.

T A C ATTACK. (Tactical Air Command) see *AERONAUTICS AND SPACE FLIGHT*

355 629.1   US   ISSN 1059-0552
▼**TACTICAL TECHNOLOGY.** 1991. fortn. $395 (foreign $420)(effective 1992). Phillips Publishing, Inc., Defense - Aviation Group, 1925 N. Lynn St., Ste. 1000, Arlington, VA 22209. TEL 703-522-8333. FAX 703-522-6448. Ed. Eric DeRitis. (looseleaf format)

356   UK   ISSN 0039-9418
TANK. 1919. q. £13. Royal Tank Regiment Publications Ltd., Regimental Headquarters Royal Tank Regiment, Bovington, Wareham, Dorset, England. FAX 0929-405131. Ed. Lt.Col. W.F. Woodhouse. adv.; bk.rev.; circ. 2,750.

TANKETTE. see *HOBBIES*

623   SZ
TECHNISCHE MITTEILUNGEN FUER SAPPEURE, PONTONIERE UND MINEURE. Abbreviated title: T M. (Text in German; summaries in French and Italian) 1936. a. 50 Fr. Gesellschaft fuer Militaerische Bautechnik, Auf der Mauer 2, CH-8001 Zurich, Switzerland. FAX 01-2521667. Ed.Bd. adv.; bk.rev.; charts; illus.; stat.; index; circ. 1,600.

355   GW
TECNOLOGIA MILITAR. (Text in Spanish) 1979. 11/yr. Moench Verlagsgesellschaft mbH, Postfach 140261, 5300 Bonn 1, Germany. TEL 0228-6483-0. FAX 0228-6483-109. TELEX 8869-429-MVB-D. Ed. M. Leibstone. adv. Indexed: Abstr.Mil.Bibl.

MILITARY

355   DR
TEMAS SOBRE LA PROFESIONALIZACION MILITAR EN LA REPUBLICA DOMINICANA. 1983. m. Editora Corripio, C. Por A., Calle A esq. Central, Zona Industrial de Herrera, Santo Domingo, Dominican Republic.

355   FR
TERRE INFORMATION. 1973. m. 50 F. Association pour le Developpement et la Diffusion de l'Information Militaire, 6 rue St. Charles, 75015 Paris, France. TEL 45-77-03-76. FAX 45-79-53-73. Ed. Joelle Lenoble. circ. 123,000.
  Description: News for active, reserve and retired members of the land army.

355   FR
TERRE MAGAZINE. m. (10/yr.). 135 F. (foreign 190 F.). Association pour le Developpement et la Diffusion de l'Information Militaire, 6 rue St. Charles, 75015 Paris, France. TEL 45-77-03-76. FAX 45-79-53-73. illus.
  Description: Covers news of the ground armies throughout the world.

TERRORISM AND POLITICAL VIOLENCE. see *POLITICAL SCIENCE*

355.115   US
TEXAN VETERAN NEWS. q. Box 7440, Ft. Worth, TX 76111-0440. TEL 817-834-7573.

355.155   US
THUNDER FROM HEAVEN. 1954. 3/yr. membership. 17th Airborne Division Association, 23 Westminster Dr., Montville, NJ 07045. TEL 201-263-2433. Ed. Joe Quade. adv.; bk.rev.; circ. 6,500.
  Description: For military veterans of WW II who served in the 17th Airborne Division.

355   GW
TICKET; tips and travel. 1985. m. $12 (outside Europe $22). Wheels Verlag, Fuertherstr. 171, 8500 Nuernberg, Germany. TEL 0911-315831. FAX 0911-316349. Ed. Thomas Derra. adv.; circ. 32,000.
  Formerly: Monthly Ticket for More Information.

355   SW   ISSN 0040-683X
TIDSKRIFT FOER KUSTARTILLERIET. 1942. q. SEK 100. Kustartilleriklubben, c/o Marinstaben, S-107 83 Stockholm, Sweden. Ed. Joergen Bergmark. adv.; bk.rev.; abstr.; illus.; cum.index; circ. 1,100.

TIDSKRIFT I FORTIFIKATION; foer fortifikationsofficerare och officerare ingenjoerer, vaeg- och vattenbyggradskaaren. see *ENGINEERING — Civil Engineering*

359   SW   ISSN 0040-6945
V5
TIDSKRIFT I SJOVASENDET. 1836. 4/yr. SEK 50. Kungl Oerlogsmannasaellskapet, P.O. Box 10186, S-100 55 Stockholm, Sweden. FAX 08-7889499. Ed. Hans von Hofsten. adv.; bk.rev.; circ. 1,000.
  Description: Journal from Royal Swedish Naval Institute

355   US   ISSN 0049-3937
TIPS;* the army personnel magazine. 1971. q. $4. U.S. Army Personnel Information Activity, Adjutant General's Office, The Pentagon, Rm. 2E532, Washington, DC 20310. TEL 317-546-9211. (Subscr. to: Supt. of Documents, U.S. Gov't Printing Office, Washington, D.C. 20402) charts; illus.; tr.lit.

355   US   ISSN 1040-9025
TOP 500 R D T & E CONTRACTORS. a. $1495. Forecast International Inc. - D M S, 22 Commerce Rd., Newtown, CT 06470. TEL 203-426-0800. FAX 203-426-1964. TELEX 467615.
  Description: Examines each company according to the last two years' contracting by the U.S. Navy, Army, and Air Force, as well as by R & D category, and by performance.

355   UK
TORCH (LONDON). 1967. s-a. $10. Royal Army Educational Corps Association, Eltham Palace, Eltham, London SE9 5QE, England. adv.; bk.rev.; illus.; circ. 1,600 (controlled).
  Formerly: R A E C Gazette (ISSN 0033-670X)

TRADING POST (GREENVILLE). see *HOBBIES*

TRANSLOG; journal of military transportation management. see *TRANSPORTATION — Roads And Traffic*

355   FR   ISSN 0036-2794
TRIOMPHE SAINT-CYR; plaquette annuelle des promotions de l'Ecole Special Militaire de St. Cyr et de l'Ecole Militaire Interarmes. 1949. a. 43 F. Ecole Speciale Militaire de Saint-Cyr, 56210 Coetquidan, France. (Co-sponsor: Ecole Militaire Interarmes) adv.; circ. 1,000.
  Formerly: Triomphe.

355   AU   ISSN 0041-3658
TRUPPENDIENST; Zeitschrift fuer Fuehrung und Ausbildung im Bundesheer. 1962. bi-m. S.290. Herold Druck und Verlag GmbH, Strozzigasse 8, A-1080 Vienna, Austria. FAX 0222-52161-5238. Ed. Horst Maeder. bk.rev.; bibl.; charts; illus.; stat.; index; circ. 12,000.

355   GW   ISSN 0041-3666
TRUPPENPRAXIS. 1957. 6/yr. DM.9.90. (Bundesministerium der Verteidigung) Verlag Offene Worte, Austrasse 19, 5300 Bonn 2, Germany. TEL 0228-340884. FAX 0228-348100. adv.; bk.rev.; circ. 33,000.
  —BLDSC shelfmark: 9058.500000.

355 629.1   US
TURBINE ENGINE OVERHAUL. a. $1495. Forecast International Inc. - D M S, 22 Commerce Rd., Newtown, CT 06470. TEL 203-426-0800. FAX 203-426-1964. TELEX 467615.
  Description: Reports and analyzes worldwide business opportunities in the turbine overhaul and upgrading market. Identifies inventories of major military and commercial turbine engines with 10-year forecast of overhaul requirements.

355 629.1   TU
▼**TURKISH DEFENCE & AEROSPACE UPDATE.** (Text in English) 1990. m. $180. Monch Media Ltd., Ahmet Mithat Efendi Sk. 20-2, 06550 Cankaya Ankara, Turkey. TEL 4-139-1937. FAX 4-139-5724. circ. 2,000. (back issues avail.)
  Description: Covers economic and industry developments in military and civil aerospace and aviation.

U N I D I R NEWSLETTER/LETTRE DE L'U N I D I R. (United Nations Institute for Disarmament Research) see *POLITICAL SCIENCE — International Relations*

355   IT   ISSN 0041-5375
U N U C I. 1964. m. membership. Unione Nazionale Ufficiali in Congedo d'Italia, Via Nomentana 313, 00162 Rome, Italy. Ed. Giovanni Spadea. adv.; bk.rev.; illus.

358.4   US
U S A F FIGHTER WEAPONS REVIEW. q. free. U.S. Air Force, F.W.S.-C.O.M., Nellis A.F.B., NV 89191-5000. **Indexed:** Air Un.Lib.Ind.

355   II   ISSN 0041-770X
U S I JOURNAL. (Text in English) 1870. q. Rs.80($24) (typically set in Oct.). United Service Institution of India, Kashmir House, Rajaji Marg, New Delhi 110011, India. TEL 301-5828. Ed. N.B. Singh. adv.; bk.rev.; illus.; circ. 5,000. **Indexed:** Abstr.Mil.Bibl., Amer.Hist.& Life, Hist.Abstr., P.A.I.S.
  —BLDSC shelfmark: 4910.650000.

355.115   US
U S J. (Uniformed Services Journal) 1968. bi-m. $8 to non-members. National Association for Uniformed Services, 5535 Hempstead Way, Springfield, VA 22151. TEL 703-750-1342. FAX 703-354-4380. Ed. Sharon Barnes. adv.; bk.rev.; charts; illus.; circ. 60,000.
  Supersedes: N A U S Newsletter.

359   US   ISSN 0041-798X
V1
U S NAVAL INSTITUTE. PROCEEDINGS. 1874. m. $28. U S Naval Institute, 118 Maryland Ave., Annapolis, MD 21402-5035. Ed. Fred H. Rainbow. adv.; bk.rev.; charts; illus.; index; circ. 119,790. (also avail. in microform from UMI; reprint service avail. from UMI) **Indexed:** Air Un.Lib.Ind., Amer.Bibl.Slavic & E.Eur.Stud, BMT, Chem.Abstr., Deep Sea Res.& Oceanogr.Abstr., DM & T, Hist.Abstr., P.A.I.S., So.Pac.Per.Ind. Key Title: Proceedings - United States Naval Institute.
  —BLDSC shelfmark: 6829.000000.

355   US
U S S HENRICO A P A -45 REUNION ASSOCIATION. NEWSLETTER. 1974. s-a. $20. U S S Henrico A P A-45 Reunion Association, 15875 Interurban Rd., Platte City, MO 64079-9185. TEL 816-431-5411. FAX 816-431-5556. Ed. Don Soper. circ. 700. (looseleaf format)
  Description: Contains history of the ship, crew and officer muster roll 1943-1968, and reunion information.

355.1   US
U S S R REPORT: MILITARY AFFAIRS. irreg. (approx. 70/yr.). $7 per no. (foreign $14.50 per no.). U.S. Joint Publications Research Service, Box 12507, Arlington, VA 22209. TEL 703-487-4630. (Orders to: NTIS, Springfield, VA 22161)
  Formerly: Translations on U S S R Military Affairs.

U S S R SERIAL REPORTS: FOREIGN MILITARY REVIEW. see *POLITICAL SCIENCE — International Relations*

U S S R SERIAL REPORTS: MILITARY HISTORY JOURNAL. see *POLITICAL SCIENCE — International Relations*

385 359   US
U S S ST. LOUIS HUBBLE BUBBLE. 1942. m. $10. U S S St. Louis CL 49 Association, Inc., 220 Otis Ave., Staten Island, NY 10306. TEL 718-351-4556. Ed. Bill Kohnle. bk.rev.; circ. 500.

355   NO   ISSN 0041-6584
UNDERVISNING OG VELFERD/EDUCATION AND WELFARE.* 1955. 10/yr. Undervisnings- og Velferdsoffiserenes Forening, Bergen, Norway.

355   US   ISSN 0041-6592
UNDERWATER LETTER. 1960. s-m. $175. Callahan Publications, Box 3751, Washington, DC 20007. TEL 703-356-1925. FAX 703-356-9614. Ed. Vincent F. Callahan, Jr. bk.rev.; charts; illus. (back issues avail.) **Indexed:** DM & T, PROMT.
  Formerly: Underwater Defense Letter.
  Description: Information on new scientific developments, research and new products in the field of underwater defense.

355   US   ISSN 0503-1982
U9
UNIFORMED SERVICES ALMANAC. 1959. a. $6. Uniformed Services Almanac, Inc., Box 4144, Falls Church, VA 22044. TEL 703-532-1631. Ed. Lt. Col. Sol Gordon, USAF-Ret.
  Description: Annual guide to pay, benefits, entitlements and other subjects of interest to military personnel.

UNION DES AVEUGLES DE GUERRE. BULLETIN MENSUEL. see *HANDICAPPED — Visually Impaired*

UNITED ARAB EMIRATES. AL-QIYADAH AL-AAMAH LIL-QUWWAT AL-MUSALLIHAH. MAJALLAH AL-TIBBIYYAH/UNITED ARAB EMIRATES. GENERAL COMMAND FOR THE ARMED FORCES. MEDICAL JOURNAL. see *MEDICAL SCIENCES*

355 539.7 320   UN   ISSN 0252-5607
UNITED NATIONS DISARMAMENT YEARBOOK. Spanish edition: Naciones Unidas sobre Desarme. Anuario (ISSN 0252-5593); French edition: Nations Unies Annuaire de Desarmement (ISSN 0252-5615); Russian edition (ISSN 0252-5585) (Text in English) 1952. irreg., latest vol.14, 1989. $45. United Nations Publications, Rm. DC2-853, New York, NY 10017. TEL 212-965-8302. FAX 212-963-3489. (Or: Distribution and Sales Section, Palais des Nations, CH-1211 Geneva 10, Switzerland) (also avail. in microfiche)
  —BLDSC shelfmark: 9096.972000.
  Former titles: United Nations. Disarmament Commission. Yearbook; United Nations. Disarmament Commission. Official Records (ISSN 0082-8076)

355 539.7 320   UN
UNITED NATIONS ECONOMIC AND SOCIAL COUNCIL. DISARMAMENT STUDY SERIES. 1981. irreg., latest no.16. price varies. United Nations Publications, Room DC2-0853, New York, NY 10017. TEL 212-963-8300. FAX 212-963-3489. (Or: Distribution and Sales Section, Palais des Nations, 1211 Geneva 10, Switzerland)

MILITARY

358 600   US
U.S. AIR FORCE GEOPHYSICS LABORATORY. A F G L (SERIES). 1960? irreg. U.S. Air Force Geophysics Laboratory, Hanscom Air Force Base, MA 01731. TEL 617-861-4441. (Dist. by: National Technical Information Service, Springfield, VA 22151) (also avail. in microform) **Indexed:** Geo.Abstr., GeoRef.
    Supersedes: U.S. Air Force Cambridge Research Laboratories. A F C R L (Series) (ISSN 0082-870X)

355 343   US   ISSN 0082-8769
JX1974.A1
U.S. ARMS CONTROL AND DISARMAMENT AGENCY. ANNUAL REPORT TO CONGRESS. 1961. a. U.S. Arms Control and Disarmament Agency, Dept. of State Bldg., Washington, DC 20451. TEL 202-632-8715. (Also avail. from: Supt. of Documents, Washington DC 20402.)

U.S. COAST GUARD MARINE SAFETY COUNCIL. PROCEEDINGS. see TRANSPORTATION — Ships And Shipping

355   US   ISSN 0082-9862
U.S. DEPARTMENT OF DEFENSE. DEFENSE PROGRAM AND DEFENSE BUDGET.* (Also called: Defense Budget and Defense Program) a. U.S. Department of Defense, The Pentagon, Washington, DC 20301. TEL 202-545-6700. (Orders to: Supt. of Documents, Washington, DC 20402) **Indexed:** DM & T.

U.S. DEPARTMENT OF DEFENSE. INDEX OF SPECIFICATIONS AND STANDARDS. see METROLOGY AND STANDARDIZATION

355.6   US   ISSN 0098-3888
UA23.2
U.S. DEPARTMENT OF DEFENSE. REPORT OF SECRETARY OF DEFENSE TO THE CONGRESS.* Cover title: Annual Defense Department Report. a. $4.00. U.S. Department of Defense, The Pentagon, Washington, DC 20301. TEL 202-545-6700. (Orders to: Supt. of Documents, Washington, DC 20402) Key Title: Report of Secretary of Defense to the Congress.

355   US
U.S. DIRECTOR OF SELECTIVE SERVICE. SEMIANNUAL REPORT. 1967. s-a. price varies. U.S. Selective Service System, Washington, DC 20435. TEL 202-724-0424. (Orders to: Supt. of Documents, Washington, DC 20402) Ed. Fred Smith. charts; stat.; circ. controlled.

355   US   ISSN 0083-1328
U.S. INDUSTRIAL COLLEGE OF THE ARMED FORCES. MONOGRAPHS. R SERIES.* 1944. irreg. U.S. Industrial College of the Armed Forces., Ft. McNeir, Washington, DC 20319-6000. TEL 202-475-0717.

359.07   US   ISSN 0500-1951
V393
U.S. OFFICE OF NAVAL RESEARCH. ANNUAL TASK SUMMARY: CONTRACT RESEARCH PROGRAM. a. U.S. Office of Naval Research, Arlington, VA 22217. TEL 202-545-6200. Key Title: Annual Task Summary, Contract Research Program.

355.11 368.4   US   ISSN 0083-3533
UB373
U.S. VETERANS ADMINISTRATION. ANNUAL REPORT. 1931. a. free. U.S. Department of Veterans Affairs, 810 Vermont Ave., N.W. (008B3), Washington, DC 20420. TEL 202-233-3557.

358.4   UK   ISSN 0956-2826
UNITED STATES AIR FORCES EUROPE YEARBOOK. 1989. a. £4. Royal Air Force Benevolent Fund, International Air Tattoo, Building 1108, RAF Fairford, Glos. GL7 4DL, England. circ. 55,000.

UNITED STATES ARMY AVIATION DIGEST. see AERONAUTICS AND SPACE FLIGHT

355   US   ISSN 0892-4023
    CODEN: UNSYE3
UNMANNED SYSTEMS. 1975. q. $25 to non-members. Association for Unmanned Vehicle Systems, 1101 14th St., N.W., Ste. 1100, Washington, DC 20005. TEL 202-371-1170. FAX 202-371-1090. adv.; circ. 2,500. **Indexed:** DM& T.
—BLDSC shelfmark: 9120.550000.
    Former titles: U V S Magazine; Remotely Piloted Magazine.

355   IT
UNUCI; rivista dell'Unione Nazionale Ufficiali in Congedo d'Italia. m. L.1000 per no. Unione Nazionale Ufficiali in Congedo d'Italia, Via Nomentana 313, 00162 Rome, Italy. TEL 869-007. Ed. Alberto Scotti. illus.
    Description: Covers the different types of Italian army activities that go on outside of Italy. It also describes each section of the Army and its responsibilities.

355.115   US   ISSN 0042-1820
V F W MAGAZINE. 1912. 11/yr. $10 to non-members. Veterans of Foreign Wars of the United States, c/o Wade W. LaDue, Broadway at 34th St., Kansas City, MO 64111. TEL 816-756-3390. Ed. Richard Kolb. adv.; bk.rev.; illus.; circ. 2,020,000. (also avail. in microfilm from UMI)

355   SW   ISSN 0042-2800
VAART FOERSVAR. 1890. 10/yr. SEK 70. Allmaenna Foersvarsfoereningen, Riddargatan 13, S-114 51 Stockholm, Sweden. Ed. Lars Killander. adv.; bk.rev.; abstr.; illus.; circ. 6,000.

355   NO   ISSN 0042-2037
VAART VERN. 1912. bi-m. NOK 150. Krigsskoleutdannede Offiserers Landsforening - Norwegian Academic Officers Association, P.O. Box 7207, Ho, N-0307 Oslo 3, Norway. TEL 02-52-15-46. FAX 02-69-56-08. Ed. Tore Hiorth Oppegaard. adv.; bk.rev.; circ. 2,000.
    Description: Directed to political, military and academic leaders to promote Norwegian national defense.

355   DK   ISSN 0109-7172
VAERN OM DANMARK. 1980. q. DKK 120. Vaern om Danmark, Trommesalen 1, 1614 Copenhagen V, Denmark. adv.; illus.; circ. 4,000.
    Formerly: Defenser.

VEILIG VLIEGEN; flight, ground and maintenance safety journal. see AERONAUTICS AND SPACE FLIGHT

355.133   RU
▼**VERSIYA.** 1990. m. 1 Rub. per issue. Mestnyi Komitet Gosudarstvennoi Bezopasnosti, Ul. Gor'kogo 32 "A", 664000 Irkutsk, Russia. Ed. Nina Voronina. circ. 60,000.

355.15   US   ISSN 0042-4765
VETERAN. (Text in Polish) 1921. m. $5. Polish Army Veterans Association of America, Inc., 17 Irving Place, New York, NY 10003. TEL 212-475-5585. Ed. Zbigniew A. Konikowski. adv.; bk.rev.; bibl.; circ. 4,500. (tabloid format) **Indexed:** Alt.Press Ind.

355.115   BE
VETERAN BELGE. (Text in Dutch, French) 1922. q. 250 Fr. (Amicale des Officiers de Campagne) F. Lepeer, Ed. & Pub., 110 Av. de Heyn, B-1090 Brussels, Belgium. adv.; bk.rev.; circ. 1,000.

355.115   US
VETERANS AFFAIRS IN WISCONSIN. 1983. s-a. free. Department of Veterans Affairs, 30 W. Mifflin St., Box 7843, Madison, WI 53707. TEL 608-266-1311. Ed. Steve L. Olson. circ. 4,000.

355.115   US
VETERAN'S OBSERVER. 1983. m. free. 7314 Deering Ave., Canoga Park, CA 91303. TEL 818-713-9447. FAX 818-713-8086. Ed. William J. Donovan. adv.; bk.rev.; circ. 220,000.

355.115   US
VETERANS OF THE VIETNAM WAR; the Veteran leader. 1980. bi-m. $12. Veterans of the Vietnam War, Inc., 2090 Bald Mountain Rd., Wilkes-Barre, PA 18702. TEL 717-825-7215. Ed. Michael Milne. circ. 10,000.

335.115   US
VETERAN'S VIEW. m. Central Newspaper, Inc., 8 South Michigan Ave., Chicago, IL 60603. TEL 312-263-5388. Ed. Michael Haddad.

355.115   US
VETS' NEWS. 1945. bi-m. free. Department of Veterans' Affairs, 700 Summer St., N.E., Salem, OR 97310-1201. TEL 503-373-2385. FAX 503-373-2362. Ed. Sharon Robertson. circ. 48,000.
    Formerly: Vets' Newsletter.

355   RM   ISSN 1018-0400
U4
VIATA ARMATEI. 1947. m. 420 lei($57) (effective Jan. 1992). Ministerul Apararii Nationale - Ministry of National Defense, Str. Cobalcescu Nr. 28A, sector 1, Bucharest 70768, Rumania. TEL 14-20-12. FAX 400-159456. (Subscr. to: Orion, Str. Calea Grivitei Nr. 64-66, sector 1, P.O. Box 12-201, Bucharest, Rumania) Ed. Ion Jianu. bk.rev.; abstr.; charts; illus.
    Former titles (until Dec. 1989): Viata Militara (ISSN 0042-5044); Imagini Militare.

355 975   US   ISSN 1046-4638
VIETNAM. 1988. bi-m. $16.95 (foreign $22.95). Empire Press, 602 S. King St., Ste. 300, Leesburg, VA 22075. TEL 703-771-9400. FAX 703-777-4627. (Subscr. to: Box 385, Mt. Morris, IL 61054-7943. TEL 815-734-1115) Ed. Harry G. Summers, Jr. circ. 238,000.
    Description: Explains the Vietnam War - from grand strategy to daily search-and destroy patrol. Covers personalities, weapons, battles, heroes, and perspectives of both North and South.

355   US   ISSN 1042-7597
DS556
VIETNAM GENERATION. 1989. q. $40 to individuals; institutions $75. Vietnam Generation, Inc., 2921 Terrace Dr., Chevy Chase, MD 20815. circ. 425.
—BLDSC shelfmark: 9236.040840.
    Description: Promotes interdisciplinary study of the Vietnam War Era and its generation.

355.115   US
VIETNAM WAR NEWSLETTER. 1979. m. $24.95. Thomas W. Hebert, Ed. & Pub., Box 469, Collinsville, CT 06022. adv.; bk.rev.; film rev.; bibl.; circ. 3,000. (looseleaf format; back issues avail.)

355   BE
VIGILO. 1960. q. 300 Fr. (Cercle des Officiers de Reserve de Bruxelles - Kring der Reserveofficieren van Brussel) F. Lepeer, Ed. & Pub., 110 Ave. de Heyn, B-1090 Brussels, Belgium. adv.; bk.rev.; circ. 1,500.

355   II   ISSN 0042-613X
VIKRANT; Asia's defence journal. (Text in English) 1970. m. Rs.85($30) Vikrant Publications, 1 Todarmal Rd., Bengali Market, New Delhi 110001, India. Ed. Krishan Kumar. adv.; charts; illus.; stat.

355   II
VIKRANT'S DEFENCE DIARY. (Text in English) 1974. w. Rs.225($52) Vikrant Publications, 1 Todarmal Rd., Bengali Market, New Delhi 110001, India. Ed. Krishan Kumar. index.

358.4   CS   ISSN 0042-7497
VITEZNA KRIDLA.* 1953. Federalni Ministerstvo Narodni Obrany, Tychonova 1, 161 00 Prague, Czechoslovakia.

355   FR
VIVAT HUSSAR. 1966. a. 120 F. Association des Amis du Musee International des Hussards, Jardin Massey, 65000 Tarbes, France. Ed.Bd. adv.; bk.rev.; bibl.; illus.; circ. 1,500. (back issues avail.)

355   RU
VOENNAYA MYSL'. 1918. m. Ministerstvo Oborony S.S.S.R., c/o A.B. Bazhenov, Ed., Kropotinskaya ul. 19, 103160 Moscow K-160, Russia. TEL 293-52-01.

VOENNO ISTORICHESKI SBORNIK. see HISTORY — History Of Europe

355   RU   ISSN 0042-9058
VOENNO-ISTORICHESKII ZHURNAL. 1959. m. 22.20 Rub. Voenizdat, Bol'shoi Kisel'nyi per., 14, Moscow, Russia. (Co-sponsor: Ministerstvo Oborony) (also avail. in microform from MIM) **Indexed:** Hist.Abstr., Numis.Lit.

355   RU   ISSN 0042-9074
VOENNYE ZNANIYA/MILITARY REVIEW. 1925. m. 4.80 Rub. Izdatel'stvo DOSAAF, Novo-Ryazanskaya ul. 26, 107066 Moscow, Russia. TEL 445-39-20. Ed. S. Sinyutin.

355   RU   ISSN 0042-9066
VOENNYI VESTNIK. 1921. m. 17.40 Rub. Voenizdat, Bolshoi Kisel'nyi per., 14, Moscow, Russia. (Co-sponsor: Ministerstvo Oborony) index. **Indexed:** Curr.Dig.Sov.Press.

MILITARY 3475

355.115 FR
VOIX DU CHEMINOT ANCIEN COMBATTANT. 1927. q. 1.80 F. Federation Nationales des Anciens Combattants, Prisonniers, Deportes, Resistants et Victimes, 46 rue Copernic, 75782 Paris Cedex 16, France. adv.; circ. 15,000.

355 YU ISSN 0042-840X
VOJNI GLASNIK; strucni casopis rodova vojske i sluzbi jna. (Text in Macedonian, Serbo-Croatian) 1947. bi-m. $20. Vojnoizdavacki Zavod, Svetozara Markovica 70, Belgrade, Yugoslavia. (Dist. by: Jugoslovenska Knjiga, P.O. Box 36, 11001 Belgrade, Yugoslavia) Ed. Sava Krstic.

355 YU ISSN 0067-5660
U4.B37
VOJNI MUZEJ, BELGRADE. VESNIK/MILITARY MUSEUM, BELGRADE. BULLETIN. (Text in Serbo-Croatian; summaries in English, French) 1954. irreg. $1 per copy. Vojni Muzej, Kalemegdan bb, 11000 Belgrade, Yugoslavia. Ed. Marijan Mozgon. bk.rev.; circ. 2,000. **Indexed:** Hist.Abstr.

355 YU ISSN 0042-8426
VOJNO DELO; opstevojni teorijski casopis. 1949. bi-m. 300000 din.($5) per no. Savazni Sekretarijat za Narodnu Odbranu, Belgrade, Yugoslavia. TEL 011-681-565. (Dist. by: Vojnoizdavacki i Novinski Centar, Svetozava Markovica 70, 11002 Belgrade, Yugoslavia) Ed. Jovan Canak.

355 YU ISSN 0042-8442
VOJNOISTORIJSKI GLASNIK. (Text in Serbo-Croatian; summaries in English, French) 1950. 3/yr. $49. Vojnoistorijski Institut - Military-Historical Institute, Bircaninova Br.5, Belgrade, Yugoslavia. (Subscr. to: Jugoslovanska Knjiga, Trg Republike 5-VIII, Belgrade, Yugoslavia) Ed. Slavko Vukcevic. bk.rev.; bibl.; charts; illus.; stat.; index, cum.index; circ. 1,000. **Indexed:** Hist.Abstr.

355 YU ISSN 0042-8469
VOJNOTEHNICKI GLASNIK. (Text in Serbo-Croatian) 1953. bi-m. 70 din.($8.50) (Savezni Sekretarijat za Narodnu Odbranu) Vojnoizdavacki Zavod, Balkanska 53, 11002 Belgrade, Yugoslavia. Ed. Nikola Zoric.

355 GW ISSN 0505-9259
VOLKSARMEE. 1956. w. DM.44.20. Militaerverlag der Deutschen Demokratischen Republik, Redaktion Volksarmee, Storkower Strasse 158, Berlin 1055, Germany. (Subscr. to: Buchexport, Leninstr. 16, 7010 Leipzig, Germany)

355 BE
VOX: HEBDOMADAIRE MILITAIRE. Dutch edition: Vox: Militair Weekblad. 1974. w. 1500 Fr. (effective Jan. 1992). Ministere de la Defense Nationale, Service de l'Information, Publication Hebdo Mil VOX, Quartier Reine Elisabeth, Block 5, Rue d'Evere, B-1050 Brussels, Belgium. FAX 02-2433931. Eds. J. Reyniers, A. Vergeynst. bk.rev.; illus.; index; circ. 30,000.
Formerly: F M (ISSN 0014-5963)

355 CN ISSN 0300-3213
VOXAIR. 1952. s-m. $3.50. Canadian Forces Base Winnipeg, Westwin, Man. R3J OTO, Canada. TEL 204-889-3963. Ed. P.J. Grossman. adv.; play rev.; circ. 3,600. (tabloid format)

W A M M NEWSLETTER. (Women Against Military Madness) see *WOMEN'S INTERESTS*

359.96 301.412 UI
W M A - NOUNCEMENTS. 1967. q. $4.50. Women Marines Association, 5030 Corinthia Way, Oceanside, CA 92056. TEL 713-367-5494. (Subscr. to: Assistant Secretary, Headquarters, WMA, P.O. Box 387 MCB, Quantico, VA 22134. TEL 703-640-6161; Editorial addr: 25N Deerfoot Cir. Woodlands, TX 77380) Ed. Jackie Treese. circ. 3,600.
Description: Includes items concerning the Marine Corps and Marine Corps Reserve, for those formerly and currently enlisted.

355 GW
DAS WAFFEN-ARSENAL. 1973. q. Podzun-Pallas Publishing GmbH, Markt 9, Postfach 314, 6360 Friedberg 3 (Dorheim), Germany. FAX 06031-62969. Ed. Horst Scheibert. adv.; circ. 12,000. (back issues avail.)

355 UK ISSN 0042-9961
WAGGONER. 1891. 6/yr. £6 (effective Jan. 1991). Royal Corps of Transport, Institution, Regimental Headquarters, Buller Barracks, Aldershot GU11 2BX, England. Ed. Lt. Col. M.H.G. Young. adv.; bk.rev.; circ. 4,000.
Description: Contains news and information for serving and retired members of the Royal Corps of Transport.

WAR AND SOCIETY. see *HISTORY*

WAR COMMUNIQUES. see *POLITICAL SCIENCE*

355 UK ISSN 0308-0676
WARFARE. 1972. s-a. Christian Defence Institute, 157 Vicarage Rd., London E1O 5DU, England. TEL 081-539-3876. Ed. Ronald King. bk.rev.

WARGAMER; analysis and review of conflict simulation. see *HOBBIES*

355 CN ISSN 0707-8056
WARRIOR. 1974. fortn. Can.$20. Canadian Forces Base, P.O. Box 190, Shearwater, N.S. B0J 3A0, Canada. TEL 902-466-1013. FAX 902-466-1796. Ed. Capt. J.L. Houston. adv.; bk.rev.; illus.; circ. 6,000.
Formerly: Shearwater Warrior (ISSN 0705-1980)

623.82 UK ISSN 0142-6222
V765
WARSHIP. 1977. a. £24. Conway Maritime Press Ltd., 101 Fleet St., London EC4Y 1DE, England. TEL 071-583 2412. Ed. Robert Gardiner. adv.; bk.rev.
—BLDSC shelfmark: 9261.868600.

623.82 US ISSN 0043-0374
V750
WARSHIP INTERNATIONAL. 1964. q. $20 (foreign $22). I N R O, Inc, (International Naval Research Organization), 1729 Lois Ct., Toledo, OH 43613. TEL 419-472-1331. Ed. Christopher C. Wright. adv.; bk.rev.; charts; illus.; stat.; circ. 4,000. (also avail. in microfilm from UMI; reprint service avail. from UMI) **Indexed:** Abstr.Mil.Bibl, Hist.Abstr.
—BLDSC shelfmark: 9261.869000.

355.115 US
WASHINGTON ACTION REPORTER. 1976. m. Veterans of Foreign Wars of the United States, National Headquarters, Broadway at 34th St., Kansas City, MO 64111. TEL 816-756-3390. illus.

355 GW
WEHRAUSBILDUNG. 1958. 6/yr. DM.8.80. (Bundesministerium der Verteidigung) Verlag Offene Worte, Austrasse 19, 5300 Bonn 2, Germany. TEL 0228-340884. FAX 0228-348100. adv.; bk.rev.; illus.; index; circ. 57,000.
Formerly: Wehrausbildung in Wort und Bild (ISSN 0043-2121)

WEHRMEDIZIN UND WEHRPHARMAZIE. see *MEDICAL SCIENCES*

WEHRTECHNIK, VEREINIGT MIT WEHR UND WIRTSCHAFT; Monatsschrift fuer wirtschaftliche Fragen der Verteidigung, Luftfahrt und Industrie. see *AERONAUTICS AND SPACE FLIGHT*

350 GW
WEISSBUCH ZUR SICHERHEIT DER BUNDESREPUBLIK DEUTSCHLAND UND ZUR LAGE DER BUNDESWEHR. 1970. irreg. price varies. Bundesministerium der Verteidigung, Fue SI 3, Postfach 1328, 5330 Bonn 1, Germany.

369.1 US
WEST VIRGINIA LEGIONNAIRE. m. $2 to non-members. (American Legion, Department of West Virginia) Record-Delta, P.O. Box 550, Buckhannon, WV 26201. TEL 304-747-2800. (Subscr. to: P.O. Box 3191, Charleston, WV 26201) Ed. Robert E. Vass. adv.; circ. 27,000.

355 GW ISSN 0083-9078
WEYERS FLOTTENTASCHENBUCH/WARSHIPS OF THE WORLD. 1900. a. DM.98. Bernard und Graefe Verlag, Karl-Mand-Str. 2, D-5400 Koblenz, Germany. TEL 0261-80706-0. TELEX 862662-SPS-D.
Former titles: Taschenbuch der Kriegsflotten; Taschenbuch der Deutschen Kriegsflotten.

355.115 US ISSN 0083-9108
WHAT EVERY VETERAN SHOULD KNOW. 1937. a. (with m. supplements). $10 (with supplements $30). Veterans Information Service, Box 111, East Moline, IL 61244. Ed. Patrick L. Murphy. index.

WHEELS & TRACKS; international historical review of military vehicles. see *TRANSPORTATION — Automobiles*

WINGS OF GOLD. see *AERONAUTICS AND SPACE FLIGHT*

355 US
WINGSPREAD RANDOLPH A F B. w. 122 E. Byrd, Box 2789, Universal City, TX 78148. TEL 512-658-7424.

355 PL
WOJSKO LUDOWE. m. $33. Wydawnictwo "Czasopisma Wojskowe", Grzybowska 77, Rembertow, 00-950 Warsaw, Poland. (Dist. by: Ars Polona-Ruch, Krakowskie Przedmiescie 7, 00-068 Warsaw, Poland) Ed. Zdzislaw Czerwinski.
Supersedes (in 1990): Wojsko Ludowe (ISSN 0043-7174)

355 PL ISSN 0043-7182
DK417
WOJSKOWY PRZEGLAD HISTORYCZNY. q. 850 Zl. per no. (Wojskowy Instytut Historyczny) Wydawnictwo "Czasopisma Wojskowe", Ul. Grzybowska 77, Rembertow, 00-950 Warsaw, Poland. Ed. Marek Tarczynski. bk.rev.; bibl.; circ. 15,000. **Indexed:** Hist.Abstr.
—BLDSC shelfmark: 9342.670000.
Description: Covers military history of Poland.

355 US ISSN 1040-2888
UG446.5
WORLD ARMORED VEHICLE INVENTORY & FORECAST. a. $1700. Forecast International Inc. - D M S, 22 Commerce Rd., Newtown, CT 06470. TEL 203-426-0800. FAX 203-426-1964. TELEX 467615.
Description: Examines the armored vehicle market: past, present, and future. Covers all active global AV programs - applications, characteristics, and manufacturers for six major component types.

355 629.133 US
WORLD HELICOPTER INVENTORY & FORECAST. a. $1700. Forecast International Inc. - D M S, 22 Commerce Rd., Newtown, CT 06470. TEL 203-426-0800. FAX 203-426-1964. TELEX 467615.
Description: Over 100 active helicopter programs are covered from concept definition through retirement. Contains performance data, systems information, historical data, milestones, price range, and production forecast for the next 10 years.

355 629.1 US ISSN 1040-2896
UG1240
WORLD MILITARY AIRCRAFT INVENTORY & FORECAST. a. $1700. Forecast International Inc. - D M S, 22 Commerce Rd., Newtown, CT 06470. TEL 203-426-0800. FAX 203-426-1964. TELEX 467615.
Description: Identifies world requirements for all types of fixed wing military aircraft and details, by country, manufacturer, mission, unit cost, technical specifications, inventory, employment trends, and ten-year production and acquisition forecasts.

355 US ISSN 1040-290X
UG1420
WORLD MILITARY AVIONICS INVENTORY & FORECAST. a. $1700. Forecast International Inc. - D M S, 22 Commerce Rd., Newtown, CT 06470. TEL 203-426-0800. FAX 203-426-1964. TELEX 467615.
Description: Covers inventory and production forecast of avionics equipment used on every military aircraft, fixed and rotary wing, outside the Soviet bloc.

MILITARY — Abstracting, Bibliographies, Statistics

355 US ISSN 0897-4667
JX1974.A1
WORLD MILITARY EXPENDITURES AND ARMS TRANSFERS. a. U.S. Arms Control and Disarmament Agency, Bureau of Nuclear and Weapons Control, Defense Program and Analysis Division, Washington, DC 20451. TEL 202-632-8715. (Also avail. from: Supt. of Documents, Washington, DC 20402) Ed. Daniel Gallik.
—BLDSC shelfmark: 9356.674650.
Formerly: World Military Expenditures (ISSN 0363-7204); Which supersedes: World Military Expenditures and Related Data (ISSN 0082-8793)
Description: Provides information on military resources by country throughout the world.

355 US ISSN 1040-2918
UG1310
WORLD MISSILES INVENTORY & FORECAST. a. $1700. Forecast International Inc. - D M S, 22 Commerce Rd., Newtown, CT 06470. TEL 203-426-0800. FAX 203-426-1964. TELEX 467615.
Description: Examines the world market for strategic, cruise, air-to-surface, anti-ship, air defense, air-to-air, and anti-tank missiles. Includes missile inventory and 10-year forecast for over 50 countries.

355 US
WORLD ORDNANCE INVENTORY & FORECAST. a. $1700. Forecast International Inc. - D M S, 22 Commerce Rd., Newtown, CT 06470. TEL 203-426-0800. FAX 203-426-1964. TELEX 467615.
Description: Covers over 100 countries, detailing current inventories of ordnance, force structure analysis, procurement histories, and future acquisitions. Includes towed and self-propelled artillery, armored vehicles, armaments, mortars, artillery ammunition, anti-tank weapons, automatic cannon, and rocket launchers.

WORLD WAR II. see *HISTORY — History Of North And South America*

WORLDWIDE REPORT: ARMS CONTROL. see *POLITICAL SCIENCE — International Relations*

355 539.7 US
WORLDWIDE REPORT: NUCLEAR DEVELOPMENTS. irreg. (approx. 30/yr.) $7 per no. (foreign $14 per no.). U.S. Joint Publications Research Service, Box 12507, Arlington, VA 22209. TEL 703-487-4630. (Orders to: NTIS, Springfield, VA 22161)
Formerly: Worldwide Report: Nuclear Development and Proliferation.

355.14 GW ISSN 0044-2852
ZEITSCHRIFT FUER HEERESKUNDE. 1929. bi-m. DM.75. Deutsche Gesellschaft fuer Heereskunde e.V., Augustin-Wibbelt-Str. 8, 4720 Beckum, Germany. Ed. Georg Ortenburg. adv.; bk.rev.; bibl.; illus.; index; circ. 1,000. Indexed: Hist.Abstr.
—BLDSC shelfmark: 9464.330000.

355 IS
ZIKA. q. Defense Department, Miltary P.O. Box 01013, Tel Aviv, Israel. adv.

355 PL ISSN 0044-4979
ZOLNIERZ POLSKI. 1945. w. $56. Wydawnictwo Czasopisma Wojskowe, Grzybowska 77, Rembertow, 00-950 Warsaw, Poland. TEL 48-22-201261. (Dist. by: Ars Polona-Ruch, Krakowskia Przedmiescie 7, 00-068 Warsaw, Poland) Ed. Wieslaw Jan Wysocki. illus.

335 909 FR
39 - 45 MAGAZINE. m. (11/yr.). 270 F. (foreign 280 F.). Editions Heimdal, Chateau de Damigny, 14400 Bayeux, France. (back issues avail.)
Description: Covers World War II.

355 US
43RD INFANTRY DIVISION VETERANS ASSOCIATION. BULLETIN. 1953. q. membership only. 43rd Infantry Division Veterans Association, 150 Lakedell Dr., E. Greenwich, RI 02818. TEL 401-884-7052. Ed. Howard F. Brown. circ. 1,900.
Description: Contains personal anecdotes and veterans' information mainly of interest to veterans of the 43rd Infantry Division.

MILITARY — Abstracting, Bibliographies, Statistics

355 016 AG
ABSTRACTS OF MILITARY BIBLIOGRAPHY. (Text in English) 1967. q. $70. Ruben A. Ramirez Mitchell, Ed. & Pub., Maipu 262, 1084 Buenos Aires, Argentina. adv.; bk.rev.; abstr.; tr.mk.; index, cum.index; circ. 2,000.
Former titles: Resumenes Analiticos sobre Defensa y Seguridad Nacional - Abstracts of Military Bibliography (ISSN 0034-5873); Resumenes Analiticos de Bibliografia Militar.

358.4 US
AIR FORCE INTERCHANGEABLE AND SUBSTITUTION REPORT. m. $3600 in U.S., Canada, Mexico; elsewhere $7200. (Department of the Air Force) U.S. National Technical Information Service, 5285 Port Royal Rd., Springfield, VA 22161. TEL 703-487-4630. (magnetic tape)

355 016 US ISSN 0002-2586
Z5063.A2
AIR UNIVERSITY LIBRARY INDEX TO MILITARY PERIODICALS. 1949. q. (plus a. cum.). free to libraries. U.S. Air Force, Air University Library, Maxwell Air Force Base, AL 36112-5564. TEL 205-953-2504. Ed. Martha M. Stewart. bk.rev.; index, cum.index; circ. 1,500.

359 090 AG ISSN 0066-7080
ARGENTINA. DEPARTAMENTO DE ESTUDIOS HISTORICOS NAVALES. SERIE J: LIBROS Y IMPRESOS RAROS. 1962. irreg., no.2, 1970. Departamento de Estudios Historicos Navales, Instituto de Publicaciones Navales, Av. Cordoba 547, Buenos Aires, Argentina.

359 AG ISSN 0066-7331
ARGENTINA. SERVICIO DE INTELIGENCIA NAVAL. BIBLIOTECAS DE LA ARMADA. BOLETIN BIBLIOGRAFICO.. 1943. a. Servicio de Inteligencia Naval, Bibliotecas de la Armada, Edificio Libertad, Comodoro Py y Corbeta Uruguay, Buenos Aires, Argentina. Ed. Juan A. Manon.

355.31 US
ARMY MANUALS AND REGULATIONS INDEX (CONSOLIDATED INDEX OF ARMY PUBLICATIONS). q. $25 in US, Canada, Mexico; elsewhere $50. (Department of the Army) U.S. National Technical Information Service, 5825 Port Royal Rd., Springfield, VA 22161. TEL 703-487-4630. (microfiche)
Description: Comprised of technical and field manuals, Army regulations, lubrication orders, and technical bulletins. Provides cross-reference of national stock number to each publication.

355 US ISSN 1040-7995
BIBLIOGRAPHIES AND INDEXES IN MILITARY STUDIES. 1988. irreg. price varies. Greenwood Press, Inc. (Subsidiary of: Greenwood Publishing Group Inc.), 88 Post Rd. W., Box 5007, Westport, CT 06881-5007. TEL 203-226-3571. FAX 203-222-1502.

355 US ISSN 1056-7410
▼**BIBLIOGRAPHIES OF BATTLES AND LEADERS.** 1990. irreg. price varies. Greenwood Press, Inc. (Subsidiary of: Greenwood Publishing Group Inc.), 88 Post Rd. W., Box 5007, Westport, CT 06881-5007. TEL 203-226-3571. FAX 203-222-1502.

355 JA ISSN 0523-8080
BOEI DAIGAKKO KYOKAN KENKYU YOROKU/NATIONAL DEFENSE ACADEMY. DIGEST OF RESEARCHES BY FACULTY MEMBERS. (Text in English and Japanese) 1956. a. Boei Daigakko - National Defense Academy, 10-20 Hashirimizu 1-chome, Yokosuka-shi, Kanagawa-ken 239, Japan.

CURRENT MILITARY AND POLITICAL LITERATURE. see *POLITICAL SCIENCE — International Relations*

335.27 US
DEFENSE INTEGRATED DATA SYSTEM TOTAL ITEM RECORD: SEGMENT V. q. $10000 for 1600 bpi in US, Canada, Mexico; elsewhere $20000. (Department of Defense, Defense Logistics Services) U.S. National Technical Information Service, 5825 Port Royal Rd., Springfield, VA 22161. TEL 703-487-4630. (magnetic tape)
Description: Features coded item characteristics data.

335.27 US
DEFENSE INTEGRATED DATA SYSTEM TOTAL ITEM RECORD: SEGMENTS A, B, C. Short title: D I D S - T I R: Segments A, B, C. q. $18000 for 1600 bpi in US, Canada, Mexico; elsewhere $36000. (Department of Defense, Defense Logistics Services) U.S. National Technical Information Service, 5825 Port Royal Rd., Springfield, VA 22161. TEL 703-487-4630. (magnetic tape)
Description: Contains the following information--Segment A: indentification data; Segment B: major organizational entity (MOE) rule data; Segment C: reference number data.

335.27 US
DEFENSE INTEGRATED SYSTEM TOTAL ITEM RECORD: MASTER REQUIREMENTS. Short title: D I D S - T I R: Master Requirements. q. $2000 for 1600 bpi in US, Canada, Mexico; elsewhere $4000. (Department of Defense, Defense Logistics Services) U.S. National Technical Information Service, 5825 Port Royal Rd., Springfield, VA 22161. TEL 703-487-4630. (magnetic tape)

351.06 US
H4 - H8 COMMERCIAL AND GOVERNMENT ENTITY PUBLICATION, SECTION A: U.S. AND CANADA. Short title: H4 - H8 C A G E Publication, Sec. A: U.S. and Canada. 6/yr. $4200 for 1600 bpi in US, Canada, Mexico; elsewhere $8400. (Department of Defense, Defense Logistics) U.S. National Technical Information Service, 5825 Port Royal Rd., Springfield, VA 22161. TEL 703-487-4630. (magnetic tape)
Description: Lists international organizations which have contracts with the Department of Defense.

351.06 US
H4 - H8 COMMERCIAL AND GOVERNMENT ENTITY PUBLICATION, SECTION B: C A G E CODE. Short title: H4 - H8 C A G E Publication, Sec. B: C A G E Code. 6/yr. $4200 for 1600 bpi in US, Canada, Mexico; elsewhere $8400. (Department of Defense, Defense Logistics Services) U.S. National Technical Information Service, 5825 Port Royal Rd., Springfield, VA 22161. TEL 703-487-4630. (magnetic tape)

351.06 US
H4 - H8 COMMERCIAL AND GOVERNMENT ENTITY PUBLICATION, SECTION C: NATO MANUFACTURERS. Short title: H4 - H8 C A G E Publication, Sec. C: NATO Manufacturers. 6/yr. $1200 in US, Canada, Mexico; elsewhere $2400. (Department of Defense, Defense Logistics Service) U.S. National Technical Information Service, 5825 Port Royal Rd., Springfield, VA 22161. TEL 703-487-4630. (magnetic tape)
Description: Lists international contractors and suppliers of the Department of Defense.

351.06 US
H4 - H8 COMMERCIAL AND GOVERNMENT ENTITY PUBLICATION, SECTION D: NATO C A G E. Short title: H4 - H8 C A G E Publication, Sec. D: NATO C A G E. 6/yr. $1200 in US, Canada, Mexico; elsewhere $2400. (Department of Defense, Defense Logistics Services) U.S. National Technical Information Service, 5825 Port Royal Rd., Springfield, VA 22161. TEL 703-487-4630. (magnetic tape)
Description: Lists international contractors and suppliers to the Department of Defense.

355 UK
IMPERIAL WAR MUSEUM, LONDON. DEPARTMENT OF PRINTED BOOKS. ACCESSIONS LIST. 1970. m. free to libraries. Imperial War Museum, Department of Printed Books, Lambeth Rd., London S.E.1, England. circ. 200. (processed)
Description: History of warfare since 1914.

351.06 US
MANAGEMENT DATA LIST (ML): ML - MARINE CORPS. q. $75 in US, Canada, Mexico; elsewhere $150. (Department of Defense, Defense Logistics Services) U.S. National Technical Information Service, 5825 Port Royal Rd., Springfield, VA 22161. TEL 703-487-4630. (microfiche)
Description: Contains supply management data to assist in acquiring and accounting for items of supply.

351.06 US
MANAGEMENT DATA LIST (ML): ML - NAVY. q. $260 in US, Canada, Mexico; elsewhere $520. (Department of Defense, Defense Logistics Services) U.S. National Technical Information Service, 5825 Port Royal Rd., Springfield, VA 22161. TEL 703-487-4630. (microfiche)
  Description: Contains supply management data to assist requisitioners in acquiring and accounting for items of supply.

351.06 US
MANAGEMENT DATA LIST CONSOLIDATED (ML-C). q. price varies. (Department of Defense, Defense Logistics Services) U.S. National Technical Information Service, 5825 Port Royal Rd., Springfield, VA 22161. TEL 703-487-4630. (magnetic tape; also avail. in microfiche)
  Description: Provides supply management data on all national stock numbers recorded in DIDS Total Item Record.

359 310 US ISSN 0894-069X
V179 CODEN: NRLOEP
NAVAL RESEARCH LOGISTICS: AN INTERNATIONAL JOURNAL. 1954. 7/yr. $275 to institutions (foreign $362.50). John Wiley & Sons, Inc., Journals, 605 Third Ave., New York, NY 10158-0012. TEL 212-850-6000. FAX 212-850-6088. TELEX 12-7063. Ed. Richard Rosenthal. bk.rev.; bibl.; charts; index, cum.index; circ. 950. (also avail. in microform from RPI; back issues avail.; reprint service avail. from RPI) **Indexed:** Appl.Mech.Rev., Compumath, Curr.Cont., Curr.Ind.Stat., Cyb.Abstr., Eng.Ind., Ind.Sci.Rev., Ind.U.S.Gov.Per., Int.Abstr.Oper.Res., Int.Aerosp.Abstr., J.Cont.Quant.Meth., Math.R., Oper.Res.Manage.Sci., Qual.Contr.Appl.Stat., Risk Abstr., Sci.Abstr., Sci.Cit.Ind., Stat.Theor.Meth.Abstr.
  —BLDSC shelfmark: 6064.995000.
  Formerly: Naval Research Logistics Quarterly (ISSN 0028-1441)
  Description: Articles on both theory and applications in key areas including: mathematical statistics, economics, tactics and strategy.

359 016 AG ISSN 0034-8775
REVISTA DE PUBLICACIONES NAVALES. 1901. q. free. Estado Mayor General de la Armada, Jefatura de Inteligencia, Buenos Aires, Argentina. Ed. Emilio J. Del Real. adv.; circ. 3,400.

943 011 GW ISSN 0036-5920
SCHARNHORST AUSLESE. 1954. q. DM.12($12) Tuermer-Verlag, Postfach, D-8137 Berg 3, Germany. Ed. E. Vowinckel. adv.; bk.rev.; bibl.; illus.; circ. 2,800.
  Formerly: Scharnhorst Mitteilungen.

011 355 II ISSN 0970-3403
UNIVERSAL MILITARY ABSTRACTS. (Text in English) 1987. bi-m. $45. 10 A Astley Hall, Dehra Dun 248 001, India. TEL 25845. Ed. S.K. Arora. adv.; bk.rev.; abstr.; charts; illus.; index.

355.115 310 US
WISCONSIN. DEPARTMENT OF VETERANS AFFAIRS. BIENNIAL REPORT. 1977. biennial. free. Department of Veterans Affairs, 30 W. Mifflin St., Box 7843, Madison, WI 53707. TEL 608-266-1311. Ed. Steve L. Olson. circ. 700.

MILITARY LAW

see Law–Military Law

MINES AND MINING INDUSTRY

see also Metallurgy

622 669 AT
A I M M SYMPOSIA SERIES. 1972. irreg. no.57, 1988. price varies. Australasian Institute of Mining and Metallurgy, Clunies Ross House, 191 Royal Parade, Parkville, Vic. 3052, Australia. TEL 03-347-3166. **Indexed:** AESIS, Chem.Abstr., GeoRef.
  Description: Publishes papers from symposia held each year on various topics covering latest developments in the mineral industry.

622 551 US ISSN 0891-6209
TN5
A M C JOURNAL. 1915. m. $36. American Mining Congress, 1920 N St., N.W., Ste. 300, Washington, DC 20036. TEL 202-861-2800. FAX 202-861-7535. Ed. Joyce Morgan. adv.; bk.rev.; circ. 12,000. (also avail. in microfilm from UMI; reprint service avail. from UMI) **Indexed:** A.S.& T.Ind., Acid Rain Abstr., Acid Rain Ind., C.I.S. Abstr., Cadscan, Chem.Abstr., Curr.Cont., Energy Info.Abstr., Eng.Ind., Environ.Per.Bibl., Excerp.Med., Fuel & Energy Abstr., Geo.Abstr., GeoRef., Ind.Sci.Rev., Lead Abstr., Ocean.Abstr., Pollut.Abstr., Zincscan.
  Formerly (until 1986): American Mining Congress Journal (ISSN 0277-8688); **Supersedes:** Mining Congress Journal (ISSN 0026-5160)

A M D E L BULLETIN. (Australia Mineral Development Laboratories) see *EARTH SCIENCES — Geology*

622 665.5 340 AT ISSN 1034-327X
A M P L A BULLETIN. 1982. q. Aus.$65. Australian Mining and Petroleum Law Association Ltd., 360 Little Bourke St., 4th Fl., Melbourne, Vic. 3000, Australia. TEL 613-670-2544. FAX 613-670-2616. circ. 700. (looseleaf format; back issues avail.) **Indexed:** AESIS.

622 665.5 340 AT ISSN 0812-857X
K1
A M P L A YEARBOOK. 1977. a. Aus.$125. Australian Mining and Petroleum Law Association Ltd., 460 Little Bourke St., 4th Fl., Melbourne, Vic. 3000, Australia. TEL 03-670-2544. FAX 03-670-2616. Ed. G. Moloney. bibl.; circ. 600. (back issues avail.) **Indexed:** AESIS, C.L.I., L.R.I.
  —BLDSC shelfmark: 1814.614000.
  Formerly (until 1983): Australian Mining and Petroleum Law Journal (ISSN 0157-2083)

622 AT ISSN 0816-942X
A M R E P DATABASE BULLETIN. 1984. m. (10/yr.). Aus.$210($165) Australian Mineral Resource Politics Pty. Ltd., 10 Hampstead Hill Rd., Aldgate, S.A. 5154, Australia. TEL 8 339 2960. Ed. Antony C. Turner. circ. 50. (looseleaf format; back issues avail.)
  ●Also available online.
  Description: Covers areas of political concern to the Australian mining and petroleum industry.

622 GW
A V INFORMATION. 1975. bi-m. Gewerkschaft Auguste Victoria, Victoriastr. 43, D-4370 Marl, Germany. TEL 02365-402851. FAX 02365-402204. TELEX 0829886-AVMAD. circ. 6,000.

622 665.5 AT ISSN 1032-8599
ACCESS (GLENSIDE); information and education for the mining and petroleum industry. (Supplement avail.: Syllabus) m. Australian Mineral Foundation, 63 Conyngham St., Glenside, S.A. 5065, Australia. TEL 08-379-0444. FAX 08-379-4634. TELEX AA87437.

549 665.5 HU ISSN 0365-8066
 CODEN: AUSEA6
ACTA UNIVERSITATIS DE ATTILA JOZSEF NOMINATAE. ACTA MINERALOGICA - PETROGRAPHICA. (Text in English) 1943. a. exchange basis. Attila Jozsef University, c/o E. Szabo, Exchange Librarian, Dugonics ter 13, P.O.B. 393, Szeged H-6701, Hungary. (Subscr. to: Kultura, P.O. Box 149, H-1389 Budapest, Hungary) Ed. Tibor Szederkenyi. bk.rev.; charts; illus.; circ. 600. **Indexed:** INIS Atomind., Met.Abstr.
  Description: Discusses geochemistry, mineralogy and petrology with studies of Hungarian topics of global interest.

622 AG ISSN 0326-6672
ACTIVIDAD MINERA. 1983. m. $24. Minera Piedra Libre S.R.L., Bolivar 187, 4 B, 1066 Buenos Aires, Argentina. TEL 30-6138 or 30-6422. Eds. Drs. Horacio Piccinini, Mario de Pablos. circ. 1,200.

622 CM ISSN 0575-7258
ACTIVITES MINERES AU CAMEROUN. 1962. a., latest 1975. Direction des Mines et de la Geologie, Ministere des Mines et de l'Energie, Yaounde, Cameroon.

AFRICA ENERGY AND MINING. see *PETROLEUM AND GAS*

MINES AND MINING INDUSTRY 3477

622 531.64 FR
AFRIQUE INDUSTRIE. m. (11/yr.). 3210 F. (foreign 3400 F.). Moreux, 190, bd. Haussmann, 75008 Paris, France. TEL 45-63-11-55. FAX 42-89-08-72. adv.

622 PL ISSN 0452-6457
AKADEMIA GORNICZO-HUTNICZA IM. STANISLAWA STASZICA. ZESZYTY NAUKOWE. GEODEZJA. (Text in Polish; summaries in English) 1956. irreg., no.113, 1991. price varies. Wydawnictwo A G H, Al. Mickiewicza 30, paw. B-5, 30-059 Krakow, Poland. (Dist. by: Ars Polona, Krakowskie Przedmiescie 7, 00-068 Warsaw, Poland) Ed. Z. Kleczek. illus.; circ. 300.

622 PL ISSN 0372-9400
AKADEMIA GORNICZO-HUTNICZA IM. STANISLAWA STASZICA. ZESZYTY NAUKOWE. GORNICTWO. (Text in English and Polish; summaries in English, Polish) 1954. irreg., no. 158, 1991. price varies. Wydawnictwo A G H, Al. Mickiewicza 30, paw. B-5, 30-059 Krakow, Poland. (Dist. by: Ars Polona, Krakowskie Przedmiescie 7, 00-068 Warsaw, Poland) Ed. Z. Kleczek. illus.; circ. 300. **Indexed:** Chem.Abstr.

622 PL ISSN 0138-0990
TN4 CODEN: GORNDL
AKADEMIA GORNICZO-HUTNICZA IM. STANISLAWA STASZICA. ZESZYTY NAUKOWE. GORNICTWO. KWARTALNIK. (Text in English and Polish; summaries in English, Polish) 1977. q. 15000 Zl. per issue (effective 1992). Wydawnictwo A G H, Al. Mickiewicza 30, paw. B-5, 30-059 Krakow, Poland. (Dist. by: Ars Polona, Krakowskie Przedmiescie 7, 00-068 Warsaw, Poland) Ed. Z. Kleczek. illus.; circ. 700.
  —BLDSC shelfmark: 9512.150000.

ALBERTA OIL & GAS DIRECTORY. see *BUSINESS AND ECONOMICS — Trade And Industrial Directories*

622 330.9 US
AMAX NEWS. 1987. bi-m. free to qualified personnel. Amax Inc., 200 Park Ave., New York, NY 10166. TEL 212-856-4200. FAX 212-856-5986. Ed. Diane Hafter. circ. 5,000. (tabloid format)
  Formerly: Headquarters News.
  Description: Focuses on company operations and employee issues.

622 338.2 669.2 US
AMERICAN GOLD NEWS AND WESTERN PROSPECTOR. 1933. m. $18. DeServices, Inc., Box 308, St. George, UT 84771-0308. FAX 801-628-7771. Ed. Mel DeYoung. adv.; bk.rev.; circ. 4,000. (also avail. in tabloid format)
  Incorporates: Western Prospector; **Formerly (until 1987):** American Gold News (ISSN 0002-8657)

549 US ISSN 0003-004X
QE351 CODEN: AMMIAY
AMERICAN MINERALOGIST. 1916. bi-m. $200 to non-members; members $50. Mineralogical Society of America, 1130 17th St. N.W., Ste. 330, Washington, DC 20036. TEL 202-775-4344. FAX 202-775-0018. Eds. Steven Bohlen, Donald Peacor. adv.; bk.rev.; bibl.; illus.; circ. 4,000. (also avail. in microfilm from PMC; back issues avail.; reprint service avail. from KTO) **Indexed:** A.S.& T.Ind., AESIS, Br.Ceram.Abstr., C.R.I. Abstr., Cadscan, Chem.Abstr., Curr.Cont., Deep Sea Res.& Oceanogr.Abstr., Eng.Ind., GeoRef., Ind.Sci.Rev., INIS Atomind., Lead Abstr., Met.Abstr., Petrol.Abstr., Photo.Abstr., Sci.Abstr., Sci.Cit.Ind., Soils & Fert., Zincscan.
  —BLDSC shelfmark: 0845.000000.
  Description: Publishes the results of original scientific research in the general fields of mineralogy, crystallography, and petrology.

622 CN
AMERICAN MINES HANDBOOK. 1989. a. Can.$38. Southam North American Magazine Group, 1450 Don Mills Rd., Don Mills, Ont. M3B 2X7, Canada. TEL 416-445-6641. FAX 416-442-2272. Ed. D. Giancola. adv.; B&W page Can.$1195.
  Description: Lists information on every mining company registered in the United States.

ANGOLA. DIRECCAO PROVINCIAL DOS SERVICOS DE GEOLOGIA E MINAS. BOLETIM. see *EARTH SCIENCES — Geology*

MINES AND MINING INDUSTRY

622   BE   ISSN 0003-4290
TN2   CODEN: ANMBAK
ANNALES DES MINES DE BELGIQUE/ANNALEN DER MIJNEN VAN BELGIE. (Text in Dutch, French; summaries in Dutch, English, French, German) 1896. 4/yr. 2200 Fr. (foreign 2500 Fr.). Administration des Mines, Departement Annales des Mines, Rue J.A. De Mot, 30, B-1040 Brussels, Belgium. adv.; bk.rev.; abstr.; charts; illus.; circ. 900. **Indexed:** Art & Archaeol.Tech.Abstr., C.I.S. Abstr., Chem.Abstr., Eng.Ind., Excerp.Med., Fuel & Energy Abstr., GeoRef.
—BLDSC shelfmark: 0985.150000.

ANNUAIRE DE L'ADMINISTRATION DES D.R.I.R.. see *ENERGY*

ANNUAL BOOK OF A S T M STANDARDS. VOLUME 05.05. GASEOUS FUELS; COAL AND COKE. see *ENGINEERING — Engineering Mechanics And Materials*

338.7   II
ANNUAL REPORT OF THE WORKING AND AFFAIRS OF MYSORE MINERALS LIMITED. (Text in English) a. Mysore Minerals Ltd., Bangalore, Karnataka, India.

622 558   CL   ISSN 0066-5096
HD9506.C5
ANUARIO DE LA MINERIA DE CHILE. 1961. a. $20 or exchange basis. Servicio Nacional de Geologia y Mineria, Casilla 10465, Santiago, Chile. FAX 56-2-372026. Ed. Juan Williams. stat.; circ. 1,000.
—BLDSC shelfmark: 1564.877000.

338.2   BL
ANUARIO MINERAL BRASILEIRO. 1972. a. Cr.$140. Departamento Nacional da Producao Mineral, Setor Autarquia Norte, Quadra 1 Bloco B, 70000 Brasilia D.F., Brazil. illus.; stat.

549   US   ISSN 0066-5487
APPLIED MINERALOGY - TECHNISCHE MINEROLOGIE. 1971. irreg., vol.12, 1981. price varies. Springer-Verlag, 175 Fifth Ave., New York, NY 10010. TEL 212-460-1500. (Also Berlin, Heidelberg, Tokyo and Vienna) (reprint service avail. from ISI) **Indexed:** GeoRef.

622   JO   ISSN 0250-9881
ARAB MINING JOURNAL. (Text in Arabic, English) 1980. q. free. Arab Mining Company, P.O. Box 20198, Amman, Jordon. TEL 663148. FAX 962-6-684114. TELEX 21489 ARMICO JO. Ed. Talal Sa'di. bk.rev.; bibl.; stat.; index; circ. 700.

ARAB PETROLEUM. see *PETROLEUM AND GAS*

622.8 631.62   GW   ISSN 0344-239X
ARBEIT UND SICHERHEIT; Zeitschrift fuer Unfallverhuetung und Grubensicherheitswesen. Short title: A S. 1947. m. DM.34. (Landesoberbergamt) Verlag Glueckauf GmbH, Franz-Fischer-Weg 61, Postfach 103945, 4300 Essen 1, Germany. FAX 0201-293630. adv.; circ. controlled.
Continues: Grubensicherheit (ISSN 0017-4858)

622   PL
TN4   CODEN: AGORAT
ARCHIVES OF MINING SCIENCES. (Text in various languages; summaries in Polish, Russian) 1956. q. $32. (Polska Akademia Nauk, Komitet Gornictwa) Panstwowe Wydawnictwo Naukowe, Miodowa 10, Warsaw, Poland. Ed. Stanislaw Knothe. bibl.; circ. 480. **Indexed:** Appl.Mech.Rev., Chem.Abstr., Eng.Ind., GeoRef., Geotech.Abstr.
Formerly: Archiwum Gornictwa (ISSN 0004-0754)

ARGENTINA. SERVICIO NACIONAL MINERO GEOLOGICO. ANALES. see *EARTH SCIENCES — Geology*

ARGENTINA. SERVICIO NACIONAL MINERO GEOLOGICO. BOLETIN. see *EARTH SCIENCES — Geology*

622 551   BN   ISSN 0518-5327
TN4   CODEN: ARUTA6
ARHIV ZA RUDARSTVO I GEOLOGIJU. vol.17, 1979. q. $15. Radna Organizacija Rudarsko-Geolosk Institut i Fakultet Tuzla, Rudarska Ulica 400, Tuzla, Bosnia Hercegovina. Ed. Odgovorni Urednik. circ. 600.

ASBESTOS PRODUCER/PRODUCTEUR D'AMIANTE. see *BUILDING AND CONSTRUCTION*

622.33   FR
ASSOCIATION TECHNIQUE DE L'IMPORTATION CHARBONNIERE. ANNUAL REPORT. a. Association Technique de l'Importation Charbonniere, 149 rue de Longchamp, 75016 Paris, France. TEL 1-5032113.

622   CN
ATLANTIC MINING JOURNAL. 1988. q. Can.$18($24) (foreign $30). N.S. Business Publishing Ltd., 2099 Gottingen St., Halifax, N.S. B3K 3B2, Canada. TEL 902-420-0437. FAX 902-423-8212. Ed. Ken Partridge. adv.; circ. 42,657. (tabloid format)

664   GW   ISSN 0004-783X
                             CODEN: AUFTAK
AUFBEREITUNGS-TECHNIK - MINERAL PROCESSING. (Text in English, French, Spanish) 1960. m. DM.276. Verlag fuer Aufbereitung GmbH, Wittelsbacherstr. 10, 6200 Wiesbaden 1, Germany. TEL 0611-74765. FAX 0611-791285. TELEX 4186792. Ed. Ing. Rolf Koehling. adv.; bk.rev.; circ. 3,600. **Indexed:** C.R.I. Abstr., Cadscan, Chem.Abstr., Chem.Eng.Abstr., Eng.Ind., Excerp.Med., Fluidex, Fuel & Energy Abstr., INIS Atomind., Lead Abstr., Met.Abstr., PROMT, T.C.E.A., World Alum.Abstr., Zincscan.
—BLDSC shelfmark: 1790.900000.

622   AT   ISSN 1034-6775
TN121   CODEN: AIBUEP
AUS I M M BULLETIN. 7/yr. Aus.$120 (foreign Aus.$200). Australasian Institute of Mining and Metallurgy, Bulletin Subsriptions, P.O. Box 122, Parkville, Vic. 3052, Australia. TEL 03-347-3166. FAX 03-347-8525. Ed. Penelope Griffiths. adv.; circ. 7,986. **Indexed:** AESIS, GeoRef., INIS Atomind., Met.Abstr., World Alum.Abstr.
—BLDSC shelfmark: 1792.932000.
Former titles: A I M M Bulletin and Proceedings (ISSN 0817-2668); A I M M Bulletin (ISSN 0158-6602); Incorporates (1898-1984): A I M M Proceedings (ISSN 0004-8364)
Description: Official organ of the Australasian Institute of Mining and Metallurgy.

622 550   AT
AUSTRALIA. BUREAU OF MINERAL RESOURCES, GEOLOGY AND GEOPHYSICS. MINERAL RESOURCE REPORT. 1987. irreg. price varies. Bureau of Mineral Resources, Geology and Geophysics, G.P.O. Box 378, Canberra, A.C.T. 2601, Australia.
Formerly: Australia. Bureau of Mineral Resouces, Geology and Geophysics. Resource Report (ISSN 0818-6278)

338.2   AT   ISSN 0067-1762
TN811.A8
AUSTRALIAN COAL INDUSTRY RESEARCH LABORATORIES. ANNUAL REPORT. 1966. a. free. Australian Coal Industry Research Laboratories Ltd., P.O. Box 83, North Ryde, N.S.W. 2113, Australia. **Indexed:** AESIS, Chem.Abstr.

622.33   AT   ISSN 0726-7819
AUSTRALIAN COAL MINER.* 1979. m. Aus.$30. Security Australia Trade News Corp., 17 Charles St., Redfern, N.S.W. 2016, Australia. Ed. Liz Symons. circ. 4,600. **Indexed:** AESIS.

531.64   AT   ISSN 0157-4566
AUSTRALIAN COAL REPORT. 1979. m. $395. J. Barlow Consultants Pty. Ltd., Ste. 227, Assembly Bldg., 44 Margaret St., Sydney, N.S.W. 2000, Australia. TEL 02-262-1652. FAX 02-262-1650. Ed. J.W. Barlow. bk.rev.; circ. 500. (back issues avail.) **Indexed:** AESIS.
Description: Includes export coal prices, news, contract and industry information, shipping news, and freight rates.

622 620.1   AT   ISSN 0705-5838
SH224.Q4
AUSTRALIAN GEOMECHANICS NEWS. 1980. 2/yr. Aus.$17($10.50) Institution of Engineers, Australia, 11 National Circuit, Barton, A.C.T. 2600, Australia. (Co-sponsor: Australasian Institute of Mining and Metallurgy) adv.; bk.rev.; circ. 650. (back issues avail.) **Indexed:** GeoRef., HRIS, Intl.Civil Eng.Abstr., Soft.Abstr.Eng.
—BLDSC shelfmark: 1801.060000.
Formerly: Australian Geomechanics Journal.
Description: News journal of Australian Geomechanics Society with news and technical papers in the general field of geomechanics.

622   AT   ISSN 0817-9646
AUSTRALIAN JOURNAL OF MINING; Australian, Asian and Pacific mining. 1986. m. Aus.$80($115) (effective Dec. 1990). G M C Studio Pty. Ltd., 8 Shelley St., Richmond North, Vic. 3121, Australia. TEL 03-429-5599. FAX 03-427-0332. Ed. Elizabeth Red. adv.; bk.rev.; circ. 7,900. (back issues avail.)
—BLDSC shelfmark: 1810.500000.
Description: Covers all aspects of minig in Asia - Pacific Region including exploration, extraction, investment, marketing, trade and politics.

AUSTRALIAN MINERALOGIST. see *EARTH SCIENCES — Geology*

622   AT   ISSN 0004-976X
TP1   CODEN: AUMNA3
AUSTRALIAN MINING. 1908. m. Aus.$66. Thomson Publications Australia, 47 Chippen St., Chippendale, N.S.W. 2008, Australia. FAX 02-698-3920. TELEX 122226. Ed. Lou Caruana. adv.; bk.rev.; illus.; mkt.; tr.lit.; index; circ. 7,103. (also avail. in microfilm from UMI,PMC) **Indexed:** AESIS, Aus.Rd.Ind., Chem.Abstr., Eng.Ind., Fuel & Energy Abstr., GeoRef., Met.Abstr., PROMT, World Alum.Abstr.
—BLDSC shelfmark: 1814.600000.
Formerly: Mining and Chemical Engineering Review.

622   AT
AUSTRALIAN MINING INDUSTRY COUNCIL. DIRECTORY. 1983. irreg. free. Australian Mining Industry Council, P.O. Box 363, Dickson, A.C.T. 2602, Australia. FAX 61-6-279-3699.

622   AT
AUSTRALIAN MINING PRODUCT REGISTER. a. Aus.$90. Thomson Publications Australia, 47 Chippen St., Chippendale, N.S.W. 2008, Australia. TEL 02-699-2411. FAX 02-698-3920. TELEX 122226. Ed. Lou Caruana. adv. (also avail. in microfiche)
Formerly: Australian Mining Year Book (ISSN 0314-7762)

338.2 332.6   AT   ISSN 1030-7915
AUSTRALIAN NUGGET JOURNAL. 1987. q. free. Goldcorp Australia, 300 Hay St., E. Perth, W.A. 6004, Australia. FAX 09-221-2258. TELEX 197171. Ed. Ron Barry. bk.rev.; circ. 4,500. (back issues avail.)
Description: Provides regular reference information on precious metals generally, precious metals investment, the Australian gold mining industry and Australia's legal tender precious metal coinage.

622   AT
AUSTRALIA'S MINING MONTHLY. 1980. m. Aus.$44. P.O. Box 78, Leederville, W.A. 6007, Australia. FAX 09-381-1848. Ed. D.E. Cake. adv.; bk.rev.; charts; circ. 7,480. **Indexed:** AESIS.
Former titles: Mining Monthly (ISSN 0725-9131); (until 1981): Mining Quarterly; Incorporates: Lodestone's Australian Oil and Gas Journal.

622   CN
B C MINE RESCUE MANUAL. base vol. (plus irreg. suppl.) Can.$17.50. Ministry of Energy, Mines and Petroleum Resources, Mineral Resources Division, Parliament Bldgs., Victoria, B.C. V8V 1X4, Canada. (Subscr. to: Crown Publications, 546 Yates St., Victoria, B.C. V8W 1K8, Canada. TEL 604-386-4636) (looseleaf format)
Description: Provides basic training in the rescue procedures to be followed in the event of an accident at a surface or underground mining operation.

622 669   AU   ISSN 0005-8912
                              CODEN: BHMMAM
B H M. BERG- UND HUETTENMAENNISCHE MONATSHEFTE.. 1841. m. DM.218($140) Springer-Verlag, Sachsenplatz 4-6, Postfach 89, A-1201 Vienna, Austria. TEL 0222-3302415-0. (Also Berlin, Heidelberg, Tokyo and New York) Ed.Bd. adv.; bk.rev.; bibl.; charts; illus.; index. (reprint service avail. from ISI) **Indexed:** Chem.Abstr., Eng.Ind., GeoRef., INIS Atomind., Sci.Abstr.
—BLDSC shelfmark: 1909.000000.
Incorporates: Montan-Berichte (ISSN 0026-9875); Montan-Rundschau (ISSN 0026-9883)

622　　　　　　　　CS
BANICKE LISTY/FOLIA MONTANA. (Text in Slovak; summaries in English, French and Russian) 1974. irreg. 9 Kcs. (Slovenska Akademia Vied, Banicky Ustav Sav) Veda, Publishing House of the Slovak Academy of Sciences, Klemensova 19, 814 30 Bratislava, Czechoslovakia. (Dist. by: Slovart, Nam. Slobody 6, 817 64 Bratislava, Czechoslovakia) illus.

BANYASZATI SZAKIRODALMI TAJEKOZTATO/MINING ABSTRACTS. see *MINES AND MINING INDUSTRY — Abstracting, Bibliographies, Statistics*

622　　　　　　　　BE
BELGIUM. ADMINISTRATION DES MINES. STATISTIQUES: HOUILLE, COKES, AGGLOMERES METALLURGIE, CARRIERES. 1954. irreg. Administration des Mines, 30 rue de Mot, 1040 Brussels, Belgium. illus.; circ. 250.
　　Formerly: Belgium. Administration des Mines. Service: Statistiques. Siderurgie, Houille, Agglomeres, Cokes (ISSN 0525-4752)

622　　　　　GW　　ISSN 0342-5681
TN3
BERGBAU;* Zeitschrift fuer Bergbau und Energiewirtschaft. m. DM.127.80 (foreign DM.74.40). (Ring Deutscher Bergingenieure e.V.) W V G Werbe- und Verlagsgesellschaft mbH, Pommernstr. 17, 4650 Gelsenkirchen, Germany. Ed. Aribert Langer. circ. 13,600. **Indexed:** INIS Atomind.
　　—BLDSC shelfmark: 1910.000000.
　　Description: Covers all branches of the mining industry.

BERGBAU-BERUFSGENOSSENSCHAFT. JAHRESBERICHT.
see *LABOR UNIONS*

622 669　　　　　SW　　ISSN 0284-0448
BERGSMANNEN. 1817. 7/yr. SEK 160($28) Moraberg Foerlag AB, Box 5, S-15121 Soedertaelje, Sweden. FAX 46-8-550-856-00. Ed. Anders M. Almgren. adv.; bk.rev.; illus.; stat.; index; circ. 4,500. (back issues avail.) **Indexed:** Appl.Mech.Rev., Chem.Abstr., Curr.Cont., Eng.Ind., INIS Atomind., Met.Abstr., World Alum.Abstr.
　　—BLDSC shelfmark: 1912.195000.
　　Formerly: Bergsmannen med Jernkontorets Annaler (ISSN 0280-4239); Supersedes in part (from vol.161, 1977): Jernkontorets Annaler (ISSN 0021-5902)

622 669　　　　　NO　　ISSN 0005-8971
BERGVERKS-NYTT; the Scandinavian journal of mining and quarrying. 1954. m. (except Jan., Jul., Dec.). NOK 250. Bergverks-Nytt, P.O. Box 1438 Strindheim, 7002 Trondheim, Norway. (Co-sponsors: Bergverkenes Landssammenslutning, Steniindustriens Landssammenslutning; Pukk- og Grusleverandorenes Landforening, Norsk Bergindustriforening) Ed. Stoerk Halstensen. adv.; bk.rev.; charts; illus.; mkt.; stat.; circ. 2,000.

622　　　　　GW　　ISSN 0935-123X
QE351
BERICHTE DER DEUTSCHEN MINERALOGISCHEN GESELLSCHAFT. (Supplement to: European Journal of Mineralogy (ISSN: 0935-1221)) 1989. s-a. price varies. E. Schweizerbart'sche Verlagsbuchhandlung, Johannesstrasse 3A, 7000 Stuttgart 1, Germany. TEL 0711-625001. FAX 0711-625005. TELEX 723363-SCHB-D. Ed. E. Althaus.

622 016　　　　　UK
BIBLIOGRAPHY OF ECONOMIC GEOLOGY. 1968. bi-m. £85($170) Geosystems, Box 40, Didcot, Oxon Ox11 9BX, England. Ed. Rosalind Templeman. adv.; bk.rev.; index.
● Also available online. Vendor(s): DIALOG.
Also available on CD-ROM.
　　Formerly: Geocom Bulletin (ISSN 0016-7053)

622　　　　　PH
BIBLIOGRAPHY ON PHILIPPINE GEOLOGY, MINING AND MINERAL RESOURCES. (Text in English) 1971. a. P.20($3) Bureau of Mines and Geo-Sciences, Sciences Mineral Economics and Information Division, Pedro Gill St., Ermita Metro Manila, Philippines. circ. 100. (back issues avail.)
　　Formerly: Philippine Geology, Mining and Mineral Resources.

622　　　　　AU
BOECKSTEINER MONTANA. irreg., no.8, 1989. varies. Verband der Wissenschaftlichen Gesellschaften Oesterreichs, Lindengasse 37, A-1070 Vienna, Austria. TEL 932166.

622　　　　　PO　　ISSN 0006-5935
TN83　　　　　　　　CODEN: PBMIBL
BOLETIM DE MINAS. (Summaries in French and English) 1912. q. Direccao-Geral de Geologia e Minas, Rua Antonio Enes 7, Lisbon 1, Portugal. Ed. Fernando Macieira. charts; illus.; circ.; 1,100. **Indexed:** GeoRef, P.A.I.S.For.Lang.Ind.
　　—BLDSC shelfmark: 2157.175000.

BOLETIN GEOLOGICO Y MINERO. see *EARTH SCIENCES — Geology*

BOLETIN GEOLOGICO Y MINERO. PUBLICACIONES ESPECIALES. see *EARTH SCIENCES — Geology*

622　　　　　BO　　ISSN 0067-9852
BOLIVIA. SERVICIO GEOLOGICO. SERIE MINERALOGICA. CONTRIBUCIONE. 1968. irreg. Servicio Geologico, Casilla 2729, La Paz, Bolivia.

622　　　　　JA
BONANZA. (Text in Japanese) Metal Mining Agency - Kinzoku Kogyo Jigyodan, c/o Tokiwa Bldg., 6-3 Shiba Nishikubo Sakuragawa-cho, Shiba, Minato-ku, Tokyo 105, Japan. illus.

662　　　　　RU
BOR'BA S GAZOM V UGOL'NYKH SHAKHTAKH. irreg. 0.61 Rub. (Nauchno-Issledovatelskii Institut po Bezopasnosti Rabot v Gornoi Promyshlennosti, Makeevka) Izdatel'stvo Nedra, Pl. Belorusskogo Vokzala, 3, 125047 Moscow, Russia. TEL 250-52-55. illus.

622 662　　　　　GW　　ISSN 0341-1060
TN831　　　　　　　CODEN: BRUKAO
BRAUNKOHLE; Zeitschrift fuer Tagebautechnik und Energieversorgung. 1902; N.S. 1949. m. DM.237 (foreign DM.269.40). Rheinische-Bergische Drueckerei- und Verlagsgesellschaft mbH, Postfach 1135, 4000 Duesseldorf 1, Germany. Ed. Dr.-Ing. Ernst-Pater Froehling. adv.; bk.rev.; abstr.; charts; maps; pat.; circ. 1,900. **Indexed:** C.I.S. Abstr., Chem.Abstr., Excerp.Med., GeoRef., Geotech.Abstr., INIS Atomind.
　　—BLDSC shelfmark: 2275.998000.
　　Formerly: Braunkohle Waerme und Energie (ISSN 0006-9299)

622　　　　　BL
BRAZIL. DEPARTAMENTO NACIONAL DA PRODUCAO MINERAL. AVULSO. 1974. irreg. free. Departamento Nacional da Produçao Mineral, Setor Autarcuia Norte, Quadra 1, Bloco B, Brasilia, D.F., Brazil.

622　　　　　BL
BRAZIL. DEPARTAMENTO NACIONAL DA PRODUCAO MINERAL. BOLETIM. 1973. irreg. price varies. Departamento Nacional da Produçao Mineral, Setor Autarcuia Norte, Quadra 1, Bloco B, Brasilia, D.F., Brazil. (back issues avail.)

622　　　　　BL
BRAZIL. DEPARTAMENTO NACIONAL DA PRODUCAO MINERAL. PROGRAMACAO. 1972. a. free. Departamento Nacional da Produçao Mineral, Setor Autarcuia Norte, Quadra 1, Bloco B, Brasilia, D.F., Brazil. TEL (061)224-2670. circ. 150 (controlled).
　　Description: Report on all planned activities of the Department: geochemical and geophysical surveys, geological mapping and more.

658 622　　　　　UK　　ISSN 0027-9773
BRITISH ASSOCIATION OF COLLIERY MANAGEMENT. NATIONAL NEWS LETTER. 1947. q. membership. British Association of Colliery Management, 317 Nottingham Rd., Old Basford, Nottingham, England. FAX 0602-422279. Ed. J.D. Meads. adv.; bk.rev.; charts; stat.; circ. 11,000.

622 665.5　　　　CN　　ISSN 0365-9356
TN27.B9　　　　　　　CODEN: BCMAA
BRITISH COLUMBIA. MINISTRY OF ENERGY, MINES AND PETROLEUM RESOURCES. ANNUAL REPORT. a. Can.$4.15. Ministry of Energy, Mines and Petroleum Resources, Publications Distribution Section, Parliament Bldgs., Victoria, B.C. V8V 1X4, Canada. TEL 604-387-5178. (Subscr. to: Crown Publications, 546 Yates St., Victoria, B.C. V8W 1K8, Canada. TEL 604-386-4636)
　　Description: Summary of ministry operations, including hydroelectric energy, mineral and petroleum and natural gas production statistics.

549　　　　　CN
BRITISH COLUMBIA. MINISTRY OF ENERGY, MINES AND PETROLEUM RESOURCES. MINERAL MARKET UPDATE. q. free. Ministry of Energy, Mines and Petroleum Resources, Parliament Bldgs., Victoria, B.C. V8V 1X4, Canada. TEL 604-387-5178. FAX 604-356-8969.
　　Description: Information on mining in B.C. Includes value and volume of B.C.'s mineral products, mine output and employment, exploration project highlights, an update on projects in the mine development review process, and news on provincial initiative of interest to the mining sector.

622　　　　　CN　　ISSN 0846-0051
BRITISH COLUMBIA MINERAL EXPLORATION REVIEW. a. Can.$5.65. Ministry of Energy, Mines and Petroleum Resources, Mineral Resources Division, Parliament Bldgs., Victoria, B.C. V8V 1K8, Canada. (Subscr. to: Crown Publications, 546 Yates St., Victoria, B.C. V8W 1K8, Canada. TEL 604-386-4636) illus.
　　Formerly (until 1985): British Columbia Exploration Review (ISSN 0828-6094)

622　　　　　UK　　ISSN 0308-2199
BRITISH MINING; memoirs and monographs. 1975. s-a. £18. Northern Mine Research Society, 41 Windsor Walk, South Anston, Sheffield S31 7EL, England. Ed. R.H. Bird. circ. 700. **Indexed:** GeoRef.
　　—BLDSC shelfmark: 2330.540000.

BULETINI I SHKENCAVE GJEOLOGJIKE. see *EARTH SCIENCES — Geology*

622　　　　　CN　　ISSN 0705-5196
CODEN: CANRD7
C A N M E T REPORTS. 1974. irreg. price varies. Canada Centre for Mineral and Energy Technology, 555 Booth St., Ottawa, Ont. K1A 0G1, Canada. FAX 613-995-3192. TELEX 053-3395. Ed. J.E. Kanasy. circ. 1,000. (also avail. in microfiche). **Indexed:** Chem.Abstr., Energy Ind., GeoRef.
　　Incorporates (in 1977): C A N M E T Review.

622　　　　　II　　ISSN 0376-7787
HD9556.I4
C C A I MONTHLY NEWS LETTER. (Text in English) 1972. m. $10. Coal Consumers Association of India, 4, India Exchange, 7th Floor, Calcutta 700 001, India. TEL 22-4488. Ed. S.S. Parikh. adv.; bk.rev.; charts; circ. 5,000.
　　Description: News and articles intended to create awareness among industrial coal consumers about the development of coal industry in India and international markets.

622　　　　　CN　　ISSN 0317-0926
TN1　　　　　　　　CODEN: CIBUBA
C I M BULLETIN. 1898. m. Can.$85($105) (foreign $115). Canadian Institute of Mining, Metallurgy & Petroleum, Xerox Tower, 3400 de Maisonneuve Blvd. W., Ste. 1210, Montreal, Que. H3Z 3B8, Canada. TEL 514-939-2710. FAX 514-939-2714. Ed. Perla Gantz. adv.; bk.rev.; bibl.; charts; illus.; index; circ. 11,000. (back issues avail.) **Indexed:** A.I.Abstr., A.S.& T.Ind., AESIS, Art & Archaeol.Tech.Abstr., CAD CAM Abstr., Cadscan, Can.B.P.I., Chem.Abstr., Chem.Eng.Abstr., Curr.Cont., Energy Info.Abstr., Environ.Abstr., Fluidex, Fuel & Energy Abstr., INIS Atomind., Lead Abstr., Sci.Abstr., Sci.Cit.Ind., T.C.E.A., Zincscan.
　　—BLDSC shelfmark: 3198.243000.
　　Description: Technical data and information on mineral engineering subjects to promote the technological interests of people involved in the development of the industry in Canada.
　　Refereed Serial

MINES AND MINING INDUSTRY

622 669   CN   ISSN 0068-9009
TN1
C I M DIRECTORY. 1967. a. Can.$80. Canadian Institute of Mining, Metallurgy & Petroleum, Xerox Tower, 3400 de Maisonneuve Blvd. W., Ste. 1210, Montreal, Que. H3Z 3B8, Canada. TEL 514-939-2710. FAX 514-939-2714. Ed. Perla Gantz. adv.; circ. 12,750.
   Description: Lists officers and members, as well as technical feature items on the mining of a territory or province of Canada.

622   CN   ISSN 0701-0710
C I M REPORTER. 3/yr. Canadian Institute of Mining, Metallurgy & Petroleum, Ste. 1200, 3400 de Maisonneuve Blvd.W., Montreal, Que. H3Z 3B8, Canada. TEL 514-939-2710. FAX 514-939-2714. Ed. Perla Gantz. adv.; circ. 10,119. **Indexed:** GeoRef.
   Description: Comprised of current mining and milling information.

622   II
C M R S ANNUAL REPORT. 1961. a. price varies. Central Mining Research Station, Barwa Rd., Dhanbad 826001, Bihar, India. TELEX 0629-208-CMRS-IN. (Affiliate: Council of Scientific and Industrial Research) Ed. M.C. Chatterjee. circ. 1,000.
   Formerly: Central Mining Research Station, Dhanbad. Progress Research (ISSN 0070-4628)
   Description: Research and development activities carried out at the Research Station.

622   II
C M R S BULLETIN. (Text in English) 1974. bi-m. Central Mining Research Station, Barwa Rd., Dhanbad 826001, Bihar, India. TELEX 0629-208-CMRS-IN. (Affiliate: Council of Scientific and Industrial Research) Ed. S.K. Gupta. circ. 3,500.

622 330   CN   ISSN 0228-1821
C R S PERSPECTIVES. 1978. irreg. Can.$10. Centre for Resource Studies, Queen's University, 100 Barrie St., Kingston, Ont. K7L 3N6, Canada. TEL 613-545-2553. FAX 613-545-6651. Ed. Margot Wojciechowski. bk.rev.; circ. 4,500.
   Description: Focuses on current mineral policy concerns in Canada.

CALIFORNIA. DIVISION OF MINES AND GEOLOGY. BULLETIN. see EARTH SCIENCES — Geology

CALIFORNIA. DIVISION OF MINES AND GEOLOGY. SPECIAL REPORT. see EARTH SCIENCES — Geology

622   US   ISSN 0008-1299
CALIFORNIA MINING JOURNAL. 1931. m. $19.95. California Mining Journal, Inc., Box 2260, Aptos, CA 95001. TEL 408-662-2899. FAX 408-662-3014. Ed. Kenneth L. Harn. adv.; bk.rev.; charts; mkt.; stat.; circ. 14,000. **Indexed:** Cal.Per.Ind. (1978-), GeoRef.
—BLDSC shelfmark: 3015.079400.
   Description: International mining publication for miners, prospectors, financiers, and others who deal with the entire mining industry. Contains articles on mining processes, mining law, and current events.

338.2   CN
CANADA. INDIAN AND NORTHERN AFFAIRS CANADA. MINES AND MINERAL ACTIVITIES (YEAR). (Text in English; summaries in French) 1967. a. free. Indian and Northern Affairs Canada, Mining Legislation and Resources Management Division, Les Terrasse de la Chaudiere, Rm. 600, 10 Wellington St., Ottawa, Ont. K1A 0H4, Canada. TEL 819-997-9828. FAX 819-997-0511. circ. 1,500.
   Formerly: Canada. Northern Natural Resources and Environment Branch. Mining Section. North of 60: Mines and Mineral Activities; **Supersedes:** Canada. Department of Indian Affairs and Northern Development. Mines and Minerals, Activities (ISSN 0590-580X)
   Description: Summary of mining and mineral exploration activities in the Yukon and Northwest territories during the calendar year.

622   CN
CANADA. MINERAL POLICY SECTOR. MINERAL BULLETINS. 1953. irreg. (approx. a.). price varies. Energy, Mines and Resources Canada, Mineral Policy Sector, Publishing Division, 460 O'Connor, Ottawa, Ont. K1A 0E4, Canada. TEL 819-956-4802. FAX 819-994-1498. (Orders to: Supply and Services Canada, Canada Communication Group - Publishing, Ottawa, Ont. K1A OS5, Canada)
   Former titles: Canada. Mineral Policy Sector. Mineral Information Bulletin; Canada. Mineral Development Sector. Mineral Information Bulletin; Canada. Mineral Resources Branch. Mineral Information Bulletin (ISSN 0068-7812)

CANADA A-Z; oil, gas, mining directory. see BUSINESS AND ECONOMICS — Trade And Industrial Directories

CANADIAN MINERALOGIST; crystallography, geochemistry, mineralogy, petrology, mineral deposits. see EARTH SCIENCES — Geology

622   CN   ISSN 0068-9270
CANADIAN MINERALS YEARBOOK/ANNUAIRE DES MINERAUX DU CANADA. 1962. a. price varies. Energy, Mines and Resources Canada, Mineral Policy Sector, Publishing Division, 460 O'Connor, Ottawa, Ont. K1A 0E4, Canada. TEL 819-956-4802. FAX 819-994-1498. (Orders to: Supply and Services Canada, Canada Communication Group - Publishing, Ottawa, Ont. K1A OS5, Canada) **Indexed:** AESIS.

622   CN   ISSN 0068-9289
HG5159.M4
CANADIAN MINES HANDBOOK. 1931. a. Can.$47. Southam North American Magazine Group, 1450 Don Mills Rd., Don Mills, Ont. M3B 2X7, Canada. TEL 416-445-6641. FAX 416-442-2272. Ed. D. Giancola. adv.; B&W page Can.$1920. circ. 15,000. (also avail. in microfilm from CML)
   Description: Lists and supplies information on every mining company registered in Canada.

622 551   CN   ISSN 0008-4492
                  CODEN: CAMJA9
CANADIAN MINING JOURNAL. 1879. bi-m. Can.$25.68($42) (foreign $45). Southam North American Magazine Group, 1450 Don Mills Rd., Don Mills, Ont. M3B 2X7, Canada. TEL 416-445-6641. FAX 416-442-2272. Ed. P. Whiteway. adv.; B&W page Can.$2240. illus.; mkt.; index; circ. 87,000. (also avail. in microfilm from PMC) **Indexed:** AESIS, C.I.S. Abstr., Cadscan, Can.B.P.I., Chem.Abstr., Curr.Cont., Eng.Ind., Environ.Per.Bibl., Excerp.Med., Fuel & Energy Abstr., GeoRef., INIS Atomind., Key to Econ.Sci., Lead Abstr., Met.Abstr., Petrol.Abstr., Zincscan.
   ●Also available online.
   —BLDSC shelfmark: 3042.000000.
   Incorporates: Mining in Canada (ISSN 0047-7494)
   Description: Provides technical oriented information and on-site coverage of mine and mill operations.

622   CN   ISSN 0315-9140
TN26
CANADIAN MINING JOURNAL'S REFERENCE MANUAL & BUYERS' GUIDE. 1891. a. Can.$22($32) Southam Business Communications Inc., 1450 Don Mills Road, Don Mills, Ontario M3B 2X7, Canada. TEL 416-445-6641. FAX 416-442-2261. Ed. Richard Fish. adv.; circ. 2,970.
   Formerly: Canadian Mining Manual (ISSN 0068-9319)

624 621.9   SP   ISSN 0008-5677
CANTERAS Y EXPLOTACIONES; revista tecnica de maquinaria para canteras, minas, cementos y obras hidraulicas. 1967. m. 5500 ptas. Pedeca Sociedad Cooperativa, Ltda., Maria Auxiliadora 5, 28040 Madrid, Spain. TEL 459 60 00. Ed. Francisco Esquitino Martin. circ. 10,000 (controlled). **Indexed:** Fluidex, Ind.SST.
   —BLDSC shelfmark: 3049.900000.

622   PE
CARTA MINERA; y panorama petrolero. 1982. w. S.200($290) includes annual directory. Andean Air Mail & Peruvian Times S.A., Pasaje Los Pinos, 156, Piso B, Of. 6, Miraflores, Lima, Peru. TEL 453-761. FAX 5114-467-888. Ed. Gustavo Ventocilla. charts; stat.
   Description: Covers mining in Peru.

622   II
CENTRAL MINE PLANNING & DESIGN INSTITUTE. MANUALS. (Text in English) 1976. irreg. free. Central Mine Planning & Design Institute Ltd. (Subsidiary of: Coal India Limited), Publications Wing, Gondwana Place, Kanke Rd., Ranchi 834008, Bihar, India.

CENTRAL QUEENSLAND NEWS. see AGRICULTURE

622   CN
CENTRE FOR RESOURCE STUDIES. ANNUAL REPORT. a. Centre for Resource Studies, Queen's University, Kingston, Ont. K7L 3N6, Canada. TEL 613-547-5957.

622   CN
CENTRE FOR RESOURCE STUDIES. PROCEEDINGS. 1978. irreg., latest 1991. price varies. Centre for Resource Studies, Queen's University, Kingston, Ont. K7L 3N6, Canada. TEL 613-545-2553. Ed. Margot Wojciechowski.

622   CN
CENTRE FOR RESOURCE STUDIES. TECHNICAL PAPERS. 1981. irreg., latest 1991. price varies. Centre for Resource Studies, Queen's University, Kingston, Ont. K7L 3N6, Canada. TEL 613-545-2553. FAX 613-545-6651. (also avail. in microfiche)

622   CN   ISSN 0226-7616
CENTRE FOR RESOURCES STUDIES. WORKING PAPERS. no.3, 1977. irreg., latest 1991. price varies. Centre for Resource Studies, Queen's University, Kingston, Ont. K7L 3N6, Canada. TEL 613-545-2553.

622 331.88   CS   ISSN 0009-0719
CESKOSLOVENSKY HORNIK A ENERGETIK. vol.5, 1965. s-m. 10.40 Kcs. (Odborovy Svaz Pracovniku Hornictvi a Energetiky) Ustredni Rada Odboru, Nam. Antonina Zapotockeho 2, 113 59 Prague 3, Czechoslovakia. Ed. Roman Fiala.

622   SA
CHAMBER OF MINES' NEWSLETTER; serving South Africa's private sector mining industry. bi-m. free to qualified personnel. Chamber of Mines of South Africa, P.O. Box 809, Johannesburg 2000, South Africa. TEL 011-838-8211. FAX 011-834-1884. TELEX 8-7057. Ed. Al Smit. bk.rev.; charts; illus. **Indexed:** INIS Atomind.
   Description: Presents articles on South Africa's mining industry and related issues.

622 550   SA   ISSN 0026-5268
TN119.S7
CHAMBER OF MINES OF SOUTH AFRICA. MINING SURVEY. (Text in English) 1946. 2/yr. free to shareholders in gold mines. Chamber of Mines of South Africa, P.O. Box 809, Johannesburg 2000, South Africa. TEL 011-838-8211. charts; illus.; stat.; circ. 21,000.
   Description: Highlights the main operations of the organization.

338.2   CM   ISSN 0069-2530
CHAMBRE DE COMMERCE, D'INDUSTRIE ET DES MINES DU CAMEROUN. RAPPORT ANNUEL. a. EAs.1000. Chambre de Commerce, d'Industrie et des Mines du Cameroun, B.P. 4011, Douala, Cameroon. circ. 350.

622   HK   ISSN 0258-3062
TN809.C47
CHINA COAL INDUSTRY YEARBOOK. (Text in English) 1982. a. HK.$250($45) Economic Information & Agency, 342 Hennessy Rd., 10th Fl., Hong Kong. (back issues avail.)

549   FR   ISSN 0182-564X
TN260   CODEN: CRMIDQ
CHRONIQUE DE LA RECHERCHE MINIERE. (Text in English, French; summaries in English, French, German) 1977. q. 600 F. Bureau de Recherches Geologiques et Minieres, Division Edition et Vente, B.P. 6009, 45060 Orleans Cedex, France. (Dist. by: Gauthier-Villars, Centrale des Revues, 11 rue Gossin, 92543 Montrouge Cedex, France. TEL 1-46-56-52-66) Ed. Philippe Lagny. index. **Indexed:** Bull.Signal., Chem.Abstr., Geo.Abstr., GeoRef., INIS Atomind., Petrol.Abstr., Ref.Zh.
   Description: Features articles and reviews on mineral deposits, including descriptions of deposits, regional or thematic geologic reviews, metallogenic reviews and more.

CLAUSTHALER GEOLOGISCHE ABHANDLUNGEN. see EARTH SCIENCES — Geology

MINES AND MINING INDUSTRY

549 666   US   ISSN 0009-8604
TN941   CODEN: CLCMAB
CLAYS AND CLAY MINERALS.* 1968. bi-m. $35 to individuals; institutions $125 (foreign $140). Clay Minerals Society, Box 880, Evergreen, CO 80439. TEL 303-674-8095. Ed. Frederick A. Mumpton. bk.rev.; bibl.; charts; illus.; circ. 1,800. (also avail. in microform from MIM; reprint service avail. from ISI; back issues avail.) **Indexed:** AESIS, Anal.Abstr., Br.Ceram.Abstr., Chem.Abstr., Curr.Cont., Deep Sea Res.& Oceanogr.Abstr., Eng.Ind., Excerp.Med., Geo.Abstr., GeoRef., Geotech.Abstr., Ind.Sci.Rev., Int.Aerosp.Abstr., Mineral.Abstr., Petrol.Abstr., Sci.Cit.Ind., Soils & Fert.
—BLDSC shelfmark: 3278.100000.
Formerly: Clay Minerals Society. Annual Proceedings.

622   JA
CLOSE EXAMINATION REPORT: JOZANKEI VALLEY REGION/SEIMITSU CHOSA HOKOKUSHO: JOZANKEI CHIIKI. (Text in Japanese) 1973. s-a. Metal Mining Agency - Kinzoku Kogyo Jigyodan, 6-3 Shiba Nishikubo Sakuragawa-cho, Shiba, Minato-ku, Tokyo 105, Japan. illus.

622   US   ISSN 1040-7820
TN799.9
COAL. 1964. m. $31.25. Maclean Hunter Publishing Company, 29 N. Wacker Dr., Chicago, IL 60606. TEL 312-726-2802. FAX 312-726-2574. TELEX 270258 EXP. Ed. Mark Sprouls. adv.; tr.lit.; index; circ. 22,307 (controlled). (also avail. in microfilm from UMI) **Indexed:** A.S.& T.Ind., Acid Rain Abstr., Acid Rain Ind., AESIS, C.I.S. Abstr., Energy Info.Abstr., Eng.Ind., Excerp.Med., Fuel & Energy Abstr., Gas Abstr., GeoRef., INIS Atomind., PROMT, Tr.& Indus.Ind.
•Also available online. Vendor(s): Mead Data Central.
—BLDSC shelfmark: 3287.945000.
Formed by the merger of (1911-1988): Coal Age (ISSN 0009-9910) & Coal Mining (ISSN 0749-1948); Which was formerly titled (until 1984): Coal Mining and Processing (ISSN 0009-9961)
Description: Covers exploration, development, underground and surface mining, preparation and distribution of anthracite, bituminous coal and ignite.

622 236.540   UK   ISSN 0143-6287
                              CODEN: CLCLEC
COAL CALENDAR. 1977. bi-m. £225 to non-members; members £75. I.E.A. Coal Research, Gemini House, 10-18 Putney Hill, London SW15 6AA, England. TEL 081-780-2111. FAX 081-780-1746. TELEX 917624. Ed. Andrew Kirchner. adv. (also avail. in microfiche) **Indexed:** AESIS.
—BLDSC shelfmark: 3289.250000.
Description: Contains over 700 entries up to the mid-1990s. Fully indexed to assist in finding events on topics of interest, held in specific locations or organized by particular institutions.

622   US   ISSN 0145-417X
HD9564
COAL DATA. a. $75 to individuals; non-profit institutions $50. National Coal Association, 1130 17th St., N.W., Washington, DC 20036. TEL 202-463-2640. **Indexed:** GeoRef., SRI.
Formerly: Bituminous Coal Data (ISSN 0067-897X)

COAL DISTRIBUTION. see *ENERGY*

338.2 622   US
COAL FACTS. 1948. a. $10. National Coal Association, 1130 17th St. N.W., Washington, DC 20036. TEL 202-463-2640. Ed. Thomas B. Johnson. index.
Formerly (until 1972): Bituminous Coal Facts (ISSN 0067-8988)

622   US
THE COAL JOURNAL. 1975. m. $36. Kentucky Coal Journal Inc., 101 E. Vine St., 5th Fl., Lexington, KY 40507. TEL 606-233-0092. FAX 606-255-9138. Ed. Wayne Masterman. adv.; bk.rev.; charts; stat.; circ. 19,326.
Formerly: Kentucky Coal Journal.

622.33   US   ISSN 1049-0574
HD9541
COAL LOCAL; national magazine of coal and energy issues. 1978. bi-m. $25. National Coal Association, 1130 17th St., N.W., Washington, DC 20036. TEL 202-463-2640. Ed. Aundrea Cika. charts; illus.; circ. 14,000. (back issues avail.)
Formerly (until Jan. 1990): Landmarc.
Description: Provides information, comments and perspective on US coal, energy and environmental issues and trends.

COAL MINING NEWSLETTER. see *OCCUPATIONAL HEALTH AND SAFETY*

622   UK   ISSN 0009-997X
COAL NEWS. 1961. m. £5. British Coal, Hobart House, Grosvenor Place, London SW1X 7AE, England. TEL 071-235-2020. (Subscr. to: Departmental sec., Internal Communications, Gartwood Hall, Eastwood, Nottingham NG16 3EB, England) Ed. Dennis Towle. adv.; bk.rev.; charts; illus.; circ. 85,000. (newspaper) **Indexed:** Fuel & Energy Abstr.

622   US
COAL NEWS. w. National Coal Association, 1130 17th St., N.W., Washington, DC 20036. TEL 202-463-2640.

622.33 531.64   US   ISSN 0162-2714
COAL OUTLOOK. 1975. w. $647 (foreign $677). Pasha Publications Inc., 1401 Wilson Blvd., Ste. 900, Arlington, VA 22209-9970. TEL 703-528-1244. FAX 703-528-1253. Ed. Barry Cassell. **Indexed:** PROMT.
•Also available online. Vendor(s): DIALOG, Mead Data Central.
Description: Reports on coal market trends.

051   US
COAL PEOPLE. 1976. m. $25. Al Skinner Enterprises Inc., Box 6247, Charleston, WV 25302. TEL 304-342-4129. FAX 304-343-3124. Ed. Al Skinner. adv.; bk.rev.; circ. 11,500.

622.33   US   ISSN 0734-9343
TN816.A1   CODEN: COAPDY
COAL PREPARATION; a multinational journal. 8/yr. (in 2 vols., 4 nos./vol.). $192. Gordon & Breach Science Publishers, 270 Eighth Ave., New York, NY 10011. TEL 212-206-8900. FAX 212-645-2459. TELEX 236735 GOPUB UR. (Subscr. to: Box 786, Cooper Sta., New York, NY 10276. TEL 800-545-8398; UK subscr. to: P.O. Box 90, Reading, Berkshire RG1 8JL, England. TEL 0734-560-080) Ed. J. Laskowski. adv.; bk.rev. (also avail. in microform) **Indexed:** AESIS.
—BLDSC shelfmark: 3291.457000.
Refereed Serial

622.33   US
COAL PRODUCTION (YEAR). Variant title: Annual Coal Production Report. 1976. a., latest 1990. $7.50. U.S. Department of Energy, Energy Information Administration, National Energy Information Center, EI-231, Rm. 1F-048, Forrestal Bldg., 1000 Independence Ave., S.W., Washington, DC 20585. TEL 202-586-8800.
Formerly: Coal Production Annual; Incorporates (in 1983): Coal-Pennsylvania Anthracite.

622   FR
COAL PROSPECTS AND POLICIES IN I E A COUNTRIES. irreg. price varies. Organization for Economic Cooperation and Development, International Energy Agency, 2 rue Andre-Pascal, 75775 Paris Cedex 16, France. TEL 45-24-82-00. (U.S. orders to: O.E.C.D. Publications and Information Center, 2001 L St., N.W., Ste. 700, Washington, DC 20036-4910. TEL 202-785-6323) (also avail. in microfiche)

622   UK
COAL RESEARCH PROJECTS. 1981. a. £500 (non-members £150). I.E.A. Coal Research, Gemini House, 10-18 Putney Hill, London SW1S 6AA, England. TEL 081-780-2111. FAX 081-780-1746. TELEX 917624. circ. 1,200. (also avail. in microfiche)
•Also available online. Vendor(s): FIZ Technik (COALRIP), STN International.
Formerly: Coal Research Projects. Coal Research Database.

622.33   NE
COAL SCIENCE AND TECHNOLOGY. 1981. irreg., vol.19, 1991. price varies. Elsevier Science Publishers B.V., Books Division, P.O. Box 211, 1000 AE Amsterdam, Netherlands. TEL 020-5803911. FAX 020-5803705. TELEX 18582 ESPA NL. (Subscr. in U.S. and Canada to: Elsevier Science Publishing Co., Inc., Box 882, Madison Sq. Sta., New York, NY 10159. TEL 212-989-5800)
Refereed Serial

622.33   UK
▼**COAL TRADES REVIEW.** 1991. 8/yr. £40. F M J International Publications, Queensway House, 2 Queensway, Redhill, Surrey RH1 1QS, England. TEL 44-737-768611. FAX 44-737-761685. adv.: B&W page #1210, color page #1925; trim 245 x 330. circ. 23,430.
Description: Covers all stages of the international coal industry.

553   US   ISSN 0069-4916
HE199.5.C6
COAL TRAFFIC ANNUAL. a. $75 to individuals; non-profit organizations $50. National Coal Association, 1130 17th St., N.W., Washington, DC 20036. TEL 202-463-2640. Ed. Bonnie L. King. **Indexed:** SRI.

622.33   US
COAL VOICE. bi-m. National Coal Association, 1130 17th St., N.W., Washington, DC 20036. TEL 202-463-2640. FAX 202-463-6152. Ed. Aundrea Cika. circ. 850.

622   US   ISSN 0149-578X
COAL WEEK. 1975. w. $792 (foreign $823). McGraw-Hill, Inc., Energy & Business Newsletters, 1221 Ave. of the Americas, 36th Fl., New York, NY 10020. TEL 212-512-6410. Ed. John K. Higgins. adv.; charts; stat.; index. (looseleaf format; reprint service avail. from UMI) **Indexed:** Fuel & Energy Abstr.
•Also available online. Vendor(s): DIALOG (File no.624/McGRAW-HILL PUBLICATIONS ONLINE), Dow Jones/News Retrieval (COW), Mead Data Central (COALWK).
Incorporates: Mine Regulation and Productivity Report (ISSN 0277-8696); Which was formerly: Mine Productivity Report (ISSN 0149-5283)

622   US
COAL WEEK INTERNATIONAL. 1984. w. $987 (foreign $1,012). McGraw-Hill, Inc., Energy & Business Newsletters, 1221 Ave. of the Americas, 36th Fl., New York, NY 10020. TEL 212-512-6410. Ed. John Higgins. (reprint service avail. from UMI)
•Also available online. Vendor(s): DIALOG (File no.624/McGRAW-HILL PUBLICATIONS ONLINE), Dow Jones/News Retrieval (CWI), Mead Data Central (COALIN).

553   UK   ISSN 0069-4991
COKE OVEN MANAGERS' ASSOCIATION. YEAR BOOK. 1917. a. £30. Waveney House, Adwick Road, Mexborough, Yorks S64 0BS, England. Ed. F.H. Metcalf. adv.; circ. 750. **Indexed:** Br.Ceram.Abstr.

622.33   GW   ISSN 0937-9258
▼**COKEMAKING INTERNATIONAL.** 1990. 2/yr. DM.52. (Verein Deutscher Kokereifachleute) Verlag Stahleisen mbH, Sohnstr. 65, Postfach 105164, 4000 Duesseldorf 1, Germany. TEL 0211-6707-0.
—BLDSC shelfmark: 3293.500000.

622   SA
COLIMPEX MINING EXECUPAD. (Text in Afrikaans and English) a. free to qualified personnel. Colimpex Africa (Pty.) Ltd., P.O. Box 5838, Johannesburg 2000, South Africa. adv.

622   UK   ISSN 0010-1281
                             CODEN: CLGUAL
COLLIERY GUARDIAN. 1860. 6/yr. £72 (foreign £100). F M J International Publications Ltd., Queensway House, 2 Queensway, Redhill, Surrey RH1 1QS, England. TEL 0737 768611. TELEX 948669-TOPJNL-G. Ed. M. Schwartz. adv. (also avail. in microform from UMI) **Indexed:** Br.Geol.Lit., Br.Tech.Ind., C.I.S. Abstr., Chem.Abstr., Eng.Ind., Excerp.Med., Fuel & Energy Abstr., GeoRef., RICS.
—BLDSC shelfmark: 3313.000000.
Incorporates: International Mining Equipment (ISSN 0020-8000)
Description: Explores coal mining and resources.

MINES AND MINING INDUSTRY

622 550 560   US   ISSN 0069-6056
CODEN: PCCOAT
COLORADO SCHOOL OF MINES. PROFESSIONAL CONTRIBUTIONS. 1965. irreg., no.11, 1983. $25. (Colorado School of Mines) Colorado School of Mines Press, Golden, CO 80401. TEL 303-273-3607. bibl.; charts; illus.; cum.index: 1953-1973; circ. 1,000. (reprint service avail. from UMI) **Indexed:** Chem.Abstr., GeoRef.
—BLDSC shelfmark: 6857.500000.

622 550   US   ISSN 0163-9153
TN210   CODEN: CSMQDN
COLORADO SCHOOL OF MINES QUARTERLY. 1905. q. $50. Colorado School of Mines Press, Golden, CO 80401. bibl.; charts; illus.; stat.; cum.index: 1953-1973; circ. 1,500. (also avail. in microform from UMI; back issues avail.) **Indexed:** AESIS, Appl.Mech.Rev., Chem.Abstr., Eng.Ind., Environ.Abstr., Fuel & Energy Abstr., GeoRef., Geotech.Abstr., INIS Atomind., Petrol.Abstr., Sci.Abstr.
—BLDSC shelfmark: 7169.600000.

COLORED STONE; the international reporter of the gemstone trade. see JEWELRY, CLOCKS AND WATCHES

COMIMEX. see BUILDING AND CONSTRUCTION

549   AT
COMMONWEALTH SCIENTIFIC AND INDUSTRIAL RESEARCH ORGANIZATION. DIVISION OF EXPLORATION GEOSCIENCE. ANNUAL REPORT. 1981. a. free. C.S.I.R.O., Division of Exploration Geoscience, P.O. Wembley, W.A. 6014, Australia. Ed. Judith Thomson. circ. controlled. **Indexed:** AESIS.
Supersedes: Commonwealth Scientific and Industrial Research Organization. Institute of Energy and Earth Resources. Division of Mineral Physics and Mineralogy. Biennial Report; Which was formerly: Commonwealth Scientific and Industrial Research Organization of Energy and Earth Resources. Division of Mineral Physics. Biennial Report (ISSN 0725-0142)

622.33   AT   ISSN 0726-6510
COMMONWEALTH SCIENTIFIC AND INDUSTRIAL RESEARCH ORGANIZATION. DIVISION OF GEOMECHANICS. GEOMECHANICS OF COAL MINING REPORT. 1978. irreg. Aus.$5 per no. C.S.I.R.O., Division of Geomechanics, Box 54, Mt. Waverley, Vic. 3149, Australia. **Indexed:** AESIS.
—BLDSC shelfmark: 4147.262000.
Description: Documentation of the research results in a range of aspects related to the coal mining industry.

624.176   AT   ISSN 0069-7249
COMMONWEALTH SCIENTIFIC AND INDUSTRIAL RESEARCH ORGANIZATION. DIVISION OF GEOMECHANICS. TECHNICAL REPORT. 1963. irreg. Aus.$5 per no. C.S.I.R.O., Division of Geomechanics, Box 54, Mt. Waverley, Vic. 3149, Australia. **Indexed:** AESIS, Biol.Abstr.
—BLDSC shelfmark: 7410.109000.
Formerly: Commonwealth Scientific and Industrial Research Organization. Division of Soil Mechanics. Technical Report.
Description: Descriptions of equipment and procedures developed during, or used in, geotechnical investigations; full details of data obtained in these investigations.

549   AT   ISSN 0729-056X
HC603.5
COMMONWEALTH SCIENTIFIC AND INDUSTRIAL RESEARCH ORGANIZATION. INSTITUTE OF ENERGY AND EARTH RESOURCES. ANNUAL REPORT. 1980. a. free. C.S.I.R.O., Institute of Energy and Earth Resources, Box 225, Dickson, A.C.T. 2602, Australia. Ed. J. North. circ. 2,000 (controlled). **Indexed:** AESIS.
—BLDSC shelfmark: 1153.013730.
Supersedes: Commonwealth Scientific and Industrial Research Organization. Institute of Earth Resources. Annual Report. (ISSN 0158-7412)
Description: Reports on institute policies and research highlights from its nine divisions.

549   AT   ISSN 0726-1780
COMMONWEALTH SCIENTIFIC AND INDUSTRIAL RESEARCH ORGANIZATION. INSTITUTE OF ENERGY AND EARTH RESOURCES. INVESTIGATION REPORT.. 1954. irreg. free. C.S.I.R.O., Institute of Energy and Earth Resources, P.O. Box 136, North Ryde, N.S.W. 2113, Australia. Ed. J. Thomson. circ. 825 (controlled). **Indexed:** Chem.Abstr.
Former titles: Commonwealth Scientific and Industrial Research Organization. Institute of Earth Resources. Investigation Report. (ISSN 0156-9953); Commonwealth Scientific and Industrial Research Organization. Minerals Research Laboratories. Investigation Report (ISSN 0084-8999); Commonwealth Scientific and Industrial Research Organization. Division of Coal Research. Investigation Report.
Description: Detailed reports of scientific investigations into mineral and hydrocarbon exploration, processing and use.

549   AT   ISSN 0159-9178
COMMONWEALTH SCIENTIFIC AND INDUSTRIAL RESEARCH ORGANIZATION. INSTITUTE OF ENERGY AND EARTH RESOURCES. MINERALS & ENERGY BULLETIN. 1980. q. free. C.S.I.R.O., Institute of Energy and Earth Resources, P.O. Box 225, Dickson, A.C.T. 2602, Australia. circ. 2,300 (controlled).
Description: Brief information items on research in progress, planned or just completed, with contact names.

549   AT   ISSN 0726-1772
CODEN: TCCRDH
COMMONWEALTH SCIENTIFIC AND INDUSTRIAL RESEARCH ORGANIZATION. INSTITUTE OF ENERGY AND EARTH RESOURCES. TECHNICAL COMMUNICATION.. 1953. irreg., approx. 2/yr. free. C.S.I.R.O., Institute of Energy and Earth Resources, Box 136, North Ryde, N.S.W. 2113, Australia. Ed. J. Thomson. circ. controlled. **Indexed:** AESIS, Chem.Abstr.
Former titles: Commonwealth Scientific and Industrial Research Organization. Institute of Earth Resources. Technical Communication (ISSN 0156-9945); Commonwealth Scientific and Industrial Research Organization. Minerals Research Laboratories. Technical Communication; Commonwealth Scientific and Industrial Research Organization. Division of Mineral Chemistry. Technical Communication.
Description: Descriptions not published elsewhere of new technical procedures developed during scientific investigations.

622 614.7   US
COMPACT. 1983. q. Interstate Mining Compact Commission, 459 Carlisle Dr. Ste. B, Herndon, VA 22070. TEL 703-709-8654. FAX 703-709-8655. Ed. Gregory E. Conrad. circ. 700.
Description: Information service for member states on mining laws, regulations and other related areas.

COMPTOIR FRANCAIS DES PRODUITS SIDERURGIQUES. BULLETIN STATISTIQUE. SERIE BLEUE. COMMERCE EXTERIEUR. see METALLURGY

COMPTOIR FRANCAIS DES PRODUITS SIDERURGIQUES. BULLETIN STATISTIQUE. SERIE ROUGE. PRODUCTION. see METALLURGY

622 551   US
COMPUTERS & MINING. 1985. m. $90 (foreign $115). Gibbs Associates, Box 706, Boulder, CO 80306. TEL 303-444-6032. Ed. Betty L. Gibbs. adv.; bk.rev.; circ. 200. (looseleaf format; back issues avail.)
Description: Computer applications for mining and geology.

622   US   ISSN 0010-6577
CONSOL NEWS.* 1962. bi-m. free. Consolidation Coal Co., 1800 Washington Rd., Pittsburgh, PA 15241. charts; illus.; index; circ. 22,500.
Description: Reports on coal mining and resources.

CONSTRUCTION AND MINING MACHINERY EN ESPANOL. see BUILDING AND CONSTRUCTION

CONSTRUCTION EQUIPMENT BUYERS' GUIDE. see BUILDING AND CONSTRUCTION

CONTRIBUTIONS TO MINERALOGY AND PETROLOGY. see EARTH SCIENCES — Geology

622 551   CU
CUBA. MINING AND GEOLOGY.* (Text in Spanish; summaries in English, Russian, Spanish) 1983. 3/yr. $21. Ediciones Cubanas, P.O. Box 605, Havana, Cuba. TEL 36655. adv.; circ. 1,000. (back issues avail.)

CURTIN UNIVERSITY OF TECHNOLOGY. MULGA RESEARCH CENTRE JOURNAL. see BIOLOGY

622   GW
D M T JOURNAL. 1981. q. free. Deutsche Montan Technologie fuer Rohstoff, Energie, Umwelt, Herner Str. 45, 4630 Bochum 1, Germany. FAX 0234-9683606. TELEX 825701. Ed. Barbara Laaser. circ. 5,000. (back issues avail.)
Formerly: W B K Journal.

DAKOTA COUNSEL. see ENERGY

622 500   US
DIRECTORY OF MINING PROGRAMS. biennial. $75 (foreign $90). Gibbs Associates, Box 706, Boulder, CO 80306. TEL 303-444-6032.
Description: Lists commercial and public domain computer programs for mining applications.

622   GW   ISSN 0012-5857
DRAEGERHEFT/DRAEGER REVIEW. (Editions in English and German) 1912. q. free. Draegerwerk AG, Moislinger Allee 53, 2400 Luebeck 1, Germany. FAX 0451-8823944. Ed. Burkard Dillig. charts; illus.; cum.index; circ. 13,000. **Indexed:** C.I.S. Abstr., Chem.Abstr.
—BLDSC shelfmark: 3622.150000.

622   CN
DRILLING AND LAND REPORT. m. Can.$110. Ministry of Energy, Mines and Petroleum Resources, Energy Resources Division, Parliament Bldgs., Victoria, B.C. V8V 1X4, Canada. TEL 604-387-5993. (Subscr. to: Crown Publications Inc., 546 Yates St., Victoria, B.C. V8W 1K8, Canada. TEL 604-386-4636) circ. 140. (back issues avail.)
Description: Outlines current drilling activity by presenting new well locations, basic data on wells drilled or completed, rig licenses issued, and descriptions of fields designated or amended quarterly.

DYNA. see ENGINEERING

622   US
E & M J INTERNATIONAL DIRECTORY OF MINING. (Engineering & Mining Journal) 1968. a. $126. Maclean Hunter Publishing Company, 29 N. Wacker Dr., Chicago, IL 60606. TEL 312-726-2802. FAX 312-726-2574. TELEX 270258 EXP. Ed. Charles Richardson. **Indexed:** Tr.& Indus.Ind.
Formerly: E & M J International Directory of Mining and Mineral Processing Operations.

E & M J MINING ACTIVITY DIGEST. (Engineering & Mining Journal) see METALLURGY

E N I ANNUAL REPORT. (Ente Nazionale Idrocarburi) see ENERGY

622 500   US
E Z SEARCH - MINING. q. $65 (foreign $75). Gibbs Associates, Box 706, Boulder, CO 80306. TEL 303-444-6032. (avail. on diskette only)
Description: Lists commercial and public domain computer programs for the mining industry.

EARTH AND MINERAL SCIENCES. see EARTH SCIENCES

EASTERN MINERAL LAW FOUNDATION. CASE UPDATE. see LAW

EASTERN MINERAL LAW FOUNDATION NEWSLETTER. see LAW

ECUADOR. MINISTERIO DE ENERGIA Y MINAS. INFORME DE LABORES. see ENERGY

549   GW
EMSER HEFTE; Magazin veber die Mineralienschatze. 1979. q. DM.62. Doris Bode Verlag GmbH, Duernberg 2, 4358 Haltern 4, Germany. TEL 02364-16107. FAX 02364-169273. Ed. Rainer Bode. circ. 2,100.

ENERGY IN VENEZUELA. QUARTERLY BULLETIN. see ENERGY

MINES AND MINING INDUSTRY   3483

ENERGY REPORT; energy policy and technology news bulletin. see *ENERGY*

622.33   CN
ENGINEERING AND INSPECTION ANNUAL REPORT. a. Can.$15. Ministry of Energy, Mines and Petroleum Resources, Mineral Resources Division, Parliament Bldgs., Victoria, B.C. V8V 1X4, Canada. (Subscr. to: Crown Publications, 546 Yates St., Victoria, B.C. V8W 1K8, Canada. TEL 604-386-4636) (back issues avail.)
 Formerly: Mining in British Columbia (ISSN 0823-1265); Which superseded in part: Geology, Exploration and Mining (ISSN 0085-1027); Which was formerly: Lode Metals in British Columbia.

---

622 620 US ISSN 0095-8948
TA1   CODEN: ENMJAK
ENGINEERING & MINING JOURNAL. Short title: E & M J. 1866. m. $60. Maclean Hunter Publishing Company, 29 W. Nacker Dr., Chicago, IL 60606. TEL 312-726-2802. FAX 312-726-2574. TELEX 270258 EXP. Ed. Robert J.M. Wyllie. adv.; bk.rev.; tr.lit.; index; circ. 32,076 (controlled). (also avail. in microform from UMI) **Indexed:** A.S.& T.Ind., Acid Rain Abstr., Acid Rain Ind., AESIS, Br.Geol.Lit., Bus.Ind., C.I.S. Abstr., CAD CAM Abstr., Cadscan, Chem.Abstr., Copper Abstr., Curr.Cont., Energy Info.Abstr., Eng.Ind., Environ.Abstr., Environ.Per.Bibl., Excerp.Med., Fuel & Energy Abstr., Geo.Abstr., GeoRef., Geotech.Abstr., Intl.Civil Eng.Abstr., Lead Abstr., Met.Abstr., Ocean.Abstr., Petrol.Abstr., Pollut.Abstr., PROMT, Soft.Abstr.Eng., Soils & Fert., SRI, Tr.& Indus.Ind., World Alum.Abstr., Zincscan.
 ●Also available online. Vendor(s): Mead Data Central.
 —BLDSC shelfmark: 3755.000000.
 Incorporates (in 1991): International Mining.
 Description: Covers exploration, development, milling, smelting, refining, and other extrative processing of metals and nonmetallics including coal.

ENVIRONMENTAL GEOCHEMISTRY AND HEALTH. see *ENVIRONMENTAL STUDIES*

EQUIPMENT ECHOES. see *BUILDING AND CONSTRUCTION*

ERDOEL UND KOHLE, ERDGAS, PETROCHEMIE; hydrocarbon technology. see *PETROLEUM AND GAS*

ERZMETALL; journal for exploration, mining and metallurgy. see *METALLURGY*

---

622 338 SP
ESTADISTICAS MINERA DE ESPANA. a. 2000 ptas. Ministerio de Industria, Direccion General de Minas y Combustibles, Paseo de la Castellana 160, Madrid 28046, Spain. FAX 259-84-80.
 Formerly: Estadisticas Minera y Metalurgica de Espana (ISSN 0071-156X)

338.2 BO ISSN 0014-1194
ESTANO. 1961. bi-m. free. Corporacion Minera de Bolivia, Departamento de Relaciones Publicas e Informacion, Avda. Mariscal Santa Cruz 1092, Casilla 349, La Paz, Bolivia. Ed. Dir. Felix R. Nieto. adv.; illus.

---

622 SZ
EUROPA STAR DIAMOND INTELLIGENCE BRIEFS. (Text in English) 1985. 20/yr. $350. Hugo Buchser S.A., Route des Acacias 25, P.O. Box 30, CH-1211 Geneva 24, Switzerland. TEL 022-3003737. FAX 022-3003748. bk.rev.

---

549 GW ISSN 0935-1221
QE351   CODEN: EJMIER
EUROPEAN JOURNAL OF MINERALOGY. (Supplement avail.: Berichte der Deutschen Mineralogischen Gesellschaft (ISSN-0935-123X)) (Text in English, French, German and Italian) 1911. 6/yr. DM.440. (Deutsche Mineralogische Gesellschaft) E. Schweizerbart'sche Verlagsbuchhandlung, Johannesstr. 3A, 7000 Stuttgart 1, Germany. TEL 0711-625001. FAX 0711-625005. TELEX 723363-SCHB-D. (Co-sponsors: Societa Italiana di Mineralogia e Petrologia; Societe Francaise de Mineralogie et de Cristallographie) Ed.Bd. adv.; bibl.; charts; illus. **Indexed:** Bull.Signal., Chem.Abstr., Excerp.Med., INIS Atomind.
 Formed by 1988 merger of: Fortschritte der Mineralogie (ISSN 0015-8186) & Rendiconti della Societa Italiana di Mineralogie e Petrologia (ISSN 0037-8828) & Bulletin de Mineralogie (ISSN 0180-9210)
 Description: Contains original papers, review articles and short notes dealing with mineralogical sciences: mineralogy, petrology, geochemistry, crystallography, ore deposits, and related fields, including applied mineralogy.
 Refereed Serial

EXPLORATION & MINING GEOLOGY. see *EARTH SCIENCES — Geology*

EXPLORATION IN BRITISH COLUMBIA. see *EARTH SCIENCES — Geology*

---

622 CN
EXTRA. 1980. w. INCO Limited Manitoba Division, Public Affairs Dept., Thompson, MB. R8N 1P3, Canada. TEL 204-778-2289. FAX 204-677-2551. Ed. Mark Tessier. circ. 2,500.
 Description: Newsletter for employees.

622.8 US
FEDERAL MINE SAFETY AND HEALTH REVIEW COMMISSION DECISIONS. 1978. m. $70. U.S. Federal Mine Safety and Health Review Commission, 1730 K St. N.W., 6th Fl., Washington, DC 20006. TEL 202-653-5633. FAX 202-653-5030. (Subscr. to Government Printing Office, Supt. of Documents, Washington, DC 20402. TEL 202-783-3238) circ. 300. **Indexed:** MEDOC.

---

690 GW
FELSBAU; journal for geomechanics, engineering geology and rock engineering in construction and mining. 1983. q. DM.88. (Oesterreichische Gesellschaft fuer Geomechanik, AU) Verlag Glueckauf GmbH, Franz-Fischer-Weg 61, Postfach 103945, 4300 Essen 1, Germany. FAX 0201-293630.

---

549 FJ ISSN 0252-2462
J961
FIJI. MINERAL RESOURCES DEPARTMENT. ANNUAL REPORT. (Text in English) 1953. a. price varies. Mineral Resources Department, P.M. Bag, Suva, Fiji. Ed. Peter Rodda. circ. 500.
 Former titles: Fiji. Mineral Resources Division. Annual Report; (until 1978): Fiji. Department of Lands and Mineral Resources. Annual Report (ISSN 0252-2470); (Until 1972): Fiji. Geological Survey. Annual Report (ISSN 0252-2489)
 Description: Summary of the year's activities, statistics of mining and exploration.

---

549 FJ
FIJI. MINERAL RESOURCES DEPARTMENT. ECONOMIC INVESTIGATION. (Text in English) 1962. irreg. price varies. Mineral Resources Department, P.M. Bag, Suva, Fiji. Ed. Peter Rodda. circ. 300. **Indexed:** GeoRef.
 Formerly: Fiji. Mineral Resources Division. Economic Investigation (ISSN 0379-296X); Supersedes (in 1972): Fiji. Geological Survey. Economic Investigation (ISSN 0428-3279)
 Description: Results of mineral explorations.

338.2 665.5 CN ISSN 0227-1656
HD9506.C2
FINANCIAL POST SURVEY OF MINES AND ENERGY RESOURCES. 1980. a. Can.$67.50. Financial Post Co., Ltd., 333 King St., E., Toronto, Ont. M5A 4N2, Canada. TEL 416-350-6477. FAX 416-350-6501. Ed. Steven Pattison. adv.; circ. 11,000.
 Formed by the merger of: Financial Post Survey of Mines (ISSN 0071-5085); Financial Post Survey of Energy Resources (ISSN 0705-7091)
 Description: Investment and financial information on publicly owned mining and resource companies in Canada.

---

622 UK ISSN 0141-3244
TN13
FINANCIAL TIMES INTERNATIONAL YEAR BOOKS: MINING. 1887. a. £115. Longman Group UK Ltd., Westgate House, The High, Harlow, Essex CM20 1YR, England. TEL 0279-442601. (Dist. in U.S. and Canada by: St. James Press, 425 N. Michigan Ave., Chicago, IL 60611)
 Formerly: Mining Year Book.

---

622 RU ISSN 0015-3273
    CODEN: FTRIAR
FIZIKO-TEKHNICHESKIE PROBLEMY RAZRABOTKI POLEZNYKH ISKOPAEMYKH. English translation: Soviet Mining Science (US ISSN 0038-5581) 1965. bi-m. 32.10 Rub. Izdatel'stvo Nauka, Fizmatlit, Leninskii prospekt, 15, 117071 Moscow, V-71, Russia. (Dist. by: Mezhdunarodnaya Kniga, ul. Dimitrova D.39, 113095 Moscow, Russia) Ed. E.I. Shemjakin. index. (tabloid format) **Indexed:** Chem.Abstr., Geotech.Abstr., INIS Atomind., Met.Abstr., World Alum.Abstr.
 —BLDSC shelfmark: 0389.990000.

FRANCE. BUREAU DE RECHERCHES GEOLOGIQUES ET MINIERES. MANUELS ET METHODES. see *EARTH SCIENCES — Geology*

FRANCE. BUREAU DE RECHERCHES GEOLOGIQUES ET MINIERES. MEMOIRES. see *EARTH SCIENCES — Geology*

---

622 GW
FUER UNSERE MITARBEITER. 1974. s-a. free. Gewerkschaft Walter, P.O. Box 101313, Stauderstr. 213, 4300 Essen-Katernberg, Germany. Ed. Degenhard Merkle. bk.rev.; circ. 3,000. (back issues avail.)
 Description: News and information on the mining company, featuring new techniques in shaft building, new projects, and more.

---

622 GW ISSN 0178-501X
DIE FUEHRUNGSKRAFT. Cover title: V D F Die Fuehrungskraft. 10/yr. DM.50. (Verband der Fuehrungskraefte in Bergbau und Energiewirtschaft) B E W Verwaltungsgesellschaft mbG, Alfredstr. 77-79, D-4300 Essen 1, Germany. TEL 0201-772011. circ. 8,000.

FUNDACION BARILOCHE. INSTITUTO DE ECONOMIA DE LA ENERGIA. PUBLICACIONES. see *ENERGY*

GAS SUPPLY AND DEMAND STUDY. see *PETROLEUM AND GAS*

338.7 ZR
GECAMINES ANNUAL REPORT/GECAMINES RAPPORT ANNUEL. (Editions in English and French) a. Generale des Carrieres et des Mines, Division des Relations Publiques, B.P. 8714, Kinshasa, Zaire. charts; stat.

---

622 ZR
GENERALE DES CARRIERES ET DES MINES. MONOGRAPHIE. irreg. (approx. 4/yr.). Generale des Carrieres et des Mines, Division des Relations Publiques, B.P. 450, Lubumbashi, Zaire.
 Formerly: Generale des Carrieres et Mines du Zaire. Monographie.

GEOLOGICAL, MINING AND METALLURGICAL SOCIETY OF INDIA. BULLETIN. see *EARTH SCIENCES — Geology*

GEOLOGICKY ZBORNIK/GEOLOGY. COLLECTION OF WORKS. see *EARTH SCIENCES — Geology*

GEOLOGIE EN MIJNBOUW/GEOLOGY AND MINING. see *EARTH SCIENCES — Geology*

M

MINES AND MINING INDUSTRY

GEOLOGISCHES JAHRBUCH. REIHE D: MINERALOGIE. PETROGRAPHIE, GEOCHEMIE, LAGERSTAETTENKUNDE. see *EARTH SCIENCES — Geology*

GEOLOGISCHES LANDESAMT BADEN-WUERTTEMBERG. JAHRESHEFTE. see *EARTH SCIENCES*

GEOLOGISCHES LANDESAMT BADEN-WUETTEMBERG. ABHANDLUNGEN. see *EARTH SCIENCES*

553   RU   ISSN 0016-7908
GEOLOGIYA RUDNYKH MESTOROZHDENII. (Text in Russian; summaries in English) 1959. bi-m. 32.10 Rub. Izdatel'stvo Nauka, 90 Profsoyuznaya ul., 117864 Moscow, Russia. TEL 234-05-84. (Dist. by: Mezhdunarodnaya Kniga, ul. Dimitrova D.39, 113095 Moscow, Russia) Ed. V.J. Smirnov. adv.; bk.rev.; bibl.; charts; illus.; index; circ. 2,750. (tabloid format) **Indexed:** Chem.Abstr., Eng.Ind., Geo.Abstr., INIS Atomind., Ref.Zh.

622 551   MX
GEOMIMET. 1973. bi-m. $25 to non-members. Asociacion de Ingenieros de Minas, Metalurgistas y Geologos de Mexico, A.C., Departamento de Circulacion, Paseo de la Reforma 51, Piso 18-801, Col. Revolucion, Delegacion Cuauhtemoc, 06030 Mexico, D.F., Mexico. Ed. Raul Morales Garcia. adv.; bk.rev.; charts; illus.; stat.; circ. 10,000. (reprint service avail. from UMI, ISI) **Indexed:** Chem.Abstr., INIS Atomind.
  Description: Covers the energy resources sector of Mexico.

GEOMINAS. see *EARTH SCIENCES*

GEOPHYSICAL DIRECTORY. see *EARTH SCIENCES — Geophysics*

338.2   US
GEORGIA GEOLOGIC SURVEY. CIRCULAR 2. MINING DIRECTORY OF GEORGIA. (Subseries of its Circular series) 18th ed., 1981. irreg., latest 1990 ed. free. Department of Natural Resources, Georgia Geologic Survey, 19 Martin Luther King Jr. Dr., S.W., Rm. 400, Atlanta, GA 30334. TEL 404-656-3214. Ed. P. Allgood.
  Description: Listing by commodity and cross-referenced by county of all materials mined in Georgia with mine locations.

622   US
GEORGIA GEOLOGIC SURVEY. CIRCULAR 3. THE MINERAL INDUSTRY OF GEORGIA. (Subseries of its Circular series) 1977. irreg., latest 1987 ed. free. Department of Natural Resources, Georgia Geologic Survey, 19 Martin Luther King Jr. Dr., S.W., Rm. 400, Atlanta, GA 30334. TEL 404-656-3214.
  Description: Information on commodities mined.

338.2   US   ISSN 0433-5473
TN24.G4
GEORGIA GEOLOGICAL SURVEY. INFORMATION CIRCULAR. 1933. irreg., no.89, 1991. price varies. Department of Natural Resources, Georgia Geologic Survey, 19 Martin Luther King Jr. Dr., S.W., Rm. 400, Atlanta, GA 30334. TEL 404-656-3214. Ed. P. Allgood.
  Description: Hydrologic or geologic reports discussing regional hydrology or mineral resources.

GEOS; quarterly concerned with the earth's resources. see *EARTH SCIENCES*

622   UK   ISSN 0960-3182
GEOTECHNICAL AND GEOLOGICAL ENGINEERING. 1983-1990; resumed 1991. q. £130 for EC (US & Canada $230). Chapman & Hall, 2-6 Boundary Row, London SE1 8HN, England. TEL 071-865-0066. FAX 071-522-9623. TELEX 263398. (Dist. by: International Thomson Publishing Services, Ltd., N. Way, Andover, Hampshire SP10 5EB, England. TEL 0264-33-2424; US addr.: Chapman & Hall, 29 W. 35th St., New York, NY 10001-2291. TEL 212-244-3336) Eds. D.G. Toll, J.M. Kemeny. index. (reprint service avail. from UMI)
—BLDSC shelfmark: 4158.921500.
  Formerly: International Journal of Mining and Geological Engineering (ISSN 0269-0136)
  Description: Provides papers relating to the planning, construction and operation of mines, both surface and underground.

622 658   FR
GERER ET COMPRENDRE/TO MANAGE AND TO UNDERSTAND. (Text in French) 4/yr. 674 F. includes Realites Industrielles (foreign 784 F.)(effective Nov. 1990). (Annales des Mines) Societe E S K A, 27 rue Dunois, 75013 Paris, France. TEL 77-32-46-13. Ed. Michel Mathieu. adv.
  Formerly: Annales des Mines. Gerer et Comprendre; Supersedes in part: Annales des Mines (ISSN 0003-4282)

622   GW   ISSN 0340-7896
TN3   CODEN: GLUEAJ
GLUECKAUF; Zeitschrift fuer Technik und Wirtschaft des Bergbaus. 1865. m. DM.426. Verlag Glueckauf GmbH, Franz-Fischer-Weg 61, Postfach 103945, 4300 Essen 1, Germany. FAX 0201-293630. adv.; bk.rev.; bibl.; illus.; pat.; stat.; circ. 6,500. **Indexed:** C.I.S. Abstr., Chem.Abstr., Dok.Arbeitsmed., Eng.Ind., Excerp.Med., Fuel & Energy Abstr., INIS Atomind.

622   GW   ISSN 0017-1387
TN3
GLUECKAUF-FORSCHUNGSHEFTE; Zeitschrift zur Verbreitung von Forschungsergebnisse im Bergbau. 1940. 6/yr. DM.550. Verlag Glueckauf GmbH, Franz-Fischer-Weg 61, Postfach 103945, 4300 Essen 1, Germany. FAX 0201-293630. bk.rev.; bibl.; charts; illus.; pat.; stat.; index; circ. 1,000. (tabloid format) **Indexed:** C.I.S. Abstr., Eng.Ind., Excerp.Med., Fuel & Energy Abstr., INIS Atomind.
—BLDSC shelfmark: 4196.007000.

622   US
▼**GOLD (YEAR).** 1990. a. $10 (foreign $20). Gold Institute, Administrative Office - Institut de l'Or, Bureau Administratif, 1112 15th St., N.W., Ste. 240, Washington, DC 20036-4823. TEL 202-835-0185. FAX 202-835-0155. TELEX 904233. (Co-sponsor: Gold Field Mineral Services Ltd.) charts.
  Description: Presents current picture of each aspect of the gold supply and demand equation in global terms.

622 610   US
GOLD INSTITUTE. INTERNATIONAL CONFERENCE ON GOLD & SILVER IN MEDICINE. PROCEEDINGS. irreg., latest 1987. $83 (foreign $90). Gold Institute, Administrative Office - Institut de l'Or, Bureau Administratif, 1112 15th St., N.W., Ste. 420, Washington, DC 20036-4823. TEL 202-835-0185. FAX 202-835-0155. TELEX 904233. (Co-sponsor: Silver Institute)
  Description: Reports on new clinical research on gold in England, Canada, the Netherlands and the United States.

338.2 669   US
GOLD NEWS/NOUVELLES DE L'OR. 1976. bi-m. $25 (foreign $30). Gold Institute, Administrative Office - Institut de l'Or, Bureau Administratif, 1112 15th St., N.W., Ste. 420, Washington, DC 20036-4823. TEL 202-835-0185. FAX 202-835-0155. TELEX 904233 GLSLAZ. Ed. John H. Lutley. circ. 5,000. (back issues avail.)

622   US
GOLD PROSPECTOR. 1968. bi-m. $2.50 per no. Gold Prospectors Association of America, Inc., 521 E. Alvarado St., Fallbrook, CA 92028. TEL 619-728-6620. FAX 619-728-4815. Eds. Perry Massie, George Massie. circ. 50,000.

GOLD STANDARD NEWS. see *BUSINESS AND ECONOMICS — Investments*

GORNIK. see *LABOR UNIONS*

622   RU   ISSN 0017-2278
TN4   CODEN: GOZHA6
GORNYI ZHURNAL. English translation: Soviet Mining Journal (NE ISSN 0970-2458) 1825. m. 31.80 Rub. (Gosudarstvennyi Komitet po Chernoi i Tsvetnoi Metallurgii) Izdatel'stvo Nedra, Pl. Belorusskogo Vokzala, 3, 125047 Moscow, Russia. TEL 250-52-55. Ed. A.V. Baronenkov. adv.; bk.rev.; charts; illus.; index; circ. 11,500. **Indexed:** C.I.S. Abstr., Chem.Abstr., Eng.Ind., Fuel & Energy Abstr., INIS Atomind.
—BLDSC shelfmark: 0051.480000.

622   US
GOWER FEDERAL SERVICE - MINING. 1962. m. $540 (renewal $315). Rocky Mountain Mineral Law Foundation, Porter Administration Bldg., 7039 E. 18th Ave., Denver, CO 80220. TEL 303-321-8100. FAX 303-321-7657. bk.rev.; circ. 250. (looseleaf format; also avail. in microfiche; back issues avail.)
●Also available online. Vendor(s): WESTLAW.

622   US
GOWER FEDERAL SERVICE - OUTER CONTINENTAL SHELF. m. $310 (renewal $150). Rocky Mountain Mineral Law Foundation, Porter Administration Bldg., 7039 E. 18th Ave., Denver, CO 80220. TEL 303-321-8100. FAX 303-321-7657. (looseleaf format; back issues avail.)
●Also available online. Vendor(s): WESTLAW.

GREAT BRITAIN. BRITISH GEOLOGICAL SURVEY. OVERSEAS GEOLOGY AND MINERAL RESOURCES. see *EARTH SCIENCES — Geology*

622.33   UK
GREAT BRITAIN. HEALTH AND SAFETY EXECUTIVE. HEALTH AND SAFETY: COAL MINES. a. H.M.S.O., P.O. Box 276, London SW8 5DT, England.

622   UK
GREAT BRITAIN. HEALTH AND SAFETY EXECUTIVE. HEALTH AND SAFETY: MINES. a. H.M.S.O., P.O. Box 276, London SW8 5DT, England.

622   UK
GREAT BRITAIN. HEALTH AND SAFETY EXECUTIVE. HEALTH AND SAFETY: QUARRIES. a. H.M.S.O., P.O. Box 276, London SW8 5DT, England.

622   SW
GRUVARBETAREN. 8/yr. SEK 120. Svenska Gruvindustriarbetarefoerbundet, Box 83, 772 01 Graengesberg 1, Sweden. FAX 240-20728. TELEX 909 TELEOPR S. adv.; circ. 9,500.

338.2   BL
GUIA ECONOMICO E INDUSTRIAL DO ESTADO DE MINAS GERAIS. a. free. Federacao das Industrias do Estado de Minas Gerais, Av. Carandai 1115, 30000 Belo Horizonte, Brazil. Ed. Paulo A.S. Passos. adv.; charts; stat.
  Supersedes (since 1979): Anuario Industrial de Minas Gerais (ISSN 0066-5231)

553   UK   ISSN 0072-8713
GUIDE TO THE COALFIELDS. 1948. a. £74. F M J International Publications Ltd., Queensway House, 2 Queensway, Redhill, Surrey RH1 1QS, England. TEL 0737-768611. TELEX 948669-TOPJNL-G. adv.

622   GY
GUYMINE NEWS. 1971. m. Guyana Mining Enterprise Ltd., Linden, Guyana. FAX 592-4-2795. TELEX GY-2245. Ed. Walter Campbell. circ. 6,000.
  Formerly: Guybau News.

HARRIS MISSOURI DIRECTORY OF MANUFACTURERS. see *BUSINESS AND ECONOMICS — Trade And Industrial Directories*

HEALTH AND SAFETY: QUARRIES. see *OCCUPATIONAL HEALTH AND SAFETY*

HERCYNICA. see *EARTH SCIENCES — Geology*

HIROSHIMA UNIVERSITY. JOURNAL OF SCIENCE. SERIES C. GEOLOGY AND MINERALOGY/HIROSHIMA DAIGAKU RIKA KIYO, CHISHITSUGAKU TO KOBUTSUGAKU. see *EARTH SCIENCES — Geology*

HOKKAIDO UNIVERSITY. FACULTY OF SCIENCE. JOURNAL. SERIES 4: GEOLOGY AND MINERALOGY. see *EARTH SCIENCES — Geology*

622 331   US
HOMESTAKE MINING. UPDATE; gold mine employee newsletter. 1981. q. Homestake Mining Company, 215 W. Main St., Lead, SD 57754-0894. TEL 605-584-4672. Ed. Scott H. Zieske. circ. 1,350. (back issues avail.)

338   JA
HONPO KOGYO NO SUSEI/MINING YEARBOOK OF JAPAN.* (Text in Japanese; captions in English or Japanese) 1906. a. Ministry of International Trade and Industry, Research and Statistics Division - Tsusho Sangyo Chosakai, 1-3-1 Kasumigaseki, Chiyoda-ku, Tokyo 100, Japan. TEL 03-501-1511. stat.

622 — **JM**
I B A REVIEW. 1975. q. $50. International Bauxite Association, P.O. Box 551, Kingston 5, Jamaica, W.I. FAX 809-926-7157. TELEX 2428 ITNLBA JA. Ed. Shirley Davis. circ. 400. **Indexed:** Met.Abstr., World Alum.Abstr., World Alum.Abstr.

622 — **GW**
I D R. (Industrie Diamanten Rundschau) 1967. q. DM.36. L.N. Schaffrath, Graphischer Betrieb, Martin-Luther-Platz 27, Postfach 11 35, D-4000 Dusseldorf 1, Germany. Ed. Walter Weiland. adv.; bk.rev.; circ. 3,000. (back issues avail.; reprint service avail.)

I E C A REPORT. (International Erosion Control Association, Inc.) see CONSERVATION

IDAHO. GEOLOGICAL SURVEY. BULLETIN. see EARTH SCIENCES — Geology

IDAHO. GEOLOGICAL SURVEY. INFORMATION CIRCULAR. see EARTH SCIENCES — Geology

338.2 553 — **US**
TN24.I3 — **CODEN: ILMNAS**
ILLINOIS MINERALS. 1954. irreg., no.104, 1990. $1.25 per no. State Geological Survey, Natural Resources Bldg., 615 E. Peabody Dr., Champaign, IL 61820. TEL 217-344-1481. abstr.; bibl.; charts; illus.; stat. **Indexed:** AESIS, Geo.Abstr., GeoRef.
 Former titles: Illinois Minerals Notes (ISSN 0094-9442); Formed by the merger of: Illinois. State Geological Survey. Industrial Mineral Notes (ISSN 0073-4853) & Illinois. State Geological Survey. Mineral Economic Briefs (ISSN 0073-5116)

622 — **US**
ILLINOIS MINING INSTITUTE. PROCEEDINGS. 1928. a. $15 (free to members, mining schools and technical libraries). Illinois Mining Institute, 615 E. Peabody, Champaign, IL 61820. TEL 217-333-5115. Ed. H.H. Damberger. adv.; circ. 1,400.

INDIAN JOURNAL OF GEOLOGY. see EARTH SCIENCES — Geology

549 — **II** — **ISSN 0019-5928**
TN103 — **CODEN: INMLA2**
INDIAN MINERALOGIST. (Text in English) 1960. s-a. Rs.75($12) Mineralogical Society of India, Manasa Gangothri, Mysore 670 006, India. Ed. A.S. Janardhan. adv.; bk.rev.; abstr.; charts; illus.; circ. 500. **Indexed:** Chem.Abstr.

549 — **II** — **ISSN 0019-5936**
TN4 — **CODEN: INMIAR**
INDIAN MINERALS. (Text in English) 1947. q. Rs.100($36) Ministry of Urban Development, Department of Publication, Civil Lines, Delhi 110 054, India. TEL 11-2517409. adv.; bk.rev.; charts; illus.; circ. 1,800. **Indexed:** C.R.I. Abstr., Chem.Abstr., Eng.Ind.

622 — **II** — **ISSN 0445-7897**
CODEN: IMYBAP
INDIAN MINERALS YEAR BOOK. (Text in English) 1959. a. $72. Indian Bureau of Mines, Controller General, Nagpur 440 001, India.

622 — **II** — **ISSN 0019-5944**
INDIAN MINING & ENGINEERING JOURNAL. (Text in English) 1962. m. Rs.60($25) I M E Publications, Esperanza Ground Floor, Colaba Causeway, Bombay 1, India. Ed. J.F. De Souza. adv.; bk.rev.; charts; illus.; mkt.; stat.; tr.lit.; index; circ. 3,500. (also avail. in microform) **Indexed:** AESIS, Fuel & Energy Abstr.
 Incorporates: Mineral Markets.

622.07 — **II** — **ISSN 0304-1158**
TN213.D52
INDIAN SCHOOL OF MINES. ANNUAL REPORT. (Text in English) 1968. a. free. Indian School of Mines, Dhanbad 826004, Bihar, India. FAX 0629-214. illus. Key Title: Annual Report - Indian School of Mines.

622 — **SP** — **ISSN 0210-2307**
CODEN: INMIDU
INDUSTRIA MINERA. 1958. m. 5500 ptas. Consejo Superior de Colegios de Ingenieros de Minas, Rios Rosas 19 Bis, 28003 Madrid, Spain. Ed. Fernando Hevia Cangas. adv.; bk.rev.; abstr.; bibl.; charts; pat.; stat.; tr.lit.; index; circ. 3,000. **Indexed:** Chem.Abstr., Ind.SST.

622 669 553 — **IT** — **ISSN 0391-1586**
INDUSTRIA MINERARIA; miniere e cave, metallurgia, geologia applicata, fonti di energia. 1927; N.S. 1950. bi-m. L.70000 (foreign L.85000). (Associazione Mineraria Italiana) Servizio Italiano Pubblicazioni Internazionali s.r.l., Viale L. Pasteur, 6, 00144 Rome, Italy. TEL 06-5918586. FAX 06-5924819. Ed.Bd. adv.; bk.rev.; charts; illus.; mkt.; stat.; index; circ. 3,000. **Indexed:** Cadscan, Chem.Abstr., INIS Atomind., Lead Abstr., Zincscan.
 —BLDSC shelfmark: 4441.500000.
 Former titles (until 1956): Industria Mineraria d'Italia e d'Oltremare (ISSN 0367-892X); (until 1936): Industria Mineraria (ISSN 0019-7696)

622 380.5 — **UK** — **ISSN 0265-5071**
INDUSTRIAL HERITAGE MAGAZINE; industry - transport - people. 1974. q. £9. Book House, Ravenstonedale, Kirkby Stephen, Cumbria CA17 4NQ, England. TEL 053-96-23634. Ed. John Keavey. adv.; bk.rev.; circ. 500. (back issues avail.)
 Former titles: Yesteryear Heritage & Industrial Past (ISSN 0307-1677)
 Description: Articles on the history of technology and transport in the UK.

338.2 660 — **US** — **ISSN 0019-8544**
CODEN: IMINBG
INDUSTRIAL MINERALS. 1967. m. $348. Metal Bulletin Inc., 220 Fifth Ave., 10 Fl., New York, NY 10001. TEL 800-638-2525. FAX 212-213-6273. Ed. Joyce Griffiths. adv.; bk.rev.; charts; illus.; stat.; index; circ. 3,600. **Indexed:** AESIS, Br.Ceram.Abstr., Br.Geol.Lit., Ceram.Abstr., Chem.Abstr., INIS Atomind., Key to Econ.Sci., Met.Abstr., PROMT, World Alum.Abstr., World Surf.Coat.
 —BLDSC shelfmark: 4458.150000.
 Description: Covers non-metallic mineral producers by country.

338.2 660 — **US** — **ISSN 0269-1701**
INDUSTRIAL MINERALS DIRECTORY - WORLD GUIDE TO PRODUCERS AND PROCESSORS. 1977. irreg. $189. Metal Bulletin Inc., 220 Fifth Ave., New York, NY 10001. TEL 212-213-6202. Ed. Joyce Griffiths. adv.
 —BLDSC shelfmark: 4458.185000.
 Formerly (until 1986): Industrial Minerals Directory (ISSN 0141-5263); Incorporates (1979): Industrial Minerals Merchants, Agents and Processors (ISSN 0143-263X)
 Description: Directory of international non-metallic mineral producers; includes a buyers guide.

622 — **GW** — **ISSN 0341-3489**
INDUSTRIE DER STEINE UND ERDEN. 6/yr. DM.98 (foreign DM.116). (Steinbruch Berufsgenossenschaft) Schlueterscher Verlagsanstalt GmbH und Co., Georgswall 4, Postfach 5440, 3000 Hannover 1, Germany. TEL 0511-1236-0. FAX 0511-1236400. circ. 10,095.

622 — **FR**
TN2 — **CODEN: INMNCA**
INDUSTRIE MINERALE MINES ET CARRIERES. 1855. m. 663.65 F. (foreign 885 F.). Societe de l'Industrie Minerale Mines et Carrieres, 41, rue de la Grange aux Belles, 75010 Paris, France. TEL 42-02-07-92. FAX 42-06-69-30. Ed.Bd. adv.; bk.rev.; abstr.; bibl.; charts; illus.; tr.lit.; index; circ. 4,300. **Indexed:** C.I.S. Abstr., Chem.Abstr., Copper Abstr., Eng.Ind., Excerp.Med., Fuel & Energy Abstr., Geotech.Abstr., INIS Atomind., Met.Abstr., World Alum.Abstr.
 Former titles: Industrie Minerale (ISSN 0302-2129); Revue de l'Industrie Minerale (ISSN 0035-1431)

549 — **FR** — **ISSN 0766-1207**
CODEN: INMTDT
INDUSTRIE MINERALE MINES ET CARRIERES. TECHNIQUES. (Text in French; summaries in English, French) 1972. 5/yr. 1633.60 F. per no. Societe de l'Industrie Minerale Mines et Carriers, 41, rue de la Grange aux Belles, 75010 Paris, France. Ed. Eric Massy-Delhotel. adv.; bibl.; charts; illus. **Indexed:** C.I.S. Abstr., Cadscan, Chem.Abstr, INIS Atomind., Lead Abstr., Met.Abstr., World Alum.Abstr., Zincscan.
 Former titles: Industrie Minerale. Techniques (ISSN 0240-9542); Industrie Minerale. Mineralurgie.

622 — **US**
INSTITUTE FOR BRIQUETTING AND AGGLOMERATION. PROCEEDINGS. s-a. Institute for Briquetting and Agglomeration, 179 Riverview Acres Rd., Hudson, WI 54016. TEL 715-549-6342.

622 — **SA** — **ISSN 0020-2983**
CODEN: JMSVAW
INSTITUTE OF MINE SURVEYORS OF SOUTH AFRICA. JOURNAL/INSTITUUT VAN MYNOPMETERS VAN SUID-AFRIKA. JOERNAAL. 1923. q. R.28. Institute of Mine Surveyors of South Africa, P.O. Box 27943, Yeoville 2143, South Africa. Ed. A.W. Harris. adv.; charts; illus.; index every vol. covering 8 issues; circ. 600. **Indexed:** Eng.Ind., Ind.S.A.Per.
 —BLDSC shelfmark: 4777.300000.

622 669 — **II** — **ISSN 0257-442X**
TN1
INSTITUTION OF ENGINEERS (INDIA). MINING ENGINEERING DIVISION. JOURNAL. (Text in English) 1920. 2/yr. Rs.40($5) Institution of Engineers (India), Mining Engineering Division, 8 Gokhale Rd., Calcutta 700 020, India. TEL 033-288334. FAX 033-288345. TELEX 0217885 IEIC IN. Ed. K.N. Majumdar. adv.; charts; illus.; index; circ. 3,000. **Indexed:** Chem.Abstr., Eng.Ind., Fluidex, INIS Atomind., Met.Abstr., Sci.Abstr.
 —BLDSC shelfmark: 4794.050000.
 Formerly (until 1984): Institution of Engineers (India). Mining and Metallurgy Division. Journal (ISSN 0020-3394)

622 669 — **UK** — **ISSN 0371-7844**
CODEN: TIMNAQ
INSTITUTION OF MINING AND METALLURGY. TRANSACTIONS. SECTION A: MINING INDUSTRY. 1892. 3/yr. £54 all three sections £137; all three sections plus Minerals Industry International £180. Institution of Mining and Metallurgy, 44 Portland Place, London W1N 4BR, England. TEL 01-580 3802. FAX 01-436-5388. TELEX 261416 IMM G. (U.S. address: I M M North American Publications Center, Old Post Rd., Broodkield, Vermont 05036) Ed. M.J. Jones. adv.; bibl.; charts; illus.; circ. 3,500. (reprint service avail. from OMP) **Indexed:** AESIS, Br.Geol.Lit., Br.Tech.Ind., Cadscan, Chem.Abstr., Copper Abstr., Energy.Info.Abstr., Eng.Ind., Environ.Abstr., Ergon.Abstr., Geo.Abstr., Lead Abstr., Met.Abstr., World Alum.Abstr., Zincscan.
 Formerly: Institution of Mining and Metallurgy. Bulletin and Transactions. Section A: Mining Industry.

622 669 550 — **UK** — **ISSN 0371-7453**
CODEN: TIAEA7
INSTITUTION OF MINING AND METALLURGY. TRANSACTIONS. SECTION B: APPLIED EARTH SCIENCES. 1892. 3/yr. £54 all three sections £137; all three sections plus Minerals Industry International £180. Institution of Mining and Metallurgy, 44 Portland Place, London W1N 4BR, England. TEL 01-580 3802. FAX 01-436-5388. TELEX 261410 IMM G. (U.S. addr.: I M M North American Publications Center, Old Post Rd., Brookfield, VT 05036) Ed. M.J. Jones. adv.; bibl.; charts; illus.; index; circ. 2,160. (reprint service avail. from OMP) **Indexed:** AESIS, Br.Geol.Lit., Br.Tech.Ind., Cadscan, Chem.Abstr., Chem.Eng.Abstr., Eng.Ind., Environ.Abstr., Ergon.Abstr., Geo.Abstr., Lead Abstr., Met.Abstr., Petrol.Abstr., World Alum.Abstr., Zincscan.
 Formerly: Institution of Mining and Metallurgy. Bulletin and Transactions. Section B: Applied Earth Sciences.

622 669 — **UK** — **ISSN 0371-9553**
CODEN: TMEMAB
INSTITUTION OF MINING AND METALLURGY. TRANSACTIONS. SECTION C: MINERAL PROCESSING & EXTRACTIVE METALLURGY. 1892. 3/yr. £54 all three sections £137; all three sections plus Minerals Industry International £180. Institution of Mining and Metallurgy, 44 Portland Place, London W1N 4BR, England. TEL 01-580 3802. FAX 01-436-5388. TELEX 261410 IMM G. (U.S. addr.: IMM North American Center, Old Post Rd., Brookfield, VT 05046) Ed. M.J. Jones. adv.; bibl.; charts; illus.; index; circ. 2,400. (reprint service avail. from OMP) **Indexed:** AESIS, Br.Geol.Lit., Br.Tech.Ind., Cadscan, Chem.Abstr., Chem.Eng.Abstr., Eng.Ind., Environ.Abstr., Ergon.Abstr., Lead Abstr., Met.Abstr., T.C.E.A., World Alum.Abstr., Zincscan.
 Formerly: Institution of Mining and Metallurgy. Bulletin and Transactions. Section C: Mineral Processing and Extractive Metallurgy.

622 382 — **US**
INTERNATIONAL COAL. a. $150 to individuals; institutions $95. National Coal Association, 1130 17th St., N.W., Washington, DC 20036. TEL 202-463-2640. **Indexed:** SRI.
 Formerly: World Coal Trade (ISSN 0084-148X)

MINES AND MINING INDUSTRY

622   UK   ISSN 0260-4299
INTERNATIONAL COAL REPORT. 1980. fortn. £559 (foreign £580). Financial Times Business Information Ltd., Tower House, Southampton St., London WC2E 7HA, England. TEL 071-240 9391. FAX 071-240-7946. TELEX 296926-BUSINF-G. Ed. Gerard McCloskey. bk.rev.; charts; stat. (back issues avail.) Indexed: Fluidex.
●Also available online. Vendor(s): Data-Star, Mead Data Central.
—BLDSC shelfmark: 4538.690000.
    Description: Provides news and analysis service for the coal industry, concentrating in price coverage for spot and contract.

622 338.2   US
INTERNATIONAL COAL REVIEW. bi-w. National Coal Association, 1130 17th St., N.W., Washington, DC 20036. TEL 202-463-2640.

INTERNATIONAL DREDGING REVIEW. see ENGINEERING — Hydraulic Engineering

622   UK
INTERNATIONAL GOLD MINING NEWSLETTER. 1974. m. £165($310) combined subscr. with International Quarterly. Mining Journal Ltd., 60 Worship St., London EC2A 2HD, England. TEL 071-377-2020. FAX 071-247-4100. TELEX 8952809-MINING-G. Ed. David Bird. circ. 750. (reprint service avail. from UMI)

INTERNATIONAL JOURNAL OF COAL GEOLOGY. see EARTH SCIENCES — Geology

622 669   NE   ISSN 0301-7516
TN500   CODEN: IJMPBL
INTERNATIONAL JOURNAL OF MINERAL PROCESSING. 1974. 12/yr. (in 3 vols.; 4 nos./vol.) fl.948 (effective 1992). Elsevier Science Publishers B.V., P.O. Box 211, 1000 AE Amsterdam, Netherlands. TEL 020-5803911. FAX 020-5803598. TELEX 18582 ESPA NL. (Subscr. in U.S. and Canada to: Elsevier Science Publishing Co., Inc. Box 882, Madison Sq. Sta., New York, NY 10159. TEL 212-989-5800) Ed.Bd. bk.rev.; bibl.; charts; illus. (also avail. in microform from RPI) Indexed: AESIS, Br.Ceram.Abstr., C.R.I. Abstr., Cadscan, Ceram.Abstr., Chem.Abstr., Curr.Cont., Fluidex, Fuel & Energy Abstr., Ind.Sci.Rev., Lead Abstr., Met.Abstr., Sci.Cit.Ind., Soils & Fert., World Alum.Abstr., Zincscan.
—BLDSC shelfmark: 4542.362000.
    Description: Covers all aspects of the processing of solid-mineral materials such as metallic and non-metallic ores, coals and other solid sources of secondary materials, etc.
    Refereed Serial

622.31   NE
INTERNATIONAL JOURNAL OF SURFACE MINING AND RECLAMATION. (Text in English) 1987. q. fl.125($70) A.A. Balkema, P.O. Box 1675, 3000 BR Rotterdam, Netherlands. TEL 010-4145822. FAX 010-4135947. Eds. R.K. Singhal, D.H. Graves.
    Formerly: International Journal of Surface Mining (ISSN 0920-8119).
    Description: Examines all aspects of surface mining technology and waste disposal systems relating to coals, oilsands, industrial minerals and metalliferous deposits. Includes computer applications and automation processes.

549   GW   ISSN 0074-7017
INTERNATIONAL MINERALOGICAL ASSOCIATION. PROCEEDINGS OF MEETINGS. (Proceedings usually published in host country) 1959. irreg. (every 4 yrs.) price varies. International Mineralogical Association, c/o Prof. Dr. S.S. Hafner, Institute of Mineralogy, Univ. of Marburg, Meerweinstr., 3550 Marburg, Germany. TELEX 482-372-UMR-D. adv. Indexed: Mineral.Abstr.

622   II   ISSN 0047-1003
INTERNATIONAL PRESS CUTTING SERVICE: MINES & MINERALS (COAL AND ORES). 1967. w. $65. International Press Cutting Service, Box 63, Allahabad 211001, India. Ed. N. Khanna. bk.rev.; index; circ. 1,200. (processed)

622   UK
INTERNATIONAL QUARTERLY. 1957. q. £165($310) combined subscription with International Gold Mining Newletter. Mining Journal Ltd., 60 Worship St., London EC2A 2HD, England. TEL 071-377-2020. FAX 071-247-4100. TELEX 8952809-MINING-G. Ed. David Bird. circ. 750. (reprint service avail. from UMI)
    Former titles: International Quarterly Review of South African Gold Shares; Quarterly Review of South African Gold Shares (ISSN 0143-3415)

622   IR   ISSN 0075-0514
IRANIAN MINERAL STATISTICS.* (Text in English and Persian) 1962. a. free. Ministry of Finance and Economic Affairs, Bureau of Statistics, Tehran, Iran.

IRON & STEELMAKER. see METALLURGY

ITOGI NAUKI I TEKHNIKI: GEOKHIMIYA - MINERALOGIYA - PETROGRAFIYA. see EARTH SCIENCES — Geology

549   RU   ISSN 0202-7437
ITOGI NAUKI I TEKHNIKI: OBOGASHCHENIE POLEZNYKH ISKOPAEMYKH. irreg., vol.23, 1989. 3.30 Rub. Vsesoyuznyi Institut Nauchno-Tekhnicheskoi Informatsii (VINITI), Baltiiskaya ul. 14, Moscow A-219, Russia. (Subscr. to: Mezhdunarodnaya Kniga, Dimitrova ul. 39, 113095 Moscow, Russia)
—BLDSC shelfmark: 0126.641000.

622   RU   ISSN 0202-7410
ITOGI NAUKI I TEKHNIKI: RAZRABOTKA MESTOROZHDENII TVERDYKH POLEZNYKH ISKOPAEMYKH. (Text in Russian) 1968. irreg., vols.44-46, 1989. price varies. Vsesoyuznyi Institut Nauchno-Tekhnicheskoi Informatsii (VINITI), Baltiiskaya ul. 14, Moscow A-219, Russia. (Subscr. to: Mezhdunarodnaya Kniga, Dimitrova ul. 39, 113095 Moscow, Russia)
—BLDSC shelfmark: 0140.230000.

622   RU   ISSN 0202-7380
TN263
ITOGI NAUKI I TEKHNIKI: RUDNYE MESTOROZHDENIYA. (Text in Russian) 1967. irreg., vols.18-20, 1988. price varies. Vsesoyuznyi Institut Nauchno-Tekhnicheskoi Informatsii (VINITI), Baltiiskaya ul. 14, Moscow A-219, Russia. (Subscr. to: Mezhdunarodnaya Kniga, Dimitrova ul. 39, 113095 Moscow, Russia)
—BLDSC shelfmark: 0154.095000.

556 338.2   IV
IVORY COAST. DIRECTION DES MINES ET DE LA GEOLOGIE. RAPPORT PROVISOIRE SUR LES ACTIVITIES DU SECTEUR. irreg. Direction des Mines et de la Geologie, c/o Ministry of Mining, BP V50, Abidjan, Ivory Coast. Indexed: GeoRef.

IZVESTIYA VYSSHIKH UCHEBNYKH ZAVEDENII. SERIYA GEOLOGIYA I RAZVEDKA. see EARTH SCIENCES — Geology

622   JM   ISSN 0254-5241
J B I JOURNAL. (Text in English, Spanish) 1980. a. $12.50 to individuals; institutions $20. Jamaica Bauxite Institute, Hope Gardens, P.O. Box 355, Kingston 6, Jamaica, W.I. TEL 809-92-72073. FAX 809-92-71159. TELEX 2309 JAMBAUX JA. Ed.Bd. adv.; bk.rev.; circ. 300. Indexed: Met.Abstr., World Alum.Abstr.
    Supersedes (1976-1979): J B I Digest.
    Description: Contains original socio-economic, legal and technical articles, highlighting development issues as they affect the Third World, with special reference to aluminium but not excluding other mineral industries.

622   GW
JAHRBUCH FUER BERGBAU, ENERGIE, MINERALOEL UND CHEMIE. 1893. a. DM.138. Verlag Glueckauf GmbH, Franz-Fischer-Weg 61, Postfach 103945, 4300 Essen 1, Germany. FAX 0201-293630. adv. Indexed: GeoRef.
    Formerly: Jahrbuch des Deutschen Bergbaus.

338.7   II   ISSN 0304-7164
HD9506.I44
JAMMU & KASHMIR MINERALS LIMITED. ANNUAL REPORT. (Text in English) a. Jammu & Kashmir Minerals Limited, Srinagar, India. Key Title: Annual Report - Jammu & Kashmir Minerals Limited.

JAPAN METAL BULLETIN. see METALLURGY

JEWELRY MAKING, GEMS AND MINERALS; gems, gem cutting, minerals, silverwork, geology. see HOBBIES

622   AT   ISSN 0075-3777
JOBSON'S MINING YEAR BOOK. 1957. a. Aus.$275. Dun & Bradstreet (Australia) Pty. Ltd., 470 St. Kilda Rd., Melbourne, Vic. 3000, Australia. TEL 03-828-3333. FAX 03-828-3300. adv.; circ. 6,000.
    Description: Covers the mining of minerals and petroleum, listed on Australian and New Zealand stock exchange.

JOBSON'S QUARTERLY. see BUSINESS AND ECONOMICS — Investments

338.2   US
JOHANNESBURG GOLD & METAL MINING ADVISOR.* 1980. m. $225. Johannesburg Publications USA, Inc., 503 Sharpsburg Cir., Birmingham, AL 35213. Ed. Brendan Ryan.
    Description: Analysis of South African gold and strategic metals mines, using present value analysis and computer generated financial forecasts.

622   DK
JOINT COMMITTEE ON MINERAL RESOURCES IN GREENLAND. ANNUAL REPORT. Eskimo edition: Kalatdlitnunane Augtitagssanik Atortugssiagssiat Pivdlugit. Faellesraadet Naluaerut. (Text in Danish and Greenlandic) 1980. a. free. Energiministeriet, Raastofforvaltningen for Groenland - Ministry of Energy, c/o Mineral Resources Administration for Greenland, Slotsholmsgade 1, 1216 Copenhagen K, Denmark. TEL 45-33 02 75 00. FAX 45-1-133017. TELEX 15505 ENRGY DK.
    Formerly: Faellesraadet Vedroerende Mineraliske Raastoffer i Groenland. Beretning (ISSN 0107-3117)
    Description: Deals with the questions concerning mineral resources in Greenland which have been discussed by the Committee during the reporting period.

JOURNAL DU MINEUR. see LABOR UNIONS

JOURNAL OF APPLIED GEOPHYSICS. see EARTH SCIENCES — Geophysics

622.33   US
JOURNAL OF COAL QUALITY. q. Center for Coal Science, 313 T C N W, Western Kentucky University, Bowling Green, KY 42101. TEL 502-745-6244. Ed. George Vourvopoulos. circ. 4,000.

JOURNAL OF MINERALOGY, PETROLOGY AND ECONOMIC GEOLOGY. see EARTH SCIENCES — Geology

622 338.2 662   II   ISSN 0022-2755
TN1   CODEN: JMMFAM
JOURNAL OF MINES, METALS AND FUELS. 1953. m. $48. Books & Journals Private Ltd., 6-2 Madan St., Calcutta 700 072, India. Ed. A.K. Ghose. adv.; bk.rev.; charts; illus.; tr.lit.; circ. 2,761. Indexed: AESIS, C.I.S. Abstr., C.R.I. Abstr., Chem.Abstr., Eng.Ind., Fuel & Energy Abstr., GeoRef.

622   GW
KALI UND STEINSALZ. 1952. 3/yr. DM.49.50. Verlag Glueckauf GmbH, Postfach 103945, 4300 Essen 1, Germany. TEL 0201-1051. FAX 0201-293630. Ed. Otto Lenz. bk.rev.; circ. 700. (back issues avail.)

622.33   CC   ISSN 1001-3946
KANCHA KEXUE JISHU/SCIENCE AND TECHNOLOGY OF PROSPECTING. (Text in Chinese) bi-m. Yejin Gongye Bu, Kancha Kexue Jishu Yanjiusuo - Ministry of Metallurgic Industry, Institute of Prospecting Science and Technology, 51 Dongfeng Zhonglu, Baoding, Hebei 071067, People's Republic of China. TEL 36001. Ed. Chen Tingzhang.

KEMISK ANALYSE AF MINERALER OG BJERGARTER. see CHEMISTRY

KEYSTONE COAL INDUSTRY MANUAL. see BUSINESS AND ECONOMICS — Trade And Industrial Directories

622   US
KEYSTONE NEWS BULLETIN. m. $120. Maclean Hunter Publishing Company, Mining Information Services, 29 N. Wacker Dr., Chicago, IL 60606. stat.; circ. 600.
    Description: Explores coal mining and resources.

622.33   US
KING'S COAL EXPORT REPORT. 1984. w. $547. King Publishing Co., Box 52210, Knoxville, TN 37950. TEL 615-584-6294. (back issues avail.)
Formerly: King's Coal Export Week (ISSN 0749-0658)
Description: Ship-by-ship listing all coal and petcoke exports from U.S. ports.

622.33 531.64   US
KING'S COALSTATS. 1987. m. $495 print ed.; floppy disk $1500. King Publishing Co., Box 52210, Knoxville, TN 37950. TEL 615-584-6294. (also avail. in magnetic tape; avail. on floppy disk)

622   US   ISSN 0749-9043
KING'S INTERNATIONAL COAL TRADE. 1984. w. $710. King Publishing Co., Box 52210, Knoxville, TN 37950. TEL 615-584-6294. (back issues avail.)
Description: Ship-by-ship listing of grain exports from the U.S. Gulf.

622.33   US   ISSN 0749-1719
KING'S NORTHERN COAL. 1980. w. $547. King Publishing Co., Box 52210, Knoxville, TN 37950. TEL 615-584-6294. (back issues avail.)
Description: Marketing report for the coal industry with emphasis on northeastern states.

622.33   US   ISSN 0749-1697
KING'S SOUTHERN COAL. 1980. w. $547. King Publishing Co., Box 52210, Knoxville, TN 37950. TEL 615-584-6294. (back issues avail.)
Description: Market report for the coal mining industry with emphasis on southern states.

622.33   US   ISSN 0749-1700
KING'S WESTERN COAL. 1983. w. $547. King Publishing Co., Box 52210, Knoxville, TN 37950. TEL 615-584-6294. (back issues avail.)
Description: Market report for the coal industry with an emphasis on western states.

622   GW   ISSN 0023-2742
KOHLE UND HEIZOEL; Fachblatt fuer den Handel. 1948. m. DM.31.60. Verlag Dr. Hoffmann KG, Tullastr. 18, Postfach 2545, 6800 Mannheim, Germany. Ed. Gerhard Sindermann. adv.; bk.rev.; bibl.; illus.; mkt.; circ. 4,000. **Indexed:** INIS Atomind.
Formerly: K W Z Kohlenwirtschaftszeitung.

662   PL   ISSN 0023-2823
TP315   **CODEN:** KSMGAA
KOKS, SMOLA, GAZ. (Text in Polish; summaries in various languages) 1956. m. $23.40. Wydawnictwo "Slask", Al. W. Korfantego 51, 40-161 Katowice, Poland. TEL 022-583221. TELEX 312326. (Dist. by: Ars Polona- Ruch, Krakowskie Przedmiescie 7, Warsaw, Poland) Ed. Henryk Zielinski. bk.rev.; circ. 1,100. **Indexed:** Chem.Abstr., Fuel & Energy Abstr., INIS Atomind.
—BLDSC shelfmark: 5101.700000.

KOMPASS; Zeitschrift fuer Sozialversicherung im Bergbau. see *INSURANCE*

KONINKLIJK NEDERLANDS GEOLOGISCH MIJNBOUWKUNDIG GENOOTSCHAP. VERHANDELINGEN. see *EARTH SCIENCES — Geology*

622.33 526.3   CC   ISSN 1001-358X
KUANGSHAN CELIANG/MINE PROSPECTING. (Text in Chinese) q. Meitan Kexueyuan, Tangshan Fenyuan - Coal Science Institute, Tangshan Branch, Xinhua Xidao, Tangshan, Hebei 063012, People's Republic of China. TEL 22145. Ed. Cui Jixian.

622.33 551   CC   ISSN 1001-5892
KUANGSHAN DIZHI. (Text in Chinese) q. Zhongguo Dizhi Xuehui, Kuangshan Dizhi Zhuanye Weiyuanhui, Sanlidian, Guilin, Guangxi 541004, People's Republic of China. TEL 444987.

622.33   CC   ISSN 1001-5809
KUANGSHAN JISHU/MINING TECHNOLOGY. (Text in Chinese) bi-m. Yejin Bu, Anshan Heise Yejin Kuangshan Sheji Yanjiusuo, Anshan, Liaoning 114002, People's Republic of China. TEL 537630. Ed. Qian Zhanxun.

KYOTO UNIVERSITY. FACULTY OF SCIENCE. MEMOIRS. SERIES OF GEOLOGY AND MINERALOGY. see *EARTH SCIENCES — Geology*

622   LB
LAMCO NEWS.* 1966. q. free. Lamco J.V. Operating Company, Box 69, Monrovia, Liberia. Ed. Louis A. Wah. circ. 5,600.

LAND AND MINERALS SURVEYING. see *ENGINEERING — Civil Engineering*

LANDESMUSEUM JOANNEUM. ABTEILUNG FUER GEOLOGIE UND PALAEONTOLOGIE. MITTEILUNGEN. see *PALEONTOLOGY*

549   GW   ISSN 0176-1285
LAPIS; die aktuelle Monatsschrift fuer Liebhaber und Sammler von Mineralien und Edelsteinen. 1976. m. DM.92.40. Christian Weise Verlag GmbH, Oberanger 6, 8000 Munich 2, Germany. TEL 089-2604018. FAX 089-2603499. Ed. Christian Weise. adv.; bk.rev.; index; circ. 15,000. (back issues avail.)
—BLDSC shelfmark: 5786.145000.
Description: Covers mineralogy, gemology and mining for collectors and dealers of minerals and gems.

300   UK   ISSN 0959-8219
LATIN AMERICAN MINING LETTER. 1982. s-m. £360($680) M I I D A Ltd., P.O. BOx 2137, London NW10 6TN, England. TEL 081-961-7407. FAX 081-961-7487. Ed. Michael Wood. bk.rev.; circ. 200.
Description: News and analysis of the metal and mineral industry of South and Central America and the Carribean.

622   CL
▼**LATINOMINERIA.** 1991. 4/yr. $20 (free to qualified personnel). G & T International, Perez Valenzuela 1098, Oficina 98 - Providencia, Santiago 09, Chile. TEL 562-225-3275. FAX 562-242-6939. Ed. Ricardo Cortes. adv.: B&W page $2700, color $3400; trim 275 x 205. charts; illus.; circ. 10,000.

622 351.823   US
▼**LEGAL QUARTERLY DIGEST OF MINE SAFETY AND HEALTH DECISIONS.** 1990. q. $295 (foreign $310). Pasha Publications Inc., 1401 Wilson Blvd., Ste. 900, Arlington, VA 22209-9970. TEL 703-528-1244. FAX 703-528-1253. Ed. Ellen Smith. index.
Description: Summarizes legal decisions, mine safety issues and health cases.

622   AU   ISSN 0259-0751
LEOBENER GRUENE HEFTE. NEUE FOLGE. irreg., no.9, 1989. price varies. (Montanhistorischer Verein fuer Oesterreich) Verband der Wissenschaftlichen Gesellschaften Oesterreichs, Lindengasse 37, A-1070 Vienna, Austria. TEL 932166.

LETTRE AFRIQUE ENERGIES. see *PETROLEUM AND GAS*

LIBERIA. MINISTRY OF LANDS, MINES AND ENERGY. ANNUAL REPORT. see *ENGINEERING — Civil Engineering*

LIGHT RAILWAY NEWS. see *TRANSPORTATION — Railroads*

LIGHT RAILWAYS. see *TRANSPORTATION — Railroads*

LITHOLOGY AND MINERAL RESOURCES. see *EARTH SCIENCES — Geology*

LITHOS; an international journal of mineralogy, petrology, and geochemistry. see *EARTH SCIENCES — Geology*

552 622   RU   ISSN 0024-497X
    CODEN: LPIKAQ
LITOLOGIYA I POLEZNYE ISKOPAEMYE. 1963. bi-m. 33.30 Rub. (Akademiya Nauk S.S.S.R., Otdelenie Nauk o Zemle) Izdatel'stvo Nauka, 90 Profsoyuznaya ul., 117864 Moscow, Russia. Ed. N.M. Strakhov. bk.rev.; bibl. (tabloid format) **Indexed:** Chem.Abstr., GeoRef., INIS Atomind.
—BLDSC shelfmark: 0098.250000.

622.184   US
LOCATING GOLD, GEMS, & MINERALS; the prospector's guide. 1947. bi-m. $6. United Prospectors Inc., 166 West H St., Benicia, CA 94510. Ed. Walter J. Price. adv.; circ. 200.
Former titles: Locating Gold (ISSN 0024-5658) & Panning Gold.

LOUISIANA STATE UNIVERSITY. LAW SCHOOL. INSTITUTE ON MINERAL LAW. PROCEEDINGS. see *LAW*

622   AT
M I M A G. 1948. 3/yr. free. M.I.M. Holdings Ltd., 410 Ann Street, Brisbane, Q'ld 4000, Australia. FAX 617-839-4009. Ed. K. Moore. circ. 12,000. (back issues avail.)
Description: Includes a blend of information on current activities and initiatives by the company, information about the metals it produces and their downstream uses as well as a variety of historical and feature articles.

338.2   II   ISSN 0377-1482
HD9506.I4
M M T C NEWS. (Text in English) 1973. q. free. Minerals and Metals Trading Corp. of India Ltd., 9 - 10 Bahadur Shah Zafar Marg, New Delhi, India. Ed. Preeti Chaturvedi. illus.; circ. 6,000.

622   SA
M S O A BULLETIN. (Text in Afrikaans, English) 1919. bi-m. R.50. Mine Surface Officials' Association of South Africa, 41 Biccard St., Braamfontein, Johannesburg, South Africa. FAX 011-403-2449. Ed. R.H. Botha. adv.; circ. 16,000.
Formerly: M S O A Journal (ISSN 0024-8428)

669   TU   ISSN 0024-9416
    CODEN: MDCKAP
MADENCILIK; maden muhendisleri odasi dergisi. (Text in Turkish; summaries in English, French, German) 1961. q. TL.60000($20) Turk Muhendis ve Mimar Odalari Birligi, Maden Muhendisleri Odasi - Union of Chambers of Engineers and Architects of Turkey, Chamber of Mining Engineers, Selanik Cad. 19-3, 06650 Ankara, Turkey. TEL 4-1251080. FAX 4-1175290. Ed. Fikret Ozbilgin. adv.; bk.rev.; abstr.; bibl.; charts; illus.; stat.; index; circ. 5,000 (controlled). (processed) **Indexed:** Chem.Abstr.
Description: Addresses technological development, working conditions and safety, mineral processing and more. Evaluates different methods and practices in production.

338.2   MY
MALAYSIAN CHAMBER OF MINES. COUNCIL REPORT. (Text in English) a. Malaysian Chamber of Mines, 8th Fl., West Block, Wisma Selanger Dredging, Jalan Ampang, P.O. Box 12560, 50782 Kuala Lumpur, Malaysia. TEL 03-2616171. FAX 03-2616179.
Formerly: States of Malaya Chamber of Mines. Council Report (ISSN 0302-6620)

338.2   MY
MALAYSIAN CHAMBER OF MINES. YEARBOOK. 1966. a. M.$10. Malaysian Chamber of Mines, 8th Fl., West Block, Wisma Selanger Dredging, Jalan Ampang, P.O. Box 12560, 50782 Kuala Lumpur, Malaysia. TEL 03-2616171. FAX 03-2616179. stat.
Formerly: States of Malaya Chamber of Mines. Yearbook.

MANITOBA. ENERGY AND MINES. ANNUAL REPORT SERIES. see *ENERGY*

MANITOBA ENERGY AND MINES. GEOLOGICAL REPORT. see *EARTH SCIENCES — Geology*

549   US   ISSN 0149-0397
TN291.5   **CODEN:** MARMDK
MARINE MINING; the journal of seafloor minerals exploration, assessment and ore processing. 1977. q. $121. Taylor & Francis, 1900 Frost Rd., Ste. 101, Bristol, PA 19007. TEL 215-785-5800. FAX 215-785-5515. Ed. J. Robert Moore. adv.; bk.rev.; abstr.; charts; index. **Indexed:** AESIS, Appl.Mech.Rev., Biol.Abstr., Chem.Abstr., Curr.Tit.Ocean, Deep Sea Res.& Oceanogr.Abstr., Eng.Ind., Environ.Abstr., Fluidex, Geo.Abstr., GeoRef., I.M.M.Abstr., Petrol.Abstr., Sci.Cit.Ind.
—BLDSC shelfmark: 5376.430000.
Description: Provides current studies on marine minerals exploration and marine mining in general, recovery and processing of ore.
Refereed Serial

622   US
MARION MILITARY INSTITUTE BULLETIN. 1904. q. Marion Military Institute, Box 420, Marion, AL 36756. TEL 205-683-9894. Ed. John K. Bibler. circ. 10,000.

MINES AND MINING INDUSTRY

622 GW
DAS MARKSCHEIDEWESEN; Fachzeitschrift fuer Lagerstaettenbearbeitung, Bergvermessung, Bergbauplanung und Raumordnung, Bergschadenkund. q. DM.116. Verlag Glueckauf GmbH, Postfach 103945, 4300 Essen 1, Germany. FAX 0201-293630. **Indexed:** INIS Atomind.

622 IT
MARMOMACCHINE. (Text in Italian; summaries in English) 1972. bi-m. free. (Assomarmi) Editrice Marmomachine di Baldini & Marabelli, C.P. 1008, Milan, Italy. (Subscr. to: Via Cenisio 50, 20154 Milan, Italy) (Co-sponsors: Assodiam e Acimm; Assofom e Assolame) Ed. Angelo Marabelli. adv.; circ. 15,000.

MATERIALS AND COMPONENTS IN FOSSIL ENERGY APPLICATIONS. see *ENERGY*

622 PL ISSN 0208-7448
TN345
MECHANIZACJA I AUTOMATYZACJA GORNICTWA; czasopismo naukowo-techniczne. (Text in Polish; summaries in English, Russian) 1962. m. 166800 Zl. Przedsiebiorstwo Obslugi Gornictwa - POMAG, A.W. Korfantego 83a, 40-161 Katowice, Poland. TEL 48-32-598-011. (Co-sponsor: Panstwowa Agencja Wegla Kamiennego) (back issues avail.)
Description: Covers electrical engineering and automation in mines.

MEITAN JINGJI YANJIU/COAL ECONOMICS STUDY. see *BUSINESS AND ECONOMICS*

622.33 CC ISSN 0253-9993
CODEN: MTHPDA
MEITAN XUEBAO/CHINA COAL SOCIETY. JOURNAL. (Text in Chinese) 1964. q. $3.80 per no. Zhongguo Meitan Xuehui - China Coal Society, Hepingli, Beijing 100013, People's Republic of China. TEL 4214931. Ed. Zhao Hongqiu. **Indexed:** Chem.Abstr.

MEMOIRES POUR SERVIR A L'EXPLICATION DES CARTES GEOLOGIQUES ET MINIERES DE LA BELGIQUE. see *EARTH SCIENCES — Geology*

622 US
METAL MINING: LATIN AMERICAN INDUSTRIAL REPORT. (Avail. for each of 20 Latin American countries) 1985. a. $235 per country report. Aquino Productions, Box 15760, Stamford, CT 06901. TEL 203-325-3138. Ed. Andres C. Aquino.

338.2 CN
METAL RESOURCES CIRCULAR. 1975. irreg. free. Ministry of Northern Development and Mines, 56 Wellesley St. W., 2nd fl., Toronto, Ont. M7A 1G2, Canada. TEL 416-965-1311. FAX 416-965-2851. Ed. G. Anders.

622 699 US
METALS ALERT. (Telex service) d. $6000. McGraw-Hill, Inc., 1221 Ave. of the Americas, New York, NY 10020. TEL 212-521-2000.

669 549 II ISSN 0026-0959
TN600 CODEN: MEMRAZ
METALS AND MINERALS REVIEW. (Text in English) 1961. m. Rs.150. L. K. Pandeya, Ed. & Pub., 105-C Block F, New Alipore, Calcutta 700053, India. **Indexed:** Chem.Abstr., GeoRef.
Description: Highlights mining, metallurgy, geology and fuel technology.

622 CN
METALS ECONOMICS GROUP STRATEGIC REPORT. bi-m. Metals Economics Group, 2000 Barrington St., Rm. 804, Halifax, N.S. B3J 3C4, Canada. TEL 902-429-2880. FAX 902-429-6593. Ed. Marilyn Wegener.

622 338.2 US ISSN 0026-0975
METALS WEEK. 1930. w. $770 (foreign $825). McGraw-Hill, Inc., Commodity Services Group, 1221 Avenue of the Americas, 42nd Fl., New York, NY 10020. TEL 212-512-2000. Ed. Ken Jacobson. mkt.; stat. (also avail. in microform from UMI) **Indexed:** Cadscan, Lead Abstr., Zincscan.
●Also available online. Vendor(s): DIALOG (File no.624/McGRAW-HILL PUBLICATIONS ONLINE), Dow Jones/News Retrieval (MW), Mead Data Central (METLWK).
Formerly: E-MJ Metal and Mineral Markets (Engineering and Mining Journal).

622 669 US
METALS WEEK INSIDER REPORT. (Telex service) 1973. d. price varies. McGraw-Hill, Inc., 1221 Ave. of the Americas, New York, NY 10020. Ed. A. Patrick Ryan.

622 669 US
METALS WEEK PRICE NOTIFICATION SERVICE. (Telex service) d., w., and m. price varies. McGraw-Hill, Inc., 1221 Ave. of the Americas, New York, NY 10020. TEL 212-521-2000.

622 UK ISSN 0369-1632
CODEN: MQRYAT
MINE AND QUARRY. 1924. m. £35 (foreign £70). Landscape Publishing LTd., Blair House, 184 High St., Toubridge Kent TN9 1BQ, England. TEL 0732-359-990. FAX 0732-770-049. Ed. Kim Burridge. adv.; bk.rev.; abstr.; charts; illus.; stat.; circ. 4,194. (reprint service avail. from UMI) **Indexed:** AESIS, Br.Geol.Lit., Br.Tech.Ind., C.I.S. Abstr., Chem.Abstr., Eng.Ind, Excerp.Med., Fluidex, Fuel & Energy Abstr., GeoRef., W.R.C.Inf.
—BLDSC shelfmark: 5775.800000.
Formerly: Mining and Minerals Engineering (ISSN 0026-5152)
Description: Explores equipment, technical articles, people, industry and company news, and project reports.

622 US
MINE & QUARRY TRADER; merchandising everything for the mining and quarry industries. 1976. m. free. Allied Publications, 7355 N. Woodland, Box 603, Indianapolis, IN 46206-0603. TEL 317-297-5500. FAX 317-299-1356. circ. 20,000.

MINE, PETROL SI GAZE. see *PETROLEUM AND GAS*

622.8 613.62 US ISSN 1040-8223
MINE REGULATION REPORTER. 1983. fortn. $725 (foreign $755). Pasha Publications Inc., 1401 Wilson Blvd., Ste. 900, Arlington, VA 22209-9970. TEL 703-528-1244. FAX 703-528-1253. Ed. Ellen Smith. index. (looseleaf format)
Formerly: Surface Mining Reporter (ISSN 0739-4020)
Description: Covers mining regulation agencies, new regulations, administrative law decisions, with analysis of recent decisions and appeals.

051 US
MINE RUN. 1979. q. Amax Coal Industries, 251 N. Illinois St., Box 6106, Indianapolis, IN 45206-6106. TEL 317-266-1500. FAX 317-266-1527. Ed. Julie L. Lewis. circ. 5,000.
Description: News and features about the company and its employees.

622 SA ISSN 0026-4504
MINE VENTILATION SOCIETY OF SOUTH AFRICA. JOURNAL. (Text in Afrikaans and English) 1948. m. R.310 (effective 1991). Mine Ventilation Society of South Africa, P.O. Box 93480, Yeoville, Johannesburg 2143, South Africa.
TEL 011-487-1049. FAX 011-648-1876. Ed. A.W. Nicoll. adv.; bk.rev.; index, cum.index every 10 yrs.; circ. 1,250. (also avail. in microform from UMI; back issues avail.; reprint service avail. from UMI) **Indexed:** C.I.S. Abstr., Eng.Ind., Fluidex, Fuel & Energy Abstr., Ind.S.A.Per., INIS Atomind.
—BLDSC shelfmark: 4826.500000.

622 AT
MINER NEWSPAPER. 1977. m. Aus.$65. Peter Isaacson Publications Pty. Ltd., 45-50 Porter St., Prahran, Vic. 3181, Australia. TEL 03-520-5555. FAX 03-521-3647. Ed. Julian Malnic. adv.; bk.rev.; circ. 5,237. (back issues avail.) **Indexed:** AESIS.
Formerly: Miner Magazine.

669 BL ISSN 0026-4520
MINERACAO METALURGIA. 1936. m. $60. (Mineracao Metalurgia) Editora Scorpio Ltda., Rua do Catete, 202, Grupo 301, CEP 22.220 Rio de Janeiro, RJ, Brazil. FAX 205-0648. Ed. Wilson Costa. adv.; bibl.; charts; illus.; stat.; circ. 15,000. **Indexed:** Chem.Abstr., GeoRef., Met.Abstr., World Alum.Abstr.

549 AT
MINERAL FACTS. 1979. irreg. Australian Mining Industry Council, Box 363, Dickson, A.C.T. 2602, Australia. FAX 61-6-279-3699.
Description: Provides vital data on mines and the mining industry in Australia.

622 AT ISSN 0313-6086
TN122.S7
MINERAL INDUSTRY QUARTERLY. 1976. q. free. Department of Mines and Energy, P.O. Box 151, Eastwood, S.A. 5063, Australia. FAX 08-272-7597. cum.index: vols.1-48. (back issues avail.) **Indexed:** AESIS, Eng.Ind., GeoRef.
—BLDSC shelfmark: 5778.150000.
Description: Current information and news items on all aspects of the South Australian mineral industry.

MINERAL INDUSTRY SURVEYS. ALUMINUM INDUSTRY. see *MINES AND MINING INDUSTRY — Abstracting, Bibliographies, Statistics*

340 622 US
MINERAL LAW NEWSLETTER. 1984. 4/yr. $60. Rocky Mountain Mineral Law Foundation, Porter Administration Bldg., 7039 E. 18th Ave., Denver, CO 80220. TEL 303-321-8100. FAX 303-321-7657. Eds. John S. Lowe, Mark J. Squillace. circ. 600.

553 II ISSN 0379-5187
MINERAL RESEARCH.* (Text in English) s-a. Rs.6. Directorate of Geology, Mining, and Groundwater Development, Old Secretariat Building, Nagpur, Maharashtra, India. illus. **Indexed:** GeoRef.

549 TU ISSN 0026-4563
HD9506.A1 CODEN: BMRXAD
MINERAL RESEARCH AND EXPLORATION INSTITUTE OF TURKEY. BULLETIN. (Editions in English and Turkish) 1953. s-a. TL.20($30) General Directorate of Mineral and Exploration, Ankara, Turkey. TEL 287-34-30. FAX 222-82-78. TELEX 42741-42040 MTATR. Eds. Ismail Seyhan, Ibrahim Selvi. circ. 1,500. **Indexed:** Biol.Abstr.

MINERAL REVIEW. see *EARTH SCIENCES — Geology*

MINERAL STATISTICS OF INDIA. see *MINES AND MINING INDUSTRY — Abstracting, Bibliographies, Statistics*

622 II ISSN 0026-4571
TN1 CODEN: MIWEA6
MINERAL WEALTH. (Text in English or Gujarati) 1965. s-a. Rs.10.10. Directorate of Geology and Mining, 0-1 New Mental Hospital Bldg., Aswara, Ahmedabad 16, India. Ed. Shri J.V. Bhatt. adv.; circ. 500. **Indexed:** Chem.Abstr., GeoRef.

622 CL ISSN 0026-458X
TN43 CODEN: MINCAN
MINERALES. (Text in Spanish; abstracts in English) 1945. q. $30. Instituto de Ingenieros de Minas de Chile, Casilla 14668, Correo 21, Santiago, Chile. Ed. Manuel Echeverria R. adv.; bk.rev.; illus.; circ. 1,000. **Indexed:** Chem.Abstr., Fluidex, GeoRef.
—BLDSC shelfmark: 5786.000000.

549 CS ISSN 0369-2086
MINERALIA SLOVACA. (Text in Czech and Slovak; abstracts and summaries in English) 1969. bi-m. 226 Kcs.($92) (Geological Research Spisska Nova Ves) Alfa, Hurbanovo nam. 3, 815 89 Bratislava, Czechoslovakia. Ed. Pavol Grecula. **Indexed:** Chem.Abstr.
—BLDSC shelfmark: 5786.100000.

549 GW ISSN 0939-6640
▼**MINERALIEN WELT**; Magazin fuer das Sammeln Schoener Steine. 1990. bi-m. DM.66. Doris Bode Verlag GmbH, Duernberg 2, 4358 Haltern 4, Germany. TEL 02364-16107.
FAX 02364-169273. Ed. Rainer Bode. circ. 4,700.

MINERALIUM DEPOSITA; international journal of geology, mineralogy, and geochemistry of mineral deposits. see *EARTH SCIENCES — Geology*

549 PL ISSN 0032-6267
QE381.P6 CODEN: MNLPBK
MINERALOGIA POLONICA. (Text in English; summaries in Polish and Russian) 1970. q. membership. Polskie Towarzystwo Mineralogiczne, Al. Mickiewicza 30, Krakow, Poland. Ed. Dr. Witold Zabinski. charts; illus.; index. **Indexed:** Chem.Abstr., GeoRef., Mineral.Abstr.

MINES AND MINING INDUSTRY 3489

549 JA ISSN 0544-2540
QE351 CODEN: MJTOAS
MINERALOGICAL JOURNAL. (Text in English) 1953. q. $43. (Mineralogical Society of Japan) Japan Scientific Societies Press, 6-2-10 Hongo, Bunkyo-ku, Tokyo 113, Japan. TEL 3814-2001. FAX 3814-2002. TELEX 2722268 BCJSP J. (Dist. by: Business Center for Academic Societies Japan, Koshin Bldg., 6-16-3 Hongo, Bunkyo-ku, Tokyo 113, Japan; Dist. in U.S. by: International Specialized Book Services, Inc., 5602 N.E. Hassalo St., Portland, OR 97213; in Asia by: Toppan Company Pvt. Ltd., 38 Liu Fang Rd., Box 22 Jurong Town, Jurong, Singapore 2262) adv.; bk.rev.; abstr.; circ. 800. **Indexed:** Chem.Abstr., GeoRef., Mineral.Abstr.
—BLDSC shelfmark: 5787.000000.

549 UK ISSN 0026-461X
QE351 CODEN: MNLMBB
MINERALOGICAL MAGAZINE. 1876. q. £114($205) Mineralogical Society, 41 Queen's Gate, London SW7 5HR, England. TEL 01-584 7516. FAX 071-823-8021. Ed. A.M. Clark. adv.; bk.rev.; charts; illus.; index; circ. 2,000. (also avail. in microfiche from BHP) **Indexed:** AESIS, Br.Ceram.Abstr., Br.Geol.Lit., Cadscan, Chem.Abstr, Curr.Cont., Deep Sea Res.& Oceanogr.Abstr., Fuel & Energy Abstr., Geo.Abstr., GeoRef., Ind.Sci.Rev., Lead Abstr., Zincscan.
—BLDSC shelfmark: 5788.000000.

549 KR ISSN 0204-3548
QE351 CODEN: MINZDR
MINERALOGICHESKII ZHURNAL; vsesoyuznyi nauchno-teoreticheskii zhurnal. (Text in Russian; summaries in English, Russian) 1979. bi-m. 7.20 Rub. (Akademiya Nauk Ukrainskoi S.S.R., Otdelenie Geologii, Geofiziki i Geokhimii) Izdatel'stvo Naukova Dumka, c/o Yu.A. Khramov, Dir, Ul. Repina, 3, Kiev 252 601, Ukraine. TEL 444-02-42. (Subscr. to: Mezhdunarodnaya Kniga, Moscow, G-200, Russia) (Co-sponsor: Akademiya Nauk S.S.S.R.) Ed. N.P. Shcherbak. **Indexed:** Chem.Abstr., GeoRef.
—BLDSC shelfmark: 0115.340000.
Formerly: Regional'naya i Geneticheskaya Mineralogiya i Konstitutsiya i Svoystva Mineralov.

549 552 AU ISSN 0930-0708
QE351 CODEN: MIPEE9
MINERALOGY AND PETROLOGY. 1872. irreg. DM.650($417) Springer-Verlag, Sachsenplatz 4-6, Postfach 89, A-1201 Vienna, Austria. TEL 0222-3302415-0-0. FAX 0222-3302426. TELEX 114506-SPRIW-A. (U.S. address: Springer-Verlag New York, 175 5th Ave., New York, NY 10010) Ed. E.F. Stumpfl. adv.; bk.rev.; charts; illus.; index. (also avail. in microfiche from UMI; back issues avail.) **Indexed:** Chem.Abstr., Curr.Cont., Eng.Ind., GeoRef., Met.Abstr.
—BLDSC shelfmark: 5790.340000.
Formerly: T M P M - Tschermaks Mineralogische und Petrographische Mitteilungen (ISSN 0041-3763)

622 US ISSN 0747-9182
CODEN: MMPRE8
MINERALS AND METALLURGICAL PROCESSING. 1984. q. $80. Society for Mining, Metallurgy and Exploration, c/o R.L. White, Pub., Box 625002, Littleton, CO 80162-5002. TEL 303-973-9550. FAX 303-973-3845. Ed. Roshan B. Bhappu. adv.; circ. 900. (also avail. in microfilm from UMI) **Indexed:** AESIS, Chem.Abstr., Eng.Ind., Excerp.Med., Soils & Fert.
—BLDSC shelfmark: 5790.620000.

MINERALS AND ROCKS; monograph series of theoretical and experimental studies. see *EARTH SCIENCES — Geology*

622 US ISSN 0892-6875
TN1 CODEN: MENGEB
MINERALS ENGINEERING; an international journal devoted to innovation and developments in mineral processing and extractive metallurgy. 1988. 12/yr. £240 (effective 1992). Pergamon Press, Inc., Journals Division, 660 White Plains Rd., Tarrytown, NY 10591-5153. TEL 914-524-9200. FAX 914-333-2444. (And: Headington Hill Hall, Oxford OX3 0BW, England. TEL 0865-794141) Ed. B.A. Wills. (also avail. in microform; back issues avail.)
—BLDSC shelfmark: 5790.678000.
Description: Reports developments in mineral processing technology and applications.
Refereed Serial

622 669 UK ISSN 0955-2847
CODEN: MINIEB
MINERALS INDUSTRY INTERNATIONAL. bi-m. £54. Institution of Mining and Metallurgy, 44 Portland Place, London W1N 4BR, England. TEL 01-580 3802. FAX 01-436-5388. TELEX 261410 IMM G. (U.S. addr.: IMM North American Publications Center, Old Post Rd., Brookfield, VT 05036) adv.; bk.rev.; circ. 5,500. **Indexed:** AESIS, Cadscan, Lead Abstr., Zincscan.
Formerly: I M M Bulletin (ISSN 0308-9789)

549 AT
MINERALS INDUSTRY SURVEY. 1978. a. Australian Mining Industry Council, Box 363, Dickson, A.C.T. 2602, Australia. FAX 61-6-279-3699. **Indexed:** AESIS.
Description: Provides statistical and financial information on the Australian mining industry.

622 918 US
MINERALS: LATIN AMERICAN INDUSTRY REPORT. 1985. a. $235 per country report. Aquino Productions, Box 15760, Stamford, CT 06901. TEL 203-325-3138. Ed. Andres C. Aquino.

549 US
MINERALS RESEARCH LABORATORY NEWSLETTER. 1959. q. free. North Carolina State University, Minerals Research Laboratory, 180 Coxe Ave., Asheville, NC 28801. TEL 704-251-6155. Ed. Louis M. Schlesinger. circ. 300. (looseleaf format)
Supersedes: Minerals Research Laboratory Bulletin (ISSN 0026-4652)
Refereed Serial

622 330.9 US
MINERALS TODAY. bi-m. $13 (foreign $16.25). U.S. Bureau of Mines, 810 Seventh St., Washington, DC 20241. TEL 202-501-9358. FAX 202-501-3933. Ed. Harold Kennedy. circ. 3,500. (back issues avail.) **Indexed:** AESIS, Amer.Stat.Ind., Cadscan, Energy Info.Abstr., Environ.Abstr., Lead Abstr., World Alum.Abstr., Zincscan.
Formerly: Minerals and Materials.

MINERAUX ET FOSSILES. see *PALEONTOLOGY*

622 PE ISSN 0026-4679
MINERIA. 1952. bi-m. $45. Instituto de Ingenieros de Minas del Peru, Las Camelias 555-2, Lima 27, Peru. TEL 51-14-424393. FAX 51-14-423190. Ed. Jorge Vargas Fernandez. adv.; illus.; mkt.; circ. 5,000. **Indexed:** Chem.Abstr.

622 669 665.5 CL ISSN 0716-1042
HD9506.C5
MINERIA CHILENA. 1980. m. $80. Ediciones Tecnicas Ltda., Perez Valenzuela 1098, Oficina 98 - Providencia, Santiago 09, Chile. TEL 225 5939. FAX 56-2-2426900. TELEX 440002 ITTPBCZ-EDITEC. (Subscr. to: P.O. Box 3074, Correo Central, Santiago, Chile) Eds. Ricardo Cortes, Roly Solis. adv.: B&W page $1350, color page $1700; trim 10 7/8 x 8 1/8. bk.rev.; index; circ. 8,000. (back issues avail.)

622 MX
LA MINERIA EN MEXICO. 1981. biennial. Mex.$1000($4.92) Instituto Nacional de Estadistica Geografia e Informatica, Secretaria de Programacion y Presupuesto, Prol. Heroe de Nacozari, 2301, Acceso 10, C.P. 20290, Aguascalientes, Ags., Mexico. TEL 91-491-81968. FAX 91-491-80739.

622.33 US
MINERIA PAN-AMERICANA. (Text in Spanish) 1982. q. $30. Mineria Pan-Americana, Inc., 9300 S. Dadeland Blvd., Ste. 103, Miami, FL 33156. TEL 305-670-4818. Ed. Juan Escalante. circ. 7,239. (back issues avail.)

622 BL
MINERIOS; extracao & processamento. (Text in Portuguese and Spanish) 1978. m. $60. E M E P Editorial Ltda., Rua Diogo Moriera 124, CEP 05423 Sao Paolo, Brazil. TEL 814-5022. FAX 813-0545. TELEX 1180007 EMED BR. (In U.S.: Box 59761, Chicago, IL 60659. TEL 708-674-7188) Ed. Joseph Young. circ. 11,800.
Description: Covers new mineral projects, advances in equipment and process technology, and improvements in prospecting and geology techniques of mineral producers of the third world.

622 MX
MINERO-NOTICIAS. 1963. m. Publi-News Latinoamericana, S.A.C.V., Colima 436, Mexico 7 D.F., Mexico. Ed. Roberto J. Marquez. adv.

622 AT
CODEN: MRSRAK
MINES AND ENERGY REVIEW, SOUTH AUSTRALIA. 1903. a. price varies. Department of Mines and Energy, P.O. Box 151, Eastwood, S.A. 5063, Australia. TEL 08-274-7597. FAX 08-272-7597. Ed. J.F. Drexel. charts; illus.; stat.; index, cum.index: vols.1-146; circ. 700. (back issues avail.) **Indexed:** AESIS, Aus.Rd.Ind., C.R.I. Abstr., Can.B.P.I., Eng.Ind., GeoRef.
Former titles: Mineral Resources Review (ISSN 0026-525X); Mining Review; Review of Mining Operations.
Description: A collection of technical articles and reviews on South Australian geology and the mineral industry; contains South Australian mineral production statistics.

622 UK
MINES & MINING EQUIPMENT AND SERVICE COMPANIES WORLDWIDE (YEAR). 1982. a. c/o Don Nelson, P.O. Box 193, Barnet, Herts EN4 8LP, England.
Formerly: Mines and Mining Equipment Companies Worldwide (ISSN 0262-7965)

622 US ISSN 0096-4859
CODEN: MMCOAW
MINES MAGAZINE. 1910. 8/yr. $30. Colorado School of Mines Alumni Association, Inc., Twin Towers, 19th & Elm, Ste. 31E, Golden, CO 80401. TEL 303-273-3291. FAX 303-273-3165. Ed. Ellen E. Glover. adv.; bk.rev.; charts; illus.; tr.lit.; circ. 6,000. **Indexed:** Chem.Abstr., Excerp.Med., GeoRef.
—BLDSC shelfmark: 5796.000000.
Formerly: Mines Golden (ISSN 0026-5055)

622 613.62 EI ISSN 0588-702X
MINES SAFETY AND HEALTH COMMISSION. REPORT/ORGANE PERMANENT POUR LA SECURITE DANS LES MINES DE HOUILLE. RAPPORT. 1967. a. free. Commission of the European Communities, 200 rue de la Loi, 1049 Brussels, Belgium.
Formerly (1959-1966): European Coal and Steel Community. Organe Permanent pour la Securite dans les Mines de Houille. Rapport.

622 II
MINETECH. (Text in English) 1976. q. free. Central Mine Planning & Design Institute Ltd. (Subsidiary of: Coal India Limited), Publications Wing, Gondwana Place, Kanke Rd., Ranchi 834008, Bihar, India.

622 FR ISSN 0026-5071
MINEURS DE FRANCE. 1949. m. 50 F. 2 rue de Metz, 57802 Freyming- Merlebach, France. FAX 87-81-75-19. Ed. Francis Schaefer. adv.; bk.rev.; film rev.; play rev.; charts; illus.; stat.; circ. 45,000.

622 FR ISSN 0989-7577
MINEURS DE FRANCE: EDITION CENTRE-MIDI. 1971. 10/yr. free. Houilleres de Bassin du Centre et du Midi, 9 av. Benoit Charvet, B.P. 534, 42007 St. Etienne cedex 1, France. adv.; bk.rev.; circ. 8,000.
Former titles: Centre Midi Magazine; Mineur d'Auvergne (ISSN 0026-5063)
Description: Explores coal mining and resources.

622 SA
MINEWORKER/MYNWERKER. 1940. m. R.3. Mineworkers' Union, Cnr. Melle & Dekorte Sts., P.O. Box 31525, Braamfontein, Johannesburg, South Africa. FAX 011-403-3930. Ed. W. Ungerer. adv.; circ. 30,000.

622 AT ISSN 0812-0293
MINFO; New South Wales mining and exploration quarterly. 1983. q. free. Department of Mineral Resources, P.O. Box 536, St. Leonards, N.S.W. 2065, Australia. TEL 02-2310922. Ed. H. Basden. circ. 3,000.

338.7 II
MINING AND ALLIED MACHINERY CORPORATION. ANNUAL REPORT. (Text in English) a. Mining and Allied Machinery Corporation, Durgapur, India. illus.

622 AT
MINING & CONSTRUCTION METHODS AND EQUIPMENT. 1973. irreg. Finecraft Publishing Co., Box 260, Neutral Bay Junction, N.S.W. 2089, Australia. Ed. Fiona Stewart.

MINES AND MINING INDUSTRY

622   GW
MINING & ENERGY; international journal for mining and mining equipment. (Text in English) 1981. irreg. (2-3/yr.). Bertelsmann Fachzeitschriften GmbH, Postfach 6666, 4830 Gutersloh 100, Germany. TEL 05241-802238. FAX 05241-73055. Ed. Aribert Langer. circ. 3,000.
   Formerly: German Mining (ISSN 0722-6675)
   Description: Covers the export of mining equipment and the mining supply industry.

622 338.2   RH
MINING AND ENGINEERING. 1959. m. Z.$44($55) (foreign Z.$50). (Zimbabwe Institution of Engineers) Thomson Publications Zimbabwe (Pvt) Ltd., Thomson House, P.O. Box 1683, Harare, Zimbabwe. TEL 736835. TELEX 24705 ZW. Ed. S. Orange. adv.; bk.rev.; index; circ. 2,000. **Indexed:** GeoRef., Ind.S.A.Per.
   Incorporates (1962-1989): Zimbabwe Engineer; (1963-1979): Chamber of Mines Journal; (1935-1963): Rhodesia Mining and Engineering.

338.2 622   SA   ISSN 1017-4249
MINING AND ENGINEERING & ELECTRONICS INDUSTRIES (YEAR). (Text in English) a. South African Foreign Trade Organisation, Publishing Division, P.O. Box 782706, Sandton 2146, South Africa. TEL 011-883-3737. FAX 011-883-6569. TELEX 4-24111 SA. adv.
   Formerly: Mining and Engineering (Year).

MINING AND MATERIALS PROCESSING INSTITUTE OF JAPAN. METALLURGICAL REVIEW. see *METALLURGY*

MINING AND PETROLEUM LEGISLATION SERVICE. see *LAW*

622   UK   ISSN 0076-8995
HD9506.U6
MINING ANNUAL REVIEW. 1935. a. £75($145) Mining Journal Ltd., 60 Worship St., London EC2A 2HD, England. TEL 071-377-2020. FAX 071-247-4100. TELEX 8952809-MINING-G. Ed. Chris Hinde. adv.; circ. 10,049. (also avail. in microfilm; microfiche; reprint service avail. from UMI) **Indexed:** AESIS, Br.Geol.Lit., Cadscan, GeoRef., Lead Abstr., Ref.Zh., Zincscan.
   ●Also available online. Vendor(s): Mead Data Central.

622   UK   ISSN 0307-9066
TN1
MINING DEPARTMENT MAGAZINE. 1948. a. £5.50. University of Nottingham, Mining Engineering Department, Nottingham NG7 2RD, England. FAX 0602-421681. Eds. S. Smith, B. Denby. adv.; circ. 5,000.

622   UK   ISSN 0026-5179
TN1   CODEN: MNEGAP
MINING ENGINEER. 1960. m. £65 to non-members. Institution of Mining Engineers, Danum House, South Parade, Doncaster DN1 2DY, England. TEL 0302-320486. FAX 0302-340554. Ed. W.J.W. Bourne. adv.; bk.rev.; bibl.; illus.; index; circ. 3,800. **Indexed:** Br.Geol.Lit., Br.Tech.Ind., C.I.S. Abstr., Chem.Abstr., Eng.Ind., Fuel & Energy Abstr., GeoRef., HRIS, Met.Abstr., W.R.C.Inf.
   —BLDSC shelfmark: 5802.950000.
   Incorporates: Institution of Mining Engineers. Transactions.
   Description: Journal serving professional and technical persons in coal and other stratified deposits.

622   US   ISSN 0026-5187
TN1   CODEN: MIENAB
MINING ENGINEERING. 1949. m. $70. Society for Mining, Metallurgy and Exploration, Box 625002, Littleton, CO 80162-5002. TEL 303-973-9550. FAX 303-973-3845. Ed. R.L. White. adv.; bk.rev.; illus.; tr.lit.; index; circ. 22,000. (also avail. in microform from UMI; reprint service avail. from UMI) **Indexed:** A.S.& T.Ind., Acid Rain Abstr., Acid Rain Ind., AESIS, Appl.Mech.Rev., C.R.I. Abstr., CAD CAM Abstr., Chem.Abstr., Comput.Abstr., Energy Info.Abstr., Eng.Ind., Environ.Abstr., Excerp.Med., Fuel & Energy Abstr., Geo.Abstr., GeoRef., INIS Atomind., Met.Abstr., Ocean.Abstr., Petrol.Abstr., Pollut.Abstr., RICS, Robomat., Sel.Water Res.Abstr., Soils & Fert., World Alum.Abstr.
   —BLDSC shelfmark: 5803.000000.
   Description: Directed to engineering professionals in the mining industry.

622   SA
MINING EQUIPMENT NEWS. Abbreviated title: M E N. 1974. m. National Publishing (Pty) Ltd., P.O. Box 2735, Johannesburg 2000, South Africa. TEL 011-835-2221. FAX 011-835-1943. TELEX 82735 SA. Ed. Charleen Clark. adv.; illus.; circ. 4,303. (tabloid format)

622 551 669   II   ISSN 0371-9588
TN1   CODEN: TMGMAL
MINING, GEOLOGICAL AND METALLURGICAL INSTITUTE OF INDIA. TRANSACTIONS. (Text in English) 1906. s-a. Rs.50 (foreign $10). Mining, Geological & Metallurgical Institute of India, 29 Chowringhee Rd., Calcutta 700016, India. Ed. S.C. Ray. adv.; bibl.; charts; illus.; circ. 2,500. **Indexed:** GeoRef.

622   CN   ISSN 0316-2281
HD9506.C2
MINING IN CANADA - FACTS & FIGURES. French edition: Mines au Canada - Faits et Chiffres (ISSN 0316-2311) 1964. a. free. Mining Association of Canada, 350 Sparks St., No. 1105, Ottawa, Ont. K1R 7S8, Canada. TEL 613-233-9391. charts; stat.; circ. 24,000. (back issues avail.) **Indexed:** CS Ind.

622   RH
MINING IN ZIMBABWE. 1950. a. Z.$17.50 (foreign Z.$22.50). Thomson Publications Zimbabwe (Pvt) Ltd., Thomson House, P.O. Box 1683, Harare, Zimbabwe. TEL 736835. TELEX 24705 ZW. Ed. S. Orange. adv.; circ. controlled.
   Formerly: Mining in Rhodesia (ISSN 0076-8987)

622   II
MINING INDUSTRY & TRADE ANNUAL. (Text in English) 1962. a. $15. Praveen Corp, Sayajiganj, Baroda 390005, India. Ed. C.M. Pandit.
   Formerly: Mining Industry and Trade Journal (ISSN 0026-5217)

622   US
MINING INDUSTRY TECHNICAL CONFERENCE. CONFERENCE RECORD. 1979. biennial. price varies. (I E E E, Industry Applications Society) Institute of Electrical and Electronics Engineers, Inc., 345 E. 47th St., New York, NY 10017-2394. TEL 212-705-7900. FAX 212-705-7682. (Subscr to: Box 1331, 445 Hoes Lane, Piscataway, NJ 08855-1331)

622   UK   ISSN 0026-5225
TN1   CODEN: MJOLAS
MINING JOURNAL. 1835. w. £225($430) combined subscription with Mining Magazine and Mining Annual Review. Mining Journal Ltd., 60 Worship St., London EC2A 2HD, England. TEL 01-377-2020. FAX 01-247-4100. TELEX 8952809-MINING-G. Eds. Roger Ellis, Chris Hinde. adv.; bk.rev.; illus.; index; circ. 4,697. (also avail. in microfiche; reprint service avail. from UMI; back issues avail.) **Indexed:** AESIS, Br.Geol.Lit., Chem.Abstr., Energy Ind., Energy Info.Abstr., Eng.Ind., Excerp.Med., Fuel & Energy Abstr., GeoRef., Key to Econ.Sci., Met.Abstr., PROMT, World Alum.Abstr.

MINING LEGISLATION: AFRICA. see *LAW — International Law*

MINING LEGISLATION: CENTRAL AMERICA & CARIBBEAN. see *LAW — International Law*

MINING LEGISLATION: EUROPE. see *LAW — International Law*

MINING LEGISLATION: FAR EAST. see *LAW — International Law*

MINING LEGISLATION: MIDDLE EAST. see *LAW — International Law*

MINING LEGISLATION: SOUTH AMERICA. see *LAW — International Law*

622   UK   ISSN 0308-6631
TN1   CODEN: MMALAD
MINING MAGAZINE. 1909. m. £55($100) Mining Journal Ltd., 60 Worship St., London EC2A 2HD, England. TEL 071-377-2020. FAX 071-247-4100. TELEX 8952809-MINING-G. Ed. Tony Brewis. adv.; bk.rev.; abstr.; bibl.; illus.; mkt.; pat.; stat.; index; circ. 12,454. (also avail. in microfiche; reprint service avail. from UMI) **Indexed:** AESIS, Art & Archaeol.Tech.Abstr., Br.Ceram.Abstr., Br.Tech.Ind., Cadscan, Chem.Abstr., Eng.Ind., Excerp.Med., Fluidex, Fuel & Energy Abstr., GeoRef., HRIS, Key to Econ.Sci., Lead Abstr., Met.Abstr., PROMT, Soils & Fert., World Alum.Abstr., Zincscan.
   ●Also available online. Vendor(s): Mead Data Central.
   —BLDSC shelfmark: 5805.000000.

622   ZA
MINING MIRROR; Zambia's mining industry newspaper. 1973. 12/yr. Z.$62.40. Zambia Consolidated Copper Mines Ltd., P.O. Box 71605, Ndola, Zambia. TELEX ZA 30104. Ed. Bd. adv.; bk.rev.; charts; illus.; circ. 35,000.
   Supersedes: Mufulira Mirror (ISSN 0047-8326) & Roan Antelope (ISSN 0048-8437)

622   SA
MINING MIRROR. q. Brooke Pattrick (pty) Ltd., P.O. Box 422, 6 Park St., Bedfordview 2008, South Africa.
   Incorporates: Drilling News.
   Description: Covers the mining industry in South Africa.

622   SA
MINING NEWS/MYNBLAD. (Text in Afrikaans and English) m. Chamber of Mines of South Africa, P.O. Box 809, Johannesburg 2000, South Africa. Ed. C. du Toit Thom. adv.; circ. controlled.
   Description: For mining industry personnel in South Africa.

MINING NEWSLETTER. see *OCCUPATIONAL HEALTH AND SAFETY*

622   US   ISSN 0026-5241
MINING RECORD. 1889. w. $39. Howell Publishing Co., Box 37510, Denver, CO 80237. TEL 303-770-6791. FAX 303-770-6796. Ed. Don E. Howell. adv.; mkt.; circ. 6,000.
   Formerly: Mining and Natural Resources Record.

622 333   AT   ISSN 0314-4607
MINING REVIEW. 1970. 6/yr. Australian Mining Industry Council, Box 363, Dickson, A.C.T. 2602, Australia. FAX 61-6-279-3699. Ed. M.A. McMillan. adv.; bk.rev.; index; circ. 5,500. **Indexed:** AESIS, Aus.Rd.Ind., Gdlns.

622   CN   ISSN 0711-3277
MINING REVIEW. 1977. bi-m. membership. (British Columbia and Yukon Chamber of Mines) Naylor Communications Ltd., 920 Yonge St., 6th fl., Toronto, Ont. M4W 3C7, Canada. TEL 604-985-8711. (Subscr. to: 100 Sutherland Ave., Winnipeg, Man. R2W 3C7, Canada) Ed. Jim Hutson. adv.; circ. 2,500. **Indexed:** GeoRef.
   Formerly: Mining Exploration and Development Review (ISSN 0318-1766)

622   UK   ISSN 0026-5276
TN1   CODEN: MNGTB7
MINING TECHNOLOGY. 1920. 10/yr. £40 (foreign £60). (Institution of Mining, Electrical & Mining Mechanical Engineers) Marylebone Press Ltd., Lloyds House, 18 Lloyds St., Manchester M2 5WA, England. TEL 061-832-6541. FAX 061-832-8129. TELEX 669362. Ed. Ernest Rhodes. adv.; bk.rev.; abstr.; charts; illus.; tr.lit.; index; circ. 3,500. **Indexed:** AESIS, Br.Tech.Ind., C.I.S. Abstr., Eng.Ind., Excerp.Med., Fuel & Energy Abstr., Met.Abstr., Sci.Abstr., World Alum.Abstr.
   —BLDSC shelfmark: 5807.400000.
   Formerly: Mining Electrical and Mechanical Engineer.

622   CN   ISSN 0317-9508
MINING - WHAT MINING MEANS TO CANADA. French edition: Mines - Pilier de l'Economie Canadienne (ISSN 0317-9524) 1964. biennial. free. Mining Association of Canada, 350 Sparks St., No. 1105, Ottawa, Ont. K1R 7S8, Canada. TEL 613-233-9391. circ. 100,000.

MINES AND MINING INDUSTRY 3491

622 US
MINING WORLD NEWS. m. Mining International Publishing Co., 90 W. Grove St., Rm. 200, Reno, NV 89509-4000. TEL 702-827-1115. FAX 702-827-1292. Ed. Ann Graham. circ. 30,000.

549 US ISSN 0272-8583
TN799.6.M6
MINNESOTA INDUSTRIAL MINERALS DIRECTORY. 1980. a. $10 (typically set in Spring). University of Minnesota, Mineral Resources Research Center, 56 East River Rd., Minneapolis, MN 55455. TEL 612-625-3344. FAX 612-625-1882. Ed. Rodney J. Lipp. circ. 400.

622 UK ISSN 0955-548X
MINTECH; annual review of international mining technology and development. a. Sterling Publishing Group PLC, 86-88 Edgware Rd., London W2 2YW, England. TEL 01-258-0066. Ed. Thomas Carr.
—BLDSC shelfmark: 5810.572000.

622.33 SA
MINTEK. SPECIAL PUBLICATIONS. 1975. irreg., latest no.13, 1989. price varies. Mintek, Private Bag X3015, Randburg 2125, South Africa. TEL 011-793-3511. FAX 011-793-2413. TELEX 4-24867 SA.
 Formerly: Council for Mineral Technology (MINTEK). Special Publication.
 Description: Covers various aspects of metallurgy and mineral technology, including research, production, and conferences.

622.33 SA
MINTEK REPORTS. 1966. irreg. (approx. 20-30/yr.). $400. Mintek, Private Bag X3015, Randburg 2125, South Africa. TEL 011-793-3511. FAX 011-793-2413. bibl.; illus. **Indexed:** Chem.Abstr., Met.Abstr., Mineral.Abstr., Nucl.Sci.Abstr.
 Former titles: M I N T E K Reports; N I M Reports.
 Description: Deals with mineral processing research.

622.33 SA ISSN 1010-2582
MINTEK RESEARCH DIGEST. 1974. bi-m. free. Mintek, Private Bag X3015, Randburg 2125, South Africa. TEL 011-793-3511. FAX 011-793-2413.
 Former titles: M I N T E K Research Digest; N I M Research Digest.

622.33 CC
MINYONG MEI KEJI. (Text in Chinese) bi-m. Wuzi Bu, Ranliao Si - Ministry of Materials, Department of Fuels, A-58, Pengzhuang, Yongdingmenwai, Beijing 100054, People's Republic of China. TEL 334461. Ed. Zhang Jitao.

549 GW
MONOGRAPH SERIES ON MINERAL DEPOSITS. (Text in English or German) 1962. irreg. price varies. Gebrueder Borntraeger Verlagsbuchhandlung, Johannesstr. 3A, 7000 Stuttgart 1, Germany. TEL 0711-625001. FAX 0711-625005. TELEX 723363-SCHB-D. Ed. G. Friedrich.

MONTANA. BUREAU OF MINES AND GEOLOGY. BULLETIN. see EARTH SCIENCES — Geology

622 US ISSN 0077-1104
MONTANA. BUREAU OF MINES AND GEOLOGY. DIRECTORY OF MINING ENTERPRISES. (Subseries of Bulletins) a. Bureau of Mines and Geology, Montana College of Mineral Science and Technology, Butte, MT 59701. TEL 406-496-4167. FAX 406-496-4133.
 Description: Each listing includes type of ore produced, mining district, property location, owners' and operators' names and addresses, mill capacity, number of employees, and yearly status.

MONTANA. BUREAU OF MINES AND GEOLOGY. MEMOIR. see EARTH SCIENCES — Geology

MONTANA. BUREAU OF MINES AND GEOLOGY. SPECIAL PUBLICATIONS. see EARTH SCIENCES — Geology

MUENCHNER GEOWISSENSCHAFTLICHE ABHANDLUNGEN. REIHE B: ALLGEMEINE UND ANGEWANDTE GEOLOGIE. see EARTH SCIENCES — Geology

622 ZR ISSN 0541-4873
MWANA SHABA; journal d'entreprise de la Gecamines. 1957. m. Generale des Carrieres et des Mines, Division des Relations Publiques, B.P. 450, Lubumbashi, Zaire.

NAMIBIA BRIEF. see BUSINESS AND ECONOMICS — International Development And Assistance

622 340 US
NATIONAL COAL ASSOCIATION. LETTER OF THE LAW. q. National Coal Association, 1130 17th St., N.W., Washington, DC 20036. TEL 202-463-2640.

622 338.2 US
NATIONAL COAL ASSOCIATION. WEEKLY STATISTICAL SUMMARY. w. National Coal Association, 1130 17th St., N.W., Washington, DC 20036. TEL 202-463-2640.

622 US ISSN 0192-7329
NATIONAL INDEPENDENT COAL LEADER; dedicated to safety in the mining industry. 1960. m. $6. National Independent Coal Operators Association, 1514 Front St., Richlands, VA 24641. TEL 703-963-9011. Ed. Louis Hunter. adv.; bk.rev.; circ. 13,000. (newspaper)
 Description: Explores coal mining and resources.

622 US
▼**NATIONAL STONE ASSOCIATION. BUYER'S GUIDE**. 1986. a. membership. National Stone Association, 1415 Elliot Pl., N.W., Washington, DC 20007. TEL 202-342-1100. FAX 202-342-0702. Ed. Frank Atlee. adv.; circ. 2,000.
 Description: For purchasing personnel in the stone aggregate quarrying industry.

622.33 551.4 US
NATIONAL SYMPOSIUM ON MINING. PROCEEDINGS. 1979. a. $45. (University of Kentucky, Office of Engineering Services - Continuing Education) O E S Publications, Office of Engineering Services, University of Kentucky, Lexington, KY 40506-0046. TEL 606-257-3343. FAX 606-257-3342. Eds. R. William DeVore, Donald H. Graves. circ. 300. (back issues avail.)
 Former titles: National Symposium on Mining, Hydrology, Sedimentology and Reclamation. Proceedings (ISSN 1046-3887); (until 1987): Symposium on Surface Mining, Hydrology, Sedimentology and Reclamation. Proceedings (ISSN 0735-0686)

NATIONAL UNION OF COAL MINE WORKERS. JOURNAL. see LABOR UNIONS

622 GW ISSN 0047-9403
TN3 CODEN: NEBBAB
NEUE BERGBAUTECHNIK; wissenschaftliche Zeitschrift fuer Bergbau, Geowissenschaften und Aufbereitung. m. DM.240. (Kammer der Technik e.V.) Deutscher Verlag fuer Grundstoffindustrie, Karl-Heine-Str. 27, 7031 Leipzig, Germany. TEL 4081011. FAX 4012571. TELEX 51451-FACHB-DD. (Co-sponsor: Bergakademie Freiberg) **Indexed:** C.I.S. Abstr., Chem.Abstr., Eng.Ind., Excerp.Med., Geotech.Abstr., Met.Abstr., World Alum.Abstr.
 Description: Contains authoritative articles on mining technology and geoscience. Includes reports of events and bibliographies.

549 GW ISSN 0077-7757
QE351 CODEN: NJMIAK
NEUES JAHRBUCH FUER MINERALOGIE. ABHANDLUNGEN. 1807. 9/yr. (in 3 vols, 3 nos./vol.). price varies. E. Schweizerbart'sche Verlagsbuchhandlung, Johannesstr. 3A, 7000 Stuttgart 1, Germany. TEL 0711-625001. FAX 0711-625005. TELEX 723363-SCHB-D. Ed.Bd. adv. (also avail. in microfiche from BHP) **Indexed:** Art & Archaeol.Tech.Abstr., Biol.Abstr., Br.Ceram.Abstr., Br.Geol.Lit., Chem.Abstr.
—BLDSC shelfmark: 6079.000000.
 Supersedes and continues volume numbering of: Neues Jahrbuch fuer Mineralogie, Geologie und Palaeontologie. Abhandlungen. Abt. B.

549 GW ISSN 0028-3649
QE351 CODEN: NJMMAW
NEUES JAHRBUCH FUER MINERALOGIE. MONATSHEFTE. (Text in English and German) 1900. 12/yr. E. Schweizerbart'sche Verlagsbuchhandlung, Johannesstr. 3a, 7000 Stuttgart 1, Germany. TEL 0711-625001. FAX 0711-625005. TELEX 723363-SCHB-D. Ed.Bd. bk.rev.; bibl.; charts; illus. **Indexed:** Art & Archaeol.Tech.Abstr., Br.Geol.Lit., Chem.Abstr., Curr.Cont., Ind.Sci.Rev., Int.Aerosp.Abstr.
—BLDSC shelfmark: 6080.200000.

NEVADA. BUREAU OF MINES AND GEOLOGY. BULLETIN. see EARTH SCIENCES — Geology

NEVADA. BUREAU OF MINES AND GEOLOGY. OPEN-FILE REPORTS. see EARTH SCIENCES — Geology

NEVADA. BUREAU OF MINES AND GEOLOGY. REPORT. see EARTH SCIENCES — Geology

NEVADA. BUREAU OF MINES AND GEOLOGY. SPECIAL PUBLICATIONS. see EARTH SCIENCES — Geology

NEVADA MINERAL INDUSTRY (YEAR). see EARTH SCIENCES — Geology

622 CN
NEW BRUNSWICK. BEACH RESOURCES - EASTERN NEW BRUNSWICK. 1975. irreg. Can.$20. Department of Natural Resources, Mines Division, Fredericton, N.B. E3B 5H1, Canada. TEL 506-453-2206. FAX 506-453-3671.
 Description: Study of the coastal zone of east New Brunswick, representing research based on aerial photography, aircraft and ground field surveys.

622 CN ISSN 0077-8109
NEW BRUNSWICK. MINERAL RESOURCES BRANCH. REPORT OF INVESTIGATIONS. 1966. irreg. price varies. Department of Natural Resources and Energy, Geology Division, Box 6000, Fredericton, N.B. E3B 5H1, Canada. TEL 506-453-2206. FAX 506-453-3671. **Indexed:** Chem.Abstr., GeoRef.
 Description: Covers studies of major stratigraphic units, important deposits or group of deposits.

622 CN
NEW BRUNSWICK. WETLANDS - PEATLANDS RESOURCES. 1975. irreg. Can.$20. Department of Natural Resources, Mines Division, Fredericton, N.B. E3B 5H1, Canada. TEL 506-453-2206. FAX 506-453-3671.
 Description: Covers study of wetlands and peatlands in New Brunswick by aerial photography and academic review.

622 NL
NEW CALEDONIA. SERVICE DES MINES ET DE L'ENERGY. RAPPORT ANNUEL. 1915. a. 110 F. Service des Mines et de l'Energie, Noumea, New Caledonia. illus.; circ. 250.

622 US
TN24.N6 CODEN: NEXBAJ
NEW MEXICO. BUREAU OF MINES AND MINERAL RESOURCES. BULLETIN. 1915. irreg., no.137, 1988. price varies. Bureau of Mines and Mineral Resources, Socorro, NM 87801. TEL 505-835-5410. **Indexed:** GeoRef.

622 US ISSN 0548-5975
CODEN: NMMMAJ
NEW MEXICO. BUREAU OF MINES AND MINERAL RESOURCES. MEMOIR. 1956. irreg., no.47, 1988. price varies. Bureau of Mines and Mineral Resources, Socorro, NM 87801. TEL 505-835-5410. **Indexed:** GeoRef.

622 US ISSN 0098-7077
TN24.N6 CODEN: NMXMB7
NEW MEXICO. BUREAU OF MINES AND MINERAL RESOURCES. PROGRESS REPORT. (First 7 nos. were designated "target exploration" reports) 1972. irreg., no.10, 1978. price varies. Bureau of Mines and Mineral Resources, Socorro, NM 87801. TEL 505-835-5410. **Indexed:** GeoRef. Key Title: Progress Report - New Mexico Bureau of Mines & Mineral Resources.

NEW MEXICO DIRECTORY OF MANUFACTURERS. see BUSINESS AND ECONOMICS — Trade And Industrial Directories

M

MINES AND MINING INDUSTRY

622   UK
NEW QUARRYING & MINING. 1976. fortn. £35. Mineral Marketing Ltd., 7 Vallet Avenue, Alcester, Warwickshire B49 6A4, England. TEL 01-733 7088. FAX 01-733-1035. Ed. D. Buntain. adv.; bk.rev.; circ. 7,000. (also avail. in microform from UMI; reprint service avail. from UMI) **Indexed:** Fluidex.
Formerly (until 1986): Quarry and Mining News (ISSN 0950-110X)
Description: News items and feature articles on technological developments in the industry, reviews of process and operational equipment, and analysis of industrial trends and the effects of legislation on the industry.

622   AT
NEW SOUTH WALES. DEPARTMENT OF MINERAL RESOURCES. ANNUAL REPORT. 1875. a. price varies. Department of Mineral Resources, P.O. Box 536, St. Leonards, N.S.W. 2065, Australia. index; circ. 475. **Indexed:** AESIS, GeoRef.
Formerly: New South Wales. Department of Minerals and Energy. Annual Report; Formed by the merger of: New South Wales. Department of Mineral Resources. Annual Report (ISSN 0727-9256); New South Wales. Department of Energy. Annual Report. Which were formerly: New South Wales. Department of Mines. Annual Report (ISSN 0077-8664); New South Wales. Energy Authority. Annual Report (ISSN 0158-0809); New South Wales. Department of Mineral Resources and Development. Annual Report.
Description: Details the activities of the department for the financial year and includes audited statements.

NEW SOUTH WALES. GEOLOGICAL SURVEY. MINERAL DEPOSIT DATA SHEETS AND METALLOGENIC STUDY. see *EARTH SCIENCES — Geology*

622 559   AT   ISSN 0077-8729
NEW SOUTH WALES. GEOLOGICAL SURVEY. MINERAL INDUSTRY SERIES. no.3, 1967. irreg., no.44, 1979. price varies. Department of Mineral Resources, P.O. Box 536, St. Leonards, N.S.W. 2065, Australia. Ed. H. Basden. circ. 400. **Indexed:** AESIS, GeoRef.

622 559   AT   ISSN 0077-8737
     CODEN: MRWGDA
NEW SOUTH WALES. GEOLOGICAL SURVEY. MINERAL RESOURCES SERIES. Variant title: Geological Survey of N.S.W. Mineral Resources. 1898. irreg., no.46, 1989. price varies. Department of Mineral Resources, P.O. Box 536, St. Leonards, N.S.W. 2065, Australia. Ed. H. Basden. index; circ. 400. **Indexed:** AESIS, GeoRef.
—BLDSC shelfmark: 5779.900000.
Description: Comprehensive treatises on the geology, distribution mining history of particular minerals.

622   AT
NEW SOUTH WALES MINERAL INDUSTRY REVIEW. 1980. a. Department of Mineral Resources, P.O. Box 536, St. Leonards, N.S.W. 2065, Australia. TEL 02-231-0922. Ed. T. Sullivan. circ. 1,000.

622   CN
NEWFOUNDLAND. GEOLOGICAL SURVEY BRANCH. INFORMATION. 1934. irreg. price varies. Department of Mines and Energy, Geological Survey Branch, P.O. Box 8700, St. John's, Nfld. A1B 4J6, Canada. TEL 709-576-6487. FAX 709-576-3493.
Formerly: Newfoundland. Mineral Development Division. Information (ISSN 0078-0340)

622   CN
NEWFOUNDLAND. GEOLOGICAL SURVEY BRANCH. INFORMATION CIRCULAR. 1934. irreg., no.15, 1974. price varies. Department of Mines and Energy, Geological Survey Branch, P.O. Box 8700, St. John's, Nfld. A1B 4J6, Canada. TEL 709-576-6487. FAX 709-576-3493.
Formerly: Newfoundland. Mineral Development Division. Information Circular (ISSN 0078-0359)

622   CN   ISSN 0078-0367
NEWFOUNDLAND. MINES BRANCH. ANNUAL REPORT SERIES. 1953. a. price varies. Department of Mines and Energy, Geological Survey Branch, P.O. Box 8700, St. John's, Nfld. A1B 4J6, Canada. TEL 709-576-6487. FAX 709-576-3493. circ. 200.

622 550   NR
NIGERIAN MINING AND GEOSCIENCES SOCIETY. JOURNAL. 1964. a. $20. Nigerian Mining and Geosciences Society, University of Nigeria, Dept. of Geology, Nsukka, Nigeria. TEL 042-771911. TELEX 51496 ULIONS NG. Ed. K. Mosto Onuoha. adv.; bk.rev.; abstr.; charts; illus.; stat.; index; circ. 750. **Indexed:** Chem.Abstr., GeoRef.
Formerly: Nigerian Mining, Geological and Metallurgical Society. Journal.

NIIGATA UNIVERSITY. FACULTY OF SCIENCE. SCIENCE REPORTS. SERIES E: GEOLOGY AND MINERALOGY. see *EARTH SCIENCES — Geology*

622 551   US   ISSN 0961-1444
▼**NONRENEWABLE RESOURCES.** 1992. q. $43 to individuals; institutions $200. (International Association for Mathematical Geology) Oxford University Press, Journals, 200 Madison Ave., New York, NY 10016. TEL 212-679-7300. FAX 212-725-2972. TELEX 6859654. (Subscr. to: Journals Fulfillment, 2001 Evans Rd., Cary, NC 27513. TEL 919-677-0977) (Co-sponsor: U.S. Geological Survey) Ed. Richard McCammon. adv.; bk.rev.; circ. 500.
—BLDSC shelfmark: 6117.340400.
Description: Covers topics in natural resource economics, management, and exploration.

622   CN   ISSN 0029-3164
HD9506.C2
THE NORTHERN MINER; devoted to the mineral resources industry of Canada. 1915. w. Can.$70. Southam North American Magazine Group, 1450 Don Mills Rd., Don Mills, Ont. M3B 2X7, Canada. TEL 416-445-6641. FAX 416-442-2272. Ed. J.S. Borland. bk.rev.; charts; illus.; mkt.; stat.; tr.lit.; circ. 28,000. (tabloid format; also avail. in microfilm from CML) **Indexed:** Can.B.P.I., Can.Per.Ind., PROMT.
●Also available online.
—BLDSC shelfmark: 6151.020000.
Description: Reports on all mines and metals.

622   CN
NORTHERN MINER MAGAZINE. 1986. m. Southam North American Magazine Group, 1450 Don Mills Rd., Don Mills, Ont. M3B 2X7, Canada. TEL 416-445-6641. FAX 416-442-2272. Ed. Olav Svela. adv.; B&W page Can.$2140. circ. 11,000.
Description: Provides broad based information for all segments of Canada's mining industry.

622   FR
O E C D. COAL INFORMATION. a. price varies. Organization for Economic Cooperation and Development, 2 rue Andre-Pascal, 75775 Paris Cedex 16, France. TEL 45-24-82-00. FAX 45-24-85-00. (U.S. orders to: O.E.C.D. Publications and Information Center, 2001 L St., N.W., Ste. 700, Washington, DC 20036-4910. TEL 202-785-6323) (also avail. in microfiche from OEC)

O E C D. URANIUM RESOURCES, PRODUCTION AND DEMAND. see *ENERGY — Nuclear Energy*

622   RU   ISSN 0202-3776
OBOGASHCHENIE RUD. 1956. bi-m. 7.20 Rub. Institut Mekhanobr, 21 Liniya, 8a, St. Petersburg B-26, Russia. TEL 213-99-05. TELEX 121419 MEOBR SU. (Subscr. to: V-O Mezdunarodnaya Kniga, ul. Dimitrova D.39, Moscow 113095, Russia) Ed. O.S. Bogdanov. adv.; bk.rev.; circ. 1,200. **Indexed:** Chem.Abstr., Ref.Zh.

622 665   US   ISSN 0271-0315
TN858.A1   CODEN: OSSPDC
OIL SHALE SYMPOSIUM PROCEEDINGS. 1964. a. $25. (Colorado School of Mines) Colorado School of Mines Press, Golden, CO 80401. TEL 303-273-3607. (reprint service avail. from UMI) **Indexed:** API Catal., API Hlth.& Environ., API Oil., API Pet.Ref., API Pet.Subst., API Transport., Chem.Abstr., GeoRef.

622   US
ON THE LEVEL. 1982. q. Homestake Mining Company, 215 W. Main St., Lead, SD 57754-0894. TEL 605-584-4672. Ed. Scott H. Zieske. circ. 2,800.

622   CN   ISSN 0708-2061
ONTARIO GEOLOGICAL SURVEY. AGGREGATE RESOURCES INVENTORY PAPER. 1979. irreg. Can.$10. Ontario Geological Survey, 77 Grenville St., Rm. 719, Toronto, Ont. M7A 1W4, Canada. TEL 416-965-6511. (Subscr. to: Natural Resources Information Centre, Rm. M1-73, MacDonald Block, 900 Bay St., Toronto, Ont. M7A 2C1, Canada) (back issues avail.)

622 551   CN
ONTARIO GEOLOGICAL SURVEY. ANNUAL REPORT OF THE REGIONAL AND RESIDENT GEOLOGISTS.. (Subseries of: Ontario. Geological Survey. Miscellaneous Paper (ISSN 0704-2752)) 1967. a. price varies. Ontario Geological Survey, 77 Grenville St., Rm. 719, Toronto, Ont. M7A 1W4, Canada. TEL 416-965-6511. (Subscr. to: Natural Resources Information Centre, Rm. M1-73, MacDonald Block, 900 Bay St., Toronto, Ont. M7A 2C1, Canada) circ. 1,000. (also avail. in microfiche; back issues avail.)

622   CN
ONTARIO GEOLOGICAL SURVEY. EXPLORATION TECHNOLOGY DEVELOPMENT FUND, SUMMARY OF RESEARCH. (Subseries of: Ontario Geological Survey. Miscellaneous Paper (ISSN 0704-2752)) 1983. a. price varies. Ontario Geological Survey, 77 Grenville St., Rm. 719, Toronto, Ont. M7A 1W4, Canada. TEL 416-965-2000. (Subscr. to: Natural Resources Information Centre, Rm. M1-73, MacDonald Block, 900 Bay St., Toronto, Ont. M7A 2C1, Canada) (back issues avail.)
Formerly: Ontario Geological Survey. Exploration Technology Development Fund Grants (ISSN 0826-791X)

622   CN   ISSN 0225-5316
QE48.C22
ONTARIO GEOLOGICAL SURVEY. GEOSCIENCE RESEARCH GRANT PROGRAM. SUMMARY OF RESEARCH. (Subseries of: Ontario Geological Survey. Miscellaneous Paper (ISSN 0704-2752)) 1979. a. price varies. Ontario Geological Survey, 77 Grenville St., Rm. 719, Toronto, Ont. M7A 1W4, Canada. TEL 416-965-2000. (Subscr. to: Natural Resources Information Centre, Rm. M1-73, MacDonald Block, 900 Bay St., Toronto, Ont. M7A 2C1, Canada) (also avail. in microfiche; back issues avail.)

ONTARIO GEOLOGICAL SURVEY. GUIDE BOOKS. see *EARTH SCIENCES — Geology*

549   CN   ISSN 0706-4551
ONTARIO GEOLOGICAL SURVEY. MINERAL DEPOSITS CIRCULAR. 1950. irreg. (1-2/yr.). price varies. Ontario Geological Survey, 77 Grenville St., Rm. 719, Toronto, Ont. M7A 1W4, Canada. TEL 416-965-2000. (Subscr. to: Natural Resources Information Centre, Rm. M1-73, MacDonald Block, 900 Bay St., Toronto, Ont. M7A 2C1, Canada) (back issues avail.) **Indexed:** GeoRef.
Formerly: Ontario. Division of Mines. Mineral Resource Circulars.

622   CN   ISSN 0704-2752
     CODEN: MPOSDQ
ONTARIO GEOLOGICAL SURVEY. MISCELLANEOUS PAPER. 1960. irreg. (approx. 3-4/yr.). price varies. Ontario Geological Survey, 77 Grenville St., Rm. 719, Toronto, Ont. M7A 1W4, Canada. TEL 416-965-2000. (Subscr. to: Natural Resources Information Centre, Rm. M1-73, MacDonald Block, 900 Bay St., Toronto, Ont. M7A 2C1, Canada) (back issues avail.) **Indexed:** GeoRef.
Formerly: Ontario. Division of Mines. Miscellaneous Papers.

622   CN   ISSN 0709-4671
TA705.4.C22
ONTARIO GEOLOGICAL SURVEY. NORTHERN ONTARIO ENGINEERING GEOLOGY TERRAIN STUDY. irreg. Can.$2. Ontario Geological Survey, 77 Grenville St., Rm. 719, Toronto, Ont. M7A 1W4, Canada. TEL 416-965-2000. (Subscr. to: Natural Resources Information Centre, Rm. M1-73, MacDonald Block, 900 Bay St., Toronto, Ont. M7A 2C1, Canada) (back issues avail.)

MINES AND MINING INDUSTRY   3493

622 557   CN
ONTARIO GEOLOGICAL SURVEY. REPORT. 1960. irreg. (3-10/yr.). price varies. Ontario Geological Survey, 77 Grenville St., Rm. 719, Toronto, Ont. M7A 1W4, Canada. TEL 416-965-2000. (Subscr. to: Natural Resources Information Centre, Rm. M1-73, MacDonald Block, 900 Bay St., Toronto, Ont. M7A 2C1, Canada) (back issues avail.) **Indexed:** Chem.Abstr., GeoRef.
  Former titles: Ontario Geological Survey. Geological Report; Ontario Geological Survey. Geological Report, Geoscience Report (ISSN 0704-2582); Ontario. Division of Mines. Geological Reports; Incorporates: Ontario. Division of Mines. Geochemical Reports.

622   CN   ISSN 0704-2590
                CODEN: OGSSD5
ONTARIO GEOLOGICAL SURVEY. STUDY. irreg. price varies. Ontario Geological Survey, 77 Grenville St., Rm. 719, Toronto, Ont. M7A 1W4, Canada. TEL 416-965-2000. (Subscr. to: Natural Resources Information Centre, Rm. M1-73, MacDonald Block, 900 Bay St., Toronto, Ont, M7A 2C1, Canada) (back issues avail.) **Indexed:** Chem.Abstr, GeoRef. —BLDSC shelfmark: 8488.450000.
  Formerly: Ontario. Division of Mines. Geological Circular, Geoscience Study.

622   CN   ISSN 0829-8203
QE191
ONTARIO GEOLOGICAL SURVEY. SUMMARY OF FIELD WORK. (Sub-series of: Ontario Geological Survey. Miscellaneous Paper (ISSN 0704-2752)) 1968. a. price varies. Ontario Geological Survey, 77 Grenville St., Rm. 719, Toronto, Ont. M7A 1W4, Canada. TEL 416-965-2000. (Subscr. to: Natural Resources Information Centre, Rm. M1-73, MacDonald Block, 900 Bay St., Toronto, Ont. M7A 2C1, Canada) (back issues avail.)

622   CN
ONTARIO GEOLOGICAL SURVEY. SUPPLEMENT TO M.P.77. (Sub-series of: Ontario Geological Survey. Miscellaneous Paper (ISSN 0704-2752)) 1978. a. price varies. Ontario Geological Survey, 77 Grenville St., Rm. 719, Toronto, Ont. M7A 1W4, Canada. TEL 416-965-2000. (Subscr. to: Natural Resources Information Centre, Rm. M1-73, MacDonald Block, 900 Bay St., Toronto, Ont. M7A 2C1, Canada) (back issues avail.)

338.2   CN   ISSN 0714-122X
HD9506.C23
ONTARIO MINERAL SCORE. 1980. a. Can.$15. Ministry of Northern Development and Mines, Planning and Information Office, 4th fl., 159 Cedar St., Sudbury, Ont. P3E 6A5, Canada. TEL 705-670-7235. FAX 705-670-7246. Eds. D. Romani, J. Webb. circ. 1,700.

622   SA   ISSN 0030-4050
HC517.S7
OPTIMA. 1951. s-a. free to shareholders. Anglo American & De Beers of South Africa, 44 Main St., Johannesburg, South Africa. FAX 011-638-3771. Ed. Ingrid Staude. charts; illus.; stat.; index; circ. 40,000. **Indexed:** AESIS, Cadscan, Field Crop Abstr., Geo.Abstr., GeoRef., Herb.Abstr., Ind.S.A.Per., Key to Econ.Sci., Lead Abstr., Met.Abstr., Mid.East: Abstr.& Ind., World Alum.Abstr., Zincscan.

OREGON. DEPARTMENT OF GEOLOGY AND MINERAL INDUSTRIES. BULLETIN. see *EARTH SCIENCES — Geology*

622   US   ISSN 1042-7902
OWLHOOTERS. m. $22. Luna Ventures, Box 398, Suisun, CA 94585. Ed. Paul Doerr. (also avail. in microfiche)
  Formerly: Owl Hooter's Gazette.
  Description: Prospecting, treasure and bounty.

622   SP
PANORAMA MINERO. 1981. a. 1500 ptas. Instituto Tecnologico Geominero de Espana, Cristobal Bordiu, 34, 28003 Madrid, Spain. TEL 441-65-00. FAX 442-62-16.
  Description: Covers the national and international industry of mining.

622   US   ISSN 0886-0912
PAY DIRT. ROCKY MOUNTAIN EDITION. 1979. m. $25. Copper Queen Publishing Co., Inc., Drawer 48, Bisbee, AZ 85603. TEL 602-432-2244. FAX 602-432-2247. adv.; circ. 3,996.
  Incorporates: Pay Dirt. Intermountain Edition (Nevada, Utah and Colorado); Pay Dirt. Big Sky Edition (Idaho, Montana and Wyoming).
  Description: Covers Colorado, Idaho, Montana, Nevada, Utah and Wyoming.

622   US   ISSN 0886-0920
PAY DIRT. SOUTHWESTERN EDITION. 1938. m. $25. Copper Queen Publishing Co., Inc., Drawer 48, Bisbee, AZ 85603. TEL 602-432-2244. FAX 602-432-2247. Ed. William C. Epler. adv.; bk.rev.; circ. 4,651.
  Incorporates: Pay Dirt. Arizona Edition; Pay Dirt. New Mexico Edition.
  Description: Covers Arizona, New Mexico and Southern California.

622   UK   ISSN 0031-3637
TN58.D4
PEAK DISTRICT MINES HISTORICAL SOCIETY. BULLETIN. 1959. s-a. £11($20) to individuals; institutions £18($34). Peak District Mines Historical Society, c/o Peak District Mining Museum, Matlock Bath, Derbyshire DE4 3NR, England. Ed. Trevor D. Ford. bk.rev.; charts; illus.; cum.index; circ. 500. **Indexed:** Br.Archaeol.Abstr., Geo.Abstr.

338.2   US
PENNSYLVANIA. DEPARTMENT OF ENVIRONMENTAL RESOURCES. ANNUAL REPORT ON MINING ACTIVITIES. 1870. a. price varies. Department of Environmental Resources, Bureau of Deep Mine Safety, Harrisburg, PA 17120. TEL 717-783-7515. FAX 717-541-7855. (Subscr. to: Pennsylvania State Bookstore, Box 1365 Harrisburg, PA 17125) Ed. Patsie Nichols. stat.; circ. 1,000.
  Former titles: Pennsylvania. Office of Mines and Land Protection. Annual Report; (until 1973): Pennsylvania. Anthracite, Bituminous Coal and Oil and Gas Divisions. Annual Report.

622   PH   ISSN 0048-3842
TN113
PHILIPPINE MINING & ENGINEERING JOURNAL. 1970. m. Business Masters International, 55 U.E. Tech. Avenue, University Hills, Subdivision Malabon, Rizal, Philippines. adv.; bk.rev.; illus.; stat.; circ. 5,000. **Indexed:** AESIS, Ind.Phil.Per.
  —BLDSC shelfmark: 6456.075000.

622   PH   ISSN 0085-4875
PHILIPPINE MINING AND ENGINEERING JOURNAL. MINING ANNUAL AND DIRECTORY. Included as July issue of Phillipine Mining and Engineering Journal. 1971. a. P.3($15) Business Masters International, 55 U.E. Tech. Avenue, University Hills, Subdivision Malabon, Rizal, Philippines. Ed. Luciano B. Quitlong. adv.; circ. 10,000.

PHOSPHORUS AND POTASSIUM; covers all aspects of world phosphate and potash fertilizer industry. see *ENGINEERING — Chemical Engineering*

549   GW   ISSN 0342-1791
QE351   CODEN: PCMIDU
PHYSICS AND CHEMISTRY OF MINERALS. 1977. 8/yr. DM.1198($681) (International Mineralogical Association) Springer-Verlag, Heidelberger Platz 3, D-1000 Berlin 33, Germany. TEL 030-8207-1. (Also Heidelberg, Tokyo, Vienna, and New York) Ed. I. Jackson. abstr.; bibl.; charts; illus.; stat.; index. (also avail. in microform from UMI; back issues avail.; reprint service avail. from ISI) **Indexed:** Br.Ceram.Abstr., Ceram.Abstr., Chem.Abstr., Curr.Cont., GeoRef., Phys.Ber., Sci.Abstr., Soils & Fert.
  —BLDSC shelfmark: 6478.217000.

622   US   ISSN 0032-0293
TN1   CODEN: PIQUAN
PIT & QUARRY. 1916. m. $25. Avanstar Communications, Inc., 7500 Old Oak Blvd., Cleveland, OH 44130. TEL 216-243-8100. FAX 216-891-2726. (Subscr. to: 1 E. First St., Duluth, MN 55802) Ed. Robert Drake. adv.; bk.rev.; charts; illus.; tr.lit.; circ. 21,672. (also avail. in microform from UMI) **Indexed:** A.S.& T.Ind., Bus.Ind., C.I.S. Abstr., C.R.I. Abstr., Chem.Abstr., Eng.Ind., Excerp.Med., GeoRef., PROMT, SRI, Tr.& Indus.Ind.
  Formerly: Cement - Mill and Quarry (ISSN 0095-9952)
  Description: Covers crushed stone, sand and gravel, cement, lime, gypsum, and related products and applications.

622   US
PIT & QUARRY HANDBOOK AND BUYERS GUIDE; equipment and technical reference manual for nonmetallic industry. 1907. a. $80. Avanstar Communications, Inc., 7500 Old Oak Blvd., Cleveland, OH 44130. TEL 216-243-8100. FAX 216-891-2726. (Subscr. to: 1 E. First St., Duluth, MN 55802) Ed. Robert Drake. adv.; index; circ. 8,700.
  Formerly: Pit and Quarry Handbook and Purchasing Guide (ISSN 0079-2128)

622   UK   ISSN 0268-7305
PLATINUM (YEAR). 1985. s-a. free. Johnson Matthey PLC, 78 Hatton Garden, London EC1N 8JP, England. TEL 071-269-8000. Ed. J.S. Coombes. circ. 25,000.
  —BLDSC shelfmark: 6538.180000.
  Description: Survey and analysis of the supply and demand for platinum and platinum group metals (palladium, rhodium, ruthenium, iridium) and developments in their markets.

622   PL   ISSN 0372-9508
TN4   CODEN: ZNSGAY
POLITECHNIKA SLASKA. ZESZYTY NAUKOWE. GORNICTWO. (Text in Polish; summaries in English, German, Russian) 1959. irreg. price varies. Politechnika Slaska, Katowicka 7, 44-100 Gliwice, Poland. FAX 371655. TELEX 036-304. (Dist. by: Ars Polona, Krakowskie Przedmiescie 7, 00-068 Warsaw, Poland) Ed. Walwry Szuscik. circ. 205. **Indexed:** Chem.Abstr.

622   PL   ISSN 0324-9670
POLITECHNIKA WROCLAWSKA. INSTYTUT GORNICTWA. PRACE NAUKOWE. KONFERENCJE. (Text in Polish; summaries in English and Russian) 1971. irreg., no.12, 1990. price varies. Politechnika Wroclawska, Wybrzeze Wyspianskiego 27, 50-370 Wroclaw, Poland. FAX 22-36-64. TELEX 712559 PWRPL. (Dist by: Ars Polona-Ruch, Krakowskie, Przedmiescie 7, Warsaw, Poland)

622   PL   ISSN 0324-9689
TN275.A1   CODEN: PIGKEF
POLITECHNIKA WROCLAWSKA. INSTYTUT GORNICTWA. PRACE NAUKOWE. MONOGRAFIE. (Text in Polish; summaries in English and Russian) 1973. irreg., no.29, 1991. price varies. Politechnika Wroclawska, Wybrzeze Wyspianskiego 27, 50-370 Wroclaw, Poland. FAX 22-36-64. TELEX 71-22-54 PWRPL. (Dist. by: Ars Polona-Ruch, Krakowskie Przediescie 7, Warsaw, Poland) illus.

622   PL   ISSN 0370-0798
POLITECHNIKA WROCLAWSKA. INSTYTUT GORNICTWA. PRACE NAUKOWE. STUDIA I MATERIALY. (Text in Polish; summaries in English and Russian) 1970. irreg., no.22, 1990. price varies. Politechnika Wroclawska, Wybrzeze Wyspianskiego 27, 50-370 Wroclaw, Poland. FAX 22-36-64. TELEX 712559 PWRPL. (Dist. by: Ars Polona-Ruch, Krakowskie Przedmiescie 7, Warsaw, Poland)

622   PL   ISSN 0079-3280
TN275 .A1
POLSKA AKADEMIA NAUK. ODDZIAL W KRAKOWIE. KOMISJA GORNICZO-GEODEZYJNA. PRACE: GORNICTWO. (Text in Polish; summaries in English and Russian) 1965. irreg., no.24, 1986. price varies. Ossolineum, Publishing House of the Polish Academy of Sciences, Rynek 9, Wroclaw, Poland. TELEX 0712771 OSS PL. (Dist. by: Ars Polona-Ruch, Krakowskie Przedmiescie 7, Warsaw, Poland) Ed. Zbigniew Strzelecki.
  —BLDSC shelfmark: 6586.570000.

PORTUGAL. SERVICOS GEOLOGICOS. COMUNICACOES. see *EARTH SCIENCES — Geology*

MINES AND MINING INDUSTRY

622   US   ISSN 0146-7204
HD9536.A1
POWELL GOLD INDUSTRY GUIDE & INTERNATIONAL MINING ANALYST. 1976. q. $120 (foreign $140). Reserve Research Ltd., Box 4135, Portland, ME 04101. TEL 207-774-4971. Ed. Larson M. Powell. charts; stat. (back issues avail.)

PRODUCCION Y EXPORTACIONES CHILENAS DE COBRE. see BUSINESS AND ECONOMICS — Production Of Goods And Services

622   CN   ISSN 1181-6414
PROSPECTOR EXPLORATION & INVESTMENT BULLETIN. 1980. 6/yr. Can.$30 for 12 issues. K W Publishing Ltd., 1268 W. Pender St., Vancouver, B.C. V6E 2S8, Canada. TEL 604-688-2038. Ed. R. MacDonald. adv.; circ. 25,000. (tabloid format)
Formerly: Northwest Prospector Miners and Developers Bulletin (ISSN 0824-6149)

622   PL   ISSN 0033-216X
TN4   CODEN: PRGOAI
PRZEGLAD GORNICZY. (Text in Polish; summaries in English, French, German and Russian) 1912. m. 144 Zl.($25.20) (Glowny Instytut Gornictwa) Wydawnictwo "Slask", Al. W. Korfantego 51, 40-161 Katowice, Poland. TEL 583221. TELEX 312326. (Dist. by: Ars Polona - Ruch, Krakowskie Przedmiescie 7, Warsaw, Poland) (Co-sponsor: Stowarzyszenie Inzynierow i Technikow Gornictwa) Ed. Jerzy Malara. adv.; bk.rev.; abstr.; bibl.; charts; illus.; index; circ. 2,800. (also avail. in microfilm; microfiche) **Indexed:** C.I.S. Abstr., Ceram.Abstr., Chem.Abstr., Eng.Ind., Geotech.Abstr.
—BLDSC shelfmark: 6942.300000.

PUBLIC LAND & RESOURCES LAW DIGEST. see LAW

622   HU   ISSN 0324-4628
TN275.A1   CODEN: PTUADT
PUBLICATIONS OF THE TECHNICAL UNIVERSITY FOR HEAVY INDUSTRY. SERIES A, MINING. (Text in English, German and Russian) irreg., vol.45, no.1-4, 1988. Nehezipari Muszaki Egyetem, Miskolc, Hungary. TEL 46-65111. FAX 46-69554. TELEX 62223-NMEMIS. Ed.Bd. bibl.; index; circ. 350.
—BLDSC shelfmark: 7113.411000.

622   AT
QUARRY. 1973. m. Aus.$50. Morgan Trade Publications, 52 St. Kilda Rd., Melbourne, Vic. 3182, Australia. TEL 03-5101242. FAX 03-510-9024. Ed. Kerrie O'Brien. adv.; bk.rev.; circ. 6,250.

622.35   UK
QUARRY MANAGEMENT. 1918. m. £30. (Institute of Quarrying) Quarry Managers' Journal Ltd., 7 Regent St., Nottingham NG1 5BY, England. TEL 0602-411315. FAX 0602-484035. Ed. Bernard Hill. adv.; bk.rev.; charts; illus.; tr.lit.; index; circ. 6,420. (reprint service avail. from UMI) **Indexed:** AESIS, Br.Geol.Lit., Br.Tech.Ind, C.I.S. Abstr., C.R.I. Abstr., Excerp.Med., Fluidex, Fuel & Energy Abstr., Geo.Abstr., GeoRef., HRIS, Intl.Civil Eng.Abstr., RICS, Soft.Abstr.Eng., W.R.C.Inf.
Formerly (until June 1984): Quarry Management and Products (ISSN 0305-9421); Incorporates: Quarry Managers' Journal (ISSN 0033-5274); Cement, Lime and Gravel (ISSN 0008-8862)
Description: For the quarrying, opencast and related industries, covering technical and management topics.

QUARTERLY COAL REPORT. see ENERGY

QUEBEC (PROVINCE). DEPARTMENT OF ENERGY AND RESOURCES. REPORT. see ENERGY

622   AT   ISSN 0033-6149
TN1   CODEN: QGMJAZ
QUEENSLAND GOVERNMENT MINING JOURNAL. 1900. m. Aus.$66. Department of Resource Industries, 61 Mary St., Brisbane, Qld. 4000, Australia. TEL 07-237-1643. FAX 07-221-9517. Ed. M. Holliday. adv.; bk.rev.; abstr.; charts; illus.; mkt.; stat.; tr.lit.; circ. 1,400. **Indexed:** AESIS, Aus.Rd.Ind., Chem.Abstr., Fuel & Energy Abstr., Geo.Abstr., GeoRef., Met.Abstr.
—BLDSC shelfmark: 7214.000000.
Description: Provides information on developments in the geological, mining and mineral processing industries in Queensland. Also covers world trends.

QUICK RELEASE TO THE MINERAL STATISTICS OF INDIA. see MINES AND MINING INDUSTRY — Abstracting, Bibliographies, Statistics

R I C INSIGHT. (Rare-earth Information Center) see METALLURGY

R I C NEWS. (Rare-earth Information Center) see METALLURGY

RAW MATERIALS REPORT; political economy of natural resources. see BUSINESS AND ECONOMICS — International Development And Assistance

622   RU   ISSN 0034-026X
CODEN: RZONAV
RAZVEDKA I OKHRANA NEDR. 1935. m. 27 Rub. (Profsoyuz Rabochikh Geologorazvedochnykh Rabot) Izdatel'stvo Nedra, Pl. Belorusskogo Vokzala, 3, 125047 Moscow, Russia. TEL 250-52-55. (Co-sponsor: Ministerstvo Geologii) Ed. V.I. Kuzmenko. bk.rev.; bibl.; charts; illus.; circ. 8,400. **Indexed:** Biol.Abstr., Chem.Abstr., Eng.Ind., GeoRef.
—BLDSC shelfmark: 0140.000000.

622 658   FR
CODEN: ANMSA3
REALITES INDUSTRIELLES. (Text in French; summaries in English, German, Russian, Spanish) 1794. m. 674 F. includes Gerer et Comprendre (foreign 784 F.)(effective Nov. 1990). (Annales des Mines) Societe E S K A, 27 rue Dunois, 75013 Paris, France. TEL 77-32-46-13. Ed. Michel Mathieu. adv.; bk.rev.; abstr.; illus.; stat.; index. cum.index every 10 yrs.; circ. 3,500. (back issues avail.) **Indexed:** C.I.S. Abstr., Chem.Abstr., Curr.Cont., Eng.Ind., Fuel & Energy Abstr., Geo.Abstr., GeoRef., INIS Atomind., Met.Abstr., Risk Abstr., World Alum.Abstr.
Formerly: Annales des Mines. Dossiers Documentaires; Supersedes in part: Annales des Mines (ISSN 0003-4282)

RECLAMATION NEWSLETTER. see ENVIRONMENTAL STUDIES

622   SA
THE REEF. (Text in Afrikaans and English) 1915. m. R.3.30. Chamber of Mines of South Africa, P.O. Box 809, Johannesburg 2000, South Africa. Ed. C. du Toit Thon. adv.; bk.rev.; circ. 45,000.
Description: For mining industry personnel in South Africa.

622   JA
REPORT OF OVERSEAS MINING INVESTIGATION: INDIA, PAKISTAN, BANGLADESH/KAIGAI KOGYO JIJO CHOSA HOKOKUSHO: INDO, PAKISUTAN, BANGURADESSHU. (Text in Japanese) irreg. Metal Mining Agency, Data Center - Kinzoku Kogyo Jigyodan, Shiryo Senta, 6-3 Nishikubo Saguragawa-cho, Shiba, Minato-ku, Tokyo 105, Japan. charts; illus.

622   JA
REPORT OF OVERSEAS MINING INVESTIGATION: MADAGASCAR, SWAZILAND/KAIGAI KOGYO JIJO CHOSA HOKOKUSHO: MADAGASUKARU, SUWAJIRANDO. (Text in Japanese) irreg. Metal Mining Agency, Data Center - Kinzoku Kogy Jigyodan. Shiryo Senta, 6-3 Shiba Nishikubo Saguragawa-cho, Shiba, Minato-ku, Tokyo 105, Japan. charts; illus.

338.2   US
REPORT ON OHIO MINERAL INDUSTRIES; with directories of reporting coal and industrial mineral operations. 1872. a. $6.54. Department of Natural Resources, Division of Geological Survey, Fountain Sq., Bldg. B, Columbus, OH 43224-1362. TEL 614-265-6605. Ed. Sherry Lopez. index; circ. 1,600.
Former titles: Ohio. Division of Mines. Report (ISSN 0078-401X); Ohio. Division of Mines. Annual Report with Coal and Industrial Mineral Directories of Reporting Firms.

RESERVES OF COAL, PROVINCE OF ALBERTA. see ENERGY

RESOURCES POLICY. see ENERGY

622   AT   ISSN 1032-0776
RESOURCES - QUARRY MINE & CONSTRUCTION NEWS. 1946. 11/yr. Aus.$70. Advanced Publishing Industries, P.M.B. 14, Ermington, N.S.W. 2115, Australia. TEL 61-2-684-2500. FAX 61-2-638-3032. Ed. Linda Vitanza. adv.; bk.rev.; charts; illus.; stat.; circ. 8,000. **Indexed:** AESIS, Aus.Rd.Ind.
Formerly: Resources Industry - Quarry Mine and Construction Equipment; Formed by the Jan. 1981 merger of: Contracting and Construction Engineer (ISSN 0010-7867); Quarry Mine and Pit (ISSN 0048-6116); Public Works and Services.

622   GW
REVIER UND WERK. 1950. bi-m. Rheinbraun AG, Stuettgenweg 2, 5000 Cologne 41, Germany. TEL 0221-4801. FAX 0221-4803333. Ed. Wolfgang Trees. bk.rev.; circ. 34,000.

338.2   TZ   ISSN 0082-1659
REVIEW OF THE MINERAL INDUSTRY IN TANZANIA. Title varies: Tanzania. Mines Division. Review of the Mineral Industry. (Former name of issuing body: Mineral Resources Division) 1965. a. free. Ministry of Water, Energy and Minerals, Mines Division, Box 903, Dodoma, Tanzania. Ed. Anthony Muze. circ. 400.

622   SP   ISSN 0210-8356
TN87
REVISTA DE MINAS. 1979. a. 2500 ptas. Universidad de Oviedo, Escuela Tecnica Superior de Ingenieros de Minas, Oviedo, Spain. (Subscr. to: Servicio de Publicaciones, Un. de Oviedo, Calle J. Arias de Velasco s/n, 33005 Oviedo, Spain) Ed. Jose Martinez Alvarez. bk.rev.; illus.; circ. 500. **Indexed:** Ind.SST.

622   CU
REVISTA DE MINERIA Y GEOLOGIA. 3/yr. $24 in N. America; S. America $25; Europe $26. (Ministerio de Mineria y Geologia, Centro de Informacion Cientifico-Tecnico) Ediciones Cubanas, Obispo No. 527, Apdo. 605, Havana, Cuba. bibl.; charts; illus. **Indexed:** GeoRef.
Formerly (until 1984): Mineria en Cuba.

622   BO
REVISTA MINERA BAMIN. no.87, Jan.-Mar., 1976. q. Banco Minero de Bolivia, Departamento de Relaciones Publicas, Casilla Correo 1410, La Paz, Bolivia.

622   FR   ISSN 0150-7516
REVUE DES INGENIEURS; des ecoles nationales superieures des mines (Paris, Saint-Etienne, Nancy). 1948. bi-m. 190 F. (foreign 210 F.). (Associations des Anciens Eleves des Ecoles des Mines) Intermines, 4 av. de Galliera, 75116 Paris, France. Ed. Henri Deniau. adv.; illus.; circ. 8,000.
—BLDSC shelfmark: 7924.258000.

622.33   SP   ISSN 0378-3316
ROCAS Y MINERALES. 1972. m. 10000 ptas. Editorial Rocas y Minerales, Arturo Baldasano, 15, 28043 Madrid, Spain. TEL 415 1804. FAX 415-1661. Eds. Laureano Fueyo, Carlos Vivas Escribano. adv.; bk.rev.; illus.; circ. 6,000 (controlled). (back issues avail.) **Indexed:** Ind.SST.

ROCK MECHANICS AND ROCK ENGINEERING. see EARTH SCIENCES — Geology

622   US   ISSN 0080-3375
CODEN: RMESDA
ROCK MECHANICS - FELSMECHANIK - MECHANIQUE DES ROCHES. SUPPLEMENT. 1970. irreg. price varies. Springer-Verlag, 175 Fifth Ave., New York, NY 10010. TEL 212-460-1500. (Also Berlin, Heidelberg, Tokyo and Vienna) (also avail. in microform from UMI; reprint service avail. from ISI) **Indexed:** Geo.Abstr., GeoRef., Geotech.Abstr.
Continues: Felsmechanik und Ingenieurgeologie. Rock Mechanics and Engineering Geology. Supplement.

MINES AND MINING INDUSTRY 3495

622   US   ISSN 0035-7464
TN950   CODEN: ROPRA5
ROCK PRODUCTS; industry's recognized authority. (International ed. avail.) 1897. m. $31.25. Maclean Hunter Publishing Company, 29 N. Wacker Dr., Chicago, IL 60606. TEL 312-726-2802. FAX 312-726-2574. TELEX 270258 EXP. Ed. Richard Hunta. adv.; illus.; tr.lit.; pat.; index; circ. 24,855. (also avail. in microform from UMI; reprint service avail. from UMI) **Indexed:** A.S.& T.Ind., AESIS, C.R.I. Abstr., Chem.Abstr., Eng.Ind., Excerp.Med., GeoRef, PROMT.
—BLDSC shelfmark: 8002.000000.
   Description: Covers the production and distribution of sand and gravel, crushed stone, cement, lime, gypsum, slag, lightweight aggregates and other nonmetallic minerals.

549 551   US   ISSN 0035-7529
QE351   CODEN: ROCMAR
ROCKS AND MINERALS; mineralogy, geology, lapidary. 1926. bi-m. $32 to individuals; institutions $53. (Helen Dwight Reid Educational Foundation) Heldref Publications, 1319 Eighteenth St., N.W., Washington, DC 20036-1802. TEL 202-296-6267. FAX 202-296-5149. Ed. Marie Huizig. adv.; bk.rev.; charts; tr.lit.; index; circ. 4,000. (also avail. in microform; back issues avail.; reprint service avail.) **Indexed:** Chem.Abstr., GeoRef., Mineral.Abstr., Petrol.Abstr.
—BLDSC shelfmark: 8002.500000.
   Description: Articles geared towards the amateurs in the field of mineralogy, geology and paleontology.
Refereed Serial

ROCKY MOUNTAIN MINERAL LAW FOUNDATION. NEWSLETTER. see *LAW*

622 340 665.5
333.33   US   ISSN 0886-747X
KF1819.A2
ROCKY MOUNTAIN MINERAL LAW INSTITUTE. PROCEEDINGS. 1955. a. $120. Matthew Bender & Co., Inc. (Oakland), 2101 Webster Ave., Box 2077, Oakland, CA 94604. TEL 415-446-7100. FAX 415-893-0160. (Subscr. addr.: 1275 Broadway, Albany, NY 12204) Ed. Karen Kaiser. circ. 1,050. (also avail. in microfilm from RRI; back issues avail.; reprint service avail. from RRI) **Indexed:** C.L.I., Leg.Per.
   Description: Covers mining, oil and gas, landmen, environmental, and water law.

ROSSING MAGAZINE. see *CONSERVATION*

622   UK   ISSN 0080-4495
ROYAL SCHOOL OF MINES, LONDON. JOURNAL. 1951. a. £1. Royal School of Mines Union, Prince Consort Road, London SW7 2BP, England. TEL 01-589 5111. Ed. Frank W.A.A. Lucas. adv.; bk.rev.; circ. 2,000. **Indexed:** Cadscan, Lead Abstr., Zincscan.

622   YU   ISSN 0035-9637
TN4.B4
RUDARSKI GLASNIK/BULLETIN OF MINES. (Text in Serbo-Croatian; summaries in English, German and Russian) 1962. q. 278 din.($26) Rudarski Institut-Beograd - Mining Institute - Belgrade, Batajnicki Put 2, Belgrade, Yugoslavia. FAX 011-614-632. TELEX 11830 YU RI. Ed. Marunic Djuro. adv.; bk.rev.; abstr.; bibl.; charts; illus.; index; circ. 1,000. **Indexed:** C.I.S. Abstr., Chem.Abstr., Eng.Ind., GeoRef., Ref.Zh.

669   XV   ISSN 0035-9645
TN4   CODEN: RMZBAR
RUDARSKO-METALURSKI ZBORNIK/MINING AND METALLURGY QUARTERLY. (Text in Serbo-Croatian or Slovenian; summaries in English) 1953. q. 1025 din.($36) Rudarski Institut, Ljubljana, Askerceva 20, Box 594, 61001 Ljubljana, Slovenia. (Co-sponsor: Univerza v Ljubljani, Fakulteta za Naravoslovje in Tehnologijo) Ed. Vasilij Gontazev. adv.; bk.rev.; charts; illus.; index; circ. 1,030. (also avail. in microform from UMI) **Indexed:** Chem.Abstr., Eng.Ind., GeoRef., Met.Abstr., World Alum.Abstr.
—BLDSC shelfmark: 8048.000000.

RUDARSTVO - GEOLOGIJA - METALURGIJA. see *METALLURGY*

622   CS   ISSN 0035-9688
RUDY. (Text in Czech; summaries in English, French, German, Russian) 1952. m. $58.30. Nakladatelstvi Technicke Literatury, Spalena 51, 113 02 Prague 1, Czechoslovakia. (Dist. by: Artia, Ve Smeckach 30, 111 27 Prague 1, Czechoslovakia) Ed. J. Malcharek. adv.; bk.rev.; bibl.; illus.; pat.; index; circ. 1,800. **Indexed:** C.I.S. Abstr., Chem.Abstr., Met.Abstr., World Alum.Abstr.

RUDY I METALE NIEZELAZNE. see *METALLURGY*

622   SA
S A MINING WORLD. m. Phase Four (Pty) Ltd., P.O. Box 784279, Sandton 2146, South Africa. TEL 011-444-4566. FAX 011-444-7888. adv.
   Formerly: Mining World S A.

622   GW
SAARBERG. 1871. bi-m. Saarbergwerke AG, Trierer Str. 1, 6600 Saarbrucken, Germany. TEL 0681-405-3425. circ. 21,000. (back issues avail.)
   Formerly: Bergmannsfreund.
   Description: Covers all aspects of mining.

622   GW
SAARBRUECKER BERGMANNSKALENDER. 1873. a. DM.12. Saarbergwerke AG, Trierer Str. 1, 6600 Saarbruecken, Germany. TEL 0681-405-3425. circ. 18,000. (back issues avail.)
   Description: Information on miners and mining.

622.33   CN
SASKATCHEWAN ENERGY & MINES. ANNUAL REPORT. 1954. a. Saskatchewan Energy & Mines, 1914 Hamilton St., Regina, Sask. S4P 4V4, Canada. TEL 306-787-2528. FAX 306-787-7338. charts; illus.
   Former titles: Saskatchewan Mineral Resources. Annual Report; Saskatchewan. Department of Mineral Resources. Annual Report (ISSN 0581-8109)

338.2 665.5   CN
SASKATCHEWAN ENERGY & MINES. MINERAL STATISTICS YEARBOOK. 1964. a. Can.$40. Saskatchewan Energy and Mines, Petroleum Statistics Branch, 1914 Hamilton St., Regina, Sask. S4P 4V4, Canada. TEL 306-787-2528. FAX 306-787-7338.
   Former titles: Saskatchewan Mineral Resources. Mineral Statistical Yearbook; Saskatchewan. Department of Mineral Resources. Statistical Yearbook (ISSN 0707-2570)
   Description: Includes a summary section on mineral production, disposition, value of disposition and provincial revenues from minerals, and a detailed section containing monthly, annual and historical data on each of fuel, industrial and metallic minerals.

SATURN FIVE'S MARKET UPDATE. see *BUSINESS AND ECONOMICS — Investments*

549 552   SZ   ISSN 0036-7699
QE351   CODEN: SMPTA8
SCHWEIZERISCHE MINERALOGISCHE UND PETROGRAPHISCHE MITTEILUNGEN/BULLETIN SUISSE DE MINERALOGIE ET PETROGRAPHIE/BOLLETINO SVIZZERO DI MINERALOGIA E PETROGRAFIA; eine europaeische Zeitschrift fuer Mineralogie, Geochemie und Petrographie. (Text in English, French, German, Italian) 1921. 3/yr. 200 Fr. Staeubli Verlag AG, Raeffelstr. 11, Postfach 237, 8045 Zurich, Switzerland. TEL 01-4615858. FAX 01-4612272. adv.; bk.rev.; charts; illus.; index. **Indexed:** Chem.Abstr., GeoRef.
—BLDSC shelfmark: 8119.000000.

338.4   GW
SECONDARY ALUMINIUM; Europe, Japan, USA. (Editions in English, French and German) 1965. a. free. Organisation of European Aluminium Smelters, Graf-Adolf-Str. 18, 4000 Duesseldorf, Germany. FAX 211-134268. TELEX 8582508. Ed. Guenter Kirchner. circ. 4,000.
   Former titles (until 1988): Aluminium Smelters; Organisation of European Aluminum Smelters. Economic Situation of the Aluminum Smelters in Europe (ISSN 0474-4829)

622   CC   ISSN 1000-1603
SHANXI KUANGYE XUEYUAN XUEBAO/SHANXI INSTITUTE OF MINING INDUSTRY. JOURNAL. (Text in Chinese) q. Shanxi Kuangye Xueyuan - Shanxi Institute of Mining Industry, 23 Yingze Dajie, Taiyuan, Shanxi 030024, People's Republic of China. TEL 665717. Ed. Sheng Jianheng.

622   JA   ISSN 0916-1740
                    CODEN: SHSOEB
SHIGEN SOZAI/MINING AND MATERIALS PROCESSING INSTITUTE OF JAPAN. JOURNAL. (Text in Japanese; summaries in English) 1885. 14/yr. 22400 Yen. Mining and Materials Processing Institute of Japan - Shigen, Sozai Gakkai, Nogizaka Bldg., 9-6-41 Akasaka, Minato-ku, Tokyo 107, Japan. TEL 03-3402-0541. FAX 03-3403-1776. Ed.Bd. adv.; bk.rev.; circ. 4,000.
—BLDSC shelfmark: 4827.700000.
   Formerly (until 1988): Nihon Kogyokaishi - Mining and Metallurgical Institute of Japan. Journal (ISSN 0369-4194)

338.2 669   US   ISSN 0730-8132
SILVER INSTITUTE LETTER; information on silver for industry. 1971. bi-m. $20 (foreign $25). Silver Institute, 1112 16th St., N.W., Ste. 240, Washington, DC 20036. TEL 202-835-0185. TELEX 904233. Ed. John H. Lutley. circ. 4,000. (back issues avail.) **Indexed:** SRI.
   Description: Covers recent developments on the uses of silver in the areas of art, finance, mining, coins and photography.

622   US   ISSN 0037-6329
TN1
SKILLINGS' MINING REVIEW. 1912. w. $30 (effective Jan. 1991). Skillings' Mining Review, Inc., c/o David N. Skillings, Jr., Ed., First Bank Pl., No. 728, 130 W. Sup. St., Duluth, MN 55802-2083. TEL 218-722-2310. FAX 218-722-0134. adv.; bk.rev.; charts; illus.; stat.; index; circ. 4,000. **Indexed:** AESIS, Geo.Abstr., PROMT.
—BLDSC shelfmark: 8295.850000.

622 943.7   CS
SLOVENSKE BANSKE MUZEUM. ZBORNIK. 1967. irreg. Vydavatel'stvo Osveta, Osloboditelov 21, 036 54 Martin, Czechoslovakia. FAX 0842-350-36. (Dist. by: Slovart, Gottwaldovo Nam. 6, 805 32 Bratislava, Czechoslovakia)

338.2   FR
SOCIETE DE L'INDUSTRIE MINERALE GUIDE DES MINES ET CARRIERES. 1855. a. 663.65 F. Societe de l'Industrie Minerale, 41-47, rue de la Grange aux Belles, 75010 Paris, France. TEL 42-02-07-92. FAX 42-06-69-30. adv.; index.
   Former titles: Societe de l'Industrie Minerale Mines et Carrieres. Annuaire; Societe de l'Industrie Minerale. Annuaire (ISSN 0081-0797)

338.7   IV   ISSN 0250-3697
SOCIETE POUR LE DEVELOPPEMENT MINIER DE LA COTE D'IVOIRE. RAPPORT ANNUEL. 1962. a. free. Societe pour le Developpement Minier de la Cote d'Ivoire, 01.B.P. 2816, Abidjan 01, Ivory Coast. FAX 011-225-440821. TELEX 26162 SODMI. illus. **Indexed:** GeoRef.

SOCIETY OF EXPLOSIVES ENGINEERS. CONFERENCE ON EXPLOSIVES AND BLASTING TECHNIQUE. PROCEEDINGS. see *ENGINEERING — Chemical Engineering*

SOCIETY OF EXPLOSIVES ENGINEERS. MEMBERSHIP DIRECTORY AND DESK REFERENCE. see *ENGINEERING — Chemical Engineering*

SOCIETY OF EXPLOSIVES ENGINEERS. SYMPOSIUM ON EXPLOSIVES AND BLASTING RESEARCH. PROCEEDINGS. see *ENGINEERING — Chemical Engineering*

MINES AND MINING INDUSTRY

622 551   SA
SOUTH AFRICA. DEPARTMENT OF MINERAL AND ENERGY AFFAIRS. ANNUAL REPORT. (Text in Afrikaans and English) N.S. 1947. a. price varies. Department of Mineral and Energy Affairs, Private Bag X59, Pretoria 0001, South Africa. (Orders to: Government Printer, Bosman St., Private Bag X85, Pretoria 0001, South Africa) circ. 1,000. **Indexed:** GeoRef.
    Formerly: South Africa. Department of Mines. Annual Report; Incorporates: South Africa. Geological Survey. Report of the Chief Director of the Geological Survey; South Africa. Minerals Buro. Report of the Chief Director of the Minerals Buro.

669   SA   ISSN 0038-2213
SOUTH AFRICAN INSTITUTE OF ASSAYERS AND ANALYSTS. JOURNAL. (Text in Afrikaans and English) 1958. q. membership. South African Institute of Assayers and Analysts, Box 61019, Marshalltown, Transvaal, South Africa. Ed. J.W. Barnett. adv.; illus.; circ. 250.

SOUTH AFRICAN INSTITUTE OF MINING AND METALLURGY. JOURNAL. see *METALLURGY*

SOUTH AFRICAN INSTITUTE OF MINING AND METALLURGY. MONOGRAPH SERIES. see *METALLURGY*

736   SA   ISSN 0038-237X
SOUTH AFRICAN LAPIDARY MAGAZINE/SUID-AFRIKAANSE LAPIDERE TYDSKRIF. 1967. 3/yr. R.4.50 per no. Federation of South African Gem & Mineralogical Societies, Box 28744, Sunnyside 0132, South Africa. Ed. L. Dreyer. adv.; bk.rev.; circ. 600. **Indexed:** GeoRef., Ind.S.A.Per.

622 620   SA
SOUTH AFRICAN MINING, COAL, GOLD AND BASE MINERALS. 1891. m. R.84 (foreign R.109)(effective 1992). Thomson Publications (Subsidiary of: Times Media Ltd.), P.O. Box 56182, Pinegowrie 2123, South Africa. TEL 011-789-2144. FAX 011-789-3196. Ed. Roy Bennetts. adv.; illus.; mkt.; stat.; index; circ. 4,978. (also avail. in microfilm from UMI) **Indexed:** AESIS, Eng.Ind., Excerp.Med., GeoRef., Ind.S.A.Per., INIS Atomind.
    Formerly: South African Mining and Engineering Journal; Incorporating: South African Mining Equipment (ISSN 0038-2477)

SOUTH AUSTRALIA. DEPARTMENT OF MINES AND ENERGY. SPECIAL PUBLICATIONS. see *EARTH SCIENCES*

622   CN
SOUTHAM MINING GROUP'S MINING SOURCEBOOK. 1981. a. $72 (foreign $89). Southam North American Magazine Group, 1450 Don Mills Rd., Don Mills, Ont. M3B 2X7, Canada. TEL 416-445-6641. FAX 416-442-2272. adv.
    Formerly: Canadian Mining Journal's Mining Sourcebook.
    Description: Contains operating data on underground mining, open pit mining and mineral processing. Includes Buyers' Guide and a list of all operating mines in Canada.

338.2 622   RU   ISSN 0038-5158
SOVETSKII SHAKHTER. 1952. m. 16.80 Rub. (Profsoyuz Rabochikh Ugol'noi Promyshlennosti S.S.S.R., Tsentral'nyi Komitet) Profizdat, Ul. Kirova, 13, Moscow, Russia. Ed. F.S. Bocharov. bk.rev.; charts; illus.; stat.; index; circ. 101,720.

622 551   US   ISSN 0038-5581
TN4   CODEN: SMNSAT
SOVIET MINING SCIENCE. English translation of: Fiziko-tekhnicheskie Problemy Razrabotki Poleznykh Iskopaemykh (RU ISSN 0015-3273) bi-m. $995 (foreign $1165)(effective 1992). (Russian Academy of Sciences, Siberian Division, RU) Plenum Publishing Corp., Consultants Bureau, 233 Spring St., New York, NY 10013-1578. TEL 212-620-8468. FAX 212-463-0742. TELEX 23-421139. Ed. E.I. Shemyakin. (also avail. in microfilm from JSC; back issues avail.) **Indexed:** Curr.Cont., Energy Ind., Energy Info.Abstr., Eng.Ind.
    —BLDSC shelfmark: 0424.550000.
    Refereed Serial

SPAIN. INSTITUTO TECNOLOGICO GEOMINERO DE ESPANA. COLECCION MEMORIAS. see *EARTH SCIENCES — Geology*

SPAIN. INSTITUTO TECNOLOGICO GEOMINERO DE ESPANA. COLECCION TEMAS GEOLOGICOS - MINEROS. see *EARTH SCIENCES*

SPAIN. INSTITUTO TECNOLOGICO GEOMINERO DE ESPANA. INFORMES. see *EARTH SCIENCES — Geology*

622   US
SPEAKERS' PAPERS: SPEECHES FROM THE GOLD AND SILVER INSTITUTES' (YEAR) ANNUAL MEETING. a. $95 (foreign $110). Gold Institute, Administrative Office - Institut de l'Or, Bureau Administratif, 1112 15th St., N.W., Ste. 420, Washington, DC 20036-4823. TEL 202-835-0185. FAX 202-835-0155. TEL 202-835-0155.
    Description: Contains current information direct from industry leaders and experts.

622   DK   ISSN 0107-430X
KDZ3371
SPECIFICATIONS OF MINERAL CONCESSIONS AND LICENSES IN GREENLAND. 1981. a. free. Ministry of Energy, Mineral Resources Administration for Greenland, Slotsholmsgade 1, 1216 Copenhagen K, Denmark. TEL 45-33-92-75-00. FAX 45-33-13-30-17. TELEX 15505 ENRGY DK.
    Formerly: Specifications of Mineral Licenses and Concessions in Greenland.
    Description: Provides information about the principles, content, etc. of the mineral resources system for Greenland; lists existing mineral concessions and prospecting licences in Greenland.

338.2   CN
STATISTICAL REVIEW OF COAL IN CANADA. 1971. a. Energy, Mines and Resources Canada, Mineral Policy Sector, 460 O'Connor St., Ottawa, Ont. K1A 0E4, Canada. TEL 613-995-1118. FAX 613-992-5565. stat.
    Formerly: Coal in Canada, Supply and Demand (ISSN 0700-284X)

622 665.5   US
HD9685.U4
STEAM - ELECTRIC PLANT FACTORS (1978). a. $125 to individuals; non-profit organizations $100. National Coal Association, 1130 17th St., N.W., Washington, DC 20036. TEL 202-463-2640. **Indexed:** SRI.
    Former titles: Steam Electric Fuels (ISSN 0090-3884); Steam - Electric Plant Factors (ISSN 0081-5411)

STEELMAKING CONFERENCE: PROCEEDINGS. see *METALLURGY*

622   GW   ISSN 0039-1018
TN950
STEINBRUCH UND SANDGRUBE; unabhaengige Fach-Zeitschrift fuer Steinbrueche, Kies- und Sandgruben, Betonsteinwerke. 1904. m. DM.60. Verlagsgesellschaft Gruetter, Postfach 910708, 3000 Hannover 91, Germany. TEL 0511-4603-300. FAX 0511-4609-320. Ed. K.-H. Mueller. adv.; bk.rev.; illus.; index; circ. 10,000.

622   US   ISSN 8750-9210
STONE REVIEW. 1985. bi-m. $48. National Stone Association, 1415 Elliot Pl., N.W., Washington, DC 20007. TEL 202-342-1100. FAX 202-342-0702. Ed. Frank E. Atlee. adv.; circ. 4,000.
    Formed by the Jan. 1985 merger of (1974-1984): Stone News; (1964-1984): Limestone.

622 943.7   CS
STUDIE Z DEJIN HORNICTVI. (Text in Czech; summaries in German) 1971. irreg. exchange basis. Narodni Technicke Muzeum, Kostelni 42, Prague 7, Czechoslovakia. bibl.; illus.

338.2 622 661.2   UK   ISSN 0039-4890
     CODEN: SULPAW
SULPHUR; covers all aspects of world sulphur and sulphuric acid industry. 1953. bi-m. £290. British Sulphur Corp. Ltd., 31 Mount Pleasant, London WC1X 0AD, England. TEL 071-837-5600. FAX 071-837-0292. TELEX 918918-SULFEX-G. Ed. K. Campbell. bk.rev.; charts; illus.; mkt.; stat.; index; circ. 639. (also avail. in microform from UMI; reprint service avail. from UMI) **Indexed:** Chem.Abstr., Soils & Fert.
    —BLDSC shelfmark: 8516.800000.

SURVEYING AUSTRALIA. see *ENGINEERING — Civil Engineering*

622   SW   ISSN 0039-6435
SVENSK BERGS- OCH BRUKSTIDNING. 1922. 6/yr. SEK 100. B & J Invest AB, P.O. Box 6040, S-20011 Malmoe, Sweden. FAX 40-79737. Ed. Joergen Dahlkvist. circ. 3,000.

T H - ERS EXPRESS; adventure bulletin. (Treasure Hunt) see *HOBBIES*

T I Z INTERNATIONAL; Powder & Bulk Magazin. see *ENGINEERING — Chemical Engineering*

622   CC   ISSN 0494-6162
TANKUANG GONGCHENG. (Text in Chinese) bi-m. Dizhi Kuangchan Bu, Kantan Jishu Yanjiusuo, 26, Baiwanzhuang Lu, Beijing 100037, People's Republic of China. TEL 8311133. Ed. Wang Decong.

622   II
TECHNICAL INFORMATION DIGEST. (Text in English) 1976. q. free. Central Mine Planning & Design Institute Ltd. (Subsidiary of: Coal India Limited), Publications Wing, Gondwana Place, Kanke Rd., Ranchi 834008, Bihar, India.

TECHNIKA POSZUKIWAN GEOLOGICZNYCH, GEOSYNOPTYKA I GOETERMIA/EXPLORATION TECHNOLOGY, GEOSYNOPTICS AND GEOTHERMAL ENERGY. see *EARTH SCIENCES — Geology*

622   GW   ISSN 0040-1501
TECHNISCHE UNIVERSITAET CLAUSTHAL. MITTEILUNGSBLATT. 1960. s-a. DM.7.50. Technische Universitaet Clausthal, Agricolastrasse 2, D-3392 Clausthal-Zellerfeld, Germany. circ. 1,800.
    Formerly: Technische Hochschule der Bergakademie Clausthal. Mitteilungsblatt.

622   CN
TECHNOLOGY FOCUS NEWSLETTER. 3/yr. free. Canada Centre for Mineral and Energy Technology, 555 Booth St., Ottawa, Ont. K1A 0G1, Canada. FAX 613-995-3192. TELEX 053-3395.

622   AA
TEKNIKA/TECHNIQUE. (Text in Albanian; summaries in French) q. $3.08. Ministere des Resources Minerales et Energetiques - Ministry of Energy and Mineral Resources, Tirana, Albania.

TEXAS ENERGY. see *ENERGY*

TIANRANQI GONGYE/NATURAL GAS INDUSTRY. see *PETROLEUM AND GAS*

TOHOKU DAIGAKU SENKO SEIREN KENKYUJO IHO/TOHOKU UNIVERSITY. RESEARCH INSTITUTE OF MINERAL DRESSING AND METALLURGY. BULLETIN. see *METALLURGY*

TRADE IN NATURAL RESOURCE-PRODUCTS. see *BUSINESS AND ECONOMICS — International Commerce*

622   FR
TRIBUNE DES MINEURS. w. 32 rue Casimir-Beugnet, 62300 Lens (Pas-de-Calais), France. adv.; circ. 78,000.

622   US   ISSN 0586-3031
TN5   CODEN: PSRMA6
U S SYMPOSIUM ON ROCK MECHANICS. PROCEEDINGS. 1977. irreg., 18th, 1977. $80. Colorado School of Mines, Golden, CO 80401. TEL 303-273-3000. Eds. Fun-Den Wang, George B. Clark. (reprint service avail. from UMI)

622 662   RU   ISSN 0041-5790
     CODEN: UGOLAR
UGOL'. 1925. m. 31.20 Rub. (Ministerstvo Ugol'noi Promyshlennosti) Izdatel'stvo Nedra, Pl. Belorusskogo Vokzala, 3, 125047 Moscow, Russia. TEL 250-52-55. Ed. G.V. Krasnikovskii. adv.; bk.rev.; bibl.; charts; illus.; stat.; index; circ. 8,945. **Indexed:** C.I.S. Abstr., Chem.Abstr., Eng.Ind., Fuel & Energy Abstr.
    —BLDSC shelfmark: 0383.000000.

622 662.6   KR   ISSN 0041-5804
     CODEN: UGOUAK
UGOL' UKRAINY. (Text in Russian) 1957. m. 22.80 Rub. Izdatel'stvo Tekhnika, Pushkinskaya 28, Kiev, Ukraine. adv.; charts; illus.; index; circ. 10,000. **Indexed:** C.I.S. Abstr., Chem.Abstr., Eng.Ind., Fuel & Energy Abstr.
    —BLDSC shelfmark: 0383.500000.

MINES AND MINING INDUSTRY 3497

622   CS   ISSN 0041-5812
TN4
UHLI/COAL. (Includes: Tuha Paliva) (Text in Czech; summaries in English, German, Russian) 1958. m. $58.30. Nakladatelstvi Technicke Literatury, Spalena 51, 113 02 Prague 1, Czechoslovakia. (Dist. by: Artia, Ve Smeckach 30, 111 27 Prague 1, Czechoslovakia) Ed. Jaroslav Siftar. adv.; bk.rev.; charts; illus.; pat.; circ. 2,800. **Indexed:** C.I.S. Abstr., Chem.Abstr., Fuel & Energy Abstr.

338.2   UK   ISSN 0957-4697
UNITED KINGDOM MINERALS YEARBOOK. 1973. a. price varies. British Geological Survey, Keyworth, Nottingham NG12 5GG, England. TEL 0602-361000. FAX 0602-362000. TELEX 378173 BGSKEY G. stat.
—BLDSC shelfmark: 9096.455000.
Supersedes (as of 1989): United Kingdom Mineral Statistics (ISSN 0308-5090)

UNITED MINE WORKERS JOURNAL. see *LABOR UNIONS*

550   UN   ISSN 0082-8114
TN1.A1   CODEN: UNEMAT
UNITED NATIONS. ECONOMIC AND SOCIAL COMMISSION FOR ASIA AND THE PACIFIC. MINERAL RESOURCES DEVELOPMENT SERIES. 1952. irreg., no.52, 1988. price varies. United Nations Economic and Social Commission for Asia and the Pacific (ESCAP), United Nations Bldg., Rajamnern Ave., Bangkok 10200, Thailand. (Dist. by: United Nations Publications, Room DC2-0853, New York, NY 10017; or Distribution and Sales Section, Palais des Nations, CH-1211 Geneva 10, Switzerland) (back issues avail.)
—BLDSC shelfmark: 5781.620000.

622   US   ISSN 0082-9129
TN23   CODEN: XBMBAJ
U.S. BUREAU OF MINES. BULLETIN. 1910. irreg. price varies. U.S. Bureau of Mines, Department of the Interior, Washington, DC 20241. (also avail. in microfiche) **Indexed:** AESIS, Petrol.Abstr.
—BLDSC shelfmark: 2431.000000.
Description: Reports final results of major projects.

622   US
U.S. BUREAU OF MINES. INFORMATION CIRCULAR. 1925. irreg. price varies. U.S. Bureau of Mines, Department of the Interior, Washington, DC 20241. (also avail. in microfiche) **Indexed:** AESIS, Chem.Abstr., GeoRef., Petrol.Abstr., Pollut.Abstr.
Description: Reports the results of various economic and special studies.

622   US   ISSN 0160-5151
HD9506.U6
U.S. BUREAU OF MINES. MINERAL COMMODITY SUMMARIES. 1957. a. free. U.S. Bureau of Mines, Department of the Interior, Washington, DC 20241. **Indexed:** AESIS.
Formerly: U.S. Bureau of Mines. Commodity Data Summaries (ISSN 0082-9137)
Description: Summarizes salient mineral data for the previous year.

549   US   ISSN 0076-8952
TN23   CODEN: MYEAAG
U.S. BUREAU OF MINES. MINERALS YEARBOOK. (In 3 vols.) 1932. a. price varies. U.S. Bureau of Mines, Department of the Interior, Washington, DC 20241. TEL 202-783-3238. (Orders to: Supt. Doc., Washington, DC 20402) (also avail. in microfiche from BHP)
Description: Mineral data on a commodity, state and foreign country basis.

622   US
U.S. BUREAU OF MINES. REPORT OF INVESTIGATIONS. 1919. irreg. free. U.S. Bureau of Mines, Department of the Interior, Washington, DC 20241. (also avail. in microfiche) **Indexed:** AESIS, Chem.Abstr., GeoRef., Petrol.Abstr., Soils & Fert.
Description: Reports research on mining and metals.

622 338.2   US   ISSN 0082-9382
U.S. BUREAU OF THE CENSUS. CENSUS OF MINERAL INDUSTRIES. (Issued in subject, geographic areas and industry series) 1840. quinquennial. price varies. U.S. Bureau of the Census, Data User Services Division, Washington, DC 20233. TEL 301-763-4100. (Dist. by: Supt. Doc., Washington, DC 20402)

U.S. ENERGY INFORMATION ADMINISTRATION. QUARTERLY COAL REPORT. see *ENERGY*

622.8   US
U.S. MINE SAFETY AND HEALTH ADMINISTRATION. INFORMATIONAL REPORT. irreg. U.S. Department of Labor, Mine Safety and Health Administration, 4015 Wilson Blvd., Arlington, VA 22203.
Formerly: U.S. Mining Enforcement and Safety Administration. Informational Report (ISSN 0097-9376)

549   IT
UNIVERSITA DEGLI STUDI DI FERRARA. ISTITUTO DI MINERALOGIA. ANNALI. NUOVA SERIE. SEZIONE: SCIENZE DELLA TERRA. (Text in Italian; summaries in English, French and Italian) vol.1, no.7, 1973. irreg. Universita degli Studi di Ferrara, Istituto di Mineralogia, C.so Ercole 1o d'Este 32, 44100 Ferrara, Italy. FAX 0532-206468. bibl.; charts.

UNIVERSITY OF TEXAS AT AUSTIN. BUREAU OF ECONOMIC GEOLOGY. MINERAL RESOURCE CIRCULARS. see *EARTH SCIENCES — Geology*

UNIWERSYTET SLASKI W KATOWICACH. PRACE NAUKOWE. PROBLEMY PRAWNE GORNICTWA. see *LAW*

622   GW   ISSN 0343-8198
UNSER BETRIEB. 1968. 3/yr. Deilmann - Haniel GmbH, Haustenbecke 1, Postfach 130163, 4600 Dortmund 13, Germany. TEL 0231-28910. FAX 0231-2891362. bk.rev.; circ. 13,000.

UTAH GEOLOGICAL SURVEY. BULLETIN. see *EARTH SCIENCES — Geology*

UTAH GEOLOGICAL SURVEY. SPECIAL STUDIES. see *EARTH SCIENCES — Geology*

UTAH GEOLOGICAL SURVEY. SURVEY NOTES. see *EARTH SCIENCES — Geology*

622   GW
V-G QUARTALSHEFTE; grubensicherheitliche Kurzberichte. 1963. q. free. Versuchsgrubengesellschaft mbH, Versuchsgrube Tremonia in Dortmund, Tremoniastr. 13, 4600 Dortmund 1, Germany. circ. 380.

V W D - MONTAN. (Vereinigte Wirtschaftsdienste GmbH) see *BUSINESS AND ECONOMICS — Investments*

622 338.2   VE
VENEZUELA. MINISTERIO DE ENERGIA Y MINAS. CARTA SEMANAL. vol.13, 1970. w. free. Ministerio de Energia y Minas, Torre Norte, Centro Simon Bolivar, Caracas, Venezuela. (Subscr. to: Ministerio de Energia y Minas, Biblioteca, Torre Oeste Piso 2, Parque Central, Caracas-Venezuela) stat.
Formerly: Venezuela. Ministerio de Minas e Hidrocarburos. Carta Semanal (ISSN 0042-3394)

622 338.2   VE
VENEZUELA. MINISTERIO DE ENERGIA Y MINAS. INFORMATIONS. (Text in French) 1967. bi-m. free. Ministerio de Energia y Minas, Torre Norte, Centro Simon Bolivar, Caracas, Venezuela. (processed)
Formerly: Venezuela. Ministerio de Minas e Hidrocarburos. Informations (ISSN 0042-3408)

622 665   VE
VENEZUELA. MINISTERIO DE ENERGIA Y MINAS. MEMORIA Y CUENTA. 1952. a. free. Ministerio de Energia y Minas, Torre piso 16, Relaciones Publicas, Caracas, Venezuela. charts; stat. **Indexed:** GeoRef.
Formerly: Venezuela. Ministerio de Minas e Hidrocarburos. Memoria y Cuenta (ISSN 0083-5374)

622 665.5   VE
VENEZUELA. MINISTERIO DE ENERGIA Y MINAS. QUARTERLY BULLETIN. Spanish edition: Actividades Petroleras (ISSN 0001-7582) (Text in English) q. Ministerio de Energia y Minas, Torre Norte, Centro Simon Bolivar, Caracas, Venezuela. (Subscr. to: Ministerio de Energia y Minas, Biblioteca Torre Oeste, Piso 2, Parque Central, Caracas, Venezuela) charts; stat.
Former titles: Venezuela. Ministerio de Energia y Minas. Monthly Bulletin; Venezuela. Ministerio de Minas e Hidrocarburos. Monthly Bulletin (ISSN 0042-3416)

622   GW
VEREIN DEUTSCHER KOHLENIMPORTEURE. JAHRESBERICHT. a. Verein Deutscher Kohlenimporteure e.V., Glockengiesserwall 19, 2000 Hamburg 1, Germany. TEL 326050. FAX 326772.

553 622   US
VIRGINIA. DIVISION OF MINERAL RESOURCES. PUBLICATIONS. 1959. irreg. price varies. Department of Mines, Minerals and Energy, Division of Mineral Resources, Box 3667, Charlottesville, VA 22903. TEL 804-293-5121. **Indexed:** GeoRef.
Former titles: Virginia. Division of Mineral Resources. Bulletin; Virginia. Division of Mineral Resources. Information Circular (ISSN 0083-632X); Virginia. Division of Mineral Resources. Mineral Resources Report (ISSN 0083-6338); Virginia. Division of Mineral Resources. Report of Investigations (ISSN 0083-6346) Virginia. Division of Mineral Resources. Reports.

VIRGINIA INDUSTRIAL DIRECTORY. see *BUSINESS AND ECONOMICS — Trade And Industrial Directories*

549   US   ISSN 0042-6652
TN24.8.V8   CODEN: VAMIAB
VIRGINIA MINERALS. 1954. q. free to residents. Department of Mines, Minerals and Energy, Division of Mineral Resources, Box 3667, Charlottesville, VA 22903. TEL 804-293-5121. bk.rev.; charts; illus.; maps; stat.; cum.index in vol.10 and vol.20. **Indexed:** Chem.Abstr., GeoRef.

622   FI   ISSN 0042-9317
VUORITEOLLISUS/BERGSHANTERINGEN.* (Text in English, Finnish, Swedish) 1943. s-a. FIM 30. Vuorimiesyhdistys-Bergsmannaforeningen r.y. - Mining and Metallurgical Society of Finland, Ins. Lars Heikel, SF-00820 Helsinki, Finland. Ed. Martti Sulonen. adv.; charts; illus.; stat.; cum.index: 1943-1969; circ. 2,300. **Indexed:** GeoRef.
—BLDSC shelfmark: 9259.500000.

WASHINGTON (STATE). DEPARTMENT OF NATURAL RESOURCES. DIVISION OF GEOLOGY AND EARTH RESOURCES. BULLETIN. see *EARTH SCIENCES — Geology*

557.97   US   ISSN 0147-1783
TN24.W2   CODEN: ICDRD3
WASHINGTON (STATE). DEPARTMENT OF NATURAL RESOURCES. DIVISION OF GEOLOGY AND EARTH RESOURCES. INFORMATION CIRCULAR. 1939. irreg., no.86, 1989. price varies. Department of Natural Resources, Division of Geology and Earth Resources, Olympia, WA 98504. TEL 206-459-6372. FAX 206-459-6380. Key Title: Information Circular - State of Washington, Department of Natural Resources, Division of Geology and Earth Resources.
Description: Provides technical geological information on the state of Washington.

WEEKLY COAL PRODUCTION. see *ENERGY*

338.2   US
WEST VIRGINIA. OFFICE OF MINER'S HEALTH, SAFETY & TRAINING. REPORT & DIGEST DIRECTORY. 1883. a. $10. Office of Miner's Health, Safety & Training, 1615 Washington St. E., Charleston, WV 25311. TEL 304-348-3500. circ. 2,500.
Formed by the merger of: West Virginia. Department of Mines. Annual Report & West Virginia. Department of Mines. Directory of Mines (ISSN 0083-8462)

338.2   US   ISSN 0091-5513
HD9547.W39
WEST VIRGINIA COAL FACTS.* 1971. a. $3. West Virginia Coal Association, 1301 Leidley Tower, Charleston, WV 25301. TEL 304-342-4153. Ed. Dan R. Fields. stat.; illus.; circ. 5,000.

622   US   ISSN 0083-842X
TN1
WEST VIRGINIA COAL MINING INSTITUTE. PROCEEDINGS. 1919. irreg. $7.50. West Virginia Coal Mining Institute, 213 White Hall, Morgantown, WV 26506. Ed. Jay Hilary Kelley.

MINES AND MINING INDUSTRY — ABSTRACTING, BIBLIOGRAPHIES, STATISTICS

622 US
WEST VIRGINIA MINERAL INDUSTRIES DIRECTORY. 1971. a. $25. Geological and Economic Survey, Box 879, Morgantown, WV 26507-0879. TEL 304-594-2331.
Former titles: West Virginia Mineral Producers and Processors Directory; West Virginia Mineral Producers Directory.
Description: Lists by commodity and county all mineral producers in West Virginia, with addresses and phone numbers.

622 AT ISSN 0510-2014
WESTERN AUSTRALIA. GEOLOGICAL SURVEY. MINERAL RESOURCES BULLETIN. 1945-1984; resumed 199?. irreg. Geological Survey of Western Australia, 100 Plain St., E. Perth, W.A. 6004, Australia. TEL 09 222-3333. circ. controlled. (back issues avail.) **Indexed:** AESIS, GeoRef.

622 549 AT ISSN 0814-9488
WESTERN CONTRACTOR. 1985. m. Aus.$50. E.P.S. Pty. Ltd., 200 Australia St., Newtown, N.S.W 20423, Australia. TEL 09-362-4344. FAX 09-470-3162. (Subscr. to: P.O. Box 609, Cloverdale, W.A. 6105, Australia) Ed. Tony Coetsee. adv.; tr.lit.; circ. 5,000. (back issues avail.)
Description: Covers news and features on engineering, earthmoving and mining, interviews, and product reviews.

622 US
WESTERN MINING DIRECTORY. 1977. a. $49. Howell Publishing Co., Box 37510, Denver, CO 80237. TEL 303-770-6794. FAX 303-770-6790. Ed. Don E. Howell. circ. 10,000. (back issues avail.)

WESTERN MINING NEWS. see *BUSINESS AND ECONOMICS — Investments*

622 AT
WHAT MINING MEANS TO AUSTRALIANS. 1978. irreg. free. Australian Mining Industry Council, Box 363, Dickson, A.C.T. 2602, Australia. FAX 61-6-279-3699.

622 AT ISSN 0817-6353
WHO'S PEGGING. 1970. w. Aus.$450 (effective Dec. 1991). Pex Publications Pty. Ltd., P.O. Box 158, Claremont, W.A. 6010, Australia. FAX 09-385-1485. Ed. Don Lipscombe. circ. 60. (back issues avail.)
Description: Australia's prospecting newsletter listing all mineral tenements by applicant, location and number.

622 PL ISSN 0043-5120
WIADOMOSCI GORNICZE. 1950. m. $39. (Stowarzyszenie Inzynierow i Technikow Gornictwa) Wydawnictwo "Slask", Al. W. Korfantego 51, 40-161 Katowice, Poland. (Dist. by: Ars Polona-Ruch, Krakowskie Przedmiescie 7, Warsaw, Poland) Ed. Marian Gustek. adv.; bk.rev.; circ. 2,850. **Indexed:** C.I.S. Abstr.

622 US
WOMEN IN MINING NATIONAL QUARTERLY. 1981. q. $10. Women in Mining National, 1801 Broadway, Ste. 400, Denver, CO 80202. TEL 303-298-1535. Ed. Jackie Beesley. circ. 600.
Description: Educates members on all aspects of the minerals industry.

338.2 US ISSN 0950-2262
WORLD COPPER DATABOOK. 1974. irreg., latest 1992. $191. Metal Bulletin Inc., 220 Fifth Ave., 10th Fl., New York, NY 10001. TEL 800-638-2525. FAX 212-213-6273. Ed. Richard Serjeantson. adv.
Supersedes: World Copper Survey (ISSN 0260-3403); Which was formerly: Copper Survey.
Description: Provides data on mines, smelters, refineries, wire rod operations, copper alloys and alloy ingot makers.

622 US
WORLD MINE PRODUCTION OF GOLD. 1979. a. $50. Gold Institute, Administrative Office - Institut de l'Or, Bureau Administratif, 1112 15th St., N.W., Ste. 420, Washington, DC 20036-4823. TEL 202-835-0185. FAX 202-835-0155. TELEX 904233. Ed. John H. Lutley. (back issues avail.)
Description: Production of each of 58 countries known to produce at least 1,000 troy ounces of gold from underground, surface and alluvial sources.

622 PL
WORLD MINING CONGRESS. REPORT. (Published in Host Country) (Text mainly in English) 1958. triennial since 1976; latest 15th, 1992, Madrid, Spain. World Mining Congress, International Organizing Committee, c/o Ing. M. Najberg, Secretary-General, Al. Ujazdowskie 1-3, 00-583 Warsaw, Poland. circ. 2,250.
Formerly: International Organizing Committee of World Mining Congresses. Report (ISSN 0074-2775)

622 US ISSN 0746-729X
TN345
WORLD MINING EQUIPMENT. 1977. 11/yr. $192. Metal Bulletin Inc., 220 Fifth Ave., New York, NY 10001. TEL 212-213-6202. Ed. Kyran Casteel. adv.; bk.rev.; circ. 24,356. (back issues avail.) **Indexed:** AESIS, Br.Geol.Lit., C.I.S. Abstr., Energy Info.Abstr., Fluidex, Fuel & Energy Abstr., Met.Abstr., Tr.& Indus.Ind.
—BLDSC shelfmark: 9356.684000.
Formed by the 1982 merger of (1977-1982): Mining Equipment International; (1974-1982): World Coal (ISSN 0361-7483); (1948-1982): World Mining (ISSN 0043-8707)
Description: Covers mines and mining equipment, decision makers with purchasing power in such companies.

622 CC ISSN 1000-8918
WUTAN YU HUATAN. (Text in Chinese) q. Dizhi Kuangchan Bu, Hangkong Wutan Yaogan Zhongxin, 29, Xueyuan Lu, Haidian-qu, Beijing 100083, People's Republic of China. TEL 2018811. Ed. Yuan Xuecheng.

622 CC ISSN 1000-9930
XIANGTAN KUANGYE XUEYUAN XUEBAO/JOURNAL OF XIANGTAN MINING INSTITUTE. (Text in Chinese; abstracts in English) 1983. s-a. Y4 (students Y2). Xiangtan Kuangye Xueyuan - Xiangtan Mining Institute, Xiangtan, Hunan 411201, People's Republic of China. TEL 22357. TELEX 64096 XMI CN. (Dist. overseas by: China National Publications Import & Export Corp., P.O. Box 88, Beijing, P.R.C.) adv.
Description: Covers mine engineering, drilling, coalfield geology and prospecting, machinery, automation, management, and the chemical coal industry. Includes information on academic developments and activities.

622.33 526.9 CC ISSN 1001-3571
XUANMEI JISHU/COAL SELECTING TECHNIQUES. (Text in Chinese) bi-m. Meitan Kexueyuan, Tangshan Fenyuan - Coal Science Institute, Tangshan Branch, Xinhua Xidao, Tangshan, Hebei 063012, People's Republic of China. TEL 22145. Ed. Wang Zurui.

622 331.8 UK
YORKSHIRE MINER. 1959. m. £4 (foreign £11). National Union of Mineworkers - Yorkshire Area, Miners' Offices, 2 Huddersfield Rd., Barnsley, S. Yorkshire S70 2LS, England. TEL 0226-284006. FAX 0226-285486. Ed. Mark Hebert. adv.; bk.rev.; circ. 17,500. (tabloid format)
Description: Covers the Yorkshire miners, their union, families and communities. Also includes articles of general interest.

622 669.3 ZA
ZAMBIA CONSOLIDATED COPPER MINES LTD. ANNUAL REPORT AND ACCOUNTS. (Text in English) a. Zambia Consolidated Copper Mines Ltd., Box 30048, Lusaka, Zambia. TELEX ZA 30104.

622 ZA
ZAMBIA INDUSTRIAL AND MINING CORPORATION. ANNUAL REPORT. (Text in English) s-a. Zambia Industrial and Mining Corp. Ltd., Zimco Information and Publicity Unit, Box 30090, Lusaka, Zambia.

338.2 ZA ISSN 0076-9010
ZAMBIA MINING YEARBOOK. 1955. a. free. Copper Industry Service Bureau, Kitwe, Zambia. (Dist. by: American Metal Climax, Inc., 1270 Ave. of the Americas, New York, NY 10026) circ. 500.
Formerly: Copperbelt of Zambia Mining Industry Year Book.

ZBORNIK RADOVA MUZEJA RUDARSTVA I METALURGIJE BOR. see *ARCHAEOLOGY*

622 CC ISSN 0253-4347
TN4 CODEN: CKYPDO
ZHONGNAN KUANGYE XUEYUAN XUEBAO/CENTRAL-SOUTH INSTITUTE OF MINING AND METALLURGY. JOURNAL. (Text in Chinese; summaries in English) 1956. bi-m. $7.50. Central-South University of Technology, Institute of Mining and Metallurgy - Zhongnan Jishu Daxue Kuangye Xueyuan, Changsha, Hunan, People's Republic of China. FAX 4731-82817. TELEX 98190. (Dist. by: China International Book Trading Corp. (Guoji Shudian), P.O. Box 2820, Beijing 100044, P.R.C.) Ed. Zuo Tieyong. adv.; circ. 2,500.

ZIMBABWE. MINISTRY OF LANDS AND NATURAL RESOURCES. REPORT OF THE SECRETARY FOR LANDS AND NATURAL RESOURCES. see *CONSERVATION*

MINES AND MINING INDUSTRY — Abstracting, Bibliographies, Statistics

A E S I S QUARTERLY. (Australian Earth Sciences Information System) see *EARTH SCIENCES — Abstracting, Bibliographies, Statistics*

338.2 CN ISSN 0380-4321
ALBERTA COAL INDUSTRY, ANNUAL STATISTICS. 1973. a. Can.$40. Energy Resources Conservation Board, 640 5th Ave. S.W., Calgary, Alta. T2P 3G4, Canada. TEL 403-297-8311. FAX 403-297-7040. TELEX 03-821717. illus.; stat.
Formerly: Cumulative Annual Statistics, Alberta Coal Industry.
Description: Statistical data on coal and the coal industry in Alberta including production, supply and disposition, plant operations and inventories.

622 SZ ISSN 0066-3808
HD9555.A1
ANNUAL BULLETIN OF COAL STATISTICS FOR EUROPE. (Text in English, French and Russian) 1966. a., vol.24, 1991. price varies. Economic Commission for Europe (ECE), Palais des Nations, 1211 Geneva 10, Switzerland. TEL 22-740-0921. (Or United Nations Publications, Rm. DC2-853, New York, NY 10017) **Indexed:** IIS.

553 AG ISSN 0066-7161
ARGENTINA. SERVICIO NACIONAL MINERO GEOLOGICO. ESTADISTICA MINERA. 1909. irreg. price varies. Servicio Nacional Minero Geologico, Bibliotheca, Av. Santa Fe 1548, Buenos Aires, Argentina. TEL 812-6879. FAX 814-4191. TELEX 27585 MINAS AR.
Formerly: Argentine Republic. Direccion Nacional de Geologia y Mineria. Estadistica Minera.

622.33 338.2 FR
ASSOCIATION TECHNIQUE DE L'IMPORTATION CHARBONNIERE. MONTHLY STATISTICS. m. Association Technique de l'Importation Charbonniere, 149 rue de Longchamp, 75016 Paris, France.

622 319.4 AT ISSN 1033-0542
AUSTRALIA. BUREAU OF STATISTICS. ACTUAL AND EXPECTED PRIVATE MINERAL EXPLORATION. 1974. q. Aus.$30 (foreign Aus.$33.60)(effective 1991). Australian Bureau of Statistics, P.O. Box 10, Belconnen, A.C.T. 2616, Australia. TEL 062-527911. FAX 062-516009. circ. 258.
Formerly (until 1989): Australia. Bureau of Statistics. Private Mineral Exploration, Australia.
Description: Actual and expected expenditure and metres drilled by private organizations exploring for minerals and petroleum.

338.2 AT ISSN 0311-8975
HD9506.A7
AUSTRALIA. BUREAU OF STATISTICS. MINERAL PRODUCTION, AUSTRALIA. 1971. a. Aus.$20 (foreign Aus.$22.25)(effective 1991). Australian Bureau of Statistics, P.O. Box 10, Belconnen, A.C.T. 2616, Australia. TEL 062-527911. FAX 062-516009. circ. 475.
Description: Covers quantity and value of production of metallic minerals, coal, petroleum (including natural gas and derivatives), construction materials and non-metallic minerals.

AUSTRALIA. BUREAU OF STATISTICS. QUEENSLAND OFFICE. CENSUS OF MINING ESTABLISHMENTS: DETAILS OF OPERATIONS BY INDUSTRY SUB-DIVISION, QUEENSLAND. see *BUSINESS AND ECONOMICS — Abstracting, Bibliographies, Statistics*

MINES AND MINING INDUSTRY — ABSTRACTING, BIBLIOGRAPHIES, STATISTICS

622   AT   ISSN 0314-1888
AUSTRALIA. BUREAU OF STATISTICS. TASMANIAN OFFICE. MINING TASMANIA. a. Aus.$8. Australian Bureau of Statistics, Tasmanian Office, G.P.O. Box 66A, Hobart, Tas. 7001, Australia.

622 669   MX   ISSN 0187-5027
AVANCE DE INFORMACION ECONOMICA. INDUSTRIA MINEROMETALURGICA. 1986. m. Mex.$77000($26) Instituto Nacional de Estadistica, Geografia e Informatica, Secretaria de Programacion y Presupuesto, Prol. Heroe de Nacozari 2301 Sur, Puerta 11, planta baja, Aguascalientes, 20290 Ags., Mexico. TEL 49-18-22-32. FAX 491-807-39. circ. 800.

622 016   HU   ISSN 0231-0651
BANYASZATI SZAKIRODALMI TAJEKOZTATO/MINING ABSTRACTS. 1949. m. 8600 Ft. Orszagos Muszaki Informacios Kozpont es Konyvtar (O.M.I.K.K.) - National Technical Information Centre and Library, Muzeum u. 17, Box 12, 1428 Budapest, Hungary. (Subscr. to: Kultura, Box 149, 1389 Budapest, Hungary) Ed. Denes Panto. index; circ. 260.
Supersedes (in 1982): Muszaki Lapszemle. Banyaszat - Technical Abstracts. Mining (ISSN 0027-495X)

312 622   GW
BERGBAU IN DER BUNDESREPUBLIK DEUTSCHLAND. 1949. a. DM.68. (Bundesministerium fuer Wirtschaft) Trans Tech Publications, Postfach 1254, 3392 Claustahl-Zellerfeld, Germany. TEL 05323-40077. FAX 05323-40079. TELEX 953713-TTP-D. stat. (tabloid format)
Formerly: Statistische Mitteilungen der Bergbehoerden der Bundesrepublik.

550 016   YU   ISSN 0351-7543
BILTEN DOKUMENTACIJE. RUDARSTVO I GEOLOGIJA/BULLETIN OF DOCUMENTATION. MINING AND GEOLOGY. 1950. bi-m. $264. Jugoslovenski Centar za Tehnicku i Naucnu Dokumentaciju - Yugoslav Center for Technical and Scientific Documentation (YCTSD), Sl. Penezica-Krcuna 29-31, Box 724, 11000 Belgrade, Yugoslavia. Ed. Ljiljana Kojic-Bogdanovic.

549   CN   ISSN 0825-6896
TN27.B9
BRITISH COLUMBIA. MINISTRY OF ENERGY, MINES AND PETROLEUM RESOURCES. MINERAL RESOURCES DIVISION. SUMMARY OF OPERATIONS. a. Can.$3.15. Ministry of Energy, Mines and Petroleum Resources, Mineral Resources Division, Parliament Bldgs., Victoria, B.C. V8V 1X4, Canada. (Subscr. to: Crown Publications, 546 Yates St., Victoria, B.C. V8W 1K8, Canada. TEL 604-386-4636) (back issues avail.)
Former titles: British Columbia. Ministry of Energy, Mines and Petroleum Resources. Mineral Resources Branch. Summary of Operations (ISSN 0825-6446); British Columbia. Ministry of Energy, Mines and Petroleum Resources. Annual Report (ISSN 0228-0078)

C A SELECTS. COAL SCIENCE AND PROCESS CHEMISTRY. see *CHEMISTRY — Abstracting, Bibliographies, Statistics*

549   CN   ISSN 0380-7797
CANADA. STATISTICS CANADA. CANADA'S MINERAL PRODUCTION: PRELIMINARY ESTIMATES. (Catalogue 26-202) (Text in English and French) 1924. a. Can.$22($26) (foreign $31). Statistics Canada, Publications Sales and Services, Ottawa, Ont. K1A 0T6, Canada. TEL 613-951-7277. FAX 613-951-1584. (also avail. in microform from MML)
Description: Early estimates on mineral production by class and province; quantities and values.

622.33   CN   ISSN 0380-6847
HD9554.C29
CANADA. STATISTICS CANADA. COAL AND COKE STATISTICS. (Catalogue 45-002) (Text in English and French) 1921. m. Can.$100($120) (foreign $140). Statistics Canada, Publications Sales and Services, Ottawa, Ont. K1A 0T6, Canada. TEL 613-951-7277. FAX 613-951-1584. (also avail. in microform from MML)
Description: Covers production, imports, exports, stocks and disposition of coal by province and supply and disposition of coke in Canada.

622.33   CN   ISSN 0705-436X
HD9554.C29
CANADA. STATISTICS CANADA. COAL MINES. (Catalogue 26-206) (Text in English and French) 1917. a. Can.$22($26) (foreign $31). Statistics Canada, Publications Sales and Services, Ottawa, Ont. K1A 0T6, Canada. TEL 613-951-7277. FAX 613-951-1584. bibl. (also avail. in microform from MML)
Description: Data on the number of mines, employment, payroll, cost of fuel and electricity, production, disposition, exports and imports and supply and demand of coal by province.

338.2   CN   ISSN 0575-8645
HD9506.C2
CANADA. STATISTICS CANADA. GENERAL REVIEW OF THE MINERAL INDUSTRIES, MINES, QUARRIES AND OIL WELLS. (Catalogue 26-201) (Text in English and French) 1949. a. Can.$22($26) (foreign $31). Statistics Canada, Publications Sales and Services, Ottawa, Ont. K1A 0T6, Canada. TEL 613-951-7277. FAX 613-951-1584. (also avail. in microform from MML)
Description: Final statistics of the mining industry, including production and value of minerals by kind and province, historical tables of values and principal statistics.

622 016   II
CENTRAL MINE PLANNING & DESIGN INSTITUTE. CURRENT AWARENESS SERVICE. (Text in English) 1976. bi-m. free. Central Mine Planning & Design Institute Ltd. (Subsidiary of: Coal India Limited), Library, Archives and Documentation Entre, Gondwana Place, Kanke Rd., Ranchi 834008, Bihar, India.

622.33   UK   ISSN 0309-4979
TP325
COAL ABSTRACTS. 1977. m. £465 to non-members; members £155. I.E.A. Coal Research, Gemini House, 10-18 Putney Hill, London SW15 6AA, England. TEL 081-780-2111. FAX 081-780-1746. TELEX 917624. index; circ. 1,200. (also avail. in microfiche) **Indexed:** AESIS.
●Also available online. Vendor(s): BELINDIS, CISTI, FIZ Technik (COAL), INKA, JICST, QL Systems Ltd., STN International.
—BLDSC shelfmark: 3287.970000.
Description: Provides details of the most recent and relevant items from the world's literature on coal.

622.33   US
COAL STATISTICS INTERNATIONAL. m. $484 (foreign $510). McGraw-Hill, Inc., Energy & Business Newsletters, 1221 Ave. of the Americas, 36th Fl., New York, NY 10020. TEL 212-512-6410. Ed. John Higgins. (reprint service avail. from UMI)

622   US   ISSN 0893-973X
COALDAT PRODUCTIVITY REPORT. (Avail. in Controlling Company Format; State - County Format) 1981. q. $545 (foreign $585). Pasha Publications Inc., 1401 Wilson Blvd., Ste. 900, Arlington, VA 22209-9970. TEL 703-528-1244. FAX 703-528-1253.
Formerly (until 1986): Productivity Report.
Description: Gives production statistics for each mine, including past performance and ownership data.

CURRENT BIBLIOGRAPHY ON SCIENCE AND TECHNOLOGY: EARTH SCIENCE, MINING AND METALLURGY/KAGAKU GIJUTSU BUNKEN SOKUHO. KINZOKU KOGAKU, KOZAN KOGAKU, CHIKYU NO KAGAKU-HEN. see *EARTH SCIENCES — Abstracting, Bibliographies, Statistics*

016 622   RU
EKONOMIKA UGOL'NOI PROMYSHLENNOSTI. irreg. 0.76 Rub. Ministerstvo Ugol'noi Promyshlennosti, Moscow, Russia. bibl.

622   EI   ISSN 0378-3472
TP325
EURO ABSTRACTS SECTION II. COAL AND STEEL. (Text in English) vol.4, 1978. irreg. $124. (European Coal and Steel Community) Office for Official Publications of the European Communities, L-2985 Luxembourg, Luxembourg. (Dist. in U.S. by: Unipub, 4611-F Assembly Dr., Lanham, MD 20706-4391) Eds. H-L. Scherff, B. Jay. abstr.; bibl.; pat.; index. **Indexed:** Br.Ceram.Abstr.

338.2   GR   ISSN 0072-7415
GREECE. NATIONAL STATISTICAL SERVICE. ANNUAL STATISTICAL SURVEY ON MINES, QUARRIES AND SALTERNS. (Text in English and Greek) 1961. a. $4. National Statistical Service of Greece, Statistical Information and Publications Division, 14-16 Lycourgou St., 10166 Athens, Greece.
TEL 3244-748. FAX 3222205. TELEX 216734 ESYE GR.

553 622 669 016   UK
I M M ABSTRACTS AND INDEX; a survey of world literature on the economic geology and mining of all minerals (except coal), mineral processing and non-ferrous extraction metallurgy. 1950. bi-m. £173.25. Institution of Mining and Metallurgy, 44 Portland Place, London W1N 4BR, England. TEL 01-580 3802. FAX 01-436-5388. TELEX 261410 IMM G. (U.S. address: IMM North American Publications Center, Old Post Rd., Brookfield, VT 05036) Ed. M. McGarr. abstr.; circ. 1,000. (reprint service avail.) **Indexed:** AESIS, Fluidex.
●Also available online. Vendor(s): Pergamon Infoline (IMMAGE).
Formerly: I M M Abstracts (ISSN 0019-0020)

338.2   II   ISSN 0027-0261
INDIAN BUREAU OF MINES. BULLETIN OF MINERAL INFORMATION. (Text in English, Hindi) 1961. q. Rs.140($50.40) Indian Bureau of Mines, New Secretariat Bldg., Civil Lines, Nagpur 400001, India. (processed) **Indexed:** Chem.Abstr.
Former titles: Indian Bureau of Mines. Bulletin of Mineral Statistics and Information; Indian Bureau of Mines. Monthly Bulletin of Mineral Statistics.

622.33 016   II
INDIAN BUREAU OF MINES. DOCUMENTATION NOTES. (Text in English) 1972. 6/yr. free. Indian Bureau of Mines, Controller General, New Secretariat Building, Civil Lines, Nagpur 440 001, India. abstr.

338.2 310   II
INDIAN GRANITE EXPORTERS' PERFORMANCE MONITOR. (Text in English, French, German, Italian) 1986. m. $500. Commercial Information Services, No.1 Beena Building, 6th Road, T.P.S. IV, Bandra, Bombay 400 050, India. TEL 91-22-6426703. Ed. C. Moonjely. circ. 300.
Description: Statistics relating to quantity, prices and turnover of each participating granite exporter in India.

622   FR
INTERGOVERNMENTAL COUNCIL OF COPPER EXPORTING COUNTRIES. STATISTICAL BULLETIN. (Text in English) a. Intergovernmental Council of Copper Exporting Countries, 39 rue de la Bienfaisance, 75008 Paris, France. TEL 42-25-00-24.

622 016   US   ISSN 0148-9062
TA706   CODEN: IRMGBG
INTERNATIONAL JOURNAL OF ROCK MECHANICS AND MINING SCIENCES & GEOMECHANICS ABSTRACTS. 1964. bi-m. £525 (effective 1992). Pergamon Press, Inc., Journals Division, 660 White Plains Rd., Tarrytown, NY 10591-5153. TEL 914-524-9200. FAX 914-333-2444. (And: Headington Hill Hall, Oxford OX3 0BW, England. TEL 0865-794141) Ed. J.A. Hudson. adv. contact: Rosemarie Fazzolari. bk.rev.; abstr.; charts; illus.; index; circ. 1,400. (also avail. in microform from MIM,UMI; reprint service avail. from UMI) **Indexed:** Appl.Mech.Rev., C.I.S. Abstr., Cadscan, Curr.Cont., Eng.Ind., Excerp.Med., Fuel & Energy Abstr., Geo.Abstr., Geotech.Abstr., HRIS, Ind.Sci.Rev., INIS Atomind., Intl.Civil Eng.Abstr., Lead Abstr., Petrol.Abstr., Sci.Abstr., Sci.Cit.Ind., Soft.Abstr.Eng., W.R.C.Inf., Zincscan.
●Also available online. Vendor(s): Pergamon Infoline.
—BLDSC shelfmark: 4542.542000.
Formerly: International Journal of Rock Mechanics and Mining Sciences (ISSN 0020-7624); Incorporating: Rock Mechanics Abstracts (ISSN 0035-7456)
Description: Original research, new developments and case studies in rock mechanics and rock engineering, for mining and civil applications, with comprehensive coverage of significant literature.
Refereed Serial

3500 MINES AND MINING INDUSTRY — ABSTRACTING, BIBLIOGRAPHIES, STATISTICS

338.2 315   KO
KOREA (REPUBLIC). NATIONAL STATISTICAL OFFICE. REPORT ON MINING AND MANUFACTURING SURVEY. (Text in English and Korean) 1967. a. 32000 Won. National Statistical Office, 90, Gyongun-dong, Jongro-gu, Seoul 110-310, S. Korea. TEL 02-720-2788. (Subscr. to: the Korean Statistical Association, Room 302, Chungok Building, 561-30, Sinsa-dong, Gangnam-gu, Seoul 135-120, S. Korea) circ. 400.
    Formerly: Korea (Republic). National Bureau of Statistics. Report on Mining and Manufacturing Survey (ISSN 0075-6849)

622 310   MY   ISSN 0126-818X
MALAYSIA. DEPARTMENT OF MINES. STATISTICS RELATING TO THE MINING INDUSTRY OF MALAYSIA. (Text in English and Malay) 1951. a. M.$6. Department of Mines - Jabatan Galian, Jalan Gurney, Kuala Lumpur, Malaysia.

549   MY
MALAYSIA. DEPARTMENT OF STATISTICS. MONTHLY TIN STATISTICS OF MALAYSIA. (Text in English) m. M.$1 per no. Department of Statistics, Wisma Statistik, Block E, Jalan Cenderasari, 50514 Kuala Lumpur, Malaysia. TEL 03-2922133.

622   US
MINERAL INDUSTRY SURVEYS. ALUMINUM INDUSTRY. m. U.S. Bureau of Mines, Production and Distribution, Cochrans Mill Rd., Box 18070, Pittsburgh, PA 15236. stat. (back issues avail.)
    Description: Statistical information on the production, import and export of aluminum.

622   US
MINERAL INDUSTRY SURVEYS. ANTIMONY. q. U.S. Bureau of Mines, Production and Distribution, Cochrans Mill Rd., Box 18070, Pittsburgh, PA 15236. TEL 412-892-4411. stat. (back issues avail.)
    Description: Statistical information on the production, import and export of antimony.

622   US
MINERAL INDUSTRY SURVEYS. BARITE. a. U.S. Bureau of Mines, Production and Distribution, Cochrans Mill Rd., Box 18070, Pittsburgh, PA 15236. TEL 412-892-4411. stat. (back issues avail.)
    Description: Statistical information on the production, import and export of barite.

622   US
MINERAL INDUSTRY SURVEYS. BAUXITE. q. U.S. Bureau of Mines, Production and Distribution, Cochrans Mill Rd., Box 18070, Pittsburgh, PA 15236. TEL 412-892-4411. stat. (back issues avail.)
    Formerly: Mineral Industry Surveys. Bauxite and Aluminum.
    Description: Statistical information on the production, import and export of bauxite.

622   US
MINERAL INDUSTRY SURVEYS. BISMUTH. a. U.S. Bureau of Mines, Production and Distribution, Cochrans Mill Rd., Box 18070, Pittsburgh, PA 15236. TEL 412-892-4411. stat. (back issues avail.)
    Description: Statistical information on the production, consumption, import and export of bismuth.

622   US
MINERAL INDUSTRY SURVEYS. BORON. a. U.S. Bureau of Mines, Production and Distribution, Cochrans Mill Rd., Box 18070, Pittsburgh, PA 15236. TEL 412-892-4411. stat. (back issues avail.)
    Description: Statistical information on the production, import and export of boron.

622   US
MINERAL INDUSTRY SURVEYS. BROMINE. a. U.S. Bureau of Mines, Production and Distribution, Cochrans Mill Rd., Box 18070, Pittsburgh, PA 15236. TEL 412-892-4411. stat. (back issues avail.)
    Description: Statistical information on the production and import and export of bromine.

622   US   ISSN 0193-0044
                 CODEN: MISCDH
MINERAL INDUSTRY SURVEYS. CADMIUM. q. and a. U.S. Bureau of Mines, Production and Distribution, Cochrans Mill Rd., Box 18070, Pittsburgh, PA 15236. TEL 412-892-4411. stat. (back issues avail.)
    Description: Statistical information on the production, distribution, consumption, import and export of cadmium.

622   US
MINERAL INDUSTRY SURVEYS. CEMENT. m. and a. U.S. Bureau of Mines, Production and Distribution, Cochrans Mill Rd., Box 18070, Pittsburgh, PA 15236. TEL 412-892-4411. stat. (back issues avail.)
    Description: Provides data and activity highlights on cement.

622   US
MINERAL INDUSTRY SURVEYS. CHROMIUM. m. U.S. Bureau of Mines, Production and Distribution, Cochrans Mill Rd., Box 18070, Pittsburgh, PA 15236. TEL 412-892-4411. stat. (back issues avail.)
    Description: Statistical information on the production, distribution, and consumption of chromium.

622   US
MINERAL INDUSTRY SURVEYS. CLAYS. a. U.S. Bureau of Mines, Production and Distribution, Cochrans Mill Rd., Box 18070, Pittsburgh, PA 15236. TEL 412-892-4411. stat. (back issues avail.)
    Description: Provides data and activity highlights on clays.

622   US
MINERAL INDUSTRY SURVEYS. COBALT. m. U.S. Bureau of Mines, Production and Distribution, Cochrans Mill Rd., Box 18070, Pittsburgh, PA 15236. TEL 412-892-4411. stat. (back issues avail.)
    Description: Statistical information on the production, consumption and distribution of cobalt.

622   US
MINERAL INDUSTRY SURVEYS. COLUMBIUM AND TANTALUM. a. U.S. Bureau of Mines, Producton and Distribution, Cochrans Mill Rd., Box 18070, Pittsburgh, PA 15236. TEL 412-892-4411. stat. (back issues avail.)
    Description: Provides data and activity highlights on columbium and tantalum.

622   US
MINERAL INDUSTRY SURVEYS. COPPER IN THE UNITED STATES. m. U.S. Bureau of Mines, Production and Distribution, Cochrans Mill Rd., Box 18070, Pittsburgh, PA 15236. TEL 412-892-4411. stat. (back issues avail.)
    Description: Statistical information on the production, distribution and consumption of copper.

622   US
MINERAL INDUSTRY SURVEYS. DIMENSION STONE. s-a. and a. U.S. Bureau of Mines, Production and Distribution, Cochrans Mill Rd., Box 18070, Pittsburgh, PA 15236. TEL 412-892-4411. stat. (back issues avail.)
    Description: Data on worldwide production of dimension stone.

622   US
MINERAL INDUSTRY SURVEYS. DIRECTORY OF PEAT PRODUCERS. irreg., latest 1989. U.S. Bureau of Mines, Production and Distribution, Cochrans Mill Rd., Box 18070, Pittsburgh, PA 15236. TEL 412-892-4411. stat. (back issues avail.)
    Description: Information on domestic producers of peat.

622   US
MINERAL INDUSTRY SURVEYS. DIRECTORY OF PHOSPHATE ROCK PRODUCERS. a. U.S. Bureau of Mines, Production and Distribution, Cochrans Mill Rd., Box 18070, Pittsburgh, PA 15236. TEL 412-892-4411. stat. (back issues avail.)
    Description: Lists companies producing phosphate rock in the United States.

622   US
MINERAL INDUSTRY SURVEYS. DIRECTORY OF SALT PRODUCERS. a. U.S. Bureau of Mines, Production and Distribution, Cochrans Mill Rd., Box 18070, Pittsburgh, PA 15236. TEL 412-892-4411. stat. (back issues avail.)
    Description: Lists salt-producing companies in the U.S.

622   US
MINERAL INDUSTRY SURVEYS. DIRECTORY OF TALC, PYROPHYLLITE, AND SOAPSTONE MINING. a. U.S. Bureau of Mines, Production and Distribution, Cochrans Mill Rd., Box 18070, Pittsburgh, PA 15236. TEL 412-892-4411. stat. (back issues avail.)
    Description: Nation-wide listing of companies mining talc, pyrophyllite and soapstone.

622   US
MINERAL INDUSTRY SURVEYS. DIRECTORY OF U.S. LIME PLANTS. a. U.S. Bureau of Mines, Production and Distribution, Cochrans Mill Rd., Box 18070, Pittsburgh, PA 15236. TEL 412-892-4411. stat. (back issues avail.)
    Description: Provides data on lime-producing plants in the U.S.

622   US
MINERAL INDUSTRY SURVEYS. END USES OF SULFUR AND SULFURIC ACID. a. U.S. Bureau of Mines, Production and Distribution, Cochrans Mill Rd., Box 18070, Pittsburgh, PA 15236. TEL 412-892-4411. stat. (back issues avail.)
    Description: Provides data on production, import, export and consumption of elemental sulfur and sulfuric acid.

622   US
MINERAL INDUSTRY SURVEYS. FELDSPAR. q. U.S. Bureau of Mines, Production and Distribution, Cochrans Mill Rd., Box 18070, Pittsburgh, PA 15236. TEL 412-892-4411. stat. (back issues avail.)
    Description: Statistical information on the production, distribution and consumption of feldspar.

622   US
MINERAL INDUSTRY SURVEYS. FLUORSPAR. q. and a. U.S. Bureau of Mines, Production and Distribution, Cochrans Mill Rd., Box 18070, Pittsburgh, PA 15236. TEL 412-892-4411. stat. (back issues avail.)
    Description: Provides data and activity highlights on fluorspar.

622   US
MINERAL INDUSTRY SURVEYS. GEM STONES. a. U.S. Bureau of Mines, Production and Distribution, Cochrans Mill Rd., Box 18070, Pittsburgh, PA 15236. TEL 412-892-4411. stat. (back issues avail.)
    Description: Provides data and activity highlights on gem stones.

622   US
MINERAL INDUSTRY SURVEYS. GOLD AND SILVER. m. U.S. Bureau of Mines, Production and Distribution, Cochrans Mill Rd., Box 18070, Pittsburgh, PA 15236. TEL 412-892-4411. stat. (back issues avail.)
    Description: Provides data on production of gold and silver.

622   US
MINERAL INDUSTRY SURVEYS. GYPSUM. m. U.S. Bureau of Mines, Production and Distribution, Cochrans Mill Rd., Box 18070, Pittsburgh, PA 15236. TEL 412-892-4411. stat. (back issues avail.)
    Description: Provides data on the production, distribution and consumption of gypsum.

622   US
MINERAL INDUSTRY SURVEYS. GYPSUM MINES AND CALCINING PLANTS IN THE U.S.. a. U.S. Bureau of Mines, Production and Distribution, Cochrans Mill Rd., Box 18070, Pittsburgh, PA 15236. TEL 412-892-4411. stat. (back issues avail.)
    Description: Provides data on the production and calcining of gypsum and its plants in the U.S.

MINES AND MINING INDUSTRY — ABSTRACTING, BIBLIOGRAPHIES, STATISTICS

622 US
MINERAL INDUSTRY SURVEYS. INDUSTRIAL EXPLOSIVES AND BLASTING AGENTS. a. U.S. Bureau of Mines, Production and Distribution, Cochrans Mill Rd., Box 18070, Pittsburgh, PA 15236. TEL 412-892-4411. stat. (back issues avail.)
Description: Statistical information on the production, distribution and consumption of blasting explosives and blasting agents.

622 US
MINERAL INDUSTRY SURVEYS. INDUSTRIAL SAND AND GRAVEL PRODUCERS IN THE U.S.. a. U.S. Bureau of Mines, Production and Distribution, Cochrans Mill Rd., Box 18070, Pittsburgh, PA 15236. TEL 412-892-4411. stat. (back issues avail.)
Description: Lists producers of sand and gravel in the U.S.

622 US
MINERAL INDUSTRY SURVEYS. IODINE. a. U.S. Bureau of Mines, Production and Distribution, Cochrans Mill Rd., Box 18070, Pittsburgh, PA 15236. TEL 412-892-4411. stat. (back issues avail.)
Description: Provides data and activity highlights on iodine.

622 US
MINERAL INDUSTRY SURVEYS. IRON AND STEEL SCRAP. m. and a. U.S. Bureau of Mines, Production and Distribution, Cochrans Mill Rd., Box 18070, Pittsburgh, PA 15236. TEL 412-892-4411. stat. (back issues avail.)
Description: Provides data on the production, distribution and consumption of iron and steel scrap.

622 US
MINERAL INDUSTRY SURVEYS. KYANITE AND RELATED MINERALS. a. U.S. Bureau of Mines, Production and Distribution, Cochrans Mill Rd., Box 18070, Pittsburgh, PA 15236. TEL 412-892-4411. stat. (back issues avail.)
Description: Provides preliminary data and activity highlights on kyanite and related minerals.

622 US
MINERAL INDUSTRY SURVEYS. LEAD INDUSTRY. m. U.S. Bureau of Mines, Production and Distribution, Cochrans Mill Rd., Box 18070, Pittsburgh, PA 15236. TEL 412-892-4411. stat. (back issues avail.)
Description: Provides worldwide data on mine production of lead, including pig metal.

622 US
MINERAL INDUSTRY SURVEYS. LIME. m. U.S. Bureau of Mines, Production and Distribution, Cochrans Mill Rd., Box 18070, Pittsburgh, PA 15236. TEL 412-892-4411. stat. (back issues avail.)
Description: Provides data on the production, import, export and consumption of lime.

622 US
MINERAL INDUSTRY SURVEYS. LIME - ANNUAL, ADVANCE SUMMARY. a. U.S. Bureau of Mines, Production and Distribution, Cochrans Mill Rd., Box 18070, Pittsburgh, PA 15236. TEL 412-892-4411. stat. (back issues avail.)
Description: Provides data on the production, distribution and consumption of lime.

622 US
MINERAL INDUSTRY SURVEYS. LIME - ANNUAL PRELIMINARY. a. U.S. Bureau of Mines, Production and Distribution, Cochrans Mill Rd., Box 18070, Pittsburgh, PA 15236. TEL 412-892-4411. stat. (back issues avail.)
Description: Provides earliest estimates of data and activity highlights on lime.

622 US
MINERAL INDUSTRY SURVEYS. MAGNESIUM. q. U.S. Bureau of Mines, Production and Distribution, Cochrans Mill Rd., Box 18070, Pittsburgh, PA 15236. TEL 412-892-4411. stat. (back issues avail.)
Description: Provides data on the production, import, export and consumption of magnesium worldwide, with emphasis on the U.S.

622 US
MINERAL INDUSTRY SURVEYS. MANGANESE. m. U.S. Bureau of Mines, Production and Distribution, Cochrans Mill Rd., Box 28070, Pittsburgh, PA 15236. TEL 412-892-4411. stat. (back issues avail.)
Description: Data on foreign and domestic manganese production, distribution and consumption.

622 US
MINERAL INDUSTRY SURVEYS. MARKETABLE PHOSPHATE ROCK. m. and a. U.S. Bureau of Mines, Production and Distribution, Cochrans Mill Rd., Box 18070, Pittsburgh, PA 15236. TEL 412-892-4411. stat. (back issues avail.)
Description: Provides data on the production, import, export and consumption of phosphate rock.

622 US
MINERAL INDUSTRY SURVEYS. MERCURY. q. and a. U.S. Bureau of Mines, Production and Distribution, Cochrans Mill Rd., Box 18070, Pittsburgh, PA 15236. TEL 412-892-4411. stat. (back issues avail.)
Description: Data on worldwide mine production, distribution and consumption of mercury.

622 US
MINERAL INDUSTRY SURVEYS. MOLYBDENUM. m. and a. U.S. Bureau of Mines, Production and Distribution, Cochrans Mill Rd., Box 18070, Pittsburgh, PA 15236. TEL 412-892-4411. stat. (back issues avail.)
Description: Data on domestic production, distribution and consumption of molybdenum.

622 US
MINERAL INDUSTRY SURVEYS. NICKEL. m. U.S. Bureau of Mines, Production and Distribution, Cochrans Mill Rd., Box 18070, Pittsburgh, PA 15236. TEL 412-892-4411. stat. (back issues avail.)
Description: Worldwide coverage of the production, distribution and consumption of nickel.

622 US
MINERAL INDUSTRY SURVEYS. PEAT. a. U.S. Bureau of Mines, Production and Distribution, Cochrans Mill Rd., Box 18070, Pittsburgh, PA 15236. TEL 412-892-4411. stat. (back issues avail.)
Description: Provides preliminary data and activity highlights on peat.

622 US
MINERAL INDUSTRY SURVEYS. PHOSPHATE ROCK - ADVANCE SUMMARY. a. U.S. Bureau of Mines, Production and Distribution, Cochrans Mill Rd., Box 18070, Pittsburgh, PA 15236. TEL 412-892-4411. stat. (back issues avail.)
Description: Statistical data on the production, distribution and consumption of marketable phosphate rock.

622 US
MINERAL INDUSTRY SURVEYS. PHOSPHATE ROCK - ANNUAL PRELIMINARY. a. U.S. Bureau of Mines, Production and Distribution, Cochrans Mill Rd., Box 18070, Pittsburgh, PA 15236. TEL 412-892-4411. stat. (back issues avail.)
Description: Provides data and activity highlights on phosphate rock.

622 US
MINERAL INDUSTRY SURVEYS. PHOSPHATE ROCK - CROP YEAR. a. U.S. Bureau of Mines, Production and Distribution, Cochrans Mill Rd., Box 18070, Pittsburgh, PA 15236. TEL 412-892-4411. stat. (back issues avail.)
Description: Provides data on the production, consumption and distribution of marketable phosphate rock.

622 US ISSN 0191-4421
CODEN: MISPDM
MINERAL INDUSTRY SURVEYS. PLATINUM - GROUP METALS. q. U.S. Bureau of Mines, Production and Distribution, Cochrans Mill Rd., Box 18070, Pittsburgh, PA 15236. TEL 412-892-4411. stat. (back issues avail.)
Description: Provides data on worldwide production, distribution and consumption of platinum, with emphasis on the United States.

622 US
MINERAL INDUSTRY SURVEYS. POTASH - ANNUAL PRELIMINARY. a. U.S. Bureau of Mines, Production and Distribution, Cochrans Mill Rd., Box 18070, Pittsburgh, PA 15236. TEL 412-892-4411. stat. (back issues avail.)
Description: Data and activity highlights on potash.

622 US
MINERAL INDUSTRY SURVEYS. POTASH - CROP YEAR. a. U.S. Bureau of Mines, Production and Distribution, Cochrans Mill Rd., Box 18070, Pittsburgh, PA 15236. TEL 412-892-4411. stat. (back issues avail.)
Description: Statistical data on worldwide production, distribution and consumption of potash.

622 US
MINERAL INDUSTRY SURVEYS. PRINCIPAL CONSTRUCTION SAND AND GRAVEL PRODUCERS IN THE U.S.. a. U.S. Bureau of Mines, Production and Distributiuon, Cochrans Mill Rd., Box 18070, Pittsburgh, PA 15236. TEL 492-892-4411. stat. (back issues avail.)
Description: Lists producers of construction sand and gravel in the U.S.

622 US
MINERAL INDUSTRY SURVEYS. PRINCIPAL CRUSHED STONE PRODUCERS IN THE U.S.. a. U.S. Bureau of Mines, Production and Distribution, Cochrans Mill Rd., Box 18070, Pittsburgh, PA 15236. TEL 412-892-4411. stat. (back issues avail.)
Description: Lists principal producers of crushed stone in the U.S.

622 US
MINERAL INDUSTRY SURVEYS. PRINCIPAL GEM STONES PRODUCERS IN THE U.S.. a. U.S. Bureau of Mines, Production and Distribution, Cochrans Mill Rd., Box 18070, Pittsburgh, PA 15236. TEL 412-892-4411. stat. (back issues avail.)
Description: Covers gem stone production in the United States.

622 US
MINERAL INDUSTRY SURVEYS. SALT. a. U.S. Bureau of Mines, Production and Distribution, Cochrans Mill Rd., Box 18070, Pittsburgh, PA 15236. TEL 412-892-4411. stat. (back issues avail.)
Description: Statistical information on the production, import, export and consumption of salt.

622 US
MINERAL INDUSTRY SURVEYS. SALT - ANNUAL PRELIMINARY. a. U.S. Bureau of Mines, Production and Distribution, Cochrans Mill Rd., Box 18070, Pittsburgh, PA 15236. TEL 412-892-4411. stat. (back issues avail.)
Description: Provides data and activity highlights on salt.

622 US
MINERAL INDUSTRY SURVEYS. SILICON. m. U.S. Bureau of Mines, Production and Distribution, Cochrans Mill Rd., Box 18070, Pittsburgh, PA 15236. TEL 492-892-4411. stat. (back issues avail.)
Description: Data on the production, import, export and consumption of silicon.

622 US
MINERAL INDUSTRY SURVEYS. SODIUM COMPOUNDS. m. U.S. Bureau of Mines, Production and Distribution, Cochrans Mill Rd., Box 18070, Pittsburgh, PA 15236. TEL 412-892-4411. stat. (back issues avail.)
Description: Provides estimates of data and activity highlights on sodium compounds.

622 US
MINERAL INDUSTRY SURVEYS. STONE - CRUSHED AND DIMENSION. a. U.S. Bureau of Mines, Production and Distribution, Cochrans Mill Rd., Box 18070, Pittsburgh, PA 15236. TEL 412-892-4411. stat. (back issues avail.)
Description: Provides estimates of data and activity highlights on stone, both crushed and dimension.

622 US
MINERAL INDUSTRY SURVEYS. SULFUR. m. U.S. Bureau of Mines, Production and Distribution, Cochrans Mill Rd., Box 18070, Pittsburgh, PA 15236. TEL 412-892-4411. stat. (back issues avail.)
Description: Provides data on the production and consumption of frasch and recovered sulfur.

M

M

622 US
MINERAL INDUSTRY SURVEYS. SULFUR - ADVANCE SUMMARY. a. U.S. Bureau of Mines, Production and Distribution, Cochrans Mill Rd., Box 18070, Pittsburgh, PA 15236. TEL 412-892-4411. stat. (back issues avail.)
Description: Data on domestic production and consumption of sulfur in all forms, frasch, recovered, and elemental.

622 US
MINERAL INDUSTRY SURVEYS. SULFUR - ANNUAL PRELIMINARY. a. U.S. Bureau of Mines, Production and Distribution, Cochrans Mill Rd., Box 18070, Pittsburgh, PA 15236. TEL 412-892-4411. stat. (back issues avail.)
Description: Provides estimates of data and activity highlights on sulfur. Most of the data estimates are based on 9 months data and are compared with final data from previous years.

622 US
MINERAL INDUSTRY SURVEYS. TIN INDUSTRY. m. U.S. Bureau of Mines, Production and Distribution, Cochrans Mill Rd., Box 18070, Pittsburgh, PA 15236. TEL 412-892-4411. stat. (back issues avail.)
Description: Data on all aspects of the tin industry.

622 US
MINERAL INDUSTRY SURVEYS. TITANIUM. q. U.S. Bureau of Mines, Production and Distribution, Cochrans Mill Rd., Box 18070, Pittsburgh, PA 15236. TEL 412-892-4411. stat. (back issues avail.)
Description: Provides data on the production and consumption of titanium internationally.

622 US
MINERAL INDUSTRY SURVEYS. TUNGSTEN. m. and a. U.S. Bureau of Mines, Production and Distribution, Cochrans Mill Rd., Box 18070, Pittsburgh, PA 15236. TEL 412-892-4411. stat. (back issues avail.)
Description: Provides data on the production and consumption of tungsten concentrate, ammonium paratungstate and intermediate products.

622 US
MINERAL INDUSTRY SURVEYS. VANADIUM. m. U.S. Bureau of Mines, Production and Distribution, Cochrans Mill Rd., Box 18070, Pittsburgh, PA 15236. TEL 412-892-4411. stat. (back issues avail.)
Description: Data on all aspects of the vanadium industry.

622 US
MINERAL INDUSTRY SURVEYS. ZINC INDUSTRY. m. U.S. Bureau of Mines, Production and Distribution, Cochrans Mill Rd., Box 18070, Pittsburgh, PA 15236. TEL 412-892-4411.
Description: Provides data on all aspects of the zinc industry.

338.2 II ISSN 0581-0000
MINERAL STATISTICS OF INDIA. 1968. s-a. Rs.100($36) Indian Bureau of Mines, Controller General, New Secretariat Bldg., Civil Lines, Nagpur 400 001, India.

549 UK ISSN 0026-4601
QE351 CODEN: MAMMAQ
MINERALOGICAL ABSTRACTS; a quarterly journal of abstracts in English, covering the world literature of mineralogy and related subjects. 1959. q. £132($235) Mineralogical Society, 41 Queen's Gate, London SW7 5HR, England. TEL 01-584 7516. (Co-sponsor: Mineralogical Society of America) Ed. R.A. Howie. bk.rev.; abstr.; index; circ. 1,800. **Indexed:** AESIS, Anal.Abstr., Br.Ceram.Abstr., Chem.Abstr., GeoRef.
● Also available online. Vendor(s): DIALOG (File no.292).
— BLDSC shelfmark: 5786.700000.

622.33 310 AT ISSN 1034-2109
NEW SOUTH WALES COAL YEARBOOK (YEAR). 1989. a. Aus.$55 (typically set in Dec.). Joint Coal Board, G.P.O. Box 3842, Sydney, N.S.W. 2001, Australia. TEL 02-235-9752. FAX 02-223-1896. circ. 2,000.
Description: Contains a comprehensive range of statistics on the N.S.W. coal industry. Includes profiles of producers, individual mines and port facilities and details of coal export brands-specifications with marketing contracts.

338.2 NZ
NEW ZEALAND ANNUAL MINING REVIEW. 1972. a. NZ.$20. Ministry of Commerce, Energy and Resources Division, Resource Information Unit, P.O. Box 1473, Wellington, New Zealand. TEL 04-472-0030. FAX 04-499-0969. Ed.Bd. circ. 800.
Former titles: New Zealand. Ministry of Energy. Annual Returns of Production from Quarries and Mineral Production Statistics (ISSN 0112-2584); New Zealand Mineral Production Statistics; New Zealand. Ministry of Energy. Mines Division. Annual Returns of Production from Quarries and Mineral Production Statistics; New Zealand. Mines Department. Annual Returns of Production from Quarries and Mineral Production Statistics.

ONTARIO MINERAL SCORE. see *MINES AND MINING INDUSTRY*

338.2 016 FR ISSN 0761-182X
P A S C A L FOLIO. F 41: GISEMENTS METALLIQUES ET NON-METALLIQUES. ECONOMIE MINIERE. 1984. 10/yr. 1330 F. (Bureau de Recherches Geologiques et Minieres) Centre National de la Recherche Scientifique, Institut de l'Information Scientifique et Technique, B.P. 54, 54514 Vandoeuvre-Les-Nancy Cedex, France. TEL 83-50-46-00.
Formerly: P A S C A L Folio. Part 41: Gisements Metalliques et Non-Metalliques. Economie Miniere; Which supersedes (1972-1984): Bulletin Signaletique: Bibliographie des Sciences de la Terre. Section 221. Gisements Metalliques et Non Metalliques. Economie Miniere; Bulletin Signaletique: Bibliographie des Sciences de la Terre. Section 221. Gisements Metalliques et Non Metalliques (ISSN 0304-1301); Which supersedes: Bulletin Signaletique: Bibliographie des Sciences de la Terre. Section 221. Cahier B. Gitologie, Economie Miniere (ISSN 0300-9270).

553.21 016 IE ISSN 0031-367X
PEAT ABSTRACTS. 1951. 3/yr. £20. Bord na Mona, Peat Research Centre, Droichead Nua, Co. Kildare, Ireland. FAX 045-33240. Ed. Tony McKenna. adv.; bk.rev.; circ. controlled. (processed) **Indexed:** Hort.Abstr.

622 317 CN
PRODUCTION OF CANADA'S LEADING MINERALS. (Text in English and French) 1979. m. free. Energy, Mines and Resources Canada, Mineral Policy Sector, Publishing Division, 460 O'Connor, Ottawa, Ont. K1A 0E4, Canada. TEL 819-956-4802. FAX 613-992-5565. (Subscr. to: Supply and Services Canada, Canada Communication Group - Publishing, Ottawa, Ont. K1A 0S9, Canada) Ed. H. Martin. stat.; circ. 1,400. (looseleaf format; back issues avail.) **Indexed:** CS Ind.

622 338.2 MY ISSN 0025-1313
QUARTERLY BULLETIN OF STATISTICS RELATING TO THE MINING INDUSTRY OF MALAYSIA. 1947. q. M.$6. Department of Mines - Jabatan Galian, Jalan Gurney, Kuala Lumpur, Malaysia. stat.; circ. 140.

622 II
QUICK RELEASE TO THE MINERAL STATISTICS OF INDIA. (Text in English) m. Rs.240($86.40) Indian Bureau of Mines, New Secretariat Bldg., Nagpur 440001, India. stat.

622 016 RU ISSN 0034-2386
REFERATIVNYI ZHURNAL. GORNOE DELO. 1964. m. 168 Rub. (196 Rub. including index). Vsesoyuznyi Institut Nauchno-Tekhnicheskoi Informatsii (VINITI), Baltiiskaya ul., 14, Moscow A-219, Russia. (Subscr. to: Mezhdunarodnaya Kniga, Dimitrova ul. 39, 113095 Moscow, Russia)

622 016 RU ISSN 0373-6415
REFERATIVNYI ZHURNAL. GORNOE I NEFTEPROMYSLOVOE MASHINOSTROENIE. 1964. m. 40 Rub. (47.40 Rub. including index). Vsesoyuznyi Institut Nauchno-Tekhnicheskoi Informatsii (VINITI), Baltiiskaya ul., 14, Moscow A-219, Russia. (Subscr. to: Mezhdunarodnaya Kniga, Dimitrova ul. 39, 113095 Moscow, Russia)
Formerly: Gornye Mashiny (ISSN 0034-2394).

REMOTE SENSING OF EARTH RESOURCES: A QUARTERLY BIBLIOGRAPHY. see *EARTH SCIENCES — Abstracting, Bibliographies, Statistics*

622 338.2 SA
SOUTH AFRICA. CENTRAL STATISTICAL SERVICE. CENSUS OF MINING. (Report No. 20-01-01) triennial. R.7.50. Central Statistical Service, Private Bag X44, Pretoria 0001, South Africa. TEL 012-310-8911. FAX 012-3108500. (Subscr. to: Government Printing Works, Private Bag X85, Pretoria 0001, South Africa)
Former titles: South Africa. Central Statistical Service. Mining: Financial Statistics; South Africa. Department of Statistics. Mining: Financial Statistics.

622 US ISSN 0498-7845
U.S. BUREAU OF MINES. MINERAL INDUSTRY SURVEYS. m. free. U.S. Bureau of Mines, Production and Distribution, Cochrans Mill Rd., Box 18070, Pittsburgh, PA 15236. TEL 412-892-4411. stat. **Indexed:** AESIS, Amer.Stat.Ind.
Description: Current data on individual mineral commodities.

622 VE
VENEZUELA. MINISTERIO DE ENERGIA Y MINAS. ANUARIO ESTADISTICO MINERO. 1965. a. free. Ministerio de Energia y Minas, Oficina de Economia Minera, Torre Oeste, Piso 4, Centro Simon Bolivar, Caracas, Venezuela.
Former titles (until 1986): Hierro; Venezuela. Ministerio de Minas e Hidrocarburos. Oficina de Economia Minera. Hierro y Otros Datos Estadisticos (ISSN 0083-5382)

VENEZUELA. MINISTERIO DE ENERGIA Y MINAS. APENDICE ESTADISTICO. see *ENERGY — Abstracting, Bibliographies, Statistics*

VENEZUELA. MINISTERO DE ENERGIA Y MINAS. MEMORIA. see *ENERGY — Abstracting, Bibliographies, Statistics*

338.2 310 UK
WORLD MINERAL STATISTICS; world production, exports and imports. 1978. a. price varies. British Geological Survey, Keyworth, Nottingham NG12 5GG, England. TEL 0602-361000. FAX 0602-362000. TELEX 378173 BGSKEY G. (Avail. from Mining Journal Books Ltd., 60 Worship St., London EC2A 2HD, England) circ. 1,000.
Supersedes: Institute of Geological Sciences, London. Statistical Summary of the Mineral Industry (ISSN 0073-9367)

549 016 GW ISSN 0514-7115
CODEN: ZMKMA5
ZENTRALBLATT FUER MINERALOGIE. TEIL I: KRISTALLOGRAPHIE, MINERALOGIE. (Text in English and German) 1807. 7/yr. E. Schweizerbart'sche Verlagsbuchhandlung, Johannesstr. 3A, 7000 Stuttgart 1, Germany. TEL 0711-625001. FAX 0711-625005. TELEX 723363-SCHB-D. Eds. B. Baader, W.H. Baur. adv.; bk.rev.; abstr.; bibl.; index. **Indexed:** Bull.Signal., Chem.Abstr., GeoRef.

549 551 016 GW ISSN 0514-7123
CODEN: ZMGMAJ
ZENTRALBLATT FUER MINERALOGIE. TEIL II: PETROGRAPHIE, TECHNISCHE MINERALOGIE, GEOCHEMIE UND LAGERSTAETTENKUNDE. (Text in English and German) 1807. 13/yr. E. Schweizerbart'sche Verlagsbuchhandlung, Johannesstr. 3A, 7000 Stuttgart 1, Germany. TEL 0711-625001. FAX 0711-625005. TELEX 723363-SCHB-D. Ed.Bd. adv.; bk.rev.; abstr.; bibl.; index. **Indexed:** Bull.Signal., Chem.Abstr., GeoRef.

ZHONGGUO DIZHI WENZHAI. see *EARTH SCIENCES — Abstracting, Bibliographies, Statistics*

MINICOMPUTERS

see *Computers–Minicomputers*

MOTION PICTURES

A F V A EVALUATIONS. (American Film & Video Association, Inc.) see *EDUCATION — Teaching Methods And Curriculum*

791.43 IT ISSN 0044-9741
A P A C INFORM. 6/yr. free. Associazione Professionale Autonoma Cineoperatori, Via P.S. Mancini, 20148 Milan, Italy. Ed. Mariso Varagnolo. circ. controlled. (tabloid format)

MOTION PICTURES 3503

791 BE ISSN 0775-9746
A S I F A NEWS. (Text in English, French, Russian) no.15, 1967. q. 175 F.($35) to non-members(effective 1992). (Association Internationale du Film d'Animation - International Association of Animated Film) Folioscope a.s.b.l., 19, Rue de la Rhetorique, 1060 Brussels, Belgium. TEL 02-5344125. FAX 02-5342279. Ed. Philippe Moins. adv.; bk.rev.
   Formerly (until 1988): International Animated Film Association. Bulletin (ISSN 0538-4281)
   Description: Aimed at professionals working in the field of animation cinema.

791.43 US
A V C VISIONS. 1973. 6/yr. $60. Association of Visual Communicators, 15125 Califa St., Ste. E, Van Nuys, CA 91411. TEL 818-787-6800. FAX 818-904-0547. Ed. Lou Ried-Scott. adv.; bk.rev.; illus.; circ. 5,000.
   Former titles: A V C Communicator; Communicator (South Pasadena); I F P A Communicator (ISSN 0099-1090); I F P A Newsletter.
   Description: Provides data to producers of corporate, industrial, educational and promotional programs in any individual medium. Focuses on the association's CINDY and VCDY competitions and on their winners.

A V GUIDE; the learning media newsletter. see EDUCATION — Teaching Methods And Curriculum

ABEL VALUE NEWS; panem et circenses/bread and circuses. see THEATER

778.5 791.43 US
ACADEMY AWARDS FOR DISTINGUISHED ACHIEVEMENTS. a. $3. Academy of Motion Picture Arts and Sciences, 8949 Wilshire Blvd., Beverly Hills, CA 90211-1972. TEL 213-278-8990. Ed. Byerly Woodward.

791.43 792 384.55 US
ACADEMY PLAYERS DIRECTORY. 3/yr. $65 per no. Academy of Motion Picture Arts and Sciences, 8949 Wilshire Blvd., Beverly Hills, CA 90211. TEL 213-247-3000. FAX 213-859-9351. Ed. Patricia L. Citrano.

791.43 380.1 US
ADAM FILM WORLD GUIDE DIRECTORY. a. $7.95. Knight Publishing Corp., 8060 Melrose Ave., Los Angeles, CA 90046. TEL 213-653-8060.
   Formerly: Adam Film World Guide.
   Description: Lists distributors, producers and other companies involved in adult video.

AGENCIES: WHAT THE ACTOR NEEDS TO KNOW. see BUSINESS AND ECONOMICS — Trade And Industrial Directories

ALLIGATOR. see MUSIC

790 RM
ALMANAHUL CINEMA. a. 25 lei. Piata Scinteii Nr. 1, Bucharest, Rumania. illus.

791.43 384.55 UK
AMATEUR FILM AND VIDEO MAKER. bi-m. £20. (Institute of Amateur Cinematographers) Film Maker Publications Ltd., 24 C W. St., Epsom, Surrey KT18 7RJ, England. FAX 081-644-0839. TELEX 934999-TXLINK-G REF:011137946. Ed. Tony Pattison. adv.; bk.rev.; circ. 3,500.
   Formerly: Amateur Film Maker.

778.534 SZ
AMATEURFILM JOURNAL. a. Alma-Verlag, Postfach 1020, 8953 Dietikon, Switzerland. Ed. Albert Haeusermann.
   Formerly: Super-8 Journal.

791.43 US ISSN 0002-7928
TR845
AMERICAN CINEMATOGRAPHER; international journal of motion picture production techniques. 1919. m. $24. (American Society of Cinematographers) A S C Holding Corporation, Box 2230, Los Angeles, CA 90078. TEL 213-969-4333. FAX 213-876-4973. (Subscr. to: Box 2230, Hollywood, CA 90078) Ed. David Heuring. adv.; bk.rev.; film rev.; charts; illus.; stat.; index, cum.index; circ. 32,000. (also avail. in microform from UMI) **Indexed:** Chem.Abstr., Film Lit.Ind. (1973-), Intl.Ind.TV.
   —BLDSC shelfmark: 0812.460000.

791.4 US ISSN 0195-8267
PN1993
AMERICAN CLASSIC SCREEN. 1977. bi-m. $15. (National Film Society, Inc.) American Classic Screen, Inc., Box 7150, Shawnee Mission, KS 66207. TEL 913-341-1919. Ed. John C. Tibbetts. adv.; bk.rev.; circ. 20,000. (back issues avail.) **Indexed:** Film Lit.Ind.

791.43 384.55 US
AMERICAN FILM AND VIDEO FESTIVAL GUIDE. 1959. a. $15. American Film & Video Association, Inc., Box 48659, Niles, IL 60648-0659. TEL 708-698-6440. FAX 708-823-1561. TELEX 403681 AFVA. Ed. Ms. Ray Rolff. adv.; index, cum.index: 1959-1963; circ. 7,000.
   Former titles: American Film Festival Guide; Festival Film Guide (ISSN 0071-4658)

791.4 384.55 US
AMERICAN FILM & VIDEO REVIEW. 1962. a. free. (American Educational Film and Video Center) Eastern College, St. Davids, PA 19087. Ed. John A. Baird, Jr. circ. 30,000.
   Formerly: American Film Review (ISSN 0065-8308)

330.1 US
AMERICAN FILM INSTITUTE MONOGRAPH SERIES. 1983. irreg. price varies. Praeger Publishers (Subsidiary of: Greenwood Publishing Group Inc.), 88 Post Rd. W., Box 5007, Westport, CT 06881-5007. TEL 203-222-3571. FAX 203-222-1502.

778.5 US
AMERICAN FILM MAGAZINE (NEW YORK).* 1974. m. $15. Eric Donne, Ed. & Pub., 250 W. 57th St., Rm. 1527, New York, NY 10019. TEL 212-582-0734. adv.; bk.rev.; film rev.; play rev.; illus. (back issues avail.) **Indexed:** Access.

778.5 US ISSN 0279-0041
PN1993.5.U6
AMERICAN PREMIERE MAGAZINE; business magazine of the film industry. 1979. bi-m. $16 (free to qualified personnel). American Premiere, Ltd., 8421 Wilshire Blvd., Penthouse Ste., Beverly Hills, CA 90211. Ed. Susan Royal. adv.; bk.rev.; film rev.; circ. 17,500. **Indexed:** Film Lit.Ind. (1982-).
   Formerly: Premiere (ISSN 0274-7766)

791.43 II
ANANDALOK. (Text in Bengali) 1975. fortn. 6 Prafulla Sarkar St., Calcutta 700 001, India. TEL 33-278000. TELEX 215468. Ed. Sevabrata Gupta. circ. 64,100.

778.53 NE
ANDERE SINEMA. bi-m. Ommeganckstraat 21, 2018 Antwerp, Netherlands. **Indexed:** Film Lit.Ind. (1980-).

778.53 384.55 UK
ANIMATOR. q. Filmcraft Publications, 13 Ringway Rd., Park St., St. Albans, Hertfords. AL2 2RE, England. **Indexed:** Film Lit.Ind. (1986-).

778.53 US
ANIMATRIX; a UCLA Animation Workshop. a. University of California at Los Angeles, Department of Theater, Film, and Television, 405 Hilgard Ave., Los Angeles, CA 90024. **Indexed:** Film Lit.Ind. (1988-).

778.5 FR
ANNEE DU CINEMA. 1977. a. price varies. Editions Calmann-Levy, 3 rue Auber, 75009 Paris, France. illus.

791.43 384.55 FR
ANNUAIRE DU CINEMA, TELEVISION, VIDEO. 1948. a. 1100 F.($82) Editions Bellefaye, 38 rue Etienne Marcel, 75002 Paris, France. TEL 42-33-52-52. FAX 42-33-39-00. TELEX 680151. adv.
   Formerly: Annuaire du Cinema et Television (ISSN 0066-2968)

778.5 US ISSN 0163-5123
PN1993
ANNUAL INDEX TO MOTION PICTURE CREDITS. 1976. a. $64. Academy of Motion Picture Arts and Sciences, 8949 Wilshire Blvd., Beverly Hills, CA 90211-1972. TEL 310-247-3000. FAX 310-859-9351. Ed. Byerly Woodward. circ. 999.
   Superseded: A M P A S Credits Bulletin; Formerly (until 1979): Screen Achievement Records Bulletin (ISSN 0147-2313)
   Description: Contains approximately 14,000 individual credits, and credits for feature films opening in LA area. Index by title, craft, individual names and distributors. Based on primary sources from producers-distributors.

791.4 LE ISSN 0003-7397
ARAB FILM AND TELEVISION CENTER NEWS. (Editions in Arabic, English and French) 1965. s-m. free to qualified personnel. Ministry of Information, Arab Film & Television Centre, Box 3434, Beirut, Lebanon. film rev.; illus.; stat.; cum.index; circ. 3,000.

ARTIBUS ET HISTORIAE; international journal for visual arts. see ART

778.53 US
ASIAN CINEMA. s-a. Box 91, Quinnipiac College, Hamden, CT 06518-0569. Ed. Mira Reym Binford. **Indexed:** Film Lit.Ind. (1986-).

791 PO
ASSOCIACAO PORTUGUESA DE EMPRESAS CINEMATOGRAFICAS. JORNAL. 1953; N.S. 1976. m. Esc.250($6.20) Associacao Portuguesa de Empresas Cinematograficas, Avenida Duque de Loule 86-2dt, 100 Lisbon, Portugal. adv.; charts; illus.; stat.; circ. 1,500.
   Formerly (until 1980): Jornal dos Espectaculos (ISSN 0041-6665)

ASSOCIATION OF TALENT AGENTS. NEWSLETTER. see THEATER

ASWAMEDHAM; the front runner. see ADVERTISING AND PUBLIC RELATIONS

778.534 GW
ATLAS FILMSZENE. 1985. q. Atlas Film & AV GmbH & Co. KG, Ludgerstr. 14-18, 4100 Duisburg 1, Germany. TEL 0203-308270. Ed. Jaimi Stueber. (back issues avail.)
   Description: Reports on new films being produced and screened.

791 IT
ATTUALITA CINEMATOGRAFICHE. 1964. a. price varies. (Parrocchia di Santa Maria della Scalla in San Fedele) Edizioni Letture, Piazza San Fedele 4, 20121 Milan, Italy. TEL 011-02-804441. FAX 001-02-72023481. circ. 1,000.

AUDIO VISUAL. see EDUCATION — Teaching Methods And Curriculum

AUDIOVISIVI. see EDUCATION — Teaching Methods And Curriculum

791.43 384.55 AT
AUSTRALIAN CATALOGUE OF NEW FILMS AND VIDEOS. a. Aus.$50 (foreign Aus.$60). Australian Catalogue, P.O. Box 204, Albert Park, Vic. 3206, Australia. TEL 03 531 2086. FAX 03-531-2411.
   Formerly: Filmviews Catalogue (ISSN 1031-4377)
   Description: Comprehensive listing of all currently released films and videos available in Australia. Includes all imported and Australian produced titles, listed alphabetically under subject headings.

791.43 AT ISSN 0313-7031
AUSTRALIAN FILM INSTITUTE NEWSLETTER. 1976. q. Aus.$40 membership. Australian Film Institute, 49 Eastern Rd., S. Melbourne, Vic. 3205, Australia. TEL 03-696-1844. FAX 03-696-7972. Ed. Vicki Molloy. bk.rev.; film rev.; tr.lit.; circ. 5,000. (back issues avail.)

AUSTRALIAN FILM, TELEVISION AND RADIO SCHOOL. ANNUAL REPORT. see COMMUNICATIONS — Television And Cable

AUSTRALIAN FILM, TELEVISION AND RADIO SCHOOL HANDBOOK. see COMMUNICATIONS — Television And Cable

M

MOTION PICTURES

AUSTRALIAN S F NEWS. (Science Fiction) see *LITERATURE — Science Fiction, Fantasy, Horror*

791.4   FR   ISSN 0045-1150
PN1993
AVANT-SCENE CINEMA. 1961. 11/yr. 600 F. Editions de l' Avant Scene, 6 rue Git-le-Coeur, 75006 Paris, France. TEL 1-46-34-28-20. FAX 1-43-54-50-14. illus.; index, cum.index: 1961-1977. (back issues avail.) **Indexed:** Arts & Hum.Cit.Ind., Curr.Cont., Film Lit.Ind. (1974-), Intl.Ind.TV, Pt.de Rep. (1979-).
—BLDSC shelfmark: 1837.118000.

AXE FACTORY REVIEW. see *LITERATURE*

778.43 384.55   US
▼**BACK STAGE - SHOOT.** 1990. w. $65. B P I Communications, Inc., 330 W. 42nd St., New York, NY 10036. TEL 212-947-0020. FAX 212-967-6786. Ed. Peter Caranicas. circ. 18,100.
Description: For the commercial production and advertising industries. Special feature issues cover industry events such as the Clio Awards, NAB Convention, ITS Convention, and SMPTE.

BARBARA EDEN INTERNATIONAL FAN CLUB NEWSLETTER. see *CLUBS*

791.43   CC
BAYI DIANYING/AUGUST 1ST FILMS. (Text in Chinese) m. $40.40. Bayi Dianying Zhipian Chang, Bayi Dianying Bianjibu, No. A-1, Liuliqiao, Guang'anwenwai, Beijing 361964, People's Republic of China. TEL 361964. (Dist. in US by: China Books & Periodicals, Inc., 2929, 24th St., San Francisco, CA 94110. TEL 415-282-2994) Ed. Zhai Junjie.

791.43   CC
BEIYING HUABAO/BEIJING FILM STUDIO PICTORIAL. (Text in Chinese) bi-m. $30.60. Beijing Dianying Zhipian Chang - Beijing Film Studio, Beijing, People's Republic of China. (Dist. in US by: China Books & Periodicals, Inc., 2929 24th St., San Francisco, CA 94110. TEL 415-282-2994) illus.

791.43   IT   ISSN 0006-0577
BIANCO E NERO. (Text in Italian; summaries in English and Italian) 1933. q. L.43000($43) (foreign L.70000). (Centro Sperimentale Cinematografia) E R I Edizioni R A I, Via Arsenale 41, 10121 Turin, Italy. TEL 011-8800. FAX 011-534732. bk.rev.; film rev.; illus.; index. **Indexed:** Arts & Hum.Cit.Ind., Curr.Cont., Film Lit.Ind. (1973-1988), Intl.Ind.TV.

778.5   US
BIG REEL. 1973. m. $25. Empire Publishing, Inc., 3130 U.S. 220, Madison, NC 27025. TEL 919-427-5850. FAX 919-427-7372. Ed. Rhonda K. Lemons. adv.; bk.rev.; film rev.; circ. 4,500. (tabloid format)
Description: Forum for film buffs to buy, trade and sell films, photographs, videotapes, publications, posters, and projectors.

778 910.03   US
BLACK FILM REVIEW. 1985. q. $12 to individuals; institutions $24. Sojourner Productions, Inc., 2025 I St. N.W., Ste. 213, Washington, DC 20006. TEL 202-466-2753. Ed. Jacquie Jones. adv.; film rev.; circ. 5,000. (back issues avail.) **Indexed:** Film Lit.Ind. (1986-).

791.43   GW
BLICKPUNKT: FILM. (Text in German; summaries in English and German) 1976. 52/yr. DM.325. Casablanca Verlag GmbH, Am Moosfeld 26, 8000 Munich 82, Germany. TEL 089-4209030. FAX 089-42090311. TELEX 5218214. Ed. Erich Kocian. adv.; bk.rev.; charts; stat.; circ. 3,500. (back issues avail.)

778.53   AU
BLIMP; Zeitschrift fuer Film. q. Griesplatz 36, A-8020 Graz, Austria. **Indexed:** Film Lit.Ind. (1988-).

BOERNEFILMKATALOGET. see *CHILDREN AND YOUTH — For*

BOMB; artists, writers, actors, directors. see *ART*

791.4   US   ISSN 0006-8527
PN1993
BOXOFFICE; the business magazine of the motion picture industry. 1920. m. $35. R L D Communications, 6640 Sunset Blvd., Ste 100, Hollywood, CA 90028. TEL 213-465-1186. FAX 213-465-5049. (Subscr. to: 1020 S. Wabash Ave., Chicago, IL 60605) Ed. Harley W. Lond. adv.; bk.rev.; film rev.; charts; illus.; stat.; circ. 8,000. **Indexed:** Film Lit.Ind. (1973-).

790   GW
BRAVO. 1956. w. $110. Heinrich Bauer Verlag (Munich), Charles de Gaulle Str. 8, 8000 Munich 83, Germany. TEL 089-6786-501. FAX 089-6702033. (Dist. in US by: German Language Publications, Inc., 560 Sylvan Ave., Englewood Cliffs, NJ 07632. TEL 201-871-1010) Ed. R. Wittner. adv.; film rev.; illus.; circ. 1,461,163.

BULAWAYO THIS MONTH. see *TRAVEL AND TOURISM*

791.43   BU   ISSN 0007-3911
BULGARIAN FILMS. Russian edition (ISSN 0204-8205); French edition (ISSN 0204-8973); English edition (ISSN 0204-8884) 1960. 8/yr. $24. Bulgarian Film Industry, 135-A Rakovski St., Sofia 1000, Bulgaria. TEL 88 32 89. TELEX 22 447 FILMEX BG. Ed. Ivan Stoyanovich. adv.; bk.rev.; film rev.; circ. 20,000 (English ed. 1,500; French ed. 1,500; Russian ed. 17,000). **Indexed:** Film Lit.Ind. (1977-), Intl.Ind.TV.
Description: Reports on films in production, screenplays and previews. Includes reviews and interviews.

THE BULLET (NASHVILLE). see *COMMUNICATIONS — Television And Cable*

BUSINESS EDUCATION FILMS CATALOG. see *BUSINESS AND ECONOMICS*

778   UK   ISSN 0068-4449
BUSINESS MONITOR: MISCELLANEOUS SERIES. M2 CINEMAS. a. price varies. (Department of Industry) H.M.S.O., P.O. Box 276, London SW8 5DT, England. (Avail. from: H.M.S.O., c/o Liaison Officer, Atlantic House, Holborn Viaduct, London EC1P 1BN, England) **Indexed:** BMT, Int.Packag.Abstr., Paper & Bd.Abstr., Rehabil.Lit.

C C U M C LEADER. (Consortium of College and University Media Centers) see *EDUCATION — Teaching Methods And Curriculum*

791   FR   ISSN 0526-6513
C.I.C.A.E. BULLETIN D'INFORMATION. 1965. irreg. $20. Confederation Internationale des Cinemas d'Art et d'Essai - International Art Cinemas Confederation, c/o Jean Lescure, 22 rue d'Artois, 75008 Paris, France. FAX 45-61-13-65. Ed. Jean Lescure. circ. 1,000.

778.53   GW
C I C I M: REVUE POUR LE CINEMA FRANCAIS. q. Institut Francais de Munich, Centro d'Information Cinematographique, Kaulbachstrasse 13, 8000 Munich 22, Germany. **Indexed:** Film Lit.Ind. (1987-).

C I L E C T NEWSLETTER. (Centre International de Liaison des Ecoles de Cinema et de Television) see *COMMUNICATIONS — Television And Cable*

791.43   II
C.T.A. JOURNAL. 1943. m. Rs.30($3) Cine Technicians' Association of South India, 150 Usman Rd., T'nagar, Madras 17, India. Ed. B. Janardana Rao. adv.; bk.rev.; illus.; tr.lit.; circ. 1,000.
Formerly (until 1973): Cine Technicians' Association of South India. Journal (ISSN 0009-6970)

791.4   US   ISSN 0007-9219
P87
C T V D: CINEMA - T V - DIGEST; a quarterly review of the serious, foreign-language cinema-T V-press. 1962. irreg. $3 for 4 nos. (foreign $4). Hampton Books, Route 1, Box 202, Newberry, SC 29108. TEL 803-276-6870. Ed. Ben Hamilton. adv.; bk.rev.; film rev.; circ. 550. (back issues avail.)

778.5   FR
CA CINEMA.* 1973. q. 110 F. Editions Albatros, 21 rue Cassette, 75006 Paris, France. Ed.Bd. bk.rev.; bibl.; cum.index: 1973-1979; circ. 1,500.

778.5   FR
CAHIERS DE LA CINEMATHEQUE. 1970. q. 130 F. Institut Jean Vigo, 21 rue Mailly, 66000 Perpignan, France. Ed. Marcel Oms. adv.; bk.rev.; film rev.; illus. **Indexed:** Film Lit.Ind. (1975-), Intl.Ind.TV.

778.5   FR   ISSN 0008-011X
PN1993
CAHIERS DU CINEMA. 1951. m. $70. Editions de l'Etoile, 9 Passage de la Boule Blanche, 75012 Paris, France. TEL 1-43-43-92-20. FAX 43-43-95-04. TELEX 215 092 F. Ed. Serge Toubiana. adv.; bk.rev.; film rev.; illus.; circ. 80,000. (also avail. in microfiche) **Indexed:** Arts & Hum.Cit.Ind., Curr.Cont., Film Lit.Ind. (1973-), Intl.Ind.TV, Pt.de Rep. (1989-).
—BLDSC shelfmark: 2948.800000.

788.53   BE
CAHIERS DU SCENARIO. q. Universite Libre de Bruxelles, Institut de Sociologie, 44 Ave. Jeanne, CP124-B, 1050 Brussels, Belgium. **Indexed:** Film Lit.Ind. (1989-).

CALIFORNIA POINTS AND AUTHORITIES. see *LAW*

778.5   US   ISSN 0270-5346
PN1995.9.W6
CAMERA OBSCURA; a journal of feminism and film theory. 1976. 3/yr. $18.50 to individuals (foreign $24.50); institutions $37 (foreign $43). Johns Hopkins University Press, Journals Publishing Division, 701 W. 40th St., Ste. 275, Baltimore, MD 21211. TEL 410-516-6987. FAX 410-516-6998. Ed.Bd. adv.; bk.rev.; film rev.; bibl.; charts; illus.; circ. 939. (also avail. in microform; back issues avail.; reprint service avail. from ISI) **Indexed:** Alt.Press Ind., Arts & Hum.Cit.Ind., Film Lit.Ind. (1976-), Int.Ind.Film Per., Intl.Ind.TV, Stud.Wom.Abstr.
—BLDSC shelfmark: 3016.149800.
Description: Presents current perspectives on the national and international film scene.

778.53   FR
CAMERA - STYLO. irreg. 18 rue des Fosses Saint Jacques, 75005 Paris, France. **Indexed:** Film Lit.Ind. (1984-).

CANADA COUNCIL ANNUAL REPORT AND SUPPLEMENT/RAPPORT ANNUEL DU CONSEIL DES ARTS DU CANADA ET SON SUPPLEMENT. see *ART*

791.43   CN   ISSN 0705-548X
CANADIAN FILM SERIES. 1976. irreg., no.6, 1981. price varies. Canadian Film Institute, 2 Daly, Ottawa, Ont. K1N 6E2, Canada. TEL 613-232-6727. FAX 613-232-6315. TELEX 0636700474.

778.534   GW   ISSN 0931-1920
CANON JAHRBUCH FUER VIDEOFILMER. 1985. a. DM.24. Fachverlag Schiele und Schoen GmbH, Markgrafenstr. 11, Postfach 610280, 1000 Berlin 61, Germany. TEL 030-2516029. Ed. Lothar Woehner. index; circ. 12,000.

778.5 700   AT   ISSN 0158-4154
PN1993
CANTRILLS FILMNOTES. 1971. q. Aus.$15($17) to individuals; institutions, libraries Aus.$23($27). Arthur & Corinne Cantrill, Eds. & Pubs., Box 1295 L, G.P.O., Melbourne, Vic. 3001, Australia. film rev.; illus.; circ. 1,000. (back issues avail.) **Indexed:** Film Lit.Ind. (1976-), Intl.Ind.TV.

CASTLE DRACULA; dedicated to the appreciation, promotion, & preservation of supernatural fiction in literature, films, theater, TV & all media. see *LITERATURE — Science Fiction, Fantasy, Horror*

791.43   IT   ISSN 0392-4440
CASTORO CINEMA. 1974. bi-m. L.60000. Nuova Italia Editrice S.p.a., Via Ernesto Codignola, 50018 Scandicci (FL), Italy. Ed. Fernaldo di Giammatteo. **Indexed:** Film Lit.Ind. (1989-).

791.43 371.912   US   ISSN 0093-7215
HV2395
CATALOG OF CAPTIONED FILMS FOR THE DEAF.* a. Associations for Education of the Deaf, Special Materials Project, c/o Assoc. Builder Contra., 4061 Powder Mill Rd., Beltsville, MD 20705-3149.

778.5 384.55   NE
CATALOGUS FILMS EN VIDEO. irreg. fl.52.50. Nederlands Filminstitut, Postbus 515, Hilversum, Netherlands. illus.
Formerly: 3 D Film Gids.

791.43 780   US
CELEBRITY DIRECTORY. 1984. a. $29.95. Axiom Information Services, Box 8015, Ann Arbor, MI 48107. TEL 313-761-4842. Ed. Terry Robinson.

CELEBRITY SERVICE INTERNATIONAL CONTACT BOOK; trade directory/entertainment industry. see *THEATER*

791.43   FR   ISSN 0397-8435
PN1993.5.F7
CENTRE NATIONAL DE LA CINEMATOGRAPHIE. BULLETIN D'INFORMATION. Cover title: Informations C N C. (Supplements avail.) 1947. 6/yr. 150 F.($3) Centre National de la Cinematographie, 12 rue de Lubeck, 75784 Paris Cedex 16, France. TEL 505-14-40. Ed. D. Wallon. bk.rev.; charts; illus.; stat.; index; circ. 10,000.

791.43   FR   ISSN 0339-8978
CHANGER LE CINEMA. 1976. m. 50 F. 15 rue des Ursulines, 75005 Paris, France. Dir. Maria Landau.

791.43   SW   ISSN 0045-6349
CHAPLIN. 1959. bi-m. SEK 198 in Scandinavia; in Europe SEK 218; elsewhere SEK 230. Svenska Filminstitutet - Swedish Film Institute, P.O. Box 27126, S-102 52 Stockholm, Sweden. TEL 08-665-1203. FAX 08-663-8009. TELEX 13326 FILMNS S. Ed. Jannike Aahlund. adv.; bk.rev.; film rev.; illus.; circ. 5,700 (controlled). **Indexed:** Film Lit.Ind. (1973-), Intl.Ind.TV.

778   US
CHICAGO FILM & VIDEO NEWS. bi-m. Real Estate News Corp., 2600 W. Peterson Ave., Chicago, IL 60659-4031. TEL 312-465-7246. FAX 312-465-7218. Ed. Donna B. Proske. adv.

791.43   CC
PN1993.5.C4
CHINA SCREEN/ZHONGGUO YINMU. (Text in Chinese, English) 1980. q. $12. Zhongguo Dianying Shuchu Shuru Gongsi - China Film Import & Export Corp., 25 Xinjiekouwai Dajie, Beijing 100088, People's Republic of China. (Dist. overseas by: China International Book Trading Corp., P.O. Box 399, Beijing, P.R.C.; Dist. in US by: China Books and Periodicals, Inc., 2929 24th St., San Francisco, CA 94110) **Indexed:** Film Lit.Ind.
Formerly: China's Screen (ISSN 0577-893X)
Description: Covers new Chinese films. Contains feature articles on actors, actresses, directors, and films.

791.43   II
CHITRALOK. (Text in Gujarati) 1952. w. Gujarat Samachar Bhavan, Khanpur, P.O. Box 254, Ahmedabad, India. Ed. Shreyans Shah. circ. 18,900.

778.534   IT
CIAO SI GIRA. m. Silvio Berlusconi Editore, Corso Europa, 5-7, 20122 Milan, Italy. TEL 02-77941. Ed. Gigi Vesigna.

791.4 790   II
CINE ADVANCE. (Text in English) 1954. w. Rs.85($50) Swadeshwari Printers and Publishers Pvt. Ltd., 74 Lenin Saranee, Calcutta 700 013, India. TELEX 215882-NEWS-IN. Ed. Ajay Agarwal. adv.; bk.rev.; film rev.; play rev.; illus.; circ. 70,000. (looseleaf format)

791.4   BE   ISSN 0771-0518
CINE & MEDIA. (Editions in English, French, Spanish) 1980. bi-m. 400 Fr.($12) International Catholic Organization for Cinema and Audiovisual - Organisation Catholique Internationale du Cinema et de l'Audiovisuel, Rue de l'Orme 8, B-1040 Brussels, Belgium. TEL 02-734-42-94. FAX 02-734-32-07. TELEX (0402) 6105905 GMA LU. Ed. Robert Molhant. adv.; bk.rev.; film rev.; video rev.; illus.
Description: Covers cinematographic productions from all over the world, especially those largely ignored by the more industrialized countries.

778.5   II
CINE BLITZ. m. Rs.130 (foreign Rs.226). Blitz Publications Private Ltd., 17-17-H, Cawasji Patel St., Fort, Bombay 400 001, India. TEL 2047166. TELEX 011-6801-BLTZ-IN. Ed. Ms. R.K. Mehta. adv.; film rev.; circ. 117,536.

778.53   CN
CINE-BULLES. q. Association des Cinemas Paralleles du Quebec, 4545 Ave. Pierre de Coubertin, CP 1000 Succ. M, Montreal, Que. H1V 3R2, Canada. **Indexed:** Film Lit.Ind. (1988-).

778.5   CU   ISSN 0009-6946
CINE CUBANO. 1960. q. C.$12($10) in N. America; S. America $12; Europe $17. Instituto Cubano del Arte e Industria Cinematograficos (ICAIC), Dpto. Publicaciones, Calle 23, No.1115, Apdo. 55, Havana, Cuba. (Dist. by: Ediciones Cubanas, Obispo No. 527, Apdo. 605, Havana, Cuba) Ed. Gloria Villazon Hernandez. circ. 20,000. **Indexed:** Film Lit.Ind. (1973-), Intl.Ind.TV.

791.4   BE   ISSN 0773-2279
CINE-FICHES DE GRAND ANGLE. 1972. m. 1400 Fr. (Centre de Documentation Cinematographique) A.S.B.L. Grand Angle-Opvac, B-5660 Mariembourg, Belgium. TEL 060-312168. FAX 060-312937. Ed. Jacques Noel. adv.; bk.rev.; film rev.; illus.; index; circ. 3,500. **Indexed:** Film Lit.Ind. (1986-).
Formerly: Grand Angle; Incorporating (as of 1983): Cinemaniac (ISSN 0770-1640)

791.43   CU
CINE-GUIA. m. Poder Popular, Empresa Exhibidora de Peliculas, Havana, Cuba.

CINE NEWS. see *PHOTOGRAPHY*

791.43   VE
CINE-OJA. 1967. 4/yr. $15. Sociedad Civil Cine al Dia, Apdo. 50446, Sabana Grande, Caracas, Venezuela. Ed. Alfredo Roffe. adv.; bk.rev.; film rev.; illus.; circ. 2,500 (controlled). (also avail. in microform from UMI) **Indexed:** Film Lit.Ind., Int.Ind.Film Per., Intl.Ind.TV.
Formerly (until no.25, 1984): Cine al Dia (ISSN 0009-692X)
Description: Includes essays on the economic and cultural development of the Venezuelan and Latinamerican cinema.

791.4   BE   ISSN 0045-6918
CINE-REVUE. 1920. w. Cine-Revue, S.A., Rue de Danemark, 1060 Brussels, Belgium. Ed. M. Leempoel. adv.; bk.rev.; film rev.; illus.; circ. 3,000,000. **Indexed:** Film Lit.Ind. (1974-).

778.53   CN
CINEACTION!. q. 40 Alexander St., Apt. 705, Toronto, Ont. M4Y 1B5, Canada. **Indexed:** Film Lit.Ind. (1985-).

791.43   US   ISSN 0009-7004
PN1993
CINEASTE. 1967. q. $15 to individuals (foreign $24); institutions $30 (foreign $37). Cineaste Publishers, Inc., 200 Park Ave. So., New York, NY 10003. TEL 212-982-1241. (Subscr. to: Box 2242, New York, NY 10009) Ed.Bd. adv.; bk.rev.; film rev.; index; circ. 7,000. (also avail. in microform from UMI; back issues avail.) **Indexed:** Alt.Press Ind., Arts & Hum.Cit.Ind., Curr.Cont., Film Lit.Ind. (1973-), Int.Ind.Film Per., Intl.Ind.TV, Left Ind. (1986-), M.L.A., Media Rev.Dig., Sociol.Abstr.
—BLDSC shelfmark: 3198.635800.
Description: Focuses on both the art and politics of the cinema.

778.534   SZ   ISSN 1018-2098
CINEBULLETIN; Zeitschrift der schweizerischen Filmbranche. (Text in French, German) 1975. m. 52 SFr. (foreign 68 SFr.). Schweizerisches Filmzentrum, Muenstergasse 18, CH-8001 Zuerich, Switzerland. TEL 01-2612860. FAX 01-2621132. TELEX 817226-SFZZ. Ed. Martin Girod. adv.; circ. 2,700.

792   IT
CINECORRIERE. 1948. m. L.15000. c/o Alberto Crucilla, Ed., Circonvallazione Clodia 80, 00195 Rome, Italy. adv.

791.43   IT   ISSN 0009-7020
CINECRONACHE.* N.S. 1967. m. Circolo del Cinema di Rovigo, Via All'ara 8, Rovigo, Italy. Dir. Gianluigi Ceruti. film rev.

791.4   AT   ISSN 0813-1600
CINEDOSSIER. 1982. w. (50/yr). Aus.$425 (foreign Aus.$450). Australian Film Institute, Research and Information Centre, 49 Eastern Rd., Melbourne, Vic. 3205, Australia. TEL 03-696-1844. FAX 03-696-7932. Ed. James Sabine. bk.rev.; film rev.; index, cum.index: 1982-1991.
Description: Press clips from over 40 Australian newspapers concerning film news, production plans, and interviews.

778.5 051   US   ISSN 0145-6032
PN1995.9.H6
CINEFANTASTIQUE. 1970. 6/yr. $21 for 4 nos. (foreign $32). Box 270, Oak Park, IL 60303. TEL 708-366-5566. Ed. Frederick S. Clarke. adv.; bk.rev.; film rev.; illus.; stat.; index; circ. 40,000. (back issues avail.) **Indexed:** Film Lit.Ind. (1973-), M.M.R.I., Media Rev.Dig.

791.43   US   ISSN 0198-1056
TR858
CINEFEX; the journal of cinematic illusions. 1980. q. $22. Cinefex, Box 20027, Riverside, CA 92516. Ed. Don Shay. adv.; circ. 15,000. **Indexed:** Film Lit.Ind. (1980-), Int.Ind.Film Per., Intl.Ind.TV.
Description: Covers motion picture special effects: optical, physical, makeup and computer.

791.43   IT   ISSN 0009-7039
PN1993
CINEFORUM; rivista di cultura cinematografica. 1960. m. (10/yr.) L.65000 (foreign L.90000)(typically set in Jan.). Federazione Italiana dei Cineforum, Via Pascoli 3, 24100 Bergamo, Italy. TEL 35-244703. FAX 35-233129. Ed. Sandro Zambetti. adv.; bk.rev.; film rev.; index; circ. 5,000. **Indexed:** Arts & Hum.Cit.Ind., Curr.Cont., Film Lit.Ind. (1973-), Intl.Ind.TV.

791.43 384.55 792   SP   ISSN 0069-4134
CINEGUIA; annuario espanol del espectaculo y audiovisuales. 1960. a. 4800 ptas. F.M. Editores, S.A., Capitan Haya, 47, oficina 909, 28020 Madrid, Spain. TEL 91-571-40-72. adv.; circ. 4,800.

778.5   BG
CINEMA. (Text in Bengali) 1974. w. Tk.0.50 per issue. 81 Motijheel C/A, Dhaka 1000, Bangladesh. Ed. Sheikh Fazlur Rahman Maruf. circ. 11,000. **Indexed:** Intl.Ind.TV.

778.5   SZ
CINEMA; unabhaengige schweizerische Filmzeitschrift - revue cinematographique independent suisse. 1951. a. 18 Fr. Stroemfeld - Roter Stern, Postfach 79, CH-4007 Basel, Switzerland. FAX 061-6912406. Ed. Janis Osolin. adv.; bk.rev.; illus.; circ. 2,600. **Indexed:** Film Lit.Ind. (1976-), Intl.Ind.TV.

791.43   IT
CINEMA. (Includes a videocassette.) m. L.235000. E R I Edizioni R A I, Via Arsenale 41, 10121 Torino, Italy. TEL 011-8800. FAX 011-534732.

791.43   TS
CINEMA. (Text in Arabic) 1988. q. exchange basis. Cultural Foundation, Culture and Arts Department, P.O. Box 2380, Abu Dhabi, United Arab Emirates. TEL 215300. FAX 336059. TELEX 22414 CULCEN EM. circ. 1,000.
Description: Covers international film news and presents an overview of world film-making activity, and discusses the department's film series.

778.5   FR   ISSN 0045-6926
PN1993
CINEMA (YEAR). 1953. m. 180 F. Societe de Presse et d'Edition, 49 rue Fg. Poissonniere, 75009 Paris, France. TEL 1-42-46-37-50. FAX 1-48-24-33-67. TELEX 290562. (Subscr. to: B.P. 63, F-77932 Perthes Cedex, France. TEL 1-64-38-01-55) Ed. Georges Montaron. adv.; bk.rev.; circ. 30,000. **Indexed:** Film Lit.Ind. (1973-), Intl.Ind.TV, Pt.de Rep.

791.43 028.5   CN   ISSN 0009-7071
PN1993.5.C2
CINEMA - CANADA. 1976. 12/yr. Can.$25. 7383 rue de la Roche, Montreal, Que. H2R 2T4, Canada. TEL 514-272-5354. FAX 514-270-5068. Ed. Connie Tadros. adv.; bk.rev.; circ. 10,000. (also avail. in microform from CML; back issues avail.) **Indexed:** Can.Per.Ind., CMI, Film Lit.Ind. (1973-1990), Int.Ind.Film Per., Intl.Ind.TV, Mag.Ind., Media Rev.Dig.

MOTION PICTURES

792   IT
CINEMA D'OGGI. 1967. fortn. L.30000. A.N.I.C.A., Viale Regina Margherita 286, 00198 Rome, Italy. Ed. Carmine Cianfarani. adv.; circ. 11,000.

791.43   PO   ISSN 0009-708X
CINEMA DE AMADORES.* 1945. q. Esc.50($2) (Portuguese Club of Cine Amateurs) Pathe Baby Portugal, R.S. Nicolau 22, Lisbon 2, Portugal. Ed. Carlos Mascarenhas Azevedo. film rev.; circ. 2,500.

791.43   IT
CINEMA DOMANI. 1961. bi-m. Rolando Jotti, Via Cerquetti 67, 00152 Rome, Italy. film rev. (back issues avail.)

791.43   IT   ISSN 0009-7152
CINEMA E SOCIETA. 1966. irreg. L.3000 per no. Giorgio Trentin, Ed. & Pub., Via Porta Maggiorea, 81, 00185 Rome, Italy. bk.rev.; film rev.; illus.; circ. 2,500. (tabloid format)

791.43   FR   ISSN 0292-7292
CINEMA FRANCAIS PRODUCTION.* 1977. a. Unifrance Film International, 77 Champs-Elysees, 75008 Paris, France.

778.53   II
CINEMA IN INDIA. q. National Film Development Corp., Ltd., 8 Dalamal Tower, 211 Nariman Point, Bombay 400 021, India. **Indexed:** Film Lit.Ind. (1988-).

791.43   US   ISSN 0009-7101
PN1993
CINEMA JOURNAL. 1961. 4/yr. $25 to individuals; institutions $32. (Society for Cinema Studies) University of Illinois Press, 54 E. Gregory Dr., Champaign, IL 61820. TEL 217-333-0950. FAX 217-244-8082. Ed. Dana Polan. adv.; bk.rev.; circ. 1,500. **Indexed:** Amer.Bibl.Slavic & E.Eur.Stud.; Arts & Hum.Cit.Ind., Curr.Cont., Film Lit.Ind. (1973-), Int.Ind.Film Per., Intl.Ind.TV, M.L.A., Mid.East Abstr.& Ind.
—BLDSC shelfmark: 3198.639000.
    Formerly: Society of Cinematologists. Journal.
    Description: Touches on history of the motion picture industry.
    Refereed Serial

778   IT
CINEMA LOMBARDIA; periodico d'informazione a cura della sezione regionale dell'A.N.E.C. 1975. m. (Associazione Nazionale Esercenti Cinema (A.N.E.C.)) A.G.I.S. Lombarda, Piazza Luigi di Savoia 24, 20124 Milan, Italy. TEL 66 90 241. Ed. Viviana Giorgi. adv.; film rev.; abstr.; charts; illus.; circ. 800. (looseleaf format)
    Description: Provides news of regional association activities and reprints news articles dealing with the film industry.

791.43   US
CINEMA NEWS. 1981. 3/yr. $7. Gateway Entertainment, Inc., 12 Moray Court, Baltimore, MD 21236. Ed. Don Dohler. adv.; bk.rev.; circ. 3,000.
    Formerly: Amazing Cinema.

791.43   IT   ISSN 0009-711X
CINEMA NUOVO; rassegna bimestrale di cultura. 1952. bi-m. L.35000 (foreign L.52500)(effective 1992). Edizioni Dedalo s.r.l., Box 362, 70100 Bari, Italy. TEL 080-371555. FAX 080-371979. Dir. Guido Aristarco. bk.rev.; bibl.; film rev.; illus.; index; circ. 14,000. **Indexed:** Film Lit.Ind. (1973-), Intl.Ind.TV.
    Description: Reviews the cinema and its future.

791.43   AT
CINEMA PAPERS. bi-m. Aus.$28 (foreign Aus.$37). M T V Publishing Ltd., 43 Charles St., Abbotsford, Vic. 3067, Australia. TEL 03-429-5511. FAX 3427-9255. adv.; bk.rev. (back issues avail.) **Indexed:** Film Lit.Ind. (1975-).
    Description: The production guide to who's making what in Australia. Includes features, interviews, news, reviews and a complete list of the latest censorship decisions.

791.43 320   FR   ISSN 0335-6280
CINEMA POLITIQUE; dans la perspective d'une vie passionnante. bi-m. 75 F. Association pour le Developpement et la Promotion par le Cinema, 20 bd. de l'Hopital, 75005 Paris, France. Ed. Dominique Loeillet. illus.

791   PK
CINEMA THE WORLD OVER. (Text in English) 1975. m. Rs.40. National Film Development Corporation, c/o K.S. Hosain, 204-205 Hotel Metropole, Karachi, Pakistan.

778.5   FR
CINEMA 9. 1969. m. 25 F. Chemin des Fosses, 77880 Moncourt-Frononville, France. Ed. Pierre Y. Dhuiege. adv.; illus.

778.5   US   ISSN 0198-1064
CINEMACABRE; an appreciation of the fantastic. 1979. irreg. $10 for 3 nos. George Stover, Ed. & Pub., Box 10005, Baltimore, MD 21285. TEL 301-828-0286. adv.; bk.rev.; film rev.; illus.; circ. 3,000. **Indexed:** Film Lit.Ind. (1979-), Media Rev.Dig.
    Supersedes: Black Oracle (ISSN 0045-2246)
    Description: Digest featuring interviews and reviews.

778.53   FR
CINEMACTION. irreg. Corlet, Imprimeur, S.A., 14110 Conde-sur-Noireau, France. **Indexed:** Film Lit.Ind. (1990-).

778.53   II
CINEMARANJANI; cine-weekly. w. Andhra Patrika, 14-14-21 Mallikarjuna Rao St., Gandhinagar, Vijayawada 520 003, India. TEL 61247. adv.

791.43   CN
CINEMASCOPE MAGAZINE. 6/yr. Vantage Publishing Inc., 609 14th St., N.W., Ste. 410, Calgary, Alta. T2N 2A1, Canada. TEL 403-270-2222. FAX 403-270-4057. Ed. Flemming Nielsen. circ. 52,000.

791.43   IT   ISSN 0009-7160
CINEMASUD; rivista neorealista di avanguardia e del cinema politico. 1958. m. L.30000 (foreign L.50000). Via Calore, 8, 83100 Avellino, Italy. Ed. Camillo Marino. adv.; illus.; charts. **Indexed:** Film Lit.Ind. (1990-).
    Description: Covers the world of cinema and film techniques.

778.5   UY
CINEMATECA REVISTA. 1977. irreg., approx. 10/yr. $20 per 10 nos. Cinemateca Uruguaya, Lorenzo Carnelli 1311, Casilla de Correo 1170, Montevideo, Uruguay. FAX 598-2-494572. TELEX 22043 CIMTECA UY. Ed.Bd. adv.; circ. 2,000. **Indexed:** Intl.Ind.TV.
    Formerly: Cinemateca.

791.43   SP   ISSN 0213-1773
CINEMATOGRAF. vol.3, 1986. a. Federacio Catalana de Cine-Clubs, Carrer d'Enric Granados, 125, 08008 Barcelona, Spain.

791.43   US   ISSN 0886-6570
CINEMATOGRAPH; a journal of film and media art. 1985. a. $9 to individuals; institutions $20; foreign $20. (Foundation of Art in Cinema) San Francisco Cinematheque, 480 Potrero, San Francisco, CA 94110. TEL 415-558-8129. FAX 415-558-0455. adv.; circ. 1,500. (also avail. in microform from UMI) **Indexed:** Film Lit.Ind. (1986-1988).

778.5   FR
CINEMATOGRAPHE. 1973. m. 220 F. Editions du Reel, 33 passage Joceffroy, 75009 Paris, France. Ed.Bd. adv.; bk.rev.; circ. 30,000. **Indexed:** Film Lit.Ind. (1974-1987), Intl.Ind.TV.

CINEMATOGRAPHERS, PRODUCTION DESIGNERS, COSTUME DESIGNERS & FILM EDITORS GUIDE. see *BUSINESS AND ECONOMICS — Trade And Industrial Directories*

778.5   US   ISSN 0162-0126
PN1993
CINEMONKEY;* a serious film journal. 1976. irreg. $7. Cinemonkey Inc., 1435 N.E. 72nd, Portland, OR 97213. TEL 503-248-0849. Ed. Douglas Holm. adv.; bk.rev.; film rev.
    Formerly: Scintillation (ISSN 0147-5789)

791.43   IT   ISSN 0024-1458
CINESCHEDARIO - LETTURE DRAMMATICHE.* vol.19, 1964. m. L.2000. Centro Salesiano Dello Spettacolo, Via M. Ausiliatrice 32, 10121 Turin, Italy. Ed. Marco Bongioanni. film rev.; play rev.; illus.
    Formerly: Letture Drammatiche.

791.43   IT
CINESCOPIO. 1980. m. L.95000. Gruppo Editoriale J C E, Via Ferri 6, 20092 Cinisello Balsamo, Italy. Ed. Ruben Castelfranchi. adv.; circ. 40,000.

791.43   AG
CINESET. 6/yr. Giribone 1325, Piso 5, Apto. 4, Buenos Aires, Argentina. adv.

791.43   FR
CINETHIQUE. 1969. s-a. Editions Cinethique, B.P. 65, 75722 Paris Cedex 15, France. Ed. Gerard Leblanc. adv.; bk.rev.; film rev.; circ. 6,000. (also avail. in microfilm; back issues avail.; reprint service avail. from UMI) **Indexed:** Film Lit.Ind., Intl.Ind.TV.

700
CINEVUE. 1986. 5/yr. $10. Asian CineVision, Inc., 32 E. Broadway, New York, NY 10002. TEL 212-925-8685. Ed. Bill J. Gee. circ. 16,000.

778.5   US
CITADEL FILM SERIES. 1959. 6/yr. Citadel Press (Subsidiary of: Lyle Stuart Inc.), 120 Enterprise Ave., Secaucus, NJ 07094. TEL 212-736-1141. FAX 212-486-2231. Ed. Allan J. Wilson.

778.5   II
CITRABIKSHANA/CHITRA-BIKSHAN. (Text in Bengali) m. Rs.1.25 per no. Cine Central, 2 Chowringhee Rd., Calcutta 700013, India.

791.43   US   ISSN 0275-8423
PN1995.9.C54
CLASSIC IMAGES. 1962. m. $27.50 (foreign $38). Muscatine Journal (Subsidiary of: Lee Enterprises, Inc.), 301 Third St. E., Box 809, Muscatine, IA 52761. TEL 319-263-2331. FAX 319-262-8042. (Subscr. to: Box 809, Muscatine, IA 52761; Editorial addr.: Box 4079, Davenport, IA 52808) Ed. Bob King. adv.; bk.rev.; film rev.; bibl.; illus.; cum.index; circ. 2,500. (tabloid format; also avail. in microfilm from UMI; back issues avail.; reprint service avail. from UMI) **Indexed:** Film Lit.Ind. (1973-), Media Rev.Dig.
    Former titles (until 1979): Classic Film - Video Images (ISSN 0164-5560); (until 1978): Classic Film Collector (ISSN 0009-8329); Eight MM Collector.

778   BL
COLECAO CINEMA. vol. 14, 1982. irreg. Editora Paz e Terra, Rua Sao Jose 90, Centro, Rio de Janeiro, RJ, Brazil.

778   SP
COLECCION DIRECTORES DE CINE. q. Ediciones J C, Monteleon, 35, Madrid-10, Spain.

778.5   FR
COLLECTION CA-CINEMA.* irreg., no. 8, 1978. Editions Albatros, 21 rue Cassette, 75006 Paris, France. Eds. Francois Barat, Joel Farges.

791.43   US
COLUMBIA FILM VIEW. 1985. 3/yr. $7.50. Columbia University, School of the Arts, Film Division, 513 Dodge Hall, New York, NY 10027. TEL 212-280-2842. Eds. Jennifer Robinson, David Wezoer. adv.; bk.rev.; circ. 1,000. **Indexed:** Film Lit.Ind. (1986-).
    Formerly: Columbia Film Review.

COMMUNICATION ARTS INTERNATIONAL. see *COMMUNICATIONS — Television And Cable*

COMPARATIVE LITERARY AND FILM STUDIES: EUROPE, JAPAN, AND THE THIRD WORLD. see *LITERATURE*

CONSORTIUM FOR DRAMA & MEDIA IN HIGHER EDUCATION. NEWSLETTER. see *THEATER*

CONTEMPORARY ART CENTRE OF SOUTH AUSTRALIA. BROADSHEET. see *ART*

778.5   US
COUNCIL ON INTERNATIONAL NONTHEATRICAL EVENTS. YEARBOOK; Golden Eagle film awards. 1962. a. $10. Council on International Nontheatrical Events, Inc., 1001 Connecticut Ave., N.W., Ste. 1016, Washington, DC 20036. TEL 202-785-1136. FAX 202-785-4114. Ed. Richard Calkins. film rev.; illus.; stat.; circ. 2,500.

791.43 070   UK   ISSN 0015-1203
CRITIC. 1950. w. £15.75. Critics' Guild, 9 Compayne Gardens, London N.W.6, England. Ed. Dore Silverman. bk.rev.; film rev.; music rev.; play rev.
Formerly: Film Critics' Guild. Bulletin.

778.53   SP   ISSN 0214-462X
CUADERNOS CINEMATOGRAFICOS. 1968. irreg., no.7, 1991. 1200 ptas. Universidad de Valladolid, Secretariado de Publicaciones, Avda. de Ramon y Cajal, 7, 47005 Valladolid, Spain.
TEL 983-423000. FAX 983-423003. TELEX 26357.

CUE SHEET. see *MUSIC*

791.43   IT
CULT MOVIE; bimestrale di cultura e politica cinematografica. (Text in Italian) 1980. bi-m. L.15000. Circolo Ricreativo ENEL, Via del Sole 10, 50123 Florence, Italy. Ed.Bd. adv.; bk.rev.; film rev.; circ. 5,000.

291.43   US   ISSN 0748-8580
PN1993
CURRENT RESEARCH IN FILM. 1985. a. price varies. Ablex Publishing Corporation, 355 Chestnut St., Norwood, NJ 07648. TEL 201-767-8450. FAX 201-767-6717. TELEX 135-393. Ed. Bruce A. Austin. **Indexed:** Film Lit.Ind. (1985-).
—BLDSC shelfmark: 3501.957600.

791.43   CS   ISSN 0011-4588
PN1993.5.C9
CZECHOSLOVAK FILM. French edition: Film Tcheocoslovaque (ISSN 0323-2972); German edition: Tschechoslowakische Film (ISSN 0139-5262); Russian edition: Chekhoslovatskoye Kino (ISSN 0323-097X); Spanish edition: Cine Checoslovaco (ISSN 0323-2964) 1947. q. $4.40. Czechoslovak Filmexport, Press Department, Vaclavske nam. 28, 111 45 Prague 1, Czechoslovakia. (Subscr. to: Artia, Ve Smeckach 30, 111 27 Prague 1, Czechoslovakia) Ed. Marie Grofova. adv.; illus.; circ. 4,200. **Indexed:** Film Lit.Ind. (1974-), Intl.Ind.TV.

791.43   GW
D D R FILM INFORMATION.* (Text in English, French and German) 1974. irreg. D E E A Studio for Shortfilms, Milastr. 2, 1058 Berlin, Germany.

DAILY VARIETY; news of the entertainment industry. see *COMMUNICATIONS — Television And Cable*

DANCE ON CAMERA NEWS. see *DANCE*

791.43   CC   ISSN 1002-4646
DANGDAI DIANYING/CONTEMPORARY CINEMA. (Text in Chinese) 1984. bi-m. Y12. China Film Art Research Centre, 25-B Xinjiekouwai Dajie, Beijing 100088, People's Republic of China. TEL 2014322. FAX 2014316. (Dist. outside China by: China National Publications Foreign Trading Corp., P.O. Box 782, Beijing, China) Ed. Chen Bo. film rev.; circ. 8,000.
Description: Covers the fields of film theory, film review, film history, film techniques, and film markets.

778.5   DK   ISSN 0418-3304
DANISH FILMS. (Text in English) 1985. a. free. Danish Film Institute, Store Soenderveldstraede, DK-1419 Copenhagen, Denmark. FAX 45-31-576700. TELEX 31465 DFILM DK. Ed. Jesper Andersen. adv.; illus.; circ. 4,000.

791.43   CC   ISSN 0492-0929
DAZHONG DIANYING/POPULAR CINEMA. (Text in Chinese) 1950. m. Y18($85.50) Zhongguo Dianying Chubanshe - China Film Press, 22, Beisanhuan Donglu, Beijing 100013, People's Republic of China. (Dist. outside China by: China International Book Trading Corp., P.O. Box 399, Beijing, P.R.C.; Dist. in US by: China Books & Periodicals, Inc., 2929 24th St., San Francisco, CA 94110. TEL 415-282-2994) Eds. Cai Shiyong, Ma Rui.

778.5   DK   ISSN 0109-4076
DENMARK. STATENS FILMCENTRAL. INFORMATION OG BERETNING. 1983. irreg. free. Statens Filmcentral, Vestergade 27, 1456 Copenhagen K, Denmark. TEL 45-33-132686. FAX 45-33-130203. illus.

791.43   DK
DENMARK. STATENS FILMCENTRAL. S F C FILM OG VIDEO CATALOGUE. 1950. biennial (plus w. supplements). free. Statens Filmcentral - National Film Board of Denmark, 27 Vestergade, 1456 Copenhagen K, Denmark. TEL 45-33-132686. FAX 45-33-130203. Eds. Else Relster, Tue Steen Mueller. circ. 25,000.
Former titles: Denmark. Statens Filmcentral. S F C Catalogue; Denmark. Statens Filmcentral. S F C Film and Video Catalogue (ISSN 0070-3621)

778.5   DK
▼**DENMARK. STATENS FILMCENTRAL. S F C VIDEO.** 1990. a. free. Statens Filmcentral - Danish Government Film Office, Vestergade 27, DK-1456 Copenhagen K, Denmark. TEL 45-33-132686. FAX 45-33-130203.

778.53   US
▼**DETROIT FILM AND VIDEO NEWS.** 1990. q. $7.50. Real Estate News Corp., 2600 W. Peterson, Ste. 100, Chicago, IL 60659. TEL 312-465-7246. FAX 312-465-7218. Ed. Donna B. Proske. adv.; circ. 3,500.
Description: Reports on the industry's progress in the Detroit Metro area and throughout Michigan. Covers trends, equipment, innovations, new facilities, services and technology.

778.53 791.4   CC   ISSN 1000-0151
DIANSHI DIANYING WENXUE/TV AND FILM LITERATURE. Short title: D D W. (Text in Chinese) 1981. bi-m. Y22.80($5) (Shanghai Shi Wenxue Yishujie Lianhehui - Shanghai Literature and Art Association) Dianshi Dianying Wenxue Zazhishe, 238 Yan'an Xilu, Shanghai 200040, People's Republic of China. TEL 21-2581568. Ed. Zhu Liang-yi. adv.; film rev.; illus.; circ. 20,000.
Description: Introduces new Chinese and foreign television, movie works, and literature. Contains stories, scripts, and biographical articles.

778.53   CC   ISSN 0257-0173
DIANYING CHUANGZUO/CINEMATIC CREATION. (Text in Chinese) 1977. m. Y7.80($61.20) (Beijing Dianying Zhipianchang - Beijing Movie Studios) Dianying Chuangzuo Zazhishe, Beisanhuan Zhonglu, Beijing 100088, People's Republic of China. (Dist. outside China by: China International Book Trade Corporation (Guoji Shudian), P.O. Box 399, Beijing, P.R.C.; Dist. in US by: China Books & Periodicals, Inc., 2929 24th St., San Francisco, CA 94110) Ed. Wang Taorui. adv.; film rev.
Description: Covers China's film industry.

791.43   CC   ISSN 0493-2374
DIANYING GUSHI/FILM STORIES. (Text in Chinese) m. $33.20. (Shanghai Dianying Faxing Fangying Gongsi - Shanghai Film Distribution and Projection Company) Dianying Gushi Bianjibu, 322 Anfu Lu, Shanghai 200031, People's Republic of China. TEL 4332839. (Dist. in US by: China Books & Periodicals, Inc., 2929 24th St., San Francisco, CA 94110. TEL 415-282-2994)

791.4   CC
DIANYING HUAKAN/FILM PICTORIAL. (Text in Chinese) m. $49.40. Shaanxi Sheng Dianying Gongsi, Wenyi Lu, Xi'an, Shaanxi 710054, People's Republic of China. TEL 719514. (Dist. in US by: China Books & Periodicals, Inc., 2929 24th St., San Francisco, CA 94110. TEL 415-282-2994) Ed. Qu Qifa.

791.43   CC
DIANYING JIESHAO. (Text in Chinese) m. Shanxi Dianying Faxing Fangying Gongsi - Shanxi Film Distribution & Projection Company, 58 Yingze Dajie, Taiyuan, Shanxi 030001, People's Republic of China. TEL 443862. Ed. Hua Zhongzhuang.

791.4   CC
DIANYING SHIJIE/FILM WORLD. (Text in Chinese) m. $40.40. Changchun Dianying Zhipianchang - Changchun Film Studio, 16 Hongqi Jie, Changchun, Jilin 130021, People's Republic of China. TEL 53511. (Dist. in US by: China Books & Periodicals, Inc., 2929 24th St., San Francisco, CA 94110. TEL 415-282-2994) Ed. Zhao Ziming.

791.43   CC   ISSN 0495-5692
DIANYING WENXUE/FILM LITERATURE. (Text in Chinese) 1958-1966; resumed 1978. m. Y19.20 (effective 1991). Changchun Dianying Zhipianchang - Changchun Film Studio, 16 Hongqi Jie, Changchun, Jilin 130021, People's Republic of China. (Dist. outside China by: China Publications Foreign Trade Corp., P.O. Box 782, Beijing, P.R.C.) Ed. Zhu Jing. circ. 190,000.

778.53   CC
DIANYING XINZUO/NEW FILMS. (Text in Chinese) bi-m. $24.80. Dianying Xinzuo Bianjibu - New Film Editorial Department, 796 Huaihai Zhonglu, Shanghai, People's Republic of China. (Dist. in US by: China Books & Periodicals, Inc., 2929 24th St., San Francisco, CA 94110) Ed.Bd. adv.

791.43   CC   ISSN 0257-0181
DIANYING YISHU/FILM ART. Variant English title: Cinema Art. (Text in Chinese) 1956. m. Y12($44) (Zhongguo Dianyingjia Xiehui - China Film Association) Zhongguo Dianying Chubanshe - China Film Press, 22 Beisanhuan Donglu, Beijing 100013, People's Republic of China. TEL 4219977. (Dist. outside China by: China International Book Trading Corp., P.O. Box 399, Beijing, P.R.C.; Dist. in US by: China Books & Periodicals, Inc., 2929 24th St., San Francisco, CA 94110) Eds. Qin Yuquan, Wang Renyin. adv.; bk.rev.; film rev.; circ. 5,000.
Formerly (until July 1959): Zhongguo Dianying.
Description: Covers all aspects of filmmaking, including scriptwriting, directing, acting, cinematography, sound recording, and editing. Critiques current Chinese filmmakers and their works, researches film history, and introduces foreign works on film theory.

791.43   CC
DIANYING YUEBAO/MOVIE MONTHLY. (Text in Chinese) bi-m. Guangxi Dianying Zhipian Chang - Guangxi Film Studio, 26 You'ai Beilu, Nanning, Guangxi 530001, People's Republic of China. TEL 34261. Ed. Gao Honghao.

791.43   CC
DIANYING ZHI YOU/FILM FANS. (Text in Chinese) 1979. m. Y7.20($4.30) Fujian Sheng Dianying Faxing Fangying Gongsi - Film Distribution and Projection Company of Fujian Province, 2 Xinan Lu, Fuzhou, Fujian 350001, People's Republic of China. TEL 551909. FAX 556749. (Dist. overseas by: Jiangsu Publications Import & Export Corp., 56 Gao Yun Ling, Nanjing, Jiangsu, P.R.C.) Eds. Sa Bendun, Zhang Xuan. adv.; bk.rev.; circ. 97,000.

791.43   CC   ISSN 1001-5582
DIANYING ZUOPIN/FILM SCRIPTS. (Text in Chinese) bi-m. E'mei Dianying Zhipian Chang - E'mei Film Studio, Chengdu, Sichuan 610072, People's Republic of China. TEL 669571. Ed. Liang Husheng.

778.53   MX
DICINE. bi-m. Leonardo da Vinci 161-A, 03700 Mexico D.F., Mexico. **Indexed:** Film Lit.Ind. (1988-).

778.53 791.43   US
DIGEST OF THE U F V A. bi-m. membership. University Film Video Association, c/o Gerry Veeder, University of N. Texas, Radio, TV, & Film Dept., Box 13108, Denton, TX 76203-3108. TEL 213-740-0832. (Alt addr.: c/o George Wehbl, School of Cinema, University of Southern California, University Park, MC 2212, Los Angeles, CA 90089) Eds. Steve Fore, Gerry Veeder.

778.534   US
DOCUMENTS IN FILM STUDIES. irreg. Peter Lang Publishing, Inc., 62 W. 45th St., 4th Fl., New York, NY 10036. TEL 212-302-6740. FAX 212-302-7574. Ed. Mark Winokur.

DRAGON. see *LITERATURE*

778.5 792 791.4   US
DRAMA-LOGUE. 1969. w. $55. Drama-Logue, Inc., Box 38771, Los Angeles, CA 90038. TEL 213-464-5079. Ed. Faye Bordy. adv.; bk.rev.; circ. 75,000.
Formerly: Hollywood Drama-Logue (ISSN 0272-2720)

DUCKBURG TIMES. see *HOBBIES*

MOTION PICTURES

778.5   NE
DUTCH FILM. (Text in English) irreg. Ministerie van Welzijn Volksgezondheid en Cultuur, Postbus 5406, 2280 HK Rijswijk, Netherlands. TEL 070-3405764. Ed. Pieter van Lierop. illus.

DZAR BICHIG/PUBLICITY HERALD. see COMMUNICATIONS — Television And Cable

791.43   GW   ISSN 0176-2044
E P D FILM. 1984. m. DM.66. Gemeinschaftswerk der Evangelischen Publizistik e.V., Postfach 170361, 6000 Frankfurt a.M. 17, Germany. TEL 069-78972177. FAX 069-78972122. TELEX 176997347. Eds. Wilhelm Roth, Bettina Thienhaus. adv.; bk.rev.; film rev.; index; circ. 6,000. (back issues avail.) **Indexed:** Film Lit.Ind. (1988-).
    Description: Articles of film theory and criticism.

791.43   US   ISSN 0891-6780
PN1993
EAST - WEST FILM JOURNAL. 1986. s-a. $15 to individuals; institutions $25. (Institute of Culture & Communication, East-West Center) University of Hawaii Press, Journal Department, 2840 Kolowalu St., Honolulu, HI 96822. TEL 808-956-8833. FAX 808-988-6052. Ed. Wimal Dissanayake. adv.; bk.rev.; circ. 300. (back issues avail.; reprint service avail. from UMI) **Indexed:** Arts & Hum.Cit.Ind., Curr.Cont., Film l it.Ind. (1986-).
    —BLDSC shelfmark: 3646.560550.
    Description: Provide a forum in which Asian cinema can be introduced to other Asian and Western audiences.
    Refereed Serial

778.5   FR
ECRAN FANTASTIQUE. 1970. m. 250 F. Editions de Tournon, 44-48 rue Brocca, 75008 Paris, France. TEL 46-37-13-90. FAX 43-36-60-87. Ed. Alain Schlockoff. adv.; bk.rev.; film rev.; illus.; circ. 50,000.

EDUCATIONAL TECHNOLOGY RESEARCH & DEVELOPMENT. see EDUCATION — Teaching Methods And Curriculum

EGYPTE - SPORTS - CINEMA. see SPORTS AND GAMES

778.5 620.2   SP   ISSN 0210-4261
EIKONOS; revista de la imagen y el sonido. (Text in Spanish) 1975. 11/yr. 100 ptas.($16) Editorial ECO, S.A., Calle de la Cruz 44, Barcelona 17, Spain. adv.; bk.rev.; film rev.; abstr.; bibl.; illus.; circ. 12,000 (controlled).
    Supersedes: Imagen y Sonida (ISSN 0445-4529)

791.43   XV   ISSN 0013-3302
PN1993
EKRAN; revija za film in televizijo. 1962. m. 1000 din. Zveza Kulturnih Organizacij Slovenije, Kidriceva 5, 61000 Ljubljana, Slovenia. Eds. Stojan Pelko, Miha Zadnikar. adv.; film rev.; illus.; circ. 2,000. **Indexed:** Film Lit.Ind. (1973-), Intl.Ind.TV.

ELVIS MONTHLY. see MUSIC

EMERSON STUDIES IN THEATRE AND FILM. see THEATER

ENCLITIC; the timely taken seriously. see LITERARY AND POLITICAL REVIEWS

ENSEMBLE; the new variety arts review. see THEATER

ENTERTAINMENT AND SPORTS LAWYER. see LAW

ENTERTAINMENT LAW REPORTER; motion pictures, television, radio, music, theater, publishing, sports. see LAW

ENTERTAINMENT MAGAZINE. see MUSIC

ENTERTAINMENT PLUS. see MUSIC

EL ESPECTACULAR. see COMMUNICATIONS — Television And Cable

778.5   US
ETIN. 1974. q. membership. National Association of Regional Media Centers, Grant Wood AEA, 4401 Sixth St., S.W., Cedar Rapids, IA 52404. TEL 319-399-6741. Ed. Jerry Cochrane. adv.; circ. 400.
    Description: Informs members of current activities in the film and video world.

791.43   FR   ISSN 0014-1992
ETUDES CINEMATOGRAPHIQUES. 1960. irreg. 165 F. for 10 nos. Lettres Modernes, 73 rue du Cardinal-Lemoine, 75005 Paris, France. TEL 1-43-54-46-09. Ed. Michel Esteve. bibl.; illus. **Indexed:** Arts & Hum.Cit.Ind., Curr.Cont., Intl.Ind.TV.

EYEPIECE. see PHOTOGRAPHY

F T T AND BETA NEWS. see LABOR UNIONS

FACE TO FACE WITH TALENT. see COMMUNICATIONS — Television And Cable

791.43   US   ISSN 0736-3745
FACETS FEATURES. 1975. bi-m. $12. Facets Multimedia, Inc., 1517 W. Fullerton Ave., Chicago, IL 60614. TEL 312-281-9075. FAX 312-929-5437. TELEX 20-6701. Ed. Milos Stehlik. adv.; bk.rev.; film rev.; illus.; circ. 50,000.
    Formerly (until 1980): Focus Chicago (ISSN 0362-0905)
    Description: Covers the world of international films and video, including new foreign, independent and classic releases.

778.53 384.55   MX
FAMA. fortn. Avda. Eugenio Garza Sada Sur 2245, Col. Roma, Apdo. 3128, Monterrey, NL, Mexico. TEL 83-59-2525. circ. 250,000.

791.43 371.33   US
FAST FOREWORD.* 1974. m. $35 to individuals; institutions $85. Association of Audio Visual Technicians, Box 603, Farmingdale, NY 11735. Ed. Elsa Kaiser. adv.; bk.rev.; circ. 1,200. (back issues avail.)

791.43   GW   ISSN 0015-0142
       CODEN: FNKTAH
FERNSEH- UND KINO-TECHNIK. 1946. 11/yr. DM.179.40. (Fernseh- und Kinotechnische Gesellschaft) Alfred Huethig Verlag GmbH, Im Weiher 10, 6900 Heidelberg 1, Germany. TEL 06221-489-281. FAX 06221-489279. TELEX 461727-HUEHDD. Ed. N. Bolewski. adv.; bk.rev.; abstr.; bibl.; charts; illus.; pat.; index; circ. 3,500. **Indexed:** Chem.Abstr., Film Lit.Ind. (1973-), Sci.Abstr.

778.5   FR   ISSN 0336-9331
FICHES DU CINEMA. 1934. w. 285 F. (foreign 405 F.). Chretien Medias, 108, rue Saint-Maur, 75011 Paris, France. TEL 43-57-93-52. FAX 47-00-83-79. Ed. Olivier Serre. film rev.; circ. 3,000.

778.53   US
FIELD OF VISION. 1976. a. $12. Island Cinema Resources, 135 St. Paul's Ave., Staten Island, NY 10301. TEL 718-727-5593. Ed. Robert A. Haller. adv.; bk.rev.; circ. 600. (back issues avail.)

791.43   US
FILAMENT. 1981. a. free. Wright State University, Department of Theatre Arts, Dayton, OH 45435. Ed. Glenn Lalich. circ. 1,500. (back issues avail.) **Indexed:** Film Lit.Ind.

791.43   PL   ISSN 0015-1033
FILM. 1946. w. Pulawska 61, 02-595 Warsaw, Poland. TEL 48-22-344215. Ed. Maciej Pawlicki. film rev.; illus.; index; circ. 149,400.

791.43   UK   ISSN 0015-1025
FILM. 1952. m. (10/yr.) £20. British Federation of Film Societies, 21 Stephen St., London W1P 1PL, England. FAX 01-436-7950. TELEX 27624 BFILDN G. Ed. Peter Cargin. adv.; bk.rev.; film rev.; illus.; index; circ. 2,500. (also avail. in microform from MIM; back issues avail.; reprint service avail. from UMI) **Indexed:** Film Lit.Ind. (1973-1987), Media Rev.Dig.
    —BLDSC shelfmark: 3925.660000.
    Description: Includes film festival articles for committees who run cinema clubs in Britain.

791.43   IR
FILM. (English supplement avail.) (Text in Farsi) 1982. m. P.O. Box 5875, Teheran 11365, Iran. TEL 021-679373. Ed. M. Mehrab.

778.53   IT
FILM. (Includes a videocassette.) m. L.235000 (effective 1991). E R I Edizioni R A I, Via Arsenale 41, 10121 Turin, Italy. TEL 011-8800. FAX 011-534732.

FILM A DIVADLO. see COMMUNICATIONS — Television And Cable

791.43   CS   ISSN 0015-1068
FILM A DOBA. (Text in Czech; summaries in English, French and Russian) 1954. m. 72 Kcs.($61.30) (Uslredni Rediteistvi Ceskoslovenskeho Filmu). Panorama, Halkova 1, 120 72 Prague 2, Czechoslovakia. Ed. Eva Zaoralova. bk.rev.; abstr.; charts; illus.; index; circ. 6,000. **Indexed:** Film Lit.Ind. (1973-), Intl.Ind.TV.

778.5   DK   ISSN 0109-2774
FILM AARBOGEN. 1949. a. DKK 49.50. Carlsen Forlag A-S, Krogshoejvej 32, DK-2880 Bagsvaerd, Denmark. FAX 44-44-36-33. TELEX 37-416-SEMIC-DK. illus.
    Formerly: Aarets Bedste Film.

778.5 900   US   ISSN 0360-3695
PN1995.2
FILM & HISTORY. 1972 N.S. q. $12 to individuals; institutions $20. Historians Film Committee, New Jersey Institute of Technology, Newark, NJ 07102. TEL 201-596-3291. Ed. John E. O'Connor. adv.; bk.rev.; film rev.; illus.; circ. 450. (tabloid format) **Indexed:** Amer.Hist.& Life, Film Lit.Ind. (1985-), Hist.Abstr., Intl.Ind.TV.
    Supersedes: Historians Film Committee Newsletter.

778 384.55   UK
FILM AND TELEVISION HANDBOOK (YEAR). a. £10.95. British Film Institute, 21 Stephen St., London W1P 1PL, England. Ed. David Leafe.

778.534 384.55   US   ISSN 1041-1933
FILM & VIDEO; the production magazine. 1984. m. $50 (N. America $75; elsewhere $90)(effective 1992). Optic Music, Inc., 8455 Beverly Blvd., Ste. 508, Los Angeles, CA 90048. TEL 213-653-8053. FAX 213-653-8190. Ed. David Swartz. adv. (back issues avail.)
    Formerly: Film and Video Production.
    Description: Covers all areas of the production and post-production process within the teleproduction, commercial, music video and motion picture industries.

791.43 658   AT
FILM AUSTRALIA BUSINESS & MANAGEMENT CATALOGUE. 1989. biennial. free. Film Australia Pty. Ltd., Eton Rd., Lindfield, N.S.W. 2070, Australia. TEL 413-8777. FAX 416-5672. TELEX 22734. circ. 30,000.

572 700 028.5 370   AT
FILM AUSTRALIA EDUCATION CATALOGUE. 1970. biennial. free. Film Australia Pty. Ltd., Eton Rd., Lindfield, N.S.W. 2070, Australia. TEL 413 8777. FAX 416-5672. TELEX 22734. circ. 20,000. (back issues avail.)
    Formerly: Film Australia Catalogue.

791.43 614.42   AT
▼**FILM AUSTRALIA HEALTH & WELFARE CATALOGUE.** 1990. biennial. free. Film Australia Pty. Ltd., Eton Rd., Lindfield, N.S.W. 2070, Australia. TEL 413-8777. FAX 416-5672. TELEX 22734. circ. 15,000.

791.43   US
FILM BILL. 1970. m. (George Fenmore, Inc.) Film Bill, Inc., 250 W. 54 St., New York, NY 10019. TEL 212-977-4140. FAX 212-977-4404. Ed. George Fenmore. adv.; bk.rev.; circ. 500,000 (controlled).

778.53   SZ
FILM BULLETIN. bi-m. Postfach 137, Hard 4, CH-8408 Winterthur, Switzerland. **Indexed:** Film Lit.Ind. (1985-).

778.534 384.55   CN   ISSN 0831-5175
FILM CANADA YEARBOOK. 1986. a. Can.$25. Cine-Communications, P.O. Box 152, Sta. R, Toronto, Ont. M4G 3Z3, Canada. TEL 416-696-2382. Ed. Patricia Thompson. adv.: B&W page Can.$825; trim 7 x 9 1/2; adv. contact: Wyndham Paul Wise.
    Description: Directories of companies and people in the film and television business in Canada. Information on film and video production companies, including post-production, labs, editing, casting and support services; distributors; exhibitors; TV and pay TV; government agencies; unions; guilds and associations.

791.43   US   ISSN 0015-119X
PN1993
FILM COMMENT. 1962. bi-m. $19.95. Film Society of Lincoln Center, 70 Lincoln Center Plaza, New York, NY 10023. TEL 212-875-5610. FAX 212-875-5636. Ed. Richard T. Jameson. adv.; bk.rev.; film rev.; illus.; index; circ. 40,000. (also avail. in microfilm from UMI; back issues avail.; reprint service avail. from UMI,ISI) **Indexed:** Acad.Ind., Arts & Hum.Cit.Ind., Bk.Rev.Ind. (1977-), Chic.Per.Ind., Child.Bk.Rev.Ind. (1977-), Curr.Cont., Film Lit.Ind. (1973-), Hum.Ind., Int.Ind.Film Per., Intl.Ind.TV, Mag.Ind., Media Rev.Dig., PMR, R.G.
—BLDSC shelfmark: 3925.690000.
Description: Covers film criticism and history.

FILM COMPOSERS GUIDE. see *BUSINESS AND ECONOMICS — Trade And Industrial Directories*

778.5   US   ISSN 0163-5069
PN1993
FILM CRITICISM. 1976. 3/yr. $9 to individuals; institutions $10. Allegheny College, Meadville, PA 16335. Ed. I. Lloyd Michaels. adv.; bk.rev.; film rev.; circ. 400. **Indexed:** Amer.Bibl.Slavic & E.Eur.Stud., Arts & Hum.Cit.Ind., Bk.Rev.Ind. (1983-), Child.Bk.Rev.Ind. (1983-), Curr.Cont., Film Lit.Ind. (1978-), Hum.Ind., Intl.Ind.TV, LCR, M.L.A., Media Rev.Dig.
—BLDSC shelfmark: 3925.705000.

791.43   US   ISSN 0015-1211
PN1993
FILM CULTURE. 1955. q. $20. Film Culture Non-Profit, Inc., c/o Film Art Fund, Inc., Box 1499, New York, NY 10001. Ed. Jonas Mekas. adv.; bk.rev.; cum.index; circ. 4,500. (also avail. in microfilm from UMI; back issues avail.; reprint service avail. from UMI) **Indexed:** Acad.Ind., Art Ind., Arts & Hum.Cit.Ind., Curr.Cont., Film Lit.Ind. (1973-), Intl.Ind.TV, Media Rev.Dig.

791.43 700   UK
FILM DIRECTIONS. 1977. q. £4. Queen's Film Theatre, 25 College Gdns., Belfast BT9 6BS, N. Ireland. FAX 0232-663733. Ed. Michael Open. adv.; bk.rev.; illus.; circ. 2,500. **Indexed:** Film Lit.Ind. (1985-), Intl.Ind.TV.

FILM DIRECTORS: A COMPLETE GUIDE. see *BUSINESS AND ECONOMICS — Trade And Industrial Directories*

791   UK   ISSN 0305-1706
FILM DOPE. 1972. irreg. (approx. 3/yr.) £3.70($9) for 4 nos. 88 Port Arthur Rd., Nottingham NG2 4GE, England. Eds. David Badder, Bob Baker. adv.; bk.rev.; circ. 1,000. (back issues avail.) **Indexed:** Film Lit.Ind. (1974-).

791.43   GW   ISSN 0015-1149
FILM-ECHO - FILMWOCHE. 1947. s-w. DM.428. Verlag Horst Axtmann GmbH und Co., Marktplatz 13, 6200 Wiesbaden, Germany. Ed. Bernd Jetschin. adv.; bk.rev.; film rev.; illus.; stat.; circ. 4,500.
Incorporating: Filmblaetter.

791.43   GW   ISSN 0071-4879
FILM-ECHO FILMWOCHE. VERLEIH-KATALOG. 1949. a. DM.85. Verlag Horst Axtmann GmbH und Co., Marktplatz 13, 6200 Wiesbaden, Germany. Ed. Horst Axtmann. adv.; bk.rev.; circ. 2,500.

791.4   BE
FILM EN TELEVISIE - VIDEO. 1956. 10/yr. 550 Fr. Katolieke Filmliga, Haachtsesteenweg 35, 1030 Brussels 3, Belgium. Ed. Jean-Pierre Wauters. adv.; bk.rev.; film rev.; circ. 60,000. **Indexed:** Film Lit.Ind. (1975-), Int.Ind.Film Per., Intl.Ind.TV.
Formerly: Film en Televisie (ISSN 0015-1084)

791.43   FR   ISSN 0397-8702
FILM FRANCAIS.* 1945. w. 1900 F. S A R L Cinema de France, 103 bd. Saint-Michel, 75005 Paris, France. Ed.Bd. adv.; bk.rev.; film rev.; illus.; circ. 15,000.
Formerly: Film Francais-Cinematographie Francais (ISSN 0015-1262)

791.43   AT   ISSN 0015-1289
FILM INDEX.* 1970. 2/yr. Aus.$80. Rastar Pty. Ltd., 47 Osborne Rd., Manly, N.S.W. 20095, Australia. TEL 977-1063. Ed. John H. Reid. adv.; bk.rev.; film rev.; illus.; stat.; circ. 2,500. (back issues avail.) **Indexed:** Film Lit.Ind.
Supersedes: Australian Film Guide.
Description: Includes complete cast lists and technical credits, release information and new reviews of English-language films from 1929 to 1979.

791.43   US   ISSN 0199-7300
FILM JOURNAL. 1934. m. $40. Pubsun Corp., 244 W. 49th St., Ste. 200, New York, NY 10019. TEL 212-246-6460. FAX 212-265-6428. adv.; film rev.; illus.; index; circ. 9,200. **Indexed:** Film Lit.Ind. (1974-).
Formerly: Independent Film Journal (ISSN 0019-3712)

791.43   IR
FILM-KHANE-YE MELLI-E IRAN. NAME-YE/NATIONAL FILM ARCHIVE OF IRAN. QUARTERLY. Variant English title: Iranian National Film Quarterly. (Text in Farsi; summaries in English) 1989. q. $19. National Film Archive of Iran - Film-khane-ye Melli-e Iran, P.O. Box 5158, Teheran 11365, Iran. TEL 021-311242. TELEX 215642 RECU IR. Eds. Mohammad Hassan Khoshnevis, Gholam Heydari. illus.

778.5   DK   ISSN 0108-772X
FILM MAGASINET. 1982. bi-m. DKK 5 per no. Ulshoejvej 16, 4400 Kalundborg, Denmark. illus.

790 659.152   II
FILM MIRROR. (Text in English) 1962. m. Rs.8. Film Mirror, 26-F Connaught Place, New Delhi 110 001, India. TEL 3312329. Ed. Harbhajan Singh. film rev.; circ. 4,000.

778.53   UK
FILM MONTHLY. m. Argus House, Boundary Way, Hemel Hempstead HP2 7ST, England. **Indexed:** Film Lit.Ind. (1989-).

778.5 780   US
FILM MUSIC BUYER'S GUIDE. 1977. a. $9.95. R T S, Box 750579, Dept. BW, Petaluma, CA 94975.
Description: Soundtrack titles, composer, record numbers, years of release and current market value of recordings.

791.43   NO   ISSN 0015-1351
FILM OG KINO; Norsk filmblad. 1930. 9/yr. NOK 220 in Scandinavia; elsewhere Kr.350. Kommunale Kinematografers Landsforbund, Stortingsgaten 16, 0161 Oslo, Norway. FAX 02-42-8949. Ed. Kalle Loechen. adv.; bk.rev.; film rev.; charts; illus.; index; circ. 3,800. **Indexed:** Film Lit.Ind. (1980-), Intl.Ind.TV.
Formerly: Norsk Filmblad.

791.43   US
FILM PREVIEW REPORTS.* 1970. m. Federation of Motion Picture Councils, 142 N. Tucker, Memphis, TN 38104. TEL 901-725-4987. adv.; film rev.; illus.

FILM PRODUCERS, STUDIOS, AGENTS AND CASTING DIRECTORS GUIDE. see *BUSINESS AND ECONOMICS — Trade And Industrial Directories*

791.43   US   ISSN 0015-1386
PN1993
FILM QUARTERLY. 1945. q. $18 to individuals (foreign $24); institutions $37 (foreign $43). University of California Press, Journals Division, Berkeley, CA 94720. TEL 510-642-4191. FAX 510-643-7127. Ed. Ann Martin. adv.; bk.rev.; film rev.; illus.; index; circ. 6,900. (also avail. in microfilm from UMI; reprint service avail. from UMI; back issues avail.) **Indexed:** Acad.Ind., Access, Amer.Bibl.Slavic & E.Eur.Stud., Art Ind., Arts & Hum.Cit.Ind., Bk.Rev.Ind. (1968-), Chic.Per.Ind., Child.Bk.Rev.Ind. (1968-), Curr.Cont., Film Lit.Ind. (1973-), Hum.Ind., Intl.Ind.TV, Mag.Ind., Media Rev.Dig., Mid.East: Abstr.& Ind., R.G.
—BLDSC shelfmark: 3925.840000.
Formerly: Quarterly of Film, Radio and Television.
Description: Articles and interviews focusing on experimental, documentary and special interest films.
Refereed Serial

MOTION PICTURES   3509

791.43   US   ISSN 0361-722X
PN1993
FILM READER. 1975. a. $8.50 to individuals; libraries $10. Dept. of Radio - TV - Film, Northwestern University, Evanston, IL 60208. TEL 708-491-7315. Ed. James Schwoch. adv.; bk.rev.; circ. 1,000. (also avail. in microfilm from UMI; reprint service avail.) **Indexed:** Arts & Hum.Cit.Ind., Curr.Cont., Film Lit.Ind., Intl.Ind.TV, Media Rev.Dig.

791.43   UK
FILM REVIEW (LONDON, 1951). 1951. m. £6.60. Spotlight Publications Ltd., Greater London House, Hampstead Rd., London NW1 7QZ, England. Ed. David Aldridge. adv.; bk.rev.; film rev.; record rev.; illus.; circ. 50,000.
Formerly: A B C Film Review (ISSN 0001-0413)

778   US   ISSN 0737-9080
PN1995
FILM REVIEW ANNUAL. 1981. a. $125. Jerome S. Ozer, Ed. & Pub., 340 Tenafly Rd., Englewood, NJ 07631. TEL 201-567-7040. index; circ. 800. (back issues avail.)
Description: Compiles film reviews from selected newspapers, magazines, and scholarly journals.

790.2 780   HU   ISSN 0015-1416
FILM, SZINHAZ, MUZSIKA. w. $54. Lapkiado Vallalat, Lenin korut 9-11, 1073 Budapest 7, Hungary. TEL 222-408. (Subscr. to: Kultura, Box 149, H-1389 Budapest, Hungary) Ed. Zoltan Iszlai. illus.; circ. 30,000.

778.53   US
FILM - TAPE WORLD. 1988. m. $25. Media Publications, Box 882433, San Francisco, CA 94188-2433. TEL 415-821-9753. circ. 5,000. (tabloid format; back issues avail.)
Description: Trade publication for the film and video commmunity of Northern California.

791.43   US   ISSN 0896-6389
FILM THREAT. 1985; N.S. 6/yr. $10.50 (foreign $20.50). Film Threat, Inc., 9171 Wilshire Blvd., Ste. 300, Beverly Hills, CA 90210. TEL 310-858-7155. FAX 310-274-7985. Ed. Christian Gore. adv.; B&W page $1520, color page $2375; adv. contact: Justin McCormack. bk.rev.; circ. 100,000. **Indexed:** Film Lit.Ind. (1988-).
Description: Unique pop culture and movie magazine. Features celebrities and coverage from big studio releases to independent films.

FILM THREAT VIDEO GUIDE. see *COMMUNICATIONS — Video*

778.53   GW   ISSN 0934-0378
FILM UND FAKTEN. 1987. q. DM.36. Spitzenorganisation der Filmwirtschaft e.V., Langenbeckstr. 9, Postfach 5129, 6200 Wiesbaden, Germany. TEL 06121-17270. adv.; bk.rev.; circ. 3,000. **Indexed:** Film Lit.Ind. (1989-).

FILM UND FERNSEHEN; Zeitschrift fuer Theorie und Praxis des Film- und Fernsehschaffens. see *ART*

791.43   GW   ISSN 0173-4970
FILM UND FERNSEHEN IN FORSCHUNG UND LEHRE. 1978. a. DM.15. Hochschule fuer Bildende Kunste Braunschweig, Postfach 2828, 3300 Braunschweig, Germany. TEL 0531-3919123. (Co-sponsor: Institut fuer Medienwissenschaft und Film Braunschweig; Siftung Deutsche Kinemathek Berlin) Eds. Helga Belach, Helmut Korte. index; circ. 1,000.
Description: Research results concerning academic instruction and writing about film and television in German-speaking countries.

791.43   GW   ISSN 0343-5571
FILM UND TV KAMERAMANN. 1950. m. DM.58. l. Weber Verlag KG, Rotbuchenstr. 21, 8000 Munich 90, Germany. TEL 089-6904981. Ed. H.-J. Weber. adv.; bk.rev.; charts; illus.; index; circ. 7,200. **Indexed:** Film Lit.Ind. (1979-).
Formerly: Deutsche Kameramann (ISSN 0012-0340)

778.5 384.55   GW
FILM UND VIDEO. bi-m. DM.36 (foreign DM.43). Verlag fuer Technik und Handwerk, Fremersbergstr. 1, 7570 Baden - Baden, Germany. TEL 07221-2107-0. FAX 07221-2107-52.

M

MOTION PICTURES

791.43   384.55   CN   ISSN 0836-1002
PN1993.5.C2
FILM - VIDEO CANADIANA; a guide to Canadian films and videos produced in (years). (Text in English and French) 1980. biennial. Can.$37($42) National Film Board of Canada, Box 6100, Sta.A, Montreal, Que. H3C 3H5, Canada. TEL 514-283-9427. FAX 514-283-7564. circ. 2,000.
●Also available online. Vendor(s): QL Systems Ltd. (FVC,FVPD), VU/TEXT Information Services, Inc..
Supersedes (1969-1980): Film Canadiana: The Canadian Film Institute Yearbook of Canadian Cinema (ISSN 0015-1173)

778   US
FILM WORLD. 1968. m. $4.95. Knight Publishing Corp., 8060 Melrose Ave., Los Angeles, CA 90046. TEL 213-653-8060. Ed. Timothy Connelly. adv.; bk.rev.; film rev.; play rev.; circ. 150,000. (back issues avail.)

FILM WORLD DIRECTORY OF ADULT FILM & VIDEO. see BUSINESS AND ECONOMICS — Trade And Industrial Directories

778   US
FILM WORLD GUIDE. bi-m. $4.95 per no. Knight Publishing Corp., 8060 Melrose Ave., Los Angeles, CA 90046. TEL 213-653-8060.

FILM WRITERS GUIDE. see BUSINESS AND ECONOMICS — Trade And Industrial Directories

791.43   SW   ISSN 0071-4925
FILMARSBOKEN/FILM YEAR BOOK (YEAR). 1968. a. $20. (Swedish Film Institute) Proprius Forlag AB, Box 10251, S-100 55 Stockholm, Sweden. TEL 08-6609602. Ed. Bertil Wredlund. adv.; circ. 1,500.
Description: Reports on the film repertoire in Sweden. Gives full data on producers, directors, scriptwriters, cinematographers, actors and Swedish release dates and a synopsis of each film. Includes TV films.

016   DK   ISSN 0107-0940
FILMATISEREDE BOEGER. 1974. a. DKK 261.25. Bibliotekscentralen, Tempovej 7-11, DK-2750 Ballerup, Denmark. TEL 2-974000. FAX 2-655310.

791.43   IT   ISSN 0015-1513
FILMCRITICA; rivista mensile di studi sul cinema. (Includes section: Lo Spettatore Critico) 1950. m. L.45000 (foreign L.60000). Editori Del Grifo, Via di Gracciano nel Corso 85, 53045 Montepulciano, Italy. Ed. Edoardo Bruno. adv.; bk.rev.; film rev.; illus.; index. (also avail. in microform from UMI; reprint service avail. from UMI) **Indexed:** Film Lit.Ind. (1973-), Intl.Ind.TV.

778.5   BL
FILME CULTURA. 1966. s-a. Empresa Brasileira de Filmes, S.A., Rua Mayrink Veiga, 28, 20090 Rio de Janeiro, RJ, Brazil. TEL 021-223-2171. Ed.Bd. bk.rev.; film rev.; illus.; circ. 3,000. **Indexed:** Film Lit.Ind. (1973-1988), Int.Ind.Film.Per., Intl.Ind.TV.
Formerly: Filme e Cultura (ISSN 0015-1521)

FILMECHANGE; droit, economie, sociologie de l'audiovisuel. see LAW

791.43   II   ISSN 0015-1548
FILMFARE. (Text in English, Hindi) 1952. fortn. Rs.240($20) Bennett, Coleman & Co. Ltd. (Bombay), Times of India Bldg., Dr. DDadabhai Naoroji Road, Bombay 400 001, India. TEL 22-4150271. TELEX 1173504. (U.S. subscr. to: M/s. Kalpana, 42-75 Main St., Flushing NY 11355) Ed. Rauf Ahmed. adv.; bk.rev.; film rev.; illus.; circ. 106,500.

778.53   GW   ISSN 0176-1110
FILMFAUST; internationale Filmzeitschrift. 1976. 6/yr. DM.98 (foreign DM.130). Filmfaust Verlag, Schumannstr. 64, 6000 Frankfurt a.M. 1, Germany. TEL 069-748305. FAX 069-7240823. Eds. Bion Steinborn, Christine von Eichel-Streiber. adv.; bk.rev.; circ. 12,500. **Indexed:** Film Lit.Ind. (1987-).

778.53   US
FILMFAX; the magazine of unusual film and television. bi-m. 1042 1/2 Michigan Ave., Evanston, IL 60202. **Indexed:** Film Lit.Ind. (1987-).

778.53   SW
FILMHAEFTET: TIDSKRIFT OM FILM OCH T V. irreg. Storgatan 15, 753 31 Uppsala, Sweden. **Indexed:** Film Lit.Ind. (1987-).

791.43   II
FILMI DUNIYA. (Text in Hindi) 1958. m. Rs.100. 16 Darya Canj, New Delhi 110 002, India. TEL 11-3278087. Ed. Narendra Kumar. adv.; circ. 119,508.

791.43   II
FILMI KALIYAN. (Text in English) 1969. m. 16-39 Subhash Nagar, New Delhi 110 027, India. TEL 11-272080. Ed. V.S. Dewan. circ. 102,700.

778.53   FI
FILMIHULLU. 8/yr. Kalevankatu 44 A 2, 00180 Helsinki, Finland. **Indexed:** Film Lit.Ind. (1973-).

791.43   NO   ISSN 0015-1556
FILMJOURNALEN; pop topp. 1940. m. NOK 60. Kaare Messel Birkelund, Ed. & Pub., Parkveien 5, Oslo 3, Norway. film rev.; play rev.; circ. 16,300.

791.43   GW   ISSN 0015-1572
PN1995
FILMKRITIK. 1957. m. DM.88. Filmkritiker Kooperative, Kreittmayrstr. 3, 8000 Munich 2, Germany. adv.; bk.rev.; film rev.; illus.; index; circ. 5,000. **Indexed:** Arts & Hum.Cit.Ind., Curr.Cont., Film Lit.Ind, Intl.Ind.TV.

791.43   HU   ISSN 0015-1580
FILMKULTURA. (Text in Hungarian; summaries in English) 1965. bi-m. $20.50. Magyar Film Intezet - Hungarian Film Institute, Stefania ut 97, 1143 Budapest, Hungary. TEL 36-1-149-136. Ed. Vera Gyurey. adv.; bk.rev.; film rev.; illus.; circ. 5,000. (tabloid format; also avail. in microfilm from UMI; reprint service avail. from UMI) **Indexed:** Film Lit.Ind. (1973-), Intl.Ind.TV.

791.43   AU   ISSN 0015-1599
FILMKUNST; Zeitschrift fuer Filmkultur und Filmwissenschaft. 1949. q. S.200($8) Oesterreichische Gesellschaft fuer Filmwissenschaft, Kommunikations- und Medienforschung, Rauhensteingasse 5, A-1010 Vienna, Austria. TEL 5129936. Ed. Ludwig Gesek. adv.; bk.rev.; film rev.; illus.; circ. 800. **Indexed:** Film Lit.Ind. (1975-).
Description: Scientific studies and essays on motion pictures and television.

778.5   UK
FILMLOG; index of feature film production and casting in Britain. 1968. m. £18 for 6 mos. P.O. Box 11, London SW15 6AY, England. TEL 081-789-0408. FAX 081-780-1977. Ed. Vaune Craig-Raymond. circ. 4,000.
Description: Lists jobs in the motion picture industry.

792   US
FILMMAKER'S REVIEW. 1976. q. $15. Columbia Filmmakers, 313 Ferris Booth Hall, Columbia University, New York, NY 10027. Ed. Jim Berger. adv.; bk.rev.; illus.; circ. 5,000.

778.53   AT
FILMNEWS. bi-m. c/o Metro Television, Paddington Town Hall, Box 299, Paddington N.S.W. 2021, Australia. **Indexed:** Film Lit.Ind. (1989-).

791.43   CS   ISSN 0015-1645
PN1998
FILMOVY PREHLED. 1939. m. 66 Kcs. Lucernafilm, Narodni Trida 28, 110 00 Prague 1, Czechoslovakia. (Subscr. to: PNS ustred ni expedice a dovoz tisku Praha, Kafkova 19, 160 00 Praha 6, Czechoslovakia) Ed. Tomas Bartosek. circ. 5,000.

778.53   PL
FILMOWY SERWIS PRASOWY. fortn. Ul. Mazowiecka 6-8, 00950 Warsaw, Poland. **Indexed:** Film Lit.Ind. (1986-).

791.43   SW   ISSN 0015-1661
FILMRUTAN. 1958. q. SEK 100($9) (typically set in Jan.). Sveriges Foerenade Filmstudios, Box 82, S-851 02 Sundwall, Sweden. FAX 0-60-129892. Ed. Roger Tereus. adv.; bk.rev.; film rev.; illus.; circ. 1,500. **Indexed:** Arts & Hum.Cit.Ind., Curr.Cont., Film Lit.Ind., Intl.Ind.TV.

791.43   CN   ISSN 0046-3825
FILMS A L'ECRAN. 1957. fortn. Can.$25 (foreign Can.$35). Office des Communications Sociales, 4005 rue de Bellechasse, Montreal, Que. H1X 1J6, Canada. TEL 514-729-6391. FAX 514-729-7375.

791.43   384.55   UK   ISSN 0015-167X
PN1993
FILMS & FILMING. 1954. m. £28. Orpheus Publications, Unit 8 Primrose Mews, 1a Sharpleshall St., London NW1 8YL, England. adv.; illus. **Indexed:** Film Lit.Ind. (1973-1991), Intl.Ind.TV.
Incorporates: Films on Screen & Video.
Description: News about film and video, interviews.

791.43   US   ISSN 0015-1688
PN1993
FILMS IN REVIEW. 1950. m. $18. National Board of Review of Motion Pictures, Inc., Box 589, New York, NY 10021. TEL 212-628-1594. Ed. Robin Little. adv.; bk.rev.; film rev.; illus.; circ. 58,600. (also avail. in microform from UMI; reprint service avail. from UMI) **Indexed:** Art Ind., Bk.Rev.Ind. (1981-), Child.Bk.Rev.Ind. (1981-), Film Lit.Ind. (1973-), Int.Ind.Film Per., Intl.Ind.TV, Media Rev.Dig., Mid.East: Abstr.& Ind., Ref.Sour.
—BLDSC shelfmark: 3926.720000.

778.5   DK   ISSN 0107-1033
PN1997.8
FILMSAESONEN: DANSK FILMFORTEGNELSE. 1980. a. DKK 248 (typically set in Dec.). (Danske Filmmuseum) Dansk BiblioteksCenter, Tempovej 7-11, DK-2750 Ballerup, Denmark. Ed. Anne Jespersen. illus.; circ. 1,200.

791.43   AU   ISSN 0015-1696
FILMSCHAU.* 1951. w. S.130. Katholische Filmkommission fuer Oesterreich, Singerstr. 7, Vienna 1, Austria. Ed. Richard Emele. adv.; film rev.; illus.; stat.; circ. 5,000.

791.43   GW   ISSN 0015-1734
FILMSPIEGEL. 1954. fortn. DM.39 (foreign DM.67.60). Henschelverlag Kunst und Gesellschaft, Oranienburger Str. 67-68, 1040 Berlin, Germany. bk.rev.

778.5   IT
FILMSTUDIA. 1974. m. free. Via Orti d'Alibert, 1c, 00165 Rome, Italy. film rev.; illus.; circ. 7,000.

778.5   DK
FILMVIDENSKABELIGT ARBOG. 1973. a. price varies. Koebenhavns Universitet, Institut for Film, TV og Kommunikation, 78 Njalsgade, DK-2300 Copenhagen S, Denmark. TEL 31-542211. FAX 31-955828. illus.; circ. 500.
Supersedes in part (as of 1978): Koebenhavns Universitet. Institut for Filmvidenskab. Skrifter.

778.53   HU
FILMVILAG. m. Bimbo ut. 55, 1022 Budapest 11, Hungary. **Indexed:** Film Lit.Ind. (1985-).

778.53   GW
FILMWAERTS. q. Seydlitzstrasse 30, 3000 Hannover 1, Germany. **Indexed:** Film Lit.Ind. (1989-).

778.5   808.8   UK
FLICKERS 'N' FRAMES. no.14, 1991. 4/yr. £5.50($14) c/o John Peters, 299 Southway Dr., Southway, Plymouth, Devon PL6 6QN, England. (Subscr. in U.S. to: Anne Marsden, 1052 Calle del Cerro, No. 708, San Clemente, CA 92672. TEL 714-361-3791) bk.rev.; film rev.; video rev.
Description: Publishes film criticism and original science fiction stories.

791.43   UK
FLICKS; magazine for moviegoers. 1985. m. £18.50 (foreign £47.50). Flicks Publications Ltd., 11 Chesilton Rd., Fulham, London SW6 5AA, England. TEL 01-731-7013. Ed. Quentin Falk. circ. 300,000. (back issues avail.)

MOTION PICTURES

778.534 384.5 — US
FLORIDA REEL.* 1989. bi-m. $15. Take 5 Publishing, Inc., PO Box 941540ia Ave., Ste. 1200, Maitland, FL 32794-1540. TEL 407-839-0642. adv.; circ. 15,275.
Description: Provides articles on the production industry, ranging from casting companies to post production. Covers computer-generated special effects, makeup professionals, editing equipment, local film commissions, professional organizations, corporate videos, financing, music and sound libraries, equipment rental, independent film producers and location shooting.

FOTO - CINE. see PHOTOGRAPHY

778.5 — AG
FOTO CINE GUIA. a. $2.50. Editorial Fotografia Universal, Muniz 1327-49, Buenos Aires, Argentina.

791.43 — YU — ISSN 0015-8704
FOTO-KINO REVIJA; jugoslovenski casopis za fotografijui amaterski film. (Text in Serbo-Croatian) 1948. m. 144 din.($5) Foto Savez Jugoslavije, Bulevar Revolucije 44, Belgrade, Yugoslavia. Ed. Milanka Saponja.

FOTOCAMARA CON POPULAR PHOTOGRAPHY. see PHOTOGRAPHY

778.53 — SP
FOTOGRAMAS. 1946. m. Comunicacion y Publicaciones, S.A., Consejo de Ciento 83, 6o, 08015 Barcelona, Spain. TEL 93-4262394. FAX 93-4261450. Dir. Elisenda Nadal Ganan. circ. 150,000.

LE FOTOGUIDE. see COMMUNICATIONS — Video

FOTOKINO-MAGAZIN; Fachzeitschrift fuer Foto- und Filmamateure. see PHOTOGRAPHY

FOTOMUNDO. see PHOTOGRAPHY

FOTON; fotografia, cine y sonida (photography, amateur movie and sound). see PHOTOGRAPHY

791.43 — UK — ISSN 0306-7661
PN1993
FRAMEWORK; a film journal. 1975. q. £10($17) to individuals; institutions £25. Sankofa Film & Video Ltd., 32-34 Gordon House Rd., Unit K, London NW5 1LP, England. Ed. Robert Crusz. adv.; bk.rev.; illus.; circ. 3,000. (reprint service avail. on UMI) Indexed: Film Lit.Ind. (1976-), Intl.Ind.TV, Media Rev.Dig.
—BLDSC shelfmark: 4032.119000.

791.43 301.412 — GW
FRAUEN UND FILM. 1974. s-a. DM.30. Stroemfeld - Roter Stern, Postfach 180147, Holzhausenstr. 4, 6000 Frankfurt a.M. 1, Germany. TEL 069-599999. FAX 069-559336. Eds. Heide Schluepmann, Gertrud Koch. adv.; bk.rev.; circ. 3,000. Indexed: Film Lit.Ind. (1986-), Intl.Ind.TV.

530 — US — ISSN 0748-5247
FREEDONIA GAZETTE; the magazine devoted to the Marx brothers. 1978. s-a. $11. Paul G. Wesolowski, Ed. & Pub., Darien 28, New Hope, PA 18938-1224. TEL 215-862-9734. FAX 215-654-0408. (Also: Raymond D. White, 137 Easterly Rd., Leeds LS8 2RY, England) adv.; bk.rev.; play rev.; illus.; circ. 400. (back issues avail.; reprint service avail. from ISI,UMI)

778.5 — CN — ISSN 0704-9536
FREEZE FRAME. 1977. q. free. Edmonton Film Society, 6243 - 112 A St., Edmonton, Alta., Canada.
Formerly: Film Edmonton.

GADNEY'S GUIDES TO INTERNATIONAL CONTESTS, FESTIVALS & GRANTS IN FILM & VIDEO, PHOTOGRAPHY, TV-RADIO BROADCASTING, WRITING & JOURNALISM. see COMMUNICATIONS

792 — IT
GALA INTERNATIONAL; rivista bimestrale di informazione visiva. 1964. 6/yr. L.15000. Amelia Colombo Editore, Via Turati 3, 20121 Milan, Italy. Ed. Mario Bendendo. adv.; play rev.; circ. 20,000.
Formerly: Gala (ISSN 0016-397X)

GAZZETTA DELLE ARTI. see ART

778.5 — HK
GOLDEN MOVIE NEWS/CHIA HO TIEN YING. m. HK.$60. (Ssu Hai Chu Pan Shih Yeh Yu Hsien Kung Ssu) Four Seas Publications Ltd., 1st Fl., 122B Argyle St., Kowloon, Hong Kong. illus.

791.43 — US — ISSN 0896-8802
GORE ZONE. 1988. bi-m. $15.99. O'Quinn Studios, Inc., 475 Park Ave. S., New York, NY 10016. TEL 212-689-2830. Ed. Anthony Timpone. adv.; bk.rev.; film rev.; circ. 180,000.

778.53 — PO
GRANDE ILUSAO; revista de cinema. irreg., no.12, 1991. price varies. Edicoes Afrontamento, Lda., Rua de Costa Cabral, 859, Apdo. 2009, 4201 Porto Codex, Portugal. TEL 489271. FAX 491777. Ed. Regina Guimaraes.

778 — UK — ISSN 0072-6958
GREAT BRITAIN. NATIONAL FILM FINANCE CORPORATION. ANNUAL REPORT. a. H.M.S.O., P.O. Box 276, London SW8 5DT, England. (reprint service avail. from UMI)

778.53 — IT
GRIFFITHIANA. irreg. Cineteca del Friuli, Via Osoppo 26, 33014 Gemona, Italy. Indexed: Film Lit.Ind. (1990-).

LE GRIOT; hebdomadaire des spectacles, du cinema et de la culture. see GENERAL INTEREST PERIODICALS — Africa

791.43 — US — ISSN 0072-8284
LB1043.Z9
GUIDE TO COLLEGE COURSES IN FILM AND TELEVISION. 1969. irreg., latest 1990. $19.95. American Film Institute, Education Services, 2021 N. Western Ave., Box 27999, Los Angeles, CA 90027. TEL 213-856-7725.
Description: Listing of film and television programs at over 500 colleges and universities.

791 — CN
GUIDE TO FILM, TELEVISION AND COMMUNICATION STUDIES IN CANADA. (Text in English and French) 1971. irreg. Can.$15.95. Canadian Film Institute, 2 Daly, Ottawa, Ont. K1N 6E2, Canada. TEL 613-232-6727. FAX 613-232-6315. TELEX 0636700474.
Former titles: Guide to Film, Television and Communications Courses in Canada; Guide to Film and Television Courses in Canada (ISSN 0383-0187)
Description: Describes relevant courses in universities and colleges in Canada.

791 355 — US
GUIDE TO GOVERNMENT-LOAN FILMS. irreg., latest 1975. $9.95. Serina Press, 70 Kennedy St., Alexandria, VA 22305. TEL 703-548-4080.
Formerly: Guide to Military-Loan Films (ISSN 0072-8586)

791.43 — NP
▼**GUZARISH-I FILM.** 1990. m. Vali Asar St., P.O. Box 15115-38, Teheran, Iran.

HECHOS DE MASCARA. see LABOR UNIONS

HISTORICAL JOURNAL OF FILM, RADIO AND TELEVISION. see HISTORY

HOLLYWOOD ACTING COACHES AND TEACHERS DIRECTORY. see EDUCATION — Teaching Methods And Curriculum

917 — US — ISSN 0018-3660
PN1993
HOLLYWOOD REPORTER. 1930. d. $142. H.R. Industries, Inc., 6715 Sunset Blvd., Hollywood, CA 90028. TEL 213-464-7411. FAX 213-469-8770. adv.; bk.rev.; film rev.; play rev.; circ. 25,000. (also avail. in microfilm from BHP,KTO)

700 — US — ISSN 0278-419X
PN1998.A1
HOLLYWOOD REPORTER STUDIO BLU-BOOK DIRECTORY. 1978. a. $55. H.R. Industries, Inc., 6715 Sunset Blvd., Hollywood, CA 90028. TEL 213-469-8770. FAX 213-464-7411. Ed. Alex Ben Block. bk.rev.; circ. 3,000.

778.5 — US
HOLLYWOOD STUNTMEN'S HALL OF FAME NEWS. 1978. 6/yr. $27.50. Hollywood Stuntmen's Hall of Fame, Inc., 111 E. 100 North, Box 277, Moab, UT 84532-0277. TEL 801-259-6100. Ed. John Gilbert Hagner. adv.; bk.rev.; circ. 375.
Formerly (until 1980): Falling for Stars News.

778.5 — US
HOLLYWOOD THEN & NOW. 1953. 12/yr. $25.97. 3960 Laurel Canyon Ave., Studio City, CA 91604-3791. TEL 818-990-5450. FAX 818-990-0524. Ed. Ralph Benner. adv.; bk.rev.; illus.; circ. 50,000. (back issues avail.) Indexed: Film Lit.Ind. (1984-).
Formerly: Hollywood Studio Magazine.

791.43 — CC
HUANQIU YINMU HUAKAN/GLOBAL SCREEN PICTORIAL. (Text in Chinese) m. Zhongguo Dianying Chubanshe - China Film Press, 22 Beisanhuan Donglu, Beijing 100013, People's Republic of China. TEL 4219977. Ed. Fu Lan.

791 384.55 — UK — ISSN 0952-7419
I V C A MAGAZINE. 1983. 10/yr. membership. International Visual Communications Association, Bolsover House, 5-6 Clipstone Street, London W1P 7EB, England. TEL 071-580-0962. FAX 071-436-2606. Ed. Tony Goodman. adv.; bk.rev.; circ. 1,500. (back issues avail.)
Formed by the 1987 merger of: B I S F A Magazine (ISSN 0263-502X) & I T V A (UK).

IMAGE (ROCHESTER, 1952); journal of photography and motion pictures. see PHOTOGRAPHY

791.4 — UK — ISSN 0950-2114
TR845 — CODEN: IMATEV
IMAGE TECHNOLOGY JOURNAL OF THE B K S T S; technology of motion picture film, sound, television, audio, visual. 1936. m. £48. British Kinematograph Sound and Television Society, 547-549 Victoria House, Vernon Place, London WC1B 4DJ, England. FAX 01-405-3560. Ed. John Gainsborough. adv.; bk.rev.; bibl.; charts; illus.; index; circ. 2,500. (also avail. in microfilm from UMI; reprint service avail. from UMI) Indexed: Br.Tech.Ind., Chem.Abstr., Film Lit.Ind. (1991-), Sci.Abstr.
—BLDSC shelfmark: 4368.992950.
Former titles: B K S T S Journal (ISSN 0305-6996) & British Kinematography, Sound and Television (ISSN 0007-1358); British Kinematography.

778.53 — IT
IMMAGINE. q. Associazione Italiana per le Ricerche di Storia del Cinema, Via Yser 8, Rome, Italy. Indexed: Film Lit.Ind. (1986-).

791.43 — FR
IMPACT. bi-m. Mad Movies, 4 rue Mansart, 75009 Paris, France. TEL 48-74-70-83. Ed. Denis Trehin. circ. 65,000.

791.43 — US
IN CINEMA.* 1980. 10/yr. $10. In Cinema, Ltd., 801 Second Ave., New York, NY 10017. TEL 212-758-5580. Ed. Harlan Jacobson. adv.; circ. 605,000.

778.534 — US
IN FOCUS (LOS ANGELES). q. membership. Friends of Visual Communications, 263 S. Los Angeles St., Ste. 307, Los Angeles, CA 90012. FAX 213-687-4848. Ed. Abraham Ferrer. film rev.; video rev.; illus.
Description: For supporters of Asian-American work in visual communications.

778.53 384.55 — US — ISSN 0889-6208
HD9697.M68
IN MOTION (ANNAPOLIS); film and video production magazine. 1981. m. $27.95. In Motion, Inc., 1203 West St., Annapolis, MD 21401. TEL 410-269-0605. FAX 410-263-4615. Ed. Allison Dollar. adv.; circ. 15,000. (back issues avail.)
Description: Reports on equipment, trends, people in the film and video production industry. Covers production, postproduction, talent, and production support services as well as surveys of segments of the industry.

3512   MOTION PICTURES

791.43 384.55   US   ISSN 0731-5198
PN1993
INDEPENDENT FILM AND VIDEO MONTHLY. 1978. m. (10/yr.). $45 to individuals; libraries $60. (Association of Independent Video and Filmmakers) Foundation for Independent Video & Film, 625 Broadway, 9th Fl., New York, NY 10012. TEL 212-473-3400. FAX 212-475-0964. Ed. Patricia Thomson. adv.; bk.rev.; circ. 22,000. (back issues avail.) **Indexed:** Alt.Press Ind., Film Lit.Ind. (1983-).
   Description: Covers the technical, legislative, marketing, and artistic facets of film and video production (especially independent production), with book reviews, conference reports, and announcements of festivals.

015   II   ISSN 0377-7359
PN1998
INDIAN FILMS. (Text in English) 1972. a. Rs.40. Motion Picture Enterprises, Alaka Talkies, Poona 411030, India. Ed B.V. Dharap. adv.; illus.; index; circ. 1,200.

791   II
INDIAN MOTION PICTURE ALMANAC. (Text in English) a. Rs.40. Shot Publications, 3-B Madan St., Calcutta 700013, India. illus.
   Incorporating: Bengal Motion Picture Diary and General Information.

791.43   SI
INDIAN MOVIE NEWS. (Text in English and Tamil) 1952. m. S.$30. Chinese Pictorial Review Ltd., Shaw Centre, Scotts Rd., Singapore 9, Singapore. Ed. I.S. Menon. film rev.; circ. 25,000. (processed)
   Former titles: Indian Malay Movie News; Indian Movie News (ISSN 0019-5979)

051   US
▼**INSIDE HOLLYWOOD.** 1991. bi-m. $22 (foreign $28). Wald Publishing Co., 990 Grove St., Evanston, IL 60201-4370. TEL 708-491-6440. (Subscr. to: Box 365, Mt. Morris, IL 61054-0365. TEL 800-877-5893) circ. 200,000.
   Description: Offers behind the scene coverage of stars, information on coming attractions, a movie trivia quiz and seasonal film calendars.

574 610   GW   ISSN 0073-8417
INSTITUT FUER DEN WISSENSCHAFTLICHEN FILM. PUBLIKATIONEN ZU WISSENSCHAFTLICHEN FILMEN. SEKTION BIOLOGIE. (Text in English, French or German; summaries in English, French and German) 1963. irreg. Institut fuer den Wissenschaftlichen Film, Nonnenstieg 72, 3400 Goettingen, Germany. FAX 0551-202200. TELEX 96691. Ed. H.K. Galle.

778.53   FR
INSTITUTE JEAN VIGO. ARCHIVES. m. Institut Jean Vigo, Palais des Congres, 66000 Perpignan, France.
Indexed: Film Lit.Ind. (1988-).

INTERNATIONAL ALLIANCE OF THEATRICAL STAGE EMPLOYES AND MOVING PICTURE MACHINE OPERATORS OF THE UNITED STATES AND CANADA. OFFICIAL BULLETIN. see LABOR UNIONS

791   US   ISSN 0074-462X
INTERNATIONAL DIRECTORY OF 16MM FILM COLLECTORS. 1971. irreg. (approx. biennial). $15. (16mm Filmland) Evan H. Foreman, Ed. & Pub., P.O. Drawer F, Mobile, AL 36601. TEL 205-432-8406. circ. 1,000. (tabloid format)

791.43 572   US   ISSN 0742-5333
PN1995.9.D6
INTERNATIONAL DOCUMENTARY. 1982. m. $15 to individuals; libraries and institutions $25. International Documentary Foundation, 1551 S. Robertson Blvd., Ste. 201, Los Angeles, CA 90035. TEL 213-655-7089. FAX 310-785-9334. Ed. Nancy Wilkan. adv.; bk.rev.; circ. 2,000. (back issues avail.) **Indexed:** Film.Lit.Ind. (1990-).
   Description: Devoted to non-fiction film and video. Provides valuable information for documentary filmmakers and their audience.

791.43   UK   ISSN 0074-6053
PN1993.3
INTERNATIONAL FILM GUIDE. 1964. a. $16.95. Variety, 34-35 Newman St., London W1P 3PD, England. FAX 071-580-5559. (Dist. in U.S. by: Samuel French Trade, 7623 Sunset Blvd., Los Angeles, CA 90046) Ed. Peter Cowie. adv.; bk.rev.
   Description: Covers film production, festivals, archives and schools in more than 60 countries.

791.43   US   ISSN 0074-7084
PN1993.3
INTERNATIONAL MOTION PICTURE ALMANAC; reference tool of the film industry. 1929. a. $81. Quigley Publishing Co., 159 W. 53 St., New York, NY 10019. TEL 212-247-3100. FAX 212-489-0871. Ed. Barry Monush. adv. (also avail. in microfilm from BHP) **Indexed:** Child.Auth.& Illus., Perf.Arts Biog.Master Ind.
   —BLDSC shelfmark: 4544.360000.

778.5   IT
INTIMITA DELLA FAMIGLIA. 1946. w. L.115000, Industrie Grafiche Cino del Duca S.p.A., Via Borgogna 5, 20122 Milan, Italy. TEL 02-781051. Eds. Giorgio Galluzzo, Sandra Rudoni. adv.; circ. 468,000.
   Former titles: Intimita; Intimita della Famiglia.

IRIS. see PHOTOGRAPHY

791.43   RU   ISSN 0021-1788
ISKUSSTVO KINO. (Text in Russian; contents page in English) 1931. m. 15.60 Rub. Soyuz Rabotnikov Kinematografii S.S.S.R., Ul. Usievicha, 9, Moscow A-319, Russia. FAX 200-4284. TELEX 411939 ECRAN SU. Ed. K.A. Cherbakov. bk.rev.; film rev.; illus.; index; circ. 53,000. **Indexed:** Film Lit.Ind. (1973-), Intl.Ind.TV.

ISLAND - EAR. see MUSIC

791
ISRAEL FILM CENTRE. INFORMATION BULLETIN. (Text in English) 1969. a. free. Israel Film Centre, P.O. Box 299, Jerusalem, Israel. TEL 750297. FAX 245110.
   Description: Provides information on local and international filmmaking in Israel. Serves as a catalogue of Israeli feature films.

778.5   IS
ISRAEL FILM INDUSTRY DIRECTORY. (Text in English) 1976. irreg., latest 1991. Israel Film Centre, P.O. Box 299, Jerusalem, Israel. TEL 750297. FAX 245110. adv.
   Formerly: Filmmakers and Film Production Services of Israel.

770   GW   ISSN 0075-2509
JAHRBUCH DES KAMERAMANNS. 1959. a. DM.25. I. Weber Verlag KG, Rotbuchenstr. 21, 8000 Munich 90, Germany. TEL 089-6904981. adv.

JANASUDHA DAILY. see LITERARY AND POLITICAL REVIEWS

JANASUDHA MONTHLY. see LITERARY AND POLITICAL REVIEWS

JANASUDHA WEEKLY. see LITERARY AND POLITICAL REVIEWS

778.534   II
JEE: FILM & T V FORTNIGHTLY. (Text in Gujarati) 1958. fortn. Rs.100($49) Madhuri Kotak, Ed. & Pub., 62 Vaju Kotak Marg, Bombay 400 001, India. TEL 91-22-2611526. FAX 22-2615895. TELEX 011-78298 JEE IN. (Subscr. to: 132 Andheri Industrial Estate, Veera Desai Road, Andheri, Bombay 400 058) adv.; circ. 95,000.
   Formerly: Jee: Film Fortnightly.

778.53   FR
JEUNE CINEMA. bi-m. Federation Jean Vigo, 8 rue Lamarck, 75018 Paris, France. **Indexed:** Film Lit.Ind. (1973-).

788.53 973   US   ISSN 1047-0476
E169.1
▼**JOE FRANKLIN'S NOSTALGIA.*** 1990. bi-m. $9.95. Joe Franklin Publications, 47-20 32nd Pl., Long Island City, NY 11101-2425. TEL 212-545-0185. FAX 212-545-0190. adv.; circ. 50,000.
   Description: Provides stories and pictures of days gone by. Articles tell of the Hollywood of yesteryear.

791.43 384.55   US   ISSN 0742-4671
PN1993
JOURNAL OF FILM AND VIDEO. 1947. q. $15 (foreign $24). University Film and Video Association, c/o Michael Selig, Ed., Div. of Mass Communication, Emerson College, Boston, MA 02116. film rev.; index, cum.index; circ. 1,300. (also avail. in microform from UMI; back issues avail.) **Indexed:** Abstr.Pop.Cult., Arts & Hum.Cit.Ind., C.I.J.E., Curr.Cont., Educ.Tech.Abstr., ERIC, Film Lit.Ind. (1973-), Intl.Ind.TV.
   Former titles (until 1984): University Film and Video Association. Journal; (until 1981): University Film Association. Journal (ISSN 0041-9311); University Film Producers Association. Journal.
   Description: Scholarly articles on film and video.

791.43   US   ISSN 0195-6051
PN1993
JOURNAL OF POPULAR FILM AND TELEVISION. 1972. q. $27 to individuals; institutions $53. (Helen Dwight Reid Educational Foundation) Heldref Publications, 1319 Eighteenth St., N.W., Washington, DC 20036-1802. TEL 202-296-6267. FAX 202-296-5149. Ed. Page Minshew. adv.; bk.rev.; bibl.; illus.; index, cum.index; circ. 800. (processed; also avail. in microform; reprint service avail.) **Indexed:** Acad.Ind., Amer.Bibl.Slavic & E.Eur.Stud., Amer.Hist.& Life, Arts & Hum,Cit.Ind., Bk.Rev.Ind. (1980-), Chic.Per.Ind., Child.Bk.Rev.Ind. (1980-), Commun.Abstr., Curr.Cont., Film Lit.Ind. (1973-), Hist.Abstr., Int.Ind.Film Per., Intl.Ind.TV, M.L.A., Ref.Sour.
   —BLDSC shelfmark: 5041.141000.
   Formerly: Journal of Popular Film (ISSN 0047-2719)
   Refereed Serial

778.5   US   ISSN 0146-5546
JUMP CUT; a review of contemporary media. 1974. irreg. (1-2/yr.). $20 (foreign $22) for 4 nos. Jump Cut Associates, Box 865, Berkeley, CA 94701. TEL 510-658-4482. Ed.Bd. adv.; bk.rev.; film rev.; illus.; circ. 6,000. (also avail. in microfilm from UMI; back issues avail.; reprint service avail. from UMI) **Indexed:** Alt.Press Ind., Chic.Per.Ind., Film Lit.Ind. (1974-), Int.Ind.Film Per., Intl.Ind.TV, Left Ind. (1986-), Media Rev.Dig., Sociol.Abstr.

JUYING YUEBAO/DRAMA & FILM MONTHLY. see THEATER

K & C. see ART

791.43   UA
KAWAKEB. 1952. w. Dar al- Hilal, 16 Sharia Muhammad Ezz el-Arab, Cairo, Egypt. TEL 02-27954. TELEX 92703. Ed. Hosn Shah. circ. 86,381.

791.43   UK
KEMPS INTERNATIONAL FILM AND TELEVISION YEAR BOOK. 1956. a. £55. Kemps Publishing Group Ltd., 11 The Swan Courtyard, Charles Edward Rd., Birmingham B26 1BU, England. TEL 021-711-4144. FAX 021-711-2866. TELEX 333786-KEMPSP-G. adv.
   Formerly: Kemps Film and Television Year Book (International) (ISSN 0075-5427)

778 384.55   UK
KEMPS PRODUCTION DIARY. 1987. a. £20($30) Kemps Publishing Group Ltd., 11 The Swan Courtyard, Charles Edward Rd., Birmingham B26 1BU, England. TEL 021-711-4144. FAX 021-711-2866. TELEX 333786-KEMPSP-G.
   Description: Presents companies involved in film, video and TV production, includes contact names.

791   JA   ISSN 0023-1460
KINDAI EIGA. 1945. m. 13000 Yen. Kindai-Eiga Co., Owaricho Bldg., 2F, 6-8-3 Ginza, Chuo-ku, Tokyo 104, Japan. TEL 03-5568-2811. FAX 03-5568-2818. Ed. Keiji Oguri. film rev.; circ. controlled. (processed)

KINDER JUGEND FILM KORRESPONDENZ. see CHILDREN AND YOUTH — For

791.43   YU
KINEMATOGRAFIJA U SRBIJI - UPOREDO S F R J.
(Subseries of: Biblioteka Dokumentacije) 1969. a. latest 1988, published in 1991. 480 din.($21) Institut za Film, Belgrade, Cika Ljubina 15, Belgrade, Yugoslavia. FAX 3811-634253. Ed. P. Golubovic. stat.; circ. 500.
Formerly: Kinematografija u Srbiji (ISSN 0350-2651)

778.53   GW
KINEMATOGRAPH. irreg. Deutsches Filmmuseum, Schaumainkai 41, 6000 Frankfurt a.M. 70, Germany. **Indexed:** Film Lit.Ind. (1986-).

778.53   CK   ISSN 0121-3776
▼**KINETOSCOPIO.** 1990. bi-m. Col.3000($10) Centro Colombo Americano, Apdo. Aereo 8734, Medellin, Colombia. TEL 574-251-4423. FAX 574-251-3326. Ed. Paul Bardwell. adv.; film rev.; circ. 3,500.
Description: Covers international cinema with a special focus on Colombian cinema. Includes information on all films currently being shown in the country.

791.43   PL   ISSN 0023-1673
PN1993
KINO. 1966. m. $13.20. Wydawnictwo Wspolczesne R S W "Prasa-Ksiazka-Ruch", Ul. Wiejska 12, 00-420 Warsaw, Poland. TEL 48-22-285330. (Dist. by: Ars Polona-Ruch, Krakowskie Przedmiescie 7, Warsaw, Poland) Ed. Ryszard Koniczek. bk.rev.; film rev.; illus.; index; circ. 30,000. **Indexed:** Film Lit.Ind. (1973-), Intl.Ind.TV.

791.43   CS
KINO. 1945. s-m. 65 Kcs. Panorama, Halkova 1, 120 72 Prague, Czechoslovakia. TEL 37 50 63. (Subscr. to: PNS, Zavod 01, Kafkova 19, 160 00 Prague 6, Czechoslovakia) Ed. Jaromira Sitarova. bk.rev.; film rev.; circ. 150,000.

778.53   GW
KINO; FILME DER BUNDESREPUBLIK DEUTSCHLAND. irreg. Export Union des Deutschen Films e.V., Tuerkenstr. 93, 8000 Munich 40, Germany. **Indexed:** Film Lit.Ind. (1982-).

778.53   GW
KINO; GERMAN FILM. 3/yr. Helgolaender Ufer 6, 1000 Berlin 21, Germany. **Indexed:** Film Lit.Ind. (1985-).

791.43   GW
KINO NEWS. 1986. m. DM.100. T und M Verlagsgesellschaft mbH, Eppendorfer Weg 169, 2000 Hamburg 20, Germany. TEL 040-4910015. FAX 040-4904122. Ed. Christoph Meier-Siem. adv.; bk.rev.; film rev.; illus.; circ. 1,500,000. (tabloid format)

791.43   GW
KINO NEWS OESTERREICH. 1989. m. DM.100. T und M Verlagsgesellschaft mbH, Eppendorfer Weg 169, 2000 Hamburg 20, Germany. TEL 040-4910015. FAX 040-4904122. Ed. Christoph Meier-Siem. adv.; bk.rev.; film rev.; illus.; circ. 241,000. (tabloid format)

778.5   BU   ISSN 0323-9993
PN1993
KINOIZKUSTVO. 1946. m. 5 lv.($10) Komitet za Izkustvo i Kultura, 7 Levsky St., 1000 Sofia, Bulgaria. (Co-sponsors: Suiuz na Kinodeitsite; Suiuz na Bulgarskite Pisatel) Ed. Emil Petrov. bk.rev.; film rev.; illus.; index; circ. 7,500. **Indexed:** Film Lit.Ind., Intl.Ind.TV.

791.43   FI
KINOLEHTI. 1932. bi-m. FIM 70. Suomen Filmikamari, Kaisaniemenkatu 3 B 29, 00100 Helsinki 10, Finland. (Co-sponsor: FK-Keskus Oy) Ed. Leo Nordberg. adv.; circ. 2,500.

778.534   GW
KINOMAGAZIN; Kino und Kultur. 1985. m. DM.10. Studio Kino GmbH, Mainzerstr. 8, 6600 Saarbruecken, Germany. TEL 0681-399297. FAX 0681-374556. adv.; circ. 10,000. (back issues avail.)

791.43   RU   ISSN 0023-1681
KINOMEKHANIK. 1937. m. 17.40 Rub. Ministerstvo Kul'tury, Moscow, Russia. Ed. Y.A. Fadeyev. **Indexed:** Chem.Abstr., Photo.Abstr.
—BLDSC shelfmark: 0089.000000.

791.43   AU
KINOSCHRIFTEN. irreg., no.1, 1988. varies. Verband der Wissenschaftlichen Gesellschaften Oesterreichs, Lindengasse 37, A-1070 Vienna, Austria. TEL 932166.

791.43   PL   ISSN 0023-169X
TR845
KINOTECHNIK. 1948. bi-m. $10.20. Krajowe Wydawnictwo Czasopism, Nowakowskiego 14, 00-666 Warsaw, Poland. (Dist. by: Ars Polona - Ruch, Krakowskie Przedmiescie 7, Warsaw, Poland) Ed. Janusz Tubek. adv.; bk.rev.; abstr.; bibl.; charts; illus.; pat.; index. (tabloid format)

791.43 384.55   DK   ISSN 0904-4159
KLIP. 1966. 4/yr. DKK 160 (typically set in Jan.). Dansk Filmlaererforening, Rypevej 22, 4000 Roskilde D, Denmark. TEL 46 755424. FAX 33-91-52-42. Ed. Frans Rasmussen. adv.; circ. 5,300.
Formerly: Film U V (ISSN 0107-9522)

778.5   KO
KOREA FILM CATALOG. a. Motion Picture Promotion Corporation, K.P.O. Box 605, Seoul, S. Korea. TEL 02-755-9291. FAX 02-774-0531. illus.

791.43   DK   ISSN 0023-4222
PN1993
KOSMORAMA. 1954. q. DKK 150. Danske Filmmuseum, Store Sondervoldstraede, 1419 Copenhagen K, Denmark. TEL 31-576500. FAX 31-541312. Ed. Kaare Schmidt. bk.rev.; illus.; index; circ. 2,000. (also avail. in microform from MIM,WMP) **Indexed:** Arts & Hum.Cit.Ind., Curr.Cont., Film Lit.Ind. (1973-), Intl.Ind.TV.
Description: Covers national and international cinema with articles, interviews and reviews.

791.43   GW   ISSN 0171-5208
KULLERAUGEN; Arbeitshilfen fuer Film-Interessierte. 1977. s-a. Verlag Brigitte Tast, Laaseweg 4, 3209 Schellerten, Germany. TEL 05123-4330. circ. 1,000. (back issues avail.)

791.43   GW   ISSN 0174-2582
KULLERAUGEN - MATERIALSAMMLUNG. 1978. s-a. Verlag Brigitte Tast, Laaseweg 4, 3209 Schellerten 1, Germany. TEL 05123-4330. circ. 1,000. (back issues avail.)

LADYSLIPPER CATALOG AND RESOURCE GUIDE OF RECORDS, TAPES, COMPACT DISCS AND VIDEOS BY WOMEN. see *WOMEN'S INTERESTS*

791.43   SA   ISSN 0023-8481
LARA LAMONT.* 1967. m. R.2. Golden Film Productions (Edms) Bpk, Dunwell-Gebou 112, Jorrissenstraat, Braamfontein, Johannesburg, South Africa.

LETTURE; libro e spettacolo, mensile di studi e rassegne. see *THEATER*

791.43   DK   ISSN 0108-5697
LEVENDE BILLEDER. 1975. m. DKK 280 (foreign DKK 380). Forlaget Sankt Peder af 1985 ApS, Meinungsgade 8D, 3.sal, DK-2200 Copenhagen N, Denmark. TEL 31-39-73-90. FAX 35-37-89-76. Ed. Peder Bundgaard. adv.; bk.rev.; film rev.; abstr.; index; circ. 10,000. **Indexed:** Film Lit.Ind. (1980-).
Supersedes: Film (ISSN 0015-1017)

LIGHTING DIMENSIONS. see *ARCHITECTURE*

801 778.5   US   ISSN 0090-4260
PN1995.3
LITERATURE - FILM QUARTERLY. 1973. q. $14 to individuals; libraries $28 (effective Jan. 1991). Salisbury State University, Salisbury, MD 21801. TEL 410-543-6556. FAX 410-543-6068. Ed. James M. Welsh. adv.; bk.rev.; film rev.; illus.; circ. 800. (also avail. in microfilm from UMI; back issues avail.) **Indexed:** Abstr.Engl.Stud., Arts & Hum.Cit.Ind., Curr.Cont., Film Lit.Ind. (1973-), Hum.Ind., Int.Ind.Film Per., Intl.Ind.TV, LCR, M.L.A., Media Rev.Dig.
—BLDSC shelfmark: 5276.721100.

778.534   US   ISSN 1047-9775
LOCATION PRODUCTION GUIDE. 1988. s-a. $12. TecSpec, Box 617024, Orlando, FL 32861-7024. Ed. Phil Flora. circ. 14,918.

778.5 384.55   US
LOCATION UPDATE; the magazine of film and video production. 1985. m. $25.95 in U.S.; Canada $39.95. Location Update, Inc., 6922 Hollywood Blvd., Ste. 612, Hollywood, CA 90028. TEL 213-461-8887. FAX 213-469-3711. adv.; circ. 30,000.
Description: Covers elements that evolve when filming and video taping on local and distant location.

778.53   US
LOCATIONS. 1987. s-a. $5 per no. Association of Film Commissioners International, I-25 and College Dr., Cheyenne, WY 82002. TEL 307-777-7777. adv.; circ. 17,000.
Description: Lists AFCI members and their services. Covers on-location productions, national and international filming, location highlights, laws and regulations, finance and budgets, news and events.

791
LOS ANGELES CINEMATHEQUE. 1973. m. $10 in L.A. county: others $5. Los Angeles Cinematheque, Inc., Box 24548, Los Angeles, CA 90024. Ed. Jared Rutter. adv.; bk.rev.; circ. 2,000.

791   IT
LUMIERE. 1984. q. L.10000. Bulzoni Editore, Via dei Liburni, 14, I-00185 Rome, Italy. Ed. Giacomo Gambetti.

M A I N. (Media Arts Information Network) see *COMMUNICATIONS — Television And Cable*

791.43   II   ISSN 0024-9432
MADHURI. (Text in Hindi) 1960. fortn. Rs.260($20) Bennett, Coleman & Co., Ltd. (Bombay), Times Bldg., Dr. D.N. Rd., Bombay 400001, India. TEL 4150271. (U.S. subscr. to: M/s Kalpana, 42-75 Main St., Flushing, NY 11355) Ed. Vinod Tiwari. adv.; bk.rev.; film rev.; circ. 115,000.

778   US
MAGILL'S CINEMA ANNUAL. a. $50. Salem Press, Box 1097, Englewood Cliffs, NJ 07632. TEL 201-871-3700. FAX 201-871-8668. Ed. F.N. Magill. film rev.
●Also available online. Vendor(s): DIALOG.

778.53 384.55   US
MARKEE. 1986. m. $24. H J K Publications, Inc., 655 Fulton St., Ste. 9, Sanford, FL 32771. TEL 407-324-1733. FAX 407-324-1766. Ed. Janet Karcher. adv.; circ. 12,200.
Description: For the Southeast and Southwest film and video industries.

MARTIN & OSA JOHNSON SAFARI MUSEUM WAIT-A-BIT NEWS. see *MUSEUMS AND ART GALLERIES*

791.43
MAYAPURI. (Text in Hindi) 1974. w. Rs.3 per no. A-5, Mayapuri, New Delhi 110 064, India. TEL 11-591439. TELEX 031-76125 MPLP IN. Ed. A.P. Bajaj. circ. 164,141.

MEDIA DIGEST; a bi-monthly media resource for education. see *EDUCATION — Teaching Methods And Curriculum*

791.43   PL
MEDIA REPORTER. 1957. fortn. $23. Ul. Miedziana 11, 00-958 Warsaw, Poland. TEL 48-22-200281. (Dist. by: Ars Polona-Ruch, Krakowskie Przedmiescie 7, Warsaw, Poland) Ed. Zygmunt Marcinczak. abstr.; circ. 100,000.
Formerly: Ekran (ISSN 0013-3299)

778.5   DK   ISSN 0903-8981
MEDIELAERERFORENINGEN FOR GYMNASIET OG H F. MEDDELELSER. 1978. irreg. (3-4/yr.). membership. Medielaererforeningen for Gymnasiet og H F, c/o Lisbet Borker, Norgesgade 31, DK 2300 Copenhagen S, Denmark. bk.rev.; illus.; circ. 200.
Formerly: Foreningen af Filmlaerer i Gymnasiet. Meddelelser (ISSN 0900-6664)

MEDIENCONCRET; Magazin fuer die paedagogische Praxis. see *COMMUNICATIONS*

MEDIENWISSENSCHAFT; Zeitschrift fuer Rezensionen ueber Veroeffentlichungen zu saemtlichen Medien. see *COMMUNICATIONS — Television And Cable*

MEDIUM (NEW YORK). see *ETHNIC INTERESTS*

MOTION PICTURES

METAPHYSICAL REVIEW. see *LITERARY AND POLITICAL REVIEWS*

METRO; media and education magazine. see *EDUCATION — Teaching Methods And Curriculum*

791.43　　　　　IO
METRU.* no.24, 1972. bi-m. Rps.100 per no. Jalan Pluit 200, Jakarta, Indonesia. Ed. B.S. Hartoyo. charts; illus.

MICHELE'S MAGIC MOMENTS. see *CLUBS*

778.53　　　　　US
MIDNIGHT MARQUEE. irreg. 4000 Glenarm Ave., Baltimore, MD 21206. **Indexed:** Film Lit.Ind. (1975-).

778.5　　　　　RU
MIFY I REAL'NOST. vol.5, 1976. 1.17 Rub. per no. (Goskino, Institut Teorii i Istorii Kino) Izdatel'stvo Iskusstvo, Vorotnikovskii pereulok 11, Moscow, Russia. Ed.Bd. film rev.; circ. 25,000.

778.53　　　　　US
MILLENNIUM FILM JOURNAL. irreg. Millennium Film Workshop, 66 E. Fourth St., New York, NY 10003. **Indexed:** Film Lit.Ind. (1978-).

778.5　　US　ISSN 0164-9655
TR845
MILLIMETER; the magazine of the motion picture and television production industries. 1973. m. $60. Penton Publishing (New York) (Subsidiary of: Pittway Company), 826 Broadway, New York, NY 10003. TEL 212-477-4700. Ed. Alison Johns. adv.; bk.rev.; film rev.; circ. 30,000. **Indexed:** Film Lit.Ind. (1974-), Intl.Ind.TV, Media Rev.Dig.
　　Description: Information on technology, craft and the use of television and film media for communication.

MODEL & PERFORMER. see *CLOTHING TRADE — Fashions*

791.43　　CI　ISSN 0026-8895
MOJ PAS. (Text in Serbo-Croatian) 1954. m. 80 din.($12.50) Kinoloski Savez SR Hrvatske, Ilica 61, Zagreb, Croatia. Ed. Vesna Sekalec.

778.53　　　　　BE
MONITEUR DU FILM EN BELGIQUE. m. Rue de Framboisier 35, 1180 Brussels, Belgium. **Indexed:** Film Lit.Ind. (1987-).

MONKEES, BOYCE & HART PHOTO FAN CLUB; the photo club. see *CLUBS*

778.53　　　　　US
MOTION PICTURE. irreg. Collective for Living Cinema, 41 White St., New York, NY 10013. **Indexed:** Film Lit.Ind. (1986-).

791.43　　　　　US
THE MOTION PICTURE GUIDE ANNUAL. 1986. a. $148. Baseline - CineBooks, R.R. Bowker, Dist., A Reed Reference Publishing Company, 121 Chanlon Rd, Box 31, New Providence, NJ 07974. TEL 800-521-8110. FAX 908-665-6688. TELEX 138 755. illus.
　　Description: Detailed entries, reviews, and anecdotes about hundreds of domestic and foreign features released in the US during the previous year.

791.43　　US　ISSN 0742-8839
MOTION PICTURE INVESTOR; newsletter on analysis of private and public values of movies and movie stock. 1984. m. $475. Paul Kagan Associates, Inc., 126 Clock Tower Place, Carmel, CA 93923. TEL 408-624-1536. FAX 408-624-1536. TELEX 408-625-3225. charts; index.
　　Description: Covers investment in public and private movie production and distribution companies. Tracks the movement and value of motion picture stocks.

MOTION PICTURE, T V & THEATRE DIRECTORY; for services & products. see *BUSINESS AND ECONOMICS — Trade And Industrial Directories*

791.43　　II　ISSN 0027-1632
MOTION PICTURES TECHNICAL BULLETIN. (Text in English) vol.12, 1969. q. Processlabs Private Ltd., S.V. Road, Dahisar, Bombay 68, India. Ed. Krishna Gopal. circ. 350.

791.43　　UK　ISSN 0027-268X
PN1993
MOVIE. 1962. q. 20s.($4) (Movie Magazine Ltd.) Orbis Publishing Ltd., 2a Roman Way, London N7 8XG, England. Ed. Ann Lloyd. film rev.; illus.; circ. 6,500. **Indexed:** Arts & Hum.Cit.Ind., Curr.Cont., Film Lit.Ind. (1975-), Intl.Ind.TV, Media Rev.Dig.

791.43　　　　　II
MOVIE. (Text in English) 1981. m. 412 Tulsiani Chambers, 212 Nariman Point, Bombay 400 021, India. TEL 22-233124. Ed. Dinesh Raheja. circ. 71,100.

384.55　　　　　US
PN1992.95
MOVIE MARKETPLACE. 1987. bi-m. $19.94 (foreign $24). World Publishing Co. (Subsidiary of: Century Publishing Company), 990 Grove St., Evanston, IL 60201-4370. TEL 708-491-6440. (Subscr. to: Box 401, Mt. Morris, IL 61054-0401) Ed. Robert Meyers. adv.; circ. 125,000.
　　Formerly (until Aug. 1990): Video Marketplace (ISSN 0895-2892)
　　Description: Includes feature articles, and video listings of over 2,500 titles available for direct purchase.

791.43　　US　ISSN 0027-271X
MOVIE MIRROR. 1957. bi-m. $9. Sterling's Magazines, Inc., 355 Lexington Ave., New York, NY 10017. TEL 212-949-6850. Ed. Joan Goldstein. adv.; bk.rev.; film rev.; record rev.

791.43　　SI　ISSN 0027-2736
MOVIE NEWS. 1948. m. S.$30. Chinese Pictorial Review Ltd., Shaw Centre, Scotts Rd., Singapore 9, Singapore. Ed. C.Y. Chan. film rev.; index; circ. 20,000. (processed; avail. on records)

791　　JA　ISSN 0047-8288
MOVIE - T V MARKETING. (Text in English) 1953. m. 30000 Yen. Movie - TV Marketing, Box 30, Central Post Office, Tokyo 100-91, Japan. TEL 03-3583-2855. FAX 03-3583-9549. TELEX J26864. Ed. Asia M. Ireton. adv.; circ. 100,000.
　　Former titles (1962-1966): Movie Marketing; (1953-1961): Far East Film News (ISSN 0425-7111)

791　　JA　ISSN 0085-3577
MOVIE - T V MARKETING GLOBAL MOTION PICTURE YEAR BOOK. (Text in English) 1955. a. 10000 Yen. Movie - TV Marketing, Box 30, Central Post Office, Tokyo 100-91, Japan. TEL 03-3587-2855. FAX 03-3583-9549. TELEX J26864. Ed. Asia M. Ireton. adv.; circ. 100,000. (also avail. in microform from UMI)

384.55　　US　ISSN 0278-5013
PN1992
MOVIE - VIDEO AGE INTERNATIONAL. 1981. 8/yr. $25. T V Trade Media Inc., 216 E. 75th St., Ste. 1W, New York, NY 10021. TEL 212-288-3933. Ed. Dom Serafini. adv.; circ. 15,000.

791.43　　US　ISSN 1055-0917
MOVIELINE. 1989. m. $15. Movieline, Inc., Attn.: B.L. Shepherd, Circ. Dir., 1141 S. Beverly Dr., Los Angeles, CA 90035. TEL 213-282-0711. Eds. Virginia Campbell, Edward Margulies. adv.; bk.rev.; circ. 100,000.
　　Description: Highlights lifestyles of film and movie makers.

791.43　　　　　US
MOVIES U S A. 1988. m. $18. Movies U S A Inc., 1100 Northmeadow Pkwy., 110, Roswell, GA 30076. TEL 404-664-1133. FAX 404-396-8373. Ed. Noe Goldwasser. adv.; circ. 1,000,000.

778.5　　　　　US
MOVIETONE NEWS.* 1971. 10/yr. $7 to individuals; institutions $10. Seattle Folklore Society, 6556 Palatine Ave., N., Seattle, WA 98103. TEL 206-782-0505. Ed. Richard T. Jameson. adv.; bk.rev.; film rev.; index; circ. 1,000. (back issues avail.) **Indexed:** Film Lit.Ind., Intl.Ind.TV.

MULTI - IMAGES. see *ADVERTISING AND PUBLIC RELATIONS*

778.5　　　　　US
N A R M C HIGHLIGHTS. 8/yr. membership. National Association of Regional Media Centers, Grant Woods AEA, 4401 Sixth St., S.W., Cedar Rapids, IA 52404. TEL 319-399-6741. Ed. Jerry Cochrane.
　　Description: Provides coverage of current activities in different states' centers.

791.43　647.968　US　ISSN 0279-120X
N A T O NEWS & VIEWS. 1967. m. $50. National Association of Theatre Owners, 4605 Lankershim Blvd., No. 340, N. Hollywood, CA 91602. TEL 818-506-1778. FAX 818-506-0269. Ed. Jim Kozak. circ. 3,000.
　　Formerly: N A T O Flash Bulletin.

791.43　　　　　NE
N F M - PROGRAMMA. 1970. m. membership. Stichting Nederlands Filmmuseum, Vondelpark 3, 1071 AA Amsterdam, Netherlands. TEL 020-5891400. FAX 020-6833401. bk.rev.; film rev.; bibl.; illus.; circ. 17,500.
　　Former titles (until 1991): N F M Programmakrant (ISSN 0922-3207); (until 1988): Filmmuseum Cinematheek Journal; (until 1974): Filmmuseum-Cinematheek (ISSN 0016-2639)
　　Description: Includes a daily program of films shown at the museum, with brief film descriptions and discussion of program themes.

791.43　　　　　NE
▼**N F M - THEMAREEKS.** 1991. 9/yr. fl.45 to non-members. Stichting Nederlands Filmmuseum, Vondelpark 3, 1071 AA Amsterdam, Netherlands. TEL 020-5891400. FAX 020-6833401. circ. 1,250.
　　Description: In-depth original articles and translations on specific film themes, directors or genres.

791.43　　　　　NZ
N Z FILM. 1980. 3/yr. New Zealand Film Commission, P.O. Box 11-546, Wellington, New Zealand. TEL 4-385-9754. FAX 64-4-384-9719. TELEX NZ-30386. circ. 4,000.
　　Description: Presents a summary of production information about New Zealand movies.

791.43　　　　　II
NANA FILM WEEKLY. (Text in Malayalam) w. R. Krishnaswamy Memorial Building, Lekshminada, Kollam 691 013, Kerala, India. TEL 3377. TELEX 0886-296 RKAY. Ed. B.A. Rajakrishnan. circ. 63,200.

NATIONAL ASSOCIATION OF PERFORMING ARTS MANAGERS AND AGENTS. NEWSLETTER. see *THEATER*

NATIONAL FILM AND SOUND ARCHIVE NEWSLETTER. see *SOUND RECORDING AND REPRODUCTION*

791.43　　　　　IR
NATIONAL FILM ARCHIVE OF IRAN. BULLETIN. (Text in English) 1989. q. free. National Film Archive of Iran - Film-khane-ye Melli-e Iran, P.O. Box 5158, Teheran 11365, Iran. TEL 021-311242. TELEX 215462 RECU IR. Eds. Mohammad Hassan Khosnevis, Fereydoun Khameneipour. illus.

791.43　　II　ISSN 0042-2444
NAV-CHITRAPAT. (Text in Hindi) 1932. m. Rs.1.50($0.40) per no. Satyendra Shyam, Ed. & Pub., 92 Daryaganj, Delhi, India. adv.; bk.rev.; film rev.; illus.; circ. 27,000. (tabloid format)

NEW ORLEANS REVIEW. see *LITERATURE*

791.43　　US　ISSN 0362-3688
PN1995
NEW YORK TIMES FILM REVIEWS. 1913. biennial. Times Books (Subsidiary of: Random House, Inc.), 201 E. 50th St., New York, NY 10022-7703. TEL 212-751-2600. illus.

778.53　　US　ISSN 0886-6511
NEWS ABOUT THE A - V SCENE. 1980. q. free. South Carolina State Library, 1500 Senate St., Box 11469, Columbia, SC 29211. TEL 803-734-8666. FAX 803-734-8676. Ed. Ronald E. Anderson. circ. 125 (controlled). (processed)

791.43　　　　　US
NEWS REEL.* 1968. m. Federation of Motion Picture Councils, 142 N. Tucker, Memphis, TN 38104. bk.rev.; film rev.; illus. **Indexed:** World Text.Abstr.

MOTION PICTURES 3515

384 US ISSN 0737-3988
NEWSBANK REVIEW OF THE ARTS: FILM AND TELEVISION. 1972. m. (plus q. and a. cum.). price varies. NewsBank, Inc., 58 Pine St., New Canaan, CT 06840-5426. TEL 203-966-1100. FAX 203-966-6254. (microfiche)
●Also available on CD-ROM.

778
NEWSLINE (DEERFIELD). 1985. q. free. Coronet - M T I Film & Video, 108 Wilmot Rd., Deerfield, IL 60015. illus.

778.53 VN
NGHE THUAT DIEN ANH/CINEMATOGRAPHY. 1984. fortn. 65 Tran Hung Dao, Hanoi, Socialist Republic of Vietnam. TEL 52473. Ed. Dang Nhat Minh.

NIKKEI ENTERTAINMENT. see COMMUNICATIONS

NOSTALGIA WORLD; for collector's and fans. see HOBBIES

778.5 IT
NOTE DI TECNICA CINEMATOGRAFICA. q. free. Associazione Tecnica Italiana per la Cinematografia, Viale Regina Margherita 286, 00198 Rome, Italy. Ed. Michele Nesci. adv.; bk.rev.

778.53 RM
NOUL CINEMA. 1963. m. Piata Presei Libere 1, 41917 Bucharest, Rumania. Ed. Adina Darian. circ. 150,000.

NUEVA LENTE; publicacion mensual de fotografia y cine. see PHOTOGRAPHY

791.4 IT
NUOVA GUIDA CINEMATOGRAFICA. 1960. w. (in 5 vols.). L.200000($3) Ente Dello Spettacolo, Via Palombini 6, 00165 Rome, Italy. circ. 6,000.
Formerly: Guida allo Spettacolo (ISSN 0017-5188)
Description: Guide to motion pictures, radio and television.

791.43 IT
NUOVO CINEMA EUROPEO. (Text in English and Italian) 1975. m. L.30000($70) Ideaform, Via Castelfidardo 20, 50137 Florence, Italy. TEL 55-611568. FAX 55-611569. Ed. Paolo di Maira. adv.; circ. 10,000.

OBJEKTIVET. see PHOTOGRAPHY

OCTOBER. see ART

791.43 AU
OESTERREICHISCHE GESELLSCHAFT FUER FILMWISSENSCHAFT, KOMMUNIKATIONS- UND MEDIENFORSCHUNG. MITTEILUNGEN. 1952. bi-m. S.5. Oesterreichische Gesellschaft fuer Filmwissenschaft, Kommunikations- und Medienforschung, Rauhensteingasse 5, A-1010 Vienna, Austria. TEL 5129936. index; circ. 600.
Formerly: Oesterreichische Gesellschaft fuer Filmwissenschaft. Mitteilungen (ISSN 0029-9146)

790.2 AU ISSN 0029-9057
DER OESTERREICHISCHE FILMAMATEUR. 1966. bi-m. S.100. Klub der Kinoamateure Oesterreichs, Neubaugasse 36, A-1070 Vienna, Austria. Ed. Peter Gruber. adv.; bk.rev.; bibl.; circ. 1,500. (looseleaf format)
Description: For the amateur filmmaker.

778.53 US
OFF-HOLLYWOOD REPORT. 8/yr. Independent Feature Project, 21 W. 86th St., New York, NY 10024.
Indexed: Film Lit.Ind. (1989-).

791.43 US
OLD TIME WESTERN FILM CLUB NEWSLETTER. 1970. bi-m. free. Old Time Western Film Club, Box 142, Siler City, NC 27344. Ed. Milo Holt. circ. 500.
Description: Encourages interest in old time Westerns.

051 US
ON LINE.* 1989. m. $9.95. Michaelson Entertainment, 250 W. 89th St., Ste. 114, New York, NY 10024-1751. TEL 212-737-8100. Ed. Orli Low. circ. 250,000.
Description: Examines plot lines of recent movie releases.

791.43 778.59 US
ON LOCATION DIRECTORY; the national film & videotape production directory. 1977. a. $75. On Location Publishing, Box 2910, Hollywood, CA 90078-2910. Ed. Steven Bernard.
Formerly: On Location: Film and Videotape Production Directory.

778.5 621.388 US ISSN 0149-7014
PN1993.5.U6
ON LOCATION MAGAZINE; the film & videotape production magazine. 1977. m. $66. On Location Publishing, Box 2910, Hollywood, CA 90078-2910. TEL 213-467-1268. Ed. Steven Bernard. adv.
Indexed: Film Lit.Ind.

778.5 621.388 US
TR899
ON PRODUCTION. 1950. bi-m. $15 (foreign $23). On Production, Inc., 17337 Ventura Blvd., Ste. 226, Encino, CA 91316. TEL 818-907-6682. Ed. Howard Kunin. adv.; charts; illus.; circ. 17,000.
Indexed: Film Lit.Ind. (1988-).
Formerly (until 1992): American Cinemeditor (ISSN 0044-7625)
Description: Describes in non-engineering terms the latest advances in production and post-production cinema and video.

778.534 US
▼**ON PRODUCTION AND POST-PRODUCTION.** 1992. bi-m. $15. On Production Inc., 17337 Ventura Blvd., Ste. 226, Encino, CA 91316. TEL 818-907-6687. Ed. Howard Kunin. circ. 15,000.
Description: For producers, technicians and film enthusiasts who need to keep current about the production and post-production industry's latest developments. Focuses on news, trends and feature stories covering the production and post-production industries.

ON THE STREET. see MUSIC

778.53 NZ
ONFILM. bi-m. Onfilm Magazine Ltd., P.O. Box 6374, Wellington, New Zealand. Indexed: Film Lit.Ind. (1989-).

791.43 UK
▼**ORIENT EXPRESS.** 1991. q. £6. Astounding Comics, 61 Pyle St., Newport, Isle of Wight PO30 1UL, England. Ed. Kevin Lyons. film rev.; video rev.; illus.
Description: Critical review of cinema from the Far East, including Japanese anime (animation), live action and monster movies, B movies from the Philippines, and Hong Kong productions, with articles on the backgrounds of individual film directors, producers and their productions.

PALMER VIDEO MAGAZINE. see COMMUNICATIONS — Video

PAST TIMES: THE NOSTALGIA ENTERTAINMENT NEWSLETTER. see COMMUNICATIONS — Television And Cable

791.43 100 US
PERSISTENCE OF VISION. 1984. a. $15 to individuals; institutions $20. City University of New York, Film Faculty, c/o Tony Pipolo, Ed., 53-24 63rd St., Maspeth, NY 11378. TEL 718-779-3936. adv.; bk.rev.; circ. 500. (back issues avail.) Indexed: Film Lit.Ind. (1985-), M.L.A.

778.534 384.55 CN
PERSISTENCE OF VISION. 1982. q. membership. Film and Video Arts Society of Alberta, 9722 102nd St., Edmonton, Alta. T5K 0X4, Canada. TEL 403-429-1671. FAX 403-424-0194. circ. 100.
Formerly: F A V A Newsletter.

791.43 II ISSN 0031-6164
PESUM PADAM. (Text in Tamil) 1942. m. Rs.60 (foreign Rs.480). Ramanath Publications Private Ltd., 325 Arcot Rd., Kodambakkam, Madras 600 024, India. Ed. K. Natarajan. adv.; film rev.; circ. 42,000.

PHOTO-CINE-EXPERT (1979); la revue suisse au service des photographes et cineastes. see PHOTOGRAPHY

791.43 US ISSN 0031-8566
PHOTO SCREEN. 1965. bi-m. $6. Sterling's Magazines, Inc., 355 Lexington Ave., New York, NY 10017. TEL 212-949-6850. Ed. Marsha Daly. adv.; illus.

770 791.43 FR
PHOTOMAGAZINE; magazine des photographes et cineastes amateurs. 1920. m. 210 F. (foreign 330 F.). Editions Denis Jacob, 103 bd. St-Michel, 75005 Paris, France. FAX 43-29-14-05. Ed. D.J. Presse. adv.; bk.rev.; film rev.; charts; illus.; mkt.; tr.lit.; index; circ. 100,000.
Former titles: Photocinema; Nouveau Photocinema (ISSN 0398-9372); Photo-Cinema, Film, Amateur-Son (ISSN 0031-8477)

791.43 US ISSN 0031-8833
PHOTON. 1963. irreg. $4. Mark Frank, Ed. & Pub., 801 Ave. C, Brooklyn, NY 11218. adv.; bk.rev.; film rev.; illus.; circ. 40,000. (back issues avail.)

791.43 II
PICTURPOST. (Text in English) 1943. m. 325 Arcot Rd., Madras 600 024, India. TEL 44-422064. Ed. K. Natarajan. circ. 11,000.

PITANJA; mjesecnik: drustvo, znanost, kultura. see LITERATURE

PLAYBACK; Canada's broadcast and production journal. see COMMUNICATIONS — Television And Cable

PLUG; maandelijks informatieblad van het Cultureel Jongeren Paspoort. see THEATER

791.43 FR ISSN 0079-2535
POINTS. FILMS. 1971. irreg. price varies. Editions du Seuil, 27 rue Jacob, 75261 Paris Cedex 06, France.

791.43 FR ISSN 0048-4911
PN1993
POSITIF. m. Societe Nouvelle des Edition Opta, 1 quai de Conti, 75006 Paris, France. Ed.Bd. adv.; bk.rev.; film rev.; illus. Indexed: Arts & Hum.Cit.Ind., Curr.Cont., Film Lit.Ind. (1973-), Intl.Ind.TV, Pt.de Rep. (1981-).
—BLDSC shelfmark: 6558.810000.

POST SCRIPT (COMMERCE); essays in film and the humanities. see HUMANITIES: COMPREHENSIVE WORKS

PRAXIS; a journal of cultural criticism. see ART

791.43 384.55 CN
PREMIERE. 1984. m. Can.$18.95($22.95) Videomania Inc., 1314 Britannia Rd. East, Mississauga, Ont. L4W 1C8, Canada. TEL 416-673-1033. Ed. Salah Bachir. adv.; film rev.; tr.lit.; circ. 17,000. (back issues avail.)

051 US
PREMIERE (NEW YORK). 1987. m. $1.95 per no. Murdoch Magazines (Subsidiary of: News America Publishing, Co.), 200 Madison Ave., New York, NY 10016. TEL 800-289-2489. FAX 212-447-4778. Ed. Susan Lyne. adv.; bk.rev.; circ. 375,000.
Indexed: Film Lit.Ind. (1987-), Mag.Ind.
Description: Fills the gap between scholarly film magazines and fan magazines. Contains interviews, investigative reports, profiles of new and old releases, and behind-the-camera looks at film production.

791.43 FR
PRESENCE DU CINEMA FRANCAIS. (Text in English, French) 1950. 6/yr. 100 F. Editions de l'Expression, 22 rue Plumet, 75015 Paris, France.
FAX 47-39-00-46. (And: French Film Office, 745 5th Ave, New York, NY 10022) film rev.; illus.
Formerly (until 1986): Cinema Francais (ISSN 0041-6746)
Description: Presents reviews of new French film releases. Profiles of actors and actresses as well as salient features pertaining to the film.

778.5 US
PREVIEW THEATER BROCHURE. m. $20. American Film Institute, John F. Kennedy Center for the Performing Arts, Washington, DC 20566. TEL 202-828-4000. film rev.; circ. controlled. (tabloid format)
Formerly: American Film Institute Theater Brochure.

3516 MOTION PICTURES

791.43 800   US   ISSN 0199-9257
P92.U5
PREVUE. Variant title: Mediascene Prevue. 1972. bi-m. $19.95. Box 4489, Reading, PA 19606. TEL 215-370-0666. FAX 215-370-0867. Ed. J. Steranko. adv.; bk.rev.; film rev.; illus.; circ. 240,000. (back issues avail.)
   Formerly (until Aug. 1980): Media Scene.

791.43   II
PRIYA. (Text in Hindi) 1956. m. Rs.1.50($0.40) per no. 92 Daryaganj, Delhi 110 002, India. TEL 11-262472. Ed. Satyendra Smyam. adv.; bk.rev.; film rev.; illus.; circ. 28,000. (tabloid format)
   Formerly (until 1960): Lalita (ISSN 0023-740X)

PRODUCER'S MASTERGUIDE; the international production manual for motion pictures, television, commercials, cable and videotape industries in the United States, Canada, the United Kingdom, Bermuda, the Caribbean Islands, Mexico, Austria, Australia and New Zealand. see BUSINESS AND ECONOMICS — Trade And Industrial Directories

778.5 791 371.3   US
▼**PRODUCERS QUARTERLY.** 1990. q. $12. (Testa Communications) Producers Quarterly Publishing Inc., 25 Willowdale Ave., Port Washington, NY 11050. TEL 516-767-2500. FAX 516-767-9335. Ed. Ken McGorry. adv.; charts; illus.; stat.; tr.lit.; circ. 15,000. (back issues avail.)
   Description: For producers, directors, editors, videographers, composers--all creative people.

778.5 792   UK
PRODUCTION AND CASTING REPORT. 1968. w. £164. P.O. Box 11, London SW15 6AY, England. TEL 081-789-0408. FAX 081-780-1977. (Subscr. to: P.O. Box 100, Broadstairs, Kent CT10 1UJ, England. TEL 0843-860885) Ed. Vaune Craig-Raymond. adv.; circ. 4,000.
   Description: Covers advance production and casting news in the film, television and theater industry.

778   GW   ISSN 0932-0393
PROFESSIONAL PRODUCTION. 1987. m. DM.59. Verlag Gerhard Spiehs, Baeckergasse 10, 8081 Kottgeisering, Germany. TEL 08144-1541. FAX 08144-1496. circ. 4,000.

PROFIFOTO; journal fuer professional photography. see PHOTOGRAPHY

791.43   FI   ISSN 0356-4096
PROJEKTIO. 1960. q. FIM 20. Suomen Elokuvakerhojen Liitto SEKL - Federation of Finnish Film Societies, Yrjonkatu 11 A 5, 00120 Helsinki 12, Finland. Ed. Jukka Vilhunen. adv.; bk.rev.; circ. 5,000.

791.43   GW   ISSN 0341-5910
PUBLIKATIONEN ZU WISSENSCHAFTLICHEN FILMEN. SEKTION ETHNOLOGIE. (Text in English, French or German; summaries in English, French and German) 1963. irreg. Institut fuer den Wissenschaftlichen Film, Nonnenstieg 72, 3400 Goettingen, Germany. FAX 0551-202200. TELEX 96691. Ed. H.K. Galle.
   Formerly: Institut fuer den Wissenschaftlichen Film. Publikationen zu Wissenschaftlichen Filmen. Sektion Voelkerkunde.

791.43 900   GW   ISSN 0341-5937
PN1993
PUBLIKATIONEN ZU WISSENSCHAFTLICHEN FILMEN. SEKTION GESCHICHTE, PUBLIZISTIK. (Text in German; summaries in English, French and German) 1963. irreg. Institut fuer den Wissenschaftlichen Film, Nonnenstieg 72, 3400 Goettingen, Germany. FAX 0551-202200. TELEX 96691. Ed. H.K. Galle.
   Formerly: Publikationen zu Wissenschaftlichen Filmen. Sektion Geschichte, Paedagogik (ISSN 0073-8441)

610 791.43   GW   ISSN 0341-5929
PUBLIKATIONEN ZU WISSENSCHAFTLICHEN FILMEN. SEKTION MEDIZIN. (Text in English, French or German; summaries in English, French and German) 1970. irreg. Institut fuer den Wissenschaftlichen Film, Nonnenstieg 72, 3400 Goettingen, Germany. FAX 0551-202200. TELEX 96691. Ed. H.K. Galle.

791.43   GW   ISSN 0344-9300
PUBLIKATIONEN ZU WISSENSCHAFTLICHEN FILMEN. SEKTION PSYCHOLOGIE, PAEDAGOGIK. (Text in English, French or German; summaries in English, French and German) 1979. irreg. Institut fuer den Wissenschaftlichen Film, Nonnenstieg 72, 3400 Goettingen, Germany. FAX 0551-202200. TELEX 96691. Ed. H.K. Galle.

500 791.43   GW   ISSN 0073-8433
T65.5.M6
PUBLIKATIONEN ZU WISSENSCHAFTLICHEN FILMEN. SEKTION TECHNISCHE WISSENSCHAFTEN, NATURWISSENSCHAFTEN. (Text in English, French or German; summaries in English, French and German) 1963. irreg. Institut fuer den Wissenschaftlichen Film, Nonnenstieg 72, 3400 Goettingen, Germany. FAX 0551-202200. TELEX 96691. Ed. H.K. Galle.

791.43   BG
PURBANI. (Text in Bengali) 1951. w. 1 Ramkrishna Mission Rd, Dhaka 1203, Bangladesh. TEL 2-256503. Ed. Khondker Shahadat Hossain. circ. 22,000.

778.5 384.55   US
PYRAMID FILM AND VIDEO CATALOG. 1960. biennial. free. Pyramid Film & Video, Box 1048, Santa Monica, CA 90406-1048. TEL 213-828-7577. FAX 213-453-9083. TELEX 678262. Ed. Denise Adams. film rev.; circ. 60,000.
   Description: Lists a variety of films and videos distributed by Pyramid.

791.43   IT   ISSN 0393-8379
PN1993
QUADERNI DI CINEMA; bimestrale di cultura e politica cinematografica. 1981. bi-m. L.39000 (foreign L.70000). Via Benedetto Varchi 57, 50132 Florence, Italy. TEL 055-243144. Ed. Gaetano Strazzulla. adv.; bk.rev.; circ. 5,000. (back issues avail.) **Indexed:** Film Lit.Ind. (1985-).

778.5 791.4   US   ISSN 1050-9208
PN1994
QUARTERLY REVIEW OF FILM AND VIDEO. Abbreviated title: Q R F V. 1976. 4/yr. (in 1 vol., 4 nos./vol.). $63. Harwood Academic Publishers, 270 Eighth Ave., New York, NY 10011. TEL 212-206-8900. FAX 212-645-2459. TELEX 236735 GOPUB UR. (Subscr. to: Box 786, Cooper Sta., New York, NY 10276. TEL 800-545-8398; UK subscr. to: P.O. Box 90, Reading, Berkshire RG1 8JL, England. TEL 0734-560-080) Ed. Michael Renov. bk.rev.; index; circ. 1,000. (also avail. in microform from MIM; reprint service avail. from UMI) **Indexed:** Amer.Bibl.Slavic & E.Eur.Stud., Bk.Rev.Ind. (1980-), Chicago Psychoanal.Lit.Ind., Child.Bk.Rev.Ind. (1980-), Curr.Cont., Film Lit.Ind. (1976-), Hum.Ind., Intl.Ind.TV, M.L.A.
   —BLDSC shelfmark: 7206.700000.
   Formerly (until 1989): Quarterly Review of Film Studies (ISSN 0146-0013)
   Refereed Serial

778.5   US
QUORUM QUOTES. 1970. q. membership. International Quorum of Film and Video, Box 2553, Charlottesville, VA 22902. TEL 804-973-4735. FAX 804-973-2761. Ed. Barbara Blair. adv.; bk.rev.; film rev.; illus.; circ. 500.

778.5   DK   ISSN 0109-0631
R F MEDLEMSBLAD. 1980. a. Romansk Filmklub, Roarsvej 18-3 tv, 2000 Copenhagen F, Denmark.
   Formerly: Romansk Filmklub. Medlemsblad (ISSN 0106-214X)

R T S VIDEO GAZETTE. see COMMUNICATIONS — Video

791.43   SU
RAABTA. (Text in Urdu) m. Transcontinental Corp., P.O. Box 9935, Jeddah, Saudi Arabia. TEL 651-3857. circ. 58,000.
   Description: Entertainment and movie news.

791.43   II
RANGBHUMI. (Text in Hindi) 1941. m. 5A-15 Ansari Rd., Darya Ganj, Delhi 110 002, India. TEL 11-274667. Ed. S.K. Gupta. circ. 30,000.

RECHERCHES IBERIQUES ET CINEMATOGRAPHIQUES. see LITERATURE

791   CN   ISSN 0085-543X
PN1995.9.E9
RECUEIL DES FILMS. 1955. a. Can.$14. Office des Communications Sociales, 4005 rue de Bellechasse, Montreal, Que. H1X 1J6, Canada. TEL 514-729-6391. FAX 514-729-7375. adv.; film rev.; circ. 1,500.

791.43   US   ISSN 0034-2238
REEL.* 1968. s-a. membership (avail. upon request to libraries, advertising agencies). Screen Actors Guild, New York Branch, 1515 Broadway, 44th Fl., New York, NY 10036-8901. Ed. Elizabeth Pennell. adv.; charts; illus.; circ. 12,000.

778   US
RELEASE PRINT. 10/yr. Film Arts Foundation, 346 Ninth St., 2nd Fl., San Francisco, CA 94103. TEL 415-552-8760. Ed. Robert Anbian. circ. 3,000.

778.5 791.43   US
REMINDER LIST OF ELIGIBLE RELEASES; annual Academy awards for distinguished achievements. a. $5. Academy of Motion Picture Arts and Sciences, 8949 Wilshire Blvd., Beverly Hills, CA 90211-1972. TEL 213-247-3000. FAX 213-859-9351. Ed. Byerly Woodward.
   Description: List of films with cast that are eligible for Academy awards consideration.

791.43   RU   ISSN 0034-4648
REPERTUAR KHUDOZHESTVENNOI SAMODEYATEL'NOSTI. 1955. s-m. $10.20. Izdatel'stvo Iskusstvo, Vorotnikovskii per. 11, Moscow, Russia. Ed. L. Gamazova. circ. 55,000.

791.43   BE   ISSN 0774-0115
PN1993.5.B4
REVUE BELGE DU CINEMA. (Text in French) 1963. q. 900 BEF (foreign 2300 BEF). A P E C, 73, av. des Coccinelles, B-1170 Brussels, Belgium. TEL 02-672-94-59. Ed. J. Debacker. illus.; circ. 2,000. (back issues avail.) **Indexed:** Film Lit.Ind. (1974-).

778.5   CN   ISSN 0843-6827
PN1993.5.C2
REVUE DE LA CINEMATHEQUE. (Text in French) 1989. 5/yr. $15 for 2 yrs. Cinematheque Quebecoise, 335 bd. de Maisonneuve E., Montreal, Que. H2X 1K1, Canada. TEL 514-842-9763. FAX 514-842-1816. Eds. Pierre Veronneau, Pierre Jutras. adv.; illus.; circ. 40,000. (back issues avail.) **Indexed:** Film Lit.Ind. (1989-), Int.Ind.Film Per., Intl.Ind.TV, Media Rev.Dig., Pt.de Rep. (1983-).
   Supersedes: Copie Zero (ISSN 0709-0471)

791.43   IT   ISSN 0035-7081
RIVISTA TECNICA DI CINEMATOGRAFIA; elettroacustica, televisione. (Text in English, French, German and Italian) 1950. s-a. free. Edizione Cinemeccanica S.p.A., Viale Campania 23, Milan, Italy. TEL 02-718941. FAX 02-70100470. TELEX 311364 CINEMC. Dir. Mariarosa Cecchi. adv.; charts; illus.; index; circ. 6,000.

791.43   JA
ROADSHOW. (Text in Japanese) 1972. m. Shueisha Inc., 5-10, 2-chome, Hitotsubashi, Chiyoda-ku, Tokyo 101-50, Japan. Ed. Mantaro Hanami. circ. 350,000.

ROLLING STONE. see MUSIC

778.53   RM
ROMANIAN FILM. irreg. Romaniafilm, 25 Juliu Fucik St., Bucharest, Rumania. **Indexed:** Film Lit.Ind. (1978-).

791.43   GW
RONDELL PROGRAMM. 1983. bi-m. Freizeitung Rondell, Lewitstr. 2b, D-4000 Dusseldorf 11, Germany. TEL 0211-588915. circ. 7,500.

778   US
RUTGERS FILMS IN PRINT SERIES. 1982. irreg., latest 1991. price varies. Rutgers University Press, 109 Church St., New Brunswick, NJ 08901. TEL 908-932-7399. FAX 908-932-7039. (Dist. by: Rutgers University Press Distribution Center, Box 4869, Hampden Sta., Baltimore, MD 21211. TEL 410-516-6947) Ed.Bd. film rev.

MOTION PICTURES 3517

778 621.385 SA
S A F T T A NEWSLETTER. bi-m. membership. South African Film and Television Technicians Association - Suid-Afrikaans Film- en Televisietegnici Associasie, No. 3 Ithaca Court, 18 Main Rd., Melville, P.O. Box 91625, Auckland Park 2006, South Africa. TEL 011-726-6924. FAX 011-726-7785. Ed. Nicola Munro. adv.; illus.; stat.
Description: Provides professional and social information for members.

791.43 AT ISSN 0036-1135
S C J.* (Sydney Cinema Journal) q. Aus.$3.50. c/o Ken Quinell & Michael Thornhill, Eds., Box 4430, Sydney, N.S.W., Australia. adv.; film rev.; illus.

791.4 US ISSN 0036-1682
TR845 CODEN: SMPJDF
S M P T E JOURNAL. 1916. m. $65. Society of Motion Picture and Television Engineers, 595 W. Hartsdale Ave., White Plains, NY 10607-1824. TEL 914-761-1100. FAX 914-761-3115. TELEX 4995348. Ed. Jeffrey B. Friedman. adv.; bk.rev.; abstr.; bibl.; illus.; index, cum.index every 5 yrs.; circ. 10,500. (also avail. in microform from UMI; reprint service avail. from UMI) **Indexed:** A.S.& T.Ind., Appl.Mech.Rev., ASCA, Chem.Abstr., Curr.Cont., Eng.Ind., Excerp.Med., Film Lit.Ind. (1973-), Graph.Arts Lit.Abstr., Photo.Abstr., Sci.Abstr.
—BLDSC shelfmark: 8313.080000.
Refereed Serial

778.5 DK
SAERRAKKE. 1978. irreg. (approx. 1/yr.). price varies. Koebenhavns Universitet, Institut for Film, TV og Kommunikation, 78 Njalsgade, DK-2300 Copenhagen S, Denmark. TEL 31-542211. FAX 31-955828.
Supersedes in part (as of 1978): Koebenhavns Universitet. Institut for Filmvidenskab. Skrifter.

791.43 384.55 US
SAN JOSE FILM & VIDEO COMMISSION DIRECTORY. 1981. a. free to industry personnel; students $5. San Jose Film & Video Commission, 333 W. San Carlos, Ste. 1000, San Jose, CA 95110. TEL 408-295-9600. FAX 408-295-3937.
Formerly: Best Performance Film and Video Directory.

SANTA ANA MOUNTAIN SERIES. see *HISTORY — History Of North And South America*

791.43 CE
SARASAVIYA. (Text in Sinhala) 1963. w. Lake House, D.R. Wijewardene Mawatha, P.O. Box 1168, Colombo 10, Sri Lanka. TEL 1-21181. Ed. Granville Silva. circ. 56,000.

778.53 US
▼**SCENE**; at the movies. 1990. m. $12. Scene, Inc., 930 Fifth Ave., New York, NY 10021. TEL 212-737-8100. adv.; circ. 75,000 (controlled).
Description: Covers new movies, actors and actresses, producers and directors.

791.43 GW
SCHMALFILM; die Zeitschrift fuer Filmamateure. 1948. 6/yr. DM.76.80. Fachverlag Schiele und Schoen GmbH, Markgrafenstr. 11, 1000 Berlin 61, Germany. TEL 030-251-6029. FAX 030-2517248. TELEX 181470-SUNDS-D. Ed. R. Rendez-Voigt. adv.; bk.rev.; film rev.; illus.; stat.; mkt.; pat.; tr.mk.; index; circ. 8,644.

SCIENCE FICTION MEDIA; Informationsdienst fuer science fiction and fantasy. see *LITERATURE — Science Fiction, Fantasy, Horror*

791.43 II ISSN 0036-9551
SCREEN. (Text in English) 1951. w. Rs.73. Indian Express Newspapers (Bombay) Pvt. Ltd., Express Towers, Nariman Point, Box 867, Bombay 400 021, India. Ed. Udaya Taranayar. adv.; film rev.; circ. 84,000.

SCREEN. see *EDUCATION — Teaching Methods And Curriculum*

791.43 JA
SCREEN. (Text in Japanese) 1946. m. 14000 Yen. Kindai-Eiga Corp., Owaricho Bldg., 2F, 6-8-3 Ginza, Chuo-kui, Tokyo 104, Japan. TEL 03-5568-2811. FAX 03-5568-2818. Ed. Hisayuki Ui.

SCREEN. see *COMMUNICATIONS — Television And Cable*

SCREEN ACTOR. see *LABOR UNIONS*

778.53 US
SCREEN ACTOR HOLLYWOOD. irreg. Screen Actors Guild, 7065 Hollywood Blvd., Los Angeles, CA 90028-6065. **Indexed:** Film Lit.Ind. (1988-).

791.4 UK ISSN 0307-4617
PN1993.5.G7
SCREEN INTERNATIONAL. 1912. w. $175. International Thomson Business Publishing, 7 Swallow Place, 249-259 Regent St., London W1R 7AA, England. TEL 01-491-9484. Ed. Paul Mungo. adv.; bk.rev.; film rev.; illus.; stat.; circ. 6,500.
Former titles: Screen International and Cinema T V Today; Cinema T V Today.
Description: For senior personnel within the entertainment industry.

791 UK
SCREEN INTERNATIONAL FILM AND T.V. YEARBOOK. 1945. a. £100. International Thomson Publishing Ltd., 7 Swallow Place, 249-259 Regent St., London W1R 7AA, England. TEL 071-491-9484. FAX 071-355-3337. Eds. Oscar Moore, Peter Noble. adv.; illus.; circ. 10,000.
Former titles: International Film and T.V. Yearbook; British Film and T.V. Yearbook (ISSN 0068-1997)

791.43 US ISSN 0080-8288
SCREEN WORLD. 1949. a. $19.95. Crown Publishers, Inc., 201 E. 50th St., New York, NY 10022. TEL 212-254-1600. Ed. John Willis.

778.53 FR
SCRIPT. q. A.F.I.C.C.A., 50 av. Marceau, 75008 Paris, France. **Indexed:** Film Lit.Ind. (1990-).

SCRIPTWRITERS MARKET. see *LITERATURE*

791 IT ISSN 0037-0932
SEGNALAZIONI CINEMATOGRAFICHE. 1934. s-m. L.25000. Ente Dello Spettacolo, Via Palombini 6, 00165 Rome, Italy. film rev.; circ. 35,000.

778.534 IT ISSN 0393-3865
PN1993
SEGNOCINEMA;* rivista cinematografica bimestrale. 1981. 6/yr. L.25000 (foreign L.35000). Cineforum di Vincenza, Via Giovanni Prati 34, 36100 Vicenza, Italy. film rev.; bibl.; illus.; index; circ. 5,000. (back issues avail.) **Indexed:** Film Lit.Ind. (1981-).

778.5 DK ISSN 0106-2484
SEKVENS; filmvidenskabelig aarbog. 1978. a. DKK 85.40. University of Copenhagen, Institut of Political Studies, Rosenborggade 15, DK-1130 Copenhagen K, Denmark. circ. 200.
Supersedes in part: Koebenhavns Universitet. Institut for Filmvidenskab. Skrifter.

778.534 FR ISSN 0996-7109
SEPTIEME ARTIFICE; les arriere-cours de la grande boutique. m. 158 F. Art of Septieme, c/o Nadja de Lesseps, 29, rue Fondary, 75015 Paris, France.

791.43 CN ISSN 0037-2412
PN1993
SEQUENCES. (Text in French) 1955. 5/yr. Can.$26 (foreign $36). 4005 rue de Bellechasse, Montreal, Que. H1X 1J6, Canada. TEL 514-729-6391. FAX 416-477-2821. (Subscr. to: C.P. 444, Outremont, PQ, H2V 9Z9, Canada) Ed. Leo Bonneville. adv.; bk.rev.; film rev.; illus.; cum.index; circ. 3,500. (also avail. in microform from MIM; back issues avail.) **Indexed:** Can.Per.Ind., Film Lit.Ind. (1973-), Intl.Ind.TV, Pt.de Rep. (1979-).

SHANGHAI YISHUJIA/SHANGHAI ARTIST. see *THEATER*

791.4 CC
SHANGYING HUABAO/SHANGHAI FILM STUDIO PICTORIAL. (Text in Chinese) m. $54. (Shanghai Dianying Zhipianchang - Shanghai Film Studio) Shangying Huabao Bianjibu, 52 Yongfu Lu, Shanghai 200031, People's Republic of China. TEL 4375215. (Dist. in US by: China Books & Periodicals, Inc., 2929 24th St., San Francisco, CA 94110. TEL 415-282-2994)

791.43 CC
SHIJIE DIANYING/WORLD FILMS. (Text in Chinese) bi-m. Zhongguo Dianyingjia Xiehui - China Film Makers Association, 22 Beisihuan Donglu, Beijing 100013, People's Republic of China. TEL 4219977.

791.43 US
SHOOT COMMERCIAL PRODUCTION DIRECTORY. 1965. a. $40. 330 W. 42nd St., New York, NY 10036. TEL 212-947-0020. FAX 212-967-6786. Ed. Theresa Piti. adv.; circ. 7,000.
Formerly: Back Stage Film - Tape Syndication Directory.
Description: B P I Communications, Inc.

791.43 UK ISSN 0037-4806
PN1993
SIGHT AND SOUND; the international film quarterly. 1932. m. £25. British Film Institute, 21 Stephen St., London W1P 1PL, England. TEL 071-636-3289. FAX 071-580-9456. TELEX 27624-BFILDNG. (Subscr. to: Tower Publishing Services, 3-4 Hardwick St., London EC1R 4RY, England. TEL 071-837-7765; U.S. subscr. to: Eastern News Distributors Inc., 1671 E. 16th St., Ste. 176, Brooklyn, NY 11229-2901) Ed. Philip Dodd. adv.; bk.rev.; film rev.; illus.; index; circ. 35,000. (also avail. in microform from MIM,WMP) **Indexed:** Acad.Ind., Art Ind., Arts & Hum.Cit.Ind., Bk.Rev.Ind. (1976-), Br.Hum.Ind., Child.Bk.Rev.Ind. (1976-), Curr.Cont., Film Lit.Ind. (1973-), Gdlns., Hum.Ind., Int.Ind.Film Per., Intl.Ind.TV, Media Rev.Dig., Mid.East: Abstr.& Ind.
—BLDSC shelfmark: 8275.270000.
Incorporates: Monthly Film Bulletin (ISSN 0027-0407)
Description: An independent, critical magazine presenting reviews, interviews, features on the film industry and more.

371 791 016 US ISSN 0037-4830
LB1044.Z9
SIGHTLINES (NILES). 1967. q. $16 to individuals; institutions $20. American Film & Video Association, Inc., Box 48659, Niles, IL 60648-0659. TEL 708-698-6440. FAX 708-823-1561. TELEX 403681 AFVA. Ed. Ms. Ray Rolff. adv.; bk.rev.; film rev.; video rev.; illus.; cum.index: vols. 1-7, 8-11; circ. 2,500. (also avail. in microform from UMI; back issues avail.; reprint service avail. from UMI) **Indexed:** Film Lit.Ind. (1973-), Lib.Lit., Media Rev.Dig.
Formed by the merger of: Filmlist (ISSN 0015-1602); E F L A Bulletin; Film Review Digest.

SILVER SCREEN. see *BUSINESS AND ECONOMICS — Investments*

778 BN ISSN 0587-0054
SINEAST/FILM MAKER; filmski casopis. (Text in Serbo-Croatian) 1967. q. $15. Kino Savez Bosne i Hercegovine, Strosmajerova 1-II, 71000 Sarajevo, Bosnia Hercegovina. TEL 071 217-002. (Co-sponsor: SIZ Kinematografije Bosne i Hercegovine) Ed. Nikola Stojanovic. adv.; bk.rev.; film rev.; cum.index: 1967-1983; circ. 2,000. (back issues avail.)
Description: Discusses film history, film makers, film events.

791.43 IT
SIPARIO.* 1946. m. L.30000. Sipario Editrice S.R.L., Via Gaffurio 2, 20124 Milan, Italy. Ed. Giacomo de Santis. adv.; circ. 23,000. **Indexed:** M.L.A.

791.43 IS ISSN 0334-6943
SIRATIM; magazine of cinema and television. (Text in Hebrew) q. Tel Aviv University, Faculty of Cinema Arts, 24 Bazel St., Tel Aviv, Israel. TEL 03-441889.

791.43 NE
SKOOP. vol.13, no.10, 1978. 8/yr. fl.49.50. Stichting Skoop, Box 5555, 1007 AN Amsterdam, Netherlands. Eds. Charles Boost, Wim Verstappen, Rogier Proper. adv.; bk.rev.; film rev.; charts; illus.; circ. 11,000. **Indexed:** Film Lit.Ind. (1973-), Intl.Ind.TV.
Formerly: Skoop Films en Filmers; Skoop Kritisch Filmblad.

778.5 384.55 770 NE
SKRIEN. 1968. 6/yr. fl.55 (foreign fl.82). (Ministerie van Welzijn, Volksgezondheid en Cultuur, Afdeling Film) Stichting Openbaar Kunstbezit, Vondelstraat 120, 1054 GS Amsterdam, Netherlands. TEL 020-854511. FAX 020-834655. Ed. Mart Dominicus. adv.; bk.rev.; film rev.; circ. 5,000. **Indexed:** Film Lit.Ind. (1973-), Intl.Ind.TV.

778.534
SMALFILM. 10/yr. Danmarks Filmamatoerer, c/o Erik Bald, Skt. Kjeldsgade 12, 2100 Copenhagen OE, Denmark. adv.; circ. 5,500.

MOTION PICTURES

778.5 384.55 DK ISSN 0107-8119
SMALFILM OG VIDEO. vol.40, nos.5-6, 1981. m. DKK 60. Danmarks Filmamatoerer, Postboks 82, 2800 Lyngby, Denmark. illus.

SMASH HITS MAGAZINE. see *MUSIC*

SMASH MAGAZINE. see *MUSIC*

778.534 SP
SOCIEDAD DE ESTUDIOS VASCOS. CUADERNOS DE SECCION. CINEMATOGRAFIA. 1986. irreg. Eusko Ikaskuntza, S.A., Legazpi, 10-1, 20004 Donostia-San Sebastian, Spain. TEL 425111.

SOUNDTRACK! INCORPORATING CINEMASCORE. see *MUSIC*

791.43 RU ISSN 0038-5395
PN1993.5.R9
SOVIET FILM/SOVETSKII FIL'M. (Editions in Arabic, English, French, German, Russian and Spanish) 1957. m. $5.50. Izdatel'stvo Pravda, Ul. Pravdy, 24, Moscow 125047, Russia. Ed. Armen Medvedev. illus.; index. **Indexed:** Arts & Hum.Cit.Ind., Curr.Cont., Film Lit.Ind. (1974-).

SPECIAL EFFECTS & STUNTS GUIDE. see *BUSINESS AND ECONOMICS — Trade And Industrial Directories*

778.53 384.55 US
SPECTATOR (LOS ANGELES). irreg. University of Southern California, School of Cinema - Television, University Park, Los Angeles, CA 90089-2211. **Indexed:** Film Lit.Ind. (1985-).

SPECTATOR (RALEIGH); at home. see *ART*

SPETTACOLO; rassegna economica e sociale degli spettacoli e delle attivita artistiche e culturali. see *THEATER*

791.43 GW ISSN 0071-4933
SPIELFILMLISTE. 1958. a. DM.10. Institut Jugend, Film, Fernsehen, Pfaelzer-Wald-Str. 64, 8000 Munich 90, Germany. Ed. Hans Strobel. adv.; circ. 3,500.
Formerly: Filmliste.

778.5 AT
SPROCKET. 1966. irreg. membership. International Film Theatre, Box 90, Subiaco, W.A. 6008, Australia. TEL 09-458-8641. circ. 300.

778.5 CE
SRI LANKA FILM ANNUAL. (Text in Sinhalese) no. 28, 1975. a. Rs.6.95. National Catholic Film Office, St. Phillip Neri's Church, Katukurunda, Kalutara, Sri Lanka. film rev.

STAGECAST-IRISH STAGE AND SCREEN DIRECTORY. see *THEATER*

791.43 II ISSN 0038-9862
STAR & STYLE. 1965. fortn. Rs.260. Eve's Weekly Ltd., J.K. Somani Bldg., Bombay Samachar Marg, Bombay 400 023, India. Ed. Mrs. Gulshan Ewing. circ. 87,000.

791.43 780
STAR GUIDE; where to contact movie, TV stars and other celebrities. 1987. a. $12.95. Axiom Information Services, Box 8015, Ann Arbor, MI 48107. TEL 313-761-4842. Ed. Terry Robinson. circ. 8,000.

STAR TREK: THE OFFICIAL FAN CLUB MAGAZINE. see *COMMUNICATIONS — Television And Cable*

STARLOG; magazine of the future. see *COMMUNICATIONS — Television And Cable*

778.534 BE ISSN 0776-0698
STARS. (Text in French) 1988. q. 600 Fr. (foreign 700 Fr.). A.S.B.L. Grand Angle-Opvac, Rue d'Arschot 29, B-5660 Mariembourg, Belgium. TEL 060-312168. FAX 060-312937. Ed. Jacques Noel. adv.; bk.rev.; film rev.; illus.; circ. 1,000. **Indexed:** Film Lit.Ind. (1990-).
Description: Covers the lives and careers of stars and other actors in the film industry.

791.43 GW
▼**STARS;** Kino, Szene, Musik. 1990. m. DM.100. T und M Verlagsgesellschaft mbH, Eppendorfer Weg 169, 2000 Hamburg 20, Germany. TEL 040-4910015. FAX 040-4904122. Ed. Christoph Meier-Siem. adv.; bk.rev.; film rev.; illus.; circ. 500,000. (tabloid format)

STELLE FILANTI. see *BIOGRAPHY*

STUDII SI CERCETARI DE ISTORIA ARTEI. SERIA TEATRU, MUZICA, CINEMATOGRAFIE/STUDIES AND RESEACH IN ART HISTORY. SERIES: THEATRE, MUSIC, CINEMATOGRAPHY. see *THEATER*

SUN BELT JOURNAL. see *BUSINESS AND ECONOMICS*

SUSHMITA. see *LITERATURE*

791.43 AT
SYDNEY FILM FESTIVAL PROGRAMME. 1954. a. Aus.$12($20) Sydney Film Festival, P.O. Box 25, Glebe, N.S.W. 2037, Australia. FAX 02-692-8793. TELEX 75111. Ed. Paul Byrnes. adv.; film rev.; circ. 4,000. (back issues avail.)

371.3 791.43 NE ISSN 0039-8330
T F C NIEUWS. (Text in Dutch) 1968. 4/yr. free. Technisch Film Centrum, Audiovisuele Media, Arnhemsestraatweg 17, 6881 NB Velp, Netherlands. TEL 085-693111. FAX 085-646818. adv.; film rev.; illus.; circ. 9,000.
Formerly: Visualeiten.

T.G.I.F. CASTING NEWS. see *OCCUPATIONS AND CAREERS*

791.4 US ISSN 0041-4492
T V AND MOVIE SCREEN. 1957. bi-m. $6. Sterling's Magazines, Inc., 355 Lexington Ave., New York, NY 10017. TEL 212-949-6850. Ed. Fran Levine. adv.; bk.rev.; film rev.; record rev.; illus.

T V COLLECTOR. see *COMMUNICATIONS — Television And Cable*

TAKE ONE; the video entertainment newspaper. see *COMMUNICATIONS — Video*

778 US
TALENT MANAGEMENT.* 1981. q. $50. T M Publishing, 917 S. Park St., Owosso, MI 48867-4422. Eds. Ben Campbell, Val Kluge. adv.; bk.rev.; film rev.; play rev.; bibl.; charts; illus.; pat.; tr.lit.; circ. 5,000. (also avail. in video cassette)
Description: Reports news about the motion picture, television and talent industries.

791.4 384.55 FR
TECHNICIEN DU FILM ET DE LA VIDEO; magazine d'information des professionnels du cinema, de la television, et de l'audio-visuel. 1954. m. 350 F. (foreign 450 F.). Editions Dujarric, 33 av. des Champs-Elysees, 75008 Paris, France. TEL 43-59-24-84. FAX 42-25-59-97. (Subscr. to: IF Diffusion, 31 Champs-Elysees, 75008 Paris, France. TEL 42-56-00-19) Ed. Henriette Dujarric. adv.; illus.; tr.lit.
Formerly: Technicien du Film (ISSN 0040-103X)

TECHTRENDS; for leaders in education and training. see *EDUCATION — Teaching Methods And Curriculum*

TEKHNIKA KINO I TELEVIDENIYA. see *COMMUNICATIONS — Television And Cable*

778.5 CN
TELEFILM CANADA ANNUAL REPORT. 1968. a. free. Canadian Film Development Corporation, Telefilm Canada, 600 de la Gauchetiere St. West, 25th Floor, Montreal, Que. H3B 4L2, Canada. TEL 514-283-6363. circ. 3,000.
Formerly: C F D C Annual Report (ISSN 0382-2273)

TELERAMA. see *COMMUNICATIONS — Television And Cable*

790 US
TIAN WAI TIAN/SKY OUTSIDE SKY. (Text in Chinese) m. $35.90. China Books & Periodicals, Inc., 2929 24th St., San Francisco, CA 94110. TEL 415-282-2994. FAX 415-282-0994.

791.43 AG ISSN 0040-7283
TIEMPO DE CINE.* 1960. m. $1.25 per no. Cineclub Nucleo, Lavalle 2016, 8 Piso, Of. 17, Buenos Aires, Argentina. Ed. Hector Vena. adv.; illus.

791.4 II ISSN 0040-7836
PN1993
TIME & TIDE; Indian journal of international films. (Text in English) 1952. fortn. $26. 1 Ansari Rd., Daryaganj, New Delhi 110 002, India. TEL 11-3272046. FAX 11-941111. Ed. Devendra Kumar. adv.; bk.rev.; film rev.; illus.; circ. 11,000. (tabloid format; also avail. in record)
Description: Details festival activities as well as socio-economic and political aspects of the Indian film industry.

791.43 CN
TORONTO FILM SOCIETY. PUBLICATION.* 1948. q. free to members, archives and libraries. Toronto Film Society, c/o Canadian Federation of Film Societies, Dept. of English, University of Saskatchewan, Saskatoon, Sask. S7N 0W0. TEL 416-921-7309. Ed. Barrie Hayne. circ. 1,000. (back issues avail.)
Description: Articles about the film industry and activities of the Society.

778.534 GW
TREFFPUNKT FILM. 1984. m. DM.20. Casablanca Verlag GmbH, Severinstr. 5, 8000 Munich 90, Germany. TEL 089-6925333. FAX 089-6970673. Ed. Peter von Schall. adv.; film rev.; circ. 205,753. (back issues avail.)

791.43 CN ISSN 0826-1210
TRIBUTE GOES TO THE MOVIES. 1984. bi-m. Can.$17.50 (in U.S. Can.$24.50, elsewhere Can.$31.50)(effective Apr. 1991). Tribute Publishing, Inc., 95 Barber Greene Rd., Ste. 201, Don Mills, Ontario M3C 3E9, Canada. TEL 416-445-0544. Ed. Allan Reznik. circ. 300,000 (controlled). (back issues avail.)
Description: Focuses on new movies, actors, and directors in the entertainment business.

ULTIMO (MUENSTER); Muensters Stadtmagazin. see *LITERARY AND POLITICAL REVIEWS*

770 UK ISSN 0267-8497
UNDERCUT. 1981. s-a. £8($30) to individuals; institutions £14. (Arts Council of Great Britain) Undercut, c/o 17 West Grove, London SE10 8QT, England. (Subscr. to: Undercut, c/o 47 George Downing Estate) Ed. Nina Danino. adv.; bk.rev.; circ. 1,000. (back issues avail.) **Indexed:** Film Lit.Ind. (1985-).
Description: Focuses on British artists working on film and video.

791.43 SG ISSN 0253-195X
UNIR CINEMA; revue du cinema africain. (Text in French) no.36, 1973. bi-m. 3000 Fr.CFA. Diocese de Saint-Louis, B.P. 160, Rue Neuville 1, Saint-Louis, Senegal. Ed. Pierre Sagna. adv.; bk.rev.; film rev.; circ. 1,000.

UNIR: ECHO DE SAINT LOUIS. see *LITERATURE*

UNIVERSITA DEGLI STUDI DI PARMA. ISTITUTO DI STORIA DELL'ARTE. CATALOGHI. see *ART*

792 US
UNIVERSITY FILM STUDY CENTER. NEWSLETTER. vol.6, 1976. bi-m. $10. University Film Study Center, c/o Museum Bldg., N52 396, M.I.T., Cambridge, MA 02139. Ed. Nancy Legge. bk.rev.; bibl.; illus.; circ. 2,000.

791.43 MY
UTUSAM FILEM DAN FESHEN. fortn. 46M Jalan Lima, Off Jalan Chan Sow Lin, Kuala Lumpur, Malaysia. TEL 03-487055. Ed. Mustafa Bin Abdul Rahim. circ. 35,000.

778.5 US
V C R AND FILM CATALOG. a. U.S. Information Agency, Television and Film Service, 301 4th St., S.W., Washington, DC 20547.

V R; mensile di videoregistrazione creativa. (Video Registrare) see *COMMUNICATIONS — Video*

VARIETY. see *THEATER*

MOTION PICTURES — ABSTRACTING, BIBLIOGRAPHIES, STATISTICS

791.43 US
VARIETY'S FILM REVIEWS. (In 22 vols.) 1907. biennial. $1750. R.R. Bowker, A Reed Reference Publishing Company, Division of Reed Publishing (USA) Inc., 121 Chanlon Rd., New Providence, NJ 07974. TEL 800-521-8110. FAX 908-665-6688. TELEX 138 755. (Subscr. to: Order Dept., Box 31, New Providence, NJ 07974)

778.53 US
VARIETY'S VIDEO DIRECTORY PLUS. a. $395. R.R. Bowker, A Reed Reference Publishing Company, Division of Reed Publishing (USA) Inc., 121 Chanlon Rd., New Providence, NJ 07974. TEL 908-665-2867. FAX 908-665-6688. (Subscr. to: Order Dept., Box 31, New Providence, NJ 07974. TEL 800-323-3288) (avail. MS-DOS version)
●Available only on CD-ROM.

791.43 US ISSN 0149-1830
PN1993 CODEN: VLTREI
VELVET LIGHT TRAP; review of cinema. 1971. s-a. $17 to individuals; institutions $32 (foreign $30.50). University of Texas Press, Box 7819, Austin, TX 78713. TEL 512-471-4531. FAX 512-320-0668. TELEX 776453 UTEXPRES AUS. Ed.Bd. adv.; bk.rev.; illus.; circ. 522. (also avail. in microform from UMI; reprint service avail. from UMI) **Indexed:** Film Lit.Ind. (1973-), Int.Ind.Film Per.
—BLDSC shelfmark: 9154.302000.
Description: Features critical essays exploring alternative methodological approaches to the analysis of American film. Studies debate about critical theoretical and historical issues.

VERONICA; weekblad voor radio en TV. see COMMUNICATIONS — Television And Cable

778.5 AT ISSN 1036-1839
VICTORIA. STATE FILM CENTRE. FILM VIDEO CATALOGUE. 1954. irreg. Aus.$19.50. State Film Centre of Victoria, 1 Macarthur St., E. Melbourne, Vic. 3002, Australia. Ed.Bd. circ. 6,000.
Former titles (until 1988): Victoria. State Film Centre. New Films and Videotapes (ISSN 0810-4476); Victoria. State Film Centre. New Films.

VIDEO AKTIV. see COMMUNICATIONS — Video

VIDEO MAGAZINE. see COMMUNICATIONS — Video

VIDEO PLUS FILM. see COMMUNICATIONS — Video

VIEWFINDER. see EDUCATION — Teaching Methods And Curriculum

791.43 CN ISSN 0840-4313
VISUAL MEDIA. (Text in English, French) 1972. 5/yr. Can.$45 (US Can.$50, elsewhere Can.$65). Ontario Film Association, Inc., 3-1750 The Queensway, Ste.1341, Etobicoke, Ont. M9C 5HS, Canada. TEL 416-761-6056. Ed. Helen Shaver. adv.; bk.rev.; film rev.; index; circ. 350. (also avail. in microform from MML)
Formerly (until 1988): Newsletter Called Fred (ISSN 0315-6923); **Supersedes:** Ontario Film Association. Bulletin (ISSN 0030-2910)

778.5 IT
VIVILCINEMA. 1985. bi-m. L.5000. Federazione Italiana Cinema d'Essai (FICE), Via dell'Ulivo 6, 50122 Florence, Italy. TEL 055 247 6625. (Co-sponsor: Cooperativa L'Atelier) adv.; bk.rev.; abstr.; bibl.; charts; film rev.; illus.; play rev.; stat.; tr.lit.; circ. 170,000. (tabloid format)
Description: Reviews of the first screening in theatres of films of high artistic standard.

778.5 FR
VIVRE LE CINEMA. 1977. irreg. Editions Jacques Glenat, 6 rue Lieutenant Chanaron, 38000 Grenoble, France. Ed. Gilbert Hus.

VYTVARNICTVO, FOTOGRAFIA, FILM; mesacnik pre zaujmovu umeleckú cinnost. see ART

791.43 US
WESTERNS & SERIALS. 1974. q. $16 (foreign $20). Norman Kietzer, Ed. & Pub., Rt. 1, Box 103, Vernon Center, MN 56090. TEL 507-549-3677. adv.; bk.rev.; circ. 2,000. (back issues avail.)
Former titles: Favorite Westerns; Serial World.
Description: Club magazine for those interested in old westerns and serials.

WHAT'S ON VIDEO AND CINEMA. see COMMUNICATIONS — Video

WHO'S WHO IN CANADIAN FILM AND TELEVISION (YEAR). see BIOGRAPHY

791.43 780 792 US
WHO'S WHO IN ENTERTAINMENT. 1988. biennial, 2nd ed., 1992. $235. Marquis Who's Who, A Reed Reference Publishing Company, Division of Reed Publishing (USA) Inc., 121 Chanlon Rd., New Providence, NJ 07974. TEL 800-521-8110. FAX 908-665-6688. TELEX 138 755. (Subscr. to: R.R. Bowker, Order Dept., Box 31, New Providence, NJ 07974) (also avail. in magnetic tape)
Description: Provides biographical coverage on more than 18,000 movers and shakers of the entertainment industry.

WHO'S WHO ON THE SCREEN. see BIOGRAPHY

778.534 US ISSN 0160-6840
PN1993
WIDE ANGLE; a film quarterly of theory, criticism and practice. 1978. q. $21 to individuals (foreign $27.10); institutions $49 (foreign $56.10). (Athens Center for Film and Video) Johns Hopkins University Press, Journals Publishing Division, 701 W. 40th St., Ste. 275, Baltimore, MD 21211. TEL 410-516-6987. FAX 410-516-6998. Ed. Jeanne Hall. adv.; bk.rev.; film rev.; illus.; index; circ. 949. (also avail. in microform from UMI; back issues avail.) **Indexed:** Arts & Hum.Cit.Ind., Curr.Cont., Film Lit.Ind. (1976-), Int.Ind.Film Per., Intl.Ind.TV, M.L.A., Media Rev.Dig.
—BLDSC shelfmark: 9315.557500.
Description: Presents current scholarship in film studies and examines topics ranging from international cinema to the history and aesthetics of film.

791.43 UK ISSN 0269-2600
WORLD CINEMA. 1986. a. £13.95. Flicks Books, 29 Bradford Rd., Trowbridge, Wilts BA14 9AN, England. TEL 0225-767728. FAX 0225-760418. Ed. Matthew Stevens. bibl.; illus.; stat.; circ. 3,000. (back issues avail.)
—BLDSC shelfmark: 9353.225000.

778.5 384.55 US
WORLDWIDE DIRECTORY OF FILM AND VIDEO FESTIVALS AND EVENTS. 1988. a. $15. Council on International Nontheatrical Events, Inc., 1001 Connecticut Ave., N.W., Ste. 1016, Washington, DC 20036. TEL 202-785-1136. FAX 202-785-4114. Ed. Richard Calkins. circ. 3,000.

791.43 UK ISSN 0043-9452
WRANGLER'S ROOST; a magazine for the B-Western aficionado. 1970. 3/yr. $7.50. Colin Momber Photography, 23 Sabrina Way, Stoke Bishop, Bristol 9, England. adv.; bk.rev.; film rev.; circ. 350. (processed)

WRITERS GUILD OF AMERICA, EAST. NEWSLETTER. see LITERATURE

XIJU YU DIANYING/THEATRE AND CINEMA. see ART

YINGJU XINZUO/NEW FILM AND PLAY SCRIPTS. see LITERATURE

791.43 792 CC
YINGJU YISHU/ART OF FILM AND DRAMA. (Text in Chinese) bi-m. Guangxi Wenhua Ting - Guangxi Bureau of Cultural Affairs, 13 Minzhu Lu, Nanning, Guangxi 530023, People's Republic of China. TEL 27924. Ed. Cai Liyang.

YINGSHI WENXUE/FILM AND TELEVISION LITERATURE. see LITERATURE

791.43 CC
YINMU NEIWAI/AROUND FILM. (Text in Chinese) m. Sichuansheng Dianying Faxing Fangying Gongsi - Sichuan Film Distribution and Projection Company, 21 Qingnian Lu, Chengdu, Sichuan 610016, People's Republic of China. TEL 22921-160.

791.43 792 CS
YOUNG CINEMA AND THEATRE/JEUNE CINEMA ET THEATRE; cultural magazine of the IUS. (Text in English, French and Spanish) q. $4. International Union of Students, 17th November St., P.O. Box 58, 110 01 Prague 1, Czechoslovakia. Ed.Bd. illus. **Indexed:** Film Lit.Ind.

778.53 NO
Z FILMTIDSSKRIFT. 5/yr. Teatergate 3, 0180 Oslo 1, Norway. **Indexed:** Film Lit.Ind. (1986-).

ZEITSCHRIFT FUER URHEBER- UND MEDIENRECHT; Film und Recht. see LAW

778.43 GW ISSN 0724-7656
ZELLULOID. 1978. irreg. (2-4/yr.). DM.18($13) Arbeitsgemeinschaft fuer Medientheorie und -praxis e.V., c/o Filmhaus, Luxemburger Str. 72, D-5000 Cologne 1, Germany. adv.; bk.rev.; circ. 1,000. (back issues avail.) **Indexed:** Film Lit.Ind. (1987-).

ZHONGGUO DIANYING NIANJIAN/CHINA FILM YEARBOOK. see MOTION PICTURES — Abstracting, Bibliographies, Statistics

ZHONGGUO GUANGBO YINGSHI/CHINESE RADIO, FILM AND TELEVISION. see COMMUNICATIONS — Radio

ZHURNAL NAUCHNOI I PRIKLADNOI FOTOGRAFII I KINEMATOGRAFII. see PHOTOGRAPHY

778 US
ZOOMING IN. q. Detroit Producers Association, 1994 Woodward Ave., No. 235, Bloomfield Hills, MI 48013. TEL 313-737-4240. FAX 313-737-8024. Ed. Genie Parker. circ. 1,200.

778.53 CN ISSN 0707-9389
24 IMAGES. (Text in French) 1979. bi-m. Can.$23.54 (US Can.$35). 3781 Rue Laval, Montreal, Que. H2W 2H8, Canada. TEL 514-286-1688. Ed. Claude Racine. circ. 9,000. (back issues avail.) **Indexed:** Film Lit.Ind. (1985-), Pt.de Rep. (1981-).

MOTION PICTURES — Abstracting, Bibliographies, Statistics

BIO-BIBLIOGRAPHIES IN THE PERFORMING ARTS. see THEATER — Abstracting, Bibliographies, Statistics

791 016 UK ISSN 0007-1552
PN1998.A1
BRITISH NATIONAL FILM CATALOGUE. 1963. q. £60. British Film Institute, 21 Stephen St., London W1P 1PL, England. TEL 071-255-1444. FAX 071-508-9456. TELEX 27624-BFILDNG. Ed. Maureen Brown. bibl.; index; circ. 1,000.
Description: Records details of films and videos available for non-theatrical hire or purchase within the UK, including educational and training films, independent productions, documentaries, tv programs and feature films.

791.43 FR
C N C STATISTIQUES. a. Centre National de la Cinematographie, 12 rue Lubeck, 75784 Paris Cedex 16, France. TEL 505-14-40.

791.43 CN ISSN 0380-6294
PN1993.5.C2
CANADA. STATISTICS CANADA. MOTION PICTURE THEATRES AND FILM DISTRIBUTORS. (Catalogue 63-207) (Text in English and French) 1930. a. Can.$20($21) (foreign $21). Statistics Canada, Publications Sales and Services, Ottawa, Ont. K1A 0T6, Canada. TEL 613-951-7277. FAX 613-951-1584. (also avail. in microform from MML)
Description: Covers motion picture theaters, regular and drive-in, film distributors and videotape production, establishments, employment, revenue and expenses, theatre capacity, amusemnts taxes.

791.43 780 US
▼**CELEBRITY BIRTHDAY DIRECTORY.** 1992. a. $4.95. Axiom Information Services, Box 8015, Ann Arbor, MI 48107. TEL 313-761-4842.

778.5 384.55 DK
DENMARK. STATENS FILMCENTRAL. STATISTIK OVER UDLEJNING OG DEPONERING AF 16 MM FILM OG VIDEO I FINANSAARET. 1976. a. Statens Filmcentral, Vestergade 27, 1456 Copenhagen K, Denmark. TEL 45-33-132686. FAX 45-33-130203.
Formerly: Denmark. Statens Filmcentral. Statistik over Udlejning af 16 MM Film i Finansaaret (ISSN 0105-5070)

791.4 US ISSN 0000-0973
LB1044.Z9
EDUCATIONAL FILM & VIDEO LOCATOR. 1978. irreg., 4th ed., 1990-91. $175. (Consortium of College and University Media Centers) R.R. Bowker, A Reed Reference Publishing Company, Division of Reed Publishing (USA) Inc., 121 Chanlon Rd., New Providence, NJ 07974. TEL 800-521-8110. FAX 908-665-6688. TELEX 138 755. (Subscr. to: Order Dept., Box 31, New Providence, NJ 07974)
 Formerly (until 3rd ed., 1986): Educational Film Locator (ISSN 0000-0590)
 Description: Lists films and videos available for rental from the Consortium members. Annotated entries are arranged alphabetically by title, with separate subject, title and audience-level index. Also contains producer-distributor listing and subject indexes.

791.43 778.59 AT ISSN 0811-1235
FILM AND VIDEO ACQUISITIONS; new film and video acquisitions of the National Film and Video Lending Collection. 1983. q. Aus.$35. National Library of Australia, Publications Section, Public Programs, Parkes Place, Canberra, A.C.T. 2600, Australia. TEL 06-262-1365. FAX 06-273-4493. circ. 1,050.

FILM & VIDEO FINDER. see *EDUCATION — Abstracting, Bibliographies, Statistics*

791.43 016 US ISSN 0093-6758
Z5784.M9
FILM LITERATURE INDEX. 1973. q. $300 (foreign $325) includes bound cum.; bound cum. only $110 (foreign $120)(effective July 1991). Film and Television Documentation Center, State University of New York at Albany, Richardson 390C, 1400 Washington Ave., Albany, NY 12222. TEL 518-442-5745. FAX 518-442-5232. bk.rev.; bibl.; circ. 500.
 —BLDSC shelfmark: 3925.800000.

FILM UND FERNSEHEN IN FORSCHUNG UND LEHRE. see *MOTION PICTURES*

778.5 DK ISSN 0106-8180
FILMREGISTRET. 1962. a. DKK 967.10. Bibliotekscentralen, Tempovej 7-11, DK-2750 Ballerup, Denmark. TEL 2-974000. FAX 2-655310.

FILMS: THE VISUALIZATION OF ANTHROPOLOGY. see *ANTHROPOLOGY — Abstracting, Bibliographies, Statistics*

791.43 GW ISSN 0071-4941
FILMSTATISTISCHES TASCHENBUCH. 1957. a. DM.20. Spitzenorganisation der Filmwirtschaft e.V., Langenbeckstr. 9, Postfach 5129, 6200 Wiesbaden, Germany. TEL 06121-17270. FAX 06121-172739. Ed. Johannes Klingsporn. circ. 700.

884.55 US
FLORIDA STATE UNIVERSITY. INSTRUCTIONAL SUPPORT CENTER. FILM AND VIDEO. 1954. biennial. free. Florida State University, Instructional Support Center, Tallahassee, FL 32306-1019. TEL 904-644-2820. FAX 904-644-3783. Ed. Peggy Stewart. circ. 5,000.
 Former titles: Florida State University. Instructional Support Center. Film; Florida State University. Media Services. Motion Pictures; Florida State University. Educational Media Center. Educational Motion Pictures (ISSN 0430-7313)

791 US ISSN 0072-8462
GUIDE TO GOVERNMENT-LOAN FILMS VOLUME 1: THE CIVILIAN AGENCIES. 1969. irreg., 6th ed., 1980. $9.95. Serina Press, 70 Kennedy St., Alexandria, VA 22305. TEL 703-548-4080. Ed. Daniel Sprecher.

478.534 384.55 US
INTERNATIONAL DIRECTORY OF FILM AND T V DOCUMENTATION CENTERS. 3rd, 1988. irreg. $45. (International Federation of Film Archives, Documentation Commission) St. James Press, 845 Penobscot Bldg., 645 Griswold St., Detroit, MI 48226-4232. TEL 800-345-0392. Ed. Frances Thorpe. bk.rev.
 Description: Describes major collections in over forty countries of published and unpublished material relating to television and film.

016.791 791.43 UK ISSN 0000-0388
Z5784.M9
INTERNATIONAL INDEX TO FILM PERIODICALS. 1972. a. £65($120) International Federation of Film Archives (F I A F), 113 Canalot Studios, 222 Kensal Rd., London W10 5BN, England. TEL 081-960 1001. Ed. Michael Moulds. (also avail. in microfiche from IFA)
 —BLDSC shelfmark: 4541.050000.

778.5 016 US ISSN 0363-7778
LB1043.Z9
MEDIA REVIEW DIGEST; the only complete guide to reviews of non-book media. 1970. a. $245. Pierian Press, Box 1808, Ann Arbor, MI 48106. TEL 313-434-5530. FAX 313-434-6409. Ed. Leslie Regan. cum.index.
 Formerly: Multi Media Reviews Index (ISSN 0091-5858)
 Description: Reviews and evaluations of all forms of non-book media appearing in 140 periodicals and reviewing services.

778.5 MX
MEXICO. CENTRO DE INFORMACION TECNICA Y DOCUMENTACION. INDICE DE PELICULAS. a. (Centro de Informacion Tecnica y Documentacion) Servicio Nacional de Adiestramiento Rapido de la Mano de Obra en la Industria, Calzada Atzcapotzalco-la Villa 209, Mexico 16, D.F., Mexico.

338 016 US
N I C E M INDEX TO A V PRODUCERS AND DISTRIBUTORS. (Audio Visual) 1971. a. $75. (National Information Center for Educational Media) Plexus Publishing, Inc., 143 Old Marlton Pike, Medford, NJ 08055-8750. TEL 609-654-4888. FAX 609-654-4309.
 Description: Provides the name, address, phone number and type of media produced and-or distributed of companies and institutions involved in non-print media.

791 371.3 US
NATIONAL UNION CATALOG. AUDIOVISUAL MATERIALS. 1953. q. $100 to N. American libraries; foreign libraries $105. (U.S. Library of Congress) Advanced Library Systems, Inc., 100 Brickstone Sq., Box 246, Andover, MA 01810. TEL 508-470-0610. FAX 508-475-1072. circ. 2,501. (also avail. in microfiche from ALS)
 Former titles: Audiovisual Materials (ISSN 0190-9827); Films and Other Materials for Projection (ISSN 0091-3294); Library of Congress Catalog. Motion Pictures and Filmstrips (ISSN 0041-7807)

PERFORMING ARTS BIOGRAPHY MASTER INDEX. see *THEATER — Abstracting, Bibliographies, Statistics*

PSYCHOLOGICAL CINEMA REGISTER; films and video in the behavioral sciences. see *PSYCHOLOGY — Abstracting, Bibliographies, Statistics*

REFERATIVNYI ZHURNAL. FOTOKINOTEKHNIKA. see *PHOTOGRAPHY — Abstracting, Bibliographies, Statistics*

016 791.4 CN ISSN 0315-7326
SIXTEEN MM FILMS AVAILABLE IN THE PUBLIC LIBRARIES OF METROPOLITAN TORONTO. 1969. irreg. Can.$80. Metropolitan Toronto Library Board, 789 Yonge St., Toronto, Ont. M4W 2G8, Canada. TEL 416-393-7160.

016 371.42 DK ISSN 0900-3479
UDDANNELSE OG ERHVERV KATALOG. 1967. a. free. Raadet for Uddannelses og Erhvervsvejledning, Aebeloegade 7, 2100 Copenhagen OE, Denmark. Ed. Bodit Sneslev. circ. 8,000.

791 371.3 016 US ISSN 0163-7320
PN1998
U.S. COPYRIGHT OFFICE. CATALOG OF COPYRIGHT ENTRIES. FOURTH SERIES. PART 4: MOTION PICTURES AND FILMSTRIPS. 1978. s-a. $5. U.S. Library of Congress, Copyright Office, Washington, DC 20559. TEL 202-783-3238. FAX 202-512-2250. (Dist. by: Supt. of Documents, Box 371954, Pittsburgh, PA 15250) bibl.; index. (microfiche)
 Formerly: U.S. Copyright Office. Catalog of Copyright Entries. Third Series. Parts 12-13. Motion Pictures and Filmstrips (ISSN 0090-8371)

778.53 CC
ZHONGGUO DIANYING NIANJIAN/CHINA FILM YEARBOOK. (Text in Chinese) a. Zhongguo Dianyingjia Xiehui - China Film Association, 15 Beihuan Xilu, Beijing 100082, People's Republic of China. TEL 66-2251. Ed. Cheng Jihua. adv.

MUNICIPAL GOVERNMENT

see *Public Administration–Municipal Government*

MUSEUMS AND ART GALLERIES

069 CN ISSN 0829-4437
A G O NEWS. 11/yr. Art Gallery of Ontario, 317 Dundas St. W., Toronto, Ont. M5T 1G4, Canada. TEL 416-977-0414. FAX 416-979-6646. charts; illus.; circ. 26,000.
 Former titles: Art Gallery of Ontario. The Gallery (ISSN 0709-8413); Art Gallery of Ontario. Coming Events (ISSN 0044-9024)

A M U NEWS. (American Malacological Union, Inc.) see *BIOLOGY — Zoology*

069 500 US ISSN 0147-7889
A S C NEWSLETTER (WASHINGTON). 1973. bi-m. $17 to individuals; institutions $32. Association of Systematics Collections, 730 11th St., N.W., 2nd Fl., Washington, DC 20001. TEL 202-347-2850. Ed. Mike Schauff. adv.; bk.rev.; circ. 1,200.
 —BLDSC shelfmark: 1739.065000.
 Description: Provides news of collections, curatorial positions, funding sources, ASC workshops, jobs, computer-software trends, profiles of member institutions and affiliate societies, biological survey activities, and legislation and regulations affecting systematists.

707.4 069.9 US
A S I POSTEN. 1969. 10/yr. membership. American Swedish Institute, 2600 Park Ave., Minneapolis, MN 55407. TEL 612-871-4907. Ed. Janice M. McElfish. adv.; circ. 7,000. (back issues avail.)
 Supersedes (as of 1982): Happenings; Which superseded: American Swedish Institute. Bulletin.

708 370 500 600 US ISSN 0895-7371
A S T C NEWSLETTER. 1974. bi-m. $30. Association of Science-Technology Centers, 1413 K St., N.W., 10th Fl., Washington, DC 20005. TEL 202-783-7200. FAX 202-783-7207. Ed. Susan McCormick. charts; illus.; circ. 3,000.

069 610 SA ISSN 0379-6531
ADLER MUSEUM BULLETIN. 1975. 3/yr. R.10. Adler Museum of the History of Medicine, P.O. Box 1038, Johannesburg 2001, South Africa. TEL 011-725-2846. (Co-sponsor: Lennon Ltd.) Ed. D.G Moyes. circ. 1,500. (back issues avail.)
 —BLDSC shelfmark: 0681.740000.

069.9 US
AFRICAN AMERICAN MUSEUMS ASSOCIATION. ANNUAL MEETING REPORT. a. African American Museums Association, 1318 Vermont Ave., N.W., Washington, DC 20005.

708.5 IT
AGARTE. (Text in Italian; summaries in English) 1950. 9/yr. free. Galleria Agarte, Via Babuino 124, 00187 Rome, Italy. Ed. Giuseppe Tedesco. illus.; mkt.; circ. 2,000.
 Formerly (until 1989): Medusa (ISSN 0025-8571)

AGENDA. see *ART*

510 JA ISSN 0385-1354
AKITA-KENRITSU HAKUBUTSUKAN KENKYU HOKOKU/AKITA PREFECTURAL MUSEUM. ANNUAL REPORT. (Text in Japanese; summaries in English, Japanese) 1976. a. Akita Prefectural Museum - Akita-kenritsu Hakubutsukan, Ushiroyama, Kanashi Niozaki, Akita-shi, Akita-ken 010-01, Japan.

MUSEUMS AND ART GALLERIES

069 500   JA
AKIYOSHIDAI KAGAKU HAKUBUTSUKAN HOKOKU/AKIYOSHIDAI MUSEUM OF NATURAL HISTORY. BULLETIN. (Text in English or Japanese; summaries in English) 1961. irreg., 1969, no. 6. Akiyoshidai Museum of Natural History - Akiyoshidai Kagaku Hakubutsukan, Akiyoshi, Shuho-cho, Mine-gun, Yamaguchi-ken 754-05, Japan. Ed. M. Ota.
   Formerly: Akiyoshi-dai Science Museum. Bulletin (ISSN 0065-5554)

069   HU   ISSN 0324-542X
ALBA REGIA. (Text in English, French, German) 1960. a. DM.70 or exchange basis. Istvan Kiraly Muzeum, P.O. Box 12, Szekesfehervar 1, Hungary. Ed. J. Fitz. bk.rev. **Indexed:** A.I.C.P.
   —BLDSC shelfmark: 0786.565000.

ALBURY & DISTRICT HISTORICAL SOCIETY. BULLETIN. see HISTORY — History Of Australasia And Other Areas

708   US   ISSN 0002-5739
N650
ALLEN MEMORIAL ART MUSEUM. BULLETIN. 1943. 2/yr. $10 (foreign $12)(effective 1992). Oberlin College, Allen Memorial Art Museum, Oberlin, OH 44074. TEL 216-775-8665. FAX 216-775-8799. Ed. Anne F. Moore. illus.; cum.index: vols.1-30; circ. 2,000. (also avail. in microform from UMI; back issues avail.; reprint service avail. from UMI) **Indexed:** Art Ind., Artbibl.Mod., RILA.
   —BLDSC shelfmark: 2384.700000.
   Description: Scholarly articles on exhibitions and objects from the permanent collection.

708.1   US   ISSN 0065-6410
ALLIED ARTISTS OF AMERICA. EXHIBITION CATALOG. 1914. a. $3. Allied Artists of America, 15 Gramercy Park S., New York, NY 10003. TEL 212-582-6411. adv.; circ. 3,000.

945   IT   ISSN 0569-1346
ALTAMURA. a. membership. Museo Civico, Biblioteca, Palazzo degli Studi, Altamura, Italy. Ed. Celio Sabini. bibl.; illus.

069   GW   ISSN 0440-1417
AM101
ALTONAER MUSEUM IN HAMBURG. NORDEUTSCHES LANDESMUSEUM. JAHRBUCH. 1963. a. DM.40. Altonaer Museum, Museumstr. 23, 2000 Hamburg 50, Germany.

069 500   US
AMERICAN MUSEUM OF NATURAL HISTORY. ANNUAL REPORT. 1870. a. American Museum of Natural History, 79th St. and Central Park W., New York, NY 10024-5192. TEL 212-769-5151. FAX 212-769-5233. Ed. Ann Breen Metcalfe. bibl.; charts; illus.; circ. 5,000.

AMERICAN MUSEUM OF NATURAL HISTORY. BULLETIN. see BIOLOGY — Zoology

069   US
AMERICAN SWEDISH HISTORICAL MUSEUM NEWSLETTER. 1957? q. $25 includes membership. American Swedish Historical Museum, 1900 Pattison Ave., Philadelphia, PA 19145. TEL 215-389-1776. FAX 215-389-7701. Ed. Ann Barton Brown. bk.rev.; illus.; circ. 800. (back issues avail.)
   Formerly (until 1987): Museum Expressen.

069.5   GR   ISSN 0302-1033
ANNALES MUSEI GOULANDRIS; contributiones ad historiam naturalem graeciae et regionis mediterraneae. (Text in English, French, German, Italian and Latin; summaries in English and Greek) 1973. a. $20. Goulandris Natural History Museum, 13 Levidou Str., 14562 Kifissia, Greece. FAX 8080-674. Ed. W.T. Stearn. circ. 1,000. **Indexed:** GeoRef.
   Description: Covers the natural history of Greece and the Mediterranean.

ANNUAL BIBLIOGRAPHY OF MODERN ART. see ART

069.9   US
APPRENTICE. 1983. 2/yr. $35. Rockport Apprenticeshop, Box 539, Rockport, ME 04856. TEL 207-236-6071. Ed. James Mays. bk.rev.; circ. 4,000.

069   GW   ISSN 0402-7817
ARBEITS UND FORSCHUNGSBERICHTE ZUR SAECHSISCHEN BODENDENKMALPFLEGE. 1953. a. price varies. (Landesmuseum fuer Vorgeschichte Dresden) VER Deutscher Verlag der Wissenschaften, Postfach 1216, 1080 Berlin, Germany. Ed. Heinz-Joachim Vogt. **Indexed:** A.I.C.P., Br.Archaeol.Abstr., NAA.

ARBEITSBLAETTER FUER RESTAURATOREN. see ARCHAEOLOGY

ARCHIVES ET BIBLIOTHEQUES DE BELGIQUE/ARCHIEF- EN BIBLIOTHEEKWEZEN IN BELGIE. see HISTORY — History Of Europe

ARCHIVIST. see HISTORY — History Of North And South America

ARGO. see HISTORY — History Of Europe

069 700   US
ARIZONA ARTISTS GUILD NEWS. m. membership. Arizona Artists Guild, 8912 N. 4th St., Phoenix, AZ 85020. Ed. Cathy McCormick. circ. 500.

700   HU   ISSN 0133-6673
ARS DECORATIVA/IPARMUVESZET. (Text in English, German, Hungarian) 1973. a. exchange basis. Iparmuveszeti Muzeum, Hopp Ferenc Keletazsiai Muveszeti Muzeum - Museum of Applied Arts, Ulloi ut 33-37, 1091 Budapest 9, Hungary. FAX 1-117-5880. Ed. Gyula Rozsa. circ. 1,000 (controlled). **Indexed:** Artbibl.Mod.
   —BLDSC shelfmark: 1697.380000.
   Supersedes: Iparmuveszeti Muzeum. Evkonyve.

069   US
ART (NEW YORK). 1988. 3/yr. membership. American Federation of Arts, 41 E. 65th St., New York, NY 10021. TEL 212-988-7700. (And: 2510 Channing Way, Ste. 4, Berkeley, CA 94704-2315) Ed. Nancy Jones. circ. 2,000. (tabloid format; back issues avail.)
   Description: Addresses issues within the museum field.

ART & ARTISTS. see ART

ART AND DESIGN. see ART

708   AT   ISSN 0066-7935
N3948
ART BULLETIN OF VICTORIA. 1968. a. price varies. National Gallery of Victoria, Victoria Arts Centre, 180 St. Kilda Rd., Melbourne, Vic. 3004, Australia. FAX 61-3-6964337. TELEX AA 151258. Ed. Sonia Dean. circ. 2,500. **Indexed:** Artbibl., Aus.P.A.I.S., RILA.
   —BLDSC shelfmark: 1733.369000.
   Supersedes (1959-1966): National Gallery of Victoria. Annual Bulletin.

ART CELLAR EXCHANGE; a service for buying and selling art. see ART

ART DEALERS ASSOCIATION OF AMERICA. DIRECTORY. see BUSINESS AND ECONOMICS — Trade And Industrial Directories

ART DEALERS ASSOCIATION OF AMERICA. UPDATE. see ART

L'ART ET LA MER. see ART

708   CN   ISSN 0082-5018
N910.T6
ART GALLERY OF ONTARIO. ANNUAL REPORT. 1967. a. Art Gallery of Ontario, 317 Dundas St. W., Toronto, Ont. M5T 1G4, Canada. TEL 416-977-0414. FAX 416-979-6646. circ. 2,500.

708   US
ART GALLERY SCENE. Title varies slightly: Art Gallery Exhibition Guide. a. Hollycroft Press, Inc., Box 278, Ivoryton, CT 06442.

708   US
ART HAPPENINGS OF HOUSTON. 1976. 5/yr. $5. Arts Publishing Co., Box 36202, Houston, TX 70036. Ed. Beth Ann Hutko. adv.; circ. 15,000.

708   US   ISSN 0069-3235
N81
ART INSTITUTE OF CHICAGO. MUSEUM STUDIES. 1966-1978; resumed 1984. s-a. $20 to individuals (foreign $27); institutions $32 (foreign $39); members $15 (foreign $22). Art Institute of Chicago, Michigan Ave. at Adams St., Chicago, IL 60603. TEL 312-443-3540. FAX 312-443-0849. Eds. Robert V. Sharp, Michael Sittenfeld. illus.; index; circ. 16,500. (back issues avail.) **Indexed:** Art Ind., Artbibl.Mod., Arts & Hum.Cit.Ind., Avery Ind.Archit.Per., Curr.Cont., RILA.
   —BLDSC shelfmark: 5989.740000.
   Description: Articles pertain to the museum's permanent collection.

ART MONTHLY. see ART

ART NEWS INTERNATIONAL DIRECTORY OF CORPORATE ART COLLECTIONS. see ART

708   US
ART NOW GALLERY GUIDE: BOSTON - NEW ENGLAND EDITION. 1981. m. (except Aug.). $20. Art Now, Inc., 87 Grayrock Rd., Box 5541, Clinton, NJ 08809. TEL 908-638-5255. FAX 908-638-8737. Ed. Lia Kudless. adv.; circ. 7,000.
   Former titles: Art Now: Boston and New England Gallery Guide; Art Now: Boston Gallery Guide.
   Description: Information about exhibitions at galleries and museums, plus gallery-area maps.

708   US
ART NOW GALLERY GUIDE: CHICAGO - MIDWEST EDITION. 1981. m. (except Aug.). $20. Art Now, Inc., 87 Grayrock Rd., Box 5541, Clinton, NJ 08809. TEL 908-638-5255. FAX 908-638-8737. Ed. Valerie Frasca. adv.; circ. 14,000.
   Formerly: Art Now: Chicago and Midwest Gallery Guide; Formed by the merger of (1981-1982): Art Now: Midwest Gallery Guide; (1980-1982): Art Now: Chicago Gallery Guide.
   Description: Information about exhibitions at galleries and museums, plus gallery-area maps.

069.5   US
ART NOW GALLERY GUIDE: INTERNATIONAL EDITION. 1982. m. (except Aug.). $35. Art Now, Inc., 87 Grayrock Rd., Box 5541, Clinton, NJ 08809. TEL 908-638-5255. FAX 908-638-8737. Ed. Bernice Shor. adv.; circ. 5,000.
   Former titles: Art Now Gallery Guide: National Edition; Art Now: U S A - National Art Museum and Gallery Guide (ISSN 0745-5720)
   Description: Information about exhibitions at galleries and museums across the US and Europe, plus gallery-area maps.

708.1   US
ART NOW GALLERY GUIDE: NEW YORK EDITION. 1969. m. (except Aug.). $30. Art Now, Inc., 87 Grayrock Rd., Box 5541, Clinton, NJ 08809. TEL 908-638-5255. FAX 908-638-8737. Ed. Bernice Shor. adv.; circ. 35,000.
   Former titles: Art Now: New York Gallery Guide; Art Now Gallery Guide.
   Description: Information about exhibitions at galleries and museums, plus gallery-area maps.

708   US
ART NOW GALLERY GUIDE: PHILADELPHIA EDITION. 1981. m. (except Aug.). $20. Art Now, Inc., 87 Grayrock Rd., Box 5541, Clinton, NJ 08809. TEL 908-638-5255. FAX 908-638-8737. Ed. Lia Kudless. adv.; circ. 7,500.
   Formerly: Art Now: Philadelphia Gallery Guide.
   Description: Information about exhibitions at galleries and museums, plus gallery-area maps.

069.5   US
ART NOW GALLERY GUIDE: SOUTHEAST EDITION. 1983. m. (except Aug.). $20. Art Now, Inc., 87 Grayrock Rd., Box 5541, Clinton, NJ 08809. TEL 908-638-5255. FAX 908-638-8737. Ed. Valerie Frasca. adv.; circ. 7,000.
   Formerly: Art Now: Southeast Gallery Guide.
   Description: Information about exhibitions at galleries and museums, plus gallery-area maps.

MUSEUMS AND ART GALLERIES

708   US
ART NOW GALLERY GUIDE: SOUTHWEST EDITION. 1981. m. (except Aug.) $20. Art Now, Inc., 87 Grayrock Rd., Box 5541, Clinton, NJ 08809. TEL 908-638-5255. FAX 908-637-8787. Ed. Susan Housewart. adv.; circ. 6,000.
    Former titles: Art Now: Southwest Gallery Guide; Art Now: Texas, Arizona, New Mexico Gallery Guide.
    Description: Information about exhibitions at galleries and museums, plus gallery-area maps.

708   US
ART NOW GALLERY GUIDE: WEST COAST EDITION. 1983. m. (except Aug.). $20. Art Now, Inc., 87 Grayrock Rd., Box 5541, Clinton, NJ 08809. TEL 908-638-5255. FAX 908-638-8737. Ed. Susan Housewart. adv.; circ. 12,000.
    Former titles: Art Now Gallery Guide: California - Northwest Edition; Art Now: California and Northwest Gallery Guide; Formed by the merger of (1980-1983): Art Now: California Gallery Guide; Art Now: Northwest Gallery Guide.
    Description: Information about exhibitions at galleries and museums, plus gallery-area maps.

ARTIFACTS (COLUMBIA). see *ART*

ARTISTS REVIEW ART. see *ART*

069 700   US
ARTSFOCUS. 1968. bi-m. membership. Colorado Springs Fine Arts Center, 30 W. Dale St., Colorado Springs, CO 80903. TEL 303-634-5581. Ed. Margaret Lew. circ. 4,000. (back issues avail.)
    Description: Covers exhibitions, performing arts series, libraries, art schools, and volunteer and staff activities.

069   FR
ASSOCIATION GENERALE DES CONSERVATEURS DE MUSEES ET COLLECTIONS PUBLIQUES DE FRANCE. ANNUAIRE. 1960. biennial. 150 F. Editions Person, 34 rue de Penthievre, 75008 Paris, France. adv.

069   UK   ISSN 0142-887X
ASSOCIATION OF INDEPENDENT MUSEUMS BULLETIN. 1977. 6/yr. £20. Association of Independent Museums, c/o Park Cottage, West Dean, Chichester, West Sussex PO18 ORX, England. TEL 0243-63364. adv.; bk.rev.; circ. 1,500.

069   CN   ISSN 0849-5858
ASSOCIATION OF MANITOBA MUSEUMS. NEWSLETTER. 6/yr. Association of Manitoba Museums, 422 - 167 Lombard Ave., Winnipeg, Man. R3B 0T6, Canada. bk.rev.; circ. 350.

591 594   NZ   ISSN 0067-0456
                               CODEN: BUKIAN
AUCKLAND INSTITUTE AND MUSEUM. BULLETIN. 1941. irreg., no.14, 1984. price varies. Auckland Institute and Museum, Private Bag, Auckland 1, New Zealand. FAX 64-9-799-956. Ed. Nigel Prickett. (back issues avail.) **Indexed:** A.I.C.P., Biol.Abstr., GeoRef.

069.7   NZ   ISSN 0067-0464
Q93   CODEN: RAUIA7
AUCKLAND INSTITUTE AND MUSEUM. RECORDS. 1930. a. price varies. Auckland Institute and Museum, Private Bag, Auckland 1, New Zealand. FAX 64-9-799-956. Ed. Nigel Prickett. index; circ. 300. (back issues avail.) **Indexed:** Biol.Abstr., Deep Sea Res.& Oceanogr.Abstr., GeoRef., Ind.N.Z.Per., So.Pac.Per.Ind.
    —BLDSC shelfmark: 7314.000000.

AUSTRALIAN COLLECTOR'S QUARTERLY. see *ANTIQUES*

AUSTRALIAN DOLL DIGEST; the magazine for the doll collector. see *ANTIQUES*

069.7   AT   ISSN 0067-1975
QH1   CODEN: RAUMAJ
AUSTRALIAN MUSEUM, SYDNEY. RECORDS. (Supplement avail.) 1890. 3/yr. Aus.$100. Australian Museum, P.O. Box A285, Sydney, N.S.W. 2000, Australia. FAX 02-339-8313. Ed. J.K. Lowry. **Indexed:** AESIS, Biol.Abstr., Deep Sea Res.& Oceanogr.Abstr., GeoRef.
    —BLDSC shelfmark: 7315.000000.
    Description: Original research in zoology, geology and anthropology in Australia, Southwest Pacific and Indian Ocean areas.

069   AT   ISSN 0812-7387
                              CODEN: RAMSEZ
AUSTRALIAN MUSEUM, SYDNEY. RECORDS SUPPLEMENTS. (Supplement to: Australian Museum, Sydney. Records) 1890. irreg. price varies. Australian Museum, P.O. Box A285, Sydney, N.S.W. 2000, Australia. Ed. Jim Lowry. **Indexed:** Biol.Abstr., GeoRef.
    Formerly (until 1983): Australian Museum, Sydney. Memoirs (ISSN 0067-1967)
    Description: Monographs in zoology, geology and anthropology in Australia, Southwest Pacific and the Indian Ocean.

069 387   AT   ISSN 0813-0523
AUSTRALIAN SEA HERITAGE. 1984. q. Aus.$4 per no. (Sydney Maritime Museum) National Publications Pty. Ltd., P.O. Box 297, Homebush West 2140, Australia. TEL 02-764-111. FAX 02-763-1699. Ed. Peter Plowman. adv.; bk.rev.; charts; illus.; stat.; circ. 6,000. (back issues avail.)
    Description: Reflects the on going work of Australia's museums in preserving maritime history.

069   US
AVISO. 1968. m. $30. American Association of Museums, 1225 Eye St., N.W., Ste. 200, Washington, DC 20005. TEL 202-289-1818. FAX 202-289-6578. Ed. Bill Anderson. tr.lit./ circ. 12,000.
    Supersedes (from 1975): A A M Bulletin (ISSN 0044-7536)
    Description: Current events covering museums; lists over 100 jobs available throughout US museums each month.

708.1   US   ISSN 0045-3242
B A C A CALENDAR OF CULTURAL EVENTS. 1971. a. $20. (Brooklyn Arts and Culture Association, Inc.) Brooklyn Arts Council, 200 Eastern Parkway, Brooklyn, NY 11238. TEL 718-783-4469. FAX 718-636-8359. Ed. Charles Reichenthal. circ. 15,000.

069   UK
B M MAGAZINE. 1969. 4/yr. £16. British Museum Society, Great Russell St., London WC1B 3DG, England. TEL 071-637 9983. adv.; bk.rev.; circ. 7,000 (controlled). **Indexed:** RILA.
    Formerly (until 1990): British Museum Society. Bulletin.

700 913   BG
BANGLADESH LALIT KALA. (Text in English) 1975. s-a. Tk.100($15) Dhaka Museum, G.P.O. Box 355, Dhaka 2, Bangladesh.

069   DK   ISSN 0109-8489
BANGSBOMUSEET. AARBOG. 1984. a. DKK 60. Bangsbo Museums Forlag, Frederikshavn, Denmark. Dir. Hans Munk Pedersen. circ. 1,000.

708   CN
BEAVERBROOK ART GALLERY. ANNUAL REPORT. 1987. a. Beaverbrook Art Gallery, P.O. Box 605, Fredericton, N.B., Canada. TEL 506-458-8545. FAX 506-459-7450. circ. 1,500.

069   GW   ISSN 0138-4279
BEITRAEGE ZUR UR- UND FRUEHGESCHICHTE DER BEZIRKE ROSTOCK, SCHWERIN UND NEUBRANDENBURG. 1967. irreg. price varies. (Museum fuer Ur- und Fruehgeschichte Schwerin) VEB Deutscher Verlag der Wissenschaften, Postfach 1216, 1080 Berlin, Germany. Ed. Horst Keiling.

708   GW
BELSER KUNSTQUARTAL; Vorschau auf Kunstausstellungen des In- und Auslandes. 1965. q. DM.44. Chr. Belser Verlag, Falkertstr. 73, 7000 Stuttgart, Germany. Ed. Guenter Beysiegel. adv.; circ. 33,000 (controlled).

069   IS
BETH HATEFUTSOTH. s-a. free. Beth Hatefutsoth - Museum of the Jewish Diaspora, P.O. Box 39359, Tel Aviv 61392, Israel. TEL 03-6462020.

069   US
BETWEEN THE LIONS. 3/yr. Bowdoin College, Museum of Art, Walker Art Bldg., Brunswick, ME 04011. TEL 207-725-3275.
    Formerly: Bowdoin College Museum of Art. Newsletter.

BIBLIOTHEQUES ET MUSEES. see *HISTORY — History Of Europe*

069   GW   ISSN 0067-9461
BODENDENKMALPFLEGE IN MECKLENBURG. 1964. a. price varies. (Museum fuer Ur- und Fruehgeschichte, Schwerin) VEB Deutscher Verlag der Wissenschaften, Postfach 1216, 1080 Berlin, Germany. Ed. E. Schuldt. **Indexed:** Br.Archaeol.Abstr., NAA.

707.4   GW
BOKULT. irreg. (2-4/yr.). Museum Bochum, Kortumstr. 147, 4630 Bochum 1, Germany.

069   US   ISSN 0084-7992
BOWDOIN COLLEGE. MUSEUM OF ART. OCCASIONAL PAPERS. 1972. irreg., no.3, 1988. price varies. Bowdoin College, Museum of Art, Walker Art Bldg., Brunswick, ME 04011. TEL 207-725-3275. **Indexed:** RILA.
    Formerly: Walker Art Museum. Bulletin.

BRAZIL. MUSEU DO INDIO. BOLETIM. DOCUMENTACAO. see *HISTORY — History Of North And South America*

BRIMLEYANA. see *BIOLOGY — Zoology*

069   UK
BRITISH ASSOCIATION OF FRIENDS OF MUSEUMS YEARBOOK. 1984. a. British Association of Friends of Museums, 548 Wilbraham Road, Manchester M21 1LB, England. TEL 061-236-7724.
    Formerly: B A F M.
    Description: Covers activities of the association, the museums they support and matters relating to volunteers in museums.

708.1   CN   ISSN 0045-3005
BRITISH COLUMBIA MUSEUMS ASSOCIATION. MUSEUM ROUND UP. 1961. m. Can.$47. British Columbia Museums Association, 514 Government St., Victoria, B.C. V8V 4X4, Canada. TEL 604-387-3315. Ed. E. Busse. adv.; bk.rev.; circ. 500.

BRITISH SCHOOL AT ROME. PAPERS. ARCHAEOLOGY, HISTORY, HISTORY OF ART. see *ARCHAEOLOGY*

708   BX   ISSN 0084-8131
BRUNEI MUSEUM. SPECIAL PUBLICATION/MUZIUM BRUNEI. PENERBITAN KHAS. (Text in English and Malay) 1972. irreg., latest no. 10. price varies. Brunei Museum, Kota Batu, Bandar Seri Begawan, Brunei Darussalam. Ed. P.M. Dato Shariffiddin. circ. 1,000.

708   BX   ISSN 0068-2918
BRUNEI MUSEUM JOURNAL. (Text in English) 1969. a. B.$10. Brunei Museum, Kota Batu, Bandar Seri Begawan, Brunei Darussalam. Ed. P.M. Dato Shariffiddin. illus.; circ. 3,000. **Indexed:** A.I.C.P., E.I.

069 708   US   ISSN 0882-651X
BUGEYE TIMES. 1976. q. membership. Calvert Marine Museum, Box 97, Solomons, MD 20688. TEL 410-326-2042. Ed. Paul L. Berry. cum.index: 1976-1990; circ. 2,000. (back issues avail.)

069 708   US
C F A NEWS (MIAMI). 1982. q. membership. Center for Fine Arts, 101 W. Flagler St., Miami, FL 33130. TEL 305-375-3000. FAX 305-375-1725. Ed. Brenda Williamson. circ. 11,000. (tabloid format; back issues avail.)
    Description: Features fine art, design, photography, and sculpture at the center.

C MAGAZINE. see *ART*

069 610   US
CADUCEUS: A MUSEUM JOURNAL FOR THE HEALTH SCIENCES. 1985. 3/yr. $34 to individuals; institutions $40. S I U School of Medicine, Dept. of the Humanities, The Pearson Museum, Box 19230, Springfield, IL 62794-9230. FAX 217-782-9132. Ed. Glen W. Davidson. adv.; bk.rev.; illus.; circ. 120. (back issues avail.) **Indexed:** Ind.Med.
    Formerly (until Jan., 1991): Caduceus: A Museum Quarterly for the Health Sciences (ISSN 0882-6447)

063   BE
CAHIERS DE MARIEMONT; bulletin du Musee royal de Mariemont. 1970. a. 200 Fr. Musee Royal de Mariemont, B-7140 Morlanwelz-Mariemont, Belgium. TEL 064-21-21-93. FAX 064-26-29-24. (Co-sponsor: Ministere de la Communaute Francaise) Ed. Guy Donnay. circ. 1,500.

069　　　　　　CN　ISSN 0701-0281
THE CAIRN. 1977. 3/yr. Can.$25. Whyte Museum of the Canadian Rockies, 111 Bear St., Box 160, Banff, Alta. TOL 0C0, Canada. TEL 403-762-2291. FAX 403-762-8919. Ed. Pat Lee. adv.; circ. 2,500. (back issues avail.)

CALIFORNIA ACADEMY OF SCIENCES. ACADEMY NEWSLETTER. see *SCIENCES: COMPREHENSIVE WORKS*

069　　　　　　　　US
CALIFORNIA MUSEUM DIRECTORY; a guide to 1,200 museums, zoos, botanic gardens, and historic buildings open to the public. 1980. irreg., 2nd ed., 1991. $25. California Institute of Public Affairs, Box 189040, Sacramento, CA 95818. TEL 916-442-CIPA. FAX 916-442-2478. (Affiliate: The Claremont Graduate School) Ed. Jennifer T. Caughman. index; circ. 1,000.
Description: Guide to approximately 1,200 museums and similar institutions in California, including many smaller and specialized museums. Indexed by geographical areas, subject, and name of institution.

069　　　　　　CN　ISSN 0820-8336
CANADIAN MUSEUM OF FLIGHT & TRANSPORTATION. MUSEUM NEWSLETTER. 1975. q. membership. Canadian Museum of Flight & Transportation, 13527 Crescent Rd., Surrey, B.C. V4A 2W1, Canada. TEL 604-535-1115. FAX 604-535-3292. Ed. Rose Zalesky. adv.; bk.rev.; circ. 2,000.

069　　　　　　　　DK
CARLSBERGFONDET AARSSKRIFT. 1974. a. DKK 188 (prices typically set in Oct.). (Carlsbergfondet) Forlaget Rhodos, H.C. Andersens Blvd. 35, DK-1553 Copenhagen K, Denmark. FAX 33156188. TELEX 33 15 61 88.
Formerly: Frederiksborgmuseet. Aarskrift (ISSN 0105-9858)

069　　　　　　　　UK
CARMARTHEN MUSEUM. PUBLICATION. 1975. irreg. price varies. Carmarthen Museum, Abergwili, Carmarthen, Wales. TEL 0267-231691. Ed. C.J. Delaney. illus.

069　　　　　　　　US
THE CARNEGIE. ANNUAL REPORT. 1898. a. The Carnegie, 4400 Forbes Ave., Pittsburgh, PA 15213. TEL 412-622-3131. FAX 412-622-1970. Ed. Janet L. McCall. circ. 5,000.
Formerly: Carnegie Institute. Annual Report.
Description: Activity reports of each of five components that comprise The Carnegie: Library of Pittsburgh, the Museum of Art, the Museum of Natural History, the Music Hall, and the Science Center, with lists of events, loans, acquisitions, contributors, programs, and visiting scholars.

069.9　　　　　　　US
CARNEGIE INTERNATIONAL. triennial. Carnegie Museum of Art, 4400 Forbes Ave., Pittsburgh, PA 15213. TEL 412-622-3204. FAX 412-622-3112.
Description: Exhibition catalogue of international contemporary art.

069　　　　　　　　DK
CARTHA. 1982. a. DKK 75. Kerteminde Museum, Strandgade, 5300 Kerteminde, Denmark. Ed. Kurt Risskov Soerensen. illus.; circ. 750.
Formerly: Kerteminde Museum. Aarsskrift (ISSN 0109-047X)

069 700　　　　　　US
CARTOON ART MUSEUM NEWSLETTER. 1986. q. $35 to individuals; families $50. Cartoon Art Museum, 665 Third St., Ste. 505, San Francisco, CA 94107. TEL 415-546-3922. Ed. Jerry Kruse. circ. 400. (back issues avail.)
Description: Provides a place to see and preserve original cartoon art.

069　　　　　　　　US
CHARLES H. MACNIDER MUSEUM NEWSLETTER. 1966. bi-m. membership. Charles H. MacNider Museum, 303 Second St., S.E., Mason City, IA 50401-3988. TEL 515-421-3666. Ed. Richard E. Leet.

CHICAGO ARCHITECTURE FOUNDATION NEWS. see *ARCHITECTURE*

CHICAGO ARTISTS' NEWS. see *ART*

CHICORA FOUNDATION RESEARCH. see *ARCHAEOLOGY*

069　　　　　　BL　ISSN 0103-2909
CIENCIAS EM MUSEUS. (Text mainly in Portuguese; abstracts in English) 1989. a. price varies. Conselho Nacional de Desenvolvimento Cientifico e Tecnologico, Museu Paraense Emilio Goeldi, Caixa Postal 399, 66000 Belem, Para, Brazil. FAX 091-299-1412. Ed.Bd. charts; illus.

708　　　　　　　　US
N550
CINCINNATI ART MUSEUM. ANNUAL REPORT. 1930; N.S. 1950. a. free. Cincinnati Art Museum, Public Service Office, Eden Park, Cincinnati, OH 45202. TEL 513-721-5204. FAX 513-721-0129. Ed. Gretchen Mehring. circ. 9,500. (also avail. in microform from UMI; reprint service avail. from UMI)
Indexed: Art Ind., Artbibl.Mod., RILA.
Formerly: Cincinnati Art Museum. Bulletin (ISSN 0069-4061)

CLARION; America's folk art magazine. see *ART*

069 745.5　　　　US　ISSN 1046-2252
COLLECTIONS (COLUMBIA). 1988. q. membership. Columbia Museum of Art, 1112 Bull St., Columbia, SC 29201. TEL 803-799-2810. FAX 803-343-2150. Ed. Salvatore G. Cilella. adv.; cum.index: 1988-1989; circ. 3,000. **Indexed:** RILA.
Description: Presents the renaissance of the Kress collection, Southern and American art.

709.5　　　　　　SZ　ISSN 0010-0781
COLLECTIONS BAUR. BULLETIN. (Text in French) 1965. s-a. 3 Fr. per no. Fondation Alfred et Eugenie Baur-Duret, 8 Rue Munier-Romilly, CH-1206 Geneva, Switzerland. TEL 022-461729. FAX 022-7891845. Ed. Frank Dunand. circ. 1,000.
Description: Features descriptions and history of objects in the collection of Japanese and Chinese artifacts. Includes museum events and activities.

COMMUNITY HISTORY. see *HISTORY — History Of Australasia And Other Areas*

069.1 920　　　　　　US
CONFLUENCE. 1984. q. price varies. North Central Washington Museum Association, 127 S. Mission St., Wenatchee, WA 98801. TEL 509-664-5989. FAX 509-664-5997. Ed. Mary L. Thomsen. adv.; bk.rev.; circ. 1,000. (tabloid format; back issues avail.)
Description: Covers regional history, association news and views, and upcoming events.

069　　　　　　　　GW
COOLIBRI; Kultur Freizeit Programm im Ruhrgebiet. 1983. m. DM.30. Roland Scherer Verlag und Werbeservice GmbH, Victoriastr. 75, Postfach 100207, 4630 Bochum 1, Germany. TEL 0234-60342-4. FAX 0234-60345. Ed. Werner Dickob. circ. 102,000.

708　　　　　　IT　ISSN 0070-0479
CORPUS VASORUM ANTIQUORUM. ITALIA. 1927. irreg., no.63, 1986. price varies. (Union Academique Internationale) L'Erma di Bretschneider, Via Cassiodoro 19, 00193 Rome, Italy. TEL 06-687-41-27. FAX 06-687-41-29. Ed. E. Mangani.

930　　　　　　　　NE
CORPUS VASORUM ANTIQUORUM (NETHERLANDS). irreg., no.4, 1991. price varies. (Rijksmuseum van Oudheiden, Leiden) E.J. Brill, P.O. Box 9000, 2300 PA Leiden, Netherlands. TEL 071-312624. FAX 071-317532. TELEX 39296 BRILL NL. (In N. America: E.J. Brill, 24 Hudson St., Kinderhook, NY 12106. TEL 800-962-4406)

CORRAL DUST. see *HISTORY*

069　　　　　　　　US
COURIER (NEWARK). bi-m. membership. Mid-Atlantic Association of Museums, Box 817, Newark, DE 19715-0817. TEL 302-731-1424.
Description: Communicates among museum personnel in the District of Columbia, Maryland, Delaware, New Jersey, Pennsylvania, and New York fostering current museum practices.

069 700　　　　　　US
COWBOY ARTISTS OF AMERICA NEWSLETTER. q. membership. Cowboy Artists of America Museum, 1550 Bandera Hwy., Box 1716, Kerrville, TX 78029. TEL 512-896-2553.

CRAS; tidsskrift for kunst og kultur. see *ART*

CRYSTAL PALACE MATTERS. see *ARCHITECTURE*

069 574　　　　US　ISSN 0011-3069
QH70　　　　　　　　CODEN: CRTRAH
CURATOR. 1958. q. $27.50 to individuals; institutions $49.50. American Museum of Natural History, Central Park W. at 79th St., New York, NY 10024-5192. TEL 212-873-1498. FAX 212-769-5233. (Subscr. to: Dept. HHH, Box 3000, Denville, NJ 07834) Ed. Thomas D. Nicholson. adv.; bk.rev.; charts; illus.; index, cum.index; circ. 1,500. (also avail. in microform from UMI; reprint service avail. from UMI) **Indexed:** Art & Archaeol.Tech.Abstr., Biol.Abstr., Br.Archaeol.Abstr., Deep Sea Res.& Oceanogr.Abstr., GeoRef., Hist.Abstr. (until 1987).
—BLDSC shelfmark: 3493.500000.

069　　　　　　　　CN
CURRENTLY: ONTARIO MUSEUM NEWS. 1972. bi-m. $9. (Ontario Museum Association) North Waterloo Publishing Ltd., 15 King St., Elmira, Ont. N3B 2R1, Canada. FAX 519-669-5928. circ. 1,500.
Formerly: Ontario Museum News (ISSN 0384-9627)
Description: Issues of interest to workers in Ontario museums.

069　　　　　　SW　ISSN 0070-2528
DAEDALUS. (Text in Swedish; summaries and occasional paper in English) 1931. a. SEK 150. Tekniska Museet - National Museum of Science and Technology, S-115 27 Stockholm, Sweden. Ed. Jan-Erik Pettersson. adv.; cum.index; circ. 5,000. **Indexed:** Acad.Ind., Amer.Bibl.Slavic & E.Eur.Stud., Arts & Hum.Cit.Ind., Curr.Cont., Educ.Admin.Abstr., G.Soc.Sci.& Rel.Per.Lit., High.Educ.Curr.Aware.Bull., M.L.A., Mag.Ind., P.A.I.S., SSCI.
—BLDSC shelfmark: 3510.000000.

069.5　　　　　　　US
N531.D38
DAVID & ALFRED SMART MUSEUM OF ART. BULLETIN. 1989. a. membership. David & Alfred Smart Museum of Art, Univeristy of Chicago, 5550 S. Greenwood Ave., Chicago, IL 60637. TEL 312-702-0180. FAX 312-702-3121. Ed. Stephanie D'Allesandro. illus.; circ. 2,000.
Formerly: David and Alfred Smart Gallery Bulletin (ISSN 1041-6005)
Description: Contains articles concerning art objects in the Smart collection; reports on exhibitions, accessions, loans, programs, and gifts to the museum.

708　　　　　　　　US
DAYTON ART INSTITUTE. ANNUAL REPORT. 1931. a. $3.50. Dayton Art Institute, Box 941, Dayton, OH 45401-0941. TEL 513-223-5277. FAX 513-223-3140. Ed. Pat Obert Koepnick. circ. 4,000. **Indexed:** Artbibl.Mod.
Supersedes in part: Dayton Art Institute. Annual Report and Bulletin; **Formerly** (until 1984): Dayton Art Institute. Annual Report (ISSN 0070-3028)

708　　　　　　　　US
DELAWARE ART MUSEUM QUARTERLY. 1984. q. membership. Delaware Art Museum, 2301 Kentmere Parkway, Wilmington, DE 19806. TEL 302-571-9590. Ed. Melissa H. Mulrooney. circ. 5,000.
Formerly: Delaware Art Museum Bulletin.

069　　　　　　DK　ISSN 0084-9308
AS281.A2
DENMARK. NATIONALMUSEET. ARBEJDSMARK. 1928. a. Nationalmuseet, Frederiksholms Kanal 12, 1220 Copenhagen K, Denmark. TEL 33-134411. FAX 33-148411.

708.8　　　　　　　DK
DENMARK. NATIONALMUSEET. WORKING PAPERS. irreg. Nationalmuseet, Frederiksholms Kanal 12, 1220 Copenhagen K, Denmark.

DESIGN QUARTERLY. see *ARCHITECTURE*

509　　　　　　GW　ISSN 0012-1339
AM101
DEUTSCHES MUSEUM. ABHANDLUNGEN UND BERICHTE. 1929. irreg. membership. R. Oldenbourg Verlag GmbH, Rosenheimerstr. 145, 8000 Munich 80, Germany. bibl.; charts; illus.; circ. 7,000. **Indexed:** Chem.Abstr.

MUSEUMS AND ART GALLERIES

069 708.1   CN   ISSN 0714-7023
AM21.B7
DIRECTORY OF MUSEUMS, ART GALLERIES AND ARCHIVES OF BRITISH COLUMBIA. a. British Columbia Museums Association, 514 Government St., Victoria, B.C. V8V 4X4, Canada. TEL 604-387-3315. Ed. Richard A. Duckles.

DOMSPATZ; Zeitschrift fuer Fulda. see *THEATER*

700   GW
DRESDENER KUNSTBLAETTER. 1956. bi-m. DM.2.50. Staatliche Kunstsammlungen Dresden, Albertinum, 8012 Dresden, Germany. TEL 4953056. TELEX 2332-SKD-DD. Ed. Karin Perssen. bk.rev.; abstr.; illus.; index; circ. 2,000. (back issues avail.) Indexed: Artbibl.Mod., Numis.Lit., RILA.

707.4   GW
DUESSELDORFER MUSEEN. 1981. q. free. Landeshauptstadt Duesseldorf, Postfach 1120, 4000 Dusseldorf 1, Germany. TEL 0211-8993131. FAX 0211-8994179. circ. 20,000.
   Description: Covers museum exhibitions in Dusseldorf.

ELECTRIC QUARTERLY. see *LIBRARY AND INFORMATION SCIENCES*

069   US
EVERSON MUSEUM OF ART BULLETIN. 1959. m. $35 to non-members. Everson Museum of Art, 401 Harrison St., Syracuse, NY 13202. TEL 315-474-6064. Ed. Thomas Piche. adv.; bibl.; illus.; circ. 3,500.

069   UK
EXETER MUSEUMS NEWS. 4/yr. free. Exeter Museums Service, Royal Albert Memorial Museum, Queen Street, Exeter, Devon EX4 3RX, England. TEL 0932-265858. FAX 0392-421252.
   Former titles: Exeter Museums Bulletin and View; Exeter Museums News Event and Exhibitors.

069   DK   ISSN 0108-3643
F R A M. (Fra Ringkoebing Amts Museer) 1982. a. DKK 98. Museumsraadet i Ringkoebing Amt, Hjerl Hedes Frilandsmuseum, Hjerl Hedevej 14, 7830 Vinderup, Denmark. Ed. Soeren Toftgaard Poulsen. illus.; circ. 3,600. Indexed: NAA.

FINGERPRINTS AND LITTLE FEATS. see *CHILDREN AND YOUTH — For*

FINSKT MUSEUM. see *ARCHAEOLOGY*

708.1 355 970   US
FORT CONCHO MEMBERS DISPATCH. 1982. m. free to qualified personnel. (Fort Concho Museum) Fort Concho Museum Press, 213 E. Ave. D, San Angelo, TX 76903-7099. TEL 915-657-4443. Ed. Robert F. Bluthardt. circ. 1,200. (back issues avail.)

FORT TICONDEROGA MUSEUM. BULLETIN. see *MILITARY*

948   DK   ISSN 0107-4849
FRA BORNHOLMS MUSEUM. 1980. a. DKK 75. Bornholms Museum, Sct. Mortensgade 29, 3700 Roenne, Denmark. Ed. Ann Vibeke Knudsen. illus.; circ. 2,000.
   Formerly: Nyt fra Bornholms Museum.

708.8 948.9   DK   ISSN 0106-8229
FRA BOV MUSEUM. vol. 2, 1979. a. DKK 60. Historisk Forening for Visherred, Bov Museum, Bovvej 2, 6330 Padborg, Denmark.
   Formerly: Fra Bov Sogns Museum.

069   GW   ISSN 0177-011X
FREUNDESKREIS BLAETTER. 1976. s-a. DM.4. Freundeskreis Freilichtmuseum Suedbayern e.V., 8119 Grossweil, Germany. TEL 08851-1850. FAX 08851-18511. circ. 2,000.

069   US
FRIENDS' QUARTERLY (ENFIELD). 1988. q. membership. Museum at Lower Shaker Village, Rt. 4A, Enfield, NH 03748. TEL 603-632-4346. Ed. Carolyn A. Smith. illus.; circ. 600.
   Description: Covers news and activities of the local museum.

FUJIAN WENBO/FUJIAN RELICS AND MUSEUM. see *ARCHAEOLOGY*

708.6 780   SP
FUNDACION LA CAIXA. PANORAMA. m. Fundacion la Caixa, Via Laietana, 56, pral., 08003 Barcelona, Spain. TEL 93-404-60-76. Ed. Jesus Val Jarrin. illus.
   Formerly: Fundacio Caixa de Pensiones. Informatiu.
   Description: Covers art exhibits and musical performances supported by the foundation.

069   IT   ISSN 0072-0070
GABINETTO DISEGNI E STAMPE DEGLI UFFIZI. CATALOGHI. 1951. irreg., no.73, 1991. price varies. Casa Editrice Leo S. Olschki, Casella Postale 66, 50100 Florence, Italy. TEL 055-6530684. FAX 055-6530214. circ. 2,000.

069
GABINETTO DISEGNI E STAMPE DEGLI UFFIZI. INVENTARIO. 1986. irreg., no.3, 1991. price varies. Casa Editrice Leo S. Olschki, Casella Postale 66, 50100 Florence, Italy. TEL 055-6530684. FAX 055-6530214.

708.9   PY   ISSN 1017-2823
GALERIA MICHELE MALINGUE. CATALOGO. (Text in English, Spanish) 1988. q. $50. Distribuidor Internacional Publicaciones Paraguayas, Torreani Viera 551, Villa Morra, Asuncion, Paraguay. Ed. Adriana Almada. circ. 1,000.

708   GW   ISSN 0072-0089
GALERIE NIERENDORF, BERLIN. KUNSTBLAETTER. 1963. irreg., no.51, 1989. price varies. Galerie Nierendorf, Hardenbergstr. 19, 1000 Berlin 12, Germany. TEL 030-7856060. FAX 030-3129327. Ed. Florian Karsch. circ. 2,000.

708   AU
GALERIE SANCT LUCAS. GEMAELDE ALTER MEISTER. 1930. a. S.400. Galerie Sanct Lucas, Josefsplatz 5, Palais Pallavicini, A-1010 Vienna, Austria. FAX 513-320316. illus.

708.5
GALLERIA DEL CAVALLINO. MOSTRE. 1956. a. $10 per no. Edizioni del Cavallino, San Marco 1725, 30124 Venice, Italy. TELEX 41-521-0642. Ed. Paolo Cardazzo. illus.; circ. 3,000.

708   AT   ISSN 0814-7833
GALLERY. 1968. m. Aus.$22. (National Gallery Society of Victoria) Mount Eagle Publications, P.O. Box 84, Heidelberg, Vic. 3084, Australia. TEL 03-618-0208. Ed. Paton Forster. adv.; index; circ. 15,000.
   Description: Monthly issue of the Victoria National Gallery Society.

069.9   US
GAZETTE (CLAYTON). 1969. q. membership. Antique Boat Museum, 750 Mary St., Clayton, NY 13624. TEL 315-686-4104. Ed. Dawn Rusho. adv.; bk.rev.; circ. 1,700.

069   JA   ISSN 0435-219X
GENDAI NO ME. (Text in Japanese) 1954. m. National Museum of Modern Art, Tokyo, 3 Kitanomaru Koen, Chiyoda-ku, Tokyo 102, Japan.
   Description: Contains articles on exhibitions and events of the three institutions, for the purpose of supplying fundamental information.

069   US
GEORGIA MUSEUM OF ART. NEWS. 1983. 4/yr. free. Georgia Museum of Art, University of Georgia, Athens, GA 30602. TEL 404-542-3255. Ed. William Eiland. circ. 10,000.

069 940   AU
GESELLSCHAFT FUER VERGLEICHENDE KUNSTFORSCHUNG IN WIEN. MITTEILUNGEN. 1930. q. S.220. Gesellschaft fuer Vergleichende Kunstforschung in Wien, Bundesdenkmalamt, Hofburg-Seulenstiege, A-1010 Vienna, Austria. (Subscr. to: Institut fuer Kunstgeschichte der Universitaet Wien, Universitaetsstr. 7, A-1010 Vienna, Austria) Ed. Eckart Vancsa. adv.; bk.rev. Indexed: Artbibl.Mod., RILA.

GIFU-KEN HAKUBUTSUKAN CHOSA KENKYU HOKOKU/GIFU PREFECTURAL MUSEUM. BULLETIN. see *SCIENCES: COMPREHENSIVE WORKS*

069   XV   ISSN 0350-2929
DR1475.G67
GORISKI LETNIK. 1974. a. 400 din. Goriski Muzej, Raziskovalna Skupnost Slovenije, Adranska 16 A, Ljubljana, Slovenia. Indexed: Amer.Hist.& Life, Hist.Abstr.

760   RU   ISSN 0077-1562
GOSUDARSTVENNYI MUZEI IZOBRAZITEL'NYKH ISKUSSTV IM. PUSHKINA. SOOBSHCHENIYA. (Text in Russian; summaries in French) 1960. irreg. Gosudarstvennyi Muzei Izobrazitel'nykh Iskusstv im. Pushkina, Volkhonka 12, 121019 Moscow, Russia.

069   JA   ISSN 0911-9892
HAKUBUTSUKAN KENKYU/MUSEUM STUDIES. (Text in Japanese) 1928. m. 6000 Yen. Japanese Association of Museums - Nihon Hakubutsukan Kyokai, Shoyu-Kaikan 3-3-1, Kasumigaseki, Chiyoda-ku, Tokyo 100, Japan. TEL 03-3591-7190. illus. Indexed: RILA.
   —BLDSC shelfmark: 5989.750000.
   Incorporates (in 1974): Hakubutsukan Nyusu.

016.9173   US   ISSN 0093-1047
Z999
HARRIS AUCTION GALLERIES. COLLECTORS' AUCTION. 1962. 6/yr. $25 for 8 nos. Harris Auction Galleries, Inc., 873-875 N. Howard St., Baltimore, MD 21201. TEL 301-728-7040. Eds. Barr Harris, Christopher Bready. circ. 1,000. Key Title: Collectors' Auction (Baltimore).

069 700   US
HEARD MUSEUM NEWSLETTER. 1960. q. membership. Heard Museum, 22 E. Monte Vista Rd., Phoenix, AZ 85004-1480. TEL 605-252-8840. FAX 602-252-9757. Ed. Mary Brennan. circ. 4,000.
   Former titles (until vol.10, no.4, 1969): Heard Museum Notes; (until vol.10, no.1, 1968): Museum Notes (Phoenix).
   Description: Covers art exhibits and educational programs.

708   UK
HEIM GALLERY CATALOGUES. 1966. 2/yr. $6. Heim Gallery (London) Ltd., 59 Jermyn St., London SW1Y 6LX, England. illus.; circ. 1,000.

069   DK   ISSN 0108-0393
HELSINGOER KOMMUNES MUSEER. AARBOG. 1981. a. DKK 120. Helsingoer Kommunes Museer, Hestemoellestraede 1, 3000 Helsingoer, Denmark. illus. Indexed: NAA.
   Formerly: Helsingoer Bymuseum. Aarbog.

069   DK   ISSN 0106-5440
HELSINGOER SOM FOTOGRAFEN SAA DET. 1980. a. DKK 25. Helsingoer Kommunes Museer, Karmeliterhuset, Hestomoellestraede 1, 3000 Helsingoer, Denmark. illus.

HERITAGE. see *ART*

069   US
HISTORIC DEERFIELD QUARTERLY. 1952. q. free. Historic Deerfield, Inc., Box 321, Deerfield, MA 01342. TEL 413-774-5581. FAX 413-773-7415. Ed. Grace Friary. circ. 3,000. (tabloid format)

HIWA KAGAKU HAKUBUTSUKAN KENKYU HOKOKU/HIWA MUSEUM FOR NATURAL HISTORY. MISCELLANEOUS REPORTS. see *SCIENCES: COMPREHENSIVE WORKS*

069   GW
HOHENLOHER FREILANDMUSEUM MITTEILUNGEN. 1980. a. DM.8. Hohenloher Freilandmuseum, Postfach 100180, 7170 Schwaebisch Hall, Germany. TEL 0791-84061.

069 952   JA   ISSN 0287-9433
HOKKAIDO KAITAKU KINENKAN KENKYU NENPO/HISTORICAL MUSEUM OF HOKKAIDO. ANNUAL REPORT. (Text in Japanese; summaries in English) 1972. a. free. Hokkaido Kaitaku Kinenkan - Historical Museum of Hokkaido, Konopporo, Atsubetsu-cho, Atsubetsu-ku, Sapporo-shi, Hokkaido 004, Japan. TEL 898-0456. FAX 898-2657. circ. 1,000.

HORIZONT; veszprem megyei kozmuvelodesi tajekoztato. see *CLUBS*

708.1   US   ISSN 0018-6708
N576.H7
HOUSTON, TEXAS. MUSEUM OF FINE ARTS BULLETIN. 1971. 3/yr. $4 per no. Museum of Fine Arts, Houston, Box 6826, 1001 Bissonnet, Houston, TX 77265. TEL 713-526-1361. Ed. Celeste Adams. charts; illus.; circ. 10,000. Indexed: Artbibl.Mod.

MUSEUMS AND ART GALLERIES 3525

707.4 US
HUNTINGTON LIBRARY, ART COLLECTIONS, AND BOTANICAL GARDENS. CALENDAR. 1936. bi-m. Huntington Library, Art Collections and Botanical Gardens, 1151 Oxford Rd., San Marino, CA 91108. TEL 818-405-2170. FAX 818-405-0225. Ed. Catherine M. Babcock. illus.; circ. 5,000.
Former titles: Huntington Library, Art Gallery and Botanical Gardens. Collections; Huntington Library, Art Gallery and Botanical Gardens. Calendar; Henry E. Huntington Library and Art Gallery. Calendar of Exhibitions (ISSN 0018-0408)

069 US
I A S M H F NEWSLETTER. 1971. bi-m. $20. International Association of Sports Museums and Halls of Fame, 101 W. Sutton Pl., Wilmington, DE 19810-4115. TEL 302-475-7068. Ed. Al Cartwright. adv.; bk.rev.; circ. 200.
Formerly: Association of Sports Museums and Halls of Fame. Newsletter.
Description: News and activities of the Association.

069.094 FR ISSN 0018-8999
I C O M NEWS. French edition: Nouvelles de l'I C O M. Spanish edition: Noticias del I C O M. 1948. q. 150 F. to non-members. International Council of Museums - Conseil International des Musees, c/o Maison de l'Unesco, 1 rue Miollis, 75732 Paris Cedex 15, France. TEL 1-47-34-05-00. FAX 33-1-43-06-78-62. TELEX UNESCO 270 602. Ed. Sabine de Valence. adv.; B&W page 6000 F.; trim 171 x 247; adv. contact: Saroj Ghose. bk.rev.; abstr.; bibl.; circ. 10,000. **Indexed:** Art & Archaeol.Tech.Abstr., Br.Archaeol.Abstr., Chem.Abstr.
—BLDSC shelfmark: 4362.060000.

069 500 US ISSN 0196-7703
E78.I18
IDAHO MUSEUM OF NATURAL HISTORY. OCCASIONAL PAPERS. 1958. irreg. price varies. Idaho Museum of Natural History, Idaho State University, Box 8096, Pocatello, ID 83209. TEL 208-236-2262. circ. 500.
Formerly: Idaho State University Museum. Occasional Papers (ISSN 0073-4551)

069 US
IDAHO MUSEUM OF NATURAL HISTORY. SPECIAL PUBLICATION. no. 2, 1971. irreg. price varies. Idaho Museum of Natural History, Idaho State University, Box 8096, Pocatello, ID 83209-0009. Ed. Barry L. Keller.

069 520 JA
IKOMAYAMA UCHU KAGAKUKAN NYUSU. (Text in Japanese) 1969. irreg. Ikomayama Uchu Kagakukan - Mount Ikoma Space Science Museum, 2312-1, Nahata-cho, Ikoma-shi, Nara-ken 630-02, Japan.
Description: News of the museum.

069 500 US ISSN 0095-2893
ILLINOIS. STATE MUSEUM. INVENTORY OF THE COLLECTIONS. 1969. irreg., no.1, pt.6, 1986. free. Illinois State Museum, Springfield, IL 62706. TEL 217-782-7386. FAX 217-782-1254.
Refereed Serial

069 355 UK ISSN 0951-3094
IMPERIAL WAR MUSEUM REVIEW. 1986. a. £8.95. Imperial War Museum, Lambeth Road, London SE1 6HZ, England. Ed. Suzanne Bardgett. illus.; circ. 2,000. (back issues avail.)
—BLDSC shelfmark: 4371.411150.

069.095 II ISSN 0019-5987
INDIAN MUSEUM BULLETIN. (Text in English) 1966. a. Rs.30($10) Indian Museum, Calcutta, 27 Jawaharlal Nehru Rd., Calcutta 700016, India. TEL 29-9902. Ed. R.C. Sharma. bk.rev.; charts, illus.; index, cum.index: 1966-1969; circ. 500. **Indexed:** Numis.Lit.

069.5 US
INDIANA UNIVERSITY ART MUSEUM. BULLETIN. irreg. Indiana University Art Museum, Bloomington, IN 47405. TEL 812-335-5445. Ed. Linda Baden.

708.7 US
INDIANAPOLIS MUSEUM OF ART. PREVIEWS MAGAZINE. 1911. bi-m. membership. Indianapolis Museum of Art, 1200 W. 38th St., Indianapolis, IN 46208. TEL 317-923-1331. FAX 317-926-8931. Ed. Judith M. Fries. illus.; circ. 15,000. **Indexed:** RILA.
Former titles: Indianapolis Museum of Art. Quarterly Magazine & Indianapolis Museum of Art. Newsletter; Indianapolis Museum of Art. Bulletin (ISSN 0004-3060); Art Association of Indianapolis. Bulletin.

069 CI ISSN 0350-2325
INFORMATICA MUSEOLOGICA. (Text in Serbo-Croatian; summaries in English) 1970. q. 350 din.($24) (effective Oct. 1990). Muzejski Dokumentacioni Centar, Mesnicka 5, 41000 Zagreb, Croatia. FAX 38-41-430-851. Ed. Branka Sulc. bk.rev.; circ. 1,000.

069 GW ISSN 0138-1989
INFORMATIONEN FUER DIE MUSEEN IN DER DDR. 1969. 6/yr. DM.10. Institut fuer Museumswesen der Deutschen Demokratischen Republik, Information-Dokumentation, Mueggelseedamm 200, 1162 Berlin, Germany. Ed. Hans Mueller. bk.rev.; circ. 900.

707.4 GW
INFORMATIONEN ZUR AUSSTELLUNGSPLANUNG. 1973. a. DM.35($1000) Institut fuer Auslandsbeziehungen - Institute for Foreign Cultural Relations, Charlottenplatz 17, 7000 Stuttgart 1, Germany. TEL 0711-542138. (Subscr. to: Helga Kleindienst, Dessauerstr. 65, 7000 Stuttgart 50) (Co-sponsor: Deutscher Museumsbund)

INSTITUTE OF DIVING. NEWSLETTER. see *SPORTS AND GAMES*

355 GW ISSN 0074-168X
INTERNATIONAL ASSOCIATION OF MUSEUMS OF ARMS AND MILITARY HISTORY. CONGRESS REPORTS. 1957. triennial, 9th, 1981, Washington. membership. International Association of Museums of Arms and Military History, c/o Ernst Aichner, Bayerisches Armeemuseum, D-8070 Ingolstadt, Neues Schloss, Paradeplatz 4, Germany. circ. controlled.

INTERNATIONAL SWIMMING HALL OF FAME HEADLINES. see *SPORTS AND GAMES*

INTERP CENTRAL CLEARINGHOUSE NEWSLETTER. see *ENVIRONMENTAL STUDIES*

INVENTAIRE GENERAL DES MONUMENTS ET DES RICHESSES ARTISTIQUES DE LA FRANCE. see *ARCHITECTURE*

IRISH ARTS REVIEW. see *ART*

069 US
IROQUOIS INDIAN MUSEUM. MUSEUM NOTES. 1981. irreg., vol.11, 1991. $20. Iroquois Indian Museum, Box 7, Caverns Rd., Howes Cave, NY 12092. TEL 518-296-8949. Ed. John P. Ferguson. circ. 1,100.
Formerly: Schoharie Museum of the Iroquois Indian. Museum Notes.

069 IS ISSN 0333-7499
N3750.J5
ISRAEL MUSEUM JOURNAL. (Text in English) 1965. a. $5. Israel Museum, P.O. Box 1299, Jerusalem, Israel. Ed.Bd. adv.; charts; illus.; circ. 3,000. **Indexed:** Artbibl.Mod., Avery Ind.Archit.Per., RILA.
Formerly: Israel Museum News (ISSN 0021-227X)

069.094 333.7 IT ISSN 0021-2822
ITALIA NOSTRA. 1956. bi-m (with monographic supplements). L.10000. Associazione Nazionale per la Tutela del Patrimonio Storico Artistico e Naturale della Nazione, Corso Vittorio Emanuele N.287, 00186 Rome, Italy. adv.; charts; illus.; index; circ. 20,000.
—BLDSC shelfmark: 4588.210000.

708 US ISSN 0362-1979
N582.M25
J. PAUL GETTY MUSEUM JOURNAL. 1974. a. $65. J. Paul Getty Museum, 17985 Pacific Coast Highway, Malibu, CA 90265. TEL 213-459-7611. FAX 213-454-8156. (Orders to: J. Paul Getty Book Distribution Center, Box 2112, Santa Monica, CA 90407-2212) Ed. John Harris. illus.; circ. 1,000. (back issues avail.) **Indexed:** Art Ind., Avery Ind.Archit.Per., RILA.
—BLDSC shelfmark: 4597.150000.

655.5 GW
JAHRBUCH DER AUKTIONSPREISE FUER BUECHER, HANDSCHRIFTEN UND AUTOGRAPHEN; Ergebnisse der Auktionen in Deutschland, den Niederlanden, Oesterreich und der Schweiz. 1950. a. DM.340. Dr. Ernst Hauswedell und Co. Verlag, Rosenbergstr. 113, Postfach 140155, 7000 Stuttgart 10, Germany. FAX 0711-6369010. Ed. Ernst Hauswedell. adv.; circ. 1,300. (back issues avail.; reprint service avail. from KTO)
Formerly: Jahrbuch der Auktionspreise (ISSN 0075-2193)

069 708 GW ISSN 0075-2207
N3
JAHRBUCH DER BERLINER MUSEEN. 1959. a. price varies. (Staatliche Museen Preussischer Kulturbesitz Berlin) Gebr. Mann Verlag GmbH, Lindenstr. 76, Postfach 110303, 1000 Berlin 61, Germany. TEL 030-2591-3589. (reprint service avail.) **Indexed:** Artbibl.Mod., Arts & Hum.Cit.Ind., Avery Ind.Archit.Per., Curr.Cont., RILA.

069.7 700 GW ISSN 0932-6251
HF5802
JAHRBUCH DER WERBUNG/ADVERTISERS ANNUAL; in Deutschland, Oesterreich und der Schweiz. 1964. a. DM.148. E C O N Verlag GmbH, Kaiserswertherstr. 282, Postfach 300321, 4000 Duesseldorf 30, Germany. FAX 0211-43906-68. TELEX 8587327-ECON-D. Ed.Bd. adv.; bk.rev.; circ. 4,000.
Formerly (until 1975): Werbung in Deutschland (ISSN 0083-8012)
Description: Provides overview of advertising developments in the German speaking world.

069 JA ISSN 0040-8948
JAPAN. NATIONAL MUSEUM NEWS. (Text in Japanese) 1947. m. 1,500 Yen. Tokyo National Museum - Tokyo Kokuritsu Hakubutsukan, 13-9 Ueno Park, Taito-ku, Tokyo 110, Japan. TEL 03-3822-1111. FAX 03-3822-9130. bk.rev.; circ. 17,000. (tabloid format)

069 GR
JEWISH MUSEUM OF GREECE. NEWSLETTER. (Text in English) 1981. q. membership. Jewish Museum of Greece, 36 Queen Amalias Ave., 105 58 Athens, Greece. TEL 323-1577. (Dist. in U.S. by: American Friends of the Jewish Museum of Greece, Box 2010, New York, NY 10185-0017. TEL 212-661-9843) Ed. N. Stavroulakis. bk.rev.; circ. 1,500.
Description: Covers the heritage of the Sephardic and Romaniot communities in the Hellenic world. Includes acquisition news.

708.1 US
N742.S5
JOHN & MABLE RINGLING MUSEUM OF ART. 1964. q. membership. John and Mable Ringling Museum of Art Foundation, Box 1838, Sarasota, FL 34230. TEL 813-355-5101. FAX 813-351-7959. Ed. Kathleen Chilson. illus.; circ. 5,000 (controlled).
Former titles: Ringling Museums (ISSN 0731-7956); Ringling Museums Newsletter (ISSN 0035-5461)

707.4 US
JOSLYN NEWS; a publication for members. 1974. bi-m. membership. Joslyn Art Museum, 2200 Dodge St., Omaha, NE 68102. TEL 402-342-3300. FAX 402-342-2376. Ed. Linda Rajcevich. illus.; circ. 7,500.
Former titles: Joslyn Art Museum Members' Calendar; Joslyn Art Museum Calendar of Events.

069 UK ISSN 0260-9126
JOURNAL OF EDUCATION IN MUSEUMS. 1980. a. £5 (foreign £6.50). Group for Education in Museums, c/o Susan Morris, 63 Navarino Rd., London E8 1AG, England. bk.rev.; illus.; circ. 800.
—BLDSC shelfmark: 4973.150500.

MUSEUMS AND ART GALLERIES

069   II
JOURNAL OF INDIAN MUSEUMS.* (Text in English) a. Museums Association of India, c/o National Museum of Natural History, F I C C I, Museum Building, Barakhamba Road, New Delhi 110002, India. **Indexed:** Art & Archaeol.Tech.Abstr.

069.095 529   CH   ISSN 0256-257X
QH1   **CODEN:** QJTMAW
JOURNAL OF TAIWAN MUSEUM. (Text in English) 1948. s-a. Taiwan Provincial Museum - Tai-wan Sheng Li Po Wu Kuan, 2 Siangyang Road, Taipei, Taiwan 100, Republic of China. FAX 3140939. Ed.Bd. charts; illus. **Indexed:** Biol.Abstr., Field Crop Abstr., Forest.Abstr., Herb.Abstr., Hort.Abstr., Rev.Appl.Entomol. Key Title: Taiwan Shengli Bowuguan Jikan.
—BLDSC shelfmark: 4905.296000.
Formerly (until 1983): Taiwan Museum. Quarterly Journal (ISSN 0039-9116)

JOURNAL OF THE AUSTRALIAN WAR MEMORIAL. see *MILITARY*

069.9   UK   ISSN 0954-6650
AM221   **CODEN:** JHCOE2
JOURNAL OF THE HISTORY OF COLLECTIONS. 1989. 2/yr. £46($90) Oxford University Press, Oxford Journals, Pinkhill House, Southfield Road, Eynsham, Oxford OX8 1JJ, England. TEL 0865-882283. FAX 0865-882890. TELEX 837330 OXPRES G. Eds. Oliver Impey, Arthur MacGregor. adv.; bk.rev.; circ. 800.
—BLDSC shelfmark: 5000.740000.
Description: Dedicated to the study of collections, ranging from the contents of palaces and accumulations in more modest households, to the most systematic collection of academic institutions.

069   GW
K I K. (Kunst in Koeln) 1965. m. free. Generaldirektion der Museen Koeln, Postfach 108020, 5000 Cologne 1, Germany. circ. 900.
Description: News from the museums of Cologne.

069 974 700   US
K W M NEWSLETTER. 1982. q. membership. Kendall Whaling Museum, 27 Everett St., Box 297, Sharon, MA 02067. TEL 617-784-5642. Ed. David C. Cruthers. circ. 850.

069   AU   ISSN 0022-7587
KAERNTNER MUSEUMSSCHRIFTEN. 1954. irreg. price varies. Landesmuseum fuer Kaernten, Museumgasse 2, A-9010 Klagenfurt, Austria. TEL 04222-536-305. circ. 200.

KAMISHIHORO-CHO HIGASHI TAISETSU HAKUBUTSUKAN KENKYU HOKOKU/HIGASHI TAISETSU MUSEUM OF NATURAL HISTORY. BULLETIN. see *SCIENCES: COMPREHENSIVE WORKS*

069   JA
KANAGAWA-KEN HAKUBUTSUKAN KYOKAI KAIHO/KANAGAWA-KEN MUSEUM GAZETTE. (Text in Japanese) 1958. irreg. Kanagawa-ken Hakubutsukan Kyokai - Museums Association of Kanagawa Prefecture, 5-60 Minami-nakadoori, Naka-ku, Yokohama-shi, Kanazawa-ken 231, Japan.

KANAGAWA-KENRITSU HAKUBUTSUKAN KENKYU HOKOKU. SHIZEN KAGAKU/KANAGAWA PREFECTURAL MUSEUM. BULLETIN. NATURAL SCIENCE. see *SCIENCES: COMPREHENSIVE WORKS*

069   KE
KENYA MUSEUM SOCIETY. CHAIRMAN'S REPORT. 1971. a. $40. Kenya Museum Society, c/o Kenya National Museums, Box 40658, Nairobi, Kenya. Ed. Chryssee Martin. adv.; circ. 2,000.

KITAKAMI-SHIRITSU HAKUBUTSUKAN KENKYU/KITAKAMI CITY MUSEUM. BULLETIN. see *SCIENCES: COMPREHENSIVE WORKS*

KITAKYUSHU-SHIRITSU SHIZENSHI HAKUBUTSUKAN KENKYU HOKOKU/KITAKYUSHU MUSEUM OF NATURAL HISTORY. BULLETIN. see *SCIENCES: COMPREHENSIVE WORKS*

708   GW   ISSN 0075-6326
KLEINE MUSEUMSHEFTE. 1967. irreg., vol.9, 1981. price varies. Rheinland Verlag GmbH, Abtei Brauweiler, Postfach 2140, 5024 Pulheim 2, Germany. TEL 02234-8051. FAX 02234-82503. (Dist. by: Dr. Rudolf Habelt GmbH, Am Buchenhang 1, 5300 Bonn, Germany)

069   DK   ISSN 0107-931X
KOEGE MUSEUM. 1976. a. DKK 80. Koege Museum, Noerregade 4, 4600 Koege, Denmark. TEL 53-65-02-62.
Formerly: Koege Museum. Aarbog.

069.094   GW   ISSN 0933-257X
AM51.C64
KOELNER MUSEUMS BULLETIN. 1961. q. plus special issues. DM.35. Museumsdienst Koeln, Richartzstr. 2-4, 5000 Cologne 1, Germany. FAX 2214005. Ed.Bd. adv.; bk.rev.; illus.; cum.index in prep. (1961-1975); circ. 2,500. **Indexed:** Artbibl.Mod., RILA.
Former titles: Museen der Stadt Koeln. Bulletin (ISSN 0178-4218); Museen in Koeln. Bulletin (ISSN 0027-3813)
Description: Reports on new acquisitions, exhibitions, and research.

500 069   JA
KOKURITSU KAGAKU HAKUBUTSUKAN NENPO. (Text in Japanese) 1972. a. Monbu-sho, Kokuritsu Kagaku Hakubutsukan - Ministry of Education, National Science Museum, 7-20 Ueno Koen, Taito-ku, Tokyo 110, Japan.
Description: Annual report of the museum.

KOMATSU-SHIRITSU HAKUBUTSUKAN KENKYU KIYO/KOMATSU CITY MUSEUM. MEMOIRS. see *SCIENCES: COMPREHENSIVE WORKS*

069 500.9   JA
KOTONOURA. (Text in Japanese) 1986. q. Wakayama-kenritsu Shizen Hakubutsukan Tomo no Kai, Wakayama-kenritsu Shizen Hakubutsukan, 370-1 Funao, Kainan-shi, Wakayama-ken 642, Japan.
Description: Publishes news of Wakayama Prefecture's natural science museum.

096   US
KRESGE FOUNDATION. ANNUAL REPORT. a. Kresge Foundation, Box 3151, 3215 W. Big Beaver Rd., Troy, MI 48007-3151. TEL 313-643-9630.

069   GW   ISSN 0344-5690
T14.7   **CODEN:** KUTEEN
KULTUR UND TECHNIK. 1977. q. DM.36 (students DM.24). (Deutsches Museum) C.H. Beck'sche Verlagsbuchhandlung, Wilhelmstr. 9, 8000 Munich 40, Germany. TEL 089-38189-1. FAX 089-38189398. TELEX 5215085-BECKD. adv.; bk.rev.; circ. 10,000.
Description: Examines the inter-relationships of culture and technology.

069 708   SW   ISSN 0282-5902
KULTURENS VAERLD. 1985. 4/yr. SEK 175. Stiftelsen Kulturens Vaerld, Box 1095, 22101 Lund, Sweden. illus.; circ. 31,000. **Indexed:** NAA, Numis.Lit.
Formerly: Kulturen.

DIE KUNST; die Kunstzeitschrift mit Tradition, Graphik, Architektur, Wohnkultur. see *ART*

KUNST EN MUSEUMJOURNAAL. see *ART*

069   GW   ISSN 0023-5474
N3
KUNSTCHRONIK; Monatsschrift fuer Kunstwissenschaft, Museumswesen und Denkmalpflege. 1948. m. DM.75.50. (Zentralinstitut fuer Kunstgeschichte in Muenchen) Verlag Hans Carl GmbH, Breite Gasse 58-60, Postfach 9110, 8500 Nuernberg 11, Germany. TEL 0911-2383-0. FAX 0911-238339. TELEX 623081. Ed. P. Diemer. adv.; bk.rev.; bibl.; charts; illus.; index; circ. 2,600. **Indexed:** Avery Ind.Archit.Per., RILA.

KUNSTREPORT. see *ART*

KURASHIKI-SHIRITSU SHIZENSHI HAKUBUTSUKAN KENKYU HOKOKU/KURASHIKI MUSEUM OF NATURAL HISTORY. BULLETIN. see *SCIENCES: COMPREHENSIVE WORKS*

069   JA   ISSN 0913-1558
KURASHIKI-SHIRITSU SHIZENSHI HAKUBUTSUKANPO. (Text in Japanese) 1986. a. free. Kurashiki-shiritsu Shizenshi Hakubutsukan - Kurashiki Museum of Natural History, 6-1 Chuo 2-chome, Kurashiki, Okayama 710, Japan. TEL 0864-25-6037. FAX 0864-25-6038. circ. 1,000.
Description: Annual report of the museum.

KUSHIRO-SHIRITSU HAKUBUTSUKAN KIYO/KUSHIRO CITY MUSEUM. MEMOIRS. see *SCIENCES: COMPREHENSIVE WORKS*

069   JA   ISSN 0288-9102
KYODO TO HAKUBUTSUKAN. (Text in Japanese) 1953. s-a. Tottori-kenritsu Hakubutsukan - Tottori Prefectural Museum, 2-124 Higashi-machi, Tottori-shi, Tottori-ken 680, Japan. FAX 0857-26-8041. circ. 1,000.

069   AU   ISSN 0007-280X
LANDESMUSEUM FUER KAERNTEN. BUCHREIHE.. 1954. irreg. price varies. Landesmuseum fuer Kaernten, Museumgasse 2, A-9010 Klagenfurt, Austria. TEL 04222-536-305. circ. 400. **Indexed:** GeoRef.

708 940   GW   ISSN 0070-7201
LANDESMUSEUM FUER VORGESCHICHTE, DRESDEN. VEROEFFENTLICHUNGEN. 1952. irreg., vol.17, 1985. price varies. VEB Deutscher Verlag der Wissenschaften, Postfach 1216, 1080 Berlin, Germany. Ed. Werner Coblenz.

708 940   GW   ISSN 0072-940X
LANDESMUSEUM FUER VORGESCHICHTE, HALLE. VEROEFFENTLICHUNGEN. 1964. irreg. price varies. (Landesmuseum fuer Vorgeschichte, Halle) VEB Deutscher Verlag der Wissenschaften, Postfach 1216, 1080 Berlin, Germany. Ed. H. Behrens.

707.4   GW
LEBENDIGES DARMSTADT; Veranstaltungsvorschau. 1950. m. DM.20. Verkehrsamt der Stadt Darmstadt, Luisenplatz 5, 6100 Darmstadt, Germany.
Description: Provides a calendar of performances and events within the city of Darmstadt.

708.2   UK   ISSN 0024-0257
LEEDS ARTS CALENDAR. 1947. s-a. membership. Leeds Arts Collections Fund, Temple Newsam House, Leeds 15, Yorkshire, England. FAX 0532-602285. Ed. Anthony Wells-Cole. adv.; illus.; circ. 750. (also avail. in microform from UMI) **Indexed:** Artbibl.Mod., Br.Hum.Ind., RILA.

LIBRARY COMPANY OF PHILADELPHIA. OCCASIONAL MISCELLANY. see *HISTORY — History Of North And South America*

069   US
LITHOPHANE COLLECTOR'S CLUB BULLETIN. 1975. bi-m. $18 includes membership. Blair Museum of Lithophanes and Carved Waxes, Lithophanes Collector's Club, 2032 Robinwood Ave., Toledo, OH 43620. TEL 419-243-4115. bk.rev.; circ. 175.
Description: For individuals interested in the history and collection of lithophanes and related art objects.

708   US   ISSN 0047-4851
LIVING HISTORICAL FARMS BULLETIN. 1970. bi-m. membership. Association for Living Historical Farms and Agricultural Museums, Washington, DC 20560. TEL 202-357-2813. FAX 202-357-1853. Ed. Stephen L. Cox. adv.; bk.rev.; bibl.; circ. 1,200.

LIVINGSTONE MUSEUM. RESEARCH NOTES. see *HISTORY — History Of Africa*

739   SW   ISSN 0024-5372
LIVRUSTKAMMAREN. (Text in English or Swedish; summaries in English, French or German) 1937. q. SEK 80($7.10) Kungliga Livrustkammaren - Royal Armoury, Kungliga Slottet, Slottsbacken 3, S-111 30 Stockholm, Sweden. FAX 08-6664487. Ed. Agneta Lundstroem. illus.

708   US
LOCUS (NEW YORK). 1975. irreg., latest 1989. $49. Filsinger and Company Ltd., 288 W. 12th St., New York, NY 10014. TEL 212-243-7421. Ed. Cheryl Filsinger.
Description: Provides cross-references to over 450 New York City galleries and their historical and contemporary artists and photographers with an index to gallery specialities, geographical sections, and a city museum list.

708   US
LOCUS SELECT. 1975? irreg., latest 1992. $49. Filsinger and Company Ltd., 288 W. 12th St., New York, NY 10014. TEL 212-243-7421.
Description: Provides cross-references to selected galleries nationwide and their artists and photographers.

MUSEUMS AND ART GALLERIES 3527

069 974   US   ISSN 0024-5828
F104.M99
LOG OF MYSTIC SEAPORT. 1948. q. membership. Mystic Seaport Museum, Inc., Mystic, CT 06355. TEL 203-572-0711. Ed. Andrew W. German. bk.rev.; illus.; index; circ. 20,000. (also avail. in microfilm from UMI) **Indexed:** Amer.Hist.& Life, Hist.Abstr.

707.4   UK   ISSN 0260-7743
LONDON FEDERATION OF MUSEUM AND ART GALLERIES. NEWSLETTER. 1979. 2/yr. membership. London Federation of Museum and Art Galleries, Museum of the Order of St. John, St. John's Gate, Clerkenwell, London C1M 4DA, England. Ed. Sue Curtis. adv.; bk.rev.; circ. 150.

708   AT   ISSN 0817-8445
LOOK MAGAZINE. 1985. m. (Art Gallery Society of New South Wales) Mount Eagle Publications, P.O. Box 84, Heidelberg, Vic. 3084, Australia. Ed. David Tunny. circ. 11,000.
   Description: A monthly sponsored by the Art Gallery Society of New South Wales.

069.097   US   ISSN 0024-6492
LORE. 1951. 2/yr. $10 membership. (Friends of the Milwaukee Public Museum) Milwaukee Public Museum, 800 W. Wells St., Milwaukee, WI 53233. TEL 414-278-2710. FAX 414-223-1396. bk.rev.; film rev.; illus.; index; circ. 10,000.

069   GW
M P Z - KOOPERATIONSPROJEKT. 1988. s-a. free. Museumspaedagogisches Zentrum, Barer Str. 29, 8000 Munich 40, Germany. TEL 089-23805192. (back issues avail.)
   Formerly: Schuler im Museum.
   Description: News about program for children and youth groups in museums and castles in Greater Munich.

069.9 296   US
MAGNES NEWS. 1968. 3/yr. $35. Judah L. Magnes Museum, 2911 Russell St., Berkeley, CA 94705. TEL 510-549-6950. FAX 510-849-3650. Ed. Paula Friedman. circ. 2,500.
   Description: Illustrated Museum newsletter; includes calendar of exhibitions.

069   II
MAHARAJA SAWAI MAN SINGH II MEMORIAL SERIES. 1971. irreg., no.8, 1987. price varies. Maharaja Sawai Man Singh II Museum, City Palace, Jaipur 302 002, India. Ed. Gopal Narayan Bahura. circ. 1,100.

069   II
MANIPUR STATE MUSEUM. BULLETIN. (Text in English) 1972. a. Rs.3. Manipur State Museum, Publications Sub-Committee, Imphal 759001, Manipur, India.

069   CN
MANITOBA MUSEUM OF MAN AND NATURE. ANNUAL REPORT. 1966. a. membership. Manitoba Museum of Man and Nature, 190 Rupert Ave., Winnipeg, Man. R3B ON2, Canada. TEL 204-956-2830. FAX 204-942-3679. TELEX 94236-79. circ. 3,000. (controlled).
   Formerly (until 1984): Manitoba Museum of Man and Nature. Biennial Report (ISSN 0076-3888)

069 708   US
MARTIN & OSA JOHNSON SAFARI MUSEUM WAIT-A-BIT NEWS. 1980. q. membership. Martin & Osa Johnson Safari Museum, Inc., 16 S. Grant, Chanute, KS 66720. TEL 316-431-2730. bk.rev.; circ. 400. (looseleaf format; back issues avail.)
   Formerly: Johnson Safari Wait-a-Bit Newsletter.

069   US
MATURANGO MUSEUM NEWSLETTER. 1964. m. membership. Maturango Museum, Box 1776, Ridgecrest, CA 93556. TEL 619-375-6900. Ed. Andrea Pelch. bk.rev.; circ. 1,500.
   Description: Covers current events, lectures, field trips as well as new exhibits of local natural and cultural history.

MAURITIANA (ALTENBURG). see *SCIENCES: COMPREHENSIVE WORKS*

MEAD ART MUSEUM MONOGRAPHS. see *ART*

069 355   SW
MEDDELANDE ARMEMUSEUM. YEARBOOK. 1938. a. SEK 150. Armemuseum - Royal Army Museum, P.O. Box 140 95, S-104 41 Stockholm, Sweden. TEL 08-660-3853. FAX 46-08-662-683. Ed. Johan Engstroem. circ. 2,000.
   Formerly (until 1976): Foereningen Armemusei Vaenner. Meddelande: Kungliga Armemuseum (ISSN 0349-1048)
   Description: Features articles on military history, particularly that of Sweden.

708.1   US
MEMPHIS BROOKS MUSEUM OF ART. NEWSLETTER. 1955. bi-m. $5. Memphis Brooks Museum of Art, Overton Park, Memphis, TN 38112. TEL 901-722-3525. Ed. Dorothy Lane. circ. 6,000.
   Formerly: Brooks Memorial Art Gallery. Newsletter.

708   US   ISSN 0077-8958
N610
METROPOLITAN MUSEUM JOURNAL. 1968. a. $60. Metropolitan Museum of Art, 1000 Fifth Ave., New York, NY 10028. (Orders to: University of Chicago Press, Journals Division, Box 37005, Chicago, IL 60637) Ed. Barbara Burn. illus. (back issues avail.) **Indexed:** Artbibl.Mod., Arts & Hum.Cit.Ind., Avery Ind.Archit.Per., Curr.Cont., RILA.
—BLDSC shelfmark: 5748.990000.
   Description: First-time investigations and critical reassessments of individual works; monographic surveys relating objects to their cultural contexts; new information drawing on archival research and technical analyses, and other scholarly articles.

708.7   US   ISSN 0026-1521
N610
METROPOLITAN MUSEUM OF ART. BULLETIN. 1905; N.S. 1942. q. $22. Metropolitan Museum of Art, 1000 Fifth Ave., New York, NY 10028. Ed. Joan Holt. illus.; index; circ. 112,000. (also avail. in microform from UMI; reprint service avail. from UMI) **Indexed:** Amer.Hist & Life, Art & Archaeol.Tech.Abstr., Art Ind, Artbibl.Mod., Arts & Hum.Cit.Ind., Avery Ind.Archit.Per., Curr.Cont., Hist.Abstr., Mid.East: Abstr.& Ind., Numis.Lit., RILA.
—BLDSC shelfmark: 5748.989000.
   Description: General information on art in the museum's collections, each issue organized around a category or an artist.

069 977.4   US   ISSN 0076-8235
MICHIGAN STATE UNIVERSITY. MUSEUM PUBLICATIONS. CULTURAL SERIES. 1961. irreg., vol.1, no.3, 1967. price varies. Michigan State University, Museum, East Lansing, MI 48824. TEL 517-355-2370. (And: Exchange Dept., MSU Library, East Lansing, MI 48824) index at end of each completed vol.; circ. 1,850.

MIDWEST MUSEUM BULLETIN. see *ART*

069.097   US
MIDWEST MUSEUMS CONFERENCE. NEWS BRIEF. bi-m. $42. Midwest Museums Conference, c/o Labor Museum, 711 N. Saginaw, Ste. 111, Flint, MI 48503-1729. TEL 313-762-0251. FAX 313-762-0204. Ed. Carl R. Hansen. bk.rev.; bibl.; charts; illus.; circ. 650. **Indexed:** GeoRef.
   Formerly (until vol.48, no.4, 1988): Midwest Museums Conference Quarterly (ISSN 0026-3443)

MILLER NOTES. see *MUSIC*

069.9 700   US
MINT MUSEUM MEMBERNEWS. 1986. bi-m. membership. Mint Museum of Art, 2730 Randolph Rd., Charlotte, NC 28207. TEL 704-337-2000. FAX 704-337-2101. Ed. Phil Busher. circ. 5,200. (looseleaf format)
   Formerly (until 1986): Mint Museum Newsletter.
   Description: Coverage of current art exhibitions, art issues affecting the museum, additions and spotlights to the collections, educational programs, films and affiliate organization news.

MISUL CHARYO/NATIONAL MUSEUM JOURNAL OF ARTS. see *ART*

708.1   US
MONTCLAIR ART MUSEUM. BULLETIN - NEWSLETTER. 1929. bi-m. free to museums & libraries. Montclair Art Museum, 3 South Mountain, Montclair, NJ 07042-1747. TEL 201-746-5555. FAX 201-746-9118. Ed. Cathy Fazekas. illus.; circ. 5,000.
   Formed by the merger of: Montclair Art Museum. Bulletin (ISSN 0027-0059); Montclair Art Museum. Newsletter.

069   RM
MONUMENTE ISTORICE SI DE ARTA. (Text in Rumanian; summaries in English, French, Russian) s-a. 100 lei($73) Ministerul Culturii, Piata Presei Libere 1, Sector 1, Bucharest, Rumania. (Subscr. to: Calea Grivitei 66-68, Box 12201, Bucharest, Rumania) illus. **Indexed:** Numis.Lit.
   Former titles: Revista Muzeelor si Monumentelor. Monumente Istorice si de Arta; Revista Muzeelor si Monumentelor. Monumente.

069.5 708.5   IT
MONUMENTI MUSEI E GALLERIE PONTIFICIE MUSEO GREGORIANO ETRUSCO. CATALOGHI. 1985. irreg., no.2, 1989. price varies. L'Erma di Bretschneider, Via Cassiodoro 19, 00193 Rome, Italy. TEL 06-687-41-27. FAX 06-687-41-29.

061   US
MOSAIC (ST. PETERSBURG). q. limited distribution. Museum of Fine Arts, St. Petersburg, 255 Beach Dr. North East, St. Petersburg, FL 33701. TEL 813-896-2667. FAX 813-894-4638. illus. **Indexed:** Abstr.Engl.Stud., Curr.Adv.Ecol.Sci.
   Description: News and announcements of art acquisitions, events, and exhibits by the Museum of Fine Arts, St. Petersburg, Florida.

707   US   ISSN 0027-3627
N11.M83
MUNSON-WILLIAMS-PROCTOR INSTITUTE. BULLETIN. 1941. m. free to members. Munson-Williams-Proctor Institute, 310 Genesee St., Utica, NY 13502-4799. TEL 315-797-0000. Ed. Joe Schmidt. illus.; circ. 5,000. (tabloid format)
   Description: Presents upcoming events and information on programming.

069.097   CN   ISSN 0820-0165
MUSE (OTTAWA). (Text in English and French) 1966. 4/yr. Can.$25($32) (foreign Can.$40)(effective Mar. 1992). Canadian Museums Association, Ste. 400, 280 Metcalfe St., Ottawa, Ont. K2P 1R7, Canada. TEL 613-233-5653. FAX 613-233-5438. Ed. Aline Michaud. adv.; bk.rev.; illus.; circ. 2,200. (back issues avail.) **Indexed:** Amer.Hist.& Life, Art & Archaeol.Tech.Abstr., Can.Per.Ind., Hist.Abstr.
   Formerly: C M A Gazette - A M C Gazette (ISSN 0317-6045)
   Description: Provides a forum for the expression of ideas, opinions and research in museology; thematic issues.

069   AT   ISSN 0728-8948
MUSE NEWS. 1982. q. Museums Association of Australia Inc., c/o Kylie Winkworth, Ed., 8 Yaralla St., Newtown, N.S.W. 2042, Australia. TEL 03-419-7092. adv.; bk.rev.; circ. 1,500. (back issues avail.)
—BLDSC shelfmark: 5986.552000.

960   FR
MUSEE DE L'HOMME, PARIS. CATALOGUES. SERIE C: AFRIQUE NOIRE. (Supplement to: Objets et Mondes) 1970. irreg., no. 2, 1976. price varies. Museum Nationale d'Histoire Naturelle, Musee de l'Homme, Palais de Chaillot, Place du Trocadero, 75116 Paris, France. TEL 45-53-70-60.

900   FR
MUSEE DE L'HOMME, PARIS. CATALOGUES. SERIE H: AMERIQUE. (Supplement to: Objets et Mondes) 1963. irreg., no. 4, 1969. price varies. Musee Nationale d'Histoire Naturelle, Musee de l'Homme, Palais de Chaillot, Place du Trocadero, 75116 Paris, France. TEL 45-53-70-60.

950   FR
MUSEE DE L'HOMME, PARIS. CATALOGUES. SERIE K: ASIE. (Supplement to: Objets et Mondes) 1969. irreg., no. 2, 1972. price varies. Museum Nationale d'Histoire Naturelle, Musee de l'Homme, Palais de Chaillot, Place du Trocadero, 75116 Paris, France. TEL 45-53-70-60.

M

MUSEUMS AND ART GALLERIES

069   FR   ISSN 0181-1525
N6490
MUSEE NATIONAL D'ART MODERNE. CAHIERS. 1979. 4/yr. Editions du Centre Georges Pompidou, Musee National d'Art Moderne, 75191 Paris cedex 04, France. FAX 42-77-29-49. TELEX MNAM 214024. Ed. Y. Michaud. adv.; bk.rev.; circ. 3,300. **Indexed:** Artbibl.Mod., Arts & Hum.Cit.Ind., Curr.Cont., RILA. —BLDSC shelfmark: 2948.388000.
Description: Specializes in contemporary art history and aesthetics. Includes information on the current activities of MNAM at the Pompidou Center.

069   PL   ISSN 0027-3791
N3160
MUSEE NATIONAL DE VARSOVIE. BULLETIN. (Text in various languages) 1960. q. $30. Muzeum Narodowe w Warszawie - National Muzeum in Warsaw, Al. Jerozolimskie 3, 00-495 Warsaw, Poland. FAX 48-22-258559. (Dist. by: Ars Polona-Ruch, Krakowskie Przedmiescie 7, 00-068 Warsaw, Poland) Ed. Agnieszka Morawinska. illus.; circ. 750. **Indexed:** Artbibl.Mod., RILA.

069   GW   ISSN 0720-7883
MUSEEN IN SCHLESWIG-HOLSTEIN; Mitteilungen aus Offentlichen Museen und Sammlungen. 1980. 3/yr. free. Amt Landesmuseumsdirektor, Schloss Gottorf, 2380 Schleswig, Germany. TEL 04621-813-0. FAX 04621-813555. (Co-sponsor: Ministerium fuer Bildung, Wissenschaft, Jugend und Kultur) Ed. Dr. Helmut Sydow. circ. 15,000. (back issues avail.)
Description: Museums and their activities in Schleswig-Holstein.

069 700   CN   ISSN 0706-098X
MUSEES. 1978. q. Can.$32.10 (effective Jan. 1991). Societe des Musees Quebecois, C.P. 8888, Succ. A, UQAM, Montreal, Que. H3C 3P8, Canada. TEL 514-987-3264. FAX 514-987-3379. Ed. Helene Panaioti. adv.; circ. 1,500. (back issues avail.) **Indexed:** Pt.de Rep. (1989-).

069.094   SZ   ISSN 0027-3821
AM68.G4   CODEN: MSGVAD
MUSEES DE GENEVE; revue des musees et collections de la ville de Geneve. 1944. m. free. Beaux-Arts et Culture, Hotel Municipal, Geneva, Switzerland. Ed. Andre Comellini. adv.; bibl.; illus.; cum.index: 1944-1964, 1965-1979; circ. 5,000. **Indexed:** Amer.Hist.& Life, Artbibl.Mod., GeoRef., Hist.Abstr., RILA.

069.094   FR   ISSN 0027-383X
AM46.A1
MUSEES ET COLLECTIONS PUBLIQUES DE FRANCE. 1932. s-a. 30 F. (Association Generale des Conservateurs de Musees et Collections Publiques de France) Editions Person, 34, rue de Penthievre, 75008 Paris, France. Ed. J.H. Person. adv.; bk.rev.; charts; illus.; index.

069.094   FR   ISSN 0521-7032
MUSEES ET MONUMENTS LYONNAIS. BULLETIN. 1952. q. 200 F. Musee de Beaux Arts, Association des Amis du Musee, Palais St. Pierre, 20 Place des Terreaux, 69001 Lyon, France. FAX 78-28-12-45. Ed. Philippe Durey. illus.; index; circ. 700. **Indexed:** Artbibl.Mod., RILA.

MUSEES ROYAUX D'ART ET D'HISTOIRE. BULLETIN/KONINKLIJKE MUSEA VOOR KUNST EN GESCHIEDENIS. BULLETIN. see HISTORY — History Of Europe

708   BE   ISSN 0027-3856
N1830
MUSEES ROYAUX DES BEAUX-ARTS DE BELGIQUE. BULLETIN/KONINKLIJKE MUSEA VOOR SCHONE KUNSTEN VAN BELGIE. BULLETIN. (Text in Dutch, English, French, German, Italian, Spanish; summaries in Dutch, French) 1952. irregg., 1985-88/1-3. price varies. Musees Royaux des Beaux-Arts de Belgique - Koninklijke Musea voor Schone Kunsten van Belgie, Museumstr. 9, 1000 Brussels, Belgium. Ed. Andre A. Moerman. illus.; index; circ. 600. **Indexed:** Art Ind., Artbibl.Mod., RILA.

069   DK   ISSN 0108-917X
MUSEET FOR HOLBAEK OG OMEGN. AARSBERETNING. 1921. a. DKK 15. Museumsforeningen for Holbaek og Omegn, Klosterstraede 14-16, 4300 Holbaek, Denmark. TEL 53-432-353. Ed. J.L. Oestergaard Christensen. adv.; illus.; circ. 1,800.
Formerly: Museet for Holbaek og Omegn.

069   IT   ISSN 0083-5447
MUSEI CIVICI VENEZIANI. BOLLETTINO. 1956. q. L.5000($15) Musei Civici Veneziani, Venice, Italy. Ed.Bd. adv.; circ. 1,650. (also avail. in microform) **Indexed:** Avery Ind.Archit.Per., RILA.

069   IT
MUSEI COMUNALI DI ROMA. BOLLETTINO. N.S. 1987. irreg., no.3, 1989. L.40000. (Associazione Amici dei Musei di Roma) L'Erma di Bretschneider, Via Cassiodoro 19, 00193 Rome, Italy. TEL 06-687-41-27. FAX 06-687-41-29.

069.094   IT   ISSN 0027-3872
MUSEI E GALLERIE D'ITALIA. 1957. s-a. L.21000. (Associazione Nazionale dei Musei Italiani) Casa Editrice Fratelli Palombi, Via dei Gracchi 181-185, 00192 Rome, Italy. Dir. Dante Bernini. bk.rev.; illus.; index. **Indexed:** RILA.

913   IT   ISSN 0391-9293
MUSEO ARCHEOLOGICO DI TARQUINIA. MATERIALI. 1980. irreg., vol.12, 1986. price varies. Giorgio Bretschneider, Via Crescenzio 43, I-00193 Rome, Italy. (back issues avail.)

708.5   IT
MUSEO BODONIANO. BOLLETTINO. 1972. irreg. L.60000 per no. Museo Bodoniano, Biblioteca Palatina, Palazzo della Pilotta, 43100 Parma, Italy. TEL 0521 282217. bk.rev.; circ. 80,000. (also avail. in microfilm)

069.5 914.5   IT
MUSEO CIVICO ARCHEOLOGICO UGO GRANAFEI DI MESAGNE. TESTI E MONUMENTI. 1977. irreg., no.6, 1988. price varies. L'Erma di Bretschneider, Via Cassiodoro 19, 00193 Rome, Italy. TEL 06-687-41-27. FAX 06-687-41-29.

069   CK
MUSEO DE ARTE COLONIAL DE BOGOTA. BOLETIN INFORMATIVO. 1975. m. free. Museo Colonial de Bogota, Carrera 6 no. 9-77, Bogota, Colombia. circ. 500.

301.2   DR
MUSEO DEL HOMBRE DOMINICANO. SERIE CATALOGOS Y MEMORIAS. 1976. irreg., no. 41. Museo del Hombre Dominicano, Calle Pedro Henriquez Urena, Plaza de la Cultura, Santo Domingo, Dominican Republic. illus.

301.2   DR
MUSEO DEL HOMBRE DOMINICANO. SERIE MESA REDONDA CONFERENCIAS. 1974. irreg., no.12, 1981. price varies. Museo del Hombre Dominicano, Calle Pedro Henriquez Urena, Plaza de la Cultura, Santo Domingo, Dominican Republic. illus.

069   SP   ISSN 0210-8143
AM101.M238
MUSEO DEL PRADO. BOLETIN. 1978. a. 2332 ptas. (foreign 2800 ptas.). Museo del Prado, Paseo del Prado, sn, 28014 Madrid, Spain. FAX 420-0794. TELEX 44949. Ed. Alfonso E. Perez Sanchez.
Description: Provides information on the activities of the Prado Museum.

708   IT
MUSEO DELLA CIVILTA ROMANA. STUDI E MATERIALI. 1938. irreg., no.13, 1989. price varies. L'Erma di Bretschneider, Via Cassiodoro, 19, 00193 Rome, Italy. TEL 06-687-41-27. FAX 06-687-41-29.
Formerly: Museo dell'Impero Romano. Studi e Materiali (ISSN 0080-3936)

    PE
MUSEO NACIONAL. REVISTA. 1932. a. $30. (Museo Nacional de la Cultura Peruana) Industrial Grafica S.A., Apdo. 3048, Lima 100, Peru. Ed. Rosalia Avalos de Matos. circ. 1,000. **Indexed:** A.I.C.P., Hisp.Amer.Per.Ind., Hist.Abstr.

500.907   CL   ISSN 0716-0224
QH119
MUSEO NACIONAL DE HISTORIA NATURAL. PUBLICACION OCASIONAL. 1963. irreg., no.45, 1989. $12. Museo Nacional de Historia Natural, Casilla 787, Santiago, Chile. Ed. Daniel Frassinetti Cabeza.

709.5   IT
MUSEO NAZIONALE D'ARTE ORIENTALE. SCHEDE. no. 6, 1974. irreg. Museo Nazionale d'Arte Orientale, Via Merulana 248, Rome 00185, Italy. bibl.

708.9   AG
MUSEO Y MONUMENTO NACIONAL "JUSTO JOSE DE URQUIZA". SERIE 3. no. 14, 1981. Museo y Monumento Nacional Justo Jose de Urquiza, Palacio San Jose, Entre Rios, Argentina.

069   CN   ISSN 0380-4623
MUSEOGRAMME. (Text in English and French) 1973. 10/yr. Can.$25 (in US Can.$32; elsewhere Can.$40). Canadian Museums Association, Ste. 400, 280 Metcalfe St., Ottawa, Ont. K2P 1R7, Canada. TEL 613-233-5653. FAX 613-233-5438. adv.
Description: Membership newsletter of the Association.

069   US   ISSN 0196-0237
MUSEOLOGY. 1975. irreg., no.7, 1986. price varies. (Texas Tech University, Museum Science Program) Texas Tech University Press, Lubbock, TX 79409-1037. TEL 806-742-2982.

MUSEU NACIONAL, RIO DE JANEIRO. ARQUIVOS. see SCIENCES: COMPREHENSIVE WORKS

069 708   UN   ISSN 0027-3996
AM1
MUSEUM. (Editions in English, French, Spanish) 1948. q. $39. 108 Cowley Rd., Oxford OX4 1JF, England. TEL 0865-791100. FAX 0865-791333. TELEX 837022 OXBOOK G. Ed. Y.R. Isar. charts; illus.; index, cum.index: 1948-1973; circ. 2,400 (English ed.); 1,500 (French ed.). **Indexed:** Art Ind., Avery Ind.Archit.Per., Chem.Abstr., Mid.East: Abstr.& Ind. —BLDSC shelfmark: 5987.010000.
Formerly: Mouseion.

069.095   JA   ISSN 0027-4003
MUSEUM. (Text in Japanese; title and contents page in English) 1951. m. $29.75. Museum Shuppan Co., Ltd., Asahi-Jinbocho Plaza, 2-14 Jinbo-cho, Chiyoda-ku, Tokyo 101, Japan. Ed. Shigeru Muramatsu. adv.; bk.rev.; illus.; index; circ. 6,000. **Indexed:** Art & Archaeol.Tech.Abstr., So.Pac.Per.Ind.

069   GW   ISSN 0341-8634
AM49
MUSEUM. 1976. m. DM.96. Georg Westermann Verlag GmbH, Georg-Westermann-Allee 66, 3300 Braunschweig, Germany. FAX 0531-708127. Ed. Andrea Kastens. adv.; bk.rev.; illus.; circ. 20,000.

708   NE   ISSN 0077-2275
MUSEUM BOYMANS-VAN BEUNINGEN. AGENDA - DIARY. (Text in Dutch and English) 1949. a. fl.25. Museum Boymans-van Beuningen, Mathenesserlaan 18-20, Postbus 2277, 3000 CG Rotterdam, Netherlands. TEL 010-4419400. FAX 010-4360500. TELEX 25572 MUBOY NL. circ. 30,000.

MUSEUM ETHNOGRAPHERS GROUP. NEWSLETTER. see ANTHROPOLOGY

MUSEUM FUER UR- UND FRUEHGESCHICHTE DER BEZIRKE POTSDAM, FRANKFURT - ODER UND COTTBUS. VEROEFFENTLICHUNGEN. see HISTORY

069 398   GW   ISSN 0075-8663
MUSEUM FUER VOELKERKUNDE, LEIPZIG. JAHRBUCH. irreg., vol.38, 1989. price varies. Akademie-Verlag Berlin, Leipziger Str. 3-4, 1086 Berlin, Germany. TELEX 114420-AVERL-DD. **Indexed:** A.I.C.P.

708 390   GW   ISSN 0075-8671
MUSEUM FUER VOELKERKUNDE, LEIPZIG. VEROEFFENTLICHUNGEN. irreg., vol. 35, 1988. price varies. Akademie-Verlag Berlin, Leipziger Str. 3-4, 1086 Berlin, Germany. TELEX 114420-AVERL-DD.

069   US
MUSEUM HIGHLIGHTS. 1982. q. membership. (Maricopa County Historical Society) Desert Caballeros Western Museum, Box 1446, Wickenburg, AZ 85358. TEL 602-684-2272. Ed. Cheryl Taylor. circ. 2,000.

069   UK
AM121
MUSEUM MANAGEMENT AND CURATORSHIP. 4/yr. £100 (Europe £110; elsewhere £120). Butterworth - Heinemann Ltd. (Subsidiary of: Reed International PLC), Linacre House, Jordan Hill, Oxford OX2 8DP, England. TEL 0865-310366. FAX 0865-310898. TELEX 83111 BHPOXF G. (Subscr. to: Turpin Transactions Ltd., Distribution Center, Blackhorse Rd., Letchworth, Herts SG6 1HN, England. TEL 0462-672555) Eds. P. Cannon-Brooks, C. Cannon-Brooks. (also avail. in microform from UMI; back issues avail.) **Indexed:** Art & Archaeol.Tech.Abstr., Br.Archaeol.Abstr., Br.Tech.Ind.
   Formerly: International Journal of Museum Management and Curatorship (ISSN 0260-4779)
   Description: Provides an international forum for the exchange of information between museum professionals. Encourages a continuous reassessment of the disciplines governing the establishment, care, presentation and understanding of museum collections.
   Refereed Serial

069.097   US   ISSN 0027-4089
AM1   CODEN: MUNSAJ
MUSEUM NEWS. 1924. bi-m. $34. American Association of Museums, 1225 Eye St., N.W., Ste. 200, Washington, DC 20005. TEL 202-289-1818. FAX 202-289-6578. Ed. Bill Anderson. adv.; bk.rev.; illus.; index; circ. 12,000. **Indexed:** Abstr.Anthropol., Art & Archaeol.Tech.Abstr., Artbibl.Mod., Arts & Hum.Cit.Ind., Avery Ind.Archit.Per., Bk.Rev.Ind. (1965-1986), Br.Archaeol.Abstr., Child.Bk.Rev.Ind. (1965-1986), Curr.Cont.
   —BLDSC shelfmark: 5987.890000.
   Description: Magazine for museum professionals.

500.907   CN   ISSN 0828-2773
MUSEUM NEWS AND VIEWS FROM THE NOVA SCOTIA MUSEUM COMPLEX; 22 branches throughout Nova Scotia. 1985. bi-m. free. Nova Scotia Museum, 1747 Summer St., Halifax, N.S. B3H 3A6, Canada. TEL 902-429-4610. Ed. Joan Waldron. circ. 10,000.
   Description: Covers events and offers information about provincial museums, historic houses, and restored mills.

069   US
N714.P7
MUSEUM NOTES (PROVIDENCE). 1913. a. $7.50. Rhode Island School of Design, Museum of Art, 224 Benefit St., Providence, RI 02903. FAX 401-831-7106. Ed. Judith A. Singsen. circ. 6,400.
   Formerly: Rhode Island School of Design. Bulletin.
   Description: Covers museum departments, museum acquisitions and news.

069 700 979   US
MUSEUM NOTES (SPOKANE). 1960? bi-m. $25. Eastern Washington State Historical Society, Cheney Cowles Museum, W. 2316 First Ave., Spokane, WA 99204. TEL 509-456-3931. Ed. Glenn Mason. circ. 1,200. (back issues avail.)
   Description: To inform members of events, programs, exhibits, acquisitions, future plans.

708   SW   ISSN 0081-5691
DS714
MUSEUM OF FAR EASTERN ANTIQUITIES. BULLETIN. 1929. a. price varies. Oestasiatiska Museet - Museum of Far Eastern Antiquities, Skeppsholmen, Box 16381, 103 27 Stockholm, Sweden. TEL 08-666-4400. FAX 08-611-2845. Ed. Jan Wirgin. circ. 600. (back issues avail.) **Indexed:** A.I.C.P., M.L.A.
   —BLDSC shelfmark: 2624.500000.

MUSEUM OF FINE ARTS, BOSTON. JOURNAL. see *ART*

069 500   US
MUSEUM OF SCIENCE MAGAZINE. 1947. bi-m. membership only. Museum of Science (Boston), Science Pk., Boston, MA 02114-1099. TEL 617-589-0246. FAX 617-589-0454. Ed. Lorraine T. Welsh. circ. 37,000.
   Incorporates: Museum of Science Newsletter.

708   US
MUSEUM OF THE CITY OF NEW YORK QUARTERLY. 1986. q. free. Museum of the City of New York, 5th Ave. at 103rd St., New York, NY 10029. TEL 212-534-1672. FAX 212-534-5974. Ed. Liz Smith. circ. 3,000 (controlled). (back issues avail.)

069.9   US
MUSEUM OF THE GREAT PLAINS NEWSLETTER. 1977. a. $15 includes Great Plains journal. Institute of the Great Plains, Box 68, Lawton, OK 73502. TEL 405-581-3460. Ed. Steve Wilson. circ. 1,000. (looseleaf format; back issues avail.)
   Description: Covers activities of Museum of the Great Plains.

MUSEUM OF VICTORIA. MEMOIRS. see *BIOLOGY — Zoology*

MUSEUM OF VICTORIA. OCCASIONAL PAPERS. see *BIOLOGY — Zoology*

069   CN   ISSN 0822-5931
MUSEUM QUARTERLY. 1971. q. Can.$16 to non-members; institutions $26. Ontario Museum Association, 50 Baldwin St., George Brown House, Toronto, Ont. M5T 1L4, Canada. TEL 416-348-8672. FAX 416-348-8689. Ed. Sonja Tanner Kaplash. adv.; bk.rev.; circ. 2,400 (controlled). (also avail. in microfilm from MML; back issues avail.; reprint service avail. from MML) **Indexed:** Art & Archaeol.Tech.Abstr., Can.Per.Ind.
   Formerly: Ontario Museum Quarterly.

MUSEUM RECORD. see *GENEALOGY AND HERALDRY*

069   UK   ISSN 0954-0423
MUSEUM REPORTER. 1988. 6/yr. free. National Museums of Scotland, Chambers St., Edinburgh EH1 1JF, Scotland. TEL 031-225-7534. FAX 031-225-7534. Ed. Barbara Buchan. bk.rev.
   Description: Collections and activities of the National Museums.

MUSEUM STORE. see *BUSINESS AND ECONOMICS — Marketing And Purchasing*

069 700   US   ISSN 0740-0403
MUSEUM YEAR. 1962. a. $3. Museum of Fine Arts, Boston, 465 Huntington Ave., Boston, MA 02115. TEL 617-267-9300. FAX 617-267-0280. Ed. Cynthia Purvis. circ. 27,000.
   Formerly: Boston Museum of Fine Arts. Museum Year. Annual Report.
   Description: Annual report of the Boston Museum of Fine Arts, focusing on annual projects and exhibits, staff activities, publications, programs, and curatorial acquisitions.

708 059   UK   ISSN 0141-6723
N1020
MUSEUMS AND GALLERIES IN GREAT BRITAIN AND IRELAND. 1955. a. £6.40. Reed Information Services Ltd. (Subsidiary of: Reed International PLC), Windsor Court, E. Grinstead House, E. Grinstead, W. Sussex RH19 1XA, England. TEL 0342-326972. FAX 0342-315130. TELEX 95127 INFSER G. Ed. Sheila Alcock. adv.; circ. 20,000.
   Formerly: Museums and Galleries (ISSN 0077-2267)
   Description: Leading guide to the local and national collections of the British Isles.

708   UN   ISSN 0077-233X
MUSEUMS AND MONUMENTS SERIES. (Editions in English, French and Spanish) 1952. irreg., vol.20, 1987. price varies. Unesco, 7-9 Place de Fontenoy, 75700 Paris, France. TEL 577-16-10. (Dist. in U.S. by: Unipub, 4611-F Assembly Dr., Lanham, MD 20706-4391) **Indexed:** GeoRef.
   —BLDSC shelfmark: 5989.915000.

069   AT
MUSEUMS ASSOCIATION OF AUSTRALIA. QUARTERLY NEWS. 1975. q. Aus.$15. Museums Association of Australia Inc., New South Wales Branch, c/o Museum of Applied Arts & Sciences, P.O. Box K346, Haymarket, N.S.W. 2000, Australia. TEL 2-217-0111. FAX 2-212-1182. Ed. Suzanne Davidson. adv.; bk.rev.; charts; illus.; tr.lit.; circ. 500. (back issues avail.)

069   AT   ISSN 0812-7883
MUSEUMS AUSTRALIA. 1983. a. Aus.$30. Museums Association of Australia Inc., c/o Kyle Winkworth, Ed., 8 Yralla St., Newtown, N.S.W. 2042. TEL 03-419-7092. adv.; circ. 1,600. (back issues avail.)

069.094   UK   ISSN 0027-416X
AM1
MUSEUMS JOURNAL. 1901. m. £30 to individuals; institutions £48. Museums Association, 34 Bloomsbury Way, London WC1A 2SF, England. TEL 071-404-4767. FAX 071-430-0167. Ed. Maurice Davies. adv.; bk.rev.; circ. 4,600. (also avail. in microform from BHP) **Indexed:** A.I.C.P., Art Ind., Artbibl.Mod., Br.Archaeol.Abstr., Br.Geol.Lit., Br.Hum.Ind., Br.Tech.Ind., RILA.
   —BLDSC shelfmark: 5990.000000.
   Incorporates (1961-1989): Museums Bulletin.
   Description: Covers new developments, opinions, technical data, historical material and reviews of museums and galleries.

069   II
MUSEUMS NEWSLETTER.* irreg. Museums Association of India, c/o National Museum of Natural History, F I C C I, Museum Building, Barakhamba Road, New Delhi 110002, India.

069 708   GW
MUSEUMS OF THE WORLD/MUSEEN DER WELT. (Text in English) 1973. irreg., 4th ed., 1992. DM.320($325) K.G. Saur Verlag KG, Ortlerstr. 8, Postfach 701620, 8000 Munich 70, Germany. TEL 089-76902-0. FAX 089-76902150. (N. America subscr. to: K.G. Saur, A Reed Reference Publishing Company, 121 Chanlon Rd., New Providence, NJ 07974. TEL 908-665-3576) adv.
   Description: Lists museums in over 180 countries, providing a broad outline of historical, geographical and ethnological information. Subject index describes museum holdings.

069   UK   ISSN 0307-7675
MUSEUMS YEARBOOK. (Includes: Directory of Museums and Art Galleries of the British Isles) 1956. a. £45 to non-members. Museums Association, 34 Bloomsbury Way, London WC1A 2SF, England. Ed. Maurice Davies. circ. 2,000.
   Formerly: Museums Calendar (ISSN 0580-2652)
   Description: Contains addresses, staff, admission fees, attendance and facilities.

069   DK   ISSN 0109-5854
MUSEUMSFORENINGEN FOR LAESOE. LITTERATURE. 1983. a. DKK 40. Laesoe Museum, Museumsforeningen for Laesoe, Oesterby Gl. Skole, 9960 Oesterby Havn, Denmark. TEL 45-8-498045. Ed. Michael Teisen. circ. 500.

069   GW   ISSN 0027-4178
MUSEUMSKUNDE. 1905. 3/yr. DM.45. Deutscher Museumsbund, Colmantstr. 14-16, 5300 Bonn 1, Germany. (Subscr. to: Rheinland Verlag, Ehrenfriedstr. 19, 5024 Pulheim 2) Ed. Christoph B. Rueger. adv.; bk.rev.; index; circ. 2,000. **Indexed:** Artbibl.Mod., RILA.

069.094   NO   ISSN 0027-4186
MUSEUMSNYTT. 1951. s-a. NOK 160. Norske Kunst- og Kulturhistoriske Museer, Ullevalsv. 11, 0165 Oslo 1, Norway. Ed.Bd. adv.; bk.rev.; bibl.; illus.; circ. 1,200. **Indexed:** Art & Archaeol.Tech.Abstr., NAA.

069   GW   ISSN 0931-4857
MUSEUMSVERBAND FUER NIEDERSACHSEN UND BREMEN. MITTEILUNGSBLATT. 1966. s-a. DM.30. Museumsverband fuer Niedersachsen und Bremen e.V., c/o Dr. Juergen Hevers, Ed., Staatliches Naturhistorisches Museum, Pockelsstr. 10a, 3300 Braunschweig, Germany. TEL 0531-3914354. (back issues avail.)
   Description: For staff members of museums in Lower Saxony and Bremen.

MUZEJ BRODSKOG POSAVLJA. VIJESTI; godisnjak. see *HUMANITIES: COMPREHENSIVE WORKS*

069   CS   ISSN 0027-5255
MUZEJNI A VLASTIVEDNA PRACE. (Text in Czech; contents page also in English, French, German and Russian) 1961. q. 27 Kcs.($13.20) (Narodni Muzeum, Ustredni Muzeologicky Kabinet) Panorama, Halkova 1, 120 72 Prague 2, Czechoslovakia. Ed. Frantiska Hyndrakova. bk.rev.; circ. 1,600. **Indexed:** Numis.Lit.

MUZEJSKI VJESNIK/MUSEUM NEWS MAGAZINE. see *ARCHAEOLOGY*

MUSEUMS AND ART GALLERIES

069 CS ISSN 0027-5263
MUZEUM; metodicky, studijny a informacny bulletin. (Text in Slovak; contents page and summaries also in English, French, German, Russian) 1954. q. exchange basis. Slovenske Narodne Muzeum, Muzeologicky Ustav, Vajanskeho Nabrezie 2, 814 36 Bratislava, Czechoslovakia. Ed. Maria Rihakova. bk.rev.; charts; illus.; circ. 500.
  Description: Guidance, information and study material for museum and art gallery workers.

MUZEUM LITERATURY IM. ADAMA MICKIEWICZA. BLOK-NOTES. see *LITERATURE*

069.5 709 PL ISSN 0208-8193
MUZEUM NARODOWE W KRAKOWIE. KATALOGI ZBIOROW/NATIONAL MUSEUM IN CRACOW. CATALOGUES OF THE COLLECTIONS. (Text in English, Polish) 1973. irreg., latest 1991. price varies. Muzeum Narodowe w Krakowie, Ul. J. Pilsudskiego 12, 31-109 Krakow, Poland. (Subscr. to: Ars-Polona, Krakowskie Przedmiescie 7, Warsaw, Poland) Ed. Ewa Harenczyk.

069 700 US
N E A GRANTMAKING PROGRAMS: MUSEUMS. a. free. National Endowment for the Arts, Public Information Office, 1100 Pennsylvania Ave., N.W., Washington, DC 20506. TEL 202-682-5400.
  Description: Grant application guidelines.

069 UK
N E M S ANNUAL REPORT. a. £2. North of England Museums Service, House of Recovery, Bath Lane, Newcastle-upon-Tyne NE4 5SQ, England. TEL 091-222-1661. FAX 091-261-4725. adv.; bk.rev.

069 UK ISSN 0267-2618
N E M S NEWS. 1983. q. £6 to non-members. North of England Museums Service, House of Recovery, Bath Lane, Newcastle upon Tyne NE4 5SQ, England. TEL 091-222-1661. FAX 091-261-4725. Ed. Martyn Ladds. adv.; bk.rev.; circ. 350.
  Description: Forum for debate and information on issues relating to the professional practice of museums in the north east region of England.

069 500 JA
N K H NAGAOKA-SHIRITSU KAGAKU HAKUBUTSUKANPO. (Text in Japanese) irreg. Nagaoka-shiritsu Kagaku Hakubutsukan - Nagaoka Municipal Science Museum, 2-1 Yanagihara, Nagaoka-shi, Niigata-ken 940, Japan.

069 500 JA ISSN 0916-6319
NAGOYA DAIGAKU FURUKAWA SOGO KENKYU SHIRYOKAN HOKOKU/NAGOYA UNIVERSITY FURUKAWA MUSEUM. BULLETIN. (Text and summaries in English and Japanese) 1985. a. free. Nagoya Daigaku, Sogo Kenkyu Shiryokan - Nagoya University, University Museum, 1 Furo-cho, Chikusa-ku, Nagoya 464-01, Japan. TEL 052-781-5111. FAX 052-781-9295.
  Formerly (until 1990): Nagoya Daigaku Sogo Kenkyu Shiryoukan Houkoku - Nagoya University Museum. Bulletin (ISSN 0912-5604)

069 900 CS ISSN 0008-7343
NARODNI MUZEUM V PRAZE. CASOPIS: RADA HISTORICKA. (Text in Czech; summaries in English, French, German, Russian) 1827. q. 20 Kcs.($12.30) Narodni Muzeum, Historicke Muzeum, Vaclavske nam. 68, 115 79 Prague 1, Czechoslovakia. FAX 02-236-9489. (Dist. by: Artia, Ve Smeckach 30, 111 27 Prague 1, Czechoslovakia) Ed. Jaroslav Cechura. bk.rev.; charts; illus.; circ. 1,000. Indexed: Amer.Hist.& Life, Hist.Abstr.

069 CS
NARODNI MUZEUM V PRAZE. CASOPIS: RADA PRIRODOVEDNA. (Text in Czech; summaries in English, German, Russian) 1827. q. 20 Kcs.($12.30) Narodni Muzeum, Prirodovedecke Muzeum, Vaclavske nam. 68, 115 79 Prague 1, Czechoslovakia. (Subscr. to: P N S - Ustredni Expedice a Dovoz Tisku Prague, Zavod 01, Administrace Vyvozu Tisku, Kafkova 19, 160 00 Prague 6, Czechoslovakia) Ed. Radvan Horny. bk.rev.; abstr.; illus.; index. Indexed: Chem.Abstr.
  Formerly: Narodni Muzeum. Casopis: Oddil Prirodovedny (ISSN 0008-7351)

600 069 CS
NARODNI TECHNICKE MUZEUM. CATALOGUES OF COLLECTIONS. (Text in English) 1956. irreg. exchange basis. Narodni Technicke Muzeum, Kostelni 42, 170 78 Prague 7, Czechoslovakia.

708 UK ISSN 0953-024X
NATIONAL GALLERIES OF SCOTLAND. BULLETIN. 1981. 6/yr. free. National Galleries of Scotland, Information Department, Belford Rd., Edinburgh EH4 3DR, Scotland. FAX 031-343-2802. Ed. Robert Dalrymple. illus.; circ. 20,000.
  Formerly (until 1987): National Galleries of Scotland. News (ISSN 0261-3220)
  Description: Photographic and informational brochure on temporary exhibits, permanent displays, new acquisitions, and current activities at the Gallery.

NATIONAL GALLERY, LONDON. TECHNICAL BULLETIN. see *ART*

354.689 RH
NATIONAL GALLERY OF ZIMBABWE. ANNUAL REPORT AND BALANCE SHEET AND INCOME AND EXPENDITURE ACCOUNT. 1953. a. free. National Gallery of Zimbabwe, P.O. Box 8155, Causeway, Harare, Zimbabwe. illus.; circ. 400.
  Former titles: National Gallery of Zimbabwe - Rhodesia. Annual Report and Balance Sheet and Income and Expenditure Account; National Gallery of Rhodesia. Annual Report and Balance Sheet and Income and Expenditure Account.

069 SA
NATIONAL MUSEUM, BLOEMFONTEIN. ANNUAL REPORT. a. National Museum, Bloemfontein - Nasionale Museum, Bloemfontein, P.O. Box 266, Bloemfontein, South Africa. TEL 051-479609. FAX 051-479681.

069 JA
NATIONAL MUSEUM OF MODERN ART. ANNUAL REPORT. (Text in English and Japanese) 1957. a. National Museum of Modern Art, Tokyo, 3 Kitanomaru Koen, Chiyoda-ku, Tokyo 102, Japan. Ed. Atsushi Tanaka. circ. 1,000.
  Description: Listing of all exhibitions, events, and collected works of the three institutions.

069 NZ ISSN 0110-9464
NATIONAL MUSEUM OF NEW ZEALAND. BULLETIN. 1906. irreg. price varies. National Museum of New Zealand, Board of Trustees, Buckle St., Box 467, Wellington, New Zealand. FAX 0064-4-384-6035. Ed. M.M. Cresswell. Indexed: Biol.Abstr.
  —BLDSC shelfmark: 6027.539000.

069 NZ ISSN 0110-1447
  CODEN: MSNZDT
NATIONAL MUSEUM OF NEW ZEALAND. MISCELLANEOUS SERIES. 1976. irreg. National Museum of New Zealand, Board of Trustees, Buckle St., Wellington, New Zealand. TEL 0064-4-384-6035. FAX 04-3857157. Ed. M.M. Cresswell. Indexed: Deep Sea Res.& Oceanogr.Abstr.

069 NZ ISSN 0110-943X
AM101.W4715 CODEN: RNMZDA
NATIONAL MUSEUM OF NEW ZEALAND RECORDS. 1975. irreg. price varies. National Museum of New Zealand, Board of Trustees, Buckle St., Wellington, New Zealand. FAX 0064-4-384-6035. Ed. M.M. Cresswell. bk.rev.; bibl.; charts; illus.; circ. 350. Indexed: Biol.Abstr., Deep Sea Res.& Oceanogr.Abstr.
  Supersedes: Dominion Museum Records; Dominion Museum Records in Ethnology.

708 TZ ISSN 0082-1675
NATIONAL MUSEUM OF TANZANIA. ANNUAL REPORT. 1966. a. National Museum of Tanzania, P.O. Box 511, Dar es Salaam, Tanzania. TEL 051-31365. circ. 1,000. Indexed: A.I.C.P.

708 PH ISSN 0076-3756
NATIONAL MUSEUM OF THE PHILIPPINES. ANNUAL REPORT. (Text in English) 1967. a. free. National Museum of the Philippines, Padre Burgos Street, Manila, Philippines. TEL 48-14-27. FAX 632-46-19-69. Ed. Rosario B. Tantoco. circ. controlled. (processed)
  Description: Contains the accomplishments of the National Museum in the fields of science, culture and education during the year under review.

709.5 CH ISSN 1011-9078
NATIONAL PALACE MUSEUM. MONTHLY OF CHINESE ART. (Text in Chinese) 1983. m. $133. National Palace Museum - Kuo Li Ku Kung Po Wu Yuan, Wai Shuang Hsi, Shih Lin, Taipei, Taiwan, Republic of China. FAX 02-882-1440. (US subscr. to: World Journal Bookstore, 141-07 20th Ave., Whitestone, NY 11367. TEL 718-746-8889) Ed. Chang Yueh-yun. bk.rev.; illus.; index; circ. 10,000. Key Title: Gugong Wenwu Yuekan.
  Description: Presents articles, analysis, and photographs of Chinese art and antiques from the museum's collection.

069.095 709.5 CH ISSN 1011-9086
N3750.T32
NATIONAL PALACE MUSEUM. NEWSLETTER. Variant title: National Palace Museum. Newsletter & Gallery Guide. (Text in Chinese and English) 1968. q. free. National Palace Museum - Kuo Li Ku Kung Po Wu Yuan, Wai Shuang Hsi, Shih Lin, Taipei, Taiwan, Republic of China. FAX 886-2-8821440. Eds. Denise R. Vetterlein, Pey-shuh Lee. charts; illus.; circ. 25,000. Key Title: Gugong Zhanlan Tongxun.
  Description: Highlights of the National Palace Museum's newest publications, exhibitions and activities.

069.095 CH ISSN 1011-906X
N3750.T32
NATIONAL PALACE MUSEUM BULLETIN. (Text in English) 1966. bi-m. $20. National Palace Museum - Kuo Li Ku Kung Po Wu Yuan, Wai Shuang Hsi, Shih Lin, Taipei, Taiwan, Republic of China. FAX 886-28821440. Ed. Su Tu-jen. bibl.; illus.; index; circ. 1,000. Indexed: Art & Archaeol.Tech.Abstr. Key Title: Gugong Tongxun Yingwen Shuangyuekan.
  Description: Articles of scholarly research on artistic and cultural subjects.

709.5 CH ISSN 1011-9094
NATIONAL PALACE MUSEUM RESEARCH QUARTERLY. (Text in Chinese) 1966. q. $54. National Palace Museum - Kuo Li Ku Kung Po Wu Yuan, Wai-Shuang-Hsi, Shih-Lin, Taipei, Taiwan, Republic of China. FAX 886-2-8821440. Ed. Fung Ming-chu. charts; illus.; index; circ. 1,000. Key Title: Gugong Xueshu Jikan.
  Formerly (until 1983): National Palace Museum Quarterly (ISSN 0454-675X)
  Description: Journal to further an atmosphere of scholarly and professional exchange.

NATIONAL SCIENCE MUSEUM. BULLETIN. SERIES E: PHYSICAL SCIENCES AND ENGINEERING/KOKURITSU KAGAKU HAKUBUTSUKAN KENKYU HOKOKU. E RUI, RIKOGAKU. see *ENGINEERING*

NATURAL HISTORY MUSEUM AND INSTITUTE, CHIBA. JOURNAL. see *HISTORY — History Of Asia*

NATURAL HISTORY RESEARCH. see *HISTORY — History Of Asia*

500.907 AU ISSN 0028-095X
NATURHISTORISCHES MUSEUM IN WIEN. MONATSPROGRAMM. 1949. m. S.3. Naturhistorisches Museum in Wien, Burgring 7, P.F. 417, A-1014 Vienna, Austria. FAX 0222-935254. circ. 4,400. (looseleaf format)

708.1 US
NELSON-ATKINS MUSEUM OF ART. CALENDAR OF EVENTS. 1934. 10/yr. membership. Nelson-Atkins Museum of Art, 4525 Oak St., Kansas City, MO 64111-1873. TEL 816-561-4000. FAX 816-561-7154. Ed. Gina O'Neal. illus.; circ. 14,500.
  Formerly: Nelson Gallery and Atkins Museum. Gallery Events (ISSN 0047-9322)

069 GW ISSN 0028-3282
AM49
NEUE MUSEUMSKUNDE; Theorie und Praxis der Museumsarbeit. (Text in German; contents page and summaries in English, French, and Russian) 1958. q. about DM.61.20. (Ministerium fuer Kultur, Rat fuer Museumswesen) Deutscher Verlag der Wissenschaften, Johannes-Dieckmann-Str. 10, 1080 Berlin, Germany. Ed. Heinz Schilling. adv.; bk.rev.; abstr.; bibl.; charts; illus.; index. (tabloid format) Indexed: Art & Archaeol.Tech.Abstr.

708 US ISSN 0077-7919
NEVADA. STATE MUSEUM, CARSON CITY. OCCASIONAL PAPERS. 1968. irreg., no.4, 1980. price varies. Nevada State Museum, Department of Anthropology, Department of Anthropology, Publications Office, Capitol Complex, Carson City, NV 89710. TEL 702-687-4810. circ. 1,000.

708 US ISSN 0077-7927
AM101
NEVADA. STATE MUSEUM, CARSON CITY. POPULAR SERIES. 1965. irreg., no.10, 1990. price varies. Nevada State Museum, Publications Office, Capitol Complex, Carson City, NV 89710. TEL 702-687-4810. Ed.Bd. circ. 1,000.

069 US
NEVADA STATE MUSEUM NEWSLETTER. 1972. bi-m. free to members. Nevada State Museum, Docent Council, Capitol Complex, Carson City, NV 89710. TEL 702-687-4810. Ed. Jack Gibson. bk.rev.; circ. 1,000.

069 974 745.1 US
NEW GLEANINGS. 1976. q. free to qualified personnel. Historic Cherry Hill, 523 1-2 S. Pearl St., Albany, NY 12202. TEL 518-434-4806. Ed. Leslie Lafrance. bk.rev.; circ. 700. (looseleaf format; back issues avail.)
Description: Covers activities of the museum including fundraising and new research.

069 US
NEW MUSEUM NEWSLETTER. 1977. q. $35. New Museum of Contemporary Art, Public Affairs, 583 Broadway, New York, NY 10012. TEL 212-219-1222. FAX 212-431-5328. Ed. Sara Palmer. circ. 15,000.
Formerly: New Museum News.

069 UK
NEW RESEARCH IN MUSEUM STUDIES: AN INTERNATIONAL SERIES. 1990. a. £45. Athlone Press Ltd., 1 Park Dr., London NW11 7SG, England. TEL 081-458-0888. (Subscr. to: B M S, Merlin Way, N. Weald Industrial Estate, N. Weald, Epping, Essex CM16 6MR, England) Ed. Susan Pearce. bk.rev.; film rev.; abstr.; bibl.; illus.; stat.; index. (back issues avail.)

069 US
NEW YORK (CITY). MUSEUM OF THE CITY OF NEW YORK. ANNUAL REPORT. 1923. a. free. Museum of the City of New York, Fifth Ave. and 103rd St., NY 10029. TEL 212-534-1672. FAX 212-534-5974. Ed. Liz Smith. charts; illus.; circ. 5,000.
Supersedes (1970?-1982): New York (City). Museum of the City of New York. Bulletin.

069.097 US
NEWARK MUSEUM. EXHIBITIONS & EVENTS. 1944. bi-m. $4 to non-members. Newark Museum Association, 49 Washington St., Box 540, Newark, NJ 07101. TEL 201-596-6550. Ed. Nina Stack. illus.; circ. 15,000. **Indexed:** Amer.Hist.& Life.
Formerly (until 1983): Newark Museum. News Notes (ISSN 0028-9256)

NEWSBANK REVIEW OF THE ARTS: FINE ARTS AND ARCHITECTURE. see ART

708.1 US ISSN 0029-2567
N715.R2
NORTH CAROLINA MUSEUM OF ART. BULLETIN. 1957. irreg. $4. North Carolina Museum of Art, c/o Anna Upchurch, 2110 Blue Ridge Blvd., Raleigh, NC 27607. TEL 919-833-1935. illus.; circ. 1,000. **Indexed:** Artbibl.Mod., RILA.

069 US
NORTH CAROLINA MUSEUM OF ART. PREVIEW. 1983. 4/yr. $25 membership. North Carolina Museum of Art, c/o Anna Upchurch, 2110 Blue Ridge Blvd., Raleigh, NC 27607. TEL 919-833-1935. Eds. Nancy Margolis, Ann Waterfall. illus.; circ. 10,000.

NOTIZIARIO VINCIANO. see ART

NYE FAMILY NEWSLETTER. see GENEALOGY AND HERALDRY

069 CN ISSN 0704-5824
OCCASIONAL; an occasional journal for Nova Scotia Museums. 1973. s-a. free. Nova Scotia Museum, 1747 Summer St., Halifax, N.S. B3H 3A6, Canada. TEL 902-429-4610. Ed. Deborah Trask. bk.rev.; index; circ. 600.

708 SZ
OEFFENTLICHE KUNSTSAMMLUNG. MUSEUM FUER GEGENWART. JAHRESBERICHT. 1904. irreg., latest 1984. price varies. Oeffentliche Kunstsammlung, Museum fuer Gegenwartskunst, Kunstmuseum Basel, St. Albangraben 16, CH-4010 Basel, Switzerland. FAX 061-220845. Ed. Paul H. Boerlin.
Formerly: Oeffentliche Kunstsammlung. Jahresbericht (ISSN 0067-4311)

708.1 AU ISSN 0029-909X
OESTERREICHISCHE GALERIE. MITTEILUNGEN. 1957. a. S.120. Oesterreichische Galerie, Prinz Eugen-Str. 27, A-1037 Vienna, Austria. FAX 784337. Ed.Bd. adv.; illus.; circ. 1,200. (tabloid format) **Indexed:** Artbibl.Mod.
Description: Includes art reviews and a report of the gallery's activities.

069 US ISSN 0090-6700
AM10.A2
OFFICIAL MUSEUM DIRECTORY. 1961. a. $179 to non-members; members $67; institutions $145. (American Association of Museums) National Register Publishing Co., A Reed Reference Publishing Company, Division of Reed Publishing (USA) Inc., 121 Chanlon Rd., New Providence, NJ 07974. TEL 800-521-8110. FAX 908-665-6688. TELEX 138 755. (Subscr. to: R.R. Bowker, Order Dept., Box 31, New Providence, NJ 07974) adv.; abstr.; circ. 4,000.
Description: Lists over 7,000 institutions in 85 categories - including museums, art associations, nature centers, aquariums, botanical gardens, planetariums, zoos, and others. Shows where they are, what they exhibit, and who manages them.

708.4 FR
OFFICIEL DES GALERIES. no.155, 1976. m. 15 rue du Temple, 75004 Paris, France. Ed. J. Wolman. adv.

069 500 JA ISSN 0385-0285
OKINAWA-KENRITSU HAKUBUTSUKAN KIYO/OKINAWA PREFECTURAL MUSEUM. BULLETIN. (Text in Japanese) 1975. a. Okinawa-kenritsu hakubutsukan - Okinawa Prefectural Museum, 1-1 Shuri Onaka-cho, Naha-shi, Okinawa-ken 903, Japan.
Description: Contains original papers.

708 NE
ORANJE-NASSAU MUSEUM. JAARBOEK. a. fl.29.50. (Vereniging "Oranje-Nassau Museum") Walburg Pers BV, P.O. Box 222, 7200 AE Zutphen, Netherlands. TEL 05750-10522. FAX 05750-41025.

069 JA ISSN 0389-8105
OSAKA-SHIRITSU SHIZENSHI HAKUBUTSUKAN KANPO/OSAKA MUSEUM OF NATURAL HISTORY. ANNUAL REPORT. (Text in Japanese) 1964. a. Osaka-shiritsu Shizenshi Hakubutsukan - Osaka Museum of Natural History, 1-23 Nagai Koen, Higashi-Sumiyoshi-ku, Osaka-shi, Osaka-fu 546, Japan. Ed. Husato Ogawa. circ. 1,200. **Indexed:** Biol.Abstr., Jap.Per.Ind.

069.094 NO ISSN 0030-6703
DL401 CODEN: OTTADD
OTTAR. 1954. 5/yr. NOK 110. Tromsoe Museum, University of Tromsoe, 9000 Tromsoe, Norway. TEL 08-45000. FAX 08-389158. Ed. Arne C. Nilssen. adv.; charts; illus.; cum.index: nos.1-190 (1954-1990); circ. 6,000. **Indexed:** GeoRef., NAA.

069 US
LAS PALABRAS. 1979. q. membership. Millicent Rogers Museum, Box A, Taos, NM 87571. TEL 505-758-2462. FAX 505-758-5751. Ed. Ione Caley. circ. 1,500.
Description: Covers the collection and interpretation of the art, history, and culture of the Native American, Hispanic, and Anglo peoples of the Southwest, focusing on Taos and northern New Mexico.

708 701.18 GW
PAN; Zeitschrift fuer Kunst und Kultur. 1980. m. DM.99.60. Burda GmbH, Arabellastr. 23, 8000 Munich 81, Germany. TEL 089-92500. (Subscr. to: Burda GmbH, Hauptstr. 130, 7600 Offenburg, Germany) Ed. Hubert Burda. adv.; illus.; circ. 100,000. (also avail. in microfilm from KTO)

069 500 US ISSN 0079-0354
AM101 CODEN: PSSEAL
PEARCE-SELLARDS SERIES. 1963. irreg., no.49, 1989. Texas Memorial Museum, University of Texas at Austin, 2400 Trinity, Austin, TX 78705. TEL 512-471-1604. **Indexed:** Biol.Abstr.

PENNSYLVANIA HERITAGE. see HISTORY — History Of North And South America

069 US ISSN 0730-5435
N577
PERCEPTIONS (INDIANAPOLIS); a scholarly publication of the Indianapolis Museum of Art. 1981. irreg. Indianapolis Museum of Art, 1200 W. 38th St., Indianapolis, IN 46208. TEL 317-923-1331. FAX 317-926-8931. illus.; circ. 1,500. **Indexed:** Artbibl.Mod., RILA.

708.1 US ISSN 0031-7160
PHAROS (ST. PETERSBURG). 1963. a. membership. Museum of Fine Arts, St. Petersburg, 255 Beach Dr. N.E., St. Petersburg, FL 33701. TEL 813-896-2667. FAX 813-894-4638. Ed. Diane Lesko. illus.; circ. 5,500. **Indexed:** RILA.
Description: Scholarly research and studies on art history, acquisitions, and collections.

708.1 US ISSN 0031-7314
N685
PHILADELPHIA MUSEUM OF ART. BULLETIN. 1903. q. $18. Philadelphia Museum of Art, Box 7646, Philadelphia, PA 19101. TEL 215-763-8100. FAX 215-236-8730. Ed. George Marcus. illus.; circ. 7,000. **Indexed:** Art & Archaeol.Tech.Abstr., Art.Ind., Artbibl.Mod., Arts & Hum.Cit.Ind., Avery Ind.Architect.Per., Curr.Cont., RILA.
—BLDSC shelfmark: 2683.580000.

500.907 GW ISSN 0343-7620
CODEN: PABKDZ
PHILIPPIA. (Text in German; summaries in English) 1970. s-a. DM.15. Naturkundemuseum der Stadt Kassel, Steinweg 2, 3500 Kassel, Germany. TEL 0561-7874014. circ. 800. (back issues avail.)

069 PH ISSN 0117-0686
▼**PHILIPPINES. REPUBLIC. NATIONAL MUSEUM PAPERS.** (Text in English) 1990. s-a. $10. National Museum, Padre Burgos St., Manila, Philippines. TEL 48-14-27. FAX 632-46-19-69. (Co-sponsor: Concerned Citizens for the National Museum, Inc.) Ed.Bd.

700 US ISSN 0032-1346
F806 CODEN: PLTUAP
PLATEAU. 1928. q. $20. (Museum of Northern Arizona) Museum of Northern Arizona Press, Rt. 4, Box 720, Flagstaff, AZ 86001. TEL 602-774-5211. FAX 602-947-2126. Ed. Diana Clark Lubick. charts; illus.; index; circ. 3,500. **Indexed:** A.I.C.P., GeoRef., Hist.Abstr.
—BLDSC shelfmark: 6537.840000.

069 US
PONY EXPRESS MAIL. 1972. m. $10 (effective 1992). Pony Express Historical Association, Inc., Box 1022, 12th and Penn, St. Joseph, MO 64502. TEL 816-232-8206. (Co-sponsors: Patee House Museum; Jesse James Home) Ed. Gary Chilcote. circ. 500. (looseleaf format)
Description: Chronicles news and activities of the Patee House Museum, headquarters of the Pony Express, and the Jesse James Home, and events pertaining to the Pony Express and Jesse James.

069.5 US ISSN 8755-2035
N719
PORTICUS. 1978. biennial. $8.50. University of Rochester, Memorial Art Gallery, 500 University Ave., Rochester, NY 14607. TEL 716-244-7032. FAX 716-473-6266. Ed. Bernard Barryte. circ. 1,500. (back issues avail.) **Indexed:** Art Ind., Artbibl.Mod., RILA.
Description: Scholarly articles on the museum's collection, exhibitions and lectures.

069 US
PORTLAND ART MUSEUM NEWSLETTER. 1949. m. membership. Oregon Art Institute, 1219 S.W. Park Ave., Portland, OR 97205. TEL 503-226-2811. FAX 503-226-2842. Ed. Diane Kantor. adv.; circ. 20,000. (controlled).
Former titles (until 1991): Oregon Art Institute Newsletter; Portland Art Association Newsletter; Portland Art Association Calendar; Portland Art Museum Calendar.

3532 MUSEUMS AND ART GALLERIES

069 708 976   US
PRESIDENTIAL MUSEUM. NEWS AND VIEWS. 1986. q. $25. Presidential Museum, 622 N. Lee, Odessa, TX 79761. TEL 915-332-7123. Ed. Rob Reese. circ. 500. (tabloid format; back issues avail.)
Description: Publicizes events of the Presidential Museum, including articles related to the Presidency and American history.

708.1   US   ISSN 0032-843X
N1
PRINCETON UNIVERSITY. ART MUSEUM. RECORD. 1942. s-a. $11. Princeton University, Art Museum, Princeton, NJ 08544-1018. TEL 609-258-4341. FAX 609-258-5949. Ed. Jill Guthrie. bibl.; illus.; cum.index every 10 yrs.; circ. 1,500. (also avail. in microform from UMI; reprint service avail. from UMI) **Indexed:** Art Ind., Artbibl.Mod., RILA.
—BLDSC shelfmark: 7313.300000.
Description: Gives history and criticism on pieces in the museum's collection.

387 979 069.9   US   ISSN 0891-2661
QUARTERDECK. 1973. q. $15. Columbia River Maritime Museum, Inc., 1792 Marine Dr., Astoria, OR 97103. TEL 503-325-2323. FAX 503-325-2331. illus.; circ. 1,900. (back issues avail.)
Formerly (until Fall 1989): Quarterdeck Review.
Description: News, historical vignettes, and announcements pertaining to the activities of the Columbia River Maritime Museum in Oregon.

069 708   AT
QUEEN VICTORIA MUSEUM AND ART GALLERY. ANNUAL REPORT. 1902. a. free. Queen Victoria Museum and Art Gallery, c/o Kay Dimmack, Wellington St., Launceston, Tas. 7250, Australia. TEL 003-316777. FAX 003-371117. Ed. C.B. Tassell. circ. 500.

069 708 500   AT   ISSN 0085-5278
AM101   CODEN: RQVMAY
QUEEN VICTORIA MUSEUM AND ART GALLERY. LAUNCESTON, TASMANIA. RECORDS. 1942. irreg., no.100, 1991. price varies. Queen Victoria Museum and Art Gallery, c/o Kaye Dimmack, Wellington Street, Launceston, Tasmania 7250, Australia. TEL 003-316777. FAX 003-371117. Ed. C.B. Tassell. circ. 250. **Indexed:** AESIS, Biol.Abstr., GeoRef.
—BLDSC shelfmark: 7324.000000.

069.7   AT   ISSN 0079-8835
QH1   CODEN: MQUMA8
QUEENSLAND MUSEUM, BRISBANE. MEMOIRS. 1912. irreg. price varies. Queensland Museum, P.O. Box 300, South Brisbane, Qld. 4101, Australia. TEL 07-840-7664. FAX 07-846-1918. Ed. P.A. Jell. circ. 650. **Indexed:** AESIS, Aus.Sci.Ind., Biol.Abstr., GeoRef., Rev.Appl.Entomol., Zoo.Rec.
—BLDSC shelfmark: 5629.800000.

069 708   US
R C H A NEWSLETTER. 1971. q. $12.50 to individuals; institutions $20 (includes: R C H A Technical Information Sheet). Regional Council of Historical Agencies, 1400 N. State St., Syracuse, NY 13208. TEL 315-475-1525. Ed. Jackie Day. adv.; bk.rev.; bibl. (tabloid format; back issues avail.)

069 708   US
R C H A TECHNICAL INFORMATION SHEET. 1971. irreg. $12.50 to individuals; institutions $20 (includes: R C H A Newsletter). Regional Council of Historical Agencies, 1400 N. State St., Syracuse, NY 13208. TEL 315-475-1525. Ed. Jackie Day. bibl. (tabloid format; back issues avail.)

R.E. OLDS TRANSPORTATION MUSEUM NEWSLETTER. see TRANSPORTATION

708   CN   ISSN 0035-7154
R.L.C.'S MUSEUM GAZETTE. 1966. irreg. Richard L. Coulton, Ed. & Pub., Bentley, Alta. T0C 0J0, Canada. adv.; bk.rev.; abstr.; charts; tr.lit.; cum.index; circ. 400. (processed)

069   US
RAWLS MUSEUM ARTS BULLETIN. 1981. m. Walter Cecil Rawls Museum, Box 318, Courtland, VA 23837. TEL 804-653-2821. Ed. K. Paul Johnson. circ. 250.

069.5   US
REDDING MUSEUM. OCCASIONAL PAPERS. 1980. irreg. $10. Redding Museum and Art Center, Box 427, Redding, CA 96099. TEL 916-243-4994. Eds. James Dotta, Margaret Kardell. circ. 1,000.

069   AG
REVISTA DEL MUSEO AMERICANISTA. 1969. a. Museo Americanista de Antropologia, Historia, Numismatica y Ciencias Naturales, Manuel Castro 254, Lomas de Zamora, Buenos Aires, Argentina.

069   RM
REVISTA MUZEELOR. (Text in Rumanian; summaries in English, French, Russian) 1964. 10/yr. 360 lei($91) Ministerul Culturii, Piata Presei Libere 1, Sector 1, Bucharest, Rumania. (Subscr. to: Calea Grivitei, 66-68, Box 12201, Bucharest, Ruamnia) Ed. Gavril Sarafoleanu. bk.rev.; bibl.; charts; illus. **Indexed:** Numis.Lit.
Former titles: Revista Muzeelor si Monumentelor. Muzee; Revista Muzeelor (ISSN 0035-0206)

708.4   FR   ISSN 0035-2608
REVUE DU LOUVRE ET DES MUSEES DE FRANCE. (Summaries in English, German) 1951. bi-m. 450 F. (foreign 550 F.). Editions de la Reunion des Musees Nationaux, 49 rue Etienne Marcel, 75001 Paris, France. TEL 40-13-48-49. FAX 40-13-48-61. Ed. Jean-Pierre Cuzin. adv.; bk.rev.; illus.; index; circ. 13,000. **Indexed:** Art & Archaeol.Tech.Abstr., Art Ind., Artbibl.Mod., Arts & Hum.Cit.Ind., Avery Ind.Archit.Per., Curr.Cont., RILA.

069   DK   ISSN 0107-928X
ROMU. 1980. a. DKK 70. Roskilde Museums Forlag, Sankt Ols Gade 17, 4000 Roskilde, Denmark. TEL 42-36 60 44. FAX 46-32-16-47. Eds. Flemming Rasmussen, Frank Birkebaek. illus.; circ. 1,000. **Indexed:** NAA.

ROYAL AUSTRALIAN HISTORICAL SOCIETY. TECHNICAL INFORMATION SERVICE. see HISTORY — History Of Australasia And Other Areas

069   CN   ISSN 0840-7681
ROYAL BRITISH COLUMBIA MUSEUM. SPECIAL PUBLICATIONS. irreg. price varies. Royal British Columbia Museum, 675 Bellville St., Victoria, B.C. V8V 1X4, Canada. TEL 604-387-3701. (Subscr. to: Crown Publications, 546 Yates St., Victoria, B.C. V8W 1K8, Canada. TEL 604-386-4636) (back issues avail.)

069 500   CN   ISSN 0843-5383
ROYAL BRITISH COLUMBIA MUSEUM MEMOIRS. 1988. irreg. price varies. Royal British Columbia Museum, 675 Bellville St., Victoria, B.C. V8V 1X4, Canada. TEL 604-387-3701. (Subscr. to: Crown Publications, 546 Yates St., Victoria, B.C. V8W 1K8, Canada. TEL 604-386-4636) (back issues avail.)

708   CN   ISSN 0082-5115
AM101
ROYAL ONTARIO MUSEUM. ANNUAL REPORT. 1949. a. free. Royal Ontario Museum, Publication Services, 100 Queen's Park, Toronto, Ont. M5S 2C6, Canada. TEL 416-586-5581. FAX 416-586-5863.

500.907 700   CN   ISSN 0316-1269
ROYAL ONTARIO MUSEUM. HISTORY, TECHNOLOGY AND ART MONOGRAPHS. 1973. irreg. price varies. Royal Ontario Museum, Publication Services, 100 Queen's Park, Toronto, Ont. M5S 2C6, Canada. TEL 416-586-5581. FAX 416-586-5863. (Subscr. to: University of Toronto Press, Order Fulfilment Division, 5201 Dufferin St., Downsview, Ont. H3H 5T8, Canada. TEL 416-667-7791) Ed.Bd. bibl.
—BLDSC shelfmark: 4318.575000.

S F E; going places with the arts. (Santa Fe East) see ART

S H S B. BULLETIN. (Societe Historique de Saint-Boniface) see HISTORY — History Of North And South America

SADO HAKUBUTSUKAN KENKYU HOKOKU/PUBLICATIONS FROM THE SADO MUSEUM. see SCIENCES: COMPREHENSIVE WORKS

708.1   US
ST. LOUIS ART MUSEUM. BULLETIN. 1914; N.S. 1965. s-a. $8. St. Louis Art Museum, Forest Park, Saint Louis, MO 63110. TEL 314-721-0067. FAX 314-721-6172. Ed. Mary Ann Steiner. illus.; circ. 14,000. **Indexed:** Artbibl.Mod., RILA.
Formerly: City Art Museum of Saint Louis. Bulletin (ISSN 0009-7691)

SAITAMA-KENRITSU SHIZENSHI HAKUBUTSUKAN KENKYU HOKOKU/SAITAMA MUSEUM OF NATURAL HISTORY. BULLETIN. see SCIENCES: COMPREHENSIVE WORKS

SAITO HO-ON KAI MUSEUM OF NATURAL HISTORY. RESEARCH BULLETIN. see SCIENCES: COMPREHENSIVE WORKS

069   II   ISSN 0304-8152
N3750.H9
SALAR JUNG MUSEUM. ANNUAL REPORT. (Text in English or Hindi) a. Salar Jung Museum, Hyderabad 500 002, Andhra Pradesh, India. TEL 523211.

069   II
SALAR JUNG MUSEUM BI-ANNUAL RESEARCH JOURNAL. (Text in English) 1970. s-a. Rs.55 price varies. Salar Jung Museum, Hyderabad 500 002, Andhra Pradesh, India. TEL 523211. Ed. M.L. Nigam. illus.

500.907   US
SANTA BARBARA MUSEUM OF NATURAL HISTORY. MUSEUM BULLETIN. 1925. m. membership. Santa Barbara Museum of Natural History, 2559 Puesta del Sol Rd., Santa Barbara, CA 93105. TEL 805-682-4711. FAX 805-569-3170. Ed. Sheryn Sears. bk.rev.; charts; illus.; circ. 3,500.
Formerly: Museum Talk.
Description: Provides a monthly notice of the museum exhibits, field trips, events, and programs; articles about natural history, American Indian studies, and the environment.

069   GW
SCHLESWIG-HOLSTEINISCHEN LANDESMUSEUM. JAHRBUCH. 1986. biennial. DM.40. (Schleswig-Holsteinischen Landesmuseum) Karl Wachholtz Verlag, Postfach 2769, 2350 Neumuenster, Germany. TEL 04321-567-20. FAX 04321-56778.

069 913   US
SCIENCE MUSEUM NEWS. 1976. s-a. free. Association of Science Museum Directors, c/o The Carnegie Museum of Natural History, 4400 Forbes Ave., Pittsburgh, PA 15213. TEL 412-622-3377. Ed. Elizabeth R. Mertz. circ. 200 (controlled).
Description: Articles directed to the natural history and science museum directors.

069   UK   ISSN 0266-6898
SCOTTISH MUSEUM NEWS. 1981. 4/yr. £10. Scottish Museums Council, County House, 20-22 Tophichen St., Edinburgh EH3 8JB, Scotland. TEL 031-229-7465. adv.; bk.rev.; circ. 1,500 (controlled).
Formerly: Omnigatherum.
Description: News and information on events in Scottish museums. Includes the work of the Council.

069 387   US
▼**SEA HISTORY'S GUIDE TO AMERICAN & CANADIAN MARITIME MUSEUMS.** 1990. irreg. $11.95. National Maritime History Society, 5 John Walsh Blvd., Charles Point, Peekskill, NY 10566-5324. TEL 914-737-7878. Ed. Joseph M. Stanford.
Description: Alphabetical listing of Maritime Museums in the U.S. and Canada.

385   US
SEASHORE TROLLEY MUSEUM DISPATCH. 1958. q. membership. New England Electric Railway Historical Society, Inc., Drawer A, Kennebunkport, ME 04046. Ed. Michael J. Carroll. bk.rev.; circ. 1,300. **Indexed:** Hist.Abstr.

SEFUNIM. see ARCHAEOLOGY

069 976   US
SHILOH MUSEUM. NEWSLETTER. 1978. q. $10 membership. Shiloh Museum, 118 W. Johnson Ave., Springdale, AR 72764. TEL 501-750-8165. Ed. Bob Besom. circ. 2,400. (looseleaf format; back issues avail.)
Description: Discusses history of Ozark Mountain region and museum programs for people of all ages.

SHIRETOKO HAKUBUTSUKAN KENKYU
HOKOKU/SHIRETOKO MUSEUM. BULLETIN. see
SCIENCES: COMPREHENSIVE WORKS

500   JA
SHIRITSU NAGOYA KAGAKUKAN NYUSU. (Text in Japanese) 1966. m. Shiritsu Nagoya Kagakukan - Nagoya Municipal Science Museum, 17-22 Sakae 2-chome, Naka-ku, Nagoya-shi, Aichi-ken 460, Japan.
  Description: Contains reviews and news of the museum.

SHIZEN KYOIKUEN HOKOKU/MINISTRY OF EDUCATION. NATIONAL SCIENCE MUSEUM. INSTITUTE FOR NATURE STUDY. MISCELLANEOUS REPORTS. see *SCIENCES: COMPREHENSIVE WORKS*

069 550.9   JA
SHIZENSHI DAYORI. (Text in Japanese) 1985. irreg. Saitama-kenritsu Shizenshi Hakubutsukan - Saitama Museum of Natural History, 1417-1 Nagatoro, Nagatoro-machi, Chichibu-gun, Saitama-ken 369-13, Japan.
  Description: News of the museum.

069 387   AT   ISSN 1033-4688
SIGNALS. q. free to qualified personnel. Australian National Maritime Museum, Public Affairs Section, G.P.O. Box 5131, Sydney, N.S.W. 2001, Australia. TEL 02-552-7777. FAX 02-552-2318. Ed. Jeffrey Mellefont. bk.rev.; circ. 5,000.
  Description: Publishes Australian maritime heritage articles, members information, museum news.

SLATE. see *ART*

SMITHSONIAN. see *SOCIAL SCIENCES: COMPREHENSIVE WORKS*

069   BP
SOLOMON ISLANDS MUSEUM ASSOCIATION. JOURNAL. 1975. a. Solomon Islands Government Printing, Box 313, Honiara, Solomon Islands.

574 500.907   US
SONORENSIS. ANNUAL REPORT. 1957. a. membership. Arizona-Sonora Desert Museum, Inc., 2021 N. Kinney Rd., Tucson, AZ 85743. TEL 602-833-1380.
  Formerly: Arizona-Sonora Desert Museum. Annual Report.

069   SA   ISSN 0370-8314
AM89.A1
SOUTHERN AFRICAN MUSEUMS ASSOCIATION. BULLETIN. (Text in Afrikaans, English) 1936. q. R.15($15) Southern African Museums Association - Suider-Afrikaanse Museumvereniging, Box 13147, Humewood 6013, South Africa. FAX 27-41-562175. (Subscr. to: S.A.M.A., P.O. Box 61, Cape Town 8000, South Africa) Ed. M.A. Raath. adv.; bk.rev.; charts; illus.; index every 2 yrs.; circ. 750.
  Formerly: Southern African Museums Association. Publication (ISSN 0036-0791)

069   US   ISSN 0073-4985
SOUTHERN ILLINOIS UNIVERSITY. UNIVERSITY MUSEUM STUDIES. 1968. irreg., no. 11, 1977. price varies. Southern Illinois University, Carbondale, University Museum, Carbondale, IL 62901. TEL 618-453-5388. FAX 618-453-3000.

623   US
SPINDRIFT (PHILADELPHIA). 1963. q. $35 membership. Philadelphia Maritime Museum, 321 Chestnut St., Philadelphia, PA 19106. TEL 215-925-5439. FAX 215-625-9635. Ed. Diane Eacret. circ. 2,000.
  Description: Carries articles on museum exhibits and programs and Delaware Valley maritime history.

SPORVEJSMUSEET SKJOLDENAESHOLM. AARSBERETNING. see *TRANSPORTATION — Railroads*

709   GW   ISSN 0075-5133
STAATLICHE KUNSTHALLE KARLSRUHE. BILDHEFTE. 1958. irreg. price varies. Staatliche Kunsthalle Karlsruhe, Hans-Thoma-Str. 2, 7500 Karlsruhe, Germany. FAX 0721-1356537.

709   GW   ISSN 0067-284X
STAATLICHE KUNSTSAMMLUNGEN IN BADEN-WUERTTEMBERG. JAHRBUCH. 1964. a. DM.60. Deutscher Kunstverlag GmbH, Nymphenbuergerstr. 84, 8000 Munich 19, Germany. FAX 089-121516-10. circ. 600. **Indexed:** Artbibl.Mod., RILA.

STAATLICHE MUSEEN ZU BERLIN. JAHRBUCH. FORSCHUNGEN UND BERICHTE. see *ART*

708 301.2   GW   ISSN 0070-7295
STAATLICHES MUSEUM FUER VOELKERKUNDE DRESDEN. ABHANDLUNGEN UND BERICHTE. 1881. irreg., vol.43, 1989. price varies. Akademie-Verlag Berlin, Leipziger Str. 3-4, 1086 Berlin, Germany. TELEX 114420-AVERL-DD. bk.rev. **Indexed:** A.I.C.P.
  Supersedes (with vol. 21, 1962): Staatliches Museum fuer Voelkerkunde und Tierkunde. Abhandlungen und Berichte.

069 792   BE   ISSN 0773-9559
NX555.A57
STAD ANTWERPEN. CULTUREEL JAARBOEK. (Text in Dutch; summaries in English, French, German) 1983. a. 150 Fr. Stad Antwerpen, 6de Directie Centraal Bestuur, Stadhuis, B-2000 Antwerp, Belgium. TEL 03-220-8211. FAX 03-220-8657. TELEX 31807 HAVANT. Ed. Gustaaf J. De Landtsheer. bk.rev.; circ. 1,500. (back issues avail.)
  Description: Presents various cultural and social events in and around Antwerp.

069   GW   ISSN 0078-2777
STADTBIBLIOTHEK NUERNBERG. AUSSTELLUNGSKATALOG. 1955. irreg., vol. 98, 1987. price varies. Stadtbibliothek, Egidienplatz 23, 8500 Nuernberg 1, Germany.

069.5   US
STANFORD ART BOOKS. 1964. irreg. (approx. a). price varies. Stanford University, Stanford Museum, Stanford, CA 94305. TEL 415-725-0460. FAX 415-725-0463.
  Description: Contains exhibition catalogues on wide-ranging subjects together with publications on the museum's history and permanent collection.

708   US   ISSN 0085-6665
STANFORD MUSEUM. 1971. biennial. $5. Stanford University, Stanford Museum, Stanford, CA 94305. TEL 415-725-0460. FAX 415-725-0463. Eds. Betsy G. Fryberger, Carol M. Osborne. circ. 3,000. **Indexed:** Artbibl.Mod., RILA.
  Description: Contains facts on selected works of art in the museum and a list of acquisitions for the two year period with descriptions of all exhibits in both the museum and nearby gallery.

069   US
THE STATESMAN. 1981. q. free. Rutherford B. Hayes Presidential Center, Spiegel Grove, Fremont, OH 43420-2796. TEL 419-332-2081. Ed. Sally B. Daubel. circ. 7,000. (back issues avail.)
  Description: News about the Hayes Presidential Center, its collections, exhibits, and programs that are available to the public.

069 797.123   US
STATION LOG. 1981. q. $10 membership. Hull Lifesaving Museum, 1117 Nantasket Ave., Box 221, Hull, MA 02045. TEL 617-925-LIFE. Ed. Lory Newmyer. film rev.; illus.; circ. 1,250. (back issues avail.)
  Description: Keeps members and visitors informed of museum activities and history.

069   NO   ISSN 0333-0656
STAVANGER MUSEUM. AARBOK. (Text in Norwegian; summaries in English) 1890. a. NOK 100. Stavanger Museum, N-4005 Stavanger, Norway.
  —BLDSC shelfmark: 1592.500000.

069   NO   ISSN 0333-0664
STAVANGER MUSEUM. SKRIFTER. (Text in Norwegian; summaries in English) 1920. irreg., vol.11, 1985. price varies. Stavanger Museum, N-4005 Stavanger, Norway. illus.

STEARNS NEWSLETTER; the Stearns collection of musical instruments at the University of Michigan. see *MUSIC*

069   HU   ISSN 0133-3046
STUDIA COMITATENSIA. (Text in Hungarian; summaries in English, German, and Russian) 1972. irreg., vol.20, 1990. price varies or on exchange basis. Pest Megyei Muzeumok Igazgatosaga, Studia Comitatensia - Direction of Pest County Museums, Fo ter 6, H-2000 Szentendre, Hungary. TEL 26-10-244. FAX 26-10-790. illus.; circ. 800. **Indexed:** A.I.C.P.
  Description: Interdisciplinary studies on Pest County. Includes art, history, sociology, culture, anthropology, archeology, literature and history.

STUDIA DO DZIEJOW DAWNEGO UZBROJENIA I UBIORU WOJSKOWEGO. see *MILITARY*

069   II   ISSN 0081-8259
STUDIES IN MUSEOLOGY. (Text in English) 1965. a. Rs.10($2.) Maharaja Sayajirao University of Baroda, Department of Museology, Sayaji Park, Baroda 390002, Gujarat, India. Ed. V.H. Bedekar. bk.rev.; circ. 400.

STUDII SI CERCETARI DE ISTORIA ARTEI. SERIA ARTA PLASTICA. see *ART*

STUTTHOF MUZEUM. ZESZYTY. see *HISTORY — History Of Europe*

069.094   SW   ISSN 0039-6885
SVENSKA MUSEER. (Text in Swedish) 1932. 4/yr. SEK 125($8.80) to non-members. Svenska Museifoereningen - Swedish Museums Association, Box 4715, S-116 92 Stockholm, Sweden. FAX 6435041. Ed. Gunilla Cedrenius. adv.; bk.rev.; charts; illus.; stat.; cum.index every 10 yrs.; circ. 4,000. **Indexed:** NAA.

708 069   SW
SWEDEN. NATIONALMUSEI SKRIFTSERIE. 1954. irreg. price varies. Nationalmusei - National Museum, Box 16176, 103 24 Stockholm, Sweden. Ed. Per Bjurstroem. adv.; circ. 2,500.
  Formerly (until 1984): Sweden. Nationalmuseum. Skriftserie (ISSN 0081-5683)

708.1   CN   ISSN 0845-8081
TABLEAU. 1970. 2/yr. free. Beaverbrook Art Gallery, P.O. Box 605, Fredericton, N.B., Canada. TEL 506-458-8545. FAX 506-459-7450. Dir. Ian G. Lumsden. circ. 1,400.
  Formerly (until 1988): Beaverbrook Art Gallery (ISSN 0045-1592)
  Description: Features a message from the director, exhibitions held, programs available, recent aquisitions, staff news, list of members, etc.

TAIDE. see *ART*

708.9   MG
TALOHA. (Text in French and Malagasy) 1965. irreg., no.10, 1987. FMG.5400. Universite de Madagascar, Musee d'Art et d'Archeologie, B.P. 564 Isoraka, Antananarivo, Malagasy Republic. **Indexed:** A.I.C.P.
  Description: Articles on the archeology, anthropology, history and art of ancient Madagascar.

700   NE   ISSN 0920-7430
TENTOONSTELLINGSBOEKJE. 1959. 10/yr. fl.39. Openbaar Kunstbezit, Postbus 5555, 1007 AM Amsterdam, Netherlands. TEL 020-852111. FAX 020-834665. circ. 5,200.
  Formerly: Tentoonstellingsagenda (ISSN 0040-3520)
  Description: Covers complete listing of exhibitions in Dutch museums, galleries and other cultural institutions, as well as a number of exhibitions in museums and galeries in nearby foreign countries.

069 574   US   ISSN 0040-3733
AM101   CODEN: TRRAB8
TERRA. 1962. q. $14 to non-members. Natural History Museum of Los Angeles County, 900 Exposition Blvd., Los Angeles, CA 90007. TEL 213-744-3330. FAX 213-742-0730. Ed. Robin A. Simpson. adv.; bk.rev.; illus.; index; circ. 25,000. **Indexed:** Abstr.Anthropol., Art & Archaeol.Tech.Abstr., Curr.Adv.Ecol.Sci., Deep Sea Res.& Oceanogr.Abstr., NAA.
  —BLDSC shelfmark: 8794.300000.
  Formerly: Museum Alliance Quarterly (ISSN 0027-402X)
  Description: Concerns natural history, anthropology, and history.

MUSEUMS AND ART GALLERIES

060   US   ISSN 0082-3074
QH105.T4   CODEN: TXMBAR
TEXAS MEMORIAL MUSEUM. BULLETIN. 1960. irreg., no.33, 1986. price varies. Texas Memorial Museum, University of Texas at Austin, 2400 Trinity, Austin, TX 78705. TEL 512-471-1604. (reprint service avail. from UMI) Indexed: Biol.Abstr., GeoRef.

069   US
TEXAS MEMORIAL MUSEUM. CONSERVATION NOTES. 1982. q. $4. University of Texas, Austin, Texas Memorial Museum, Materials Conservation Laboratory, 2400 Trinity, Austin, TX 78705. Ed. Georg Zapper. circ. 1,600.

069 500   US   ISSN 0082-3082
CODEN: TMMMBI
TEXAS MEMORIAL MUSEUM. MISCELLANEOUS PAPERS. 1968. irreg., no. 6, 1981. price varies. Texas Memorial Museum, University of Texas at Austin, 2400 Trinity, Austin, TX 78705. TEL 512-471-1604. (reprint service avail. from UMI) Indexed: Biol.Abstr., GeoRef.

060   US
TEXAS MEMORIAL MUSEUM. MUSEUM NOTES. 1938. irreg., no. 12, 1974. price varies. Texas Memorial Museum, University of Texas at Austin, 2400 Trinity, Austin, TX 78705. TEL 512-471-1604. Ed. Georg Zappler. (reprint service avail. from UMI)

TEXAS MEMORIAL MUSEUM. SPELEOLOGICAL MONOGRAPHS. see *EARTH SCIENCES — Geology*

TEXAS TECH UNIVERSITY. MUSEUM. SPECIAL PUBLICATIONS. see *BIOLOGY*

677   US
TEXTILE MUSEUM BULLETIN. 1971. q. membership. Textile Museum, 2320 S St., N.W., Washington, DC 20008. TEL 202-667-0441. Ed. George Rogers. circ. 4,500.
Formerly: Textile Museum Newsletter.
Description: Includes exhibition information, calendar of events, development, travel, education, special events, and Museum Shop news.

709   DK   ISSN 0085-7262
N1925
THORVALDSENS MUSEUM. MEDDELELSER. (Text in Danish; summaries in English, French, German) 1917. irreg., latest 1989. price varies. Thorvaldsens Museum, Porthusgade 2, 1213 Copenhagen K, Denmark. TEL 33-321532. FAX 33-32-17-71. illus.; index; circ. 1,200.

069   SZ
THURGAUISCHE MUSEUM. MITTEILUNGEN. 1946. irreg., latest 1974. 3 Fr. Thurgauische Museumsgesellschaft, CH-8500 Frauenfeld, Switzerland. Ed. H. Guhl-Widmer.

069   AU   ISSN 0379-0231
DB761
TIROLER LANDESMUSEUM FERDINANDEUM, INNSBRUCK. VEROEFFENTLICHUNGEN. 1825. a. S.450. Tiroler Landesmuseum Ferdinandeum, Museumstr. 15, A-6010 Innsbruck, Austria. FAX 0512-59489-88. Ed. Josef Riedmann. circ. 400.

TOCHIGI-KENRITSU HAKUBUTSUKAN KENKYU HOKOKUSHO/TOCHIGI PREFECTURAL MUSEUM. MEMOIRS. see *SCIENCES: COMPREHENSIVE WORKS*

TOKEN BIJUTSU/JOURNAL OF JAPANESE FINE ARTS SWORDS. see *ART*

TOKYO DAIGAKU SOGO KENKYU SHIRYOKAN GYOSEKISHU/UNIVERSITY OF TOKYO. UNIVERSITY MUSEUM. COLLECTED REPRINTS. see *SCIENCES: COMPREHENSIVE WORKS*

TOKYO-TO TAKAO SHIZEN KAGAKU HAKUBUTSUKAN KENKYU HOKOKU/TAKAO MUSEUM OF NATURAL HISTORY. SCIENCE REPORT. see *SCIENCES: COMPREHENSIVE WORKS*

069   US
TORCH (WASHINGTON). 1954. m. free. Smithsonian Institution, Office of Public Affairs, 900 Jefferson Dr., Rm. 2410, Washington, DC 20560. TEL 202-357-2627. Ed. Mary Combs. bk.rev.; illus.; circ. 10,400. (tabloid format)
Formerly: Smithsonian Torch (ISSN 0037-7341)

TOTTORI-KENRITSU HAKUBUTSUKAN KENKYU HOKOKU/TOTTORI PREFECTURAL MUSEUM. BULLETIN. see *SCIENCES: COMPREHENSIVE WORKS*

500   JA
TOYAMA TO SHIZEN. (Text in Japanese) q. Toyama-shi Kagaku Bunka Senta - Toyama Science Museum, 1-19 Nishi-Nakano-machi 3-chome, Toyama-shi, Toyama-ken 939, Japan.
Description: Contains news of the center.

069   SA   ISSN 0496-1102
TRANSVAAL MUSEUM. BULLETIN. 1955. irreg., no.22, 1987. price varies. Transvaal Museum, P.O. Box 413, Pretoria 0001, South Africa.
TEL 012-322-7632. FAX 012-332-7939. Indexed: Art & Archaeol.Tech.Abstr., Biol.Abstr.
Description: Comprises articles in zoology, in particular systematics and newsworthy contributions on activities of museum staff.

069   SA   ISSN 0255-0172
CODEN: TMMOER
TRANSVAAL MUSEUM. MONOGRAPHS. 1983. irreg., no.6, 1988. Transvaal Museum, P.O. Box 413, Pretoria 0001, South Africa. TEL 012-322-7632. FAX 012-322-7939. Ed. Dippenaar.
Description: Contributions in zoology, and systematics in particular.

707.4   US   ISSN 0733-463X
TRAVELING EXHIBITION INFORMATION SERVICE. NEWSLETTER. (Editions in English and French)) 1980. bi-m. $35. Humanities Exchange, Inc., Box 1608, Largo, FL 34649. TEL 813-581-7328. FAX 813-585-6398. Ed. S.R. Howarth. adv.; circ. 600.

069.9   US
TROLLEY FARE. 1953. bi-m. membership. Pennsylvania Railway Museum Association, Box 832, Pittsburgh, PA 15230. TEL 412-734-5780. Ed. Harold M. Englund. circ. 500. (back issues avail.)
Description: Covers streetcar preservation and restoration.

708.1   US
U A B VISUAL ARTS GALLERY. SELECTIONS FROM THE PERMANENT SELECTION. 1981. irreg. free. University of Alabama at Birmingham, Visual Arts Gallery, 101 Honors House, Birmingham, AL 35294. TEL 205-934-4941. FAX 205-975-6639. TELEX 888826 UAB BHM. Ed. John M. Schnorrenberg. circ. 2,200. (back issues avail.)
Description: Illustrated catalogue with essays about works in the Gallery.

708.1   US
U A B VISUAL ARTS GALLERY PAPERS. 1977. irreg. (6-10/yr.). free. University of Alabama at Birmingham, Visual Arts Gallery, 101 Honors House, Birmingham, AL 35294. TEL 205-934-4941. FAX 205-975-6639. TELEX 888826 UAB BHM. Eds. John M. Schnorrenberg, Antoinette Spanos Johnson. circ. 475. (back issues avail.)
Description: Biographies of artists exhibiting in the Gallery.

708.7   CN   ISSN 0824-5991
UKRAINIAN CULTURAL AND EDUCATIONAL CENTRE. VISTI - NEWS. (Text in English and Ukrainian) 1976. q. membership. Ukrainian Cultural and Educational Centre, 184 Alexander Ave. East, Winnipeg, Man. R3B 0L6, Canada. TEL 204-942-0218. FAX 204-943-2857. Ed. Eugene Cherwick. circ. 2,000.

708.9   BL   ISSN 0041-8803
UNIVERSIDADE DE SAO PAULO. MUSEU DE ARTE CONTEMPORANEA. BOLETIM INFORMATIVO. 1963. s-m. free. Universidade de Sao Paulo, Museu de Arte Contemporanea, Caixa Postal 22031, CEP 01499-Sao Paulo, Brazil. Ed. Aracy Amarali. circ. 250. (looseleaf format)

069.9   BL
UNIVERSIDADE DE SAO PAULO. MUSEU PAULISTA. COLECAO. SERIE DE MOBILIARIO. irreg. Universidade de Sao Paulo, Museu Paulista, Caixa Posta 42503, Parque da Independencia, 04263 Sao Paulo, Brazil. Ed. Setembrino Petri.
Supersedes in part (in 1975): Museu Paulista. Colecao (ISSN 0080-6382)

069   US   ISSN 0093-7436
AM101.F3
UNIVERSITY OF ALASKA MUSEUM. ANNUAL REPORT. a. University of Alaska Museum, 907 Yukon Dr., Fairbanks, AK 99775-1200. TEL 907-474-7505. FAX 907-474-5469. circ. controlled.

069 700   US
UNIVERSITY OF CALIFORNIA, LOS ANGELES. FOWLER MUSEUM OF CULTURAL HISTORY. OCCASIONAL PAPERS. 1969. irreg., no.5, 1985. price varies. University of California, Los Angeles, Fowler Museum of Cultural History, Los Angeles, CA 90024. TEL 213-825-4361. FAX 213-206-7007.
Formerly: University of California, Los Angeles. Museum of Cultural History. Occasional Papers (ISSN 0068-628X)

069 700   US
UNIVERSITY OF KENTUCKY ART MUSEUM NEWSLETTER. 1986. s-a. free. University of Kentucky Art Museum, Rose and Euclid Sts., Lexington, KY 40506-0241. TEL 606-257-5716. FAX 606-257-4000. Ed. Harriet Fowler. circ. 3,000. (tabloid format)
Description: Information on acquisitions, exhibitions and programs of the Museum.

708   US   ISSN 0270-1642
UNIVERSITY OF MICHIGAN. MUSEUMS OF ART AND ARCHAEOLOGY. BULLETIN. 1978. a. $8. University of Michigan Museum of Art, Alumni Memorial Hall, 525 S. State St., Ann Arbor, MI 48109-1354. TEL 313-764-0395. (Co-sponsors: Kelsey Museum of Archaeology, Department of the History of Art) Ed. Marvin Eisenberg. circ. 500. Indexed: Avery Ind.Archit.Per., RILA.
Supersedes (N.S. 1965-1977): University of Michigan. Museum of Art. Bulletin (ISSN 0076-8391)

708   US   ISSN 0077-8583
N512.A5
UNIVERSITY OF NEW MEXICO ART MUSEUM. BULLETIN. 1965. irreg., latest no.14, 1981-83. $7. University of New Mexico, Art Museum, FAC 1017, Albuquerque, NM 87131. TEL 505-277-4001. Ed. Peter Walch. circ. 1,000. Indexed: Artbibl.Mod., RILA.
Description: Provides information and illustrations on recent acquisitions.

069   US
VALENTINE MUSEUM. NEWS. 1898. bi-m. $35 to members. Valentine Museum, 1015 E. Clay St., Richmond, VA 23219. TEL 804-649-0711. FAX 804-643-3510. Ed. Michael McGrann. circ. 3,000. (back issues avail.)
Formerly (until 1985): Visitor.

708   CN   ISSN 0083-5161
VANCOUVER ART GALLERY. ANNUAL REPORT. 1932. a. free. Vancouver Art Gallery, 750 Hornby St., Vancouver, B. C. V6Z 2H7, Canada. TEL 604-682-4668. circ. 9,000.

069   SW   ISSN 0083-5536
AM101
VARBERGS MUSEUM. AARSBOK. 1950. a. SEK 40. Hallands Laensmuseer, 432 44 Varberg, Sweden. FAX 0340-14722. Ed. Bengt-Arne Person. adv.; bk.rev.

954.9 069   BG
VARENDRA RESEARCH MUSEUM. JOURNAL. (Text in English) 1972. a. Tk.15($3) Varendra Research Museum, University of Rajshahi, Rajshahi, Bangladesh.

069   CI   ISSN 0042-6083
VIJESTI MUZEALACA I KONZERVATORA HRVATSKE. (Text in Croatian, summaries in German; index in English, French) 1960. bi-m. $12. Muzejsko Drustvo Hrvatske, Mesnicka 5, 41000 Zagreb, Croatia. (Co-sponsor: Drustvo Konzervatora Jugoslavije) Ed. Zdenko Kuzmic. bk.rev.; bibl.; illus.
Supersedes: Drusto Muzejsko-Konzervatorskih Radnika N.R. Hrvatske. Vijesti.

MUSEUMS AND ART GALLERIES

708 US ISSN 0363-3519
N716.V45
VIRGINIA MUSEUM OF FINE ARTS BULLETIN. 1940. bi-m. $5 to non-members. Virginia Museum of Fine Arts, Publications Dept., 2800 Grove Ave., Richmond, VA 23221-2466. TEL 804-367-0534. Ed. Monica S. Rumsey. illus.; circ. 17,500.
  Formerly: Virginia Museum Bulletin (ISSN 0042-6687)
  Description: Newsletter and calendar of art exhibitions and related events held at the Virginia Museum and at affiliated arts organizations throughout Virginia.

VISITOR BEHAVIOR. see *PSYCHOLOGY*

708 CN ISSN 0712-9238
VISTA. 1973. 4/yr. free. Norman Mackenzie Art Gallery, 3475 Albert St., Regina, Sask. S4S 6X6, Canada. TEL 306-522-4242. FAX 306-569-8191. Eds. Jeanette Groenendyk, Bonnie Schaffer. bk.rev.; illus.; circ. 4,500.
  Former titles: Mackenzie M A G & N - M A G; N M A G Review (ISSN 0384-1022); Norman Mackenzie Art Gallery. Newsletter (ISSN 0384-1014)
  Description: Information on exhibitions, permanent collection, events, education classes and volunteer news.

069.5 US
VISTAS. 1979. irreg. price varies. V.O.L.N. Press, Box 93, Merion Station, Montgomery County, PA 19066. FAX 215-664-4026. Ed. Ellen Homsey. circ. 2,000.

VISUAL RESOURCES; an international journal of documentation. see *ART*

600 NO ISSN 0048-2277
T183
VOLUND. Represents: Norsk Teknisk Museum. Yearbook. (Text in Norwegian; summaries in English) 1953. a. NOK 100. Norsk Teknisk Museum - Norwegian Museum of Science and Technology, Kjelsaasveien 143, 0491 Oslo 4, Norway. TEL 02-22-25-50. FAX 02-222950. Eds. Torleif Lindtveit, Merete K. Skogheim. adv.; bk.rev.; illus.; circ. 2,500.

090 CS
VYROCNE SPRAVY O CINNOSTI SLOVENSKYCH MUZEI A GALERII. 1966. a. free. Slovenske Narodne Muzeum, Muzeologicky Ustav, Vajanskeho Nabrezie 2, 814 36 Bratislava, Czechoslovakia. Ed. A. Korcekova.
  Former titles: Ustredna Sprava Muzei a Galerii. Vyrocne Spravy o Cinnosti Slovenskych Muzei; Slovenske Narodne Muzeum. Muzeologicky Kabinet. Vyrocne Spravy o Cinnosti Slovenskych Muzei.

WALTERS ART GALLERY BULLETIN. see *ART*

069 708 US
WARD FOUNDATION NEWS.* q. Ward Foundation, Box 3416, Salisbury, MD 21802-3416. TEL 301-742-4988. adv.; circ. 8,000.

069 US
WELLESLEY COLLEGE FRIENDS OF ART NEWSLETTER. 1965. a. membership. Wellesley College Museum, Wellesley College, Wellesley, MA 02181. TEL 617-235-0320. FAX 617-235-7361. Ed. Nancy Gunn. circ. 2,500.
  Description: Current information on acquisitions, benefits, curriculum and alumnae activity.

069 913 CC ISSN 1000-7954
WEN BO/JOURNAL OF MUSEUMS & ARCHAEOLOGY. Variant English title: Relics and Museology. (Text in Chinese) 1984. bi-m. $36. Shaanxi Sheng Wenwu Shiye Guanli-ju - Shaanxi Provincial Administration of Archaeological Data, Beilin Bowuguan, Sanxue Jie, Xi'an, Shaanxi 710001, People's Republic of China. (Dist. in US by: China Books & Periodicals, Inc., 2929 24th St., San Francisco, CA 94110. TEL 415-282-2994) Ed. Chen Quanfang.

WEST COAST PEDDLER; oldest journal of antiques, art & collectibles in the Pacific states. see *ANTIQUES*

069 708 AT ISSN 0312-3162
QH1 CODEN: REMUDY
WESTERN AUSTRALIAN MUSEUM. RECORDS. 1974. irreg. Aus.$7.50. Western Australian Museum, Francis St., Perth, W.A. 6000. Ed.Bd. circ. 150. **Indexed:** Aus.Sci.Ind., Biol.Abstr., So.Pac.Per.Ind.
  —BLDSC shelfmark: 7325.306000.
  Formerly: Western Australia. Public Library, Museum and Art Gallery. Record.

069 AT ISSN 0313-122X
WESTERN AUSTRALIAN MUSEUM. RECORDS. SUPPLEMENT. 1975. irreg. Aus.$7.50. Western Australian Museum, Francis St., Perth, W.A. 6000, Australia. FAX 09-328-8686. **Indexed:** Aus.Sci.Ind, Biol.Abstr.

069 AT
WESTERN AUSTRALIAN MUSEUM, PERTH. ANNUAL REPORT. 1960. a. Western Australian Museum, Perth, W.A., Australia. FAX 328-8686. circ. 1,000. **Indexed:** GeoRef.
  Formerly: Western Australia Museum, Perth. Report of the Museum Board (ISSN 0083-8721)

069.9 US
WHISPERS NEAR THE INGLENOOK. 1978. q. $15. 1890 House Museum and Center for Victorian Arts, 37 Tompkins St., Cortland, NY 13045. Dir. John H. Nozynski. circ. 1,300.

069 US
WHITNEY MUSEUM OF AMERICAN ART. BULLETIN. 1961. a. $5 (membership). Whitney Museum of American Art, 945 Madison Ave., New York, NY 10021. TEL 212-570-3657. FAX 212-570-1807. Ed. Sheila Schwartz. circ. 8,000. (back issues avail.)

WHO'S WHO IN AMERICAN ART. see *BIOGRAPHY*

708 069 US
WILDFOWL ART JOURNAL. q. $25. Ward Foundation, Box 3416, Salisbury, MD 21802-3416. TEL 301-742-4988. Ed. Curtis J. Badger. adv.; circ. 8,000. (back issues avail.)
  Description: Wildfowl art with emphasis on carving.

069 US
WILLIAM HAMMOND MATHERS MUSEUM. OCCASIONAL PAPERS AND MONOGRAPHS. 1974. irreg. Indiana University, William Hammond Mathers Museum, 601 E. Eighth St., Bloomington, IN 47405. TEL 812-335-7224.
  Formerly: Indiana University Museum. Occasional Papers and Monographs.

708 709 US ISSN 0084-0416
N9
WINTERTHUR PORTFOLIO: A JOURNAL OF AMERICAN MATERIAL CULTURE. 1964. 3/yr. $30 to individuals; institutions $64; students $24. (Henry Francis Du Pont Winterthur Museum) University of Chicago Press, Journals Division, 5801 S. Woodlawn Ave., Chicago, IL 60637. TEL 312-753-3347. FAX 312-702-0694. TELEX 25-4603. (Subscr. to: Box 37005, Chicago, IL 60637) Ed. Catherine E. Hutchins. adv.; bk.rev.; charts; illus.; index; circ. 1,600. (back issues avail.; reprint service avail. from UMI,ISI) **Indexed:** Amer.Hist.& Life, Archit.Per.Ind., Art Ind., Artbibl.Mod., Artbibl., Arts & Hum.Cit.Ind., Avery Ind.Archit.Per., Br.Tech.Ind., Curr.Cont., Hist.Abstr., Ind.Bk.Rev.Hum., M.L.A., RILA.
  —BLDSC shelfmark: 9319.800000.
  Incorporates: Winterthur Conference Report (ISSN 0084-0408)
  Description: Articles on the arts in America and the historical context in which they developed. Emphasizes analytical studies that integrates artifacts into their cultural framework.
  Refereed Serial

069.9 US
WOODROW WILSON BIRTHPLACE NEWSLETTER. 1973. q. membership. Woodrow Wilson Birthplace Foundation, Inc., Box 24, Staunton, VA 24401. TEL 703-885-0897. FAX 703-886-9874. Ed. Susan E. Klaffky. bk.rev.; circ. 1,000. (tabloid format; back issues avail.)
  Description: Coverage of Presidential museum activities, including exhibits, seminars, lectures, collections, and school programs.

708 US ISSN 0084-3539
N10
YALE UNIVERSITY ART GALLERY BULLETIN. 1926. a. $7 per no. Yale University Art Gallery, 2006 Yale Sta., New Haven, CT 06520. TEL 203-432-0660. FAX 203-432-7159. Ed. Leslie Baier. circ. 2,100. (also avail. in microform from UMI; reprint service avail. from UMI) **Indexed:** Artbibl.Mod., Artbibl., Avery Ind.Archit.Per., RILA. **Key Title:** Bulletin - Yale University Art Gallery.
  Formerly: Yale Art Gallery Bulletin (ISSN 0360-3180)
  Description: Articles and notes relating to works in the Gallery's collection. Includes annual director's report and a complete acquisitions list for the previous year.

069 500 JA
YAMA TO HAKUBUTSUKAN/MOUNTAIN AND MUSEUM. (Text in Japanese) 1956. m. 1230 Yen. Omachi-shiritsu Omachi Sangaku Hakubutsukan - Omachi Alpine Museum, 8056-1, Kamisakae-cho, Omachi-shi, Nagano-ken 398, Japan. FAX 0261-22-0211. circ. 1,000.
  Description: Contains reviews and news of the museum.

YAMAGUCHI-KENRITSU YAMAGUCHI HAKUBUTSUKAN KENKYU HOKOKU/YAMAGUCHI PREFECTURAL YAMAGUCHI MUSEUM. BULLETIN. see *SCIENCES: COMPREHENSIVE WORKS*

YOKOSUKA-SHI HAKUBUTSUKAN KENKYU HOKOKU. SHIZEN KAGAKU/YOKOSUKA CITY MUSEUM. SCIENCE REPORT. see *SCIENCES: COMPREHENSIVE WORKS*

YOKOSUKA-SHI HAKUBUTSUKAN SHIRYOSHU/YOKOSUKA CITY MUSEUM. MISCELLANEOUS REPORT. see *SCIENCES: COMPREHENSIVE WORKS*

069 500 JA ISSN 0385-8472
QH188
YOKOSUKA-SHI HAKUBUTSUKANPO/YOKOSUKA CITY MUSEUM. ANNUAL REPORT. (Text in Japanese) a. Yokosuka-shi Shizen Hakubutsukan - Yokosuka City Museum, 95, Fukadadai, Yokosuka-shi, Kanagawa-ken 238, Japan.

708 ZA ISSN 0084-4977
ZAMBIA. NATIONAL MUSEUMS BOARD. REPORT. a. K.1. National Museums Board, Livingstone Museum, Box 498, Livingstone, Zambia.

069 ZA
ZAMBIA MUSEUMS JOURNAL. 1970. irreg. K.8. National Museums Board, Livingstone Museum, Box 60498, Livingstone, Zambia. Ed. F.B. Musonda. circ. 500.

069 BS
ZEBRA'S VOICE; lentswe la pitse ya naga. (Text in English; summaries in Setswana) q. free to S A D C C countries. National Museum, Monuments and Art Gallery, Independence Ave., P.B. 114, Gaborone, Botswana. TEL 374616. Ed. S.A. Hughes. circ. 5,000. (back issues avail.)

069 CC
ZHONGGUO BOWUGUAN/CHINESE MUSEUMS. (Text in Chinese) q. Zhongguo Bowuguan Xuehui - China Museum Society, 29 Wusi Dajie, Beijing 100009, People's Republic of China. TEL 4015577. Ed. Su Donghai.

ZOO - NACHRICHTEN; Allwetterzoo - Nachrichten. see *BIOLOGY — Zoology*

THE 13TH STREET JOURNAL. see *ART*

MUSEUMS AND ART GALLERIES —
Abstracting, Bibliographies, Statistics

060 US
CATALOG OF MUSEUM PUBLICATIONS AND MEDIA; a directory and index of publications and audiovisuals available from U.S. and Canadian institutions. 1972. irreg., latest ed. 1979. $275. Gale Research Inc., 835 Penobscot Bldg., Detroit, MI 48226. TEL 313-961-2242. FAX 313-961-6083. TELEX 810-221-7086. Eds. Paul Wasserman, Esther Herman. index.
Former titles: Museum Catalog of Publications and Media; Museum Media.
Description: Compendium of books, periodicals, audio and audiovisual material available from American and Canadian museums.

069.5 011 II
CONCISE DESCRIPTIVE CATALOGUE OF ARABIC MANUSCRIPTS IN THE SALAR JUNG MUSEUM AND LIBRARY. (Text in English) 1957. irreg., lastest vol.6, 1989. Rs.50. Salar Jung Museum, Hyderabad 500 002, Andhra Pradesh, India. TEL 523211. Ed. Mohamed Ashraf.
Formerly: Catalogue of Arabic Manuscripts in Salar Jung Museum.

069.5 011 II
CONCISE DESCRIPTIVE CATALOGUE OF THE PERSIAN MANUSCRIPTS IN THE SALAR JUNG MUSEUM AND LIBRARY. (Text in English) 1965. irreg., latest vol.9, 1988. Rs.72 price varies. Salar Jung Museum, Hyderabad 500 002, Andhra Pradesh, India. Ed. Mohmed Ashraf. illus.
Formerly: Catalogue of Persian Manuscripts in Salar Jung Museum.

HERITAGE RECORD SERIES. see BIBLIOGRAPHIES

069 700 US
LIBRARY CATALOG OF THE METROPOLITAN MUSEUM OF ART. 1980. irreg. $600 (foreign $660). G.K. Hall & Co., 70 Lincoln St., Boston, MA 02111. TEL 617-423-3990. FAX 617-423-3999. TELEX 94-0037.
Description: Lists materials cataloged by the Metropolitan Museum of Art Library. Lists bound books, exhibition catalogs, dealer's catalogs, serial publications, magazines, and catalogs of important public and private collections.

069 UK ISSN 0267-8594
MUSEUM ABSTRACTS. 1985. 12/yr. £35. Routledge, 11 New Fetter Lane, London EC4P 4EE, England.
Description: Covers museums and museum management, heritage interpretation, exhibit design and display, tourism, conservation, and the arts.

708 010 AU
OESTERREICHISCHES MUSEUM FUER VOLKSKUNDE. KATALOGE. 1946. irreg. price varies. Verlag Ferdinand Berger und Soehne GmbH, Wiener Str. 21-23, A-3580 Horn, Austria. TEL 02982-2317-0.

016 CS
VYBEROVA BIBLIOGRAFIA MUZEOLOGICKEJ LITERATURY. 1962. a. exchange basis. Slovenske Narodne Muzeum, Muzeologicky Ustav, Vajanskeho Nabrezie 2, 814 36 Bratislava, Czechoslovakia. TEL 335460. Ed. Viera Schnappova.

MUSIC

see also Dance; Sound Recording and Reproduction

780 US ISSN 0360-7178
A A M O A REPORTS.* 1961. q. $10. Afro-American Music Opportunities Association, 2809 Wayzata Blvd., Minneapolis, MN 55405. Ed. C. Edward Thomas. adv.; bk.rev.; bibl.; circ. 12,000.
Formerly: A A M O A News.

780.23 US ISSN 0002-0990
A G M A ZINE.* 1936. 5/yr. free. American Guild of Musical Artists, 1727 Broadway, New York, NY 10019-5214. Ed. Gene Boucher. illus.; circ. 6,000.

A H A! HISPANIC ARTS NEWS. (Association of Hispanic Arts) see ART

780 US
A I M S BULLETIN. 1969. biennial. free. American Institute of Musical Studies, c/o AIMS, 3500 Maple Ave., Ste. 120, LB 22, Dallas, TX 75219-3901. TEL 214-528-9234. FAX 214-521-3383. TELEX 403872 RESDESK. Ed. Nora Sands. illus.; circ. 10,000.

784 CN ISSN 0700-3900
A L'ECOUTE. vol.5, 1979. q. Can.$21.40. Alliance des Chorales du Quebec, 4545 Av. Pierre-de-Coubertin, C.P. 1000 Succursale M, Montreal, Que. H1V 3R2, Canada. TEL 514-252-3020. FAX 514-251-8038. TELEX 05-829647 SECADMIBEC. Ed. Christine Dumas. adv.; bk.rev.; rec.rev.; illus.; index; circ. 6,000. (back issues avail.)
Description: Covers choral music and singers.

789 US
A M I C A BULLETIN.* vol.7, 1970. m. membership. Automatic Musical Instrument Collectors' Association, c/o Tom Beckett, 1111 Via Malibu, Aptos, CA 95003-1721. (Subscr. to: A.N. Johnson, Membership Sec., Box 666, Grand Junction, CO 81501) Ed. Mrs. Virginia Billings. adv.; bk.rev.; index; circ. 950. (processed)
Formerly: Amica (ISSN 0003-1712)

780 US
A M S NEWSLETTER (PHILADELPHIA). 1971. 2/yr. free with subscr. to journal. American Musicological Society, 201 S. 34th St., Philadelphia, PA 19104-6313. TEL 215-898-8698.

789.91 US ISSN 0361-2147
A P M MONOGRAPH SERIES. (Antique Phonograph Monthly) 1973. 4/yr. $15. A P M Press, 502 E. 17th St., Brooklyn, NY 11226. TEL 718-941-6835. Ed. Allen Koenigsberg. adv.; bk.rev.; circ. 2,000.
Description: Devoted to the history of the phonograph and popular music.

780 800 070.5 920 US
A S C A P BIOGRAPHICAL DICTIONARY. irreg., 4th ed. 1980. $41.95. American Society of Composers, Authors and Publishers, One Lincoln Plaza, New York, NY 10023. TEL 212-621-6222. FAX 212-721-0955. **Indexed:** Child.Auth.& Illus., Perf.Arts Biog.Master Ind.

780.23 US
A S C A P IN ACTION. 1967. 4/yr. free. American Society of Composers, Authors and Publishers, One Lincoln Plaza, New York, NY 10023. TEL 212-595-3050. FAX 212-721-0955. Ed. Murdoch McBride. circ. 40,000. (also avail. in microfilm from UMI; reprint service avail. from UMI) **Indexed:** Music Artic.Guide, Music Ind.
Former titles (until 1979): A S C A P Today; A S C A P (ISSN 0001-2424)

786.97 US ISSN 0001-2734
A T G BULLETIN. Variant title: Accordion Teachers' Guild Newsletter. 1946. q. membership. Accordion Teachers' Guild, Inc., 632 Hevey St., Manchester, NH 03102. TEL 603-645-4327. Ed. Lisa Cleveland. circ. 200. (processed; back issues avail.)

780 US
A W C NEWS FORUM. 1977. a. $13.50. American Women Composers, Inc., 1690 36th St., N.W., Ste. 409, Washington, DC 20007. TEL 202-342-8179. adv.; bk.rev.; circ. 500. (back issues avail.) **Indexed:** Music Artic.Guide.
Description: Provides articles on women in the field of music.

ABHANDLUNGEN ZUR KUNST-, MUSIK- UND LITERATURWISSENSCHAFT. see ART

792 UK ISSN 0001-3242
ML5
ABOUT THE HOUSE. 1962. 3/yr. £9 to non-members. Friends of Covent Garden Ltd., Royal Opera House, Covent Garden, London WC2E 9DD, England. FAX 071-836-1762. Ed. Phyllida Ritter. adv.; dance rev.; illus.; circ. 22,000. (also avail. in microfilm from UMI) **Indexed:** Arts & Hum.Cit.Ind., Br.Tech.Ind., Curr.Cont., Music Ind., RILM.
—BLDSC shelfmark: 0049.730000.
Description: Discusses cultural events; specifically opera and ballet.

780 IT
ACCADEMIA DEI CONCORDI ROVIGO. COLLANA DI MUSICHE. no.12, 1977. irreg. price varies. Giardini Editori e Stampatori, Via Santa Bibbiana 28, 56100 Pisa, Italy. TEL 050 502531.

787 US ISSN 1049-9261
ML1015.G9
▼**ACOUSTIC GUITAR.** 1990. bi-m. $23.95 in U.S.; Canada $31.45; elsewhere $38.95. String Letter Press, Inc., Box 767, San Anselmo, CA 94979-0767. TEL 415-485-6946. FAX 415-485-0831. Ed. Jeffrey Pepper Rodgers. adv.; bk.rev.; rec.rev.; circ. 17,000.
Description: Written by and for musicians to cover a variety of musical styles including transcriptions from recordings and solo pieces for guitars.

781.7 AT
ACROSS COUNTRY; Australian national country music magazine. m. Box 177, Ferntree Gully, Vic. 3156, Australia. Eds. James Jazzer Smith, Christine Whyte. adv.; illus. (back issues avail.)

789.5 DK ISSN 0105-6255
ACTA CAMPANOLOGICA. s-a. DKK 100. Scriptor Publisher ApS, Gasvaerksvej 15, DK-1656 Copenhagen V, Denmark. **Indexed:** NAA.

780 920 GW ISSN 0001-6233
ACTA MOZARTIANA. 1954. q. DM.60 membership. Deutsche Mozart-Gesellschaft e.V., Karlstr. 6, 8900 Augsburg, Germany. TEL 0821-518588. Ed. Dr. Erich Valentin. adv.; bk.rev.; charts; illus.; circ. 2,900. **Indexed:** Arts & Hum.Cit.Ind., Curr.Cont., Music Ind., RILM.

780.01 GW ISSN 0001-6241
ML5
ACTA MUSICOLOGICA. (Text in English, French, German) 1928. 3/yr. DM.135 membership. (International Musicological Society, SZ) Baerenreiter Verlag, Heinrich Schuetz Allee 31-37, 3500 Kassel-Wilhelmshoehe, Germany. TEL 0561-3105-0. FAX 0561-3105240. (U.S. subscr.: Foreign Music Distributors, 13 Elkay Dr., Chester, NY 10918) Ed. Helmut Federhofer. adv.; bibl.; illus.; index, cum.index: vols.1-25 (1928-1953). **Indexed:** Curr.Cont., Music Ind., RILM.

786.5 GW ISSN 0567-7874
ML5
ACTA ORGANOLOGICA. 1967. a. (Gesellschaft der Orgelfreunde e.V.) Verlag Merseburger Berlin GmbH, Motz Str. 13, 3500 Kassel, Germany. illus. **Indexed:** RILM.

780 GW ISSN 0001-6942
ACTA SAGITTARIANA. (Text in English, French and German) 1963. a. membership. Internationale Heinrich Schuetz-Gesellschaft e.V., Heinrich-Schuetz-Allee 35, 3500 Kassel-Wilhelmshoehe, Germany. TEL 0561-3105-0. FAX 0561-3105-240. TELEX 992376-BAERRD. Ed. Sieglinde Froehlich. adv.; bk.rev.; illus.; circ. 1,500. **Indexed:** Music Ind.

781.7 GW ISSN 0001-7965
AD MARGINEM; Randbemerkungen zur musikalischen Volkskunde. 1964. 2/yr. free. Universitaet zu Koeln, Institut fuer Musikalische Volkskunde, Gronewaldstr. 2, 5000 Cologne 41, Germany. TEL 0221-470-5269. Eds. Guenther Noll, Wilhelm Schepping. bk.rev.; abstr.; circ. controlled. (looseleaf format; back issues avail.)

ADAM INTERNATIONAL REVIEW. see LITERATURE

780 BE ISSN 0001-8171
ADEM; driemaandelijks tijdschrift voor muziekkultuur. 1965. q. 950 Fr. Madrigaal V.Z.W., Herestraat 53, B-3000 Leuven, Belgium. FAX 016-22-2477. Ed. P. Schollaert. adv.; bk.rev.; circ. 1,800. (reprint service avail. from UMI) **Indexed:** Music Ind., RILM.
—BLDSC shelfmark: 0680.420000.

780 681 374   US
ADVANCE BAND MAGAZINE; the international voice of adult bands. 1977. q. membership. Association of Concert Bands, 3020 E. Majestic Ridge, Las Cruces, NM 88001. TEL 505-522-8723. FAX 505-646-5421. Ed. Steve Walker. adv.; bk.rev.; bibl.; illus.; circ. 2,000. (back issues avail.)
Former titles (until 1991): A B C Newsmagazine; (until 1987): A B C Newsletter.
Description: For band directors and band music enthusiasts and music educators. Focuses on community concert and band advancement in America and abroad.

780   US
AESTHETICS IN MUSIC SERIES. 1983. irreg., no.5, 1987. Pendragon Press, R.R. 1, Box 159, Stuyvesant, NY 12173-9720. TEL 518-828-3008. FAX 518-828-2368.

780   SA   ISSN 0065-4019
ML5
AFRICAN MUSIC. (Text in English, French) 1948. irreg. (approx. a.), vol.7, no.1, 1991. R.20($15) International Library of African Music, Institute of Social and Economic Research, Rhodes University, Grahamstown 6140, South Africa. TEL 0461-22023. FAX 0461-23948. Ed. Andrew Tracey. adv.; bk.rev.; cum.index per vol.; circ. 500. (back issues avail.; reprint service avail. from SWZ) **Indexed:** A.I.C.P., Curr.Cont.Africa, Curr.Cont., Ind.S.A.Per., Music Ind., RILM.
—BLDSC shelfmark: 0732.900000.
Supersedes (in 1954): African Music Society. Newsletter.

781.7   KE
AFRICAN MUSICOLOGY. 1983. a. $5. (University of Nairobi, Institute of African Studies) Eleza Services Ltd., P.O. Box 14925, Nairobi, Kenya. Eds. A. Darkwa, W.A. Omondi. **Indexed:** M.L.A.

780   US
AFRO-AMERICAN MUSIC OPPORTUNITIES ASSOCIATION. RESOURCE PAPERS. irreg. price varies. Afro-American Music Opportunities Association, 2909 Wayzata Blvd., Minneapolis, MN 55440. TEL 612-377-3730.

781.7   IR
AHANG. (Text in Farsi) 1988. q. Rs.960 per no. Center of Music and Revolutionary Songs, Vahdat Hall, Arfa St., Hafiz Ave., Teheran, Iran.
Description: Covers Iranian music.

780   PL
AKADEMIA MUZYCZNA. PRACE SPECJALNE. 1984. irreg. exchange basis. Akademia Muzyczna, Ul. Zacisze 3, 40-025 Katowice, Poland. TEL 48 32 155-4017. (Distr. by: Ars Polona Ruch, Krakowskie Przedmiescie 7, 00-068 Warsaw, Poland)
Formerly: Panstwowa Wyzsza Szkola Muzyczna. Prace Specjalne.

780   PL
AKADEMIA MUZYCZNA. SKRYPTY. 1984. irreg. exchange basis. Akademia Muzyczna, Ul. Zacisze 3, 40-025 Katowice, Poland. TEL 48 32 155-4017. (Distr. by: Ars Polona Ruch, Krakowskie Przemiescie 7, 00-068 Warsaw, Poland)
Formerly: Panstwowa Wyzsza Szkola Muzyczna. Skrypty.

780   PL
AKADEMIA MUZYCZNA. SPRAWOZDANIA. a. exchange basis. Akademia Muzyczna, Ul. Zacisze 3, 40-025 Katowice, Poland. TEL 48 32 155-4017. (Dist. by: Ars Polona-Ruch, Krakowskie Przedmiescie 7, 00-068 Warsaw, Poland)
Formerly: Panstwowa Wyzsza Szkola Muzyczna. Sprawozdania.

780   PL
AKADEMIA MUZYCZNA. WYDAWNICTWA OKOLICZNOSCIOWE. irreg. exchange basis. Akademia Muzyczna, Ul. Zacisze 3, 40-025 Katowice, Poland. TEL 48 32 155-4017. (Dist. by: Ars Polona Ruch, Krakowskie Przedmiescie 7, 00-068 Warsaw, Poland)
Formerly: Panstwowa Wyzsza Szkola Muzyczna. Wydawnictwa Okolicznosciowe.

780   AJ
AKADEMIYA NAUK AZERBAIDZHANSKOI S.S.R. MUZEI ISTORII. TRUDY. (Text in Azerbaijani and Russian) vol.9, 1973. irreg. 1.50 Rub. per no. Izdatel'stvo Elm, Ul. Narimanova, 31, Baku 370073, Azerbaijan. Ed. P. Azizbekova. illus.; circ. 500.

780   CN
ALL ACCESS PASS. m. 3 Manorcrest Street, Bramlea, Ont. L6S 2W6, Canada. TEL 416-791-5574. (tabloid format)

ALLEGRO. see *LABOR UNIONS*

783 282   GW
ALLGEMEINER CAECILIEN-VERBAND. SCHRIFTENREIHE. irreg., latest no.15. price varies. Allgemeiner Caecilien-Verband, Andreasstr. 9, 8400 Regensburg, Germany. TEL 0941-84339.

780 621.389 778   US
ALLIGATOR.* 1983. m. $12. See You Later, Alligator, c/o Coppersmith, Box 50842, New Orleans, LA 70150-0842. TEL 504-866-2367. Ed. Roy Lambert. bk.rev.; film rev.; circ. 25,000. (tabloid format; back issues avail.)

ALTA FEDELTA. see *SOUND RECORDING AND REPRODUCTION*

780   GW
ALTE MUSIK AKTUELL; aktuelle Information fuer alte Musik. 1985. m. (11/yr.) DM.34. Pro Musica Antiqua, Luitpoldstr. 3, 8400 Regensburg, Germany. TEL 0941-52687. FAX 0941-53094. Ed. Stephan Schmid. index; circ. 1,000. (back issues avail.)

ALTERNATE ROOTS NEWSLETTER. see *THEATER*

780   US
AMATEUR CHAMBER MUSIC PLAYERS. ANNUAL NEWSLETTER. 1947. a. membership. Amateur Chamber Music Players, Inc., 545 Eight Ave., New York, NY 10018. TEL 212-244-2778. Eds. Susan M. Lloyd, Robert K. McIntosh. circ. 6,000.

780   US   ISSN 0065-6704
AMATEUR CHAMBER MUSIC PLAYERS. DIRECTORY. (Overseas Directory or North American Directory published in alternate years) 1949. a. contribution. Amateur Chamber Music Players, Inc., 545 Eighth Ave., New York, NY 10018. TEL 212-244-2778. Ed. Susan M. Lloyd. circ. 4,500.

780   RU
AMATEUR MUSIC ACTIVITIES. 8/yr. 17.80 Rub. Izdatel'stvo Muzyka, Ul. Neglinnaya 14, Moscow 103031, Russia. TEL 924-81-63. FAX 921-83-53.

780   CN
AMATEUR MUSICIAN/MUSICIEN AMATEUR. irreg. (3-4/yr.). $25 to individuals; students $13. Canadian Amateur Musicians (CAMMAC), P.O. Box 353, Westmount, Que. H3Z 2T5, Canada. TEL 514-932-8755. Ed. Claire Heistek. adv.; circ. 2,000.

789.5   US   ISSN 0093-1330
ML27.U5
AMERICAN BELL ASSOCIATION. DIRECTORY. a. (some vols. accompanied by supplemental directory). $12 to members. American Bell Association, Route 1, Box 286, Natrona Heights, PA 15065. TEL 412-295-9623. Key Title: Directory - American Bell Association.

780.6   US   ISSN 8756-8357
ML410.B81
AMERICAN BRAHMS SOCIETY. NEWSLETTER. 1983. s-a. $20. American Brahms Society, University of Washington, School of Music DN-10, Seattle, WA 98195. TEL 206-543-0400. Ed. Virginia Hancock. bk.rev.; circ. 1,500. (back issues avail.) **Indexed:** Music Artic.Guide.
Description: Essays on Brahms and his music; reports on new publications and research on Brahms and his circle.

784   US   ISSN 0002-788X
AMERICAN CHORAL FOUNDATION. RESEARCH MEMORANDUM SERIES. 1959. s-a. $30 (Canada $32.50; elsewhere $35) includes American Choral Review. American Choral Foundation, Inc., c/o Chorus America (APVE), 2111 Sansom St., Philadelphia, PA 19103. TEL 215-563-2430. FAX 215-563-2431. Ed. Walter Collins. bibl.; circ. 2,000. (processed) **Indexed:** Music Artic.Guide.

MUSIC 3537

784   US   ISSN 0002-7898
AMERICAN CHORAL REVIEW. 1958. s-a. membership only. American Choral Foundation, Inc., c/o Chorus America (APVE), 2111 Sansom St., Philadelphia, PA 19103. TEL 215-563-2430. FAX 215-563-2431. Ed. Alfred Mann. adv.; bk.rev.; bibl.; charts; illus.; circ. 2,000. (back issues avail.) **Indexed:** Arts & Hum.Cit.Ind., Curr.Cont., Music Artic.Guide, Music Ind., RILM.

780 331.8   US   ISSN 0036-407X
AMERICAN FEDERATION OF MUSICIANS LOCAL 325. 1945. m. $6. American Federation of Musicians, Local 325 Music Association of San Diego County, A F L-C I O, 1717 Morena Blvd., San Diego, CA 92110. TEL 619-276-4324. Ed. Earl Smith. adv.; illus.; circ. 1,500.

780   US   ISSN 0888-8701
AMERICAN HANDEL SOCIETY. NEWSLETTER. 1986. 3/yr. $30. American Handel Society, Inc., c/o University of Maryland, Department of Music, College Park, MD 20742. TEL 301-405-5523. circ. 170.
Description: Conducts research in the life and work of the composer.

787.5   US   ISSN 0002-869X
ML1
AMERICAN HARP JOURNAL. 1967. s-a. $25 to individuals; libraries $15. American Harp Society, Inc., 1374 Academy Ln., Teaneck, NJ 07666. TEL 201-836-8909. (Subscr. to: c/o Charles Jensen, Business Mgr., 187 W. Palisade Ave., Englewood, NJ 07631) Ed. Jane Weidensaul. adv.; bibl.; illus.; circ. 3,300. (back issues avail.) **Indexed:** Music Artic.Guide.
—BLDSC shelfmark: 0816.550000.

780   GW   ISSN 0065-8855
AMERICAN INSTITUTE OF MUSICOLOGY. MISCELLANEA. 1951. irreg. (American Institute of Musicology, US) Haenssler Verlag, Postfach 1220, Bismarckstr. 4, 7303 Neuhausen-Stuttgart, Germany. TEL 07158-177-114. FAX 07158-177119. TELEX 715816-HAENSLR. (Dist. by: Laudate GmbH, Bismarkstrasse 4, 7303 Neuhausen-Stuttgart, Germany) Ed. Armen Carapetyan.

780.6   US   ISSN 0749-341X
AMERICAN LISZT SOCIETY. NEWSLETTER. 1984. s-a. $25. American Liszt Society, Inc., 4540 46th St., N.W., Washington, DC 20016. (Subscr. to: c/o Nancy Hallsted, ALS Memb. Sec., 9212 Villa Dr., Bethesda, MD 20817) Ed. John R. Anderson. circ. 500.

780   US
▼**AMERICAN LISZT SOCIETY STUDIES SERIES.** 1990. irreg. Pendragon Press, R.R. 1, Box 159, Stuyvesant, NY 12173-9720. TEL 518-828-3008. FAX 518-828-2368.

787   US   ISSN 1041-7176
AMERICAN LUTHERIE. 1973. q. $30 includes membership. Guild of American Luthiers, 8222 S. Park, Tacoma, WA 98408. TEL 206-472-7853. Ed. Tim Olsen. adv.; bk.rev.; illus.; circ. 2,000.
Former titles (until 1985): Guild of American Luthiers. Quarterly; (until vol.4): G.A.L. Newletter.
Description: Information sharing system for string instrument makers and repairers of all interests and skill levels.

780   US   ISSN 0734-4392
ML1
AMERICAN MUSIC. 1983. q. $28 to individuals; institutions $38. (Sonneck Society) University of Illinois Press, 54 E. Gregory Dr., Champaign, IL 61820. TEL 217-333-0950. FAX 217-244-8082. Ed. Wayne Shirley. adv.; bk.rev.; rec.; rev.; illus.; circ. 1,900. (also avail. in microform from UMI) **Indexed:** Arts & Hum.Cit.Ind., Curr.Cont., Music Artic.Guide, Music Ind.
—BLDSC shelfmark: 0845.800000.
Refereed Serial

MUSIC

780 US ISSN 0003-0104
AMERICAN MUSIC CENTER. NEWSLETTER. 1959. 2/yr. $15 (foreign $20). American Music Center, Inc., 30 W. 26th St., Ste. 1001, New York, NY 10010-2011. TEL 212-366-5260. FAX 212-366-5265. Ed. Heidi Waleson. adv.; circ. 2,000. **Indexed:** Music Artic.Guide, RILM.
Formerly: Music Today Newsletter.
Description: Contains articles relating to contemporary music and publicizes member premieres, commissions, new recordings, and other activities.

780.7 US ISSN 0003-0112
ML1
AMERICAN MUSIC TEACHER. 1951. bi-m. to libraries. Music Teachers National Association, Inc., 617 Vine St., Ste. 1432, Cincinnati, OH 45202-2434. TEL 513-421-1420. FAX 513-421-2503. Ed. Robert J. Elias. adv.; bk.rev.; circ. 27,000. (also avail. in microform from UMI; microfiche from MUE; back issues avail.; reprint service avail. from UMI) **Indexed:** Bk.Rev.Ind. (1980-), Child.Bk.Rev.Ind. (1980-), Educ.Ind., Music Artic.Guide, Music Ind.
—BLDSC shelfmark: 0845.850000.
Description: Presents features articles on aesthetics, composition, criticism, interpretation, musicology and performances.

781.9 US ISSN 0362-3300
ML1
AMERICAN MUSICAL INSTRUMENT SOCIETY. JOURNAL. 1975. a. $35 includes membership. American Musical Instrument Society, c/o Shrine to Music Museum, 414 E. Clark St., Vermillion, SD 57069-2390. TEL 605-677-5306. FAX 605-677-5073. Ed. Arthur Lawrence. adv.; bk.rev.; bibl.; charts; illus.; circ. 1,000. **Indexed:** Arts & Hum.Cit.Ind., Curr.Cont., Music Artic.Guide, Music Ind., RILM. Key Title: Journal of the American Musical Instrument Society.

781.9 US ISSN 0160-2365
ML1
AMERICAN MUSICAL INSTRUMENT SOCIETY. NEWSLETTER. 1971. 3/yr. $35 includes membership. American Musical Instrument Society, c/o Shrine to Music Museum, 414 E. Clark St., Vermillion, SD 57069-2390. TEL 605-677-5306. FAX 605-677-5073. Ed. Andre P. Larson. **Indexed:** Curr.Cont., Music Ind.

780 US ISSN 0003-0139
ML27.U5
AMERICAN MUSICOLOGICAL SOCIETY. JOURNAL. 1948. 3/yr. $36 to members. American Musicological Society, 201 S. 34th St., Philadelphia, PA 19104-6316. TEL 215-898-8698. Ed. William P. Prizer. adv.; bk.rev.; charts; illus.; index; circ. 4,500. **Indexed:** Arts & Hum.Cit.Ind., Curr.Cont., Hum.Ind., Ind.Bk.Rev.Hum., Music Artic.Guide, Music Ind., RILM.
—BLDSC shelfmark: 4689.150000.

780 US
AMERICAN MUSICOLOGICAL SOCIETY. STUDIES AND DOCUMENTS. 1948. irreg., no.6, 1972. price varies. American Musicological Society, 201 S. 34th St., Philadelphia, PA 19104-6316. TEL 215-898-8698.

786.6 US ISSN 0164-3150
ML1
AMERICAN ORGANIST. 1967. m. $40 to non-members (foreign $40). American Guild of Organists, 475 Riverside Dr., Ste. 1260, New York, NY 10115. FAX 212-870-2163. (Co-sponsor: Royal Canadian College of Organists) Ed. Anthony Baglivi. adv.; bk.rev.; charts; illus.; stat.; tr.lit.; index, cum.index; circ. 25,000. (also avail. in microfilm from UMI) **Indexed:** Music Artic.Guide, Music Ind.
Incorporates (in 1979): A G O Times (ISSN 0362-5907); Formerly (until 1978): Music (ISSN 0027-4208)

789.91 US ISSN 0003-0716
ML1
AMERICAN RECORD GUIDE. 1935 (not published 1972-75). bi-m. $24 to individuals; institutions $36. Record Guide Productions, 4412 Braddock St., Cincinnati, OH 45204. TEL 513-941-1116. Ed. Donald R. Vroon. adv.; bk.rev.; rec.rev.; illus.; index; circ. 9,000. (also avail. in microform; reprint service avail. from UMI) **Indexed:** Access, Bk.Rev.Ind. (1965-1982), Child.Bk.Rev.Ind. (1965-1982), Mag.Ind., Music Artic.Guide, Music Ind., PMR, R.G.
Formerly: American Music Lover.
Description: Reviews 400 classical recordings per issue.

788.53 US ISSN 0003-0724
AMERICAN RECORDER. 1960. q. $24 (foreign $28). American Recorder Society, Inc., 580 Broadway, Ste. 1107, New York, NY 10012-3223. TEL 212-966-1246. Ed. Benjamin Dunham. adv.; bk.rev.; music rev.; record rev.; illus.; cum.index every 2 yrs.; circ. 4,300. (also avail. in microform from UMI; back issues avail.; reprint service avail. from UMI) **Indexed:** Music Artic.Guide, Music Ind., RILM.
—BLDSC shelfmark: 0853.530000.

780 US
AMERICAN RECORDER SOCIETY MEMBERS' LIBRARY. 1986. a. membership. American Recorder Society, 580 Broadway, Ste. 1107, New York, NY 10012-3223. TEL 212-966-1246. Ed. Jennifer W. Lehmann. circ. 4,200. (looseleaf format; back issues avail.)
Description: Covers music for recorder consort.

780 US
AMERICAN RECORDER SOCIETY NEWSLETTER. 1980. 3/yr. membership. American Recorder Society, Inc., 580 Broadway, Ste. 1107, New York, NY 10012-3223. TEL 212-966-1246. Ed. Benjamin Dunham. circ. 4,200. (looseleaf format)
Description: Calendar of recorder and early music events worldwide, and news of society's activities.

AMERICAN REVIEW. see ART

787 780.7 US ISSN 0003-1313
ML27.U5
AMERICAN STRING TEACHER. 1950. q. $35 includes membership. American String Teachers Association, c/o Jody Atwood, Ed., Box 170639, Hialeah, FL 33017-0639. FAX 214-490-4219. (Subscr. to: ASTA National Office, 4020 McEwan, Ste. 105, Dallas, TX 75244. TEL 214-233-3116) adv.; bk.rev.; music rev.; circ. 7,500. **Indexed:** Music Artic.Guide., Music Ind.

780 US ISSN 0193-5372
AMERICAN SUZUKI JOURNAL.* 1972. 6/yr. $32 to members. Suzuki Association of the Americas, Box 17310, Boulder, CO 80308-7310. TEL 319-263-3071. Ed. Robert Klein Reinsager. adv.; bk.rev.; circ. 5,500. **Indexed:** Music Artic.Guide.
Description: Publication of interest to teachers, parents, and educators dedicated to the advancement of the Suzuki method of music education in the western world.

781.7 US
AMERICAN VERNACULAR MUSIC. 1968. q. $15 to individuals; institutions $20. Middle Tennessee State University, Center for Popular Music, Box 41, Murfreesboro, TN 37132. TEL 615-898-2449. bk.rev.; rec.rev.; bibl.; index; circ. 700. (processed; also avail. in microfilm from UMI; back issues avail.; reprint service avail. from UMI) **Indexed:** Amer.Hist.& Life (until 1985), Arts & Hum.Cit.Ind., Curr.Cont., Hist.Abstr. (until 1985), M.L.A., Music Ind., Ref.Sour., RILM.
Former titles (until 1985): J E M F Quarterly (John Edwards Memorial Forum); J E M F Newsletter (ISSN 0021-3632)
Description: Covers all forms of American vernacular music, particular emphasis on commercially disseminated forms of folk musics.

787 US ISSN 0898-5987
AMERICAN VIOLA SOCIETY. JOURNAL. 1973. irreg. (approx. s-a). $25. American Viola Society, Brigham Young University, Provo, UT 84602. TEL 801-378-4953. Ed. David Dalton. adv.; bk.rev.; circ. 1,000. (back issues avail.) **Indexed:** Music Artic.Guide.
Supersedes (after no.28, 1985): American Viola Society. Newsletter.

780 US
AMERICAN WAGNER ASSOCIATION. NEWSLETTER. 1984. 3/yr. membership. American Wagner Association, Inc., 82 W. 82nd St., Apt. 6C, New York, NY 10024. TEL 212-874-4504. (And: 77 Cooper Ln., Larchmont, NY 10538. TEL 914-834-7239) Ed. Warren F. Michon. illus.; circ. 125. (looseleaf format; back issues avail.)
Description: News about fundraising and educational events concerning the American Wagner Association, and scholarly and review-type articles on the German composer.

780 US
AMERICAS BOYCHOIR - INTERNATIONAL CHILDREN'S CHOIR FEDERATION. NEWSLETTER. 1953. q. $12. (Americas Boychoir Federation) Shallway Foundation, Shallway Bldg., Connellsville, PA 15425. TEL 412-628-3939. (Co-sponsor: International Children's Choir Federation) Ed. John B. Shallenberger. circ. 1,400. (looseleaf format; back issues avail.)
Formerly: Children's Choir Newsletter.

780 FR ISSN 0154-7283
AMIS DE L'OEUVRE ET LA PENSEE DE GEORGES MIGOT. BULLETIN D'INFORMATION. 1976. 2/yr. 120 F. (Amis de l'Oeuvre et la Pensee de Georges Migot) Institut de Musicologie, 22, rue Descartes, 67084 Strasbourg Cedex, France. Ed. Dr. Marc Honegger. circ. 200.

780 CN ISSN 0826-7464
ANACRUSIS. (Text in English, French) 1980. q. Can.$45($30) Association of Canadian Choral Conductors, 250 Heath St. W., Ste. 1504, Toronto, Ont. M5B 3L4, Canada. TEL 416-488-7842. Ed. Gary Fisher. adv.; bk.rev.; circ. 500. (back issues avail.)
Description: For choral conductors in schools, churches, communities and universities.
Refereed Serial

780 GW ISSN 0569-9827
ANALECTA MUSICOLOGICA. (Vols. 1-11 published by Boehlau-Verlag) 1963. irreg., vol.27, 1991. price varies. (Deutsches Historisches Institut in Rom, Musikgeschichtliche Abteilung, IT) Laaber-Verlag, Regensburger Str. 19, 8411 Laaber, Germany. illus.

780 FR ISSN 0295-3722
ML5
ANALYSE MUSICALE. q. 290 F. (foreign 340 F.). Societe Francaise d'Analyse Musicale, 83 bd de Sebastopol, 75002 Paris, France. TEL 1-40-28-45-72. (back issues avail.)

785 US ISSN 0091-7176
ML1
ANCIENT TIMES. 1973. q. $10 (membership). Company of Fifers & Drummers, Inc., Box 525, Ivoryton, CT 06442. Ed. Maurice A. Schoos. adv.; bk.rev.; illus.; circ. 1,300. (newspaper)

781.57 US
AND ALL THAT JAZZ. 1973. 2/yr. New Orleans Jazz Club of California, Box 1225, Kerrville, TX 78029. TEL 512-896-2285. circ. 4,000.

780 US
ANDY'S FRONT HALL. (Includes: Buyer's Guide & Source Book) 1977. s-a. $2. Front Hall Enterprises, Inc., Wormer Rd., Box 307, Voorheesville, NY 12186. TEL 518-765-4193. FAX 518-765-4193. Ed. Kay L. Spence. bk.rev.; circ. 8,000.
Description: Covers books and recordings of folk and traditional music.

780 SZ
ANNALES PADEREWSKI. 1979. irreg., approx. 1/yr. 10 Fr. Societe Paderewska a Morges, Centre Culturel, CH-1110 Morges, Switzerland. Ed. Maurice Giordani. bk.rev.; circ. 1,000.
Description: Publication containing reminiscences about the life of the Polish pianist. Includes society's news.

780 US
ANNOTATED REFERENCE TOOLS IN MUSIC SERIES. (Text in English, French and German) 1978. irreg., vol.3, 1990. Pendragon Press, Rt. 1, Box 159, Stuyvesant, NY 12173-9720. TEL 518-828-3008. FAX 518-828-2368. (back issues avail.)

780 US
ANNOUNCED...; this month in classical recordings. 1988. m. $26 (foreign $42). Bushnell Corporation, 880 W. Williams Rd., Bloomington, IN 47404. TEL 812-339-2258. TELEX 966420. Ed. Vinson Bushnell. adv.; circ. 200.
Description: Provides a current source of information about new recordings of classical music in the United States.

384.554 FR ISSN 0066-3565
ANNUAIRE O.G.M. (Partie 1: Radio-Television-HiFi-Electronique-Electroacoustique; Partie 2: Musique) a. 620 F. per vol. (Office General de la Musique) Editions Louis Johanet, 68 rue Boursault, 75017 Paris, France. adv.

780 UK
ANNUAL CHART SUMMARIES. 1983. a. $4. Chart Watch, 8 Worcester House, Bumpstead Rd., Haverhill, Suffolk CB9 8QB, England. circ. 70.

786 US
ANNUAL ORGAN HANDBOOK; regional survey of historical pipe organs. 1956. a. $25 (includes subscr. to: Tracker). Organ Historical Society, Inc., Box 26811, Richmond, VA 23261. TEL 804-353-9226. FAX 804-353-9266. Ed. Alan Laufman. adv.; illus.; circ. 3,000.
Supersedes: Organ Historical Society. National Convention (Proceedings).

780 IT
ANNUARIO MUSICALE ITALIANO. 1981. biennial. L.75000. Comitato Nazionale Italiano Musica (CIDIM), Via Vittoria Colonna 18, 00193 Rome, Italy. TEL 06-6833741. FAX 06-6874989. TELEX 625412 CIDIM I. Ed. Marcello Ruggieri. adv.; circ. 6,000.

780 745.1 US ISSN 0361-2147
TS2301
ANTIQUE PHONOGRAPH MONTHLY. 1973. q. $15. A P M Press, 502 E. 17th St., Brooklyn, NY 11226. TEL 718-941-6835. Ed. Allen Koenigsberg. adv.; bk.rev.; charts; illus.; cum.index: 1973-1990; circ. 2,000. (back issues avail.) **Indexed:** RILM.
Description: Covers the history of recorded sound from 1877 to 1930, and restoration of antique phonographs.

780 SP ISSN 0211-3538
ML32.S7
ANUARIO MUSICAL. 1946. a. 3000 ptas. (foreign 4500 ptas.). Consejo Superior de Investigaciones Cientificas (C.S.I.C.), Institucion "Mila I. Fontanals", Vitruvio, 8, 28006 Madrid, Spain. TEL 93-2429123. FAX 93-2429123. **Indexed:** Music Ind.
Description: Covers musicology, ethnomusicology and musical investigation.

780 GW
ARBEITSGEMEINSCHAFT FUER RHEINISCHE MUSIKGESCHICHTE. MITTEILUNGEN. 1955. q. membership. Arbeitsgemeinschaft fuer Rheinische Musikgeschichte e.V., c/o Musikwissenschaftliches Institut der Universitaet zu Koln, Albertus-Magnus-Platz, 5000 Cologne 41, Germany. TEL 0221-470-2249. FAX 0221-470-5151. TELEX 888-2291-UNIK-G. Ed. K.W. Niemoeller. bk.rev.; cum.index; circ. 400. **Indexed:** RILM.

780 GW ISSN 0003-9292
ML5
ARCHIV FUER MUSIKWISSENSCHAFT. (Supplement avail.) (Text in English and German) 1918. q. DM.128. Franz Steiner Verlag Wiesbaden GmbH, Birkenwaldstr. 44, Postfach 101526, 7000 Stuttgart 1, Germany. TEL 0711-2582-0. FAX 0711-291450. TELEX 723636-DAZD. Ed. H.H. Eggebrecht. adv.; charts; illus.; index; circ. 800. (back issues avail.) **Indexed:** Arts & Hum.Cit.Ind., Curr.Cont., Music Ind., RILM.
—BLDSC shelfmark: 1621.100000.

780 GW ISSN 0570-6769
ARCHIV FUER MUSIKWISSENSCHAFT. BEIHEFTE. (Text in English and German) irreg., vol.32, 1991. price varies. Franz Steiner Verlag Wiesbaden GmbH, Birkenwaldstr. 44, Postfach 101526, 7000 Stuttgart 1, Germany. TEL 0711-2582-0. FAX 0711-2582290. TELEX 723636-DAZD.
—BLDSC shelfmark: 1621.150000.

780.903 IT
ARCHIVUM MUSICUM; collana di testi rari. 1978. irreg. price varies. Studio per Edizioni Scelte, Lungarno Guicciardini 9, 50125 Florence, Italy. Ed.Bd.

ARISTOS; devoted to the preservation and advancement of traditional values (as opposed to modernism and post-modernism) in the arts. see ART

780 US
ARIZONA MUSIC NEWS. 1956. 3/yr. $15 to non-members. Arizona Music Educators Association, Inc., 8455 N. La Oesta, Tucson, AZ 85704. TEL 602-544-0929. Ed. Carol Vogt. tr.; lit.; circ. 1,000.
Description: Covers issues in music education at all levels.

ARKANSAS COUNTRY DANCER. see DANCE

783 028.5 IT ISSN 0391-5425
ARMONIA DI VOCI. 1946. bi-m. L.31000. (Centro Catechistico Salesiano) Editrice Elle Di Ci, Corso Francia 214, 10096 Leumann (Turin), Italy. TEL 011 95-91-091. Ed. Antonio Fant. adv.; circ. 1,500.

780 US ISSN 0146-5856
ML410.S283
ARNOLD SCHOENBERG INSTITUTE. JOURNAL. 1976. 2/yr. $15 (foreign $20). Arnold Schoenberg Institute, c/o University of Southern California, University Park, MC-1101, Los Angeles, CA 90089-1101. TEL 213-740-4090. Ed. Juliane Brand. bk.rev.; bibl.; circ. 800. (also avail. in microfilm; back issues avail., reprint service avail. from UMI) **Indexed:** Arts & Hum.Cit.Ind., Curr.Cont., Music Artic.Guide, Music Ind., RILM.
—BLDSC shelfmark: 4701.050000.
Supersedes: Arnold Schoenberg Institute. Bulletin.

410 US ISSN 1043-3848
ARS LYRICA: JOURNAL OF LYRICA. 1981. irreg., approx 1/yr. $15 to individuals; libraries $25. Society for Word-Music Relations, 90 Church St., Guilford, CT 06437. Ed. Louis E. Auld. bk.rev.; circ. 250 (controlled).
Description: Articles and other works dealing with relations of words and music in any aspect.

780 SA ISSN 0379-6485
ARS NOVA. (Text in Afrikaans, English) 1969. a. R.6.60($4.50) University of South Africa, Department of Musicology, P.O. Box 392, Pretoria 0001, South Africa. FAX 012-429-3221. TELEX 350068. Ed. Bernard van der Linde. adv.; bk.rev.; circ. 450. (back issues avail.)

786.6 GW ISSN 0004-2919
ARS ORGANI; Zeitschrift fuer das Orgelwesen. 1951. q. DM.7 per no. (Gesellschaft der Orgelfreunde e.V.) Verlag Merseburger Berlin GmbH, Motzstrasse 13, 3500 Kassel, Germany. adv.; bk.rev.; music rev; illus. **Indexed:** Music Ind., RILM.
—BLDSC shelfmark: 1697.660000.

700 793 BL ISSN 0102-3357
ART.* (Text occasionally in English) 1981. 2/yr. $20 (foreign $30). (Universidade Federal da Bahia, Escola de Musica e Artes Cenicas) Grafica Universitaria, Rua Augusto Viana s-n, Canela, 40000 Salvador BA, Brazil. Ed. Paulo Lima. abstr.; circ. 500. **Indexed:** Music Ind.

ART AND CULTURE. see ART

ARTES. see ART

780 CI ISSN 0587-5455
ML5
ARTI MUSICES/MUSICOLOGICAL YEARBOOK. (Text in Croatian; summaries in English, German) 1969. a. $18. Muzicka Akademija u Zagrebu, Muzikoloski Zavod - Zagreb Academy of Music, Institute of Musicology, Berislaviceva 16, 41000 Zagreb, Croatia. Ed.Bd. adv.; bk.rev.; bibl.; illus. **Indexed:** Music Ind., RILM.
—BLDSC shelfmark: 1734.075500.

700 GW ISSN 0004-3885
ARTIST; Fachzeitschrift fuer Musiker. 1883. s-m. DM.90. Zeitschriften Verlag RBDV, Pressehaus Am Martin-Luther-Platz, Postfach 1135, 4000 Duesseldorf 1, Germany. TEL 0211-505-2616. FAX 0211-505-2555. TELEX 8582495. Ed. Helmut Schwanen. adv.; bk.rev.; illus.; circ. 3,000. **Indexed:** Artbibl.Mod.

786.97 789 FR ISSN 0004-3907
ARTISTES ET VARIETES; revue de l'accordeoniste et des instrumentistes de rythme. 1945. 8/yr. 95 F. Enterprise Generale de Fabrication et de Publicite, 2 bis rue de la Baume, 75008 Paris, France. Ed. Henri Dufourg. adv.; bk.rev.; music rev.; play rev.; illus.; circ. 25,000.
Formerly: Revue de l'Accordeoniste et des Instrumentistes de Rythme.

ARTS ADDRESS BOOK; a classified guide to national (U.K. & Ireland) and international arts organizations with details of their activities and publications. see ART

ARTS BULLETIN. see ART

ARTS MANAGEMENT. see THEATER

ARTSBOARD. see THEATER

ARTSFOCUS. see MUSEUMS AND ART GALLERIES

ARTSPACE (COLUMBUS). see ART

780 950 US ISSN 0044-9202
ML1
ASIAN MUSIC. 1968. 2/yr. $30 (typically set in July). Society for Asian Music, Dept. of Asian Studies, Cornell University, 388 Rockefeller Hall, Ithaca, NY 14853. TEL 607-255-5049. FAX 607-255-1454. Ed.Bd. adv.; bk.rev.; rec.; rev.; circ. 600. **Indexed:** Arts & Hum.Cit.Ind., Curr.Cont., M.L.A., Music Artic.Guide, RILM.
—BLDSC shelfmark: 1742.701000.

780 US ISSN 0081-1319
ASIAN MUSIC PUBLICATIONS. SERIES A: BIBLIOGRAPHIC AND RESEARCH AIDS. 1970. irreg., no.3, 1974. price varies. (Society for Asian Music) Asian Music Publications, c/o Theodore Front Musical Literature, Inc., 16122 Cohasset St., Van Nuys, CA 91406. TEL 818-994-1902. FAX 818-994-0419. Ed. Fredric Lieberman. circ. 400. (back issues avail.) **Indexed:** RILM.
Formerly: Society for Asian Music. Publication Series. Series A: Bibliographic and Research Aids.

780 US ISSN 0081-1327
ASIAN MUSIC PUBLICATIONS. SERIES B. TRANSLATIONS. irreg. price varies. (Society for Asian Music) Asian Music Publications, c/o Theodore Front Musical Literature, Inc., 16122 Cohasset St., Van Nuys, CA 91406. TEL 818-994-1902. FAX 818-994-0419. Ed. Fredric Lieberman. **Indexed:** RILM.
Formerly: Society for Asian Music. Publication Series. Series B: Translations.

780 US ISSN 0081-1335
ASIAN MUSIC PUBLICATIONS. SERIES C: REPRINTS. irreg. price varies. (Society for Asian Music) Asian Music Publications, c/o Theodore Front Musical Literature, Inc., 16122 Cohasset St., Van Nuys, CA 91406. TEL 818-994-1902. FAX 818-994-0419. Ed. Fredric Lieberman. **Indexed:** RILM.
Formerly: Society for Asian Music. Publication Series. Series C: Reprints.

780 US ISSN 0081-1343
ASIAN MUSIC PUBLICATIONS. SERIES D: MONOGRAPHS. 1969. irreg., no.3, 1977. price varies. (Society for Asian Music) Asian Music Publications, c/o Theodore Front Musical Literature, Inc., 16122 Cohasset St., Van Nuys, CA 91406. TEL 818-994-1902. FAX 818-994-0419. Ed. Fredric Lieberman. circ. 400 (approx.). **Indexed:** RILM.
Formerly: Society for Asian Music. Publications Series. Series D: Monographs.

780.6 SP
ASOCIACION DE COMPOSITORES SINFONICOS ESPANOLES. BOLETIN. 1978. s-a. Asociacion de Compositores Sinfonicos Espanoles, Francisco de Rojas 5, Madrid 10, Spain. adv.; circ. 1,500.

783 CN ISSN 0335-5012
ASSEMBLEE NOUVELLE.* 1969. q. 20 F. Editions du Levain, 205 rue Laurier Oeust, Montreal, Que H2T 2N9, Canada. Ed. Claude Truchot. adv.; bk.rev.; rec.; rev.

ASSOCIATION OF PERFORMING ARTS PRESENTERS BULLETIN. see THEATER

789.91 612.381 US
AUDIO. 1947. m. $21.94. Hachette Magazines, Inc., 1633 Broadway, New York, NY 10009. TEL 212-767-6000. (Subscr. to: Box 52548, Boulder, CO 80321-2548. TEL 800-274-8808) Ed. Eugene Pitts III. adv.; bk.rev. **Indexed:** A.S.& T.Ind., Acad.Ind., Mag.Ind., Music Ind.

780 GW
AUGSBURGER JAHRBUCH FUER MUSIKWISSENSCHAFT. 1984. a. Verlag Dr. Hans Schneider GmbH, Mozartstr. 6, 8132 Tutzing, Germany. TEL 08158-3050. FAX 08158-7636. Ed. Franz Krautwurst.

MUSIC

780 792 US
AUSTIN CHRONICLE. 1981. w. $55. Austin Chronicle Corporation, Box 49066, Austin, TX 78765. TEL 512-454-5766. FAX 512-458-6910. adv.; bk.rev.; circ. 72,000.
Description: Focuses on local entertainment, culture and politics.

785.1 AT ISSN 0084-6953
AUSTRALASIAN BANDSMAN. 1955. m. Aus.$3. Victorian Bands League, c/o G.H. Gearside, Lithgow, N.S.W. 2790, Australia. (Co-sponsor: Queensland Band Associations)

781.7 AT
AUSTRALIAN COUNTRY MUSIC NEWSLETTER. no.36, May 1979. 3/yr. $2.50. Don & Noela Gresham, Box 186, Murwillumbah, N.S.W. 2484, Australia. illus.

780 AT
AUSTRALIAN MUSIC INDUSTRY: AN ECONOMIC EVALUATION. 1987. irreg. Aus.$25. Australian Music Centre Ltd., P.O. Box N690, Grosvenor Pl., Sydney, N.S.W. 2000, Australia. TEL 61-2-247-4677. FAX 61-2-241-2873. Ed. Hans Hoegh Guldberg.

781.7 AT ISSN 0726-1292
AUSTRALIAN SONGS. SERIES. 1986. irreg. Aus.$6 per no.; catalogue Aus.$2. Sound Austral, 34 Lucerne Cres., Frankston, Vic. 3199, Australia. TEL 03-789-2205. Ed. Frank Hinz. (back issues avail.; catalogue of titles avail.)
Description: Collection of folkloric and community songs of Australia.

780.7 374 AT
AUSTRALIAN STRING TEACHER. 1976. s-a. Aus.$30. Australian String Teachers Association, 16 Clapham St., Balwyn, Vic. 3103, Australia. Ed. Maureen Higgs. adv.; bk.rev.; circ. 1,000.

787 US ISSN 0736-3796
AUTOHARPOHOLIC. 1980. q. $14.50 (foreign $18)(effective Jun. 1991). I.a.d. Publications, Box 504, Brisbane, CA 94005. TEL 415-467-1700. Ed. Becky Blackley. adv.; bk.rev.; rec.; rev.; circ. 2,000. (back issues avail.)
Description: Covers all areas of interest to autoharp (chorded zither) players: music, instruction, interviews, events and listings.

AUTORES. see *THEATER*

780 FR ISSN 0764-2873
AVANT-SCENE OPERA. (Text in language of author and French) 1976. 7/yr. 520 F. (foreign 650 F.)(effective 1992). Editions Premieres Loges, 15 rue Tiquetonne, 75002 Paris, France. TEL 1-42-33-51-51. FAX 1-42-33-80-91. **Indexed:** Curr.Cont.

780 US
B A MAGAZINE. vol.6, 1977. irreg. Brooklyn Academy of Music, 30 Lafayette Ave., Brooklyn, NY 11217. TEL 718-636-4100. illus.

780 UK ISSN 0144-9621
B A S C A NEWS. no.117, 1980. q. British Academy of Songwriters, Composers & Authors, 34 Hanway St., London W1P 9DE, England. FAX 071-436-1913. adv.; bk.rev.; illus.; circ. 2,900.
Incorporates: Songwriter's Guild News.

780 398 US ISSN 0897-2907
B D A A NEWSLETTER. 1978. q. $15 includes membership. Balalaika and Domra Association of America, 2225 Madison Sq., Philadelphia, PA 19146. TEL 215-985-4678. Ed. Stephen M. Wolownik. adv.; film rev.; illus.; circ. 500. (tabloid format; back issues avail.)
Description: Perpetuates the playing of the balalaika and domra, and related instruments.

780.7 370 US
B D GUIDE. (Band Director) 1987. 5/yr. (during the school yr.). $15. Village Press, 2779 Aero Park Dr., Traverse City, MI 49684. TEL 616-946-3712. FAX 616-946-3289. (Subscr. to: Box 629 Traverse City, MI 49685) Ed. Kenneth Neidig. adv.; bk.rev.; circ. 20,000. (back issues avail.)
Description: In-service education publication for high school, junior high, community and four-year college, and military band directors.

780 US
B M I: MUSIC WORLD. 1962. 4/yr. free to qualified personnel. Broadcast Music Inc., 320 W. 57th St., New York, NY 10019. TEL 212-586-2000. Ed. Robin Ahrold. abstr.; circ. 100,000. (processed; also avail. in microfilm from UMI) **Indexed:** Music Artic.Guide, Music Ind.
Formerly (until 1987): B M I: The Many Worlds of Music (ISSN 0045-317X)

780.6 GW
B M R - CORRESPONDENZ; Informationen - Berichte - Kommentare. 1979. bi-m. free. Bayerischer Musikrat e.V., Linprunstr. 16 Rgb., 8000 Munich 2, Germany. TEL 089-5234054. FAX 089-529704. Ed. Peter-Klaus Schwiedel.

781.57 FI ISSN 0784-7726
B N. (Blues News) (Text in Finnish) 1968. bi-m. FIM 150. Finnish Blues Society, PL 257, 00531 Helsinki 53, Finland. TEL (358 0) 760 755. Ed. Pertti Nurmi. adv.; bk.rev.; rec.rev.; circ. 1,300.
Description: Covers all forms of Afro-American music.

780 US ISSN 0005-3600
M410.B1
BACH. 1970. 2/yr. $20 membership (libraries $26). Riemenschneider Bach Institute, Baldwin-Wallace College, Berea, OH 44017. TEL 216-826-2207. FAX 216-826-2329. (Co-sponsor: American Bach Society) Ed. Elinore L. Barber. charts; illus.; index; circ. 800. (tabloid format) **Indexed:** Arts & Hum.Cit.Ind., Curr.Cont., Music Artic.Guide, Music Ind., RILM.
—BLDSC shelfmark: 1854.625000.
Description: Provides articles concerned with Bach styles, forms, and performance practices, with a historical background.

780 GW ISSN 0084-7682
ML410.B1
BACH-JAHRBUCH. 1904. a. price varies. New Bach Society, Thomaskirchhof 16, Postfach 1349, 7010 Leipzig, Germany. FAX 03741-275308. Eds. H.-J. Schulze, C. Wolff. bk.rev.; bibl.; charts; illus.; circ. 4,700. **Indexed:** RILM.
—BLDSC shelfmark: 1854.630000.
Description: Contains scientific findings, bibliographies, facsimiles, Bach Society reports.

BACKBOARD. see *LITERATURE — Poetry*

780.42 US
BACKSTAGE PASS MAGAZINE. m. Loftus Communications Inc., 3800 N. Wilke, Ste.300, Arlington Heights, IL 60004. TEL 708-818-0111. FAX 708-818-0367. Ed. Donna Siclair. circ. 50,000.

780.42 US ISSN 0746-990X
ML420.S77
BACKSTREETS. 1980. q. $15 (foreign $20). Backstreets Publishers Inc., Box 51225, Seattle, WA 98115. FAX 206-728-8827. Ed. Charles R. Cross. adv.; bk.rev.; circ. 20,000. (back issues avail.)
Description: Deals with the music and performances of Bruce Springsteen and other Jersey shore acts.

784 GW
BADISCHE SAENGERZEITUNG; Organ des Badischen Saengerbundes. 1972. m. DM.23.54. Badischer Saengerbund e.V., Brauerstr. 1B, 7500 Karlsruhe 1, Germany. TEL 0721-849669. FAX 0721-853886. Ed. Bernd J. Schorn. circ. 8,000.

780 NO
BALLADE; ballade tidsskrift for ny musikk. 1977. q. NOK 120 (foreign NOK 170) to individuals; institutions NOK 200 (foreign NOK 250); students NOK 60 (foreign NOK 110). Ny Musikk, Toftesgate 69, N-0552 Oslo 5, Norway. TEL 2-370810. FAX 2-376027. Ed. Morten Eide Pedersen. adv.; bk.rev.; rec.rev.; circ. 20,000. **Indexed:** Music Ind.

780.6 US ISSN 0885-7113
BALUNGAN. 1984. 2/yr. $15 to individuals (foreign $20); institutions $30. American Gamelan Institute, Box A-36, Hanover, NH 03755. TEL 603-643-5321. Ed. Jody Diamond. adv.; bk.rev.; circ. 800.
Description: Focuses on all forms of gamelan, Indonesian performing arts, and their international counterparts.

780.42 US
BAM: THE CALIFORNIA MUSIC MAGAZINE. 1976. fortn. $18. Bam Publications, Inc., 3470 Buskirk Ave., Pleasant Hill, CA 94523. TEL 510-934-3700. FAX 510-934-2417. Ed. Steve Stolder. adv.; bk.rev.; circ. 130,000. (tabloid format)
Formerly (until 1977): B A M: Bay Area Music.
Description: Covers developments in popular music from a California perspective.

785 US
BAND FAN. 1972. q. $15. Detroit Concert Band, Inc., 7443 E. Butherus, Ste. 100, Scottsdale, AZ 85260. TEL 602-948-9870. Ed. John Stafford. adv.; bk.rev.; circ. 10,000.
Description: Contains editorials, concert reviews and classified ads.

785.067 JA ISSN 0005-4933
BAND JOURNAL. (Text in Japanese) 1959. m. 720 Yen. Ongaku no Tomo Sha Corp., Kagurazaka 6-30, Shinjuku-ku, Tokyo 162, Japan. TEL 03-3235-2111. FAX 03-3235-5731. TELEX J23718 ONTOA. adv.: B&W page 204000 Yen, color page 444000 Yen; trim 275 x 210. bk.rev.; illus.; circ. 72,000.
Description: Contains commentaries, lectures, analysis of compositions and reports on items of interest. Also includes scores for parts in the supplement of each issue to make the publication practical.

785 US ISSN 0084-7704
BAND MUSIC GUIDE. 1959. irreg. $28. Instrumentalist Co., 200 Northfield Rd., Northfield, IL 60093-3390. TEL 708-446-5000.

780 US ISSN 0190-1559
ML1
BANJO NEWSLETTER; the 5-string banjo magazine. 1973. m. $20 (foreign $48). Banjo Newsletter, Inc., Box 364, Greensboro, MD 21639. TEL 410-482-6278. FAX 410-482-7252. Ed. Hub Nitchie. adv.; bk.rev.; illus.; index; circ. 6,900. **Indexed:** Music Ind.
Description: Contains information on the 5-string banjo, a musical instrument used in folk and classical music. Includes tablature for the instrument.

787 US
BASS MAGAZINE HALL OF FAME YEARBOOK (YEAR). a. $24.95 (foreign $49.95). (International Bassists' - Bass Players Hall of Fame Museum) First Bass International, 33 Essex St., Hackensack, NJ 07601. TEL 201-488-2055. FAX 201-489-5057. circ. 41,188.
Description: Educational tool for teachers and students to enhance and maintain levels of music education and history for the electric and string bass instrument players.

780 US ISSN 1050-785X
BASS PLAYER; for electric and string bass musicians. 1988. 8/yr. $19.97. G P I Publications (Subsidiary of: Miller Freeman, Inc.), 20085 Stevens Creek, Cupertino, CA 95014. TEL 408-446-1105. FAX 408-446-1088. (Subscr. to: Box 57324, Boulder, CO 80322-7324) Ed. Jim Roberts. adv.; circ. 40,000. (also avail. in microfilm from UMI; reprint service avail. from UMI)
Description: For professional, semi-pro and amateur bass players in all styles.

BATON. see *PHILATELY*

780 UK
BAX SOCIETY BULLETIN.* 1969. q. Bax Society, Ed. Paul Podro, 103 Cheyneys Ave., Canons Park, Edgware, Middlesex, England. bk.rev.; bibl.

780 US
BEAT (HIGHLAND). 1977. m. Lounges Publications, 2613 41st St., Highland, IN 46322. TEL 219-924-4027. Ed. Tom Lounges. circ. 20,000.

780 US
THE BEAT (LOS ANGELES); Reggae, African, Caribbean, world music. 1982. bi-m. $12. Bongo Productions, Box 65856, Los Angeles, CA 90065. TEL 818-569-3061. Ed. C.C. Smith. adv.; bk.rev.; circ. 15,000. (back issues avail.)
Formerly: Reggae and African Beat.
Description: Popular and traditional music of the Caribbean, Africa and Brazil, and the new world beat movement.

780.42 US ISSN 0274-6905
BEATLEFAN. 1978. bi-m. $14. Goody Press, Box 33515, Decatur, GA 30033. TEL 404-633-5587. Ed. William King. adv.; bk.rev.; circ. 9,000.
Description: News and features for fans and collectors of the Beatles and the group's individual members: John Lennon, Paul McCartney, George Harrison, Ringo Starr.

780.42 UK ISSN 0261-1600
BEATLES BOOK. 1963. m. $40. Beat Publications, 43-45 St. Mary's Rd., Ealing, London W5 5RQ, England. TEL 01-579-1082. Ed. Johnny Dean. adv.; illus.; circ. 11,000.

780.42 NE
BEATLES VISIE. 1980. q. $12. Vereniging Nederlandse Beatles Fanclub, Box 1464, 1000 BL Amsterdam, Netherlands. Ed. Bertus Elzenaar. adv.; bk.rev.; circ. 600. (microfiche)
Formerly: Nota Beatles.

780 US
BEATS MAGAZINE. 1987. m. free. The Wiz, 1300 Federal Blvd., Carteret, NJ 07008. TEL 908-602-1900. FAX 908-602-0030. Ed. Lori Senger. adv.; circ. 85,000.
Description: Provides news, artist interviews, and concert and product reviews of all genres of music, including video.

780 GW ISSN 0522-5949
BEETHOVEN-JAHRBUCH. 1954. biennial. price varies. Verein Beethoven-Haus, Postfach 2463, 5300 Bonn 1, Germany. bk.rev.; bibl.; circ. 1,000. **Indexed:** RILM.
—BLDSC shelfmark: 1876.490000.

780 US ISSN 0898-6185
BEETHOVEN NEWSLETTER. 1986. 3/yr. membership. San Jose State University, Center for Beethoven Studies, One Washington Sq., San Jose, CA 95192-0171. (Co-sponsor: American Beethoven Society) Ed. William Meredith. bk.rev.; circ. 1,000. **Indexed:** Music Artic.Guide, Music Ind., RILM.
Description: Devoted to the life and music of the composer.

780 CN
BEETLE. 1970. m. Can.$7.50. Entertainment Publications, Inc., Box 5696, Postal Stn. A, Toronto, Ont., Canada. Ed. Debbie Brioux. adv.; bk.rev.; film rev.; play rev.; circ. 150,000.

780 CC
BEIFANG YINYUE/NORTHERN MUSIC. (Text in Chinese) bi-m. (Heilongjiang Sheng Wenlian) Beifang Yinyue Zazhishe, 16, Yaojingjie, Nangang-qu, Harbin, Heilongjiang 150006, People's Republic of China. TEL 30847. Ed. Shu Feng.

780 GW ISSN 0233-0105
ML410.B1
BEITRAEGE ZUR BACH-FORSCHUNG. 1982. s-a. DM.19.90. Nationale Forschungs- und Gedenkstaetten Johann Sebastian Bach, Postfach 1349, 7010 Leipzig, Germany. TELEX 512928. circ. 1,000.

780 AU ISSN 0067-5067
BEITRAEGE ZUR HARMONIKALEN GRUNDLAGENFORSCHUNG. 1968. irreg., no.11, 1980. price varies. Musikverlag Elisabeth Lafite, Hegelgasse 13-22, A-1010 Vienna, Austria.

780 AU
BEITRAEGE ZUR JAZZFORSCHUNG/STUDIES IN JAZZ RESEARCH. (Text in German) 1969. irreg., vol.8, 1986. price varies. (International Society for Jazz Research) Akademische Druck- und Verlagsanstalt Dr. Paul Struzl, Schoenaugasse 6, 8010 Graz, Styria, Austria. TEL 81-34-60. Eds. Alfons M. Dauer, Franz Kerschbaumer. (back issues avail.) **Indexed:** RILM.

789 US ISSN 0092-8666
ML1
BELL TOWER. 9/yr. membership. American Bell Association, Box 286, RD 1, Natrona Heights, PA 15065. TEL 412-295-9623. illus.; circ. 2,600.

780 FR
BEST; le mensuel du rock. 1968. m. 200 F. (foreign 300 F.). Editions Mericourt, 23 rue d'Antin, 75002 Paris, France. TEL 47-42-33-56. FAX 47-42-68-86. Ed. Sylvie Boutin.

780.42 JA
BEST HIT. (Text in Japanese) 1983. m. 5880 Yen. Gakken Co., Ltd., 40-5, 4 chome, Kamiikedai, Ohta-ku, Tokyo 145, Japan. Ed. Kin'ichi Iina.

BIBLIOGRAFICKY KATALOG C S F R: CESKE HUDEBNINY, GRAMOFONOVE DESKY A C D. see BIBLIOGRAPHIES

780 PL
BIBLIOTEKA CHOPINOWSKA. 1959. irreg. price varies. Polskie Wydawnictwo Muzyczne, Al. Krasinskiego 11a, 31-111 Krakow, Poland. TEL 22-70-44. FAX 22-01-74. Ed. Mieczyslaw Tomaszewski.
Description: Survey of the books on Chopin's life and work.

780 PL ISSN 0208-9963
BIBLIOTEKA RES FACTA. 1970. irreg. price varies. Polskie Wydawnictwo Muzyczne, Al. Krasinskiego 11a, 31-111 Krakow, Poland. TEL 22-70-44. FAX 22-01-74. (Dist. by: Ars Polona-Ruch, Krakowskie Przedmiescie 7, 00-068 Warsaw, Poland) Ed. Michal Bristiger. **Indexed:** RILM.

780 PL ISSN 0067-7779
BIBLIOTEKA SLUCHACZA KONCERTOWEGO. SERIA WPROWADZAJACA. 1954. irreg. price varies. Polskie Wydawnictwo Muzyczne, Al. Krasinskiego 11a, 31-111 Krakow, Poland. TEL 22-70-44. FAX 22-01-74. Ed. Mieczyslaw Tomaszewski.
Description: Covers popular way famous symphonic and concert works.

780 NE
▼**BIBLIOTHEEK NEDERLANDSE MUZIEK.** 1991. a. fl.39.50. Walburg Pers BV, P.O. Box 222, 7200 AE Zutphen, Netherlands. TEL 05750-10522. FAX 05750-41025. (Co-sponsor: Centrum Nederlandse Muziek)

781.57 GW
BIELEFELDER KATALOG - JAZZ. a. DM.26.80. Motor-Presse Stuttgart, Leuschnerstr. 1, Postfach 106036, 7000 Stuttgart 1, Germany. TEL 0711-18201. FAX 0711-1821669.

789.91 GW
BIELEFELDER KATALOG - KLASSIK. 1954. s-a. DM.26.80. Motor-Presse Stuttgart, Leuschnerstr. 1, Postfach 106036, 7000 Stuttgart 1, Germany. TEL 0711-18201. FAX 0711-1821669. Ed. H. Hartmann. adv.; circ. 14,000.
Formerly: Bielefelder Katalog (ISSN 0006-2103)

780 US
BIG APPLE BLUES. 1981. irreg. $10. Eric Lesselbaum, Ed. & Pub., c/o Dr. Boogie, Box 655, Bronxville, NY 10708. adv.; bk.rev.; music rev.; circ. 250.
Description: Covers blues performances in New York metro area.

BIG BOPPER. see CHILDREN AND YOUTH — For

791 US ISSN 0006-2510
PN2000
BILLBOARD (NEW YORK). 1894. w. $209. B P I Communications, Inc. (New York) (Subsidiary of: Affiliated Publications, Inc.), 1515 Broadway, 39th Fl., New York, NY 10036. TEL 212-764-7300. FAX 212-944-1719. (Alt. addr.): 9107 Wilshire Blvd., Beverly Hills, CA 90210) Ed. Ken Schlager. circ. 46,675. (also avail. in microform from UMI,KTO; microfilm from BHP,KTO; reprint service avail. from UMI) **Indexed:** Bus.Ind., Music Ind., PMR, Tr.& Indus.Ind.
●Also available online. Vendor(s): DIALOG.
—BLDSC shelfmark: 2060.700000.
Description: Newsweekly for the music and home entertainment industries.

780.42 US
▼**BILLBOARD HISTORY OF ROCK 'N ROLL.** 1992. a. $100. B P I Information & Research Group, 1515 Broadway, New York, NY 10010. rec.rev.
●Available only on CD-ROM.
Description: Combines CD-Audio and CD-ROM technologies to list top-selling recording artists by year, and also includes a feature article section.

780 US ISSN 0067-8600
BILLBOARD'S INTERNATIONAL BUYER'S GUIDE OF THE MUSIC-RECORD-TAPE INDUSTRY. 1958. a. $75. B P I Communications, Inc. (New York) (Subsidiary of: Affiliated Publications, Inc.), 1515 Broadway, 39th Fl., New York, NY 10036. TEL 212-764-7300. FAX 212-944-1719. (And: 9000 Sunset Blvd., Los Angeles, CA 90069. TEL 800-344-7119) (also avail. in microfilm from KTO; reprint service avail. from UMI)
Formerly (until 1960): Billboard. International Buyer's Guide of the Music-Record Industry.
Description: Worldwide music and video business to business directory.

780 US ISSN 0732-0124
ML1
BILLBOARD'S INTERNATIONAL TALENT AND TOURING DIRECTORY; the music industry's worldwide reference source: talent, talent management, booking agencies, promoters, venue facilities, venue services and products. 1978. a. $67. B P I Communications, Inc. (New York) (Subsidiary of: Affiliated Publications, Inc.), 1515 Broadway, 39th Fl., New York, NY 10036. TEL 212-764-7300. FAX 212-944-1719. (And: 9000 Sunset Blvd., Los Angeles, CA 90069. TEL 800-344-7119) circ. 15,000. (also avail. in microfilm from KTO)
Formerly: Billboard's International Talent Directory (ISSN 0190-9649); Incorporates: Billboard's on Tour (ISSN 0361-5383); Campus Attractions (ISSN 0067-8597); Which was formerly (1964-1968): Billboard. Music on Campus.
Description: Source for US and interntional talent, booking agencies, facilities, services and products.

792 US
BILLBOARD'S YEAR-END AWARDS ISSUE. 1970. a. $9.95. B P I Communications, Inc. (New York) (Subsidiary of: Affiliated Publications, Inc.), 1515 Broadway, 39th Fl., New York, NY 10036. TEL 212-764-7300. FAX 212-944-1719. (And: 9000 Sunset Blvd., Los Angeles, CA 90069. TEL 800-344-7119) circ. 45,000. (also avail. in microfilm from KTO)
Former titles: Billboard's Year-End Issue Talent in Action; Billboard's Year-End Awards - Talent in Action; Billboard's Talent in Action.

781.7 367 US
BILLIE JO WILLIAMS INTERNATIONAL FAN CLUB. 1982. q. $10 to individuals; senior citizens $7. Box 1408, N. Wilkesboro, NC 28659. Ed. Billie Jo Williams. (back issues avail.)
Description: Provides news of the artist, including his show dates, merchandise price list and photos.

BLACK BEAT. see CHILDREN AND YOUTH — For

780 910.03 US ISSN 0276-3605
ML3556
BLACK MUSIC RESEARCH JOURNAL. 1980. s-a. $15 (foreign $20). Center for Black Music Research, Columbia College Chicago, 600 S. Michigan Ave., Chicago, IL 60605. TEL 312-663-1600. FAX 312-663-9019. Ed. Samuel A. Floyd, Jr. index; circ. 808. **Indexed:** Arts & Hum.Cit.Ind., Music Artic.Guide, Music Ind., RILM.
—BLDSC shelfmark: 2105.965600.
Description: Broad range of research in black music.

780.65 910.03 US ISSN 1043-9455
ML2999
BLACK SACRED MUSIC; a journal of theomusicology. 1987. s-a. $15 to individuals (foreign $19); institutions $30 (foreign $34). Duke University Press, 6697 College Station, Durham, NC 27708. TEL 919-684-2173. FAX 919-684-8644. Ed. Jon Michael Spencer. **Indexed:** Music Artic.Guide.
—BLDSC shelfmark: 2107.130000.
Formerly (until 1989): Journal of Black Sacred Music (ISSN 0891-9321)
Refereed Serial

BLAETTER DER FREIEN VOLKSBUEHNE BERLIN. see THEATER

780 GW
DIE BLASMUSIK. 1950. m. DM.25.20. (Bund Deutscher Blasmusikverbaende e.V.) Blasmusikverlag, Am Maerzengraben 6, 7800 Freiburg 33, Germany. Ed. K. Schulz. adv.; bk.rev.; bibl.; illus.; stat.; circ. 6,200. (back issues avail.)
Formerly: Allgemeine Volksmusikzeitung.

MUSIC 3541

M

MUSIC

780.904 — US
BLITZ; the rock and roll magazine for thinking people. 1975. q. $15 for 6 issues. Box 48124, Los Angeles, CA 90048-0124. TEL 818-360-3262. Ed. Mike McDowell. adv.; bk.rev.; charts; illus.; stat.; circ. 5,000. (back issues avail.)
Description: Focus on obscure and underrated artists in rock and roll music, with a record collector's perspective.

781.57 — NE
BLOCK; magazine for blues. 1975. q. fl.22.50 (foreign fl.32.50). c/o M.A. Wisse, Postbus 244, 7600 AE Almelo, Netherlands. TEL 011-31-5490-19976. FAX 011-31-5490-20106. Ed. Rien Wisse. adv.; bk.rev.; circ. 4,000. (back issues avail.) **Indexed:** Alt.Press Ind.

780 — IT
BLU AND BLU; mensile di musica tutta italiana. m. (Athena 2001 Coop. a.r.l.) Edizioni L.E.T.I. s.r.l., Via E.Q. Visconti, 20, 00193 Rome, Italy. TEL 06-3144512. circ. 80,500.

781.7 — GW — ISSN 0936-2479
ML3519
BLUEGRASS - BUEHNE; old time and bluegrass magazine. 1981. bi-m. DM.25($15) Eberhardtstr. 14-4, 7900 Ulm, Germany. TEL 0731-28642. Ed. Eberhard Finke. adv.; bk.rev.; circ. 600.

780 681 — US
BLUEGRASS DIRECTORY. 1981. biennial. $7.50. B D Products, Box 412, Murphys, CA 95247. TEL 209-728-3379. Ed. Betty Deakins. adv.; circ. 1,000. (back issues avail.)
Description: Lists over 500 suppliers of instruments, repairs, accessories, services, and instructional tapes for bluegrass and folk musicians.

781.7 — US — ISSN 0006-5129
BLUEGRASS MUSIC NEWS. 1950. 4/yr. $8 to non-members (foreign $12). Kentucky Music Educators Association, c/o Hazel O. Carver, Ed., 1007 Granville Ln., Russellville, KY 42276. TEL 502-726-6427. adv.; bk.rev.; charts; illus.; circ. 2,000.
Description: Articles on music education.

781.7 — US — ISSN 0006-5137
ML1
BLUEGRASS UNLIMITED. 1966. m. $20 (foreign $27). Bluegrass Unlimited Inc., Box 111, Broad Run, VA 22014. TEL 703-349-8181. Ed. Peter V. Kuykendall. adv.; bk.rev.; record rev.; illus.; circ. 21,540. **Indexed:** Music Ind., Pop.Mus.Per.Ind.
Description: Covers old-time, traditional country music and bluegrass.

780 — US
BLUEMONT MUSE. 1979. bi-m. Bluemont Concert Series, Box 208, Leesburg, VA 22075. TEL 703-777-0574. Ed. Peter H. Dunning. circ. 5,000.

781.57 — IT
IL BLUES. 1982. q. L.20000. Editori Blues e Dintorni, Piazza Grandi 12, I-20135 Milan, Italy. (Subscr. to: c/o Mario Grandi, viale Tunisia 15, 20124 Milan, Italy) Ed.Bd. adv.; bk.rev.; circ. 2,000. (tabloid format; back issues avail.)

781.57 — US
BLUES ACCESS. no.8, 1991. 4/yr. $12 (Canada $14; elsewhere $18). Cary Wolfson, Ed. & Pub., 1514 North St., Boulder, CO 80304. TEL 303-443-7245. FAX 303-939-9729. adv.

781.57 — UK
BLUES & RHYTHM; the gospel truth. every 5 weeks. £2.85 (foreign £3.15) per issue. 16 Bank St., Cheadle, Cheshire SK8 2AZ, England. FAX 0532-531960. (Subscr. to: c/o Tony Watson, 13 Ingleborough Dr., Morley, Leeds, LS27 9DY, England) record rev.
Description: Covers all aspects of blues, R&B, and gospel; and includes articles, discographies, and letters.

781 — US — ISSN 0045-2297
BLUES & SOUL MUSIC REVIEW. 1966. fortn. £71. Napfield Ltd., 153 Praed St., London W2 RL, England. TEL 071-402-6869. FAX 071-224-8227. Ed. R. Killbourn. adv.; bk.rev.; illus.; circ. 65,000.
Incorporates: Black Music and Jazz Review (ISSN 0307-2169)

781.57 — US
BLUES AT THE FOUNDATION. q. free to members. Blues Foundation, 174 Beale St., Memphis, TN 38103. TEL 901-527-2583. FAX 901-529-4030. circ. 3,000 (controlled).

781.57 — AU — ISSN 0250-4421
ML3521
BLUES LIFE; oesterreichische Fachzeitschrift fuer Bluesmusik. 1977. q. S.200. Blues Life Verlag, Kegelgasse 40-1-17, A-1030 Vienna, Austria. TEL 0222-7123765. FAX 0222-7123765. Ed. Fritz Svacina. adv.; bk.rev.; circ. 5,000. (back issues avail.)

781.57 — US
BLUES RESEARCH. 1959. irreg., no.17, 1975. $1 per no. Record Research, 65 Grand Ave., Brooklyn, NY 11205. TEL 718-857-7003. Eds. Anthony Rotante, Paul Sheatsley. charts; illus.

781.573 — UK — ISSN 0006-5153
ML5
BLUES UNLIMITED. 1963. 4/yr. £7.50($15) B U Publications Ltd., 36 Belmont Park, Lewisham, London S.E. 13, England. Ed.Bd. adv.; bk.rev.; illus.; circ. 4,000. **Indexed:** M.L.A.

780 793 — PE
BOLETIN DE MUSICA Y DANZA.* 1978. Instituto Nacional de Cultura, Departamental Ancash, Oficion Numero. 363, Huaras, Peru. Dir. Domingo Sanchez. bk.rev. (processed)

783 — IT — ISSN 0006-663X
BOLLETTINO CECILIANO; rivista di musica sacra. 1905. m. (10/yr.) L.30000($25) Associazione Italiana Santa Cecilia, Piazza S. Agostino 20A, 00186 Rome, Italy. TEL 06-654-.0461. Ed.Bd. adv.; bk.rev.; index.

BOMBAY ART SOCIETY'S ART JOURNAL. see ART

780 — US
BOMP. 1966. 6/yr. $12 for 8 issues. Bomp Magazine, Box 7112, Burbank, CA 91510. Ed. Gregory Shaw. adv.; bk.rev.; circ. 40,000.
Formerly: Who Put the Bomp (ISSN 0039-7873)

789.91 070.5 — NE — ISSN 0166-1426
BOOGIE WOOGIE AND BLUES COLLECTOR. (Text in Dutch and English) 1968. q. fl.7.50($4) (Blues Record Centre) Dutch Blues and Boogie Organisation, Postbus 12538, 1100 AM Amsterdam, Netherlands. TEL 20-6961111. (Subscr. to: Maasdrielhof 175, 1106 NG Amsterdam, Netherlands) Ed. Martin van Olderen. adv.; bk.rev.; circ. 4,500. (back issues avail.)

785 — US — ISSN 8755-5832
BOOMBAH HERALD; a band history newsletter. 1973. s-a. $10. 15 Park Blvd., Lancaster, NY 14086. Ed. Loren D. Geiger. adv.; bk.rev.; illus.; tr.lit.; rec.rev.; cum.index; circ. 100. (tabloid format; back issues avail.)
Description: Seeks to preserve the heritage of the concert band in the USA and around the world. Articles cover band histories and composer biographies.

781.973 — US — ISSN 0006-7598
BOOSEY AND HAWKES NEWSLETTER. 1965. 3/yr. free. Boosey and Hawkes, Inc., 24 E. 21st St., New York, NY 10010-7200. TEL 212-228-3300. FAX 212-473-5730. TELEX 650-284-8790 MCI. Ed. Steven Swartz. bk.rev.; illus.; music rev.; circ. 10,000.
Description: Provides articles and information about the work of composers published by Boosey and Hawkes and its affiliates.

BOP. see CHILDREN AND YOUTH — For

786 — US
BOSTON ORGAN CLUB NEWSLETTER.* 1965. irreg. $5. Organ Historical Society, Boston Organ Club, Box 863, Claremont, NH 03743. Ed. E.A. Boadway. adv.; bk.rev.; circ. 300.

780.15 — US
BOSTON SYMPHONY ORCHESTRA PROGRAM. 1882. w. during season. $65. Boston Symphony Orchestra, Program Office, Symphony Hall, Boston, MA 02115. TEL 617-266-1492. FAX 617-638-9367. TELEX TWX-710-321-9283. Ed. Marc Mandel. adv.; bk.rev.; index; circ. 234,000. (also avail. in microform from UMI,BHP; microfilm from KTO; reprint service avail. UMI)
Formerly: Boston Symphony Orchestra Program Book-Notes (ISSN 0006-8020)

780 — NE
DE BOUWBRIEF. 1975. q. fl.57 (effective 1992). Vereniging voor Muziek en Instrumentenbouw, Huismuziek, Utrechtsestraat 77, P.O. Box 350, 3400 AJ Ijsselstein, Netherlands. Ed. A. Riesthuis. adv.; bk.rev.; illus.; circ. 1,500.
Description: Devoted to the building and designing of musical instruments. Covers materials, tools, and measurements. Includes announcements of events, exhibitions, and courses.

780 920 — GW
BRAHMS STUDIEN. 1976. biennial. DM.30. J. Brahms-Gesellschaft, Internationale Vereinigung e.V., Trostbruecke 4, 2000 Hamburg 11, Germany. adv.; bk.rev.; illus.; circ. 500.
Formerly: Brahms-Gesellschaft Hamburg. Jahresgabe.

BRAILLE MUSIC MAGAZINE. see HANDICAPPED — Visually Impaired

780 — SZ — ISSN 0303-3848
ML5
BRASS BULLETIN; international magazine for brass players. (Text in English, French and German) 1971. 4/yr. $38 to individuals; students $30. P.O. Box, CH-1630 Bulle, Switzerland. TEL 029-24422. FAX 029-21350. Ed. Jean-Pierre Mathez. adv.; bk.rev.; bibl.; illus.; circ. 7,000. (back issues avail.) **Indexed:** Music Ind.
—BLDSC shelfmark: 2273.640000.

780 — US
BRASS PLAYERS GUIDE (YEAR). 1975. a. $4 (effective 1992). Robert King Music Sales, Inc., Shovel Shop Sq., 28 Main St., Bldg. 15, N. Easton, MA 02356-1499. FAX 508-238-2571. Ed. Dennis Hugh Avey. adv.; circ. 20,000.

780 — US — ISSN 0363-454X
BRASS RESEARCH SERIES. irreg. Brass Press, c/o RKMS, 28 Main St., N. Easton, MA 02356. FAX 508-238-2571. Ed. Stephen L. Glover.
Description: Music history and research.

BRAVO. see MOTION PICTURES

BRAVURA STUDIES IN MUSIC. see MUSIC — Abstracting, Bibliographies, Statistics

BRIO. see LIBRARY AND INFORMATION SCIENCES

785 — UK — ISSN 0007-0319
BRITISH BANDSMAN. 1887. w. $71. British Bandsman Ltd., London End, Beaconsfield, Bucks, England. Ed. Peter Wilson. adv.; bk.rev.; illus.
Incorporates: Brass Band News & International Bandsman.

781.97 016 — UK — ISSN 0068-1407
BRITISH CATALOGUE OF MUSIC. 1957. 3/yr. (annual cum. incorporates contents of 2 previous issues). £60($130) (foreign £70). (British Library, Bibliographic Services) Bowker-Saur Ltd. (Subsidiary of: Reed International Books), 59-60 Grosvenor St., London W1X 9DA, England. TEL 071-493-5841. FAX 071-499-1590. (Subscr. to: Order Processing Dept., Butterworth Services, Borough Green, Sevenoaks, Kent TN15 8PH, England. TEL 0732-884567) Patrick Mills. bibl.; index; circ. 600.
● Also available online.
—BLDSC shelfmark: 2292.600000.
Description: Lists music recently published in the UK and received by the Copyright Receipt Office of the British Library, music available in the UK via a sole agent, and post-1980 acquisitions of the British Library.

780.7 CN ISSN 0705-9019
BRITISH COLUMBIA MUSIC EDUCATOR. 1959. s-a. Can.$50 to non-members; members Can.$25; students Can.$12. B.C. Music Educators' Association, 1734 Evelyn St., North Vanouver, B.C. V7K 1V1, Canada. TEL 604-985-5722. FAX 604-985-5770. (Subscr. to: B.C. Teachers' Federation, 2235 Burrard St., Vancouver, B.C. V6J 3H9 Canada) adv.; bk.rev.; illus.; stat.; index; circ. 1,200. **Indexed:** Can.Educ.Ind.
Description: Covers the study and teaching of music.

780 UK
BRITISH FEDERATION OF FESTIVALS. YEARBOOK. 1921. a. £8.50. British Federation of Festivals, 198 Park Lane, MacClesfield, Cheshire SK11 6UD, England. FAX 0625-503229. adv.; circ. 2,500.
Formerly: British Federation of Music Festivals. Yearbook (ISSN 0309-8044)
Description: Contains detailed information about affiliated festivals in the UK, Hong Kong, and Bermuda - like music, dance, speech, and drama festivals for amateurs.

650 UK ISSN 0265-0517
ML5
BRITISH JOURNAL OF MUSIC EDUCATION. 1984. 3/yr. $35 to individuals; institutions $55. Cambridge University Press, Edinburgh Bldg., Shaftesbury Rd., Cambridge CB2 2RU, England. TEL 0223-312393. FAX 0223-315052. TELEX 851817256. (North American addr.: Cambridge University Press, 40 W. 20th St., New York, NY 10011) Eds. John Paynter, Keith Swanwick. (also avail. in microform from UMI; reprint service avail. from SWZ) **Indexed:** Cont.Pg.Educ.
—BLDSC shelfmark: 2311.890000.
Description: Covers classroom music teaching, individual instrumental teaching and group teaching, music in higher education.

780 UK ISSN 0007-1463
BRITISH MOUTHPIECE; brass & military band journal. 1958. w. £11. Mechanics Institute, Spring St., Shuttleworth, Nr. Ramsbottom, Lancashire, England. Ed. E.C. Buttress. adv.; bk.rev.; abstr.; charts; illus.; record rev.; tr.lit.; circ. 4,000.

780.6 UK ISSN 0958-5664
BRITISH MUSIC. 1979. a. £5. British Music Society, 7 Tudor Gardens, Upminster, Essex RM14 3DE, England. Ed. Brian Blyth Daubney. adv.; circ. 500.
—BLDSC shelfmark: 2330.620000.
Formerly (until vol.10, 1988): British Music Society. Journal (ISSN 0143-7402)
Description: Covers British opera, chamber music, orchestral music; reviews of artists, works, interviews and more.

780.7 UK ISSN 0266-2329
BRITISH MUSIC EDUCATION YEARBOOK. 1984. a. £11.50. Rhinegold Publishing Ltd., 241 Shaftesbury Ave., London WC2H 8EH, England. TEL 071-836-2383. FAX 071-528-7991. Ed. Annabel Carter.
—BLDSC shelfmark: 2330.700000.
Description: Complete guide to music education at all levels from pre-school to post-graduate.

780 UK ISSN 0954-1802
BRITISH MUSIC WORLDWIDE. a. £15. Rhinegold Publishing Ltd., 241 Shaftesbury Ave., London WC2H 8EH, England. TEL 071-240-5749. FAX 071-528-7991. Ed. Keith Clarke. adv.

780 UK ISSN 0306-5928
ML21
BRITISH MUSIC YEARBOOK. 1972. a. £12.95. Rhinegold Publishing Ltd., 241 Shaftesbury Ave., London WC2H 8EH, England. TEL 071-836-2383. FAX 071-528-7991. Ed. Annabel Carter. adv.; stat.; index. **Indexed:** RILA.
Formerly: Music Yearbook.
Description: Comprehensive directory of British classical music.

BRITISH PERFORMING ARTS YEARBOOK. see *DANCE*

780 616.89 UK ISSN 0953-7511
BRITISH SOCIETY FOR MUSIC THERAPY. BULLETIN. 1987. 3/yr. (included to members free with subscr. of "Journal"). British Society for Music Therapy, 69 Avondale Ave., E. Barnet, Herts. EN4 8NB, England. Ed. Denise Christophers.
—BLDSC shelfmark: 2425.300000.

780.42 US
BUDDY. m. 5705 Oram, Dallas, TX 75206-7227. TEL 214-823-1867. Ed. Stoney Burns. circ. 100,000.

BUEHNE. see *THEATER*

780 BU
BULGARSKA MUSIKA; organ na suyuza no Bulgarskite kompositiry i na komiteta za kultura. 10/yr. 7. Komiteta a Kultura, Iv. Vazov 2, Sofia, Bulgaria. Ed. Dimitr Zenginor. **Indexed:** Music Ind.

780.1 US ISSN 0739-5639
ML1
BULLETIN OF HISTORICAL RESEARCH IN MUSICAL EDUCATION. 1980. s-a. $15. University of Kansas, A M E M T Department, 311 Baily Hall, Lawrence, KS 66045-2344. TEL 913-864-4784. Ed. George Heller. bk.rev.; bibl.; circ. 205. (back issues avail.) **Indexed:** Music Ind.
Description: Emphasizes music education in the United States as well as musical works worldwide.
Refereed Serial

780 GW
BUNDESBRUDER SAENGERSCHAFT FRANCO-PALATIA BAYREUTH. 1917. 5/yr. not for sale. Altherrenverband der Saengerschaft Franco-Palatia Bayreuth, Richthofenhoehe 50, 8580 Bayreuth, Germany. Ed. Kurt Schimmel. index; circ. 300.

780.7 GW
BUNDESSCHULMUSIKWOCHE. 1972. biennial. price varies. (Verband Deutscher Schulmusikerzieher) Musikverlag B. Schott's Soehne, Weihergarten 5, 6500 Mainz, Germany. TEL 06131-2246815. Ed. Karl Heinrich Ehrenforth. circ. 800. (back issues avail.)
Formerly: Kongressbericht Bundesschulmusikwoche (ISSN 0172-9624)

780 026 CN ISSN 0383-1299
C A M L NEWSLETTER/A C B M NOUVELLES. (Text in English and French) 1972. 3/yr. Can.$65($20) to individuals; institutions Can.$75; student Can.$25. Canadian Association of Music Libraries, c/o Faculty of Music Library, University of Toronto, Toronto, Ont. M5S 1A1, Canada. TEL 416-978-6920. FAX 416-978-5771. Ed. Kathleen McMorrow. adv.: B&W page Can.$30. bk.rev.; circ. 170. (back issues avail.)
Supersedes: Canadian Music Library Association. Newsletter (ISSN 0383-1280)
Description: Features association news, conference reports, book and music reviews and library articles.

780 US ISSN 1053-7694
ML1
C A S JOURNAL. 1964. s-a. $35 to individuals (foreign $40); libraries $50. Catgut Acoustical Society, c/o Carleen M. Hutchins, Sec., 112 Essex Ave., Montclair, NJ 07042. Ed. Daniel W. Haines. bk.rev.; charts; illus.; index; circ. 800. (back issues avail.) **Indexed:** Forest Prod.Abstr.
Former titles: Catgut Acoustical Society. Journal (ISSN 0882-2212); (until 1984): Catgut Acoustical Society Newsletter (ISSN 0576-9280)

780 CN
C B C CLASSICAL RECORD REFERENCE BOOK. (Text in English and French) 1980. a. Canadian Broadcasting Corporation, 7925 Cote St. Luc Rd., Montreal, Que. H4W 1R5, Canada. TEL 514-285-3211.

780 910.03 US ISSN 1042-8836
C B M R MONOGRAPHS. 1989. a. $10 (foreign $13). Center for Black Music Research, Columbia College Chicago, 600 S. Michigan Ave., Chicago, IL 60605. TEL 312-663-1600. FAX 312-663-9019. Ed. Samuel A. Floyd, Jr. circ. 450.
Description: Covers broad range of research in black music.

783 US
C C M UPDATE. (Contemporary Christian Music) 1983. 25/yr. $110. C C M Communications, 1913 21st Ave., S., Nashville, TN 37212. TEL 800-333-9643. (Subscr. to: Box 55995, Boulder, CO 80322) Ed. John W. Styll. adv.; circ. 5,000.
Formerly (until 1986): MusicLine (ISSN 0746-7656)
Description: Contains news and information about the contemporary gospel music industry, including airplay and sales reports.

C C T NEWSLETTER. (Choreographers Theatre) see *DANCE*

C D GUIDE. (Compact Disc) see *SOUND RECORDING AND REPRODUCTION*

780 AU ISSN 0574-9468
C I A REVUE. 1953. a. Confederation Internationale des Accordeonistes, c/o Walter Mauer, Sec. Gen., Dietrichgasse 51-19, 1030 Vienna, Austria. FAX 1-74830320. circ. 1,000.

370 US ISSN 0007-8638
C M E A NEWS. 1947. q. $10. California Music Educators Association, 3924 Cottonwood Dr., Concord, CA 94519. TEL 510-685-3237. Ed. Jerri Burke. adv.; circ. 3,100. **Indexed:** Music Artic.Guide.

780.42 384.55 US
C M J NEW MUSIC REPORT. (College Media Journal) 1978. w. $250. College Media Inc., 245 Great Neck Rd., 3rd Fl., Great Neck, NY 11021-3308. TEL 516-466-6000. FAX 516-466-7159. Ed: Robert Haber. adv.; bk.rev.; film rev.; circ. 3,000. (back issues avail.)
Former titles: Progressive Media (ISSN 0731-5708); C M J Progressive Media (ISSN 0195-7430)

780 US ISSN 0162-6973
ML3505.8
CADENCE (REDWOOD); the review of jazz & blues: creative improvised music. 1976. m. $25. Cadence Jazz & Blues Magazine Ltd., Cadence Bldg., Redwood, NY 13679. TEL 315-287-2852. FAX 315-287-2860. Ed. Robert Rusch. adv.; bk.rev.; index; circ. 7,500. **Indexed:** Abstr.Pop.Cult, Microcomp.Ind., Music Ind., Pop.Mus.Per.Ind.
Description: Features interviews, oral histories, news and coverage of record scenes.

780 RU
CADENCIES TO MOZART'S CONCERTS. a. 3.60 Rub. Izdatel'stvo Muzyka, Ul. Neglinnaya 14, Moscow 103031, Russia. TEL 924-81-63. FAX 921-83-53.

780.7 US ISSN 0007-9405
CADENZA. 1942. 3/yr. $8 to non-members. Montana Music Educators Association, Thayer Rd., Mill Creek, Lolo, MT 59847. TEL 406-273-2112. Ed. Joseph Mussulman. adv.; illus.; circ. 1,000.
Description: Forum covering the study and teaching of music.

780.7 CN ISSN 0703-8380
CADENZA. q. Can.$30. (Saskatchewan Music Educators' Association) Saskatchewan Teachers' Federation, Box 1108, Saskatoon, Sask. S7K 3N3, Canada. Ed. Doug Millington. adv.
Former titles: S M E A. Journal (ISSN 0317-5073) & S M E A. Newsletter (ISSN 0381-9051)

780.92 FR ISSN 0395-1200
ML140.D28
CAHIERS DEBUSSY. 1974. a. 120 F. Centre de Documentation Claude Debussy, IRCAM, 31, rue Saint-Merri, 75004 Paris, France. TEL 42-77-06-39. Ed. Francois Lesure. adv.; illus. **Indexed:** RILM.

780 US
CALENDAR FOR NEW MUSIC. 1979. m. (9/yr.). $11 to individuals; students $7. SoundArt Foundation, Inc., Box 850, Philmont, NY 12565-0850. FAX 518-672-4775. adv.; circ. 6,500.
Formerly (until 1981): New Music News.

782.1 UK ISSN 0954-5867
ML1699
CAMBRIDGE OPERA JOURNAL. 1988. 3/yr. £32 to individuals; institutions £59. Cambridge University Press, Edinburgh Bldg., Shaftesbury Rd., Cambridge CB2 2RU, England. TEL 0223-312393. (North American addr.: Cambridge University Press, Journals Dept., 40 W. 20th St., New York, NY 10011) Eds. J. Groos, R. Parker.
—BLDSC shelfmark: 3015.966900.
Description: Addresses audiences from a variety of disciplines, ranging from musicology to literature, theater, and history.

CANADA'S ATLANTIC FOLKLORE AND FOLKLIFE SERIES. see *FOLKLORE*

MUSIC

785.06   CN
CANADIAN BAND ASSOCIATION (ONTARIO). NEWSLETTER. 1971. q. membership. Canadian Band Association (Ontario) Inc., 21 Tecumseh St., Brantford, Ont. N3S 2B3, Canada. TEL 519-753-1858. Ed. Frank McKinnon. adv.; circ. 170. (processed)
   Formerly: Canadian Band Directors Association. Newsletter (ISSN 0381-9159)
   Description: Promotes and develops the musical, educational and cultural values of bands in Ontario.

785   CN   ISSN 0703-9077
CANADIAN BAND JOURNAL. 1975. q. Can.$15. Unison, Inc., P.O. Box 5005, Red Deer, Alta. T4N 5H5, Canada. TEL 403-342-3216. FAX 403-341-5474. Ed. K. Mann. adv.; bk.rev.; music rev.; index; circ. 3,500. (CD reviews)
   Description: A professional journal for instrumental music educators and performers.

780   CN   ISSN 0045-4575
CANADIAN COIN BOX. 1946. 10/yr. Can.$28. N C C Publishing, 106 Lakeshore Rd. E., Ste. 209, Mississauga, Ont. L5G 1E38, Canada. TEL 519-376-9680. FAX 416-271-6373. Ed. Sandra Anderson. adv.: adv.: B&W page Can.$770; trim 8 1/2 x 11. circ. 2,200.
   Description: News for the coin-operated entertainment industry.

781.6   CN   ISSN 0008-3259
ML27.C3
CANADIAN COMPOSER/COMPOSITEUR CANADIEN. (Text in English and French) 1965; N.S. 1990. q. $10. Society of Composers, Authors and Music Publishers of Canada (SOCAN) - Societe Canadienne des Auteurs, Compositeurs et Editeurs de Musique, 41 Valleybrook Dr., Don Mills, Ont. M3B 2S6, Canada. TEL 416-445-8700. FAX 416-445-7108. Ed. Rick MacMillan. bk.rev.; illus.; rec.rev.; circ. 14,000. (also avail. in microform from MML) Indexed: Can.Per.Ind., CMI, Mag.Ind., Music Ind., Pt.de Rep. (1990-), RILM.

780 371.3   CN
CANADIAN FEDERATION OF MUSIC TEACHERS' ASSOCIATIONS. NEWSLETTER. q. membership. Canadian Federation of Music Teachers' Associations, 616 Andrew St., Thunder Bay, Ont. P7B 2C9, Canada. Ed. L. Gresch. adv.; bk.rev.; circ. 4,000.

781.7   CN   ISSN 0829-5344
ML3563
CANADIAN FOLK MUSIC BULLETIN. (Text in English, French) 1965. q. Can.$18($18) to individuals; students and seniors Can.$14($14); institutions Can.$20($20); subscribers receive both Journal and Bulletin. Canadian Society for Musical Traditions, P.O. Box 4232, Sta. C, Calgary, Alta. T2T 5N1, Canada. Ed. Lynn Whidden. bk.rev.; circ. 900. **Indexed:** M.L.A.
   Formerly: Canadian Folk Music Society Newsletter (ISSN 0576-5234)

780   CN   ISSN 0068-8746
CANADIAN FOLK MUSIC JOURNAL. (Text in English and French) 1973. a. Can.$18($18) to individuals; students and seniors Can.$14($14); institutions Can.$20($20); subscribers receive both Journal and Bulletin. Canadian Society for Musical Traditions, P.O. Box 4232, Sta. C, Calgary, Alta. T2T 5N1, Canada. Ed. Lynn Whidden. bk.rev.; circ. 900. **Indexed:** M.L.A., Music Ind.

CANADIAN MUSIC DIRECTORY. see *BUSINESS AND ECONOMICS — Trade And Industrial Directories*

780.7   CN
CANADIAN MUSIC EDUCATOR. 1959. 4/yr. membership (Can.$20) includes newsletter and journal. Canadian Music Educators Association, National Office, 16 Royaleigh Ave., Etobicoke, Ont. M9P 2J5, Canada. TEL 416-235-1833. Ed. Robert Walker. adv.; bk.rev.; charts; illus.; stat.; index; circ. 2,800.

780.7   CN   ISSN 0045-5172
CANADIAN MUSIC EDUCATORS ASSOCIATION. NEWSLETTER. 1967. 3/yr (includes the Canadian Music Educator) Can.$35 (foreign Can.$42). Canadian Music Educators Association - L'Association Canadienne des Educateurs de Musique, National Office, 16 Royaleigh Ave., Etobicoke, Ont. M9P 2J5. TEL 416-235-1833. Ed. Jane Atkinson. adv.; bk.rev.; circ. 3,000.

780.7   CN   ISSN 0319-6356
ML5
CANADIAN MUSIC TEACHER. 1935. 3/yr. membership. Canadian Federation of Music Teachers' Associations, 616 Andrew St., Thunder Bay, Ont. P7B 2C9, Canada. Ed. Laura Gresch. adv.; bk.rev.; circ. 4,000.
   Incorporates: Canadian Federation of Music Teachers' Associations. News Bulletin (ISSN 0008-3534)

780   CN   ISSN 0225-9435
CANADIAN MUSIC TRADE. 1979. bi-m. Can.$10($16) Norris Publications, 3284 Yonge St., Toronto, Ont. M4N 3M7, Canada. TEL 416-485-8284. FAX 416-485-8924. Ed. Lisa Ferguson. adv.; circ. 3,000 (controlled). (back issues avail.)

780   CN   ISSN 0708-9635
ML3848
CANADIAN MUSICIAN. 1979. bi-m. Can.$16($21) Norris Publications, 3284 Yonge St., Toronto, Ont. M4N 3M7, Canada. TEL 416-485-8284. FAX 416-485-8924. Ed. Lisa Ferguson. adv.; circ. 28,000. **Indexed:** Can.Per.Ind., CMI, Music Ind.

782.1   CN
CANADIAN OPERA COMPANY MAGAZINE. 1978. National Theatre Publications, 30 St. Clair Ave. W. No. 805, Toronto, Ont. M4V 3A1, Canada. TEL 416-926-7595. FAX 416-926-0407.

782.1   CN
CANADIAN OPERA COMPANY NEWS. 1982. 3/yr. Can.$50. Canadian Opera Company, 227 Front St. E., Toronto, Ont. M5A 1E8, Canada. TEL 416-363-6671. FAX 416-363-5584. circ. 14,000.
   Description: Information on forthcoming productions, as well as other activities and events.

780   CN   ISSN 0710-0353
ML5
CANADIAN UNIVERSITY MUSIC REVIEW/REVUE DE MUSIQUE DES UNIVERSITES CANADIENNES. (Text in English and French) 1971. N.S. 1980. s-a. Can.$30 (foreign Can.$35). University of Toronto Press, Journals Department, P.O. Box 1280, 1011 Sheppard Ave. W., Downsview, Ont. M3H 5V4, Canada. TEL 613-545-2066. Ed. Alan Lessem. adv.; bk.rev.; circ. 400. (also avail. in microfilm from UMI; back issues avail.; reprint service avail. from UMI) **Indexed:** Music Ind., RILM.
—BLDSC shelfmark: 3046.092000.
   Formerly: Canadian Association of University Schools of Music. Journal. (ISSN 0315-3541)

780   SP
CANCIONES CIFRADAS - J L A.* m. 330 ptas.($7) Ediciones Anel, San Vicente Ferrer 13, Granada, Spain. adv.; charts; illus.; circ. 38,750. (back issues avail)
   Formerly: Acordes Cifrados para Guitarra.

781.7 398   UK
CANU GWERIN/FOLK SONG. 1909. a. membership. Welsh Folk-Song Society, c/o Mrs. B.L. Roberts, Hafan, Cricieth, Gwynedd, Wales. Eds. Rhidian Griffiths, Rhiannon Ifans. bk.rev.; circ. 250. (back issues avail.)
   Formerly (until 1978): Welsh Folk-Song Society. Journal.

781.7   AT
CAPITAL NEWS. 1975. m. Aus.$24 (foreign Aus.$90). B.A.L. Marketing, P.O. Box 497, Tamworth, N.S.W. 2340, Australia. FAX 067-652762. TELEX AA 163166. adv.; bk.rev.; circ. 6,000.

780   IT
CAR AUDIO & FM; la prima rivista di musica in auto. 1986. m. L.50000 (foreign L.180000). Editore Progest s.r.l., Via Rovereto, 6, 00198 Rome, Italy. TEL 06-868885. Ed. Gianni Caserta.

789.5   US   ISSN 0730-5001
ML1039
CARILLON NEWS. 1969. s-a. $4. Guild of Carillonneurs in North America, c/o Margo Halsted, Ed., University of Michigan, 900 Burton Tower, Ann Arbor, MI 48109. TEL 313-764-2539. circ. 525.
   Formerly: Randschriften; a Newsletter for the Guild of Carillonneurs (ISSN 0085-5383)

CARNEGIE MAGAZINE; dedicated to art, science, literature and music. see *ART*

784   IT   ISSN 1120-4621
CARTELLINA; rivista bimestrale di didattica e musica corale. 1977. bi-m. L.40000 (foreign L.50000). Edizioni Suvini Zerboni S.p.A., Via M.F. Quintiliano 40, 20138 Milan, Italy. FAX 5084261. TELEX 321063. Ed. Giovanni Acciai. adv.; bk.rev.; bibl.; cum.index; circ. 3,000. (back issues avail.)

789.91   US   ISSN 0008-7289
ML1
CASH BOX; the international music-record weekly. 1942. w. $185. Cash Box Publishing Co., Inc., 157 W. 57th St., Ste. 1402, New York, NY 10019. TEL 212-586-2640. Ed. Fred Goodman. adv.; illus.; rec.; rev.; index; circ. 20,339. **Indexed:** Music Ind.

CASSETTE GAZETTE; audio magazine. see *LITERATURE*

780   FR
CATALOGUE GENERAL CLASSIQUE. a. 295 F. Diapason - Harmonie, 9-13 rue Colonel Pierre Avia, 75754 Paris Cedex 15, France.

780   AT
CATALOGUE OF AUSTRALIAN BRASS MUSIC. 1985. irreg. Aus.$10. Australian Music Centre Ltd., P.O. Box N690, Grosvenor Pl., Sydney, N.S.W. 2000, Australia. TEL 61-2-247-4677. FAX 61-2-241-2873.
   Formerly (until 1989): Catalogue of Australian Brass and Concert Band Music.
   Description: Information on music written by Australian composers for brass and concert bands.

780   AT
CATALOGUE OF AUSTRALIAN CHORAL MUSIC. 1985. irreg. Aus.$12. Australian Music Centre Ltd., P.O. Box N690, Grosvenor Pl., Sydney, N.S.W. 2000, Australia. TEL 61-2-247-4677. FAX 61-2-241-2873.
   Description: Information on choral music with two or more parts written by Australian composers.

786   AT
CATALOGUE OF AUSTRALIAN KEYBOARD MUSIC. 1989. irreg. Aus.$16. Australian Music Centre Ltd., P.O. Box N690, Grosvenor Pl., Sydney, N.S.W. 2000, Australia. TEL 61-2-247-4677. FAX 61-2-241-2873.
   Description: Information on Australian musical works for piano, electronic keyboard, harpsicord, organ, piano accordion.

781.7   UK
CATALOGUE OF CONTEMPORARY WELSH MUSIC. irreg. £3 per no. Guild for the Promotion of Welsh Music, 94 Walter Rd., Swansea SA1 5QA, Wales. Ed. Robert Smith.

780   GW   ISSN 0069-116X
CATALOGUS MUSICUS. 1963. irreg. price varies. (International Association of Music Libraries). Baerenreiter Verlag, Heinrich-Schuetz-Allee 31-37, 3500 Kassel-Wilhelmshoehe, Germany. TEL 0561-3105 0. FAX 0561 3105240. (U.S. subscr. addr.: Foreign Music Distributors, 13 Elkay Dr., Chester, NY 10918) (Co-sponsor: International Musicological Society) Ed.Bd.

783   IT   ISSN 0008-8706
CELEBRIAMO; rivista bimestrale di musica vocale per la liturgia. 1970. m. L.45000. Casa Musicale Edizioni Carrara, Casella Postale 158, Via Calepio 4, 24100 Bergamo, Italy. Dir. Vinicio Carrara. adv.
   Supersedes: Organista; Musica Sacra; Scholare Assemblea & Lodiamo Il Signore & Fiori dell'Organo. Maestri dell'Urgano.

CELEBRITY DIRECTORY. see *MOTION PICTURES*

CENTER MAGAZINE. see *ART*

CENTRE CULTUREL FRANCAIS DE YAOUNDE. PROGRAMME SAISON. see *ART*

781.7 398   VE
CENTRO PARA LAS CULTURAS POPULARES Y TRADICIONALES. BOLETIN. 1987. 2/yr. Centro para las Culturas Populares y Tradicionales, Apdo. 81015, Prados del Este, Caracas, Venezuela. TEL 62-72-96. bk.rev.; illus.
   Supersedes (1975-1986, no.6): Instituto Interamericano de Etnomusicologia y Folklore. Revista.

783 XV ISSN 0351-496X
CERKVENI GLASBENIK. (Text in Slovenian; summaries in English) 1878. q. 1200 din.($5) (Sovenske Rimskokatoliske Skofije) Druzina, Cankarjevo Nabrezje 3-I, 61101 Ljubljana, Slovenia. TEL 061-221-324. Ed. Edo Skulj. circ. 1,500.

780 US ISSN 8755-0725
ML1
CHAMBER MUSIC MAGAZINE. 1984. q. $50. Chamber Music America, 545 Eighth Ave., New York, NY 10018. TEL 212-244-2772. FAX 212-244-2776. Ed. Clair W. Van Ausdall. adv.; bk.rev.; circ. 12,500. **Indexed:** Music Artic.Guide, Music Ind.
Former titles: Chamber Music; American Ensemble.
Description: News, features, profiles, events, and lists pertaining to chamber orchestras, string trios and quartets, duo recitalists, instrumental ensembles, vocal ensembles, jazz ensembles, concert presenters, and audiences.

781.7 CN ISSN 0227-5023
CHANSONS D'AUJOURD'HUI. 1984. bi-m. Can.$12. Office des Communications Sociales, 4005 rue de Bellechasse, Montreal, Que. H1X 1J6, Canada. TEL 514-729-6391. FAX 514-729-7375. (back issues avail.)
Description: Covers music from francophone countries.

784 FR
CHANT CHORAL MAGAZINE. bi-m. 130 F. (effective Jan. 1992). A Coeur Joie, Les Passerelles, 24 ave J. Masset, 69337 Lyon Cedex 09, France. TEL 78-83-19-61. Ed. Francois Harquel. adv.; circ. 13,500. (back issues avail.)

780.7 028.5 FR
CHANTE ET RIS. q. 52 F. (effective Jan. 1992). A Coeur Joie, Les Passerelles, 24 ave J. Masset, 69337 Lyon Cedex 09, France. TEL 78-83-19-61. Ed. Monique Gelas. adv.; circ. 4,000. (back issues avail.)

780 UK ISSN 0262-9577
CHART WATCH. 1981. q. $22.60. ChartWatch, 8 Worcester House, Bumpstead Rd., Haverhill, Suffolk CB9 8QB, England. Eds. Neil Rawlings, John Hancock. adv.; bk.rev.; charts; circ. 300.

380.1 IT
CHI E DOVE. (Special issue of Musica e Dischi) 1971. a. L.20000. Musica e Dischi, Via De Amicis 47, 20123 Milan, Italy. FAX 39-2-8323843. Ed. Mario de Luigi.
Description: Lists addresses of people and companies operating in the Italian music business.

CHI SONO. see *BIOGRAPHY*

CHICAGO. see *TRAVEL AND TOURISM*

787 US
CHICAGO SYMPHONY ORCHESTRA. q. Orchestral Association, 220 South Michigan Ave., Chicago, IL 60604-2559. TEL 312-435-8122. FAX 312-435-0126. Ed. Denise Wagner.

780 IT ISSN 0069-3391
CHIGIANA; rassegna annuale di studi musicologici. 1964. a. price varies. Accademia Musicale Chigiana, Siena, Via di Citta 89, 53100 Siena, Italy. FAX 0577-46152. (Dist. by: Casa Editrice Leo S. Olschki, Casella Postale 66, 50100 Florence, Italy. TEL 055-6350684) Ed. G. Turchi. bk.rev.; circ. 500. **Indexed:** RILM.
Formerly: Accademia Musicale Chigiana. Quaderni (ISSN 0065-0714)

780 RU
CHILDREN - MUSICIANS. 3/yr. 9.70 Rub. Izdatel'stvo Muzyka, Ul. Neglinnaya 14, Moscow 103031, Russia. TEL 924-81-63. FAX 921-83-53.

781.7 US ISSN 0192-3749
ML336
CHINESE MUSIC. 1978. q. $25 to individuals; institutions $41. Chinese Music Society of North America, One Heritage Plaza, Woodridge, IL 60517. TEL 708-910-1551. FAX 708-910-1561. Ed. Sin-Yan Shen. adv.; bk.rev.; rec.; rev.; index; circ. 1,200. (also avail. in microform from UMI; back issues avail.) **Indexed:** Music Artic.Guide, Music Ind., RILM.
—BLDSC shelfmark: 3181.020000.
Formerly: Chinese Music General Newsletter.
Description: Covers all phases of research and performance activities in Chinese music. Provides a forum for original papers concerned with musicology, composition, acoustics, analysis, orchestration, musicians, global interactions, intercultural studies, and musical instruments.

780.01 HK
CHINESE UNIVERSITY OF HONG KONG. CHUNG CHI COLLEGE. MUSIC DEPARTMENT. HOLDINGS OF THE CHINESE MUSIC ARCHIVES. (Text in English and Chinese) 1974. a. Chinese University of Hong Kong, Chung Chi College, Music Department, Shatin, New Territories, Hong Kong. illus.

787 IT
CHITARRE; rivista di tecnica musicale e chitarristica. 1986. m. L.60000 (Europe L.80000; elsewhere L.120000). Edizioni Lakota, Via Pietro Mascagni 3-5, 00199 Rome, Italy. FAX 6-8608930. Ed. Andrea Carpi. adv.; bk.rev.; circ. 20,000.

784 US
CHOIR HERALD. m. $28. Lorenz Publishing Co., 501 E. 3rd St., Box 802, Dayton, OH 45401-0802. TEL 513-228-6118. Ed. Hughs Livingston, Jr.

784 CN ISSN 0822-4749
CHOIRS ONTARIO. 4/yr. membership. Ontario Choral Federation, Maison Chalmers House, 20 St. Joseph St., Toronto, Ont. M4Y 1J9, Canada. Ed. Bev. Jahnke. adv.
Description: Information and articles of interest to Ontario Choirs and other choral enthusiasts.

784 GW
CHOR. 1947. q. DM.2. Deutschen Allgemeinen Saengerbundes e.V., Barbarastr. 7, Postfach 150423, 4600 Dortmund 15, Germany. TEL 0231-333352.

784 US ISSN 0009-5028
ML1
CHORAL JOURNAL. 1959. m. (Aug.-May). $25 to libraries. American Choral Directors Association, Box 6310, Lawton, OK 73506-0310. TEL 405-355-8161. FAX 405-248-1465. Ed. Francisco G. Rodriquez. adv.; bk.rev.; rec.; rev.; illus.; index, cum.index vols.1-18; circ. 15,000. (also avail. in microform from UMI; microfiche from UMI; reprint service avail. from UMI) **Indexed:** Music Artic.Guide, Music Ind., RILM.

780 US ISSN 0069-3758
CHORD AND DISCORD. 1933. irreg. (every 3-4 yrs.). free. Bruckner Society of America Inc., 2150 Dubuque Rd., Iowa City, IA 52244. TEL 319-351-5758. Ed. Charles Eble. circ. 750.

784 GW ISSN 0009-5036
DER CHORDIRIGENT; Nachrichtenblatt fuer Chorleiter. 1951. irreg. free. B. Schott's Soehne, Weihergarten 5, Postfach 3640, 6500 Mainz 1, Germany. TEL 06131-246830. Ed. Hilger Schallehn. circ. 20,000.
Description: Presentation and discussion about new publications of choral music in print for hire and for sale.

784 028.5 US
CHORISTERS GUILD LETTERS. 1949. 10/yr. $40 (effective June 1991). Choristers Guild, 2834 W. Kingsley Rd., Garland, TX 75041. TEL 214-271-1521. FAX 214-840-3113. Ed. Donald F. Jensen. adv.; bk.rev.; bibl.; charts; illus.; index; circ. 8,500. (back issues avail.) **Indexed:** Music Artic.Guide.
Description: Focuses on music with young people. Includes articles, news releases, reviews, and study plans pertaining to choral compositions; with announcements and news on the members and activities of the guild.

784 658.048 AU
CHORMAGAZIN. 1974. q. S.4. Oesterreichischer Arbeiter-Saengerbund, Arndtstr. 27, A-1120 Vienna, Austria. TEL 0222-830220. FAX 0222-67660127. Ed. Georg Stockreiter. charts; illus.
Formerly: Oesterreichische Arbeitersaenger.

780 GW ISSN 0172-2255
DER CHORSAENGER. 1951. q. membership. Mitteldeutscher Saengerbund e.V., Ulmenstr. 16, 3500 Kassel, Germany. Ed. Helmuth Breiter. adv.; bk.rev.; circ. 3,800.

784 GW
CHORSZENE. 1980. s-a. free. Staedtischen Musikvereins zu Duesseldorf e.V., Heinrich-Heine-Allee 22, 4000 Duesseldorf 1, Germany. TEL 0211-329191. circ. 5,000. (back issues avail.)

784 CN ISSN 0821-1108
CHORUS. 1976. q. membership. Nova Scotia Choral Federation, 5516 Spring Garden Rd., Ste. 304, Halifax, N.S. B3J 1G6, Canada. Ed. Dena Simon. adv.: B&W page Can.$100. circ. 350.
Description: Articles of interest to members and choral music enthusiasts. Information on federation programs and services.

780 US ISSN 1044-7857
CHORUS!. 1989. m. $19.95. D S C Publishing, 2131 Pleasant Hill Rd., Ste. 151-121, Duluth, GA 30136. TEL 404-623-0358. Ed. Mark Gresham. adv.; bk.rev.; circ. 3,000. (tabloid format; back issues avail.) **Indexed:** Music Artic.Guide.
Description: For the choral music enthusiast, whether singer, listener, educator, conductor, and composer; contains interviews, articles, reviews, concert calendar.

780.1 US
CHRISTIAN MUSIC DIRECTORIES: PRINTED MUSIC. 1976. a. (plus q. updates). $160. Resource Publications, Inc., 160 E. Virginia St., San Jose, CA 95112. TEL 408-286-8505. circ. 950.
Formerly: Music Locator (ISSN 0899-0115)
Description: Lists religious music by title, composer and theme or use.

783 621.389 200 US ISSN 1048-6844
CHRISTIAN MUSIC DIRECTORIES: RECORDED MUSIC. 1974. q. $160 (effective 1992). Resource Publications, Inc., 160 E. Virginia St., No. 290, San Jose, CA 95112. TEL 408-286-8505. circ. 1,200.
Former titles (until 1989): Recording Locator (ISSN 0899-0123); (Until 1981): Musicatalog.
Description: Lists religious music available in recorded form by artist, title and album name.

783 UK ISSN 0307-6334
ML5
CHURCH MUSIC QUARTERLY. 1963. q. membership. Royal School of Church Music, Addington Palace, Croydon CR9 5AD, England. FAX 081-340-0021. Ed. Trevor Ford. adv.; bk.rev.; rec.; rev.; bibl.; charts; illus.; circ. 14,500 (controlled). (reprint service avail. from UMI)
Formerly: Promoting Church Music (ISSN 0033-1112)

783 200 US
THE CHURCH MUSIC REPORT. 1984. m. $39.95. William H. Rayborn, Ed. & Pub., Box 1179, Grapevine, TX 76051-1179. TEL 817-488-0141. FAX 817-481-4191. adv.; bk.rev.; circ. 6,600.

783 US ISSN 0009-6466
ML1
CHURCH MUSICIAN. 1950. m. $20.25. Southern Baptist Convention, Sunday School Board, 127 Ninth Ave., N., Nashville, TN 37234. TEL 800-458-2772. circ. 20,000. **Indexed:** Chr.Per.Ind., Music Ind., South.Bap.Per.Ind.

786 US
CHURCH PIANIST. bi-m. $14.95. Lorenz Publishing Co., 501 E. Third St., Box 802, Dayton, OH 45401-0802. TEL 513-228-6118. Ed. Hugh S. Livingston, Jr.

784 US
CI KAN/VERSES. (Text in Chinese) bi-m. $17.10. China Books & Periodicals, Inc., 2929 24th St., San Francisco, CA 94110. TEL 415-282-2994. FAX 415-282-0994.

3546 MUSIC

CIAO 2001. see *CHILDREN AND YOUTH — For*

780.7 SP
CICLO VIDA Y OBRA. no.6, 1983. Asociacion de Compositores Sinfonicos Espanoles, Teatro Real, Calle Carlos III, Madrid, Spain.

786.6 UK
CINEMA ORGAN. 1953. q. membership. Cinema Organ Society, 3 Dorothy Farm Rd., Rayleigh, Essex SS6 8RE, England. Ed. Tony Bernard Smith. adv.; bk.rev.; illus.; circ. 2,050.

791.3 US
CIRCUS. 1969. m. $22. Circus Enterprises Corp., 3 W. 18th St., New York, NY 10011. TEL 212-685-5050. Ed. Gerald Rothberg. adv. contact: Gary Victor. bk.rev.; film rev.; rec.rev.; illus.; circ. 307,092. (also avail. in microform from UMI)
Former titles (until 1979): Circus Weekly (ISSN 0164-9248); Until 1978: Circus (ISSN 0009-7365)
Description: Popular music publication that covers music news and rock-and-roll personalities.

780 UK
CITY OF BIRMINGHAM SYMPHONY ORCHESTRA. ANNUAL PROSPECTUS. a. free. City of Birmingham Symphony Orchestra, Paradise Place, Birmingham B3 3RP, England. FAX 021-223-2423. TELEX 334231-CBSORC-G. circ. 200,000.

780 UK
CITY OF BIRMINGHAM SYMPHONY ORCHESTRA. SUMMER SEASON BROCHURE. a. free. City of Birmingham Symphony Orchestra, Paradise Place, Birmingham B3 3RP, England. FAX 021-233-2423. TELEX 334231-CBSORC-G. circ. 60,000.
Formerly: City of Birmingham Symphony Orchestra. Prom Prospectus.

780 IT
CIVICA SCUOLA DI MUSICA. QUADERNI. 1980. q. free. Civica Scuola di Musica, Via Stilicone 36, 20142 Milan, Italy. TEL 02-313334. FAX 02-29400457. Ed. Sergio Marzorati. circ. 2,500.
●Also available online.

780 US ISSN 0361-5553
ML1
CLARINET. 1973. q. $25 (foreign $40). International Clarinet Society-Clarinetwork International, College of Music, University of North Texas, Denton, TX 76203. TEL 817-565-4096. FAX 817-565-4919. Ed. James Gillespie. adv.; bk.rev.; charts; illus.; stat.; circ. 3,000. (back issues avail.) **Indexed:** Music Artic.Guide, Music Ind.
Description: Contains articles and a wide range of subjects written by the world's leading performers, teachers and scholars. Topics include performance and pedagogy, care and repair, acoustics and instrument design, repertoire, history, and reviews of new publications and recordings. Also includes reports on clinics, master classes, and activities of the membership.

788 UK ISSN 0260-390X
CLARINET AND SAXOPHONE. vol.5, 1980. q. membership. Clarinet and Saxophone Society of Great Britain, 26 Monks Orchard, Wilmington, Kent, England. illus.
—BLDSC shelfmark: 3274.376500.
Formerly: C A S S News (ISSN 0308-9053)

780 FR ISSN 0761-9553
ML929
CLARINETTE MAGAZINE. (Text in French; summaries in English) 1984. q. 180 Fr. Clarinette Magazine, 5 rue des Fleurs, 67550 Vendenheim, France. Ed. Jean-Marie Paul. adv.; bk.rev.; circ. 700.
Description: All aspects about the Clarinet; interviews with players, information on composers, special events, competitions, new records and scores.

780 US ISSN 1048-4507
ML1
CLASSICAL.* m. $29. Unique Communications, P.O. Box 1234, Rahway, NJ 07065. TEL 212-308-6666. Ed. Charles Passy. bk.rev.; circ. 100,000. **Indexed:** Music Artic.Guide.
Incorporates (1985-1989): Stevenson Classical Compact Disc Guide.
Description: Profiles leading classical artists. Includes news of the classical music world and reviews of recent recordings, videos, and high-tech components.

780 UK
ML156.2
THE CLASSICAL CATALOGUE. 1953. 2/yr. £224.35 includes supplements. General Gramophone Publications Ltd., 177-179 Kenton Rd., Harrow, Middlesex HA3 0HA, England. adv.; circ. 8,000.
Former titles: Gramophone Classical Catalogue (ISSN 0309-4367) & Gramophone Classical Record Catalogue.
Description: Lists classical CDs, LPs and cassettes available in the UK issued since 1985.

787 UK ISSN 0950-429X
CLASSICAL GUITAR. 1982. m. £28.50($58.50) Ashley Mark Publishing Co., Olsover House, 43 Sackville Rd., Newcastle Upon Tyne NE6 5TA, England. TEL 091-276-0448. FAX 091-276-1623. Ed. Colin Cooper. adv.; circ. 7,500. (back issues avail.)
Description: Aimed at a player, a teacher, or a listener. Devoted to the classical guitar, with some flamenco and some lute coverage.

780 UK ISSN 0961-2696
CLASSICAL MUSIC. 1976. fortn. £55. Rhinegold Publishing Ltd., 241 Shaftesbury Ave., London WC2H 8EH, England. TEL 071-836-2383. FAX 071-528-7991. (Subscr. to: P.O. Box 47, Gravesend, Kent DA12 2AN, England) Ed. Keith Clarke. adv.; bk.rev.
Former titles: Classical Music and Album Reviews; (until Sept. 1978): Classical Music Weekly (ISSN 0308-9762)

787 CN
CLASSICAL MUSIC MAGAZINE. 5/yr. Box 313, Port Credit Postal Sta., Mississauga, Ontario L5G 4L8, Canada. TEL 416-271-0339. FAX 416-271-9748. Ed. Rick Macmillian.

780 RU
CLASSICS OF WORLD MUSIC CULTURE. a. 3.10 Rub. Izdatel'stvo Muzyka, Ul. Neglinnaya 14, Moscow 103031, Russia. TEL 924-81-63. FAX 921-83-53.

786 US ISSN 0009-854X
ML1
CLAVIER; a magazine for pianists and organists. 1962. 10/yr. $18. Instrumentalist Co., 200 Northfield Rd., Northfield, IL 60093-3390. TEL 708-446-5000. Ed. Kingsley Day. adv.; bk.rev.; rec.; rev.; illus.; index; circ. 19,000. **Indexed:** Amer.Bibl.Slavic & E.Eur.Stud, Arts & Hum.Cit.Ind., Curr.Cont., Educ.Ind., Music Artic.Guide, Music Ind., RILM.

786 US ISSN 0279-0858
ML3930.A2
CLAVIER'S PIANO EXPLORER. 1981. 10/yr. $6. Instrumentalist Co., 200 Northfield Rd., Northfield, IL 60093-3390. TEL 708-446-5559. Ed. Ann Rohner. circ. 73,000.

780.7 US
CLEVELAND INSTITUTE OF MUSIC (NEWSLETTER). 1973. m. (Sep.-Jun.). free. Cleveland Institute of Music, 11021 E. Boulevard, Cleveland, OH 44106. TEL 216-791-5000. Ed. Paul Bunker. illus.; circ. 8,000.
Formerly: C I M Notes (ISSN 0007-845X)

780 US
▼**CLIP.** 1991. m. David Bernstein, Ed. & Pub., Box 17705, Irvine, CA 92713. TEL 714-262-9336. adv.

CLOCKWATCH REVIEW; a journal of the arts. see *LITERATURE*

781.7 US ISSN 0896-372X
ML1
CLOSE UP MAGAZINE. Running title: C M A Close Up. 1959. m. membership only. Country Music Association, Inc., One Music Circle S., Nashville, TN 37203-4383. TEL 615-244-2840. FAX 615-726-0314. Ed. Teresa George. bk.rev.; illus.; circ. 8,000.
Formerly: Close-Up (ISSN 0009-9449)
Description: Profiles of radio stations, broadcasters, country music artists and songwriters.

781.57 CN ISSN 0820-926X
ML5
CODA MAGAZINE; the journal of jazz and improvised music. 1958. 6/yr. Can.$25.68 (foreign $24). Coda Publications, P.O. Box 87, Sta. J, Toronto, Ont. M4J 4X8, Canada. TEL 416-593-7230. FAX 416-593-7230. Ed. Bill Smith. adv.; bk.rev.; rec.; rev.; circ. 3,500. (also avail. in microfilm from UMI,MML; back issues avail.; reprint service avail. from UMI, MML) **Indexed:** Can.Per.Ind., CMI, Music Ind, New Per.Ind., Pop.Mus.Per.Ind.
Formerly: Coda (ISSN 0010-017X)
Description: Contains articles and interviews covering the entire spectrum of the music.

780 700 SP
COLECCION ETHOS - ARTE. no.4, 1981. irreg. Universidad de Oviedo, Departamento de Arte - Musicologia, Servicio de Publicaciones, Oviedo, Spain.

780 IT
COLLANA DI MUSICHE VENEZIANE INEDITE O RARE. 1962. irreg., no. 8, 1973. price varies. Casa Editrice Leo S. Olschki, Casella Postale 66, 50100 Florence, Italy. TEL 055-6530684. FAX 055-6530214.

780 FR
COLLECTION PSYCHOLOGIE ET PEDAGOGIE DE LA MUSIQUE. 1978. irreg. price varies. Editions Scientifiques et Psychologiques, 6 bis, rue Andre-Chenier, 92130 Issy-les-Moulineaux, France. TEL 46-45-38-12. FAX 40-95-73-32. TELEX 370 105 F. (back issues avail.)

780 UK ISSN 0261-2550
COLLECTORS ITEMS. 1980. 6/yr. £17 (Europe £19.50; America £25; elsewhere £26). John A. Holley, Pub., 10 Rydens Rd., Walton-on-Thames, Surrey KT12 3BX, England. TEL 0932-242862. Ed. Howard Rye. bk.rev.; bibl.; circ. 1,000. (back issues avail.)

785 US ISSN 0742-8480
ML1299
COLLEGE BAND DIRECTORS NATIONAL ASSOCIATION JOURNAL.* 1984. s-a. $15. College Band Directors National Association, c/o A-R Editions Inc., 801 Deming Way, Madison, WI 53717. Ed. James Arrowood. circ. 1,100.

780 US ISSN 0069-5696
ML1
COLLEGE MUSIC SYMPOSIUM. 1961. s-a. $25. College Music Society, 202 W. Spruce St., Missoula, MT 59802. TEL 406-721-9616. Ed. Margaret Barela. adv.; bk.rev.; cum.index in vol. 12; circ. 6,500. (also avail. in microfiche) **Indexed:** Arts & Hum.Cit.Ind., Curr.Cont., Music Artic.Guide, Music Ind., RILM.
—BLDSC shelfmark: 3311.175000.

780 US ISSN 0147-0108
M2
COLLEGIUM MUSICUM: YALE UNIVERSITY. 1955. irreg. price varies. (Yale University, Department of Music) A-R Editions, Inc., 801 Deming Way, Madison, WI 53717. TEL 608-836-9000. Ed. Leon Plantinga. circ. 800. (back issues avail.) **Indexed:** Music Ind., RILM.

COLOQUIO: ARTES; revista de artes visuais musica e bailado. see *ART*

780.7 370 US ISSN 0010-1672
COLORADO MUSIC EDUCATOR. 1953. q. $1.75 to non-members. Colorado Music Educators Association, 165 Iroquois Dr., Boulder, CO 80303. Ed. Kevin J. McCarthy. adv.; bk.rev.; illus.; circ. 2,200. **Indexed:** Music Artic.Guide.
Description: Presents study and teaching methods.

780 PL
COMPENDIUM MUSICUM. 1983. irreg. price varies. Polskie Wydawnictwo Muzyczne, Al. Krasinskiego 11a, 31-111 Krakow, Poland. TEL 22-70-44. FAX 22-01-74.
Description: Series of elementary textbooks covering all fields of music.

780 US
COMPOSER - U S A. 1932. 3/yr. $15. National Association of Composers - U S A, Box 49652, Barrington Sta., Los Angeles, CA 90049. TEL 213-541-8213. Ed. Charles Dvorak. adv.; bk.rev.; circ. 600. (tabloid format) **Indexed:** Music Artic.Guide.

MUSIC 3547

780 927   US   ISSN 0069-8016
COMPOSERS OF THE AMERICAS/COMPOSITORES DE AMERICA. 1955. a. $7. Organization of American States, 1889 F St., N.W., Washington, DC 20006. TEL 703-941-1617. circ. 2,000.

789.91   NE
COMPOSERS' VOICE; Dutch contemporary music on compact discs. 1975. irreg. Donemus Amsterdam, Paulus Potterstraat 14, 1071 CZ Amsterdam, Netherlands. TEL 020-764436. (Dist. in U.S. and Canada by: Records International, Box 1140, Goleta, CA 93116)
   Formerly: Donemus Audio-Visual Series.

780   GW
CONCENTUS MUSICUS. 1973. irreg., vol.8, 1989. price varies. (Deutsches Historisches Institut in Rom, Musikgeschichtliche Abteilung, IT) Laaber-Verlag, Regensburger Str. 19, 8411 Laaber, Germany. FAX 09498-2543. illus.

780   US
CONCERT SHOTS. bi-m. Tempo Publishing Company, Inc., 475 Park Ave. S., New York, NY 10016. TEL 212-213-8620.

780   US
CONCERTINA & SQUEEZEBOX; international journal for reed musicians. 1983. q. $15. J.M. Cowan, Ed. & Pub., Box 6706, Ithaca, NY 14851. adv.; bk.rev.; circ. 750.
   Former titles: Concertina and Free Reed; Concertina.

745   UK
THE CONDUCTOR. 1947. q. £8 to non-members. National Association of Brass Band Conductors, Marrey, 7 Carr View Rd., Hepworth, Huddersfield HD7 7HN, England. TEL 0484-6833793. Ed. Jeffrey Turner. adv.; bk.rev.; music rev.; circ. 250. (back issues avail.)
   Description: Assists members with problems, stimulates interest, and improves the standards of musicianship, also enhances prestige.

780   US   ISSN 0734-1032
ML457
CONDUCTORS' GUILD. JOURNAL. 1980. q. $30. Conductors' Guild, Inc., Box 3361, Westchester, PA 19381. TEL 215-436-4904. FAX 215-692-9737. Ed. Jacques Voois. adv.; bk.rev.; circ. 1,300. **Indexed:** Music Artic.Guide.

780   FR
CONFEDERATION MUSICALE DE FRANCE. JOURNAL. 10/yr. Confederation Musicale de France, 121 rue la Fayette, 75010 Paris, France.

781.7   ZR   ISSN 0010-5775
CONGO DISQUE;* revue de la musique congolaise moderne. vol.5, 1967. B.P. 6112, Kinshasa 6, Zaire. adv.; illus.

780.7   SZ   ISSN 0010-6550
CONSERVATOIRE DE MUSIQUE DE GENEVE. BULLETIN. 1933. 10/yr. 20 Fr. Conservatoire de Musique de Geneve, Case Postale 181, CH-1211 Geneva 11, Switzerland. TEL 022-217633. FAX 022-3121810. Ed.Bd. adv.; circ. 3,500.

780   UK
CONSORT. 1929. a. plus Bulletin 3/yr. £12 (foreign £15). Dolmetsch Foundation Inc., 15 Hamlyn Ave., Hull HU4 6BT, England. Ed. Gwilym Beechey. adv.; bk.rev.; charts; illus.; cum.index: 1929-1987; circ. 900. (also avail. in microfilm; reprint service avail. from UMI) **Indexed:** Br.Hum.Ind., Music Ind., RILM.

780   CN
CONSORT; a journal for early music lovers. 1980. 3/yr. Can.$12 (typically set in Sep.). Early Music Society of Nova Scotia, Dept. of Music, Dalhousie University, Halifax, N.S. B3H 3J5, Canada. TEL 902-494-2418. Ed. David F. Wilson. adv.; bk.rev.; circ. 200.
   Description: Articles of historic early music news, concerts and artists to come.

CONTACTS & FACILITIES IN THE AUSTRALIAN ENTERTAINMENT INDUSTRY. see *THEATER*

780   US
CONTEMPORARY CHRISTIAN MUSIC. Short title: C C M. 1978. m. $18. C C M Communications, 1913 21st Ave., S., Nashville, TN 37212. TEL 800-333-9643. (Subscr. to: Box 55995, Boulder, CO 80322) Ed. John W. Styll. adv.; bk.rev.; rec.; rev.; circ. 50,000. (back issues avail.)
   Former titles: Contemporary Christian (ISSN 0746-0066); Contemporary Christian Music.

780   US   ISSN 0749-4467
ML197
CONTEMPORARY MUSIC REVIEW. 1984. 2/yr. $63 to individuals; library $98; corporate $142. Harwood Academic Publishers, 270 Eighth Ave., New York, NY 10011. TEL 212-206-8900. FAX 212-645-2459. TELEX 236735 GOPUB UR. (Subscr. to: Box 786, Cooper Sta., New York, NY 10276. TEL 800-545-8398; UK subscr. to: P.O. Box 90, Reading, Berkshire RG1 8JL, England. TEL 0734-560-080) Ed. Nigel Osborne. (also avail. in microform; back issues avail.)
   —BLDSC shelfmark: 3425.192200.
   Description: Covers composition today - its techniques, aesthetics, technology and its relationship to other disciplines as well as current thought.
   Refereed Serial

780   US   ISSN 0891-5415
CONTEMPORARY MUSIC STUDIES. irreg. Harwood Academic Publishers, 270 Eighth Ave., New York, NY 10011. TEL 212-206-8900. FAX 212-645-2459. TELEX 236735 GOPUB UR. (Subscr. to: Box 786, Cooper Sta., New York, NY 10276. TEL 800-545-8398; UK subscr. to: Box 90, Reading, Berkshire RG1 8JL, England. TEL 0734-560-080) Ed. Nigel Osborne. (also avail. in microform)
   —BLDSC shelfmark: 3425.192250.
   Refereed Serial

920   US   ISSN 1044-2197
ML385
CONTEMPORARY MUSICIANS. 1989. s-a. $54 (effective June 1992). Gale Research Inc., 835 Penobscot Bldg., Detroit, MI 48226. TEL 313-961-2242. FAX 313-961-6083. TELEX 810-221-7086. (Subscr. to: Box 33477, Detroit, MI 48232-5477. TEL 800-877-GALE)
   ●Also available online. Vendor(s): Mead Data Central.
   Description: Contains approximately 100 biographical entries on artists in the music business.

780   US
CONTEMPORARY RECORD SOCIETY. SOCIETY NEWS. 1983. s-a. $25 (foreign $45). Contemporary Record Society, 724 Winchester Rd., Broomall, PA 19008. TEL 215-544-5920. FAX 215-544-5921. Ed. David Meyer. adv.; bk.rev.; music rev.; rec.rev.; index; circ. 90,000. (back issues avail.)

780   US
CONTINUO; an early music magazine. 1977. 6/yr. $35. Matthew James Redsell, Ed.& Pub., Box 327, Hammondsport, NY 14840. TEL 607-569-2489. adv.; bk.rev.; circ. 1,200.

780   AT   ISSN 0310-6802
ML26
CONTINUO. 1970. s-a. Aus.$35. International Association of Music Libraries Archives & Documentation Centres (Australian Branch), Performing Arts Library, University of Adelaide, Adelaide, S.A. 5001, Australia. TEL 08-2285489. FAX 08-232-3689. TELEX UNIVD AA 89141. Ed. Gordon Abbott. adv.; bk.rev.; circ. 90. (back issues avail.) **Indexed:** Aus.P.A.I.S.

780   US   ISSN 0190-4922
ML1
CONTRIBUTIONS TO MUSIC EDUCATION. 1972. a. $5 to individuals; institutions $7.50. Ohio Music Education Association, c/o John Kratus, Dept. of Music, Case Western Reserve Univ., Cleveland, OH 44106. TEL 216-368-2431. bk.rev.; circ. 500. **Indexed:** Music Ind.
   —BLDSC shelfmark: 3461.026000.
   Description: Covers research in experimental, descriptive, theoretical, and speculative research in music education.

780   US   ISSN 0193-9041
CONTRIBUTIONS TO THE STUDY OF MUSIC AND DANCE. 1981. irreg. price varies. Greenwood Press, Inc. (Subsidiary of: Greenwood Publishing Group Inc.), 88 Post Rd. W., Box 5007, Westport, CT 06881-5007. TEL 203-226-3571. FAX 203-222-1502.

780   GW   ISSN 0070-0363
CORPUS MENSURABILIS MUSICAE. 1948. irreg. (American Institute of Musicology, US) Haenssler Verlag, Postfach 1220, Bismarckstr. 4, 7303 Neuhausen-Stuttgart, Germany. TEL 07158-177-149. FAX 07158-177119. Ed. Frank D'Accone.
   Description: Examines Medieval and Renaissance compositions.

780   GW
CORPUS OF EARLY KEYBOARD MUSIC; transcription of all known sources of keyboard music of the 14th and 15th centuries. 1963. irreg. price varies. (American Institute of Musicology, US) Haenssler Verlag, Postfach 1220, Bismarckstr. 4, 7303 Neuhausen-Stuttgart, Germany. TEL 07158-177-149. FAX 07158-177119. Ed. John Caldwell.

780   GW   ISSN 0070-0460
ML170
CORPUS SCRIPTORUM DE MUSICA. (Text mainly in Latin) 1950. irreg. (American Institute of Musicology, US) Haenssler Verlag, Postfach 1220, Bismarckstr. 4, 7303 Neuhausen-Stuttgart, Germany. TEL 07158-177-149. FAX 07158-177119. Ed. Gilbert Reaney.

780.7 370   US   ISSN 0010-9894
ML1
COUNCIL FOR RESEARCH IN MUSIC EDUCATION. BULLETIN. 1963. q. $15 to individuals; institutions $22.50; student $9 (effective Mar. 1992; typically set in Jan.). University of Illinois at Urbana-Champaign, School of Music, 1114 W. Nevada, Urbana, IL 61801. TEL 217-333-1027. Ed. Marilyn P. Zimmerman. bk.rev.; charts; index; circ. 2,000. (also avail. in microform from UMI; back issues avail.; reprint service avail. from UMI) **Indexed:** Arts & Hum.Cit.Ind., Child Devel.Abstr., Cont.Pg.Educ., Curr.Cont., Educ.Ind., Mid.East: Abstr.& Ind., Music Artic.Guide, Music Ind., Psychol.Abstr., Res.High.Educ.Abstr., RILM. Key Title: Bulletin of the Council for Research in Music Education.
   —BLDSC shelfmark: 2462.570000.
   Description: Presents articles, critiques of doctoral dissertations, conference papers, and reviews of books of interest to the music eduction profession.

781.7 051   US
COUNTRY AMERICA. 1989. 10/yr. $14.97. Meredith Corporation, 1716 Locust St., Des Moines, IA 50336. TEL 515-284-3000. Ed. Danita Allen. circ. 750,000.
   Description: Entertainment and lifestyle magazine targeted to people who opt for country music and the country way of life.

781.7   UK   ISSN 0011-0094
COUNTRY AND WESTERN ROUNDABOUT.* 1962. q. 15s.($2.) c/o R.F. Benson, Ed., 21 Roseacres, Takeley, Dunmow, Essex, England. adv.; bk.rev.; rec.; rev.; illus.; circ. 1,000.

781.7   US
COUNTRY CRAZY. 1976. 3/yr. $6. Jammie Ann Club - Rebel International Fan Club, Box 3525, York, PA 17402. FAX 717-792-3060. circ. 3,500.

COUNTRY DANCE AND SONG. see *DANCE*

780   US   ISSN 0733-8759
ML459 .D6
COUNTRY HERITAGE. 1982. bi-m. $9.25. Country Heritage Productions, RR 1, Box 320, Madill, OK 73446. Ed. Matt Noyzolio. adv.; illus.; circ. 400.
   Incorporates (1976-1982): Resophonic Echoes (ISSN 0273-3242); Which was formerly (1974-1976): Dobro Nut.
   Description: 2/92 publ states this may cease with May June 92 issue.

MUSIC

780   CN   ISSN 0714-8356
COUNTRY MUSIC NEWS; the voice of country music in Canada. 1980. m. Can.$20($32) 97594 Canada Ltd., P.O. Box 7323, Vanier Terminal, Ottawa, Ont. K1L 8E4, Canada. TEL 613-745-6006. FAX 613-745-0576. Ed. Larry Delaney. adv.; bk.rev.; circ. 4,500. (tabloid format; back issues avail.)
Description: Covers the country music scene in Canada; aimed at both fans and the industry.

784   AT
COUNTRY MUSIC NEWSLETTER. 1970. 3/yr. Earl Heywood Fan Club, P.O. Box 186, Murwillumbah, N.S.W. 2484, Australia. Ed. Don Gresham, Noela Gresham. (newspaper)

781.7   UK   ISSN 0591-2237
ML5
COUNTRY MUSIC PEOPLE. 1970. m. £28. Music Farm Ltd., 225A Lewisham Way, London SE4, England. TEL 81-692-1106. FAX 81-469-3091. Ed. Craig Baguley. adv.; bk.rev.; circ. 30,000.
Description: Reports on American country music, including artist features and record reviews.

781.7   UK   ISSN 0140-5721
COUNTRY MUSIC ROUND UP. 1976. m. £21.50. Country Music Round-up Publishing Co., 286-287 High St., Upper Precinct, Lincoln LN2 1AL, England. TEL 0522-541546. FAX 0522-512621. Ed. John Emptage. adv.; bk.rev.; circ. 30,120.
Description: Country music magazine for Britain and Europe. Includes artist profiles, record reviews, tour schedules and regional reports.

780   US   ISSN 0273-1428
ML18
COUNTRY MUSIC SOURCEBOOK. Variant title: Billboard's Country Music Sourcebook. a. $33. B P I Communications, Inc. (New York) (Subsidiary of: Affiliated Publications, Inc.), 1515 Broadway, 39th Fl., New York, NY 10036. TEL 212-764-7300. FAX 212-944-1719. (And: 9000 Sunset Blvd., Los Angeles, CA 90069. TEL 800-344-7119) adv.; circ. 47,000. (also avail. in microfilm from KTO)
Description: Radio stations, performing artists, booking agents, personal managers and recording companies listed.

781.7   US   ISSN 0011-0248
COUNTRY SONG ROUNDUP. 1947. m. $25. Country Song Roundup Publications, Inc., 40 Violet Ave., Poughkeepsie, NY 12601. TEL 201-487-6124. Ed. Celeste Gomes. adv.; bk.rev.; rec.; rev.; illus.; circ. 75,000.
Formerly: Country Song Roundup. Yearbook (ISSN 0277-1292)
Description: Covers country songs, lyrics, and music and articles about singers and songwriters.

780 200   US   ISSN 1045-0815
CREATOR; the bimonthly magazine of balanced music ministries. 1978. bi-m. $29.95 (Canada and Mexico $45.95; elsewhere $69.95). Church Music Associates, Inc., 123 S. High St., Box 100, Dublin, OH 43017. TEL 614-889-0012. FAX 614-792-3585. Ed. Marcia C. Daugherty. adv.; bk.rev.; index; circ. 5,500. (back issues avail.)
Description: Focuses on music and worship in the local church.

780   US   ISSN 0011-1147
ML1
CREEM. 1969-198?; resumed 1990. 10/yr. $35. Alternative Media, Inc., 519 Eighth Ave., New York, NY 10018. TEL 212-967-6262. FAX 212-967-6288. Ed. Marvin Jarrett. adv.; bk.rev.; film rev.; illus.; tr.lit.; circ. 120,000. (also avail. in microform from UMI) *Indexed:* Access, Media Rev.Dig.

780   CN
CRESCENDO. 1958. bi-m. Toronto Musicians' Association, 101 Thorncliffe Park Dr., Toronto, Ont. M4H 1M2, Canada. TEL 416-421-1020. FAX 416-421-7011. Ed. George Zarras. adv.; circ. 5,600 (controlled).

780   MX   ISSN 0185-1896
CUADERNOS DE MUSICA. 1981. irreg., latest 1985. price varies. Universidad Nacional Autonoma de Mexico, Instituto de Investigacion Esteticas, Circuito Mtro. Mario de la Cueva, Ciudad de la Investigacion en Humanidades - Zona Cultural, 04000 Mexico, D.F., Mexico.

780 791.43   US   ISSN 0888-9015
ML2074
CUE SHEET. 1984. q. membership. Society for the Preservation of Film Music, Box 93536, Los Angeles, CA 90093-0536. TEL 213-474-5225. FAX 213-474-2132. Eds. Leslie T. Zador, Clifford McCarty. adv.; bk.rev.; circ. 300. (back issues avail.) *Indexed:* Film Lit.Ind. (1988-).
Description: Provides news and studies on the art of composing for film. Features interviews with film composers.

781.7   IT
CULTURE MUSICALE; quaderni di etnomusicologia. 1982. s-a. L.25000. (Societa Italiana di Etnomusicologia) Bulzoni Editore, Via del Liburni 14, 00185 Rome, Italy. Ed. D. Carpitella. abstr.

CURRENT ISSUES IN MUSIC EDUCATION. see *EDUCATION — Teaching Methods And Curriculum*

780.01   US   ISSN 0011-3735
ML1
CURRENT MUSICOLOGY. 1965. s-a. $16 to individuals; institutions $22; students $12. Columbia University, Department of Music, New York, NY 10027. TEL 212-280-3826. Ed. Edmund Goehring. adv.; bk.rev.; abstr.; bibl.; charts; illus.; stat.; cum.index every 5 yrs.; circ. 1,000. (also avail. in microfilm from UMI; back issues avail.; reprint service avail. from UMI) *Indexed:* Amer.Bibl.Slavic & E.Eur.Stud, Arts & Hum.Cit.Ind., Curr.Cont., Hum.Ind., Ind.Bk.Rev.Hum., Mid.East: Abstr.& Ind., Music Artic.Guide, Music Ind., RILM.
—BLDSC shelfmark: 3500.500000.

780   US   ISSN 0895-6936
CYMBIOSIS; the marriage of music and magazine. 1986. q. $39.98. Cymbiosis, Inc., 6201 W. Sunset Blvd., Ste. 80, Hollywood, CA 90028-8704. TEL 213-463-3808. FAX 213-463-5426. Ed. Ric Levine. adv.; bk.rev.; circ. 15,000. (audio cassette)
●Also available on CD-ROM.
Description: Articles feature six new age, jazz and progressive artists included in a one-hour music sampler.

780   FR
D I S C INSTRUMENTS INTERNATIONAL. 1973. 7/yr. 200 F. Editions Mediapresse, 148 rue de Paris, 92100 Boulogne, France. Ed. Alain Douarche. adv.; bk.rev.; circ. 35,000.
Formerly: D I S C International.

780.42   US
D J TIMES. m. Testa Communications, 25 Willowdale Ave., Port Washington, NY 11050-3716. TEL 516-767-2500. FAX 516-767-9335. Ed. Chuck Arnold. circ. 13,000.

DAILY VARIETY; news of the entertainment industry. see *COMMUNICATIONS — Television And Cable*

DANCE AND MUSIC SERIES. see *DANCE*

DANCING U S A. see *DANCE*

780   DK   ISSN 0905-6300
▼**DANSK MUSIK AARBOG (YEAR).** 1991? a. Dansk Musik Aarbog ApS, Vendersgade 25, DK-1363 Copenhagen K, Denmark. TEL 33-93-97-00. FAX 33-14-51-75. Ed. Flemming Madsen.
Description: Contains articles and statistics on the Danish popular music industry. Directories of the Danish record industry, sheet music publishing, composers and performers.

780   DK   ISSN 0105-8045
DANSK MUSIKFORTEGNELSE/DANISH NATIONAL BIBLIOGRAPHY: MUSIC. 1933. a. DKK 384.25. (Kongelige Bibliotek, Musikafdeling) Bibliotekscentralen, Tempovej 7-11, DK-2750 Ballerup, Denmark. TEL 2-974000. FAX 2-655310.

780   UK   ISSN 0306-0373
ML410.D35
DELIUS. 1973. q. £10($21) Delius Society Journal, 85A Farley Hill, Luton LU1 5EG, Bedfordshire, England. Ed. Stephen Lloyd. bk.rev.; circ. 460. *Indexed:* Music Ind.
—BLDSC shelfmark: 3547.840000.

DENVER ARTS CENTER PROGRAMS. see *THEATER*

780   US
DETROIT MONOGRAPHS IN MUSICOLOGY. STUDIES IN MUSIC. 1971. irreg. price varies. Harmonie Park Press, 23630 Pinewood, Warren, MI 48091-4759. TEL 313-755-3080.
Formerly: Detroit Monography in Musicology.
Description: Monographs on musicology.

780   GW   ISSN 0417-2051
ML5
DEUTSCHE GESELLSCHAFT FUER MUSIK DES ORIENTS. MITTEILUNGEN. (Text in English and German) 1962. irreg. DM.28. (Deutsche Gesellschaft fuer Musik des Orients) Verlag der Musikalienhandlung Karl Dieter Wagner, Rothenbaumchaussee 1, 2000 Hamburg 13, Germany. illus. (back issues avail.) *Indexed:* A.I.C.P.

782.1   GW
DEUTSCHE OPER BERLIN AKTUELL. 1961. m. Deutsche Oper Berlin, Richard-Wagner-Str. 10, 1000 Berlin 10, Germany. TEL 030-34381. FAX 030-3438232. adv.; circ. 30,000.
Formerly: Opernjournal.

780   GW
DEUTSCHES MOZARTFEST. 1954. 4/yr. DM.60 membership. Deutsche Mozart-Gesellschaft e.V., Karlstr. 6, 8900 Augsburg, Germany. TEL 0821-518588. Ed. Dr. Erich Valentin. *Indexed:* Music Ind.

780   GW   ISSN 0415-7435
DEUTSCHES MUSIKLEBEN (YEAR). English edition: Music in Germany (ISSN 0173-5136) 1954. a. free. Inter Nationes e.V., Kennedyallee 91-103, 5300 Bonn 2, Germany. TEL 0228-880-0. FAX 0228-880-457. TELEX 17228308. Ed. Marianne Goebel. circ. 9,500.
Description: Chronological list of the year's most important music festivals and competitions, and events of musicological interest.

781.7   US
DEVIL'S BOX. vol.17, 1983. q. $7. Tennessee Folklore Society, 305 Stella Dr., Madison, AL 35758. Ed. Stephen F. Davis. rec.; rev. *Indexed:* M.L.A.

780   US
DEVOTEE; magazine for chamber music players and listeners. q. $12. Devotee Publications Inc., 28 24th Street, Troy, NY 12180. Ed. Paul Elistta. *Indexed:* Music Artic.Guide, Music Ind.

DIALOGUE IN INSTRUMENTAL MUSIC EDUCATION. see *EDUCATION — Teaching Methods And Curriculum*

786.6   US   ISSN 0012-2378
ML1
DIAPASON; devoted to the organ, the harpsichord, the carillon and church music. 1909. m. $15. Scranton Gillette Communications, Inc., 380 E. Northwest Hwy., Des Plaines, IL 60016-2282. TEL 312-298-6622. FAX 708-390-0408. TELEX 206041 MSG RLY. Ed. Jerome Butera. adv.; bk.rev.; illus.; circ. 5,000. (also avail. in microform from UMI; reprint service avail. from UMI) *Indexed:* Music Artic.Guide, Music Ind., RILM.
—BLDSC shelfmark: 3580.210500.
Description: Technical reviews and compositional analysis on the organ, the harpsichord, and church music, with recital announcements, reviews of new releases and instruments, and classified ads.

780   FR
DIAPASON. (Supplement avail.) 1955. 11/yr. 274 F. (with supplement 354 F.). Diapason - Harmonie, 9-13 rue Colonel Pierre Avia, 75754 Paris Cedex 15, France. TEL 1-46-62-20-00. FAX 1-46-62-25-33. adv.; bk.rev.; circ. 70,000. (also avail. in microfilm) *Indexed:* Music Ind., RILA, RILM.

780   AT   ISSN 0815-5232
DIRECTORY OF AUSTRALIAN COMPOSERS. 1985. biennial. Aus.$10. Australian Music Centre Ltd., P.O. Box N690, Grosvenor Pl., Sydney, N.S.W. 2000, Australia. TEL 61-2-247-4677. FAX 61-2-241-2873. circ. 600.
Description: Lists names, addresses and telephone numbers of Australian composers.

780 AT ISSN 0157-6402
DIRECTORY OF AUSTRALIAN MUSIC ORGANISATIONS. 1980. irreg. Aus.$8. Australian Music Centre Ltd., P.O. Box N690, Grosvenor Pl., Sydney, N.S.W. 2000, Australia. TEL 61-2-247-4677. FAX 61-2-241-2873. Ed. Bill Flemming.
Description: Lists names, addresses and telephone numbers of Australian musical organizations.

785 CN ISSN 0705-6249
DIRECTORY OF CANADIAN ORCHESTRAS AND YOUTH ORCHESTRAS/ANNUAIRE CANADIEN DES ORCHESTRES ET ORCHESTRES DES JEUNES. (Text in English, French) 1976. a. Can.$13. Association of Canadian Orchestras, 56 The Esplanade, Suite 311, Toronto, Ont. M5E 1A7, Canada. TEL 416-366-8834. (Co-sponsor: Ontario Federation of Symphony Orchestras)
Description: Current list of orchestra personnel.

780 370 US
DIRECTORY OF INTERNATIONAL MUSIC EDUCATION DISSERTATIONS IN PROGRESS. (Not published in 1990) 1963. biennial. $10. Council for Research in Music Education, University of Illinois, 1114 W. Nevada, Urbana, IL 61801. Ed. Marilyn P. Zimmerman. circ. 1,500. (back issues avail.)
Formerly: Approved Doctoral Dissertations in Progress in Music Education.

780 US ISSN 0098-664X
ML13
DIRECTORY OF MUSIC FACULTIES IN COLLEGES & UNIVERSITIES U S AND CANADA. 1967. biennial. $25 to individuals; institutions $45. C M S Publications, Inc., Box 8208, Missoula, MT 59807. TEL 406-728-2002. FAX 406-721-9419. Ed. Catherine Butler. circ. 4,000. Indexed: Music Ind., RILM.
Formerly: Directory of Music Faculties in American Colleges and Universities (ISSN 0419-3040)
Description: Includes approximately 30,000 music faculty and 1,745 postsecondary institutions.

780 621.389 US ISSN 0731-843X
ML1
DISC COLLECTOR. 1950. m. $5 (foreign $10). Disc Collector Publications, Box 315, Cheswold, DE 19936. TEL 302-674-3149. Ed. Lou Deneumoustier. adv.; bk.rev.; circ. 1,100. (processed)
Formerly: Disc Collector's Newsletter (ISSN 0070-6655)

DISCO & DANCING. see DANCE

781.57 UK ISSN 0012-3544
DISCOGRAPHICAL FORUM. 1960. q. £3($4) c/o Malcolm Walker, Ed., 44 Belleville Rd., London SW11 6QT, England. Ed. Malcom Walker. adv.; bk.rev.; bibl.; stat.; circ. 600. (processed)
Description: Focuses on jazz music.

780.1 US ISSN 0095-8115
DISCOGRAPHY SERIES. 1969. irreg. no.20, 1990. price varies. J.F. Weber, Ed. & Pub., 194 Roosevelt Dr., Utica, NY 13502. TEL 315-732-4747. bibl.; circ. 300.

789.91 IT
DISCOTECA HI FI.* 1959. m. Casa Editrice Discoteca s.r.l., Via Monforte 15, 20122 Milan, Italy. Ed. Ornella Zanuso Mauri. adv.; bk.rev.; illus.; circ. 20,000.
Former titles: Discoteca Alta Fedelta (ISSN 0012-3560); Discoteca.

780 745.1 US ISSN 0896-8322
DISCOVERIES (PORT TOWNSEND); the music world trade center. 1987. m. $19. Discoveries Publications, Inc., Box 255, Port Townsend, WA 98368. TEL 206-385-1200. FAX 206-385-6572. Ed. Jon E. Johnson. adv.; bk.rev.; circ. 15,000.
Description: Devoted to the hobby of music collecting: buy, sell, trade records, CDs and related memoribilia.

780.42 GW ISSN 0724-6978
DISCRET; Fach-Journal der Unterhaltungsgastronomie. 1983. m. DM.84. Brigitte Tecklenborg Verlag, Lindenstr. 4, 4430 Steinfurt, Germany. TEL 02552-3933. Ed. Hubert Tecklenborg. circ. 5,900.

781.57 US
DISC'RIBE; a journal of discographical information. 1980. irreg. (approx. a.). $5 for 4 issues. Wildmusic Company, 3040 Midvale Ave., Los Angeles, CA 90034-3408. Ed. David Wild. adv.; circ. 200.

780 NE
DIVITIAE MUSICAE ARTIS. SERIES A. vol.3, 1975. irreg. price varies. Uitgeverij Frits Knuf B.V., Box 720, 4116 ZJ Buren, Netherlands.

781.57 NE ISSN 0166-2309
DOCTOR JAZZ MAGAZINE. (Text in Dutch; occasionally in English) 1963. q. fl.25. Vijverweg 4, 5461 AL Veghel, Netherlands. TEL 04130-63542. (Subscr. to: van Lynden van Sandenburglaan 5, 3571 BA Utrecht, Netherlands) Ed.Bd. adv.; bk.rev.; circ. 850 (controlled). (back issues avail.)
Description: Contains information and research on traditional and classic jazz, blues and related music.

780 PL
DOCUMENTA CHOPINIANA. (Text in English and Polish) 1970. irreg. price varies. Polskie Wydawnictwo Muzyczne, Al. Krasinskiego 11a, 31-111 Krakow, Poland. TEL 22-70-44. FAX 22-01-74. Ed. Mieczyslaw Tomaszewski.
Description: Covers Chopin's life and work.

780 BE
DOCUMENTA MUSICAE NOVAE; critical edition of contemporary music sources. (Text in English, Flemish, French) 1968. irreg. vol.6, 1980. $12. Rijksuniversiteit te Gent, Seminarie voor Musicologie, Blandijnberg 2, B-9000 Ghent, Belgium. Ed. Herman Sabbe. circ. 200. Indexed: RILM.

DOMSPATZ; Zeitschrift fuer Fulda. see THEATER

782.1 UK ISSN 0307-1448
ML410.D7
DONIZETTI SOCIETY. JOURNAL. 1974. s-a. $15. Donizetti Society, 56 Harbut Rd., London SW11 2RB, England. illus.

780 UK
DONIZETTI SOCIETY NEWSLETTER. 1973. q. £8($15) Donizetti Society, c/o John R. Carter, 56 Harbut Rd., London SW11 2RB, England. bibl.

780.42 GW
DOORS QUARTERLY MAGAZINE. (Text in English, French, German) 1983. q. DM.30($20) Am Oelvebach 5, 4150 Krefeld 12, Germany. TEL 02151-571862. Ed. Rainer Moddemann. adv.; bk.rev.; circ. 1,000. (back issues avail.)
Description: Examines rock music of the 60's.

788.705 US ISSN 0741-7659
ML929
DOUBLE REED. 1978. q. membership. International Double Reed Society, c/o Lowry Riggins, 626 Lakeshore Dr., Monroe, LA 71203-4032. Eds. Daniel Stolper, Ron Klimko. adv.; bk.rev.; illus.; circ. 3,200. Indexed: Music Artic.Guide.
Former titles: International Double Reed Society (Publication); To the World's Oboists (ISSN 0091-9683); To the World's Bassoonists; International Double Reed Society Journal (ISSN 0092-0827)

780.904 US ISSN 0012-5768
ML1
DOWN BEAT; jazz, blues, and beyond. 1934. m. $26 (foreign $35). Maher Publications, Inc., 180 W. Park Ave., Elmhurst, IL 60126. TEL 708-941-2030. FAX 708-941-3210. (Subscr. to: Box 1071, Skokie, IL, 60076) Eds. Frank Alkyer, John Ephland. adv.; bk.rev.; rec.rev.; illus.; circ. 88,253. (also avail. in microform from UMI; reprint service avail. from UMI) Indexed: Acad.Ind., Arts & Hum.Cit.Ind., Bk.Rev.Ind. (1977-), Child.Bk.Rev.Ind. (1977-), Curr.Cont., Mag.Ind., Music Artic.Guide, Music Ind., PMR, R.G., RILM.
Description: Articles for musicians and listeners interested in contemporary music.

780 621.389 US
DOWN HOME MUSIC NEWSLETTER. 1978. irreg. (approx. 5/yr.). $6 (foreign $10). Down Home Music Inc., 6921 Stockton Ave., El Cerrito, CA 94530. TEL 415-525-1494. FAX 415-525-2904. Ed. Franklyn Scott. adv.; bk.rev.; rec.rev, video rev.; circ. 13,000.
Description: Features reviews of blues, country and jazz music.

MUSIC   3549

DRAGON. see LITERATURE

DREAM GUYS. see CHILDREN AND YOUTH — For

789.1 US
▼**DRUM!.** 1991. bi-m. free to qualified personnel. 12 S. First St., Ste. 417, San Jose, CA 95113. TEL 408-971-9794. FAX 408-971-0382. Ed. Andy Doerschuk. circ. 30,000 (controlled).
Description: For California drummers and music enthusiasts.

785.067 US ISSN 0012-6748
DRUM CORPS NEWS.* 1961. s-m. (Jun.-Aug.); 4/mo. (Sep.-May). $10.50. Tri-Star Enterprises, Inc., Box 108, Prudential Ctr., Boston, MA 02199. TEL 617-266-0299. Ed. Andy Uzarins. adv.; illus.; circ. 15,000. Indexed: Music Artic.Guide.

780 US ISSN 0164-3223
ML1306
DRUM CORPS WORLD. 1971. 20/yr. $42 (effective Jan. 1991). Drum Corps Sights & Sounds, Inc., Box 8052, Madison, WI 53708. TEL 608-241-2292. FAX 608-241-4974. Ed. Steven Don Vickers. adv.; bk.rev.; illus.; stat.; circ. 5,300. (tabloid format; back issues avail.)
Description: Provides information on the worldwide drum and bugle corps activity; includes schedules, contest reviews and results, news and press releases.

780 GW
DRUMS & PERCUSSION. bi-m. DM.40. Spezial Zeitschrift Verlag, Schellingstr. 39, Postfach 401629, 8000 Munich 40, Germany. TEL 0221-121080. FAX 0221-132740. Ed. Manni Von Bohr. adv.; circ. 7,000.

DUE SOUTH; the biggest guide to what's on in the South. see ARTS AND HANDICRAFTS

787.9 US ISSN 0098-3527
ML1
DULCIMER PLAYERS NEWS. 1975. q. $15. Madeline MacNeil, Ed. & Pub., Box 2164, Winchester, VA 22601. adv.; bk.rev.; illus.; index; circ. 3,200.
Description: For players and builders of hammered and mountain dulcimers.

785.0671 CS
DYCHOVA HUDBA. irreg. vol.17, 1976. 8 Kcs. per no. Opus, Bratislava, Czechoslovakia.

780 NE ISSN 0012-7418
DYNAMITE INTERNATIONAL. (Text in English) 1961. bi-m. $11. International Cliff Richard Movement, P.O. Box 4164, 1009 AD Amsterdam, Netherlands. Ed. Anton Husmann. adv.; illus.; circ. 10,500.
Formerly: Dynamite.
Description: Provides international news of interest to fans of Cliff Richard, a British singer.

780.42 GW
E B - METRONOM; Musik magazin. 1984. bi-m. DM.22($16) E B - Metronom Verlag, Hospeltstr. 66, 5000 Cologne 30, Germany. TEL 0221-543506. FAX 0221-542620. Ed. Gisela Lobisch. adv.; bk.rev.; circ. 12,000. (back issues avail.)

780 US ISSN 0893-9500
ML197
EAR: MAGAZINE OF NEW MUSIC. 1973. m. (10/yr.). $25 (foreign $45). Ear, Inc., 131 Varick St., Rm. 905, New York, NY 10013. TEL 212-807-7944. FAX 212-807-7963. adv.; bk.rev.; bibl.; illus.; index, cum.index: 1973-1989; circ. 20,000. (back issues avail.) Indexed: Access, Music Artic.Guide.
Formerly (until 1976): Ear (New York) (ISSN 0734-2128)
Description: Presents international contemporary, experimental, avant-garde and world music from a multi-ethnic and multi-media perspective.

EARLY DRAMA, ART, AND MUSIC REVIEW. see THEATER

784 US ISSN 0899-8132
ML549.8
EARLY KEYBOARD JOURNAL. 1982. a. $18 to members; institutions $25; students $9. Southeastern Historical Keyboard Society & Midwestern Historical Keyboard Society, Box 32022, Charlotte, NC 28232-2022. Eds. Lilian Pruett, Thomas G. MacCracken. adv.; bk.rev.; circ. 500. Indexed: RILM.

3550 MUSIC

786 371.3   US   ISSN 0882-0201
ML549.8
EARLY KEYBOARD STUDIES NEWSLETTER. 1985. q. $30. Westfield Center for Early Keyboard Studies, One Cottage St., Easthampton, MA 01027. TEL 413-527-7664. adv.; bk.rev.; illus.; circ. 750. (back issues avail.)
  Description: Fosters appreciation and understanding of early music from the Renaissance through the Baroque, Classical, and Romantic eras. Emphasis is on the keyboard, and on historical performance practices and circumstances.
  Refereed Serial

780   UK   ISSN 0306-1078
ML5
EARLY MUSIC. 1973. q. £38($72) Oxford University Press, Oxford Journals, Pinkhill House, Southfield Road, Eynsham, Oxford OX8 1JJ, England. TEL 0865-882283. FAX 0865-882890. TELEX 837330 OXPRES G. Ed. Nicholas Kenyon. adv.; bk.rev.; illus.; index, cum.index; circ. 4,200. (also avail. in microform from UMI; reprint service avail. from UMI) **Indexed:** Amer.Hist.& Life, Arts & Hum.Cit.Ind., Curr.Cont., Hist.Abstr., Music Ind., RILM.
  —BLDSC shelfmark: 3642.993000.
  Description: Covers the field of Medieval, Renaissance, Baroque and Classical music history, critical surveys and performance practice.

780   UK   ISSN 0261-1279
ML169.8
EARLY MUSIC HISTORY. 1982. a. $42 to individuals; institutions $75. Cambridge University Press, Edinburgh Bldg., Shaftesbury Rd., Cambridge CB2 2RU, England. TEL 0223-312393. FAX 0223-315052. TELEX 851817256. (N. American subscr. to: Cambridge University Press, 40 W. 20th St., New York, NY 10011) Ed. Iain Fenlon. bk.rev. (also avail. in microform from UMI) **Indexed:** Amer.Hist.& Life (1992-), Arts Hum.Cit.Ind., Curr.Cont., Hist.Abstr. (1992-).
  —BLDSC shelfmark: 3642.998100.
  Description: Encourages British, American and European work in manuscript studies, analytical work, iconography, textual criticism, and the relationship between music and society before 1700.

788   US
EARLY MUSIC NEWSLETTER. vol.16, 1976. m. (Sep.-June). $20. New York Recorder Guild, c/o Eleanor Brodkin, Ed., 197 New York Ave., Dumont, NJ 07628. adv.; bk.rev.; circ. 185.

780   UK   ISSN 0144-8072
EARLY MUSIC RECORD SERVICES. MONTHLY REVIEW. 1980. m. £4.25. Early Music Record Services, 53 Ashton St., Saffron Walden, Essex CB10 2AQ, England.

780.42   US
EAST COAST ROCKER. w. Arts Weekly, Inc., 7 Oak Pl., Montclair, NJ 07042-3824. TEL 201-783-4346. FAX 201-783-5057. Ed. James Rensenbrink. circ. 40,000.

785.067   US   ISSN 0012-8902
EASTERN REVIEW (BROOKLYN); the voice of drum & bugle corps. 1956. m. $20 (Canada $28). Eastern Review, Inc., Box 495, Brooklyn, NY 11201. Ed. R.P. Bellarosa. adv.; bk.rev.; music rev.; charts; illus.; stat.; circ. 4,000. (also avail. in tabloid format)
  Formerly (until vol.20, no.3): Drum Corps Review (ISSN 0094-3649)

780   US   ISSN 0147-345X
MT4.R6
EASTMAN NOTES. 1966. q. free to qualified personnel. University of Rochester, Eastman School of Music, 26 Gibbs St., Rochester, NY 14604. illus.; circ. 11,000. **Indexed:** Music Artic.Guide.
  Former titles: Notes from Eastman (1979); Eastman Notes (1976); Notes from Eastman (ISSN 0550-0958)

780   US
EASY REEDING. 1985. q. $10 one time fee. Hohner Inc., 101 Sycamore Dr., Ashland, VA 23005. TEL 804-550-2700. FAX 804-550-9625. (Subscr. to: Hohner Inc., Dept. HNL, Box 9375, Richmond, VA 23227) Ed. Jack C. Kavoukian. circ. 5,000.

780.7   FR   ISSN 0013-1415
EDUCATION MUSICALE; revue culturelle et pedagogique de tout l'enseignement de la musique. (5 supplements yearly) 1945. 10/yr. 320 F. (foreign 380 F.). 23 rue Benard, 75014 Paris, France. TEL 45-42-34-07. FAX 45-43-26-74. Ed. C. Negiar. adv.; rec.rev.; charts; circ. 7,000. **Indexed:** RILM.
  Description: Presents study and teaching methods.

780   US   ISSN 0363-4558
EDWARD H. TARR SERIES. irreg. Brass Press, c/o RKMS, 28 Main St., N. Easton, MA 02356. FAX 508-238-2571.
  Description: Music for trumpet.

783 200   FR   ISSN 0013-2357
EGLISE QUI CHANTE. 1957. bi-m. 145 F. (foreign 180 F.). (Association Saint-Ambroise) Editions du Cerf, 29 bd. Latour-Maubourg, 75340 Paris Cedex 07, France. TEL 44-18-12-12. FAX 45-56-04-27. (Subscr. to: Service Abonnements, 3 chemin des Prunais, 94350 Villiers-sur-Marne, France) Ed. J. Lebon. adv.; charts; index.

EIGHTEENTH-CENTURY STUDIES. see *HISTORY*

780   GW
EISERNE LERCHE; Hefte fuer eine demokratische Musikkultur. q. DM.8. Verlag Plaene GmbH, Postfach 827, 4600 Dortmund 1, Germany. illus.

789   US   ISSN 0884-4720
ML1380
ELECTRONIC MUSICIAN. 1976. m. $24 (foreign $44). Act III Publishing, 6400 Hollis, Ste. 12, Emeryville, CA 94608. TEL 510-653-3307. FAX 510-635-5142. (Subscr. to: Box 41094, Nashville, TN 37204. TEL 800-888-5139) Ed. Bob O'Donnell. adv.; bk.rev.; rec.rev.; software rev.; circ. 50,677. (back issues avail.) **Indexed:** Amer.Hist.& Life, Music Ind.
  Formerly (until 1985): Polyphony (ISSN 0163-4534)
  Description: High-tech music equipment and applications magazine.

780 621.3   US   ISSN 0160-1148
ELECTRONOTES. 1972. m. $25. Musical Engineering Group, One Pheasant Ln., Ithaca, NY 14850. TEL 607-272-8030. Ed. Bernie Hutchins. bk.rev.; abstr.; bibl.; charts; illus.; circ. 1,000. (back issues avail.)
  Formerly: Electronotes Newsletter.

780.92   UK   ISSN 0143-1269
ELGAR SOCIETY. JOURNAL. 1973. 3/yr. £10. Elgar Society, c/o John Greig, Treasurer, Orchard Barn, Derringstone St., Barham, Canterbury, Kent CT4 6QB, England. TEL 0227-831841. Ed. geoffrey Hodgkins. adv.; bk.rev.; circ. 1,200.
  Formerly: Elgar Society. Newsletter (ISSN 0309-4405)

780   UK   ISSN 0013-6484
ELVIS MONTHLY. 1958. m. £12($24) Heanor Record Centre Ltd., 47 Derby Rd., Heanor, Derbyshire DE7 7QH, England. TEL 0533-537271. FAX 0533-531875. (Subscr. to: Spotlight Magazine Distribution Ltd., 1 Benwell Rd., Holloway, London N7 7AX, England) Ed. Todd Slaughter. adv.; bk.rev.; film rev.; illus.; circ. 50,000.
  Description: Provides news of Elvis, his music and his fans.

ELVIS NOW FAN CLUB. see *CLUBS*

780   US
ELVIS WORLD. 1986. q. $12. Burk Enterprises, Box 16792, Memphis, TN 38186-0792. TEL 901-327-1128. FAX 901-323-1528. Ed. Connie Lauridsen Burk. adv.; bk.rev.; circ. 5,300. (back issues avail.)
  Description: Features rare photos and stories (factual) of Elvis Presley.

781.7   UK   ISSN 0013-8231
ML5
ENGLISH DANCE AND SONG. 1936. 4/yr. £12 (includes Folk Music Journal). English Folk Dance and Song Society, Cecil Sharp House, 2 Regents Park Rd., England. Ed. Dave Arthur. adv.; bk.rev.; rec.rev.; illus.; circ. 9,000. (also avail. in microform from UMI; reprint service avail. from UMI) **Indexed:** A.I.C.P., M.L.A., Music Ind., RILM.
  Incorporates: E F D S S News (ISSN 0012-7647)

ENTERTAINMENT AND SPORTS LAWYER. see *LAW*

ENTERTAINMENT BITS. see *DANCE*

780.42   US
ENTERTAINMENT EYES. 1979. m. $12.60. Alsaman Rec. and Comm. Group, Inc., Box 8263, Haledon, NJ 07508. TEL 201-942-6810. Eds. Maureen Ellis, Samuel Cummings. adv.; bk.rev.; bibl.; charts; circ. 10,000. (back issues avail.)

780 791.43   US   ISSN 0742-9568
ENTERTAINMENT MAGAZINE. 1977. m. $20 (foreign $35). S W Alternatives, Inc., Box 3355, Tucson, AZ 85722. TEL 602-623-3733. Ed. Robert E. Zucker. adv.; bk.rev.; circ. 20,000. (back issues avail.)
  Description: Explores music, theatre, video, film and the arts with articles and interviews; plus comprehensive Arizona calendar of events, new music, and video release guide; includes national and Southwest regional coverage

780 792   CN
ENTERTAINMENT MAGAZINE. 1978. 6/yr. $1.50. 752 King St., E., Hamilton, Ont. L8M 1A5, Canada. TEL 416-523-5566. circ. 15,000.

780 791.43   US
ENTERTAINMENT PLUS. w. Box 11707, Rock Hill, SC 29731. TEL 803-329-4000.

782   FR   ISSN 0013-8975
ENTR'ACTE;* la revue des theatres lyriques. 1955. s-m. 36 F. 29 Bd. Voltaire, 75011 Paris, France. Ed. Stephane Wolff. adv.; illus.

780 793.3   NE   ISSN 0924-560X
ML5
ENTR'ACTE; muziek journal. vol.3, 1977. m. (10/yr.). fl.72.50 to individuals; students fl.57.50. S D U - Openbaar Kunstbezit, Postbus 5555, 1007 AN Amsterdam, Netherlands. TEL 20-523511. FAX 20-5235197. Ed. Sytze Smit. adv.; bk.rev.; illus.; circ. 12,500. **Indexed:** Excerp.Med.
  Former titles (until Sep. 1989): Muziek en Dans (ISSN 0166-0535); M D.

780   US
ERNEST BLOCH SOCIETY. BULLETIN. 1967. a. $3.50. Ernest Bloch Society, c/o Susan Bloch, Ed., 448 Riverside Dr., New York, NY 10027. bk.rev.; circ. 2,000.
  Former titles: Ernest Bloch Society. Newsletter; (until 1983): Ernest Bloch Society. Bulletin (ISSN 0071-1195)
  Description: Devoted entirely to correspondence between the composer and his friends and colleagues.

780   US
ERTONG YINYUE/CHILDREN'S MUSIC. (Text in Chinese) bi-m. $10.30. China Books & Periodicals, Inc., 2929 24th St., San Francisco, CA 94110. TEL 415-282-2994. FAX 415-282-0994.

780.42   AG
▼**ESCENARIOS;** de musica popular argentina. 1990. m. Editorial Escenarios, Juncal 971, 4o A, Buenos Aires, Argentina. TEL 393-6298.

EL ESPECTACULAR. see *COMMUNICATIONS — Television And Cable*

ESSAYS ON ASIAN THEATER, MUSIC AND DANCE. see *THEATER*

ESTETICKA VYCHOVA. see *EDUCATION*

781.7   US
ETHNOMUSICOLOGY NEWSLETTER. 1966. 4/yr. membership. Society for Ethnomusicology, Morrison Hall 005, Indiana University, Bloomington, IN 47405-2501. TEL 812-855-6672. Ed. Laurel Sercombe. circ. 2,000. (processed; also avail. in microform from UMI; reprint service avail. from UMI) **Indexed:** A.I.C.P., Music Artic.Guide, Music Ind.
  Former titles: Society for Ethnomusicology Newsletter; S E M Newsletter (ISSN 0036-1291)

783   FR   ISSN 0071-2086
ETUDES GREGORIENNES; revue de musicologie religieuse. (Text in English, French and Italian) 1954. irreg. latest vol.20, 1981. price varies. Editions Abbaye Saint-Pierre de Solesmes, 72300 Sable sur Sarthe, France. Dir. D. Jean Claire. bk.rev.; circ. 500. **Indexed:** RILM.

780 KO
EUMAK DONG-A. 1984. m. Dong-A Ilbo, 139 Sejongno, Chongno-gu, Seoul, S. Korea. TEL 02-721-7114. Ed. Kwon O-Kie. circ. 85,000.

786.23 GW ISSN 0014-2387
EURO PIANO; information & service. (Text in English, French, German, Italian) 1960. q. DM.57. (Union Europaeischer Pianomacher-Fachverbaende) Verlag Erwin Bochinsky GmbH, Muenchenerstr. 45, 6000 Frankfurt a.M. 1, Germany. TEL 069-239521. Ed. Rita Orgel. adv.; charts; illus.; stat.; circ. 3,100.
  Description: Information and workshop service for piano manufacturers. Features latest technology, computerization, association news and events, readers' comments.

786 SZ
EUROPIANO. q. Schweizerischer Verband der Klavierbauer und -stimmer, c/o E. Schoeckle, Lindenfeldweg 9, 4106 Therwil, Switzerland. TEL 031-840036.

781.57 DK
EVELYN BOOSTER. 1980. m. free. Fajabefa Aarhus, Guldsmedgade 23 og 2th, DK-8000 Aarhus C, Denmark. TEL 86 19 36 97. adv.; circ. 800.
  Formerly: Fajabefa Nyt (ISSN 0105-5933)

781.7 AT ISSN 0159-1991
EVERYONE'S SONGS. SERIES. 1977. irreg. Aus.$6 per no.; catalogue Aus.$2. Sound Austral, 34 Lucerne Cres., Frankston, Vic. 3199, Australia. TEL 03-789-2205. Ed. Frank Hinz. (back issues avail.; catalogue of titles avail.)
  Description: Collection of folkloric and community songs of Australia.

780.01 US ISSN 0276-6795
ML1
EX TEMPORE. 1981. s-a. $10 to individuals; institutions $14. c/o Deptartment of Music, Texas Christian University, Ft. Worth, TX 76129. adv.; circ. 200. (back issues avail.)

EXETER STUDIES IN AMERICAN & COMMONWEALTH ARTS. see *LITERATURE*

781 US ISSN 0883-0754
EXPERIMENTAL MUSICAL INSTRUMENTS. 1985. q. $25. Experimental Musical Instruments, Box 784, Nicasio, CA 94946. TEL 415-662-2182. Ed. Bart Hopkin. adv.; bk.rev.; bibl.; charts; illus.; cum.index; circ. 650. (back issues avail.) **Indexed:** Music Artic.Guide.
  —BLDSC shelfmark: 3839.790000.
  Description: Devoted to new and unusual acoustic and electro-acoustic musical instruments and sound sculpture.

783 NE
EXPRESSIE. 1975. a. $15. Continental Sound, Postbus 80165, 3009 GB Rotterdam, Netherlands. FAX 010-4559022. Ed. Leen la Riviere. adv.; bk.rev.; circ. 1,500.
  Formerly: Gospel Informatie-Handboek.

787 US
F I G A. 1960. bi-m. $15 (foreign $27.50). Fretted Instrument Guild of America, 2344 S. Oakley Ave., Chicago, IL 60608. TEL 312-376-1143. Ed. Glen Lemmer. adv.; bibl.; circ. 2,000.
  Formerly (until 1980): F I G A News (ISSN 0014-5890)

F M GUIDE. see *COMMUNICATIONS — Radio*

780.42 UK ISSN 0263-1210
THE FACE. 1980. m. $48. Wagadon Ltd., Old Laundry, Ossington Buildings, Moxon St., London W1, England. FAX 01-935-2237. (Subscr. to: Alan Wells International, P.O. Box 500, Leicester LE99 0AA, England) Ed. Nick Logan. adv.; bk.rev.; illus.; circ. 80,000.
  Description: Primary focus is on music. Includes interviews and fashion items.

780.42 US
FACES ROCKS. 1983. irreg., latest Apr. 1992. $19 (foreign $25). Faces Magazines, Inc., 63 Grand Ave., Ste. 115, River Edge, NJ 07661-1912. TEL 201-487-3255. FAX 201-487-9360. Ed. Lorena Alexander. adv.; illus.; circ. 100,000.
  Description: Features hard rock and heavy metal music.

780.42 GW
FACHBLATT MUSIC MAGAZIN. m. DM.60. S Z V Verlag, Falltorstr. 13-15, 5060 Bergisch-Gladbach 1, Germany. Ed. Horst Stachelhaus.

FACILITIES DIRECTORY/REPERTOIRE DES SALLES DE SPECTACLE. see *DANCE*

789.91 US ISSN 0148-9364
ML156.9
FANFARE; the magazine for serious record collectors. 1977. bi-m. $34. Fanfare, Inc., 273 Woodland St., Tenafly, NJ 07670. (Subscr. to: Box 720, Tenafly, NJ 07670) Ed. Joel Flegler. adv.; bk.rev.; circ. 26,000. (back issues avail.) **Indexed:** Music Artic.Guide, Music Ind.

780 UK
FANFARE. 1968. a. £3($10) Royal Military School of Music, Kneller Hall, Twickenham, Middx. TW2 7DU, England. Ed. Major Gordon Turner. adv.; bk.rev.; circ. 4,500.

781.57 IT
FARE MUSICA. 1980. m. L.60000. Ediscreen s.r.l., Via Calderini, 68, 00196 Rome, Italy. Dir. Enzo Perilli. adv.; circ. 80,000. (back issues avail.)

781.7 US ISSN 8755-9137
ML3551
FAST FOLK MUSICAL MAGAZINE. 1984. 10/yr. $65. Fast Folk Musical Magazine, Inc., Box 938, New York, NY 10014. FAX 212-927-1831. Ed. Richard Meyer. adv.; bk.rev.; circ. 1,500. (also avail. in record)

FAVES. see *CHILDREN AND YOUTH — For*

781.57 US
FEDERATION JAZZ. 1985. 6/yr. $25 to non-members. Federation of Jazz Societies, 2787 Del Monte St., W. Sacramento, CA 95691. TEL 916-372-5277. adv.; bk.rev.; illus.; circ. 300 (controlled).

780 GW ISSN 0939-4664
FERMATE; rheinisches Musikmagazin. 1982. q. DM.20. Verlag Petra Dohr, Johann-Brinck-Platz 1, 5000 Cologne - Bickendorf, Germany. TEL 0221-532720. FAX 0221-531790. Ed. Christoph Dohr. adv.; bk.rev.

780.1 US
FESTSCHRIFT SERIES. 1977. irreg., vol.8, 1989. Pendragon Press, Rt. 1, Box 159, Stuyvesant, NY 12173-9720. TEL 518-828-3008. FAX 518-828-2368. (back issues avail.) **Indexed:** RILM.

781.7 AG
FICTA-DIFUSORA DE MUSICA ANTIQUA. 1977. s-a. Centro de Musica Antiqua, Mexico 1208, 1097 Buenos Aires, Argentina. Ed. Jorge V. Gonzalez. adv.; bk.rev.; circ. 1,500.

FILM MUSIC BUYER'S GUIDE. see *MOTION PICTURES*

FILM, SZINHAZ, MUZSIKA. see *MOTION PICTURES*

787 US
FIRST BASS. 1987. q. $14.95 (foreign $24.95). (Bass Players Hall of Fame Museum) First Bass International, 33 Essex St., Hackensack, NJ 07601. TEL 201-488-2055. FAX 201-489-5057. Ed. Joe Campagna. bk.rev.; circ. 86,000.
  Description: Directed to the electric and acoustic bass player of all ages, levels and backgrounds with emphasis on the intelligent creative reader, thinker and music lover. Educational tool for students and guide for consumers.

780 AT ISSN 0311-0559
FLAUTIST. 1971. 4/yr. Aus.$30. Victorian Flute Guild, Inc., Box 95, Malvern, Vic. 3144, Australia. Ed. P. Burke. adv.; circ. 600.
  Description: Publishes articles relevent to flute players.

FLORIDA FOLKLIFE RESOURCE DIRECTORY. see *FOLKLORE*

784 US ISSN 0160-5119
ML1
FLORIDA FRIENDS OF BLUEGRASS SOCIETY. NEWSLETTER. bi-m. Florida Friends of Bluegrass Society, 7318 Sequaia Dr., Tampa, FL 33617. illus.

780.7 US ISSN 0046-4155
ML1
FLORIDA MUSIC DIRECTOR. 1947. 10/yr. $12. Florida Music Educators Association, c/o Vicki Miazga, Man. Ed., 207 Office Plaza Dr., Tallahassee, FL 32301. (Co-sponsor: Florida State Music Teachers Association) adv.; bk.rev.; illus.; circ. 4,875. **Indexed:** Music Artic.Guide.
  Formerly: Music Director (ISSN 0027-4313); Incorporates: Florida Music Teacher.

780 US
FLUTE TALK; a magazine for flutists and flute teachers. 1980. 10/yr. $15. Instrumentalist Co., 200 Northfield Rd., Northfield, IL 60093-3390. TEL 708-446-5559. Ed. Kathleen Goll-Wilson. adv.; bk.rev.; rec.rev.; circ. 12,000. **Indexed:** Music Artic.Guide.

780 US ISSN 8756-8667
ML27.U5
FLUTIST QUARTERLY. 1974. q. $30. National Flute Association, Inc., c/o Phyllis Pemberton, Box 800597, Santa Clarita, CA 91380-0597. TEL 805-297-5287. Ed. Susan Phelps. adv.; bk.rev.; circ. 4,500. **Indexed:** Music Artic.Guide.
  Formerly: National Flute Association. Newsletter.

FOLIO (NORTH HOLLYWOOD). see *COMMUNICATIONS — Radio*

781.7 US
FOLK ERA TODAY!. 1981. q. $8. Folk Era Productions, Inc., 17 Middle Dunstable Rd., Nashua, NH 03062. TEL 603-888-3457. Ed. Bob Grand. adv.; bk.rev.; circ. 15,000. (back issues avail.)
  Former titles: Folk Era Newsletter; Kingston Korner Newsletter.
  Description: Covers popular acoustic folk music.

780 US ISSN 0094-8934
ML1
FOLK HARP JOURNAL. 1973. q. $16 to institutions; free to members. International Society of Folk Harpers and Craftsmen, Inc., 4718 Maychelle Dr., Anaheim, CA 92807-3040. TEL 714-998-5717. FAX 805-962-2841. Ed. Nadine Bunn. adv.; bk.rev.; bibl.; charts; illus.; circ. 1,400. **Indexed:** Music Ind.
  Description: Covers folk (nonpedal) harp playing, construction, and history. Aims to provide communication among harpers and builders.

FOLK IN KENT. see *DANCE*

781.7 GW ISSN 0934-6449
ML3544
FOLK-MICHEL. 1977. bi-m. DM.25($20) Losemund Verlag, Postfach 300531, Hermannstr. 18, 5300 Bonn, Germany. TEL 0228-474387. (Subscr. to: Ilse Bast, Kircheichstr. 136, 5120 Herzogenrath) Ed. Bernhard Hanneken. adv.; bk.rev.; cum.index; circ. 1,500.
  Formerly (until 1987): Michel - Zeitschrift fuer Volksmusik.

781.7 793.31 UK ISSN 0531-9684
FOLK MUSIC JOURNAL. 1965. a. English Folk Dance and Song Society, Cecil Sharp House, 2 Regents Park Rd., London NW1 7AY, England. Ed. Ian Russell. adv.; bk.rev.; cum.index; circ. 9,000. (also avail. in microform from UMI; reprint service avail. from UMI,KTO) **Indexed:** Arts & Hum.Cit.Ind., Br.Hum.Ind., Curr.Cont., M.L.A., Music Ind.
  —BLDSC shelfmark: 3974.572000.
  Supersedes: English Folk Dance and Song Society. Journal.

781.7 793.31 UK
FOLK NORTH-WEST. 1977. 4/yr. £4.25. North-West Federation of Folk Clubs, 118 Bolton Rd., Aspull, Wigan WN2 1XF, England. TEL 0942-833292. (Subscr. to: 7 Sunleigh Rd., Hindley, Wigan, Lancashire, England) Ed. Nigel Firth. adv.; bk.rev.; play rev. (back issues avail.)
  Formerly: North-West Federation of Folk Clubs Newsletter.
  Description: News and articles on folk music in Northwest England.

781.7 UK ISSN 0951-1326
FOLK ROOTS. 1979. m. £23.20 (foreign £28.50). Southern Rag Ltd., P.O. Box 337, London N4 1TW, England. TEL 081-340-9651. FAX 081-348-5626. Ed. Ian A. Anderson. adv.; bk.rev.; circ. 13,000. (back issues avail.)
  Formerly: Southern Rag.

3552 MUSIC

FOLKBLAD PIBROCH. see *FOLKLORE*

781.7   GW
FOLKBRIEF; news & views. (Supplement avail.) (Text in German; summaries in English, French) 1979. m. DM.33.80. Folk-Edition, Burgstr. 9, 4405 Nottuln, Germany. TEL 02502-6151. FAX 02502-1825. bk.rev. (back issues avail.)
Formerly (until 1986): Folkblatt.

781.7   US
FOLKLORICA PUBLICATIONS IN FOLKSONG AND BALLADRY. irreg., no.3, 1981. Folklorica Press, Inc., 301 E. 47 St., New York, NY 10017. Ed. Kenneth S. Goldstein.

781.7 398   US
FOLKSONG IN THE CLASSROOM; a network of teachers of history, literature, music and the humanities - a newsletter. 1980. 3/yr. $7 to individuals (foreign $8); institutions $12. Box 264, Holyoke, MA 01041. Ed.Bd. bk.rev.; rec.rev.; circ. 1,500. (back issues avail.) Indexed: ERIC.
Description: Contains sheet music and lyrics, historical analysis, correspondence from readers; instructional guidance and materials for classroom teaching.

780   SP
FONO 2; * la revista de los jovenes y de la musica. m. 480 ptas.($9) Ediciones Anel, San Vicente Ferrer 13, Granada, Spain. adv.; bk.rev.; film rev.; charts; illus.; circ. 30,000. (back issues avail.)
Formerly (1963-1969): Fonorama.

789.91 621.389   GW   ISSN 0015-6140
FONOFORUM. 1957. m. DM.54. S Z V KG, Schellingstr. 39-43, 8000 Munich 40, Germany. TEL 089-23726-0. FAX 089-23726-125. Ed. Soeren Meyer-Eller. adv.; bk.rev.; rec.rev.; illus.; tr.lit.; index; circ. 38,000.
—BLDSC shelfmark: 3976.300000.

784   RU
FOR A LOVER OF VOCAL MUSIC. a. 2.10 Rub. Izdatel'stvo Muzyka, Ul. Neglinnaya 14, Moscow 103031, Russia. TEL 924-81-63. FAX 921-83-53.

FORCED EXPOSURE. see *LITERARY AND POLITICAL REVIEWS*

780   RU
FOREIGN COMPOSERS. 2/yr. 2.10 Rub. per issue. Izdatel'stvo Muzyka, Ul. Neglinnaya 14, Moscow 103031, Russia. TEL 924-81-63. FAX 021-83-53.

780.01   UK
FORMGHI QUARTERLY. 1975. q. £7.50. Fellowship of the Makers and Researchers of Historical Instruments, Faculty of Music, St. Aldate's, Oxford OX1 1DB, England. FAX 0365-276128. bk.rev.; cum.index.; circ. 700 (controlled). (back issues avail.)

780.01   AU
FORSCHUNGEN ZUR AELTEREN MUSIKGESCHICHTE. 1976. irreg., no.5, 1984. price varies. (Universitaet Wien, Musikwissenschaftliches Institut) W. Braumueller, Servitengasse 5, A-1092 Vienna, Austria. Ed. Walter Pass. circ. 500.

780   GW   ISSN 0173-5187
ML110
FORUM MUSIKBIBLIOTHEK; Beitraege und Informationen aus der musikbibliothekarischen Praxis. 1980. q. DM.38. Deutsches Bibliotheksinstitut, Abt. 1-Publikationen, Bundesallee 184-185, 1000 Berlin 31, Germany. TEL 030-8505-0. FAX 030-8505-100. Ed.Bd. circ. 280.

781.7   US   ISSN 0887-1892
FOUNDER SOUNDER. 1979. s-a. $5. (Middle Atlantic Regional) M A R Press, 100 Bryant St., N.W., Washington, DC 20001. TEL 202-265-7609.
Description: Covers African American gospel music.

780   US
FRENCH OPERA IN THE 17TH AND 18TH CENTURIES. 1984. irreg., no.5 1990. Pendragon Press, R.R. 1, Box 159, Stuyvesant, NY 12173-9720. TEL 518-828-3008. FAX 518-828-2368.

780   US
FRIENDS OF JULIO INTERNATIONAL NEWSLETTER. Abbrivated title: F O J I Newsletter. 1986. q. membership. Friends of Julio International, 28 Farmington Ave., Longwood, MA 01106. TEL 413-567-0845. Ed. Isabel Butterfield. circ. 150. (looseleaf format)
Description: Reports on Julio's concerts, albums, tour schedules, benefits; includes photos of Julio.

787   IT
FRONIMO; rivista trimestrale di chitarra e liuto. 1972. q. L.30000 (foreign L.40000). Edizioni Suvini Zerboni, Via M.F. Quintiliano, 40, 20138 Milan, Italy. FAX 5084261. TELEX 321063. Ed. Ruggero Chiesa. adv.; bk.rev.; bibl.; charts; illus.; index; circ. 7,000.

780.42   US
▼**FULL EFFECT!.** 1991. 6/yr. $14.95 (foreign $19.95). Pilot Communications, Inc., 831 Federal Rd., Box 304, Brookfield, CT 06804. TEL 203-775-0190. FAX 203-775-1931. (And: 25 W. 39th St., New York NY 10018. TEL 212-302-2626) Ed. Steve Korte. circ. 225,000.
Description: Covers today's rap, rhythm and blues and soul music scene for teenagers.

FUNDACION LA CAIXA. PANORAMA. see *MUSEUMS AND ART GALLERIES*

789.5   US   ISSN 0827-5955
ML1
G C N A BULLETIN. 1940. a. Guild of Carillonneurs in North America (San Antonio), c/o George Gregory, Ed., 132 Linda Dr., San Antonio, TX 78216. adv.; bk.rev.; circ. 500.
Description: Covers the carillon, the players and their music.

780 382   JA
G S R. (Gakki Shoho Review) 1980. bi-m. $36. Gakki Shoho-Sha Co., Ltd., Gakki Kaikan Bldg., 5th Fl., 2-18-21 Sotokanda, Chiyoda-ku, Tokyo 101, Japan. Ed. Toshio Suganuma. adv.

780   US
G. SCHIRMER HIGHLIGHTS. m. G. Schirmer Inc., 225 Park Ave. S., 18th Fl., New York, NY 10023. TEL 212-254-2100. FAX 212-254-2013. (Co-publisher: Associated Music Publisher Inc.) Ed. Eric Gordon.

780   DK   ISSN 0109-0097
GAFFA. 1983. m. free. Musikmagasinet Gaffa, Guldsmedegade 23, 8000 Aarhus C, Denmark. FAX 42-123501. Ed. Arne Vollertsen. adv.; bk.rev.; illus.; circ. 82,000.

781.91   JA
GAKKI SHOHO/MUSIC TRADE IN JAPAN. (Text in Japanese) 1950. m. 10000 Yen($50) Gakki Shoho-Sha Co., Ltd., Gakki Kakan, 5th Fl., 2-18-21, Sotokanda, Chiyoda-ku, Tokyo 101, Japan. Ed. Yuichi Sayama. adv.; bk.rev.; mkt.; stat.; circ. 5,000.
Formerly: Musical Instruments News (ISSN 0016-3945)

780.01   UK   ISSN 0072-0127
ML5
GALPIN SOCIETY JOURNAL; for the study of musical instruments. 1948. a. £15 (foreign £20) to individuals; institutions £25. Galpin Society, c/o Miss Pauline Holden, 38 Eastfield Rd., Western Park, Leicester LE3 6FE, England. Ed. David Rycroft. adv.; bk.rev.; index; circ. 1,400. (also avail. in microfilm from UMI; reprint service avail. from SWZ,UMI) Indexed: Arts & Hum.Cit.Ind.; Br.Hum.Ind.; Curr.Cont.; Music Ind., RILM.
—BLDSC shelfmark: 4067.550000.

784.96   NE   ISSN 0016-5239
GAUDEAMUS. 1945. 6/yr. fl.7.50($2.) Vereniging Het Maastrichts Mannenkoor - Maastricht Male Choir, Arkebijsruwe 87, 6218 RW Maastricht, Netherlands. adv.; illus.

780.904   NE   ISSN 0533-9235
GAUDEAMUS INFORMATION. ENGLISH EDITION. 1966. 6/m. free. Gaudeamus Foundation, Swammerdamstr. 38, 1091 RV Amsterdam, Netherlands. TEL 020-6947349. FAX 020-6947258. Ed. H. Heuvelmans. adv.; bk.rev.; music rev.; circ. 11,000.
Description: Devoted to contemporary music; contains information on concerts, festivals, competitions, records and scores.

780.65   US
THE GAVIN REPORT. w. 140 Second St., 2nd Fl., San Francisco, CA 94105-3727. TEL 415-495-1990. FAX 415-495-2580. Ed. Ron Fell.

GAZZETTA DELLE ARTI. see *ART*

784   GW
DER GEMEINDECHOR. 1879. bi-m. DM.7.50. Christlicher Saengerbund e.V., Westfalenweg 207, 5600 Wuppertal 1, Germany. TEL 0202-750633. Ed. Max Koehler.

781.7   RU
GEMS OF RUSSIAN AND SOVIET MUSIC. a. 3.50 Rub. per issue. Izdatel'stvo Muzyka, Ul. Neglinnaya 14, Moscow 103031, Russia. TEL 924-81-63. FAX 921-93-53.

780   US   ISSN 0046-5798
ML1
GEORGIA MUSIC NEWS. 1940. q. $4. Georgia Music Educators Association, c/o Mary Leglar, Ed., University of Georgia School of Music, Athens, GA 30602. TEL 404-542-2763. adv.; bk.rev.; circ. 2,472. Indexed: Music Artic.Guide.

784   CC   ISSN 0454-0816
GEQU/SONGS. (Text in Chinese) 1952. m. $23.30. Renmin Yinyue Chubanshe, Beijing, People's Republic of China. (Dist. in US by: China Books & Periodicals, Inc., 2929 24th St., San Francisco, CA 94110. TEL 415-282-2994)

781.57   GW
GERMAN BLUES CIRCLE INFO. 1976. m. DM.20. Fritz Marschall, Ed. & Pub., Ringelstr. 1, 6000 Frankfurt a.M. 60, Germany. Ed.Bd. bk.rev.; film rev.; illus.; circ. 600. (back issues avail.)

780   IT   ISSN 1120-6195
IL GIORNALE DELLA MUSICA. 1985. m. L.60000($80) E.D.T. s.r.l., Via Alfieri 19, 10121 Torino, Italy. TEL 011-511496. FAX 011-545296. Ed. Alberto Sinigaglia. adv.; bk.rev.; circ. 20,000.
Description: Contains information about musical events, new recordings and music publications, Italian university musicological activities.

GIORNALE DELLO SPETTACOLO. see *DANCE*

GIORNO POETRY SYSTEMS L P'S, C D'S, CASSETTES & GIORNO VIDEO PAK SERIES. see *LITERATURE — Poetry*

780   GW   ISSN 0172-9683
GITARRE & LAUTE; das Magazin fuer alle Gitarristen und Lautenisten. 1979. bi-m. DM.49.50. Gitarre & Laute Verlags GmbH, Friedrich-Schmidt-Str. 46A, Postfach 410408, 5000 Cologne 41, Germany. TEL 0221-493477. FAX 0221-4973716. Ed. Peter Paeffgen. adv.; circ. 6,500.

780 028.5   IS
GITIT. 1957. q. $18. Israel Youth and Music, Rehov Huberman 1, Tel Aviv 64 075, Israel. TEL 03-202333. Ed. Bat-Sheva Rozenvasser. adv.; bk.rev.; circ. 2,000.

780   SZ
GLAREANA. 1951. s-a. membership. Gesellschaft der Freunde alter Musikinstrumente, Oberwilerstr. 122, CH-4054 Basel, Switzerland. Ed. Veronika Gutmann. adv.; bk.rev.; bibl. Indexed: RILM.
Description: Contains news and information concerning old and ancient musical instruments. Features reports of events, exhibitions, museums, history.

780 620.2   US   ISSN 1045-5027
GLASS AUDIO. 1988. s-a. $10. Audio Amateur Publications, Box 176, Peterborough, NH 03458. TEL 603-924-9464. FAX 603-924-9467. Ed. Edward T. Dell, Jr. adv.; circ. 2,500. (back issues avail.) Indexed: Ind.How To Do It (1988-).
Description: Covers high quality audio reproduction using vacuum tube technology; hands-on; and project orientation.

286 780   US   ISSN 0731-0781
GLORY SONGS. q. $6.75. Southern Baptist Convention, Sunday School Board, 127 Ninth Ave., N., Nashville, TN 37234. TEL 800-458-2772.

782.1   UK   ISSN 0434-1066
GLYNDEBOURNE FESTIVAL PROGRAMME BOOK. 1952. a. £8. (Glyndebourne Festival Opera) Glyndebourne Productions Ltd., Glyndebourne, Lewes, E. Sussex BN8 5UU, England. TEL 0273-812321. FAX 0273-812783. TELEX 877862 GLYOP G. Ed. Helen O'Neill. adv.; circ. 30,000.

780   UK
GODOWSKY SOCIETY NEWSLETTER. 1980. s-a. $12. Godowsky Society, Ettrick, Main St., W. Linton, Peeblesshire EH46 7EE, Scotland. Ed. H.S. Winstanley. bk.rev.; circ. 200.

780   US   ISSN 8750-2577
GOLDMINE; the record collector's marketplace. 1974. bi-w. $35. Krause Publications, Inc., 700 E. State St., Iola, WI 54990. TEL 715-445-2214. FAX 715-445-4087. TELEX 556461 KRAUSE PUB UD. Ed. Jeff Tamarkin. adv.; bk.rev.; illus.; circ. 29,200. (also avail. in microform from UMI)
   Description: Articles on collecting and selling recordings (LPs, tapes, and CDs) in all music fields. Market information on rare and out-of-print records as well as new releases. Offers dealer lists and private sources of sales, and also features discographies, interviews, and record reviews.

GONG. see CHILDREN AND YOUTH — For

780.42   US   ISSN 1041-4118
GOOD DAY SUNSHINE. 1980. bi-m. £10($10) (foreign $20). Liverpool Productions, 397 Edgewood Ave., New Haven, CT 06511-4013. TEL 203-865-8131. FAX 203-562-5260. Ed. Charles F. Rosenay. adv.; bk.rev.; film rev.; play rev.; illus.; tr.lit.; circ. 3,800. (back issues avail.)
   Incorporates: Dark Horse & Here, There and Everywhere.
   Description: For Beatles fans, collectors and appreciators of music from the 60's, including news, reviews, convention reports, and photos.

780.7   US   ISSN 0017-2235
GOPHER MUSIC NOTES. 1930. q. $8. Minnesota Music Educators Association, c/o Robert I. Iverson, Ed., 1104 Pine View Rd., Alexandria, MN 56308. TEL 612-763-6135. adv.; bk.rev.; tr.lit.; circ. 4,600. (tabloid format) **Indexed:** Music Artic.Guide.

GOSPEL CHOIR. see RELIGIONS AND THEOLOGY — Protestant

783.7   US
GOSPEL MUSIC ASSOCIATION. RESOURCE GUIDE. 1971. a. Gospel Music Association, Inc., Box 23201, Nashville, TN 37202. TEL 615-255-1907. FAX 615-254-9755. Ed. Donald W. Butler. adv.; illus.; circ. 15,000.
   Former titles: Gospel Music Official Directory; Complete Guide to Gospel Music; Gospel Music (ISSN 0197-2715); Gospel Music Association. Annual Directory. Gospel Music Association. Annual Directory and Yearbook (ISSN 0362-7330); Gospel Music Directory and Yearbook.

783   DK   ISSN 0106-9586
GOSPEL TIME. 6/yr. DKK 60. Nonnetittvoenget 4, DK-5270 Odense, Denmark.

783   GW   ISSN 0017-2499
ML5
GOTTESDIENST UND KIRCHENMUSIK. 1951. bi-m. DM.15. (Gesellschaft fuer Innere und Aeussere Mission im Sinne der Lutherischen Kirche e.V.) Druckhaus Pastyrik, Kleiner Johannes 8, 8570 Pegnitz, Germany. Ed. Friedrich Hofmann. adv.; bk.rev.; abstr.; index; circ. 2,300. **Indexed:** Music Ind.
   —BLDSC shelfmark: 4203.300000.

780   UK   ISSN 0141-5085
ML410.G75
GRAINGER SOCIETY JOURNAL. 1978. s-a. £9.50($25) Percy Grainger Society, 6 Fairfax Crescent, Aylesbury, Buckinghamshire HP20 2ES, England. TEL 0296-28609. Ed. Barry Peter Ould. adv.; bk.rev.; circ. 500. **Indexed:** Music Ind.
   Formerly: Grainger Journal.
   Description: To promote the life and works of Percy Grainger.

780.42   SP
GRAN MUSICAL. 1969. m. $110. (Sociedad Espanola de Radiodifusion) Nuevas Ediciones, S.A., Gran Via 32-2, Madrid 28013, Spain. FAX 341-347-0709. TELEX 27638 SER E. Ed. Rafael Revert. adv.; bk.rev.; illus.; circ. 60,000.
   Formerly (until 1972): Musical.

780   US   ISSN 0434-3336
LE GRAND BATON. 1964. irreg. $15 (foreign $15). Sir Thomas Beecham Society, Inc., Box 340, Camden, NC 27921. Ed. Joseph G. Ayers. bk.rev.; charts; illus.; circ. 704. **Indexed:** Music Artic.Guide.
   Description: For music lovers and collectors, focusing on life and times of Sir Thomas Beecham.

LE GRAND HUIT. see THEATER

780.42   US
▼**GRAY AREAS.** 1992. q. $18 (foreign $26). Gray Areas, Inc., Box 808, Broomall, PA 19008-0808. TEL 215-353-8238. adv.; music rev.
   Description: Focuses on live music and taping.

781.7   US   ISSN 0272-0264
GREENWOOD ENCYCLOPEDIA OF BLACK MUSIC. 1981. irreg. price varies. Greenwood Press, Inc. (Subsidiary of: Greenwood Publishing Group Inc.), 88 Post Rd. W., Box 5007, Westport, CT 06881-5007. TEL 203-226-3571. FAX 203-222-1502.

780.7   XV   ISSN 0017-4343
GRLICA/TURTLEDOVE; revija za glasbeno vzgojo. 1969. bi-m. 200 din.($7) Zveza Drustev Glasbenih Pedagogov Slovenije, Kidriceva 5, Ljubljana, Slovenia. Ed. Jakob Jez. bk.rev.; circ. 1,300.
   Description: Covers the study and teaching of music.

780.01   GW
▼**GROSSE KOMPONISTEN.** 1990. fortn. DM.12.90 per no. c/o Marshall Cavendish, Paulstr. 3, 2000 Hamburg 1, Germany. TEL 040-322175. FAX 040-338769.

GUIDE TO RECORDING IN THE UK. see BUSINESS AND ECONOMICS — Trade And Industrial Directories

GUILDNOTES. see ART

787   US   ISSN 0270-9325
ML1
GUITAR AND MANDOLIN. 1978. bi-m. $12. Michael I. Holmes, Ed. & Pub., 15 Arnold Place, New Bedford, MA 02740. TEL 617-993-0156. adv.; bk.rev.; illus.; circ. 3,000.
   Formerly (until 1980): Mandolin Notebook (ISSN 0148-5482)

787   US
GUITAR EXTRA. q. Cherry Lane Music Co., 10 Midland Ave., Port Chester, NY 10573. TEL 914-935-5200. FAX 914-937-0614. Ed. Andy Aledort. circ. 75,000.

787   US   ISSN 0738-937X
GUITAR FOR THE PRACTICING MUSICIAN. 1983. m. $27.50. Cherry Lane Music Co., Inc., 10 Midland Ave., Port Chester, NY 10573. TEL 914-937-8601. FAX 914-937-0614. (Subscr. to: Mail Box Music, Box 341, Rye, NY 10580) Ed. Lorena Alexander. adv.; circ. 1,000,000.
   Description: Contains note-for-note transcriptions to todays best-selling songs. Features interviews, instructional playing tips and informative guitar techniques.

787   UK   ISSN 0958-6342
GUITAR INTERNATIONAL. 1972. m. $80. Purestop Ltd., Manor Rd., Mere, Wiltshire, England. Ed. George Clinton. adv.; bk.rev.; illus.; tr.lit.
   Formerly (until Aug. 1984): Guitar (ISSN 0301-7214)
   Description: For acoustic fingerstyle players.

787.61   US   ISSN 0017-5463
ML1
GUITAR PLAYER; for professional and amateur guitarists. 1967. m. $19.97. G P I Publications (Subsidiary of: Miller Freeman, Inc.), 20085 Stevens Creek, Cupertino, CA 95014. TEL 408-446-1105. FAX 408-446-1088. (Subscr. to: Box 58590, Boulder, CO 80322-8590) Ed. Dominic Milano. adv.; bk.rev.; charts; illus.; cum.index; circ. 135,003. (also avail. in microfilm from UMI; reprint service avail. from UMI) **Indexed:** Mag.Ind., Music Artic.Guide, Music Ind., PMR.
   Description: For professional, semi-pro and amateur guitar players in all styles.

787.61   US   ISSN 0017-5471
ML1
GUITAR REVIEW. 1946. q. $24 (foreign $28). Albert Augustine, Ltd., 40 W. 25th St., New York, NY 10010. TEL 212-924-4651. FAX 212-242-2220. Ed. Rose L. Augustine. adv.; bk.rev.; rec.rev.; illus.; circ. 4,000. (back issues avail.) **Indexed:** Arts & Hum.Cit.Ind., Curr.Cont., Music Artic.Guide, Music Ind., RILM.
   —BLDSC shelfmark: 4230.231000.

787 780.7   US
GUITAR SCHOOL. 1989. bi-m. $10.50. Harris Publications, Inc., 1115 Broadway, New York, NY 10010. TEL 212-807-7100. Ed. Brad Tolinski. adv.; circ. 100,688.
   Description: Contains sheet music with instructional lessons and transcriptions to today's songs and classic songs.

787   US
GUITAR WORLD. 1980. 9/yr. $19.85. Harris Publications, Inc., 1115 Broadway, 8th fl., New York, NY 10010. TEL 212-807-7100. FAX 212-627-4678. Ed. Brad Tolinski. circ. 132,317.
   Description: Contains interviews and transcriptions.

780   UK
GUITARIST. 1984. m. £18 (foreign £21). Music Maker Publications Ltd., Alexander House, Forehill, Ely, Cambs CB7 4AF, England. TEL 0353-665577. FAX 0353-662489. (U.S. addr.: Music Maker Publications, Inc., 22024 Lassen St., Ste. 118, Chatsworth, CA 91311) Ed. Nev Marten. circ. 30,000.

787   US
GUITARRA MAGAZINE. 1979. bi-m. $15.50. Sherry - Brener, Inc., 3145 W. 63rd St., Chicago, IL 60629. Ed: James Sherry. adv.; bk.rev.; circ. 4,500. (back issues avail.) **Indexed:** Music Artic.Guide.
   Description: Classic and flamenco guitar and music.

H D K INFO. (Hochschule der Kunste Berlin) see ART

780 621.389   IT
H.M. HEAVY METAL & HARD ROCK; quindicinale di musica specializzata. fortn. (Athena 2001 Coop a.r.l.) Edizioni L.E.T.I. s.r.l., Via E.Q. Visconti, 20, 00193 Rome, Italy. TEL 06-386353. circ. 120,000.

781.57   NE   ISSN 0017-632X
HAAGSE JAZZ CLUB. 1951. m. membership. Haagse Jazz Club - Hague Jazz Club, Laan van Heldenburg 7, Voorburg, Netherlands. adv.; circ. 250 (controlled).

780 700   US
HADASHOT. 1975. q. membership. America-Israel Cultural Foundation, 41 E. 42nd St., Ste. 608, New York, NY 10017. TEL 212-557-1600. FAX 212-557-1611. Ed.Bd. circ. 2,500.

780.6   UK
HALLE NEWS. 1946. s-a. 30p. Halle Concerts Society, 30 Cross St., Manchester M2 7BA, England. TEL 061-834-8363. TELEX 666140. Ed. William Lennon. adv.; circ. 11,500.
   Formerly: Halle Magazine.

MUSIC

780.6   UK
HALLE YEAR BOOK. 1858. a. £2.50. Halle Concerts Society, 30 Cross St., Manchester M2 7BA, England. TEL 061-834-8363. Ed. William Lennon. adv.; circ. 6,500.
Formerly: Halle Prospectus.
Description: Program of activities of the Halle Orchestra. Includes a preview of the season's concerts, news of the sponsoring society and sponsorships, lists of members and patrons, and articles on music.

780   GW
HAMBURGER JAHRBUCH FUER MUSIKWISSENSCHAFT. 1974. a. DM.82. Verlag der Musikalienhandlung Karl Dieter Wagner, Rothenbaumchaussee 1, 2000 Hamburg 13, Germany. **Indexed:** RILM.

780 286   US   ISSN 8756-7407
M147
HANDBELLS; for directors and ringers. 1985. q. $19.75. Southern Baptist Convention, Sunday School Board, 127 Ninth Ave., N., Nashville, TN 37234. TEL 800-458-2772. FAX 615-251-3866. Ed. Sharon Lyon. circ. 1,500.
Description: Contains music for beginning and advanced handbell choirs. Includes articles for leadership and ringers regarding all aspects of handbell usage: inspirational, practical, and technical.

780   GW   ISSN 0440-2863
ML410.P32
HANS - PFITZNER - GESELLSCHAFT. MITTEILUNGEN. 1954. s.a. free to members. (Hans-Pfitzner-Gesellschaft e.V.) Verlag Dr. Hans Schneider GmbH, Mozartstr. 6, 8132 Tutzing, Germany. TEL 08158-3050. Ed. Reinhard Seebohm. bk.rev.; play rev.; bibl.; illus.; circ. 250. **Indexed:** Music Ind., RILM.

HARD ROCK VIDEO. see *COMMUNICATIONS — Video*

786.9   GW   ISSN 0938-6629
HARMONIKA INTERNATIONAL. 1931. q. DM.24. Deutscher Harmonikaverband e.V., Postfach 1150, 7218 Trossingen, Germany. FAX 07425-20-521. TELEX 760727-HOHN-D. Ed. Wolfgang Layer. adv.; bk.rev.; illus.; circ. 32,000.
Formerly (until 1989): Harmonika-Revue.

784.96   US   ISSN 0017-7849
HARMONIZER. 1942. 6/yr. $18 to non-members (foreign $27). (Society for the Preservation and Encouragement of Barber Shop Quartet Singing in America, Inc.) SPEBSQSA, Inc., 6315 Third Ave., Kenosha, WI 53140-5199. TEL 414-653-8440. FAX 414-654-4048. Ed. Dan Daily. adv.; music rev.; illus.; index; circ. 36,000.

780   US
HARMONOLOGIA - STUDIES IN MUSIC THEORY. 1978. irreg., no.3 1990. Pendragon Press, R.R. 1, Box 159, Stuyvesant, NY 12173-9720. TEL 518-828-3008. FAX 518-828-2368.

786.221   UK
HARPSICHORD AND FORTEPIANO.* 1973. s.a. £2($6) c/o W.H. Cole, Little Tatchley, Prestbury Rd., Prestbury, Cheltenham, Glos. GL52 3DD, England. adv.; bk.rev.; illus.; circ. 800. (back issues avail.)
Supersedes (in 1987): Harpsicord Magazine (ISSN 0306-4395)

780   US   ISSN 0073-0629
HARVARD PUBLICATIONS IN MUSIC. 1967. irreg., no.16, 1991. price varies. Harvard University Press, 79 Garden St., Cambridge, MA 02138. TEL 617-495-2600. FAX 617-495-5898.
Refereed Serial

780   UK
HAYDN SOCIETY NEWSLETTER. 1980. a. £5($10) Haydn Society, University of Lancaster, Music Dept., Bailrigg, Lancaster LA1 4YW, England. TEL 0524-65420. Ed. Denis McCaldin. circ. 200.

780 920   GW   ISSN 0440-5323
HAYDN - STUDIEN. (Text in English and German) 1965. a. price varies. (Joseph Haydn-Institut e.V.) G. Henle Verlag, Forstenrieder Allee 122, Postfach 710466, 8000 Munich 71, Germany. FAX 089-7598240. (U.S. dist. by: G. Henle USA, Inc., 2446 Centerline Industrial Drive, Maryland Heights, MO 63043) Ed. Georg Feder. adv.; bk.rev.; illus.; index; circ. 750. **Indexed:** Arts & Hum.Cit.Ind., Curr.Cont., RILM.

783 200   US   ISSN 0889-5252
ML3529
HEARTSONG REVIEW; resource guide for New Age music of the spirit. 1986. s-a. $8 (foreign $13)(effective 1991). Box 1084, Cottage Grove, OR 97424. Ed. Wahaba Heartsun. adv.; bk.rev.; film rev.; index; circ. 9,000. (back issues avail.)
Description: Reviews of vocal and instrumental music for inspirational and therapeutic purposes; a consumer's resource guide.

780.42   US
HEAVY METAL THUNDER. q. $3.95 per no. Starlog Group, Inc, 475 Park Ave. S., New York, NY 10016. TEL 212-689-2830. FAX 212-889-7933.

DER HEIMATPFLEGER; Zeitschrift fuer Volkstanz, Volksmusik, Brauchtum und Heimatpflege. see *FOLKLORE*

HEMBYGDEN; tidning foer folkdans och folkmusik. see *DANCE*

780   MX   ISSN 0018-1137
ML5
HETEROFONIA; revista musical trimestral. (Text in Spanish; summaries in English) 1968. q. Mex.$200($22) Conservatorio Nacional de Musica, Department of Musicology, Masaryk 582, Mexico 5, D.F., Mexico. Ed. Esperanza Pulido. adv.; bk.rev.; abstr.; index; circ. 1,500. **Indexed:** Arts & Hum.Cit.Ind., Curr.Cont., Music Ind., RILM.

780   DK   ISSN 0441-5833
HI FI AARBOGEN. 1973. a. DKK 119.50. Forlaget Audio A-S, St. Kongensgade 72, DK-1264 Copenhagen K, Denmark. Ed.Bd. adv.; illus.; tr.lit.; circ. 20,000. (back issues avail.)

780   UK   ISSN 0142-6230
HI-FI NEWS AND RECORD REVIEW. 1956. m. £35. Link House Magazines Ltd., Link House, Dingwall Ave., Croydon, Surrey CR9 2TA, England. TEL 01-686-2599. FAX 01-760-0973. TELEX 947709. (Subscr. to: U M S, Stephenson House, 1st Fl., Brunel Centre, Bletchley, Milton Keynes, MK2 2EW) Ed. Steve Harris. adv.; bk.rev.; rec.rev.; charts; illus.; tr.lit.; index; circ. 35,100. (also avail. in microform from UMI) **Indexed:** Br.Tech.Ind.
Incorporates: Audio Record Review (ISSN 0018-1226)
Description: Explores classical, pop and jazz music. Includes hi-fi equipment reviews and ratings, articles, and news of product developments.

HI-FI STEREO; la rivista di musica e alta fedelta. see *SOUND RECORDING AND REPRODUCTION*

789.91 621.389   BE
HIFI MUSIQUE. REVUE DES DISQUES ET DE LA HAUTE FIDELITE. 1950. bi-m. 950 Fr. Editions Dereume, Rue Golden Hope,1, 1620 Drogenbos, Belgium. Ed. Serge Martin. adv.; bk.rev.; charts; illus.; circ. 5,000.
Formerly: Revue des Disques et de la Haute Fidelite (ISSN 0035-1970)

HIFI & MUSIK. see *SOUND RECORDING AND REPRODUCTION*

789.91   GW   ISSN 0178-6156
HIFI VISION. 1985. m. DM.93. R. van Acken GmbH, Josefstr. 35, 4450 Lingen-Ems, Germany. TEL 0591-7008. Ed. Heinz Schmitt. circ. 125,464.

780   DK
HIGH FIDELITY. 1967. m. DKK 345. Forlaget Audio A-S, St. Kongensgade 72, DK-1264 Copenhagen K, Denmark. Ed. Klaus Nordfeld. adv.; illus.; tr.lit.; index; circ. 21,000. (back issues avail.) **Indexed:** Acad.Ind.

780.42   US
HIGH VOLTAGE. bi-m. $2.95 per no. Michael John Publishing, 102 Triangle Rd., Somerville, NJ 08876. TEL 908-906-0500.

780.904
HINDEMITH - JAHRBUCH/ANNALES HINDEMITH. 1971. a. DM.22.40 (single copy, DM. 28). (Paul-Hindemith-Institut) B. Schott's Soehne, Weihergarten 5, Postfach 3640, 6500 Mainz 1, Germany. TEL 06131-246815. Ed. Dieter Rexroth. bk.rev.; circ. 1,200. **Indexed:** RILM.

HISPANIC AMERICAN ARTS; all you want or must know, about everything, in all the fields of Hispanic American arts. see *ART*

780   SP
HISTORIA DE LA MUSICA POP ESPANOLA.* m. 3800 ptas. Ediciones Anel, San Vicente Ferrer 13, Granada, Spain. adv.; circ. 20,000.

780   IT   ISSN 0073-2516
HISTORIAE MUSICAE CULTORES BIBLIOTECA. 1952. irreg., vol.60, 1991. price varies. Casa Editrice Leo S. Olschki, Casella Postale 66, 50100 Florence, Italy. TEL 055-6530684. FAX 055-6530214. circ. 1,000.

780   US   ISSN 1045-4616
HISTORIC BRASS SOCIETY JOURNAL. 1989. a. $15. Historic Brass Society, Inc., 148 W. 23rd St., No. 2A, New York, NY 10011. TEL 212-627-3820. Ed. Stewart Carter. adv.; bk.rev.; bibl.; charts; illus.; circ. 700. (back issues avail.) **Indexed:** Music Ind., RILM.
Description: Scholarly articles on the entire range of historic brass music subjects.
Refereed Serial

780   US   ISSN 1045-4594
HISTORIC BRASS SOCIETY NEWSLETTER. 1989. a. $15. Historic Brass Society, Inc., 148 West 23rd St., No. 2A, New York, NY 10011. TEL 212-627-3820. Ed. Stewart Carter. bk.rev.; rec.rev.; bibl.; charts; illus.; circ. 700. (back issues avail.) **Indexed:** Music Ind., RILM.
Description: Practical articles concerning the early brass music field.
Refereed Serial

780   US
HISTORICAL HARPSICHORD SERIES. 1984. irreg., vol.2, 1985. Pendragon Press, R.R. 1, Box 159, Stuyvesant, NY 12173-9720. TEL 518-828-3008. FAX 518-828-2368.

780   US   ISSN 0898-8587
ML1
HISTORICAL PERFORMANCE; the journal of early music America. 1988. s-a. $30. Early Music America, 30 W. 26th St., Ste. 1001, New York, NY 10010-2011. TEL 212-366-5643. FAX 212-366-5265. Ed. Timothy Pfaff. adv.; bk.rev.; charts; illus.; cum.index; circ. 3,000. (back issues avail.) **Indexed:** Music Artic.Guide.
Description: Covers current news, scholarship, and events in the field of early-music performance in North America.

780   US   ISSN 0162-0266
HIT PARADER. 1954. m. $29.50. Hit Parader Publications, Inc., 40 Violet Ave., Poughkeepsie, NY 12601. Ed. Andy Secher. adv.; bk.rev.; charts; illus.; tr.lit.; circ. 150,000. **Indexed:** PMR.

780.7   GW   ISSN 0936-2940
HOCHSCHULE FUER MUSIK KOELN. JOURNAL. 1982. s-a. free. Hochschule fuer Musik Koeln, Dagobertstr. 38, 5000 Cologne, Germany. TEL 0221-124033. FAX 0221-131204. Ed. Franz Mueller-Heuser. adv.
Description: Music and reports on the school and the world of musicology and teaching methods.

HOLIDAYS AT THE KINDERGARTEN. see *CHILDREN AND YOUTH — For*

780   UK
HOME KEYBOARD REVIEW. 1985. m. £14.50 (foreign £16.50). Music Maker Publications Ltd., Alexander House, Forehill, Ely, Cambs CB7 4AF, England. TEL 0353-665577. FAX 0353-662489. (U.S. addr.: Music Maker Publications, Inc., 22024 Lassen St., Ste. 118, Chatsworth, CA 91311) Ed. Malcolm Harrison. circ. 20,000.

780   UK
HOME ORGANIST & KEYBOARD UPDATE.* 1977. m. 90p. Northern & Shell Publications, Northern & Shell Bldg, P.O. Box 381, Millharbour, London E14 9TW, England. adv.; bk.rev.; circ. 25,000.
Formerly: Home Organist and Leisure Music.

780.7   US   ISSN 0046-7928
ML1
HORN CALL. 1971. s-a. $25. International Horn Society, 2227 Gershwin Dr., P.O. Box 1724, Durant, OK 74702. TEL 405-924-5859. FAX 405-924-7313. Ed. Paul Mansur. adv.; bk.rev.; index; circ. 3,000. (also avail. in looseleaf format; back issues avail.) **Indexed:** Music Artic.Guide.
Description: Covers reviews, horn, new music, recordings, history, biography, and research at all educational levels.

786 US
HORN CALL ANNUAL. a. $25 (membership). International Horn Society, c/o Ellen Powley, Exc. Secretary, 2220 N. 140 E., Provo, UT 84604. TEL 801-377-3026.
 Description: Covers detailed and scholarly research studies pertaining to the horn.
 Refereed Serial

780.42 US
HOT!. 1983. irreg. $21.95. Pilot Communications, Inc., 831 Federal Rd., Box 304, Brookfield, CT 06804. TEL 203-775-0190. FAX 203-775-1931. (And: 25 W. 39th St., New York, NY 10018. TEL 212-302-2626) Ed. Susan Freeman. adv.; circ. 134,759.
 Former titles (until 1990): Smash Hits (ISSN 0899-9392); Star Hits (ISSN 8750-7234)

780 US
HOT LINE NEWS. 1980. bi-m. membership. Musicians National Hot Line Association, 277 E. 6100 S., Salt Lake City, UT 84107. Ed. Nancy Zitting. circ. 1,000.
 Description: Helps musicians find bands and helps bands find musicians and gigs.

780.43 US
HOUSTON SYMPHONY MAGAZINE. 1914. 10/yr. (Houston Symphony Orchestra) A R C Communications, Inc., 5615 Kirby Dr., Ste. 600, Houston, TX 77005. TEL 713-524-3000. FAX 713-524-8213.
 Description: Contains program notes for the month's concerts, biographies, interviews, history, social events, corporate sponsor articles, symphony and city news.

780 CC
HUANG ZHONG. (Text in Chinese) q. Wuhan Yiyue Xueyuan, No. 255, Jiefang Lu, Wuchang, Wuhan, Hubei 430060, People's Republic of China. TEL 872026. Ed. Kuang Xuefei.

780 CS ISSN 0323-1283
ML5
HUDEBNI NASTROJE. (Summaries in English, German, Russian) 1964. bi-m. 30 Kcs.($22.10) Ceskoslovenske Hudebni Nastroje, Skroupova 9, 501 97 Hradec Kralove, Czechoslovakia. TELEX 194-260. (Subscr. to: Artia, Ve Smeckach 30, 111 27 Prague 1, Czechoslovakia) Ed. Vaclav Korbel. adv.; bk.rev.; bibl.; charts; illus.; index; circ. 3,000. (also avail. in microfilm) **Indexed:** RILM.
 Description: Devoted to researching, developing and using musical instruments. Deals with acoustics, musicology and musical pedagogy.

780 CS ISSN 0018-6996
HUDEBNI ROZHLEDY. 1948. m. 120 Kcs. Asociace Hudebnich Umelcu a Vedcu, Maltezske nam. 1, 118 00 Prague 1, Czechoslovakia. TEL 0422-312-1366. (Dist. by: PNS, zav.01, Administrace Vyvozu Tisku, Kovpakova 26, 160 00 Prague 6, Czechoslovakia) Ed. Jan Smolik. adv.; bk.rev.; bibl.; illus.; index; circ. 4,000. **Indexed:** Music Ind., RILM.

780 CS ISSN 0018-7003
ML5
HUDEBNI VEDA/MUSICOLOGY. (Text mainly in Czech; summaries in English, German, Russian) 1964. q. DM.141. (Czechoslovak Academy of Sciences, Institute of Theory and History of Arts, Section of Musicology) Academia, Publishing House of the Czechoslovak Academy of Sciences, Vodickova 40, 112 29 Prague 1, Czechoslovakia. TEL 26-63-92. (Dist. in Western countries by: Kubon & Sagner, P.O. Box 34 01 08, 8000 Munich 34, Germany) bk.rev.; rec.; rev.; bibl.; illus.; index. **Indexed:** Arts & Hum.Cit.Ind., CERDIC, Curr.Cont., Music Ind., RILM.
 Description: Deals with various branches of the musical sciences, e.g., the history of music, aesthetics and musical theory as well as the musical sociology and popular music.

780 CS
HUDOBNY ARCHIV. (Text in Slovak; summaries also in German and Russian) 1974. irreg. price varies. Matica Slovenska, Archiv Literatury a Umenia, Ul. Novomeskeho 32, 036 52 Martin, Czechoslovakia. TEL 31371. FAX 0842-324-54. TELEX 075331. Eds. Emanuel Muntag, Eleonora Oravcova.

781.57 780.42 CS
HUDOBNY ZIVOT. s-m. $60. (Slovkoncert) Obzor, Ceskoslovenskej Armady 35, 815 85 Bratislava, Czechoslovakia. **Indexed:** RILM.

780 NE ISSN 0018-7097
HUISMUZIEK. 1951. bi-m. fl.70. Vereniging voor Muziek en Instrumentenbouw, Huismusiek, Utrechtsestraat 77, P.O. Box 350, 3400 AJ Ijsselstein, Netherlands. TEL 03408-85678. FAX 03408-70028. Ed. D.J. Horringa. adv.; bk.rev.; illus.; circ. 6,500.
 Description: Covers music history, building of musical instruments, music interpretation, music making, musicians, association news, and reports of music events. Includes list of courses and activities, classified adds.

780 HU ISSN 0238-9401
ML248
HUNGARIAN MUSIC QUARTERLY. (Text in English) 1970. q. $13.50. (Ministry of Culture) Editio Musica Budapest, Vorosmarty ter 1, P.O. Box 80, 1366 Budapest 5, Hungary. FAX 138-2732. TELEX 225500. Ed. Antal Boronkay. adv.; bk.rev.; circ. 5,000.
 Formerly (until 1989): Hungarian Music News (ISSN 0441-5973)

786 US ISSN 0191-6785
HURDY GURDY. 1972. 4/yr. $18. Amateur Organists & Keyboard Association International, 6436 Penn Ave., S., Minneapolis, MN 55423. TEL 612-866-0463. Ed. Crane J. Bodine. adv.; illus.; circ. 5,000.

783.9 US ISSN 0018-8271
ML1
HYMN; a journal of congregational song. 1949. q. $35 (membership). Hymn Society in the United States and Canada, Headquarters, Texas Christian University, Box 30854, Fort Worth, TX 76129. TEL 817-921-7608. Ed. David Music. adv.; bk.rev.; index; circ. 3,500. (back issues avail.) **Indexed:** Chr.Per.Ind., Music Artic.Guide, Music Ind., Rel.& Theol.Abstr. (1978-), Rel.Ind.One.

780 UK
HYMN SOCIETY OF GREAT BRITAIN AND IRELAND. 1937. q. £8($16) Hymn Society of Great Britain and Ireland, c/o Re. Michael Garland, St. Nicholas Rectory, Curdworth, Sutton Coldfield, West Midlands B76 9ES, England. TEL 0675-470-384. Ed. Bernard Massey. bk.rev.; rec.rev.; cum.index every 3 yrs.; circ. 228. (back issues avail.)
 Refereed Serial

HYMNOLOGISKE MEDDELELSER; tidsskrift om salmer. see *RELIGIONS AND THEOLOGY — Protestant*

781.57 US ISSN 0098-9487
ML156.9
I A J R C JOURNAL. 1967. q. $10 to libraries; individuals $20. International Association of Jazz Record Collectors, 127 Briarcliff La., Bel Air, MD 21014. FAX 410-638-0497. (Subscr. to: Attn: Murray Slochover, Box 855, Tenafly, NJ 07670) Ed. Phil Oldham. adv.; bk.rev.; circ. 1,450. (back issues avail.) **Indexed:** Music Ind.
 Description: Covers news, reviews and research articles on the subject of jazz music and musicains and related fields of interest to the collector and interested public.

782.1 GW
I B S AKTUELL. 1981. 5/yr. DM.25. Interessenvereins des Bayerische Staatsopernpublikums e.V., Gartenstr. 22, 8000 Munich 40, Germany. TEL 089-3003798. Ed. Helga Schmidt. circ. 850.

780 US
I M A BULLETIN. 1984. bi-m. $40. International MIDI Association, 5316 W. 57th St., Los Angeles, CA 90056. TEL 213-649-6434. FAX 213-215-3880. bk.rev.; circ. 2,500. (back issues avail.)
 Description: Covers all aspects of MIDI: musical instruments and digital interface.

780 US
I T G JOURNAL. 1976. q. $26. International Trumpet Guild, Drawer 2025, Columbia, SC 29202. (Subscr. to: Bryan Goff, School of Music, Florida State University, Tallahasse, FL 32306. TEL 904-385-0639) Ed. Anne F. Hardin. adv.; bk.rev.; abstr.; circ. 5,000. **Indexed:** Music Artic.Guide, Music Ind.
 Formerly: International Trumpet Guild. Journal (ISSN 0363-2849); Incorporates (1974?-1988): International Trumpet Guild. Newsletter (ISSN 0363-2857)

IDOL OF MY HEART ELVIS PRESLEY FAN CLUB NEWSLETTER. see *CLUBS*

MUSIC 3555

780 US
ILLINOIS ENTERTAINER. 1974. m. $25. 101 W. Locust, Fairbury, IL 61739. FAX 312-298-7973. Ed. Michael Harris. adv.; bk.rev.; circ. 80,000.

780.7 US ISSN 0019-2147
ILLINOIS MUSIC EDUCATOR.* vol.30, 1970. 5/yr. membership. Illinois Music Educators Association, R.R. No. 4, Box 68, Murphyside, IL 62966. TEL 618-453-3736. Ed. Charles Taylor. adv.; bk.rev.; illus.; circ. 3,000.
 Description: Presents teaching methods.

780 975 US ISSN 0255-8831
ML85
IMAGO MUSICAE; international yearbook of musical iconography. (Text in English, French, German, Italian) 1984-1990; resumed in 1991. a. price varies. Duke University Press, 6697 College Sta., Durham, NC 27708. TEL 919-684-2173. FAX 919-684-3200. (In Italy: Libreria Musicale Italiana Editrice, P.O. Box 198, 55100 Lucca, Italy. TEL 0538-39-44-64) (Co-publisher: Barenreiter-Verlag Basel) Ed. Tilman Seebass. circ. 2,000. (back issues avail.) **Indexed:** RILM.

781.57 US
IMBAT. 1984. bi-m. $8 to non-members. International Association of Jazz Appreciation, Box 48146, Los Angeles, CA 90048. TEL 213-673-7541. FAX 213-673-0757. Eds. Stuart O'Gilvie, James Luther. adv.; bk.rev.; circ. 5,000 (controlled). (tabloid format; back issues avail.)

780 US
IMPROMTU. 1982. q. U.S. Library of Congress, Research Services, Music Division, Washington, DC 20540. bk.rev.

IN THE GROOVE. see *ANTIQUES*

780 US ISSN 0360-4365
ML1
IN THEORY ONLY. 1975. irreg. $15 (foreign $20). Michigan Music Theory Society, c/o School of Music, University of Michigan, 700 Burton Memorial Tower, Ann Arbor, MI 48109-1270. TEL 313-936-0425. FAX 313-763-5097. Ed. Kristin Y. DeKoster. adv.; bk.rev.; bibl.; charts; illus.; index; circ. 500. (also avail. in microform from UMI; reprint service avail. from UMI) **Indexed:** Music Artic.Guide, Music Ind., RILM.
 —BLDSC shelfmark: 4372.465000.

780 UK ISSN 0951-6220
INCORPORATED SOCIETY OF MUSICIANS YEARBOOK. 1898. a. £20. Incorporated Society of Musicians, 10 Stratford Place, London W1N 9AE, England. TEL 071-629-4413. FAX 071-408-1538. circ. 7,500.
 Formerly: Incorporated Society of Musicians Handbook.
 Description: Reports activities of the society; lists membership in the UK and overseas.

690 UK ISSN 0073-5744
INCORPORATED SOCIETY OF ORGAN BUILDERS. JOURNAL. 1949. irreg. £3.50. Incorporated Society of Organ Builders, Petersfield, Hants GU32 3AT, England. Ed. C.J. Gordon Wells. circ. 400.

780 II ISSN 0019-5995
ML5
INDIAN MUSIC JOURNAL; devoted to general reader and student. (Text in English, Tamil, and Sanskrit; summaries in English) 1964. a. Rs.25($9) Tyaga Bharati Music Education Mission, Melkote-571 431, India. Ed. Sri Rama Bharati. adv.; bk.rev.; charts; illus.; circ. 1,300.

780 II ISSN 0251-012X
ML5
INDIAN MUSICOLOGICAL SOCIETY. JOURNAL. 1970. s-a. $12.50. Indian Musicological Society, Jambu Bet, Dandia Bazar, Baroda 390 001, India. TEL 555388. Ed. Prof. R.C. Mehta. adv.; bk.rev.; circ. 1,000. (also avail. in microform from UMI; reprint service avail. from UMI) **Indexed:** Arts & Hum.Cit.Ind., Curr.Cont., Music Ind., RILM.
 Formerly: Sangeet Kala Vihar (ISSN 0036-4320)

INDIAN RECORDS; film, classical, popular. see *SOUND RECORDING AND REPRODUCTION*

MUSIC

780 US ISSN 0742-2490
INDIANA DIRECTORY OF MUSIC TEACHERS. 1941. a. $16 (educators $12). Indiana University, School of Music, Music Education Department, Bloomington, IN 47405. TEL 812-855-2051. Ed. Joe R. Casar. index; circ. 220.
   Description: Lists faculties-teachers of music at Indiana public and parochial schools, colleges and universities, and state schools and hospitals. Addresses and telephone numbers included.

780.7 US ISSN 0273-9933
INDIANA MUSICATOR. 1945. q. $15 to non-members. Indiana Music Educators Association, Ball State University, School of Music, Muncie, IN 47306. TEL 317-285-5496. adv.; bk.rev.; circ. 2,000. **Indexed:** Music Artic.Guide.

780.7 US ISSN 0271-8022
MT6
INDIANA THEORY REVIEW. 1977. 2/yr. $10. Indiana University, School of Music, Graduate Theory Association, Bloomington, IN 47405. TEL 812-855-0168. Ed. Clair Wallarab. bk.rev.; abstr.; charts; circ. 175. (back issues avail.) **Indexed:** Music Ind., RILM.
   —BLDSC shelfmark: 4431.870000.
   Description: Articles on music theory.

780.904 NE
INFORMATIEBLAD 2112. q. fl.15. 2112 Productions, Postbus 906, 6800 AX Arnhem, Netherlands. adv.; bk.rev.; circ. 300.

INFORMAZIONI E STUDI VIVALDIANI. see *BIOGRAPHY*

780 AU
INNSBRUCKER BEITRAEGE ZUR MUSIKWISSENSCHAFT. 1977. irreg. price varies. Edition Helbling KG, Kaplanstr. 9, Postfach 416, A-6021 Innsbruck Neu Rum, Austria. Ed. Walter Salmen. charts; illus.; index.

781.7 US
INSIDE BLUEGRASS. 1974. m. $15. Minnesota Bluegrass and Old Time Music Association, Box 11419, Saint Paul, MN 55111-0419. TEL 612-378-0377. Ed. William Nicholson. adv.; bk.rev.; circ. 800. (back issues avail.)

200 US
INSIDE MUSIC; excellence in Christian music. Short title: I M. (Supplement avail.) vol.2, 1990. m. Strang Communications Company, 600 Rinehart Rd., Lake Mary, FL 32746. TEL 407-333-0600. FAX 407-333-9753. Ed. Suzanne Schwalb. adv.; music rev.; circ. 100,000.

780 CN
INSIDE TRACKS. bi-m. 93 Goulding Ave., N. York, Ont. M2M 1L3, Canada. TEL 416-229-9213. Ed. Stephen Hubbard. circ. 5,000 (controlled).

780 IT ISSN 0073-8611
INSTITUTA ET MONUMENTA. SERIE I: MONUMENTA. 1954. irreg. vol.7, 1973. price varies. (Universita degli Studi di Pavia, Scuola di Paleografia e Filologia Musicale) Fondazione "Claudio Monteverdi", Via Ugolani Dati 4, 26100 Cremona, Italy. TEL 372-26580.

780 IT ISSN 0392-629X
INSTITUTA ET MONUMENTA. SERIE II: INSTITUTA. 1969. irreg., vol.12, 1989. price varies. (Universita degli Studi di Pavia, Scuola di Paleografia e Filologia Musicale) Fondazione "Claudio Monteverdi", Via Ugolani Dati 4, 26100 Cremona, Italy. TEL 0372-26580. circ. 500 (controlled).

781.5 US
INSTITUTE FOR STUDIES IN AMERICAN MUSIC. MONOGRAPHS. 1973. irreg., no.32, 1991. price varies. Institute for Studies in American Music, Conservatory of Music, Brooklyn College, City University of New York, Brooklyn, NY 11210. TEL 718-780-5655. FAX 718-951-6140. Ed. H. Wiley Hitchcock.

780 US ISSN 0145-8396
ML28.B81
INSTITUTE FOR STUDIES IN AMERICAN MUSIC. NEWSLETTER. Short title: I S A M Newsletter. 1971. s-a. free. Institute for Studies in American Music, Conservatory of Music, Brooklyn College, City University of New York, Brooklyn, NY 11210. TEL 718-780-5655. FAX 718-951-6140. Ed. H. Wiley Hitchcock. adv.; bk.rev.; bibl.; circ. 4,200. **Indexed:** Music Artic.Guide.
   —BLDSC shelfmark: 6107.390500.

INSTITUTO BRASIL - ESTADOS UNIDOS. BOLETIM. see *EDUCATION*

780.7 US ISSN 0020-4331
INSTRUMENTALIST; a magazine for school and college band and orchestra directors, professional instrumentalists, teacher-training specialists in instrumental music education and instrumental teachers. 1946. m. $22. Instrumentalist Co., 200 Northfield Rd., Northfield, IL 60093-3390. TEL 708-446-5000. Ed. Jack Zimmerman. adv.; bk.rev.; rec.rev.; illus.; index, cum.index; circ. 20,000. **Indexed:** Educ.Ind., Jun.High.Mag.Abstr., Music Artic.Guide, Music Ind., RILM.
   —BLDSC shelfmark: 4528.900000.

780 GW ISSN 0936-014X
INSTRUMENTENBAU REPORT; aktuelle Informationen fuer Musikfreunde und Instrumentenbauer. 1984. s-a. DM.15.60 for 3 nos. Laerchenstr. 23, 8011 Zorneding, Germany. TEL 08106-22476. Ed. Wilhelm Erlewein. adv.; bk.rev.; circ. 1,200. (back issues avail.)

780 PL
INSTRUMENTY OD A DO Z. 1966. irreg. price varies. Polskie Wydawnictwo Muzyczne, Al. Krasinskiego 11a, 31-111 Krakow, Poland. TEL 22-70-44. FAX 22-01-74.
   Description: Series about musical instruments: their history, description, sound properties, orchestral use.

780 100 US
INTEGRAL. 1987. a. $12 to individuals (foreign $16); institutions $16 (foreign $20). c/o Elizabeth Sayrs, Eastman School of Music, 26 Gibbs St., Rochester, NY 14604. Eds. Gerald Krumbholz, Yayoi Uno. bk.review. **Indexed:** Music Artic.Guide.

780 US ISSN 0195-6655
INTER-AMERICAN MUSIC REVIEW. s-a. $16. Theodore Front Musical Literature, 16122 Cohasset St., Van Nuys, CA 91406. TEL 818-994-1902. FAX 818-994-0419. Ed. Robert Stevenson. bk.rev.; bibl.; illus.; circ. 500. **Indexed:** Curr.Cont, Music Ind., RILM.
   —BLDSC shelfmark: 4531.891530.

780 NE ISSN 0303-3902
ML5 CODEN: IFCEBC
INTERFACE; journal of new music research. (Text in English, French and German) 1972. 4/yr. $180. Swets Publishing Service (Subsidiary of: Swets en Zeitlinger B.V.), Heereweg 347, 2161 CA Lisse, Netherlands. TEL 31-2521-35111. FAX 31-2521-15888. TELEX 41325. (Dist. in N. America by: Swets & Zeitlinger, Box 517, Berwyn, PA 19312. TEL 215-644-4944) Ed.Bd. bk.rev.; bibl.; charts; circ. 500. (also avail. in microform from SWZ; reprint service avail. from SWZ) **Indexed:** Music Ind., Sci.Abstr.
   —BLDSC shelfmark: 4533.440000.
   Formed by the merger of: Electronic Music Reports; Instituut voor Psychoakoestiek en Elektronische Muziek. Jaarboek.

781.57 US
INTERMISSION (BUENA PARK). 1968. m. $6 (non-musicians $15). New Orleans Jazz Club of Southern California, Box 15212, Long Beach, CA 90815. Ed. Norman Burnham. adv.; bk.rev.; circ. 400-600. (back issues avail.)
   Description: Preservation and education of Dixieland jazz. Information on scheduled jazz shows and places to perform jazz music.

780 US
INTERNATIONAL ALBAN BERG SOCIETY NEWSLETTER. 1968. a. $10 to individuals; libraries $15; students $6. International Alban Berg Society, Ph.D. Program in Music, City University of New York, 33 W. 42 St., New York, NY 10036. TEL 212-642-2389. Ed. Joan Allen Smith. circ. 300. (back issue avail.) **Indexed:** RILM.

780 US ISSN 0272-2062
INTERNATIONAL BANJO.* 1980. q. $16. International Banjo, Inc., 3431 Snowbell Ct., Orlando, FL 32810-2970. Ed. Pat Terry, Jr. adv.; bk.rev.; charts; illus.; tr.lit.; circ. 2,000.

781.57
INTERNATIONAL BLUEGRASS. 1985. bi-m. $20. International Bluegrass Music Association, 326 St. Elizabeth St., Owensboro, KY 42301. TEL 502-684-9025. FAX 502-926-4404. Ed. Dan Hays. bk.rev.; circ. 3,500. (back issues avail.)
   Description: Business news for the bluegrass music industry.

784 US ISSN 0896-0968
INTERNATIONAL CHORAL BULLETIN. (Text in English, French, German, Spanish) 1981. q. $25 to individuals; libraries $15. International Federation for Choral Music, University of Illinois at Chicago, Dept. of Music, Box 4348, Chicago, IL 60680. TEL 312-996-8714. FAX 312-996-0954. Ed. Jean-Claude Wilkens. adv.; bk.rev.; circ. 1,200. (back issues avail.) **Indexed:** Music Artic.Guide.
   Description: Articles dealing with choral music and choral activities throughout the world. Lists festivals, workshops and competitions.

780 IT
INTERNATIONAL CONGRESS OF VERDI STUDIES. PROCEEDINGS.. (Text in English, French, German, Italian, Spanish) irreg. price varies. Istituto Nazionale di Studi Verdiani, Strada della Repubblica 56, 43100 Parma, Italy. TEL 0521-286044. FAX 0521-287949.

781.7 US ISSN 0739-1390
ML26
INTERNATIONAL COUNCIL FOR TRADITIONAL MUSIC. BULLETIN. (Text in English, French and German) 1948. s-a. $35. International Council for Traditional Music, c/o Department of Music, Columbia University, New York, NY 10027. TEL 212-678-0332. FAX 212-749-0397. TELEX 220094 COLU UR. Ed. Dieter Christensen. circ. 1,300. (back issues avail.) **Indexed:** A.I.C.P., RILM.
   Formerly (until 1981): International Folk Music Council. Bulletin (ISSN 0020-6768)

781.7 SW
INTERNATIONAL FOLK MUSIC COUNCIL. INTERNATIONALE ARBEITSTAGUNG DER STUDY GROUP ON FOLK MUSICAL INSTRUMENTS. (Supplement to: Musikhistoriska Museets Skrifter) 6th, 1977. irreg. $57. Almqvist & Wiksell International, Box 638, S-101 28 Stockholm, Sweden. Ed. Erich Stockmann. illus.

786 US
INTERNATIONAL HORN SOCIETY. DIRECTORY. a. $25 (membership). International Horn Society, c/o Ellen Powley, Exe. Secretary, 2220 N. 1400 E., Provo, UT 84604. TEL 801-377-3026.

786 US
INTERNATIONAL HORN SOCIETY. NEWSLETTER. q. $25 (membership). International Horn Society, c/o Ellen Powley, Exe. Secretary, 2220 N. 1400 E., Provo, UT 84604. TEL 801-377-3026.
   Description: Keeps members informed of immediate horn news and activities.

780 GW ISSN 0723-9769
INTERNATIONAL JOSEPH MARTIN KRAUS-GESELLSCHAFT. MITTEILUNGEN. 1983. irreg. membership. Internationale Joseph Martin Kraus-Gesellschaft e.V., Kellereistr. 25, Postfach 1422, 6967 Buchen, Germany. TEL 06281-8898. bk.rev.

780.7 UK ISSN 0255-7614
INTERNATIONAL JOURNAL OF MUSIC EDUCATION. (Abstracts in French, German, and Spanish) 1967. s-a. $12 (typically set in Jan.). International Society for Music Education, University of Reading, Music Education Centre, Bulmershe Court, Reading RG6 1HY, England. TEL 0734-318846. FAX 0734-352080. Eds. Jack Dobbs, Anthony Kemp. adv.; bk.rev.; music rev.; illus.; circ. 2,500. (also avail. in microform from UMI; microfiche from KTO; back issues avail.; reprint service avail. from UMI) **Indexed:** Aus.Educ.Ind., Cont.Pg.Educ., Music Ind., RILM.
   Formerly (until 1983): Australian Journal of Music Education (ISSN 0004-9484)
   Description: Reports on various aspects of music education throughout the world.

MUSIC

780.6 US ISSN 0748-5735
INTERNATIONAL LEAGUE OF WOMEN COMPOSERS. NEWSLETTER. 1975. 3/yr. $20 to individuals; students and senior citizens $10; institutions $30. International League of Women Composers, c/o Elizabeth Hayden Pizer, Box 670, S. Shore Rd., Pr. Peninsula, NY 13693. TEL 315-649-5086. Ed. Mary Chaves. adv.; bk.rev.; illus.; circ. 400. (looseleaf format; back issues avail.) **Indexed:** Music Artic.Guide.
Description: Promotes serious concert music composed by women. Informs readers of activities, opportunities, and events.

331.8 780 US ISSN 0020-8051
ML1
INTERNATIONAL MUSICIAN. 1901. m. $20 to non-members. American Federation of Musicians of the United States and Canada, 1501 Broadway, New York, NY 10036. TEL 212-869-1330. FAX 212-764-6134. Ed. Stephen R. Sprague. adv.; bk.rev.; illus.; circ. 180,000. (tabloid format; also avail. in microform from UMI; reprint service avail. from UMI) **Indexed:** Music Artic.Guide, Music Ind., PMR.

780 UK
INTERNATIONAL MUSICIAN & RECORDING WORLD.* 1975. m. £1. Northern & Shell Publications, Northern & Shell Bldg., P.O. Box 381, MillHarbour, London E14 9TW, England. Ed. Pavi Ashford. adv.; bk.rev.; circ. 55,000.

780.65 IT
INTERNATIONAL RECORDS NEWS. (Text in English) 1982. m. L.30000($35) Fini Editions, 18 Via Monte Battaglia, 40046 Inola, Italy. Ed. Francesco Fini. bibl.; charts.

780 CI ISSN 0351-5796
INTERNATIONAL REVIEW OF THE AESTHETICS AND SOCIOLOGY OF MUSIC. (Text in English, French, German; summaries in English and Croatian) 1970. s-a. $28. Muzicka Akademija u Zagrebu, Muzikoloski Zavod, Berlislaviceva 16, 41001 Zagreb, Croatia. Ed. Ivo Supicic. adv.; bk.rev.; bibl.; circ. 1,250. (reprint service avail. from SWZ) **Indexed:** Curr.Cont., Music Ind., RILM.
—BLDSC shelfmark: 4545.980000.
Formerly: International Review of Music Aesthetics and Sociology (ISSN 0047-1208)

INTERNATIONAL SINATRA SOCIETY NEWSLETTER. see *CLUBS*

780 US ISSN 0892-0532
ML920
INTERNATIONAL SOCIETY OF BASSISTS. JOURNAL. 1982. 3/yr. $30 (foreign $35). International Society of Bassists, 4020 McEwen, No. 105, Dallas, TX 75244. TEL 214-233-9107. Ed. David Bjur. adv.; bk.rev.; bibl.; illus.; circ. 1,600. **Indexed:** Music Artic.Guide.
Formed by the 1982 merger of: International Society of Bassists. Newsletter; Bass World; Which was formerly: Probas.

790 US
INTERNATIONAL SOCIETY OF PERFORMING ARTS ADMINISTRATORS. FORUM. vol.9, 1984. bi-m. $25. International Society of Performing Arts Administrators, Inc., 6065 Pickerel Dr., Rockford, MI 49341. TEL 616-874-6200. FAX 616-874-5723. Dir. Michael C. Hardy. adv.; bk.rev.; circ. 500. (back issues avail.; reprint service avail. from ISI,UMI)
Formerly: Performing Arts Forum (ISSN 0739-1161); **Supersedes:** I S P A A Bulletin; (1949-19??): International Association of Concert and Festival Managers. Bulletin.
Description: Covers member news, arts update and ISPAA conference and congress reports

780 US ISSN 0145-3513
ML1
INTERNATIONAL TROMBONE ASSOCIATION. JOURNAL. 1971. 3/yr. $20. International Trombone Association, Music Department, North Texas State University, TX 76203. Ed. Vern Kagarice. adv.; bk.rev.; circ. 3,500. **Indexed:** Music Ind.
Formerly (until 1981): International Trombone Association. Newsletter.

780 US ISSN 0363-5708
INTERNATIONAL TROMBONE ASSOCIATION SERIES. irreg. Brass Press, c/o RKMS, 28 Main St., N. Easton, MA 02356. FAX 508-238-2571. Ed. Stephen L. Glover.

787 US
INTERNATIONAL VIOLIN AND GUITAR MAKERS ASSOCIATION. JOURNAL. 1958-1978; resumed 1980. a. $10. International Violin and Guitar Makers Association, c/o Bill Reid, Ed., 4459 Olive Ave., Long Beach, CA 90807. adv.; bk.rev.; illus.; tr.lit.; circ. 1,200.

780 UK ISSN 0307-2894
INTERNATIONAL WHO'S WHO IN MUSIC AND MUSICIANS' DIRECTORY. 1935. triennial. price varies. Melrose Press Ltd., 3 Regal Lane, Soham, Ely, Cambridgeshire CB7 5BA, England. TEL 0353-721091. FAX 0353-721839. (Dist. in U.S. by: International Publication Services, Taylor-Francis, Inc., 1900 Frost Rd., Ste.101, Bristol, PA 19007-1598) **Indexed:** Child.Auth.& Illus., Perf.Arts Biog.Master Ind.
Formerly: Who's Who in Music and Musicians' International Directory (ISSN 0083-9647)

780 AU ISSN 0020-9325
INTERNATIONALE STIFTUNG MOZARTEUM. MITTEILUNGEN. 1952. s-a. S.300. Internationale Stiftung Mozarteum, Schwarzstr. 26, A-5020 Salzburg, Austria. TEL 0662-88940-10. FAX 0662-882419. Ed. Rudolph Angermueller. adv.; bk.rev.; illus.; index; circ. 2,000. **Indexed:** Music Ind., RILM.
Description: Features historical and musical information, reviews and analysis of his works, Mozart's contemporaries, foundation news, and news of Mozart societies. Includes announcement of events and exhibitions.

780.6 GW ISSN 0579-8353
INTERVALLE; A M J Informationen. s-a. Arbeitskreis Musik in der Jugend, Adersheimer Str. 60, 3340 Wolfenbuettel, Germany. TEL 05331-46016. FAX 05331-43723. Ed. Rolf Pasdzierny. adv.; bk.rev. (back issues avail.)
Description: Reports on the activities of the Arbeitskreis.

780.7 US ISSN 0021-0609
IOWA MUSIC EDUCATOR. 1946? 3/yr. $9. Iowa Music Educators Association, c/o Dorothy McDonald, Ed., School of Music, University of Iowa, Iowa City, IA 52242. adv.; bk.rev.; tr.lit.; circ. 1,400.

780 IE
IRISH FOLK MUSIC STUDIES. 1972. irreg. £3. Folk Music Society of Ireland, 15 Herietta St., Dublin 1, Ireland. Ed. Hugh Shields. adv.; bk.rev.; bibl.; circ. 1,000. **Indexed:** RILM.

781.7 793.31 US
IRISH MUSIC AND DANCE ASSOCIATION NEWSLETTER. (Text in English, Gaelic) 1983. m. $10. Irish Music and Dance Association, Box 65187, St. Paul, MN 55165. TEL 612-721-7452. Ed. Sean T. Kelly. circ. 225. (looseleaf format)

780 791.43 US
ISLAND - EAR. 1978. bi-w. $48. Island - Ear Inc., Box 309, Island Park, NY 11558. TEL 516-889-6045. FAX 516-889-5513. Ed. Arie Nadboy. adv.; circ. 32,000. (tabloid format; back issues avail.)
Description: Provides articles on music, movies, comedy and videos.

ISLENSK HLJODRITASKRA/BIBLIOGRAPHY OF ICELANDIC SOUND RECORDINGS. see *BIBLIOGRAPHIES*

781.7 IS ISSN 0334-2026
ISRAEL STUDIES IN MUSICOLOGY. 1978. irreg. $15. Israel Musicology Society, P.O. Box 503, Jerusalem, Israel. bk.rev.; circ. 1,000. **Indexed:** RILM.
—BLDSC shelfmark: 4583.915500.

783 IT
ISTITUTO DI MUSICA "VINCENZO AMATO". QUADERNI; teologia,filologia ed estetica nella musica sacra. 1985. irreg. Istituto di Musica "Vincenzo Amato", Via SS. Salvatore, No.1, 90134 Palermo, Italy. TEL 091-323392. Ed. Gino Lo Galbo.
Description: Contains a collection of didactic and cultural initiatives unfolded in the course of each year of musical activity. Also publishes contributions from institutions that research and perform music.

780 US
J A L S. 1977. 2/yr. $25 to institutions. American Liszt Society, c/o Virginia Tech, Music Department, Blacksburg, VA 24061. Ed. Michael Saffle. adv.; bk.rev.; abstr.; bibl.; circ. 550. (also avail. in microform from UMI; reprint service avail. from UMI,ISI) **Indexed:** Amer.Bibl.Slavic & E.Eur.Stud, Music Artic.Guide, Music Ind., RILM.
Formerly: American Liszt Society. Journal (ISSN 0147-4413)

782.1 GW
JAHRBUCH DER BAYERISCHEN STAATSOPER. 1959. a. DM.28. (Gesellschaft zur Foerderung der Muenchner Opernfestspiele) F. Bruckmann Munich, Verlag und Druck GmbH, Nymphenburger Str. 86, 8000 Munich 2, Germany. TEL 089-1257322. circ. 5,000. (back issues avail.)

JAHRBUCH FUER LITURGIK UND HYMNOLOGIE. see *RELIGIONS AND THEOLOGY*

780 398 GW ISSN 0075-2703
ML5
JAHRBUCH FUER MUSIKALISCHE VOLKS- UND VOELKERKUNDE. 1968. irreg. price varies. (Freie Universitaet Berlin, Vergleichende Musikwissenschaft) Baerenreiter Verlag, Heinrich-Schuetz-Allee 31-37, 3500 Kassel-Wilhelmshoehe, Germany. TEL 0561-3105-0. Ed. Josef Kuckertz. **Indexed:** A.I.C.P., RILM.

782 GW ISSN 0724-8156
ML1699
JAHRBUCH FUER OPERNFORSCHUNG. (Text in English, French, and German) 1985. a. DM.49. Verlag Peter Lang, Eschborner Landstr. 42-50, 6000 Frankfurt a.M. 90, Germany. TEL 069-7807050.

784.4 398 GW ISSN 0075-2789
ML3630
JAHRBUCH FUER VOLKSLIEDFORSCHUNG. 1928. a. price varies. (Deutsches Volksliedarchiv) Erich Schmidt Verlag GmbH & Co. (Bielefeld), Viktoriastr. 44A, Postfach 7330, 4800 Bielefield 1, Germany. TEL 0521-583080. Ed. Rolf Wilhelm Brednich. adv.; bk.rev.; index. (back issues avail.) **Indexed:** Curr.Cont., M.L.A.

780 GW ISSN 0323-8105
ML5
JAHRBUCH PETERS. 1980. a. Verlag C. F. Peters, Kennedyallee 101, Postfach 700906, 6000 Frankfurt a.M. 70, Germany. FAX 069-635401. (U.S. dist. by: C. F. Peters Corp., 373 Park Ave. S., New York, NY 10016) Ed. Eberhard Klemm. **Indexed:** RILM.
—BLDSC shelfmark: 4632.038000.
Supersedes (1973-1977): Deutsches Jahrbuch der Musikwissenschaft (ISSN 0070-4504)

780 US
JAM RAG. 1985. fortn. $36. Jam Rag Press, Box 20076, 573 Meadowdale, Ferndale, MI 48220. TEL 313-542-8090. Ed. Tom Ness. adv.; music rev.; play rev.; circ. 16,000.
Description: For ages 15-40, covers rock bands, politics, environmental issues, and local news.

780 792 JM
JAMAICA PICTORIAL. bi-m. Jam.$15($14) for 12 issues. J. S. M. Press, 121 King St., Kingston, Jamaica.

785 NO
JANITSJARN. bi-m. Bjarne H. Reenskaug A-S, Box 130, 2261 Kirkenaer, Norway. adv.; circ. 6,000.

JAUNA GAITA. see *ART*

781.57 PL ISSN 0021-5600
ML5
JAZZ. 1956. m. $6.60. Krajowe Wydawnictwo Czasopism, Nowakowskiego 14, 00-666 Warsaw, Poland. (Dist. by: Ars Polona - Ruch, Krakowskie Przedmiescie 7, Warsaw, Poland) Ed. Jozef Balcerak. index; circ. 40,000. **Indexed:** RILM.

781.5 SZ
JAZZ. (Text in German) 1968. m. 30 Fr.($10.) Hochuli AG, Box 4132, Muttuez, Switzerland. Ed. Freddy J. Angstman. adv.; bk.rev.; rec.rev.; bibl.; charts; illus.; stat.; index, cum.index; circ. 10,000 (controlled).
Formerly: Jazz - Rhythm and Blues (ISSN 0021-5619)

MUSIC

781.57 US
JAZZ ARCHIVIST. 1986. s-a. Hogan Jazz Archive, Howard-Tilton Memorial Library, Tulane University, New Orleans, LA 70118. TEL 504-865-5688. Ed. Dr. John J. Joyce.

781.57 GW
JAZZ CLUB KARLSRUHE E.V.; termine, veranstaltungen, news. 1985. bi-m. DM.17.50($10) Piduch Verlag, Am Hang 21, 7550 Rastatt 21, Germany. TEL 07222-53514. Ed. Georg Kleinert. adv.; bk.rev.; circ. 8,000.

781.57 AT
JAZZ DOWN UNDER. no.19, 1977. bi-m. Aus.$3.60. Box 202, Camden, N.S.W, 2570, Australia. Ed. Peter Hume. adv.; illus.

780.7 US ISSN 0730-9791
ML1
JAZZ EDUCATORS JOURNAL. 1968. 4/yr. $20 (effective Jul. 1991). International Association of Jazz Educators, Box 724, Manhattan, KS 66502. TEL 913-776-8744. FAX 913-776-6190. Ed. John Kuzmich, Jr. adv.; bk.rev.; film rev.; bibl.; cum.index; circ. 6,000. (back issues avail.) **Indexed:** Music Ind.
Former titles: National Association of Jazz Educators. Newsletter; N A J E Educator (ISSN 0047-8741)

781.57 DK ISSN 0900-064X
JAZZ FESTIVALS AND RELATED MAJOR JAZZ EVENTS. DIRECTORY. biennial. DKK 50. Danish Jazz Center, Borupvej 66 B, DK-4683 Roennede, Denmark.

781.57 PL ISSN 0021-5635
ML3505.8
JAZZ FORUM; the European jazz magazine. (Supplements avail.) (Editions in English, Polish) 1965. bi-m. $18 in Europe; elsewhere $20. For Jazz, Inc., Nowogrodzka 49, 00-695 Warsaw, Poland. TEL 48-22-219451. Ed. Pawel Brodowski. adv.; bk.rev.; rec.rev.; illus.; circ. 10,000 (Eng.ed.), 12,000 (Polish ed.). (also avail. in microform from UMI; back issues avail.; reprint service avail. from UMI) **Indexed:** Music Ind.

781.57 FR ISSN 0021-5643
ML5
JAZZ HOT; la revue internationale de jazz. 1934. 11/yr. 350 F. (effective 1992). Jazz Hot Publications, 191 rue des Pyrenees, B.P. 405, 75969 Paris Cedex 20, France. TEL 43-66-74-88. FAX 43-66-72-60. Ed. Yves Sportis. adv.; rec.rev.; illus. **Indexed:** Music Ind.

781.57 UK
JAZZ IN THE MIDLANDS. 1984. q. £7.50. (Jazz Central) Jazz Central Ltd., 29/30 Guildhall Buildings, Navigation Street, Birmingham B2 4BT, England. TEL 0 273 571536. Ed. Alan James. adv.; circ. 15,000. (back issues avail.)
Description: Features news of tours, festivals, workshops, performances, record reviews and competitions. Also contains performance guide for local jazz music.

781.57 658.048 US ISSN 8756-6540
JAZZ INTERACTIONS. 1965. s-m. $25. Jazz Interactions, Inc., Box 268, Glen Oaks, NY 11004. TEL 718-465-7500. Ed. R. Neufeld. adv.; circ. 300. (back issues avail.)
Description: Comprehensive listing of jazz clubs and artists in NYC and its vicinity. Includes information on free summer jazz park concerts.

781.57 UK ISSN 0140-2285
ML5
JAZZ JOURNAL INTERNATIONAL. 1948. m. £27($55) (foreign £33). Jazz Journal Ltd., 113-117 Farringdon Rd., London EC1R 3BT, England. TEL 071-278-0631. FAX 071-833-5720. Ed. Eddie Cook. adv.; bk.rev.; rec.rev.; illus.; index; circ. 14,000. (also avail. in microform from UMI; back issues avail.) **Indexed:** Music Ind.
—BLDSC shelfmark: 4663.433400.
Formerly (until April 1977): Jazz Journal (ISSN 0021-5651); Incorporates: Jazz and Blues.
Description: Various issues contain: personal interviews with leading Jazz musicians, career appraisals, discographical information, readers' letters, news previews and reports, of interest to jazz enthusiasts as well as musicians.

781.57 FR ISSN 0021-566X
ML5
JAZZ MAGAZINE. 1954. m. 265 F. (foreign 327 F.). Compagnie Generale d'Edition et de Presse (COGEDIPRESSE), 63 Champs-Elysees, 75008 Paris, France. TEL 33-1-40-74-74-55. FAX 33-1-40-74-74-91. Ed. Philippe Carles. adv.; bk.rev.; rec.rev.; illus.; circ. 25,000. (also avail. in microform from UMI; reprint service avail. from UMI) **Indexed:** Music Ind.

781.57 US
JAZZ NEWSLETTER. m. New Orleans Jazz Club of California, Box 1225, Kerrville, TX 78029. TEL 512-896-2285.

781.57 NE ISSN 0166-7025
JAZZ NU; maandblad voor jazz en geimproviseerde muziek. 1978. m. fl.100. Stichting Jazzonderzoek, Postbus 6072, 7401 JB Deventer, Netherlands. TEL 05700-15233. Ed. Lo Reizevoort. adv.; bk.rev.; illus.; index; circ. 5,000. (back issues avail.)

781.57 SZ
JAZZ PASSION. (Text in French) m. Rue a Ornette, CH-1333 Lussy-sur-Morges, Switzerland. TEL 021-701-1071. (Subscr. to: c/o Catherine Montandon, Rue de l'Industrie 35, CH-1030 Bussigny) adv.; bk.rev.; illus.
Description: Provides festival coverage, interviews and information to jazz fans of Switzerland.

781.57 GW ISSN 0021-5686
ML5
JAZZ PODIUM. 1952. m. DM.46.20 (foreign DM.58.30). Jazz Podium Verlags GmbH, Vogelsangstr. 32, 7000 Stuttgart 1, Germany. TEL 0711-631530. FAX 0711-632893. Ed. Gudrun Endress. adv.; bk.rev.; circ. 11,000. **Indexed:** Music Ind.

781.57 UK ISSN 0021-5716
JAZZ TIMES. 1964. m. membership. British Jazz Society, 10 Southfield Gardens, Twickenham, Middlesex, England. Ed. John G. Boddy. adv.; film rev.; rec.rev.; illus.; circ. 10,000.

781.57 US
JAZZ WORLD. 1972. bi-m $35 includes supplement. World Jazz Society, Box 777, Times Square Sta., New York, NY 10108-0777. TEL 201-939-0836. Ed. Jan A. Byrczek. adv.; bk.rev.; circ. 6,000. (back issues avail.) **Indexed:** Music Ind.
Former titles: Jazz World Index; (until 1981): Jazz Echo (ISSN 0277-5980); (until 1979): Swinging Newsletter.

781.57 GW
JAZZ ZEITUNG. 1976. m. DM.25. Titurelstr. 9, 8000 Munich 81, Germany. TEL 089-983360. FAX 089-981886. Ed. Hans Ruland. adv.; bk.rev.; circ. 7,000.
Description: Jazz portaits, record reviews, information about concerts and musicians in and around Munich.

785.4 AG
JAZZBAND. 1972. bi-m. $7. c/o Alberto Miguel Consiglio, 2291 Yerbal, Buenos Aires, Argentina. adv.; bk.rev.; illus.; circ. 10,000.

780 AU ISSN 0075-3572
ML5
JAZZFORSCHUNG/JAZZ RESEARCH. (Text and summaries in English and German) 1969. a. price varies; free to members. (International Society for Jazz Research) Akademische Druck- und Verlagsanstalt Dr. Paul Struzl, Schoenaugasse 6, A-8010 Graz, Austria. TEL 811096. (Co-sponsors: Hochschule fuer Musik und Institut fuer Jazz Darstellende Kunst) **Indexed:** Music Ind., RILM.
—BLDSC shelfmark: 4663.435500.

781.57 GW ISSN 0021-5724
ML5
DER JAZZFREUND; Mitteilungsblatt fuer Jazzfreunde in Ost und West. 1956. q. DM.21.20. Gerhard Conrad, Von-Stauffenberg-Str. 24, 5750 Menden 1, Germany. TEL 02373-63776. bk.rev.; rec.rev. (processed)

781.57 US
JAZZIZ. 1983. bi-m. $12.95. Jazziz Magazine, Inc., 3620 N.W. 43rd St. Ste. D, Gainesville, FL 32606. TEL 904-375-3705. FAX 904-375-7268. Ed. Michael Fagien. adv.; bk.rev.; circ. 95,000. (reprint service avail.) **Indexed:** Music Artic.Guide.
Description: Focuses on the latest in recorded music spanning all aspects of adult-oriented music. Includes free CDs twice a year.

781.57 973 US ISSN 0890-6440
ML3505.8
JAZZLETTER. 1981. 12/yr. $40 (foreign $50). Box 240, Ojai, CA 93023. TEL 818-646-5332. Ed. Gene Lees. adv.; bk.rev.; cum.index; circ. 2,000. (also avail. in looseleaf format; back issues avail.)
Description: Biographical portraits of major artists, and articles on the evolution and contemporary state of American jazz.

781.57 AT
JAZZLINE. 1975. q. Aus.$3.00 per no. Victorian Jazz Club, P.O. Box 2421v, Melbourne, Vic. 3001, Australia. Ed. Judi Anderson. adv.; bk.rev.; circ. 500.

781.57 US ISSN 8756-6540
JAZZLINE. 1965. s-m. $25. Jazz Interactions, Inc., Box 268, Glen Oaks, NY 11004. TEL 718-465-7500. Ed. R. Neufeld. circ. 250.
Description: Provides information on jazz and jazz events in the New York metropolitan area.

781.57 US
JAZZMEN'S REFERENCE BOOK; Jazz World Direct. 1973. a. $95 to non-members. Jazz World Society, Box 777, Times Square Sta., New York, NY 10108-0777. Ed. Jan Byrczek. adv.; circ. 8,000.

780 SW
JAZZNYTT. 1965. 4/yr. SEK 50. Svenska Jazzriksfoerbundet - Swedish Jazz Federation, P.O. Box 4020, 102 61 Stockholm, Sweden. FAX 8-7022118. adv.; illus.; circ. 13,000.
Formerly: S J R.

781.57 US
JAZZOLOGIST. 1963. irreg. (4-6/yr.). $8. New Orleans Jazz Club of California, Box 1225, Kerrville, TX 78029. TEL 512-896-2285. Ed. Mort Enob. adv.; bk.rev.; rec.rev.; bibl.; circ. 5,000.

781.57 US ISSN 0272-572X
ML1
JAZZTIMES; America's jazz magazine. 1972. 10/yr. $21.95 Canada $35.95; elsewhere $59.95. Jazz Times Inc., 7961 Eastern Ave., Ste. 303, Silver Spring, MD 20910-4898. TEL 301-588-4114. FAX 301-588-5531. Ed. Mike Joyce. adv.; bk.rev.; illus.; circ. 65,000. (also avail. in microform from UMI; reprint service avail. from UMI) **Indexed:** Music Artic.Guide.
Supersedes: Radio Free Jazz (ISSN 0145-5125)
Description: Comprehensive consumer jazz publication covering swing and big band to Brazilian, blues and contemporary jazz.

781 SW ISSN 0345-5653
ML5
JEFFERSON; Scandanavian magazine for blues and related music. 1968. 4/yr. SEK 130. Scandinavian Blues Association, c/o Tommy Loefgren, Zetterlunds Vaag 90 B, 186 51 Vallentuna, Sweden. Ed. Tommy Loefgren. adv.; bk.rev.; bibl.; circ. 2,000.
Description: Contains related music styles like zydeco, rock 'n roll, gospel, and reggae.

781.57 US ISSN 0740-5928
JERSEY JAZZ. 1973. 11/yr. $25. New Jersey Jazz Society, 836 W. Inman Ave., Rahway, NJ 07065. Ed. Warren W. Vache. adv.; bk.rev.; illus.; circ. 1,500 (controlled).
Description: Covers traditional and mainstream jazz.

780 US
JET LAG MAGAZINE. m. $12. 8419 Halls Ferry, St. Louis, MO 63147. TEL 314-383-5841.
Description: Presents articles, interviews and reviews of new records and performance artists. Covers rock, progressive and classical music.

780 CC
JIANGSU YINYUE/JIANGSU MUSIC. (Text in Chinese) m. Jiangsu Wenxue Yishu Jie Lianhehui - Jiangsu Literary and Art Circle Association, 126 Ninghai Lu, Nanjing, Jiangsu 210024, People's Republic of China. TEL 306362. Ed. Xie Hua.

780　　　　　　UK　ISSN 0951-5143
JOCKS. 1986. m. £18($65) Spotlight Publications Ltd., Greater London House, Hampstead Rd., London NW1 7QZ, England. TEL 01-387-6611. (Subscr. to: Royal Sovereign House, 10 Beresford St., London SE18 6BQ, England) Ed. Philip Chapman.

783　　　　　　IE
JOINT COMMITTEE FOR CHURCH MUSIC IN IRELAND. NEWSLETTER. 1977. q. free. Joint Committee for Church Music in Ireland, R.E. Resource Centre, Mount Argus Rd., Dublin 6, Ireland. Ed. David Bedlow. adv.; bk.rev.; circ. 1,000.

780　　　　　　US
JOLSON JOURNAL. 1950. 2/yr. $15. International Al Jolson Society, c/o Michael Modero, 476 Colonial Rd., Roselle Park, NJ 07204. Ed. Harold E. Rhinehart. bk.rev.; illus.; circ. 1,000.

780　　　　　　US
JOLSON JOURNALETTE. q. membership. International Al Jolson Society, c/o Michael Modero, 476 Colonial Rd., Roselle Park, NJ 07204.

780　　　　　　GW　ISSN 0446-9577
JOSEPH HAAS GESELLSCHAFT. MITTEILUNGENSBLATT. 1950. a. membership. Joseph Haas Gesellschaft e.V., Veroneserstr. 4, 8000 Munich 90, Germany. Ed. Siegfried Bissinger. bk.rev.; bibl.; index; circ. 300.

781.7　　　　　　US
JOURNAL FOR ETHNOMUSICOLOGY. 1953. 3/yr. $50 to individuals & institutions $50; students $25. Society for Ethnomusicology, Morrison Hall 005, Indiana University, Bloomington, IN 47405-2051. TEL 812-855-6672. Ed. Jeff Titon. bk.rev.; film rev.; rec.rev.; bibl.; charts; illus.; index, cum.index: vols.1-10, 11-20, 21-30; circ. 2,000. (also avail. in microform from UMI; reprint service avail. from UMI) Indexed: A.I.C.P., Abstr.Anthropol., Amer.Bibl.Slavic & E.Eur.Stud, Arts & Hum.Cit.Ind., Chic.Per.Ind., Curr.Cont.Africa, Curr.Cont., Hum.Ind., Ind.Bk.Rev.Hum., M.L.A., Mid.East: Abstr.& Ind., Music Ind., Ref.Sour., RILM, So.Pac.Per.Ind., SSCI.
　Formerly: Ethnomusicology (ISSN 0014-1836)
　Description: Explores the music of people worldwide.
　Refereed Serial

JOURNAL OF AESTHETICS AND ART CRITICISM. see *ART*

786.067　　　　　　US　ISSN 0021-9207
JOURNAL OF BAND RESEARCH. 1964. s-a. $7. (American Bandmasters Association) Troy State University Press, Troy, AL 36082. TEL 205-670-3259. FAX 205-566-6500. (Co-sponsors: College Band Directors National Association; National Band Association; American School Band Directors Association) Ed. Frankie D. Muller. bk.rev.; abstr.; bibl.; charts; illus.; stat.; cum.index: vols.1-8; circ. 2,000. (also avail. in microform from UMI; reprint service avail. from UMI) Indexed: Arts & Hum.Cit.Ind., Curr.Cont., Music Artic.Guide, Music Ind., RILM.

JOURNAL OF BRITISH MUSIC THERAPY. see *EDUCATION — Special Education And Rehabilitation*

780.01　　　　　　US　ISSN 0092-0517
ML1
JOURNAL OF COUNTRY MUSIC. 1970. 3/yr. $15. Country Music Foundation, Inc., 4 Music Square E., Nashville, TN 37203. TEL 615-256-1639. FAX 615-255-2245. Ed. Paul F. Kingsbury. adv.; bk.rev.; rec.rev, bibl.; circ. 1,300. (back issues avail.) Indexed: Arts & Hum.Cit.Ind., Curr.Cont., M.L.A., RILM.
　Formerly: Country Music Foundation News Letter.
　Description: Presents biographical reviews of performers and their musical development, question-and-answer interviews with performers and music business people, and overview essays on historical development of specific styles of music.

783.02　　　　　　US　ISSN 0197-0100
ML3195
JOURNAL OF JEWISH MUSIC AND LITURGY. (Text in English and Hebrew) 1976. a. $7. Cantorial Council of America, c/o Yeshiva University, 500 W. 185th St., New York, NY 10033. TEL 212-960-5353. Ed. Macy Nulman. bk.rev.; circ. 300.
　Description: Informs the professional and layman of aspects of Jewish music and liturgy from the Biblical period to present.

781　　　　　　US　ISSN 0022-2909
ML1
JOURNAL OF MUSIC THEORY. 1957. s-a. $21 to individuals; institutions $27 (effective Jan. 1990). Yale University, School of Music, New Haven, CT 06520. TEL 203-436-8740. Ed. Martha M. Hyde. adv.; bk.rev.; bibl.; charts; illus.; index; circ. 1,700. (also avail. in microform from MIM,UMI; reprint service avail. from UMI) Indexed: Arts & Hum.Cit.Ind., Curr.Cont., Ind.Bk.Rev.Hum., Music Artic.Guide, Music Ind., RILM, SSCI.

615.837　　　　　　US　ISSN 0022-2917
ML1　　　　　　　CODEN: JMUTA2
JOURNAL OF MUSIC THERAPY.* 1964. q. $24 (foreign $28). National Association for Music Therapy, Inc., 8455 Colesville Rd, K930, Silver Spring, MD 20910-3319. Ed. Richard M. Graham. bk.rev.; charts; illus.; index; circ. 6,000. (also avail. in microform from UMI; reprint service avail. from UMI) Indexed: Arts & Hum.Cit.Ind., Curr.Cont., Educ.Ind., Except.Child Educ.Abstr., Hosp.Lit.Ind., Music Artic.Guide, Music Ind., Psychol.Abstr., RILM.
　—BLDSC shelfmark: 5021.160000.
　Description: Reports research in the area of music therapy and the use of music in treatment and rehabilitation settings.
　Refereed Serial

780.7　　　　　　US　ISSN 0141-1896
ML5
JOURNAL OF MUSICOLOGICAL RESEARCH. 1974. 4/yr. (in 1 vol., 4 nos./vol.). $91. Gordon and Breach Science Publishers, 270 Eighth Ave., New York, NY 10011. TEL 212-206-8900. FAX 212-645-2459. TELEX 236735 GOPUB UR. (Subscr. to: Box 786, Cooper Sta., New York, NY 10276. TEL 800-545-8398; UK subscr. to: P.O. Box 90, Reading, Berkshire RG1 8JL, England. TEL 0734-560-080) Ed. Ralph P. Locke. adv.; bk.rev.; illus. (also avail. in microform from MIM) Indexed: Arts & Hum.Cit.Ind., Br.Hum.Ind., Curr.Cont., Ind.Bk.Rev.Hum., Music Artic.Guide, Phil.Ind., RILM.
　—BLDSC shelfmark: 5021.163000.
　Formerly: Music and Man (ISSN 0306-2082)
　Description: Focuses on study and teaching.
　Refereed Serial

780.01　　　　　　US　ISSN 0277-9269
ML1
JOURNAL OF MUSICOLOGY; a quarterly review of music history, criticism, analysis, and performance practice. 1982. q. $26 to individuals (foreign $32); institutions $52 (foreign $57); students $19 (foreign $24). University of California Press, Journals Division, 2120 Berkeley Way, Berkeley, CA 94720. TEL 510-642-6221. FAX 510-643-7127. Ed. Marian C. Green. adv.; bk.rev.; circ. 1,400. Indexed: Arts & Hum.Cit.Ind., Curr.Cont., Music Artic.Guide, Music Ind., RILM.
　—BLDSC shelfmark: 5021.163700.
　Description: Examines music history, criticism, analysis and performance practice.
　Refereed Serial

780.7　　　　　　US　ISSN 0022-4294
ML1
JOURNAL OF RESEARCH IN MUSIC EDUCATION. 1953. q. $22. (Society for Research in Music Education) Music Educators National Conference, 1902 Association Dr., Reston, VA 22091-1597. TEL 703-860-4000. FAX 703-860-1531. Ed. Rudolf E. Radocy. bibl.; charts; index; circ. 4,000. (also avail. in microform from UMI; reprint service avail. from UMI,KTO) Indexed: Arts & Hum.Cit.Ind., C.I.J.E., Cont.Pg.Educ., Curr.Cont., Educ.Ind., Music Artic.Guide, Music Ind, Psychol.Abstr., RILM, SSCI.
　Description: Covers the study and teaching of music.
　Refereed Serial

784　　　　　　US
JOURNAL OF RESEARCH IN SINGING AND APPLIED VOCAL PEDAGOGY. 1977. s-a. $25 (foreign $30). International Association for Research in Singing, Texas Christian University, Department of Music, Box 32887, Ft. Worth, TX 76129-0001. TEL 817-921-7602. FAX 817-92107333. Ed. Vincent Russo. adv.; bk.rev.; circ. 500. Indexed: Music Artic.Guide, Music Ind., RILM.
　Formerly: Journal of Research in Singing (ISSN 0272-6440)
　Description: Intends to increase the knowledge of the singing voice and the practical application of that knowledge.

780　　　　　　US　ISSN 0364-2216
ML1
JOURNAL OF THE GRADUATE MUSIC STUDENTS AT THE OHIO STATE UNIVERSITY. 1969. irreg., no.6, 1977. Ohio State University, School of Music, 1899 N. College Rd., Columbus, OH 43210. TEL 614-422-6571.

780　　　　　　US
JUBILATION. q. membership. Paul Anka Admiration Society, 2136 Lincoln Ave., Apt. J, Alameda, CA 94501. TEL 415-769-9562.
　Description: News and information on the life and performing career of singer and songwriter Paul Anka.

780　　　　　　IT　ISSN 0022-5711
JUCUNDA LAUDATIO. 1963. q. L.10000. Padri Benedettini, Isola di Giorgio Maggiore, 30124 Venice, Italy. charts.

780.7　　　　　　US
MT4.N3
JUILLIARD JOURNAL; monthly newspaper. 1962. 8/yr. $10 (free to qualified personnel). Juilliard School, Lincoln Center, New York, NY 10023. TEL 212-799-5000. FAX 212-724-0263. Ed. Charissa M. Sgoures. adv.; bk.rev.; illus.; circ. 12,000. (also avail. in microform from UMI; reprint service avail. from UMI) Indexed: Music Artic.Guide.
　Formerly (until 1985): Juilliard News Bulletin (ISSN 0022-6173)

780　　　　　　US
JUILLIARD PERFORMANCE GUIDES. 1983. irreg., no.3 1990. Pendragon Press, R.R. 1, Box 159, Stuyvesant, NY 12173-9720. TEL 518-828-3008. FAX 518-828-2368.

781.57　　　　　　UK
JUKE BLUES. 1985. q. $20. P.O. Box 148, London W9 1DY, England. FAX 44-85-572-4119. (In U.S.: c/o Dick Shurman, 3S 321 Winfield Rd., Warrenville, IL 60555) adv.; bk.rev.; circ. 5,000.
　Description: Continues tradition of British blues journalism.

JUKEBOX COLLECTOR. see *HOBBIES*

780　　　　　　US　ISSN 0022-6629
ML1
JUNIOR KEYNOTES. 1927. 4/yr. $4. National Federation of Music Clubs, 1336 N. Delaware St., Indianapolis, IN 46202. TEL 317-638-4003. Ed. Mary Alice Cox. adv.; bk.rev.; illus.; circ. 6,000.
　Description: Contains organization news.

JUNKANOO. see *THEATER*

780.7　　　　　　US　ISSN 0022-8702
ML1
KANSAS MUSIC REVIEW. 1938. 4/yr. $3 to non-members. Kansas Music Educators Association, Wichita State University, School of Music, Wichita, KS 67208. TEL 316-689-3103. FAX 316-689-3795. Ed. James Hardy. adv.; bk.rev.; illus.; music rev.; circ. 3,000. Indexed: Music Artic.Guide, Music Ind.
　Description: Presents study and teaching methods.

780　　　　　　RU
KAZANSKII GOSUDARSTVENNYI PEDAGOGICHESKII INSTITUT. VOPROSY ISTORII, TEORII MUZYKI I MUZYKAL'NOGO VOSPITANIYA. SBORNIK. 1970. irreg. price varies. Kazanskii Gosudarstvennyi Pedagogicheskii Institut, Ul. Mezjlauk, 1, 420021 Kazan, Russia. Ed.Bd. circ. 600.
　Description: Contains the research of theoretical and historical materials about professional training of the school musical teachers.

780　　　　　　UK
KEMPS INTERNATIONAL MUSIC BOOK. 1965. a. £25. Kemps Publishing Group Ltd., 11 The Swan Courtyard, Charles Edward Rd., Birmingham B26 1BU, England. TEL 021-711-4144. FAX 021-711-2866. TELEX 333786-KEMPSP-G. adv.
　Former titles: Kemps International Music and Recording Industry Yearbook; Kemps International Music and Recording Yearbook; Kemps Music and Record Industry Year Book International (ISSN 0305-7100); Kemps Music and Record Industry Year Book (ISSN 0075-5451)

MUSIC

780   KE
KENYA CONSERVATOIRE OF MUSIC. NEWSLETTER. (Text in English) 1945. irreg. K.150 (typically set in Jan.). Kenya Conservatoire of Music, Box 41343, Nairobi, Kenya. TEL NAIROBI222933. Ed. Trevor Walshaw. circ. 400.
Description: Provides information about the activities of the Kenya Conservatoire of Music, and the musical life of Nairobi.

786   US   ISSN 0735-8660
ML552
KERAULOPHON. 1968. q. $5. Organ Historical Society, Greater New York City Chapter, Box 194, Pepperell, MA 01463. (Subscr. to: Box 104, Harrisville, NH 03450) Ed. John Ogasapian. adv.; bk.rev.; bibl.; circ. 100. (looseleaf format; back issues avail.) **Indexed:** RILM.
Description: Articles, reviews, research queries, notices pertaining to the history of organs and organ building in New York City.

780   UK   ISSN 0262-6624
KERRANG!. w. $104. Spotlight Publications Ltd., Greater London House, Hampstead Rd., London NW1 7QZ, England. TEL 01-387 6611. Ed. Geoff Barton. circ. 67,649.
Description: Covers heavy metal music for young men.

780.42 793   US
KEY & B P M ANNUAL GUIDE TO DANCE MUSIC.* a. $19.95. Time Warp Publishing, 5802 Halbrent Ave., Van Nuys, CA 91411-3024. TEL 818-344-2286. Ed. Joseph Brosta.

780 790.13   US
THE KEY-NOTE (WESTMINSTER). 1960. q. $5. Harmony, Inc., 143 S. Ashburnham Rd., Westminster, MA 01473. TEL 617-874-5817. Ed. Diane A. Lorion. adv.; circ. 2,550. (back issues avail.)

786   AT
KEY VIVE. 1973. q. Aus.$3.50. Australian Society for Keyboard Music, 9 Glenroy Ave., Middle Cove, N.S.W. 2068, Australia. Ed.Bd. adv.; bk.rev.; charts; illus.; circ. 700.

786   US   ISSN 0730-0158
ML1
KEYBOARD; for all keyboard players. 1975. m. $19.97. G P I Publications (Subsidiary of: Miller Freeman, Inc.), 20085 Stevens Creek, Cupertino, CA 95014. TEL 408-446-1105. FAX 408-446-1088. (Subscr. to: Box 58528, Boulder, CO 80322-8528) Ed. Dominic Milano. adv.; bk.rev.; charts; illus.; cum.index; circ. 72,000. (also avail. in microfilm from UMI; reprint service avail. from UMI) **Indexed:** Music Artic.Guide, Music Ind., RILM.
Formerly (until 1981): Contemporary Keyboard (ISSN 0361-5820)
Description: For keyboard musicians of all styles and levels of ability.

786   US   ISSN 0273-9526
KEYBOARD CLASSICS; the magazine you can play. 1981. bi-m. $15.47. Keyboard Classics, Inc., 223 Katonah Ave., Katonah, NY 10536. (Subscr. to: Box 58629, Boulder, CO 80322. Tel.: 800-759-3036) Ed. Stuart Isacoff. adv.; bk.rev.; illus.; circ. 50,000. **Indexed:** Music Artic.Guide, Music Ind.

786   UK   ISSN 0269-3836
KEYBOARD PLAYER;* keyboards, organs, pianos, synthesizers. 1979. m. £15. Bookrose Ltd., 330 Hertford Rd., London N9 7HB, England. Ed. Julie Hahnes. adv.; bk.rev.; circ. 14,500.
Formerly (until 1985): Organ Player and Keyboard Review (ISSN 0144-8331)

786.6   US
KEYBOARD TEACHER. 1964. bi-m. (except Jul. and Aug.). membership. Keyboard Teachers Association International, Inc., 361 Pin Oak Ln., Westbury, NY 11590. circ. 2,000.
Former titles: Organ Teacher; N A O T Notes (ISSN 0027-5948)

786   US   ISSN 0199-3313
ML549
KEYBOARD WORLD.* German edition: Tasten Welt. 1972. m. $14.50. (International Association of Organ Teachers) Keyboard World, Inc., Box 3407, Palm Desert, CA 92260-3407. (Co-sponsor: Young Organists Association International) Ed. Anthony Ramos. adv.; bk.rev.; circ. 18,000. **Indexed:** Music Artic.Guide.
Formerly (until Jan., 1977): Organist.

780   US   ISSN 0199-6657
KICKS. 1979. a. Norton Records, Box 646, Cooper Station, New York, NY 10003. TEL 718-789-4438. FAX 718-398-9215. Eds. Billy Miller, Miriam Linna. adv.; bk.rev.; film rev.; rec.rev.; circ. 6,000.
Description: Covers rock & roll and popular culture.

783   GW   ISSN 0023-1800
ML5
DER KIRCHENCHOR. 1940. bi-m. DM.12. (Verband Evangelischer Kirchenchoere Deutschlands) Baerenreiter Verlag, Heinrich-Schuetz-Allee 31-37, 3500 Kassel-Wilhelmshoehe, Germany. TEL 0561-3105-0. FAX 0561-3105240. (U.S. subscr. addr.: Foreign Music Distributors, 13 Elkay Dr., Chester, NY 10918) Ed. Otto Brodde. adv.; bk.rev.; index; circ. 5,000. **Indexed:** Music Ind.
—BLDSC shelfmark: 5097.337300.

783   GW   ISSN 0174-2116
KIRCHENMUSIKALISCHE MITTEILUNGEN. 1967. q. Amt fuer Kirchenmusik, St. Meinradweg 6, 7407 Rottenburg 1, Germany. TEL 07472-169430. circ. 3,500.

780 200   GW   ISSN 0939-4761
ML5
KIRCHENMUSIKALISCHE NACHRICHTEN. 1950. q. DM.10. Evangelische Kirche in Hessen und Nassau in Frankfurt, Amt fuer Kirchenmusik, Miquelallee 7, 6000 Frankfurt a.M. 90, Germany. TEL 069-2477190. bk.rev.; circ. 1,800.

780   GW   ISSN 0075-6199
KIRCHENMUSIKALISCHES JAHRBUCH. 1876. a. price varies. Allgemeiner Caecilien-Verband, Andreasstr. 9, 8400 Regensburg, Germany. TEL 0941-84339. Ed. Prof. Guenther Massenkeil. bk.rev. **Indexed:** Music Ind., RILM.

783   GW   ISSN 0023-1819
DER KIRCHENMUSIKER. 1950. bi-m. DM.18. (Verband Evangelischer Kirchenmusiker Deutschlands) Verlag Merseburger Berlin GmbH, Motz Str. 13, 3500 Kassel, Germany. Ed. D. Schuberth. adv.; bk.rev.; rec.rev.; illus.; index; circ. 5,600. **Indexed:** RILM.
—BLDSC shelfmark: 5097.350000.

780   NE   ISSN 0030-3836
KLANK EN WEERKLANK. 1970. irreg. (7-8/yr.). fl.3. Stichting Vrienden van het Brabants Orkest - Foundation Friends of the Brabant Orchestra, Postbus 310, 5600 AE Eindhoven, Netherlands. TEL 01131-73-138500. FAX 01131-73-125170. Ed.Bd. adv.; bk.rev.; illus.; circ. 4,500.
Supersedes: Opmaat.

789.5   NE   ISSN 0023-2181
KLOK EN KLEPEL. 1959. s-a. fl.20. Nederlandse Klokkenspel-Vereniging, Wielengahof 21, 2625 LJ Delft, Netherlands. TEL 31-15-563034. Ed. Loek Boogert. adv.; bk.rev.; illus.; circ. 500. **Indexed:** Music Ind.
Description: Covers carillons, carillon music and the history of bells.

780   US
KODALY ENVOY. 1975. q. $25 to libraries. Organization of American Kodaly Educators, Nicholls State University, Thibodaux, LA 70310. TEL 504-448-4602. FAX 504-448-4927. Ed. Alan Strong. adv.; bk.rev.; illus.; index; circ. 1,600. **Indexed:** Music Ind.

780.7   CN   ISSN 1180-1344
KODALY SOCIETY OF CANADA. ALLA BREVE. (Text in English and French) 1976. 3/yr. Can.$15 to libraries; members Can.$10. Kodaly Society of Canada, Department of Visual & Performing Arts, Keyano College, 8115 Franklin Ave., Ft. McMurray, Alta. T9H 2H7, Canada. TEL 403-791-8981. Ed. Eila Peterson. adv.; bk.rev.; circ. 550. (back issues avail.)
Former titles: Kodaly Society of Canada. Notes; Kodaly Institute of Canada. Notes (ISSN 0700-3269)

780   GW
▼**KOELN KONTAKTER;** ein Handbuch durch die Musikpresse Koeln. 1991. biennial. DM.10. E B - Metronom Verlag, Hospeltstr. 66, 5000 Cologne 30, Germany. TEL 0221-543506. FAX 0221-542620. Ed. Gisela Lobisch. circ. 4,000.

780   GW
KOELNER BEITRAEGE ZUR MUSIKFORSCHUNG. irreg., vol.163, 1990. price varies. Gustav Bosse Verlag, Von-der-Tann-Str. 38, Postfach 417, 8400 Regensburg 1, Germany. Ed. Michael Trapp.

780.6   SW   ISSN 0023-3560
KONSERTNYTT. 1965. m. SEK 140($16) Stockholms Konsertusstiftelse - Stockholm Concert Hall Foundation, Box 7083, S-103 87 Stockholm, Sweden. TEL 08-221800. FAX 08-7917330. Ed. Lotta Hoejer. circ. 5,000.

780.7   SA   ISSN 0023-3579
KONSERVATORIUM NUUS. 1963. s-a. free. Konservatorium-Vereniging, Konservatorium vir Musiek, Private Bag 315, Pretoria, South Africa. adv.; illus.; circ. 2,000.

780   GW   ISSN 0721-5398
KONZERT ALMANACH; Termine, Programme, Sitzplaene und Preise klassischer Konzerte in der BRD. 1981. a. DM.39.80. Heel-Verlag GmbH, Hauptstr. 354, 5330 Koenigswinter 1, Germany. FAX 02223-23028. adv.; circ. 6,000.

780   JA
KUNITACHI ONGAKU DAIGAKU KENKYU KIYO/KUNITACHI COLLEGE OF MUSIC. MEMOIRS. (Text in Japanese) 1966. a. 2500 Yen. Kunitachi Ongaku Daigaku - Kunitachi College of Music, 5-1 Kashiwa-cho 5-chome, Tachikawa-shi, Tokyo 190, Japan. Ed.Bd. illus.; circ. 800.

780.6   US   ISSN 0899-6407
KURT WEILL NEWSLETTER. 1983. 2/yr. free. Kurt Weill Foundation for Music, 7 E. 20th St., New York, NY 10003-1106. TEL 212-505-5240. FAX 212-353-9663. TELEX 650 2966674. Ed. David Farneth. bk.rev.; circ. 6,000.

780.7   JA   ISSN 0388-7502
KYOIKU ONGAKU, CHUGAKU KOKO-BAN/EDUCATIONAL MUSIC, JUNIOR HIGH AND HIGH SCHOOL. (Text in Japanese) m. 720 Yen. Ongaku no Tomo Sha Corp., Kagurazaka 6-30, Shinjuku-ku, Tokyo 162, Japan. TEL 03-3235-2111. FAX 03-3235-5731. TELEX J23718 ONTOA. adv.: B&W page 120000 Yen, color page 300000 Yen; trim 257 x 182. circ. 35,000.
Formerly: Educational Music, Secondary School.
Description: Presents study and teaching methods.

780.7   JA   ISSN 0388-7480
KYOIKU ONGAKU, SHOGAKU-BAN/EDUCATIONAL MUSIC, ELEMENTARY SCHOOL. (Text in Japanese) 1946. m. 720 Yen. Ongaku no Tomo Sha Corp., Kagurazaka 6-30, Shinjuku-ku, Tokyo 162, Japan. TEL 03-3235-2111. FAX 03-3235-5731. TELEX J23718 ONTOA. adv.: B&W page 120000 Yen, color page 300000 Yen; trim 257 x 182. circ. 35,000.
Description: Presents study and teaching methods.

783   SW   ISSN 0281-286X
ML5
KYRKOMUSIKERNAS TIDNING. Short title: K M T. 1935-1982; resumed 1984. 17/yr. SEK 215 (typically set in Jan.). Kyrkomusikernas Riksfoerbund, Sveriges Laerarfoerbund, P.O. Box 12229, S-102 26 Stockholm, Sweden. FAX 8-696-9415. Ed. Stellan Sagvik. adv.; bk.rev.; illus.; circ. 4,300.
Formerly: Svensk Kyrkomusik (Edition AB for Church Musicians); Incorporates: Kyrkomusikernas Tidning; Kyrkosaangsfoerbundet (ISSN 0347-416X)

780 IT
LABORATORIO MUSICA. vol.2, 1980. m. L.16000. Cooperativa Nuova Comunicazione s.r.l., Via F. Carrara 27, 00196 Rome, Italy. Ed. Luigi Nono.

LADYSLIPPER CATALOG AND RESOURCE GUIDE OF RECORDS, TAPES, COMPACT DISCS AND VIDEOS BY WOMEN. see WOMEN'S INTERESTS

780.7 GW ISSN 0047-3979
LANDESVERBAND DER TONKUENSTLER UND MUSIKLEHRER. MITTEILUNGSBLATT. vol.26, 1976. q. membership. Landesverband der Tonkuenstler und Musiklehrer, Neue Musikzeitung, Husumer Str. 31, 2000 Hamburg 20, Germany. Ed. Walter Gehlert. adv.; bk.rev.; bibl.
Description: Covers the study and teaching of music.

789.91 US
LASERLOG REPORTER. 1986. fortn. $228. Phonolog Publishing (Subsidiary of: Trade Service Corporation), 10996 Torreyana Rd., Box 85007, San Diego, CA 92138. TEL 619-457-5920. Ed. Bonnie J. Dudley. (looseleaf format)

781.7 US ISSN 0163-0350
ML199
LATIN AMERICAN MUSIC REVIEW/REVISTA DE MUSICA LATINO AMERICANA. 1980. s-a. $19 to individuals; institutions $30. University of Texas Press, Box 7819, Austin, TX 78713. TEL 512-471-4531. Ed. Gerard H. Behague. adv.; bk.rev.; index; circ. 450. (also avail. in microform from MIM,UMI; reprint service avail. from UMI) Indexed: Arts & Hum.Cit.Ind., Chic.Per.Ind., Curr.Cont., Hisp.Amer.Per.Ind, M.L.A., Music Ind., RILM.
—BLDSC shelfmark: 5160.083000.
Description: Examines all aspects of the written and oral musical traditions of Latin America.

781.7 JA
LATINA. (Text in Japanese) 1952. m. 6360 Yen. Musica Iberoamericana Co., 1-13-6 Ebisu, Shibuya-ku, Tokyo, Japan. FAX 03-443-7123. Ed. Kenji Honda. adv.; illus.; circ. 30,000.
Formerly: Musica Iberoamericana (ISSN 0027-4534)

781.7 US
LATVJU MUZIKA. (Text in Latvian) 1968. a. $8. Latvian Choir Association in the United States, Inc., 7886 Anita Dr., Philadelphia, PA 19111. (Subscr. to: 3322 St. Antoine Ave., Kalamazoo, MI 49007) Ed. Roberts Zuika. bk.rev.; circ. 1,200. (back issues avail.)

787 US ISSN 1056-5329
▼**LEAD BELLY LETTER**; to appreciate and celebrate Lead Belly music. 1990. 4/yr. $15. Lead Belly Society, Box 6679, Ithaca, NY 14851. TEL 607-273-6615. Ed. Sean Killeen. circ. 3,000.

780 UK ISSN 0960-6297
LEADING NOTES; journal of the National Early Music Association. 1984. s-a. £5 (free to members). National Early Music Association, 8 Covent Garden, Cambridge CB1 2HR, England. TEL 0223-315681. adv.; bk.rev.; circ. 1,000.
Formerly (until 1991): N E M A Journal (ISSN 0951-6573)

780 US
LEBLANC BELL. 1977. q. free. G. Leblanc Corporation, 7001 30th Ave., Kenosha, WI 53141-1415. TEL 414-658-1644. FAX 414-658-2824. Ed. Mike Johnson. bk.rev.; circ. 30,000. (back issues avail.)

780.42 US ISSN 0892-1830
LEFSETZ LETTER; first in music analysis. 1986. bi-w. $110. 2128 Oak St., Ste. B, Santa Monica, CA 90405. TEL 213-450-3798. Ed. Robert Scott Lefsetz.

LEISURE INDUSTRY REPORT. see LEISURE AND RECREATION

780 US ISSN 0961-1215
ML3807
▼**LEONARDO MUSIC JOURNAL.** (Includes compact disc of recorded music) 1991. a. $35 to individuals; institutions $90 (effective 1992). Pergamon Press, Inc., Journals Division, 660 White Plains Rd., Tarrytown, NY 10591-5153. TEL 914-524-9200. FAX 914-333-2444. (And: Headington Hill Hall, Oxford OX3 0BW, England. TEL 0865-794141) Indexed: Music Artic.Guide.
—BLDSC shelfmark: 5182.620000.
Description: Addresses the role of science and technology in contemporary music and multimedia art forms using sound.
Refereed Serial

780.7 RU
LESSONS OF MASTERSHIP. a. 1.70 Rub. Izdatel'stvo Muzyka, Ul. Neglinnaya 14, Moscow 103031, Russia. TEL 924-81-63. FAX 921-83-53.

780.42 US
LETTER FROM EVANS. bi-m. C S C S Publications, 2712 Cady Way, Winter Park, FL 32792-4856. TEL 407-678-7113. FAX 407-678-7049. Ed. Win Hinkle. circ. 500.

780 FR ISSN 0766-916X
LETTRE DU MUSICIEN. 1984. 15/yr. 260 F. (foreign 310 F.). 12 rue Jacob, 75006 Paris, France. TEL 47-34-06-91. FAX 42-73-18-47. Ed. Michele Worms. adv.; circ. 5,000.

LIAISON; revue culturelle de l'Ontario francais. see ART

784 GW ISSN 0024-290X
ML5
LIED UND CHOR; Zeitschrift fuer das gesamte Chorwesen. 1908. m. DM.24. (Deutscher Saengerbund e.V.) Verlag Deutsche Saengerzeitung GmbH, Luepertzenderstr. 14, Postfach 1355, 4050 Moenchengladbach 1, Germany. Ed. Franz R. Miller. adv.; bk.rev.; illus.; circ. 21,000.

780 US
LIGHTNING STRIKES. 1977. 2/yr. $10. (Lou Christie International Fan Club) Universal Mind Press, c/o Harry Young, Ed., Box 748, Chicago, IL 60690-0748. TEL 312-241-5412. adv.; bk.rev.; circ. 650. (back issues avail.)
Description: Covers all aspects of the career and music of Lou Christie.

781.7 ZR
LIKEMBE. bi-m. K.350. Maison d'Editions "Jeunes pour Jeunes", B.P. 9624, Kinshasa 1, Zaire. Ed. Mulongo Mulunda Mukena. illus.

780 US
LINGNAN YINYUE/LINGNAN MUSIC. (Text in Chinese) bi-m. $9. China Books & Periodicals, Inc., 2929 24th St., San Francisco, CA 94110. TEL 415-282-2994. FAX 415-282-0994.

780 BN ISSN 0024-4244
LIRA. 1974. m. 3 din. per no. Opstinska Konferencija Muzicke Omladine, AVNOJ-a 5, Bihac, Bosnia Hercegovina. Ed. Safet Curtovic.

781.57 DK ISSN 0109-1212
LISTE OVER RYTMISKE SPILLESTEDER I DANMARK. 1982. a. DKK 30. Danske Jazzcenter, Borupvej 66, 4683 Roennede, Denmark. Eds. Arnvid Meyer, Birgit Kabelmann. circ. 2,500.
Formerly: Liste over Danske Jazzklubber og Huse.

780.92 SW ISSN 0263-0249
LISZT SAECULUM. (Text in English, German) 1978. s-a. SEK 150 membership. International Liszt Centre, Synaalsvaegen 5, S-161 49 Bromma, Sweden. TEL 08-251716. FAX 08-251736. Ed. Lennart Rabes. adv.; bk.rev.; circ. 400.
Formerly: I.L.C. Quarterly.

780 UK ISSN 0141-0792
LISZT SOCIETY. JOURNAL. (Supplement avail.) 1976. a. £15 (foreign £18) membership. Liszt Society Ltd., 135 Stevenage Road, Fulham, London SW6 6PB, England. TEL 071-381-9751. FAX 071-381-2406. Ed. Dudley Newton. bk.rev.; bibl.; circ. 300.
Formerly: Liszt Society, London. Newsletter (ISSN 0459-5084)
Description: Contains original articles and reviews.

LITERARNO - MUZEJNY LETOPIS. see LITERATURE

780 DK
LITTLE RICHARD NEWS. 1986. irreg. (2-3/yr.). DKK 100. Mjoelner Edition, Oeregaardsvaengevej 15, DK-4720 Praestoe, Denmark. FAX 53-79-30-28. Ed. John Garodkin. adv.; bk.rev.; circ. 400.

LITURGY 90. see RELIGIONS AND THEOLOGY — Roman Catholic

780 GW
LIVE IN CONCERT. 1984. m. DM.30. I S E Verlag, Hohenwaldstr. 21, D-8024 Deisenhofen, Germany. TEL 089-6131015. FAX 089-6133439. TELEX 5216850-ISE-D. Ed. Dankmar Isleib. circ. 328,475.
Formerly: Concert.

781.573 US ISSN 0024-5232
ML1
LIVING BLUES; a journal of the African American blues tradition. 1970. 6/yr. $18. University of Mississippi, Center for the Study of Southern Culture, University, MS 38677-9836. TEL 601-232-5742. FAX 601-232-5740. Ed. Peter Lee. adv.; bk.rev.; rec.rev.; illus.; circ. 16,000. (also avail. in microfilm from UMI; back issues avail.) Indexed: Abstr.Folk.Stud., M.L.A., Music Ind., Pop.Mus.Per.Ind., RILM.
Description: Features interviews with blues musicians, record reviews, upcoming festivals and more.

780 UK
LONDON COLLEGE OF MUSIC MAGAZINE. 1960. 2/yr. London College of Music, Polytechnic of West London, St. Mary's Rd., Ealingi London W5 5RF, England. TEL 081-579-5000. FAX 081-566-1353. adv.; bk.rev.; circ. controlled. (processed)
Description: For students, staff and LCM Society members.

780 US ISSN 1049-4340
LOOK BACK. 1984. q. $25 (foreign $35). Box 857, Chardon, OH 44024. adv.; bk.rev.; film rev.; bibl.; charts; illus.; circ. 800. (back issues avail.)
Description: Covers Bob Dylan, current news, music reviews, collectors news, and lyric interpretation.

780 US
LOS ANGELES SONGWRITERS SHOWCASE MUSEPAPER. Cover title: Songwriters Musepaper. 1986. m. $19 in US; Canada $29; elsewhere $50. Music & Arts Foundation of America, Los Angeles, Box 93759, Hollywood, CA 90093. FAX 213-467-0531. Ed. John Braheny. adv.; circ. 20,000.

780 RM
LUCRARI DE MUZICOLOGIE. (Text in Rumanian; summaries in English, or French, or German) 1965. a. price varies. Academia de Muzica "Gheorge Dima", Str. I.C. Bratianu 25, 3400 Cluj-Napoca, Rumania. Ed. Dan Voiculescu. circ. 300. Indexed: RILM.

780 UK ISSN 0952-0759
ML5
THE LUTE. 1959. a. £20. Lute Society, 103 London Rd., Oldham, Lancs OL1 4BW, England. TEL 061-624-4369. Ed. M. Spring, J. Craig-McFeely. adv.; bk.rev.; circ. 400. (back issues avail.) Indexed: RILM.
Formerly (until 1982): Lute Society Journal (ISSN 0460-007X)

780 US ISSN 0076-1524
ML1
LUTE SOCIETY OF AMERICA. JOURNAL. 1968. a. membership. Lute Society of America, c/o Beedle Hinely, Box 1328, Lexington, VA 24450. TEL 703-463-5812. Ed. Victor Coelho. adv.; bk.rev.; index; circ. 600. Indexed: RILM.

780 US
LUTE SOCIETY OF AMERICA. QUARTERLY. q. membership. Lute Society of America, c/o Beedle Hinely, Box 1328, Lexington, VA 24450. TEL 703-463-5812. Ed. Bryan Prud'Homme. Indexed: Music Artic.Guide.
Formerly: Lute Society of America. Newsletter.

784.61 US
LYRIC AND MELODY NEWSLETTER. 1984. a. membership. Songwriter and Lyricist Club, Box 023304, Brooklyn, NY 11202-0066. TEL 718-855-5057. Ed. Robert Makinson. adv.; bk.rev.; circ. 60. (looseleaf format)

MUSIC

782.1 US ISSN 0024-7839
LYRIC OPERA NEWS. 1956. 2/yr. membership. Lyric Opera of Chicago, 20 N. Wacker Dr., Chicago, IL 60606. TEL 312-332-2244. FAX 312-419-8345. Ed. Alfred Glasser. adv.; bk.rev.; music rev.; illus.; circ. 23,000. **Indexed:** Music Artic.Guide.

780.42 CN
M E A T. 1989. m. Can.$25($30) M E A T Communications, Inc., P.O. Box 35, Sta. O, Toronto, Ont. M4A 2M8, Canada. TEL 416-699-8486. FAX 416-690-6697. Ed. Drew Masters. circ. 35,000 (controlled).

780 375 US ISSN 1056-4039
M E N C SOUNDPOST. 1984. 3/yr. membership. Music Educators National Conference, 1902 Association Dr., Reston, VA 22091-1597. TEL 703-860-4000. FAX 703-860-1531. Ed. Greg Ross. adv.; illus.; circ. 60,000. (back issues avail.)

780 GW ISSN 0722-9119
M M BRANCHEN HANDBUCH. 1980. a. DM.45.80. (Musik Markt) Josef Keller Verlag, Postfach 1440, 8130 Starnberg, Germany. TEL 08151-7710. Ed.Bd. index.

780.903 IT
MADRIGALISTI DELL'ITALIA CENTRO-SETTENTRIONALE. 1980. irreg., no.5, 1991. price varies. Casa Editrice Leo S. Olschki, Casella Postale 66, 50100 Florence, Italy. TEL 055-6530684. FAX 055-6530214.

781.7 HU ISSN 0025-0384
ML5
MAGYAR ZENE. 1960. q. $18. (Magyar Zenemuveszek Szovetsege) Lapkiado Vallalat, Lenin korut 9-11, 1073 Budapest 7, Hungary. TEL 222-408. (Subscr. to: Kultura, Box 149, H-1389 Budapest, Hungary) bk.rev.; abstr.; bibl. **Indexed:** Arts & Hum.Cit.Ind., Curr.Cont.

780 792 AT
MAJOR ATTRACTIONS. ANNUAL DIARY. 1978. a. Sydney Opera House Trust, G.P.O. Box 4274, Sydney N.S.W. 2001, Australia. TEL 02-250-7414. FAX 02-252-1161.

780 PL
MALA BIBLIOTEKA OPEROWA. 1955. irreg. price varies. Polskie Wydawnictwo Muzyczne, Al. Krasinskiego 11a, 31-111 Krakow, Poland. TEL 22-70-44. FAX 22-01-74. Ed. Mieczyslaw Tomaszewski.
Description: Covers the most popular Polish and foreign operas: music, libretto, work's origin.

780 PL
MALE MONOGRAFIE MUZYCZNE; monografie popularne. 1952. irreg. price varies. Polskie Wydawnictwo Muzyczne, Al. Krasinskiego 11a, 31-111 Krakow, Poland. TEL 22-70-44. FAX 22-01-74. Ed. Stanislaw Haraschin.
Description: Presents life and work of great composers.

MANNHEIMER LIEDERTAFEL. MITTEILUNGEN. see CLUBS

780.42 US ISSN 0364-815X
ML1
MARQUEE (NORWALK). m. $6. World Wide Publishing Co., Box 509, Norwalk, CA 90650. TEL 213-864-2741. illus. **Indexed:** Avery Ind.Archit.Per.

780.7 US ISSN 0025-4312
MARYLAND MUSIC EDUCATOR. 1954. 4/yr. $8 to non-members. Maryland Music Educators Association, c/o Thomas W. Fugate, Ed., 27 Meadow Ln., Thurmont, MD 21788. adv.; bk.rev.; illus.; circ. controlled. **Indexed:** Music Artic.Guide.
Description: Presents study and teaching methods.

780.42 CS
MASARYKOVA UNIVERZITA. FILOZOFICKA FAKULTA. SBORNIK PRACI. H: RADA HUDEBNEVEDNA. 1966. irreg. (approx. a). price varies. Masarykova Univerzita, Filozoficka Fakulta, A. Novaka 1, 660 88 Brno, Czechoslovakia.
Formerly: Univerzita J.E. Purkyne. Filozoficka Fakulta. Sbornik Praci. H: Rada Hudebnevedna (ISSN 0231-522X)
Description: Series Musicologica provides articles in the various fields of the theory and history of music: Czech, Russian, Italian, modern, folk and more.

780.7 US ISSN 0147-2550
MASSACHUSETTS MUSIC NEWS. 1953. q. $6. Massachusetts Music Educators Association, Inc. (Subsidiary of: Music Educators National Conference), c/o J. Anthony DiGiore, Ed., Box 532, W. Springfield, MA 01090-0532. TEL 413-739-9065. FAX 413-788-9251. adv.; bk.rev.; music rev.; illus.; stat.; circ. 1,600. **Indexed:** Music Artic.Guide.
Formerly: M.M.E.A. Music News (ISSN 0024-8258)
Description: Documents the progress of music education in Massachusetts.

780 UK
MASSENET SOCIETY. NEWSLETTER. no.2, 1975. q. £4. Massenet Society, c/o Stella J. Wright, Flat 2, 79 Linden Gardens, London W2 4EU, England. Ed. Frank Granville Barker.

786.2 US ISSN 0360-8484
ML423.M42
THE MATTHAY NEWS. 1927. 2/yr. $30. American Matthay Association, 100 Minty Dr., Dayton, OH 45415. Ed. Elizabeth Vandevander. bk.rev.; illus.; circ. 250.

780.42 US
MEAN MOUNTAIN MUSIC; records of the 50's. 1975. s-a. $8. Mountain Productions, Box 04352, Milwaukee, WI 53204. Ed. Mike Muskovitz. adv.; bk.rev.; circ. 4,000.

789 US
MECHANICAL MUSIC. 1954. 3/yr. $30. Musical Box Society International, 887 E. Orange Ave., St. Paul, MN 55106. TEL 612-772-2464. Ed. Angelo Rulli. adv.; bk.rev.; illus.; circ. 3,000. **Indexed:** Music Ind.
Former titles: Musical Box Society International Technical Journal & Musical Box Society International. Bulletin; Musical Box Society. Bulletin (ISSN 0027-4577)
Description: Technical articles about the restoration of antique musical mechanical instruments.

MEDICAL PROBLEMS OF PERFORMING ARTISTS. see MEDICAL SCIENCES

MEDIUM (NEW YORK). see ETHNIC INTERESTS

781.5 CS ISSN 0025-8997
MELODIE; monthly for jazz and pop music. 1962. m. 60 Kcs.($52.10) Panorama, Halkova 1, 120 72 Prague 2, Czechoslovakia. Ed. Jan Dobias. adv.; bk.rev.; charts; illus.; index; circ. 90,000. (tabloid format)

784.3 787.61 CS
MELODIE PRE VAS. irreg, vol.7, 1974. 7 Kcs. per no. Opus, Bratislava, Czechoslovakia.

781.5 GW ISSN 0025-9004
MELODIE UND RHYTHMUS; devoted to light music song and jazz. 1957. m. DM.35.40 (foreign DM.46.20). Henschelverlag Kunst und Gesellschaft, Oranienburger Str. 67-68, 104 Berlin, Germany. adv.; charts; illus.

780 UK ISSN 0025-9012
ML5
MELODY MAKER. 1926. w. $80. I P C Magazines Ltd., Holborn Group (Subsidiary of: Reed Business Publishing Ltd.), Commonwealth House, 1-19 New Oxford St., London WC1 1NG, England. TEL 01-404-0700. Ed. Alan Jones. adv.; bk.rev.; charts; film rev.; illus.; play rev.; circ. 68,300. (also avail. in microform from UMI) **Indexed:** Music Ind.

780 GW ISSN 0174-7207
MELOS; Vierteljahreszeitschrift fuer zeitgenoessische Musik. 1984. m. DM.48. B. Schott's Soehne, Weihergarten 1-9, Postfach 3640, D-6500 Mainz, Germany. TEL 06131-246812. Ed.Bd. adv.; bk.rev.; bibl.; charts; illus.; index; circ. 2,500.

789.91 UK ISSN 0266-8033
MEMORY LANE. 1968. q. £11($30) (typically set in Feb.). Memory Lane, 226 Station Rd., Leigh-on-Sea, Essex SS9 3BS, England. Ed. Ray Pallett. adv.; bk.rev.; circ. 2,000.
Description: Covers popular music from 1920-1950: jazz, dance bands, big bands.

780 792 US
MEMPHIS STAR.* m. $10. 1315 Peabody Ave., Memphis, TN 38104-3518. TEL 901-452-7827. Ed. David Wayne Brown. adv.; bk.rev.
Description: Looks at music, theater, and the movies, mainly from an entertainment perspective. Includes record industry news.

780 NE ISSN 0025-9462
MENS EN MELODIE. 1946. m (10/yr.). fl.57.50. Wegener Tijl Tijdschriften Groep B.V., Postbus 9943, 1006 AP Amsterdam, Netherlands. TEL 020-5182828. FAX 020-5182843. Ed. Peter Peters. adv.; bk.rev.; bibl.; illus.; index; circ. 5,000. **Indexed:** Music Ind., RILM.
—BLDSC shelfmark: 5678.461000.

780.904 UK
METAL HAMMER; the international hard rock & heavy metal magazine. 1984. m. £2.50 per no. Rock Team Publishing and Productions Ltd., 134B King St., Hammersmith, London W6 ORQ, England. TEL 081-748-1200. FAX 081-748-1131. (In Germany: Ernst-Mehlich-Str. 6, 4600 Dortmund 1) Ed. Chris Welch. adv.; bk.rev.; circ. 40,000. (back issues avail.)

780 US
METAL MANIA. 9/yr. Tempo Publishing Company, Inc., 475 Park Ave. S., New York, NY 10016. TEL 212-213-8620.

780 US
METAL REVOLUTION. q. Flip Magazines, Inc., 801 Second Ave., New York, NY 10017. TEL 212-661-7878.

780.42 US
METALLIX. 6/yr. $14.95. Pilot Communications, Inc., 831 Federal Rd., Box 304, Brookfield, CT 06804. TEL 203-775-0190. FAX 203-775-1931. (And: 25 W. 39th St., New York, NY 10018. TEL 212-302-2626) Ed. Chris Nadler. circ. 143,000.
Description: Covers rock & roll and heavy metal music for mid- to late teens.

783 UK ISSN 0047-6919
METHODIST CHURCH MUSIC SOCIETY BULLETIN. 1970. 2/yr. £2. Methodist Church Music Society, c/o Peter Essex, Ed., 3 St. John's, North Holmwood, Dorking RH5 4JG, England. adv.; bk.rev.; circ. 1,000. (also avail. in microform from WMP)

780 US
METRONOME MAGAZINE. 1986. m. $20. Metronome Publishing, 3 Karen Circle, Ste. 7, Billerica, MA 01821. Ed. Brian M. Owens. rec.rev.; circ. 15,000. (tabloid format; back issues avail.)
Description: Focuses on music and entertainment. Contains interviews with national and international musicians.

METRU. see MOTION PICTURES

700 AG ISSN 0026-2676
MICROCRITICA; arte-musica-teatro-literatura. 1965. bi-m. General Hornos 1110, Buenos Aires, Argentina. Ed. Eve Benasso. bk.rev.; music rev.; play rev.; illus.

781.6 CN
LE MILIEU. English edition: Probe. m. free to members. Society of Composers, Authors and Music Publishers of Canada (SOCAN) - Societe Canadienne des Auteurs, Compositeurs et Editeurs de Musique, 41 Valleybrook Dr., Don Mills, Ont. M3B 2S6, Canada. TEL 416-445-8700. FAX 416-445-7108. (also avail. in microform from MML)
Description: Newsletter of the organization.

785 069 US
MILLER NOTES. 1975. 5/yr. membership. Glenn Miller Birthplace Society, Box 61, Clarinda, IA 51632. TEL 712-542-2461. Ed. Wilda Martin. adv.; bk.rev.; circ. 700. (looseleaf format)
Description: Presents news of personnel associated with big band leader Glenn Miller, his records, and the Society's festival.

781.6 US
MILWAUKEE SYMPHONY ORCHESTRA. ENCORE. 1980. s-m. free. Milwaukee Symphony Orchestra, 4532 N. Oakland Ave., Milwaukee, WI 53211. TEL 414-964-5669. Ed. Rose DeFontes. adv.
Formerly: Milwaukee Symphony Orchestra. Stagebill.

781.7 CC
MINZU MINJIAN YINYUE/NATIONAL AND FOLK MUSIC.
(Text in Chinese) q. Y4.80. (Guangdongsheng
Minjian Yinyue Yanjiushi - Guangdong Folk Music
Research Office) Minzu Minjian Yinyue Bianjibu, 79
Wende Lu, 7th Floor, Guangzhou, Guangdong
510030, People's Republic of China. TEL 340465.
Eds. Lin Yun, Ma Ming.
 Description: Introduces folk music popular among
nationalities in Guangdong Province.

780 CS ISSN 0544-4136
ML3797
MISCELLANEA MUSICOLOGICA. (Text in Czech;
summaries in German) 1956. irreg. (approx. a.).
19.50 Kcs. per no. Universita Karlova, Filosoficka
Fakulta, Katedra Dejin Hudby, Divadla a Filmu, Nam.
Krasnoarmejcu 1, 116 38 Prague 1,
Czechoslovakia. Ed. Frantisek Muzik. illus.; circ. 770.
Indexed: A.I.C.P., CERDIC.

780.7 US
MISSISSIPPI MUSIC EDUCATOR. 1941. 3/yr. $6.
Mississippi Music Educators Association, c/o Larry
W. Newell, Ed., 2106 Bob White Dr., Tupelo, MS
38801-6181. TEL 601-842-7909. adv.; bk.rev.;
film rev.; illus.; stat.; tr.lit.; circ. 550.
 Formerly: Mississippi Notes (ISSN 0026-6353)

781.57 US ISSN 0742-4612
MISSISSIPPI RAG; the voice of traditional jazz and
ragtime. 1973. m. $18 (foreign $20). Mississippi
Rag, Inc., 6500 Nicollet Ave. S., Minneapolis, MN
55423. TEL 612-861-2446. FAX 612-861-4621.
Ed. Leslie Carole Johnson. adv.; bk.rev.; rec.rev.;
illus.; circ. 3,800. (tabloid format; back issues avail.)
Indexed: Music Ind., Pop.Mus.Per.Ind.
 Description: Historical articles, current jazz and
ragtime news, photos and articles on performers and
festivals.

780 US ISSN 0085-350X
ML1
**MISSOURI JOURNAL OF RESEARCH IN MUSIC
EDUCATION.** 1962. a. $2. Missouri Music Educators
Association, 1113 E. Meadowlark, Springfield, MO
65810. TEL 417-887-5252. FAX 314-882-5071.
(Subscr. to: 138 Fine Arts Center, University of
Missouri at Columbia, Columbia, MO 65211. TEL
314-882-3238) Ed. Wendy L. Sims. circ. 200.
Indexed: Music Artic.Guide, Music Ind.
 —BLDSC shelfmark: 5829.073000.
 Description: Reports of original research related to
music teaching and learning.

780.7 US ISSN 0026-6701
MISSOURI SCHOOL MUSIC. 1945. 4/yr. $6. Missouri
Music Educators Association (Marshfield), Box 690,
Marshfield, MO 65706. adv.; illus.; circ. 3,000.

780 FR ISSN 1159-070X
MODAL. s-a. 450 F. Geste Editions, Maison des
Ruralies, B.P. 1, 79230 Vouille, France.
TEL 49-75-67-71. Ed. Jean-Loic Le Quellec.
 Description: Covers ethnomusicology, French
tradition music and dance.

780 US ISSN 0194-4533
ML1035
MODERN DRUMMER; a contemporary publication
exclusively for drummers. 1977. m. $27.95.
Modern Drummer Publications, Inc., 870 Pompton
Ave., Cedar Grove, NJ 07009. TEL 201-239-4140.
FAX 201-239-7139. Ed. Ronald L. Spagnardi. adv.;
bk.rev.; illus.; circ. 102,000. **Indexed:** Music Ind.
 Incorporates (in 1988): Modern Percussionist
(ISSN 8750-7838)
 Description: Articles, news, profiles, advice, and
equipment specs for the contemporary percussionist.

781.57 IT
MODERN JAZZ. (Text in English) irreg. Ruggero Stiassi,
Ed. & Pub., Via Putti 3, Bologna, Italy. adv.; rec.rev.
(processed)

786.6 US
MODERN KEYBOARD. 1988. bi-m. $2.95 per no. Harris
Publications, Inc., 1115 Broadway, 8th fl., New York,
NY 10010. TEL 212-807-7100. adv.; circ. 65,000.
 Description: Combines rock & roll music with new
technology. Features include interviews profiling top
keyboard artists and MIDI technology for the
beginner. Covers the basics from home studio and
computer music to sequencers and synthesizers.

781.7 US
MODERN SCREEN'S COUNTRY MUSIC SPECIAL. bi-m.
$2.50 per no. Sterling's Magazines, Inc., 355
Lexington Ave., New York, NY 10017.
TEL 212-973-3220.

MOLODEZHNAYA ESTRADA. see CHILDREN AND
YOUTH — For

780.904 CN ISSN 0823-0498
MONDE DU ROCK. m. Can.$9.75. Monde du Rock Entr.,
558 6E Rue, Quebec, Que. G1J 2S4, Canada. (Distr.
by: Distributions Eclair, 8320 Place de Lorraine,
Anjou, Que. H1J 1E6, Canada) Ed. Michel Jacques.

780.42 US
MONDO 2000. q. Box 10171, Berkeley, CA 94709.
TEL 415-845-9018. Ed. Alison Kennedy.

MONKEES, BOYCE & HART PHOTO FAN CLUB; the photo
club. see CLUBS

780.01 US
MONOGRAPHS IN MUSICOLOGY SERIES. 1983. irreg.,
vol.9, 1988. Pendragon Press, Rt. 1, Box 159,
Stuyvesant, NY 12173-9720. TEL 518-828-3008.
FAX 518-828-2368.

780 US ISSN 0275-5866
MONOGRAPHS ON MUSICOLOGY. 1979. irreg., vol.10,
1989. Gordon & Breach Science Publishers, 270
Eighth Ave., New York, NY 10011.
TEL 212-206-8900. FAX 212-645-2459. TELEX
236735 GOPUB UR. (Subscr. to: Box 786, Cooper
Sta., New York, NY 10276. TEL 800-545-8398; UK
subscr. to: P.O. Box 90, Reading, Berkshire RG1
8JL, England. TEL 0734-560-080) Ed. F.J. Smith.
 —BLDSC shelfmark: 5990.891000.
 Refereed Serial

780 SP ISSN 0210-4083
ML5
MONSALVAT. 1973. m. 5000 ptas. Ediciones de Nuevo
Arte Thor, Plaza Gala Placidia 1-16, 08006
Barcelona, Spain. TEL 93 218 11 97.
FAX 932184638. Ed. Jose Manuel Infiesta
Monterde. adv.; bk.rev.; illus.; circ. 20,000.

780 PL
**MONUMENTA MUSICAE IN POLONIA. SERIES A: WORKS
BY POLISH COMPOSERS.** (Text mainly in Latin;
occasionally in Polish and other languages) 1966.
irreg. price varies. (Polska Akademia Nauk, Instytut
Sztuki) Polskie Wydawnictwo Muzyczne, Al.
Krasinskiego 11a, 31-111 Krakow, Poland.
TEL 22-70-44. FAX 22-01-74. Ed. Zygmunt M.
Szweykowski.
 Supersedes in part: Monumenta Musicae in Polonia
(ISSN 0077-1465)

780 PL
**MONUMENTA MUSICAE IN POLONIA. SERIES B:
COLLECTANEA MUSICAE ARTIS.** 1964. irreg. (Polska
Akadmia Nauk, Instytut Sztuki) Polskie Wydawnictwo
Muzyczne, Al. Krasinskiego 11a, 31-111 Krakow,
Poland. TEL 22-70-44. FAX 22-01-74. Ed. Jozef M.
Chominski.
 Formerly: Monumenta Musicae in Polonia. Series
B: Fontes Artis Musicae; **Supersedes in part:**
Monumenta Musicae in Polonia (ISSN 0077-1465)

780 PL
**MONUMENTA MUSICAE IN POLONIA. SERIES C:
TRACTATUS DE MUSICA.** 1984. irreg. (Polska
Akademia Nauk, Instytut Sztuki) Polskie
Wydawnictwo Muzyczne, Al. Krasinskiego 11a,
31-111 Krakow, Poland. TEL 22-70-44.
FAX 22-01-74. Ed. Henryk Kowalewicz.
 Supersedes in part: Monumenta Musicae in Polonia
(ISSN 0077-1465)

780 PL
**MONUMENTA MUSICAE IN POLONIA. SERIES D:
BIBLIOTHECA ANTIQUA.** 1975. irreg. (Polska
Akademia Nauk, Instytut Sztuki) Polskie
Wydawnictwo Muzyczne, Al. Krasinskiego 11a,
31-111 Krakow, Poland. TEL 22-70-44.
FAX 22-01-74. Ed. Jerzy Morawski.
 Supersedes in part: Monumenta Musicae in Polonia
(ISSN 0077-1465)
 Description: Contains the reprints of the treatises
and music editions from the 16th and 17th
centuries.

780 US ISSN 0077-1503
MONUMENTS OF RENAISSANCE MUSIC. 1967. irreg.,
vol.7, 1986. price varies. University of Chicago
Press, 5801 S. Ellis Ave., Chicago, IL 60637.
TEL 312-702-7899. Ed. Howard M. Brown. (reprint
service avail. from UMI,ISI)
 Refereed Serial

780.7 RU
MONUMENTS OF WORLD MUSICAL SCIENCE. a.
4.60 Rub. Izdatel'stvo Muzyka, Ul. Neglinnaya 14,
Moscow 103031, Russia. TEL 924-81-63.
FAX 921-83-53.

781.7 US ISSN 0278-0763
ML1
MORAVIAN MUSIC JOURNAL. (Supplement to: Moravian
Music Foundation Newsletter) 1957. q. $10.
Moravian Music Foundation, 20 Cascade Ave.,
Winston-Salem, NC 27127. TEL 919-725-0651.
Ed. Richard Starbuck. adv.; bk.rev.; bibl.; circ. 4,000.
(back issues avail.) **Indexed:** Music Artic.Guide, Music
Ind.
 Former titles: Moravian Music Foundation. Bulletin
(ISSN 0147-7013); Moravian Music Foundation.
News Bulletin (ISSN 0027-1020)

MOVEMENTS IN THE ARTS. see ART

780 GW ISSN 0077-1805
MOZART - JAHRBUCH. (Text in English, French and
German) 1950. a. price varies. (Internationale
Stiftung Mozarteum, AU) Baerenreiter Verlag,
Heinrich-Schuetz-Allee 29-37, 3500
Kassel-Wilhelmshoehe, Germany. TEL 0561-3105-0.
FAX 0561-3105240. (U.S. subscr. addr.: Foreign
Music Distributors, 13 Elkay Dr., Chester, NY
10918) Ed.Bd. adv.; index; circ. 1,000. **Indexed:**
RILM.
 —BLDSC shelfmark: 5980.708000.

781.7 780.42 IT
IL MUCCHIO SELVAGGIO; mensile di musica e cultura.
1977. m. Editore Lakota, Via Pietro Mascagni, 3-5,
00199 Rome, Italy. TEL 06-837879. Ed. Massimo
Stefani. illus.

780 GW
MUENCHNER PHILHARMONIKER. 1985. s-m. DM.26.
Muenchner Philharmoniker, Gasteig Kulturzentrum,
8000 Munich 80, Germany.

784.4 AT ISSN 0157-3381
MULGA WIRE. 1954. 6/yr. Aus.$5. Bush Music Club,
P.O. Box 433, Sydney, N.S.W. 2001, Australia. Ed.
Don Richmond. adv.; bk.rev.; illus.; circ. 300.
 Incorporates (in 1979): Singabout; Journal of
Australian Folksong (ISSN 0037-5632)

780 IS
MUSEIKA. 1987. m. Music Publications Ltd., P.O.B.
28144, Tel Aviv 61 281, Israel. TEL 03-615538.

780.01 572 GW
**MUSEUM FUER VOELKERKUNDE, BERLIN.
VEROEFFENTLICHUNGEN. NEUE FOLGE. ABTEILUNG:
MUSIKETHNOLOGIE.** 1961. irreg., vol.7, 1990. price
varies. Staatliche Museen Preussischer Kulturbesitz,
Berlin, Generalverwaltung, Stauffenbergstr. 41,
1000 Berlin 30, Germany. TEL 030-266-6.
FAX 030-2662612.

780 US ISSN 0895-1543
ML128.P63
MUSI - KEY; the reference guide of note. 1987. bi-m.
$288. 1505 Kirkwood Dr., Ft. Collins, CO 80525.
TEL 303-484-1062. FAX 303-484-8080. Eds.
Randy Rucker, Linda Rucker. circ. 1,000.
 Description: Lists popular and standard music
currently in print, both sheets and collections.

780 IT
MUSIC. 1978. m. L.60000. (Athena 2001 Coop.)
Edizioni L.E.T.I. s.r.l., Viale E. Q. Visconti, 20, 00198
Rome, Italy. FAX 06-3210651. Ed. Salvatore Puzzo.
adv.; circ. 200,000.
 Description: Covers various topics in music.

780 II
MUSIC ACADEMY. CONFERENCE SOUVENIR. (Text in
English, Sanskrit or Tamil) 1940. a. Rs.15. Music
Academy, 306 T.T.K. Rd., Royapettah, Madras
600014, India.
 Description: Contains articles on music contributed
by international writers, and documented
programmes of music and dance recitals.

MUSIC

780   II
MUSIC ACADEMY. JOURNAL. (Text in English, Sanskrit, Tamil) 1929. a. Rs.15($3) Music Academy, 306 T.T.K. Rd., Royapettah, Madras 600014, India.
    Description: Devoted to the advancement of the science and art of music.

780   US
▼**MUSIC ACCESS DIRECTORY.** 1990. m. $12. Music Access, Inc., 90 Fifth Ave., Brooklyn, NY 11217. TEL 718-398-2146. FAX 718-230-5539. (Subscr. to: Box 179022, Times Plaza Sta., Brooklyn, NY 11217-9022. TEL 718-398-2166) Ed. Bar Biszick. music rev.
    Description: Listings of all independently produced recorded music accessible through the Music Access interactive telephone network. Categories include classical, rock and pop, jazz and blues, country and folk, contemporary, children's, and experimental.

780   UK   ISSN 0262-5245
MUSIC ANALYSIS. 1982. 3/yr. £35($60) to individuals; institutions £81.50($172.50). Basil Blackwell Ltd., 108 Cowley Rd., Oxford OX4 1JF, England. TEL 0865-791100. FAX 0865-791347. TELEX 837022-OXBOOK-G. Ed. Derrick Puffett. adv.; bk.rev.; circ. 800. (reprint service avail. from SWZ,UMI) **Indexed:** Arts & Hum.Cit.Ind., Curr.Cont.
    —BLDSC shelfmark: 5990.185300.

780.42   US
MUSIC & AUDIO REVIEWS. m. $2.95 per no. W G E Publishing, Inc., Forest Rd., Box 278, Hancock, NH 03449-0278. TEL 800-227-1053. FAX 603-525-4660.

780   UK   ISSN 0262-8260
ML1049.8
MUSIC & AUTOMATA; from horology to mechanical musical instruments. 1983. s-a. £18($30) Music & Automata Publications, 24 Shepherds Lane, Guildford, Surrey GU2 6SL, England. TEL 0483-574460. FAX 0483-301884. Ed. Arthur W.J.G. Ord-Hume. adv.; bk.rev.; illus.; circ. 2,500.
    —BLDSC shelfmark: 5990.185400.

780.7   US
MUSIC AND ENTERTAINMENT INDUSTRY EDUCATORS' NOTES. Short title: M I E A Notes. 1978. q. $6. Music Industry Educators Association, c/o Music Department, New York State University, Oneonta, NY 13820. TEL 703-568-6863. Ed. Janet Nepkie. circ. 500. (looseleaf format)
    Formerly: Music Industry Educators' Notes.

780   UK
MUSIC & EQUIPMENT MART. m. £13.20 (foreign £38). Maze Media Ltd., 89 East Hill, Colchester, Essex CO1 2QN, England. TEL 0206-871450. FAX 0206-871537. Ed. Steve Wright. adv.

780.07   UK   ISSN 0027-4224
ML5
MUSIC AND LETTERS. 1920. q. £40($82) Oxford University Press, Oxford Journals, Pinkhill House, Southfield Road, Eynsham, Oxford OX8 1JJ, England. TEL 0865-882283. FAX 0865-882890. TELEX 837330 OXPRES G. Ed.Bd. adv.; bk.rev.; music rev.; illus.; index, cum.index: vols.1-40, 1920-1959; circ. 1,850. (also avail. in microform from UMI; reprint service avail. from SWZ) **Indexed:** Abstr.Engl.Stud., Arts & Hum.Cit.Ind., Br.Hum.Ind., Can.Rev.Comp.Lit., Curr.Cont., Hum.Ind., Ind.Bk.Rev.Hum., M.L.A., Music Ind., RILM.
    —BLDSC shelfmark: 5990.190000.
    Description: Covers all fields of musical enquiry, from earliest times to present day. Includes wide range of reviews: scholarly editions of music of the past; new music.

780   UK   ISSN 0085-3607
MUSIC AND LIFE. 1950. irreg. (3-4/yr.). £1.20. Music Group of the Communist Party, c/o George Burn, Ed., 17 Huntingdon Rd., London N.2, England. circ. 300. (processed)

784   UK   ISSN 0305-4438
ML5
MUSIC AND LITURGY. 1974. 6/yr. £15 (foreign £18). Society of St. Gregory, 30 North Terrace, Mildenhall, Suffolk IP28 7AB, England. FAX 0638-7165799. Ed. Stephen Dean. adv.; bk.rev.; circ. 1,250. (also avail. in microform from UMI) **Indexed:** Br.Hum.Ind., Cath.Ind., CERDIC.
    —BLDSC shelfmark: 5990.200000.
    Formed by the merger of: Church Music (ISSN 0009-644X) & Life and Worship (ISSN 0024-5119)

780 621.389 658   US   ISSN 0894-1238
ML1092
MUSIC AND SOUND RETAILER; the newsmagazine for musical instrument and sound product merchandisers. 1978. m. $18 free to qualified personnel. Testa Communications, Inc., 25 Willowdale Ave., Port Washington, NY 11050. TEL 516-767-2500. FAX 516-767-9335. Ed. Jon Mayer. adv.; charts; illus.; stat.; tr.lit.; circ. 10,000. (tabloid format; back issues avail.)
    Former titles: Music and Sound Electronics Retailer; Sound Arts Merchandising Journal.
    Description: For professional musicians and retailers.

MUSIC AND THE TEACHER. see EDUCATION — Teaching Methods And Curriculum

780   IE
MUSIC ASSOCIATION OF IRELAND. ANNUAL REPORT. 1975. a. Music Association of Ireland, 5 North Frederick St., Dublin 1, Ireland. TEL 01-746060. stat.

780 028.5   RU
MUSIC AT THE KINDERGARTEN. a. 3 Rub. Izdatel'stvo Muzyka, Ul. Neglinnaya 14, Moscow 103031, Russia. TEL 924-81-63. FAX 921-83-53.

780 681   UK   ISSN 0269-0292
MUSIC BUSINESS; musical instrument retailers and allied trade. 1986. m. £10 (foreign £20). Feedback Publications Ltd., 10 Farmfield Rd., Great Tey, Colchester CO6 1AB, England. TEL 0206 211243. FAX 081-950-0302. (Subscr. to: Grosvenor House, Police Station Ln., Bushey, Hertfordshire WD2 1BR, England) Ed. Peter Pulham. adv.; circ. 3,600. (back issues avail.)

MUSIC CATALOGING BULLETIN. see LIBRARY AND INFORMATION SCIENCES

781.5   US   ISSN 0027-4291
MUSIC CITY NEWS. 1963. m. $23.50 (typically set in Jan.). Music City News Publishing Co., Inc., Box 22975, 50 Music Sq. W., Nashville, TN 37202. TEL 615-329-2200. Ed. Lydia Dixon-Harden. adv.; bk.rev.; illus.; circ. 150,000.
    Description: Focuses on country music and entertainers.

780   US   ISSN 0161-2654
ML1
MUSIC CLUBS MAGAZINE. 1922. 4/yr. $6. National Federation of Music Clubs, 1336 N. Delaware St., Indianapolis, IN 46202. TEL 317-638-4003. Ed. Bryan Blackwell. adv.; bk.rev.; film rev.; music rev.; circ. 4,000(approx.). (also avail. in microform from UMI) **Indexed:** Music Artic.Guide, Music Ind.

780.65   US
MUSIC CONNECTION. 1977. fortn. $35. Music Connection Inc., 6640 Sunset Blvd., Ste. 201, Hollywood, CA 90028. FAX 213-462-3123. Ed. Michael Dolan. adv.; bk.rev.; circ. 35,000.

780   CN   ISSN 0820-0416
ML21.C3
MUSIC DIRECTORY CANADA. 1983. biennial. Can.$26.95. Norris Publications, 3284 Yonge St., Toronto, Ont. M4N 3M7, Canada. TEL 416-485-1049. FAX 416-485-8924. Ed. Jim Norris. circ. 6,000.

780.7   US   ISSN 0027-4321
ML1
MUSIC EDUCATORS JOURNAL. 1914. 9/yr. $41 (institutional subscriptions only.). Music Educators National Conference, 1902 Association Dr., Reston, VA 22091. TEL 703-860-4000. FAX 703-860-1531. Ed. Michael Blakeslee. adv.; bk.rev.; illus.; index; circ. 60,000. (also avail. in microform from UMI; reprint service avail. from UMI) **Indexed:** Arts & Hum.Cit.Ind., Bk.Rev.Ind. (1965-), C.I.J.E., Child.Bk.Rev.Ind. (1965-), Cont.Pg.Educ., Curr.Cont., Educ.Ind., Except.Child.Educ.Abstr., Music Artic.Guide, Music Ind., PMR, RILM, So.Pac.Per.Ind., Sp.Ed.Needs Abstr.
    —BLDSC shelfmark: 5990.270000.
    Description: Presents study and teaching methods.

780   CN
MUSIC EXPRESS. 1976. m. Can.$25($27) (foreign $30). Rock Express Communications Inc., 219 Dufferin, Toronto, Ont. M6K 3J1, Canada. TEL 416-538-7500. FAX 416-538-7503. Ed. Mary Dickie. film rev.; charts; circ. 195,000. (back issues avail.)
    Former titles: Rock Express (ISSN 0710-6076); Music Express.

MUSIC FILE. see EDUCATION — Teaching Methods And Curriculum

780   CN
MUSIC FOR ONE MUSIC FOR ALL. 1988. a. Can.$14. Saskatchewan Music Festival Association, 201 - 1819 Cornwall St., Regina, Sask. S4P 2K4, Canada. Ed. Doris Covey Lazecki. circ. 2,500.
    Description: The written history of the Association.

780.1   US
MUSIC FORUM. 1967. irreg., vol.4, 1977. price varies. Columbia University Press, 562 W. 113th St., New York, NY 10025. TEL 212-678-6777. Ed. Felix Salzer. illus. **Indexed:** Music Ind., RILM.

780   US
▼**MUSIC FROM CHINA. NEWS/CHANG FENG YUE XUN.** (Text in Chinese and English) 1991. q. $10. Music from China - Chang Feng Zhongyuetuan, 170 Park Row, Ste. 12-D, New York, NY 10038. TEL 212-962-5698. Eds. Paul Shackman, Chen Yi. music rev.; circ. 1,200. (back issues avail.)
    Description: Aims to foster interest in Chinese music. Introduces musicians, works, and events.

780   US
MUSIC IN AMERICAN LIFE. irreg. University of Illinois Press, 54 E. Gregory Dr., Champaign, IL 61820. TEL 217-333-0950. FAX 217-244-8082. (reprint service avail. from UMI)
    Refereed Serial

780 057.85   PL   ISSN 0860-911X
MUSIC IN POLAND. (Text in English) 1966. s-a. free. Polish Music Council, Fredry 8, 00-097 Warsaw, Poland. (Co-sponsor: Ministry of Culture and Arts) bk.rev.; bibl.; circ. 900.
    —BLDSC shelfmark: 5990.381250.
    Description: Contains articles especially on Polish music and musical life in Poland.

780   AU
MUSIC IN THE MEDIA - I M Z BULLETIN. (Text in English, French, German) 1961. m. (10/yr.). International Music Centre - Internationales Musikzentrum, Lothringerstr. 20, A-1030 Vienna, Austria. TEL 7130777. FAX 7130777-17. TELEX 75311745-IMZ. Ed. Monika Gelbmann. bk.rev.; circ. 1,500. **Indexed:** RILM.
    Former titles: Music and Media - I M Z Bulletin; I M Z Bulletin (ISSN 0019-0071); I M Z Information (ISSN 0538-8783)

780   IS
MUSIC IN TIME. 1984. a. $6. Jerusalem Rubin Academy of Music and Dance, Campus Givat Ram, Jerusalem 91904, Israel. TEL 02-636232. FAX 02-527713. Ed. Tzvi Avni. circ. 1,000.
    Description: Concerns subjects of interest to the music and dance world. Presents contributions from internationally-known musicians and music educators.

780.65   US
MUSIC INC.. 11/yr. Maher Publications, Inc., 180 Park Ave., Elmhurst, IL 60126. TEL 708-941-2030. FAX 708-941-3210. Ed. Gerry Clark. circ. 10,800.

780 793.3	US	ISSN 1048-1400
▼MUSIC INTERNATIONAL. Russian edition: Musika Mneznonarodnia (ISSN 1048-1494) 1990. q. $19.95 (foreign $29). (Gosconcert, RU) Kompass Intercontinental Publishing, 418 Commonwealth Ave., Boston, MA 02215. TEL 617-266-1214. FAX 617-247-3008. Ed. Sam Chase. adv.; bk.rev.; circ. 50,000. (back issues avail.)
 Description: Focuses on classical music and other performing arts in the US and Russia.

780	UK	ISSN 0951-5135
ML5
MUSIC JOURNAL. 1929. m. £20. Incorporated Society of Musicians, 10 Stratford Place, London W1N 9AE, England. TEL 071-629 4413. FAX 071-408-1538. Ed. Neil Hoyle. circ. 5,000. (back issues avail.)
 Description: Carries general musical news and reports of members' activities.

780	US	ISSN 0027-4372
ML1
THE MUSIC LEADER. q. $9.75. Southern Baptist Convention, Sunday School Board, Church Music Department, 127 Ninth Ave., Nashville, TN 37234. TEL 800-458-2772.
 Formerly: Children's Music Leader.

780	US	ISSN 0580-289X
MUSIC LIBRARY ASSOCIATION. NEWSLETTER. Variant title: M L A Newsletter. 1969. q. Music Library Association, Box 487, Canton, MA 02021. TEL 617-828-8450. Ed. James Farington. Key Title: Newsletter - Music Library Association.
 —BLDSC shelfmark: 5879.715470.

MUSIC LIBRARY ASSOCIATION. NOTES. see LIBRARY AND INFORMATION SCIENCES

MUSIC LIBRARY ASSOCIATION. TECHNICAL REPORTS; information for music media specialists. see LIBRARY AND INFORMATION SCIENCES

780	JA
MUSIC LIFE. (Text in Japanese) 1952. m. 6000 Yen. Shinko Music Publishing Co. Ltd., 2-1, Ogawa-machi, Kanda, Chiyoda-ku, Tokyo, Japan. Ed. Kaoruko Togo.

780	CN	ISSN 0705-4009
ML5
MUSIC MAGAZINE. 1978. 5/yr. Can.$16 (foreign $20). Future Perfect Publishing, P.O. Box 96, Station "R", Toronto, Ont. M4G 3Z3, Canada. TEL 416-323-9790. Ed. Rick MacMillan. adv.; bk.rev.; circ. 15,000. Indexed: CMI, Music Ind.
 Incorporates (in 1987): R C M Bulletin.
 Description: National magazine on classical music. Written for lovers of classical music as well as professionals and music educators.

MUSIC MAKERS (NASHVILLE). see RELIGIONS AND THEOLOGY — Protestant

780.42	US
MUSIC MAKERS (REDWOOD CITY).* m. $28 (foreign $36). The Personics Corporation, 981 Bing St., San Carlos, CA 94070-5381. TEL 415-368-1700. Ed. Kevin Berger.

780 658	DK	ISSN 0108-5328
MUSIC MANAGEMENT & INTERNATIONAL PROMOTION; the magazine behind the business news. Variant title: M M I P. 1983. bi-m. DKK 21.25 per no. Music Management International, Postbox 77, 2650 Hidovre, Denmark. illus.

789.91	UK
MUSIC MASTER CATALOGUE. 1974. a. (with m. supplements). £199.50. Music Master, Music House, One De Cham Ave., Hastings, Sussex TN37 6HE, England. TEL 0424 715181. FAX 0424-422805. adv.; circ. 3,500.
 Formerly: Music Master (ISSN 0308-9347); Incorporates: Singles Master; Record Prices.
 Description: Lists albums, casettes, compact discs and videos; all recorded popular music with details and format included.

789.91	UK
MUSIC MASTER LABELS LIST. 1980. a. £14.95. Music Master, Music House, 1 De Cham Ave., Hastings, Sussex TN37 6HE, England. TEL 0424 715181. FAX 0424-422805. circ. 8,000.
 Description: List names, addresses and contacts of record companies and distributors, with product checklists.

780	CN	ISSN 0702-9012
MUSIC MCGILL. 1976. s-a. free. McGill University, Faculty of Music, 555 Sherbrooke St. W., Montreal, Que. H3A 1E3, Canada. TEL 514-398-4535. Ed. John Grew. circ. 4,500.

780	US	ISSN 0891-1002
ML1
MUSIC NEWS (WASHINGTON);* the monthly report. 1984. m. $20. Keyboard Press, Ltd., 3829 Legation St., N.W., Washington, DC 20015-2701. TEL 301-474-0050. Eds. Bradford Gowen, Maribeth Gowen. bk.rev.; circ. 700.

780	CS	ISSN 0027-4410
ML5
MUSIC NEWS FROM PRAGUE. (Text in English) 1964. 6/yr. $20 in Europe; overseas $25. Czech Music Fund, Music Information Centre, Besedni 3, 118 00 Prague 1, Czechoslovakia. FAX 422-539-720. Ed. Nina Vseteckova. adv.; bk.rev.; illus.; index; circ. 14,000. Indexed: Music Ind.
 Description: Contains calendar of symphony concerts, interviews and record reviews.

780	US	ISSN 0027-4437
MUSIC NOW. 1951. 4/yr. membership. Southeastern Composers' League, Mississippi University for Women, Box W-70, Colombus, MS 39701. TEL 601-329-7203. Ed. Richard Montalto. adv.; bk.rev.; circ. 600. (processed) Indexed: Music Artic.Guide.

MUSIC O C L C USERS GROUP. NEWSLETTER. see LIBRARY AND INFORMATION SCIENCES

MUSIC OF THE SPHERES; a quarterly magazine of art and music for the New Age. see NEW AGE PUBLICATIONS

780	US
MUSIC PAPER. 1979. m. $12. Sound Resources, Box 304, Manhassett, NY 11030. TEL 516-883-8898. FAX 516-883-2577. Ed. Karen A. Cavill. adv.; bk.rev.; circ. 70,000.

780.01	US	ISSN 0730-7829
ML1
MUSIC PERCEPTION. 1983. q. $38 to individuals (foreign $44); institutions $81 (foreign $87). University of California Press, Journals Division, 2120 Berkeley Way, Berkeley, CA 94720. TEL 510-642-4191. FAX 510-643-7127. Ed. Diana Deutsch. adv.; bk.rev.; illus.; index; circ. 900. (back issues avail.) Indexed: Arts & Hum.Cit.Ind., Curr.Cont., Music Ind., Psychol.Abstr.
 —BLDSC shelfmark: 5990.381000.
 Description: Focuses on scientific and musical approaches to the study of musical phenomena. Refereed Serial

MUSIC REFERENCE SERVICES QUARTERLY. see LIBRARY AND INFORMATION SCIENCES

780	JA
MUSIC RESEARCH/ONGAKU KENKYU. 1972. a. free. Osaka College of Music, Music Research Institute - Osaka Ongaku Daigaku Ongaku Kenkyujo, 1-1-4 Meishinguchi, Toyonaka, Osaka 561, Japan. FAX 06-866-8490. Ed. Kiyoshi Inobe. adv.; bk.rev.; illus.; circ. 1,000.
 Former titles (until 1982): Music Culture; (until 1978): Data of Music in Western Japan; (until 1975): Data of Music in Kansai District.
 Description: Contains papers on music culture, modern music, folk music, acoustics, music physiology, and music education.

780.7	CN	ISSN 0700-3838
MUSIC RESEARCH NEWS. 1976. s-a. membership. Canadian Music Research Council, c/o Robert Walker, Simon Fraser University, Faculty of Education, Burnaby, B.C., Canada. TEL 604-291-3192. bk.rev.; bibl.; circ. 100.

658	US	ISSN 1051-1822
ML3790
▼MUSIC RETAILING. 1990. bi-w. $95. Out to Launch Communications Inc. (Subsidiary of: International Data Group), Forest Rd., Hancock, NH 03449. TEL 603-525-4201. Ed. Mark Lo. circ. 12,000 (controlled).
 Description: Covers current news and advice on the techniques and equipment of managing a successful music business.

780	UK	ISSN 0027-4445
ML5
MUSIC REVIEW. 1940. q. £50. Black Bear Press Ltd., Kings Hedges Rd., Cambridge CB4 2PQ, England. Ed. A.F. Leighton Thomas. adv.; bk.rev.; music rev.; rec.rev.; index; circ. 1,000. (also avail. in microform from UMI; reprint service avail. from KTO) Indexed: Arts & Hum.Cit.Ind., Br.Hum.Ind., Curr.Cont., Hum.Ind., Ind.Bk.Rev.Hum., Music Ind., RILM.
 —BLDSC shelfmark: 5990.400000.

780.42	SZ
MUSIC SCENE; das Schweizer Musikmagazin. m. 50 Fr. Gjuchstrasse 15, CH-8935 Dietikon, Switzerland. TEL 061-661111. (Subscr. to: Zeitschriften der Basler Zeitung, Hocherbergstr. 15, CH-4002 Basel, Switzerland) Ed. Paul Casutt.

780.7	UK	ISSN 0027-4461
ML5
MUSIC TEACHER. 1909. m. £31. Rhinegold Publishing Ltd., 241 Shaftesbury Ave., London WC2H 8EH, England. TEL 071-836-2384. FAX 071-528-7991. (Subscr. to: P.O. Box 47, Gravesend, Kent DA12 2AN, England) Ed. Tim Homfray. adv.; bk.rev.; music rev. (also avail. in microform from UMI) Indexed: Cont.Pg.Educ., Music Ind.
 —BLDSC shelfmark: 5990.420000.
 Formerly: Music Teacher and Piano Student.
 Description: Presents study and teaching methods.

MUSIC TEACHERS' ASSOCIATION OF N.S.W. QUARTERLY MAGAZINE. see EDUCATION — Teaching Methods And Curriculum

780.7	RU
MUSIC TEACHERS LIBRARY. 2/yr. 1.50 Rub. per issue. Izdatel'stvo Muzyka, Ul. Neglinnaya 14, Moscow 103031, Russia.

780 621.389	UK	ISSN 0891-7264
ML73
MUSIC TECHNOLOGY. (U.K. Edition) 1981. m. £18 (foreign £21). Music Maker Publications Ltd., Alexander House, Forehill, Ely, Cambs CB7 4AF, England. TEL 0353-665577. FAX 0353-662489. (U.S. addr.: Music Maker Publications Inc., 22024 Lassen St., Ste. 118, Chatsworth, CA 91311) Ed. Tim Goodyear. adv.; bk.rev.; circ. 50,000.
 Formerly (until 1986): Electronics and Music Maker.
 Description: Latest technology in music, covering keyboards, guitars, drums, woodwinds, and other types of musical instruments. Includes articles on sound recording and reproduction, performance reviews, interviews, and profiles of industry leaders.

780	US	ISSN 0195-6167
MT6
MUSIC THEORY SPECTRUM. 1979. s-a. $40. Society for Music Theory, School of Music, Florida State University, Tallahassee, FL 32306-2098. TEL 812-855-7346. FAX 904-644-6100. Ed. James Baker. adv.; bk.rev.; circ. 1,100. Indexed: Music Artic.Guide, Music Ind., RILM.
 —BLDSC shelfmark: 5990.425000.

780	US	ISSN 0734-7367
ML3920
MUSIC THERAPY. 1981. a. $15 to individuals; institutions and libraries $25. American Association for Music Therapy, Box 80012, Valley Forge, PA 19484-0012. TEL 215-265-4006. Ed. David Marcus. bk.rev.; circ. 1,000. (back issues avail.) Indexed: Psychol.Abstr.
 —BLDSC shelfmark: 5990.429000.

780 286	US	ISSN 0164-7180
MUSIC TIME. q. $6.75. Southern Baptist Convention, Sunday School Board, 127 Ninth Ave., N., Nashville, TN 37234. TEL 800-458-2772.

780	US	ISSN 0027-4488
ML1
MUSIC TRADES. 1890. m. $12 (includes Purchaser's Guide to the Music Industries). Music Trades Corporation, c/o Paul A. Majeski, Ed., Box 432, 80 West St., Englewood, NJ 07631. TEL 201-871-1965. adv.; charts; illus.; circ. 7,200. (also avail. in microform from UMI; reprint service avail. from UMI) Indexed: Music Ind., PROMT.

MUSIC

780 310　　　US
MUSIC U S A; annual statistical review of the musical instrument industry. 1957? a. $15. American Music Conference, 303 E. Wacker Dr., Ste. 1214, Chicago, IL 60601. TEL 312-856-8820.
FAX 312-856-8807. Ed. Paul Bjorneberg. circ. 1,750.

658.8 789.91　　UK　　ISSN 0265-1548
MUSIC WEEK. 1959. w. $215. Spotlight Publications Ltd., Greater London House, Hampstead Rd., London NW1 7QZ, England. Ed. David Dalton. adv.; bk.rev.; rec.rev.; charts; circ. 12,509.
Former titles: Music and Video Week; (until Jul. 1981) Music Week; Record Retailer (ISSN 0034-1606)
Description: News for the music industry and music retailer.

780　　　UK
MUSIC WEEK DIRECTORY. 1976. a. $14. Spotlight Publications Ltd., Greater London House, Hampstead Rd., London NW1 7QZ, England.
Former titles: Music and Video Week Directory (ISSN 0264-3383); Music and Video Week Yearbook; Music Week Industry Year Book.
Description: Directory of UK record and music industry institutions, companies and individuals.

780　　UK　　ISSN 0077-2453
MUSIC WORLD YEAR BOOK. 1981. a. £1.25. (Music Trade Association) Turret-Wheatland Ltd., 12 Greycaine Rd., Watford, Herts. WD2 4JP, England. Ed. Peter Pulham. circ. 3,000.

780　　GW　　ISSN 0027-4518
ML5
MUSICA; Zweimonatsschrift fuer alle Gebiete des Musiklebens. 1946. bi-m. DM.50. Baerenreiter Verlag, Heinrich-Schuetz-Allee 31-37, 3500 Kassel-Wilhelmshoehe, Germany. TEL 0561-3105-0. FAX 0561-3105240. (U.S. subscr. addr.: Foreign Music Distributors, 13 Elkay Dr., Chester, NY 10918) Ed.Bd. adv.; bk.rev.; bibl.; illus.; index; circ. 11,000. Indexed: Music Ind., RILM.

780 789.91　　IT　　ISSN 0392-5544
MUSICA; informazione musicale e discografica. 1977. bi-m. L.45000 (foreign L.80000). Edizioni Diapason Milano, Via Ampere 60, 20131 Milan, Italy. TEL 02.23.67.615. Dir. Umberto Masini. adv.; bk.rev.; film rev.; index; circ. 35,000. (back issues avail.)

780　　CU
MUSICA. q. Ministerio de Cultura, UNEAC, Casa de las Americas, 3 y G, Vedado, Havana, Cuba.

780.902　　BE　　ISSN 0771-7016
MUSICA ANTIQUA. 1984. q. 600 Fr.($21) (foreign 700Fr.). (Flemish Centre for Early Music) Alamire, P.O. Box 45, 3990 Peer, Belgium.
TEL 011-632-164. FAX 011-63-49-11. Ed. H. Baeten. adv.; bk.rev.; music rev.; circ. 1,000.
Description: Scholarly and general coverage of early music, including musicology topics, interviews, reports on music fairs, festivals, and conferences.

780 950　　US　　ISSN 0140-6078
MUSICA ASIATICA. 1978. irreg. (approx. a.), vol.3, 1981. price varies. Oxford University Press, 200 Madison Ave., New York, NY 10016.
TEL 212-679-7300. Ed. Laurence Picken. illus. Indexed: RILM.
—BLDSC shelfmark: 5990.535000.

780　　UK　　ISSN 0580-2954
MUSICA BRITANNICA; a national collection of music. 1951. irreg. price varies. (Musica Britannica Trust) Stainer and Bell Ltd., P.O. Box 110, Victoria House, 23 Gruneisen Rd., London N3 1DZ, England. FAX 081-343-3024. Ed. Paul Doe. circ. 1,100.

780 700 792　　IT
MUSICA, CINEMA, IMMAGINE, TEATRO. irreg., latest no.8. price varies. Angelo Longo Editore, Via Paolo Costa 33, P.O. Box 431, 48100 Ravenna, Italy. TEL 0544-217026. Ed. Gianfranco Casadio. circ. 1,500.
Former titles: Musica, Cinema, Teatro; Musica, Immagine, Teatro.

780　　IT
MUSICA D'OGGI; periodico di cultura musica spettacolo. 1975. m. L.20000. Musica d'Oggi, Via Romolo Balzani, 64-6, 00177 Rome, Italy. Ed. Dino Cafaro. adv.; bk.rev.; circ. 30,000. (tabloid format)

780.9　　GW　　ISSN 0077-2461
MUSICA DISCIPLINA; yearbook of the history of music, Medieval and Renaissance. (Text in English; occasionally in French, German, Italian) 1946. a. DM.81.50. (American Institute of Musicology, US) Haenssler Verlag, Postfach 1220, Bismarckstr. 4, 7303 Neuhausen-Stuttgart, Germany.
TEL 07158-177-149. FAX 07158-177119. Eds. Gilbert Reaney, Frank D'Accone. Indexed: Arts & Hum.Cit.Ind., Curr.Cont., Music Ind., RILM.

780.904 780.7　　IT　　ISSN 0391-4380
MT3.18
MUSICA DOMANI; trimestrale di cultura e pedagogia musicale. 1971. q. L.24000 (foreign L.29000). G. Ricordi & C. S.p.A., Via Berchet 2, Milan, Italy. FAX 8881212. TELEX 310177 RICOR I. Ed. Andrea Talmelli. adv.; bk.rev.; circ. 4,500. (back issues avail.)

789.91　　IT　　ISSN 0027-4526
MUSICA E DISCHI. (Includes supplements) 1945. m. L.80000. Musica e Dischi, Via De Amicis 47, 20123 Milan, Italy. FAX 39-2-8323843. Ed. Mario de Luigi. adv.; rec.rev.; illus.; bibl. Indexed: Music Ind.
Description: Information on music industry, audio (professional) and home video.

780　　IT
MUSICA E DOSSIER. m. L.57000. Giunti Gruppo Editoriale S.p.A., Via Vincenzo Gioberto, 34, 50121 Florence, Italy. TEL 055-66791. FAX 055-268312. Ed. Francesco Cristino.

781.57　　IT　　ISSN 0027-4542
ML5
MUSICA JAZZ. 1945. m. L.115200($35) (foreign L.200000). (Messaggerie Musicali) Rusconi Editori Associati S.p.A., Servizio Abbonamenti, Via Vitruvio 43, 20124 Milan, Italy. TEL 02-67561.
FAX 67562732. Dir. Pino Candini. adv.; bk.rev.; film rev.; music rev.; play rev.; rec.rev.; illus.; index; circ. 9,500. (back issues avail.) Indexed: Music Ind.

781.7　　US　　ISSN 0147-7536
ML1
MUSICA JUDAICA. (Text in English and Hebrew) 1976. a. $25. American Society for Jewish Music, 155 Fifth Ave., New York, NY 10010.
TEL 212-533-2601. FAX 212-533-2601. Ed. Israel J. Katz. adv.; bk.rev.; circ. 1,500. Indexed: Ind.Jew.Per., Music Ind., RILM.
—BLDSC shelfmark: 5990.665000.

780　　PL　　ISSN 0077-247X
ML170
MUSICA MEDII AEVI. (Text in Polish; summaries in English) 1965. irreg. price varies. (Polska Akademia Nauk, Instytut Sztuki) Polskie Wydawnictwo Muzyczne, Al. Krasinskiego 11a, 31-111 Krakow, Poland. TEL 22-70-44. FAX 22-01-74. Ed. Jerzy Morawski. Indexed: RILM.
Description: Covers the field of Medieval music.

786　　JA　　ISSN 0289-3630
MUSICA NOVA. (Text in Japanese) m. 700 Yen. Ongaku no Tomo Sha Corp., Kagurazaka 6-30, Shinjuku-ku, Tokyo 162, Japan.
TEL 03-3235-2675. FAX 03-3260-6415. TELEX J23718 ONTOA. adv.; B&W page 174000 Yen, color page 360000 Yen; trim 257 x 182. circ. 65,000.
Description: Directed at pianists and piano instructors.

783　　GW　　ISSN 0179-356X
MUSICA SACRA. bi-m. DM.49. Allgemeiner Caecilien-Verband, Andreasstr. 9, 8400 Regensburg, Germany. TEL 0941-84339. Indexed: RILM.

780　　IT
MUSICA VIVA. 1977. m. L.70000. Sigel S.r.l., Via Leopardi 1, 20123 Milan, Italy. FAX 48008443. TELEX 321118 NIM I. Ed. Lorenzo Arruga. adv.; bk.rev.; rec.rev.; illus.; circ. 20,000. (back issues avail.)

783　　IT　　ISSN 0027-4569
MUSICAE SACRAE MINISTERIUM. 1964. irreg. $10 to non-members. Consociatio Internationalis Musicae Sacrae, c/o PIMS, Via di Torre Rossa 21, 00165 Rome, Italy. FAX 396-6985378. TELEX 504-2024 DIRGENTEL VA. Ed. Rudolf Pohl. bk.rev.; abstr.; index; circ. 5,000. Indexed: RILM.

790　　US　　ISSN 0735-7788
ML12
MUSICAL AMERICA INTERNATIONAL DIRECTORY OF THE PERFORMING ARTS. 1960. a. $75. Musical America Publishing Inc., 825 Seventh Ave., 8th Fl., New York, NY 10019. TEL 212-887-8383.
FAX 212-586-1364. (Subscr. to: Box 3238, Harlan, IA 51537. TEL 800-666-3977) Ed. Charles Passy. adv.; circ. 11,500.
—BLDSC shelfmark: 5990.739000.
Formerly (until 1968): Musical America Annual Directory Issue (ISSN 0580-308X)

780　　DK　　ISSN 0027-4585
MUSICAL DENMARK. 1952. s-a. DKK 60 (free elsewhere). Danish Cultural Institute, Kultorvet 2, 1175 Copenhagen K, Denmark. TEL 33-13-54-48. FAX 45-33-15-10-91. (Co-sponsor: Danish Music Information Centre) bibl.; illus.; circ. 6,000. (back issues avail.) Indexed: Music Ind.

780　　US　　ISSN 0160-3876
ML1
MUSICAL HERITAGE REVIEW MAGAZINE. 1977. 18/yr. membership only. Musical Heritage Society, 1710 Highway 35, Ocean, NJ 07712.
TEL 201-531-7000. adv.; bk.rev.; circ. controlled.

781.7　　KE
MUSICAL INSTRUMENTS OF EAST AFRICA. 1975. irreg. EAs.0.80. Nelson Africa Ltd., Box 73146, Nairobi, Kenya.

780 001.3　　SW　　ISSN 0349-988X
MUSICAL INTERPRETATION RESEARCH. Short title: M I R. 1982. irreg. price varies. Mirage, Raadmansgatan 3, 4tr., S-11425 Stockholm, Sweden.
TEL 08-108052. Ed. Nils-Goran Sundin. bk.rev. (back issues avail.) Indexed: RILM.
Description: Concerns the artistic aspects of musical performance, particularly the aesthetics of conductors.

MUSICAL MAINSTREAM (LARGE PRINT EDITION). see HANDICAPPED — Visually Impaired

658.8 781.91　　US　　ISSN 0027-4615
ML1
MUSICAL MERCHANDISE REVIEW; pianos, musical instruments, organs, accessories. 1879. m. $24. Larkin-Pluznick-Larkin, Inc., 100 Wells Ave., Box 9103, Newton, MA 02159-9103.
TEL 617-964-5100. Ed. Don Johnson. adv.; bk.rev.; film rev.; rec.rev.; illus.; mkt.; pat.; tr.lit.; tr.mk.; index; circ. 12,000 (controlled).

780.7　　UK　　ISSN 0027-4623
ML5
MUSICAL OPINION; serious music journal. 1877. m. £23 (foreign £35) (subscr. includes bi-m newsletter of National Federation of Music Societies, UK and section of Organ World). Serious Music Ltd., 2 Princes Rd., St. Leonards-on-Sea, East Sussex TN37 6EL, England. FAX 0424-730052. Ed. Denby Richards. adv.; bk.rev.; music rev.; rec.rev.; illus.; circ. 5,000. (also avail. in microform from UMI) Indexed: Br.Hum.Ind., Music Ind., RILM.
—BLDSC shelfmark: 5990.770000.
Description: Covers classical music for the music enthusiast and for the professional musician.

780　　US　　ISSN 0027-4631
ML1
MUSICAL QUARTERLY. 1915. q. $34 to individuals (foreign $48); institutions $44 (foreign $59). Oxford University Press, Journals, 200 Madison Ave., New York, NY 10016. TEL 212-679-7300. FAX 212-725-2972. TELEX 6859654. (Subscr. to: Journals Fulfillment, 2001 Evans Rd., Cary, NC 27513. TEL 919-677-0977) Ed. Paul Wittke. adv.; bk.rev.; bibl.; illus.; index, cum.index: 1915-1959, vols.1-45; circ. 3,500. (also avail. in microform from MIM,UMI) Indexed: Acad.Ind., Amer.Bibl.Slavic & E.Eur.Stud., Arts & Hum.Cit.Ind., Bk.Rev.Dig., Bk.Rev.Ind. (1965-), Can.Rev.Comp.Lit., Child.Bk.Rev.Ind. (1965-), Curr.Cont., Hum.Ind., Ind.Bk.Rev.Hum., Mag.Ind., Music Artic.Guide, Music Ind., R.G., RILM.
Description: Contains original articles covering the entire range of musical composition and performance, from early music to the Classical-Romantic tradition to twentieth-century jazz and pop to the latest developments in theory and practice.

MUSICAL SALVATIONIST. see RELIGIONS AND THEOLOGY — Protestant

MUSIC   3567

MUSICAL SHOW; devoted to the amateur presentation of Broadway musical shows on the stage. see *THEATER*

780   UK   ISSN 0027-4666
ML5
MUSICAL TIMES; a monthly journal for serious music lovers. 1844. m. $60. Orpheus Publications Ltd., Centro House, Mandela St., London NW1 0DU, England. TEL 071-387-3848. FAX 071-388-8532. Ed. Basil Ramsey. adv. contact: adv. contact: Jon Williams. bk.rev.; music rev.; rec.rev.; index; circ. 6,000. (also avail. in microform from UMI; reprint service avail. from UMI) **Indexed:** Arts & Hum.Cit.Ind., Br.Hum.Ind., Curr.Cont., Ind.Bk.Rev.Hum., Music Ind., RILM.
—BLDSC shelfmark: 5990.810000.

780.7   301.412   US   ISSN 0737-0032
ML82
MUSICAL WOMAN. 1983. irreg., latest 1992. price varies. Greenwood Press, Inc. (Subsidiary of: Greenwood Publishing Group Inc.), 88 Post Rd. W., Box 5007, Westport, CT 06881-5007. TEL 203-226-3571. FAX 203-222-1502.

780   UK
MUSICAL WORLD; the definitive music trade magazine. 1979. bi-m. £22. (Music Retailers Association) Turret-Wheatland Ltd., 12 Greycaine Rd., Watford, Herts. WD2 4JP, England. Ed. Peter M.G. Pulham. adv.; bk.rev.; circ. 3,500. (also avail. in microform from UMI; reprint service avail. from UMI)
Incorporates: Music Trades International.

780   IT   ISSN 0027-4674
MUSICALBRANDE; arvista Piemontese. (Text in Italian and Piemontais) 1959. q. L.3500. Corso Palermo 11, 10152 Turin, Italy. Ed. Alfredo Nicola. adv.; bk.rev.; illus.

MUSICALS; das Musicalmagazin. see *THEATER*

780.903   IT
▼**MUSICHE DEL RINASCIMENTO ITALIANO**. 1990. irreg., no.2, 1990. price varies. Casa Editrice Leo S. Olschki, Casella Postale 66, 50100 Florence, Italy. TEL 055-6530684. FAX 055-6530214.

780.01   IT
MUSICHE RINASCIMENTALI SICILIANE. no.7, 1978. irreg., no.11, 1988. price varies. Casa Editrice Leo S. Olschki, Casella Postale 66, 50100 Florence, Italy. TEL 055-6530684. FAX 055-6530214. circ. 1,000.

780   US   ISSN 0733-5253
ML1
MUSICIAN. 1976. 12/yr. $17. Billboard Publications, Inc., 33 Commercial St., Gloucester, MA 01930. TEL 617-281-3110. Ed. Bill Flanagan. adv.; illus.; circ. 115,000. (also avail. in microform from UMI; reprint service avail. from UMI) **Indexed:** Music Artic.Guide, Music Ind., New Per.Ind.
Former titles (until 1982): Musician, Player and Listener (ISSN 0161-9543); (until 1977): Music America (ISSN 0145-5419)

780   CN   ISSN 0844-479X
MUSICIEN QUEBECOIS. 1989. bi-m. Can.$18. Musicien Quebecois Inc., 1165 Gouin, Ste. 140, Quebec, Que. G1N 1T3, Canada. TEL 418-681-6254. FAX 418-681-1437. Ed. Ralph Angelillo. circ. 20,000. (back issues avail.)
Description: Covers profiles of Quebec musicians, music education, technology, recording studios and records.

780   CN
MUSICK. 1979. q. Can.$10($10) Vancouver Society for Early Music, 1254 West 7th Ave., Vancouver, B.C. V6H 1B6, Canada. TEL 604-732-1610. FAX 604-732-1602. Ed. John Glofcheskie. adv.; bk.rev.; circ. 4,000.
Description: Covers medieval, renaissance, baroque and classical music.

780   US
MUSICK OF THE FIFES & DRUMS SERIES. 1976. irreg., latest 1981. price varies. Colonial Williamsburg Foundation, Box 1776, Williamsburg, VA 23187-1776. TEL 804-220-7349. Ed. John C. Moon.

780   NE
MUSICMAKER; maandblad voor de muziekbeoefenaar. (Text in Dutch) m. fl.79. Audet Tijdschriften bv, Postbus 16, 6500 AA Nijmegen, Netherlands. TEL 080-228316. FAX 080-239561. TELEX 48633. Ed. Jaap van Eik. adv.: B&W page fl.2980; trim 215 x 285; adv. contact: Cor van Nek. circ. 21,183.
Description: For amateur and professional musicians in the Netherlands and Belgium.

780.1 781.7   SP
MUSICOLOGIA ESPANOLA. 1975. irreg. Ministerio de Educacion y Ciencia, Comisaria Nacional de la Musica, Madrid 3, Spain.

780.01   BE
MUSICOLOGICA NEOLOVANIENSIA STUDIA. 1980. irreg., no.7, 1989. price varies. Association des Diplomes Histoire Art et Archeologie, College Erasme, Place Blaise Pascal 1, B-1348 Louvain-la-Neuve, Belgium. FAX 10-472579.

780   CS   ISSN 0581-0558
MUSICOLOGICA SLOVACA. 1969. irreg. price varies. (Slovenska Akademia Vied, Umenovedny Ustav) Veda, Publishing House of the Slovak Academy of Sciences, Klemensova 19, 814 30 Bratislava, Czechoslovakia. (Dist. by: Slovart, Nam. Slobody 6, 817 64 Bratislava, Czechoslovakia) **Indexed:** Music Ind., RILM.

780   AT   ISSN 0155-0543
MUSICOLOGICAL SOCIETY OF AUSTRALIA. NEWSLETTER. 1977. 3/yr. membership. Musicological Society of Australia, G.P.O. Box 2404, Canberra, A.C.T. 2601, Australia. Ed. Lisa - Jane Ward. circ. 400. (back issues avail.)
Description: Carries news of Australian musicology and musicologists as well as international matters of interest to members.

780   GW   ISSN 0077-2496
MUSICOLOGICAL STUDIES AND DOCUMENTS. (Text in English; occasionally in French) 1948. irreg. (American Institute of Musicology, US) Haenssler Verlag, Postfach 1220, Bismarckstr. 4, 7303 Neuhausen-Stuttgart, Germany. TEL 07158-177-149. FAX 07158-177119. Ed. Armen Carapetyan.
—BLDSC shelfmark: 5990.880000.

450   AT   ISSN 0814-5857
ML5
MUSICOLOGY AUSTRALIA. 1965. a. Aus.$30. Musicological Society of Australia, G.P.O. Box 2404, Canberra, A.C.T. 2601, Australia. Ed. Peter Platt. adv.; bk.rev.; circ. 350. (back issues avail.) **Indexed:** Aus.P.A.I.S., Music Ind., RILM.
—BLDSC shelfmark: 5990.890100.
Formerly: Musicology (ISSN 0077-250X)
Description: Features articles on the music of Europe, America, Asia, Indian Ocean, Pacific Ocean, Australian Aborigines and Australian musical composition.

780.7   SA   ISSN 0256-8837
MUSICUS. (Text in Afrikaans and English) 1973. 2/yr. R.22($13) University of South Africa, Department of Music, P.O. Box 392, Pretoria 0001, South Africa. FAX 012-429-2533. TELEX 350068. Ed. H.H. van der Spuy. adv.; bk.rev.; circ. 2,000. (reprint service avail. from UMI)
Description: Presents articles written on different aspects of music and music examinations and their success.

780 700   CN   ISSN 0225-686X
ML5
MUSICWORKS; Canadian audio-visual journal of sound explorations. (Text in English, French; occasionally Inuit, Micmac) 1978. 3/yr. Can.$30 to individuals; institutions Can.$47. Music Gallery, 1087 Queen St. W., Toronto, Ont. M6J 1H3, Canada. TEL 416-533-0192. FAX 416-536-1849. Ed. Gayle Young. adv.; bibl.; charts; illus.; circ. 3,000. (also avail. in microfilm from MML; includes cassette; back issues avail.)
Description: Explores, from the artist's perspective, contemporary (including ethnic and indigenous) notions of music and sound.

780.5   FI   ISSN 0355-1059
MUSIIKKI. 1971. q. Fmk.70. Suomen Musiikkitieteellinen Seura, Vironkatu 1, 00170 Helsinki 17, Finland. Ed. Erkki Salmenharra. adv.; bk.rev.; circ. 600.

780   GW   ISSN 0930-8954
ML21.G3
MUSIK - ALMANACH; Musikleben in der Bundesrepublik Deutschland. triennial. (German Music Council) Gustav Bosse Verlag GmbH & Co. KG, Postfach 417, 8400 Regensburg 1, Germany. TEL 0941-794091. Ed.Bd.

780 792   SZ
MUSIK & THEATER; die aktuelle Kulturzeitschrift. 1979. m. (10/yr.). 75 Fr. Aemtlerstr. 201, CH-8040, Switzerland. TEL 071-235555. (Subscr. to: Kuenzler Bachman AG, Geltenwilenstr. 8A, 9001 St. Gallen, Switzerland) Ed. Andrea Meuli. adv.; rec.rev.; illus.
Description: News and information from the music and theater world. Includes lists of new records and performances, announcements of events, and classified ads.

780   GW
MUSIK AUS DER STEIERMARK. 1959. irreg. (4-6/yr.). price varies. (Styrian Composers Society) Musikverlag Fritz Schulz GmbH, Am Maerzengraben 6, 7800 Freiburg-Tiengen, Germany. FAX 07664-5123. Ed. Wolfgang Suppan. circ. 200.
Description: Publication of contemporary music by young composers. Features musical arrangements for all instruments. Each issue includes a single piece of music.

780   GW
MUSIK EXPRESS; sounds. 1967. m. DM.60. Medien Verlagsgesellschaft mbH, Werinherstr. 71, D-8000 Munich 90, Germany. TEL 089-9234-367. FAX 089-6913064. TELEX 523854. Ed.Bd. adv.; circ. 168,000.

780   SW   ISSN 0077-2518
MUSIK I SVERIGE. (Text in English, German and Swedish) 1969. irreg. price varies. Svenskt Musikhistoriskt Arkiv, Box 16326, S-103 26 Stockholm, Sweden. TEL 8-6664560. (Co-sponsor: Svenska Samfundet foer Musikforskning) **Indexed:** RILM.

780   GW   ISSN 0937-583X
MUSIK IN BAYERN. s-a. Verlag Dr. Hans Schneider GmbH, Mozartstr. 6, 8132 Tutzing, Germany.

780.7   GW   ISSN 0027-4704
ML5
MUSIK IN DER SCHULE; Zeitschrift fuer Theorie und Praxis des Musikunterrichts. 1949. m. DM.34. Volk und Wissen Verlag GmbH, Lindenstr. 54A, 1086 Berlin, Germany. TEL 0372-20343-0. Ed. Wolfgang Wunder. adv.; bk.rev.; abstr.; illus.; index; circ. 6,500. **Indexed:** Music Ind., RILM.
—BLDSC shelfmark: 5991.053000.
Description: Presents study and teaching methods.

789.91   GW
MUSIK - INFO. 1958. m. DM.75.60. Sigert Verlag GmbH, Ekbertstr. 14, 3300 Braunschweig, Germany. Ed. Guenter Hennemann. adv.; illus.; rec.rev.; circ. 5,000.
Formerly: Musik-Informationen (ISSN 0027-4712)

781.91   GW
MUSIK INTERNATIONAL; Instrumentenbau Zeitschrift. 1880. m. DM.73.90 (foreign DM.88.20). (Musik International Instrumentenbau) Verlag Franz Schmitt, Kaiserstr. 99-101, Postfach 1831, 5200 Siegburg, Germany. TEL 02241-64030. FAX 02241-53891. Ed.Bd. adv.; charts; illus.; index; circ. 5,000. **Indexed:** RILM.
Formerly: Instrumentenbau-Zeitschrift (ISSN 0020-4390)

780   GW   ISSN 0931-3311
MUSIK - KONZEPTE; die Reihe ueber Komponisten. 1977. 4/yr. DM.62. Edition Text und Kritik GmbH, Levelingstr. 6a, 8000 Munich 80, Germany. TEL 089-432929. FAX 089-433997. Eds. Heinz-Klaus Metzger, Rainer Riehn. **Indexed:** RILM.

780.7   GW   ISSN 0027-4747
ML5
MUSIK UND BILDUNG; Zeitschrift fuer Theorie und Praxis der Musikerziehung. 1969. m. DM.58.80. (Verband Deutscher Schulmusikerzieher) B. Schott's Soehne, Weihergarten 5, Postfach 3640, 6500 Mainz 1, Germany. TEL 06131-246850. Ed.Bd. adv.; bk.rev.; music rev.; rec.rev.; bibl.; charts; illus.; index; circ. 8,200. **Indexed:** Music Ind., RILM.
—BLDSC shelfmark: 5991.055000.
Supersedes: Musik im Unterricht, Ausgaben A and B.

MUSIC

780   GW   ISSN 0027-4755
ML5
MUSIK UND GESELLSCHAFT. 1951. m. DM.35.40 (foreign DM.49.80). (Verband der Komponisten und Musikwissenschaftler der DDR) Henschelverlag Kunst und Gesellschaft, Oranienburger Str. 67-68, 104 Berlin, Germany. adv.; bk.rev.; abstr.; illus.; index; circ. 4,500. **Indexed:** Music Ind., RILM.
—BLDSC shelfmark: 5969.055000.

780 301   AU   ISSN 0259-076X
MUSIK UND GESELLSCHAFT. 1967. irreg., no.21, 1990. price varies. Verband der Wissenschaftlichen Gesellschaften Oesterreichs, Lindengasse 37, A-1070 Vienna, Austria. TEL 932166.

783   SZ   ISSN 0027-4763
MUSIK & GOTTESDIENST. 1947. bi-m. 60 Fr. Gotthelf Verlag, Badenerstr. 69, CH-8026 Zurich, Switzerland. FAX 01-2418242. Eds. Heinz-Roland Schneeberger, Andreas Marti. adv.; bk.rev.; circ. 3,800. (also avail. in microform from UMI; reprint service avail. from UMI) **Indexed:** Music Ind, RILM.
—BLDSC shelfmark: 5991.065000.
Incorporates: Der Evangelische Kirchenchor.

783   GW   ISSN 0027-4771
ML5
MUSIK UND KIRCHE. 1930. bi-m. DM.50. Baerenreiter Verlag, Heinrich-Schuetz-Allee 31-37, 3500 Kassel-Wilhelmshoehe, Germany. TEL 0561-3105-0. FAX 0561-3105240. (U.S. subscr. addr.: Foreign Music Distributors, 13 Elkay Dr., Chester, NY 10918) Ed.Bd. adv.; bk.rev.; bibl.; illus.; circ. 4,000. **Indexed:** Arts & Hum.Cit.Ind.; Curr.Cont., Music Ind., RILM.

780   GW   ISSN 0077-2526
MUSIKALISCHE DENKMAELER. 1955. irreg. price varies. (Akademie der Wissenschaften und der Literatur, Mainz) B. Schott's Soehne Musikverlag, Weihergarten, 6500 Mainz 1, Germany. TEL 06131-240-0. FAX 06131-246211. TELEX 4187821.
Description: Studies the history of German music and composers.

787   GW   ISSN 0172-8989
ML3469
MUSIKBLATT; Zeitschrift fuer Gitarre, Folklore und Lied. 1974. bi-m. DM.42. W. Ulrichs Musikblattverlag, Tannenweg 14, 3400 Goettingen, Germany. TEL 0551-796606. FAX 0551-792681. Ed. Wieland Ulrichs. adv.; bk.rev.; bibl.; illus.; index; circ. 3,000. (back issues avail.)

780   DK   ISSN 0108-0040
MUSIKBRANCHENS AARBOG. 1982. a. DKK 29.75. Danplay, Krohsgade 1, 2100 Copenhagen OE, Denmark. Ed. Uffe Egekvist. adv.; bk.rev.; illus.; circ. 7,000.

780   DK
MUSIKEREN. 1911. m. (11/yr.). DKK 308. Musikeren ApS, Vendersgade 25, 1363 Copenhagen K, Denmark. FAX 33-337517. Ed. Henrik Strube. adv.; circ. 6,000.
Formerly: Dansk Musiker Tidende.

780   SW   ISSN 0027-478X
ML5
MUSIKERN. 1907. 10/yr. SEK 160. Svenska Musikerfoerbundet - Swedish Musicians Union, Box 43, 10120 Stockholm, Sweden. Ed. Ammi Lennander. adv.; bk.rev.; charts; illus.; mkt.; circ. 11,000. **Indexed:** Music Ind.
—BLDSC shelfmark: 5991.080000.

780   AU   ISSN 0027-4798
MUSIKERZIEHUNG; Zeitschrift der Musikerzieher Oesterreichs. 1947. 5/yr. S.300. Oesterreichischer Bundesverlag Gesellschaft mbH, Schwarzenbergstr. 5, Postfach 79, A-1010 Vienna, Austria. adv.; bk.rev.; rec.rev.; bibl.; charts; illus.; index; circ. 1,800. **Indexed:** Arts & Hum.Cit.Ind., Music Ind., RILM.
—BLDSC shelfmark: 5991.100000.

780.01   GW   ISSN 0027-4801
ML5
DIE MUSIKFORSCHUNG. 1947. q. DM.110 or membership. (Gesellschaft fuer Musikforschung) Baerenreiter Verlag, Heinrich-Schuetz-Allee 31-37, 3500 Kassel-Wilhelmshoehe, Germany. TEL 0561-3105-0. FAX 0561-3105240. (U.S. subscr. addr.: Foreign Music Distributors, 13 Elkay Dr., Chester, NY 10918) Eds. C-H. Mahling, W. Doemling. adv.; bk.rev.; abstr.; bibl.; charts; illus.; index; circ. 2,500. **Indexed:** Curr.Cont., Music Ind., RILM.

780   GW
ML5.I579
MUSIKFORUM - REFERATE UND INFORMATIONEN DES DEUTSCHEN MUSIKRATES. no.9, 1968. 3/yr. free. Deutscher Musikrat, Am Michaelshof 4-a, 5300 Bonn-Bad Godesberg, Germany. FAX 0228-352650. Eds. Richard Jakoby, Andreas Eckhardt.
Formerly: International Music Council. German Committee. Referate Informationen (ISSN 0538-8791)

780   GW   ISSN 0027-481X
ML5
MUSIKHANDEL. 1949. 8/yr. DM.36. (Gesamtverband Deutscher Musikfachgeschaefte e.V.) Musikhandel Verlagsgesellschaft mbH, Friedrich-Wilhelm-Str. 31, 5300 Bonn, Germany. FAX 0228-235916. (Co-sponsor: Deutsches Musikverleger-Verband e.V.) adv.; bk.rev.; rec.rev.; charts; illus.; circ. 2,450. **Indexed:** Music Ind.
—BLDSC shelfmark: 5991.113500.
Description: Trade publication for sheet music, musical instruments and record retailers. Features news, record reviews, new publications, and available positions.

780   DK   ISSN 0109-2618
MUSIKHISTORISK MUSEUM OG CARL CLAUDIUS' SAMLING. MEDDELELSER. 1982. biennial. DKK 30. Musikhistorisk Museum, Aabenraa 30, DK-1124 Copenhagen K, Denmark. Ed. Mette Mueller. adv.; illus.

681.8   GW   ISSN 0027-4828
ML5
DAS MUSIKINSTRUMENT. (Text in English, French, German, Italian) 1952. m. DM.101.10. Verlag Erwin Bochinsky GmbH, Muenchenerstr. 45, 6000 Frankfurt a.M. 1, Germany. TEL 069-239521. Ed.Bd. adv.; bk.rev.; charts; illus.; pat.; index; circ. 5,500. **Indexed:** RILM.
Description: International trade magazine devoted to the manufacturing, trade, handicraft and research of musical instruments and musical electronics. Includes book and magazine reviews.

780   NO
MUSIKK OG SKOLE. 1956. 8/yr. NOK 200. Landslaget Musikk i Skolen, Toftesgt. 69, 0552 Oslo 5, Norway. Ed. Elf Nesheim. adv.; bk.rev.; circ. 4,500. **Indexed:** RILM.

780   SW   ISSN 0027-4836
MUSIKLIVET - VAAR SAANG. 1928. q. SEK 60. (Sveriges Koerfoerbund) Sveriges Koerfoerbunds Foerlag, Rosenlundsgatan 54, 11863 Stockholm, Sweden. Ed. Inger Laurell. adv.; bk.rev.; bibl.; charts; illus.; circ. 15,000.
Formerly: Musiklivet.

780 658.8   GW   ISSN 0047-8474
DER MUSIKMARKT. 1959. s-m. DM.211.20. Josef Keller Verlag, Postfach 1440, 8130 Starnberg, Germany. Ed. Uwe Lencher. adv.; bk.rev.; circ. 9,300.

780   SW   ISSN 0282-8952
MUSIKMUSEETS SKRIFTER. 1964. irreg., no.21, 1991. price varies. Statens Musiksamlingar, Musikmuseet, Box 16326, S-10326 Stockholm, Sweden. FAX 46-86639181. circ. 1,000. **Indexed:** RILM.
Formerly: Musikhistoriska Museets. Skrifter (ISSN 0081-5675)

780   GW
MUSIKPAEDAGOGISCHE BIBLIOTHEK. 1962. irreg., vol.35, 1987. DM.24. Florian Noetzel Verlag, Heinrichshofen Buecher, Valoisstrasse 11, 2940 Wilhelmshaven, Germany. (Dist. in U.S. by: C.F. Peters Corp., 373 Park Ave. S., New York, N.Y. 10016) Ed. Walter Kolneder.

780   GW   ISSN 0177-350X
ML3830
MUSIKPSYCHOLOGIE. 1984. irreg. DM.44. (Deutsche Gesellschaft fuer Musikpsychologie) Florian Noetzel Verlag, Heinrichshofen Buecher, Postfach 580, 2940 Wilhelmshaven, Germany. Ed.Bd. circ. 1,000. (back issues avail.)

789.91   SW   ISSN 0027-4844
ML5
MUSIKREVY; allmaen musiktidsskrift. (Editions in English and German at irregular intervals) 1946. 8/yr. SEK 275. Bengt Pleijel, Ed. & Pub., P.O. Box 10 284, S-100 55 Stockholm, Sweden. adv.; bk.rev.; music rev.; rec.rev.; illus.; index; circ. 14,000.
—BLDSC shelfmark: 5991.114000.

MUSIKSTADT COLOGNE; Musik-Termine. see *TRAVEL AND TOURISM*

780   GW   ISSN 0178-8884
MUSIKTEXTE; Zeitschrift fuer neue Musik. 1983. 5/yr. DM.40($25) Verlag MusikTexte, Postfach 10 13 48, D-5000 Cologne 1, Germany. Ed.Bd. adv.; bk.rev.; circ. 1,200.

780   GW   ISSN 0177-4182
ML5
MUSIKTHEORIE. 1986. 3/yr. DM.70 (foreign DM.82). Laaber-Verlag, Regensburger Str. 19, 8411 Laaber, Germany. TEL 09498-2307. index. (back issues avail.)
—BLDSC shelfmark: 5991.114310.

780   SW   ISSN 0345-7699
MUSIKTIDNINGEN. 1973. bi-m. SEK 50. Torgil Rosenberg Reportage, Radarvagen 7, 183 04 Taby, Sweden. adv.; bk.rev.; illus.; circ. 1,500.

780   SW
MUSIKTIDNINGEN MUSIKOMANEN. 1980. 6/yr. SEK 100($15) Nya Mediaplan AB, P.O. Box 6903, 10239 Stockholm, Sweden. circ. 100,020. (back issues avail.)

780   DK
MUSIKVEJVISER FOR VEJLE AMT. 1981. a. free. Amtsmusikudvalget of Vejle Amt, Undervisnings- og kulturforvaltningen, Damhaven 12, 7100 Vejle, Denmark. TEL 05-835333. Ed. Lars Kristiansen. circ. 2,500.
Formerly: Musikvejleder for Vejle Amt.
Description: An index of the musical activity in Vejle Amt.

780.01   GW   ISSN 0005-8106
ML5
MUSIKWISSENSCHAFT. BEITRAEGE. 1959. q. DM.50. (Gesellschaft fuer Musikwissenschaft) Academia Verlag GmbH, Postfach 1663, 5205 St. Augustin 1, Germany. TEL 2241-333349. FAX 2241-341528. adv.; bk.rev.; illus.; index; circ. 800. **Indexed:** RILM.
—BLDSC shelfmark: 1885.700000.

780   CN
MUSIMAGAZINE. 6/yr. Publiart, Inc., 1741 Leprohon, Montreal, Que. H4E 1P3, Canada. TEL 514-769-7032. FAX 514-769-5884. Ed. Andre Boulet. circ. 12,000.

780   FR
MUSIQUE EN JEU. 1970. q. 120 F. Editions du Seuil, 27 rue Jacob, 75261 Paris Cedex 06, France. Ed. Dominique Jameux. adv.; rec.rev.; bibl.; index, cum.index; circ. 4,000. **Indexed:** Curr.Cont., RILM.

780   FI   ISSN 0356-7923
MUUSIKKO/MUSICIAN. 1922. m. Fmk.160. Suomen Muusikkojen Liitto r.y. - Finnish Musicians' Union, Uudenmaankatu 36 D21, 00120 Helsinki, Finland. TEL 90-640758. FAX 90-611282. Ed. Aslak Allinniemi. adv.; bk.rev.; rec.rev.; circ. 4,500.

780   RM   ISSN 0580-3713
ML5
MUZICA. (Text in Rumanian; summaries in French) 1950. m. 184 lei($38) (Uniunea Compozitorilor din Republica Socialista Romania) Editura Stiintifica si Enciclopedica, R. 71341, Piata Scinteii 1, Bucharest 33, Rumania. (Subscr. to: ROMPRESFILATELIA, P.O. Box 12-201, Calea Grivitei 64-66, Bucharest, Rumania) (Co-sponsor: Consiliul Culturii si Educatiei Socialiste) Ed. Vasile Tomescu. bk.rev.; circ. 1,400. **Indexed:** RILM.

780 370 NE ISSN 0378-0651
MUZIEK EN ONDERWIJS. 1962. bi-m. fl.15. Vereniging Leraren Schoolmuziek, Lageweg 10, 3815 VG Amersfoort, Netherlands. Ed. Max de Boer. adv.; bk.rev.; bibl.; illus.; index; circ. 1,000.

028.5 NE ISSN 0027-528X
MUZIEK EXPRES. 1956. s-m. Geillustreerde Pers, Postbus 63, Haarlem, Netherlands. TEL 023-304304. FAX 023-304704. TELEX 41371-41653. Ed. Rick Tawfik. adv.; bk.rev.; illus.; circ. 100,000.

783 NE
MUZIEKBODE.* 1932. m. fl.16. Nederlandse Federatie van Christelijke Muziekbonden, Postbus 204, 7100 AE Winterswijk, Netherlands, Netherlands. Ed. Wim Dragstra. adv.; bk.rev.; play rev.; abstr.; bibl.; illus.; stat.; tr.lit.; circ. 4,500.
Formerly: Christelijke Muziekbode (ISSN 0009-5176)

658.8 781.91 NE ISSN 0027-5301
MUZIEKHANDEL. 1950. m. free. Nederlandse Muziek Federatie, Eikbosserweg 181, 1213 RX Hilversum, Netherlands. TEL 035-48104. FAX 02159-46173. Ed. C. Smit. adv.; bk.rev.; bibl.; mkt.; tr.lit.; circ. 700 (controlled).
Description: Trade publication for the music industry. Covers sheet music publishing as well as musical instruments. Includes reports and announcements of meetings and events.

780.7 CI ISSN 0027-531X
ML5
MUZIKA. 1956. bi-m. 30 din.($3) Udruzenje Muzickih Pedagoga Hrvatske, Socijalisticke Revolucije, 17, Zagreb, Croatia. Ed. Andrija Tomasek. adv.; bk.rev.; abstr.; bibl.; charts; illus.; stat.; index, cum.index; circ. 1,300. (microform)
Formerly: Muzika i Skola.

780 XV ISSN 0580-373X
MUZIKOLOSKI ZBORNIK/MUSICOLOGICAL ANNUAL. (Text in various languages; summaries in English and Slovene) 1965. a. price varies. Univerza v Ljubljani, Filozofska Fakulteta, Oddelek za Muzikologijo, Askerceva 12, 61000 Ljubljana, Slovenia. TEL 061-150-001. FAX 061-159-337. Ed. Andrej Rijavec. illus.; index; circ. 500. **Indexed:** RILM.

781.7 US
MUZIKOS ZINIOS/MUSIC NEWS. (Text in Lithuanian) 1911. s-a. $10 membership. Lithuanian Music Alliance, c/o Antanas Giedraitis, 7310 S. California Ave., Chicago, IL 60629. TEL 312-737-2421. Ed. Stasys Slizys. circ. 250.
Description: Contains news of composers, musicians and singers from Lithuania. Provides information on programs and concerts.

780 HU ISSN 0027-5336
MUZSIKA. 1958. m. $23. Lapkiado Vallalat, Lenin korut 9-11, 1073 Budapest 7, Hungary. TEL 121-5440. (Subscr. to: Kultura, Box 149, H-1389 Budapest, Hungary) Ed. Maria Feuer. adv.; bk.rev.; illus.; circ. 7,500. **Indexed:** Music Ind., RILM.

781 PL ISSN 0027-5344
ML5
MUZYKA; kwartalnik poswiecony historii i teorii muzyki. (Text in Polish; summaries in English) 1956. q. $25. (Polska Akademia Nauk, Instytut Sztuki) Ossolineum, Publishing House of the Polish Academy of Sciences, Rynek 9, 50-106 Wroclaw, Poland. TELEX 0712771 OSS PL. Ed. Elzbieta Dziebowska. bk.rev.; music rev.; rec.rev.; bibl.; illus. (reprint service avail. for UMI) **Indexed:** Music Ind., RILM.
Description: History and theory of music.

781.71 PL
MUZYKA POLSKA W DOKUMENTACJACH I INTERPRETACJACH. 1980. irreg. price varies. Polskie Wydawnictwo Muzyczne, Al. Krasinskiego 11a, 31-111 Krakow, Poland. TEL 22-70-44. FAX 22-01-74. Ed.Bd.
Description: Papers on Polish music, devoted to composers, material and folklore papers.

780 398 RU
MUZYKAL'NAYA FOL'KLORISTIKA. (Text in Russian; summaries in English and German) 1973. irreg. 2 Rub. (Soyuz Kompozitorov Rossiiskoi S.F.S.R., Fol'klornaya Komissiya) Izdatel'stvo Sovetskii Kompozitor, 14-12, Sadovaya-Triumfalnaya St., 103006, Moscow, Russia. illus. **Indexed:** M.L.A.

780 RU ISSN 0027-5352
MUZYKAL'NAYA ZHIZN'. 1957. s-m. 22.80 Rub. (Soyuz Kompozitorov S.S.S.R.) Izdatel'stvo Sovetskii Kompozitor, 14-12, Sadovaya-Triumfalnaya St., 103006, Moscow, Russia. TEL (095) 209-75-24. Ed. I.E. Popov. index.

N A C CALENDAR OF EVENTS. (National Arts Centre) see *DANCE*

780.7 US ISSN 0027-576X
ML27.U5
N A C W P I JOURNAL. 1952. q. $25 to non-members. (National Association of College Wind & Percussion Instructors) Simpson Publishing Co., c/o Dr. R. Weerts, Ed., Division of Fine Arts, Northeast Missouri State University, Kirksville, MO 63501. TEL 816-785-4442. adv.; bk.rev.; charts; illus.; circ. 6,000 (controlled). (also avail. in microform from UMI; reprint service avail. from UMI) **Indexed:** Music Artic.Guide, Music Ind., RILM.
—BLDSC shelfmark: 6011.332000.

658.8 780 US ISSN 0027-5913
ML3790
N A M M MUSIC RETAILER NEWS. 1947. 4/yr. membership. National Association of Music Merchants Inc., 5140 Avenida Encinas, Carlsbad, CA 92008. TEL 619-438-8001. Ed. Richard Hallabrin. adv.; mkt.; stat.; tr.lit.; circ. 10,500 (controlled).
Formerly: N A M M Members Monthly Bulletin.

789.91 US
N A R M SOUNDING BOARD. s-m. National Association of Recording Merchandisers, 3 Eves Dr., Ste. 307, Marlton, NJ 08053.

784.9 US ISSN 0884-8106
ML27.U5
N A T S JOURNAL. 1944. 5/yr. $23 (foreign $27)(effective Sep. 1991). National Association of Teachers of Singing, Inc., 2800 University Blvd. N., JU Sta., Jacksonville, FL 32211. TEL 904-744-9022. Ed. James McKinney. adv.; bk.rev.; music rev.; rec.rev.; charts; illus.; index; circ. 6,000. (also avail. in microfilm from UMI; reprint service avail. from UMI) **Indexed:** Music Artic.Guide, Music Ind.
Formerly (until May 1985): N A T S Bulletin (ISSN 0027-6073)
Description: Presents study and teaching methods.

780 US
N E A GRANTMAKING PROGRAMS: MUSIC. a. free. National Endowment for the Arts, Public Information Office, 1100 Pennsylvania Ave., N.W., Washington, DC 20506. TEL 202-682-5400.
Description: Grant application guidelines.

N E A GRANTMAKING PROGRAMS: OPERA - MUSICAL THEATER. (National Endowment for the Arts) see *THEATER*

780 AT ISSN 0811-7497
N M A. (New Music Articles) 1982. 2/yr. Aus.$35 to individuals; institutions Aus.$75. N.M.A. Publications, 42 Canterbury St., Richmond, Vic. 3121, Australia. (Subscr. to: P.O. Box 185, Brunswick, Vic. 3056, Australia) Ed. Rainer Linz. adv.; bk.rev.; circ. 600. (back issues avail.)

787 NE
N N O MAGAZINE. 1989. bi-m. fl.20. Noord - Nederlands Orkest, Emmaplein 2, P.O. Box 818, 9700 AV Groningen, Netherlands. TEL 31-50-126200. FAX 31-50-138164. Eds. H.J. Smink, J. van Wouwe. circ. 3,500 (controlled).

782.1 US
N O A NEWSLETTER. 1977. q. $40 to non-members; institutions $50. National Opera Association, RD4, 393A, Clinton, NY 13323. TEL 315-853-6292. (Subscr. to: National Opera Assocaition, c/o Marajean Marvin, Ohio State University School of Music, 1866 College Road, Columbus, OH 43210.) Ed. JoElyn Wakefield-Wright. adv.; circ. 1,000. (tabloid format)
Description: Opera convention information, notices of competitions for members of the association, articles concerning opera, and news of member activit ies.

780 US ISSN 0146-9975
ML1
N S O A BULLETIN. 1959. q. membership; libraries $8. National School Orchestra Association, c/o University of Northern Colorado, Greeley, CO 80639. Ed. Donn L. Mills. bk.rev.; circ. 1,200-1,400. (back issues avail.) **Indexed:** Music Artic.Guide, Music Ind.

016.78 US ISSN 0093-0288
-ML1
N U QUARTER NOTES. 1972. 4/yr. free. Northwestern University, Music Library, Evanston, IL 60208. TEL 708-491-3434. Ed. Deborah Campana. bk.rev.; bibl.; circ. 350.
Formerly (until 1981): 1810 Overture.

780 GW ISSN 0170-8791
N Z: NEUE ZEITSCHRIFT FUER MUSIK. 1834. m. DM.56. B. Schott's Soehne, Weihergarten 1-9, Postfach 3640, 6500 Mainz, Germany. TEL 06131-246890. Ed.Bd. adv.; bk.rev.; music rev.; rec.rev.; charts; illus.; index; circ. 6,000. (also avail. in microfilm from BHP) **Indexed:** Curr.Cont., Music Ind., RILM.
Former titles: Melos (ISSN 0025-9020); Neue Zeitschrift fuer Musik (ISSN 0028-3509)

780 AU
NACHRICHTEN ZUR MAHLER FORSCHUNG. (Text in English and German) 1976. s-a. S.210($20) Internationale Gustav Mahler Gesellschaft, Wiedner Guertel 6, A-1040 Vienna, Austria. TEL 0222-5057330. circ. 1,000. (back issues avail.)

780 792 US
NASHVILLE SCENE.* w. 301 Broadway, Nashville, TN 37201-2005. TEL 615-371-9357.
Description: Covers entertainment, arts and leisure.

781.7 NE
NASHVILLE TENNESSEE. 1984. 11/yr. fl.45. Karel van der Kemp, P.O. Box 570, 2800 AN Gouda, Netherlands. TEL 01682-4877. Ed.Bd. adv.; bk.rev.; circ. 9,000.
Description: Devoted to country and rock and roll music, featuring articles and interviews with singers, international news, reports and lists of events and new records, photos.

780 XV ISSN 0027-8270
NASI ZBORI. (Text in Slovenian; summaries in English) vol.18, 1966. w. 300 din.($30) Zveza Kulturnih Organizacij Slovenije, Kidriceva 5, 61000 Ljubljana, Slovenia. Ed. M. Gobec.

780 US ISSN 0547-4175
ML27.U5
NATIONAL ASSOCIATION OF SCHOOLS OF MUSIC. DIRECTORY. 1950. a. $16. National Association of Schools of Music, 11250 Roger Bacon Dr., No. 21, Reston, VA 22090. TEL 703-437-0700.
Description: Lists accredited institutions and degree programs, with addresses, telephone numbers, and music executives of all member institutions.

780 US ISSN 0164-2847
ML27.U5
NATIONAL ASSOCIATION OF SCHOOLS OF MUSIC. HANDBOOK. 1930. biennial. $14. National Association of Schools of Music, 11250 Roger Bacon Dr., No. 21, Reston, VA 22090. TEL 703-437-0700. circ. 2,200.

780.7 US ISSN 0077-3409
NATIONAL ASSOCIATION OF SCHOOLS OF MUSIC. PROCEEDINGS OF THE ANNUAL MEETING. 1934. a. $18. National Association of Schools of Music, 11250 Roger Bacon Dr., No. 21, Reston, VA 22090. TEL 703-437-0700. **Indexed:** Music Ind.

NATIONAL BRAILLE ASSOCIATION. MUSIC CATALOG. see *HANDICAPPED — Visually Impaired*

786 US
NATIONAL CONFERENCE ON PIANO PEDAGOGY. PROCEEDINGS.* Variant title: Journal of the Proceedings. 1980. biennial. $20. National Conference on Piano Pedagogy, c/o Felsher, 36 Dead Tree Run Rd., Belle Mead, NJ 08502-5901. TEL 201-924-3969. circ. 1,000.

MUSIC

786.3 US ISSN 0077-4642
NATIONAL GUILD OF PIANO TEACHERS. GUILD SYLLABUS. 1943. a. $1. National Guild of Piano Teachers, Box 1807, Austin, TX 78767. TEL 512-478-5775. Ed. Richard Allison. circ. 14,000.

NATIONAL JEWISH ARTS NEWSLETTER. see ETHNIC INTERESTS

780.65 US
NATIONAL MUSIC PUBLISHERS' ASSOCIATION. NEWS & VIEWS. 1965. q. National Music Publishers' Association, 205 E. 42nd St., New York, NY 10017. TEL 212-370-5330. TELEX 237441 HAFOX UR. Ed. Margaret A. O'Keeffe. illus.; circ. 4,000.
Formerly (until 1991): National Music Publishers' Association. Bulletin.

786 US
NATIONAL PIANO MANUFACTURERS ASSOCIATION OF AMERICA. NEWSLETTER. s-a. National Piano Manufacturers Association of America, c/o Donald W. Dillon Associates, 4020 McEwen St., Dallas, TX 75244.

NATIONAL RADIO GUIDE; guide to C B C radio and C B C stereo. see COMMUNICATIONS — Radio

787.9 US
NATIONAL SACRED HARP NEWSLETTER; covering the country like kudzu. 1985. bi-m. $8. Sacred Harp Publishing Co., Inc., Box 551, Temple, GA 30179. (Subscr. to: Box 1828, Carrollton, GA 30117) Eds. Hugh McGraw, Richard DeLong. circ. 1,500.

780 US
NEBRASKA MUSIC EDUCATOR. 1940. q. $10. Nebraska Music Educators Association, 2325 S. 24th St., Lincoln, NE 68502-4099. Ed. Michael H. Veak. adv.; bk.rev.; circ. 1,950 (controlled). **Indexed:** Music Artic.Guide.
Description: Membership journal including columns by officers, music reviews, feature articles.

780.65 US
NETWORK NEWS (NEW YORK). 1982. q. $10 or membership. Composers' Forum, Inc., 596 Broadway, Ste. 602A, New York, NY 10012. TEL 212-334-0216. Ed. Bernadette Speach. adv.; circ. 2,500. (tabloid format; back issues avail.) **Indexed:** Music Artic.Guide.
Description: Announcements, opportunities, and items of interest pertaining to members, other composers, and performers worldwide.

780 GW
NETWORK PRESS; das deutschsprachige Magazin fuer Disco und Dance. 1985. bi-w. DM.108 (foreign DM.190). M.N.S. Hamburg, Deichstr. 23, D-2000 Hamburg 11, Germany. TEL 040-3600603. FAX 040-36006-111. Ed. Ruediger Kutz. circ. 20,000. (back issues avail.)

780 GW ISSN 0077-7714
NEUE MUSIKGESCHICHTLICHE FORSCHUNGEN. 1968. irreg. price varies. Breitkopf und Haertel, Walkmuehlstr. 52, Postfach 1707, 6200 Wiesbaden 1, Germany. TEL 0611-4903-0. FAX 0611-490359. TELEX 4182647-EB-D. Ed. Lothar Hoffmann-Erbrecht.

780 GW ISSN 0028-3290
NEUE MUSIKZEITUNG; musikalische Jugend - jeunesses musicales. 1952. bi-m. DM.25. (Verband Deutscher Musikschulen) Gustav Bosse Verlag, Von-der-Tann-Str. 38, Postfach 417, 8400 Regensburg 1, Germany. TEL 0941 941-794096. Ed. Theo Geissler. adv.; bk.rev.; play rev.; illus.; circ. 30,000. (tabloid format; also avail. in microfilm from BHP,KTO) **Indexed:** Music Ind.
Formerly: Musikalische Jugend.

780 US ISSN 0028-4181
ML156.9
NEW AMBEROLA GRAPHIC. 1971. q. $8 for 2 yrs. (foreign $10). New Amberola Phonograph Co., 37 Caledonia St., St. Johnsbury, VT 05819. Ed. Martin Bryan. adv.; bk.rev.; circ. 975.
Description: For collectors of records and phonographs from 1895-1935.

NEW CULTURE; a review of contemporary African arts. see ART

780.42 UK ISSN 0260-3330
NEW GANDY DANCER; the magazine for instrumental rock music. 1976. s-a. $3 per no. Instrumental Disc Services, 85-87 Napier Rd., Swalwell, Newcastle-upon-Tyne NE16 3BT, England. Ed. David Peckett. adv.; bk.rev.; charts, rec.rev.; circ. 1,000.
Description: Devoted to instrumental rock music. Includes features and artist profiles.

780.7 US ISSN 0028-5315
ML1
NEW HAMPSHIRE QUARTER NOTES.* vol.20, 1977. a. $10. New Hampshire Music Educators Association, Rt. 5, Box 240, Penacook, NH 03303. Ed. Nan Arnstein. adv.; bk.rev.; circ. 750 (controlled). **Indexed:** Music Artic.Guide.

780.7 US ISSN 0028-6265
NEW MEXICO MUSICIAN. 1954. 3/yr. $7. New Mexico Music Educators Association, 93 Mimbres Dr., Los Alamos, NM 87544. Ed. Donald E. Gerheart. adv.; bk.rev.; charts; illus.; circ. 1,700.
Description: Presents study and teaching methods.

780 UK ISSN 0028-6362
NEW MUSICAL EXPRESS. 1952. w. $97. I P C Magazines Ltd., Holborn Group (Subsidiary of: Reed Business Publishing Ltd.), King's Reach Tower, Stamford St., London SE1 9LS, England. TEL 01-261 5000. Ed. Neil Spencer. record rev.; circ. 123,200. (tabloid format)

780 US ISSN 0276-7031
ML18
NEW ON THE CHARTS. 1976. m. $185 (limited distribution). Music Business Reference, Inc., 70 Laurel Pl., New Rochelle, NY 10801. TEL 914-632-3349. FAX 914-633-7690. Ed. Leonard Kalikow. adv.; circ. 2,500 (controlled).

780.7 US
NEW OXFORD HISTORY OF MUSIC. irreg. price varies. Oxford University Press, 200 Madison Ave., New York, NY 10016. TEL 212-679-7300. Ed.Bd.

780 US
NEW ROUTE. 1986. q. $5. New Route Publishing, Inc., 67-73 Spring St., New York, NY 10012. TEL 212-941-5600. FAX 212-941-5664. Ed. Douglas Joseph. adv.; circ. 250,000. (back issues avail.)
Description: Music magazine written by college radio programmers for the young adult market.

NEW YORK ON STAGE. see THEATER

782.1 US
NEW YORK OPERA NEWSLETTER. m. Box 278, Maplewood, NJ 07040. TEL 201-378-9549. FAX 201-278-2372. Ed. David D. Wood.

781.7 398 US ISSN 1041-4150
NEW YORK PINEWOODS FOLK MUSIC CLUB NEWSLETTER. 1965. m. (except Aug.). $15. Folk Music Society of New York, 31 W. 95th St., New York, NY 10025. Ed. Eileen Pentel. adv.; bk.rev.; circ. 1,200.

783 UK ISSN 0263-2306
NEWS OF HYMNODY; noh. 1981. q. £2($5.50) Grove Books, Ltd., Bramcote, Nottinghamshire NG9 3DS, England. TEL 0602-430786. FAX 0602-220134. circ. 1,000.

780 621.389 IT
▼**NEWSFOR;** moda, modi, tecnologie, spettacolo professionale per discoteche, meeting, American bar. 1990. m. (11/yr.). L.66000 (foreign L.130000). Editecno s.r.l., Viale Abruzzi, 25, 20131 Milan, Italy. TEL 02-225291. FAX 02-29514395. Ed. Alfonso Graziano. adv.; bk.rev.; music rev.; illus.; circ. 7,800.
Description: Covers music, dance, technology, interior design, bartending, disc jockeying, and management for discotheques and bars.

NIKKEI ENTERTAINMENT. see COMMUNICATIONS

780 UK
NO. 1. 1983. w. I P C Magazines Ltd., Holborn Group (Subsidiary of: Reed Business Publishing Ltd.), Commonwealth House, 1-19 New Oxford St., London WC1 1NG, England. TEL 01-404-0700. Ed. Phil McNeil. circ. 232,400.

780 DK
NORDIC SOUNDS. 1982. 4/yr. free. (Nordic Council of Ministers) Danish Music Information Center, Vimmelskaftet 48, DK-1161 Copenhagen K, Denmark. Ed. Knud Ketting. circ. 5,000. **Indexed:** Music Ind.

780 NO ISSN 0029-2044
NORSK MUSIKERBLAD. 1914. 10/yr. NOK 160 in Scandinavia; elsewhere Kr.180. Norsk Musikerforbund - Norwegian Musicians' Union, Youngsgt. 11, 0181 Oslo, Norway. TEL 02-401-050. FAX 02-40-14-90. Ed. Tore Nordvik. adv.; bk.rev.; circ. 2,700. **Indexed:** Music Ind.
—BLDSC shelfmark: 6144.100000.

780 NO ISSN 0332-5482
NORSK MUSIKKTIDSSKRIFT. 1964. q. NOK 85($8) Norske Musikklaereres Landsforbund, Youngsgt. 11, 0181 Oslo 1, Norway. Ed. Joerg Johnsen. adv.; bk.rev.; circ. 1,700. **Indexed:** RILM.

780.7 US ISSN 0029-2753
NORTH DAKOTA MUSIC EDUCATOR. 1961. q. $10. North Dakota Music Educator's Association, 2103 E. Capitol Ave., Bismarck, ND 58501. TEL 701-221-3570. Ed. Angie Koppang. adv.; bk.rev.; circ. 834.

780 UK ISSN 0261-5096
NORTHUMBRIAN PIPERS' SOCIETY MAGAZINE. 1980. a. £1.35. Northumbrian Pipers' Society, c/o The Literary and Philosophical Society, Westgate Rd., Newcastle-upon-Tyne NE1, England. adv.; bk.rev.; rec.rev.; circ. 550.
Description: News items, articles, and reviews relating to Northumbrian bagpipes and Northumbrian music.

780 NO ISSN 0801-1087
NORWEGIAN MUSIC INFORMATION CENTER. BULLETIN. 1980. a. free. Norwegian Music Information Centre, Toftesgt. 69, N-0552 Oslo 5, Norway. TEL 02-37-09-09. FAX 02-356938. Ed. Lisbeth Risnes.

NOSTALGIA. see SOUND RECORDING AND REPRODUCTION

780.7 US ISSN 0029-3946
NOTES A TEMPO; the official publication of the West Virginia Music Educators Association. 1950. m. (Sep.-May). $3 (typically set in June). West Virginia Music Educators Association, Inc., Hall of Fine Arts, West Liberty State College, West Liberty, WV 26074-0335. TEL 304-336-8263. FAX 304-336-8285. Ed. Edward C. Wolf. adv.; stat. (processed)
Description: Covers all aspects of music education within the state of West Virginia.

780 RU ISSN 0029-4462
NOTNAYA LETOPIS'. 1931. q. $6.60. (Komitet po Pechati Soveta Ministrov) Izdatel'stvo Kniga, 50, Gorky St., 125047 Moscow, Russia. bibl.; index; circ. 930. (also avail. in microfiche from MUE; back issues avail.)

787 GW ISSN 0254-9565
NOVA GIULIANIAD; Saitenblaetter fuer die Gitarre und Laute. 1983. s-a. DM.14($10) (Internationale Gitarristische Vereinigung Freiburg e.V.) Orlando Syrg Verlag, Lessingstr. 4, 7800 Freiburg, Germany. TEL 0761-77407. Ed. Joerg Sommermeyer. adv.; bk.rev.; circ. 9,000. (back issues avail.)

780 IT
NUOVA RASSEGNA DI STUDI MUSICALI. 2/yr. L.40000. (Universita degli Studi di Padova, Centro di Studi Musicali Aggregati) Giardini Editori e Stampatori, Via Santa Bibbiana 28, 56100 Pisa, Italy. TEL 050-502531. Ed. Franco Piva.

780 IT ISSN 0029-6228
ML5
NUOVA RIVISTA MUSICALE ITALIANA; trimestrale di cultura e informazione musicale. 1967. q. L.60000 (foreign L.85000). E R I Edizioni R A I, Via Arsenale 41, 10121 Turin, Italy. TEL 011-8800. FAX 011-534732. Ed. Dir. Leonardo Pinzauti. adv.; bk.rev.; record rev.; bibl.; circ. 3,500. **Indexed:** Arts & Hum.Cit.Ind., Curr.Cont., Music Ind., RILM.

MUSIC

780.904 SW ISSN 0029-6597
ML5
NUTIDA MUSIK/CONTEMPORARY MUSIC. 1957. 4/yr. SEK 180. International Society for Contemporary Music, Swedish Section, c/o Svenska Rikskonserter, P.O. Box 1225, S-111 82 Stockholm, Sweden. FAX 08-784-1500. TELEX 10000 SRCENT S. Ed. Goeran Persson. bk.rev.; illus.; cum.index. **Indexed:** Music Ind., RILM.

780 GW ISSN 0179-8170
ML929
OBOE - KLARINETTE - FAGOTT. 1986. q. DM.44 (students DM.38). Verlag Karl Hofmann, Steinwasenstr. 6-8, Postfach 1360, 7060 Schorndorf, Germany. TEL 07181-7811. adv.; bk.rev.; index.
Formerly: Klarinette.
Description: For those interested in the clarinet.

780 PL
OBRZEDY I ZWYCZAJE LUDOWE. 1985. irreg. price varies. Polskie Wydawnictwo Muzyczne, Al. Krasinskiego 11, 31-111 Krakow, Poland. TEL 22-70-44. FAX 22-01-74. Ed. Alexandra Bogucka. illus.
Description: Publishes documents; ethnographic descriptions of traditional rites and customs. Includes narration, quotations of ritual text in dialect, songs and couplets with music.

780 AU ISSN 0023-3048
OESTERREICHISCHE AKADEMIE DER WISSENSCHAFTEN. KOMMISSION FUER MUSIKFORSCHUNG. MITTEILUNGEN. 1956. irreg. price varies. Verlag der Oesterreichischen Akademie der Wissenschaften, Dr. Ignaz-Seipel-Platz 2, A-1010 Vienna, Austria. FAX 0222-5139541.

OESTERREICHISCHE AUTORENZEITUNG. see *PATENTS, TRADEMARKS AND COPYRIGHTS*

780 GW ISSN 0078-3471
OESTERREICHISCHE GESELLSCHAFT FUER MUSIK. BEITRAEGE. 1967. irreg. price varies. Baerenreiter Verlag, Heinrich-Schuetz-Allee 31-37, 3500 Kassel-Wilhelmshoehe, Germany. TEL 0561-3105-0. FAX 0561-3105240. (U.S. subscr. address: Foreign Music Distributors, 13 Elkay Dr., Chester, NY 10918) Eds. R. Klein, K. Roschitz. **Indexed:** RILM.

780 920 AU ISSN 0078-3501
OESTERREICHISCHE KOMPONISTEN DES 20. JAHRHUNDERTS. 1964. irreg. price varies. Musikverlag Elisabeth Lafite, Hegelgasse 13-22, A-1010 Vienna, Austria. (And: Oesterreichischer Bundesverlag, Schwarzenbergstr. 5, 1015 Vienna 1, Austria)

780 AU ISSN 0029-9316
ML5
OESTERREICHISCHE MUSIKZEITSCHRIFT. 1946. m. S.410. Musikverlag Elisabeth Lafite, Hegelgasse 13-22, A-1010 Vienna, Austria. Ed. Christian Baier. adv.; bk.rev.; music rev.; rec.rev.; illus.; index. **Indexed:** Music Ind., RILM.
—BLDSC shelfmark: 6308.170000.
Incorporates (in 1979): Komponist.

780.01 AU
OESTERREICHISCHER MUSIKRAT - BULLETIN. 1965. s-a. Oesterreichischer Musikrat, Lothringer Str. 18, A-1030 Vienna, Austria. FAX 5872897. (Co-sponsor: Ministry for Education, Arts and Sports) Ed. Sigrid Wiesmann. bk.rev.; circ. 900. (back issues avail.)

784 AU ISSN 0473-8624
OESTERREICHISCHES VOLKSLIEDWERK. JAHRBUCH. 1952. a. S.200. Oesterreichisches Volksliedwerk, Fuhrmannsgasse 18, A-1080 Vienna, Austria. TEL 0222-420140. FAX 0222-4085148. Ed. Maria Walcher. bk.rev.; index; circ. 600. **Indexed:** RILM.
Formerly: Volkslied, Volkstanz, Volksmusik.

780.42 US
OFFENSE NEWSLETTER.* 1982. 12/yr. $7.20. Tet Offensive Productions, Box 12614, Columbus, OH 43212. Ed. Timothy K. Anstaett. bk.rev.; rec.rev.; circ. 500. (back issues avail.)
Supersedes (1980-1982): Offense.

786.6 US
OFFICIAL ELECTRONIC KEYBOARD BLUEBOOK;* used electronic keyboard valuation guide. 1967. a. $65. Sight & Sound Music Software, Inc., 1220 Mound Ave., Racine, WI 53404-3336. TEL 414-784-5850. FAX 414-784-5853. TELEX 910-262-3029. Ed. Deborah Nelson. illus.; stat.; index. cum.index; circ. 2,500.
Formerly (until 1985): Official Organ Blue Book (ISSN 0048-1513)

781.7 US
OKLAHOMA BLUEGRASS GAZETTE. 1975. m. membership. Oklahoma Bluegrass Club Inc., 8700 Hillview, Midwest City, OK 73150. Ed. Charles Blackwell. adv.; bk.rev.; illus.; tr.lit.; circ. 1,000. (tabloid format)

781.7 US ISSN 1044-1042
OLD TIME COUNTRY. q. $10 (foreign $20). University of Mississippi, Center for the Study of Southern Culture, University, MS 38677. TEL 601-232-5742. FAX 601-232-5740. Ed. W.K. McNeil. bk.rev.; record rev.
Incorporates: Jimmie Rodgers Memorial Association Newsletter.
Description: Contains musician profiles and conference information.

780 US
OLD-TIME HERALD; a magazine dedicated to old-time music. 1989. q. $15. Old-Time Music Group, Inc., 1812 House Ave., Durham, NC 27707. Ed. Alice Gerrard. adv.; illus.

780.5 GW
OLDIE - MARKT. 1977. m. DM.120($200) New Media Verlag, Mozartstr. 10, Postfach 1144, A-2090 Winsen-Luhe, Austria. TEL 04171-64243. FAX 04171-64355. Ed. Martin Reichold. adv.; bk.rev.; circ. 15,000.

780 US ISSN 1057-9893
ML1
▼**ON THE AIR MAGAZINE.** 1990. m. $20. Classical Guide, Inc., Box 19600, Denver, CO 80219. TEL 303-969-9021. FAX 303-988-1871. adv.; music rev.; circ. 6,700. (back issues avail.) **Indexed:** Music Artic.Guide.
Description: Contains program listings for classical music stations in eight major markets as well as articles about composers, performing artists, and other items of interest to classical music lovers.

780.42 US ISSN 0196-1446
ON THE ROCK. 1979. m. $15. Pumpernickel Press, Box 24-8741, Miami, FL 33124. Ed. Chris Freeman. adv.; bk.rev.; circ. 2,150.

780 778.534 AT
ON THE STREET. 1980. w. Aus.$52. 8 Bellevue St., Surry Hills, N.S.W. 2010, Australia. FAX 02-2115162. Ed. Manaser N. Crabbe. adv.; bk.rev.; film rev.; play rev.; charts; illus.; circ. 30,901. (back issues avail.)

780.42 US
ONE SHOT; the magazine of one hit wonders. 1986. s-a. $9 for 3 nos. One Shot Enterprises, Contract Sta. E, Box 145, 1525 Sherman St., Denver, CO 80203. TEL 303-744-6360. Ed. Steven Rosen. adv.; bk.rev.; circ. 250. (back issues avail.)
Description: Study and appreciation of now-obscure one-hit wonders of rock and pop music.

780 UK
ONE-TWO-TESTING. 1982. m. $24. I P C Magazines Ltd., Kings Reach Tower, Stamford St., London SE1 9LS, England. Ed. Paul Colbert. circ. 20,000.

780.01 JA ISSN 0030-2597
ONGAKU GAKU/JAPANESE MUSICOLOGICAL SOCIETY. JOURNAL. (Text in Japanese; summaries in English) 1954. 3/yr. 7000 Yen($60) Nippon Ongaku Gakkai - Musicological Society of Japan, c/o Tokyo National University of Fine Arts and Music, Department of Musicology, Ueno Park, Taito-ku, Tokyo 110, Japan. (Subscr. to: Academia Music Ltd. 3-16-5 Hongo, Bunkyo-ku, Tokyo 113, Japan) adv.; bk.rev.; abstr.; bibl.; charts; illus.; circ. 1,000. **Indexed:** RILM.
—BLDSC shelfmark: 6260.282000.
Description: Aims to present original articles in the field of musicology.

780.01 JA ISSN 0030-2600
ONGAKU GEIJUTSU/ART OF MUSIC. 1946. m. 770 Yen. Ongaku no Tomo Sha Corp., Kagurazaka 6-30, Shinjuku-ku, Tokyo 162, Japan. TEL 03-3235-2111. FAX 03-3235-2119. TELEX J23718 ONTOA. Ed. Yukio Kurosawa. adv.: B&W page 108000 Yen, color page 320400 Yen; trim 227 x 152. bk.rev.; circ. 36,000. **Indexed:** RILM.
Description: Specialized in the study and critics of music. Includes research on composers, their works, musical history and aesthetics of music.

780.7 JA ISSN 0289-3657
ONGAKU KYOIKU KENKYU/STUDY OF MUSICAL EDUCATION. q. 770 Yen. Ongaku no Tomo Sha Corp., Kagurazaka 6-30, Shinjuku-ku, Tokyo 162, Japan. TEL 03-3235-2111. FAX 03-3235-5731. TELEX J23718 ONTOA. adv.: B&W page 57600 Yen; trim 210 x 148. circ. 27,000.
Description: Theoretical study of multiphase problems in musical education for music instructors in elementary, secondary schools and colleges.

780 JA ISSN 0289-3606
ONGAKU NO TOMO/FRIENDS OF MUSIC. 1941. m. 770 Yen. Ongaku no Tomo Sha Corp., Kagurazaka 6-30, Shinjuku-ku, Tokyo 162, Japan. TEL 03-3235-2111. FAX 03-3235-2129. TELEX J23718 ONTOA. adv.: B&W page 288000 Yen, color page 552000; trim 277 x 210. illus.; circ. 120,000.
Description: Contains commentary and explanations of outstanding works and performances, stories of great composers and musicians, movements of music circles in the world as well as in Japan.

780.42 US
ONLINE DIGITAL MUSIC REVIEW. fortn. B B S Press Service Inc., 8125 S.W. 21st St., Topeka, KS 66615-1515. TEL 913-478-3157. Ed. Alan Bechtold. circ. 275,000.

780 US ISSN 0276-8747
OP; independent music. 1978. bi-m. $8. Lost Music Network, Box 2391, Olympia, WA 98507. Ed. John Foster. adv.; bk.rev.; illus.; circ. 10,000. (also avail. in microform from BLH)

780 GW ISSN 0030-3518
ML5
OPER UND KONZERT. 1963. m. DM.83. Industrie- und Handelswerbung A. Hanuschik, Ungererstr. 19-VI (Fuchsbau), 8000 Munich 40, Germany. Ed. Hans Huber. adv.; bk.rev.; music rev.; play rev.; rec.rev.; charts; illus.; circ. 4,150. **Indexed:** Music Ind.
—BLDSC shelfmark: 6266.350000.

782 IT ISSN 0030-3542
OPERA;* a magazine dedicated to the International Lyric Theatre. (Text mainly in Italian; some articles in English, French, German and Spanish) 1965. q. L.15000($24). Editoriale Fenarete, Via Beruto 7, Milan, Italy. Ed. Francesco Montuoro. circ. 10,000. **Indexed:** Music Ind.

782.1 UK ISSN 0030-3526
ML5
OPERA. 1950. m. £41($68) Opera Magazine, 1A Mountgrove Rd., London N5 2LU, England. TEL 071-359-1037. FAX 071-354-2700. (Subscr. to: DSB, 2A Sopwith Cres., Shotgate, Wickford, Essex SS11 8YU, England) Ed. Rodney Milnes. adv.; bk.rev.; music rev.; rec.rev.; illus.; index; circ. 12,000. (also avail. in microform from UMI; reprint service avail. from UMI) **Indexed:** Br.Hum.Ind., Hum.Ind., Music Ind., RILM.
—BLDSC shelfmark: 6266.400000.

782.1 IT
L'OPERA (MILAN). m. L.80000 (foreign L.100000). Edizioni di Sabino Lenoci, Via Carlo Botta, 4, 20135 Milan, Italy. TEL 02-5460154. FAX 02-54-60-154.

780 792 US
OPERA AMERICA. REPERTOIRE SURVEY. a. $20 to non-members; members $12. Opera America, 777 14th St., N.W., Ste. 520, Washington, DC 20005. TEL 202-347-9262. FAX 202-393-0735. Ed. Martha Perry. **Indexed:** Music Artic.Guide.
Description: Catalogs productions presented by Opera America companies during the preceeding season, with analysis of trends in operatic repertoire.

MUSIC

780 792 370   US
OPERA AMERICA NEWSLINE. 1972. m. (10/yr.). membership. Opera America, 777 14th St., N.W., Ste. 520, Washington, DC 20005. TEL 202-347-9262. FAX 202-393-0735. Ed. Martha Perry. adv.; bk.rev.; abstr.; stat.; circ. 2,100. (back issues avail.)
    Formerly (until 1991): Intercompany Announcements.
    Description: Reports on opera company activities and information currently affecting the field. Covers legislation, research, and management techniques, conferences, new publications, job listings and auditions.

782.1   US
OPERA ANNUAL U S (YEAR). 1988. a. $48. Jerome S. Ozer, Ed. & Pub., 340 Tenafly Rd., Englewood, NJ 07631. TEL 201-567-7040.
    Description: Examines opera sources throughout the U.S.

782.1   AT   ISSN 0155-4980
OPERA AUSTRALIA. 1978. m. Aus.$32($26) Pellinor Pty. Ltd., Level 2, 44 Bridge St., Sydney, N.S.W. 2000, Australia. TEL 02-247-2264. FAX 02-247-2269. Ed. David Gyger. adv.; bk.rev.; index, cum.index: 1978-1981, 1982-1985, 1986-1989; circ. 2,039. (tabloid format; back issues avail.)
    Description: Covers the opera and music theatre in Australia, with some reference to the international scene.

782.1   AT   ISSN 0810-8021
OPERA AUSTRALIA LIBRETTO SERIES. 1982. irreg. Aus.$8.80. Pellinor Pty. Ltd., Level 2, 44 Bridge St., Sydney, N.S.W. 2000, Australia. TEL 02-247-2264. FAX 02-247-2269. Ed. David E. Gyger. circ. 1,000. (back issues avail.)

782.1   CN   ISSN 0030-3577
ML5
OPERA - CANADA. 1960. 4/yr. Can.$18. Opera Canada Publications, Ste. 433, 366 Adelaide St. E., Toronto, Ont. M5A 3X9, Canada. TEL 416-363-0395. FAX 416-363-0395. Ed. Harvey Chusid. adv.; bk.rev.; rec.rev.; illus.; circ. 7,500. (also avail. in microform from UMI; back issues avail.; reprint avail. from UMI) **Indexed:** Can.Per.Ind., CMI, Music Ind., RILM.
    —BLDSC shelfmark: 6266.730000.

782.1   US
OPERA DIGEST. 1980. 6/yr. $12. Opera Index, 315 W. 23rd St., New York, NY 10011. TEL 212-691-0552. Ed. William H. Wells. adv.; bk.rev.; circ. 1,200. **Indexed:** Music Ind.

782.1   US
OPERA FANATIC; the magazine for lovers of expressive singing. q. $20 (foreign $25). Bel Canto Society, Inc., New York, NY 10023. TEL 800-341-1522. Ed. Stefan Zucker.

782.1   US   ISSN 0030-3585
ML1
OPERA JOURNAL. 1968. q. $20. National Opera Association, Inc., West Texas State University, WT Box 879, Canyon, TX 79016. TEL 806-656-2844. FAX 806-656-2076. Ed. Robert Hansen. adv.; bk.rev.; music rev.; illus.; index, cum.index; circ. 1,000. (also avail. in microfilm from UMI; reprint service avail. from UMI) **Indexed:** Music Artic.Guide, Music Ind.
    —BLDSC shelfmark: 6267.100000.
    Description: Articles on opera, and reviews.

786   US   ISSN 0897-6554
ML1699
OPERA MONTHLY. 1988. m. $25. That New Magazine, Inc., 28 W. 25th St., 4th Fl., New York, NY 10010. TEL 212-627-2120. FAX 212-727-9321. (And: Box 816, Madison Sq. Sta., New York, NY 10159) Ed. Thomas E. Steele. adv.; bk.rev.; circ. 5,000. (back issues avail.)
    Description: Includes reviews and interviews for the opera lover.

782.1   US   ISSN 0030-3607
ML1
OPERA NEWS. 1936. m. (May-Nov.); fortn. (Dec.-Apr.). $30. Metropolitan Opera Guild, Inc., 70 Lincoln Center Plaza, New York, NY 10023. TEL 212-769-7080. FAX 212-769-7007. TELEX 277504. Ed. Patrick J. Smith. adv.; bk.rev.; music rev.; rec.rev.; bibl.; illus.; index; circ. 120,000. (also avail. in microform from UMI; reprint service avail. from UMI) **Indexed:** Amer.Bibl.Slavic & E.Eur.Stud., Arts & Hum.Cit.Ind., Biog.Ind., Bk.Rev.Ind. (1965-), Child.Bk.Rev.Ind. (1965-), Curr.Cont., Hum.Ind., Mag.Ind., Music Artic.Guide, Music Ind., PMR, R.G., RILM.
    —BLDSC shelfmark: 6267.500000.
    Description: Contains interviews with prominent singers and conductors, historical background articles, performance reviews worldwide, plus cast lists, photographs, and plot summaries for weekly Metropolitan Opera radio broadcasts.

782.1   UK
OPERA NOW. 1989. m. £46. Rhinegold Publishing Ltd., 241 Shaftesbury Ave., London WC2H 8EH, England. TEL 071-836-2534. FAX 071-528-8786. Ed. Graeme Kay. adv.; bk.rev.; music rev.; rec.rev.; circ. 20,070.
    Description: Covers personalities: singers, performers, directors, producers, designers, and sponsors.

780   US   ISSN 0736-0053
ML1699
OPERA QUARTERLY. 1983. q. $36 to individuals; institutions $48. Duke University Press, Box 6697, College Station, Durham, NC 27708. TEL 919-684-2173. FAX 919-684-8644. Ed. Bruce Burroughs. adv.; bk.rev.; rec.rev.; illus.; circ. 6,000. (back issues avail.) **Indexed:** Arts & Hum.Cit.Ind., Curr.Cont., Music Artic.Guide, Music Ind.
    —BLDSC shelfmark: 6267.512000.
    Refereed Serial

782.1   DK   ISSN 0900-6354
ML1
OPERABLADET ASCOLTA. 1982. 8/yr. DKK 135. Operaens Venner, Anemonevej 4, 3500 Vaerloese, Denmark. TEL 42987166. Ed. J. Krisand. adv.; bk.rev.; illus.; circ. 3,800.
    Formerly: Ascolta (ISSN 0108-2124)

782.1   GW   ISSN 0935-6398
OPERNGLAS. 1980. m. DM.82.50($80) Opernglas Verlagsgesellschaft mbH, Lappenbergsallee 45, 2000 Hamburg 20, Germany. TEL 040-850-33-95. FAX 040-858112. Ed. Michael Lehnert. adv.; bk.rev.; rec.rev.; circ. 14,000.
    Description: Features opera reviews, interviews, information, artist information and calendar.

782.1   SZ   ISSN 0030-3690
ML5
OPERNWELT; die internationale Opernzeitschrift. 1963. m. 195 Fr. Orell Fuessli & Friedrich Verlag, Dietzingerstr. 3, CH-8036 Zurich, Switzerland. TEL 041-4667711. FAX 041-4667457. TELEX 813575. adv.; illus.; circ. 10,000 (controlled).
    Indexed: Music Ind.

780.01   US   ISSN 0882-178X
ML1
OPTION MAGAZINE. 1985. bi-m. $15.95. Sonic Options Network, 2345 Westwood Blvd., Ste. 2, Los Angeles, CA 90064. TEL 310-474-2600. Ed. Scott Becker. adv.; bk.rev.; illus.; circ. 20,500. (back issues avail.)
    Description: Covers non-mainstream music.

OPUS. see *SOUND RECORDING AND REPRODUCTION*

780   CS   ISSN 0862-8505
OPUS MUSICUM. 1969. 10/yr. 90 Kcs.($30) Statni Filharmonie Brno, Radnicka 10, 60200 Brno, Czechoslovakia. (Foreign subscr. to: Kubon and Sagner, P.O. Box 340108, 8000 Munich, P.O. Box 34108, Germany) (Co-sponsor: Asociace Hudebnich Umelcu a Vedcu) Ed. Eva Drlikova. adv.; bk.rev.; illus.; circ. 1,500. **Indexed:** Music Ind., RILM.

780.01   IS   ISSN 0303-3937
ORBIS MUSICAE; Assaph studies in the arts. (Text in English, French, German) 1971. biennial. $18.50. Tel Aviv University, Department of Musicology, Ramat Aviv, Tel Aviv, Israel. FAX 3-419513. (Dist. by: Theodore Front Musical Literature, Inc., 16122 Cohasset St., Van Nuys, CA 19406; And: Theodore Front Musical Literature, Inc., 16122 Cohasset St., Van Nuys, CA 19406, USA. TEL 818-994-1902) Ed.Bd. bk.rev.; circ. 500. (back issues avail.) **Indexed:** Music Ind.
    —BLDSC shelfmark: 6277.867000.
    Description: Articles in musicology and ethnomusicology by international scholars.

785   GW   ISSN 0030-4468
ML5
DAS ORCHESTER; Zeitschrift fuer deutsche Orchesterkultur und Rundfunk-Chorwesen. 1953. m. DM.84. (Deutsche Orchestervereinigung) B. Schott's Soehne, Weihergarten 1-9, Postfach 3640, 6500 Mainz 1, Germany. TEL 06131-246850. Eds. R. Duennwald, G. Engelmann. adv.; bk.rev.; charts; illus.; index; circ. 12,400. **Indexed:** Music Ind., RILM.
    —BLDSC shelfmark: 6277.925000.

780.6   CN   ISSN 0380-1799
ORCHESTRA CANADA/ORCHESTRES CANADA. (Text in English, French) 1974. 8/yr. Can.$15.50. Association of Canadian Orchestras, 56 The Esplanade, Ste. 311, Toronto, Ont. M5E 1A7, Canada. TEL 416-366-8834. (Co-sponsor: Ontario Federation of Symphony Orchestras) Ed. Jack Edds. adv.; circ. 3,000.
    Description: Contains reviews of government legislation, cultural issues, news, people, and orchestras.

780.7   US   ISSN 0030-4743
OREGON MUSIC EDUCATOR.* vol.25, 1973. 3/yr. $2 to non-members. 337 W. Riverside Dr., Roseburg, OR 97470. TEL 503-673-6353. Ed. Robert E. Robins. adv.; bk.rev.; illus.; music rev.; circ. 2,000. **Indexed:** Music Artic.Guide.
    Description: Presents study and teaching methods.

780   US   ISSN 0095-2613
ML1
ORFF ECHO. 1968. 4/yr. $35 to individuals; libraries $40. American Orff-Schulwerk Association, 332 Gerard Ave., Elkins Park, PA 19117. TEL 215-635-2622. FAX 215-625-2415. (Subscr. to: c/o Cindi Wobig, Box 391089, Cleveland, OH 44139-1089. TEL 216-543-5366) Ed. Tossi Aaron. adv.; bk.rev.; circ. 4,800. **Indexed:** Music Artic.Guide.

780   AT
ORFF-SCHULWERK ASSOCIATION OF QUEENSLAND. BULLETIN.* 1968. m. Aus.$3. Orff-Schulwerk Association of Queensland, c/o Australian National Council of Orff-Schulwerk Association, 32 Cuthbert St., Heathmont, Vic. 3135, Australia.

786.6   UK   ISSN 0030-4883
ORGAN; review for its makers, its players and its lovers. 1921. q. £13 (foreign £17.50). T.G. Scott & Son Ltd., 30-32 Southampton St., London WC2E 7HR, England. TEL 071-240-2032. FAX 071-379-7155. TELEX 299181. Ed. D. Carrington. adv.; rec.rev.; charts; illus.; circ. 2,000. **Indexed:** Arts & Hum.Cit.Ind., Br.Hum.Ind., Curr.Cont., Music Ind., RILM.
    —BLDSC shelfmark: 6285.300000.

780   GW
ORGAN BUILDING PERIODICAL/ZEITSCHRIFT FUER ORGELBAU; I S O information. (Text in English and German) 1969. irreg. DM.45 for 3 issues. (International Society of Organbuilders - Internationale Orgelbauer-Vereinigung) Orgelbau-Fachverlag, Postfach 226, 7128 Lauffen-N., Germany. FAX 07133-7058. Ed. Richard Rensch. bk.rev.; circ. 2,200. **Indexed:** Music Ind.
    Formerly: I S O Information (ISSN 0579-5613)

786   UK   ISSN 0306-0357
ORGAN CLUB JOURNAL. 1964. bi-m. $14. Organ Club, c/o Philip Weston, Gen. Sec., 36 Fortismere Ave., London N10 3BL, England. (Subscr. to: James Treloar, 29 Columbine Close, Huntingdon, Chester CH3 6BQ, England) bk.rev.; circ. controlled.

MUSIC 3573

786 US
ORGAN PORTFOLIO. bi-m. $14.95. Lorenz Publishing Co., 501 E. Third St., Box 802, Dayton, OH 45401-0802. TEL 513-228-6118. Ed. Dorothy Wells.
   Description: Includes arrangements for the trained organist.

780 NE ISSN 0078-6098
ORGAN YEARBOOK; a journal for the players and historians of keyboard instruments. (Text in English, French and German) 1970. a. fl.49. Uitgeverij Frits Knuf B. V., Box 720, 4116 ZJ Buren, Netherlands. FAX 31-349-2617. Ed. Peter Williams. adv.; bk.rev.; circ. 3,000. (back issues avail.) **Indexed:** Music Ind., RILM.
   —BLDSC shelfmark: 6285.800000.

786 US
ORGANIST. bi-m. $14.95. Lorenz Publishing Co., 501 E. Third St., Box 802, Dayton, OH 45401-0802. TEL 513-228-6118. Ed. James Mansfield.
   Description: Arrangements for the organist with little or no training.

786 UK
ORGANISTS' BENEVOLENT LEAGUE. ANNUAL REPORT. 1909. a. free. Organists' Benevolent League, c/o R.C. Lyne, Ed., 10 Stratford Place, London W1N 9AE, England. circ. 2,500.

786.6 UK ISSN 0048-2161
ORGANISTS' REVIEW. 1913. q. £12 (elsewhere £13.50). (Incorporated Association of Organists) Marcus Knight, 6 Homefield Close, Chelmsford, Essex CM1 2HE, England. TEL 0245-259120. Ed. Paul Hale. adv.; bk.rev.; rec.rev.; tape rev.; circ. 6,500. (also avail. in microform from UMI; reprint service avail. from UMI) **Indexed:** Music Ind.
   Description: Contents include articles on pipe organs, organ music, organ builders, association news, record and tape reviews.

786 786 IT ISSN 0474-6376
ORGANO; rivista di cultura organaria e organistica. (Text in Italian; summaries in English, French, German and Italian) 1960. s-a. L.60000($20) Patron Editore, Via Badini 12, Quarto Inferiore, 40127 Bologna, Italy. Eds. Oscar Mischiati, Luigi Tagliavini. bk.rev.; index. (back issues avail.) **Indexed:** RILM.
   —BLDSC shelfmark: 6291.059000.

786.6 FR ISSN 0030-5170
ML5
ORGUE; histoire-technique-esthetique-musique. (Supplement avail: Cahiers et Memoires de l'Orgue) 1929. q. 330 F. Association des Amis de l'Orgue, 70 rue de Rivoli, 75004 Paris, France. TEL 42-78-60-23. Ed. Brigitte De Leersnyder. adv.; bk.rev.; bibl.; charts; illus. **Indexed:** Music Ind., RILM.

781.57 SW ISSN 0030-5642
ML5
ORKESTER JOURNALEN. 1933. m. SEK 340. Stiftelsen Orkester Journalen, Box 4204, Oestgoetagatan 44, 10263 Stockholm, Sweden. Ed. Lars Westin. adv.; bk.rev.; rec.rev.; circ. 3,000. (back issues avail.) **Indexed:** Music Ind.
   Description: Focuses on jazz music.

780 GW
ORPHEUS. 1972. m. DM.137. Neue Gesellschaft fuer Musikinformation mbH, Livlaendischestr. 27, 1000 Berlin 31, Germany. TEL 030-8532387. FAX 030-8542207. Ed. Geerd Heinsen. adv.; bk.rev.; index. (back issues avail.; reprint service avail. from KTO)

780.904 AT
OSSIA; a journal of contemporary music. 1989. 3/yr. Aus.$18 to non-members. Fellowship of Australian Composers, P.O. Box 522, Strathfield, N.S.W. 2134, Australia. Ed. Paul Brown. circ. 250.

780 US
OVERTURE (BALTIMORE). 1977. 5/yr. free. Baltimore Symphony Orchestra, Inc., c/o Marjorie Cassel, Adv. Mgr., 1212 Cathedral St., Baltimore, MD 21201-5545. TEL 301-783-8100. FAX 301-783-8077. TELEX 87770 BAL. Ed. Jan Bedell. adv.; circ. 300,000.
   Description: Covers news, upcoming events and interviews with guest artists and members of the Baltimore Symphony Orchestra.

780 331.8 US ISSN 0030-7556
ML1
OVERTURE (LOS ANGELES). 1919. m. $20 to non-members. American Federation of Musicians, Musicians' Union, Local 47, A F L - C I O, 817 N. Vine St., Los Angeles, CA 90038. TEL 213-462-2161. Ed. Serena Kay Williams. adv.; charts; illus.; circ. 12,000.

OVERTURES; the magazine devoted to the musical on stage and record. see *THEATER*

780 US
OXFORD MONOGRAPHS ON MUSIC. irreg. price varies. Oxford University Press, 200 Madison Ave., New York, NY 10016. TEL 212-679-7300.

780 US ISSN 0078-7264
OXFORD STUDIES OF COMPOSERS. irreg. no.19, 1982. price varies. Oxford University Press, 200 Madison Ave., New York, NY 10016. TEL 212-679-7300. Ed. Colin Mason.

780.7 US ISSN 0030-8102
P M E A NEWS. 1952. 4/yr. $8. Pennsylvania Music Educators Association, Inc., c/o R. Merrell, 823 Old Westtown Rd., West Chester, PA 19382. TEL 215-436-9281. adv.; bk.rev.; charts; illus.; index; circ. 5,000. **Indexed:** Music Artic.Guide.
   Description: Professional journal for Pennsylvania music educators.

780 US ISSN 0030-8153
P.M.O. NOTES. 1943. q. $25. Purdue University Musical Organizations, Edward C. Elliott Hall of Music, W. Lafayette, IN 47907. TEL 317-494-3941. Ed. Dave Lamie. illus.; circ. 1,500. (processed)
   Description: Features articles and pictures on recent events, including musical shows, concerts, tours and student organization activities.

780 UK ISSN 0964-9875
▼**P R S MEMBERS HANDBOOK.** 1991. irreg. membership. Performing Right Society Ltd., c/o Terri Anderson, 29-33 Berners St., London W1P 4AA, England. TEL 071-580-5544. circ. 27,000.

780 UK
P R S NEWS. 1976. 2/yr. membership. Performing Right Society Ltd., c/o Terri Anderson, 29-33 Berners St., London W1P 4AA, England. TEL 071-580-5544. circ. 27,000. **Indexed:** Music Ind.
   Former titles: Performing Right News (ISSN 0309-0019); Performing Right (ISSN 0031-5257)
   Description: For organizations related to the music industry, and their members.

780 CN
▼**PAGEANTRY ONTARIO.** 1991. m. Can.$25 to non-members. Ontario Drum Corps Association, 258 King St. N., Ste. 12 J, Waterloo, Ont. N2J 2Y9, Canada. TEL 519-746-0042. FAX 519-746-4936. Ed. Lynne Sosnowski. adv.; circ. 150. (back issues avail.)
   Description: Registry of North American parades.

780 PL ISSN 0137-3935
PAGINE; Polsko-Wloskie materialy muzyczne - argomenti musicali Polacco-Italiani. (Text in Italian and Polish; summaries in Italian) irreg. irreg. price varies. (Polish Music Council, Warsaw) Polskie Wydawnictwo Muzyczne, Al. Krasinskiego 11a, 31-111 Krakow, Poland. TEL 22-70-44. FAX 22-01-74. Ed. Michal Bristiger. bk.rev.; index. **Indexed:** RILM.
   Description: Articles about Italian music by Polish, Italian and other authors.

PALACE PEEPER. see *THEATER*

780 CN
PARADES & PAGEANTRY. 1972. m. Can.$25 to non-members. Ontario Drum Corps Association, 258 King St., N., Ste. 12 J, Waterloo, Ont. N2J 2Y9, Canada. TEL 519-746-0042. FAX 519-746-4936. Ed. Lynne Sosnowski. adv.; circ. 450. (back issues avail.)
   Formerly: Information Drum Corps.

780 FR ISSN 0247-0357
PAROLES ET MUSIQUE; le mensuel de toutes les musiques. 1980. m. 275 F. Editions de l'Araucaria, 1 rue du Pont-De-Lodi, 75006 Paris, France. Ed. Fred Hidalgo.

PAST TIMES: THE NOSTALGIA ENTERTAINMENT NEWSLETTER. see *COMMUNICATIONS — Television And Cable*

783 US ISSN 0363-6569
ML1
PASTORAL MUSIC. 1976. bi-m. $27 to libraries. National Association of Pastoral Musicians, 225 Sheridan St., N.W., Washington, DC 20011. TEL 202-723-5800. Ed. Virgil Funk. adv.; bk.rev.; illus.; circ. 9,500. (also avail. in microfilm from UMI; back issues avail.; reprint service avail. from UMI) **Indexed:** Cath.Ind., CERDIC, Music Artic.Guide, Music Ind.
   Supersedes: Musart (ISSN 0027-3724)

783 US ISSN 0145-6636
ML2999
PASTORAL MUSIC NOTEBOOK. 1977. bi-m. membership. National Association of Pastoral Musicians, 225 Sheridan St. N.W., Washington, DC 20011. TEL 202-723-5800. Ed. Gordon E. Truitt. circ. 8,500.

789.9 US ISSN 0360-2109
ML156.9
PAUL'S RECORD MAGAZINE. 1975. irreg. nos.17-18, 1978. $5 per no. Paul E. Bezanker, Ed. & Pub., Box 843, Enfield, CT 06083-0843. adv.; bk.rev.; rec.; rev.; illus.; stat.; index, cum.index; circ. 1,500. **Indexed:** Pop.Mus.Per.Ind.

PEABODY NEWS. see *COLLEGE AND ALUMNI*

787 US
PEDAL STEEL NEWSLETTER. 1973. 10/yr. $20 (foreign $30). Pedal Steel Guitar Association, Inc., Box 248, Floral Park, NY 11001. Ed. Doug Mack. adv.; circ. 1,200. (back issues avail.)
   Description: Concerns the pedal steel guitar, how it is played, and those who play it.

786 286 US ISSN 0272-9199
ML2999
PEDALPOINT. q. $31.75. Southern Baptist Convention, Sunday School Board, 127 Ninth Ave., N., Nashville, TN 37234. TEL 800-458-2772.

780.6 US
PEOPLE'S SONGLETTER. 4/yr. membership. Newsong Network, 61 Wurts St., Kingston, NY 12401. TEL 914-338-8587.

780 US
PERCUSSION NEWS. bi-m. $40 (students $20); includes Percussive Notes. Percussive Arts Society, Inc., Box 25, Lawton, OK 73502-0025. TEL 405-353-1455. FAX 405-353-1456. Ed. S. Beck.

789 US ISSN 0553-6502
ML1
PERCUSSIVE NOTES. 1961. 6/yr. $40 (students $20); includes Percussion News. Percussive Arts Society, Inc., Box 25, Lawton, OK 73502-0025. TEL 405-353-1455. FAX 405-353-1456. Ed. James Lambert. adv.; bk.rev.; illus.; index, cum.index; circ. 5,500. (also avail. in microform from UMI; reprint service avail. from UMI) **Indexed:** Music Artic.Guide., Music Ind., RILM.
   —BLDSC shelfmark: 6423.560000.
   Formerly: Percussionist (ISSN 0553-6499); Incorporates: Percussionist and Percussive Notes (ISSN 0031-5168)

780 US ISSN 1044-1638
ML1
PERFORMANCE PRACTICE REVIEW. 1988. s-a. $16 to individuals; institutions $32; students $8. Claremont Graduate School, Music Department, 105 E. 10th St., Claremont, CA 91711-6160. TEL 714-621-8000. Ed. Roland Jackson. adv.; bk.rev.; circ. 600. **Indexed:** Music Artic.Guide.
   —BLDSC shelfmark: 6423.833000.
   Description: Addresses the concerns of musicians.

PERFORMING ARTS; the theatre & music magazine. see *THEATER*

PERFORMING ARTS IN CANADA. see *THEATER*

780   UK   ISSN 0309-0884
ML27.G7
PERFORMING RIGHT YEAR BOOK. 1977. a. membership. Performing Right Society Ltd., c/o Terri Anderson, 29-33 Berners St., London W1P 4AA, England. TEL 071-580-5544.
  Description: Reviews the previous year's activities, including the society's annual report and accounts.

780   US   ISSN 0191-1554
ML1
PERFORMING WOMAN; a national directory of professional women musicians. 1978. a. $5. J.D. Dinneen, Ed. & Pub., 26910 Grand View Ave., Hayward, CA 94542. circ. 4,000.

780   US
PERGOLESI STUDIES/STUDI PERGOLESIANI. 1986. irreg. (vol.2, 1989). Pendragon Press, R.R. 1, Box 159, Stuyvesant, NY 12173-9720. TEL 518-828-3008. FAX 518-828-2368.

781.7   RU
PERSONALITIES. EVENTS. TIMES; albums. 1982. a. 15 Rub. Izdatel'stvo Muzyka, Ul. Neglinnaya 14, Moscow 103031, Russia.

780.904   US   ISSN 0031-6016
ML1
PERSPECTIVES OF NEW MUSIC. 1962. s-a. $30 to individuals; institutions $60. Perspectives of New Music, Inc., School of Music DN-10, University of Washington, Seattle, WA 98195. TEL 206-543-0196. FAX 206-543-9285. Ed. John Rahn. adv.; bk.rev.; rec.rev.; charts; illus.; index, cum.index; circ. 1,500. (also avail. in microform from UMI; back issues avail.; reprint service avail. from UMI) **Indexed:** Amer.Bibl.Slavic & E.Eur.Stud, Arts & Hum.Cit.Ind., Curr.Cont., Ind.Bk.Rev.Hum., Music Artic.Guide, Music Ind., RILM.
—BLDSC shelfmark: 6428.145900.

780   UK   ISSN 0266-366X
PETER WARLOCK SOCIETY NEWSLETTER. 1965. 6/m. £8 membership. Peter Warlock Society, 100 Boileau Rd., London W5 3AJ, England. Ed. David Cox. bk.rev.; circ. 150. (processed)

784   GW   ISSN 0031-6687
PFAELZER SAENGER. 1949. m. DM.9. (Pfaelzischer Saengerbund) Pfaelzer Saenger, Hauptstr. 80, Postfach 1343, 6757 Waldfischbach-Burgalben, Germany. Ed. H.J. Hoffmann. adv.; circ. 5,000.

781.7
PHILADELPHIA FOLKSONG SOCIETY NEWSLETTER. m. (excl. July-Sept.). membership. Philadelphia Folksong Society, 7113 Emlen St., Philadelphia, PA 19119. TEL 215-247-1300. Ed. Rosemarie Urbano. circ. 1,575.
  Formerly: Tune Up (ISSN 0161-3081)
  Description: Covers community news, membership information, and concert and event listings.

780.6   GW
PHILHARMONISCHE BLAETTER (BERLIN). 1960? 6/yr. DM.18. Berliner Philharmonisches Orchester, Matthaeikirchstr. 1, 1000 Berlin 30, Germany. TEL 030-254880. FAX 030-261-4887. Ed. Helge Gruenewald. adv.; illus.; circ. 30,000. (back issues avail.)

780   GW
PHILHARMONISCHE BLAETTER (MUNICH). 1985. m. DM.20. Muenchener Philharmoniker, Kellerstr. 4, 8000 Munich 80, Germany. TEL 089-480980. FAX 089-48098525. TELEX 523400. adv.
  Description: News about the Munich Philharmonic Orchestra.

780   BE
PHILIPPE DE MONTE OPERA. SERIES A, MOTETS. 1975. irreg., vol.7, 1986. Leuven University Press, Krakenstraat 3, B-3000 Leuven, Belgium. TEL 016-284175. FAX 016-284176.

780   BE
PHILIPPE DE MONTE OPERA. SERIES B, MASSES. 1976. irreg., vol.2, 1979. Leuven University Press, Krakenstraat 3, B-3000 Leuven, Belgium. TEL 016-284175. FAX 016-284176.

780   BE
PHILIPPE DE MONTE OPERA. SERIES D, MADRIGALS. 1977. irreg., vol.4, 1988. Leuven University Press, Krakenstraat 3, B-3000 Leuven, Belgium. TEL 016-284175. FAX 016-284176.

789.91   US
PHILLIP EDWARDS MILLION DOLLAR RECORD REVIEW; gospel, jazz, slow jams, reggae, R&B, dance hip hop, videos, house, socalypso. m. $1 per no. Box 6400, Bridgeport, CT 06606. TEL 203-335-4557. FAX 203-335-3911. Ed. Phillip Edwards.

780.65   GW
PHONO PRESS. 1973. s-a. free. Bundesverband Phono e.V., Grelckstr. 36, 2000 Hamburg 54, Germany. TEL 040-580258. FAX 040-582842. circ. 2,000.

789.91   US
PHONOLOG REPORTER. 1948. w. $480. Phonolog Publishing (Subsidiary of: Trade Service Corporation), 10996 Torreyana Rd., Box 85007, San Diego, CA 92138. TEL 619-457-5920. Ed. Bonnie J. Dudley. (looseleaf format)

780.42   IT
PHOTOROCK & RECORDS.* 12/yr. L.20000. Gruppo Editoriale Suono s.r.l., Via Capo Peloro, 30, 00141 Rome, Italy. TEL 893608.

786   FR   ISSN 0999-5404
PIANO. a. 65 F. (foreign 70 F.). 12 rue Jacob, 75006 Paris, France. TEL 47-34-06-91. FAX 42-73-18-47. Ed. Michele Worms.

786.3   US   ISSN 0031-9546
PIANO GUILD NOTES. 1945. bi-m. $10. National Guild of Piano Teachers, Box 1807, Austin, TX 78767. TEL 512-478-5775. Ed. Barbara Stooksberry. adv.; bk.rev.; illus.; circ. 14,000. (also avail. in microfilm from UMI; reprint service avail. from UMI)

786   GW   ISSN 0173-8607
ML650
PIANO-JAHRBUCH; das deutschsprachige Klavierperiodikum. 1977. irreg. DM.58($14) Piano-Verlag Recklinghausen, Koernerplatz 8, 4350 Recklinghausen, Germany. Ed. Rainer M. Klaas. adv.; bk.rev.; bibl.; illus.; index; circ. 1,300. (back issues avail.)

786   UK   ISSN 0267-7253
ML5
PIANO JOURNAL. 1980. 3/yr. £6($12) European Piano Teachers' Association (E.P.T.A.), 28 Emperor's Gate, London SW7 4HS, England. TEL 071-373-7307. Ed. Carola Grindea. adv.; bk.rev.; music rev.; tr.lit.; circ. 3,250. (back issues avail.)
  —BLDSC shelfmark: 6498.264000.
  Description: Includes articles on pianists and piano teaching, reviews, and association news.

786.3   US   ISSN 0031-9554
ML1
PIANO QUARTERLY. 1952. q. $28 in U.S.; Canada $34; elsewhere $38. String Letter Press, Inc., Box 767, San Anselmo, CA 94979-0706. TEL 415-485-6946. FAX 415-485-0831. Ed. Robert Joseph Silverman. adv.; bk.rev.; music rev.; rec.rev.; illus.; cum.index every 3 yrs.; tr.; circ. 13,000. (also avail. in microform from UMI; reprint service avail. from UMI,ISI) **Indexed:** Arts & Hum.Cit.Ind., Curr.Cont., Music Artic.Guide., Music Ind., RILM.
  Description: Interviews with leading pianists, composers and conductors, lessons, reviews of new music, and articles of historical interest to teachers, performers and amateurs who play the piano.

786.23   US   ISSN 0031-9562
ML1
PIANO TECHNICIANS JOURNAL. 1958. m. $85. Piano Technicians Guild, Inc., Box 22529, Kansas City, MO 64113. Ed. Larry Goldsmith. adv.; bk.rev.; charts; illus.; index; circ. 3,900. **Indexed:** Music Ind.

786   IT
PIANO TIME. 1983. m. L.70000. Ediscreen s.r.l., Via Calderini, 68, 00196 Rome, Italy. Dir. Enzo Perilli.

PIANO-TUNERS QUARTERLY. see HANDICAPPED — Visually Impaired

787   US
PITCH; for the international microtonalist. 1986. q. $62 (Canada $66; elsewhere $70). American Festival of Microtonal Music, Inc., 318 E. 70th St., Ste. 5FW, New York, NY 10021. TEL 212-517-3550. Ed. Johnny Reinhard. bk.rev.; circ. 500. (audio cassette)

780 331.8   US   ISSN 0032-034X
PITTSBURGH MUSICIAN. 1949. bi-m. membership. Pittsburgh Musical Society, Local No.60-471, A.F.M., 709 Forbes Ave., Pittsburgh, PA 15219. TEL 412-281-1822. Ed. Amy C. Movic. adv.; charts; illus.; circ. 1,500 (controlled). (newspaper)

785.06   US   ISSN 0032-0358
PITTSBURGH SYMPHONY ORCHESTRA PROGRAM. 1926. w. (Sept.-May). $45. Pittsburgh Symphony Society, Heinz Hall, 600 Penn Ave., Pittsburgh, PA 15222. TEL 412-392-4800. FAX 412-392-4909. Ed. Bruce Carr. adv.; index; circ. 8,550. **Indexed:** Music Ind.

789.91   DK   ISSN 0109-534X
PLADEANMELDELSER, RYTMISK MUSIK. 1984. fortn. DKK 1854.50. Bibliotekscentralen, Tempovej 7-11, 2750 Ballerup, Denmark. TEL 2-974000. FAX 2-655310.

783   UK   ISSN 0143-4918
PLAINSONG & MEDIAEVAL MUSIC SOCIETY. JOURNAL. 1978. a. £10($24) to individuals; institutions £20($48). Plainsong & Mediaeval Music Society, 72 Brewery Rd., London N7 9NE, England. Ed. David Hiley. adv.; bk.rev.; circ. 400.
—BLDSC shelfmark: 4842.180000.

PLATEAU. see ART

PLAY METER. see SPORTS AND GAMES

786   UK
PLAYER PIANO GROUP BULLETIN. 1959. q. £10. Player Piano Group, 36 Yarm Court Rd., Leatherhead, Surrey KT22 8PA, England. TEL 0372-376034. Ed. Julien Dyer. adv.; bk.rev.; circ. 275. (back issues avail.)

781.7   PL   ISSN 0032-2946
ML5
POLISH MUSIC/POLNISCHE MUSIK. (Text in English and German) 1966. q. $14. Agencja Autorska - Authors' Agency, Hipoteczna 2, P.O. Box 133, 00-950 Warsaw, Poland. TEL 22-27-83-96. FAX 22-27-58-82. TELEX ZAIKS PL 812470. Ed. Jan Grzybowski. adv.; bk.rev.; circ. 1,200. **Indexed:** Music Ind., RILM.
●Available only online.
—BLDSC shelfmark: 6543.705000.

781.7   US   ISSN 0741-9945
POLISH MUSIC HISTORY SERIES. 1982. irreg. price varies. Friends of Polish Music, University of Southern California, School of Music, Los Angeles, CA 90089-0851. TEL 213-887-1906. Ed. Wanda Wilk. circ. 1,000.

780.55   US
POLLSTAR. 50/yr. Promoters On-Line Listings, 4838 N. Blackstone Ave, 2nd Fl., Fresno, CA 93726-0110. TEL 209-224-2631. FAX 209-224-2674. Ed. Gary Bongiovanni. circ. 15,000.

781.7   PL   ISSN 0079-3612
POLSKA PIESN I MUZYKA LUDOWA. ZRODLA I MATERIALY. (Text in English and Polish) 1974. irreg. price varies. (Polska Akademia Nauk, Instytut Sztuki) Polskie Wydawnictwo Muzyczne, Al. Krasinskiego 11a, 31-111 Krakow, Poland. TEL 22-70-44. FAX 22-01-74. Ed. Ludwik Bielawski.
  Description: Folklore materials collected from 1945-1962: transcription from tape recordings, critical commentaries.

780.42   CN
POP ROCK. (Text in French) 1971. m. $16. Ultra Monde, 3646 St. Germain, Montreal, Que. H1W 2V5, Canada. TEL 514-521-3262. circ. 18,500.

784.61   NE
POPFOTO. 1945. m. fl.38.40. Geillustreerde Pers, Postbus 63, Haarlem, Netherlands. TEL 023-304304. FAX 023-304704. TELEX 41371-41653. Ed. Rick Tawfik. adv.; bk.rev.; illus.; circ. 100,000.
  Formerly: Pop-Foto-Tuney Tunes (ISSN 0032-4345)

780.904   IT
POPSTER.* 1976. m. L.15000($31) Gruppo Editoriale Suono s.r.l., Via Capo Peloro, 30, 00141 Rome, Italy. TEL 893608. adv.; illus.; circ. 11,500.

MUSIC 3575

780.42 CS
POPULAR. m. $33. Obzor, Ceskoslovenskej Armady 35, 815 85 Bratislava, Czechoslovakia.

780.42 UK ISSN 0261-1430
ML3469
POPULAR MUSIC. 1982. 3/yr. $40 to individuals; institutions $84. Cambridge University Press, Edinburgh Bldg., Shaftesbury Rd., Cambridge CB2 2RU, England. TEL 0223-312393. FAX 0223-315052. TELEX 851817256. (North American addr.: 40 W. 20th St., New York, NY 10011) Eds. Richard Middleton, David Horn. adv.; bk.rev. (also avail. in microform from UMI; reprint service avail. from SWZ) **Indexed:** Music Ind.
—BLDSC shelfmark: 6550.760800.
Description: Multi-disciplinary coverage of all aspects of popular music: musicology, literary studies, sociology, economic and social history.

780 301 US ISSN 0300-7766
ML1
POPULAR MUSIC & SOCIETY. 1972. q. $20. (Bowling Green State University) Popular Press, Bowling Green State University, Bowling Green, OH 43403. TEL 419-372-7866. Ed. R. Serge Denisoff. adv.; bk.rev.; stat.; index; circ. 5,000. (processed; also avail. in microform from UMI; reprint service avail. from UMI) **Indexed:** Arts & Hum.Cit.Ind., Bk.Rev.Ind. (1980-), Child.bk.Rev.Ind. (1980-), Commun.Abstr., Curr.Cont., Ind.Bk.Rev.Hum., Music Ind., RILM, Sage Fam.Stud.Abstr.
—BLDSC shelfmark: 6550.761000.

780 PL
PRACE ARCHIVUM SLASKIEJ KULTURY MUZYCZNEJ. 1972. irreg., no.8, 1980. exchange basis. Akademia Muzyczna, Biblioteka Glowna, Ul. Zacisze 3, 40-025 Katowice, Poland. TEL 32-155-4017. (Dist. by: Ars Polona-Ruch, Krakowskie Przedmiescie 7, 00-68 Warsaw, Poland)

780 CN ISSN 0822-7500
PRAIRIE SOUNDS. 1980. q. free. Canadian Music Centre, Prairie Region, 911 Library Tower, 2500 University Dr., N.W., Calgary, Alta T2N 1N4, Canada. TEL 403-220-7403. FAX 403-282-0085. Ed. John C. Reid. adv.; circ. 2,000. (back issues avail.)
Description: Focuses on music composed by Canadian composers.

PRESS PRESS MAGAZINE; the Tasmanian quarterly on music and the performing arts. see THEATER

780 SZ
PRESTO. (Text in French, German) 1915. m. (11/yr.). 25 Fr. (foreign 30 Fr.). Schweizerischer Musikerverband, Elisabethenstr. 2, CH-4051 Basel, Switzerland. Ed. Bernard Schenkel. adv.; bk.rev.; circ. 2,200.
Formerly: Schweizer Musikerblatt - Bulletin Musical Suisse.

PREVUE. see MOTION PICTURES

780 700 500 IT
PRIMI PIANI. 1964. m. L.2000. Via Bolzano 32, 00198 Rome, Italy. Ed. Fernando Luciani. adv.; illus.; stat.; tr.lit.
Formerly: Pentagramma (ISSN 0031-4889)

782.1 US
PRINCETON SERIES IN OPERA. irreg. price varies. Princeton University Press, 3175 Princeton Pike, Lawrenceville, NJ 08648. TEL 609-896-1344. FAX 609-895-1081.

PRODUCTIV'S HANDBUCH FUER MUSIKER. see SOUND RECORDING AND REPRODUCTION

PRODUCTIV'S SOLO. see SOUND RECORDING AND REPRODUCTION

780 CN ISSN 1186-1797
▼**PROFESSIONAL SOUND.** 1990. q. Norris Publications, 3284 Yonge St., Toronto, Ont. M4N 3M7, Canada. TEL 416-485-8284. FAX 416-485-8924. Ed. Lisa Ferguson. adv.; circ. 10,500.

780 792 US
PROFILE (WASHINGTON). a. $25 to non-members; members $15. Opera America, 777 14th St., N.W., Ste. 520, Washington, DC 20005. TEL 202-347-9262. FAX 202-393-0735. Ed. Martha Perry.
Description: provides an overview of Opera America and the professional opera field, with analysis of the most recent professional opera survey, and descriptions of individual Opera America companies.

780.42 US ISSN 0738-8861
PROGRESSIVE PLATTER MUSIC REVIEW.* 1976. m. $15. (New England D J Association) Progressive Platter, 72-74 E. Dedham St., No. 5, Boston, MA 02118-2417. TEL 617-247-1144. (Subscr. to: Kenmore Station, Box 638, Boston, MA 02215) Ed. Cosmo Wyatt. adv.; bk.rev.; circ. 10,000.

786 GW
PROLIX; Wochenzeitung im Dreyeckland. (Text in English, French, German) 1975. w. Prolix Verlag GmbH, Goethestr. 23, 7800 Freiburg, Germany. Ed. Daniel Jaeger. circ. 5,000. (back issues avail.)

PROTOKOLLE; Wiener Halbjahresschrift fuer Literatur, Bildende Kunst und Musik. see LITERATURE

780 CN
PROVINCIAL NEWSLETTER. 3/yr. British Columbia Registered Music Teachers' Association, 1 - 8560 162nd St., Surrey, B.C. V3S 3V4, Canada. TEL 604-492-8944. (Subscr. to: 197 Vancouver Ave., Penticton, B.C. V2A 1A1, Canada) Ed. Ernst Schneider. adv.; bk.rev.; circ. 779 C. (looseleaf format; back issues avail.)
Description: Presents articles on the teaching of music and reports of the branches of the Association.

781.15 UK ISSN 0305-7356
ML5
PSYCHOLOGY OF MUSIC. 1973. s-a. £13($35) Society for Research in Psychology of Music and Music Education, Department of Music, Southlands College, Roehampton Institute of Higher Education, London SW19 5NN, England. Ed. David Hargreaves. adv.; bk.rev.; cum.index every 5 vols.; circ. 700. **Indexed:** Psychol.Abstr., RILM.
—BLDSC shelfmark: 6946.536000.

780.01 US ISSN 0275-3987
ML3830
PSYCHOMUSICOLOGY; a journal of research in music cognition. 1981. s-a. $21 (foreign $25). Illinois State University, Office of Research in Arts Technology, Normal, IL 61761. TEL 309-438-3575. FAX 309-438-8318. Ed. David Brian Williams. adv.; bk.rev.; bibl.; charts; stat.; circ. 300. **Indexed:** Educ.Ind., Music Ind., Psychol.Abstr., RILM.
—BLDSC shelfmark: 6946.540070.

PUBLICUM; Innsbrucker Theater- und Konzertspiegel. see THEATER

780 792 JM
PULSE. q. Pulse Ltd., P.O. Box 200, Kingston 5, Jamaica, W.I. Ed. Kingsley Cooper.

780 US ISSN 1047-4528
PUNCTURE; a magazine of music and the arts. 1982. q. $10. Puncture Magazine, 1592 Union St., Ste. 431, San Francisco, CA 94123. TEL 415-771-5127. Ed. Katherine Spielmann. adv.; bk.rev.; circ. 6,000. (back issues avail.)
Description: Presents articles and reviews covering new developments in contemporary music (especially rock & roll).

780 US
PURCHASER'S GUIDE TO THE MUSIC INDUSTRIES. 1897. a. free with subscription to Music Trades. Music Trades Corporation, c/o Paul A. Majeski, Box 432, 80 West St., Englewood, NJ 07631. TEL 201-871-1965. Ed. Brian T. Majeski. adv.; circ. 8,000. (reprint service avail. from UMI)

780.6 CC
QING YINYUE/LIGHT MUSIC. (Text in Chinese) bi-m. Jilin Sheng Yinyuejia Xiehui - Jilin Musicians' Association, Fu 111, Stalin St., Bldg. No. 14, Changchun, Jilin 130021, People's Republic of China. TEL 884953. Ed. Wang Guanqun.

QU YI/VARIETY SHOW. see THEATER

780 IT
QUADERNI PUCCINIANI. 1982. a. L.25000. Istituto di Studi Pucciniani, Via Circo 18, Milan, Italy. bk.rev.

780 IT
QUADERNI ROSSINIANI. 1954. irreg., no.19, 1976. price varies. (Fondazione Rossini) Casa Editrice Leo S. Olschki, Casella Postale 66, 50100 Florence, Italy. TEL 055-6530684. FAX 055-6530214.

780 UK
QUARTERNOTE. 1979. q. free to members. Bournemouth Orchestras, Centre for the Arts, Poole, Dorset BH15 1UF, England. TEL 0202-670611. FAX 0202-687235. Eds. Terry Barfoot, James Pestell. illus.; circ. 2,500.
Formerly (until 1988): W O S News.

780 331.8 US
QUARTERNOTE. 1976. q. $4. American Musicians Union, Inc., 8 Tobin Ct., Dumont, NJ 07628. TEL 201-384-5378. Ed. Ben Intorre. adv.; bk.rev.; illus.; circ. 350 (controlled).
Description: Provides information of interest to members of the union.

780 GW ISSN 0079-905X
QUELLENKATALOGE ZUR MUSIKGESCHICHTE. 1966. irreg., vol.22, 1989. Florian Noetzel Verlag, Heinrichshofen Buecher, Valoisstrasse 11, 2940 Wilhelmshaven, Germany. (Dist. in U.S. by C. F. Peters Corp., 373 Park Ave. S., New York, N.Y. 10016) Ed. Richard Schaal.

784 US
QUODLIBET. 1967. 3/yr. membership. Intercollegiate Musical Council, Department of Music, Wabash College, Crawfordsville, IN 47933. TEL 317-364-4398. (Subscr. to: Fr. Richard H. Trame, S.J., Exec. Sec., Department of Music, Loyola Marymount University, Los Angeles, CA 90045) Ed. Stanley A. Malinowski. bk.rev.; circ. 75. (looseleaf format; back issues avail.)

780 US
▼**R & B MUSIC & ENTERTAINMENT MONTHLY.*** (Rhythm and Blues) 1990. m. $22.95. 501 Colorado Ave, No. 305. 200, Santa Monica, CA 90401-2426. TEL 818-843-7225. Ed. Deborah Gipson-Young.
Description: Covers jazz, dance, rap and new age music.

780.7 UK ISSN 0033-684X
ML5
R C M MAGAZINE. 1904. 3/yr. £5 to non-members. Royal College of Music, Prince Consort Rd., London SW7 2BS, England. FAX 071-589-7740. Ed. Angela Escott. adv.; bk.rev.; music rev.; illus.; circ. 3,000. **Indexed:** Br.Hum.Ind., Music Ind.
Description: Journal of general musical interest for undergraduate and post graduate students and professional musicians and musicologists.

780 US ISSN 0889-6607
ML85
R I D I M - R C M I INVENTORY OF MUSIC ICONOGRAPHY. irreg. (Repertoire Internationale d'Iconographie Musicale. Research Center for Music Iconography) City University of New York, Research Center for Music Iconography, Graduate School and University Center, 33 W. 42nd St., New York, NY 10036. TEL 212-642-2336. FAX 212-642-2642. Ed. Zdravko Blazekovic.
Description: Catalogues of the music iconography in individual museums.

780 US ISSN 0360-8727
ML26
R I D I M - R C M I NEWSLETTER. 1975. s-a. $7.50 to individuals; institutions $15. (Repertoire Internationale d'Iconographie Musicale. Research Center for Music Iconography) City University of New York, Research Center for Musical Iconography, Graduate School and University Center, 33 W. 42nd St., New York, NY 10036. TEL 212-642-2336. FAX 212-642-2642. Ed. Zdravko Blazekovic. bk.rev.; circ. 500. **Indexed:** RILM.

789.91 UK
R M. 1954. w. $85. Spotlight Publications Ltd., Greater London House, Hampstead Rd., London NW1 7QZ, England. Ed. Betty Page. adv.; bk.rev.; rec.; rev.; charts; circ. 43,945.
Formerly: Record Mirror (ISSN 0144-5804)
Description: Weekly magazine for young men interested in pop and disco dance music.

3576 MUSIC

780   NO   ISSN 0800-0549
R - O - C - K. (Text in Norwegian and Swedish) 1978. 4/yr. NOK 100($11) Rock and Roll Society of Scandinavia, P.O. Box 115, 1344 Haslum, Norway. Ed. Folke Myrvang. adv.; bk.rev.; illus.; circ. 2,000.
     Supersedes (1972-1977): Rock and Roll International Magazine; Whole Lotta Rockin.

789.91   CN   ISSN 0033-7064
R P M WEEKLY. (Records - Promotion - Music); music, television, radio, film, records, theatre. 1964. w. $126. R P M Music Publications Ltd., 6 Brentcliffe Rd., Toronto, Ont. M4G 3Y2, Canada. TEL 416-425-0257. Ed. Walt Grealis. adv.; bk.rev.; film rev.; play rev.; abstr.; bibl.; charts; illus.; index; circ. 5,000 (controlled). (tabloid format)

789.91   US
R T S MUSIC GAZETTE. 1973. bi-m. $15 to individuals; institutions $10. R T S, Box 750579, Dept. BW, Petaluma, CA 94975. Ed. I. Nii. adv.; bk.rev.; illus.; tr.lit.
     Description: Information about film music and soundtrack recordings, soundtracks for sale.

RADAR; international magazine for creativity. see *ART*

RADIO & RECORDS. see *COMMUNICATIONS — Radio*

780   US
RADIO FREE ROCK. vol.2, 1978. m. free. Cyco Publishing, 900 E. 79th St., Indianapolis, IN 46240. Ed. David F. Myers. adv.; illus.; circ. 10,000. (tabloid format)
     Incorporates: Gulcher.

785.4   US   ISSN 0090-4570
ML1
RAG TIMES. 1967. bi-m. $10 (foreign $13). Maple Leaf Club, 15522 Ricky Ct., Grass Valley, CA 95949. Ed. Richard Zimmerman. adv.; bk.rev.; illus.; circ. 600. (back issues avail.)
     Description: News, articles, announcements, and reviews pertaining to rag-time music and musicians across the nation.

781.572   CN   ISSN 0033-8672
ML5
RAGTIMER. 1962. bi-m. Can.$8. Ragtime Society, Box 520, Station A, Weston, Ont. M9N 3N3, Canada. bk.rev.; rec.rev.; circ. 500. **Indexed:** Music Ind.

RAMPIKE MAGAZINE. see *ART*

780.42   US
RAP EXPRESS. q. $3.50 per no. Circus Enterprise Corp., 3 W. 18th St., New York, NY 10011. TEL 212-685-5050.

780.42   US
RAP MASTER. m. $24. Word Up! Publications, Inc., 63 Grand Ave., Ste. 230, River Edge, NJ 07661. TEL 201-487-6124. Ed. Kate Ferguson.

781.57   US
▼**RAPPAGES.** 1991. bi-m. $9.95 (foreign $19.95). Larry Flynt Publications, Inc., 9171 Wilshire Blvd., Ste. 300, Beverly Hills, CA 90210. TEL 310-858-7100. FAX 310-275-3857. Ed. Dane Webb. adv.
     Description: Covers rap music releases and performers.

782.1   IT   ISSN 0033-9784
RASSEGNA MELODRAMMATICA; corriere de musica. 1890. s-m. L.40000. Via Alfredo Oriani 4, 20122 Milan, Italy. Ed. Vittore Deliliers. adv.; abstr.; illus.; circ. 3,500. (newspaper)

782.1   IT   ISSN 0033-9806
RASSEGNA MUSICALE CURCI; periodico di cultura e attualita musicali. 1948. 3/yr. free. Edizioni Curci s.r.l., Galleria del Corso 4, 20122 Milan, Italy. Ed. Giuseppe Gramitto Ricci. adv.; bk.rev.; music rev.; rec.rev.; illus.; circ. 7,000. **Indexed:** Music Ind., RILM.
     Description: Covers classical and contemporary music; lists new publications and musical competitions.

RASSEGNA SOVIETICA; rivista bimestrale di cultura. see *ART*

780   US
RAVINIA FESTIVAL. 1936. 12/yr. Midwest Publishing Co., 8328 N. Lincoln Ave., Skokie, IL 60077. TEL 312-539-8540. Ed. Charlis McMillan. circ. 140,000.
     Description: Program book for the viewers of the concert programs in Ravinia Park Pavilion of Chicago's North Shore, during the Ravinia Festival Season each summer.

917.1   CN
REARGARDE. 1986. m. $15. Squishy Music, Box 1421, Stn. H, Montreal, Que. H3G 2N4, Canada. TEL 514-483-5372. Ed. Paul Gott. (tabloid format)

780   US   ISSN 0147-0078
RECENT RESEARCHES IN AMERICAN MUSIC. 1975. q. $31.95. A-R Editions, Inc., 801 Deming Way, Madison, WI 53717. TEL 608-836-9000. Ed. H. Wiley Hitchcock. (back issues avail.)

780   US   ISSN 0484-0828
M2
RECENT RESEARCHES IN THE MUSIC OF THE BAROQUE ERA. 1964. q. $31.95. A-R Editions, Inc., 801 Deming Way, Madison, WI 53717. TEL 608-836-9000. Ed. Christoph Wolff. (back issues avail.)

780   US   ISSN 0147-0086
M2
RECENT RESEARCHES IN THE MUSIC OF THE CLASSICAL ERA. 1973. q. $31.95. A-R Editions, Inc., 801 Deming Way, Madison, WI 53717. TEL 608-836-9000. Ed. Eugene K. Wolf. (back issues avail.)
     Formerly: Recent Researches in the Music of the Classical and Early Romantic Era.

780   US   ISSN 0362-3572
M2
RECENT RESEARCHES IN THE MUSIC OF THE MIDDLE AGES AND EARLY RENAISSANCE. 1973. q. $31.95. A-R Editions, Inc., 801 Deming Way, Madison, WI 53717. TEL 608-836-9000. Ed. Charles M. Atkinson. (back issues avail.)

780.904   US   ISSN 0193-5364
M2
RECENT RESEARCHES IN THE MUSIC OF THE NINETEENTH AND EARLY TWENTIETH CENTURIES. 1979. q. $31.95. A-R Editions, Inc., 801 Deming Way, Madison, WI 53717. TEL 608-836-9000. Eds. Rufus Hallmark, D. Kern Holoman. (back issues avail.)

780   US   ISSN 0486-123X
M2
RECENT RESEARCHES IN THE MUSIC OF THE RENAISSANCE. 1964. q. $31.95. A-R Editions, Inc., 801 Deming Way, Madison, WI 53717. TEL 608-836-9000. Ed. James Haar. (back issues avail.)

780   IT   ISSN 1120-5741
RECERCARE; rivista per lo studio e la pratica della musica antica - journal for the study and practice of early music. (Text in English, French, German, Italian, Spanish) 1971. s-a. L.35000. (Fondazione Italiana per la Musica Antica) Liberia Musicale Italiana Editrice, P.O. Box 198, 55100 Lucca, Italy. TEL 0583-39-44-64. FAX 0538-39-44-69. Ed. Marco Di Pasquale. adv.; bk.rev.; abstr.; circ. 5,000. **Indexed:** RILM.
     Formerly (until 1988, no.17-18): Flauto Dolce.

780   UK   ISSN 0309-0574
RECOMMENDED RECORDINGS. 1966. 2/yr. £6.95($12.60) General Gramophone Publications Ltd., 177-179 Kenton Rd., Harrow, Middlesex HA3 0HA, England. adv.; circ. 5,000.
     Description: Details of outstanding recordings and performances of the standard repertoire: CDs, LPs & cassettes.

780   CN   ISSN 0712-8290
THE RECORD. 1981. w. Can.$225($325) P.O. Box 201, Sta. M, Toronto, Ont. M6S 4T3, Canada. TEL 416-533-9417. FAX 416-533-0367. Ed. David Farrell. adv.; circ. 1,600.

780.42   US   ISSN 0745-2594
RECORD (NEW YORK, 1967). m. $12. Straight Arrow Publishers, Inc., 1290 Ave. of Americas, New York, NY 10104. TEL 212-484-1616. Ed. David McGee. adv.; illus.; circ. 75,000. (also avail. in microfiche from UMI) **Indexed:** C.I.S. Abstr., Music Ind.

789.9   UK   ISSN 0261-250X
RECORD COLLECTOR. 1980. m. $110. Parker Publishing Group Ltd., 43-45 St. Mary's Rd., Ealing, London W5 5RQ, England. TEL 081-579-1082. FAX 081-566-2024. Ed. Peter Doggett. illus. (back issues avail.)

789.91   UK   ISSN 0034-1568
RECORD COLLECTOR (BROOMFIELD); a magazine for collectors of recorded vocal art. 1946. q. $34. c/o Larry Lustig, Ed., 111 Longshots Close, Broomfield, Chelmsford CM1 5DU, England. TEL 0245-441661. adv.; bk.rev.; rec.rev.; .charts; illus.; index; circ. 850. **Indexed:** Music Ind.

RECORD COLLECTOR (LEICESTER). see *SOUND RECORDING AND REPRODUCTION*

780   US   ISSN 8755-6154
RECORD COLLECTOR'S MONTHLY. 1982. irreg. (4-5/yr.). $15 for 10 issues (foreign $23 for 6 issues). Record Collector's Monthly, Inc., Box 75, Mendham, NJ 07945. TEL 201-543-9520. FAX 201-543-6033. Ed. Don Mennie. adv.; bk.rev.; rec.rev.; circ. 5,000. (tabloid format; back issues avail.)
     Description: Covers collectible recordings from the 1950's and 1960's of vocal groups, blues, R & B, and rock & roll, with emphasis on 45's and LP's.

780 621.389   US   ISSN 0557-9147
RECORD EXCHANGER. 1969. q. $11.95. Vintage Records, Box 6144, Orange, CA 92667. TEL 714-639-3383. Ed. Art Turco. adv.; bk.rev.; charts; illus.; index; circ. 22,000.

789.91   JA   ISSN 0289-3614
RECORD GEIJUTSU/ART OF RECORDS, DISCOGRAPHY REVIEW. 1952. m. 870 Yen. Ongaku no Tomo Sha Corp., Kagurazaka 6-30, Shinjuku-ku, Tokyo 162, Japan. TEL 03-3235-2111. FAX 03-3235-2129. TELEX J23718 ONTOA. adv.: B&W page 312,000 Yen, color page 624,000 Yen; trim 257 x 182. circ. 150,000.
     Description: Carries critical commentaries by authorities in the field that serve as guidelines for new record selections as well as enhances the knowledge of music.

780   UK
RECORD MART. 1968. m. £7.50. 16 London Hill, Rayleigh, Essex, England. Ed. Frank K. Bailey. adv.; tr.lit.; circ. 900.

789.91   US   ISSN 0034-1592
ML1
RECORD RESEARCH; the magazine of record statistics and information. 1955. bi-m. $10 for 10 issues. 65 Grand Ave., Brooklyn, NY 11205. TEL 718-857-7003. Ed. Len Kunstadt. bk.rev.; illus.; mkt.; stat. (processed) **Indexed:** Music Ind.

RECORD RETAILING DIRECTORY. see *BUSINESS AND ECONOMICS — Trade And Industrial Directories*

780   GW
RECORD-SERIE. 1962. s-m. DM.52.80. VEB Lied der Zeit Musikverlag, Rosa-Luxemburg-Str. 41, 102 Berlin, Germany.
     Formerly: Standard-Serie (ISSN 0038-9617)

789.91   UK   ISSN 0961-3544
ML5
RECORDER MAGAZINE. 1963. q. £6($15) Schott & Co. Ltd., 48 Great Marlborough St., London W1V 2BN, England. TEL 0353-612105. FAX 0353-762639. (Subscr. to: Brunswick Rd., Ashford, Kent, England) Ed. Eve O'Kelly. adv.; bk.rev.; music rev.; circ. 2,500. **Indexed:** Music Ind., RILM.
—BLDSC shelfmark: 7326.685000.
     Former titles: Recorder and Music Magazine (ISSN 0306-4409); Recorder and Music (ISSN 0034-1665); **Incorporates:** Recorder News.

MUSIC

786 US ISSN 0736-9549
REED ORGAN SOCIETY BULLETIN. Short title: R O S Bulletin. 1982. q. $12.50. (Reed Organ Society, Inc.) Reed Organ Society Publications, 6907 Rix St., S.E., Ada, MI 49301. TEL 616-676-1188. (Subscr. to: Reed Organ Society, Inc., Musical Museum, Deansboro, NY 13328. TEL 315-841-8774) Ed. Edward A. Peterson. adv.; bk.rev.; bibl.; circ. 750. (back issues avail.)
Formerly: Reed Organ Society Newsletter.
Description: For musicians, historians, collectors and restorers of all types of reed instruments, including melodeons, "pump" organs, harmoniums and more.

780 GW
REGER-STUDIEN. 1978. irreg. price varies. (Max-Reger-Institut, Bonn) Breitkopf und Haertel, Walkmuehlstr. 52, Postfach 1707, 6200 Wiesbaden 1, Germany. TEL 0611-4903-0. FAX 0611-490359. TELEX 4182647-EB-D. Ed.Bd.

780 HU ISSN 0080-0562
REGI MAGYAR DALLAMOK TARA/CORPUS MUSICAE POPULARIS HUNGARICAE. (Text in Hungarian; occasional summaries in German) 1958. irreg. price varies. (Magyar Tudomanyos Akademia, Nepzenekutato Csoport) Akademiai Kiado, Publishing House of the Hungarian Academy of Sciences, P.O. Box 24, H-1363 Budapest, Hungary.

780 UK ISSN 0953-5330
REGISTER OF MUSICIANS IN EDUCATION. 1986. a. £6. Incorporated Society of Musicians, 10 Stratford Place, London W1N 9AE, England. TEL 071-629-4413. FAX 071-408-1538. circ. 3,000.
Description: Directory of members working in all fields of music education.

780 UK
REGISTER OF PERFORMERS & COMPOSERS. 1976. a. £8.50. Incorporated Society of Musicians, 10 Stratford Place, London W1N 9AE, England. TEL 071-629-4413. FAX 071-408-1538. circ. 4,000.
Formerly: Professional Register of Artists.
Description: Directory of members working professionally as performers, conductors, and composers.

780 UK ISSN 0951-6239
REGISTER OF PROFESSIONAL PRIVATE MUSIC TEACHERS. 1987. a. £10. Incorporated Society of Musicians, 10 Stratford Place, London W1N 9AE, England. TEL 071-629-4413. FAX 071-408-1538. circ. 6,000.
Formerly: Professional Register of Private Teachers of Music.
Description: Directory of professional teachers of music to private pupils.

780 200 US
REJOICE!; the gospel music magazine. 1988. bi-m. $12 (foreign $21.95). University of Mississippi, Center for the Study of Southern Culture, University, MS 38677. TEL 601-232-5742. FAX 601-232-5740. Eds. Pepper Smith, Edwin Smith.

780.42 US ISSN 0146-3489
RELIX; music for the mind. Variant title: Dead Relix. 1974. bi-m. $23 (foreign $27). Relix Magazine, Inc, Box 94, Brooklyn, NY 11229. TEL 718-258-0009. FAX 718-692-4345. Ed. Toni A. Brown. adv.; bk.rev.; film rev.; charts; illus.; stat.; circ. 100,000. (back issues avail.) **Indexed:** Music Ind.
Description: Specializes in music from San Francisco during the 1960s, with a focus on the Grateful Dead. Also covers current blues, folk, reggae and rock music.

780 GW ISSN 0196-7037
ML169.8
RENAISSANCE MANUSCRIPT STUDIES. 1973. irreg., latest vol.1. (American Institute of Musicology, US) Haenssler Verlag, Postfach 1220, Bismarckstr. 4, 7303 Neuhausen-Stuttgart, Germany. TEL 07158-177-149. FAX 07158-177119. Ed. Charles Hamm.

RENFRO VALLEY BUGLE. see *GENERAL INTEREST PERIODICALS — United States*

780 CC ISSN 0447-6573
IN PROCESS
RENMIN YINYUE/PEOPLE'S MUSIC. (Text in Chinese; table of contents in English) 1950. bi-m. Y1.50 (foreign $24.30). Zhongguo Yinxie Zazhishe, No. 10, Nongzhanguan Nanli, Beijing 100026, People's Republic of China. (Dist. outside China by: China International Book Trading Corp., P.O. Box 2399, Beijing, P.R.C.; Dist. in US by: China Books & Periodicals, Inc., 2929 24th St., San Francisco, CA 94110. TEL 415-282-2994)

780 FR
REPERTOIRE DES MANUSCRIPTS MEDIEVAUX (CORBIN). a. price varies. Editions du C N R S, 1 Place Aristide Briand, 92195 Meudon Cedex, France. TEL 1-45-34-75-50. FAX 1-46-26-28-49. TELEX LABOBEL 204 135 F. (Subscr. to: Presses du C N R S, 20-22, rue Saint Amand, 75015 Paris, France. TEL 1-45-33-16-00) adv.; bk.rev.; index; circ. 1,500 (controlled).

784 US ISSN 0360-7348
ML1
REPLAY; a professional publication for the coin-operated amusement industry. 1975. m. $60 per no. Replay Publishing, Inc., Box 2550, Woodland Hills, CA 91365. TEL 818-347-3820. Ed. Key Snodgrass. adv.; illus.; circ. 4,400. Key Title: RePlay Magazine.

780.42 US
REQUEST. 1989. m. $20. Request Media Inc., 7630 Excelsior Blvd., Minneapolis, MN 55426. TEL 612-932-7740. FAX 612-932-7797. Ed. Keith Moerer. circ. 450,000.
Description: Covers pop, rock, R

780.01 PL ISSN 0486-4689
ML5
RES FACTA; teksty o muzyce wspolczesnej. (Text in English, German and Polish) 1967. irreg. price varies. Polskie Wydawnictwo Muzyczne, Al. Krasinskiego 11a, 31-111 Krakow, Poland. TEL 22-70-44. FAX 22-01-74. Ed. Michal Bristiger. **Indexed:** RILM.
Description: Covers problems of modern music, writings of Polish and foreign musicologists and composers.

780.01 US
RESEARCH SYMPOSIUM ON THE PSYCHOLOGY AND ACOUSTICS OF MUSIC. PROCEEDINGS. 1977. a. price varies. University of Kansas, A M E M T Department, 311 Bailey Hall, Lawrence, KS 66045-2344. TEL 913-864-4784. FAX 913-864-3566. Ed. George L. Duerksen. circ. 300.

781 US ISSN 0749-2472
RESOUND. 1982. q. $20. Indiana University, Archives of Traditional Music, Morrison Hall 117, Bloomington, IN 47405-2501. TEL 812-855-8632. FAX 812-855-5678. Ed. Marilyn Graf. index; circ. 500.
Description: Reports on the Archives' collections of traditional music from all regions of the world.

780 UK
RESOURCES OF MUSIC SERIES. 1969. irreg., no.21, 1985. price varies. Cambridge University Press, Edinburgh Bldg., Shaftesbury Rd., Cambridge CB2 2RU, England. TEL 0223-312393. FAX 0223-315052. TELEX 851817256. Ed. John Paynter.
Formerly: Resources of Music (ISSN 0080-1828)

781.7 BL
REVISTA BRASILEIRA DE MUSICA. 1934-1947; resumed 1981. irreg., latest 1986. Universidade Federal de Rio de Janeiro, Escola de Musica, Rua de Passeio 98-Lapa, 20021 Rio de Janeiro, Brazil. adv.; circ. 1,000. **Indexed:** Music Ind.
Description: Covers folk music of Brazil.

780.01 CK
REVISTA COLOMBIANA DE INVESTIGACION MUSICAL. 1985. 2/yr. exchange basis. Universidad Nacional de Colombia, Instituto de Investigaciones Esteticas, Seccion de Musicologia, Bogota, Colombia. Eds. Ellie Duque, Egberto Bermudez. bk.rev.; circ. 1,000.

780.01 SP ISSN 0210-1459
REVISTA DE MUSICOLOGIA. s-a. 700 ptas. Sociedad Espanola de Musicologia, Ordonez, 1, Madrid-29, Spain. Ed. Dionisio Preciado. bibl. **Indexed:** RILM.

780 BL ISSN 0103-5525
▼**REVISTA MUSICA.** 1990. s-a. exchange basis. Universidade de Sao Paulo, Departamento de Musica, Av. Prof. Lucio Martins Rodrigues 443, 05508 Butanta SP, Brazil. TEL 813-3222. FAX 815-4272. TELEX 80629 UVSI BR. —BLDSC shelfmark: 7867.248000.

780.7 CL ISSN 0716-2790
ML5
REVISTA MUSICAL CHILENA. 1945. s-a. $40. Universidad de Chile, Facultad de Artes, Compania 1264, Casilla 2100, Santiago, Chile. TEL 6965767. Ed. Luis Merino. adv.; bk.rev.; bibl.; charts; illus.; index, cum.index; circ. 1,000. **Indexed:** Hisp.Amer.Per.Ind., Music Ind., RILM.
Description: Review of Chilean and Latin American art and music from the colonial epoch to present.

780.01 BE
REVUE BELGE DE MUSICOLOGIE/BELGISCH TIJDSCHRIFT VOOR MUZIEKWETENSCHAP. (Text in Dutch, English, French, and German) 1945. a. 700 Fr.($14) Societe Belge de Musicologie, 30 rue de la Regence, 1000 Brussels, Belgium. Eds. H. Vanhulst, R. Wangermee. adv.; bk.rev.; illus.; circ. 600. **Indexed:** Music Ind., RILM.

780.01 FR ISSN 0035-1601
REVUE DE MUSICOLOGIE. 1917. s-a. 200 F. Societe Francaise de Musicologie, 2 rue de Louvois, 75002 Paris, France. Eds. Christian Meyer, Georgie Durosoir. adv.; bk.rev.; illus.; cum.index; circ. 1,250. (also avail. in microform from UMI; reprint service avail. from UMI,KTO) **Indexed:** Arts & Hum.Cit.Ind., Curr.Cont., Ind.Bk.Rev.Hum., Music Ind., RILM.

REVUE DES ARCHEOLOGUES ET HISTORIENS D'ART DE LOUVAIN. see *ART*

780.1 FR ISSN 0035-3736
REVUE MUSICALE; revue d'esthetique musicale. 1920. 10/yr. 1200 F. Editions Richard Masse, 7 place Saint Sulpice, 75006 Paris, France. Dir. Albert Richard. circ. 1,500. (also avail. in microfilm from BHP; reprint service avail. from SWZ) **Indexed:** Arts & Hum.Cit.Ind., Curr.Cont., Music Ind., RILM.
Formerly: Polyphonie (ISSN 0032-4019)

780 SZ ISSN 0035-3744
REVUE MUSICALE DE SUISSE ROMANDE; courrier suisse du disque. 1948. q. 40 Fr. for Europe; elsewhere 50 Fr. Case Postale 3074, CH-1401 Yverdon-les-Bains, Switzerland. TEL 024-212606. FAX 024-217310. Ed. H. Cornaz. adv.; bk.rev.; music rev.; rec.rev.; charts; illus.; circ. 3,000. **Indexed:** Music Ind., RILM.

780 UK
RHYTHM; for the contemporary drummer, percussionist and programmer. (U.K. Edition) 1987. m. £16.50 (foreign £19). Music Maker Publications Ltd., Alexander House, Forehill, Ely, Cambs CB7 4AF, England. TEL 0353-665577. FAX 0353-662489. (U.S. addr.: Music Maker Publications Inc., 22024 Lassen St, Ste. 118, Chatsworth, CA 91311) circ. 20,000.
Description: For the contemporary drummer, percussionist and programmer. Includes new electronic drum technology, interviews with rhythm professionals and drumming news.

780.42 US
RHYTHM & NEWS.* vol.5, 1989. m. Tune-In Publications, Inc., 9800 Richmond Ave., Ste. 300, Houston, TX 77042.

780.65 UK
RHYTHM RAG. no.4, 1977. 4/yr. £1.50 for 5 nos. Cunningham, 190 Camrose Ave., Edgware, Middlesex, England. adv.

780 GW
RICHARD STRAUSS-BLAETTER; neue Folge. (Text in English, German) 1979. s-a. (Internationale Richard Strauss-Gesellschaft, AU) Verlag Dr. Hans Schneider GmbH, Mozartstr. 6, 8132 Tutzing, Germany.

780 GW
RICHARD WAGNER BLAETTER. (Text in French, German) s-a. (Aktionskreis fuer das Werk Richard Wagners e.V.) Verlag Dr. Hans Schneider GmbH, Mozartstr. 6, 8132 Tutzing, Germany.

MUSIC

789.5   UK   ISSN 0035-5453
RINGING WORLD. 1911. w. £33. (Central Council of Church Bell Ringers) Ringing World Ltd., Penmark House, Woodbridge Meadows, Guildford GU1 1BL, Surrey, England. TEL 0483 69535. Ed. D.G. Thorne. adv.; bk.rev.; circ. 5,000.

780.42   US   ISSN 0889-5791
RIP. m. $22.95 (foreign $32.95). Larry Flynt Publications, Inc., 9171 Wilshire Blvd., Ste. 300, Beverly Hills, CA 90210. TEL 310-858-7100. FAX 310-275-3857. Ed. Lonn Friend.
Description: Covers heavy metal music for young adults.

780.42   US
RIP PHOTO SPECIALS. q. $2.95 per no. Larry Flynt Publications, Inc., 9171 Wilshire Blvd., Ste. 300, Beverly Hills, CA 90210. TEL 213-858-7100. FAX 213-275-3857.

780.42   US
RIP PRESENTS. q. $2.95 per no. Larry Flynt Publications, Inc., 9171 Wilshire Blvd., Ste. 300, Beverly Hills, CA 90210. TEL 213-858-7100. FAX 213-275-3857.

780.6   IT
RISVEGLIO MUSICALE. 1982. bi-m. L.10000($12) Anbima, Via Marianna Dionigi 43, 00193 Rome, Italy. Ed. Orazio Giuri. adv.; bk.rev.; circ. 15,000.
Formerly: Risveglio Bandistico.

783   IT   ISSN 0394-6282
ML2999
RIVISTA INTERNAZIONALE DI MUSICA SACRA/INTERNATIONAL CHURCH MUSIC REVIEW/INTERNATIONALE ZEITSCHRIFT FUER KIRCHENMUSIK/REVUE INTERNATIONALE DE MUSIQUE SACREE/REVISTA INTERNACIONAL DE MUSICA SAGRADA. (Text in English, French, German, Italian, Spanish) 1980. q. $31. Editrice Internazionale Musica e Arte s.r.l., Viale Gorizia 5, 20144 Milan, Italy. Ed. Natale Ghiglione. **Indexed:** RILM.

780.01   IT   ISSN 0035-6867
ML5
RIVISTA ITALIANA DI MUSICOLOGIA. 1966. s-a. L.63000 (foreign L.80000). (Societa Italiana di Musicologia) Casa Editrice Leo S. Olschki, Casella Postale 66, 50100 Florence, Italy. TEL 055-6530684. FAX 055-6530214. Ed.Bd. adv.; bk.rev.; circ. 1,000. **Indexed:** Arts & Hum.Cit.Ind., Curr.Cont., Music Ind., RILM.

780.01   IT
RIVISTA ITALIANA DI MUSICOLOGIA. QUADERNI. 1966. irreg., no.25, 1991. price varies. Casa Editrice Leo S. Olschki, Casella Postale 66, 50100 Florence, Italy. TEL 055-6530684. FAX 055-6530214.

ROAR; tapebook series. see *LITERARY AND POLITICAL REVIEWS*

781   FR   ISSN 0048-8445
ROCK & FOLK; pop music, rhythm & blues, jazz chanson. 1966. m. 220 F. (foreign 270 F.). Editions Lariviere, 15-17 quai de l'Oise, 75166 Paris Cedex 19, France. TEL 1-40-34-22-07. FAX 1-40-35-84-41. TELEX 211 678 F. Dir. Christian de la Tullaye. adv.; bk.rev.; film rev.; charts; illus.; circ. 115,000. **Indexed:** Pt.de Rep. (1991-).

780.42   GW   ISSN 0930-6994
ROCK & POP L P - PREISKATALOG. 1983. a. Vereinigte Motor-Verlage GmbH und Co. KG, Leuschnerstr. 1, Postfach 106036, 7000 Stuttgart 10, Germany. TEL 0711-18201. FAX 0711-1821756. Ed. Frank-Michael Goldmann. bk.rev.; bibl.; charts; illus.; circ. 6,000.

780.42   UK
ROCK & POP STARS. 1979. m. £0.75 per no. Moore Harness Ltd., Gaddline House, Whyteleafe, Surrey, England. Ed. Leonard Holdsworth. adv.; circ. 70,000.

780.42   US
ROCK & ROLL CONFIDENTIAL. 1983. m. $21. Dept. RB, Box 1073, Maywood, NJ 07607. bk.rev.; circ. 6,000. (back issues avail.)
Description: Exposes Rock & Roll as an industry whose chief aim is profit. Payola, more equitable royalties and behind-the-scenes activities are included.

780.42   US
ROCK & ROLL DISC. 1987. bi-m. $24. Tag Enterprises, Box 17601, Memphis, TN 38187-0601. TEL 901-386-4954. Ed. Tom Graves. adv.; bk.rev.; circ. 5,233. (tabloid format; avail. in CD)
Description: Features renowned music critics on compact discs.

780.42   US
ROCK FEVER. 5/yr. $2.95. Comics World, 475 Park Ave. S., New York, NY 10016. TEL 212-689-2830.

784   US   ISSN 0090-3353
ML1
ROCK SCENE. 1973. m. Tempo Publishing Company, Inc., 475 Park Ave. S., New York, NY 10016. Ed. Richard Robinson. adv.; bk.rev.; illus.

780   JA
ROCK SHOW. (Text in Japanese) 1976. bi-m. 3480 Yen. Shinko Music Publishing Co. Ltd., 2-1, Ogawa-machi, Kanda, Chiyoda-ku, Tokyo, Japan. Ed. Mariko Miyazaki.

780.42*   US
ROCKBILL.* 1982. m. $15. Rave Communications, Inc., 228 E. 45th St., New York, NY 10017. TEL 212-925-7560. Ed. Mike Hammer. adv.; circ. 250,000.
Description: Covers pop-rock music and industry.

781.7   JM
ROCKERS. 1982. bi-m. Rockers Productions, P.O. Box 46, Hagley Park P.O., Jamaica, W.I. Ed. Lynval Gibbons.

780.42   US
ROCKET. 1979. m. $12. Murder, Inc. Publishers, 2028 Fifth Ave., Seattle, WA 98121. TEL 206-728-7625. Ed. Charles Cross. adv.; circ. 64,479.
Description: Covers music, entertainment, popular culture, film and lifestyles in the Pacific Northwest.

780.42 790.2 150   US
ROCKHEAD; for rockers with brains. 1973. q. $12. Performing Arts Social Society, Inc., Box 421713, San Francisco, CA 94102-9991. TEL 415-759-4625. FAX 415-759-2490. Ed. Eve Furchgott. adv.; bk.rev.; film rev.; bibl.; charts; illus.; tr.lit.; circ. 36,000. (also avail. in microfilm from UMI; back issues avail.) **Indexed:** New Per.Ind.
Supersedes (since 1987): Utopian Classroom; Formerly: Utopian Psychology (ISSN 0882-0317); Formed by the June 1981 merger of: Utopian Eyes; Storefront Classroom.

780 745.1   US
ROCKIN' RECORDS; buyers - sellers reference book and price guide. 1986. a. $29.95. Jellyroll Publishing, Box 29, Boyne Falls, MI 49713. TEL 616-582-6852. Ed. Jerry Osborne. adv.; circ. 10,000.
Description: Covers the hobby of record collecting, with price information for all size records.

780.904   US   ISSN 0738-7717
ROCKIN' 50'S;* dedicated to the true rock 'n' roll era. 1976. bi-m. $21. (Buddy Holly Memorial Society) William F. Griggs, Ed.& Pub., 3806 55th St., Lubbock, TX 79413-4620. TEL 806-799-4299. (Subscr. to: Box 6123, Lubbock, TX 79493) adv.; bk.rev.; film rev.; play rev.; stat.; circ. 5,450. (back issues avail.)
Formerly (until Jun. 1986): Reminiscing.
Description: For 1950's record collectors. Covers the artists and fads of the 1950's rock and roll era.

780   IT
ROCKYSSIMO. 1987. m. L.3000 per no. Edizioni Coop Athena 2001 a.r.l., Via E. Q. Visconti, 20, 00193 Rome, Italy. TEL 06-314451. Ed. Salvatore Puzzo. adv.; illus.; circ. 122,200.

786   PL   ISSN 0208-5992
ML410.C54
ROCZNIK CHOPINOWSKI. 1956. a. price varies. Towarzystwo im. F. Chopina - Frederick Chopin Society, Ul. Okolnik 1, 00-368 Warsaw, Poland. TEL 48-22-275471. FAX 48-22-279599. TELEX 816598.

780.42   US
ROGUES GALLERY. m. Box 1464, Reseda, CA 91337. TEL 818-781-4104. Ed. Nannette Freeman. circ. 10,000.

781.5   US   ISSN 0035-791X
AP2
ROLLING STONE. 1967. fortn. $25.95. Straight Arrow Publishers, Inc., 1290 Ave. of Americas, New York, NY 10104. TEL 800-876-8138. FAX 212-759-2966. (Subscr. to: Box 51933, Boulder, CO 80321-1933) Ed. Jann Wenner. adv.; bk.rev.; rec.rev.; circ. 1,070,858. (tabloid format; also avail. in microform from UMI; Braille) **Indexed:** Acad.Ind., Bk.Rev.Ind. (1976-), Chic.Per.Ind., Child.Bk.Rev.Ind. (1976-), Curr.Lit.Fam.Plan., Film Lit.Ind. (1973-), Jun.High.Mag.Abstr., Mag.Ind., Media Rev.Dig., Music Ind., PMR, Pop.Per.Ind., TOM.
Description: Covers all aspects of the pop/rock music industry. Articles, interviews, reviews. Includes features on politics, movies and fashion.

780 791.43   AT
ROLLING STONE. 1972. 13/yr. Aus.$35($50) Front Publishers, 46-54 Foster St., 3rd Fl., Surrey Hills, N.S.W. 2010, Australia. TEL 02-281-3177. FAX 02-281-4154. Ed. Toby Creswell. circ. 35,000.

780   UK   ISSN 0080-4320
ROYAL COLLEGE OF ORGANISTS. YEAR BOOK. 1864. a. £5. Royal College of Organists, 7 St. Andrew St., Holborn, London EC4A 3LQ, England. adv.; circ. 3,000.

780   IE
ROYAL IRISH ACADEMY OF MUSIC. PROSPECTUS. 1973. a. free. Royal Irish Academy of Music, 36-38 Westland Row, Dublin, 2, Ireland. circ. 1,000.

780.01   UK   ISSN 0269-0403
ML28.L8
ROYAL MUSICAL ASSOCIATION. JOURNAL. 1874. 2/yr. £36($72) (Royal Musical Association) Oxford University Press, Oxford Journals, Pinkhill House, Southfield Road, Eynsham, Oxford OX8 1JJ, England. TEL 0865-882283. FAX 0865-882890. TELEX 837330 OXPRES G. Ed. Mark Everist. adv.; bk.rev.; cum.index: vols.1-99; circ. 1,450. (also avail. in microfilm from BHP; reprint service avail. from KTO) **Indexed:** Arts & Hum.Cit.Ind., Br.Hum.Ind., Curr.Cont., Music Ind., RILM.
—BLDSC shelfmark: 4862.125000.
Supersedes (in 1987): Royal Musical Association, London. Proceedings (ISSN 0080-4452)
Description: Addresses new research into all branches of musical scholarship - historical musicology and ethnomusicology, theory and analysis, textural criticism, archival research, organology and performing practice.

780   UK   ISSN 0080-4460
ML5
ROYAL MUSICAL ASSOCIATION. R.M.A. RESEARCH CHRONICLE. 1961. a. £16 to non-members. Royal Musical Association, c/o Chris Banks, Tne British Library, Music Library, Great Russell St., London WC1B 3DG, England. TEL 071-323-7527. FAX 071-323-7751. Ed. Simon McVeigh. circ. 600. **Indexed:** Br.Hum.Ind., Music Ind., RILM.
Description: Comprises articles on the history of music, reviews and musicological documentation.

780   PL
ROZPRAWY I SZKICE FILOZOFICZNO-ESTETYCZNE O MUZYCE. 1972. irreg. price varies. Polskie Wydawnictwo Muzyczne, Al. Krasinskiego 11a, 31-111 Krakow, Poland. TEL 22-70-44. FAX 22-01-74.
Description: Covers dissertations and essays about music by Polish authors.

780   PL   ISSN 0035-9610
ML5
RUCH MUZYCZNY; a musical review. 1957. fortn. $16.90. Wydawnictwo Wspolczesne R S W "Prasa-Ksiazka-Ruch", Ul. Wiejska 12, 00-420 Warsaw, Poland. TEL 22-285330. (Dist. by: Ars Polona-Ruch, Krakowskie Przedmiescie 7, Warsaw, Poland) Ed. Ludwik Erhardt. bk.rev.; illus.; music rev.; record rev.; index; circ. 10,000. **Indexed:** Music Ind., RILM.
—BLDSC shelfmark: 8047.340000.

780   RU
RUSSIAN CLASSICAL MUSICAL CRITICS. a. 2.20 Rub. Izdatel'stvo Muzyka, Ul. Neglinnaya 14, Moscow 103031, Russia.

781.7 US
RUSSIAN MUSIC STUDIES. irreg., vol.20, 1988. University of Rochester Press, c/o Robert Easton, Man. Ed., Box 41026, Rochester, NY 14604. TEL 716-275-4019.

786 RU
RUSSIAN PIANO MUSIC. a. 9.70 Rub. Izdatel'stvo Muzyka, Ul. Neglinnaya 14, Moscow 103031, Russia. TEL 924-81-63. FAX 921-83-53.

780 RU
RUSSIAN SYMPHONIC MUSIC. 2/yr. 20 Rub. per issue. Izdatel'stvo Muzyka, Ul. Neglinnaya 14, Moscow 103031, Russia. TEL 924-81-63. FAX 921-83-53.

780 792 DK ISSN 0107-6280
RYTME; nyt om folkemusik, rock, jazz og teater i Nordjylland. 1981. m. DKK 25. Skraaen, Strandvejen 19, DK-9000 Aalborg, Denmark. TEL 8-122189. Ed. Jorgen Nissen. adv.; bk.rev.; illus.; circ. 15,000.

786 US
S A B CHOIR. (Soprano, Alto, Bass) 1981. 8/yr. $18. Lorenz Publishing Co., 501 E. Third St., Box 802, Dayton, OH 45401-0802. TEL 513-228-6118. Ed. Hugh S. Livingston, Jr.
 Description: Concerns three-part music.

780 US
S C I JOURNAL OF MUSIC SCORES. Variant title: Journal of Music Scores. 1973. irreg. (2-3/yr.). price varies. (Society of Composers International) European American Music Corporation, Box 850, Valley Forge, PA 19482-0650. TEL 215-648-0506. FAX 215-889-0242. Ed. Bruce Taub. circ. 175. **Indexed:** Music Ind.
 Formerly: A S U C Journal of Music Scores.

780 US
S C MUSICIAN. 1948. 3/yr. $5. (South Carolina Music Educators Association) Wentworth Publishing Co., c/o Mrs. Johnnie Price, Ed., Rt. 5, Box 1352, Orangeburg, SC 29115. adv.; circ. 1,774.

S V ZEITUNG. (Sondenhaeuser Verband) see COLLEGE AND ALUMNI

783 US ISSN 0036-2255
SACRED MUSIC. 1874. q. $10. Church Music Association of America, 548 Lafond Ave., St. Paul, MN 55103. Ed. Rev. Richard J. Schuler. adv.; bk.rev.; charts; index; circ. 1,100. (also avail. in microform from UMI; reprint service avail. from UMI,ISI) **Indexed:** Arts & Hum.Cit.Ind., Cath.Ind., Curr.Cont., Music Artic.Guide, Music Ind.
 —BLDSC shelfmark: 8062.740000.
 Incorporates: Caecilia; Catholic Choirmaster.

786 US ISSN 0036-2263
SACRED ORGAN JOURNAL. 1966. bi-m. $14.95. Lorenz Publishing Co., 501 E. Third St., Box 802, Dayton, OH 45401-0802. TEL 513-228-6118. Ed. James Mansfield.
 Description: Arrangements for liturgical church services.

SADLER'S WELLS THEATRE PROGRAMME. see THEATER

784 GW
SAENGER-TASCHENKALENDER. 1955. a. price varies. (Deutscher Saengerbund e.V.) Verlag Deutsche Saengerzeitung GmbH, Luepertzenderstr. 14, Postfach 1355, 4050 Moenchengladbach 1, Germany. adv.; circ. 12,000.

781.7 GW ISSN 0036-2328
ML5
SAENGER- UND MUSIKANTENZEITUNG; Zweimonatschrift fuer Volksmusik. 1958. bi-m. DM.41.10. B L V Verlagsgesellschaft mbH, Lothstr. 29, 8000 Munich 40, Germany. Ed. Maria Hildebrandt. adv.; bk.rev.; illus.

784 US ISSN 0036-2336
SAENGER-ZEITUNG.* (Text in English and German) vol.41, 1965. q. membership. Federation of Worker's Singing Societies of the U.S.A, 1729 Springfield Ave., Maplewood, NJ 07040. Ed. Walter Hoops. adv.; music rev.; circ. 600.

780 GW
SAITENSPIEL. 1961. 6/yr. DM.25($20) Deutscher Zithermusik-Bund e.V., Ysenburgstr. 9, 8000 Munich 19, Germany. TEL 089-1688846. FAX 089-131438. Ed. Michael Brandlmeier. adv.; bk.rev.; circ. 1,600.
 Description: All about the zither: composition, instruction, recordings.

780 DK ISSN 0109-8438
SAMFUNDET TIL UDGIVELSE AF DANSK MUSIK. BULLETIN. 1981. irreg. free. Samfundet til Udgivelse af Dansk Musik - Society for Publication of Danish Music, Grlaabroedrestraede 18, I, DK-1156 Copenhagen K, Denmark. TEL 45-33-13-54-45. FAX 45-33-93-30-44.

780.01 GW ISSN 0085-588X
SAMMLUNG MUSIKWISSENSCHAFTLICHER ABHANDLUNGEN/COLLECTION D'ETUDES MUSICOLOGIQUES. (Text in English, French, and German) 1932. irreg., no.83, 1992. price varies. Verlag Valentin Koerner, H.-Sielcken-Str. 36, Postfach 304, 7570 Baden Baden 1, Germany. TEL 07221-22423. FAX 07221-38697.
 Description: Monographs on musicological studies.

780 792 II ISSN 0036-4339
SANGEET NATAK; journal of Indian music, dance, theatre. (Text in English) 1965. q. Rs.30 to individuals; institutions Rs.50 (foreign $15). Sangeet Natak Akademi - National Academy of Music, Dance and Drama, Rabindra Bhavan, Ferozeshah Rd., New Delhi 110001, India. TELEX 031-65466-SNA-IN. Ed. Abhijit Chatterjee. bk.rev.; illus.; circ. 750.

SANGER-HILSEN/SINGERS GREETINGS. see ETHNIC INTERESTS

780 CN
SASKATCHEWAN MUSIC FESTIVAL ASSOCIATION OFFICIAL SYLLABUS. 1909. a. Can.$14. Saskatchewan Music Festival Association, 201 - 1819 Cornwall St., Regina, Sask. S4P 2K4, Canada. Ed. Doris Covey Lazecki. adv.; circ. 2,500.

780 US
SASSAFRAS.* s-a. membership. People's Music Network for Songs of Freedom and Struggle, Box 295, Norwich, VT 05055-0295.

780 YU
SAVEZ ORGANIZACIJA KOMPOZITORA JUGOSLAVIJE. BILTEN. English edition: Union of Yugoslav Composers' Organizations. Bulletin. (Text in Serbo-Croatian) 1972. q. free. Savez Organizacija Kompozitora Jugoslavije - Union of Yugoslav Composers' Organizations, Misarska 12-14, 1000 Belgrade, Yugoslavia. TEL 38-11-334771. FAX 38-11-336-168. Ed. Ivan Kovac. circ. free. **Indexed:** Music Ind.
 Description: Publishes news on union's activities: copyright protection, international cooperation, major music events in the country, news on first performances, awards.

SAVEZ ORGANIZACIJA KOMPOZITORA JUGOSLAVIJE. BILTEN. see LABOR UNIONS

780 US ISSN 0276-4768
SAXOPHONE JOURNAL. 1980. 6/yr. $25 (foreign $32). Box 206, Medfield, MA 02052. (back issues avail.) **Indexed:** Music Artic.Guide.
 Formerly: Saxophone Sheet.
 Description: Provides news to improve playing with regular columns on jazz improvisation, techniques, doubling, career management, new publications, writing and teaching ideas, plus reviews.

SCENARIA. see THEATER

780 792 US
SCENERY, COSTUMES, AND MUSICAL MATERIALS DIRECTORY. a. $25 to non-members; members $15. Opera America, 777 14th St., N.W., Ste. 520, Washington, DC 20005. TEL 202-347-9262. FAX 202-393-0735. Ed. Martha Perry.
 Description: Listing of materials available for rent or purchase from Opera America companies.

SCENES MAGAZINE; mesuel suisse d'information culturelle. see ART

780 028.5 US ISSN 1048-2180
SCHERZO; a magazine for music students. 1989. q. $10. Jimm Omodt Music Studio, 3016 N.E. 19th, Portland, OR 97212. TEL 503-287-7009. Ed. Jimm A. Omodt. bk.rev.; circ. 500. (back issues avail.)
 Description: Articles and activities for beginning to intermediate music students.

780 FR
SCHERZO - GUIDE MUSICAL. 1970. 10/yr. 70 F. Vie Musicale, 27 rue Dareau, 75014 Paris, France. adv.; bk.rev.; circ. 12,000.
 Formed by the 1975 merger of: Scherzo & Guide Musical.

780 US
SCHIRMER - NEWS. 1987. irreg. (1-4/yr.). free. G. Schirmer Inc., 225 Park Ave. S., 18th Fl., New York, NY 10003. TEL 212-254-2100. TELEX 428351. (Co-publisher: Associated Music Publishers Inc.)

780 GW ISSN 0036-6137
SCHLAGER FUER DICH. 1954. q. Lied der Zeit Musikverlag, Rosa-Luxemburg-Str.41, 1020 Berlin, Germany.

780 US ISSN 0036-6668
ML1
SCHOOL MUSIC NEWS. 1936. 8/yr. (Sep.-May). $16 to non-members. New York State School Music Association, 151 Sweetwater Hills Dr., Hendersonville, NC 28739-8003. Ed. Robert Campbell. adv.; bk.rev.; music rev.; bibl.; illus.; index; circ. 50,000. (also avail. in microform from UMI; reprint service avail. from UMI) **Indexed:** Music Artic.Guide.

791 GW
SCHOTT AKTUELL. 1961. irreg. free. B. Schott's Soehne, Weihergarten 1-9, Postfach 3640, 6500 Mainz 1, Germany. TEL 06131-246886. Ed.Bd. circ. 2,800. (tabloid format)
 Formerly: Schott-Kurier (ISSN 0036-6919)

SCHUBERT DURCH DIE BRILLE. see BIOGRAPHY

780 GW ISSN 0174-2345
SCHUETZ-JAHRBUCH. 1979. a. membership. (Internationale Heinrich Schuetz-Gesellschaft e.V.) Baerenreiter Verlag, Heinrich-Schuetz-Allee 31-37, 3500 Kassel-Wilhelmshoehe, Germany. TEL 0561-3105-0. FAX 0561-3105240. (U.S. subscr. address: Foreign Music Distributors, 13 Elkay Dr., Chester, NY 10918) **Indexed:** Music Ind., RILM.
 Supersedes (1966-1973): Sagittarius (ISSN 0080-5408)

780 SZ
SCHWEIZER BEITRAGE ZUR MUSIKWISSENSCHAFT. (Text in German; summaries vary) 1972. irreg. price varies. Paul Haupt AG, Falkenplatz 14, CH-3001 Berne, Switzerland. TEL 031-232425. Ed. Ernst Lichtenhahn.

780 SZ ISSN 0036-7419
SCHWEIZER MUSIKER-REVUE. vol.41, 1965. m. 8 Fr. R. Stocker, Ed. & Pub., Postfach 193, CH-8029 Zurich, Switzerland. Ed. Beat Braendli. adv.; music rev.; circ. 4,000.

785 SZ
SCHWEIZERISCHE BLASMUSIKZEITUNG. (Text in French, German, Italian) 11/yr. 28 SFr. (foreign 33 SFr.). (National Society of Music from Switzerland) Zollikofer AG, Fuerstenland Str. 122, CH-9001 St. Gallen, Switzerland. TEL 071-297777. FAX 071-257487. TELEX 77537. circ. 22,000. (back issues avail.)

784 SZ
SCHWEIZERISCHE CHORZEITUNG/REVUE SUISSE DES CHORALES. (Text in French, German, Italian) 1978. m. 21 Fr. (foreign 26 fr.) Union Suisse des Chorales - Schweizerische Chorvereinigung, Scheuchzerstr. 14, CH-8006 Zurich, Switzerland. TEL 01-3612855. Ed. Sibylle Ehrismann. adv.

780 SZ ISSN 0080-7354
SCHWEIZERISCHE MUSIKFORSCHENDE GESELLSCHAFT. PUBLIKATIONEN. SERIE 2. 1952. irreg., no.34, 1991. price varies. Paul Haupt AG, Falkenplatz 14, CH-3001 Berne, Switzerland. TEL 031-232425.

MUSIC

200   US
▼**SCORE (BROOKLYN);*** your gospel music connection. 1990. m. $17. Harvest Press, 182 Gates Ave., Brooklyn, NY 11238-1902. TEL 718-858-2771. Ed. Teresa Hairston.
    Description: Keeps lovers of gospel music from the church informed of activities in the music industry. Includes news on new records, and keeps the pastors and ministers abreast on current issues related to music.

781.7   UK
SCOTTISH FOLK ARTS DIRECTORY. 1973. a. £4.25. 49 Blackfriars St., Edinburgh EH1 1NB, Scotland. adv.; bk.rev.; circ. 650.
    Formerly: Scottish Folk Directory.

SEATTLE FOLKLORE SOCIETY NEWSLETTER. see *FOLKLORE*

781.57   US   ISSN 0037-0576
ML1
SECOND LINE. 1950. q. $25 membership. New Orleans Jazz Club, 828 Royal St., Ste. 265, New Orleans, LA 70116. TEL 504-455-6847. Ed. Carolyn Stafford. adv.; bk.rev.; bibl.; charts; illus.; stat.; index. cum.index; circ. 1,000. **Indexed:** Music Ind.

781.7   US   ISSN 0361-6622
ML3799
SELECTED REPORTS IN ETHNOMUSICOLOGY. 1966. irreg. vol. 8, 1989. price varies. University of California, Los Angeles, Department of Ethnomusicology and Systematic Musicology, Los Angeles, CA 90024. TEL 213-825-5947. FAX 213-206-6958. Ed. Eran Fraenkel. illus.; circ. 800. **Indexed:** A.I.C.P., M.L.A., Music Ind., RILM.
—BLDSC shelfmark: 8235.030000.

780.01   IT
SEMINARIO DI STUDI E RICERCHE SUL LINGUAGGIO MUSICALE. ATTI. 1971. a. Istituto Musicale F. Canneti, Villa Cordellina-Lombardi, Montecchio Maggiore, Vincenza, Italy. illus.

SENSIBLE SOUND. see *SOUND RECORDING AND REPRODUCTION*

780.904   US
SERIOUS HIP HOP. bi-m. Hip Hop, Inc., Box 838, Philadelphia, PA 16105. TEL 215-629-9992. FAX 215-625-9719. Ed. Andrea Pringle.

SEVENTEENTH CENTURY FRENCH STUDIES. see *LITERATURE*

780.6 920   US   ISSN 1054-6022
SEVENTEENTH - CENTURY MUSIC. 1984. 2/yr. $10 to non-members. American Heinrich Schutz Society, c/o Steven Saunders, Dept. of Music, Colby College, Waterville, ME 04901. FAX 207-872-3237. adv.; bk.rev.; circ. 120.
    Former titles: Schutz Society Reports; Archer.
    Description: Deals with all aspects of the study and performance of music in the Seventeenth century.

783   US
SHALSHELET: THE CHAIN. vol.11, 1976. irreg. membership. Hebrew Union College - Jewish Institute of Religion (New York), One W. 4th St., New York, NY 10012. TEL 212-674-5300. Ed. B. Ostfeld Horowitz. circ. 200.

780   US   ISSN 0741-7780
SHEET MUSIC EXCHANGE. 1983. bi-m. $30 (foreign $40). Sheet Music Exchange, Box 69, Quicksburg, VA 22847-0069. TEL 703-740-3080. Ed. Pat Cleveland. adv.; bk.rev.; bibl.; illus.; index; circ. 500. (back issues avail.)
    Description: Information exchange for collectors of sheet music.

780.42   US   ISSN 0273-6462
ML1
SHEET MUSIC MAGAZINE. STANDARD PIANO-GUITAR EDITION. 1977. bi-m. $15.97. Sheet Music Magazine, Inc., 223 Katonah Ave., Katonah, NY 10536. TEL 914-232-8108. (Subscr. to: Box 58629, Boulder, CO 80322) Ed. Josephine Slendorio. adv.; bk.rev.; circ. 240,000.
    Description: Contains articles and features of interest to musicians, amateur and professional, together with instructional material and sheet music for several songs.

781.57   UK   ISSN 0583-1296
SHOUT. 1967. m. £2.25($6) c/o Clive Richardson, Ed., 46 Slades Drive, Chislehurst, Kent BR7 6JX, England. adv.; film rev.; index; circ. 2,000. (processed)
    Formerly: Soul Music.

780.65   GW
SHOW; independent music media service. 1968. w. DM.513.69($360) Show Organisation Dieter Liffers GmbH, Stumpf 15, 5204 Lohmar 21, Germany. TEL 02205-6869. FAX 02205-6879. Ed. Dieter Liffers. adv.; bk.rev.; circ. 1,600. (looseleaf format; back issues avail.)

789.91 792   US   ISSN 8755-9560
ML1699
SHOW MUSIC; the musical theatre magazine. 1981. q. $17. 900 D Speed Opera House, P.O. Box 466, East Haddam, CT 06423-0466. TEL 203-813-8664. FAX 203-873-2329. Ed. Max O. Preeo. adv.; bk.rev.; circ. 3,600. (back issues avail.)
    Description: Reviews new, original cast recordings and related-interest records, videos, and compact disc releases; contains articles on musical theatre personalities and creators.

780 790   UK
SHOWCALL. 1973. a. £5.50 for 2 parts. Carson and Comerford Ltd., Stage House, 47 Bermondsley St., London SE1 3XT, England. adv.; illus.; index.

780   US   ISSN 0889-7581
SIGMA ALPHA IOTA QUARTERLY: PAN PIPES. vol.63, 1970. 4/yr. $15. Sigma Alpha Iota, International Music Fraternity, c/o Margaret Maxwell, Ed., 8466 N. Lockwood Ridge Rd., Ste. 312, Sarasota, FL 34243. TEL 813-794-0623. (Subscr. to: Executive Office of Sigma Alpha Iota, 4119 Rollins Ave., Des Moines, IA 50312) adv.; bk.rev.; music rev.; rec.rev.; illus.; circ. 20,000. **Indexed:** Music Artic.Guide, Music Ind. Key Title: Pan Pipes.
    Formerly (until 1980): Pan Pipes of Sigma Alpha Iota (ISSN 0031-0611)

SINATRA INTERNATIONAL. see *BIOGRAPHY*

784   US   ISSN 0037-5624
ML1
SING OUT!; the folksong magazine. 1950. q. $18 to individuals (foreign $21); institutions $25 (foreign $28) (effective 1992). Sing Out Corporation, Box 5253, Bethlehem, PA 18015-5253. TEL 215-865-5366. FAX 215-865-5129. Ed. Mark D. Moss. adv.; bk.rev.; illus.; music rev.; cum.index; circ. 8,000. (also avail. in microform from UMI; back issues avail.; reprint service avail. from UMI) **Indexed:** Access, Alt.Press Ind., Curr.Cont.; Mag.Ind., Music Artic.Guide, Music Ind., New Per.Ind.
    Description: Selection of songs and articles reflecting a diversity of folk music styles: blues, blue-grass, country, gospel contemporary folk, Celtic traditional, women's, topical children's, and seasonal.

783   AU   ISSN 0037-5721
ML5
SINGENDE KIRCHE; Zeitschrift fuer katholische Kirchenmusik. 1953. q. S.55. Oesterreichische Bischofskonferenz, Oesterreichische Kirchenmusikkommission, Stock-im-Eisen Platz 3-IV, A-1010 Vienna, Austria. TEL 0222-51552-641. FAX 0222-51552-640. Ed. Walter Sengstschmid. adv.; bk.rev.; abstr.; bibl.; illus.; circ. 3,500. **Indexed:** Music Ind., RILM.
—BLDSC shelfmark: 8285.560000.

780 792   US
SINGER'S GUIDE TO THE PROFESSIONAL OPERA COMPANIES. biennial. $25 to non-members; members $15. Opera America, 777 14th St., N.W., Ste. 520, Washington, DC 20005. TEL 202-347-9262. FAX 202-393-0735. Ed. Martha Perry.
    Formerly: Opera America. Survey of Professional Training-Apprentice Programs.
    Description: Provides information on training, apprenticeship, and artist-in-residence programs at opera companies in North America and elsewhere, with company casting policies and application procedures.

784   US
SINGING NEWS; the printed voice of gospel music. 1969. m. $24. Singing News, Inc., Box 2810, Boone, NC 28607-2810. TEL 704-264-3700. FAX 704-264-4621. Ed. Jerry Kirksey. adv.; bk.rev.; bibl.; illus.; circ. 160,000.

781.7   CS
SLOVAK MUSIC. (Text in English) 1969. s-a. free. Slovensky Hudobny Fond, Hudobne Informacne Stredisko - Slovak Music Found, Music Information Center, Fucikova 29, 811 02 Bratislava, Czechoslovakia. TEL 07-333-569. FAX 07-331-380. Ed. Olga Smetanova. bk.rev.; circ. 4,000. **Indexed:** Music Ind.
    Description: Contains information on new compositions, composers, musical history and musical education.

SLOVENSKA NARODNA BIBLIOGRAFIA SERIA H: HUDOBNINY. see *MUSIC — Abstracting, Bibliographies, Statistics*

784.7691 786.97   CS
SLOVENSKE LUDOVE PIESNE PRE AKORDEON. irreg., vol.3, 1974. 8 Kcs. per no. Opus, Bratislava, Czechoslovakia.

780.7   CN
SLUR; a smooth connection between notes. 1988. q. free. Saskatchewan Band Association, 1840 McIntyre St., Regina, Sask. S4P 2P9, Canada. TEL 306-522-2263. FAX 306-565-2177. Ed. Carol J. McNabb. adv.; circ. 300.
    Description: Contains articles and events pertaining to instrumental music programs in Saskatchewan.

780.42   UK   ISSN 0260-3004
SMASH HITS. fortn. £19.50 (foreign £23.50). E M A P National Publications Ltd., 20-22 Station Rd., Kettering, Northants NN15 7HH. TEL 0536-416416. FAX 0536-415748. Ed. Mike Soutar. adv.; circ. 602,156.

781.57 791.43   AT
SMASH HITS MAGAZINE. 1984. fortn. Aus.$48.98 (foreign Aus.$73. Mason Stewart Publishing Pty. Ltd., P.O. 746, Darlinghurst, N.S.W. 2010, Australia. FAX 02-360-5367. Ed. James Manning. adv.; bk.rev.; circ. 63,000.
    Description: Entertainment magazine covering music, movies and TV.

789.42   AT   ISSN 0815-4740
SMASH HITS YEARBOOK. a. Mason Stewart Publishing Pty. Ltd., P.O. Box 746, Darlinghust, N.S.W., Australia. TEL 02-331-5006. FAX 02-360-5367.

780.42   CN
SMASH MAGAZINE. 1987. m. Can.$24. Breakaway Media, 401 Richmond St., W., Toronto, Ont. M5V 1X3, Canada. TEL 416-971-6498. Ed. Lynne Shuttleworth. adv.; circ. 25,000. (tabloid format)
    Formerly: Toronto Teen.
    Description: Focuses on popular culture: music, movies, personalities.

780   SP   ISSN 0213-0815
ML315.7.B37
SOCIEDAD DE ESTUDIOS VASCOS. CUADERNOS DE SECCION. MUSICA. 1983. irreg. Eusko Ikaskuntza, S.A., Legazpi, 10-1, 20004 Donostia-San Sebastian, Spain. TEL 425 111.

780   US
SOCIETY OF COMPOSERS NEWSLETTER. (Former name of issuing body: American Society of University Composers) 1968. 6/yr. membership. Society of Composers, Inc., Box 296, New York, NY 10011-9998. Ed. Ting Ho. bk.rev.; bibl.; circ. 900.
    Former titles: American Society of University Composers Newsletter; American Society of University Composers News Bulletin; American Society of University Composers Newsletter.

SOCIOLOGY OF MUSIC SERIES. see *SOCIOLOGY*

SON!. see *ART*

780.904   SP
SONDA;* problema y panorama de la musica contemporanea. 1973. q. Sonda, Juventudes Musicales, San Bernardo 44, Madrid 8, Spain. Ed. Ricardo Parado.

MUSIC 3581

783 US ISSN 0273-2920
SONG OF ZION; newsletter for LDS musicians. 1980. 4/yr. free. Jackman Music Corp., Box 1900, Orem, UT 84059-5900. TEL 801-225-0859. FAX 801-225-0851. Ed. Jerry R. Jackman. adv.; bk.rev.; bibl.; illus.; tr.lit.; circ. 13,000 (controlled).

781.7 AT ISSN 0726-1306
SONGS OF NEW SOUTH WALES. SERIES. 1988. irreg. Aus.$6 per no.; catalogue Aus.$2. Sound Austral, 34 Lucerne Cres., Frankston, Vic. 3199, Australia. TEL 03-789-2205. Ed. Frank Hintz. (back issues avail.; catalogue of titles avail.)
 Description: Collection of folkloric and community songs of New South Wales.

781.7 AT ISSN 1035-6355
▼**SONGS OF NEW ZEALAND**. 1990. irreg. Aus.$6 per no.; catalogue Aus.$2. Sound Austral, 34 Lucerne Cres., Frankston, Vic. 3199, Australia. TEL 03-789-2205. Ed. Frank Hinz. (back issues avail.; catalogue of titles avail.)
 Description: Collection of folkloric and community songs of New Zealand.

781.7 AT ISSN 0726-1365
SONGS OF NORTHERN TERRITORY. SERIES. 1988. irreg. Aus.$6 per no.; catalogue Aus.$2. Sound Austral, 34 Lucerne Cres., Frankston, Vic. 3199, Australia. TEL 03-789-2205. Ed. Frank Hinz. (back issues avail. catalogue of titles avail.)

781.7 AT ISSN 0726-1330
SONGS OF QUEENSLAND. SERIES. 1986. irreg. Aus.$6 per no.; catalogue Aus.$2. Sound Austral, 34 Lucerne Cres., Frankston, Vic. 3199, Australia. TEL 03-789-2205. Ed. Frank Hinz. (back issues avail.; catalogue of titles avail.)
 Description: Collection of folkloric and community songs of Queensland.

781.7 AT ISSN 0726-1322
SONGS OF SOUTH AUSTRALIA. SERIES. 1988. irreg. Aus.$6 per no.; catalogue Aus.$2. Sound Austral, 34 Lucerne Cres., Frankston, Vic. 3199, Australia. TEL 03-789-2205. Ed. Frank Hinz. (back issues avail.; catalogue of titles avail.)
 Description: Collection of folkloric and community songs of South Australia.

781.7 AT ISSN 0726-1357
SONGS OF TASMANIA. SERIES. 1986. irreg. Aus.$6 per no.; catalogue Aus.$2. Sound Austral, 34 Lucerne Cres., Frankston, Vic. 3199, Australia. TEL 03-789-2205. Ed. Frank Hinz. (back issues avail.; catalogue of titles avail.)
 Description: Collection of folkloric and community songs of Tasmania.

781.7 AT ISSN 0726-1314
SONGS OF VICTORIA. SERIES. 1977. irreg. Aus.$6 per no.; catalogue Aus.$2. Sound Austral, 34 Lucerne Cres., Frankston, Vic. 3199, Australia. TEL 03-789-2205. Ed. Frank Hinz. (back issues avail.; catalogue of titles avail.)
 Description: Collection of folkloric and community songs of Victoria.

781.7 AT ISSN 0726-1349
SONGS OF WESTERN AUSTRALIA. SERIES. 1988. irreg. Aus.$6 per no.; catalogue Aus.$2. Sound Austral, 34 Lucerne Cres., Frankston, Vic. 3199, Australia. TEL 03-789-2205. Ed. Frank Hinz. (back issues avail.; catalogue of titles avail.)
 Description: Collection of folkloric and community songs of Western Australia.

780 US
SONGTALK; the songwriter's newspaper. 1986. q. $30 for 2 yrs. National Academy of Songwriters, 6381 Hollywood Blvd., Ste. 780, Hollywood, CA 90028. TEL 213-463-7178. FAX 213-463-2146. Ed. Paul Zollo. adv.; circ. 25,000.
 Description: In-depth coverage of songwriting and songwriters, with interviews and feature articles.

780 US
SONGWRITER'S CONTACTS. 1980. bi-m. $6 for 5 nos. Music-by-Mail, Box 6101, Long Island City, NY 11106. TEL 718-728-2972. Ed. Sydney Berman.

780.65 US ISSN 0161-5971
MT67
SONGWRITER'S MARKET. 1979. a. $19.95. F & W Publications, Inc., 1507 Dana Ave., Cincinnati, OH 45207. TEL 513-531-2222. Ed. Michael Oxley. (reprint service avail. from UMI)
 Description: Lists 2000 listings of music publishers, record companies, producers, AD/AV firms, managers, booking agents.

780 AT ISSN 0729-9389
SONICS. 1980. bi-m. Aus.$19.50. Federal Publishing Company, 180 Bourke Rd., Alexandria, N.S.W. 2015, Australia. Ed. Henry Pepper. cum.index; circ. 10,000. (back issues avail.)

780 MX
SONIDO;* revista musical. 1976. m. Mex.$200($25) Corporacion Editorial S.A., Lucio Blanco 435, Col. San Juan Tlihuaca, 02400 Mexico D.F., Mexico. circ. 100,000.

780 US
SONNECK SOCIETY BULLETIN; for American music. 1975. 3/yr. membership. (Sonneck Society) Ohio State University, 4240 Campus Dr., Lima, OH 45804. TEL 419-221-1641. FAX 419-221-0450. Ed. Susan L. Porter. adv.; bk.rev.; bibl.; circ. 1,000. (also avail. in microform from UMI; reprint service avail. from UMI) **Indexed:** Music Artic.Guide, Music Ind.
 Formerly (until vol.13, 1987): Sonneck Society Newsletter (ISSN 0196-7967)
 Description: Contains brief articles of current interest, essays, news of performances and publications. Includes editorials, notes and queries.

780 US ISSN 0739-229X
ML1
SONUS. 1980. s-a. $20 to individuals; institutions $25; students $15. 24 Avon Hill, Cambridge, MA 02140. Ed. Pozzi Escot. adv.; circ. 350. **Indexed:** Music Artic.Guide, RILM.
 —BLDSC shelfmark: 8327.964000.

781.57 FR ISSN 0398-9089
ML5
SOUL BAG; le magazine du Blues et de la Soul. 1970. bi-m. 70 F.($13) Edit 71, 22 rue d'Annam, 75020 Paris, France. (Subscr. to: C.L.A.R.B., 35 rue Trezel, 92300 Levallois-Perret, France) adv.; circ. 1,000. (back issues avail.)

789.91 621.38 GR ISSN 1105-1302
SOUND & HI FI/IHOS. 1973. m. $42.50. Technical Press S.A., 6 Gorgiou St., Athens 11636, Greece. TEL 01-92-30-832. FAX 01-92-30-836. TELEX 222189 TECH GR. Ed. Costas Cavathas. adv.; circ. 16,000.
 Description: Music and presentation of hi-fi equipment.

SOUND & IMAGE. see *SOUND RECORDING AND REPRODUCTION*

780.7 GW ISSN 0936-0689
SOUND CHECK. 1984. m. DM.57. Presse Project Verlag, Detmoldstr. 2, 8000 Munich, Germany. TEL 089-3512011. FAX 089-3543838. TELEX 5215477-PPV-D. Ed. Michael van Almsick. circ. 58,000.

780 US ISSN 8756-6176
ML3469
SOUND CHOICE. 1985. q. $10. Audio Evolution Network, Box 1251, Ojai, CA 93023. TEL 805-646-6814. Ed. David Ciaffardini. adv.; bk.rev.; circ. 7,500. (back issues avail.)
 Description: Covers all types of music, reggae to funk, old-time country to salsa, electronic to rock.

780 MY
SOUND OF MALAYSIAN'S MUSICIAN/TA MA KO YU CHIH SHENG. (Text in Chinese) 1971. s-a. M.$0.30 per no. 18 Dato Koyah Rd., Penang, Malaysia. illus.

780 621.389 UK ISSN 0951-6816
SOUND ON SOUND. 1985. m. £25 (Europe £35; world £45). S O S Publications Ltd., Media House, Burrel Rd., St. Ives, Cambridgeshire PE17 4LE, England. TEL 0480-61244. FAX 0480-492422. Ed. Ian L. Gilby. adv.; index; circ. 27,000. (back issues avail.)

381.7 US ISSN 0749-0755
ML1
SOUND POST; dedicated to Scandinavian folk music and dance. 1984. q. $10. Hardanger Fiddle Association of America, 2745 Winnetka Ave. N., Ste. 211, Minneapolis, MN 55427. TEL 612-724-5540. (Subscr. to: c/o Carol Sersland, Rt. 120 G-7, Merrifield, MN 56465) Ed. Stephen Tabor. adv.; bk.rev.; index; cum.index: 1984-1988; circ. 360. (back issues avail.)
 Description: Presents Scandinavian folk music and dance with emphasis on the Norwegian Hardanger fiddle.

787 US
SOUNDBOARD. 1974. q. $25. Guitar Foundation of America, c/o Gunnar Eisel, Gen. Mgr., Box 878, Claremont, CA 91711. Ed. Peter Danner. adv.; bk.rev.; bibl.; illus.; circ. 1,800. (also avail. in microfiche; back issues avail.) **Indexed:** Music Artic.Guide, Music Ind.
 Formerly: Guitar Foundation of America Soundboard (ISSN 0145-6237)

780 UK ISSN 0144-5774
SOUNDS. 1970. w. $100. Spotlight Publications Ltd., Greater London House, Hampstead Rd., London NW1 7QZ, England. Ed. Tony Stewart. adv.; bk.rev.; record rev.; charts; circ. 58,417. (tabloid format)
 Description: Weekly magazine for young men interested in rock music.

780 AT ISSN 0811-3149
SOUNDS AUSTRALIAN JOURNAL. 1983. q. Aus.$40 to individuals; institutions Aus.$55. Australian Music Centre Ltd., P.O. Box N690, Grosvenor Pl., Sydney, N.S.W 2000, Australia. TEL 61-2-247-4677. FAX 61-2-241-2873. Ed. Richard Letts. adv.; bk.rev.; rec.rev.; circ. 1,200.
 Description: Covers issues in contemporary composition and current activities in contemporary Australian music.

780 AT ISSN 1030-4916
SOUNDS AUSTRALIAN UPDATE. 1977. m. free with subscription to Sounds Australian Journal. Australian Music Centre Ltd., P.O. Box N690, Grosvenor Pl., Sydney, N.S.W. 2000, Australia. TEL 61-2-247-4677. FAX 61-2-241-2873. Ed. Richard Letts. adv.; bk.rev.; circ. 1,200.
 Formerly (until 1987): A M C News.
 Description: Covers current events in Australian music: concerts, performances, competitions, festivals, etc.

780 621.389 US ISSN 1042-0649
SOUNDTRACK. 1988. bi-m. $58. (Independent Music Association) Soundtrack Publishing, 317 Skyline Lake Dr., Box 609, Ringwood, NJ 07456. TEL 201-831-1317. Ed. Don Kulak. adv.; bk.rev.; circ. 5,000. (back issues avail.)
 Description: Provides promotion, marketing and distribution information for independent record labels. Covers co-op marketing programs, recording techniques and acoustics, and includes independent record label and musician profiles, business tips and news of members.

786 778.5 BE ISSN 0771-6303
SOUNDTRACK! INCORPORATING CINEMASCORE. 1975. q. 500 Fr.($15) Belgian Film Music Society, Astridlaan 171, B-2800 Mechelen, Belgium. TEL 15-41-41-07. (Subscr. in U.S. to: Roger Feigelson, 1370 Third St. Apt. 103, Alameda, CA 94501) Ed. Luc Van de Ven. adv.; bk.rev.; rec.rev.; film rev.; circ. 3,000. **Indexed:** Film Lit.Ind. (1983-), Int.Ind.Film Per.
 —BLDSC shelfmark: 8330.555000.
 Incorporates: CinemaScore (ISSN 0277-9803); Former titles: Soundtrack! The Collector's Quarterly; (until vol.6, 1980): Soundtrack Collector's Newsletter.

780 US
▼**THE SOURCE (NEW YORK)**; magazine of hip-hop music, culture and politics. 1991. m. $19.95 (Canada $40.95; elsewhere $69.95). 594 Broadway, Ste. 510, New York, NY 10012-3233. TEL 212-274-0464. Ed. Jon Shecter. adv.; illus.

780 975 US
SOURCES OF MUSIC AND THEIR INTERPRETATION, DUKE STUDIES IN MUSIC. 1987. irreg. price varies. Duke University Press, 6697 College Station, Durham, NC 27708. TEL 919-684-2173. FAX 919-684-8644. Ed. Peter Williams.

M

MUSIC

780.01 SA ISSN 0258-509X
ML5
SOUTH AFRICAN JOURNAL OF MUSICOLOGY/SUID-AFRIKAANSE TYDSKRIF VIR MUSIEKWETENSKAP. (Text in Afrikaans, English) 1981. a. R.40($20) Musicological Society of Southern Africa, P.O. Box 29958, Sunnyside, Pretoria 0132, South Africa. Ed. R.W. Walton. bk.rev.; cum.index; circ. 300. (back issues avail.)

780.7 SA ISSN 0038-2493
ML5
SOUTH AFRICAN MUSIC TEACHER/SUID-AFRIKAANSE MUSIEKONDERWYSER. (Text in Afrikaans, English) 1931. s-a. free. South African Society of Music Teachers, 20 Erica Place, Bergvliet 7945, South Africa. TEL 021-72-4682. Ed. Michael Whiteman. adv.; bk.rev.; music rev.; circ. 2,000. **Indexed:** Ind.S.A.Per., Music Ind.
   Description: Presents information and articles of interest and use to music teachers in South Africa.

SOUTH DAKOTA MUSICIAN. see *EDUCATION*

780.7 US ISSN 0162-380X
SOUTHWESTERN MUSICIAN COMBINED WITH THE TEXAS MUSIC EDUCATOR. 1915. m. (Aug.-May). $15 (effective Jul. 1989). Texas Music Educators Association, Box 49469, Austin, TX 78765. TEL 512-452-0710. FAX 512-451-9213. Ed. Bill R. Cormack. adv.; bk.rev.; illus.; index; circ. 8,498. (processed; also avail. in microfiche; reprint service avail. from UMI)
   Formerly: Southwestern Musician (ISSN 0038-4895); Incorporating: Texas Music Educator.

780 RU ISSN 0038-5085
ML5
SOVETSKAYA MUZYKA. 1933. m. 33 Rub. (Soyuz Kompozitorov S.S.S.R.) Izdatel'stvo Sovetskii Kompozitor, 14-12, Sadovaya Triumfalnaya St., 103006 Moscow, Russia. (Co-sponsor: Ministerstvo Kul'tury S.S.S.R.) Ed. Yu.S. Korev. bk.rev.; bibl.; illus.; music rev.; index. **Indexed:** Curr.Dig.Sov.Press, Music Ind., RILM.

780 SP
SPAIN. DIRECCION GENERAL DE BELLAS ARTES. SEMANA DE MUSICA EN LA NAVIDAD. irreg. Direccion General de Bellas Artes, Murcia, Spain. illus.

SPECTATOR (RALEIGH); at home. see *ART*

780 IT ISSN 0038-7401
SPETTATORE MUSICALE.* 1966. bi-m. L.3000. Via Nizza 45, 00198 Rome, Italy. Ed.Bd. circ. 1,100.

789.9 US ISSN 0886-3032
ML3533.8
SPIN. 1985. m. $18. Camouflage Associates, 6 W. 18th St., New York, NY 10011. TEL 212-633-8200. FAX 212-633-2668. Ed. Bob Guccione, Jr. adv.; bk.rev.; circ. 300,000. (also avail. in microform from UMI) **Indexed:** Access (1986-).

780 PL
SPOTKANIA (KRAKOW). 1985. irreg. price varies. Polskie Wydawnictwo Muzyczne, Al. Krasinskiego 11, 31-111 Krakow, Poland. TEL 22-70-44. FAX 22-01-74.
   Description: Literary text connected with music, engravings and musical text.

780 YU ISSN 0490-6659
SRPSKA AKADEMIJA NAUKA I UMETNOSTI. ODELJENJE LIKOVNE I MUZICKE UMETNOSTI. MUZICKA IZDANJA. 1953. irreg. exchange basis. Srpska Akademija Nauka i Umetnosti, Odeljenje Likovne i Muzicke Umetnosti, Knez Mihailova 35, 11001 Belgrade, Serbia, Yugoslavia. FAX 38-11-182-825. TELEX 72593 SANU YU. (Dist. by: Prosveta Export Import Terazije 16, 11001 Belgrade, Serbia, Yugoslavia) circ. 300.

SRPSKA AKADEMIJA NAUKA I UMETNOSTI. ODELJENJE LIKOVNE I MUZICKE UMETNOSTI. POSEBNA IZDANJA. see *ART*

783 US ISSN 0196-2337
ML1
STANZA. vol.2, 1978. s-a. membership. Hymn Society in the United States and Canada, Headquarters, Texas Christian University, Box 30854, Fort Worth, TX 76129. TEL 817-921-7608. illus.

STAR GUIDE; where to contact movie, TV stars and other celebrities. see *MOTION PICTURES*

780 RU
STARS OF MUSIC WORLD. a. 5 Rub. Izdatel'stvo Muzyka, Ul. Neglinnaya 13, Moscow 103031, Russia. TEL 924-81-63. FAX 921-83-53.

780 RU
STARS OF WORLD VARIETY. a. 3.50 Rub. Izdatel'stvo Muzyka, Ul. Neglinnaya 14, Moscow 103031, Russia. TEL 924-81-63. FAX 921-83-53.

780 069 US ISSN 1046-4387
STEARNS NEWSLETTER; the Stearns collection of musical instruments at the University of Michigan. 1986. 3/yr. $30. University of Michigan, Music Department, Ann Arbor, MI 48109. TEL 313-763-4389. FAX 313-763-5097. circ. 400. (back issues avail.)

786 US
STEINWAY NEWS. 1935. q. free to libraries, colleges and conservatories. Steinway & Sons, Steinway Place, Long Island City, NY 11105. TEL 718-721-2600. Ed. Leo Spellman. bk.rev.; illus.; circ. 45,000.
   Description: Provides "how-to" tips on caring for your Steinway and information on piano competitions. Profiles new Steinway artists.

STEREO. see *SOUND RECORDING AND REPRODUCTION*

STEREO REVIEW. see *SOUND RECORDING AND REPRODUCTION*

789.91 US ISSN 0585-2544
TK7881.8
STEREOPHILE; for the high-fidelity stereo perfectionist. 1962. 12/yr. $35 (foreign $75). Box 5529, Santa Fe, NM 87502. TEL 505-982-2366. FAX 505-989-8791. Ed. John Atkinson. adv.; bk.rev.; index; circ. 56,000.
   —BLDSC shelfmark: 8464.364000.

780 GR ISSN 1105-1345
STEREOPHONY AND MUSIC. 1975. a. Technical Press, S.A., 6 Gorgiou St., 11636 Athens, Greece. TEL 01-9230832. FAX 01-9230836. TELEX 222189 TECH GR. Ed. Costas Cavathas. circ. 15,000.
   Description: Guide for purchasing of hi-fi equipment.

780 GW ISSN 0172-388X
STEREOPLAY; das internationale HiFi-Magazin. m. DM.90 (foreign DM.102). (Stereoplay) Vereinigte Motor-Verlage GmbH und Co. KG, Leuschnerstr. 1, 7000 Stuttgart 1, Germany. TEL 0711-18201. FAX 0711-1821756. Ed. Karl Breh. adv.; charts; illus.; circ. 75,000. **Indexed:** Music Ind.
   Incorporating: HiFi Stereophonie (ISSN 0018-1382); Which was formerly: HiFi Stereopraxis.

780 SW ISSN 0283-3190
STIM NYTT. 1984. s-a. free. Swedish Performing Rights Society, P.O. Box 27327, S-102 54 Stockholm, Sweden. Ed. Margita Jardfelt. charts; illus.; circ. 24,000.
   Formerly: Ord och Ton.

781.57 UK ISSN 0039-2030
ML5
STORYVILLE. 1965. q £10($20) Storyville Publications & Co. Ltd., 66 Fairview Dr., Chigwell, Essex 1G7 6HS, England. TEL 01-500-6098. Ed. Laurie Wright. adv.; bk.rev.; illus, record rev.; index; circ. 2,000. (processed)
   Description: Covers classic jazz and blues.

787.01 UK ISSN 0039-2049
ML5
STRAD; a monthly journal for professionals and amateurs of all stringed instruments played with the bow. 1890. m. $72. Orpheus Publications Ltd., Centro House, Mandela St., London NW1 0DU, England. TEL 071-387-3848. FAX 071-388-8532. Ed. Helen Wallace. adv. contact: adv. contact: Stephen Jocelyn. bk.rev.; illus.; music rev.; record rev.; circ. 11,000. (also avail. in microform from UMI; reprint services avail. from UMI) **Indexed:** Arts & Hum.Cit.Ind., Br.Hum.Ind., Curr.Cont., Music Ind.
   —BLDSC shelfmark: 8467.600000.

STREET ARTISTS' NEWSLETTER. see *ART*

780 CN ISSN 0841-2650
STREETSOUND; North America's international D.J. authority. 1988. m. Can.$2.98. 174 Spadina Ave., Ste. 506, Toronto, Ont. M5T 2C2, Canada. TEL 416-369-0070. FAX 416-369-1702. Ed. Michael Mannix. adv.; bk.rev.; circ. 16,000.

781.57 US
STRICTLY NOTHING BUT; the blues. 1989. m. $15 (effective Nov. 1991). J & M Publishing, Box 81383, San Diego, CA 92138. TEL 619-469-9102. Eds. Michael Dollins, Jo Ann Dollins. adv.; bk.rev.; play rev.; bibl.; illus.; tr.lit.; circ. 1,000. (tabloid format)
   Description: Focuses on American blues music and related topics.

787 US ISSN 0888-3106
ML749.5
STRINGS; the magazine for players and makers of bowed instruments. 1986. bi-m. $36 in U.S.; Canada $43.50; elsewhere $51. String Letter Press, Inc., Box 767, San Anselmo, CA 94979-0767. TEL 415-485-6946. FAX 415-485-0831. Ed. David M. Brin. adv.; bk.rev.; illus.; music rev.; circ. 10,000. **Indexed:** Music Artic.Guide, Music Ind.
   Description: Directed to the practicing and performing musician who wants to play with greater knowledge and craft.

793.31 DK ISSN 0906-1061
STRINGS AND SQUARES; bladet for traditionel amerikansk musik og dans i Danmark. 1984. bi-m. DKK 35 (typically set in Oct.). Strings and Squares, Hasselvej 18, DK-2830 Virum, Denmark. TEL 45-83-99-83. (Subscr. to: Bent Hjortshoej, Gedevasevej 17, DK-3520 Farum, Denmark) (Co-sponsors: Oldtime, Bluegrass & Country i Danmark; Midtjysk Old Time Music Association; Dansk-Amerikansk Folkemusik Forening; Square Dance Partners) Ed. Margot Gunzenhauser. adv.; bk.rev.; illus, rec.rev.; circ. 800.
   Former titles: Lydhullet (ISSN 0109-2480) & Broken Strings (ISSN 0107-4172)
   Description: Covers square dancing, bluegrass, and old-time music events in Denmark plus other general interest articles and U.S. news.

781.91 IT ISSN 0039-260X
STRUMENTI & MUSICA. 1947. m. L.3000. Berben Editore, Via Redipuglia 65, 60100 Ancona, Italy. Ed. Bio Boccosi. adv.

780 IT ISSN 0392-890X
STRUMENTI MUSICALI. 1979. m. L.77000 (foreign L.154000). Gruppo Editoriale Jackson S.p.A., Via Pola 9, 20124 Milan, Italy. TEL 39-2-69481. FAX 39-2-6948238. TELEX 316213 GEJIT 1. Ed. Pado Reina. adv.; circ. 11,938.
   Description: Offers special reports, audiotests, reviews and monographs about acoustic and electronic instruments. Also includes interviews with famous musicians.

780 IT
STUDI DI MUSICA VENETA. 1968. irreg., no.18, 1991. price varies. (Fondazione Giorgio Cini) Casa Editrice Leo S. Olschki, Casella Postale 66, 50100 Florence, Italy. TEL 055-6530684. FAX 055-6530214.

780 IT
STUDI DI MUSICA VENETA. QUADERNI VIVALDIANI. 1980. irreg., no.6, 1991. price varies. (Fondazione Giorgio Cini) Casa Editrice Leo S. Olschki, Casella Postale 66, 50100 Florence, Italy. TEL 055-6530684. FAX 055-6530214.

780.903 IT
STUDI E TESTI PER LA STORIA DELLA MUSICA. 1979. irreg., no.9, 1990. price varies. Casa Editrice Leo S. Olschki, Casella Postale 66, 50100 Florence, Italy. TEL 055-6530684. FAX 055-6530214.

780 IT ISSN 0391-7789
STUDI MUSICALI. 1972. s-a. L.63000 (foreign L.80000). (Accademia Nazionale di Santa Cecilia di Roma) Casa Editrice Leo S. Olschki, Casella Postale 66, 50100 Florence, Italy. TEL 055-6530684. FAX 055-6530214. Ed. Nino Pirrotta. bk.rev.; circ. 1,000. **Indexed:** Arts & Hum.Cit.Ind., RILM.

STUDI PIEMONTESI. see *LITERATURE*

782.1 IT ISSN 0393-2532
STUDI VERDIANI. (Text in English, German, Italian) 1982. a. L.28000($15) Istituto Nazionale di Studi Verdiani, Strada della Repubblica 56, 43100 Parma, Italy.

780 PL
STUDIA I MATERIALY DO DZIEJOW MUZYKI POLSKIEJ. 1955. irreg. price varies. Polskie Wydawnictwo Muzyczne, Al. Krasinskiego 11a, 31-111 Krakow, Poland. TEL 22-70-44. FAX 22-01-74. Ed. Tadeusz Strumillo.
  Formerly: Muzyka Polska w Dokumentacjach i Interpretacjach.
  Description: Covers Polish composers' lives and work.

780.01 HU ISSN 0039-3266
STUDIA MUSICOLOGICA ACADEMIAE SCIENTIARUM HUNGARICAE. (Text in English, French, German, Russian) 1961. q. $62. (Magyar Tudomanyos Akademia) Akademiai Kiado, Publishing House of the Hungarian Academy of Sciences, P.O. Box 24, H-1363 Budapest, Hungary. Ed. J. Ujfalussy. adv.; bk.rev.; bibl.; charts; index. **Indexed:** Music Ind., RILM.

780.01 NO ISSN 0332-5024
ML3797.1
STUDIA MUSICOLOGICA NORVEGICA. (Text in English and Norwegian) 1968. a. $39. Unviersitetsforlaget, P.O. Box 2959-Toeyen, 00-068 Oslo, Norway. (U.S. addr.: Publications Expediting Inc., 200 Meacham Ave., Elmont, NY 11003) Ed. Harald Herresthal. **Indexed:** Music Ind., RILM.

780 SW ISSN 0081-6744
STUDIA MUSICOLOGICA UPSALIENSIA. NOVA SERIES. (1952-58, vols. 1-8; 1965 designated as Nova Series and issued in Acta Universitatis Upsaliensis) irreg., vol.10, 1987. price varies. (Uppsala Universitet) Almqvist and Wiksell International, Box 638, S-101 28 Stockholm, Sweden. Ed. Ingmar Bengtsson.
  —BLDSC shelfmark: 0586.580000.

780 GW ISSN 0081-7341
STUDIEN ZUR MUSIKGESCHICHTE DES NEUNZEHNTEN JAHRHUNDERTS. irreg. price varies. Gustav Bosse Verlag, Postfach 417, 8400 Regensburg 1, Germany. TEL 0941-794091.

780.01 GW
STUDIEN ZUR MUSIKWISSENSCHAFT; Beihefte der Denkmaeler der Tonkunst in Oesterreich. biennial. Verlag Dr. Hans Schneider GmbH, Mozartstr. 6, 8132 Tutzing, Germany. Ed. Othmar Wessely.

780 HU
STUDIES IN CENTRAL AND EASTERN EUROPEAN MUSIC. (Text in English) 1967. irreg., vol.4, 1989. price varies. (Magyar Tudomanyos Akademia) Akademiai Kiado, Publishing House of the Hungarian Academy of Sciences, P.O. Box 24, H-1363 Budapest, Hungary. Ed. Zoltan Falvy.
  Formerly (until 1980): Musicologica Hungarica (ISSN 0077-2488)

780 AT ISSN 0081-8267
ML5
STUDIES IN MUSIC. 1967. a. Aus.$20 plus postage. University of Western Australia, Department of Music, Nedlands, 6009 W.A., Australia. Ed.Bd. circ. 950. **Indexed:** Aus.P.A.I.S., Music Ind., RILM.
  —BLDSC shelfmark: 8491.140000.

780 CN ISSN 0703-3052
ML5
STUDIES IN MUSIC. 1976. a. University of Western Ontario, Department of Music History, London, Ont., Canada. Ed. Richard Semmens. circ. 300. **Indexed:** Music Ind.
  —BLDSC shelfmark: 8491.141000.

780.01 US
STUDIES IN MUSIC. irreg., vol.101, 1988. University of Rochester Press, c/o Robert Easton, Man. Ed., Box 41026, Rochester, NY 14604. TEL 716-275-4019.
  Formerly: Studies in Musicology.

780 900 US
STUDIES IN THE HISTORY AND INTERPRETATION OF MUSIC. 1980. irreg., latest no.36. $39.95 per no. Edwin Mellen Press, 240 Portage Rd., Box 450, Lewiston, NY 14092. TEL 716-754-8566. FAX 716-754-4335.

781.7 JA ISSN 0039-3851
STUDIES ON ORIENTAL MUSIC/TOYO ONGAKU KENKYU. (Text in Japanese; summaries in English) 1937. price varies. Japan Publications Trading Co. Ltd., Box 5030, Tokyo International, Tokyo 100-31, Japan. (Or: 1255 Howard St., San Francisco, CA 94103) Ed. Masao Tanabe. adv.; bk.rev.; illus.; circ. 4,000. **Indexed:** RILM.

STUDII SI CERCETARI DE ISTORIA ARTEI. SERIA TEATRU, MUZICA, CINEMATOGRAFIE/STUDIES AND RESEACH IN ART HISTORY. SERIES: THEATRE, MUSIC, CINEMATOGRAPHY. see *THEATER*

STUDIO; tjedni informativni list za televiziju, radio, film, teatar i muziku. see *COMMUNICATIONS — Television And Cable*

SUOSIKKI. see *CHILDREN AND YOUTH — For*

780.42 CL
SUPER ROCK. 1985. w. Luis Thayer Ojeda 1626, Casilla 3092, Providencia, Santiago, Chile. TEL 2-74-8231. TELEX 341194. Dir. Dario Rojas Morales. illus.; circ. 40,000.
  Description: Covers Latin American and European rock music.

780 II
SURCHHANDA. (Text in Bengali) 1955. m. Rs.30. Nilratan Banerji, Ed. & Pub., Nirala, 2B, Jadar Ghosh Bye Lane, Calcutta 700 061, India. adv.; bk.rev.; illus.; circ. 1,200.

780 310 US
SURVEY OF OPERATING PERFORMANCE FOR MUSIC DEALERS. a. $35 to members; non-members $60. National Association of Music Merchants Inc., 5140 Avenida Encinas, Carlsbad, CA 92008-4391. TEL 619-438-8001. (back issues avail.)
  Description: Reports statistical data supplied by music products retailers on sales volume and product line.

367 781.7 US
SUZI DEVERAUX INTERNATIONAL FAN CLUB. 1975. q. $5. 201 Waters Ave., Watertown, TN 37184. TEL 615-237-3020. Ed. Cheryl Ellison. circ. 2,000. (back issues avail.)
  Description: For country music fans interested in Suzi Deveraux's career.

780.01 SW ISSN 0081-9816
SVENSK TIDSKRIFT FOER MUSIKFORSKNING/SWEDISH JOURNAL OF MUSICOLOGY. (Text in Swedish; occasionally in English and German; summaries in English) 1919. a. SEK 150. Svenska Samfundet foer Musikforskning - Swedish Society for Musicology, Statens Musiksamligar, Box 16326, S-103 26 Stockholm, Sweden. Eds. Hans Bernskioeld, Ola Stockfelt. adv.; bk.rev.; index, cum.index: 1919-68 (vols. 1-50); circ. 600. (reprint service avail. from SWZ) **Indexed:** Arts & Hum.Cit.Ind., Curr.Cont., Music Ind., RILM.
  Description: Consists of articles covering various fields of musicology. Reports are given of unpublished theses in musicology, of research projects and congresses. Also a review section on literature and scholarly editions of music.

780 016 SW ISSN 0586-0709
SVENSKT MUSIKHISTORISKT ARKIV. BULLETIN. (Text in Swedish; glossary in English) 1966. irreg. (approx. 1/yr.). free. Svenskt Musikhistoriskt Arkiv, Box 16326, S-103 26 Stockholm, Sweden. TEL 8-6664560. circ. 300. **Indexed:** RILM.
  Description: Acquisitions and holdings of the Svenskt Musikhistoriskt Arkiv.

780 CI
SVETA CECILIJA; casopis za duhovnu glazbu. 1877. q. 1000 din. (Institut za Crkvenu Glazbu u Zagrebu) Hrvatsko Knjizevno Drustvo Cirila i Metoda, Trg Kralja Tomislava 21, 41000 Zagreb, Croatia. TEL 041-431-950. Ed. A. Milanovic. adv.; bk.rev.; illus.; circ. 1,200.

781.57 JA ISSN 0039-744X
SWING JOURNAL. (Text in Japanese) 1947. m. 18000 Yen. Swing Journal Co. Ltd., 3-6-24, Shibakoen, Minato-ku, Tokyo 105, Japan. FAX 03-3432-7758. Ed. Kiyoshi Koyama. adv.; bk.rev.; record rev.; illus.; circ. 250,000.

782.1 792 AT
SYDNEY OPERA HOUSE. DIARY. 1973. bi-m. $12 (foreign Aus.$20). Sydney Opera House Trust, G.P.O. Box 4274, Sydney, N.S.W. 2001, Australia. TEL 02-250-7414. FAX 02-221-1161. Ed. Warner Whiteford. circ. 50,000. (back issues avail.)
  Description: Calendar of events at Sydney Opera House.

786 AT ISSN 0817-2285
SYDNEY ORGAN JOURNAL. 1970. bi-m. Aus.$27 membership. Organ Society of Sydney, Box 2348, G.P.O., Sydney, N.S.W. 2001, Australia. Ed. G. Bock. adv.; bk.rev.; circ. 700.

780 US ISSN 0275-9381
ML27.U5
SYMPHONY GOLD BOOK. a. $35. American Symphony Orchestra League, 777 14th St., N.W., Ste. 500, Washington, DC 20005. TEL 202-628-0099. FAX 202-783-7228. circ. 600.
  Description: A compendium of successful volunteer projects in the areas of ticket sales, fundraising, and educational programs.

785.066 US ISSN 0271-2687
ML1
SYMPHONY MAGAZINE. 1948. bi-m. $35 includes membership. American Symphony Orchestra League, 777 14th St., N.W., Ste. 500, Washington, DC 20005. TEL 202-628-0099. FAX 202-783-7228. Eds. Chester Lane, Matthew Sigman. adv.; bk.rev.; bibl.; charts; illus.; stat.; tr.lit.; index; circ. 16,000. (also avail. in microform from UMI; back issues avail; reprint service avail. from UMI) **Indexed:** Music Artic.Guide, Music Ind.
  Former titles (until Apr. 1980): Symphony News (ISSN 0090-5380); American Symphony Orchestra League. Newsletter (ISSN 0003-1372)
  Description: Provides news of the orchestra field, the music world, and the League itself.

780 PL
SYNTEZY. 1972. irreg. price varies. Polskie Wydawnictwo Muzyczne, Al. Krasinskiego 11a, 31-111 Krakow, Poland. TEL 22-70-44. FAX 22-01-74.
  Description: Covers history of music, composers.

780 PL ISSN 0239-9148
SZKICE O KULTURZE MUZYCZNEJ XIX WIEKU. STUDIA I MATERIALY. (Text in Polish; summaries in English) irreg., vol.4, 1981. price varies. (Polska Akademia Nauk, Instytut Sztuki) Panstwowe Wydawnictwo Naukowe, Miodowa 10, 00-251 Warsaw, Poland. (Dist. by: Ars Polona, Krakowskie Przedmiescie 7, 00-068 Warsaw, Poland) Ed. Z. Chechlinska. charts; illus.

781.57 US
T - J TODAY. (Traditional Jazz) 1981. q. $15. 732 Cynthia Ct., Watsonville, CA 95076. TEL 408-728-3948. Ed. Alice Leyland. adv.; bk.rev.; circ. 1,000. (back issues avail.)

T R U K P A C T INFO. (Transvaalse Raad vir die Uitvoerende Kunste) see *THEATER*

780.6 US ISSN 0363-4787
ML1
T.U.B.A. JOURNAL. 1973. 4/yr. $25 for libraries. Tubists Universal Brotherhood Association, 444 North County St., Waukegan, IL 60085. Ed. Tom Gillette. adv.; bk.rev.; bibl.; charts; illus.; tr.; lit.; index; circ. 1,800. (back issues avail.)
  Formerly: T.U.B.A. Newsletter (ISSN 0363-4779)

T V PICTURE LIFE - METAL EDGE. see *COMMUNICATIONS — Television And Cable*

780.43 943 US
▼**TANNECK.** 1992. a. $30 to non-members; members $25; institutions $35. Wilhelm Furtwaengler Society of America, Box 620702, Woodside, CA 94062. TEL 415-851-3808. FAX 415-851-3151. (Subscr. to: Editor, Dept. of Lang. and Lit., Univ. of Utah, Salt Lake City, UT 84112) Ed. Charles Schlacks, Jr.

TAPE - DISC DIRECTORY (YEAR); for the record, CD and audio-video tape industries. see *COMMUNICATIONS — Video*

MUSIC

780 GW ISSN 0082-1969
TASCHENBUECHER ZUR MUSIKWISSENSCHAFT. 1969. irreg., vol.111, 1987. DM.23.80. Florian Noetzel Verlag, Heinrichshofen Buecher, Valoisstrasse 11, 2940 Wilhelmshaven, Germany. (Dist. in U.S. by: C. F. Peters Corp., 373 Park Ave. S., New York, N.Y. 10016) Ed. Richard Schaal.

786 SZ
TASTEN WELT. 1978. bi-m. 27 Fr. Buehler's Tasten Welt Verlag, Postfach 111, CH-2558 Aegerten, Switzerland. FAX 032-533891. Ed. A. Buehler. adv.; bk.rev.; circ. 9,400.

TEATRO E STORIA. see THEATER

TEEN BEAT. see CHILDREN AND YOUTH — For

781.57 SZ
TELEJAZZ (YEAR); schweizer Jazz Handbuch. (Text in German) 1986. a. 16 Fr. Jazztime-Verlag, CH-5425 Schneisingen, Switzerland. TEL 056-51-25-28. Ed. Eduard Keller.

780 UK ISSN 0040-2982
ML5
TEMPO (LONDON, 1939); a quarterly review of modern music. 1939. q. £6. Boosey & Hawkes Music Publishers Ltd., 295 Regent St., London W1R 8JH, England. (U.S. addr.: Boosey & Hawkes, Inc., Oceanside, NY 11572) Ed. C. MacDonald. adv.; bk.rev.; record rev.; charts; illus. **Indexed:** Br.Hum.Ind., Ind.Bk.Rev.Hum., Music Ind., RILM. —BLDSC shelfmark: 8790.042000.

780.1 US ISSN 0040-3334
TENNESSEE MUSICIAN. 1948. q. $6 to non-members. Tennessee Music Educators Association, c/o Carl H. Kauffman, Ed., 500 Holly Hill Ct., Nashville, TN 37221. adv.; bk.rev.; circ. 2,130.

THEATER HEUTE. see THEATER

THEATER IN GRAZ. see THEATER

786.6 US ISSN 0040-5531
THEATRE ORGAN. vol.17, 1975. bi-m. $25 membership. American Theatre Organ Society, c/o Douglas Fisk, Box 417490, Sacramento, CA 95841. FAX 916-966-3172. Ed. Grace McGinnis. adv.; bk.rev.; illus.; record rev.; index; circ. 6,200.

786.6 UK ISSN 0040-5558
THEATRE ORGAN REVIEW.* 1947. q. 10s.($3.50) Theatre Organ Review, 127 Stratford St., Leeds LS11 6JG, Yorkshire, England. (U.S. subscr. addr.: Bobby Clark, 939 Green St., Orangeburg, SC 29115) Ed. Frank Hare. adv.; illus.; record rev. (tabloid format)

780 US
THEMATIC CATALOGUE SERIES. (Text in English, French and German) 1972. irreg., no.15, 1990. Pendragon Press, Rt. 1, Box 159, Stuyvesant, NY 12173-9720. TEL 518-828-3008. FAX 518-828-2368.

780 US ISSN 0741-6156
THEORY AND PRACTICE. 1975. a. $18 to individuals; libraries $25. Music Theory Society of New York State, Inc., School of Music, Ithaca College, Ithaca, NY 14850. TEL 607-274-3350. Ed. Frank Samarotto. bk.rev.; bibl.; circ. 250. (back issues avail.) **Indexed:** RILM.
—BLDSC shelfmark: 8814.628300.

784 CC
TIANJIN GESHENG/SONGS OF TIANJIN. (Text in Chinese) m. $21.50. Tianjin Gesheng Bianjibu, Tianjin, People's Republic of China. (Dist. in US by: China Books & Periodicals, Inc., 2929 24th St., San Francisco, CA 94110. TEL 415-282-2994)

780 GW ISSN 0176-6511
TIBIA; Magazin fuer Freunde alter und neuer Blaesermusik. 1976. 4/yr. DM.33 (foreign DM.37). Moeck Verlag & Musikinstrumentenwerk, Postfach 143, 3100 Celle 1, Germany. FAX 05141-885342. Ed.Bd. adv.; bk.rev.; circ. 4,000. (back issues avail.) **Indexed:** RILM.

780.9031 NE ISSN 0920-0649
TIJDSCHRIFT VOOR OUDE MUZIEK. 1986. q. fl.35. Organisatie Oude Muziek, Postbus 734, 3500 AS Utrecht, Netherlands. TEL 30-340921. FAX 30-322798. circ. 4,500.
Description: Covers topics in early music.

780 UK
TOCCATA. 1978. £10($28) (typically set in Apr.). Leopold Stokowski Society, 12 Market St., Deal, Kent CT1 6HS, England. Ed.Bd. adv.; film rev.; play rev.; rec.rev.; abstr.; bibl.; charts; illus.; tr.lit.; index; circ. 250. (back issues avail.)

780.7 375
TODAY'S MUSIC EDUCATOR. Short title: T M E. 1988. q. $12. Drum Corps Sights & Sounds, Inc., Box 8052, Madison, WI 53708. TEL 608-241-2292. FAX 608-241-4974. Ed. Steve Vickers. adv.; circ. 29,500. (back issues avail.)
Description: For instrumental music educators, drum and bugle corps directors and music enthusiasts.

TON - REPORT. see SOUND RECORDING AND REPRODUCTION

780 SW ISSN 0346-329X
TONFALLET. 1968. irreg. (10/yr.). SEK 150. Svenska Rikskonserter - The Swedish Concert Institute, Box 1225, 111 82 Stockholm, Sweden. FAX 10-99-92. Ed. Cecilia Aare. adv.; bk.rev.; bibl.; illus.; circ. 6,000.

780.42 CC
TONGSU GEQU/POPULAR SONGS. (Text in Chinese) m. Hebei Sheng Yishu Yanjiusuo - Hebei Art Research Institute, 41, Beima Lu, Shijiazhuang, Hebei 050071, People's Republic of China. TEL 743726. Ed. Li Jiang.

780 920 UK ISSN 0260-7425
ML410.S587
TONIC. 1980. irreg. membership. Robert Simpson Society, c/o Licensed Victuallers' School, London Rd., Ascot, Berks SL5 8DR, England. Ed. Christine Skinner. adv.; bk.rev.; circ. 200. (back issues avail.)
Description: Discusses the music of Robert Simpson.

780.42 KO
▼**TOP 10.** (Text in English, Korean) 1990. m. 20 Won($30) Sangji Music Publishing Co., Ltd., 83-4 Guro 2-Dong, Guro-Ku, Seoul, Korea. TEL 82-2-867-4544. FAX 82-2-868-5179. TELEX K24393. Ed. Saehoon Oh. adv. (also avail. in talking book; back issues avail.)
Description: Includes the top 10 Korean and foreign hit songs in piano and guitar arrangements.

785 CN
TORONTO SYMPHONY MAGAZINE.* 1968. 7/yr. free. National Theatre Publications, 30 St. Clair Ave. W. No. 805, Toronto, Ont. M4V 3A1, Canada. TEL 416-926-7595. FAX 416-926-0407. circ. 30,000.
Formerly: Toronto Symphony News (ISSN 0049-4224)

784 200 US ISSN 0884-738X
TOTALLY GOSPEL.* vol.4-4, 1989. m. $12. Hemphill Publication, 17400 Manderson Rd., Detroit, MI 48203-1712.

786.63 US ISSN 0041-0330
ML1
TRACKER; journal of American pipe organ progress, history, preservation, organbuilding, and performance. 1956. q. $25. Organ Historical Society, Inc., Box 26811, Richmond, VA 23261. TEL 804-253-9226. FAX 804-353-9266. Ed. Jerry Morton. adv.; bk.rev.; charts; illus.; stat.; index; circ. 3,000. (also avail. in microfilm from UMI) **Indexed:** Music Artic.Guide.

781.7 US
TRADITION (WALNUT). 1976. bi-m. $12. (National Traditional Country Music Association, Inc.) Prairie Press Ltd., Box 438, Walnut, IA 51577. TEL 712-784-3001. Ed. Robert P. Everhart. adv.; bk.rev.; film rev.; charts; illus.; cum.index: 1976-1989; circ. 2,500. (back issues avail.)
Description: Publication for acoustic music lovers, supporters, performers, fans, preservationists and promoters of all forms of traditional acoustic music: folk, bluegrass, traditional country, western swing, ragtime, hillbilly, etc.

780 UK ISSN 0306-7440
ML5
TRADITIONAL MUSIC. 1975. 3/yr. £1.20($3) Alan Ward, Ed. & Pub, 90 St. Julian's Farm Rd., London SE27 ORS, England. adv.; bk.rev.; illus. **Indexed:** M.L.A., Music Ind.

780 US ISSN 1059-5953
THE TRADITIONAL MUSICLINE. 1987. m. $17.50 (Canada $20). Stephanie P. Ledgin, Ed. & Pub., Box 10598, New Brunswick, NJ 08906. TEL 908-572-3429. circ. 2,500.
Description: A comprehensive calendar magazine for traditional music concerts, dances and festivals in a six-state area covering Rhode Island, eastern Pennsylvania, northern Delaware, midstate New York, New Jersey and Connecticut; subscriptions includes a semi annual radio program and resource guide.

780 US ISSN 1041-7494
ML935
TRAVERSO; baroque flute newsletter. 1989. q. $12 (foreign $15). Folkers & Powell, c/o Ardal Powell, Ed., RD 3 Box 56, Hudson, NY 12534-3508. TEL 518-828-9779. TELEX 23-6503624777 MCI UW. bk.rev.
Description: Covers news, information and ideas for all interested in the baroque flute and its music.

780.42 US
TRAX DANCE MUSIC GUIDE. bi-m. Trax Entertainment, 111 N. La Cienega Blvd., Beverly Hills, CA 90211-2206. TEL 213-659-7852. Ed. Jimmy Kim. circ. 5,000.

781.7 IE ISSN 0790-004X
ML5
TREOIR; Irish folk music, song, dance, customs and heritage. 1968. q. £5($15) Comhaltas Ceoltoiri Eireann, 32, Belgrave Sq., Monkstown, Co. Dublin, Ireland. (U.S. orders to: Head Office, 32-33 Belgrave Sq., Monkstown, Co. Dublin, Ireland) Ed. Labhras O'Murchu. adv.; bk.rev.; illus.; index; circ. 13,000.

781.7 US
TRI-SON NEWS; biggest little news sheet in country music. 1963. m. $10. Tri-Son, Inc., Box 40328, Nashville, TN 37204-0328. TEL 615-371-9596. Ed. Loudilla Johnson. charts; illus.; tr.lit.; circ. 1,200. (looseleaf format)
Description: Covers entertainment with a strong emphasis on country music.

785 US
TRI-STATE BLUEGRASS ASSOCIATION BAND AND FESTIVAL GUIDE. 1981. a. $10. Tri-State Bluegrass Association, R.R. 1, Kahoka, MO 63445. TEL 314-853-4344. Ed. Erma Spray. circ. 5,000. (back issues avail.)
Description: Contains information on bluegrass music bands and related materials.

780.7 US ISSN 0041-2511
ML1
TRIAD (WOOSTER). 1928. 6/yr. $15. Scheide Music Center, College of Wooster, Wooster, OH 44691. TEL 216-263-2052. Ed. Nancy E. Ditmer. adv.; illus.; circ. 4,900. **Indexed:** Music Ind.
Description: Articles and columns address issues and concerns relevant to music education.

780 US ISSN 0041-2600
ML1
TRIANGLE OF MU PHI EPSILON. 1906? q. $6. Mu Phi Epsilon International Professional Music Fraternity, c/o Mimi A. Altman, International Executive Office, 730 Waukegan Rd., Ste. 108, Deerfield, IL 60015-4304. TEL 708-940-1222. Ed. Gerri Flynn. bk.rev.; illus.; circ. 10,000. **Indexed:** Music Ind.

780 AG ISSN 0041-2767
TRIBUNA MUSICAL. 1965. s-a. Arg.$20000. Pablo Luis Bardin Ed. & Pub., Av. Libertador 3576, Buenos Aires, Argentina. adv.; illus.; circ. 1,500. (tabloid format)

780 SZ
TRIBUNE DE L'ORGUE. 1948. q. 30 Fr. Maison du Prieur, CH-1323 Romainmotier, Switzerland. TEL 24-531446. FAX 24-531150. Ed. Guy Bovet. adv.; bk.rev.; circ. 2,000. **Indexed:** Music Ind.
Description: Devoted to the organ and its music.

780.01 UK
TRINITY MAGAZINE. 1966. 3/yr. £10 (effective 1990). Trinity College of Music London, 16 Park Cres., London W1N 4AH, England. TEL 071-323-2320. Ed. Charles Franklyn. adv.; bk.rev.; rec.rev.; circ. 3,000.

780 UK
TRITSCH - TRATSCH. 1966. s-a. £2 per no. Johann Strauss Society of Great Britain, 12 Bishams Court, Church Hill, Caterham, Surrey CR3 6SE, England.

780.42 GW
TRUST; Hardcore Magazin. 1986. bi-m. DM.20. Trust Verlag, Salzmannstr. 53, 8900 Augsburg, Germany. TEL 0821-665088. FAX 0821-666964. Ed. Hermann Staedter. circ. 2,200.

TUITION, ENTERTAINMENT, NEWS, VIEWS. see ART

780 GW
DER TURNERMUSIKER. 6/yr. Deutscher Turnerbund e.V., c/o Westharzer Musikhaus Wilhelm Watermann, P.O. Box 370, 3353 Bad Gandersheim, Germany. TEL 05382-5021.

TURTLE QUARTERLY MAGAZINE. see ETHNIC INTERESTS

780.7 UK
TUTOR & TEXTBOOK - ELEMENTARY PIPING & DRUMMING. 1963. £5. Royal Scottish Pipe Band Association, 45, Washington Street, Glasgow, G3 8AZ, Scotland. adv.

780 FR ISSN 0222-3074
TUTTI. 1978. 4/yr. 100 F. Domaine Musiques, 2, rue des Buisses, 59800 Lille, France. TEL 20-55-01-58. FAX 20-06-56-52. Ed. Pierre Host.
 Description: Covers musical patrimony, composers, dance, choral singing, new music.

780 IT
TUTTI FRUTTI. 1982. m. L.30000($50) Abroma House Coop.r.l., Via Ouidio 10, 00193 Rome, Italy. TEL 06-6833665. FAX 06-6832688. Ed. Massimo Bassoli. adv.; bk.rev.; circ. 112,000. (back issues avail.)

780 IT
TUTTO MUSICA E SPETTACOLO. 1977. m. L.24000. Silvio Berlusconi Editore S.p.A., Corso Europa 5-7, 20122 Milan, Italy. Ed. Gherardo Gentili. adv.; circ. 310,000. (back issues avail.)

780 IT
TUTTO STRUMENTI. 1985. s-a. L.15000 per no. Ediscreen s.r.l., Via Calderini, 68, 00196 Rome, Italy. TEL 06-3233204. Dir. Enzo Perilli.

784 288 US
U U M N NOTES. 1983. 3/yr. $10. Unitarian Universalist Musician's Network, c/o D.L. Jackson, 1234 Oak Knoll Dr., Cincinnati, OH 34224. TEL 513-729-4183. Ed. Betty Wylder. adv.; bk.rev.; circ. 1,000. (back issues avail.)

780 GW
UEBEN & MUSIZIEREN; Zeitschrift fuer Musikschule, Studium und Berufspraxis. 1983. m. DM.36. B. Schott's Soehne, Weihergarten 1-9, Postfach 3640, 6500 Mainz, Germany. TEL 06131-246850. Ed.Bd. adv.; bk.rev.; bibl.; charts; illus.; index; circ. 5,000.

780 US
ULTIMATE EARLY CHILDHOOD MUSIC RESOURCE. 1984. a. $19.95 (foreign $29.50). Miss Jackie Music Co., 10001 El Monte, Overland Park, KS 66207. TEL 913-381-3672. Ed. Emily A. Smith. adv.; bk.rev.; index; circ. 1,000. (back issues avail.)
 Supersedes (in 1990): Early Childhood Music Quarterly; Which was formerly: Early Childhood Music (ISSN 0747-5446)
 Description: Features, news, exercises, programs, and original music, as a guide for teaching pre- and early-schoolers.

ULTIMO (MUENSTER); Muensters Stadtmagazin. see LITERARY AND POLITICAL REVIEWS

780.42 IT
ULTIMO BUSCADERO; mensile d'informazione rock. 1980. m. L.35000($70) Ultimo Buscadero S.r.l., Casella Postale 56, 21010 Aeroporto Malpensa, Italy. TEL 0331 223065. adv.; bk.rev.; circ. 25,000. (back issues avail.)

780 BU
UNION OF BULGARIAN COMPOSERS. NEWS BULLETIN. (Editions in English and Russian) 1970. q. free. Soyuz na Bulgarski Kompozitori - Union of Bulgarian Composers, 2, Ivan Vazov St., 1000 Sofia, Bulgaria. Ed. Evgueni Pavlov. circ. 600.
 Formerly: Music News Bulletin (ISSN 0566-9197)
 Description: Features composer awards, Bulgarian music abroad and discographies.

780.01 UY
UNIVERSIDAD DE LA REPUBLICA. FACULTAD DE HUMANIDADES Y CIENCIAS. REVISTA. SERIE MUSICOLOGIA. irreg. exchange basis. Universidad de la Republica, Facultad de Humanidades y Ciencias, Seccion Revista, Tristan Narvaja 1674, Montevideo, Uruguay. Dir. Beatriz Martinez Osorio.
 Supersedes in part: Universidad de la Republica. Facultad de Humanidades y Ciencias. Revista.

UNIVERSIDAD NACIONAL DE COLOMBIA. CENTRO DE ESTUDIOS FOLKLORICOS. MONOGRAFIAS. see FOLKLORE

780 AT
UNIVERSITY OF WESTERN AUSTRALIA. DEPARTMENT OF MUSIC. MUSIC MONOGRAPH. no.2, 1975. irreg. University of Western Australia, Department of Music, Nedlands, W.A. 6009, Australia. TEL 09-380-3838. Ed. David Tunley.

UNIVERZITA KOMENSKEHO. FILOZOFICKA FAKULTA. ZBORNIK: MUSAICA. see ART

785.06 US
UPBEAT. LEXINGTON PHILHARMONIC SOCIETY NEWSLETTER. 1965. 5/yr. free. Lexington Philharmonic Society, 161 N. Mill St., Lexington, KY 40517-1125. adv.; bk.rev.; circ. 6,000. (processed)
 Formerly: Lexington Philharmonic Society Newsletter (ISSN 0024-161X)
 Description: Contains organization news.

780 371.3 US
UPDATE (RESTON); applications of research in music education. 1982. 2/yr. $11. Music Educators National Conference, 1902 Association Dr., Reston, VA 22091-1597. FAX 703-860-1531. adv.; bk.rev.; circ. 1,350. Indexed: Music Artic.Guide.
 Description: Contains articles to help music educators use research results in their teaching.

780 US ISSN 0506-306X
V D G S A NEWS. 1964. q. $20 in US and Canada; elsewhere $30. Viola da Gamba Society of America, Inc., c/o John A. Whisler, Exec.Sec., 1308 Jackson, Charleston, IL 61920-2242. Ed. Newton Blakeslee. adv.; bk.rev.; circ. 850. Indexed: Music Ind.

780 RU
V MIRE MUZYKI; Kalendar' a. 1.50 Rub. Izdatel'stvo Sovetskii Kompozitor, 14-12, Sadovaya Triumfalnaya St., 103006 Moscow, Russia. illus.

780 IT ISSN 0042-3734
ML410.V4
VERDI. (Text in English, Italian) 1960. irreg. price varies. Istituto Nazionale di Studi Verdiani, Strada della Repubblica 56, 43100 Parma, Italy. illus.; index. cum.index every 3 nos. Indexed: RILM.
 Description: Discusses origin, musical aspects, libretto, staging, performances and singers of a single opera.

780 920 US ISSN 0160-2667
ML410.V4
VERDI NEWSLETTER. (Text in English and Italian) 1976. a. $15. (American Institute for Verdi Studies) New York University, Department of Music, 24 Waverly Pl., New York, NY 10003. TEL 212-998-8300. FAX 212-995-4147. Eds. Martin Chusid, Andrew Porter. adv.; bk.rev.; bibl.; charts; illus.; circ. 500. (back issues avail.) Indexed: RILM.
 Description: Research into the music, life and times of Giuseppe Verdi.

MUSIC 3585

780.9 NE ISSN 0042-3874
VERENIGING VOOR NEDERLANDSE MUZIEKGESCHIEDENIS. TIJDSCHRIFT. (Text in Dutch, English; summaries in English) 1882. a. $50. Swets Publishing Service (Subsidiary of: Swets en Zeitlinger B.V.), Hereweg 347, 2161 CA Lisse, Netherlands. TEL 31-2521-35111. FAX 31-2521-15888. TELEX 41325. (Dist. in N. America by: Swets & Zeitlinger, Box 517, Berwyn, PA 19312. TEL 215-644-4944) Ed. Arend Jan Gierveld. bk.rev.; cum.index: vols. 1-30; circ. 800. (also avail. in microfiche; back issues avail.; reprint service avail. from SWZ)
 Indexed: Arts & Hum.Cit.Ind., Curr.Cont., Music Ind., RILM.

780 GW ISSN 0543-1735
VEROEFFENTLICHUNGEN DES MAX-REGER-INSTITUTES. 1966. irreg. price varies. (Max-Reger-Institut) Ferd. Duemmlers Verlag, Kaiserstr. 32, 5300, Bonn 1, Germany.

780 GW
VEROEFFENTLICHUNGEN ZUR MUSIKFORSCHUNG. 1973. irreg., vol.9, 1990. price varies. Florian Noetzel Verlag, Heinrichshofen Buecher, Valoisstrasse 11, 2940 Wilhelmshaven, Germany. (Dist. in U.S. by C.F. Peters Corp., 373 Park Ave. S., New York, NY 10016) Ed. Richard Schaal.

VERONICA; weekblad voor radio en TV. see COMMUNICATIONS — Television And Cable

VICE VERSA MAGAZINE. see LITERATURE

780 US
VICTORY MUSIC REVIEW. 1976. m. $20. Victory Music, Box 7515, Bonney Lake, WA 98390. TEL 206-863-6617. Ed. Chris Lunn. adv.; bk.rev.; rec.; rev.; circ. 5,500.
 Description: Covers folk, jazz, new acoustic, songwriter, children's, women's, old time dance, blues, and other acoustic music through reviews.

VIDEO & MUSIC BUSINESS. see BUSINESS AND ECONOMICS — Marketing And Purchasing

780 FR ISSN 0083-6109
VIE MUSICALE EN FRANCE SOUS LES ROIS BOURBONS. SERIE 1: ETUDES. (Text in English; summaries in French) 1954. irreg. price varies. Editions A. et J. Picard, 82 rue Bonaparte, 75006 Paris, France. FAX 43-26-42-64. TELEX 305-551 BSC PICAREDIT.

780 FR ISSN 0080-0139
VIE MUSICALE EN FRANCE SOUS LES ROIS BOURBONS. SERIE 2: RECHERCHES SUR LA MUSIQUE FRANCAISE CLASSIQUE. (Text in English, French; summaries in French) 1960. a. price varies. Editions A. et J. Picard, 82 rue Bonaparte, 75006 Paris, France. FAX 43-26-42-64. TELEX 305-551 BSC PICAREDIT. Ed. Nobert Dufourcq. Indexed: RILM.

780 US
VIERUNDZWANZIGSTENJAHRSSCHRIFT DER INTERNATIONALEN MAULTROMMELVIRTUOSENGENOSSENSCHAFT. (Text in English, French, German, Italian) 1982. irreg. $12 for 2 nos. V I M, 930 Talwrn Ct., Iowa City, IA 52246. Ed. Frederick Crane. adv.; bk.rev.; rec.; rev.; circ. 75. (back issues avail.) Indexed: RILM.
 Description: Articles, reviews, checklists, discographies, bibliographies relating to the Jew's Harp.

781.57 UK ISSN 0042-6369
VINTAGE JAZZ MART. 1953. q. $19.50. c/o M. Berresford, R. Sher, 1 Station Cottages, Moor Rd., Bestwood Village, Nottingham NG6 8SZ, England. TEL 0602-264465. (Distr. addr. in U.S.: Box 184, Radnor PA 19087) adv.; bk.rev.; circ. 1,200.
 ●Also available on CD-ROM.
 Description: Jazz record trading magazine.

VINTAGE RECORD MART. see SOUND RECORDING AND REPRODUCTION

787 US
VIOLA D'AMORE SOCIETY OF AMERICA. NEWSLETTER. (Text in English; summaries in German) 1977. s-a. $12. Viola d'Amore Society of America, 39-23 47th St., Sunnyside, NY 11104. TEL 718-729-3138. Eds. Myron Rosenblum, Daniel Thomason. adv.; bk.rev.; bibl.; tr.lit.; circ. 200. (processed; back issues avail.)
 Description: Furthers the research, history and performance of the Viola d'Amore.

MUSIC

780 US ISSN 0507-0252
ML1
VIOLA DA GAMBA SOCIETY OF AMERICA. JOURNAL. 1964. a. $20 in U.S. and Canada; elsewhere $30. Viola da Gamba Society of America, Inc., c/o John A. Whisler, 1308 Jackson, Charleston, IL 61820-2242. Ed. Ann Viles. adv.; bk.rev.; bibl.; illus.; circ. 850. (back issues avail.) Indexed: Music Ind., RILM.
—BLDSC shelfmark: 4912.510000.

787 US ISSN 0892-5437
ML749.5
VIOLEXCHANGE; * a quarterly journal of string literature and repertoire. 1986. q. $25. L.F.S. Publications, Inc., 4825 CMU Frew St., Ste. 136, Pittsburgh, PA 15213-3890. TEL 313-930-6297. Ed. Louise C. Sciannameo. adv.; bk.rev.; circ. 2,500. Indexed: Music Artic.Guide.
Description: Articles of interest for violinists, violists, and cellists. Focuses on musical repertoire for all string instruments.

787 US ISSN 0148-6845
ML1
VIOLIN SOCIETY OF AMERICA. JOURNAL. 1973. q. $35. (Violin Society of America) Queens College Press, 65-30 Kissena Blvd., Flushing, NY 11367. TEL 718-520-7773. (Subscr. to: Norman Pickering, 23 Culver Hill, Southampton, NY 11968) Ed. Albert Mell. adv.; bk.rev.; illus.; circ. 1,400. (back issues avail.) Indexed: Arts & Hum.Cit.Ind., Curr.Cont., Music Artic.Guide, Music Ind., RILM. Key Title: Journal of the Violin Society of America.
Formerly: Violin Society of America. Bulletin.

VLAANDEREN; tijdschrift voor kunst en letteren. see ART

784 US
VOICE OF CHORUS AMERICA. 1978. q. membership. Chorus America (APVE), 2111 Sansom St., Philadelphia, PA 19103. TEL 215-563-2430. FAX 215-563-2431. Ed. Wilson M. Jeffreys. adv.; bk.rev.; circ. 3,600. Indexed: Music Artic.Guide.

780 US ISSN 0147-4367
ML1
VOICE OF WASHINGTON MUSIC EDUCATORS. 1956. 4/yr. $3. Washington Music Educator's Association, c/o Tom Bourne, Ed., 817 E. Third Ave, Ellensburg, WA 98926. TEL 509-925-3609. FAX 509-925-7150. adv.; illus.; circ. 1,500. Indexed: Music Artic.Guide.
Supersedes: Washington Music Educator (ISSN 0043-065X)

784 US
VOLUNTEER CHOIR. m. $28. Lorenz Publishing Co., 501 E. Third St., Box 802, Dayton, OH 45401-0802. TEL 513-228-6118. Ed. Eugene McCluskey.

780.42 920 US
VOODOO CHILD. 1985. q. $12. Jimi Hendrix Information Management Institute, Box 374, Des Plaines, IL 60016. TEL 708-803-8373. Ed. Ken Voss. adv.; bk.rev.; film rev.; circ. 1,600. (back issues avail.)
Description: Accumulates and disseminates information regarding the legend and legacy of rock guitarist Jimi Hendrix.

784 RU
VOPROSY UCHEBNO-VOSPITATEL'NOI RABOTY V SAMODEYATEL'NYKH KOLLEKTIVAKH. (Subseries of the Institute's Trudy) 1972. irreg. 0.33 Rub. (Nauchno-Issledovatel'skii Institut Kul'tury, Otdel Narodnogo Tvorchestva) Izdatel'stvo Sovetskaya Rossiya, Proezd Sapunova 13-15, Moscow K-12, Russia.

780 AT
VOX. 1960. m. Aus.$12($18) Theater Organ Society of Australia, Victorian Division, 19 Beatty St., Ivanhoe, Vic. 3079, Australia. Ed. Eric Wicks. adv.; bk.rev.; circ. 850. (back issues avail)

790.2 US ISSN 0092-4113
ML28.W2
W P A S MUSELETTER. 1970. irreg. $25 membership. Washington Performing Arts Society, 2000 L St., N.W., No. 810, Washington, DC 20036-4907. TEL 202-833-9800. FAX 202-331-7678. Ed. Christina King. circ. 9,000.
Description: Contains membership events, development updates, WPAS news, and a calendar.

782.1 920 UK
WAGNER. 1980. q. £12 institutions (£17 individuals). Wagner Society, c/o Dr. J.J. Pritchard, 15 David Ave., Wickford, Essex SS11 7BG, England. (The Wagner Society, 4 Lucastes Road, Haywards Heath, West Sussex RH16 1JL, England. TEL 0444-450829) Ed. Stewart Spencer. adv.; bk.rev.; circ. 1,100.
Description: Contains items of a scholarly nature about the life and works of the composer Richard Wagner.

782.1 920 UK ISSN 0261-3468
ML410.W1
WAGNER NEWS. 1980. 8/yr. £5 institutions (£15 individuals). Wagner Society, c/o Dr. J.J. Pritchard, 15 David Ave., Wickford, Essex SS11 7BG, England. (The Wagner Society, 4 Lucastes Road, Haywards Heath, West Sussex RH16 1JL, England. TEL 0444-450829) Ed. Martin Hunt. adv.; bk.rev.; rec.; rev.; circ. 1,000.
Description: Includes news of forthcoming events, reviews and articles of general interest about the works of Richard Wagner.

780.904 NE
WAPKRANT. m. free. Westlandse Associatie van Popmuzikanten, Langestraat 38, 2691 BH 's-Gravenzande, Netherlands. adv.; bk.rev.; circ. 1,500.

780 792 US
WASHINGTON OPERA MAGAZINE. 1974. q. Washington Opera Guild, Kennedy Center, Washington, DC 20566. TEL 202-416-7850. FAX 202-416-7857. Ed. Eleanor Forrer. adv.; circ. 10,000.
Description: Information on the opera productions presented at the Kennedy Center by the Washington Opera. Includes interviews with guest artists, synopsis of the operas and a calendar of events.

780.42 US ISSN 0741-2460
WAVELENGTH (NEW ORLEANS). 1980. m. $15 (foreign $32). Box 15667, New Orleans, LA 70175. FAX 504-891-7996. Ed. Connie Atkinson. adv.; bk.rev.; circ. 30,000.
Description: Contains news, reviews, interviews and stories of the late greats and the immortal moments of New Orleans music.

DIE WEBEREIZEITUNG. see GENERAL INTEREST PERIODICALS — Germany

781.7 UK ISSN 0043-244X
WELSH MUSIC/CERDDORIAETH CYMRU. (Text mainly in English) 1959. 3/yr. £2 per no. Guild for the Promotion of Welsh Music, 94 Walter Rd., Swansea SA1 5QA, Wales. Ed. A.J. Heward Rees. adv.; bk.rev.; music rev.; record rev.; charts; illus.; circ. 450. Indexed: RILM.

WEST COAST LINE; a journal of contemporary writing and criticism. see LITERATURE

784 US
WESTERN PENNSYLVANIA BLUEGRASS COMMITTEE. NEWSLETTER. 1969. m. $10. Western Pennsylvania Bluegrass Committee, Box 5295, Pittsburgh, PA 15206-5295. Ed. G.P. Corey. adv.; bk.rev.; circ. 2,000.

WESTWIND (LOS ANGELES); U C L A's journal of the arts. see ART

780 US ISSN 0043-4752
WHEEL OF DELTA OMICRON. 1915. 4/yr. $5. Delta Omicron International Music Fraternity, c/o Jane Wiley Kuckuk, 1352 Redwood Ct., Columbus, OH 43229. Ed. Carolyn Goodman. illus.; circ. 5,500.
Description: Contains organization news.

WHO'S WHO IN ENTERTAINMENT. see MOTION PICTURES

780 PL
WIEDZA O MUZYCE. 1983. irreg. price varies. Polskie Wydawnictwo Muzyczne, Al. Krasinskiego 11a, 31-111 Krakow. TEL 22-70-44. FAX 22-01-74.
Description: Series of text-books for students; it covers various fields of music.

780 AU ISSN 0084-0017
WIENER MUSIKHOCHSCHULE. PUBLIKATIONEN. 1967. irreg., no.7, 1978. price varies. Musikverlag Elisabeth Lafite, Hegelgasse 13-22, A-1010 Vienna, Austria.

780.43 943 US
WILHELM FURTWAENGLER SOCIETY OF AMERICA. NEWSLETTER. 1989. q. $20 (effective 1991). Wilhelm Furtwaengler Society of America, Box 620702, Woodside, CA 94062. TEL 415-851-3808. FAX 415-851-3151. Ed. Charles Schlacks, Jr. circ. 500. (back issues avail.)
Description: Covers German and European musical life with emphasis on Furtwaengler and his times.

780 US ISSN 1051-0788
WILLEM MENGELBERG SOCIETY. NEWSLETTER. 1970. 4/yr. $6 (foreign $8). Willem Mengelberg Society, 6954 Crocus Ct., Apt. 2, Greendale, WI 53129. Ed. Ronald Klett. bk.rev.; rec.; rev.
Description: Covers all aspects of the life, recordings and concerts of the orchestral and choral conductor.

780 US ISSN 0895-1527
WINDPLAYER. 1985. bi-m. $12.95. Windplayer Publications, Box 46370, Los Angeles, CA 90046. TEL 818-891-0551. Ed. Daniel Miller. adv.; bk.rev.; tr.; lit.; circ. 16,000. (back issues avail.)

780 UK ISSN 0952-0686
THE WIRE. 1982. m. £20($50) Wire Magazine Ltd., Units G & H, 115 Cleveland St., London W1P 5PN, England. TEL 071-580-7522. FAX 071-323-6905. Ed. Richard Cook. adv.; bk.rev.; film rev.; charts; illus.; circ. 20,000.

780.7 US ISSN 0043-6658
ML1
WISCONSIN SCHOOL MUSICIAN. 1926. 4/yr. $12. Wisconsin School Music Association, Inc., 4797 Hayes Rd. No. 3, Madison, WI 53704-3288. TEL 608-249-4566. FAX 608-249-4973. Ed. Michael George. adv.; bk.rev.; illus.; circ. 4,200. Indexed: Music Artic.Guide.

780 US
WOMEN'S MUSIC PLUS; directory of resources in women's music & culture. 1977. a. $15. Empty Closet Enterprises, 5210 N. Wayne, Chicago, IL 60640. TEL 312-769-9009. Eds. Toni Armstrong Jr., Lynn Siniscalchi. circ. 2,000.
Description: Contact information (names, addresses, phone numbers, descriptions) for women's music and culture industry (music, publishing, film and video, theatre, and periodicals).

WOMEN'S NETWORK; national newsletter for women. see WOMEN'S INTERESTS

780.42 US ISSN 0891-9585
WOODSTOCK SERIES; popular music of today. 1976. irreg., latest 1991. price varies. Borgo Press, Box 2845, San Bernardino, CA 92406. TEL 714-884-5813.
Description: Monographs on popular musicians and music groups of the twentieth century, with discographies and bibliographies.

780.42 028.5 US
WORD UP!. 1987. 12/yr. $24. Word Up! Publications, Inc., 63 Grand Ave., Ste. 230, River Edge, NJ 07661. TEL 201-487-6124. FAX 207-487-9360. Ed. Kate Ferguson. adv.; bk.rev.; circ. 200,000.

781.7 JA
WORKS BY JAPANESE COMPOSERS (YEAR). biennial. Japan Federation of Composers, 602 Shinano-machi Bldg., 33 Shinano-machi, Shinjuku-ku, Tokyo 160, Japan. TEL 03-3359-2927. FAX 03-3359-3916.

784 US
WORLD CHORAL CENSUS. (Text in English, French, German) 1984. a. $25. International Federation for Choral Music, University of Illinois at Chicago, Dept. of Music, Box 4348, Chicago, IL 60680. TEL 312-996-8744. FAX 312-996-0954. Ed. Claude Tagger. circ. 2,000.
Description: Attempts to list all choral organizations in the world.

780 US ISSN 1049-0140
WORLD MUSIC CONNECTIONS. 1988. q. $15 (effective Jan. 1991). White Cliffs Media Company, Box 561, Crown Point, IN 46307. TEL 219-322-5537. FAX 219-322-5537. Ed. Larry W. Smith. adv.; bk.rev.; circ. 3,000 (controlled).

780   GW   ISSN 0043-8774
ML5
THE WORLD OF MUSIC. (Text in English) 1958. 3/yr. $27 to individuals; institutions $33. International Institute for Traditional Music, Winklerstr. 20, 1000 Berlin 33, Germany. FAX 04421-42985. TELEX 182875-IICMS-D. (Subscr. to: Florian Noetzel Verlag, "Heirichshofen-Books", P.O. Box 580, 2940 Wilhelmshaven, Germany) Ed. M.P. Baumann. adv.; bk.rev.; music rev.; record rev.; illus.; circ. 2,000. (reprint service avail. from SWZ) **Indexed:** Arts & Hum.Cit.Ind., Curr.Cont., Music Ind., RILM.
—BLDSC shelfmark: 9356.730000.

780   PL
WSPOLCZESNA PUBLICYSTYKA POLSKA. 1971. irreg. price varies. Polskie Wydawnictwo Muzyczne, Al. Krasinskiego 11a, 31-111 Krakow, Poland. TEL 22-70-44. FAX 22-01-74.
Description: Contemporary Polish music publicists' writings about music.

780   GW   ISSN 0177-6487
ML5
WUERTTEMBERGISCHE BLAETTER FUER KIRCHENMUSIK. 1927. bi-m. DM.20. Evangelische Kirchenmusik in Wuerttemberg, Gerokstr. 19, 7000 Stuttgart 1, Germany. FAX 0711-6403976. Ed. Helmut Voelkl. bk.rev.; circ. 3,700. (back issues avail.)

780   PL   ISSN 0512-4255
WYCHOWANIE MUZYCZNE W SZKOLE. 1956. 5/yr. $15. (Ministerstwo Edukacji Narodowej) Wydawnictwa Szkolne i Pedagogiczne, Pl. Dabrowskiego 8, 00-950 Warsaw, Poland. TEL 48-22-26-89-71. (Dist.by: Ars Polona-Ruch, Krakowskie Przedmiescie 7, Warsaw, Poland) circ. 9,746. **Indexed:** RILM.
Description: For music teachers who direct vocal and instrumental groups in schools and other educational institutions. Publishes articles dealing with music and related fields of knowledge, such as psychology, sociology, music pedagogy, aesthetics, including both Polish and foreign traditions and ideas of music education.

780   US   ISSN 0740-1558
ML1
YEARBOOK FOR TRADITIONAL MUSIC. (Text in English, French, German) 1949. a. $35. International Council for Traditional Music, c/o Department of Music, Columbia University, New York, NY 10027. TEL 212-678-0332. FAX 212-749-0397. TELEX 220094 COLU UR. Ed. Dieter Christensen. bk.rev.; rec.; rev.; circ. 1,300. (reprint service avail. from SWZ) **Indexed:** A.I.C.P., M.L.A., Music Ind., RILM.
Former titles (until 1980): International Folk Music Council. Yearbook; International Folk Music Council Journal (ISSN 0074-6096)

780   CC
YINXIANG SHIJIE/AUDIO-VISUAL WORLD. (Text in Chinese) m. Shanghai Changpian Zonggongsi - Shanghai Record Corporation, 739 Hengshan Road, Shanghai 200030, People's Republic of China. TEL 4373230. Ed. Liu Senmin.

780   CC
YINYUE AIHAOZHE/MUSIC LOVER. (Text in Chinese) bi-m. $20.30. Shanghai Yiyue Chubanshe - Shanghai Music Publishing Company, 74 Shaoxing Lu, Shanghai 200020, People's Republic of China. TEL 021-4372608. FAX 021-4332452. TELEX 33384. (Dist. in US by: China Books & Periodicals, Inc. 2929 24th St., San Francisco, CA 94110. TEL 415-282-2994) Ed. Chen Xueya. circ. 50,000.
Description: Presents popular music knowledge with illustrations.

780   US
YINYUE CHUANGZUO/MUSICAL CREATION. (Text in Chinese) q. $27.90. China Books & Periodicals, Inc., 2929 24th St., San Francisco, CA 94110. TEL 415-282-2994. FAX 415-282-0994.

780   CC   ISSN 0512-7920
YINYUE SHENGHUO/MUSIC LIFE. (Text in Chinese) m. $35.90. (Zhongguo Yinyuejia Xiehui, Liaoning Fenhui - Chinese Musicians Association, Liaoning Chapter) Yinyue Shenghuo Bianjibu, 74 Bajing Jie, Heping-qu, Shenyang, Liaoning 110003, People's Republic of China. TEL 24778. (Dist. in US by: China Books & Periodicals, Inc., 2929 24th St., San Francisco, CA 94110. TEL 415-282-2994) Ed. Ding Ming.

780   CC
YINYUE SHIJIE/MUSIC WORLD. (Text in Chinese) m. (China Musicians Association, Sichuan Branch) Yiyue Shijie Bianjibu, 85 Hongxing Zhonglu Erduan (Sec. 2), Chengdu, Sichuan 610012, People's Republic of China. TEL 29323.

780.7   CC
YINYUE TANSUO/EXPLORATIONS IN MUSIC; the academic periodical of Sichuan Conservatory. Variant title: Sichuan Yinyue Xueyuan Xuebao. (Text in Chinese; table of contents in English) q. Sichuan Yinyue Xueyuan - Sichuan Conservatory of Music, 2, Xinsheng Lu, Xinnan Menwai, Chengdu, Sichuan 610012, People's Republic of China. TEL 552181. Ed. Song Daneng.

780   CC
YINYUE TIANDI/MUSIC WORLD. (Text in Chinese) m. $24.20. Zhongguo Yinyuejia Xiehui, Shaanxi Fenhui - China Musicians Association, Shaanxi Chapter, Wenyi Lu, Tuanjiefang, Building No. 7, Xi'an, Shaanxi 710054, People's Republic of China. TEL 712616. (Dist. in US by: China Books & Periodicals, Inc., 2929 24th St., San Francisco, CA 94110. TEL 415-282-2994) Ed. Wang Yan.

780.7   CC
YINYUE YANJIU/MUSIC RESEARCH. Variant English title: Music Study. (Text in Chinese; table of contents in English) q. $19.50. Renmin Yinyue Chubanshe, Beijing, People's Republic of China. (Dist. outside China by: China International Book Trading Corp., P.O. Box 2820, Beijing, P.R.C.; Dist. in US by: China Books & Periodicals, Inc., 2929 24th St., San Francisco, CA 94110. TEL 415-282-2994) Eds. Zhao Feng, Li Yedao.

780   CC   ISSN 1000-4270
ML5
YINYUE YISHU/ART OF MUSIC. (Text in Chinese; table of contents in English) 1979. q. $16.50. Shanghai Conservatory of Music - Shanghai Yinyue Xueyuan, 20 Fenyang Lu, Shanghai, People's Republic of China. (Dist. outside China by: China International Book Trading Corp., P.O. Box 2820, Beijing, P.R.C.; Dist. in US by: China Books & Periodicals, Inc., 2929 24th St., San Francisco, CA 94110. TEL 415-282-2994)

780.42   US
YO! MAGAZINE. m. $2.95 per no. Ashley Communications, Inc., Box 88427, Los Angeles, CA 90009. TEL 818-885-6800. (And: 19431 Business Center Dr., Northridge, CA 91324) Ed. Dedi Fee.

780   JA
YOUNG AUDIO NOW. (Text in Japanese) 1974. a. 680 price varies. Gakken Co. Ltd., 40-5, 4-chome, Kamiikedai, Ohta-ku, Tokyo 145, Japan. Ed. Akira Ohuchi.

780   JA
YOUNG GUITAR. (Text in Japanese) 1969. m. 6000 Yen. Shinko Music Publishing Co. Ltd., 2-1 Ogawa-machi, Kanda, Chiyoda-ku, Tokyo, Japan. Ed. Takashi Yamamoto.

780   UK
YOUNG MUSICIAN. 1981. bi-m. £2.50. Young Musicians Enterprises, St. Albans Lane, Golders Green, London EC4Y 1PN, England. adv.

783.7   US   ISSN 0044-0841
ML1
YOUNG MUSICIANS. q. $7. Southern Baptist Convention, Sunday School Board, 127 Ninth Ave., N., Nashville, TN 37234. TEL 800-458-2772. charts; illus.
Formerly: Junior Musician.

780   CC   ISSN 1001-5736
YUEFU XIN SHENG. Variant title: Shenyang Yinyue Xueyuan Xuebao. (Text in Chinese) 1983. q. Y6. Shenyang Yinyue Xueyuan - Shenyang Conservatory of Music, No. 1, Sanhao Jie Sec. 2, Heping Qu, Shenyang, Liaoning 110003, People's Republic of China. FAX 0086-24-394193. music rev.; circ. 5,000. (back issues avail.)
Description: Covers music theory, music education, theory of composition technique, music history, music science and technology, research on performance art and ethnomusicology.

780   IS   ISSN 0084-439X
ML3776
YUVAL. (Text in English, French and Hebrew; summaries in English and Hebrew) 1968. irreg. price varies. (Jewish Music Research Centre) Magnes Press, The Hebrew University, Jerusalem, Israel. Ed. Israel Adler. **Indexed:** Ind.Heb.Per., RILM.

780   PL   ISSN 0084-442X
Z DZIEJOW MUZYKI POLSKIEJ. 1960. irreg. Bydgoskie Towarzystwo Naukowe, Jezuicka 4, Bydgoszcz, Poland. (Dist. by Ars Polona-Ruch, Krakowskie Przedmiescie 7, Warsaw, Poland)

780   GW   ISSN 0232-9387
ML120.G3
ZEITGENOESSISCHES MUSIKSCHAFFEN IN DER DEUTSCHEN DEMOKRATISCHEN REPUBLIK. URAUFFUEHRUNGEN. (Text in German) 1976. a. Saechsische Landesbibliothek, Marienalle 12, 8060 Dresden, Germany. Ed. Ludwig Mueller.
Formerly: Sozialistisches Musikschaffen der Deutschen Demokratischen Republik.

780.7   GW
ZEITSCHRIFT FUER MUSIKPAEDAGOGIK. 1976. 6/yr. DM.73. Erhard Friedrich Verlag GmbH, Im Brande 15, Postfach 100150, 3016 Seelze 6, Germany. index; circ. 2,300. (back issues avail.)

781.7   US
ZHONGGUO YINYUE/CHINESE MUSIC. (Text in Chinese) q. $16.50. China Books & Periodicals, Inc., 2929 24th St., San Francisco, CA 94110. TEL 415-282-2994. FAX 415-282-0994.

780.01   CC
ZHONGGUO YINYUEXUE/MUSICOLOGY IN CHINA. (Text in Chinese; table of contents and summaries in English) 1985. q. (Zhongguo Yishu Yanjiuyuan, Yinyue Yanjiusuo) Wenhua Yishu Chubanshe, 17, Qianhai Xijie, Xicheng Qu, Beijing 100009, People's Republic of China. Ed. Guo Naian. bk.rev.

780.904   CC   ISSN 1001-9871
ZHONGYANG YINYUE XUEYUAN XUEBAO/CENTRAL CONSERVATORY OF MUSIC. JOURNAL. (Text in Chinese; table of contents in English) no.36, 1989. q. Y6($20.40) Central Conservatory of Music - Zhongyang Yinyue Xueyuan, 43 Baojia Jie, Xi Cheng Qu (West City District), Beijing, People's Republic of China. (Dist. by: China International Book Trading Corporation (Guoji Shudian), P.O. Box 339, Beijing 100044, P.R.C.; Dist. in US by: China Books & Periodicals, Inc., 2929 24th St., San Francisco, CA 94110) Ed. Yu Run-yang. bk.rev.
Description: Publishes research papers on music history, theory of ethnomusicology, composition and conducting, and vocal and instrumental performance; articles on music teaching; selected foreign papers on music; and reviews of performances. Also includes recent vocal and instrumental composition scores.

780   PL
ZRODLA PAMIETNIKARSKO-LITERACKIE DO DZIEJOW MUZYKI POLSKIEJ. 1956. irreg. price varies. Polskie Wydawnictwo Muzyczne, Al. Krasinskiego 11a, 31-111 Krakow, Poland. TEL 22-70-44. FAX 22-01-74. Ed. Tadeusz Strumillo.
Description: Letters, memoirs, diaries and opinions about Polish musical culture.

780   GW   ISSN 0176-0971
ZUPFMUSIK MAGAZIN. q. DM.24. (Bund Deutscher Zupfmusiker e.V.) Oertel & Spoerer, Burgstr. 1-7, 7410 Reutlingen, Germany. TEL 07121-302563. Ed. Ruediger Grambow. adv.; illus.
Incorporates: Gitarre.

780   YU   ISSN 0044-555X
ML5
ZVUK; Jugoslovenska muzicka revija. (Text in Serbo-Croatian; summaries in English) 1955. q. DM.10 per no. Savez Organizacija Kompozitora Jugoslavije (SOKOJ), Misarska 12-14, 11000 Belgrade, Yugoslavia. TEL 38-11-334771. FAX 38-11-336-168. Ed. Erika Krpan. adv.; bk.rev.; rec.rev.; circ. 1,500. **Indexed:** Music Ind., RILM.
Description: Provides reviews on the most significant music events, musicologial studies, interviews

MUSIC — ABSTRACTING, BIBLIOGRAPHIES, STATISTICS

780　　　　　　　　US
ML3809
1 - 1 JOURNAL. 1985. q. $15 to individuals; libraries $25. Just Intonation Network, 535 Stevenson St., San Francisco, CA 94103. TEL 415-864-8123. FAX 415-864-8726. Ed. David B. Doty. adv.; bk.rev.; circ. 500. **Indexed:** RILM.
　Formerly: 1 - 1 Quarterly (ISSN 8756-7717)
　Description: Devoted solely to music theory and practice, and instrument construction and modification relating specifically to just intonation.

781.57　　　　　　AT　　ISSN 0313-0797
2 M B S - F M STEREO F M RADIO PROGRAM GUIDE. 1975. m. Aus.$55. Music Broadcasting Society of N.S.W. Co-op Ltd., 76 Chandos St., St. Leonards, N.S.W. 2065, Australia. TEL 439 4777. FAX 612-439-4064. Ed. Nicole Aristidis. adv.; circ. 8,000. (back issues avail.)
　Description: Features mostly classical, specialist jazz, blues, folk, contemporary-experimental and Afro-American music.

780　　　　　　　US　　ISSN 0148-2076
ML1
19TH CENTURY MUSIC. 1977. 3/yr. $25 to individuals (foreign $30); institutions $51 (foreign $56). University of California Press, Journals Division, 2120 Berkeley Way, Berkeley, CA 94720. TEL 510-642-4191. FAX 510-643-7127. Eds. Walter Frisch, D. Kern Holoman. adv.; bk.rev.; index. cum.index; circ. 1,350. (also avail. in microform from UMI; microfiche; back issues avail.; reprint service avail. from UMI) **Indexed:** Curr.Cont., Hum.Ind., Ind.Bk.Rev.Hum., Music Artic.Guide, Music Ind., RILM.
　Description: Explores music history and criticism, analysis and theory, as well as reviews and commentary by guest columnists.
　Refereed Serial

MUSIC — Abstracting, Bibliographies, Statistics

780 016　　　　US　　ISSN 0893-7486
ML156.2
ARTIST ISSUE. 1975. a. $16. Schwann Publications, Box 5529, Santa Fe, NM 87502. Ed. Donna Hieken. adv.; circ. 30,000.
　Formerly: Schwann Artist Issue (ISSN 0582-1487)
　Description: Reference to over 55,000 classical music compact discs, LPs, cassette tapes and CD-Videos, organized by name of artist, conductor, and orchestra.

780　　　　　　　　PL
BIBLIOGRAFIA MUZYCZNA POLSKICH CZASOPISM NIEMUZYCZNYCH. 1962. irreg. price varies. Polskie Wydawnictwo Muzyczne, Al. Krasinskiego 11a, 31-111 Krakow, Poland. TEL 22-70-44. FAX 22-01-74. Ed. Kornel Michalowski.
　Description: Lists literature about music in 19th and 20th century Poland.

780　　　　　　　　PL
BIBLIOGRAFIA POLSKICH CZASOPISM MUZYCZNYCH. 1955. irreg. price varies. Polskie Wydawnictwo Muzyczne, Al. Krasinskiego 11a, 31-111 Krakow, Poland. TEL 22-70-44. FAX 22-01-74. Ed. Kornel Michalowski.
　Description: Reveals valuable and hitherto not fully exploited material based on sources, contained in Polish musical journals.

016 780　　　　　NE　　ISSN 0084-7844
ML113
BIBLIOGRAPHIA MUSICOLOGICA; a bibliography of musical literature. (Text in various languages) 1970. irreg., vol.3, 1976. fl.500($300) Joachimsthal Publishers, Box 2218, 1180 EE Amstelveen, Netherlands. Ed. A.M. Joachimsthal. (back issues avail.)

016.78　　　　　　US　　ISSN 0360-2753
ML136.N5
BIBLIOGRAPHIC GUIDE TO MUSIC. (Text in various languages) a. $190 cloth (foreign $220). G.K. Hall & Co., 70 Lincoln St., Boston, MA 02111. TEL 617-423-3990. FAX 617-423-3999. TELEX 94-0037.
　—BLDSC shelfmark: 1964.895000.
　Formerly: Music Book Guide (ISSN 0360-1943)
　Description: Covers musical subjects in book and non-book form.

780　　　　　　　FR　　ISSN 0150-5971
Z2165
BIBLIOGRAPHIE DE LA FRANCE. SUPPLEMENT 3: MUSIQUE. 3/yr. Bibliotheque Nationale, 58 rue de Richelieu, 75002 Paris, France. TEL 42-74-22-22. FAX 42-96-84-47.

780　　　　　　　GW　　ISSN 0232-7678
BIBLIOGRAPHIE MUSIK. (Text in German) 1975. a. DM.90. Saechsische Landesbibliothek, Marienalle 12, 8060 Dresden, Germany. Ed. Maria Scholze.

780 016　　　　　US
BIBLIOGRAPHIES IN AMERICAN MUSIC. 1974. irreg. price varies. (College Music Society) Harmonie Park Press, 23630 Pinewood, Warren, MI 48091-4759. TEL 313-755-3080. Ed. Bunker J. Clark.
　Description: Bibliographies in the field of American music.

780　　　　　　　US　　ISSN 0742-6968
BIO-BIBLIOGRAPHIES IN MUSIC. 1985. irreg. price varies. Greenwood Press, Inc. (Subsidiary of: Greenwood Publishing Group Inc.), 88 Post Rd. W., Box 5007, Westport, CT 06881-5007. TEL 203-226-3571. FAX 203-222-1502.
　—BLDSC shelfmark: 2066.804400.

016　　　　　　　DK　　ISSN 0106-729X
BOERNEBIBLIOTEKSKATALOG. GRAMMOFONPLADER, KASSETTEBAAND. 1979. a. (plus supplements). DKK 1147.50. Bibliotekscentralen, Tempovej 7-11, DK-2750 Ballerup, Denmark. TEL 2-974000. FAX 2-655310.
　●Also available online.
　Formerly: Boerneplader Boernekassetter.

780　　　　　　　UK
BRAVURA STUDIES IN MUSIC. 1979. a. price varies. Bravura Publications, 2 Clovelly Park, Clovelly Drive, Hindhead, Surrey GU26 6RS, England. Ed. Alan Poulton. bibl.; circ. 250. (back issues avail.)

015 789.91　　　　BU　　ISSN 0323-9365
BULGARSKI GRAMOFONNI PLOCHI. 1974. a. $27. Narodna Biblioteka Kiril i Metodii, 11, V. Levski Blvd., Sofia, Bulgaria. Ed. V. Magneva. bibl.; circ. 300.

780 011　　　　　US　　ISSN 1045-0114
ML156.9
C D REVIEW DIGEST - CLASSICAL; the international indexing service - a guide with excerpts to English language reviews of all music recorded on compact and video laser discs. 1983. q. with a. cumulation. $79. Peri Press, Hemlock Ridge, Box 348, Voorheesville, NY 12186-0348. TEL 518-765-3163. FAX 518-765-3158. Ed. Janet Grimes. adv. (back issues avail.)
　Supersedes in part (in 1988): C D Review Digest (ISSN 0890-0213)

780 011　　　　　US　　ISSN 1045-0122
ML156.4.J3
C D REVIEW DIGEST - JAZZ, POPULAR, ETC.; the international indexing service - a guide with excerpts to English language reviews of all music recorded on compact and video laser discs. 1983. q. with a. cumulation. $79. Peri Press, Hemlock Ridge, Box 348, Voorheesville, NY 12186-0348. TEL 518-765-3163. FAX 518-765-3158. Ed. Janet Grimes. adv. (back issues avail.)
　Supersedes in part (in 1988): C D Review Digest (ISSN 0890-0213)

CELEBRITY BIRTHDAY DIRECTORY. see *MOTION PICTURES* — *Abstracting, Bibliographies, Statistics*

780　　　　　　　DK　　ISSN 0107-9816
DANSK LYDFORTEGNELSE. 1982. q. DKK 527. Bibliotekscentralen, Tempovej 7-11, DK-2750 Ballerup, Denmark. TEL 2-974000. FAX 2-655310.
　●Also available online.

784　　　　　　　DK　　ISSN 0108-2272
DANSK SANGINDEKS; register til sange for boern og voksne. 1982. a. DKK 1134. Bibliotekscentralen, Tempovej 7-11, DK-2750 Ballerup, Denmark. TEL 2-974000. FAX 2-655310.

780 016　　　　　US　　ISSN 0070-3885
DETROIT STUDIES IN MUSIC BIBLIOGRAPHY. 1961. irreg., no.65, 1990. price varies. (Information Coordinators, Inc.) Harmonie Park Press, 23630 Pinewood, Warren, MI 48091-4759. TEL 313-755-3080.
　—BLDSC shelfmark: 3561.640000.
　Description: Bibliographies in the field of American music.

780 015　　　　　GW
DEUTSCHE NATIONALBIBLIOGRAPHIE: VERZEICHNIS DER MUSIKALIEN UND MUSIKSCHRIFTEN. 1976. m. DM.270. (Deutsche Bibliothek, Deutsches Musikarchiv) Buchhaendler-Vereinigung GmbH, Grosser Hirschgraben 17-21, Postfach 100442, 6000 Frankfurt a.M. 1, Germany. TEL 069-1306-0. TELEX 413573-BUCHV-D.
　Formerly: Deutsche Bibliographie: Musikalien-Verzeichnis (ISSN 0170-124X)
　Description: Bibliography that lists music scores from German-speaking countries available at the Music Archive.

780 016　　　　　GW　　ISSN 0015-6191
ML5
FONTES ARTIS MUSICAE. (Text in English, French, German) 1953. 4/yr. membership. (International Association of Music Libraries) Baerenreiter Verlag, Heinrich-Schuetz-Allee 31-37, 3500 Kassel-Wilhelmshoehe, Germany. TEL 0561-3105-0. FAX 0561-3105240. (U.S. subscr. addr.: Foreign Music Distibutors, 13 Elkay Dr., Chester, NY 10918) Ed.Bd. adv.; bk.rev.; bibl.; index; circ. 2,200. **Indexed:** Arts & Hum.Cit.Ind., Curr.Cont., Lib.Lit., Music.Ind., RILM.
　—BLDSC shelfmark: 3976.850000.

780 016　　　　　GW　　ISSN 0075-2959
Z6811
JAHRESVERZEICHNIS DER MUSIKALIEN UND MUSIKSCHRIFTEN. (In 2 Vols: Teil 1 Alphabetischer Teil; Teil 2 Systematischer Teil und Registerteil) a. DM.160 for both vols. Friedrich Hofmeister Musikverlag GmbH, Karlstr. 10, 7010 Leipzig, Germany.
　Formerly: Jahresverzeichnis der Musikalien und Musikschriften.

780 016　　　　　JA
JAPAN FEDERATION OF COMPOSERS. CATALOGUE OF PUBLICATIONS. (Text in Japanese, English) 1970. a. free. Japan Federation of Composers, 602 Shinano-machi Bldg., 33 Shinano-machi, Shinjuku-ku, Tokyo 160, Japan. TEL 03-3359-3916. FAX 03-3359-2927. Ed.Bd. circ. 1,000.

780　　　　　　　　PL
KATALOG POLSKICH DRUKOW MUZYCZNYCH 1800-1963. (Text in English and Polish) 1968. irreg. price varies. Polskie Wydawnictwo Muzyczne, Al. Krasinskiego 11a, 31-111 Krakow, Poland. TEL 22-70-44. FAX 22-01-74.
　Description: Bibliography of music publications printed in Poland and Polish historical documents published abroad.

780 016　　　　　HU　　ISSN 0133-5782
ML120.H9
MAGYAR NEMZETI BIBLIOGRAFIA. ZENEMUVEK BIBLIOGRAFIAJA. (Supplement to: Magyar Nemzeti Bibliografia. Konyvek Bibliografiaja (HU 0133-6843)) 1977. q. Orszagos Szechenyi Konyvtar, Budavari Palota F epulet, 1827 Budapest, Hungary. TEL 36-1-175-0096. FAX 36-1-202-0804. TELEX 224226 BIBLN H. (Subscr. to: Kultura Kulkereskedelmi Vallalat, 1389 Budapest Pf. 149, Hungary) Ed. Veronika Vavrinecz. circ. 1,200.
　—BLDSC shelfmark: 5345.006000.
　Supersedes in part: Magyar Nemzeti Bibliografia (ISSN 0373-1766); Also supersedes (1970-1977): Magyar Zenemuvek Bibliografiaja (ISSN 0200-0679)
　Description: Bibliography of musical compositions and recordings published in Hungary and officially deposited in the National Szechenyi Library.

780 PL
MATERIALY DO BIBLIOGRAFII MUZYKI POLSKIEJ. 1954. irreg. price varies. Polskie Wydawnictwo Muzyczne, Al. Krasinskiego 11a, 31-111 Krakow, Poland. TEL 22-70-44. FAX 22-01-74. Ed. Tadeusz Strumillo.
   Description: Covers publications concerning music published and copied in Polish and Polish authors' works published in foreign languages.

MEDIA REVIEW DIGEST; the only complete guide to reviews of non-book media. see *MOTION PICTURES — Abstracting, Bibliographies, Statistics*

780 US
MELLEN OPERA REFERENCE INDEX. irreg. Edwin Mellen Press, 240 Portage Rd., Box 450, Lewiston, NY 14092. TEL 716-754-8566. FAX 716-754-4335.

780 793 US
MUSIC AND DANCE PERIODICALS; an international directory and guide book. 1989. irreg. $65. Peri Press, Hemlock Ridge, Box 348, Voorheesville, NY 12186-0348. TEL 518-765-3163. FAX 518-765-3158. Ed. Doris Robinson.

MUSIC & MUSICIANS: BRAILLE SCORES CATALOG - CHORAL (LARGE PRINT EDITION). see *HANDICAPPED — Abstracting, Bibliographies, Statistics*

MUSIC & MUSICIANS: BRAILLE SCORES CATALOG - INSTRUMENTAL (LARGE PRINT EDITION). see *HANDICAPPED — Abstracting, Bibliographies, Statistics*

MUSIC & MUSICIANS: BRAILLE SCORES CATALOG - ORGAN (LARGE PRINT EDITION). see *HANDICAPPED — Abstracting, Bibliographies, Statistics*

MUSIC & MUSICIANS: BRAILLE SCORES CATALOG - PIANO (LARGE PRINT EDITION). see *HANDICAPPED — Abstracting, Bibliographies, Statistics*

MUSIC & MUSICIANS: BRAILLE SCORES CATALOG VOCAL PART I: CLASSICAL (LARGE PRINT EDITION). see *HANDICAPPED — Abstracting, Bibliographies, Statistics*

MUSIC & MUSICIANS: BRAILLE SCORES CATALOG VOCAL PART II: POPULAR (LARGE PRINT EDITION). see *HANDICAPPED — Abstracting, Bibliographies, Statistics*

MUSIC & MUSICIANS: INSTRUCTIONAL CASSETTE RECORDINGS CATALOG (LARGE PRINT EDITION). see *HANDICAPPED — Abstracting, Bibliographies, Statistics*

MUSIC & MUSICIANS: INSTRUCTIONAL DISC RECORDINGS CATALOG (LARGE PRINT EDITION). see *HANDICAPPED — Abstracting, Bibliographies, Statistics*

MUSIC & MUSICIANS: LARGE-PRINT SCORES AND BOOKS CATALOG (LARGE PRINT EDITION). see *HANDICAPPED — Abstracting, Bibliographies, Statistics*

780 016 US ISSN 0027-4240
ML1
MUSIC ARTICLE GUIDE; annotated guide to feature articles in American music periodicals with special emphasis on the special needs of school and college music educators. 1965. q. $47. Information Services, Inc., Box 27066, Philadelphia, PA 19118. Ed. Morris Henken. index. (also avail. in microfilm from UMI; reprint service avail. from UMI)

780 011 US ISSN 0092-2838
Z881.A1
MUSIC, BOOKS ON MUSIC AND SOUND RECORDINGS. (Text in various languages) 1953. a. $105. U.S. Library of Congress, Catalog Management and Publication Division, Washington, DC 20540. TEL 202-707-6100. (Dist. by: Cataloging Distribution Service, Library of Congress, Washington, DC 20541)
   —BLDSC shelfmark: 5198.190000.
   Formerly: U.S. Library of Congress Catalog - Music and Phonorecords (ISSN 0041-7793)

780 US ISSN 0146-7883
MUSIC-IN-PRINT SERIES. 1974. irreg. price varies. Musicdata, Inc., Box 48010, Philadelphia, PA 19144-8010. TEL 215-842-0555. Ed.Bd. adv.; bibl.; circ. 2,000.
   Description: Goal is to locate and catalog all printed music published throughout the world, and to keep the information current by publishing supplements and revised editions.

780 016 US ISSN 0027-4348
ML118
MUSIC INDEX; a subject-author guide to over 300 current international periodicals. (Supplement avail. Music Index Subject Heading List) (Entries are in language of country of origin) 1949. m. $1,125 (includes Subject Heading List). Harmonie Park Press, 23630 Pinewood, Warren, MI 48091-4759. TEL 313-755-3080. Ed. Nadia Stratelak. bk.rev.; bibl.; cum.index; circ. 500.
   Description: Bibliography-guide to current music periodicals worldwide.

780 029.5 US ISSN 0094-6478
MUSIC LIBRARY ASSOCIATION. INDEX AND BIBLIOGRAPHY SERIES. 1964. irreg. price varies. Music Library Association, Box 487, Canton, MA 02021. TEL 617-828-8450. circ. 250.
   Formerly: Music Library Association. Index Series (ISSN 0077-2445)
   Description: Analytical indexes to music serials and music materials.

780 US ISSN 0736-7740
MUSIC REFERENCE COLLECTION. 1983. irreg. Greenwood Press, Inc. (Subsidiary of: Greenwood Publishing Group Inc.), 88 Post Rd. W., Box 5007, Westport, CT 06881-5007. TEL 203-226-3571. FAX 203-222-1502.
   —BLDSC shelfmark: 5990.401500.

780 016 DK ISSN 0085-3623
MUSIKALIER I DANSKE BIBLIOTEKER (ANNUAL)/MUSIC IN DANISH LIBRARIES; accessionskatalog/union catalogue. (Text in Danish and English) 1970. a. price varies. Bibliotekscentralen, Tempovej 7-11, DK-2750 Ballerup, Denmark. (also avail. in microfiche)
   ●Also available online.

780 016 JA
ONGAKU BUNKEN YOSHI MOKUROKU. 1973. a. 2,000 Yen (effective since 1991). R I L M National Committee of Japan, Musashino Music College, 1-13 Hazawa, Nerima-ku, Tokyo 176, Japan. (Affiliate: International Repertory of Music Literature) adv.; bk.rev.; circ. 1,000.
   Formerly: Nihon Ongaku Bunken Yoshi Mokuroku.
   Description: Annotated bibliography of music literature in Japan.

780.42 UK ISSN 0951-1318
ML3470
P O M P I. (Popular Music Periodicals Index) 1988. a. £20 (foreign £23.50). British Library, National Sound Archive, 29 Exhibition Rd., London SW7 2AS, England. TEL 071-589-6603. FAX 071-823-8970. Ed.Bd. adv.; circ. 500.
   —BLDSC shelfmark: 6550.766000.
   Description: Index of articles in over 90, mainly English-language, jazz, pop, folk and other music periodicals.

780 016 US ISSN 0033-6955
ML1
R I L M ABSTRACTS OF MUSIC LITERATURE. 1967. q. $90 to individuals; institutions $330. (Repertoire International de Litterature Musicale - International Repertory of Music Literature) R I L M Abstracts, City University of New York, 33 W. 42nd St., New York, NY 10036. TEL 212-642-2709. FAX 212-642-2642. (Co-sponsors: International Association of Music Libraries, International Musicological Society, American Council of Learned Societies) Ed. Barry S. Brook. bk.rev.; abstr.; index. cum.index; circ. 1,500 (controlled).
   ●Also available online. Vendor(s): DIALOG (File no.97).
Also available on CD-ROM.
   —BLDSC shelfmark: 7971.466000.

780 011 US
REPERTOIRE INTERNATIONAL DE LA PRESSE MUSICALE. 1987. q. University Microfilms International, 300 N. Zeeb Rd., Box 34, Ann Arbor, MI 48106. TEL 800-521-0600. Ed. H. Robert Cohen.
   Description: Indexes 19th-Century music periodicals in Europe and North America.

780 CS
SLOVENSKA NARODNA BIBLIOGRAFIA SERIA H: HUDOBNINY. (Text in German, Slovak; summaries in English, French, German, Slovak) 1981. a. Matica Slovenska, Slovenska Narodna Kniznica, Ul. L. Novomeskeho 32, 036 52 Martin, Czechoslovakia. TEL 0842-313-71. FAX 0842-324-54. TELEX 075 331. (Subscr. to: Slovart, Gottwaldovo nam, 48, 805 32 Bratislava, Czechoslovakia) Ed. Anna Kucianova. (back issues avail.)

016 US ISSN 1047-2371
ML156.2
SPECTRUM (BOSTON). 1949. q. $24.95. Schwann Publications (Subsidiary of: Stereophile), 535 Boyleston Rd., Boston, MA 02116. TEL 617-437-1350. (Subscr. to: Box 55442, Boulder, CO 80322. TEL 800-234-3373) Ed. Paul Crapo. adv.; bibl.; circ. 30,000. (also avail. in microfilm)
   Former titles (until 1990): Schwann-2 Record and Tape Guide (ISSN 0271-5783); Schwann-2, Records and Tapes (ISSN 0099-0167)

MUSIC — Computer Applications

see also Computers–Computer Music

780 US
A T M I TECHNOLOGY DIRECTORY. a. $20 (foreign $30) includes Newsletter. Association for Technology in Music Instruction, c/o Ohio State University, School of Music, 1866 College Dr., Columbus, OH 43210-1170. bk.rev.
   Description: Includes listings and information about hardware, software, video discs, and other materials related to technology-based music instruction.

780 US
ASSOCIATION FOR TECHNOLOGY IN MUSIC INSTRUCTION NEWSLETTER. 1977. q. $20 (foreign $30) includes Technology Directory. Association for Technology in Music Instruction, c/o Ohio State University, School of Music, 1866 College Dr., Columbus, OH 43210-1170. TEL 614-292-4654. Ed. Barbara Murphy. bk.rev.; circ. 325. (tabloid format) **Indexed:** ERIC.
   Formerly: National Consortium for Computer-Based Music Instruction. Newsletter.

780 620.2 US ISSN 0148-9267
ML1 CODEN: CMUJDY
COMPUTER MUSIC JOURNAL. 1977. q. $38 to individuals (foreign $52); institutions $80 (foreign $94); students $30 (foreign $44). M I T Press, 55 Hayward St., Cambridge, MA 02142. TEL 617-253-2889. FAX 617-258-6779. TELEX 921473. (Editorial addr.: 1836 Webster St., Palo Alto, CA 94301-3855) Ed. Stephen Pope. adv.; bk.rev.; illus.; circ. 4,000. (also avail. in microfilm from UMI; back issues avail.; reprint service avail. from UMI) **Indexed:** Arts & Hum.Cit.Ind., Compumath, Comput.& Contr.Abstr., Comput.Cont., Comput.Rev., Curr.Cont., Eng.Ind., Ind.Sci.Rev., Inform.Sci.Abstr., LAMP, Music Artic.Guide, Music Ind., RILM, Sci.Abstr., Sci.Cit.Ind.
   ●Also available online.
   —BLDSC shelfmark: 3394.113000.
   Description: Resource for musicians, composers, scientists, engineers and computer enthusiasts interested in contemporary and electronic music and computer-generated sound.

780 US ISSN 1046-1744
ML73
COMPUTERS IN MUSIC RESEARCH. 1989. a. $16. Wisconsin Center for Music Technology, School of Music, University of Wisconsin, Madison, WI 53706. TEL 608-263-1900. Ed. John W. Schaffer. bk.rev.; circ. 230. (back issues avail.) **Indexed:** Music Ind., RILM.
   —BLDSC shelfmark: 3394.925330.
   Description: Application of computers and technology to the study of music.
   Refereed Serial

3590 MYSTERY AND DETECTIVE

789.99 370   US
▼**MUSIC & COMPUTER EDUCATOR.*** 1990. 10/yr. $19.25. T A M E E Publications, 16 N. Broadway, Hicksville, NY 11801-2913. TEL 516-549-3200. FAX 516-385-7104. Ed. Nill Stephen. adv.; bk.rev.; circ. 20,000 (controlled). Indexed: Music Artic.Guide.
   Description: For music teachers integrating technology into their classrooms. Includes profiles of instructors and innovators.

MYSTERY AND DETECTIVE

see Literature-Mystery and Detective

NEEDLEWORK

746   US
ALL TIME FAVORITE CROCHET. 1985. a. Harris Publications, Inc., 1115 Broadway, 8th fl., New York, NY 10010. TEL 212-807-7100. Ed. Barbara Jacksier. bk.rev. (back issues avail.)
   Description: Covers needlework patterns.

746   US   ISSN 8756-6591
TT835
AMERICAN QUILTER. 1985. q. $15 includes membership. American Quilter's Society, Box 3290, Paducah, KY 42002-3290. TEL 502-898-7903. FAX 502-898-8890. Ed. Victoria Faoro. adv.; bk.rev.; circ. 70,000.
   Description: Serves today's quilters with articles on quilt designing techniques, study, exhibition, issues, events.

746   NE
ARIADNE. 1947. m. fl.63. Uitgeverij Spaarnestad B.V., Europalaan 93, 3526 KP Utrecht, Netherlands. TEL 030-822511. FAX 030-898388. Ed. Rozemarijn de Witte. adv.; index; circ. 144,000.
   Formerly: Handwerken Ariadne (ISSN 0017-7415)
   Description: Resource for creative leisure activities including home decoration, crafts, sewing, fahsions for children and adults, and more.

746   UK   ISSN 0268-5175
AUDREY BABINGTON'S WORKBOX. 1984. 4/yr. $9. Workbox Enterprises, 40, Silver St., Wiveliscombe, Somerset TA4 2NY, England. TEL 0984-24033. Ed. Audrey Babington. adv.; bk.rev.; circ. 40,000.
   Description: For needlecraft enthusiasts: news about embroidery, dollmaking, patchwork and quilting.

746   NE
BIJVOORBEELD. 1968. q. fl.48.50. Spanjaardsgat b.v., Pieterskerkhof 22, 2300 AB Leiden, Netherlands. Ed. Marjan Unger. adv.; circ. 7,000.

746   US
BLANKET STATEMENTS. q. American Quilt Study Group, 660 Mission St., Ste. 400, San Francisco, CA 94105-4007. TEL 415-495-0163.
   Description: Circulates news of AQSG and publishes research queries.

746   IT
BRAVA-CASA. m. L.36000. Rizzoli Editore-Corriere della Sera, Via A. Rizzoli 2, 20132 Milan, Italy. Ed. C. Giagnoni.
   Formerly: Brava.

746   GW
BURDA BABYMASCHEN. s-a. Verlag Aenne Burda, Am Kestendamm 2, Postfach 1160, 7600 Offenburg, Germany. TEL 0781-8402. Ed. Iris Hanle-Schmidt. circ. 180,000.

746   GW
BURDA FILETHAEKELN. a. Verlag Aenne Burda, Am Kestendamm 2, Postfach 1160, 7600 Offenburg, Germany. TEL 0781-8402. Ed. Maria Blumrich. circ. 225,000.

746   GW
BURDA KINDERMASCHEN. q. Verlag Aenne Burda, Am Kestendamm 2, Postfach 1160, 7600 Offenburg, Germany. TEL 0781-8402. Ed. Iris Hanle-Schmidt. circ. 150,000.

746   GW
BURDA KREUZSTICH. a. Verlag Aenne Burda, Am Kestendamm 2, Postfach 1160, 7600 Offenburg, Germany. TEL 0781-8402. Ed. Maria Blumrich. circ. 120,000.

746   GW
BURDA MASCHENMUSTER. q. Verlag Aenne Burda, Am Kestendamm 2, Postfach 1160, 7600 Offenburg, Germany. TEL 0781-8402. Ed. Iris Hanle-Schmidt. circ. 180,000.

BURDA MODEN (ARABIC EDITION). see *BEAUTY CULTURE*

677 746   CN
CANADA QUILTS MAGAZINE. 1975. 5/yr. Can.$15.50($19) (Canada Quilts) Deborrah Sherman, Ed. & Pub., P.O. Box 39, Sta. A, Hamilton, Ont. L8N 3A2, Canada. TEL 416-549-1055. FAX 416-523-7440. adv.; bk.rev.; circ. 3,500. (back issues avail.)
   Formerly: Canada Quilts (ISSN 0381-7369)
   Description: Contains patterns, instructions, quilting news from across Canada, color photos, product reviews, an antique column and events listed by region.

746   JA
CHARM. (Text in Japanese) 1975. bi-m. 2320 Yen. Shufu-to-Seikatsusha Ltd., 5-7, 3-chome, Kyobashi, Chuo-ku, Tokyo 104, Japan. Ed. Tsuguo Nakamura.

746 745.5   US
CHRISTMAS: YEAR ROUND NEEDLEWORK & CRAFT IDEAS. bi-m. $2.95 per no. Oxmoor Publishing, 2100 Lakeshore Dr., Birmingham, AL 35209. TEL 205-877-6000.

746   SP
CLARA. 1986. m. Hogar y la Moda, S.A., Diputacion, 211, 08011 Barcelona, Spain. TEL 254 10 04. Ed. Dona Eulalia Ubach Nuet. adv.; bk.rev.; charts; illus.; circ. 115,416.

746   US
CLASSIC CROSS-STITCH. 1988. bi-m. $17.70. P J S Publications, Inc., New Plaza, Box 1790, Peoria, IL 61656. TEL 309-682-6626.

746   US   ISSN 8755-2655
THE CLOTH DOLL; the finest quality cloth doll magazine. 1982. q. $13.95. Bergman Publishing, 20 Kennedy Dr., Box 1089, Mt. Shasta, CA 96067. TEL 916-926-5009. Ed. Leta Bergman. adv.; bk.rev.; circ. 4,800. **Indexed:** Ind.How To Do It (1984-).
   Description: Contains how-to articles, supply sources, features on doll makers, and patterns.

746   US
COUNTRY STITCH. bi-m. $2.95 per no. Oxmoor Publishing, 2100 Lakeshore Dr., Birmingham, AL 35209. TEL 205-877-6000.

746   US   ISSN 0887-9818
TT159
CRAFT & NEEDLEWORK AGE ANNUAL TRADE DIRECTORY. a. $40. Hobby Publications, Inc., 225 Gordons Corner Plaza, Box 420, Manalapan, NJ 07726. TEL 908-446-4900. FAX 908-446-5488. Ed. Karen Ancona. circ. 25,000.
   Former titles: Annual Basic Industry Trade Directory; Craft, Model and Hobby Industry Annual Trade Directory; Craft and Needlework Age - World of Miniatures Annual Trade Directory.

746   US
▼**CREATIVE MACHINE.** 1990. q. $15 (effective 1992). Open Chain Publishing, Inc., Box 2634, Menlo Park, CA 94026. TEL 415-366-4440. Ed. Robbie Fanning. adv.; bk.rev.; illus.; circ. 20,000.
   Description: Projects and advice for sewing machine lovers.

CREATIVE PRODUCTS NEWS; new products for crafts/needlework/art supplies/miniatures. see *ARTS AND HANDICRAFTS*

746   US   ISSN 0887-3690
CREATIVE QUILTING. 1986. $21. Grass Roots Publishing Co., Inc., 950 Third Ave., 16th Fl., New York, NY 10022. TEL 212-888-1855. adv.; bk.rev.; circ. 280,000.
   Description: Features step-by-step instructions and diagrams for various levels of quilters. Each issue contains patterns for different types of quilts. Includes a buyer's guide and articles on well-known quilters.

746   US
CROCHET. 1981. q. $2.50 per no. Harris Publications, Inc., 1115 Broadway, 8th fl., New York, NY 10010. TEL 212-807-7100. Ed. Georgiana Heyda. adv.; illus.
   Description: Contains illustrations and detailed instructions for a variety of crochet projects, some submitted by readers.

746   FR
CROCHET D'ART.* 1974. m. 97 F. Editions E.G.E., B.P. 7085, 69007 Lyon, France. TEL 78-72-06-88. Ed. J. Deschavanne. circ. 66,000.
   Formerly: Tout le Tricot - Le Crochet et le Tricot d'Art (ISSN 0183-3898)

746   US   ISSN 8750-8877
CROCHET FANTASY. 1983. 8/yr. $28. All American Crafts, Inc., 243 Newton-Sparta Rd., Newton, NJ 07860-2748. TEL 201-383-8080. Eds. Karen Manthey, Janice Edsall. adv.; bk.rev.; illus.; circ. 198,000.
   Description: Publication for crochet enthusiasts featuring photographs, instructions, and diagrams for traditional and contemporary garments, asccessories, and home decor.

746   US   ISSN 1046-719X
CROCHET HOME. 1987. bi-m. $12.95. Jerry Gentry, Inc., 206 West St., Big Sandy, TX 75755. TEL 903-636-4011. FAX 903-636-2288. (Subscr. to: 23 Old Pecan Rd., Big Sandy, TX 75755) Ed. Loretta Blevins. circ. 50,000. (back issues avail.)
   Formerly (until 1989): Crochet Fun.
   Description: Crochet patterns and instructions for home decorating, toys, and clothing for the beginner and experienced stitcher alike.

746   US
CROCHET PATTERNS. bi-m. P J S Publications, Inc., New Plaza, Box 1790, Peoria, IL 61656. TEL 309-682-6626. Ed. Sylvia Miller. circ. 200,000.

746   US
CROCHET WORLD. 1978. bi-m. $12.97. House of White Birches Publishing, 306 E. Parr Rd., Berne, IN 46711. TEL 219-589-8741. Ed. Susan Foster. illus.; circ. 88,250.
   Description: Contains 15 to 25 patterns for afghans and doilies, plus contests and question and answers.

746   US   ISSN 1041-0759
CROCHET WORLD SPECIAL. 1978. q. $9.95. House of White Birches Publishing, 306 E. Parr Rd., Berne, IN 46711. TEL 219-589-8741. Ed. Susan Foster. circ. 58,662.
   Former titles: Crochet Today Fashions; Crochet World Omnibook.
   Description: Contains 15 to 25 needlework patterns, plus contests and question and answers.

746 745.5   US
CROSS QUICK - CROSS STITCH. m. $3.50 per no. Meredith Corporation, 1716 Locust St., Des Moines, IA 50366. TEL 515-284-2484. FAX 515-284-2700. (Subscr. to: 70 W. 36th St., 15th Fl., New York, NY 10018)

746   US
CROSS STITCH & COUNTRY CRAFTS. bi-m. Meredith Corporation, Special Interest Publications, 1716 Locust St., Des Moines, IA 50336. TEL 515-284-3000. (Alt. addr.: 4118 Lakeside Dr., Richmond, CA 94806) circ. 2,000,000.

746   US   ISSN 1056-7542
▼**CROSS STITCH! MAGAZINE.** 1990. bi-m. $12.95. Jerry Gentry, Inc., 206 West St., Big Sandy, TX 75755. TEL 903-636-4011. FAX 903-636-2288. (Subscr. to: 23 Old Pecan Rd., Big Sandy, TX 75755) Ed. Cindy Wambach. circ. 75,000. (back issues avail.)
   Description: Presents cross stitch patterns and instructions for home decorating and clothing.

746   US   ISSN 1054-3430
CROSS-STITCH PLUS. 1983. bi-m. $12.97. House of White Birches Publishing, 306 E. Parr Rd., Berne, IN 46711. TEL 219-589-8741. Ed. Lana Schurb. adv.; circ. 86,012. (back issues avail.)
   Former titles: Women's Circle Counted Cross-Stitch; Women's Circle Counted Cross-Stitch and Candlewicking.
   Description: Contains 20 or more patterns, interviews with designers and reference material.

NEEDLEWORK

746 745.5   US
CROSS STITCH PLUS. bi-m. $2.95. House of White Birches Publishing, 306 E. Parr Rd., Berne, IN 46711. TEL 219-589-8741. FAX 219-589-8093.

746   US
CROSS-STITCHER. 1983. 6/yr. $14.97. Clapper Communications Companies, 701 Lee St., Ste. 1000, Des Plaines, IL 60016-4570. TEL 708-297-7400. FAX 708-297-8328. Ed. B.J. McDonald. circ. 50,000. (back issues avail.)

746   US
ELIZABETH ZIMMERMANN'S WOOL GATHERING. 1964. s-a. $12.50 in Can.; Elsewhere. Schoolhouse Press, 6899 Cary Bluff, Pittsville, WI 54466. TEL 715-884-2799. FAX 715-884-2829. Ed. Meg Swansen. bk.rev.; circ. 9,000. (back issues avail.)
   Formerly: Wool Gathering.

746.44   UK   ISSN 0013-6611
EMBROIDERY. 1932. q. $27. (Embroiderers' Guild) E G Enterprises Ltd., P.O. Box 42B, E. Molesey, Surrey KT8 9BB, England. FAX 081-977-9882. Ed. Valerie Campbell-Harding. adv.; bk.rev.; illus.; index; circ. 14,500. Indexed: Artbibl.Mod.
   Description: Features current embroidery, both amateur and professional techniques, historical and ethnographic subjects and design.

746   SP
ESPECIAL LABORES. 1954. q. $17.50. Hogar y la Moda, S.A., Diputacion, 211, 08011 Barcellona, Spain. TEL 254 10 04. Ed. D. Julio Bou Gibert. adv.; circ. 67,000.

746   IT
FANTASTICA MAGLIA. 1982. m. Curcio Periodici S.p.A., Via Corsica 4, 00198 Rome, Italy. Ed. Rosanna Falconi. adv.; circ. 245,000.

FASHION AND CRAFT. see *CLOTHING TRADE — Fashions*

746   US
FASHION KNITTING. 1981. bi-m. $23.70. All American Crafts, Inc., 243 Newton-Sparta Rd., Newton, NJ 07860-2748. TEL 201-383-8080. Ed. Sally V. Klein. adv.; illus.; circ. 102,000.
   Description: Publication for knitting enthusiasts featuring contemporary knitted garment designs, photographs, instructions, diagrams and more.

FASHION POETRY PATTERNS & RECITALS NEWS. see *WOMEN'S INTERESTS*

746   US   ISSN 0270-2959
TT740
FLYING NEEDLE. 1971. q. $25. Council of American Embroiderers, 588 St. Charles Ave., N.E., Atlanta, GA 30308. (Subscr. to: c/o Judy Royner, 10200 Dechaux Re., E., Puyallup, WA 98371) Ed. Jeane Hutchins. adv.; bk.rev.; circ. 3,500. (back issues avail.)
   Description: Covers all areas of fiber using a threaded needle. Includes artists' profiles, information on exhibitions, and how-to articles.

746   US
FOR THE LOVE OF CROSS STITCH. 1988. 6/yr. $12.95. Leisure Arts, Box 56099, Little Rock, AR 72215-6099. Ed. Anne Van Wagner Young.

746   DK
HAANDARBEJDE TRIN FOR TRIN. 1974. m. DKK 34.50. Bonniers Specialmagasiner A-S, Strandboulevarden 130, 2100 Copenhagen OE, Denmark. Ed. Merete Rude. circ. 120,000.
   Formerly: Alt om Haandarbejde.
   Description: Features articles on knitting, sewing and crocheting for women, men and children.

746   DK   ISSN 0107-1769
HAANDARBEJDETS FREMME/DANISH HANDCRAFT GUILD. 1934. q. DKK 275($46) Selskabet til Haandarbejdets Fremme, Glentevej 70 B, DK-2400 Copenhagen NV, Denmark. TEL 31 10 20 88. FAX 31-106798. adv.; bk.rev.; circ. 6,000.

746   GW   ISSN 0017-7156
HANDARBEIT. 1964. q. DM.9.60. Zeitschriftenverlag fuer die Frau, Friedrich-Ebert-Str. 76-78, 7010 Leipzig, Germany.

746   US
HANDWORKER. 1953. bi-m. $9. Suennen Publications, Rt. 1, Box 239, Wausaukee, WI 54177. TEL 715-732-6327. Ed. Lucille Suennen. adv.; bk.rev.; circ. 2,000. (back issues avail.)

746   CN
HEDDLE. bi-m. $7.50. Muskoka Publications Group, 27 Dominion St., Box 1906, Bracebridge, Ont. P0B 1C0, Canada. TEL 705-645-5710. FAX 705-645-3928. adv.; bk.rev.
   Description: Magazine for spinners and weavers containing personality profiles, features and instructional articles.

HOBBY MERCHANDISER ANNUAL TRADE DIRECTORY. see *HOBBIES*

746   US   ISSN 0893-1879
HOOKED ON CROCHET!. 1987. bi-m. $12.95. Jerry Gentry, Inc., 206 West St., Big Sandy, TX 75755. TEL 903-636-4011. FAX 903-636-6288. (Subscr. to: 23 Old Pecan Rd., Big Sandy, TX 75755) Ed. Loretta Blevins. circ. 110,000. (back issues avail.)

746   US
HOUSEWIVES' HANDY HINTS, SMALL BUSINESSWOMAN'S NEWSLETTER. 1980. bi-m. $8. Box 66, Mount Dora, FL 32757. Ed. Jackie Barlow. circ. 150.

746   US
INSIDE A H S C A. 5/yr. membership. American Home Sewing & Craft Association, 1375 Broadway, New York, NY 10018. TEL 212-302-2150. Ed. Joan Katz. circ. 1,600.
   Description: News of consumer motivation, education, membership and government relations programs. Includes fashion and home decorating trends and industry news.

746   US
KEEPSAKE CALENDAR; (year) cross-stitch collection. 1988. a. $9.97. Craftways Corporation, 418 Lakeside Dr., Richmond, CA 94806. TEL 510-262-7700. FAX 510-223-6431. (Subscr. to: Dept. KC92, 111 Tenth St., Box 11447, Des Moines, IA 50336-1447) Ed. Joan Cravens. charts; circ. 150,000. (back issues avail.)
   Description: Cross-stitch patterns, articles and instructions themed to each month for the needlework hobbyist.

746   II   ISSN 0023-107X
KHATOON MASHRIQ. (Text in Urdu) 1937. m. Rs.48. 423, Matia Mahal, Ama Masjid, Delhi-6, India. Ed. Taufiq Farooqi. adv.; illus.; circ. 81,000.

746.43   US   ISSN 0747-9026
KNITTERS. 1984. q. $16 (foreign $20). Golden Fleece Publications, Box 1525, Sioux Falls, SD 57101. TEL 605-338-2450. FAX 605-338-2994. Ed. Elaine Rowley. adv.; bk.rev.; tr.lit.; charts; illus. (back issues avail.)
   Description: Features techniques and instructions for innovative fashion knitting projects, plus interviews with designers and craftspeople.

KNITTING TECHNIQUE. see *TEXTILE INDUSTRIES AND FABRICS*

746.43   US   ISSN 0194-8083
KNITTING WORLD. bi-m. $12.97. House of White Birches Publishing, 306 E. Parr Rd., Berne, IN 46711. TEL 219-589-8741. Ed. Anne Jefferson. circ. 37,321.
   Description: Contains 25 to 30 patterns, reviews, regular and feature articles.

746   US
KURENAI: JAPANESE EMBROIDERY JOURNAL. 4/yr. $18. Embroidery Research Press Inc., No.200 G-4, 10800 Alpharetta Hwy., Roswell, GA 30076. TEL 404-390-0617. FAX 404-512-7837. Ed. Dolly Norton Fehd. bk.rev.; circ. 400.
   Description: Devoted to traditional Japanese embroidery. Articles on symbolism, color usage and design elements.

746   SP   ISSN 0047-3863
LABORES DEL HOGAR. 1926. m. $42.50. Hogar y la Moda, S.A., Diputacion 211, 08011 Barcelona, Spain. TEL 254 10 04. FAX 254-13-22. Ed. Eulalia Ubach Nuet. adv.; bk.rev.; charts; illus.; circ. 75,839.

746   US
LACE & CRAFTS. 1987. q. $20. Laces and Lace Making, 3201 E. Lakeshore Dr., Tallahassee, FL 32312. TEL 904-385-5093. FAX 904-422-3646. Ed. Eunice Sein-Jurado. adv.; tr.; lit.; circ. 30,000 (controlled). (back issues avail.)
   Formerly: Lace Crafts Quarterly.
   Description: Covers lacemaking, fine sewing and crafts. Contains how tos and full size patterns.

746   US
LADY'S CIRCLE PATCHWORK QUILTS. bi-m. Lopez Publications, Inc., 152 Madison Ave., Ste. 905, New York, NY 10016. TEL 212-689-3933. FAX 212-725-2239.
   Description: Features present-day quilts and interviews with quilters around the U.S., and provides instructions for selected designs.

746   US   ISSN 0024-8924
MCCALL'S NEEDLEWORK & CRAFTS. 1935. bi-m. $13.97. (McCall Pattern Co.) P J S Publications, Inc., News Plaza, Box 1790, Peoria, IL 61656. TEL 309-682-6626. FAX 309-682-7394. Ed. Helene Rush. adv.; bk.rev.; illus.; circ. 600,112. Indexed: Ind.How To Do It (1978-), MELSA.
   Description: Contains instructions for a variety of craft projects, including knitting and crocheting, embroidery, sewing and other home-based crafts, to produce fashion items as well as decorative objects.

746   UK   ISSN 0269-9761
MACHINE KNITTING MONTHLY. 1986. m. £18 (U.S. £27). Machine Knitting Monthly Ltd., 3 Bridge Avenue, Maidenhead, Berks. SL6 1RR, England. TEL 0628-770289. FAX 0628-777335. Ed. Sheila Berriff. adv.; bk.rev.; circ. 47,000. (back issues avail.)
   Description: The latest patterns, features and news for all machine knitters.

746.43 687   UK   ISSN 0266-8505
MACHINE KNITTING NEWS. 1984. m. £20 in UK; elsewhere £42. Litharne Ltd., P.O. Box 9, Stratford-upon-Avon, Warwickshire CV37 8RS, England. TEL 07-89-720133. FAX 07-89-720888. Ed. Jean Ryder. adv.; circ. 50,000.

746   FR   ISSN 0246-5957
MAGIC CROCHET. no.25, 1983. bi-m. $16.25. Editions de Saxe, 20 rue Croix Barret, 69364 Lyon Cedex 7, France. (U.S. addr.: Robin Hill Park, Rt. 22, Patterson, NY 12563)

MANEQUIM. see *CLOTHING TRADE — Fashions*

746   NE   ISSN 0025-3383
MARION; fashion and home sewing patterns. (Text in Dutch) 1948. m. fl.61.80. Eska Tijdschriften B.V., Europalaan 93, 3526 KP Utrecht, Netherlands. Ed. E. Kiezebrink. adv.; circ. 180,000.

MEYERS MODEBLATT. see *CLOTHING TRADE — Fashions*

746   US
MINIATURE QUILTS. q. Chitra Publications, 2 Public Ave., Montrose, PA 18801. TEL 717-278-1984. FAX 717-278-2223. Ed. Patti Bacheldor. Indexed: Ind.How To Do It (1991-).

746.434   IT
MIO UNCINETTO. m. 1978. L.21600. Via Corsica 4, 00198 Rome, Italy. Ed. Rosanna Falconi. adv.; circ. 197,000.

746 687   UK   ISSN 0957-6673
MODERN MACHINE KNITTING. m. £18 (foreign £27). Modern Machine Knitting Ltd., 3 Bridge Ave., Maidenhead, Berkshire Sl6 1RR, England. TEL 0628-777289. FAX 0628-777335. Ed. Sue Watson. adv.; bk.rev. (back issues avail.)
   Description: Presents the latest patterns, features and news, plus letters, hints and tips by UK's leading experts in the field.

MODUS. see *HOME ECONOMICS*

746   US   ISSN 0273-0197
NK9100
NEEDLE AND BOBBIN CLUB BULLETIN. 1916. a. $20 to non-members. Needle and Bobbin Club, c/o Mrs. P. Guth, 955 Fifth Ave., New York, NY 10021. TEL 212-288-5525. Ed. Anne Dahlgren Hecht. adv.; bk.rev.; charts; illus.; circ. 375. Indexed: Artbibl.Mod.

3592 NEEDLEWORK

746.44 US ISSN 0047-925X
NEEDLE ARTS. 1970. q. $24 (effective Jan. 1991). Embroiderers Guild of America, 335 W. Broadway, Ste. 100, Louisville, KY 40202. TEL 203-426-2665. FAX 502-589-3242. Ed. Bruce Allar. adv.; bk.rev.; charts; illus.; tr.lit.; circ. 21,000. **Indexed:** Art & Archaeol.Tech.Abstr., Text.Tech.Dig.

746 US
NEEDLEPOINT BULLETIN. 1973. m. $12. Needlepoint, Inc., Box 13165, N. Palm Beach, FL 33408. Ed. Sharlene Weldon. bk.rev.

746 US ISSN 1040-5518
NEEDLEPOINT PLUS. 1974. bi-m. $15. E G W Publishing Co., 1320 Galaxy Way, Concord, CA 94520. TEL 510-671-9852. (Subscr. to: Box 5967, Concord, CA 94524) Ed. Judy Swager. adv.; bk.rev.; cum.index; circ. 30,000. (back issues avail.) **Indexed:** Ind.How To Do It (1990-).
Formerly: Needlepoint News (ISSN 0145-8256)

746 US ISSN 1050-9518
OLD TIME CROCHET. 1978. q. $9.95. House of White Birches Publishing, 306 E. Parr Rd., Berne, IN 46711. TEL 219-589-8741. Ed. Anne Jefferson. circ. 80,420.
Formerly (until 1989): Old Time Crochet Patterns and Designs (ISSN 0195-2013)
Description: Contains reprints of popular patterns and signs from fifty years ago.

746 FR
OUVRAGES AU CROCHET.* 1976. m. 130 F. Editions E.G.E., B.P. 7085, 69007 Lyon, France. Ed. J. Deschavanne. circ. 51,000.
Formerly: Tout le Tricot - Ouvrages au Crochet (ISSN 0183-391X)

746 UK ISSN 0957-381X
PATTERNS GALORE. 1989. 4/yr. £6.80($14) Litharne Publishing Ltd., P.O. Box 9, Stratford-upon-Avon, Warwickshire CV37 8RS, England. FAX 0789-720-888. Ed. Viv Paine. circ. 28,000.
Description: Provides styles and ideas for the home dress-maker.

746 US
PEACEFUL PIECES. 1983. s-a. $6. Boise Peace Quilt Project, 1110 Warm Springs Ave., Boise, ID 83712. TEL 208-375-6709. (Subscr. to: Box 6469, Biose, ID 83707) Ed. Lyn McCollum.
Description: Connects those who make or support fabric arts for peace, justice, and the environment.

746 JA
PICHI. (Text in Japanese) 1977. bi-m. 2340 Yen. Gakken Co. Ltd., 40-5, 4-chome, Kamiikedai, Ohta-ku, Tokyo 145, Japan. Ed. Junko Horibe.

746 US
PINGOUIN KNITTING. irreg. (8-12/yr.). $51 for 12 nos. Pingouin, 476 Longpoint Rd., Mt. Pleasant, SC 29464. TEL 803-881-1277. FAX 803-881-2025. circ. 7,200.
Description: Features illustrated instructions for fashion items using Pingouin-brand yarns.

745.5 US ISSN 1045-1854
PLASTIC CANVAS! MAGAZINE. 1989. bi-m. $12.95. Jerry Gentry, Inc., 206 West St., Big Sandy, TX 75755. TEL 903-636-4011. FAX 903-636-2288. (Subscr. to: 23 Old Pecan Rd., Big Sandy, TX 75755) Ed. Janet Tipton. circ. 200,000. (back issues avail.)
Description: Plastic canvas needlework patterns and instructions for home decorating, toys, and wearables.

746 745.5 US
PLASTIC CANVAS WORLD. bi-m. $2.95 per no. House of White Birches Publishing, 306 E. Parr Rd., Berne, IN 46711. TEL 219-589-8741. FAX 219-589-8093.

PROFESSIONAL QUILTER; your source of information for the business of quilting. see BUSINESS AND ECONOMICS — Small Business

746 US ISSN 1048-3659
QUICK & EASY CRAFTS. 1967. bi-m. $12.97. House of White Birches Publishing, 306 E. Parr Rd., Berne, IN 46711. TEL 219-589-8741. Ed. Beth Schwartz. circ. 162,675.
Formerly (until 1990): Women's Circle Country Needlecraft (ISSN 0892-8223)
Description: Contains 20 to 30 patterns, offers designs in various crafts.

746 US
QUICK AND EASY CROCHET. bi-m. Grass Roots Publishing Co., Inc., 950 Third Ave., 16th Fl., New York, NY 10022-2705. TEL 212-888-1855. FAX 212-838-8420. circ. 425,000.

745.5 US ISSN 1048-5341
QUICK & EASY PLASTIC CANVAS. 1989. bi-m. $12.95. Jerry Gentry, Inc., 206 West St., Big Sandy, TX 75755. TEL 903-636-4011. FAX 903-636-2288. (Subscr. to: 26 Old Pecan Rd., Big Sandy, TX 75755) Ed. Janet Tipton. circ. 100,000. (back issues avail.)
Description: Plastic canvas needlework patterns and instructions for home decorating, toys and wearables.

746 US ISSN 1045-5965
QUICK & EASY QUILTING. 1978. q. $9.95. House of White Birches Publishing, 306 E. Parr Rd., Berne, IN 46711. TEL 219-589-8741. Ed. Sandra Hatch. bk.rev.; circ. 102,937.
Formerly: Quilt World Omnibook.
Description: Contains patterns and a directory of quilt shows.

746 US
QUILT. q. Harris Publications, Inc., 1115 Broadway, 8th Fl., New York, NY 10010. TEL 212-807-7100. FAX 212-627-4678. Ed. Jean Eitel. circ. 94,500.

746 US
▼**QUILT CRAFT.** 1991. bi-m. $11.97. Lopez Publications, Inc., 152 Madison Ave., Ste. 905, New York, NY 10016. TEL 212-689-3933. FAX 212-725-2239. Ed. Karen O'Dowd. circ. 175,000.
Description: Focuses on quilts of the 1920s and '30s.

746 US ISSN 0740-4093
QUILT DIGEST.* 1983. irreg. price varies. Quilt Digest Press, Box 1331, Gualala, CA 95445-1331. Ed. Michael M. Kile.

646 US ISSN 0149-8045
TT835
QUILT WORLD. 1974. bi-m. $12.97. House of White Birches Publishing, 306 E. Parr Rd., Berne, IN 46711. TEL 219-589-8741. Ed. Sandra Hatch. adv.; illus.; tr.lit.; circ. 71,414.
Description: Contains 15 to 20 patterns, plus features and a directory of quilt shows.

746 677 UK
THE QUILTER. 1979. q. £3.50 per no. to non-members. Quilters Guild, P.O. Box 66, Dean Clough, Halifax HX3 5AX, England. TEL 0422-345631. FAX 0422-347256. Ed. Vivien Finch. adv.; bk.rev.; illus.; circ. 6,000.
Formerly: Quilters Guild. Newsletter (ISSN 0261-7420)

746 677 US ISSN 0274-712X
TT835
QUILTER'S NEWSLETTER MAGAZINE; the magazine for quilt lovers. 1969. m. $18.95. Leman Publications, Inc. (Subsidiary of: Rodale Press, Inc.), 6700 W. 44th Ave., Wheatridge, CO 80033. TEL 303-420-4272. FAX 303-420-7358. (Subscr. to: Box 394, Wheatridge, CO 80034-0394) Ed. Bonnie Leman. adv.; bk.rev.; charts; illus.; cum.index: 1969-1988; circ. 175,000. (back issues avail.) **Indexed:** Ind.How To Do It (1990-).

746 US
QUILTING INTERNATIONAL; the ultimate quilt magazine. 1987. bi-m. $23.70. All American Crafts, Inc., 243 Newton-Sparta Rd., Newton, NJ 07860-2848. TEL 201-383-8080. Ed. Marion Buccieri. adv.; bk.rev.; illus.; circ. 121,000.
Formerly: Quilting U S A.
Description: Publication for quilting enthusiasts featuring traditional and contemporary quilting patterns, techniques, interviews, show listing, reviews, history, and tips.

746 US ISSN 1040-4457
QUILTING TODAY. bi-m. Chitra Publications, 2 Public Ave., Montrose, PA 18801. TEL 717-278-1984. FAX 717-278-2223. Ed. Patti Bacheider. **Indexed:** Ind.How To Do It (1990-).

746 677 US ISSN 1047-1634
QUILTMAKER; the pattern magazine for today's quiltmakers. 1982. 4/yr. $14.95. Leman Publications, Inc. (Subsidiary of: Rodale Press, Inc.), 6700 W. 44th Ave., Wheatridge, CO 80033. TEL 303-420-4272. FAX 303-420-7358. (Subscr. to: Box 394, Wheatridge, CO 80034-0394) Ed. Bonnie Leman. adv.; illus.; cum.index: 1982-1986; circ. 70,000. (back issues avail.) **Indexed:** Ind.How To Do It (1990-).

RAKAM; mensile di moda e lavori femminili. see WOMEN'S INTERESTS

746 687 US
ROUND BOBBIN. 1965. m. $25 in U.S.; $35 in Canada; $80 elsewhere. Independent Sewing Machine Dealers Association, Box 338, Hilliard, OH 43026. TEL 614-870-7211. Ed. Carole Harris. adv.; bk.rev.; circ. 7,800. (tabloid format)
Description: Provides business, marketing, and other information of relevance to independent sewing machine and vacuum cleaner dealers. Includes association and industry developments.

S A G A NEWS. (Smocking Arts Guild) see ARTS AND HANDICRAFTS

746 GW
SANDRA; tolle Strickmode. (Editions in English, French, German, Italian and Spanish) m. Gruner und Jahr AG und Co., Am Baumwall 11, 2000 Hamburg 11, Germany. TEL 040-3703-0. FAX 040-37035631. Ed. Johnnes Haller. (back issues avail.)

746 646.4 US
SEW BEAUTIFUL. 1987. 5/yr. $23. Martha Pullen Co., Inc., 518 Madison St., Huntsville, AL 35801. TEL 205-533-9586. FAX 205-533-9630. Ed. Scott Wright. adv.; circ. 45,000.
Description: How-to articles and patterns. Features include heirloom sewing, smockery, embroidery, applique and cross stitch designs, with emphasis on sewing for children.

746 US
SEW IT SEAMS. 1986. q. $22. Sharon Lewis, Ed. & Pub., c/o Sew it Seams, 333 11th Pl., Kirkland, WA 98033.

SEW NEWS; the newspaper for people who sew. see CLOTHING TRADE — Fashions

640 745.5 US ISSN 0080-9446
TS1490
SHUTTLE CRAFT GUILD. MONOGRAPHS. 1960. irreg., latest no.37. price varies. Shuttle Craft Books, Inc., Box 550, Coupeville, WA 98239. TEL 206-678-4648. Ed. Jim Anderst.
Description: Provides monographs on weaving.

476 US
▼**SIMPLY CROSS STITCH.** 1990. bi-m. $12.95. Jerry Gentry, Inc., 206 West Street, Big Sandy, TX 75755. TEL 903-636-4011. FAX 903-636-2288. (Subscr. to: 26 Old Pecan Rd., Big Sandy, TX 75755) Ed. Cindy Wambach. circ. 50,000. (back issues avail.)
Description: Presents cross stitch patterns and instructions for home decorating, toys and clothing.

746 745.5 US
STITCH & SEW CRAFTS. bi-m. $2.95 per no. House of White Birches Publishing, 306 E. Parr Rd., Berne, IN 46711. TEL 219-589-8741. FAX 219-589-8093.

746 US ISSN 0744-1649
STITCH 'N SEW QUILTS. 1981. bi-m. $12.97. House of White Birches Publishing, 306 E. Parr Rd., Berne, IN 46711. TEL 219-589-8741. Ed. Sandra Hatch. circ. 65,042.

STITCHES. see CLOTHING TRADE

746 US ISSN 0194-4193
STUMPWORK SOCIETY CHRONICLE. 1979. q. $15. Stumpwork Society, Box 122, Bogota, NJ 07603. TEL 201-224-3622. FAX 201-224-3075. Ed. Sylvia C. Fishman. bk.rev. (back issues avail.)

746 FI ISSN 0355-2098
SUURI KASITYOKERHO. 1974. m. Fmk.229. (Sanomaprint) Sanoma Corporation, PL. 113, SF-00381 Helsinki 38, Finland. TEL 358-0-1221. Ed. Tina Toetterman. circ. 111,079.

TAITO. see *ARTS AND HANDICRAFTS*

746   GW
TEXTIL STUNDE; Lehrblaetter fuer Textiles Gestalten und Werken. 1977. s-a. DM.18. A L S Verlag GmbH, Justus-von-Liebig-Str. 19, 6057 Dietzenbach, Germany. TEL 06074-25051. FAX 06074-27322. Ed. Ingrid Kreide. cum.index 1977-1990; circ. 24,000. (looseleaf format; back issues avail.)

746   US
THREADS. 1985. bi-m. $24. Taunton Press, Inc., 63 S. Main St., Box 5506, Newtown, CT 06470-5506. TEL 203-426-8171. FAX 203-426-3434. Ed. Amy Yanagi. adv.; bk.rev.; illus.; index; circ. 145,000. **Indexed:** Ind.How To Do It (1985-).
 Description: Devoted to the design, materials and techniques of fashion sewing, knitting, quilting and other needle arts.

746.43   FR   ISSN 0183-4738
TOUS LES OUVRAGES - TOUTE LA BRODERIE.* 1950. m. 120 F. Editions E.G.E., B.P. 7085, 69007 Lyon, France. Ed. J. Deschavanne. circ. 53,000.

746.43   FR   ISSN 0183-3901
TOUT LE TRICOT.* 1963. m. 120 F. Editions E.G.E., B.P. 7085, 69007 Lyon, France. Ed. J. Deschavanne.

746.43   FR   ISSN 0183-3928
TOUT LE TRICOT - TRICOT D'ART.* 1977. q. 95 F. Editions E.G.E., B.P. 7085, 69007 Lyon, France. Ed. J. Deschavanne. circ. 45,000.

746.44   FR   ISSN 0183-3944
TOUTE LA BRODERIE - POINT DE CROIX.* 1969. m. Editions E.G.E., B.P. 7085, 69007 Lyon, France. Ed. J. Deschavanne. circ. 30,000.

746   US   ISSN 1050-0073
TRADITIONAL QUILTER;* the leading teaching magazine for creative quilters. 1989. bi-m. $21 (effective Sep. 1990). M S C Publishing, Inc., 243 Newton Sparta Rd., Newton, NJ 07860-2748. TEL 201-729-4477. FAX 201-729-5426. (Subscr. to: Box 507, Mt. Morris, IL 61054) Ed. Phyllis Barbieri. adv.; bk.rev. (back issues avail.)
 Description: Teaches quilting, advanced techniques and design. Offers news on quilters and exhibits.

746   US   ISSN 1050-4435
TRADITIONAL QUILTWORKS. bi-m. Chitra Publications, 2 Public Ave., Montrose, PA 18801. TEL 717-278-1984. FAX 717-278-2223. Ed. Patti Bachelder. **Indexed:** Ind.How To Do It (1990-).

746 646.2   FR   ISSN 0241-0702
TRICOT PRESTIGE. 1979. 4/yr. 105 F. Societe Generale de Publications Illustrees, 10 rue St. Marc, 75002 Paris, France. illus.

746 646.2   FR
TRICOTS CHICS; layette, adults. 1948. 4/yr. (foreign 105 F.). Societe Generale de Publications Illustrees, 10 rue St. Marc, 75002 Paris, France.

746.43   DK   ISSN 0901-1056
ULRICKS STRIKKEIDEER. 3/yr. DKK 24.75. Ulricks Forlag, Uldveyen, DK-2970 Horsholm, Denmark.

746.434   IT
UNCINETTO SELEZIONE. 1979. m. L.12000. Curcio Periodici S.p.A., Via Corsica 4, 00198 Rome, Italy. Ed. Rosanna Falconi. adv.; circ. 165,000.

UNCOVERINGS; research papers. see *WOMEN'S INTERESTS*

746   GW
VERENA; Mode - Maschen - Ideen. 1986. m. DM.67.20. Verlag Aenne Burda, Am Kestendamm 2, Postfach 1160, 7600 Offenburg, Germany. TEL 0781-8402. Ed. Marianne Muesch. circ. 560,000.

746   US
VOGUE KNITTING. vol.7, 1988. 3/yr. $4.50 per no. Butterick Company, Inc., 161 Ave. of the Americas, New York, NY 10013. TEL 212-620-2500.

746   US   ISSN 1042-7643
TT848
WEAVERS. 1981; N.S. 1988. q. $18 (foreign $22). Golden Fleece Publications, Box 1525, Sioux Falls, SD 57101. TEL 605-338-2450. FAX 605-338-2994. Ed. A. David Xenakis. adv.; bk.rev.; charts; illus.; tr.lit.; index; circ. 4,300. (back issues avail.)
 Formerly (until vol.5, no.2): Prairie Wool Companion (ISSN 0743-8907)

793   US
WOMAN'S DAY CHRISTMAS CRAFTS. 1973. a. $2.25. Hachette Magazines, Inc., Woman's Day Special Publications, 1633 Broadway, 45th Fl., New York, NY 10019. TEL 201-767-6000. Ed. Carolyn Galla. adv.; bk.rev.; charts; illus.; tr.lit. (back issues avail.)
 Former titles: Woman's Day Holiday Craft and Granny Square; Granny Square and Craft Ideas; Woman's Day Granny Squares.

746.4
WOMAN'S DAY CHRISTMAS TRADITIONS. 1981. a. Hachette Magazines, Inc., Woman's Day Special Publications, 1633 Broadway, 45th Fl., New York, NY 10019. TEL 212-767-6000. Ed. Theresa Capuana. adv.; bk.rev.; charts; illus.; tr.lit.; circ. 763,000. (back issues avail.)
 Former titles: Woman's Day 101 Sweater and Craft Ideas; Woman's Day 101 Needlework and Sweater Ideas; Woman's Day 101 Sweaters You Can Knit and Crochet.
 Description: For the home knitter, contains instructions for sweaters and other knit and crochet items, plus other types of needle crafts

746   US   ISSN 0279-1978
WOMEN'S CIRCLE CROCHET. 1981. q. $9.95. House of White Birches Publishing, 306 E. Parr Rd., Berne, IN 46711. TEL 219-589-8741. Ed. Anne Jefferson. circ. 49,763.
 Description: Contains patterns, fashion tips and other items for the crochet lover.

746   US   ISSN 0745-0575
WOMEN'S HOUSEHOLD CROCHET. q. $9.95. House of White Birches Publishing, 306 E. Parr Rd., Berne, IN 46711. TEL 219-589-8741. Ed. Susan Foster. circ. 44,873.
 Formerly: Crochet for Women Only.

746   US   ISSN 0162-9123
TT697
WORKBASKET; and home arts magazine. 1935. bi-m. $12.95. K C Publishing Inc., 4251 Pennsylvania Ave., Kansas City, MO 64111-9990. TEL 816-531-5730. FAX 816-531-3873. Ed. Roma Jean Rice. adv.; bk.rev.; illus.; circ. 1,784,529. (also avail. in microfilm from UMI; reprint service avail. from UMI) **Indexed:** Ind.How To Do It (1978-), Mag.Ind., MELSA, PMR.
 ●Also available online. Vendor(s): DIALOG.
 Description: Provides easy-to-follow instructions and guidance on needlework (knitting, tatting, crocheting, stitching, and sewing), crafts, recipes and gardening.

NEW AGE PUBLICATIONS

see also Astrology; Parapsychology and Occultism

100   US
A U R A NEWSLETTER.* vol.3, no.2, 1981. 12/yr. $10. Association for Unity, Research and Awareness, c/o Bob Mahlman, Ed., 8539 Morning Glory Ln., Lincoln, NE 68505-3156.

200   US
AGAPE (LOS ANGELES). 1971. bi-m. donation. Truth Center, 506 Crestview Dr., Ojai, CA 93023-3204. TEL 213-876-6295. Ed. Val Schorre. circ. 2,500. (back issues avail.)
 Description: Articles dealing with the discovery of the divine Self within, and its by-product: the living of selfless love expressed to others.

133.9   GW   ISSN 0934-4535
ALLGEMEINE ZEITSCHRIFT FUER PARANORMOLOGIE. 1976. q. DM.38. Thraenstr. 13, 7900 Ulm, Germany. TEL 0731-33057. Ed. Hildegund Zehmke. bk.rev.; circ. 1,000.
 Formerly (until 1988): Allgemeine Zeitschrift fuer Parapsychologie (ISSN 0174-0288)

NEW AGE PUBLICATIONS   3593

AMMONITE. see *LITERATURE — Poetry*

ANCIENT SKIES. see *AERONAUTICS AND SPACE FLIGHT*

001.3 301.4   US   ISSN 0097-1146
AP2
ANIMA; the journal of human experience. 1974. s-a. $9.95. (Conocheague Associates, Inc.) Anima Publications, 1053 Wilson Ave., Chambersburg, PA 17201-1247. TEL 717-267-0087. Ed. Barbara D. Rotz. adv.; bk.rev.; circ. 1,000. (also avail. in microform from UMI) **Indexed:** Rel.& Theol.Abstr. (1988-), Rel.Ind.One, Rel.Per.
 —BLDSC shelfmark: 0902.919000.
 Description: Concentrates on the quest for human wholeness through values traditionally labeled "feminine." Presents critical new ideas in feminism, psychology and religion.

ANUBIS; Zeitschrift fuer praktische Magie und Psychonautik. see *PARAPSYCHOLOGY AND OCCULTISM*

AQUARIAN VOICES. see *ASTROLOGY*

051   US
ARIZONA NETWORKING NEWS. q. $10 (foreign $15). Tri-Pyramids, Inc., Box 5477, Scottsdale, AZ 85261-5477. TEL 602-951-1275. Ed. Joanne Henning Tedesco. adv.; bk.rev.; circ. 20,000. (tabloid format; back issues avail.)
 Description: Focuses on holistic health.

294.54   CN   ISSN 0315-8179
ASCENT (KOOTENAY BAY). 1970. 3/yr. $8. Yasodhara Ashram Society, Box 9, Kootenay Bay, B.C. V0B 1X0, Canada. TEL 604-227-9224. FAX 604-227-9494. Ed. Swami Gopalananda. bk.rev.; bibl.; charts; illus.; circ. 1,600.
 Description: Offers an integration of modern Western psychological tools with the practice of Yoga.

ASTROFLASH. see *ASTROLOGY*

133 110   US
THE BEACON (MIAMI SHORES). 1974. m. $5. Roundtable of the Light Centers, Inc., Box 531212, Miami Shores, FL 33153-1212. TEL 305-270-4778. Ed. Jay Johnson. adv.; bk.rev.; circ. 450. (tabloid format)

142   US
BETTER WORLD. 1985. bi-m. $17.95. Intergroup for Planetary Oneness, 17211 Orozco St., Granada Hills, CA 91344-1132. TEL 800-266-6624. FAX 818-360-2059. Ed. Tricia Harbula. adv.; bk.rev.; music rev.; circ. 30,000. (reprint service avail.)
 Formerly: Meditation.
 Description: Presents articles on personal, social and environmental issues with opinions and inspiration from leaders in those fields.

BIOFEEDBACK & SELF REGULATION. see *PSYCHOLOGY*

133.91   US
BODY, MIND & SPIRIT MAGAZINE. 1982. bi-m. $18. Island Publishing Company, Inc., Box 701, Providence, RI 02901. TEL 401-351-4320. FAX 401-272-5767. Ed. Paul Zuromski. adv.; bk.rev.; circ. 160,000. (back issues avail.)
 Supersedes: Body, Mind and Spirit; Which was formerly: Psychic Guide (ISSN 0745-8746)
 Description: Provides news and information on all aspects of New Age, from spirit channeling to nutritional supplements.

133   US   ISSN 0006-8233
BOTH SIDES NOW; an alternative journal of aquarian - new age transformations. 1969. irreg., latest no.27. $9 for 10 issues. Free People, Rt. 6, Box 28, Tyler, TX 75704-9712. TEL 903-592-4263. Ed. Elihu Edelson. adv.; bk.rev.; circ. 2,000. (also avail. in microform from UMI)

133   PY   ISSN 1017-2777
▼**BUHARDILLA.** 1990. m. Distribuidor Internacional Publicaciones Paraguayas, Torreani Viera 551, Villa Morra, Asuncion, Paraguay. adv.; circ. 1,000.

NEW AGE PUBLICATIONS

133   US
CATALYST (MARIETTA); a publication resource of New Age newsletters, book reviews, personals, holistic health, and psychic connections. 1985. a. $7.95 (foreign $12.95). Catalyst, Box 670022, Marietta, GA 30066. bk.rev. (back issues avail.)
    Formerly: Psychic Connections.

658   US
CATALYST DIRECTORY NEWSLETTER. 1985. a. $7.95. Catalyst, Box 670022, Marietta, GA 30066. adv.; bk.rev.; circ. 2,000. (back issues avail.)
    Formerly: Catalyst Perspective.
    Description: Lists metaphysical, New Age newsletters.

133   US
CELEBRATE LIFE!. 1988. q. $8. Unimedia Corporation, Box 247, 18395 Gulf Blvd., Ste. 201, Indian Rocks Beach, FL 34635. TEL 813-595-4141. Ed. Marty Johnson. adv.; circ. 10,000.
    Description: Focuses on positive awareness and self-discovery. Features include unique vacations, health-related travel and leisure, culture, the arts, retreats, workshops and New Thought.

CHRISTIAN NEW AGE QUARTERLY. see *RELIGIONS AND THEOLOGY*

110 133.5   US   ISSN 0009-6520
CHURCH OF LIGHT QUARTERLY. 1925. q. $10. Church of Light Inc., 2341 Coral St., Los Angeles, CA 90031-2916. TEL 213-226-0453. Ed. Lea Riffle. bk.rev.; charts; illus.; circ. 1,000.

327   US   ISSN 0896-8071
CLARION CALL;* the voice of transcendence. vol.2, 1989. q. $15 (foreign $18). Gaudiya Vaishnava Society, 815 Arnold Dr., Ste. 124, Martinez, CA 94553-6500. TEL 415-327-6002. (back issues avail.)

051   US
COMING CHANGES NEWSLETTER. Variant title: Changes Newsletter. 1979. 6/yr. $17.95. Changes Publishing Co., 937 St. Mary's St., DePere, WI 54115. TEL 414-336-4769. Richard C. Green. bk.rev.; illus.; circ. 1,500. (back issues avail.)
    Description: Covers current events and Christian prophecy.

COMMUNITIES; journal of cooperation. see *BUSINESS AND ECONOMICS — Cooperatives*

100   GW   ISSN 0932-5565
CONNECTION; fuer Spiritulitaet und Lebenskunst. 1985. m. DM.60. Connection Medien GmbH, Hauptstr. 5, 8267 Niedertaufkirchen, Germany. TEL 08639-600911. FAX 08639-1219. Ed. Sugata W. Schneider. adv.; bk.rev.; circ. 20,000. (back issues avail.)

133   US
COSMIC VOICE; cosmic revelations for the New Age. 1955. m. $16. Aetherius Society, 6202 Afton Pl., Hollywood, CA 90028-8298. TEL 213-465-9652. Ed. George King. adv.; illus.; circ. 700.
    Supersedes: Aetherius Society Newsletter; Cosmic Voice.

110   US
CREATIONS; a showcase of Long Island's creative spirit. vol.2, 1988. q. Creations Magazine, Box 295, Roslyn, NY 11576. TEL 516-484-5384. Ed. Zed J. Director.

100 808   CN   ISSN 0735-6501
CRITIQUE (WEST VANCOUVER); the juicy embrace between information and transformation. 1980. 4/yr. $15. Critique Publishing, Box 91980, W. Vancouver, B.C. V7V 4S4, Canada. TEL 604-925-0069. Ed. Bob Banner. adv.; bk.rev.; circ. 25,000. Indexed: Arts & Hum.Cit.Ind., Hum.Ind.

CRYSTAL RAINBOW. see *RELIGIONS AND THEOLOGY*

DA'AT; Jewish philosophy and Kabbalah. see *PHILOSOPHY*

DESIGN SPIRIT. see *ARCHITECTURE*

333.7   AT
DOWN TO EARTH NORTH EAST AUSTRALIA NEWSLETTER. Short title: D T E - N E A Newsletter. 1977. m. Aus.$25 (foreign Aus.$35). P.O. Box 341, Spring Hill, Qld. 4004, Australia. Ed. Dik Freestun. adv.; bk.rev.; circ. 750. (back issues avail.)
    Description: Presents information on a wide variety of events and techniques for raising awareness of real needs both personal and global. Special interest in total health and nature.

135.3 154.63   US   ISSN 1054-6707
BF1074
DREAM NETWORK; a quarterly journal exploring dreams and myth. 1982. q. $22 (Canada $26; $32 elsewhere). 1337 Powerhouse Ln., Ste. 22, Moab, UT 84532. TEL 801-259-5936. Ed. H. Roberta Ossana. bk.rev.; cum.index: 1982-1991; circ. 2,000. (back issues avail.)
    Formerly (until 1989): Dream Network Bulletin.
    Description: Provides a forum for exchange of ideas among individuals interested in understanding the symbologic language of dreams, with a focus on dream sharing and exploring relationships between dream and mythology.

EAR: MAGAZINE OF NEW MUSIC. see *MUSIC*

ELEMENTE; zur Metapolitik - fuer die Europaeische Wiedergeburt. see *PHILOSOPHY*

614.7   US
ELYSIUM: JOURNAL OF THE SENSES. Abbreviated title: J O T S. 1961. 4/yr. $4. (Elysium Institute, Inc.) Elysium Growth Press, 814 Robinson Rd., Topanga, CA 90290. TEL 213-455-1000. FAX 213-455-2007. TELEX 6975129. Ed. Art Kunkin. adv.; bk.rev.; circ. 15,000.
    Former titles: Journal of the Senses (ISSN 0741-8787); Elysium.

100   US   ISSN 0890-538X
EMERGING. 1987. s-a. $25. (Teleos Institute) L P Publications, Box 7601, San Diego, CA 92167-0601. TEL 619-225-0133. FAX 619-225-8109. Ed. Mariamne Paulus. illus.; circ. 600.
    Supersedes (1982-1986): Seeker Magazine (ISSN 0886-1285); (1972-1981): Seeker Newsletter (ISSN 0145-8361); (1969-1971): New Focus (ISSN 0047-9683)
    Description: Essays and commentary on spiritual consciousness and evolution, stressing the importance of universal and unconditional love, the study of wisdom teachings, and living life with purpose.

133 100   US
EMSHOCK LETTER. 1977. irreg. (7-12/yr.). $25. Vongrutnorv Og Press, Inc., Box 411, Randall Flat Rd., Troy, ID 83871-0411. TEL 208-835-4902. Ed. Steven E. Erickson. bk.rev.; circ. 25. (back issues avail.)
    Description: Provides an "experiment in consciousness", with no limit on variables. A positive yet realistic approach to human existence.

130   GW   ISSN 0003-2921
ESOTERA; neue Dimensionen des Bewusstseins. 1949. m. DM.72. Verlag Hermann Bauer KG, Kronenstr. 2-4, Postfach 167, 7800 Freiburg, Germany. TEL 761-7082109. Ed. Gert Geisler. adv.; bk.rev.; bibl.; charts; illus.; circ. 48,000.
    Formerly: Andere Welt.

181.45   US
EXPANDING LIGHT PROGRAM GUIDE. 1981. 3/yr. free. Ananda Church of God-Realization, 14618 Tyler Foote Rd., Nevada City, CA 95959. TEL 916-292-3494. Ed. Richard McCord. adv.; circ. 16,000.
    Former titles: Ananda Program Guide; Ananda.
    Description: Describes retreat programs in spiritual growth offered at Ananda Village.

100   US
FAITHIST JOURNAL. 1968. bi-m. $12 (foreign $20). Kosmon Publishing, Inc., 2324 Suffock Ave., Kingman, AZ 86401. TEL 602-757-4569. Eds. Charles W. Benfield, Kasandra Kares. bk.rev.; abstr.; charts; illus.; circ. 275. (back issues avail.)
    Description: New Age magazine discussing a variety of subjects such as UFO's, spiritualism, life after death, vegetarianism, astral travel, crystal power and I-Ching.

133   US   ISSN 1046-6029
FIREHEART; a journal of magic and spiritual transformation. 1988. s-a. $8.50. EarthSpirit Community, Box 462, Maynard, MA 01754. TEL 617-395-1023. (And: Box 365, Medford, MA 02155) Ed. Myrriah Lavin. adv.; bk.rev.; circ. 3,000. (back issues avail.)
    Description: Devoted to magic and nature spirituality and to exploring various traditions such as Wicca, Paganism, Shamanism and New Age spirituality.

FORESIGHT (BIRMINGHAM). see *PARAPSYCHOLOGY AND OCCULTISM*

FREE SPIRIT (BROOKLYN); a directory and journal of new realities. see *PHILOSOPHY*

133.5 100   US   ISSN 0894-6159
BL624
GNOSIS; a journal of the Western inner traditions. 1985. q. $20 to individuals; libraries $25. (Lumen Foundation) Jay Kinney, Box 14217, San Francisco, CA 94114-0217. TEL 415-255-0400. FAX 415-255-6329. Ed. Richard Smoley. adv.; bk.rev.; illus.; circ. 13,500.
    Description: Features non-sectarian articles and reviews on the mystical and esoteric spiritual paths of the Western world, from the perspectives of comparative religion, history and Jungian psychology.

615.53 613.2   US
GOOD LIFE TIMES;* choices in health, education and the arts. 1978. m. $20. Association for Wholistic Living, 6970 Central Ave., Lemon Grove, CA 91945-2110. Ed. Dr. Mark Solomon. adv.; bk.rev.; circ. 50,000.
    Formerly: Wholistic Living News.

DAS GROSSE LEBEN; Makrobiotik-Magazin. see *NUTRITION AND DIETETICS*

613.7 135   CN   ISSN 0827-7982
GUIDE RESSOURCES; nouvelles tendances, nouvelles valeurs. 1985. m. (10/yr.) Can.$29.95($52) S W A A Communications Inc., 4388 St-Denis St., Ste. 305, Montreal, Que. H2J 2L1, Canada. TEL 514-847-0060. FAX 514-847-0062. Ed. Christian Lamontagne. adv.; bk.rev.; circ. 26,928. Indexed: Pt.de Rep. (1989-).
    Description: Devoted to New Age topics: nutrition, environmental issues, psychology, health and spirituality.

619   US
HEALTH CONSCIOUSNESS; an holistic magazine. 1980. bi-m. $18. Dr. Roy Kupsinel, Ed. & Pub., Shangri-La Ln., Box 550, Oviedo, FL 32765. TEL 407-365-6681. FAX 407-365-1834. adv.; bk.rev.; illus.; circ. 2,000. (back issues avail.)
    Formerly: Kup's Komments.

HEARTSONG REVIEW; resource guide for New Age music of the spirit. see *MUSIC*

612   US
HOLISTIC LIVING; a celebration of life. 1983. bi-m. $12. Holistic Health Association of the Princeton Area, 360 Nassau St., Princeton, NJ 08540. TEL 609-924-8580. Ed. Jackie Schilder. adv.; bk.rev.; circ. 22,000.
    Description: Explores healing processes, environmental legislation and common health problems.

289.9 100   US
INNER JOURNEYS. 1987. q. $5. (Institute for the Development of the Harmonious Human Being, Inc.) Gateways Books and Tapes, Box 370, Nevada City, CA 95959. TEL 916-477-1116. FAX 916-432-1810. Ed. Iven Lourie. bk.rev.; circ. 2,500. (back issues avail.)
    Description: Promotional material and news for bookstores and retailers of metaphysical books.

181.45   US   ISSN 0149-6026
BL624
INNER PATHS. 1977. 12/yr. $15. Inner Paths Publications, Inc., 26 Reichert Circle, Westport, CT 06880. Ed. Louis Rogers. adv.; bk.rev.; circ. 33,500.

NEW AGE PUBLICATIONS

100   NR   ISSN 0794-7968
INSIGHT MAGAZINE; a magazine for spiritual development. (Text in English) 1987. m. $2 per no. OAL Research Publications Ltd., Cleanjohn House, 90 Ladipo House, P.O. Box 9802, Lagos, Nigeria. TEL 01-523-420. TELEX 27358. Ed. O.A. Lawal. adv.; circ. 25,000. (back issues avail.)

100   CN   ISSN 0712-7685
INTEGRITY INTERNATIONAL; honoring a gathering of light in 1992. 1972. q. Can.$22($22) Integrity International, P.O. Box 9, 100 Mile House, B.C. V0K 2E0, Canada. TEL 416-395-2026. Ed. Chris Foster. bk.rev.; circ. 1,750.
  Description: A quarterly publication in practical spirituality.

JOURNAL FOR THE STUDY OF CONSCIOUSNESS. see *PHILOSOPHY*

JOURNAL OF REGRESSION THERAPY. see *PSYCHOLOGY*

KARUNA: A JOURNAL OF BUDDHIST MEDITATION. see *RELIGIONS AND THEOLOGY — Buddhist*

100 289.9   US
KOOKS MAGAZINE. 1989. q. $15. Out-of-Kontrol Data Institute, Box 953, Allston, MA 02134. TEL 617-782-5602. Ed. Donna Kossy. adv.; bk.rev.; charts; illus.; circ. 750 (controlled). (back issues avail.)
  Formerly (until Feb. 1990): Original Donna Kossy's Kooks Magazine (ISSN 1045-103X)
  Description: Covers fringe beliefs and those who hold them, including religious and political cults and extremists, schizophrenics, visionaries, and weird science.

KWAN UM ZEN SCHOOL NEWSLETTER. see *RELIGIONS AND THEOLOGY — Buddhist*

613.7   US
L A RESOURCES. 1981. 4/yr. $10. Community Resource Publications, 18822 Beach Blvd., Ste. 211, Huntington Beach, CA 92648-2055. TEL 714-963-7697. FAX 719-963-4794. Ed. Brian Enright. adv.; bk.rev.; circ. 80,000. (back issues avail.)
  Formerly (until 1983): Light Directory.

133.9   AT   ISSN 1033-0186
LIFESTYLES SEASON. 1986. q. Aus.$25. Queensland Awareness Centre Pty. Ltd., P.O. Box 1201, Runaway Bay, Gold Coast, Qld. 4216, Australia. TEL 075-771-322. FAX 085-773-947. Eds. Jonathan Sherwood, Anne Boyd. index; circ. 1,500.
  Description: Covers relaxation, advanced healing techniques, courses on ESP and channeling, workshop and private appointments available in U.S.A.

301   US
LIVING FREE; a personal journal of self liberation. 1979. bi-m. $9. Living Free, Box 29, Hiler Branch, Buffalo, NY 14223. Ed. Jim Stumm. adv.; bk.rev.; circ. 200. (also avail. in microfiche; back issues avail.)
  Description: Survivalists, homesteaders and anarchists discuss self-reliant living.

101
LOVE; the journal of the human spirit. 1978. irreg. free. Box 9, Prospect Hill, NC 27314-0009. Eds. Bob Love, Pat Warren. circ. 100.

LYNX; a quarterly journal of renga. see *ORIENTAL STUDIES*

179.3   US   ISSN 0147-1201
M A I N. (Mark-Age Inform-Nations) 1960. q. $20 (foreign $25). Mark-Age, Inc., Box 290368, Ft. Lauderdale, FL 33329. TEL 305-587-5555. Ed. Pauline Sharpe. bk.rev.; film rev.; play rev.; bibl.; circ. 1,000. (back issues avail.)
  Description: Contains news, educational articles and guidelines for linking of light workers and groups as preparation for the Second Coming and New Age of Aquarius.

133.9   US
MAD SCIENTIST. m. $25. Heritage Institute of Psychic Science, Box 114, Plainfield, WI 54966.
  Description: Devoted exclusively to self-help information and instruction for the "New Ager".

700   US   ISSN 1040-4287
MAGICAL BLEND; a transformative journey. 1980. q. $14 (foreign $16). Magical Blend Publishers, Box 11303, San Francisco, CA 94101. TEL 415-673-1001. FAX 415-673-0323. Ed. Jerry Snyder. adv.; bk.rev.; film rev.; charts; illus.; tr.lit.; circ. 40,000. (back issues avail.)
  Description: Contains articles on new age metaphysics, healing, anciet mysticism, human potentials, transformational psychology, holistic health, interspecies communication as well as fantasy, comics, art and poetry.

MAGICKAL UNICORN MESSENGER. see *PARAPSYCHOLOGY AND OCCULTISM*

133   US
MANY HANDS; resources for personal and social transformation. 1979. q. $10. c/o Beyond Words Bookshop, 150 Main St., Northhampton, MA 01060. TEL 413-586-5037. Ed. Polly S. Baumer. adv.; bk.rev.; film rev.illus.; circ. 30,000. (back issues avail.)

100   US
MASTER OF LIFE. 1976. q. free. Valley of the Sun Publishing Co., Box 38, Malibu, CA 90265. TEL 818-889-1575. FAX 818-706-3606. Ed. Dick Sutphen. adv.; bk.rev.; circ. 250,000.
  Formerly: Self-Help Update.
  Description: Promotes mental, physical and philosophical self-sufficiency through awareness and reprogramming techniques.

156   GW
MERIDIAN;* Zeitschrift fuer Kosmobiologie, Astrologie und angewandte Psychologie. 1979. 6/yr. DM.52. Ebertin-Verlag, Kronenstr. 2, Postfach 167, 7800 Freiberg, Germany.
  Incorporates: Kosmobiologie (ISSN 0023-4214) & Kosmischer Beobachter.

METAPSICHICA; rivista italiana di parapsicologia. see *PARAPSYCHOLOGY AND OCCULTISM*

METASCIENCE ANNUAL; a New Age journal of parapsychology. see *PARAPSYCHOLOGY AND OCCULTISM*

MONTHLY PLANET. see *POLITICAL SCIENCE — International Relations*

700 780   US   ISSN 0892-2721
MUSIC OF THE SPHERES; a quarterly magazine of art and music for the New Age. 1988. q. $14. Music of the Spheres Publishing, Box 1751, Taos, NM 87571. TEL 505-758-0405. Ed. John Patrick Lamkin. adv.; bk.rev.; film rev.; play rev.; illus.; circ. 10,000.
  Description: Focuses on promoting and networking the art and music of the New Age, and to promote world peace.

301   AG   ISSN 0326-0666
MUTANTIA; cuadernos eco-espirituales. 1980. q. $30. Ediciones Mutantia, Casilla 260, Sucursal 12, 1412 Buenos Aires, Argentina. FAX 541-3311033. Dir. Miguel Grinberg. adv.; bk.rev.; illus.; circ. 12,000. (also avail. in microfilm; back issues avail.)
  Description: Covers documents exploring the building of the 21st century's society, transformational education, focusing on human potentials and alternative ways of living.

NATURAL HEALING & NUTRITION ANNUAL. see *PHYSICAL FITNESS AND HYGIENE*

NEW AGE ASTROLOGY GUIDE (YEAR). see *ASTROLOGY*

133   US
NEW AGE DIGEST. 1983. irreg. donation or exchange basis. New Age Press, Box 1373, Keala Kekua, HI 96750. TEL 808-328-8013. Ed. Jim Butler. circ. 400.

110   US
NEW AGE EXCHANGE;* a magazine of contemporary metaphysical thought. 1986. 6/yr. $18. Zoan Publishing Co., Inc., 88 Shefield St., Old Saybrook, CT 06475. Ed. S. Jasinski. adv.; bk.rev.; circ. 1,000. (back issues avail.)

051   US   ISSN 0746-3618
NEW AGE JOURNAL. 1974. bi-m. $24. Rising Star Associates, Ltd. Partnership, 342 Western Ave., Brighton, MA 02135. TEL 617-787-2005. FAX 617-787-2879. (Subscr. to: Box 53275, Boulder, CO 80321-327553) Ed. Peggy Taylor. adv.; bk.rev.; illus.; circ. 150,835. (also avail. in microfiche from UMI) **Indexed:** Alt.Press Ind., Bk.Rev.Ind. (1981-), Child.Bk.Rev.Ind. (1981-), New Per.Ind.
  Former titles (until 1983): New Age Magazine (ISSN 0164-3967); New Age Journal.
  Description: Explores holistic health, personal growth and social change.

070.5   US   ISSN 1042-6566
NEW AGE RETAILER; books, music, merchandise. 1987. bi-m. $15 (foreign $24). Continuity Publishing, Inc., Box 224, Greenbank, WA 98253. TEL 206-678-7772. FAX 206-678-8803. Ed. Duane Sweeney. adv.; bk.rev.; circ. 5,800 (controlled).
  Formerly (until 1989): Monthly Report to Booksellers.
  Description: Trade journal focusing on quality material for retailers of new age books, and music. Includes articles and reviews.

299   US
NEW AGE TEACHINGS. 1967. bi-m. contribution. New Age Teaching Center of Learning, 37 Maple St., Brookfield, MA 01506. TEL 508-867-3754. Ed. Anita Afton. bk.rev.; circ. 3,000.

133   US
NEW CONSCIOUSNESS SOURCEBOOK;* spiritual community guide. 1972. biennial. $8.95. Arcline Publishing, c/o Highpoint Type-Graphics, 131 Spring St., Claremont, CA 91711-4930. TEL 714-623-1738. Eds. P.S. & D.K. Khalsa. adv.; circ. 10,000. (back issues avail.)

100   US   ISSN 1040-2047
NEW DAY HERALD. 1975. bi-m. $25 (effective Mar. 1991). (Church of the Movement of Spiritual Inner Awareness) Mandeville Press, Box 3935, Los Angeles, CA 90051. FAX 213-737-5680. Ed. Victoria Marine. adv.; circ. 6,000. (tabloid format; back issues avail.)
  Formerly (until 1988): Movement Newspaper.

301   US
NEW ENVIRONMENT BULLETIN. 1974. m. $7.50 in N. America; elsewhere $11.50. New Environment Association, 270 Fenway Dr., Syracuse, NY 13224. TEL 315-446-8009. Ed. Harry Schwarzlander. bk.rev.; circ. 150.
  Description: Articles, reviews and announcements dealing with a wide range of ecological and social topics; includes reports on activities of the New Environment Association.

100   US   ISSN 0886-4616
NEW FRONTIER; magazine of transformation. 1981. m. $18. New Frontier Education Society, 46 N. Front St., Philadelphia, PA 19106. TEL 215-627-5683. FAX 215-440-9945. Ed. Sw. Virato. adv.; bk.rev.; film rev.; music rev.; circ. 60,000. (back issues avail.)
  Description: Presents informative articles by, and interviews with, internationally respected leaders in the New Age field. Covers holistic helath, metaphysics, yoga, natural foods, astrology and events.

613   US
NEW LIFE; for those who want to make a change. bi-m. $10. Serenity Health Organization, Inc., Box 1408, Ansonia Sta., New York, NY 10023. TEL 212-496-0354. Ed. Mark Becker. circ. 60,000.
  Formerly: Serenity's New Life.
  Description: Reference and resource guide for holistic health, environment and New Age. Examines consciousness and the human potential, and provides information on products and services.

100   US   ISSN 1044-2782
NEW TIMES (SEATTLE); the Northwest's monthly new age community newspaper. 1985. m. $12. Silver Owl Publications, Inc., Box 51186, Seattle, WA 98115-1186. TEL 206-524-9071. Ed. Krysta Gibson. adv.; bk.rev.; film rev.; circ. 17,000. (back issues avail.)
  Incorporates (in 1991): Inner Woman; Which was formerly: Spiritual Women's Times.
  Description: Examines human potential, peace and numerous spiritual alternatives.

NEW AGE PUBLICATIONS

100   US   ISSN 1040-8185
NEW WAVES (WASHINGTON). 1985. m. membership. Proutist Universal, Inc., 1354 Montague St., N.W., Box 56466, Washington, DC 20040. TEL 202-829-2278. FAX 202-829-0462. Ed. D. Dhruva. bk.rev.; illus.; circ. 4,000. (back issues avail.)
     Description: Informs members of developments in the PROUT (Progressive Utilization Theory) movement, social projects, and activities of other progressive organizations.

NEW YORK BODIES. see *PHYSICAL FITNESS AND HYGIENE*

133   DK   ISSN 0108-3503
NYT ASPEKT; magazine for alternative living and thinking. 1983. bi-m. DKK 260. Nyt Aspekt, Griffenfeldsgade 7A, 2200 Copenhagen N, Denmark. TEL 35-37-60-63. FAX 31-39-1789. Ed. Steen Landsy. adv.; bk.rev.; circ. 10,000.
     Formed by the merger of: Psykisk Forum (ISSN 0108-7800); U F O Aspekt (ISSN 0107-0258)
     Description: Covers spiritual science, personal growth, health, parapsychology and alternative thinking and living.

133   US
O P R A NEWSLETTER. 1975. 12/yr. $10. Organization of Psychic Research Associates, Box 60901, Oklahoma City, OK 73146-0901. TEL 405-557-8048. adv.; bk.rev.; circ. 500.

ODYSSEY; an adventure in more conscious living. see *PHILOSOPHY*

OMEGA NEW AGE DIRECTORY. see *BUSINESS AND ECONOMICS — Trade And Industrial Directories*

100   US
ON COURSE; weekly perspectives on the inner journey. 1983. 40/yr. $2.50 per week. Interfaith Fellowship, 459C Carol Dr., Monroe, NY 10950. TEL 914-783-0383. FAX 914-873-0383. Ed. Jon Mundy. adv.; bk.rev.; bibl.; illus.; circ. 1,200. (back issues avail.)
     Formerly: Mustard Seed.
     Description: Helps bring people of different faiths together. Includes daily meditations, quotations, jokes, parables, prayers, poems, and seasonal perspectives.

133   CN   ISSN 0845-471X
ONTARIO'S COMMON GROUND MAGAZINE. 1975. 4/yr. Can.$15 (foreign Can.$22). 320 Danforth Ave., Ste.204, Toronto, Ont. M4K 1P3, Canada. TEL 416-463-6677. Ed. Julia Woodford. adv.; bk.rev.; circ. 39,000 (controlled). (back issues avail.)
     Description: Ontario's guide to personal growth and natural living.

615.53   US
ORANGE COUNTY RESOURCES. 1984. q. $10. Community Resource Publications, 18822 Beach Blvd., Ste. 211, Huntington Beach, CA 92648-2055. TEL 714-963-7697. FAX 714-963-4794. Ed. Brian Enright. bk.rev.; circ. 40,000. (tabloid format; back issues avail.)
     Description: Community New Age and holistic resource guide for healing, growth and transformation.

100   US
PERSPECTIVE ON CONSCIOUSNESS & PSI RESEARCH. 1979. 12/yr. membership. A.R.E. Press, Box 595, Virginia Beach, VA 23451. TEL 804-428-3588. Ed. Henry Reed. circ. 70,000.

110   US
PHENOMENEWS; exploring human potential, holistic health and living. 1978. m. $14. PhenomeNews Inc., 18444 W. 10 Mile Rd., No. 105, Southfield, MI 48075-2626. TEL 313-569-3888. Ed. Cindy Saul. adv.; bk.rev.; circ. 20,000. (tabloid format)

179.3   US
POLY. m. $22. Luna Ventures, Box 398, Suisun, CA 94585. Ed. Paul Doerr.
     Description: Covers line marriage, polygamy and other alternate lifestyles, with articles on the law and living arrangements, and readers' letters.

100   BE
PRESSE-INTER. 1981. w. 1000 Fr. (effective 1992). Centre d'Inter-Action Culturelle, 4 rue de la Procession, B-1331 Rosieres, Belgium. TEL 02-653-53-24. Ed. Pierre Houart. adv.; bk.rev.
     Formerly: Alternatives (ISSN 0770-4437)
     Description: Examines peace and non-violence in culture and spirituality.

PRIMARY POINT. see *RELIGIONS AND THEOLOGY — Buddhist*

133 616.89   US   ISSN 0893-8148
PSYCH IT; the sophisticated newsletter for everyone. 1986. q. $8 (foreign $21). c/o Charlotte Babicky, Ed., 6507 Bimini Ct., Apollo Beach, FL 33572. adv.; illus.; circ. 100. (back issues avail.)
     Description: Attempts to further psychology and increase one's awareness through creativity. Includes writers, poets, artists, caroonists and crossword puzzle creators.

PSYCHIC READER. see *PARAPSYCHOLOGY AND OCCULTISM*

PSYCHICAL STUDIES. see *PARAPSYCHOLOGY AND OCCULTISM*

200   US   ISSN 1040-533X
THE QUEST (WHEATON). 1988. q. $14 (foreign $17). Theosophical Society in America, 1926 N. Main St., Box 270, Wheaton, IL 60189-0270. TEL 708-668-1571. FAX 708-665-8791. Ed. William Metzger. adv.; bk.rev.; circ. 20,000.
     Description: A journal of philosophy, religion, science, and the arts.

299   US
▼**QUINTILE**. 1991. 4/yr. free. Box 89, Hales Corners, WI 53130. TEL 414-529-0411. bk.rev.

133   US   ISSN 1040-5836
THE RADIANCE TECHNIQUE JOURNAL. 1980. 3/yr. $4 per no. (free to members). The Radiance Technique Association International, Inc., Box 40570, St. Petersburg, FL 33743-0570. Dir. Fred W. Wright, Jr. adv.; bk.rev.; circ. 5,000. (back issues avail.)
     Formerly: Reiki Journal.
     Description: Features alumni sharing of their use of the Radiance Technique; includes the latest articles on the subject.

100   US
RAINBOW RAY FOCUS. 6/yr. $12. Magnificent Consummation Inc., Box 1188, Sedona, AZ 86336. Ed. Angel Violet.
     Formerly: Ruby Focus.

610   GW   ISSN 0722-7949
RAUM UND ZEIT; die neue Dimension der Wissenschaft. 1981. bi-m. DM.75 (foreign DM.83). Ehlers Verlag GmbH, Daimlerstr. 5, 8029 Sauerlach, Germany. TEL 08104-2269. FAX 08104-2127. Ed. Hans-Joachim Ehlers. adv.; bk.rev.; circ. 20,000. (back issues avail.)

100 133   US   ISSN 0886-036X
REALITY CHANGE; a magazine for people who want to change their lives. 1980. q. $18 (typically set in Aug.). Austin Seth Center, Box 7786, Austin, TX 78713-7786. TEL 512-479-8909. Ed. Maude Cardwell. bk.rev.; circ. 700. (back issues avail.)

REFLECTIONS QUARTERLY RESOURCE DIRECTORY. see *BUSINESS AND ECONOMICS — Trade And Industrial Directories*

808.81   US
RESONANCE (NEW YORK); new voices for a new age. 1988. q. $12. Box 215, Beacon, NY 12508. TEL 914-838-1217. Ed. Evan T. Pritchard. adv.; bk.rev.; circ. 2,000.
     Description: Presents articles on dreams, spiritual fiction, greenhouse effect, New Age music as medicine., poetry, art and humor.

100   US
REVELATIONS OF AWARENESS. 1972. 17/yr. $42. Cosmic Awareness Communications, Box 115, Olympia, WA 98507. Ed. Avaton. bk.rev.; circ. 3,100.
     Description: Explains UFOs, the alien presence, other mysteries, plus spiritual philosophy, and life-after-death.

301   US   ISSN 0275-6935
BF309
REVISION; the journal of consciousness and change. 1978. q. $26 to individuals; institutions $44. (Helen Dwight Reid Education Foundation) Heldref Publications, 1319 Eighteenth St., N.W., Washington, DC 20036-1802. TEL 202-296-6267. FAX 202-296-5149. Ed. Slyvia Nothman. adv.; bk.rev.; abstr.; bibl.; charts; stat.; tr.lit.; circ. 5,400. (also avail. in microform from UMI; back issues avail.) **Indexed:** Alt.Press Ind., Psychol.Abstr. —BLDSC shelfmark: 7800.565000.
     Refereed Serial

051   US
▼**SAN DIEGO RESOURCES**. 1991. q. $12. Community Resource Publications, 18822 Beach Blvd., Ste. 211, Huntington Beach, CA 92648-2955. TEL 714-963-7697. FAX 714-963-4794. Ed. Brian Enright. circ. 40,000. (tabloid format; back issues avail.)
     Description: Community New Age and historical resource guide for healing, growth and transformation.

SELF & SOCIETY; European journal of humanistic psychology. see *PSYCHOLOGY*

SELF-REALIZATION. see *RELIGIONS AND THEOLOGY*

133   UK   ISSN 0266-8599
BD511
SHADOW. 1984. 2/yr. £1.50 per no. Traditional Cosmology Society, School of Scottish Studies, University of Edinburgh, 27 George Square, Edinburgh EH8 9LD, Scotland. TEL 031-667-1011. —BLDSC shelfmark: 8254.560910.
     Description: Studies myth; religion, and cosmology.

100   UK   ISSN 0262-9356
SHARE IT; a magazine to celebrate & promote awareness of our true identity. 1979. irreg. £1.50 per no. Roots Church Ln., Playford, Ipswich IP6 9DS, England. TEL 0473-624556. Ed. Ann Seward. bk.rev.; illus.; circ. 500. (back issues avail.)
     Formerly: Nacton Newsletter.

300   US
SPECTRUM MAGAZINE (LOS ANGELES). (Includes World Directory) 1965. q. $8. Unity-and-Diversity World Council, 1010 S. Flower St., No. 500, Los Angeles, CA 90015-1428. TEL 213-742-6832. FAX 213-748-2432. Ed. Louis K. Acheson. adv.; bk.rev.; circ. 1,000. (tabloid format) **Indexed:** Abstr.Engl.Stud.
     Formerly: Unity-in-Diversity Centers Bulletin (ISSN 0038-7037)
     Description: Focuses toward creating a new universal person and civilization

133   US
SPIRITUAL EMERGENCE NETWORK NEWSLETTER. * 1982. s-a. membership. Spiritual Emergence Network, 5905 Soquel Dr., Ste. 650, Soquel, CA 94073-2850. TEL 415-327-2776. bk.rev.; bibl.; tr.; lit.; circ. 8,000. (tabloid format; back issues avail.)

131   UK   ISSN 0038-7622
THE SPIRITUAL HEALER; journal of spiritual healing and philosophy. 1953. bi-m. free. Harry Edwards Spiritual Healing Sanctuary Trust, Burrows Lea, Shere, Guildford, Surrey GU5 9QG, England. Ed. Ramus Branch. adv.; illus.; index; circ. 6,750.

133.5   US
STAR BEACON. 1987. m. $14. (U F O Contact Center International, Delta County) Earth Star Publications, Box 117, Paonia, CA 81428. TEL 303-872-4678. Ed. Ann Ulrich. adv.; bk.rev.; circ. 500. (looseleaf format; back issues avail.; reprint service avail.)
     Description: For UFO percipients offering a wide variety of metaphysical information and promoting spiritual awareness.

STAR TECH; the real cosmic connection. see *ASTRONOMY*

100   US
STARLITE TIMES; * a publication for body, mind & spirit. 1988. bi-m. $15. Under the Stars Publishing Co., c/o Life Quest, Box 268, Boonton, NJ 07005. TEL 201-843-4455. Eds. Ernest D. Chu, Sharon L. Tesauro. adv.; bk.rev.; circ. 70,000.

301.1 150 613.7   US
STRESS MASTER. 1983. s-a. $1. Conscious Living Foundation, Inc., Box 9, Drain, OR 97435. TEL 503-836-2358. FAX 503-836-2930. Ed. Tim Lowenstein. adv.; bk.rev.; circ. 80,000. (back issues avail.)
 Formerly: Gentle Places and Quiet Spaces.
 Description: Self-improvement through biofeedback, stress management, and relaxation.

135
SUBCONSCIOUSLY SPEAKING; you can change your life through the power of your mind. 1985. bi-m. $12 (foreign $15). Harriman Publishing Co. (Subsidiary of: Infinity Institute International, Inc.), 4110 Edgeland, Dept. 800, Royal Oak, MI 48073-2251. TEL 313-549-5594. Ed. Anne H. Spencer. adv.; bk.rev.; circ. 3,500.
 Description: To elevate the consciousness of all who read through current information regarding hypnosis, imagery, and healing of body, mind and spirit.

100   US
SUPPORTIVE LIFESTYLES NEWS. 1972. 12/yr. $25. Fellowship of the Inner Light, 620 14 St., Virginia Beach, VA 23451. TEL 703-896-3673. FAX 804-428-6648. Ed. Myrrh Haslam. adv.; bk.rev. (tabloid format)

100 370.15   US   ISSN 0743-1384
TALK OF THE MONTH. 1983. m. $150. (Institute for the Development of the Harmonious Human Being, Inc.) Gateways Books and Tapes, Box 370, Nevada City, CA 95959. TEL 916-477-1116. FAX 916-432-1810. Ed. Iven Lourie. cum.index 1983-1985; 1986-1988; circ. 150. (back issues avail.)
 Description: Studies metaphysical and transformational ideas.

100 152   US
TAROT NETWORK NEWS. 1981. s-a. $10. Taroco, P.O. Box 104, Sausalito, CA 94966. TEL 415-332-9254. Ed. Gary W. Ross. adv.; bk.rev.; circ. 350. (back issues avail.)
 Description: A guide to the content and application of the Tarot.

133   US
TERRITORIAL HERALD. 1981. q. $3 (foreign $5). Ministry of the Interior, RP 200-0203, Box 7075, Laguna Niguel, CA 92677. TEL 714-240-8472. circ. 200. (back issues avail.)

TO YOUR HEALTH!; the magazine of healing and hope. see *PHYSICAL FITNESS AND HYGIENE*

133 200 615.53   US
TRANSFORMATION TIMES; New Age journal. 1982. 10/yr. $8. (Christ Light Community Church) Life Resources Unlimited, Box 425, Beavercreek, OR 97004. TEL 503-632-7141. Ed. Connie L. Faubel. adv.; bk.rev.; circ. 8,000. (tabloid format)

TRANSFORMERS NOTEBOOK. see *DRUG ABUSE AND ALCOHOLISM*

100   US
TRUTH JOURNAL. 1968. 10/yr. $10. Center for Spiritual Awareness, Lake Rubun Rd., Lakemont, GA 30552. TEL 404-782-4723. Ed. Roy E. Davis. bk.rev.; illus.; circ. 7,500. **Indexed:** CERDIC.

ULTIMO (KIEL); Kiel's Stadtmagazin. see *GENERAL INTEREST PERIODICALS — Germany*

100   US
UNARIUS LIGHT MAGAZINE. 1974. 4/yr. $20. Unarius Academy of Science Publications, 145 S. Magnolia Ave., El Cajon, CA 92020-4522. TEL 619-447-4170. FAX 619-447-6485. Eds. Ruth E. Norman, Barbara Reynolds. adv.; bk.rev.; circ. 500.
 Description: Presents dialogs or communications about a range of topics, from intelligent minds of more advanced people who once lived on Earth, to incorporating the interdimensional physics of energy and of the consciousness.

133   US
THE UNEXPLAINED; mysteries of life explained. 1960. q. $10. (M U - Metaphysical Union) Krastman Productions, Box 16790, Encino, CA 91416. TEL 818-705-8865. Ed. Hank Krastman. adv.; bk.rev.; circ. 10,000 (paid); 20,000 (controlled). (also avail. in video cassette; back issues avail.)

334   US
UTOPIA 2; commune co-operation as a global dynamic. 1985. q. $24. Kerista Consciousness Church, 547 Frederick St., San Francisco, CA 94117. TEL 415-759-4625. FAX 415-759-2490. Ed.Bd. circ. 500.
 Former titles: Kerista Book Series; Kerista: Journal of the U S Utopian Movement and the International Kibbutz Movement (ISSN 0743-3301)

200 133   US   ISSN 0748-3406
VENTURE INWARD. 1984. bi-m. membership. Association for Research and Enlightenment, Inc., Box 595, Virginia Beach, VA 23451. TEL 804-428-3588. FAX 804-422-4631. Ed. A. Robert Smith. bk.rev.; index; circ. 75,000.
 Supersedes: A.R.E. Journal.
 Description: Publishes articles that relate to the parapsychology, metaphysical and spiritual concepts contained in the readings of the late psychic Edgar Cdyce.

133   US
VISIONS (MIAMI). 1988. m. $15. Edie & Michael Moser, 3250 N.W. 77th Ct., Ste. 707, Miami, FL 33122. TEL 305-599-9242. Ed. Michael Moser. adv.; bk.rev.; music rev. (back issues avail.)
 Description: Explores the realms of relationships, wellness, addictions and recovery, and the environment through a New Age perspective; also includes a calendar of events.

VITA NUOVA; realta spiritica. see *SCIENCES: COMPREHENSIVE WORKS*

133.9   GW
WEGE MAGAZIN; zur Integration von Natur und Mensch. 1982. bi-m. DM.15. (Frankfurter Ring e.V.) Verlag Aviva W. Dahlberg, Kobbachstr. 12, 6000 Frankfurt a.M. 50, Germany. TEL 089-782123. FAX 089-784601. Ed. Wolfgang Dahlberg. adv.; circ. 13,000.
 Formerly: Wege... (ISSN 0177-4891)

WELCOME TO PLANET EARTH; journal of new astrology in the contemporary world. see *ASTROLOGY*

327   AU
WELT SPIRALE UND AGNI YOGA; Zeitschrift fuer Fortschritt und Welterneuerung. 1961. m. S.500. Welt-Spirale - Ethische Gesellschaft fuer Forschritt und Welterneuerung, Wienerstr. 12, A-4020 Linz, Austria. Ed. Willy Augustat. circ. 1,500.
 Formerly: Welt Agni (ISSN 0043-2555)
 Description: Comments on politics, economics, technical problems, religion, and philosophy on the basis of the theosophical teaching.

051   US   ISSN 0749-5056
AP2
WHOLE EARTH REVIEW. 1974. q. $20. Point Foundation, 27 Gate Five Rd., Sausalito, CA 94965. TEL 415-332-1716. FAX 415-332-2416. Ed. Howard Rheingold. bk.rev.; film rev.; charts; illus.; index; circ. 50,000. (also avail. in microform from UMI; back issues avail.) **Indexed:** Acad.Ind., Access (1978-), Alt.Press Ind., Bk.Rev.Ind. (1989-), CAD CAM Abstr., Child.Bk.Ind. (1989-), Consum.Ind., Energy Rev., Fut.Surv., Hum.Ind., Microcomp.Ind., New Per.Ind.
 ●Also available online. Vendor(s): DIALOG. Also available on CD-ROM.
 —BLDSC shelfmark: 9311.953670.
 Formed by the 1984 merger of: Whole Earth Software Review; CoEvolution Quarterly (ISSN 0095-134X); Which superseded (1969-1974): Whole Earth Catalog (ISSN 0043-5031)
 Description: Features cover a broad variety of holistic topics. Each issue offers computer-related articles.

613.2 614.7   US   ISSN 0279-5590
          CODEN: CMMOD9
WHOLE LIFE TIMES.* 1979. 8/yr. $11.95. Whole Life Company, Inc., 7 Hundred Oaks Ln., Ashland, MA 01721-2341. Ed. Kimberly French. adv.; bk.rev.; circ. 140,000. (tabloid format) **Indexed:** Alt.Press Ind., Hlth.Ind.

133.5   US
WINGED CHARIOT; a tarot newsletter. 1981. irreg. $10. MoonStar Enterprises, Box 1718, Milwaukee, WI 53201-1718. Ed. Tracey A. Hoover. adv.; bk.rev.; circ. 100. (looseleaf format; back issues avail.)

WINGED MERCURY MISSIVE. see *SOCIOLOGY*

WINGSPAN: JOURNAL OF THE MALE SPIRIT. see *MEN'S STUDIES*

WITCHES INTERNATIONAL CRAFT ASSOCIATES. W I C A NEWSLETTER. see *PARAPSYCHOLOGY AND OCCULTISM*

160   US   ISSN 0898-5839
WITHIN AND BEYOND. 1984. q. $10. National Alliance for Spiritual Growth, Box 2683, Lafayette, LA 70502. TEL 318-235-6535. Eds. Dan Latour, Melissa Latour. adv.; bk.rev.; circ. 875. (looseleaf format)
 Former titles: National Alliance for Spiritual Growth. Bulletin; National Association for Metaphysics. Bulletin.
 Description: Covers issues pertaining to health, counseling and teaching, and reviews products and services.

133   US   ISSN 0740-6754
THE WORD. 1986. q. $15. Word Foundation, Inc., Box 180340, Dallas, TX 75218. TEL 214-348-5006. Ed. Neil F. Avery. (tabloid format; back issues avail.)
 Description: Sheds light on problems of human living for individuals seeking to make progress through self - improvement.

181.45   US   ISSN 1055-7911
B132.Y6
YOGA INTERNATIONAL. 1981. bi-m. $15 (Canada $20; elsewhere $25). (Himalayan International Institute of Yoga Science and Philosophy) Yoga International, Inc., RR 1, Box 407, Honesdale, PA 18431. TEL 717-253-6241. FAX 717-253-9078. TELEX 510 600 1805. Ed. Deborah Willoughby. illus.; circ. 5,000. (back issues avail.)
 Supersedes (in July 1991): Dawn (Honesdale) (ISSN 0277-4461)

613   US   ISSN 0191-0965
YOGA JOURNAL; for health and conscious living. 1975. bi-m. $18. California Yoga Teachers Association, 2054 University Ave., No. 601, Berkeley, CA 94704-1082. TEL 510-841-9200. FAX 510-644-3101. (Subscr. to: Box 3755, Escondido, CA 92033-3755) Ed. Stephan Bodian. adv.; bk.rev.; circ. 66,000. (also avail. in microform from UMI; back issues avail.) **Indexed:** New Per.Ind.
 Description: Covers yoga, holistic health, psychology, New Age consciousness, meditation and Eastern spirituality.

133.323   GW
ZEITSCHRIFT FUER RADIAESTHESIE UND HARMONIEFINDUNG. 1949. q. DM.26. (Zentrum fuer Radiaesthesie) Herold-Verlag Dr. Franz Wetzel und Co. KG, Kirchbachweg 16, 8000 Munich 71, Germany. Ed. Claus Wetzel. adv.; bk.rev.; bibl.; charts; illus.; index, cum.index: 1950-1961; circ. 2,000.
 Formerly: Zeitschrift fuer Radiaesthesie (ISSN 0044-3425)

NUCLEAR ENERGY

see *Energy-Nuclear Energy*

NUCLEAR PHYSICS

see *Physics-Nuclear Physics*

NUMISMATICS

737   US
A N S NEWSLETTER. 1979. q. American Numismatic Society, Broadway at 155th St., New York, NY 10032. TEL 212-234-3130. Ed. Elam Martin. circ. 1,400.

737   CS   ISSN 0862-1195
ACTA MUSEI MORAVIAE. SUPPLEMENTUM: FOLIA NUMISMATICA. (Text in Czech; summaries in English, French, German, Russian) 1965? a. $17.50. Moravske Zemske Muzeum, Numismaticke Oddeleni, Zelny trh 6, 65937 Brno, Czechoslovakia. TEL 42-5-22241. FAX 42-5-25279. illus.; index; circ. 700.
 Incorporates: Moravskie Numismaticke Zpravy (ISSN 0077-152X)

NUMISMATICS

737.4 US
CJ1
AMERICAN JOURNAL OF NUMISMATICS. SERIES 2. 1866. a. $30. American Numismatic Society, Broadway at 155th St., New York, NY 10032. TEL 212-345-3130. circ. 2,400. (back issues avail.)
 Former titles (until 1989): American Journal of Numismatics (ISSN 1053-8356); (until 1924): Museum Notes (New York) (ISSN 0145-1413)
 Description: Academic analysis of numismatic objects contributing to the understanding and interpretation of history, political science, archaeology, and art history.

737 US ISSN 0569-6720
CJ15
AMERICAN NUMISMATIC SOCIETY. ANNUAL REPORT. a. free. American Numismatic Society, Broadway at 155th St., New York, NY 10032. TEL 212-234-3130. Ed. M.H. Martin. illus.

737.4 US ISSN 0271-4019
ANCIENT COINS IN NORTH AMERICAN COLLECTIONS. 1969. irreg. price varies. American Numismatic Society, Broadway at 155th St., New York, NY 10032. TEL 212-234-3130. Eds. M.H. Martin, L.A. Elam. (reprint service avail. from UMI)
 —BLDSC shelfmark: 0900.317000.
 Formerly: Greek Coins in North American Collections (ISSN 0072-744X)
 Description: Covers public and private collections not generally available for inspection.

737 954 II
ANDHRA PRADESH, INDIA. DEPARTMENT OF ARCHAEOLOGY AND MUSEUMS. MUSEUM SERIES. (Text in English) 1961. irreg., no.18, 1975-76. price varies. Department of Archaeology and Museums, Hyderabad 500001, Andhra Pradesh, India. (Or: Publications Bureau, Directorate of Government Printing, Chanchalguda, Hyderabad, Andhra Pradesh, India)
 Former titles: Andhra Pradesh, India. Department of Archaeology and Museums. Museum Objects and Numismatics Series; Andhra Pradesh, India. Department of Archaeology. Museum Series (ISSN 0066-166X)

737 AG ISSN 0004-4873
ASOCIACION NUMISMATICA ARGENTINA. REVISTA.* vol.11, 1966. s-a. Asociacion Numismatica Argentina, Casilla de Correo 496, Buenos Aires, Argentina. Ed. Jorge Von Stremayr. adv.; bk.rev.; bibl.; charts; illus.; tr.lit.

737 FR ISSN 0004-5543
ASSOCIATION INTERNATIONALE DES NUMISMATES PROFESSIONELS. BULLETIN-CIRCULAR. (Text in English, French) no.49, 1969. membership. International Association of Professional Numismatists, c/o Michel Kampmann, 49 rue de Richelieu, 75001 Paris, France. Ed. J.P. Divo.

737 CN ISSN 0044-9903
ATLANTIC PROVINCES NUMISMATIC ASSOCIATION. NEWSLETTER.* m. Atlantic Provinces Numismatic Association, 25 Honeydale Cresc., Halifax, N.S., Canada. Ed. N.C. Boltz.

737.4 AT ISSN 0004-8887
AUSTRALIAN COIN REVIEW. 1964. m. Aus.$28($67) Jesat Pty. Ltd., P.O. Box 5, Wombarra, N.S.W. 2515, Australia. TEL 042-68-1434. FAX 042-68-1435. Ed. J. Sykes. adv.; bk.rev.; circ. 7,222. **Indexed:** Numis.Lit, Pinpointer.
 Description: Devoted to the numismatic world of coins, medallions, medals, tokens, banknotes and share scrips.

AUSTRALIAN NUGGET JOURNAL. see *MINES AND MINING INDUSTRY*

737 AT ISSN 0004-9875
AUSTRALIAN NUMISMATIC JOURNAL; devoted to the study of coins, tokens, paper money and medals, particularly the issues of Australia. 1949. a. membership. South Australian Numismatic Society, G.P.O. Box 80, Adelaide, S.A., Australia. Ed. D.J. Rampling. bk.rev.; index, cum.index; circ. 200. **Indexed:** Numis.Lit.

737 US ISSN 0164-0828
BANK NOTE REPORTER; your news and marketplace for all paper money. 1973. m. $23.95. Krause Publications, Inc., 700 E. State St., Iola, WI 54990. TEL 715-445-2214. FAX 715-445-4087. TELEX 55 6461 KRAUSE PUB UD. Ed. David C. Harper. adv.; circ. 5,226. (tabloid format; also avail. in microform from UMI) **Indexed:** Numis.Lit.
 Description: News source and marketplace for collectors of U.S. and world paper money, notes, checks and related fiscal paper. Provides current prices for bank notes of the U.S. and world. Includes active buy-sell marketplace for paper money collectors.

737.4 NE ISSN 0165-8654
BEELDENAAR; munt- en penningkundig nieuws. 1977. bi-m. fl.32. (Koninklijk Nederlands Genootschap voor Munt- en Penningkunde) Vonk Uitgevers b.v., Postbus 420, Zeist, Netherlands. TEL 03404-54000. (Co-sponsor: Vereniging voor Penningkunst) Ed.Bd. adv.; bk.rev.; illus.; circ. 3,000.

737 PL ISSN 0006-4017
BIULETYN NUMIZMATYCZNY/NUMISMATIC BULLETIN. 1965. q. $30. Polskie Towarzystwo Numizmatyczne, Ul. Jezuicka 6, P.O. Box 2, 00-958 Warsaw, 40, Poland. (Dist. by: Ars Polona, Krakowskie Przedmiescie 7, 00-068 Warsaw, Poland) Ed. Janusz Kurpiewski. adv.; bk.rev.; abstr.; bibl.; illus.; cum.index; circ. 2,500. **Indexed:** Numis.Lit.

737 UK
BRITISH NUMISMATIC JOURNAL. (Includes the Society's Annual Proceedings) 1905. a. £12($25) membership. British Numismatic Society, c/o W. Slayter, Hon. Sec., 63 West Way, Edgeware, Middx. HA8 9LA, England. Eds. M. Delme-Radcliffe, N.J. Mayhew. adv.; bk.rev.; bibl.; charts; illus.; index, cum.index every 10 vols.; circ. 650. **Indexed:** Br.Archaeol.Abstr., Br.Hum.Ind., Numis.Lit.

737 370 US ISSN 0010-1443
C N L. (Colonial Newsletter) 1960. q. $12. Colonial Newsletter Foundation, Inc., Box 4411, Huntsville, AL 35815. Ed. James C. Spilman. bk.rev.; charts; illus.; stat.; circ. 350. (back issues avail.) **Indexed:** Numis.Lit.

737 FR ISSN 0008-0373
CAHIERS NUMISMATIQUES. 1964. q. 120 F. (foreign 130 F.). Societe d'Etudes Numismatiques et Archeologiques, 3 rue des Arts, 92100 Boulogne Billancourt, France. adv.; bk.rev.; bibl.; charts; illus.; stat.; circ. 380. **Indexed:** Numis.Lit.
 —BLDSC shelfmark: 2950.080000.

737 US ISSN 0008-0616
CALCOIN NEWS. 1946. q. membership. California State Numismatic Association, Box 499, Colton, CA 92324. Ed. Virginia Hall. bk.rev.; charts; illus.; circ. 1,500. **Indexed:** Numis.Lit.

737 CN ISSN 0702-3162
CANADIAN COIN NEWS. 1963. fortn. Can.$19.98. Metroland Printing, Publishing and Distributing Ltd., North York Mirror Division, 10 Tempo Ave., Willowdale, Ont. M2H 2N8, Canada. TEL 416-493-4400. Ed. Don Atanasoff. adv.; bk.rev.; illus.; stat.; circ. 18,500. **Indexed:** CMI, Numis.Lit.
 Formerly: Coin, Stamp, Antique News (ISSN 0010-0439)

737 CN ISSN 0008-4573
CANADIAN NUMISMATIC JOURNAL. 1956. m. (Jul. and Aug. combined). Can.$25. Canadian Numismatic Association, P.O. Box 226, Barrie, Ont. L4M 4T2, Canada. TEL 705-737-0845. Ed. Robert C. Willey. adv.; bk.rev.; bibl.; illus.; stat.; index; circ. 2,250. (also avail. in microform; back issues avail.) **Indexed:** CMI, Numis.Lit.
 Description: Aims to encourage and promote the science of numismatics by acquirement and study of coins, paper money, medals, tokens and all other numismatic items, with special emphasis on material pertaining to Canada.

737 CN ISSN 0045-5202
CANADIAN NUMISMATIC RESEARCH SOCIETY. TRANSACTIONS. (Text mainly in English, occasionally in French) 1965. a. Can.$16. Canadian Numismatic Research Society, P.O. Box 1263, Guelph, Ont. N1H 6N6, Canada. Ed. R.W. Irwin. bk.rev.; circ. 50. **Indexed:** Numis.Lit.

737 CN ISSN 0703-895X
CANADIAN TOKEN. 1972. bi-m. membership. Canadian Association of Token Collectors, 10 Wesanford Place, Hamilton, Ont. L8P 1N6, Canada. Ed. K.A. Palmer. bk.rev.; circ. 300. **Indexed:** Numis.Lit.

737.4 700 US ISSN 1048-0986
THE CELATOR; numismatic art of antiquity. 1987. m. $24. Clio's Cabinet, Box 123, Lodi, WI 53555. TEL 608-592-4684. Ed. Wayne G. Sayles. adv.; bk.rev.; bibl.; charts; illus.; tr.lit.; circ. 1,800.
 Incorporates: Roman Coins and Culture.
 Description: Articles and features about ancient coins and artifacts, connoisseurship and market news.

737 BE ISSN 0009-0344
CERCLE D'ETUDES NUMISMATIQUES. BULLETIN. 1964. q. 800 BEF. Cercle d'Etudes Numismatiques, 4 Bd. de l'Empereur, B-1000 Brussels, Belgium. adv.; bk.rev.; charts; illus.; cum.index.

737 BE ISSN 0069-2247
CERCLE D'ETUDES NUMISMATIQUES. TRAVAUX. 1964. irreg. price varies. Cercle d'Etudes Numismatiques, 4 Bd. de l'Empereur, B-1000 Brussels, Belgium.

737.4 US
CERTIFIED COIN DEALER NEWSLETTER. 1986. w. $99. Coin Dealer Newsletter, Box 11099, Torrance, CA 90510-1099. TEL 310-515-7369. FAX 310-515-7534. Ed. Dennis R. Baker.

737 US
CHECK COLLECTOR; devoted to the study of security paper. 1974. q. $10. American Society of Check Collectors, c/o Charles Kemp, Sec., Box 71892, Madison Heights, MI 48071. Ed. Robert A. Spence. adv.; bk.rev.; charts; illus.; circ. 350.
 Formerly: Check List.

737.4 CN ISSN 0045-7019
CITY OF OTTAWA COIN CLUB. MONTHLY BULLETIN. 1968. m. membership. City of Ottawa Coin Club, Box 2180, Sta. D, Ottawa, Ont. K1P 5W4, Canada. (Co-sponsor: Canadian Numismatic Association) Ed. Tom McFerran. adv.; bk.rev.; circ. 125.

737 UK
CJ1
CLASSICAL NUMISMATIC REVIEW. 1936. 10/yr. £15. Seaby Coins, 7 Davies St., London W1Y 1LL, England. TEL 071-495-1888. FAX 071-499-5916. Eds. B. Reeds, S. Mitchell. bk.rev.; illus.; tr.bibl.; index. **Indexed:** Br.Archaeol.Abstr., Numis.Lit.
 Formerly: Seaby's Coin and Medal Bulletin (ISSN 0037-0053)

737.4 US
COIN DEALER NEWSLETTER. 1963. w. $89. Box 11099, Torrance, CA 90510. TEL 310-515-7369. FAX 310-515-7534. Ed. Dennis R. Baker.

737 UK ISSN 0140-1149
COIN HOARDS. irreg. membership. Royal Numismatic Society, British Museum, London WC1B 3DG, England. (Dist. by: Spink & Son Ltd., 5-7 King St., St. James, London SW1, England) Ed. M.J. Price. **Indexed:** Br.Archaeol.Abstr.

737.4 UK
COIN MONTHLY (1980). 1966. m. £44.60. Numismatic Publishing Co., Sovereign House, Brentwood, Essex CM14 4SE, England. adv.; bk.rev.; charts; illus.; mkt.; stat.; circ. 10,534.
 Former titles: Coin (ISSN 0143-5485); Coin Monthly (ISSN 0010-0390)

737 UK ISSN 0955-4386
CJ1
COIN NEWS. 1979. m. £22($35) Token Publishing Ltd., 84 High St., Honiton, Devon EX14 8JW, England. TEL 0404-45414. FAX 0404-45313. (Dist. by: Seymour Press Ltd., Windsor House, 1270 London Rd., Norbury, London SW16 4DH) Ed. John W. Mussell. adv.; index; circ. 12,000.
 Formerly: Coin and Medal News; **Incorporates:** Medals International.
 Description: Monthly information for collectors of coins and banknotes.

737 332.6   US
COIN PREVIEWER; numismatic investment newsletter. 1974. m. $19.95. 500 N.W. 101st Ave., Coral Springs, FL 33071. TEL 305-755-7930. (Subscr. to: Box 8655, Coral Springs, FL 33075) Ed. Robert J. Leuchten. adv.; bk.rev.; circ. 200. (back issues avail.)

737.4   US   ISSN 0010-0412
COIN PRICES. 1967. bi-m. $16.95. Krause Publications, Inc., 700 E. State St., Iola, WI 54990. TEL 715-445-2214. FAX 715-445-4087. TELEX 556461 KRAUSE PUB UD. Ed. Bob Wilhite. adv.; circ. 83,175. (also avail. in microform from MIM,PMC,UMI)
   Description: Current market information for U.S. coin investors and collectors, featuring market analysis and auction results.

737.4   US   ISSN 0045-7280
COIN WHOLESALER.* 1970. m. $10. World-Wide Coin Investments Ltd., 3763 Roswell Rd. N.E., Atlanta, GA 30342-4414. TEL 404-262-1810. Ed. Michael G. Nugent. adv.; bk.rev.; illus.; stat.; circ. 30,000. (tabloid format)

737.4   US   ISSN 0010-0447
COIN WORLD. 1960. w. $26. Amos Press Inc., Box 4315, Sidney, OH 45365. TEL 513-498-0800. FAX 513-498-0812. Ed. Beth Deisher. adv.; bk.rev.; illus.; stat.; circ. 75,000. (newspaper; also avail. in microform from UMI; reprint service avail. from UMI) **Indexed:** Numis.Lit.
   Formerly: Numismatic Scrapbook (ISSN 0029-6058)

737.4   US   ISSN 0361-0845
CJ1
COIN WORLD ALMANAC. 1976. triennial. $29.95. Amos Press Inc., Box 150, Sidney, OH 45365. TEL 513-498-0800. FAX 513-498-0812. illus.

737 332.6   US
COIN WORLD ANNUAL PRICE GUIDE. 1989. a. $4.95. Signet Books, Penguin USA, 375 Hudson St., New York, NY 10014. TEL 212-366-2594. Ed. Donna Cullen.

737.4   UK   ISSN 0307-6571
CJ2471
COIN YEARBOOK. 1968. a. £10.95. Numismatic Publishing Co., Sovereign House, Brentwood, Essex CM14 4SE, England. illus.; circ. 20,000.

737.4   US   ISSN 0010-0455
COINAGE. 1964. m. $23. Miller Magazines, Inc., 4880 Market St., Ventura, CA 93003-2888. TEL 805-644-3824. Ed. James L. Miller. (also avail. in microform from UMI) **Indexed:** Numis.Lit.
   Description: History and human stories about coins and coin collecting and investing, plus coverage of medals, ancient coins and currency. Most articles deal with U.S. coins and medals.

737.4   US   ISSN 8756-6265
COINAGE OF THE AMERICAS CONFERENCE. PROCEEDINGS. a. price varies. American Numismatic Society, Broadway at 155th St., New York, NY 10032. TEL 212-234-3130. Ed. L.A. Elam.

737   US
COINFIDENTIAL REPORT. 1963. m. (except Jul. & Aug.). $25. Bale Publications, Box 2727, New Orleans, LA 70176. Ed. Don Bale, Jr. adv.; bk.rev.; film rev.; charts; illus.; stat.; tr.lit.; circ. 1,000. (processed; back issues avail.)
   Description: Highlights in-depth analyses of coins that should be lucrative long and/or short-term investments, and stock recommendations on the major U.S. markets. Includes inside look at the coin and stock markets, and current news briefs and trends in both fields.

737.4   US   ISSN 0010-0471
COINS. 1955. m. $19.95. Krause Publications, Inc., 700 E. State St., Iola, WI 54990. TEL 715-445-2214. FAX 715-445-4087. TELEX 55 6461 KRAUSE PUB UD. Ed. Arlyn G. Sieber. adv.; bk.rev.; illus.; circ. 74,726. (also avail. in microform from UMI) **Indexed:** Numis.Lit.
   Description: Provides in-depth features on U.S. coins accompanied by full-color photographs, helpful collector columns, and U.S. and world coin hobby news.

737.4   UK   ISSN 0069-4983
COINS MARKET VALUES. a. £3.50. Link House Magazines Ltd., Link House, Dingwall Ave, Croydon, Surrey CR9 2TA, England. TEL 01-686 2599. FAX 01-760-0973. (Subscr. to: U M S, Stephenson House, 1st Fl., Brunel Centre, Bletchley, Milton Keynes, MK2 2EW) Ed. Richard West. **Indexed:** Numis.Lit.
   Formerly: Coins Annual.
   Description: Examines ancient and modern British coins.

COLLECTORS' SHOWCASE. see *ANTIQUES*

737.4 332.6   US
DAVID HALL'S INSIDE VIEW. 1979. bi-m. $97. David Hall's Rare Coins and Collectibles, 1936 E. Deere Ave., Ste. 102, Santa Ana, CA 92705-5723. TEL 714-261-0509. FAX 714-252-0541. Ed. David Hall.

DEUTSCHE BRIEFMARKEN - REVUE; SD - Sammlerdienst. see *PHILATELY*

737   GW
DEUTSCHES MUENZEN MAGAZIN. 1987. bi-m. DM.34.50. E M S - Verlag, Birkenhofstr. 10, 7000 Stuttgart 70, Germany. TEL 0711-454098. FAX 0711-4570666. Ed. Wolfgang Erzinger. circ. 200,000.

737.4 380.1   US
DIRECTORY OF COIN COLLECTORS. irregg. 53 Beverly Blvd., San Jose, CA 95116. TEL 408-272-8265.

737.4   US
EDMUNDS UNITED STATES COIN PRICES. 1980. 4/yr. $13.40. Edmund Publications Corp., 200 Baker Ave., Ste. 309, Concord, MA 01742. TEL 508-371-9788. FAX 508-371-9806. Ed. Robert Belloch.
   Description: Gives comprehensive price breakdowns on all coins circulated, as well as commemorative grading information. Includes photographs.

737   US
ERROR TRENDS COIN MAGAZINE. 1968. m. $15. Box 158, Oceanside, NY 11572. TEL 516-764-8063. Ed. Arnold Margolis. adv.; bk.rev.; illus.; circ. 2,000. (back issues avail.)
   Description: Devoted entirely to coin collectors who specialize in numismatic error coins.

737   US
ERRORSCOPE.* 1963. m. membership. Combined Organizations of Numismatic Error Collectors of America, c/o J.T. Stanton, Pres., Box 15487, Savannah, GA 31416. TEL 912-232-8655. Ed. Stella Teiglang. adv.; bk.rev.; circ. 550.
   Formerly: Errorgram.

737   NE   ISSN 0014-3030
EUROPEAN NUMISMATICS.* (Text in Dutch, English) 1968. bi-m. fl.7.50.($2.10) Uitgeverij Numismatica Nederland N.V., Darwinplantsoen 26, Amsterdam 6, Netherlands. Ed. S.A.M. Le Loux. adv.; bk.rev.; bibl.; illus.; stat.; tr.lit. **Indexed:** Numis.Lit.

737   US   ISSN 0014-7745
FARE BOX. 1947. m. $16. American Vecturist Association, Box 1204, Boston, MA 02104. TEL 617-277-8111. Ed. John M. Coffee, Jr. adv.; bk.rev.; charts; stat.; circ. 825. **Indexed:** Numis.Lit.
   Description: For collectors of transportation fare tokens and those interested in urban transportation history.

737.4   US
▼**FELL'S U S COINS QUARTERLY INVESTMENT GUIDE.** 1991. q. Blockbuster Periodicals, Inc., 2131 Hollywood Blvd., Hollywood, CA 33020. TEL 305-925-5242. Ed. Barbara Newman. circ. 75,000.
   Description: For collectors and investors. Highlights numismatic news and expands upon basic beginner information for the advanced collector.

737 700   US   ISSN 0092-5039
CJ5813
FRANKLIN MINT ALMANAC. 1970. 6/yr. free. (Franklin Mint Collectors Society) Franklin Mint, Franklin Center, PA 19091. TEL 215-459-6000. FAX 215-459-6880. Ed. Jack Wilkie. adv.; illus.; stat.; index, cum.index: 1970-1984; circ. 1,020 (controlled).

737   SP   ISSN 0210-2137
GACETA NUMISMATICA. 1966. q. membership. Asociacion Numismatica Espanola, Gran via de les Corts Catalanes, 627, 08010 Barcelona, Spain. adv.; bk.rev.; cum.index in vol.101; circ. 2,000. **Indexed:** Numis.Lit.

737   SZ   ISSN 0016-5565
GAZETTE NUMISMATIQUE SUISSE/SCHWEIZER MUENZBLAETTER. (Text in English, French, German) 1949. q. 100 SFr. Societe Suisse de Numismatique - Schweizerische Numismatische Gesellschaft, Niederdorfstr. 43, CH-8001 Zuerich, Switzerland. adv.; illus.; cum.index every 5 yrs.; circ. 1,000. **Indexed:** Numis.Lit.
   —BLDSC shelfmark: 8112.370000.

737   GW   ISSN 0931-0681
DER GELDSCHEINSAMMLER; Zeitschrift fuer Papiergeld. 1986. bi-m. DM.36($26) Heinrich Gietl Verlag, Am Grasigen Weg 8, Postfach 166, 8413 Regenstauf, Germany. TEL 09402-5856. FAX 09402-6635. Ed. Alexander Persijn. adv.; bk.rev.; index; circ. 3,000. (back issues avail.)

737   GW
GOLD UND SILBER ZUM SAMMELN. a. Dresdner Bank AG, Juergen-Ponto-Platz 2, 6000 Frankfurt a.M. 11, Germany. TEL 069-263-2841. FAX 069-263-7892. circ. 50,000.

737.4   US   ISSN 0072-8829
CJ1826
GUIDEBOOK OF UNITED STATES COINS. 1946. a. $9.95. Western Publishing Co., Inc., 1220 Mound Ave., Racine, WI 53404. TEL 414-633-2431. Ed. R.S. Yeoman. illus.; index.
   Description: Retail guide of all U.S. coins from 1616 to the present.

737   GW   ISSN 0072-9523
HAMBURGER BEITRAEGE ZUR NUMISMATIK. 1947. a. DM.100. Hamburger Museumsverein, Holstenwall 24, 2000 Hamburg 36, Germany. FAX 03497-3103. Eds. Walter Haevernick, Gert Hatz. bk.rev.; circ. 200. **Indexed:** Numis.Lit.
   —BLDSC shelfmark: 4241.320000.
   Description: Articles and reviews on scientific numismatics.

737.4   US   ISSN 0072-9949
HANDBOOK OF UNITED STATES COINS. 1941. a. $5.50. Western Publishing Co., Inc., 1220 Mound Ave., Racine, WI 53404. TEL 414-633-2431. Ed. R.S. Yeoman. illus.; index.
   Description: Contains up-to-date wholesale values for all U.S. coins from 1616 to the present.

737   SZ   ISSN 0073-0963
HAUTES ETUDES NUMISMATIQUES. 1966. irreg., no.2, 1967. (Ecole Pratique des Hautes Etudes, Centre de Recherches d'Histoire et de Philologie, FR) Librairie Droz S.A., 11, rue Massot, CH-1211 Geneva 12, Switzerland. TEL 022-466666. FAX 022-472391. circ. 1,000.
   Description: Examines ancient coins.

737   US
HIGH PROFITS FROM RARE COIN INVESTMENT. irreg., 13th ed., 1991. $19.95. Bowers and Merena Publications, Box 1224, Wolfeboro, NH 03894. TEL 603-569-5095. Ed. Q. David Bowers.

737 980   AG   ISSN 0325-7622
INSTITUTO DE NUMISMATICA E HISTORIA DE SAN NICOLAS DE LOS ARROYOS. BOLETIN. 1965. q. Arg.$20($10) Casilla de Correo 44, 2900 San Nicolas, Buenos Aires, Argentina. circ. 300. (back issues avail.)

INTERPHILA; international directory of philately and numismatics. see *PHILATELY*

INVESTMENT COIN REVIEW. see *BUSINESS AND ECONOMICS — Investments*

737   IS   ISSN 0021-2288
ISRAEL NUMISMATIC JOURNAL. (Text in English) 1963. irreg. (approx. a.). $30. Israel Numismatic Society, P.O. Box 750, Jerusalem, Israel. TEL 02-249779. TELEX 26598. Ed.Bd. bk.rev.; bibl.; charts; illus.; stat.; circ. 300. **Indexed:** New Test.Abstr., Numis.Lit.

NUMISMATICS

737   IT   ISSN 0578-9923
ISTITUTO ITALIANO DI NUMISMATICA. ANNALI. 1954. a. L.80000 (typically set in May). Istituto Italiano di Numismatica, Palazzo Barberini, Via Quattro Fontane 13, 00195 Rome, Italy. TEL 06-4743603. adv.; bk.rev.; circ. 500. (back issues avail.)

737.4   NE
JAARBOEK VOOR MUNT- EN PENNINGKUNDE. (Text in Dutch, occasionally in English, French, German; summaries in English) 1914. a. price varies. Koninklijk Nederlands Genootschap voor Munt- en Penningkunde - Royal Dutch Society of Numismatics, c/o The Netherlands Bank, Postbus 98, 1000 AB Amsterdam, Netherlands. Ed.Bd. cum.index; circ. 500.

737   GW   ISSN 0075-2711
CJ31
JAHRBUCH FUER NUMISMATIK UND GELDGESCHICHTE. (Text mainly in German; occasionally in English and French) 1949. irreg. price varies. (Bayerische Numismatische Gesellschaft) Verlag Michael Lassleben, Lange Gasse 19, Postfach 20, 8411 Kallmuenz, Germany. Ed. J. Kellner. **Indexed:** Br.Archaeol.Abstr., Numis.Lit.

737   US   ISSN 0308-8677
L A N S A. (Former name of publishing body: Latin American Paper Money Society) (Text in English, Spanish) 1973. 3/yr. $8. Latin American Bank Note Society, 3304 Milford Mill Rd., Baltimore, MD 21207. Ed. Arthur C. Matz. adv.; bk.rev.; illus.; index; circ. 300. (back issues avail.)
Description: Covers articles on paper money and related items of Latin America and Iberia for the collector.

LANDESMUSEUM FUER KAERNTEN. BUCHREIHE. see MUSEUMS AND ART GALLERIES

737 900   AU   ISSN 0255-2809
LITTERAE NUMISMATICAE VINDOBONENSES. 1979. irreg. price varies. Verlag der Oesterreichischen Akademie der Wissenschaften, Dr. Ignaz-Seipel-Platz 2, A-1010 Vienna, Austria. FAX 0228-5139541.

737   PL   ISSN 0024-5771
LODZKI NUMIZMATYK.* 1961. q. membership. Polskie Towarzystwo Archeologiczne i Numizmatyczne, Oddzial w Lodzi, Plac Wolnosci 14, Lodz, Poland. Ed. Anatol Gupieniec. bk.rev.; abstr.; bibl.; charts; illus.; stat.; index; cum.index. **Indexed:** Numis.Lit.

737   IQ   ISSN 0002-4058
AL-MASKUKAT.* 1969. a. ID.5000($12) Ministry of Culture and Information, State Organization of Antiquities and Heritage, Jamal Abdul Nasr St., Baghdad, Iraq. TEL 4158355.

737   IT   ISSN 0392-5439
MEDAGLIA. (Text in Italian; summaries in English, French, German) 1971. a. L.45000 (foreign L.55000). Edizioni S. Johnson Milano, Via Terraggio, 15, 20123 Milan, Italy. TEL 02-86452792. FAX 02-72002758. TELEX 323562 JOHNME I. Ed. Mariangela Johnson. adv.; bk.rev.; bibl.; illus.; cum.index. (back issues avail.)
Description: Dedicated to collectors of antique and modern medals. Articles are written by specialists in this field. Includes historical profiles of specific kinds of medals.

737 709   UK   ISSN 0263-7707
CJ5501
THE MEDAL. 1982. 2/yr. £20 (foreign £25). British Art Medal Trust, c/o Mark Jones, Ed., Dept. of Coins and Medals, British Museum, London WC1B 3DG, England. TEL 071-323-8170. FAX 071-323-8171. adv.; bk.rev.; index every 10 issues; circ. 900. **Indexed:** Artbibl.Mod., RILA.
—BLDSC shelfmark: 5424.628800.

737 355   SA
MILITARY MEDAL SOCIETY OF SOUTH AFRICA. JOURNAL. (Text in English) 1974. 2/yr. R.40($17) Military Medal Society of South Africa, 1 Jacqueline Ave., Northcliff, Johannesburg 2195, South Africa. TEL 011-888-5797. Ed. C.H. Loots. bk.rev.; cum.index; circ. 200. (back issues avail.)

737.4   US
MODERN GOLD COINAGE (YEAR). 1976. a. $50. Gold Institute, Administrative Office - Institut de l'Or, Bureau Administratif, 1112 15th St., N.W., Ste. 420, Washington, DC 20036-4823. TEL 202-835-0185. FAX 202-835-0155. TELEX 904233. Ed. John H. Lutley. circ. 600. (back issues avail.)
Description: Data on all gold coins issued in the world in each year.

737   US
MODERN SILVER COINAGE (YEAR). 1973. a. $40. Silver Institute, 1112 16th St., N.W., Ste. 240, Washington, DC 20036-4823. TEL 202-783-0500. TELEX 904233. Ed. John H. Lutley. (back issues avail.)
Description: Data on all silver coins issued worldwide, with names and addresses of mints from which they can be acquired.

737   DK   ISSN 0900-1409
MOENTSAMLEREN. 1984. s-a. DKK 26. Moentsamlaren, Noerregade 48, 7400 Herning, Denmark. TEL 97-22-08-45. Ed. Preben Eriksen. adv.; bk.rev.; illus.; circ. 4,000.

737   VB   ISSN 0958-1545
MONETA INTERNATIONAL; coins and treasures monthly. 1988. m. $20. c/o Vernon W. Pickering, P.O. Box 704, Road Town - Tortola, British Virgin Islands. TEL 809-49-43510. FAX 809-494-4540. Ed. Giorgio Migliavacca. adv.; bk.rev.; index; circ. 6,000. (tabloid format; back issues avail.)
Description: Covers coin collecting and numismatic research from ancient to modern coins.

737.4 769.56   US
MONEY TALKS. 1970. 4/yr. $5. Superior Stamp and Coin Co. Inc., 9478 W. Olympic Blvd., Beverly Hills, CA 90212-4299. FAX 213-203-0496. Ed. Mark Goldberg. adv.; bk.rev.; illus.; circ. 12,000.

737   SZ
MUENZEN-REVUE. 1969. 12/yr. 72 Fr. Verlag Muenzen-Revue, Blotzheimerstr. 40, CH-4055 Basel, Switzerland. FAX 061-445542. adv.; bk.rev.; bibl.; circ. 20,000.
Description: Features news, history, values, new coins, trade as well as reports of events and auctions for coin hobbyists.

737   SZ   ISSN 0027-3007
MUENZEN UND MEDAILLEN/MONNAIES ET MEDAILLES. 1942. m. free. Muenzen und Medaillen AG, Malzgasse 25, CH-4002 Basel, Switzerland. illus.; circ. 12,500.

737   GW   ISSN 0179-3683
MUENZEN- UND MEDAILLENSAMMLER BERICHTE. (Text in English, French and German) 1961. bi-m. DM.48. Kricheldorf Verlag, Guenterstalstr. 16, 7800 Freiburg, Germany. TEL 0761-73913. bk.rev.; circ. 1,000. (back issues avail.)

737   RM
MUZEUL NATIONAL DE ISTORIE A ROMANIEI. CERCETARI NUMISMATICE. 1978. irreg. Muzeul National de Istorie a Romaniei, Calea Victoriei, 12, Bucharest, Rumania.
Formerly: Muzeul de Istorie al Republicii Socialiste Romania. Cercetari Numismatice.

737.4   PL   ISSN 0208-5062
MUZEUM ARCHEOLOGICZNE I ETNOGRAFICZNE, LODZ. PRACE I MATERIALY. SERIA NUMIZMATYCZNA I KONSERWATORSKA. (Text in Polish; summaries in English) 1981. a. price varies. Panstwowe Wydawnictwo Naukowe, Ul. Miodowa 10, 00-251 Warsaw, Poland. (Dist. by: Ars Polona, Krakowskie Przedmiescie 7, 00-068 Warsaw, Poland) Ed. A. Mikolajczyk. circ. 600.

737   US   ISSN 0027-6006
N A S C QUARTERLY. 1959. q. $10 (effective 1992). Numismatic Association of Southern California, Box 2123, Sepulveda, CA 91393. Ed. Jeff Oxman. adv.; bk.rev.; charts; illus.; stat.; circ. 700.
Description: Contains articles, coin club and association news.

737   PO
N U M M U S. (Text in English, French and Portuguese; summaries in English and French) 1952. a. $25. Sociedade Portuguesa de Numismatica, Rua de Costa Cabral, 664, 4200 Porto, Portugal. Ed.Bd. bk.rev.; bibl.; charts; illus.; cum.index 1968-1972; circ. 2,000.
Formerly: N U M U S Numismatica, Medalhistica, Arqueologia (ISSN 0085-364X)

737   US
NEW JERSEY NUMISMATIC JOURNAL. 1975. q. membership. Garden State Numismatic Association, Inc., Box 787, Pearl River, NY 10965. TEL 201-827-2482. (Subscr. to: Judith Kessler, Correspondence Sec., Box 331, Millville, NJ 08332; Box 3462, Toms River, NJ 08756-3462) Ed. James K. Brandt. adv.; bk.rev.; bibl.; illus.; circ. 1,000.

737   GR
NOMISMATIKA CHRONICA. (Summaries in English) 1972. irreg. $6. Hellenic Numismatic Society, Box 736, Athens, Greece. circ. 1,000. **Indexed:** Numis.Lit.

NORDISK FILATELI. see PHILATELY

737   SW
NORDISK FILATELI MED MYNT - MAGAZINET. 1937. 10/yr. $35. Nordisk Filateli AB, Box 141, S-182 16 Danderyd, Sweden. Ed. Sven Olof Forselius. adv.; bk.rev.; illus.; circ. 8,000. **Indexed:** Numis.Lit.
Supersedes in part: Skandinaviska Mynt Magasinet; Which was formerly: Skandinavisk Numismatik (ISSN 0346-0479)

NORDISK JULEMAERKE KATALOG; Nordic Christmas seal catalogue. see PHILATELY

737   DK   ISSN 0025-8539
NORDISK NUMISMATISK UNION MEDLEMSBLAD. 1936. 8/yr. DKK 100. Nordisk Numismatisk Union - Nordic Numismatic Union, c/o Royal Collection of Coins and Medals, National Museum, DK-1220 Copenhagen K, Denmark. FAX 33-155521. Ed. Joergen Steen Jensen. adv.; bk.rev.; illus.; circ. 2,700. **Indexed:** NAA, Numis.Lit.

737 769.56   IT
NOTIZIARIO STORICO NUMISMATICO FILATELICO. m. Casella Postale 136, 55100 Lucca, Italy. Ed. Giorgi Giorgi.

737.4   SZ
NUMIS-POST; Monatszeitschrift fuer den Muenzensammier. 1968. 12/yr. 35 Fr. Numis-Post, Postfach, CH-7310 Bad Ragaz, Switzerland. FAX 085-95984. Ed. Ruth Niedermann.

737   FI   ISSN 0355-5615
NUMISMAATIKKO. 1965. 6/yr. Fmk.165. Suomen Numismaatikkoliitto, Box 895, 00101 Helsinki, Finland. Ed. Erkki Rautiainen. adv.; bk.rev.; cum.index: 1965-1974; circ. 2,500. **Indexed:** Numis.Lit.

737 900   UK   ISSN 0078-2696
NUMISMATIC CHRONICLE AND JOURNAL. 1839. a. membership. Royal Numismatic Society, British Museum, London, WC1B 3DG, England. (Dist. by: Spink & Son Ltd., 5-7 King St., St. James, London SW1, England) Ed. K. Rutter. adv.; bk.rev.; circ. 1,400. **Indexed:** Br.Hum.Ind., NAA.
—BLDSC shelfmark: 6184.719000.

737   UK   ISSN 0029-6023
NUMISMATIC CIRCULAR. 1892. 10/yr. £10 (foreign £25). Spink & Son Ltd., 5 King St., St. James's, London S.W. 1, England. TEL 071-930-7888. FAX 071-839-4853. Ed. Douglas Saville. bk.rev.; bibl.; tr.list.; index; circ. 3,000. **Indexed:** Numis.Lit.

737   US   ISSN 0029-6031
Z6866
NUMISMATIC LITERATURE. 1947. s-a. $10. American Numismatic Society, Broadway at 155th St., New York, NY 10032. TEL 212-234-3130. Ed. L.A. Elam. adv.; abstr.; bibl.; index. (reprint service avail. from UMI) **Indexed:** Amer.Bibl.Slavic & E.Eur.Stud, Br.Archaeol.Abstr., Numis.Lit.

NUMISMATICS

737 US ISSN 0029-604X
CJ1
NUMISMATIC NEWS. 1952. w. $27.95. Krause Publications, Inc., 700 E. State St., Iola, WI 54990. TEL 715-445-2214. FAX 715-445-4087. TELEX 55 6461 KRAUSE PUB UD. Ed. Bob Wilhite. adv.; bk.rev.; bibl.; charts; illus.; mkt.; stat.; tr.lit.; circ. 37,836. (tabloid format; also avail. in microform from UMI)
 Description: Guide to coin collecting hobby, serving collectors of U.S. coins with news and advertising marketplace where coin collectors can buy and sell through the mail.

737 US ISSN 0078-2718
NUMISMATIC NOTES AND MONOGRAPHS. 1920. irreg., no.165, 1991. price varies. American Numismatic Society, Broadway at 155th St., New York, NY 10032. TEL 212-234-3130. Eds. M.H. Martin, L.A. Elam. (reprint service avail. from UMI) **Indexed:** Numis.Lit.

737 II ISSN 0029-6066
NUMISMATIC SOCIETY OF INDIA. JOURNAL. (Text in English) 1910. s-a. Rs.200($30) Numismatic Society of India, Banaras Hindu University, Varanasi 221005, India. TEL 311074. Ed.Bd. bk.rev.; bibl.; charts; illus.; stat. (back issues avail.) **Indexed:** Numis.Lit.

737 US ISSN 0517-404X
NUMISMATIC STUDIES. 1938. irreg. price varies. American Numismatic Society, Broadway at 155th St., New York, NY 10032. TEL 212-234-3130. Eds. M.H. Martin, L.A. Elam. circ. 800. (back issues avail.; reprint service avail. from UMI) **Indexed:** Numis.Lit.
 —BLDSC shelfmark: 6184.743000.
 Description: Scholarly monographs analysizing numismatic materials and their relationship to the understanding and interpretation of history, archaeology, political science, and art history.

737 IT
NUMISMATICA; mensile di scienza, storia, arte, economia delle monete. 1970. m. L.50000($70) Gino Manfredini, Ed. & Pub., Via Ferramola 1-A, 25121 Brescia, Italy. TEL 030-56211. adv.; bk.rev.; illus. **Indexed:** Numis.Lit.

737 SZ
NUMISMATICA E ANTICHITA CLASSICHE. (Supplements avail.) (Text in English, French, German, Italian) 1972. a. 145 Fr. Amici dei Quaderni Ticinesi di Numismatica e Antichita Classiche, Secretariat, C.P. 3157, CH-6901 Lugano, Switzerland. index; circ. 500. (back issues avail.)

737 BE
NUMISMATICA LOVANIENSIA. 1977. irreg., no.14, 1989. price varies. Universite Catholique de Louvain, Seminaire de Numismatique Marcel Hoc, College Erasme, 1 place Blaise Pascal, B-1348 Louvain-la-Neuve, Belgium. TEL 10-47-48-80. FAX 10-472999. Ed. T. Hackens. circ. 2,000.

737 CS ISSN 0078-2726
NUMISMATICA MORAVICA. (Text in Czech; summaries also in English or in French, German, Russian) 1965. irreg., no.7, 1986. price varies. Moravske Zemske Muzeum, Numismaticke Oddeleni, Zelny trh 6, 659 37 Brno, Czechoslovakia. TEL 42-5-22241. FAX 42-5-25279. illus.; index; circ. 1,200. **Indexed:** Numis.Lit.
 Description: Monographs and materials from the conferences dealing with the questions of the history of the Moravian coinage.

737 CS ISSN 0029-6074
NUMISMATICKE LISTY. (Text in Czech; summaries in English, French, German, Russian) 1945. bi-m. 32.20 Kcs.($24) (Narodni Muzeum) Panorama, Halkova 1, 120 72 Prague 2, Czechoslovakia. (Dist. by: Artia, Ve Smeckach 30, 111 27 Prague 1, Czechoslovakia) Ed. Jarmila Haskova. bk.rev.; abstr.; bibl.; illus.; index; circ. 7,500. **Indexed:** Numis.Lit.
 —BLDSC shelfmark: 6184.745000.

737.4 943.7 CS ISSN 0546-9414
CJ9
NUMISMATICKY SBORNIK. (Text mainly in Czech and Slovak; occasionaly in German and other languages) 1953. irreg., vol.18, 1989. Academia, Publishing House of the Czechoslovak Academy of Sciences, Vodickova 40, 112 29 Prague 1, Czechoslovakia. TEL 23-63-065. (Subscr. to: Artia, Ve Smeckach 30, 111 27 Prague 1, Czechoslovakia) Ed. Jiri Sejbal. illus.; circ. 1,000. **Indexed:** Numis.Lit.

737 FR ISSN 0335-1971
NUMISMATIQUE & CHANGE. 1972. m. 185 F. S E P S, 12 rue Poincare, 55800 Revigny, France. Ed. R.L. Martin. adv.; bk.rev.; charts; stat.; circ. 15,000.
 Indexed: Numis.Lit.
 Formerly: Change (ISSN 0009-1367)

737 GW ISSN 0323-8962
NUMISMATISCHE BEITRAEGE. q. DM.40. (Gesellschaft fuer Heimatgeschichte, Zentraler Fachausschuss fuer Numismatik) V E B Deutsche Verlag der Wissenschaften, Johannes-Dieckmann-Str. 10, 1080 Berlin, Germany. (Orders to: Buchexport, Leninstr. 16, 7010 Leipzig, Germany) Ed. J. Gottschalk.

737 GW ISSN 0937-6488
NUMISMATISCHES NACHRICHTENBLATT. 1952. m. DM.27.50. Deutsche Numismatische Gesellschaft, Leharstr. 17, 6720 Speyer, Germany. TEL 06232-35752. Ed. Helfried Ehrend. adv.; bk.rev.; abstr.; bibl.; illus.; index; circ. 4,500. (back issues avail.) **Indexed:** Numis.Lit.

737 SW ISSN 0078-2734
NUMISMATISKA MEDDELANDEN/NUMISMATIC COMMUNICATIONS. (Text in Swedish; summaries in English, French and occasionally German) 1874. irreg. price varies. Svenska Numismatiska Foereningen, Sandhamnsgatan 50 A, S-115 28 Stockholm, Sweden. Ed.Bd. index; circ. 1,000. **Indexed:** NAA, Numis.Lit.

737 US ISSN 0029-6090
THE NUMISMATIST. 1888. m. $26 to non-members (foreign $33). American Numismatic Association, 818 N. Cascade Ave., Colorado Springs, CO 80903-3279. TEL 719-632-2646. Ed. Barbara Gregory. adv.; bk.rev.; charts; illus.; stat.; index; cum.index: vols. 1-51, 52-71; circ. 31,000. (also avail. in microfiche) **Indexed:** Amer.Bibl.Slavic & E.Eur.Stud, Numis.Lit.
 —BLDSC shelfmark: 6184.749000.
 Incorporates: First Strike (ISSN 0896-4432); (1951-1981): A N A Club Bulletin (ISSN 0001-1991)

737 BU
NUMIZMATIKA. 1969. q. $1. Suiuz na Bulgarski Filatelisti, Sofia, Bulgaria. (Dist. by: Hemus, 6, Rouski Blvd., 1000 Sofia, Bulgaria) circ. 2,000. **Indexed:** Numis.Lit.

737 AU
OESTERREICHISCHE AKADEMIE DER WISSENSCHAFTEN. NUMISMATISCHE KOMMISSION. VEROEFFENTLICHUNGEN. (Subseries of: Oesterreichische Akademie der Wissenschaften. Philosophisch-Historische Klasse. Denkschriften) 1973. irreg. Verlag der Oesterreichischen Akademie der Wissenschaften, Dr. Ignaz-Seipel-Platz 2, A-1010 Vienna, Austria. FAX 0222-5139541. illus.

737 AU ISSN 0029-9359
OESTERREICHISCHE NUMISMATISCHE GESELLSCHAFT. MITTEILUNGEN. 1883. 6/yr. S.215. Oesterreichische Numismatische Gesellschaft, Burgring 5, A-1010 Vienna, Austria. Ed. Karl Schulz. adv.; bk.rev.; abstr, illus.; cum. index; circ. 700.

737 CN ISSN 0048-1815
ONTARIO NUMISMATIST.* 1961. m. Box 33, Waterloo, Ont., Canada.

PHILA-REPORT; die Sammlerfreundliche Briefmarkenzeitung. see *PHILATELY*

THE PHILATELIC EXPORTER; world's greatest stamp trade journal. see *PHILATELY*

737 US
PROOF COLLECTORS CORNER. 1964. bi-m. $15 (Junior $10). World Proof Numismatic Association, Box 4094, Pittsburgh, PA 15201. TEL 412-781-4557. FAX 412-782-4477. bk.rev.
 Description: Current coverage of numismatic issues, with information on the history and background of coins.

793 US ISSN 0095-263X
CJ1
RARE COIN REVIEW. 1969. m. $19. Bowers and Merena Galleries, Inc., Box 1224, Wolfeboro, NH 03894. TEL 603-596-5095. FAX 603-569-5319. Ed. Q. David Bowers. adv.; bk.rev.; bibl.; illus.; circ. controlled.

737 BE
REVUE BELGE DE NUMISMATIQUE ET DE SIGILLOGRAPHIE. 1842. a. 2000 Fr. Societe Royale de Numismatique de Belgique, 28a Av. Leopold, B-1330 Rixensart, Belgium. FAX 32-10-472999. Ed. Tony Hackens. adv.; bk.rev.; cum.index; circ. 500. **Indexed:** Numis.Lit.

737 FR ISSN 0484-8942
REVUE NUMISMATIQUE. 1836. a. 330 F. (Societe Francaise de Numismatique) Societe d'Edition les Belles Lettres, 95 Boulevard Raspail, 75006 Paris, France. bk.rev. **Indexed:** Numis.Lit.
 —BLDSC shelfmark: 7938.600000.

737 SZ ISSN 0035-4163
REVUE SUISSE DE NUMISMATIQUE/SCHWEIZERISCHE NUMISMATISCHE RUNDSCHAU. (Text in English, French and German) 1890. a. 100 SFr. Societe Suisse de Numismatique - Schweizerische Numismatische Gesellschaft, Niederdorfstr. 43, CH-8001 Zuerich, Switzerland. adv.; illus.; circ. 1,000. **Indexed:** Numis.Lit.
 —BLDSC shelfmark: 7953.385400.

737 UK ISSN 0080-4487
ROYAL NUMISMATIC SOCIETY. SPECIAL PUBLICATIONS. irreg. Royal Numismatic Society, British Museum, London WC1B 3DG, England.

737 US ISSN 0036-4053
SAN DIEGO NUMISMATIC SOCIETY. BULLETIN. 1947. m. membership. San Diego Numismatic Society Inc., 611 Oakwood Way, El Cajon, CA 92021. (Subscr. to: Box 1145, San Diego, CA 92112) Ed. Dorothy Baber. charts; illus.; circ. 150.

737.4 UK
SEABY'S STANDARD CATALOGUE OF BRITISH COINS. 1929. a. £12.95. B.A. Seaby Ltd., 7 Davies St., London W1Y 1LL, England. TEL 071-495-2590. FAX 071-491-1595. illus.

737 296 US
SHEKEL. 1968. 6/yr. $15 (foreign $22). American Israel Numismatic Association, 5150 W. Copans Rd., Ste. 1193, Margate, FL 33063. TEL 305-891-4315. FAX 305-895-1258. Ed. Edward Schuman. bk.rev.; circ. 3,000. **Indexed:** Numis.Lit.

737.4 DK ISSN 0586-4496
SIEG'S MOENTKATALOG. DANMARK (YEAR); Groenland, Faeroerne, Island og Dansk Vestindien 1740-1913. (Text in Danish; summaries in English) 1968. a. DKK 90. Frovin Sieg, Ulbjerg Gl. Skole, DK-8832 Skals, Denmark. TEL 86-697102. (Dist. by: Danske Boghandleres Kommissionsanstalt, Siljangade 6, DK-2300 Copenhagen S, Denmark) illus.

737.4 DK ISSN 0900-9310
SIEG'S MOENTKATALOG - NORDEN (YEAR). 1969. a. DKK 120. Frovin Sieg, Ulbjerg Gl. Skole, DK-8832 Skals, Denmark. TEL 86-697102. (Dist. by: Danske Boghandleres Kommissionsanstalt, Siljansgade 6, DK-2300, Copenhagen S. Denmark)

737 US ISSN 0037-5616
SINFORMATION. (Text in English; occasionally in French, German and Spanish) vol.9, 1970. q. $10. Society for International Numismatics, Box 943, Santa Monica, CA 90406. TEL 213-396-4662. Ed. Keith Laumer. adv.; bk.rev.; index; circ. 500. (also avail. in microfilm from UMI)

737 CS ISSN 0081-0088
SLOVENSKA NUMIZMATIKA. (Text in Slovak; summaries in German) 1970. approx. biennial. 35 Kcs. (Slovenska Akademia Vied) Veda, Publishing House of the Slovak Academy of Sciences, Klemensova 19, 814 30 Bratislava, Czechoslovakia. (Dist. by: Slovart, Nam. Slobody 6, 817 64 Bratislava, Czechoslovakia) Ed. Eva Kolnikova. **Indexed:** Numis.Lit.

SLOVENSKE NARODNE MUZEUM. ZBORNIK. see *HISTORY — History Of Europe*

737 FR ISSN 0037-9344
SOCIETE FRANCAISE DE NUMISMATIQUE. BULLETIN. 1946. 10/yr. 180 F. Societe Francaise de Numismatique, 58 rue de Richelieu, 75084 Paris Cedex 2, France. Ed. S. de Turckheim-Pey. bk.rev.; charts; illus.; cum. index every 5 yrs.; circ. 950. **Indexed:** Numis.Lit.

NUMISMATICS — ABSTRACTING, BIBLIOGRAPHIES, STATISTICS

737   IT
SOLDI NUMISMATICA. 1966. m. L.1500 per no. Audiovisivi e Periodici s.r.l., Via Taranto 21, 00182 Rome, Italy. Ed. Mariella Storoni. adv.; circ. 65,000.

STAMP & COIN MART INTERNATIONAL. see *PHILATELY*

737   CS   ISSN 0081-6779
STUDIA NUMISMATICA ET MEDAILISTICA. (Text in Czech; summaries English or in French, German and Russian) 1970. irreg., no.7, 1988. price varies. Moravske Zemske Muzeum, Numismaticke Oddeleni, Zelny trh 6, 659 37 Brno, Czechoslovakia. TEL 42-5-22241. FAX 42-5-25279. illus.; index; circ. 1,200.
   Description: Papers on numismatics and the art of medals.

737   RM   ISSN 0081-8887
STUDII SI CERCETARI DE NUMISMATICA. 1957. irreg., vol.8, 1984. (Academia Romana) Editura Academiei Romane, Calea Victoriei 125, 79717 Bucharest, Rumania. (Subscr. to: Artexim, Export-Import Presa, Str. Piata Presei Libere nr.1, P.O. Box 33-16, 70055 Bucharest, Rumania) **Indexed:** Numis.Lit.

737.4   SW   ISSN 0283-071X
SVENSK NUMISMATISK TIDSKRIFT. 1972. 8/yr. SEK 150. Svenska Numismatiska Foereningen, Sandhamnsgatan 50 A, S-115 28 Stockholm, Sweden. bk.rev.; illus. **Indexed:** NAA, NAA, Numis.Lit.
   Formerly: Myntkontakt.

737   US   ISSN 0271-3993
SYLLOGE NUMMORUM GRAECORUM. Short title: S N G A N S. 1972. irreg., vol.7, 1989. price varies. American Numismatic Society, Broadway at 155th St., New York, NY 10032. TEL 212-234-3130. Eds. M.H. Martin, L.A. Elam. (reprint service avail. from UMI)

737   US   ISSN 0039-8233
T A M S JOURNAL. 1961. bi-m. $20. Token and Medal Society, Box 366, Bryantown, MD 20617. TEL 301-274-3441. Ed. David E. Schenkman. adv.; bk.rev.; charts; illus.; index; cum.index; circ. 2,000. **Indexed:** Numis.Lit.
   Formerly: Token and Medal Society. Journal.

737   AT   ISSN 0817-4075
TASMANIAN NUMISMATIST. 1985. s-a. Aus.$10($12) Tasmanian Numismatic Society, Inc., G.P.O. Box 884 J, Hobart, Tas. 7001, Australia. bk.rev.; circ. 120.

737   US
TIPSICO BULLETIN. 1972. bi-m. $6. Tipsico Coin Co., Box 1128, 2141 Broadway, N. Bend, OR 97459. TEL 503-756-7111. Ed. J. Richard Wagner. adv.; bk.rev.; illus.; circ. 1,000 (controlled).
   Formerly: Collector's Choice Bulletin.

TRIBUNA DEL COLLEZIONISTA; mensile culturale di attualita e cronaca filatelica e numismatica. see *PHILATELY*

TRIDENT - VISNYK. see *PHILATELY*

TRIERER ZEITSCHRIFT FUER GESCHICHTE UND KUNST DES TRIERER LANDES UND SEINER NACHBARGEBIETE. see *ARCHAEOLOGY*

UKRAINIAN PHILATELIST. see *PHILATELY*

069.9 737   BL
UNIVERSIDADE DE SAO PAULO. MUSEU PAULISTA. COLECAO. SERIE DE NUMISMATICA. 1975. irreg. Universidade de Sao Paulo, Museu Paulista, Caixa Postal 42503, Parque da Independencia, 04263 Sao Paulo SP, Brazil. Ed. Antonio Rocha Penteado.
   Supersedes in part (in 1975): Museu Paulista. Colecao (ISSN 0080-6382)

737   CN   ISSN 0049-5824
VANCOUVER NUMISMATIC SOCIETY. NEWS BULLETIN. 1961. m. (except July-Aug.). membership. Vancouver Numismatic Society, Box 67737, Sta. O, Vancouver, B.C. V5W 3V2, Canada. Ed. P.N. Moogk. adv.; bk.rev.; circ. 225. (processed)

737   BE
VIE NUMISMATIQUE. 1966. m. 300 Fr. Cercle d'Etudes Numismatiques, 4 bd. de l'Empereur, B-1000 Brussels, Belgium. (Co-sponsor: Alliance Europeene Numismatique) bibl.; illus. **Indexed:** Numis.Lit.
   Supersedes (in 1973): Jeunesses Numismatiques (ISSN 0021-6224)

737   PL   ISSN 0043-5155
WIADOMOSCI NUMIZMATYCZNE/NUMISMATIC NEWS. 1957. q. $30. Polska Akademia Nauk, Instytut Historii Kultury Materialnej, Al. Solidarnosci 105, 00-190 Warsaw, Poland. (Subscr. to: Ossolineum Pulishing House, Foreign Trade Department, Rynek 9, 50-106 Wroclaw, Poland) Eds. Marta Meclewska, Stanislaw Suchodolski. charts; illus.; index; circ. 740. **Indexed:** Numis.Lit.
   Formerly: Wiadomosci Numizmatyczno-Archeologiczne.

737.4   US   ISSN 0145-9090
WORLD COIN NEWS. 1973. fortn. $24.95. Krause Publications, Inc., 700 E. State St., Iola, WI 54990. TEL 715-445-2214. Ed. Dave Harper. adv.; bk.rev.; bibl.; charts; illus.; circ. 9,393. (also avail. in microfilm from PMC) **Indexed:** Numis.Lit.
   Description: News and classified-display advertisements for international coin investors and collectors, featuring question-answer and reader-opinion forums.

737.4 769.56   IT
WORLD COLLECTIONS NEWS; mensile di informazioni numismatiche e filateliche. 1982? m. (11/yr.). $30. World Wide Collections S.r.l., Corso Buenos Ayres, 20-4, 16129 Genoa, Italy. TEL 010-581463. FAX 010-561855. adv.; circ. 5,000.

737.4   CC
ZHONGGUO QIANBI/CHINA NUMISMATICS. (Text in Chinese) 1983. q. Y20($46.50) (Zhongguo Qianbi Xuehui) Zhongguo Jinrong Chubanshe, Xijiaomin Xiang 17, Beijing 100031, People's Republic of China. TEL 653858. (Dist. in US by: China Books & Periodicals, Inc., 2929 24th St., San Francisco, CA 94110. TEL 415-282-2994)
   Description: Publishes research on numismatics or the history of coins, news of excavations, and interesting anecdotes about coins. Introduces historic coins, presents the experiences of coin collectors, and reports on related events in China and the world.

NUMISMATICS — Abstracting, Bibliographies, Statistics

NUMISMATIC BOOKS IN PRINT. see *BIBLIOGRAPHIES*

769.56 737   US
▼**STAMPS, COINS, POSTCARDS & RELATED MATERIALS;** a directory of periodicals. 1991. irreg. $29. Peri Press, Hemlock Ridge, Box 348, Voorheesville, NY 12186-0348. TEL 518-765-3163. FAX 518-765-3158. Ed. Doris Robinson.
   Description: Includes data in annotated listings of about 700 current periodicals.

NURSES AND NURSING

see *Medical Sciences–Nurses and Nursing*

NUTRITION AND DIETETICS

616.39   GW   ISSN 0720-7522
A I D VERBRAUCHERDIENST; Zeitschrift fuer Fach-, Lehr- und Beratungskraefte im Bereich Ernaehrung. 1956. m. DM.20. Auswertungs- und Informationsdienst fuer Ernaehrung, Landwirtschaft und Forsten e.V., Postfach 200153, 5300 Bonn 2, Germany. TEL 0228-84990. FAX 0228-8499177. TELEX 886323-AIDNB-D. circ. 13,000.
   —BLDSC shelfmark: 9155.778000.

613.2   CN
ACHIEVING HEALTH. q. O'Brien Publishing, 311 Richmond Rd., Ste. 200, Ottawa, Ont. K1Z 6X3, Canada. TEL 514-227-1923. FAX 514-227-5836. Ed. John Moore. adv.; circ. 1,500,000.

ADVANCES. see *PHYSICAL FITNESS AND HYGIENE*

613.2 641.1   US
TX537   CODEN: AFREAW
ADVANCES IN FOOD AND NUTRITION RESEARCH. 1948. irreg., vol.34, 1990. Academic Press, Inc., 1250 Sixth Ave., San Diego, CA 92101. TEL 619-231-0926. FAX 619-699-6715. Eds. E.M. Mrak, George F. Stewart. index. (reprint service avail. from ISI) **Indexed:** Abstr.Hyg., Biol.Abstr., Biol.& Agr.Ind., Chem.Abstr., Dairy Sci.Abstr., Excerpt.Med., Food Sci.& Tech.Abstr., Ind.Med., INIS Atomind., Nutr.Abstr., Trop.Dis.Bull.
   Formerly (until 1990): Advances in Food Research (ISSN 0065-2628)

613.2   US   ISSN 0149-9483
QP141.A1   CODEN: ANURD9
ADVANCES IN NUTRITIONAL RESEARCH. 1977. irreg., vol.8, 1990. Plenum Publishing Corp., 233 Spring St., New York, NY 10013-1578. TEL 212-620-8000. FAX 212-463-0742. TELEX 23-421139. Ed. Harold H. Draper. (back issues avail.) **Indexed:** Chem.Abstr., Ind.Med., Ind.Sci.Rev., Sci.Cit.Ind.
   Description: Provides authoritative accounts of the current state of knowledge regarding major topics of research in the nutritional sciences.
   Refereed Serial

613.26   US
AHIMSA. 1960. 4/yr. $18. American Vegan Society, 501 Old Harding Highway, Malaga, NJ 08328. TEL 609-694-2887. Ed. H. Jay Dinshah. adv.; bk.rev.; index, cum.index.
   Description: Presents total-vegetarian diet, lifestyle, and philosophies.

610 641.1   GW   ISSN 0341-0501
CODEN: AEKPDQ
AKTUELLE ERNAEHRUNGSMEDIZIN; Klinik und Praxis. 1976. bi-m. DM.164 for students and members of the Arbeitsgemeinschaft fuer klinische Diaetetik, Diaetassistentinnen DM.95.40. Georg Thieme Verlag, Ruedigerstr. 14, Postfach 104853, 7000 Stuttgart 10, Germany. Ed.Bd. index; circ. 2,400. (reprint service avail. from UMI) **Indexed:** Chem.Abstr., Curr.Cont., Excerp.Med., Potato Abstr., Triticale Abstr.
   —BLDSC shelfmark: 0785.735000.

641.1   FR
ALIMENTATION ET LA VIE - NOUVELLE PRESENTATION. 1942. q. 65 F. Societe Scientifique d'Hygiene Alimentaire, 16 rue de l'Estrapade, 75005 Paris, France. (Co-sponsor: Association Francaise des Techniciens de l'Alimentation Animale) Ed. Georges le Moan. adv.; bibl.; charts; stat. **Indexed:** Dairy Sci.Abstr., Ind.Vet., Nutr.Abstr., Vet.Bull.
   Formerly: Alimentation et la Vie (ISSN 0065-6267)

613.2   IT   ISSN 0392-7512
CODEN: ANMTD9
ALIMENTAZIONE NUTRIZIONE METABOLISMO; rivista trimestrale di studi nutrizionali ed endocrino-metabolici. (Text in English, French, Italian; summaries in English, Italian) 1979. q. L.64000($35.70) Societa Editrice Universo, Via Morgagni 1, 00161 Rome, Italy. Ed. Michelangelo Cairella. adv.; bk.rev.; bibl.; charts; illus.; index; circ. 500. (tabloid format; back issues avail.) **Indexed:** Biol.Abstr., Chem.Abstr.
   —BLDSC shelfmark: 0787.952000.

612.3 664   SP   ISSN 0212-6400
ALIMENTEC. 1981. m. 4500 ptas. Francisco Javier Goyoaga Perez, Ed. & Pub., Modesto Lafuente, 16, bajo A., Madrid, Spain. TEL (91)445 55 50. FAX 4455600. TELEX SDMAE 46422.

ALIMENTOS E NUTRICAO. see *FOOD AND FOOD INDUSTRIES*

ALIVE; Canadian journal of health and nutrition. see *PHYSICAL FITNESS AND HYGIENE*

AMERICAN CHIROPRACTOR. see *MEDICAL SCIENCES — Chiropractic, Homeopathy, Osteopathy*

616.39   US   ISSN 0731-5724
RC620.A1   CODEN: JONUDL
AMERICAN COLLEGE OF NUTRITION. JOURNAL. 1982. 6/yr. $175 to institutions (foreign $236). John Wiley & Sons, Inc., Journals, 605 Third Ave., New York, NY 10158-0012. TEL 212-850-6000. FAX 212-850-6088. TELEX 12-7063. Ed. Mildred S. Seelig. adv.; bk.rev. (also avail. in microform from RPI) **Indexed:** Biol.Abstr., Chem.Abstr., Curr.Adv.Biochem., Curr.Adv.Ecol.Sci., Curr.Cont., Excerp.Med., Ind.Med., NRN, Sci.Cit.Ind.
—BLDSC shelfmark: 4685.780000.
Description: Covers nutrition research as it applies to patient care.
Refereed Serial

613.2   US   ISSN 0002-8223
RM214   CODEN: JADAAE
AMERICAN DIETETIC ASSOCIATION. JOURNAL. 1925. m. $94. American Dietetic Association, 216 W. Jackson Blvd., Ste. 800, Chicago, IL 60606-6995. TEL 312-899-0040. FAX 312-899-1757. Ed. Elaine R. Monsen. adv.; bk.rev.; abstr.; bibl.; charts; index; circ. 62,000. (also avail. in microform from PMC,UMI; back issues avail.; reprint service avail. from UMI) **Indexed:** Abstr.Health Care Manage.Stud., Abstr.Hyg., Behav.Med.Abstr., Biol.Abstr., Biol.& Agr.Ind., C.I.S. Abstr., Chem.Abstr., Curr.Adv.Biochem., Curr.Adv.Ecol.Sci., Curr.Cont., Dairy Sci.Abstr., Dent.Ind., Dok.Arbeitsmed., Environ.Per.Bibl., Excerp.Med., Food Sci.& Tech.Abstr., Gen.Sci.Ind., Helminthol.Abstr., Hlth.Ind., Hosp.Lit.Ind., Ind.Med., INIS Atomind., Int.Nurs.Ind., NRN, Nutr.Abstr., Potato Abstr., Poult.Abstr., Psychol.Abstr., Risk Abstr., Soc.Work Res.& Abstr.
—BLDSC shelfmark: 4686.130000.
Formerly: American Dietetic Association. Bulletin.
Description: Publishes reports of original research and other papers covering all aspects of dietetics, including nutrition and diet therapy, community nutrition, education, and administration.
Refereed Serial

612.3 613.2   US   ISSN 0002-9165
RC584   CODEN: AJCNAC
AMERICAN JOURNAL OF CLINICAL NUTRITION; a journal reporting the practical application of our world-wide knowledge of nutrition. (Supplement avail.) 1952. m. $80 to non-members; members $40 (foreign $60); institutions $120 (foreign $140). American Society for Clinical Nutrition, Inc., 9650 Rockville Pike, Bethesda, MD 20814-3998. TEL 301-530-7110. FAX 301-571-8303. Ed. Dr. Norman Kretchmer. adv.; bibl.; charts; illus.; index; circ. 7,900. (also avail. in microfilm from PMC,UMI; back issues avail.) **Indexed:** A.S.& T.Ind., Abstr.Hyg., Abstr.Inter.Med., Anim.Breed.Abstr., Behav.Med.Abstr., Bibl.Dev.Med.& Child.Neur., Biol.Abstr., Biol.& Agr.Ind., Chem.Abstr., Curr.Adv.Biochem., Curr.Cont., Dairy Sci.Abstr., Dent.Ind., Dok.Arbeitsmed., Energy Rev., Environ.Per.Bibl., Excerp.Med., Food Sci.& Tech.Abstr., Helminthol.Abstr., Ind.Med., Ind.Sci.Rev., Ind.Vet., INIS Atomind., NRN, Nutr.Abstr., Potato Abstr., Psychol.Abstr., Rev.Plant Path., Rice Abstr., Sci.Cit.Ind., So.Pac.Per.Ind., Soyabean Abstr., Triticale Abstr., Trop.Dis.Bull., Vet.Bull., World Agri.Econ.& Rural Sociol.Abstr.
—BLDSC shelfmark: 0823.000000.

AMERICAN JOURNAL OF HEALTH PROMOTION. see *PUBLIC HEALTH AND SAFETY*

ANALES DE BROMATOLOGIA. see *FOOD AND FOOD INDUSTRIES*

616.39   SZ   ISSN 0250-6807
CODEN: ANUMDS
ANNALS OF NUTRITION AND METABOLISM; European journal of nutrition, metabolic diseases and dietetics. (Supplement: Bibliotheca Nutritio et Dieta) (Text in English, French, German) 1959. bi-m. 373 Fr.($249) per vol. (Federation of European Nutrition Societies) S. Karger AG, Allschwilerstr. 10, P.O. Box, CH-4009 Basel, Switzerland. TEL 061-3061111. FAX 061-3061234. TELEX CH 962652. Ed. N. Zoellner. adv.; bibl.; charts; illus.; index; circ. 1,250. (also avail. in microform from RPI) **Indexed:** Abstr.Hyg., Anim.Breed.Abstr., Biol.Abstr., Biotech.Abstr., Cadscan, Chem.Abstr., Curr.Adv.Ecol.Sci., Curr.Cont., Dairy Sci.Abstr., Dent.Ind., Excerp.Med., Food Sci.& Tech.Abstr., Ind.Med., Ind.Sci.Rev., Lead Abstr., NRN, Nutr.Abstr., Poult.Abstr., Sci.Cit.Ind, Soyabean Abstr., Zincscan.
—BLDSC shelfmark: 1043.250000.
Incorporating (1947-1980): Annales de la Nutrition et de l'Alimentation (ISSN 0003-4037); **Former titles (until 1980):** Nutrition and Metabolism (ISSN 0029-6678); (until 1970): Nutritio et Dieta.
Description: Reports of basic research, primarily on the biochemical and physiological aspects of nutrition.

613.2 664 613.7   US
ANNUAL EDITIONS: NUTRITION. 1988. a. $10.95. Dushkin Publishing Group, Inc., Sluice Dock, Guilford, CT 06437-9989. TEL 203-453-4351. FAX 203-453-6000. Ed. Charlotte Cook-Fuller. illus.
Refereed Serial

613.2   US   ISSN 0199-9885
QP141.A1   CODEN: ARNTD8
ANNUAL REVIEW OF NUTRITION. 1981. a. $45 (foreign $50)(effective Jan. 1992). Annual Reviews Inc., 4139 El Camino Way, Box 10139, Palo Alto, CA 94303-0897. TEL 800-523-8635. FAX 415-855-9815. TELEX 910-290-0275. Ed. Robert E. Olson. bibl.; index. cum.index. (also avail. in microform from UMI; back issues avail.) **Indexed:** Abstr.Hyg., Biol.Abstr., Chem.Abstr., Curr.Adv.Ecol.Sci., Dent.Ind., Ind.Med., Ind.Sci.Rev., Pig News & Info., Potato Abstr., Sci.Cit.Ind.
—BLDSC shelfmark: 1524.300000.
Description: Original reviews of critical literature and current developments in nutrition.
Refereed Serial

613.2   UK   ISSN 0195-6663
QP136   CODEN: APPTD4
APPETITE; the journal for research on intake, and dietary practices, their control and consequences. 1980. bi-m. (2 vols./yr.). $218. Academic Press Ltd., 24-28 Oval Rd., London NW1 7DX, England. TEL 071-267-4466. Ed.Bd. adv.; bk.rev.; index. **Indexed:** Chem.Abstr., Curr.Adv.Ecol.Sci., Dent.Ind., Excerp.Med., Ind.Med., Ind.Sci.Rev., NRN, Nutr.Abstr., Potato Abstr., Poult.Abstr., Psychol.Abstr., Sci.Cit.Ind.
—BLDSC shelfmark: 1570.200000.
Description: Covers the determinants and consequences of eating and drinking disorders. Includes dietary intake, attitudes, and practices.

AQUARIAN ALCHEMIST. see *PARAPSYCHOLOGY AND OCCULTISM*

612.3   GT   ISSN 0004-0622
TX341   CODEN: ALANBH
ARCHIVOS LATINOAMERICANOS DE NUTRICION. (Text in English, French, Portuguese, Spanish) 1966. q. $60 per vol. Latin American Nutrition Society, Institute of Nutrition of Central America and Panama, Carretera Roosevelt, Apdo. Postal 11-88, Guatemala, Guatemala. TELEX 5696 INCAP-GU. Ed. Ricardo Bressani. adv.; bk.rev.; abstr.; bibl.; charts; index; circ. 1,000. (reprint service avail. from ISI) **Indexed:** Biol.Abstr., Chem.Abstr., Curr.Adv.Ecol.Sci., Curr.Cont., Dairy Sci.Abstr., Dent.Ind., Excerp.Med., Food Sci.& Tech.Abstr., Helminthol.Abstr., Ind.Med., Maize Abstr., NRN, Nutr.Abstr., Potato Abstr., Triticale Abstr.
—BLDSC shelfmark: 1655.300000.
Formerly: Archivos Venezolanos de Nutricion.

613.2 610   AT   ISSN 0812-3896
AUSTRALASIAN HEALTH & HEALING; journal of alternative medicine. 1981. q. Aus.$42($21.40) Trim-Keg Party Ltd, 29 Terrace St, Kingscliff, N.S.W. 2487, Australia. TEL 066-742-407. Ed. Maurice Finkel. adv.; bk.rev.; abstr.; circ. 12,000. (back issues avail.)

NUTRITION AND DIETETICS 3603

641 613.2   AT   ISSN 1032-1322
TX341
AUSTRALIAN JOURNAL OF NUTRITION AND DIETETICS. 1944. q. Aus.$40 (foreign Aus.$50). Dietitians Association of Australia, P.O. Box 11, O'Connor, A.C.T. 2601, Australia. TEL 062-472555. FAX 062-572-184. Ed. Nancy E. Hichcock. adv.; bk.rev.; abstr.; circ. 2,400. **Indexed:** Curr.Cont., Dairy Sci.Abstr., Food Sci.& Tech.Abstr., Nutr.Abstr.
—BLDSC shelfmark: 1810.700000.
Former titles (until Mar. 1989): Journal of Food and Nutrition (ISSN 0728-4713); Food and Nutrition Notes and Reviews (ISSN 0015-6329)

613.26   AT
AUSTRALIAN VEGETARIAN. 1962. bi-m. Aus.$4. Vegetarian Society, South Australia, P.O. Box 46, Rundle Sta., Adelaide, S.A. 5000, Australia. Eds. T. Allen, E.M. Fearnside. adv.; bk.rev.; circ. 1,000.
Description: Covers cooking methods and philosophies.

AUSTRALIAN WELL BEING; personal and planetary healing. see *PHYSICAL FITNESS AND HYGIENE*

B A S H MAGAZINE. (Bulimia Anorexia Self-Help) see *MEDICAL SCIENCES — Psychiatry And Neurology*

613   CN
B C D N A NEWS. m. British Columbia Dietitians' and Nutritionists' Association, 306 - 1037 W. Broadway, Vancouver, B.C. V6H 1E3, Canada. circ. 725. (back issues avail.)
Description: Provides members with current information on topics and events of interest.

641.4 664   UK   ISSN 0141-9684
CODEN: BNUBD6
B N F NUTRITION BULLETIN. 1968. 3/yr. £16. British Nutrition Foundation, 15 Belgrave Sq., London SW1X 8PS, England. TEL 071-235-4904. FAX 071-235-5336. Ed. Margaret Ashwell. index; circ. 1,300. **Indexed:** Abstr.Hyg., Biol.Abstr., Chem.Abstr, Curr.Adv.Ecol.Sci., Dairy Sci.Abstr., Food Sci.& Tech.Abstr., Nutr.Abstr., Packag.Sci.Tech., Trop.Dis.Bull.
—BLDSC shelfmark: 2116.298000.
Description: Covers the present state of knowledge in clinical nutrition, food processing, food safety and food policy.

612.3 617.1   US
BARIATRICIAN. 1986. q. $36 (foreign $48). American Society of Bariatric Physicians, 5600 S. Quebec, Ste. 160D, Englewood, CO 80111-2210. FAX 303-779-4834. Ed. James F. Merker. adv.; circ. 1,000. (back issues avail.)

641   US
BASIC AND CLINICAL NUTRITION. 1980. irreg., vol.3, 1981. price varies. Marcel Dekker, Inc., 270 Madison Ave., New York, NY 10016. TEL 212-696-9000. FAX 212-685-4540. TELEX 421419. **Indexed:** Biol.Abstr., Chem.Abstr.
Refereed Serial

613.2   US
BETTER HOMES AND GARDENS LOW-CALORIE RECIPES. 1982. a. $3.50 per. no. Meredith Corporation, Special Interest Publications, 1716 Locust St., Des Moines, IA 50309. TEL 515-284-3000. circ. 500,000.
Formerly: Diet and Exercise (ISSN 0163-0334)

641.1   US
TX341
BETTER NUTRITION FOR TODAY'S LIVING. m. $20 (foreign $90). Communication Channels, Inc., 6255 Barfield Rd., Atlanta, GA 30328-4369. TEL 404-256-9800. FAX 404-256-3116. TELEX 4611075 COMCHANI. Ed. Frank Murray. adv.; illus. (also avail. in microform from UMI; reprint service avail. from UMI) **Indexed:** Hlth.Ind., PMR.
●Also available online.
Formerly (until 1990): Better Nutrition (ISSN 0405-668X); Incorporates (in 1990): Today's Living (ISSN 0743-7285)
Description: Discusses health foods, vitamin supplements, herbs, cosmetics and bodycare, diet and new products. Includes menus and recipes.

NUTRITION AND DIETETICS

641.1　　　　　　SZ　　ISSN 0067-8198
TX341　　　　　　　　　CODEN: BNDSA3
BIBLIOTHECA NUTRITIO ET DIETA. (Supplement avail.: Annals of Nutritional Metabolism) (Text in English, French and German) 1960. irreg. (approx. 1/yr). price varies. S. Karger AG, Allschwilerstr. 10, P.O. Box, CH-4009 Basel, Switzerland. TEL 061-3061111. FAX 061-3061234. TELEX CH 962652. Ed. J.C. Somogyi. (back issues avail.; reprint service avail. from ISI) **Indexed:** Biodet.Abstr., Biol.Abstr., Chem.Abstr., Curr.Cont., Dairy Sci.Abstr., Food Sci.& Tech.Abstr., Ind.Med., Nutr.Abstr.
—BLDSC shelfmark: 2019.200000.

BIO NACHRICHTEN. see *AGRICULTURE — Crop Production And Soil*

BIOLOGICAL TRACE ELEMENT RESEARCH. see *BIOLOGY — Biological Chemistry*

612.3　　　　　　AT　　ISSN 0729-2759
BREASTFEEDING REVIEW. 1982. s-a. Aus.$25. Nursing Mothers' Association of Australia, P.O. Box 231, Nunawading, Vic. 3131, Australia. Ed. Ellen McIntyre. adv.; bk.rev.; circ. 1,500. (back issues avail.)
—BLDSC shelfmark: 2277.494260.
Description: For medical, nursing and allied health professionals, contains current research and developments in all aspects of human lactation.

BRITISH FOOD JOURNAL. see *FOOD AND FOOD INDUSTRIES*

612.3　　　　　　UK　　ISSN 0007-1145
TX501　　　　　　　　　CODEN: BJNUAV
BRITISH JOURNAL OF NUTRITION. (Supplement avail.: Nutrition Research Review (ISSN 0954-4224)) 1947. 6/yr. $419 (includes supplement). (Nutrition Society) Cambridge University Press, Edinburgh Bldg., Shaftesbury Rd., Cambridge CB2 2RU, England. TEL 0223-312393. FAX 0223-315052. TELEX 851817256. (North American orders to: Cambridge University Press, 40 W. 20th St., New York, NY 10011) Ed. M.I. Gurr. adv.; bibl.; charts; index. (also avail. in microform from SWZ,UMI,PMC) **Indexed:** Abstr.Hyg., Anal.Abstr., Anim.Breed.Abstr., ASCA, Behav.Med.Abstr., Biol.Abstr., Biol.& Agr.Ind., Biotech.Abstr., Chem.Abstr., Curr.Adv.Biochem., Curr.Adv.Ecol.Sci., Curr.Cont., Dairy Sci.Abstr., Dent.Ind., Environ.Per.Bibl., Excerp.Med., Food Sci.& Tech.Abstr., Helminthol.Abstr., Ind.Med., Ind.Sci.Rev., Ind.Vet., INIS Atomind., Maize Abstr., NRN, Nutr.Abstr., Pig News & Info., Potato Abstr., Poult.Abstr., Protozool.Abstr., Rice Abstr., Sci.Cit.Ind, Small Anim.Abstr., Sorghum & Millets Abstr., Soyabean Abstr., Triticale Abstr., Trop.Dis.Bull., Vet.Bull.
—BLDSC shelfmark: 2312.000000.
Description: Devoted to the advancement of the scientific study of nutrition and its application to the maintenance of human and animal health. Includes papers on clinical and human nutrition, as well as general nutrition.

613.2　　　　　　UK
BRITISH NUTRITION FOUNDATION BRIEFING PAPERS. 1980. irreg. £2. British Nutrition Foundation, 15 Belgrave Square, London SW1X 8PS, England. TEL 071-235-4904.
Description: Topics include nutrition during pregnancy, salt, energy balance, food and behavior, dietary information.

613.2　　　　　　UK
BRITISH NUTRITION FOUNDATION MONOGRAPH. 1980. irreg. British Nutrition Foundation, 15 Belgrave Sq., London SW1X 8PS, England. TEL 071-235-4904. FAX 071-235-5336. **Indexed:** Nutr.Abstr.
Formerly: British Nutrition Foundation Newsletter.
Description: Monographs on nutrition and diet.

613.2　　　　　　UK
BRITISH NUTRITION FOUNDATION TASK FORCE REPORTS. 1983. irreg. British Nutrition Foundation, 15 Belgrave Sq., London SW1X 8PS, England. TEL 071-235-4904. FAX 071-235-5336.
Description: Reports on nutrition in medical education, food intolerance and food aversion, sugars and syrups, trans-fatty acids.

613.2　　　　　　US　　ISSN 0007-7364
BUXOM BELLE COURIER.* 1959. m. $1. Buxom Belles International, Inc., 619 Spencer, Ferndale, MI 48220. Ed. Mrs. Dee Phillips. charts; illus.; stat.; circ. 2,800. (processed)

BWINO: HEALTH CARE NEWS. see *PHYSICAL FITNESS AND HYGIENE*

C M U JOURNAL OF SCIENCE. (Central Mindanao University) see *AGRICULTURE*

641.1 613.7　　　US　　ISSN 0741-739X
C S C REPORTS. 1977. 4/yr. $16. (Cooking for Survival Consciousness) C S C Press, Box 26762, Elkins Park, PA 19117-0672. TEL 215-635-1022. Ed. Beatrice Wittels. adv.; bk.rev.; circ. 39,000.
Description: News briefs, articles, and recipes on health-through-nutrition, and changes in lifestyle.

641　　　　　　　FR　　ISSN 0007-9960
　　　　　　　　　　　CODEN: CNDQA8
CAHIERS DE NUTRITION ET DE DIETETIQUE. 1966. bi-m. 370 F. (EEC 55 ECU, elsewhere $72). (Societe de Nutrition et de Dietetique de Langue Francaise) S.P.P.I.F. (Subsidiary of: Masson), 7 rue Laromiguiere, 75005 Paris, France. TEL 33-1-46-34-21-60. FAX 33-1-45-87-29-99. TELEX 202 671 F. Ed. Robert Feron. adv.; bk.rev.; charts; illus.; circ. 3,000 (controlled). **Indexed:** Biol.Abstr., Chem.Abstr., Curr.Adv.Biochem., Curr.Adv.Ecol.Sci., Curr.Adv.Genetics & Molec.Biol., Curr.Cont., Dairy Sci.Abstr., Excerp.Med., Food Sci.& Tech.Abstr., Rural Recreat.Tour.Abstr., World Agri.Econ.& Rural Sociol.Abstr.
—BLDSC shelfmark: 2950.200000.

613.2　　　　　　JM　　ISSN 0376-7655
CAJANUS. 1967. q. free to Caribbean and Latin American countries; $6 to Third World countries; $12 to U.S and other developed countries. Caribbean Food and Nutrition Institute, U.W.I. Mona Campus, P.O. Box 140, Kingston 7, Jamaica, W.I. TEL 809-927-1540. FAX 809-927-2657. TELEX 3705. (Co-sponsors: Pan American Health Organization, World Health Organization) Ed. Clare Forrester. bk.rev.; bibl.; charts; index; circ. 2,028. **Indexed:** Dairy Sci.Abstr., Food Sci.& Tech.Abstr., Nutr.Abstr., Rural Ext.Educ.& Tr.Abstr.
—BLDSC shelfmark: 2952.570000.
Description: Research articles on nutrition and dietary intake, focusing on the population of the Caribbean.

613.2　　　　　　US　　ISSN 1049-1791
CALORIE CONTROL COMMENTARY. 1979. irreg. (2-3/yr). free. Calorie Control Council, 5775 Peachtree-Dunwoody Rd., Ste. 500-G, Atlanta, GA 30342. TEL 404-252-3663. FAX 404-252-0774. Ed. Keith C. Keeney. charts; illus.; stat.; circ. 12,000. (back issues avail.)
Description: Newsletter summarizing scientific, regulatory and other developments relating to sweeteners, fat replacers, dieting, weight control and dietary foods and beverages.

641　　　　　　　CN　　ISSN 0008-3399
　　　　　　　　　　　CODEN: JCDTAH
CANADIAN DIETETIC ASSOCIATION. JOURNAL/ASSOCIATION CANADIENNE DES DIETETISTES. REVUE. (Text in English, French) 1939. q. Can.$45 (foreign $50). Canadian Dietetic Association - Association Canadienne des Dietetistes, 480 University Ave., Ste. 601, Toronto, Ont. M5G 1V2, Canada. TEL 416-596-0857. FAX 416-596-0603. Ed. Kathleen Harrison. adv.; bk.rev.; charts; illus.; index; circ. 5,500. (also avail. in microfilm from UMI) **Indexed:** Biol.Abstr., Chem.Abstr., Curr.Cont., Food Sci.& Tech.Abstr., NRN, Nutr.Abstr.
—BLDSC shelfmark: 4723.020000.
Description: Articles and research reports in nutrition, dietetics, food administration and management.
Refereed Serial

613.2　　　　　　VI
CARIBBEAN DIET DIGEST. Cover title: Dr. Carter's Caribbean Diet Digest. q. $18. Caribbean Diet Institute, PO Box 191, Frederiksted, St. Croix, Virgin Islands.

613.2　　　　　　US
CARNATION NUTRITION EDUCATION SERIES. 1989. irreg., latest vol.3. price varies. Raven Press, 1185 Ave. of the Americas, New York, NY 10036. TEL 212-930-9500. FAX 212-869-3495.

613　　　　　　　UK　　ISSN 0267-3851
CATERING AND HEALTH; the international journal of hygiene and nutrition in catering (food service). 1987. 4/yr. £79($159) A B Academic Publishers, P.O. Box 42, Bicester, Oxon OX6 7NW, England. TEL 0869-320949. Ed. Dr. Robert Charles.
—BLDSC shelfmark: 3092.885000.
Description: Concerned with the nutritional and hygienic aspects of foodservice.

CEYLON JOURNAL OF MEDICAL SCIENCE. see *MEDICAL SCIENCES*

CHICAGO HEALTHCARE. see *PHYSICAL FITNESS AND HYGIENE*

CHILE PEPPER; spicy world cuisine. see *HOME ECONOMICS*

613.2　　　　　　IT
CLINICA DIETOLOGICA. q. L.18000. Societa Editrice Universo, Via G.B. Morgagni 1, 00161 Rome, Italy. Ed. Michelangelo Cairella. **Indexed:** Biol.Abstr., Soyabean Abstr.

613.2　　　　　　UK　　ISSN 0261-5614
　　　　　　　　　　　CODEN: CLNUDP
CLINICAL NUTRITION. 1982. 7/yr. £152($296) (European Society of Parenteral and Enteral Nutrition) Churchill Livingstone Medical Journals, Robert Stevenson House, 1-3 Baxter's Pl., Leith Walk, Edinburgh EH1 3AF, Scotland. TEL 031-556-2424. FAX 031-558-1278. TELEX 727511. (Subscr. to: Longman Group, Journals Subscr. Dept, P.O. Box 77, Fourth Ave., Harlow, Essex CM19 5AA, England; U.S. subscr. to: Churchill Livingstone, 650 Ave. of the Americas, New York, NY 10011. TEL 212-206-5000) Ed. S.P. Allison. adv.; bk.rev. (also avail. in microform from UMI; back issues avail.) **Indexed:** Chem.Abstr., Curr.Adv.Ecol.Sci., Excerp.Med., NRN.
—BLDSC shelfmark: 3286.314500.

613.2　　　　　　US　　ISSN 1053-0452
RM214
▼**CLINICS IN APPLIED NUTRITION.** 1990. 4/yr. $55 to individuals (foreign $75); institutions $75 (foreign $92). Andover Medical Publishers Inc., 125 Main St., Reading, MA 01867. TEL 617-438-8464. FAX 617-438-1479. (Dist. by: Butterworth - Heinemann Ltd., 80 Montvale Ave., Stoneham, MA 02180. TEL 800-366-2665) Ed. Ronni Chernoff.
—BLDSC shelfmark: 3286.543000.
Description: Focuses on current research and issues in clinical nutrition.

COLLEGE - UNIVERSITY FOODSERVICE WHO'S WHO. see *BUSINESS AND ECONOMICS — Trade And Industrial Directories*

COMMENTS FROM C A S T. see *AGRICULTURE*

CONSUMING PASSIONS. see *WOMEN'S INTERESTS*

COOKING LIGHT; the magazine of food and fitness. see *HOME ECONOMICS*

616.39　　　　　US　　ISSN 0191-2453
　　　　　　　　　　　CODEN: CTNDDU
CURRENT TOPICS IN NUTRITION AND DISEASE. 1977. irreg., vol.22, 1990. price varies. Wiley-Liss, Inc., 41 E. 11th St., New York, NY 10003. TEL 212-475-7700. bibl.; illus.; index. **Indexed:** Biol.Abstr., Chem.Abstr.
Refereed Serial

641.1　　　　　　US　　ISSN 0011-5568
　　　　　　　　　　　CODEN: DACDAK
DAIRY COUNCIL DIGEST; an interpretive review of recent nutrition research. 1929. bi-m. $12 (foreign $16). National Dairy Council, 6300 N. River Rd., Rosemont, IL 60018-4233. TEL 708-696-1020. FAX 708-696-1033. index; circ. 25,000. (back issues avail.) **Indexed:** CHNI, Hlth.Ind., Nutr.Abstr.
Description: Covers recent nutrition research information for professional people. Each issues examines a single topic.

641.5　　　　　　US
DELICIOUS!; guide to natural living. 8/yr. $20 (foreign $24). New Hope Communications, Inc., 1301 Spruce St., Boulder, CO 80302-4832. TEL 303-939-8440. FAX 303-939-9559. Ed. Sue Frederick.
Description: Articles on personal care, fitness, natural foods, herbs, vitamins and lifestyles.

NUTRITION AND DIETETICS

DIABETES, NUTRITION & METABOLISM, CLINICAL AND EXPERIMENTAL. see *MEDICAL SCIENCES — Endocrinology*

DIET & HEALTH MAGAZINE. see *PHYSICAL FITNESS AND HYGIENE*

616.39   IT
DIETETICA CLINICA E MALATTIE DELLA NUTRIZIONE. q. Casa Editrice Idelson, Via A. DeGasperi, 55, 80133 Naples, Italy. TEL 081-5524733. FAX 5518295. Ed. Giovanni Iacono.

641.1 640   SA   ISSN 0378-5254
DIETETICS & HOME ECONOMICS/DIEET- EN HUISHOUDKUNDE. (Text in Afrikaans, English) 1973. 3/yr. R.21. South Africa Dietetics & Home Economics Association (SADHEA), P.O. Box 35269, Menlo Park, Pretoria 0102, South Africa. Ed. E. Boshoff. adv.; bk.rev.; circ. 1,300. **Indexed:** INIS Atomind., Nutr.Abstr.

612.3   CN   ISSN 0834-3160
DIETETIQUE EN ACTION. 1986. 4/yr. $50 to individuals; institutions $70. Corporation Professionelle des Dietetistes du Quebec, 1425 boul. Rene-Levesque Ouest, Bureau 402, Montreal, Que. H3G 1T7, Canada. TEL 514-393-3733. FAX 514-844-9601. Ed. Gisele Fournier. adv.; circ. 2,500. **Indexed:** Pt.de Rep. (1989-).

641.1   SW
DIETISTEN. 1949. m. (11/yr.). SEK 198. Svensk Dietistfoerening, P.O. Box 12069, S-102 22 Stockholm, Sweden. Ed. Anne-Marie Tidholm. adv.; circ. 2,396.

616   US   ISSN 1048-6984
▼**EATING DISORDERS REVIEW;** current clinical information for the professional treating eating disorders. 1990. bi-m. $59. P.M. Inc., Box 10172, Van Nuys, CA 91410. TEL 213-873-4399. Ed. Mary K. Stein. (back issues avail.)

613.2   FR
ECOLE NATIONALE SUPERIEURE DE BIOLOGIE APPLIQUEE A LA NUTRITION ET A L'ALIMENTATION. CAHIERS. Cover title: E N S B A N A Cahiers. 1976. a. price varies. Ecole Nationale Superieure de Biologie Appliquee a la Nutrition et a l'Alimentation (ENSBANA), 11 rue Lavoisier, 75384 Paris cedex 08, France. TEL 42-65-39-95. FAX 42-65-02-46. TELEX LAVOISI 649404 F. Ed. Denise Simatos. adv.; bk.rev.; bibl.; charts; illus.; circ. 3,000. **Indexed:** Bull.Signal., Chem.Abstr.
Former titles: Amis de l'E.N.S.B.A.N.A; Amis de l'I.B.A.N.A. (Publication) (ISSN 0003-1801)

613.2   US   ISSN 0367-0244
TX341   CODEN: ECFNBN
ECOLOGY OF FOOD AND NUTRITION. 1971. 8/yr. (in 2 vol., 4 nos./vol.). $236. Gordon and Breach Science Publishers, 270 Eighth Ave., New York, NY 10011. FAX 212-645-2459. TELEX 236735 GOPUB UR. (Subscr. to: Box 786, Cooper Sta., New York, NY 10276. TEL 800-545-8398; UK subscr. to: P.O. Box 90, Reading, Berkshire RG1 8JL, England. TEL 0734-560-080) Ed.Bd. adv.; bk.rev.; bibl.; charts; illus.; index. (also avail. in microform from MIM) **Indexed:** A.I.C.P., Abstr.Anthropol., Abstr.Hyg., Agroforest.Abstr., Biol.Abstr., Cadscan, Chem.Abstr., Curr.Adv.Ecol.Sci., Curr.Cont., Dairy Sci.Abstr., Energy Ind., Energy Info.Abstr., Environ.Per.Bibl., Excerp.Med., Field Crop Abstr., Food Sci.& Tech.Abstr., Geo.Abstr., Herb.Abstr., Ind.Sci.Rev., Lead Abstr., Maize Abstr., NRN, Nutr.Abstr., Potato Abstr., Rice Abstr., Rural Sociol.Abstr., Sci.Cit.Ind., So.Pac.Per.Ind., Soils & Fert., Trop.Dis.Bull., World Agri.Econ.& Rural Sociol.Abstr., Zincscan.
—BLDSC shelfmark: 3650.043000.
Description: Emphasizes foods and their utilization in satisfying the nutritional needs of mankind, but also extends to nonfood contributions, to obesity and leanness, malnutrition, vitamin requirements, and mineral needs.
Refereed Serial

614   BE   ISSN 0004-5144
EDUCATION SANITAIRE ET NUTRITIONNELLE D'AFRIQUE CENTRALE. 1927. q. 100 Fr. Centre d'Education Sanitaire et Nurtritionnelle d'Afrique Centrale, 11 rue Brialmont, B-1030 Brussels, Belgium. Ed. M. M. Moeremans d'Emaus. circ. 1,000.
Formerly: Assistance aux Maternites et Dispensaires en Afrique Centrale.

641.1   UA   ISSN 1110-0192
EGYPTIAN JOURNAL OF FOOD SCIENCE/MAJALLAH AL-MISRIYAH LI-ULUM AL-AGHDHIYA. (Text in English; summaries in Arabic and English) 1973. 3/yr. $45. (Society of Food Science and Technology, Research Department) National Information and Documentation Centre (NIDOC), Tahrir St., Dokki, Awqaf P.O., Cairo, Egypt. Ed. A. Alian. illus.; circ. 1,000. **Indexed:** Biol.Abstr., Chem.Abstr., Curr.Pack.Abstr., Dairy Sci.Abstr., Food Sci.& Tech.Abstr., Hort.Abstr., Nutr.Abstr., Packag.Sci.Tech.

641.1   US   ISSN 0893-4452
ENVIRONMENTAL NUTRITION; the professional newsletter of diet, nutrition and health. 1977. m. $36 to libraries (foreign $49). Environmental Nutrition, Inc., 2112 Broadway, Ste. 200, New York, NY 10023. TEL 212-362-0424. (Subscr. to: Box 3000, Dept. BBB, Denville, NJ 07834) Ed. Denise Webb. bk.rev.; index; circ. 10,000. (looseleaf format; back issues avail.) **Indexed:** CHNI, Hlth.Ind.
●Also available on CD-ROM.
Formerly: Environmental Nutrition Newsletter (ISSN 0195-4024)

ENVIRONMENTAL OPPORTUNITIES. see *ENVIRONMENTAL STUDIES*

641.1   IT
ERBORISTERIA DOMANI. 1978. m. (11/yr.). L.21000 for 10 nos. Giulio Benelli, Ed. & Pub., Via F. Denti 2, 20133 Milan, Italy. adv.; circ. 20,000. **Indexed:** Apic.Abstr.

641.1   GW   ISSN 0340-2371
                            CODEN: ERUMAT
ERNAEHRUNGS UMSCHAU; Forschung und Praxis. (Includes supplement: Ernaehrungslehre- und Praxis) 1954. m. DM.112.20 (student DM.91.80). (Deutsche Gesellschaft fuer Ernaehrung) Umschau Verlag Breidenstein GmbH, Stuttgarter Str. 18-24, 6000 Frankfurt a.M. 1, Germany. TEL 069-2600-0. FAX 069-2600-609. TELEX 411964. (Co-sponsors: Verband Deutscher Diaetassistenten; Guetegemeinschaft Diaetverpflegung) Ed. Sabine Fankhaenel. adv.; bk.rev.; charts; illus.; stat.; index; circ. 9,900. (back issues avail.) **Indexed:** Biol.Abstr., Chem.Abstr., Curr.Adv.Ecol.Sci., Curr.Cont., Dairy Sci.Abstr., Excerp.Med., Food Sci.& Tech.Abstr., INIS Atomind., Nutr.Abstr.

ERNAEHRUNGSDIENST; deutsche Getreidezeitung; Boersen- u. Handelsblatt fuer Getreide u. Landesprodukte. see *AGRICULTURE — Feed, Flour And Grain*

641.1   GW   ISSN 0071-1179
                            CODEN: ERNFA7
ERNAEHRUNGSFORSCHUNG; aktuelle Informationen aus Wissenschaft und Praxis. 1956. bi-m. DM.100.20. (Akademie der Wissenschaften der DDR, Zentralinstitut fuer Ernaehrung) Akademie-Verlag Berlin, Leipziger Str. 3-4, 1086 Berlin, Germany. TELEX 114420-AVERL-DD. Ed. H.-A. Ketz. charts; illus.; index. **Indexed:** Biol.Abstr., Chem.Abstr, Dairy Sci.Abstr., Excerp.Med., Food Sci.& Tech.Abstr., Maize Abstr., Pig News & Info.

612.3   GW   ISSN 0721-5118
ERNAEHRUNGSRUNDBRIEF. 1970. q. DM.24. Arbeitskreis fuer Ernaehrungsforschung e.V., Zwerweg 19, 7263 Bad Liebenzell, Germany. Ed. U. Reuzenbrink. adv.; bk.rev.; index; circ. 4,000. (back issues avail.)

613.2   DK
ERNAERINGSNYT. 6/yr. free. Sundhedsministeriet, Levnedsmiddelsesstyrelsen, Moerkehoej Bygade 19, DK-2860 Soeborg, Denmark. TEL 39-69-66-00.

EXERCISE PHYSIOLOGY: CURRENT SELECTED RESEARCH. see *PHYSICAL FITNESS AND HYGIENE*

EXTENDED CARE PRODUCT NEWS. see *PHYSICAL FITNESS AND HYGIENE*

613.2   UN   ISSN 1014-3181
F A O FOOD AND NUTRITION SERIES. (Text in English, French and Spanish) irreg., no.24. 1991. price varies. Food and Agriculture Organization of the United Nations, c/o UNIPUB, 4611-F Assembly Dr., Lanham, MD 20706-4391. FAX 301-459-0056. **Indexed:** Ind.Med., Nutr.Abstr., World Agri.Econ.& Rural Sociol.Abstr.
Formerly: F A O Nutritional Study (ISSN 0071-7088)

613.2   GW   ISSN 0933-6680
FEINSCHMECKER FUER AERZTE. 1987. m. DM.96. Pharma Verlag Frankfurt GmbH, August-Schanz-Str. 21, 6000 Frankfurt a.M. 50, Germany. TEL 069-5480000. FAX 069-548000-77. Ed. Peter Hoffmann. circ. 20,000. (back issues avail.)

613.2   US   ISSN 0895-0040
FELIX LETTER; a commentary on nutrition. 1981. 6/yr. $11 (effective Feb. 1991). Clara Felix, Ed. & Pub., Box 7094, Berkeley, CA 94707. bk.rev.; circ. 2,000 (controlled). (back issues avail.)
Description: Critical review and commentary on nutrition research. Promotes nutrition as an alternative to or adjunctive to medical approaches to illness.

572 900   US   ISSN 0740-9710
TX341   CODEN: FOFWEC
FOOD AND FOODWAYS; explorations in the history and culture of human nutrition. 4/yr. (in 1 vol., 4 nos./vol.). $91. Harwood Academic Publishers, 270 Eighth Ave., New York, NY 10011. TEL 212-206-8900. FAX 212-645-2459. TELEX 236735 GOPUB UR. (Subscr. to: Box 786, Cooper Sta., New York, NY 10276. TEL 800-545-8398; UK Subscr. to: P.O. Box 90, Reading, Berkshire RG1 8JL. TEL 0734-560-080) Ed. Steven L. Kaplan. adv. (also avail. in microform)
—BLDSC shelfmark: 3977.038450.
Refereed Serial

612.3   US   ISSN 0046-4384
TX341
FOOD AND NUTRITION. 1971. q. $5. U.S. Department of Agriculture, Food and Nutrition Service, Alexandria, VA 22302. TEL 202-447-8046. (Subscr. to: Supt. of Documents, Govt. Printing Office, Washington, DC 20402) Ed. Jan A. Kern. charts; illus.; circ. 5,000. (also avail. in microform from MIM,UMI) **Indexed:** Biol.& Agr.Ind., Food Sci.& Tech.Abstr., Hlth.Ind., Ind.U.S.Gov.Per., Mag.Ind., MEDOC, Rural Devel.Abstr., World Agri.Econ.& Rural Sociol.Abstr.
Description: Information on family assistance and child nutrition programs administered by the service.

641.1   UN   ISSN 0379-5721
TX341   CODEN: FNBPDV
FOOD AND NUTRITION BULLETIN. (Text in English) 1978. q. $40 (developing countries $25). United Nations University Press, Toho Seimei Bldg., 15-1, Shibuya 2-chome, Shibuya-ku, Tokyo 150, Japan. TEL 03-3499-2811. FAX 03-3499-2828. TELEX J25442 UNATUNIV. Ed. Dr. Nevin S. Scrimshaw. bk.rev.; cum.index, vols.1-3; circ. 3,800. (also avail. in microfiche; back issues avail.) **Indexed:** Agroforest.Abstr., Chem.Abstr, Food Sci.& Tech.Abstr., I D A, IIS, Rice Abstr., Rural Devel.Abstr., Sorghum & Millets Abstr., World Agri.Econ.& Rural Sociol.Abstr.
Supersedes: Protein-Calorie Advisory Group of the United Nations System. P A G Bulletin.

FOOD AND NUTRITION IN HISTORY AND ANTHROPOLOGY. see *ANTHROPOLOGY*

641   US   ISSN 0015-6310
FOOD & NUTRITION NEWS. 1930. 5/yr. free. National Live Stock and Meat Board, 444 N. Michigan Ave., Chicago, IL 60611. TEL 312-467-5520. FAX 312-467-9729. Ed. E. Urenos. bk.rev.; index; circ. 55,000. (reprint service avail. from UMI) **Indexed:** CHNI, Hlth.Ind., Ind.Free Per.
—BLDSC shelfmark: 3977.045000.

641.1   GW   ISSN 0721-6912
FOOD COMPOSITION AND NUTRITION TABLES/ZUSAMMENSETZUNG DER LEBENSMITTEL, NAEHRWERT TABELLEN. (Text in English, French and German) irreg. (2-3/yr.). Wissenschaftliche Verlagsgesellschaft mbH, Postfach 105339, 7000 Stuttgart 10, Germany. TEL 0711-2582-0. FAX 0711-2582-290.
—BLDSC shelfmark: 3977.289000.

FOOD HYGIENIC SOCIETY OF JAPAN. JOURNAL/SHOKUHIN EISEIGAKU ZASSHI. see *PUBLIC HEALTH AND SAFETY*

FOOD, NUTRITION & HEALTH NEWSLETTER. see *FOOD AND FOOD INDUSTRIES*

NUTRITION AND DIETETICS

581 UK
CODEN: JPFOD4
FOOD SCIENCE. 1973-19??; resumed 1992. q. £22 to individuals; institutions £45. Macmillan Press Ltd., Houndmills, Basingstoke, Hampshire RG2 2XS, England. Eds. J.W.T. Dickerson, A.R. Leeds. circ. 1,000 (controlled). **Indexed:** Abstr.Hyg., Chem.Abstr., Curr.Pack.Abstr., Food Sci.& Tech.Abstr., Hort.Abstr., Nutr.Abstr., Trop.Dis.Bull.
Former titles (until 1992): Journal of Plant Foods (ISSN 0142-968X); Plant Foods for Man (ISSN 0306-2686)

664 UK ISSN 0950-9623
FOOD SCIENCE AND TECHNOLOGY TODAY. 1987. q. £52($125) Institute of Food Science and Technology, 210 Shepherd's Bush Rd., London W6 7LR, England. FAX 071-522-9623. Ed. H. Paine. adv.; bk.rev. **Indexed:** Br.Tech.Ind., Dairy Sci.Abstr. —BLDSC shelfmark: 3983.090000.
Description: Provides the food community with proceedings and symposia, articles, opinions, research, and review articles about food science.

613.2 664 US ISSN 1046-705X
TX543 CODEN: FSTUE2
FOOD STRUCTURE. 1982. q. $65 (foreign $70). Scanning Microscopy International, Inc., Box 66507, AMF O'Hare, Chicago, IL 60666-0507. TEL 312-529-6677. FAX 312-980-6698. Ed. Om Johari. bk.rev.; illus.; cum.index; circ. 300. (back issues avail.) **Indexed:** ASCA, Biol.Abstr., Chem.Abstr., Curr.Adv.Ecol.Sci., Curr.Cont., Dairy Sci.Abstr., Food Sci.& Tech.Abstr., Ind.Sci.Rev., Sci.Cit.Ind, SSCI. —BLDSC shelfmark: 3983.600000.
Formerly (until vol.8, no.2, 1989): Food Microstructure (ISSN 0730-5419)
Description: Covers the structure of foods and feeds with special emphasis on the relation between processing, molecular properties, microstructure and macroscopic behavior.
Refereed Serial

612.3 616.3 US ISSN 0890-507X
G I G NEWSLETTER. 1974. q. $22.50 (foreign $30). Gluten Intolerance Group of North America, Box 23053, Seattle, WA 98102-0353. TEL 206-325-6980. Ed. Elaine I. Hartsook. bk.rev.; index; circ. 1,500. (looseleaf format; back issues avail.)

641.1 635 US
GARLIC TIMES;* the newsletter of lovers of the stinking rose. 1976. a. $21 for 2 yrs. (Lovers of the Stinking Rose) Harris Publishing, 1563 Solan Ave., Ste. 201, Berkeley, CA 94707-2116. Ed. L. John Harris. adv.; bk.rev.; circ. 5,000. (back issues avail.)

GASTRONOMIE; Fachzeitschrift fuer Restaurant, Kueche und Hotel. see *HOTELS AND RESTAURANTS*

GATHERED VIEW. see *MEDICAL SCIENCES*

641.1 IO ISSN 0436-0265
GIZI INDONESIA. (Text in English, Indonesian) q. Rps.1200. (Indonesian Nutrition Association) Akedemi Gizi, J1. Hang Jebat III/F3, P.O. Box 8 KBB, Kebayoran Baru, Jakarta, Indonesia. Ed. Ig. Tarnotjo. adv.; bk.rev.; illus.

641.1 US ISSN 0897-7275
GOLDBECKS' TRUE FOOD; wholefoods for modern times. 1988. q. $14. Ceres Press, Box 87, Woodstock, NY 12498. TEL 914-679-8561. Ed. David Goldbeck. circ. 750. (also avail. in microform from UMI; back issues avail.)
Description: Keeps consumers current on the whole food world: food additives, pesticides, irradiation, biotechnology, and agriculture.

GOOD HEALTH. see *PHYSICAL FITNESS AND HYGIENE*

GOOD LIFE TIMES; choices in health, education and the arts. see *NEW AGE PUBLICATIONS*

613.2 US
▼**GOOD-NEWS-LETTER.** 1990. bi-m. $10. American Institute for Cancer Research (AICR), 1759 R St., N.W., Washington, DC 20009. TEL 202-328-7744. FAX 202-328-7226. circ. 1,000.
Description: For children ages 7-10. Contains games and puzzles that teach children about good nutrition in an entertaining manner.

GOURMED; magazine for doctors. see *MEDICAL SCIENCES*

GREAT BODY. see *PHYSICAL FITNESS AND HYGIENE*

613.2 GW ISSN 0932-2981
DAS GROSSE LEBEN; Makrobiotik-Magazin. 1986. q. DM.34. Ost-West-Bund Verlag, Auf der Juchhoeh 21, 6620 Voelklingen 9, Germany. TEL 06802-202. FAX 06802-1248. Ed. Richard Theobald. adv.; bk.rev.; circ. 3,000. (back issues avail.)

641.1 SW ISSN 0345-4797
HAELSA. 1940. m. (11/yr.). SEK 248. Tidskrift foer Haelsa, P.O. Box 1001, 181 21 Lidingoe, Sweden. TEL 08-765 27 60. Eskil Svensson. adv.; circ. 52,279.
Description: Focuses on health, physical fitness, hygiene, consumer education and protection.

HEALTH CONSCIOUSNESS; an holistic magazine. see *NEW AGE PUBLICATIONS*

613.2 641.1 US ISSN 1055-8241
▼**HEALTH DIET & NUTRITION.** (Supplement avail.) 1991. a. $23.99. Publishing & Business Consultants, 951 S. Oxford, No. 109, Los Angeles, CA 90006. TEL 213-732-3477. (Subscr. to: Box 75392, Los Angeles, CA 90075) Ed. Atia Napoleon. adv.; circ. 100,000.
Description: Covers basic nutrition information, dietary habits, and personal health care.

613.2 US
HEALTH EXPRESS (LAS VEGAS).* 12/yr. $12. International Academy of Nutritional Consultants, 2375 Tropicana, Ste. 270, Las Vegas, NV 90109. TEL 702-454-1665. adv.

664 US ISSN 0149-9602
HD9001 CODEN: HFBUED
HEALTH FOODS BUSINESS; the business publication of the natural foods industry. 1954. m. $30. Howmark Publishing Corp., 567 Morris Ave., Elizabeth, NJ 07208. TEL 908-353-7373. FAX 908-353-8221. Ed. Ging Geslewitz. adv.; bk.rev.; circ. 11,950. —BLDSC shelfmark: 4275.015950.
Description: Reaches health and natural foods retailers with news, information, purchasing guide and surveys.

613.2 616.39 II
HEALTH FOR THE MILLIONS. bi-m. Rs.30($18) to individuals; Rs.48 or $25 to institutions. Voluntary Health Association of India, 40 Institutional Area, South of IIT, New Delhi 110 016, India. bk.rev.; circ. 3,000. **Indexed:** Curr.Adv.Ecol.Sci.

613 US
HEALTH NEWS & REVIEW. 1983. bi-m. $6.95. Keats Publishing Inc., 27 Pine St., Box 876, New Canaan, CT 06840. TEL 203-966-8721. FAX 203-972-3991. Ed. Nathan Keats. adv.; bk.rev.; circ. 135,000. (tabloid format) **Indexed:** Hlth.Ind.

613 UK ISSN 0144-4948
HEALTH NOW. 1977. 6/yr. Health Now Publishing Co. Ltd., Seymour House, South St., Godalming, Surrey GU7 1BZ, England. TEL 0483 426064. FAX 0483-426005. Ed. Alice Peet. adv.; bk.rev.; circ. 400,000.

613.2 613.7 CN
HEALTH WATCH. 1989. 5/yr. Can.$12.95. Telemedia Procom Inc., 50 Holly St., Toronto, Ont. M4S 3B3, Canada. TEL 416-482-9399. FAX 416-482-8153. Ed. Patrisha Robertson. adv.; circ. 450,000.

612 US ISSN 0888-7330
HEALTH WORLD. 1982. q. $10.50 (foreign $30). Health World, Inc., 1540 Gilbreath Rd., Burlingame, CA 94010-1605. TEL 415-697-8038. FAX 415-697-7937. Ed. Lawrence E. Badgley. adv.; bk.rev.; circ. 65,000. (back issues avail.)
Formerly: International Journal of Holistic Health and Medicine.
Description: Provides information on different health therapies, remedies, and practices around the world with emphasis on homeopathy, Chinese medicine, herbs, acupuncture and chiropractic.

HEALTHCARE FOODSERVICE WHO'S WHO. see *BUSINESS AND ECONOMICS — Trade And Industrial Directories*

HEALTHCARE NEW ORLEANS. see *PHYSICAL FITNESS AND HYGIENE*

641.1 US ISSN 0897-9251
HEALTHWAYS. 1987. 3/yr. $25 (foreign $30). International Macrobiotic Shiatsu Society, 1122 M St., Eureka, CA 95501-2442. TEL 707-445-2290. FAX 707-445-2391. Ed. Patrick McCarty. bk.rev.; circ. 600.

613.26 AT
HEALTHY LIFE NEWS. bi-m. Aus.$12. Marketing Factory Pty. Ltd., 501-13 Spring St., Chatswood, N.S.W., Australia. TEL 02-411-2944. Ed. K. Richards. adv.; circ. 200,000.
Description: Covers preventive medicine and health issues.

HEALTHY TIMES. see *PHYSICAL FITNESS AND HYGIENE*

HERE'S HEALTH; a monthly guide to health, nutrition, natural food and natural therapy. see *PHYSICAL FITNESS AND HYGIENE*

613.2 664 US ISSN 0893-0627
HIPPOCRATES NEWS. vol.5, 1987. 3/yr. $25. Hippocrates Health Institute, 1443 Palmdale Court, W. Palm Beach, FL 33411. TEL 305-471-8876. FAX 407-471-9464. Ed. Marilyn Willison. adv.; bk.rev.; index; circ. 50,000.

HOLISTIC LIVING; a celebration of life. see *NEW AGE PUBLICATIONS*

HOME ECONOMICS ASSOCIATION OF VICTORIA. NEWSLETTER. see *HOME ECONOMICS*

HOME ECONOMICS, HOUSING AND NUTRITION. BULLETINS. see *HOME ECONOMICS*

HOME ECONOMICS, HOUSING AND NUTRITION. REPORT SERIES. see *HOME ECONOMICS*

HOME ECONOMICS, HOUSING AND NUTRITION. SPECIAL REPORTS. see *HOME ECONOMICS*

HUMAN ECOLOGY. ANNUAL REPORT. see *SOCIAL SCIENCES: COMPREHENSIVE WORKS*

HUMAN ECOLOGY & ENERGY BALANCING SCIENTIST. see *MEDICAL SCIENCES*

613.2 US ISSN 0886-6848
QP141.A1 CODEN: HNUTEP
HUMAN NUTRITION. 1979. irreg., vol.7, 1991. $95. Plenum Publishing Corp., 233 Spring St., New York, NY 10013-1578. TEL 212-620-8468. FAX 212-463-0742. TELEX 23421139. Eds. Roslyn B. Alfin-Slater, David Kritchev. (back issues avail.)
Refereed Serial

616.39 US ISSN 0740-1116
HUNGER NOTES. 1976. 4/yr. $18 to individuals; institutions $45. World Hunger Education Service, P.O. Box 29056, Washington, DC 20017. Ed. P. Kutzner. bk.rev.; illus.; circ. 1,000. **Indexed:** HR Rep.
Description: Presents facts and insights on hunger, development and related topics for policy makers, educators and activists. Acts as a guide to organizations and print resources on the specific focus of each issue.

613.2 US
I A P N H NEWSLETTER. 1985. q. $12 to non-members. International Association of Professional Natural Hygienists, 204 Stambaugh Bldg., Youngstown, OH 44503. TEL 216-746-5000. Ed. Mark A. Huberman. bk.rev.; circ. 55. (looseleaf format; back issues avail.)
Description: For primary care doctors.

I B F A N NEWS. (International Baby Food Action Network) see *CHILDREN AND YOUTH — About*

616.39 US
I L S I HUMAN NUTRITION REVIEWS. 1986. irreg. price varies. Springer-Verlag, 175 Fifth Ave., New York, NY 10010. TEL 212-460-1500. (Also Berlin, Heidelberg, Tokyo, Vienna) (reprint service avail. from ISI)

641.1 II ISSN 0022-3174
TX341 CODEN: IJNDAN
INDIAN JOURNAL OF NUTRITION AND DIETETICS. (Text in English) 1964. m. Rs.150($40) Avinashilingam Institute for Home Science and Higher Education for Women, c/o Rajammal P. Devadas, Ed., Coimbatore 641 043, India. TEL 40241. TELEX 855 459 ADU IN. adv.; bk.rev.; bibl.; charts; stat.; index; circ. 620. **Indexed:** Abstr.Hyg., Biol.Abstr., Chem.Abstr., Curr.Cont., Dairy Sci.Abstr., Field Crop Abstr., Food Sci.& Tech.Abstr., Helminthol.Abstr., INIS Atomind., Maize Abstr., Nutr.Abstr., Plant Breed.Abstr., Poult.Abstr., Seed Abstr., Sorghum & Millets Abstr., Soyabean Abstr., Triticale Abstr., Trop.Dis.Bull., Trop.Oil Seeds Abstr.
—BLDSC shelfmark: 4417.450000.
Formerly (until vol.7, 1970): Journal of Nutrition and Dietetics.
Description: Research papers and review articles in the fields of nutrition and dietetics.
Refereed Serial

613.26 II ISSN 0019-6460
INDIAN VEGETARIAN CONGRESS QUARTERLY. 1968. q. $6. Indian Vegetarian Congress, The Grove, No. 1, Eldams Road, Madras 600 018, India. TEL 450-364. Ed. Surendra M. Mehta. adv.; bk.rev.; charts; illus.; circ. 1,500.

641 FR ISSN 0020-0034
INFORMATION DIETETIQUE. 1964. 4/yr. 145 F. (foreign 210F.). Association des Dieticiens de Langue Francaise, 14 rue Saint-Benoit, 75006 Paris, France. TEL 42-86-99-80. Ed.Bd. adv.; bk.rev.; circ. 3,000.
—BLDSC shelfmark: 4493.538350.

613.2 SZ ISSN 1011-6966
CODEN: INFUEW
INFUSIONSTHERAPIE. (Supplements avail.: Beitraege zur Infusionstherapie und Klinischen Ernaehrung - Forschung und Praxis) (Text in German; summaries in English and German) 1974. bi-m. 124 Fr.($83) (Deutsche Arbeitsgemeinschaft fuer Kuenstliche Ernaehrung) S. Karger AG, Allschwilerstr. 10, P.O. Box, CH-4009 Basel, Switzerland. TEL 061-3061111. FAX 061-3061234. TELEX CH 962652. (Co-sponsors: Oesterreichische Arbeitsgemeinschaft fuer klinische Ernaehrung; Deutsche Gesellschaft fuer Transfusionsmedizin und Immunhaematologie) Ed.Bd. adv.; illus.; index; circ. 20,000. **Indexed:** Biol.Abstr., Chem.Abstr., Curr.Cont., Dent.Ind., Excerp.Med., Ind.Med., Ind.Sci.Rev., Nutr.Abstr., Sci.Cit.Ind.
—BLDSC shelfmark: 4499.550000.
Former titles: Internationale Zeitschrift fuer Infusionstherapie, Klinische Ernaehrung und Transfusionsmedizin & Infusionstherapie und Klinische Ernaehrung - Forschung und Praxis (ISSN 0378-0791); Infusionstherapie und Klinische Ernaehrung (ISSN 0301-3243); Infusionstherapie.

641 UN ISSN 0533-4179
INSTITUTO DE NUTRICION DE CENTRO AMERICA Y PANAMA (INCAP). INFORME ANUAL. (Editions in English and Spanish) 1950. a. exchange basis. Institute of Nutrition of Central America and Panama (INCAP) - Instituto de Nutricion de Centro America y Panama, Carretera Roosevelt Zona 11, Apdo. Postal 1188, 01901 Guatemala City, Guatemala. TEL 723762. FAX 715658. TELEX 5696 INCAP GU. Ed. Grace H. de Munoz. circ. 550. **Indexed:** Biol.Abstr., Nutr.Abstr.

INSTITUTO DE TECNOLOGIA DE ALIMENTOS. COLETANEA. see *FOOD AND FOOD INDUSTRIES*

INSTITUTO DE TECNOLOGIA DE ALIMENTOS. INSTRUCOES PRATICAS. see *FOOD AND FOOD INDUSTRIES*

INSTITUTO DE TECNOLOGIA DE ALIMENTOS. INSTRUCOES TECNICAS. see *FOOD AND FOOD INDUSTRIES*

612 NG ISSN 0534-4700
INTER-AFRICAN CONFERENCE ON FOOD AND NUTRITION. PROGRAMA E INFORMACOES.* (Text in English, French and Portuguese) irreg. (Commission for Technical Co-Operation in Africa South of the Sahara) Maison de l'Afrique, B.P. 878, Niamey, Niger.

641 NG ISSN 0538-2785
INTER-AFRICAN CONFERENCE ON FOOD AND NUTRITION. REPORT.* 1949. irreg. (Commission for Technical Co-Operation in Africa, South of the Sahara) Maison de l'Afrique, B.P. 878, Niamey, Niger.

641.1 AT ISSN 0725-7090
CODEN: ICNRDJ
INTERNATIONAL CLINICAL NUTRITION REVIEW. 1981. q. Aus.$49($63) Integrated Therapies Pty. Ltd., P.O. Box 370, Manly, N.S.W. 2095, Australia. FAX 02-977-0267. Ed. Robert A. Buist. bk.rev.; circ. 2,000. **Indexed:** Chem.Abstr., Curr.Adv.Ecol.Sci., Dairy Sci.Abstr., NRN, Nutr.Abstr.
—BLDSC shelfmark: 4538.673500.
Incorporates: Orthomolecular Review.
Description: Reports recent nutritional research from journals worldwide with original articles emphasizing potential clinical applications.

INTERNATIONAL JOURNAL FOR VITAMIN AND NUTRITION RESEARCH. see *PHARMACY AND PHARMACOLOGY*

614.7 612.3 370 US ISSN 1044-811X
BF1 CODEN: IJMREU
INTERNATIONAL JOURNAL OF BIOSOCIAL AND MEDICAL RESEARCH; bridging the gap between the natural and social sciences to better understand human behavior. 1979. 2/yr. $25 to individuals; institutions and foreign $50. (Foundation for Biosocial Research) Life Sciences Press, Box 1174, Tacoma, WA 98401-1174. TEL 206-922-0442. FAX 206-922-0479. Ed. Alexander G. Schauss. adv.; bk.rev.; circ. 3,500. (back issues avail.) **Indexed:** Excerp.Med., Lang.& Lang.Behav.Abstr., Neurosci.Abstr., Nutr.Abstr., Psychol.Abstr., Sociol.Abstr.
—BLDSC shelfmark: 4542.155090.
Formerly (until 1989): International Journal for Biosocial Research (ISSN 0731-9169)
Description: Publishes studies on behavior as it relates to nutrition, neurotoxicology and environmental health.
Refereed Serial

616.37 US ISSN 0276-3478
RC552.A72 CODEN: INDIDJ
INTERNATIONAL JOURNAL OF EATING DISORDERS. 1981. 8/yr. $320 to institutions (foreign $420). John Wiley & Sons, Inc., Journals, 605 Third Ave., New York, NY 10158-0012. TEL 212-850-6000. FAX 212-850-6088. TELEX 12-7063. Ed. Dr. Michael Strober. adv.; bk.rev.; bibl.; stat.; circ. 1,050. (also avail. in microfiche from RPI) **Indexed:** Adol.Ment.Hlth.Abstr., Biol.Abstr., Curr.Adv.Ecol.Sci., Excerp.Med., NRN, Psychol.Abstr., Risk Abstr., Sp.Ed.Needs Abstr., Stud.Wom.Abstr.
—BLDSC shelfmark: 4542.195500.
Description: Basic research, clinical and theoretical articles of scholarly substance on a variety of aspects of anorexia nervosa, bulimia, obesity and other atypical patterns of eating behavior and body weight regulation.

613 UK ISSN 0307-0565
RC628 CODEN: IJOBDP
INTERNATIONAL JOURNAL OF OBESITY. 1977. m. £165 to institutions. (Association for the Study of Obesity) Macmillan Press Ltd., Houndmills, Basingstoke, Hampshire RG21 2XS, England. (Co-sponsor: North American Association for the Study of Obesity) Ed. Per Bjorntorp. adv.; bk.rev.; cum.index; circ. 1,000. **Indexed:** Abstr.Hyg., Chem.Abstr, Curr.Adv.Ecol.Sci., Curr.Cont., Dent.Ind., Excerp.Med., Ind.Med., Ind.Sci.Rev., NRN, Nutr.Abstr., Risk Abstr., Sci.Cit.Ind, Soyabean Abstr., Trop.Dis.Bull.
—BLDSC shelfmark: 4542.410000.
Description: Reports of animal and human studies in the areas of metabolism, genetics, endocrinology, treatment of obesity, and exercise physiology.

613.2 617.1 US ISSN 1050-1606
RC1235
▼**INTERNATIONAL JOURNAL OF SPORT NUTRITION.** Short title: I J S N. 1991. q. $32 to individuals (foreign $36); institutions $64 (foreign $68); students $20 (foreign $24). Human Kinetics Publishers, Inc., Box 5076, Champaign, IL 61825-5076. TEL 217-351-5076. FAX 217-351-2674. Ed. Melvin H. Williams. adv.; abstr.; bibl.; charts; stat.; index; circ. 740. (back issues avail.)
—BLDSC shelfmark: 4542.680800.
Description: Advances understanding of nutritional aspects of human physical and athletic performance.
Refereed Serial

IRON METABOLISM. see *BIOLOGY — Biological Chemistry*

612.3 US ISSN 0148-6071
RM224 CODEN: JPENDU
J P E N: JOURNAL OF PARENTERAL AND ENTERAL NUTRITION. 1979. bi-m. $75 to individuals; institutions $100. American Society of Parenteral and Enteral Nutrition, 8630 Fenton St., Ste. 412, Silver Spring, MD 20910-3805. TEL 301-587-6315. FAX 301-587-3323. Ed. Dr. John L. Rombeau. adv.; circ. 7,600. (also avail. in microform; reprint service avail. from ISI) **Indexed:** CINAHL, I.P.A., Ind.Med., INIS Atomind., Soyabean Abstr.
●Also available online.
—BLDSC shelfmark: 5029.100000.
Description: Research on nutritional deficiency and its treatment, including administration, risks and complications.

613.2 JA ISSN 0485-1412
CODEN: RNEYAW
JAPANESE JOURNAL OF CLINICAL NUTRITION/RINSHO EIYO. (Text in Japanese) 1952. m. 700 Yen per no. Ishiyaku Publishers, Inc., 7-10 Honkomagome 1-chome, Bunkyo-ku, Tokyo 113, Japan. Ed. Hiroshi Miura. adv.; bk.rev.; charts; illus.; circ. 16,500. **Indexed:** Chem.Abstr.
—BLDSC shelfmark: 4651.377000.

641 JA ISSN 0021-5147
CODEN: EYGZAD
JAPANESE JOURNAL OF NUTRITION/EIYOGAKU ZASSHI. (Text in Japanese, title in English) 1941. bi-m. 3708 Yen. (National Nutrition Society - Kokumin Eiyo Shinkokai) Daiichi Shuppan K. K., 1-39 Kanda Jimbo-cho, Chiyoda-ku, Tokyo 101, Japan. FAX 03-3291-4579. (Subscr. to: Japan Publications Trading Co. Ltd., PO Box 5030, Tokyo International, Tokyo 100-31, Japan) Ed. Shuhei Kobayashi. **Indexed:** Biol.Abstr., Chem.Abstr., Dairy Sci.Abstr., Field Crop Abstr., Food Sci.& Tech.Abstr., INIS Atomind., Maize Abstr., Nutr.Abstr., Rice Abstr., Seed Abstr.

641 JA ISSN 0287-3516
CODEN: NESGDC
JAPANESE SOCIETY OF NUTRITION AND FOOD SCIENCE. JOURNAL/NIPPON EIYO SHOKURYO GAKKAISHI. (Text in Japanese; summaries in English) 1947. 6/yr. 6,300 Yen for members; students 4,200 Yen; others 18,000 Yen. (Japanese Society of Nutrition and Food Science - Nippon Eiyo Shokuryo Gakkai) Center for Academic Publications, Japan, 2-4-16 Yayoi, Bunkyo-ku, Tokyo 113, Japan. FAX 81-3-3817-5820. Ed. Yousuke Seyama. adv.; bk.rev.; circ. 4,300. **Indexed:** Biol.Abstr., Chem.Abstr., Food Sci.& Tech.Abstr., So.Pac.Per.Ind.
—BLDSC shelfmark: 4809.474000.
Formerly: Food and Nutrition - Eiyo to Shokuryo (ISSN 0021-5376)

613.26 UK ISSN 0021-681X
JEWISH VEGETARIAN. 1965. q. £8($15) International Jewish Vegetarian Society, 855, Finchley Rd., London NW11 8LX, England. Ed. Philip L. Pick. adv.; bk.rev.; circ. 8,000. (tabloid format)

613 US
TX392
JEWISH VEGETARIANS. 1983. q. $12. Jewish Vegetarians of North America, Box 1463, Baltimore, MD 21203. TEL 410-366-8343. Eds. Charles Stahler, Debra Wasserman. adv.; bk.rev.; circ. 800.
Formerly: Jewish Vegetarians of New York (ISSN 0883-1904)
Description: Discusses Judaism and vegetarianism. Topics include health, ecology, world hunger, and animal rights.

JIANKANG BAO/HEALTH GAZETTE. see *PHYSICAL FITNESS AND HYGIENE*

NUTRITION AND DIETETICS

641.1   US   ISSN 0021-8960
CODEN: JNAPAX
JOURNAL OF APPLIED NUTRITION. 1947. q. $60 to individuals (foreign $75); students $30. International Academy of Nutrition and Preventive Medicine, Box 18433, Asheville, NC 28814-0433. TEL 704-258-3243. Ed. Dr. Brian Leibovitz. adv.: B&W page $250; adv. contact: Elizabeth Pavka. bk.rev.; abstr.; charts; illus.; cum.index: 1947-1984; circ. 1,500. (also avail. in microform from UMI; back issues avail.; reprint service avail. from UMI) **Indexed:** Biol.Abstr., Biol.& Agr.Ind., Chem.Abstr., Environ.Per.Bibl., Excerp.Med., Nutr.Abstr.
Incorporates: International Academy of Preventive Medicine. Journal (ISSN 0094-324X)
Description: Scientific reports and reviews that stress practical human applications of macro and micro nutrients in treatment and prevention of diseases.
Refereed Serial

JOURNAL OF CLINICAL NUTRITION AND GASTROENTEROLOGY. see *MEDICAL SCIENCES — Gastroenterology*

612.3   US
JOURNAL OF HEALTH SCIENCE.* 1981. q. $10. Health News Network, Inc., 2700 Timberline Dr., Eugene, OR 97405-1270. Ed. Cameron Stauth. adv.; illus.

JOURNAL OF HUMAN LACTATION. see *MEDICAL SCIENCES — Obstetrics And Gynecology*

613.2   UK   ISSN 0952-3871
CODEN: JHNDEO
JOURNAL OF HUMAN NUTRITION AND DIETETICS. 1988. q. £84 (foreign £92). (British Dietetic Association) Blackwell Scientific Publications Ltd., Osney Mead, Oxford OX2 0EL, England. TEL 0865-240201. FAX 0865-721205. TELEX 833355-MEDBOK-G. Ed. P.A. Judd. adv.; bk.rev.; illus.; index. (back issues avail.)
—BLDSC shelfmark: 5003.419300.
Formerly (until 1987): Human Nutrition. Applied Nutrition (ISSN 0263-8495) Which supersedes in part (in 1981): Journal of Human Nutrition (ISSN 0308-4329); Which was formerly (until 1976): Nutrition (ISSN 0029-6600).

JOURNAL OF MUSCLE FOODS. see *FOOD AND FOOD INDUSTRIES*

641 613   US   ISSN 0022-3166
RM214   CODEN: JONUAI
JOURNAL OF NUTRITION. 1928. m. $90 to non-members; members $45; institutions $175; students $25. American Institute of Nutrition, 9650 Rockville Pike, Bethesda, MD 20814. TEL 301-530-7027. FAX 301-571-1892. Ed. Dr. Willard Visek. adv.; bk.rev.; abstr.; bibl.; charts; illus.; index; circ. 4,430. (also avail. in microform from UMI; back issues avail.; reprint service avail. from UMI) **Indexed:** Abstr.Anthropol., Abstr.Hyg., Anim.Breed.Abstr., Biol.Abstr., Biol.& Agr.Ind., Biol.Dig., Biotech.Abstr., Cadscan, Chem.Abstr., Curr.Adv.Cancer Res., Curr.Adv.Ecol.Sci., Curr.Cont., Dairy Sci.Abstr., Dent.Ind., Environ.Per.Bibl., Excerp.Med., Food Sci.& Tech.Abstr., Gen.Sci.Ind., Helminthol.Abstr., Ind.Med., Ind.Sci.Rev., Ind.Vet., Ind.Vet., INIS Atomind., Lead Abstr., Maize Abstr., Nutr.Abstr., Pig News & Info., Plant Breed.Abstr., Poult.Abstr., Rev.Appl.Entomol., Rice Abstr., Sorghum & Millets Abstr., Soyabean Abstr., Triticale Abstr., Trop.Dis.Bull., Trop.Oil Seeds Abstr., Vet.Bull., Zincscan.
—BLDSC shelfmark: 5024.000000.
Description: Reports of original research in all aspects of nutrition.
Refereed Serial

641.1   US   ISSN 0022-3182
QP141.A1
JOURNAL OF NUTRITION EDUCATION. 1969. bi-m. $70 to individuals (foreign £90); institutions $85 (foreign $105). (Society for Nutrition Education) Williams & Wilkins, 428 East Preston St., Baltimore, MD 21202-3993. TEL 301-528-4000. FAX 301-528-4312. Ed. Audrey N. Maretzki. adv.; bk.rev.; index; circ. 4,800. (also avail. in microform from UMI; reprint service avail. from UMI,ISI) **Indexed:** Behav.Med.Abstr., C.I.J.E., Cont.Pg.Educ., Curr.Cont., Educ.Ind., Environ.Per.Bibl., Gen.Sci.Ind., Ind.Sci.Rev., Nutr.Abstr., Risk Abstr., Sp.Ed.Needs Abstr., Stud.Wom.Abstr.
—BLDSC shelfmark: 5024.700000.
Description: Designed to stimulate interest and research in applied nutritional sciences and to disseminate information to educators and others concerned about positive nutritional practices and policies.

JOURNAL OF NUTRITION FOR THE ELDERLY. see *GERONTOLOGY AND GERIATRICS*

612.3   US   ISSN 0736-8283
RC261.A1   CODEN: JNGCDR
JOURNAL OF NUTRITION, GROWTH AND CANCER. 1983. q. $92. (International Association for Vitamins and Nutritional Oncology) Food & Nutrition Press, Inc., 2 Corporate Dr., Box 374, Trumbull, CT 06611. TEL 203-261-8587. Ed. George P. Tryfiates.
Indexed: Chem.Abstr, Curr.Adv.Ecol.Sci.
Description: Original, biochemically oriented papers relating nutrition and nutrients to cell growth whether normal or neoplastic.
Refereed Serial

641.1   US   ISSN 1055-1379
▼**JOURNAL OF NUTRITION IN RECIPE & MENU DEVELOPMENT;** innovations in new nutritional product development, dietary substitutes, medically-related issues in food service. 1992. q. $18 to individuals; institutions $24; libraries $32. Haworth Press, Inc., Food Products Press, 10 Alice St., Binghamton, NY 13904-1580. TEL 800-342-9678. FAX 607-722-1424. TELEX 4932599. Ed. Mahmood A. Khan. adv.; bk.rev. (also avail. in microfiche from HAW; reprint service avail. from HAW) **Indexed:** Food Sci.& Tech.Abstr.
Description: Publishes research and practice papers relating directly to new recipe and menu concepts which are aimed at health promotion.
Refereed Serial

641   US   ISSN 0955-2863
QP141.A1   CODEN: JNBIEL
JOURNAL OF NUTRITIONAL BIOCHEMISTRY. 1970. m. $280 (foreign $325). Butterworth - Heinemann Ltd. (Subsidiary of: Reed International PLC), 80 Montvale Ave., Stoneham, MA 02180. TEL 617-438-8464. FAX 617-438-1479. TELEX 880052. Ed. Dr. Steven H. Zersel. adv.; charts; illus.; index. (also avail. in microfilm from UMI; reprint service avail.; back issues avail.) **Indexed:** Anim.Breed.Abstr., Biol.Abstr., Cadscan, Chem.Abstr., Curr.Adv.Biochem., Curr.Adv.Ecol.Sci., Curr.Cont., Dairy Sci.Abstr., Environ.Per.Bibl., Excerp.Med., Food Sci.& Tech.Abstr., Helminthol.Abstr., Herb.Abstr., Ind.Sci.Rev., Ind.Vet., Lead Abstr., Maize Abstr., Nutr.Abstr., Pig News & Info., Poult.Abstr., Protozool.Abstr., Rice Abstr., Risk Abstr., Sorghum & Millets Abstr., Soyabean Abstr., Triticale Abstr., Trop.Oil Seeds Abstr., Vet.Bull., Weed Abstr., Zincscan.
—BLDSC shelfmark: 5024.730000.
Supersedes (in 1990): Nutrition Reports International (ISSN 0029-6635)
Description: Forum for advances and issues in nutrition, nutritional biochemistry and food sciences.

JOURNAL OF NUTRITIONAL IMMUNOLOGY. see *MEDICAL SCIENCES — Allergology And Immunology*

616.39   UK   ISSN 0955-6664
CODEN: JNMEEU
▼**JOURNAL OF NUTRITIONAL MEDICINE.** 1990. q. $106 to individuals; institutions $264. Carfax Publishing Co., P.O. Box 25, Abingdon, Oxfordshire OX14 3UE, England. TEL 0235-555335. FAX 0235-553559. (U.S. subscr. addr.: Carfax Publishing Co., Box 2025, Dunnellon, FL 32630) Ed. Stephen Davies, Damien Downing.
—BLDSC shelfmark: 5024.740000.
Description: Aimed at physicians, surgeons, dietitians, nutritionists, clinical biochemists, clinical psychologists, as well as students in these fields. Covers the field of nutrition and its relationship to clinical medicine.

615.328   JA   ISSN 0301-4800
CODEN: JNSVA5
JOURNAL OF NUTRITIONAL SCIENCE AND VITAMINOLOGY. 1954. bi-m. $100. (Japanese Society of Nutrition and Food Science) Japan Scientific Societies Press, 6-2-10 Hongo, Bunkyo-ku, Tokyo 113, Japan. TEL 3814-2001. FAX 3814-2002. TELEX 2722268 BCJSP J. (Dist. by: Business Center for Academic Societies Japan, Koshin Bldg., 6-16-3 Hongo, Bunkyo-ku, Tokyo 113, Japan; Dist. in U.S. by: International Specialized Book Services, Inc., 5602 Hassalo St., Portland, OR 97213; in Asia by: Toppan Company Pvt. Ltd., 38. Liu Fang Rd., Box 22 Jurong Town, Jurong, Singapore 2262) (Co-sponsor: Vitamin Society of Japan) bk.rev.; bibl.; charts; illus.; index; circ. 1,500. **Indexed:** Biol.Abstr., Biotech.Abstr., Chem.Abstr., Curr.Adv.Ecol.Sci., Curr.Cont., Dairy Sci.Abstr., Excerp.Med., Food Sci.& Tech.Abstr., Ind.Med., Ind.Sci.Rev., Ind.Vet., INIS Atomind., Nutr.Abstr., Rice Abstr., Soyabean Abstr., Vet.Bull.
—BLDSC shelfmark: 5024.750000.
Formerly (until 1972): Journal of Vitaminology (ISSN 0022-5398)

612.3   US
JOURNAL OF PARENTERAL AND ENTERAL NUTRITION. bi-m. Williams & Wilkins, 428 E. Preston St., Baltimore, MD 21202-3923. TEL 301-528-4000. FAX 301-528-4132. Ed. Harry Shizgal. circ. 7,856.

JOURNAL OF PEDIATRIC & PERINATAL NUTRITION. see *MEDICAL SCIENCES — Pediatrics*

JOURNAL OF PEDIATRIC GASTROENTEROLOGY AND NUTRITION. see *MEDICAL SCIENCES — Gastroenterology*

616.39 616.6   US
▼**JOURNAL OF RENAL NUTRITION.** 1991. q. $52. W.B. Saunders Co., Curtis Center, Independence Sq. W., Philadelphia, PA 19106. TEL 215-238-7807. Ed. Dr. Judith A. Beto. adv.; circ. 1,754.
Description: Disseminates renal nutrition-related research and professional education related to renal nutrition.

JOURNAL OF SENSORY STUDIES. see *MEDICAL SCIENCES — Psychiatry And Neurology*

JOURNAL OF TEXTURE STUDIES; an international journal of rheology, psychorheology, physical and sensory testing of foods and pharmaceuticals. see *FOOD AND FOOD INDUSTRIES*

574.13   JA   ISSN 0368-5209
TX341
KOKURITSU KENKO EIYO KENKYUJO HOKOKU/NATIONAL INSTITUTE OF HEALTH AND NUTRITION. ANNUAL REPORT. (Text in Japanese) 1949. a. exchange basis. Kosei-sho, Kokuritsu Kenko Eiyo Kenkyujo - National Institute of Health and Nutrition, 1-23-1 Toyama-cho, Shinjuku-ku, Tokyo 162, Japan. FAX 03-3203-3278. **Indexed:** Biol.Abstr.
—BLDSC shelfmark: 1364.711000.
Formerly: Kokuritsu Eiyo Kenkyujo Hokoku - National Institute of Nutrition. Annual Report.

613.2   JA   ISSN 0913-5537
CODEN: KDKAEH
KOSHIEN UNIVERSITY. DEPARTMENT OF NUTRITION. BULLETIN. (Text in English, Japanese) 1970. a. Koshien University, Department of Nutrition, 10-1 Momiji-ga-oka, Takarazuka 665, Japan. TEL 0797-87-5111. Ed. Hiroyuki Masutani. circ. 500.

KOST OG ALLERGI NYT. see *MEDICAL SCIENCES*

NUTRITION AND DIETETICS   3609

KRAUT UND RUEBEN; das Magazin fuer biologischen Gaertnern und naturgemaesses Leben. see *GARDENING AND HORTICULTURE*

L S T NYT. see *MEDICAL SCIENCES*

LET'S LIVE. see *PHYSICAL FITNESS AND HYGIENE*

LIFELINES (TORONTO); the voice of the Toronto vegetarian community. see *PHYSICAL FITNESS AND HYGIENE*

613.7   US
LOSE WEIGHT NATURALLY NEWSLETTER. m. $18. Rodale Press, Inc., 33 E. Minor St., Emmaus, PA 18098. TEL 215-967-5171. TELEX 847338.
  Description: Provides information on natural ways to lose weight, including exercise programs, nutritional advice, and body makeovers.

MAA BRA. see *PHYSICAL FITNESS AND HYGIENE*

641.1   US
MACROBIOTIC WORLD DIRECTORY. 1986. s-a. $3 per no. Kushi Foundation, Inc., Box 7, Beeket, MA 02146. TEL 413-623-5742.

641.1   US
MACROBIOTICS TODAY. 1960. 6/yr. $15. George Ohsawa Macrobiotic Foundation, 1511 Robinson St., Oroville, CA 95965. TEL 916-533-7702. Ed. Bob Ligon. adv.; bk.rev.; circ. 3,000.
  Formerly (until 1984): G O M F News.
  Description: Articles and news events concerning macrobiotics and the George Ohsawa Macrobiotic Foundation.

613   FR
MEDECINE ET NUTRITION. 1965. 6/yr. 300 F. (foreign 330 F.)(effective 1991). (Societe d'Hygiene de Langue Francaise) Editions la Simarre, Z.I. No. 2 - rue Joseph-Cugnot, 37300 Joue-les-Tours, France. TEL 47-53-53-66. FAX 47-67-45-05. adv.; bibl.; charts; illus.; circ. 10,000. **Indexed:** Biol.Abstr., C.I.S. Abstr., Chem.Abstr., Dairy Sci.Abstr., Excerp.Med., Food Sci.& Tech.Abstr., Nutr.Abstr., Soyabean Abstr.
  Formerly: Annales d'Hygiene de Langue Francaise (ISSN 0003-4363)
  Description: Publishes original studies on the fundamental and applied aspects of food and nutrition.

MEDICINE, EXERCISE, NUTRITION AND HEALTH. see *MEDICAL SCIENCES*

MEMPHIS HEALTH CARE NEWS. see *PHYSICAL FITNESS AND HYGIENE*

MILITAER-KUECHENCHEF. see *MILITARY*

616.39 612.015   SZ   ISSN 0026-6841
RA421   CODEN: MGLHAE
MITTEILUNGEN AUS DER GEBIETE DER LEBENSMITTELUNTERSUCHUNG UND HYGIENE/TRAVAUX DE CHIMIE ALIMENTAIRE ET D'HYGIENE. (Text mainly in French and German; occasionally in English and Italian) 1910. 6/yr. 62 Fr. Bundesamt fuer Gesundheitswesen, Postfach, CH-3000 Bern 14, Switzerland. (Co-sponsors: Schweizerische Gesellschaft fuer Analytische und Angewandte Chemie; Schweizerische Gesellschaft fuer Lebensmittelhygiene) adv.; bk.rev.; bibl.; illus.; index; circ. 2,000. **Indexed:** Anal.Abstr., Biol.Abstr., Biotech.Abstr., Chem.Abstr., Excerp.Med., Food Sci.& Tech.Abstr., Ind.Med., Nutr.Abstr., Packag.Sci.Tech., Potato Abstr., Vet.Bull.
—BLDSC shelfmark: 5878.000000.

613.2   US
MODERN NUTRITION NEWS. q. $7. Connaught Press Inc., 212 Hillside Ave., Hillside, NJ 07205. TEL 201-926-0816. Ed. E. Gerald Kay. (newspaper)
  Description: Provides a variety of health-related information, viewpoints and new discoveries.

613.2   US
N A A F A NEWSLETTER. 1969. m. membership. National Association to Advance Fat Acceptance, Inc., P.O. Box 188620, Sacramento, CA 95818. TEL 916-443-0303. Ed. Sally E. Smith. adv.; bk.rev.; circ. 4,000. (back issues avail.)
  Description: Provides information regarding obesity research, size discrimination, and advances in size acceptance movement.

612.3   US
N C P: NUTRITION IN CLINICAL PRACTICE. m. $35. American Society of Parenteral and Enteral Nutrition, 8630 Fenton St., Ste. 412, Silver Spring, MD 20910. TEL 301-587-6315. FAX 301-587-3323.
  Description: Multidisciplinary clinical journal providing information on nutritional and metabolic therapy for personnel associated with oral and IV nutrition therapy. Features articles, clinical observations, case reports, techniques and procedures.

613.2   US
N N F A MONITOR. 1986. m. membership. National Nutritional Foods Association, 150 E. Paulerino, Ste. 285, Costa Mesa, CA 92626. TEL 714-966-6632. Ed. Burton Kallman. adv.; bk.rev.; circ. controlled.
  Supersedes (1981?-1984): Food for Thought (Oceanside).

613.2   US
N O H A NEWS. 1976. q. $8. Nutrition for Optimal Health Association, Box 380, Winnetka, IL 60093. TEL 312-835-5030. Eds. Marjorie Fisher, Lynn Lawson. bk.rev.; circ. 700. (back issues avail.)
  Description: Reports on nutritional information and research findings culled from a wide range of scientific sources; includes a column written by members of the professional advisory board.

612.3 641   GW   ISSN 0027-769X
TX341   CODEN: NAHRAR
DIE NAEHRUNG/FOOD; chemistry, biochemistry, microbiology, technology, nutrition. (Supplement) (Text in English and German; summaries in English, German and Russian) 1957. 10/yr. DM.307. (Akademie der Wissenschaften der DDR, Zentralinstitut fuer Ernaehrung) Akademie-Verlag Berlin, Leipziger Str. 3-4, 1086 Berlin, Germany. TELEX 114420-AVERL-DD. Ed. J. Voigt. bk.rev.; charts; illus.; index. **Indexed:** Anal.Abstr., Biol.Abstr., Cadscan, Chem.Abstr., Curr.Adv.Ecol.Sci., Curr.Cont., Curr.Pack.Abstr., Dairy Sci.Abstr., Excerp.Med., Field Crop Abstr., Food Sci.& Tech.Abstr., Herb.Abstr., Ind.Med., Ind.Vet., Lead Abstr., Mass Spectr.Bull., Nutr.Abstr., Rev.Plant Path., Soils & Fert., Vet.Bull., Zincscan.
—BLDSC shelfmark: 6015.300000.

612.3   SW   ISSN 0346-7104
    CODEN: NRFSA3
NAERINGSFORSKNING. (Text in English and Swedish) 1958. q. SEK 215. Swedish Nutrition Foundation, Ideon, S-22370 Lund, Sweden. TEL 46-46-182280. FAX 46-46-182281. Ed. Bo Hallgren. circ. 2,500 (controlled). (back issues avail.)
—BLDSC shelfmark: 6015.349000.

NATIONAL FLUORIDATION NEWS; covering reports on research into the toxicity of fluoride, news on accidents, election outcomes and general information on the issue. see *ENVIRONMENTAL STUDIES*

641.1   II   ISSN 0377-3744
NATIONAL INSTITUTE OF NUTRITION. ANNUAL REPORT. (Text in English) 1946. a. free. National Institute of Nutrition, Indian Council of Medical Research, Jamai-Osmania, Hyderabad 500 007, India. circ. 1,400.
  Formerly: Nutrition Research Laboratories. Annual Report.

613.2   GW   ISSN 0721-8982
NATUERLICH UND GESUND; Das Magazin fuer Ganzheitliche Lebensfuehrung. 1979. bi-m. DM.30($25) Verlag Helmut Preussler, Rothenburger Str. 25, D-8500 Nuremberg, Germany. TEL 0911-26 23 23. Ed. Eberhard Coelle. circ. 35,000.

613.2   GW   ISSN 0932-3503
NATUR UND HEILEN; die Monatszeitschrift fuer gesundes Leben. 1924. m. DM.60 (foreign DM.72). Verlag Natur und Heilen, Neuveutherstr. 1, 8000 Munich 40, Germany. TEL 089-2725046. FAX 089-2722816. Ed. Hansjoerg Volkhardt. adv.; bk.rev. (back issues avail.)
—BLDSC shelfmark: 6033.868000.

613.2 631   US
NATURAL FOOD & FARMING. 1953. 12/yr. $20. Natural Food Associates, Box 210, Atlanta, TX 75551. Ed. Bill Francis. adv.; bk.rev.; circ. 10,000.

641.1   UK
NATURAL FOOD TRADER. 1960. m. £36 (foreign £48). I B T M Ltd., Queensway House, 2 Queensway, Redhill, Surrey RH1 1QS, England. TEL 0737-768611. FAX 0737-760425. Ed. Paul Rouse. adv.; bk.rev.; illus.; circ. 4,500 (controlled).
  Formerly: Health Food Trader (ISSN 0046-7049)
  Description: Monthly trade magazine for health food store professionals.

NATURAL FOODS MERCHANDISER; new ideas, trends, products for the natural and organic foods industry. see *BUSINESS AND ECONOMICS — Marketing And Purchasing*

612.3   AT   ISSN 0816-2751
NATURAL HEALTH. 1961. bi-m. Aus.$32 (foreign Aus.$44). Natural Health Society of Australia Ltd., Ste. 28, 541 High St., Penrith, N.S.W. 2750, Australia. TEL 047-215068. Ed. Roger French. adv.; bk.rev.; circ. 6,000. (back issues avail.)
  Description: To promote health and well-being through a more natural way of living, recognizing that prevention is far better than cure.

616.39   US
NATURAL HYGIENE SOCIETY OF NEW JERSEY. NEWSLETTER. 1981. 8/yr. $15. Natural Hygiene of New Jersey, Inc., Box 142, Pompton Plains, NJ 07444. TEL 201-839-5919. Ed. John R. Chorba. abstr.; circ. 350. (looseleaf format; back issues avail.)
  Formerly: American Natural Hygiene Society. New Jersey Chapter. Newsletter.
  Description: Covers various issues in health and hygiene, includes exercise, diet and behavior.

612.3   AT   ISSN 0158-9911
NATURE AND HEALTH. 1977. q. Aus.$27.80 (foreign Aus.$ 32). Kenvale Pty. Ltd., 2a Blakesley St., Chatswood, N.S.W 2067, Australia. TEL 02-411-1766. FAX 02-413-2689. Ed. Pamela Allardice. adv.; bk.rev.; circ. 21,000.
  Description: Covers a wide spectrum of topics - natural health, self improvement body care, relationships, organic gardening, natural beauty and fitness, oriental herbs, whole foods, science, social change and spirituality.

NAUTILUS (INDEPENDENCE). see *PHYSICAL FITNESS AND HYGIENE*

613.2 616.39   SZ
NESTLE FOUNDATION. ANNUAL REPORT. 1969. a. free. Nestle Foundation, 4 Place de la Gare, CH-1003 Lausanne, Switzerland. FAX 41-21203392. Ed. B. Schuerch. circ. 1,500.

613.2   US
NESTLE NUTRITION SERIES. 1982. irreg., latest vol.29. price varies. Raven Press, 1185 Ave. of the Americas, New York, NY 10036. TEL 212-930-9500. FAX 212-869-3495.

641.1   US
NEW YORK STATE. ASSEMBLY SUBCOMMITTEE ON FOOD, FARM AND NUTRITION POLICY. REPORT.* a. Subcommittee on Food, Farm and Nutrition Policy, Empire State Plaza, 13th Fl., A-4, Albany, NY 12248-0001.

613.2   NR   ISSN 0189-0913
    CODEN: NJNSEP
NIGERIAN JOURNAL OF NUTRITIONAL SCIENCES. 1980. s-a. £N10. (Nutritional Society of Nigeria) Ibadan University Press, Department of Human Nutrition, University of Ibadan, Ibadan, Nigeria. Ed. Dr. Tola Atinmo. circ. 2,000.

641   JA   ISSN 0029-0572
NINGEN IGAKU/HUMAN MEDICINE. (Text in Japanese) 1938. m. 2000 Yen($7) Ningen Igakusha, 5-16-23 Senrioka, Settsu-shi 564, Japan. Ed. Takaaki Oura. adv.; bk.rev.; illus.; tr.lit.; circ. 20,000.

NISARG ANE AROGYA. see *PHYSICAL FITNESS AND HYGIENE*

NUTRITION AND DIETETICS

641.1   NO   ISSN 0332-5083
CODEN: FSSEDG
NORWAY. FISKERIDIREKTORATET. SKRIFTER. SERIE ERNAERING. (Text in English) 1976. irreg. free. Fiskeridirektoratet - Directorate of Fisheries, Box 185, 5002 Bergen, Norway. Ed. Leif Rein Njaa. **Indexed:** Biol.Abstr., Chem.Abstr., Nutr.Abstr.
—BLDSC shelfmark: 3946.900000.
Description: Reports on nutrition investigations concerning Norwegian Fisheries Research.

613.2   CN   ISSN 0078-236X
NOVA SCOTIA. DEPARTMENT OF HEALTH. NUTRITION DIVISION. ANNUAL REPORT. a. free to qualified personnel. Department of Health, Nutrition Division, Box 488, Halifax, N.S. B3J 2R8, Canada. TEL 902-424-4034.

612.3   SP   ISSN 0211-6057
CODEN: NUTCDF
NUTRICION CLINICA; dietetica hospitalaria. 6/yr. 5500 ptas. (Sociedad Espanol de Nutricion (S.E.N.)) Alpe Editores, S.A., Pedro Rico, 27, 28029 Madrid, Spain. TEL 733 88 11. FAX 315-96-52. adv.; charts. **Indexed:** Chem.Abstr, Excerp.Med., Ind.Med.Esp., Triticale Abstr.
—BLDSC shelfmark: 6187.650000.

641.1   II   ISSN 0550-404X
NUTRITION. 1966. q. Rs.2. National Institute of Nutrition, Indian Council of Medical Research, Jamai-Osmania, Hyderabad 500 007, India. Ed. M. Mohanram. circ. 4,000.
Description: Popular magazine concerning food and nutrition.

613.2   US
NUTRITION; an international journal of applied and basic nutritional science. 1985. bi-m. $99. Nutrition, Inc., Box 3748, 3001 N. San Fernando Blvd., Burbank, CA 91510. TEL 818-845-3748. FAX 315-464-6238. Ed. Dr. Michael Meguid. adv.; circ. 20,112.
Description: Publishes news of current research and practice in the field of applied and basic nutrition.
Refereed Serial

641.1   US
NUTRITION ACTION HEALTHLETTER. 1974. 10/yr. $19.95. Center for Science in the Public Interest, 1875 Connecticut Ave., N.W., Ste. 300, Washington, DC 20009-5728. TEL 202-332-9110. FAX 202-265-4954. Ed. Stephen B. Schmidt. bk.rev.; abstr.; bibl.; circ. 200,000. (back issues avail.; reprint service avail.) **Indexed:** Alt.Press Ind., CHNI, Hlth.Ind.
Formerly: Nutrition Action (ISSN 0199-5510); Incorporating (1976-1980): Intake (New Hyde Park) (ISSN 0732-6920)
Description: News, commentary, features, letters, and advocacy on nutrition and food policy, in order to promote good health.

NUTRITION AND CANCER; an international journal. see *MEDICAL SCIENCES — Cancer*

613.2   US
NUTRITION & DIETARY CONSULTANT; America's only journal for the practicing professional. 1981. m. $15.96. American Association of Nutritional Consultants, 1641 E. Sunset Rd., B 117, Las Vegas, NV 89119. TEL 702-361-1132. FAX 702-739-7225. Ed. Myra E. Zelikovics. adv.; circ. 46,000.
Incorporating: Herald of Holistic Health Newsletter; **Formerly:** Nutritional Consultant.

641 664   UK   ISSN 0034-6659
CODEN: NFSCD7
NUTRITION AND FOOD SCIENCE. 1966. bi-m. £17.50 (foreign £21). M C B University Press Ltd., 62 Toller Ln., Bradford, W. Yorks BD8 9BY, England. TEL 0274-499821. FAX 0274-574143. TELEX 51317 MCBUNI G. Ed. Dilys Wells. adv.; bk.rev.; abstr.; charts; stat.; index; circ. 3,500. **Indexed:** Br.Tech.Ind., Chem.Abstr., Curr.Adv.Ecol.Sci., Dairy Sci.Abstr., Food Sci.& Tech.Abstr., Nutr.Abstr., Rural Recreat.Tour.Abstr., World Agri.Econ.& Rural Sociol.Abstr.
—BLDSC shelfmark: 6188.070000.
Formerly: Review of Nutrition and Food Science.

613   UK   ISSN 0260-1060
CODEN: NUHEDT
NUTRITION AND HEALTH. 1982. 4/yr. £89($179) (McCarrison Society) A B Academic Publishers, P.O. Box 42, Bicester, Oxon OX6 7NW, England. TEL 0869-320949. Ed. Edward Kirby. adv.; bk.rev. (also avail. in microform) **Indexed:** ASSIA, Curr.Adv.Ecol.Sci., Dairy Sci.Abstr., Environ.Per.Bibl., Excerp.Med., Ind.Med.
—BLDSC shelfmark: 6188.073000.
Description: Covers preventive medical and nutrition education.

618   US
NUTRITION AND THE BRAIN. 1975. irreg., latest vol.8. price varies. Raven Press, 1185 Ave. of the Americas, New York, NY 10036. TEL 212-930-9500. FAX 212-869-3495. TELEX 640073. Eds. Richard J. and Judith J. Wurtman. **Indexed:** Biol.Abstr., Curr.Cont., Sci.Cit.Ind.

613 641   US   ISSN 0732-0167
NUTRITION & THE M.D.; a continuing education service for physicians and nutritionists. 1974. m. $46. P.M. Inc., Box 10172, Van Nuys, CA 91410. TEL 213-873-4399. Ed. Gerald McKee. circ. 10,000. (back issues avail.)
Description: Each issue covers a single topic from several aspects.

641.7   US   ISSN 0888-3483
QP141.A1
NUTRITION CLINICS. 1986. bi-m. $40 to individuals (foreign $45); insitututions $50 (foreign $55). J.B. Lippincott Co., E. Washington Sq., Philadelphia, PA 19105. TEL 215-238-4200. Ed. Eleanor N. Whitney. circ. 1,000.

613.2   US
NUTRITION COUNSELOR. 1989. q. $24.95. HealthTeam Interactive Communications, Inc., 246 5th Ave., No. 207, New York, NY 10001. TEL 212-689-1520. FAX 212-779-2094. circ. 30,000.
Description: Provides educational articles for the nutritionist and includes tear-out information guides.

641.4   CN
NUTRITION FORUM/FORUM DE NUTRITION. 1966. s-a. membership. Canadian Society for Nutritional Sciences, Department of Foods and Nutrition, University of Manitoba, Winnipeg, Man. R3T 2N2, Canada. TEL 613-993-4484. (Dist. by: Department de Nutrition, Universite de Montreal, Que. H30 3J7, Canada) Ed. Vivian Bruce. bk.rev.; circ. controlled.

641.1   US   ISSN 0748-8165
NUTRITION FORUM. 1984. bi-m. $40 to individuals (foreign $45); institutions $50 (foreign $55). J.B. Lippincott Co., E. Washington Sq., Philadelphia, PA 19105. TEL 215-238-4200. Ed. Stephen Barrett, M.D. bk.rev.; circ. 2,000. **Indexed:** Hlth.Ind.
—BLDSC shelfmark: 6188.285000.
Description: Uses biomedical research and investigative journalism to give an informative, easily-digested collection of items in a newsletter format.

612   US   ISSN 0892-1474
NUTRITION FUNDING REPORT; a monthly guide to locating resources. 1986. m. $41.95. Nutrition Legislation Services, Box 75035, Washington, DC 20013. TEL 202-488-8879. Ed. Lenora Moragne.
Description: Itemizes available resources for nutrition activities: grants, contracts, scholarships, publications, all from charities, corporations, foundations, government and others.

613   US   ISSN 0164-7202
NUTRITION HEALTH REVIEW. 1976. q. $18 for 2 yrs. Vegetus Publications, 171 Madison Ave., New York, NY 10016. TEL 212-679-3590. FAX 212-679-3597. Eds. A. Rifkin, F.R. Rifkin. adv.; bk.rev.; illus.; circ. 181,000. (tabloid format) **Indexed:** Hlth.Ind.

613.2   US   ISSN 0884-5336
CODEN: NCPREH
NUTRITION IN CLINICAL PRACTICE. 1986. bi-m. $35 to individuals; institutions $75. American Society for Parenteral and Enteral Nutrition, 8630 Fenton St., Ste. 412, Silver Spring, MD 20910. TEL 301-587-6315. FAX 301-587-3323. Ed. Philip J. Schneider, M.S. adv.; circ. 8,124. (also avail. in microform)
—BLDSC shelfmark: 6188.130000.
Description: Articles of intermediate clinical interest for all members of the nutrition support community, including physicians, dieticians and nurses.

612.3   US
NUTRITION JOURNAL. bi-m. 3001 N. San Fernando Blvd., Burbank, CA 91504-2525. TEL 818-845-3748. FAX 818-954-8916. Ed. Michael Meguid. circ. 12,000.

612 340   US   ISSN 8756-6060
NUTRITION LEGISLATION NEWS; a twice-monthly report of United States government activities. 1985. s-m. $150. Nutrition Legislation Services, Box 75035, Washington, DC 20013. TEL 202-488-8879. Ed. Lenora Moragne.
Description: Offers regulatory and legislative information covering all areas of nutrition: research, education, international food assistance, manpower training, surveillance and monitoring, and food quality and safety.

613   US   ISSN 8756-5919
NUTRITION NEWS (RIVERSIDE). 1978. m. $18. Nutrition News, 4108 Watkins Dr., Riverside, CA 92507-4752. Ed. Siri Khalsa. circ. 90,000. (tabloid format; back issues avail.)

641.1   US   ISSN 0369-6464
TX501
NUTRITION NEWS (ROSEMONT). 1937. 3/yr. $4 (foreign $5). National Dairy Council, 6300 N. River Rd., Rosemont, IL 60018-4233. TEL 708-696-1020. FAX 708-696-1033. circ. 25,000. (back issues avail.) **Indexed:** CHNI, Nutr.Abstr.
—BLDSC shelfmark: 6188.480000.
Description: Provides updates on recent developments in nutrition research, and the latest educational resources. Contains teaching ideas of interest to elementary and secondary teachers and nurses.

NUTRITION NEWS IN ZAMBIA. see *FOOD AND FOOD INDUSTRIES*

613.2   US
NUTRITION NOTES. 1965. q. $24. American Institute of Nutrition, 9650 Rockville Pike, Bethesda, MD 20814. TEL 301-530-7050. FAX 301-571-1892. Ed. Phylis Moser-Veillon. circ. 2,750. (back issues avail.)
Description: Information on awards, publications, reports, meetings; updates readers (nutrition scientists) on legislation.

612.3   US   ISSN 0740-8684
NUTRITION REPORT. 1983. m. $48. Health Media of America, Inc., 11300 Sorrento Valley Rd., Ste. 103, San Diego, CA 92121. TEL 619-453-3887. Ed.Bd. abstr.; bibl.; circ. 4,000.
Description: Provides concise summaries of recently published scientific research on vitamins and minerals.

616.39   US   ISSN 0271-5317
QP141.A1   CODEN: NTRSDC
NUTRITION RESEARCH; the international medium for rapid publication of communications in the nutritional sciences. 1981. 12/yr. £265 (effective 1992). Pergamon Press, Inc., Journals Division, 660 White Plains Rd., Tarrytown, NY 10591-5153. TEL 914-524-9200. FAX 914-333-2444. (And: Headington Hill Hall, Oxford OX3 0BW, England. TEL 0865-794141) Ed. Ranjit K. Chandra. (also avail. in microform from MIM,UMI) **Indexed:** Abstr.Hyg., Chem.Abstr., Curr.Adv.Ecol.Sci., Curr.Cont., Dairy Sci.Abstr., Excerp.Med., Ind.Sci.Rev., Maize Abstr., Nutr.Abstr., Pig News & Info., Poult.Abstr., Rice Abstr., Soyabean Abstr., Triticale Abstr., Trop.Oil Seeds Abstr.
—BLDSC shelfmark: 6188.950000.
Description: Reports on basic and applied research on all aspects of the nutritional sciences, including concerns of the social sciences. Also includes information from readers.
Refereed Serial

NUTRITION AND DIETETICS

641.1 US ISSN 0736-0037
NUTRITION RESEARCH NEWSLETTER; a monthly update for food, nutrition, and health professionals. 1983. m. $96. Lyda Associates, Box 700, Palisades, NY 10964. TEL 914-359-8282. FAX 914-359-1229. Ed. Lillian Langseth. index; circ. 5,000. (reprint service avail. from ISI) **Indexed:** Hlth.Ind.
Description: Geared to food, nutrition and health professionals, with articles on diet in health and disease.

612.3 UK ISSN 0954-4224
QP141.A1 CODEN: NREREX
NUTRITION RESEARCH REVIEWS. (Supplement to: British Journal of Nutrition. (ISSN 0007-4224)) 1988. a. $79 (free with subscr. to The British Journal of Nutrition). Cambridge University Press, Edinburgh Building, Shaftesbury Rd., Cambridge CB2 2RU, England. TEL 0223-312393. FAX 0223-315052. (N. American subscr. to: Cambridge University Press, 40 W. 20th St., New York, NY 10011) Ed. Roy H. Smith. (also avail. in microform from UMI) **Indexed:** Environ.Per.Bibl.
—BLDSC shelfmark: 6188.975000.
Description: Reviews of research on a variety of nutritional problems.

NUTRITION REVIEW. see *MEDICAL SCIENCES*

641 US ISSN 0029-6643
TX341 CODEN: NUREA8
NUTRITION REVIEWS. 1942. 12/yr. $66. (International Life Sciences Institute - Nutrition Foundation) Springer-Verlag, Journals, 175 Fifth Ave., New York, NY 10010. TEL 212-460-1500. Ed. Robert E. Olson. adv.; bk.rev.; abstr.; bibl.; index; circ. 10,000. (also avail. in microfilm from UMI; reprint service avail. from UMI) **Indexed:** Abstr.Hyg., Acad.Ind., Biol.Abstr., Biol.& Agr.Ind., Cadscan, Chem.Abstr., Curr.Adv.Biochem., Curr.Adv.Ecol.Sci., Curr.Cont., Dairy Sci.Abstr., Dent.Ind., Environ.Per.Bibl., Excerp.Med., Food Sci.& Tech.Abstr., Gen.Sci.Ind., Helminthol.Abstr., Hlth.Ind., Ind.Med., Ind.Sci.Rev., Ind.Vet., Lead Abstr., Nutr.Abstr., Protozool.Abstr., Rev.Plant Path., Risk Abstr., Trop.Dis.Bull., Vet.Bull.
—BLDSC shelfmark: 6189.000000.
Description: Reports of research in clinical and experimental nutrition.

641 UK ISSN 0029-6651
TX501 CODEN: PNUSA4
NUTRITION SOCIETY. PROCEEDINGS. 1941. 3/yr. $190. Cambridge University Press, Edinburgh Bldg., Shaftesbury Rd., Cambridge CB2 2RU, England. TEL 0223-312393. FAX 0223-315052. TELEX 851817256. (N. American subscr. to: Cambridge University Press, 40 W. 20th St., New York, NY 10011) Ed. R.H. Smith. adv.; bibl.; charts; index. (also avail. in microform from SWZ,UMI) **Indexed:** Abstr.Hyg., Anim.Breed.Abstr., Biol.Abstr., Biol.& Agr.Ind., Biotech.Abstr., Cadscan, Chem.Abstr., Curr.Adv.Ecol.Sci., Curr.Cont, Dairy Sci.Abstr., Energy Ind., Energy Info.Abstr., Field Crop Abstr., Food Sci.& Tech.Abstr., Helminthol.Abstr., Herb.Abstr., Ind.Med., Ind.Vet., Lead Abstr., Nutr.Abstr., Risk Abstr., Rural Recreat.Tour.Abstr., Triticale Abstr., Trop.Dis.Bull., Vet.Bull., World Agri.Econ.& Rural Sociol.Abstr., Zincscan.
—BLDSC shelfmark: 6780.000000.
Description: Papers presented by invitation at symposia of the Society, and abstracts of original communications presented at other meetings.

613.2 612.3 AT ISSN 0314-1004
CODEN: PNSADB
NUTRITION SOCIETY OF AUSTRALIA. PROCEEDINGS. 1976. a. Aus.$15. Nutrition Society of Australia, c/o C S I R O, Private Bag, PO, Wembley, W.A. 6014, Australia. Ed. J.R. Mercer. index; circ. 1,000. (back issues avail.) **Indexed:** Biol.Abstr., Chem.Abstr., Curr.Cont.
—BLDSC shelfmark: 6779.400000.

641.4 630 II
NUTRITION SOCIETY OF INDIA. PROCEEDINGS. 1967. a. Rs.50($15) Nutrition Society of India, c/o National Institute of Nutrition, PO-Jamai Osmania, Hyderabad 500007, India. Ed.Bd. circ. 1,500. (back issues avail.) **Indexed:** Agroforest.Abstr., Rice Abstr., Soyabean Abstr., Trop.Oil Seeds Abstr.

641 US ISSN 0029-666X
RA784
NUTRITION TODAY. 1966. bi-m. $27.50 to individuals; institutions $46. Williams and Wilkins, 428 E. Preston St., Baltimore, MD 21202. TEL 301-528-4000. FAX 301-528-4312. TELEX 87669. Ed. Helen A. Guthrie. adv.; bk.rev.; index; circ. 6,700. (also avail. in microform; reprint service avail.) **Indexed:** A.S.& T.Ind., Bibl.Agri., Biol.Abstr., CHNI, Curr.Cont., Gen.Sci.Ind., Hlth.Ind., Nutr.Abstr.
—BLDSC shelfmark: 6190.100000.
Description: Articles on new developments in nutrition for dieticians, nutritionists and physicians.

641.1 US ISSN 0736-0096
NUTRITION WEEK. 1970. w. $75 to individuals; students $40. Community Nutrition Institute, 2001 S St., N.W., Washington, DC 20009. FAX 202-462-5241. Ed. Rod Leonard. bk.rev.; bibl.; index; circ. 4,800.
Former titles: C N I Weekly Report (ISSN 0191-0833); C N I Report.

641 JM ISSN 0255-8203
NYAM NEWS. 1975. m. free. Caribbean Food and Nutrition Institute, U.W.I. Mona Campus, P.O. Box 140, Kingston 7, Jamaica, W.I. TEL 809-927-1540. FAX 809-927-2657. TELEX 3705. (Co-sponsors: Pan American Health Organization, World Health Organization) Eds. Sadie Campbell, Claire Forrester. circ. 700. **Indexed:** Nutr.Abstr.

612.3 613.2 US ISSN 1044-1522
OBESITY & HEALTH; journal of research, news, issues. 1986. bi-m. $59 to individuals (foreign $98); institutions $89 (foreign $168). (Healthy Living Institute) Frances M. Berg, Ed. & Pub., 402 S. 14th St., Hettinger, ND 58639. TEL 701-567-2646. (Subscr. to: RR2, Box 905, Hettinger, ND 58639. TEL 701-567-2845) adv.; bk.rev.; index; circ. 1,400. (back issues avail.) **Indexed:** CINAHL, Nurs.Abstr., Soc.Work Res.Abstr.
Former titles (until 1989): International Obesity Newsletter (ISSN 0893-2204); Obesity Newsletter (ISSN 0891-4028)
Description: Reports research and information on obesity including causes, prevalence, treatment, prevention, health risks, impact on individuals, social and political issues and the weight loss industry.

641.1 633 US
ON YOUR MARK. 1976. q. Sugar Association, Inc., 1101 15th St., N.W., No. 600, Washington, DC 20005. TEL 202-785-1122. FAX 202-785-5019. Ed. Sarah Barnett. circ. 10,000.
Formerly: Sugar and Health.
Description: Covers nutrition, fitness and the role of sugar in nutrition and health.

613.2 051 US
ONE PEACEFUL WORLD. 1989. 4/yr. $30 to individuals; families $50. One Peaceful World, Inc., Box 10, Becket, MA 01223. TEL 413-623-2322. FAX 413-623-8827. Ed. Alex Jack. adv.; bk.rev.; circ. 5,000.
Formerly: Return to Paradise.

ONTARIO WRESTLER MAGAZINE. see *SPORTS AND GAMES*

641.1 US
ORGANIC CONSUMER REPORT. w. $5. Eden Ranch, Box 370, Topanga, CA 90290. TEL 213-455-2065. Ed. Judith Eagan. bk.rev.; circ. controlled.

613.2 GW ISSN 0178-7624
ORTHOMOLEKULAR; Fachzeitschrift fuer Ernaehrung, Gesundheit und Umwelt. (Text in Dutch, German) 1985. bi-m. DM.139 (foreign DM.159). Ortho-Communications, Lindemannstr. 47, D-4000 Dusseldorf, Germany. TEL 0211-684422. FAX 0211-684946. Ed. Diana Evans von Metternich. adv.; bk.rev.; circ. 3,250.

664 641 US ISSN 0748-8394
OUTPOST EXCHANGE; Milwaukee's food and wellness magazine. 1971. m. $10. (Outpost Natural Foods) Outpost Exchange, 102 E. Capitol Dr., Milwaukee, WI 53212. TEL 414-964-7789. Ed. Art Blair. adv.; bk.rev.; circ. 24,000.

OVER THE GARDEN FENCE; natural living in North Texas. see *GARDENING AND HORTICULTURE*

PERSONAL FITNESS. see *PHYSICAL FITNESS AND HYGIENE*

641 PH ISSN 0031-7640
TX501 CODEN: PJNUAF
PHILIPPINE JOURNAL OF NUTRITION. 1949. q. $12. Philippine Association of Nutrition, c/o Nutrition Foundation of the Philippines, 107 E. Rodriguez., Sr. Blvd., Quezon City, Philippines. Ed. Velona A. Corpus. adv.; bk.rev.; abstr.; charts; illus.; index; circ. 2,000. (also avail. in microform from UMI; reprint service avail. from UMI) **Indexed:** Biol.Abstr., Chem.Abstr., Dairy Sci.Abstr., Food Sci.& Tech.Abstr., Nutr.Abstr., Philip.Abstr., Rural Recreat.Tour.Abstr., World Agri.Econ.& Rural Sociol.Abstr.
Formerly: Nutrition News.

641.1 PH
PHILIPPINES. FOOD AND NUTRITION RESEARCH INSTITUTE. ANNUAL REPORT. (Text in English) 1950. a. free. Food and Nutrition Research Institute, 727 Pedro Gil St., P.O. Box EA-467, Ermita, Manila, Philippines. TEL 595113. FAX 632-59-22-75. Ed. Alma M. Jose. circ. controlled.
Formerly: Philippines. Food and Nutrition Research Center. Annual Report (ISSN 0071-7142)
Description: A detailed compilation of the institute's various projects and activities. Includes completed research, research in progress, public services, staff papers and publications, staff development, cooperative activities, foreign visitors, financial resources, and technical staff.

PHYSICIANS FOOD ADVISOR. see *FOOD AND FOOD INDUSTRIES*

641.1 NE ISSN 0921-9668
TX341 CODEN: PFHNE8
PLANT FOODS FOR HUMAN NUTRITION. (Text in English) 1952. 4/yr. fl.287($163) Kluwer Academic Publishers, Postbus 17, 3300 AA Dordrecht, Netherlands. TEL 078-334267. FAX 078-334254. TELEX 29245. (Dist. by: Kluwer Academic Publishers Group, Box 322, 3300 AH Dordrecht, Netherlands; N. Americ dist. addr.: Box 358, Accord Station, Hingham, MA 02018-0358. TEL 617-871-6600) Ed. Constance V. Kies. adv.; bk.rev.; bibl.; charts; illus.; circ. 500. (reprint service avail. from SWZ) **Indexed:** Biol.Abstr., Chem.Abstr., Curr.Adv.Biochem., Curr.Adv.Ecol.Sci., Excerp.Med., Field Crop Abstr., Food Sci.& Tech.Abstr., Herb.Abstr., Hort.Abstr., I.P.A., Maize Abstr., Nutr.Abstr., Plant Breed.Abstr., Potato Abstr., Poult.Abstr., Rice Abstr., Seed Abstr., Soils & Fert., Soyabean Abstr., Triticale Abstr., Trop.Oil Seeds Abstr., VITIS.
Former titles: Qualitas Plantarum (ISSN 0377-3205); Qualitas Plantarum et Materiae Vegetabiles (ISSN 0033-5134)

PLENTY BULLETIN. see *AGRICULTURE — Agricultural Economics*

664 331.88 CS ISSN 0032-566X
POTRAVINAR. m. 9.60 Kcs.($13.20) (Odborovy Svaz Pracovniku Potravinarskeho Prumyslu) Ustredni Rada Odboru, Nam. Antonina Zapotockeho 2, 113 59 Prague 3, Czechoslovakia. (Dist. by: Artia, Ve Smeckach 30, 111 27 Prague 1, Czechoslovakia) Ed. Jaroslav Pikard.

PROFESSIONEALLEVATORE. see *AGRICULTURE — Poultry And Livestock*

641 US ISSN 0306-0632
QP141.A1 CODEN: PFNSDI
PROGRESS IN FOOD & NUTRITION SCIENCE. 1975. 4/yr. £220 (effective 1992). Pergamon Press, Inc., Journals Division, 660 White Plains Rd., Tarrytown, NY 10591-5153. TEL 914-524-9200. FAX 914-333-2444. (And: Headington Hill Hall, Oxford OX3 0BW, England. TEL 0865-794141) Ed. Ranjit K. Chandra. index. (also avail. in microform from MIM,UMI) **Indexed:** Biol.Abstr., Chem.Abstr., Curr.Adv.Ecol.Sci., Curr.Cont., Energy Ind., Energy Info.Abstr., Excerp.Med., Food Sci.& Tech.Abstr., Ind.Med., Ind.Sci.Rev., Nutr.Abstr.
—BLDSC shelfmark: 6868.400000.
Formerly: International Encyclopedia of Food and Nutrition (ISSN 0074-4700)
Description: Critical reviews of topical subjects within the general area of food and nutrition science. *Refereed Serial*

RACE ACROSS AMERICA PROGRAM. see *SPORTS AND GAMES — Bicycles And Motorcycles*

REPORT ON INSTITUTIONAL FOODSERVICE. see *FOOD AND FOOD INDUSTRIES*

NUTRITION AND DIETETICS

REVISTA DE INVESTIGACION CLINICA. see *MEDICAL SCIENCES*

616.1 616.39   AG   ISSN 0034-8600
REVISTA DE NUTRICION Y ATEROSCLEROSIS. 1958. bi-m. free. c/o Mario Campagnoli, Juan B. Alberdi 3255, Buenos Aires, Argentina. adv.; illus.; circ. 15,000.

REVUE DE L'INDUSTRIE ALIMENTAIRE. see *FOOD AND FOOD INDUSTRIES*

613.2   FR   ISSN 0556-7793
REVUE FRANCAISE DE DIETETIQUE. 1957. q. 28 F. Syndicat National des Techniciens Superieurs en Dietetique, 95 rue de la Loubiere, 13005 Marseille, France. adv. **Indexed:** Food Sci.& Tech.Abstr., Nutr.Abstr.
—BLDSC shelfmark: 7903.300000.

613.2   IT
RIVISTA ITALIANA DI NUTRIZIONE CLINICA E PREVENTIVA. 3/yr. L.90000($150) (effective 1992). Casa Editrice Idelson, Via A. De Gasperi 55, 80133 Naples, Italy. TEL 081-5524733. FAX 081-5518295. Ed. Flaminio Fidanza.

641.1   IT   ISSN 0393-5582
RIVISTA ITALIANA DI NUTRIZIONE PARENTERALE ED ENTERALE. (Text in Italian; summaries in English) 3/yr. L.90000($90) (effective 1992). Wichtig Editore s.r.l., Via Friuli, 72-74, 20135 Milan, Italy. TEL 02-5452306. FAX 02-5451843.
—BLDSC shelfmark: 7987.442500.

612.3   US
RODALE'S FOOD & NUTRITION LETTER. m. Rodale Press, Inc., 33 E. Minor St., Emmaus, PA 18049-4113. TEL 215-967-5171. Ed. Mark Bricklin. circ. 65,000.

RUNNING & FITNEWS. see *PHYSICAL FITNESS AND HYGIENE*

613   US
RX WEIGHT CONTROL;* the multidisciplinary newsletter designed to reduce health risk. 1984. bi-m. $18. Nutritional Management, c/o Herbert Kahn, 114 State St., 4th Fl., Boston, MA 02109-2402. Ed.Bd. illus.

SANTE. see *PHYSICAL FITNESS AND HYGIENE*

SCHOOL FOODSERVICE WHO'S WHO. see *BUSINESS AND ECONOMICS — Trade And Industrial Directories*

641.1   IT
SCUOLA DELLA SALUTE. m. L.36000. Curcio Periodici S.p.A., Via Corsica 4, 00198 Rome, Italy. Ed. Rosanna Falconi. adv.

664   MX
SECTOR ALIMENTARIO EN MEXICO (YEAR). 1981. irreg. Mex.$3000($18.50) Instituto Nacional de Estadistica, Geografia e Informatica, Secretaria de Programacion y Presupuesto, Prol. Heroe de Nacozari, 2301, Acceso 10, C.P. 20290, Aguascalientes, Ags., Mexico. TEL 91-491-81968. FAX 91-491-80739. (Subscr. to: Rio Rhin No. 56, Col. Cuauhtemoc, 06500 Mexico, D.F., Mexico) circ. 1,000.

SEMINARS IN PEDIATRIC GASTROENTEROLOGY AND NUTRITION. see *MEDICAL SCIENCES — Gastroenterology*

641.1 664   CC
SHIPIN KE-JI/FOOD SCIENCE. (Text in Chinese) m. $0.40 per no. Guoji Shudian, Qikan Bu, P.O. Box 399, Beijing 100044, People's Republic of China.

613.2   UK   ISSN 0144-8129
SLIMMING. 1969. 8/yr. £15.90 outside Europe. E M A P Elan, Victory House, 14 Leicester Place, London WC2H 7BP, England. FAX 071-434-0656. Ed. Kandy Shepherd. adv.; bk.rev.; circ. 210,964.
Formerly (until Mar. 1979): Slimming and Nutrition (ISSN 0049-075X)

616.39 610   UK   ISSN 0264-5807
SOCIETY FOR ENVIRONMENTAL THERAPY. NEWSLETTER. 1981. q. £10 to libraries; students £5; scientists £14. Society for Environmental Therapy, c/o Mrs. Hilary Davidson, 521 Foxhall Rd., Ipswich, Suffolk IP3 8LW, England. Ed. V. Rippere. adv.; bk.rev.; circ. 350.
—BLDSC shelfmark: 6108.344340.

SOUTH PACIFIC FOODS LEAFLET. see *FOOD AND FOOD INDUSTRIES*

641.1   US   ISSN 0894-072X
SOYA INTERNATIONAL. 1979. 4/yr. $20 free to qualified personnel. Soyatech, Inc., Box 84, Bar Harbour, ME 04609. FAX 207-288-5264. adv.; bk.rev.; circ. 1,500 (controlled).
Formerly: Soyfoods.

614.53   US
SPECIALTY COOKING; cookbook magazine. 1989. bi-m. $3.95 per no. Blockbuster Periodicals, Inc., 2131 Hollywood Blvd., Hollywood, FL 33020. TEL 305-925-5242. Ed. Barbara Newman. circ. 65,000.
Incorporates: Cookbook Series & Good Cooking Series.
Description: Covers diabetic and low-cholesterol cooking.

641.1 790.1 617.1   US   ISSN 0741-3696
SPORTS - NUTRITION NEWS; incorporating the latest in health and fitness. 1982. s-m. $43. Healthmere Press, Inc., Box 986, Evanston, IL 60204. TEL 708-251-5950. Ed. Joan Fishman. bk.rev.; index. (back issues avail.)

613.26   US   ISSN 0744-9860
SPROUTLETTER. 1980. q. $10. Sprouting Publications, Box 62, Ashland, OR 97520. TEL 503-488-2326. Ed. Michael Linden. adv.; bk.rev.; charts; illus.; tr.lit.; cum.index; circ. 3,000. (back issues avail.)
Description: Explores nutrition, holistic health, vegetarianism, sprouting, live foods, blue-green algae, acidophillus, enzymes, indoor food gardening; includes recipes and product listings.

641 613   US   ISSN 0039-5382
SUNFLOWER (MANHATTAN). 1946. 6/yr. $20 (elsewhere $30). Kansas Dietetic Association, c/o Dept. of Hotel, Restaurant, Institution Management and Dietetics, Justin Hall 104, Kansas State University, Manhattan, KS 66103. TEL 913-532-5521. FAX 913-532-5504. Ed. Carole Stephens. bk.rev.; circ. 800.
Description: Covers professional and educational activities of the association's members.

641   SW   ISSN 0082-0415
                        CODEN: SSNFAW
SWEDISH NUTRITION FOUNDATION. SYMPOSIA. (Text in English) 1962. irreg., latest vol.15. price varies. Almqvist & Wiksell International, PO Box 638, S-101 28 Stockholm, Sweden. Ed. Gunnar Blix. **Indexed:** Biol.Abstr.
—BLDSC shelfmark: 8585.050000.

T O P S NEWS. (Take Off Pounds Sensibly, Inc.) see *PHYSICAL FITNESS AND HYGIENE*

613.2   US   ISSN 0883-5691
TOPICS IN CLINICAL NUTRITION. 1986. q. $59. Aspen Publishers, Inc., 200 Orchard Ridge Dr., Gaithersburg, MD 20878. TEL 301-417-7500. FAX 301-417-7550.
—BLDSC shelfmark: 8867.432800.

613.2 614.58   US
TOTAL HEALTH. 1979. bi-m. $13. Trio Publications, 6001 Topanga Canyon Blvd., No. 300, Woodland Hills, CA 91367. TEL 818-887-6484. FAX 818-887-7960. Ed. Robert L. Smith. adv.; bk.rev.; circ. 95,000. **Indexed:** Hlth.Ind.
Formerly: Trio.
Description: Preventive health care lifestyle magazine covering nutrition, diet, fitness, travel, psychological-spiritual health encompassing mind, body, and spirit.

TRENDS IN FOOD SCIENCE AND TECHNOLOGY. see *FOOD AND FOOD INDUSTRIES*

513.2   US
TUFTS UNIVERSITY DIET AND NUTRITION LETTER. 1983. m. $20. W.H. White Publications, Inc., 53 Park Pl., 8th Fl., New York, NY 10007. TEL 212-608-6515. FAX 212-732-2360. (Subscr. to: Box 57857, Boulder, CO 80322) Ed. Stanley N. Gershoff. bk.rev.; circ. 280,000. (also avail. in microfilm) **Indexed:** Hlth.Ind.

664   BL
UNIVERSIDADE ESTADUAL DE CAMPINAS. FACULDADE DE TECNOLOGIA DE ALIMENTOS. INFORMATIVO ANNUAL. (Text in English or Portuguese) a. Universidade Estadual de Campinas, Faculdade de Tecnologia de Alimentos, Ciudade Universitaria, Barao Geraldo, Caixa Postal 1170, Campinas, Sao Paulo, Brazil.
Formerly: Universidade Estadual de Campinas. Faculdade de Engenharia de Alimentos e Enpenhoria Agricola. Informativo Annual.

UNIVERSITY OF CALIFORNIA, BERKELEY. WELLNESS LETTER; the newsletter of nutrition, fitness, and stress management. see *PHYSICAL FITNESS AND HYGIENE*

UNIVERSITY OF TEXAS LIFETIME HEALTH LETTER. see *PHYSICAL FITNESS AND HYGIENE*

613.2   SW   ISSN 0042-2657
TX341   CODEN: VAFOAS
VAAR FOEDA. (Text in Swedish; summaries in English) 1949. 10/yr. SEK 190($25) Statens Livsmedelsverk - National Food Administration, PO Box 622, S-751 26 Uppsala, Sweden. FAX 46-18-105848. TELEX 76121 SLVUPS. Ed. L. Boija. bk.rev.; charts; illus.; circ. 7,000. **Indexed:** Chem.Abstr., Dairy Sci.Abstr., Food Sci.& Tech.Abstr., Nutr.Abstr.
Description: Covers activities in food control projects, new regulations and current research.

613.2   SW   ISSN 0346-7341
VAAR FOEDA. SUPPLEMENT. 1973. irreg. (3-5/yr.). price varies. Statens Livsmedelsverk - National Food Administration, PO Box 622, S-751 26 Uppsala, Sweden. Ed. Leif Chrona. bk.rev.; circ. 2,500.
—BLDSC shelfmark: 9146.020000.
Description: Contains complete NFA investigation results with comprehensive table material.

637   SW   ISSN 0042-2681
VAAR NAERING; tidskrift foer upplysning om livsmedlen, kosten och haelsan. 1923. 4/yr. SEK 85. S-105 33 Stockholm, Sweden. Ed. Margriet Pieters. bk.rev.; circ. 20,000.
Formerly: Mjolkpropagandan.

613.26 179.3   UK   ISSN 0307-4811
VEGAN. 1946. q. £6. Vegan Society, 7 Battle Rd., St. Leonards-on-Sea, E. Sussex TN37 7AA, England. Ed. Richard Farhall. adv.; bk.rev.; circ. 6,000. (back issues avail.)
Description: Information on animal rights, vegan nutrition, health and ecology.

VEGETARIAN ASTROLOGER. see *ASTROLOGY*

919.204   UK
VEGETARIAN HANDBOOK. 1956. biennial. £3.95. Vegetarian Society, c/o Publications Mgr., Parkdale, Dunham Rd., Altrincham, Cheshire WA14 4QG, England. TEL 061-928-0793. Ed. Jane Bowler. adv.; circ. 20,000.
Former titles: International Vegetarian Health Food Handbook; Vegetarian Handbook (ISSN 0083-5315); Food Reformers' Yearbook.
Description: Comprehensive list of where to eat, stay, and products available.

613.26   US   ISSN 0885-7636
VEGETARIAN JOURNAL. 1982. bi-m. $20. Vegetarian Resource Group, P.O. Box 1463, Baltimore, MD 21203. TEL 401-366-8343. Eds. Charles Stahler, Debra Wasserman. adv.; bk.rev.; film rev.; illus.; circ. 20,000. (reprint service avail. from UMI)
Formerly: Baltimore Vegetarians.
Description: Covers various aspects of vegetarianism including health, recipes, ethics, ecology, world hunger and animal rights.

VEGETARIAN TIMES. see *PHYSICAL FITNESS AND HYGIENE*

613.26   US   ISSN 0271-1591
VEGETARIAN VOICE. 1974. q. $15 to individuals; free to libraries. North American Vegetarian Society, Box 72, Dolgeville, NY 13329. TEL 518-568-7636. Ed. Jennie O. Collura. bk.rev.; illus.; circ. 7,000.
Description: Information on nutrition, cooking, health, animal and environmental protection for people interested in vegetarianism, with organization new and reports on annual conferences.

613.26 GW ISSN 0178-9104
DER VEGETARIER; Zeitschrift fuer ethische Lebensgestaltung und Lebensreform. 1949. bi-m. DM.30. Vegetarier Bund Deutschlands e.V., Blumenstr. 3, 3000 Hannover 1, Germany. TEL 0511-3632050. Eds. Judith Baumgartner, Peter Schmitt. adv.; bk.rev.; circ. 4,000. (back issues avail.)

613.26 DK ISSN 0109-8861
VEGETARISK TIDSSKRIFT. irreg. (1-2/yr.), vol.77, 1983. DKK 30. Dansk Vegetar-og Raakostforening, Ny Vestergaardsvej 6, 3500 Vaerloese, Denmark. illus.
Formerly: V F (ISSN 0109-8845)

VIBRANT LIFE (HAGERSTOWN); a Christian guide to total health. see PHYSICAL FITNESS AND HYGIENE

VIE ET SANTE. see PHYSICAL FITNESS AND HYGIENE

613.2 IT
VITALITY. m. L.43000. Rusconi Editore Associati S.p.A., Viale Sarca 235, 20126 Milan, Italy. TEL 02-66191. FAX 02-66192686. (back issues avail.)

VITALITY MAGAZINE; Toronto's monthly wellness journal. see PHYSICAL FITNESS AND HYGIENE

613.2 613.7 CN
VITASANA.* (Text in English, Italian) 1984. m. (10/yr.) $25. VitaSana Magazine Inc., 1100 Caledonia Rd., Ste. 200, Toronto, Ont. M6A 2W5, Canada. TEL 416-785-4975. FAX 416-785-4329. Ed. Elena Caprile. adv.: B&W page Can.$1495, color page Can.$1990; trim 8 1/2 x 11. circ. 21,618.

641.1 IT
VIVERE - GUARIRE. 1952. q. L.7000. Editrice Guarire di Fausto Pistarino, San Felice, Centro Commerciale, Torre 7, 20090 Segrate (Milan), Italy. adv.; circ. 50,000.

641 613 FR ISSN 0042-7608
VIVRE EN HARMONIE. 1952. m. 130 F. (effective 1991). Centre Fraternel Vivre en Harmonie, B.P. 492, 95005 Cergy Pontoise Cedex, France. FAX 1-34-64-46-45. Ed. Raymond Dextreit. bk.rev.; bibl.; charts; illus.

641 NE ISSN 0042-7926
TX341 CODEN: VOEDAK
VOEDING; Netherlands journal of nutrition. (Occasional articles in English, French or German) 1939. m. fl.65. Stichting Voeding Nederland, Postbus 84154, 2508 AD The Hague, Netherlands. FAX 070-3547049. Ed. Dr. W.Th.J.M. Hekkens. adv.; bk.rev.; charts; illus.; index; circ. 5,000. **Indexed**: Biol.Abstr., Chem.Abstr., Dairy Sci.Abstr., Food Sci.& Tech.Abstr., Ind.Med., Nutr.Abstr., Rural Recreat.Tour.Abstr., World Agri.Econ.& Rural Sociol.Abstr.
—BLDSC shelfmark: 9251.000000.

612 641 RU ISSN 0042-8833
CODEN: VPITAR
VOPROSY PITANIYA/PROBLEMS OF NUTRITION. 1932. bi-m. 12.90 Rub.($10.20) (Vsesoyuznoe Nauchnoe Obshchestvo Gigienistov) Izdatel'stvo Meditsina, Petroverigskii pereulok 6-8, 101838 Moscow, Russia. (Co-sponsor: Ministerstvo Zdravookhraneniya S.S.S.R.) Ed. V.A. Shaternikov. index. **Indexed**: Abstr.Hyg., Biol.Abstr., Chem.Abstr., Dairy Sci.Abstr., Dent.Ind., Dok.Arbeitsmed., Food Sci.& Tech.Abstr., Ind.Med., Int.Aerosp.Abstr., Maize Abstr., Nutr.Abstr., Seed Abstr., Triticale Abstr., Trop.Dis.Bull.
—BLDSC shelfmark: 0043.930000.
Description: Publishes original and survey articles, reflecting joint work done by physiologists, biochemists, hygienists, pathophysiologists, clinicians and technologists dealing with problems of nutrition.

641.1 CS
VYZIVA/NUTRITION. (Supplements avail.: Vyziva v Rodine; Vyziva a Spotreba Pozivatin v Cislech) 1946. m. 8 Kcs.($1) (effective Jan. 1991). Spolecnost pro Racionalni Vyzivu - Society for Rational Nutrition, Narodni tr. 24, Nove Mesto, 110 00 Prague, Czechoslovakia. TEL 29-01-91. (Dist. by: Artia, Ve Smeckach 30, 111 27 Prague 1, Czechoslovakia) Ed. Milan Starnovsky. circ. 5,500 (controlled). **Indexed**: Biol.Abstr., Chem.Abstr., Dairy Sci.Abstr., Food Sci.& Tech.Abstr., Rural Recreat.Tour.Abstr., World Agri.Econ. & Rural Sociol.Abstr.
Formerly (until 1991): Vyziva Lidu (ISSN 0042-9414)

613.2 641 CS ISSN 0042-9406
VYZIVA A ZDRAVIE/NUTRITION AND HEALTH; journal for rational nutrition. (Text in Slovak; summaries also in English and Russian) 1956. m. 24 Kcs.($16) Slovenska Spolecnost pre Racionalnu Vyzivu - Slovak Society for Rational Nourishment, Leningradska 19, Bratislava, Czechoslovakia. (Subscr. to: Slovart, Gottwaldovo nam. 48, 805 32 Bratislava, Czechoslovakia) Ed. Vojtech Spanko. adv.; bk.rev.; charts; illus.; circ. 9,000. **Indexed**: Chem.Abstr.

WARSAW AGRICULTURAL UNIVERSITY. S G G W. ANNALS. FOOD TECHNOLOGY AND NUTRITION. see FOOD AND FOOD INDUSTRIES

613.2 US ISSN 0043-2180
RM222.2
WEIGHT WATCHERS MAGAZINE. 1968. m. $15.97. Weight Watchers-Twenty-First Corporation, 360 Lexington Ave., New York, NY 10017. TEL 212-370-0644. FAX 212-687-4398. Ed. Lee Haiken. adv.; bk.rev.; circ. 1,000,000. (also avail. in microform from UMI; microfiche from KTO) **Indexed**: CHNI, Mag.Ind.
Description: For women who want to change their lives for the better. Provides "how-to" tips on smart eating, beauty, fashion, fitness, health and nutrition.

THE WELLNESS NEWSLETTER; offering a better way to better health. see PHYSICAL FITNESS AND HYGIENE

641.1 US
WELLNESS NOTES.* 1981. 4/yr. $4. (Circle of Life) Lifecircle Publications, 72 N. Thomas Rd., Ste. 8B, Tallmadge, OH 44278-1720. Ed. Jonathon Miller. bk.rev.; circ. 2,000.
Formerly (until 1982): Fruit.

WHOLE LIFE TIMES. see NEW AGE PUBLICATIONS

613.2 US
WOMAN'S DAY 101 WAYS TO LOSE WEIGHT AND STAY HEALTHY. 1973. a. Hachette Magazines, Inc., Woman's Day Special Publications, 1633 Broadway, 45th Fl., New York, NY 10019. TEL 212-767-6000. Ed. Andrea Levine. adv.; illus.

612.3 UN ISSN 1010-9099
WORLD FOOD PROGRAMME JOURNAL. (Editions in English, French and Spanish) 1963. 6/yr. free. Food and Agriculture Organization of the United Nations, Sales & Distribution Section, Via delle Terme di Caracalla, 00100 Rome, Italy. **Indexed**: Environ.Abstr., IIS, Nutr.Abstr., Rural Recreat.Tour.Abstr., World Agri.Econ.& Rural Sociol.Abstr.
—BLDSC shelfmark: 9355.548000.
Formerly (until 1987): World Food Programme News (ISSN 0049-8084)

641.1 SZ ISSN 0084-2230
QP141.A1 CODEN: WRNDAT
WORLD REVIEW OF NUTRITION AND DIETETICS. (Text in English) 1964. irreg. price varies. S. Karger AG, Allschwilerstr. 10, P.O. Box, CH-4009 Basel, Switzerland. TEL 061-3061111. FAX 061-3061234. TELEX CH 962652. Ed. A.P. Simopoulos. (reprint service avail. from ISI) **Indexed**: Abstr.Hyg., Biol.Abstr., Chem.Abstr., Curr.Cont., Dairy Sci.Abstr., Dent.Ind., Food Sci.& Tech.Abstr., Ind.Med., Nutr.Abstr., Rice Abstr., Triticale Abstr., Trop.Dis.Bull.

Y M C A WEEKLY NEWS (VANCOUVER, BC). (Vancouver Downtown Young Men's Christian Association) see PHYSICAL FITNESS AND HYGIENE

613.2 CC ISSN 0512-7955
YINGYANG XUEBAO/JOURNAL OF NUTRITION. (Text in Chinese) q. Zhongguo Yingyang Xuehui - China Nutrition Society, 1 Dali Dao, Heping Qu, Tianjin 300050, People's Republic of China. TEL 390149. Ed. Gu Jingfan.

614.8 US
YOUR HEALTH. bi-m. $30 membership. International Academy of Nutrition and Preventive Medicine, Box 18433, Asheville, NC 28814-0433. TEL 704-258-3243. Ed. Carroll Thompson. adv.; bk.rev.; circ. 1,000. (tabloid format; back issues avail.)
Description: Written for lay people to inform readers of developments in nutrition and preventive medicine.

ZAMBIA. NATIONAL FOOD AND NUTRITION COMMISSION. ANNUAL REPORT. see FOOD AND FOOD INDUSTRIES

641 GW ISSN 0044-264X
QP141.A1 CODEN: ZERNAL
ZEITSCHRIFT FUER ERNAEHRUNGSWISSENSCHAFT/JOURNAL OF NUTRITIONAL SCIENCES/JOURNAL DES SCIENCES DE LA NUTRITION. (Text, title and summaries in English, French and German) 1960. q. DM.260. Dr. Dietrich Steinkopff Verlag, Saalbaustr. 12, Postfach 111442, 6100 Darmstadt 11, Germany. TEL 06151-26538. FAX 06151-20849. Eds. K.H. Baessler, H.F. Erbersdobler. adv.; bk.rev.; charts; illus.; index; circ. 1,500. **Indexed**: Biol.Abstr., Chem.Abstr., Curr.Adv.Biochem., Curr.Adv.Cell & Devel.Biol., Curr.Adv.Ecol.Sci., Curr.Cont., Dairy Sci.Abstr., Excerp.Med., Food Sci.& Tech.Abstr., Ind.Med., Nutr.Abstr., Poult.Abstr., Soyabean Abstr.
—BLDSC shelfmark: 9458.860000.

614 PL
CODEN: ZCMEDQ
ZYWIENIE CZLOWIEKA. 1974. q. $52. (Instytut Zywnosci i Zywienia) Panstwowy Zaklad Wydawnictw Lekarskich, Ul. Dluga 38-40, Warsaw, Poland. TEL 31-42-81. (Dist. by: Ars Polona-Ruch, Krakowskie Przedmiescie 7, Warsaw, Poland) Ed. Swiatoslaw Ziemlanski. **Indexed**: Chem.Abstr., Nutr.Abstr.
Formerly: Zywienie Czlowieka (ISSN 0209-164X)

NUTRITION AND DIETETICS — Abstracting, Bibliographies, Statistics

ABSTRACTS FROM CURRENT SCIENTIFIC AND TECHNICAL LITERATURE. see FOOD AND FOOD INDUSTRIES — Abstracting, Bibliographies, Statistics

641.1 016 GW
BIBLIOGRAPHIE NUTRIS, SERIES: ERNAEHRUNGSWISSENSCHAFT. 1971. m. DM.450. Zentralinstitut fuer Ernaehrung, Arthur-Scheunert-Allee 114-116, 1505 Bergholz-Rehbruecke, Germany. Ed. Peter Klingenberg. index.
Formerly: Bibliographie "Nahrung und Ernaehrung der Menschen": Ernaehrung (ISSN 0138-208X)

641.1 016 GW
BIBLIOGRAPHIE NUTRIS, SERIES: LEBENSMITTELWISSENSCHAFT. 1971. m. DM.550. Zentralinstitut fuer Ernaehrung, Arthur-Scheunert-Allee 114-116, 1505 Bergholz-Rehbruecke, Germany. Ed. Peter Klingenberg. index.
Formerly: Bibliographie "Nahrung und Ernaehrung der Menschen": Lebensmittelwissenschaft (ISSN 0138-2136)

612.3 016 UK
C.A.B. INTERNATIONAL BUREAU OF NUTRITION. ANNOTATED BIBLIOGRAPHIES. irreg, no.2, 1967. price varies. C.A.B. International, Wallingford, Oxon OX10 8DE, England. TEL 0491-32111. FAX 0491-33508. TELEX 847964 COMAGG G. (U.S. subscr. to: C.A.B. International - North American Office, 845 N. Park Ave., Tucson, AZ 85719. TEL 800-528-4841) bk.rev. **Indexed**: Nutr.Abstr.
●Also available online. Vendor(s): BRS, CISTI, DIMDI, DIALOG, European Space Agency.
Formerly: Commonwealth Bureau of Nutrition. Annotated Bibliographies (ISSN 0069-6935)

COMPLEMENTARY MEDICINE INDEX. see MEDICAL SCIENCES — Abstracting, Bibliographies, Statistics

OBSTETRICS AND GYNECOLOGY

613.2   US   ISSN 0883-1963
CONSUMER HEALTH AND NUTRITION INDEX. 1985. q with a. cum. $105 (foreign $120). Oryx Press, 4041 N. Central at Indian School Rd., Phoenix, AZ 85012-3397. TEL 602-265-2651. FAX 602-265-6250. Ed. Alan M. Rees. bibl. (back issues avail.)
● Also available on CD-ROM.
Description: Comprehensive index to articles on health topics in general and specialized publications, for researchers and medical librarians.

011 613.2   FR   ISSN 0998-478X
HORIZON. BULLETIN BIBLIOGRAPHIQUE O R S T O M SANTE. 1989. s-a. 100 F. (Institut Francais de Recherche Scientifique pour le Developpement en Cooperation) Editions de l' O R S T O M, 72 Route d'Aulnay, 93143 Bondy Cedex, France. TEL 48-47-31-95. FAX 48-47-30-88. circ. 250.

NUTRICION EN SALUD PUBLICA. see *PUBLIC HEALTH AND SAFETY — Abstracting, Bibliographies, Statistics*

641 016   UK   ISSN 0309-1295
QP141.A1
NUTRITION ABSTRACTS AND REVIEWS. SERIES A: HUMAN AND EXPERIMENTAL. Incorporating separate section: Reviews in Clinical Nutrition. 1977. m. £389($702) C.A.B. International, Wallingford, Oxon OX10 8DE, England. TEL 0491 32111. FAX 0491-33508. TELEX 847964 COMAGG G. (U.S. subscr. to: C.A.B. International, North American Office, 845 N. Park Ave., Tucson, AZ 85719. TEL 800-528-4841) Ed.Bd. adv.; bk.rev.; index. cum.index: vols.1-10 (in 2 vols.); circ. 1,750. (also avail. in microfiche; back issues avail.) **Indexed:** Abstr.Hyg., Anim.Breed.Abstr., Biol.Abstr., Chem.Abstr., Dairy Sci.Abstr., Forest.Abstr., Ind.Med., JAMA, Trop.Dis.Bull.
● Also available online. Vendor(s): BRS (NUTR), CISTI, DIMDI, DIALOG, European Space Agency (File nos.16 & 124/CAB).
Supersedes in part: Nutrition Abstracts and Reviews (ISSN 0029-6619)
Description: Aimed at research workers, consultants, public health specialists, advisors and general practitioners.

NUTRITION DE SANTE PUBLIQUE. see *PUBLIC HEALTH AND SAFETY — Abstracting, Bibliographies, Statistics*

PUBLIC HEALTH NUTRITION. see *PUBLIC HEALTH AND SAFETY — Abstracting, Bibliographies, Statistics*

613.2   US   ISSN 0360-4594
HV696.F6
U.S. FOOD AND NUTRITION SERVICE. FOOD AND NUTRITION PROGRAMS. a. U.S. Department of Agriculture, Food and Nutrition Service, Alexandria, VA 22302. TEL 202-447-8046. Key Title: Food and Nutrition Programs.

OBSTETRICS AND GYNECOLOGY

see *Medical Sciences–Obstetrics and Gynecology*

OCCUPATIONAL HEALTH AND SAFETY

614.85   CN   ISSN 0044-5878
ACCIDENT PREVENTION. 1952. 10/yr. Industrial Accident Prevention Association, 2 Bloor St. W., Toronto, Ont. M4W 3N8, Canada. TEL 416-965-8888. bk.rev.; abstr.; illus.; charts; circ. 68,000. **Indexed:** C.I.S. Abstr.

AEROSPACE NEWSLETTER. see *AERONAUTICS AND SPACE FLIGHT*

614.7   US
AMERICAN CONFERENCE OF GOVERNMENTAL INDUSTRIAL HYGIENISTS. TRANSACTIONS OF THE ANNUAL MEETING. vol.39, 1976. a. $40. American Conference of Governmental Industrial Hygienists, Inc., 6500 Glenway Ave., Bldg. D-7, Cincinnati, OH 45211. TEL 513-661-7881. circ. 3,500. (back issues avail.)

613.62   US   ISSN 0002-8894
RC963   CODEN: AIHAAP
AMERICAN INDUSTRIAL HYGIENE ASSOCIATION JOURNAL. 1940. m. $75. American Industrial Hygiene Association, 345 White Pond Dr., Box 8390, Akron, OH 44320-1155. TEL 216-873-2442. FAX 216-873-1642. Ed. Samuel Elkin. adv.; bibl.; charts; illus.; index; circ. 11,000. (also avail. in microfiche; microfilm; reprint service avail. from UMI) **Indexed:** A.S.& T.Ind., Abstr.Hyg., Anal.Abstr., API Catal., API Hlth.& Environ., API Oil., API Pet.Ref., API Pet.Subst., API Transport., B.C.I.R.A., Bibl.Ind., Biodet.Abstr., Biol.Abstr., Br.Ceram.Abstr., C.I.S. Abstr., Cadscan., Chem.Abstr., Curr.Adv.Ecol.Sci., Curr.Cont., Energy Ind., Energy Info.Abstr., Excerp.Med., Fuel & Energy Abstr., Ind.Hyg.Dig., Ind.Med., Ind.Sci.Rev., Ind.Vet., INIS Atomind., Lab.Haz.Bull., Lead Abstr., Maize Abstr., Noise Pollut.Publ.Abstr., Ocean.Abstr., Pollut.Abstr., Poult.Abstr., Protozool.Abstr., Rev.Med.& Vet.Mycol., Risk Abstr., Sci.Cit.Ind., Trop.Dis.Bull., Vet.Bull., Zincscan.
—BLDSC shelfmark: 0819.995000.
Former titles (1946-1957): American Industrial Hygiene Association Quarterly (ISSN 0096-820X); Industrial Hygiene.
Description: Offers a broad spectrum of peer reviewed articles together with literature and book reviews, new products, meeting announcements, committee activities, AIHA news and the Industrial Hygiene Forum.
Refereed Serial

613.62   US   ISSN 0271-3586
               CODEN: AJIMD8
AMERICAN JOURNAL OF INDUSTRIAL MEDICINE. 1980. m. $519 (foreign $948). John Wiley & Sons, Inc., Journals, 605 Third Ave., New York, NY 10158. TEL 212-850-6000. FAX 212-850-6088. TELEX 12-7063. Ed. Irving J. Selikoff. adv.; bibl.; charts; illus.; index. **Indexed:** Abstr.Hyg., Biol.Abstr., Br.Ceram.Abstr., Cadscan, Chem.Abstr., Curr.Adv.Ecol.Sci., Curr.Cont., Dent.Ind., Excerp.Med., Ind.Med., INIS Atomind., Lab.Haz.Bull., Lead Abstr., Rev.Med.& Vet.Mycol., Zincscan.
● Also available online.
—BLDSC shelfmark: 0826.750000.
Description: Presents both clinical and laboratory findings, as well as general academic and scientific contributions in the fundamental or applied study of occupational disease.
Refereed Serial

614.85 338   US   ISSN 1047-9090
AMERICAN WINDOW CLEANER; voice of the professional window cleaner. 1986. bi-m. $35 to individuals (Canada $40); institutions and foreign $60. (International Window Cleaning Association) Richard Fabry, Ed. & Pub., 27 Oak Creek Rd., El Sobrante, CA 94803. TEL 510-222-7080. FAX 510-223-7080. adv.; bk.rev.; circ. 9,000. (back issues avail.)
Formerly: American Window Cleaner Newsletter.
Description: Provides an industry-wide communication link on new products, techniques, association news, interviews, business advice, and upcoming events.

AMERISURE SAFETY NEWS. see *PUBLIC HEALTH AND SAFETY*

ANGEWANDTE ARBEITSWISSENSCHAFT. see *BUSINESS AND ECONOMICS — Labor And Industrial Relations*

614.85   JA
ANZEN NO SHIHYO/BAROMETER OF OCCUPATIONAL SAFETY. (Text in Japanese) a. 470 Yen (effective 1990). Japan Industrial Safety and Health Association, Research and Survey Division, 5-35-1 Shiba, Minato-ku, Tokyo 108, Japan.
Description: Educational and promotional booklet for Japan's annual Safety Week.

614.8   NO   ISSN 0332-7124
HD7200
ARBEIDERVERN; working environment journal. 1973. 6/yr. NOK 100. Direktoratet for Arbeidstilsynet - Directorate of Labour Inspection, Fr. Nansens vei 14, Box 8103 Dep., 0032 Oslo 1, Norway. TEL 02-957000. TELEX 02-466214. adv.; illus.; circ. 36,427 (controlled). **Indexed:** C.I.S. Abstr.
—BLDSC shelfmark: 1584.023000.

614.85   NO   ISSN 0332-9127
ARBEIDSMILJOE. 1951. 8/yr. NOK 200. Arbeidsmiljoesenteret, P.O. Box 82 Korsvoll, N-0808 Oslo 8, Norway. Ed. Bjorn Skogmo. adv.; bk.rev.; circ. 10,489.
Formerly: Vern og Velferd (ISSN 0049-5964)

614.8   NE
ARBEIDSOMSTANDIGHEDEN/WORKING ENVIRONMENT. (Text mainly in Dutch; summaries in English) 1927. m. fl.135. (Veiligheidsinstituut) Uitgeverij Kluwer BV, P.O.B. 23, 7400 AR Amsterdam, Netherlands. adv.; bk.rev.; bibl.; illus.; stat.; circ. 6,500. **Indexed:** C.I.S. Abstr., Chem.Abstr., Excerp.Med.
Formerly: De Veiligheid - Safety (ISSN 0042-3149)

614.85   BE
ARBEIDSVEILIGHEID. (Text in Flemish) s-m. 5380 Fr. C E D Samson (Subsidiary of: Wolters Samson Belgie n.v.), Louizalaan 485, B-1050 Brussels, Belgium. TEL 02-7231111. FAX 02-6498480. TELEX CEDSAM 64130. index.
Description: Focuses on latest developments in workers' safety.

ARBEIT UND SICHERHEIT; Zeitschrift fuer Unfallverhuetung und Grubensicherheitswesen. see *MINES AND MINING INDUSTRY*

613   DK
ARBEJDSBETINGEDE LIDELSER. YEARBOOK. (Illness at Work) 1983. a. DKK 50. Arbejdskaderegister - Directorate of National Labor Inspection, Postboks 858, 2100 Copenhagen OE, Denmark. Ed. Kirsten Joergensen. circ. 1,000.

614.8   NE
ARBO JAARBOEK. 1959. a. fl.116. (Nederlands Instituut voor Arbeidsomstandigheden - Dutch Institute for the Working Environment) Kluwer B.V., Postbus 23, 7400 GA Deventer, Netherlands. FAX 020-462310. Eds. J.E. Alderlieste, G. Korstjens. adv.; bk.rev.; circ. 4,000.
Formerly: Veiligheidsjaarboek (ISSN 0083-534X)
Description: Yearbook for those professionally occupied with the working environment.

ARCHIVES BELGES DE MEDECINE SOCIALE ET D'HYGIENE. see *MEDICAL SCIENCES*

613.62 614   FR   ISSN 0003-9691
                 CODEN: AMPMAR
ARCHIVES DES MALADIES PROFESSIONNELLES DE MEDECINE DU TRAVAIL ET DE SECURITE SOCIALE. (Text in French; summaries in English) 1938. 8/yr. 165 ECU($201) (typically set in Jan.). (Societe de Medecine et d'Hygiene du Travail de France) Masson, 120 bd. Saint-Germain, 75280 Paris Cedex 06, France. TEL 1-46-34-21-60. FAX 1-45-87-29-99. TELEX 202 671 F. Ed. Patrick Hadengue. adv.; bk.rev.; illus.; index; circ. 3,200. (also avail. in microform from UMI; reprint service avail. from ISI) **Indexed:** Abstr.Hyg., Biol.Abstr., C.I.S. Abstr., Chem.Abstr., Curr.Adv.Ecol.Sci., Ergon.Abstr., Excerp.Med., Helminthol.Abstr., Ind.Med., INIS Atomind., Nutr.Abstr., Rev.Plant Path., Trop.Dis.Bull.
—BLDSC shelfmark: 1637.400000.

ARHIV ZA HIGIJENU RADA I TOKSIKOLOGIJU/ARCHIVES OF INDUSTRIAL HYGIENE AND TOXICOLOGY. see *ENVIRONMENTAL STUDIES — Toxicology And Environmental Safety*

613.62   US   ISSN 0197-7903
ART HAZARDS NEWS. 1978. 10/yr. $21. Center for Safety in the Arts, 5 Beekman St., New York, NY 10038. TEL 212-227-6220. Ed. Michael McCann. bk.rev.; index; circ. 2,500.
Description: News on research and education pertaining to hazards in the arts (including visual and performing arts, and museums and educational facilities), covering such topics as precautions, legislation and regulations, lawsuits, and calendars of events.

ASBESTOS CASE LAW QUARTERLY. see *LAW*

ASBESTOS WATCH. see *ENVIRONMENTAL STUDIES*

ASIAN ENVIRONMENT; journal of environmental science and technology for balanced development. see *ENVIRONMENTAL STUDIES*

OCCUPATIONAL HEALTH AND SAFETY

613.62 FR ISSN 0066-927X
ASSOCIATION FRANCAISE DES TECHNICIENS ET INGENIEURS DE SECURITE ET DES MEDECINS DU TRAVAIL. ANNUAIRE. 1965. a. 360 F. Association Francaise des Techniciens et Ingenieurs de Securite et des Medecins du Travail (AFTIM), 1 place Vranie, 94340 Joiuville le Pont, France.
TEL 33-1-48-85-70-59. FAX 33-1-48-85-02-99. adv.

613.62 CN ISSN 0226-9422
AT THE CENTRE/AU CENTRE. (Text in English, French) 1979. 3/yr. free. Canadian Centre for Occupational Health and Safety (CCOHS), 250 Main St., E., Hamilton, Ont. L8N 1H6, Canada.
TEL 416-572-2981. FAX 416-572-2206. TELEX 061-8532. Ed. David Cohen. adv.; bk.rev.; circ. 7,000 (controlled).
—BLDSC shelfmark: 1765.352900.
Description: Serves as a national forum for new developments, useful information and opinions related to occupational health and safety.

613 340 AT
AUSTRALIAN INDUSTRIAL SAFETY, HEALTH & WELFARE. (In 3 vols.) 1979. 10/yr. C C H Australia Ltd., P.O. Box 230, North Ryde, N.S.W. 2113, Australia.
TEL 888-2555. FAX 02-888-7324. Ed.Bd.

620.86 US
AUTOMOTIVE, TOOLING, METALWORKING, AND ASSOCIATED INDUSTRIES. NEWSLETTER. bi-m. $19 to non-members; members $15. National Safety Council, Industrial Section, 444 N. Michigan Ave., Chicago, IL 60611. TEL 800-621-7619.
Former titles: Safety Newsletter: Automotive, Tooling, Metalworking and Associated Industries; Safety Newsletter: Automotive and Machine Shop Section.
Description: Information and recommendations on various safety issues within the field.

614.85 US
B C S P NEWSLETTER. 1975. 3/yr. membership only. Board of Certified Safety Professionals, 208 Burwash, Savoy, IL 61874. TEL 217-359-9263. Ed. Michael K. Orn. (back issues avail.)
Description: Professional certification in safety, demographics of safety engineers, and regulatory activities.

B G W MITTEILUNGEN. (Berufsgenossenschaft fuer Gesundheitsdienst und Wohlfahrtspflege) see INSURANCE

614.7 FR
BATIMENT - ENTRETIEN. 1968. bi-m. 72 F. 91 rue du Faubourg Saint Denis, 75010 Paris, France. Ed. Bernard Abenesdra. adv.; circ. 10,500.

613.62 GW ISSN 0341-096X
BAU; Mitteilungsblatt. 1949. q.
Bau-Berufsgenossenschaft Wuppertal, Eulenbergstr. 15-21, 5000 Cologne 80, Germany.
TEL 0221-6703-157.

614.85 GW ISSN 0931-2862
BAU-BERUFSGENOSSENSCHAFT HANNOVER. MITTEILUNGSBLATT. 1976. q. free.
Bau-Berufsgenossenschaft Hannover, Hildesheimer Str. 309, 3000 Hannover 81, Germany.
TEL 0511-83801. FAX 0511-8380440. bk.rev.; circ. 52,000. (back issues avail.)

614.85 US ISSN 0090-7480
T55.A1
BEST'S SAFETY DIRECTORY; safety-industrial hygiene-security. 1946. a. $35. A.M. Best Co., Ambest Rd., Oldwick, NJ 08858.
TEL 908-439-2200. FAX 908-439-3363. TELEX 837744. Ed. K. Guindon. adv.; circ. 19,500.

690 NE ISSN 0926-7859
BEVEILIGING; onafhankelijk vakblad voor de beveiligingsector. vol.4, 1991. m. fl.75. Uitgeverij P.C. Noordervliet B.V., Mississippidreef 85, 3565 CE Utrecht, Netherlands.

613.62 RU
BEZOPASNOST' TRUDA V PROMYSHLENNOSTI/LABOUR SAFETY IN INDUSTRY. 1932. m. Izdatel'stvo Nedra, Pl. Belorusskogo Vokzala, 3, 125047 Moscow, Russia.

614.85 CS
BEZPECNA PRACA. (Text in Czech or Slovak; summaries in English, German, Russian) bi-m. $39. (Research Institute of Work Security) Obzor, Ceskoslovenskej Armady 35, 815 85 Bratislava, Czechoslovakia. (Dist. by: Slovart, Gottwaldovo nam. 48, 805 32 Bratislava, Czechoslovakia) Indexed: C.I.S. Abstr.

614.85 GW ISSN 0935-9451
BILAG BRIEF. 1982. 2/yr. DM.10. Berliner Infoladen fuer Arbeit und Gesundheit e.V., Gneisenausstr. 2a, 1000 Berlin 61, Germany. TEL 030-6932090. Ed. Eberhard Goebel, Beate Guthke. adv.; bk.rev.; bibl.; illus.; circ. 1,200. (back issues avail.)

614.85 IS
BITECHUT. (Text in Hebrew) bi-m. Safety and Hygiene Institute, 22 Mazeh St., Tel Aviv, Israel.
TEL 03-297311.

613.7 US
BODY BULLETIN NEWSLETTER. m. Rodale Press, Inc., 33 E. Minor St., Emmaus, PA 18098.
TEL 215-967-5171. TELEX 847338.
Description: Introduces employees to safe and sensible ways to deal with common health problems.

BRITISH COLUMBIA. MINISTRY OF LABOUR AND CONSUMER SERVICES. NEGOTIATED WORKING CONDITIONS. see BUSINESS AND ECONOMICS — Labor And Industrial Relations

613.62 616.98 UK ISSN 0007-1072
RC963 CODEN: BJIMAG
BRITISH JOURNAL OF INDUSTRIAL MEDICINE. 1944. m. £114. B M J Publishing Group, B.M.A. House, Tavistock Sq., London WC1H 9JR, England.
TEL 071-387-4499. Ed. H.A. Waldron. adv.; bk.rev.; abstr.; charts; illus.; index. cum.index: 1944-1960. (also avail. in microform from UMI; reprint service avail. from UMI) Indexed: Abstr.Hyg., API Abstr., API Catal., API Hlth.& Environ., API Oil, API Pet.Ref., API Pet.Subst., API Transport, B.C.I.R.A., Biol.Abstr., Br.Ceram.Abstr., C.I.S. Abstr., CAD CAM Abstr., Cadscan, Chem.Abstr., Cott.& Trop.Fibr.Abstr., Curr.Adv.Ecol.Sci., Curr.Cont., Dent.Ind., Energy Rev., Environ.Per.Bibl., Ergon.Abstr., Excerp.Med., Helminthol.Abstr., Ind.Med., Ind.Sci.Rev., Ind.Vet., Lab.Haz.Bull., Lead Abstr., Nutr.Abstr., Paint Breed.Abstr., Poult.Abstr., Risk Abstr., Sci.Cit.Ind., Trop.Dis.Bull., Vet.Bull., World Surf.Coat., World Text.Abstr., Zincscan.
—BLDSC shelfmark: 2310.000000.

614.85 UK
BUILDING FIRE AND SECURITY DESIGN. 1982. 3/yr. £3. Health and Safety Publishing, 32 Portland St., Cheltenham, Glos. GL52 2PB, England. Ed. John Bennett. adv.; circ. 15,266.
Formerly: What's New in Fire and Security. Product Information Cards.

613.62 620 US
C S P DIRECTORY. 1975. biennial. $30. Board of Certified Safety Professionals, 208 Barwash Ave., Savoy, IL 61874. TEL 217-359-9263. Ed. Michael K. Orn. adv.; circ. 8,500.

614.85 CN ISSN 0713-3421
C S S E CONTACT. (Text in English, French) 1978. bi-m. Can.$35. Canadian Society of Safety Engineering, 6519 - B Mississauga Rd., Mississauga, Ont. L5N 1A6, Canada. TEL 416-567-7192.
FAX 416-567-7191. Ed. Peter Fletcher. circ. 2,300.

613.62 US ISSN 1054-1209
CAL - O S H A REPORTER. (Occupational Safety and Health Association) 1973. w. $185. Sten-O-Press, 1862 23rd St., Box 36, San Pablo, CA 94806.
TEL 415-233-1880. FAX 415-233-1249. Ed. Anne Bell. bk.rev.; index; circ. 1,600. (looseleaf format; back issues avail.)
Former titles: California - O S H A Reporter; Cal - O S H A Reporter.
Description: For occupational safety and health practitioners primarily in California. Covers workers' compensation, toxics, hazardous waste, risk management and other related issues. Provides detailed coverage of laws, regulations and court cases.

CALIFORNIA. DEPARTMENT OF INDUSTRIAL RELATIONS. BIENNIAL REPORT. see BUSINESS AND ECONOMICS — Labor And Industrial Relations

344 613.62 CN
CANADIAN EMPLOYMENT SAFETY AND HEALTH GUIDE. m. Can.$615. C C H Canadian Ltd., 6 Garamond Ct., Don Mills, Ont. M3C 1Z5, Canada.
TEL 416-441-2992. FAX 416-444-9011.
Description: Reports on federal and provincial legislation on employment safety and health plus relevant case law.

CANADIAN MINING JOURNAL. see MINES AND MINING INDUSTRY

614.8 CN ISSN 0709-5252
CANADIAN OCCUPATIONAL HEALTH & SAFETY NEWS. 1978. w. Can.$337. Corpus Information Services, Division of Southam Business Communications Inc., 1450 Don Mills Rd., Don Mills, Ont. M3B 2X7, Canada. TEL 416-445-6641. FAX 416-442-2200. TELEX 06-966612. Ed. Angela Stelmakovich. quarterly index.
Formerly: Canadian Industrial Health and Safety News (ISSN 0701-8983)

614.85 CN ISSN 0008-4611
CANADIAN OCCUPATIONAL SAFETY. 1963. 6/yr. Can.$24($36) Clifford Elliot & Associates Ltd., 277 Lakeshore Rd., E., Oakville, Ont. L6J 6J3, Canada. TEL 416-842-2884. FAX 416-842-8226. Ed. Jackie Roth. adv.; charts; illus.; stat.; tr.lit.; circ. 10,039. Indexed: C.I.S. Abstr., Can.B.P.I.
—BLDSC shelfmark: 3043.140000.
Description: Features in-depth articles to inform and educate Canadian safety professionals on a wide variety of safety topics, practices, and concerns in today's workplace.

614 340 CN ISSN 0704-3724
CANADIAN OCCUPATIONAL SAFETY & HEALTH LAW. 1978. 6/yr. Can.$869. Corpus Information Services, Division of Southam Business Communications Inc., 1450 Don Mills Rd., Don Mills, Ont. M3B 2X7, Canada. TEL 416-445-6641. FAX 416-442-2200. TELEX 06-966612. Ed. Mark Sabourin. bk.rev.; cum.index. (looseleaf format)

620.86 US
CEMENT, QUARRY AND MINERAL AGGREGATES NEWSLETTER. bi-m. $19 to non-members; members $15. National Safety Council, Industrial Section, 444 N. Michigan Ave., Chicago, IL 60611.
TEL 800-621-7619.
Formerly: Safety Newsletter: Cement, Quarry and Mineral Aggregates Section.
Description: Information and recommendations on various safety issues within the field.

614.85 PL ISSN 0509-6510
CODEN: PCIOAP
CENTRALNY INSTYTUT OCHRONY PRACY. PRACE. (Text in Polish; summaries English, French, Russian) 1951. q. 25000 Zl. Centralny Instytut Ochrony Pracy, Ul. Tomka 1, 00-349 Warsaw, Poland.
TEL 48-22-267061. FAX 48-22-279612. circ. 1,000. Indexed: C.I.S.Abstr.
Description: Covers occupational safety and ergonomics for research workers.

613.62 540 UK ISSN 0265-5721
CODEN: CHINEK
CHEMICAL HAZARDS IN INDUSTRY. 1984. m. £215($470) Royal Society of Chemistry, Thomas Graham House, Science Park, Milton Rd., Cambridge CB4 4WF, England. TEL 0462-672555.
FAX 0462-480947. TELEX 825372. (Subscr. to.: Distribution Centre, Blackhorse Rd., Letchworth, Herts SG6 1HN, England) Ed. Michael Hannant. cum.index. Indexed: Chem.Abstr., World Surf.Coat.
•Also available online. Vendor(s): Data-Star (CHIN), DIALOG (File no.317), STN International.
—BLDSC shelfmark: 3146.588000.
Description: Covers such topics as health and safety, chemical and biological hazards, plant safety, legislation, protective equipment and storage relating to the chemical and allied industries.

330.280 US
CHEMICAL NEWSLETTER. bi-m. $19 to non-members; members $15. National Safety Council, Industrial Section, 444 N. Michigan Ave., Chicago, IL 60611. TEL 800-621-7619.
Formerly: Safety Newsletter: Chemical Section.

CHEMICAL SAFETY SHEETS. see CHEMISTRY

OCCUPATIONAL HEALTH AND SAFETY

613.62 US ISSN 0073-7488
CHEMICAL-TOXICOLOGICAL SERIES. BULLETINS. 1947. irreg., no.8, 1969. price varies. Industrial Health Foundation, Inc., 34 Penn Circle West, Pittsburgh, PA 15206. TEL 412-363-6600.
 Formerly: Industrial Hygiene Foundation. Chemical-Toxicological Series. Bulletin (ISSN 0537-5215)

613.62 614.85 NE
CHEMIEKAARTEN; gegevens voor veilig werken met chemicalien. (Text in Dutch) 1977. a. fl.189.50. (Nederlandse Instituut voor Arbeidsomstandigheden - Dutch Institute for the Working Environment) Samsom Uitgeverij B.V., Postbus 316, 2400 AH Alphen aan den Rijn, Netherlands.
TEL 01720-66822. FAX 01720-66639. (Co-sponsors: Nederlandse Vereniging voor Veiligheidskunde; Vereniging van de Nederlandse Chemische Industrie) circ. 10,000.
 Description: Standard work on the effects of chemicals on the human being and prevention possibilities.

614.85 US ISSN 8755-2566
 CODEN: CIHNEM
CHILTON'S INDUSTRIAL SAFETY & HYGIENE NEWS; news of safety, health and hygiene, environmental, fire, security and emergency protection equipment. 1967. m. $35. Chilton Co., One Chilton Way, Radnor, PA 19089. TEL 215-964-4028. Ed. Dave Johnson. adv.; charts; illus.; tr.lit.; circ. 60,060. (tabloid format; also avail. in microform from UMI; reprint service avail. from UMI) **Indexed:** Curr.Pack.Abstr.
 Former titles (until 1982): Industrial Safety and Hygiene News; (until 1981): Industrial Safety Product News (ISSN 0192-8325); (until 1978): Safety Products News (ISSN 0278-8217)

613.62 US
▼**CLEANROOMS INTERNATIONAL.** 1990. bi-m. $33 (free to qualified personnel). Witter Publishing Co., Inc., 84 Park Ave., Flemington, NJ 08822.
TEL 908-788-0343. FAX 908-788-3782. Ed. Linda Bell. circ. 25,000 (controlled). (tabloid format)
 Description: For engineering, research, quality control and management personnel who serve industries that require controlled manufacturing environments. Includes technical articles, product information and industry news from the United States and abroad.

331.204 US
COAL MINING NEWSLETTER. bi-m. $19 to non-members; members $15. National Safety Council, Industrial Section, 444 N. Michigan Ave., Chicago, IL 60611. TEL 800-621-7619.
 Formerly: Safety Newsletter: Coal Mining Section.
 Description: Information and recommendations on various safety issues within the coal mining industry.

614 MX
CONDICIONES DE TRABAJO; cuadernos de medicina, seguridad e higiene. (Text in Spanish; summaries in English and French) 1976. 3/yr. Secretaria del Trabajo y Prevision Social, Direccion General de Medicina y Seguridad en el Trabajo, Calzada Azcapotzalco la Villa No. 209, Junto Metro Ferreria, 02020 Mexico, D.F., Mexico. TEL 394-33-44. Dir. Dr. Juan Antonio Legaspi Velasco. bibl.; charts; illus.; stat.; circ. 4,000.
 Description: Covers general medicine, health insurance, hygiene, and work conditions in the work force.

658.3 US
CONSTRUCTION NEWSLETTER. bi-m. $19 to non-members; members $15. National Safety Council, Industrial Section, 444 N. Michigan Ave., Chicago, IL 60611. TEL 800-621-7619.
 Formerly: Safety Newsletter: Construction Section.
 Description: Information and recommendations on various safety issues in construction.

614.85 CN
CORPUS OCCUPATIONAL HEALTH AND SAFETY MANAGEMENT HANDBOOK. 1985. biennial. Can.$59. Corpus Information Services, Division of Southam Business Communications Inc., 1450 Don Mills Road, Don Mills, Ont. M3B 2X7, Canada. TEL 416-445-6641. FAX 416-442-2200. TELEX 06-966612. Ed. Frances Makedessian. charts; graphs.; illus.; circ. 1,600.

613 669 CN ISSN 0712-4724
COULEE CONTINUE. 1972. bi-m. Sidbec - Dosco Inc., C.P. 2000 Succ. Place-du-Parc, Montreal, Que. H2W 2S7, Canada. TEL 514-286-8662.
FAX 514-286-8649. TELEX 05-24515 (SIDBEC MTL). Eds. Benoit Rocheleau, Gilles Monette. circ. 5,000. (tabloid format)

614.85 UK
CRONER'S DANGEROUS SUBSTANCES. 1983. bi-m. £127 (effective 1992). Croner Publications Ltd., Croner House, London Road, Kingston, Surrey KT2 6SR, England. TEL 081-547-3333.
FAX 081-547-2637. Ed. Sarah Tullett. (looseleaf format)
 Description: Covers European requirements for dangerous substance classification, packaging and labelling, with emphasis on the United Kingdom.

614.85 340 UK
CRONER'S HEALTH AND SAFETY AT WORK. 1979. bi-m. £103.20 (effective 1992). Croner Publications Ltd., Croner House, London Road, Kingston, Surrey KT2 6SR, England. TEL 081-547-3333.
FAX 081-547-2637. Ed. Sarah Tullett. (looseleaf format)
 Description: Provides information on health and safety legislation, legal requirements, and related topics.

613.62 US ISSN 0270-3777
T55.3.H3 CODEN: DPIRDU
DANGEROUS PROPERTIES OF INDUSTRIAL MATERIALS REPORT. 1980. bi-m. $195 (Canada $235). Van Nostrand Reinhold, 115 Fifth Ave., New York, NY 10003. TEL 212-254-3232. FAX 212-673-1239. Ed. N. Irving Sax. adv.; bk.rev.; bibl.; charts; illus.; stat.; cum.index; circ. 2,000. (back issues avail.)
Indexed: Abstr.Bull.Inst.Pap.Chem., C.I.S. Abstr., CAD CAM Abstr., Chem.Abstr., Corros.Abstr., Dent.Ind., Environ.Abstr., Lab.Haz.Bull.
—BLDSC shelfmark: 3518.820000.

DELO IN VARNOST; revija za varstvo pri delu. see BUSINESS AND ECONOMICS — Labor And Industrial Relations

DIAGNOSTIC ENGINEERING. see ENGINEERING — Mechanical Engineering

DICTIONNAIRE PERMANENT SECURITE ET CONDITIONS DE TRAVAIL. see BUSINESS AND ECONOMICS — Labor And Industrial Relations

614.85 FR ISSN 0339-6517
DOCUMENTS POUR LE MEDECIN DU TRAVAIL. 1973. q. 330 F. Institut National de Recherche et de Securite pour la Prevention des Accidents du Travail et des Maladies Professionnelles, Ministere du Travail, Direction des Relations du Travail, 30 rue Olivier-Noyer, 75680 Paris Cedex 14, France.
TEL 40-44-30-00. FAX 40-44-30-99. bk.rev.; index. cum.index; circ. 9,000. **Indexed:** C.I.S.Abstr.
—BLDSC shelfmark: 3609.113080.
 Description: Scientific and medical publication for occupational medical practitioners.

614.85 GW
DOKUMENTATION ARBEITSSCHUTZ UNFALLVERHUETUNG ARBEITSMEDIZIN. (Text in English and German) 1970. irreg. DM.30. Berufsgenossenschaft der Chemischen Industrie, Abteilung IuD, Gaisbergstr. 11, Postfach 101480, 6900 Heidelberg 1, Germany. bk.rev.; circ. 1,900.

E R G A. BIBLIOGRAFICO. see OCCUPATIONAL HEALTH AND SAFETY — Abstracting, Bibliographies, Statistics

614.85 613.62 AT ISSN 0013-6832
EMPLOYERS' REVIEW. 1928. 23/yr. Aus.$25. Employers' Federation of New South Wales, 313 Sussex St, Sydney, N.S.W. 2001, Australia.
FAX 61-2-2642000. Ed. Len Read. adv.; bk.rev.; circ. 3,300.

331 313.62 US ISSN 0093-1535
EMPLOYMENT SAFETY AND HEALTH GUIDE. 3/yr. (plus w. reports). $710. Commerce Clearing House, Inc., 4025 W. Peterson Ave., Chicago, IL 60646.
TEL 312-583-8500.

613.62 US
ENVIRONMENTAL HEALTH AND SAFETY NEWS. 1951. m. free. University of Washington, Department of Environmental Health, School of Public Health and Community Medicine, F-461 Health Sciences Building, Seattle, WA 98195. TEL 206-543-4252. FAX 206-543-8123. Ed. Thomas Burbacher. circ. 3,000. (processed)
 Former titles: Environmental Health and Safety News; Occupational Health Newsletter (ISSN 0029-7925)

EVERYONE'S BACKYARD. see ENVIRONMENTAL STUDIES — Waste Management

613.62 US ISSN 0738-6583
EXECUTIVE HOUSEKEEPING TODAY. 1980. m. $18. National Executive Housekeepers Association, 1001 Eastwind Dr., Ste. 301, Westerville, OH 43081. TEL 614-895-7166. FAX 614-895-1248. Ed. Linda K. Gambaiani. adv.; bk.rev.; index; circ. 9,164.
 Description: Geared to management professionals responsible for institutional housekeeping.

FEDERATION NEWS (SYDNEY). see BUSINESS AND ECONOMICS — Labor And Industrial Relations

620.86 US
FERTILIZER AND AGRICULTURAL CHEMICAL NEWSLETTER. bi-m. $19 to non-members; members $15. National Safety Council, Industrial Section, 444 N. Michigan Ave., Chicago, IL 60611.
TEL 800-621-7619.
 Former titles: Safety Newsletter: Fertilizer and Agricultural Chemical Section; Safety Newsletter: Fertilizer Section.
 Description: Information and recommendations on various safety issues in the field of fertilizer and agricultural chemicals.

614.8 US
FOOD & BEVERAGE NEWSLETTER. bi-m. $19 to non-members; members $15. National Safety Council, Industrial Section, 444 N. Michigan Ave., Chicago, IL 60611. TEL 800-621-7619.
 Formerly: Safety Newsletter: Food and Beverage Section.
 Description: Information and recommendations on various safety issues in food and beverages.

634.9 US
FOREST INDUSTRIES NEWSLETTER (CHICAGO). bi-m. $19 to non-members; members $15. National Safety Council, Industrial Section, 444 N. Michigan Ave., Chicago, IL 60611. TEL 800-621-7619.
 Formerly: Safety Newsletter: Forest Industries Section.
 Description: Information and recommendations on various safety issues in forest industries.

614.8 FR ISSN 0007-9952
 CODEN: CNDBIJ
FRANCE. INSTITUT NATIONAL DE RECHERCHE ET DE SECURITE POUR LA PREVENTION DES ACCIDENTS DU TRAVAIL ET DES MALADIES PROFESSIONNELLES. CAHIERS DE NOTES DOCUMENTAIRES; securite et hygiene du travail. 1956. q. 350 F. Institut National de Recherche et de Securite pour la Prevention des Accidents du Travail et des Maladies Professionnelles, 30 rue Olivier Noyer, 75680 Paris Cedex 14, France. TEL 40-44-30-00.
FAX 40-44-30-99. TELEX 203594F INRSPAR. abstr.; charts; illus.; index. cum.index; circ. 10,000.
Indexed: C.I.S. Abstr., Chem.Abstr., INIS Atomind., Ref.Zh.
—BLDSC shelfmark: 2950.000000.
 Description: Scientific and technical publication in the field of occupational safety and health.

614.85 DK ISSN 0109-5129
FRAVAER VED ANMELDTE ARBEJDSULYKKER. 1981. quinquennial. free. Direktoratet for Arbejdstilsynet, Landskrongade 33-35, DK-2100 Copenhagen Oe, Denmark. TEL 31180088.

613.62 GW
GEGENGIFT; Hamburger Hefte fuer Arbeit und Gesundheit. 1986. 3/yr. DM.15 for 5 nos. Gruppe Arbeit und Gesundheit, Informationsstelle Arbeit und Gesundheit, Schanzenstr. 75, 2000 Hamburg 36, Germany. TEL 4940-4392858. Ed. Henning Wriedt. adv.; bk.rev.; circ. 1,500. (back issues avail.)
 Description: Covers all areas of occupational health; aimed at safety activists and employees.

OCCUPATIONAL HEALTH AND SAFETY

613.62 669 EI
GENERAL COMMISSION ON SAFETY AND HEALTH IN THE IRON AND STEEL INDUSTRY. REPORT. (First edition in French only; later editions in Dutch, French, German and Italian) 1966. a. General Commission on Safety and Health in the Iron and Steel Industry, Rue de la Loi 200, 1040 Brussels, Belgium. circ. controlled.

614.85 GW
GERMANY (FEDERAL RPUBLIC, 1949-) BUNDESANSTALT FUER ARBEITSSCHUTZ. AMTLICHE MITTEILUNGEN. 1984. q. Bundesanstalt fuer Arbeitsschutz, Vogelpothsweg 50-52, Postfach 17 02 02, D-4600 Dortmund, Germany. TEL 0231-17631.

614 RU ISSN 0016-9919
CODEN: GTPZAB
GIGIENA TRUDA I PROFESSIONAL'NYE ZABOLEVANIYA/INDUSTRIAL HYGIENE AND OCCUPATIONAL DISEASES. 1957. m. 22.20 Rub.($16.20) (Vsesoyuznoe Nauchnoe Obshchestvo Gigienistov) Izdatel'stvo Meditsina, Petroverigskii pereulok 6-8, 101838 Moscow, Russia. (Co-sponsor: Ministerstvo Zdravookhraneniya S.S.S.R.) Ed. A.V. Roshchin. index. **Indexed:** Abstr.Hyg., Bioeng.Abstr., Biol.Abstr., C.I.S. Abstr., Chem.Abstr., Dent.Ind., Excerp.Med., Ind.Med., INIS Atomind., Int.Aerosp.Abstr., Trop.Dis.Bull., World Bibl.Soc.Sec.
—BLDSC shelfmark: 0048.200000.
Description: Covers hygiene in industry and agriculture, physiology of labor, industrial toxicology, clinical picture of occupational diseases.

GIORNALE ITALIANO DI MEDICINA DEL LAVORO. see MEDICAL SCIENCES

GREAT BRITAIN. DEPARTMENT OF EDUCATION AND SCIENCE. SAFETY IN EDUCATION. see PUBLIC HEALTH AND SAFETY

613.62 JA
GUIDEBOOK ON INDUSTRIAL SAFETY. (Text in Japanese) a. 470 Yen. Japan Industrial Safety and Health Association, 5-35-1 Shiba, Minato-ku, Tokyo 108, Japan.
Description: Educational and promotional booklet for Japan's annual National Safety Week.

613.62 IS
HABITECHUT. (Text in Arabic) q. Safety and Hygiene Institute, 7 Solomon St., Tel Aviv 66 023, Israel. TEL 03-374933.

HAZARDOUS MATERIALS NEWSLETTER. see PUBLIC HEALTH AND SAFETY

613.62 UK
HAZARDOUS SUBSTANCES. 10/yr. £110 (foreign £125). Monitor Press, Rectory Road, Great Waldingfield, Sudbury, Suffolk CO10 OTL, England. TEL 0787-78607. FAX 0787-880201. (back issues avail.)
Description: Covers the storage, transportation, processing, disposal, and laboratory research use of hazardous substances.

614 UK ISSN 0267-7296
HAZARDS. 1976. 5/yr. £6 to individuals; institutions £15. Hazards Publications Ltd., P.O. Box 199, Sheffield S1 1FQ, England. Ed.Bd. bk.rev.; abstr.; charts; illus.; stat.; index; circ. 4,500. (back issues avail.) **Indexed:** Br.Tech.Ind.
—BLDSC shelfmark: 4274.451570.
Formerly (until 1984): Hazards Bulletin (ISSN 0140-0525)
Description: Aims to help all people in all workplaces to organize, through their union, for health and safety.

614 UK
HEALTH AND SAFETY IN INDUSTRY AND COMMERCE; news bulletin. 1977. m. £82.50 (foreign £87.50). Springfield Information Services, Cross Street Court, Ground Fl. Office, Cross St., Peterborough, Cambs. PE1 1XA, England. TEL 0733-52454. Ed. John Franks. bk.rev.; abstr.; tr.lit. (back issues avail.) **Indexed:** Int.Packag.Abstr., Lab.Haz.Bull., Mgmt.& Market.Abstr.

340 613.62 UK
HEALTH & SAFETY MONITOR. m. £104 (foreign £119). Monitor Press, Rectory Rd., Great Waldingfield, Sudbury, Suffolk CO10 OTL, England. TEL 0787-78607. FAX 0787-880201. (back issues avail.) **Indexed:** Cadscan, Lead Abstr., Mgmt.& Market.Abstr., Zincscan.
Description: For senior executives and safety officers, company secretaries and legal representatives as well as union officials.

614 UK ISSN 0954-5972
HEALTH AND SAFETY OFFICER'S HANDBOOK. 1983. a. £25. Millbank Publications Ltd., 25 Catherine St., London WC2B 5JW, England. TEL 071-379-3036. FAX 071-240-6840. adv.; charts; illus.; circ. 4,000.

622 613.62 UK ISSN 0263-3094
HEALTH AND SAFETY: QUARRIES. 1979. a. price varies. H.M.S.O., P.O. Box 276, London SW8 5DT, England.

613.62 AT ISSN 1033-1425
HEALTH AT WORK; newsletter. q. Aus.$10 to individuals; institutions Aus.$30. National Heart Foundation of Australia, Royal Insurance Building, 25 London Circuit, Canberra, A.C.T. 2601, Australia. TEL 062-82-2144. FAX 06-246-7100.

614.8 US
HEALTH CARE NEWSLETTER. bi-m. $19 to non-members; members $15. National Safety Council, Industrial Section, 444 N. Michigan Ave., Chicago, IL 60611. TEL 800-621-7619.
Former titles: Safety Newsletter: Health Care Section; Safety Newsletter: Hospital-Health Care Section.
Description: Information and recommendations on safety issues in the health care field.

613.62 CN
HEALTH IN WORK PLACE. 12/yr. $160. Carswell Publications, Corporate Plaza, 2075 Kennedy Rd., Scarborough, Ont. M1T 3V4, Canada. TEL 416-609-8000. FAX 416-298-5094.

613.62 US
HEALTH PLUS. 1989. m. $7.08. Bureau of Business Practice, 24 Rope Ferry Rd., Waterford, CT 06386. TEL 203-442-4365. FAX 203-434-3341. TELEX 966420. Ed. Monica DiGangi.

HEALTHCARE HAZARDOUS MATERIALS MANAGEMENT. see HOSPITALS

HOPE HEALTH LETTER. see PHYSICAL FITNESS AND HYGIENE

613.62 JA ISSN 0911-3363
HOPPO SANGYO EISEI/JOURNAL OF NORTHERN OCCUPATIONAL HEALTH. (Text in English or Japanese; summaries in English) 1938. biennial. Association of Northern Occupational Health - Hoppo Sangyo Eisei Kyoukai, c/o Department of Hygiene and Preventive Medicine, Hokkaido University School of Medicine, Kita-15 nishi-7, Kita-ku, Sapporo 060, Japan. TEL 011-716-2111. FAX 011-717-1140. Ed.Bd. (back issues avail.)
Formerly: Hoppo Sangyo Eisei Kyoukai Kaishi.

HOSPITAL EMPLOYEE HEALTH. see HOSPITALS

HOSPITAL SAFETY INFORMATION SERVICE. see HOSPITALS

331 US
HUMAN RESOURCES MANAGEMENT - O S H A COMPLIANCE. a. (plus m. reports). $335. Commerce Clearing House, Inc., 4025 W. Peterson Ave., Chicago, IL 60646. TEL 312-583-8500.
Formerly: C C H - O S H A Compliance Guide.

613.62 FR ISSN 0335-0274
I N R S BULLETIN DE DOCUMENTATION. 8/yr. 250 Fr. Institut National de Recherche et de Securite pour la Prevention des Accidents du Travail et des Maladies Professionnelles, 30 rue Olivier Noyer, 75680 Paris Cedex 14, France. TEL 40-44-30-00. FAX 40-44-30-99. TELEX 203594F INRSPAR. index. cum.index; circ. 3,000.
Description: Bibliographic information about occupational safety and health.

614.8 628 331.8 SZ
I Z A. (Illustrierte Zeitschrift fuer Arbeitssicherheit) (Text and summaries in German) 1953. s-m. 25 Fr. Ott Verlag und Druck AG, Laenggasse 57, Postfach 22, CH-3607 Thun, Switzerland. TEL 033 22 16 22. FAX 033-22-20-06. Ed. Alfred Lauchli-Wyss. circ. 3,500.

INDIAN JOURNAL OF INDUSTRIAL MEDICINE. see MEDICAL SCIENCES

613.62 II ISSN 0019-5391
RC963
INDIAN JOURNAL OF OCCUPATIONAL HEALTH. (Text in English) 1958. m. Rs.12. Society for the Study of Industrial Medicine, Bombay Branch, c/o Dr. S.V. Bhatt, 243 Khetwadi, Main Rd., Bombay 4, India. Ed. Dr. R.L. Mendonca. adv.; bk.rev.; abstr.; bibl.; charts; illus.; index. **Indexed:** C.I.S. Abstr., INIS Atomind.

613 614 331 IO
INDONESIAN JOURNAL OF INDUSTRIAL HYGIENE, OCCUPATIONAL HEALTH-SAFETY AND SOCIAL SECURITY/MAJALAH HIGENE PERUSAHAAN, KESEHATAN-KESELAMATAN KERJA, DAN JAMINAN SOSIAL. (Text in English and Indonesian) q. National Institute of Industrial Hygiene and Occupational Health - Lembaga Nasional Higene Perusahaan dan Kesehatan Kerja, Jl. Jend. A. Yani 69-70, Jakarta, Indonesia. Ed.Bd. charts; stat. (also avail. in microfilm from UMI; reprint service avail. from UMI)

814.85 US ISSN 8755-8270
KF3568.36
INDUSTRIAL ACCIDENT LAW BULLETIN.* m. $37.50. Quinlan Publishing Co., Inc., 23 Drydock Ave., 2nd Fl., Boston, MA 02210-2307. index. (looseleaf format; back issues avail.)
Formerly: O S H A Litigation.

614.85 CN ISSN 0073-7305
INDUSTRIAL ACCIDENT PREVENTION ASSOCIATION. ANNUAL REPORT. 1918. a. Industrial Accident Prevention Association, 2 Bloor St. W., Toronto, Ont. M4W 3N8, Canada. TEL 416-965-8888. circ. 10,000.

613.62 JA ISSN 0019-8366
RC963
INDUSTRIAL HEALTH. (Text in English) 1963. q. membership. National Institute of Industrial Health - Rodo-sho Sangyo Igaku Sogo Kenkyujo, 21-1 Nagao 6-chome, Tama-ku, Kawasaki-shi, Kanagawa-ken 214, Japan. TEL 81-044-865-6111. FAX 81-044-865-6116. Ed. Sohei Yamamoto. charts; illus.; index; circ. 1,100. **Indexed:** Abstr.Hyg., Art & Archaeol.Tech.Abstr., Biol.Abstr., C.I.S. Abstr., Chem.Abstr., Curr.Cont., Dent.Ind., Excerp.Med., Ind.Med., INIS Atomind., Trop.Dis.Bull.
●Also available online. Vendor(s): DIALOG, JICST.
—BLDSC shelfmark: 4454.700000.
Description: Contains research articles in the area of industrial health.

613.2 US ISSN 0073-7496
INDUSTRIAL HEALTH FOUNDATION. ENGINEERING SERIES. BULLETINS. 1936. irreg., no.8, 1971. price varies. Industrial Health Foundation, Inc., 34 Penn Circle West, Pittsburgh, PA 15206. TEL 412-363-6600.

331.8 613.62 US ISSN 0073-750X
INDUSTRIAL HEALTH FOUNDATION. LEGAL SERIES BULLETINS. 1936. irreg., no.9, 1972. price varies. Industrial Health Foundation, Inc., 34 Penn Circle West, Pittsburgh, PA 15206. TEL 412-363-6600.
Formerly: Industrial Hygiene Foundation of America. Legal Series Bulletin.

331 614 US
INDUSTRIAL HEALTH FOUNDATION. MANAGEMENT SERIES. 1971. irreg., no.2, 1978. price varies. Industrial Health Foundation, Inc., 34 Penn Circle West, Pittsburgh, PA 15206. TEL 412-363-6600. (back issues avail.)

613.62 US ISSN 0073-7518
HD7260
INDUSTRIAL HEALTH FOUNDATION. MEDICAL SERIES. BULLETINS. 1937. irreg., no.21, 1982. price varies. Industrial Health Foundation, Inc., 34 Penn Circle West, Pittsburgh, PA 15206. TEL 412-363-6600.

OCCUPATIONAL HEALTH AND SAFETY

613.62 US ISSN 0073-7526
INDUSTRIAL HEALTH FOUNDATION. NURSING SERIES. BULLETINS. 1965. irreg., no.3, 1971. price varies. Industrial Health Foundation, Inc., 34 Penn Circle West, Pittsburgh, PA 15206. TEL 412-363-6600.

331 US ISSN 0147-5401
INDUSTRIAL HYGIENE NEWS. 1978. bi-m. $200 (free to qualified personnel). Rimbach Publishing, Inc., 8650 Babcock Blvd., Pittsburgh, PA 15237. TEL 412-364-5366. Ed. David C. Lavender. adv.; bk.rev.; circ. 61,000. (tabloid format)
Description: Information on occupational health and high technology safety.

614.85 UK
INDUSTRIAL MAINTENANCE; for factory managers and maintenance professionals. 1957. 10/yr. £30. A.G.B. Hulton Ltd., Walwick House, Azalea Dr., Swanley, Kent BR8 8JF, England. TEL 0322-69411. Ed. Graham Hadfield. circ. 23,363. (back issues avail.)

614.85 II ISSN 0301-4746
T55.A1
INDUSTRIAL SAFETY CHRONICLE. (Text in English) 1969. q. Rs.40($8) National Safety Council, Central Labour Institute Bldg., Sion, Bombay 400022, India. Ed. A.A. Krishnan. adv.; bk.rev.; illus.; circ. 1,500.
Indexed: C.I.S. Abstr.

614.85 UK ISSN 0262-3226
INDUSTRIAL SAFETY DATA FILE. 1982. m. £48($152) United Trade Press Ltd., U.T.P. House, 33-35 Bowling Green Ln., London EC1R 0DA, England. TEL 01-837 1212. Ed. Dina Chase. illus.; s-a. index; circ. 2,500. (looseleaf format) *Indexed:* Br.Tech.Ind., C.I.S. Abstr.
—BLDSC shelfmark: 4462.330000.
Supersedes: Industrial Safety (ISSN 0019-8757)

INDUSTRIAL VENTILATION; A MANUAL OF RECOMMENDED PRACTICE. see *HEATING, PLUMBING AND REFRIGERATION*

614.85 NO
INDUSTRIVERN-NYTT. (Text in Norwegian) 1955. q. free. Industrivernet, Drammensveien 40, 0255 Oslo 2, Norway. FAX 2-446995. Ed. Harald Johan Bergmann. adv.; bk.rev.; circ. 6,000. (back issues avail.)

613.62 UK
INSTITUTE OF OCCUPATIONAL HEALTH. PROCEEDINGS. irreg. University of Birmingham, Institute of Occupational Health, P.O. Box 363, Edgbaston, Birmingham B15 2TT, England. TEL 021-414-6030. FAX 021-471-5208.

620.86 US
INTERNATIONAL AIR TRANSPORT NEWSLETTER. 1952. bi-m. $19 to non-members; members $15. National Safety Council, Industrial Section, 444 N. Michigan Ave., Chicago, IL 60611. TEL 800-621-7619.
Former titles: Air Transport Newsletter; Safety Newsletter: Air Transport Section (ISSN 0470-2832)
Description: Information and recommendations on various safety issues in the field of international air transport.

613.62 GW ISSN 0340-0131
RC963.A1 CODEN: IAEHDW
INTERNATIONAL ARCHIVES OF OCCUPATIONAL AND ENVIRONMENTAL HEALTH. (Text in English or German) 1930. 8/yr. DM.1318($748) Springer-Verlag, Heidelberger Platz 3, 1000 Berlin 33, Germany. TEL 030-8207-1. (Also Heidelberg, Tokyo, Vienna, and New York) Ed. G. Lehnert. adv.; bibl.; charts; illus.; index. (also avail. in microform from UMI; back issues avail.; reprint service avail. from ISI) *Indexed:* Abstr.Hyg., ASCA, Biol.Abstr., C.I.S. Abstr., Cadscan, Chem.Abstr., CINAHL, Curr.Adv.Cancer Res., Curr.Adv.Ecol.Sci., Curr.Cont., Dent.Ind., Excerp.Med., Ind.Med., Ind.Sci.Rev., Lab.Haz.Bull., Lead Abstr., NRN, Nutr.Abstr., Risk Abstr., Sci.Cit.Ind., Trop.Dis.Bull., Zincscan.
—BLDSC shelfmark: 4536.128000.
Former titles (until vols.26-34, 1970-75): International Archives of Occupational Health (ISSN 0020-5923); (until vols.19-25, 1962-68): Internationales Archiv fuer Gewerbepathologie und Gewerbehygiene; (until vols.1-18, 1930-61): Archiv fuer Gewerbepathologie und Gewerbehygiene.
Description: Covers occupational, environmental, and social medicine, and their subdisciplines.

613.62 AT ISSN 0074-3828
INTERNATIONAL CONGRESS OF OCCUPATIONAL THERAPY. PROCEEDINGS. 1974. irreg., 7th, 1978, Jerusalem. World Federation of Occupational Therapists, 20 Syree Court, Marmion, W.A. 6020, Australia. circ. 1,500.

613.62 331 US
IOWA. DIVISION OF LABOR. OCCUPATIONAL INJURIES AND ILLNESSES SURVEY. 1973. a. free. Division of Labor, Bureau of Labor Statistics Section, 1000 E. Grand Ave., Des Moines, IA 50319. TEL 515-281-3606. stat.; circ. 300. (processed)
Formerly: Iowa. Bureau of Labor. Occupational Injuries and Illnesses Survey (ISSN 0092-6299)

614.85 JA
JAPAN INDUSTRIAL SAFETY AND HEALTH ASSOCIATION. ANNUAL REPORT. a. Japan Industrial Safety & Health Association, 5-35-1 Shiba, Minato-ku, Tokyo 108, Japan. TEL 03-452-6841. FAX 03-453-8034.

613.62 JA
JAPAN INDUSTRIAL SAFETY AND HEALTH ASSOCIATION. INTERNATIONAL COOPERATION DEPARTMENT. GUIDEBOOK ON OCCUPATIONAL HEALTH. (Text in Japanese) a. 470 Yen. Japan Industrial Safety and Health Association, International Cooperation Department, 5-35-1 Shiba, Minato-ku, Tokyo 108, Japan. TEL 03-452-6841. FAX 03-453-8034.
Description: Educational and promotional booklet for Japan's annual occupational Health Week.

613.62 JA
JAPAN INDUSTRIAL SAFETY AND HEALTH ASSOCIATION. INTERNATIONAL COOPERATION DEPARTMENT. OCCUPATIONAL HEALTH. (Text in Japanese) m. 8400 Yen. Japan Industrial Safety and Health Association, International Cooperation Department, 5-35-1 Shiba, Minato-ku, Tokyo 108, Japan. TEL 03-452-6841. FAX 03-453-8034.
Description: Magazine for occupational health managers, specialists and practitioners.

614.85 JA
JAPAN INDUSTRIAL SAFETY AND HEALTH ASSOCIATION. INTERNATIONAL COOPERATION DEPARTMENT. SAFETY. (Text in Japanese) m. 7920 Yen. Japan Industrial Safety and Health Association, International Cooperation Department, 5-35-1 Shiba, Minato-ku, Tokyo 108, Japan. TEL 03-452-6841. FAX 03-453-8034.
Description: Magazine for occupational safety managers, specialists and practitioners.

614.85 JA
JAPAN INDUSTRIAL SAFETY AND HEALTH ASSOCIATION. INTERNATIONAL COOPERATION DEPARTMENT. YEARBOOK OF INDUSTRIAL SAFETY AND HEALTH. (Text in Japanese) a. 5000 Yen. Japan Industrial Safety and Health Association, International Cooperation Department, 5-35-1 Shiba, Minato-ku, Tokyo 108, Japan. TEL 03-452-6841. FAX 03-453-8034.
Formerly: Japan Industrial Safety and Health Association. Research and Survey Division. Yearbook of Industrial Safety.
Description: Covers activities and relevant information in the field of industrial safety and health in Japan.

614.8 JA ISSN 0047-1879
CODEN: SAIGBL
JAPANESE JOURNAL OF INDUSTRIAL HEALTH/SANGYO IGAKU. (Text in English or Japanese; summaries in English) 1959. 7/yr. 4200 Yen. Japan Association of Industrial Health - Nihon Sangyo Eisei Gakkai, Public Health Bldg., 1-29-8 Shinjuku, Shinjuku-ku, Tokyo 160, Japan. Ed. Yutaka Hosoda. adv.; bk.rev.; illus.; index; circ. 2,500. (processed) *Indexed:* Abstr.Hyg., C.I.S. Abstr., Chem.Abstr., Curr.Cont., Excerp.Med., Ind.Med., Trop.Dis.Bull.
—BLDSC shelfmark: 4655.500000.

658.3 US ISSN 0149-7510
JOB SAFETY & HEALTH (WASHINGTON). (Subseries of: B N A Policy and Practice Series, and Environment, Safety, and Health Series) 1977. bi-w. $570. The Bureau of National Affairs, Inc., 1231 25th St., N.W., Washington, DC 20037. TEL 202-452-4200. FAX 202-822-8092. TELEX 285656 BNAI WSH. (Subscr. to: 9435 Key West Ave., Rockville, MD 20850. TEL 800-372-1033) Ed. Eileen Z. Joseph. index. (looseleaf format; back issues avail.)
●Also available online. Vendor(s): Human Resources Information Network (CDD, HDD).

614.8 US ISSN 1040-4198
JOB SAFETY CONSULTANT. 1973. m. $169. Business Research Publications, Inc., 817 Broadway, New York, NY 10003. TEL 212-673-4700. FAX 212-475-1790. Ed. Gail Hayden. bibl.; index.
Formerly: O S H A Report.
Description: Tells you what you need to know to comply with OSHA and other government safety regulations and how to reduce worker injuries - and reduce your production losses, medical bills and workers' compensation costs. Includes a monthly safety talk for worker safety training sessions.

613.62 UK ISSN 0954-576X
JOURNAL OF HEALTH AND SAFETY. 1981. 3/yr. £7.50. British Health and Safety Society, c/o Health & Safety Unit, Aston University, Aston Triangle, Birmingham B4 7ET, England. TEL 021-359 3611. FAX 021-359-3758. TELEX 336997 UNIAST G. Ed. Roger C. Clarke. adv.; bk.rev.; circ. 400. (back issues avail.)
—BLDSC shelfmark: 4996.725000.
Formed by the 1988 merger of: British Health and Safety Society. Newsletter (ISSN 0268-0580) & British Health and Safety Society. Reviews Bulletin (ISSN 0268-0572)
Description: Articles, conference papers, and more relating to all aspects of occupational health and safety.

613 AT ISSN 0815-6409
JOURNAL OF OCCUPATIONAL HEALTH AND SAFETY: AUSTRALIA AND NEW ZEALAND. 1985. bi-m. C C H Australia Ltd., P.O. Box 230, North Ryde, N.S.W. 2113, Australia. TEL 02-888-2555. FAX 02-888-7324. Eds. Anne Wyatt, Gabrielle Grammeno. adv.; bk.rev.; film rev.; illus.; index; cum.index. (back issues avail.)
—BLDSC shelfmark: 5026.092000.
Description: Information for occupational health and safety professionals and managers.

JOURNAL OF OCCUPATIONAL MEDICINE. see *MEDICAL SCIENCES*

614.85 US ISSN 1052-2263
HD7255.A2
▼**JOURNAL OF VOCATIONAL REHABILITATION.** 1991. q. $48 to individuals (foreign $60); institutions $72 (foreign $84). Andover Medical Publishers Inc., 125 Main St., Reading, MA 01867. TEL 617-438-8464. FAX 617-438-1479. TELEX 880052. (Dist. by: Butterworth - Heinemann Ltd., 80 Montvale Ave., Stoneham, MA 02180. TEL 800-366-2665) Ed. Paul Wehman. (back issues avail.)
—BLDSC shelfmark: 5072.512400.
Description: Topics range from supported employment to psychiatric impairment, vocational training, and physical disability.

KOKUTETSU CHUO HOKEN KANRIJOHO; health control. see *PUBLIC HEALTH AND SAFETY*

614 US
LABOR OCCUPATIONAL HEALTH PROGRAM MONITOR. 1974. 4/yr. $15. University of California, Berkeley, School of Public Health, Labor Occupational Health Program, 2515 Channing Way, Berkley, CA 94720. TEL 510-642-5507. Ed. Eugene S. Darling. bk.rev.; film rev.; charts; illus.; circ. 2,500. (back issues avail.)

614.85 661 UK ISSN 0261-2917
CODEN: LHBUD2
LABORATORY HAZARDS BULLETIN. 1981. m. £110($240) Royal Society of Chemistry, Thomas Graham House, Science Park, Milton Rd., Cambridge CB4 4WF, England. TEL 0462-672555. FAX 0462-480947. TELEX 825372. (Subscr. to: Distribution Centre, Blackhorse Rd., Letchworth, Herts SG6 1HN, England) Ed. Mike Hannant. adv.; index. cum.index.
●Also available online. Vendor(s): Data-Star (CSNB), DIALOG (File no.317), European Space Agency (File no.90/LABORATORY HAZARDS BULLETIN), STN International (LHB).
—BLDSC shelfmark: 5139.870000.
Description: Reports on safety measures, potential hazards and new legislation affecting the well-being of employees working in laboratories.

LABOUR RESOURCER. see *BUSINESS AND ECONOMICS — Labor And Industrial Relations*

OCCUPATIONAL HEALTH AND SAFETY

614.82   FR
LETTRE D'INFORMATION SUR LA RECHERCHE HYGIENE ET SECURITE. English Edition: Safety Research News (ISSN 0765-913X) 1982. irreg. free. Institut National de Recherche et de Securite pour la Prevention des Accidents du Travail et des Maladies Professionnelles, 30 rue Olivier Noyer, 75680 Paris Cedex 14, France. TEL 40-44-30-00.
FAX 40-44-30-99. TELEX 203-594 INSPAR.
(Co-sponsors: International Social Security Association; International Section for Research on Prevention of Occupational Risks) Ed. B. Moncelon. bk.rev.
Formerly: I N R S Lettre d'Information sur la Recherche.

620.86   US
MARINE NEWSLETTER. bi-m. $19 to non-members; members $15. National Safety Council, Industrial Section, 444 N. Michigan Ave., Chicago, IL 60611. TEL 800-621-7619.
Formerly: Safety Newsletter: Marine Section.
Description: Information and recommendations on various safety issues in the marine industry.

613.62   FR   ISSN 0025-6757
MEDECINE ET TRAVAIL. 1961. q. 1100 F. Syndicat National Professionnel des Medecins du Travail, 12 Impasse Mas, F-31000 Toulouse, France. adv.; bk.rev.; circ. 1,700. *Indexed:* C.I.S. Abstr., Excerp.Med.
—BLDSC shelfmark: 5487.733200.
Description: Publishes articles on occupational medicine, industrial health, hygienics, and safety at work.

613.62   SP
MEDICINA DE EMPRESA; publicacion dedicada a la seguridad y medicina del trabajo. 1963. q. 500 ptas.($8) Sociedad Catalana de Seguridad y Medicina del Trabajo, Tapineria, 10, 2, Barcelona 2, Spain. Ed. Vicente Sanjose Capella. adv.; bk.rev.; illus.; circ. controlled. *Indexed:* C.I.S. Abstr.

613.62   IT   ISSN 0025-7818
RC963   CODEN: MELAAD
MEDICINA DEL LAVORO. (Text in Italian; summaries in English and Italian) 1901. bi-m. L.90000. Istituti Clinici di Perfezionamento, Via Daverio 6, 20122 Milan, Italy. Ed. Enrico C. Vigliani. adv.; bk.rev.; illus.; stat.; index; circ. 1,200. *Indexed:* Abstr.Hyg., Biol.Abstr., C.I.S. Abstr., Chem.Abstr., Ergon.Abstr., Excerp.Med., Ind.Med., INIS Atomind., Nutr.Abstr., Trop.Dis.Bull.
—BLDSC shelfmark: 5533.600000.

620.86   US
METALS NEWSLETTER. bi-m. $19 to non-members; members $15. National Safety Council, Industrial Section, 444 N. Michigan Ave., Chicago, IL 60611. TEL 800-621-7619.
Formerly: Safety Newsletter: Metals Section.
Description: Information and recommendations on safety issues in the field of metals.

613.62   US   ISSN 0026-251X
MICHIGAN'S OCCUPATIONAL HEALTH. 1955. s-a. free. Department of Public Health, Division of Occupational Health, Box 30195, Lansing, MI 48909. TEL 517-335-8250. charts; illus.; circ. 4,500.
Description: Articles pertaining to industrial hygiene, toxicology, engineering controls and interpretations of federal and state occupational health standards.

610 613.62   SA
MINE MEDICAL OFFICERS' ASSOCIATION OF SOUTH AFRICA. JOURNAL. (Text in English) 1921. irreg. membership. Chamber of Mines of South Africa, P.O. Box 61809, Marshalltown 2107, South Africa. TEL 011-838-8211. Ed. R.L. Cowie. charts; illus.; cum.index; circ. 500. (back issues avail.) *Indexed:* Abstr.Hyg., Excerp.Med., Ind.Med., Ind.S.A.Per., Trop.Dis.Bull.
Formerly: Mine Medical Officers' Association of South Africa. Proceedings (ISSN 0026-4490)

MINE REGULATION REPORTER. see *MINES AND MINING INDUSTRY*

MINES SAFETY AND HEALTH COMMISSION. REPORT/ORGANE PERMANENT POUR LA SECURITE DANS LES MINES DE HOUILLE. RAPPORT. see *MINES AND MINING INDUSTRY*

620.86   US
MINING NEWSLETTER. bi-m. $19 to non-members; members $15. National Safety Council, Industrial Section, 444 N. Michigan Ave., Chicago, IL 60611. TEL 800-621-7619.
Formerly: Safety Newsletter: Mining Section.
Description: Information and recommendations on safety issues in mining.

331 614.5   HU   ISSN 0027-3619
T55.A1   CODEN: MMUZDM
MUNKAVEDELEM/LABOR SAFETY. (Text in Hungarian; summaries in English, German, Russian) 1955. q. $20. (Szakszervezetek Orszagos Tanacsa, Munkavedelmi Tudomanyos Kutatointezet) Nepszava Lapkiado Vallalat, Rakoczi ut 54, 1964 Budapest 7, Hungary. TEL 222-408. (Subscr. to: Kultura, Box 149, H-1389 Budapest, Hungary) (Co-sponsor: Orszagos Munkaegeszsegugyi Intezet) Ed. Gyula Nagy. adv.; bk.rev.; circ. 5,000. *Indexed:* Abstr.Hyg., Chem.Abstr., Trop.Dis.Bull.

614.85   US
N I O S H T I C DATABASE. q. price varies. (National Institute for Occupational Safety and Health Technical Information Center, Priorities and Research Analysis Branch) U.S. National Technical Information Service, 5285 Port Royal Rd., Springfield, VA 22161. TEL 703-487-4630. bibl.
●Also available online. Vendor(s): DIALOG, Orbit Information Technologies.
Also available on CD-ROM.
Description: Bibliographic database which cites over 125,000 cases involving hazards and resultant injuries and illnesses in the workplace.

N R W - INTERNATIONAL. (Nord - Rhein Westfalen) see *BUSINESS AND ECONOMICS — Labor And Industrial Relations*

614.85 616.2   SA   ISSN 0374-9800
NATIONAL CENTRE FOR OCCUPATIONAL HEALTH. ANNUAL REPORT. 1957. irreg. free. Department of National Health and Population Development, National Centre for Occupational Health, Box 4788, Johannesburg 2000, South Africa.
FAX 011-720-6608. TELEX 422251. Ed. Dr. A.C. Cantrell. circ. 400 (controlled).
Formerly: National Institute for Occupational Diseases. Annual Report.

614.8 368   AU
NEUE B S; Sicherheitsmagazin. 1965. 10/yr. S.240. Allgemeine Unfallversicherungsanstalt Abteilung HUB, Adalbert-Stifter-Str. 65, A-1200 Vienna, Austria. Eds. Wilfried Friedl, Ilse Zembaty. adv.; bk.rev.; abstr.; illus.; stat.; index; circ. 270,000. *Indexed:* C.I.S. Abstr.
Formerly: Betriebssicherheit - B S (ISSN 0005-3287)

NEW HAMPSHIRE MUNICIPAL PRACTICE SERIES. VOL. 3: PUBLIC HEALTH, SAFETY AND HIGHWAYS. see *PUBLIC ADMINISTRATION — Municipal Government*

NEW SOLUTIONS; a journal of environmental and occupational health policy. see *ENVIRONMENTAL STUDIES*

614.8 374.013   NO
NORWAY. DIREKTORATET FOR ARBEIDSTILSYNET. FORSKRIFTER/REGULATIONS. irreg. free. Direktoratet for Arbeidstilsynet - Directorate of Labour Inspection, Fr. Nansens vei 14, Box 8103 Dep., 0032-Oslo 1, Norway. TEL 02-95-70-00. TELEX 02-46-62-14. charts; illus.
Formerly: Norway. Statens Arbeidstilsyn Direktoratet. Verneregler.

613.62   US
NOTICIAS DE SEGURIDAD. (Text in Spanish) 1938. m. $32. Inter-American Safety Council, 33 Park Pl., Englewood, NJ 07631. FAX 201-871-2074. TELEX 135407. Ed.Bd. adv.; circ. 10,000.

613.62   CN   ISSN 0827-4576
O H & S CANADA. (Occupational Health & Safety) 1985. bi-m. Can.$79. Corpus Information Services, Division of Southam Business Communications Inc., 1450 Don Mills Rd., Don Mills, Ont. M3B 2X7, Canada. TEL 416-445-6641. FAX 416-442-2200. TELEX 06-966612. Ed. Margaret Nearing. adv.; bk.rev.; charts; stat.; tr.lit.; index; circ. 7,000. (back issues avail.) *Indexed:* Can.Per.Ind.
—BLDSC shelfmark: 6228.859000.

O S H A TRAINING BULLETIN FOR SUPERVISORS. (Occupational Safety and Health Administration) see *ENVIRONMENTAL STUDIES*

613.62   US
O S H A UP TO DATE NEWSLETTER. (U.S. Occupational Safety & Health Administration) m. $31 to non-members; members $25. National Safety Council, Industrial Section, 444 N. Michigan Ave., Chicago, IL 60611. TEL 800-621-7619. Ed. Kathleen Knowles. circ. 30,000.

613.62 614.85   US
O S H A WEEK. (Occupational Safety and Health) w. Stevens Publishing Corporation, 225 N. New Rd., Waco, TX 76710-6931. TEL 817-776-9000. Ed. Stephen G. Minter.

613.62   BE   ISSN 0771-2634
OBJECTIF PREVENTION. 1964. m. 750 Fr. Association Nationale pour la Prevention des Accidents du Travail (ANPAT), 88 Rue Gachard, Bte. 4, B-1050 Brussels, Belgium. TEL 02-648-03-37. circ. 27,000. (tabloid format)

614.85   US   ISSN 0029-7909
    CODEN: OCHAAZ
OCCUPATIONAL HAZARDS; magazine of health & environment. 1938. m. $45 (free to qualified personnel). Penton Publishing (Subsidiary of: Pittway Company), 1100 Superior Ave., Cleveland, OH 44114-2543. TEL 216-696-7000.
FAX 216-696-8765. (Subscr. to: Box 95759, Cleveland, OH 44101) Ed. Stephen G. Minter. adv.; bk.rev.; charts; illus.; stat.; tr.lit.; index; circ. 60,000 (controlled). (also avail. in microform from UMI; reprint service avail. from UMI) *Indexed:* ABI Inform, B.P.I., BPIA, Bus.Ind., C.I.S. Abstr., Chem.Abstr., Hlth.Ind., Ind.Hyg.Dig., Lab.Haz.Bull., Pers.Manage.Abstr., PROMT, Tr.& Indus.Ind., Work Rel.Abstr.
—BLDSC shelfmark: 6228.000000.
Description: News on industrial safety, occupational health, environmental control, insurance, first aid, medical care, and hazardous material control.

613.62   US   ISSN 0362-4064
RC963   CODEN: OHSADQ
OCCUPATIONAL HEALTH & SAFETY. m. $40. Stevens Publishing Corporation, 225 N. New Rd., Waco, TX 76710. TEL 817-776-9000. FAX 817-776-9018. Ed. Margaret Leary. adv.; bk.rev.; charts; circ. 88,000. (also avail. in microform from UMI; reprint service avail. from UMI) *Indexed:* Abstr.Hyg., B.P.I., Biol.Abstr., C.I.S. Abstr., Chem.Abstr., Dent.Ind., Ergon.Abstr., Hosp.Lit.Ind., Ind.Med., Lab.Haz.Bull., Noise Pollut.Publ.Abstr., Pers.Lit., Sci.Abstr., Trop.Dis.Bull.
Former titles (until vol.45, 1976): International Journal of Occupational Health and Safety (ISSN 0093-2205); Industrial Medicine and Surgery (ISSN 0019-8536)
Refereed Serial

614.85   US
▼**OCCUPATIONAL HEALTH & SAFETY ASBESTOS CONTROL BUYER'S GUIDE.** 1990. a. Stevens Publishing Corporation, 225 N. New Rd., Waco, TX 76710. TEL 817-776-9000. adv.; circ. 46,550.
Description: Contains industrial, corporate, government, legal and school personnel, listings of products, equipment and services available from manufacturers, distributors, contractors and consultants.

OCCUPATIONAL HEALTH AND SAFETY LAW. see *LAW*

614   US   ISSN 0196-058X
OCCUPATIONAL HEALTH & SAFETY LETTER; ...towards productivity and peace of mind. 1971. fortn. $254.54 (effective Sep. 1992). Business Publishers, Inc., 951 Pershing Dr., Silver Spring, MD 20910-4464. TEL 301-587-6300.
FAX 301-585-9075. Ed. Bryan Morris. (looseleaf format)
●Also available online. Vendor(s): NewsNet.
Former titles: Workplace Health Safety and Liability Report; Workplace Health and Job Safety Report; Workplace Health; Job Safety and Health Report; Job Safety and Health (Silver Spring) (ISSN 0148-4079)
Description: News for workplace managers on maintaining staff safety; includes Americans with Disabilities Act regulations.

OCCUPATIONAL HEALTH AND SAFETY

613.62 614.85   US
OCCUPATIONAL HEALTH & SAFETY NEWS. m. $59. Stevens Publishing Corporation, 225 N. New Rd., Waco, TX 76710. TEL 817-776-9000. adv.

613.62   CN   ISSN 0706-5043
OCCUPATIONAL HEALTH AND SAFETY TOPICS/SUJETS SE RAPPORTANT A LA SANTE ET LA SECURITE AU TRAVAIL. m. free. Ministry of Labour, Library, 400 University Ave., 10th fl., Toronto, Ont. M7A 1T7, Canada. TEL 416-326-7840.

614.8   CN   ISSN 0705-9388
OCCUPATIONAL HEALTH IN ONTARIO. (Text in English; summaries in English, French) 1979. q. Can.$16. Ministry of Labor, Occupational Health and Safety Division, 400 University Ave., Toronto M7A 1T7, Ont., Canada. TEL 416-326-1404. FAX 416-326-1439. Ed. Dr. Mark A. Nazar. bk.rev.; index; circ. 1,000. (back issues avail.)
—BLDSC shelfmark: 6228.960000.

613.62   US
▼**OCCUPATIONAL HEALTH MANAGEMENT.** 1991. m. $189. American Health Consultants, Inc., Six Piedmont Center, Ste. 400, 3525 Piedmont Rd., N.E., Atlanta, GA 30305. TEL 404-262-7436. FAX 800-284-3291. (Subscr. to: Box 740056, Atlanta, GA 30374-9822. TEL 800-688-2421) Ed. Christi Reynolds. circ. 1,200.

658.3   US
OCCUPATIONAL HEALTH NURSING NEWSLETTER. bi-m. $19 to non-members; members $15. National Safety Council, Industrial Section, 444 N. Michigan Ave., Chicago, IL 60611. TEL 800-621-7619.
Formerly: Safety Newsletter: Occupational Health Nursing Section (ISSN 0466-499X)
Description: Information and recommendations on safety issues in the field of occupational health nursing.

613.62   UK   ISSN 0951-4600
OCCUPATIONAL HEALTH REVIEW. 1987. 6/yr. £95 (foreign £105). Eclipse Publications Ltd., 18-20 Highbury Place, London N5 1QP, England. TEL 01-354-5858. FAX 071-359-4000. Ed. John Ballard. circ. 1,400. (back issues avail.)
—BLDSC shelfmark: 6228.990000.
Description: For specialists and non-specialists in the area of occupational medicine and employee welfare.

613.62   UK   ISSN 0141-7568
            CODEN: OHMOD4
OCCUPATIONAL HYGIENE MONOGRAPHS. 1978. irreg. price varies. Science and Technology Letters, P.O. Box 81, Northwood, Middlesex HA6 3DN, England. TEL 09274-23586. FAX 09274-25066. Ed. Dr. Donald Hughes. circ. 5,000. (back issues avail.)

OCCUPATIONAL MEDICINE. see *MEDICAL SCIENCES*

613.62   US   ISSN 0885-114X
RC963.A1   CODEN: SAOME4
OCCUPATIONAL MEDICINE; state of the art reviews. q. $74 (foreign $84). Hanley & Belfus, Inc., 210 S. 13th St., Philadelphia, PA 19107. TEL 215-546-7293. FAX 215-790-9330. circ. 2,500. (back issues avail.)
—BLDSC shelfmark: 6229.620000.
Refereed Serial

344   US   ISSN 0092-3435
KF3568.3.A2
OCCUPATIONAL SAFETY AND HEALTH DECISIONS. 1973. irreg. $37.50. Commerce Clearing House, Inc., 4025 W. Peterson Ave., Chicago, IL 60646. TEL 312-583-8500.

331   US   ISSN 0095-3237
KF3570.A1
OCCUPATIONAL SAFETY & HEALTH REPORTER. 1971. w. $870. The Bureau of National Affairs, Inc., 1231 25th St., N.W., Washington, DC 20037. TEL 202-452-4200. FAX 202-822-8092. TELEX 285656 BNAI WSH. (Subscr. to: 9435 Key West Ave., Rockville, MD 20850. TEL 800-372-1033) Ed. Mary R. Worobec. charts; stat.; index. (looseleaf format; back issues avail.) Indexed: Ind.Hyg.Dig.
●Also available online. Vendor(s): DIALOG (Laborlaw, File 244), Human Resources Information Network (CDD, HDD).
—BLDSC shelfmark: 6231.205000.
Description: Notification and reference service which provides information on federal and state regulation of occupational safety and health, standards, legislation, enforcement activities, research, and legal decisions.

613.62   UN   ISSN 0078-3129
            CODEN: OSHSDY
OCCUPATIONAL SAFETY AND HEALTH SERIES. (Editions in English, French and Spanish) 1963. irreg. price varies. (International Labour Office) I L O Publications, CH-1211 Geneva 22, Switzerland. TEL 022-799-6111. FAX 022-799-6358. TELEX 415647-ILO-CH. (Dist. in U.S. by: I L O Publications Center, 49 Sheridan Ave., Albany, NY 12210)

614.8   US   ISSN 0198-7208
HD7260
OHIO MONITOR. 1928. m. free to qualified personnel. Industrial Commission, Division of Safety and Hygiene, 246 N. High St., Columbus, OH 43215. TEL 614-466-3385. Ed. Robert L. McCullough. bk.rev.; abstr.; charts; illus.; stat.; circ. 75,000.
Formerly: Monitor (ISSN 0026-9751)

614.85   US
ON THE SAFE SIDE. 1979. m. $35.40. Bureau of Business Practice, 24 Rope Ferry Rd., Waterford, CT 06386. TEL 203-442-4365. FAX 203-434-3341. TELEX 966420. Ed. Paulette Zander.

658.3   US
PETROLEUM NEWSLETTER. bi-m. $19 to non-members; members $15. National Safety Council, Industrial Section, 444 N. Michigan Ave., Chicago, IL 60611. TEL 800-621-7619. Indexed: AESIS.
Formerly: Safety Newsletter: Petroleum Section.
Description: Information and recommendations on safety issues in the petroleum industry.

658.5   UK
PLANT ENGINEERING & MAINTENANCE; the magazine of factory and plant management. 1977. 10/yr. £48($100) Trinity Publishing Ltd., Times House, Station Approach, Ruislip, Middlesex HA4 8NB, England. TEL 0895-677677. FAX 0895-676027. Ed. Geoff Bone. illus.; tr.lit.; circ. 20,000. (back issues avail.) Indexed: BMT, Fluidex, Int.Build.Serv.Abstr., World Surf.Coat., World Text.Abstr.
Description: Maintenance and management of industrial and commercial plant.

PLANT SECURITY. see *CRIMINOLOGY AND LAW ENFORCEMENT — Security*

613.85   PL
            CODEN: PJOMEY
POLISH JOURNAL OF OCCUPATIONAL MEDICINE AND ENVIRONMENTAL HEALTH. (Text in English; summaries in English, Polish) 1988. q. 100000 Zl.($200) Institute of Occupational Medicine, P.O. Box 199, Ul. Teresy 8, 90-950 Lodz, Poland. TEL 42-569632. FAX 42-348331. (Co-sponsor: Polish Association of Occupational Medicine) adv.; bk.rev.; index; circ. 1,000. (back issues avail.) Indexed: Excerp.Med., Ind.Med.
Formerly: Polish Journal of Occupational Medicine (ISSN 0860-6536)
Description: Publishes papers concerning industrial hygiene, preventive medicine, diagnosis and treatment of occupational diseases, physiology and psychology of work, toxicological research, environmental toxicology, environmental epidemiology and epidemiological studies devoted to occupational problems.
Refereed Serial

658.3   US
POWER PRESS AND FORGING NEWSLETTER. bi-m. $19 to non-members; members $15. National Safety Council, Industrial Section, 444 N. Michigan Ave., Chicago, IL 60611. TEL 800-621-7619.
Formerly: Safety Newsletter: Power Press and Forging Section.
Description: Information and recommendations on safety issues in the field.

PRACOVNI LEKARSTVI. see *MEDICAL SCIENCES*

614.8   FR
PREVENIR LES RISQUES DU METIER. 1959. q. 33 F. Institut National de Recherche et de Securite pour la Prevention des Accidents du Travail et des Maladies Professionnelles, 30 rue Olivier Noyer, 75680 Paris Cedex 14, France. TEL 40-44-30-00. FAX 40-44-30-99. TELEX 203594F INRSPAR. Ed. J. Laurin. circ. 380,000. Indexed: C.I.S. Abstr.
Formerly: Risques du Metier (ISSN 0048-8321)

613.62   FR
PREVENTIQUE. 6/yr. 410 F. (foreign 550 F.). Preventique S.a.r.l., 7, Chemin de Gordes, 38100 Grenoble, France. TEL 76-43-28-64. FAX 76-56-94-09.

614.8   HT
PREVOYANCE. 1981. s-a. free. Office d'Assurance Accidents du Travail, Maladie et Maternite, B.P. 1324, Port-au-Prince, Haiti. Ed. Gerson Alexis. charts; illus.; stat.; circ. 2,000.
Formerly (until 1980): Prevention (ISSN 0048-5241)

658.3   US
PRINTING AND PUBLISHING NEWSLETTER. bi-m. $19 to non-members; members $15. National Safety Council, Industrial Section, 444 N. Michigan Ave., Chicago, IL 60611. TEL 800-621-7619.
Formerly: Safety Newsletter: Printing and Publishing Section.
Description: Information and recommendations on safety issues in printing and publishing.

614.85   US   ISSN 0099-0027
T55.A1   CODEN: PRSAD5
PROFESSIONAL SAFETY. 1956. m. $43. American Society of Safety Engineers, 1800 E. Oakton St., Des Plaines, IL 60018-2187. TEL 708-692-4121. FAX 708-296-3769. Ed. Neal Lorenzi. adv.; bk.rev.; charts; illus.; tr.; lit.; index; circ. 25,000. (also avail. in microform from UMI; reprint service avail. from UMI) Indexed: A.S.& T.Ind., ABI Inform, C.I.S. Abstr., Eng.Ind., Environ.Per.Bibl., ISMEC, Met.Abstr., Mgmt.& Market.Abstr.
Formerly (until 1974): American Society of Safety Engineers. Journal (ISSN 0003-1208)
Description: For safety professionals. Features information on developments in the research and technology of accident prevention.

613.62   BE   ISSN 0771-2782
PROMOSAFE. Dutch Ed. (ISSN 0771-2839) (Supplement avail.: annual catalogue) (Text in Dutch, French) 1974. bi-m. 2200 Fr. Wolters Kluwer, Louizalaan 485, B-1050 Brussels, Belgium. TEL 02-641-7411. FAX 02-647-4342. TELEX 62067 WOSABE. Eds. B. Schoenmacchers, M. De Block. adv.; bk.rev.; circ. 3,000. Indexed: C.I.S. Abstr., Ergon.Abstr.
—BLDSC shelfmark: 6925.155000.
Description: Features information on safety and safety education.

658.382   US
PUBLIC EMPLOYEE NEWSLETTER. bi-m. $19 to non-members; members $15. National Safety Council, Industrial Section, 444 N. Michigan Ave., Chicago, IL 60611. TEL 800-621-7619.
Formerly: Safety Newsletter: Public Employee Section (ISSN 0470-2840)
Description: Information and recommendations on safety issues for public employees.

PUBLIC SERVICE ASSOCIATION JOURNAL. see *PUBLIC ADMINISTRATION*

OCCUPATIONAL HEALTH AND SAFETY

350.162 US
PUBLIC UTILITIES NEWSLETTER. bi-m. $19 to non-members; members $15. National Safety Council, Industrial Section, 444 N. Michigan Ave., Chicago, IL 60611. TEL 800-621-7619.
Formerly: Safety Newsletter: Public Utilities Section (ISSN 0466-5007)
Description: Information and recommendations on safety issues in public utilities.

620.86 US
RAILROAD NEWSLETTER. bi-m. $19 to non-members; members $15. National Safety Council, Industrial Section, 444 N. Michigan Ave., Chicago, IL 60611. TEL 800-621-7619.
Formerly: Safety Newsletter: Railroad Section.
Description: Information and recommendations on safety issues for the railroad industry.

615 US ISSN 0361-2546
RA1215
REGISTRY OF TOXIC EFFECTS OF CHEMICAL SUBSTANCES. Short title: R T E C S. 1971. q. Department of Health and Human Services, National Institute of Occupational Safety and Health, Attn.: Doris Sweet, Ed. (C-28), 4676 Columbia Pkwy., Cincinnati, OH 45226. TEL 513-533-8317. (Dist. by: Supt. of Documents, U.S. Government Printing Office, Washington, DC 20402) abstr.; bibl.; index; circ. 10,000. (microfiche; also avail. in magnetic tape)
●Also available online. Vendor(s): Chemical Information Systems, DIALOG (File no.336). Also available on CD-ROM. Producer(s): SilverPlatter.
Description: Provides information on known toxic and biological effects of chemical substances for use by employers, employees, physicians, industrial hygienists, toxicologists, researchers, and others concerned with the safe handling of chemicals. The absence of a substance from the registry does not indicate that it is not toxic. Includes CODEN files.

613.63 US
RESCUE - E M S NEWS. bi-m. Life Saving Communications, Box 165, Milford, DE 19963-0165. TEL 302-422-2772. FAX 302-422-2772. Ed. Lou Jordan. circ. 25,817.

620.86 US
RESEARCH AND DEVELOPMENT NEWSLETTER. bi-m. $19 to non-members; members $15. National Safety Council, Industrial Section, 444 N. Michigan Ave., Chicago, IL 60611. TEL 800-621-7619.
Formerly: Safety Newsletter: Research and Development.
Description: Information and recommendations on safety issues pertaining to research and development.

614.85 JA
RESEARCH INSTITUTE OF INDUSTRIAL SAFETY. ANNUAL REPORT. (Text in Japanese) 1968. a. free. Research Institute of Industrial Safety, 35-1, 5-chome, Shiba, Minato-ku, Tokyo 108, Japan. circ. 2,000. (back issues avail.)

613.62 539.7 US
RESPIRATORY PROTECTION NEWSLETTER. 1985. bi-m. $119 in N. America; elsewhere $129. Radiation Safety Associates, Inc., Box 107, Hebron, CT 06248. TEL 203-228-0487. FAX 203-228-4402. Ed. Paul R. Steinmeyer. bk.rev.; circ. 150. (looseleaf format; back issues avail.)
Formerly (until Nov. 1988): Radiological Respiratory Protection Newsletter (ISSN 0882-0953)

614.85 US
RESPONSE (FAIRFAX). q. Box 3709, Fairfax, VA 22038. TEL 703-352-1349. FAX 703-352-0309. Ed. Tom Vines.

331 613 FR ISSN 0035-1261
T55.A1
REVUE DE LA SECURITE.* 1883. m. 270 F. A.I.F. Services, 10, rue de Calais, 75441 Paris Cedex 09, France. Ed. Paul Germaix. adv.; bk.rev.; bibl.; charts; illus.; stat.; tr.lit.; index; circ. 8,500. *Indexed:* C.I.S. Abstr.
Formerly: Protection, Securite, Hygiene du Travail.

613.62 FR ISSN 0300-0559
REVUE DE MEDECINE DU TRAVAIL. (Summaries in English, French) 1972. bi-m. 450 F.($95) (effective 1992). Groupement National des Medecins du Batiment et des Travaux Publics, 7 rue la Perouse, 75116 Paris, France. TEL 1-40-69-53-77. FAX 1-45-53-58-77. Eds. M. Blaizot, M. Amphoux. adv.; bk.rev.; index; circ. 2,000. (back issues avail.)
—BLDSC shelfmark: 7931.800000.
Description: Covers all subjects concerning occupational health, medicine, and ergonomics industrial toxicologies.

613.62 368 IT ISSN 0035-5836
HD7816.I8 CODEN: RIMPAA
RIVISTA DEGLI INFORTUNI E DELLE MALATTIE PROFESSIONALI. 1914. bi-m. L.42000. Istituto Nazionale per l' Assicurazione Contro gli Infortuni Sul Lavoro, Via 4 Novembre 144, 00187 Rome, Italy. adv.; bk.rev.; abstr.; bibl.; charts; illus.; stat.; index; cum.index; circ. 8,000. *Indexed:* C.I.S. Abstr., Chem.Abstr., World Bibl.Soc.Sec.

613.62 IT ISSN 0391-2825
RIVISTA DI MEDICINA DEL LAVORO ED IGIENE INDUSTRIALE. q. L.40000($65) (effective 1992). Casa Editrice Idelson, Via A. DeGasperi, 55, 80133 Naples, Italy. TEL 081-5524733. FAX 5518295. Ed. Luciano Rossi.

610 JA ISSN 0022-443X
CODEN: ROKAAV
RODO KAGAKU (KAWASAKI, 1924)/JOURNAL OF SCIENCE OF LABOUR. (Text in English, Japanese) 1924. m. 8800 Yen. Institute for Science of Labour - Rodo Kagaku Kenkyujo, 2-8-14 Sugao, Miyamae-ku, Kawasaki 213, Japan. Ed. Akira Nishioka. adv.; bk.rev.; abstr.; bibl.; index; circ. 2,000. (also avail. in microfilm) *Indexed:* Abstr.Hyg., C.I.S. Abstr., Chem.Abstr., Ergon.Abstr., Ind.Hyg.Dig., Nutr.Abstr., Occup.Saf.& Health Abstr., Psychol.Abstr., Trop.Dis.Bull.
—BLDSC shelfmark: 5056.230000.

610 JA ISSN 0035-7774
CODEN: ROKAAV
RODO NO KAGAKU (KAWASAKI, 1946)/DIGEST OF SCIENCE OF LABOUR. (Text in Japanese) 1946. m. 11000 Yen. Institute for Science of Labour - Rodo Kagaku Kenkyujo, 2-8-14 Sugao, Miyamae-ku, Kawasaki 213, Japan. Ed. Akira Nishioka. adv.; bk.rev.; circ. 3,000. *Indexed:* Chem.Abstr.

660.280 US
RUBBER AND PLASTICS NEWSLETTER. bi-m. $19 to non-members; members $15. National Safety Council, Industrial Section, 444 N. Michigan Ave., Chicago, IL 60611. TEL 800-621-7619.
Formerly: Safety Newsletter: Rubber and Plastics Section.
Description: Information and recommendation on safety issues pertaining to rubber and plastics.

613.62 UK ISSN 0144-4301
S P A I D NEWS. 1980? irreg. £5. Society for the Prevention of Asbestosis and Industrial Diseases, 38 Drapers Rd., Enfield, Middx. EN2 8LU, England. TEL 0707-8730250. Ed. Nancy Tait. circ. 2,000.

331 US
SAFE WORKER. m. $19 to non-members; members $15. National Safety Council, Industrial Section, 444 N. Michigan Ave., Chicago, IL 60611. TEL 800-621-7619. Ed. Kathleen Knowles. circ. 160,000.

SAFETY & INDUSTRY LAW SERVICE N S W. see *LAW*

614.8 US ISSN 1040-4236
SAFETY & SECURITY FOR SUPERVISORS. 1973. m. price varies. Business Research Publications, Inc., 817 Broadway, New York, NY 10003. TEL 212-673-4700. FAX 212-475-1790. Eds. Gail Hayden, Albert Sce. circ. 80,000.
Description: Includes safety checklists, case decisions covering the legal problems of safety and security, "Questions and Answers" that probe all aspects of industrial safety and security, and safety and security ideas that work.

614.8 US
SAFETY COMPLIANCE LETTER; with OSHA highlights. s-m. $82.80. Bureau of Business Practice, 24 Rope Ferry Rd., Waterford, CT 06386. TEL 203-442-4365. FAX 203-434-3341. TELEX 966420. Ed. Shelley Wolf.
Formerly: O S H A Compliance Letter (ISSN 0092-5799)

614.85 SA ISSN 0377-8592
T55.A1
SAFETY MANAGEMENT/VEILIGHEIDSBESTUUR. (Text in Afrikaans, English) 1958. m. (foreign $24). National Occupational Safety Association (NOSA) - Nasionale Beroepsveiligheidsvereniging, P.O. Box 26464, Arcadia 0007, South Africa. TEL 012-217736. FAX 021-325-6056. TELEX 3-22262 SA. (Co-sponsor: Association of Societies for Occupational Safety and Health) Ed. Henri Heyns. adv.; bk.rev.; film rev.; illus.; stat.; tr.lit.; circ. 25,516. *Indexed:* C.I.S. Abstr., Lab.Haz.Bull.
Formerly: Safety in Industry (ISSN 0036-2484); *Incorporates:* Safety Digest (ISSN 0036-2468)
Description: Explores the various echelons of management and the workforce in industrial, commercial, financial and governmental undertakings. Emphasis on all aspects of occupational health and safety.

613.62 658 US
SAFETY MANAGEMENT. 1975. m. $75. Bureau of Business Practice, 24 Rope Ferry Rd., Waterford, CT 06386. TEL 203-442-4365. FAX 203-434-3341. TELEX 966420. Ed. Margot Loomis. *Indexed:* Br.Tech.Ind.

SAFETY NEWS (DENVER). see *WATER RESOURCES*

614.85 US
SAFETY RESOURCES. bi-m. Box 8068, Lakeland, FL 33802. TEL 813-683-9377. FAX 813-687-0921. Ed. Ernie Neff.

331 613 NE ISSN 0925-7535
HD7262 CODEN: SSCIEO
SAFETY SCIENCE. (Text in English, French and German) 1976. 6/yr. fl.446 (effective 1992). Elsevier Science Publishers B.V., P.O. Box 211, 1000 AE Amsterdam, Netherlands. TEL 020-5803911. FAX 020-5803598. TELEX 18582 ESPA NL. (Subscr. in U.S. and Canada to: Elsevier Science Publishing Co., Inc., Box 882, Madison Sq. Sta., New York, NY 10159. TEL 212-989-5800) Eds. H.S. Eisner, A.R. Hale. adv.; bk.rev.; charts; illus.; index. (also avail. in microform from RPI) *Indexed:* Abstr.Hyg., Agri.Eng.Abstr., Biol.Abstr., C.I.S. Abstr., Curr.Cont., Eng.Ind., Excerp.Med., HRIS, INIS Atomind., Risk Abstr., Trop.Dis.Bull.
—BLDSC shelfmark: 8069.124900.
Formerly (until vol.15, 1992): Journal of Occupational Accidents (ISSN 0376-6349)
Description: For safety engineers and inspectors, industrial engineers, research scientists, industrial psychologists and ergonomists. Presents research papers on aspects of work-related risks of various occupations.
Refereed Serial

614.85 AT
SAFETY W A. 1972. q. Aus.$10. Industrial Foundation for Accident Prevention, Box 339, Willetton, W.A. 6155, Australia. FAX 09-332-3511. Ed. R. Moore. adv.; bk.rev.; circ. 1,700.
Former titles: I F A P Bulletin; I F A P News (ISSN 0311-0311)

620.8 JA ISSN 0911-8063
SANGYO ANZEN KENKYUJO GIJUTSU SHISHIN/RESEARCH INSTITUTE OF INDUSTRIAL SAFETY. TECHNICAL RECOMMENDATION. (Text in Japanese) 1972. irreg. Research Institute of Industrial Safety - Sangyo Anzen Kenkyujo, 35-1, 5-chome, Shiba, Minato-ku, Tokyo 108, Japan. circ. 450. (back issues avail.)
—BLDSC shelfmark: 8710.750000.

613.62 614.7 JA ISSN 0911-6923
SANGYO ANZEN KENKYUJO KENKYU HOKOKU/RESEARCH INSTITUTE OF INDUSTRIAL SAFETY. RESEARCH REPORT. (Text in Japanese; summaries in English) 1968. a. Research Institute of Industrial Safety - Sangyo Anzen Kenkyujo, 35-1, 5-chome, Shiba, Minato-ku, Tokyo 108, Japan. circ. 450. (back issues avail.)
—BLDSC shelfmark: 7762.851000.
Formerly: Sangyo Anzen Kenkyujo Hokoku (ISSN 0911-6915)

OCCUPATIONAL HEALTH AND SAFETY

614.7   FI   ISSN 0355-3140
RC963.A1   CODEN: SWEHDO
SCANDINAVIAN JOURNAL OF WORK, ENVIRONMENT & HEALTH. (Includes supplement) (Text in English) 1975. bi-m. Fmk.700. Finnish Institute of Occupational Health, Topeliuksenkatu 41 a A, SF-00250 Helsinki, Finland. (Co-sponsors: National Institutes of Occupational Health for Sweden, Norway and Denmark) Ed. Sven Hernberg. bk.rev.; illus.; index; circ. 1,600. **Indexed:** Abstr.Hyg., ASCA, ASSIA, Biol.Abstr., C.I.S. Abstr., Chem.Abstr., Curr.Adv.Cancer Res., Curr.Cont., Dent.Ind., Ergon.Abstr., Excerp.Med., Ind.Med., Lab.Haz.Bull., Psychol.Abstr., Sci.Cit.Ind., Trop.Dis.Bull., World Surf.Coat.
—BLDSC shelfmark: 8087.568000.
Formed by the merger of: Nordisk Hygienisk Tidskrift (ISSN 0029-1374) & Work - Environment - Health (ISSN 0300-3221)

614   FR
SECURITE ET MEDECINE DU TRAVAIL. 1969. 4/yr. 100 F. Association Francaise des Techniciens et Ingenieurs de Securite et des Medecins du Travail (AFTIM), 1 place Vranie, 94340 Joinville le Pont, France. Ed. Jacqy Bellaguet. adv.; bibl.; charts; illus. **Indexed:** C.I.S. Abstr.

614.85 613.62   CC
SHIJIE LAODONG ANQUAN WEISHENG DONGTAI/WORLD INDUSTRIAL SAFETY AND HYGIENE DEVELOPMENT. (Text in Chinese) m. Zhongguo Laodong Anquan Weisheng Qingbao Zhongxin - China Industrial Safety and Hygiene Information Center, A-1 Xibahe, Chaoyang-qu, Beijing 100028, People's Republic of China. TEL 4219190. Ed. Wang Zhixin.

614.85   GW   ISSN 0037-4504
SICHER IST SICHER; Zeitschrift fuer Arbeitsschutz. 1949. m. DM.77. (Verein Deutscher Sicherheitsingenieure e.V.) Verlag Wilhelm Kluge, Saalmannstr. 9, 1000 Berlin 51, Germany. FAX 030-2132745. Ed. W. Koch. adv.; bk.rev.; abstr.; charts; illus.; stat.; index.; cum.index; circ. 9,500. **Indexed:** C.I.S. Abstr., Dok.Arbeitsmed.

614.85 331   AU   ISSN 0037-4512
SICHERE ARBEIT; Zeitschrift fuer Arbeitsschutz. 1947. bi-m. S.462. Allgemeine Unfallversicherungsanstalt Abteilung HUB, Adalbert-Stifter-Str. 65, A-1200 Vienna, Austria. adv.; bk.rev.; charts; illus.; stat.; index; circ. 13,000. **Indexed:** C.I.S. Abstr.
—BLDSC shelfmark: 8271.500000.

011   US
SOCIETY FOR HEALTH SYSTEMS. JOURNAL. q. Institute of Industrial Engineers, 25 Technology Park-Atlanta, Norcross, GA 30092. TEL 404-449-0460. circ. 1,000.
Formerly: I E News: Health Services.

STEEL INDUSTRY SAFETY AND HEALTH COMMISSION. INFORMATION BULLETIN. see METALLURGY

613.62   GW   ISSN 0178-0182
SUEDDEUTSCHE EISEN- UND STAHL-BERUFSGENOSSENSCHAFT. MITTEILUNGEN. 1947. q. membership. Sueddeutsche Eisen- und Stahl-Berufsgenossenschaft, Wilhelm-Theodor-Roemheld Str. 15, D-6500 Mainz, Germany. TEL 06131-802-1. FAX 06131-802-232. TELEX FS-4187-433.

331.1   JA   ISSN 0081-928X
CODEN: SSEIBV
SUMITOMO SANGYO EISEI/SUMITOMO BULLETIN OF INDUSTRIAL HEALTH. (Text in Japanese; summaries in English) 1965. a. Sumitomo Hospital, Institute of Industrial Health - Sumitomo Byoin Sangyo Eisei Kenkyujo, 5-2-2 Nakanoshima, Kita-ku, Osaka 530, Japan. TEL 06-443-1261. FAX 06-444-3975. Ed. Tatsuo Shirasaki. bk.rev. (also avail. in microfiche) **Indexed:** Biol.Abstr., C.I.S. Abstr., Chem.Abstr., Excerp.Med., Ind.Med.

614.8   GW
T U - TECHNISCHE UEBERWACHUNG. SICHERHEIT ZUVERLAESSIGKEIT UND UMWELTSCHUTZ IN WIRTSCHAFT UND VERKEHR. 1960. m. DM.299($131.50) (Verband der Technischen Ueberwachungsvereine e.V.) V D I-Verlag Gmbh, Heinrichstr. 24, Postfach 101054, 4000 Duesseldorf 1, Germany. TEL 0211-6188-0. FAX 0211-6188-112. TELEX 8587-743. Ed. E. Zimmermann. adv.; bk.rev.; charts; illus, pat.; tr.mk.; index; circ. 6,000. **Indexed:** Chem.Abstr.
Former titles: T U Sicherheit und Zuverlaessigkeit in Betrieb und Verkehr (ISSN 0376-1185); T U Technische Ueberwachung (ISSN 0040-1498)

TAASIOT. see BUSINESS AND ECONOMICS — Labor And Industrial Relations

TALLYBOARD. see FORESTS AND FORESTRY

658.382   US
TEXTILE NEWSLETTER. bi-m. $19 to non-members; members $15. National Safety Council, Industrial Section, 444 N. Michigan Ave., Chicago, IL 60611. TEL 800-621-7619.
Formerly: Safety Newsletter: Textile Section.
Description: Information and recommendations on safety issues pertaining to the textile industry.

613   US   ISSN 0734-3302
HD7260
TODAY'S SUPERVISOR. 1935. m. $23 to non-members; members $18. National Safety Council, Industrial Section, 444 N. Michigan Ave., Chicago, IL 60611. TEL 800-621-7619. Ed. Kathleen Knowles. circ. 137,000. (also avail. in microform from UMI; reprint service avail. from UMI)
Formerly (until 1982): Industrial Supervisor (ISSN 0019-879X)

613.62   US
TOPHEALTH; the health promotion and wellness letter. (Editions in English, Spanish) 1987. m. price varies. Health Source Corporation, 74 Clinton Pl., Box 203, Newton, MA 02159. TEL 617-244-6965. Ed. Dr. Arnon I. Dreyfuss, M.D.
Description: Promotes the good health of members and employees of organizations and corporations.

613.62   US
▼**TOPHEALTH EN ESPANOL;** the health promotion and wellness letter. (Text in Spanish) 1990. m. price varies. Health Source Corporation, 74 Clinton Pl., Box 203, Newton, MA 02159. TEL 617-244-6965. Ed. Dr. Arnon Dreyfuss.
Description: Promotes the good health of members and employees of organizations and corporations.

658.382   US
TRADES AND SERVICES NEWSLETTER. bi-m. $19 to non-members; members $15. National Safety Council, Industrial Section, 444 N. Michigan Ave., Chicago, IL 60611. TEL 800-621-7619.
Formerly: Safety Newsletter: Trades and Services Section.
Description: Information and recommendations on safety issues pertaining to trade and services.

613.62 628   US   ISSN 0737-5743
TRANSMISSION - DISTRIBUTION HEALTH & SAFETY REPORT. 1983. 10/yr. $350 (foreign $25). (Interdisciplinary Environmental Associates, Inc.) Robert S. Banks Associates, 2701 University Ave., S.E., Ste. 203, Minneapolis, MN 55414-3236. TEL 612-623-4600. FAX 612-623-3645. (Subscr. to: Box 14501, University Sta., Minneapolis, MN 55414) Ed. Robert S. Banks. bibl.; charts; circ. 500. (looseleaf format; back issues avail.)
Formerly: T and D Health and Safety Report (ISSN 0736-5047)

TRANSPORTATION SAFETY SPECIAL REPORTS. see PUBLIC HEALTH AND SAFETY

613.62   CN
TRAVAIL ET SANTE. 1985. 4/yr. $20. Group de Communication Sansectra Inc., P.O. Box 1089, Napierville, Que. J0J 1L0, Canada. TEL 514-245-7285. Ed. Robert Richards. adv.; circ. 1,904. **Indexed:** Agri.Eng.Abstr., Pt.de Rep. (1989-).

614 331   FR   ISSN 0373-1944
HD7262
TRAVAIL ET SECURITE. 1949. m. 210 F. Institut National de Recherche et de Securite pour la Prevention des Accidents du Travail et des Maladies Professionnelles, 30 rue Olivier-Noyer, 75680 Paris Cedex 14, France. TEL 40-44-30-00. FAX 40-44-30-99. TELEX 203594F INRSPAR. Ed. J. Laurin. bk.rev.; film rev.; bibl.; illus.; cum.index; circ. 63,000. **Indexed:** C.I.S. Abstr., World Surf.Coat.
—BLDSC shelfmark: 9027.000000.

613.62   FI   ISSN 0041-4816
TYO - TERVEYS - TURVALLISUUS/WORK - HEALTH - SAFETY.* 1971. 15/yr. Fmk.315. Finnish Institute of Occupational Health, Topeliuksenkatu 41 a A, 00250 Helsinki, Finland. Ed. Matti Tapiainen. adv.; bk.rev.; illus.; circ. 88,523. **Indexed:** C.I.S. Abstr., Ergon.Abstr.
—BLDSC shelfmark: 9077.460000.

DER UNFALLCHIRURG; gesamte Unfallchirurgie Einschliesslich Sporttraumatologie. see MEDICAL SCIENCES — Orthopedics And Traumatology

363.1   US
RC965.R25
U.S. NUCLEAR REGULATORY COMMISSION. OCCUPATIONAL RADIATION AT COMMERCIAL NUCLEAR POWER REACTORS AND OTHER FACILITIES. ANNUAL REPORT. 1970. a. U.S. Nuclear Regulatory Commission, Office of Nuclear Regulatory Research, Washington, DC 20555. TEL 301-492-7000. circ. 1,000. **Indexed:** Geo.Abstr. Key Title; Occupational Radiation Exposure, Annual Report.
Former titles: U.S. Nuclear Regulatory Commission. Occupational Radiation Exposure. Annual Report (ISSN 0198-8360) & U.S. Nuclear Regulatory Commission. Annual Occupational Radiation Exposure Report.

344   US   ISSN 0094-7776
KF3568.3.A2
U.S. OCCUPATIONAL SAFETY AND HEALTH REVIEW COMMISSION. ADMINISTRATIVE LAW JUDGE AND COMMISSION DECISIONS. 1975. m. $43. U.S. Occupational Safety and Health Review Commission, 1825 K St. N.W., Washington, DC 20006. TEL 202-634-7960. (Orders to: Supt. of Documents, G.P.O., Washington, D.C. 20402) Ed. Linda A. Smith. circ. 700. (microfiche) Key Title: O.S.A.H.R.C. Reports.

613.62   UK
UNIVERSITY OF BIRMINGHAM. INSTITUTE OF OCCUPATIONAL HEALTH. BULLETIN. 1986. s-a. University of Birmingham, Institute of Occupational Health, P.O. Box 363, Edgbaston, Birmingham B15 2TT, England. TEL 021-414-6030. FAX 021-471-5208. (back issues avail.)

613.62   JA   ISSN 0387-821X
CODEN: JOUOD4
UNIVERSITY OF OCCUPATIONAL AND ENVIRONMENTAL HEALTH. JOURNAL. (Text in English and Japanese; summaries in English) 1979. q. $48. University of Occupational and Environmental Health, Japan, Iseigaoka 1-1, Yahatanishi-ku, Kita-Kyushu 807, Japan. FAX 093-692-4876. Ed. Atsuo Sugita. bk.rev.; circ. 900 (controlled). (back issues avail.) **Indexed:** Abstr.Hyg., Biol.Abstr., C.I.S. Abstr., Excerp.Med., Trop.Dis.Bull. Key Title: Journal of U O E H.
—BLDSC shelfmark: 4912.250000.
Description: Focuses on occupational and environmental health sciences, but includes articles in other fields of medicine and humanities.

614.85   NE
UOORKOMEN. 1951. 6/yr. fl.70. Nederlands Instituut voor Arbeidsomstandigheden - Dutch Institute for the Working Environment, Postbus 75665, 1070 AR Amsterdam, Netherlands. TEL 020-5498611. FAX 020-462310. pat.; circ. 160,000.
Former titles (until 1991): Doen en Laten - Working Safely; Veilig Werken (ISSN 0042-3130)
Description: For workers and scholars; seeks to increase interest and motivation concerning the working environment.

613.62   GW
VERWALTUNGSBERICHT (YEAR). a. Berufsgenossenschaft fuer Gesundheitsdienst und Wohlfahrtspflege, Pappelallee 35-37, 2000 Hamburg 76, Germany. TEL 040-20207-0. FAX 040-20207-525.

OCCUPATIONAL HEALTH AND SAFETY — ABSTRACTING, BIBLIOGRAPHIES, STATISTICS

614.85   CN
W H M I S COMPLIANCE MANUAL. (Workplace Hazardous Materials Information Systems) 1989. 3/yr. Can.$139. Thomson Professional Publishing Canada, Corporate Plaza, 2075 Kennedy Rd., Scarborough, Ont. M1T 3V4, Canada. TEL 416-609-8000. FAX 416-298-5094. Ed. R. Ferguson. circ. 2,000.
    Description: For companies developing a program to comply with WHMIS requirements throughout Canada.

614.85   UK
W R A P. m. £13.50. Royal Society for the Prevention of Accidents, Cannon House, the Priory Queensway, Birmingham B4 6BS, England. Ed. Jacqui Heath. circ. 7,669. (tabloid format)
    Formerly: Safety Representative.

614.85   US   ISSN 1051-9815
RM735.A1
▼**WORK (READING)**; a journal of prevention, assessment & rehabilitation. 1990. q. $48 to individuals (foreign $60); institutions $72 (foreign $84). Andover Medical Publishers Inc., 125 Main St., Reading, MA 01867. TEL 617-438-8464. FAX 617-438-1479. TELEX 880052. (Dist. by: Butterworth - Heinemann Ltd., 80 Montvale Ave., Stoneham, MA 02180. TEL 800-366-2665) Ed. Karen Jacobs.
    —BLDSC shelfmark: 9348.040100.
    Description: Each issue is devoted to one topic within the scope of work practice, such as injury prevention, work assessment, and the older worker.

WORK AND STRESS. see *PSYCHOLOGY*

WORKERS' COMPENSATION LAW REPORTER. see *INSURANCE*

WORKLIFE REPORT. see *BUSINESS AND ECONOMICS — Labor And Industrial Relations*

613.62   AT
WORKPLACE HEALTH AND SAFETY MANUAL. 1988. q. C C H Australia Ltd., P.O. Box 230, North Ryde, N.S.W. 2113, Australia. TEL 02-888-2555. FAX 02-888-7324.

614.8   SZ   ISSN 0084-165X
WORLD CONGRESS ON THE PREVENTION OF OCCUPATIONAL ACCIDENTS AND DISEASES. PROCEEDINGS. (Proceedings published by national organizing committee) 1955. triennial, 12th, 1990 Hamburg. International Social Security Association, P.O. Box 1, 1211 Geneva 22, Switzerland.

331   YU   ISSN 0044-1880
ZASTITA RADA. 1959. m. 40 din.($2.67) Jelene Cetkovic 3, Box 723, Belgrade, Yugoslavia. Ed. Katarina Todorovic.

613.62   GW   ISSN 0340-7047
CODEN: ZAAPDJ
ZENTRALBLATT FUER ARBEITSMEDIZIN, ARBEITSSCHUTZ UND PROPHYLAXE. 1951. m. DM.186. Dr. Curt Haefner Verlag, Bachstr. 14, Postfach 106060, 6900 Heidelberg, Germany. TEL 06221-49064. Ed.Bd. adv.; bk.rev.; abstr.; bibl.; charts; illus.; pat.; index; circ. 2,500. **Indexed:** Abstr.Hyg.; Biol.Abstr.; C.I.S. Abstr., Chem.Abstr., Chem.Infd., Ergon.Abstr., Excerp.Med., Ind.Med., Trop.Dis.Bull.
    Formed by the merger of: Zentralblatt fuer Arbeitsmedizin und Arbeitsschutz (ISSN 0044-4049) & Prophylaxe (Heidelberg) (ISSN 0033-1368).

OCCUPATIONAL HEALTH AND SAFETY — Abstracting, Bibliographies, Statistics

613.62   US
AMERICAN INDUSTRIAL HYGIENE ASSOCIATION. CONFERENCE ABSTRACTS. a. $20. American Industrial Hygiene Association, 345 White Pond Dr., Box 8390, Akron, OH 44320-1155. TEL 216-873-2442.
    Description: Abstracts of papers presented at the annual meeting of the American Industrial Hygiene Conference.

614.8 016   GW   ISSN 0932-2876
ARBEITSMEDIZIN. (Text in English and German) 1975. irreg. (3-4/yr.). Institut fuer Dokumentation und Information, Sozialmedizin und Oeffentliches Gesundheitswesen, Westerfeldstr. 35-37, Postfach 201012, 4800 Bielefeld 1, Germany. TEL 0521-86033. Ed. H. Lange. bk.rev.; circ. 600.
    Indexed: Ergon.Abstr.
    Former titles: Beruf und Gesundheit - Occupational Health; (until 1985): Dokumentation Arbeitsmedizin - Documentation Occupational Health (ISSN 0340-3238).

614.85 011   DK   ISSN 0905-9539
ARBEJDSMILJOET - NETOP NU. 1978. 10/yr. DKK 1200. Arbejdstilsynet, Bibliotek og Dokumentation, Landskronagade33-35, 2100 Copenhagen Oe, Denmark. TEL 45-31-18-00-88. FAX 45-31-18-35-60. TELEX 45-16-149 AMI DK. Ed. Tove Bruum. circ. 1,000.
    Former titles (until 1991): Dok (ISSN 0903-6083); (until 1988): S D A - Nyt (ISSN 0108-5417)
    Description: Presents occupational safety and health abstracts.

614.85   DK   ISSN 0106-9683
HD7262.5.D4
ARBEJDSULYKKER. AARSSTATISTIK. 1977. biennial. free. Arbejdstilsynet, Statistik Kontor, Postbox 858, 2100 Copenhagen OE, Denmark. Eds. Ole Brunn, Joergen Raffansoe. circ. 1,000.

613.62   AT   ISSN 1032-5352
AUSTRALIA. BUREAU OF STATISTICS. QUEENSLAND OFFICE. EMPLOYMENT INJURIES, QUEENSLAND. 1966. a. Aus.$11.50 (foreign Aus.$16.50). Australian Bureau of Statistics, Queensland Office, 313 Adelaide St., Brisbane, Qld. 4000, Australia. TEL 07-222-6022. FAX 07-229-6171. TELEX AA 40271.
    Formerly: Australia. Bureau of Statistics. Queensland Office. Industrial Accidents.
    Description: Lists by industry group and occupation group, extent and duration of disability, type of accident, nature of injury, and agency related to the accident.

613.62   US   ISSN 0190-9398
CODEN: CSCSDD
C A SELECTS. CHEMICAL HAZARDS, HEALTH & SAFETY. s-w. $195. Chemical Abstracts Service (Subsidiary of: American Chemical Society), 2540 Olentangy River Rd., Box 3012, Columbus, OH 43210. TEL 614-447-3600. FAX 614-447-3713. TELEX 6842086.
    Description: Covers safety in chemical laboratories and in the chemical and nuclear industries; health and safety of personnel working in these areas or working with hazardous substances.

613.62 011   US   ISSN 1047-8124
C A SELECTS. OCCUPATIONAL EXPOSURE & HAZARDS. 1988. s-w. $195. Chemical Abstracts Service (Subsidiary of: American Chemical Society), 2540 Olentangy River Rd., Box 3012, Columbus, OH 43210. TEL 614-447-3600. FAX 614-337-3713. TELEX 6842986.
    Formerly (until 1989): BIOSIS CAS Selects: Occupational Exposure.
    Description: Covers occupational exposure and related hazards. Includes epidemiological studies on workplace exposure of humans to chemicals, biological agents, radiation, and noise.

331.11   US   ISSN 0164-1530
HD7262.5.U62
CALIFORNIA WORK INJURIES AND ILLNESSES. 1945. a. free. Department of Industrial Relations, Division of Labor Statistics and Research, Box 420603, San Francisco, CA 94142-0603. TEL 415-703-5971.
    Supersedes in part (in 1975): California Work Injuries.

614 016   SP   ISSN 0213-943X
E R G A. BIBLIOGRAFICO. 1973. m. 3180 ptas. Instituto Nacional de Seguridad e Higiene en el Trabajo, Ministerio de Trabajo y Seguridad Social, Calle Dulcet 2-10, 08034 Barcelona, Spain. FAX 343-280-36-42. Ed.Bd. bk.rev.; index. cum.index; index: 1975-1988; circ. 2,000.
    Former titles (until 1988): Instituto Nacional de Seguridad e Higiene en el Trabajo. Boletin Bibliografico (ISSN 0212-2359); (until 1981): Spain. Servicio Social de Higiene y Seguridad del Trabajo. Boletin Bibliografico (ISSN 0210-069X)

HEALTH AND SAFETY SCIENCE ABSTRACTS. see *PUBLIC HEALTH AND SAFETY — Abstracting, Bibliographies, Statistics*

613.62 016   US   ISSN 0019-8382
CODEN: IHYDA
INDUSTRIAL HYGIENE DIGEST. 1937. m. $150. Industrial Health Foundation, Inc., 34 Penn Circle West, Pittsburgh, PA 15206. TEL 412-363-6600. bk.rev.; abstr.; index. cum.index every 10 yrs.; circ. 1,000. **Indexed:** C.I.S. Abstr., JAMA.
    —BLDSC shelfmark: 4456.480000.

331.8 016 613   UN   ISSN 0074-2147
INTERNATIONAL CATALOGUE OF OCCUPATIONAL SAFETY AND HEALTH FILMS. (Subseries of Occupational Safety and Health Series) (Text in English, French and Spanish) 1969. irreg. (International Labour Office) I L O Publications, CH-1211 Geneva 22, Switzerland. (U.S. Distributor: I L O Publications, 49 Sheridan Ave., Albany, NY 12210)

MEXICO. CENTRO DE INFORMACION TECNICA Y DOCUMENTACION. INDICE DE ARTICULOS SOBRE SEGURIDAD E HIGIENE INDUSTRIAL. see *INSURANCE — Abstracting, Bibliographies, Statistics*

331.11   US
OCCUPATIONAL DISEASE IN CALIFORNIA. (Formerly published by California Department of Health) 1979. a. free. Department of Industrial Relations, Division of Labor Statistics and Research, Box 420603, San Francisco, CA 94141-0603. TEL 415-703-5971.

OCCUPATIONAL HEALTH. see *PHYSICS — Abstracting, Bibliographies, Statistics*

614.8 016   UN   ISSN 1010-7053
T55.A1   CODEN: SHWOEV
SAFETY AND HEALTH AT WORK. French edition: Securite et Sante au Travail (ISSN 1010-7061) (Editions in English, French,) 1974. 6/yr. $200. International Labour Office, International Occupational Safety and Health Information Centre, CH-1211 Geneva 22, Switzerland. TEL 799-65-40. TELEX 415-647-ILO-CH. Ed.Bd. adv.; bk.rev.; abstr.; index; cum.index; circ. 20,000. (tabloid format) **Indexed:** Ergon.Abstr., Lab.Haz.Bull.
    ●Also available online. Vendor(s): European Space Agency (File no.40/CISDOC), IST-INFORMATHEQUE, Orbit Information Technologies, Telesystemes - Questel.
    Also available on CD-ROM. Producer(s): SilverPlatter.
    —BLDSC shelfmark: 8065.717000.
    Former titles: C I S Abstracts (ISSN 0302-7651); Occupational Safety and Health Abstracts (ISSN 0029-7984)

614.8 016   UN   ISSN 1010-7061
SECURITE ET SANTE AU TRAVAIL. English edition: Safety and Health at Work (ISSN 1010-7053) (Editions in English and French) 1974. 6/yr. $200. International Labour Office, International Occupational Safety and Health Information Centre - Bureau International du Travail, Centre International d'Infromations de Securite et de Sante au Travail, CH-1211 Geneva 22, Switzerland. TEL 22-799-6740. FAX 41-22-798-8685. TELEX 415-647-ILO-CH. Ed.Bd. adv.; bk.rev. **Indexed:** Ergon.Abstr., Lab.Haz.Bull., Occup.Saf.& Health Abstr.
    ●Also available online. Vendor(s): European Space Agency, IST-INFORMATHEQUE, Orbit Information Technologies, Telesystemes - Questel.
    Also available on CD-ROM. Producer(s): SilverPlatter.
    Former titles: Bulletin C I S (ISSN 0250-4235); Bulletin Bibliographique de la Prevention (ISSN 0045-3498)

610 613.62   UK
SELECTED ABSTRACTS ON OCCUPATIONAL DISEASES. 1982. q. £8. Departments of Health and Social Security, Hannibal House, Elephant and Castle, London SE1 6TE, England. (Subscr. to: DHSS (Leaflets), P.O. Box 21, Stanmore, Middlesex HA7 1AY, England) Ed. John Lehane.

613.62 016   RU   ISSN 0202-8905
SIGNAL'NAYA INFORMATSIYA. TEKHNIKA BEZOPASNOSTI. SANITARNAYA TEKHNIKA. 1971. s-m. 17.60 Rub. Vsesoyuznyi Institut Nauchno-Tekhnicheskoi Informatsii (VINITI), Baltiiskaya ul. 14, Moscow A-219, Russia. (Dist. by: Mezhdunarodnaya Kniga, Dimitrova ul. 39, 113095 Moscow, Russia)

OCCUPATIONS AND CAREERS

614.852 310   US   ISSN 0195-9344
WESTERN WOOD PRODUCTS ASSOCIATION. QUARTERLY INJURY & ILLNESS INCIDENCE REPORT. q. $18. Western Wood Products Association, Yeon Bldg., 512 S.W. Fifth Ave., Portland, OR 97236. TEL 503-761-0134. FAX 503-224-3934. (back issues avail.)

OCCUPATIONS AND CAREERS

see also Business and Economics—Labor and Industrial Relations

A G H E EXCHANGE. (Association for Gerontology in Higher Education) see *GERONTOLOGY AND GERIATRICS*

331.1   US
A I M CAREER EXCHANGE CLEARINGHOUSE.* 1978. m. membership. Association for Information Management, 6348 Munhall, Mc Lean, VA 22101-4116. TEL 703-490-4246. FAX 703-490-8615. Ed. Norm Sims.

331.1   US
A S A EMPLOYMENT BULLETIN. m. $22 (foreign $28); effective 1992. American Sociological Association, 1722 N St., N.W., Washington, DC 20036. TEL 202-833-3410. FAX 202-785-0146.
   Description: Contains current position vacancy listings in academic, applied, and fellowship settings.

A S P P NEWSLETTER. (American Society of Plant Physiologists) see *BIOLOGY — Botany*

371.42 658.3   IS   ISSN 0792-0490
ADAM VEAVODA/MAN AND WORK; journal in labor studies. (Text in English and Hebrew) 1987. s-a. $12. Association of Vocational and Career Counseling in Israel, P.O. Box 9006, Haifa 31090, Israel. TEL 04-527785. Ed. Edgar Krau. adv.; bk.rev.; circ. 400.

371.42   US
ADVANCE (LIBERTY). 1985. s-a. Target Marketing, Inc., 115 Blue Jay Dr., Box 217, Liberty, MO 64068. TEL 800-331-2496. FAX 816-792-3892. (816-781-7557) adv.; circ. 250,000. (controlled).
   Description: For college and university career planning and job placement advisors.

331   US   ISSN 0146-2113
AFFIRMATIVE ACTION REGISTER; the E E O recruitment publication. 1974. m. $15 to individuals; free to qualified personnel. (Affirmative Action, Inc.) Warren H. Green, Ed.& Pub., 8356 Olive Blvd., St. Louis, MO 63132. TEL 314-991-1335. FAX 314-997-1788. adv.; circ. 60,000 (controlled). **Indexed:** Rehabil.Lit.
   Description: All-personnel recruitment publication for female, minority, handicapped, native American and Veteran candidate sources and pools.

371.42   US
AFTER COLLEGE. m. (July-Aug. combined). Earls Court Publishing Company, 4324 Barringer Dr., Ste. 114, Charlotte, NC 28217-1500. TEL 704-529-6866. FAX 704-529-6696. Ed. Elaine Wilson. circ. 200,000.

AGENDA. see *ART*

371.42   FR
AGENT DE VOYAGES; defense et soutien de la profession. 1968. bi-m. 240 F. A P I-Publication, 400 rue St. Honore, 75001 Paris, France. Eds. C. Lea Kadouch, R.R. Leroux. adv.; bk.rev.; circ. 3,200.

371.42   US
AIM (KANSAS CITY). 1985. s-a. $3. Communications Publishing Group, Inc., 250 Mark Twain Tower, 106 W. 11th St., Ste. 250, Kansas City, MO 64105-1806. TEL 816-221-4404. FAX 816-221-1112. adv.; circ. 350,000.
   Description: Assists vocational-technical graduates ages 21-35 in their search for career opportunities.

331.1   US
AIR JOBS DIGEST. vol.6, no.6, 1991. m. $96. World Air Data, Box 70127, Washington, DC 20088. TEL 301-984-0002. (newspaper)
   Description: Contains current open positions that are aviation, aerospace, and space oriented within the federal government and corporate employment market.

370.15   US
ALABAMA ASSOCIATION FOR COUNSELING AND DEVELOPMENT JOURNAL. 1974. s-a. $5 to non-members. (Alabama Association for Counseling & Development) University of South Alabama, Publication Services, c/o Dr. Ervin L. Word, Station No. 36, Livingston University, Livingston, AL 35470. TEL 205-652-9661. FAX 205-652-9661. Ed. Roger C. Du Mars. adv.; bk.rev.; charts; circ. 2,000. (back issues avail.)
   Formerly: Alabama Personnel and Guidance Journal.

AMBULANCE INDUSTRY JOURNAL. see *BUSINESS AND ECONOMICS — Trade And Industrial Directories*

AMERICAN COLLEGE OF SPORTS MEDICINE. CAREER SERVICES BULLETIN. see *MEDICAL SCIENCES — Sports Medicine*

AMERICAN WINDOW CLEANER; voice of the professional window cleaner. see *OCCUPATIONAL HEALTH AND SAFETY*

AMERICAN WORKER. see *BUSINESS AND ECONOMICS — Labor And Industrial Relations*

371.42 917.306   US
ANUARIO HISPANO. (Text in English, Spanish) 1985. a. T I Y M Publishing Company, Inc., 8379 Greensboro Dr., No. 1009, McLean, VA 22102. TEL 703-734-1632. Ed. Angela Zavala. adv.; circ. 25,000.
   Description: Covers career opportunities for hispanics. Includes statistical information, self-marketing strategies and listings of employment services, Hispanic organizations and publications.

331.1   II
APPOINTMENTS MARKET WEEKLY.* 1971. w. Rs.1.60. C-7 Chauptain Colony, Lucknow 5, India. Ed. K.G. Srivastava. adv.; tr.lit.

331.1   US
ARKANSAS. DEPARTMENT OF LABOR. EMPLOYMENT SECURITY DIVISION. ANNUAL REPORT. 1946? a. free. Department of Labor, Employment Security Division, Box 2981, Little Rock, AR 72203. TEL 501-682-3119. charts; stat.; circ. controlled.

ARKANSAS. DEPARTMENT OF LABOR. EMPLOYMENT SECURITY DIVISION. STATISTICAL REVIEW. see *BUSINESS AND ECONOMICS — Abstracting, Bibliographies, Statistics*

700   US   ISSN 0730-9023
ARTSEARCH; the national employment service bulletin for the performing arts. 1981. 23/yr. $48 to individuals; institutions $60; foreign $100. Theatre Communications Group, Inc., 355 Lexington Ave., New York, NY 10017. TEL 212-697-5230. FAX 212-983-4847. Ed. Ann Marie Rogone. adv.; circ. 5,000. (also avail. in looseleaf format)
   Description: Lists jobs in theater, dance, opera companies, symphony orchestras, universities, arts councils, performing arts centers, and more.

331.1   US
ATHLETICS EMPLOYMENT WEEKLY. 1986. 48/yr. $65. R D S T Enterprises, Box 103, Basco, IL 62313. TEL 217-357-3615. circ. 1,400. (tabloid format)
   Description: Lists job openings for athletic directors, coaches, assistant coaches and graduate assistants. Covers all sports and all sizes of colleges throughout the United States.

ATTORNEYS PERSONNEL REPORT. see *BUSINESS AND ECONOMICS — Personnel Management*

DER AUSBILDER. see *EDUCATION — Adult Education*

373.246   FR   ISSN 0005-1969
HF5382
AVENIRS. 1947. 10/yr. 280 F. (foreign 350 F.) (effective Oct. 1991). Office National d'Information sur les Enseignements et les Professions (ONISEP), 46, 52 rue Albert, 75013 Paris, France. TEL 40-77-60-00. FAX 45-86-60-85. TELEX 202 962 F ONISEP N. bk.rev.; bibl.; charts; illus.; stat.; index. **Indexed:** Int.Lab.Doc.

AVIATION EMPLOYMENT MONTHLY. see *AERONAUTICS AND SPACE FLIGHT*

371.42   GW
B F Z - INFO. 1986. q. Berufsfoerderungszentrum Essen e.V., Altenessenerstr. 80-84, 4300 Essen 12, Germany. TEL 0201-3204-27. FAX 0201-3204-276. Ed. Herbert Schneider. circ. 12,000.

371.42 332.1   US
BANK EMPLOYMENT NEWS. s-m. Maracom, 128 C N. State St., Concord, NH 03301. TEL 603-225-8940.
   Description: For displaced bankers.

371.42 663.1   UK
BARTENDER INTERNATIONAL. 1982. bi-m. £13 to members & qualified personnel. (U K Bartenders' Guild) Adpress Ltd., 29 Cavendish Rd., Redhill, Surrey RH11 4AH, England. adv.; circ. 1,700.

371.42   DK   ISSN 0901-313X
BARTENDEREN. 1950. 6/yr. free. Dansk Bartender Laug, Chr. Richardtsvej 6, 1951 Frederiksberg C, Denmark. TEL 31-355882. Ed. Per Valet. adv.; circ. 1,000.

331.1   GW   ISSN 0173-6574
HD5777
BEITRAEGE ZUR ARBEITSMARKT- UND BERUFSFORSCHUNG. (Text in German) 1970. irreg. (approx. 10/yr.). price varies. Institut fuer Arbeitsmarkt- und Berufsforschung (IAB), Regensburger Str. 104, 8500 Nuremberg, Germany. TEL 0911-1793017. FAX 0911-1792123. TELEX 622348-BA-D. circ. 1,400. (back issues avail.)

371.42   GW   ISSN 0931-8895
BERUFLICHE REHABILITATION. 1987. q. DM.42. (Bundesarbeitsgemeinschaft der Berufsbildungswerke) Lambertus-Verlag GmbH, Woelfinstr. 4, 7800 Freiburg, Germany. TEL 0761-31566. FAX 0761-37064. Ed. Philibert Magin. adv.; bk.rev.; circ. 1,600.

371.42   GW
BERUFSPLANUNG FUER DEN MANAGEMENT NACHWUCHS. 1974. a. $10. Institut fuer Berufs- und Ausbildungsplanung Koeln GmbH, Konrad-Adenauer-Ufer 21, 5000 Cologne 1, Germany. TEL 0221-124038. Ed. Joerg Staufenbiel. circ. 15,000.

371.42   US   ISSN 0006-4122
BLACK CAREERS. 1965. bi-m. $20. Project Magazine Inc., Box 8214, Philadelphia, PA 19101. TEL 215-387-1600. Ed. Emory W. Washington. adv.; bk.rev.; charts; illus.; circ. 275,000.
   Formerly (until vol.5, no.4, Jul. 1969): Project - Guidelines to Equal Opportunity (ISSN 0033-0892)
   Description: Provides job search information and guidance on career preparation, development and advancement to working professionals nationwide in industry, government, business and technology.

BLACK EMPLOYMENT AND EDUCATION. see *ETHNIC INTERESTS*

371.4   UK   ISSN 0306-9885
LB1027.5   CODEN: BJGCDD
BRITISH JOURNAL OF GUIDANCE AND COUNSELLING. 1973. 3/yr. £24.95. (Careers Research and Advisory Centre) Hobsons Publishing Plc., Bateman Street, Cambridge CB2 1LZ, England. TEL 0223-354551. FAX 0223-323154. TELEX 81546-HOBCAM-G. Ed.Bd. adv.; bk.rev.; abstr.; circ. 750. **Indexed:** ASSIA, FAMLI, High.Educ.Curr.Aware.Bull., Psychol.Abstr., Res.High.Educ.Abstr., Sociol.Educ.Abstr., Stud.Wom.Abstr.

331.4   CN   ISSN 0045-3587
BUSINESS AND PROFESSIONAL WOMAN (CANADA). (Text in English, French) 1930. 4/yr. Can.$3. (Canadian Federation of Business and Professional Women's Clubs) Val Publications Ltd., 95 Leeward Glenway, Unit 121, Don Mills, Ont. M3C 2Z6, Canada. TEL 416-424-1393. FAX 416-424-4393. (Subscr. to: 56 Sparks St., Ste. 308, Ottawa, Ont. K1P 5A9, Canada) Ed. Valerie Dunn. adv.; bk.rev.; circ. 5,000.
   Description: Issues, news, self-help and management skills for businesswomen.

331.4 UK ISSN 0045-3595
BUSINESS AND PROFESSIONAL WOMAN (ENGLAND). 1938. q. £0.60. United Kingdom Federation of Business & Professional Women, 23 Ansdell St., London W8 5BN, England. Ed. Linda Findlay. adv.; bk.rev.; illus.; circ. 14,000.

C E I P FUND. CONNECTIONS. see *ENVIRONMENTAL STUDIES*

331.7 US ISSN 0749-7474
HF5382.5.U5
C P C ANNUAL; a guide to employment opportunities for college graduates. (In 4 vols.) 1957. a. $39.95. College Placement Council, Inc., 62 Highland Ave., Bethlehem, PA 18017. TEL 215-868-1421. FAX 215-868-0208. Ed. Joan M. Bowser. adv.; illus.; circ. 1,122,000.
Formerly: College Placement Annual (ISSN 0069-5734)
Description: Contains information on career planning, the job search, work-related education, graduate schools; administration, business and other nontechnical career options; engineering, sciences, computer field and other technical career options; medical, nursing, and allied health career options.

331.1 US ISSN 1046-1183
C P C CAREER & JOB FAIR FINDER. 1989. a. $29.95 to non-members; members $19.95. College Placement Council, Inc., 62 Highland Ave., Bethlehem, PA 18017. TEL 215-868-1421. FAX 215-868-0208. Ed. Marian R. Szakacs. circ. 1,000.
Description: Contains information on over 1,750 career days, job fairs, and consortiums happening nationwide. Includes contact people, addresses, phone numbers, dates of events. Consists of a geographical section listing information on 830 schools alphabetically by state followed by seven public events; an institutional index; a chronological index; and a special index by type or major.

371.42 US ISSN 8755-8378
LB2343.5
C P C NATIONAL DIRECTORY; who's who in career planning, placement, and recruitment. 1985. a. $47.95 to non-members; members $32.95. College Placement Council, Inc., 62 Highland Ave., Bethlehem, PA 18017. TEL 215-868-1421. FAX 215-868-0208. Ed. Marian R. Szakacs. circ. 4,200.
Description: Contains information on 2,200 colleges, 2,100 employers and 9,400 personnel people in the field. Includes names, addresses, phone numbers, interview schedules, and minority enrollments.

371 US ISSN 0196-1004
C P C SALARY SURVEY; a study of beginning salary offers. 1960. 4/yr. $220 to non-members. College Placement Council, Inc., 62 Highland Ave., Bethlehem, PA 18017. TEL 215-868-1421. FAX 215-868-0208. Ed. Dawn L. Oberman. circ. 4,000. Indexed: SRI.

CALIFORNIA CONNECTIONS; a directory of private and public sector employment opportunities. see *BUSINESS AND ECONOMICS — Trade And Industrial Directories*

371.42 US
CALIFORNIA PERSONNEL & GUIDANCE ASSOCIATION. MONOGRAPHS. 1960. irreg., no.11, 1977. price varies. California Personnel & Guidance Association, 2555 E. Chapman Ave., Ste. 201, Fullerton, CA 92631-3617. TEL 714-871-6460. FAX 714-871-5132.

371.42 II
CAREER & COMPETITION TIMES. (Text in English) 1981. m. Rs.190. Bennett, Coleman & Co. Ltd. (New Delhi), c/o Times of India, 10 Daryaganj, New Delhi 110002, India. TEL 11-3276567. FAX 11-3323346. TELEX 3161337. (U.S. subscr. addr.: Ms. Kalpana, 42-75 Main St., Flushing NY 11355) Ed. Bidyut Sarkar. circ. 57,000.

371.42 US ISSN 0738-7075
CAREER CENTER BULLETIN. 1979. q. $29. Columbia University, Center for Research in Career Development, 316 Uris Hall, New York, NY 10027. TEL 212-854-2830. FAX 212-316-1473. bk.rev.; circ. 3,500. Indexed: Pers.Lit.
—BLDSC shelfmark: 3051.690000.
Formerly (until vol.3, no.4): Career Development Bulletin.
Description: Disseminates information on news practices, trends, research in the field of career development and human resources.

371.42 US ISSN 0889-4019
HF5381.A1
CAREER DEVELOPMENT QUARTERLY. 1952. 4/yr. $20. (National Career Development Association) American Association for Counseling and Development, 5999 Stevenson Ave., Alexandria, VA 22304. TEL 703-823-9800. FAX 703-823-0252. Ed. Mark L. Savickas. adv.; bibl.; charts; index; circ. 8,000. (also avail. in microform from UMI; reprint service avail. from UMI) Indexed: BPIA, C.I.J.E., Coll.Stud.Pers.Abstr., Cont.Pg.Educ., Curr.Cont., Educ.Ind., High.Educ.Curr.Aware.Bull., Int.Lab.Doc., Psychol.Abstr., Psycscan, Soc.Work Res.& Abstr., SSCI, Stud.Wom.Abstr., Yrbk.Assoc.Educ.& Rehab.Blind.
—BLDSC shelfmark: 3051.706000.
Formerly: Vocational Guidance Quarterly (ISSN 0042-7764)
Description: Concerned with research, theory, and practice in career development, career counseling, occupational resources, labor market dynamics, and career education.

371.42 US
CAREER DIRECTIONS. (Editions avail. for Great Lake states.) 1989. q. Directions Publishing, Inc., 21 N. Henry St., Edgerton, WI 53534. TEL 608-884-3367. adv.; circ. 112,000.
Description: Directed to college juniors, seniors, and graduate students.

CAREER EDUCATION. see *EDUCATION — Adult Education*

371.42 US
CAREER FOCUS. 1988. bi-m. $28.95. Communications Publishing Group, Inc., 250 Mark Twain Tower, 106 W. 11th St., Ste. 250, Kansas City, MO 64105-1806. TEL 816-221-4404. FAX 816-221-1112. Ed. Georgia Lee Clark. adv.; bk.rev.; circ. 750,000.
Description: Informs and motivates Black and Hispanic young adults, ages 21-35, on preparing, developing and advancing their careers.

371.42 US
CAREER FUTURES MAGAZINE. 1989. 4/yr. $10.50. Career Information Services, Inc., 21 Charles St., Westport, CT 06880. TEL 203-227-1775. FAX 203-226-8988. adv.; circ. 650,000.
Description: Gives practical guidance on achieving career objectives.

371.42 US ISSN 0891-0596
HF5382.5.U5
THE CAREER GUIDE. a. $450 to commercial institutions; libraries $395. Dun and Bradstreet Information Services (Subsidiary of: Dun & Bradstreet, Inc.), 3 Sylvan Way, Parsippany, NJ 07054-3896. TEL 201-605-6000.
Formerly (until 1985): Dun's Employment Opportunities Directory (ISSN 0740-7289)
Description: Describes career opportunities and hiring practices of 5,000 companies actively seeking resumes.

371.42 US ISSN 0739-5043
CAREER OPPORTUNITIES NEWS. 1983. 6/yr. $30. Garrett Park Press, Box 190F, Garrett Park, MD 20896. TEL 301-946-2553. Ed. Robert Calvert, Jr. bk.rev.; charts; illus.

CAREER PLANNING & ADULT DEVELOPMENT JOURNAL. see *EDUCATION — Adult Education*

CAREER PLANNING AND ADULT DEVELOPMENT NETWORK NEWSLETTER; a newsletter for career counselors, educators, and human resource specialists. see *EDUCATION — Adult Education*

OCCUPATIONS AND CAREERS 3625

371.42 US
CAREER SUCCESS. 1987. 3/yr. $0.50. Target Marketing, Inc., 115 Blue Jay Dr., Box 217, Liberty, MO 64068. TEL 816-781-7557. FAX 816-792-3892. adv.; circ. 600,000.
Description: Reflects the benefits of vocational education. Covers career opportunities, job outlook, success stories and financial aid.

CAREER VISION. see *COLLEGE AND ALUMNI*

CAREER WOMAN MAGAZINE. see *WOMEN'S INTERESTS*

374 US ISSN 0361-8994
HF5381.A1
CAREER WORLD. 1972. m. (Sept.-May.) $5.25. General Learning Corporation, Curriculum Innovations Group, 60 Revere Dr., Northbrook, IL 60062-1563. TEL 800-323-5471. Ed. Joyce Lain Kennedy. bk.rev. (also avail. in microform from UMI) Indexed: Ind.Child.Mag.
Incorporating: Real World.
Description: Informational articles, essays, and photographs on job markets, job search techniques, and prospective business trends pertaining to vocational planning, for the high school student.

371.42 AT
CAREERS. 1955. a. free. Careers Publishing Pty Ltd., 8 Elliott St., Ascot Vale, Vic. 3032, Australia.

371.42 US
CAREERS; the magazine of choices for today's young achievers. 1981. 5/yr. $8.75. E.M. Guild, Inc., 1001 Ave. of the Americas, New York, NY 10018. TEL 212-354-8877. Ed. Mary Dalheim. adv.; bk.rev.; illus.; circ. 600,000. (back issues avail.; reprint service avail.)
Description: Provides coverage on higher education, career paths, college choices, financial aid, and role models. Distributed to juniors and seniors in high school.

371.42 UK
CAREERS ADVISER.* 1973. bi-m. £6. Dominion Press Ltd., Signal House, Lyon Rd., Harrow, Middx. HA1 2QE, England. adv.; circ. 15,000.

371.42 378.0025 US ISSN 1059-5856
CAREERS & MAJORS. 1989. s-a. Oxendine Publishing, Inc., Box 14081, Gainesville, FL 32604-2081. TEL 904-373-6907. Ed. W.H. Oxendine, Jr. circ. 18,000 (controlled).
Description: Focuses on career opportunities in relation to the college major of choice.

371.42 US
CAREERS AND THE COLLEGE GRAD. 1987. a. $12.95. Bob Adams, Inc., 260 Center St., Holbrook, MA 02343. TEL 617-767-8100. FAX 617-767-0994. adv.; circ. 17,941.
Description: Lists employers, profiles, current needs, industry reports, feature articles and career opportunities for recruitment purposes.

CAREERS & THE DISABLED. see *HANDICAPPED*

371.42 620 US
CAREERS AND THE ENGINEER. 1989. 2/yr. $12.95 per no. Bob Adams, Inc., 260 Center St., Holbrook, MA 02343. TEL 617-767-8100. FAX 617-767-0994. adv.; circ. 21,014.
Description: Lists employers, profiles, current needs, feature articles, industry reports and career opportunities.

371.42 330 US
CAREERS AND THE M B A. (Masters of Business Administration) 1969. 2/yr. $12.95. Bob Adams, Inc., 260 Center St., Holbrook, MA 02343. TEL 617-767-8100. FAX 617-767-0994. adv.; circ. 14,327.
Description: Lists employers, profiles, current needs, feature articles, industry reports and career trends for recruitment purposes.

CAREERS COP: I S C O CAREERS BULLETIN. (Independent Schools Careers Organisation) see *EDUCATION*

331.1 II
CAREERS DIGEST. (Text in English) 1963. m. 21 Shankar Market, Delhi 110 001, India. TEL 11-44726. Ed. O.P. Varma. circ. 35,000.

OCCUPATIONS AND CAREERS

371.42 UK
CAREERS ENCYCLOPAEDIA. 1952. a. £28. Cassell Plc., Villiers House, 41-47 Strand, London WC2N 5JE, England. (Subscr. to: Fleets Lane, Poole, Dorset BH15 3AJ) Ed. Audrey Segal. adv.
Description: Provides career information to graduates, parents, teachers and career advisers. Covers courses and qualifications in future and higher education and how it relates to particular career areas.

371.42 AT
CAREERS GUIDE. 1956. a. Aus.$5.95. David Boyce Publishing and Associates, 44 Regent St., Redfern, N.S.W. 2016, Australia.

371.42 US ISSN 0069-0449
CAREERS IN DEPTH; exploring careers. 1960. irreg. $11.95. Rosen Publishing Group, Inc., 29 E. 21 St., New York, NY 10010. TEL 212-777-3017. FAX 777-0277. Ed. Ruth C. Rosen.

371.42 AT
CAREERS IN HOSPITALS AND HEALTH SERVICES IN VICTORIA. 1969. biennial. Aus.$3.50. Health Department, Victoria, Mayfield Centre, 11-27 Mayfield Ave., Malvern, Vic. 3144, Australia. Ed. Leigh Brown. circ. 2,500.

331.1 621.38 US
CAREERS IN THE COMMUNICATION ARTS & SCIENCES. 1976. biennial. $1. Association for Communication Administration, 311 Wilson Hall, Murray State University, Murray, KY 42071. TEL 502-762-3411. Ed. Robert N. Hall.
Description: Information on careers in all areas of the communication arts and sciences.

371.42 UK
CAREERS OFFICER. 1980. q. £8 (typically set in Apr.). Institute of Careers Officers, 27a Lower High St., Stourbridge, West Midlands DY8 1TA, England. FAX 0384-440830. adv.; bk.rev.; circ. 4,000.
Indexed: High.Educ.Curr.Aware.Bull.
Formerly: Careers Journal; Which superseded (in Jul. 1989): Careers Quarterly.

371.42 AT
CAREERS WEEKLY. w. Aus.$45 to individuals and schools; companies Aus.$110. Monash University, Course and Career Centre, Clayton, Vic. 3168, Australia. TEL 03-565-3150. FAX 03-565-3168. Ed. L.H. Parrott. circ. 1,000.
Description: Contains job advertisements and career-related news.

371.42 UK
CAREERSCOPE. 1981. 3/yr. £1.50. Hamilton House Publishing, 17 Staveley Way, Brixworth Industrial Park, Northampton NN6 9EU, England. Eds. Tony Attwood, Sue Hesse. circ. 5,000.

331.1 FR
CARREFOUR DES METIERS. 1965. bi-m. 66 F. Chambre de Metiers du Rhone, 58 av. Marechal Foch, 69453 Lyon cedex 06, France. Eds. M. Laroche, I. Laforet. adv.; bk.rev.; circ. 19,590.

CHICAGO SCHOOLS AND CAREERS. see *EDUCATION — Guides To Schools And Colleges*

371.42 US ISSN 0746-7761
CHIEF - CIVIL SERVICE LEADER. 1897. w. $20. New York Civil Service Employees Publishing Co., Inc., 150 Nassau St., New York, NY 10038. TEL 212-962-2690. Ed. Frank J. Prial. adv.; circ. 58,146.
Formerly: Chief (ISSN 0009-3807)
Description: Concentrates on the civil services field, reaching police officers, firefighters, school teachers, sanitation and postal employees.

CLERICAL SALARY REVIEW. see *BUSINESS AND ECONOMICS — Personnel Management*

371.42
COLLEGE PLANNING - SEARCH BOOK. 1975. a. $10. American College Testing, 2201 N. Dodge, Box 168, Iowa City, IA 52243. TEL 319-337-1429.

COLORADO JOB FINDER. see *PUBLIC ADMINISTRATION — Municipal Government*

331.1 US ISSN 0195-1157
COMMUNITY JOBS (WASHINGTON).* (Former name of issuing body: Community Careers Resource Center) 1977. m. $15 to individuals; institutions $30. Access, 50 Beacon St., Boston, MA 02108. TEL 617-720-5627. Ed. Barry Sims. adv.; bk.rev.; circ. 3,000. *Indexed:* Alt.Press Ind.
Description: Nationwide listing of socially responsible job and internship opportunities.

371.42 US
CONNECTIONS (SPRINGFIELD). 3/yr. free. Fairfax County Career Development Center for Women, 5501 Backlick Rd., Ste. 110, Springfield, VA 22151. TEL 703-750-0633. circ. 3,000. (back issues avail.)

331.1 US
CONSTRUCTION EMPLOYMENT GUIDE IN THE NATIONAL AND INTERNATIONAL FIELD. irreg., 7th ed., 1990. $16.50. World Trade Academy Press, Inc., 50 E. 42nd St., Ste. 509, New York, NY 10017-5480. TEL 212-697-4999.

CONSULTING OPPORTUNITIES JOURNAL. see *BUSINESS AND ECONOMICS — Management*

331.1 330 US
CONSULTING RATES AND BUSINESS PRACTICES. ANNUAL SURVEY. 1979. biennial. $25. Professional and Technical Consultants Association, 1330 S. Bascom Ave., Ste. D, San Jose, CA 95128. Eds. Gary Cunningham, John Stormes. circ. 2,000.

658 US
CONTEMPORARY TIMES. 1982. q. $100 to non-members; members $50; non-profit $75. National Association of Temporary Services, Inc., 119 S. Saint Asaph St., Alexandria, VA 22314. TEL 703-549-6287. FAX 703-549-4808. Ed. Louise Gates Seghers. adv.; bk.rev.; charts; illus.; stat.; index, cum.index; circ. 5,000. (back issues avail.)
Formerly: N A T S News.
Description: Presents management support articles for the temporary help industry, and current information on Association and industry activities.

CONTRACT EMPLOYMENT WEEKLY. see *BUSINESS AND ECONOMICS — Trade And Industrial Directories*

331.1 US ISSN 0892-5232
HF5382.5.U5
CORPORATE JOBS OUTLOOK!. 1986. bi-m. $159.99. Corporate Jobs Outlook!, Drawer 100, Boerne, TX 78006-0100. TEL 512-755-8810. FAX 512-755-2410. Ed. Jack W. Plunkett. cum.index: 1986-1992; circ. 1,000. (looseleaf format; back issues avail.)
●Also available online. Vendor(s): NewsNet (File no.GB.41).
Description: Objective reports on growing, hiring employers. Includes ratings for salaries, benefits, and advancement opportunities. Covers training, corporate growth, financial stability, marketing, products and services, and mid-term outlook for America's top employers.

371.2 US ISSN 1041-7877
COUNTY CARE. vol.11, 1975. 7/yr. membership. Health Care Foundation, c/o Lloyd R. Chase, Ed., Box 323, Houlton, ME 04730-0323. TEL 207-532-2176. FAX 207-764-0311. adv.; bk.rev.; film rev.; play rev.; bibl.; charts; illus.; stat.; tr.lit.; circ. 800. (processed)
Former titles: Administrative News and Notes; Maine School Administrative District No. 70 News and Notes; Maine School Administrative District No. 29 News and Notes.

371.42 US ISSN 1055-8292
▼**CURRENT EMPLOYMENT.** (Supplement avail.) 1991. a. $23.99. Publishing & Business Consultants, 951 S. Oxford, No. 109, Los Angeles, CA 90006. TEL 213-732-3477. (Subscr. to: Box 75932, Los Angeles, CA 90075) Ed. Atia Napoleon. adv.; circ. 100,000.
Description: Provides updated information on government jobs, with employment trends and forecasts.

331.1 UK
CURRENT VACANCIES FOR GRADUATES. 1972. fortn. £6 for 6 issues. Central Services Unit, Armstrong House, Oxford Rd., Manchester M1 7ED, England. TEL 061-2369816. Ed. Julia Warburton. adv.; circ. 45,000.
Description: Contains list of immediate vacancies for graduates, featuring jobs, career opportunities, and vocational training.

371.42 UK
D O G CAREER GUIDES SERIES.* (Directory of Opportunities for Graduates) 1974. a. £2.25. Newpoint Publishing Ltd., 76 St. James' Lane, London N10 3DF, England. circ. 12,000.

DIMENSIONS (RIMROCK). see *PARAPSYCHOLOGY AND OCCULTISM*

920 CK
DIRECTORIO NACIONAL DE PROFESIONALES. irreg. E C O C Ltda., Calle 17 no. 5-43, Apdo. Aereo 30969, Bogota, Colombia. illus.

DIRECTORY OF INTERNSHIPS, RESIDENCIES AND REGISTRARSHIPS AVAILABLE IN VICTORIAN HOSPITALS. see *HOSPITALS*

DIRECTORY OF MODEL - TALENT AGENCIES AND SCHOOLS USA AND INTERNATIONAL. see *BUSINESS AND ECONOMICS — Trade And Industrial Directories*

DIRECTORY OF OPPORTUNITIES FOR GRADUATES. VOL.6: BUYING, MARKETING, SELLING. see *BUSINESS AND ECONOMICS — Trade And Industrial Directories*

DIRECTORY OF OVERSEAS SUMMER JOBS. see *BUSINESS AND ECONOMICS — Trade And Industrial Directories*

DIRECTORY OF POSTGRADUATE STUDY. see *BUSINESS AND ECONOMICS — Trade And Industrial Directories*

DIRECTORY OF PUBLIC VOCATIONAL TECHNICAL SCHOOLS AND INSTITUTES. see *BUSINESS AND ECONOMICS — Trade And Industrial Directories*

DIRECTORY OF SUMMER JOBS ABROAD. see *BUSINESS AND ECONOMICS — Trade And Industrial Directories*

DIRECTORY OF SUMMER JOBS IN BRITAIN. see *BUSINESS AND ECONOMICS — Trade And Industrial Directories*

DIRECTORY OF TECHNICAL AND FURTHER EDUCATION. see *BUSINESS AND ECONOMICS — Trade And Industrial Directories*

DIRECTORY OF WOMEN IN BUSINESS, PROFESSIONS & MANAGEMENT. see *BUSINESS AND ECONOMICS — Trade And Industrial Directories*

E M A JOURNAL. (Employment Management Association) see *BUSINESS AND ECONOMICS — Personnel Management*

EDUCATION & CAREERS IN SOUTH AFRICA. see *EDUCATION*

371.42 GW
EDUCATIONAL AND VOCATIONAL GUIDANCE - BULLETIN A I O S P, I A E V G, I V S B B. (Text in English, French and German) 1959. s-a. $10 per no. Association Internationale d'Orientation Scolaire et Professionelle - International Association for Educational and Vocational Guidance - Internationale Vereinigung fuer Schul- und Berufsberatung, c/o Friedrichstr. 34, 1000 Berlin 61, Germany. TEL 030-2532-2600. Ed. B. Jenschke. adv.; bk.rev.; bibl.; charts; illus.; circ. 1,600.
Former titles: Bulletin A I O S P-I A E V G-I V S B B (ISSN 0251-2513) & A I O S P Bulletin (ISSN 0044-9504)
Description: Discusses new methods of counseling, guidance systems in various countries, and information for the evryday work of counselors.

EMERGING PATTERNS OF WORK AND COMMUNICATIONS IN AN INFORMATION AGE. see *COMMUNICATIONS*

OCCUPATIONS AND CAREERS

331.1   SZ
L'EMPLOI/STELLE/POSTO. (Text in German, French and Italian) 1974. w. 44 Fr. (foreign 54 Fr.). (Office Federal du Personnel, Service de Placement) Staempfli und Cie AG, Postfach, CH-3001 Bern, Switzerland. TEL 031-276666. FAX 031-276699. illus.; tr.lit. (tabloid format)

333.78   US
EMPLOY. 9/yr. $25 to non-members; members $15; institutions $50. National Recreation and Park Association, 3101 Park Center Dr., Alexandria, VA 22302. TEL 703-820-4940. FAX 703-671-6772. Ed. Robert Kauffman.
    Description: Provides employment resource information for many traditional and non-traditional employment opportunites within the parks and recreation field.

EMPLOYERS OF NEW COMMUNITY COLLEGE GRADUATES: DIRECTORY. see *BUSINESS AND ECONOMICS — Trade And Industrial Directories*

EMPLOYERS OF NEW UNIVERSITY GRADUATES: DIRECTORY. see *BUSINESS AND ECONOMICS — Trade And Industrial Directories*

EMPLOYMENT IN ALBERTA; a guide to conditions of work and employee benefits. see *LAW*

EMPLOYMENT IN BRITISH COLUMBIA; a guide to conditions of work and employee benefits. see *LAW*

EMPLOYMENT IN ONTARIO; a guide to conditions of work and employee benefits. see *LAW*

EMPLOYMENT LEADER. see *BUSINESS AND ECONOMICS — Personnel Management*

331.1   II
EMPLOYMENT NEWS. (Editions in English, Hindi, Urdu) 1976. w. Rs.130 (effective Apr. 1992). Government of India, East Block IV, Level 7, R.K. Puram, New Delhi 110 066, India. TEL 11-603856. Ed. Nagendra Mishra. circ. 426,000.
    Description: Strives to upgrade the awareness of the job seeking fraternity about suitable openings in public and private sector and provides a useful component of guidance materail designed to assist them in coping with the prescribed tests.

331.1   US
EMPLOYMENT OPPORTUNITIES (CLEVELAND). q. $55. National Association of Business Economists, 28790 Chagrin Blvd., Ste. 300, Cleveland, OH 44122. TEL 216-464-7986. FAX 216-464-6350. (back issues avail.)
    Description: A listing of job openings in business and economics, including description of job, qualifications, salary information, and contact person.

331.1   US
EMPLOYMENT OPPORTUNITIES (ENGLEWOOD). m. $60 (includes Guildnotes). National Guild of Community Schools of the Arts, Box 8018, Englewood, NJ 07631. TEL 201-871-3337.
    ●Also available online. Vendor(s): NewsNet.
    Description: Announcements of administrative openings in the field of community arts education.

331.1   US
EMPLOYMENT OUTLOOK FOR NEW ENGLAND COLLEGE GRADUATES. 1986. a. U.S. Bureau of Labor Statistics, New England Regional Office, 1603 JFK Bldg., Boston, MA 02203. TEL 617-565-2327. Ed. Mary M. Sullivan. circ. 1,000.

331.1   US
EMPLOYMENT PRACTICE GUIDE. 1965. s-m. $680. Commerce Clearing House, Inc., 4025 W. Peterson Ave., Chicago, IL 60646. TEL 312-583-8500. Ed. D. Newquist.

331.1 368   US
EMPLOYMENT SERVICE AND UNEMPLOYMENT INSURANCE OPERATIONS; a monthly summary. m. Employment Security Commission, Labor Market Information Division, 532 Kendal Bldg., 700 Wade Ave., Box 25903, Raleigh, NC 27611. TEL 919-733-2936.

ENTREPRENEURIAL WOMAN. see *BUSINESS AND ECONOMICS — Small Business*

ENTREPRISE ET CARRIERES. see *BUSINESS AND ECONOMICS*

331.1   US
▼**ENVIRONMENTAL CAREERS.** 1990. m. P H Publishing, Inc., 760 Whalers Way, Ste. 100-A, Fort Collins, CO 80525. TEL 303-229-0029. Ed. David Hill. circ. 60,000 (controlled).
    Description: Covers career opportunities in the environmental field.

EQUAL OPPORTUNITY. see *ETHNIC INTERESTS*

371.42   UK   ISSN 0951-1806
ESCAPE: THE CAREER CHANGE MAGAZINE. 1986. 6/yr. £17.50. Weavers Press Publishing, Tregeraint House, Zennor, St. Ives, Cornwall TR26 3DB, England. TEL 0736-797061. Ed. John T. Wilson. circ. 4,000.
    Formerly: Escape Committee.
    Description: Articles and features on career change and self-employment.

EXECUTIVE SEARCH SERVICE NEWS. see *SOCIAL SERVICES AND WELFARE*

371.42   US
EXPERIENTIAL EDUCATION. 1973. bi-m. $70. National Society for Internships and Experiential Education, 3509 Haworth Dr., Ste. 207, Raleigh, NC 27609-7229. Ed. Anne Kaplan. adv.; bk.rev.; circ. 2,000. (back issues avail.)
    Description: Covers college and K-12 programs for experiential education, internships, community-service learning, field education, cooperative education, community-based learning, and action research.

371.42   US
▼**EXPRESSMALE.** 1992. m. $21. S A Publishing Inc., 120 Webster St., Ste. 326, Louisville, KY 40206. TEL 502-589-2719. Ed. Cameron Mason Steele. adv.; B&W page $6100. circ. 60,000.
    Description: Targets 21-to 35-year-old males who are starting their careers.

331.1   US   ISSN 0279-2230
FEDERAL CAREER OPPORTUNITIES. 1974. fortn. $160. Federal Research Service, Inc., 243 Church St., N.W., Box 1059, Vienna, VA 22183-1059. TEL 703-281-0200. Ed. Judelle A. McArdle.
    Description: Updated listings of federal government job vacancies. Includes articles on how to get a federal job.

370   US   ISSN 0145-9376
LC1046.F6
FLORIDA VOCATIONAL JOURNAL. 1975. 4/yr. $10. Florida State University, Center for Instructional Development and Services, Tallahassee, FL 32306. TEL 904-487-2054. Ed. Donald Caswell. adv.; bk.rev.; circ. 20,000. (also avail. in microform from UMI; reprint service avail. from UMI). **Indexed:** C.I.J.E., Cont.Pg.Educ., ERIC.

FORDYCE LETTER; commentary and information provided exclusively for those involved in the personnel, search, employment, recruiting and outplacement professions. see *LAW — Corporate Law*

371.42   IT   ISSN 0015-7767
FORMAZIONE E LAVORO. 1963. bi-m. L.7000($15.) Ente Nazionale A C L I Istruzione Professionale, Via Giuseppe Marcora 18-20, 00153-Rome, Italy. adv.; bibl.; charts; illus.; stat.; circ. 3,000.
    —BLDSC shelfmark: 4008.350000.

FREELANCERS OF NORTH AMERICA. see *PUBLISHING AND BOOK TRADE*

371.42   UK
FUTURE VACANCIES FOR THE FINALIST; jobs for those graduating in (Year). 1976. 5/yr. £12 (foreign £16.50. Central Services Unit, Armstrong House, Oxford Rd., Manchester M1 7ED, England. TEL 061-2369816. Ed. Julia Warburton. circ. 70,000.
    Formerly: Foward Vacancies.
    Description: Publication of use during student's final year of degree, containing vacancies for which applications can be made in advance of exams.

G C C A NEWSLETTER. (Graduate Careers Council of Australia Ltd.) see *EDUCATION — Higher Education*

331.1 334   US
G E O: GRASSROOTS ECONOMIC ORGANIZING NEWSLETTER. 1984. q. $9.95 to individuals; institutions $19.95. GEO, Box 5065, New Haven, CT 06525. TEL 203-389-6194. Ed. Len Krimerman. adv.; bk.rev.; film rev.; play rev.; illus.; circ. 1,000. (back issues avail.)
    Formerly (until 1990): Changing Work (ISSN 0883-1416)
    Description: News articles, interviews, departments, and informational documents in pursuit of democratizing the workplace and effecting worker-community ownership.

371.42   UK   ISSN 0017-2804
GRADUATE CAREERS.* 1961. q. £1.($2.50) Dominion Press Ltd., Dominion House, Signal House, Lyon Rd., Harrow, Middx HA1 2QE, England. Ed. Alex Taylor. adv.; bk.rev.; illus.
    Description: Career opportunities for university graduates.

371.42   AT   ISSN 0314-0679
GRADUATE OUTLOOK. 1977. a. Hobsons Press Australia Pty Ltd., 270 Pitt St., Sydney, N.S.W. 2000, Australia. Eds. C. Etteridge, M. Lord. adv.; circ. 68,000.

GRADUATING ENGINEER. see *ENGINEERING*

GUIDE TO CAMPUS RECRUITING. see *EDUCATION — Guides To Schools And Colleges*

GUIDE TO THE TORONTO REGION'S TOP EMPLOYERS. see *BUSINESS AND ECONOMICS*

371.42   US   ISSN 0017-5323
GUIDEPOST. 1958. 14/yr. $30. American Association for Counseling and Development, 5999 Stevenson Ave., Alexandria, VA 22304. TEL 703-823-9800. FAX 703-823-0252. adv.; bk.rev.; film rev.; circ. 60,000. (tabloid format; reprint service avail. from UMI)

H R D I ADVISORY. (Human Resources Development Institute) see *BUSINESS AND ECONOMICS — Labor And Industrial Relations*

371.42   IS
HADASSAH CAREER COUNSELING INSTITUTE. ANNUAL REPORT FOR THE YEAR. (Editions in English, Hebrew) 1948. a. free. Hadassah Career Counseling Institute, P.O. Box 1406, Jerusalem, Israel. TEL 02-244344. (Co-sponsor: Hadassah Women Zionist Organization of America) Ed. Y. Garty. circ. 1,200.
    Former titles: Hadassah Career Guidance Institute. Annual Report for the Year; Hadassah Vocational Guidance Institute. Annual Report for the Year; Hadassah Vocational Guidance Institute. Report (ISSN 0072-9248)

HEALTH CAREER POST. see *HOSPITALS*

HEALTH WAGE MONITOR. see *MEDICAL SCIENCES*

371.42 610   US
HEALTHCARE TRENDS AND TRANSITION. 6/yr. Nex, Inc., Box 48, Eden, MD 21822. TEL 800-541-9129. FAX 301-749-8769. Ed. Karen Flynn.

HELPING OUT IN THE OUTDOORS; a directory of volunteer jobs and internships in parks and forests nationwide. see *BUSINESS AND ECONOMICS — Trade And Industrial Directories*

331.1 629.1   US   ISSN 0749-2960
HIGH TECHNOLOGY CAREERS. 1984. bi-m. $29. High Technology Careers, 4701 Patrick Henry Dr., Ste. 1901, Santa Clara, CA 95054. TEL 408-970-8800. Ed. Greg Bahue. adv.; bk.rev.; tr.lit.; circ. 350,000. (tabloid format; reprint service avail.)
    Description: For the technical community.

371.42 374   AT
HINTS FOR JOB HUNTERS. 1980. a. Monash University, Careers & Appointments Service, Wellington Rd., Clayton, Vic. 3168, Australia. TEL 03- 565 4000. Ed. Linel Parrott.
    Description: Provides tips on planning a job seeking strategy, resume writing and interviews.

HISPANIC ENGINEER. see *ENGINEERING*

OCCUPATIONS AND CAREERS

331.1 917.306   US   ISSN 0892-1369
HD8081
HISPANIC TIMES MAGAZINE; the nation's only career and business magazine for Hispanics, American Indians and Native Americans. (Text in English, Spanish) 1978. 5/yr. $30. Hispanic Times Enterprises, Box 579, Winchester, CA 92596. FAX 818-579-3572. Ed. Gloria J. Davis. adv.; bk.rev.; circ. 35,000. (back issues avail.) **Indexed:** Chic.Per.Ind.

658   FR   ISSN 0752-4676
I C A EXECUTIVE SEARCH NEWSLETTER. (Text in various European languages) 1974. 40/yr. $185. International Classified Advertising (I C A), 3 rue d'Hauteville, 75010 Paris, France. FAX 47-70-08-77. (Dist. in U.S. by: I C A, Inc., 575 Madison Ave., New York, NY 10022) Ed. Michel Manley. adv.; bk.rev.; circ. 20,000.
   Formerly: International Executive Search Newsletter (ISSN 0220-6862)
   Description: Databank and research service for those seeking job positions as well as those seeking employees.

I E E E CAREERS CONFERENCE. CONFERENCE RECORD. see ENGINEERING — Electrical Engineering

371.42   US   ISSN 0279-0491
LC1041
ILLINOIS VOCATIONAL EDUCATION JOURNAL. vol.37, 1981. 3/yr. free. State Board of Education, 100 N. First St., Springfield, IL 62777. TEL 217-782-7084. Ed. Michael Whalen. circ. 4,000(controlled). **Indexed:** C.I.J.E.
   Former titles: Illinois Career Education Journal; Illinois Vocational Progress.

371.42 760 686   US   ISSN 8756-6664
IMAGE WORLD; careers in graphic communications. 1986. bi-m. (except during summer) $10 to industry; students and teachers free. Technical and Education Center of the Graphic Arts, c/o Rochester Institute of Technology, 50 W. Main St., Rochester, NY 14614. TEL 716-475-2549. FAX 716-475-5571. Ed. Sandy Richolson. circ. 150,000. (back issues avail.)
   Description: Information on career opportunities in graphic communications for high school and college students.

371.42   US
INDEPENDENT SCHOLAR;* a newsletter for independent scholars and their organizations. 1987. q. $10 (foreign $12). Natoinal Coalition of Independent Scholars, 2312 Blake St., Berkeley, CA 94704-2802. TEL 415-549-1922. Ed. Georgia S. Wright. adv.; bk.rev.; circ. 350. (looseleaf format; back issues avail.)
   Description: Lists grants, institutional resources, profiles (individual, institutional), and covers news.

INDIAN JOURNAL OF TRAINING & DEVELOPMENT. see BUSINESS AND ECONOMICS — Personnel Management

INFORMATIONEN ZUM ARBEITSLOSENRECHT UND SOZIALHILFERECHT. see SOCIAL SERVICES AND WELFARE

371.42   GW
INFORMATIONEN ZUR BERUFLICHEN BILDUNG. 1970. m. DM.38.04. Deutscher Instituts Verlag GmbH, Gustav-Heinemann-Ufer 84-88, Postfach 510670, 5000 Cologne 51, Germany. TELEX 8882768-IWKD. Ed. Winfried Schlaffke.

371.42   GW   ISSN 0721-1295
INFORMATIONSDIENST ZUR AUSLAENDERARBEIT. 1979. q. DM.40. Institut fuer Sozialarbeit und Sozialpaedagogik (ISS), Am Stockborn 5-7, 6000 Frankfurt a.M. 50, Germany. TEL 069-582025. FAX 069-582029. Ed. Gerd Stuwe. adv.; bk.rev.; film rev.; abstr.; bibl.; circ. 2,500. (back issues avail.)

331.1   FR
INNOVATION AND EMPLOYMENT. 4/yr. 170 F. (25 ECU). Organization for Economic Cooperation and Development, 2 rue Andre Pascal, 75775 Paris Cedex 16, France. FAX 45-24-82-00. (U.S. subscr. to: O.E.C.D. Publications and Information Center, 2001 L St., N.W., Ste. 700, Washington, DC 20036-4095. TEL 202-785-6323) (Co-sponsor: Commission of the European Communities) (also avail. in microfiche)

371.42   CE
INSTITUTE OF BANKERS OF SRI LANKA. JOURNAL. 1981. s-a. Rs.50 (foreign Rs.100). Institute of Bankers of Sri Lanka, No. 5, Milepost Avenue, Colombo 3, Sri Lanka. TEL 573625. Ed. H.B. Illankone. adv.; circ. 5,000.
   Formerly (until 1981): Bankers' Training Institute (Sri Lanka). Bulletin.

371.42   IE   ISSN 0332-3641
INSTITUTE OF GUIDANCE COUNSELLORS. JOURNAL. vol.4, 1981. 2/yr. £7. Institute of Guidance Counsellors, c/o H. O'Brien, Curriculum Development Unit, Trinity College, Dublin, Ireland. Ed. Finian Buckley. adv.; bk.rev.; cum.index vols.1-14; circ. 750.
   —BLDSC shelfmark: 4776.101000.
   Formerly: Career Guidance and Counselling.
   Description: The chief aim of the journal is to disseminate both practical and theoretical ideas among Guidance Counselors and others involved in education, careers and counselling.

371.42 368 332   US
INSURANCE AND FINANCIAL SERVICES CAREERS. 1960. a. Wallace Witmer Company, 1509 Madison Ave., Memphis, TN 38104. TEL 901-276-5424. adv.; circ. 50,650.
   Description: Contains career guidance for college students interested in the insurance and financial services industry.

INTERNATIONAL ASSOCIATION FOR EDUCATIONAL AND VOCATIONAL INFORMATION. STUDIES AND REPORTS. see EDUCATION

INTERNATIONAL EDUCATOR. see EDUCATION — International Education Programs

371.42 331.1   US   ISSN 0748-8890
INTERNATIONAL EMPLOYMENT HOTLINE. 1980. m. $36. Cantrell Corporation, Box 3030, Oakton, VA 22124. TEL 703-620-1972. Ed. Will Cantrell. adv.; circ. 5,000. (looseleaf format)
   Description: Reports on developments in the international job market, covering a wide range of overseas job openings for US citizens.

331.1   US   ISSN 0890-2305
INTERNATIONAL EMPLOYMENT OPPORTUNITIES DIGEST. 1970. q. $15. International Publications (Subsidiary of: Mid-America Marketing, Inc.), Box 5730, Pompano Beach, FL 33074-5730. Ed. M.W. Vail. (back issues avail.)
   Description: Lists a wide variety of specific overseas employment opportunities with contact name and address.

658.3   UK   ISSN 0955-6214
HF5549.5.C35
INTERNATIONAL JOURNAL OF CAREER MANAGEMENT. 4/yr. $499.94. M C B University Press Ltd., 62 Toller Ln., Bradford, W. Yorks BD8 9BY, England. TEL 0274-499821. FAX 0274-547143. TELEX 51317-MCBUNI-G. (N. American subscr. to: M C B University Press Limited, Box 1943, Birmingham, AL 35202) Ed. Rod Davies.
   —BLDSC shelfmark: 4542.161200.
   Description: Covers theory and practice of all aspects of career management.

658.3   US   ISSN 0272-5460
L901
INTERNSHIPS; 38,000 on-the-job training opportunities for all types of careers. 1981. a. $24.95. Peterson's Guides, Inc., 202 Carnegie Center, Box 2123, Princeton, NJ 08543-2123. TEL 609-243-9111. FAX 609-243-9150. Ed. Brian Rushing.
   —BLDSC shelfmark: 4557.251200.
   Description: Current information on 38,000 training opportunities in fields ranging from business to science to theater.

371.42 362.7   US
J A C S VOLUNTEER. 1968. q. free. Joint Action in Community Services, Inc., 5225 Wisconsin Ave. N.W., Ste. 404, Washington, DC 20015. TEL 202-537-0996. FAX 202-363-0239. Ed. Shirley A. Gravely-Currie. circ. 6,000.
   Description: Directed to volunteers across the U.S. providing help for ex-Job Corps (disadvantaged youth 16-21 yrs.) students.

J C A H P O OUTLOOK. (Joint Commission on Allied Health Personnel in Ophthalmology) see MEDICAL SCIENCES — Ophthalmology And Optometry

JAPANESE NURSING ASSOCIATION RESEARCH REPORT. see MEDICAL SCIENCES — Nurses And Nursing

371.42   US   ISSN 0278-5706
HF5382.75.U6
JOB CATALOG;* where to find that creative job in Washington DC and Baltimore. 1979. a. $9.50. Mail Order USA, 1255 Wisconsin Ave, N.W., No. 6, Washington, DC 20007. Ed. Dorothy O'Callaghan. circ. 5,000.

JOB EXPRESS. see COMPUTERS

331.1   US
JOB EXPRESS REGISTRY. 1984. m. $33 to non-members; members $18 for 3 mos. American Dance Guild, 31 W. 21st St., 3rd Fl., New York, NY 10010. TEL 212-627-3790.
   Description: Lists positions for teachers in colleges, universities, public schools, administrations.

658.3   US
JOB FINDER; a checklist of openings for administrative and government research employment in the West. 1957. m. $20. Western Government Research Association, c/o Graduate Center for Public Policy and Administration, California State University at Long Beach, 1250 Bellflower Blvd., Long Beach, CA 90840. TEL 310-985-5419. FAX 310-985-1624. Ed. Mel D. Powell. circ. 2,000. (back issues avail.)

331.1   US
JOB MARKET. 1987. s-a. $14. American Vocational Association, 1410 King St., Alexandria, VA 22314. TEL 703-683-3111. FAX 703-683-7424. Ed. Jerry Rehm. circ. 40,000.
   Description: Guide to emerging careers for classroom use in high schools.

331 330   US
JOB OPENINGS FOR ECONOMISTS. 1974. bi-m. $25 to non-members and institutions; members $15. American Economic Association, 2014 Broadway, Ste. 305, Nashville, TN 37203. TEL 615-322-2595. tr.lit.
   Description: Lists job vacancies.

331.128   US
JOB PROSPECTOR: NEW ENGLAND EDITION. 1978. m. Prospector Research Services, Inc., 751 Main St., Waltham, MA 02154. TEL 617-899-1271.
   Description: Contains job opportunities in New England.

331.1   US
JOB SEEKER. 1988. fortn. $60 to individuals; institutions $84. Rt. 2, Box 16, Warrens, WI 54666. FAX 608-378-4290. Ed. Becky Potter.

331.1   US
JOB SERVICE OPENINGS AND STARTING WAGES REPORTS. m. free. Department of Employment and Training Services, Labor Market Information, 10 Senate Ave., Rm. 101, Indianapolis, IN 46204. TEL 317-232-8536. FAX 317-232-6950.
   Description: Lists occupations in local offices by occupational category.

331.1   US
JOBMART. 22/yr. membership only. American Planning Association, 1313 E. 60th St., Chicago, IL 60637. TEL 312-955-9100. FAX 312-955-8312. (And: 1776 Massachusetts Ave., N.W., Washington, DC 20036. TEL 202-872-0611) adv. (reprint service avail. from UMI)

331.1 100   US
JOBS FOR PHILOSOPHERS. 1973. 5/yr. $30 to individuals; free to members. American Philosophical Association, University of Delaware, Newark, DE 19716. TEL 302-451-1112. FAX 302-451-8690. circ. 4,750.

371.42   US
▼**JOBS FROM RECYCLABLES POSSIBILITY NEWSLETTER**. 1991. a. $4.50. Sought After Publications, Box 570213, Houston, TX 77257. (Dist. by: Prosperity and Profits Unlimited, Box 570213, Houston, TX 77257-0213) Ed. A.C. Doyle. circ. 2,000. (tabloid format)

331.1   US   ISSN 1053-654X
▼**JOBS IN RECESSIONARY TIMES POSSIBILITY NEWSLETTER**. 1990. a. $7. Continnuus, c/o Prosperity & Profits Unlimited, Box 570213, Houston, TX 77257. TEL 713-867-3438. Ed. A.C. Doyle. circ. 1,500. (looseleaf format)

OCCUPATIONS AND CAREERS

371.42   UK
JOBS IN THE 'GAP' YEAR. 1969. biennial, 9th ed., 1989. £2. Independent Schools Careers Organisation, 12a-18a Princess Way, Camberley, Surrey GU15 3SP, England. Ed. Anna Alston. circ. 4,000.
   Formerly: Temporary Occupations and Employment (ISSN 0264-7761)

371.42   US   ISSN 0894-8453
LC1037.5
JOURNAL OF CAREER DEVELOPMENT. 1972. q. $115 (foreign $135). Human Sciences Press, Inc. (Subsidiary of: Plenum Publishing Corp.), 233 Spring St., New York, NY 10013-1578. TEL 212-620-8000. FAX 212-463-0742. Ed. Norman C. Gysbers. adv.; bk.rev.; bibl.; charts; illus.; stat.; index. (also avail. in microform from UMI; reprint service avail. from UMI) **Indexed:** Bus.Educ.Ind., C.I.J.E., Coll.Stud.Pers.Abstr., Cont.Pg.Educ., Psychol.Abstr., Soc.Work Res.& Abstr. —BLDSC shelfmark: 4954.876000.
   Formerly (until 1984): Journal of Career Education (ISSN 0164-2502)
   Description: Covers career education, adult career development, career development of special needs population, and career and leisure, focusing on impact of theory and research on practice.
   Refereed Serial

371.42 378   US   ISSN 0884-5352
LB2343.5
JOURNAL OF CAREER PLANNING & EMPLOYMENT; the international magazine of placement and recruitment. 1940. 4/yr. $65 to non-members, includes Spotlight newsletter. College Placement Council, Inc., 62 Highland Ave., Bethlehem, PA 18017. TEL 215-868-1421. FAX 215-868-0208. Ed. Mimi Collins. adv.; bk.rev.; charts; illus.; index; circ. 4,200. (also avail. in microform from UMI; reprint service avail. from UMI) **Indexed:** Account.Ind. (1974-), C.I.J.E., Educ.Ind., High.Educ.Curr.Aware.Bull., P.A.I.S., Pers.Lit., Pers.Manage.Abstr., Work Rel.Abstr.
—BLDSC shelfmark: 4954.878500.
   Formerly: Journal of College Placement (ISSN 0021-9770)

371.4   US   ISSN 0748-9633
HF5381.A1
JOURNAL OF COUNSELING & DEVELOPMENT. 1922. bi-m. $40. American Association for Counseling and Development, 5999 Stevenson Ave., Alexandria, VA 22304. TEL 703-823-9800. FAX 703-823-0252. Ed. Charles D. Claiborn. adv.; index; circ. 58,000. (also avail. in microform from UMI; reprint service avail. from UMI,SCH) **Indexed:** Acad.Ind., ASSIA, Bk.Rev.Ind. (1965-1984, 1986-1987), C.I.J.E., Child.Bk.Rev.Ind. (1965-1984, 1986-1987), Coll.Stud.Pers.Abstr., Curr.Cont., Educ.Admin.Abstr., Educ.Ind., Except.Child.Educ.Abstr., Hlth.Ind., Human Resour.Abstr., Mag.Ind., Past.Care & Couns.Abstr., Psychol.Abstr., Psycscan, Rehabil.Lit., Risk Abstr., Sage Fam.Stud.Abstr., Sage Pub.Admin.Abstr., Soc.Work Res.& Abstr., Sp.Ed.Needs Abstr., SSCI, Work Rel.Abstr.
—BLDSC shelfmark: 4965.445000.
   Formerly (until 1984): Personnel and Guidance Journal (ISSN 0031-5737)
   Description: Publishes archival materials and contains authoritative in-depth articles on professional and scientific issues, research of interest to practitioners, and new techniques or practices.

371.42   US   ISSN 0022-0787
HF5382.5.U5   CODEN: JECODE
JOURNAL OF EMPLOYMENT COUNSELING. 1965. 4/yr. $11. (National Employment Counselors Association) American Association for Counseling and Development, 5999 Stevenson Ave., Alexandria, VA 22304. TEL 703-823-9800. FAX 703-823-0252. Ed. Robert Drummond. adv.; bk.rev.; index; circ. 2,700. (also avail. in microform from UMI; reprint service avail. from UMI) **Indexed:** ASSIA, BPIA, C.I.J.E., Curr.Cont., Int.Lab.Doc., Psychol.Abstr., Sage Fam.Stud.Abstr., Soc.Work Res.& Abstr., SSCI.
—BLDSC shelfmark: 4977.700000.
   Description: Focuses on developing trends in organizational behavior and state-of-the-art personnel practices.

JOURNAL OF STUDIES IN TECHNICAL CAREERS. see *EDUCATION — Higher Education*

371   US
JOURNALISM CAREER GUIDE FOR MINORITIES. 1985. a. free. Dow Jones Newspaper Fund, Inc., Box 300, Princeton, NJ 08543-0300. TEL 609-452-2820. FAX 609-520-5804.
   Description: Offers information on financial aid and programs specifically geared to minorities for the study of print journalism as well as information on journalism careers.

658.3   US   ISSN 0891-2572
KENNEDY'S CAREER STRATEGIST; a monthly guide to career planning success and job satisfaction. 1986. m. $59. Career Strategies, 1153 Wilmette Ave., Wilmette, IL 60091. TEL 708-251-1661. FAX 708-251-5191. Ed. Marilyn Moats Kennedy. index; circ. 2,000. (back issues avail.)
   Description: Covers mid-level management on careers, office politics, job hunting for mid-career people in all fields.

KEY - A GUIDE TO COLLEGE AND CAREERS. see *EDUCATION — Guides To Schools And Colleges*

331.1   SW   ISSN 0024-0230
LEDIGA PLATSER. 1961. w. SEK 84. Jiells Bokfoerlag, PO Box 1527, 701 15 Oerebro, Sweden. Ed. John H. Larsson. adv.; bk.rev.; circ. 12,500.

371.42   GW   ISSN 0172-1658
LITERATURINFORMATIONEN ZUR BERUFLICHEN BILDUNG. 1974. 6/yr. DM.100. Bundesinstitut fuer Berufsbildung, Fehrbellinerplatz 3, 1000 Berlin 31, Germany. TEL 8683230. bk.rev. (back issues avail.)

371.42   US
LOOKING FOR EMPLOYMENT IN FOREIGN COUNTRIES. 1970. irreg., 8th ed., 1990. $16.50. World Trade Academy Press, Inc., 50 East 42nd St., New York, NY 10017. TEL 212-697-4999. Ed. Sara Gonzalez. circ. 10,000.

331.1 410   US
M L A JOB INFORMATION LISTS. (In 2 editions: English Edition; Foreign Language Edition) 1971. q. $35. Modern Language Association of America, 10 Astor Pl., New York, NY 10003. TEL 212-614-6321. FAX 212-477-9863. Ed. Roy Chustek. circ. 6,000. (reprint service avail. from UMI)
   Description: Lists available college teaching positions in English, comparative literature, linguistics and foreign languages.

MAGAZINE AFFAIRES PLUS. see *BUSINESS AND ECONOMICS — Investments*

MAGAZINE AVENIR; pour mieux gerer et former vos ressources humaines. see *EDUCATION — Adult Education*

331.1   BA
MIDDLE AND FAR EAST EXPATRIATE. (Text in English) 1983. m. 9500 din.($25) Al Hilal Publishing & Marketing Group, P.O. Box 224, Manama, Bahrain. TEL 293131. FAX 234175. TELEX 8981 HILAL BN. (In Singapore: Al Hilal Publishing (Far East) Pte Ltd, 50 Jalan Sultan, 20-06 Jalan Sultan Centre, Singapore 0719. TEL 2939233) Ed. John Rowles. adv.; circ. 20,334. (back issues avail.)
   Description: Covers topics of interest to expatriates living and working in the Middle East and Far East.

054.1   FR   ISSN 0026-3591
MIGRATIONS; revue des possibilites d'emploi-outre-mer, etranger. 1963. m. 5 F. per issue. Editions Lafayette, 3 rue de Montyon, 75429 Paris 9, France. Dir. Yves Andre. adv.; circ. 45,000. **Indexed:** CERDIC.
   Formerly: France Vie.

371.42   US
▼**MINORITY EMPLOYMENT JOURNAL.** 1990. bi-m. $2 per no. C.L. Lovick and Associates, 1341 Ocean Ave., Ste. 228, Santa Monica, CA 90401. TEL 213-338-8444. FAX 213-338-0901. adv.; circ. 25,000.
   Description: Provides information on career opportunities in several areas for minority professionals, executives, community leaders, scholars and students.

371.42 330   US
MINORITY M B A. 1988. a. $8.95. Peterson's - C O G Publishing, 16030 Ventura Blvd., Ste. 560, Encino, CA 91436. TEL 818-789-5293. FAX 818-789-5488. adv.; bk.rev.; circ. 13,381 (controlled).
   Description: Provides career and job placement information for African-American, Hispanic, Asian-American and women graduate students enrolled in business programs nationwide.

371.42 659.152   US
▼**MODEL CALL.** 1991. q. $14. Richard Poirier Model and Talent Agency, 3575 Cahuenga Blvd. W., No. 254, Los Angeles, CA 90068-1341. TEL 213-969-9990. FAX 213-850-3382. adv.; circ. 20,000.
   Description: Covers the business activities of professional models and talents who work in advertising print media.

MODEL NEWS. see *CLOTHING TRADE — Fashions*

371.42   SA   ISSN 0027-5425
MY CAREER/MY LOOPBAAN; yearly on vocational information/jaarlikse publikasie oor beroepsinligting. 1950. a. free. Department of Manpower - Departement van Mannekrag, Private Bag X117, Pretoria 0001, South Africa. Ed. E. Jeffery. abstr.; bibl.; charts; index, cum.index; circ. 25,000. **Indexed:** Ind.S.A.Per.
   Description: Intended for juvenile workseekers in need of vocational guidance and placement.

N S B E BRIDGE. (National Society of Black Engineers) see *ENGINEERING*

331.1 301.16   US
N Y - A B C EMPLOYMENT LETTER. 1972. m. $30. N Y - A B C, ISO, 160 Water St., New York, NY 10038. TEL 212-487-4796. Ed. Bob Adler. circ. 2,000. (back issues avail.)

331.1   US   ISSN 0744-7140
NATIONAL AD SEARCH. 1968. 50/yr. $235. National Ad Search, Inc., Box 2083, Milwaukee, WI 53201. TEL 414-351-1398. Ed. Doris M. Morey. (tabloid format)
   Former titles: Ad Search: The Weekly National Want Ad Digest; Ad Search: The National Want Ad Newspaper.
   Description: Lists over 2,000 want ads, categorized into 55 areas of expertise, compiled from 75 major newspapers throughout the U.S.

371.42   US
NATIONAL BUSINESS EMPLOYMENT WEEKLY. 1980. w. $52 for 10 weeks. Dow Jones & Co., Inc. (Princeton), Box 300, Princeton, NJ 08543-0300. TEL 609-520-4305. Ed. Tony Lee. adv.; circ. 35,000. (tabloid format; back issues avail.)
   Description: Aimed at Wall Street Journal readers. Provides career guidance and job-hunting advice.

NATIONAL DIRECTORY OF INTERNSHIPS, RESIDENCIES & REGISTRARSHIPS. see *BUSINESS AND ECONOMICS — Trade And Industrial Directories*

NATIONAL EMPLOYMENT LISTING SERVICE (N E L S) BULLETIN. see *CRIMINOLOGY AND LAW ENFORCEMENT*

NATIONAL PARALEGAL EMPLOYMENT & SALARY SURVEY. see *LAW*

331.1   US   ISSN 0896-3002
HD4904.25
NATIONAL REPORT ON WORK & FAMILY. 1987. fortn. $475 (foreign $497). Buraff Publications (Subsidiary of: Millin Publications, Inc.), 1350 Connecticut Ave. N.W., Ste. 1000, Washington, DC 20036. TEL 202-862-0992. FAX 202-862-0999. Ed. Richard Hagan. (back issues avail.)
   ●Also available online. Vendor(s): Human Resources Information Network.
   Description: Covers work and family issues, such as parental leave, elder care, care for sick children, and flexible work time.

NEW SETTLER'S GUIDE FOR WASHINGTON, D.C. AND COMMUNITIES IN NEARBY MARYLAND AND VIRGINIA. see *TRAVEL AND TOURISM*

NEWS ON WOMEN IN GOVERNMENT. see *WOMEN'S INTERESTS*

OCCUPATIONS AND CAREERS

371.42　　　　　UK　ISSN 0307-8477
NEWSCHECK; with careers service bulletin. 1975. m. free. Careers and Occupational Information Centre, Virginia House, Foulsham, Dereham, Norfolk NR20 5RX, England. Ed. Janet Widmer. adv.; bk.rev.; circ. 20,000. **Indexed:** Build.Manage.Abstr., High.Educ.Curr.Aware.Bull.
—BLDSC shelfmark: 6106.245703.

331.1 378　　　　US
NORTHWESTERN LINDQUIST ENDICOTT REPORT; salary schedules and employment trends on the employment of college and university graduates in business and industry. 1946. a. $35. Northwestern University, Placement Center, Evanston, IL 60208. TEL 708-491-3707. circ. 18,000. **Indexed:** ERIC, PROMT, SRI.
Former titles: Northwestern Endicott Lindquist Report; Northwestern Endicott Report; Endicott Report.
Description: Investigates various employment practices and policies.

371.4 340　　　　US
NOW HIRING; government jobs for lawyers. 1952. a. $14.95 to non-members; members $9.95. American Bar Association, Law Student Division, 750 N. Lake Shore Dr., Chicago, IL 60611. TEL 312-988-5000.
Former titles: Washington Want Ads & Federal Government Legal Career Opportunities (ISSN 0065-7476)

371.42　　　　　FR
O N I S E P COMMUNIQUE. 20/yr. 100 F. (foreign 125 F.)(effective Oct. 1991). Office National d'Information sur les Enseignements et les Professions (ONISEP), 46-52 rue Albert, 75013 Paris, France. TEL 40-77-60-00, FAX 45-86-60-85. TELEX 202 962 F ONISEP N.

OCCUPATIONAL PROGRAMS IN CALIFORNIA PUBLIC COMMUNITY COLLEGES. see *EDUCATION — Guides To Schools And Colleges*

OFFICE SKILLS WORKSHOP. see *BUSINESS AND ECONOMICS — Office Equipment And Services*

331.1　　　　　US
OFFICIAL GUIDE TO AIRLINE CAREERS. 1977. irreg., latest 1985. $9.95. International Publishing Company of America, 665 La Villa Dr., Miami Springs, FL 33166. TEL 305-887-1700. FAX 305-885-1923. Ed. Alex Morton. adv.; circ. 25,000.

371.42 387.7　　　　US
OFFICIAL GUIDE TO FLIGHT ATTENDANTS CAREERS. 1968. biennial. $9.95. International Publishing Company of America, 665 La Villa Dr., Miami Springs, FL 33166. TEL 305-887-1700. FAX 305-885-1923. Ed. Alexander C. Morton. circ. 25,000.
Former titles: Airline Guide to Stewardess and Stewards Career (ISSN 0065-4914); Annual Guide to Stewardess Career.

331.1　　　　　US
OFFICIAL GUIDE TO FOOD SERVICE AND HOSPITALITY MANAGEMENT CAREERS. 1982. irreg; latest 2nd ed. $9.95. International Publishing Company of America, 665 La Villa Dr., Miami Springs, FL 33166. TEL 305-887-1700. FAX 305-885-1923. Ed. Alexander C. Morton. circ. 25,000.

331.1 387.7　　　　US
OFFICIAL GUIDE TO TRAVEL AGENT & TRAVEL CAREERS. 1980. irreg., latest 1986. $9.95. International Publishing Company of America, 665 La Villa Dr., Miami Springs, FL 33166. TEL 305-887-1700. Ed. Alexander C. Morton. illus.; circ. 25,000.

331.1　　　　　AT
ON STARTING WORK. irreg. Monash University, Careers and Appointments Service, Wellington Road, Clayton, Vic. 3168, Australia. TEL 03 565 4007. Ed. Lionel Parrot.
Description: Manual for students making the transition from tertiary studies to the workforce.

OPERATION ENTERPRISE NEWS. see *BUSINESS AND ECONOMICS — Management*

OPPORTUNITIES IN SCIENCE AND ENGINEERING. see *ENGINEERING*

371.42 658.3　　　　US　ISSN 0734-1776
ORGANIZE YOUR LUCK!. 1976. irreg. $18. Behavioral Images, Inc., Carrage House, Ste. A4, 901 E. Grove St., Bloomington, IL 61701. TEL 309-829-3931. FAX 309-829-9677. Ed. Stephen C. Johnson. adv.; bk.rev.; circ. 3,000. (also avail. in talking book)
Description: Assists people in finding, getting and keeping their jobs through self-marketing methods.

371.42　　　　　CN　ISSN 0833-0530
L'ORIENTATION.* (Text in English, French) 1964. 4/yr. Can.$20 to individuals; institutions Can.$40. Corporation Professionnelle des Conseillers d'Orientation du Quebec, 1100 Avenue Beuamont, Mont-Royal, Que. H3P 3E5, Canada. TEL 514-337-3366. Ed. Lucille Bilodeau-Morcency. adv.; bk.rev.; charts; cum.index; circ. 1,500. **Indexed:** C.I.J.E., Pt.de Rep. (1983-).
Formerly (until 1987): Orientation Professionnelle - Vocational Guidance (ISSN 0030-5413)

371.42　　　　　UK
OXBRIDGE CAREERS HANDBOOK. 1979. a. £7.95. Oxford University Students Union, New Barnet House, Little Clarendon St., Oxford OX1 2HU, England. FAX 0865-270778. Ed. Jan West. adv.; circ. 20,000.

371.42 658　　　　US
▼**P B L BUSINESS LEADER.** 1991. 3/yr. $9. Future Business Leaders of America, Phi Beta Lambda, 1908 Association Dr., Reston, VA 22091. TEL 703-860-3334. Ed. Angela Angerosa. adv.; circ. 19,735.

331　　　　　UN
P R E A L C NEWSLETTER. (Text and summaries in English and Spanish) 1985. irreg. (approx. 3/yr.). free. Programa Regional del Empleo para America Latina y el Carige, Casilla 19034, Correo 19, Santiago, Chile. (Affiliate: International Labour Office) circ. 1,300. (looseleaf format)

333.78 371.42
PARK AND RECREATION OPPORTUNITIES JOB BULLETIN. s-m. $30 to members only. National Recreation and Park Association, 3101 Park Center Dr., Alexandria, VA 22302. TEL 703-820-4940. FAX 703-671-6772.
Description: Provides specific position vacancy listings received by NRPA.

658.3　　　　　US
PART-TIME PROFESSIONAL. 1981. m. $45. Association of Part-Time Professionals, Crescent Plaza, Ste. 216, 7700 Leesburg Pike, Falls Church, VA 22043. TEL 703-734-7975. circ. 1,500. (back issues avail.)
Formerly: Association of Part-Time Professionals. National Newsletter (ISSN 0739-2931)
Description: Trends in part-time employment, employer policies, employee profiles and job search information.

331.1　　　　　US　ISSN 0161-2425
PERSONNEL CONSULTANT. 1968. bi-m. $60. National Association of Personnel Consultants, 3133 Mt. Vernon Ave., Alexandria, VA 22305. TEL 703-684-0180. FAX 703-684-0071. adv.; bk.rev.; circ. 2,500 (controlled). (tabloid format)
Formerly: Placement Age.

331.1　　　　　US　ISSN 1048-3411
HF5382.5.U5
PETERSON'S JOB OPPORTUNITIES FOR BUSINESS AND LIBERAL ARTS GRADUATES (YEAR). 1984. a. $20.95. Peterson's Guides, Inc., 202 Carnegie Center, Box 2123, Princeton, NJ 08543-2123. TEL 609-243-9111. FAX 609-243-9150. circ. 12,000.
Former titles: Peterson's Business and Management Jobs (Year) (ISSN 0894-9433); Peterson's Guide to Business and Management Jobs (Year) (ISSN 0749-5021)
Description: Presents information from hundreds of organizations that recruit employees in the areas of business and management.

331.1 620　　　　US　ISSN 1048-342X
PETERSON'S JOB OPPORTUNITIES FOR ENGINEERING, SCIENCE, AND COMPUTER GRADUATES (YEAR). 1980. a. $20.95. Peterson's Guides, Inc., 202 Carnegie Center, Box 2123, Princeton, NJ 08543-2123. TEL 609-243-9111. FAX 609-243-9150. circ. 23,000.
—BLDSC shelfmark: 6430.193500.
Former titles: Peterson's Engineering, Science, and Computer Jobs (Year) (ISSN 0894-9425); Peterson's Guide to Engineering, Science and Computer Jobs (Year) (ISSN 0730-0980); Peterson's Annual Guide to Careers and Employment for Engineers, Computer Scientists, and Physical Scientists (ISSN 0190-4213)
Description: Contains data from about 1,000 manufacturing, research, consulting and government organizations hiring technical graduates.

658.3　　　　　US
PROFESSIONAL PLACEMENT NEWSNOTES. 1962. q. free. Catholic Medical Mission Board, Inc., 10 W. 17th St., New York, NY 10011. TEL 212-242-7757. FAX 212-807-9161. Ed. Leo T. Tarpey. circ. 5,000.

371.42　　　　　US　ISSN 0190-1796
HD6278.U5　　　　CODEN: PWMIDY
PROFESSIONAL WOMEN AND MINORITIES; a manpower data resource service. (Former name of issuing body: Scientific Manpower Commission) 1975. a. $100. Commission on Professionals in Science & Technology, 1500 Massachusetts Ave., N.W., Ste. 813, Washington, DC 20005. TEL 202-223-6995. Eds. B. Vetter, E. Babco. bibl.; charts; index; circ. 1,000. (reprint service avail. from UMI) **Indexed:** SRI.

PROWOMAN. see *WOMEN'S INTERESTS*

371.42　　　　　US　ISSN 0742-9770
PRYOR REPORT. 1984. m. $69. Imagine, Inc., Box 1766, Clemson, SC 29633. FAX 803-654-7275. Ed. Paul G. Friedman. bk.rev.; circ. 27,000.

REAL TALK. see *CHILDREN AND YOUTH — For*

331.1　　　　　AT
REASONS FOR CHOOSING. irreg. Monash University, Careers and Appointments Service, Wellington Road, Clayton, Vic. 3168, Australia. TEL 03 565 4000. FAX 03-565-4007. Ed. Lionel Parrott.
Description: Guide for students preparing to choose an employer and suitable employment.

371.42 613　　　　US
RECRUITMENT DIRECTIONS. 1985. 10/yr. $125. National Association for Healthcare Recruitment, Box 5769, Akron, OH 44372. FAX 216-867-1630. Ed. Karen Hart. adv.; bk.rev.; circ. 1,900.

REHABILITATION COUNSELING BULLETIN. see *HANDICAPPED*

331.1　　　　　US
RESUMES FOR EMPLOYMENT IN THE U S AND OVERSEAS. irreg., 3rd ed., 1988. $16.50. World Trade Academy Press, Inc., 50 E. 42nd St., Ste. 509, New York, NY 10017-5480. TEL 212-697-4999.
Description: Contains general resumes and cover letter formats, with examples for jobs ranging from administrative assistant to video producer; sources of mailing lists to fit individual skills; requirements for work permits in foreign countries; tips for the interview and after.

REVIEW OF THE ECONOMY AND EMPLOYMENT. see *BUSINESS AND ECONOMICS — Economic Situation And Conditions*

371.4　　　　　CN
S C W E A NEWSLETTER. 1981. 3/yr. Can.$15. (Saskatchewan Career - Work Education Association) Saskatchewan Teachers' Federation, Box 1108, Saskatoon, Sask. S7K 3N3, Canada.

331.1　　　　　US　ISSN 0146-5015
Q149.U5
SALARIES OF SCIENTISTS, ENGINEERS AND TECHNICIANS; a summary of salary surveys. 1965. biennial. $75. Commission on Professionals in Science & Technology, 1500 Massachusetts Avenue, N.W., Ste. 831, Washington, DC 20005. TEL 202-223-6995. Ed. Eleanor L. Babco. charts; illus.; stat.; circ. 1,000. (reprint service avail. from UMI) **Indexed:** SRI.

OCCUPATIONS AND CAREERS — ABSTRACTING, BIBLIOGRAPHIES, STATISTICS

620 US ISSN 0036-8768
TA157
SCIENTIFIC, ENGINEERING, TECHNICAL MANPOWER COMMENTS. 1963. m. (10/yr.). $90. Commission on Professionals in Science & Technology, 1500 Massachusetts Ave. N.W., Ste. 831, Washington, DC 20005. TEL 202-223-6995. Ed. Betty M. Vetter. bk.rev.; abstr.; bibl.; charts; stat.; index; circ. 1,500. (also avail. in microfilm from UMI; reprint service avail. from UMI) **Indexed:** Pers.Lit.

371.42 AT ISSN 1035-1116
SMART START. 1967. a. Hobson's Press Australia Pty Ltd., 270 Pitt St., Sydney, N.S.W. 2000, Australia. Ed. C. Etteridge. adv.; circ. 10,000.
Former titles (until 1990): Jobs, Careers and Further Studies; Australian School Leavers Yearbook; (until 1981): Opportunities for School Leavers in Australia.

331.1 360 US
SOCIAL SERVICE JOBS. 1975. fortn. $118. Employment Listings for the Social Services, 10 Angelica Dr., Framingham, MA 01701. TEL 508-626-8644. FAX 508-626-8389. Ed. M.B. Sack. circ. 5,000.
Description: National listings of current job openings for social workers, psychologists and counselors.

331.1 US ISSN 0162-1068
SPOTLIGHT (BETHLEHEM); bi-weekly newsletter covering career planning, placement, and recruitment. 1977. fortn. $65 to non-members (includes Journal of Career Planning & Employment). College Placement Council, Inc., 62 Highland Ave., Bethlehem, PA 10817. TEL 215-868-1421. FAX 215-868-0208. Ed. Mimi Collins.

371.42 AU ISSN 0038-9951
START UND AUFSTIEG. 1961. m. S.30.($1.50) Oesterreichischer Gewerkschaftsbund, Berufsfoerderungsinstitut, Altmannsdorfer Strasse 154-56, A-1232 Vienna, Austria. Ed. Josef Eksl. adv.; bk.rev.; abstr.; bibl.; charts; illus.; stat.; circ. 12,000. (processed)

STREET ARTISTS' NEWSLETTER. see ART

650 150 US ISSN 0745-2489
CODEN: SUCSEY
SUCCESS (NEW YORK); the magazine for achievers. 1954. m. (10/yr.). $19.97 (effective 1993). Success Magazine Company, 230 Park Ave., 7th Fl., New York, NY 10169-0014. TEL 212-551-9500. FAX 212-922-2919. Ed. Scott DeGarmo. adv.; bk.rev.; charts; illus.; circ. 475,000. (back issues avail.)
—BLDSC shelfmark: 8503.719500.
Formerly: Success Unlimited (ISSN 0039-4424)

SUMMER EMPLOYMENT DIRECTORY OF THE UNITED STATES. see BUSINESS AND ECONOMICS — Trade And Industrial Directories

331.1 US
SUMMER JOBS FOR (YEAR); Opportunities in the Federal Government. a. U.S. Office of Personnel Management, 1900 E. St., N.W., Washington, DC 20415. TEL 202-606-0597.

SURVEY OF FINAL YEAR ACCOUNTING STUDENTS. see BUSINESS AND ECONOMICS — Accounting

790 US
T.G.I.F. CASTING NEWS. 1973. bi-w. $10. T.G.I.F. Enterprise, Box 1683, Hollywood, CA 90028. Ed. R. H. Smith, Jr. adv.; bk.rev.; film rev.; play rev.; circ. 20,000.

TEACHER SUPPLY - DEMAND. see EDUCATION — School Organization And Administration

TEACHERS' GUIDE TO OVERSEAS TEACHING; a complete and comprehensive guide of English-language schools and colleges overseas. see EDUCATION — International Education Programs

TEACHING OPPORTUNITIES OVERSEAS - BULLETIN. see EDUCATION

331.1 US
TECHNOLOGICAL MARKETPLACE: SUPPLY AND DEMAND FOR SCIENTISTS AND ENGINEERS. 1977. irreg. $25. Commission on Professionals in Science & Technology, 1500 Massachusetts Ave., N.W., Ste. 831, Washington, DC 20005. TEL 202-223-6995. Ed. Betty M. Vetter. charts.
Formerly: Supply and Demand for Scientists and Engineers (ISSN 0732-2631)

371.42 US
TOMORROW'S BUSINESS LEADER. 1969. q. membership. Future Business Leaders of America - Phi Beta Lambda, 2800 Shirlington Rd., Ste. 706, Arlington, VA 22206. Ed. Angela M. Angerosa. adv.; bk.rev.; circ. 220,000.

TRAINING TODAY. see EDUCATION

371.42 US
TRENDS (LIBERTY); you and your future. 1985. s-a. Target Marketing, Inc., 115 Blue Jay Dr., Box 217, Liberty, MO 64068. TEL 816-781-7557. FAX 816-792-3892. Ed. Lyle Kraft. adv.; circ. 500,000.
Description: Focuses on the opportunities available in career schools, two and four year colleges, and the military.

371.42 GW
UNI PERSPEKTIVEN FUER BERUF UND ARBEITSMARKT. 1977. 7/yr. DM.45.50. (Bundesanstalt fuer Arbeit) TransMedia Mannheim Projekt und Verlag GmbH, Kolpingstr. 18, 6800 Mannheim 1, Germany. TEL 0621-440000. FAX 0621-4400011. TELEX 462924-TRANS-D. (Subscr. to: DSB Zeitschriften-Abonnements-Verwaltungsgesellschaft mbH, Postfach 1163, 7107 Neckarsulm) Ed. Hans Wohlfarth. circ. 250,000. (back issues avail.)
Formerly (until 1991): Uni Berufswahl-Magazin.

371.42 AT
UNIVERSITY OF NEW SOUTH WALES. FACULTY HANDBOOKS: PROFESSIONAL STUDIES. a? Aus.$5. University of New South Wales, P.O. Box 1, Kensington, N.S.W. 2033, Australia. TEL 02-697-2840. FAX 02-662-2163.

VACATURE; nieuws- en advertentieblad voor het onderwijs. see EDUCATION

371.42 373.246 GW
VOCATIONAL TRAINING. 3/yr. (European Center for the Development of Vocational Training) C E D E F O P, P.O. Box 31 05 29, D-1000 Berlin 15, Germany. TEL (030)88-41-20. FAX 884-12-222. TELEX 184-163 EUCEN D.
Description: Specialized source of reference for all those involved in vocational training (decision making, program planning, and administration).

371.42 EI
VOCATIONAL TRAINING INFORMATION BULLETIN. (Text in English) 3/yr. $12. Office for Official Publications of the European Communities, L-2985 Luxembourg, Luxembourg. (Dist. in the U.S. by: Unipub, 4611-F Assembly Dr., Lanham, MD 20706-4391)

371.426 US
VOCATIONAL TRAINING NEWS; the independent weekly report on employment, training & vocational education. 1970. w. $280 (foreign $330). Capitol Publications Inc., 1101 King St., Ste. 444, Box 1455, Alexandria, VA 22314. TEL 703-683-4100. FAX 703-739-6517. Ed. David Harrison. charts; stat.; s-a. index. (looseleaf format)
●Also available online. Vendor(s): NewsNet.
Formed by the 1984 merger of: Manpower and Vocational Education Weekly (ISSN 0047-5785); (1975-1984): Education and Work (ISSN 0194-231X)
Description: Provides current reports on the federal Job Training Partnership Act and the Carl D. Perkins Vocational Education Act. Includes coverage of adult literacy, dropout prevention, and state education and training initiatives.

331.1 US
WASHINGTON. EMPLOYMENT SECURITY DEPARTMENT. ANNUAL DEMOGRAPHIC INFORMATION. 1976. a. free. Employment Security Department, LMEA Mailstop 6001, Box 9046, Olympia, WA 98507-9046. TEL 206-438-4800. FAX 206-438-4846. Ed. Jack Schillinger. circ. 400.

371.42 US
WASHINGTON COUNSELETTER. 1963. m. (Oct.-May). $37.44. Chronicle Guidance Publications, Inc., Box 1190, Moravia, NY 13118. TEL 315-497-0330. Ed. Samuel Kavruck. bk.rev.; film rev.; circ. 5,250. (looseleaf format)

WINDS OF CHANGE; American Indian education & opportunity. see ETHNIC INTERESTS

371.42 GW ISSN 0341-339X
WIRTSCHAFT UND BERUFS - ERZIEHUNG; Zeitschrift fuer Berufsbildung. 1949. m. DM.169.20. W. Bertelsmann Verlag KG, Auf dem Esch 4, Postfach 1020, 4800 Bielefeld 1, Germany. TEL 0521-9110126. FAX 0521-9110179. Ed. A. Kieslinger.
—BLDSC shelfmark: 9325.413000.

640 338 US
WORK-AT-HOME SOURCEBOOK; how to find "at-home" work that's right for you. 1987. a. $14.95. Live Oak Publications, Box 2193, Boulder, CO 80306. TEL 303-447-1087. Ed. Lynie Arden. illus.; index.
Description: Provides names, addresses and complete information on over 1,000 companies that have work-at-home programs.

331.1 610 US
WORK PROGRAMS; special interest section newsletter. (Consists of 7 sections: Administration and Management; Developmental Disabilities; Gerontology; Mental Health; Physical Disabilities; Sensory Integration; Work Programs) vol.3, no.4, 1989. q. $15. American Occupational Therapy Association, Inc., 1383 Piccard Dr., Box 1725, Rockville, MD 20850-0822. TEL 301-948-9626. FAX 301-948-5512.

WORK TIMES. see BUSINESS AND ECONOMICS — Economic Situation And Conditions

371.42 910.09 US ISSN 0895-3678
WORKAMPER NEWS; America's guide to working while camping. 1987. bi-m. $18. Workamper News, 201 Hiram Rd., Heber Springs, AR 72543. TEL 501-362-2637. Ed. Greg Robus. circ. 6,000.
Description: Provides information on seasonal & year-round employment opportunities in parks and resort areas.

375 SW ISSN 0513-6261
HF5382.5.S8
YRKE OCH FRAMTID. 1972. biennial. SEK 85. (Arbetsmarknadsstyrelsen) National Board of Education, 106 42 Stockholm, Sweden. illus.

354.689 ZA ISSN 0514-5457
ZAMBIA. EDUCATIONAL AND OCCUPATIONAL ASSESSMENT SERVICE. ANNUAL REPORT. a. 20 n. Government Printer, P.O. Box 30136, Lusaka, Zambia. stat.
Description: Annual report on the selection process of talent for Zambia's secondary schools.

ZENTRALER BEWERBERANZEIGER MARKT UND CHANCE. see SOCIAL SERVICES AND WELFARE

371 NP
100 LIVELIHOOD OCCUPATIONS. 1984. q. $50. Siveast Consultants, Inc., USA, c/o P.O. Box 1755, Kathmandu, Nepal. (UK subscr to: Dr. Ramasastry, c/o Overseas Customer Service, Midland Bank Blc., Poultry and Princes St., London EC2, England) Ed. C.V. Ramasastry. circ. 50 (controlled). (looseleaf format)
Formerly: Matrimonial, Overseas Jobs and Real Estate International Newsletter (ISSN 0742-8944)

OCCUPATIONS AND CAREERS — Abstracting, Bibliographies, Statistics

AMERICAN SALARIES AND WAGES SURVEY. see BUSINESS AND ECONOMICS — Abstracting, Bibliographies, Statistics

371.42 331.1 US ISSN 0276-0355
Z7164.V6
CHRONICLE CAREER INDEX. a. $17.81. Chronicle Guidance Publications, Inc., Box 1190, Moravia, NY 13118. TEL 315-497-0330. circ. 6,150.
Former titles: Chronicle Career Index Annual (ISSN 0190-4663); Career Index (ISSN 0576-7296)

OCEANOGRAPHY

331.1 317.2   MX
▼CLASIFICACION MEXICANA DE OCUPACIONES. 1990. irreg. Instituto Nacional de Estadistica, Geografia e Informatica, Secretariado de Programacion e Presupuesto, Av. Prol. Heroe de Nacozari 2301 S., Puerta 11, planta baja, Aguascalientes, 20290 Ags., Mexico.

331.1   CN
CLERICAL SALARY SURVEY & EMPLOYMENT PRACTICES (YEAR). a. Can.$350 to non-members; members Can.$300. Board of Trade of Metropolitan Toronto, P.O. Box 60, 1 First Canadian Place, Toronto, Ont. M5X 1C1, Canada. TEL 416-366-6811.

371.42   US   ISSN 0161-0562
Z7164.V6
CURRENT CAREER AND OCCUPATIONAL LITERATURE (YEAR). 1973. biennial. $35. H.W. Wilson Co., 950 University Ave., Bronx, NY 10452. TEL 800-367-6770. FAX 212-538-2716. TELEX 4990003HWILSON. Ed. Leonard H. Goodman.

331.1   CN
DATA PROCESSION SALARY SURVEY & EMPLOYMENT PRACTICES (YEAR). a. Can.$350 to non-members; members Can.$300. Board of Trade of Metropolitan Toronto, P.O. Box 60, 1 First Canadian Place, Toronto, Ont. M5X 1C1, Canada. TEL 416-366-6811.

331.1   HK
EMPLOYMENT AND VACANCIES STATISTICS IN: WHOLESALE, RETAIL AND IMPORT - EXPORT TRADES, RESTAURANTS AND HOTELS. (Text in English) a. price varies. (Census and Statistics Department) Government Publication Centre, G.P.O. Building, Ground Floor, Connaught Place, Hong Kong, Hong Kong. (Subscr. to: Director of Information Services, Information Services Dept., 1 Battery Path, G-F, Central, Hong Kong) Ed.Bd.

331   HK
EMPLOYMENT AND VACANCY STATISTICS IN: TRANSPORT, STORAGE AND COMMUNICATION FINANCING, INSURANCE, REAL ESTATE AND BUSINESS SERVICES, COMMUNITY, SOCIAL AND PERSONAL SERVICES. (Text in English) a. price varies. (Census and Statistics Department) Government Publication Centre, G.P.O. Building, Ground Floor, Connaught Place, Hong Kong, Hong Kong. (Subscr. to: Director of Information Services, Information Services Dept., 1 Battery Path, G-F, Central, Hong Kong) Ed.Bd.

331.1 690   HK
EMPLOYMENT, WAGES AND MATERIAL PRICES IN THE CONSTRUCTION INDUSTRY. (Text in English) q. HK.$12. (Census and Statistics Department) Government Publication Centre, G.P.O. Bldg., Ground Fl., Connaught Place, Hong Kong, Hong Kong. (Subscr. to: Director of Information Services, Information Services Dept., 1 Battery Path, G-F, Central, Hong Kong) Ed.Bd.

331.1   CN
EXECUTIVE COMPENSATION SURVEY (YEAR). a. Can.$450 to non-members; members Can.$370. Board of Trade of Metropolitan Toronto, P.O. Box 60, 1 First Canadian Place, Toronto, Ont. M5X 1C1, Canada. TEL 416-366-6811.

331.1 312   JA   ISSN 0911-8527
JAPAN. MINISTRY OF HEALTH AND WELFARE. STATISTICS AND INFORMATION DEPARTMENT. REPORT ON SURVEY OF OCCUPATIONAL STATISTICS ON VITAL EVENTS. (Text in English and Japanese) 1951. quinquennial. 6000 Yen. Ministry of Health and Welfare, Statistics and Information Department - Kosei-sho Daijin Kanbo Tokei Joho-bu, 7-3 Ichigaya-Honmura cho, Shinjuku-ku, Tokyo 162, Japan. TEL 03-260-3181. (Order from: Health & Welfare Statistics Association, 5-13-14 Roppongi, Minato-ku, Tokyo, Japan) Key Title: Shokugyo, Sangyobetsu Jinko Dotai Tokei.

331.1   CN
MIDDLE MANAGEMENT & PROFESSIONAL COMPENSATION SURVEY (YEAR). a. Can.$450 to non-members; members Can.$370. Board of Trade of Metropolitan Toronto, P.O. Box 60, 1 First Canadian Place, Toronto, Ont. M5X 1C1, Canada. TEL 416-366-6811.

MONASH UNIVERSITY. CAREERS & APPOINTMENTS SERVICE. SURVEY OF GRADUATE STARTING SALARIES AS OF 30 APRIL (YEAR). see *BUSINESS AND ECONOMICS — Abstracting, Bibliographies, Statistics*

NETHERLANDS. CENTRAAL BUREAU VOOR DE STATISTIEK. STATISTIEK VAN HET BEROEPSONDERWIJS: TECHNISCH EN NAUTISCH ONDERWIJS/STATISTICS OF VOCATIONAL TRAINING. see *EDUCATION — Abstracting, Bibliographies, Statistics*

NETHERLANDS. CENTRAAL BUREAU VOOR DE STATISTIEK. STATISTIEK VAN HET HOGER BEROEPSONDERWIJS: AGRARISCH ONDERWIJS. see *EDUCATION — Abstracting, Bibliographies, Statistics*

371.42 317   US
U.S. BUREAU OF LABOR STATISTICS. OCCUPATIONAL OUTLOOK HANDBOOK. 1946. biennial. price varies. U.S. Bureau of Labor Statistics, 441 G. St., N.W., Washington, DC 20212. TEL 202-272-5282. (Dist. by: Supt. of Documents, Washington, DC 20402) Ed. Michael Pilot.

OCEANOGRAPHY

see *Earth Sciences–Oceanography*

OFFICE EQUIPMENT AND SERVICES

see *Business and Economics–Office Equipment and Services*

OPHTHALMOLOGY AND OPTOMETRY

see *Medical Sciences–Ophthalmology and Optometry*

OPTICS

see *Physics–Optics*

ORGANIC CHEMISTRY

see *Chemistry–Organic Chemistry*

ORIENTAL STUDIES

see also *History–History of Asia; Linguistics*

950   II   ISSN 0304-6214
DS401
A I I S QUARTERLY NEWSLETTER. (Text in English) 1974. q. American Institute of Indian Studies, D-176 Defence Colony, New Delhi 110024, India. Ed. P.R. Mehendiratta. adv.; bk.rev.; bibl.; illus.; circ. 1,500.

500   GW   ISSN 0343-7051
ABHANDLUNGEN AUS DEM GEBIET DER AUSLANDSKUNDE. SERIES B & C. (Text in English and German) irreg., vol.74, 1975. price varies. (Universitaet Hamburg, Seminar fuer Kultur und Geschichte Indiens) Franz Steiner Verlag Wiesbaden GmbH, Birkenwaldstr. 44, Postfach 101526, 7000 Stuttgart 1, Germany. TEL 0711-2582-0. FAX 0711-2582290. TELEX 723636-DAZ-D. **Indexed:** Excerp.Med.

956   GW   ISSN 0173-1904
ABHANDLUNGEN DES DEUTSCHEN PALAESTINAVEREINS. 1969. irreg., vol.15, 1990. price varies. Verlag Otto Harrassowitz, Taunusstr. 14, Postfach 2929, 6200 Wiesbaden 1, Germany. TEL 0611-530-0. FAX 0611-530570. TELEX 4186135. Ed. Arnulf Kuschke.

950   GW   ISSN 0567-4980
ABHANDLUNGEN FUER DIE KUNDE DES MORGENLANDES. (Text in English, French, and German) irreg., vol.50, no.2, 1991. price varies. (Deutsche Morgenlaendische Gesellschaft) Franz Steiner Verlag Wiesbaden GmbH, Birkenwaldstr. 44, Postfach 101526, 7000 Stuttgart 1, Germany. TEL 0711-2582-0. FAX 0711-2582290. TELEX 723636-DAZD. Ed. Ewald Wagner. (also avail. in microfiche from BHP; reprint service avail. from KTO)

950   LE   ISSN 0002-3973
AS595.A6
AL-ABHATH. (Text in Arabic and English) 1948. a. $18. American University of Beirut, P.O. Box 1786, Beirut, Lebanon. Ed. Ramzi Baalbaki. bk.rev.; bibl.; circ. 1,000. **Indexed:** Hist.Abstr., Numis.Lit.

950   BE   ISSN 0065-0382
PJ3001
ABR-NAHRAIN. (Text in English, French, German) 1959. a. 1200 Fr. (University of Melbourne, Department of Classical and Near Eastern Studies, AT) Editions Peeters s.p.r.l., Bondgenotlenlaan 153, B-3000 Leuven, Belgium. TEL 016-235170. FAX 016-228500. Ed. T. Muraoka.
—BLDSC shelfmark: 0549.749300.

950   HU   ISSN 0001-6446
DS1
ACADEMIA SCIENTIARUM HUNGARICA. ACTA ORIENTALIA. (Text in English, French, German, Russian) 1950. 3 nos. per vol. $62. (Magyar Tudomanyos Akademia) Akademiai Kiado, Publishing House of the Hungarian Academy of Sciences, P.O. Box 24, H-1363 Budapest, Hungary. Ed. F. Tokei. adv.; bk.rev.; illus.; index. **Indexed:** M.L.A., Old Test.Abstr.

ACADEMIA SINICA. INSTITUTE OF ETHNOLOGY. BULLETIN. see *ANTHROPOLOGY*

950   JA   ISSN 0567-7254
DS12
ACTA ASIATICA. (Text in English) 1961. s-a. 4000 Yen. Institute of Eastern Culture - Toho Gakkai, 4-1, Nishi-Kanda 2-chome, Chiyoda-ku, Tokyo 101, Japan. FAX 03-3262-7227. Ed.Bd. bibl.; circ. 1,000. **Indexed:** M.L.A.
—BLDSC shelfmark: 0596.700000.

950   DK   ISSN 0001-6438
PJ1
ACTA ORIENTALIA. (Text in English, French or German) a. DKK 435. Munksgaard International Publishers Ltd., 35 Noerre Soegade, P.O Box 2148, DK-1016 Copenhagen K, Denmark. TEL 33-127030. FAX 33-129387. TELEX 19431-MUNKS-DK. Ed. Soeren Egerod. bk.rev.; circ. 500. (reprint service avail. from ISI,KTO) **Indexed:** Curr.Cont., M.L.A., Mid.East: Abstr.& Ind.
—BLDSC shelfmark: 0641.900000.

950 492   FR
ADYATAN. irreg., latest no.5. price varies. Institut National des Langues et Civilisations Orientales, Centre de Recherche et d'Etudes sur le Sous-Continent Indien Contemporain, 2 rue de Lille, 75343 Paris Cedex 07. TEL 49-26-42-74.
Description: Aims to inform and intensify interest in modern India.

950   GW   ISSN 0720-9061
AEGYPTEN UND ALTES TESTAMENT; Studien in Geschichte, Kultur und Religion Aegypten und des Alten Testaments. 1979. irreg., vol.20, 1990. price varies. Verlag Otto Harrassowitz, Taunusstr. 14, Postfach 2929, 6200 Wiesbaden 1, Germany. TEL 0611-530-0. FAX 0611-530570. TELEX 4186135. Ed. Manfred Goerg.

956   GW   ISSN 0568-0476
AEGYPTOLOGISCHE ABHANDLUNGEN. 1960. irreg., vol.52, 1991. price varies. Verlag Otto Harrassowitz, Taunusstr. 14, Postfach 2929, 6200 Wiesbaden 1, Germany. TEL 0611-530-0. FAX 0611-530570. TELEX 4186135. Ed. Wolfgang Helck.

950   GW   ISSN 0931-282X
AETAS MANJURICA. 1987. irreg., vol. 2, 1991. price varies. Verlag Otto Harrassowitz, Taunusstr. 14, Postfach 2929, 6200 Wiesbaden 1, Germany. TEL 0611-530-0. FAX 0611-530570. Ed.Bd.

ORIENTAL STUDIES

950   GW   ISSN 0170-3196
AETHIOPISTISCHE FORSCHUNGEN. (Text in English and German) irreg., vol.33, 1992. price varies. Franz Steiner Verlag Wiesbaden GmbH, Birkenwaldstr. 44, Postfach 101526, 7000 Stuttgart 1, Germany. TEL 0711-2582-0. FAX 0711-2582290. TELEX 723636-DAZD. Ed. Ernst Hammerschmidt.

AFRO-ASIA. see *HISTORY*

950   GW   ISSN 0568-4447
AKADEMIE DER WISSENSCHAFTEN UND DER LITERATUR, MAINZ. ORIENTALISCHE KOMMISSION. VEROEFFENTLICHUNGEN. (Text in French and German) irreg., vol.40, 1990. price varies. Franz Steiner Verlag Wiesbaden GmbH, Birkenwaldstr. 44, Postfach 101526, 7000 Stuttgart 1, Germany. TEL 0711-2582-0. FAX 0711-291450. TELEX 723636-DAZD.

956   GW   ISSN 0342-0329
AKTUELLER INFORMATIONSDIENST MODERNER ORIENT/ORIGINAL NEWS AND COMMENTS FROM MIDDLE EASTERN NEWSPAPERS. (Text in English, French, German) 1975. bi-w. DM.110. Deutsches Orient-Institut, Mittelweg 150, 2000 Hamburg 13, Germany. Ed.Bd. adv.; circ. 160.

950   II   ISSN 0970-0994
ALIGARH JOURNAL OF ORIENTAL STUDIES. (Text in English; summaries in Arabic, Persian, Sanskrit) 1984. s-a. Rs.100($20) Viveka Publications, 3-364 Samad Rd., Aligarh 202 001, India. TEL 24681. Ed. Umesh Chandra Sharma. adv.; bk.rev.; circ. 500. (back issues avail.)
—BLDSC shelfmark: 0787.821500.

950   NE   ISSN 0065-6593
ALTBABYLONISCHE BRIEFE IM UMSCHRIFT UND UEBERSETZUNG. 1964. irreg., vol.12, 1990. price varies. E.J. Brill, P.O. Box 9000, 2300 PA Leiden, Netherlands. TEL 071-312624. FAX 071-317532. TELEX 39296 BRILL NL. (In N. America: E.J. Brill, 24 Hudson St., Kinderhook, NY 12106. TEL 800-962-4406) Ed. F.R. Kraus.

DAS ALTERTUM. see *CLASSICAL STUDIES*

ALTORIENTALISCHE FORSCHUNGEN. see *HISTORY — History Of The Near East*

950   US   ISSN 0065-9541
AMERICAN ORIENTAL SERIES. 1925. irreg. price varies. American Oriental Society, Harlan Hatcher Graduate Library, University of Michigan, Ann Arbor, MI 48109-1205. TEL 313-747-4760. (Subscr. to: Eisenbrauns, Box 275, Winona Lake, IN 46590. TEL 219-269-2011) bk.rev. (reprint service avail. from KTO)

950   US   ISSN 0003-0279
PJ2
AMERICAN ORIENTAL SOCIETY. JOURNAL. (Text in English, French and German) 1842. q. $65. American Oriental Society, Harlan Hatcher Graduate Library, University of Michigan, Ann Arbor, MI 48109-1205. TEL 313-747-4760. Ed. Edwin Gerow. adv.; bk.rev.; charts; illus.; index; circ. 2,300. (also avail. in microform from UMI,PMC; back issues avail.; reprint service avail. from UMI) **Indexed:** Amer.Bibl.Slavic & E.Eur.Stud, Arts & Hum.Cit.Ind., Curr.Cont., Hum.Ind., Ind.Bk.Rev.Hum., New Test.Abstr., Numis.Lit, Old Test.Abstr., Rel.& Theol.Abstr. (1973-), Rel.Ind.One.
—BLDSC shelfmark: 4689.390000.

950   US   ISSN 0003-097X
DS101
AMERICAN SCHOOLS OF ORIENTAL RESEARCH. BULLETIN. Abbreviated title: B A S O R. 1919. q. $42 to individuals (foreign $53); institutions $57 (foreign $68). (American Schools of Oriental Research) Scholars Press, Box 15399, Atlanta, GA 30333-0399. TEL 404-636-4757. FAX 404-636-8301. Ed. James W. Flanagan. bk.rev.; charts; illus.; index; circ. 2,100. (also avail. in microform from UMI; reprint service avail. from SWZ,UMI) **Indexed:** A.I.C.P., New Test.Abstr., Numis.Lit, Old Test.Abstr., Rel.& Theol.Abstr. (1968-), Rel.Ind.One, Rel.Per.
—BLDSC shelfmark: 2392.700000.

951 952   US   ISSN 0361-6029
DS101
AMERICAN SCHOOLS OF ORIENTAL RESEARCH. NEWSLETTER. 1938. q. $16 to individuals (foreign $16.50); institutions $23 (foreign $23.50). (American Schools of Oriental Research (ASOR)) Scholars Press, Box 15399, Atlanta, GA 30333-0399. TEL 404-636-4757. FAX 404-636-8301. Ed. James A. Sauer. bibl.; circ. 1,500. (also avail. in microform from UMI; reprint service avail. from UMI) **Indexed:** A.I.C.P., Rel.Ind.One.
—BLDSC shelfmark: 0856.457000.
Formerly: Archeological Newsletter.
Description: Intended as a means of communicating news to members of the American Schools of Oriental Research (ASOR) and others interested in ASOR's activities in the Middle East.

950   VC
ANALECTA ORIENTALIA. 1931. irreg., no.53, 1986. price varies. (Pontificio Istituto Biblico) Biblical Institute Press, Piazza della Pilotta 35, 00187 Rome, Italy.

954   II
ANANDA VARTA. (Text in English) 1953. q. Rs.12($8) Shree Shree Anandamayee Charitable Society, 31 Ezra Mansion, 10 Govt. Place East, Calcutta 700 069, India.

950   US
ANCIENT NEAR EASTERN SOCIETY. JOURNAL. Short title: J A N E S. 1968. a. $10 to individuals; institutions $20. Ancient Near Eastern Society, Jewish Theological Seminary, 122nd & Broadway, New York, NY 10027. TEL 212-678-8847. FAX 212-678-8947. Eds. Edward L. Greenstein, David Marcus. adv.; illus.; circ. 400. (also avail. in microfilm; back issues avail.) **Indexed:** Mid.East: Abstr.& Ind., Old Test.Abstr., Rel.& Theol.Abstr. (1973-), Rel.Ind.One.
Formerly: Columbia University. Ancient Near Eastern Society. Journal (ISSN 0010-2016)
Description: Presents articles on all aspects of the ancient Near East.

954 913   NP
ANCIENT NEPAL. (Text in English and Nepali) 1967. bi-m. Rs.10. Department of Archaeology, Kathmandu, Nepal. TEL 215358. Ed. Saphalya Amatya. circ. 500. **Indexed:** Avery Ind.Archit.Per.

956 297   UA   ISSN 0570-1716
ANNALES ISLAMOLOGIQUES. (Text in Arabic, English, French) 1954. a. £E25($35) Institut Francais d'Archeologie Orientale du Caire, P.O. Box 11562 Kasr-el-Aini, 37 Sharia Sheikh Aly Youssef, Mounira, Cairo, Egypt. circ. 800. (back issues avail.)
Description: Research of history, archaeology and linguistics from the beginning of Islam to the 19th century.

950   II
ANNALS OF ORIENTAL RESEARCH. (Text in English or various Indian languages) s-a. University of Madras, Chepauk, Triplicane, Madras 600005, Tamil Nadu, India.

068.549 954   BG
ANNUAL GENERAL MEETING OF THE ASIATIC SOCIETY OF BANGLADESH: REPORT OF THE GENERAL SECRETARY. (Text in English) a. Asiatic Society of Bangladesh, 5 Old Secretariat Rd., Ramna, Dhaka, Bangladesh.

ARAB HISTORY AND CIVILIZATION; studies and texts. see *HISTORY — History Of The Near East*

ARAB STRUGGLE. see *HISTORY — History Of The Near East*

953   NE   ISSN 0570-5398
PJ6001
ARABICA; revue d'etudes Arabes. 1954. 3/yr. fl.155 (effective 1992). E.J. Brill, P.O. Box 9000, 2300 PA Leiden, Netherlands. TEL 071-312624. FAX 071-317532. TELEX 39296 BRILL NL. (In N. America: E.J. Brill, 24 Hudson St., Kinderhook, NY 12106. TEL 800-962-4406) Ed. M. Arkoun. bk.rev.; bibl.; index. (also avail. in microform from SWZ; reprint service avail. from SWZ) **Indexed:** Amer.Hist.& Life, Hist.Abstr., M.L.A., Numis.Lit.
Description: Studies, documents and notes on the language, literature, history and civilization of the Arab world.

950   FR   ISSN 0044-8613
ARCHIPEL. (Text in English, French, Indonesian) 1971. s-a. 195 F. Association Archipel, Ehess Bureau 732, 54 bd. Raspail, 75270 Paris Cedex 06, France. FAX 45-44-93-11. Ed.Bd. adv.; bk.rev.; bibl.; charts; illus.; circ. 1,000. **Indexed:** Amer.Hist.& Life, Bull.Signal., E.I.
—BLDSC shelfmark: 1597.657000.

950 960   NE   ISSN 0044-8699
DS1
ARCHIV ORIENTALNI/ORIENTAL ARCHIVES; quarterly journal of African, Asian and Latin-American studies. (Text in English, French, German, Russian) 1929. q. fl.285($157) (effective 1992). (Czechoslovak Academy of Sciences, Oriental Institute, CS) John Benjamins Publishing Co., Amsteldijk 44, P.O. Box 75577, 1070 AN Amsterdam, Netherlands. TEL 020-6738156. FAX 020-6739797. (In N. America: 821 Bethlehem Pike, Philadelphia, PA 19118. TEL 215-836-1200) Eds. B. Hruska, B. Richova. bk.rev.; bibl.; charts; illus.; circ. 1,200. (back issues avail.) **Indexed:** A.I.C.P., Amer.Hist.& Life, E.I., Hist.Abstr., M.L.A., Mid.East: Abstr.& Ind., Old Test.Abstr.
—BLDSC shelfmark: 1621.570000.
Description: Original papers, review articles and book reviews pertaining to the history, economy, culture and society of African, Asian and Latin American countries.

956   GW   ISSN 0724-8822
DS327
ARCHIVUM EURASIAE MEDII AEVI. (Text in English, French) 1975. irreg., no.6, 1986. price varies. Verlag Otto Harrassowitz, Taunusstr. 14, Postfach 2929, 6200 Wiesbaden 1, Germany. TEL 0611-530-0. FAX 0611-530570. TELEX 4186135. Ed.Bd. bk.rev. **Indexed:** Numis.Lit.

950   US
ARIZONA STATE UNIVERSITY. CENTER FOR ASIAN STUDIES. MONOGRAPH SERIES. 1967. s-a. $10 per vol. Arizona State University, Center for Asian Studies, Tempe, AZ 85287-1702. TEL 602-965-7184. FAX 602-965-8317. Ed. John Timothy Wixted. circ. 500.
Formerly: Arizona State University. Center for Asian Studies. Occasional Papers.

950 709   US   ISSN 0571-1371
ARS ORIENTALIS; the arts of Asia, Southeast Asia and Islam. 1954. a. $30. Department of History of Art, Tappan Hall, University of Michigan, Ann Arbor, MI 48109-1357. TEL 313-747-3307. Ed. Margaret Lourie. bk.rev.; circ. 500. **Indexed:** Avery Ind.Archit.Per.
—BLDSC shelfmark: 1697.670000.
Supersedes: Ars Islamica.

950   IT
ARTE ORIENTALE IN ITALIA. (Subseries of: Rome (City). Museo Nazionale d'Arte Orientale. Pubblicazione) 1971. irreg. price varies. Museo Nazionale d'Arte Orientale, Via Merulana 248, Rome 00185, Italy. Ed. Giovanni Poncini. illus.; circ. 1,000.

ARTIBUS ASIAE; quarterly of Asian art and archaeology for scholars and connoisseurs. see *ART*

ARTIBUS ASIAE SUPPLEMENTA. see *ART*

ARTS ASIATIQUES. see *ART*

ARYANA. see *HISTORY — History Of Asia*

950   US   ISSN 0890-4464
N7280.A1
ASIA INSTITUTE. BULLETIN. (Text in English, French, German, Spanish) 1987. a. $35 to individuals; institutions $50. (Asia Institute) Iowa State University Press, 2121 S. State Ave., Ames, IA 50010. TEL 515-292-0140. bk.rev.; circ. 500. (back issues avail.)
—BLDSC shelfmark: 2396.260000.
Description: For historians, collectors, connoisseurs, and museums. Promotes current studies in the arts, archaeology, history, and culture of early Iran and its interconnections with Greater Asia, the Mediterranean and Europe.

ORIENTAL STUDIES

950 960 490 890   CS   ISSN 0571-2742
DS1
ASIAN AND AFRICAN STUDIES. (Text in English) 1965. a. price varies. (Slovenska Akademia Vied, Ustav Historickych Vied) Veda, Publishing House of the Slovak Academy of Sciences, Klemensova 19, 814 30 Bratislava, Czechoslovakia. (Dist. in Western countries by: Curzon Press Ltd., 42 Gray's Inn Rd., London WC1, England) Ed. Jozef Genzor. bk.rev.; index. **Indexed:** Curr.Cont.Africa, E.I.
—BLDSC shelfmark: 1742.290000.

700   US   ISSN 0894-234X
N7262
ASIAN ART. 1988. 4/yr. $35 to individuals; institutions $77. Oxford University Press, Journals, 200 Madison Ave., New York, NY 10016. TEL 212-679-7300. FAX 212-725-2972. TELEX 6859654. (Subscr. to: Journals Fulfillment, 2001 Evans Rd., Cary, NC 27513. TEL 919-677-0977) Ed. Karen Sagstetter.
—BLDSC shelfmark: 1742.385000.

ASIAN BULLETIN/BULLETIN D'ASIE. see *HISTORY — History Of Asia*

950   UN
ASIAN CULTURAL CENTRE FOR UNESCO. ORGANIZATION AND ACTIVITIES. (Text in English) biennial. Asian Cultural Centre for Unesco, 6 Fukuro-machi, Shinjuku-ku, Tokyo 162, Japan. TEL 3-269-4435. illus.

ASIAN CULTURAL STUDIES. see *HISTORY — History Of Asia*

950   UN
ASIAN PACIFIC CULTURE; cross-cultural magazine. Short title: A P C. (Text in English) 1972. irreg. $4.20 per issue. Asian Cultural Centre for Unesco, 6, Fukuro-machi, Shinjuku-ku, Tokyo 162, Japan. TEL 03-269-4435. Ed. Taichi Sasaoka. illus.; circ. 2,000.
Formerly: Asian Culture (ISSN 0385-6402)

950   CH
ASIAN PACIFIC CULTURE QUARTERLY. (Text in English) 1973. q. Asian-Pacific Cultural Center, Asian-Pacific Parliamentarians' Union, 6-F, 66 Aikuo East Rd., Taipei, Taiwan, Republic of China. TEL 02-322-2139. FAX 02-322-2138. Ed. Tai-chu Chen. adv.; bk.rev.; index; circ. 3,000.
Formerly: Asian Culture Quarterly (ISSN 0378-8911)
Description: General articles on Asian-Pacific culture and creative writings.

ASIAN PHILOSOPHY. see *PHILOSOPHY*

950   HK   ISSN 0304-8675
DS1
ASIAN PROFILE. (Text in English) 1973. bi-m. $45 to individuals; institutions $75. Asian Research Service, G.P.O. Box 2232, Hong Kong. TEL 5707227. FAX 5128050. TELEX 63899-HX. Ed. Nelson Leung. adv.; bk.rev. (back issues avail.) **Indexed:** Amer.Hist.& Life, Geo.Abstr., Hist.Abstr., Mid.East: Abstr.& Ind., Rural Devel.Abstr., Rural Ext.Educ.& Tr.Abstr., Rural Recreat.Tour.Abstr., Soils & Fert., World Agri.Econ.& Rural Sociol.Abstr.

950   JA
ASIAN RESEARCH TRENDS: A HUMANITIES AND SOCIAL SCIENCE REVIEW. (Text in English) 1962. a. $18.20 (effective 1991). Centre for East Asian Cultural Studies, Toyo Bunko (Oriental Library), 2-28-21 Honkomagome, Bunkyo-ku, Tokyo 113, Japan. TEL 03-942-0124. FAX 03-942-0120. Ed. Yoneo Ishii. circ. 1,000. **Indexed:** Rural Devel.Abstr., World Agri.Econ.& Rural Sociol.Abstr.
Formerly (until vol.29 1990): East Asian Cultural Studies (ISSN 0012-8414)
Description: Presents resent trends in the research on Asia and North Africa done by regional specialists in the various disciplines concerning these areas.

950   PH   ISSN 0004-4679
DS1
ASIAN STUDIES. 1963. a. $12.50 (effective since 1989). University of the Philippines, Asian Center, Diliman, Quezon City 1101, Philippines. FAX 992863. TELEX 2231 UPDIL PU. charts; illus.; stat.; circ. 500. **Indexed:** E.I., M.L.A.
—BLDSC shelfmark: 1742.747000.

950   AT   ISSN 0156-0182
ASIAN STUDIES ASSOCIATION OF AUSTRALIA. CONFERENCE PAPERS. 1978. biennial. price varies. (Asian Studies Association of Australia) University of New South Wales Library, P.O. Box 1, Kensington, N.S.W. 2033, Australia. FAX 02-313-7196. (microfiche)

ASIAN STUDIES MONOGRAPHS SERIES. see *HISTORY — History Of Asia*

950   US
ASIAN STUDIES NEWSLETTER. 1955. 5/yr. $20 to institutions. Association for Asian Studies, Inc., 1 Lane Hall, University of Michigan, Ann Arbor, MI 48109. TEL 313-665-2490. FAX 313-665-3801. adv.; circ. 7,000. (back issues avail.; reprint service avail. from UMI) **Indexed:** A.I.C.P., E.I.
Formerly: Association for Asian Studies. Newsletter (ISSN 0004-5403)
Description: Contains association news, and information on grants, publications, study programs, meetings, exhibits, and jobs available.

ASIAN STUDIES REVIEW. see *HISTORY — History Of Asia*

ASIAN SURVEY. see *POLITICAL SCIENCE*

ASIAN THEATRE JOURNAL. see *THEATER*

950   US   ISSN 0893-6870
ASIAN THOUGHT AND CULTURE. irreg. Peter Lang Publishing, Inc., 62 W. 45th St., 4th Fl., New York, NY 10036. TEL 212-302-6740. FAX 212-302-7574. Ed. Charles Wei-hsun Fu.

950   II   ISSN 0571-3161
ASIATIC SOCIETY, CALCUTTA. JOURNAL. (Text in English) vol.18, 1976. a. $9. Asiatic Society, Calcutta, 1 Park St., Calcutta 16, India. bk.rev.; bibl.; charts; illus. (also avail. in microfilm from UMI; reprint service avail. from UMI) **Indexed:** A.I.C.P., Numis.Lit.

950   II
ASIATIC SOCIETY, CALCUTTA. MONOGRAPH SERIES. irreg. $10 per vol. Asiatic Society, Calcutta, One Park St., Calcutta 16, India.

950   II
ASIATIC SOCIETY, CALCUTTA. SEMINAR SERIES. irreg. Asiatic Society, Calcutta, One Park St., Calcutta 16, India.

950   BG
ASIATIC SOCIETY OF BANGLADESH. JOURNAL. (Text in English) vol.16, 1971. 5/yr. $10. Asiatic Society of Bangladesh, 5 Old Secretariat Rd., Ramna, Dhaka, Bangladesh. TEL 2-239390. bk.rev.; bibl.; charts; illus.; circ. 500. **Indexed:** Amer.Hist.& Life, Hist.Abstr.
Formerly: Asiatic Society of Pakistan. Journal.

ASIATIC SOCIETY OF BANGLADESH. JOURNAL. SCIENCE. see *SCIENCES: COMPREHENSIVE WORKS*

950   II   ISSN 0004-4709
ASIATIC SOCIETY OF BOMBAY. JOURNAL. 1925. a. price varies. Asiatic Society of Bombay, Town Hall, Bombay 400 023, India. (Subscr. to: Arthur Probsthain, 41 Great Russell St., London, W.C. 1, England) Ed.Bd. bk.rev.; illus.; circ. 1,000. **Indexed:** A.I.C.P., Amer.Hist.& Life, Hist.Abstr.

950 952   JA   ISSN 0287-6051
ASIATIC SOCIETY OF JAPAN. TRANSACTIONS. (Text in English) 1872. a. 4000 Yen. Asiatic Society of Japan, C.P.O. Box 592, Tokyo, Japan. TEL 03-586-1548. Ed. Derek Massarella. adv.; circ. 500. (also avail. in microfilm from BHP; back issues avail.; reprint service avail. from KTO)

956   GW   ISSN 0571-320X
ASIATISCHE FORSCHUNGEN. 1959. irreg., vol.115, 1991. price varies. Verlag Otto Harrassowitz, Taunusstr. 14, Postfach 2929, 6200 Wiesbaden 1, Germany. TEL 0611-530-0. FAX 0611-530570. TELEX 4186135. Ed.Bd.

950   SZ   ISSN 0004-4717
DS1
ASIATISCHE STUDIEN/ETUDES ASIATIQUES. (Text & summaries in English, French and German) 1947. s-a. $40.80. (Schweizerische Gesellschaft fuer Asienkunde) Verlag Peter Lang AG, Jupiterstr. 15, CH-3000 Bern 15, Switzerland. TEL 031-321122. FAX 031-321131. TELEX 912651-PELA-CH. Ed.Bd. bk.rev.; bibl.; illus.; index; circ. 800. **Indexed:** M.L.A.
—BLDSC shelfmark: 3816.770000.

950   GW   ISSN 0721-5231
DS1
ASIEN; deutsche Zeitschrift fuer Politik, Wirtschaft und Kultur. 1981. 4/yr. DM.50. Deutsche Gesellschaft fuer Asienkunde e.V., Rothenbaumchaussee 32, 2000 Hamburg 13, Germany. TEL 040-445891. Ed. Angelika Pathak. adv.; bk.rev.; circ. 1,300. **Indexed:** Forest.Abstr., Rural Devel.Abstr.

950   SP   ISSN 0571-3692
DS1
ASOCIACION ESPANOLA DE ORIENTALISTAS. BOLETIN. (Text in language of authors) 1965. a. 6000 ptas. Asociacion Espanola de Orientalistas, Universidad Autonoma, Edificio Rectorado, 28049 Madrid, Spain. TEL 397-41-12. Ed. F. Valderrama. bk.rev.; charts; illus.; circ. 500. (back issues avail.) **Indexed:** Amer.Hist.& Life, Hist.Abstr.

950   US   ISSN 0883-8909
ASSOCIATION FOR ASIAN STUDIES. SOUTHEAST CONFERENCE. ANNALS. 1979. A. $10 to non-members; members $5. Association for Asian Studies, Southeast Region, c/o Reference Department, Duke University Library, Durham, NC 27706-2597. TEL 919-684-2373. FAX 919-684-2855. Ed. Kenneth W. Berger. adv.; circ. 200.

950 320 300   AT   ISSN 0156-7365
DS701
AUSTRALIAN JOURNAL OF CHINESE AFFAIRS. 1979. 2/yr. Aus.$25($25) to individuals; institutions Aus.$30($30); students Aus.$20($20). Australian National University, Research School of Pacific Studies, Contemporary China Centre, G.P.O. Box 4, Canberra, A.C.T. 2601, Australia. FAX 06-257-3642. Ed. Jonathan Unger. adv.; bk.rev.; circ. 700. **Indexed:** Amer.Hist.& Life, Aus.P.A.I.S., Geo.Abstr., Hist.Abstr., Int.Polit.Sci.Abstr., Rural Recreat.Tour.Abstr., Sage Urb.Stud.Abstr., World Agri.Econ.& Rural Sociol.Abstr.
—BLDSC shelfmark: 1806.090000.
Description: Publishes articles that analyze and study different aspects of China's development since 1949.

955   IR
AYANDEH; Persian journal of Iranian studies. (Text in Farsi) 1926. m. $50. Iraj Afshar, Ed. & Pub., P.O. 19575-583 Niyavaran, Teheran, Iran. TEL 021-283254. adv.; bk.rev.; circ. 4,000.

BANGALORE THEOLOGICAL FORUM. see *RELIGIONS AND THEOLOGY*

950 490   AU   ISSN 0259-0654
BEIHEFTE ZUR WIENER ZEITSCHRIFT FUER DIE KUNDE DES MORGENLANDES. irreg., no.15, 1989. price varies. Verband der Wissenschaftlichen Gesellschaften Oesterreichs, Lindengasse 37, A-1070 Vienna, Austria. TEL 932166. Ed. Arne A. Ambros.

BEIRUT REVIEW. see *POLITICAL SCIENCE — International Relations*

952   AU   ISSN 0522-6759
BEITRAEGE ZUR JAPANOLOGIE. (Text in English and German, summaries in English and Japanese) 1955. irreg., vol.29, 1991. price varies. Universitaet Wien, Institut fuer Japanologie, Universitaetsstr. 7-IV, A-1010 Vienna, Austria. FAX 0222-4020533. Eds. Alexander Slawik, Sepp Linhart. bk.rev.; circ. 300. **Indexed:** A.I.C.P.

950   GW   ISSN 0138-4228
BERLINER TURFANTEXTE. (Text in English and German) 1971. irreg., vol.15, 1985. (Akademie der Wissenschaften der DDR) Akademie-Verlag Berlin, Leipziger Str. 3-4, 1086 Berlin, Germany.

ORIENTAL STUDIES

954 II
BHANDARKAR ORIENTAL RESEARCH INSTITUTE. ANNALS. (Text in English) 1919. a. price varies. Bhandarkar Oriental Research Institute, Deccan Gymkhana, Poona 411 004, India. TEL 336932. Eds. R.N. Dandekar, S.D. Laddu. bk.rev.; circ. 1,250. **Indexed:** A.I.C.P., M.L.A.

954 II
BHARATYA VIDYA. (Text in English and Sanskrit) 1939. m? Rps.60. Bharatiya Vidya Bhavan, Kulapnati K.M. Munshi Marg, Bombay 400 007, India. Eds. J.H. Dave, S.A. Upadhyaya. (back issues avail.) **Indexed:** M.L.A.

BIBLICA ET ORIENTALIA. see *RELIGIONS AND THEOLOGY — Roman Catholic*

BIBLICAL ARCHAEOLOGIST. see *ARCHAEOLOGY*

BIBLIOTECA DEGLI STUDI CLASSICI E ORIENTALI. see *CLASSICAL STUDIES*

BIBLIOTHECA ISLAMICA. see *RELIGIONS AND THEOLOGY — Islamic*

BIBLIOTHECA ORIENTALIS. see *HISTORY — Abstracting, Bibliographies, Statistics*

950 490   HU   ISSN 0067-8104
BIBLIOTHECA ORIENTALIS HUNGARICA. (Text in English, French and German) 1955. irreg., vol.32, 1989. price varies. (Magyar Tudomanyos Akademia) Akademiai Kiado, Publishing House of the Hungarian Academy of Sciences, P.O. Box 24, H-1363 Budapest, Hungary. **Indexed:** New Test.Abstr., Old Test.Abstr.

500   GW   ISSN 0170-0006
BOCHUMER JAHRBUCH ZUR OSTASIENFORSCHUNG. 1978. a. DM.89.80. Universitaetsverlag Dr. N. Brockmeyer, Querenburger Hoehe 281, 4630 Bochum 1, Germany. TEL 0234-706978. circ. 80.

BOSTON THIRD WORLD LAW JOURNAL. see *LAW — International Law*

954   II   ISSN 0001-902X
BP500
BRAHMAVIDYA. Variant title: Adyar Library Bulletin. (Text in English and Sanskrit; occasionally French and German) 1937. a. Rs.100($20) (effective 1990). Adyar Library and Research Centre, Theosophical Society, Adyar, Madras 600 020, India. Ed.Bd. adv.; bk.rev.; cum.index: vols.1-51; circ. 300. (back issues avail.) **Indexed:** M.L.A.

934   NE   ISSN 0925-2916
BRILL'S INDOLOGICAL LIBRARY. 1991. irreg., vol.7, 1992. price varies. E.J. Brill, P.O. Box 9000, 2300 PA Leiden, Netherlands. TEL 071-312624. FAX 071-317532. TELEX 39296 BRILL NL. (In N. America: E.J. Brill, 24 Hudson St., Kinderhook, NY 12106. TEL 800-962-4406) Ed. Johannes Bronkhorst.
Description: Scholarly monographs on topics in Indian religion, language, history and philosophy.

952   NE
BRILL'S JAPANESE STUDIES LIBRARY. 1989. irreg., latest 1990. price varies. E.J. Brill, P.O. Box 9000, 2300 PA Leiden, Netherlands. TEL 071-312624. FAX 071-317532. TELEX 39296 BRILL NL. (In N. America: E.J. Brill, 24 Hudson St., Kinderhook, NY 12106. TEL 800-962-4406)

950   HU   ISSN 0139-4614
BUDAPESTI ORIENTAL REPRINTS, SERIES A-2. 1977. irreg. price varies or exchange basis. (Korosi Csoma Tarasag) Magyar Tudomanyos Akademia Konyvtara, Aranyjanos u.1, P.O. Box 7, 1361 Budapest, Hungary. Eds. E. Schutz, Eva Apor.

BULLETIN CRITIQUE DES ANNALES ISLAMOLOGIQUES. see *RELIGIONS AND THEOLOGY — Islamic*

950   FR   ISSN 0007-4349
BULLETIN DE L'OEUVRE D'ORIENT. 1856. bi-m. 10 F.($1) Association de l'Oeuvre d'Orient, 20 rue du Regard, 75006 Paris, France. Ed. J. Andre Boissonnet. circ. 210,000.

BULLETIN OF CONCERNED ASIAN SCHOLARS. see *POLITICAL SCIENCE — International Relations*

952   GW   ISSN 0932-268X
BUNKEN; Studien und Materialen zur japanischen Literatur. 1987. irreg. Verlag Otto Harrassowitz, Taunusstr. 14, Postfach 2929, 6200 Wiesbaden, Germany. TEL 0611-530-0. FAX 0611-530-570. TELEX 4186135. Ed. Ekkehard May.

949.5   GW   ISSN 0007-7704
BYZANTINISCHE ZEITSCHRIFT. (Text in several languages) 1892. s-a. DM.189. C.H. Beck'sche Verlagsbuchhandlung, Wilhelmstr. 9, 8000 Munich 40, Germany. TEL 089-38189-338. FAX 089-38189-398. TELEX 5215085-BECK-D. Ed. A. Hohlweg. adv.; bk.rev.; bibl.; illus.; index. cum.index: vols.1-12; circ. 1,000. (reprint service avail. from SCH) **Indexed:** Curr.Cont., M.L.A., Numis.Lit, RILA.

956 939   NE   ISSN 0007-7712
CB231
BYZANTINOSLAVICA; revue internationale des etudes byzantines. (Text in English, French, German, Italian, Russian) 1929. s-a. fl.240($131) (Czechoslovak Academy of Sciences, Institute of Greek, Roman and Latin Studies, CS) John Benjamins Publishing Co, Amsteldijk 44, P.O. Box 75577, 1070 AN Amsterdam, Netherlands. TEL 020-6738156. FAX 020-6739773. (In N. America: 821 Bethlehem Pike, Philadelphia, PA 19118. TEL 215-836-1200) Ed. Vladimir Vavrinek. bk.rev.; bibl.; illus.; maps; index; circ. 1,100. (back issues avail.) **Indexed:** CERDIC, Curr.Cont., M.L.A., Numis.Lit.
—BLDSC shelfmark: 2942.530000.
Description: International journal devoted to Byzantine studies.
Refereed Serial

900   BE
BYZANTION; revue internationale des etudes Byzantines. (Text in English, French, German, Greek, Italian) 1924. s-a. 1500 Fr.($42) ASBL Byzantion, Boulevard de l'Empereur 4, B-1000 Brussels, Belgium. Eds. Alice Leroy-Molinghen, Justin Mossay. bk.rev.; bibl. (reprint service avail. from KTO) **Indexed:** M.L.A., Numis.Lit, RILA.

950   LE
C E M A M REPORTS. 1974. a. price varies. (Universite Saint-Joseph, Center for the Study of the Modern Arab World) Dar el-Mashreq S.A.R.L., 2 rue Huvelin, PO Box 946, Beirut, Lebanon. (Subscr. to: Librairie Orientale, PO Box 946, Beirut, Lebanon)

950 491   FR
CAHIERS D'ETUDES ARABES. irreg., latest no.4. price varies. Institut National des Langues et Civilisations Orientales, Centre de Documentation et de Recherches en Etudes Arabes, 2 rue de Lille, 75343 Paris Cedex 07, France. TEL 49-26-42-74.
Description: Studies the Arabic language and classical and contemporary Islamic civilization.

951 495.1   FR
CAHIERS D'ETUDES CHINOISE. irreg., latest no.9. price varies. Institut National des Langues et Civilisations Orientales, Centre d'Etudes Chinoises, 2 rue de Lille, 75343 Paris Cedex 07, France. TEL 49-26-42-74.
Description: Presents the results of research of members.

950 495   FR
CAHIERS DE L'ASIE DU SUD-EST. 1977. irreg., latest no.27. price varies. Institut National des Langues et Civilisations Orientales, 2 rue de Lille, 75343 Paris Cedex 07, France. TEL 49-26-42-74.
Description: Presents articles, translations, summaries and bibliographies on the languages, literatures and civilizations of South-East Asia.

950   FR   ISSN 0767-6468
DS36
CAHIERS DE L'ORIENT. q. 300 F. (Centre de Reflexion sur le Proche-Orient) Societe Francaise d'Edition, d'Impression et de Realisation, 80 rue Saint Dominique, 75007 Paris, France. Ed. Antoine Sfeir. adv.; bk.rev.; circ. 1,986.

890 808.81   FR
CAHIERS DE POETIQUE COMPAREE. irreg., latest no.20. price varies. Institut National des Langues et Civilisations Orientales, 2 rue de Lille, 75343 Paris Cedex 07, France. TEL 49-26-42-74.
Description: Studies the theories of rhythms and translation and systems of versification.

CAHIERS DU MONDE RUSSE ET SOVIETIQUE. see *HISTORY — History Of Europe*

CELESTINESCA; boletin informativo internacional. see *LITERATURE*

958   PK
CENTRAL ASIA. (Text in English) 1978. 3/yr. Rs.90($25) University of Peshawar, Area Study Center (Central Asia), Peshawar, Pakistan. Ed. Mohammad Anwar Khan. circ. 200.

950 490 890   GW   ISSN 0008-9192
DS785
CENTRAL ASIATIC JOURNAL; international periodical for the languages, literatures, history and archaeology of Central Asia. (Text in English, French, German) 1955. s-a. Verlag Otto Harrassowitz, Taunusstr. 14, Postfach 2929, 6200 Wiesbaden 1, Germany. TEL 0611-530-0. FAX 0611-530570. TELEX 4186135. Ed. G. Stary. adv.; bk.rev.; bibl.; charts; illus.; index; circ. 550. (back issues avail.) **Indexed:** Arts & Hum.Cit.Ind., Curr.Cont., Mid.East: Abstr.& Ind., Numis.Lit.
—BLDSC shelfmark: 3105.970000.

959 490   CN   ISSN 0839-4555
CENTRE D'ETUDES DE L'ASIE DE L'EST. CAHIERS; recherche sur l'Asie de l'Est. (Text in English, French) 1980. s-a. Can.$10 per no. Universite de Montreal, Faculte des Arts et des Sciences, Centre d'Etudes de l'Asie de l'Est, C.P. 6128, Succ. A, Montreal, Que. H3C 3J7, Canada. TEL 514-343-5970. FAX 514-343-7716. Ed. Claude Comtois. bk.rev.; circ. 300. (back issues avail.)
Description: Presents a multidisciplinary forum that covers all aspects of the Far East. Publishes original manuscripts, notes, essays, documents, bibliographical studies in the field of humanities by specialists of East and Southeast Asia.
Refereed Serial

CENTRE FOR SOUTH-EAST ASIAN STUDIES. OCCASIONAL PAPERS. see *HISTORY — History Of Asia*

950   JA   ISSN 0009-1537
GT2910
CHANOYU QUARTERLY; tea and the arts of Japan. (Text in English) 1970. q. 4,400 Yen($25) Urasenke Foundation, Ogawa Teranouchi Agaru, Kamikyo-ku, Kyoto 602, Japan. FAX 075-432-4553. (Subscr. to: Urasenke Chanoyu Center, 153 E. 69th St., New York, NY 10021, USA) Ed. Gretchen Mittwer. bk.rev.; bibl.; illus, charts; circ. 2,000. (processed; also avail. in microform from UMI; reprint service avail. from ISI) **Indexed:** Artbibl.Mod., Arts & Hum.Cit.Ind., Curr.Cont.
—BLDSC shelfmark: 3129.669500.
Description: Covers art, cultural history, literature and philosophy of Japan, in relation to the "tea ceremony".

950   II
CHAUKHAMBHA ORIENTAL RESEARCH STUDIES. 1976. irreg., no.35, 1989. price varies. Chaukhambha Orientalia, Gokul Bhawan, K 37-109 Gopal Mandir Lane, Varanasi 221001, India.

950 700 370   US
CHINA INSTITUTE IN AMERICA. BULLETIN.. q. membership only. China Institute in America, Inc., 125 E. 65th St., New York, NY 10021. TEL 212-744-8181. Ed. Helen Geraghty. bk.rev.; circ. 1,700.

951   UK   ISSN 0009-4439
CHINA QUARTERLY. 1960. q. $48 (students $24). University of London, School of Oriental and African Studies, Thornhaugh St., Russell Sq., London WC1H OXG, England. TEL 071-637-2388. FAX 071-436-3844. Ed. David Shambaugh. adv.; bk.rev.; bibl.; charts; maps; index; circ. 3,000. (also avail. in microform from UMI) **Indexed:** A.B.C.Pol.Sci., Acad.Ind., Amer.Hist.& Life, ASSIA, Curr.Cont., E.I., Hist.Abstr., Int.Lab.Doc., Key to Econ.Sci., M.L.A., Mid.East: Abstr.& Ind., P.A.I.S., Ref.Sour., Rural Recreat.Tour.Abstr., Soc.Sci.Ind., SSCI, World Agri.Econ.& Rural Sociol.Abstr.
—BLDSC shelfmark: 3180.230000.
Description: Covers all aspects of modern China studies.

951   US
CHINESE AMERICA; history and perspectives. 1987. a. membership. Chinese Historical Society of America, 650 Commercial St., San Francisco, CA 94111. TEL 415-391-1188. illus.

ORIENTAL STUDIES

951 CH ISSN 0009-4544
DS701
CHINESE CULTURE. (Text in English) 1957. q. NT.$600($20) China Academy, Institute for Advanced Chinese Studies, PO Box 12, Yang Ming Shan, Taiwan, Republic of China. Ed. Dr. Chang Chi-Yun. adv.; bk.rev.; index; circ. 2,000. (also avail. in microform from UMI)

951 HK
CHINESE CULTURE QUARTERLY/CHIU CHOU HSUEH K'AN. (Text in Chinese; table of contents in English) q. HK.$80 in Hong Kong; Taiwan NT.$450; elsewhere $15 to individuals (institutions HK.$120; NT.$600; $25). Hong Kong Institute for Promotion of Chinese Culture, Rm. 1001-5, Shun Tak Centre, 200 Connaught Rd., Central, Hong Kong. TEL 5-594904. (Subscr. to: Far East Book Company, G.P.O. Box 4892, Hong Kong; Editorial addr.: Kwan-Fong Institute of East Asian Studies, Pace University, New York, NY 10038, USA. TEL 212-488-1832) Ed. Pei-kai Cheng. bk.rev.

950 US
CHINESE HISTORIAN. 1987. s-a. $6 to individuals; institutions $8. Chinese Historians in the United States, Inc., Ohio University, Dept. of History, Athens, OH 45701. Eds. Zhaohui Hong, Qiang Zhai. bk.rev.; circ. 200.
Formerly: Historian (Athens).
Description: Provides a forum for Chinese historians in the United States to share their views and exchange ideas.

CHINESE LITERATURE; fiction, poetry, art. see *LITERATURE*

951 001.3 US
CHINESE SCHOLARLY WORKS IN ENGLISH. irreg. Peter Lang Publishing, Inc., 62 W. 45th St., 4th Fl., New York, NY 10036. TEL 212-302-6740. FAX 212-302-7574. Ed. Stephen Ohlander.

CHINESE SCIENCE. see *SCIENCES: COMPREHENSIVE WORKS*

CHINESE STUDIES IN HISTORY; a journal of translations. see *HISTORY*

951 HK
CHINESE UNIVERSITY OF HONG KONG. INSTITUTE OF CHINESE STUDIES. JOURNAL. 1968. a. HK.$50($8.70) Chinese University of Hong Kong, Institute of Chinese Studies, Shatin, New Territories, Hong Kong. Ed.Bd. adv.; bk.rev.; bibl.; charts; illus.; circ. 500. **Indexed:** Amer.Hist.& Life, Hist.Abstr.

CHINESISCHE MEDIZIN; theoretische Grundlagen, Diagnostik, Akupunktur, Arzneimittel, Taiji, Qigong. see *MEDICAL SCIENCES*

CHING FENG; a journal on the encounter of religion and culture in Asia. see *RELIGIONS AND THEOLOGY*

951 895.1 US ISSN 0193-7774
PL2253
CHINOPERL PAPERS. (Text in Chinese and English) 1969. a. $15 to individuals; institutions $25; students $10. Conference on Chinese Oral and Performing Literature, c/o Susan Blader, Asian Studies Department, 202 Bartlett Hall, Dartmouth College, NH 03755. Eds. Samuel H.N. Cheung, Lindy Li Mark. bk.rev.; bibl.; circ. 200. (back issues avail.)
Formerly: Chinoperl News.
Description: Deals primarily with oral Chinese literature (popular storytelling, opera, ceremonial chanting and folksongs) and various genres of Chinese verse and prose.

CHRISTELIJK OOSTEN. see *RELIGIONS AND THEOLOGY*

CHRISTIAN INSTITUTE FOR ETHNIC STUDIES IN ASIA. BULLETIN. see *RELIGIONS AND THEOLOGY*

962 BE ISSN 0009-6067
CHRONIQUE D'EGYPTE. (Text in English, French, German, Italian) 1925. s-a. 2200 Fr. Fondation Egyptologique Reine Elisabeth, Parc du Cinquantenaire 10, 1040 Brussels, Belgium. TEL 02-74-17-364. Eds. J. Bingen, H. de Meulenaere. bk.rev.; bibl.; illus.; circ. 1,000. **Indexed:** M.L.A.

CODEX: JOURNAL OF THE CENTRE FOR THE STUDY OF CHRISTIANITY IN ISLAMIC LANDS. see *RELIGIONS AND THEOLOGY*

950 GW ISSN 0340-6393
CODICES ARABICI ANTIQUI. 1972. irreg., vol.4, 1986. price varies. Verlag Otto Harrassowitz, Taunusstr. 14, Postfach 2929, 6200 Wiesbaden 1, Germany. TEL 0611-530-0. FAX 0611-530570. TELEX 4186135. Ed. R.G. Khoury.

950 AG
COLECCION ORIENTE-OCCIDENTE. 1976. irreg. price varies. Universidad del Salvador, Instituto Latinoamericano de Investigaciones Comparadas Oriente-Occidente, Callao 853, 1023 Buenos Aires, Argentina. Ed. I. Quiles. circ. 2,000.

954 UK ISSN 0141-0156
COLLECTED PAPERS ON SOUTH ASIA.* 1978. irreg. price varies. (University of London, School of Oriental and African Studies) Curzon Press Ltd., 7 Caledonian Rd., London N1 9DX, England.

COLLECTIONS BAUR. BULLETIN. see *MUSEUMS AND ART GALLERIES*

951 FR
COLLEGE DE FRANCE. INSTITUT DES HAUTES ETUDES CHINOISES. MEMOIRS.* 1975. irreg. Diffusion de Boccard, 11 Rue du Medicis, 75006 Paris, France. illus. (reprint service avail. from KTO)

950 FR
COLLOQUES LANGUES'O. irreg. price varies. Institut National des Langues et Civilisations Orientales, 2 rue de Lille, 75343 Paris Cedex 07, France. TEL 49-26-42-74.

950 US
COLUMBIA UNIVERSITY. EAST ASIAN INSTITUTE. STUDIES. 1962. irreg. price varies. Columbia University Press, 562 W. 113th St., New York, NY 10025. TEL 212-678-6777.

COMMONWEALTH NOVEL IN ENGLISH. see *LITERATURE*

954 959.8 NE
COMPARATIVE HISTORY OF INDIA AND INDONESIA. irreg., vol.4, 1989. price varies. E.J. Brill, P.O. Box 9000, 2300 PA Leiden, Netherlands. TEL 071-312624. FAX 071-317532. TELEX 39296 BRILL NL. (In N. America: E.J. Brill, 24 Hudson St., Kinderhook, NY 12106. TEL 800-962-4406)

COMPUTER AIDED RESEARCH IN NEAR EASTERN STUDIES. see *HISTORY — Computer Applications*

951 UK ISSN 0085-2856
CONTEMPORARY CHINA INSTITUTE PUBLICATIONS. 1970. irreg., latest 1986. price varies. (Contemporary China Institute, School of Oriental and African Studies, University of London) Cambridge University Press, Edinburgh Bldg., Shaftesbury Rd., Cambridge CB2 2RU, England. TEL 0223-312393. FAX 0223-315052. TELEX 851817256. Ed.Bd.

950 US ISSN 1053-1866
▼**CONTRIBUTIONS IN ASIAN STUDIES.** 1991. irreg. price varies. Greenwood Press, Inc. (Subsidiary of: Greenwood Publishing Group Inc.), 88 Post Rd. W., Box 5007, Westport, CT 06881-5007. TEL 203-226-3571. FAX 203-222-1502.

CONTRIBUTIONS TO NEPALESE STUDIES. see *HISTORY — History Of Asia*

950 US ISSN 0734-449X
Z688.A75
CORMOSEA BULLETIN. vol.7, 1974. s-a. $10. Association for Asian Studies, Inc., Committee for Research Materials on Southeast Asia, University of Michigan, One Lane Hall, Ann Arbor, MI 48109. TEL 313-665-2490. Ed. Carol Mitchell. bk.rev.; bibl.; circ. 200. **Indexed:** E.I.
Formerly: Cormosea Newsletter.
Description: Bibliographies and reviews of research materials in Southeast Asian Studies.

950 US ISSN 1050-2955
CORNELL EAST ASIA SERIES. 1973. irreg., no.52, 1990. price varies. Cornell University, East Asia Program, 140 Uris Hall, Ithaca, NY 14853. TEL 607-255-6222. FAX 607-255-1388. Ed. David McCann. circ. 2,000.
Formerly: Cornell East Asia Papers (ISSN 8756-5293)
Description: Publishes manuscripts on a wide variety of scholarly topics pertaining to East Asia.

959 011 US ISSN 0589-7300
CORNELL UNIVERSITY. MODERN INDONESIA PROJECT PUBLICATIONS. MONOGRAPHS, TRANSLATIONS, BIBLIOGRAPHIES, INTERIM REPORTS. 1958. irreg., no.70, 1989. price varies. Cornell University, Cornell Modern Indonesia Project, 102 West Ave., Ithaca, NY 14850. TEL 607-255-4359. FAX 607-254-5000. TELEX WUI 6713054. Ed. Audrey R. Kahin.
—BLDSC shelfmark: 7127.250000.
Former titles: Cornell University. Modern Indonesia Project Publications. Monographs, Translations, Bibliographies; Cornell University. Modern Indonesia Project. Monographs.

950 US
▼**CORNELL UNIVERSITY. SOUTHEAST ASIA PROGRAM. TRANSLATION SERIES.** 1990. irreg. price varies. Cornell University, Southeast Asia Program, 102 West Ave., Ithaca, NY 14850. TEL 607-255-8038. FAX 607-255-7116. TELEX WUI-6713054. (Subscr. to: S E A P Publications, Cornell University, E. Hill Plaza, Ithaca, NY 14850)

CORPUS SCRIPTORUM CHRISTIANORUM ORIENTALIUM: AETHIOPICA. see *RELIGIONS AND THEOLOGY — Other Denominations And Sects*

CORPUS SCRIPTORUM CHRISTIANORUM ORIENTALIUM: ARABICA. see *RELIGIONS AND THEOLOGY — Other Denominations And Sects*

CORPUS SCRIPTORUM CHRISTIANORUM ORIENTALIUM: ARMENIACA. see *RELIGIONS AND THEOLOGY — Other Denominations And Sects*

CORPUS SCRIPTORUM CHRISTIANORUM ORIENTALIUM: COPTICA. see *RELIGIONS AND THEOLOGY — Other Denominations And Sects*

CORPUS SCRIPTORUM CHRISTIANORUM ORIENTALIUM: IBERICA. see *RELIGIONS AND THEOLOGY — Other Denominations And Sects*

CORPUS SCRIPTORUM CHRISTIANORUM ORIENTALIUM: SUBSIDIA. see *RELIGIONS AND THEOLOGY — Other Denominations And Sects*

CORPUS SCRIPTORUM CHRISTIANORUM ORIENTALIUM: SYRIACA. see *RELIGIONS AND THEOLOGY — Other Denominations And Sects*

956 297 NE ISSN 0169-8257
DE GOEJE STICHTING. UITGAVEN/DE GOEJE FUND. PUBLICATIONS.* 1956. irreg., vol.26, 1988. price varies. De Goeje Stichting - De Goeje Fund, c/o Prof. R. Roolvink, Prins Bernhardtlaan 70, 2252 GZ Voorschoten, Netherlands. FAX 071-317532. (Dist. by: Nederlands Instituut voor het Nabije Oosten, Witte Singel 24, P.O. Box 9515, 2300 RA Leiden, Netherlands)

950 GW ISSN 0341-0137
PJ5
DEUTSCHE MORGENLAENDISCHE GESELLSCHAFT. ZEITSCHRIFT. (Supplement avail.) (Text in English and German) 1847. s-a. DM.140. Franz Steiner Verlag Wiesbaden GmbH, Birkenwaldstr. 44, Postfach 101526, 7000 Stuttgart 1, Germany. TEL 0711-2582-0. FAX 0711-2582290. TELEX 723636-DAZD. Ed. Ewald Wagner. adv.; bk.rev.; bibl.; index; circ. 1,200. (also avail. in microfiche from BHP; back issues avail.; reprint service avail. from KTO) **Indexed:** Numis.Lit.

950 GW ISSN 0341-0803
DS57
DEUTSCHE MORGENLAENDISCHE GESELLSCHAFT. ZEITSCHRIFT. SUPPLEMENTA. irreg., vol.8, 1990. price varies. Franz Steiner Verlag Wiesbaden GmbH, Birkenwaldstr. 44, Postfach 101526, 7000 Stuttgart 1, Germany. TEL 0711-2582-0. FAX 0711-2582290. TELEX 723636-DAZ-D.

956 GW ISSN 0012-1169
DEUTSCHER PALAESTINA-VEREIN. ZEITSCHRIFT. (Text in English, French and German) 1878. 2/yr. price varies. (Deutscher Verein zur Erforschung Palaestinas) Verlag Otto Harrassowitz, Taunusstr. 14, Postfach 2929, 6200 Wiesbaden 1, Germany. TEL 0611-530-0. FAX 0611-530570. TELEX 4186135. Eds. Manfred Weippert, Siegfried Mittmann. adv.; bk.rev.; illus.; circ. 600. (back issues avail.; reprint service avail. from KTO) **Indexed:** Mid.East: Abstr.& Ind.

954　　　　　II
DHANIRAM BHALLA GRANTHAMALA. (Text in Hindi and Sanskrit) irreg., vol.19, 1972. price varies. Vishveshvaranand Vedic Research Institute, P.O. Sadhu Ashram, Hoshiarpur 146021, Punjab, India. Ed. Vishva Bandhu.

950 895 495　　CS
DISSERTATIONES ORIENTALES. (Text in Chinese and English) vol.35, 1975. irreg. price varies. (Ceskoslovenska Akademie Ved, Orientalni Ustav) Academia, Publishing House of the Czechoslovak Academy of Sciences, Vodickova 40, 112 29 Prague 1, Czechoslovakia. TEL 23-63-065. Ed. Jaroslav Cesar.

950　　　　　FR
DOCUMENTS D'HISTOIRE MAGHREBINE. irreg. Librairie Orientaliste Paul Geuthner, 12 rue Vavin, 75006 Paris, France. TEL 33-1-46-34-71-30. FAX 33-1-43-29-75-64. Ed. Chantal de la Veronne.

890　　　　　KO
DONG-A MUNHUA/EAST ASIA CULTURE. (Text in Korean; summaries in English) 1963. irreg, latest no.29. 1500. Seoul National University, Institute of Asian Studies, College of Humanities, San 56-1, Sinlim-Dong, Kwanak-ku, Seoul 151, S. Korea. FAX 02-871-7244. bk.rev.; circ. 500.

DONGFANG SHIJIE/ORIENTAL WORLD. see HISTORY — History Of Asia

950　　　　　CC
DONGNAN YA YANJIU/SOUTHEAST ASIAN STUDIES. (Text in Chinese) q. Jinan Daxue - Jinan University, Shipai, Guangzhou, Guangdong 510632, People's Republic of China. TEL 516511. Ed. Chen Senhai.

950　　　　　MP
DORNODAHINY SUDLAL/ORIENTAL STUDIES. (Text in Mongolian, summaries in English, Russian) 1978. q. Academy of Sciences, Institute of Oriental Studies, P.O. Box 48-17, Ulan Bator, Mongolia. Ed. Sh. Sandag.
　Description: Socio-political journal featuring history, culture and foreign relations.

EAST. see GENERAL INTEREST PERIODICALS — Japan

950　　　　　IT　　ISSN 0012-8376
AP37
EAST AND WEST. (Text in English) 1951. q. $100. (Istituto Italiano per il Medio ed Estremo Oriente) Herder Editrice e Libreria s.r.l., Piazza Montecitorio 120, 00186 Rome, Italy. TEL 67 94 628. FAX 678-47-51. TELEX 621427 NATEL. adv.; bk.rev.; bibl.; charts; illus.; index; circ. 1,500. Indexed: Amer.Hist.& Life, Hist.Abstr., Numis.Lit.
　—BLDSC shelfmark: 3645.400000.

950　　　　　US
EAST ASIAN HISTORICAL MONOGRAPHS. irreg. Oxford University Press, 200 Madison Ave., New York, NY 10016. TEL 212-679-7300. Ed. Wang Gungwu.

950　　　　　US
EAST ASIAN RESEARCH AIDS AND TRANSLATIONS. (Text in English or Oriental languages) 1984. irreg., vol.2, 1989. price varies. Western Washington University, Center for East Asian Studies, Bellingham, WA 98225. TEL 206-676-3041. Ed. Henry G. Schwarz.

950　　　　　FR　　ISSN 0336-1519
DS531
ECOLE FRANCAISE D'EXTREME-ORIENT. BULLETIN. 1901. irreg., latest vol.77, 1988. price varies. Editions d' Amerique et d'Orient, 11 rue St. Sulpice, 75006 Paris, France. FAX 33-1-43-54-59-54. Indexed: A.I.C.P., Amer.Hist.& Life, E.I., Hist.Abstr.
　—BLDSC shelfmark: 2496.900000.

950　　　　　MX　　ISSN 0185-0164
DS1
ESTUDIOS DE ASIA Y AFRICA. 1966. 3/yr. Mex.$2500($32) to individuals (foreign $42); institutions $50 (foreign $60). Colegio de Mexico, A.C., Departamento de Publicaciones, Camino al Ajusco 20, Codigo Postal 01000, Mexico, D.F., Mexico. TEL 568 6033. FAX 6526233. TELEX 1777585 COLME. Ed.Bd. adv.; bk.rev.; cum.index; circ. 1,500. (back issues avail.) reprint service avail. from UMI) Indexed: Amer.Hist.& Life, Hist.Abstr., M.L.A.
　—BLDSC shelfmark: 3812.660000.
　Supersedes: Estudios Orientales.

959　　　　　BE　　ISSN 0531-1926
ETUDES ORIENTALES. 1963. irreg., no.11, 1983. price varies. Librairie-Editions Thanh-Long, 34 rue Dekens, B-1040 Brussels, Belgium. (back issues avail.)

ETUDES PRELIMINAIRES AUX RELIGIONS ORIENTALES DANS L'EMPIRE ROMAIN. see RELIGIONS AND THEOLOGY

955 297　　　IR　　ISSN 0014-7788
DS251
FARHANG-E IRAN ZAMIN. (Text mainly in Farsi: occasionally in English, French) 1952. q. $40. Iraj Afshar, Ed. & Pub., Box 19575-583 Niyavaran, Teheran, Iran. TEL 021-283254. bk.rev.; circ. 2,000. (also avail. in microfiche) Indexed: M.L.A.

950　　　　　AT　　ISSN 0085-0586
FLINDERS ASIAN STUDIES LECTURE. 1970. a. price varies. Flinders University of South Australia, School of Social Sciences, Director of Asian Studies, G.P.O. Box 2100, Adelaide, S.A. 5001, Australia. TEL 08-201-2404. FAX 08-210-2566. Ed. L. Brennan.

950　　　　　AT
FLINDERS ASIAN STUDIES MONOGRAPH. 1981. irreg. price varies. Flinders University of South Australia, School of Social Sciences, Director of Asian Studies, G.P.O. Box 2100, Adelaide, S.A. 5001, Australia. TEL 08-201-2404. FAX 08-201-2566.

950　　　　　PL　　ISSN 0015-5675
FOLIA ORIENTALIA. (Text in English, French and German) 1959. a. price varies. (Polska Akademia Nauk, Oddzial w Krakowie, Komisja Orientalistyczna - Polish Academy of Sciences, Cracow Section, Commission of Orientalistics) Ossolineum, Publishing House of the Polish Academy of Sciences, Rynek 9, 50-106 Wroclaw, Poland. TEL 386-25. (Dist. by: Ars Polona, Krakowskie Przedmiescie 7, 00-068 Warsaw, Poland) Ed. Stanislaw Stachowski. bk.rev.; abstr.; bibl.; circ. 590. Indexed: M.L.A., Numis.Lit.
　Description: Monographs and research reports from Oriental studies in Poland.

FREE PALESTINE. see POLITICAL SCIENCE — Civil Rights

950　　　　　GW　　ISSN 0170-3307
FREIBURGER ALTORIENTALISCHE STUDIEN. irreg., vol.18, 1989. price varies. Franz Steiner Verlag Wiesbaden GmbH, Birkenwaldstr. 44, Postfach 101526, 7000 Stuttgart 1, Germany. TEL 0711-2582-0. FAX 0711-2582290. TELEX 723636-DAZD. Ed. Burkhart Kienast.

956　　　　　GW　　ISSN 0340-6261
FREIBURGER BEITRAEGE ZUR INDOLOGIE. 1968. irreg., vol.25, 1991. price varies. Verlag Otto Harrassowitz, Taunusstr. 14, Postfach 2929, 6200 Wiesbaden 1, Germany. TEL 0611-530-0. FAX 0611-530570. TELEX 4186135. Ed. Ulrich Schneider.

950　　　　　GW　　ISSN 0724-4703
FREIBURGER FERNOESTLICHE FORSCHUNGEN. 1983. irreg., vol.1, 1983. price varies. Verlag Otto Harrassowitz, Taunusstr. 14, Postfach 2929, 6200 Wiesbaden 1, Germany. TEL 0611-530-0. FAX 0611-530570. TELEX 4186135. Ed. Peter Greiner.

956 297　　　GW　　ISSN 0170-3285
FREIBURGER ISLAMSTUDIEN. irreg., vol.15, 1992. price varies. Franz Steiner Verlag Wiesbaden GmbH, Birkenwaldstr. 44, Postfach 101526, 7000 Stuttgart 1, Germany. TEL 0711-2582-0. FAX 0711-2582290. TELEX 723636-DAZD. Ed. Hans Robert Roemer.

951　　　　　GW
FREIES ASIEN. 1959. s-m. Deutsch-Chinesische Gesellschaft e.V., Villichgasse 17, 5300 Bonn 2, Germany. TEL 0228-356535. FAX 0228-357520. circ. 1,200. (looseleaf format; back issues avail.)

FU JEN STUDIES; literature & linguistics. see LITERATURE

950　　　　　II
GANGANATHA JHA KENDRIYA SANSKRIT VIDYAPEETHA. JOURNAL. (Text in English, Hindi, Sanskrit) 1943. q. Rs.120($15) Ganganatha Jha Kendriya Sanskrit Vidyapeetha, Chandrashakhar Azad Park, Allahabad 211002, Uttar Pradesh, India. TEL 0532-600957. FAX 532-606121. Eds. G.C. Tripathi, Maya Malaviya. bk.rev.; illus.; index; circ. 1,000.
　Formerly: Ganganatha Jha Research Institute. Journal (ISSN 0016-4461)
　Description: Devoted to Oriental studies in general.

890 297　　　BN　　ISSN 0350-1418
DB240.5
GAZI HUSREVBEGOVA BIBLIOTEKA. ANALI. (Text in Serbocroatian; summaries in English) 1972. a. Gazi Husrevbegova Biblioteka, Obala Pariske Komune 4, 71000 Sarajevo, Bosnia Hercegovina. (Co-sponsor: Starjesinstvo Islamske Zajednice) Ed. Abdurahman Hukic. circ. 1,500. Indexed: Amer.Hist.& Life, Hist.Abstr.

950　　　　　GW　　ISSN 0016-9080
GESELLSCHAFT FUER NATUR- UND VOELKERKUNDE OSTASIENS. NACHRICHTEN; Zeitschrift fuer Kultur und Geschichte Ostasiens. (Text in English and German) s-a. DM.60 (members DM.50). Universitaet Hamburg, Seminar fuer Sprache und Kultur Japans, Von Melle Park 6-7, 2000 Hamburg 13, Germany. Ed.Bd. bk.rev.; bibl.; charts; illus.; circ. 750. Indexed: Amer.Hist.& Life, Hist.Abstr.

GHANTA. see EDUCATION — International Education Programs

950　　　　　GW　　ISSN 0170-3455
GLASENAPP-STIFTUNG. irreg., vol.32, 1991. price varies. (Glasenapp-Stiftung) Franz Steiner Verlag Wiesbaden GmbH, Birkenwaldstr. 44, Postfach 101526, 7000 Stuttgart 1, Germany. TEL 0711-2582-0. FAX 0711-2582290. TELEX 723636-DAZD.

954 300　　　II　　ISSN 0970-1427
GLORY OF INDIA; quarterly on Indology. (Text in English and Hindi) 1977. q. Rs.40($22) Motilal Banarsidass (Delhi), 40, U.A., Bungalow Rd., Jawahar Nagar, Delhi 110007, India. TEL 11-2911985. FAX 011-2930689. TELEX 031-66053-ENKY-JN. Ed. Sunil Dutt. adv.; bk.rev.; abstr.; bibl.

935 950　　　GW　　ISSN 0340-6326
GOETTINGER ORIENTFORSCHUNGEN. REIHE I: SYRIACA. irreg., vol.34, 1991. price varies. Verlag Otto Harrassowitz, Taunusstr. 14, Postfach 2929, 6200 Wiesbaden 1, Germany. TEL 0611-530-0. FAX 0611-530570. TELEX 4186135.

950　　　　　GW　　ISSN 0173-2358
GOETTINGER ORIENTFORSCHUNGEN. REIHE II: STUDIEN ZUR SPAETANTIKEN UND FRUEHCHRISTLICHEN KUNST. 1980. irreg., vol.9, 1986. price varies. Verlag Otto Harrassowitz, Taunusstr. 14, Postfach 2929, 6200 Wiesbaden 1, Germany. TEL 0611-530-0. FAX 0611-530570. TELEX 4186135.

932　　　　　GW　　ISSN 0340-6342
GOETTINGER ORIENTFORSCHUNGEN. REIHE IV: AEGYPTEN. 1973. irreg., vol.22, 1991. price varies. Verlag Otto Harrassowitz, Taunusstr. 14, Postfach 2929, 6200 Wiesbaden 1, Germany. TEL 0611-530-0. FAX 0611-530570. TELEX 4186135. Eds. Friedrich Junge, Wolfhart Westendorf.

951 915.134　　CC
GUIZHOU MINZU YANJIU/STUDY OF GUIZHOU NATIONALITIES. (Text in Chinese) q. $20.40. Guizhou Sheng Minzu Yanjiusuo - Guizhou Nationality Research Institute, No. 16, Bianjing Xiang, Bajiaoyan, Guiyang, Guizhou 550001, People's Republic of China. TEL 625623. (Dist. in US by: China Books & Periodicals, Inc., 2929 24th St., San Francisco, CA 94110. TEL 415-282-2994) Ed. Wu Yongqing.

930.1 950　　　NE
HANDBUCH DER ORIENTALISTIK. (In 8 Sections) 1952. irreg., latest 1992. price varies. E.J. Brill, P.O. Box 9000, 2300 PA Leiden, Netherlands. TEL 071-312624. FAX 071-317532. TELEX 39296 BRILL NL. (In N. America: E.J. Brill, 24 Hudson St., Kinderhook, NY 12106. TEL 800-962-4406) Ed. B. Spuler. illus.
　Description: Scholarly monographs on all aspects of Oriental studies.

ORIENTAL STUDIES

HANDBUCH DER ORIENTALISTIK. 1. ABTEILUNG. DER NAHE UND DER MITTLERE OSTEN. see *HISTORY — History Of The Near East*

954   NE   ISSN 0169-9377
HANDBUCH DER ORIENTALISTIK. 2. ABTEILUNG. INDIEN. 1966. irreg., latest 1992. price varies. E.J. Brill, P.O. Box 9000, 2300 PA Leiden, Netherlands. TEL 071-312624. FAX 071-317532. TELEX 39296 BRILL NL. (In N. America: E.J. Brill, 24 Hudson St., Kinderhook, NY 12106. TEL 800-962-4406) Ed. B. Spuler.
—BLDSC shelfmark: 4254.055000.

959   NE   ISSN 0169-9571
HANDBUCH DER ORIENTALISTIK. 3. ABTEILUNG. INDONESIEN, MALAYSIA UND DIE PHILIPPINEN. 1972. irreg. price varies. E.J. Brill, P.O. Box 9000, 2300 PA Leiden, Netherlands. TEL 071-312624. FAX 071-317532. TELEX 39296 BRILL NL. (In N. America: E.J. Brill, 24 Hudson St., Kinderhook, NY 12106. TEL 800-962-4406) Ed. B. Spuler.

951   NE   ISSN 0169-9520
HANDBUCH DER ORIENTALISTIK. 4. ABTEILUNG. CHINA. 1976. irreg., latest 1989. price varies. E.J. Brill, P.O. Box 9000, 2300 PA Leiden, Netherlands. TEL 071-312624. FAX 071-317532. TELEX 39296 BRILL NL. (In N. America: E.J. Brill, 24 Hudson St., Kinderhook, NY 12106. TEL 800-962-4406) Ed. B. Spuler.

952   NE   ISSN 0921-5239
HANDBUCH DER ORIENTALISTIK. 5. ABTEILUNG. JAPAN. 1988. irreg., latest 1991. price varies. E.J. Brill, P.O. Box 9000, 2300 PA Leiden, Netherlands. TEL 071-312624. FAX 071-317532. TELEX 39296 BRILL NL. (In N. America: E.J. Brill, 24 Hudson St., Kinderhook, NY 12106. TEL 800-962-4406) Ed. B. Spuler.

950 700   NE   ISSN 0169-9474
HANDBUCH DER ORIENTALISTIK. 7. ABTEILUNG. KUNST UND ARCHAEOLOGIE. 1970. irreg., latest 1992. price varies. E.J. Brill, P.O. Box 9000, 2300 PA Leiden, Netherlands. TEL 071-312624. FAX 071-317532. TELEX 39296 BRILL NL. (In N. America: E.J. Brill, 24 Hudson St., Kinderhook, NY 12106. TEL 800-962-4406) Ed. B. Spuler.

494   NE
HANDBUCH DER ORIENTALISTIK. 8. ABTEILUNG. HANDBOOK OF URALIC STUDIES. 1988. irreg. price varies. E.J. Brill, P.O. Box 9000, 2300 PA Leiden, Netherlands. TEL 071-312624. FAX 071-317532. TELEX 39296 BRILL NL. (In N. America: E.J. Brill, 24 Hudson St., Kinderhook, NY 12106. TEL 800-962-4406) Ed. B. Spuler.

HANDES AMSORYA; Zeitschrift fuer Armenische Philologie. see *LINGUISTICS*

HARVARD ARMENIAN TEXTS AND STUDIES. see *HISTORY — History Of The Near East*

950   US   ISSN 0073-0548
DS501
HARVARD JOURNAL OF ASIATIC STUDIES. 1936. s-a. $30 to individuals; institutions $45 (effective 1992). Harvard-Yenching Institute, 2 Divinity Ave., Cambridge, MA 02138. TEL 617-495-2758. FAX 617-495-7798. Ed. Howard S. Hibbett. bk.rev.; cum.index: 1936-80; index every 5 yrs.; circ. 1,200. (also avail. in microform from UMI,MIM; reprint service avail. from UMI,SCH) Indexed: Amer.Hist.& Life, Arts & Hum.Cit.Ind., Bk.Rev.Ind., Curr.Cont., Hist.Abstr., Hum.Ind., Ind.Bk.Rev.Hum., M.L.A., Mid.East: Abstr.& Ind., Soc.Sci.Ind
—BLDSC shelfmark: 4267.300000.
Description: Covers the languages, literatures, cultures, and histories of the countries in Eastern and Central Asia.

410   SZ   ISSN 0073-0971
HAUTES ETUDES ORIENTALES. 1968. irreg., no.27, 1991. (Ecole Pratique des Hautes Etudes, Centre de Recherches d'Histoire et de Philologie, FR) Librairie Droz S.A., 11, rue Massot, CH-1211 Geneva 12, Switzerland. TEL 022-3466666. FAX 022-3472391. circ. 600.
Description: Discusses studies of military, literature and poetry from the Far East.

HENRY MARTYN INSTITUTE OF ISLAMIC STUDIES. BULLETIN. see *RELIGIONS AND THEOLOGY — Islamic*

950   MR   ISSN 0018-1005
DT301
HESPERIS - TAMUDA. (Text in English, French, Spanish) N.S. 1960. 3/yr. DH.45.($9) per no. Universite Mohammed V, Faculte des Lettres et des Sciences Humaines, Association des Sciences de l'Homme, Avenue Moulay Cherif, B.P. 1040, C.C.P. 45631, Rabat, Morocco. bk.rev.; bibl.; charts; illus. **Indexed:** A.I.C.P., Amer.Hist.& Life, Hist.Abstr.

950   GW   ISSN 0232-3001
HILPRECHT: SAMMLUNG. 1961. irreg., vol.3, 1976. (Friedrich-Schiller-Universitaet, Prof. Hilprecht Sammlung Vorderasiatischer Altertuemer) Akademie-Verlag Berlin, Leipziger Str. 3-4, 1086 Berlin, Germany. TELEX 114420-AVERL-DD. Eds. Rudolf Heyer, Friedmar Kuhnert.

958   NP
HIMALAYAN CULTURE. (Text in English or Nepali) 1978. q. Rs.38($6) Hari Bangsha Kirant, 20-136 Kamal Pokhari, Kathmandu 711000, Nepal.

890   TI   ISSN 0018-862X
AS653
I B L A. (Text in French) 1937. s-a. 15000 din.($22.50) Institut des Belles Lettres Arabes, 12 rue Jamaa el Haoua, 1008 Tunis, Tunisia. TEL 560-133. Ed. Jean Fontaine. adv.; bk.rev.; bibl.; index; circ. 850. (also avail. in microfiche) **Indexed:** A.I.C.P., Bull.Signal., Lang.& Lang.Behav.Abstr., M.L.A.
Description: Covers questions in the field of arts and human sciences concerning the Arab-Muslim world, with special reference to Tunisia.

954 800   II
IMAGE. (Text in English) vol.2, 1977. s-a. Rs.10($3) Image Publication, Sahadevkhunta, Balasore 756001, Orissa, India. Ed. Indu Bhusan Kar. adv.; bk.rev.

INDIAN HORIZONS. see *HISTORY — History Of Asia*

954   II   ISSN 0019-686X
DS401
INDICA. (Text in English) 1964. s-a. Rs.35($10) Heras Institute of Indian History and Culture, St. Xavier's College, Bombay 400 001, India. TEL 22-262-0661. Ed. John Correia-Afonso. adv.; bk.rev.; illus.; index, cum.index; circ. 400. (back issues avail.) **Indexed:** Amer.Hist.& Life, Hist.Abstr.
—BLDSC shelfmark: 4432.300000.
Description: Articles on history, literature, archeology, art and religion.

INDICES VERBORUM LINGUAE MONGOLIAE MONUMENTIS TRADITORUM. see *LINGUISTICS*

INDO-ASIA; fuer Politik, Kultur und Wirtschaft Indiens und Suedost Asiens. see *POLITICAL SCIENCE*

INDO-IRAN JOURNAL. see *POLITICAL SCIENCE*

950   NE   ISSN 0019-7246
PK1   CODEN: IIRJAU
INDO-IRANIAN JOURNAL. 1957. q. $161.50. Kluwer Academic Publishers, Postbus 17, 3300 AA Dordrecht, Netherlands. TEL 078-334911. FAX 078-334254. TELEX 29245. (Dist. by: Kluwer Academic Publishers Group, P.O. Box 322, 3300 AH Dordrecht, Netherlands; N. America dist. addr.: Box 358, Accord Station, Hingham, MA 02018-0358. TEL 617-871-6600) Eds. J.W. De Jong, M. Witzel. adv.; bk.rev.; index. (reprint service avail. from SWZ) **Indexed:** Curr.Cont., Ind.Bk.Rev.Hum., Lang.& Lang.Behav.Abstr., M.L.A., Mid.East: Abstr.& Ind.
—BLDSC shelfmark: 4437.590000.
Description: Publishes original scholarship on ancient and medieval Indian and Iranian languages, literatures and linguistics, as well as related philosophical and textual issues.

954   NE
INDOLOGICA TAURINENSIA. (Text in various languages) 1973. a. L.25000. (C E S M E O) E.J. Brill, P.O. Box 9000, 2300 PA Leiden, Netherlands. TEL 071-312624. FAX 071-317532. TELEX 39296 BRILL NL. (Orders in N. America to: 24 Hudson St., Kinderhook, NY 12106. TEL 800-962-4406) (back issues avail.)

991   US   ISSN 0019-7289
DS611
INDONESIA (ITHACA). 1966. s-a. $18 (foreign $23). Cornell University, Southeast Asia Program, 102 West Ave., Ithaca, NY 14850. TEL 607-255-8038. FAX 607-254-5000. TELEX WUI-6713054. (Subscr. to: S E A P Publications, Cornell University, E. Hill Plaza, Ithaca, NY 14850) Ed. Audrey Kahin. bk.rev.; bibl.; charts; illus.; stat.; index every 3 yrs.; circ. 900. (also avail. in microform from UMI; reprint service avail. from UMI; back issues avail.) **Indexed:** E.I.
—BLDSC shelfmark: 4437.630000.
Description: Interdisciplinary journal devoted to Indonesia's culture, history and socio-political problems.

INDONESIAN STUDIES. see *POLITICAL SCIENCE — International Relations*

INKSTONE; a magazine of haiku. see *LITERATURE — Poetry*

INSTITUT DOMINICAIN D'ETUDES ORIENTALES DU CAIRE. MELANGES. see *HISTORY — History Of The Near East*

950   II   ISSN 0073-8352
INSTITUT FRANCAIS DE PONDICHERY. DEPARTEMENT D'INDOLOGIE. PUBLICATIONS. (Text in English, French) 1956. irreg.(approx. 4/yr.). price varies. Institut Francais de Pondichery, Box 33, Pondicherry 605 001, India. TEL 24170. FAX 91-413-29534. TELEX 469224 FRAN IN. (Dist. outside India: Librairie Adrien Maisonneuve, 11 rue Saint Sulpice, 75006 Paris, France) Ed. F. Grimalal. bk.rev.; index; circ. 500. **Indexed:** Bull.Signal.
Formerly: Institut Francais d'Indologie. Publications.

956   GW   ISSN 0073-8387
INSTITUT FUER ASIENKUNDE. SCHRIFTEN. (Text in German; summaries in English) 1957. irreg., no.47, 1986. price varies. Verlag Otto Harrassowitz, Taunusstr. 14, Postfach 2929, 6200 Wiesbaden 1, Germany. TEL 0611-530-0. FAX 0611-530570. TELEX 4186135.

INSTITUTE OF ASIAN STUDIES. JOURNAL. see *SOCIOLOGY*

950 001.3 300   JA   ISSN 0538-6012
PJ21
INTERNATIONAL CONFERENCE OF ORIENTALISTS IN JAPAN. TRANSACTIONS. (Text in English) 1957. a. 2300 Yen. Toho Gakkai - Institute of Eastern Culture, 4-1, Nishi-Kanda 2-chome, Chiyoda-ku, Tokyo 101, Japan. Ed.Bd. (back issues avail.) **Indexed:** M.L.A.

INTERNATIONAL DIRECTORY OF CENTERS FOR ASIAN STUDIES. see *BUSINESS AND ECONOMICS — Trade And Industrial Directories*

950 300   CN   ISSN 0847-3471
▼**INTERNATIONAL JOURNAL OF INDIAN STUDIES.** 1990. a. $15. McGill University, Religious Studies, 3520 University St., Montreal, Que. H3A 2A7, Canada. Ed. Sushil Mittal. bk.rev.
Description: Interdisciplinary forum for the scholarly analysis of all aspects of Indian society and culture of the past and present.

956   UK   ISSN 0020-7438
DS41
INTERNATIONAL JOURNAL OF MIDDLE EAST STUDIES. 1970. q. $104 (includes 2 issues of MESA Bulletin). (Middle East Studies Association of North America (MESA), US) Cambridge University Press, Edinburgh Bldg., Shaftesbury Rd., Cambridge CB2 2RU, England. TEL 0223-312393. FAX 0223-315052. TELEX 851817256. (North American orders to: Cambridge University Press, 40 W. 20th St., New York, NY 10011) Ed. Leila Fawaz. adv.; bk.rev. (also avail. in microform from UMI; reprint service avail. from SWZ,UMI) **Indexed:** A.B.C.Pol.Sci., Amer.Hist.& Life, Commun.Abstr., Curr.Cont., Geog.Abstr., Hist.Abstr., I D A, M.L.A., Mid.East: Abstr.& Ind., Rural Recreat.Tour.Abstr., Soc.Sci.Ind., SSCI, World Agri.Econ.& Rural Sociol.Abstr.
—BLDSC shelfmark: 4542.358000.
Description: Research on the Middle East from the seventh century to the present day: history, politics, economics, anthropology, sociology, literature and folklore, comparative religion, law.

950　　　　　　　HK
INTERNATIONAL SYMPOSIA ON ASIAN STUDIES. PROCEEDINGS. 1979. a. $125. Asian Research Service, G.P.O. Box 2232, Hong Kong. TEL 5707227. FAX 5128050. TELEX 63899-HX. Ed. Nelson Leung.

955　　　　　　　US　　ISSN 0021-0862
　　　　　　　　　　　　　　CODEN: IRSTEK
IRANIAN STUDIES. 1968. q. $35. Society for Iranian Studies, Middle East Institute, Columbia University, 1113 International Affairs Bldg., New York, NY 10027. TEL 212-854-3996. Ed. Richard Bulliet. adv.; bk.rev.; bibl.; charts; illus.; index; circ. 1,000. (tabloid format; also avail. in microform from MIM) **Indexed:** Ind.Islam., M.L.A., Mid.East: Abstr.& Ind.
—BLDSC shelfmark: 4567.534000.

IRANICA ANTIQUA. see ARCHAEOLOGY

IRANICA ANTIQUA SUPPLEMENTA. see ARCHAEOLOGY

955　　　　　　　GW
IRANISTISCHE MITTEILUNGEN. (Text in English and German) 1967. irreg. (2-3/yr.). DM.40 per no. Antigone-Verlag, Postfach 1147, 3559 Allendorf-Eder, Germany. TEL 06452-1800. Ed. Helmhart Kanus-Crede. bk.rev.; circ. 50. (back issues avail.)
Description: Iranian studies.

IRAQ. see ARCHAEOLOGY

AL-ISLAAM. see RELIGIONS AND THEOLOGY — Islamic

297　　　　　　　GW　　ISSN 0021-1818
DS36
DER ISLAM; Zeitschrift fuer Geschichte und Kultur des Islamischen Orients. (Text in English, French and German) 1910. 2/yr. $87. Walter de Gruyter und Co., Genthiner Str. 13, 1000 Berlin 30, Germany. TEL 030-26005-0. FAX 030-26005251. TELEX 184027. (U.S. addr.: Walter de Gruyter, Inc., 200 Saw Mill Rd., Hawthorne, NY 10532) Eds. Albercht Noth, Bertold Spuler. adv.; bk.rev.; bibl.; illus.; circ. 300. **Indexed:** Curr.Cont., E.I., M.L.A., Numis.Lit, Rel.Ind.One.
—BLDSC shelfmark: 4583.013000.

297 892.7　　　II　　ISSN 0021-1834
DS36
ISLAMIC CULTURE. (Text in English) 1927. q. $8. Islamic Culture Board, Opposite Osmania University Post Office, Hyderabad 7, India. Ed. Syed Sirajuddin. adv.; bk.rev.; bibl.; illus.; index; circ. 700. (also avail. in microform from UMI; reprint service avail. from KTO) **Indexed:** Amer.Hist.& Life, Hist.Abstr., Ind.Bk.Rev.Hum., Mid.East: Abstr.& Ind.

ISLAMIC EDUCATION. see EDUCATION

297 892.7　　　UK　　ISSN 0021-1842
D198
ISLAMIC QUARTERLY; a review of Islamic Culture. 1954. q. £18.50 (foreign £23). Islamic Cultural Centre, 146 Park Rd., London NW8 7RG, England. TEL 01-724-3363-7. Ed. Bashir Ebrahim-Khan. bk.rev.; circ. 1,000. (back issues avail.) **Indexed:** Amer.Hist.& Life, Hist.Abstr.
—BLDSC shelfmark: 4583.030000.

956　　　　　　　MY　　ISSN 0126-5636
DS36.85
ISLAMIYYAT. (Text in English and Malay) 1977. a. M.10($10) Penerbit Universiti Kebangsaan Malaysia, Fakulti Pegajian Islam, 43600 UKM Bangi Selangor, Malaysia. TEL 8250001. TELEX UNIKEB-MA-31496. Ed. Muda Ismail Ab. Rahman. circ. 500.

ISRAEL EXPLORATION JOURNAL. see ARCHAEOLOGY

492　　　　　　　NE　　ISSN 0334-4401
PJ3001
ISRAEL ORIENTAL STUDIES. (Text in Arabic, English, French, German) 1971. irreg., vol.12, 1991. (Tel Aviv University, Faculty of Humanities, IS) E.J. Brill, P.O. Box 9000, 2300 PA Leiden, Netherlands. TEL 071-312624. FAX 071-317532. TELEX 39296 BRILL NL. (In N. America: E.J. Brill, 24 Hudson St., Kinderhook, NY 12106. TEL 800-962-4406) Ed. S. Somekh. bk.rev.; circ. 1,000.

ISSUES & STUDIES. see POLITICAL SCIENCE — International Relations

ISTANBULER MITTEILUNGEN. see ARCHAEOLOGY

950　　　　　　　IT
ISTITUTO UNIVERSITARIO ORIENTALE DI NAPOLI. ANNALI. (Text in English, Italian) 1940; N.S. 1944. q. (plus 4 suppl.). L.100000($100) Herder Editrice e Libreria s.r.l., Piazza Montecitorio 120, 00186 Rome, Italy. TEL 67 94 628. FAX 678-47-51. TELEX 621427 NATEL. Ed. Luigi Cagni. bk.rev.; bibl. (back issues avail.)
Supersedes: Istituto Orientale di Napoli. Annali.

ISTITUTO UNIVERSITARIO ORIENTALE DI NAPOLI. SEMINARIO DI STUDI DEL MONDO CLASSICO. ANNALI. SEZIONE LINGUISTICA. see CLASSICAL STUDIES

952　　　　　　　GW　　ISSN 0937-2008
IZUMI; Quellen, Studien und Materialen zur Kultur Japans. 1989. irreg., vol.1, 1989. Verlag Otto Harrassowitz, Taunusstr. 14, Postfach 2929, 6200 Wiesbaden 1, Germany. TEL 0611-530-0. FAX 0611-530-570. TELEX 4186135. Ed. Klaus Kracht.

JAPAN-AMERICA SOCIETY OF WASHINGTON. BULLETIN. see POLITICAL SCIENCE — International Relations

952 059.956　　JA　　ISSN 0385-2318
DS821
JAPAN FOUNDATION NEWSLETTER. (Text in English) 1973. bi-m. free. Japan Foundation, Park Bldg., 3-6, Kioi-cho, Chiyoda-ku, Tokyo 102, Japan. bk.rev.; circ. 8,000. (back issues avail.)
Description: Features cultural highlights, research reports, conference reports and foundation activities. Intended for those interested in Japanese culture and international cultural exchange.

JAPAN LETTER. see BUSINESS AND ECONOMICS — Economic Situation And Conditions

JAPANESE JOURNAL OF RELIGIOUS STUDIES. see RELIGIONS AND THEOLOGY — Buddhist

952　　　　　　　GW　　ISSN 0934-9995
JAPANISCHE FACHTEXTE. 1980. irreg., vol.3, 1988. Verlag Otto Harrassowitz, Taunusstr. 14, Postfach 2929, 6200 Wiesbaden 1, Germany. TEL 0611-530-0. FAX 0611-530-570. TELEX 4186135. Ed. Bruno Lewin.

952　　　　　　　US
JAPANOPHILE. 1974. q. $14. Japanophile, Box 223, Okemos, MI 48864. TEL 517-349-1795. Ed. Earl R. Snodgrass. adv.; bk.rev.; circ. 400. (back issues avail.)

JAPANWIRTSCHAFT. see BUSINESS AND ECONOMICS — Economic Situation And Conditions

950　　　　　　　FR　　ISSN 0021-762X
PJ4
JOURNAL ASIATIQUE. 1822. 4/yr. (two double nos./yr.). price varies. (Societe Asiatique) Librairie Orientaliste Paul Geuthner, 12 rue Vavin, 75006 Paris, France. TEL 33-1-46-34-71-30. FAX 33-1-43-29-75-64. TELEX 250 303 PUBLIC PARIS. bk.rev.; illus.; index. (reprint service avail. from SCH) **Indexed:** E.I., M.L.A.

JOURNAL OF ARABIC LITERATURE. see LITERATURE

950　　　　　　　US　　ISSN 1044-2979
DS1
JOURNAL OF ASIAN AND AFRICAN AFFAIRS. 1989. s-a. $25 to individuals; students $15. Box 44843, Washington, DC 20026-4843. TEL 703-491-9231. Ed. Aftab Kazi. bk.rev.; circ. 1,000. **Indexed:** Amer.Hist.& Life, Hist.Abstr., Int.Polit.Sci.Abstr., P.A.I.S.
Description: Encourages research distinguishing between established stereotype and actual sociopolitical realities in Asia and Africa.
Refereed Serial

950　　　　　　　US　　ISSN 0162-6795
DS1
JOURNAL OF ASIAN CULTURE. 1977. a. $10. University of California, Los Angeles, Department of East Asian Languages and Cultures, Graduate Students in Asian Studies, 290 Royce Hall, Los Angeles, CA 90024. TEL 213-206-8235. Ed. Adam Schorr. adv.; bk.rev.; charts; illus.; circ. 500. **Indexed:** Amer.Hist.& Life, Hist.Abstr., Sociol.Abstr., Sociol.Abstr.
Description: Annual publication of graduate students whose research involves various aspects of Asian studies.

ORIENTAL STUDIES　3639

950　　　　　　　US　　ISSN 0021-9118
DS501
JOURNAL OF ASIAN STUDIES. 1941. 4/yr. $95 includes Bibliography of Asian Studies and Doctoral Dissertations on Asia. Association for Asian Studies, Inc., 1 Lane Hall, University of Michigan, Ann Arbor, MI 48109. TEL 313-665-2490. Ed. David Buck. adv.; bk.rev.; bibl.; charts; illus.; stat.; index; circ. 7,000. (also avail. in microform from UMI; back issues avail.; reprint service avail. from UMI) **Indexed:** A.B.C.Pol.Sci., Acad.Ind., Amer.Bibl.Slavic & E.Eur.Stud., Amer.Hist.& Life, Bk.Rev.Ind. (1965-), Child.Bk.Rev.Ind. (1965-), Curr.Cont., E.I., Hist.Abstr., Hum.Ind., Ind.Bk.Rev.Hum., M.L.A., Ref.Sour., Rural Devel.Abstr., SSCI, Stud.Wom.Abstr.
—BLDSC shelfmark: 4947.250000.
Description: Contains articles about the humanities and social sciences in reference to Asia.

950　　　　　　　KO　　ISSN 0021-9126
DS1
JOURNAL OF ASIATIC STUDIES. (Text in Korean; occasionally in English) 1958. s-a. $20. (Korea University, Asiatic Research Center) Korea University Press, Seoul, S. Korea. TEL 02-9261926. FAX 02-9249132. TELEX KOREA-KU-K34138. Ed. Eom Tae-am. adv.; bk.rev.; bibl.; charts; cum. index; circ. 1,000. **Indexed:** Amer.Hist.& Life, Hist.Abstr., Mid.East: Abstr.& Ind.

JOURNAL OF CHINESE LAW. see LAW

JOURNAL OF CHINESE RELIGIONS. see RELIGIONS AND THEOLOGY — Buddhist

495.1 951　　US
JOURNAL OF CHINESE STUDIES. 1984. s-a. $16. American Association for Chinese Studies, 300 Bricker Hall, Ohio State Univerity, Columbus, OH 43210. Ed. Fred Sturm. adv.; bk.rev.; circ. 500.
Former titles: American Association for Chinese Studies. Bulletin; American Association for Chinese Studies Newsletter; American Association of Teachers of Chinese Language and Culture. Newsletter.

JOURNAL OF CUNEIFORM STUDIES. see ARCHAEOLOGY

950　　　　　　　PH　　ISSN 0022-0450
JOURNAL OF EAST ASIATIC STUDIES. 1951. s-a. $12. University of Manila, 546 Dr. M.V. de los Santos St., Manila D-403, Philippines. Ed. Charles O. Houston, Jr. adv.; charts; illus.; index; circ. 500. **Indexed:** A.I.C.P., Hist.Abstr.

JOURNAL OF FUKIEN HISTORY. see HISTORY — History Of Asia

JOURNAL OF INDIAN PHILOSOPHY. see PHILOSOPHY

952　　　　　　　US　　ISSN 0095-6848
DS801
JOURNAL OF JAPANESE STUDIES. 1974. s-a. $25. Society for Japanese Studies, Thomson Hall, DR-05, University of Washington, Seattle, WA 98195. TEL 206-543-9302. FAX 206-685-0668. Ed. Susan B. Hanley. adv.; bk.rev.; circ. 1,800. (back issues avail.) **Indexed:** Amer.Hist.& Life, Arts & Hum.Cit.Ind., Curr.Cont., Hist.Abstr., M.L.A.
Description: Multi-disciplinary study of Japan.
Refereed Serial

950　　　　　　　II　　ISSN 0022-3301
PK101
JOURNAL OF ORIENTAL RESEARCH. (Text in English and Sanskrit) 1927. irreg. (approx. a.). Kuppuswami Sastri Research Institute, 84 Royapettah High Rd., Madras 600 004, Mylapore, India. TEL 847320. Ed. S.S. Janaki. bk.rev.; illus.; index; circ. 500.
Description: Contributions to Sanskrit and Indological research.

950　　　　　　　HK　　ISSN 0022-331X
DS501
JOURNAL OF ORIENTAL STUDIES. (Text in Chinese and English) 1954. s-a. HK.$150 to individuals; institutions HK.$200. University of Hong Kong, Centre of Asian Studies, Pokfulam Rd., Hong Kong. FAX 559-5884. Ed. E.K.Y. Chen. adv.; bk.rev.; index; circ. 300. (also avail. in microform from UMI; back issues avail.; reprint service avail. from UMI) **Indexed:** Amer.Hist.& Life, Hist.Abstr., Ind.Bk.Rev.Hum.
Description: Covers research from China, Japan and Southeast Asia concerning traditional and contemporary issues in various social sciences.

ORIENTAL STUDIES

294.6   II   ISSN 0379-8194
BL2017
JOURNAL OF SIKH STUDIES. (Text in English) 1974. s-a. Rs.30 to individuals; institutions Rs.40($15). (Guru Nanak Dev University, Department of Guru Nanak Studies) Guru Nanak Dev University Press, Amritsar 143 005, India. TEL 62450. Ed. Jaswinder Kaur Dhillon. adv.; bk.rev.; circ. 1,000.
    Description: Aims to promote Sikh studies as a scientific discipline.

951   JA
JOURNAL OF SINOLOGICAL STUDIES/SHINAGAKU KENKYU. (Text in Japanese; summaries in English) 1948. s-a. Sinological Society of Hiroshima - Hiroshima Shinagakkai, c/o Hiroshima University, Faculty of Literature, 1-1-89 Higashi-Senda-machi, Hiroshima, Japan.

JOURNAL OF SOUTHEAST ASIAN STUDIES. see *HISTORY — History Of Asia*

951   US
DS751
JOURNAL OF SUNG-YUAN STUDIES. (Text in Chinese and English) 1970. a. $15 to individuals; institutions $25. c/o James M. Hargett, Ed., Department of East Asian Studies, HU 285, State University of New York, Albany, Albany, NY 12222. FAX 518-442-4188. adv.; bk.rev.; bibl.; illus.; circ. 300.
    Former titles (until no.22, 1989): Bulletin of Sung-Yuan Studies (ISSN 0049-254X); (until vol.14, 1978): Sung Studies Newsletter.

950   CH
JOURNAL OF SUNOLOGY. (Text in Chinese) 1985. q. free. National Sun Yat-sen University, Sun Yat-sen Institute, Kaohsiung, Taiwan 800, Republic of China. TEL 07-531-2022. Ed. Richard Yang. bk.rev.; circ. 1,000.

JOURNAL OF THE ECONOMIC AND SOCIAL HISTORY OF THE ORIENT/JOURNAL DE L'HISTOIRE ECONOMIQUE ET SOCIALE DE L'ORIENT. see *HISTORY — History Of Asia*

JOURNAL OF TRADITIONAL ACUPUNCTURE. see *MEDICAL SCIENCES*

KADMONIOT; quarterly for the antiquities of Eretz-Israel and Biblical lands. see *ARCHAEOLOGY*

KARATE AND ORIENTAL ARTS. see *SPORTS AND GAMES*

954   II   ISSN 0022-9210
KASHMIR AFFAIRS. (Text in English) 1959. bi-m. Rs.7.50. Karan Nagar, Jammu, India. Ed. Balraj Puri. adv.; bk.rev.; charts; cum.index.

KEILSCHRIFFTEXTE AUS BOGHAZKOI. see *ARCHAEOLOGY*

KEIRAKU SHINRYO. see *MEDICAL SCIENCES*

950   HU   ISSN 0133-6193
KELETI TANULMANYOK/ORIENTAL STUDIES. (Text in English, French, German, Hungarian, Russian and Oriental languages) 1976. irreg. price varies or exchange basis. Magyar Tudomanyos Akademia Konyvtara, Aranyjanos u.1, P.O. Box 7, 1361 Budapest 5, Hungary. Ed. Eva Apor. circ. 800.
    Description: Oriental studies and papers on the documents and the history of the Oriental collection of the Academy Library of Hungary.

950   NE   ISSN 0169-8907
KERN INSTITUTE, LEIDEN. MEMOIRS. irreg., latest 1991. price varies. E.J. Brill, P.O. Box 9000, 2300 PA Leiden, Netherlands. TEL 071-312624. FAX 071-317532. TELEX 39296 BRILL NL. (In N. America: E.J./Brill, 24 Hudson St., Kinderhook, NY 12106. TEL 800-962-4406)

950   GW   ISSN 0937-2105
KHOJ; a series of modern South Asian studies. 1988. irreg., vol.3, 1991. Verlag Otto Harrassowitz, Taunusstr. 14, Postfach 2929, 6200 Wiesbaden 1, Germany. TEL 0611-530-0. FAX 0611-530-570. TELEX 4186135. Eds. Richard Barz, Monika Thiel-Horstmann.

950   PH   ISSN 0115-6012
KINAADMAN/WISDOM; a journal of the Southern Philippines. 1979. s-a. P.100($10) Xavier University, Cagayan de Oro 9000, Philippines. (Dist. by: Bookmark Inc., Box 1171, Manila, Philippines; Dist. in U.S. by: Cellar Book Shop, 18090 Wyoming Ave., Detroit, MI 48221) Ed. Miguel A. Bernad. bk.rev.; bibl.; circ. 800. **Indexed:** Ind.Phil.Per.
    Description: Covers the Southern Philippines and Mindanao topics.

956   GW   ISSN 0343-1088
KLEINE AEGYPTISCHE TEXTE. 1969. irreg., vol.10, 1986. price varies. Verlag Otto Harrassowitz, Taunusstr. 14, Postfach 2929, 6200 Wiesbaden 1, Germany. TEL 0611-530-0. FAX 0611-530570. TELEX 4186135. Ed. Wolfgang Helck. circ. 350.

950   GW   ISSN 0722-1789
KOELN SARASVATI SERIES. irreg., vol.7, 1985. price varies. Franz Steiner Verlag Wiesbaden GmbH, Birkenwaldstr. 44, Postfach 101526, 7000 Stuttgart 1, Germany. TEL 0711-2582-0. FAX 0711-2582290. TELEX 723636-DAZD. Ed. Klaus Ludwig Janert.

KOKUSAI KORYU. see *ETHNIC INTERESTS*

KONGZI YANJIU/STUDIES ON CONFUCIUS. see *PHILOSOPHY*

951.9   KO   ISSN 0023-3919
KOREA OBSERVER. 1968. q. $40. Institute of Korean Studies, C.P.O. Box 3410, Seoul 100-634, S. Korea. TEL 02-278-1198. FAX 278-1198. Ed. Myong Whai Kim. adv.; bk.rev.; abstr.; charts; stat.; circ. 3,500. (processed)
    Description: Covers the fields of the humanities and social sciences, and promotes cultural exhcanges with other nations.

KOREA UPDATE. see *POLITICAL SCIENCE — Civil Rights*

950   US   ISSN 0145-840X
DS901   CODEN: KOSTEL
KOREAN STUDIES. 1977. a. $13.50 (foreign $15) per vol. (University of Hawaii, Center for Korean Studies) University of Hawaii Press, Journals Department, 2840 Kolowalu St., Honolulu, HI 96822. TEL 808-956-8833. FAX 808-988-6052. Ed. Edward Shultz. adv.; bk.rev.; circ. 125. (back issues avail.; reprint service avail. from UMI,ISI) **Indexed:** Amer.Hist.& Life, Hist.Abstr.
—BLDSC shelfmark: 5113.609000.
    Description: Features interdisciplinary and multicultural articles on Korea and the Korean community abroad.
    Refereed Serial

KOREANA; a quarterly on Korean culture. see *POLITICAL SCIENCE*

950 895   II
LALBHAI DALPATBHAI INSTITUTE OF INDOLOGY. PUBLICATIONS. (Text in various languages) irreg. price varies. Lalbhai Dalpatbhai Institute of Indology, Near Gujarat University, P.O. Navarangpura, Ahmedabad 380009, India.

LEBANON REPORT. see *POLITICAL SCIENCE — International Relations*

LEVANT MORGENLAND. see *RELIGIONS AND THEOLOGY*

LIBRARY RESEARCH IN ASIA, AFRICA & AUSTRALIA. see *LIBRARY AND INFORMATION SCIENCES*

954   UK   ISSN 0142-601X
LONDON STUDIES ON SOUTH ASIA.* 1980. irreg. price varies. (University of London, School of Oriental and African Studies) Curzon Press Ltd., 7 Caledonian Rd., London N1 9DX, England. bibl.; index.

950 179.3   US   ISSN 1049-4502
LYNX; a quarterly journal of renga. 1986. q. $15 (foreign $20). Eruptions Ink, Box 169, Toutle, WA 98649. TEL 206-274-6661. Ed. Terri Lee Grell. adv.; bk.rev.; circ. 1,000. (back issues avail.)
    Formerly (until 1988): A P A - Renga.
    Description: Devoted to renga, the poetry form from which haiku is derived. Contributors include Hiroaki Sato, Jane Reichhold, James Penha, Alexis Rotella, J.I. Lipscomb, Marlene Mountain and Richard Witherspoon.

297 954   II
M A A S JOURNAL OF ISLAMIC SCIENCE. (Text in English) 1985. s-a. Rs.60($20) to individuals; institutions Rs.100($60). Muslim Association for the Advancement of Science, Al-Homera, Muzzammil Manzil Complex, Civil Lines, Aligarh 202 002, India. TEL 0571-29209. Ed. M. Zaki Kirmani. adv.; bk.rev.; circ. 1,000.
    Formerly: M A A S Journal of Islamic Studies (ISSN 0970-1672)

950   PK   ISSN 0002-4015
AL-MA'ARIF. (Text in Urdu) 1968. q. Rs.15($4) Institute of Islamic Culture, 2 Club Rd., Lahore 3, Pakistan. TEL 363127. Ed. Muhammad Suheyl Umar. bk.rev.; circ. 1,000.
    Formerly: Thaqafat.

954   II
MADHYA PRADESH ITIHASA PARISHAD. JOURNAL. (Text in English or Hindi) 1959. irreg. (approx. a.). Rs.20. Madhya Pradesh Itihasa Parishad, 34-14, South T.T. Nagar, Bhopal 462003, India. Ed. S.D. Guru. bk.rev.; circ. 500. (also avail. in microfilm)
    Description: History, art, archaeology and civilization of Madya Pradesh.

952 001.3 300   BE   ISSN 0495-7725
MAISON FRANCO-JAPONAISE. BULLETIN. (Text in French; summaries in English, French) 1927; N.S. 1951. irreg. (every 2-3 yrs.). price varies. (Maison Franco-Japonaise, JA) Editions Peeters s.p.r.l., Bondgenotenlaan 153, B-3000 Leuven, Belgium. TEL 016-235170. FAX 016-228500. Ed.Bd. bibl.; circ. 7,000. (reprint service avail. from KTO)
Indexed: MLA.

MAJALLAH-I TAHQIQAT-I TARIKHI/JOURNAL OF HISTORICAL RESEARCH. see *HISTORY — History Of The Near East*

MANUSCRIPTS OF THE MIDDLE EAST; journal devoted to the study of handwritten materials of the Middle East. see *HISTORY — History Of The Near East*

572 915.16   CC   ISSN 1000-7873
MANYU YANJIU/MANCHU LANGUAGE STUDIES. (Text in Chinese) 1985. s-a. $20.40. Heilongjiang Manyu Yanjiusuo - Heilongjiang Institute for Manchu Studies, 26 Qingbin Lu, Harbin. TEL 63931. (Dist. in US by: China Books & Periodicals, Inc., 2929 24th St., San Francisco, CA 94110. TEL 415-282-2994) Ed. Liu Jingxian.
    Description: Studies on Manchu culture and language.

MANZU WENXUE/MANCHU LITERATURE. see *LITERATURE*

950   IT
MATERIALI PER IL VOCABOLARIO NEOSUMERICO. COLLANA. 1974. a. L.25000. (Unione Accademica Nazionale) Multigrafica Editrice, Viale Quattro Venti 52-A, 00152 Rome, Italy. (back issues avail.)

MATERIALIEN ZUM INTERNATIONALEN KULTURAUSTAUSCH/STUDIES IN INTERNATIONAL CULTURAL RELATIONS. see *POLITICAL SCIENCE — International Relations*

MATRIX (URBANA). see *LITERATURE — Poetry*

956 950   GW   ISSN 0543-1719
MAX FREIHERR VON OPPENHEIM-STIFTUNG. SCHRIFTEN. 1955. irreg., vol.14, 1988. price varies. Gebr. Mann Verlag GmbH, Lindenstr. 76, Postfach 110303, 1000 Berlin 61, Germany. (reprint service avail.)

950   GW   ISSN 0138-3663
MEROITICA. (Text in English, French, German) 1973. irreg., vol.11, 1989. (Humboldt-Universitaet zu Berlin, Bereich Aegyptologie und Sudan Archaeologie) Akademie-Verlag Berlin, Leipziger Str. 3-4, 1086 Berlin, Germany. TELEX 114420-AVERL-DD.
    Description: Monographs and source material on ancient Sudanese history and archaeology.

MIDDLE EAST STUDIES ASSOCIATION BULLETIN. see *SOCIAL SCIENCES: COMPREHENSIVE WORKS*

ORIENTAL STUDIES

950 GW ISSN 0177-1647
MIDDLE EASTERN CULTURE CENTER, JAPAN. BULLETIN. 1984. irreg., vol.4, 1991. price varies. Verlag Otto Harrassowitz, Taunusstr. 14, Postfach 2929, 6200 Wiesbaden 1, Germany. TEL 0611-530-0. FAX 0611-530570. TELEX 4186135. Ed. H.I.H. Prince Takahito Mikasa.

950 US ISSN 0147-037X
DS753
MING STUDIES. 1975. s-a. $15 to individuals; institutions $20. Hobart & William Smith Colleges, Department of History, Geneva, NY 14456-3397. TEL 315-781-3349. FAX 315-781-3560. Ed. William S. Atwell. adv.; bk.rev.; bibl.; circ. 250. (back issues avail.) **Indexed:** Amer.Hist.& Life, Hist.Abstr.
 Formerly: Ming Studies Newsletter.

MINZU HUABAO/NATIONALITY PICTORIAL. see ETHNIC INTERESTS

951 300 CC ISSN 0256-1891
MINZU YANJIU/STUDY IN NATIONALITIES. (Text and summaries in Chinese; table of contents in English) 1979. bi-m. Y6.60($26.10) Zhongguo Shehui Kexueyuan, Minzu Yanjiusuo - Chinese Academy of Social Sciences, Institute of Nationalities, 27 Baishiqiao Lu, Beijing 100081, People's Republic of China. TEL 8022288. (Dist. outside China by: China International Book Trading Corporation, P.O. Box 399, Beijing, P.R.C.; Dist. in US by: China Books & Periodicals, Inc., 2929 24th St., San Francisco, CA 94110. TEL 415-282-2994) Ed. Du Rongkun. bk.rev.; circ. 5,000 (controlled).
 Description: Contains historical, social, and economic studies of minority nationalities.

950 SP ISSN 0544-408X
PJ3001
MISCELANEA DE ESTUDIOS ARABES Y HEBRAICOS. 1952. 2/yr. 5180 ptas. Universidad de Granada, Servicio de Publicaciones, Antiguo Colegio Maximo, Campus de Cartuja, 18071 Granada, Spain. TEL 2813566. Eds. Angel Badillos, Jose Besteiro. **Indexed:** Amer.Hist.& Life, Hist.Abstr.

MITHILA INSTITUTE OF POST GRADUATE STUDIES AND RESEARCH IN SANSKRIT LEARNING. BULLETIN. see LINGUISTICS

950 IS ISSN 0017-7083
DS41
HA-MIZRAH HEHADASH/NEW EAST. (Text in Hebrew; summaries in English) 1949. q. $30. Israel Oriental Society, Hebrew University, Jerusalem, Israel. Ed. Aharon Layish. bk.rev.; bibl.; charts; stat.; index; circ. 2,500 (controlled). **Indexed:** A.B.C.Pol.Sci., Ind.Heb.Per., Old Test.Abstr.

950 UK ISSN 0026-749X
DS1
MODERN ASIAN STUDIES. 1967. q. $71 to individuals; institutions $142. Cambridge University Press, Edinburgh Bldg., Shaftesbury Rd., Cambridge CB2 2RU, England. TEL 0223-312393. FAX 0223-315052. TELEX 851817256. (North American addr.: Cambridge University Press, 40 W. 20th St., New York, NY 10011) Ed. G. Johnson. adv.; bk.rev. (also avail. in microform from UMI; reprint service avail. from SWZ) **Indexed:** A.B.C.Pol.Sci., Amer.Hist.& Life, Curr.Cont, E.I., Hist.Abstr., Mid.East: Abstr.& Ind., Rice Abstr., Rural Devel.Abstr., Rural Recreat.Tour.Abstr., Soc.Sci.Ind., SSCI, World Agri.Econ.& Rural Sociol.Abstr.
 —BLDSC shelfmark: 5883.650000.
 Description: Covers Asia from Pakistan to Japan; studies the impact of modernization during the nineteenth and twentieth centuries on the ancient cultures of these nations.

MODERN CHINA; an international quarterly of history and social science. see HISTORY — History Of Asia

MODERN CHINESE LITERATURE. see LITERATURE

MODERN MIDDLE EAST SERIES. see HISTORY — History Of Asia

951 IT
MONDO CINESE; rivista trimestrale. (Text in Italian; summaries in Chinese, English, Italian) 1973. q. L.45000 (effective Jan. 1992). Istituto Italo Cinese per gli Scambi Economici e Culturali, Via Carducci, 18, 20123 Milan, Italy. TEL 8057384. FAX 72000236. TELEX 334384 ITCINA I. Ed.Bd. adv.; bk.rev.; bibl.; charts; stat.; circ. 1,200. (back issues avail.) **Indexed:** Amer.Hist.& Life, Hist.Abstr.
 Description: Covers the development of relations between the Chinese and Italian cultures.

950 US
MONGOLIAN STUDIES. 1974. a. $25. Mongolia Society, Inc., 321-322 Goodbody Hall, Indiana University, Bloomington, IN 47405-2401. TEL 812-335-4078. FAX 812-855-7500. Ed. John R. Krveger. adv.; bk.rev.; abstr.; bibl.; charts; stat.; circ. 400. **Indexed:** Amer.Bibl.Slavic & E.Eur.Stud, Amer.Hist.& Life, Hist.Abstr., M.L.A.
 Supersedes: Mongolian Society Bulletin (ISSN 0026-9654)
 Description: Scholarly research articles and multidisciplinary approaches to Mongolia, past and present.

954 GW ISSN 0170-8864
MONOGRAPHIEN ZUR INDISCHEN ARCHAEOLOGIE, KUNST UND PHILOLOGIE. irreg., vol.6, 1987. price varies. (Stiftung Ernst Waldschmidt) Franz Steiner Verlag Wiesbaden GmbH, Birkenwaldstr. 44, Postfach 101526, 7000 Stuttgart 1, Germany. TEL 0711-2582-0. FAX 0711-2582290. TELEX 723636-DAZD. Ed. Marianne Yaldiz.

MONUMENTA GRAECA ET ROMANA. see ART

MONUMENTA LINGUAE MONGOLICAE COLLECTA. see LINGUISTICS

952 390 JA ISSN 0027-0741
DS821.A1
MONUMENTA NIPPONICA; studies in Japanese culture. (Text in English) 1938. q. 4200 Yen($30) Sophia University - Jochi Daigaku, 7-1 Kioi-cho, Chiyoda-ku, Tokyo 102, Japan. Ed. Michael Cooper. bk.rev.; illus.; index, cum.index: vols.1-45; circ. 1,150. (also avail. in microform from UMI) **Indexed:** Amer.Hist.& Life, Arts & Hum.Cit.Ind., Curr.Cont., Hist.Abstr., Ind.Bk.Rev.Hum., M.L.A., SSCI.

950 GW ISSN 0254-9948
MONUMENTA SERICA; journal of Oriental studies. (Text in English, French, German) 1934. irreg., vol.39, 1990-91. DM.158. Steyler Verlag, Bahnhofstr. 9, 4054 Nettetal 2, Germany. TEL 02157-1202-20. FAX 02157-1202-22. Ed. Roman Malek. bk.rev.; circ. 500. (also avail. in microfilm from UMI) **Indexed:** Amer.Hist.& Life, Hist.Abstr.
 Description: Scholarly journal dealing with China and neighboring countries.

950 GW ISSN 0179-261X
MONUMENTA SERICA MONOGRAPH SERIES. (Text in English, French and German) 1937. a. Monumenta Serica, Arnold-Janssen-Str. 20, 5205 Sankt Augustin 1, Germany. TEL 02241-237431. FAX 02241-29142. TELEX 889559-STEYL-D. Ed. Roman Malek. circ. 400. (back issues avail.)

950 RU
MOSKOVSKII UNIVERSITET. VESTNIK. SERIYA 14: VOSTOKOVEDENIE. s-a. 12.80 Rub. Moskovskii Universitet, Ul. Gertsena 5-7, 103009 Moscow, Russia. bk.rev.; bibl.; index. **Indexed:** Int.Aerosp.Abstr.

956 GW ISSN 0077-1880
MUENCHENER INDOLOGISCHE STUDIEN. 1955. irreg., vol.6, 1969. price varies. Verlag Otto Harrassowitz, Taunusstr. 14, Postfach 2929, 6200 Wiesbaden 1, Germany. TEL 0611-530-0. FAX 0611-530570. TELEX 4186135. Ed. H. Hoffmann.

950 GW ISSN 0170-3668
MUENCHENER OSTASIATISCHE STUDIEN. (Text in English and German) irreg., vol.59, 1991. price varies. Franz Steiner Verlag Wiesbaden GmbH, Birkenwaldstr. 44, Postfach 101526, 7000 Stuttgart 1, Germany. TEL 0711-2582-0. FAX 0711-2582290. TELEX 723636-DAZD. Ed.Bd.

950 GW ISSN 0170-3676
MUENCHENER OSTASIATISCHE STUDIEN. SONDERREIHE. (Text in English and German) irreg., vol.4, 1991. price varies. Franz Steiner Verlag Wiesbaden GmbH, Birkenwaldstr. 44, Postfach 101526, 7000 Stuttgart 1, Germany. TEL 0711-2582-0. FAX 0711-2582290. TELEX 723636-DAZD. Ed.Bd.

MUSEO NAZIONALE D'ARTE ORIENTALE. SCHEDE. see MUSEUMS AND ART GALLERIES

950 BE ISSN 0771-6494
LE MUSEON; revue d'etudes orientales. (Supplement avail.: Bibliotheque du Museon, Publications de l'Institut Orientaliste de Louvain) (Text in English, French) 1881. 4/yr. 3000 Fr. Editions Peeters s.p.r.l., Bondgenotenlaan 153, B-3000 Leuven, Belgium. TEL 016-235170. FAX 016-228500. Ed. B. Coulie. bk.rev.; bibl.; cum.index 1882-1931, 1932-1973. (back issues avail.) **Indexed:** New Test.Abstr., Numis.Lit.
 —BLDSC shelfmark: 5986.950000.
 Description: Studies all aspects of the Christian Near East.

MUSEUM OF FAR EASTERN ANTIQUITIES. BULLETIN. see MUSEUMS AND ART GALLERIES

MUSICA ASIATICA. see MUSIC

954 II ISSN 0580-4396
PK401
MYSORE ORIENTALIST. (Text in English and Sanskrit) 1967. a. $5. University of Mysore, Oriental Research Institute, Mysore 5, Karnataka, India. Ed. R.S. Shivaganesha Murthy. bk.rev.; circ. 300.
 Description: Contains studies on Indic peoples.

950 DK ISSN 0904-4337
N I A S - NYTT. (Text in Danish, English, Norwegian and Swedish) 1983. irreg. free. Nordic Institute of Asian Studies, Njalsgade 84, DK-2300 Copenhagen S, Denmark. FAX 32-96-25-30. Eds. Karl Haellquist, Leena Hoskuldsson. circ. 2,500.
 Former titles: C I N A - Nytt (ISSN 0109-4203) & Asien-Studier i Skandinavien (ISSN 0105-7340)
 Description: Contains short scholarly reports, conference and symposia reports, information on new and current journals and series of books and forthcoming conferences.

960 DK ISSN 0904-597X
DS32.9.S34
N I A S REPORT. 1968. irreg. free. Nordic Institute of Asian Studies, Njalsgade 84, DK-2300 Copenhagen S, Denmark. Ed. Jens Chr. Soerensen. bk.rev.; circ. 300. **Indexed:** So.Pac.Per.Ind.
 —BLDSC shelfmark: 6109.726000.
 Formerly (until 1989): Scandinavian Institute of Asian Studies. Annual Newsletter (ISSN 0106-3871)

954 CC ISSN 1004-1508
NANYA YANJIU JIKAN/SOUTH ASIAN STUDIES QUARTERLY. (Text in Chinese) 1979. q. Y6($2.50) Sichuan University, South Asian Research Institute, Sichuan Daxue Nei, Jiuyanqiao, Chengdu, Sichuan 610064, People's Republic of China. TEL 583875. Eds. Iei Qihuai, Li Dechang. circ. 1,000.

950 CC
NANYANG WENTI YANJIU/SOUTHEAST ASIAN STUDIES. (Text in Chinese) q. Xiamen Daxue, Nanyang Yanjiusuo - Xiamen University, Institute of Southeast Asian Studies, Xiamen, Fujian 361005, People's Republic of China. TEL 27414. Ed. Wang Muheng.

950 CC
NANYANG ZILIAO YICONG. (Text in Chinese) q. Xiamen Daxue, Nanyang Yanjiusuo - Xiamen University, Institute of Southeast Asian Studies, Xiamen, Fujian 361005, People's Republic of China. TEL 27414. Ed. Zhou Shixiong.

NANZAN INSTITUTE FOR RELIGION AND CULTURE. BULLETIN. see RELIGIONS AND THEOLOGY

ORIENTAL STUDIES

950 960   RU   ISSN 0130-6995
DS1
NARODY AZII I AFRIKI: ISTORIYA, EKONOMIKA, KUL'TURA. (Text in Russian; summaries in English, content pages in English and French) 1955. bi-m. 50.70 Rub. (Akademiya Nauk S.S.S.R., Institut Vostokovedeniya) Izdatel'stvo Nauka, 90 Profsoyuznaya ul., 117864 Moscow, Russia. (Dist. by: Mezhdunarodnaya Kniga, ul. Dimitrova D.39, 113095 Moscow, Russia) (Co-sponsor: Institut Afriki) Ed. A.A. Kutzenkov. bk.rev.; bibl.; charts; illus.; index; circ. 3,700. **Indexed:** Amer.Hist.& Life, Bull.Signal., Hist.Abstr., Int.Lab.Doc., Numis.Lit., Polit.Sci.Abstr., World Agri.Econ.& Rural Sociol.Abstr.
    Former titles: Narody Azii i Afriki (ISSN 0027-8041); (1959-1961): Problemy Vostokovedeniya.

NATIONAL PALACE MUSEUM. NEWSLETTER. see MUSEUMS AND ART GALLERIES

950   GW   ISSN 0932-2728
NEAR AND MIDDLE EAST MONOGRAPHS. 1987. irreg., vol.3, 1990. Verlag Otto Harrassowitz, Taunusstr. 14, Postfach 2929, 6200 Wiesbaden 1, Germany. TEL 0611-530-0. FAX 0611-530-570. TELEX 4186135. Ed.Bd.

959 320   NP
NEPAL - ANTIQUARY; journal of social-historical research and digest. 1974. bi-m. $30 per no. Office of Nepal-Antiquary, 20-401 Naxal, Kathmandu, Nepal. Ed. Jagadish C. Regmi. circ. 75. (back issues avail.)

950   GW   ISSN 0720-6615
NEPAL RESEARCH CENTRE. JOURNAL. (Text in English) 1977. a. DM.58. Franz Steiner Verlag Wiesbaden GmbH, Birkenwaldstr. 44, Postfach 101526, 7000 Stuttgart 1, Germany. TEL 0711-2582-0. FAX 0711-2582290. TELEX 723636-DAZD. Ed. Albrecht Wezler.

956   US   ISSN 0081-8291
NEW YORK UNIVERSITY. STUDIES IN NEAR EASTERN CIVILIZATION. 1968. irreg., latest no.12. New York University Press, 70 Washington Square S., New York, NY 10012. TEL 212-998-2575. FAX 212-995-3833. TELEX 235128 NYU UR. Ed. Peter Chelkowski.

320.956   II
NEWS REVIEW ON WEST ASIA. (Text in English) 1971. m. Rs.66. Institute for Defence Studies and Analyses, Sapru House, Barkhamba Rd., New Delhi 110001, India. Ed. Jasjit Singh. circ. 250.
    Supersedes in part (1970-1972): News Review on East Asia, Australasia and West Asia.

950   CH   ISSN 0253-2875
NEWSLETTER FOR RESEARCH IN CHINESE STUDIES. 1982. q. $40. Center for Chinese Studies, c/o National Central Library, 20 Chung Shan S. Rd., Taipei, Taiwan 10040, Republic of China. TEL 02-314-7321. FAX 02-371-2126. Ed. Pei-ling Tsai. adv.; bk.rev.; circ. 2,400.

950   CS   ISSN 0029-5302
DS1
NOVY ORIENT/NEW ORIENT. (Text in Czech) 1946. 10/yr. DM.99. (Czechoslovak Academy of Sciences, Oriental Institute) Academia, Publishing House of the Czechoslovak Academy of Sciences, Vodickova 40, 112 29 Prague 1, Czechoslovakia. TEL 53-25-29. (Subscr. to: Artia, Ve Smeckach 30, 111 27 Prague 1, Czechoslovakia) Ed. Jan Filipovsky. bk.rev.; charts, illus, maps; index; circ. 3,500. **Indexed:** Hist.Abstr.
    Description: Deals with the cultures and civilizations of Asia and Africa; regularly includes studies on developing countries and information about current problems of the Third World.

950 320   UK   ISSN 0960-7935
O I O C NEWSLETTER. 1974. 2/yr. free. Oriental and India Office Collections, British Library, 197 Blackfriars Rd., London SE1 8NG, England. TEL 071-412-7000. FAX 071-412-7858. Ed. David Plumb. adv.; bk.rev.; bibl.; circ. 880.
    Former titles: India Office Library and Records Oriental Collections Newsletter (ISSN 0265-1386); India Office Library and Records Newsletter (ISSN 0307-6008)
    Description: News of activities of the library and articles pertaining to its collections, recent publications and research in progress.

ORBIS MUSICAE; Assaph studies in the arts. see MUSIC

950   NE   ISSN 0078-6527
DS1
ORIENS. (Text in English, French, German) 1948. irreg., vol.32, 1991. price varies. (Internationale Gesellschaft fuer Orientforschung) E.J. Brill, P.O. Box 9000, 2300 PA Leiden, Netherlands. TEL 071-312624. FAX 071-317532. TELEX 39296 BRILL NL. (In N. America: E.J. Brill, 24 Hudson St., Kinderhook, NY 12106. TEL 800-962-4406) Ed. R. Sellheim. bk.rev.; cum.index: vols.1-10. **Indexed:** Hist.Abstr.
    Description: Studies in the culture of Asia and North Africa from antiquity to the present focusing on language, literature, religion and art.

913   IT   ISSN 0030-5189
DS56
ORIENS ANTIQUUS. (Text in English, French, German, Italian, Spanish) 1961. s-a. L.40000($80) (Istituto per l'Oriente) Herder Editrice e Libreria s.r.l., Piazza Montecitorio, 120, 00186 Rome, Italy. TEL 67-94-628. FAX 678-47-51. (Co-sponsor: Centro per le Antichita e la Storia dell'Arte del Vicion Oriente) Ed. Giovanni Pettinato. bk.rev.; bibl.; charts, illus.; maps; index; circ. 400. **Indexed:** Numis.Lit.

950 490 890   GW   ISSN 0030-5197
DS501
ORIENS EXTREMUS; Zeitschrift fuer Sprache, Kunst und Kultur der Laender des fernen Ostens. (Text mainly in German; occasionally in English and French) 1954. 2/yr. Verlag Otto Harrassowitz, Taunusstr. 14, Postfach 2929, 6200 Wiesbaden 1, Germany. TEL 0611-530-0. FAX 0611-530570. TELEX 4186135. Ed.Bd. charts; illus.; index; circ. 350. (back issues avail.) **Indexed:** E.I., Hist.Abstr., M.L.A.

950   GW   ISSN 0030-5227
DS41
ORIENT; Deutsche Zeitschrift fuer Wirtschaft und Politik des Orients - German journal for politics and economics of the Middle East. (Title and Contents Page in English, French and German) 1960. q. DM.90. (Deutsches Orient-Institut) Leske Verlag und Budrich GmbH, Gerhart-Hauptmann-Str.27, Postfach 300551, 5090 Leverkusen 3, Germany. adv.; bk.rev.; bibl.; charts; illus.; maps. **Indexed:** Curr.Cont.M.E., Key to Econ.Sci., P.A.I.S.For.Lang.Ind.
    Description: Deals with the politics, economy and society of the modern Near and Middle East.

950   FR   ISSN 1161-0344
▼**ORIENT EXPRESS.** 1991. 2/yr. Institut d'Art et d'Archeologie, 3, rue Michelet, 75006 Paris, France.
    Description: European bulletin specializing in oriental archaeology.

709.5   UK   ISSN 0030-5278
N8
ORIENTAL ART; devoted to the study of all forms of Oriental art. N.S. 1955. q. £24($48) Oriental Art Magazine Ltd., 12 Ennerdale Rd., Richmond, Surrey TW9 3PG, England. Ed. Ann Butler. adv.; bk.rev.; bibl.; illus.; index. (reprint service avail. from KTO) **Indexed:** Art & Archaeol.Tech.Abstr., Art Ind, Artbibl.Mod., Artbibl, Arts & Hum.Cit.Ind., Avery Ind.Archit.Per., Curr.Cont., Ind.Bk.Rev.Hum.
    —BLDSC shelfmark: 6291.163000.

950   II   ISSN 0030-5324
PJ25
ORIENTAL INSTITUTE. JOURNAL. (Text in English and Sanskrit) 1951. q. Rs.30($10) Oriental Institute, Maharaja Sayajirao University of Baroda, Baroda 390 002, Gujarat, India. Ed. R.T. Vyas. adv.; bk.rev.; abstr.; bibl.; illus.; index; circ. 550. **Indexed:** E.I.
    Description: Publishes research articles on all subjects related to Oriental studies.

950   AT   ISSN 0030-5340
DS41
ORIENTAL SOCIETY OF AUSTRALIA. JOURNAL. 1961. a. Aus.$15. Oriental Society of Australia, University of Sydney, School of Asian Studies, Sydney, N.S.W. 2006, Australia. Ed. A.D. Stefanowska. adv.; bk.rev.; charts; circ. 500. **Indexed:** Aus.P.A.I.S, E.I.
    —BLDSC shelfmark: 4837.600000.

950   VC   ISSN 0030-5367
PJ6
ORIENTALIA. (Text in English, French, German, Italian) 1920. q. L.100000($90) (Pontificio Istituto Biblico) Biblical Institute Press, Piazza Pilotta 35, 00187 Rome, Italy. Ed. Rev. R. Caplice S.J. bk.rev.; bibl.; charts; illus.; index; circ. 650. (back issues avail.) **Indexed:** New Test.Abstr., Old Test.Abstr., Rel.Ind.One.
    Description: Consists of Near Eastern studies.

950 200   VC
ORIENTALIA CHRISTIANA ANALECTA. (Text in English, French, German, Italian) 1923. irreg. price varies. (Pontificio Istituto Orientale) Edizioni Orientalia Cristiana, Piazza S. Maria Maggiore 7, 00185 Rome, Italy. TEL 06-446-5589. FAX 06-446-5576. Ed. Robert Taft. circ. 1,000.
    Continues (since 1935): Orientalia Christiana.

950   SW   ISSN 0078-656X
ORIENTALIA GOTHOBURGENSIA. (Subseries of: Acta Universitatis Gothoburgensis) 1969. irreg., no.9, 1986. price varies; also exchange basis. Acta Universitatis Gothoburgensis, Box 5096, S-402 22 Goeteborg, Sweden. Ed. Fathi Talmoudi.

950   BE   ISSN 0085-4522
ORIENTALIA LOVANIENSIA PERIODICA. (Supplement avail.: Orientalia Lovaniensia Analecta) (Text in English, French, German; summaries in English) 1970. a. 1600 Fr. Katholieke Universiteit te Leuven, Departement Orientalistiek, Blijde Inkomststraat 21, B-3000 Leuven, Belgium. (Subscr. to: Editions Peeters s.p.r.l., Bondgenotenlaan 153, B-3000 Leuven, Belgium. TEL 016-235170) Ed. G. Pollet. bk.rev.; abstr.; charts; illus.; cum.index; circ. 500. (back issues avail.) **Indexed:** M.L.A., Numis.Lit., Old Test.Abstr.
    —BLDSC shelfmark: 6291.187400.

950   NE   ISSN 0169-9504
ORIENTALIA RHENO-TRAIECTINA. 1949. irreg., vol.37, 1991. price varies. E.J. Brill, P.O. Box 9000, 2300 PA Leiden, Netherlands. TEL 071-312624. FAX 071-317532. TELEX 39296 BRILL NL. (In N. America: E.J. Brill, 24 Hudson St., Kinderhook, NY 12106. TEL 800-962-4406) Ed. J. Gonda.

950   SW   ISSN 0078-6578
DS1
ORIENTALIA SUECANA. 1952. a. SEK 75($15) (Uppsala Universitet) Almqvist & Wiksell International, Box 638, S-101 28 Stockholm, Sweden. Ed. Tryggue Kronholm. circ. 600. **Indexed:** M.L.A., Numis.Lit.
    —BLDSC shelfmark: 6291.191000.

890   GW   ISSN 0030-5383
PJ5
ORIENTALISTISCHE LITERATURZEITUNG; Zeitschrift fuer die Wissenschaft vom ganzen Orient und seinen Beziehungen zu den angrenzenden Kulturkreisen. (Text in English, French, German, Italian) 1898. bi-m. M.220.20. (Akademie der Wissenschaften der DDR, Zentralinstitut fuer Alte Geschichte und Archaeologie) Akademie-Verlag Berlin, Leipziger Str. 3-4, 1086 Berlin, Germany. TELEX 114420-AVERL-DD. Ed. H. Klengel. adv.; bk.rev.; bibl. **Indexed:** New Test.Abstr., Old Test.Abstr.

ORIENTATIONS. see ART

950   IT   ISSN 0030-5472
D461
ORIENTE MODERNO; revista mensile d'informazione e di studi per la conoscenza dell'Oriente. 1921. m. L.50000($60) (Istituto per l'Oriente) Herder Editrice e Libreria s.r.l., Piazza Montecitorio, 120, 00186 Rome, Italy. TEL 67-94-628. FAX 678-47-51. (Alt. addr.: via a Carconcini 190, 00197 Rome) Ed. Giovanni Oman. bk.rev.; index, cum.index: 1921-1973; circ. 800. **Indexed:** Hist.Abstr.

950 410   II   ISSN 0474-9030
OUR HERITAGE. (Text in English, Bengali or Sanskrit) vol.19, 1972. s-a. Sanskrit College, Department of Postgraduate Training and Research, 1 Bankim Chatterjee St., Calcutta 12, India. Ed. B. Bhattacharya. bibl.
    Description: Covers literary subjects.

PAPERS ON FAR EASTERN HISTORY. see HISTORY — History Of Asia

950 GW ISSN 0232-3257
PAPYRI AUS DEN STAATLICHEN MUSEEN ZU BERLIN. 1978. irreg. (Staatliche Museen zu Berlin) Akademie-Verlag Berlin, Leipziger Str. 3-4, 1086 Berlin, Germany. TELEX 114420-AVERL-DD.

894 494 947.87 US ISSN 0031-5508
PERMANENT INTERNATIONAL ALTAISTIC CONFERENCE (PIAC). NEWSLETTER. 1966. irreg. (2-3/yr.). free. Indiana University, Permanent International Altaistic Conference, Goodbody Hall 101, Bloomington, IN 47405. TEL 812-855-0959. FAX 812-855-7500. Ed. Prof. Denis Sinor. adv.; bibl.; circ. 750. (processed)

PHOENIX. see ARCHAEOLOGY

950 572 PP ISSN 0253-2913
POINT SERIES. 1982-1988; resumed 1989. s-a. $14. Melanesian Institute for Pastoral & Socio-Economic Service, P.O. Box 571, Goroka EHP, Papua New Guinea. FAX 675-721-070. Ed. Paul Roche. bk.rev.; circ. 1,000. (back issues avail.) **Indexed:** Rel.Ind.One.
—BLDSC shelfmark: 6541.858000.

950 PL ISSN 0079-4783
POLSKA AKADEMIA NAUK. KOMITET NAUK ORIENTALISTYCZNYCH. PRACE ORIENTALISTYCZNE. (Text and summaries in English, French, German, Polish, and Russian) 1954. irreg., vol.28, 1984. price varies. Panstwowe Wydawnictwo Naukowe, Ul. Miodowa 10, 00-251 Warsaw, Poland. (Dist. by: Ars Polona, Krakowskie Przedmiescie 7, 00-068 Warsaw, Poland) circ. 1,200.

950 PL ISSN 0079-3426
POLSKA AKADEMIA NAUK. ODDZIAL W KRAKOWIE. KOMISJA ORIENTALISTYCZNA. PRACE. (Text in English, French, German, Polish) 1962. irreg., no.19, 1987. price varies. Ossolineum, Publishing House of the Polish Academy of Sciences, Rynek 9, 50-106 Wroclaw, Poland. TELEX 0712771 OSS PL. (Dist. by: Ars Polona-Ruch, Krakowskie Przedmiescie 7, Warsaw, Poland) Ed. Stanislaw Stachowski. circ. 700.
—BLDSC shelfmark: 6588.147300.
Description: Presents Arabic sources concerning the history of Central and Eastern Europe. Also important literary and linguistic works on Oriental subjects.

PORTA LINGUARUM ORIENTALIUM. see LINGUISTICS

954 II
PRACHYA PRATIBHA. (Text in English, Hindi, Sanskrit) 1973. s-a. Rs.100. Birla Institute of Art and Music, Prachya Niketan, Birla Museum, P.O. Vallabh Bhavan, Bhopal 462004, India. Ed. K.D. Bajpai. bk.rev.; circ. 500. (also avail. in microfilm)
Description: A research journal which carries contributions from scholars and savants on indology. Regular features include indian history and culture, archaeology, epigraphy, museology and numismatics.

950 490 US
PRINCETON LIBRARY OF ASIAN TRANSLATIONS. irreg. price varies. Princeton University Press, 3175 Princeton Pike, Lawrenceville, NJ 08648. TEL 609-896-1344. FAX 609-895-1081.

PRINCETON STUDIES ON THE NEAR EAST. see HISTORY — History Of The Near East

956 NE ISSN 0169-9601
PROBLEME DER AEGYPTOLOGIE. 1953. irreg, vol.7, 1991. price varies. E.J. Brill, P.O. Box 9000, 2300 PA Leiden, Netherlands. TEL 071-312624. FAX 071-317532. TELEX 39296 BRILL NL. (In N. America: E.J. Brill, 24 Hudson St., Kinderhook, NY 12016. TEL 800-962-4406) Ed. W. Helck.
Description: Interpretations of religious, historical and cultural topics in Egyptology.

954 II
PUNJAB UNIVERSITY INDOLOGICAL SERIES. no.24, 1979. irreg. price varies. Vishvshavranand Vedic Research Institute, P.O. Sadhu Ashram, Hoshiarpur 146021, Punjab, India. Ed. S. Bhaskaran Nair.

950 GW ISSN 0931-9158
PURANA RESEARCH PUBLICATIONS, TUEBINGEN. 1987. irreg., vol.2, 1989. price varies. Verlag Otto Harrassowitz, Taunusstr. 14, Postfach 2929, 6200 Wiesbaden 1, Germany. TEL 0611-530-0. FAX 0611-530570. Ed. Heinrich von Stietencron.

951.47 300 CC
QINGHAI MINZU XUEYUAN XUEBAO/QINGHAI INSTITUTE OF NATIONALITIES. JOURNAL. (Text in Chinese) q. Y6. Qinghai Minzu Xueyuan - Qinghai Institute of Nationalities, 25 Bayi Lu, Xining, Qinghai 810007, People's Republic of China.
Description: Focuses on local and ethnic history, minority languages and literatures (including folk literature), economics, education, government policy, religion, law, and arts pertaining to nationalities in Qinghai Province.

QUARTERLY INDEX ISLAMICUS; current books, articles, and papers on Islamic Studies. see HISTORY — Abstracting, Bibliographies, Statistics

QUINTESSENCE. see MEDICAL SCIENCES

RECORDS OF CIVILIZATION. SOURCES AND STUDIES. see HISTORY

932 950 GW ISSN 0340-8450
RECORDS OF THE ANCIENT NEAR EAST. (Text in English) 1972. irreg., vol.2, 1976. price varies. Verlag Otto Harrassowitz, Taunusstr. 14, Postfach 2929, 6200 Wiesbaden 1, Germany. TEL 0611-530-0. FAX 0611-530570. TELEX 4186135.

950 HK ISSN 0377-3515
RENDITIONS; a Chinese-English translation magazine. 1973. s-a. $15. Chinese University of Hong Kong, Research Centre for Translation, Shatin, New Territories, Hong Kong. FAX 6035149. TELEX 50301-CUHK-HX. Ed. Eva Hung. adv.; bk.rev.; bibl.; index; circ. 1,500. (back issues avail.) **Indexed:** Arts & Hum.Cit.Ind., Curr.Cont., M.L.A.
Description: Offers translations of traditional and modern Chinese literature. Special issues include poetry, fiction, and prose, as well as regional studies.

956 FR
REVUE D'ASSYRIOLOGIE ET D'ARCHEOLOGIE ORIENTALE. 1904. s-a. 320 F. (foreign 410 F.). Presses Universitaires de France, Departement des Revues, 14 av. du Bois-de-l'Epine, B.P.90, 91003 Evry Cedex, France. TEL 1-60-77-82-05. FAX 1-60-79-20-45. TELEX PUF 600 474 F. (reprint service avail. from KTO) **Indexed:** Mid.East: Abstr.& Ind., Old Test.Abstr.

REVUE D'EGYPTOLOGIE. see ARCHAEOLOGY

951.9 UN
REVUE DE COREE. (Text in French) 1969. q. 5400 Won. Unesco, Korean National Commission for Unesco, B.P. 64 Poste Centrale, Seoul, S. Korea. TEL 02-776-3950. FAX 02-774-3956. TELEX MOCNDM-K-23231-2. Ed. Paik Syeung-gil. adv.; bk.rev.; index, cum.index; circ. 1,800.
Description: Aspects of Korean language, culture, history, education, science and society.

221 FR ISSN 0035-1725
BM487.A62
REVUE DE QUMRAN. (Text in English, French, German, Italian, Latin, Spanish) 1958. s-a. 568 F. J. Gabalda et Cie, 18 rue P.et M. Curie, 75005 Paris, France. Ed. E. Purch. bk.rev.; circ. 1,000. **Indexed:** New Test.Abstr., Old Test.Abstr., Rel.& Theol.Abstr. (1968-), Rel.Ind.One, Rel.Per.
Description: Examines the Dead Sea scrolls.

REVUE DES ETUDES ARMENIENNES NOUVELLE SERIE. see HISTORY — History Of The Near East

297 FR ISSN 0336-156X
BP1
REVUE DES ETUDES ISLAMIQUES. 1927. 2/yr. Librairie Orientaliste Paul Geuthner, 12 rue Vavin, 75006 Paris, France. TEL 33-1-46-34-71-30. FAX 33-1-43-29-75-64. TELEX 250 303 PUBLIC PARIS. Ed. D. Sourdel. abstr.; charts. (back issues avail.; reprint service avail. from KTO) **Indexed:** E.I., M.L.A.
Continues: Revue du Monde Musulman.
Description: Cultural, sociological and historical studies of Islamic world.

950 CC
RIBEN WENTI YANJIU/JOURNAL OF JAPANESE STUDIES. (Text in Chinese) q. Hebei Daxue - Hebei University, Baoding, Hebei 071002, People's Republic of China. TEL 22921. Ed. Sun Zhizhong.

950 IT ISSN 0392-4866
PJ6
RIVISTA DEGLI STUDI ORIENTALI. (Text in English, French, German, Italian, Spanish.) 1907. q. L.80000($80) (Universita degli Studi di Roma, Dipartimento di Studi Orientali) Bardi Editore, Salita de'Crescenzi, 16, 00186 Rome, Italy. FAX 06-4451209. Ed. Paolo Daffina. adv.; bk.rev.; bibl.; circ. 300. **Indexed:** Int.Z.Bibelwiss., M.L.A.
Description: Covers all fields of Oriental studies, from the ancient Near East to modern Japan.

950 PL ISSN 0080-3545
ROCZNIK ORIENTALISTYCZNY. (Text in English, French, German, Polish and Russian) 1914. irreg., vol.46, 1989. price varies. (Polska Akademia Nauk, Komitet Nauk Orientalistycznych) Panstwowe Wydawnictwo Naukowe, Ul. Miodowa 10, 00-251 Warsaw, Poland. (Dist. by: Ars Polona, Krakowskie Przedmiescie 7, 00-068 Warsaw, Poland) Ed. E. Tryjarski. circ. 470. **Indexed:** Hist.Abstr., M.L.A.

950 HK ISSN 0085-5774
DS1
ROYAL ASIATIC SOCIETY. HONG KONG BRANCH. JOURNAL. 1961. a. $15 (typically set in Apr.). Royal Asiatic Society, Hong Kong Branch, 20, 10th St., Hong Lok Yuen, Tai Po, New Territories, P.O. Box 3864. TEL 848-2551. FAX 845-4389. Ed. Patrick Hase. bk.rev.; cum.index: vols. 1-10, 11-20; circ. 1,000. (back issues avail.) **Indexed:** A.I.C.P., Amer.Hist.& Life, Hist.Abstr.
Description: Specialises in Hong Kong and South China studies, especially local history, social anthropology, and natural history.

950 UK ISSN 0035-869X
AS122
ROYAL ASIATIC SOCIETY OF GREAT BRITAIN AND IRELAND. JOURNAL. 1834. 3/yr. $49. (Royal Asiatic Society of Great Britain and Ireland) Cambridge University Press, Edinburgh Bldg., Shaftesbury Rd., Cambridge CB2 2RU, England. TEL 0223-312393. Ed. D.O. Morgan. adv.; bk.rev.; illus.; index; circ. 1,600. (also avail. in microform; reprint service avail. from SCH) **Indexed:** A.I.C.P., Amer.Hist.& Life, Arts & Hum.Cit.Ind., Br.Hum.Ind, Curr.Cont., Hist.Abstr., Mid.East: Abstr.& Ind., Numis.Lit.
—BLDSC shelfmark: 4853.810000.
Description: Covers Asian languages, literatures, history, archaeology, arts, philosophies & religions.

RTAM. see LINGUISTICS

950 II
SAMBODHI. (Text in English, Gujarati, Hindi, Prakrit and Sanskrit) 1972. q. Rs.25($6.50) Lalbhai Dalpatbhai Institute of Indology, Near Gujarat University, P.O. Navarangpura, Ahmedabad 380009, India. Ed.Bd. bk.rev.; circ. 150.

950 GW ISSN 0940-0265
▼**SANTAG;** Arbeiten und Untersuchungen zur Keilschriftkunde. 1990. irreg., vol.2, 1990. Verlag Otto Harrassowitz, Taunusstr. 14, Postfach 2929, 6200 Wiesbaden 1, Germany. TEL 0611-530-0. FAX 0611-530-570. TELEX 4186135. Eds. Karl Hecker, Walter Sommerfeld.

930 950 UK ISSN 0069-1712
SCANDINAVIAN INSTITUTE OF ASIAN STUDIES. MONOGRAPH SERIES.* (Text in English) 1969. irreg. price varies. (Scandinavian Institute of Asian Studies, DK) Curzon Press Ltd., 7 Caledonian Rd., London N1 9DX, England. circ. 1,100.
—BLDSC shelfmark: 8087.479000.

958 UK ISSN 0266-206X
SCANDINAVIAN INSTITUTE OF ASIAN STUDIES. OCCASIONAL PAPERS.* 1987. irreg. (Scandinavian Institute of Asian Studies, DK) Curzon Press Ltd., 7 Caledonian Rd., London N1 9DX, England.
—BLDSC shelfmark: 8087.480000.

SCHRIFTEN ZUR GESCHICHTE UND KULTUR DES ALTEN ORIENTS. see HISTORY — History Of Asia

SCRIPTA MEDITERRANEA. see HISTORY — History Of The Near East

ORIENTAL STUDIES

950 296　　　　NE　　ISSN 0169-9911
SEMITIC STUDY SERIES. (Text in English) 1902; N.S. 1952. irreg., vol.6, 1987. E.J. Brill, P.O. Box 9000, 2300 PA Leiden, Netherlands. TEL 071-312624. FAX 071-317532. TELEX 39296 BRILL NL. (In N. America: E.J. Brill, 24 Hudson St., Kinderhook, NY 12106. TEL 800-962-4406) Eds. R.J.M. Gottmeil, M. Jastrow, Jr.

950　　　　　　　II
SHREYE; international research quarterly. (Text in English or Hindi) 1971. q. free to members. Bharatiya Sahityakar Sangh, 51-1 New Market, Guru Gavind Singh Marg, New Delhi 110 005, India. TEL 11-5725707. Ed. Dr. Mohan Lal Srivastava. adv.; bk.rev.; circ. 1,000.

951　　　　GW　　ISSN 0170-3706
SINOLOGICA COLONIENSIA; Ostasiatische Beitraege der Universitaet zu Koeln. irreg., vol.14, 1990. price varies. (Universitaet zu Koeln) Franz Steiner Verlag Wiesbaden GmbH, Birkenwaldstr. 44, Postfach 101526, 7000 Stuttgart 1, Germany. TEL 0711-2582-0. FAX 0711-2582290. TELEX 723636-DAZD. Ed. Martin Gimm.

950　　　　　　　CH
SINOLOGICAL STUDIES.* (Text in Chinese) vol.15, 1973. bi-m. Wen-Tsai-Lee, 162 Ho-Ping E. Rd., Sec. 1, Taipei, Taiwan, Republic of China. Ed. Hsueh-Chuen Sha. bibl.

950　　　　　　　FR
SLOVO. 1979. irreg., latest no.13. price varies. Institut National des Langues et Civilisations Orientales, 2 rue de Lille, 75343 Paris Cedex 07, France. TEL 49-26-42-74.
　Description: Studies the culture and civilization of the people occupying the Soviet territory.

SOCIETE FRANCAISE D'EGYPTOLOGIE. BULLETIN. see ARCHAEOLOGY

950　　　　UK　　ISSN 0262-7280
DS331
SOUTH ASIA RESEARCH. 1981. 2/yr. £7 to individuals; institutions £12. South Asia Research Editorial Association, School of Oriental and African Studies, Room 472, Thornhaugh St., Russell Square, London WC1H OXG, England. TEL 071-323-6352. FAX 071-436-3844. Ed.Bd. adv.; bk.rev.; circ. 350. (also avail. in microfiche; back issues avail.) Indexed: Hist.Abstr.
　—BLDSC shelfmark: 8348.584000.

950　　　　GW　　ISSN 0170-7787
SOUTH ASIAN DIGEST OF REGIONAL WRITING. (Text in English) irreg., vol.11, 1986. price varies. (Universitaet Heidelberg, Suedasien Institut) Franz Steiner Verlag Wiesbaden GmbH, Birkenwaldstr. 44, Postfach 101526, 7000 Stuttgart 1, Germany. TEL 0711-2582-0. FAX 0711-2582290. TELEX 723636-DAZD. Ed. Guenther D. Sontheimer.

950　　　　　II　　ISSN 0970-3764
SOUTH ASIAN SOCIAL SCIENTIST. (Text in English) 1985. s-a. $15 individuals; institutions $23. South Asian Social Scientists Association, Department of Anthropology, University of Madras, Tamil Nadu, Madras 600 005, India. TEL 568778. TELEX 41-6376-UNOM-IN. Ed. N. Subba Reddy. adv.; bk.rev.; circ. 325.
　Description: Offers a forum for discussions between researchers and scholars on the theoretical and empirical on various aspects of the social sceinces.
　Refereed Serial

950 954　　　II　　ISSN 0038-285X
DS335
SOUTH ASIAN STUDIES. (Text in English) 1965. s-a. Rs.60($72) University of Rajasthan, South Asian Studies Centre, Research Centre Building, Jaipur 302 004, India. Ed. Dr. Ramakaut. bk.rev.; bibl. Indexed: A.B.C.Pol.Sci.; I D A, Int.Polit.Sci.Abstr.

954　　　　GW　　ISSN 0584-3170
SOUTH ASIAN STUDIES. (Text in English) irreg., vol.24, 1989. price varies. (Universitaet Heidelberg, Suedasien Institut, New Delhi, II) Franz Steiner Verlag Wiesbaden GmbH, Birkenwaldstr. 44, Postfach 101526, 7000 Stuttgart 1, Germany. TEL 0711-2582-0. FAX 0711-2582290. TELEX 723636-DAZD. Indexed: I D A.

SOUTH EAST ASIA LIBRARY GROUP NEWSLETTER. see LIBRARY AND INFORMATION SCIENCES

959　　　　　　　US
SOUTHEAST ASIA PAPERS. (Text in English) 1973. irreg. (1-2/yr.). price varies. University of Hawaii, Southeast Asian Studies Program, Honolulu, HI 96822. TEL 808-948-8324. Ed. Walter F. Vella. bibl.; circ. 150. Indexed: HR Rep., Seed Abstr.
　Formerly: Southeast Asian Studies Working Paper Series.

959　　　　　　　US
SOUTHEAST ASIA PROGRAM SERIES; monographs, translations, bibliographies. 1986. irreg. price varies. Cornell University, Southeast Asia Program, 102 West Ave., Ithaca, NY 14850. TEL 607-255-8038. FAX 607-254-5000. TELEX WUI-6713054. (Subscr. to: S E A P Publications, Cornell University, E. Hill Plaza, Ithaca, NY 14850)

953　　　　　　　IT
STUDI ARABI. QUADERNI. (Text in English, French, Italian) 1983. a. L.50000. (Universita degli Studi di Venezia, Dipartimento di Scienze Storico-Archeologiche e Orientalistiche) Herder Editrice e Libreria s.r.l., Piazza Montecitorio, 117-120, 00186 Rome, Italy. TEL 6794628. FAX 678-47-51. Ed. F. Picchetti Lucchetta.

950　　　　　　　IT
STUDI ORIENTALI. 1943. irreg., no.9, 1990. price varies. (Universita degli Studi di Roma, Dipartimento di Studi Orientali) Bardi Editore, Salita de Crescenzi 16, 00186 Rome, Italy. FAX 06-4451209.

955　　　　BE　　ISSN 0772-7852
STUDIA IRANICA. (Supplements avail.: Abstracta Iranica; Cahiers de Studia Iranica) (Text in French) 1972. 2/yr. 1800 Fr. (Association pour l'Avancement des Etudes Iraniennes) Editions Peeters s.p.r.l., Bondgenotenlaan 153, B-3000 Leuven, Belgium. TEL 016-235170. FAX 016-228500. Eds. M.P. Gignoux, R. Gyselen. adv.; bk.rev.; bibl.; illus.; stat. Indexed: M.L.A.

950　　　　FI　　ISSN 0039-3282
PJ9
STUDIA ORIENTALIA. (Text in English, French and German) 1925. irreg. Fmk.200. Finnish Oriental Society, c/o University of Helsinki, Department of Asian and African Studies, SF-00100 Helsinki, Finland. Ed. Harry Halen. bk.rev.; charts; illus.; cum.index; circ. 700.

STUDIA ORIENTALIA LUNDENSIA. see LINGUISTICS

950　　　　　　　VC
STUDIA POHL. (Text in language of author) 1967. irreg. price varies. (Pontificio Istituto Biblico) Biblical Institute Press, Piazza della Pilotta 35, 00187 Rome, Italy.

950　　　　　　　VC
STUDIA POHL: SERIES MAIOR. 1969. irreg. price varies. (Pontificio Istituto Biblico) Biblical Institute Press, Piazza della Pilotta 35, 00187 Rome, Italy. charts; illus.

950　　　　GW　　ISSN 0171-9378
STUDIEN ZU NICHTEUROPAEISCHEN RECHTSTHEORIEN. 1979. irreg., vol.2, 1986. price varies. Franz Steiner Verlag Wiesbaden GmbH, Birkenwaldstr. 44, Postfach 101526, 7000 Stuttgart 1, Germany. TEL 0711-2582-0. FAX 0711-2582290. TELEX 723636-DAZD. Eds. Theodor Viehweg, Reinhard May.

STUDIEN ZUR OSTASIATISCHEN SCHRIFTKUNST. see ART

STUDIES IN CENTRAL AND EAST ASIAN RELIGIONS. see RELIGIONS AND THEOLOGY — Buddhist

950 390　　　US　　ISSN 0081-8321
STUDIES IN ORIENTAL CULTURE. 1967. irreg., latest no.14. Columbia University Press, 562 W. 113th St., New York, NY 10025. TEL 212-678-6777.

954　　　　UK　　ISSN 0142-6028
STUDIES ON ASIAN TOPICS.* 1980. irreg. price varies. (Scandinavian Institute of Asian Studies, DK) Curzon Press Ltd., 7 Caledonian Rd., London N1 9DX, England.

950　　　　　　　US
STUDIES ON EAST ASIA. (Text in English or Oriental languages) 1971. irreg., vol.17, 1984. price varies. Western Washington University, Center for East Asian Studies, Bellingham, WA 98225. TEL 206-676-3041. Ed. Henry G. Schwarz.
　Formerly (until vol.13): Western Washington State College. Program in East Asian Studies. Occasional Papers.

959　　　　　　　US
STUDIES ON SOUTHEAST ASIA. 1985. irreg. price varies. Cornell University, Southeast Asia Program, 102 West Ave., Ithaca, NY 14850. TEL 607-255-8038. FAX 607-254-5000. TELEX WUI-6713054. (Subscr. to: S E A P Publications, Cornell University, E. Hill Plaza, Ithaca, NY 14850)

SUI YUAN WEN HSIEN. see ETHNIC INTERESTS

950 613.7　　US　　ISSN 0730-1049
T'AI CHI; perspectives of the way and its movement. 1977. bi-m. $20 (foreign $30). Wayfarer Publications, Box 26156, Los Angeles, CA 90026. TEL 213-665-7773. FAX 213-665-1627. Ed. Marvin Smalheiser. adv.; bk.rev.; circ. 5,500. (back issues avail.)
　Description: Comparative look at the different styles of T'ai Chi Ch'uan practice, Qigong, and the Chinese philosophy and health principles.

TAMKANG REVIEW; a journal mainly devoted to comparative studies between Chinese and foreign literatures. see LITERATURE

950　　　　US　　ISSN 0737-5034
T'ANG STUDIES. 1982. a. $10 to individuals; institutions $15. T'ang Studies Society, c/o Prof. Michael R. Drompp, Rhodes College, Department of History, 2000 N. Parkway, Memphis, TN 38112. Ed. Paul W. Kroll. circ. 250.
　Description: Surveys scholarly articles relating to China's T'ang Dynasty (618-907).

TEL AVIV JOURNAL OF ARCHAEOLOGY. see ARCHAEOLOGY

951.5　　　　II　　ISSN 0970-5368
THE TIBET JOURNAL. (Text in English) 1975. q. $20. Library of Tibetan Works and Archives, Dharamshala 176 215, India. TELEX TF 2467. Ed. Karma Gyatsho. adv.; bk.rev.; bibl.; charts; circ. 1,000. (back issues avail.)
　—BLDSC shelfmark: 8820.637000.
　Description: Provides international information on the study of Tibet.

950　　　　US　　ISSN 0735-1364
DS785.A1
TIBET SOCIETY. JOURNAL. (Text in English, French, German and Tibetan) 1981. a. $20 (foreign $24). Tibet Society, Inc., Box 1968, Bloomington, IN 47402. TEL 812-335-8222. Ed. Elliot Sperling. bk.rev.; circ. 450.
　Description: Devoted to all areas of research on Tibet and regions influenced by Tibetan culture.

958　　　　GW　　ISSN 0935-7505
TIBETAN AND INDO-TIBETAN STUDIES. irreg., vol.4, 1990. price varies. (University of Hamburg, Institute for the Culture and History of India and Tibet) Franz Steiner Verlag Wiesbaden GmbH, Birkenwaldstr. 44, Postfach 101526, 7000 Stuttgart 1, Germany. TEL 0711-2582-0. FAX 0711-2582290.

950 297　　　JA　　ISSN 0304-2448
TOHO GAKUHO/DONGFANG XUEBAO. (Text in Japanese; occasionally in Chinese) 1931. a. Kyoto University, Institute for Research in Humanities - Kyoto Daigaku Jinbun Kagaku Kenkyujo, Ushinomiya-cho, Yoshida, Sakyo-ku, Kyoto 606, Japan. illus.
　—BLDSC shelfmark: 5027.410000.
　Description: Covers humanities in East Asia.

900　　　　JA　　ISSN 0495-7199
TOHOGAKU/EASTERN STUDIES. (Text in Japanese) 1951. s-a. 1900 Yen. Toho Gakkai - Institute of Eastern Culture, 4-1, Nishi-Kanda 2-chome, Chiyoda-ku, Tokyo 101, Japan. Ed.Bd. bk.rev. (back issues avail.) Indexed: M.L.A.

TOKEN BIJUTSU/JOURNAL OF JAPANESE FINE ARTS SWORDS. see ART

ORIENTAL STUDIES

950   NE   ISSN 0082-5433
DS501
T'OUNG PAO; revue internationale de sinologie. (Supplement avail.: T'oung Pao. Monographies (ISSN 0169-832X)) (Text in English, French, German) vol.78, 1992. 4/yr. fl.160($91.43) (effective 1992). E.J. Brill, P.O. Box 9000, 2300 PA Leiden, Netherlands. TEL 071-312624. FAX 071-317532. TELEX 39296 BRILL NL. (In N. America: E.J. Brill, 24 Hudson St., Kinderhook, NY 12106. TEL 800-962-4406) Eds. J. Gernet, E. Zuercher. (also avail. in microfilm from BHP; reprint service avail. from KTO) **Indexed:** Arts & Hum.Cit.Ind., Hist.Abstr., M.L.A.
—BLDSC shelfmark: 8870.900000.

950   NE   ISSN 0169-832X
T'OUNG PAO. MONOGRAPHIES. (Supplement to: T'oung Pao) (Text in English, French, German) 1954? irreg., vol. 16, 1989. price varies. E.J. Brill, P.O. Box 9000, 2300 PA Leiden, Netherlands. TEL 071-312624. FAX 071-317532. TELEX 39296 BRILL NL. (In N. America: E.J. Brill, 24 Hudson St., Kinderhook, NY 12106. TEL 800-962-4406)

950   GW   ISSN 0938-0051
TRAVAUX DU GROUPE DE RECHERCHES ET D'ETUDES SEMITIQUES ANCIENNES. 1982. irreg., vol.3, 1990. Verlag Otto Harrassowitz, Taunusstr. 14, Postfach 2929, 6200 Wiesbaden 1, Germany. TEL 0611-530-0. FAX 0611-530-570. TELEX 4186135.

950   GW   ISSN 0344-5542
TUNGUSICA. 1978. irreg., vol.3, 1985. price varies. Verlag Otto Harrassowitz, Taunusstr. 14, Postfach 2929, 6200 Wiesbaden 1, Germany. TEL 0611-530-0. FAX 0611-530570. TELEX 4186135. Ed. Michael Weiers.

950   GW   ISSN 0177-4743
TURCOLOGICA. 1985. irreg., vol.7, 1991. price varies. Verlag Otto Harrassowitz, Taunusstr. 14, Postfach 2929, 6200 Wiesbaden 1, Germany. TEL 0611-530-0. FAX 0611-530570. TELEX 4186135. Ed. Lars Johanson.

TURK TARIH KURUMU. BELGELER. see HISTORY — History Of The Near East

TURK TARIH KURUMU. BELLETEN. see HISTORY — History Of The Near East

TURKOLOGISCHER ANZEIGER/TURKOLOGY ANNUAL. see ORIENTAL STUDIES — Abstracting, Bibliographies, Statistics

UNIVERSITAETSBIBLIOTHEK GIESSEN. KURZBERICHTE AUS DEN PAPYRUS-SAMMLUNGEN. see HISTORY

UNIVERSITE CATHOLIQUE DE LOUVAIN. INSTITUT ORIENTALISTE. PUBLICATIONS. see HISTORY — History Of Asia

955 200   LE
UNIVERSITE SAINT-JOSEPH. FACULTE DES LETTRES ET DES SCIENCES HUMAINES. RECHERCHES. SERIE B: ORIENT CHRETIEN. (Previously published by its Institut des Lettres Orientales in 4 series) 1956; N.S. 1971. irreg. price varies. Dar el-Mashreq S.A.R.L., 2 rue Huvelin, Box 946, Beirut, Lebanon. (Subscr. to: Librairie Orientale, Box 946, Beirut, Lebanon)

950 011   UK   ISSN 0307-0654
UNIVERSITY OF DURHAM. CENTRE FOR MIDDLE EASTERN AND ISLAMIC STUDIES. OCCASIONAL PAPERS SERIES.. 1972. irreg., latest no.41. price varies. University of Durham, Centre for Middle Eastern and Islamic Studies, South End House, South Rd., Durham City DH1 3TG, England. TEL 091-374-2823. Eds. J.C. Dewdney, C.H. Bleaney. bibl.

950   HK   ISSN 0378-2689
UNIVERSITY OF HONG KONG. CENTRE OF ASIAN STUDIES. OCCASIONAL PAPERS AND MONOGRAPHS. (Text in Chinese or English) 1970. irreg., no.96, 1991. price varies. University of Hong Kong, Centre of Asian Studies, Pokfulam Rd., Hong Kong. FAX 559-5884. TELEX 71919-CEREB-HX. Ed. Edward K.Y. Chen. (processed; reprint service avail. from UMI) Key Title: Occasional Papers and Monographs - Centre of Asian Studies.
—BLDSC shelfmark: 3106.467000.

951   UK   ISSN 0308-6119
UNIVERSITY OF LONDON. CONTEMPORARY CHINA INSTITUTE. RESEARCH NOTES AND STUDIES. 1976. irreg. price varies. University of London, School of Oriental and African Studies, Thornhaugh St., Russell Sq., London WC1H OXG, England. TEL 071-637-2388. FAX 071-436-3844. (Co-sponsor: Contemporary China Institute)

915.4   II
UNIVERSITY OF RAJASTHAN. SOUTH ASIAN STUDIES CENTRE. ANNUAL REPORT. (Text in English) 1966. irreg., latest 1973. University of Rajasthan, South Asian Studies Centre, Gandhi Nagar, Jaipur 302004, India.

UNIVERZITA KOMENSKEHO. FILOZOFICKA FAKULTA. ZBORNIK: GRAECOLATINA ET ORIENTALIA. see CLASSICAL STUDIES

VARENDRA RESEARCH MUSEUM. JOURNAL. see MUSEUMS AND ART GALLERIES

890 967   MF
VASANTA. (Text in Hindi) 1978. q. Rs.20. Mahatma Gandhi Institute, Library, Moka, Mauritius. TEL 464-8022. Ed. Abhimanyu Unnuth. bk.rev.; circ. 700.
Description: Provides a representation of Hindi literature being written in Maruitius consolidating a geographical indentity while keeping in touch with trends of world Hindi literature.

950   GW   ISSN 0506-7936
VERZEICHNIS DER ORIENTALISCHEN HANDSCHRIFTEN IN DEUTSCHLAND. Short title: V O H D. (Text in English and German) irreg., vol.33, 1991. price varies. (Deutsche Morgenlaendische Gesellschaft) Franz Steiner Verlag Wiesbaden GmbH, Birkenwaldstr. 44, Postfach 101526, 7000 Stuttgart 1, Germany. TEL 0711-2582-0. FAX 0711-2582290. TELEX 723636-DAZD. Eds. Dieter George, Hartmut-Ortwin Feistel.

950   GW   ISSN 0506-7944
VERZEICHNIS DER ORIENTALISCHEN HANDSCHRIFTEN IN DEUTSCHLAND. SUPPLEMENTBAENDE. Abbreviated title: V O H D Supplementbaende. (Text in English and German) irreg., vol.31, 1989. price varies. (Deutsche Morgenlaendische Gesellschaft) Franz Steiner Verlag Wiesbaden GmbH, Birkenwaldstr. 44, Postfach 101526, 7000 Stuttgart 1, Germany. TEL 0711-2582-0. FAX 0711-2582290. TELEX 723636-DAZD. Eds. Dieter George, Hartmut-Ortwin Feistel.

VESTNIK DREVNEI ISTORII/JOURNAL OF ANCIENT HISTORY. see HISTORY

VIETNAMESE STUDIES. see HISTORY — History Of Asia

954   II
VISHVA VICHARAMALA. (Text in Hindi and Sanskrit) irreg. price varies. Vishveshvaranand Vedic Research Institute, P.O. Sadhu Ashram, Hoshiarpur 146021, Punjab, India. Ed. S. Bhaskaran Nair.

954   II
VISHVESHVARANAND VEDIC RESEARCH INSTITUTE. RESEARCH AND GENERAL PUBLICATIONS. (Text in English, Hindi, and Sanskrit) 1921. irreg. price varies. Vishveshvaranand Vedic Research Institute, P.O. Sadhu Ashram, Hoshiarpur 146021, Punjab, India.

VOORAZIATISCH-EGYPTISCH GENOOTSCAP "EX ORIENTE LUX". JAARBERICHT; annuaire de la Societe Orientale Neerlandaise "Ex Oriente Lux". see HISTORY — History Of Asia

VOORAZIATISCH-EGYPTISCH GENOOTSCAP "EX ORIENTE LUX". MEDEDELINGEN EN VERHANDELINGEN. see HISTORY — History Of Asia

950   GW   ISSN 0138-4449
VORDERASIATISCHE SCHRIFTDENKMALER DER STAATLICHEN MUSSEN ZU BERLIN. 1971. irreg., vol.8, 1987. (Vorderasiatisches Museum DDR) Akademie-Verlag Berlin, Leipziger Str. 3-4, 1086 Berlin, Germany. TELEX 114420-AVERL-DD. (Alt. ed. addr.: Bodestr. 1-3, Germany)

WAQA'I DAWLAT AL-IMARAT/EMIRATES EVENTS. see HISTORY — History Of The Near East

AL-WATHA'IQ AL-FILASTINIYYAH/PALESTINIAN DOCUMENTS. see HISTORY — History Of The Near East

WATHA'IQ DAWLAT AL-IMARAT/EMIRATES DOCUMENTS. see HISTORY — History Of The Near East

AL-WATHIQA. see HISTORY — History Of The Near East

956 297   NE   ISSN 0043-2539
DS36
DIE WELT DES ISLAMS/WORLD OF ISLAM; internationale Zeitschrift fuer die Geschichte des Islams in der Neuzeit - international journal for the history of modern Islam. (Text in English, French, German) 1955. 2/yr. fl.100($57.14) E.J. Brill, P.O. Box 9000, 2300 PA Leiden, Netherlands. TEL 071-312624. FAX 071-317532. TELEX 39296 BRILL NL. (In N. America: E.J. Brill, 24 Hudson St., Kinderhook, NY 12106. TEL 800-962-4406) Eds. S. Wild, W. Ende. (also avail. in microform from SWZ; reprint service avail. from SWZ) **Indexed:** Hist.Abstr.
—BLDSC shelfmark: 9294.710000.

951   CC
WENHUA CHUNQIU. (Text in Chinese) m. Y18. Zhongguo Zuojia Xiehui, Fujian Fenhui - China Writers' Association, Fujian Chapter, Wenlian Dalou, Xihong Lu, Fuzhou, Fujian 350002, People's Republic of China. TEL 712657. (Dist. overseas by: Jiangsu Publications Import & Export Corp., 56 Gao Yun Ling, Nanjing, Jiangsu, P.R.C.) Ed. Zhang Shilian.
Description: Includes cultural mysteries, historical stories, and cultural collections.

WENSHI ZHISHI/KNOWLEDGE OF LITERATURE AND HISTORY. see SOCIAL SCIENCES: COMPREHENSIVE WORKS

956   AU   ISSN 0084-0076
Z2831
WIENER ZEITSCHRIFT FUER DIE KUNDE DES MORGENLANDES. (Text in English, French, German and Italian) 1887. a. price varies. Universitaet Wien, Institut fuer Orientalistik, Universitaets Str. 7-V, A-1010 Vienna, Austria. FAX 0222-4020533. Ed.Bd. adv.; bk.rev.; circ. 400. **Indexed:** M.L.A.
—BLDSC shelfmark: 9074.480000.

WISCONSIN CHINA SERIES. see HISTORY — History Of Asia

951 915.12   CC   ISSN 1001-5558
XIBEI MINZU YANJIU/NORTHWEST MINORITIES STUDIES. (Text in Chinese) s-a. $27.20. Xibei Minzu Yanjiusuo - Northwest Minorities Institute, 4, Xibei Xincun, Lanzhou, Gansu 730030, People's Republic of China. TEL 464011. (Dist. in US by: China Books & Periodicals, Inc., 2929 24th St., San Francisco, CA 94110. TEL 415-282-2994)

XIZANG WENXUE/TIBETAN LITERATURE. see LITERATURE

951 915.12   CC   ISSN 1000-0003
XIZANG YANJIU/TIBETAN STUDIES. (Editions in Chinese, English, Tibetan) 1981. q (English ed. s-a). $24 for Chinese ed.; Tibetan ed. $21. Xizang Zizhiqu Shehui Kexueyuan - Tibetan Autonomous Region Academy of Social Sciences, Lhasa, Xizang (Tibet) 850000, People's Republic of China. TEL 22638. (Dist. in US by: China Books & Periodicals, Inc., 2929 24th St., San Francisco, CA 94110. TEL 415-282-2994) Ed. Shilai Daoji.
Description: Covers Tibetan politics, economics, history, religion, literature, art, language, medicine, law and archaeology.

951   CC   ISSN 1003-7942
XUEYU WENHUA/TIBETAN CULTURE. (Editions in Chinese and Tibetan) 1989. q. Y10. Xueyu Wenhua Zazhishe, 2 Dolsingar Road, Lhasa, Xizang (Tibet) 850000, People's Republic of China. TEL 22024. FAX 26689. (Dist. overseas by: Guoji Shudian - China International Book Trade Corp., P.O. Box 399, Beijing, P.R.C.) Ed. Gyamco. adv. contact: Zhong Zhang. circ. 7,000.
Description: Features Tibetan customs, arts, religion, ancient relics and tourism.

ORIENTAL STUDIES — ABSTRACTING, BIBLIOGRAPHIES, STATISTICS

950 US ISSN 0513-4501
YALE SOUTHEAST ASIA STUDIES. MONOGRAPH SERIES. 1961. irreg., no.33, 1989. Yale University, Council on Southeast Asia Studies, Box 13A, 85 Trumbull St., New Haven, CT 06520. TEL 203-432-3431. FAX 203-432-3296. Ed. M.K. Mansfield. adv. (reprint service avail. from UMI)
—BLDSC shelfmark: 9371.210000.

951 CC ISSN 1003-7527
YANG GUAN. (Text in Chinese) 1979. bi-m. Y3.6. (Jiuquan Diqu Wenlian) Yang Guan Zazhishe, Xi Dajie, Jiuquan, Guansu 735000, People's Republic of China. TEL 0937-4283. (Dist. overseas by: Jiangsu Publications Import & Export Corp., 56 Gao Yun Ling, Nanjing, Jiangsu, P.R.C.) Ed. Zhao Shuming. adv.; bk.rev.; circ. 4,000.
Description: Includes literary works, profiles of historical figures, legends, and ancient relics and art works along the Silk Road in Western China.

YAQEEN INTERNATIONAL. see *RELIGIONS AND THEOLOGY — Islamic*

950 GW ISSN 0932-3201
YARMOUK UNIVERSITY. INSTITUTE OF ARCHAEOLOGY AND ANTHROPOLOGY. SERIES. 1987. irreg., vol.2, 1989. Verlag Otto Harrassowitz, Taunusstr. 14, Postfach 2929, 6200 Wiesbaden 1, Germany. TEL 0611-530-0. FAX 0611-530-570. TELEX 4186135. Ed. M.M. Ibrahim.
—BLDSC shelfmark: 9371.582460.

294.3 JA ISSN 0386-4251
YOUNG EAST; a quarterly on Buddhism and Japanese culture. (Text in English) 1925-1966; N.S. 1975. q. 2000 Yen($10) (Young East Association) Tohokai, Inc., 6-2-17 Nishitenma, Kita-ku, Osaka 530, Japan. Ed. Nara Yasuaki. circ. 20,000.

951.35 301 CC ISSN 1001-8913
YUNNAN MINZU XUEYUAN XUEBAO/YUNNAN INSTITUTE OF NATIONALITIES. JOURNAL. (Text in Chinese) 1983. q. Y4.80. Yunnan Minzu Xueyuan - Yunnan Institute of Nationalities, Lianhua Chi, Kunming, Yunnan 650031, People's Republic of China. TEL 0871-54458. (Dist. overseas by: China International Book Trading Corp., P.O. Box 399, Beijing, P.R.C.) adv.; bk.rev.
Description: Contains research papers and reports on political science, philosophy, economics, literature, history, and linguistics relating to ethnic groups in Yunnan Province.

962 490 GW ISSN 0044-216X
PJ1004
ZEITSCHRIFT FUER AEGYPTISCHE SPRACHE UND ALTERTUMSKUNDE. (Text in English and German) 1863. 2/yr. DM.115.60. Akademie-Verlag Berlin, Leipziger Str. 3-4, 1086 Berlin, Germany. TELEX 114420-AVERL-DD. Eds. F. Hintze, E. Blumenthal. bk.rev.; bibl.; illus.; index.

956 GW ISSN 0179-4639
ZEITSCHRIFT FUER GESCHICHTE DER ARABISCH-ISLAMISCHEN WISSENSCHAFTEN. (Text in Arabic, English, French and German) 1984. a. price varies. Institut fuer Geschichte der Arabisch-Islamischen Wissenschaften, Beethovenstrasse 32, Frankfurt, Germany. TEL 069-756009-0. Ed. Fuat Sezgin. bk.rev.

956.1 GW ISSN 0934-0696
HC491
ZEITSCHRIFT FUER TUERKEISTUDIEN. s-a. DM.60. Leske und Budrich GmbH, Gerhart-Hauptmann-Str. 27, Postfach 300406, 5090 Leverkusen 3, Germany. TEL 02171-2079. Ed.Bd.

951 CC ISSN 1001-0882
ZHONGGUO SHAOSHU MINZU. (Subseries of: Fuyin Baokan Ziliao) (Text in Chinese) m. Y29.40. Zhongguo Renmin Daxue, Shubao Ziliao Zhongxin - China People's University, Book & Newspaper Information Center, P.O. Box 1122, Beijing 100007, People's Republic of China. TEL 441792.
Description: Reprints papers and articles on China's minority groups.

ZHONGGUO SHEHUI JINGJISHI YANJIU/JOURNAL OF CHINESE SOCIAL AND ECONOMIC HISTORY. see *HISTORY — History Of Asia*

951 915.12 US
ZHONGGUO ZANGXUE/STUDY - TIBETAN NATIONALITIES. (Editions in Chinese and Tibetan) q. $22.50. China Books & Periodicals, Inc., 2929 24th St., San Francisco, CA 94110. TEL 415-282-2994. FAX 415-292-0994.

951 CC
ZHONGGUOXUE DAOBAO/SINOLOGICAL PIONEER. (Text mostly in Chinese; summaries and table of contents in English) 1987. bi-m. $9 per no. Zhongguo Wenhua Shuyuan, Zhongguoxue Zixun Zhongxin - International Academy of Chinese Culture, Consultation Center for Chinese Studies, P.O. Box 9058, Beijing, People's Republic of China. Ed. Yang Jing. bibl.
Description: Publishes materials concerning ancient and contemporary Chinese literature, art, architecture, political systems, law, legal ideology, economics, economic ideology, religion, philosophy, and folk conventions. Also lists relevant publications.

ORIENTAL STUDIES — Abstracting, Bibliographies, Statistics

ANNUAL EGYPTOLOGICAL BIBLIOGRAPHY/BIBLIOGRAPHIE EGYPTOLOGIQUE ANNUELLE/JAEHRLICHE AEGYPTOLOGISCHE BIBLIOGRAPHIE. see *HISTORY — Abstracting, Bibliographies, Statistics*

950 015 II ISSN 0006-1212
BIBLIOGRAPHIA ASIATICA. 1968. m. Rs.1800($250) K.K. Roy (Private) Ltd., 55 Gariahat Rd., P.O. Box 10210, Calcutta 700 019, India. Ed. K.K. Roy. abstr.; bibl.; index; circ. 1,600. (tabloid format; also avail. in microform)

950 US ISSN 1046-8765
DS504.5
▼**BIBLIOGRAPHIC GUIDE TO EAST ASIAN STUDIES.** 1990. a. $160 (foreign $180). G.K. Hall & Co., 70 Lincoln St., Boston, MA 02111. TEL 617-423-3990. FAX 617-423-3999. TELEX 94-0037.
Description: Covers China, Hong Kong, Taiwan, North and South Korea, and Japan, with approximately 3500 listings from LCMARC tapes and the Oriental Division of the New York Public Library. Includes publications about East Asia, materials published in any of the relevant countries, and publications in Chinese, Korean, and Japanese (transliterated into Roman letters).

956 US ISSN 1058-644X
▼**BIBLIOGRAPHIC GUIDE TO MIDDLE EASTERN STUDIES.** 1991. a. $200 (foreign $225). G.K. Hall & Co., 70 Lincoln St., Boston, MA 02111. TEL 617-423-3990. FAX 617-423-3999. TELEX 94-0037.
Description: Lists all the materials cataloged during the past year by the Library of Congress, the Middle East section of the New York Public Library's Oriental Division, and modern Hebrew language books in the NYPL's Jewish Division.

950 JA ISSN 0524-0654
Z3001
BOOKS AND ARTICLES ON ORIENTAL SUBJECTS PUBLISHED IN JAPAN. (Text in English, Japanese) 1956. a. 4700 Yen. Toho Gakkai - Institute of Eastern Culture, 4-1, Nishi-Kanda 2-chome, Chiyoda-ku, Tokyo 101, Japan. Ed.Bd. (back issues avail.)

BULLETIN D'ARABE CHRETIEN. BIBLIOGRAPHIE DES AUTEURS ARABES CHRETIENS. see *HISTORY — Abstracting, Bibliographies, Statistics*

950 016 US ISSN 0008-9044
Z7043
CENTER FOR CHINESE RESEARCH MATERIALS. NEWSLETTER. 1968. s-a. free. Center for Chinese Research Materials, Box 3090, Oakton, VA 22124. TEL 703-281-7731. Ed. Pingfeng Chi. bibl.; charts; circ. 1,400.

950 016 NE ISSN 0920-203X
CHINA INFORMATION. 1967. q. fl.70 to individuals; institutions fl. 90; students fl. 50. Rijksuniversiteit te Leiden, Sinologisch Instituut, Documentation and Research Centre for Contemporary China, Postbus 9515, 2300 RA Leiden, Netherlands. TEL 071-272516. FAX 071-272615. Ed. W.L. van Woerkom-Chong. adv.; bk.rev.; circ. 375. **Indexed:** Key to Econ.Sci.
—BLDSC shelfmark: 3180.170700.
Formerly (until 1986): China Informatie (ISSN 0577-8832)
Description: Scholarly coverage of contemporary China.

950 016 US
CORNELL UNIVERSITY. LIBRARY. JOHN M. ECHOLS COLLECTION ON SOUTHEAST ASIA. ACCESSIONS LIST. 1959. m. $20. Cornell University, Southeast Asia Program, 102 West Ave., Ithaca, NY 14850. TEL 607-255-8038. FAX 607-255-7116. TELEX WUI-6713054. (Subcsr. to: S E A P Publications, Cornell University, E. Hill Plaza, Ithaca, NY 14850) Ed. John Badgeley. bibl.; circ. 400. (back issues avail.)
Formerly (until 1978): Cornell University. Library. Wason Collection. Southeast Asia Accessions List (ISSN 0589-7351)

011 950 US ISSN 0098-4485
Z3001
DOCTORAL DISSERTATIONS ON ASIA; an annotated bibliographical journal of current international research. 1975. a. $20. Association for Asian Studies, Inc., 1 Lane Hall, University of Michigan, Ann Arbor, MI 48109. TEL 313-665-2490. FAX 313-665-2490. Ed. Frank J. Shulman. bibl.; circ. 2,500. (back issues avail.)
—BLDSC shelfmark: 3607.200000.

950 016
INDEX ASIA SERIES IN HUMANITIES. 1965. irreg. price varies. Centre for Asian Dokumentation, K-15, CIT Bldg., Christopher Rd., Calcutta 700 014, India. Ed. S. Chaudhuri. bk.rev.; index.
Description: Cumulative index to writings in journals on all aspects of South Asian and Buddhistic studies as well as bibliographies on specific topics.

954 015 II ISSN 0019-3844
INDEX INDIA; a quarterly documentation list of selected articles, editorials, notes, and letters, etc., from periodicals and newspapers published in the English language all over the world. (Text in English) 1967. q. Rs.800($85) Rajasthan University Library, Gandhi Nagar, Jaipur 302004, India. TEL 511866. Ed. Pawan K. Gupta. adv.; bk.rev.; bibl.; index; circ. 400.

950 015 II ISSN 0019-3852
INDEX INDO-ASIATICUS. (Text in Bengali, English, Hindi, Sanskrit and other European languages) 1968. q. Rs.150($600) Centre for Asian Dokumentation, K-15, CIT Bldg., Christopher Rd., Calcutta 700 014, India. (Subscr. to: Central News Agency, P.O. Box 374, New Delhi 110 001, India) Ed. Sibadas Chaudhuri. adv.; bk.rev.; bibl.; cum.index; circ. 400.
Description: Indexes international periodicals of all languages, whose topics relate to the culture of India and ancient Asia.

650 II
INDEX INTERNATIONALIS INDICUS. 1970. triennial. price varies. Centre for Asian Dokumentation, K-15, CIT Bldg., Christopher Rd., Calcutta 700 014, India. (Distr. by: Verlag Otto Harrassowitz, Taunusstr. 14, P.O. Box 2929, 6200 Wiesbaden 1, Germany) Ed. S. Chaudhuri. adv.; circ. 500.
Description: Lists cumulative articles on indological and buddhistic sutdies published in Indian and foreign periodicals.

959 016 SI ISSN 0046-984X
INSTITUTE OF SOUTHEAST ASIAN STUDIES. LIBRARY. ACCESSIONS LIST. 1968. irreg. vol.4, no.14. free. Institute of Southeast Asian Studies, Heng Mui Keng Terrace, Pasir Panjang, Singapore 0511, Singapore. TEL 7780955. FAX 7781735. TELEX RS 37068 ISEAS. bibl. (processed)

954 011   II   ISSN 0970-1435
M L B D NEWSLETTER; monthly of indological bibliography. (Text in English and Hindi) 1979. m. Rs.15($10) Motilal Banarsidass (Delhi), 41 U.A. Bungalow Rd., Jawahar Nagar, Delhi 110 007, India. TEL 2911985. FAX 011-2930689. TELEX 031-66053 ENKY IN. (Dist. in U.S. by: South Asia Books, Box 502, Columbia, MO 65205; in U.K. by: M S Motilal Books Ltd., 52 Crown Rd., Wheatley, Oxford OX9 1UL, England. TEL 314-449-1359) Ed. Sunil Dutt. adv.; bk.rev.; abstr.; bibl.; illus.
    Description: Focuses on Vedic and Buddhist works of literature and research.

011   SU
MARKAZ AL-MALIK FAISAL LIL-BUHUTH WAL-DIRASAT AL-ISLAMIYYAH. FIHRIS AL-MAKHTUTAT/KING FAISAL CENTER FOR RESEARCH AND ISLAMIC STUDIES. MANUSCRIPT CATALOGUE. 1985. irreg. King Faisal Center for Research and Islamic Studies, P.O. Box 5149, Riyadh 11543, Saudi Arabia. TEL 4652255. TELEX 205470.

951 011   NP
NEPAL - ANTIQUARY. BIBLIOGRAPHICAL SERIES. 1976. irreg. Rs.250($30) Office of Nepal-Antiquary, 20-401 Naxal, Kathmandu, Nepal.

950   GW   ISSN 0720-2695
NEUERWERBUNG SUEDASIEN. 1977. 7/yr. DM.28. Universitaetsbibliothek Tuebingen, Orientalabteilung, Postfach 2620, Wilhelmstr. 32, 7400 Tuebingen, Germany. index; circ. 120.
    Description: Collects new literature focusing on language and culture of Southern Asia received in the University of Tuebingen library.

950   GW   ISSN 0720-2741
NEUERWERBUNGEN VORDERER ORIENT. 1977. m. DM.28. Universitaetsbibliothek Tuebingen, Orientalabteilung, Postfach 2620, Wilhelmstr. 32, 7400 Tuebingen, Germany. TEL 07071-292587. FAX 07071-293123. index; circ. 240.
    Description: Contains new literature about ancient history, language, and modern regional studies of the Near and Middle East as well as North Africa.

950   RU   ISSN 0132-7348
OBSHCHESTVENNYE NAUKI ZA RUBEZHOM. VOSTOKOVEDENIE I AFRIKANISTIKA; referativnyi zhurnal. 1972. bi-m. 4.20 Rub. Akademiya Nauk S.S.S.R., Institut Nauchnoi Informatsii po Obshchestvennym Naukam, Ul. Krasikova 28-21, 117418 Moscow V-418, Russia. Ed. S.N. Kuznetsova.

950   AU
TURKOLOGISCHER ANZEIGER/TURKOLOGY ANNUAL. (Text in English, French and German) 1975. a. S.400($32) Orientalisches Institut, Universitaet Wien, A-1010 Vienna, Austria. TEL 0222-40103-2593. FAX 0222-4020533. (Co-sponsor: Unesco) Eds. Georges Hazai, Andreas Tietze. circ. 400. (back issues avail.)
    Description: Provides bibliographic information on new publications on Turkish language, literature, and history.

950 016   HK   ISSN 0441-1900
Z3107.H7
UNIVERSITY OF HONG KONG. CENTRE OF ASIAN STUDIES. BIBLIOGRAPHIES AND RESEARCH GUIDES. (Text in Chinese or English) 1970. irreg., no.24, 1987. price varies. University of Hong Kong, Centre of Asian Studies, Pokfulam Rd., Hong Kong. FAX 559-5884. TELEX 71919-CEREB-HX. Ed. Edward K.Y. Chen. (processed)

ORNITHOLOGY

see Biology–Ornithology

ORTHOPEDICS AND TRAUMATOLOGY

see Medical Sciences–Orthopedics and Traumatology

OTORHINOLARYNGOLOGY

see Medical Sciences–Otorhinolaryngology

OUTDOOR LIFE

see Sports and Games–Outdoor Life

PACKAGING

660.29 658.7 670   GW
TP244.A3   CODEN: AERRBV
AEROSOL SPRAY REPORT. (Text in English and German) 1961. 11/yr. DM.368. Dr. Alfred Huethig Verlag GmbH, Im Weiher 10, Postfach 102869, 6900 Heidelberg 1, Germany. TEL 06221-489-281. FAX 06221-489279. TELEX 461727-HUEHDD. charts; illus.; circ. 3,851. Indexed: Chem.Abstr., Curr.Pack.Abstr., Eng.Ind., Excerp.Med., Int.Packag.Abstr., Met.Abstr., Packag.Sci.Tech., World Alum.Abstr.
    Formerly: Aerosol Report (ISSN 0001-9313)

ALCAN INFORMIERT. see METALLURGY

658.788   US
AMERICAN FASTENER JOURANL. bi-m. 293 Hopewell Dr., Powell, OH 43065-9350. TEL 614-848-3232. FAX 614-848-5045. Ed. Carol McGuire.

ANNUAL BOOK OF A S T M STANDARDS. VOLUME 15.09. PAPER; PACKAGING; FLEXIBLE BARRIER MATERIALS; BUSINESS COPY PRODUCTS. see ENGINEERING — Engineering Mechanics And Materials

658.7884   US
ANNUAL CAN SHIPMENTS REPORT. 1972. a. $75. Can Manufacturers Institute, 1625 Massachusetts Ave., N.W., Washington, DC 20036. TEL 202-232-4677. circ. 500.
    Formerly: Can Manufacturers Institute. Annual Metal Can Shipments Report (ISSN 0068-7014)
    Description: Covers domestic can shipments by market, product, technology and material used.

ANYAGMOZGATAS-CSOMAGOLAS. see TRANSPORTATION — Ships And Shipping

AUSTRALIAN LITHOGRAPHER, PRINTER, AND PACKAGER. see PRINTING

658.7   AT   ISSN 0004-9921
AUSTRALIAN PACKAGING. 1952. m. Aus.$55. Business Press International Pty. Ltd., 162 Goulburn St., Darlinghurst, N.S.W. 2010, Australia. TEL 266-9711. FAX 267-1223. Ed. A. Craven. adv.; bk.rev.; charts; illus.; pat.; tr.lit.; tr.mk.; circ. 5,000. Indexed: Abstr.Bull.Inst.Pap.Chem., Curr.Pack.Abstr., Int.Packag.Abstr., Packag.Sci.Tech.
    —BLDSC shelfmark: 1817.400000.

658.7   AU   ISSN 0005-0563
AUSTROPACK; Zeitschrift fuer alle Gebiete des Verpackungswesens fuer Transport und Verkehr. 1964. m. DM.100. Verlag Dr. A. Schendl, Karlsgasse 15, Postfach 29, A-1041 Vienna, Austria. TEL 0222-5055593. FAX 0222-5055596. Ed. Franz Oegg. adv.; bk.rev.; abstr.; charts; illus.; stat.; circ. 1,500. (tabloid format) Indexed: Int.Packag.Abstr.

658.788   FR
B I C - CODE. (Text in English, French) 1970. a. 130 Fr. per no. Bureau International des Containers - International Container Bureau, 16 rue Jean Rey, F-75015 Paris, France. TEL 47-34-68-13. FAX 42-73-01-40. TELEX 270835 UNINFER. Ed. P. Fournier. charts.

621   US   ISSN 0360-8689
TS195.A1
BEST IN PACKAGING. (Subseries of: Print Casebooks) 1975. biennial. $27.95. R C Publications, Inc., 104 Fifth Ave., 9th Fl., New York, NY 10011. TEL 212-463-0600. FAX 212-989-9891. (Subscr. to: 3200 Tower Oaks Blvd., Rockville, MD 20852. TEL 301-770-2900) illus.

658.788   JA
▼**BEST OF PACKAGING IN JAPAN.** 1990. a. 16000 Yen. Nippo Co. Ltd., 1-19 Misaki-cho 3-chome, Chiyoda-ku, Tokyo 101, Japan. TEL 03-3262-3461. FAX 03-3263-2560.
    Description: Information on packaged goods: food, drugs, cosmetics, confectioneries and daily necessities.

BEVERAGE DIGEST. see BEVERAGES

676.3   US
BOARD CONVERTING NEWS. 1984. w. $110. N V Business Publishers Corp., 43 Main St., Avon By Sea, NJ 07717. TEL 908-502-0500. FAX 908-502-9606. Ed. Jim Curley. circ. 4,450. (back issues avail.)
    Description: Covers product and current news.

676.3   US
BOARD CONVERTING NEWS INTERNATIONAL. fortn. $110. N V Business Publishers Corp, 43 Main St., Avon By Sea, NJ 07717. TEL 908-502-0500. FAX 908-502-9606. (U.K. addr.: Walton House, 90 London Rd., Hooks, Hampshire RG27 9LF, England) Ed. Michael Brunton. circ. 3,075. (back issues avail.)
    Description: Covers product news and general news.

BOTTLE - CAN RECYCLING UPDATE. see ENVIRONMENTAL STUDIES — Waste Management

676.3 658.7   US   ISSN 0006-8489
BOXBOARD CONTAINERS. 1892. m. $26. Maclean Hunter Publishing Company, 29 N. Wacker Dr., Chicago, IL 60606. TEL 312-726-2802. FAX 312-726-2574. TELEX 270258 EXP. Ed. Charles Huck. adv.; charts; illus.; tr.lit.; circ. 14,025. (also avail. in microform from UMI; reprint service avail. from UMI) Indexed: Curr.Pack.Abstr., Graph.Arts Lit.Abstr., Key to Econ.Sci., Packag.Sci.Tech., PROMT.
    —BLDSC shelfmark: 2265.100000.
    Description: Covers corrugated and solid fibre shipping container, folding carton, setup paper box, transparent, fiber can, drum and tube and paperboard mills.

CAN MAKERS REPORT. see FOOD AND FOOD INDUSTRIES

658.788   US
CAN SHIPMENTS REPORT. (Annual edition avail.) 1975. m. $250. Can Manufacturers Institute, 1625 Massachussets Ave., N.W., Washington, DC 20036. TEL 202-232-4677. circ. 750. (back issues avail.)
    Description: Lists domestic (US and US controlled territories) shipment by market, product, material used and technology.

658.7 670   CN   ISSN 0008-4654
                              CODEN: CPAKAN
CANADIAN PACKAGING. 1948. 11/yr. Can.$33. Maclean-Hunter Ltd., Business Publication Division, Maclean-Hunter Bldg., 777 Bay St., Toronto, Ont. M5W 1A7, Canada. TEL 416-596-5745. Ed. Jack Homer. adv.; illus.; circ. 12,000. (also avail. in microform from UMI) Indexed: Abstr.Bull.Inst.Pap.Chem., Art & Archaeol.Tech.Abstr., Can.B.P.I., Chem.Abstr., Curr.Pack.Abstr., Int.Packag.Abstr., Key to Econ.Sci., Packag.Sci.Tech.
    —BLDSC shelfmark: 3043.350000.

PACKAGING

658.7 676.3   FR   ISSN 0247-8390
CARTONNAGES & EMBALLAGES MODERNES. 1940. m.
620 F. Editions Technorama, 31 place St. Ferdinand, 75017 Paris, France. TEL 1-45-74-67-43. FAX 45-72-63-21. Ed. R. Baschet. adv.; charts; illus.; circ. 7,300. **Indexed:** Graph.Arts Lit.Abstr., Key to Econ.Sci.
Formed by the merger of: Emballage Moderne (ISSN 0013-6565); Cartonnages.

658.7   SP
CATALOGO ESPANOL DEL ENVASE, EMBALAJE Y ARTES GRAFICAS APLICADAS. vol.5, 1972. s-a.
22500 ptas. per no. Instituto Espanol del Envase y Embalaje, Breton de los Herreros, 57, bajo H, 28003 Madrid, Spain. TEL 442-34-81. FAX 5383718. TELEX 27307 E. Ed. Luis Sicre. circ. 15,000. (reprint service avail.)
Formerly: Catalogo Nacional del Envase, Embalaje y Artes Graficas Aplicadas (ISSN 0008-7610)

676   IT
CATALOGO GUIDA DELL'IMBALLAGGIO (YEAR). (Text in English, Italian) 1987. a. L.22000. Gruppo Editoriale Faenza Editrice S.p.A., Via Pier. de Crescenzi, 44, 48018 Faenza, Italy.
TEL 0546-663488. FAX 0546-660440. TELEX 550387 EDITFA I. Ed. Franco Rossi. adv.; circ. 15,000. (back issues avail.)

658.788 660   US   ISSN 1054-5131
TP201
▼**THE CHEMICAL PACKAGING REVIEW**; the journal of hazardous materials regulation and distribution. 1990. bi-m. $195 ($205 to Canada and Mexico; elsewhere $220)(effective 1992). Packaging Research International Inc., Box 3144, W. Chester, PA 19381-3144. TEL 215-436-8292. FAX 215-436-9422. Ed. Vincent Vitollo. adv.; circ. 605.
Description: Covers packaging and distribution issues related to the transport of hazardous materials. Covers U.S. DOT and international regulations and EPA guidelines.

380.5   CN
CONTAINERIZATION AND MATERIAL HANDLING ANNUAL.
a. Anchor Press, 1056 Chemin du Golf, Nun's Island, Verdun, Que. H3E 1H4, Canada.
TEL 514-766-8650. FAX 514-766-5559. Ed. O. J. Silva. adv.; illus.

658.88   FR
CONTAINERS. 1933. 6/yr. 200 F. Bureau International des Containers - International Container Bureau, 16 rue Jean Rey, F-75015 Paris, France.
TEL 47-34-68-13.

CONVERTING TODAY. see *PAPER AND PULP*

677.7   FR
CORDERIE FRANCAISE. 1950. m. 120 Fr. Chambre Syndicale Generale de la Corderie, 11 rue du Canal, C U Strasbourg-Illkirch, Boite Postale 271, 67400 Strasbourg, France. Ed. R. Weiss. adv.; circ. 700.

676.3   US   ISSN 1058-0883
CORRUGATED CONTAINERS CONFERENCE (YEAR). Title varies slightly--Corrugated Conference Proceedings. (1981 held jointly with Testing Conference Proceedings) a. price varies. Technical Association of the Pulp and Paper Industry, Inc., Technology Park-Atlanta, Box 105113, Atlanta, GA 30348. TEL 404-446-1400. FAX 404-446-6947.
Formerly: Technical Association of the Pulp and Paper Industry. Corrugated Containers Conference. Proceedings (Year) (ISSN 1046-4166)
Refereed Serial

DIRECTORY OF U S AND CANADIAN SCRAP PLASTICS PROCESSORS AND BUYERS. see *PLASTICS*

658.788   AT
DRUMBEAT. 1971. s-a. Pak Pacific Corporation Pty. Ltd., Dougharty Road, Heidelberg West, Vic. 3081, Australia. Ed. R.J. Bonney. circ. 4,000.

E E C - TIN IN TINPLATE. (European Economic Community) see *METALLURGY*

658.7   BL   ISSN 0013-6530
HF5770.A1
EMBALAGEM. 1970. bi-m. $25. Editora Metodos Ltda, Caixa Postal 15085, Rua Cardoso Marinho, 42, 20220 Rio de Janeiro RJ, Brazil. Ed. J.M. Lopez Barreto. adv.; bk.rev.; circ. 3,000.

658.788   SP   ISSN 0210-1084
EMBALAJES Y PLASTICOS Y MANUFACTURAS. m.
3000 ptas. P G, San Romualdo 26, s-n (Edificio Astygi, Planta 7), Madrid-17, Spain. Ed. Manuel Suarez Alonso. adv.; charts; illus.; circ. 3,000.
Indexed: Ind.SST.
Formerly: Embalajes (ISSN 0210-0770)

658.7 670   FR   ISSN 0013-6557
EMBALLAGE DIGEST. (Text in English, French, German and Italian) 1958. m. 180 F. Societe Europeenne de Presse et d'Edition, 142 rue d'Aguesseau, 92100 Boulogne, France. Ed. Emmanuel C. Pottier. adv.; illus.; circ. 12,000. **Indexed:** Int.Packag.Abstr., Met.Abstr., Packag.Sci.Tech., World Alum.Abstr.
—BLDSC shelfmark: 3732.970000.

658.7   FR   ISSN 0013-6573
TS158
EMBALLAGES. 1932. 10/yr. 365 F. (foreign 507 F.) (effective Jan. 1992). Groupe Usine Nouvelle, 1 cite Bergere, 75009 Paris, France.
TEL 48-24-23-24. FAX 40-22-02-70. TELEX 650702. Eds. Philippe-Edouerd Grardel, Claude Reny. adv.; bk.rev.; bibl.; illus.; pat.; stat.; circ. 10,000. **Indexed:** Abstr.Bull.Inst.Pap.Chem., Curr.Pack.Abstr., Dairy Sci.Abstr., Food Sci.& Tech.Abstr., Int.Packag.Abstr., Key to Econ.Sci., PROMT, World Alum.Abstr.

658.7   NO   ISSN 0013-6581
EMBALLERING. 1939. m. (10/yr.). NOK 235. Selvig Publishing A-S, Postboks 9070 Vaterland, 0134 Oslo 1, Norway. TEL 02-364440. FAX 02-360550. Ed. Terje Luende. adv.; illus.; circ. 4,350. **Indexed:** Abstr.Bull.Inst.Pap.Chem., Int.Packag.Abstr.
Formerly: Norske Esker.

663   AG   ISSN 0325-0415
ENVASAMIENTO. 1969. m. $150. Editorial Tecnica Siglo XXI, S.A., Talcahuano 374-1p. B, 1013 Buenos Aires, Argentina. Ed. G. Oliveti. adv.; bk.rev.; bibl.; stat.; circ. 6,000.
Description: Raw materials, machines, design and confections, analysis of markets, regulations, adhesion and events.

676.3   SP
ENVASPRES; equipos y materiales para el envase, embalaje, acondicionamiento, y su presentacion. 11/yr. 4500 ptas. Pedeca Sociedad Cooperativa, Ltda., Maria Auxiliadora 5, 28040 Madrid, Spain. TEL 459 60 00.

676   SP   ISSN 0212-5226
EQUIPACK; revista bimestral de los equipos y medios de produccion y envasado. 1983. bi-m. 6,000 ptas. Ediciones Alfil, S.A., C-Zancoeta No. 9, 5 Planta, 48013 Bilbao, Spain. TEL 344-441-0766. FAX 344-442-5116. Ed. Ignacio Echevarria. adv.; circ. 6,000.

670   US   ISSN 1052-2131
CODEN: EPANEO
EUROPEAN PACKAGING NEWSLETTER AND WORLD REPORT. 1961. m. $240 (foreign $255). (International Packaging Club, FR) E P N Inc., 669 S. Washington St., Alexandria, VA 22314-4109. TEL 703-519-3907. FAX 703-519-7732. Ed. Pierre J. Louis.
—BLDSC shelfmark: 3829.768230.
Description: Serves the packaging industry as a clearinghouse for information on techniques, new machinery, and processes from Europe and Asia.

658.788   FR   ISSN 0765-3204
FLEXO-EUROPE. 1983. 6/yr. 380 Fr. Editions Technoroma, 31 Place Saint Ferdinand, 75017 Paris, France. FAX 45-72-63-21. Ed. R. Baschet. adv.; bk.rev.; circ. 3,300.

676.3   UK
FOLDING CARTON INDUSTRY. 1974. q. Brunton Business Publications Ltd., Thruxton Down House, Thruxton Down, Andover, Hampshire SP11 8PR, England. TEL 0264-889533. FAX 0264-889524. Ed. Michael D. Brunton. adv. **Indexed:** Abstr.Bull.Inst.Pap.Chem., Int.Packag.Abstr., Packag.Sci.Tech.
Description: Covers all technical aspects of folding carton production.

658.7 664.09   US   ISSN 0015-6272
CODEN: FDPGAZ
FOOD AND DRUG PACKAGING. 1959. m. $45. Avanstar Communications, Inc., 7500 Old Oak Blvd., Cleveland, OH 44130. TEL 216-826-2839. FAX 216-891-2726. (Subscr. to: 1 E. First St., Duluth, MN 55802) Ed. Sophia Dilberakis. adv.; charts; illus.; tr.lit.; index; circ. 77,365. (also avail. in microform) **Indexed:** Int.Packag.Abstr., PROMT.
—BLDSC shelfmark: 3977.033000.
Description: Industry journal covering new products, marketing trends and regulatory developments in the food, drug, pharmaceutical and cosmetic industries.

658.788 668.4   UK   ISSN 0951-4554
FOOD, COSMETICS AND DRUGS PACKAGING; an international newsletter. 1978. m. £269 (effective 1992). Elsevier Science Publishers Ltd., Crown House, Linton Rd., Barking, Essex IG11 8JU, England. TEL 081-594-7272. FAX 081-594-5942. TELEX 896950 APPSCI G. (Subscr. in U.S. and Canada to: Elsevier Science Publishing Co., Inc., Box 882, Madison Sq. Sta., New York, NY 10159. TEL 212-989-5800) Ed. P. Barnes, R. Coles. bk.rev.; illus.; pat.; stat. (back issues avail.) **Indexed:** Curr.Pack.Abstr.
●Also available online. Vendor(s): DIALOG.
—BLDSC shelfmark: 3977.292000.
Former titles: F C D Packaging; (until Apr. 1983): Plastics in Retail Packaging Bulletin (ISSN 0140-878X)
Description: Presents practical information in concise, readable form, helping management to make well-infomed decisions on the developments, application, planning and forecasting of the role of FCD packaging within their own organizations.

FOOD SAFETY AND SECURITY. see *FOOD AND FOOD INDUSTRIES*

658.7884 663.19   US
GLASS PACKAGING INSTITUTE. ANNUAL REPORT. 1957. a. free. Glass Packaging Institute, 1801 K St., N.W., Ste. 1105-L, Washington, DC 20006.
FAX 202-785-5377. circ. 24,000. **Indexed:** Br.Ceram.Abstr.
Formerly: Glass Containers (ISSN 0072-4637)

658.7   US   ISSN 1049-3158
TS2301.C8   CODEN: GPMAEX
GOOD PACKAGING MAGAZINE. 1940. m. $30 includes annual Western Packaging Directory. Pacific Trade Journals, 1315 E. Julian St., San Jose, CA 95116-1094. TEL 408-286-1661. FAX 408-275-8071. Ed. J.E. Erich. adv.; illus.; tr.lit.; circ. 9,600. **Indexed:** Curr.Pack.Abstr., Int.Packag.Abstr.
Formerly: Good Packaging (ISSN 0017-2170)
Description: Focuses on innovative products, equipment and packaging methods in a variety of industries, including cosmetics, film, food processing, machinery, materials handling, pharmaceuticals and plastics.

670   US   ISSN 1053-6418
CODEN: GREEEJ
▼**GREEN 2000.** 1991. m. $327. Packaging Strategies, 122 S. Church St., West Chester, PA 19382. TEL 215-436-4220. FAX 215-436-6277. Ed. Ben Miyares.
Description: News and analysis of technological, legislative and economic issues relating to the development of environmental packaging strategies for the 1990s.

658.788   BL
GUIA DA EMBALAGEM. a. Editora Quimica e Derivados Ltda., Rua Dr. Gabriel dos Santos, 55, Santa Cecilla CEP 01231, Sao Paulo, Brazil. TEL 011-826-6899. FAX 011-825-8192. TELEX 11-21801. Ed. Emanoel Fairbanks.

670   MX
GUIA DEL ENVASE Y EMBALAJE. 1975. a.
Mex.$100000($50) Informatica Cosmos, S.A. de C.V., Fernandez Arrieta 5-101, Col. Los Cipreses, 04830 Mexico D.F, Mexico. TEL 677-48-68. FAX 679-35-75. Ed. Cesar Macazaga. adv.
Formerly: Envase y Embalaje.

658.788   UK
HANDLING AND PACKAGING PRODUCT INFORMATION CARDS. 1982. q. Trinity Publishing Ltd., Times House, Station Approach, Ruislip, Middx. HA4 8NB, England. TEL 0895-677677. FAX 0895-676027. adv.; circ. 20,000.

PACKAGING 3649

HOUSEHOLD & PERSONAL PRODUCTS INDUSTRY; the magazine for the detergent, soap, cosmetic and toiletry, wax, polish and aerosol industries. see ENGINEERING — Chemical Engineering

670   SP   ISSN 0300-4171
I D E. (Informacion de Envase y Embalaje) 1959. m. 8000 ptas. (foreign 11000 ptas.). Instituto Espanol del Envase y Embalaje, Breton de los Herreros, 57, bajo H, 28003 Madrid, Spain. TEL 442-34-81. FAX 5383718. TELEX 27307 E. Ed. Luis Sicre Canut. adv.; bibl.; index; circ. 8,000. **Indexed:** Ind.SST, Int.Packag.Abstr.
Incorporates (in 1990): Instituto Espanol del Envase y Embalaje. B I U. Boletin Informativo Urgente.
Description: Covers the industry and users of packaging.

I D: INTERNATIONAL DESIGN MAGAZINE; planning-design-marketing. see INTERIOR DESIGN AND DECORATION

658.7 670   IT   ISSN 0019-2708
IMBALLAGGIO. 1950. m. L.100000 (foreign L.155000). Etas s.r.l., Via Mecenate 91, 20138 Milan, Italy. TEL 02-580841. FAX 02-5064867. Ed. Stefano Lavorini. circ. 6,908. (back issues avail.) **Indexed:** Chem.Abstr., Dairy Sci.Abstr., Food Sci.& Tech.Abstr., Int.Packag.Abstr., Packag.Sci.Tech.
—BLDSC shelfmark: 4369.050000.

658.788   IT
IMBALLAGGIO NEWS. 1960. m. L.100000 (included with Imballaggio). Etas s.r.l., Via Mecenate, 91, 20138 Milan, Italy. TEL 02-580841. FAX 02-5064867. Ed. Stefano Lavorini. circ. 10,860. (back issues avail.)
Formerly: Giornale dell'Imballaggio.

663.19   IT   ISSN 0392-792X
IMBOTTIGLIAMENTO. bi-m. L.30000 (foreign L.85000)(effective 1992). Tecniche Nuove s.p.a., Via C. Menotti 14, 20129 Milan, Italy. TEL 02-75701. FAX 02-7570205. circ. 4,600.
—BLDSC shelfmark: 4369.057000.
Description: Various technologies for the production of alcoholic and non-alcoholic beverages.

658.788   DK   ISSN 0106-9403
IN-PAK; packaging and handling: from process to shelf. 1980. 9/yr. DKK 375. Jante-Forlaget ApS, Box 15, Kongstrupvej 3, DK-4390 Vipperoed, Denmark. TEL 45-53-482800. FAX 45-53-482205. Ed. Gitte Soendergaard. circ. 8,356.

INDUSTRIA GRAFICA Y ARTES GRAFICAS. see PRINTING

INTERNATIONAL BOTTLER AND PACKER. see BEVERAGES

676.2   US
INTERNATIONAL CONTAINER DIRECTORY. a. $40. Avanstar Communications, Inc., 7500 Old Oak Blvd., Cleveland, OH 44130. TEL 216-826-2839. FAX 216-891-2726. (Subscr. to: 1 E. First St., Duluth, MN 55802) Ed. Nancy Page. adv.; circ. 1,540.

INTERNATIONAL JOURNAL OF RADIOACTIVE MATERIALS TRANSPORT. see TRANSPORTATION

676   US   ISSN 0020-8191
TS1135
INTERNATIONAL PAPER BOARD INDUSTRY. 1956. m. $55. N V Business Publishers Corp., 43 Main St., Avon By Sea, NJ 07717. TEL 908-502-0500. FAX 908-502-9606. Eds. Michael Brunton, Ted Vilardi. adv.; charts; illus.; tr.lit.; circ. 9,494. **Indexed:** Abstr.Bull.Inst.Pap.Abstr., Int.Packag.Abstr., Key to Econ.Sci., Paper & Bd.Abstr.
—BLDSC shelfmark: 4544.860000.

INTERNATIONAL PRODUCT ALERT. see FOOD AND FOOD INDUSTRIES

ISRAEL INSTITUTE OF PACKAGING. PACKAGING DIRECTORY. see BUSINESS AND ECONOMICS — Trade And Industrial Directories

660.29 658.7 670   US   ISSN 0021-8502
QC882   CODEN: JALSB7
JOURNAL OF AEROSOL SCIENCE. (Also contains selections from: Journal of Aerosol Research, Japan) 1970. 8/yr. £415 (effective 1992). (Gesellschaft fuer Aerosolforschung - Association for Aerosol Research) Pergamon Press, Inc., Journals Division, 660 White Plains Rd., Tarrytown, NY 10591-5153. TEL 914-524-9200. FAX 914-333-2444. (And: Headington Hill Hall, Oxford OX3 0BW, England. TEL 0865-794141) Eds. G. Kasper, J.H. Vincent. adv.; bk.rev.; circ. 1,000. (also avail. in microform from MIM,UMI; reprint service avail. from UMI) **Indexed:** Appl.Mech.Rev., Biotech.Abstr., C.I.S. Abstr., Cadscan, Chem.Abstr., Chem.Eng.Abstr., Curr.Cont., Eng.Ind., Environ.Abstr., Environ.Ind., Excerp.Med., Ind.Sci.Rev., INIS Atomind., Lead Abstr., Sci.Abstr., Sci.Cit.Ind, T.C.E.A., Zincscan.
—BLDSC shelfmark: 4919.060000.
Description: Publishes original papers in basic and applied aerosol research.
Refereed Serial

658.7   US   ISSN 0892-029X
                     CODEN: JPATET
JOURNAL OF PACKAGING TECHNOLOGY.* 1987. m. $49 (foreign $69). Technical Publications, Inc., 85 N. St., No. 15, Danbury, CT 06810-5636. TEL 201-529-3380. Ed. Tom Farley. circ. 28,000. (back issues avail.)
—BLDSC shelfmark: 5027.770000.
Description: Covers all aspects of the packaging industry.

676.3 658.7   NE
KARTOFLEXMARKT. 1947. 6/yr. fl.20($8) (Vereniging van Kartonnagefabrikanten - Association of Paper Box and Carton Manufacturers) Barneveldse Drukkerij & Uitgeverij B.V., Postbus 67, 3770 AB Barneveld, Netherlands. TEL 03420-94911. FAX 03420-13141. Ed. Hans Oskamp. adv.; bk.rev.; illus.; circ. 4,000 (controlled).
Former titles: Kartonnagemarkt; Cartonnagebedrijf (ISSN 0008-705X)

676   CN
L M NEWS. 1971. s-a. (Mardon Packaging International) Lawson Mardon Group Ltd., Corporate Office, 6711 Mississauga Rd., Ste. 401, Mississauga, Ont. L5N 2W3, Canada. TEL 416-821-9711. FAX 416-821-1454. TELEX 06-218572. circ. 7,000.
Former titles: M P I News; Mardon Packaging Review.
Description: Employee publication.

676.2 658.7   UK   ISSN 0143-2192
LABELS AND LABELLING INTERNATIONAL. Running title: Labels and Labelling. 1979. bi-m. $72. Labels and Labelling Publishers, The White House, 60 High St., Potters Bar, Herts EN6 5AB, England. TEL 0707-56828. FAX 0707-45322. TELEX 892623-LABELX-G. Ed. M.C. Fairley. adv.; bk.rev.; circ. 6,500. **Indexed:** Int.Packag.Abstr., Packag.Sci.Tech., Print.Abstr.
—BLDSC shelfmark: 5137.892000.

676   DK
LEVERANDOERHAANDBOGEN (SKOVLUNDE); emballage og pakkemaskiner. 1979. biennial. DKK 180 (typically set in Jan.). Emballage & Transportinstituttet, Meterbuen 15, 2740 Skovlunde, Denmark. FAX 42-846010. Ed. Lars G. Hansen. circ. 10,000.
Formerly: Emballageinstituttets Leverandoerhaandbog (ISSN 0107-3737)
Description: Lists Danish suppliers of packaging materials, machinery and equipment.

LEVNEDSMIDDELBLADET - SUPERMARKEDET/FOODSTUFF MAGAZINE - THE SUPERMARKET. see FOOD AND FOOD INDUSTRIES — Grocery Trade

676   US
M T J RECYCLING MARKETS. 1963. w. $90. N V Business Publishers Corp., 43 Main St., Avon By Sea, NJ 07717. TEL 908-502-0500. FAX 908-502-9606. Ed. Ted Vilardi. adv.; bk.rev.; abstr.; charts; illus.; pat.; stat.; tr.lit.
Formerly: Mill Trade Journal (ISSN 0047-7427)

658.7   CS
MANIPULACE, SKLADOVANI, BALENI/MATERIAL HANDLING, STORAGE PACKAGING. (Text in Czech; summaries in English, German, Russian) 1970. m. 60 Kcs.($52.50) (Institute of Handling, Transport, Packaging and Storage Systems) Nakladatelstvi Technicke Literatury, Spalena 51, 113 02 Prague 1, Czechoslovakia. (Dist. by: Artia, Ve Smeckach 30, 111 27 Prague 1, Czechoslovakia) Ed. K. Langhammerova. adv.; bk.rev.; illus.; circ. 3,000. (also avail. in microfilm) **Indexed:** Abstr.Bull.Inst.Pap.Chem., Dairy Sci.Abstr., Food Sci.& Tech.Abstr., Int.Packag.Abstr., Packag.Abstr., Packag.Sci.Tech., Ref.Zh.
Supersedes: Obaly.

MANIPULACION DE MATERIALES EN LA INDUSTRIA. see BUILDING AND CONSTRUCTION

670   BE
MANUTENTION EMBALLAGES/BEHANDELING VERPAKKINGEN. (Text in Flemish and French) m. (11/yr.). (Institut Belge de l'Emballage) Imprimerie et Publicite du Marais S.A., Rue de Flandre 169, 1000 Brussels, Belgium. Ed. A. Levoz. adv.; circ. 6,844.

676.3   US
MARI-BOARD CONVERTING NEWS. (Text in English, Spanish) 1989. bi-m. $45. Ted Vilardi, c/o N V Business Publishers Corp., 602 Main St., Belmar, NJ 07719. TEL 908-280-1900. FAX 908-280-1717. adv.; bk.rev.; circ. 2,380.
Formerly: Mari.

676   US
MARI-BOARD CONVERTING NEWS ESPANOL. (Text in English, Spanish) 1989. bi-m. $45. N V Business Publishers Corp., 43 Main St., Belmar, NJ 07717. TEL 908-502-0500. FAX 908-502-9606. Ed. Ted Vilardi. adv.; circ. 2,234.
Formerly: Board Converting News Espanol.

MATERIAL HANDLING ENGINEERING; technical magazine for material handling, packaging and shipping specialists. see MACHINERY

MATERIAL HANDLING ENGINEERING HANDBOOK AND DIRECTORY. see MACHINERY

663.19   US
MID-CONTINENT BOTTLER. 1947. bi-m. $9. Fan Publications, Inc., 10741 El Monte, Overland Park, KS 66211. TEL 913-341-0020. FAX 913-341-3025. Ed. Floyd E. Sageser. adv.; bk.rev.; circ. 3,585.
Description: Coverage of the soft drink industry in a 21-state area bounded on the east by Ohio and the west by Colorado-Wyoming.

670   NE
MISSETS PAKBLAD. 1970. m. fl.182.50. Uitgeversmaatschappij C. Misset B.V., Hanzestr. 1, 7006 RH Doetinchem, Netherlands. TEL 08340-49911. FAX 08340-43839. TELEX 45481. (Subscr. to: Postbus 4, 7000 BA Doetinchem, Netherlands) Ed. P.P. Roessel. adv.: B&W page fl.2671; unit 185 x 270; adv. contact: Cor van Nek. bk.rev.; charts; illus.; circ. 6,180. **Indexed:** Excerp.Med., Key to Econ.Sci., Packag.Sci.Tech.
Formerly: Industrieel Verpakken.
Description: Information on packaging for managers of selfpacking industries, product and marketing managers, designers and product engineers.

658.788   II
MODERN PACKAGING TRENDS. (Text in English) 1984. q. Rs.80($30) Eastern Trade Press Co., 43 Sunder Mahal, Churchgate, Bombay 400 020, India. adv.; bk.rev.; circ. 5,000.

658.788 380.1   US
N S T A ANNUAL SAFE TRANSIT CONFERENCE. PROCEEDINGS. 1987. a. $85 to non-members; members $40. National Safe Transit Association, Box 10744, Chicago, IL 60610-0744. TEL 312-645-0083. FAX 312-645-1078.
Description: Technical papers presented at the Conference.

PACKAGING

658.788   GW   ISSN 0341-0390
TS195.A1
N V. (Neue Verpackung) 1946. m. DM.300.60. Verlag fuer Fachliterature GmbH, Im Weiher 10, Postfach 102869, 6900 Heidelberg 1, Germany. TEL 06221-489-0. FAX 06221-489279. TELEX 461727-HUEHDD. Ed. Collin Weber. adv.; circ. 14,059.
—BLDSC shelfmark: 6077.820000.
Description: Package engineering in both food and non-food areas.

664.09   US
NATIONAL PACKING NEWS. m. $25. Box 1349, Murphys, CA 95247. TEL 209-728-1455. FAX 209-728-3277. Ed. Jack W. Soward. adv.; bk.rev.; stat.; tr.lit.; circ. 2,400.
Incorporates (1989-1991): Eastern Packing News; (1937-1991): Western Packing News.
Description: News for and about staff and line management personnel in the food processing industries.

NEW ZEALAND PACKAGING YEARBOOK. see *BUSINESS AND ECONOMICS — Trade And Industrial Directories*

658.788   PH
NEWSPACK. 12/yr. Packaging Institute of the Philippines, Comfoods Bldg., no.216, Sen Gil J Puyat Ave., Makati MM, Philippines. TEL 885422. Ed. Lorenzo Ligot.

NIEUWSBLAD TRANSPORT. see *TRANSPORTATION*

658.788   NR   ISSN 0794-7054
NIGERIAN PACKAGING NEWS. 1987. bi-m. $60. Nigerian Printer Publications, P.O. Box 632, Yaba, Nigeria. TEL 082-221782. Ed. Austin Odiadi. circ. 3,000.
Description: Technological articles and current technology and applications.

658.7   SW   ISSN 0039-6494
NORD-EMBALLAGE. 1934. 10/yr. SEK 380. Foerlags AB Thorsten Fahlskog, Box 25, S-162 11 Vaellingby, Sweden. TEL 46-8-870280. FAX 46-8-874815. Ed. Kerstin Fahlskog. adv.; bk.rev.; bibl.; charts; illus.; mkt.; pat.; stat.; tr.lit.; tr.mk.; index; circ. 3,023. *Indexed:* Int.Packag.Abstr.
Formerly: Svensk Emballagetidskrift - Emballage.
Description: Directed towards the five Nordic countries. Covers developments in consumer packaging, aerosols, printing and design techniques as well as transport handling. The editorial features also cover important business events within the industry and other organisations in Sweden and internationally.

658.7   AU
O V Z - MITTEILUNGEN. 1956. bi-m. membership. Bundeskammer der Gewerblichen Wirtschaft, Wirtschaftsfoerderungsinstitut, Oesterreichisches Verpackungszentrum, Box 130, Wiedner Hauptstr. 63, A-1045 Vienna, Austria. TEL 0222-50105-3045. FAX 0222-50206-253. TELEX 111871-BUKA. bk.rev.; illus.; stat.; circ. 6,400. *Indexed:* Int.Packag.Abstr., Packag.Sci.Tech.
Formerly (until Oct. 1976): Besser Verpacken (ISSN 0005-9595)

676   US   ISSN 0030-0284
OFFICIAL BOARD MARKETS; "the yellow sheet". 1925. w. $130. Avanstar Communications, Inc., 233 N. Michigan Ave., 24th Fl., Chicago, IL 60601. FAX 312-938-4854. Ed. Mark Arzoumanian. adv.; charts; mkt.; stat.; circ. 5,500. (also avail. in microform) *Indexed:* Abstr.Bull.Inst.Pap.Chem.
Description: Covers corrugated container, folding carton and paper recycling industries.

658.7   US   ISSN 0030-0292
OFFICIAL CONTAINER DIRECTORY. 1913. s-a. $50. Avanstar Communications, Inc., 7500 Old Oak Blvd., Cleveland, OH 44130. TEL 216-826-2839. FAX 216-891-2726. (Subscr. to: 1 E. First St., Duluth, MN 55802) Ed. Mark Arzoumanian. adv.; circ. 3,179.

ONTARIO RECYCLING UPDATE. see *ENVIRONMENTAL STUDIES — Waste Management*

658.7   PL   ISSN 0030-3348
OPAKOWANIE. (Text in Polish; summaries in English) 1955. m. $20. Wydawnictwo Czasopism i Ksiazek Technicznych SIGMA - NOT, Ul. Biala 4, P.O. Box 1004, 00-950 Warsaw, Poland. (Dist. by: SIGMA NOT Ltd., Ul. Bartycka 20, 00-716 Warsaw, Poland) adv.; bk.rev.; abstr.; bibl.; charts; illus.; stat.; index; circ. 700. *Indexed:* Food Sci.& Tech.Abstr., Packag.Sci.Tech.
—BLDSC shelfmark: 6265.800000.

P A T E F A NEWS BULLETIN. (Printing & Allied Trades Employers Federation of Australia) see *PRINTING*

658.788   US
P H L BULLETIN. (Packaging, Handling, Logistics) 1956. m. $40. National Institute of Packaging, Handling and Logistic Engineers, 6902 Lyle St., Lanham, MD 20706-3454. FAX 301-459-4925. Ed. James A. Russell. adv.; bk.rev.; bibl.; circ. 300.

658.7 670   UK   ISSN 0030-9060
PACKAGING. 1930. bi-m. $94. Turret Group Plc., Turret House, 171 High St., Rickmansworth, Herts. WD3 1SN, England. TEL 0923-777000. FAX 0923-771297. TELEX 888095-DX. Ed. Norman Shepherd. adv.; illus. (also avail. in microfilm from UMI; reprint service avail. from UMI) *Indexed:* Br.Tech.Ind, Bus.Ind., Curr.Pack.Abstr., Food Sci.& Tech.Abstr., Int.Packag.Abstr., Key to Econ.Sci., PROMT.

658.7 670   US   ISSN 0746-3820
TS195.A1   CODEN: PACKD6
PACKAGING. 1956. 13/yr. (plus a. Packaging Casebook Directory). $84.95 (Canada $123; Mexico $114.95; elsewhere $149.95). Cahners Publishing Company (Des Plaines) (Subsidiary of: Reed International PLC), Division of Reed Publishing (USA) Inc., 1350 E. Touhy Ave., Box 5080, Des Plaines, IL 60017-5080. TEL 708-635-8800. FAX 708-635-6856. (Subscr. to: 44 Cook St., Denver, CO 80826. TEL 800-662-7776) Ed. Greg Erickson. adv.; bk.rev.; charts; illus.; tr.lit.; index; circ. 105,000. (also avail. in microform from RPI; reprint service avail. from UMI) *Indexed:* A.S.& T.Ind., Abstr.Bull.Inst.Pap.Chem., Biol.Abstr., Bus.Ind., Chem.Abstr., Curr.Pack.Abstr., Eng.Ind, I.P.A., Int.Packag.Abstr., ISMEC, PROMT, SRI, Tr.& Indus.Ind.
•Also available online.
Formerly (until 1983): Package Engineering (ISSN 0030-9044); *Incorporates (in 1980):* Modern Packaging (ISSN 0026-8224)
Description: For managers in production and engineering, corporate and general management, marketing package design and purchasing. Provides business news and information on technical design, innovations, consumer protection concerns and trends.

676.3 658.788   SA   ISSN 1011-8519
PACKAGING (YEAR). a. South African Foreign Trade Organisation, Publishing Division, P.O. Box 782706, Sandton 2146, South Africa. TEL 011-883-3737. FAX 011-883-6569. TELEX 4-24111 SA.
Description: Provides information on packaging products and services available for export from South Africa.

658.788   US
PACKAGING AND CONVERTING TECHNOLOGY SERIES. 1981. irreg., vol.4, 1991. price varies. Marcel Dekker, Inc., 270 Madison Ave., New York, NY 10016. TEL 212-696-9000. FAX 212-685-4540. TELEX 421419.
Formerly: Packaging Technology Series.

658.7   US
PACKAGING CASEBOOK DIRECTORY. a. $30. Cahners Publishing Company (Des Plaines) (Subsidiary of: Reed International PLC), Division of Reed Publishing (USA) Inc., 1350 E. Touhy Ave., Box 5080, Des Plaines, IL 60017-5080. TEL 708-635-8800. FAX 708-635-6856. (Subscr. to: 44 Cook St., Denver, CO 80206. TEL 800-662-7776)
Former titles (until 1992): Packaging Product Sources Guide; *(until 1991):* Packaging Buyers Guide.

658.7 670   US   ISSN 0030-9117
PACKAGING DIGEST; packaging management, marketing, design, equipment, materials. 1963. m. $75 (free to qualified personnel). Delta Communications, Inc. (Chicago) (Subsidiary of: Elsevier Business Press, Inc. (New York)), 400 N. Michigan Ave., Ste. 1200, Chicago, IL 60611. TEL 312-222-2000. Ed. Robert W. Heitzman. adv.; illus.; tr.lit.; circ. 105,062. (tabloid format; also avail. in microform from UMI; reprint service avail. from UMI) *Indexed:* Curr.Pack.Abstr., Graph.Arts Lit.Abstr., Int.Packag.Abstr., Tr.& Indus.Ind.
—BLDSC shelfmark: 6332.651000.
Description: Articles for makers and prime users of packaging.

658.7   II   ISSN 0030-9125
     CODEN: PINDDS
PACKAGING INDIA. (Text in English) 1968. bi-m. Rs.100($35) Indian Institute of Packaging, E-2 Marol Industrial Estate, MIDC, Post Box 9432, Chakala, Andheri East, Bombay 400 093, India. TEL 6324670. TELEX 011-79042. Ed. M.R. Subramamian. adv.; bk.rev.; circ. 1,000.
Incorporates: Packaging Digest; Formed by the 1989 merger of: Packaging Institute; Packaging India.
Description: Covers technical and economic aspects of the packaging industry as well as new product information.

658.788   UK   ISSN 0269-9834
PACKAGING INDUSTRY DIRECTORY. a. £56 (foreign £67). Benn Business Information Services Ltd., P.O. Box 20, Sovereign Way, Tonbridge, Kent TN9 1RW, England. TEL 0732-362666. FAX 0732-770483. TELEX 95162-BENTON-G. Ed. Cheryl Whitehead. circ. 1,600.
—BLDSC shelfmark: 6332.780000.
Formerly: Packaging Review Directory.
Description: Features 5 buyers' guides (A-Z listings of: Packaging Equipment; Containers and Closures; Packaging Materials; Packaging Services; Handling Equipment) all cross-referenced to the master alphabetical listing of over 6,000 companies manufacturing, supplying or distributing materials, products and services to the packaging and related industries.

658.7   JA   ISSN 0288-3864
     CODEN: PAJAEC
PACKAGING JAPAN. 1980. bi-m. $47. Nippo Co. Ltd., 4-5 Iidabashi 4-Chome, Chiyoda-ku, Toyko 102, Japan. TEL 03-3263-2560. TELEX 2322348 PJNIPOJ. Ed. Katsushi Kawamura. adv.; bk.rev.; charts; illus.; circ. 10,000.
—BLDSC shelfmark: 6332.810000.
Formerly: New Packaging (ISSN 0004-6469)

658.7884   US   ISSN 0078-7698
PACKAGING MACHINERY MANUFACTURERS INSTITUTE. OFFICIAL PACKAGING MACHINERY DIRECTORY. Cover title: Packaging Machinery Directory. 1954. biennial. $3. Packaging Machinery Manufacturers Institute, 1343 L St., N.W., Washington, DC 20005. TEL 202-347-3838. FAX 202-628-2471. Ed. Claude S. Breeden, Jr. index; circ. 50,000.

658.788   US
PACKAGING MARKETPLACE; the practical guide to packaging sources. 1978. irreg. $140. Gale Research Inc., 835 Penobscot Bldg., Detroit, MI 48226. TEL 313-961-2242. FAX 313-961-6083. TELEX 810-221-7086. Ed. Joseph F. Hanlon.
Description: Directory of packaging manufacturers and jobbers.

658.7   AT   ISSN 0048-2676
PACKAGING NEWS. 1959. m. Aus.$58 (foreign Aus.$145)(effective Apr. 1992). Yaffa Publishing Group, 17-21 Bellevue St., Surry Hills, N.S.W. 2010, Australia. TEL 02-281-2333. FAX 02-281-2750. Ed. Patrick Giorgi. adv.; B&W page Aus.$1790, color page Aus.$2560; trim 297 x 210. circ. 5,524 (controlled). *Indexed:* Int.Packag.Abstr., Key to Econ.Sci.
—BLDSC shelfmark: 6332.870000.
Description: For Australian packaging industry management.

PACKAGING

658.7   UK   ISSN 0030-9133
CODEN: PKGNAY
PACKAGING NEWS. 1954. m. £84. Maclean Hunter Ltd., Maclean Hunter House, Chalk Lane, Cockfosters Rd., Barnet, Herts EN4 0BU, England. TEL 081-975-9759. FAX 081-440-1796. TELEX 299072-MACHUN-G. Ed. Michael Maddox. adv.; bk.rev.; charts; illus.; tr.lit.; circ. 19,191. (newspaper) **Indexed:** Abstr.Bull.Inst.Pap.Chem., Curr.Pack.Abstr., Int.Packag.Abstr., Packag.Sci.Tech.
—BLDSC shelfmark: 6332.840000.

658.7   UK
PACKAGING NEWS PRODUCT INFORMATION CARDS. 1967. 5/yr. free. Maclean Hunter Ltd., Maclean Hunter House, Chalk Lane, Cockfosters Rd., Barnet, Herts EN4 0BU, England. TEL 081-975-9759. FAX 081-440-1796. TELEX 299072 MACHUN G. adv.; circ. 15,494.

677.7   GW   ISSN 0933-4165
PACKAGING PRODUCTION INTERNATIONAL. (Text in English and German) 1988. bi-m. DM.96. Verlag fuer Fachliteratur GmbH, Im Weiher 10, Postfach 10 28 69, D-6900 Heidelberg, Germany. TEL 06221-489280. FAX 06221-489279. TELEX 461727-HUEHD-D. Eds. Peter Haberstolz, Collin Weber. adv.; illus.; circ. 15,000. (back issues avail.)

658.788   SA
PACKAGING REVIEW SOUTH AFRICA. 1975. bi-m. R.45 (foreign R.75). (Institute of Packaging, South Africa) National Publishing (Pty) Ltd., P.O. Box 2735, Johannesburg 2000, South Africa. TEL 011-835-2221. FAX 011-835-1943. TELEX 82735 SA. (Co-sponsor: Packaging Council) Ed. Gill Loubser. adv.; illus.; circ. 2,407. **Indexed:** Dairy Sci.Abstr., Ind.S.A.Per., Int.Packag.Abstr., Packag.Sci.Tech.

670   US   ISSN 8755-6189
CODEN: PASTEC
PACKAGING STRATEGIES. 1983. s-m. $297 (foreign $339). Packaging Strategies, 122 S. Church St., West Chester, PA 19382. TEL 215-436-4220. FAX 215-436-6277. Ed. William H. LeMaire. (looseleaf format; back issues avail.)
Description: An intelligence service on critical trends and new developments in packaging materials, containers and machinery.

676 335   UK   ISSN 0894-3214
TS195.A1   CODEN: PTSCEQ
PACKAGING, TECHNOLOGY AND SCIENCE. 1988. bi-m. $335 (effective 1992). John Wiley & Sons Ltd., Journals, Baffins Lane, Chichester, Sussex PO19 1UD, England. TEL 0243-779777. FAX 0243-775878. TELEX 86290 WIBOOK G. Ed. F.A. Paine.
—BLDSC shelfmark: 6333.018500.
Description: Provides an international forum for the rapid publication of articles about new developments in this field.

614.7   AT
PACKAGING TODAY. 1979. q. Aus.$25. Packaging Council of Australia, 15-17 Park St., South Melbourne, Vic. 3250, Australia. FAX 03-690-3514. circ. 3,000. **Indexed:** Int.Packag.Abstr.
Supersedes: Packaging Council of Australia. Legislation and Metrication Newsletter.

658.7   II
PACKAGING UPDATE. (Text in English) 1975. m. Rs.35. Indian Institute of Packaging, E-2 Marol Industrial Estate, MIDC, Andheri East, Bombay 400093, India. abstr.

658.7 670   UK
PACKAGING WEEK. 1897. w. £65 (foreign £95). Benn Publications Ltd., Sovereign Way, Tonbridge, Kent TN9 1RW, England. TEL 0732-364422. Ed. Mary Murphy. adv.; bk.rev.; illus.; stat.; circ. 14,720. (also avail. in microform from UMI; reprint service avail. from UMI) **Indexed:** Curr.Pack.Abstr., Dairy Sci.Abstr., Food Sci.& Tech.Abstr., Int.Packag.Abstr., Key to Econ.Sci., PROMT.
Formerly: Packaging Review (ISSN 0048-2684)

658.788   SW
PACKMARKNADEN SCANDINAVIA. 1978. 10/yr. SEK 425. Aller Specialtidningar AB, S-251 85 Haelsingborg, Sweden. TEL 46-42-17-35-00. FAX 46-42-17-36-00. Ed. Peter Schulz. adv.; circ. 6,000.
Description: Focuses on the packaging industry as well as the needs and uses of packaging in various industries.

660 670   GW   ISSN 0343-7183
PACKUNG UND TRANSPORT; Fachmagazin fuer Verpackung, Materialfluss und Logistik. 1968. m. DM.108. Handelsblatt GmbH, Kasernenstr. 67, Postfach 102717, 4000 Dusseldorf 1, Germany. TEL 0211-8870. FAX 0211-133522. Ed. H. Sprinhorn. circ. 7,400. (reprint service avail. from UMI) **Indexed:** Key to Econ.Sci.
—BLDSC shelfmark: 6333.087000.
Former titles: Packung und Transport in der Chemischen Industrie; Packung und Transport im Chemiebetrieb (ISSN 0030-9184)

658.7   FI   ISSN 0031-0131
PAKKAUS. (Text in Finnish; summaries in English) 1964. m. Fmk.200. Suomen Pakkausyhdistys - Finnish Packaging Association, Ritarikatu 3, 00170 Helsinki 17, Finland. Ed. Jorma Hamalainen. adv.; bk.rev.; charts; illus.; mkt.; circ. 2,900. **Indexed:** Int.Packag.Abstr., Packag.Sci.Tech.

676.3   UK
PAPER AND PACKAGING ANALYST; a quarterly review of production, markets, etc. 1955. q. £465($895) (Economist Intelligence Unit) Business International Ltd., 40 Duke St., London W1A 1DW, England. TEL 071-499-2278. FAX 071-499-9767. TELEX 266353 EIUG. (US addr.: Business International Corp., 215 Park Ave. S., New York, NY 10003. TEL 212-460-0600) charts; stat.; cum.index. **Indexed:** Int.Packag.Abstr., Key to Econ.Sci., Paper & Bd.Abstr., PROMT.
Former titles: Paper and Packaging Bulletin (ISSN 0142-5307); Paper Bulletin (ISSN 0031-1111)
Description: Research information and forecasts for major markets and end uses, with emphasis on the UK and the EEC.

676   US   ISSN 0031-1138
CODEN: PFFCAT
PAPER, FILM AND FOIL CONVERTER. 1927. m. $50. Maclean Hunter Publishing Company, 29 N. Wacker Dr., Chicago, IL 60606. TEL 312-726-2802. FAX 312-726-2574. TELEX 270258 EXP. Ed. James Martin. adv.; bk.rev.; charts; illus.; stat.; tr.lit.; index; circ. 40,220 (controlled). (also avail. in microfilm from UMI; reprint service avail. from UMI) **Indexed:** Abstr.Bull.Inst.Pap.Chem., Art & Archaeol.Tech.Abstr., Chem.Abstr., Curr.Pack.Abstr., Graph.Arts Lit.Abstr., Int.Packag.Abstr., Key to Econ.Sci., Packag.Sci.Tech., Paper & Bd.Abstr., PROMT.
—BLDSC shelfmark: 6362.000000.
Former titles (until 1953): American Paper Converter (ISSN 0096-090X); (until 1944): Converter (ISSN 0097-4080)

676 658.7   US   ISSN 0031-1227
HF5770
PAPERBOARD PACKAGING. 1916. m. $25. Avanstar Communications, Inc., 7500 Old Oak Blvd., Cleveland, OH 44130. TEL 216-826-2839. FAX 216-891-2726. (Subscr. to: 1 E. First St., Duluth, MN 55802) Ed. Mark Arzoumanian. adv.; charts; illus.; mkt.; stat.; index; circ. 13,797. (also avail. in microform; back issues avail.) **Indexed:** Abstr.Bull.Inst.Pap.Chem., B.P.I., Bus.Ind., Chem.Abstr., Curr.Pack.Abstr., Graph.Arts Lit.Abstr., Int.Packag.Abstr., Packag.Sci.Tech., Paper & Bd.Abstr., PROMT, SRI, Tr.& Ind.Ind.
—BLDSC shelfmark: 6366.300000.
Description: News about corporate management, production management, sales-marketing and engineering.

PAPERPRINTPACK INDIA. see *PAPER AND PULP*

PLASTICS RECYCLING UPDATE. see *ENVIRONMENTAL STUDIES — Waste Management*

PNEUMATIC PACKAGING. see *ENGINEERING — Mechanical Engineering*

658.788 380.5   US   ISSN 1043-2841
PRESHIPMENT TESTING. 1977. m. membership. National Safe Transit Association, Box 10744, Chicago, IL 60610-0744. TEL 312-645-0083. FAX 312-645-1078. Ed. Ellis Murphy. adv.; bk.rev.; circ. 3,200 (controlled).
Description: Discusses packaging and transportation issues such as preshipment testing of packaged products, hazardous material transport, quality control and customer service.

PREVISIONS GLISSANTES DETAILLEES EN PERSPECTIVES SECTORIELLES (VOL.23): EMBALLAGES. see *BUSINESS AND ECONOMICS — Economic Situation And Conditions*

664.09   GW
PRINTING & PACKAGING; with Arabian food and packaging. (Text in Arabic and English) 1977. q. DM.52. Verlag Peter Wranesch, Postfach 810645, 7000 Stuttgart 81, Germany. TEL 0711-713781. Ed. Peter Wranesch. circ. 5,300.

PRINTING PRODUCT INTERNATIONAL. see *PRINTING*

PRODUCE MARKETING ASSOCIATION MEMBERSHIP DIRECTORY & BUYER'S GUIDE. see *FOOD AND FOOD INDUSTRIES*

664.09   US
PRODUCE PACKAGING HANDLING DIGEST. a. $5. Vance Publishing Corporation, 7950 College Blvd., Shawnee Mission, KS 66210. TEL 913-451-2200. FAX 913-451-5821. Ed. Bill O'Neill. adv.; circ. 16,000. (back issues avail.)
Formerly: Produce Packaging and Materials Handling Digest.

658.788   GW   ISSN 0724-5661
PRODUKTIONSMENGE UND PRODUKTIONSWERT DER VERPACKUNGSINDUSTRIE IN DER BUNDESREPUBLIK. 1954. a. DM.73. R G Verpackung im R K W, Duesseldorferstr. 40, Postfach 5867, 6236 Eschborn 1, Germany. TEL 06196-495200. stats.; index; circ. 400. (back issues avail.)

658.788   IT   ISSN 1120-6136
RASSEGNA DELL'IMBALLAGGIO. 1979. fortn. L.24000 (foreign L.200000). Editrice Arti Poligrafiche Europee, Via Casella 16, 20156 Milan, Italy. TEL 02-330221. FAX 02-39214341. Ed. Antonio Ghiorzo. adv.; charts; illus.; circ. 10,000 (controlled).
—BLDSC shelfmark: 7294.227500.

RESEARCH & DEVELOPMENT ASSOCIATES FOR MILITARY FOOD AND PACKAGING SYSTEMS. ACTIVITIES REPORT. see *MILITARY*

658.788   UK
RETAIL PACKAGING. m. L.24.90. Turret-Wheatland Ltd., 12 Greycaine Rd., Watford, Herts. WD2 4JP, England. Ed. Jane Farrow. circ. controlled. **Indexed:** Abstr.Bull.Inst.Pap.Chem.
Formerly: Packaging.

658.788 681   US   ISSN 0890-7900
S M T TRENDS. (Surface Mount Technology) m. $295. Market Intelligence Research Company, 2525 Charleston Rd., Mountain View, CA 94043. TEL 415-389-8671. FAX 415-389-8671. Ed. Sarah Collings.
•Also available online. Vendor(s): Data-Star, DIALOG, NewsNet.
Description: Covers markets for surface mount technology and electronic packaging technology.

ST. REGIS NEWS. see *PAPER AND PULP*

670   SZ
SCHWEIZER VERPACKUNGSKATALOG. (Text in French and German) 1942. a. 29 Fr. Verlag Binkert AG, CH-4335 Laufenburg, Switzerland. TEL 064-697272. FAX 064-697333. Ed. Walter Meier-Schmid. adv.; circ. 4,200.

676.3   CC
SHANGHAI BAOZHUANG/SHANGHAI PACKAGING. (Text in Chinese) q. Zhongguo Chukou Shangpin Baozhuang Yanjiusuo, Shanghai Fensuo - Chinese Institute of Export Commodities Packaging, Shanghai Branch, 97 Yuanmingyuan Lu, Shanghai 200002, People's Republic of China. TEL 3212999.

PACKAGING — ABSTRACTING, BIBLIOGRAPHIES, STATISTICS

676 668.4   UK
SKYLON. 1980. q. Publications in Business Ltd., 30 Rathbone Place, London W1P 1AD, England. Ed. J. Nutting. circ. 1,000. (tabloid format; back issues avail.)

SOUTH AFRICAN FOOD REVIEW. see FOOD AND FOOD INDUSTRIES

660.29 658.7   US   ISSN 1055-2340
TS198.P7   CODEN: STEMEJ
SPRAY TECHNOLOGY & MARKETING; the magazine of spray pressure packaging. 1956. m. $20. Industry Publications, Inc. (Fairfield), 389 Passaic Ave., Fairfield, NJ 07006. TEL 201-227-5151. FAX 201-227-9219. Ed. M. SanGiovanni. adv.; charts; illus.; pat.; tr.mk. (also avail. in microform from UMI; reprint service avail. from UMI) Indexed: B.P.I., Biotech.Abstr., Chem.Abstr., Curr.Pack.Abstr., I.P.A., Int.Packag.Abstr., Key to Econ.Sci., PROMT.
●Also available online.
—BLDSC shelfmark: 8422.610000.
Formerly (until Apr.1991): Aerosol Age (ISSN 0001-9291)

670   FR
TECH-EMBAL; annuaire des fournisseurs de l'emballage. 1966. a. 300 F. Editions Technorama, 31 Place Saint Ferdinand, 75017 Paris, France. TEL 1-45-74-67-43. FAX 45-72-63-21. Ed. R. Baschet. circ. 2,000.

676   US   ISSN 0892-7146
TECHPAK. 1955. bi-w. $417 (foreign $457). McGraw-Hill, Inc., Chemical & Plastics Information Services, 1221 Ave. of the Americas, 43rd Fl., New York, NY 10020. TEL 800-537-9213. FAX 609-426-7116. Ed. Stuart Kahan. circ. 300. (back issues avail.)
Formerly: Packaging Letter (ISSN 0277-9722)

670 658.788   IT
TECNICHE DELL'IMBALLAGGIO. 1970. m. L.96000 (foreign L.140000)(effective 1992). Franco Angeli Editore, Viale Monza 106, 20127 Milan, Italy. TEL 02-28-27-651. adv.; bk.rev.; abstr.; charts; illus.; stat.; tr.lit.; index; circ. 6,000.

TIN INTERNATIONAL. see METALLURGY

TRANSPORT, FOERDER- UND LAGERTECHNIK; Schweizerische Fachzeitschrift fuer rationellen Gueterumschlag, Logistik, Transport, Lagerhaltung und Foerdertechnik. see TRANSPORTATION

TRANSPORT 2000 AND INTERMODAL WORLD. see TRANSPORTATION

655   GW   ISSN 0042-4269
TS158
VERPACKUNG; Zeitschrift fuer neuzeitliches Verpackungswesen. (Text in German; index and summaries in English and Russian) 1960. 6/yr. DM.10 per no. Fachbuchverlag GmbH, Karl-Heine-Str. 16, 7031 Leipzig, Germany. TEL 49500. FAX 470280. TELEX 51451-FACHB-D. bk.rev. Indexed: Food Sci.& Tech.Abstr., Int.Packag.Abstr., Nutr.Abstr., Packag.Sci.Tech.
Description: Trade publication for the packaging industry, featuring technology, machinery, materials, industrial design, industrial news, and report of events. Includes bibliographies.

658.7   SZ   ISSN 0042-4277
DIE VERPACKUNG; schweizerische Fachzeitschrift fuer Verpackung, Technologie, Verpackungspsychologie, Package Design, Marketing. 1945. m. 90 Fr. (foreign 110 Fr.). S H Z Fachverlag AG, Alte Landstr. 43, CH-8700 Kusnacht-Zurich, Switzerland. TEL 01-910 80 22. FAX 01-9105155. Ed. R. Walser. adv.; bk.rev.; charts; illus.; stat.; circ. 4,650. Indexed: Int.Packag.Abstr., Key to Econ.Sci., Nutr.Abstr.

658.7   GW   ISSN 0042-4293
VERPACKUNGS BERATER. 1956. m. DM.156 (foreign DM.166.80). P. Keppler Verlag GmbH und Co. KG, Industriestr. 2, 6056 Heusenstamm, Germany. TEL 06104-6060. FAX 06104-606144. TELEX 410131. Ed. Susanna Stock. adv.; charts; illus.; circ. 14,089. Indexed: Int.Packag.Abstr., Key to Econ.Sci., Packag.Sci.Tech.
—BLDSC shelfmark: 9194.720000.

658.7 670   GW   ISSN 0042-4307
VERPACKUNGS-RUNDSCHAU. (Text in German; contents page in English and German) 1950. m. DM.291. P. Keppler Verlag GmbH und Co. KG, Industriestr. 2, P.O. Box 1353, 6056 Heusenstamm, Germany. TEL 06104-6060. FAX 06104-606323. Ed. F. Heydorn. adv.; bk.rev.; charts; illus.; pat.; index. cum.index; circ. 14,000. Indexed: Abstr.Bull.Inst.Pap.Chem., Chem.Abstr., Curr.Cont., Curr.Pack.Abstr., Dairy Sci.Abstr., Eng.Ind., Excerp.Med., Food Sci.& Tech.Abstr., Int.Packag.Abstr., Key to Econ.Sci., Met.Abstr.
—BLDSC shelfmark: 9194.740000.

658.7   NE   ISSN 0042-4315
VERPAKKEN. 1948. bi-m. fl.88. (Nederlands Verpakkingscentrum) Wegener Tijl Tijdschriften Groep B.V., P.B. 9943, 1006 AP Amsterdam, Netherlands. TEL 020-5182828. FAX 020-177143. TELEX 15230. Ed. O. Y. Van Bochove. circ. 9,000. Indexed: Excerp.Med., Packag.Sci.Tech.

677.7   US   ISSN 0740-1809
WIRE ROPE NEWS AND SLING TECHNOLOGY. 1979. 6/yr. $20 (Canada $25; elsewhere $30). Box 871, Clark, NJ 07066. TEL 908-486-3221. FAX 908-396-4215. Ed. Conrad Miller. adv.; circ. 3,100.

658.788   US
ZHONGGUO BAOZHUANG/CHINA PACKAGING. (Text in Chinese) q. $44.40. China Books & Periodicals, Inc., 2929 24th St., San Francisco, CA 94110. TEL 415-282-2994. FAX 415-282-0994.

PACKAGING — Abstracting, Bibliographies, Statistics

ANYAGMOZGATASI ES CSOMAGOLASI SZAKIRODALMI TAJEKOZTATO/ABSTRACT JOURNAL FOR MATERIALS HANDLING AND PACKAGING. see TRANSPORTATION — Abstracting, Bibliographies, Statistics

658.788 016   US   ISSN 0890-4227
CURRENT PACKAGING ABSTRACTS. 1969. s-m. $120. Rutgers University, Ira S. Gotscho Packaging Information Center, Busch Campus, Bldg. 3529, Piscataway, NJ 08855. TEL 201-932-3044. FAX 201-932-5636. circ. 250. (looseleaf format; back issues avail.)
Formerly: Packaging Bulletin (ISSN 0030-9095)

658.788 016   RU   ISSN 0131-0526
EKSPRESS-INFORMATSIYA. TARA I UPAKOVKA. KONTEINERY. 1962. 48/yr. 38.40 Rub. Vsesoyuznyi Institut Nauchno-Tekhnicheskoi Informatsii (VINITI), Baltiiskaya ul., 14, Moscow A-219, Russia. (Subscr. to: Mezhdunarodnaya Kniga, Dimitrova ul. 39, 113095 Moscow, Russia)
Formerly: Ekspress-Informatsiya. Tara i Upakovka (ISSN 0013-3825)

658.788 016   UK   ISSN 0260-7409
INTERNATIONAL PACKAGING ABSTRACTS. 1944. m. $946.50. (Research Association for the Paper and Board, Printing and Packaging Industries) Pira International, Randalls Rd., Leatherhead, Surrey KT22 7RU, England. TEL 0372-376161. Ed. Sarah-Jane Sutton. bk.rev.; abstr.; index; circ. 955. (also avail. in microform from UMI; reprint service avail. from UMI) Indexed: Abstr.Bull.Inst.Pap.Chem., Curr.Pack.Abstr., World Surf.Coat., World Text.Abstr.
●Also available online. Vendor(s): Data-Star, European Space Agency, FIZ Technik, Orbit Information Technologies (PIRA).
—BLDSC shelfmark: 4544.857200.
Formerly: Packaging Abstracts (ISSN 0030-9087)

658.788 011   GW   ISSN 0722-3218
PACKAGING SCIENCE AND TECHNOLOGY ABSTRACTS/REFERATEDIENST VERPACKUNG. (Text in English and German) 1982. 6/yr. DM.550. (Fraunhofer Institut fuer Lebensmitteltechnologie und Verpackung) International Food Information Service GmbH, Melibocusstr. 52, 6000 Frankfurt a.M. 71, Germany. TEL 069-6690070. FAX 069-66900710. pat.; index.
●Also available online. Vendor(s): CISTI, DIMDI, DIALOG (File no.252), European Space Agency (File no.55/PACKABS), FIZ Technik, Orbit Information Technologies.
Description: Abstracts from journals, books, conference proceedings in packaging technology and engineering.

PAINTS AND PROTECTIVE COATINGS

ADVANCES IN ORGANIC COATINGS SCIENCE AND TECHNOLOGY. see CHEMISTRY — Organic Chemistry

667.6   SW
AKTUELLT MAALERI.* 1911. m. (11/yr.). SEK 75. (Maalarmaestarnas Riksoferening) L M P Foerlagsgruppen, Box 630, 10128 Stockholm, Sweden. Ed. Birgitta Aahs. adv.; circ. 2,681 (controlled).

667.6   US   ISSN 0098-5430
TP934   CODEN: APCJDB
AMERICAN PAINT & COATINGS JOURNAL. 1916. w. $25. American Paint Journal Co., 2911 Washington Ave., St. Louis, MO 63103. TEL 314-530-0301. Ed. Chuck Reitter. adv.; mkt.; tr.lit.; tr.mk.; index; circ. 5,936. Indexed: Anal.Abstr., Bus.Ind., Chem.Abstr, Key to Econ.Sci., PROMT, Tr.& Indus.Ind., World Surf.Coat.
—BLDSC shelfmark: 0847.829000.
Formerly: American Paint Journal (ISSN 0003-0317)

698   US   ISSN 0003-0325
AMERICAN PAINTING CONTRACTOR. 1924. m. $24. American Paint Journal Co., 2911 Washington Ave., St. Louis, MO 63103. TEL 314-530-0301. Ed. Paul Stoecklein. adv.; illus.; tr.lit.; index; circ. 24,754. Indexed: Corros.Abstr.
Formerly (1924-1963): American Painter and Decorator (ISSN 0096-0918)
Description: Aimed at industrial, commercial and residential painters.

ANNUAL BOOK OF A S T M STANDARDS. VOLUME 06.01. PAINT - TESTS FOR FORMULATED PRODUCTS AND APPLIED COATINGS. see ENGINEERING — Engineering Mechanics And Materials

ANNUAL BOOK OF A S T M STANDARDS. VOLUME 06.02. PAINT - PIGMENTS, RESINS AND POLYMERS. see ENGINEERING — Engineering Mechanics And Materials

ANNUAL BOOK OF A S T M STANDARDS. VOLUME 06.03. PAINT - FATTY OILS AND ACIDS, SOLVENTS, MISCELLANEOUS; AROMATIC HYDROCARBONS. see ENGINEERING — Engineering Mechanics And Materials

698   SZ
APPLICA; Zeitschrift fuer das Maler- und Gipsergewerbe. 1893. s-m. 105 Fr. (foreign 150 Fr.). Schweizerischer Maler und Gipsermeister Verband, Grindelstr. 2, CH-8304 Wallisellen, Switzerland. TEL 01-8305959. FAX 01-8301176. adv. Indexed: C.I.S. Abstr., World Surf.Coat.

698   AT   ISSN 0816-3596
AUSTRALIAN PAINT AND PANEL. 1982. bi-m. Aus.$34 (foreign Aus.$85)(effective Apr. 1992). Yaffa Publishing Group, 17-21 Bellevue St., Surry Hills, N.S.W. 2010, Australia. TEL 02-281-2333. FAX 02-281-2750. Ed. Henny Berich. adv.: B&W page Aus.$1720, color page Aus.$2475; trim 273 x 210. circ. 4,644 (controlled).
Description: Keeps body repair shops in touch with latest trends, developments, techniques and new products.

667.6   UK
B A S A ADHESIVES & SEALANTS YEARBOOK AND DIRECTORY. a. £51. (British Adhesives and Sealants Association) F M J International Publications Ltd., Queensway House, 2 Queensway, Redhill, Surrey RH1 1QS, England. TEL 0737-768611. FAX 0737-761685. TELEX 948669-TOPJNL-G.
Description: Provides chemical and technical information on adhesives and sealants and raw materials, as well as comprehensive listings of suppliers and manufacturers.

698   IT
BOTTEGA DEL COLORE. 1966. m. L.50000($45) (effective 1992). (Federcolor Association of Paint Stores) Gest. Ed. di Daniele Paolucci, Via Menotti, 33, 20129 Milan, Italy. TEL 02-29512541. FAX 02-29404950. adv.; index; circ. 14,000. (back issues avail.)

PAINTS AND PROTECTIVE COATINGS

698 UK
BRITISH DECORATORS ASSOCIATION. MEMBERS REFERENCE HANDBOOK. 1932. a. British Decorators Association, 6 Haywra Street, Harrogate, North Yorkshire, HG1 5BL, England. Ed. S.M. Boroughton. adv.; abstr.; charts; circ. 2,500.

679.6 GW
BROSSAPRESS-NACHRICHTENBLATT FUER DIE BUERSTEN- UND PINSELINDUSTRIE. (Text in English, French and German) 1925. bi-m. DM.160. Verlag Dr. Grueb, Nachf., Oelbergweg 8, 7801 Bollschweil, Germany. TEL 07633-7025. FAX 07633-82129. TELEX 772730-BROS-D. Ed. Rainer Grueb. adv.; bk.rev.; charts; illus.; pat.; stat.; tr.lit.; circ. 4,500. (tabloid format)
  Formerly: Nachrichtenblatt fuer die Buersten- und Pinselindustrie (ISSN 0027-7487)

BRUSHWARE. see *BUILDING AND CONSTRUCTION — Hardware*

667.6 FR ISSN 0396-1214
CATALOGUE NATIONAL DU TRAITEMENT DES SURFACES DE L'ANTICORROSION ET DES TRAITEMENTS THERMIQUES.* 1963. a. 175 F. Editions du Cartel, 1 pl. d'Estienne-d'Orves, 75009 Paris, France. TEL 42-36-00-66. Ed. A.L. Savu. adv.; circ. 10,000.
  Description: Covers the entire French market of surface coatings.

667.6 SP
CHAPA Y PINTURA. 9/yr. 8000 ptas. (foreign 11000 ptas.). Tecnipublicaciones, S.A., Fernando VI, 27, 28004 Madrid, Spain. TEL 1-319-7889. FAX 1-410-2041. TELEX 43905 YEBE E.

698 CN ISSN 0225-6363
COATINGS. 1979. bi-m. Can.$22($36) Kay Publishing Company Ltd., 86 Wilson St., Suite A, Oakville, Ont. L6K 3G5, Canada. TEL 416-844-9773. FAX 416-844-5672. Ed. G. Barry Kay. circ. 7,600. (back issues avail.)
  —BLDSC shelfmark: 3292.580000.

COLOR RESEARCH AND APPLICATION. see *ENGINEERING — Chemical Engineering*

667.6 II ISSN 0588-5094
TP934 CODEN: COSJAZ
COLOUR SOCIETY. JOURNAL. (Text in English) 1962. bi-m. Rs.5 per no. Colour Society, c/o S. P. Potnis, Department of Chemical Technology, Matunga, Bombay 400019, India. Ed. V. Gowrishankar. adv.; bk.rev.; abstr.; index; circ. 400. Indexed: Art & Archaeol.Tech.Abstr., Chem.Abstr., World Surf.Coat.

667.6 SA ISSN 0377-8711
TA418.74 CODEN: CCSADT
CORROSION AND COATINGS. (Text in English) 1973. bi-m. R.92. (South African Corrosion Institute) George Warman Publications (Pty.) Ltd., Box 3847, Cape Town 8000, South Africa. TEL 021-24-5320. FAX 021-26-1332. TELEX 5-21849 SA. Ed. Tony Walker. adv.; circ. 2,400. Indexed: Chem.Abstr., Corros.Abstr., Ind.S.A.Per., INIS Atomind., Met.Abstr., W.R.C.Inf., World Alum.Abstr.
  —BLDSC shelfmark: 3473.350000.
  Description: Covers the corrosion prevention and surface coatings industry in South Africa.

667.6 SA
CORROSION AND COATINGS BUYER'S GUIDE. 1984. a. R.110. George Warman Publications (Pty.) Ltd., P.O. Box 704, Cape Town 8000, South Africa. TEL 021-24-5320. FAX 021-26-1332. TELEX 5-21849 SA.
  Description: Lists suppliers, representatives, manufacturers, corrosion related products and services.

667 DK ISSN 0905-6440
DANSKE MALERMESTRE. 1963. m. DKK 285 (typically set in Jan.). Bygeriets Arbejdsgivere, Kejsergade 2, 1155 Copenhagen K, Denmark. FAX 45-33-15-31-11. Ed. Adam Pade. adv.; bk.rev.; circ. 3,200 (controlled).
  Formerly (until 1990): Malermesteren (ISSN 0025-1364)
  Description: Provides technical, political and legal information. Features outstanding work by individuals and independent painting companies.

DECORATING PRODUCTS TRENDS ADVISORY; marketing newsletter for the decorating products industry. see *INTERIOR DESIGN AND DECORATION*

667.6 GW ISSN 0012-009X
TP934 CODEN: DFZTBF
DEFAZET.* (Supplement: Blaetter fuer den Nachwuchs) 1947. m. DM.54. Lack und Chemie Verlag Elvira Moeller GmbH, Postfach 1168, 7024 Filderstadt 1, Germany. Ed. Elvira Moeller. adv.; bk.rev.; abstr.; illus.; pat.; tr.lit.; index; circ. 4,500. Indexed: Chem.Abstr., Excerp.Med., PROMT.
  Formerly: Deutsche Farben-Zeitschrift.

698 GW
DEUTSCHE MALER- UND LACKIERERZEITSCHRIFT DIE MAPPE. 1880. m. DM.114. Callwey Verlag, Streitfeldstr. 35, 8000 Munich 80, Germany. FAX 08841-99511. Ed. Konrad Gatz. adv.; bk.rev.; circ. 30,000. (back issues avail.)

698 GW ISSN 0012-0448
TT300
DAS DEUTSCHE MALERBLATT. (Supplements avail.) 1928. m. DM.124.80 (students DM.94.20). (Hauptverband des Deutschen Maler- und Lackiererhandwerks) Deutsche Verlags-Anstalt GmbH, Neckarstr. 121, Postfach 106012, 7000 Stuttgart 10, Germany. TEL 0711-2631-0. FAX 0711-2631-292. Ed. Karl Apel. adv.; bk.rev.; charts; illus.; tr.lit.; index; circ. 19,000. Indexed: Art & Archaeol.Tech.Abstr., Biodet.Abstr., World Surf.Coat.
  —BLDSC shelfmark: 3572.700000.

698 GW
DEUTSCHES TASCHENBUCH FUER MALER UND LACKIERER (YEAR). 1952. a. DM.18. Verlag Georg D.W. Callwey, Streitfeldstr. 35, Postfach 800409, 8000 Munich 80, Germany. TEL 089-436005-0. Eds. Konrad Gatz, Klaus Halmburger. circ. 10,000.

698 667 FR ISSN 0012-5709
CODEN: DOLIA8
DOUBLE LIAISON; chimie des peintures. (Text and summaries in English and French) 1954. m. 521 F. (Etude et Realisations de la Couleur) E R E C, 68 rue Jean Jaures, 92800 Puteaux, France. Ed. Annik Chauvel. adv.; abstr.; bibl.; charts; illus.; stat.; index; circ. 4,700. (back issues avail.) Indexed: Anal.Abstr., Art & Archaeol.Tech.Abstr., Chem.Abstr., PROMT, World Alum.Abstr., World Surf.Coat.
  Description: Information on paints, varnishes, printing inks and adhesives.

698 NE
EISMA'S VAKPERS; algemeen vakblad voor het schildersbedrijf. 1899. fortn. fl.210. Eisma B.V. Publishers, Celsiusweg 37, Box 340, 8901 BC Leeuwarden, Netherlands. TEL 058-152545. FAX 058-154000. adv.; bk.rev.; index; circ. 7,000.
  Formerly: Eisma's Schildersblad (ISSN 0013-287X)

667.6 GW ISSN 0930-3847
EUROPEAN COATINGS JOURNAL. (Text in English and French) 1986. m. DM.190.35. Curt R. Vincentz Verlag, Schiffgraben 41-43, 3000 Hannover 1, Germany. TEL 0511-99098-0. FAX 0511-9909899. TELEX 923846. Ed. Juergen Nowak. adv.; bk.rev.; bibl.; charts; illus.; circ. 8,753. (tabloid format; reprint service avail. from UMI) Indexed: Biodet.Abstr., Chem.Abstr., Curr.Cont., Eng.Ind., Met.Abstr., Phys.Ber., Sci.Cit.Ind., World Surf.Coat.
  —BLDSC shelfmark: 3829.609000.

667.6 UK ISSN 0266-7800
EUROPEAN PAINT AND RESIN NEWS. 1957. m. $355. Information Research Ltd., 262 Regent St., London W1R 5DA, England. FAX 071-287-9322. Ed. Cvetka Fuller. pat.; tr.lit.; circ. 500. (processed; reprint service avail. from UMI) Indexed: World Surf.Coat.
  —BLDSC shelfmark: 3829.768400.
  Formerly: Continental Paint and Resin News (ISSN 0010-7735); Incorporates: Phosphating News.
  Description: Industry developments, marketing news and statistics, technology developments, symposia and exhibition news of the European paint and resin industry.

667.6 SW ISSN 0427-9107
FAERG OCH FERNISSA. vol.35, 1971. q. free. Becker Industrifaerg AB, Box 2041, 195 02 Maersta, Sweden. FAX 760-16949. Ed. Birgitta Karlsson. adv.; charts; illus.; tr.lit.; cum.index every 5 yrs.; circ. 10,000. Indexed: World Surf.Coat.

667.6 DK ISSN 0037-6094
TP934 CODEN: STFLAH
FAERG OCH LACK SCANDINAVIA. (Text in Danish, Norwegian and Swedish; summaries in English) 1955. m. DKK 380. (Federation of Scandinavian Paint and Varnish Technicians) Forlaget Folia ApS, Store Kongensgade 62 A, DK-1264 Copenhagen K, Denmark. Eds. Helge Meyer, Mike Symes. adv.; bk.rev.; charts; illus.; index; circ. 1,802. Indexed: Chem.Abstr.

DIE FARBE; Zeitschrift fuer alle Zweige der Farbenlehre und ihre Anwendung. see *PHYSICS — Optics*

667.6 GW ISSN 0014-7699
FALAAA
FARBE UND LACK. 1893. m. DM.128. (Gesellschaft Deutscher Chemiker) Curt R. Vincentz Verlag, Schiffgraben 41-43, Postfach 6247, 3000 Hannover, Germany. TEL 0511-990980. (Co-sponsor: Schweizerische Vereinigung der Lack- und Farbenchemiker (SVLFC)) Ed.Bd. adv.; bk.rev.; abstr.; bibl.; charts; illus.; pat.; circ. 5,796. (tabloid format; also avail. in microform from UMI; reprint service avail. from UMI) Indexed: Anal.Abstr., Art & Archaeol.Tech.Abstr., Biodet.Abstr., C.I.S. Abstr., Cadscan, Chem.Abstr., Curr.Cont., Excerp.Med., INIS Atomind., Int.Packag.Abstr., Key to Econ.Sci., Lead Abstr., Packag.Sci.Tech., Sci.Cit.Ind., World Surf.Coat., Zincscan.
  —BLDSC shelfmark: 3869.000000.

667.6 AU ISSN 0014-7737
FARBENKREIS, OESTERREICHISCHE MALERZEITUNG. m. S.200. (Landesinnung Wien der Maler, Anstreicher und Lackierer) Eugen Ketterl, Anastasius-Grun-Gasse 43, A-1180 Vienna, Austria. Ed. Erwin Berger. circ. 4,000.

667.6 667.7 FR ISSN 0071-416X
FEDERATION D'ASSOCIATIONS DE TECHNICIENS DES INDUSTRIES DES PEINTURES, VERNIS, EMAUX ET ENCRES D'IMPRIMERIE DE L'EUROPE CONTINENTALE. ANNUAIRE OFFICIEL. OFFICIAL YEARBOOK. AMTLICHES JAHRBUCH. (Text in English, French, German) 1955. biennial. Federation d'Associations de Techniciens des Industries des Peintures, Vernis, Emaux et Encres d'Imprimerie de l'Europe Continentale, Maison de la Chimie, 28 rue Saint Dominique, 75007 Paris, France. adv.; circ. 3,000.

698 UK ISSN 0264-2506
TS670.A1 CODEN: FINIE2
FINISHING. 1948. m. $118. Turret Group Plc., Turret House, 171 High St., Rickmansworth, Herts. WD3 1SN, England. TEL 0923-777000. FAX 0923-771297. TELEX 888095-DX. Ed. Glenn Tomkins. adv.; bk.rev. (also avail. in microfilm from UMI; reprint service avail. from UMI) Indexed: Br.Tech.Ind., Cadscan, Chem.Abstr., Eng.Ind., Excerp.Med., Int.Packag.Abstr., ISMEC, Lead Abstr., Met.Abstr., PROMT, Sci.Abstr., World Alum.Abstr., World Surf.Coat., Zincscan.
  —BLDSC shelfmark: 3928.204000.
  Formerly: Finishing Industries (ISSN 0309-3018); Incorporates: Industrial Finishing and Surface Coatings (ISSN 0039-6001) & Electroplating and Metal Finishing (ISSN 0013-5305) & Industrial Finishing (ISSN 0019-8315) & Surface Coatings.

667.6 531 011 US
FINISHING LINE; quarterly on finishing and coating technology. 1983. q. $60. Society of Manufacturing Engineers, Association for Finishing Process, One SME Dr., Box 930, Dearborn, MI 48121-0930. TEL 313-271-1500. FAX 313-271-2861. TELEX 2977422 SME UR (VIA RCA). Ed. Sherry Caruso. bk.rev.; circ. 3,000.

667.6 FR ISSN 0071-9048
FRANCE - PEINTURE. 1953. biennial. 240 F. Creations, Editions et Productions Publicitaires, 1 Place d'Estienne d'Orves, 75009 Paris, France. TEL 42-80-67-62. FAX 42-82-99-30. Ed. Georges Prieux. adv.; circ. 9,100.
  Description: Directory of paint varnish and allied industries.

667.6 676.284 UK
HOME DECOR. 1955. m. £50. Wallpaper Paint & Wallcovering Retailers Association, Box 44, Walsall WS3 1TD, England. TEL 0922-31134. FAX 0922-723703. Ed. Christina Gregory. adv.; bk.rev.; circ. 8,500. Indexed: World Surf.Coat.
  Former titles: W P W Decor; Wallpaper, Paint and Wallcovering (ISSN 0043-0153)

PAINTS AND PROTECTIVE COATINGS

698 US ISSN 0019-8323
TT325.A1 CODEN: IFIIAJ
INDUSTRIAL FINISHING; the management and engineering magazine for better finishing systems. 1924. m. $50. Hitchcock Publishing (Subsidiary of: Capital Cities - A B C, Inc.), 191 S. Gary Ave., Carol Stream, IL 60188. TEL 708-665-1000. FAX 708-462-2225. Ed. Steve Suslik. adv.; bk.rev.; abstr.; charts; illus.; circ. 38,000. (also avail. in microform from UMI; reprint service avail. from UMI) **Indexed**: A.S.& T.Ind., Bus.Ind., CAD CAM Abstr., Ceram.Abstr., Chem.Abstr., Eng.Ind., Excerp.Med., Ind.Sci.Rev., Met.Abstr., Robomat., Tr.& Indus.Ind., World Alum.Abstr.
●Also available online. Vendor(s): DIALOG.
—BLDSC shelfmark: 4450.950000.

667.6 US
INDUSTRIAL FINISHING BUYER'S GUIDE. 1984. a. Hitchcock Publishing (Subsidiary of: Capital Cities - A B C, Inc.), 191 S. Gary Ave., Carol Stream, IL 60188. TEL 708-665-1000. FAX 708-462-2225. TELEX 72-0404. adv.; circ. 36,000.

667.6 GW ISSN 0019-9109
CODEN: ILBEAE
INDUSTRIE LACKIERBETRIEB. 1933. m. DM.115.80. (European Coil Coating Association - ECCA) Curt R. Vincentz Verlag, Schiffgraben 41-43, Postfach 6247, 3000 Hannover, Germany.
TEL 0511-990980. Ed. Olaf Lueckert. adv.; bk.rev.; abstr.; bibl.; charts; illus.; pat.; circ. 3,089. (tabloid format) **Indexed**: C.I.S. Abstr., Chem.Abstr., Excerp.Med., Packag.Sci.Tech., World Surf.Coat.
—BLDSC shelfmark: 4469.000000.

667.6 II
INTERNATIONAL PRESS CUTTING SERVICE: PAINT - COLOUR - VARNISH - INKS. 1967. w. $65. International Press Cutting Service, Box 63, Allahabad 211001, India. Ed. N. Khanna. bk.rev.; index; circ. 1,200. (processed)

698 GW
INTERSTANDOX; information for the world of the car repair painter. (Editions in various languages) 1978. s-a. free. Herberts GmbH, Christbusch 25, Postfach 200244, 5600 Wuppertal 2, Germany.
TEL 0202-529-0. FAX 0202-529-2810. TELEX 17202174. (back issues avail.)

698 GW
INTERSTANDOX EXTRA. 1978. q. free. Herberts GmbH, Christbusch 25, Postfach 200244, 5600 Wuppertal 2, Germany. TEL 0202-529-0.
FAX 0202-529-2810. TELEX 17202174. circ. 18,000. (back issues avail.)
Description: Information for body shops and car repair painters.

667.6 US ISSN 0361-8773
TP934 CODEN: JCTEDL
J C T: JOURNAL OF COATINGS TECHNOLOGY. 1922. m. $30. Federation of Societies for Coatings Technology, 492 Norristown Rd., Blue Bell, PA 19422-2307. TEL 215-940-0777.
FAX 215-940-0292. Ed. Patricia D. Viola. adv.; bk.rev.; charts; illus.; index; circ. 10,000. (also avail. in microform from UMI; reprint service avail. from UMI) **Indexed**: A.S.& T.Ind., Anal.Abstr., Art & Archaeol.Tech.Abstr., BMT, Chem.Abstr., Corros.Abstr., Curr.Cont., Energy Ind., Energy Info.Abstr., Excerp.Med., Graph.Arts Lit.Abstr., Ind.Sci.Rev., Int.Packag.Abstr., Key to Econ.Sci., Met.Abstr., PROMT, Sci.Cit.Ind., World Alum.Abstr., World Surf.Coat.
—BLDSC shelfmark: 4958.796000.
Former titles: J.P.T. Journal of Paint Technology (ISSN 0022-3352); Federation of Societies for Paint Technology. Official Digest.

JOURNAL OF COATED FABRICS. see *TEXTILE INDUSTRIES AND FABRICS*

667.6 US ISSN 8755-1985
TP934
JOURNAL OF PROTECTIVE COATINGS AND LININGS. 1984. m. $45 (foreign $75). (Steel Structures Painting Council) Technology Publishing Co., 2100 Wharton St., Ste. 31, Pittsburgh, PA 15203. TEL 412-431-8300. FAX 412-431-5428. Ed.Bd. adv.; bk.rev.; charts; illus.; index; circ. 13,000 (controlled). **Indexed**: Corros.Abstr., Excerp.Med., World Surf.Coat.
—BLDSC shelfmark: 5042.940000.

698 NE ISSN 0169-0930
KLEUR; vakblad voor het schilders-, afwerkings- en glaszettersbedrijf. 1983. m. (11/yr.). fl.80. Stichting Ondernemersuitgaven Schilders-, Afwerkings- en Glaszettersbedrijf, Postbus 651, 2800 AR Gouda, Netherlands. TEL 01820-71444.
FAX 01820-72083. Ed. Mr. van Donk. adv.; bk.rev.; circ. 5,500.
Supersedes (1975-1982): Intrex; Which was formerly (1880-1974): Schilder (ISSN 0036-6072)

KOLORISZTIKAI ERTESITO/COLORISTICAL REVIEW. see *ENGINEERING — Chemical Engineering*

667.6 540 HU ISSN 0133-2546
CODEN: KOFIDO
KORROZIOS FIGYELO. (Text in Hungarian; summaries in English) 1961. bi-m. $20 (effective 1991). N E V I K I - V E K O R - Research Institute for Heavy Chemical Industries, Corrosion Protection Organization for Chemical Industry, Wartha Vince u.1-3, P.O. Box 160, 8201 Veszprem, Hungary. TEL 80-25-011. FAX 80-25-810. TELEX 32-608 NKIV H. adv.; bk.rev.; abstr.; bibl.; illus.; index; circ. 600. **Indexed**: Corros.Abstr., INIS Atomind., Met.Abstr.

677.6 RU ISSN 0023-737X
LAKOKRASOCHNYE MATERIALY I IKH PRIMENENIE. 1960. bi-m. 25.20 Rub. Gosudarstvennyi Komitet po Khimii pri Sovete Ministrov, Moscow, Russia. bibl.; index. **Indexed**: Art & Archaeol.Tech.Abstr., Chem.Abstr., INIS Atomind., World Surf.Coat.

698 FI ISSN 0024-8568
MAALARILEHTI. (Text in Finnish; summaries in Swedish) 1917. m. Fmk.160. Suomen Maalarimestariliitto - National Federation of Finnish Master Painters, Vuorikatu 4A4, SF-00100 Helsinki, Finland. TEL 01-299254. FAX 01-299252. Ed. Tapio Kari. adv.; abstr.; charts; illus.; stat.; index, cum.index; circ. 6,000. (processed)

698 GW ISSN 0464-7777
DER MALER UND LACKIERERMEISTER. 1950. m. DM.30. Verlag W. Sachon, Schloss Mindelburg, Postfach 1463, 8948 Mindelheim, Germany.
TEL 08261-999-0. FAX 08261-999-132. TELEX 539624. Ed. Peter Hartmann. adv.; charts; illus.; tr.lit.; circ. 21,555.

698 NO
MALEREN. 1908. m. (10/yr.). NOK 360. Malermestrenes Landsforbund, Gjerdrumsvej 10c, 0486 Oslo 4, Norway. TEL 02-950650.
FAX 02-950241. Ed. Knut Randem. adv.; bk.rev.; circ. 2,000. **Indexed**: C.I.S. Abstr.
Description: Articles about the construction industry and painting as a trade.

698 DK
MALERTIDENDE. m. Centralforeningen af Malermestre i Danmark, Allegade 33-37, 6500 Vojens, Denmark. adv.; circ. 2,491.

698 GW ISSN 0025-2697
NK1700
DIE MAPPE; Deutsche Maler- und Lackierer-Zeitschrift. 1881. m. DM.136.80 (students DM.108). Verlag Georg D.W. Callwey, Streitfeldstr. 35, Postfach 800409, 8000 Munich 80, Germany. Ed. Klaus Halmbuerger. adv.; bk.rev.; bibl.; illus.; stat.; index; circ. 30,000. **Indexed**: Art & Archaeol.Tech.Abstr., World Surf.Coat.
—BLDSC shelfmark: 5369.350000.

667.6 US ISSN 0098-7786
TP934 CODEN: MPCODM
MODERN PAINT AND COATINGS. 1910. m. $45 (foreign $115). Communication Channels, Inc., 6255 Barfield Rd., Atlanta, GA 30328-4369. TEL 404-256-9800. FAX 404-256-3116. TELEX 4611075 COMCHANI. Ed. Larry Anderson. adv.; bk.rev.; charts; illus.; pat.; tr.lit.; circ. 14,500. (also avail. in microform from UMI; reprint service avail. from UMI) **Indexed**: A.S.& T.Ind., Art & Archaeol.Tech.Abstr., Chem.Abstr., Excerp.Med., Ind.Sci.Rev., Int.Packag.Abstr., Key to Econ.Sci., Lead Abstr., PROMT, World Surf.Coat., Zincscan.
●Also available online.
—BLDSC shelfmark: 5890.765000.
Formerly: Paint and Varnish Production (ISSN 0030-9478)
Description: Covers current technical developments in the manufacture and use of paints and coatings, including processes, raw materials, equipment and products.

MODERN PAINT & COATINGS PAINT RED BOOK; directory of the paint and coatings industry. see *BUSINESS AND ECONOMICS — Trade And Industrial Directories*

667.6 US
NAVAL STORES REVIEW. 1890. bi-m. $58. Kriedt Enterprises, Ltd., 4640 S. Carrollton Ave., Ste. 1D, New Orleans, LA 70119. TEL 504-482-3914. Ed. Don E. Neighbors. adv.; bk.rev.; charts; illus.; mkt.; circ. 600. **Indexed**: Chem.Abstr., P.A.I.S., SRI.
Formerly: Naval Stores Review and Terpene Chemicals (ISSN 0028-1468)

698 SZ ISSN 0048-1270
CODEN: OBSUA7
OBERFLAECHE/SURFACE; internationale Fachzeitschrift fuer das gesamte Gebiet der Oberflaechentechnik und des Korrosionsschutzes von Metallen und anderen Werkstoffen. (Text in French, German) 1959. m. 95 Fr. (foreign 116 Fr.). (Schweizerische Galvanotechnische Gesellschaft) S H Z Fachverlag AG, Alte Landstr. 43, CH-8700 Kusnacht-Zurich, Switzerland. TEL 01-910 80 22. FAX 01-9105155. (Co-sponsor: Verband Galvano Betriebe der Schweiz) Ed. Helmut Tannenberger. adv.; bk.rev.; illus.; index; circ. 4,150. **Indexed**: Art & Archaeol.Tech.Abstr., Chem.Abstr., Excerp.Med., Met.Abstr., World Alum.Abstr., World Surf.Coat.
—BLDSC shelfmark: 6196.750000.

667.6 US ISSN 0884-3848
PAINT & COATINGS INDUSTRY. (Includes annual Raw Material & Equipment Directory & Buyers Guide) 1918. 9/yr. $36. Business News Publishing, Co., Box 2600, Troy, MI 48007. TEL 313-362-3700. FAX 313-362-0317. Ed. Larry P. Dill. adv.; illus.; pat.; stat.; tr.lit.; index; circ. 17,050 (controlled). **Indexed**: Chem.Abstr.
—BLDSC shelfmark: 6334.249900.
Former titles (until 1985): Industry Section of Western Paint and Decorating; Decorative Products World; Paint and Decorating; Western Paint and Decorating; Western Paint Review (ISSN 0043-4027)
Description: Serves manufacturers, suppliers, distributors in the paint and coatings field with industry news, technology and product coverage.

667.6 686 UK
PAINT AND INK INTERNATIONAL. q. £64.10 (foreign £79.80). F M J International Publications Ltd., Queensway House, 2 Queensway, Redhill, Surrey RH1 1QS, England. TEL 0737-768611.
FAX 0737-761685. TELEX 948669-TOPJNL-G. Ed. Tom Mulligan.
Description: Covers worldwide developments in the paint and printing ink industries, from raw materials to manufacturing processes, equipment and applications.

667.6 UK ISSN 0261-5746
TP934 CODEN: PTRNDJ
PAINT AND RESIN. 1931. 6/yr. Turret Group Plc., Turret House, 171 High St., Rickmansworth, Herts. WD3 1SN, England. TEL 0923-777000.
FAX 0923-771297. TELEX 888095. Ed. Lloyd Arkill. adv.; bk.rev.; abstr.; bibl.; charts; illus.; stat.; index. **Indexed**: Art & Archaeol.Tech.Abstr., Br.Tech.Ind., C.I.S. Abstr., Cadscan, Chem.Abstr., Excerp.Med., Lead Abstr., World Surf.Coat., Zincscan.
—BLDSC shelfmark: 6334.700000.
Former titles: Paint Manufacture and Resin News; Paint Manufacture (ISSN 0030-9508)

667.6 658 US
▼**PAINT DEALER**. 1992. 10/yr. $25. 13850 Manchester Rd., St. Louis, MO 63011.
TEL 314-256-3214. FAX 314-227-3351. adv.: B&W page $3275; trim 8 x 10 3/4. circ. 20,000.
Description: Covers product innovations, merchandising ideas, store management and industry news.

667.6 II ISSN 0030-9540
TP934 CODEN: PIDABZ
PAINTINDIA. (Text in English) 1951. m. Rs.200($100) Colour Publications Pvt. Ltd., 126-A Dhurunadi, Off. Dr. Nariman Rd., Bombay 400 025, India.
TEL 430-9318. TELEX 71242 CEPE IN. Ed. R.V. Raghavan. adv.; bk.rev.; illus.; stat.; circ. 5,096. (also avail. in microfilm from UMI; reprint service avail. from UMI) **Indexed**: Art & Archaeol.Tech.Abstr., Chem.Abstr., W.R.C.Inf., World Surf.Coat.

PAINTS AND PROTECTIVE COATINGS

698 US
PAINTING AND DECORATING CRAFTSMAN MANUAL AND TEXTBOOK. irreg., 5th ed., 1975. $9.75. Painting and Decorating Contractors of America, 3913 Old Lee Hwy., Ste. 33B, Fairfax, VA 22030. TEL 703-359-0826. FAX 703-359-2576. charts; illus.

698 US ISSN 0735-9713
TT300
PAINTING AND WALLCOVERING CONTRACTOR. 1938. bi-m. $12. Finan Publishing Company, Inc., 8730 Big Bend Blvd., St. Louis, MO 63119. TEL 314-961-6644. FAX 314-961-4809. Ed. Jeffery Beckner. adv.; stat.; circ. 40,000. **Indexed:** Corros.Abstr.
   Former titles: P D C A Magazine; Professional Decorating and Coating Action (ISSN 0099-0310); P D C A 74 (ISSN 0038-8416); Spotlights.

667.6 GW
PHAENOMEN FARBE; aktuelle Informationen fuer die Lackindustrie. 1981. m. DM.158. R L - Press Renate Wittsack, Ostlandstr. 1, 5000 Cologne 40, Germany. TEL 02234-73488. FAX 02234-73598. circ. 1,000.

667.6 UK ISSN 0369-9420
TP934 CODEN: PGRTBC
PIGMENT AND RESIN TECHNOLOGY. 1936. m. $87. Sawell Publications Ltd., 127 Stanstead Rd., London SE23 1JE, England. Ed. J. Bean. adv.; bk.rev.; abstr.; charts; illus.; tr.lit.; index; circ. 1,419. **Indexed:** Anal.Abstr., Br.Tech.Ind., Cadscan, Chem.Abstr., Excerp.Med., Graph.Arts Lit.Abstr., Lead Abstr., PROMT, World Surf.Coat., Zincscan.
   —BLDSC shelfmark: 6500.145000.
   Formerly: Paint Technology (ISSN 0030-9524)

667.5 SP ISSN 0031-9945
PINTORES. 1961. m. 1200 ptas. Asociacion de Maestros Pintores de Barcelona, Diputacion 297, Pral., Barcelona, Spain. Ed. Jose Bollo Feu. adv.; illus.; stat.; circ. 6,000.

667.6 SP ISSN 0031-9953
TT300 CODEN: PACIDY
PINTURAS Y ACABADOS INDUSTRIALES. 1958. 8/yr. 8800 ptas.($106) Ediciones CEDEL, C. Mallorca 257, Barcelona 8, Spain. TEL 343-215-6039. FAX 343-215-6088. adv.; bk.rev.; bibl.; charts; illus.; tr.lit.; index; circ. 4,000. **Indexed:** Chem.Abstr., Ind.SST, World Surf.Coat.
   —BLDSC shelfmark: 6501.510000.

698 IT ISSN 0048-4245
CODEN: PIVEAY
PITTURE E VERNICI. 1925. m. L.96000. On-edit s.a.s., Via Natale Battaglia 10, 20127 Milan, Italy. Dir. Annamaria Zambrini. adv.; bk.rev.; abstr.; circ. 3,500. **Indexed:** Art & Archaeol.Tech.Abstr., Biodet.Abstr., Chem.Abstr., Corros.Abstr., World Surf.Coat.
   —BLDSC shelfmark: 6506.000000.

667.6 UK ISSN 0370-1158
TP934 CODEN: PPCJA3
POLYMERS PAINT AND COLOUR JOURNAL. 1879. fortn. £91 (foreign £110.80). F M J International Publications Ltd., Queensway House, 2 Queensway, Redhill, Surrey RH1 1QS, England. TEL 0737-768611. FAX 0737-761685. TELEX 948669-TOPJNL-G. Ed. J. Ward. adv.; bk.rev.; abstr.; charts; mkt.; pat.; s-a. index; circ. 2,002. **Indexed:** Anal.Abstr., Art & Archaeol.Tech.Abstr., BMT, Chem.Abstr., Chem.Eng.Abstr., Excerp.Med., Key to Econ.Sci., PROMT, T.C.E.A., W.R.C.Inf., World Surf.Coat.
   —BLDSC shelfmark: 6547.744000.
   Formerly: Paint Oil and Colour Journal (ISSN 0030-9516)

667.6 UK ISSN 0078-7817
POLYMERS PAINT AND COLOUR YEAR BOOK. 1961. a. £75. F M J International Publications Ltd., Queensway House, 2 Queensway, Redhill, Surrey RH1 1QS, England. TEL 0737-768611. FAX 0737-761685. TELEX 948669-TOPJNL-G. Ed. J. Ward. adv.
   Formerly: Paint, Oil Colour Year Book.

698 US ISSN 0032-9940
TS200 CODEN: PRFCAB
PRODUCTS FINISHING. 1936. m. $24 (foreign $48). Gardner Publications, Inc., 6600 Clough Pike, Cincinnati, OH 45244-4090. TEL 513-231-8020. FAX 513-231-2818. Ed. G. Thomas Robison. adv.; bibl.; illus.; tr.lit.; circ. 50,000. (also avail. in microform from UMI; reprint service avail.) **Indexed:** Cadscan, Chem.Abstr., Eng.Ind., Lead Abstr., Met.Abstr., World Alum.Abstr., World Surf.Coat., Zincscan.
   —BLDSC shelfmark: 6854.000000.

698 US ISSN 0478-4251
PRODUCTS FINISHING DIRECTORY. a. $10. Gardner Publications, Inc., 6600 Clough Pike, Cincinnati, OH 45244-4090. TEL 513-231-8020. FAX 513-231-2818. Ed. G. Thomas Robison. adv.; circ. 30,000.

698 683 IT
PROFESSIONAL. 1987. 8/yr. L.80000. (Editoriale Tecnica Macchine) E T M, S.r.l, Via Roncaglia 14, 20146 Milan, Italy. TEL 02-48010095. FAX 02-48010011. circ. 12,000.
   Description: Review for hardware and paint stores, wood-shop and do-it-yourself supermarkets.

698 US
PROFESSIONAL SPRAYING. q. Graco Inc., Box 1441, Minneapolis, MN 55440. TEL 612-623-6000. Ed. Mick Lee.

547 698 SZ ISSN 0033-0655
PROGRESS IN ORGANIC COATINGS; an international review journal. (Text in English, French and German) 1972. 4/yr. 370 SFr. (effective 1992). Elsevier Sequoia S.A., P.O. Box 564, CH-1001 Lausanne, Switzerland. TEL 021-207381. FAX 021-235444. TELEX 450620 ELSA CH. (Subscr. in U.S. and Canada to: Elsevier Science Publishing Co., Inc., Box 882, Madison Sq. Sta., New York, NY 10159. TEL 212-989-5800) Ed.Bd. adv.; bk.rev.; charts; illus.; index. (tabloid format; also avail. in microform from UMI) **Indexed:** Chem.Abstr., Corros.Abstr., Curr.Cont., Eng.Ind., Met.Abstr., Phys.Ber., Sci.Cit.Ind., World Alum.Abstr., World Surf.Coat.
   —BLDSC shelfmark: 6872.200000.
   Description: Analyzes and publicizes the progress and current state of knowledge in the field of organic coatings and related materials.
   Refereed Serial

698 FR
QUI FABRIQUE ET FOURNIT QUOI. 1973. a. 190 F. Editions Ampere, Groupe C.E.P.P., 25, rue Dagorno, 75012 Paris, France. TEL 43-47-30-20.
   Description: Directory for surface treatments in industry, paints and coatings.

698 IT ISSN 0048-8348
CODEN: RCLRA3
RIVISTA DEL COLORE; verniciatura industriale. 1968. m. L.70000. Rivista del Colore s.r.l., Via degli Imbriani 10, 20158 Milan, Italy. Ed. Dr. Danilo O. Malavolti. adv.; bk.rev.; abstr.; tr.lit.; index; circ. 3,000. **Indexed:** Chem.Abstr., World Surf.Coat.

698 US
S S P C BULLETIN. 1955. q. membership. Steel Structures Painting Council, 4400 Fifth Ave., Pittsburgh, PA 15213-2683. TEL 412-268-3326. FAX 412-268-7048. Ed. Janet Rex. circ. 6,500.
   Formerly (until 1988): Steel Structures Painting Bulletin.
   Description: Serves members of SSPC by informing them of SSPC initiative in research, standards, and education.

SCAFFOLD INDUSTRY ASSOCIATION. NEWSLETTER. see *BUILDING AND CONSTRUCTION*

382 II ISSN 0304-8179
HD9769.L33
SHELLAC EXPORT PROMOTION COUNCIL. ANNUAL REPORT. (Text in English) a. Shellac Export Promotion Council, 14-1-B Ezra St., Calcutta 1, India. stat.

SUPATIMBA TECHNICAL REVIEW. see *ENGINEERING — Engineering Mechanics And Materials*

SURFACE COATING & RAW MATERIAL DIRECTORY. see *BUSINESS AND ECONOMICS — Trade And Industrial Directories*

667.6 AT ISSN 0815-709X
SURFACE COATINGS AUSTRALIA. 1964. 11/yr. Aus.$55 (foreign Aus.$90). Surface Coatings Association - Australia, 13 Melby Ave., Balaclava, Vic. 3183, Australia. Ed. L.A. Hill. adv.; bk.rev.; circ. 1,000. **Indexed:** Aus.Sci.Ind., Chem.Abstr., Corros.Abstr., World Surf.Coat.
   —BLDSC shelfmark: 8547.793000.
   Formerly (until 1984): Australian O.C.C.A. Proceedings and News (ISSN 0045-0774)

667.6 UK
TP934
SURFACE COATINGS INTERNATIONAL. 1918. m. £88($185) Oil & Colour Chemists' Association, Priory House, 967 Harrow Rd., Wembley, Middlesex HA0 2SF, England. FAX 081-908-1086. TELEX 922670-OCCA-G. Ed. J.R. Taylor. adv.; bk.rev.; illus.; index; circ. 3,420. **Indexed:** Art & Archaeol.Tech.Abstr., BMT, Br.Tech.Ind., Cadscan, Chem.Abstr., Excerp.Med., Graph.Arts Lit.Abstr., Lead Abstr., Met.Abstr., Print.Abstr., RAPRA, RICS, World Alum.Abstr., World Surf.Coat., Zincscan.
   Formerly (until 1991): Oil and Colour Chemists' Association. Journal (ISSN 0030-1337)

698 FR ISSN 0585-9840
TS653.A1 CODEN: SUFPA2
SURFACES (PARIS); finition et protection. 8/yr. 370 F. (foreign 520 F.). Editions Ampere, Groupe C.E.P.P., 25, rue Dagorno, 75012 Paris, France. TEL 43-47-30-20. circ. 7,000. **Indexed:** Chem.Abstr., Met.Abstr., World Alum.Abstr., World Surf.Coat.
   —BLDSC shelfmark: 8548.070000.
   Incorporates (in 1984): Email Metal.
   Description: Surface treatments, coatings and painting in general industry.

667.6 SW ISSN 0039-6516
SVENSK FAERGHANDEL. 1907. 8/yr. SEK 430. Sveriges Faerghandlares Riksfoerbund, Kungsgatan 19, 105 61 Stockholm, Sweden. TEL 08-7915390. FAX 08-103126. Ed. Axel Wennerholm. adv.; bk.rev.; illus.; stat.; circ. 1,800.
   Description: Analysis and debate concerning products and people in the paint, wallpaper and perfume trades in Sweden.

667.6 GW ISSN 0340-8167
TASCHENBUCH FUER LACKIERBETRIEBE (YEAR). 1943. a. DM.28. Curt R Vincentz Verlag, Schiffgraben 41-43, Postfach 6247, 3000 Hannover 1, Germany. TEL 0511-990980. Eds. Dieter Ondratschek, Konrad Ortlieb. circ. 7,000.

TOLE WORLD. see *ART*

669 698 IT
TRATTAMENTI E FINITURE; rivista tecnica dei trattamenti, processi, finiture delle superfici. 1961. m. (8/yr.). L.70000 (foreign L.95000). E T M S.r.l., Via Roncaglia, 14, 20146 Milan, Italy. TEL 02-48010095. FAX 02-48010011. adv.; bk.rev.; charts; illus.; tr.lit.; index; circ. 15,000. (back issues avail.) **Indexed:** Met.Abstr.
   Formerly: Trattamenti e Finitura - Superfici (ISSN 0041-1833)
   Description: Technical review concerning treatment processing, protection and finishing of metals as well as processes for treating the metal surface, finishing, protection and paintings.

667.6 NE ISSN 0042-3904
CODEN: VERFAL
VERFKRONIEK. 1928. m. fl.80. Vereniging van Verf- en Drukinktfabrikanten - Association of Paint and Ink Manufacturers in the Netherlands, c/o Mrs. J. van der Kley, Schuttersveld 10, Postbus 248, 2300 AE Leiden, Netherlands. FAX 071-223279. adv.; bk.rev.; abstr.; charts; illus.; stat.; circ. 1,000. **Indexed:** Art & Archaeol.Tech.Abstr., C.I.S. Abstr., Chem.Abstr., Key to Econ.Sci., World Surf.Coat.
   —BLDSC shelfmark: 9156.000000.

PAINTS AND PROTECTIVE COATINGS — Abstracting, Bibliographies, Statistics

667.6   US   ISSN 0275-7036
CODEN: CCIPDO
C A SELECTS. COATINGS, INKS, & RELATED PRODUCTS. s-w. $195. Chemical Abstracts Service (Subsidiary of: American Chemical Society), 2540 Olentangy River Rd., Box 3012, Columbus, OH 43210. TEL 614-447-3600. FAX 614-447-3713. TELEX 6842086.
   Description: Covers the chemistry, chemical and physical properties, and analysis of decorative and protective coatings.

667.6   US   ISSN 0749-7296
CODEN: CASCEM
C A SELECTS. CORROSION-INHIBITING COATINGS. s-w. $195. Chemical Abstracts Service (Subsidiary of: American Chemical Society), 2540 Olentangy River Rd., Box 3012, Columbus, OH 43210. TEL 614-447-3600. FAX 614-447-3713. TELEX 6842086.
   Description: Covers the formulation and application of coatings intended to prevent corrosion of metallic surfaces.

667.6   US   ISSN 0734-8762
CODEN: CAPADY
C A SELECTS. PAINT ADDITIVES. s-w. $195. Chemical Abstracts Service (Subsidiary of: American Chemical Society), 2540 Olentangy River Rd., Box 3012, Columbus, OH 43210. TEL 614-447-3600. FAX 614-447-3713. TELEX 6842086.
   Description: Covers materials added to paints (pigmented coatings) other than the basic polymeric binder, solvents, pigments.

667   US   ISSN 0749-7369
CODEN: CSWCEW
C A SELECTS. WATER-BASED COATINGS. s-w. $195. Chemical Abstracts Service (Subsidiary of: American Chemical Society), 2540 Olentangy River Rd., Box 3012, Columbus, OH 43210. TEL 614-447-3600. FAX 614-447-3713. TELEX 6842086.
   Description: Covers formulation, application, and performance of water-borne coatings, water-soluble coatings, latex coatings, aqueous coatings.

667.6 016   UK   ISSN 0144-4425
PAINT TITLES. 1984. w. £430 (effective 1992). (Paint Research Association) Pergamon Press plc, Headington Hill Hall, Oxford OX3 0BW, England. TEL 0865-794141. FAX 0865-743911. TELEX 83177 PERGAP. (And: 660 White Plains Rd., Tarrytown, NY 10591-5153. TEL 914-524-9200) Ed. S.C. Haworth. bibl.; circ. 300. **Indexed:** Curr.Cont.
   Refereed Serial

REFERATIVNYI ZHURNAL. KORROZIYA I ZASHCHITA OT KORROZII. see *METALLURGY — Abstracting, Bibliographies, Statistics*

667.6 016   RU   ISSN 0202-8697
SIGNAL'NAYA INFORMATSIYA. LAKI - KRASKI - ORGANICHESKIE POKRYTIYA. 1970. s-m. 15.20 Rub. Vsesoyuznyi Institut Nauchno-Tekhnicheskoi Informatsii (VINITI), Baltiiskaya ul. 14, Moscow A-219, Russia. (Subscr. to: Mezhdunarodnaya Kniga, Dimitrova ul. 39, 113095 Moscow, Russia)

667.6 016   UK   ISSN 0043-9088
Z7914.P15
WORLD SURFACE COATING ABSTRACTS. 1960. 13/yr. £895 (effective 1992). (Paint Research Association) Pergamon Press plc, Headington Hill Hall, Oxford OX3 0BW, England. TEL 0865-794141. FAX 0865-743911. TELEX 83177 PERGAP. (And: 660 White Plains Rd., Tarrytown, NY 10591-5153. TEL 914-524-9200) Ed. N. Morgan. (also avail. in magnetic tape) **Indexed:** Abstr.Bull.Inst.Pap.Chem., Anal.Abstr., BMT, Curr.Cont., Int.Packag.Abstr.
   ●Also available online. Vendor(s): Orbit Information Technologies (WSCA), Pergamon Infoline (WSCA).
   —BLDSC shelfmark: 9360.043000.
   Refereed Serial

PALEONTOLOGY

A M U NEWS. (American Malacological Union, Inc.) see *BIOLOGY — Zoology*

ACTA PALAEOBOTANICA. see *BIOLOGY — Botany*

560   PL   ISSN 0567-7920
QE755.P7   CODEN: APGPAC
ACTA PALAEONTOLOGICA POLONICA. (Text in English, French, Polish; summaries in Polish) 1956. q. $44. Polska Akademia Nauk, Instytut Paleobiologii, Al. Zwirki i Wigury 93, 02-089 Warsaw. (Dist. by: Ars Polona, Krakowskie Przedmiescie 7, 00-068 Warsaw, Poland) Ed. J. Dzik. bk.rev.; bibl.; illus.; circ. 710. **Indexed:** Biol.Abstr., Deep Sea Res.& Oceanogr.Abstr., GeoRef., Petrol.Abstr., Vet.Bull.
   —BLDSC shelfmark: 0642.500000.

560   AT   ISSN 0311-5518
QE758.A1   CODEN: ALCHDB
ALCHERINGA. 1975. s-a. Aus.$65. Geological Society of Australia, Association of Australasian Palaeontologists, 301 George St., Sydney, N.S.W. 2000, Australia. FAX 02-290-2198. Ed. J.W. Pickett. bk.rev.; circ. 600. **Indexed:** Curr.Cont., Geo.Abstr., GeoRef., Petrol.Abstr.
   —BLDSC shelfmark: 0786.752000.

ALTENBURGER NATURWISSENSCHAFTLICHE FORSCHUNGEN. see *BIOLOGY*

560   AG   ISSN 0002-7014
QE752.A7   CODEN: AMGHB2
AMEGHINIANA. (Text in English and Spanish; summaries in English) 1957. 4/yr. $45. Asociacion Paleontologica Argentina, Maipu 645, 1r piso, 1006 Buenos Aires, Argentina. (Co-sponsor: Consejo Nacional de Investigaciones Cientificas y Tenicas) Ed. Dr. Sergio Archangelsky. adv.; bk.rev.; bibl.; index; circ. 1,000. **Indexed:** AESIS, Biol.Abstr., GeoRef.

551   US   ISSN 0160-8843
CODEN: ASPLCY
AMERICAN ASSOCIATION OF STRATIGRAPHIC PALYNOLOGISTS. CONTRIBUTIONS SERIES. irreg., no.27, 1991. American Association of Stratigraphic Palynologists Foundation, c/o Robert T. Clarke, Mobil R & D Corp.-D R L, Box 819047, Dallas, TX 75381. TEL 214-851-8481. FAX 214-851-8185. **Indexed:** Biol.Abstr., GeoRef.
   —BLDSC shelfmark: 3461.370000.

AMERICAN ASSOCIATION OF STRATIGRAPHIC PALYNOLOGISTS. NEWSLETTER. see *EARTH SCIENCES — Geology*

560   US   ISSN 0192-737X
AMERICAN ASSOCIATION OF STRATIGRAPHIC PALYNOLOGISTS FOUNDATION. FIELD TRIP GUIDE. 1971. a. American Association of Stratigraphic Palynologists Foundation, c/o Robert T. Clarke, Mobil R & D Corp.-D R L, Box 819047, Dallas, TX 75381. TEL 214-851-8481. FAX 214-851-8185.

560   FR   ISSN 0753-3969
ANNALES DE PALEONTOLOGIE (VERT - INVERT). (Text in French; summaries in English) 1906. q. 235 ECU($285) (typically set in Jan.). E S I Publications, 5 et 7 rue Laromiguiere, 75005 Paris, France. TEL 1-46-34-21-60. FAX 1-45-87-29-99. TELEX 202 671 F. Ed. B. Badre. circ. 430. (also avail. in microform from UMI; reprint service avail. from ISI) **Indexed:** Biol.Abstr., Deep Sea Res.& Oceanogr.Abstr., GeoRef.
   —BLDSC shelfmark: 0991.000000.
   Formed by the merger of: Annales de Paleontologie: Vertebres (ISSN 0570-1627); Annales de Paleontologie: Invertebres (ISSN 0570-1619); Which superseded in part: Annales de Paleontologie (ISSN 0003-4142)

560 572   GW   ISSN 0066-4723
ANTHROPOS; studie z oboru anthropologie, paleoethnologie, paleontologie a kvarterni geologie. (Text in Czech and German) 1959 (N.S.). irreg., no.16, 1990. price varies. (Moravske Museum, Brno, CS) Dr. Rudolf Habelt GmbH, Am Buchenhang 1, 5300 Bonn 1, Germany. **Indexed:** CERDIC, Curr.Cont.Africa, E.I., Rel.Ind.One.

ARGENTINA. MUSEO PROVINCIAL DE CIENCIAS NATURALES. COMUNICACIONES. NUEVA SERIE. see *BIOLOGY*

560   AT   ISSN 0810-8889
ASSOCIATION OF AUSTRALASIAN PALEONTOLOGISTS. MEMOIRS. 1983. irreg. price varies. Geological Society of Australia, Association of Australasian Palaeontologists, 301 George St., Sydney, N.S.W. 2000, Australia. FAX 02-290-2198. Ed. P.A. Jell. (back issues avail.)
   —BLDSC shelfmark: 5577.283000.

560 551   GW   ISSN 0077-2070
QE701   CODEN: BSPGBT
BAYERISCHE STAATSSAMMLUNG FUER PALAEONTOLOGIE UND HISTORISCHE GEOLOGIE. MITTEILUNGEN. (Text and summaries in English and German) 1961. a. price varies. Bayerische Staatssammlung fuer Palaeontologie und Historische Geologie, Richard-Wagner-Strasse 10, 8000 Munich 2, Germany. TEL 089-5203361. FAX 089-5203286. Ed. Dietrich Herm. **Indexed:** Biol.Abstr.

560   AU
BEITRAEGE ZUR PALAEONTOLOGIE VON OESTERREICH. (Text and summaries in English, German) 1976. a. Institut fuer Palaeontologie, Universitaetsstr. 7-II, A-1010 Vienna, Austria. FAX 0222-4020533. Ed.Bd. circ. 200. (back issues avail.) **Indexed:** Biol.Abstr.

566   US   ISSN 0272-8869
Z6033.V45
BIBLIOGRAPHY OF FOSSIL VERTEBRATES. 1902. a. $135. Society of Vertebrate Paleontology, W. 436 Nebraska Hall, University of Nebraska, Lincoln, NE 68588-0542. TEL 402-472-4604. **Indexed:** GeoRef.

BOREAS; an international journal of quaternary research. see *EARTH SCIENCES — Geology*

BRIMLEYANA. see *BIOLOGY — Zoology*

BUDOWA GEOLOGICZNA POLSKI. see *EARTH SCIENCES — Geology*

BULLETIN SCIENTIFIQUE DE BOURGOGNE. see *SCIENCES: COMPREHENSIVE WORKS*

560   US   ISSN 0007-5779
CODEN: BAPLAJ
BULLETINS OF AMERICAN PALEONTOLOGY. 1895. 2/yr. $60. Paleontological Research Institution, 1259 Trumansburg Rd., Ithaca, NY 14850-1398. Ed. Dr. Peter R. Hoover. (reprint service avail. from KTO) **Indexed:** Biol.Abstr., GeoRef.
   —BLDSC shelfmark: 2827.750000.

560   FR   ISSN 0068-5054
QE719
CAHIERS DE MICROPALEONTOLOGIE. 1965. q. (Ecole Pratique des Hautes Etudes, Laboratoire de Micropaleontologie) Editions du C N R S, 1 Place Aristide Briand, 92195 Meudon Cedex, France. TEL 1-45-34-75-50. FAX 1-46-26-28-49. TELEX LABOBEL 204 135 F. (Subscr. to: Presse du C N R S, 20-22, rue Saint Amand, 75015 Paris, France. TEL 1-45-33-16-00) adv.; bk.rev.; index; circ. 1,500. **Indexed:** Br.Geol.Lit., Geo.Abstr., GeoRef.
   —BLDSC shelfmark: 2949.810000.

560 572   FR   ISSN 0293-1176
CAHIERS DE PALEOANTHROPOLOGIE. a. price varies. (Centre National de la Recherche Scientifique) Editions du C N R S, 1 Place Aristide Briand, 92195 Meudon Cedex, France. TEL 1-45-34-75-50. FAX 1-46-26-28-49. TELEX LABOBEL 204 135 F. (Subscr. to: Presses du C N R S, 20-22, rue Saint Amand, 75015 Paris, France. TEL 1-45-33-16-00) adv.; bk.rev.; index; circ. 1,250 (controlled).

560   FR   ISSN 0766-0502
CAHIERS DE PALEONTOLOGIE. a. price varies. (Centre National de Recherche Scientifique) Editions du C N R S, 1 Place Aristide Briand, 92195 Meudon Cedex, France. TEL 1-45-34-75-50. FAX 1-46-26-28-49. TELEX LABOBEL 204 135 F. (Subscr. to: Presses du C N R S, 20-22, rue Saint Amand, 75015 Paris, France. TEL 1-45-33-16-00) adv.; bk.rev.; index; circ. 1,500 (controlled).

560   FR   ISSN 0298-248X
CAHIERS DE PALEONTOLOGIE EST-AFRICAINE. a. price varies. (Centre National de la Recherche Scientifique) Editions du C N R S, 1 Place Aristide Briand, 92195 Meudon Cedex, France. TEL 1-45-34-75-50. FAX 1-46-26-28-49. TELEX LABOBEL 204 135 F. (Subscr. to: Presses du C N R S, 20-22, rue Saint Amand, 75015 Paris, France. TEL 1-45-33-16-00) adv.; bk.rev.; index; circ. 1,500 (controlled).

CARNEGIE MUSEUM OF NATURAL HISTORY. ANNALS OF CARNEGIE MUSEUM. see *SCIENCES: COMPREHENSIVE WORKS*

CARNEGIE MUSEUM OF NATURAL HISTORY. BULLETIN. see *SCIENCES: COMPREHENSIVE WORKS*

PALEONTOLOGY

CENTRAL TEXAS ARCHEOLOGIST. see *ARCHAEOLOGY*

CEPHALOPOD NEWSLETTER. see *BIOLOGY — Zoology*

CHRONOLOGY & CATASTROPHISM REVIEW. see *EARTH SCIENCES — Geology*

COLLANA DI STUDI PALEONTOLOGICI. see *ANTHROPOLOGY*

COLORADO SCHOOL OF MINES. PROFESSIONAL CONTRIBUTIONS. see *MINES AND MINING INDUSTRY*

CONTRIBUTIONS IN BIOLOGY AND GEOLOGY. see *BIOLOGY*

CURRENT RESEARCH IN THE PLEISTOCENE. see *ARCHAEOLOGY*

563   US   ISSN 0070-2242
CODEN: SPCFAO
CUSHMAN FOUNDATION FOR FORAMINIFERAL RESEARCH. SPECIAL PUBLICATION. 1952. irreg. price varies. Cushman Foundation for Foraminiferal Research, Rm. E-206, MRC NHB 121, National Museum of Natural History, Washington, DC 20560. TEL 202-357-2405. Ed. Stephen J. Culver. circ. 600. **Indexed:** Biol.Abstr., Deep Sea Res.& Oceanogr.Abstr., GeoRef.
—BLDSC shelfmark: 8378.000000.

560 591   US   ISSN 0886-3806
CYPRIS; international ostracoda newsletter. 1983. a. membership. International Research Group on Ostracoda, c/o Elisabeth M. Brouwers, Ed., U.S. Geological Survey, Federal Center, MS 919, Denver, CO 80225. bibl.; circ. 400.
Description: To improve international contacts between ostracode workers.

560 560.17   NE
DEVELOPMENTS IN PALAEONTOLOGY AND STRATIGRAPHY. 1975. irreg., vol.13, 1990. Elsevier Science Publishers B.V., Books Division, P.O. Box 211, 1000 AE Amsterdam, Netherlands. TEL 020-5803911. FAX 020-5803705. TELEX 18582 ESPA NL. (Subscr. in U.S. and Canada to: Elsevier Science Publishing Co., Inc., Box 882, Madison Sq. Sta., New York, NY 10159. TEL 212-989-5800) (back issues avail.)
Refereed Serial

DISTRICT MEMOIR. see *EARTH SCIENCES — Geology*

DORTMUNDER BEITRAEGE ZUR LANDESKUNDE. see *BIOLOGY*

EHIME DAIGAKU KYOIKUGAKUBU KIYO. DAI-3-BU. SHIZEN KAGAKU/EHIME UNIVERSITY. FACULTY OF EDUCATION. MEMOIRS. SERIES 3: NATURAL SCIENCES. see *EARTH SCIENCES — Geology*

560   GW   ISSN 0424-7116
QE696   CODEN: EZGWAB
EISZEITALTER UND GEGENWART. 1951. a. (Deutsche Quartaervereinigung) E. Schweizerbart'sche Verlagsbuchhandlung, Johannesstr. 3a, 7000 Stuttgart 1, Germany. TEL 0711-625001. FAX 0711-625005. TELEX 723363-SCHB-D. Ed. H.D. Lang. (reprint service avail. from SWZ) **Indexed:** Geo.Abstr.

560   GW   ISSN 0932-4739
QH274   CODEN: EJPREZ
EUROPEAN JOURNAL OF PROTISTOLOGY. (Text in English, French) 1965. q. DM.445. (Centre National de la Recherche Scientifique, FR) Gustav Fischer Verlag, Wollgrasweg 49, Postfach 720143, 7000 Stuttgart 70, Germany. TEL 0711-458030. FAX 0711-4580334. TELEX 7111488-FIBUCH. (U.S. subscr. to: V C H Publishers, Inc., 303 N.W. 12th Ave., Deerfield Beach, FL 33442-1705) Ed. A. Hollande. abstr.; bibl.; charts; illus.; circ. 450. **Indexed:** Abstr.Hyg., Biol.Abstr., Chem.Abstr., Curr.Adv.Ecol.Sci., Curr.Cont., Deep Sea Res.& Oceanogr.Abstr., Helminthol.Abstr., Ind.Vet., Protozool.Abstr., Soils & Fert., Trop.Dis.Bull., Vet.Bull.
—BLDSC shelfmark: 3829.737600.
Formerly: Protistologica (ISSN 0033-1821)

F A C E N A. (Facultad de Ciencias Exactas y Naturales y Agrimensura) see *BIOGRAPHY*

FACIES. see *EARTH SCIENCES*

560   PL   ISSN 0015-573X
QE696   CODEN: FOQUAN
FOLIA QUATERNARIA. (Text in English, German) 1960. irreg., no.58, 1988. price varies. (Polska Akademia Nauk, Oddzial w Krakowie) Ossolineum, Publishing House of the Polish Academy of Sciences, Rynek 9, Wroclaw, Poland. TELEX 0712771 OSS PL. Ed. Kazimierz Kowalski. **Indexed:** Biol.Abstr., Geo.Abstr., GeoRef., NAA.
—BLDSC shelfmark: 3973.700000.
Description: Paleography of the Quaternary, mainly of Poland. Papers concern geomorphology, stratigraphy, paleobotany and paleozoology, archaeology of Quaternary sediments.

560   GW   ISSN 0175-5021
FOSSILIEN; Zeitschrift fuer Sammler und Hobbypalaeontologen. 1984. bi-m. DM.86.40 (foreign DM.87.60). Goldschneck Verlag, Birkenweg 5, Postfach 1265, 7054 Korb 2, Germany. TEL 07151-660119. FAX 07151-660778. Ed. Werner Karl Weidert. adv.; bk.rev.; circ. 3,000. (back issues avail.)
Description: For collectors and amateur fossil hunters.

560   JA   ISSN 0022-9202
QE701   CODEN: KASKAS
FOSSILS/KASEKI. (Text in Japanese) 1960. s-a. 2300 Yen. Palaeontological Society of Japan - Nihon Koseibutsu Gakkai, c/o Business Center for Academic Societies, 2-4-16 Yayoi, Bunkyo-ku, Tokyo 113, Japan. Ed.Bd. adv.; bk.rev.; circ. 400. **Indexed:** GeoRef.

560   NO
FOSSILS AND STRATA; a monograph series in palaeontology and biostratigraphy. (Text in English) 1972. irreg. price varies. Universitetsforlaget, Box 2959-Toeyen, N-0608 Oslo 1, Norway. (U.S. address: Publication Expediting Inc., 200 Meacham Ave., Elmont, NY 11003) Ed. Stefan Bengtson. (back issues avail.) **Indexed:** Biol.Abstr., Br.Geol.Lit.

FREIBERGER FORSCHUNGSHEFTE. MONTANWISSENSCHAFTEN: REIHE C. GEOWISSENSCHAFTEN. see *EARTH SCIENCES*

FUNDGRUBE; populaerwissenschaftliche Zeitschrift fuer Geologie, Mineralogie, Palaeontologie und Spelaeologie. see *EARTH SCIENCES — Geology*

560.17   FR   ISSN 0016-6995
CODEN: GEBSAJ
GEOBIOS; paleontology, stratigraphy, paleoecology. (Text and summaries in English, French) 1968. bi-m. 800 F.($130) (Association de Paleontologie Prehistoire) Universite de Lyon I, Departement de Sciences de la Terre, 43 bd. du 11 Novembre, 69622 Villeurbanne, France. TEL 72-44-84-16. Ed. A. Schaaf. adv.; bk.rev.; index; circ. 850. **Indexed:** Biol.Abstr., Bull.Signal., Curr.Cont., Geo.Abstr., Helminthol.Abstr., SSCI.
—BLDSC shelfmark: 4116.902000.

GEOLOGICA ET PALAEONTOLOGICA. see *EARTH SCIENCES — Geology*

GEOLOGISCHE ABHANDLUNGEN HESSEN. see *EARTH SCIENCES — Geology*

GEOLOGISCHE BUNDESANSTALT, VIENNA. JAHRBUCH. see *EARTH SCIENCES — Geology*

GEOLOGISCHES JAHRBUCH. REIHE A: ALLGEMEINE UND REGIONALE GEOLOGIE B.R. DEUTSCHLAND UND NACHBARGEBIETE, TEKTONIK, STRATIGRAPHIE, PALAEONTOLOGIE. see *EARTH SCIENCES — Geology*

GEOLOGISCHES JAHRBUCH HESSEN. see *EARTH SCIENCES — Geology*

GEOLOGISCHES LANDESAMT BADEN-WUERTTEMBERG. JAHRESHEFTE. see *EARTH SCIENCES*

GEOLOGISCHES LANDESAMT BADEN-WUETTEMBERG. ABHANDLUNGEN. see *EARTH SCIENCES*

561.05   II   ISSN 0376-5156
QE901   CODEN: GPHTAR
GEOPHYTOLOGY; a journal of palaeobotany and allied sciences. (Text in English) 1971. s-a. Rs.300($45) Palaeobotanical Society, 53 University Rd., Lucknow 7, India. Ed.Bd. bk.rev.; illus.; circ. 240. **Indexed:** AESIS, Biol.Abstr., Soils & Fert.

GESELLSCHAFT DER GEOLOGIE- UND BERGBAUSTUDENTEN. MITTEILUNGEN. see *EARTH SCIENCES — Geology*

566   CC   ISSN 1000-3118
GUJIZHUI DONGWU XUEBAO/VERTEBRATA PALASIATICA. (Text in Chinese; summaries in English) 1959. q. Y14.80($10) per no. (Zhongguo Kexueyuan, Gujizhui Dongwu yu Gurenlei Yanjiusuo - Academia Sinica, Institute of Vertebrata Palasiatica) Science Press, Marketing and Sales Department, 16 Donghuangchenggen Beijie, Beijing 100707, People's Republic of China. TEL 4010642. FAX 4012180. TELEX 210247-SPBJ-CN. adv.; circ. 10,000.
—BLDSC shelfmark: 9216.500000.
Description: Publishes research papers and brief notes on vertebrate paleontology, especially on vertebrates found in Asia.
Refereed Serial

560   CC   ISSN 1001-4306
GUSHENGWU XUE WENZHAI. (Text in Chinese) q. Zhongguo Kexueyuan, Nanjing Dizhi Gushengwu-suo, 39 Beijing Donglu, Nanjing, Jiangsu 210008, People's Republic of China. TEL 637537. Ed. Zhang Wentang.

560   CC   ISSN 0001-6616
QE701   CODEN: KSWHAT
GUSHENGWU XUEBAO/ACTA PALAEONTOLOGICA SINICA. (Text in Chinese; summaries in English) 1950. bi-m. Y14($10) per no. (Zhongguo Kexueyuan, Nanjing Dizhi Gushengwu-suo) Science Press, Marketing and Sales Department, 16 Donghuangchenggen Beijie, Beijing 100707, People's Republic of China. TEL 4010642. FAX 4012180. TELEX 210247-SPBJ-CN. adv.; bk.rev.; circ. 7,000. **Indexed:** Biol.Abstr., Curr.Adv.Ecol.Sci., GeoRef.
—BLDSC shelfmark: 0643.000000.
Description: Contains theses on paleontology, academic discussions, and comments. Introduces new methodology and techniques.
Refereed Serial

574 572   US   ISSN 0891-2963
QE701   CODEN: HIBIEW
▼**HISTORICAL BIOLOGY;** an international journal of paleobiology. 1991. 4/yr. $67. Harwood Academic Publishers, 270 Eighth Ave., New York, NY 10011. TEL 212-206-8900. FAX 212-645-2459. TELEX 236735 GOPUB UR. (Subscr. to: Box 786, Cooper Sta., New York, NY 10011. TEL 800-545-8398; UK subscr. to: P.O. Box 90, Reading, Berkshire RG1 8JL, England. TEL 0734-560-080) Ed. E. Buffetaut. (also avail. in microform)
—BLDSC shelfmark: 4316.155000.
Refereed Serial

560 551   JA   ISSN 0912-7798
HOBETSU-CHORITSU HAKUBUTSUKAN KENKYU HOKOKU/HOBETSU MUSEUM. BULLETIN. (Text in Japanese; summaries in English) 1984. a. free to institutions. Hobetsu Museum - Hobetsu-choritsu Hakubutsukan, 80-6 Hobetsu, Hobetsu-cho, Yufutsu-gun, Hokkaido 054-02, Japan.
Description: Contains mainly paleontological and geological studies of the Hobetsu area of Hokkaido. Includes studies on late Cretaceous-Neogene vertebrate and invertebrate fossils.

560   CC   ISSN 1000-3185
HUASHI/FOSSILS. (Text in Chinese) 1973. q. Y4. (Zhongguo Kexueyuan, Gujizhui Dongwu yu Gurenlei Yanjiusuo - Academia Sinica, Institute of Vertebrate Palasiatica) Science Press, Marketing and Sales Department, 16 Donghuangchenggen Beijie, Beijing 100707, People's Republic of China. TEL 4010642. FAX 4012180. TELEX 210247-SPBJ-CN. adv.; circ. 100,000.
—BLDSC shelfmark: 4024.365000.
Description: For popular reading. Covers the evolution of living things from a paleontological point of view: evolution of plants, invertebrates, vertebrates, and mankind. Also reports on activities, museums, primitive clan customs, and interesting tidbits.

PALEONTOLOGY

560 US ISSN 0096-1191
QL368.F6 CODEN: JFARAH
JOURNAL OF FORAMINIFERAL RESEARCH. 1971. q. $80 (effective Jan. 1991). Cushman Foundation for Foraminiferal Research, Rm. E-206, MRC NHB 121, National Museum of Natural History, Washington, DC 20560. TEL 202-357-2405. Ed. Paul Loubere. adv.; bk.rev.; charts; illus.; index; circ. 800. (back issues avail.) **Indexed:** AESIS, Biol.Abstr., Br.Geol.Lit., Deep Sea Res.& Oceanogr.Abstr., Geo.Abstr., GeoRef., Ind.Sci.Rev., Petrol.Abstr., Sci.Cit.Ind.
—BLDSC shelfmark: 4984.575000.
Supersedes: Cushman Foundation for Foraminiferal Research. Contributions (ISSN 0011-409X)
Refereed Serial

561.1 574 NE ISSN 0921-2728
CODEN: JOUPE8
JOURNAL OF PALEOLIMNOLOGY. bi-m. fl.504($287) Kluwer Academic Publishers, Postbus 17, 3300 AA Dordrecht, Netherlands. TEL 078-334911. FAX 078-334254. TELEX 29245. (Dist. by: Kluwer Academic Publishers Group, P.O. Box 322, 3300 AH Dordrecht, Netherlands; N. America dist. addr.: Box 358, Accord Station, Hingham, MA 02018-0358. TEL 617-871-6600) Ed. J.P. Smol. (reprint service avail. from SWZ)
—BLDSC shelfmark: 5027.995500.

560 US ISSN 0022-3360
QE701 CODEN: JPALAZ
JOURNAL OF PALEONTOLOGY. 1927. bi-m. $99 to non-members. Paleontological Society, Business Office, 1261 Trumansburg Rd., Ithaca, NY 14850-1313. TEL 607-273-6623. Ed.Bd. adv.; bk.rev.; bibl.; charts; illus.; index, cum.index; circ. 3,500. (also avail. in microform from UMI; back issues avail.) **Indexed:** AESIS, Biol.Abstr., Br.Geol.Lit., Curr.Adv.Ecol.Sci., Curr.Cont., Deep Sea Res.& Oceanogr.Abstr., Geo.Abstr., GeoRef., Ind.Sci.Rev., Petrol.Abstr., Sci.Cit.Ind.
—BLDSC shelfmark: 5028.000000.
Description: Publishes contributions in all fields of paleontology, including invertebrate and vertebrate paleontology, micropaleontology, and paleobotany, emphasizing taxonomic, biostratigraphic, paleoecological, paleoclimatological or paleobiogeographic aspects.
Refereed Serial

560 US ISSN 0272-4634
QE841 CODEN: JVPADK
JOURNAL OF VERTEBRATE PALEONTOLOGY. 1981. q. $85. Society of Vertebrate Paleontology, W. 436 Nebraska Hall, University of Nebraska, Lincoln, NE 68588-0542. TEL 402-472-4604. adv. (back issues avail.)
—BLDSC shelfmark: 5072.320000.
Refereed Serial

KYUSHU UNIVERSITY. DEPARTMENT OF EARTH AND PLANETARY SCIENCES. SCIENCE REPORTS/KYUSHU DAIGAKU RIGAKUBU KENKYU HOKOKU CHIKYU-WAKUSEI-KAGAKU. see *EARTH SCIENCES — Geology*

560 622 551 AU
LANDESMUSEUM JOANNEUM. ABTEILUNG FUER GEOLOGIE UND PALAEONTOLOGIE. MITTEILUNGEN. 1937. irreg. (approx. 1/yr.). price varies. Landesmuseum Joanneum, Abteilung fuer Geologie und Palaeontologie, Raubergasse 10, A-8010 Graz, Austria. illus.
Former titles: Landesmuseum Joanneum. Abteilung fuer Geologie, Palaeontologie und Bergbau. Mitteilungen; (until 1972): Joanneum. Museum fuer Bergbau, Geologie und Technik. Mitteilungen.

560.17 NO ISSN 0024-1164
QE701 CODEN: LETHAT
LETHAIA; official journal of the International Palaeontological Association, specializing in palaeobiology and ecostratigraphy. (Text in English) 1968. q. $60 to members; institutions $125. (International Palaeontological Association) Universitetsforlaget, P.O. Box 2959-Toeyen, N-0608 Oslo 1, Norway. (U.S. addr.: Publications Expediting Inc., 200 Meacham Ave., Elmont, NY 11003) Ed. Lars Ramskoeld. illus.; circ. 1,300. (also avail. in microform from UMI; back issues avail.; reprint series avail. from ISI) **Indexed:** Abstr.Anthropol., AESIS, Biol.Abstr., Br.Geol.Lit., Curr.Adv.Ecol.Sci., Curr.Cont., Curr.Tit.Ocean., Deep Sea Res.& Oceanogr.Abstr., GeoRef., Ind.Sci.Rev., Petrol.Abstr.
—BLDSC shelfmark: 5184.950000.

MAINZER GEOWISSENSCHAFTLICHE MITTEILUNGEN. see *EARTH SCIENCES — Geology*

MAN & ENVIRONMENT. see *ANTHROPOLOGY*

560 NE ISSN 0377-8398
QE719 CODEN: MAMIDH
MARINE MICROPALEONTOLOGY. 1976. 8/yr.(in 2 vols.; 4 nos./vol.). fl.692 (effective 1992). Elsevier Science Publishers B.V., P.O. Box 211, 1000 AE Amsterdam, Netherlands. TEL 020-5803911. FAX 020-5803598. TELEX 18582 ESPA NL. (Subscr. in U.S. and Canada to: Elsevier Science Publishing Co., Inc., Box 882, Madison Sq. Sta., New York, NY 10159. TEL 212-989-5800) Eds. J. Lipps, H. Thierstein. (also avail. in microform from RPI; reprint service avail. from SWZ) **Indexed:** AESIS, Biol.Abstr., Curr.Cont., Deep Sea Res.& Oceanogr.Abstr., Geo.Abstr., GeoRef., Ind.Sci.Rev., Mar.Sci.Cont.Tab., Petrol.Abstr., So.Pac.Per.Ind.
—BLDSC shelfmark: 5376.400000.
Description: Publishes results of research in all fields of marine micropalaentology of the ocean basins and continents, including paleoceanography, evolution, ecology and paleoecology, biology and paleobiology, biochronology, paleoclimatology, taphonomy, and the systematic relationships of higher taxa.
Refereed Serial

560 US
MICHIGAN STATE UNIVERSITY. MUSEUM PUBLICATIONS. PALEONTOLOGICAL SERIES. 1972. irreg. price varies. Michigan State University, Museum, East Lansing, MI 48824. TEL 517-335-2370. Ed.Bd. bibl.; charts; illus.; circ. 1,500.

563 US ISSN 0026-2803
QE701 CODEN: MCPLAI
MICROPALEONTOLOGY. 1954. q. $60 to individuals; institutions $120. American Museum of Natural History, Central Park W. at 79th St., New York, NY 10024-5192. TEL 212-769-5656. FAX 212-769-5233. Ed. Dr. John A. Van Couvering. bk.rev.; charts; illus.; circ. 1,000. (also avail. in microform from MIM,UMI; microfilm; back issues avail.; reprint service avail. from UMI) **Indexed:** AESIS, Biol.Abstr., Chem.Abstr., Deep Sea Res.& Oceanogr.Abstr., Geo.Abstr., GeoRef., Ocean.Abstr., Petrol.Abstr., Pollut.Abstr.
—BLDSC shelfmark: 5759.500000.
Description: Contains international research on stratigraphy, systematics, morphology, paleobiology and paleoecology of all microorganisms with fossilized hard parts.
Refereed Serial

563 US ISSN 0160-2071
CODEN: MSPUDO
MICROPALEONTOLOGY SPECIAL PAPERS. 1970. irreg., no.4, 1983. American Museum of Natural History, Central Park W. at 79th St., New York, NY 10024-5192. TEL 212-769-5656. FAX 212-769-5233. Ed. John A. Van Couvering. charts; illus.; maps; circ. 625. (reprint service avail. from UMI) **Indexed:** Deep Sea Res.& Oceanogr.Abstr., GeoRef.
Description: Monographs on micropaleontology, including biostratigraphy, paleo-ecology, and systematics in all microfossil groups.

560 622 FR ISSN 0335-6566
MINERAUX ET FOSSILES. 1974. m. 250 F. S E P S, 12 rue Poincare, 558700 Revigny, France. adv.; bk.rev.

MISSISSIPPI GEOLOGY. see *EARTH SCIENCES — Geology*

560 NE ISSN 0168-6151
QE696
MODERN QUATERNARY RESEARCH IN SOUTHEAST ASIA. 1975. a. fl.85($45) A.A. Balkema, P.O. Box 1675, 3000 BR Rotterdam, Netherlands. TEL 10-4145822. FAX 10-4135947. (And: Old Post Road, Brookfield, VT 05036, USA) Eds. G.-J. Bartstra, W.A. Casparie. **Indexed:** GeoRef.

560 US ISSN 0736-3907
QE701.M68
MOSASAUR. 1983. irreg. price varies. Delaware Valley Paleontological Society, c/o Stephen J.G. Farrington, Bus. Mgr., Box 42078, Philadelphia, PA 19101-2078. Ed. William B. Gallagher. circ. 500.
—BLDSC shelfmark: 5967.483650.

560 551 GW ISSN 0177-0950
QE1
MUENCHNER GEOWISSENSCHAFTLICHE ABHANDLUNGEN. REIHE A: GEOLOGIE UND PALAEONTOLOGIE. (Text in English, French, German) 1984. irreg. price varies. Verlag Dr. Friedrich Pfeil, P.O. Box 65 00 86, 8000 Munich 65, Germany. TEL 089-8888-196. Ed. Friedrich H. Pfeil. circ. 500.
Description: Covers geology and paleontology.

560 AG ISSN 0524-9511
QE752.A7
MUSEO ARGENTINO DE CIENCIAS NATURALES "BERNARDINO RIVADAVIA." INSTITUTO NACIONAL DE INVESTIGACION DE LAS CIENCIAS NATURALES. REVISTA. PALEONTOLOGIA. 1964. irreg. Museo Argentino de Ciencias Naturales "Bernardino Rivadavia", Instituto Nacional de Investigacion de las Ciencias Naturales, Avda. Angel Gallardo 470, Casilla de Correo 220-Sucursal 5, Buenos Aires, Argentina. **Indexed:** GeoRef.

560 UY
MUSEO NACIONAL DE HISTORIA NATURAL. COMUNICACIONES PALEONTOLOGICAS. (Summaries in English, Spanish) 1970. irreg. exchange basis. Museo Nacional de Historia Natural, Casilla de Correos 399, 11 000 Montevideo, Uruguay. illus.; circ. 1,200.

560 551.6 US
▼**NATIONAL OCEANIC AND ATMOSPHERIC ADMINISTRATION. NATIONAL GEOPHYSICAL DATA CENTER. PALEOCLIMATE PUBLICATIONS SERIES.** 1991. irreg. exchange basis. National Oceanic and Atmospheric Administration, National Geophysical Data Center, 325 Broadway, Boulder, CO 80303-3328. TEL 303-497-6280. FAX 303-497-6513. TELEX 592811 NOAA MASC BDR. stat.
Description: Publishes research results in fields relevant to paleoclimatology.

NATURAL HISTORY CONTRIBUTIONS. see *BIOLOGY*

NATURHISTORISCHES MUSEUM BASEL. VEROEFFENTLICHUNGEN. see *SCIENCES: COMPREHENSIVE WORKS*

NATURWISSENSCHAFTLICHER VEREIN FUER SCHWABEN. BERICHTE. see *BIOLOGY*

NATUURHISTORISCH GENOOTSCHAP IN LIMBURG. PUBLICATIES. see *BIOLOGY*

NEUES JAHRBUCH FUER GEOLOGIE UND PALAEONTOLOGIE. ABHANDLUNGEN. see *EARTH SCIENCES — Geology*

NEUES JAHRBUCH FUER GEOLOGIE UND PALAEONTOLOGIE, MONATSHEFTE. see *EARTH SCIENCES — Geology*

560 AT
NEW SOUTH WALES. GEOLOGICAL SURVEY. MEMOIRS: PALEONTOLOGY. 1888. irreg., no.19, 1982. price varies. Department of Mineral Resources, P.O. Box 536, St Leonards, N.S.W. 2065, Australia. TEL 02 240 4259. Ed. H. Basden. circ. 400. **Indexed:** GeoRef.
Formerly: New South Wales. Department of Mines. Memoirs: Palaeontology (ISSN 0077-8699)

560 NZ ISSN 0114-2283
NEW ZEALAND GEOLOGICAL SURVEY. PALEONTOLOGICAL BULLETIN. Short title: Paleontological Bulletins. 1913. irreg., no.63, 1990. price varies. (Geological Survey) D S I R Geology & Geophysics, P.O. Box 30368, Lower Hutt, New Zealand. TEL 04-4699-059. FAX 04-4695-016. Ed. J.G. Gregory. circ. 500. (back issues avail.) **Indexed:** Biol.Abstr., Geo.Abstr., GeoRef., Petrol.Abstr.
—BLDSC shelfmark: 6345.322000.
Formerly: New Zealand. Department of Scientific and Industrial Research. Paleontological Bulletin (ISSN 0078-8589)
Description: Monographs about New Zealand fossils and stratigraphy.

560 AT ISSN 0159-818X
NOMEN NUDUM. a. Geological Society of Australia, Association of Australasian Palaeontologists, 301 George St., Sydney, N.S.W. 2000, Australia. FAX 02-290-2198. Ed. J.R. Laurie. **Indexed:** AESIS.

OESTERREICHISCHE GEOLOGISCHE GESELLSCHAFT. MITTEILUNGEN. see *EARTH SCIENCES — Geology*

560   PK   ISSN 0078-8155
PAKISTAN. GEOLOGICAL SURVEY. MEMOIRS; PALEONTOLOGIA PAKISTANICA. (Text in English) 1956. irreg. price varies. Geological Survey of Pakistan, c/o Chief Librarian, Box 15, Quetta, Pakistan. TEL 73055. circ. 1,500. **Indexed:** GeoRef.

566   GW   ISSN 0724-6331
                     CODEN: PICHEK
PALAEO ICHTHYOLOGICA. (Text in English, French, German) 1983. irreg. price varies. Verlag Dr. Friedrich H. Pfeil, P.O. Box 65 00 86, 8000 Munich 65, Germany. TEL 089-8888196. Ed. Friedrich H. Pfeil. abstr.; bibl.; charts; illus.; circ. 500. (back issues avail.)
   Description: Neontological and paleontological works on systematics, ecology, and stratigraphy of fishes.

560 550   NE   ISSN 0031-0182
QE500   CODEN: PPPYAB
PALAEOGEOGRAPHY, PALAEOCLIMATOLOGY, PALAEOECOLOGY; an international journal for the geo-sciences. (Includes supplement: Global and Planetary Change (ISSN 0921-8181)) (Text in English, French and German) 1965. 32/yr.(in 8 vols.; 4 nos./vol.) fl.3008 (effective 1992). Elsevier Science Publishers B.V., P.O. Box 211, 1000 AE Amsterdam, Netherlands. TEL 020-5803911. FAX 020-5803598. TELEX 18582 ESPA NL. (Subscr. in U.S. and Canada to: Elsevier Science Publishing Co., Inc., Box 882, Madison Sq. Sta., New York, NY 10159. TEL 212-989-5800) Eds. F. Surlyk, E.J. Barron. adv.; bk.rev.; abstr.; bibl.; charts; illus.; index. (also avail. in microform from RPI; reprint service avail. from ISI,SWZ) **Indexed:** AESIS, Biol.Abstr., Br.Archaeol.Abstr., Br.Geol.Lit., Bull.Signal., Chem.Abstr., Curr.Adv.Ecol.Sci., Curr.Cont., Deep Sea Res.& Oceanogr.Abstr., Environ.Abstr., Geo.Abstr., GeoRef., Ocean Abstr., Petrol.Abstr., Pollut.Abstr.
   —BLDSC shelfmark: 6343.450000.
   Description: Publishes original studies and comprehensive reviews in the field of palaeo-environmental geology.
   Refereed Serial

551   GW   ISSN 0375-0442
                     CODEN: PGABA8
PALAEONTOGRAPHICA. ABT. A: PALAEOZOOLOGIE - STRATIGRAPHIE. (Text in English and German; summaries in English, French, German) 1846. 8/yr. (in 4 vols.). price varies. E. Schweizerbart'sche Verlagsbuchhandlung, Johannesstr. 3A, 7000 Stuttgart 1, Germany. TEL 0711-625001. FAX 0711-625005. TELEX 723363-SCHB-D. Ed. W. Haas. illus. **Indexed:** Biol.Abstr., Br.Geol.Lit., GeoRef.
   —BLDSC shelfmark: 6343.603000.

560   GW   ISSN 0375-0299
                     CODEN: PABPAD
PALAEONTOGRAPHICA. ABT. B: PALAEOPHYTOLOGIE. (Text in English, French and German) 1846. 10/yr. (in 5 vols.). E. Schweizerbart'sche Verlagsbuchhandlung, Johannesstr. 3A, 7000 Stuttgart 1, Germany. TEL 0711-625001. FAX 0711-625005. TELEX 723363-SCHB-D. Ed. H.J. Schweitzer. bibl.; charts; illus.; index. **Indexed:** AESIS, Biol.Abstr., Br.Geol.Lit., Curr.Adv.Ecol.Sci., GeoRef.
   —BLDSC shelfmark: 6343.605000.

560   GW   ISSN 0085-4611
                     CODEN: PLTGAH
PALAEONTOGRAPHICA. SUPPLEMENTBAENDE. irreg. price varies. E. Schweizerbart'sche Verlagsbuchhandlung, Johannesstr. 3A, 7000 Stuttgart 1, Germany. TEL 0711-625001. FAX 0711-625005. TELEX 723363-SCHB-D. **Indexed:** GeoRef.

560   US   ISSN 0078-8546
QE701   CODEN: PALAAI
PALAEONTOGRAPHICA AMERICANA. 1916. irreg., no.54, 1984. price varies. Paleontological Research Institution, 1259 Trumansburg Road, Ithaca, NY 14850. TEL 607-273-6623. Ed. Dr. Peter R. Hoover. bibl.; charts; illus.; stat.; circ. 250. (back issues avail.) **Indexed:** Biol.Abstr., GeoRef.
   —BLDSC shelfmark: 6343.610000.
   Refereed Serial

560   IT
PALAEONTOGRAPHICA ITALICA. vol.78, 1991. a. L.100000 (foreign L.110000)(effective 1992). Pacini Editore s.r.l., Via Gherardesca 1, 56014 Ospedaletto (Pisa), Italy. TEL 050-982439. FAX 050-983906. Ed. M. Tongiorgi.

PALAEONTOGRAPHICAL SOCIETY. MONOGRAPHS (LONDON). see *EARTH SCIENCES — Geology*

560   SA   ISSN 0078-8554
QE757.A1   CODEN: PBPRAS
PALAEONTOLOGIA AFRICANA. (Text in English) 1953. irreg., vol.26, 1985-87. price varies. University of the Witwatersrand, Johannesburg, Bernard Price Institute for Palaeontological Research, Wits 2050, South Africa. TEL 011-716-2727. FAX 27-11-403-1926. Ed.Bd. bk.rev.; cum.index: vols.1-20 (1953-1977); circ. 600. (back issues avail.) **Indexed:** Biol.Abstr., Bull.Signal., Geo.Abstr., GeoRef., Ind.S.A.Per.

560   CC
PALAEONTOLOGIA CATHAYANA/HUAXIA GUSHENGWU. (Text in English) 1983. irreg., no.4, 1989. price varies. Kexue Chubanshe, Qikan Bu, 16 Donghuangchenggen Beijie, Beijing 100707, People's Republic of China. TEL 4010642. FAX 4012180. TELEX 210247-SPBJ-CN. (US office: Science Press New York, Ltd., 63-117 Alderton St., Rego Park, NY 11374. TEL 718-459-4638) Ed. Lu Yan-hao. illus.
   Description: Publishes papers on all aspects of paleontology, stratigraphy, and paleobiogeography. Includes review articles, short papers of description or discussion of important flora and fauna, news of current research, and occasional translations.
   Refereed Serial

560   CI   ISSN 0552-9352
                     CODEN: PLJUA9
PALAEONTOLOGIA JUGOSLAVICA. (Text and summaries in Croatian, English, French and German) 1958. a. $20. Jugoslavenska Akademija Znanosti i Umjetnosti, Brace Kavurica 1, 41000 Zagreb, Croatia. TEL 041 449-867. circ. 800. (back issues avail.) **Indexed:** Biol.Abstr., GeoRef., Zent.Math.

560   PL   ISSN 0078-8562
                     CODEN: PLPOAL
PALAEONTOLOGIA POLONICA. (Text in English or French; summaries in Polish) 1929. irreg., no.50, 1991. price varies. (Polska Akademia Nauk, Zaklad Paleobiologii) Panstwowe Wydawnictwo Naukowe, Miodowa 10, 00-251 Warsaw, Poland. (Dist. by: Ars Polona, Krakowskie Przedmiescie 7, 00-068 Warsaw, Poland) Ed. Zofia Kielan-Jaworowska. charts; illus.; circ. 560. **Indexed:** Biol.Abstr., GeoRef.

560   JA   ISSN 0031-0204
QE756.J29   CODEN: TPPJAA
PALAEONTOLOGICAL SOCIETY OF JAPAN. TRANSACTIONS AND PROCEEDINGS. (Text in English; summaries in Japanese) 1935. q. $75. (Palaeontological Society of Japan) Japan Scientific Societies Press, 6-2-10 Hongo, Bunkyo-ku, Tokyo 113, Japan. TEL 3814-2001. FAX 3814-2002. TELEX 2722268 BCJSP J. (Dist. by: Business Center for Academic Societies Japan, Koshin Bldg., 6-16-3 Hongo, Bunkyo-ku, Tokyo 113, Japan; Dist. in U.S. by: International Specialized Book Services, Inc., 5602 N.E. Hassalo St., Portland, OR 97213; in Asia by: Toppan Company Pvt. Ltd., 38 Liu Fang Rd., Box 22 Jurong Town, Jurong, Singapore 2262) bibl.; charts; illus.; index; circ. 550. **Indexed:** Biol.Abstr., GeoRef., Petrol.Abstr.

560   GW   ISSN 0031-0220
                     CODEN: PAZEAW
PALAEONTOLOGISCHE ZEITSCHRIFT. (Text in English and German; summaries in English and French) 1914. s-a. price varies. (Palaeontologische Gesellschaft e.V.) E. Schweizerbart'sche Verlagsbuchhandlung, Johannesstr. 3A, 7000 Stuttgart 1, Germany. TEL 0711-625001. FAX 0711-625005. TELEX 723363-SCHB-D. Ed. W.E. Reif. adv.; bibl.; charts; illus. (back issues avail.) **Indexed:** Biol.Abstr., Br.Geol.Lit., Curr.Adv.Ecol.Sci., Deep Sea Res.& Oceanogr.Abstr., GeoRef.
   —BLDSC shelfmark: 6345.250000.

560   UK   ISSN 0031-0239
                     CODEN: PONTAD
PALAEONTOLOGY. (Supplement avail.: Special Papers in Palaeontology) 1957. q. £28 to individuals; institutions £60. (Palaeontological Association) Cambridge University Press, The Edinburgh Bldg., Shaftesbury Rd., Cambridge CB2 2RU, England. (Subscr. to: c/o Dr. H.A. Armstrong, Department of Geology, University of Newcastle, Newcastle upon Tyne NE1 7RV, England) Ed.Bd. circ. 2,000. **Indexed:** AESIS, Curr.Adv.Ecol.Sci., Deep Sea Res.& Oceanogr.Abstr.
   —BLDSC shelfmark: 6345.200000.

560   FR   ISSN 0031-0247
QE841   CODEN: PLVTAW
PALAEOVERTEBRATA. (Text and summaries in English, French, German, Spanish) 1967. q. 450 F. (foreign 500 F.($100)). U S T L, Laboratoire de Paleontologie, Place E. Bataillon, F-34095 Montpellier Cedex 5, France. TEL 67-14-38-90. FAX 67-04-20-32. Dir. Henri Cappetta. bk.rev.; bibl.; charts; illus.; stat.; tr.lit.; circ. 200. (tabloid format) **Indexed:** Bull.Signal., GeoRef.
   —BLDSC shelfmark: 6345.210000.

560   US   ISSN 0883-1351
                     CODEN: PALAEM
PALAIOS. 1986. bi-m. $95. S E P M, Box 4756, Tulsa, OK 74159-0756. TEL 918-743-9765. Ed. David J. Bottjer. bk.rev.; circ. 1,300. (back issues avail.) **Indexed:** AESIS, Curr.Adv.Ecol.Sci., Deep Sea Res.& Oceanogr.Abstr.
   —BLDSC shelfmark: 6345.214500.
   Description: Contains comprehensive articles, short papers, invited editorials, and essays devoted to the applications of paleontology in solving geologic problems.

560   US   ISSN 0094-8373
QE701   CODEN: PALBBM
PALEOBIOLOGY. 1975. q. $65 (effective 1992). Paleontological Society, Business Office, 1261 Trumansburg Rd., Ithaca, NY 14850-1313. TEL 607-273-6623. Eds. R. Cowen, P. Signor. adv.; bk.rev.; abstr.; bibl.; charts; illus.; pat.; stat.; index; circ. 2,400. (also avail. in microform from UMI; back issues avail.; reprint service avail. from UMI) **Indexed:** Biol.Abstr., Br.Archaeol.Abstr., Curr.Adv.Ecol.Sci., Curr.Cont., Deep Sea Res.& Oceanogr.Abstr., GeoRef., Petrol.Abstr., Sci.Cit.Ind., So.Pac.Per.Ind.
   —BLDSC shelfmark: 6345.280000.
   Refereed Serial

560 551   US   ISSN 0031-0298
QE701   CODEN: PLBIA
PALEOBIOS. 1967. irreg. $8. University of California, Berkeley, Museum of Paleontology, Berkeley, CA 94720. TEL 510-642-1821. Ed. Robert G. Dundas. bibl.; charts; illus.; circ. 800. (back issues avail.) **Indexed:** Biol.Abstr., Deep Sea Res.& Oceanogr.Abstr., GeoRef.

560 551.6   US
▼**PALEOCLIMATE DATA RECORD.** 1990. irreg., 2-3/yr. free. National Oceanic and Atmospheric Administration, National Geophysical Data Center, 325 Broadway, Boulder, CO 80303-3328. TEL 303-498-6280. FAX 303-497-6513. TELEX 592811 NOAA MASC BDR. Ed. Bruce Bauer.
   Description: Presents news of paleoclimatology projects supported by the NOAA and the National Geophysical Data Center, and lists new data and research materials available.

560   NE   ISSN 0168-6208
QE993   CODEN: PLEABR
PALEOECOLOGY OF AFRICA. 1966. a. fl.140($75) A.A. Balkema, P.O. Box 1675, 3000 BR Rotterdam, Netherlands. TEL 10-4145822. FAX 10-4135947. (And: Old Post Road, Brookfield, VT 05036, USA) Ed. K. Heine. **Indexed:** GeoRef.
   —BLDSC shelfmark: 6343.428000.
   Former titles: Paleoecology of Africa and the Surrounding Islands; Paleoecology of Africa and the Surrounding Islands and Antarctica (ISSN 0078-8538)

PALEONTOLOGY

560 US ISSN 0031-0301
QE701 CODEN: PJOUA
PALEONTOLOGICAL JOURNAL. English translation of: Paleontologicheskii Zhurnal (UR ISSN 0031-031X) 1967. q. $395 (foreign $439). (Akademii Nauk S.S.S.R., UR) Scripta Technica, Inc. (Subsidiary of: John Wiley & Sons, Inc.), 7961 Eastern Ave., Silver Spring, MD 20910. TEL 301-588-0484.
FAX 301-588-5278. (Dist. by: John Wiley & Sons, Inc., Periodicals Division, 650 Third Ave., New York, NY 10158. TEL 212-692-6000) (Co-sponsor: American Geological Institute) Ed. Matthew Nitecki. adv.; circ. 425. (also avail. in microform from UMI; reprint service avail. from KTO) **Indexed:** GeoRef.
—BLDSC shelfmark: 0416.675000.
 Description: Deals with the anatomy, morphology and taxonomy of extinct animals and plants.
 Refereed Serial

560 US ISSN 0078-8597
 CODEN: PSMECR
PALEONTOLOGICAL SOCIETY. MEMOIR. 1968. irreg. $8 per no. Paleontological Society, Box 115, Jacksonville, NY 14854. TEL 607-273-6623. Ed. Richard D. Hoare. circ. 3,200. **Indexed:** Biol.Abstr., Deep Sea Res.& Oceanogr.Abstr., GeoRef.

560 RU ISSN 0031-031X
QE701 CODEN: PAZHA7
PALEONTOLOGICHESKII ZHURNAL. English translation: Paleontological Journal (US ISSN 0031-0301) 1959. q. 27 Rub. (Akademiya Nauk S.S.S.R., Institut Paleontologii) Izdatel'stvo Nauka, 90 Profsoyuznaya ul., 117864 Moscow, Russia. (Dist. by: Mezhdunarodnaya Kniga, ul. Dimitrova D.39, 113095 Moscow, Russia) Ed. L.P. Tatarinov. index; circ. 1,200. (tabloid format) **Indexed:** ASCA, Biol.Abstr., Deep Sea Res.& Oceanogr.Abstr., GeoRef.
—BLDSC shelfmark: 0128.940000.
 Incorporates: Akademiya Nauk S.S.S.R. Institut Paleontologii. Trudy.

560 BU
PALEONTOLOGIIA, STRATIGRAFIIA I LITOLOGIIA. (Text in various languages; summaries in Bulgarian, English, French, German) 1975. irreg. price varies. (Bulgarska Akademiia na Naukite, Geologicheski Institut) Publishing House of the Bulgarian Academy of Sciences, Acad. G. Bonchev St., Bldg. 6, 1113 Sofia, Bulgaria. Ed. C. Spasov. illus.; circ. 470. **Indexed:** Biol.Abstr., BSL Geo., GeoRef.
 Supersedes in part: Bulgarska Akademiia na Naukite. Geologicheski Institut. Izvestiia.

560 FR
PALEORIENT. 1973. biennial. price varies. (Universite de Paris, Laboratoire de Paleontologie Humaine et de Paleontologie des Vertebres) Editions du C N R S, 1 Place Aristide Briand, 92195 Meudon Cedex, France. TEL 1-45-34-75-50. FAX 1-46-26-28-49. TELEX LABOBEL 204 135 F. (Subscr. to: Presses du C N R S, 20-22, rue Saint Amand, 75105 Paris, France. TEL 1-45-33-16-00) Ed. S. Renimel. adv.; bk.rev.; bibl.; index; circ. 1,500 (controlled). **Indexed:** A.I.C.P., GeoRef., Mid.East: Abstr.& Ind.

561 560 US ISSN 0191-6122
QE993 CODEN: PALYDP
PALYNOLOGY. 1977. a. $20. American Association of Stratigraphic Palynologists Foundation, c/o Robert T. Clarke, Mobil R & D Corp-D R L, Box 819047, Dallas, TX 75381. TEL 214-851-8481.
FAX 214-851-8185. Ed. David G. Goodman. circ. 950. **Indexed:** Biol.Abstr., Br.Geol.Lit., Geo.Abstr., GeoRef., Ocean.Abstr., Petrol.Abstr., Pollut.Abstr.
—BLDSC shelfmark: 6345.580000.
 Supersedes (in 1977): Geoscience and Man (ISSN 0072-1395); **Incorporates** (1970-1976): American Association of Stratigraphic Palynologists. Proceedings of the Annual Meeting (ISSN 0270-1316)
 Refereed Serial

PANSTWOWY INSTYTUT GEOLOGICZNY. PRACE. see *EARTH SCIENCES — Geology*

PRIRODNJACKI MUZEJ U BEOGRADU. GLASNIK. SERIJA A: MINEROLOGIJA, GEOLOGIJA, PALEONTOLOGIJA. see *EARTH SCIENCES — Geology*

QUARTAERPALAEONTOLOGIE. see *EARTH SCIENCES*

560 US ISSN 0033-5894
QE696 CODEN: QRESAV
QUATERNARY RESEARCH; an interdisciplinary journal. (Text mainly in English; occasionally in French, German or Russian) 1970. bi-m. $192 (foreign $232). Academic Press, Inc., Journal Division, 1250 Sixth Ave., San Diego, CA 92101.
TEL 619-230-1840. FAX 619-699-6800. TELEX 181726. Ed. Stephen C. Porter. bk.rev.; index. (back issues avail.) **Indexed:** AESIS, Biol.Abstr., Br.Archaeol.Abstr., Br.Geol.Lit., Chem.Abstr., Curr.Cont., Curr.Cont.Africa, Curr.Tit.Ocean., Deep Sea Res.& Oceanogr.Abstr., Forest.Abstr., Forest Prod.Abstr., Geo.Abstr., GeoRef., Sci.Abstr., So.Pac.Per.Ind., Soils & Fert.
—BLDSC shelfmark: 7210.100000.
 Refereed Serial

560 JA ISSN 0418-2642
QUATERNARY RESEARCH. (Text in English and Japanese; summaries in English) 1957. 5/yr. $72. (Japan Association for Quaternary Research) Japan Scientific Societies Press, 6-2-10 Hongo, Bunkyo-ku, Tokyo 113, Japan. TEL 3814-2001.
FAX 3814-2002. TELEX 2722268 BCJSP J. (Dist. by: Business Center for Academic Societies Japan, Koshin Bldg., 6-16-3 Hongo, Bunkyo-ku, Tokyo 113, Japan; Dist. in U.S. by: International Specialized Book Services, Inc., 5602 N.E. Hassalo St., Portland, OR 97213; in Asia by: Toppan Company Pvt. Ltd., 38 Liu Fang Rd., Box 22 Jurong Town, Jurong, Singapore 2262) bk.rev.; index; circ. 1,900. (back issues avail.) **Indexed:** AESIS, Biol.Abstr.

RENLEIXUE XUEBAO/ACTA ANTHROPOLOGICA SINICA. see *ANTHROPOLOGY*

560 UK ISSN 0266-4755
REPORT ON BRITISH PALAEOBOTANY & PALYNOLOGY. 1976. biennial. £2.50. National Museum of Wales, Department of Botany, Cathays Park, Cardiff CF1 3NP, England. TEL 0222-397951.
FAX 0222-373219. Ed.Bd. bibl.; circ. 125. **Indexed:** Biol.Abstr.
 Description: Reports on work in progress, publications.

561 NE ISSN 0034-6667
QE993 CODEN: RPPYAX
REVIEW OF PALAEOBOTANY AND PALYNOLOGY; an international journal. (Text in English, French and German) 1967. 16/yr.(in 4 vols.; 4 nos./vol.). fl.1444 (effective 1992). Elsevier Science Publishers B.V., P.O. Box 211, 1000 AE Amsterdam, Netherlands. TEL 020-5803911.
FAX 020-5803598. TELEX 18582 ESPA NL. (Subscr. in U.S. and Canada to: Elsevier Science Publishing Co., Inc., Box 882, Madison Sq. Sta., New York, NY 10159. TEL 212-989-5800) Ed. W. Punt. adv.; bk.rev.; abstr.; bibl.; charts; illus.; index. (also avail. in microform from RPI; reprint service avail. from SWZ) **Indexed:** Abstr.Anthropol., AESIS, Biol.Abstr., Br.Geol.Lit., Bull.Signal., Curr.Adv.Ecol.Sci., Curr.Cont., Deep Sea Res.& Oceanogr.Abstr., Geo.Abstr., GeoRef., Plant Breed.Abstr., Soils & Fert.
—BLDSC shelfmark: 7793.830000.
 Description: Aims to stimulate wide interdisciplinary cooperation and understanding among workers in the fields of palaeobotany and palynology.
 Refereed Serial

560 SP ISSN 0556-655X
QE719 CODEN: RTEMB5
REVISTA ESPANOLA DE MICROPALEONTOLOGIA. 1969. 3/yr. 8500 ptas. Empresa Nacional Adaro de Investigaciones Mineras S.A. (ENADIMSA), Doctor Esquerdo 138, 28007 Madrid, Spain.
TEL 34-1-552-9900. adv.; bk.rev.; circ. 700. **Indexed:** Biol.Abstr., Deep Sea Res.& Oceanogr.Abstr., GeoRef., Ind.SST.
—BLDSC shelfmark: 7854.110000.

563 FR ISSN 0035-1598
 CODEN: RMCPAM
REVUE DE MICROPALEONTOLOGIE. 1958. q. 200 F. to individuals (foreign 240 F.); institutions 360 F. (foreign 420 F.)(effective June 1991). Maison de la Geologie, B.P. 11705, 75224 Paris Cedex 05, France. Ed. M. Neumann. adv.; bk.rev.; bibl.; charts; illus.; circ. 550. **Indexed:** Br.Geol.Lit., Bull.Signal., Curr.Adv.Ecol.Sci., Deep Sea Res.& Oceanogr.Abstr., Geo.Abstr., GeoRef., Petrol.Abstr., Zoo.Rec.
—BLDSC shelfmark: 7933.500000.
 Description: Original scientific contributions, review papers and short communications, congress and symposium reports dealing with any micropaleontological theme.

REVUE DE PALEOBIOLOGIE. see *EARTH SCIENCES — Geology*

560 NE
RIJKSUNIVERSITEIT TE UTRECHT. DEPARTMENT OF STRATIGRAPHY AND PALEONTOLOGY. SPECIAL PUBLICATIONS. (Text in English) 1974. irreg., no.5, 1989. price varies. Rijksuniversiteit te Utrecht, Department of Stratigraphy and Paleontology, Working Group of Mammal Paleontology - State University of Utrecht, c/o C.W. Drooger, Ed., Budapestlaan 4, P.O. Box 80.021, 3508 TA Utrecht, Netherlands. (Subscr. to: c/o T. van Schaik, Budapestlaan 4, 3584 CD Utrecht, Netherlands) (back issues avail.)

560.17 IT ISSN 0035-6883
QE701 CODEN: RPLSAT
RIVISTA ITALIANA DI PALEONTOLOGIA E STRATIGRAFIA. (Text in English, French, German, Italian; summaries in English, French, German) 1895. q. L.100000. Via Mangiagalli 34, 20133 Milan, Italy. TEL 236981. bk.rev.; abstr.; bibl.; charts; illus.; index, cum.index; circ. 450. (reprint service avail. from SWZ) **Indexed:** Biol.Abstr., Deep Sea Res.& Oceanogr.Abstr., Geo.Abstr., GeoRef.
—BLDSC shelfmark: 7987.480000.

S.I.S. CHRONOLOGY & CATASTROPHISM WORKSHOP. (Society for Interdisciplinary Studies) see *EARTH SCIENCES — Geology*

560 CS ISSN 0036-5297
QE755.C95 CODEN: SGPABC
SBORNIK GEOLOGICKYCH VED: PALEONTOLOGIE/JOURNAL OF GEOLOGICAL SCIENCES: PALEONTOLOGY. (Text in English, French or German; summaries also in Russian) 1949. irreg. Ustredni Ustav Geologicky, Malostranske nam. 19, 118 21 Prague 1, Czechoslovakia. (Dist. by: Artia, Ve Smeckach 30, 111 27 Prague 1, Czechoslovakia) Ed. Vladimir Havlicek. charts; illus.; circ. 600. (back issues avail.) **Indexed:** Bull.Signal., GeoRef., Ref.Zh.
—BLDSC shelfmark: 4992.600000.

560 SZ ISSN 0080-7389
 CODEN: SPAAAX
SCHWEIZERISCHE PALAEONTOLOGISCHE ABHANDLUNGEN/MEMOIRES SUISSE DE PALEONTOLOGIE. (Text in English, French, German, Italian) 1874. irreg. price varies. (Schweizerische Naturforschende Gesellschaft) Birkhaeuser Verlag, P.O. Box 133, CH-4010 Basel, Switzerland.
TEL 061-737740. FAX 061-737950. TELEX 963475 BIRKH CH. (Dist. in N. America by: Springer-Verlag New York, Inc., Journal Fulfillment Services, Box 2485, Secaucus, NJ 07096-2491. TEL 201-348-4033) Ed. B. Engesser. index. **Indexed:** Biol.Abstr., GeoRef.
—BLDSC shelfmark: 8119.200000.

560 GW ISSN 0037-2110
QE701 CODEN: SLETAE
SENCKENBERGIANA LETHAEA. (Text and summaries in English, French and German) 1919. 6/yr. DM.95. Senckenbergische Naturforschende Gesellschaft, Abt. Schriftentausch, Senckenberganlage 25, 6000 Frankfurt a.M. 1, Germany. TEL 069-7542-1.
FAX 069-746238. TELEX 413129. Ed. W. Struve. bibl.; charts; illus.; maps; index, cum.index; circ. 850. **Indexed:** Biol.Abstr., Br.Geol.Lit., Chem.Abstr., Curr.Adv.Ecol.Sci., Deep Sea Res.& Oceanogr.Abstr., GeoRef.
—BLDSC shelfmark: 8241.000000.

560   US   ISSN 0081-0266
QE701   CODEN: SPBYA8
SMITHSONIAN CONTRIBUTIONS TO PALEOBIOLOGY.
1969. irreg., no.68, 1990. Smithsonian Institution Press, 470 L'Enfant Plaza, Ste. 7100, Washington, DC 20560. TEL 202-287-3738.
FAX 202-287-3138. Ed. Barbara T. Spann. circ. 2,500. (reprint service avail. from UMI) **Indexed:** AESIS, Biol.Abstr., Deep Sea Res.& Oceanogr.Abstr., GeoRef.

560   IT   ISSN 0375-7633
SOCIETA PALEONTOLOGICA ITALIANA. BOLLETTINO.
(Text in English, French and Italian) 1960. q. L.45000. (Consiglio Nazionale delle Ricerche (CNR) - Italian Council for Scientific Research) Mucchi Stampati, Via Emila Est, 1525, 41100 Modena, Italy. FAX 053-218212. (Subscr. to: Dr. Stefano Conti, Treasurer S.P.I., c/o Istituto di Geologia di Modena, Corso Vittorio Emanuele II, 59, 4110 Modena, Italy) cum.index: 1960-1983; circ. 700. **Indexed:** Deep Sea Res.& Oceanogr.Abstr.
—BLDSC shelfmark: 2231.700000.

SOCIETE BELGE DE GEOLOGIE. BULLETIN/BELGISCHE VERENIGING VOOR GEOLOGIE. BULLETIN. see *EARTH SCIENCES — Geology*

560   US   ISSN 0096-9117
QE701   CODEN: SVPNAJ
SOCIETY OF VERTEBRATE PALEONTOLOGY. NEWS BULLETIN. 1941. 3/yr. $22. Society of Vertebrate Paleontology, W. 436 Nebraska Hall, University of Nebraska, Lincoln, NE 68588-0542.
TEL 402-472-4604. circ. 1,300. **Indexed:** Biol.Abstr., GeoRef.

SOUTH AFRICAN MUSEUM. ANNALS/SUID-AFRIKAANSE MUSEUM. ANNALE. see *BIOLOGY*

SOUTH AUSTRALIAN MUSEUM, ADELAIDE. RECORDS. see *ANTHROPOLOGY*

SPELEOLOGICAL SOCIETY OF JAPAN. JOURNAL. see *EARTH SCIENCES*

560   IT
STUDI E RICERCHE SUI GIACIMENTI TERZIARI DI BOLCA.
(Text and summaries in English, French, Italian) 1969. irreg. L.30000 per no. Museo Civico di Storia Naturale di Verona, Lungadige Porta Vittoria 9, 37129 Verona, Italy. TEL 045-8001987. circ. 600. (back issues avail.)

STUDI PER L'ECOLOGIA DEL QUATERNARIO. see *ANTHROPOLOGY*

TOHOKU DAIGAKU RIGAKUBU CHISHITSUGAKU KOSEIBUTSUGAKU KYOSHITSU KENKYU HOBUN HOKOKU/TOHOKU UNIVERSITY. FACULTY OF SCIENCE. INSTITUTE OF GEOLOGY AND PALEONTOLOGY. CONTRIBUTIONS. see *EARTH SCIENCES — Geology*

TOHOKU UNIVERSITY. FACULTY OF SCIENCE. INSTITUTE OF GEOLOGY AND PALEONTOLOGY. SCIENCE REPORTS. SECOND SERIES. see *EARTH SCIENCES — Geology*

TRENDS IN ECOLOGY AND EVOLUTION. see *BIOLOGY — Botany*

565   NO   ISSN 0085-7386
TRILOBITE NEWS. (Text in English) 1971. a. free. Universitet i Oslo, Paleontologiska Museum, Sarsgate 1, Oslo 5, Norway. Ed. D.L. Bruton. bk.rev.; abstr.; bibl.; index; circ. 250. **Indexed:** Biol.Abstr., GeoRef.

TULANE STUDIES IN GEOLOGY AND PALEONTOLOGY. see *EARTH SCIENCES — Geology*

560   IT
UNIVERSITA DEGLI STUDI DI FERRARA. ISTITUTO DI GEOLOGIA. ANNALI. SEZIONE 15. PALEONTOLOGIA UMANA E PALETNOLOGIA. (Text and summaries in English, French, Italian) 1959. irreg. exchange basis. Universita degli Studi di Ferrara, Istituto di Geologia, C.So Ercole 1 d'Este 32, Ferrara, Italy. circ. 450.
Formerly: Universita degli Studi di Ferrara. Istituto di Geologia, Paleontologia e Paleontologia Umana. Annali. Sezione 15. Paleontologia Umana e Paleontologia (ISSN 0071-4542)

UNIVERSITA DEGLI STUDI DI FERRARA. ISTITUTO DI GEOLOGIA. PUBBLICAZIONI. see *EARTH SCIENCES — Geology*

UNIVERSITAET HAMBURG. GEOLOGISCH-PALAEONTOLOGISCHES INSTITUT. MITTEILUNGEN. see *EARTH SCIENCES — Geology*

UNIVERSITAET STUTTGART. INSTITUT FUER GEOLOGIE UND PALAEONTOLOGIE ARBEITEN NEUE FOLGE. see *EARTH SCIENCES*

560   US   ISSN 1046-8390
QE701   CODEN: KUPABM
UNIVERSITY OF KANSAS. PALEONTOLOGICAL CONTRIBUTIONS. NEW SERIES. 1947. irreg. price varies. University of Kansas, Paleontological Institute, 121 Lindley Hall, Lawrence, KS 66045.
TEL 913-864-3338. (Subscr. to: University of Kansas Libraries, Exchange & Gifts Dept., Lawrence, KS 66045) Ed. Roger L. Kaesler. abstr.; bibl.; circ. 700. (back issues avail.) **Indexed:** AESIS, Biol.Abstr., Geo.Abstr.
Formed by the 1992 merger of: University of Kansas. Paleontological Contributions. Articles (ISSN 0075-5044) & University of Kansas. Paleontological Contributions. Papers. (ISSN 0075-5052) & University of Kansas. Paleontological Contributions. Monographs (ISSN 0278-9744)
Refereed Serial

560   US   ISSN 0041-9834
UNIVERSITY OF MICHIGAN. MUSEUM OF PALEONTOLOGY. CONTRIBUTIONS. 1924. irreg., vol.26, nos.7-13, 1983. price varies. University of Michigan, Museum of Paleontology, Museums Bldg., Ann Arbor, MI 48109. TEL 313-764-0489. Ed. Gerald R. Smith. circ. 500. **Indexed:** Biol.Abstr.
Refereed Serial

560   US   ISSN 0148-3838
QE701   CODEN: PPUMD3
UNIVERSITY OF MICHIGAN. MUSEUM OF PALEONTOLOGY. PAPERS ON PALEONTOLOGY. 1972. irreg. University of Michigan, Museum of Paleontology, Ann Arbor, MI 48109.
TEL 313-764-0489. **Indexed:** GeoRef.
Refereed Serial

UNIVERSITY OF WYOMING. CONTRIBUTIONS TO GEOLOGY. see *EARTH SCIENCES — Geology*

550   CS
USTREDNI USTAV GEOLOGICKY. ROZPRAVY. (Text in English or German; summaries in Czech and English) 1926. irreg. Ustredni Ustav Geologicky, Malostranske nam. 19, 118 21 Prague 1, Czechoslovakia. (Dist by: Artia, Ve Smeckach 30, 111 27 Prague 1, Czechoslovakia) charts; illus.; circ. 650. (back issues avail.) **Indexed:** Bull.Signal., GeoRef., Ref.Zh.

560   NE   ISSN 0083-4963
QE719   CODEN: UTMBAA
UTRECHT MICROPALEONTOLOGICAL BULLETINS. (Text in English) 1969. irreg., no.40, 1991. price varies. Rijksuniversiteit te Utrecht, Department of Stratigraphy and Paleontology - State University of Utrecht, Budapestlaan 4, P.O. Box 80.021, 3508 TA Utrecht, Netherlands. (Subscr. to: Sales Office, c/o T. van Schaik, Budapestlaan 4, 3584 CD Utrecht, Netherlands) Ed. C.W. Drooger. (back issues avail.) **Indexed:** GeoRef.

560 551   GW   ISSN 0373-9627
QE701   CODEN: ZTLAAN
ZITTELIANA; Abhandlungen der Bayerischen Staatssammlung fuer Palaeontologie und historische Geologie. 1969. irreg. price varies. Bayerische Staatssammlung fuer Palaeontologie und Historische Geologie, Richard-Wagner-Strasse 10, 8000 Munich 2, Germany. FAX 089-5203286. Ed. Dietrich Herm. **Indexed:** Biol.Abstr., GeoRef.
—BLDSC shelfmark: 9514.667000.

PALEONTOLOGY — Abstracting, Bibliographies, Statistics

AMERICAN ASSOCIATION OF STRATIGRAPHIC PALYNOLOGISTS. ABSTRACTS OF PAPERS PRESENTED AT THE ANNUAL MEETINGS.. see *EARTH SCIENCES — Abstracting, Bibliographies, Statistics*

560 016   US   ISSN 0300-7227
BIBLIOGRAPHY AND INDEX OF MICROPALEONTOLOGY.
(Text in original language with English translation; summaries in English) 1971. m. $75 to individuals; corporations $660. American Museum of Natural History, Central Park W. at 79th St., New York, NY 10024-5192. TEL 212-769-5656.
FAX 212-769-5233. Eds. Susan Carroll, Sharon Tahirkeli. abstr.; bibl.; index; circ. 250. (looseleaf format; reprint service avail. from UMI)
Description: Survey of world literature in all fields of micropaleontology, with annual subject and author index.

560 016   FR   ISSN 0761-1889
P A S C A L FOLIO. F 47: PALEONTOLOGIE. 1985. 10/yr. 815 F. (Bureau de Recherches Geologiques et Minieres) Centre National de la Recherche Scientifique, Institut de l'Information Scientifique et Technique, B.P. 54, 54514 Vandoeuvre-Les-Nancy Cedex, France. TEL 83-50-46-00. abstr.; index, cum.index.
Formerly: P A S C A L Folio. Part 47: Paleontologie; Which superseded (1972-1984): Bulletin Signaletique: Bibliographie des Sciences de la Terre. Section 227: Paleontologie (ISSN 0300-9335)

560 016   GW   ISSN 0044-4189
                                     CODEN: ZGPGA4
ZENTRALBLATT FUER GEOLOGIE UND PALAEONTOLOGIE. TEIL II: PALAEONTOLOGIE. 1807. 7/yr. price varies. E. Schweizerbart'sche Verlagsbuchhandlung, Johannesstr. 3A, 7000 Stuttgart 1, Germany. TEL 0711-625001. FAX 0711-625005. TELEX 723363-SCHB-D. Eds. Adolf Seilacher, E. Seilacher. adv.; bk.rev.; abstr.; bibl.; index. **Indexed:** Chem.Abstr., Deep Sea Res.& Oceanogr.Abstr.

PAPER AND PULP

see also Packaging

676   GW   ISSN 0002-5917
A P R. (Allgemeine Papier-Rundschau) (Text in German; summaries in English) 1876. w. DM.239.40 (foreign DM.276). P. Keppler Verlag GmbH und Co. KG, Industriestr. 2, 6056 Heusenstamm, Germany. TEL 06104-6060. FAX 06104-606333. TELEX 410131. Ed. Frank Koether. adv.; bk.rev.; abstr.; bibl.; charts; illus.; pat.; stat.; index; circ. 6,508. **Indexed:** Abstr.Bull.Inst.Pap.Chem., Int.Packag.Abstr., Packag.Sci.Tech., Paper & Bd.Abstr., PROMT.
—BLDSC shelfmark: 0791.900000.

676   MX
A T C P REVISTA. (Text in Spanish; summaries in English) 1960. bi-m. Mex.$64500($50) (Asociacion Mexicana de Tecnicos de las Industrias de la Celulosa y del Papel, A.C.) G S A Publicidad, Av. Insurgentes No. 3493, Poseidon No. 504, 14020 Mexico, D.F., Mexico. TEL 568-74-08. FAX 568-7408. TELEX 1773608 CNCPME. Ed. Octavio Tirado. adv.; bk.rev.; bibl.; charts; illus.; stat.; tr.lit.; circ. 1,700. (also avail. in microform; back issues avail.)
Description: Information on the technology, manufacture and business administration of the pulp and paper trade industry worldwide.

ADHESIVE TRENDS. see *RUBBER*

ADVANCES IN DRYING. see *ENGINEERING — Mechanical Engineering*

676   US   ISSN 0897-2524
ALKALINE PAPER ADVOCATE. 1988. 6/yr. $30 to individuals; institutions $40. Abbey Publications, Inc., 320 E. Center St., Provo, UT 84606.
TEL 801-373-1598. FAX 801-375-4423. Ed. Ellen McCrady. index; circ. 500. (tabloid format; back issues avail.)
Description: For those interested (papermakers, librarians and paper industry suppliers) in trends in conversion to alkaline papermaking.

676   US
AMERICAN PAPER INSTITUTE. CAPACITY SURVEY. 1958. a. $375 (foreign $395). American Paper Institute, Inc., 260 Madison Ave., New York, NY 10016. TEL 212-340-0600. circ. 2,500. **Indexed:** SRI.

3662 PAPER AND PULP

676   CN
AMERICAN PAPERMAKER. vol.50, 1987. m. $30 (foreign $45)(free to qualified personnel). Maclean Hunter Ltd., 777 Bay St., Toronto, Ont. M5W 1A7, Canada. TEL 416-596-5897. FAX 416-593-3170. Ed. Jerome Knocel. adv.; circ. 30,500.

676   GW
ANNUAIRE BIRKNER FRANCE. 1975. a. 255 F. Birkner & Co. Verlag, Winsbergring 38, Postfach 520662, 2000 Hamburg 52, Germany. TEL 040-85308-401. FAX 040-85308381. Ed. Harry von Hofmann. adv.; circ. 3,000.

ANNUAL BOOK OF A S T M STANDARDS. VOLUME 15.09. PAPER; PACKAGING; FLEXIBLE BARRIER MATERIALS; BUSINESS COPY PRODUCTS. see ENGINEERING — Engineering Mechanics And Materials

676   AT   ISSN 0003-6757
TS1080   CODEN: APPIA2
APPITA. 1947. bi-m. Aus.$55 to non-members (effective 1992). Technical Association of the Australian and New Zealand Pulp and Paper Industry, Inc., Clunies Ross House, 191 Royal Pde., Parkville, Vic. 3052, Australia. FAX 61-3-348-1206. Ed. P.J. Brown. adv.: B&W page Aus.$930; trim 297 x 210. bk.rev.; charts; illus.; index; circ. 1,900. (also avail. in microform from UMI) **Indexed:** Abstr.Bull.Inst.Pap.Chem., Anal.Abstr., Biol.Abstr., Chem.Abstr., Chem.Eng.Abstr., Curr.Cont., Energy Ind., Energy Info.Abstr., Forest.Abstr., Forest Prod.Abstr., Ind.Sci.Rev., P.I.R.A., Paper & Bd.Abstr., Sci.Cit.Ind., T.C.E.A.

676   FR   ISSN 0004-5896
     CODEN: ATIPBH
ASSOCIATION TECHNIQUE DE L'INDUSTRIE PAPETIERE. REVUE. 1947. 8/yr. membership. Association Technique de l'Industrie Papetiere, 154 bd. Haussmann, 75008 Paris, France. FAX 33-1-45-63-53-09. adv.; bk.rev.; charts; illus.; circ. 2,050. **Indexed:** C.I.S. Abstr., Chem.Abstr., Forest Prod.Abstr.

AUSTRALIAN LITHOGRAPHER, PRINTER, AND PACKAGER. see PRINTING

BERITA SELULOSA. see FORESTS AND FORESTRY

BOARD CONVERTING NEWS. see PACKAGING

BOARD CONVERTING NEWS INTERNATIONAL. see PACKAGING

634.9 676   US
BOISE CASCADE INSIGHT. 1986. 3/yr. qualified personnel only. Boise Cascade Corporation, One Jefferson Sq., Box 50, Boise, ID 83728. TEL 208-384-7809. FAX 208-384-7224. Ed. Karla Haun. circ. 31,000.
     Formerly: Boise Cascade Quarterly.
     Description: News and information for employees and retirees of Boise Cascade Corporation.

676   CU   ISSN 0138-8940
BOLETIN TECNICO PULPA Y PAPEL. 1984. s-a. exchange basis. Union del Papel, Departamento Tecnico, Calle Perla y Primera, Los Pinos, Havana 18, Cuba. TEL 448651. TELEX 512121. Ed. Francisco Cabrera. bk.rev.; circ. 2,000.
     Description: Offers updated information on pulp, paper and converting issues from both domestic and international industries.

676.2   UK   ISSN 0068-2330
BRITISH PAPER AND BOARD INDUSTRY FEDERATION. TECHNICAL ASSOCIATION. TECHNICAL PAPERS. 1960. a. price varies. Paper Industry Technical Association, Pira House, Randalls Rd., Leatherhead KT22 7RU, England. TEL 0372-376161. Ed. M. Marley. index.

051   US
BRUNSWICK MONTHLY. 1988. m. free. Georgia - Pacific, Brunswick Operations, Box 1438, Brunswick, GA 31521. FAX 912-265-8060. Ed. Curtis H. Carter. circ. 1,000 (controlled).
     Formerly: Brunswick Week.

676   RU   ISSN 0007-5817
     CODEN: BUMPAK
BUMAZHNAYA PROMYSHLENNOST'. 1922. m. 26.40 Rub. Ministerstvo Tsellyulozno-bumazhnoi Promyshlennosti, Ul. 25 Oktyabrya, Moscow K-12, Russia. Ed. V.N. Shul'gin. bk.rev.; charts; illus.; index. **Indexed:** Abstr.Bull.Inst.Pap.Chem., Chem.Abstr., Forest Prod.Abstr.

676 658.8   IT
C L. (CartoLibraio) 1965. m. L.60000. A P I Editrice srl., Via Pezzotti, 4, 20141 Milan, Italy. TEL 02-8321087. FAX 02-8323710. Ed. Antonio Spagnoli. adv.; bk.rev.; circ. 15,500. **Indexed:** CERDIC.
     Description: Covers the market of selling Italian school supplies, gift articles, stamps, stationery, office supplies and more both on the national and international scale.

676   CN   ISSN 0705-6710
CANADIAN PAPER ANALYST. 1978. 9/yr. $195. J.D.R. Publications, P.O. Box 300, Westmount Station, Westmount, Que. H3Z 2V5, Canada. TEL 514-933-8749. FAX 514-849-8367. Ed. Jim Rowland. (back issues avail.)

676   CN
CANADIAN PULP AND PAPER ASSOCIATION. ANNUAL REPORT. a. free. Canadian Pulp and Paper Association, Sun Life Bldg., 19th Fl., 1155 Metcalfe St., Montreal, Que. H3B 4T6, Canada. TEL 514-886-6621. FAX 514-866-3035. circ. 5,000. **Indexed:** CS Ind.
     Formerly: Canadian Pulp and Paper Association. Pulp and Paper Report (ISSN 0068-9505)

676   CN
CANADIAN PULP AND PAPER ASSOCIATION. MONTHLY NEWSPRINT STATISTICS. m. Canadian Pulp and Paper Association, Sun Life Bldg., 19th Fl., 1155 Metcalfe St., Montreal, Que. H3B 4T6, Canada. TEL 514-866-6621. FAX 514-866-3035.

676.1   CN
CANADIAN PULP AND PAPER ASSOCIATION. TECHNICAL SECTION. PROCEEDINGS. 1915. a. Can.$65 to non-members; members Can.$50. Canadian Pulp and Paper Association, Sun Life Bldg., 19th Fl., 1155 Metcalfe St., Montreal, Que. H3B 4T6, Canada. TEL 514-866-6621. FAX 514-866-3035. index; circ. 100. **Indexed:** Abstr.Bull.Inst.Pap.Chem.

676   CN
▼**CANADIAN WOODPROCESSING NEWS.** 1990. 6/yr. 831 Helmcken St., Vancouver, B.C. V6Z 1B1, Canada. TEL 604-689-2804. FAX 604-682-8347. Ed. Toni Dabbs. adv.; circ. 15,000.

CELLULOSA E CARTA. see FORESTS AND FORESTRY — Lumber And Wood

676   RM   ISSN 0008-879X
TS1080   CODEN: CLOZA8
CELULOZA SI HIRTIE. (Text in Rumanian; summaries in English, French, German, Russian) 1951. q. $53. Departamentul Industriei Lemnului, Officiul de Informare Documentara, B-dul Magheru, 31, sect. 1, 70162 Bucharest, Rumania. TELEX 10944 ICHIM. (Dist. by: Rompresfilatelia, Sector Export-Import Presa, P.O. Box 12-201, Calea Grivitei nr.64-66, Bucharest, Rumania) adv.; bk.rev.; abstr.; bibl.; illus.; pat.; index; circ. 1,000. **Indexed:** Chem. Abstr.
     Supersedes in part: Revista Padurilor-Industria Lemnului-Celuloza si Hirtie (ISSN 0035-029X)

676   FR
CENTRE TECHNIQUE DU PAPIER. FEUILLETS BIBLIOGRAPHIQUES. 1969. m. 985. Centre Technique du Papier, B.P. 7110, 38020 Grenoble Cedex, France. bibl.; circ. 200.
     Formerly: Association Technique de l'Industrie Papetiere. Feuillets Bibliographiques. (ISSN 0004-5888)

COMPUTER PAPER; Western Canada's computer information source. see COMPUTERS

676   UK   ISSN 0010-8189
CONVERTER.* 1964. m. £17.50. Faversham House Group Ltd., 111 St. James's Rd., Croydon, Surrey CR9 2TH, England. Ed. Alan J. Buckton. adv.; bk.rev.; charts; illus.; stat.; tr.lit.; index; circ. 4,257. (also avail. in microform from UMI; reprint service avail. from UMI) **Indexed:** Abstr.Bull.Inst.Pap.Chem., Art & Archaeol.Tech.Abstr., Curr.Pack.Abstr., Int.Packag.Abstr., Paper & Bd.Abstr., Print.Abstr.
     —BLDSC shelfmark: 3463.600000.

676   US   ISSN 0746-7141
CONVERTING MAGAZINE. 1979. m. $55 (free to qualified personnel). Delta Communications, Inc. (Chicago) (Subsidiary of: Elsevier Business Press, Inc. (New York)), 400 N. Michigan Ave., Ste. 1200, Chicago, IL 60611. TEL 312-222-2000. FAX 312-222-2026. Ed. Yolanda Simonsis. circ. 40,363.
     —BLDSC shelfmark: 3463.612000.
     Former titles: Converting Product News (ISSN 0279-4187); Paper and Converting Product News.
     Description: For industries which convert paper, paperboard, plastic, film and foil via printing, coating, laminating, extruding, slitting, forming, sealing and related processes.

676.3   UK   ISSN 0264-715X
CONVERTING TODAY. 1987. m. $146. Angel Publishing Ltd., Kingsland House, 361 City Rd., London EC1v 1LR, England. TEL 071-417-7400. FAX 071-417-7500. Ed. Pauline Covell. circ. 7,122.

CORRUGATED CONTAINERS CONFERENCE (YEAR). see PACKAGING

676   GW   ISSN 0070-4296
     CODEN: DPAWA2
DEUTSCHE PAPIERWIRTSCHAFT; magazine for economy and technology of manufacturing, finishing and converting of pulp, paper, substitution products and of the printing world. Short title: D P W. (Text in English and German) 1958. q. DM.130 (foreign DM.118). D P W Verlag GmbH, Postfach 1353, 6056 Heusenstamm, Germany. TEL 06104-6060. FAX 06104-606317. Ed. Martin Swayne. bk.rev.; circ. 7,500. **Indexed:** Abstr.Bull.Inst.Pap.Chem., Chem.Abstr.
     —BLDSC shelfmark: 3573.210000.

676   IT
DICARTA.* 1980. q. L.16000. Raddicchi Editore S.R.L., Piazza Vesuvio 23, 20144 Milan, Italy. Ed. Lino Radicchi. adv.; circ. 7,800.

676   US
E S P NEWS. bi-m. Conservatree Paper Company, 10 Lombard St., Ste.250, San Francisco, CA 94111. TEL 415-433-1000. FAX 415-391-7890. Ed. David Assmann. circ. 25,000.

676   GW
EUROPAEISCHER WIRTSCHAFTSDIENST. INFORMATIONSBRIEF HOLZ - ZELLSTOFF - PAPIER. m. DM.420. Casimir Katz Verlag, Bleichstr. 20-22, 7562 Gernsbach, Germany. TEL 07224-3091. FAX 07224-3094. TELEX 78915-DBV-D.

676   GW
EUROPAEISCHER WIRTSCHAFTSDIENST. PAPIER- UND ZELLSTOFF-DIENST. 1926. w. DM.650. Casimir Katz Verlag, Bleichstr. 20-22, 7562 Gernsbach, Germany. TEL 07224-3091. FAX 07224-3094. TELEX 78915-DBV-D. Ed. Ellen Streckel. circ. 1,400.

676   GW
EUROPAEISCHER WIRTSCHAFTSDIENST. PULP AND PAPER SERVICE. (Text in English) 1926. w. DM.830. Casimir Katz Verlag, Bleichstr. 20-22, 7562 Gernsbach, Germany. TEL 07224-3091. FAX 07224-3094. TELEX 78915-DBV-D. Ed. Annette Steinmetz. circ. 520.

FOREST INDUSTRY AFFAIRS; information for decision. see FORESTS AND FORESTRY — Lumber And Wood

676   GW
G P MAGAZIN. 1987. m. DM.20. Industriegewerkschaft Chemie - Papier - Keramik, Koenigswoerther Pl. 6, 3000 Hannover 1, Germany. TEL 0511-7631324. circ. 682,517.
     Formerly: Gewerkschaftpost.

PAPER AND PULP

676   GW
GEWERKSCHAFTLICHE UMSCHAU. 1957. bi-m. DM.18. Industriegewerkschaft Chemie - Papier - Keramik, Koenigsworther Pl. 6, 3000 Hannover, Germany. TEL 0511-7631324. TELEX 922608. circ. 52,000.
    Formerly: Industriegewerkschaft Chemie - Papier - Keramik. Umschau.

GREATER BATON ROUGE MANUFACTURERS DIRECTORY. see *BUSINESS AND ECONOMICS — Trade And Industrial Directories*

676.2   CC   ISSN 1001-3911
GUOWAI ZAOZHI/PAPER MANUFACTURING IN FOREIGN COUNTRIES. (Text in Chinese) bi-m. Zhongguo Zaozhi Xuehui - China Paper Manufacturing Society, 12 Guanghua Lu, Chaoyang-qu, Beijing 100020, People's Republic of China. TEL 5022561. Ed. Li Jiawan.

676.2 745.5   US   ISSN 0887-1418
HAND PAPERMAKING. (Includes quarterly newsletter) 1986. s-a. $25 (effective July 1991). Box 10571, Minneapolis, MN 55458. TEL 612-788-9440. Eds. Amanda Degener, Michael Durgin. adv.; bk.rev.; circ. 2,000. (back issues avail.) **Indexed:** Ind.How To Do It (1989-).
    —BLDSC shelfmark: 4241.594000.
    Description: Devoted to advancing traditional and contemporary ideas in the art of Eastern and Western papermaking. Provides information for readers at all levels of expertise and from all perspectives of interest.

676   NE
HANDBOOK OF PAPER SCIENCE; the science and technology of papermaking, paper properties and paper usage. 1980. irreg., vol.2, 1982. price varies. Elsevier Science Publishers B.V., Books Division, P.O. Box 211, 1000 AE Amsterdam, Netherlands. TEL 020-5803911. FAX 020-5803705. TELEX 18582 ESPA NL. (Subscr. in U.S. and Canada to: Elsevier Science Publishing Co., Inc., Box 882, Madison Sq. Sta., New York, NY 10159. TEL 212-989-5800)
    Refereed Serial

676   SP
I N S. (International Stationery) q. 5000 ptas. Reclamo Tecnico, S.A., Casanova 212, 1-2, 08036 Barcelona, Spain. TEL 3212149. FAX 3223812. circ. 9,000.

676 700   SP
IMPREMPRES; tecnicas equipos para las artes graficas e industrias de la transformacion del papel y carton. 12/yr. 4500 ptas. Pedeca Sociedad Cooperativa, Ltda., Maria Auxiliadora 5, 28040 Madrid, Spain. TEL 459 60 00.

INDIAN PRINT & PAPER; a journal for printers, papermakers and the allied industries. see *PRINTING*

676   II   ISSN 0019-6231
TS1171   CODEN: IPPAAW
INDIAN PULP AND PAPER; India's leading journal on paper, printing and packaging. (Text in English) 1946. bi-m. Rs.30($9) R.N. Chatterjee, Ed. & Pub., 15 India Exchange Pl., 3rd Floor, Calcutta 700001, India. adv.; bk.rev.; charts; illus.; index; circ. 3,500. **Indexed:** Abstr.Bull.Inst.Pap.Chem., Chem.Abstr., Cott.& Trop.Fibr.Abstr., Field Crop Abstr., Forest.Abstr., Forest Prod.Abstr.

676
INDIAN PULP & PAPER INDUSTRY DESKBOOK. (Text in English) 1978. biennial. $45. Technical Press Publications, 5-1 Convent Street, Colaba, Bombay 400 039, India. TEL 2021446. TELEX 011-3479-CHEM-IN. Ed. J.P. Sousa. adv.; bk.rev.; abstr.; charts; illus.; circ. 6,400. (also avail. in microform from UMI)

676   IT   ISSN 0019-7548
    CODEN: ICAMA4
INDUSTRIA DELLA CARTA. (Text in Italian; summaries in English and Italian) 1962. m. (10/yr.) L.90000 (foreign L.200000). Editrice Arti Poligrafiche Europee, Via Casella 16, 20156 Milan, Italy. TEL 02-330221. FAX 02-39214341. Dir. Osvaldo Gigliotti. adv.; bk.rev.; illus.; stat.; index; circ. 4,000. **Indexed:** Abstr.Bull.Inst.Pap.Chem., Chem.Abstr., PROMT.
    —BLDSC shelfmark: 4438.466000.

INFORMACION TECNICO ECONOMICA. see *BUSINESS AND ECONOMICS*

676   US   ISSN 0361-4719
    CODEN: IPPICO
INSTRUMENTATION IN THE PULP AND PAPER INDUSTRY. 1960. irreg. price varies. Instrument Society of America, 67 Alexander Dr., Box 12277, Research Triangle Park, NC 27709. TEL 919-549-8411. FAX 919-549-8288. TELEX 802540 ISA DURM. (reprint service avail. from ISI,UMI)
    Refereed Serial

INTERNATIONAL PAPER BOARD INDUSTRY. see *PACKAGING*

676   II   ISSN 0047-1038
INTERNATIONAL PRESS CUTTING SERVICE: PAPER - PULP - BOARD - STRAW. 1967. w. $65. International Press Cutting Service, Box 63, Allahabad 211001, India. Ed. N. Khanna. bk.rev.; index; circ. 1,200. (processed)

676 670   US   ISSN 0097-2509
HD9820.3
INTERNATIONAL PULP & PAPER DIRECTORY. 1974. biennial. $157 (Business Travel Editions - Europe $177; Asia-Australasia $177). Miller Freeman, Inc. (Subsidiary of: United Newspapers), 600 Harrison St., San Francisco, CA 94107. TEL 415-905-2200. FAX 415-905-2232. TELEX 278273. Ed. Vincent M. Ridley.
    —BLDSC shelfmark: 4545.440000.

676   SP
INVESTIGACION Y TECNICA DEL PAPEL. (Text in Spanish; summaries in English, French, German and Spanish) 1964. q. 4800 ptas.($50) (Asociacion de Investigacion Tecnica de la Industria Papelera Espanola) Instituto Papelero Espanol, Avda. Padre Huidobro s-n, Carr. de la Coruna, Km. 7, 28040 Madrid, Spain. adv.; bk.rev.; bibl.; stat.; index; circ. 1,000. (back issues avail.) **Indexed:** Abstr.Bull.Inst.Pap.Chem., Chem.Abstr., Forest.Abstr., Forest Prod.Abstr., Ind.SST.

676   JA
JAPAN PULP AND PAPER. 4/yr. $53. Intercontinental Marketing Corp., I.P.O. Box 5056, Tokyo 100-31, Japan. FAX 81-3-3667-9646.

676   JA   ISSN 0022-815X
    CODEN: KAGIAU
JAPAN T A P P I JOURNAL/KAMI PA GIKYOSHI. (Text in Japanese; summaries in English) 1947. m. 18000 Yen. Japan Technical Association of the Pulp and Paper Industry, Kami Pulp Kaikan Building, 5-6 Hisamatsu-cho, Nihombashi, Chuo-ku, Tokyo 103, Japan. TEL 03-3249-4841. FAX 03-3249-4843. Ed. Atsuo Fuse. adv.; bk.rev.; abstr.; bibl.; charts; illus.; pat.; stat.; circ. 5,500. **Indexed:** Abstr.Bull.Inst.Pap.Chem., Chem.Abstr., INIS Atomind., Paper & Bd.Abstr.
    —BLDSC shelfmark: 4650.260000.

676   CN   ISSN 0830-887X
JOURNAL DES PATES ET PAPIERS. bi-m. Can.$17($37) (effective Jan. 1990). Maclean-Hunter Ltd., Business Publication Division, 1001 de Maisonneuve O., Ste. 1000, Montreal, Que. H3A 3E1, Canada. TEL 514-845-5141. FAX 514-845-4393. Ed. Pierre Deschamps. adv.; circ. 4,000.

676   CN   ISSN 0826-6220
    CODEN: JPUSDN
JOURNAL OF PULP & PAPER SCIENCE. (Text in English and French) 1975. bi-m. Can.$64.20. Canadian Pulp & Paper Association, Technical Section, Sun Life Bldg., 19th Fl., 1155 Metcalfe St., Montreal, Que. H3B 4T6, Canada. TEL 514-866-6621. FAX 514-866-3035. Ed. D.H. Paterson. charts; illus.; index; circ. 7,500. **Indexed:** Abstr.Bull.Inst.Pap.Chem., Chem.Abstr., Eng.Ind., Paper & Bd.Abstr., Sci.Abstr.
    Formerly: Canadian Pulp and Paper Association. Technical Section. Transactions (ISSN 0317-882X)

676   JA   ISSN 0022-8168
KAMI PARUPU TOKEI GEPPO/PAPER & PULP STATISTICAL MONTHLY.* (Text in Japanese) 1953. m. 7680 Yen. Ministry of International Trade and Industry, Research and Statistics Division - Tsusho Sangyo-sho Daijin Kanbo Chosa Tokei-bu, 1-3-1 Kasumigaseki, Chiyoda-ku, Tokyo 100, Japan. TEL 03-3501-1511. charts; stat.; circ. 700.

338.4   JA   ISSN 0453-1515
KAMI PARUPU TOKEI NENPO/YEARBOOK OF PULP AND PAPER STATISTICS. (Editions in English and Japanese) 1947. a. Japan Paper Association, Kami-Parupu Kaikan Bldg., 9-11 Ginza 3-chome, Chuo-ku, Tokyo, Japan. TEL 03-3501-1511.

KOEHLER RUNDSCHAU. see *ADVERTISING AND PUBLIC RELATIONS*

LOCKWOOD - POST'S DIRECTORY OF THE PULP, PAPER AND ALLIED TRADES. see *BUSINESS AND ECONOMICS — Trade And Industrial Directories*

M T J RECYCLING MARKETS. see *PACKAGING*

MARI-BOARD CONVERTING NEWS. see *PACKAGING*

MARI-BOARD CONVERTING NEWS ESPANOL. see *PACKAGING*

676   NE   ISSN 0077-1414
MONUMENTA CHARTAE PAPYRACEAE HISTORIAM ILLUSTRANTIA/COLLECTION OF WORKS AND DOCUMENTS ILLUSTRATING THE HISTORY OF PAPER. (Text mainly in English; occasionally in other languages) 1950. irreg., vol.15, 1992. price varies. Paper Publications Society, Universiteits-Bibliotheek, Singel 425, 1012 W P Amsterdam, Netherlands. Ed. J.S.G. Simmons. circ. 500.

676   US   ISSN 0739-2214
N P T A MANAGEMENT NEWS. 1959. m. $15. National Paper Trade Association, Inc., 111 Great Neck Rd., Ste. 603, Great Neck, NY 11021. TEL 516-829-3070. Ed. William H. Frohlich. adv.; bk.rev.; charts; stat.; circ. 17,000. **Indexed:** SRI.
    Formerly: Current (Great Neck).

NONWOVENS INDUSTRY; the international magazine for the nonwoven fabrics and disposable soft goods industry. see *TEXTILE INDUSTRIES AND FABRICS*

676   NO
NORWEGIAN PULP AND PAPER ASSOCIATION. ANNUAL REVIEW/TREFOREDLINGINDUSTRIENS LANDSFORENING. AARSOVERSIKT. (Text in English, Norwegian) 1981. a. free. Norwegian Pulp and Paper Association - Treforedlingsindustriens Landsforening, Drammensvn 30, P.O. Box 2854 Solli, N-0230 Oslo 2, Norway. TEL 47-2-55-42-10. FAX 47-2-55-42-19.
    Formerly: Papirindustriens Sentralforbund. Annual Review.

OFFICIAL BOARD MARKETS; "the yellow sheet". see *PACKAGING*

OFFICIAL CONTAINER DIRECTORY. see *PACKAGING*

P A T E F A NEWS BULLETIN. (Printing & Allied Trades Employers Federation of Australia) see *PRINTING*

676 651.3   AU   ISSN 0030-784X
P B S AKTUELL. (Papierwaren, Buerobedarf, Schreibwaren) 1948. s-m. S.300. Johann L. Bondi und Sohn, Industriestr. 2, A-2380 Perchtoldsdorf, Austria. Ed. Franz Bondi. circ. 3,500.

676   AU
P F. (Papierhandelsfachblatt) m. Bundesgremium des Papierhandels, Wiedner Haupstr. 63, A-1045 Vienna, Austria. TEL 635763.

676   US   ISSN 1046-4352
TS1080   CODEN: PMAGDY
P I M A MAGAZINE. 1919. m. $50. Paper Industry Management Association, 2400 E. Oakton St., Arlington Heights, IL 60005. TEL 708-956-0250. FAX 708-956-0520. Ed. Alan Rooks. adv.; bk.rev.; abstr.; charts; illus.; stat.; index; circ. 19,357 (controlled). (also avail. in microform from UMI) **Indexed:** A.S.& T.Ind., Abstr.Bull.Inst.Pap.Chem., Eng.Ind, Paper & Bd.Abstr., PROMT. Key Title: Pima.
    Former titles: P I M A (ISSN 0161-1364); (until 1978): Paper Industry (ISSN 0197-3991); (until 1977): American Paper Industry (ISSN 0003-0333)
    Description: Articles on operations and management, training and staff development written in non-technical language, including interviews with industry executives. Columns focus on management issues or key mill technical processes. Departments focus on news and trends, new products, application stories and personnel changes.

PAPER AND PULP

676 686.2 UK ISSN 0262-8600
P I R A ANNUAL REVIEW OF RESEARCH & SERVICES.
1977. a. membership. Paper, Printing & Packaging Industries Research Association, Randalls Rd., Leatherhead, Surrey KT22 7RU, England. illus. **Indexed:** Curr.Pack.Abstr.

676 BL ISSN 0031-1057
TS1080 CODEN: PAPLA3
PAPEL. (Text in Portuguese; summaries in English) 1939. m. $250. (Associacao Tecnica Brasileira de Celulose e Papel) Editora Orientador Ltda., Caixa Postal 1430, Sao Paulo, Brazil. TEL 220-4610. FAX 222-6056. Ed. Paulo Jorge Engelberg. adv.; illus.; stat.; tr.lit.; circ. 3,000. **Indexed:** Chem.Abstr., Corros.Abstr.

676.2 UK ISSN 0306-8234
TS1080 CODEN: PAPRCN
PAPER. (Summaries in French and German) 1879. m. £70 (foreign £100). Benn Publications Ltd., Sovereign Way, Tonbridge, Kent TN9 1RW, England. Ed. David Price. adv.; bk.rev.; abstr.; bibl.; charts; illus.; pat.; stat.; tr.mk.; circ. 12,000. (also avail. in microform from UMI; reprint service avail. from UMI) **Indexed:** Abstr.Bull.Inst.Pap.Chem., Br.Tech.Ind., Chem.Abstr., Excerp.Med., Graph.Arts Lit.Abstr., Paper & Bd.Abstr., PROMT.
—BLDSC shelfmark: 6358.600000.
Incorporating: World's Paper Trade Review (ISSN 0043-9320); Paper-Maker (ISSN 0031-1154)
Description: International pulp and paper industry's journal.

676 US ISSN 0031-1081
PAPER AGE. 1884. m. $20 (foreign $75)(typically set in Sep). Global Publications, 400 Old Hook Rd., Ste. G6, Westwood, NJ 07675. TEL 201-666-2262. FAX 201-666-9046. Ed. Mark McCready. adv.; bk.rev.; charts; illus.; circ. 31,400 (controlled). **Indexed:** Abstr.Bull.Inst.Pap.Chem., Graph.Arts Lit.Abstr., Int.Packag.Abstr., Paper & Bd.Abstr.
—BLDSC shelfmark: 6358.850000.
Description: For global manufacturers and converters of paper, pulp and paperboard products. Provides information about corporate strategies, and plant operations. Profiles the world's pulp and paper companies and suppliers to the industry.

676 SI
PAPER ASIA. (Text in English) 1985. bi-m. $90. Toucan Publications Pte. Ltd., 322-C King George's Ave., Singapore 0820, Singapore. TEL 65-2997121. FAX 65-2997545. Ed. Andrew Loh. adv.; circ. 4,100.
Description: Covers the pulp, paper and conversion industry in Asia for Asian executives.

676 UK ISSN 0950-4478
PAPER EUROPEAN DATA BOOK. 1985. a? £170 (foreign £190). Benn Business Information Services Ltd., P.O. Box 20, Sovereign Way, Tonbridge, Kent TN9 1RW, England. TEL 0732-362666. FAX 0732-770483. TELEX 95162-BENTON-G. Ed. John Vincent. circ. 600.
—BLDSC shelfmark: 6396.832300.
Description: For all top decision makers involved with the European paper industry. Provides vital statistical analysis of the economies, raw material resources and pulp and paper industries of Western Europe; global, regional and national data; trends in demand, capacity developments, corporate performance and price movements; financial results, product range and capacity of the market leaders.

676.2 UK ISSN 0031-112X
PAPER FACTS AND FIGURES. 1961. bi-m. £65 (foreign £81). Benn Business Information Services Ltd., P.O. Box 20, Sovereign Way, Tonbridge, Kent TN9 1RQ, England. TEL 0732-362666. FAX 0732-770483. TELEX 95162-BENTON-G. Ed. Janet Seal. adv.; stat.; circ. 3,500. **Indexed:** Paper & Bd.Abstr.
—BLDSC shelfmark: 6361.500000.
Description: Links paper and board manufacturers, agents and merchants.

PAPER, FILM AND FOIL CONVERTER. see PACKAGING

676 US
PAPER INDUSTRY MAGAZINE. 1984. bi-m. Hatton-Brown Publishers, Inc., 225 Hanrick St., Montgomery, AL 36104. TEL 205-834-1170. FAX 205-834-4525. (Subscr. to: Box 2268, Montgomery, AL 36102) adv.; circ. 19,200. (reprint service avail.)
Formerly: Paper Industry Equipment.

676 UK
PAPER INDUSTRY TECHNICAL ASSOCIATION. FUNDAMENTAL RESEARCH INTERNATIONAL SYMPOSIA. 1958. quadrennial. price varies. Paper Industry Technical Association, Pira House, Randalls Rd., Leatherhead KT22 7RU, England. TEL 0372-376161. **Indexed:** Abstr.Bull.Inst.Pap.Chem.
Formerly: British Paper and Board Industry Federation. Technical Association. Fundamental Research International Symposia (ISSN 0068-2322)

676 US
PAPER MERCHANT PERFORMANCE. 1935. a. $300. National Paper Trade Association, Inc., 111 Great Neck Rd., Ste. 603, Great Neck, NY 11021. TEL 516-829-3070. Ed. George Cain. charts; stat.; circ. 2,500. **Indexed:** SRI.

338.4 US
PAPER MERCHANT SALES REPORT. 1940. m. membership only. National Paper Trade Association, Inc., 111 Great Neck Rd., Ste. 603, Great Neck, NY 11021. TEL 516-829-3070. Ed. George Cain. circ. 5,000. **Indexed:** SRI.

676 US
▼**PAPER RECYCLER.** 1990. m. $327. Miller Freeman, Inc. (Subsidiary of: United Newspapers), 600 Harrison St., San Francisco, CA 94107. TEL 415-905-2200. FAX 415-905-2232. Ed. Debra Adams Garcia.

676 UK ISSN 0302-4180
HD9820.1
PAPER REVIEW OF THE YEAR.* 1973. a. free with "Paper" subscription. Benn Publications Ltd., Sovereign Way, Tonbridge, Kent TN9 1RW, England. Ed. David Price. index; circ. 8,175.

676.3 US ISSN 0031-1170
TS1080
PAPER SALES. 1940. m. $15. Avanstar Communications, Inc., 7500 Old Oak Blvd., Cleveland, OH 44130. TEL 216-826-2839. FAX 216-891-2726. (Subscr. to: 1 E. First St., Duluth, MN 55802) Ed. Jane Seybolt. adv.; illus.; mkt.; tr.lit.; circ. 12,932.
●Also available online. Vendor(s): Data-Star, DIALOG.
Description: Focuses on improving selling skills and increasing sales for paper distributors and paper, pulp and paperboard manufacturers and converters.

676 330 US
PAPER SALES CONVENTION NEWS. 1952. a. Avanstar Communications, Inc., 7500 Old Oak Blvd., Cleveland, OH 44130. TEL 216-826-2839. FAX 216-891-2683. (Subscr. to: 1 E. First St., Duluth, MN 55802) Ed. Jane Seybolt. circ. 3,550.

676 SA ISSN 0254-3494
PAPER SOUTHERN AFRICA; devoted exclusively to the pulp, paper & board industries in Southern Africa. (Text in English) 1980. bi-m. R.84. (Technical Association of the Pulp and Paper Industry of Southern Africa) George Warman Publications (Pty.) Ltd., Box 3847, Cape Town 8000, South Africa. TEL 021-24-5320. FAX 021-26-1332. TELEX 5-21849 SA. Ed. Debbie Welsh. adv.; circ. 1,200. **Indexed:** Abstr.Bull.Inst.Pap.Chem., Ind.S.A.Per., Paper & Bd.Abstr.
Description: Technical journal on pulp, paper and board production and processing.

676.142 US
▼**PAPER STOCK REPORT.** 1990. w. $85. McEntee Media Corp., 1327 Holland Rd., Cleveland, OH 44142-3290. TEL 216-362-7979. FAX 216-362-4623. Ed. Ken McEntee. stat.
Description: Covers developments in the paper recycling industry.

676 UK
PAPER TECHNOLOGY. 1960. 12/yr. £76 to non-members. Paper Industry Technical Association, Pira House, Randalls Rd., Leatherhead KT22 7RU, England. TEL 0372-376161. Ed. M. Marley. adv.; bk.rev.; abstr.; bibl.; charts; illus.; index, cum.index; circ. 3,700. **Indexed:** Abstr.Bull.Inst.Pap.Chem., Br.Tech.Ind., C.I.S. Abstr., Chem.Abstr., Eng.Ind., Excerp.Med., Graph.Arts Lit.Abstr., Paper & Bd.Abstr., Sh.& Vib.Dig.
Former titles: Paper Technology and Industry (ISSN 0306-252X); Paper Technology (ISSN 0031-1189)

PAPER TREE LETTER; independent analysis of forest products economics. see FORESTS AND FORESTRY — Lumber And Wood

PAPER YEAR BOOK. see BUSINESS AND ECONOMICS — Trade And Industrial Directories

676 FI ISSN 0031-1243
HD9765.F4 CODEN: PAPUAU
PAPERI JA PUU/PAPER AND TIMBER. (Text and title in English, Finnish) 1919. m. $140. (Suomen Metsateollisuuden Keskusliitto) Finnish Paper and Timber Journal Publishing Co., P.O. Box 154, 00131 Helsinki 13, Finland. FAX 0-630-365. (Co-sponsors: Finnish Woodworking Engineers' Association; Finnish Paper Engineers' Association) Ed. Marja Korpinvaara. adv.; bibl.; charts; illus.; stat.; index; circ. 4,000. **Indexed:** Abstr.Bull.Inst.Pap.Chem., C.I.S. Abstr., Chem.Abstr., Curr.Cont., Forest.Abstr., Forest Prod.Abstr., Graph.Arts Lit.Abstr., Paper & Bd.Abstr., PROMT, Risk Abstr.
—BLDSC shelfmark: 6366.500000.

676 II ISSN 0048-2862
PAPERPRINTPACK INDIA. (Text in English) 1963. m. Rs.60 (foreign Rs.400). (Shantarani Sons & Co.) Smt. S. Tikku, Pub., 7-104 Nariman Passage, Prabhadevi P.O., Bombay 400 025, India. TEL 4220906. Ed. Somnath Tikku. adv.; charts; illus.; circ. 6,000. **Indexed:** Packag.Sci.Tech.
Description: Devoted to developments in the paper, printing, packaging, and other affiliated industries in India. Includes calendar of relevant events.

PAPERWORKER. see LABOR UNIONS

676 338.4 US
▼**PAPERWORLD.** 1991. m. free to qualified personnel. 6 Piedmont Center, Ste. 300, Atlanta, GA 30305. TEL 404-841-3333. FAX 404-841-3332. circ. 40,000 (controlled).

676 FR ISSN 0031-1308
CODEN: PPTRDD
PAPETERIE; fabrications, transformation, distribution. (Text in French; summaries in English) 1878. m. 910 F. Groupement d'Activites de Presse (GRAP), 21 rue d'Hauteville, 75010 Paris, France. TEL 33-1-42-46-32-32. FAX 33-1-45-23-41-44. Ed. Ginette Blery. adv.; bk.rev.; abstr.; charts; illus.; mkt.; index; circ. 3,500. **Indexed:** Chem.Abstr., Paper & Bd.Abstr., PROMT.
—BLDSC shelfmark: 6401.000000.

676 SZ ISSN 0031-1316
PAPETERIST/PAPETIER/CARTOLAIO. (Text in French and German) 1919. m. 40 Fr. (Verband Schweizerischer Papeteristen) Buri Druck und Verlag, Eigerstr. 71, 3001 Berne, Switzerland. adv.; illus.; mkt.

676.2 CN ISSN 0048-2889
PAPETIER. (Text in French) 1964. 4/yr. free. Association des Industries Forestieres du Quebec, Ltee., 1200 Ave. Germain-des-Pres, Ste-Foy, Que. G1V 3M7, Canada. TEL 418-651-9352. FAX 418-651-4622. Ed. Andre Duchesne. circ. 25,000. **Indexed:** Pt.de Rep. (1979-).

676 CN ISSN 0847-2645
▼**PAPETIERES DU QUEBEC.** 1990. bi-m. Can.$29($35) (foreign Can.$55). Guy Fortin, 3300 Cote Vertu, Ste. 410, St. Laurent, Que. H4R 2B7, Canada. TEL 514-339-1399. FAX 514-339-1396. Ed. Yves Lavertu. adv.; circ. 5,600.
●Also available online.
Description: Addresses the scientific and technical information needs of the pulp and paper industry.

676 GW ISSN 0031-1340
TS1080 CODEN: PAERAY
DAS PAPIER; Zeitschrift fuer die Erzeugung von Holzstoff, Zellstoff, Papier und Pappe, Chemische Technologie der Cellulose. (Text in German; summaries in English) 1947. m. DM.176. Eduard Roether Verlag, Berliner Allee 56, 6100 Darmstadt, Germany. TEL 06151-3001-17. Ed. R. Weidenmueller. adv.; bk.rev.; bibl.; charts; illus.; mkt.; pat.; stat.; tr.lit.; index; circ. 4,000. (also avail. in microform from UMI; reprint service avail. from UMI) **Indexed:** Abstr.Bull.Inst.Pap.Chem., Chem.Abstr., Curr.Cont., Excerp.Med., Forest.Abstr., Forest Prod.Abstr., Packag.Sci.Tech., Paper & Bd.Abstr., PROMT, World Text.Abstr.

PAPER AND PULP

676   AU
PAPIER AUS OESTERREICH. (Text in English and German) 1964. m. S.630. Vereinigung Oesterreichischer Papierindustrieller - Association of Austrian Paper Manufacturers, Gumpendorfer Str. 6, A-1061 Vienna, Austria. TEL 0222-58886-0. FAX 0222-58886-222. Ed. Viktor Bauer. adv.; bk.rev.; illus.; stat.; index; circ. 5,000. **Indexed:** Abstr.Bull.Inst.Pap.Chem.
   Formerly: Oesterreichische Papier (ISSN 0473-8322)

676   FR   ISSN 0031-1367
                           CODEN: PCCLAK
PAPIER CARTON ET CELLULOSE. 1952. m. 570 F. (foreign 670 F.)(effective Jan. 1991). Pacacel, 18 rue Saint-Fiacre, 75002 Paris, France. TEL 1-42-36-95-59. FAX 33-1-42-33-83-24. Ed. Charley Sifaoui. adv.; bk.rev.; abstr.; bibl.; charts; illus.; stat.; circ. 2,500. **Indexed:** Abstr.Bull.Inst.Pap.Chem., Chem.Abstr., Excerp.Med., Paper & Bd.Abstr.
   Description: Includes producers in Europe, suppliers, converters, merchants and agents.

676   FR
PAPIER, CARTON ET CELLULOSE. ANNUAIRE. a. 610 F. (foreign 640 F.). Pacacel, 18 rue Saint Fiacre, 75002 Paris, France. TEL 33-1-42-36-95-59. FAX 33-1-42-33-83-24.
   Description: Identifies participants, partners and companies in all involved sectors of activity.

338.4   FR
PAPIER, CARTON ET CELLULOSE. ANNUAIRE FINANCIER. a. 1957 Fr. Pacacel, 18 rue Saint Fiacre, 75002 Paris, France. TEL 33-1-42-36-95-59. FAX 33-1-42-33-83-24.
   Description: Provides financial profiles of more than 400 companies in the paper industry.

676   FR
PAPIER, CARTON ET CELLULOSE. CATALOGUE DES MATERIELS ET EQUIPEMENTS. a. 280 Fr. Pacacel, 18 rue Saint Fiacre, 75002 Paris, France. TEL 33-1-42-36-95-59. FAX 33-1-42-33-83-24.
   Description: Covers market offerings of equipment and manufacturers.

676 658.7   FR
PAPIER, CARTON ET CELLULOSE. GUIDE DU PAPIER. a. 400 Fr. Pacacel, 18 rue Saint Fiacre, 75002 Paris, France. TEL 33-1-42-36-95-59. FAX 33-1-42-33-83-24.
   Description: Offers a complete list of products in the industry for purchasers.

676   AU   ISSN 0259-7454
PAPIER UND DRUCK. 1895. 24/yr. S.590. Verlagsbuchhandlung Brueder Hollinek und Co. GmbH, Feldgasse 13, A-1238 Vienna, Austria. TEL 0222-8893646. FAX 0222-8893647-24. TELEX 1-13353. Ed. K. Patschka. adv.; bibl.; charts; illus.; stat.; circ. 4,800.
   Incorporates (1949-1986): Papier- und Buchgewerbe-rundschau (ISSN 0031-1359); Formerly (until 1986): Oesterreichische Papier-Zeitung (ISSN 0029-9391)

676   GW   ISSN 0031-1375
TS1080
PAPIER UND DRUCK; Fachzeitschrift fuer Typografie, polygrafische Technik und Papierverarbeitung. (Text in German; index in English and Russian) 1952. m. DM.84 (foreign DM.104.40). Fachbuchverlag, Karl-Heine-Str. 16, 7031 Leipzig, Germany. adv.; bk.rev.; abstr.; illus.; pat.; tr.lit.; tr.mk.; index. **Indexed:** Abstr.Bull.Inst.Pap.Chem., Bibl.Cart., C.I.S. Abstr., Chem.Abstr.
   Description: Trade publication for the printing and paper manufacturing industries, featuring book production and design, graphic arts, book binding, production development, screen printing, industry news, and reports of events and exhibitions.

676   GW   ISSN 0048-2897
PAPIER UND KUNSTSTOFF VERARBEITER; die fachzeitschrift fuer druck, veredelung und weiterverarbeitung von papier, vollpappe, wellpape, zellglas, kunststoff und folien aller art. 1965. m. DM.151. Deutscher Fachverlag GmbH, Mainzer Landstr. 251, Postfach 100606, 6000 Frankfurt a.M. 1, Germany. Ed. B. Wassmann. circ. 4,300. **Indexed:** Abstr.Bull.Inst.Pap.Chem., Int.Packag.Abstr., Packag.Sci.Tech., Paper & Bd.Abstr.
   Formerly: Papier Verarbeiter.

676   GW   ISSN 0031-1405
DER PAPIERMACHER. 1951. 13/yr. (Vereinigung der Arbeitgeberverbaende der Deutschen Papierindustrie e.V.) Dr. Curt Haefner Verlag, Bachstr. 14, Postfach 106060, 6900 Heidelberg, Germany. TEL 06221-49064. circ. 70,000. **Indexed:** Abstr.Bull.Inst.Pap.Chem., Paper & Bd.Abstr.
   —BLDSC shelfmark: 6403.126000.

676   CS   ISSN 0031-1421
TS1080   CODEN: PCELAU
PAPIR A CELULOZA. (Text in Czech or Slovak; summaries in English, German, Russian) 1945. m. $54.70. (Vyskumny Ustav Papiera a Celulozy) Nakladatelstvi Technicke Literatury, Spalena 51, 113 02 Prague 1, Czechoslovakia. (Dist. by: Artia, Ve Smeckach 30, 111 27 Prague 1, Czechoslovakia) Ed. Josef Korda. adv.; bk.rev.; charts; illus.; pat.; circ. 1,700. **Indexed:** Abstr.Bull.Inst.Pap.Chem., C.I.S. Abstr., Chem.Abstr., Forest Prod.Abstr., Paper & Bd.Abstr.

676   NO
PAPIRHANDLEREN. 1929. m. NOK 420. Norske Papirhandleres Landsforbund, Oevre Vollgt. 15, 0158 Oslo 1, Norway. FAX 02-333269. Ed. Dag Helland. adv.; circ. 1,300.

676   HU   ISSN 0031-1448
                           CODEN: PAPIBT
PAPIRIPAR. (Text in Hungarian; summaries in German and Russian) 1957. bi-m. $25. Papir- es Nyomdaipari Mueszaki Egyesuelet, H-1371 Budapest pf. 433, Hungary. (Subscr. to: Kultura, Box 149, H-1389 Budapest, Hungary) Ed. G. Vamos. adv.; bk.rev.; abstr.; bibl.; charts; illus.; index; circ. 1,900. **Indexed:** Abstr.Bull.Inst.Pap.Chem., Chem.Abstr., Forest Prod.Abstr., Graph.Arts Lit.Abstr.

PAPIRIPARI ES NYOMDAIPARI SZAKIRODALMI TAJEKOZTATO/PAPER INDUSTRY & PRINTING ABSTRACTS. see *PAPER AND PULP — Abstracting, Bibliographies, Statistics*

658   US   ISSN 0899-6008
PARTY & PAPER RETAILER. 1986. m. $31. 4Ward Corporation, 500 Summer St., Ste. 300, Stamford, CT 06901. TEL 203-964-0900. FAX 203-964-1816. (Subscr. to: P.O. Box 925, Darien, CT 06820) Ed. Trisha McMahon Drain. adv.; circ. 22,000. (also avail. in microfilm; back issues avail.)
   Description: Covers the retailing of party supplies including balloons, plastics and paper tableware, gift wrap, and greeting cards.

676   UK   ISSN 0954-8521
TS1088
PHILLIPS' INTERNATIONAL PAPER DIRECTORY (PAPER). 1904. a. £90 (foreign £100). Benn Business Information Services Ltd., P.O. Box 20, Sovereign Way, Tonbridge, Kent TN9 1RQ, England. TEL 0732-362666. FAX 0732-770483. TELEX 95162-BENTON-G. Ed. George Hutton. adv.; index; circ. 3,000.
   —BLDSC shelfmark: 6461.293500.
   Formerly: Phillips' Paper Trade Directory - Europe-Mills of the World (ISSN 0079-158X); Incorporates: Papermakers' and Merchants' Directory of All Nations (ISSN 0078-9038)
   Description: Comprehensive guide to the world's pulp, paper and paperboard mills including details of mill executives, machines, products and output.

PRESSURE SENSITIVE TAPE COUNCIL. TECHNICAL SEMINAR. PROCEEDINGS. see *RUBBER*

PREVISIONS GLISSANTES DETAILLEES EN PERSPECTIVES SECTORIELLES (VOL.22): INDUSTRIE DES PATES, PAPIERS ET CARTONS. see *BUSINESS AND ECONOMICS — Economic Situation And Conditions*

676   US   ISSN 0033-4081
TS1080   CODEN: PUPAA8
PULP AND PAPER. 1927. m. (s-m. Nov.). $90 (free to qualified personnel). Miller Freeman, Inc., (Subsidiary of: United Newspapers), 600 Harrison St., San Francisco, CA 94107. TEL 415-905-2200. FAX 415-905-2232. TELEX 278273. Ed. Ken L. Patrick. adv.; bk.rev.; charts; illus.; mkt.; stat.; tr.lit.; index; circ. 34,000 (controlled). (also avail. in microform from UMI; reprint service avail. from UMI) **Indexed:** Abstr.Bull.Inst.Pap.Chem., B.P.I., Bus.Ind., Chem.Abstr., Curr.Pack.Abstr., Excerp.Med., Forest.Abstr., Forest Prod.Abstr., Key to Econ.Sci., Ocean.Abstr., Paper & Bd.Abstr., Pollut.Abstr., PROMT, SRI, Tr.& Indus.Ind., W.R.C.Inf.
   —BLDSC shelfmark: 7157.000000.

676   US
PULP & PAPER BUYERS GUIDE. a. $55. Miller Freeman, Inc. (Subsidiary of: United Newspapers), 600 Harrison St., San Francisco, CA 94107. TEL 415-905-2200. FAX 415-905-2232. TELEX 278273. Ed. Ken L. Patrick. circ. 34,000. (also avail. in microfilm; reprint service avail. from UMI)

676.12 674   CN   ISSN 0316-4004
TS1080   CODEN: PPCAAA
PULP & PAPER CANADA. 1903. m. Can.$49($56) (foreign $120). (Canadian Pulp and Paper Association) Guy Tortolano, 3300 Cote Vertu, Suite 410, St. Laurent, Que. H4R 2B7, Canada. TEL 514-339-1399. FAX 514-339-1396. Ed. Peter Williamson. adv.; bk.rev.; charts; illus.; mkt.; stat.; tr.lit.; index; circ. 9,500. (also avail. in microfiche from UMI) **Indexed:** Abstr.Bull.Inst.Pap.Chem., Acid Rain Abstr., Agri.Eng.Abstr., Bibl.Agri., CAD CAM Abstr., Can.B.P.I., Chem.Abstr., Curr.Cont., Energy Info.Abstr., Environ.Abstr., Excerp.Med., Forest.Abstr., Forest Prod.Abstr., Graph.Arts Lit.Abstr., Paper & Bd.Abstr., Sci.Abstr., Sel.Water Res.Abstr., W.R.C.Inf.
   ●Also available online.
   —BLDSC shelfmark: 7157.050000.
   Formerly: Pulp and Paper Magazine of Canada (ISSN 0033-4103); Incorporating: Woodlands Review.
   Description: Addresses the scientific and technical information needs of the pulp and paper industry.

676   CN   ISSN 0708-501X
TS1088
PULP & PAPER CANADA DIRECTORY. 1907. a. Can.$88($65) Guy Tortolano (Subsidiary of: Southam Inc.), 3300 Cote Vertu, Suite 410, St. Laurent, Que. H4R 2B7, Canada. TEL 514-339-1399. FAX 514-339-1396. TELEX 058-24168. Ed. P. Williamson. adv.; index; circ. 1,700. **Indexed:** Abstr.Bull.Inst.Pap.Chem.
   Former titles: Pulp and Paper Canada Business Directory (ISSN 0317-3550); Canada's Pulp and Paper Business Directory (ISSN 0079-7936)

676   CN   ISSN 1181-6562
▼**PULP & PAPER CANADA GRADE DIRECTORY.** 1990. a. Can.$99.95. Guy Tortolano, 3300 Cote Vertu, Ste. 410, St. Laurent, Que. H4R 2B7, Canada. TEL 514-339-1399. FAX 514-399-1396. Ed. Peter N. Williamson. adv.
   ●Also available online.
   Description: Gives details of the Canadian-made pulp and paper products by brand name, end use and technical specifications. Includes details of Canadian pulp and paper companies.

676   CN   ISSN 0709-2563
TS1088
PULP & PAPER CANADA'S ANNUAL & DIRECTORY. 1930. a. Can.$80 (foreign $100). Guy Tortolano, 3300 Cote Vertu, Ste. 410, St. Laurent, Que. H4R 2B7, Canada. TEL 514-339-1399. FAX 514-339-1396. Ed. Peter N. Williamson. adv.; index; circ. 1,500.
   ●Also available online.
   Former titles: Pulp and Paper Canada's Reference Manual and Buyers' Guide; Pulp and Paper Magazine of Canada's Reference Manual and Buyers' Guide (ISSN 0079-7952)
   Description: Gives corporate and technical information (equipment lists and flow charts) of Canada's pulp and paper companies and their mills. Lists suppliers and products plus copmlete address information. Also lists allied and related organizations.

PAPER AND PULP

676   US
PULP & PAPER FORECASTER. 1988. bi-m. $985. Miller Freeman, Inc. (Subsidiary of: United Newspapers), 600 Harrison St., San Francisco, CA 94107. TEL 415-905-2200. FAX 415-905-2232. TELEX 278273. Ed. Will Mies.

338.47   FR
PULP AND PAPER INDUSTRY IN O E C D MEMBER COUNTRIES/INDUSTRIE DES PATES ET PAPIERS DANS LES PAYS MEMBRES DE L'O C D E. (Text in English, French) 1954. a. price varies. Organization for Economic Cooperation and Development, 2 rue Andre-Pascal, 75775 Paris Cedex 16, France. TEL 45-24-82-00. FAX 45-24-85-00. (U.S. Orders to: O.E.C.D. Publications and Information Center, 2001 L St., N.W., Ste. 700, Washington, DC 20036-4910. TEL 202-785-6323) (also avail. in microfiche from OEC)
Formerly: Pulp and Paper Industry in O E C D Member Countries and Finland - Industrie des Pates et Papiers dans les Pays Membres de l'O C D E et la Finlande (ISSN 0474-5485)

676   US   ISSN 0190-2172
TS1109   CODEN: CRCFDZ
PULP AND PAPER INDUSTRY TECHNICAL CONFERENCE. CONFERENCE RECORD. Variant title: Annual Pulp and Paper Industry Technical Conference. Conference Record. a. (I E E E, Industry Applications Society) Institute of Electrical and Electronics Engineers, Inc., 345 E. 47th St., New York, NY 10017-2394. TEL 212-705-7900. FAX 212-705-7682. (Subscr. to: Box 1331, 445 Hoes Ln., Piscataway, NJ 08855-1331)
—BLDSC shelfmark: 4362.859800.
Formerly: Pulp and Paper Industry Technical Conference. Record (ISSN 0079-7944)
Description: Development and application of electrical systems related to the manufacture and fabrication of products.

676   US   ISSN 0033-409X
PULP & PAPER INTERNATIONAL. (Annual editions in Chinese, Russian) 1958. m. $115 free to qualified personnel. Miller Freeman, Inc. (Subsidiary of: United Newspapers), 600 Harrison St., San Francisco, CA 94107. TEL 415-905-2200. FAX 415-905-2232. TELEX 278273. (Alt.addr.: 123A Chausee de Charleroi, Box 5, B-1060 Brussels, Belgium) Ed. Peter G. Sutton. adv.; bk.rev.; charts; illus.; stat.; index; circ. 11,500. **Indexed:** Abstr.Bull.Inst.Pap.Chem., B.P.I., Bus.Ind., Chem.Abstr., Curr.Pack.Abstr., Eng.Ind., Excerp.Med., Forest.Abstr., Forest Prod.Abstr., Key to Econ.Sci., Ocean.Abstr., Paper & Bd.Abstr., Pollut.Abstr.
—BLDSC shelfmark: 7157.700000.
Description: Technical and operational reports for improved operations.

676   US
PULP & PAPER INTERNATIONAL FACT & PRICE BOOK. 1980. a. $260. Miller Freeman Inc., 600 Harrison St., San Francisco, CA 94107. TEL 415-905-2200. Ed. Heide Matussek. circ. 500.
Formerly: Pulp and Paper International Factbook.

676   CN   ISSN 0713-5807
TS1080   CODEN: PPAJDU
PULP & PAPER JOURNAL. 1948. 11/yr. Can.$28. Maclean Hunter Ltd., Business Publication Division, Maclean Hunter Bldg., 777 Bay St., Toronto, Ont. M5W 1A7, Canada. TEL 416-596-5831. Ed. John Mullinder. adv.; bk.rev.; abstr.; charts; illus.; mkt.; pat.; stat.; tr.lit.; index; circ. 7,606. (also avail. in microform from UMI; reprint service avail. from UMI) **Indexed:** Abstr.Bull.Inst.Pap.Chem., Can.B.P.I., Chem.Abstr., P.A.I.S., PROMT.
Supersedes in part (as of 1982): Canadian Pulp and Paper Industry (ISSN 0008-4867)

676   US
PULP & PAPER NORTH AMERICAN INDUSTRY FACTBOOK. 1980. biennial. $285. Miller Freeman, Inc. (Subsidiary of: United Newspapers), 600 Harrison St., San Francisco, CA 94107. TEL 415-905-2200. FAX 415-905-2232. TELEX 278273. Ed. Willard E. Mies. circ. 600. (reprint service avail. from UMI) **Indexed:** SRI.

676.2   US
PULP & PAPER PROJECT REPORT. 1982. m. $369. Miller Freeman, Inc. (Subsidiary of: United Newspapers), 600 Harrison St., San Francisco, CA 94107. TEL 415-905-2200. FAX 415-905-2232. TELEX 278273. Ed. Carl P. Espe. (reprint service avail. from UMI)

676   CN   ISSN 0079-7960
TS1080
PULP AND PAPER RESEARCH INSTITUTE OF CANADA. ANNUAL REPORT. 1968. a. free. Pulp and Paper Research Institute of Canada, 570 bvd. St. Jean, Pointe Claire, Que. H9R 3J9, Canada. TEL 514-630-4100. FAX 514-630-4134. TELEX 05-821541. Ed. P.M. Nobbs. circ. 2,500.

676   US
PULP & PAPER WEEK. 1979. w. $617. Miller Freeman, Inc. (Subsidiary of: United Newspapers), 600 Harrison St., San Francisco, CA 94107. TEL 415-905-2200. FAX 415-905-2232. TELEX 278273. Ed. Willard E. Mies. stat.; index. (looseleaf format; back issues avail.; reprint service avail. from UMI) **Indexed:** Abstr.Bull.Inst.Pap.Chem.

REPRODUCTION BULLETIN. see *PRINTING*

REVISTA FORESTAL BARACOA. see *FORESTS AND FORESTRY — Lumber And Wood*

676   SW   ISSN 0348-2650
S T F I MEDDELANDE. SERIES A. 1969. irreg. exchange basis. Svenska Traeforskningsinstitutet (STFI) - Swedish Pulp and Paper Research Institute, Box 5604, S-114 86 Stockholm, Sweden. FAX 8-115518. TELEX 10880. illus.; cum.index: 1969-1983; circ. 500. **Indexed:** Abstr.Bull.Inst.Pap.Chem., Forest.Abstr., Forest Prod.Abstr.
—BLDSC shelfmark: 8464.749500.
Formerly: Svenska Traeforskningsinstitutet. Meddelande. Series A (ISSN 0085-6983)

676   US
ST. REGIS NEWS.* 1965. m. free to qualified personnel. Champion International, 1 Champion Plaza, Stamford, CT 06921. TEL 203-358-7000. Ed. Ron Martin. circ. 31,000. (tabloid format)
Formerly: St. Regis News, Southern Edition (ISSN 0036-3189)

676.3   BE
SCRIPT/PAPIERHANDEL. (Text in Flemish, French) 1986. bi-m. 1500 Fr. Uitgevery E.G.P. Editions, F. Lenoirstr. 23, B-1090 Brussels, Belgium. FAX 2-4259312. Ed. Marc Bruynseraede. adv.; bk.rev.; circ. 4,500.
Formerly: Papetier.

SEKUNDAER-ROHSTOFFE; Fachzeitschrift fuer Rohstoffhandel, Wiederverwertung und Recycling-Technik. see *MACHINERY*

676   AT   ISSN 0310-4389
SOMETHING ON PAPER. 1973. q. free. Associated Pulp and Paper Mills Ltd., P.O. Box 558, Camberwell, Vic. 3124, Australia. FAX 03-811-9629. Ed. N. Heydon. circ. 5,000.

676   US   ISSN 0081-2129
SOURCES OF SUPPLY - BUYERS GUIDE. 1924. a. $80. Advertisers and Publishers Service, Inc., Drawer 795, Park Ridge, IL 60068. TEL 708-823-3145. Ed. L.B. Cowan. adv.; circ. 1,500.
Formerly: Source of Supply Directory.

676.2   US   ISSN 0270-5222
TS1080   CODEN: SOPPDD
SOUTHERN PULP & PAPER.* (Annual Review Number) 1938. m. $18. Ernest H. Abernethy Publishing (Subsidiary of: A-S-M Communications, Inc.), 6 Pidemont Ctr. N.E., Ste. 300, Atlanta, GA 30305-1515. Ed. John C. Cook. adv.; bk.rev.; charts; illus.; tr.lit.; index; circ. 10,000. (back issues avail.) **Indexed:** Abstr.Bull.Inst.Pap.Chem., Chem.Abstr., Paper & Bd.Abstr.
—BLDSC shelfmark: 0850.050000.
Formerly: Southern Pulp and Paper Manufacturer (ISSN 0038-4488)

676   SW   ISSN 0283-6831
TS1080
SVENSK PAPPERSTIDNING - NORDISK CELLULOSA. (Text in Swedish) 1898. 18/yr. SEK 605 within the Nordic countries; elewhere SEK 730. (Svenska Cellulosa- och Papperbruksfoereningen) Arbor Publishing AB, Midskogsgraend 5, S-115 43 Stockholm, Sweden. TEL 08-6643400. FAX 08-6642124. (Co-sponsor: Svenska Papers- och Cellulosaingenioersfoereningen) Ed. A. Forsstroem. adv.; bk.rev.; abstr.; bibl.; charts; illus.; pat.; stat.; index; circ. 7,687 (controlled). **Indexed:** Abstr.Bull.Inst.Pap.Chem., ASCA, Biol.Abstr., Chem.Abstr., Curr.Cont., Curr.Pack.Abstr., Forest.Abstr., Forest Prod.Abstr., Paper & Bd.Abstr., PROMT, World Text.Abstr.
Formerly: Svensk Papperstidning (ISSN 0039-6680)
Description: Trade journal for the pulp and paper industry.

676   US   ISSN 0734-1415
TS1080   CODEN: TAJODT
T A P P I JOURNAL. 1949. m. membership. Technical Association of the Pulp and Paper Industry, Inc., Technology Park-Atlanta, Box 105113, Atlanta, GA 30348. TEL 404-446-1400. FAX 404-446-6947. adv.; bk.rev.; charts; illus.; mkt.; pat.; tr.lit.; index; circ. 38,000. (also avail. in microform from MIM) **Indexed:** A.S.& T.Ind., Abstr.Bull.Inst.Pap.Chem., Acid Rain Abstr., Acid Rain Ind., Anal.Abstr., Art & Archaeol.Tech.Abstr., ASCA, Biol.Abstr., CAD CAM Abstr., Chem.Abstr., Chem.Eng.Abstr., Curr.Biotech.Abstr., Curr.Cont., Curr.Pack.Abstr., Energy Info.Abstr., Eng.Ind., Environ.Abstr., Excerp.Med., Fluidex, Forest.Abstr., Graph.Arts Lit.Abstr., Int.Packag.Abstr., Mass Spectr.Bull., Packag.Sci.Tech., Paper & Bd.Abstr., Risk Abstr., Robomat., Sh.& Vib.Dig., Soils & Fert., T.C.E.A., Text.Tech.Dig., W.R.C.Inf., World Surf.Coat., World Text.Abstr.
—BLDSC shelfmark: 8603.948000.
Formerly: T A P P I (ISSN 0039-8241)
Refereed Serial

676   US   ISSN 1046-4166
T A P P I PROCEEDINGS. 1985. a. price varies. Technical Association of the Pulp and Paper Industry, Inc., Technology Park-Atlanta, Box 105113, Atlanta, GA 30348. TEL 404-446-1400. FAX 404-446-6947.
—BLDSC shelfmark: 8603.947500.
Formerly (until 1988): Technical Association of the Pulp and Paper Industry. Annual Meeting Proceedings (ISSN 0272-7269)
Refereed Serial

676   US   ISSN 1045-618X
TS1109
T A P P I TEST METHODS. 1926. biennial. membership. Technical Association of the Pulp and Paper Industry, Inc., Technology Park-Atlanta, Box 105113, Atlanta, GA 30348. TEL 404-446-1400. FAX 404-446-6947. index.
—BLDSC shelfmark: 8604.256500.
Former titles: T A P P I Standards and Provisional Methods; T A P P I Standards and Suggested Methods.
Refereed Serial

676   US   ISSN 1047-305X
TECHNICAL ASSOCIATION OF THE PULP AND PAPER INDUSTRY. COATING CONFERENCE. PROCEEDINGS (YEAR) 1987. a. price varies. Technical Association of the Pulp and Paper Industry, Inc., Technology Park-Atlanta, Box 105113, Atlanta, GA 30348. TEL 404-446-1400. FAX 404-446-6947.
Refereed Serial

676   US   ISSN 0734-1415
TS1088
TECHNICAL ASSOCIATION OF THE PULP AND PAPER INDUSTRY. DIRECTORY. Running title: T A P P I Directory. 1931. a. Technical Association of the Pulp and Paper Industry, Inc., Technology Park-Atlanta, Box 105113, Atlanta, GA 30348. TEL 404-446-1400. FAX 404-446-6947. adv.; circ. 31,000. Key Title: Directory - Technical Association of the Pulp and Paper Industry.

PAPER AND PULP — ABSTRACTING, BIBLIOGRAPHIES, STATISTICS

676   US   ISSN 0271-9959
TS1080   CODEN: ECOPD8
TECHNICAL ASSOCIATION OF THE PULP AND PAPER INDUSTRY. ENGINEERING CONFERENCE PROCEEDINGS (YEAR). (In 3 books) a. Technical Association of the Pulp and Paper Industry, Inc., Technology Park-Atlanta, Box 105113, Atlanta, GA 30348. TEL 404-446-1400. FAX 404-446-6947.
Refereed Serial

676   US   ISSN 1050-4265
TS1118.F5   CODEN: PACFEQ
TECHNICAL ASSOCIATION OF THE PULP AND PAPER INDUSTRY. FINISHING AND CONVERTING CONFERENCE. PROCEEDINGS (YEAR). a. Technical Association of the Pulp and Paper Industry, Inc., Technology Park-Atlanta, Box 105113, Atlanta, GA 30348. TEL 404-446-1400. FAX 404-446-6947. adv.
Formerly: Technical Association of the Pulp and Paper Industry. Paper Finishing and Converting Conference. Proceedings (Year) (ISSN 0738-0313)
Refereed Serial

676   US   ISSN 1046-4166
TECHNICAL ASSOCIATION OF THE PULP AND PAPER INDUSTRY. INTERNATIONAL PROCESS & PRODUCT QUALITY CONFERENCE PROCEEDINGS (YEAR). (Each year held jointly with a different TAPPI section) a. $70 to non-members; members $47. Technical Association of the Pulp and Paper Industry, Inc., Technology Park-Atlanta, Box 105113, Atlanta, GA 30348. TEL 404-446-1400. FAX 404-446-6947. circ. 500. **Indexed:** Chem.Abstr., Eng.Ind.
Former titles: Technical Association of the Pulp and Paper Industry. International Process and Materials Quality Evaluation Proceedings (Year); Technical Association of the Pulp and Paper Industry. Testing Conference Proceedings.
Refereed Serial

676   US
TECHNICAL ASSOCIATION OF THE PULP AND PAPER INDUSTRY. NONWOOD PLANT FIBER PULPING PROGRESS REPORT. 1975. irreg. $72 to non-members; members $48. Technical Association of the Pulp and Paper Industry, Inc., Technology Park-Atlanta, Box 105113, Atlanta, GA 30348. TEL 404-446-1400. FAX 404-446-6947.
Refereed Serial

676   US
TECHNICAL ASSOCIATION OF THE PULP AND PAPER INDUSTRY. NONWOVENS CONFERENCE. PROCEEDINGS (YEAR). a. price varies. Technical Association of the Pulp and Paper Industry, Inc., Box 105113, Atlanta, GA 30348. TEL 404-446-1400. FAX 404-446-6947.
Refereed Serial

676   US   ISSN 0197-5153
TS1080   CODEN: TPCPDY
TECHNICAL ASSOCIATION OF THE PULP AND PAPER INDUSTRY. PAPERMAKERS CONFERENCE PROCEEDINGS (YEAR). a. price varies. Technical Association of the Pulp and Paper Industry, Inc., Technology Park-Atlanta, Box 105113, Atlanta, GA 30348. TEL 404-446-1400.
Refereed Serial

676   US   ISSN 1047-3033
TECHNICAL ASSOCIATION OF THE PULP AND PAPER INDUSTRY. POLYMERS, LAMINATIONS & COATINGS CONFERENCE. PROCEEDINGS (YEAR). a. price varies. Technical Association of the Pulp and Paper Industry, Inc., Box 105113, Atlanta, GA 30348. TEL 404-446-1400. FAX 404-446-6947.
Refereed Serial

676   US
TECHNICAL ASSOCIATION OF THE PULP AND PAPER INDUSTRY. PROCESS CONTROL CONFERENCE. PROCEEDINGS (YEAR). a. price varies. Technical Association of the Pulp and Paper Industry, Inc., Box 105113, Atlanta, GA 30348. TEL 404-446-1400. FAX 404-446-6947.
Refereed Serial

676   US   ISSN 0275-0899
TS1171   CODEN: PUCPDP
TECHNICAL ASSOCIATION OF THE PULP AND PAPER INDUSTRY. PULPING CONFERENCE PROCEEDINGS (YEAR). a. Technical Association of the Pulp and Paper Industry, Inc., Technology Park-Atlanta, Box 105113, Atlanta, GA 30348. TEL 404-446-1400.
Refereed Serial

676   US
TRANSPORT AND HANDLING IN THE PULP AND PAPER INDUSTRY; proceedings. 1975. irreg. (Pulp & Paper International Symposium) Miller Freeman, Inc. (Subsidiary of: United Newspapers), 600 Harrison St., San Francisco, CA 94107. TEL 415-905-2200. FAX 415-905-2232. TELEX 278273. illus.; index. (reprint service avail. from UMI)

676   GW   ISSN 0042-3939
VERHUETET UNFAELLE. 1935. 13/yr. (Papiermacher Berufsgenossenschaft) Dr. Curt Haefner Verlag, Bachstr. 14, Postfach 106060, 6900 Heidelberg, Germany. TEL 06221-49064. Ed. H. Gross. illus.; circ. 75,000. **Indexed:** Abstr.Bull.Inst.Pap.Chem.

VORWAERTS. see *LABOR UNIONS*

676   US   ISSN 0083-7024
WALDEN'S A B C GUIDE AND PAPER PRODUCTION YEARBOOK. 1885. a. $92.50. Walden-Mott Corporation, 225 N. Franklin Tpke., Ramsey, NJ 07446-1600. TEL 201-818-8630. FAX 201-818-8720. Ed. Theresa J. Dougherty. adv.; index.

676   US
WALDEN'S FIBER & BOARD REPORT. fortn. Walden-Mott Corporation, 225 N. Franklin Tpke., Ramsey, NJ 07446-1600. TEL 201-261-2630. FAX 201-261-2814. Ed. Gregg Fales.

676   US
WALDEN'S PAPER REPORT. 1971. s-m. $140. Walden-Mott Corporation, 225 N. Franklin Tpke., Ramsey, NJ 07446-1600. TEL 201-818-8630. FAX 201-818-8720. Ed. Sylvia Peremes. adv.; bk.rev.
Formerly: Walden-Mott Paper Report.

676.284 747   US   ISSN 1055-4394
WALLCOVERINGS, WINDOWS & INTERIOR FASHION. 1919. m. $18. Publishing Dynamics Inc., 15 Bank St., Ste. 101, Stamford, CT 06901. TEL 203-357-0028. FAX 203-357-0075. Ed. G. Lisa Cutler. adv.; illus.; stat.; tr.lit.; circ. 17,000. (back issues avail.)
Former titles (until 1991): Wallcoverings Magazine (ISSN 8750-8184); Wallpaper and Wallcoverings (ISSN 0043-0145)

WEYERHAEUSER TODAY. see *FORESTS AND FORESTRY — Lumber And Wood*

676   UK
WHO'S WHO IN CORRUGATED. a. £35. (International Paper Board Industry) Brunton Business Publications Ltd., Thruxton Down House, Thruxton Down, Andover, Hampshire SP11 8PR, England. Ed. Michael D. Brunton.

676   US
WHO'S WHO IN PAPER DISTRIBUTION. 1903. a. $50. National Paper Trade Association, Inc., 111 Great Neck Rd., Ste. 603, Great Neck, NY 11021. TEL 516-829-3070. Ed. William H. Frohlich. adv.; charts; stat.; circ. 2,500.
Former titles: Who's Who in Paper Distribution and Factbook; Who's Who in Paper Distribution.

676   GW   ISSN 0043-7131
TS1080   CODEN: WBPFAZ
WOCHENBLATT FUER PAPIERFABRIKATION; Fachzeitschrift fuer die Papier-, Pappen- und Zellstoff-industrie. 1871. s-m. DM.151.80. Deutscher Fachverlag GmbH, Postfach 100606, 6000 Frankfurt a.M. 1, Germany. TEL 069-7595-1232. FAX 069-7595-1230. (Co-sponsors: Akademischer Papieringenieur-Verein an der TH Darmstadt; Vereinigter Papierfachverband Munchen e.V.; Papiermacher-Berufsgenossenschaft Mainz; Vereinigung Gernsbacher Papiermacher e.V.) Ed. Dr. Manhart Schlegel. adv.; bk.rev.; abstr.; charts; illus.; pat.; stat.; tr.lit.; index; circ. 3,900. (reprint service avail. from ISI) **Indexed:** Abstr.Bull.Inst.Pap.Chem., Chem.Abstr., Curr.Cont., Excerp.Med., Paper & Bd.Abstr., PROMT, Sel.Water Res.Abstr.
—BLDSC shelfmark: 9342.000000.

WOODWORKING INTERNATIONAL. see *FORESTS AND FORESTRY — Lumber And Wood*

676   GW   ISSN 0044-3867
TS1080   CODEN: ZLPAAL
ZELLSTOFF UND PAPIER; wissenschaftlich-technische Zeitschrift fuer die Zellstoff-, Papier- und Pappenindustrie. (Text in German; summaries in English and Russian) 1952. 6/yr. DM.42 (foreign DM.52.20). Fachbuchverlag, Karl-Heine-Str. 16, 7031 Leipzig, Germany. adv.; bk.rev.; abstr.; bibl.; charts; illus.; pat.; tr.lit.; index. **Indexed:** Abstr.Bull.Inst.Pap.Chem., Chem.Abstr., Curr.Cont., Paper & Bd.Abstr.
—BLDSC shelfmark: 9499.400000.
Description: Trade publication for the pulp and paper industry. Covers science and technology, industry news, reports of events, and international news.

676   CC   ISSN 1001-6309
ZHI HE ZAOZHI/PAPER AND PAPER MANUFACTURING. (Text in Chinese) q. Zhongguo Zaozhi Xuehui - China Paper Manufacturing Society, 12 Guanghua Lu, Chaoyang-qu, Beijing 100020, People's Republic of China. TEL 5022561. Ed. Zhou Zhili.

676.2   CC   ISSN 0254-508X
ZHONGGUO ZAOZHI/CHINESE JOURNAL OF PAPER MANUFACTURING. (Text in Chinese) bi-m. Zhongguo Zaozhi Xuehui - China Paper Manufacturing Society, 12 Guanghua Lu, Chaoyang-qu, Beijing 100020, People's Republic of China. TEL 5022561. Ed. Zhu Yice.
—BLDSC shelfmark: 3180.225000.

PAPER AND PULP — Abstracting, Bibliographies, Statistics

676   US   ISSN 0003-0341
HD9824
AMERICAN PAPER INSTITUTE. PAPER, PAPERBOARD, & WOOD PULP MONTHLY STATISTICAL SUMMARY. (Includes Fact Sheet) 1921. m. $415 (foreign $445). American Paper Institute, Inc., 260 Madison Ave., New York, NY 10016. TEL 212-340-0600. Ed. Dr. Benjamin Slatin. charts; mkt.; circ. 800. **Indexed:** Abstr.Bull.Inst.Pap.Chem., SRI.

676   US
AMERICAN PAPER INSTITUTE. PAPER PRODUCTION RATIO WEEKLY REPORT. w. $195 (foreign $215). American Paper Institute, Inc., 260 Madison Ave., New York, NY 10016. TEL 212-340-0600.

676   US   ISSN 0731-8863
HD9839.P33
AMERICAN PAPER INSTITUTE. STATISTICS OF PAPER, PAPERBOARD AND WOOD PULP. 1947. a. $345 (foreign $360). American Paper Institute, Inc., 260 Madison Ave., New York, NY 10016. TEL 212-340-0600. **Indexed:** SRI.
Former titles: Statistics of Paper and Paperboard (ISSN 0097-4730); Paperboard Industry Statistics.

676   US   ISSN 0734-8711
CODEN: CSPAEP
C A SELECTS. PAPER ADDITIVES. s-w. $195. Chemical Abstracts Service (Subsidiary of: American Chemical Society), 2540 Olentangy River Rd., Box 3012, Columbus, OH 43210. TEL 614-447-3600. FAX 614-447-3713. TELEX 6842086.
Description: Covers noncellulosic materials added during papermaking; chemicals used for treating freshly formed sheets.

676.3 634.9   CN   ISSN 0835-0094
HD9834.C2
CANADA. STATISTICS CANADA. PAPER AND ALLIED PRODUCTS INDUSTRIES. (Catalogue 36-250) (Text in English and French) 1917. a. Can.$35($42) (foreign $49). Statistics Canada, Publications Sales and Services, Ottawa, Ont. K1A OT6, Canada. TEL 613-951-7277. FAX 613-951-1584. (also avail. in microform from MML)
Supersedes: Paper and Allied Products Industries (ISSN 0384-4633)
Description: Annual census of manufactures.

338.4   CN   ISSN 0316-4241
HD9839.N4
CANADIAN PULP AND PAPER ASSOCIATION. ANNUAL NEWSPRINT SUPPLEMENT. a. free. Canadian Pulp and Paper Association, Sun Life Building, 19th Fl., 1155 Metcalfe St., Montreal, Que. H3B 4T6, Canada. TEL 514-866-6621. FAX 514-866-3035. stat.

PARAPSYCHOLOGY AND OCCULTISM

676   FR
EUROPEAN PAPER INSTITUTE. ANNUAL STATISTICS. a. European Paper Institute, 42 rue Galilee, 75116 Paris, France. TEL 47-20-43-83. FAX 47-20-37-20. TELEX 610 498.

676   FR
FRANCE. SERVICE D'ETUDE DES STRATEGIES ET DES STATISTIQUES INDUSTRIELLES. RESULTATS TRIMESTRIELS DES ENQUETES DE BRANCHE. FABRICATION D'ARTICLES DE PAPETERIE. q. 180 F. (foreign 210 F.)(effective 1991). Service d'Etude des Strategies et des Statistiques Industrielles (SESSI), 85 Bd. du Montparnasse, 75270 Paris Cedex 06, France. TEL 45-56-42-34. FAX 45-56-40-71. stat.
   Description: Provides detailed industry-wide performance statistics for comparative evaluations.

676 016   US
Z7914.P2
INSTITUTE OF PAPER SCIENCE AND TECHNOLOGY. ABSTRACT BULLETIN. (Former name of issuing body: Institute of Paper Chemistry) 1930. m. price varies. Institute of Paper Science and Technology, 575 14th St., N.W., Atlanta, GA 30318. TEL 404-853-9500. Ed. Rosana Bechtel. bk.rev.; index, cum.index.; circ. 800. (microfilm; back issues avail,; reprint service avail.) **Indexed:** Anal.Abstr., Biol.Abstr., Forest.Abstr., Forest Prod.Abstr., Graph.Arts Lit.Abstr., Int.Packag.Abstr., Paper & Bd.Abstr., World Surf.Coat.
   ●Also available online. Vendor(s): DIALOG (File nos.240 & 840/PAPERCHEM).
   Formerly (until July 1989): Institute of Paper Chemistry. Abstract Bulletin (ISSN 0020-3033)

676   JA   ISSN 0044-0663
MONTHLY STATISTICS OF PAPER DISTRIBUTION/KAMI RYUTSU TOKEI GEPPO.* m. 12000 Yen. Ministry of International Trade and Industry, 1-3-1 Kasumigaseki, Chiyoda-ku, Tokyo 100, Japan. TEL 03-501-1511. Ed.Bd. charts; stat.; circ. 600.

676   NE   ISSN 0168-4361
HD9835.N4
NETHERLANDS. CENTRAAL BUREAU VOOR DE STATISTIEK. PRODUKTIESTATISTIEKEN: PAPIER- EN KARTONINDUSTRIE. a. Centraal Bureau voor de Statistiek, Prinses Beatrixlaan 428, Voorburg, Netherlands. (Orders to: SDU - Publishers, Christoffel Plantijnstraat, The Hague)
   Formed by the merger of: Netherlands. Centraal Bureau voor de Statistiek. Produktiestatistiek van de Papierindustries & Netherlands. Centraal Bureau voor de Statistiek. Produktiestatistiek Strokartonindustrie.

676 016   UK   ISSN 0307-0778
PAPER AND BOARD ABSTRACTS.* 1965. m. $830. (Research Association for the Paper and Board, Printing and Packaging Industries) Pira International, Randalls Rd., Leatherhead, Surrey KT22 7RU, England. Ed. Diana Deavin. bk.rev.; abstr.; index. (also avail. in microfilm from UMI; reprint service avail. from UMI) **Indexed:** Curr.Cont., World Text.Abstr.
   ●Also available online. Vendor(s): Orbit Information Technologies (PIRA), Pergamon Infoline.
   —BLDSC shelfmark: 6358.900000.
   Formerly (until 1976): Kenley Abstracts.

676.3 338.4   US
▼**PAPER DISTRIBUTION DATA SOURCE**; market research for the paper and plastics industries. 1990. a. $240. National Paper Trade Association, Inc., 111 Great Neck Rd., Ste. 603, Great Neck, NY 11021. TEL 516-829-3070. Ed. George Cain. stat.
   Description: Provides current information on changes in the US paper industry compiled from government, NPTA and other sources, including information on gross sales volume, state by state evaluations, specific product types, and market projections.

674 676 016   HU   ISSN 0231-0740
PAPIRIPARI ES NYOMDAIPARI SZAKIRODALMI TAJEKOZTATO/PAPER INDUSTRY & PRINTING ABSTRACTS. 1949. m. 7000 Ft. Orszagos Muszaki Informacios Kozpont es Konyvtar (O.M.I.K.K.) - National Technical Information Centre and Library, Muzeum u. 17, Box 12, 1428 Budapest, Hungary. (Subscr. to: Kultura, Box 149, 1389 Budapest, Hungary) Ed. Peter Kalmar. abstr.; index; circ. 230.
   Supersedes (in 1983): Muszaki Lapszemle. Faipar, Papir-es Nyomdaipar - Technical Abstracts. Wood and Paper Industry, Printing (ISSN 0027-4992)

676 016   PL   ISSN 0033-2291
TS1080   CODEN: PRZPAE
PRZEGLAD PAPIERNICZY/POLISH PAPER REVIEW. 1945. m. $82. Wydawnictwo Czasopism i Ksiazek Technicznych SIGMA - NOT, Ul. Biala 4, P.O. Box 1004, 00-950 Warsaw, Poland. (Dist. by: SIGMA NOT Ltd., Ul. Bartycka 20, 00-716 Warsaw, Poland) adv.; bk.rev.; abstr.; charts; illus.; stat.; index; circ. 1,400. **Indexed:** Abstr.Bull.Inst.Pap.Chem., Biol.Abstr., Chem.Abstr., Packag.Sci.Tech.
   —BLDSC shelfmark: 6944.000000.

676 310   FR
STATISTIQUES DE L'INDUSTRIE FRANCAISE DES PATES. PAPIERS ET CARTONS. a. 40 F. C.O.P.A.C.E.L., 154, Boulevard Haussmann, 75008 Paris, France. TEL 1-45-62-87-07. FAX 1-45-62-82-47. TELEX 290 544 F. illus.
   Continues: Quelques Donnees Statistiques sur l'Industrie Francaise des Pates, Papiers, Cartons (ISSN 0481-0112)

PARAPSYCHOLOGY AND OCCULTISM

see also New Age Publications

133   US
A A - E V P NEWS. 1982. q. $20. American Association - Electronic Voice Phenomena, 726 Dill Rd., Severna Park, MD 21146. TEL 301-647-8742. Ed. Sarah Wilson Estep. illus.; circ. 300. (back issues avail.)
   Description: Evidence of death survival as presented through electronic instruments such as: tape recorders, televisions, and computers.

133.91   US   ISSN 0044-7919
A S P R NEWSLETTER. 1968. q. $15 to non-members. American Society for Psychical Research, Inc., 5 W. 73rd St., New York, NY 10023. TEL 212-799-5050. FAX 212-496-2497. illus.; circ. 2,000.

133   US
ABRASAX. 1988. q. $20. Ordo Templi Baphe-Metis, Box 1219, Corpus Christi, TX 78403-1219. (Dist. by: Abyss Books, Box 1022, Easthampton, MA 01027) Ed. James M. Martin. adv.; bk.rev.; circ. 200.
   Description: Devoted to the study of all aspects of the occult, emphasizing a non-judgemental attitude towards the so-called Left Hand Path (black magic, Satanism).

133 200   US
ACADEMY OF RELIGION AND PSYCHICAL RESEARCH. PROCEEDINGS. 1980. a. $5. Academy of Religion and Psychical Research, Box 614, Bloomfield, CT 06002. TEL 203-242-4593. (Co-sponsor: Spiritual Frontiers Fellowship) Ed. Mary Carmen Rose. circ. 300. (also avail. in microfiche; back issues avail.)
   Description: Interfaces religion and psychical research.

133   US
AKHADEN; the Atlantean news journal. 1987. m. $18. Atlantean Antiquities Company, c/o Michael Morgan, 230 W. 76th St., Ste. 2A, New York, NY 10023.

ALLGEMEINE ZEITSCHRIFT FUER PARANORMOLOGIE. see *NEW AGE PUBLICATIONS*

133.91   US   ISSN 0003-1070
AMERICAN SOCIETY FOR PSYCHICAL RESEARCH. JOURNAL. 1907. q. $35 to individuals; institutions $60; students and senior citizens $20. American Society for Psychical Research, Inc., 5 W. 73rd St., New York, NY 10023. TEL 212-799-5050. FAX 212-496-2497. Ed. Rhea A. White. bk.rev.; abstr.; charts; stat.; index; circ. 2,000. (also avail. in microform from UMI; back issues avail.; reprint service avail. from UMI) **Indexed:** Mid.East: Abstr.& Ind., Psychol.Abstr., Soc.Sci.Ind., SSCI.
   —BLDSC shelfmark: 4693.050000.
   Description: Discusses clairvoyance, extrasensory perception, precognition, psychokinesis psychic healing.

133.323   FR   ISSN 0003-1798
AMIS DE LA RADIESTHESIE. 1930. q. 60 F. Association des Amis de la Radiesthesie, 70 rue du General de Gaulle, B.P. 3, 95620 Parmain, France. Ed. H. de France. adv.; bibl.; charts; circ. 500.

ANTHROPOLOGY OF CONSCIOUSNESS. see *ANTHROPOLOGY*

133.4   AU
ANUBIS; Zeitschrift fuer praktische Magie und Psychonautik. 1985. 4/yr. S.280($30) Postfach 45, A-1203 Vienna, Austria. adv.; bk.rev.; circ. 800.

133 100 613.2   US
AQUARIAN ALCHEMIST. 1980. q. contributions. Academy Research Associates, Box 1867, Santa Monica, CA 90406-1867. Ed. Daniel Fritz. bk.rev.; circ. 10,000.

133   UK   ISSN 0141-0121
AQUARIAN ARROW. 1977. irreg. (approx. 3/yr.). £5($10) for 4 nos. Neopantheist Society, BCM-OPAL, London WC1N 3XX, England. Ed. Zachary Cox. adv.; bk.rev.; circ. 300. (back issues avail.)
   Description: Libertarian magazine with a Thelemic/Nietzschean orientation. Focuses on speculative ethics and irony. Contains articles, essays, creative writing, and reader correspondence on the relationship between pantheistic, spiritual philosophies and cultural, psychological and civic development.

133 150.19   US   ISSN 0895-1268
R726.5
ARCHAEUS. 1983. biennial. $20 (includes 4 nos. of Artifex). Archaeus Project, 2402 University Ave., St. Paul, MN 55114. TEL 612-781-5012. Eds. Gail Duke, Dennis Stillings. charts; illus.; circ. 800. (back issues avail.) **Indexed:** Psychol.abstr.
   Description: Examines alternative medicine, science and anomalies such as parapsychological phenomena, from a Jungian point of view.

133 150.19   US   ISSN 0895-125X
ARTIFEX; journal of cyberbiology. 1982. q. $20 (includes Archaeus). Archaeus Project, 2402 University Ave., St. Paul, MN 55114. TEL 612-781-5012. Eds. Gail Duke, Dennis Stillings. adv.; bk.rev.; illus.; circ. 800. (back issues avail.)
   Description: Examines alternative medicine, science and anomalies such as parapsychological phenomena, from a Jungian point of view.

133 150   AT   ISSN 1035-9621
AUSTRALIAN PARAPSYCHOLOGICAL REVIEW. 1983. 3/yr. Aus.$18. Australian Institute of Parapsychological Research Inc., P.O. Box 445, Lane Cove, N.S.W. 2066, Australia. TEL 02-6607232. Ed. Harvey Irwin. bk.rev.; charts; illus.; cum.index; circ. 350. (back issues avail.)
   Former titles: Australian Institute of Parapsychological Research Bulletin & Australian Institute of Psychic Research Bulletin (ISSN 0813-2194)
   Description: Promotes scientific study of parapsychological and related phenomena. Emphasis on Australian studies.

133   FR
AUTRE MONDE. 1978. m. 90 F. G. Gourdon, Ed. & Pub., 10 rue de Crussol, 75011 Paris, France. adv.; illus.; circ. 60,000.

THE BEACON (MIAMI SHORES). see *NEW AGE PUBLICATIONS*

BEACON (NEW YORK). see *PHILOSOPHY*

133   US
BEYOND REALITY; the latest discoveries in ESP, UFO's & psychic phenomena. 1972. bi-m. $18. Beyond Reality Magazine, Inc., Box 428, Nanuet, NY 10954. Ed. Harry Belil. adv.; bk.rev.; illus.; circ. 40,000. (reprint service avail. from UMI)

BODY, MIND & SPIRIT MAGAZINE. see *NEW AGE PUBLICATIONS*

133.323   UK   ISSN 0007-179X
BRITISH SOCIETY OF DOWSERS. JOURNAL. 1933. q. $37 (typically set in July). British Society of Dowsers, Sycamore Cottage, Hastingleigh, Ashford, Kent TN25 5HW, England. TEL 0233-75-253. Ed. Deidre N. Rust. bk.rev.; abstr.; index; circ. 1,250. (also avail. in microfilm from UMI; reprint service avail. from UMI)
   —BLDSC shelfmark: 4719.200000.

CATALYST (MARIETTA); a publication resource of New Age newsletters, book reviews, personals, holistic health, and psychic connections. see *NEW AGE PUBLICATIONS*

PARAPSYCHOLOGY AND OCCULTISM

133   US
CENTRIC. 1974. 7/yr. $8. Esoteric Philosophy Center, Inc., 10085 Westpark Dr., Apt. B, Houston, TX 77042-5928. TEL 713-952-9909. Ed. Brett Chandler. adv.; bk.rev.; illus.; circ. 15,000.

CHAMP CHANNELS. see *BIOLOGY — Zoology*

CHURCH OF LIGHT QUARTERLY. see *NEW AGE PUBLICATIONS*

133.4 110   US
CINCINNATI JOURNAL OF MAGIC. 1976. a. $6. Black Moon Publishing, Box 19469, Cincinnati, OH 45219-0469. FAX 812-988-8518. Eds. Joe Bounds, Louis Martinie. bk.rev.; circ. 1,000.
Description: Collection of night side magicks.

133   AG   ISSN 0010-6291
CONOCIMIENTO DE LA NUEVA ERA. 1938. m. Arg.$2. Viamonte 1716, 1055 Buenos Aires, Argentina. Ed. Adolfo Bruzikis. bk.rev.; circ. 8,000.

COSMIC VOICE; cosmic revelations for the New Age. see *NEW AGE PUBLICATIONS*

130   IT
DIMENSIONE PSI; rivista internazionale di parapsicologia. (Text and summaries in English, French, German, Italian, Spanish) 1946. s-a. $6 membership or exchange basis. Associazione Italiana Studi del Paranormale, Via Puggia 47, 16131 Genoa, Italy. Ed.Bd. adv.; bk.rev.; abstr.; bibl.; charts; illus.; index; circ. 3,000.

133 370.15 150 371.42   US
DIMENSIONS (RIMROCK). 1980. bi-m. $10. Delphi Publications, Box 211, Rimrock, AZ 86335. TEL 602-634-2390. Ed. Jay Harris. adv.; bk.rev.; circ. 2,500.

133.4   US
DRUID HENGE. 1979. 12/yr. $15 to individuals; pagans $12. Craeftgemot Witancoveyne, Inc., Box 499, Deerfield Beach, FL 33441. TEL 305-428-9713. Ed. Janice Scot-Reeder. adv.; bk.rev.

ECLECTIC THEOSOPHIST; following the Blavatsky and Point Loma traditions. see *PHILOSOPHY*

133   US   ISSN 0731-7840
ENCYCLOPEDIA OF OCCULTISM AND PARAPSYCHOLOGY. 1978. irreg., 3rd ed., 1990. $295. Gale Research Inc., 835 Penobscot Bldg., Detroit, MI 48226. TEL 313-961-2242. FAX 313-961-6083. TELEX 810-221-7086. Ed. Leslie Shepard. **Indexed:** Child.Auth.& Illus.

ESOTERA; neue Dimensionen des Bewusstseins. see *NEW AGE PUBLICATIONS*

133   US   ISSN 0741-8795
ESOTERIC REVIEW;* an eclectic newsletter for modern occultists. 1983. bi-m. $15. Support of Nature, Box 9518, Hickory, NC 28603-9518. TEL 704-728-5431. Ed. Timothy L. Bost. bk.rev.; circ. 200. (looseleaf format; back issues avail.)

133   GW   ISSN 0170-4249
ESOTERIK UND WISSENSCHAFT. 1966. 3/yr. DM.13.50($10) OARCA - Freie Akademie zur Koordinierung von Esoterik und Wissenschaft e.V., Donnersbergerstr. 11-I, 8000 Munich 19, Germany. adv.; circ. 1,100.

133   US
ESSENTIA. 4/yr. $8. Paracelsus College, 3555 S. 700 East, Salt Lake City, UT 84106. TEL 801-486-6730. Ed. Mary Adams. adv.; illus.

ESSERE. see *PHILOSOPHY*

133   IT
L'ETA DELL'ACQUARIO; the magazine of the new plane of consciousness. 1971. q. L.30000($30) Via Torchio 16, 28075 Grignasco (NO), Italy. TEL 011-585214. Ed. Isabella Bresci. bk.rev.; circ. 1,200. (back issues avail.)

130   NE
EUROPEAN JOURNAL OF PARAPSYCHOLOGY. (Text in English) 1974. s-a. fl.30($10) University of Utrecht, Parapsychology Laboratory, Sorbonnelaan 16, 3584 CA Utrecht, Netherlands. Ed.Bd. circ. 250. **Indexed:** Psychol.Abstr.

133   US
FANGORIA. 1979. 10/yr. $18.98. Starlog Group, Inc., 475 Park Ave. S., New York, NY 10016. TEL 212-689-0230. (Subscr. to: Box 142, Mt. Morris, IL 61054) Ed. David McDonnell. adv.; circ. 150,000.
Formerly: Fantastica (ISSN 0164-2111)

130   US   ISSN 0014-8776
BF1995
FATE; the world's mysteries explored. 1948. m. $17. Llewellyn Publications, 84 S. Wabasha St., Box 64383, St. Paul, MN 55164. TEL 612-291-1970. FAX 612-291-1908. adv.; bk.rev.; abstr.; illus.; circ. 140,000. (also avail. in microform from UMI; back issues avail.; reprint service avail. from UMI) **Indexed:** Access (1975-), Hlth.Ind., Mag.Ind.
Description: Presents true stories, personal vignettes, and biographical profiles pertaining to strange, mystical, and parapsychological experiences.

FIREHEART; a journal of magic and spiritual transformation. see *NEW AGE PUBLICATIONS*

133   UK
FORESIGHT (BIRMINGHAM). 1970. q. £2.50. 44 Brockhurst Rd., Hodge Hill, Birmingham B36 8JB, England. Eds. John W.B. Barklam, Mrs. J. Barklam. adv.; bk.rev.; charts; illus.; circ. 1,500.
Description: Examines UFO's, occult and psychic phenomena, and new age subjects.

001.94   UK   ISSN 0308-5899
FORTEAN TIMES; the journal of strange phenomena. 1973. 6/yr. $30. P.O. Box 2409, London NW5 4NP, England. FAX 071-485-5002. Eds. Robert J.M. Rickard, Paul Sieveking. adv.; bk.rev.; bibl.; illus.; index; circ. 15,000.
Description: Provides accounts of strange phenomena, experiences, curiosities, mysteries, prodigies and portents.

133   US   ISSN 0886-6791
THE GATE; explore the mysteries. 1985. q. $8. Box 43518, Richmond Hts., OH 44143. Ed. Beth Robbins. adv.; bk.rev.; illus.; circ. 200. (back issues avail.)

133   US
GHOST TRACKERS NEWSLETTER. 1982. 3/yr. $12. Ghost Research Society, Box 205, Oaklawn, IL 60454-0205. TEL 708-425-5163. Ed. Dale Kaczmarek. adv.; bk.rev.; circ. 200. (looseleaf format; back issues avail.)

133 016   US   ISSN 0888-0433
BF1434.U6
GUIDE TO THE AMERICAN OCCULT; directory and bibliography. a. $24.95. Laird Wilcox, Box 2047, Olathe, KS 66061. TEL 913-829-0609. FAX 913-829-0609. circ. 700.
Description: Directory of over 1,200 occult organizations and serials. Includes a bibliography.

133   US
HARVEST (SOUTHBORO). 1980. 8/yr. $11. Box 378, Southboro, MA 01772. adv.; bk.rev.
Description: Includes articles, news, reviews, art, and letters on modern Wicca and Neo-Paganism.

133.4   UK
HARVEST MOON. 1987. 6/yr. £4. 36 Dawes House, Orb Street, London SE17 1RE, England. TEL 071-708-4629. adv.; bk.rev.
Formerly: Odinn Magazine.

133   US
HECHIZOS. (Text in Spanish) 1987. m. $2.50 per no. 614 Franklin St., Elizabeth, NJ 07206. TEL 908-355-8835. Ed. Jose Tenreiro Napoles. adv.; circ. 45,000.
Description: Covers parapsychology, spiritualism, science fiction and astrology.

THE HERMETIC JOURNAL. see *RELIGIONS AND THEOLOGY — Other Denominations And Sects*

133.91   UK
HIDDEN HISTORY. 1965. q. $25. Anomalous Phenomenon Research Association, 5 Frederick Ave., Carlton NG4 1HP, England. TEL 0602-860010. Ed. S.W. Henley. adv.; bk.rev.; illus.; index; circ. 457.
Former titles (until 1987): Anomalous Phenomenon Review; U F O Research Review (ISSN 0306-9915); N U F O I S Newsletter.
Description: Contains information about various earth mysteries, folklore, archaeological curiosities, and other super natural phenomena.

133   IC
HUGINN AND MUNINN; interstellar messenger. (Text in English) 1966-1974; resumed 1979. 4/yr. $5. (Felag Nyalssinna) Bioradii Publications, P.O. Box 1159, Reykjavik, Iceland. TEL 354-1-35683. FAX 354-1-45341. Ed. Thorsteinn Gudjonsson. bk.rev.; circ. 400. (processed)
Former titles: Interstellar Bulletins; Interstellar Communication (ISSN 0020-9740)
Description: Focuses on philosophy, parapsychology, old Norse religion and lore.

HUMANSPACE BOOKS. NEWSLETTER. see *HOMOSEXUALITY*

IMAGINATION, COGNITION AND PERSONALITY. see *PSYCHOLOGY*

133.91   FR   ISSN 0338-8190
INCONNU; revue des phenomenes et des sciences paralleles. (Includes supplements) 1975. m. 162 F. Editions H C L, 18-20 rue Claude Tillier, 75012 Paris, France. TEL 43-72-61-02. FAX 43-72-80-40. Ed. Marc Tripier. adv.; bk.rev.; charts; illus.; circ. 75,000.

133   US
INNERGY NEWS.* 4/yr. free. Source of Innergy, Ltd., c/o Flanagan, Box 2285, Sedona, AZ 86336. Ed. Patrick Flanagan. illus. (tabloid format)

130   US
INSIGHTS (MORRISTOWN).* vol. 5, 1976. 10/yr. $10. Jersey Society of Parapsychology, Box 2071, Morristown, NJ 07960. TEL 201-539-1466. Ed. B.J. McKay. bk.rev.; circ. 700.

133   US
INTERNATIONAL DIRECTORY OF PSYCHIC SCIENCES. 1986. a. $7. Ghost Research Society, Box 205, Oaklawn, IL 60454-0205. TEL 708-425-5163. Ed. Dale Kaczmarek. circ. 200. (looseleaf format; back issues avail.)
Description: Lists organizations, groups and individuals associated with the occult in general.

IO. see *ANTHROPOLOGY*

133   US
IRIDIS. 12/yr. California Society for Psychical Study, Box 844, Berkeley, CA 94701. Ed. Donald McQuilling. bk.rev.

133   US
JOURNAL OF BORDERLAND RESEARCH. 1945. bi-m. $25. Borderland Sciences Research Foundation, Box 429, Garberville, CA 95440. TEL 707-986-7211. FAX 707-986-7272. Ed. Thomas Joseph Brown. bk.rev.; charts; illus.; circ. 1,000. (back issues avail.)

130   US   ISSN 0022-3387
BF1001   CODEN: JPRPAU
JOURNAL OF PARAPSYCHOLOGY; a scientific quarterly dealing with extrasensory perception, the psychokinetic effect and related topics. 1937. q. $30 to individuals; institutions $40. (Foundation for Research on the Nature of Man) Parapsychology Press, Box 6847 College Sta., Durham, NC 27708. TEL 919-688-8241. FAX 919-683-4338. Ed. K.R. Rao. adv.; bk.rev.; abstr.; bibl.; charts; illus.; index; circ. 1,000. (also avail. in microform from UMI; back issues avail.; reprint service avail. from UMI, ISI) **Indexed:** ASSIA, Biol.Abstr., Curr.Cont., Excerp.Med., Mid.East: Abstr.& Ind., Psychol.Abstr., Soc.Sci.Ind., SSCI.

PARAPSYCHOLOGY AND OCCULTISM

133 200   US   ISSN 0731-2148
BL65.P3
JOURNAL OF RELIGION & PSYCHICAL RESEARCH; a scholarly quarterly dealing with religion, psychical research, and related topics. 1979. q. $8 to libraries. Academy of Religion and Psychical Research, Box 614, Bloomfield, CT 06002. TEL 203-242-4593. Ed. Mary Carmen Rose. bk.rev.; index; circ. 300. (back issues avail.) Indexed: Rel.Ind.One.
—BLDSC shelfmark: 5049.352000.

JOURNAL OF SCIENTIFIC EXPLORATION. see *SCIENCES: COMPREHENSIVE WORKS*

154   UK
KABBALIST. 1974. q. £4. International Order of Kabbalists, 25 Circle Gardens, Merton Park, London SW19 3JX, England. Ed. J. Sturzaker. adv.; bk.rev.; bibl.; circ. 4,000.

133.91   GR   ISSN 0023-4257
KOSMOS TIS PSYCHIS/WORLD OF SOUL. 1947. m. Dr.100($3.50) Psychic Society of Athens, 32 Tsiller St., Athens 905, Greece. Ed. Georgos Sakellaropoulos. bk.rev.; abstr.; bibl.; illus.; tr.mk.; index; circ. 1,000.

133.91   UK   ISSN 0047-4649
LIGHT (LONDON, 1881); a journal of psychic and spiritual studies. 1881. 3/yr. £7($16) College of Psychic Studies, 16 Queensberry Pl., London SW7 2EB, England. Ed. Brenda Marshall. bk.rev.; circ. 2,600.

133 133.5 398 200   US
LIGHT BEARER.* 1975. 12/yr. $10. Healing Light Center, Box 758, Sierra Madre, CA 91025-0758. TEL 818-244-8807. Ed. Wendy Jo Block. adv.; bk.rev.; circ. 7,600.

133.9   US
LIGHT - LINES. 1982. q. donations only. Rock Creek Research & Development Labs, Inc., Box 5195, Louisville, KY 40205. TEL 502-245-6495. Ed. James McCarty. circ. 1,500. (looseleaf format; back issues avail.)

MAD SCIENTIST. see *NEW AGE PUBLICATIONS*

133   US
MAGICKAL UNICORN MESSENGER.* 1980. 4/yr. $9. Temple of Wicca, 817 1-2 Park St., Findlay, OH 45840. Ed. Samantha Pugh. adv.; bk.rev.; illus.; circ. 200. (tabloid format)
    Description: Informative publication concerning wicca and paganism. Includes articles, news, reviews and forthcoming events.

133   GW
MESCALITO - SPRUNG IN DIE UNMOEGLICHKEIT; Magazin fuer Magie und Schamanismus. 1979. q. DM.48. Indianisches Netzwerk BRD, Zornstr. 11A, 6520 Worms 1, Germany. TEL 06241-56099. Ed. Berthold Roeth. bibl.; illus.; tr.lit.

133   UK
METAMORPHIC ASSOCIATION PROGRAMME. 1981. 3/yr. £1. Metamorphic Association, 67 Ritherdon Rd., London SW17 8QE, England. TEL 081-672-5951. Ed. Gaston St. Pierre. illus.; circ. 5,000.
    Supersedes in part (as of 1983): Metamorphic Association Newsletter (ISSN 0262-1533)
    Description: Lists activities and members of the Association.

133   UK
METAMORPHOSIS. 1981. 2/yr. £7. Metamorphic Association, 67 Ritherdon Rd., London SW17 8QE, England. TEL 081-672-5951. Ed. Gaston St. Pierre. bk.rev.; illus.; circ. 1,200. (back issues avail.)
    Supersedes in part (as of 1983): Metamorphic Association Newsletter (ISSN 0262-1533)
    Description: Articles on the theory and principles behind Metamorphosis and the Metamorphic technique, an approach to self-healing and creative growth.

133.91   IT   ISSN 0026-1076
METAPSICHICA; rivista italiana di parapsicologia. 1946. q. L.45000 or exchange basis. Associazione Italiana Scientifica di Metapsichica, Via S. Vittore 19, 20123 Milan, Italy. TEL 02-4980365. (Co-sponsor: Centro Studi Parapsicologici) Ed. Pierangelo Garzia. adv.; bk.rev.; circ. 1,000.
    Description: Journal dealing with parapsychological research from world wide conferences. Includes articles contributed by Italian authors interested in this field.

133   US
METASCIENCE ANNUAL; a New Age journal of parapsychology. 1979. a. $25. MetaScience Foundation, Box 32, Kingston, RI 02881. TEL 401-294-2414. Ed. Marc J. Seifer. adv.; bk.rev.; abstr.; bibl.; charts; illus.; stat.; index; circ. 2,500. (back issues avail.)
    Formerly: MetaScience Quarterly; Which supersedes (1977-1978): Journal of Occult Studies.
    Description: Academic journal which objectively studies a broad range of parapsychological topics.

MOONCIRCLES. see *WOMEN'S INTERESTS*

MUTANTIA; cuadernos eco-espirituales. see *NEW AGE PUBLICATIONS*

133   UK
NEOMETAPHYSICAL DIGEST. 1952. q. £8($20) to non-members. Society of Metaphysicians Ltd., Archers' Court, Stonestile Lane, the Ridge, Hastings, E.Sussex TN35 4PG, England. TEL 0424-751577. Ed. Eleanor Swift. adv.; bk.rev.; circ. 60,000.
    Formerly: Metaphysical Digest.
    Description: Seeks functional solutions to human problems, understanding of consciousness and its manifestations in mysticism, esoterica, psychic phenomena.

NEW CONSCIOUSNESS SOURCEBOOK; spiritual community guide. see *NEW AGE PUBLICATIONS*

NEWS EXTRA. see *CLOTHING TRADE — Fashions*

133   US
NEWS NOVEL. 1969. irreg. Box 3232, Riverside, CA 92519. Ed. Darlene Wheeler.

NNIDNID: SURREALITY. see *ART*

133   IT
NUOVO MONDO OCCULTO. vol.3, 1971. m. L.15,000. (Tayu Center) Istituto Ricerche exo Mediche, Via Dalbono, 30/b, 80055 Portici, Codice Fiscale 94064860631. bk.rev.; bibl.; illus.
    Formerly: Mondo Occulto (ISSN 0047-7869)

350 320 792   IT
OGGI E DOMANI. 1973. m. L.40000. EDIARS S.A.S., Via C. Battisti 162, Pescara, Italy. FAX 3985-381298. Ed. Edoardo Tiboni. adv.; bk.rev.; circ. 5,000.
    Description: Includes articles on relevant issues in the field of public administration, political sciences and economics.

133.91   SA
PARAPSYCHOLOGICAL JOURNAL OF SOUTH AFRICA. (Text in English) 1980. s-a. R.18($21) South African Society for Psychical Research, P.O. Box 23154, Johannesburg 2044, South Africa. Ed. V.M. Neppe. bk.rev.; circ. 350. Indexed: Psychol.Abstr.

133   US   ISSN 0078-9437
PARAPSYCHOLOGICAL MONOGRAPHS. 1958. irreg., latest no.18. price varies. Parapsychology Foundation, 228 E. 71st St., New York, NY 10021. TEL 212-628-1550. Indexed: Psychol.Abstr.
—BLDSC shelfmark: 6404.920000.

133   US
PARAPSYCHOLOGY FOUNDATION. PROCEEDINGS OF INTERNATIONAL CONFERENCES. 1953. a. price varies. Parapsychology Foundation, 228 E. 71st St., New York, NY 10021. TEL 212-628-1550.

133   US
PARAPSYCHOLOGY-PSYCHIC SCIENCE REPORTS; magazine of psychic phenomena. 1973. m. $18. Gibbs Publishing Company, Box 600927, N. Miami Beach, FL 33160. Ed. James Calvin Gibbs. adv.; bk.rev.; circ. 10,000.
    Former titles: Parapsychology-Psychic Science Journal; Parapsychology.

133   US
PARINFO. 1972. m. $10 to non-members. Parapsychology Association of Riverside, Inc., 7111 Magnolia Ave., Ste. G, Riverside, CA 92504. TEL 714-684-2242. Ed. Janet Taylor. bk.rev.

133 289.9   US
PORTAL. q. Hermetic Society of the Golden Dawn, 31849 Pacific Hwy. S., Ste.107, Federal Way, WA 98003.

POWER PLACES OF CALIFORNIA. see *EARTH SCIENCES — Geophysics*

133   UK   ISSN 0032-7182
PREDICTION. 1936. m. £24. Link House Magazines Ltd., Link House, Dingwall Ave., Croydon, Surrey CR9 2TA, England. TEL 01-686-2599. FAX 01-760-0973. TELEX 947709. (Subscr. to: U M S, Stephenson House, 1st Fl., Brunel Centre, Bletchley, Milton Keynes, MK2 2EW) Ed. Jo Logan. adv.; bk.rev.; illus.; circ. 25,275.
    Description: Explores astrology, palmistry, tarot, graphology, dream interpretations and methods used to interpret character and events in life. Includes articles, news briefs, questions and answers, and personal advertisements.

133.324   UK   ISSN 0079-4953
PREDICTION ANNUAL. a. Link House Magazines Ltd., Link House, Dingwall Ave., Croydon, Surrey CR9 2TA, England. TEL 01-686-2599. FAX 01-760-0973. TELEX 947709. (Subsccr. to: U M S, Stephenson House, 1st Fl., Brunel Centre, Bletchley, Milton Keynes, MK2 2EW) Ed. Jo Logan. adv.; bk.rev.
    Description: Presents astrological forecasts for each sign of the Zodiac; includes Tarot card projections.

133 001.94   UK   ISSN 0260-8189
PROBE REPORT. 1980. q. £3.40($6.60) Probe, 16 Marigold Walk, Ashton, Bristol BS3 2PD, England. Ed. Ian Mrzyglod. adv.; bk.rev.; illus.; stat.; circ. 500. (back issues avail.)

100   US   ISSN 0197-2138
PSI - M. 10/yr. $12. Psychic Science Special Interest Group, Inc., 7514 Belleplaine Dr., Dayton, OH 45424-3229. TEL 513-236-0361. Ed. Rich Strong.

133   US
PSYCHIC MESSENGER.* 4/yr. Shafenberg Research Foundation, c/o Alice Shiver, Ed., 3411 Regatta Pl., Oxnard, CA 93030-6416.

133.91   UK   ISSN 0033-2801
PSYCHIC NEWS. 1932. w. £25($45) Psychic Press Ltd., 2 Tavistock Chambers, Bloomsbury Way, London WC1A 2SE, England. TEL 071-405-3340. Ed. Tony Ortzen. adv.; bk.rev.; bibl.; charts; illus.; tr.lit.; circ. 13,000.
    Description: Newspaper covering spiritualism and the paranormal.

133   US
PSYCHIC READER. 1975. m. $10. (Church of Divine Man) Deja Vu Publishing, 95 Belvedere St., San Rafael, CA 94901. TEL 415-459-3551. FAX 415-459-5539. Ed. Sandra Kovacs. adv.; bk.rev.; circ. 60,000. (tabloid format; back issues avail.)
    Formerly: Psychic Life.
    Description: New age publication that discusses parapsychology, alternative healing, religions and theology.

133.91   US   ISSN 0276-1610
PSYCHIC STUDIES. 1982. irreg., vol.4, 1980. price varies. Gordon & Breach Science Publishers, 270 Eighth Ave., New York, NY 10011. TEL 212-206-8900. FAX 212-645-2459. TELEX 236735 GOPUB UR. (Subscr. to: Box 786, Cooper Sta., New York, NY 10276. TEL 800-545-8398; UK subscr. to: P.O. Box 90, Reading, Berkshire RG1 8JL, England. TEL 0734-560-080) Eds. Stanley Krippner, Irene Hall.
    Refereed Serial

133.91   UK
PSYCHICAL STUDIES. 1968. 2/yr. £5. c/o Mrs. F.I. Hornby, Waterbarrow, High Cunsey, Via Ambleside, Cumbria LA22 0LH, England. TEL 05394-46629. bk.rev.; circ. 200.
    Formerly: Beyond.
    Description: Examines the relation of psychical studies to religion.

500 133 US
PURSUIT - S I T U. vol.2, 1969. q. $12 to individuals; libraries $10. Society for the Investigation of the Unexplained, Box 265, Little Silver, NJ 07739. TEL 201-842-5229. Ed. Robert C. Warth. bk.rev.; bibl.; charts; illus.; index; circ. 1,500. (also avail. in microform from UMI; reprint service avail. from UMI) **Indexed:** Abstr.Folk.Stud.
Formerly: Pursuit (ISSN 0033-4685)

133 IT
QUADERNI DI PARAPSICOLOGIA. (Text in Italian; abstracts in English, Italian) 1970. s-a. L.50000($40) includes Bollettino. Centro Studi Parapsicologici, Via L. Valeriani, 39, 40134 Bologna, Italy. TEL 051-411885. Ed. Piero Cassoli. bk.rev.; abstr.; circ. 450. (back issues avail.)
Incorporates: Centro Studi Parapsicologici. Bollettino.

133
QUADERNI GNOSIS. (Includes 3/yr. supplement: Fogli Gnosis) (Text in Italian; summaries in English and French) 1963. a. L.20000. Istituto Gnosis per la Ricerca sulla Ipotesi della Sopravvivenza, Via Belvedere 87, 80127 Naples, Italy. Ed. Giorgio di Simone. adv.; bk.rev.; bibl.; illus.; circ. 600.
Supersedes (in 1981): Informazioni di Parapsicologia (ISSN 0046-9491)

133 200 800 FR
QUESTION DE. 1973. q. 330 F. (Edition Albin Michel) Edition Question de, B.P. 21, 84220 Gordes, France. FAX 90-72-08-38. Dir. Marc de Smedt. adv.; bk.rev.; bibl.; charts; illus.; circ. 12,000.
Former titles: Question de Racines, Pensees, Sciences Eclairees; Question de Spiritualite, Tradition, Litteratures.

130 SZ
RADIAESTHESIE. 1950. q. 35 Fr.($6) Verlag R G S, Postfach 944, CH-9001 St. Gallen, Switzerland. TEL 071-226621. Ed. L. Buergi. adv.; bk.rev.; circ. 4,000.
Formerly: Radiaesthesie - Geopathie - Strahlenbiologie (ISSN 0033-7552)

REALITY CHANGE; a magazine for people who want to change their lives. see *NEW AGE PUBLICATIONS*

RELIGIOUS FREEDOM REPORTER. see *POLITICAL SCIENCE — Civil Rights*

133.9 FR ISSN 0151-4016
RENAITRE 2000; revue des investigations psychiques et des recherches theoriques et experimentales sur la survivance humaine. 1977. 5/yr. 210 F. Andre Dumas, Ed. & Pub., 29 Av. des Sablons, 77230 Dammartin-en-Goele, France. bk.rev.; circ. 2,000.
Supersedes (1858-1977): Revue Spirite; Formerly: Survie de l'Ame Humaine (ISSN 0049-2655)

133 JA
RESEARCH FOR RELIGION & PARAPSYCHOLOGY. (Issuing body also known as: Institute for Religious Psychology) 1975. irreg. (1-2/yr.). price varies. International Association for Religion & Parapsychology, 4-11-7 Inokashira, Mitaka, Tokyo 181, Japan. FAX 0422-48-3548.
Formerly: International Association for Religion and Parapsychology Journal.

133 US ISSN 0094-7172
RESEARCH IN PARAPSYCHOLOGY; abstracts and papers from the annual convention. 1972. a. price varies. (Parapsychological Association) Scarecrow Press, Inc., 52 Liberty St., Metuchen, NJ 08840. TEL 800-537-7107. Ed. Linda Henkel.
—BLDSC shelfmark: 7755.048000.
Formerly (1957-1971): Parapsychological Association. Proceedings.
Description: Original presentations on empirical, methodological, philosophical, and historical themes.

133.9 294 II
REVIEW OF INDIAN SPIRITUALISM. (Text in English) vol.6, 1974. m. Rs.6($3) Sinha Publishing House, 39 S. R. Das Rd., Calcutta 700026, India. Ed. Amiya Kumar Sinha. adv.; bk.rev.; circ. 1,000.

133 FR ISSN 0294-2623
REVUE DE PARAPSYCHOLOGIE. (Text in French; summaries occasionally in English) 1975. irreg. 220 F. Groupe d'Etude et de Recherche en Parapsychologie, 8 rue Octave Dubois, 95150 Taverny, France. Ed. Gisele Titeux. bk.rev.; charts; circ. 1,000. (back issues avail.)

133.91 FR ISSN 0338-2079
REVUE DU MAGNETISME-ETUDE DU PSYCHISME EXPERIMENTAL. 1975. bi-m. 240 F. 1 rue des Moulins de Garance, 59800 Lille, France. Ed. Jean Magnes. bk.rev.; index.
Description: Offers an experimental approach to psychic phenomena. Covers magnetism, hypnotism, suggestion, and mediums.

133 FR ISSN 0484-8934
REVUE METAPSYCHIQUE. 1920. irreg., vol.17, 1983. 40 F. per no. Institut Metapsychique International, 1 Place de Wagram, 75017 Paris, France. TEL 47-63-65-48. Ed. Hubert Larcher. bk.rev.; circ. 500.

133.91 UK
S P R NEWSLETTER. (Supplement avail.) 1981. 4/yr. membership. Society for Psychical Research, 49 Marloes Rd., Kensington, London W8 6LA, England. TEL 071-937-8984. Ed. Jane Henry. circ. 900. (back issues avail.)

133 AT
THE SKEPTIC. 1981. q. Aus.$28. P.O. Box E324, St. James, N.S.W. 2000, Australia. Ed. Barry Williams. bk.rev.; circ. 1,000. (back issues avail.)
Description: Scientific articles on paranormal issues: psychics, astrology, UFOs, alternative medicine.

133 US ISSN 1060-216X
▼**SKEPTICAL BRIEFS.** 1991. q. $15. Committee for the Scientific Investigation of Claims of the Paranormal, Box 703, Buffalo, NY 14226-0703. TEL 716-636-1425. FAX 716-636-1733. Ed. Doris Doyle. circ. 2,100.

133 US ISSN 0194-6730
BF1001
SKEPTICAL INQUIRER. 1976. q. $25. Committee for the Scientific Investigation of Claims of the Paranormal, Box 703, Buffalo, NY 14226-0703. TEL 716-636-1425. FAX 716-636-1733. Ed. Kendrick Frazier. bk.rev.; charts; illus.; stat.; cum.index; circ. 40,000. (back issues avail.)
Indexed: Lang.& Lang.Behav.Abstr.
Formerly (until 1977): Zetetic (ISSN 0148-1096)
Description: Contains articles, news and comments.

133.91 UK ISSN 0037-9751
BF1011
SOCIETY FOR PSYCHICAL RESEARCH. JOURNAL. 1884. 4/yr. £20($36) Society for Psychical Research, 49 Marloes Rd., Kensington, London W8 6LA, England. TEL 071-937-8984. Ed. John Beloff. bk.rev.; charts; index. cum.index published irregularly. **Indexed:** Br.Hum.Ind., Psychol.Abstr.

133 UK ISSN 0081-1475
BF1011 CODEN: PPSRA5
SOCIETY FOR PSYCHICAL RESEARCH. PROCEEDINGS. 1882. irreg. membership. Society for Psychical Research, 49 Marloes Rd., Kensington, London W8 6LA, England. TEL 071-937-8984. Ed. John Beloff. **Indexed:** Br.Hum.Ind., Psychol.Abstr.

130 SW ISSN 0038-0504
SOEKAREN. 1964. 8/yr. SEK 175. Sven Magnusson, Ed. & Pub., Oestra Kanalgatan 18, S-652 20 Karlstad, Sweden. TEL 054-111689. adv.; bk.rev.; illus.; circ. 3,000.

133 US
SPHINX (WINNISQUAM). 4/yr. $6. Coven of Isis, Box 231, Winnisquam, NH 03289. TEL 603-722-5668. illus.

133.9 US
SPIRIT SPEAKS. 1985. bi-m. $24. Spirit Speaks, Inc., Box 84304, Los Angeles, CA 90073. TEL 800-856-9104. FAX 213-826-9197. Ed. Molli Nickell. adv.; circ. 10,000.
Description: Covers topics pertaining to daily life via spiritual psychology.

SPIRITUAL EMERGENCE NETWORK NEWSLETTER. see *NEW AGE PUBLICATIONS*

SUBCONSCIOUSLY SPEAKING; you can change your life through the power of your mind. see *NEW AGE PUBLICATIONS*

133 MX
SUPERMENTE; nuevo sendero al naturismo. s-m. Editorial Posada, S.A., Oculistas No. 43, Col. El Sifon, 09400 Mexico, D.F., Mexico.

133 UK ISSN 0143-5418
SUT ANUBIS. irreg. £10($20) Occultique, 73 Kettering Rd., Northampton NN1 4AW, England. TEL 0604-27727. adv.; bk.rev.; circ. 500.
Description: Original articles on witchcraft, Crowleyanity, ceremonial magic, paganism.

133.91 US ISSN 0040-6066
BF1001
THETA (CARROLLTON); exploring human potential in life and death. 1963. 3/yr. $18 (foreign $28). Parapsychological Services Institute, Inc., c/o W.G. Roll, Ed., Department of Psychology, W. Georgia College, Carrollton, GA 30118-0001. adv.; bk.rev.; circ. 900. **Indexed:** Psychol.Abstr.
—BLDSC shelfmark: 8820.101000.

TRANSFORMATION TIMES; New Age journal. see *NEW AGE PUBLICATIONS*

130 FR ISSN 0049-4666
TRIBUNE PSYCHIQUE.* vol. 75, 1972. q. 5 F. Societe Francaise d'Etude des Phenomenes Psychiques, 1 rue des Gatines, 75020 Paris, France. Ed. M. Lemoine. bk.rev.; bibl.

THE UNEXPLAINED; mysteries of life explained. see *NEW AGE PUBLICATIONS*

133 US
UNICORN (NORTHRIDGE). 1977. 8/yr. $10. Rowan Tree Church, Box 383, Northridge, CA 91328-0383. TEL 818-709-7618. Ed. Rev. Paul Beyerl. bk.rev.; illus.; circ. 150.
Description: Covers modern Neo-Pagan Revival literature.

133 US
UNIVERSALIAN; dedicated to expanding conscious awareness. 1985. bi-m. contributions. Universalia, Inc., Box 6243, Denver, CO 80206. Ed. Jan Martin. circ. 1,200.

133 US ISSN 1042-7899
UNKNOWN. 1969. m. $22. Luna Ventures, Box 398, Suisun, CA 94585. Ed. Paul Doerr. adv.; bk.rev. (also avail. in microfiche)
Description: Covers anomalies, the mysterious, and the unusual from witchcraft and appearances to Bigfoot and UFOs.

133 GW ISSN 0174-3538
V T F-POST. 1975. q. DM.50. Verein fuer Tonbandstimmenforschung e.V., Hoehscheider Str. 2, 4000 Duesseldorf 13, Germany. TEL 0211-786439. Ed. Fidelio Koeberle. bk.rev.; circ. 2,000. (back issues avail.)

VENTURE INWARD. see *NEW AGE PUBLICATIONS*

133 UK
VIEWPOINT AQUARIUS. 1972. bi-m. $13. Box 97, Camberley, Surrey GU15 2LH, England. TEL 0276-21531. Ed. Jean Coulsting. bk.rev. (processed)
Description: Study of occult, yoga, meditation, flying saucers.

133 110 US
VISIONS (AGOURA HILLS). 1975. 6/yr. free. Antonia Rodriguez, Ed. & Pub., 5809 N. Kanan Rd., Ste. 263, Agoura Hills, CA 91301. TEL 805-523-1483. adv.; bk.rev.; circ. 1,000.

133.9 MX
VOZ INFORMATIVA; revista bimestral de filosofia, ciencia y moral. 1952. bi-m. Mex.$120($6) Pino 129, Mexico 4, D.F., Mexico. (And Apdo. Postal M-7057, Mexico 1, D.F., Mexico) Ed. Jose Castol Gonzalez. circ. 1,000.

133 NE
WICCAN REDE. (Text in Dutch and English) 1980. q. fl.22.50($15) Silver Circle, P.O. Box 473, 3700 AL Zeist, Netherlands. Eds. Merlin and Morgana. adv.; bk.rev.; circ. 250.
Description: Discusses the heritage, symbolism, archetypes, natural magic, elements and seasonal tides of witchcraft.

PARAPSYCHOLOGY AND OCCULTISM — ABSTRACTING, BIBLIOGRAPHIES, STATISTICS

133.4   UK   ISSN 0952-522X
WICCAN WORKSHOP NEWS. 1982. 2/yr. £2. Aurora Aurea, BM Deosil, London WC1N 3XX, England.

THE WISE WOMAN. see *WOMEN'S INTERESTS*

133.4   US   ISSN 0085-8250
WITCHCRAFT DIGEST. (Supplement to: W I C A Newsletter) 1970. a. $2. (Witches International Craft Associates) Hero Press, 153 W. 80th St., Ste. 1B, New York, NY 10024. (Co-sponsor: Witches Liberation Movement) Ed. Leo Louis Martello. adv.; bk.rev.; circ. 3,000.
    Formerly: Witchcraft (ISSN 0014-2840)

133.4   US   ISSN 0049-7754
WITCHES INTERNATIONAL CRAFT ASSOCIATES. W I C A NEWSLETTER. Issued with: Witchcraft Digest (ISSN 0085-8250) 1970. m. $4 for 10 nos. Hero Press, 153 W. 80th St., Ste. 1B, New York, NY 10024. Ed. Leo Louis Martello. adv.; bk.rev.; film rev.; illus.; circ. 2,500. (processed)
    Formerly: Witches Newsletter (ISSN 0028-4173); Supersedes: New Age Intellectual Newsletter.

133.91   GW   ISSN 0028-3479
BF1003
ZEITSCHRIFT FUER PARAPSYCHOLOGIE UND GRENZGEBIETE DER PSYCHOLOGIE. 1957. q. DM.80. (Wissenschaftliche Gesellschaft zur Foederung der Parapsychologie e.V.) W G F P Geschaeftsstelle, Hildastr. 64, 7800 Freiburg, Germany. TEL 0761-77202. Ed.Bd. adv.; bk.rev.; illus.; circ. 1,600. Indexed: Excerp.Med., Psychol.Abstr., SSCI. —BLDSC shelfmark: 9475.900000.
    Supersedes: Neue Wissenschaft.

ZEITSCHRIFT FUER RADIAESTHESIE UND HARMONIEFINDUNG. see *NEW AGE PUBLICATIONS*

133   US   ISSN 0741-6229
BF1001
ZETETIC SCHOLAR. 1978. irreg. $15 to individuals; institutions $20; foreign $30. Center for Scientific Anomalies Research, Box 1052, Ann Arbor, MI 48106. FAX 517-522-3555. (Subscr. to: Department of Sociology, Eastern Michigan University, Ypsilanti, MI 48197) Ed. Marcello Truzzi. bk.rev.; bibl.; circ. 600. (back issues avail.) Indexed: Lang.& Lang.Behav.Abstr., Sociol.Abstr.

PARAPSYCHOLOGY AND OCCULTISM — Abstracting, Bibliographies, Statistics

133   US   ISSN 1053-4768
BF1001
EXCEPTIONAL HUMAN EXPERIENCE; studies of the psychic - spontaneous - intangible. 1983. s-a. $35 to individuals; institutions $50. Parapsychology Sources of Information Center, 2 Plane Tree Ln., Dix Hills, NY 11746. TEL 516-271-1243. Ed. Rhea A. White. bk.rev.; abstr.; film rev.; index; circ. 350.
●Also available online.
    Formerly (until 1990): Parapsychology Abstracts International (ISSN 0740-7629)
    Description: Information resource for literature recording parapsychological and unusual phenomena, including profiles of investigators, accounts of experiences, methodological and theoretical articles, and abstracts from a broad range of journals covering anomalies, as well as relevant publications in anthropology, philosophy, sociology and other fields.

133   US
OCCULT PUBLICATIONS DIRECTORY. irreg. $7. Ghost Research Society, Box 205, Oaklawn, IL 60454-0205. TEL 708-425-5163.
    Description: Lists newsletters, directories, and tabloids dealing with the occult in general.

133   US
WITCHCRAFT - PAGANISM DIRECTORY. irreg. $6.50. Ghost Research Society, Box 205, Oaklawn, IL 60454-0205. TEL 708-425-5163.
    Description: Lists groups, organizations, and publications dealing specifically with witchcraft and paganism.

PATENTS, TRADEMARKS AND COPYRIGHTS

602.7   US
A A S R C NEWS.* 1972. q. free. American Association of Small Research Companies, c/o Ventures Corp., 222 Third St., Cambridge, MA 02142. Ed. Joanne Martin. adv.; bk.rev.; circ. 17,000.

A I P L A BULLETIN. (American Intellectual Property Law Association) see *LAW*

602.7 608.7 340   JA   ISSN 0385-8863
A.I.P.P.I. JAPANESE GROUP. JOURNAL (INTERNATIONAL EDITION). (Text and summaries in English) 1976. bi-m. 12900 Yen. International Association for the Protection of Industrial Property, Japanese Group, 8-1, 2-chome, Toranomon, Minato-ku, Tokyo 105, Japan. FAX 03-3591-1510. Ed.Bd. adv.; cum.index: 1976-1986; circ. 3,000. (back issues avail.) Key Title: Journal of the Japanese Group of A.I.P.P.I. International Edition.

ANNUAL FRANCHISE HANDBOOK DIRECTORY. see *BUSINESS AND ECONOMICS — Trade And Industrial Directories*

608.7   AT
ANNUAL RECORD OF PATENT OFFICE PROCEEDINGS. 1904. a. Aus.$55. Patent Office, Attn: Publications Officer, Scarborough House, Phillip, A.C.T. 2606, Australia. TEL 06-2832481. FAX 06-285-3593. (Subscr. to: Patent Office, P.O. Box 200, Woden, A.C.T. 2606, Australia) circ. 137. (back issues avail.)
    Description: Includes names of applicants for patents; assignments and changes of name recorded.

602.7   AT
ANNUAL RECORD OF TRADE MARKS OFFICE PROCEEDINGS. 1906. a. Aus.$55. Patent Office, Scarborough House, Phillip, A.C.T 2606, Australia. TEL 06-2832481. FAX 06-2853593. TELEX COMPAT AA 61517. (Subscr. to: Patent Office, P.O. Box 200, Woden, A.C.T 2606, Australia) circ. 129.
    Description: Includes names of applicants for trade marks, assignments and changes of name recorded, applications accepted.

346.73 608.7   US   ISSN 0361-3844
KF3165.A3
ATTORNEYS AND AGENTS REGISTERED TO PRACTICE BEFORE THE U.S. PATENT AND TRADEMARK OFFICE. irreg. $17. U.S. Patent and Trademark Office, Washington, DC 20231. TEL 703-557-1728. (Orders to: Supt. of Documents, Washington, DC 20402)
    Former titles: Attorneys and Agents Registered to Practice Before the U.S. Patent Office (ISSN 0092-5934); Roster of Attorneys and Agents Registered to Practice Before the U.S. Patent Office; Directory of Registered Patent Attorneys and Agents (ISSN 0565-9582)

608.7   AT
AUSTRALIA. DESIGNS OFFICE. ANNUAL RECORD OF DESIGNS OFFICE PROCEEDINGS. 1907. a. Aus.$50. Patent Office, P.O. Box 200, Woden, A.C.T. 2606, Australia. TEL 06-2832481. FAX 06-2853593. TELEX COMPAT AA 61518. circ. 100. (back issues avail.)
    Former titles: Australia. Designs Office. Registered Owners of Designs and Articles in Respect of Which Designs Have Been Registered; Australia. Designs Office. Registered Owners of Designs and Articles in Respect of Which Designs Have Been Registered Under the Designs Act in Australia; Australia. Designs Office. Registered Owners of Designs.
    Description: Contains names of applicants for designs, names of subsequent owners entered in the register and name changes.

608.7   AT
AUSTRALIA. PATENT, TRADE MARKS AND DESIGNS OFFICES. ACTIVITIES REPORT. 1972. a. Aus.$15 (typically set in Sep.). Patent Office, P.O. Box 200, Woden, A.C.T. 2606, Australia. FAX 06-2853593. TELEX COMPAT AA61517. illus.; circ. 214.
    Former titles: Australia. Patent Office. Annual Report of Activities (ISSN 0311-2152); Australia. Patent Office. Report.

340   AT   ISSN 0311-2934
AUSTRALIAN COPYRIGHT COUNCIL. BULLETIN. 1973. 4/yr. Aus.$37. Australian Copyright Council, Ste. 3, 245 Chalmers St., Redfern, N.S.W. 2061, Australia. Ed. Libby Baulch. circ. 600.

608.7 340   AT   ISSN 1038-0671
AUSTRALIAN OFFICIAL JOURNAL OF DESIGNS. 1907. fortn. Aus.$220 (effective 1992). Patent Office, Scarborough House, Phillip A.C.T. 2606, Australia. TEL 06-2832481. FAX 2853593. TELEX COMPAT AA 61517. (Subscr. to: Patent Office, P.O. Box 200, Woden A.C.T. 2606, Australia) circ. 93. (back issues avail.) Indexed: Chem.Abstr., Petrol.Abstr., RAPRA.
    Formerly (until 1982): Australian Official Journal of Patents, Trade Marks and Designs (ISSN 0004-9891)
    Description: Covers proceedings under the Designs Act, including design applications lodged and registered.

608.7 602.7   AT   ISSN 0819-1794
AUSTRALIAN OFFICIAL JOURNAL OF PATENTS. 1904. w. Aus.$355. Patent Office, P.O. Box 200, Woden, A.C.T. 2606, Australia. TEL 06-2832481. FAX 06-2853593. TELEX COMPAT AA 61517. circ. 270. (back issues avail.)
    Incorporates: Patent Abridgements.
    Description: Proceedings under the Patents Act, including applications lodged, applications open to public inspection, complete specifications accepted, patents renewed.

608.7 602.7   AT   ISSN 0819-1808
AUSTRALIAN OFFICIAL JOURNAL OF TRADE MARKS. 1906. w. Aus.$380. Patent Office, P.O. Box 200, Woden, A.C.T. 2606, Australia. TEL 06-2832481. FAX 06-2853593. TELEX COMPAT AA 61517. circ. 206. (back issues avail.)
    Formerly: Australian Official Journal of Patents, Trade Marks and Design. Trade Marks Supplement.
    Description: Proceedings under the Trade Marks Act, including applications lodged, accepted, registered, and renewed.

608.7   GW
AUSZUEGE AUS DEN EUROPAEISCHEN PATENTANMELDUNGEN. TEIL 1. GRUND- UND ROHSTOFFINDUSTRIE, CHEMIE UND HUETTENWESEN, BAUWESEN, BERGBAU. 1968. w. DM.150 per mo. Wila Verlag Wilhelm Lampl GmbH, Landsberger Str. 191A, 8000 Munich 21, Germany. TEL 089-5795-0. FAX 089-5706693. circ. 1,000.
●Also available online.

608.7   GW   ISSN 0177-963X
AUSZUEGE AUS DEN EUROPAEISCHEN PATENTANMELDUNGEN. TEIL 2. ELEKTROTECHNIK, PHYSIK, FEINMECHANIK UND OPTIK, AKUSTIK. 1985. w. DM.150 per mo. Wila Verlag Wilhelm Lampl GmbH, Landsberger Str. 191A, 8000 Munich 21, Germany. TEL 089-5795-0. FAX 089-5706693. circ. 1,500.
●Also available online.

608.7   GW   ISSN 0177-9648
AUSZUEGE AUS DEN EUROPAEISCHEN PATENTANMELDUNGEN. TEIL 3. UEBRIGE VERARBEITUNGSINDUSTRIE UND ARBEITSVERFAHREN, MASCHINEN- UND FAHRZEUGBAU, ERNAEHRUNG, LANDWIRTSCHAFT. 1985. w. DM.150 per mo. Wila Verlag Wilhelm Lampl GmbH, Landsberger Str. 191A, 8000 Munich 21, Germany. TEL 089-5795-0. FAX 089-5706693. circ. 1,000.
●Also available online.

810.7   GW   ISSN 0720-9339
AUSZUEGE AUS DEN EUROPAEISCHEN PATENTSCHRIFTEN. TEIL 1. GRUND- UND ROHSTOFFINDUSTRIE, CHEMIE UND HUETTEN-WESEN, BAUWESEN UND BERGBAU. 1980. w. DM.120 per mo. Wila Verlag Wilhelm Lampl GmbH, Landsberger Str. 191A, 8000 Munich 21, Germany. TEL 089-5795-0. FAX 089-5706693. abstr.; pat.; circ. 500.
●Also available online.

608.7   GW
AUSZUEGE AUS DEN EUROPAEISCHEN PATENTSCHRIFTEN. TEIL 2. ELEKTROTECHNIK, PHYSIK, FEINMECHANIK UND OPTIK, AKUSTIK. 1980. w. DM.120. Wila Verlag Wilhelm Lampl GmbH, Landsbergerstr. 191A, 8000 Munich 21, Germany. TEL 089-5795-0. FAX 089-5706693. circ. 500.

PATENTS, TRADEMARKS AND COPYRIGHTS

608.7 GW
AUSZUEGE AUS DEN EUROPAEISCHEN PATENTSCHRIFTEN. TEIL 3. UEBRIGE VERARBEITUNGSINDUSTRIE UND ARBEITSVERFAHREN, MASCHINEN- UND FAHRZEUGBAU, ERNAEHRUNG, LANDWIRTSCHAFT. 1980. w. DM.120. Wila Verlag Wilhelm Lampl GmbH, Landsbergerstr. 191A, 8000 Munich 21, Germany. TEL 089-5795-0. FAX 089-5706693. circ. 500.

608.7 GW ISSN 0005-0571
AUSZUEGE AUS DEN GEBRAUCHSMUSTERN. 1964. w. DM.120 per mo. Wila Verlag Wilhelm Lampl GmbH, Landsberger Str. 191A, 8000 Munich 21, Germany. TEL 089-5795-0. FAX 089-5706693. abstr.; illus.; pat.; circ. 1,000.
●Also available online.

608.7 GW ISSN 0340-0816
AUSZUEGE AUS DEN OFFENLEGUNGSSCHRIFTEN. TEIL 1. GRUND- UND ROHSTOFFINDUSTRIE, CHEMIE UND HUETTEN-WESEN, BAUWESEN UND BERGBAU. 1968. w. DM.140 per month. Wila Verlag Wilhelm Lampl GmbH, Landsberger Str. 191a, 8000 Munich 21, Germany. TEL 089-5795-0. FAX 089-5706693.
●Also available online.

608.7 GW ISSN 0340-0867
AUSZUEGE AUS DEN OFFENLEGUNGSSCHRIFTEN. TEIL 2. ELEKTROTECHNIK, PHYSIK, FEINMECHANIK UND OPTIK, AKUSTIK. 1968. w. DM.140 per mo. Wila Verlag Wilhelm Lampl GmbH, Landsberger Str. 191A, 8000 Munich 21, Germany. TEL 089-5795-0. FAX 089-5706693. circ. 1,500.
●Also available online.

608.7 GW ISSN 0340-0913
AUSZUEGE AUS DEN OFFENLEGUNGSSCHRIFTEN. TEIL 3. UEBRIGE VERARBEITUNGSINDUSTRIE UND ARBEITSVERFAHREN, MASCHINEN- UND FAHRZEUGBAU, ERNAEHRUNG, LANDWIRTSCHAFT. 1968. w. DM.140 per mo. Wila Verlag Wilhelm Lampl GmbH, Landsberger Str. 191A, 8000 Munich 21, Germany. TEL 089-5795-0. FAX 089-5706693. circ. 1,000.
●Also available online.

608.7 GW ISSN 0178-4250
AUSZUEGE AUS DEN PATENTSCHRIFTEN. 1955. w. DM.140 per mo. Wila Verlag Wilhelm Lampl GmbH, Landsberger Str. 191A, 8000 Munich 21, Germany. TEL 089-5795-0. FAX 089-5706693. circ. 1,500.
●Also available online.
Former titles: Auszuege aus den Auslegeschriften; Auszuege aus den Patentanmeldungen (ISSN 0005-058X)

AWISHKARA. see *SCIENCES: COMPREHENSIVE WORKS*

340 608.7 US ISSN 0148-7965
B N A'S PATENT, TRADEMARK & COPYRIGHT JOURNAL. 1970. w. $880. Bureau of National Affairs, 1231 25th St., N.W., Washington, DC 20037. TEL 202-452-4200. FAX 202-833-8092. TELEX 285656 BNAI WSH. (Subscr. to: 9435 Key West Ave., Rockville, MD 20850. TEL 800-372-1033) Ed. Jeffrey M. Samuels. bk.rev.; abstr.; pat.; stat.; index, cum.index. (looseleaf format; back issues avail.)
●Also available online. Vendor(s): Mead Data Central, WESTLAW (BNA-PTCJ).
Description: Provides an in-depth review of current developments in the intellectual property field. Covers congressional activity, court decisions, relevant conferences, professional associations, international developments, and actions of the Patent and Trademark Office and the Copyright Office.

608.7 FR ISSN 0750-7674
T271 CODEN: BOPBEN
B.O.P.I. BREVETS D'INVENTION - ABREGES ET LISTES. (Bulletin Officiel de la Propriete Industrielle) w. 2500 F. Institut National de la Propriete Industrielle, 26 bis rue de Leningrad, 75800 Paris Cedex 08, France. TEL 42-94-52-52. FAX 42-94-21-93. TELEX 290-368INPI PARIS. pat.; index; circ. 1,900. (also avail. in microfiche; back issues avail.)
Formerly: B.O.P.I. Abreges (ISSN 0151-0592)
Description: Contains fac-similes of trademarks registered in France with the bibliographical data and the list of products designated in the registration.

608.7 FR ISSN 0223-3401
B.O.P.I. MARQUES. (Bulletin Officiel de la Propriete Industrielle) 1884. w. 1150 F. Institut National de la Propriete Industrielle, 26 bis rue de Leningrad, 75800 Paris Cedex 08, France. TEL 42-94-52-52. FAX 42-94-21-93. TELEX 290-368INPA PARIS. tr.mk.; index; circ. 700. (back issues avail.)

608.7 FR
B.O.P.I. STATISTIQUES. (Bulletin Officiel de la Propriete Industrielle) 1958. a. 50 F. per no. Institut National de la Propriete Industrielle, 26 bis rue de Leningrad, 75800 Paris Cedex 08, France. TEL 42-94-52-52. FAX 42-94-21-93. TELEX 290-368INPI PARIS. index; circ. 1,200. (back issues avail.)
Description: Contains the statistical data concerning patents, industrial designs, trademarks, trade and business register and the trade directory.

347.7 NE ISSN 0006-2251
BIJBLAD BIJ DE INDUSTRIELE EIGENDOM. 1933. m. fl.80. Bureau voor de Industriele Eigendom, Octrooiraad, Patentlaan 2, 2288 EE Rijswijk (Z.H.), Netherlands. Ed.Bd. bk.rev.; bibl.; charts; stat.; index; circ. 900.

BLAKES REPORT - INTELLECTUAL PROPERTY. see *LAW*

608.7 602.7 GW ISSN 0930-2980
BLATT FUER PATENT, MUSTER- UND ZEICHENWESEN. 1898. m. DM.84.40. (Deutsches Patentamt) Carl Heymanns Verlag KG, Luxemburgerstr. 449, 5000 Cologne 41, Germany. TEL 0221-46010-0. FAX 0221-4601069. adv.; pat.; stat.; tr.mkt.; index, cum.index; circ. 2,300. (tabloid format)

608.7 VE ISSN 0006-6338
BOLETIN DE LA PROPIEDAD INDUSTRIAL. 1931. m. free. Ministerio de Fomento, Officina de Registro de la Propiedad Industrial, Centro Simon Bolivar, Edificio Sur, Caracas, Venezuela. Ed. Ricardo Pages. index; circ. 600.

608.7 SP ISSN 0211-0105
BOLETIN OFICIAL DE LA PROPIEDAD INDUSTRIAL. 1: MARCAS Y OTROS SIGNOS DISTINTIVOS. 1886. fortn. 33600 ptas. for hardcopy; microfiche 703000 ptas. Ministerio de Industria, Comercio y Turismo, Registro de la Propiedad Industrial, Panama, 1, 28071 Madrid, Spain. TEL 458-22-00. charts; illus.; pat.; index. (also avail. in microfiche)
Superseded in part (in 1965): Boletin Oficial de la Propiedad Industrial (ISSN 0038-6413)

608.5 SP ISSN 0211-0121
BOLETIN OFICIAL DE LA PROPIEDAD INDUSTRIAL. 2: PATENTES Y MODELOS DE UTILIDAD. 1886. fortn. 26100 ptas. for hardcopy; microfiche 8000 ptas. Ministerio de Industria, Comercio y Turismo, Registro de la Propiedad Industrial, Panama, 1, 28071 Madrid, Spain. TEL 458-22-00. charts; illus.; pat.; index. (also avail. in microfiche)
Supersedes in part: Boletin Oficial de la Propiedad Industrial. 2: Patentes, Modelos y Dibujos (ISSN 0211-0113); Which superseded in part (in 1965): Boletin Oficial de la Propiedad Industrial (ISSN 0038-6413)

608.5 SP ISSN 0211-013X
BOLETIN OFICIAL DE LA PROPIEDAD INDUSTRIAL. 3: MODELOS Y DIBUJOS INDUSTRIALES Y ARTISTICOS. 1886. fortn. 7900 ptas. for hardcopy; microfiche 2400 ptas. Ministerio de Industria, Comercio y Turismo, Registro de la Propiedad Industrial, Panama, 1, 28071 Madrid, Spain. TEL 458-22-00. charts; illus.; pat.; index.
Supersedes in part: Boletin Oficial de la Propiedad Industrial. 2: Patentes, Modelos y Dibujos (ISSN 0211-0113); Which superseded in part (in 1969): Boletin Oficial de la Propiedad Industrial (ISSN 0038-6413)

602.7 608.7 SP
BOLETIN OFICIAL DE LA PROPIEDAD INDUSTRIAL. 4: RESUMENES DE PATENTES. 1980. fortn. Ministerio de Industria, Comercio y Turismo, Registro de la Propiedad Industrial, Panama, 1, 28071 Madrid, Spain. TEL 458-22-00.
Formerly (until 1989): Boletin Oficial de la Propiedad Industrial. Informacion Tecnologica de Patentes (ISSN 0211-187X)

608.7 IT ISSN 0006-6664
BOLLETTINO DEI BREVETTI PER INVENZIONI, MODELLI E MARCHI. 1902. s-m. Ministero dell'Industria, del Commercio e dell'Artigianato, 00100 Rome, Italy. illus.; pat.; tr.mk.

602.7 US
T223.V4
BRANDS AND THEIR COMPANIES. (Supplement avail.) 1976. irreg., 9th ed., 1990. $345 (in 2 vols.). Gale Research Inc., 835 Penobscot Bldg., Detroit, MI 48226. TEL 313-961-2242. FAX 313-961-6083. TELEX 810-221-7086. Ed. Susan Stitler.
●Also available online. Vendor(s): DIALOG.
Formerly: Trade Names Dictionary (ISSN 0272-8818)
Description: Identifies more than 230,000 consumer products and their manufacturers. Entries are arranged alphabetically by trade name and include contact information for product inquiries or complaints.

602.7 US
T223.V4
BRANDS AND THEIR COMPANIES SUPPLEMENT. 1976. a. (except during the publication of Brands and Their Companies). $260. Gale Research Inc., 835 Penobscot Bldg., Detroit, MI 48226. TEL 313-961-2242. FAX 313-961-6083. TELEX 810-221-7086. Ed. Susan Stetler.
Formerly: New Trade Names (ISSN 0272-8826)
Description: Adds 18,000 new trade names and their companies to the listings in the main volumes.

340 IT ISSN 0393-5981
BREVETTI & INVENZIONI. 1979. q. L.50000. Mostra Brevetti & Invenzioni, Viale Ronchi, 18, 00177 Rome, Italy. TEL 06-290256. Ed.Bd. circ. 5,000. (back issues avail.)

BRITISH GLASS MANUFACTURERS CONFEDERATION. DIGEST OF INFORMATION AND PATENT REVIEW. see *CERAMICS, GLASS AND POTTERY*

602.7 608.7 RM ISSN 1220-6105
BULETIN OFICIAL DE PROPRIETATE INDUSTRIAL/OFFICIAL BULLETIN FOR INDUSTRIAL PROPERTY. (Issued in 2 sections: Inventions and Trademarks) (Text in Rumanian; summaries in English, French) 1961. m. $70 or exchange basis. Oficiul de Stat pentru Inventii si Marci (OSIM) - State Office for Inventions and Trademarks, 5, Ioan Ghica St., Sect.3, 70418 Bucharest, Rumania. FAX 15-90-66. TELEX 11370-ROPAT R. (Subscr. to: Rompresfilatelia, Foreign Trade Rumanian Entreprise, Calea Grivitei 64-66, Sect.1, P.O. Box 12-201, Bucharest, Rumania) (Co-sponsor: Rumanian Institute for Inventions and Trademarks) adv. contact: Dima Sofia Liliana.
Formerly (until 1991): Buletinul de Informare pentru Inventii si Marci - Bulletin for Inventions and Trademarks.

602 608 UK ISSN 0261-023X
BULLETIN OF INVENTIONS AND SUMMARY OF PATENT SPECIFICATIONS. 1981. q. £24($30) Okikiolu Scientific & Industrial Co., 377 Edgware Rd., London W2 1BT, England. Ed. G.O. Okikiolu. illus.; pat.; index. cum.index. (back issues avail.)
Description: Reports on new discoveries and inventions.

BUTTERWORTHS LEGAL SERVICES DIRECTORY. see *LAW*

608.7 UK ISSN 0306-0314
C I P A. 1971. m. £40 to non-members. Chartered Institute of Patent Agents, Staple Inn Bldgs., High Holborn, London WC1V 7PZ, England. Ed. G.F. Arthur. bk.rev.

608.7 US
CALIFORNIA INVENTOR. 1978. m. $45 (foreign $60). Inventors of California, Box 6158, Rheem Valley, CA 94570. TEL 415-376-7541. FAX 415-376-7762. Ed. Dorothy D. Parrish. bk.rev.; circ. 150. (looseleaf format; back issues avail.)

602.7 608.7 CN ISSN 0825-7256
CANADIAN INTELLECTUAL PROPERTY REVIEW. 1984. s-a. Can.$45. Patent and Trademark Institute of Canada, P.O. Box 1298, Station "B", Ottawa, Ont. K1P 5R3, Canada. TEL 613-234-0516. circ. 800.
Indexed: Ind.Can.L.P.L.
Formerly: Patent and Trademark Institute of Canada. Bulletin.
Description: Contains papers presented at spring and annual meetings of the institute.

CANADIAN PATENT REPORTER. see *LAW*

PATENTS, TRADEMARKS AND COPYRIGHTS

608.7   US
CATALOG FOR GOVERNMENT INVENTIONS AVAILABLE FOR LICENSING. Issued with: Abstract Newsletter. Government Inventions Available for Licensing. a. $59. U.S. National Technical Information Service, 3285 Port Royal Rd., Springfield, VA 22161. TEL 703-487-4630. FAX 703-321-8547. TELEX 64617. Ed. Ed Lehmann. (back issues avail.)
   Former titles: Catalog for Government Inventions for Licensing; Catalog of Government Patents Available for Licensing.
   Description: Provides inventor and back-up information to those interested in patent licensing opportunities.

COMPRESSOR NEWS AND PATENTS. see *MACHINERY*

340   UN   ISSN 0010-8626
LAW
COPYRIGHT. French edition: Droit d'Auteur (ISSN 0012-6365) 1965. m. 160 Fr. World Intellectual Property Organization (WIPO) - Organisation Mondiale de la Propriete Intellectuelle, Publications and Public Information Section, 34 Chemin des Colombettes, 1211 Geneva 20, Switzerland. TEL 022-730-9111. FAX 022-733-5428. TELEX 412912 OMPI CH. adv.; bk.rev.; charts; index; circ. 700. (also avail. in microfiche; back issues avail.)
—BLDSC shelfmark: 3468.600000.
   Description: Covers the developments, theory and practical applications of international copyright and neighboring rights law. Includes national, regional, multilateral laws and treaties.

COPYRIGHT BULLETIN; quarterly review. see *LAW*

COPYRIGHT CLEARANCE CENTER. REPORT. see *PUBLISHING AND BOOK TRADE*

COPYRIGHT LAW IN BUSINESS AND PRACTICE. see *LAW*

320   US
COPYRIGHT LAW REPORTS. 2 base vols. (plus m. updates). $455. Commerce Clearing House, Inc., 4025 W. Peterson Ave., Chicago, IL 60646. TEL 312-583-8500.

347.7   US   ISSN 0069-9950
KF3035.A75
COPYRIGHT LAW SYMPOSIUM. 1950. irreg., no.25, 1980. price varies. (American Society of Composers, Authors, and Publishers) Columbia University Press, 562 W. 113th St., New York, NY 10025. TEL 212-678-6777. Indexed: C.L.I., L.R.I., Leg.Per.
—BLDSC shelfmark: 3468.960000.

340   UN
COPYRIGHT LAWS AND TREATIES OF THE WORLD. 3 base vols. (plus irreg. suppl.). $665 includes Supplement. Unesco, 7-9 Place de Fontenoy, 75700 Paris, France. TEL 577-16-10. (Dist. in U.S. by: Barnan, 4611-F Assembly Dr., Lanham, MD 20706-4391; and by: BNA Customer Service Center, 9435 Key West Ave., Rockville, MD 20850-3397. TEL 800-372-1033) (Co-sponsor: World Intellectual Property Organization) (looseleaf format)
   Description: Presents the copyright laws, orders, and regulations of more than 150 countries, from Afghanistan to Zimbabwe.

340   UN   ISSN 0069-9969
COPYRIGHT LAWS AND TREATIES OF THE WORLD. SUPPLEMENT. irreg., 25th, 1989. $245. Unesco, 7-9 Place de Fontenoy, 75700 Paris, France. TEL 577-16-10. (Dist. in U.S. by: Unipub, 4611-F Assembly Dr., Lanham, MD 20706-4391; and by: BNA Customer Service Center, 9435 Key West Ave., Rockville, MD 30850-3397. TEL 800-372-1033) (Co-sponsor: World Intellectual Property Organization) (also avail. in looseleaf format)

340   AT   ISSN 0725-0509
COPYRIGHT REPORTER. 1981. 4/yr. Aus.$120. Australian Copyright Council, Ste. 3, Chalmers St., Redfern, N.S.W. 2016, Australia. Ed. Susan Bridge.
—BLDSC shelfmark: 3470.150000.

608.7   CU   ISSN 0011-2615
CUBA. OFICINA NACIONAL DE INVENCIONES, INFORMACION TECNICA Y MARCAS. BOLETIN OFICIAL. Short title: O N I I T E M. Boletin. 1906. q. $8. Oficina Nacional de Invenciones, Informacion Tecnica y Marcas, Picota no. 15 c/o Luz y Acosta, Havana Vieja, Havana 1, C.P. 10100, Cuba. index; circ. 200. (also avail. in microfilm)
   Formerly: Cuba. Registro de la Propriedad Industrial. Boletin Oficial.

608.7   DK   ISSN 0903-8825
DANSK MOENSTERTIDENDE. 1970. fortn. DKK 600. Patentdirektoratet, Helgeshoej Alle 81, DK-2630 Taastrup, Denmark. TEL 43 71 71 71. FAX 43-71-71-70. TELEX 16046 DPO DK.

608.7   DK   ISSN 0011-6416
   CODEN: DAPAA8
DANSK PATENTTIDENDE. 1894. w. DKK 1000. Patentdirektoratet, Helgeshoej Alle 81, DK-2630 Taastrup, Denmark. TEL 43 71 71 71. FAX 43-71-71-70. TELEX 16046 DPO DK.

602.7   DK
DANSK VAREMAERKETIDENDE. 1879. w. DKK 1000. Patentdirektoratet, Helgeshoj Alle 81, DK-2630 Taastrup, Denmark. TEL 43 71 71 71. FAX 43-71-71-70. TELEX 16046 DPO DK.

340   US   ISSN 0070-3176
KF2994.A1
DECISIONS OF THE UNITED STATES COURTS INVOLVING COPYRIGHTS. (Subseries of U.S. Copyright Office. Bulletin) 1910. a. price varies. U.S. Library of Congress, Copyright Office, The Library of Congress, Washington, DC 20559. TEL 202-783-3238. FAX 202-512-2250. (Dist. by: Supt. of Documents, P.O. Box 371954, Pittsburgh, PA 15250) cum.index.

608.7   DK
DENMARK. PATENTDIREKTORATET. AARSBERETNING. 1975. a. free. Patentdirektoratet - Danish Patents and Trademark Office, Helgeshoj Alle 81, DK-2630 Taastrup, Denmark. FAX 45-43717170. TELEX 16046-DPO-DK. Ed. P.L. Thoft. circ. 5,000.
   Former titles: Denmark. Patentdirektoratet. Direktorat under Forandring & Denmark. Direktoratet for Patent- og Varemaerkevaesenet. Aarsberetning.

608.7   GW   ISSN 0232-7643
▼**DEUTSCHES PATENTAMT. BEKANNTMACHUNGEN 1. GRUND- UND ROHSTOFFINDUSTRIE, CHEMIE UND HUETTENWESEN, BAUWESEN UND BERGBAU.** 1991. w. DM.65 for 3 months. Deutsches Patentamt, Gitschinerstr. 97, 1000 Berlin 61, Germany. FAX 030-2594693.

608.7   GW   ISSN 0232-7694
▼**DEUTSCHES PATENTAMT. BEKANNTMACHUNGEN 2. ELEKTROTECHNIK, PHYSIK, FEINMECHANIK UND OPTIK, AKUSTIK.** 1991. w. DM.65 for 3 months. Deutsches Patentamt, Gitschinerstr. 97, 1000 Berlin 61, Germany. FAX 030-2594693.

608.7   GW   ISSN 0232-7740
▼**DEUTSCHES PATENTAMT. BEKANNTMACHUNGEN 3. UEBRIGE VERARBEITUNGSINDUSTRIE UND ARBEITSVERFAHREN, MASCHINEN- UND FAHRZEUGBAU, ERNAEHRUNG, LANDWIRTSCHAFT.** 1991. w. DM.65 for 3 months. Deutsches Patentamt, Gitschinerstr. 97, 1000 Berlin 61, Germany. FAX 030-2594693.

DIRECTORY OF CANADIAN CONSULTANTS, COPYWRITERS & CONTRACT PUBLISHERS. see *PUBLISHING AND BOOK TRADE*

340   IT   ISSN 0012-3420
DIRITTO DI AUTORE. (Text in French and Italian) 1930. q. L.50000 (foreign L.75000). Casa Editrice Dott. A. Giuffre, Via Busto Arsizio 40, 20151 Milan, Italy. TEL 02-38000905. FAX 02-38009582. Ed. Mario Fabiani. adv.; bk.rev.; abstr.; bibl.; index; circ. 900.

340   UN   ISSN 0012-6365
DROIT D'AUTEUR. English edition: Copyright (ISSN 0010-8626) 1888. m. 160 Fr. World Intellectual Property Organization (WIPO) - Organisation Mondiale de la Propriete Intellectuelle, Publications and Public Information Section, 34 Chemin des Colombettes, 1211 Geneva 20, Switzerland. TEL 022-730-9111. FAX 022-733-5428. TELEX 412912 OMPI CG. adv.; bk.rev.; charts; index; circ. 700. (also avail. in microfiche; back issues avail.)
   Description: Covers the developments, theory and practical applications of international copyright and neighboring rights law. Includes national, regional, multilateral laws and treaties.

E P M ENTERTAINMENT MARKETING SOURCEBOOK. see *BUSINESS AND ECONOMICS — Marketing And Purchasing*

ENERGY INFORMATION DIRECTORY. see *ENERGY*

ENTERTAINMENT MARKETING LETTER. see *BUSINESS AND ECONOMICS — Marketing And Purchasing*

608.7   GW
ERFINDER UND NEUHEITENDIENST. 1949. m. DM.33. Deutscher Erfinderring e.V., Schlegelstr. 25, 8500 Nuremberg, Germany. Ed. H. Hammermann. adv.; bk.rev.; circ. 1,000.
   Formerly: Neuheiten und Erfinderdienst (ISSN 0028-3711)

608.7   GW
EUROPAEISCHES PATENTBLATT. (Text in English, French and German) w. DM.430. Europaeischen Patentamt, Erhardtstr. 27, 8000 Munich 2, Germany. TEL 089-23990. FAX 089-23994465.

608.7   GW   ISSN 0170-9291
EUROPAISCHES PATENTAMT. AMTSBLATT/EUROPEAN PATENT OFFICE. OFFICIAL JOURNAL. m. DM.175. European Patent Office, Erhardtstrasse 27, 8000 Munich 2, Germany. FAX 089-2399-4465. TELEX 523656. adv.; circ. 3,500.

608.7   GW   ISSN 0724-7729
EUROPEAN PATENT OFFICE. ANNUAL REPORT. (Text in English, French and German) 1978. a. free. European Patent Office, Erhardtstrasse 27, 8000 Munich 2, Germmany. FAX 089-2399-4465. TELEX 523656. adv.; circ. 7,000. (back issues avail.)
   Description: Annual review detailing patent growth, international patent cooperation, new patents and judicial developments.

608.7 341   UK   ISSN 0269-0802
EUROPEAN PATENT OFFICE REPORTS. 1986. 8/yr. £215. (E S C Publishing Ltd.) Sweet & Maxwell, South Quay Plaza, 8th Fl., 183 Marsh Wall, London E14 9FT, England. TEL 071-538-8686. FAX 071-538-8625. Eds. Brian Reid, Jonathan Turner. adv.; bk.rev. (back issues avail.)
   Description: Provides the patent practitioner with ready access to EPO decisions. For all those advising on the European route to patent protection.

608.7   UK
EUROPEAN PATENTS HANDBOOK. irreg. £370. (Chartered Institute of Patent Agents) Longman Group UK Ltd., Law, Tax and Finance Division, 21-27 Lamb's Conduit St., London WC1N 3NJ, England. TEL 071-242-2548. FAX 071-831-8119. TELEX 295445. (looseleaf format)
   Description: Practical guide to intricacies of processing an application and patent in the European Patent Office.

608.7   FI   ISSN 0355-4481
FINLAND. PATENTTI- JA REKISTERIHALLITUS. MALLIOIKEUSLEHTI. (Text in Finnish and Swedish) 1971. m. FIM 590. Patentti- ja Rekisterihallitus - National Board of Patents and Registration, Albertinkatu 25, SF-00180 Helsinki 18, Finland. FAX 358-0-6953-204. (Dist. by: VAPK - Kustannus, P.O. Box 516, SF-00101 Helsinki 10, Finland) circ. 285.

608.7   FI   ISSN 0031-2916
FINLAND. PATENTTI- JA REKISTERIHALLITUS. PATENTTILEHTI. (Text in Finnish and Swedish) 1889. s-m. FIM 850. Patentti- ja Rekisterihallitus - National Board of Patents and Registration, Albertinkatu 25, 00180 Helsinki 18, Finland. FAX 358-0-6953-204. (Dist. by: VAPK - Kustannus, P.O. Box 516, SF-00101 Helsinki 10, Finland) index; circ. 520.

PATENTS, TRADEMARKS AND COPYRIGHTS 3675

608.7 602.7   FI   ISSN 0039-9922
FINLAND. PATENTTI- JA REKISTERIHALLITUS. TAVARAMERKKILEHTI. (Text in Finnish and Swedish) 1889. s-m. FIM 510. Patentti- ja Rekisterihallitus - National Board of Patents and Registration, Albertinkatu 25, SF-00180 Helsinki 18, Finland. FAX 358-0-6953-204. (Dist. by: VAPK - Kustannus, P.O. Box 516, SF-00101 Helsinki 10, Finland) charts; tr.mk.; circ. 230.
  Former titles: Tavaraleimalehti; Tavaraleimarekisteri Rekisterilehti.

346   UK
FLEET STREET REPORTS. 1963. m. £280. (European Law Centre Ltd.) Sweet & Maxwell, South Quay Plaza, 8th Floor, 183 Marsh Wall, London E14 9FT, England. TEL 071-538-8686. FAX 071-538-9508. Ed. Michael Fysh. adv.; index. (back issues avail.)
  Formerly: Fleet Street Patent Law Reports (ISSN 0430-6457)
  Description: Reference to all major cases on industrial property law.

FOGRA-PATENTSCHAU. see *PRINTING*

LA FRANCE DE L'INDUSTRIE ET SES SERVICES. see *BUSINESS AND ECONOMICS — Trade And Industrial Directories*

FRIDAY MEMO. see *COMPUTERS*

608.7   US   ISSN 0083-3029
GENERAL INFORMATION CONCERNING TRADEMARKS. irreg. $1.50. U.S. Patent and Trademark Office, Washington, DC 20231. TEL 703-557-3158. (Orders to: Supt. of Documents, Washington, DC 20402)

608.7   GW   ISSN 0934-7062
GESCHMACKSMUSTERBLATT. 1988. s-m. DM.48. (Deutsches Patentamt) Wila Verlag Wilhelm Lampl GmbH, Landsbergerstr. 191a, 8000 Munich 21, Germany. FAX 5706693. TELEX 5212943-WILA-D. circ. 600.

608.7 340   GW   ISSN 0016-9420
GEWERBLICHER RECHTSSCHUTZ UND URHEBERRECHT. 1896. m. DM.538. (Deutsche Vereinigung fuer Gewerblichen Rechtsschutz und Urheberrecht) V C H Verlagsgesellschaft mbH, Postfach 101161, 6940 Weinheim, Germany. TEL 06201-602-0. FAX 06201-602328. TELEX 465516-VCHWH-D. (US addr.: V C H Publishers Inc., 220 E. 23rd St., New York, NY 10010-4606. TEL 212-683-8333) Eds. R. Jacobs, U. Krieger. adv.; bk.rev.; bibl.; pat.; tr.lit.; index; circ. 2,500. (also avail. in microfilm from VCI; reprint service avail. from ISI,SCH) *Indexed:* INIS Atomind.

608.7 340   GW   ISSN 0435-8600
GEWERBLICHER RECHTSSCHUTZ UND URHEBERRECHT. INTERNATIONALER TEIL. (Text in German; summaries in English) 1952. m. DM.538. (Deutsche Vereinigung fuer Gewerblichen Rechtsschutz und Urheberrecht) V C H Verlagsgesellschaft mbH, Postfach 101161, 6940 Weinheim, Germany. TEL 06201-602-0. FAX 06201-602328. TELEX 465516-VCHWH-D. (US addr.: V C H Publishers Inc., 220 E. 23rd St., New York, NY 10010-4606) Ed.Bd. circ. 2,425. (also avail. in microfilm from VCI)

608.7   UK   ISSN 0072-5706
GREAT BRITAIN. DEPARTMENT OF TRADE. PATENTS, DESIGN AND TRADE MARKS (ANNUAL REPORT). a. H.M.S.O., P.O. Box 276, London SW8 5DT, England. (reprint service avail. from UMI)

GUIDE TO AVAILABLE TECHNOLOGIES; an annual guide to business opportunities in technology. see *TECHNOLOGY: COMPREHENSIVE WORKS*

HANDBUCH DER DATENBANKEN FUER NATURWISSENSCHAFT, TECHNIK, PATENTE. see *COMPUTERS — Data Base Management*

608.7   CN
HUGHES AND WOODLEY ON PATENTS. s-a. Can.$160. Butterworths Canada Ltd., 75 Clegg Rd., Markham, Ont. L6G 1A1, Canada. TEL 416-479-2665. FAX 416-479-2826. Eds. Roger T. Hughes, John M. Woodley. (looseleaf format)
  Description: Canadian Patent Office practice and procedures.

340   CN
HUGHES ON COPYRIGHT AND INDUSTRIAL DESIGN. a. Can.$160. Butterworths Canada Ltd., 75 Clegg Rd., Markham, Ont. L6G 1A1, Canada. TEL 416-479-2665. FAX 416-479-2826. Ed. Roger T. Hughes. (looseleaf format)
  Description: Covers law and procedure issues on copyrights.

602.7   CN
HUGHES ON TRADEMARK. s-a. Can.$160. Butterworths Canada Ltd., 75 Clegg Rd., Markham, Ont. L6G 1A1, Canada. TEL 416-479-2665. FAX 416-479-2826. Ed. Roger T. Hughes. (looseleaf format)
  Description: Covers trademarks and unfair competition.

608   GW   ISSN 0018-9855
K9
I I C. (International Review of Industrial Property and Copyright Law) (Text in part selected from German and international editions of the journal Gewerblicher Rechtsschutz und Urheberrecht) (Text in English) 1969. 6/yr. DM.394. (Max-Planck-Institute for Foreign and International Patent, Copyright and Competitition Law, Munich) V C H Verlagsgesellschaft mbH, Postfach 101161, 6940 Weinheim, Germany. TEL 06201-602-0. FAX 06201-602328. TELEX 465516-VCHWH-D. (US addr.: V C H Publishers Inc., 220 E. 23rd St., New York, NY 10010-4606. TEL 212-683-8333) Eds. F.-K. Beier, G. Schricker. bk.rev.; index; circ. 1,250. (also avail. in microfilm from VCI; reprint service avail. from ISI) *Indexed:* Curr.Cont., SSCI.
  —BLDSC shelfmark: 4363.680000.

608.7   HK   ISSN 1011-3649
LAW
I P ASIA; intellectual property marketing and communications law. 1988. 10/yr. HK.$3625($465) Asia Law & Practice Ltd., 2-F, 29 Hollywood Rd., Central, Hong Kong. TEL 544-9918. FAX 544-0040. Ed. David Shannon.

IMPACT PUMP NEWS PATENTS. see *MACHINERY*

608.7 697   US   ISSN 1056-1544
IMPACT VALVES NEWS AND PATENTS. 1962. 10/yr. $150. Impact Publications, Box 3113, Ketchum, ID 83340-3113. TEL 208-726-2133. bk.rev.; pat.; circ. 100. (back issues avail.)
  Former titles: Impact Valves (ISSN 0883-7619); Valve Information Report (ISSN 0042-2436)
  Description: Contains recent patent gazette information.

608.7   UN   ISSN 0019-8625
INDUSTRIAL PROPERTY. French edition: Propriete Industrielle (ISSN 0033-1430) 1962. m. 180 Fr. World Intellectual Property Organization (WIPO) - Organisation Mondiale de la Propriete Intellectuelle, Publications and Public Information Section, 34 Chemin des Colombettes, 1211 Geneva 20, Switzerland. TEL 022-730-9111. FAX 022-733-5428. TELEX 412912 OMPI CH. bk.rev.; index; circ. 1,350. (also avail. in microfiche; back issues avail.)
  Description: Covers developments in industrial property in all fields of technology at national and international levels. Includes all major national, regional, and multilateral industrial property laws.

608.7   NE   ISSN 0019-9249
INDUSTRIEEL EIGENDOM. 1912. s-m. fl.350. Bureau voor de Industriele Eigendom, Octrooiraad - Netherlands Patent Office, Patentlaan 2, 2288 EE Rijswijk (Z.H.), Netherlands. index. *Indexed:* Key to Econ.Sci.

602.7   CU
INFORMACION DE PATENTES. fortn. Academia de Ciencias, Instituto de Documentacion e Informacion Cientifico-Tecnica (I D I C T), Capitolio Nacional, Prado y San Jose, Habana 2, Havana, Cuba.

INFORMATION SOURCES (YEAR). see *COMPUTERS*

INFORMATION TIMES. see *LIBRARY AND INFORMATION SCIENCES — Computer Applications*

608.7   GW   ISSN 0863-2790
T273
INNOVATION & MANAGEMENT. 1952. m. DM.108.60. Verlag Die Wirtschaft Berlin GmbH, Am Friedrichshain 22, 1055 Berlin, Germany. TEL 43870. FAX 4361249. Ed. Klaus Brunne. adv.; bk.rev.; bibl.; charts; illus.; pat.; tr.lit.
  Formerly: Neuerer. Ausgaben A-C (ISSN 0028-3584)

338   US   ISSN 1058-8523
INNOVATIVE PRODUCTS. Variant title: Innovative Products Letter. 1988. q. $19. Innovation Groups, Inc., Box 16645, Tampa, FL 33687. TEL 813-622-8484. FAX 813-664-0051. adv.; bk.rev.; circ. 2,500.
  Description: Discussed new products of interest to local governments.

340   AT
INSTITUTE OF PATENT ATTORNEYS OF AUSTRALIA. ANNUAL PROCEEDINGS. 1919. irreg., every 3-5 yrs. membership. Institute of Patent Attorneys of Australia, Quantas House, 2 Railway Parade, Camberwell, Vic. 3124, Australia. TEL 03-882-8041. FAX 613-882-8087. Ed. R.J. Strickland. bk.rev.; circ. 250.

340   AT
INTELLECTUAL PROPERTY - COPYRIGHT. base vol. (plus q. updates). $355. Butterworths Pty. Ltd., 271-273 Lane Cove Rd., P.O. Box 345, N. Ryde, N.S.W. 2113, Australia. TEL 02-335-4444. FAX 02-335-4655. (looseleaf format)

340   AT
INTELLECTUAL PROPERTY IN AUSTRALIA: PATENTS, DESIGNS & TRADEMARKS. 2 base vols. (plus updates 4/yr.). $385. Butterworths Pty. Ltd., 271-273 Lane Cove Rd., P.O. Box 345, N. Ryde, N.S.W. 2113, Australia. TEL 02-335-4444. FAX 02-335-4655. (looseleaf format)

INTELLECTUAL PROPERTY JOURNAL. see *LAW*

608.7   US   ISSN 0193-4864
KF3114.A1
INTELLECTUAL PROPERTY LAW REVIEW. 1969. a. $85. Clark - Boardman - Callaghan Company Ltd., 375 Hudson St., New York, NY 10014. TEL 212-929-7500. FAX 212-924-0460. Ed. Thomas E. Costner. index. *Indexed:* C.L.I., L.R.I., Leg.Per.
  —BLDSC shelfmark: 4531.824000.
  Formerly: Patent Law Review (ISSN 0079-0168)

341.758   FR   ISSN 0074-2899
INTERNATIONAL CONFEDERATION OF SOCIETIES OF AUTHORS AND COMPOSERS. irreg., no.186, 1976. International Confederation of Societies of Authors and Composers, 11 rue Keppler, 75116 Paris, France.

608.7   UN   ISSN 0250-7730
TS171.A1
INTERNATIONAL DESIGNS BULLETIN; bulletin des dessins et modeles internationaux. (Text in English and French) 1979. m. 300 Fr. World Intellectual Property Organization (WIPO) - Organisation Mondiale de la Propriete Intellectuelle, Publications and Public Information Section, 34 Chemin des Colombettes, 1211 Geneva 20, Switzerland. TEL 022-730-9111. FAX 022-733-5428. TELEX 412912 OMPI CH. adv.; illus.; circ. 400. (back issues avail.)
  Formerly: Dessins et Modeles Internationaux (ISSN 0011-9520).

602.7   US   ISSN 1050-8376
INTERNATIONAL DIRECTORY OF BRANDS AND THEIR COMPANIES; international consumer products and their manufacturers, importers and distributors with addresses. 1988. biennial. Gale Research Inc., 835 Penobscot Bldg., Detroit, MI 48226-4094. TEL 800-877-GALE. FAX 313-961-6083. Ed. Susan Stetler. (also avail. in magnetic tape; also avail. on diskette)
  ●*Also available online. Vendor(s):* DIALOG.
  Formerly: International Trade Names Directory.

INTERNATIONAL LICENSING. see *TECHNOLOGY: COMPREHENSIVE WORKS*

P
Q

PATENTS, TRADEMARKS AND COPYRIGHTS

608.7   US
INTERNATIONAL PATENT LITIGATION; a county-by-county analysis. 1983. base vol. (plus irreg. suppl.). $195. B N A Books (Subsidiary of: The Bureau of National Affairs, Inc.), 1231 25th St., N.W., Washington, DC 20037. TEL 908-225-1900. FAX 908-417-0482. (Subscr. to: BNA Books Distribution Center, 300 Raritan Center Parkway, Box 7816, Edison, NJ 08818-7816. TEL 800-372-1033) Ed. Michael N. Meller. (looseleaf format)
   Description: Covers patent laws and procedures of 23 industrial nations.

608.7   US
▼**INTERNATIONAL PATENT LITIGATION. SUPPLEMENT.** 1990. a. $85. B N A Books (Subsidiary of: The Bureau of National Affairs, Inc.), 1231 25th St., N.W., Washington, DC 20037. TEL 908-225-1900. FAX 908-417-0482. (Subscr. to: BNA Books Distribution Center, 300 Raritan Center Parkway, Box 7816, Edison, NJ 08818-7816. TEL 800-372-1033) Ed. Michael N. Meller.

608   II
INTERNATIONAL PRESS CUTTING SERVICE: LIST OF INDUSTRIAL LICENCES ISSUED. 1977. 3-4/m. $65. International Press Cutting Service, Box 63, Allahabad 211001, India. Ed. Nandi Khanna. (looseleaf format)

340   AU   ISSN 0539-1512
INTERNATIONALE GESELLSCHAFT FUER URHEBERRECHT. YEARBOOK.* (Text in English, French, German, Italian and Spanish) irreg., vol.5, 1984. Nomos Verlagsgesellschaft mbH und Co. KG, Waldseestr. 3-5, Postfach 610, 7570 Baden-Baden. TEL 07221-20140. FAX 07221-210427. circ. 1,200.

608.7   US
▼**INVENTING AND PATENTING SOURCEBOOK.** 1990. irreg., 2nd ed., 1992. $79. Gale Research Inc., 835 Penobscot Bldg., Detroit, MI 48226. TEL 800-877-4253. FAX 313-961-6083. TELEX 810-221-7086. Ed. Robert J. Hoffman.
   Description: Guide for inventors, innovators, and marketers of new products. Provides information on how to get funding for your ideas, how to patent or trademark a product without an attorney's assistance, and how to select a company to approach for licensing.

INVENTION INTELLIGENCE. see *SCIENCES: COMPREHENSIVE WORKS*

608.7   UK   ISSN 0579-8388
INVENTOR.* 1928. q. £10. Institute of Patentees and Inventors, 189 Regent St., London WC1R 7WF, England. Ed.Bd. adv.; bk.rev.; bibl.; circ. 2,000.

608.7   US   ISSN 0883-9859
INVENTORS' DIGEST. 1985. bi-m. $20 (Canada $25; elsewhere $38). Affiliated Inventors Foundation, 2132 E. Bijou St., Colorado Springs, CO 80909. TEL 719-635-1234. Ed. Joanne Hayes. adv.; bk.rev.; circ. 3,000. (back issues avail.)
   Description: Informs inventors who want to know how to develop and protect their ideas.

608.7   US   ISSN 0899-8841
INVENTOR'S GAZETTE.* 1986. m. $24. Inventors Association of America, 7780 Klusman Ave., Box 1531, Rancho Cucamonga, CA 91730. TEL 714-980-6446. Ed. L. Troy Hall. adv.; circ. 480,000. (tabloid format; back issues avail.)
   Description: Articles on inventors and their latest inventions.

608.7 607.7   IS   ISSN 0021-2326
ISRAEL. MINISTRY OF JUSTICE. PATENT OFFICE. PATENTS AND DESIGNS JOURNAL. (Part A: Patents, Trademarks and Copyrights; Part B: Patents and Designs) (Text in English and Hebrew) 1968. m. IS.465. Ministry of Justice, Patent Office, P.O. Box 717, Jerusalem, Israel. (Subscr. to: Distribution Service of Government Publications, 29-B St., Hakirya, Tel-Aviv, Israel) Ed.Bd. abstr.; circ. 150. **Indexed:** Chem.Abstr.

340   IT
ITALY. OFFICIO DELLA PROPRIETA LETTERARIA, ARTISTICA E SCIENTIFICA. BOLLETTINO.* m. L.3500. Italy. Istituto Poligrafico dello Stato, Piazza Verdi 10, 00198 Rome, Italy.

608.7   RU   ISSN 0130-1802
T201
IZOBRETATEL' I RATSIONALIZATOR. 1929. m. 16.80 Rub. (Society of Soviet Inventors and Innovators, Central Council) Profizdat, Ul. Kirova, 13, Moscow, Russia. Ed. Nina Karaseva. adv.; circ. 400,000.
—BLDSC shelfmark: 0085.800000.

608.7   FI
HF5565
KAUPPAREKISTERILEHTI/HANDELSREGISTERTIDNING. (Text in Finnish, Swedish) 1896. w. FIM 590. Board of Patents and Registration, Albertilkatu 25, 00180 Helsinki 18, Finland. FAX 358-0-6953204. (Susbcr. to: Government Printing Centre, Aikakauslehtien Tilaukset, PL 516, 00101 Helsinki, Finland) Ed. Oscar Wilder. index; circ. 200.
   Formerly: Kaupparekisteri (ISSN 0022-9504)

608.7   US   ISSN 0047-4576
L E S NOUVELLES. 1966. 4/yr. membership; libraries $35. Licensing Executives Society (U.S. & Canada), Inc., c/o Jack Stuart Ott, Ed., 1444 W. 10th St., Ste. 403, Cleveland, OH 44113. TEL 216-771-2600. FAX 216-771-8478. bk.rev.; pat.; index; circ. 6,300.
   Formerly: Nouvelles (ISSN 0270-174X)

340   US
LATMAN'S THE COPYRIGHT LAW. irreg., 7th ed., 1990. $75. B N A Books (Subsidiary of: The Bureau of National Affairs, Inc.), 1231 25th St., N.W., Washington, DC 20037. TEL 908-225-1900. FAX 908-417-0482. (Subscr. to: BNA Books Distribution Center, 300 Raritan Center Parkway, Box 7816, Edison, NJ 08818-7816. TEL 800-372-1033) Ed. William F. Patry.
   Description: Reviews statutes, regulations, international conventions, and judicial and administrative rulings on copyrightability; publication and notice; registration and deposit; infringement and remedies; interaction of federal and state laws; historical background; and international issues.

608.7 658   US
LICENSING BOOK. 1983. m. $36. Adventure Publishing, 264 W. 40th St., New York, NY 10018. TEL 212-575-4510. Ed. Milt Shulman. adv.; circ. 25,000.

602.7   US   ISSN 0890-135X
KF3145.A15
LICENSING JOURNAL. 1982. m. $150 (foreign $165). G B Enterprises, Box 1169, Stamford, CT 06904-1169. TEL 203-358-0848. FAX 203-348-2720. Eds. Charles W. Grimes, Gregory J. Battersby. adv.; bk.rev.; index; circ. 1,000.
   Formerly (until vol.7, no.5): Merchandising Reporter.

608 658.8   US   ISSN 8755-6235
LICENSING LETTER. 1977. m. $235 (foreign $265). E P M Communications, Inc., 488 E. 18th St., Brooklyn, NY 11226. TEL 718-469-9330. FAX 718-469-7124. Ed. Karen Raugust. (back issues avail.)
   Incorporates: Licensing Industry Newsletter.
   Description: News on licensed properties, licensing representatives, manufacturer licenses and statistical data and contact lists.

608.7 658   US
LICENSING TODAY.* 1983. m. $60. Toy & Hobby World (Subsidiary of: V S D Communications), 41 Madison Ave., New York, NY 10010-2202. TEL 212-594-4237. Ed. Thomas X. Hurn. adv.; circ. 18,106.

608.7   MW   ISSN 0025-1267
MALAWI PATENT JOURNAL AND TRADE MARKS JOURNAL. 1966. m. K.2 per no. Ministry of Finance, Government Printer, Box 37, Zomba, Malawi. pat.; tr.mk.

608.7   UN   ISSN 0025-3936
MARQUES INTERNATIONALES. 1893. m. 410 Fr. World Intellectual Property Organization (WIPO) - Organisation Mondiale de la Propriete Intellectuelle, Publications and Public Information Section, 34 Chemin des Colombettes, 1211 Geneva 20, Switzerland. adv.; charts; tr.mk.; index; circ. 1,600. (also avail. in microfiche; back issues avail.)
   Description: Covers all marks, registered, renewed, modified, transferred, refused or otherwise. Includes countries of origin and destination, with reproduction of the actual trademarks or service marks.

608.7   US
MEDICAL DEVICE PATENTS LETTER. 1988. m. $597. Washington Business Information, Inc., 1117 N. 19th St., Ste. 200, Arlington, VA 22209-1798. TEL 703-247-3434. FAX 703-247-3421. Ed. Sean Oberle.

608.7   NE   ISSN 0026-007X
MERKENBLAD BENELUX/MARQUES BENELUX RECUEIL. (Editions in Dutch and French) 1971. m. fl.220. Benelux Merkenbureau - Bureau Benelux des Marques, Bankastraat 151, The Hague, Netherlands. circ. 300.

608.7 340   GW   ISSN 0026-6884
MITTEILUNGEN DER DEUTSCHEN PATENTANWAELTE. 1909. m. DM.136. (Patentanwaltskammer) Carl Heymanns Verlag KG, Luxemburgerstr. 449, 5000 Cologne 41, Germany. TEL 0221-46010-0. FAX 0221-4601069. adv.; bk.rev.; abstr.; pat.; index; circ. 1,300. (tabloid format)

340 608.7   JA
MOJI SHOHYOSHU. (Text in Japanese) 1985. a. (Benrishikai) Nihon Benrishi Kyodo Kumiai, Stanley Bldg. 3F, 5-3, 3-Chome, Kasumigaseki, Chiyoda-Ku, Tokyo 100, Japan. circ. 830.

340.5   NE
MONOGRAPHS ON INDUSTRIAL PROPERTY AND COPYRIGHT LAW. (Text in English) 1976. irreg. Kluwer Academic Publishers, Postbus 17, 3300 AA Dordrecht, Netherlands. TEL 078-334911. FAX 078-334254. TELEX 29245.

608.7   GW
NAMENSVERZEICHNIS ZUM EUROPAEISCHEN PATENTBLATT. (Text in English, French and German) a. DM.50 (foreign DM.60). Europaeischen Patentamt, Erhardtstr. 27, 8000 Munich 2, Germany. TEL 089-23990. FAX 089-23994465.

NONWOVENS PATENT NEWS. see *TEXTILE INDUSTRIES AND FABRICS*

608.7   NO   ISSN 0029-2206
                   CODEN: NOTIAM
NORSK TIDENDE FOR DET INDUSTRIELLE RETTSVERN. DEL 1: PATENTER. 1911. w. NOK 300($30) Styret for det Industrielle Rettsvern - The Norwegian Patent Office, Koebenhavngate 10, P.O. Box 8160 Dep., N-0033 Oslo, Norway. TEL 472-387300. FAX 47-2-387301. TELEX 19152 NOPAT R. abstr.; pat.; index; circ. 600. **Indexed:** Chem.Abstr.

608.7   NO   ISSN 0029-2184
NORSK TIDENDE FOR DET INDUSTRIELLE RETTSVERN. DEL 3: MOENSTRE. 1971. 25/yr. NOK 300($30) Styret for det Industrielle Rettsvern - The Norwegian Patent Office, Koebenhavngate 10, P.O. Box 8160, Dep., N-0033 Oslo, Norway. TEL 472-387300. FAX 472-387301. TELEX 19152 NOPAT R. illus.; pat.; circ. 350.

602.7   NO
                   CODEN: NTAV-A
NORSK VAREMERKETIDENDE. 1911. w. NOK 300($30) Styret for det Industrielle Rettsvern - The Norwegian Patent Office, Koebenhavngate 10, P.O. Box 8160, Dep., N-0033 Oslo, Norway. TEL 472-387300. FAX 472-387301. TELEX 19152 NOPAT R. illus.; tr.mk.; index; circ. 425.
   Formerly (until 1992): Norsk Tidende for det Industrielle Rettsvern. Del 2: Varemerker (ISSN 0029-2192)

340   AU   ISSN 0029-8883
OESTERREICHISCHE AUTORENZEITUNG. 1896. q. free. Staatlich Genehmigte Gesellschaft der Autoren, Baumannstr. 8-10, 1030 Vienna 3, Austria. TEL 71714. FAX 71714107. Ed. Manfred Brunner. adv.; bk.rev.; illus.; index; circ. 16,000. **Indexed:** Music Ind., RILM.

PATENTS, TRADEMARKS AND COPYRIGHTS

340 AU ISSN 0029-8921
OESTERREICHISCHE BLAETTER FUER GEWERBLICHEN RECHTSSCHUTZ UND URHEBERRECHT. 1952. bi-m. (4/yr. with Rundfunkrecht). S.1870. (Oesterreichische Vereinigung fuer Gewerblichen Rechtsschutz und Urheberrecht) Manzsche Verlags- und Universitaetsbuchhandlung, Kohlmarkt 16, A-1014 Vienna, Austria. TEL 0222-531610. FAX 0222-5316181. Ed. Gerhard Friedl. adv.; bk.rev.; index; circ. 900. (also avail. in microfilm; microfiche)

602.7 AU ISSN 0029-9782
OESTERREICHISCHER MARKENANZEIGER. 1948. m. S.850. Oesterreichisches Patentamt, Kohlmarkt 8-10, A-1014 Vienna, Austria. FAX 53-424-520. TELEX 136847. tr.mk.; index; circ. 250.

608.7 AU
OESTERREICHISCHER PATENTINHABER- UND ERFINDERVERBAND; Ideen, Erfindungen, Neuheiten. 1909. q. S.80. Oesterreichischer Patentinhaber- und Erfinderverband, Arsenal, Objekt 219, A-1030 Vienna 1, Austria. TEL 0222-789371. FAX 0222-789371.

608.7 AU ISSN 0029-9944
CODEN: ORPBAD
OESTERREICHISCHES PATENTBLATT. 1899. m. (in 2 parts). S.2000. Oesterreichisches Patentamt, Kohlmarkt 8-10, A-1014 Vienna, Austria. FAX 53-424-520. TELEX 136847. bibl.; charts; illus.; pat.; index; circ. 450.
Description: Decisions and statistics concerning patents, trademarks and industrial designs.

608.7 US ISSN 0098-1133
T223 CODEN: OGUPE7
OFFICIAL GAZETTE OF THE UNITED STATES PATENT AND TRADEMARK OFFICE. PATENTS. 1872. w. $375 priority; $270 non-priority. U.S. Patent and Trademark Office, U.S. Dept. of Commerce, Washington, DC 20231. TEL 703-557-3794. (Orders to: Supt. of Documents, Washington, DC 20402) annual indexes sold separately. (also avail. in microform from RPI) Indexed: Abstr.Bull.Inst.Pap.Chem., Chem.Abstr., Petrol.Abstr., RAPRA, World Text.Abstr.
Supersedes in part: U.S. Patent Office. Official Gazette (ISSN 0041-8021)

602.7 US ISSN 0360-5132
T223.V13
OFFICIAL GAZETTE OF THE UNITED STATES PATENT AND TRADEMARK OFFICE. TRADEMARKS SUPPLEMENTS. w. $238. U.S. Patent and Trademark Office, U.S. Dept. of Commerce, Washington, DC 20231. TEL 703-557-3341. (Orders to: Supt. of Documents, Washington, DC 20402) Indexed: Petrol.Abstr.
Supersedes in part: U.S. Patent Office. Official Gazette (ISSN 0041-8021)

608.7 UK ISSN 0030-0330
T257 CODEN: OFJBAZ
OFFICIAL JOURNAL (PATENTS). 1986. w. £234. Patent Office, St. Mary Cray, Orpington, Kent BR5 3RD, England. adv.; index; circ. 1,400. Indexed: Br.Ceram.Abstr., Chem.Abstr., Petrol.Abstr., RAPRA, World Text.Abstr.

608.7 602.7 IE ISSN 0030-0349
OFFICIAL JOURNAL OF INDUSTRIAL AND COMMERCIAL PROPERTY. 1928. fortn. £95. Government Publications Sales Office, Sun Alliance House, Molesworth St., Dublin 2, Ireland. charts; pat.; tr.mk.; index.

608.7 RU ISSN 0208-287X
T285.A2 CODEN: OTIZDX
OTKRYTIYA, IZOBRETENIYA. 1924. 4/m. р907. Vsesoyuznyi Nauchno-Issledovatel'skii Institut Patentnoi Informatsii (VNIIPI), Raushskaya Nab. 4, 113834 Moscow, Russia. TEL 233 58 58. TELEX 411093 POISK SU. (Subscr. to: NPO "Poisk", Raushskaya nab., 4, Moscow, Russia) Ed. V.A. Lukanin. adv.; illus.; pat.; tr.mk.; index; circ. 11,125. (also avail. in microfiche; microfilm) Indexed: Abstr.Bull.Inst.Pap.Chem., Chem.Abstr.
—BLDSC shelfmark: 0128.434500.
Supersedes in part (in 1983): Otkrytiya, Izobreteniya, Promyshlennye Obraztsy, Tovarnye Znaki (ISSN 0007-4020); Formerly: Bulleten' Izobretenii, Promyshlennykh Obraztsov i Tovarnykh Znakov.
Description: Publishes formulas and drawings of scientific inventions and discoveries listed in the U.S.S.R. Federal Register. Contains information about any changes in their legal status and description.

340 US ISSN 0736-8232
KF2972
P T C NEWSLETTER. 1982. q. membership only. American Bar Association, Patent, Trademark and Copyright Law Section, 750 N. Lake Shore Dr., Chicago, IL 60611. TEL 312-988-5555. FAX 312-988-5500. Ed. Thomas I. O'Brien.
Description: Recent developments in intellectual property law, Section activities, calendar of events.

602.7 608.7 CN ISSN 0849-3154
P T I C BULLETIN. 1967. 10/yr. membership. Patent and Trademark Institute of Canada, Box 1298, Sta. B, Ottawa, Ont. K1P 5R3, Canada. TEL 613-234-0516. Ed. W.J. Galloway. circ. controlled. (looseleaf format)
Formerly: P T I C Newsletter (ISSN 0380-6375)

608.7 CN ISSN 0079-015X
PATENT AND TRADEMARK INSTITUTE OF CANADA. ANNUAL PROCEEDINGS. 1928. a. membership. Patent and Trademark Institute of Canada, Box 1298, Sta. B, Ottawa, Ont. K1P 5R3, Canada. TEL 613-234-0516. circ. controlled.

340 US
PATENT AND TRADEMARK OFFICE NOTICES. w. $57. U.S. Patent and Trademark Office, Washington, DC 20231. TEL 703-557-3341.

643.3 608.7 US
PATENT DIGEST. 1946? m. $60. Gas Appliance Manufacturers Association, 1901 N. Moore St., Ste. 1100, Arlington, VA 22209. TEL 703-525-9565. FAX 703-525-8159.
Description: Reports on relevant patents. Excerpted from Offical Gazette of the U.S. Patent Office.

608.7 602.7 SA ISSN 0031-286X
T319.S7 CODEN: PASDEW
PATENT JOURNAL INCLUDING TRADEMARKS AND MODELS. (Text in Afrikaans, English) 1948. m. R.12.50. Government Printer, Bosman St., Private Bag X85, Pretoria 0001, South Africa. TELEX 3230009. charts; illus.; pat.; tr.mk. Indexed: RAPRA.

340 US ISSN 0192-8198
KF3114
PATENT LAW HANDBOOK. a. $75. Clark - Boardman - Callaghan Company, Ltd., 375 Hudson St., New York, NY 10014. TEL 212-929-7500. FAX 212-924-0460.
—BLDSC shelfmark: 6410.543000.

608.7 CN ISSN 0008-4670
CODEN: PORCCI
PATENT OFFICE RECORD (CANADA)/GAZETTE DU BUREAU DES BREVETS. (Text and title in English and French) 1873. w. Can.$63($75.60) Department of Consumer and Corporate Affairs, Patent Office, 50 Victoria St., Hull, Que. K1A 0C9, Canada. TEL 819-997-2525. (Subscr. to: Supply and Services Canada, Order Adjustment Section, Rm. 2202, 45 Sacre Coeur Blvd., Hull, Que. K1A 0S9) adv.; bk.rev.; pat.; index; circ. 1,000. Indexed: Abstr.Bull.Inst.Pap.Chem., Chem.Abstr. Petrol.Abstr.
●Also available online.
Also available on CD-ROM.
Formerly: Canadian Patent Office Record.

608.7 II
PATENT OFFICE TECHNICAL SOCIETY. JOURNAL. (Text in English) vol.10, 1976. irreg. Rs.15. Patent Office Technical Society, 214, Acharya Jagadish Bose Rd., Calcutta 700 017, India. Ed. N.R. Seth. adv.; bk.rev.; pat.; stat.; circ. 250. (also avail. in microfilm from WSH) Indexed: C.L.I., Leg.Per., SSCI.

608.7 UK ISSN 0950-2513
CODEN: PAWOEH
PATENT WORLD. 1987. 10/yr. $245. Intellectual Property Publishing Ltd., 2 Parkside, Ravenscourt Park, London W6, England. TEL 01-386-5366. FAX 081-746-3400. Ed. Andrew Armstrong. adv.; bk.rev.; circ. 1,750.
—BLDSC shelfmark: 6412.250000.

608.7 GW ISSN 0031-2894
PATENTBLATT. 1877. w. DM.896. (Deutsches Patentamt) Carl Heymanns Verlag KG, Luxemburgerstr. 449, 5000 Cologne 41, Germany. TEL 0221-46010-0. FAX 0221-4601069. circ. 1,850. Indexed: Abstr.Bull.Inst.Pap.Chem., Chem.Abstr.

602.7 608.7 DK ISSN 0904-275X
PATENTDIREKTORATET ORIENTERER. q. free. Patentdirektoratet, Helgeshoej Alle 81, DK-2630 Taastrup, Denmark. TEL 43 71 71 71. FAX 43-71-71-70. TELEX 16046 DPO DK.

608.7 YU ISSN 0031-2908
PATENTNI GLASNIK; Sluzbeni list Saveznog Zavoda za Patente. 1921. bi-m. 350 din. Savezni Zavod za Patente, Uzun Mirkova 1, 11000 Belgrade, Yugoslavia. TEL 011-636-466. FAX 011-639-761. TELEX 12761 SZPAT YU. adv.; illus.; pat.; index; circ. 700.

608.7 JA ISSN 0388-7081
PATENTS AND LICENSING. (Text in English) 1971. bi-m. $90. Japan Engineering News, Inc., Room 202, Sun Mansion, 1-11, Azabudai 1-Chome, Minato-ku, Tokyo 106, Japan. TEL 03-589-4749. FAX 03-291-3764. Ed. Osahito Makiyama. adv.; circ. 8,000. Indexed: JTA.
Formerly: Patents and Engineering.
Description: Offers the latest information and data concerning legal protection.

608.7 340 US
PATENTS AND THE FEDERAL CIRCUIT. (Supplement avail.) 1982. irreg., latest 1988. $87. B N A Books (Subsidiary of: The Bureau of National Affairs), 1231 25th St., N.W., Washington, DC 20037. TEL 908-225-1900. FAX 908-417-0482. (Subscr. to: BNA Books Distribution Center, 300 Raritan Center Parkway, Box 7816, Edison, NJ 08818-7816. TEL 800-372-1033) Ed. Robert L. Harmon.

608.7 340 US
PATENTS AND THE FEDERAL CIRCUIT. SUPPLEMENT. 1989. a. $40. B N A Books (Subsidiary of: The Bureau of National Affairs, Inc.), 1231 25th St., N.W., Washington, DC 20037. TEL 908-225-1900. FAX 908-417-0482. (Subscr. to: BNA Books Distribution Center, 300 Raritan Center Parkway, Box 7816, Edison, NJ 08818-7816. TEL 800-372-1033) Ed. Robert L. Harmon.

608.7 PL ISSN 0137-8015
POLAND. URZAD PATENTOWY. BIULETYN/POLAND. PATENT OFFICE. BULLETIN. 1973. bi-w. 390000 Zl.($520) Urzad Patentowy, Al. Niepodleglosci 188, Warsaw, Poland. TEL 48 22 25-05-84. FAX 48-22-250581. (Dist. by: Ars Polona-Ruch, Krakowskie Przedmiescie 7, Warsaw, Poland) illus.; circ. 2,400.

608.7 PL ISSN 0043-5201
POLAND. URZAD PATENTOWY. WIADOMOSCI/POLAND. PATENT OFFICE. NEWS. (Text in Polish; summaries in English and Russian) 1924. m. 156000 Zl.($153) Urzad Patentowy, Al. Niepodleglosci 188, Warsaw, Poland. TEL 48 22 25-05-84. (Dist. by: Ars Polona-Ruch, Krakowskie Przedmiescie 7, Warsaw, Poland) adv.

PATENTS, TRADEMARKS AND COPYRIGHTS

608.7   RU   ISSN 0208-2888
PROMYSHLENNYE OBRAZTSY. TOVARNYE ZNAKI. 1924. 4/yr. Vsesoyuznyi Nauchno-Issledovatel'skii Institut Patentnoi Informatsii (VNIIPI), Raushskaya nab. 4, 113834 Moscow, Russia. TEL 233 58 58. TELEX 411093 POISK SU. (Subscr. to: NPO "Poisk", Raushskaya nab. 4, 113834, Moscow, Russia) Ed. V.A. Lukanin. adv.; circ. 6,375. (also avail. in microfiche; microfilm)
    Supersedes in part (as of 1983): Otkrytiya, Izobreteniya, Promyshlennye Obraztsy, Tovarnye Znaki (ISSN 0007-4020)
    Description: Publishes information about industrial designs, trademarks; contains their graphic representation; also includes information about any relevant changes.

608.7   UN   ISSN 0033-1430
PROPRIETE INDUSTRIELLE. English edition: Industrial Property (ISSN 0019-8625) 1885. m. 180 Fr. World Intellectual Property Organization (WIPO) - Organisation Mondiale de la Propriete Intellectuelle, Publications and Public Information Section, 34 Chemin des Colombettes, 1211 Geneva 20, Switzerland. TEL 022-730-9111. FAX 022-733-5428. TELEX 412912 OMPI CH. adv.; pat.; stat.; charts; index; circ. 1,100. (also avail. in microfiche; back issues avail.)
    —BLDSC shelfmark: 6927.380000.
    Description: Covers developments in industrial property in all fields of technology at national and international levels. Includes special studies and collection of all major national, regional, multilateral industrial property laws and treaties.

381   FR   ISSN 0338-6473
PROPRIETE INDUSTRIELLE BULLETIN DOCUMENTAIRE. 24/yr. 610 F. (Institut National de la Propriete Industrielle) Documentation Francaise, 124 rue Henri Barbusse, 93308 Aubervilliers Cedex, France. TEL 1-40-15-70-00. abstr.; pat.; circ. 1,200. (also avail. in microfiche; back issues avail.)
    Description: Contains information and reports of French and foreign case law and literature in the field of industrial property.

608.7   BE   ISSN 0034-1851
T267   CODEN: REBIA8
RECUEIL DES BREVETS D'INVENTION. (Text in Dutch or French) 1854. m. 12000 Fr. Ministry of Economic Affairs, Office de la Propriete Industrielle - Dienst voor Industriele Eigendom, 24-26 rue de Mot, B-1040 Brussels, Belgium. FAX 02-2310256. Ed.Bd. illus.; pat.; index; circ. 1,000. **Indexed:** RAPRA.
    ●Also available online. Vendor(s): BELINDIS.
    —BLDSC shelfmark: 7328.000000.

608.7   UK
REGISTER OF PATENT AGENTS. 1889. a. £2. Chartered Institute of Patent Agents, Staple Inn Bldgs., High Holborn, London WC1V 7PZ, England. adv.; circ. 2,500.

608.7   DK   ISSN 0107-590X
REGISTER OVER DANSKE PATENTER UDSTEDT. 1970. a. DKK 400. Patentdirektoratet, Helgeshoej Alle 81, DK-2630 Tasstrup, Denmark. FAX 45-43717170.

608.7   UK   ISSN 0080-1364
REPORTS OF PATENT, DESIGN, TRADE MARK AND OTHER CASES. 1884. irreg. £110.50. Patent Office, St. Mary Cray, Orpington, Kent, BR5 3RD, England. Ed. Michael Fysh. circ. 1,800.

608.7 338   UK   ISSN 0374-4353
                             CODEN: RSDSBB
RESEARCH DISCLOSURE. 1960. m. £70($120) Kenneth Mason Publications Ltd., 12 North St., Emsworth, Hants. PO10 7DQ, England. TEL 0243-377977. FAX 0243-379136. **Indexed:** Abstr.Bull.Inst.Pap.Chem., Dairy Sci.Abstr., Food Sci.& Tech.Abstr., Int.Packag.Abstr., Paper & Bd.Abstr., Text.Tech.Dig., World Text.Abstr.
    —BLDSC shelfmark: 7738.873000.

340 608.7   MX   ISSN 0035-0044
REVISTA MEXICANA DE LA PROPIEDAD INDUSTRIAL Y ARTISTICA. 1963. s-a. Mex.$250($14) David Rangel Medina, Ed. & Pub., Cerrada de Xitle No. 19, Pedregal San Angel, Mexico 20, D.F., Mexico. bk.rev.; illus.; pat.; tr.mk.; index; circ. 1,000.

340   RM   ISSN 1220-3009
▼**REVISTA ROMANA DE PROPRIETATE INDUSTRIALA/ROMANIAN REVIEW FOR INDUSTRIAL PROPERTY.** (Text in Rumanian; summaries in English, French, German, Russian) 1991. q. $100 or exchange basis. Oficiul de Stat pentru Inventii si Marci (OSIM) - State Office for Inventions and Trademarks, 5, Ion Ghica St., Sect. 3, Bucharest, Rumania. FAX 15-90-66. TELEX 11370 ROPAT R. adv. contact: Nicolae Mihailescu.

608   FR   ISSN 0035-337X
REVUE INTERNATIONALE DE LA PROPRIETE INDUSTRIELLE ET ARTISTIQUE. 1883. q. 360 F. (effective 1991). Union des Fabricants pour la Protection de la Propriete Industrielle et Artistique, 16 rue de la Faisanderie, 75116 Paris, France. Ed. A. Thrierr. bk.rev.; illus.; tr.mk.; index; circ. 1,800.

340 070 850   FR   ISSN 0035-3515
REVUE INTERNATIONALE DU DROIT D'AUTEUR. (Text in English, French and Spanish) 1953. q. 650 F. 225 av. Charles de Gaulle, 92200 Neuilly, France. FAX 47-45-12-94. bk.rev.; abstr.; index.

340   SZ   ISSN 1011-0240
K1411.2
RIGHTS; copyright and related rights in the service of creativity. q. $45. International Publishers Association, Ave. de Miremont 3, CH-1206 Geneva, Switzerland. TEL 22-3464018. FAX 22-3475717. (Co-publisher: International Group of Scientific, Technical and Medical Publishers (STM)) Ed. Susan Wagner.
    —BLDSC shelfmark: 7970.684950.
    Description: Contains opinions, news and analysis of current developments in the world of publishing and copyright.

608.7   SZ   ISSN 0036-7974
SCHWEIZERISCHES PATENT-, MUSTER- UND MARKENBLATT/FEUILLE SUISSE DES BREVETS, DESSINS ET MARQUES/FOGLIO SVIZZERO DEI BREVETTI, DISEGNI E MARCHI. (Text in French, German and partly in Italian) 1962. s-m. 405 Fr. for all sections (Edition C); 208 Fr. for trademark section (Edition B); 228 Fr. for patent and design section (Edition A). Bundesamt fuer Geistiges Eigentum - Intellectual Property Office, Einsteinstr. 2, CH-3003 Bern, Switzerland. TEL 031-614990. FAX 031-614895. TELEX 912805-BAGE-CH. (Subscr. to: Binkert AG, Druck und Verlag, CH-4335 Laufenberg, Switzerland.) Ed. Kurt Wuethrich. adv.; charts; illus.; pat.; index; circ. 255.

602.7   IT
SIGLARIO ITALIANO/ITALIAN TRADE-MARKS. 1983. a. L.52000. Guida Monaci S.p.A., Via Vitorchiano 107, 00189 Rome, Italy. TEL 06-3288805. FAX 063275693. TELEX 623234 MONACI.
    Description: Trade marks of the most important Italian firms.

608.7   SW   ISSN 0348-324X
SVENSK VARUMAERKESTIDNING - SWEDISH TRADEMARK JOURNAL. PART A (PUBLICATIONS FOR OPPOSITION). 1885. w. SEK 800. Patent- och Registreringsverket - Royal Patent and Registration Office, Box 5055, S-102 42 Stockholm, Sweden. illus.; stat.; tr.mk.; circ. 640.
    Formerly: Registreringstidning foer Varumaerken. Part A (Publications for Opposition) (ISSN 0347-3449)

608.7   SW   ISSN 0348-3258
SVENSK VARUMAERKESTIDNING - SWEDISH TRADEMARK JOURNAL. PART B (PUBLICATIONS OF REGISTRATIONS). 1885. w. SEK 800. Patent- och Registreringsverket - Royal Patent and Registration Office, Box 5055, S-102 42 Stockholm, Sweden. illus.; circ. 640.
    Formerly: Registreringstidning foer Varumaerken. Part B (Publications of Registrations) (ISSN 0347-3465)

608.87   SW   ISSN 0348-3266
SVENSK VARUMAERKESTIDNING - SWEDISH TRADEMARK JOURNAL. PART C (RENEWALS, CHANGES OF OWNERSHIP). 1885. w. SEK 600. Patent- och Registreringsverket - Royal Patent and Registration Office, Box 5055, S-102 42 Stockholm, Sweden. illus.; circ. 480.
    Formerly: Registreringstidning foer Varumaerken. Part C (Renewals, Changes of Ownership) (ISSN 0347-3457)

602.7   SW
SVENSKT VARUMAERKESARKIV/SWEDISH TRADEMARK ARCHIVE; computer-indexed microfiche archive including full information about registered trademarks and pending applications. 1976. a. (with updates weekly). SEK 6400. Patent- och Registreringsverket - Royal Patent and Registration Office, Box 5055, S-102 42 Stockholm, Sweden.

602.7   SW
SVENSKT VARUMAERKESLEXIKON/SWEDISH TRADE MARK DICTIONARY; registered trademarks in alphabetical order. 1972. s-a. SEK 2900. Patent- och Registreringsverket - Royal Patent and Registration Office, Box 5055, S-102 42 Stockholm, Sweden. TEL 46-8-782-25-00. FAX 46-8-783-01-63. TELEX PATOREG S 17978. (also avail. in microfiche)

608   SW
SWEDEN. PATENT- OCH REGISTERERINGSVERKET. AARSBERAETTELSE. 1965. a. free. Patent- och Registreringsverket, Box 5055, S-102 42 Stockholm, Sweden. pat.; stat.; circ. 3,000.

608.7 602.7   HU   ISSN 0039-8071
T265.5
SZABADALMI KOZLONY ES VEDJEGYERTESITO/PATENT AND TRADE MARK REVIEW. (Text in Hungarian; summaries in English, French, German and Russian) 1896. m. $63. (Orszagos Szabadalmi Hivatal) Lapkiado Vallalat, Lenin korut 9-11, 1073 Budapest 7, Hungary. TEL 222-408. (Subscr. to: Kultura, Box 149, H-1389 Budapest, Hungary) Ed. Laszlo Mezey. pat. (avail. on records)

T M A TRADEMARK REPORT. (Tobacco Merchants Association of the United States, Inc.) see TOBACCO

608.7   SP   ISSN 0040-179X
TECNICA E INVENCION. 1954. m. $10. Princesa 14, Madrid-8, Spain. Ed. Garcia Cabrerizo. adv.; bibl.; illus.; pat.; circ. 3,000 (controlled).

608.7 602.7   CN   ISSN 0041-0438
T226.V1
TRADE MARKS JOURNAL/JOURNAL DES MARQUES DE COMMERCE; consumer and corporate affairs. (Catalogue no. RG42-2) (Text in English and French) 1954. w. Can.$72($86.40) Supply and Services Canada, Ottawa, Ont. K1A 0S9, Canada. TEL 819-997-2560. illus.; tr.mk.; circ. 799.

608.7 602.7   UK   ISSN 0041-0446
TRADE MARKS JOURNAL. 1876. w. £275. Patent Office, St. Mary Cray, Orpington, Kent BR5 3RD, England. adv.; illus.; circ. 900. **Indexed:** RAPRA.

608.7 340   IS   ISSN 0334-2425
TRADE MARKS JOURNAL. (Text in English and Hebrew) 1968. m. Distribution Service of Government Publications, 29-B St., Hakirya, Tel Aviv, Israel.

608.7   US   ISSN 0082-5786
T223.V4
TRADEMARK REGISTER OF THE UNITED STATES. 1958. a. $312. Trademark Register, National Press Bldg., 1297, Washington, DC 20045. TEL 202-662-1233. Ed. Cyril W. Sernak. cum.index: 1881-1991.
    ●Also available on CD-ROM.
    Description: Lists all trademarks registered with the U.S. patent and trademark office; also includes owners' data and product information

602.7   US   ISSN 0041-056X
K24
TRADEMARK REPORTER. 1911. bi-m. membership. United States Trademark Association, 6 E. 45th St., New York, NY 10017. TEL 212-986-5880. FAX 212-687-8267. TELEX 175662 USTA UT. Ed. Allan S. Pilson. bk.rev.; charts; index, cum.index: 1937-1950, 1951-1960; every 5 yrs. thereafter; circ. 2,700. (also avail. in microfilm from UMI) **Indexed:** C.L.I., L.R.I., Leg.Per.

608.7   GW   ISSN 0041-1310
TRANSPATENT. 1949. 18/yr. DM.576. Transpatent GmbH, Postfach 105027, 4000 Duesseldorf 1, Germany. FAX 0211-319784. TELEX 8587428-TTKR. Ed. H.-Jochen Krieger. adv.; bk.rev.; pat.

340   US   ISSN 0090-2845
U.S. COPYRIGHT OFFICE. ANNUAL REPORT OF THE REGISTER OF COPYRIGHTS. 1910. a. price varies. U.S. Library of Congress, Copyright Office, Library of Congress, Washington, DC 20559. TEL 202-783-3238. FAX 202-512-2250. (Dist. by: Supt. of Documents, P.O. Box 371954, Pittsburgh, PA 15250) Key Title: Annual Report of the Register of Copyrights.

608.7   US   ISSN 0083-3002
U.S. PATENT AND TRADEMARK OFFICE. ANNUAL REPORT OF THE COMMISSIONER OF PATENTS. 1837. a. price varies. U.S. Patent and Trademark Office, Washington, DC 20231. TEL 703-557-3341. (Orders to: Supt. of Documents, Washington, DC 20402)

608.7   US   ISSN 0083-3010
U.S. PATENT AND TRADEMARK OFFICE. CLASSIFICATION BULLETINS. irreg. price varies. U.S. Patent and Trademark Office, Washington, DC 20231. TEL 703-557-3341. (Orders to: Supt. of Documents, Washington, DC 20402)

608.7   US   ISSN 0041-803X
UNITED STATES PATENTS QUARTERLY. 1929. w. $1080. The Bureau of National Affairs, Inc., 1231 25th St., N.W., Washington, DC 20037. TEL 202-452-4200. FAX 202-822-8092. TELEX 285656 BNAI WSH. (Subscr. to: 9435 Key West Ave., Rockville, MD 20850. TEL 800-372-1033) Ed. Cynthia J. Bolbach. abstr.; pat.; tr.mk.; index, cum.index every 5 yrs. (back issues avail.)
●Also available online. Vendor(s): DIALOG (Patlaw, File 243), Pergamon Infoline.
Description: Reports on decisions dealing with patents, trademarks, copyrights, unfair competition, trade secrets, and computer chip protection.

608.7   GW
VIERTELJAEHRLICHES NAMENSVERZEICHNIS ZUM PATENTBLATT. 1950. q. DM.168. Carl Heymanns Verlag KG, Luxemburgerstr. 449, 5000 Cologne 41, Germany. TEL 0221-46010-0. FAX 0221-4601069. circ. 950.

608.7 658.57   CS
VYNALEZY A ZLEPSOVACI NAVRHY/INVENTIONS AND IMPROVEMENT SUGGESTIONS. (Text in English, French, German, Russian) 1952. m. 72 Kcs.($33) Urad pro Vynalezy a Objevy, Vaclavske nam. 19, 113 47 Prague 1, Czechoslovakia. (Subscr. to: Postovni Novinova Sluzba, Jindrisska 14, 125 05 Prague 1) Eds. Parina Brzobohata, Petr Linka. bk.rev.; bibl.; charts; illus.; stat.; index; circ. 5,000. Indexed: Chem.Abstr.
Formerly: Vynalezy (ISSN 0042-935X)

608   GW   ISSN 0323-5394
WARENZEICHEN- UND MUSTERBLATT; eingetagene Warenkennzichen, industrielle Muster und Veraenderungen. 1955. 8/yr. DM.38.40. (Deutsches Patentamt) Verlag Die Wirtschaft Berlin GmbH, Am Friedrichshain 22, 1055 Berlin, Germany. TEL 43870. FAX 4361249. Ed. Klaus Brunne. illus.
Formerly: Germany, Democratic Republic. Amt fuer Erfindungs - und Patentwessen. Warenzeichenblatt.
Description: Contains patent information on new trademarks and product inventions.

608.7   GW   ISSN 0043-0331
WARENZEICHENBLATT. TEIL 1: ANGEMELDETE ZEICHEN. 1950. s-m. DM.40. (Deutsches Patentamt) Wila Verlag Wilhelm Lampl GmbH, Landsberger Str. 191A, 8000 Munich 21, Germany. adv.; illus.; tr.mk.; index; circ. 2,000.

608.7   GW   ISSN 0043-034X
WARENZEICHENBLATT. TEIL 2: EINGETRAGENE ZEICHEN. 1950. s-m. DM.48. (Deutsches Patentamt) Wila Verlag Wilhelm Lampl GmbH, Landsberger Str. 191A, 8000 Munich 21, Germany. TEL 089-5795-0. FAX 089-5706693. adv.; illus.; tr.mk.; index; circ. 1,000.

608.7   US
▼**WHO'S INVENTING WHAT?;** tracking US patenting activities and trends. 1990. q. (includes a. cum.). $195. Gale Research Inc., 835 Penobscot Bldg., Detroit, MI 48226. TEL 800-877-4253. FAX 313-961-6083. TELEX 810-221-7086. Ed. Donna Wood.
Description: Reporting service on the 80,000-100,000 patents granted by the US Patent and Trademark Office each year. Entries are alphabetically listed by name of company or individual to whom the patents were assigned.

602.7 608.7   UK   ISSN 0952-7613
K1401.A13
WORLD INTELLECTUAL PROPERTY REPORT. 1987. m. £288($518) B N A International, Inc. (Subsidiary of: The Bureau of National Affairs, Inc.), 17 Dartmouth St., London SW1H 9BL, England. TEL 222-8831. FAX 222-0294. (US addr.: 1231 25th St., N.W., Washington, DC 20037. TEL 202-542-4200) Ed. Joel Kolko. pat.; index. (back issues avail.)
Description: Provides information on copyright, trademark, and unfair competition issues worldwide.

608.7   US   ISSN 0172-2190
T210   CODEN: WPAID2
WORLD PATENT INFORMATION; international journal for patent documentation, classification & statistics. 1979. 4/yr. £130 (effective 1992). (Commission of the European Communities) Pergamon Press, Inc., Journals Division, 660 White Plains Rd., Tarrytown, NY 10591-5153. TEL 914-524-9200. FAX 914-333-2444. (And: Headington Hill Hall, Oxford OX3 0BW, England. TEL 0865-794141) (Co-sponsor: World Intellectual Property Organization) Ed. V.S. Dodd. (also avail. in microform from UMI,MIM; reprint service avail. from ISI,UMI) Indexed: BPIA, Sci.Abstr., World Surf.Coat.
—BLDSC shelfmark: 9356.973000.
Refereed Serial

WORLD TECHNOLOGY; patent licensing gazette. see TECHNOLOGY: COMPREHENSIVE WORKS

608.7 778.1   US   ISSN 0361-4190
T212
XEROX DISCLOSURE JOURNAL. 1976. bi-m. Xerox Corporation (Rochester), Xerox Sq. 021, Rochester, NY 14644. TEL 716-423-3255. Ed. Carole Ann Banke. illus.; index; circ. 500 (controlled). Indexed: Graph.Arts Lit.Abstr.

608.7   US
ZHONGGUO ZHUANLI BAO/PATENT REVIEW OF CHINA. (Text in Chinese) d. $62.70. China Books & Periodicals, Inc., 2929 24th St., San Francisco, CA 94110. TEL 415-282-2994. FAX 415-282-0994. (newspaper)

PATENTS, TRADEMARKS AND COPYRIGHTS — Abstracting, Bibliographies, Statistics

608.7   UK
ABSTRACTS AND ABRIDGEMENTS OF PATENT SPECIFICATIONS. 1883. w. price varies. Patent Office, Sales Branch, Orpington, Kent BR5 3RD, England. TEL 0689-892146. FAX 0689-78375. circ. 400.

608.7   FR   ISSN 0223-3398
B.O.P.I. DESSINS & MODELES. (Bulletin Officiel de la Propriete Industrielle) 1910. q. 60 F. Institut National de la Propriete Industrielle, 26 bis rue de Leningrad, 75800 Paris Cedex 08, France. TEL 42-94-52-52. FAX 42-94-21-93. TELEX 290-368INPA PARIS. index; circ. 400. (back issues avail.)
Description: Contains the bibliographical data on the published industrial designs, arranged according to the international classification of industrial designs.

C A SELECTS. CERAMIC MATERIALS (PATENTS). see CERAMICS, GLASS AND POTTERY — Abstracting, Bibliographies, Statistics

540   US   ISSN 0734-8819
CODEN: CAPPEC
C A SELECTS. NOVEL POLYMERS FROM PATENTS. s-w. $195. Chemical Abstracts Service (Subsidiary of: American Chemical Society), 2540 Olentangy River Rd., Box 3012, Columbus, OH 43210. TEL 614-447-3600. FAX 614-447-3713. TELEX 6842086.
Description: Covers patents mentioning newly reported polymeric materials.

C A SELECTS. PHARMACEUTICAL CHEMISTRY (PATENTS). see PHARMACY AND PHARMACOLOGY — Abstracting, Bibliographies, Statistics

340   US   ISSN 1050-5156
Z642
COPYRIGHT DIRECTORY: ATTORNEYS, PROFESSORS, GOVERNMENT AGENCIES, CONGRESSIONAL COMMITTEES, SEARCHERS, CLEARINGHOUSES, HOTLINES & ASSOCIATIONS, (YEAR). biennial. $79.95. Copyright Information Services, 1025 Vermont Ave., N.W., Ste. 820, Washington, DC 20005. TEL 206-378-5218. Ed.Bd.

016 608.7   KO
FOREIGN PATENTS INFORMATION BULLETIN. (Text in Korean) 1963. s-m. Korea Institute for Economics and Technology, P.O.B. 250, Seoul, S. Korea. pat.; circ. 450. (reprint service avail. from UMI)
Former titles: Current List on Foreign Patents; Current Bibliography on Foreign Patents.

608.7   US   ISSN 0362-0719
T223
INDEX OF PATENTS ISSUED FROM THE UNITED STATES PATENT AND TRADEMARK OFFICE. 1920. a. price varies. U.S. Patent and Trademark Office, Washington, DC 20231. TEL 703-557-3341. (Orders to: Supt. of Documents, Washington, DC 20402)
Formerly: U.S. Patent Office. Index of Patents Issued from the United States Patent Office (ISSN 0083-3037).

608.7   US   ISSN 0099-0809
T223.V4
INDEX OF TRADEMARKS ISSUED FROM THE U.S. PATENT AND TRADEMARK OFFICE. a. price varies. U.S. Patent and Trademark Office, Washington, DC 20231. TEL 703-557-3341. (Orders to: Supt. of Documents, Washington, DC 20402)
Formerly: Index of Trademarks Issued from the United States Patent Office (ISSN 0083-3045).

608.7   US
INDEX TO THE U.S. PATENT CLASSIFICATION. a. U.S. Patent and Trademark Office, Washington, DC 20231.

608.7   UN   ISSN 1013-8374
T201
INDUSTRIAL PROPERTY, STATISTICS B. PART 1 - PATENTS/PROPRIETE INDUSTRIELLE, STATISTIQUES B. PARTIE 1 - BREVETS. (Text in English and French) a. 50 Fr. World Intellectual Property Organization (WIPO) - Organisation Mondiale de la Propriete Intellectuelle, Publications and Public Information Section, 34 Chemin des Colombettes, 1211 Geneva 20, Switzerland. TEL 022-730-9111. FAX 022-733-5428. TELEX 412912 OMPI CH. charts; circ. 250. (back issues avail.) Indexed: IIS.
Supersedes in part (in 1985): Industrial Property, Statistics B (ISSN 0377-0044)
Description: Covers year in question, with complete statistics on patent applications and patents granted to residents and non-residents.

PATENTS, TRADEMARKS AND COPYRIGHTS — ABSTRACTING, BIBLIOGRAPHIES, STATISTICS

602.7 608.7   UN   ISSN 1013-8382
INDUSTRIAL PROPERTY, STATISTICS B. PART 2 - TRADEMARKS AND SERVICE MARKS, UTILITY MODELS, INDUSTRIAL DESIGNS, VARIETIES OF PLANTS, MICROORGANISMS/PROPRIETE INDUSTRIELLE, STATISTIQUES B. PARTIE 2 - MARQUES DE PRODUITS ET DES SERVICES, MODELES D'UTILIT. (Text in English and French) a. 50 Fr. World Intellectual Property Organization (WIPO) - Organisation Mondiale de la Propriete Intellectuelle, Publications and Public Information Section, 34 Chemin des Colombettes, 1211 Geneva 20, Switzerland. TEL 022-730-9111. FAX 022-733-5428. TELEX 412912 OMPI CH. charts. (back issues avail.)
   Supersedes in part (in 1985): Industrial Property, Statistics B (ISSN 0377-0044).
   Description: Covers year in question with complete statistics on trademark and service mark applications and registrations by residents and non-residents.

608.7 016   US
N A S A PATENT ABSTRACTS BIBLIOGRAPHY: A CONTINUING BIBLIOGRAPHY. SECTION 1. ABSTRACTS. 1969. s-a. $17 per no. U.S. National Aeronautics and Space Administration, Box 8757, Baltimore-Washington International Airport, MD 21240. index.

608.7 016   US
N A S A PATENT ABSTRACTS BIBLIOGRAPHY: A CONTINUING BIBLIOGRAPHY. SECTION 2. INDEXES. 1969. s-a. $50 per no. U.S. National Aeronautics and Space Administration, Center for Aerospace Information, Box 8757, Baltimore-Washington International Airport, MD 21240. TEL 301-621-0153. index.

608.7   UN   ISSN 0250-7757
P C T GAZETTE. (Patent Cooperation Treaty) French edition: Gazette du P C T (ISSN 0250-7749) 1978. fortn. 460 Fr. World Intellectual Property Organization (WIPO) - Organisation Mondiale de la Proprieté Intellectuelle, Publications and Public Information Section, 34 Chemin des Colombettes, 1211 Geneva 20, Switzerland. TEL 022-730-9111. FAX 022-733-5428. TELEX 412912 OMPI CG. adv.; cum.index; circ. 1,000. (also avail. in magnetic tape; back issues avail.) **Indexed:** Potato Abstr.
●Also available online.
   Description: Contains bibliographic data on applicant, inventor, origin and destination of application published, title, abstract and drawing or formula of invention, arranged in order of International Patent Classification indexes by filing and publication numbers, designated countries, applicant's names and IPC classes.

608.7 602.7   AT
PATENT ABSTRACTS SUPPLEMENT TO THE AUSTRALIAN OFFICIAL JOURNAL OF PATENTS. 1981. w. Aus.$950. Patent Office, P.O. Box 200, Woden, A.C.T. 2606, Australia. TEL 06-2832481. FAX 06-2853593. TELEX COMPAT AA 61517. circ. 50. (back issues avail.)
   Formerly (until 1987): Patent Abstracts Supplement to the Australian Official Journal of Patents, Trade Marks and Designs.
   Description: Abstracts of unaccepted complete patent specifications as laid open to public inspection; search materials for the public.

011   US   ISSN 0163-7290
Z642
U.S. COPYRIGHT OFFICE. CATALOG OF COPYRIGHT ENTRIES. FOURTH SERIES. PART 1: NONDRAMATIC LITERARY WORKS; excluding serials and periodicals. 1978. q. $14. U.S. Library of Congress, Copyright Office, Washington, DC 20559. TEL 202-783-3238. FAX 202-512-2250. (Dist. by: Supt. of Documents, P.O. Box 371954, Pittsburgh, PA 15250) index. (microfiche)
   Supersedes in part: U.S. Copyright Office. Catalog of Copyright Entries. Third Series. Part 1. Books and Pamphlets (ISSN 0041-7815).

050 011   US   ISSN 0163-7304
Z642
U.S. COPYRIGHT OFFICE. CATALOG OF COPYRIGHT ENTRIES. FOURTH SERIES. PART 2: SERIALS AND PERIODICALS. 1978. s-a. $5. U.S. Library of Congress, Copyright Office, Washington, DC 20559. TEL 202-783-3238. FAX 202-512-225-. (Dist. by: Supt. of Documents, P.O. Box 371954, Pittsburgh, PA 15250) (microfiche)
   Formerly: U.S. Copyright Office. Catalog of Copyright Entries. Third Series. Part 2. Periodicals (ISSN 0041-784X); Supersedes in part: U.S. Copyright Office. Catalog of Copyright Entries. Third Series. Part 1. Books and Pamphlets, Including Serials and Contributions to Periodicals (ISSN 0041-7815).

800 016   US   ISSN 0163-7312
Z653
U.S. COPYRIGHT OFFICE. CATALOG OF COPYRIGHT ENTRIES. FOURTH SERIES. PART 3: PERFORMING ARTS. 1978. q. $14. U.S. Library of Congress, Copyright Office, Washington, DC 20559. TEL 202-783-3238. FAX 202-512-2250. (Dist. by: Supt. of Documents, P.O. Box 371954, Pittsburgh, PA 15250) index. (microfiche)
   Formerly: U.S. Copyright Office. Catalog of Copyright Entries. Third Series. Parts 3-4. Drama and Works Prepared for Oral Delivery (ISSN 0041-7858); U.S. Copyright Office Catalog of Copyright Entries. Third Series. Part 5. Music (ISSN 0041-7866)

U.S. COPYRIGHT OFFICE. CATALOG OF COPYRIGHT ENTRIES. FOURTH SERIES. PART 4: MOTION PICTURES AND FILMSTRIPS. see MOTION PICTURES — Abstracting, Bibliographies, Statistics

U.S. COPYRIGHT OFFICE. CATALOG OF COPYRIGHT ENTRIES. FOURTH SERIES. PART 5: VISUAL ARTS EXCLUDING MAPS. see ART — Abstracting, Bibliographies, Statistics

U.S. COPYRIGHT OFFICE. CATALOG OF COPYRIGHT ENTRIES. FOURTH SERIES. PART 6: MAPS. see GEOGRAPHY — Abstracting, Bibliographies, Statistics

001.5   US   ISSN 0163-7355
Z655.6
U.S. COPYRIGHT OFFICE. CATALOG OF COPYRIGHT ENTRIES. FOURTH SERIES. PART 7: SOUND RECORDINGS. 1978. s-a. $7.50. U.S. Library of Congress, Copyright Office, Washington, DC 20559. TEL 202-783-3238. FAX 202-512-2250. (Dist. by: Supt. of Documents, P.O. Box 371954, Pittsburgh, PA 15250) (microfiche)

011   US   ISSN 0163-7363
Z642
U.S. COPYRIGHT OFFICE. CATALOG OF COPYRIGHT ENTRIES. FOURTH SERIES. PART 8: RENEWALS. 1978. s-a. $5. U.S. Library of Congress, Copyright Office, Washington, DC 20559. TEL 202-783-3238. FAX 202-512-2250. (Dist. by: Supt. of Documents, P.O. Box 371954, Pittsburgh, PA 15250) (microfiche)

PEDIATRICS

see Medical Sciences–Pediatrics

PERFUMES AND COSMETICS

see Beauty Culture–Perfumes and Cosmetics

PERSONAL COMPUTERS

see Computers–Personal Computers

PERSONNEL MANAGEMENT

see Business and Economics–Personnel Management

PETROLEUM AND GAS

666.5 553.282   US   ISSN 0149-1423
TN860   CODEN: AABUD2
A A P G BULLETIN. Microform edition (ISSN 0364-9849) 1917. m. $120 domestic; foreign $145. American Association of Petroleum Geologists, Box 979, Tulsa, OK 74101. TEL 918-584-2555. Ed. Susan A. Longacre. adv.; bk.rev.; bibl.; illus.; maps; stat.; index, cum.index every 5 yrs.; circ. 42,000. (also avail. in microform from PMC,UMI) **Indexed:** A.S.& T.Ind., AESIS, ASCA, Bibl.& Ind.Geol., Biol.Abstr., Br.Geol.Lit., Chem.Abstr., Curr.Cont., Curr.Tit.Ocean, Deep Sea Res.& Oceanogr.Abstr., Energy Info.Abstr., Eng.Ind., Fuel & Energy Abstr., Gas Abstr., Geo.Abstr., Geotech.Abstr., Ind.Sci.Rev., INIS Atomind., Petrol.Abstr., Sci.Cit.Ind.
—BLDSC shelfmark: 0537.502000.
   Formerly: American Association of Petroleum Geologists. Bulletin (ISSN 0002-7464)
   Description: Technical journal of petroleum geology; worldwide in scope and contributions.
   Refereed Serial

666.5   US   ISSN 0195-2986
A A P G EXPLORER. 1979. m. $25. American Association of Petroleum Geologists, Box 979, Tulsa, OK 74101. TEL 918-584-2555. Ed. Vern Stefanic. adv.; circ. 40,000. **Indexed:** Petrol.Abstr.
—BLDSC shelfmark: 0537.502300.
   Description: News periodical for the petroleum industry.
   Refereed Serial

666.5   US   ISSN 0271-8510
    CODEN: ASTGD6
A A P G STUDIES IN GEOLOGY SERIES. 1975. irreg., no.29, 1989. price varies. American Association of Petroleum Geologists, Box 979, Tulsa, OK 74101. TEL 918-584-2555. cum.index: 1971-75, 1976-80, 1981-85. **Indexed:** AESIS, Bibl.& Ind.Geol., Biol.Abstr., Chem.Abstr.
   Description: Book series that documents current, state-of-the-art advances in research applicable to the geological community.
   Refereed Serial

665.5   TS
A D N O C NEWS/AKHBAR A D N O C. (Text in Arabic, English) 1978. m. free. Abu Dhabi National Oil Company, Public Relations Department, P.O. Box 898, Abu Dhabi, United Arab Emirates. TEL 666000. FAX 655745. TELEX 22215 EM. Ed. Khalifa al-Hossani. circ. 5,000 (paid); 3,500 (controlled).
   Formerly (until Dec. 1988): Petroleum Community - Mujtama' al-Bitrul.
   Description: Discusses ADNOC activities and all petroleum projects in Abu Dhabi and the U.A.E.

A F P - AUTO; bulletin quotidien d'informations. (Agence France-Presse) see TRANSPORTATION — Automobiles

PETROLEUM AND GAS

665.7   US
TP700   CODEN: AGAMAC
A G A AMERICAN GAS. 1919. 11/yr. $39 (foreign $70). American Gas Association, 1515 Wilson Blvd., Arlington, VA 22209. TEL 703-841-8400. FAX 703-841-8406. (Subscr. to: Dept. 0765, McLean, VA 22109-0765) Ed. Lois Whetzel. bk.rev.; charts; illus.; stat.; ind; circ. 6,200. (also avail. in microfilm) **Indexed:** A.S.& T.Ind., Chem.Abstr., Energy Info.Abstr., Eng.Ind., Environ.Abstr., Fuel & Energy Abstr., Gas Abstr., INIS Atomind., Petrol.Abstr., PROMT.
   Former titles (until 1989): A G A Monthly (ISSN 0885-2413); American Gas Association Monthly (ISSN 0002-8584)

665.7   US
A G A GAS ENERGY REVIEW. m. $50 to non-members; members $40. American Gas Association, 1515 Wilson Blvd., Arlington, VA 22209. TEL 703-841-8400. FAX 703-841-8406. (Subscr. to: Dept. 0765, McLean, VA 22109-0765)

338.47 665.74   US
A G A RATE SERVICE. 1919. s-a. $300 to non-members; members $175. American Gas Association, 1515 Wilson Blvd., Arlington, VA 22209. TEL 703-841-8400. FAX 703-841-8406. (Subscr. to: Dept. 0765, McLean, VA 22109-0765) Ed. Sheila Rana. circ. 500. (looseleaf format)

665.54   US
A G A SYNTHETIC PIPELINE GAS SYMPOSIUM. PROCEEDINGS. vol.7, 1975. irreg., latest Boston, 1991. $50. American Gas Association, 1515 Wilson Blvd., Arlington, VA 22209. TEL 703-841-8400. FAX 703-841-8406. (Subscr. to: Dept. 0765, McLean, VA 22109-0765) (Co-sponsors: U.S. Energy Research; Development Administration; International Gas Union)

665.7   US
A G A THE NATURAL RESOURCE NEWSLETTER. q. $56 to non-members (foreign $66); members $28 (foreign $38). American Gas Association, 1515 Wilson Blvd., Arlington, VA 22209. TEL 703-841-8400. FAX 703-841-8406. (Subscr. to: Dept. 0765, McLean, VA 22109-0765)

665.5   US
A G A TRAINING UPDATE. q. $20 to non-members; members $10. American Gas Association, 1515 Wilson Blvd., Arlington, VA 22209. TEL 703-841-8400. FAX 703-841-8406. (Subscr. to: Dept. 0765, McLean, VA 22109-0765)

A M P L A BULLETIN. (Australian Mining and Petroleum Law Association Ltd.) see *MINES AND MINING INDUSTRY*

A M P L A YEARBOOK. (Australian Mining and Petroleum Law Association Ltd.) see *MINES AND MINING INDUSTRY*

A M R E P DATABASE BULLETIN. (Australian Mineral Resource Politics Pty. Ltd.) see *MINES AND MINING INDUSTRY*

665.538   CN   ISSN 0822-2509
CODEN: AJREEU
A O S T R A JOURNAL OF RESEARCH. 1984. q. Can.$30 to individuals (foreign Can.$47); institutions Can.$60 (foreign Can.$7). (Alberta Oil Sands Technology and Research Authority) 500 Highfield Place, 10010-106 Street, Edmonton, Alta. T5J 3L8, Canada. TEL 403-427-7623. FAX 403-422-9112. TELEX 037-3519. Eds. R.G. Bentsen, L.G. Hepler. abstr.; bibl.; circ. 250.
—BLDSC shelfmark: 1567.727700.
   Description: Publishes papers dealing with oil sands, heavy oils, enhanced oil recovery, upgrading and refining of bitumens and heavy oils, and related technology such as steam generation orminimization of environmental problems.

665.5   UY   ISSN 0253-6005
A R P E L BOLETIN TECNICO. (Text in Spanish; summaries in English, French, Spanish and Portuguese) 1972. q. $56. Asistencia Reciproca Petrolera Estatal Latinoamericana, Box 1006, Montevideo, Uruguay. TEL 407454. FAX 237023. abstr.; bibl.; charts; illus.; stat. **Indexed:** API Abstr., API Catal., API Hlth.& Environ., API Oil., API Pet.Ref., API Pet.Subst., API Transport.
—BLDSC shelfmark: 2219.085000.
   Formerly: Asistencia Reciproca Petrolera Estatal Latinoamericana. Revista Tecnica.

665.5   UY
A R P E L HOY. 1967. bi-m. free. Asistencia Reciproca Petrolera Estatal Latinoamericana, Box 1006, Montevideo, Uruguay. FAX 598-2-237023. TELEX 22560 ARPEL UY.
   Supersedes (since Sep. 1989): A R P E L Boletin Informativo.

665.5   UK   ISSN 0263-5054
ABERDEEN PETROLEUM REPORT. 1981. w. £345 (Europe £350; elsewhere £360) includes Europetroleum with Aberdeen Petroleum Quarterly. Aberdeen Petroleum Publishing Ltd., 37 Huntly St., Aberdeen AB1 1TJ, Scotland. TEL 0224-644725. FAX 0224-647574. Ed. Ted Strachan. (back issues avail.)
   Description: Covers North Sea oil and gas activities.

ABERDEEN PORT HANDBOOK. see *BUSINESS AND ECONOMICS — Trade And Industrial Directories*

ACCESS (GLENSIDE); information and education for the mining and petroleum industry. see *MINES AND MINING INDUSTRY*

ACTA UNIVERSITATIS DE ATTILA JOZSEF NOMINATAE. ACTA MINERALOGICA - PETROGRAPHICA. see *MINES AND MINING INDUSTRY*

ADVANCED FOSSIL ENERGY TECHNOLOGIES. see *ENERGY*

665.5 531.64   US
ADVANCED OIL AND GAS RECOVERY TECHNOLOGIES. m. $90 in U.S., Canada, Mexico; elsewhere $180. (Department of Energy) U.S. National Technical Information Service, 5285 Port Royal Rd., Springfield, VA 22161. TEL 703-487-4630. Ed. Rivers.
   Description: Disseminates international information on all aspects of enhanced and unconventional recovery of petroleum and natural gas. Includes oil shales and tar sands, natural gas production from coal mines, gas hydrates and geopressured systems.

665.5 551   US
ADVANCES IN PETROLEUM GEOCHEMISTRY. 1984. irreg., vol.2, 1987. Academic Press, Inc., 2150 Sixth Ave., San Diego, CA 92101. TEL 619-231-6616. FAX 619-699-6715. Eds. Jim Brooks, Dietrich Welte. (back issues avail.)
Refereed Serial

665.538 549   FR
AFRICA ENERGY AND MINING. French edition: Lettre Afrique Energies. 1983. 23/yr. 3350 F.($620) Indigo Publications, 10, rue du Sentier, 75002 Paris, France. TEL 45-08-14-80. TELEX LOI 215405F. Ed. Antoine Glaser.

665.5   PL   ISSN 0860-1860
TN871.2
AKADEMIA GORNICZO-HUTNICZA IM. STANISLAWA STASZICA. ZESZYTY NAUKOWE. WIERTNICTWO NAFTA GAS/STANISLAW STASZIC UNIVERSITY OF MINING AND METALLURGY. SCIENTIFIC BULLETINS. DRILLIGN OIL GAS. (Text in English and Polish; summaries in English, Polish) 1985. irreg., no.8, 1991. price varies. Wydawnictwo A G H, Al. Mickiewicza 30, paw. B-5, 30-059 Krakow, Poland. (Dist. by: Ars Polona, Krakowskie Przedmiescie 7, 00-068 Warsaw, Poland) Ed. Z. Kleczek. illus.; circ. 550.

552   TS
AKHBAR AL-BUTRUL WAL-SINA'A/PETROLEUM AND INDUSTRY NEWS. (Text in Arabic) 1970. m. Ministry of Petroleum and Mineral Wealth, P.O. Box 59, Abu Dhabi, United Arab Emirates. TEL 651810. FAX 663414. TELEX 22544 MPMR EM. Ed. Manaa Said al-Otaiba. circ. 2,000 (controlled).
   Description: Discusses current developments and news in petroleum and industry, with a focus on the U.A.E.

552   BA
AKHBAR B A P C O. (Text in Arabic; summaries in English) 1957. w. free. Bahrain Petroleum Co. Ltd., Public Relations Department, P.O. Box 25149, Awali, Bahrain. TEL 755055. FAX 755999. TELEX 8214 BAPCO BN. Ed. Khalid Fahad Mehmas. bk.rev.; circ. 8,000.
   Formerly (until 1981): Weekly Star - An-Najma al-Usbou'

665.5   US
ALABAMA PROPANE GAS NEWS. 1950. m. Alabama Propane Gas Association, 660 Adams Ave., Ste. 394, Montgomery, AL 36104-4336. TEL 205-264-9630. adv.; circ. 500.

665   US
ALASKA SUMMARY REPORT - INDEX. 1980. a. free. Outer Continental Shelf Information Program, Offshore Information and Publications Office, Minerals Management Service, 381 Elden St., No. 1400, Herndon, VA 22070-4817. TEL 703-787-1080. circ. 4,000.
   Formed by the 1985 merger of: Arctic Summary Report; Bering Sea Summary Report; Alaska Index.
   Description: Documents with status of federal offshore oil and gas leasing, exploration, development and production activities.

665.538 634.9   CN
ALBERTA OIL & FORESTRY REVIEW. 1988. q. Can.$18. Alberta Publications, 10234 124th St., Ste. 105, Edmonton, Alta. T5N 1P9, Canada. TEL 403-488-7484. FAX 403-482-7481.

ALBERTA OIL & GAS DIRECTORY. see *BUSINESS AND ECONOMICS — Trade And Industrial Directories*

665.74 531.64   CN   ISSN 0229-8546
TN873.C22
ALBERTA'S RESERVE OF GAS: COMPLETE LISTING. (Avail. only on microfiche) 1979. a. Can.$250. Energy Resources Conservation Board, 640 5th Ave.S.W., Calgary, Alberta T2P 3G4, Canada. FAX 403-297-7040. TELEX 03-821717.

665.5   LY
AL-FATEH UNIVERSITY. FACULTY OF PETROLEUM. BULLETIN. a. Al-Fateh University, Faculty of Petroleum, P.O. Box 13040, Tripoli, Libya. TEL 36010. TELEX 20629.

AMERICAN ASSOCIATION OF PETROLEUM GEOLOGISTS. MEMOIR. see *EARTH SCIENCES — Geology*

665.7   US   ISSN 0362-4994
TN880.A1   CODEN: POAGAB
AMERICAN GAS ASSOCIATION. OPERATING SECTION. PROCEEDINGS. 1965. a. $10. American Gas Association, 1515 Wilson Blvd., Arlington, VA 22209. TEL 703-841-8400. FAX 703-841-8406. (Subscr. to: Dept. 0765, McLean, VA 22109-0765) illus. **Indexed:** API Abstr., Bibl.& Ind.Geol., Chem.Abstr, Gas Abstr. Key Title: Operating Section Proceedings.

665.5   US   ISSN 0145-9198
TN872
AMERICAN OIL & GAS REPORTER. 1958. 12/yr. $28. National Publishers Group, Inc., Box 343, Derby, KS 67037-0343. FAX 316-788-7568. Ed. Bill Campbell. adv.; bk.rev.; tr.lit.; circ. 11,413. **Indexed:** Petrol.Abstr.
—BLDSC shelfmark: 0847.320000.
   Formerly: Mid-America Oil and Gas Reporter.

AMERICAN PETROLEUM INSTITUTE. MONTHLY COMPLETION REPORT. see *PETROLEUM AND GAS — Abstracting, Bibliographies, Statistics*

665.75   US
AMERICAN PUBLIC GAS ASSOCIATION. NEWSLETTER. 1962. bi-w. American Public Gas Association, 11094-D Lee Hwy., Ste. 102, Fairfax, VA 22030. TEL 703-352-3890. Ed. Carole Curtis. circ. 1,000.
   Formerly: American Public Gas Association. Memorandum Bulletins (ISSN 0065-9894)

665.7   US
ANALYSES OF NATURAL GASES. (Subseries of: Information Circular) 1917. a. price varies. U.S. Bureau of Mines, Department of the Interior, Washington, DC 20241.
   Formerly: Analyses of Natural Gases of the United States (ISSN 0066-149X)
   Description: Tables of analyses of natural gases. Purpose of analysis is to identify the helium content of these gases.

ANNUAL BOOK OF A S T M STANDARDS. VOLUME 05.01. PETROLEUM PRODUCTS AND LUBRICANTS (1). see *ENGINEERING — Engineering Mechanics And Materials*

PETROLEUM AND GAS

ANNUAL BOOK OF A S T M STANDARDS. VOLUME 05.02. PETROLEUM PRODUCTS AND LUBRICANTS (2). see ENGINEERING — Engineering Mechanics And Materials

ANNUAL BOOK OF A S T M STANDARDS. VOLUME 05.03. PETROLEUM PRODUCTS AND LUBRICANTS (3); CATALYSTS. see ENGINEERING — Engineering Mechanics And Materials

ANNUAL BOOK OF A S T M STANDARDS. VOLUME 05.05. GASEOUS FUELS; COAL AND COKE. see ENGINEERING — Engineering Mechanics And Materials

665.5   US
ANNUAL REVIEW OF CALIFORNIA - ALASKA OIL AND GAS EXPLORATION. 1944. a. $45. Munger Oil Information Service, Inc., 9800 S. Sepulveda Blvd., Ste. 723, Box 45738, Los Angeles, CA 90045. TEL 213-776-3990. FAX 213-645-9147. Ed. Averill H. Munger. circ. 300.
    Formerly: Annual Review of California Oil and Gas Exploration.

APPLIED ENERGY. see ENERGY

665   FR   ISSN 0031-6369
ARAB OIL & GAS. French edition: Petrole et Gaz Arabes. (Text in English) 1969. fortn. 8600 F.($1240) Arab Petroleum Research Center, 7 av. Ingres, 75781 Paris Cedex 16, France. FAX 45-20-16-85. TELEX 613497 OIL. Ed. Nicolas Sarkis. bk.rev.; bibl.; stat.; index; circ. 1,800. **Indexed:** Fuel & Energy Abstr.
    —BLDSC shelfmark: 6430.670000.
    Description: Provides news, sutdies, comments, interviews, texts of laws and agreements on all aspects of the development of the oil and gas industry in the Middle East and Africa.

338.2   FR   ISSN 0304-8551
HD9578.A55
ARAB OIL & GAS DIRECTORY. (Text in English) 1974. a. $395. Arab Petroleum Research Center, 7 av. Ingres, 75781 Paris Cedex 16, France. FAX 45-20-16-85. TELEX 613497 OIL. Ed. Nicolas Sarkis. adv.: B&W page $2840, color page $3310; trim 180 x 245; adv. contact: Anne-Marie Happey. illus.; stat.; circ. 5,250.
    —BLDSC shelfmark: 1583.258000.
    Description: Provides complete coverage of Arab oil and gas exporting countries, new products, investment figures, survey of all oil producing surveys, addresses of oil companies.

338.2   665.538   FR
ARAB OIL & GAS MAGAZINE (MONTHLY). (Text in Arabic) 1966. m. Arab Petroleum Research Center, 7 av. Ingres, 75781 Paris Cedex 16, France. FAX 45-20-16-85. TELEX 613497 OIL. adv.: B&W page $2840, color page $4250; trim 190 x 250; adv. contact: Anne-Marie Happey. circ. 16,200.

665   LY   ISSN 0003-7435
ARAB OIL REVIEW. (Text in English and Arabic) 1964. bi-m. £L7. 4 Sharia Omar Ibn Abdulaziz, Tripoli, Libya. Ed. Naim El-Arady. adv.; illus.; mkt.; tr.lit.; index.

665   622   LY   ISSN 0003-7443
ARAB PETROLEUM. 1964. m. Arab Federation of Petroleum Mining & Chemical Workers, P.O. Box 1905, Tripoli, Libya.

ARAMCO WORLD. see ETHNIC INTERESTS

665.5   IT
ARGOMENTI ESSO. 1974. m. free. Esso Italiana, Stampa Informazione, Viale Castello della Magliana 25, 00148 Rome, Italy. TEL 06 59952318. Ed. Carlo Angelo Guareschi. charts; illus.; stat.; circ. 10,000.
    Formerly (until 1988): Esso Italiana. Informazioni Economiche.
    Description: Analysis of relations between the oil industry and environment. Covers safe industrial activity, measures for the protection of the environment and actions toward a more rational order of marketing.

665.5   US   ISSN 0570-9520
ARIZONA. OIL & GAS CONSERVATION COMMISSION. OIL, GAS & HELIUM PRODUCTION. 1958. m. $16. (Oil & Gas Conservation Commission) Arizona Geological Survey, 845 N. Park Ave, Ste. 100, Tuscon, AZ 85719-4816. TEL 602-882-4795. FAX 602-628-5106. stat.; index; circ. 150. (processed)

557   622   US
ARIZONA. OIL AND GAS CONSERVATION COMMISSION. SPECIAL PUBLICATION. irreg., no.6, 1990. (Oil and Gas Conservation Commission) Arizona Geological Survey, 845 N. Park Ave., Ste. 100, Tucson, AZ 85719-4816. TEL 602-882-4795. FAX 602-628-5106.

665.7   US
ARKANSAS PROPANE GAS NEWS. vol.24, 1972. bi-m. $2. Arkansas Propane Gas Association, Inc., 103 E. 7th St., Ste. 1012, Little Rock, AR 72201. TEL 501-374-8396. Ed. J.P. Lybrand, Jr. adv.; circ. 561. (processed)
    Formerly: Arkansas L P News (ISSN 0044-8893)

665   US   ISSN 0273-4931
TN867
ARMSTRONG OIL DIRECTORIES: LOUISIANA, MISSISSIPPI, ARKANSAS, TEXAS GULF COAST AND EAST TEXAS EDITION. (In 4 regional eds.) 1958. a. $50. Armstrong Oil Directories, c/o Alan Armstrong, Ed., 1606 S. Jackson St., Amarillo, TX 79102-9660. TEL 806-374-1818. FAX 806-374-1838.
    Formerly (until 1980): Armstrong Oil Directories - Louisiana, Texas Gulf Coast, East Texas, Arkansas and Mississippi (ISSN 0073-0254)

665
ARMSTRONG OIL DIRECTORIES: MINI BRIEFCASE EDITION; nation-wide coverage. (In 4 regional eds.) a. $130. Armstrong Oil Directories, c/o Alan Armstrong, Ed., 1606 S. Jackson St., Amarillo, TX 79102-9660. TEL 800-375-1838. FAX 806-374-1838.

665   US   ISSN 0273-5229
TN867
ARMSTRONG OIL DIRECTORIES: ROCKY MOUNTAIN - CENTRAL UNITED STATES EDITION. (In 4 regional eds.) 1961. a. $50. Armstrong Oil Directories, c/o Alan Armstrong, Ed., 1606 S. Jackson St., Amarillo, TX 79102-9660. TEL 806-374-1818. FAX 806-374-1838.
    Former titles (until 1980): Armstrong Oil Directory - Central United States; Hank Seale Oil Directory - Central United States (ISSN 0073-0238)

665   US   ISSN 0277-2280
ARMSTRONG OIL DIRECTORIES: TEXAS INCLUDING SOUTHEAST NEW MEXICO EDITION. (In 4 regional eds.) 1957. a. $50. Armstrong Oil Directories, c/o Alan Armstrong, Ed., 1606 S. Jackson St., Amarillo, TX 79102-9660. TEL 806-374-1818. FAX 806-374-1838.
    Formerly (until 1980): Hank Seale Oil Directory - Texas Including Southeast New Mexico (ISSN 0073-0262)

665.5   US
ASHLAND NEWS. 1961. m. free. Ashland Oil, Inc., Box 391, Ashland, KY 41114. TEL 606-329-3333. Ed. Lesli S. Christian. charts; illus.; circ. 32,000. **Indexed:** Energy Info.Abstr.

665.5   338.7   US   ISSN 0748-4089
HD9576.A1
ASIA - PACIFIC - AFRICA - MIDDLE EAST PETROLEUM. 1979. a. $115 (or $210 as a 2 volume set with European Petroleum Directory). PennWell Publishing Co., Box 1260, Tulsa, OK 74101. TEL 918-835-3161. FAX 918-831-9497. TELEX 211012. Ed. Jonelle Moore. adv.
    Formerly: Asia - Pacific Petroleum Directory (ISSN 0270-1235); Incorporating (as of 1985): Africa - Middle East Petroleum Directory (ISSN 0197-7830); Which superseded in part: Eastern Hemisphere Petroleum Directory (ISSN 0070-8224)
    Description: Lists companies involved in drilling, refining, exploration, pipelines, engineering, field services, construction and other petroleum related operations.

665.5   JA
ASIAN OIL AND GAS. (Text in English) m. $100. Intercontinental Marketing Corp., I.P.O. Box 5056, Tokyo 100-31, Japan. FAX 81-3-3667-9646.

338.47   HK
ASIAN OIL AND GAS. (Text in English) 1980. m. Publications Ltd., 14th Fl., 200 Lockhart Rd., Hong Kong. TEL 8921301. FAX 8344620. Ed. Andrew Burns. circ. 6,042.
    Description: Oil industry trade journal.

ASPHALT EMULSION MANUFACTURERS ASSOCIATION. NEWSLETTER. see TRANSPORTATION — Roads And Traffic

665.5   US
ASPHALT ROOFING MANUFACTURERS ASSOCIATION. NEWSLETTER. 6/yr. Asphalt Roofing Manufacturers Association, 6288 Montrose Rd., Rockville, MD 20852. TEL 301-231-9050. FAX 301-881-6572.

665.5   551   US
ATLANTIC SUMMARY REPORT - INDEX. 1980. a. Outer Continental Shelf Information Program, Offshore Information and Publications Office, Minerals Management Service, 381 Elden St., No. 1400, Herndon, VA 22070-4817. TEL 703-787-1080. circ. 4,000.
    Formed by the 1985 merger of: Atlantic Index; Mid-Atlantic Summary Report; Atlantic Summary Report; Which was formerly (until 1983): South Atlantic Summary Report.

ATOMO PETROLIO ELETTRICITA. see ENERGY

665.5   550   AT   ISSN 0817-9263
AUSTRALIA. BUREAU OF MINERAL RESOURCES, GEOLOGY AND GEOPHYSICS. AUSTRALIAN PETROLEUM ACCUMULATIONS REPORT. 1986. irreg. price varies. Bureau of Mineral Resources, Geology and Geophysics, G.P.O. Box 378, Canberra, A.C.T. 2601, Australia. FAX 062-725161.

696   AT   ISSN 0727-3541
THE AUSTRALIAN GAS INDUSTRY DIRECTORY (YEAR). a. Aus.$30. Australian Gas Association, G.P.O. Box 323, Canberra, A.C.T. 2601, Australia. TEL 06-247-3955. FAX 06-249-7402. TELEX AA62137. Ed. Naomi Donohue.
    Former titles: Directory of the Australian Gas Industry (ISSN 0706-666X); Australian Gas Association. Directory.
    Description: List members of The Australian Gas Association, and suppliers to the gas industry.

665.7   AT   ISSN 0004-9166
TP700
THE AUSTRALIAN GAS JOURNAL. 1936. q. Aus.$35. Australian Gas Association, G.P.O. Box 323, Canberra, A.C.T. 2601, Australia. TEL 06-247-3955. FAX 06-249-7402. TELEX AA62137. Ed. Morag Cameron. adv.; bk.rev.; circ. 1,900. **Indexed:** AESIS, Bibl.& Ind.Geol., Chem.Abstr., Fuel & Energy Abstr., GeoRef.
    —BLDSC shelfmark: 1800.600000.

553   AT   ISSN 0314-3171
AUSTRALIAN INSTITUTE OF PETROLEUM. ANNUAL REPORT. 1977. a. free. Australian Institute of Petroleum, Ltd., 257 Collins St., Melbourne, Vic. 3000, Australia.

AUTOMOTIVE ENGINEER. see TRANSPORTATION — Automobiles

338.47   US
AUTOMOTIVE FUEL ECONOMY PROGRAM. ANNUAL REPORT TO THE CONGRESS. 1977. a. U.S. Department of Transportation, National Highway Traffic Safety Administration, Washington, DC 20590. TEL 202-655-4000. circ. 200.

665   BA
B A P C O NEWS. (Text in English) w. free. Bahrain Petroleum Co. B.S.C., P.O. 25149, Awali, Bahrain. TEL 755047. FAX 755999. TELEX 8214 BAPCO BN. Ed. Samuel Knight. circ. 1,000. (newspaper)
    Formerly: B A P C O Daily News.

665.5   FR   ISSN 0300-4554
B I P. (Bulletin de l'Industrie Petroliere) 1964. d. 11600 F. Societe d' Information et de Documentation, Bureau d'Informations Professionnelles, 142 rue Montmartre, 75002 Paris, France. FAX 40-39-97-52. TELEX 220528F. Ed. Jacques Marie. bk.rev.; stat.; circ. 1,000. (processed) **Indexed:** Chem.Abstr., Petrol.Energy B.N.I., Sci.Cit.Ind.
    —BLDSC shelfmark: 2862.090000.
    Description: Daily news and comments on oil and gas in the world.

PETROLEUM AND GAS 3683

665.5 UK
B P NEWS. m. free to qualified personnel. British Petroleum Company p.l.c., Britannic House, 1 Finsbury Circus, London EC2M 7BA, England. Ed. Diana Ching. circ. 21,000.
Description: Tabloid newspaper for BP staff in the London area.

665.5 UK
B P SHIPPING REVIEW. 1986. q. free. B P Shipping Ltd., B P House, Third Ave., Harlow, Essex CM19 5AQ, England. FAX 0279-414722. Ed. Allan Carter. bk.rev.; circ. 4,500. **Indexed:** BMT.
Formerly: B P Fleet News.
Description: Publicity magazine for clients and potential clients of BP Shipping.

665.5 US
B T U HANDBOOK.* (British Thermal Unit) a. $71 (foreign $81). B T U Publishing, Inc. (Subsidiary of: Waterman & Barrett Publishing), 65 Mechanic St., Red Bank, NJ 07701-1803.

665.5 US
B T U WEEKLY.* (British Thermal Unit) w. $427 (foreign $550). B T U Publishing, Inc. (Subsidiary of: Waterman & Barrett Publishing), 65 Mechanic St., Red Bank, NJ 07701-1803.
Description: For producers and users of natural gas.

BASIC OIL LAWS & CONCESSION CONTRACTS: ASIA & AUSTRALASIA. see *LAW — International Law*

BASIC OIL LAWS & CONCESSION CONTRACTS: CENTRAL AMERICA & CARIBBEAN. see *LAW — International Law*

BASIC OIL LAWS & CONCESSION CONTRACTS: EUROPE. see *LAW — International Law*

BASIC OIL LAWS & CONCESSION CONTRACTS: MIDDLE EAST. see *LAW — International Law*

BASIC OIL LAWS & CONCESSION CONTRACTS: NORTH AFRICA. see *LAW — International Law*

BASIC OIL LAWS & CONCESSION CONTRACTS: SOUTH AMERICA. see *LAW — International Law*

BASIC OIL LAWS & CONCESSION CONTRACTS: SOUTH & CENTRAL AFRICA. see *LAW — International Law*

629.286 FI ISSN 0045-1738
BENSIINI UUTISET.* 1958. m. free. Suomen Bensiinikauppiaitten Liitto r.y., Mannerheimintie 40 D 86, 00100 Helsinki 10, Finland. Ed. Orjo Pattiniemi.

665.77 DK ISSN 0005-8858
BENZIN & OLIE BLADET.* 1931. m. (except Jul.). $10. Centralforeningen af Benzinforhandlere i Danmark, Gl. Kongevej 135A, DK-1850 Frederiksberg C, Denmark. Ed. Ole Holm. adv.; charts; illus.; mkt.; circ. 3,000.

665.5 658.3 SI ISSN 0005-9153
BERITA SHELL. (Text in English and Malay) 1955. m. free to employees. Shell Eastern Petroleum Pty. Ltd., Shell Tower, 50 Raffles Place, 1 Singapore, Singapore. Ed. Chua Swee Kiat. bk.rev.; circ. 3,800.

665.5 CN
BIO-JOULE. 1978. 4/yr. $40. Biomass Energy Institute, 1329 Niakwa Rd. East, Winnipeg, Man. R2J 3T4, Canada. TEL 204-257-3891. FAX 204-945-1784. Ed. Beth Candlish. adv.; bk.rev.; circ. 2,000. **Indexed:** Energy Info.Abstr., Environ.Abstr.
Formerly: Bio-Joule Newsletter (ISSN 0708-1936); Supersedes: Biomass Energy Institute. Newsletter (ISSN 0315-3223)
Description: Dedicated to raising public awareness of biomass production and technologies.

665 UA
AL-BITRUL. m. Egyptian General Petroleum Corporation, Sharia Filastin, P.O. Box 2130, New Maadi, Cairo, Egypt. TEL 02-3531340. TELEX 92049.

665 BL ISSN 0102-9304
BOLETIM DE GEOCIENCIAS DA PETROBRAS. (Summaries in English and Portuguese) 1957. 4/yr. free to qualified personnel. Petroleo Brasileiro S.A., Centro de Pesquisas e Desenvolvimento "Leopoldo A. Miguez de Mello", Setor de Informacao Tecnica e Propriedade Industrial, Cidade Universitaria, Quadra 7-Ilha do Fundao, C.P. 809, 21910 Rio de Janeiro, Brazil. TEL 021-598-6114. Eds. Affonso Celso M. de Paula, Fani Knoploch. abstr.; bibl.; charts; illus.; stat.; index; circ. 2,000. **Indexed:** API Abstr., API Catal., API Hlth.& Environ., API Oil., API Pet.Ref., API Pet.Subst., API Transport., Bibl.& Ind.Geol., Chem.Abstr., Petrol.Abstr.
Formerly (until 1987): Boletim Tecnico da Petrobras (ISSN 0006-6117)
Description: Covers all aspects of the petroleum industry worldwide with emphasis on Brazil.

665.7 UK ISSN 0006-7601
BOOST. 1962. every 6 wks. free. British Gas West Midlands, 5 Wharf Ln., Solihull, West Midlands, England. Ed. Norma Frankham. charts; illus.; circ. 13,500.

665.5 GW ISSN 0342-6580
HD9553.1
BRENNSTOFFSPIEGEL. 1947. m. DM.72. Ceto Verlag GmbH, Goethestr. 34, Postfach 104029, 3500 Kassel, Germany. FAX 0561-772562. TELEX 992452. Ed. Hans-Colin Wulff. adv.; bk.rev.; circ. 4,500.
Formerly: Brennstoffhandel.

BRITISH COLUMBIA. MINISTRY OF ENERGY, MINES AND PETROLEUM RESOURCES. ANNUAL REPORT. see *MINES AND MINING INDUSTRY*

BRITISH COLUMBIA. MINISTRY OF ENERGY, MINES AND PETROLEUM RESOURCES. BULLETIN. see *EARTH SCIENCES — Geology*

665.5 UK
BRITISH FLEET. 1968. q. Shell Tankers (UK) Ltd., Shell Centre, London SE1 7PQ, England. Ed. Terence Ryan. circ. 3,500.
Formerly: British Fleet News.

665.7 UK
BRITISH GAS. ANNUAL REPORT AND ACCOUNTS. 1948. a. free. British Gas PLC, Rivermill House, 152 Grosvenor Rd., London SW1V 3JL, England. TEL 071-821-1444. TELEX 938529. Ed. Richard Batson. circ. 2,700,000.
Former titles: British Gas. Report and Accounts & British Gas Corporation. Report and Accounts (ISSN 0072-0216); Gas Council (Great Britain) Report and Accounts

665.5 531.64 UK
BRITISH GAS. MONITOR. 1985. a. free. British Gas Plc., Rivermill House, 152 Grosvenor Rd., London SW1V 3JL, England. TEL 071-821-1444. FAX 071-630-7538. TELEX 938529. Ed. J.S. Carmichael. charts; illus.; pat.; circ. 25,000.
Formerly: British Gas Corporation. Monitor (ISSN 0268-3296)

665.5 UK
BRITISH PUMP MARKET. 1981. irreg. £33.50. C H W Roles & Associates Ltd., P.O. Box 25, Sunbury-on-Thames, Middlesex TW16 5QB, England. TEL 081-783 0088. Ed. Richard R.S. Tomes. adv.
Description: Practical reference book and buyer's guide to manufacturers and suppliers of pumps and auxiliary equipment available in the UK.

662.6 UK
BRITOIL. ANNUAL REPORT. 1983. a. Britoil PLC, 301 St. Vincent St., Glasgow, G2 5DD, Scotland. TEL 041-204 2525. circ. 50,000.
Description: Britoil Plc and subsidiaries' annual report for the year;, includes chairman's statement, financial statements and more.

665.7 US ISSN 0197-8098
TP714
BROWN'S DIRECTORY OF NORTH AMERICAN AND INTERNATIONAL GAS COMPANIES. 1887. a. $225. Avanstar Communications, Inc., 7500 Old Oak Blvd., Cleveland, OH 44130. TEL 216-826-2839. FAX 216-891-2726. (Subscr. to: 1 E. First St., Duluth, MN 55802) Ed. Dean Hale. adv.; circ. 962.
Formerly (until 1978): Brown's Directory of North American Gas Companies (ISSN 0068-2888)
Description: Indexes data concerning personnel, plants and facilities, sales, revenue and other aspects of North American and international gas companies.

662 627 UK ISSN 0305-0122
BULK CARRIER REGISTER. 1969. a. £160($288) Clarkson Research Studies Ltd., 12 Camomile St., London EC3A 7BP, England. TEL 071-283 8955. adv.

665.7 FR ISSN 0007-7240
BUTANE PROPANE; la revue des gaz de petrole. (Summaries in English and French) 1957. q. 197 F. Butane - Propane News, Inc., 16 ave. Kelber, 75116 Paris, France. FAX 47-235279. (US addr.: 338 E. Foothill Blvd., Box 419, Arcadia, CA 91006. TEL 818-357-2168) Ed. Jacques A. Meggle. adv.; charts; illus.; circ. 5,000.

665.7 US ISSN 0007-7259
TP761.B8
BUTANE - PROPANE NEWS. 1939. m. $20 to qualified personnel; others $30. Butane - Propane News, Inc., 338 E. Foothill Blvd., Box 419, Arcadia, CA 91006. TEL 818-357-2168. FAX 818-303-2854. Ed. Steve Prowler. adv.; charts; illus.; tr.lit.; index; circ. 18,000. (also avail. in microform from UMI; reprint service avail. from UMI) **Indexed:** Chem.Abstr, Fuel & Energy Abstr.

338.47 665.5 US
C I-G WORLD. 1943. 6/yr. free to qualified personnel. Colorado Interstate Gas Co., Box 1087, Colorado Springs, CO 80944. TEL 719-520-4451. FAX 719-520-4318. (Street addr.: 2 N. Nevada, Colorado Springs, CO 80903) Ed. Wayne K. Tiller. circ. 1,500 (controlled).
Formerly: Gasser.

665.5 330.9 US
C R A PETROLEUM ECONOMICS MONTHLY. m. $2,000. Charles River Associates Incorporated, John Hancock Tower, 200 Clarendon St., Boston, MA 02116. TEL 617-266-0500. FAX 617-266-0698.
Description: Featuring in-depth articles on world petroleum market.

665.5 US ISSN 0273-3250
TJ563
C T I JOURNAL. 1980. s-a. $20 to libraries. Cooling Tower Institute, Box 73383, Houston, TX 77273. TEL 713-583-4087. FAX 713-537-1721. Ed. Dorothy Garrison. adv.; bk.rev.; illus.; circ. 6,000. (back issues avail.) **Indexed:** Corros.Abstr.
—BLDSC shelfmark: 4732.150000.

665.5 US ISSN 0362-1243
TN872.C2 CODEN: CDOOAL
CALIFORNIA. DIVISION OF OIL AND GAS. ANNUAL REPORT OF THE STATE OIL AND GAS SUPERVISOR. 1915. a. free. Divison of Oil and Gas, 1416 Ninth St., Rm. 1310, Sacramento, CA 95814. FAX 916-323-0424. Ed. Susan Hodgson. illus.; circ. 2,400. **Indexed:** Bibl.& Ind.Geol.

622.33 CN
TN873.C22
CANADA. ENERGY, MINES AND RESOURCES CANADA. INDIAN AND NORTHERN AFFAIRS. CANADA OIL AND GAS LANDS ADMINISTRATION FRONTIER LANDS RELEASED INFORMATION. 1981. a. free. Oil and Gas Lands Administration, 355 River Road, Ottawa, Ont. K1A 0E4, Canada. TEL 613-993-3760. FAX 613-993-9897. circ. 1,000.
Former titles: Canada. Energy, Mines and Resources Canada. Indian and Northern Affairs. Canada Oil and Gas Lands Administration Released Geophysical-Geological Data (ISSN 0317-4085); Canada. Northern Natural Resources and Environment Branch. Oil and Mineral Division. North of 60: Oil and Gas Technical Reports; Supersedes: Canada. Northern Economic Development Branch. Oil and Gas Technical Reports- North of 60.

3684 PETROLEUM AND GAS

CANADA. ENVIRONMENT CANADA. ENVIRONMENTAL PROTECTION SERIES REPORTS. see *ENVIRONMENTAL STUDIES*

CANADA A-Z; oil, gas, mining directory. see *BUSINESS AND ECONOMICS — Trade And Industrial Directories*

665.5   US
CANADA PETROLEUM INDUSTRY. a. $40. Midwest Register, Inc., 601 S. Boulder, Ste. 1001, Tulsa, OK 74119-1301. TEL 918-582-2000.
   Formerly: Oil Directory of Canada (ISSN 0474-0114)
   Description: Supplies company name, address, phone and fax numbers, division offices, office location, U.S. office if any. Divided by sections.

CANADIAN ENERGY NEWS. see *ENERGY*

665.5   CN   ISSN 0316-3547
HD9581.C3
CANADIAN GAS FACTS. a. Can.$40 to non-members; members Can.$15. Canadian Gas Association, 55 Scarsdale Road, Don Mills, Ont. M3B 2R3, Canada. TEL 416-447-6465. FAX 416-447-7067.

CANADIAN NATIONAL ENERGY FORUM PROCEEDINGS. see *ENERGY*

340 665.5   CN
CANADIAN OIL & GAS. 6/yr. Can.$895. Butterworths Canada Ltd., 75 Clegg Rd., Markham, Ont. L6G 1A1, Canada. TEL 416-479-2665.
FAX 416-479-2826. Eds. Bennett Jones Verchere, Nigel Bankes. (looseleaf format)
   Description: Statutes, regulations and case law for eleven jurisdictions.

CARTA MINERA; y panorama petrolero. see *MINES AND MINING INDUSTRY*

551 665.5   FR   ISSN 0396-2687
QE1   CODEN: BCREDP
CENTRES DE RECHERCHES EXPLORATION - PRODUCTION ELF AQUITAINE. BULLETIN. (Text and summaries in French, English) 1967. s-a. 170 F.($35) exchange basis. Elf-Aquitaine, F-31360 Boussens, France. TEL 61-97-86-24.
FAX 61-97-80-49. TELEX SNEA 530385F. Ed. R. Curnelle. abstr.; bibl.; charts; illus.; circ. 2,000.
Indexed: AESIS, Bibl.& Ind.Geol., Bull.Signal., Chem.Abstr., INIS Atomind., Petrol.Abstr.
—BLDSC shelfmark: 2439.270000.
   Formerly (until 1977): Societe Nationale des Petroles d'Aquitaine. Centre de Recherches de Pau. Bulletin (ISSN 0008-9672)
   Description: Publishes the results of general interest arising from research undertaken by Elf Aquitaine particularly at the research centers, or by scientists working in collaboration with Elf Aquitaine.

"CHECK THE OIL!" MAGAZINE; the publication devoted exclusively to Petroliana. see *HOBBIES*

CHEMECA - AUSTRALASIAN CONFERENCE ON CHEMICAL ENGINEERING. PROCEEDINGS. see *ENGINEERING — Chemical Engineering*

CHEMICAL AND PETROLEUM ENGINEERING. see *ENGINEERING — Chemical Engineering*

665.5 668.4   UK
CHEMICALS & POLYMERS NEWS. 1981. m. I C I Chemicals & Polymers Ltd., P.O. Box 54, Weton, Middl., Cleveland TS6 8JA, England.
   Formerly (until 1987): Petrochemicals and Plastics News.

662   US   ISSN 0009-3092
TP315   CODEN: CTFCAK
CHEMISTRY AND TECHNOLOGY OF FUELS AND OILS. English translation of: Khimiya i Tekhnologiya Topliv i Masel (RU ISSN 0023-1169) 1965. m. $1175 (foreign $1375)(effective 1992). (Russian Academy of Sciences, RU) Plenum Publishing Corp., Consultants Bureau, 233 Spring St., New York, NY 10013-1578. TEL 212-762-8468.
FAX 212-463-0742. TELEX 23-421139. Ed. E.D. Radchenko. (also avail. in microfilm from JSC; back issues avail.) **Indexed:** Cadscan, Chem.Eng.Abstr., Chem.Titles, Curr.Cont., Eng.Ind., Excerp.Med., INIS Atomind., ISMEC, Lead Abstr., T.C.E.A., Zincscan.
—BLDSC shelfmark: 0410.490000.
   Refereed Serial

665.5   US   ISSN 0148-3102
HD9569.S82
CHEVRON WORLD. 1913. q. free. Chevron Corporation, Corporate Communications, 225 Bush St., San Francisco, CA 94104. TEL 415-894-2574.
FAX 415-894-0066. Ed. R.K. Leaper. charts; illus.; circ. 300,000. **Indexed:** Ind.Free Per., INIS Atomind., PROMT.
   Formerly (until 1977): Standard Oil Company of California Bulletin.
   Description: Features, news, and statistics of interest to the stockholders and employees of the corporation.

662.338   UK
CHINTHE. 1970. 3/yr. Burmah Oil Trading Ltd., Burmah House, Pipers Way, Swindon SN3 1RE, England. TEL 0793-511521. FAX 0793-513506.
TELEX 449221. Ed. Simon Elliott. circ. 6,000. (back issues avail.)
   Former titles: Burmah Chinthe; Burmah International.

665.5   BE
COMBUSTIBLES. (Text in Flemish and French) 1946. m. Federation Belge des Negociants-Detaillants en Combustibles, Centre International Rogiers, 12th Fl., Passage International 6, B.P. 202, B-1000 Brussels, Belgium. TEL 2-2175704. FAX 2-2196012. adv.; circ. 3,800.

665.5 333.91   UY
COMISION DE INTEGRACION ELECTRICA REGIONAL. RECURSOS ENERGETICOS DE LOS PAISES DE LA C I E R. (Text in Portuguese, Spanish) 1968. irreg. Comision de Integracion Electrica Regional, Bulevar Artigas 996, Montevideo, Uruguay. index.

COMITE DE CONTROLE DE L'ELECTRICITE ET DU GAZ. RAPPORT ANNUEL. see *ENGINEERING — Electrical Engineering*

665.5   US
COMPOSITE CATALOG OF OIL FIELD EQUIPMENT & SERVICES. 1929. biennial. Gulf Publishing Co., Box 2608, Houston, TX 77252-2608.
TEL 713-529-4301. FAX 713-520-4433. TELEX 287330 GULF UR. Ed. Robert Rust. adv.; tr.lit.; index; circ. 20,000. (reprint service avail.)

665.5 660   US   ISSN 1042-508X
COMPOUNDINGS. 1988. m. $800 to non-members; members $45. Independent Lubricant Manufacturers Association, 651 S. Washington St., Alexandria, VA 22314. TEL 703-684-5574.
FAX 703-836-8503. Ed. Alice E. Green. adv.; circ. 1,300.
   Description: Features new products and technology, new plant operations, people in the industry, legislative and regulatory developments, meetings, news and employment and business opportunities.

CUBA. MINISTERIO DEL COMERCIO EXTERIOR. BOLETIN SEMANAL DE PRECIOS. PETROLEO Y METALES. see *BUSINESS AND ECONOMICS — International Commerce*

665.54 690   US
D C A NEWS. 1961. m. membership. Distribution Contractors Association, 101 W. Renner Rd., Ste. 250, Richardson, TX 75082. TEL 214-680-0261.
FAX 214-680-0461. Ed. Dennis J. Kennedy.

665.5   YU   ISSN 0352-0870
D I T; strucni casopis. (Text in Serbo-Croatian) 1982. q. $10. Drustvo Inzenjera i Tehnicara "Nafta - Gas", Sutjeska 1, 21000 Novi Sad, Yugoslavia. TEL 021 615-144. FAX 021-27-157. TELEX 14196. Ed. Milan Mladenovic. adv.; bk.rev.; circ. 700. (back issues avail.)

531.64   US
D R I - MCGRAW-HILL ENERGY REVIEW: COAL INDUSTRY FOCUS. q. D R I - McGraw-Hill, 24 Hartwell Ave., Lexington, MA 02173. TEL 617-863-5100.
FAX 617-860-6332. TELEX 200 284.

665.7 531.64   US
D R I - MCGRAW-HILL ENERGY REVIEW: NATURAL GAS REVIEW. q. D R I - McGraw-Hill, 24 Hartwell Ave., Lexington, MA 02173. TEL 617-863-5100.
FAX 617-860-6332. TELEX 200 284.

665.5   US
DAILY MUNGER OILOGRAM. d. $624. Munger Oil Information Service, Inc., 9800 S. Sepulveda Blvd., Ste. 723, Box 45738, Los Angeles, CA 90045. TEL 213-776-3990. Ed. Averill H. Munger. stat.
   Description: Provides information on exploration wells, abandonments, map revisions, and developments affecting the industry, with a focus on California, Alaska, Arizona, Nevada, Oregon, and Washington.

665.7   DK
DANISH OFFSHORE GUIDE AND YEARBOOK. 1983. a. DKK 175. Bjoerndal & Gundestrup A-S, Oestre Havnevej, 6700 Esbjerg, Denmark. Ed. Kurt Bjoerndal. adv.; illus.; circ. 7,500.
   Former titles: Danish Offshore Guide & Westcoast Offshore Guide (ISSN 0108-9161)

622   IS
DELEK. ANNUAL REPORT. (Text in English and Hebrew) a. free. Delek, Israel Fuel Corporation, 6 Ahuzat Bayit St, Tel Aviv, Israel. FAX 03-653664. TELEX 33671.

665.5   NE
DEVELOPMENTS IN PETROLEUM SCIENCE. 1976. irreg., vol.37, 1992. Elsevier Science Publishers B.V., Books Division, P.O. Box 211, 1000 AE Amsterdam, Netherlands. TEL 020-5803911.
FAX 020-5803705. TELEX 18582 ESPA NL. (Subscr. in U.S. and Canada to: Elsevier Science Publishing Co., Inc., Box 882, Madison Sq. Sta., New York, NY 10159. TEL 212-989-5800) (back issues avail.) **Indexed:** Chem.Abstr.
   Refereed Serial

662   RU
DINAMIKA IZLUCHAYUSCHEGO GAZA. 1974. irreg. 0.51 Rub. (Akademiya Nauk S.S.S.R., Vychislitel'nyi Tsentr) Izdatel'stvo Nauka, 90 Profsoyuznaya ul., 117864 Moscow, Russia. TEL 234-05-84.

665.5   CN   ISSN 0847-527X
DIRECTORY OF CERTIFIED APPLIANCES AND ACCESSORIES. a. Can.$24 (yearly revision service Can.$70). Canadian Gas Association, 55 Scarsdale Rd., Don Mills, Ont. M3B 2R3, Canada.
TEL 416-447-6465. FAX 416-447-1026.

DIRECTORY OF ELECTRIC UTILITY INDUSTRY. see *ENGINEERING — Electrical Engineering*

665.7   US
DIRECTORY OF MUNICIPAL NATURAL GAS SYSTEMS. a. $17. American Public Gas Association, 11094-D Lee Hwy., Ste. 102, Fairfax, VA 22030.
TEL 703-352-3890. Ed. Carole Curtis. adv.; circ. 750.

665.54 338.47   CN
TP714
DIRECTORY OF NATURAL GAS COMPANY OPERATIONS. 1955. a. Can.$40 to non-members; members Can.$15. Canadian Gas Association, 55 Scarsdale Rd., Don Mills, Ont. M3B 2R3, Canada.
TEL 416-447-6465. FAX 416-447-7067.
   Former titles: Directory of Gas Distribution, Transmission and Production Companies (ISSN 0840-9455); Former titles: Canadian Gas Association Directory; Canadian Gas Utilities Directory (ISSN 0576-5269); Directory of Gas Utilities (ISSN 0315-8349)

662.338   CN   ISSN 0228-5630
DRILLING ACTIVITY REPORT. 1953. m. $120. Saskatchewan Energy and Mines, 1914 Hamilton St., Regina, Sask. S4P 4V4, Canada.
TEL 306-787-2528. FAX 306-787-7338.
   Description: Lists by production and disposition areas and classification of wells.

665.5   US
DRILLING & WELL SERVICING CONTRACTORS. a. $40. Midwest Register, Inc., 601 S. Boulder, Ste. 1001, Tulsa, OK 74119-1301. TEL 918-582-2000.
   Formerly: Directory of Oil Well Drilling Contractors (ISSN 0415-9764)
   Description: Supplies company name, address, phone and fax number and personnel.

PETROLEUM AND GAS

622.338   US   ISSN 0046-0702
TN860
DRILLING CONTRACTOR. 1944. bi-m. $30 (effective Jan. 1991). Drilling Contractor Publications, Inc., Box 4287, Houston, TX 77210. TEL 713-578-7171. FAX 713-578-0589. Ed. Alvaro Franco. adv.; charts; illus.; stat.; tr.lit.; circ. 17,000 (controlled). **Indexed:** Fuel & Energy Abstr., Petrol.Abstr.
—BLDSC shelfmark: 3627.005000.
   Description: Articles feature new technology and promote cooperation among drilling contractors, operators and oilfield suppliers.

665.5   US
DRILLING PERMITS. d. $325. Offshore Data Services, Inc., Box 19909, Houston, TX 77224-9909. TEL 713-781-2713. FAX 713-781-9594.
   Description: Provides current information on new oil drilling permits filed for the U.S. Gulf of Mexico and S. Louisiana.

662.338   US
DRILLING - THE WELLSITE MAGAZINE. 6/yr. Energy Publications, Box 1589, Dallas, TX 75221-1589. TEL 214-691-3911.
   Description: Covers wellsite operations in the energy industry.

665.5 620.85   US   ISSN 1054-6464
TD195.M5
▼**E & P ENVIRONMENT.** (Exploration & Production) 1990. fortn. $347 (foreign $362). Pasha Publications Inc., 1401 Wilson Blvd., Ste. 900, Arlington, VA 22209-9970. TEL 703-528-1244. FAX 703-528-1253. Ed. Jerry Grisham.
   Description: Covers environmental issues affecting the oil and gas industries, including news of federal and state actions, enforcement and regulation, as well as trends in risk management and liability.

622 665   FR   ISSN 0012-7701
E L F AQUITAINE; bulletin mensuel d'informations. 1966. m. free. E L F - Aquitaine, Direction des Relations Publiques et de la Communication, Tour ELF, Cedex 45, 92078 Paris la Defense, France. FAX 47-44-68-21. Ed. B. Lefranc. illus.; stat.; circ. 18,500. **Indexed:** Georef.
   Former titles: E L F; E R A P. Bulletin Mensuel d'Informations.

622 665   FR   ISSN 0249-1729
E L F - AQUITAINE NEWS. (Text in English) 1982. m. free. E L F - Aquitaine, Directions des Relations Publiques et de la Communication, Tour ELF, 92078 Paris La Defense Cedex 45, France. FAX 47-44-32-32. Ed. Brice Lefranc. adv.; charts; illus.; stat.; circ. 8,000.

665.5   SP
ENCICLOPEDIA NACIONAL DEL PETROLEO PETROLQUIMICA Y GAS. 1970. a. $150. Oilgas S.A., Paseo de la Habana, 48, 28003 Madrid, Spain. Ed. Carlos Martin. circ. 6,000.
   Description: Spanish national encyclopedia on the petroleum, petrochemical and gas activities.

ENERGIEWIRTSCHAFTLICHE TAGESFRAGEN; Zeitschrift fuer Energie-Wirtschaft, Recht und Technik. see *ENERGY*

ENERGY ANALECTS. see *ENERGY*

665.5   SI
ENERGY ASIA; weekly newsletter on Asia's energy industry. (Text in English) 1979. w. $150. Petroleum News Publishing Pte. Ltd., 43 Middle Road, 04-00, Singapore 0718, Singapore. TEL 3367128. FAX 3367919. Ed. Julie Bundy. circ. 6,000. (back issues avail.)

ENERGY DIGEST. see *ENERGY*

ENERGY IN JAPAN. see *ENERGY*

ENERGY POLICY; international journal of the political, economic, planning and social aspects of energy. see *ENERGY*

ENERGY PROCESSING - CANADA. see *ENERGY*

ENERGY REPORT. see *ENERGY*

ENERGY REPORT; energy policy and technology news bulletin. see *ENERGY*

ENERGY SOURCES; an international interdisciplinary journal of science and technology. see *ENERGY*

ENERGY TODAY. see *ENERGY*

ENERGY TRENDS. see *ENERGY*

ENERGY WORLD. see *ENERGY*

665.5 620   US   ISSN 0160-337X
ENHANCED OIL-RECOVERY FIELD REPORTS. 1975. s-a. $35 to non-members (typically set in June). Society of Petroleum Engineers, Inc., Box 833836, Richardson, TX 75083-3836. TEL 214-669-3377. FAX 214-669-0135. TELEX 730989 SPEDAL. charts; circ. 1,500. (back issues avail.) **Indexed:** Petrol.Abstr.
—BLDSC shelfmark: 3775.410000.
   Formerly: Improved Oil-Recovery Field Reports. *Refereed Serial*

665.7   IT   ISSN 0071-0687
ENTE NAZIONALE IDROCARBURI. REPORT AND STATEMENT OF ACCOUNTS. a. Ente Nazionale Idrocarburi, Piazzale Enrico Mattei 1, 00144 Rome, Italy.

665 338.2   AU
ERDOEL. 1969. 6/yr. free. Shell Austria AG, Rennweg 12, A-1030 Vienna, Austria. TEL 431-79797-206. FAX 431-79797-201. TELEX 133241-SHEL-A. Ed. G. Krutina. index; circ. 4,800.
   Supersedes: Shell Erdoel-Informationen (ISSN 0037-3567)

665.5   GW   ISSN 0179-3187
TN860   CODEN: EEKOEY
ERDOEL - ERDGAS - KOHLE; Aufsuchung und Gewinnung, Verarbeitung und Anwendung, Petrochemie, chemische Kohlenveredlung. (Annual Directory number avail.) (Summaries in English and German) 1884. m. DM.316. (German Scientific Society of Petroleum, Gas and Coal Chemistry) Urban-Verlag GmbH, Postfach 701606, 2000 Hamburg 70, Germany. TEL 040-6567071. FAX 040-6567075. (Co-sponsors: Austrian Society of Petroleum Sciences) Eds. T. Vieth, H.J. Mager. adv.; bk.rev.; abstr.; bibl.; charts; illus.; stat.; index; circ. 4,140. **Indexed:** API Abstr, API Catal., API Hlth.& Environ., API Oil., API Pet.Ref., API Pet.Subst., API Transport., Bibl.& Ind.Geol., Br.Geol.Lit., Chem.Abstr., Eng.Ind., Fuel & Energy Abstr., Gas Abstr., Petrol.Abstr.
—BLDSC shelfmark: 3799.720000.
   Former titles: Erdoel-Erdgas (ISSN 0724-8555); Erdoel-Erdgas Zeitschrift (ISSN 0014-004X)

ERDOEL-INFORMATIONSDIENST. see *ENERGY*

665.5 662.6   GW   ISSN 0014-0058
   CODEN: EKEPAB
ERDOEL UND KOHLE, ERDGAS, PETROCHEMIE; hydrocarbon technology. (Text in German and English) 1947. m. DM.358.20 (foreign DM.366). Konradin-Industrieverlag GmbH, Ernst-Mey-Str. 8, Postfach 100252, 7022 Leinfelden-Echterdingen, Germany. TEL 0711-75940. Ed. Dr. Kambam Ritapal. adv.; bk.rev.; bibl.; charts; illus.; stat.; tr.lit.; index; circ. 4,087. **Indexed:** Anal.Abstr., API Abstr., API Catal., API Hlth.& Environ., API Oil., API Pet.Ref., API Pet.Subst., API Transport., C.I.S. Abstr., Chem.Abstr., Chem.Eng.Abstr., Chem.Infd., Energy Info.Abstr., Excerp.Med., Fluidex, Fuel & Energy Abstr., Gas Abstr., INIS Atomind., Key to Econ.Sci., Petrol.Abstr., PROMT, Risk Abstr., Sci.Cit.Ind, T.C.E.A.
—BLDSC shelfmark: 3800.010000.
   Incorporated: Brennstoffchemie (ISSN 0006-9620)
   Description: Covers current topics, science and technology, industry news and information. Includes abstracts and calendar of events.

665   MY
ESSO IN MALAYSIA. (Text in English, Malay) 1962. m. free. Esso Malaysia Berhad, P.O. Box 10601, Kuala Lumpur, Malaysia. TEL 03-2428760. FAX 03-2422521. (Co-sponsor: Esso Production Malaysia Inc.) Ed. Chan Soon Ching. illus.; circ. 3,900.
   Formerly: Esso News (ISSN 0014-102X)

665   NE   ISSN 0014-1046
ESSOBRON. 1951. 4/yr. DM.35. Esso Nederland B.V., Jan van Nassaustraat 129-131, The Hague, Netherlands. FAX 070-324-3319. Ed. Joh. Diepraam. illus.; circ. 10,000 (controlled). **Indexed:** Key to Econ.Sci.

665.5   SP
ESTADISTICO DEL PETROLEO. BOLETIN. Short title: B E P. 1986. m. free. Ministerio de Economia y Hacienda, Delegacion del Gobierno en Campsa, Capitan Haya, 41, 28020 Madrid, Spain. TEL 582 52 06.

665.5   NO   ISSN 0802-9474
EUROIL; European oil and gas journal. (Text in English) 1973. m. £80($198) Noroil Publishing House Ltd. AS, P.O. Box 480, 4001 Stavanger, Norway. (Subscr. to: Richard Fry and Associates, Ste. 225, Surrey House, 34 Eden St., Kingston upon Thames, Surrey KT1 1ER, England. TEL 081-549-3444) Ed. Ole-Jacob Kvinnsland. adv.; bk.rev.; charts; illus.; stat.; tr.lit.; circ. 13,000. **Indexed:** Bibl.& Ind.Geol., BMT, Br.Geol.Lit., Br.Tech.Ind., Energy Info.Abstr., Petrol.Abstr.
—BLDSC shelfmark: 3829.268800.
   Formerly (until 1990): Noroil (ISSN 0332-544X)

338.2 665   GW   ISSN 0014-2824
EUROPE OIL-TELEGRAM. 1963. 2/w. DM.1265. KG Oil-Telegram GmbH und Co., Carl-Petersen-Str. 70-76, Postfach 261712, 2000 Hamburg 26, Germany. FAX 040-256392. Ed. Dieter W. Gripp. adv.; bk.rev.; circ. 1,000.
—BLDSC shelfmark: 3829.480500.

665.5   NO   ISSN 0332-5210
EUROPEAN OFFSHORE PETROLEUM NEWSLETTER. (Text in English) 1976. w. £495($935) Noroil Publishing House Ltd. AS, P.O. Box 480, 4001 Stavanger, Norway. (Subscr. to: Richard Fry and Associates, Ste. 225, Surrey House, 34 Eden St., Kingston upon Thames, Surrey KT1 1ER, England. TEL 081-549-3444) Ed. Dan Rigden.

665.5   US   ISSN 0275-3871
HD9575.A12
EUROPEAN PETROLEUM DIRECTORY. 1979. a. $115 (or $210 as a 2 volume set with Asia-Pacific-Africa-Middle East Directory). Pennwell Publishing Co., Box 1260, Tulsa, OK 74101. TEL 918-835-3161. FAX 918-831-9497. TELEX 211012. Ed. Jonelle Moore. adv.
   Supersedes in part: Eastern Hemisphere Petroleum Directory (ISSN 0070-8224)
   Description: Lists companies involved in drilling, refining, exploration, pipelines, engineering, field services, construction and any other petroleum-related operations.

665.5   GW   ISSN 0342-6947
HD9575.A1
EUROPEAN PETROLEUM YEARBOOK/JAHRBUCH DER EUROPAEISCHEN ERDOELINDUSTRIE/ANNUAIRE EUROPEEN DU PETROLE. Variant title: A N E P. (Text in English, French and German) 1963. a. DM.168. Urban Verlag Hamburg-Wien GmbH, Postfach 701606, 2000 Hamburg 70, Germany. FAX 040-6567071. Ed. Thomas Vieth. adv.; circ. 2,000.
—BLDSC shelfmark: 0900.450000.

665.5   UK   ISSN 0956-6333
EUROPETROLEUM; with Aberdeen Petroleum Quarterly. 1989. q. £40. Aberdeen Petroleum Publishing Ltd., 37 Huntly St., Aberdeen AB1 1TJ, Scotland. TEL 0224-644725. FAX 0224-647574. Ed. Ted Strachan. circ. controlled.
   Formerly: Aberdeen Petroleum Quarterly.
   Description: News and business intelligence about the petroleum industry.

EXPERIMENTAL PETROLEUM GEOLOGY. see *EARTH SCIENCES — Geology*

665.5   US
EXPLORATION DAILY. d. $50 (fax delivery avail.). Petroleum Information Corporation, Box 2162, Denver, CO 80201-2162. TEL 303-740-7100. FAX 303-694-1754.
   Description: Covers important petroleum exploration news, including wildcats, new discoveries, and land plays.

665.538   US
F M A TODAY. 1976. fortn. membership. Fuel Merchants Association of New Jersey, 66 Morris Ave., Springfield, NJ 07081. TEL 201-467-1400. FAX 201-467-4066. Ed. Marjorie R. Krampf. circ. 900.

FACTS & FIGURES; a graphical analysis of world energy. see *ENERGY*

PETROLEUM AND GAS

665.5 US
FEDERAL COAL MANAGEMENT REPORT. 1977. a. U.S. Department of the Interior, Bureau of Land Management, Washington, DC 20240. TEL 202-343-5717. circ. 1,800.
Description: Discusses status of Federal Coal Program for preceding fiscal year.

665.5 531.64 US
FEDERAL TAXATION OF OIL AND GAS TRANSACTIONS. 1958. a. Matthew Bender & Co., Inc., 11 Penn Plaza, New York, NY 10001. TEL 212-967-7707. (Subscr. to: 1275 Broadway, New York, NY 12201) Eds. Cecil L. Smith, Robert Poleroi. (looseleaf format)

665.5 UK
FIELD & PRODUCTION REPORT. m. £500. Arthur Andersen & Co., Petroleum Services Group, 1 Surrey St., London WC2R 2PS, England. TEL 071-438-3888. FAX 071-438-3881. TELEX 8812711.
Description: Presents summary of monthly production rates from the producing fields of Northwest Europe. Provides production figures for all the oil, gas and condensate fields in the North Sea and onshore UK.

FILTRATION NEWS. see *ENVIRONMENTAL STUDIES*

665.5 UK ISSN 0141-3228
HG4821
FINANCIAL TIMES INTERNATIONAL YEAR BOOKS: OIL AND GAS. 1910. a. £115. Longman Group UK Ltd., Westgate House, The High, Harlow, Essex CM20 1YR, England. TEL 0279-442601. (Dist. in U.S. and Canada by: St. James Press, 425 North Michigan Ave., Chicago IL 60611)
—BLDSC shelfmark: 3927.005000.
Formerly: Oil and Petroleum Year Book.

668 UK ISSN 0141-3236
HD9560.3
FINANCIAL TIMES INTERNATIONAL YEAR BOOKS: WHO'S WHO IN WORLD OIL AND GAS. a. £95. Longman Group UK Ltd., Westgate House, The High, Harlow, Essex CM20 1YR, England. TEL 0279-442601.
—BLDSC shelfmark: 9312.560000.

665.5 AT
FLAME. 1976. q. free. Australian Gas Light Co., 111 Pacific Highway Nth., Sydney, N.S.W. 2000, Australia. Ed. M. Tesoriero. circ. 4,000.

665.5 UK
FLEET LIST. 1981. q. free. Shell Tankers (UK) Ltd., Shell Centre, London SE1 7PQ, England. Ed. Terence Ryan. adv.; circ. 3,500.
Formerly (until 1988): British Fleet List.

FLUESSIGGAS. see *ENERGY*

622 FR ISSN 0046-4481
FORAGES. 1958. q. $25. Association Amicale des Anciens Eleves des Ecoles de Maitres-Sondeurs et des Sessions de Perfectionnement Forage Production de l'Institut Francais du Petrole, B.P. 311, 92506 Rueil-Malmaison Cedex, France. Ed J.M. Thirault. adv.; bibl.; charts; illus.; stat.; tr.lit.; index, cum.index; circ. 3,300.

662 US ISSN 0095-1587
KF1870.A15
FOSTER NATURAL GAS REPORT. 1956. w. $925. Foster Associates, 1015 15th St., N.W., Washington, DC 20005-2605. TEL 202-408-7710. FAX 202-408-7723. Ed. M.W. Rockefeller. index; circ. 1,100.
● Also available online. Vendor(s): Mead Data Central.

665.5 VE
FRENTE NACIONAL PRO-DEFENSA DEL PETROLEO VENEZOLANO. ACTUACIONES. 1970. irreg. $5 per no. Frente Nacional Pro Defensa del Petroleo Venezolano, Apto. 50514, Caracas 105, Venezuela. circ. 3,000.

662.6 UK ISSN 0016-2361
CODEN: FUELAC
FUEL; science and technology of fuel and energy. 1922. m. £525 (Europe £570). Butterworth - Heinemann Ltd. (Subsidiary of: Reed International PLC), Linacre House, Jordan Hill, Oxford OX2 8DP, England. TEL 0865-310366. FAX 0865-310898. TELEX 83111 BHPOXF G. (Subscr. to: Turpin Transactions, Distribution Centre, Blackhorse Rd., Letchworth, Herts SG6 1HN, England. TEL 0462-672555) Ed.Bd. adv.; bk.rev.; illus.; index, cum.index: 1922-1981. (also avail. in microfilm from UMI; back issues avail.) **Indexed:** Acid Rain Abstr., Acid Rain Ind., AESIS, API Abstr., API Catal., API Hlth.& Environ., API Oil., API Pet.Ref., API Pet.Subst., API Transport., Appl.Mech.Rev., Br.Ceram.Abstr., Br.Tech.Ind., Cadscan, Chem.Abstr., Curr.Cont., Energy Abstr., Energy Info.Abstr., Energy Rev., Eng.Ind., Environ.Abstr., Excerp.Med., GeoRef, Ind.Sci.Rev., Lead Abstr., Mass Spectr.Bull., Petrol.Abstr., Sci.Cit.Ind, Zincscan.
—BLDSC shelfmark: 4048.000000.
Description: Studies the nature, conservation, preparation, use, physical and nuclear properties of gaseous, liquid and solid fuels.
Refereed Serial

388.324 665.538 UK
FUEL OIL NEWS AND ROAD TANKER TRANSPORT. 1977. m. £40.85. Fuel Oil News Ltd., Regent House, Bexton Lane, Knutsford, Cheshire WA16 9AB, England. TEL 0565-53283. FAX 0565-55607. Ed. James Smith. adv.
Description: News, views and information for the oil fuel distribution trade.

662.6 NE ISSN 0378-3820
TP315 CODEN: FPTEDY
FUEL PROCESSING TECHNOLOGY; an international journal devoted to all aspects of processing coal, oil shale, tar sands and peat. (Text in English) 1978. 9/yr. (in 3 vols.; 3 nos./vol.) fl.993 (effective 1992). Elsevier Science Publishers B.V., P.O. Box 211, 1000 AE Amsterdam, Netherlands. TEL 020-5803911. FAX 020-5803598. TELEX 18582 ESPA NL. (Subscr. in U.S. and Canada to: Elsevier Science Publishing Co., Inc., Box 882, Madison Sq. Sta., New York, NY 10159. TEL 212-989-5800) Ed.Bd. (also avail. in microfilm from RPI) **Indexed:** AESIS, Chem.Abstr., Curr.Cont., Energy Ind., Energy Info.Abstr., Energy Rev., Eng.Ind., Environ.Abstr., Environ.Per.Bibl., Excerp.Med., Fuel & Energy Abstr., Gas Abstr., Ind.Sci.Rev., Petrol.Abstr., Sci.Cit.Ind.
—BLDSC shelfmark: 4052.760000.
Description: Deals with the scientific and technological aspects of processing fuels to other fuels, chemicals and by-products.
Refereed Serial

665.538 US
▼**FUEL REFORMULATION.** 1991. bi-m. $149. Information Resources, Inc., 499 S. Capitol St., S.W., Ste. 406, Washington, DC 20003. TEL 202-554-0614. FAX 202-554-0613. Ed. Richard A. Corgett. adv.; circ. 8,000.
Description: Analyzes the business, technical and regulatory circumstances associated with the manufacture, supply and use of transportation fuels, reformulated to improve air quality worldwide.

665.7 662 US
TP690.A1
FUELOIL & OIL HEAT. 1922. m. $20. Industry Publications, Inc. (Fairfield), 389 Passaic Ave., Fairfield, NJ 07006. TEL 201-227-5151. FAX 201-227-9219. Ed. Paul Geiger. adv.; illus.; stat.; circ. 13,300. (also avail. in microfilm from UMI; back issues avail.; reprint service avail.) **Indexed:** B.P.I, Bus.Ind., Chem.Abstr., Fuel & Energy Abstr., Tr.& Indus.Ind.
Former titles: Fueloil and Oil Heat and Solar Systems (ISSN 0148-9801); (until vol.36, no.8, Aug. 1977): Fueloil and Oil Heat (ISSN 0016-2418)

665.5 620 US
G P S A ENGINEERING DATA BOOK. (In 2 vols.) irreg., latest 10th ed. $65 to non-members; members $35. Gas Processors Suppliers Association, Box 35584, Tulsa, OK 74153. TEL 918-493-3872. FAX 918-493-3875. TELEX 910-845-2191.
Description: Compiles basic design information, current technical data, and approved procedures for use by gas processing personnel to determine operating and design parameters for hydrocarbon processing and related facilities.

665.7 US
G R I D. (Gas Research Institute Digest) 1976. q. free. Gas Research Institute, Technical Communications Department, 8600 W. Bryn Mawr Ave., Chicago, IL 60631. TEL 312-399-8100. FAX 312-399-8170. TELEX 253812. Ed. Cheryl G. Drugan. index; circ. 14,000 (controlled). (back issues avail.) **Indexed:** Energy Info.Abstr., Environ.Abstr., Gas Abstr.
Description: Natural gas research of a technical nature explained in simplified terms.

665.7 628 SZ
CODEN: GWASA4
G W A/G E E U - GAZ EAUX EAUX USEES. (Text in English, French and German) 1921. m. 190 Fr. Schweizerischer Verein des Gas- und Wasserfaches - Societe Suisse de l'Industrie du Gaz et des Eaux, Gruetlistr. 44, CH-8027 Zurich, Switzerland. TEL 01-2883333. FAX 01-2021633. Ed. C. Nagel. adv.; bk.rev.; bibl.; charts; illus.; stat.; index; circ. 1,600. (back issues avail.) **Indexed:** C.I.S. Abstr., Chem.Abstr.
Former titles: G W A - Gas Wasser Abwasser (ISSN 0036-8008); Schweizerischer Verein von Gas und Wasserfachmaennern. Monatsbulletin.

665.7 NE ISSN 0016-4828
TP700
GAS. (Text in Dutch; summaries in English) 1880. m. (11/yr.) fl.95. Stichting Tijdschrift Openbare Gasvoorziening, Postbus 137, 7300 AC Apeldoorn, Netherlands. TEL 055-494-949. FAX 055-418963. TELEX 49456. Ed. P. Moody. adv.; bk.rev.; charts; illus.; pat.; stat.; index; circ. 2,600. (also avail. in microfilm from UMI; reprint service avail. from UMI) **Indexed:** A.S.& T.Ind., Chem.Abstr., Eng.Ind., Excerp.Med., Gas Abstr., Int.Build.Serv.Abstr., Key to Econ.Sci., Met.Abstr.
Description: Contains information on the gas industry; distribution, applications and supply.

665.538 GW ISSN 0343-2092
TN880.A1
GAS; internationale Zeitschrift fuer wirtschaftliche und umweltfreudliche Energieanwendung. 1949. 6/yr. DM.103. (Bundesverband der deutschen Gas-und Wasserwirtschaft e.V.) R. Oldenbourg Verlag GmbH, Postfach 801360, Rosenheimerstr. 145, 8000 Munich 80, Germany. (Co-sponsors: Deutscher Verein des Gas-und Wasserfaches; Fachverband Heiz-und Kochgeraete Industrie; Technische Vereinigung der Firmen im Gas-und Wasserfach) adv.; bk.rev.; circ. 5,500. **Indexed:** Key to Econ.SCi.
—BLDSC shelfmark: 4073.100000.
Description: Trade publication for the natural gas industry covering technology, air pollution control, energy savings, economics and international news.

662 AT ISSN 0072-0208
GAS AND FUEL CORPORATION OF VICTORIA. ANNUAL REPORT. 1851. a. free. Gas and Fuel Corporation of Victoria, 171 Flinders St., Melbourne 3000, Vic., Australia. FAX 03-652-4801. TELEX AA31422. Ed. L.E. Curnow. circ. 9,500.

665.5 US ISSN 0897-8778
CODEN: GBGUEX
GAS BUYERS GUIDE. 1974. w. $427 (foreign $457). Pasha Publications Inc., 1401 Wilson Blvd., Ste. 900, Arlington, VA 22209-9970. TEL 703-528-1244. FAX 703-528-1253. Daniel Macey. stat.; circ. 350. (back issues avail.)
Formerly (until 1984): Inside Oil and Gas.
Description: Covers legal, technological and legislative matters affecting the gas industry.

665.7 US ISSN 0885-5935
GAS DAILY. 1974. d. (5/wk.). $897 (foreign $985). Pasha Publications Inc., 1401 Wilson Blvd., Ste. 900, Arlington, VA 22209-9970. TEL 703-528-1244. Ed. Daniel Macey. circ. 1,400. (back issues avail.)
● Also available online. Vendor(s): Data-Star, DIALOG.
Formerly (until 1985): Inside Gas Markets.

662 US ISSN 0161-4851
TP700
GAS DIGEST; the magazine of gas operations. 1975. q. $12 to qualified personnel; others $20. Tri-Plek Productions, Box 35819, Houston, TX 77035. TEL 713-723-7456. Ed. Ken Kridner. adv.; bk.rev.; circ. 3,500. **Indexed:** Fuel & Energy Abstr., Petrol.Abstr.

665.7 UK ISSN 0306-6444
TP700 CODEN: GEMABL
GAS ENGINEERING & MANAGEMENT. 1961. 10/yr. £30 to non-members. Institution of Gas Engineers, 17 Grosvenor Crescent, London SW1X 7ES, England. Ed. Barrie Atkinson. adv.; bibl.; charts; illus.; stat.; index; circ. 6,000. (also avail. in microform from UMI; reprint service avail. from UMI) **Indexed:** API Abstr., API Catal., API Hlth.& Environ., API Oil., API Pet.Ref., API Pet.Subst., API Transport., Br.Ceram.Abstr., Br.Tech.Ind., C.I.S. Abstr., Eng.Ind., Excerp.Med., Fuel & Energy Abstr., Gas Abstr., Int.Build.Serv.Abstr., Met.Abstr., W.R.C.Inf., World Alum.Abstr.
—BLDSC shelfmark: 4077.550000.
Formerly: Institution of Gas Engineers. Journal (ISSN 0020-3432)

665.7 628 338.2 GW ISSN 0016-4909
CODEN: GWGEAQ
GAS - ERDGAS - G W F; das Gas- und Wasserfach. 1858. m. DM.312 to non-members; members DM.208. (Deutsche Verein der Gas -und Wasserfaches Bundesverband der Deutscher Gas- und Wasserwirtschaft (DVGW)) R. Oldenbourg Verlag GmbH, Rosenheimerstr. 145, 8000 Munich 80, Germany. adv.; bk.rev.; abstr.; charts; illus.; mkt.; tr.lit.; tr.mk.; index. **Indexed:** API Abstr., API Catal., API Hlth.& Environ., API Oil., API Pet.Ref., API Pet.Subst., API Transport., C.I.S. Abstr., Chem.Abstr., Eng.Ind., Excerp.Med., Fuel & Energy Abstr.
—BLDSC shelfmark: 4085.050000.
Description: Trade publication for the gas industry featuring gas production, distribution, installation and technology. Includes events, patents and positions available.

665 US
GAS FACTS; a statistical record of the gas utility industry. 1946. a. $50 to non-members; members $25. American Gas Association, Department of Statistics, 1515 Wilson Blvd., Arlington, VA 22209. TEL 703-841-8490. FAX 703-841-8406. (Subscr. to: Dept 0765, McLean, VA 22109-0765) circ. 3,000. **Indexed:** SRI.

665.7 US
TP350
GAS INDUSTRIES MAGAZINE; the operations engineering management magazine of gas energy pipeline transmission, utility distribution. 1956. m. $20 (foreign $90). Gas Industries Inc., Box 558, Park Ridge, IL 60068. TEL 708-693-3682. FAX 708-696-3445. Ed. Ruth W. Stidger. adv.; bk.rev.; circ. 11,000. **Indexed:** Corros.Abstr., Gas Abstr.
Formerly: Gas Industries E and A News (ISSN 0194-2468); **Incorporates:** Better Schools (Chicago) (ISSN 0363-373X); Industrial Energy (ISSN 0094-1646); Gas in Industry (ISSN 0016-4933)

665.7 UK ISSN 0954-853X
GAS INDUSTRY DIRECTORY (YEAR). 1896. a. £60 (foreign £70). Benn Business Information Services Ltd., P.O. Box 20, Sovereign Way, Tonbridge, Kent TN9 1RQ, England. TEL 0732-362666. FAX 0732-770483. TELEX 95162-BENTON-G. Ed. Ann Black. adv.; stat.; index; circ. 1,500.
—BLDSC shelfmark: 4077.940000.
Former titles: Gas Directory and Who's Who (ISSN 0307-3084); Gas Directory and Undertakings of the World; **Incorporates:** Gas Journal Directory (ISSN 0072-0240); Gas Industry Directory (ISSN 0072-0232); Who's Who in the Gas Industry (ISSN 0083-9779)
Description: Complete guide to the gas industry; includes a classified buyers guide, trade names and trade associations.

665.7 IT ISSN 0016-495X
GAS LIQUEFATTI - LE APPARECCHIATURE.* vol.16, 1970. bi-m. L.3000. Editrice Sfera, Via Aurelio Saffi 26, 20123 Milan, Italy.

665.7 UK ISSN 0308-7026
GAS MARKETING.* 1922. m. £45 (foreign £58). Benn Publications Ltd., Sovereign Way, Tonbridge, Kent TN9 1RW, England. TEL 0732-364422. Ed. W. Bentley. adv.; illus.; circ. 14,075. (also avail. in microform from UMI; reprint service avail. from UMI)
Former titles: Gas Marketing (ISSN 0016-4984); Gas Showroom (ISSN 0016-4992); Domestic Gas.

665.5 US
GAS PRICE INDEX. w. $295. Intelligence Press Inc., 425B Carlisle St., Herndon, VA 22070. TEL 703-318-8848. FAX 703-318-0597. (Subscr. to: Box 70587, Washington, DC 20024)
Description: Reports on trading activity and pricing within the domestic spot natural gas market.

665.5 US ISSN 0096-8870
TN880.A1 CODEN: PGPAAC
GAS PROCESSORS ASSOCIATION. ANNUAL CONVENTION. PROCEEDINGS. Title varies: Natural Gas Processors Association. Annual Convention. Proceedings. 1921. a. price varies. Gas Processors Association, 6526 E. 60th St., Tulsa, OK 74145. TEL 918-493-3872. FAX 918-493-3875. TELEX 910-845-2191. circ. 5,000. **Indexed:** API Catal., API Hlth.& Environ., API Oil., API Pet.Ref., API Pet.Subst., API Transport., Chem.Abstr, Fuel & Energy Abstr., Gas Abstr.

665.5 US
GAS PROCESSORS ASSOCIATION. RESEARCH REPORTS. 1971. irreg., latest RR-120. $25 to non-members; members $10. Gas Processors Association, 6526 E. 60th St., Tulsa, OK 74145. TEL 918-493-3872. FAX 918-493-3875. TELEX 910-845-2191.

665.5 US
GAS PROCESSORS ASSOCIATION. TECHNICAL PUBLICATIONS. irreg., latest TP-19. Gas Processors Association, 6526 E. 60th St., Tulsa, OK 74145. TEL 918-493-4872. FAX 918-493-3875. TELEX 910-845-2191.

665.5 CN
GAS SAFETY CODE. base vol. (plus irreg. suppl.). Can.$8.90. Ministry of Municipal Affairs, Recreation and Culture, Victoria, B.C., Canada. (Subscr. to: Crown Publications, 546 Yates St., Victoria, B.C. V8W 1K8, Canada. TEL 604-386-4636) (looseleaf format)

665.5 US ISSN 1057-2279
▼**GAS STORAGE REPORT.** 1991. m. $347 (foreign $362). Pasha Publications Inc., 1401 Wilson Blvd., Ste. 900, Arlington, VA 22209-9970. TEL 703-528-1244. FAX 703-528-1253. Ed. Daniel Macey.
Description: Monitors natural gas storage inventories, withdrawals and injections, open-access storage programs, federal and state regulatory actions, new business ventures, technological innovations and business trends.

622 531.64 AT
GAS SUPPLY AND DEMAND STUDY. 1985. triennial. Aus.$200 for participants report; public report Aus.$10. Australian Gas Association, G.P.O. Box 323, Canberra, A.C.T. 2601, Australia. TEL 06-247-3955. FAX 06-249-7402. TELEX AA62137. Ed. J.C.M. Jones. charts; illus.; stat.
Description: Guide for industry and government to the study of Australia's long-term supply and demand for natural gas.

665.5 DK ISSN 0106-4355
GAS-TEKNIK. 1911. bi-m. DKK 250 (typically set in Jan.). Dansk Gasteknisk Forening, Naturgassens Hus, Dr. Neergaards Vej 5A, DK-2970 Hoersholm, Denmark. TEL 45-766995. FAX 42-57-16-44. Ed. Erik Hansen. adv.; bk.rev.; circ. 1,100.
—BLDSC shelfmark: 4081.700000.

GAS TURBINE WORLD. see *ENGINEERING — Engineering Mechanics And Materials*

665.5 US
GAS UTILITY INDUSTRY. a. $40. Midwest Register, Inc., 601 S. Boulder, Ste. 1001, Tulsa, OK 74119-1301. TEL 918-582-2000.
Formerly: Directory of Gas Utility Companies.
Description: Supplies company name, address, phone and fax number. Includes personnel with their titles.

665.7 628 697 AU ISSN 0016-5018
CODEN: GAWWA6
GAS, WASSER, WAERME. 1947. m. S.1390. Oesterreichische Vereinigung fuer das Gas- und Wasserfach, Ebendorferstr. 10, A-1010 Vienna, Austria. FAX 0222-438693. (Co-sponsor: Fachverband der Gas- und Waermeversorgungsunternehmungen) adv.; bk.rev.; bibl.; charts; illus.; circ. 1,800. **Indexed:** Chem.Abstr., Eng.Ind., Excerp.Med., Fuel & Energy Abstr., Gas Abstr., W.R.C.Inf.
—BLDSC shelfmark: 4086.000000.

665.7 UK
TP700
GAS WORLD INTERNATIONAL.* 1884. m. £52 (foreign £65). Benn Publications Ltd., Sovereign Way, Tonbridge, Kent TN9 1RW, England. TEL 0732-364422. Ed. Alan Bakalor. adv.; bk.rev.; charts; illus.; mkt.; tr.lit.; circ. 3,200. (also avail. in microform from UMI; reprint service avail. from UMI) **Indexed:** Br.Ceram.Abstr., Br.Tech.Ind., C.I.S. Abstr., Chem.Abstr., Eng.Ind., Fuel & Energy Abstr., Gas Abstr., Key to Econ.Sci., Met.Abstr., Petrol.Abstr., PROMT, W.R.C.Inf.
Former titles: Gas World (ISSN 0308-7654); Gas World and Gas and Coke.

665.7 US ISSN 0016-4976
GASCOPE. 1964. q. free. Institute of Gas Technology, 3424 S. State St., Chicago, IL 60616. TEL 312-567-3650. Ed. Carl Sauer. illus.; circ. 15,000. (back issues avail.) **Indexed:** Energy Info.Abstr.
Description: Provides information about the R & D and educational activities of the Institute.

665.5 AT
GASCOR NEWS. 1950. q. free. Gas and Fuel Corporation of Victoria, 171 Flinders St., Melbourne, Vic. 3000, Australia. TEL 03-652-5056. FAX 03-652-4801. TELEX AA31422. Ed. Lin Curnow. circ. 6,000. (back issues avail.)

665.7 SW ISSN 0039-6834
GASNYTT. 1970. q. SEK 320 (foreign Kr.400). Svenska Gasfoereningen, Norrtullsgatan 6, P.O. Box 6405, S-113 82 Stockholm 6, Sweden. FAX 46-8-7288635. Ed. Rolf Johansson. adv.; bk.rev.; charts; illus.; maps; index; circ. 4,000. **Indexed:** Fuel & Energy Abstr., Gas Abstr.
—BLDSC shelfmark: 4087.500000.
Supersedes: Svenska Gasfoereningens Maanadsblad.

665.538 II
GASOIL. (Text in English and Hindi) 1968. q. free. Oil & Natural Gas Commission, Western Regional Business Centre, Department of PR & Communication, Makarpura Rd., Baroda 390 009, India. TEL 550324. FAX 0265-65996. TELEX 0175-363-576. Eds. S.K. Panigrahy, T. Premnak. circ. 6,000.
Description: Contains news and information about the commission for employees. Attempts to reflect the future trends of the organization as well as divergent views on its various activities.

665.7 FR ISSN 0016-5328
TP700
GAZ D'AUJOURD'HUI. 1877. 10/yr. 700 F. Association Technique de l'Industrie du Gaz en France, 62 rue de Courcelles, 75008 Paris, France. Eds. Alain Thibault, Claude Bureau. adv.; bk.rev.; abstr.; illus.; stat.; index; circ. 4,000. **Indexed:** C.I.S. Abstr., Eng.Ind., Gas Abstr., PROMT.
Formerly: Journal des Industries du Gaz.

662 FR ISSN 0072-0321
GAZ DE FRANCE. SECRETARIAT GENERAL. SCHEMA D'ORGANISATION PROFOR.* 1966. a. Gaz de France, 23 rue Philibert, 75804 Paris, France.

662.6 RU ISSN 0016-5581
CODEN: GZVPAJ
GAZOVAYA PROMYSHLENNOST/GAZ INDUSTRY. 1956. m. 22.20 Rub. (Nauchno-Tekhnicheskoe Obshchestvo Neftyanoi i Gazovoi Promyshlennosti) Izdatel'stvo Nedra, Pl. Belorusskogo Vokzala, 3, 125047 Moscow, Russia. TEL 250-52-55. (Co-sponsor: Ministerstvo Gazovoi Promyshlennosti) Ed. S.F. Gudkov. bibl.; charts; illus.; stat.; circ. 8,000. **Indexed:** Chem.Abstr., Fuel & Energy Abstr., Gas Abstr., INIS Atomind.
—BLDSC shelfmark: 0047.020000.

GEOBYTE. see *COMPUTERS*

PETROLEUM AND GAS

553.28   RU   ISSN 0016-7894
CODEN: GENGA9
GEOLOGIYA NEFTI I GAZA. (Text in Russian; contents page in English) 1957. m. 25.20 Rub. (Ministerstvo Geologii) Izdatel'stvo Nedra, Pl. Belorusskogo Vokzala, 3, 125047 Moscow, Russia.
TEL 250-52-55. (Co-sponsors: Ministerstvo Gazovoi Promyshlennosti S.S.S.R.; Ministerstvo Neftedobyvayushchei Promyshlennosti S.S.S.R.; Ministerstvo Geologii S.S.S.R.) Ed. S.P. Maksimov. adv.; bk.rev.; abstr.; bibl.; charts; illus.; stat.; index; circ. 5,000. (tabloid format) Indexed: Chem.Abstr., Eng.Ind, INIS Atomind., Petrol.Abstr.
—BLDSC shelfmark: 0047.620000.

GEOPHYSICAL DIRECTORY. see EARTH SCIENCES — Geophysics

051   US
GO DEVIL. 1941. bi-m. Shell Pipe Line Co., Box 2648, Houston, TX 77252-2648. Ed. Dillon R. Scott. circ. 3,000.
Description: For the employees and retirees of the Company.

GOSPODARKA PALIWAMI I ENERGIA/FUEL AND ENERGY MANAGEMENT. see ENERGY

338.8 531.6   UK
GREAT BRITAIN. DEPARTMENT OF ENERGY. DEVELOPMENT OF THE OIL AND GAS RESOURCES OF THE UNITED KINGDOM. a. Department of Energy, 1 Palace St., London SW1E 5HE, England.
TEL 071-873-0011. (Avail. from: H.M.S.O., P.O. Box 276, London SW8 5DT, England) illus.
Description: Covers exploration and production; includes economic, industrial and environmental aspects.

GUIDE TO U S G S GEOLOGIC AND HYDROLOGIC MAPS. see EARTH SCIENCES

665.5   US   ISSN 0884-7967
HD9567.A13
GULF COAST OIL WORLD. 1981. 9/yr. $39 (foreign $89). Hart Publications, Inc., 1900 Grant St., Ste. 400, Box 1917, Denver, CO 80201.
TEL 303-837-1917. (back issues avail.)
Formerly (until 1985): Gulf Coast Oil Reporter (ISSN 0744-9070)
Description: Covers Louisiana, Mississippi, Florida, Alabama, and East and South Texas.

665.5 662.6   US
▼**GULF COAST PETROPROCESS DIRECTORY.** (Includes Buyer's Guide) 1990. a. I E I, 1635 W. Alabama, Houston, TX 77006. TEL 713-529-1616. FAX 713-529-0936. Ed. Janis Jamieson. adv.; circ. 4,000.
Description: Covers the petrochemical and refining industry.

665.538   US
GULF OF MEXICO DRILLING REPORT. w. $1250. Offshore Data Services, Inc., Box 19909, Houston, TX 77224-9909. TEL 713-781-2713.
FAX 713-781-9594.
Description: Provides performance and statistical information on drilling activity in the U.S. Gulf of Mexico.

665.5   US
GULF OF MEXICO FIELD DEVELOPMENT LOCATOR. m. $250. Offshore Data Services, Inc., Box 19909, Houston, TX 77224-9909. TEL 713-781-2713. FAX 713-781-9594.
Description: Covers new project developments from the planning stages through final installation.

665.5   US   ISSN 1058-5885
GULF OF MEXICO NEWSLETTER. 1986. w. $77. Offshore Data Services, Inc., Box 19909, Houston, TX 77224-9909. TEL 713-781-2713.
FAX 713-781-9594. Ed. Tom Marsh. circ. 2,175.
Description: Follows opportunities, projects, and people in the petroleum drilling and exploration industry along the U.S. Gulf Coast.

665.5 338.2   US
GULF OF MEXICO RIG LOCATOR. w. $500. Offshore Data Services, Inc., Box 19909, Houston, TX 77224-9909. TEL 713-781-2713.
FAX 713-781-9594.
Description: Provides information on all U.S. offshore rigs operating in the Gulf of Mexico.

665   US
GULF OF MEXICO SUMMARY REPORT - INDEX. 1980. a. free. Outer Continental Shelf Information Program, Offshore Information and Publications Office, Minerals Management Service, 381 Elden St., No. 1400, Herndon, VA 22070-4817.
TEL 703-787-1080. circ. 4,000.
Formed by the merger of: Gulf of Mexico Index & Gulf of Mexico Summary Report.
Description: Documents on the federal offshore oil and gas leasing, exploration, development and production.

GUOWAI YOUQI KANTAN. see EARTH SCIENCES — Geology

658.8   US   ISSN 0018-4764
HOOSIER INDEPENDENT. 1934. q. membership. Indiana Oil Marketers Association, Inc., 8780 Purdue Rd., Ste. 4, Indianapolis, IN 46268. FAX 317-875-6721. Ed. Charlene Hillman. adv.; bk.rev.; charts; illus.; tr.lit.; circ. 1,400 (controlled).
Description: For independent oil marketers.

HOUSTON BUSINESS JOURNAL. see BUSINESS AND ECONOMICS — Economic Situation And Conditions

665.5 670   US
HOUSTON OIL DIRECTORY. 1971. a. $39. (International Exhibitions, Inc.) I E I, Publishing Division, 1635 W. Alabama, Houston, TX 77006. TEL 713-529-1616. FAX 713-529-0936. Ed. Janis Jamieson. adv.; circ. 4,000.

665.5 338.2   US
HOUSTON PETROLEUM INDUSTRY. a. $40. Midwest Register, Inc., 15 W. Sixth St., Ste. 1308, Tulsa, OK 74119-1505. TEL 918-582-2000.
Formerly: Oil Directory of Houston, Texas (ISSN 0471-3877)
Description: Supplies company name, address, phone and fax numbers and personnel information, producers, drilling and well service, pipelines, refineries, gas processing, petrochemical, engineering, equipment manufacturers and suppliers.

HUADONG SHIFAN DAXUE XUEBAO (ZHEXUE SHEHUI KEXUE BAN)/EAST CHINA NORMAL UNIVERSITY. JOURNAL. (SOCIAL SCIENCE EDITION). see SOCIAL SCIENCES: COMPREHENSIVE WORKS

HUAGONG ZHI YOU/FRIEND OF CHEMICAL INDUSTRY. see CHEMISTRY

HUAXUE YU NIANHE/CHEMISTRY AND BINDING. see ENGINEERING — Chemical Engineering

HUNTING GROUP REVIEW. see GENERAL INTEREST PERIODICALS — Great Britain

665.5   US
HUTTLINGER'S NATURAL GAS BULLETIN. w. $360. Huttlinger's Energy News, Box 409, Pooolesville, MD 20837. TEL 301-972-8100. Ed. Stan Janet. bibl.; stat. (looseleaf format; back issues avail.)

665.5   US
HUTTLINGER'S OIL REPORT. w. $360. Huttlinger's Energy News, Box 409, Poolesville, MD 20837. TEL 301-972-8100. Ed. Stan Janet. bibl.; stat. (looseleaf format; back issues avail.)

665.5 690   US
HUTTLINGER'S PIPELINE REPORT. w. $360. Huttlinger's Energy News, Box 409, Poolesville, MD 20837. TEL 301-972-8100. Ed. Stan Janet. bibl.; stat. (looseleaf format; back issues avail.)

552   CN
HYDROCARBON AND BYPRODUCT RESERVES. a. Ministry of Energy, Mines and Petroleum Resources, Energy Resources Division, Parliament Bldgs., Victoria, B.C. V8V 1X4, Canada. (Subscr. to: Crown Publications, 546 Yates St., Victoria, B.C. V8W 1K8, Canada. TEL 604-386-4636) (back issues avail.)
Description: Contains tables of the reserves estimated by the division at the end of the year with an explanation of the definitions used throughout. A copy of the stratigraphic correlation chart and a map showing the location of the fields in the province is also included.

665.5   US   ISSN 0018-8190
TP690.A1   CODEN: IHPRBS
HYDROCARBON PROCESSING. 1922. m. $20. Gulf Publishing Co., Box 2608, Houston, TX 77252-2608. TEL 713-529-4301.
FAX 713-520-4433. TELEX 287330 GULF UR. Ed. Harold L. Hoffman. adv.; bk.rev.; charts; illus.; tr.lit.; index; circ. 32,538. (also avail. in microfilm from UMI; back issues avail.; reprint service avail.)
Indexed: A.S.& T.Ind., AESIS, API Abstr., API Catal., API Hlth.& Environ., API Oil., API Pet.Ref., API Pet.Subst., API Transport., Chem.Abstr., Chem.Eng.Abstr., Chem.Infd., Curr.Cont., Energy.Info.Abstr., Energy Rev., Eng.Ind., Excerp.Med., Fluidex, Foul.Prev.Res.Dig., Fuel & Energy Abstr., Gas Abstr., HRIS, Ind.Sci.Rev., INIS Atomind., ISMEC, Ocean.Abstr., Petrol.Abstr., Pollut.Abstr., PROMT, Risk Abstr., Sci.Cit.Ind, Sel.Water Res.Abstr., Soils & Fert., T.C.E.A.
—BLDSC shelfmark: 4343.100000.
Formerly: Hydrocarbon Processing - Petroleum Refiner.

552   CN
HYDROCARBONS RESERVE TAPE. a. Can.$250. Ministry of Energy, Mines and Petroleum Resources, Energy Resources Division, Parliament Bldgs., Victoria, B.C. V8V 1X4, Canada. (Subscr. to: Crown Publications, 546 Yates St., Victoria, B.C. V8W 1K8, Canada. TEL 604-386-4636) (magnetic tape)
Description: Shows all oil and gas reserves in BC and estimates how much has been used and how much is left.

665.5 540 330   CI
I N A VJESNIK INDUSTRIJE NAFTE. (Text in Croatian) 1964. I N A - Industrija Nafte, Proleterskih b.78, 41000 Zagreb, Croatia. TEL 516-411. Ed. Branko Franjic. circ. 25,000.

655.5   US
I U P I W VIEWS. 1945. bi-m. $5. International Union of Petroleum & Industrial Workers, 8131 E. Rosecrano Ave., Paramount, CA 90723. FAX 213-408-1073. Ed. Robert Davidson. circ. 9,000.

665.5   US
ILLINOIS PETROLEUM. 1926. irreg., no.132, 1989. price varies. State Geological Survey, Natural Resources Bldg., 615 E. Peabody Dr., Champaign, IL 61820. TEL 217-344-1481. abstr.; bibl.; charts; illus.; stat.; circ. 3,100. Indexed: AESIS, Bibl.& Ind.Geol., Geo.Abstr., Petrol.Abstr.

665.5   CN   ISSN 0700-5156
IMPERIAL OIL REVIEW/REVUE DE L'IMPERIALE. (Text in English, French) 1917. q. free. Imperial Oil Ltd., 111 St. Clair Ave., W., Toronto, Ont. M5W 1K3, Canada. TEL 416-968-4111. Ed. Wynne Thomas. illus.; index; circ. 60,000. Indexed: Can.Per.Ind., Pt.de Rep. (1989-).
Former titles: Imperial Oil Limited. Review (ISSN 0380-903X); Imperial Oil Review (ISSN 0019-2910)

665.5 531.64 310   US
IMPORTED CRUDE OIL AND PETROLEUM PRODUCTS. 1977. m. $330 to non-members; members $275; Canada and Mexico $363; elsewhere $429. American Petroleum Institute, Publications Department, 1220 L St., N.W., Washington, DC 20005. TEL 202-682-8378. (Subscr. to: 1970 Chain Bridge Rd., McLean, VA 22109-6000) Ed. Claudette Reid. circ. 350. (also avail. in magnetic tape; back issues avail.)

INDEPENDENT ENERGY; the industry's business magazine. see ENERGY

665.5 350   US
INDEPENDENT GASOLINE MARKETING. 1973. bi-m. membership. Society of Independent Gasoline Marketers of America, 11911 Freedom Dr., No. 590, Reston, VA 22090-5602.
TEL 703-709-7007. FAX 703-379-4561. Ed. Angela M. Angerosa. adv.; circ. 4,000 (controlled).
Former titles (until 1987): S I G M A Update; Capitol Digest.
Description: Covers gasoline legislation and issues.

665.5 US
INDEPENDENT LIQUID TERMINALS ASSOCIATION. DIRECTORY OF BULK LIQUID AND STORAGE FACILITIES. 1975. a. $95 (includes Newsletter). Independent Liquid Terminals Association, 1133 15th St., N.W., Ste. 204, Washington, DC 20005. TEL 202-659-2301. FAX 202-466-4166. Ed. E. Bruce Calvert. index; circ. 700.
  Description: Locates 325 bulk liquid terminals and storage facilities, commodities handled and modes served.

665.5 US
INDEPENDENT LIQUID TERMINALS ASSOCIATION. DIRECTORY OF SUPPLIERS OF GOODS & SERVICES. 1982. a. $20. Independent Liquid Terminals Association, 1133 15th St., N.W., Ste. 204, Washington, DC 20005. TEL 202-659-2301. FAX 202-466-4166. Ed. E. Bruce Calvert. index; circ. 700.
  Description: Covers suppliers of goods and services for terminal and tank farm industry.

665.5 US
INDEPENDENT LIQUID TERMINALS ASSOCIATION. NEWSLETTER. 1975. m. $95 (includes Directory). Independent Liquid Terminals Association, 1133 15th St., N.W., Ste. 204, Washington, DC 20005. TEL 202-659-2301. FAX 202-466-4166. Ed. John Prokop. circ. 1,000.
  Description: Covers legislation and regulations affecting terminals, the tank farm industry and related industries.

662.338 II
▼**INDIAN JOURNAL OF PETROLEUM GEOLOGY.** (Text in English) 1992. q. Rs.600($80) Indian Petroleum Publishing Co., 100-9, Naishville Road, Dehra Dun 248 001, India. Ed. A.T.R. Raju.
  Description: Provides a forum for the exchange of scientific and technical information concerning petroleum exploration in Southeast Asian countries in particular and the world in general.

665.5 II
INDIAN PETROCHEMICAL INDUSTRY DESKBOOK. (Text in English) 1984. biennial. $45. Technical Press Publications, 5-1 Convent Street, Colaba, Bombay 400 039, India. TEL 2021446. TELEX 011-3479-CHEM-IN. Ed. J.P. Sousa. adv.; bk.rev.; abstr.; charts; illus.; circ. 6,400.

338.7 II
INDO-BURMA PETROLEUM COMPANY. ANNUAL REPORT. (Text in English) a. Indo-Burma Petroleum Company, Gillander House, Netaji Subhas Rd., P.O. Box 952, Calcutta 700 001, India. stat.

665.5 IT ISSN 0073-7275
INDUSTRIA DEL PETROLIO IN ITALIA. a. Direzione Generale delle Fonti di Energia e Industrie di Base, Via Molise 2, 00187 Rome, Italy. charts; stat.

665.5 338.2 MX ISSN 0187-487X
INDUSTRIA PETROLERA EN MEXICO. 1979. irreg. Mex.$2500($22) Instituto Nacional de Estadistica, Geografia e Informatica, Secretaria de Programacion y Presupuesto, Prol. Heroe de Nacozari, 2301, Acceso 10, C.P. 20290, Aguascalientes, Ags., Mexico. TEL 91-491-81968. FAX 91-491-80739. (Subscr. to: Rio Rhin No. 56, Col. Cuauhtemoc, 06500 Mexico, D.F., Mexico) circ. 1,000.

665.5 GW ISSN 0341-3756
DIE INDUSTRIEFEUERUNG. Short title: I F. 3/yr. price varies. Vulkan-Verlag GmbH, Hollestr. 1G, Postfach 103962, 4300 Essen, Germany. TEL 0201-82002-0. FAX 0201-82002-40.
  —BLDSC shelfmark: 4474.753000.

665.5 MX
INGENIERIA PETROLERA. 1959. m. $76. Asociacion de Ingenieros Petroleros de Mexico A.C., Apdo. Postal 53-013, CP-11490 Mexico, D.F., Mexico. Ed. Eduardo Lozano Vistuer. adv.; circ. 2,000.

665.5 US
INSIDE F E R C'S GAS MARKET REPORT. (U.S. Federal Energy Regulatory Commission) 1985. bi-w. $715 (foreign $740). McGraw-Hill, Inc., Energy & Business Newsletters, 1221 Ave. of the Americas, 36th Fl., New York, NY 10020. TEL 212-512-6410. Ed. Larry Foster. (reprint service avail. from UMI)
  ●Also available online. Vendor(s): DIALOG (File no.624/McGRAW-HILL PUBLICATIONS ONLINE), Dow Jones/News Retrieval (GSMR), Mead Data Central (GASMKT).

665.5 FR ISSN 0073-8360
TN860 CODEN: IPTCBP
INSTITUT FRANCAIS DU PETROLE. COLLECTION COLLOQUES ET SEMINAIRES. 1964. irreg., vol.49, 1991. price varies. Editions Technip, 27 rue Ginoux, 75737 Paris Cedex 15, France. TEL 45-77-11-08. FAX 45-75-37-11. TELEX EDITECP 200375F. circ. 1,250. **Indexed:** Bull.Signal., Chem.Abstr., Geophys.Abstr., Petrol.Abstr.

665.5 FR ISSN 0073-8379
INSTITUT FRANCAIS DU PETROLE. RAPPORT ANNUEL. (Text in English, French) 1963. a. free. Institut Francais du Petrole (IFP), 1 et 4 av. de Bois-Preau, B.P. No. 311, 92506 Rueil-Malmaison Cedex, France. TEL 47-49-02-14. FAX 33-1-47-49-04-11. TELEX IFPA 203 050 F. circ. 8,000. **Indexed:** Ocean.Abstr., Petrol.Abstr.

665 FR
INSTITUT FRANCAIS DU PETROLE. REVUE. (Text in English, French; summaries in English, French, Spanish) 1946. 6/yr. 1230 F. Editions Technip, 27 rue Ginoux, 75737 Paris Cedex 15, France. TEL 45-77-11-08. FAX 45-75-37-11. TELEX EDITECP 200375F. bk.rev.; bibl.; charts; illus.; index, cum.index: 1946-1960, 1961-1965, 1966-1970, 1971-1975, 1976-1980, 1981-1985, 1986-1990; circ. 1,400. **Indexed:** API Abstr., API Catal., API Hlth.& Environ., API Oil., API Pet.Ref., API Pet.Subst., API Transport., Appl.Mech.Rev., Bibl.& Ind.Geol., C.I.S. Abstr., Chem.Abstr., Chem.Eng.Abstr., Curr.Cont., Deep Sea Res.& Oceanogr.Abstr., Eng.Ind., Excerp.Med., Geo.Abstr., Petrol.Abstr., T.C.E.A.
  Formerly: Institut Francais du Petrole. Revue et Annales des Liquides Combustibles (ISSN 0020-2274)

665.5 BE ISSN 0020-2185
CODEN: AIBPD9
INSTITUT ROYAL BELGE DU PETROLE. ANNALES/KONINKLIJK BELGISCH PETROLEUM INSTITUUT. ANNALEN. (Text in Dutch, English, French, German) 1967. q. 1000 Fr. Institut Royal Belge du Petrole, 4 rue de la Science, 1040 Brussels, Belgium. Ed. Joris De Smet. bk.rev.; circ. 1,000.
  Description: Contains information concerning all aspects of the petroleum industry in Belgium.

665.5 551 IS ISSN 0073-8832
INSTITUTE FOR PETROLEUM RESEARCH AND GEOPHYSICS, HOLON, ISRAEL. REPORT. irreg. Institute for Petroleum Research and Geophysics, Box 1717, Holon, Israel.

INSTITUTE OF ENERGY. JOURNAL. see *ENERGY*

662 US
INSTITUTE OF GAS TECHNOLOGY. ANNUAL REPORT. a. free. Institute of Gas Technology, 3424 S. State St., Chicago, IL 60616. TEL 312-567-3650. Ed. Colleen Taylor Sen. stat.
  Formerly: Institute of Gas Technology. Director's Report.

665.5 340 US
INSTITUTE ON OIL AND GAS LAW AND TAXATION. PROCEEDINGS. 1949. a. $11. Southwestern Legal Foundation, Attn: Carol Holgren, Ed., Box 830707, Richardson, TX 75083. TEL 214-690-2370. index. (also avail. in microfilm from RRI; reprint service avail. from RRI)

665 UK ISSN 0367-7850
CODEN: IGECBN
INSTITUTION OF GAS ENGINEERS. PROCEEDINGS. 1971. s-a. Institution of Gas Engineers, 17 Grosvenor Crescent, London SW1X 7ES, England. Ed. Barrie Atkinson. **Indexed:** F.A.C.T., Gas Abstr.
  —BLDSC shelfmark: 3351.880000.

665.5 MX ISSN 0538-1428
TN873.M6 CODEN: RVMPAX
INSTITUTO MEXICANO DEL PETROLEO. REVISTA. (Text in Spanish; summaries in English) 1969. q. $40. Instituto Mexicano del Petroleo, Eje Central Lazaro Cardenas Norte 152, Col. San Bartolo Atepehuacan Mexico 07730, D.F., Mexico. TEL 398-17-99. Ed. Armando Comaduran Cordova. abstr.; charts; illus.; cum.index; circ. 1,500. (back issues avail.) **Indexed:** API Abstr, API Catal., API Hlth.& Environ., API Oil., API Pet.Ref., API Pet.Subst., API Transport., Bibl.& Ind.Geol., Chem.Abstr., Fuel & Energy Abstr., Petrol.Abstr.
  —BLDSC shelfmark: 7819.865000.

665.5 622 553.28 PL ISSN 0209-0724
INSTYTUT GORNICTWA NAFTOWEGO I GAZOWNICTWA. PRACE. (Text in Polish; summaries in English and Russian) 1950. irreg. (5-7/yr.). price varies. Instytut Gornictwa Naftowego i Gazownictwa, Ul. Lubicz 25A, 31-503 Krakow, Poland. TELEX 0325276 IGNG PL. charts; illus.; circ. 1,000. **Indexed:** Chem.Abstr.
  —BLDSC shelfmark: 6581.030000.
  Formerly: Instytut Naftowy. Prace (ISSN 0032-6232)

665.7 US
INTERNATIONAL BUTANE - PROPANE NEWSLETTER. 1977. s-m. $195. Butane - Propane News, Inc., 338 E. Foothill Blvd., Box 419, Arcadia, CA 91006. TEL 818-357-2168. FAX 818-303-2854. Ed. Ann Rey.

665.7 US
INTERNATIONAL CONFERENCE ON LIQUEFIED NATURAL GAS. PAPERS. (Papers in English, some in French; abstracts in English and French) 1968. triennial. $100 for 1989 edition. Institute of Gas Technology, 3424 South State St., Chicago, IL 60616. TEL 312-567-3650. (Co-sponsors: International Gas Union; International Institute of Refrigeration) Ed. Bonnie Feingold. **Indexed:** Chem.Abstr., Gas Abstr.
  Formerly: International Conference on Liquefied Natural Gas. Proceedings (ISSN 0538-611X)

662.6 CY ISSN 1010-1179
INTERNATIONAL CRUDE OIL AND PRODUCT PRICES. 1971. s-a. $560. Middle East Petroleum and Economic Publications, P.O. Box 4940, Nicosia, Cyprus. TEL 445431. FAX 474988. TELEX 2198 MEES CY. charts, stat.
  Description: Review and analysis of oil price trends in world markets.

665.5 US ISSN 0736-5721
TP345.A1 CODEN: PGRCDV
INTERNATIONAL GAS RESEARCH CONFERENCE. PROCEEDINGS. 1980. irreg., latest 1989. $175. (Gas Research Institute) Government Institutes, Inc., 966 Hungerford Dr., No. 24, Rockville, MD 20850. TEL 301-251-9250. FAX 301-251-0638. **Indexed:** Chem.Abstr.
  —BLDSC shelfmark: 4540.502000.

665.7 US ISSN 0276-4040
INTERNATIONAL GAS TECHNOLOGY HIGHLIGHTS. 1971. fortn. $90 (foreign $100). Institute of Gas Technology, 3424 S. State St., Chicago, IL 60616. TEL 312-567-3650. FAX 312-567-5209. Ed. Colleen Taylor Sen. circ. 2,500.

338.39 SZ
INTERNATIONAL GAS UNION. PROCEEDINGS OF WORLD GAS CONFERENCES. (Text in English and French) 1931. triennial; 17th, 1988, Washington. International Gas Union - Union Internationale de l'Industrie du Gaz, Grutlistrasse 44, Case Postale 658, CH-8027 Zurich, Switzerland. Ed. J.P. Lauper.
  Formerly: International Gas Union. Proceedings of Conferences (ISSN 0074-6126)

INTERNATIONAL JOURNAL OF OFFSHORE AND POLAR ENGINEERING. see *ENGINEERING — Mechanical Engineering*

INTERNATIONAL JOURNAL OF SURFACE MINING AND RECLAMATION. see *MINES AND MINING INDUSTRY*

INTERNATIONAL OFFSHORE FINANCIAL CENTRES. see *BUSINESS AND ECONOMICS — International Commerce*

PETROLEUM AND GAS

665.5 US ISSN 1058-6008
HD9563
INTERNATIONAL OFFSHORE RIG OWNERS DIRECTORY. a. $125. Offshore Data Services, Inc., Box 19909, Houston, TX 77224-9909. TEL 713-781-2713. FAX 713-781-9594.
Formerly: Offshore Rig Owners Directory.
Description: Provides corporate, personnel, and rig information for US and foreign owned offshore rigs, including US and overseas addresses.

665.5 US
INTERNATIONAL OIL AND GAS DEVELOPMENT YEARBOOK. 1930. a. price varies. International Oil Scouts Association, Box 272949, Houston, TX 77277-2949. circ. 1,500. (back issues avail.)

665 622 US
INTERNATIONAL OIL NEWS: MANAGEMENT EDITION; weekly news report of significant and timely business intelligence for oil industry executives. 1954. w. $397. William F. Bland, Co., Box 16666, Chapel Hill, NC 27516-6666. TEL 919-490-0700. FAX 919-490-3002. TELEX 965952-BLAND. Ed. Chris R. Schultz. (back issues avail.) **Indexed:** Bibl.& Ind.Geol.
Former titles (until 1986): International Oil News (ISSN 0043-8855); (until 1970): World Petroleum Report.
Description: For top executives managing international oil and gas activities.

INTERNATIONAL OIL NEWS: SUPPLIERS EDITION; the weekly news report of significant and timely business intelligence for suppliers to the industry. see BUSINESS AND ECONOMICS — Trade And Industrial Directories

553.28 US ISSN 0277-6812
INTERNATIONAL OIL SCOUTS ASSOCIATION. OFFICIAL PUBLICATION. 1956. q. $10. International Oil Scouts Association, Box 272949, Houston, TX 77277-2949. adv.; bk.rev.; charts; illus.; circ. 1,500.
Formerly: International Oil Scouts Association. Official Newsletter (ISSN 0047-0864)

INTERNATIONAL OIL SCOUTS ASSOCIATION DIRECTORY. see BUSINESS AND ECONOMICS — Trade And Industrial Directories

665.5 US ISSN 0148-0375
HD9560.1
INTERNATIONAL PETROLEUM ENCYCLOPEDIA. 1968. a. $95. PennWell Publishing Co., Box 1260, Tulsa, OK 74101. TEL 918-835-3161. FAX 918-831-9497. Ed. John C. McCaslin. adv. **Indexed:** SRI.
Description: Provides plans, activities, statistics, technology and analysis in all segments of today's worldwide oil and gas businesses. Features new maps, updated country-by-country reports and brand new features on the most timely petroleum industry developments.

665.5 332 US ISSN 0193-9270
INTERNATIONAL PETROLEUM FINANCE; earnings, finances and management strategies in the petroleum industry. 1978. s-m. $580 in N. America (elsewhere $595)(typically set. in Oct.). Petroleum Analysis Ltd., Box 130, F.D.R. Sta., New York, NY 10150-0130. TEL 212-755-7484.
FAX 212-750-0189. Ed. Dillard Spriggs. stat.; index. (back issues avail.) **Indexed:** Petrol.Energy B.N.I.
Description: Covers financial and regulatory trends and developments affecting the petroleum industry, including exploration projects, acquisitions and investment evaluations.

665.5 US
INTERNATIONAL PETROLEUM INDUSTRY. a. $40. Midwest Register, Inc., 601 S. Boulder, Ste. 1001, Tulsa, OK 74119-1301. TEL 918-582-2000.
Formerly: Oil Directory of Companies Outside the U.S. and Canada (ISSN 0472-7711)
Description: Supplies company name, address, phone and fax numbers, telex number, division offices, office locations and U.S. office if known. Divided by sections.

665.5 II ISSN 0047-1046
INTERNATIONAL PRESS CUTTING SERVICE: PETROLEUM - PETROCHEMICALS - FERTILISERS - AGRICULTURAL CHEMISTRY. 1967. w. $75. International Press Cutting Service, P.O. Box 63, Allahabad 211001, India. Ed. N. Khanna. bk.rev.; index; circ. 1,200. (processed)

INTERNATIONAL TAXATION SERIES. see BUSINESS AND ECONOMICS — Public Finance, Taxation

665.5 US
INTERNATIONAL TRENDS IN OIL AND GAS. m. $300 (foreign $360). Petroleum Information Corporation, Box 2612, Denver, CO 80201-2612. TEL 303-740-7100. FAX 303-694-1754.
Description: Covers oil and gas exploration worldwide.

665.5 531.64 US
INTERSTATE NATURAL GAS ASSOCIATION OF AMERICA WASHINGTON REPORT. 1962. w. $495. Interstate Natural Gas Association of America (INGAA), 555 13th St., N.W., Ste. 300 W., Washington, DC 20004. TEL 202-626-3200. FAX 202-626-3239. Ed. Cheryl W. Hoffman. index; circ. 800. (looseleaf format; back issues avail.)
Formerly: Interstate Natural Gas Association of America Weekly Report.
Description: Covers congressional and regulatory developments of interest to the natural gas pipeline industry. Includes company news.

665 US ISSN 1046-2333
TN872
INTERSTATE OIL COMPACT COMMISSION. COMPACT & COMMITTEE BULLETIN. 1958. s-a. free. Interstate Oil Compact Commission, Box 53127, Oklahoma City, OK 73152. TEL 405-525-3556. charts; illus.
Indexed: INIS Atomind., Petrol.Abstr.
Formed by the merger of (1942-1986): Oil and Gas Compact Bulletin; (1958-1986): Interstate Oil Compact Commission. Committee Bulletin (ISSN 0020-9732)

338.47 US
INTERSTATE OIL COMPACT COMMISSION ANNUAL REPORT. 1974. a. free. Interstate Oil Compact Commission, Box 53127, Oklahoma City, OK 73152. TEL 405-525-3556.

665.773 US
INVENTORIES OF NATURAL GAS LIQUIDS & LIQUIFIED REFINERY GASES. 1956. m. $220. American Petroleum Institute, Publications and Distributions, 1220 L St., N.W., Washington, DC 20005. Ed.Bd. circ. 150.
Formerly (until Apr., 1985): Liquified Petroleum Gas Report (ISSN 0024-421X)

665.5 US
IOWA OIL SPOUT. 6/yr. Petroleum Marketers of Iowa, 321 Sixth Ave., Des Moines, IA 50309-4102. TEL 515-244-6273. Ed. E.A. Kistenmacher. circ. 1,000.

665.5 US
IOWA PETROLEUM DISTRIBUTOR NEWSLETTER. m. Petroleum Marketers of Iowa, 321 Sixth Ave., Des Moines, IA 50309-1903. TEL 515-244-6273. FAX 515-244-1051. Ed. Ron Marr.

665 IR ISSN 0021-079X
IRAN OIL JOURNAL. French edition: Iran Petrole. Farsi edition: Nameh Sanaat-e-Naft. (Editions in English, Farsi, French) q. free. Petroleum Ministry, Public Relations & Guidance Department, P.O. Box 1863, Central NIOC Bldg., Taleghani Ave., Teheran, Iran. TEL 021-6151. TELEX 212514. Ed. Yegandokht Mostofian.

665.5 IR
IRAN OIL NEWS. 1984. m. free. Petroleum Ministry, Public Relations & Guidance Department, P.O. Box 1863, Central NIOC Bldg., Taleghani Ave., Tehran, Iran. TEL 6153823.
Formerly: Petroleum Newsletter.
Description: Promotes a better understanding of the Petroleum Ministry of Iran and its policies, as well as providing analysis of the accomplishments within the industry. Addresses energy issues and international petroleum affairs.

665.5 IQ
IRAQ OIL NEWS. (Text in English) no. 55, 1980. Ministry of Oil, Baghdad, Iraq.

665.5 RU ISSN 0202-7429
CODEN: IRNGAK
ITOGI NAUKI I TEKHNIKI: RAZRABOTKA NEFTYANYKH I GAZOVYKH MESTOROZHDENII. 1968. irreg., vol.21, 1989. 6.60 Rub. Vsesoyuznyi Institut Nauchno-Tekhnicheskoi Informatsii (VINITI), Baltiiskaya ul. 14, Moscow A-219, Russia. (Subscr. to: Mezhdunarodnaya Kniga, Dimitrova ul. 39, 113095 Moscow, Russia)
—BLDSC shelfmark: 0140.236000.

665.5 US ISSN 0149-2136
TN860 CODEN: JPTJAM
J P T: JOURNAL OF PETROLEUM TECHNOLOGY. 1949. m. $30 to non-members. Society of Petroleum Engineers, Inc., Box 833836, Richardson, TX 75083-3836. TEL 214-669-3377.
FAX 214-669-0135. TELEX 730989 SPEDAL. Ed. Jim McInnis. adv.; bk.rev.; abstr.; bibl.; charts; illus.; index, cum.index; circ. 52,500. (also avail. in microform from UMI; back issues avail.; reprint service avail. from SPE) **Indexed:** A.S.& T.Ind., AESIS, API Abstr., API Catal., API Hlth.& Environ., API Oil., API Pet.Ref., API Pet.Subst., API Transport., Appl.Mech.Rev., Bibl.& Ind.Geol., Cadscan, Chem.Abstr., Curr.Cont., Deep Sea Res.& Oceanogr.Abstr., Energy Ind., Energy Info.Abstr., Energy Rev., Eng.Ind., Environ.Abstr., Environ.Per.Bibl., Excerp.Med., Fuel & Energy Abstr., Gas Abstr., INIS Atomind., Lead Abstr., Met.Abstr., Ocean.Abstr., Petrol.Abstr., Pollut.Abstr., Risk Abstr., Sh.& Vib.Dig., W.R.C.Inf., Zincscan.
Formerly: Journal of Petroleum Technology (ISSN 0022-3522)
Refereed Serial

665.5 NE
JAARBOEK VAN DE OPENBARE GASVOORZIENING. 1971. a. fl.35. Vereniging van Exploitanten van Gasbedrijven in Nederland, Postbus 137, 7300 AC Apeldoorn, Netherlands. FAX 055-418963. (Co-sponsor: VEG-Gasinstituut N.V.) circ. 2,000.

665.5 JA ISSN 0916-2623
JAPAN PETROLEUM AND ENERGY TRENDS. (Text in English) 1966. bi-w. (26/yr.). 180000 Yen($1200) Japan Petroleum and Energy Consultants, Ltd. - Nihon Sekiyu Konsarutanto K.K., P.O. Box 1185, Tokyo Central, Tokyo 100-91, Japan.
FAX 03-3351-9755. Ed. K. Kurokawa. mkt.; stat.; index; circ. 1,200. (looseleaf format)
Former titles: Japan Petroleum and Energy Weekly & Japan Petroleum Weekly (ISSN 0386-6165)

665.53 CC ISSN 1003-9384
JINGXI SHIYOU HUAGONG/SPECIALTY PETROCHEMICALS. (Text in Chinese) 1984. bi-m. Y15. Zhongguo Shiyou Huagong Zonggongsi, Jinling Shiyou Huagong Gongsi - SINOPEC, Specialty Petrochemical S & T Information Center, Shanggulin, Dagang-qu, Tianjin 300061, People's Republic of China. TEL 756622. Ed. Sun Luhou.

665.5 CN ISSN 0021-9487
CODEN: JCPMAM
JOURNAL OF CANADIAN PETROLEUM TECHNOLOGY. 1962. 6/yr. Can.$55($65) (foreign $75). Canadian Institute of Mining, Metallurgy and Petroleum, Petroleum Society, Xerox Tower, 3400 de Maisonneuve Blvd. W., Ste. 1210, Montreal, Que. H3Z 3B8, Canada. TEL 514-939-2710.
FAX 514-939-2714. Ed. Perla Gantz. adv.; bk.rev.; abstr.; bibl.; charts; illus.; tr.lit.; index; circ. 5,700. **Indexed:** AESIS, API Abstr, API Catal., API Hlth.& Environ., API Oil., API Pet.Ref., API Pet.Subst., API Transport., Bibl.& Ind.Geol., CAD CAM Abstr., Chem.Abstr., Curr.Cont., Energy Info.Abstr., Eng.Ind., Environ.Abstr., Environ.Per.Bibl., Fuel & Energy Abstr., Gas Abstr., INIS Atomind., Petrol.Abstr., Risk Abstr.
—BLDSC shelfmark: 4954.750000.
Description: Contains news and technical information of specific interest to the petroleum, oil and gas industries.

665.5 UK ISSN 0141-6421
TN870.5 CODEN: JPEGD9
JOURNAL OF PETROLEUM GEOLOGY. 1978. q. $240. Scientific Press Ltd., P.O. Box 21, Beaconsfield, Bucks. HP9 1NS, England. TEL 0494-675139. FAX 0494-670155. TELEX 94016686-SSP-G. Ed. E.N. Tiratsoo. adv.; bk.rev. **Indexed:** AESIS, Bibl.& Ind.Geol., Br.Geol.Lit., Chem.Abstr, Deep Sea Res.& Oceanogr.Abstr., Geo.Abstr., Petrol.Abstr.
—BLDSC shelfmark: 5030.990000.

PETROLEUM AND GAS

665.54 US
JOURNAL OF PETROLEUM MARKETING. 1988. 7/yr. B M T Publications, Inc., 7 Penn Plaza, New York, NY 10001-3900. TEL 212-594-4120. FAX 212-714-0514. Ed. Greg Pitkoff. circ. 19,600.

665.5 IQ ISSN 1012-3369
JOURNAL OF PETROLEUM RESEARCH. 1982. s-a. ID.10($15) to individuals; institutions $50. Scientific Research Council, Petroleum Research Centre, P.O. Box 10039, Jadiriyah, Baghdad, Iraq. FAX 7768929. TELEX 213976 SRC. Ed. A.H. Mohammed. circ. 500. Indexed: Chem.Abstr., Eng.Ind., Petrol.Abstr.
—BLDSC shelfmark: 5030.995000.

665.5 NE ISSN 0920-4105
TN860 CODEN: JPSEE6
JOURNAL OF PETROLEUM SCIENCE AND ENGINEERING. (Text in English) 1987. 8/yr. (in 2 vols.; 4 nos./vol.) fl.602 (effective 1992). Elsevier Science Publishers B.V., P.O. Box 211, 1000 AE Amsterdam, Netherlands. TEL 020-5803911. FAX 020-5803598. TELEX 18582 ESPA NL. (Subscr. in U.S. and Canada to: Elsevier Science Publishing Co., Inc., Box 882, Madison Sq. Sta., New York, NY 10159. TEL 212-989-5800) Ed.Bd. adv.; bk.rev.; charts; illus.; stat. (back issues avail.). Indexed: Curr.Cont., Eng.Ind., Geo.Abstr., Petrol.Abstr.
—BLDSC shelfmark: 5030.998000.
Description: Covers the fields of petroleum geology, exploration and engineering.
Refereed Serial

665.538 UK ISSN 0265-6582
CODEN: JSLUE6
JOURNAL OF SYNTHETIC LUBRICATION; research, development and application of synthetic lubricants and functional fluids. 1984. q. £95($160) Leaf Coppin Publishing Co., P.O. Box 111, Deal, Kent CT14 6SX, England. TEL 33-2187-2521. FAX 33-2187-0511. TELEX 96118 ANZEEK G. Ed. Stephen Godfree. adv.; bk.rev.; circ. 400. Indexed: Chem.Abstr., Eng.Ind.
—BLDSC shelfmark: 5068.042000.
Refereed Serial

665.538 US ISSN 0742-4787
TJ1075.A2 CODEN: JOTRE9
JOURNAL OF TRIBOLOGY. 1967. q. $120 to non-members; members $29. American Society of Mechanical Engineers, 345 E. 47th St., New York, NY 10017. TEL 212-705-7722. Ed. W.O. Winer. adv.; bk.rev.; charts; illus.; index; circ. 3,547. (also avail. in microform from UMI; reprint service avail. from UMI) Indexed: A.S.& T.Ind., API Abstr., API Catal., API Hlth.& Environ., API Oil., API Pet.Ref., API Pet.Subst., API Transport., Appl.Mech.Rev., Br.Rail.Bd., Chem.Abstr., Curr.Cont., Eng.Ind., Fluidex, Ind.Sci.Rev., INIS Atomind., Int.Aerosp.Abstr., ISMEC, Met.Abstr., Nucl.Sci.Abstr., Sh.& Vib.Dig., World Alum.Abstr.
Formerly (until 1983): Journal of Lubrication Technology (ISSN 0022-2305) Supersedes in part (1880-1958): American Society of Mechanical Engineers. Transactions (ISSN 0097-6822).
Description: Details lubrication and lubricants.
Refereed Serial

665.5 US
KANSAS OIL MARKETER.* 1920. 6/yr. membership. Kansas Oil Marketeers Association, P.O. Box 8479, Topeka, KS 66608-0479. TEL 913-233-9655. Ed. C.A. Hutton. circ. 700.

KELLY'S OIL & GAS INDUSTRY DIRECTORY. see *BUSINESS AND ECONOMICS — Trade And Industrial Directories*

KHIMICHESKOE I NEFTYANOE MASHINOSTROENIE/CHEMICAL AND OIL INDUSTRY. see *ENGINEERING — Chemical Engineering*

665.5 547.8 RU ISSN 0023-1169
CODEN: KTPMAG
KHIMIYA I TEKHNOLOGIYA TOPLIV I MASEL. English translation: Chemistry and Technology of Fuels and Oils (US ISSN 0009-3092) 1956. m. 27 Rub. Izdatel'stvo Khimiya, Novaya ul., 10, Moscow K-12, Russia. Ed. I.S. Polyakov. bibl.; charts; illus.; index; circ. 3,270. Indexed: Bibl.& Ind.Geol., Chem.Abstr., INIS Atomind., Pollut.Abstr.
—BLDSC shelfmark: 0394.000000.

665.7 US
KING'S NORTH AMERICAN GAS. 1986. w. $547. King Publishing Co., Box 52210, Knoxville, TN 37950. TEL 615-584-6294. (back issues avail.)
Formerly: King's Midwest Gas (ISSN 0888-9449)
Description: Market report for the natural gas industry.

338.2 UK ISSN 0141-4305
HD9571.1
KNOW MORE ABOUT OIL WORLD STATISTICS. a. 60p. (first copy free). Institute of Petroleum, 61 New Cavendish St., London W1M 8AR, England. TEL 01-636-1004. FAX 01-255-1472. TELEX 264380.
Formerly: Oil World Statistics (ISSN 0306-770X)

KOKS, SMOLA, GAZ. see *MINES AND MINING INDUSTRY*

665.5 KU ISSN 0023-5792
KUWAITI. (Text in Arabic) 1961. m. free. Kuwait Oil Company (K.S.C.), Supdt. Press and Publications Division, P.O. Box 9758 Ahmadi, 61008 Ahmadi, Kuwait. TEL 3989111. FAX 3983661. TELEX 44226 KUOCO. Ed. Salem R. Al Roomi. film rev.; play rev.; illus.; tr.lit.; circ. 6,300.
Description: Articles on economics, energy, oil industry and science.

KYUSHU UNIVERSITY. DEPARTMENT OF EARTH AND PLANETARY SCIENCES. SCIENCE REPORTS/KYUSHU DAIGAKU RIGAKUBU KENKYU HOKOKU CHIKYU-WAKUSEI-KAGAKU. see *EARTH SCIENCES — Geology*

665.7 US ISSN 1053-6949
▼ **L N G OBSERVER.** 1990. q. $100. Institute of Gas Technology, 3424 S. State St., Chicago, IL 60616. TEL 312-567-3650. FAX 312-567-5209. Ed. Colleen Taylor. circ. 2,500.
Description: Provides information about the worldwide liquified natural gas industry.

658.8 US
L O M A LINE. m. membership. Louisiana Oil Marketers Association, 2354 S. Acadian Thwy. Ste. G., Baton Rouge, LA 70808. TEL 504-344-6968. adv.; circ. 600. (processed)
Formerly: L O M A Bulletin.

665.7 US ISSN 0024-7103
TP761.P4
L P - GAS. 1941. m. (with annual supplement). $15 (supplement $8). Avanstar Communications, Inc., 7500 Old Oak Blvd., Cleveland, OH 44130. TEL 216-826-2839. FAX 216-891-2726. (Subscr. to: 1 E. First St., Duluth, MN 55802) Ed. Zane Chastain. adv.; illus.; stat.; tr.lit.; circ. 15,337. Indexed: Gas Abstr.
Description: Covers gas production, storage, utilization and marketing.

665.5 UK ISSN 0309-3077
L P GAS REVIEW. 1977. bi-m. £33 (foreign £45). Bouverie Publishing Company Ltd., 4th fl., 58 Fleet St., Entrance 3 Pleydell St., London EC4Y 1JU, England. TEL 071-353-4881. FAX 071-583-6069. Ed. Peter Hancox. circ. 4,585.
—BLDSC shelfmark: 5300.125000.
Description: Covers every aspect of liquefied petroleum gas from bulk containerization to site transfer and consumer containers.

665.5 US ISSN 0023-7418
HD9560.1
LAMP (NEW YORK). 1918. q. Exxon Corporation, 225 E. John W. Carpenter Freeway, Irving, TX 75062-2298. TEL 214-444-1116. FAX 214-444-1139. Ed. James B. Davis. illus.; index every 3 yrs.; circ. 650,000 (controlled). Indexed: Chem.Abstr., Environ.Abstr., Ind.Free Per., P.A.I.S., PROMT.

665.5 US
LAND RIG NEWSLETTER. m. Slaton & Associates, Box 59065, Dallas, TX 75229. TEL 214-620-2046. Ed. Mike Slaton.

665.5 621.3 FR ISSN 0754-5215
LETTRE AFRIQUE ENERGIES. English edition: Africa Energy and Mining. 1983. 23/yr. 3350 F.($620) Indigo Publications, 10, rue du Sentier, 75002 Paris, France. TEL 45-08-14-80. FAX 45-08-59-83. TELEX LOI 215405F. Dir. Maurice Botbol.

665.5 AT ISSN 0817-6191
LIPSCOMBE REPORT. w. (by telex) and every 2-3 mos. (newsletter). Aus.$2950. Pex Publications Pty. Ltd., P.O. Box 158, Claremont, W.A. 6010, Australia. TEL 09-383-3477. FAX 385-1485. Ed. Don Lipscombe. index. (back issues avail.)
Description: Provides information on energy and on exploration and development of Australian natural resources.

662 627 UK ISSN 0305-1803
HE566.T3
LIQUID GAS CARRIER REGISTER. 1966. a. £92($160) Clarkson Research Studies Ltd., 12 Camomile St., London EC3A 7BP, England. TEL 071-283 8955.
—BLDSC shelfmark: 5221.935000.

LIQUIDS HANDLING. see *ENGINEERING*

LITERATURE ABSTRACTS: CATALYSTS & CATALYSIS. (American Petroleum Institute) see *CHEMISTRY — Abstracting, Bibliographies, Statistics*

665.5 US ISSN 0024-581X
CODEN: LGALAS
LOG ANALYST. 1962. bi-m. $90. Society of Professional Well Log Analysts, 6001 Gulf Fwy., Ste. C 129, Houston, TX 77023. TEL 713-928-8925. FAX 713-928-9061. adv.; bk.rev.; circ. 4,500. Indexed: AESIS, Bibl.& Ind.Geol., Eng.Ind., Petrol.Abstr., W.R.C.Inf.
—BLDSC shelfmark: 5292.304500.

LOUISIANA OIL AND GAS LAW. see *LAW*

665.53 338 US
LUBRICANTS WORLD. m. Oil Daily Company, 1401 New York Ave. N.W., No. 500, Washington, DC 20005. TEL 202-662-0715. FAX 202-783-5918. Ed. John A. Moore. circ. 10,000.

665.5 US
LUNDBERG LETTER. 1974. s-m. $399. Lundberg Survey, Incorporated, Box 3996, N. Hollywood, CA 91609. TEL 818-768-5111. FAX 818-768-1883.

665 HU
MAGYAR OLAJIPARI MUZEUM. EVKONYV. 1974. irreg. 117 Ft. Magyar Olajipari Muzeum, Zalaegerszeg, Hungary. illus.; circ. 1,000.

665.5 UK
MAJOR CHEMICAL AND PETROCHEMICAL COMPANIES OF EUROPE. a. $299. Graham & Trotman Ltd., Sterling House, 66 Wilson Rd., London SW1V 1DE, England. (Dist. in US and Canada by: Gale Research Inc., Dept. 77748, Detroit, MI 48277-0748)
Description: Describes the finances, personnel, structure, products, and locations of such companies in Western Europe.

MARINE AND PETROLEUM GEOLOGY. see *EARTH SCIENCES — Geology*

665.5 CN ISSN 0826-8371
MARITIME INDUSTRIES. (Supplement to: Offshore Resources) 1985. bi-m. I.B.I.S. Publishing Inc., P.O. Box 91760, W. Vancouver, B.C. V7V 4S1, Canada. Ed. Duncan Cumming. adv.; bk.rev.

665.5 QA
AL-MASH'AL/TORCH. (Text in Arabic, English) 1986. s-m. Qatar General Petroleum Corporation, P.O. Box 3212, Doha, Qatar. TEL 491491. FAX 811125. TELEX 4343. circ. 4,000.

MATERIALS AND COMPONENTS IN FOSSIL ENERGY APPLICATIONS. see *ENERGY*

AL-MAWARID AL-TABI'IYYAH/NATURAL RESOURCES. see *CONSERVATION*

665.5 US
MICHIGAN OIL & GAS NEWS. w. 206 W. Michigan, Ste.200, Mt. Pleasant, MI 48858. TEL 517-772-5181. Ed. Jack Westbrook.

665.538 658.7 UK
MID-WEEK PETROLEUM ARGUS. w. £590($890) Petroleum Argus Ltd., 93 Shepperton Rd., London N1 3DF, England. TEL 071-359-8792. FAX 071-226-0695. TELEX 21277.

PETROLEUM AND GAS

665.5 US ISSN 0883-7325
MIDCONTINENT OIL WORLD. 1985. bi-m. $39 (foreign $89). Hart Publications, Inc., 1900 Grant St., Ste. 400, Box 1917, Denver, CO 80201. TEL 303-837-1917. adv.; bk.rev. (reprint service avail. from UMI)
Description: Covers Oklahoma, Kansas, Nebraska, North Texas, the Panhandle, Western Arkansas and Missouri.

380 US
MIDCONTINENT PETROLEUM INDUSTRY. 1945. a. $40. Midwest Register, Inc., 601 Boulder, Ste. 1001, Tulsa, OK 74119-1001. TEL 918-582-2000.
Formed by the 1992 merger of: Directory of Producers and Drilling Contractors: Kansas; Directory of Producers and Drilling Contractors: Oklahoma.
Description: Supplies company name, address, phone and fax numbers, personnel, division offices, offshore operations, whether producer of oil or gas and if drilling contractor with rotary or cable tools.

338.47 CY ISSN 0544-0424
HD9576.N36
MIDDLE EAST ECONOMIC SURVEY. Short title: M E E S. 1957. w. $1,375. Middle East Petroleum and Economic Publications, P.O. Box 4940, Nicosia, Cyprus. TEL 445431. FAX 474988. TELEX 2198 MEES CY. Ed. Ian Seymour. bk.rev.; charts; stat.; index. **Indexed:** Key to Econ.Sci., Petrol.Energy B.N.I.
Description: Review of oil, finance, banking, and political developments in the Middle East and North Africa.

665 622 RM
MINE, PETROL SI GAZE. (Text in Rumanian; summaries in English, French, German and Russian) 1950. m. 160 lei. Ministerul Minelor Petrolului si Geologiei, Oficiul de Informare Documentara, Str. Mendeleev 36-38, Sector 1, Bucharest, Rumania. adv.; bk.rev.; bibl.; charts; illus.; circ. 1,500. **Indexed:** Bibl.& Ind.Geol., C.I.S. Abstr., Chem.Abstr, Corros.Abstr., Petrol.Abstr.
Formed by the merger of: Petrol si Gaze (ISSN 0031-6350) & Revista Minelor (ISSN 0035-0168)

665.5 GW ISSN 0544-2524
MINERALOEL - MINERALOELRUNDSCHAU; Zeitschrift fuer die Deutsche Mineraloelwirtschaft. 1953. m. DM.55. Uniti Bundesverband Mittelstaendischer Mineraloelunternehmen e.V., Buchstr. 10, 2000 Hamburg 76, Germany. TEL 040-2270030. FAX 040-22700338. TELEX 212776-UNITI-D. Ed. Wolfgang Stichler. adv.; bk.rev.; pat.; circ. 1,200.
—BLDSC shelfmark: 5790.360000.
Former titles: Mineraloelrundschau; (until 1972): Uniti.

MINERIA CHILENA. see MINES AND MINING INDUSTRY

662.6 GW ISSN 0341-1893
CODEN: MTCKAZ
MINEROELTECHNIK. 1956. m. DM.111.20. Beratungsgesellschaft fuer Mineraloel-Anwendungstechnik mbH, Buchstr. 10, D-2000 Hamburg 76, Germany. TEL 040-22700344. FAX 040-2270-0338. TELEX 212776-UNITI-D. Ed. Wolfgang Heine. adv.; bk.rev.; index; circ. 2,000. (back issues avail.)
—BLDSC shelfmark: 5786.420000.
Description: Reports on mineral oil usage, research results on oil products, fuels, heating oils, lubricants.

MINING AND PETROLEUM LEGISLATION SERVICE. see LAW

MINING RECORD. see MINES AND MINING INDUSTRY

353.9 US ISSN 0095-3024
HD9579.G5
MINNESOTA. DEPARTMENT OF REVENUE. PETROLEUM DIVISION. ANNUAL REPORT. 1973. a. Department of Revenue, Petroleum Division, Centennial Office Bldg., St. Paul, MN 55145. TEL 612-296-3781. Key Title: Annual Report - Petroleum Division.

665.5 US
MISSOURI PIPELINE. 1936. m. membership. Missouri Petroleum Marketers Association, 238 E. High St., Jefferson City, MO 65101. TEL 314-635-7117. FAX 314-635-3575. Ed. Jim Keown. adv.; bk.rev.; tr.lit.; circ. 1,400. (controlled).
Formerly: Missouri Oil Jobber.

665.5 UK
MODERN LIVING AT THE HOME OF GAS. 1938. s-a. British Gas North Thames, North Thames House, London Rd., Staines, Middx. TW18 4AE, England. Ed. Michael Purdie. circ. 1,800,000.
Formerly: Modern Living with Gas.

662.6 US ISSN 0047-794X
MONTANA OIL JOURNAL.* 1921. w. $26. Montana Oil Journal, Inc., 1580 Lincoln St., No. 1270, Denver, CO 80203-1514. Ed. Roy Boles. adv.; circ. 4,000. (tabloid format)

665.5 IO
MONTHLY BULLETIN OF THE PETROLEUM AND NATURAL GAS INDUSTRY OF INDONESIA. 1973. m. Directorate General of Oil and Gas, Programming and Reporting Division - Direktorat Jenderal Minyak dan Gas Bumi, Jalan M.H. Thamrin No. 1, Jakarta 10110, Indonesia. TEL 62-21-351215.
FAX 62-21-354987. TELEX 44363. charts; stat.; circ. 400.

665.5 US
MONTHLY CRUDE OIL PRODUCTION. m. $75. Railroad Commission, Oil and Gas Publications, Drawer 12967, Capitol Sta., Austin, TX 78711. TEL 512-463-7255.
Former titles: Monthly Production of Crude Oil Allowable, Production and Removal from Leases in the State of Texas; Preliminary Statement of Crude Oil Allowable, Production and Removal from Leases in the State of Texas.

665.5 JA ISSN 0016-5069
MONTHLY GASOLINE STAND/GEKKAN GASORIN SUTANDO. (Text in Japanese) 1959. m. 4800 Yen($13) Gekkan Gasorin Sutandosha, 3-2-3 Shinbashi, Minato-ku, Tokyo 105, Japan. Ed. Yoshihide Yoshitake. adv.; bk.rev.; abstr.; charts; illus.; stat.; tr.lit.; index; circ. 80,000.

665 JA ISSN 0016-5964
MONTHLY JOURNAL OF GASOLINE SERVICE STATIONS/GEKKAN KYUSHO NIHON. (Text in Japanese) 1965. m. 6000 Yen($20) Yugyo Hochi Shinbunsha, 2-15-19 Shinkawa, Chuo-ku, Tokyo 104, Japan. Ed. Yoshio Takeda. adv.; bk.rev.; abstr.; bibl.; charts; illus.; pat.; stat.; tr.lit.; index; circ. 30,000.

665.5 US ISSN 0094-2766
TN881.T4
MONTHLY SUMMARY OF TEXAS NATURAL GAS. 1949. m. $19. Railroad Commission, Oil and Gas Publications, Drawer 12967, Capitol Sta., Austin, TX 78711. TEL 512-463-7255. charts; stat.; circ. 500. (looseleaf format)

665.5 MR
MOROCCO. MINISTERE DE L'ENERGIE ET DES MINES. ACTIVITE DU SECTEUR PETROLIER. (Text in French) 1956. irreg. $10. Direction des Mines et de la Geologie, Direction de l'Energie, Rabat, Morocco. stat.
Formerly: Morocco. Direction des Mines et de la Geologie. Activite du Secteur Petrolier.

665.5 UK ISSN 0952-6846
MULTIPHASE UPDATE. 1987. bi-m. $260 (foreign £150). S T I Ltd., 4 Kings Meadow, Ferry Hinksey Rd., Oxford OX2 0DU, England. TEL 0865-798898. FAX 0865-798788. (Dist. in U.S. by: Air Science Co., P.O. Box 143, Corning, NY 14830. TEL 607-962-5591) Ed. Barry Morgan. (back issues avail.)
Description: News about petroleum and gas pipelines, subsea engineering and platforms.

665.5 US
MUNGER MAP BOOK. a. vol. 35, 1991. $100. Munger Oil Information Service, Inc., 9800 S. Sepulveda Blvd., Ste. 723, Box 75738, Los Angeles, CA 90045. TEL 213-776-3990. FAX 213-645-9147. Ed. Averill H. Munger.
Description: Provides a comprehensive atlas with pages for each oil, gas and geothermal field in California and Alaska; also wildcat areas: information on current drilling wells, producers and dry holes.

665.538 US ISSN 0027-6782
TJ1077.A1 CODEN: NLGIA4
N L G I SPOKESMAN. 1937. m. $18 (foreign $48). National Lubricating Grease Institute, 4635 Wyandotte St., Kansas City, MO 64112. TEL 816-931-9480. FAX 816-753-5026. Ed. Duane J. Fike. adv.; bk.rev.; pat.; index; circ. 2,600. (also avail. in microfilm from UMI; reprint service avail. from UMI) **Indexed:** API Abstr., API Catal., API Hlth.& Environ., API Oil., API Pet.Ref., API Pet.Subst., API Transport., Appl.Mech.Rev., Chem.Abstr, Eng.Ind., Fluidex.
—BLDSC shelfmark: 6113.800000.
Description: Contains original articles on the manufacture of lubricating grease or new developments in application methods, as well as other items related to the industry.

655.5 US ISSN 0099-4294
N P N FACTBOOK. (National Petroleum News) a. $50. Hunter Publishing Limited Partnership, 950 Lee St., Des Plaines, IL 60016. TEL 708-296-0770. FAX 708-803-3328. stat.

665.5 UK
N W EUROPE PETROLEUM DATABASE. 1986. s-a. £1,750. Arthur Andersen & Co., Petroleum Services Group, 1 Surrey St., London WC2R 2PS, England. TEL 071-438-3888. FAX 071-438-3881. TELEX 8812711.
Description: Provides information on licences, drilling activity and reserves for the offshore sectors of Norway, the Netherlands, Denmark, Ireland and West Germany, as well as onshore Denmark and Ireland.

665.5 NZ ISSN 0113-0501
N Z PETROLEUM EXPLORATION NEWS. q. NZ.$80. Ministry of Commerce, Energy and Resources Division, P.O. Box 1473, Wellington, New Zealand. TEL 04-472-0030. FAX 04-499-0968. circ. 1,000.
Description: Magazine on petroleum exploration in New Zealand.

665.5 IQ
NAFT WAL ALAM. 1973. m. Ministry of Oil, Baghdad, Iraq. Ed. Tayeh Abdel Karim. adv.

665 PL ISSN 0027-7541
TN860 CODEN: NAFPAB
NAFTA. (Text in Polish; summaries in English and Russian) 1945. bi-m. $30. Instytut Gornictwa Naftowego i Gazownictwa, Ul. Lubicz 25A, 31-503 Krakow, Poland. (Dist. by: Ars Polona- Ruch, Krakowskie Przedmiescie 7, Warsaw, Poland) (Co-sponsor: Stowarzyszenie Inzynierow i Technikow Przemyslu Naftowego) Ed. Jozef Raczkowski. adv.; bk.rev.; abstr.; bibl.; charts; illus.; stat.; index; circ. 1,460. **Indexed:** Chem.Abstr., Energy Info.Abstr., Environ.Abstr., Petrol.Abstr.
—BLDSC shelfmark: 6012.600000.

665 CI ISSN 0027-755X
NAFTA. (Contents page and abstracts in English and Russian) 1950. m. $102. Jugoslavenski Komitet Svjetskog Kongresa za Naftu - Yugoslav Committee of the World Petroleum Congresses, Savska Cesta 64, Zagreb, Croatia. TEL 518-111. Ed. Ifet Ibrahimpasic. adv.; bk.rev.; charts; illus.; index, cum.index; circ. 2,100. **Indexed:** Chem.Abstr., Petrol.Abstr., Ref.Zh.

NANJING DAXUE XUEBAO (ZHEXUE SHEHUI KEXUE BAN)/NANJING UNIVERSITY. JOURNAL (SOCIAL SCIENCE EDITION). see SOCIAL SCIENCES: COMPREHENSIVE WORKS

NANKAI XUEBAO. ZHEXUE SHEHUI KEXUE BAN/NANKAI UNIVERSITY. JOURNAL. PHILOSOPHY AND SOCIAL SCIENCES EDITION.. see SOCIAL SCIENCES: COMPREHENSIVE WORKS

665.5 TS
NASHRAT A D M A/A D M A BULLETIN. (Text in Arabic) 1984. w. Abu Dhabi Marine Operating Company, P.O. Box 303, Abu Dhabi, United Arab Emirates. TEL 776600. FAX 720028. TELEX 22284 ADMA EM. Ed. Ahmed el-Tayeb Ahmed. circ. 2,400 (controlled).
Description: News of the company's activities and employees.

NATIONAL DRILLERS BUYERS GUIDE. see WATER RESOURCES

PETROLEUM AND GAS

665.5   JM
NATIONAL ENERGY OUTLOOK. irreg., 3rd ed. Jam.$40 per no. Petroleum Corporation of Jamaica, Energy Economics Department, 36 Trafalgar Rd., P.O. Box 579, Kingston 10, Jamaica, W.I. TEL 809-929-5380. TELEX 2356 PETCORP.
Description: Provides a brief analysis of the international energy environment and world energy outlook.

665.5   US   ISSN 0149-5267
NATIONAL PETROLEUM NEWS. 1909. 13/yr. $60 (Canada $69; elsewhere $75). Hunter Publishing Limited Partnership, 950 Lee St., Des Plaines, IL 60016. TEL 708-296-0770. FAX 708-803-3328. Ed. Peggy Smedley. adv.; bk.rev.; charts; illus.; mkt.; stat.; tr.lit.; s-a cum.index; circ. 19,100. (also avail. in microform from UMI; reprint service avail. from UMI) **Indexed:** B.P.I., Chem.Abstr., Petrol.Energy B.N.I., PROMT, SRI, Tr.& Indus.Ind.
●Also available online. Vendor(s): DIALOG.

662.338   US   ISSN 0470-3219
TN872
NATIONAL STRIPPER WELL SURVEY. 1951. a. free. Interstate Oil Compact Commission, Box 53127, Oklahoma City, OK 73152. TEL 405-525-3556.

665.5   US
NATIONAL WILDCAT MONTHLY. m. $40. Petroleum Information Corporation, Box 2162, Denver, CO 80201-2612. TEL 303-740-7100. FAX 303-694-1754.
Description: Covers new field discoveries, with operating and production details, and a statistical evaluation of activity.

665.7   UK
NATURAL GAS.* 1928. bi-m. £40 (foreign £53). Benn Publications Ltd., Sovereign Way, Tonbridge, Kent TN9 1RW, England. TEL 0732-364422. Ed. Geoff Clarke. adv.; bk.rev.; illus.; circ. 29,270. (also avail. in microform from UMI) **Indexed:** BMT, Br.Tech.Ind.
Formerly: Industrial and Commercial Gas; Incorporating: Gas in Industry and Commerce (ISSN 0016-4925)

338.47 665.7   US
NATURAL GAS. 1949. m. $252 in US and Canada; elsewhere $337 (effective 1992). Executive Enterprises Publications Co., Inc., 22 W. 21st St., New York, NY 10010-6904. TEL 212-645-7880. FAX 212-645-1160. **Indexed:** Energy Info.Abstr., Environ.Abstr.
Former titles (1979-1983): Oil and Gas Regulation Analyst (ISSN 0199-3410); Oil and Gas Price Regulation Analyst.
Description: Articles on financial and regulatory concerns: contracts pricing, purchasing, merging, acquisitions and financing. Examines federal and state regulation.

665.7   US
NATURAL GAS ANNUAL. a., latest 1989. $12. U.S. Department of Energy, Energy Information Administration, National Energy Information Center, EI-231, Rm. 1F-048, Forrestal bldg., 1000 Independence Ave., S.W., Washington, DC 20585. TEL 202-586-8800. **Indexed:** Energy Info.Abstr.
Supersedes (as of 1979): Natural Gas Production and Consumption (ISSN 0732-6629)

665.5   US
NATURAL GAS INTELLIGENCE; weekly gas market newsletter. 1981. w. $595 includes Gas Price Index. Intelligence Press Inc., 425B Carlisle St., Herndon, VA 22070. TEL 703-444-4505. FAX 703-318-0597. (Subscr. to: Box 70587, Washington, DC 20024) Ed. Ellen Beswick. circ. 800.

665.5   US
NATURAL GAS MARKETING PIPELINE GUIDE. 1987. irreg. (plus w. updates). $567 (renewals $492). Pasha Publications Inc., 1401 Wilson Blvd., Ste. 900, Arlington, VA 22209-9970. TEL 703-528-1244. FAX 703-528-1253. Ed. Tom Castleman.
Description: Covers the major gas pipelines, with information on prices, policies, suppliers, and an industry marketing directory.

665.7   US
NATURAL GAS MONTHLY. Variant titles: Natural and Synthetic Gas. Natural Gas Monthly Report. m. $87. U.S. Department of Energy, Energy Information Administration, National Energy Information Center, EI-231, Rm. 1F-048, Forrestal bldg., 1000 Independence Ave., S.W., Washington, DC 20585. TEL 202-586-8800. **Indexed:** Chem.Abstr, Energy Info.Abstr., PROMT.
Formerly (until 1981): Natural Gas.

665.7   US
NATURAL GAS POLICY ACT NOTICES OF DETERMINATION (F E R C FORM 121). (Federal Energy Regulatory Commission) m. $500 for 1600 bpi in US, Canada, Mexico; elsewhere $1000. (Department of Energy, Energy Information Administration) U.S. National Technical Information Service, 5825 Port Royal Rd., Springfield, VA 22161. TEL 703-487-4630. (magnetic tape)
Description: Contains seller codes instead of names.

NATURAL GAS VEHICLE. see TRANSPORTATION — Automobiles

665.5   US
NATURAL GAS WEEK. 1985. w. $697. Oil Daily Co., 1401 New York Ave., N.W., Ste. 500, Washington, DC 20005. TEL 202-662-0700. FAX 202-347-8089. Ed. John H. Jennrich. bk.rev.

665.7   US   ISSN 1042-1440
NATURAL GAS YEARBOOK. 1988. a. $252 in N. America; elsewhere $337. Executive Enterprises Publications Co., Inc., 22 W. 21st St., New York, NY 10010-6990. TEL 212-645-7880. FAX 212-645-1160. Ed. Jeffrey Longcope. (also avail. in microform from UMI)
Description: Reports on the financial and regulatory concerns of the natural gas industry.

665.7   DK   ISSN 0108-3422
NATURGAS NYT; den afhaengige nyhedsbrev om naturgassens indfoerelse i Danmark. 1982. m. DKK 346. Naturgas Nyt, Enighedsvej 3, 2920 Charlottenlund, Denmark. Ed. Jorgen Erik Fokdal. illus.; circ. 1,000.

665.54   US
NEBRASKA PETROLEUM MARKETER. 1917. m. Nebraska Petroleum Marketers, Inc., 1320 Lincoln Mall, Lincoln, NE 68508. TEL 402-474-6691. FAX 402-474-2510. Ed. Fred R. Stone. adv.; tr.; lit.; circ. 1,860.
Formerly: Nebraska Oil Jobber.

665.5   RU
NEFT', GAZ I NEFTEKHIMIYA ZA RUBEZHOM/OIL, GAS AND PETROCHEMISTRY ABROAD. (Russian version of three US journals: World Oil (ISSN 0043-8790), Pipe Line (ISSN 0032-0145), Hydrocarbon Processing (ISSN 0018-8190)) 1979. m. Izdatel'stvo Nedra, Pl. Belorusskogo Vokzala, 3, 125047 Moscow, Russia. TEL 250-52-55.
Description: Covers scientific-technology and production.

665.5   RU
NEFTEGAZONOSNYE I PERSPEKTIVNYE KOMPLEKSY TSENTRAL'NYKH I VOSTOCHNYKH OBLASTEI RUSSKOI PLATFORMY. (Subseries of: Vsesoyuznyi Nauchno-Issledovatel'skii Geologorazvedochnyi Neftyanoi Institut. Trudy) irreg. 1.65 Rub. per issue. (Vsesoyuznyi Nauchno-Issledovatel'skii Geologorazvedochnyi Neftyanoi Institut) Izdatel'stvo Nedra, Pl. Belorusskogo Vokzala, 3, 125047 Moscow, Russia. TEL 250-52-55. illus.

665.5 547.8   RU   ISSN 0028-2421
TP690.A1   CODEN: NEFTAH
NEFTEKHIMIYA. 1961. bi-m. 33.30 Rub. (Akademiya Nauk S.S.S.R.) Izdatel'stvo Nauka, 90 Profsoyuznaya ul., 117864 Moscow, Russia. Ed. P.L. Sanin. index. (tabloid format) **Indexed:** API Abstr., API Catal., API Hlth.& Environ., API Oil., API Pet.Ref., API Pet.Subst., API Transport., Chem.Abstr, Chem.Infd., Curr.Chem.React, Ind.Chem.
—BLDSC shelfmark: 0124.280000.

NEFTENA I VUGLISTNA GEOLOGIIA/PETROLEUM AND COAL GEOLOGY. see EARTH SCIENCES — Geology

665.53   KR   ISSN 0548-1406
TP690.A1   CODEN: NEFNBY
NEFTEPERERABOTKA I NEFTEKHIMIYA; respublikanskii mezhvedomstvennyi sbornik nauchnykh trudov. (Text in Russian) 1965. s-a. (Akademiya Nauk Ukrainskoi S.S.R., Institut Fiziko-Organicheskoi Khimii i Uglekhimii, Otdelenie Neftekhimii) Izdatel'stvo Naukova Dumka, c/o Yu.A. Khramov, Dir, Ul. Repina, 3, Kiev 252 601, Ukraine. (Subscr. to: Mezhdunarodnaya Kniga, ul. Dimitrova 39, Moscow G-200, Russia) (Co-sponsor: Ministerstvo Neftepererabatyvayushchei Promyshlennosti S.S.S.R.) Ed. V.T. Sklyar. **Indexed:** Chem.Abstr.
—BLDSC shelfmark: 0124.230000.

665   RU   ISSN 0028-243X
TN860   CODEN: NFTYA7
NEFTYANIK (MOSCOW, 1956). 1956. m. 16.20 Rub. (Ministerstvo Neftyanoi Promyshlennosti) Izdatel'stvo Nedra, Pl. Belorusskogo Vokzala, 3, 125047 Moscow, Russia. TEL 250-52-55. (Dist. by: Mezhdunarodnaya Kniga, ul. Dimitrova 39, Moscow G-200, Russia) charts; illus.; index. **Indexed:** Chem.Abstr.
—BLDSC shelfmark: 0124.380000.

665 622   RU   ISSN 0028-2448
TN860   CODEN: NEKHA6
NEFTYANOE KHOZYAISTVO. 1920. m. $57. (Ministerstvo Neftyanoi Promyshlennosti) Izdatel'stvo Nedra, Pl. Belorusskogo Vokzala 3, 125047 Moscow, Russia. TEL 250-52-55. Ed. V Philanovsky. adv.; bk.rev.; bibl.; charts; illus.; index; circ. 8,600. (reprint service avail. from UMI) **Indexed:** Bibl.& Ind.Geol., Chem.Abstr., Curr.Cont., Eng.Ind., Petrol.Abstr., Risk Abstr.
—BLDSC shelfmark: 0124.400000.

NEW WORLDWIDE TANKER NOMINAL FREIGHT SCALE; code name worldscale. see TRANSPORTATION — Ships And Shipping

NEW ZEALAND GEOLOGICAL SURVEY BASIN STUDIES. see EARTH SCIENCES — Geology

338.2   NR
HD9577.N5
NIGERIAN NATIONAL PETROLEUM CORPORATION. MONTHLY PETROLEUM INFORMATION. m. Nigerian National Petroleum Corporation, P.M.B. 12701, Lagos, Nigeria. circ. 2,000.
Formerly: Nigeria. Federal Department of Petroleum Resources. Monthly Petroleum Information (ISSN 0549-2513)

665.7   JA   ISSN 0029-0211
   CODEN: NIPGAM
NIHON GASU KYOKAISHI/JAPAN GAS ASSOCIATION. JOURNAL. (Text in Japanese) 1948. m. 4200 Yen. Nihon Gasu Kyokai - Japan Gas Association, 15-12, Toranomon 1-chome, Minato-ku, Tokyo 105, Japan. Ed. Kazutomo Mukoyama. adv.; circ. 5,000. **Indexed:** Fuel & Energy Abstr., Gas Abstr., JTA.
—BLDSC shelfmark: 4805.000000.

NONRENEWABLE RESOURCES. see MINES AND MINING INDUSTRY

655.5   NO
NOROIL CONTACTS - OFFSHORE DIRECTORY. 1976. 3/yr. £60. Noroil Publishing House Ltd. AS, P.O. Box 480, 4001 Stavanger, Norway. (Subscr. to: Richard Fry and Associates, Ste. 225, Surrey House, 34 Eden St., Kingston upon Thames, Surrey KT1 1ER, England. TEL 081-549-3444) adv.; circ. 5,292.
Formerly: Noroil Contacts.

665.5 338.2   NO
NOROIL NEWSWIRE. (Text in English) 1978. s-w. £1150($1882) Noroil Publishing House Ltd. AS, P.O. Box 480, 4001 Stavanger, Norway. (Subscr. to: Richard Fry and Associates, Ste. 225, Surrey House, 34 Eden St., Kingston upon Thames, Surrey KT1 1ER, England. TEL 081-549-3444) Ed. N. Terdre.

665.5   NO
NORSK PETROLEUMSFORENING. AARBOK/NORWEGIAN PETROLEUM SOCIETY. YEARBOOK. (Text in Norwegian) 1979. a. Norsk Petroleumsforening, P.O. Box 1897, Vika, 0214 Oslo 2, Norway.

665.7   US
NORTH CAROLINA PROPANE GAS NEWS. m. North Carolina Propane Gas Association, 5112 Bur Oak Circle, Raleigh, NC 27612-3101. TEL 919-787-8485. Ed. Romaine Holt. circ. 800.

PETROLEUM AND GAS

665.5 332   UK
NORTH SEA LETTER. w. £547 (foreign £586). Financial Times Business Information Ltd., Tower House, Southampton St., London WC2E 7HA, England. TEL 071-240 9391. FAX 071-240-7946. TELEX 296926-BUSINF-G.
● Also available online. Vendor(s): Data-Star, Mead Data Central.
Description: Provides news and commentary on events in the oil and gas industry on Europe's NW Continental Shelf.

665.5   UK   ISSN 0265-5039
NORTH SEA OIL & GAS DIRECTORY. 1972. a. £52. Benn Business Information Services Ltd., P.O. Box 20, Sovereign Way, Tonbridge, Kent TN9 1RQ, England. TEL 0732-362666. adv.; circ. 3,250.

665.538   US   ISSN 0884-4771
TN860
NORTHEAST OIL WORLD. 1981. m. $39 (foreign $89). Hart Publications, Inc., 1900 Grant St., Ste. 400, Box 1917, Denver, CO 80201. TEL 303-837-1917. adv. (back issues avail.) **Indexed:** Petrol.Abstr.
Formerly (until 1985): Northeast Oil Reporter (ISSN 0279-7798)
Description: Covers the Appalachian, Illinois and Michigan Basin areas.

380   US
NORTHEAST PETROLEUM INDUSTRY. 1945. a. $40. Midwest Register, Inc., 601 S. Boulder, Ste. 1001, Tulsa, OK 74119-1301. TEL 918-582-2000.
Formerly: Directory of Producers and Drilling Contractors Northeast: Michigan, Indiana, Illinois, Kentucky.
Description: Supplies company name, address, phone and fax number, personnel, division offices, offshore operations, producers of oil or gas and if drilling contractor with rotary or cable tools, pipelines, refineries, petrochemical, gas processing, manufacturers and suppliers, petroleum engineers, landmen.

NOZZLE. see TRANSPORTATION — Automobiles

665 338.2   SA
NUTSHELL. (Text in English) 1938. m. Shell South Africa (Pty) Ltd., P.O. Box 2231, Cape Town 8000, South Africa. TEL 021-408-4911. FAX 021-253807. circ. 7,500 (controlled).
Formerly (until 1982): Shell Chronicle (ISSN 0037-3524)

665.5   UK
NWY NEWS. 1960. bi-m. free. British Gas Wales, Public Relations Dept., Helmont House, Churchill Way, Cardiff CF1 4NB, Wales. TEL 0222-239290. FAX 0222-290738. Ed. Andy Weltch. circ. 6,300 (controlled).

338.47   KU
O A P E C ENERGY RESOURCES MONITOR. (Text in Arabic) 1981. q. free. Organization of Arab Petroleum Exporting Countries, P.O. Box 20501, Safat 13066, Kuwait. TEL 965-2448200. FAX 965-2426885. TELEX 22166 NAFARAB KT. circ. 250.
Description: Coverage of Arab and world developments in petroleum exploration, drilling, production, field development and in alternative energy technology.

382.42   KU
O A P E C MONTHLY BULLETIN. (Editions in Arabic, English) 1975. m. $24 to individuals; institutions $48. Organization of Arab Petroleum Exporting Countries, Information Department, P.O. Box 20501, Safat 13066, Kuwait. TEL 965-2448200. FAX 965-242-6885. TELEX 22166 NAFARAB KT. adv.; bk.rev.; stat.; circ. 3,000. **Indexed:** Key to Econ.Sci., Mid.East: Abstr.& Ind., World Bank.Abstr.
Formerly: O A P E C News Bulletin; Incorporating (after 1988): Organization of Arab Petroleum Exporting Countries. Current Awareness; Which was formerly: O A P E C Monthly Bulletin of Current Awareness.
Description: Coverage of activities of OAPEC and its sponsored ventures. Arab and world developments in petroleum and energy, statistics, and Arab and international conferences.

665.5   US
O & A MARKETING NEWS. bi-m. McAnally & Associates, Inc., Box 765, La Canada, CA 91012-0765. TEL 818-790-6554. FAX 818-248-9051. Ed. Don McAnally. circ. 9,000.

665.5   FR
O E C D. ANNUAL OIL MARKET REPORT. a. price varies. Organization for Economic Cooperation and Development, 2 rue Andre-Pascal, 75775 Paris Cedex 16, France. TEL 45-24-82-00. FAX 45-24-85-00. (U.S. orders to: O.E.C.D. Publications and Information Center, 2001 L St., N.W., Ste. 700, Washington, DC 20036-4910. TEL 202-785-6323) (also avail. in microfiche from OEC)

665.5   UK   ISSN 0277-0180
HD9560.1   CODEN: OPECDI
O P E C REVIEW; an energy and economic forum. (Text in English) 1976. q. £75 (effective 1992). (Organization of the Petroleum Exporting Countries, Public Information Department, AU) Pergamon Press plc, Headington Hill Hall, Oxford OX3 0BW, England. TEL 0865-794141. FAX 0865-743911. TELEX 83177 PERGAP. (And: 660 White Plains Rd., Tarrytown, NY 10591-5153. TEL 914-524-9200) Ed. James Audu. circ. 2,000. **Indexed:** AESIS, C.R.E.J., Energy Info.Abstr., IIS, Key to Econ.Sci., World Bank.Abstr.
—BLDSC shelfmark: 6265.943000.
Refereed Serial

665.5   US   ISSN 0029-8026
GC1   CODEN: OCIDAF
OCEAN INDUSTRY. 1966. 10/yr. $22 (free to qualified personnel). Gulf Publishing Co., Box 2608, Houston, TX 77252-2608. TEL 713-529-4301. FAX 713-520-4433. TELEX 287330 GULF UR. Ed. Robert Snyder. adv.; bk.rev.; abstr.; charts; illus.; stat.; circ. 30,148. (also avail. in microfilm from UMI; reprint service avail. from UMI) **Indexed:** AESIS, API Abstr., API Catal., API Hlth.& Environ., API Oil., API Pet.Ref., API Pet.Subst., API Transport., Bibl.& Ind.Geol., BMT, Br.Geol.Lit., Bus.Ind., Deep Sea Res.& Oceanogr.Abstr., Energy Rev., Excerp.Med., Fluidex, Fuel & Energy Abstr., J.of Ferroc., Ocean.Abstr., Ocean.Ind., Petrol.Abstr., Pollut.Abstr.

662   US   ISSN 0029-8042
OCEAN OIL WEEKLY REPORT. 1966. w. $335 (outside N. America $395). PennWell Publishing Co. (Houston), Box 1941, Houston, TX 77251. TEL 713-621-9720. FAX 713-963-6285. Ed. Michael Crowden. cum.index; circ. 1,000. (looseleaf format)
● Also available online.
Description: Provides news and developments in the world's offshore oil and gas industry.

665.5   US
OCTANE WEEK. 1986. w. $895. Information Resources, Inc., 499 S. Capitol St., S.W., No. 406, Washington, DC 20003. TEL 800-USA-FUEL. FAX 202-554-0613. Ed. Dan McKay.
● Also available online. Vendor(s): Data-Star, DIALOG.

338.47   AU
OE M V ANNUAL REPORT (YEAR). (Text in English) 1956. a. free. Oe M V Aktiengesellschaft, Oeffentlichkeitsarbeit, Otto Wagner-Platz 5, A-1090 Vienna, Austria. FAX 0222-40440-91. TELEX 114801.

621.3   US   ISSN 0078-3706
OFF-SHORE TECHNOLOGY CONFERENCE. RECORD.* a. Offshore Technology Conference, Program Department, Box 833836, Richardson, TX 75083-3836.

665.5   UK
OFFSHORE BUSINESS; engineering and project management. £180 (foreign £190). Smith Rea Energy Analysts Limited, Hunstead House, Nickel, Chartham, Kent, Canterbury, Kent CT4 7PL, England.

665.7   US
OFFSHORE CONTRACTORS AND EQUIPMENT WORLDWIDE DIRECTORY. 1969. a. $125. PennWell Publishing Co., Box 1260, Tulsa, OK 74101. TEL 918-835-3161. (Alternate addr.: 1421 S. Sheridan, Tulsa, OK 74112) Ed. Jonell Moore. adv. (back issues avail.)
Former titles: Offshore Contractors and Equipment Directory (ISSN 0475-1310); Worldwide Offshore Contractors Directory (ISSN 0084-2575)
Description: Lists over 3500 companies and personnel in the drilling, construction, geophysical diving, service and supply manufacturing and transportation industries.

665.5 620   UK   ISSN 0305-876X
TC1501
OFFSHORE ENGINEER. 1975. m. £64 (foreign £68). (Institution of Civil Engineers) Thomas Telford Ltd., Thomas Telford House, 1 Heron Quay, London E14 4JD, England. TEL 071-987-6999. FAX 071-537-2443. TELEX 298105-CIVILS-G. Ed. Jenny Gregory. adv.; charts; illus.; circ. 16,500. (back issues avail.) **Indexed:** AESIS, Bibl.& Ind.Geol., BMT, Br.Geol.Lit., Br.Tech.Ind., Excerp.Med., Fluidex, Fuel & Energy Abstr., Key to Econ.Sci., Ocean.Abstr., Petrol.Abstr., Pollut.Abstr.
—BLDSC shelfmark: 6244.225000.
Incorporating: Northern Offshore (ISSN 0332-5237)
Description: Covers engineering, technical and operational facets of offshore oil and gas exploration and production worldwide.

OFFSHORE ENGINEERING. see ENGINEERING — Civil Engineering

665.5 338.2   US   ISSN 1058-5869
OFFSHORE FIELD DEVELOPMENT INTERNATIONAL. 1979. m. $445 (foreign $480). Offshore Data Services, Inc., Box 19909, Houston, TX 77224-9909. TEL 713-781-2713. FAX 713-781-9594. Ed. Paul Hillegeist. circ. 900. (also avail. in magnetic tape; also avail. on diskette)
Formerly (until 1991): Ocean Construction Locator (ISSN 0276-3680)
Description: Lists information on all offshore platform, pipeline, and mooring terminal projects worldwide, from the planning stages to final installation.

387   US   ISSN 0266-3112
OFFSHORE FLEET ECONOMICS. 1984. fortn. $250. Offshore Data Services, Inc., Box 19909, Houston, TX 77224-9909. TEL 713-781-2713. FAX 713-781-9594. Ed. Susanne Pagano. circ. 130.
Description: Focuses on opportunities and developments affecting the workboat and marine support services industries.

338.2 622   US
TN871.3   CODEN: OFSHAU
OFFSHORE INCORPORATING THE OILMAN. 1954. 12/yr. $55 (foreign $72). PennWell Publishing Co., Box 1260, Tulsa, OK 74101. TEL 918-835-3161. Ed. Leonard Le Blanc. adv.; charts; illus.; tr.lit.; circ. 25,600. (also avail. in microform from UMI; reprint service avail. from UMI) **Indexed:** A.S.& T.Ind., BMT, Br.Tech.Ind., Deep Sea Res.& Oceanogr.Abstr., Energy Rev., Environ.Per.Bibl., J.of Ferroc., Key to Econ.Sci., Ocean.Abstr., Petrol.Abstr., Pollut.Abstr., SRI, Tr.& Indus.Ind.
● Also available online. Vendor(s): Mead Data Central.
Incorporates (1973-1988): Offshore (Tulsa) (ISSN 0030-0608); **Formerly:** Oilman (ISSN 0143-6694)
Description: Serves the worldwide petroleum industry in its marine operations, engineering and technology. Includes information pertaining to seismic services, exploration, drilling, production, process, transportation (pipeline, marine, and air), marine and underwater engineering and communications, naval architecture, design and construction, diving services, marine support facilities, and research in oceanography and meteorology.

665.5   US   ISSN 1058-5842
OFFSHORE INTERNATIONAL NEWSLETTER. 1973. w. $475 (foreign $510). Offshore Data Services, Inc., Box 19909, Houston, TX 77224-9909. TEL 713-781-2713. FAX 713-781-9594. Ed. Susanne S. Pagano. circ. 695.
Former titles (until 1991): Offshore Construction Report (ISSN 0147-152X); Ocean Construction and Engineering Report.
Description: Follows offshore oil developments and related concerns worldwide.

338.47   US
OFFSHORE PETROLEUM INDUSTRY. q. $1800 first year; thereafter $950. Barrows Co., Inc., 116 E. 66th St., New York, NY 10021. TEL 212-772-1199. FAX 212-288-7242. TELEX 4971238/BARROWS. Ed. Marta Guerra.
Description: Follows world oil and gas offshore operations in all countries. Emphasis on world investment, geological favorability, production, technology and economics.

PETROLEUM AND GAS

665.5 CN ISSN 0820-0858
OFFSHORE RESOURCES; Canada's offshore oil & gas and oceanic industries magazine. 1983. 6/yr. I.B.I.S. Publishing Inc., P.O. Box 91760, W. Vancouver, B.C. V7V 4S1, Canada. TEL 604-986-9501. Ed. Duncan Cumming. adv.; bk.rev.; circ. 8,767.

665.5 338.2 US
OFFSHORE RIG LOCATOR. 1974. m. $485 (foreign $525). Offshore Data Services, Inc., Box 19909, Houston, TX 77224-9909. TEL 713-781-2713. FAX 713-781-9594. Ed. John Chadderdon. circ. 700. (also avail. in magnetic tape; also avail. on diskette)
Formerly (until 1984): Offshore Rig Location Report (ISSN 0733-0928)
Description: Provides location information and operating statistics on the activity of all offshore drilling rigs, with analyses of market conditions.

665.5 US ISSN 0147-1481
OFFSHORE RIG NEWSLETTER. 1974. m. $190 (foreign $205). Offshore Data Services, Inc., Box 19909, Houston, TX 77224-9909. TEL 713-781-2713. FAX 713-781-9594. Ed. Tom Marsh. circ. 1,650.
Description: Reports news and events affecting the international offshore drilling market.

665.5 US
OFFSHORE RIG REPORT. 1984. m. $360. PennWell Publishing Co., Box 1260, Tulsa, OK 74101. TEL 918-835-3161. Ed. Mary J. Lutz. (avail. on diskette)
Formerly: Worldwide Offshore Rigfinder.

662 627 UK ISSN 0309-040X
OFFSHORE SERVICE VESSEL REGISTER. 1977. a. £145($240) Clarkson Research Studies Ltd., 12 Camomile St., London EC3A 7BP, England. TEL 071-283 8955. adv.

665.5 US ISSN 1058-5877
OFFSHORE U S OIL COMPANY OPERATING PERSONNEL DIRECTORY. a. $125. Offshore Data Services, Inc., Box 19909, Houston, TX 77224-9909. TEL 713-781-2713. FAX 713-781-9594.
Formerly: Oil Company Operating Personnel Directory.
Description: Lists personnel at 267 oil companies operating in the Gulf of Mexico.

665.5 CN
OIL ACTIVITY REVIEW. 1982. a. free. Manitoba Energy and Mines, Petroleum Branch, 555-330 Graham Ave., Winnipeg, Man. R3C 4E3, Canada. TEL 204-945-6315. FAX 204-945-0586. Ed. L.R. Dubreuil. charts; illus.; stat.; circ. 1,000.
Description: Review of petroleum industry activity in Manitoba.

665.5 KU
OIL AND ARAB COOPERATION. (Text in Arabic; summaries in English) 1975. q. $20 to individuals; $40 to institutions. Organization of Arab Petroleum Exporting Countries, Information Department, P.O. Box 20501, Safat 13066, Kuwait. TEL 965-2448200. FAX 965-2426885. TELEX 22166 NAFARAB KT. Ed. Abdelaziz Alwattari. bk.rev.; bibl.; circ. 1,500. Indexed: Mid.East: Abstr.& Ind.
Description: Articles on petroleum sector and economic and social development in Arab countries.

OIL & CHEMICAL WORKER. see *LABOR UNIONS*

665.5 UK ISSN 0950-1045
HD9560.4
OIL AND ENERGY TRENDS. 1975. m. £300. Basil Blackwell Ltd., 108 Cowley Rd., Oxford OX4 1JF, England. TEL 0865-791100. FAX 0865-791347. TELEX 837022 OXBOOK G. Ed. F.R. Parra. charts; stat.; circ. 1,000.
Supersedes: Petroleum Industry Trends.

665.5 557 US
OIL AND GAS; monthly report on drilling in Illinois. 1936. m. $15. State Geological Survey, Natural Resources Bldg., 615 E. Peabody Dr., Champaign, IL 61820. TEL 217-344-1481. bibl.; stat.; circ. 600.

OIL AND GAS ACCOUNTING. see *BUSINESS AND ECONOMICS — Accounting*

665.5 531.64 US
OIL AND GAS DEVELOPMENTS IN PENNSYLVANIA. 1951. a. price varies. (Bureau of Topographic and Geologic Survey, Department of Environmental Resources) Pennsylvania Geological Survey, c/o John Harper, 121 S. Highland Ave., Pittsburgh, PA 15206-3988. TEL 717-787-2169. (Subscr. to: State Book Store, Box 1365, Harrisburg, PA 17105) (back issues avail.)

338.2 US ISSN 0471-380X
OIL & GAS DIRECTORY. 1970. a. $60 (foreign $75). Geophysical Directory, Inc., 2200 Welch Ave., Box 130508, Houston, TX 77219. TEL 713-529-8789. FAX 713-529-3646. Ed. Claudia La Calli. adv.; circ. 5,000.
Description: Lists oil companies, key personnel as well as service and supply companies in the petroleum industry.

OIL AND GAS FIELD DESIGNATIONS. see *EARTH SCIENCES — Geology*

665.5 657 UK ISSN 0962-3752
OIL & GAS FINANCE AND ACCOUNTING. 1986. q. £115($200) Langham Publishing, 21 Pointers Close, Isle of Dogs, London E14 3AP, England. TEL 071-987-8631. Ed. Tudor David. adv.; bk.rev.; index. (back issues avail.) Indexed: Account.Ind. (1987-).
—BLDSC shelfmark: 6249.844500.
Formerly: Journal of Oil and Gas Accountancy (ISSN 0267-4920)

665.5 US
OIL & GAS INTERESTS NEWSLETTER. m. Tamarack Consulting Company, Box 218162, Houston, TX 77218-8162. TEL 713-579-2782. FAX 713-579-8895. Ed. Jack Stevenson.

665.5 US ISSN 0744-5881
HD9561
OIL AND GAS INVESTOR. 1981. m. $195 (foreign $277). Hart Publications, Inc., 1900 Grant St., Ste. 400, Box 1917, Denver, CO 80201. TEL 303-837-1917. adv.; charts; illus.; circ. 6,500. (back issues avail.) Indexed: ABI Inform.
—BLDSC shelfmark: 6249.958000.
Description: Written for the sophisticated petroleum investor. Topics cover financial and money management and petroleum investment in nontechnical language.

665.5 US ISSN 0030-1388
TN860 CODEN: OIGJAV
OIL & GAS JOURNAL. 1902. w. $48.50 to qualified personnel (foreign $82); non-operational personnel $95. PennWell Publishing Co., Box 1260, Tulsa, OK 74101. TEL 918-835-3161. Ed. Gene T. Kinney. adv.; bk.rev.; charts; illus.; mkt.; stat.; tr.lit.; index; circ. 62,000. (also avail. in microform from UMI; reprint service avail. from UMI) Indexed: A.S.& T.Ind., Acid Rain Abstr., Acid Rain Ind., AESIS, API Abstr., API Catal., API Hlth.& Environ., API Oil., API Pet.Ref., API Pet.Subst., API Transport., Bibl.& Ind.Geol., Br.Geol.Lit., Bus.Ind., C.I.S. Abstr., CAD CAM Abstr., Chem.Abstr., Chem.Eng.Abstr., Chem.Infd., Corros.Abstr., Curr.Cont., Deep Sea Res.& Oceanogr.Abstr., Dok.Arbeitsmed., Energy Info.Abstr., Energy.Info.Abstr., Eng.Ind., Environ.Abstr., Excerp.Med., Fluidex, Fuel & Energy.Abstr., Gas Abstr., HRIS, Key to Econ.Sci., Met.Abstr., Mid.East: Abstr.& Ind., Ocean.Abstr., Petrol.Abstr., Petrol.Energy B.N.I., Pollut.Abstr., PROMT, Risk Abstr., Soils & Fert., SRI, T.C.E.A., Tr.& Indus.Ind., W.R.C.Inf., World Alum.Abstr.
●Also available online. Vendor(s): Mead Data Central.
—BLDSC shelfmark: 6250.000000.
Description: Covers all segments of the petroleum industry: exploration, drilling, production, refining, processing and pipeline transportation.

338.2 665 UK ISSN 0263-5070
K3911.2
OIL & GAS: LAW AND TAXATION REVIEW. 1982. m. £235. E S C Publishing Ltd., Mill St., Oxford OX2 0JU, England. TEL 0865-249248. FAX 0865-792301. adv.; bk.rev.; index; circ. 350. (back issues avail.)
—BLDSC shelfmark: 6250.023000.

665.5 SI ISSN 0217-6602
OIL AND GAS NEWS. w. $495 (effective 1991). Al Hilal Publishing & Marketing Group, P.O. Box 224, Manama, Bahrain. TEL 293131. FAX 293400. TELEX 8981 HILAL BN. (In Singapore: Al Hilal Publishing (Far East) Pte Ltd, 50 Jalan Sultan, 20-06 Jalan Sultan Centre, Singapore 0719. TEL 2939233) Ed. Gurdip Singh. adv.; circ. 5,050.
Description: Covers news of trends, products, events and other information for senior personnel in all sectors of the petroleum industry, including oil companies, exploration, supply, marine and offshore contractors, and government agencies.

OIL AND GAS POOL DESCRIPTIONS. see *EARTH SCIENCES — Geology*

665.5 CN
OIL AND GAS PRODUCTION REPORT. m. Can.$125. Ministry of Energy, Mines and Petroleum Resources, Energy Resources Division, Parliament Bldgs., Victoria, B.C. V8V 1X4, Canada. TEL 604-356-2743. (Subscr. to: Crown Publications, 546 Yates St., Victoria, B.C. V8W 1K8, Canada. TEL 604-386-4636) circ. 125. (back issues avail.)
Description: Includes a statistical summary of the drilling activity, well count, production and injection of all fluids on a pool basis, disposition of production gas plant and refinery operations, and nominations and estimated requirements by the refineries.

665.5 US ISSN 0472-7630
KF1845.A2
OIL AND GAS REPORTER. 1952. m. $540. Southwestern Legal Foundation, Box 830707, Richardson, TX 75083. TEL 214-690-2370. (Subscr. to: 1275 Broadway, Albany, NY 12201.) Ed. Carol Holgren. index; cum. index. (looseleaf format)
Description: Reporter of oil and gas judicial decisions with editorial comments and case digests.

OIL AND GAS TAX QUARTERLY. see *BUSINESS AND ECONOMICS — Public Finance, Taxation*

665.5 665.74 II
OIL AND NATURAL GAS COMMISSION. BULLETIN. (Text in English) 1964. s-a. $65. (Oil & Natural Gas Commission) Indian Petroleum Publishing Company, 100-9, Naishville Road, Dehra Dun 248 001, India. Ed. B.S. Venkataachala. bk.rev.; circ. 1,400. (back issues avail.) Indexed: Petrol.Abstr.

662 US
OIL BUYERS' GUIDE. vol. 5, 1975. w. $695 (foreign $795). Bloomberg Financial Markets, 100 Business Park Dr., Box 888, Princeton, NJ 08542-0888. TEL 609-497-3500. FAX 609-683-7523. Ed. Vincent Sgro. charts; stat.

665.5 US
OIL BUYERS' GUIDE INTERNATIONAL. 1981. w. $775 (foreign $875). Bloomberg Financial Markets, 100 Business Park Dr., Box 888, Princeton, NJ 08542-0888. TEL 609-497-3500. FAX 609-683-7523. Ed. Vincent Sgro. charts; stat.

665 US
OIL CAN. 1926. bi-m. $18 to non-members; members $8. Illinois Petroleum Marketers Association, Box 12020, Springfield, IL 62791-2020. TEL 217-544-4609. FAX 217-789-0222. (Co-sponsor: Illinois Association of Convenience Stores) Ed. William R. Deutsch. adv.; illus.; circ. 1,250. (back issues avail.)
Description: Contains news about products and personnel in Illinois' petroleum industry.

OIL CHEMICAL RUBBER WORKERS TRADE UNION OF TURKEY. YEARBOOK. see *LABOR UNIONS*

665.5 338.2 US ISSN 0030-1434
HD9561
OIL DAILY; daily newspaper of the petroleum industry. 1951. d. $597. Oil Daily Co., 1401 New York Ave., N.W., Ste. 500, Washington, DC 20005. TEL 202-662-0700. FAX 202-783-8320. Ed. Marshall Thomas. adv.; charts; mkt.; stat. (tabloid format; also avail. in microform from UMI; reprint service avail. from UMI) Indexed: Bus.Ind., Petrol.Energy B.N.I., Tr.& Indus.Ind.
●Also available online. Vendor(s): DIALOG.
—BLDSC shelfmark: 6250.750000.

PETROLEUM AND GAS

665.5 338.2 US
OIL DAILY WEEKLY EDITION. w. $397. Oil Daily Co., 1401 New York Ave., N.W., Ste 500, Washington, DC 20005. TEL 202-662-0700. FAX 202-783-8320. Ed. Mike Zastodil.

665.5 US
OIL EXPRESS; exclusive report giving informed petroleum marketers nationwide. w. $247. United Communications Group, 11300 Rockville Pike, Ste. 1100, Rockville, MD 20852-3030. TEL 301-816-8950. Ed. Carole Donoghue.
  Description: Provides petroleum marketers with the latest news in the industry, plus new approaches in oil marketing.

622 665 US ISSN 0030-1353
TN871.5
OIL, GAS & PETROCHEM EQUIPMENT. 1954. m. free to qualified personnel; others $30. PennWell Publishing Co., Box 1260, Tulsa, OK 74101. TEL 918-835-3161. Ed. J.B. Avants. adv.; circ. 36,000 (controlled). (tabloid format) **Indexed:** Petrol.Abstr.
  Formerly: Oil and Gas Equipment.
  Description: Serves the operating phases (except marketing) of the petroleum industry, including: exploration, drilling, drilling and well services contracting, production, natural gas processing, refining, petrochemical manufacturing, process plant contracting, design, engineering, oil and gas pipeline contracting, design, engineering and construction.

665.5 US
OIL, GAS & PETROCHEMICALS ABROAD. (Text in Russian) m. Gulf Publishing Co., Box 2608, Houston, TX 77252-2608. TEL 713-529-4301.
  Description: Covers technical articles for people in the gas and oil business.

665.5 GW ISSN 0342-5622
TN860
OIL GAS EUROPEAN MAGAZINE. (Text in English) 1975. 4/yr. DM.96. Urban-Verlag GmbH, Postfach 701606, 2000 Hamburg 70, Germany. TEL 040-6567071. FAX 040-6567075. Eds. Thomas Vieth, Hans Joerg Mager. circ. 5,000. **Indexed:** Gas Abstr.
  —BLDSC shelfmark: 6252.025000.
  Formerly: European Oil and Gas Magazine.

665.5 US
OIL IN THE ROCKIES. m. $33.50. Petroleum Information Corporation, Box 2612, Denver, CO 80201-2612. TEL 303-740-7100. FAX 303-694-1754. stat.
  Description: Regional activity summary featuring exploration highlights, land and leasing information, pipeline and refining activity, completion and production statistics, and more.

665.5 US
OIL INDUSTRY COMPARATIVE APPRAISALS 1. 1948. m. $1030 (foreign $1095). 5 Edgewood Ave., Greenwich, CT 06830. TEL 203-869-2585. Ed. Charles Andrew. charts; illus.; stat.
  Description: Provides appraisal reports and updates on the largest U.S. and international public oil and gas companies.

665.5 US
OIL INDUSTRY COMPARATIVE APPRAISALS 2. m. $1030 (foreign $1095). John S. Herold, Inc., 5 Edgewood Ave., Greenwich, CT 06830. TEL 203-869-2585.
  Description: Appraises the independent exploration and production companies of the US, and the Master Limited Partnership and Royalty Trust industry sectors.

665.5 US
OIL INDUSTRY COMPARATIVE APPRAISALS 3. $1030 (foreign $1095). John S. Herold, Inc., 5 Edgewood Ave., Greenwich, CT 06830. TEL 203-869-2585.
  Description: Appraises Canadian oils and foreign domiciled, integrated and independent oils.

388.47 330.9 US ISSN 0741-3343
HD9561
OIL INDUSTRY OUTLOOK FOR THE U S A. 1984. a. $150 (foreign $187.50). PennWell Publishing Co., Box 1260, Tulsa, OK 74101. TEL 918-835-3161. Ed. Robert J. Beck.

665 US
OIL MARKETER; official voice of petroleum marketers in Oklahoma. 1964. q. $12. Oklahoma Oil Marketers Association, 5115 N. Western, Oklahoma City, OK 73118. TEL 405-842-6625. FAX 405-842-9564. Ed. Heard Broderick. adv.; circ. 1,300 (controlled).
  Formerly: Oklahoma Oil Marketer.

665.5 US
THE OIL MARKETING BULLETIN. w. $695. United Communications Group, 11300 Rockville Pike, Ste. 1100, Rockville, MD 20852-3030. TEL 301-816-8950. Ed. Brian Crotty.
  Description: Directed to oil company executives providing information on buying trends, pricing and industry news.

655.5 658.8 US
OIL MARKETING INDUSTRY. 1945. a. $40. Midwest Register, Inc., 601 S. Boulder, Ste. 1001, Tulsa, OK 74119-1301. TEL 918-582-2000.
  Formerly: Directory of Oil Marketing and Wholesale Distributors (ISSN 0070-5993)
  Description: Supplies company name, address, phone and fax number. Includes personnel with their titles.

665.5 338.2 IR ISSN 0030-1450
OIL NEWS. fortn. free. Petroleum Ministry, Public Relations & Guidance Department, P.O. Box 1863, Central NIOC Bldg., Taleghani Ave., Teheran, Iran. TEL 021-6151. TELEX 212514. **Indexed:** Fuel & Energy Abstr.

665.5 UK
OIL NEWS SERVICE NEWSLETTER. 1972. fortn. £97($185) Oil News Service, Springfield House, Dollar, Clackmannanshire, Scotland. Ed. David Gibson. adv.; bk.rev.; circ. 800. (back issues avail.)

665.538 UK
OIL PACKER INTERNATIONAL. 1988. q. $50. Binsted Publications Ltd., Walton House, 90 London Rd., Hook, Hants RG27 9LF, England. FAX 0256-766102. Ed. Edward C. Binsted. circ. 8,000.

338.47 US ISSN 0279-7801
OIL PRICE INFORMATION SERVICE. w. $545. United Communications Group, 11300 Rockville Pike, Ste. 1100, Rockville, MD 20852-3030. TEL 301-816-8950. Ed. Ben Brockwell.
  ●Also available online. Vendor(s): United Communications Group (PETROSCAN).
  Description: Gives actual wholesale and spot gasoline, distillate and propane prices each week, plus trends, new sources, and new markets.

OIL SHALE SYMPOSIUM PROCEEDINGS. see MINES AND MINING INDUSTRY

665.5 US ISSN 0195-3524
TD427.P4
OIL SPILL INTELLIGENCE REPORT; the weekly newsletter on oil spill control and cleanup worldwide. 1978. w. $527 (foreign $627). Cutter Information Corp., 37 Broadway, Arlington, MA 02174. TEL 617-648-8700. FAX 617-648-8707. TELEX 650 100 9891 MCI UW.
  ●Also available online. Vendor(s): Data-Star, DIALOG, NewsNet.
  Description: News and information for professionals worldwide - government agencies, oil and shipping companies, research labs, spill-control equipment manufacturers, environmental consultants, legislators, and litigators.

OIL SPILL U S LAW REPORT; legislation, litigation, regulations & enforcement actions. see LAW

665.5 UK ISSN 0261-3247
OIL SPOT. 1978. m. Britoil PLC, 301 St. Vincent St., Glasgow G2 5DD, Scotland. TEL 041-204 2525. illus.
  Description: Company newsletter; includes news of company developments, business activities and employees.

OIL TECHNOLOGISTS' ASSOCIATION OF INDIA. JOURNAL.
see CHEMISTRY — Organic Chemistry

665.5 US
OIL WELL SUPPLY INDUSTRY. a. $40. Midwest Register, Inc., 601 S. Boulder, Ste. 1001, Tulsa, OK 74119-1301. TEL 918-582-2000.
  Formerly: Directory of Oil Well Supply Companies (ISSN 0415-9772)
  Description: Supplies company name, address, phone and fax number, and personnel information.

665.5 551 NE ISSN 0923-1730
OILFIELD REVIEW. 1950. 4/yr. fl.296 (effective 1992). (Schlumberger-Doll Research) Elsevier Science Publishers B.V., P.O. Box 211, 1000 AE Amsterdam, Netherlands. TEL 020-5803911. FAX 020-5803598. TELEX 18582 ESPA NL. (Subscr. in U.S. and Canada to: Elsevier Science Publishing Co., Inc., Box 882, Madison Sq. Sta., New York, NY 10159. TEL 212-989-5800) Ed. Henry N. Edmundson. bk.rev.; illus.; circ. 4,100. (back issues avail.)
  —BLDSC shelfmark: 6252.274680.
  Formed by the 1990 merger of: Schlumberger Limited. Technical Review & Drilling and Pumping Journal.
  Description: Source of information on seismic surveying, drilling, MWD, well logging, well testing, reservoir stimulation and completion practices.
  Refereed Serial

665.5 SP ISSN 0030-1493
OILGAS. 1968. m. 7500 ptas.($115) in Europe; elsewhere $140. (Spanish Petroleum Association) Oilgas S.A., Paseo de la Habana, 48, 28036 Madrid, Spain. Ed. Carlos Martin. circ. 6,500. **Indexed:** Gas Abstr., Ind.SST.
  Description: Discusses the petroleum, petrochemical and gas industries' activities.

665.5 CN ISSN 0164-887X
OILPATCH MAGAZINE; the natural resources magazine. 1976. m. Can.$42.95. c/o Master Publications, 2nd Fl., 17560 - 107th Ave., Edmondton, Alta. T5S 1E9, Canada. TEL 403-486-1295. FAX 403-484-0884. Ed. Leah Hyman. adv.; circ. 12,000.

665.5 338.2 CN ISSN 0030-1515
CODEN: OLWKAX
OILWEEK. 1954. 51/yr. Can.$79. Maclean-Hunter Ltd. (Calgary), 200-1015 Centre St. N., Calgary, Alta. T2E 2P8, Canada. TEL 403-276-7881. FAX 403-276-5026. Ed. Greg Gilbertson. adv.; bk.rev.; charts; illus.; maps; mkt.; stat.; circ. 10,088. (also avail. in microform from UMI; reprint service avail. from UMI) **Indexed:** API Abstr., API Catal., API Hlth.& Environ., API Oil., API Pet.Ref., API Pet.Subst., API Transport., Bibl.& Ind.Geol., Can.B.P.I., Chem.Abstr., Petrol.Abstr., PROMT.
  —BLDSC shelfmark: 6252.620000.

338.47 DK ISSN 0109-3916
OLIEBERETNING. 1979. a. free. Oliebranchens Faellesrepraesentation - Danish Petroleum Industry Association, Vognmagergade 7, P.O. Box 120, DK-1004 Copenhagen K, Denmark. TEL 45-33 11 30 77. FAX 45-33-32-16-18. illus.
  Formerly: Oliebranchens Faellesrepraesentation. Beretning.

553 US ISSN 0078-5741
TN872.07 CODEN: OGOGAE
OREGON. STATE DEPARTMENT OF GEOLOGY AND MINERAL INDUSTRIES. OIL AND GAS INVESTIGATIONS.* 1963. irreg., no.16, 1989. price varies. Department of Geology and Mineral Industries, 800 N.E. Oregon St., Portland, OR 97232-2109. TEL 503-229-5580. FAX 503-229-5639.

341.7 KU
ORGANIZATION OF ARAB PETROLEUM EXPORTING COUNTRIES. SECRETARY GENERAL'S ANNUAL REPORT. 1974. a. free. Organization of Arab Petroleum Exporting Countries, P.O. Box 20501, Safat 13066, Kuwait. TEL 965-2448200. FAX 965-2426885. TELEX 22166 NAFARAB KT. charts; stat.; circ. 2,500.
  Description: Review of Arab and world economics and energy developments plus description of activities of OPEC and its sponsored ventures.

PETROLEUM AND GAS

665.5   AU   ISSN 0474-6279
HD9560.1
ORGANIZATION OF THE PETROLEUM EXPORTING COUNTRIES. BULLETIN. (Text in English) 1969. 10/yr. free. Organization of the Petroleum Exporting Countries Publications, Public Information Department, Obere Donaustr. 93, A-1020 Vienna, Austria. TEL 222-22112-0. FAX 222-264320. TELEX 134474. Ed. Keith Jinks. bk.rev.; charts; illus.; stat.; index; circ. 8,500. (microfiche) **Indexed:** Energy Info.Abstr., Energy Rev., Environ.Abstr.
—BLDSC shelfmark: 6265.940000.
Description: Includes organization reports, market reviews, statistics, energy news and surveys, OPEC publications and fund news, new publications in the OPEC library, announcements of events.

665.5   AT   ISSN 0310-4184
P E X: AUSTRALIA'S PETROLEUM EXPLORATION NEWSLETTER. 1972. 11/yr. Aus.$200 (effective Dec. 1991). Pex Publications Pty. Ltd., P.O. Box 158, Claremont, W.A. 6010, Australia. TEL 09-383-3477. FAX 09-385-1485. Ed. Don Lipscombe. bk.rev.; circ. 500. **Indexed:** AESIS.
Description: Publishes news, views, comments and analysis.

665.5   US
P G W NEWSLINE. 1928. m. free. Philadelphia Gas Works, 800 W. Montgomery Ave., Philadelphia, PA 19122. TEL 215-684-6564. Ed. Peter A. Hussie. circ. 4,500 (controlled).
Formerly: P G W News.

662.6 338   US
PACIFIC COAST OIL DIRECTORY. 1983. a. Petroleum Publishers, Inc., 753 W. Lambert Rd., Box 129, Brea, CA 92621. FAX 714-990-4061.

PACIFIC - MOUNTAIN OIL DIRECTORY. see *BUSINESS AND ECONOMICS — Trade And Industrial Directories*

665.5   US   ISSN 0008-1329
TN860
PACIFIC OIL WORLD. 1908. m. $30. (Petroleum Publishers, Inc.) Petroleum Publishers, Inc., 753 W. Lambert Rd., Box 129, Brea, CA 92621. FAX 714-990-4061. Ed. Jack M. Rider. adv.; illus.; circ. 3,065. (also avail. in microform from UMI; reprint service avail. from UMI) **Indexed:** Cal.Per.Ind. (1978-), Chem.Abstr., GeoRef, Petrol.Abstr.
—BLDSC shelfmark: 6330.600000.
Formerly: California Oil World.

665   US
PACIFIC SUMMARY REPORT - INDEX. 1980. a. free. Outer Continental Shelf Information Program, Offshore Information and Publications Office, Minerals Management Service, 381 Elden St., No. 1400, Herndon, VA 22070-4817. TEL 703-787-1080. circ. 4,000.
Formed by the merger of: Pacific Index; Pacific Summary Report.
Description: Documents with status of federal offshore oil and gas leasing, exploration, development and production activities.

665   PK   ISSN 0552-9115
PAKISTAN PETROLEUM LIMITED. ANNUAL REPORT. (Text in English) 1952. a. $6. Pakistan Petroleum Ltd., PIDC House, Dr. Ziauddin Ahmad Rd., Karachi 4, Pakistan. Ed. Ahsan Halim. circ. 5,000.
Description: Presents a complete picture of the company's finances and operations.

665.7   US   ISSN 0031-076X
PANHANDLE MAGAZINE. 1964. q. free. Panhandle Eastern Corporation, 3000 Bissonnet Ave., Box 1642, Houston, TX 77001-1642. TEL 713-664-3401. Ed. Dan Mullis. charts; illus.; circ. 26,000.

665.5   BL
PETROBRAS. CONSOLIDATED REPORT. (Text in English) a. Petroleo Brasileiro S.A., Servico de Relacoes Publicas, Av. Republica do Chile, 65 S-2056, Rio de Janeiro RJ, Brazil. charts; illus.; stat.

665.5   BL
PETROBRAS NEWS. (Text in English) q. Petroleo Brasileiro S.A., Public Affairs (SERCOM), Caixa Posta 15521, 20132 Rio de Janeiro, RJ, Brazil. TEL 021-262-7126. FAX 021-220-5052. TELEX 021-23335. Ed. Lanning Elwis. charts; illus.; stat. (looseleaf format) **Indexed:** Energy Info.Abstr.
Description: Covers news in the petroleum and drilling field.

PETROCHEMICAL EQUIPMENT. see *ENGINEERING — Chemical Engineering*

380   US
▼**PETROCHEMICAL INDUSTRY.** 1991. a. $40. Midwest Register, Inc., 601 Boulder, Ste. 1001, Tulsa, OK 74119-1301. TEL 918-582-2000.

665.5   US
PETROFAX. (Avail in 4 reports: Canada, Products, LPG, Crude) d. $97. Bloomberg Financial Markets, 100 Business Park Dr., Box 888, Princeton, NJ 08542-0888. TEL 609-497-3500. FAX 609-683-7523.

665.5   US
PETROFLASH. d. $2,495. Bloomberg Financial Markets, 100 Business Park Dr., Box 888, Princeton, NJ 08542-0888. TEL 609-497-3500. FAX 609-683-7523.
●Available only online.
Description: Computerized daily oil price reporting service.

665.5   FR   ISSN 0761-2095
PETROLE ET GAZ. (Text in English, French) 1984. 10/yr. (plus index) 1175 Fr. (with index 1465 F.). (Centre de Documentation Scientifique et Technique (CDST)) Editions Technip, 27 rue Ginoux, 75737 Paris cedex 15, France. TEL 45-77-11-08. FAX 45-75-37-11. TELEX EDITECP 200375F. (Co-sponsor: Institut Francais du Petrole. Centre de Documentation et d'Analyse de l'Information) index.
Formerly: Institut Francais du Petrole. Fiches de Documentation.

665.5   FR
PETROLE ET LE GAZ EN AFRIQUE. irreg., latest 1986. 1190 F. I C Publications, 10 rue Vineuse, 75116 Paris, France. TEL 1-45-27-30-82. FAX 1-45-20-81-74.

665.5   FR   ISSN 0152-5425
TN860   CODEN: PETEDX
PETROLE ET TECHNIQUES. no.241, Feb.1977. m. 550 F. (foreign 590 F.). Association Francaise des Techniciens du Petrole, 3, rue E et A Peugeot, B.P. 282, 92505 Rueil Malmaison Cedex. TEL 47-08-08-06. FAX 47-14-10-55. Ed. Ph. Seng. adv.; charts; illus.; circ. 4,000. **Indexed:** API Abstr, API Catal., API Hlth.& Environ., API Oil., API Pet.Ref., API Pet.Subst., API Transport., Bibl.& Ind.Geol., Chem.Abstr, Petrol.Abstr.
—BLDSC shelfmark: 6430.680000.
Formerly: Association Francaise des Techniciens du Petrole. Revue (ISSN 0004-5470)

665.5   FR   ISSN 0755-561X
TN864
PETROLE INFORMATIONS INTERNATIONAL (EDITION BILINGUE). m. 980 F. Societe d'Information et de Documentation, Bureau d'Informations Professionnelles, 142 rue Montmartre, 75002 Paris, France. FAX 40-39-97-52. TELEX 220528F. Ed. Elisabeth Liegeois. adv.; illus.; tr.lit.; circ. 7,757. **Indexed:** API Abstr., API Catal., API Hlth.& Environ., API Oil, API Pet.Ref., API Pet.Subst., API Transport., Petrol.Abstr.
—BLDSC shelfmark: 6430.700000.
Former titles (until 1982): Petrole Informations (ISSN 0150-6463); (until 1969): Petrole Informations, la Revue Petroliere (ISSN 0150-6471)
Description: Comprehensive analysis of developments in the international oil and gas industries.

665.5   FR   ISSN 0762-0357
PETROLE INFORMATIONS INTERNATIONAL (ENGLISH EDITION). 1983. m. Societe d'Information et de Documentation, Bureau d'Informations Professionnelles, 142 rue Montmartre, 75002 Paris, France. FAX 40-39-97-52. TELEX 220 528 F.
Formerly: Petrole Informations (International Edition) (ISSN 0756-8371)

665.5   SP   ISSN 0213-8360
PETROLEO. 1973. w. 27500 ptas.($265) (Spanish Petroleum Association) Oilgas S.A., Paseo de la Habana, 48, 28036 Madrid, Spain. Ed. Carlos Martin. circ. 2,000.
Description: Deals with international activities of the petroleum, petrochemical and gas markets.

665.5   US   ISSN 0093-7851
TN860   CODEN: PTRIB2
PETROLEO INTERNACIONAL. (Text in Spanish) 1943. bi-m. free to qualified personnel. Keller International Publishing Corporation, 150 Great Neck Rd., Great Neck, NY 11021. TEL 516-829-9210. FAX 516-829-5414. TELEX 221-574 KELLE. Ed. Victor Prieto. adv.; bk.rev.; charts; illus.; stat.; circ. 8,511. (processed) **Indexed:** Chem.Abstr., GeoRef, Petrol.Abstr., PROMT.
—BLDSC shelfmark: 6430.780000.
Former titles: Petroleo y Petroquimica Internacional; Petroleo Interamericano (ISSN 0031-6407)

665.5   VE
PETROLEUM. 1977. 12/yr. Bs.3000($60) Petroleum Editores, S.A., Apdo. 379, Maracaibo 4001-A, Venezuela. TEL 58-61-529435. FAX 58-61-522302. TELEX 64336 PEMIN UC. Ed. Jorge Zajia. adv.; bk.rev.; circ. 5,000.
Formerly (until 1983): Petroleo y Tecnologia.
Description: For professionals and technicians. Covers Latin American oil industry.

PETROLEUM AND CHEMICAL INDUSTRY CONFERENCE. RECORD OF CONFERENCE PAPERS. see *ENGINEERING — Chemical Engineering*

662.6   II
PETROLEUM ASIA JOURNAL. (Text in English) 1978. q. Rs.60($30) Himachal Times Group of Newspapers, 57-B Rajpur Rd., P.O. Box 50, Dehra Dun 248001, India. Ed. Dev Kumar Pandhi. adv.; circ. 10,000.

665.5   US   ISSN 0899-6369
PETROLEUM - C-STORE PRODUCTS; new products for oil marketing, c-stores, car washes, truck stops. 1979. 10/yr. $18 (Canada and Mexico $27; elsewhere $48). Hunter Publishing Limited Partnership, 950 Lee St., Des Plaines, IL 60016. TEL 708-296-0770. FAX 708-803-3328. Ed. Peggy Smedley. adv.; tr.lit.; circ. 38,000. (tabloid format)
Formerly: Petroleum Equipment.

661   US   ISSN 0031-6458
TP690.A1   CODEN: PECHAM
PETROLEUM CHEMISTRY U.S.S.R. English translation of: Neftekhimiya (UR ISSN 0028-2421) 1962. 4/yr. £560 (effective 1992). Pergamon Press, Inc., Journals Division, 660 White Plains Rd., Tarrytown, NY 10591-5153. TEL 914-524-9200. FAX 914-333-2444. (And: Headington Hill Hall, Oxford OX3 0BW, England. TEL 0865-794141) Ed. E.V. Whitehead. adv.; bk.rev.; abstr.; bibl.; charts; circ. 1,025. (also avail. in microform from MIM,UMI; back issues avail.) **Indexed:** Curr.Cont.
—BLDSC shelfmark: 0416.688000.
Refereed Serial

PETROLEUM CONCESSION HANDBOOK. see *LAW — International Law*

665.5   UK   ISSN 0306-395X
HD9560.1   CODEN: PEECDK
PETROLEUM ECONOMIST; the international energy journal. (Editions in English and Japanese) 1934. m. $355. Petroleum Economist Ltd., P.O. Box 105, 25-31 Ironmonger Row, London EC1V 3PN, England. TEL 01-251 3501. FAX 01-253-1224. TELEX 27161. Ed. Ian Bourne. adv.; bk.rev.; charts; mkt.; stat.; index; circ. 3,700. (also avail. in microform from UMI; reprint service avail. from UMI) **Indexed:** AESIS, Bibl.& Ind.Geol., BMT, Br.Geol.Lit., Bus.Ind., Energy Info.Abstr., Fuel & Energy Abstr., Gas.Abstr., Geo.Abstr., Key to Econ.Sci., P.A.I.S., Petrol.Energy B.N.I., PROMT, Tr.& Indus.Ind.
—BLDSC shelfmark: 6431.680000.
Formerly: Petroleum Press Service (ISSN 0031-6504)
Description: Informational articles, editorial commentary, news items, and statistical data pertaining to the marketing, exploratory, technological, and production aspects of the international oil, gas, and other energy-source industries with company profiles.

3698 PETROLEUM AND GAS

622 US ISSN 0031-6466
PETROLEUM ENGINEER INTERNATIONAL; the international magazine of methods for engineering-operating people. Includes section: Energy Management Report (ISSN 0013-7537) 1929. m. $20. Avanstar Communications, Inc., 7500 Old Oak Blvd., Cleveland, OH 44130. TEL 216-826-2839. FAX 216-891-2726. (Subscr. to: 1 E. First St., Duluth, MN 55802) Ed. Steven Moore. adv.; charts; illus. (also avail. in microform) **Indexed:** A.S.& T.Ind., AESIS, Bibl.& Ind.Geol., Eng.Ind, Excerp.Med., Gas Abstr., ISMEC, Petrol.Abstr., SRI.
  Supersedes (in 1970): Hydrocarbon News (ISSN 0018-8182); Petro-Chem Engineer (ISSN 0031-6326)
  Description: Provides practical engineering, operating and methods technology to maximize profits in oil and gas drilling and production worldwide.

665.5 US
PETROLEUM EQUIPMENT DIRECTORY. 1955. a. $50. Petroleum Equipment Institute, Box 2380, Tulsa, OK 74101. TEL 918-494-9696. Ed. Robert N. Renkes. adv.; circ. 3,000.

665.5 US
PETROLEUM FRONTIERS. q. $200. Petroleum Information Corporation, Box 2612, Denver, CO 80201-2612. TEL 303-740-7100. FAX 303-694-1754.
  Description: Each issue examines petroleum explorations within a particular geographical region, covering stratigraphic and structural analyses, mineralogy, drilling and discovery history, discussions of leasing history and future outlook, and more.

553 AT ISSN 0048-3591
TN860
PETROLEUM GAZETTE. 1952. q. free. Australian Institute of Petroleum Ltd., 257 Collins St., Melbourne, Vic. 3000, Australia. Ed. D.A. Rose. **Indexed:** AESIS, Aus.Rd.Ind., Bibl.& Ind.Geol., GdIns.

553
PETROLEUM GEOLOGY: A DIGEST OF RUSSIAN LITERATURE ON PETROLEUM GEOLOGY. vol.2, 1959. m. $40. Box 171, McLean, VA 22101. Ed. Grace Carrington. charts; illus.; circ. 300. **Indexed:** AESIS, GeoRef, Petrol.Abstr.

665.5 552 CH
PETROLEUM GEOLOGY OF TAIWAN/T'AIWAN SHIH-YU TI-CHIH. (Text in English) 1962. a. Chinese Petroleum Corporation, Exploration Division, 46 Chung Cheng Rd., Miaoli, Taiwan, Republic of China. **Indexed:** Bibl.& Ind.Geol., Deep Sea Res.& Oceanogr.Abstr.

665.5 551 CN
▼**PETROLEUM GEOLOGY SPECIAL PAPER SERIES.** 1990. a. price varies. Ministry of Energy, Mines and Petroleum Resources, Energy Resources Division, Parliament Bldgs., Victoria, B.C. V8V 1X4, Canada. (Subscr. to: Crown Publications, 546 Yates St., Victoria, B.C. V8W 1K8, Canada. TEL 604-386-4636)

665.5 US ISSN 0747-2528
HD9561
PETROLEUM INDEPENDENT. (Statistical issue avail.: Oil & Natural Gas Producing Industry in Your State) 1929. 10/yr. $100 to non-members. (Independent Petroleum Association of America) Petroleum Independent Publishers, Inc., 1101 16th St., N.W., Washington, DC 20036. TEL 800-433-2851. FAX 202-857-4799. Ed. Bruce A. Wells. adv.; charts; illus.; stat.; circ. 10,000. **Indexed:** Gas Abstr., PROMT.
  —BLDSC shelfmark: 6433.570000.

665.5 US
PETROLEUM INDUSTRY IN ILLINOIS. (Subseries of: Illinois Petroleum) 1933. a. $1.25 per no. State Geological Survey, Natural Resources Bldg., 615 E. Peabody Dr., Champaign, IL 61820. TEL 217-344-1481. stat. (back issues avail.)

665.5 JA
PETROLEUM INDUSTRY IN JAPAN. (Text in English) 1955. a. 4500 Yen($35) membership. World Petroleum Congress, Japanese National Committee - Sekai Sekiyu Kaigi Nihon Kokunai Iinkai, Kasahara Bldg., 1-6-10 Uchi Kanda, Chiyoda-ku, Tokyo 101, Japan. FAX 03-294-3103. TELEX 2223316 JNCWPC J. stat.; circ. 2,000.

665.5 US ISSN 0480-2160
HD9560.1
PETROLEUM INTELLIGENCE WEEKLY. 1961. w. $1375. Petroleum Energy & Intelligence Weekly, Inc., 575 Broadway, New York, NY 10012-3230. TEL 212-941-5500. FAX 212-941-5508. TELEX 62371 PETROIN. Ed. Sarah Miller. **Indexed:** Fuel & Energy Abstr., Petrol.Energy B.N.I.
  —BLDSC shelfmark: 6433.630000.
  Description: Provides market insights for oil and natural gas executives and government leaders. Includes information and analysis of major industry developments, issues and trends.

665.5 918 US
PETROLEUM: LATIN AMERICAN INDUSTRIAL REPORT. (Avail. for each of 22 Latin American countries) 1985. a. $435 per country report. Aquino Productions, Box 15760, Stamford, CT 06901. TEL 203-325-3138. Ed. Andres C. Aquino.

PETROLEUM LEGISLATION. see *LAW — International Law*

658.8 US ISSN 0362-7799
HD9561
PETROLEUM MARKETER. 1933. bi-m. $18. McKeand Publications, Inc., 636 First Ave., Box 507, West Haven, CT 06516. TEL 203-934-5288. Ed. Keith B. Tuerk. adv.; charts; illus.; stat.; tr.lit.; circ. 17,000 (controlled). (processed; reprint service avail. from UMI) **Indexed:** Chem.Abstr.
  Formerly: Petroleum and TBA Marketer (ISSN 0031-644X)

662 US
PETROLEUM MARKETER'S HANDBOOK. 1977. a. $127 (foreign $139). Bloomberg Financial Markets, 100 Business Park Dr., Box 888, Princeton, NJ 08542-0888. TEL 609-497-3500. FAX 609-683-7523.
  Description: Lists brokers and traders in petroleum products.

338 US ISSN 0741-9643
CODEN: PMMOEH
PETROLEUM MARKETING MONTHLY. 1983. m. $65. U.S. Department of Energy, Energy Information Administration, National Energy Information Center, EI-231, Rm. 1F-048, Forrestal bldg., 1000 Independence Ave., S.W., Washington, DC 20585. TEL 202-586-8800. **Indexed:** Energy Info.Abstr.

338.2 HK ISSN 0250-7765
PETROLEUM NEWS; Asia's energy journal. 1969. m. $100. Petroleum News Southeast Asia Ltd., 6th Floor, 146 Prince Edward Road West, Kowloon, Hong Kong. TEL 3-805294. Ed. Andrew Burns. adv.; bk.rev.; illus.; circ. 8,000. (back issues avail.) **Indexed:** AESIS, Bibl.& Ind.Geol., Key to Econ.Sci., Petrol.Energy B.N.I.
  —BLDSC shelfmark: 6433.790000.
  Formerly (until vol. 9, Dec. 1978): Petroleum News, Southeast Asia.

PETROLEUM NEWSLETTER. see *OCCUPATIONAL HEALTH AND SAFETY*

665.5 AT ISSN 0312-9837
TN878.A1 CODEN: PNGGD3
PETROLEUM NEWSLETTER; a summary of petroleum exploration activity in Australia. no.67, 1976. s-a. price varies. Bureau of Mineral Resources, Geology and Geophysics, G.P.O. Box 378, Canberra, A.C.T. 2601, Australia. FAX 062-725161. **Indexed:** Bibl.& Ind.Geol.

665.5 338.2 US ISSN 0031-6490
HG6047.P47
PETROLEUM OUTLOOK. 1948. m. $520 (foreign $560). John S. Herold, Inc., 5 Edgewood Ave., Greenwich, CT 06830. TEL 203-869-2585. Ed.Bd. adv.; illus.; stat.; circ. 2,500. **Indexed:** Petrol.Energy B.N.I.
  —BLDSC shelfmark: 6433.850000.
  Description: Corporate and industry developments of 150 oil and gas service companies.

665.5 UK ISSN 0020-3076
TP690.A1 CODEN: PETRB2
PETROLEUM REVIEW. 1947. m. £50 (foreign £62). Institute of Petroleum, 61 New Cavendish St., London W1M 8AR, England. TEL 071-636-1004. FAX 071-255-1472. TELEX 264380. Ed. Carol Reader. adv.; bk.rev.; illus.; stat.; tr.lit.; Bibl.& Ind.Geol.; circ. 8,500. (also avail. in microfilm from UMI; reprint service avail. from UMI) **Indexed:** AESIS, API Abstr., API Catal., API Hlth.& Environ., API Oil, API Pet.Ref., API Pet.Subst., API Transport., Bibl.& Ind.Geol., BMT, Br.Geol.Lit., Br.Tech.Ind., Chem.Abstr., Eng.Ind., Excerp.Med., Fluidex, Fuel & Energy Abstr., Geo.Abstr., HRIS, Petrol.Abstr., RAPRA.
  —BLDSC shelfmark: 6435.190000.
  Formerly: Institute of Petroleum Review.

665.5 UK
PETROLEUM SERVICES. ANNUAL PETROLEUM REVIEW. 1986. a. £100 (free to subscribers of other services). Arthur Andersen & Co., Petroleum Services Group, 1 Surrey St., London WC2R 2PS, England. TEL 071-438-3888. FAX 071-438-3881. TELEX 8812771.
  Description: Covers the upstream petroleum activities of the oil in Northwest Europe. Details license changes and awards, drilling activity, production rates, field activity, and deals made during the year.

665.5 UK
PETROLEUM SERVICES. WEEKLY SERVICE. 1972. w. £1,400. Arthur Andersen & Co., Petroleum Services Group, 1 Surrey St., London WC2R 2PS, England. TEL 071-438-3888. FAX 071-438-3881. TELEX 8812711. Ed. Simon Roper.
  Former titles (until 1986): Weekly Exploration Service; Offshore Petroleum Exploration Service (ISSN 0140-5268)
  Description: Covers drilling activity, rig movements and licence changes in the North Sea region and onshore UK and France.

665.5 UK
PETROLEUM SERVICES. WEEKLY SERVICE (OFFSHORE). 1982. w. £1100. Arthur Andersen & Co., Petroleum Services Group, 1 Surrey St., London WC2R 2PS, England. TEL 071-438-3888. FAX 071-438-3881. TELEX 8812711. Ed. Simon Roper. (back issues avail.)
  Former titles: Petroleum Services. Weekly Service. Offshore Report; (until 1986): Offshore Drilling Report (Year).
  Description: Highlights current drilling activity, rig movements and license changes in the offshore sectors of North Sea region.

665.5 UK
PETROLEUM SERVICES. WEEKLY SERVICE (ONSHORE). 1982. w. £500. Arthur Andersen & Co., Petroleum Services Group, 1 Surrey St., London WC2R 2PS, England. TEL 071-438-3888. FAX 071-438-3881. TELEX 8812711. Ed. Simon Roper. (back issues avail.)
  Former titles: Petroleum Services. Weekly Service. Onshore Report; (until 1986): Onshore Activity Report (Year).
  Description: Highlights current drilling activity, rig movements and license changes for onshore UK, Ireland and France.

PETROLEUM SOFTWARE DIRECTORY. see *COMPUTERS — Software*

665.5 US
PETROLEUM SUPPLY ANNUAL. a. (in 2 vols.), latest 1990. $40. U.S. Department of Energy, Energy Information Administration, National Energy Information Center, EI-231, Rm. 1F-048, Forrestal bldg., 1000 Independence Ave., S.W., Washington, DC 20585. TEL 202-586-8800. **Indexed:** Energy Info.Abstr.
  Former titles: Deliveries of Fuel Oil and Kerosene; Sales of Liquid Petroleum Gases and Ethane; Petroleum Refineries in the United States and U.S. Territories; Petroleum Statement.

665.5   US   ISSN 0733-0553
HD9561   CODEN: PSMODO
PETROLEUM SUPPLY MONTHLY. 1982. m. $60. U.S. Department of Energy, Energy Information Administration, National Energy Information Center, EI-231, Rm. 1F-048, Forrestal bldg., 1000 Independence Ave., S.W., Washington, DC 20585. TEL 202-586-8800. (Dist. by: Supt. of Documents, Washington, DC 20402) **Indexed:** Chem.Abstr, Energy Info.Abstr., PROMT.
  Formed by the merger of: Monthly Petroleum Statement. Availability of Heavy Fuel Oils by Sulfur Levels & U.S. Energy Information Administration. Monthly Petroleum Statistics Report.
  Description: Current statistics on production, import, export, transportation, and supply and disposition of petroleum. Includes occasional feature articles on energy-related subjects.

338.2 665
PETROLEUM TAXATION & LEGISLATION REPORT. 1957. bi-m. $1300 first year; thereafter $1050. Barrows Co., Inc., 116 E. 66th St., New York, NY 10021. TEL 212-772-1199. FAX 212-288-7242. TELEX 4971238/BARROWS. Ed. Gordon H. Barrows. bk.rev.; charts; mkt.; tr.lit.; circ. 6,000.
  Formerly: Petroleum Taxation Report (ISSN 0031-6539)
  Description: Reviews changes in world oil and gas laws and tax regulations by country.

665.5   UK   ISSN 0261-3883
PETROLEUM TIMES PRICE REPORT. 1899. fortn. £132 (avail. as package with Petroleum Times Business Reviews). Whitehall Press Ltd., Earl House, Maidstone ME14 1PE, England. TEL 0622-759841. FAX 0622-675734. Ed. Bonnie Downing. **Indexed:** PROMT.
  —BLDSC shelfmark: 6436.015000.

665.5   IT   ISSN 0031-6563
PETROLIERI D'ITALIA. 1954. m. L.20000. Italia Editoriale, Via Andrea Doria 3, 20124 Milan, Italy. Ed. Enzo Fassitelli. adv.; bk.rev.; circ. 3,200.

665.5   IT
PETROLIERI INTERNATIONAL. 1954. m. L.20000($17.) Italia Editoriale, Via Andrea Doria 3, 20124 Milan, Italy. Ed. Enzo Fassitelli. adv.; bk.rev.; charts; illus.; mkt.; pat.; circ. 3,000. **Indexed:** Chem.Abstr, Petrol.Abstr.

665.5 338.2   IT   ISSN 0031-6571
PETROLIO;* economia e tecnica degli idrocarburi. (Text in Italian; summaries in English & French) 1950. m. (11/yr.). L.10000. Publicazioni Petrolifere S.p.A., Piazza della Lega 14, Alessandria, Italy. Ed. Dir. Giovanni Spantigati. adv.; charts; illus.; stat.; index.

665.5   AG   ISSN 0031-6598
PETROTECNICA.* 1960. bi-m. Arg.$750.($12.) Victor Sulimovich, Ed. & Pub., Maipu 645, Buenos Aires, Argentina. adv.; charts; illus.; index; circ. 3,500.

665   US
PHILNEWS. 1937; N.S. 1976. m. free to qualified personnel. Phillips Petroleum Company, Corporate Affairs, 16 D3 PB, Bartlesville, OK 74004. TEL 918-661-6600. FAX 918-662-2926. Ed. Bill Miller. illus.; circ. 35,000.

665.54   US   ISSN 0032-0145
TJ930
PIPE LINE INDUSTRY; crude oil and products pipelines, gas transmission and gas distribution. (International Edition avail.) 1954. m. $20 (free to qualified personnel). Gulf Publishing Co., Box 2608, Houston, TX 77252-2608. TEL 713-529-4301. FAX 713-520-4433. TELEX 287330 GULF UR. Ed. William Quarles. adv.; bk.; rev.; charts; illus.; index; circ. 26,539. (also avail. in microfilm from UMI; reprint service avail.) **Indexed:** A.S.& T.Ind., API Abstr, API Catal., API Hlth.& Environ., API Oil., API Pet.Ref., API Pet.Subst., API Transport., Corros.Abstr., Eng.Ind., Fuel & Energy Abstr., Gas Abstr., Met.Abstr., Petrol.Abstr., World Alum.Abstr.
  —BLDSC shelfmark: 6502.000000.

622   US   ISSN 0032-0188
PIPELINE & GAS JOURNAL; energy construction, transportation and distribution. Includes section: Energy Management Report (ISSN 0013-7537) 1859. m. $20. Oildom Publishing Co. of Texas, Inc., 3314 Mercer St., Houston, TX 77027. TEL 713-622-0676. FAX 712-623-4768. Ed. Jim Watts. adv.; charts; illus. (also avail. in microform) **Indexed:** A.S.& T.Ind., AESIS, API Abstr, API Catal., API Hlth.& Environ., API Oil., API Pet.Ref., API Pet.Subst., API Transport., Bus.Ind., Chem.Eng.Abstr., Corros.Abstr., Energy Ind., Energy Info.Abstr., Environ.Abstr., Fluidex, Fuel & Energy Abstr., Gas Abstr., Met.Abstr., Petrol.Abstr., PROMT, SRI, Tr.& Indus.Ind., W.R.C.Inf., World Alum.Abstr.
  Incorporates (in 1990): Pipeline (Houston) (ISSN 0148-4443); **Formerly:** Pipe Line News (ISSN 0032-0153); Pipeline & Gas Journal was formed by the merger of: Pipeline Engineer (ISSN 0096-8293); American Gas Journal.
  Description: Covers engineering and operating methods on cross-country pipelines that transport crude oil products and natural gas.

665.5   US
PIPELINE & GAS JOURNAL ANNUAL DIRECTORY OF PIPELINES AND EQUIPMENT. 1928. a. $60. Oildom Publishing Co. of Texas, Inc., 3314 Mercer St., Houston, TX 77027. TEL 713-622-0676. FAX 713-623-4768. Ed. James Watt. adv.; stat.; circ. 24,000.
  Former titles: Pipe Line Annual Directory of Pipelines; Pipeline Annual Directory.

665.54   US
PIPELINE & UTILITIES CONSTRUCTION. 1945. 13/yr. $40. Oildom Publishing Co. of Texas, Inc., 3314 Mercer St., Houston, TX 77027. TEL 713-622-0676. FAX 713-623-4768. Ed. Oliver Klinger, Jr. adv.; bk.rev.; tr.lit.; circ. 23,000. (back issues avail.) **Indexed:** Fuel & Energy Abstr., Geotech.Abstr., Petrol.Abstr.
  Formerly: Pipeline and Underground Utilities Construction (ISSN 0032-0196)
  Description: Covers all aspects of underground systems construction as applied to pipelines and distribution systems: water, gas, sewers, and storm drains.

665.5   US
PIPELINE AND UTILITY CONTRACTORS DIRECTORY. a. $60. Oildom Publishing Co. of Texas, Inc., 3314 Mercer, Houston, TX 77027. Ed. Oliver Klinger. adv.
  Formerly: Pipeline Contractors Directory.

665.54   US   ISSN 0197-1506
TJ930
PIPELINE DIGEST. 1963. s-m. $43 (foreign $50)(effective Jan. 1992). 45-45 Post Oak Place, Ste. 210, Houston, TX 77027. TEL 713-468-2626. FAX 713-465-2224. Ed. Judy R. Clark. adv.; bk.rev.; circ. 27,000. **Indexed:** Corros.Abstr., Fluidex.
  Formerly: Universal News (ISSN 0041-820X)

665.54   US
PIPELINE INDUSTRY (HOUSTON). 1954. m. Gulf Publishing Co., Box 2608, Houston, TX 77252. TEL 713-529-4301. TELEX 287330. Ed. Bill Quaries. circ. 11,901. **Indexed:** Energy Rev.

665.54   US
PIPELINE INDUSTRY (TULSA). a. $40. Midwest Register, Inc., 601 S. Boulder, Ste. 1001, Tulsa, OK 74119-1301. TEL 918-582-2000.
  Formerly: Pipe Line & Pipe Line Contractors.
  Description: Supplies company name, address, phone and fax numbers, personnel, division offices, size and length of pipes and type of lines, equipment manufacturers and suppliers.

665.54 627   UK   ISSN 0032-020X
TS280   CODEN: PPIIAU
PIPES AND PIPELINES INTERNATIONAL; pipes, hoses, tubes, pumps, valves. 1956. bi-m. £54($119) Scientific Surveys Ltd., P.O. Box 21, Beaconsfield, Bucks HP9 1NS, England. TEL 0494-675139. FAX 0494-670155. Ed. J.N.H. Tiratsoo. adv.; bk.rev.; charts; illus.; pat.; tr.lit.; index. **Indexed:** AESIS, BMT, Br.Tech.Ind., Chem.Abstr., Chem.Eng.Abstr., Eng.Ind., Excerp.Med., Fluidex, Fuel & Energy Abstr., Gas Abstr., Met.Abstr., Petrol.Abstr., World Alum.Abstr.
  —BLDSC shelfmark: 6502.350000.
  Incorporates (1958-1990): Pipeline Industries Guild Journal (ISSN 0308-3098)
  Description: Technical information on pipes and pipelines research.

665.5 531.64 US
PLATT'S ASIA - PACIFIC - ARAB GULF MARKETSCAN. (Telex service) d. price varies. McGraw-Hill, Inc., 1221 Ave. of the Americas, New York, NY 10020. TEL 212-521-2000.

665.5 531.64 US
PLATT'S CRUDE OIL MARKET WIRE. (Telex service) w. price varies. McGraw-Hill, Inc., 1221 Ave. of the Americas, New York, NY 10020. TEL 212-521-2000.

665.5 531.64 US
PLATT'S CRUDE TANKERWIRE. (Telex service) d. price varies. McGraw-Hill, Inc., 1221 Ave. of the Americas, New York, NY 10020. TEL 212-521-2000.

665.5 531.64 US
PLATT'S EUROPEAN PETROCHEMICALSCAN. (Telex service) w. price varies. McGraw-Hill, Inc., 1221 Ave. of the Americas, New York, NY 10020. TEL 212-521-2000.

665.5 531.64 US
PLATT'S FAR EASTERN PETROCHEMICAL SCAN. (Telex service) w. price varies. McGraw-Hill, Inc., 1221 Ave. of the Americas, New York, NY 10020. TEL 212-521-2000.

665.5   US
PLATT'S INTERNATIONAL PETROCHEMICAL REPORT. w. $920. McGraw-Hill, Inc., 1221 Avenue of the Americas, New York, NY 10020.
  ●Also available online. Vendor(s): DIALOG (File no.624/McGraw-HILL PUBLICATIONS ONLINE), Dow Jones/News Retrieval, Mead Data Central.
  Description: Aimed at executives who manufacture, market and distribute petroleum products.

PLATT'S L P GASWIRE. see ENERGY

665.5   US   ISSN 0277-0415
PLATT'S OIL MARKETING BULLETIN. 1983. 51/yr. $427. McGraw-Hill, Inc., 1221 Ave. of the Americas, New York, NY 10020. Ed. Joseph L. Link. (looseleaf format) **Indexed:** Petrol.Energy B.N.I.
  ●Also available online. Vendor(s): Mead Data Central.

665.5   US
PLATT'S OIL PRICE HANDBOOK. a. $165. McGraw-Hill, Inc., Commodity Services Group, 1221 Ave. of the Americas, 42nd Fl., New York, NY 10020. TEL 212-512-2000. Ed. Halsey Peckworth.

PLATT'S OILGRAM BUNKERWIRE. see ENERGY

PLATT'S OILGRAM MARKETSCAN. EUROPEAN EDITION. see ENERGY

PLATT'S OILGRAM MARKETSCAN. U S EDITION. see ENERGY

665.5   US   ISSN 0163-1284
HD9561
PLATT'S OILGRAM NEWS. 1923. d. $1,347 (foreign $1,457). McGraw-Hill, Inc., Commodity Services Group, 1221 Ave. of the Americas, 42nd Fl., New York, NY 10020. TEL 212-512-2000. Ed. Onnic Marashian. (also avail. in microform from UMI; back issues avail.) **Indexed:** Bus.Ind., Petrol.Energy B.N.I., Tr.& Indus.Ind.
  ●Also available online. Vendor(s): DIALOG (File no.624/McGRAW-HILL PUBLICATIONS ONLINE), Dow Jones/News Retrieval (PON), Mead Data Central (PONEWS).
  Former titles: Platt's Oilgram News Service; Oilgram News Service.

PLATT'S OILGRAM NEWS - WIRE. see ENERGY

665.5   US
PLATT'S OILGRAM PRICE REPORT; an international daily oil-gas price and marketing letter. 1923. d. $1,517 (foreign $1,767). McGraw-Hill, Inc., 1221 Ave. of the Americas, New York, NY 10020. Ed. Joseph Link. (also avail. in microform from UMI)
  ●Also available online. Vendor(s): DIALOG (File no.624/McGRAW-HILL PUBLICATIONS ONLINE), Dow Jones/News Retrieval (POP), Mead Data Central (PPRICE).
  Former titles: Platts Oilgram Price Service; Oilgram Price Service.

665.5 531.64 US
PLATT'S OLEFINSCAN. (Telex service) w. price varies. McGraw-Hill, Inc., 1221 Ave. of the Americas, New York, NY 10020. TEL 212-521-2000.

PETROLEUM AND GAS

PLATT'S PETROCHEMICALSCAN. see *ENERGY*

665.5 531.64 US
PLATT'S PRODUCT TANKERWIRE. (Telex service) d. price varies. McGraw-Hill, Inc., 1221 Ave. of the Americas, New York, NY 10020. TEL 212-521-2000.

665.5 531.64 US
PLATT'S SOLVENTWIRE. (Telex service) w. price varies. McGraw-Hill, Inc., 1221 Ave. of the Americas, New York, NY 10020. TEL 212-521-2000.

665.7 CS ISSN 0032-1761
CODEN: PVZTAK
PLYN/GAS; manufacture, distribution and utilization of gas. (Text in Czech; summaries in English, German, Russian) 1920. m. $54.70. K P K - Knizni Podnikatelsky Klub, spol. s.r.o., Mimonska 643, 190 00 Prague 9, Czechoslovakia. Ed. Karel Zelenka. adv.; bk.rev.; abstr.; charts; illus.; stat.; index; circ. 2,000. (also avail. in microform) **Indexed:** C.I.S. Abstr., Chem.Abstr., Fuel & Energy Abstr., Gas Abstr., Met.Abstr., World Alum.Abstr.
Supersedes: Paliva.

553 RU
PRIRODNYI GAZ SIBIRI. 1969. irreg. Vsesoyuznyi Nauchno-Issledovatelskii Institut Prirodnykh Gazov, Tyumenskii Filial, Tyumen, Russia. illus.

665.5 FR
PROFILS I F P. 1989. 3/yr. free. Institut Francail du Petrole, 1 et 4 ave. de Bois Preau, B.P. 311, 92506 Rueil-Malmaison Cedex, France.
TEL 33-1-47-49-02-14. FAX 33-1-47-49-04-11. TELEX 203 050 F. circ. 2,000.

665.5 PK ISSN 0033-0574
PROGRESS. (Text in English) 1956. m. Rs.120. Pakistan Petroleum Ltd., c/o Nusrat Nasarullah, Ed., P I D C House, Dr. Ziauddin Ahmed Rd., P.O. Box 3942, Karachi 75530, Pakistan. TEL 21-511338. FAX 21-510005. TELEX 2869 PPETK PK. bk.rev.; charts; illus.; stat.; circ. 5,000. (tabloid format)
Description: Provides news about the activities of the company in particular, and the Pakistani oil and gas industry in general. Includes activities and achievements of the company's employees.

665.77 CN ISSN 0033-1260
PROPANE - CANADA. 1968. 6/yr. Can.$30($35) Northern Star Communications, 801 - 825 8th Ave. S.W., Calgary, Alta. T2P 2T3, Canada.
TEL 403-265-4750. FAX 403-263-2172. Ed. Scott Jeffrey. adv.; abstr.; charts; stat.; tr.lit.; circ. 5,106. (processed) **Indexed:** Fuel & Energy Abstr., Gas Abstr.
—BLDSC shelfmark: 6927.200000.

PUBLIC UTILITIES FORTNIGHTLY. see *ENGINEERING — Electrical Engineering*

665.5 SU
AL-QAFILAH/CARAVAN. (Text in Arabic) 1959. m. free. Saudi Aramco, P.O. Box 5000, Dhahran 31311, Saudi Arabia. Ed. Abdullah Y. Al-Hussaini. circ. 12,500. (tabloid format)
Formerly: Oil Caravan Weekly (ISSN 0030-1418)

QUENTIN CAMERON'S OIL & GAS BULLETIN. see *BUSINESS AND ECONOMICS — Investments*

665.5 US
R G D A NEWS.* 1945. m. free. Retail Gasoline and Garage Dealers Association, 3865 W. Henrietta Rd., Rochester, NY 14623-3703. TEL 716-328-3950. Ed. Diane M. Kearns. adv.; circ. 1,500.
Description: For the retail gasoline and repair shop industry in Monroe, Ontario, Wayne and Livingston counties.

622 CI
RAFINERIJSKI LIST. 1974. fortn. free. Rafinerija Nafte, Sisak, Sisak, Croatia. Ed. Bozidar Babic.

RANLIAO HUAXUE XUEBAO/JOURNAL OF FUEL CHEMISTRY AND TECHNOLOGY. see *ENGINEERING — Chemical Engineering*

665.5 UK ISSN 0033-9822
RASSEGNA PETROLIFERA.* 1934. w. L.120000. C E S P E T R O L, c/o Arthur James Chambers, 33 The Avenue, Beckenham, Kent, England. Ed. Giuseppe Jacono. adv.; charts; illus.; mkt.; stat.; index; cum.index.

665.53 US
REFINING & GAS PROCESSISNG. a. $40. Midwest Register, Inc., 601 S. Boulder, Ste. 1001, Tulsa, OK 74119-1301. TEL 918-582-2000.
Formerly: Refining, Construction, Petrochemical & Natural Gas Processing Plants of the World.
Description: Supplies company name, address, phone and fax numbers, personnel, capacities and refined product, and equipment manufacturers and suppliers.

665.5 US ISSN 0190-8715
TP690.A1
REPORTS ON RESEARCH ASSISTED BY THE PETROLEUM RESEARCH FUND. a. American Chemical Society, 1155 16th St., N.W., Washington, DC 20036.
TEL 202-872-4600. FAX 202-872-4615. TELEX 440159 ACSP UI.
Formerly: American Chemical Society. Reports of Research Supported by the Petroleum Research Fund.
Refereed Serial

662 US
RESOURCES (FORT WORTH). vol.22, 1975. 2/yr. free. Union Pacific Resources Company, Box 7, Ft. Worth, TX 76101-0007. TEL 817-737-1000. Ed. James L. Sailer. charts; illus.; circ. 12,000.
Formerly: Cycler.

665.5 US
RESULTS (HOUSTON). 1935. q. Exxon Company, U.S.A., 800 Bell St., Box 2180, Houston, TX 77252-2180. TEL 713-656-8477.
FAX 713-656-9742. Ed. Sue Berniard. circ. 30,000. (back issues avail.)
Formerly (until 1988): Oilways.
Description: Articles about various industrial concerns, Exxon products, and general technical interest items.

662.338 US ISSN 0270-7527
TN860
RESUME; a review of oil and gas activity in the United States. a. $95. Petroleum Information Corporation, Box 2612, Denver, CO 80201-2612.
TEL 303-740-7100. FAX 303-694-1754. stat.
Description: Reference for oil and gas statistics, including well drilling highlights, new field discoveries, well completions, and comparative analysis.

665.5 BL
REVISTA DO GAS. 1970. q. free. Associacao Brasileira dos Distribuidores de Gas Liquefeito de Petroleo, Av. Paulista 1009-16, Caixa Postal 6132, 01311 Sao Paulo, Brazil. Ed. Maria Carlota Portella Carmeiro. adv.; bk.rev.; charts; illus.; tr.lit.; circ. 20,000.

665.5 MX
REVISTA MEXICANA DEL PETROLEO. (Includes annual special issue) (Text in English and Spanish) 1958. bi-m. $16. Morelos 31 Desp. 303, Mexico 1, D.F., Mexico. Ed. Roberto Navarrete Espinosa. adv.; charts; illus.; stat.; tr.lit.; circ. 15,000. (back issues avail.) **Indexed:** Gas Abstr.

REVISTA PROFESIONAL DEL GREMIO DE ESTACIONES DE SERVICIO. see *LABOR UNIONS*

662.338 UK
RIG MARKET FORECAST. m. £400 (foreign £418). Financial Times Business Information Ltd., Tower House, Southampton St., London WC2E 7HA, England. TEL 071-240-9391. FAX 071-240-7946. TELEX 296926-BUSINF-G.
●Also available online. Vendor(s): Data-Star, Mead Data Central.
Description: Charts Northwestern Europe market trends in the offshore rig business.

665 338 IT ISSN 0035-5852
LA RIVISTA DEI COMBUSTIBILI. 1947. m. L.70000 (effective Jan. 1992). Stazione Sperimentale per i Combustibili, Viale A. de Gasperi 3, 20097 S. Donato Milanese (Milan), Italy. TEL 02-510031. FAX 02-514286. TELEX SSC 321622. Ed. A. Fiumara. adv.; bk.rev.; abstr.; illus.; stat.; index; circ. 1,500. (reprint service avail. from UMI) **Indexed:** API Catal., API Hlth.& Environ., API Oil., API Pet.Ref., API Pet.Subst., API Transport., C.I.S. Abstr., Chem.Abstr., Chem.Eng.Abstr., T.C.E.A.

ROCKY MOUNTAIN MINERAL LAW INSTITUTE. PROCEEDINGS. see *MINES AND MINING INDUSTRY*

380 US
ROCKY MOUNTAIN PETROLEUM INDUSTRY. 1945. a. $40. Midwest Register, Inc., 601 S. Boulder, Ste. 1001, Tulsa, OK 74119-1301.
TEL 918-582-2000.
Formerly: Directory of Producers and Drilling Contractors: Rocky Mountain Region, Williston Basin, Four Corners New Mexico.
Description: Supplies information on producing, drilling and well service, pipelines, refineries, gas procesing, petrochemicals, engineering, equipment, manufacturers and suppliers, company names, addresses, phone and fax numbers, and personnel.

665 CS ISSN 0035-8231
CODEN: ROUHAY
ROPA A UHLIE. (Text in Czech or Slovak; summaries in English, French, German, Russian) 1959. m. $116. (Research Institute of Crude Oil and Hydrocarbon Gases) Obzor, Ceskoslovenskej Armady 35, 815 85 Bratislava, Czechoslovakia. (Dist. by: Slovart, Gottwaldovo nam. 48, 805 32 Bratislava, Czechoslovakia) Ed. Xeno Liebl. adv.; bk.rev.; abstr.; charts; pat.; stat.; index; circ. 2,000. **Indexed:** Chem.Abstr., Gas Abstr., Met.Abstr., Ref.Zh., World Alum.Abstr.
—BLDSC shelfmark: 8023.400000.

665.5 CN
ROUGHNECK. 1952. m. Can.$27. Tacher Enterprises Ltd., 700 4th Ave. SW, Ste. 1600, Calgary, Alta. T2P 3J4, Canada. FAX 403-263-6886. Ed. David Yager. adv.; bk.rev.; circ. 6,600.
Description: Trade magazine for the oil industry.

665.5 UK
ROUSTABOUT. 1972. m. £50. Roustabout Publications Ltd., Suite 5, International Base, Greenwell Rd., Tullos, Aberdeen AB1 4AX, Scotland.
FAX 0224-879757. Ed. Lorna Anderson. adv.; circ. 10,000.

660 SZ
RUSSIAN PETROLEUM PRESS REVIEW.* (Text in English) 1973. P.O. Box 670, CH-1211 Geneva 1, Switzerland. charts; stat.

665.5 US ISSN 0885-9744
TN871.2
S P E DRILLING ENGINEERING. 1986. q. $40 to nonmembers; members $20. Society of Petroleum Engineers, Inc., Box 833836, Richardson, TX 75083-3836. TEL 214-669-3377.
FAX 214-669-0135. TELEX 730989 SPEDAL. adv.; index; circ. 8,000. (back issues avail.) **Indexed:** A.S.& T.Ind., AESIS, Eng.Ind.
—BLDSC shelfmark: 8361.841000.
Refereed Serial

665.5 US ISSN 0885-923X
TN871.35 CODEN: SFEVEG
S P E FORMATION EVALUATION. 1986. q. $40 to non-members; members $20. Society of Petroleum Engineers, Inc., Box 833836, Richardson, TX 75083-3836. TEL 214-669-3377.
FAX 214-669-0135. TELEX 730989 SPEDAL. adv.; index; circ. 8,000. (back issues avail.) **Indexed:** A.S.& T.Ind., AESIS, Eng.Ind.
—BLDSC shelfmark: 8361.842000.
Refereed Serial

665.5 US ISSN 0885-9221
TN870 CODEN: SPENES
S P E PRODUCTION ENGINEERING. 1986. q. $40 to non-members; members $20. Society of Petroleum Engineers, Inc., Box 833836, Richardson, TX 75083-3836. TEL 214-669-3377.
FAX 214-669-0135. TELEX 730989 SPEDAL. adv.; index; circ. 9,000. (back issues avail.) **Indexed:** A.S.& T.Ind., AESIS, Eng.Ind.
—BLDSC shelfmark: 8361.863000.
Refereed Serial

665.5 US ISSN 0885-9248
CODEN: SREEEF
S P E RESERVOIR ENGINEERING. 1986. q. $40 to non-members; members $20. Society of Petroleum Engineers, Inc., Box 833836, Richardson, TX 75083-3836. TEL 214-952-9393.
FAX 214-952-9435. TELEX 730989 SPEDAL. adv.; index; circ. 8,000. (back issues avail.) **Indexed:** A.S.& T.Ind., AESIS, Eng.Ind.
—BLDSC shelfmark: 8361.866000.
Refereed Serial

665.5 BX
SALAM. (Text in English, Malay) 1953. m. free to employees. Brunei Shell Petroleum Co Sdn Bhd, Seria 7082, Brunei Darussalam. TEL 037-8624. FAX 037-8494. circ. 9,000.

SASKATCHEWAN ENERGY & MINES. ANNUAL REPORT. see MINES AND MINING INDUSTRY

SASKATCHEWAN ENERGY & MINES. MINERAL STATISTICS YEARBOOK. see MINES AND MINING INDUSTRY

553 665 CN
SASKATCHEWAN ENERGY & MINES. PETROLEUM AND NATURAL GAS RESERVOIR ANNUAL. 1963. a. Can.$60. Saskatchewan Energy & Mines, Petroleum and Natural Gas Branch, 1914 Hamilton St., Regina, Sask. S4P 4V4, Canada. TEL 306-787-2528. FAX 306-787-7338.
Former titles: Saskatchewan Mineral Resources. Petroleum and Natural Gas Reservoir Annual (ISSN 0707-2562); Saskatchewan. Department of Mineral Resources. Petroleum and Natural Gas Reservoir Annual.
Description: Contains oil and gas reserves data, development and production data, information concerning enhanced recovery projects and related reservoir information.

338.7 CN
SASKATCHEWAN OIL AND GAS CORPORATION. ANNUAL REPORT. 1974. a. free. Saskatchewan Oil and Gas Corporation, 1777 Victoria Ave., P.O. Box 1550, Regina, Sask. S4P 3C4, Canada. TEL 306-781-8200. FAX 306-781-8364. Ed.Bd. charts; illus.; circ. 55,000.

665.5 NO ISSN 0332-5334
SCANDINAVIAN OIL - GAS MAGAZINE. (Text in English) 1973. bi-m. NOK 700. Scandinavian Oil-Gas Publishing, P.O. Box 6865, St. Olavs Plass, N-0130 Oslo, Norway. TEL 47-2-44-72-70. FAX 47-2-44-72-87. TELEX 72737 SCAND N. Eds. Odd E. Pedersen, Terje Dahl. adv.; bk.rev.; circ. 12,800. Indexed: Petrol.Abstr.
—BLDSC shelfmark: 8087.569700.

665.5 UK
SCOTTISH PETROLEUM ANNUAL. 1982. a. £8.95. Aberdeen Petroleum Publishing Ltd., 37 Huntly St., Aberdeen AB1 1TJ, Scotland. TEL 0224-644725. FAX 0224-647574. Ed. Ted Strachan. adv.

665.5 US
SEVENTY SIX. 1921. q. free. Unocal Corporation, Box 7600, Los Angeles, CA 90051. TEL 213-977-7600. Ed. Tim Smight. circ. 42,000 (controlled). Indexed: Energy Info.Abstr.

SHANXI DAXUE XUEBAO (SHEHUI KEXUE BAN)/SHANXI UNIVERSITY. JOURNAL (SOCIAL SCIENCE EDITION). see SOCIAL SCIENCES: COMPREHENSIVE WORKS

SHELL BITUMEN REVIEW. see ENGINEERING

665.5 NE
SHELL-POST. (Text in Dutch; summaries in English) 1959. fortn. free. Shell Nederland B.V., Carel van Bylandtlaan 30, 2596 HR The Hague, Netherlands. Eds. Hanneke Foppes, Samalina Hoorn. bk.rev.; illus.; circ. 8,100. (tabloid format)
Formerly: Koninklijke Shell-Post (ISSN 0023-3390)

665.5 NE
SHELL-VENSTER. 1917. bi-m. free. Shell Nederland B.V., Dept. PAC/1, Hofplein 20, Rotterdam, Netherlands. Ed. P. de Wit. bk.rev.; charts; illus.; stat.; index; circ. 51,000 (controlled).
Formerly: Olie (ISSN 0030-2112)

665.5 UK
SHIELD. 1924. 4/yr. free to qualified personnel. British Petroleum Company plc., Britannic House, 1 Finsbury Circus, London EC2M 7BA, England. FAX 071-496-4528. (U.S. dist.: BP America Inc., 200 Public Sq., Cleveland, Ohio 44114-2373) Ed. Valerie Shepard. charts; illus.; circ. 100,000. Indexed: Fluidex, Geo.Abstr.
Former titles: B P Shield; B P Shield International (ISSN 0045-1274)
Description: Covers business issues relating to activities of the BP group throughout the world.

665.6 500 CC ISSN 1000-5870
SHIYOU DAXUE XUEBAO (ZIRAN KEXUE BAN)/UNIVERSITY OF PETROLEUM, CHINA. JOURNAL (NATURAL SCIENCE EDITION). (Text in Chinese; table of contents in English) 1959. bi-m. Y24. Shiyou Daxue, Xuebao Bianjibu, Dongying, Shandong 257062, People's Republic of China. (Dist. overseas by: China Educational Publications Import & Export Corp., No. 15, Xueyuan Lu, Beijing, P.R.C.) Ed. Li Lanzhi.
—BLDSC shelfmark: 4911.950000.

SHIYOU DILI WULI KANTAN. see EARTH SCIENCES — Geology

665.5 CC ISSN 1001-2206
SHIYOU GONGCHENG JIANSHE/PETROLEUM ENGINEERING CONSTRUCTION. (Text in Chinese) 1975. bi-m. $2.50. Zhongguo Shiyou Tianranqi Zong Gongqi, Shigong Jishu Yanjiusuo - China Petroleum and Gas Corporation, Engineering Technology Research Institute, No.40, Jin-Tang Gonglu, Tanggu Qu, Tianjin 300451, People's Republic of China. TEL 983589. FAX 022-987876. (Dist. outside China by: Guoji Shudian - China International Book Trading Corp., P.O. Box 399, Beijing, P.R.C.) Ed. Meng Qingfu. adv.; circ. 8,000.
Description: Covers news in engineering construction, including, construction, installation, management and results of research programs.

665.5 CC ISSN 1000-8144
TP692.3 CODEN: SHHUE8
SHIYOU HUAGONG/PETROCHEMICAL TECHNOLOGY. 1970. m. $60. Ministry of Chemical Industry, Beijing Research Institute of Chemical Industry - Huaxue Gongye Bu, Beijing Huagong Yanjiuyuan, P.O. Box 1442, Hepingli, Beijing, People's Republic of China. TEL 4216131. FAX 4228661. (Co-sponsor: Chemical Industry & Engineering Society of China, Institute of Petrochemicals) Ed. Jiang Xuequan. adv.; circ. 9,500.
—BLDSC shelfmark: 6430.395000.
Description: Publishes scientific research papers, technical reports, and reviews on the petrochemical and organic chemical industries.

665.5 CC
SHIYOU KANTAN YU KAIFA/PETROLEUM EXPLORATION AND DEVELOPMENT. (Text in Chinese) bi-m. $1.30 per no. Guoji Shudian, Qikan Bu, P.O. Box 399, Beijing 100044, People's Republic of China.

665.5 CC ISSN 1001-6112
SHIYOU SHIYAN DIZHI. (Text in Chinese) q. Dizhi Kuangchan-bu, Shiyou Dizhi Zhongxin Shiyanshi, P.O. Box 916, Wuxi, Jiangsu 214151, People's Republic of China. TEL 668043. Ed. Zhu Xia.
—BLDSC shelfmark: 3840.035000.

665.5 CC ISSN 1000-1441
SHIYOU WUTAN. (Text in Chinese) q. Dizhi Kuangchan-bu, Shiyou Wutan Yanjiusuo, 21 Weigang, Nanjing, Jiangsu 210014, People's Republic of China. TEL 432191. Ed. Ou Qingxian.
—BLDSC shelfmark: 4156.100000.

665.5 CC
SHIYOU XUEBAO/ACTA PETROLEI SINICA. (Text in Chinese) q. $3.80 per no. Guoji Shudian, Qikan Bu, P.O. Box 399, Beijing 100044, People's Republic of China. Indexed: Bibl.& Ind.Geol., Chem.Abstr, Fluidex, Petrol.Abstr.

665.5 FR
SOCIETE NATIONALE E L F AQUITAINE. RAPPORT ANNUEL. a. free. E L F - Aquitaine, Direction des Relations Publiques et de la Communication, Tour ELF, Cedex 45, 92078 Paris La Defense, France. charts; illus.; stat.

665.5 622 US
SOCIETY OF PETROLEUM ENGINEERS. REPRINT SERIES. 1958. irreg. price varies. Society of Petroleum Engineers, Inc., Box 833836, Richardson, TX 75083-3836. TEL 214-659-3377. FAX 214-669-0135. TELEX 730989 SPEDAL. Ed. Jim McInnis. Indexed: Eng.Ind., Ocean.Abstr.
Formerly: Society of Petroleum Engineers of American Institute of Mining, Metallurgical and Petroleum Engineers. Petroleum Transactions Reprint Series (ISSN 0081-1688)
Description: Anthologies of classic and important recent technical reports on broad oil and gas drilling, exploration and production topics.
Refereed Serial

665.5 US ISSN 0081-1696
TN1 CODEN: TPTEAF
SOCIETY OF PETROLEUM ENGINEERS. TRANSACTIONS. 1925. a. $70 to non-members. Society of Petroleum Engineers, Inc., Box 833836, Richardson, TX 75083-3836. TEL 214-669-3377. Ed. Jim McInnis. charts; illus.; index; circ. 5,000. (back issues avail.) Indexed: Bibl.& Ind.Geol., Chem.Abstr., Eng.Ind., Gas Abstr., Petrol.Abstr.
—BLDSC shelfmark: 9008.700000.
Formerly: Society of Petroleum Engineers of American Institute of Mining, Metallurgical and Petroleum Engineers. Transactions.
Description: Selection of technical reports from five Society journals.
Refereed Serial

622.338 US ISSN 0081-1718
CODEN: SPWLA6
SOCIETY OF PROFESSIONAL WELL LOG ANALYSTS. S P W L A ANNUAL LOGGING SYMPOSIUM TRANSACTIONS. 1960. a. price varies. Society of Professional Well Log Analysts, 6001 Gulf Frwy, Ste. C 129, Houston, TX 77023. TEL 713-928-8925.
FAX 713-928-9061. adv.; bibl.; charts; illus.; circ. 2,500. (also avail. in microfiche) Indexed: GeoRef, Petrol.Abstr.

665.773 US ISSN 0038-1500
SOONER L P G TIMES. 1963. m. free. Oklahoma LP-Gas Association, 4200 N. Lindsay, Oklahoma City, OK 73105. TEL 405-424-1775. Ed. Kurt S. Winden. adv.; bk.rev.; charts; illus.; stat.; circ. 1,450. (processed)

665.5 US
SOUTH DAKOTA PETROLEUM MARKETER. m. Box 1058, Pierre, SD 57501-1058. TEL 605-224-8606. Ed. Curt Newharth. circ. 500.

665.538 US
SOUTH LOUISIANA DRILLING REPORT; drilling activity below the 31st parallel. w. $400. Offshore Data Services, Inc., Box 19909, Houston, TX 77224-9909. TEL 713-781-2713. FAX 713-781-9594.
Formerly: South Louisiana Land Report.
Description: Covers developments in the oil drilling industry in Louisiana.

380 US
SOUTHEAST PETROLEUM INDUSTRY. 1945. a. $40. Midwest Register, Inc., 601 S. Boulder, Ste. 1001, Tulsa, OK 74119-1301. TEL 918-582-2000.
Formerly: Directory of Producers and Drilling Contractors Southeast: Louisiana, Arkansas, Florida, Georgia.
Description: Supplies company name, address, personnel, division offices, offshore operations, producer of oil or gas and if drilling contractor with rotary or cable tools, pipelines, refineries, petrochemical, gas processing, equipment manufacturers and suppliers, engineers.

665.5 US
SOUTHEASTERN OIL REVIEW. 1926. w. $30. Oil Review Publishing Co., Box 145, Jackson, MS 39205. TEL 601-353-6213. Ed. J. Ishee. adv.; circ. 3,200.
Description: Covers oil and gas exploration and devlopment, drilling and production activities in the Southeastern States.

665 338.2 US ISSN 0884-6219
TN860
SOUTHWEST OIL WORLD. 1976. bi-m. $39 (foreign $89). Hart Publications, Inc., 1900 Grant St., Ste. 400, Box 1917, Denver, CO 80201.
TEL 303-837-1917. adv.; bk.rev.; illus.; tr.lit./; circ. 4,467. (back issues avail.) Indexed: Bibl.& Ind.Geol., Petrol.Abstr.
—BLDSC shelfmark: 8356.715000.
Formerly (until 1985): Drill Bit (ISSN 0012-6225)
Description: Covers the Permian Basin area.

665.5 SP
SPAIN. MINISTERIO DE ECONOMIA Y HACIENDA, DELEGACION DEL GOBIERNO EN CAMPSA. EL PETROLERO EN LA C E E. (Comunidad Economica Europea) 1986. a. free. Ministerio de Economia y Hacienda, Delegacion del Gobierno en Campsa, Capitan Haya, 41, 28020 Madrid, Spain. TEL 582-5206. FAX 5561819.

PETROLEUM AND GAS

665.5   SP
SPAIN. MINISTERIO DE ECONOMIA Y HACIENDA. DELEGACION DEL GOBIERNO EN CAMPSA. MEMORIA. 1969. a. free. Ministerio de Economia y Hacienda, Delegacion del Gobierno en Campsa, Capitan Haya, 41, 28020 Madrid, Spain. TEL 582.52.06. Ed. J.A. Entrent. illus.; circ. 2,000.
   Description: Provides information on the petroleum industry and trade.

665.5   US   ISSN 0584-8016
TN860
SPAN. 1961. q. free. Amoco Corporation, 200 E. Randolph Dr., Chicago, IL 60601. TEL 312-856-6614. FAX 312-856-3155. Ed. Tom W. Seslar. charts; illus.; circ. 225,000. **Indexed:** Curr.Adv.Ecol.Sci., Excerp.Med., Helminthol.Abstr., Herb.Abstr., Ind.Vet., Rev.Appl.Entomol., Seed Abstr.

665.5   IT
STAFFETA QUOTIDIANA PETROLIFERA; e delle altre fonti di energia. 1933. d. L.180000. Goffredo Cozzi, Ed. & Pub., Via Aventina 19, 00153 Rome, Italy. FAX 06-57554906. TELEX 611674 RIVPE.

STEAM - ELECTRIC PLANT FACTORS (1978). see *MINES AND MINING INDUSTRY*

STEELMAKING CONFERENCE: PROCEEDINGS. see *METALLURGY*

665 338.47   RU   ISSN 0039-2448
STROITEL'STVO TRUBOPROVODOV. 1956. m. 22.20 Rub. Izdatel'stvo Nedra, Pl. Belorusskogo Vokzala, 3, 125047 Moscow, Russia. TEL 250-52-55. bk.rev.; charts; illus.; index. **Indexed:** Chem.Abstr, Gas Abstr., Geotech.Abstr.
—BLDSC shelfmark: 0174.200000.
   Description: Covers the pipe-line construction industry.

665.5   UK   ISSN 0266-2205
SUBSEA ENGINEERING NEWS; including pipeline and floater update. 1984. s-m. £180 in Europe £185; elsewhere £200. Knighton Enterprises Ltd., 2 Marlborough St., Faringdon, Oxon SN7 7JP, England. TEL 0793-71-303. FAX 079371-433. TELEX 449703-TELSER-G. Ed. Steven Sasanow. adv.; bk.rev.; circ. 350. (back issues avail.) **Indexed:** Petrol.Abstr.
   Former titles: S E N Incorporating Oil and Gas Pipeline News; O G P N.
   Description: Covers market information and technical details on subsea and underwater engineering, pipelines, and floating production systems.

665   US
SUN MAGAZINE. 1923. 4/yr. free. Sun Company, Inc. (Radnor), 100 Matsonford Rd., Radnor, PA 19087. TEL 215-293-6000. Ed. B.M Dotter. circ. 317,763. **Indexed:** Ocean.Abstr., Pollut.Abstr.
   Formerly: Our Sun.

338.2 665   US   ISSN 0039-8403
HD9567.T3
T I P R O REPORTER. 1948. q. $25 to non-members. Texas Independent Producers & Royalty Owners Association, 515 Congress Ave., Ste. 1910, Austin, TX 78701. TEL 512-477-4452. FAX 512-476-8070. Ed. Larry Springer. adv.; circ. 4,500. (back issues avail.)

665.5   UK   ISSN 0958-8787
TANKER CHARTER RECORD. 12/yr. Basil Blackwell Ltd., 108 Cowley Rd., Oxford OX4 1JF, England. TEL 0865-791100. FAX 0865-791347. TELEX 837022-OXBOOK-G.

662 627   UK   ISSN 0305-179X
TANKER REGISTER. 1960. a. £155($280) Clarkson Research Studies Ltd., 12 Camomile St., London EC3A 7BP, England. TEL 071-283 8955.
—BLDSC shelfmark: 8602.517000.

665.5   TS
AL-TAWZI/DISTRIBUTION. (Text in Arabic) 1984. m. free. Abu Dhabi National Oil Company, Distribution Division - Sharikat Bitrul Abu Dhabi al-Wataniyyah lil-Tawzi', P.O. Box 4188, Abu Dhabi, United Arab Emirates. TEL 771300. TELEX 22358 FUDIST EM. Ed. Abdullah Majid al-Mansouri. circ. 1,000.
   Description: News of company activities.

665.538   US
TEXAS. RAILROAD COMMISSION. OIL AND GAS DIVISION. ANNUAL REPORT. a. $15. Railroad Commission, Oil and Gas Publications, Drawer 12967, Capitol Station, Austin, TX 78711. TEL 512-463-7255.

665.5   US
TEXAS. RAILROAD COMMISSION. OIL AND GAS DIVISION. CRUDE OIL AND GAS NOMINATIONS. (Subseries of: Statewide Oil and Gas Stocks and Nominations) m. $28. Railroad Commission, Oil and Gas Publications, Drawer 12967, Capitol Sta., Austin, TX 78711. TEL 512-463-7255.
   Formerly: Texas. Railroad Commission. Oil and Gas Division. Recapitulation of Crude Oil Nominations and Purchases by Company.

665.5   US
TEXAS. RAILROAD COMMISSION. OIL AND GAS DIVISION. CRUDE OIL NOMINATIONS AND PURCHASES. m. $32. Railroad Commission, Oil and Gas Publications, Drawer 12967, Capitol Sta., Austin, TX 78711. TEL 512-463-7255.
   Formerly: Texas. Railroad Commission. Oil and Gas Division. Summary of Crude Oil Nominations and Purchases by District.

665.538   US
TEXAS. RAILROAD COMMISSION. OIL AND GAS DIVISION. GAS PRORATION SCHEDULE. (Avail. by RRC district) s-a. $202. Railroad Commission, Oil and Gas Publications, Drawer 12967, Capitol Sta., Austin, TX 78711. TEL 512-463-7255.

665.538   US
TEXAS. RAILROAD COMMISSION. OIL AND GAS DIVISION. OIL PRORATION SCHEDULE. (Avail. by RRC district) s-a. $292. Railroad Commission, Oil and Gas Publications, Drawer 12967, Capitol Sta., Austin, TX 78711. TEL 512-463-7255.

665.538   US
TEXAS. RAILROAD COMMISSION. OIL AND GAS DIVISION. PRORATED GAS FIELDS - MONTHLY SCHEDULE. (Avail. by RRC district) m. $241. Railroad Commission, Oil and Gas Publications, Drawer 12967, Capitol Sta., Austin, TX 78711. TEL 512-463-7255.
   Formerly: Texas. Railroad Commission. Oil and Gas Division. Gas Monthly Proration Schedule.

665.773   US   ISSN 0040-4454
TEXAS L P - GAS NEWS. 1944. m. (11/yr.). $24. Texas L P - Gas Association, Box 140735, Austin, TX 78714-0735. TEL 512-836-8620. FAX 512-834-0758. Ed. Ellen Terry. adv.; illus.; circ. 1,259 (controlled).
   Formerly: Texas Butane News.
   Description: Covers new laws and regulations, both state and federal, affecting the industry, new technology and products, marketing opportunities, and safety issues.

TEXAS LAW OF OIL AND GAS. see *LAW*

TEXAS NATURAL RESOURCES REPORTER. see *WATER RESOURCES*

665 338.2   US   ISSN 0896-8969
TEXAS OIL MARKETER. 1951. q. $20. Texas Oil Marketers Association, 701 W. 15th St., Austin, TX 78701. TEL 512-476-9547. Ed. Cheryl Lockhart. adv.; illus.; circ. 1,400.
   Formerly: Texas Oil Jobber (ISSN 0040-4527)

380   US
TEXAS PETROLEUM INDUSTRY. 1945. a. $40. Midwest Register, Inc., 601 S Boulder, Ste. 1001, Tulsa, OK 74119-1301. TEL 918-582-2000.
   Formerly: Directory of Producers and Drilling Contractors: Texas.
   Description: Supplies company name, address, phone and fax numbers, personnel, division offices, offshore operations, whether producer of oil or gas and if drilling contractor with rotary or cable tools, pipelines, refineries, petrochemical, gas processing, equipment manufacturers and suppliers, engineers, landman.

TEXAS PUBLIC UTILITY NEWS. see *ENERGY*

665.7   CC   ISSN 1000-0976
TN880.A1   CODEN: BM 944
TIANRANQI GONGYE/NATURAL GAS INDUSTRY. (Text mainly in Chinese; summaries in Chinese, English) 1981. bi-m. Y1.50 per no. (effective 1992). (Sichuan Shiyou Guanli-ju - Sichuan Petroleum Administration) Tianranqi Gongye Zazhishe - Natural Gas Industry Journal Agency, No.3, Sec. 1, Fuqing Lu, Chengdu, Sichuan 610051, People's Republic of China. TEL 334911. (Subscr. to: Guoji Shudian - China International Book Trading Corporation, P.O. Box 399, Beijing 100044, P.R.C.) Ed. Zhao Dingzhong. adv.; charts; illus.; stat.; index; circ. 5,000. (back issues avail.)
—BLDSC shelfmark: 6037.315000.
   Description: Contains articles on exploration and development, drilling-production technology and equipment, storage, transportation, surface construction, gas processing and utilization, reforms and management in the industry.

665.773   US   ISSN 1048-0935
TODAY'S REFINERY. 1987. m. $25 in U.S. and Canada; elsewhere $60 (free to qualified personnel). Percy Publishing Company, Inc., 170 King St, Box 287, Chappaqua, NY 10514. TEL 914-238-0205. FAX 914-238-0210. Ed. James D. Wall. adv.; circ. 7,000 (controlled).
   Description: Contains articles, column, abstracts and reviews of interest to petroleum refiners in the USA and Canada.

354   TR
TRINIDAD AND TOBAGO. MINISTRY OF ENERGY. ANNUAL REPORT. 1964. a. free. Ministry of Energy, P.O. Box 96, Port-of-Spain, Trinidad & Tobago, W.I. illus.; stat.; circ. 500.
   Former titles: Trinidad and Tobago. Ministry of Energy and Natural Resources. Annual Report; Trinidad and Tobago. Ministry of Energy and Energy-Based Industries. Annual Report; Trinidad and Tobago. Ministry of Petroleum and Mines. Annual Report.

622 338.2   TR
TRINIDAD AND TOBAGO. MINISTRY OF ENERGY. MONTHLY BULLETIN. 1964. m. free. Ministry of Energy, P.O. Box 96, Port-of-Spain, Trinidad & Tobago, W.I. charts; mkt.; index, cum.index; circ. 570.
   Former titles: Trinidad and Tobago. Ministry of Energy and Natural Resources. Monthly Bulletin; Trinidad and Tobago. Ministry of Energy and Energy-Based Industries. Monthly Bulletin; Trinidad and Tobago. Ministry of Petroleum and Mines. Monthly Bulletin (ISSN 0026-5322)

TURKIYE PETROL KIMYA, LASTIK ISCILEERI SENDIKASI. MAGAZINE. see *RUBBER*

665.5   UK
U K UPSTREAM PETROLEUM DATABASE. 1984. s-a. £1,300. Arthur Andersen & Co., Petroleum Services Group, 1 Surrey St., London WC2R 2PS, England. TEL 071-438-3888. FAX 071-438-3881. TELEX 8812711.
●Available only online.
   Description: Provides information on licences, drilling activity and reserves both onshore and offshore UK.

665.5   US   ISSN 0082-8599
HD9563
U S A OIL INDUSTRY DIRECTORY. 1962. a. $125. PennWell Publishing Co., Box 1260, Tulsa, OK 74101. TEL 918-835-3161. Ed. Jonelle Moore. adv.; circ. 5,000.
   Description: Lists headquarters and provides company profiles of the domestic oil industry.

665.5   US
U S A OILFIELD SERVICE, SUPPLY, AND MANUFACTURERS DIRECTORY. 1983. a. $115. PennWell Publishing Co., Box 1260, Tulsa, OK 74101. TEL 918-835-3161. Ed. Jonelle Moore. adv.; circ. 1,500.
   Former titles: Oilfield Service, Supply, and Manufacturers Worldwide Directory (ISSN 0736-038X); Oilfield Service, Supply, and Manufacturers Directory.
   Description: Provides oilfield services, the wholesale and retail sale of oilfield products as well as information on companies engaged in the design, manufacture and construction of equipment used in the oilfield.

PETROLEUM AND GAS

665.5   US
U S CRUDE OIL, NATURAL GAS, AND NATURAL GAS LIQUIDS. a. $6.50. U.S. Department of Energy, Energy Information Administration, National Energy Information Center, EI-231, Rm. 1F-048, Forrestal bldg., 1000 Independence Ave., S.W., DC 20585. TEL 202-586-8800. (Dist. by: Supt. of Documents, Washington, DC 20402) charts.

665.5   US   ISSN 0502-9767
U S OIL WEEK; inside report on trends in petroleum marketing without the influence of advertising. 1967. w. $259 (foreign $309) includes Fuel Oil Update; C-Store Digest; and U S Oil Week's Price Monitor. Capitol Publications Inc., 1101 King St., Ste. 444, Alexandria, VA 22314. TEL 703-683-4100. FAX 703-739-6517. Ed. Tom Guay. index.
- Also available online. Vendor(s): DIALOG.
  Incorporates (in 1989): C-Store Week (ISSN 0887-4700)
  Description: Competitive coverage of profit opportunities and market trends for petroleum marketers across the country. Focuses on ways to thrive in a changing marketpalce. Covers industry news; current and pending government regulations; underground tank, insurance and environmental issues.

UIT EUROPOORTKRINGEN; magazine voor het bedrijfsleven in Rotterdam/Botlek/Europoort/Delta. see *TRANSPORTATION — Ships And Shipping*

UNITED KINGDOM OFFSHORE LEGISLATION GUIDE. see *LAW*

665.538   US
U.S. DEPARTMENT OF ENERGY. STRATEGIC PETROLEUM RESERVE OFFICE. ANNUAL REPORT. a. U.S. Department of Energy, Strategic Petroleum Reserve Office, Washington, DC 20545. TEL 202-252-5000.

665.5   US
U.S. ENERGY INFORMATION ADMINISTRATION. WEEKLY PETROLEUM STATUS REPORT. w. $47. U.S. Department of Energy, Energy Information Administration, National Energy Information Center, EI-231, Rm. 1F-048, Forrestal bldg., 1000 Independence Ave., S.W., Washington, DC 20585. TEL 202-586-8800. (Dist. by: Supt. of Documents, Washington, DC 20402) charts. **Indexed:** Energy Info.Abstr.
- Also available online.
  Description: Provides up-to-date information on the petroleum supply situation in the context of historical information, selected prices, and forecasts.

URJA. see *ENERGY*

665.5   II   ISSN 0971-2038
▼**URJA OIL AND GAS INTERNATIONAL.** (Text in English) 1992. m. Rs.125($40) Urja, P.O. Box 3008, G-82, Sujan Singh Park, New Delhi 110-003, India. TEL 91-11-611536. FAX 91-11-462-8251. Ed. Dipak Basu Chaudhuri.
  Description: Devoted to petroleum and petrochemicals in South Asia. Also covers the world energy scene and developments in India's near-west.

UTILITY REPORTER: FUELS ENERGY & POWER. see *ENERGY*

V W D - OELE UND FETTE. (Vereinigte Wirtschaftsdienste GmbH) see *BUSINESS AND ECONOMICS — Investments*

VENEZUELA. MINISTERIO DE ENERGIA Y MINAS. CARTA SEMANAL. see *MINES AND MINING INDUSTRY*

VENEZUELA. MINISTERIO DE ENERGIA Y MINAS. INFORMATIONS. see *MINES AND MINING INDUSTRY*

VENEZUELA. MINISTERIO DE ENERGIA Y MINAS. MEMORIA Y CUENTA. see *MINES AND MINING INDUSTRY*

VENEZUELA. MINISTERIO DE ENERGIA Y MINAS. QUARTERLY BULLETIN. see *MINES AND MINING INDUSTRY*

665 553.28 622   SZ   ISSN 0042-1901
VEREINIGUNG SCHWEIZERISCHER PETROLEUM-GEOLOGEN UND -INGENIEURE. BULLETIN/ASSOCIATION SUISSE DES GEOLOGUES ET INGENIEURS DU PETROLE. BULLETIN. Cover title: V S P Bulletin. (Text in English, French, German) 1934. s-a. 50 Fr. Vereinigung Schweizerischer Petroleum-Geologen und -Ingenieure, c/o V. Gschwind, Shell (Switzerland), Bederstr. 66, Postfach, CH-8021 Zurich, Switzerland. FAX 41-1-2062209. Ed.Bd. adv.; bk.rev.; bibl.; charts; illus.; cum.index; circ. 650. **Indexed:** Bibl.& Ind.Geol.
  —BLDSC shelfmark: 2404.050000.

655 658.3   US   ISSN 0042-5087
VICKERS VOICE. 1954. q. free. Vickers Petroleum Corporation, c/o Total Petroleum, Box 500, Denver, CO 80230. Eds. Derald Linn, Dick Snider. illus.; circ. 2,000.

665.5   CI
VJESNIK I N A - NAFTAPLIN. (Text in Croatian) 1974. fortn. I N A - Naftaplin, Subiceva 29, 41000 Zagreb, Croatia. TEL 418-011. Ed. Ivo Decak. circ. 8,000.

665.5   GW
VORAN. 1932. 6/yr. Aral AG, Wittener Str. 45, 4630 Bochum 1, Germany. FAX 0234-3152364. Ed. Roland Mielke. adv.; index; circ. 5,500.
  Formerly: Voran Aktuell.

WAERMETECHNIK; internationales Fachorgan fuer Feuerungs- und Haustechnik. see *HEATING, PLUMBING AND REFRIGERATION*

WASHINGTON STATE ENERGY OFFICE DISPATCH; a bi-monthly journal of Washington's energy and environmental issues and programs. see *ENERGY*

665.538 658.7   UK   ISSN 0268-7844
WEEKLY PETROLEUM ARGUS. 1969. w. £895($1475) Petroleum Argus Ltd., 93 Shepperton Rd., London N1 3DF, England. TEL 071-359-8792. FAX 071-226-0695. TELEX 21277. Ed. Adrian Binks. bk.rev.; index; circ. controlled. (looseleaf format; back issues avail.)
  Formerly (until 1985): Europ-Oil Prices.
  Description: An analysis of the oil markets and the news and events that affect them.

665.7   US
WEEKLY PROPANE NEWSLETTER. 1971. w. $150 (effective Jan. 1991). Butane - Propane News, Inc., 338 E. Foothill Blvd., Box 419, Arcadia, CA 91066. TEL 818-357-2168. FAX 818-303-2854. Ed. Hal McWilliams.

662.338   CN
WEEKLY WELL ACTIVITY REPORT. 1980. w. Can.$75. Manitoba Energy and Mines, Petroleum Branch, 555-330 Graham Ave., Winnipeg, Man. R3C 4E3, Canada. TEL 204-945-6574. FAX 204-945-0586. Ed. J.N. Fox. circ. 50.
  Description: Information on field activities in Manitoba: wells licensed, drilling information and well status.

622.338   US
WELL SERVICING. 1961. bi-m. free to qualified personnel. (Association of Oilwell Servicing Contractors) Workover-Well Servicing Publications, Inc., 6060 N. Central Expy., Ste. 428, Dallas, TX 75206. TEL 214-692-0771. Ed. Polly S. Henderson. adv.; bk.rev.; illus.; pat.; stat.; tr.lit.; circ. 12,000 (controlled). (back issues avail.) **Indexed:** Petrol.Abstr.

665 338.2   US
WESTERN OIL WORLD. 1944. m. $39 (foreign $89). Hart Publications, Inc., 1900 Grant St., Ste. 400, Box 1917, Denver, CO 80201. TEL 303-892-1917. adv.; bk.rev.; charts; illus.; stat.; circ. 7,175. (back issues avail.) **Indexed:** GeoRef, Petrol.Abstr.
  Formerly (until 1985): Western Oil Reporter (ISSN 0043-3985)
  Description: Covers the Rocky Mountain region.

380   US
WESTERN PETROLEUM INDUSTRY. 1945. a. $40. Midwest Register, Inc., 601 S. Boulder, Ste. 1001, Tulsa, OK 74119-1301. TEL 918-582-2000.
  Formerly: Directory of Producers and Drilling Contractors: California.
  Description: Supplies company name, address, phone and fax number, personnel, division offices, offshore operations, whether producer of oil or gas and if drilling contractor with rotary or cable tools, pipeline companies, refineries, gas processing, petrochemical and equipment manufacturers and suppliers.

665.5   US
THE WHOLE WORLD OIL DIRECTORY. a. $229. National Register Publishing Co., A Reed Reference Publishing Company, Division of Reed Publishing (USA) Inc., 121 Chanlon Rd., New Providence, NJ 07974. TEL 800-521-8110. FAX 908-665-6688. TELEX 138 755. (Subscr. to: R.R. Bowker, Order Dept., Box 31, New Providence, NJ 07974)
  Description: Profiles over 35,000 key decision-makers from 8,700 comapnies worldwide.

507.1 531.64   AT   ISSN 0159-1878
WHO'S DRILLING. 1979. w. Aus.$670 (effective Dec. 1991). Pex Publications Pty. Ltd., P.O. Box 158, Claremont, W.A. 6010, Australia. TEL 09-383-3477. FAX 09-385-1485. Ed. Don Lipscombe. circ. 300.
  Description: National exploration newsletter analysing all current and pending wells, rig and boat movements, and seismic surveys.

665.7   US
▼**WORLD GAS INTELLIGENCE.** 1990. m. $585. Petroleum & Energy Intelligence Weekly, Inc., 575 Broadway, New York, NY 10012-3230. TEL 212-941-5500. FAX 212-941-5508. TELEX 62371 PETROIN. Ed. Patrick Heren.
  Description: Provides concise news and analysis of developments in the international gas industry.

665.5   US   ISSN 1053-9859
WORLD GEOPHYSICAL NEWS. 1984. s-m. $240 (foreign $300). Petroleum Information Corporation, Box 2162, Denver, CO 80201-2162. TEL 303-340-7100. FAX 303-794-1694. stat.
  Description: Includes crew location reports, statistical summaries, and industry news.

WORLD L N G - GAS CONTRACTS. see *LAW — International Law*

WORLD NATIONAL OIL COMPANY STATUTES. see *LAW. — International Law*

665 338.2   US   ISSN 0043-8790
TN860   CODEN: WOOIAS
WORLD OIL. 1916. m. $24 (free to qualified personnel). Gulf Publishing Co., Box 2608, Houston, TX 77252-2608. TEL 713-529-4301. FAX 713-520-4433. TELEX 287330 GULF UR. Ed. T.R. Wright, Jr. adv.; bk.rev.; charts; illus.; tr.lit.; index; circ. 37,582. (also avail. in microfilm from UMI; reprint service avail.) **Indexed:** A.S.& T.Ind., AESIS, API Abstr., API Oil., Bibl.& Ind.Geol., Bus.Ind., Chem.Abstr., Curr.Cont., Energy Info.Abstr., Energy Rev., Eng.Ind., Environ.Per.Bibl., Fuel & Energy Abstr., Gas Abstr., Mid.East: Abstr.& Ind., Ocean.Abstr., Petrol.Abstr., Pollut.Abstr., PROMT, Risk Abstr., So.Pac.Per.Ind., Tr.& Indus.Ind.
  —BLDSC shelfmark: 9356.950000.
  Formerly: Oil Weekly.

662.338 382   UK   ISSN 0950-1029
WORLD OIL TRADE. 2/yr. Basil Blackwell Ltd., 108 Cowley Rd., Oxford OX4 1JF, England. TEL 0865-791100. FAX 0865-791347. TELEX 837022-OXBOOK-G.

665.5   UK
WORLD PETROLEUM TRENDS. a. Petroconsultants Ltd., Europa House, 266 Upper Richmond Rd., Putney,London SW15 6TQ, England. TEL 081-780-2500. FAX 081-780-2036. TELEX 94018027-PUKL.

665.54   UK
WORLD PIPELINES. 1983. a. £25. P.O. Box 21, Beaconsfield, Bucks HP9 1NS, England. TEL 0494-675139. FAX 0494-670155. TELEX 94016686-SSSP-G. Ed. John Tiratsoo.

PETROLEUM AND GAS — ABSTRACTING, BIBLIOGRAPHIES, STATISTICS

665.5   US   ISSN 0084-2583
TP692.3
WORLDWIDE PETROCHEMICAL DIRECTORY. 1962. a. $140. PennWell Publishing Co., Box 21288, Tulsa, OK 74121. TEL 918-835-3161. Ed. Jonelle Moore. adv.
   Incorporates in part (in 1987): Refining and Petrochemical Technology Yearbook.

665.73   US   ISSN 0277-0962
TN867
WORLDWIDE REFINING AND GAS PROCESSING DIRECTORY. 1942. a. $140. PennWell Publishing Co., Box 21288, Tulsa, OK 74121. TEL 918-835-3161. (Alternate addr.: 1421 S. Sheridan, Tulsa, OK 74101) Ed. Jonelle Moore. adv.; circ. 2,500. (back issues avail.)
   Incorporates in part (in 1987): Refining and Petrochemical Technology Yearbook.
   Description: Lists over 14,000 personnel in over 3,000 plant sites in the United States, Canada, Europe, Latin America, Asia-Pacific, Africa and the Middle East.

300 100   CC   ISSN 0439-8041
XUESHU YUEKAN/ACADEMIC MONTHLY. (Text in Chinese) 1957. m. Y14.40($54) (Shanghai Shi Zhexue Shehui Kexue Xuehui, Lianhehui - Shanghai Society for Philosophy and Social Sciences) Shanghai Shehui Kexue Chubanshe, No.7, Alley 622, Huaihai Zhonglu, Shanghai 200020ic of China, People's Republic of China. (Dist. outside China by: China International Book Trading Corp., P.O. Box 399, Beijing, P.R.C.; Dist. in US by: China Books & Periodicals, Inc., 2929 24th St., San Francisco, CA 94110. TEL 415-282-2994) Eds. Huang Yingshu, Gu Mouzhong.

XUEXI YU TANSUO/STUDY & EXPLORATION. see *SOCIAL SCIENCES: COMPREHENSIVE WORKS*

665   US   ISSN 0044-0205
YANKEE OILMAN. 1955. m. $12. New England Fuel Institute, Box 457, Swampscott, MA 01907. TEL 617-598-2074. FAX 617-595-2915. Ed. Scott Rolph. adv.; bk.rev.; stat.; circ. 6,843.
   Description: Contains news and features about the oil heating and petroleum distribution industries in the northeast United States.

665.5   IS
YEDA. (Text in Hebrew) 1960. bi-m. free. Paz Oil Co., Ltd., Business Information Unit, P.O. Box 434, Haifa 31003, Israel. TEL 04-567111. FAX 04-567366. circ. 2,500.

662.338   CC   ISSN 1001-697X
YOUTIAN DIMIAN GONGCHENG/SURFACE STRUCTURE OF OIL FIELDS. (Text in Chinese) bi-m. Daqing Shiyou Guanliju - Daqing Bureau of Petroleum Administration, Ranghu Lu, Daqing, Heilongjiang 163712, People's Republic of China. TEL 55524. Wang Daoman.

665.5 665.7   CC
ZHONGGUO HAISHANG YOUQI (DIZHI). (Text in Chinese) bi-m. Nengyuan Bu, Haiyang Shiyou Kantan Kaifa Yanjiusuo - Ministry of Energy, Offshore Petroleum Exploration Institute, Xincheng, Hebei 074010, People's Republic of China. TEL 2799. Ed. Yan Haozhi.

665.5   CC   ISSN 1001-7682
ZHONGGUO HAISHANG YOUQI (GONGCHENG). (Text in Chinese) bi-m. Nengyuan-bu, Bohai Gongcheng Sheji Gongsi - Ministry of Energy, Bohai Engineering Design Company, P.O. Box 536, No. 13, Tanggu, Tianjin 300452, People's Republic of China. TEL 975661. Ed. Liu Chufan.

665.5   CC   ISSN 1001-4500
ZHONGGUO HAIYANG PINGTAI. (Text in Chinese) bi-m. Zhongguo Guoji Haiyang Shiyou Gongcheng Gongsi - China International Marine Drilling Engineering Corporation, No.851, Zhongshan Nan 2 Lu, Shanghai 200032, People's Republic of China. TEL 4399626. Ed. Qian Xixiang.

665.5   CC
ZHONGGUO SHIYOU HUABAO/CHINA OIL PICTORIAL. (Text in Chinese) q. No. 3-15 A, Xinkai Lu, Langfang, Hebei 102800, People's Republic of China. TEL 25111.
   Description: Introduces the Chinese petroleum industry and other energy industries.

ZHONGNAN MINZU XUEYUAN XUEBAO (SHEHUI KEXUE BAN)/SOUTH-CENTRAL COLLEGE FOR NATIONALITIES. JOURNAL (SOCIAL SCIENCE EDITION). see *SOCIAL SCIENCES: COMPREHENSIVE WORKS*

662.6   CC   ISSN 1001-5620
ZUANJING YE YU WANJING YE. (Text in Chinese) q. Huabei Shiyou Guanli-ju - North China Bureau of Petroleum Administration, P.O. Box 19, Renqiu, Hebei 062550, People's Republic of China. TEL 2396. Ed. Pan Shikui.

666.5   VE
ZUMAQUE.* 1976. q. Sociedad Venezolana de Ingenieros de Petroleo, c/o Colegio de Engenieros de Venezuela, Apdo. 2006, Caracas, Venezuela.

665.5   GW
3 R - INTERNATIONAL. (Text in German; summaries in English, French) 1951. m (10/yr.). DM.265. (Rohrleitungsverband e.V.) Vulkan-Verlag GmbH, Hollestr. 1G, Postfach 103962, 4300 Essen, Germany. TEL 0201-82002-0. FAX 0201-82002-40. Ed.Bd. adv.
   Formerly: Rohre-Rohrleitungsbau-Rohrleitungstransport (ISSN 0035-7855)

PETROLEUM AND GAS — Abstracting, Bibliographies, Statistics

665.5   US
A G A GAS INDUSTRY TRAINING DIRECTORY. a. $70 to non-members; members $35. American Gas Association, 1515 Wilson Blvd., Arlington, VA 22209. TEL 703-841-8400. FAX 703-841-8406. (Subscr. to: Dept. 0765, McLean, VA 22109-0765)

665.5   US
A G A GAS STATS; monthly gas utility statistical report. m. $16 to non-members (foreign $24); members $8 (foreign $16). American Gas Association, Department of Statistics, 1515 Wilson Blvd., Arlington, VA 22209. TEL 703-841-8400. FAX 703-841-8406. (Subscr.to: Dept. 0765, McLean, VA 22109-0765)

665.5   US
A G A GAS STATS QUARTERLY. q. $16 to non-members (foreign $24); members $8 (foreign $16). American Gas Association, Department of Statistics, 1515 Wilson Blvd., Arlington, VA 22209. TEL 703-841-8400. FAX 703-841-8406. (Subscr. to: Dept. 0765, McLean, VA 22109-0765)

622 338.2   CN
ALBERTA DRILLING PROGRESS WEEKLY REPORT. 1950. w. Can.$325. Energy Resources Conservation Board, 640 5th Ave., S.W., Calgary, Alta. T2P 3G4, Canada. TEL 403-297-8311. FAX 403-297-7040. TELEX 03-821717.
   Former titles: Alberta Drilling Progress and Pipeline Receipts. Weekly Report (ISSN 0227-3357); Weekly Production and Drilling Statistics (ISSN 0032-9827)
   Description: Summary of oil pipeline gathering operations and drilling activity in the province of Alberta.

665.5 016   US   ISSN 0002-6441
ALPHABETIC SUBJECT INDEX TO PETROLEUM ABSTRACTS. 1961. a. service basis. University of Tulsa, Petroleum Abstracts, 600 South College, Tulsa, OK 74104. TEL 800-247-8678. FAX 918-599-9361. TELEX 497543. bibl.; cum.index; circ. 500. (also avail. in microform)

025.3 665.5   US
Z695.1.P43
AMERICAN PETROLEUM INSTITUTE. CENTRAL ABSTRACTING & INFORMATION SERVICES. THESAURUS. 1964. a. $100 ($75 to non-profit organizations). American Petroleum Institute, Central Abstracting & Information Services, 275 Seventh Ave., New York, NY 10001. TEL 212-366-4040. FAX 212-366-4298. TELEX 4938591 API UI. Key Title: Thesaurus - American Petroleum Institute.
   Formerly: American Petroleum Institute. Central Abstracting and Indexing Service. Thesaurus (ISSN 0193-5151); Supersedes: American Petroleum Institute. Information Retrieval System, Subject Authority List.
   Description: Guide to the indexing system and controlled vocabulary used to prepare the petroleum refining and petrochemicals industries technology databases.

665.5 338.2   US
AMERICAN PETROLEUM INSTITUTE. DIVISION OF STATISTICS. WEEKLY STATISTICAL BULLETIN. Variant title: American Petroleum Institute. Weekly Statistical Bulletin and Monthly Statistical Report. (Includes Monthly Statistical Report) w. $110 to non-members; members $55; Canada and Mexico $121; elsewhere $143. American Petroleum Institute, Publications Department, 1220 L St., N.W., Washington, DC 20005. TEL 202-682-8378. (Subscr. to: 1970 Chain Bridge Rd., McLean, VA 22109-6000) charts; stat.; circ. 2,500. **Indexed:** SRI.
   ●Also available online.
   Formerly: American Petroleum Institute. Division of Statistics and Economics. Weekly Statistical Bulletin (ISSN 0003-0457)

AMERICAN PETROLEUM INSTITUTE. HEALTH AND ENVIRONMENTAL SCIENCES DEPARTMENT. REPORTS AND OTHER PUBLICATIONS, INDEX AND ABSTRACTS. see *PUBLIC HEALTH AND SAFETY — Abstracting, Bibliographies, Statistics*

665.5   US
AMERICAN PETROLEUM INSTITUTE. MONTHLY COMPLETION REPORT. 1970. m. $105 to non-members; members $55; Canada and Mexico $115.50; elsewhere $136.50. American Petroleum Institute, Publications Department, 1220 L St., N.W., Washington, DC 20005. TEL 202-682-8518. (Subscr. to: 1970 Chain Bridge Rd., McLean, VA 22109-6000) Ed. Valoria Boone. circ. 500.
   Former titles: Monthly Drilling Completion Report; Monthly Report on Drilling Activity in the U.S.
   Description: Provides data on the cumulative number of completions and related footage drilled, by month, for two prior years.

310   US
AMERICAN PETROLEUM INSTITUTE. MONTHLY STATISTICAL REPORT. 1977. m. $55 to non-members; members $30; Canada and Mexico $60.50; elsewhere $71.50. American Petroleum Institute, Publications Department, 1220 L St., N.W., Washington, DC 20005. TEL 202-682-8378. (Subscr. to: 1970 Chain Bridge Rd., McLean, VA 22109-6000) charts; stat. (looseleaf format) **Indexed:** SRI.
   Description: Analyzes trends and developments in U.S. petroleum supply and demand.

622.338 338.2   US
AMERICAN PETROLEUM INSTITUTE. QUARTERLY COMPLETION REPORT. q. $210 to non-members; members $110; Canada and Mexico $231; elsewhere $273. American Petroleum Institute, Publications Department, 1220 L St., N.W., Washington, DC 20005. TEL 202-682-8378. (Subscr. to: 1970 Chain Bridge Rd., McLean, VA 22109-6000) stat. **Indexed:** GeoRef.
   Former titles: Quarterly Drilling Completions; Quarterly Review of Drilling Statistics (ISSN 0033-5789)

665.7   UN   ISSN 0066-3824
HD9581.E8
ANNUAL BULLETIN OF GAS STATISTICS FOR EUROPE/BULLETIN ANNUEL DE STATISTIQUES DE GAZ POUR L'EUROPE. (Text in English, French and Russian) 1955. a. price varies. Economic Commission for Europe (ECE), Palais des Nations, 1211 Geneva 10, Switzerland. TEL 734-6011. FAX 733-9879. TELEX 412962. (Or United Nations Publications, Rm. DC2-853, New York, NY 10017) (also avail. in microfiche) **Indexed:** IIS.

665.5 338.2   US   ISSN 0004-1874
ARKANSAS OIL AND GAS STATISTICAL BULLETIN. 1942. m. free. Oil and Gas Commission, Box 1472, El Dorado, AR 71731-1472. TEL 501-862-4965. circ. 350 (controlled). (looseleaf format) **Indexed:** SRI.

662.338   CN
B C WELL TAPE. m. Can.$1500. Ministry of Energy, Mines and Petroleum Resources, Energy Resources Division, Parliament Bldgs., Victoria, B.C. V8V 1X4, Canada. TEL 604-387-5178. (Subscr. to: Crown Publications, 546 Yates St., Victoria, B.C. V8W 1K8, Canada. TEL 604-386-4636) (magnetic tape)
   Description: Lists every oil and gas well in BC and all drilling and analysis on these wells, such as cores, distance, and formation taps.

PETROLEUM AND GAS — ABSTRACTING, BIBLIOGRAPHIES, STATISTICS

338.2   UK
B P STATISTICAL REVIEW OF WORLD ENERGY. a. £8. British Petroleum Company plc., Britannic House, 1 Finsbury Circus, London EC2M 7BA, England. FAX 071-496-4528. (Dist. in U.S. by: B P America Inc., 200 Public Sq., Cleveland, Ohio 44114-2375) circ. 35,000.
Formerly: Statistical Review of the World Oil Industry (ISSN 0081-5039)
Description: Compendium of energy statistics covering the previous 10 years.

665.5   US
BASIC PETROLEUM DATA BOOK. 1974. 3/yr. $110 (non-members $140; foreign $182). American Petroleum Institute, Statistical Publications Section, 1220 L St., N.W., Washington, DC 20005. TEL 202-682-8000. (Subscr. to: 1970 Chain Bridge Rd., McLean, VA 22109-6000) Ed. Julie Scott.
Indexed: PROMT, SRI.
Supersedes: Petroleum Facts and Figures; Incorporates: American Petroleum Institute. Division of Statistics and Economics. Annual Statistical Review (ISSN 0569-6852)

665.5   TS
AL-BUTRUL WAL-SINA'A FI ABU DHABI/PETROLEUM AND INDUSTRY IN ABU DHABI. (Text in Arabic) 1970. a. exchange basis. Ministry of Petroleum and Mineral Wealth, P.O. Box 59, Abu Dhabi, United Arab Emirates. TEL 651810. FAX 663414. TELEX 22544 MPMR EM. circ. 1,000.
Description: Statistical review of petroleum and industrial activity in Abu Dhabi.

665   US   ISSN 0749-730X
                                 CODEN: CADMEB
C A SELECTS. DRILLING MUDS. fortn. $195. Chemical Abstracts Service (Subsidiary of: American Chemical Society), 2540 Olentangy River Rd., Box 3012, Columbus, OH 43210. TEL 614-447-3600. FAX 614-447-3713. TELEX 6842086.
Description: Covers formulation, properties, and performance of aqueous suspensions used in drilling of oil and gas wells.

665.5   US   ISSN 0734-8746
                                  CODEN: CAEREV
C A SELECTS. ENHANCED PETROLEUM RECOVERY. s-w. $195. Chemical Abstracts Service (Subsidiary of: American Chemical Society), 2540 Olentangy River Rd., Box 3012, Columbus, OH 43210. TEL 614-447-3600. FAX 614-447-3713. TELEX 6842086.
Description: Covers means for stimulating production of oil wells; secondary and tertiary recovery techniques; in-situ retorting of oil shales and tar sands.

C A SELECTS. FUEL & LUBRICANT ADDITIVES. see CHEMISTRY — *Abstracting, Bibliographies, Statistics*

665.7   CN   ISSN 0068-7103
HD9574.C2
CANADA. STATISTICS CANADA. CRUDE PETROLEUM AND NATURAL GAS INDUSTRY. (Catalogue 26-213) (Text in English and French) 1926. a. Can.$26($31) (foreign $36). Statistics Canada, Publications Sales and Services, Ottawa, Ont. K1A 0T6, Canada. TEL 613-951-7277. FAX 613-951-1584. (also avail. in microform from MML)
Description: Presents data on the number of establishments, employment, payroll, production, disposition, exports and imports.

665.5   CN   ISSN 0702-6846
HD9574.C2
CANADA. STATISTICS CANADA. CRUDE PETROLEUM AND NATURAL GAS PRODUCTION. m. Can.$100($120) (foreign $140). Statistics Canada, Publications Division, Ottawa, Ont. K1A 0T6, Canada. TEL 613-951-7277. FAX 613-951-1584.
Description: Estimates the production and disposition of crude petroleum and natural gas, by province, monthly and cumulative.

665.5   CN   ISSN 0527-5318
HD9581.C3
CANADA. STATISTICS CANADA. GAS UTILITIES, TRANSPORT AND DISTRIBUTION SYSTEMS. (Catalogue 57-205) (Text in English and French) 1959. a. Can.$27($32) (foreign $38). Statistics Canada, Publications Sales and Services, Ottawa, Ont. K1A 0T6, Canada. TEL 613-951-7277. FAX 613-951-1584. stat. (also avail. in microform from MML)
Description: Covers receipts and disposition of natural gas by month and province, pipeline distance, balance sheet, property account, income account, employees and earnings.

665.54   CN   ISSN 0380-4615
CANADA. STATISTICS CANADA. OIL PIPE LINE TRANSPORT. 1951. m. Can.$100($120) (foreign $140). Statistics Canada, Publications Division, Ottawa, Ont. K1A 0T6, Canada. TEL 613-951-7277. FAX 613-951-1584.
Description: Receipts and deliveries by source and by movement of crude oil and refined petroleum products by gathering and trunk lines, by provinces; barrel-miles, operating revenues. Includes data analysis.

662.338   CN
DAILY LIST OF WELL AUTHORIZATIONS. 3/wk. Can.$72. Ministry of Energy, Mines and Petroleum Resources, Energy Resources Division, Parliament Bldgs., Victoria, B.C. V8V 1X4, Canada. (Subscr. to: Crown Publications, 546 Yates St., Victoria, B.C. V8W 1K8, Canada. TEL 604-386-4636) (back issues avail.)
Description: Presents relevant data on wells authorized by the Petroleum Resources Division.

EMENTARIO DA LEGISLACAO DO PETROLEO. see LAW — *Abstracting, Bibliographies, Statistics*

ENERGY REVIEW (SANTA BARBARA). see ENERGY — *Abstracting, Bibliographies, Statistics*

665.5   US   ISSN 0739-3075
HD9502.A1
ENERGY STATISTICS. 1978. q. $100 (foreign $147). Institute of Gas Technology, 3424 S. State St., Chicago, IL 60616. TEL 312-567-3650. Ed. Harold L. Mensch. circ. 1,000. **Indexed:** INIS Atomind.
●Also available online.

310   SP
ESTADISTICA DE PROSPECCION Y PRODUCCION DE HIDROCARBUROS. a. 1000 ptas. Ministerio de Industria, Paseo de la Castellana, 160, Madrid 28046, Spain. FAX 259-84-80.

665.538 662 016   UK   ISSN 0140-6701
TP315   CODEN: FEABDN
FUEL AND ENERGY ABSTRACTS; a summary of world literature on all scientific, technical, commercial and environmental aspects of fuel and energy. 1960. 12/yr. £525 (Europe £570). (Institute of Energy) Butterworth - Heinemann Ltd. (Subsidiary of: Reed International PLC), Linacre House, Jordan Hill, Oxford OX2 8DP, England. TEL 0865-310366. FAX 0865-310898. TELEX 83111 BHPOXF G. (Subscr. to: Turpin Transactions, Distribution Centre, Blackhorse Rd., Latchworth, Herts SG6 1HN, England. TEL 0462-672555) Ed.Bd. (also avail. in microform from UMI; back issues avail.) **Indexed:** Anal.Abstr., Br.Ceram.Abstr., Chem.Abstr., Fluidex.
Formerly: Fuel Abstracts and Current Titles (ISSN 0016-2388)
Description: Each issue contains 1500 abstracts and titles from the international literature dealing with fuel and energy.
Refereed Serial

665.7 016   US   ISSN 0016-4844
TP700   CODEN: GAABA3
GAS ABSTRACTS. 1945. m. $130 (foreign $160). Institute of Gas Technology, 3424 S. State St., Chicago, IL 60616. TEL 312-567-3650. Ed. J.L. Schaeffer. bk.rev.; index; circ. 700. (also avail. in microform from UMI; reprint service avail. from UMI) **Indexed:** Chem.Abstr., Corros.Abstr., Eng.Ind.
●Also available online.
—BLDSC shelfmark: 4075.000000.

531.64 622   AT   ISSN 0157-731X
GAS INDUSTRY STATISTICS (YEAR). 1979. a. Aus.$10. Australian Gas Association, G.P.O. Box 323, Canberra, A.C.T. 2601, Australia. TEL 06-247-3955. FAX 06-249-7402. TELEX AA62137. Ed. O. DiIulio. charts.
Description: Australian gas industry statistics and world energy resources.

665.5   US
GUIDE TO PETROLEUM STATISTICAL INFORMATION. a. $120 to non-members; members $60. American Petroleum Institute, Central Abstracting & Information Services, 275 Seventh Ave., New York, NY 10001. TEL 212-366-4040. FAX 212-366-4298. TELEX 4938591 API UI.
Description: Lists the recurring statistical features in four sections that regularly appear in 120 energy-related publications and 350 databases.

338.2   US   ISSN 0073-2656
HISTORICAL STATISTICS OF THE GAS INDUSTRY. 1956. irreg. $25 (non-members $50). American Gas Association, Department of Statistics, 1515 Wilson Blvd., Arlington, VA 22209. TEL 703-841-8490. FAX 703-841-8406. (Subscr. to: Dept. 0765, McLean, VA 22109-0765) circ. 1,000.

665.5   II
INDIAN PETROLEUM AND NATURAL GAS STATISTICS. (Text in English) 1976. a. free. Ministry of Petroleum & Chemicals, Department of Petroleum & Natural Gas, Economics and Statistics Division, Shastri Bhawan, New Delhi 110 001, India. FAX 66235. stat.; circ. controlled.
Former titles: Indian Petroleum and Petrochemicals Statistics; Indian Petroleum and Chemicals Statistics.

338.27   IO
INDONESIA OIL STATISTICS/STATISTIK PERMINYAKAN INDONESIA. (Text in English) 1971. q. (with a. cum.). Directorate General Oil and Gas, Programming & Reporting Division - Direktorat Jenderal Minyak Dan Gas Bumi, Jln. M.H. Thamrin No. 1, Jakarta 10110, Indonesia. TEL 62-21-30541. FAX 62-21-354987. TELEX 44363. circ. 400.

INDUSTRIA PETROLERA EN MEXICO. see PETROLEUM AND GAS

338.4   US   ISSN 0163-3724
HD9560.4
INTERNATIONAL ENERGY STATISTICAL REVIEW. 1978. m. U.S. Central Intelligence Agency, Washington, DC 20505. (Avail. from: Document Expediting (DOCEX) Project, Library of Congress, Washington, DC 20540; or from NTIS, 5285 Port Royal Rd., Springfield, VA 22161) (also avail. in microfiche) **Indexed:** Amer.Stat.Ind., Energy Info.Abstr.
Former titles: International Energy Biweekly Statistical Review (ISSN 0160-1512); (Until Oct. 1977): International Oil Developments: Statistical Survey.

665.5 016   UK   ISSN 0309-4944
TN860   CODEN: IPMABI
INTERNATIONAL PETROLEUM ABSTRACTS. 1973. q. $645 (effective 1992). (Institute of Petroleum) John Wiley & Sons Ltd., Baffins Lane, Chichester, Sussex PO19 1UD, England. TEL 0243-779777. FAX 0243-775878. TELEX 86290 WIBOOK G. Ed. Gretchen E. Taylor. **Indexed:** AESIS, Fuel & Energy Abstr.
●Also available online. Vendor(s): Pergamon Infoline (IPA).
Incorporates: Offshore Abstracts.
Description: provides an extensive review of the onshore/offshore oil and gas industry.

665.5   IT
ITALY. MINISTERO DELL'INDUSTRIA DEL COMMERCIO E DELL'ARTIGIANATO; Direzione generale delle fonti di energia e delle industrie di base, bollettino Petrolifero. vol. 30, 1987. q? Ministero dell'Industria del Commercio dell'Artigianato, Direzione Generale delle Fonti di Energia e delle Industrie di Base, Rome, Italy. stat.
Description: Provides statistical data resulting from surveys of the petroleum firms in various regions of Italy.

PETROLEUM AND GAS — ABSTRACTING, BIBLIOGRAPHIES, STATISTICS

665.5 — US
JOINT ASSOCIATION SURVEY ON DRILLING COSTS. 1959. a. $105 to non-members; members $55; Canada and Mexico $115.50; elsewhere $136.50). American Petroleum Institute, Publications Department, 1220 L St., N.W., Washington, DC 20005. TEL 202-682-8378. (Subscr. to: 1970 Chain Bridge Rd., McLean, VA 22109-6000) circ. 1,600.
Description: Provides annual information pertaining to the cost of drilling oil and gas wells and dry holes by state and by depth interval.

665.5 — LY — ISSN 0075-9260
LIBYA. CENSUS AND STATISTICS DEPARTMENT. REPORT OF THE ANNUAL SURVEY OF PETROLEUM MINING INDUSTRY. (Text in Arabic and English) 1965. a. free. Secretariat of Planning, Census and Statistics Department, P.O. Box 600, Tripoli, Libya.

665.5 338.2 — LY
LIBYA. CENSUS AND STATISTICS DEPARTMENT. REPORT OF THE ANNUAL SURVEY OF UNITS PROVIDING TECHNICAL SERVICES TO THE PETROLEUM MINING INDUSTRY. (Text in Arabic and English) 1965. a. free. Secretariat of Planning, Census and Statistics Department, P.O. Box 600, Tripoli, Libya.

665.5 016
LITERATURE ABSTRACTS. 1954. w. price varies. American Petroleum Institute, Central Abstracting & Information Services, 275 Seventh Ave., New York, NY 10001-6708. TEL 212-366-4040. FAX 212-366-4298. TELEX 4938591 API UI. Ed. M. Pronin.
●Also available online. Vendor(s): DIALOG, STN International.
Former titles: A P I Abstracts - Literature; (until 1978): Abstracts of Refining Literature (ISSN 0003-0422) Until 1961: A.P.I. Technical Abstracts (ISSN 0096-5073); Incorporating: Abstracts of Health and Environment Literature; Abstracts of Petroleum Refining and Petrochemical Literature; Abstracts of Petroleum Substitutes Literature; Which was formerly titled: Abstracts of Petroleum Substitutes Literature and Patents (ISSN 0003-0414); and Abstracts of Transportation and Storage Literature; Which was formerly: Abstracts of Transportation and Storage Literature and Patents (ISSN 0003-0449).
Description: Abstracts of journal papers; trade magazine articles, meeting papers; dissertations, technical reports; news articles; and other documents on science and technology related to the work of the petroleum refining and petrochemical industry.

665.5 — US
LITERATURE AND PATENT ABSTRACTS: OILFIELD CHEMICALS. 1981. m. $900. American Petroleum Institute, Central Abstracting & Information Services, 275 Seventh Ave., New York, NY 10001-6708. TEL 212-366-4040. FAX 212-366-4298. TELEX 4938591 API UI.
●Also available online. Vendor(s): Orbit Information Technologies, STN International.
Formerly: A P I Abstracts - Oilfield Chemicals.
Description: Covers the manufacturing and use of chemicals in the oil and gas fields for drilling, well completion and stimulation, oil production, and enhanced recovery. Covers trade magazine articles and scientific journal papers published worldwide, as well as conference papers and patents.

531.64 665.5 — CN
MANITOBA. DEPARTMENT OF ENERGY AND MINES. PRODUCTION STATISTICS REPORT.. 1955. m. Can.$90. Department of Energy and Mines, 330 Graham Ave., Ste. 555, Winnipeg, Man. R3C 4E3, Canada. TEL 204-945-6578. FAX 204-945-0586. circ. 150. (back issues avail.)
Formerly: Manitoba. Department of Energy and Mines. Production Statistics and Activity Report.

665.5 — CN
MANITOBA PETROLEUM ROYALTY AND TAX INFORMATION. 1982. irreg. free. Manitoba Energy and Mines, Petroleum Branch, 555-330 Graham Ave., Winnipeg, Man. R3C 4E3, Canada. TEL 204-945-6577. FAX 204-945-0586. Ed. L.R. Dubreuil. circ. 400.
Description: Irregularly issued booklet with a general overview of petroleum royalty-tax structure and incentive programs operating in Manitoba, Canada.

016 665 — FR — ISSN 0752-5508
MEDIAGAZ. 1927. 11/yr. 750 F. Association Technique de l'Industrie du Gaz en France, 62 rue de Courcelles, 75008 Paris, France. Ed. Alain Thibault. bk.rev.; abstr.; pat.; stat.; circ. 300.
Indexed by: Fuel & Energy Abstr.
Formerly (until 1982): Association Technique de l'Industrie du Gaz en France. Bulletin Bibliographique Mensuel.

665.7 — US — ISSN 0085-3429 — CODEN: MGSDA3
MICHIGAN'S OIL AND GAS FIELDS: ANNUAL STATISTICAL SUMMARY. 1964. a. price varies. Department of Natural Resources, Geological Survey Division, Information Services Center, Box 30028, Lansing, MI 48909. TEL 517-334-6907.

665.5 — RU
NEFTYANIK (MOSCOW, 1974). (Abstracts from Petroleum Engineer and Pipeline & Gas Journal) 1974. m. 21 Rub. Izdatel'stvo Nedra, Pl. Belorusskogo Vokzala, 3, 125047 Moscow, Russia. TEL 250-52-55. adv.; circ. 3,000.
Formerly: Inzhener - Naftyanik.

338.4 — NO — ISSN 0377-1806
TN867
NORWEGIAN OFFSHORE INDEX. (Text in English) 1974. a. free. (Export Council of Norway) Selvig Publishing A-S, Box 9070 Vaterland, 0134 Oslo 1, Norway. TEL 02-364440. FAX 02-360550. (Co-sponsor: Federation of Norwegian Industries) circ. controlled.

338.47 011 — KU
O A P E C ENERGY BIBLIOGRAPHY. (Text in Arabic, English) 1977. a. free. Organization of Arab Petroleum Exporting Countries, P.O. Box 20501, Safat 13066, Kuwait. TEL 965-2448200. FAX 965-2426885. TELEX 22166 NAFARAB KT. circ. 350.
Description: Subject classification of books recieved by OAPEC's library on energy and petroleum plus a list of publisher's addresses and an author index.

338.47 011 — KU
O A P E C LIBRARY INDEX OF PERIODICAL ARTICLES. (Text in Arabic, English) 1982. q. free. Organization of Arab Petroleum Exporting Countries, P.O. Box 20501, Safat 13066, Kuwait. TEL 965-2448200. FAX 965-2426885. TELEX 22166 NAFARAB KT. circ. 350.
Formerly: O A P E C Library Index.
Description: Subject index of periodical articles received by OAPEC's library on energy, petroleum and economic development.

338.2 665.5 — FR — ISSN 0474-6007
HD9575.A12
O E C D. OIL STATISTICS. SUPPLY AND DISPOSAL. (Text in English, French) 1961. irreg. Organization for Economic Cooperation and Development, 2 rue Andre-Pascal, 75775 Paris Cedex 16, France. TEL 45-24-82-00. FAX 45-24-85-00. (U.S. orders to: O.E.C.D. Publications and Information Center, 2001 L St., N.W., Ste. 700, Washington, D.C. 20036-4910. TEL 202-785-6323) (also avail. in microfiche)

665.5 — FR — ISSN 1013-9362
O E C D. QUARTERLY OIL STATISTICS AND ENERGY BALANCES. (Text in English, French) vol.2, 1978. q. 750 F.($158) Organization for Economic Cooperation and Development, 2 rue Andre-Pascal, 75775 Paris Cedex 16, France. TEL 45-24-82-00. FAX 45-24-85-00. (U.S. Orders to: O.E.C.D. Publications and Information Center, 2001 L St., N.W., Ste. 700, Washington, D.C. 20036-4910. TEL 202-785-6323) (also avail. in microfiche from OEC)
●Also available online.
Former titles: Organization for Economic Cooperation and Development. Quarterly Oil and Gas Statistics; Organization for Economic Cooperation and Development. Quarterly Oil Statistics (ISSN 0378-6536).
Description: Provides detailed data on production of crude oil, natural gas, liquids as well as refinery feedstocks, crude oil and product trades; refinery intake and output; final consumption; stock levels and changes.

665.5 338.2 — FR
O E C D OIL AND GAS INFORMATION. (Text in English, French) 1970. a. price varies. Organization for Economic Cooperation and Development, 2 rue Andre-Pascal, 75775 Paris Cedex 16, France. TEL 45-24-82-00. FAX 45-24-85-00. (U.S. orders to: O.E.C.D. Publications and Information Center, 2001 L St., N.W., Ste. 700, Washington, DC 20036-4910. TEL 202-785-6323) charts; stat. (also avail. in microfiche from OEC; back issues avail.)
Former titles: O E C D. Annual Oil and gas Statistics - O C D E. Statistiques Annuelles des Hydrocarbures et du Gaz Naturel; Organization for Economic Cooperation and Development. Oil Statistics - Statistiques Petrolieres; Organization for Economic Cooperation and Development. Provisional Oil Statistics - Statistiques Petrolieres Provisoires (ISSN 0029-7062)

338.47 — US
HD9561
OIL & NATURAL GAS PRODUCING INDUSTRY IN YOUR STATE. (Statistical issue of: Petroleum Independent (ISSN 0747-2528)) 1939. a. $75. (Independent Petroleum Association of America) Petroleum Independent Publishers, Inc., 1101 16th St., N.W., Washington, DC 20036. TEL 800-433-2851. FAX 202-857-4799. Ed. Deborah Rowell. adv.; charts; illus.; stat.; circ. 12,000.
Former titles: Oil and Gas Producing Industry in Your State; (until 1984): Oil Producing Industry in Your State.

665.538 — US
OIL - ENERGY STATISTICS BULLETIN; and Canadian oil reports. 1923. bi-w. $185. Oil Statistics Company, Box 189, Whitman, MA 02382. Ed. John J. McGilvray. circ. 1,500.

OIL IMPORTS INTO THE UNITED STATES AND PUERTO RICO (E I A 814). (Energy Information Administration) see *BUSINESS AND ECONOMICS — Abstracting, Bibliographies, Statistics*

338.2 665.5 — AU — ISSN 0475-0608
HD9560.4
ORGANIZATION OF THE PETROLEUM EXPORTING COUNTRIES. ANNUAL STATISTICAL BULLETIN. 1965. a. S.350. Organization of the Petroleum Exporting Countries, Obere Donaustr. 93, A-1020 Vienna, Austria. TEL 222-21112-0.
—BLDSC shelfmark: 1531.944000.
Description: Contains oil and gas data, summary tables and basic indicators of imports, exports, oil reserves, and refined products. Also covers oil transportation, oil prices and the major oil companies. Includes maps.

665.5 016 — US
PATENTS ABSTRACTS. 1960. w. price varies. American Petroleum Institute, Central Abstracting & Information Services, 275 Seventh Ave., New York, NY 10001-6708. TEL 212-366-4040. FAX 212-366-4298. TELEX 4938591 API UI.
●Also available online. Vendor(s): Orbit Information Technologies, STN International.
Formerly: A P I Abstracts - Patents; Supersedes (in 1977): A P I Patent Alert; Formerly (until 1971): American Petroleum Institute. Abstracts of Refining Patents (ISSN 0003-0430)
Description: Reports worldwide patents related to the work of the petroleum refining and petrochemical industry with coverage in the chemicals and polymers areas.

665.5 — MX — ISSN 0186-3401
PEMEX. BOLETIN BIBLIOGRAFICO. (Text in English) vol.31, 1986. m. free. Petroleos Mexicanos, Unidad de Servicios Sociales y Culturales, Biblioteca Central, Marina Nacional 329, Edif. A, Mezzanine, 11300 Mexico, D.F., Mexico. circ. 3,000.
Formerly: Petroleos Mexicanos. Boletin Bibliografico.
Description: Abstracts from scientific and technical journals.

665.5 016   US   ISSN 0031-6423
TN860
PETROLEUM ABSTRACTS. 1961. w. service basis. University of Tulsa, Information Services Division, 600 South College, Tulsa, OK 74104. TEL 800-247-8678. FAX 918-599-9361. TELEX 497543. illus.; stat.; index, cum.index; circ. 1,800. (also avail. in microform)
●Also available online. Vendor(s): Orbit Information Technologies (TULSA).
Description: Abstracts from worldwide petroleum-related literature dealing with exploration and production.

665.5   CN
PETROLEUM AND NATURAL GAS PRODUCTION TAPE. m. Can.$1500. Ministry of Energy, Mines and Petroleum Resources, Energy Resources Division, Parliament Bldgs., Victoria, B.C. V8V 1X4, Canada. (Subscr. to: Crown Publications, 546 Yates St., Victoria, B.C. V8W 1K8, Canada. TEL 604-386-4636) (magnetic tape)
Description: Lists all oil and gas wells ever drilled in BC, historical production records for all wells from 1954, amounts produced and number of days productive.

665.5 016   US
PETROLEUM-ENERGY BUSINESS NEWS INDEX. 1975. m. $750. American Petroleum Institute, Central Abstracting & Information Services, 275 Seventh Ave., New York, NY 10001. TEL 212-366-4040. FAX 212-366-4298. TELEX 4938591 API UI.
●Also available online. Vendor(s): Data-Star (PEAB), DIALOG, Orbit Information Technologies.
Description: Provides access to political, economic, and social news and economic studies that may affect the petroleum, petrochemical, and energy industries.

666.5 338.2   US
PETROLEUM MARKET INTELLIGENCE. (Supplementary data diskettes avail.) 1987. m. $575. Petroleum Energy & Intelligence Weekly, Inc., 575 Broadway, New York, NY 10012-3230. TEL 212-941-5500. FAX 212-941-5508. TELEX 62371 PETROIN. Ed. Thomas Wallin. charts; illus.; stat.
Description: Provides analyses of regional pricing, production figures, and key statistics on the oil market.

665.5   CN
PETROLEUM TITLES DATA TAPE. m. Can.$4200. Ministry of Energy, Mines and Petroleum Resources, Energy Resources Division, Parliament Bldgs., Victoria, B.C. V8V 1X4, Canada. (Subscr. to: Crown Publications, 546 Yates St., Victoria, B.C. V8W 1K8, Canada. TEL 604-386-4636) (magnetic tape)
Description: Contains information on each active provincial petroleum and natural gas tenure inclusive of term, tenure holder, location, rights conveyed, continuation and renewals.

665.5 627   UK   ISSN 0265-3990
TJ930
PIPELINES ABSTRACTS. 1983. bi-m. $260 (foreign £145). S T I Ltd., 4 Kings Meadow, Ferry Hinksey Rd., Oxford OX2 0DU, England. TEL 0865-798898. FAX 0865-798788. (Dist. in U.S. by: Air Science Co., P.O. Box 143, Corning, NY 14830. TEL 607-962-5591) Ed. Lindsay Gale. bk.rev.; abstr.; index, cum.index.
●Also available online. Vendor(s): DIALOG (File no.96/FLUIDEX), European Space Agency (File no.48/FLUIDEX).
Description: Covers all aspects of planning, construction and operation of pipelines for the transport of liquids, gases and multiphase flow - also pipe protection and leakage testing.

665.7 338.39   US
PROPANE INDUSTRY PROFILE; statistical handbook of the LP-gas industry. 1950. a. National Propane Gas Association, 1600 Eisenhower Ln., Ste. 100, Lisle, IL 60532. Ed. M.A. Spear. index. **Indexed:** SRI.
Formerly (until 1992): L P - Gas Market Facts (ISSN 0075-9759)
Description: Presents market research information about the industry on a historical basis.

665.7   NE   ISSN 0081-5225
TP733.N4
STATISTIEK VAN DE GASVOORZIENING IN NEDERLAND. 1953. a. Centraal Bureau voor de Statistiek, Prinses Beatrixlaan 428, Voorburg, Netherlands. (Orders to: SDU - Publishers, Christoffel Plantijnstraat, The Hague) circ. 375.

338.4   FR
STATISTIQUES DE L'INDUSTRIE GAZIERE EN FRANCE. a. Direction du Gaz, de l'Electricite du Charbon, 97-99, rue de Grenelle, 75700 Paris Cedex, France. TELEX DIGEC 250 757 F. charts; stat.
Continues: France. Direction du Gaz et de l'Electricite. Statistiques Officielles de l'Industrie Gaziere en France (ISSN 0429-3843)
Description: Covers statistics in the French gas industry.

SUMMARY OF RATE SCHEDULES OF NATURAL GAS PIPELINE COMPANIES. see ENERGY — Abstracting, Bibliographies, Statistics

665.8 338.2   US
TRANSPORTATION ACCIDENT BRIEFS. PIPELINE. (Subseries of: Transportation Accident Briefs) irreg. (approx. 6/yr.). $16.50 per issue in US, Canada, Mexico; elsewhere $33. (Department of Transportation, National Transportation Safety Board) U.S. National Technical Information Service, 5825 Port Royal Rd., Springfield, VA 22161. TEL 703-487-4630.

665.8 338.2   US
TRANSPORTATION ACCIDENT REPORTS. PIPELINE. (Subseries of: Transportation Accident Reports) irreg. (approx. 6/yr.). $70 in US, Canada, Mexico; elsewhere $140. (Department of Transportation, National Transportation Safety Board) U.S. National Technical Information Service, 5825 Port Royal Rd., Springfield, VA 22161. TEL 703-487-4630.

665.538 310   US   ISSN 0196-0806
U.S. FEDERAL HIGHWAY ADMINISTRATION. MONTHLY MOTOR GASOLINE REPORTED BY STATES. m. U.S. Federal Highway Administration, 400 Seventh St., S.W., Washington, DC 20590. TEL 202-426-0600. **Indexed:** Amer.Stat.Ind. Key Title: Monthly Motor Gasoline Reported by States.

338.2   VE
VENEZUELA. MINISTERIO DE ENERGIA Y MINAS. PETROLEO Y OTROS DATOS ESTADISTICOS. English edition: Venezuelan Petroleum Industry. Statistical Data. a. free. Ministerio de Energia y Minas, Oficina de Estudios Economicos Energeticos, Torre Norte, Caracas, Venezuela. (Subscr. to: Ministerio de Energia y Minas, Biblioteca Torre Oeste Piso 9, Parque Central, Caracas-Venezuela)
Formerly: Venezuela. Ministerio de Minas e Hidrocarburos. Oficina de Economia Petrolera. Petroleo y Otros Datos Estadisticos (ISSN 0083-5390)

PETS

see also Animal Welfare

636.8   US   ISSN 0744-9631
A C F A BULLETIN. 1955. bi-m. $15 to non-members. American Cat Fanciers Association, Inc., Box 203, Point Lookout, MO 65726. TEL 417-334-5430. FAX 417-334-5540. Ed. Wini Kewler. adv.; circ. 2,000. (processed)

636.8   AT
A C I YEAR BOOK. 1978. a. Aus.$3.50 per no. Australian Cat Federation, Inc., c/o Ms. J. Ruasack, 32 Tarrant St., Prospect, S.A. 5082, Australia. adv.; circ. 1,000. (back issues avail)

636
A M C CENTERSCOPE. 3/yr. donation. Animal Medical Center, 510 E. 62nd St., New York, NY 10021. TEL 212-838-8100. FAX 212-832-9630. Ed. Joan M. Foster. circ. 10,000.

636.7
A M S C O P E NEWSLETTER. m. American Miniature Schnauzer Club, 302 Southwood, Lancaster, TX 75146. Ed. Carma Ewer. circ. 500.

599   AT
ABYSSINIAN. 1967. s-a. Aus.$8. Abyssinian Cat Club of Australasia, G.P.O. Box 2323, Sydney, N.S.W. 2001, Australia. Ed. Ms. E. Outram. adv.; bk.rev.; circ. 350.

636.7   US
ADVOCATE (OLD BROOKVILLE). 1967. q. $10. Owner Handler Association of America, c/o Mildred Mesh, Six Michaels Ln., Old Brookville, NY 11545. circ. 2,000.

636.7   US
AFGHAN HOUND CLUB OF AMERICA. BULLETIN. 3/yr. Afghan Hound Club of America, c/o Norma Cozzoni, Ed., 2408 A Rt. 31, Oswego, IL 60543. TEL 312-554-8339.

636.7   US   ISSN 8750-9776
AFGHAN HOUND REVIEW. 1974. bi-m. $36. Showdogs Publications, Box 30430, Santa Barbara, CA 93130-0430. TEL 805-966-7270. Ed. Bo Bengtson. adv.; bk.rev.; circ. 2,000.
Description: Information and photographs of Afghan Hound showdogs.

636.7   US
AIREDALE TERRIER CLUB OF AMERICA. NEWSLETTER. 1900. 5/yr. membership. Airedale Terrier Club of America, c/o Aletta Moore, Epoch Farm, 14181 County Rd.-40, Carver, MN 55315. Ed. Richard Schlicht. circ. 700.

636.7   US
AKITA DOG. 1973. m. $15. Akita Club of America, 2155 Hackamore Pl., Riverside, CA 92506. Ed. Jackie Costello. adv.; circ. 600.
Formerly: Akita Magazine.

636.7   US
AKITA WORLD. bi-m. $42. Hoflin Publishing Ltd., 4401 Zephyr St., Wheat Ridge, CO 80033-3259. TEL 303-467-0089. FAX 303-420-1076.

636.7   US
ALASKAN GANGLINE. 1979. 8/yr. $16. 400 Denali, Wasilla, AK 99687. FAX 907-326-2081. Ed. Lavon Barve. adv.; circ. 500.
Description: Explores the sport of dog sledding.

636.7   US
ALASKAN MALAMUTE CLUB OF AMERICA. NEWSLETTER. m. membership. Alaskan Malamute Club of America, Inc., c/o Kris Campes, Ed., 14134 Walton Dr., Manassas, VA 22111. TEL 703-791-5567. adv.; bk.rev.; circ. 800.

636   GW   ISSN 0720-2849
ALLES FUER DIE KATZ. 1981. bi-m. DM.8.50($4.30) Gabriele Sparrenberger, Ed. & Pub., Postfach 800627, 6230 Frankfurt a.M. 80, Germany. (looseleaf format; back issues avail.)

636.7   US
ALPENHORN. 1967. bi-m. $15 to non-members. Bernese Mountain Dog Club of America, 1825 Grant St., Downers Grove, IL 60515. TEL 708-852-8850. Ed. Elizabeth Pearson. adv.; circ. 950.
Former titles: B M D C A; Bernese Mountain Dog Club of America. Newsletter.
Description: Contains dog-related articles, club news and information.

636.7   US   ISSN 0199-7297
SF429.B78
AMERICAN BRITTANY. 1948? m. membership. American Brittany Club, Inc., Box 616, Marshfield, MO 65706. TEL 417-468-6249. FAX 417-468-5860. Ed. Ronnie C. Smith. adv.; bk.rev.; circ. 4,000.
Description: Covers field trails, shows, hunting and general information on Brittanys.

636.7   US
AMERICAN BULLMASTIFF ASSOCIATION. BULLETIN. 6/yr. $35 membership. American Bullmastiff Association, c/o Chris Lezotte, 28011 Old Colony, Farmington Hills, MI 48334. Ed. Helma Weeks. adv.; bk.rev.; circ. 425.

AMERICAN CAGE-BIRD MAGAZINE. see BIOLOGY — Ornithology

636.932   US
AMERICAN CHECKERED GIANT RABBIT CLUB. NEWS BULLETIN. bi-m. American Checkered Giant Rabbit Club, Box 481, Grand Prarie, TX 75051. TEL 214-264-1099.

636.7   US
AMERICAN CHESAPEAKE CLUB. BULLETIN. bi-m. c/o Patricia A. Puwal, 4439 Sargent Ave., Castro Valley, CA 94546.

636.7   US
AMERICAN CHOW CHOW. q. $20. American Chow Chow, 2915 Skyview Dr., Wylie, TX 75098-8340.

PETS

636.7 US ISSN 0279-358X
AMERICAN COCKER MAGAZINE. 1981. bi-m. $30. American Cocker Magazine, Inc., 14531 Jefferson St., Midway City, CA 92655. TEL 714-893-0053. Ed. Michael Allen. adv.; bk.rev.; circ. 4,000.

598 US
AMERICAN DOVE ASSOCIATION NEWSLETTER. 1955. bi-m. $10 to individuals; juniors $5; senior citizens $7.50; families $12.50. American Dove Association, c/o Rita M. Courtney, Ed., Box 21, Milton, KY 40045. adv.; bk.rev.; illus.; circ. 400.
Formerly: American Dove Association. Monthly Bulletin.

636 658.048 US
AMERICAN FANCY RAT AND MOUSE ASSOCIATION YEARBOOK. 1985. a. membership. American Fancy Rat and Mouse Association, 9230 64th St., Riverside, CA 92509. TEL 714-685-2350. Ed. Karen Hauser. adv.; circ. 200.
Description: List of members, officers, champions, show results, trophy winners and dates, veterinarian referrals, addresses of similar clubs, upcoming show and display dates.

636.7 US
AMERICAN FOX TERRIER CLUB. NEWSLETTER.* bi-m. c/o Mrs. James A. Farrell, 2105 Chester Village W., Chester, CT 06412-1040. adv.; circ. 500.

636.7 US ISSN 0888-627X
AMERICAN KENNEL CLUB AWARDS; new titles, shows, obedience trials, tracking tests, field trials and hunting tests. 1981. m. $36 (foreign $44). American Kennel Club, Inc., 51 Madison Ave., New York, NY 10010. TEL 212-696-8330. FAX 212-696-8299. circ. 18,000. (also avail. in microfilm from UMI)
Formerly: American Kennel Club. Show, Obedience and Field Trial Awards (ISSN 0272-4383)

636.7 US
AMERICAN MANCHESTER TERRIER CLUB. NEWSLETTER. 1961. bi-m. membership. c/o Muriel S. Henkel, 4961 N.E. 193 St., Seattle, WA 98155. adv.; circ. 200.

636.596 US ISSN 0003-0511
AMERICAN PIGEON JOURNAL; devoted to all branches of pigeon raising--fancy, utility and racing. 1912. m. $18 (foreign $22). William L. Worley, Ed. & Pub., Box 278, Warrenton, MO 63383. TEL 314-456-2122. adv.; bk.rev.; illus.; circ. 8,000.

636.7 US
AMERICAN SALUKI ASSOCIATION. NEWSLETTER.* 1963. q. c/o Sally Bell, 14118 228th St., S.E., Snohomish, WA 98290. circ. 600.

636.7 US
AMERICAN SHETLAND SHEEPDOG ASSOCIATION. BULLETIN BOARD. q. membership. American Shetland Sheepdog Association, 2516 Country Club Dr., Odessa, TX 79762. Ed. Diana Rockwell. circ. 714.
Formerly: American Shetland Sheepdog Association. Bulletin.

636.7 US
AMERICAN SPANIEL CLUB. BULLETIN. 1951. q. membership. American Spaniel Club, 848 Old Stevens Creek Rd., Martinez, GA 30907-9277. FAX 706-860-0881. Ed. Barbara J. Hoops. circ. 1,500.

636.932 US
AMERICAN STANDARD CHINCHILLA RABBIT ASSOCIATION. NEWSLETTER. bi-m. American Standard Chinchilla Rabbit Association, c/o Patricia Gest, 1607 Ninth St. W., Palmetto, FL 34221. TEL 813-729-1184.

ANIMAL FINDERS' GUIDE. see AGRICULTURE — Poultry And Livestock

636 US ISSN 0003-360X
ANIMALDOM. 1930. m. (except Aug.). $2 to non-members. Pennsylvania S.P.C.A., 350 E. Erie Ave., Philadelphia, PA 19134. TEL 215-426-6300. Ed. Charlene W. Peters. bk.rev.; illus.; circ. 42,000.

636 US ISSN 0899-045X
AQUARIUM FISH MAGAZINE; your guide to successful fishkeeping. 1988. m. $23.97. Fancy Publications, Inc., Box 6050, Mission Viejo, CA 92690. TEL 714-855-8822. FAX 714-855-3045. (Subscr. to: Box 6040, Mission Viejo, CA 92690) Ed. Edward Bauman. adv.; circ. 75,000. (back issues avail.)
Description: Covers freshwater and saltwater aquariums and ponds and pond fish. Provides information on the hobby for beginners and experienced hobbyists.

636.7 US
ARISTOCRAT. 1903. q. $30 to non-members. Borzoi Club of America, c/o Sandy Zeboski, Corres. Sec., 8310 Autumn Willow, Tomball, TX 77375. adv.; bk.rev.; circ. 600.
Description: Covers all aspects of living with and raising purebred Borzoi dogs.

636.7 US
ARK (COLORADO SPRINGS).* 1974. bi-m. $15. American Rottweiler Club, c/o W.M. Gruenerwald & Associates, Box 60669, Colorado Springs, CO 80960-0669. Ed. Dorothea Gruenerwald. circ. 1,200.

636.7 US
ASSOCIATION OF OBEDIENCE CLUBS AND JUDGES. NEWSLETTER. 1950. q. Association of Obedience Clubs and Judges, c/o Patricia Scully, 328 Parkside Dr., Suffern, NY 10901. circ. 500.

598 AT
AUSTRALIAN CANARY BREEDER. 1970. m. Aus.$1 per no. Canary Breeders' Association of Australia, 13 Robina Rd., Eaglemont, Vic. 3084, Australia. Ed. S.J. Leaney.

636.7 US
AUSTRALIAN TERRIER CLUB OF AMERICA NEWSLETTER. 1959. q. $6 to non-members. Australian Terrier Club of America, c/o Mrs. Milton Fox, 1411 Dorsett Dock Rd., Pt. Pleasant, NJ 08742. TEL 201-899-0557. Ed. Mae Roo. adv.; circ. 250. (processed)

636 UK
BARBARA WOODHOUSE ANIMAL ANNUAL. a. Grandreams Ltd., Jadwin Hse., 205/211 Kentish Town Rd., London, NW5 2JH, England.

636.7 US
BARKS.* 1977? q. $10. Bull Terrier Club of America, 6239 Genoa Rd., Belvidere, IL 61008. Ed. Mary Jung. circ. 400.

636.7 US ISSN 0094-9744 SF429.B15
BASENJI. 1964. m. $20. Jon and Susan Coe, Eds. & Pubs., 789 Linton Hill Rd., Newtown, PA 18940-1207. TEL 215-860-8254. adv.; bk.rev.; illus.; stat.; circ. 1,500. (back issues avail.)

636.7 US
BASENJI CLUB OF AMERICA. OFFICIAL BULLETIN. 1942. bi-m. Basenji Club of America, 2435 Hibiscus Dr., Hayward, CA 94545. circ. 600.

636.7 US ISSN 0736-9743
BETTER BEAGLING. 1977. m. $14. Box 142, Essex, VT 05451. TEL 802-878-3616. Ed. Pearl N. Baker. adv.; bk.rev.; circ. 6,000.
Formerly: Large Pack.
Description: Covers breeding and care of beagle hunting hounds.

636.7 US
BICHON FRISE REPORTER. 1979. q. $30. Reporter Publications, Box 6369, Los Osos, CA 93412. bk.rev.

179.3 US
BIDE-A-WEE NEWS. 1969. q. contribution. Bide-A-Wee Home Association, 410 E. 38th St., New York, NY 10016. FAX 212-532-4210. circ. 40,000. (back issues avail.)

636 598.2 US ISSN 0891-771X
BIRD TALK. 1982. m. $25.97. Fancy Publications, Inc., Box 6050, Mission Viejo, CA 92690. TEL 714-855-8822. FAX 714-855-3045. (Subscr. to: Box 57347, Boulder, CO 80322-7347) Ed. Karyn New. adv.; circ. 146,000.
Description: Contains information on understanding and caring for all types of cage and aviary birds. Covers species, medical aspects, bird care and behavior, and special birds. Includes questions and answers.

BIRD WORLD. see BIOLOGY — Ornithology

636.569 UK
BIRDKEEPER. 1988. bi-m. £8.75($18) I P C Magazines Ltd., Kings Reach House, Stamford St., London SE1 9LS, England. TEL 071-261-5849. FAX 071-261-7851. (US Subscr. to: 205 E. 42nd St., New York, NY 10017. TEL 212-867-2080) Ed. Peter Moss.
Description: All aspects of birdkeeping for the beginner and enthusiast.

636 US
▼**BIRDS U S A.** 1989. a. $5.95. Fancy Publications, Inc., Box 6050, Mission Viejo, CA 92690. TEL 714-855-8822. FAX 714-855-3045. Ed. Karyn New. adv.; circ. 110,500.
Description: Contains articles on the basics of bird care for the pet bird owner.

636 SW ISSN 0006-4076
BLAA STJAERNAN. 1965. 4/yr. SEK 30 to non-members. Svenska Blaa Stjaernan, Riddarg. 13, 114 51 Stockholm, Sweden. Ed. Karin Wiebe. adv.; bk.rev.; illus.; circ. 9,000.

636.932 GW
DAS BLAUE JAHRBUCH; Ein praktischer Wegweiser fuer den Kaninchenzuechter. 1955. a. (Deutscher Kleintier Zuechter) Oertel & Spoerer, Burgstr. 1-7, 7410 Reutlingen, Germany. TEL 07121-302555. circ. 10,000.

636.7 US
BLOODHOUND BULLETIN. 1958. 3/yr. 7275 Jennings Rd., Whitmore Lake, MI 48189. adv.; circ. 400.

636.7 US
BLOODLINES. 1905. 7/yr. $12 (foreign $23). United Kennel Club, Inc., 100 E. Kilgore Rd., Kalamazoo, MI 49001. TEL 616-343-9020. FAX 616-343-7037. Ed. John J. Miller. adv.; bk.rev.; circ. 5,000.
Formerly: Bloodlines Journal (ISSN 0006-5013)
Description: Devoted to dog sports and family dogs; covers obedience, breeding, tracking, agility, service dogs, therapy dogs, and herding dogs.

636 338 US
BOARDERLINE MAGAZINE. 1979. bi-m. $50 membership. American Boarding Kennels Association, 4575 Galley Rd., Ste. 400A, Colorado Springs, CO 80915. TEL 719-591-1113. FAX 719-579-0006. Ed. Pat Colt. adv.; bk.rev.; circ. 1,500.
Description: Covers the pet industry and small business person.

636.7 US
BORDERLINE.* q. membership. Border Terrier Club of America, c/o Patricia Quinn, Ed., Box 545, Silverhill, AL 36576-0545. circ. 200.

636 US
BORZOI INTERNATIONAL; for people who love Borzoi. 1988. q. $25. Borzoi International, Inc., 33594 Overland Lane, Solon, OH 44139. TEL 216-248-0067. FAX 216-946-0664. Ed. Sue Vasick-Croley. adv.; bk.rev.; circ. 1,492. (back issues avail.)
Description: Covers all aspects of Borzoi ownership worldwide.

636.7 US
BORZOI QUARTERLY. 1974. q. $36. Hoflin Publishing Ltd., 4401 Zephyr St., Wheat Ridge, CO 80033-3299. TEL 303-467-0089. FAX 303-420-1076. circ. 1,500.

636.7 US
BOSTON BULLETIN. 1957? m. $12 to non-members. Boston Terrier Club of America, Box 235, Bronx, NY 10466. Ed. Carl Gomes. circ. 200.

PETS

636.7 US
BOSTON QUARTERLY. q. $36. Hoflin Publishing Ltd., 4401 Zephyr St., Wheat Ridge, CO 80033-3299. TEL 303-467-0089. FAX 303-420-1076.

636.7 US
BOXER REVIEW. m. $9.25. M. D. Drucker, 8760 Appian Way, Los Angeles, CA 90046. (Subscr. to: Box 6900, Beverly Hills, CA 90213) Ed. Kris Dahl.

636.7 US
BRITTANY WORLD; a quarterly magazine for Brittany lovers. q. $36. Hoflin Publishing Ltd., 4401 Zephyr St., Wheat Ridge, CO 80033-3299. TEL 303-467-0089. FAX 303-420-1076.

636.7 SW
BRUKSHUNDEN. bi-m. Svenska Brukshundklubben, Box 349, 123 03 Farsta 3, Sweden. Ed. Arne Sundblad. adv.; circ. 37,279.

636.7 US
BRUSSELS GRIFFON QUARTERLY. q. c/o Mrs. E.H. Hellweman, 541 Old Oak Rd., Severn, MD 21144. circ. 80.

BUDGERIGAR BULLETIN. see *BIOLOGY — Ornithology*

636 UK
BUDGERIGAR WORLD. 1974. m. $49. Budgerigar World Ltd., County Press Buildings, Bala, Gwynedd LL23 7PG, Wales. TEL 0678-520262. Ed. G.S. Binks.

636.7 US
BULL SHEET.* 1973. irreg. (4-5/yr.). Obedience Steward Club, c/o Maria Coon, Box 1463, Riverhead, NY 11901-0952. circ. 75.

636.7 US
BULLDOGGER. 3/yr. Bulldog Club of America, c/o Rita L. Phethean, 133 Wild Oak Dr., Birmingham, AL 35210-2605. circ. 1,600.

636 GW ISSN 0341-9770
BUNTE TIERWELT; Ratgeber fuer Tierfreunde. 1964. m. DM.26. Hortus Verlag GmbH, Rheinallee 4B, 5300 Bonn 2, Germany. TEL 0228-353030. FAX 0228-364533. Ed. Rolf Doermann. adv.; bk.rev.; index; circ. 22,000.
Description: Animal lover magazine.

CAGE & AVIARY BIRDS. see *BIOLOGY — Ornithology*

636 CN ISSN 0045-4052
CALQUARIUM. 1959. m. membership. Calgary Aquarium Society, Box 63180, Calgary, Alta. T2N 4S5, Canada. Ed. Gary Stevenson. adv.; bk.rev.; circ. 175.
Description: Articles and news on aquarium keeping. Subject matter is aimed at the average hobbyist.

636.7 US
CANINE CHRONICLE.* 1975. s-w. $40. Routledge Publications, Inc., 605 2nd Ave., N., No. 203, Columbus, MS 39701-4552. Ed. Fran Bir. adv.; circ. 7,000.

636.7 364.4 US
CANINE COURIER. 1979. q. $30. United States Police Canine Association, Inc., Rt. 2, Box 221 J, Angier, NC 27501. TEL 919-639-0490. Ed. Richard Rogers. adv.; bk.rev.; circ. 3,000.

CANINE LISTENER. see *HANDICAPPED — Hearing Impaired*

636.7 US
CASSETTE. 1970. q. $7. c/o Anne Lively, Ed., 2 Hemlock Cove Rd., R.R. No.3, Falmouth, ME 04105. TEL 207-797-9635. adv.; circ. 500.
Description: Articles, letters, and interviews pertaining to dog-breeding and showing, with show results. Focus is on Collies and Shetland sheepdogs.

636.8 UK ISSN 0008-7599
CAT. 1934. bi-m. membership. Cats Protection League, 17 Kings Rd., Horsham, West Sussex RH13 5PP, England. TEL 0403-65566. FAX 0403-218414. Ed. H.E. Boothby. adv.; bk.rev.; circ. 35,000.

179.3 AT
CAT CALL. 1968. q. membership. Feline Control Council of W.A., P.O. Box 232, Gosnells, W.A. 6110, Australia. TEL 3841933. Ed. P. Parish. adv.; circ. 300.
Description: News of interest to members of the council.

CAT COLLECTORS. see *HOBBIES*

636.8 US
CAT COMPANION FROM FRISKIES. 1985. bi-m. $9.98. Quarton Group Publishers, Inc., 2155 Butterfield, Ste. 200, Troy, MI 48084. TEL 313-649-1110. FAX 313-649-2306. adv.; bk.rev.; circ. 160,000.
Formerly: Friskies Cat Companion.
Description: Contains articles on pet health, nutrition, grooming, basic medicine and first aid for cats.

636.8 US
CAT FANCIERS' ASSOCIATION. ANNUAL YEARBOOK. 1958. a. $35 (foreign $40). Cat Fanciers Association, Inc., 1805 Atlantic Ave., Manasquan, NJ 08736. TEL 908-528-9797. Ed. Marna Fogarty. adv.; bk.rev.; circ. 7,500.

636.8 AT
CAT FANCIERS' MAGAZINE. 1971. irreg. free. Cat Fanciers' Club of Tasmania, P.O. Box 114, North Hobart, Tas. 7002, Australia. Ed. Danny Cool.

595 US ISSN 0892-6514
SF441
CAT FANCY. 1966. m. $21.97. Fancy Publications, Inc., Box 6050, Mission Viejo, CA 92690. TEL 714-855-8822. (Subscr. addr.: Box 52864, Boulder, CO 80322-2864) Ed. Kathryn Segnar. circ. 230,000.
Supersedes: International Cat Fancy (ISSN 0199-0640)
Description: Contains information on how to better understand and care for cats. Covers medical problems, care technique, purebreds, personal and fictional stories. Includes questions and answers.

636.8 US
▼**CAT LOVER**. 1991. q. $12. (Cat Lovers of America) Fancy Publications, Inc., 2401 Beverly Blvd., Los Angeles, CA 90057. TEL 213-385-2222. FAX 213-385-8565. adv.; B&W page $1200, color page $1800; trim 8 x 10 7/8; adv. contact: Norman Ridker. circ. 10,200.
Description: Covers care and nutrition, feline products and services, news, history, and trivia.

636 US ISSN 0163-1926
CAT WORLD. 1973. bi-m. $7.95. Thompson Bureau, Box 35635, Phoenix, AZ 80401. Ed. Pauline Thompson. adv.; bk.rev.; index; circ. 2,500. (back issues avail.)

636.8 UK ISSN 0952-2875
CAT WORLD. 1982. m. £24.60. Cat World Ltd., 10 Western Rd., Shoreham-by-Sea, West Sussex BN43 5WD, England. TEL 0273 462000. Ed. Joan Moore. adv.; bk.rev.; circ. 19,000. (back issues avail.)
Description: All about cats: information guides, veterinary articles, handicraft items, breeders and trade advertisements.

636.8 UK
CAT WORLD ANNUAL. 1982. a. £6.50. Cat World Ltd., 10 Western Rd., Shoreham-by-Sea, West Sussex BN43 5WD, England. TEL 0273 462000. Ed. Joan Moore. circ. 10,000.
Description: Informational articles, stories and photographs for cat lovers.

636.8 UK ISSN 0260-3837
CATS. 1981. w. £95. Our Dogs Publishing Co. Ltd., 5 James Leigh St., Manchester M1 6EX, England. TEL 061-236-0577. FAX 061-236-5534. Ed. Brian W. Doyle. bk.rev.; illus.; circ. 7,000 (controlled).

636.8 US ISSN 0008-8544
CATS MAGAZINE. 1945. m. $18.97. Cats Magazine, Inc., Box 290037, Port Orange, FL 32129. TEL 904-788-2770. Ed. Linda J. Walton. adv.; bk.rev.; illus.; index; circ. 149,000. (also avail. in microfilm from UMI; reprint service avail. from UMI)
Indexed: A.I.P.P.

636.7 US
CAVALIER KING CHARLES SPANIEL CLUB, U S A. BULLETIN. 1964. q. $10. Cavalier King Charles Spaniel Club, U S A, Inc., c/o Courtney Carter, Sec., 2 Brynwood Ln., Newtown, PA 18940. Ed. Jesse Cleveland. bk.rev.; circ. 750.
Formerly: Cavalier King Charles Spaniel Club of America. Bulletin.

636.7 SZ
LE CHIEN MAGAZINE; revue mensuelle specialisee du chien. m. 34 Fr. (foreign 44 Fr.). Presses Centrale Lausanne SA, Rue de Geneve 7, 1003 Lausanne, Switzerland. Ed. Liliane Mordesike. adv.; illus.
Formerly: Chien.

636.7 FR
CHIENS 2000.* 1973. bi-m. 69 rue St-Nicolas, B.P. 1, 78600 Maisons Lafitte, France.

636.7 US
CHIHUAHUA NEWS.* 1981. 10/yr. $12. Dudgeon Publications, 5100 E. Rosehill Ave., Terre Haute, IN 47805. TEL 812-466-3361. Ed. Mollie Dudgeon. adv.; illus.; circ. 500.
Description: Discusses dog care and breeding.

636 US ISSN 0273-2335
LOS CHIHUAHUAS.* 1976. bi-m. $15. Myrle Hale, Ed.& Pub., 12860 Thonotosassa Rd., Dover, FL 33527. circ. 650. (back issues avail.)

636.7 179.3 AT ISSN 0819-5862
CLUMBER SPANIEL CORRESPONDENCE. 1987. bi-m. Aus.$13 (foreign Aus.$19). Erinrac Enterprises, Foott Rd., Upper Beaconsfield, Vic. 3808, Australia. TEL 059-44-3383. Ed. Miss Jan Irving. adv.; bk.rev.; illus.; stat.; circ. 80. (back issues avail.)

636.7 US
COLLIE CLUB OF AMERICA. BULLETIN. bi-m. membership. Collie Club of America, Rt. 2, Ledge Hill Farm, Easton, ME 04740. Ed. Ronald Dow. circ. 3,500.

636.73 US
COLLIE REVIEW. m. $9.25. M. D. Drucker, 8760 Appian Ave., Los Angeles, CA 90046. (Subscr. to: Box 6900, Beverly Hills, CA 90213) stat.; circ. 4,000. (back issues avail.)
Formerly: Collie-Shetland Sheepdog Review.

636.7 US
COLLIE VARIETY; a quarterly magazine for Collie lovers. q. $36. Hoflin Publishing Ltd., 4401 Zephyr St., Wheat Ridge, CO 80033-3299. TEL 303-467-0089. FAX 303-420-1076.

636.596 FR
COLOMBOPHILIE; bulletin nationale. q. 54 bd. Carnot, 59042 Lille Cedex, France. Ed. Marie L. Lesecq.

636 US
COLONIAL ROTTWEILER CLUB NEWSLETTER. 1954. 6/yr. $25 to non-members. Colonial Rottweiler Club, E. Lake Rd., RD 2, Westfield, NY 14787. TEL 716-326-2370. Ed. Norma Dikeman. adv.; circ. 400. (back issues avail.)

COMMON SENSE PEST CONTROL QUARTERLY. see *BIOLOGY — Entomology*

636 US
COMPANION ANIMAL NEWS. 1981. 3/yr. free. Morris Animal Foundation, 45 Inverness Dr. E., Englewood, CO 80112. TEL 303-790-2345. FAX 303-790-4066. Ed. Janice Rooney. bk.rev.; circ. 140,000. (tabloid format)
Description: Articles on pet health studies.

636.932 IT
CONGLIO. bi-m. Associazione Nazionale Coniglicultori Italiani, Via A. Torlonia 19, 00161 Rome, Italy. TEL 06-854903.

636.7 US
COONHOUND BLOODLINES. 1973. m. $14 (foreign $25). United Kennel Club, Inc., 100 E. Kilgore, Kalamazoo, MI 49001. TEL 616-343-9020. FAX 616-343-7037. Ed. John J. Miller. adv.; bk.rev.; circ. 25,000.
Description: Contains information about raccoon, bobcat and bear hunting, and coonhound field trials.

PETS

636.7 US
CORGI QUARTERLY. q. $36. Hoflin Publishing Ltd., 4401 Zephyr St., Wheat Ridge, CO 80033-3299. TEL 303-467-0089. FAX 303-420-1076.

COUNTRYSIDE AND SMALL STOCK JOURNAL. see *AGRICULTURE — Poultry And Livestock*

636.753 GW ISSN 0011-5231
DACHSHUND. 1946. m. DM.30. Deutscher Teckelklub e.V., Postfach 10 03 62, Prinzenstr. 38, 4100 Duisburg 1, Germany. adv.; bk.rev.; circ. 29,000.
Description: Highlights dog care and breeding.

636.7 US
DALMATIAN QUARTERLY. q. $36. Hoflin Publishing Ltd., 4401 Zephyr St., Wheat Ridge, CO 80033-3299. TEL 303-467-0089. FAX 303-420-1076.

636 DK
DENMARK. STATENS HUSDYRBRUGSFORSOEG. AARSRAPPORT. 1974. a. free. Statens Husdyrbrugsforsoeg - National Institute of Animal Science, Research Center Foulum, P.O. Box 39, DK-8830 Tjele, Denmark.

636 GW
DEUTSCHER JAGDTERRIERCLUB. NACHRICHTENBLATT. 1946. q. DM.12. Deutscher Jagdterrierclub e.V., Wolbecker Str. 7, 4415 Sendenhorst 2, Germany. TEL 02535-8074. circ. 2,800.

636.932 GW
DEUTSCHER KANINCHENZUECHTER. bi-w. Zentralverband Deutscher Kaninchenzuechter e.V., Landenburger Str. 62, 7000 Stuttgart 40, Germany.

636.7 US
DEW CLAW.* 1928. bi-m. $9 to non-members. Briard Club of America, c/o Jack McLeroth, 6715 Maysville Rd., No. 15, Fort Wayne, IN 46815-8225. Ed. Diane McLeroth. adv.; bk.rev.; circ. 700.

636 NE
DIBEVO VAKBLAD. 1947. m. (11/yr.). fl.63.60. Landelijke Organisatie DIBEVO - Netherlands Organisation of Pet Retailers and Suppliers and Fishing Tackle Trade Organization, Postbus 94, 3800 AB Amersfoort, Netherlands. TEL 033-550433. FAX 033-552835. Ed. G.T. Ebert. adv.; bk.rev.; charts; illus.; stat.; circ. 6,500 (controlled). *Indexed:* Key to Econ.Sci.
Formerly: Dibevo (ISSN 0012-2416)

636.7 US ISSN 1046-1043
DOBEDITION. 1989. bi-m $36 (foreign $48). Leslie Hall, Ed. & Pub., Box 600, Georgetown, CT 06829. TEL 203-762-2484. adv.; circ. 890.
Description: Includes news and current information on the Doberman.

636.7 US
DOBERMAN WORLD; a bimonthly magazine for Doberman lovers. 1979. bi-m. $36. Hoflin Publishing Ltd., 4401 Zephyr St., Wheat Ridge, CO 80033-3299. TEL 303-467-0089. FAX 303-420-1076.

636.7 US ISSN 0194-9756
DOG (MARSHALL). 1979. fortn. Ringside Publications, 4977 Midway Lane, Marshall, WI 53559.

636 US
DOG BREEDING. 1988. q. $59. Simone Publications, 2 Gilbert Pl., West Orange, NJ 07052. Ed. Peter Simone. adv.; bk.rev.

636.7 US ISSN 0892-6522
SF421
DOG FANCY. 1970. m. $21.97. Fancy Publications, Inc., Box 6050, Mission Viejo, CA 92690. TEL 714-855-8822. FAX 714-855-3045. (Subscr. address: Box 53264, Boulder, CO 80322-3264) Ed. Kim Thornton. adv.; bk.rev.; illus.; circ. 143,000. (back issues avail.)
Description: For the dog lover - including professional breeders, show exhibitors and, especially, general pet owners. Covers information on canine diet, grooming, exotic and domestic breeds, medical news and tips for showing.

636.7 UK ISSN 0309-1031
DOG NEWS AND FAMILY PETS.* vol.6,1970. q. National Dog Owners' Association, 39-41 North Rd., Islington, London N7 9DP, England. Ed. Joan Palmer. adv.; bk.rev.; illus.; circ. 12,000.
Formerly: Dog News (ISSN 0012-4850)

636.7 790.1 US ISSN 0194-6706
DOG SPORTS. 1979. m. $44. D S M Publishing, Inc., 940 Tyler St., Studio 17, Benicia, CA 94519-2916. TEL 707-745-6897. FAX 707-745-4581. Ed. Michael E. McKown. adv.; bk.rev.; circ. 3,200.
Description: Covers the world of the working dog. Includes canine search and rescue, dogs used for personal and industrial security and working dog sports.

636.7 US
DOG WATCH. w. $120. B & E Publications, Inc., 11331 Ventura Blvd., Ste. 301, Studio City, CA 91604. TEL 818-761-3647. FAX 818-761-7586. Ed. Frank T. Sabella. bk.rev.; circ. 5,000 (controlled).

636.7 UK ISSN 0012-4885
DOG WORLD. 1919. w. $122. M.J. Boulding, Ed. & Pub., 9 Tufton St., Ashford, Kent TN23 1QN, England. (also avail. in microform from UMI; reprint service avail. from UMI)

636.7 US ISSN 0012-4893
DOG WORLD. 1916. m. $28. Maclean Hunter Publishing Company, 29 N. Wacker Dr., Chicago, IL 60606. TEL 312-726-2802. FAX 312-726-2574. TELEX 270258 EXP. Ed. Enid Bergstrom. adv.; bk.rev.; illus.; circ. 58,624. (also avail. in microform from UMI)
Description: Covers purebreds for breeders, exhibitors and trainers.

636.8 UK ISSN 0070-7015
DOG WORLD ANNUAL. 1930. a. $18. M.J. Boulding, Ed. & Pub., 9 Tufton St., Ashford, Kent TN23 1QN, England. index.

636.7 CN ISSN 0317-1485
DOGS IN CANADA. 1889. m. Can.$27. Apex Publishers & Publicity Ltd., 43 Railside Rd., Don Mills, Ont. M3A 3L9, Canada. TEL 416-441-3228. FAX 416-441-3212. Ed. Susan E. Pearce. adv.; bk.rev.; illus.; circ. 22,000. *Indexed:* CMI.

636.7 CN
DOGS IN CANADA ANNUAL. a. Apex Publishers & Publicity Ltd., 43 Railside Rd., Don Mills, Ont. M3A 3L9, Canada. TEL 416-441-3228. FAX 416-441-3212. Ed. Susan E. Pearce. adv.; circ. 88,000.

636.7 US ISSN 0895-5581
DOGS U S A. 1986. a. $5.95. Fancy Publications, Inc., Box 6050, Mission Viejo, CA 92690. TEL 714-855-8822. Ed. Connie Jankowski. adv.; circ. 170,000.

630 GW ISSN 0341-5759
DU UND DAS TIER. 1971. 6/yr. DM.21.40 (foreign DM.31.40). (Deutscher Tierschutzbund e.V.) Verlag M. und H. Schaper, Kalandstr. 4, Postfach 1642, 3220 Alfeld, Germany. adv.; bk.rev.; illus.; index; circ. 15,000. *Indexed:* Agri.Eng.Abstr., Ind.Vet., Nutr.Abstr., Vet.Bull.

636.8 GW ISSN 0013-0826
DIE EDELKATZE; illustrierte Fachzeitschrift fuer Rassekatzenzucht. 1922. bi-m. DM.54. Erster Deutscher Edelkatzenzuechter Verband e.V., Berlinerstr. 13, 6334 Asslar, Germany. Ed. W. Sattler. adv.; bk.rev.; bibl.; circ. 15,000.

636 591 FI ISSN 0357-8747
ELAINMAAILMA. 1979. m. FIM 209. Sanoma Corporation, PL. 113, SF-00381 Helsinki 38, Finland. TEL 358-0-1221. Ed. Jyrki Leskinen. circ. 36,613.
Description: For school-aged children and adults. Articles vary from pets to wildlife and nature.

636.7 US
ELKHOUND QUARTERLY. q. $36. Hoflin Publishing Ltd., 4401 Zephyr St., Wheat Ridge, CO 80033-3299. TEL 303-467-0089. FAX 303-420-1076.

636.7 US
ENGLISH COCKER QUARTERLY. q. $36. Hoflin Publishing Ltd., 4401 Zephyr St., Wheat Ridge, CO 80033-3299. TEL 303-467-0089. FAX 303-420-1076.

636.7 US
ENGLISH SETTER ASSOCIATION OF AMERICA. NEWSLETTER. m. membership. English Setter Association of America, c/o Dawn Ronyak, Sec., 114 Burlington Oval, Chardon, OH 44024-1452. FAX 216-729-8413. circ. 1,000.

636 US
FAMILY PET.* 1971. q. $2. c/o M. Linda Sabella, Box 25353, Tampa, FL 33622-5353. adv.; bk.rev.; circ. 3,000. (back issues avail.)

636.7 US
FIELD ADVISORY NEWS.* 1971. bi-m. $20. American Sighthound Field Association, Inc., c/o Bunny Reed, Ed., 316 S. Marshall, Boone, IA 50036. adv.; bk.rev.; circ. 600.

636.7 US
FLUSHING WHIP. 1956. m. $15 to individuals; free to libraries. National Red Setter Field Trial Club, RR1, Box 71C, Cypress Inn, TN 38752-9801. TEL 615-724-5458. Ed. Robert Sprouse. adv.; bk.rev.; circ. 250.
Description: For breeders, owners, bird hunters, and professional trainers of field Irish Red Setters.

636.7 US
FRENCH BULLDOG CLUB OF AMERICA. NEWSLETTER.* bi-m. French Bulldog Club of America, c/o Richard M. Hover, 86 Gold Rd., Wappingers Falls, NY 12590-3534. circ. 100.

636 US ISSN 0160-4317
SF456
FRESHWATER AND MARINE AQUARIUM. 1978. m. $22. R-C Modeler Corp., 144 W. Sierra Madre Blvd., Sierra Madre, CA 91024. TEL 818-355-1476.

636.7 JA
FRIENDS OF DOG/AIKEN NO TOMO. (Text in Japanese) 1952. m. 25940 Yen. Seibundo Shinkosha Publishing Co. Ltd., 1-5-5 Kanda Nishiki-Cho, Chiyoda-Ku, Tokyo 101, Japan. Ed. Mitsuo Shoji.

636.7 US
FRONT AND FINISH: THE DOG TRAINER'S NEWS. 1970. m. $20. H and S Publications, Inc., Box 333, Galesburg, IL 61402. Ed. Robert T. Self. adv.; bk.rev.; index; circ. 6,500. (also avail. in microform)

FUND FOR ANIMALS QUARTERLY. see *CONSERVATION*

636.7 US
G S P C A "SHORTHAIR". 1954. m. $25. German Shorthaired Pointer Club of America, 18151 Harrison St., Omaha, NE 68136. Ed. Art and Jean Armbrust. adv.; bk.rev.; circ. 2,550.
Formerly (until 1986): G S P C A Newsletter.
Description: Reports on breed activities in show, field trial, hunt test and obedience. Covers training, dog care, nutrition, new products and industry news,

636 GW ISSN 0016-5824
GEFLUEGEL-BOERSE. 1879. s-m. DM.120. (Bund Deutscher Rassegefluegelzuechter e.V) Verlag Juergens KG, Industriestr. 13, 8034 Germering-McH., Germany. FAX 089-8402351. Ed. D. Juergens. adv.; bk.rev.; circ. 45,000.

636.7 US
GERMAN SHEPHERD DOG REVIEW. 1922. m. $25. German Shepherd Dog Club of America, c/o Lois Fryslin, Ed., 30 Far View Rd., Chalfont, PA 18914. adv.; bk.rev.; circ. 5,700.

636.7 US
GERMAN SHEPHERD QUARTERLY. q. $36. Hoflin Publishing Ltd., 4401 Zephyr St., Wheat Ridge, CO 80033-3299. TEL 303-467-0089. FAX 303-420-1076.

636.7 US
GERMAN SHORTHAIRED POINTER NEWS. 1954. m. $20. Shirley L. Carlson, Ed. & Pub., 86 N. Heck Hill Rd., Box 850, Saint Paris, OH 43072. TEL 513-663-4773. adv.; bk.rev.; stat.; circ. 1,500. (back issues avail.)
Description: Focuses on breeding, puppies, competition; includes articles on training.

636.7 US
GOLDEN RETRIEVER WORLD; a quarterly magazine for Golden lovers. q. $36. Hoflin Publishing Ltd., 4401 Zephyr St., Wheat Ridge, CO 80033-3299. TEL 303-467-0089. FAX 303-420-1076.

636.7 US
GOOD DOG!. 6/yr. 2945 Dove Haven Court, Ste. H, Charleston, SC 29414. TEL 803-763-8750. FAX 803-763-1788. Ed. Lidia Murdy. circ. 50,000.

636.7 US
GORDON SETTER NEWS. 1947. m. membership. Gordon Setter Club of America, Inc., 10120 DeWitt, DeWitt, MI 48820. Ed. Dianne Avery. adv.; bk.rev.; circ. 1,000.

636.7 US
GREAT DANE CLUB OF AMERICA. MONTHLY BULLETIN. m. Great Dané Club of America, c/o Pattie Glanz, Gage Rd., RR 5, Brewster, NY 10509. circ. 2,000.

636.7 US
GREAT DANE REPORTER. 1976. bi-m. $40. Marlo Publications, Dept. DW, Box 5284, Beverly Hills, CA 90209-5284. Ed. Lynn Lowy. adv.; bk.rev.; circ. 2,000.

636 796 AT
GREYHOUND ADVISER. 1970. m. Aus.$30. Greyhound Racing Control Board (Victoria), 1 Queens Rd., Melbourne, Vic., Australia. FAX 03-266-2494. (Co-sponsor: National Coursing Association of Victoria) Ed. G.F. Allen. adv.; bk.rev.; circ. 6,000.

636.7 UK ISSN 0017-4165
GREYHOUND OWNER & BREEDER. 1946. w. £6.50 for 6 mos. Greyhound Owner Ltd., 8 Greenford Ave., London W7 3QP, England. Ed. Jim Shepherd. adv.; stat.; cum.index; circ. 9,800. (tabloid format)

636 976 AT
GREYHOUND RECORDER. 1935. w. Aus.$125 per no. 9 East St., Lidcombe 2141, Australia. circ. 11,000.

636.7 US ISSN 0199-8366
SF427.5
GROOM & BOARD. 1980. 9/yr. $25. H.H. Backer Associates, Inc., 207 S. Wabash Ave., Ste. 504, Chicago, IL 60604. TEL 312-663-4040. FAX 312-663-5676. Ed. Karen Long MacLeod. adv.; circ. 17,968. (back issues avail.)

636.7 NE
▼**GROOMERS EUROPE**; for professional dog groomers. (Text in Dutch, English, French, German) 1991. 4/yr. fl.35. InterMedium Publishers, P.O. Box 1318, 3800 BH Amersfoort, Netherlands. TEL 33-947672. FAX 33-945886. Ed. Reinder Sterenborg. adv.; illus.

636.7 US
GROOMERS VOICE. 1969. q. membership. National Dog Groomers Association of America, c/o Jeffrey L. Reynolds, Box 101, Clark, PA 16113. TEL 412-962-2711. adv.; circ. 2,500.

636.596 GW ISSN 0935-5405
DAS GRUENE JAHRBUCH; Ein praktischer Wegweiser fuer den Gefluegel- und Taubenzuechter. 1953. a. (Deutscher Kleintier Zuechter) Oertel & Spoerer, Burgstr. 1-7, 7410 Reutlingen, Germany. TEL 07121-302555. circ. 7,000.

636.7 362.41 US
GUIDE DOG NEWS. 1950. q. membership. Guide Dogs for the Blind, Inc., Box 151200, San Rafael, CA 94915-1200. FAX 415-499-4023. Ed. Jennifer Conroy. circ. 55,000.

636.7 362.41 US
GUIDE LINES (YORKTOWN HTS.). 1954. q. free. Guiding Eyes for the Blind, 611 Granite Springs Rd., Yorktown Hts., NY 10598-3499.

GUN DOG; upland bird and waterfowl dogs. see SPORTS AND GAMES — Outdoor Life

HANDBOOK OF LIVE ANIMAL TRANSPORT. see TRANSPORTATION

636.7 US
HARP & HOUND.* s-a. $25. Irish Wolfhound Club of America, c/o Mrs. Hector P. Siat, 325 Deer Run Dr., Grafton, OH 44044. circ. 700.

636 US ISSN 0193-1997
HEART OF AMERICA AQUARIUM SOCIETY NEWS. vol.24, 1979. m. (11/yr.). $12 to members. Heart of America Aquarium Society, 2029 W. 84th Terr., Leawood, KS 66206. Ed. Betty Ryne. adv.; circ. 300.
    Description: Provides current news and information on all species of fish, tropical and native.

HENSTON VETERINARY VADE MECUM (SMALL ANIMALS). see VETERINARY SCIENCE

636.7 NE ISSN 0018-4527
HONDENWERELD. 1946. m. fl.64. Stichting de Hondenwereld, Burg. Wijnenstraat 44, Postbus 8, 5720 AA Asten, Netherlands. TEL 04936-91345. FAX 04936-95005. Ed. B. Bosch. adv.; bk.rev.; abstr.; illus.; index; circ. 13,000.

636.7 US ISSN 0018-6384
HOUNDS AND HUNTING. 1903. m. $14. Hounds and Hunting Publishing Co., Box 372, Bradford, PA 16701. TEL 814-368-6154. FAX 814-368-3522. Ed. Robert F. Slike. adv.; bk.rev.; illus.; circ. 12,000.

636.7 SZ
HUNDE HALTUNG ZUCHT SPORT. 1883. fortn. 81 Fr. (Schweizerischen Kynologischen Gesellschaft) Paul Haupt AG, Falkenplatz 11, CH-3001 Berne, Switzerland. TEL 031-232434. Ed. Hans Raeber. adv.; charts; illus.; circ. 23,000.
    Formerly: Schweizer Hundesport (ISSN 0036-7354)

636.7 DK
HUNDEN. 10/yr. Dansk Kennel Klub, Parkvej 1, Jersie Strand, 2680 Solroed Strand, Denmark. adv.; circ. 27,000.

636.7 NO
HUNDESPORT. m. (10/yr.). Norsk Kennel Klub, Teglverksgate 8, Oslo 5, Norway.

636.7 GW ISSN 0018-7682
DIE HUNDEWELT.* 1928. m. DM.22.20. Minerva-Verlag, Eichenstr. 72, Postfach 100702, 4060 Viersen, Germany. Ed. R. Wadewitz. circ. 47,500.

636.7 SW ISSN 0018-7690
HUNDSPORT. 1887. m. SEK 195. Svenska Kennel Klubben - Swedish Kennel Club, Box 11043, 161 11 Bromma, Sweden. FAX 08-808595. Ed. Torsten Widholm. adv.; bk.rev.; circ. 100,015.

636.7 US ISSN 8750-6629
HUNTING RETRIEVER. 1984. bi-m. $15 membership. United Kennel Club, Inc., 100 E. Kilgore Rd., Kalamazoo, MI 49001. TEL 616-343-9020. FAX 616-343-7037. Ed. Andy Johnson. adv.; bk.rev.; circ. 2,400.
    Description: Official organ of the Hunting Retriever Club, an organization devoted to retriever performance testing.

636.7 362.41 US
I G E NEWS. irreg. free. International Guiding Eyes, 13445 Glenoaks Blvd., Sylmar, CA 91342.
    Formerly: International Guiding Eyes. Newsletter.

636.8 US ISSN 0899-9570
I LOVE CATS. 1988. bi-m. $21. Grass Roots Publishing Co., Inc., 950 Third Ave., 16th Fl., New York, NY 10022. TEL 212-888-1855. circ. 200,000.
    Description: Features information necessary for cat owners to help their cats live healthier and happier lives. Includes proper nutrition, veterinarian advice, dental care and stories about cat lovers and their adventures with cats.

INFO (NORDMAN). see SPORTS AND GAMES — Outdoor Life

636.7 US
IRISH TERRIER CLUB OF AMERICA. NEWSLETTER. 1970. 6/yr. membership. Irish Terrier Club of America, Box 889, Route 2, Scurry, TX 75158. TEL 617-263-2314. Ed. Beth Childers. bk.rev.; circ. 350.

636.7 US
IRISH WATER SPANIEL CLUB OF AMERICA. NEWSLETTER. m. membership only. Irish Water Spaniel Club of America, c/o Susan Tapp, 434 Webster Ave., Washington Township, NJ 07675.

636.7 US ISSN 0164-8675
IRISH WOLFHOUND QUARTERLY. 1978. q. $36. Hoflin Publishing Ltd., 4401 Zephyr St., Wheat Ridge, CO 80033-3299. TEL 303-467-0089. FAX 303-420-1076.

636.752 GW ISSN 0021-3950
DER JAGDSPANIEL. 1907. 6/yr. DM.32. Jagdspaniel-Klub, Trainsjochstr. 6, 8000 Munich 82, Germany. TEL 089-4316172. Ed. Bruno Richter. adv.; charts; illus.; stat.; tr.lit.

JAGTHUNDEN. see SPORTS AND GAMES — Outdoor Life

636 AU ISSN 0022-8117
KAMERAD TIER. 1965. irreg. (4-6/yr.). membership. Tierschutzaktion "der Blaue Kreis", Goldschlagerstr. 15, A-1150 Vienna, Austria. TEL (0222)9218573. Ed. Dr. Kurt Kolar. adv.; bk.rev.; illus. (looseleaf format)

KANARIENFREUND. see BIOLOGY — Ornithology

636.8 GW ISSN 0176-4853
KATZEN EXTRA. 1979. m. DM.70. Symposion Verlag, Wagnerstr. 12, 7300 Esslingen, Germany. TEL 0711-350001. FAX 0711-386766. Ed. H.A. Siegler. circ. 50,000. (back issues avail.)

636.7 US
KEEZETTE. 1976. bi-m? $10. c/o Carol Cash, Ed. & Pub., 15646 Creekwood Ln., Strongsville, OH 44136. adv.

636 UK
KENNEL AND CATTERY MANAGEMENT. 1983. m. £14. Gladeside - Ardent Ltd., P.O. Box 45, Dorking, Surrey RH5 5YZ, England. Ed. Carol Andrews. adv.; bk.rev.; circ. 4,500. (back issues avail.)
    Description: Covers nutrition, hygiene, veterinary advice, breeding, and management.

636.7 UK
KENNEL CLUB YEARBOOK. (Published in three parts) a. £1 for each part. Kennel Club, 1 Clarges Street, Piccadilly, London W1Y 8AB, England. Ed. Charles Colborn. circ. 3,000.

636.7 UK ISSN 0022-9962
KENNEL GAZETTE. 1880. m. £27. Kennel Club, 1 Clarges St., London W1Y 8AB, England. Ed. C. Colborn. adv.; bk.rev.; illus.; circ. 11,000.
    Description: Dog care and breeding.

636.7 US ISSN 0164-4289
SF425.15
KENNEL REVIEW. 1898. 11/yr. $55. B & E Publications, Inc., 11331 Ventura Blvd., Ste. 301, Studio City, CA 91604. TEL 818-761-3647. FAX 818-761-7586. Ed. Rita Davis. adv.; bk.rev.; circ. 8,500. (controlled).

636.7 US
KERRY BLUEPRINTS. q. $15 (foreign $18). United States Kerry Blue Terrier Club, 602 W. Fernwood Dr., Toronto, OH 43964. Ed. JoAnn Custer. adv.; circ. 400.

636.7 FI ISSN 0355-7235
KOIRAMME - VAARA HUNDAR. 1896. 10/yr. FIM 125. Suomen Kennelliitto - Finska Kennelklubben, Kamreerintie 8, 02770 Espoo, Finland. FAX 358-0-8054603. Ed. Oejvind Semenius. adv.; circ. 100,000.

636.7 US
KOMONDOR KOMMENTS. 1971. q. $16. Komondor Club of America, 26036 S.E. 27th St., Issaquah, WA 98027. adv.; circ. 200.

636.7 US
LABRADOR QUARTERLY. q. $36. Hoflin Publishing Ltd., 4401 Zephyr St., Wheat Ridge, CO 80033-3299. TEL 303-467-0089. FAX 303-420-1076.

636.73 UK ISSN 0260-5627
LABRADOR RETRIEVER CLUB OF WALES. YEARBOOK. 1980. a. £2. Labrador Retriever Club of Wales, c/o M. Williams, 6 Dan-y-Felin, Llantrisant, Pontyclun, Mid Glam CF7 8EH, Wales. adv.; bk.rev.; illus.; circ. 500.

636.7 US
LAKELANDER. bi-m. $10. United States Lakeland Terrier Club, 4259 Bear Hollow Trail, Haymarket, VA 22069. circ. 200.

636.7 US ISSN 0273-8333
LHASA APSO REPORTER. 1973. b-m. $36. Kachina Publications, Box 889, Dalzell, SC 29040. TEL 803-499-4664. Ed. Sally Ann Vervaeke-Helf. adv.; bk.rev.; circ. 750.

636.7 US
LHASA BULLETIN.* q. membership. c/o Ann Lanterman, 1746 Bellevue Way N.E., Bellevue, WA 98004. circ. 600.

LIVE ANIMAL TRADE & TRANSPORT MAGAZINE. see *TRANSPORTATION*

LIVESTOCK ADVISER; an English monthly dedicated to improve the animal wealth of India. see *AGRICULTURE — Poultry And Livestock*

636.7   MX
LOS PERROS DEL MUNDO; la revista de la canofilia Mexicana. 1985. m. Mex.$72,000. Publitecnic S.A., Calle 4, no. 188, Box 74-290, C.P. 09070, Mexico 13, D.F., Mexico. TEL 685-28-19. FAX 67-06318. Ed. Fernando Ulacia Esteve. adv.; circ. 10,000 (controlled). (back issues avail.)
   Formerly: Xolo.

636   GW
MAGAZIN DER TIERFREUNDE. 1955. bi-m. free. Zentralverband Zoologischer Fachbetriebe Deutschlands, Fischerfeldstr. 4, 6000 Frankfurt a.M. 1, Germany. Ed. Ivo Baumann. circ. 104,000.

636.7   US
MALAMUTE QUARTERLY. 1982. q. $36. Hoflin Publishing Ltd., 4401 Zephyr St., Wheat Ridge, CO 80033-3299. TEL 303-467-0089. FAX 303-420-1076.

636.7   US
MALTESE MAGAZINE. 4/yr. $28. Reporter Publications, Box 6369, Los Osos, CA 93412. illus.
   Description: News and information of interest to Maltese owners.

636.7   US
MASTIFF JOURNAL.* 1970. q. $25. (Mastiff Club of America) Moore and Ahlers Publishing, c/o Robert Goldblatt, P.O. Box 578, Freedom, CA 95019-0578. Ed. Deborah Ahlers. adv.; bk.rev.; circ. 600.

636.7   US
MATCH SHOW BULLETIN. 1969. m. $20. Myrna Lieber, Ed.& Pub., Box 214, Massapequa, NY 11758. TEL 516-541-3442. FAX 516-541-3442. circ. 6,700. (back issues avail.)
   Description: Lists locations and details of dog shows, seminars, and training classes.

179.3   AU
MENSCH UND TIER. 1910. q. membership. Liga gegen Tierquaelerei und Missbrauch der Tierversuche, Blindengasse 38, A-1080 Vienna, Austria. Ed. J. Koenig. bk.rev.; circ. 16,000.

MERIGAL; a voice for the dingo. see *CONSERVATION*

636.8   US
MORRIS REPORT. 1987. q. $7.50. 9-Lives Cat Food - Hogan Communications, 150 E. Olive Ave., Ste. 208, Burbank, CA 91502. FAX 818-848-4995. adv.; bk.rev.

636.7   US
MUSTARD AND PEPPER. 1973. q. $24. Dandie Dinmont Terrier Club of America, 12109 Piney Glen Ln., Potomac, MD 20854. Ed. Cathy Nelson. circ. 300.

179.3   US
N A C A NEWS. 1978. bi-m. $15. National Animal Control Association, Box 1600, Indianola, WA 98342. TEL 800-828-6474. Ed. Martin Prince. adv.; bk.rev.; film rev.; charts; stat.; tr.lit.; circ. 3,500.

636.7   US
NATIONAL BELGIAN NEWSLETTER. 1953. bi-m. $25. Belgian Sheepdog Club of America, c/o Kimball, 211 W. Elm St., Pembroke, MA 02359. Ed. Terry Coughlin. adv.; bk.rev.; circ. 550.

NATIONAL GREYHOUND NEWS. see *SPORTS AND GAMES*

636   US   ISSN 0028-0267
NATIONAL STOCK DOG. 1954. bi-m. $18. National Stock Dog Registry, Box 402, Butler, IN 46721-0402. TEL 219-868-2670. Ed. J.R. Russell. adv.; abstr.; illus.; circ. 5,000.
   Description: For the preservation and advancement of the livestock working breeds of America and the world.

636.7   US   ISSN 0194-7206
NEWF-TIDE.* 1969? q. $25. Newfoundland Club of America, 61 Ridge Rd., Hopewell, NJ 08525-2606. Eds. Allan Saeger, Peggy Saeger. adv.; bk.rev.; circ. 3,200.

636.7   US
NORSK ELGHUND QUARTERLY. 1979. q. $20. Norsk Elghund Quarterly, 31 Peck St., Rehoboth, MA 02769. adv.; circ. 400.
   Description: Articles on Norwegian Elkhounds.

636.7   179.3   US
NORTHEAST CANINE COMPANION. 1986. m. $18. Companion Publishing Co., Box 357, Sudbury, MA 01776. TEL 508-443-8387. FAX 508-443-0183. Ed. Christine Harris. adv.; bk.rev.; circ. 12,000. (back issues avail.)
   Description: For dog fanciers, especially show dogs.

636.7   US
NORWEGIAN ELKHOUND NEWS. 1975? bi-m. $7. Norwegian Elkhound Association of America, Rt. 9 Box 58B, Jonesboro, AR 72401. Ed. Robin L. Anderson. circ. 600.

636.7   US
NORWICH & NORFOLK NEWS. 1962. s-a. $5. Norwich and Norfolk Terrier Club, c/o Mrs. Susan Elay, Mountain Top Rd., Bernardsville, NJ 07924. bk.rev.; circ. 700.

636   IT   ISSN 0029-3784
NOSTRI CANI. 1955. m. L.20000 (foreign L.40000)(effective 1992). Ente Nazionale della Cinofilia Italiana, Viale Premuda 21, 20129 Milan, Italy. TEL 02-76021706. FAX 02-783127. (Affiliate: Federation Cynologique Internationale) adv.; circ. 75,700.

636.7   US   ISSN 0094-0186 SF431
OFF-LEAD; the dog training monthly. 1972. m. $20. Arner Publications, Inc., 100 Bouck St., Rome, NY 13440. TEL 315-339-2033. Ed. Lorenz D. Arner. adv.; bk.rev.; illus.; stat.; index; circ. 5,000. (back issues avail.; reprint service avail. from UMI)

636.7   US
OLD ENGLISH TIMES. 1972. bi-m. $20. Old English Sheepdog Club of America, Inc., c/o Kathryn Bunnell, Corresponding Sec., 14219 E. 79th St., S., Derby, KS 67037. Ed. Carol Cooke. adv.; bk.rev.; circ. 1,000.

636.7   NE
ONZE BOSTONS. 5/yr. fl.30. Boston Terrier Club Nederland, c/o Spitaal 27, 8602 VR Sneek, Netherlands. Ed. G.B.L. Legtenberg. bk.rev.; circ. 250.

636   DK   ISSN 0106-6714
OPDRAETTERVEJVISEREN. vol.46, 1980. irreg. free. Dansk Kennel Klub, Parkvej 1, Jersie Strand, 2680 Solroed Strand, Denmark. illus.

636.7   US
ORIENT EXPRESS. bi-m. $20. Southern California Chinese Shar Pei Club, 4430 Arista Dr., San Diego, CA 92103.

636.7   US
OUR AFGHANS. 1968. m. $20. Weddle Publications, 22235 Parthenia St., Canoga Park, CA 91304. Ed. Ruth Weddle. adv.; bk.rev.; circ. 1,000.

636.7   UK
OUR DOGS. 1895. w. £96. Our Dogs Publishing Co. Ltd., 5 Oxford Rd., Station Approach, Manchester M60 1SX, England. TEL 061-236-2660. FAX 061-236-5534. Ed. William Moores. adv.; bk.rev.; tr.lit.; circ. 22,000. (tabloid format; back issues avail.)

636.7   US
PEKINGESE CLUB OF AMERICA. BULLETIN. q. Pekingese Club of America, Inc., 3 Carolyn ter., Southboro MA 01772. Ed. Hetty Orringer. circ. 225.

636.7   US
PEKINGESE NEWS.* 1972. 10/yr. $15. Dudgeon Publications, 5100 E, Rosehill Ave., Terre Haute, IN 47805. TEL 812-466-3361. Ed. Mollie Dudgeon. adv.; illus.; circ. 1,000.

636.7   US
PEMBROKE WELSH CORGI CLUB OF AMERICA. NEWSLETTER.* 1967. q. $10. Pembroke Welsh Corgi Club of America, c/o Bryce Beasley, 420 FM 2934, Forney, TX 75126. adv.; bk.rev.; circ. 850.

636   US
PEOPLE, ANIMALS, NATURE. 1983. q. $35 to individuals (foreign $45); libraries $50 (foreign $60). Delta Society, 321 Burnett Ave., S., Third fl., Renton, WA 98055. TEL 206-226-7357. FAX 206-235-1076. (Subscr. to: Box 1080, Renton, WA 98057-1080) Ed. Linda M. Hines. adv.; bk.rev.; circ. 5,000.
   Formerly (until 1992): People, Animals, Environment (ISSN 8755-5875)
   Description: Covers interactions of people, animals, and the nature, animal-assisted therapy, and community people-pet programs.

636.7   US
PEPPER 'N SALT. 1965. 3/yr. $26. Standard Schnauzer Club of America, Rt. 2, Box 208, Galesburg, IL 61401. Eds. John Pazereskis, Dorothy Pazereskis. adv.; circ. 500 (controlled).
   Description: Pictures, advertisements, lists of breeders, dog show results and other available club publications pertaining to the Standard Schnauzer dog species.

636.7   US
PERSIAN QUARTERLY. q. $36. Hoflin Publishing Ltd., 4401 Zephyr St., Wheat Ridge, CO 80033-3299. TEL 303-467-0089. FAX 303-420-1076.

636   US   ISSN 0098-5406
PET AGE. 1971. m. $25. H.H. Backer Associates, Inc., 207 S. Wabash Ave., Ste. 504, Chicago, IL 60604. TEL 312-663-4040. FAX 312-663-5676. Ed. Karen Long MacLeod. adv.; charts, illus.; stat.; index; circ. 18,026. (back issues avail.)

636 658   US   ISSN 0191-4766
PET BUSINESS. 1973. m. $24 (foreign $72). Pet Business of Florida, Inc., 13506 Dallas Ln., Ste. 100, Carmel, IN 46032-9312. TEL 317-571-9007. FAX 317-571-9022. Ed. Karen Payne. adv.; bk.rev.; tr.lit.; circ. 16,000.
   Formerly: Aquarium Industry.

PET BUSINESS WORLD. see *BUSINESS AND ECONOMICS — Small Business*

636   US
PET CARE REPORT. q. Whittle Communications L.P., 333 Main Ave., Knoxville, TN 37902. TEL 615-595-5300. Ed. Anne Krueger.
   Description: Offers tips to owners of small animals. Features include "how-to" articles dealing with specific problems such as pregnancy, disease and immunization, and the needs of special pet breeds.

636   US   ISSN 0553-8572 SF411
PET DEALER. 1952. m. $22. Howmark Publishing Corp., 567 Morris Ave., Elizabeth, NJ 07208. TEL 201-353-7373. FAX 201-353-8221. Ed. Donna Eastman. adv.; circ. 16,100.
   Description: Reaches pet shop retailers with news, information, purchasing guide and surveys.

636   US   ISSN 1046-2112
PET FOCUS; practical information for people who love pets. 1989. bi-m. $30 (Canada & Mexico $40; elsewhere $45). Dermvet, Inc., Box 608, Mesa, AZ 85211-0608. Ed. Dr. Lowell J. Ackerman. bibl.; illus.
   Description: For the layperson, covers pet health issues.

636   UK   ISSN 0262-5849
PET PRODUCT MARKETING; the pet trade journal. 1954. m. £21. Frontline Ltd. (Subsidiary of: E M A P - Haymarket Ltd.), Park House, 117 Park Rd., Peterborough PE1 2TR, England. TEL 0733-555161. FAX 62788. TELEX 329292 FRONT G. Ed. Bob Stonebridge. adv.; bk.rev.; illus.; mkt.; pat.; circ. 4,427. (tabloid format)
   Former titles: Pet Product Marketing and Garden Supplies - The Pet Trade Journal; Pet Trade Journal.

636 US
PET PRODUCT NEWS. 1988. bi-m. $18. Fancy Publications, Inc., Box 6050, Mission Viejo, CA 92690. TEL 714-855-8822. FAX 714-855-3045. adv.; circ. 1,055.
  Description: For pet store operators. Covers industry news, including trade shows, legal issues, corporate takeovers and personnel changes, with emphasis on new products.

636 US
PET STUFF. 1985. bi-m. Tanis Group, Inc., Box 697, Fallbrook, CA 92028-0697. TEL 619-723-3633. FAX 619-723-3638. adv.; tr.lit.; circ. 17,500. (looseleaf format)

PET VETERINARIAN. see *VETERINARY SCIENCE*

PETFOOD INDUSTRY. see *FOOD AND FOOD INDUSTRIES*

636 NE
PETS EUROPE. (Former issuing body: International Pet Trade Organization) (Text in English, French, German) 1980. s-m. fl.98. InterMedium Publishers, P.O. Box 1318, 3800 BH Amersfoort, Netherlands. TEL 33-947672. FAX 33-945886. Ed. Reinder Sterenborg. adv.; bk.rev.; circ. 7,000.
  Formerly (until 1989): I P T O Bulletin.

636 CN ISSN 0715-8947
PETS MAGAZINE. 1985. bi-m. Can.$15($18) Moorshead Publications Ltd., 1300 Don Mills Rd., Toronto, Ont. M3B 3M8, Canada. TEL 416-445-5600. Ed. Marie Hubbs. circ. 60,000.
  Indexed: CMI.
  Description: For the concerned and caring pet owner.

PETS, SUPPLIES, MARKETING. see *BUSINESS AND ECONOMICS — Marketing And Purchasing*

PETS WELCOME; animal lovers' holiday guide. see *TRAVEL AND TOURISM*

636 US
PETTPOURI. q. c/o Andrea Pett, Ed. & Pub., 5907 Cahill Ave., Tarzana, CA 91356-1207. TEL 818-343-1249. circ. 2,500.

636.4 US ISSN 1054-5123
PIG TAIL TIMES. 1989. bi-m. $18. (International Gold Star Pot Belly Pig Register) Kiyoko and Company, Box 1478, Pacifica, CA 94044. TEL 415-738-8659. FAX 415-359-8768. Ed. Kiyoko Hancock. adv.; bk.rev.; illus.; circ. 2,500. (back issues avail.)
  Description: Provides news and information for pot belly pig owners and enthusiasts.

636.7 362.41 US
PILOT DOGS. 1950. q. free. Pilot Light, 625 W. Town St., Columbus, OH 43215.

636.7 US
PIPELINE (ROY). 1976. 3/yr. free to qualified personnel only. Doberman Pinscher Club of America, 29604 24th Ave. S., Roy, WA 98580. Ed. Barbara Gaines. circ. 2,000 (controlled).

636.7 US
POINTER POINTS. q. $8. American Pointer Club, Inc., 1082 Ocean Blvd., Coronado, CA 92118-2801. Ed. Lucy Goodman. circ. 200.

636 NE
POLITIE, DIER EN MILIEU.* 1925. m. fl.30 (effective 1992). B.V. Uitgeverij J.B. van den Brink & Co., Postbus 14, 7240 BA Lochem, Netherlands. TEL 05730-53651. FAX 05730-56724. adv.; bk.rev.; illus.; circ. 15,000.
  Former titles: Politie Dieren- en Milieubescherming; Politie-Dierenbescherming (ISSN 0032-3322)

636.7 US
POMERANIAN REVIEW.* q. $16. American Pomeranian Club, c/o Judy Blocker, 612 Woodrow Ave., Modesto, CA 95350.

636.7 US ISSN 0477-5449
SF429.P85
POODLE REVIEW.* 1955. bi-m. $30 (foreign $35). 2003 E. Illini Airport Rd., Urbana, IL 61801-7561. TEL 217-328-7375. Eds. Del and Sara Dahl. adv.; bk.rev.; illus.; circ. 1,700.
  Description: Dedicated to poodle breeders and those interested in showing their poodles in competitions.

636.7 US ISSN 0882-2816
POODLE VARIETY. 1977. bi-m. $36. Showdogs Publications, Box 30430, Santa Barbara, CA 93130-0430. TEL 805-966-7270. Ed. Bo Bengtson. adv.; bk.rev.; circ. 1,800.
  Description: Informtion and photographs of poodle showdogs.

636.7 US
PORTUGUESE WATER DOG CLUB OF AMERICA. NEWSLETTER. bi-m. Portuguese Water Dog Club of America, c/o Diana H. Metcalf, 243 Cheswold Ln., Haverford, PA 19041.

636 US
▼**POT-BELLIED PIGS;** a journal for breeders & pet owners. 1990. bi-m. $25. Sarnan Publications, Box 853, Ooltewah, TN 37363. Eds. Nancy Cardillo, Sara Oster. adv.; illus.

PRATIQUE MEDICALE ET CHIRURGICALE DE L'ANIMAL DE COMPAGNIE. see *VETERINARY SCIENCE*

636 GW
DER PUDEL SPIEGEL. 1952. q. DM.34.20($20) Verband der Pudelfreunde Deutschland e.V., Dorfstr. 27, Postfach 144, 2055 Wohltorf, Germany. circ. 2,400.

636.7 US
PUG DOG CLUB OF AMERICA. BULLETIN. 1966. q. $10. Pug Dog Club of America, c/o Polly J. Lamarine, 61 Fairfax Ave., Meriden, CT 06450. Ed. Alice Faye Sproul. circ. 410.

636.7 US
PULI NEWS. bi-m. Puli Club of America, c/o Laurel Colton, 655 Amesbury Dr., Dixon, CA 95620.

636 US ISSN 0033-4561
SF421
PURE-BRED DOGS, AMERICAN KENNEL GAZETTE. 1889. m. $24 (foreign $32). American Kennel Club, Inc., 51 Madison Ave., New York, NY 10010. TEL 212-696-8331. FAX 212-696-8299. Ed. Elizabeth Bodner. adv.; bk.rev.; bibl.; illus.; circ. 58,200. (also avail. in microform from UMI; reprint service avail. from UMI)

636 IT
QUATTRO ZAMPE. 1987. m. L.5000 per no. Fabbri Rizzoli Edizioni Periodiche srl, Via Mecenate, 87-6, 20138 Milan, Italy. TEL 02-580841. FAX 02-5062865. Ed. Giovanni Giovannini.

RABBIT GAZETTE. see *AGRICULTURE — Poultry And Livestock*

636.596 UK ISSN 0033-7404
RACING PIGEON PICTORIAL. 1970. m. $35. Racing Pigeon Publishing Co. Ltd., Unit 13, 21 Wren St., London WC1X 0HF, England. TEL 071-833-5959. FAX 071-833-3151. Ed. Colin Osman. adv.; bk.rev.; circ. 10,000.

636.7 US ISSN 0899-1111
RANCH DOG TRAINER. 1986. bi-m. $17. Stonehedge Publishing Co., Inc., Rt. 2, Box 333, W. Plains, MO 65775. FAX 417-256-2801. Ed. Kathleen Conner. adv.; circ. 1,800.
  Description: For the livestock producer who uses the stockdog as a livestock-handling tool.

636 US
RAT AND MOUSE TALES. 1984. bi-m. membership. American Fancy Rat and Mouse Association, 9230 64th St., Riverside, CA 92509. TEL 714-685-2350. Ed. Karen Hause. circ. 200. (back issues avail.)
  Description: Club newsletter with technical, informative, helpful as well as human interest stories, and articles about rats and mice.

636.7 US ISSN 0279-9693
RETRIEVER FIELD TRIAL NEWS. 1964. 10/yr. $40. 4213 S. Howell Ave., Milwaukee, WI 53207. FAX 414-481-2743. (Co-sponsors: National Retriever Club; National Amateur Retriever Club) Ed. Mary C. Knapp. adv.; circ. 3,800.

636.7 US
RHODESIAN RIDGEBACK QUARTERLY. q. $36. Hoflin Publishing Ltd., 4401 Zephyr St., Wheat Ridge, CO 80033-3299. TEL 303-467-0089. FAX 303-420-1076.

636.7 US
RIDGEBACK.* q. Rhodesian Ridgeback Club of the United States, c/o Trish Reynolds, 2589 Rittmer Ln., Seneca Falls, NY 13148. adv.

636.7 US ISSN 1040-8037
ROTTWEILER QUARTERLY. (Text mainly in English; occasionally in German) 1987. q. $30 (effective Jan. 1991). G R Q Publications, 3355 Conant Ln., Watsonville, CA 95076. TEL 408-728-8461. FAX 408-728-4708. (Subscr. to: Box 900, Aromas, CA 95004) Ed. Robin Stark. adv.; circ. 4,000.
  Description: Covers showing, breeding, working, health issues, statistics, training and humor for Rottweiler owners.

636.7 US
SAINT FANCIER. bi-m. membership. Saint Bernard Club of America, c/o Joanne Alstede, RR 5, Box 206, Old Turnpike Rd., Califon, NJ 07830. TEL 201-832-9317. Ed. Robert Bostrom. adv.; circ. 800.

636.7 US
SALUKI CLUB OF AMERICA. NEWSLETTER. q. Saluki Club of America, 3816 E. Waterloo Rd., Akron, OH 44312. circ. 108.

636.7 US ISSN 0194-5297
SALUKI QUARTERLY. 1978. q. $36. Hoflin Publishing Ltd., 4401 Zephyr St., Wheat Ridge, CO 80033-3299. TEL 303-467-0089. FAX 303-420-1076.

636.7 US
SAMOYED QUARTERLY. 1976. q. $36. Hoflin Publishing Ltd., 4401 Zephyr St., Wheat Ridge, CO 80033-3299. TEL 303-467-0089. FAX 303-420-1076.

636.932 US
SATIN NEWS. bi-m. American Satin Rabbit Breeders Association, 2019 N. 13th St., Kansas City, KS 66104. TEL 913-371-4197.

636.7 US
SCHIPPERKE CLUB OF AMERICA. BULLETIN.* q. $7.50 to members; non-members $10. Schipperke Club of America, 1094 Nootka Dr., Fox Island, WA 98333. Ed. Joie Chandler. adv.; circ. 350.

636.7 GW ISSN 0178-2177
SCHOTTISCHE TERRIER GAZETTE. 1985. q. DM.20. Libertas Verlag, Hintere Gasse 35-1, 7032 Sindelfingen, Germany. TEL 07031-81855. FAX 07031-83693. Ed. Claudine Vigouroux. adv.; bk.rev.; circ. 1,300. (back issues avail.)

636.7 US
SETTERS, INCORPORATED. 1975. bi-m. $24. 12 Bay Path Ct., Huntington, NY 11743. Ed. Marilyn Sturz. adv.; bk.rev.; circ. 1,000.
  Formerly: Setters.

636.7 US
SHELTIE INTERNATIONAL. 6/yr. $38. Reporter Publications, Box 6369, Los Osos, CA 93412. illus.
  Description: News and information of interest to Sheltie owners.

636.7 US ISSN 0744-6608
SHELTIE PACESETTER. 1977. bi-m. $39. Sheltie Pacesetter, Box 3310, Palos Verdes, CA 90274-3310. TEL 213-541-7820. Ed. Nancy Lee Marshall. adv.; bk.rev.; circ. 3,600.
  Description: Informative articles and photos on the Sheltie.

636.7 US
SHELTIE PACESETTER TRADE SECRETS BOOK. 1982. quinquennial. $14.50 (foreign $15.50). Sheltie Pacesetter, Box 3310, Palos Verdes, CA 90274-3310. TEL 213-541-7820. Ed. Nancy Lee Marshall.
  Description: 770 hints for the novice or professional owner, trainer or breeder of Shelties; 70 topics are covered.

636 US
SHIH TZU BULLETIN. 1951. q. $30 to non-members. American Shih Tzu Club, Inc., 2500 E. Fender Ave., Fullerton, CA 92631. FAX 714-879-3738. Ed. Bruce Lane. adv.; illus.; circ. 850.

636.7 US
SHIH TZU REPORTER. 1975. bi-m. $36. Reporter Publications, Box 6369, Los Osos, CA 93412.

636.8 US
SIAMESE NEWS QUARTERLY. 1960. q. membership. Siamese Cat Society of America, Inc., Box 1149, Green Valley, AZ 85622. TEL 602-967-4459. (Subscr. to: Z. Kozaczka, 917B S. Acapulco, Tempe AZ 85281) Ed. Shirley Johnson. adv.; bk.rev.; circ. 600.
 Description: Provides Siamese cat owners and breeders with the latest information on breeding, genetics, general care and health problems.

636 US ISSN 0583-1776
SF429.S65
SIBERIAN HUSKY CLUB OF AMERICA NEWSLETTER.* vol. 6, 1972. bi-m. $10. Siberian Husky Club of America, Inc., c/o Ken Gentry, 1408 N.E. Tudor Rd., Lee's Summit, MO 64063. Ed. Debbie Swindlehurst. bk.rev.; charts; illus.; circ. 800.

636.7 US ISSN 0274-7286
SIBERIAN QUARTERLY. 1980. q. $36. Hoflin Publishing Ltd., 4401 Zephyr St., Wheat Ridge, CO 80033-3299. TEL 303-467-0089. FAX 303-420-1076.

636.7 US
SIGHTHOUND REVIEW. 1984. bi-m. $36. Showdogs Publications, Box 30430, Santa Barbara, CA 93130-0430. TEL 805-966-7270. Ed. Bo Bengtson. adv.; bk.rev.; circ. 1,500.
 Description: Information and photographs of the Sighthound-Greyhound breeds.

636.7 US
SILKY TERRIER CLUB OF AMERICA NEWSLETTER. 1953. m. membership. Silky Terrier Club of America, Inc., Box 1132, Alameda, CA 94501-1132. Eds. Shelby Rust, Janet Aslett. bk.rev.; illus.; stat.; circ. 400. (processed)

636.7 US
SILKY TERRIER QUARTERLY. q. $28. Reporter Publications, Box 6369, Los Osos, CA 93412. illus.
 Description: News and information of interest to owners of Silky Terriers.

636 US ISSN 0037-539X
SIMIAN.* 1958. m. $10. Simian Society of America, Inc., 147 School St., Salem, NH 03079-2681. Ed. Barbara E. O'Brien. adv.; bk.rev.; film rev.; bibl.; illus.; index; circ. 3,000.
 Formerly: Monkey Business.

SINGLE PET LOVERS. see SINGLES' INTERESTS AND LIFESTYLES

636.7 US
SKYE TERRIER CLUB OF AMERICA. BULLETIN. q. $17. Skye Terrier Club of America, 12109 Piney Ln., Potomac, CO 20854. Ed. Catherine B. Nelson. adv.; circ. 400.

636.7 US
SPANIELS IN THE FIELD. 1980. q. $28. On the Line, Ltd., 10714 Escondido Dr., Cincinnati, OH 45249. TEL 513-489-2727. adv.; circ. 1,500.
 Former titles: On the Line (Cincinnati) & Springers on the Line.
 Description: Dedicted to the advancement and promotion of all field-bred spaniels.

636.596 GW ISSN 0490-5687
SPORTAUBE. m. DM.25.80. Deutscher Bauernverlag, Reinhardstr. 14, 1040 Berlin, Germany.

636.7 US
SPOTTER. 1971. q. membership only. Dalmatian Club of America, 10119 Charmont, LaPorte, TX 77571. Ed. Tim Robbins. adv.; bk.rev.; circ. 1,000.

636.7 US
STAFFORDSHIRE BULL TERRIER CLUB OF AMERICA. NEWSLETTER.* 3/yr. Staffordshire Bull Terrier Club of America, 5240 Long Island Dr., N.W., Atlanta, GA 30327. adv.

636.7 US
STODGHILL'S ANIMAL RESEARCH FOUNDATION COWDOG MAGAZINE.* 196? m. $12. Stodghill Animal Research Foundation, Box 40, Quinlan, TX 75474-0040. TEL 214-356-2267. Ed. Tom Stodghill.

636 DK ISSN 0039-4165
STUEKULTURER; naturen og hjemmet. 1903. 10/yr. Kr.90. Selskabet for Stuekulturer i Danmark, Buddingevej 244-F, DK-2860 Soeborg, Denmark. Eds. Borge Strandberg, H.-U.C. Laursen. adv.; bk.rev.; film rev.; illus.; circ. 3,000.

636.7 US
TALLY-HO.* bi-m. membership. Basset Hound Club of America, 2009 Adeline Ct., Wayzata, MN 55391. Ed. Sherry Neiberger. circ. 800.

636.7 US
TASSELS AND TAILS. 3/yr. $10. Bedlington Terrier Club of America, 12 Irma Pl., Oceanport, NJ 07757. circ. 330.

636.7 US
TEAM AND TRAIL; the musher's monthly news. 1963. m. $24 Canada $20 (foreign $30). Team & Trail Publishers, Box 128, Center Harbor, NH 03226-0128. TEL 603-253-6265. FAX 603-253-9513. Ed. Cynthia J. Molburg. adv.; bk.rev.; circ. 1,200.
 Description: Provides worldwide sled dog racing news and information on other related events.

636.7 US ISSN 0199-6495
TERRIER TYPE. 1961. 10/yr. $20. Dan Kiedrowski, Ed. & Pub., Drawer A, LaHonda, CA 94020.

636.7 179.31 US
THERAPY DOGS INTERNATIONAL. MINI-NEWSLETTER. 1980. q. Therapy Dogs International, 1536 Morris Pl., Hillside, NJ 07205. circ. 70.

TIDSSKRIFT FOR KANINAVL. see AGRICULTURE — Poultry And Livestock

636.7 AT
▼TOP DOGS. 1992. m. Aus.$24 (foreign Aus.$48). Erinrac Enterprises, Foott Rd., Upper Beaconsfield, Vic. 3808, Australia. TEL 059-44-3383. Ed. Jan Irving. adv.; bk.rev.; illus.; stat.; circ. 2,000.

179.3 US ISSN 0082-5441
TOURING WITH TOWSER. 1948. biennial. $1.50. Quaker Professional Services, Box 9001, Chicago, IL 60604-9001. (Orders to: Quaker Professional Services, 585 Hawthorne Court, Galesburg, IL 61401) Ed. Tom O'Shea. circ. 22,500.

636.7 GW
UNSERE WINDHUNDE. 1983. m. DM.50. Deutscher Windhundzucht- und Rennverbands e.V., Brandenburger Weg 9, 3201 Soehlde 01, Germany. TEL 05129-7341. Ed. August C. Brendel. circ. 4,000.

636 AT
V C A KENNEL GAZETTE. 1932. m. Aus.$50. Victorian Canine Association Inc., Royal Showgrounds, Epsom Rd., Ascot Vale, Vic. 3032, Australia. Ed. Ian R. Hunter. adv.; bk.rev.; circ. 26,000.
 Formerly: K C C Kennel Gazette.

636 AT
VICTORIAN CANINE ASSOCIATION GAZETTE DOGS. 1934. m. free to members. Victorian Canine Association Inc., Royal Showgrounds, Epsom Road, Ascot Vale, Vic. 3032, Australia. TEL 03-376-3733. FAX 03-376-1772. Ed. I.R. Hunter. adv.; bk.rev.; circ. 25,000.
 Formerly: Kennel Control Council Gazette Dogs.
 Description: Lists pure-bred dog shows, trial and performance tests.

636.7 AT
VICTORIAN CANINE ASSOCIATION JOURNAL. 1957. m. membership. Victorian Canine Association Inc., Royal Showgrounds, Epsom Rd., Ascot Vale, Vic. 3032, Australia. TEL 03-376-3733. FAX 03-376-1772. Ed. I. Hunter. adv.; bk.rev.; illus.; stat.; circ. 21,000.
 Formerly: R A S Kennel Control Journal (ISSN 0033-6777)

636.7 US ISSN 0162-315X
WEIMARANER MAGAZINE. 1949. m. $22 to non-members. Weimaraner Club of America, P.O. Box 110708, Nashville, TN 37222-0708. TEL 615-832-9115. Ed. Dorothy Derr. adv.; bk.rev.; film rev.; illus.; circ. 1,800.
 Formerly: Weimaraner (ISSN 0049-710X)

636.7 NE
WELSH SPRINGER. 1976. bi-m. membership. Welsh Springer Spaniel Club, 2e Valthermond 2, 7877 TB Tweede Valthermond, Netherlands. adv.; bk.rev.; circ. 700.

636.7 US
WESTIE IMPRINT. q. $15. West Highland White Terrier Club of America, 604 Arlic St., Richmond, VA 23226. TEL 804-288-7424. Ed. Daphne Gentry. adv.; circ. 900.
 Formerly (until 1985): West Highland White Terrier Club of America. Bulletin.

636.7 US
WHERE TO BUY, BOARD OR TRAIN A DOG. biennial. $1.50. Quaker Professional Services, Box 9001, Chicago, IL 60604-9001. (Orders to: Quaker Professional Services, 585 Hawthorne Court, Galesburg, IL 61401)

636.7 US
WHIPPET NEWS.* m. American Whippet Club, 2300 Hillside Ave., Orange City, FL 32763. circ. 210.

636.7 US
WHIPPET NEWSLETTER. m. $8. 1462 Granger Rd., Medina, OH 44256.

WHO'S WHO IN LIVE ANIMAL TRADE & TRANSPORT. see TRANSPORTATION

635 US
WILD BIRD. m. $2.95 per no. Fancy Publications, Inc., 2401 Beverly Blvd., Los Angeles, CA 90057. TEL 213-385-2222. FAX 213-285-8565.

636.7 US
WINDHOUND. 1981. q. $32. Hoflin Publishing Ltd., 4401 Zephyr St., Wheat Ridge, CO 80033-3299. TEL 303-467-0089. FAX 303-420-1076.

636.7 US
THE WORKING BORDER COLLIE. 1988. 6/yr. $25 (foreign $30). 14933 Kirkwood Rd., Sidney, OH 45365. TEL 513-492-2215. Ed. Casey Fogt. adv.; bk.rev.; illus.; circ. 2,000.
 Description: Helps farmers and ranchers to train stock dogs. For beginners through top handlers.

636.932 IT
WORLD RABBIT SCIENCE ASSOCIATION. NEWSLETTER. q. World Rabbit Science Association, Via A. Torlonia 19, 00161 Rome, Italy. TEL 06-854903. TELEX 613440.

636.7 US
YORKIE EXPRESS. 1951. bi-m. membership. Yorkshire Terrier Club of America, 80 Soundview Avenue, Mattituck, NY 11952. Ed. Dorothy DeMaula. circ. 500.

636.7 GW ISSN 0343-2963
YORKSHIRE TERRIER JOURNAL. 1978. q. DM.20. Libertas Verlag, Hintere Gasse 35-1, 7032 Sindelfingen, Germany. TEL 07031-81855. FAX 07031-83693. Ed. Claudine Vigouroux. adv.; bk.rev.; circ. 2,100. (back issues avail.)

636 GW
ZUCHTBUCH FUER DEUTSCHE SCHAEFERHUNDE. 1901. a. DM.45.90. Verein fuer Deutsche Schaeferhunde, Steinerne Furt 71-71a, 8900 Augsburg 1, Germany. TEL 0821-74002-0. FAX 0821-709298. Ed.Bd. circ. 2,450.

PHARMACY AND PHARMACOLOGY

see also Drug Abuse and Alcoholism

615 378 US
A A C P NEWS. 1972. m. $25. American Association of Colleges of Pharmacy, 1426 Prince St., Alexandria, VA 22314-2815. TEL 703-739-2330. Ed. Jacqueline L. Eng. adv.; bibl.; illus.; circ. 2,500.

615.9 SP
A C O F A R. m. 2000 ptas.($35) (Asociacion de Cooperativas Farmaceuticas) Editorial Garsi, S.A., Londres, 17, 28028 Madrid, Spain. TEL 256-08-00. FAX 361-10-07. Ed. Luis Ayanz. circ. 17,500.

PHARMACY AND PHARMACOLOGY

615.19   US
A D R I D. (Adverse Drug Reactions & Interactions Database) 1965. bi-m. $795. Paul De Haen International, 2750 S. Shoshone St., Englewood, CO 80110. TEL 800-438-0296. FAX 303-789-2534. Ed. Faye N. Richendifer. index. (also avail. in microfiche; back issues avail.)
●Also available online. Vendor(s): DIALOG.
   Formerly: A D R I S.
   Description: Reports of adverse reactions and interactions of international and approved drugs.
Refereed Serial

615.19   US
A I H P NOTES. 1955. q. membership. American Institute of the History of Pharmacy, Pharmacy Bldg., 425 N. Charter St., Madison, WI 53706. TEL 608-262-5635. Ed. Rosemary Zurlo-Cuva. circ. 1,200. (back issues avail.)
   Description: News and information on the history of pharmacy and about activities of the institute.

615.1   US
A P P M UPDATE. 1966. q. membership. (Academy of Pharmacy Practice & Management) American Pharmaceutical Association, 2215 Constitution Ave., N.W., Washington, DC 20037. TEL 202-628-4410. FAX 202-783-2351. Ed. Naomi U. Kaminsky. abstr.; circ. 19,000. (processed)
   Former titles (until 1989): Pharmacy Practice; Academy - G P.

615   US   ISSN 1050-5725
A S C P UPDATE. 1969. m. $24 includes membership. American Society of Consultant Pharmacists, 2300 Ninth St. S., Ste. 515, Arlington, VA 22204. TEL 703-920-8492. FAX 703-486-2997. Ed. Joanne Kaldy. bk.rev.; circ. 5,600. (looseleaf format; back issues avail.)
   Description: News on issues and legislation relevant to members of the American Society of Consultant Pharmacists.

615.1   US   ISSN 0001-2483
A S H P NEWSLETTER. 1968. m. membership. American Society of Hospital Pharmacists, c/o Jean Rogers, Dir., Mkt. Svcs., 4630 Montgomery Ave., Bethesda, MD 20814. TEL 301-657-3000. illus.; circ. 23,000. (reprint service avail. from UMI)
   Description: Contains articles on pharmacy and member news.

615   FR
ACCESSOIREX. (Medical accessories available in pharmacies) 1971. a. (with 11 supplements). 442 F. Societe d'Editions Medico-Pharmaceutiques (SEMP), 26 rue le Brun, 75013 Paris, France. TEL 1-43-37-83-50. FAX 43-31-94-11. TELEX 203046F. circ. 11,000 (controlled). (looseleaf format; also avail. in microfiche)

615.1 370.58   US
ACCREDITED PROFESSIONAL PROGRAMS OF COLLEGES AND SCHOOLS OF PHARMACY. 1940. a. free. American Council on Pharmaceutical Education, 311 W. Superior St., Chicago, IL 60610. TEL 312-664-3575. FAX 312-664-4652. Ed. Dr. Daniel A. Nona. circ. 10,000.
   Formerly: Accredited Colleges of Pharmacy (ISSN 0065-7980)
Refereed Serial

ACTA BIOLOGICA IUGOSLAVICA. SERIJA C: IUGOSLAVICA PHYSIOLOGICA ET PHARMACOLOGICA ACTA. see *BIOLOGY*

615.1   HU   ISSN 0001-6659
                        CODEN: APHGAO
ACTA PHARMACEUTICA HUNGARICA. (Text mainly in Hungarian; occasionally in English; abstracts in English) 1925. bi-m. $38. Magyar Gyogyszereszeti Tarsasag - Hungarian Pharmaceutical Association, Hogyes E. U. 4, 1092 Budapest, Hungary. FAX 1-1473-973. TELEX 22-5067. (Subscr. to: Kultura, Box 149, H-1389 Budapest, Hungary) Ed. Prof. Sandor Gorog. adv.; bk.rev.; charts; illus.; circ. 1,500. Indexed: Anal.Abstr., Biol.Abstr., Biotech.Abstr., Chem.Abstr., Dent.Ind., Excerp.Med., Hort.Abstr., I.P.A., Ind.Med.
●Also available online.
—BLDSC shelfmark: 0645.000000.

615.1   CI   ISSN 0001-6667
                        CODEN: APJUA8
ACTA PHARMACEUTICA JUGOSLAVICA. (Text in English) 1951. q. 40000 din.($40) Savez Farmaceutskih Drustava Jugoslavije - Federation of Yugoslav Pharmaceutical Associations, Masary Kova 2, 41000 Zagreb, Croatia. FAX 041-431-301. Ed. Dr. Franc Kozjek. adv.; bk.rev.; charts; illus.; index, cum.index; circ. 1,000. (reprint service avail. from ISI) Indexed: Anal.Abstr., ASCA, Biol.Abstr., Biotech.Abstr., Bull.Signal., Chem.Abstr., Curr.Adv.Ecol.Sci., Curr.Cont., Excerp.Med., Hort.Abstr., I.P.A., Ind.Sci.Rev., INIS Atomind., Ref.Zh, Sci.Cit.Ind.
●Also available online.
—BLDSC shelfmark: 0646.000000.
   Description: Publishes review articles, original papers and preliminary communications dealing with pharmacy and related fields.

615.1   SW   ISSN 1100-1801
RS1   CODEN: APNOEE
ACTA PHARMACEUTICA NORDICA. (Text and summaries in English) 1938. 4/yr. SEK 600($110) in Nordic countries; elsewhere SEK 700. (Swedish Academy of Pharmaceutical Sciences) Swedish Pharmaceutical Press, P.O. Box 1136, S-111 81 Stockholm, Sweden. TEL 46-08-24-50-80. FAX 46-08-14-95-80. adv.; index; circ. 1,000. Indexed: Biol.Abstr., Biotech.Abstr., I.P.A., INIS Atomind.
—BLDSC shelfmark: 0646.200000.
   Incorporates (1973-1988): Farmaci. Scientific Edition; Which was formerly: Archiv for Pharmaci og Chemi. Scientific Edition (ISSN 0302-248X); Dansk Tiddskrift for Farmaci (ISSN 0011-6513); Former titles: Norwegica Pharmaceutica Acta (ISSN 0800-2606); Norsk Farmaceutisk Selskap. Meddelelser (ISSN 0029-1927)

615.19   TU
ACTA PHARMACEUTICA TURCICA. (Text in English, Turkish; summaries in English) 1954. q. TL.5000($10) Istanbul Universitesi, Eczacilik Facultesi - Istanbul University, Faculty of Pharmacy, Beyazit, Istanbul, Turkey. FAX 1-5221870. Ed. Kasim C. Guven. adv.; circ. 1,125. (back issues avail.) Indexed: Anal.Abstr., Biol.Abstr., Chem.Abstr., I.P.A.
   Formerly: Eczacilik Bulteni.

ACTA PHYSIOLOGICA ET PHARMACOLOGICA BULGARICA. see *BIOLOGY — Physiology*

615.1   PL   ISSN 0001-6837
                        CODEN: APPHAX
ACTA POLONIAE PHARMACEUTICA. (Text in Polish; summaries in English and Russian) 1937. bi-m. (Polskie Towarzystwo Farmaceutyczne) Wydawnictwo Polskiego Towarzystwa Farmaceutycznego, Dluga 16, 00-238 Warsaw, Poland. TEL 31-02-41. Ed. Maksym Nikonorow. charts; illus.; index. Indexed: ASCA, Biol.Abstr., Biotech.Abstr., Chem.Abstr., Curr.Adv.Ecol.Sci., Curr.Chem.React., Excerp.Med., Helminthol.Abstr., Hort.Abstr., I.P.A., Ind.Chem., Ind.Med., Ind.Sci.Rev., INIS Atomind., Nutr.Abstr., Sci.cit.Ind.
—BLDSC shelfmark: 0659.000000.

ACTA TOXICOLOGICA ET THERAPEUTICA; international journal of toxicology, pharmacology and therapy. see *ENVIRONMENTAL STUDIES — Toxicology And Environmental Safety*

615   FR   ISSN 0515-3700
ACTUALITES PHARMACEUTIQUES. 1961. m. 580 F. S.U.T.I.P., 175 rue du Faubourg Poissonniere, 75009 Paris, France. FAX 42-82-98-00. adv. Indexed: Biotech.Abstr., Chem.Abstr., I.P.A., INIS Atomind.
●Also available online.
—BLDSC shelfmark: 0677.324000.
   Supersedes: Officine et Techniques Pharmaceutiques.

615   UK   ISSN 0950-0502
ADRENERGIC RECEPTORS. s-m. £115. Sheffield University Biomedical Information Service (SUBIS), The University, Sheffield S10 2TN, England. TEL 0742-768555. FAX 0742-739826. TELEX 547216-UGSHEF-G.
   Supersedes (in 1987): Catecholamines and Adrenergic Receptors (ISSN 0261-4987)
   Description: Current awareness service for researchers in clinical and life sciences.

615.19   NE   ISSN 0169-409X
                        CODEN: ADDREP
ADVANCED DRUG DELIVERY REVIEWS. (Text in English) 1987. 6/yr.(in 2 vols; 3 nos./vol.). fl.1012 (effective 1992). Elsevier Science Publishers B.V., P.O. Box 211, 1000 BM Amsterdam, Netherlands. TEL 002-5803911. FAX 020-5803598. TELEX 18582 ESPA NL. (Subscr. in U.S. and Canada to: Elsevier Science Publishing Co., Inc., Box 882, Madison Sq. Sta., New York, NY 10159. TEL 212-989-5800) Ed.Bd. adv.; bk.rev.; index. Indexed: Biol.Abstr., Chem.Abstr., Curr.Cont., Excerp.Med.
—BLDSC shelfmark: 0696.845000.
   Description: Publishes critical review articles on current and emerging aspects of research into the design and development of advanced drug delivery systems and their application to experimental and clinical therapeutics.
Refereed Serial

615 616.8   US   ISSN 0065-2229
RM315   CODEN: ABPYBL
ADVANCES IN BIOCHEMICAL PSYCHOPHARMACOLOGY. 1969. irreg., latest vol.46. price varies. Raven Press, 1185 Ave. of the Americas, New York, NY 10036. TEL 212-930-9500. FAX 212-869-3495. TELEX 640073. Eds. E. Costa, P. Greengard. Indexed: Biol.Abstr., Chem.Abstr., Curr.Cont., Ind.Med., Ind.Sci.Rev.
—BLDSC shelfmark: 0699.930000.
Refereed Serial

ADVANCES IN CLINICAL CHEMISTRY. see *BIOLOGY — Biological Chemistry*

615.1   US   ISSN 0065-2490
RS1
ADVANCES IN DRUG RESEARCH. 1964. irreg., vol.19, 1990. Academic Press, Inc., 1250 Sixth Ave., San Diego, CA 92101. TEL 619-231-0926. FAX 619-699-6715. Ed. B. Testa. index. (reprint service avail. from ISI) Indexed: Biol.Abstr., Biotech.Abstr., Ind.Med., Ind.Vet., Vet.Bull.
—BLDSC shelfmark: 0704.300000.
Refereed Serial

615.7   UK   ISSN 0272-068X
RC483   CODEN: AHPSDD
ADVANCES IN HUMAN PSYCHOPHARMACOLOGY; a research annual. 1980. a? $88. Jessica Kingsley Publishers, 118 Pentonville Rd., London N1 9JN, England. TEL 071-833-2307. FAX 071-837-2917. (Dist. in U.S. by: Taylor & Francis, 1900 Frost Rd., Ste. 101, Bristol PA 19007-1598. TEL 215-785-5800) Eds. Graham D. Burrows, John S. Werry. Indexed: Chem.Abstr., Excerp.Med. (1992-), Psychol.Abstr.
Refereed Serial

ADVANCES IN NEUROPSYCHIATRY AND PSYCHOPHARMACOLOGY. see *MEDICAL SCIENCES — Psychiatry And Neurology*

615.19   US
ADVANCES IN PARENTERAL SCIENCES. 1985. irreg., vol.4, 1990. price varies. Marcel Dekker, Inc., 270 Madison Ave., New York, NY 10016. TEL 212-696-9000. FAX 212-685-4540. TELEX 421419. Ed. Joseph R. Robinson.

615   US   ISSN 0065-3136
RS1   CODEN: APHMA8
ADVANCES IN PHARMACEUTICAL SCIENCES. 1964. irreg., vol.5, 1982. Academic Press, Inc., 1250 Sixth Ave., San Diego, CA 92101. TEL 619-231-0926. FAX 619-699-6715. Eds. H.S. Bean, A.H. Beckett. index. (reprint service avail. from ISI) Indexed: Biol.Abstr., Biotech.Abstr., I.P.A., Ind.Med.
●Also available online.
—BLDSC shelfmark: 0709.740000.
Refereed Serial

615.1   US
RM30   CODEN: AVPCAQ
ADVANCES IN PHARMACOLOGY. 1962. irreg., vol.21, 1990. Academic Press, Inc., 1250 Sixth Ave., San Diego, CA 92101. TEL 619-231-0926. FAX 619-699-6715. Ed. S. Garattini. index. (reprint service avail. from ISI) Indexed: Biol.Abstr., Biotech.Abstr., Chem.Abstr., Ind.Med., Ind.Sci.Rev., Ind.Vet., Sci.Cit.Ind, Vet.Bull.
   Former titles (until 1991): Advances in Pharmacology and Chemotherapy (ISSN 0065-3144); Advances in Pharmacology; Advances in Chemotherapy.
Refereed Serial

PHARMACY AND PHARMACOLOGY

ADVERSE DRUG REACTION BULLETIN. see *MEDICAL SCIENCES*

ADVERSE DRUG REACTIONS AND TOXICOLOGICAL REVIEWS. see *MEDICAL SCIENCES*

615   DK   ISSN 0900-3142
AFHAENGING. 1984. q. free. Landsforeningen for Human Narkobehandling, Lundtofteparken 32, 2800 Kgs. Lyngby, Denmark. Ed. P.T. Pedersen.

615   NR   ISSN 0044-6564
                                   CODEN: 002161
AFRICAN JOURNAL OF PHARMACY AND PHARMACEUTICAL SCIENCES. 1970. q. L.5.25($100) African Journal of Pharmacy and Parmaceutical Sciences, 21 Wharf Rd., P.O. Box 399, Apapa, Lagos, Nigeria. Ed. Bode Ladejobi. adv.; bk.rev.; illus.; circ. 40,000. **Indexed:** Excerp.Med., I.P.A.
    Description: Reviews and reports the research and other aspects of those sciences which contribute to the discovery, evaluation and development of medicinal substances.

615   SZ   ISSN 0065-4299
RM1   CODEN: AGACBH
AGENTS AND ACTIONS. (Supplements avail.) (Text in English) 1969. 12/yr. 858 Fr.($585) (European Histamine Research Society) Birkhaeuser Verlag, P.O. Box 133, CH-4010 Basel, Switzerland. TEL 061-737740. FAX 061-737950. TELEX 963475-BIRKH-CH. (Dist. in N. America by: Springer-Verlag New York, Inc., Journal Fulfillment Services, Box 2485, Secaucus, NJ 07096-2491, USA. TEL 201-348-4033) (Co-sponsors: European Workshop on Inflammation; American Inflammation Research Association; British Inflamation Research Association) Ed. K. Brune. index. **Indexed:** Biol.Abstr., Biotech.Abstr., Chem.Abstr., Curr.Adv.Biochem., Curr.Adv.Cancer Res., Curr.Adv.Ecol.Sci., Curr.Cont., Dairy Sci.Abstr., Dent.Ind., Excerp.Med., Helminthol.Abstr., Ind.Med., Ind.Sci.Rev., Nutr.Abstr., Rev.Plant Path., Sci.Cit.Ind.
   —BLDSC shelfmark: 0736.255500.

AGRESSOLOGIE; revue internationale de physiobiologie et de pharmacologie appliquees aux effets de l'agression. see *MEDICAL SCIENCES*

ALKALOIDS; chemistry and pharmacology. see *CHEMISTRY — Organic Chemistry*

615.1   US   ISSN 0002-5690
ALLEGHENY COUNTY PHARMACIST. 1947. m. membership. Allegheny County Pharmaceutical Association, 111 Two Parkway Center, Pittsburgh, PA 15220. TEL 412-922-2440. Ed. Carole F. Ladik. adv.; illus.; circ. 800.

ALTERNATIVE METHODS IN TOXICOLOGY SERIES. see *ENVIRONMENTAL STUDIES — Toxicology And Environmental Safety*

615   US
AMERICAN ASSOCIATION OF COLLEGES OF PHARMACY. (YEAR) PROFILE OF PHARMACY FACULTY. 1980. a. $20. American Association of Colleges of Pharmacy, Office of Academic Affairs, 1426 Prince St., Alexandria, VA 22314-2815. FAX 703-836-8982. Ed. Susan M. Meyer. circ. 2,500.
    Formerly: American Association of Colleges of Pharmacy. Annual Survey of Faculty Salaries.

AMERICAN COLLEGE OF TOXICOLOGY. JOURNAL. PART A. see *ENVIRONMENTAL STUDIES — Toxicology And Environmental Safety*

615.9   US   ISSN 1044-2049
RA1190   CODEN: ATDAEI
AMERICAN COLLEGE OF TOXICOLOGY. JOURNAL. PART B; acute toxicity data. bi-m. $167 (foreign $220); with Part A $280 (foreign $380). Mary Ann Liebert, Inc., 1651 Third Ave., New York, NY 10128. TEL 212-289-2300. FAX 212-289-4697. Ed. Richard A. Parent. cum.index.
   —BLDSC shelfmark: 0678.080000.
    Description: Compilation of experimental data published with brief experimental procedures. Compounds are indexed by chemical names and CAS numbers.

615.1   US   ISSN 0190-5279
RS1   CODEN: AMDREK
AMERICAN DRUGGIST. 1871. m. $36. Hearst Corp., American Druggist, 60 E. 42nd St., No. 449, New York, NY 10165-0449. TEL 212-297-9680. FAX 212-286-9886. Ed. Leonard Gross. adv.; charts; illus.; mkt.stat.; tr.lit.; circ. 84,400. (also avail. in microform from UMI; reprint service avail.)
Indexed: B.P.I., Bus.Ind., Excerp.Med., Hlth.Ind., I.P.A., PROMT, Tr.& Indus.Ind.
●Also available online.
   —BLDSC shelfmark: 0812.900000.
    Formerly: American Druggist Merchandising (ISSN 0090-6638)

615.1   US   ISSN 0364-7471
HD9666.4
AMERICAN DRUGGIST BLUE BOOK. a. $45. Hearst Corp., American Druggist, 60 E. 42nd St., No. 449, New York, NY 10165-0449. TEL 212-297-9680. circ. 60,000.
    Formerly: American Druggist Blue Price Book.

AMERICAN HERB ASSOCIATION NEWSLETTER. see *GARDENING AND HORTICULTURE*

615   US
AMERICAN HOSPITAL FORMULARY SERVICE DRUG INFORMATION. 1959. base vol. (plus 3 supplements/yr.). $95. American Society of Hospital Pharmacists, c/o Jean Rogers, Dir., Mkt. Svcs., 4630 Montgomery Ave., Bethesda, MD 20814. TEL 301-657-3000. Ed. Gerald K. McEvoy. (reprint service avail. from UMI)
●Also available online. Vendor(s): BRS (DIFT), BRS/Saunders Colleague, DIALOG (File no.229), Mead Data Central.
Also available on CD-ROM. Producer(s): University Microfilms International.
    Formerly (until 1984): American Hospital Formulary Service.

615.1   US   ISSN 0002-9289
                                  CODEN: AJHPA9
AMERICAN JOURNAL OF HOSPITAL PHARMACY. 1945. m. $105. American Society of Hospital Pharmacists, c/o Jean Rogers, Dir., Mkt. Svcs., 4630 Montgomery Ave., Bethesda, MD 20814. TEL 301-657-3000. Ed. William A. Zellmer. adv.; bk.rev.; abstr.; bibl.; charts; illus.; tr.lit.; index; circ. 28,000. (also avail. in microform from UMI; back issues avail.; reprint service avail. from ISI,UMI) **Indexed:** Abstr.Health Care Manage.Stud., Abstr.Hosp.Manage.Stud., Biol.Abstr., Biotech.Abstr., Chem.Abstr., CINAHL, Curr.Adv.Ecol.Sci., Curr.Cont., Dairy Sci.Abstr., Excerp.Med., Helminthol.Abstr., Hosp.Lit.Ind., I.P.A., Ind.Med., Ind.Sci.Rev., Med.Care Rev., Nutr.Abstr., Sci.Cit.Ind.
●Also available online.
   —BLDSC shelfmark: 0824.850000.
Refereed Serial

615.1 370   US   ISSN 0002-9459
RS110   CODEN: AJPDAD
AMERICAN JOURNAL OF PHARMACEUTICAL EDUCATION. 1937. 4/yr. $40 to individuals (foreign $65); libraries $100. American Association of Colleges of Pharmacy, 1426 Prince St., Alexandria, VA 22314-2815. TEL 703-739-2330. Ed. George H. Cocolas. bk.rev.; bibl.; charts; illus.; index, cum.index every 10 yrs.; circ. 2,300. (also avail. in microform from UMI,PMC; back issues avail.) **Indexed:** Biol.Abstr., C.I.J.E., Chem.Abstr., Curr.Pg.Educ., Curr.Adv.Ecol.Sci., Curr.Cont., Excerp.Med., High.Educ.Curr.Aware.Bull., Hosp.Lit.Ind., I.P.A., Ind.Sci.Rev., Sci.Cit.Ind.
●Also available online.
   —BLDSC shelfmark: 0830.000000.
Refereed Serial

615.1 614   US   ISSN 0730-7780
                                      CODEN: APSHDH
AMERICAN JOURNAL OF PHARMACY (1981); and the sciences supporting public health. 1825-1980; resumed 1981. q. Philadelphia College of Pharmacy and Science, 43rd St. & Kingsessing Mall, Philadelphia, PA 19104. TEL 215-596-8800. Ed. A.R. Gennaro. adv.; bk.rev.; abstr.; bibl.; charts; illus.; tr.bibl.; index; circ. 2,500. (also avail. in microform from UMI,PMC; reprint service avail. from UMI) **Indexed:** Biol.Abstr., Chem.Abstr., Curr.Cont., Excerp.Med., I.P.A., Ind.Med, Nutr.Abstr.
●Also available online.
   —BLDSC shelfmark: 0831.100000.
    Former titles (until 1980): Pharmacy Management (ISSN 0163-464X); (until 1979): American Journal of Pharmacy and the Sciences Supporting Health (ISSN 0002-9467); American Journal of Pharmacy (ISSN 0093-4712)
Refereed Serial

615.1   US   ISSN 0160-3450
RS1   CODEN: AMPHDF
AMERICAN PHARMACY. 1912. m. $50 to non-members. American Pharmaceutical Association, 2215 Constitution Ave., N.W., Washington, DC 20037. TEL 202-628-4410. Ed. Marlene Bloom. adv.; bk.rev.; charts; illus.; index; circ. 48,800. (also avail. in microform from UMI,PMC) **Indexed:** Biol.Abstr., Chem.Abstr., Curr.Adv.Ecol.Sci., Curr.Cont., Excerp.Med., Helminthol.Abstr., I.P.A., Ind.Med., Med.Care Rev., MEDSOC, Nutr.Abstr.
●Also available online.
   —BLDSC shelfmark: 0850.576000.
    Formerly: American Pharmaceutical Association. Journal (ISSN 0003-0465)
Refereed Serial

615.1   BL   ISSN 0003-2441
RS1   CODEN: AFQUEB
ANAIS DE FARMACIA E QUIMICA DE SAO PAULO. (Text in Portuguese; summaries in English) 1924-1964; resumed 1978. s-a. Sociedade de Farmacia e Quimica de Sao Paulo, Avda. Brigadeiro Luis Antonio 393, 7 andar, CEP 01317, Sao Paulo, Brazil. Ed.Bd. adv.; bk.rev.; cum.index every 10 yrs. (1924-1964); circ. 1,500. **Indexed:** Biol.Abstr., Chem.Abstr., I.P.A., Ind.Med.
●Also available online.
    Formerly (until 1953): Annaes de Sociedade de Pharmacia e Chimica de Sao Paulo (ISSN 0365-7086)
    Description: Presents original research in pharmacology and chemistry.

615.19   US   ISSN 0099-5428
RS189   CODEN: APDSB7
ANALYTICAL PROFILES OF DRUG SUBSTANCES. 1972. irreg., vol.19, 1990. Academic Press, Inc., 1250 Sixth Ave., San Diego, CA 92101. TEL 619-231-0926. FAX 609-699-6715. Ed. Klaus Florey. (reprint service avail. from ISI) **Indexed:** Chem.Abstr.
Refereed Serial

615.1   FR   ISSN 0003-4509
RS1   CODEN: APFRAD
ANNALES PHARMACEUTIQUES FRANCAISES. (Text in French; summaries in English) 1943. bi-m. 185 ECU($215) (typically set in Jan.). (Academie de Pharmacie) Masson, 120 bd. Saint-Germain, 75280 Paris Cedex 06, France.
TEL 1-46-34-21-60. FAX 1-45-87-29-99. TELEX 202 671 F. Ed. G. Deysson. adv.; bk.rev.; illus.; index; circ. 1,000. (reprint service avail. from ISI) **Indexed:** Anal.Abstr., Biol.Abstr., Biotech.Abstr., C.I.S. Abstr., Chem.Abstr., Curr.Adv.Ecol.Sci., Curr.Chem.React., Curr.Cont., Excerp.Med., Helminthol.Abstr., I.P.A., Ind.Chem., Ind.Med., Ind.Sci.Rev., INIS Atomind., Rev.Med.& Vet.Mycol., Sci.Cit.Ind.
●Also available online.
   —BLDSC shelfmark: 0992.000000.

615.1   PL   ISSN 0867-0609
ANNALES UNIVERSITATIS MARIAE CURIE-SKLODOWSKA. SECTIO DDD. PHARMACIA. (Text in English or Polish; summaries in English) 1988. a. price varies. Uniwersytet Marii Curie-Sklodowskiej, Wydawnictwo, Pl. M. Curie-Sklodowskiej 5, 20-031 Lublin, Poland. TEL 48-81-375304. FAX 48-81-336699. TELEX 0643223. Ed. R. Langwinski. circ. 600.

615 FR ISSN 0396-0625
ANNUAIRE DES FOURNISSEURS DE LABORATOIRES PHARMACEUTIQUES ET COSMETIQUES. vol.2, 1976. a. Agence de Diffusion et de Publicite, 24 Place du General Catroux, 75017 Paris, France.
Formerly: Annuaire des Fournisseurs de Laboratoires Pharmaceutiques (ISSN 0517-8991)

ANNUAIRE FOURNI-LABO PHARMACIE (YEAR); cosmetique et alimentaire. see BUSINESS AND ECONOMICS — Trade And Industrial Directories

615.19 UK ISSN 0260-955X
ANNUAL REGISTER OF PHARMACEUTICAL CHEMISTS. 1869. a. £65. Royal Pharmaceutical Society of Great Britain, 1 Lambeth High St., London SE1 7JN, England. TEL 071-735-9141. index; circ. 1,000.
Description: Contains an alphabetical list of names and addresses of all registered pharmacists; corporate bodies operating retail pharmacy businesses with the names of their superintendents; and the business titles and addresses of all registered retail pharmacies in country, county and town order.

615.1 US ISSN 0065-7743
RS402 CODEN: ARMCBI
ANNUAL REPORTS IN MEDICINAL CHEMISTRY. 1966. irreg., vol.25, 1990. (American Chemical Society, Division of Medicinal Chemistry) Academic Press, Inc., 1250 Sixth Ave., San Diego, CA 92101. TEL 619-231-0926. FAX 619-699-6715. Ed. Denis M. Bailey. (reprint service avail. from ISI) **Indexed:** Biol.Abstr., Chem.Abstr., Curr.Cont., Dairy Sci.Abstr., Ind.Sci.Rev., Sci.Cit.Ind.
—BLDSC shelfmark: 1513.050000.
Refereed Serial

651 US ISSN 0743-9539
RS201.C64 CODEN: ANRCEI
ANNUAL REVIEW OF CHRONOPHARMACOLOGY.* 1984. a. price varies. Raven Press, 1185 Ave. of the Americas, New York, NY 10036. TEL 212-930-9500. FAX 212-869-3495. TELEX 640073. Ed. Dr. Michael Smolensky. adv. (also avail. in microform from MIM,UMI) **Indexed:** Curr.Adv.Ecol.Sci., Curr.Cont., Excerp.Med.
—BLDSC shelfmark: 1522.230000.
Refereed Serial

615.1 US ISSN 0362-1642
RM16 CODEN: ARPTDI
ANNUAL REVIEW OF PHARMACOLOGY AND TOXICOLOGY. 1961. a. $44 (foreign $49)(effective Jan. 1992). Annual Reviews Inc., 4139 El Camino Way, Box 10139, Palo Alto, CA 94303-0897. TEL 415-493-4400. FAX 415-855-9815. TELEX 910-290-0275. Ed. Arthur K. Cho. bibl.; index, cum.index. (also avail. in microfilm from PMC; back issues avail.; reprint service avail. from ISI) **Indexed:** Biol.Abstr., Biotech.Abstr., Chem.Abstr., Curr.Adv.Ecol.Sci., Curr.Cont., Excerp.Med., Helminthol.Abstr., Ind.Med., Ind.Sci.Rev., Ind.Vet., M.M.R.I., Psychol.Abstr., Sci.Cit.Ind., Vet.Bull.
Formerly: Annual Review of Pharmacology (ISSN 0066-4251)
Description: Original reviews of critical literature and current developments in pharmacology and toxicology.
Refereed Serial

615.1 SZ ISSN 0066-4758
RM260 CODEN: ANBCB3
ANTIBIOTICS AND CHEMOTHERAPY. (Text in English) 1954. irreg. (approx. 1/yr.). price varies. S. Karger AG, Allschwilerstr. 10, P.O. Box, CH-4009 Basel, Switzerland. TEL 061-3061111. FAX 061-3061234. TELEX CH 962652. Ed. H. Schoenfeld. (reprint service avail. from ISI) **Indexed:** Biol.Abstr., Chem.Abstr., Curr.Adv.Ecol.Sci., Curr.Cont., Ind.Med.
—BLDSC shelfmark: 1546.980000.

615.329 RU ISSN 0235-2990
RM265 CODEN: ANKHEW
ANTIBIOTIKI I KHIMIOTERAPIYA/ANTIBIOTICS AND CHEMOTERAPY. 1956. m. 40.80 Rub.($21) (Ministerstvo Meditsinskoi Promyshlennosti, Nauchnoe Obshchestvo "Antibiotiki") Izdatel'stvo Meditsina, Petroverigskii pereulok 6-8, 101838 Moscow, Russia. Ed. S.M. Navashin. **Indexed:** Anal.Abstr., Biol.Abstr., Biotech.Abstr., Chem.Abstr., Curr.Biotech.Abstr., Curr.Chem.React., Curr.Cont., Dairy Sci.Abstr., Excerp.Med., Helminthol.Abstr., Ind.Chem., Ind.Med., Ind.Sci.Rev., Nutr.Abstr., Rev.Med.& Vet.Mycol., Rev.Plant Path., Sci.Cit.Ind.
—BLDSC shelfmark: 0007.013000.
Former titles: Antibiotiki i Meditsinskaya Biotekhnologiya (ISSN 0233-7525); Antibiotiki (ISSN 0003-5637)
Description: Covers research and chemical transformation of antibiotics, relation between structure and function, experimental and clinical antibiotic therapy, molecular mechanisms of action of antimicrobial antibiotics, antibiotic resistance mechanisms, antitumour, and more.

ANTIBODY, IMMUNOCONJUGATES, AND RADIOPHARMACEUTICALS. see MEDICAL SCIENCES — Cancer

ANTIMICROBIAL AGENTS AND CHEMOTHERAPY. see BIOLOGY — Microbiology

615 UK ISSN 0956-3202
CODEN: ACCHEH
▼**ANTIVIRAL CHEMISTRY & CHEMOTHERAPY.** 1990. bi-m. £109.50 (foreign £132). Blackwell Scientific Publications Ltd., Osney Mead, Oxford OX2 0EL, England. TEL 0865-240201. FAX 0865-721205. TELEX 833355-MEDBOK-G. Eds. J.F. Oxford, K. Broadhurst. adv.; bk.rev.; illus.; index. (back issues avail.)
—BLDSC shelfmark: 1552.828000.

615.19 NO
APOTEK - TEKNIKEREN. 1938. m. (11/yr.). NOK 200. Norsk Apotekerforbund, Snorresgate 10, Oslo 1, Norway. adv.; bk.rev.; circ. 1,931.

615.19 SW
APOTEKSTJAENSTEMANNEN. 1931. m. (11/yr.). SEK 250. Apotekstjaenstemannafoerbundet, Vaestmannagatan 66, 113 25 Stockholm, Sweden. FAX 08-342147. Ed. Anita Westin-Jameson. adv.; circ. 7,856.
Formerly (until 1983): Apotekstekniker.

615.1 US ISSN 0003-6560
APOTHECARY; the business journal for pharmacy. 1888. 6/yr. $18 (free to qualified personnel). (Massachusetts College of Pharmacy and Allied Health Sciences) Health Care Marketing Services, H C M S Inc., Box AP, Los Altos, CA 94023-0179. FAX 415-941-2303. Ed. Jerold K. Karabensh. adv.; bk.rev.; charts; illus.; index; circ. 67,335 (controlled). (also avail. in microform from UMI; reprint service avail. from UMI) **Indexed:** I.P.A.
●Also available online.
Incorporates: Mid-Atlantic Apothecary (ISSN 0026-2943)
Refereed Serial

135 GW ISSN 0173-1882
APOTHEKE HEUTE. (Supplement to: Deutsche Apotheker Zeitung) 1950. q. DM.13.60 free with subscr. to Deutsche Apotheker Zeitung. Deutscher Apotheker Verlag, Postfach 101061, 7000 Stuttgart 10, Germany. TEL 0711-2582-0. FAX 0711-2582290. TELEX 723636-DAZ-D. Ed. Peter Ditzel.
Former titles: Das Schaufenster (Stuttgart) (ISSN 0173-2110) & Aktuelle Schaufenster (ISSN 0568-7632)
Description: Explores store window-dressing and advertising in pharmacies.

615.19 GW ISSN 0177-9591
APOTHEKE UND KRANKENHAUS. 1985. q. DM.44. (Bundesverband Krankenhausversorgender Apotheker e.V.) Deutscher Apotheker Verlag, Postfach 101061, 7000 Stuttgart 10, Germany. TEL 0711-25820. FAX 0711-2582290. TELEX 723636-DAZ-D. Ed. Dieter Steinbach. circ. 2,000.
Description: For hospital pharmacists.

615.19 GW
APOTHEKEN KURIER. 1985. m. Pharma-Kurier Verlag GmbH, Borsigstr. 1-3, D-6056 Heusenstamm, Germany. TEL 06104-6060. FAX 06104-606117. TELEX 410131.

615 GW ISSN 0939-3331
APOTHEKENHELFERIN HEUTE. (Supplement to: Deutsche Apotheker Zeitung) 1952. 6/yr. DM.16.20 free with subscr. to Deutsche Apotheker Zeitung. Deutscher Apotheker Verlag, Postfach 101061, 7000 Stuttgart 10, Germany. TEL 0711-2582-0. FAX 0711-2582290. TELEX 723636-DAZ-D. Ed. Michael Schmidt.
Formerly: Die Apothekenhelferin (ISSN 0570-4723)
Description: Aimed at enlightening pharmaceutical assistants.

615.1 GW ISSN 0066-5347
APOTHEKER - JAHRBUCH. 1915. a. price varies. (Deutscher Apotheker Verein) Wissenschaftliche Verlagsgesellschaft mbH, Postfach 105339, 7000 Stuttgart 10, Germany. TEL 0711-2582-0. FAX 0711-2582-290. TELEX 723636-DAZD. Ed.Bd. adv.; index.; cum.index.
—BLDSC shelfmark: 1568.914300.
Description: Focuses on new pharmaceutical laws and decrees, jurisdiction, statistical data and important addresses.

615.19 GW ISSN 0720-1028
APOTHEKER JOURNAL; Magazin aus Wissenschaft und Praxis. 1979. m. DM.72. Otto Hoffmanns Verlag GmbH, Platenstr. 6, 8000 Munich 2, Germany. Ed. Helmut Becker. adv.; bk.rev.; circ. 17,800.

615 GW
APOTHEKERKAMMER NIEDERSACHSEN. MITTEILUNGSBLATT. 1947. m. DM.61.60. Verlag Fritz Eberlein GmbH, Kestnerstr. 44, 3000 Hannover 1, Germany. TEL 0511-810592. circ. 4,800.

615.1 BE ISSN 0003-6579
APOTHEKERSBLAD. 1950. m. 2381 Fr.($16) (foreign 2846 Fr.). Algemene Pharmaceutische Bond, Archimedesstraat 11, Brussels 1040, Belgium. FAX 02-2306681. TELEX 61833APBB. Ed. D. Broeckx. adv.; bk.rev.; index; circ. 4,000. **Indexed:** I.P.A.
—BLDSC shelfmark: 1568.950000.

615.7 US
APPROVED DRUG PRODUCTS WITH THERAPEUTIC EQUIVALENCE EVALUATIONS. q. $800 in US, Canada, Mexico; elsewhere $1600. (Department of Health and Human Services, Food and Drug Administration) U.S. National Technical Information Service, 5825 Port Royal Rd., Springfield, VA 22161. TEL 703-487-4630. (magnetic tape)
Description: Contains information required to identify a particular drug product. Includes NDA and ANDA number for each entry.

615.1 GR ISSN 0003-8148
ARCHEIA TES PHARMAKEUTIKES (ATHENS). (Text in English, French and Greek) 1932. irreg. Dr.150($3) Greek Pharmaceutical Society, Emm. Benakis 30, Athens 10678, Greece. Ed. N.H. Choulis. adv.; bk.rev.; bibl.; charts; illus.; index; circ. 1,000. **Indexed:** Biol.Abstr., Chem.Abstr.

615.1 GW ISSN 0365-6233
CODEN: ARPMAS
ARCHIV DER PHARMAZIE. (Text in English, German) 1822. m. DM.618($315) (Deutsche Pharmazeutische Gesellschaft, GW) V C H Verlagsgesellschaft mbH, Postfach 101161, 6940 Weinheim, Germany. TEL 06201-602-0. FAX 06201-602328. TELEX 465516-VCHWH-D. (US addr.: V C H Publishers, Inc., 220 E. 23rd St., New York, NY 10010-4606. TEL 212-683-8333) Ed. W. Wiegrebe. adv.; bk.rev.; charts; illus.; index; circ. 940. (also avail. in microfilm from VCl; microfiche from BHP; reprint service avail. from ISI) **Indexed:** Anal.Abstr., Biol.Abstr., Chem.Abstr., Crop Physiol.Abstr., Curr.Adv.Ecol.Sci., Curr.Chem.React., Excerp.Med., Helminthol.Abstr., Hort.Abstr., I.P.A., Ind.Chem., Ind.Med., Ind.Sci.Rev., Mass Spectr.Bull., Protozool.Abstr., Sci.Cit.Ind.
—BLDSC shelfmark: 1622.800000.

PHARMACY AND PHARMACOLOGY

615.1   BE   ISSN 0003-9780
CODEN: AIPTAK
ARCHIVES INTERNATIONALES DE PHARMACODYNAMIE ET DE THERAPIE/INTERNATIONAL ARCHIVES OF PHARMACOLOGY. (Text in English) 1894. bi-m. 8000 Fr.($240) (effective 1992). Heymans Institute of Pharmacology, De Pintelaan 185, B-9000 Ghent, Belgium. FAX 32-91-40-49-88. Ed.Bd. bk.rev.; charts; circ. 1,000. (also avail. in microfilm from PMC) **Indexed:** Anim.Breed.Abstr., Biol.Abstr., Biotech.Abstr., Chem.Abstr., Curr.Adv.Ecol.Sci., Curr.Chem.React., Curr.Cont., Dairy Sci.Abstr., Excerp.Med., Helminthol.Abstr., I.P.A., Ind.Chem., Ind.Med., Ind.Sci.Rev., Ind.Vet., Pig News & Info., Sci.Cit.Ind., Vet.Bull.
—BLDSC shelfmark: 1636.000000.

615   KO   ISSN 0253-6269
CODEN: APHRDQ
ARCHIVES OF PHARMACAL RESEARCH. (Text in English) 1978. s-a. $30. Pharmaceutical Society of Korea, c/o Natural Products Research Institute, Seoul National University, Seoul 110-460, S. Korea. Ed. Eun Bang Lee. circ. 1,300. (back issues avail.) **Indexed:** Biol.Abstr., Chem.Abstr., Ind.Med.
—BLDSC shelfmark: 1638.975000.

615.9   GW   ISSN 0340-5761
CODEN: ARTODN
ARCHIVES OF TOXICOLOGY. 1930. 10/yr. DM.1458($850) (effective 1992). (Deutsche Pharmakologische Gesellschaft) Springer-Verlag, Heidelberger Platz 3, 1000 Berlin 33, Germany. TEL 030-8207-1. (Also Heidelberg, Tokyo, Vienna, and New York) (Co-sponsor: Deutsche Gesellschaft fuer Rechtsmedizin) Ed. H.M. Bolt. adv.; bibl.; charts; illus. (also avail. in microform from UMI; back issues avail.; reprint service avail. from ISI) **Indexed:** Biol.Abstr., Biotech.Abstr., C.I.S. Abstr., Chem.Abstr., Curr.Adv.Ecol.Sci., Curr.Cont., Dairy Sci.Abstr., Dent.Ind., Dok.Arbeitsmed., Excerp.Med., Helminthol.Abstr., Ind.Med., Ind.Sci.Rev., Ind.Vet., INIS Atomind., Lab.Haz.Bull., Nutr.Abstr., Pollut.Abstr., Protozool.Abstr., Rev.Med.& Vet.Mycol., Sci.Cit.Ind., Vet.Bull.
—BLDSC shelfmark: 1643.510000.
Former titles: Archiv fuer Toxikologie (ISSN 0003-9446); Fuehner-Wieland's Sammlung von Vergiftungsfaellen.

615.9   GW   ISSN 0171-9750
RA1190   CODEN: ATSUDG
ARCHIVES OF TOXICOLOGY. SUPPLEMENT. 1978. irreg., vol.10, 1987. price varies. Springer-Verlag, Heidelberger Platz 3, D-1000 Berlin 33, Germany. TEL 030-8207-1. (Also Heidelberg, Tokyo, Vienna, and New York) (also avail. in microfilm from UMI; reprint service avail. from ISI) **Indexed:** Chem.Abstr., Dent.Ind., Ind.Med., NRN, Nutr.Abstr.

615.1   SP   ISSN 0304-8616
CODEN: AFTOD7
ARCHIVOS DE FARMACOLOGIA Y TOXICOLOGIA. 1949. irreg. (about 3/yr.). 2120 ptas.($35) Universidad Complutense de Madrid, Facultad de Medicina, Departamento Coordinado de Farmacologia, Pabellon, Madrid 3, Spain. **Indexed:** Biol.Abstr., Chem.Abstr., Excerp.Med., Ind.Med.Esp., Ind.Med., Ind.SST.
—BLDSC shelfmark: 1655.020000.
Formerly (until 1975): Spain. Consejo Superior de Investigaciones Cientificas. Instituto de Farmacologia Experimental. Archivos (ISSN 0024-9629)

615.1   FR   ISSN 0004-1203
ARGUS DES PHARMACIENS;* journal professionnel et documentaire. 1927. s-m. 24. F. 26 rue Brey, Paris (17), France.

615.328 615.7   LE
ARGUS PHARMA REPORT. (Text in English) m. $270. Bureau of Lebanese and Arab Documentation, P.O. Box 165403, Beirut, Lebanon. (Subscr. to: Bureau of Lebanese and Arab Documentation, c/o Marcel Tawil, Postfach 2412, 7850 Loerrach, Germany)
Description: Report on health care projects in the Arab countries.

615.1   YU   ISSN 0004-1963
ARHIV ZA FARMACIJU. (Text in Serbo-Croatian; summaries in English, French, German or Russian) 1951. 6/yr. 60 din.($23.70) Farmaceutsko Drustvo Srbije, Terazije 12, Box 664, Belgrade, Yugoslavia. adv.; bk.rev.; abstr.; bibl.; charts; illus.; index. **Indexed:** Biol.Abstr., Chem.Abstr., Hort.Abstr., I.P.A.
●Also available online.
—BLDSC shelfmark: 0009.900000.

ARHIV ZA HIGIJENU RADA I TOKSIKOLOGIJU/ARCHIVES OF INDUSTRIAL HYGIENE AND TOXICOLOGY. see *ENVIRONMENTAL STUDIES — Toxicology And Environmental Safety*

615.1   US
ARIZONA PHARMACIST.* 1947. m. $15 to non-members. (Arizona Pharmaceutical Association) State Pharmaceutical Editorial Association, 223 W. Jackson Blvd., No. 1000, Chicago, IL 60606-6906. TEL 602-258-8121. Ed. Warren Ellison. adv.; illus.; circ. 1,300.
Former titles: New Arizona Pharmacist; Arizona Pharmacist (ISSN 0004-1602)

615.9 610   US
ARIZONA POISON CONTROL SYSTEM NEWSLETTER. 1980. q. free. Arizona Poison Control System, University of Arizona, College of Pharmacy, Tucson, AZ 85721. TEL 602-626-7899, FAX 602-626-4063. Ed. Dr. Theodore G. Tong. circ. 3,000. (tabloid format)
Description: Updates and reviews about clinical toxicology and poisonings, for physicians, pharmacists and pharmacologists.

615.1   SP   ISSN 0004-2927
CODEN: APHRAN
ARS PHARMACEUTICA. (Text in Spanish; summaries in English) 1960. 4/yr. 3650 ptas. Universidad de Granada, Facultad de Farmacia, Servicio de Publicaciones, Antiguo Colegio Maximo, Campus de Cartuja, 18071 Granada, Spain. TEL 281356. Ed. Jesus Cabo Torres. adv.; bk.rev.; bibl.; charts; illus.; index; circ. 1,000. **Indexed:** Biol.Abstr., Chem.Abstr., Excerp.Med., I.P.A., Ind.Med.Esp., Ind.SST.
●Also available online.
—BLDSC shelfmark: 1697.700000.

ARTERE. see *HOSPITALS*

615   GW   ISSN 0066-8192
ARZNEI-TELEGRAMM. 1970. m. DM.75 individuals; institutions DM.139. Arzneimittel Information Berlin GmbH (A.T.I.), Petzower Str. 7, 1000 Berlin 39, Germany. TEL 030-8054044. FAX 030-8054203. Ed. U.M. Moebius. bk.rev.; circ. 29,000.

615.1   GW   ISSN 0004-4172
RM301.25   CODEN: ARZNAD
ARZNEIMITTEL-FORSCHUNG/DRUG RESEARCH. (Text in English and German) 1951. m. DM.490. Editio Cantor, Postfach 1255, 7960 Aulendorf, Germany. TEL 07525-2060. FAX 07525-20680. Eds. H.G. Classen, V. Schramm. adv.; bk.rev.; charts; illus.; tr.lit.; index; circ. 5,200. (reprint service avail. from ISA) **Indexed:** Anal.Abstr., Biol.Abstr., Biotech.Abstr., Chem.Abstr., Chem.Infd., Curr.Adv.Biochem., Curr.Adv.Cancer Res., Curr.Adv.Cell & Devel.Biol., Curr.Adv.Ecol.Sci., Curr.Adv.Genetics & Molec.Biol., Curr.Biotech.Abstr., Curr.Cont., Dairy Sci.Abstr., Dent.Ind., Excerp.Med., Helminthol.Abstr., I.P.A., Ind.Chem., Ind.Med., Ind.Sci.Rev., Ind.Vet., INIS Atomind., Mass Spectr.Bull, Nutr.Abstr., Protozool.Abstr., Rev.Plant Path., Sci.Cit.Ind., Vet.Bull.
●Also available online.
—BLDSC shelfmark: 1738.000000.

615.19   GW   ISSN 0935-2767
ARZNEIMITTEL ZEITUNG. 1988. fortn. DM.90. Aerzte Zeitung Verlags GmbH, Am Forsthaus Gravenbruch 5, 6078 Neu-Isenburg 2, Germany. TEL 06102-5060. FAX 06102-5870. Ed. Dieter Eschenbach. adv.; bk.rev.; circ. 8,000.
Description: Information for employers in the pharmaceutical industry.

615   GW
DER ARZNEIMITTELBRIEF; unabhaengiges Informationsblatt fuer den Arzt. 1967. m. DM.69. Westkreuz Druckerei und Verlag, Toepchiner Weg 198-200, 1000 Berlin 49, Germany. Ed.Bd.

615.19   GW   ISSN 0723-6913
ARZNEIMITTELTHERAPIE. 1983. m. DM.36 (students DM.24). Wissenschaftliche Verlagsgesellschaft mbH, Postfach 105339, 7000 Stuttgart 1, Germany. TEL 0711-2582-0. FAX 0711-2582290. Ed.Bd. adv.; bk.rev.; circ. 16,600. **Indexed:** Chem.Abstr.
—BLDSC shelfmark: 1738.120000.

615.19   SI   ISSN 0217-9687
CODEN: APJPEV
ASIA PACIFIC JOURNAL OF PHARMACOLOGY. 4/yr. S.$250 (renewal S$160). Singapore University Press Pte. Ltd., 10 Kent Ridge Crescent, Singapore 0511, Singapore. TEL 7761148. FAX 7740652. TELEX RS-55370-SKAT.
—BLDSC shelfmark: 1742.260800.
Description: Covers all aspects of experimental and clinical research on synthetic and natural drugs.

615.1   CN   ISSN 0066-9555
ASSOCIATION OF FACULTIES OF PHARMACY OF CANADA. PROCEEDINGS. 1970. a. Can.$10 to non-members. Association of Faculties of Pharmacy, Faculty of Pharmaceutical Sciences, University of British Columbia, Vancouver, B.C. V6T 1Z3, Canada. FAX 604-822-4451. Ed. K.M. McErlane. circ. 200.
Formerly (until vol.26, 1969): Canadian Conference of Pharmaceutical Faculties. Proceedings.

ATRIAL NATRIURETIC FACTORS. see *MEDICAL SCIENCES — Endocrinology*

617.7   SP   ISSN 0213-9014
AUDIOPTICA. 1987. q. 3700 ptas.($50) (Asociacion de Farmaceuticos Especialistas en Optica, Optometria y Audiologia Protesica) Editorial Garsi, S.A., Londres, 17, 28028 Madrid, Spain. TEL 256-08-00. FAX 361-10-07. Ed. Vicente Vilas Sanchez. circ. 3,000.

615   AT   ISSN 0706-3202
AUSTRALIAN INSTITUTE OF PHARMACY MANAGEMENT NEWSLETTER. 1981. bi-m. free to members. Pharmacy Guild of Australia, P.O. Box 36, Deakin, A.C.T. 2600, Australia. TEL 062 81-0911. FAX 062-824745. Ed. Ewan D. Brown. circ. 5,000.

615   AT   ISSN 0310-6810
CODEN: AUHPAI
AUSTRALIAN JOURNAL OF HOSPITAL PHARMACY. 1966. bi-m. Aus.$75 (foreign Aus.$85). Society of Hospital Pharmacists of Australia, Ste. 2, 31 Coventry St., South Melbourne, Vic. 3205, Australia. TEL 03-690-6733. FAX 03-696-7634. Ed. A. Paul Hargreaves. adv.: B&W page Aus.$930, color page Aus.$1,425; trim 272 x 206. bk.rev.; abstr.; illus.; stat.; circ. 2,100. **Indexed:** Biol.Abstr., Chem.Abstr., Excerp.Med., I.P.A.
—BLDSC shelfmark: 1808.700000.
Description: The AJHP aims to assist the development of the practice of hospital pharmacy in Australia.

615.1   AT   ISSN 0004-8399
AUSTRALIAN JOURNAL OF PHARMACY. 1886. m. Aus.$69. Australian Pharmaceutical Publishing Co. Ltd., 40 Burwood Rd., Hawthorn , Vic. 3122, Australia. TEL 03-810-98700. FAX 03-819-1706. Ed. Stuart Dickson. adv.; bk.rev.; illus.; mkt.; index; circ. 7,600. (also avail. in microfilm from UMI; back issues avail.) **Indexed:** Aus.Sci.Ind., Biol.Abstr., Biotech.Abstr., Chem.Abstr., Excerp.Med., I.P.A.

615   AT   ISSN 0728-4632
AUSTRALIAN PHARMACIST. 1982. 6/yr. Aus.$46 (typically set Jan.). Pharmaceutical Society of Australia, P.O. Box 21, Curtin, A.C.T. 2605, Australia. FAX 61-6-2854869. Ed. W.J. Kelly. adv.; bk.rev.; circ. 10,021.
—BLDSC shelfmark: 1817.685000.
Description: Contains news and information, therapeutic management reviews, promotional and advertising material, continuing education material.

AUSTRALIAN PHYSIOLOGICAL AND PHARMACOLOGICAL SOCIETY. PROCEEDINGS. see *BIOLOGY — Physiology*

615   AT   ISSN 0312-8008
AUSTRALIAN PRESCRIBER. 1975. q. free. Commonwealth Department of Community Health, Housing and Services, P.O. Box 100, Woden, A.C.T. 2606, Australia. TEL 06-289-7038. circ. 68,000 (controlled).
—BLDSC shelfmark: 1818.260000.
Formerly: Prescriber's Journal (ISSN 0085-5103)

615.19   US
AZOAN.* 1923. a. free. Alpha Zeta Omega Pharmaceutical Fraternity, c/o Coleman Levin, 9026 Germantown Ave., Philadelphia, PA 19113-2702. circ. 2,000. (back issues avail.)
Description: Fraternity news, officers' reports, chapter reports, and professional articles.

PHARMACY AND PHARMACOLOGY

615   BF
BAHAMAS PHARMACEUTICAL ASSOCIATION. NEWSLETTER. m. Bahamas Pharmaceutical Association, P.O. Box 3730, Nassau NP, Bahamas.

615   BG   ISSN 0301-4606
CODEN: BPJLAQ
BANGLADESH PHARMACEUTICAL JOURNAL. (Text in English) 1972. q. Bangladesh Pharmaceutical Society, University of Dhaka, Ramna, Dhaka 2, Bangladesh. **Indexed:** Chem.Abstr., Excerp.Med., I.P.A.
●Also available online.

615 540   GW   ISSN 0005-6960
BAYER BERICHTE/BAYER REPORTS. (Editions in English, French, German, Italian, Japanese, Portuguese and Spanish) 1958. s-a. free to stockholders. Bayer AG, Public Relations Dept., 5090 Leverkusen, Germany. TEL 0214-3081759. Ed. Gerti-Rose Beckmann. abstr.; bibl.; charts; illus.; stat.; circ. 520,000. **Indexed:** RAPRA, Text.Tech.Dig.
—BLDSC shelfmark: 1871.139000.

615 150   UK   ISSN 0955-8810
▼**BEHAVIOURAL PHARMACOLOGY.** 1990. bi-m. £80($144) to individuals; institutions £145($261). Rapid Communications of Oxford Ltd., The Old Malthouse, Paradise St., Oxford OX1 1LD, England. TEL 0865-790447. FAX 0865-244012. Ed. Paul Willner. (reprint service avail.) **Indexed:** Psychol.Abstr.
—BLDSC shelfmark: 1877.630000.

615.1   US   ISSN 0006-2952
QP901   CODEN: BCPCA6
BIOCHEMICAL PHARMACOLOGY. 1958. 24/yr. £1410 (effective 1992). Pergamon Press, Inc., Journals Division, 660 White Plains Rd., Tarrytown, NY 10591-5153. TEL 914-524-9200. FAX 914-333-2444. (And: Headington Hill Hall, Oxford OX3 0BW, England. TEL 0865-794141) Eds. Alan C. Sartorelli, P. Alexander. adv.; bk.rev.; charts; illus.; index; circ. 1,150. (also avail. in microform from MIM,UMI; back issues avail.; reprint service avail. from UMI) **Indexed:** Abstr.Inter.Med., Anal.Abstr., Biol.Abstr., Biotech.Abstr., C.I.S. Abstr., Chem.Abstr., Curr.Adv.Biochem., Curr.Adv.Cancer Res., Curr.Adv.Cell & Devel.Biol., Curr.Adv.Ecol.Sci., Curr.Adv.Genetics & Molec.Biol., Curr.Cont., Dairy Sci.Abstr., Dent.Ind., Excerp.Med., Helminthol.Abstr., Hort.Abstr., I.P.A., Ind.Med., Ind.Sci.Rev., Ind.Vet., INIS Atomind., Mass Spectr.Bull., Nutr.Abstr., Protozool.Abstr., Psychol.Abstr., Rev.Plant Path., Sci.Cit.Ind., Vet.Bull., Weed Abstr.
—BLDSC shelfmark: 2067.700000.
Refereed Serial

BIOLOGIZACE A CHEMIZACE ZIVOCISNE VYROBY - VETERINARIA/BIOLOGICAL AND CHEMICAL FACTORS IN ANIMAL PRODUCTION - VETERINARIA/BIOLOGISATION UND CHEMISATION DER TIERERZEUGUNG - VETERINARIA/FACTEURS BIOLOGIQUES ET CHIMIQUES DANS LA PRODUCTION DES ANIMAUX - VETERINARIA/FACTORES BIOLOGICOS Y QUIMICOS DE LA PRODUCTION ANIMAL - VETERINARIA. see *VETERINARY SCIENCE*

BIOMEDICAL AND ENVIRONMENTAL SCIENCES. see *MEDICAL SCIENCES*

615   US   ISSN 1040-8304
CODEN: BPRME5
BIOPHARM. 1987. 9/yr. $59 (foreign $117). Aster Publishing Corporation, 859 Willamette St., Box 10955, Eugene, OR 97440. TEL 503-343-1200. FAX 503-343-3641. TELEX 510-597-0365. Ed. M. Jane Ganter. adv.; circ. 20,000. (reprint service avail.) **Indexed:** Telegen.
—BLDSC shelfmark: 2089.353500.
Formerly: Biopharm Manufacturing.
Description: Meets the growing need in the biopharmaceutical, diagnostics, and intermediates industries for information regarding scale-up from the research and development stage to full-scale manufacturing.

615   UK   ISSN 0142-2782
CODEN: BDDID8
BIOPHARMACEUTICS & DRUG DISPOSITION. 1979. 9/yr. $555 (effective 1992). John Wiley & Sons Ltd., Baffins Lane, Chichester, Sussex PO19 1UD, England. TEL 0243-779777. FAX 0243-775878. TELEX 86290 WIBOOK G. Ed.Bd. (reprint service avail. from ISI,SWZ,UMI) **Indexed:** Anal.Abstr., Biotech.Abstr., Chem.Abstr., Curr.Adv.Ecol.Sci., Curr.Cont., Dairy Sci.Abstr., Excerp.Med., I.P.A., Ind.Med., Ind.Sci.Rev., Mass Spectr.Bull., Sci.Cit.Ind.
—BLDSC shelfmark: 2089.355000.
Description: Presents original reports of studies in biopharmaceutics, drug disposition and pharmacokinetics, especially those which have a direct relation to the therapeutic use of drugs.

BIOSYNTHETIC PRODUCTS FOR CANCER CHEMOTHERAPY. see *MEDICAL SCIENCES — Cancer*

BIOTECHNOLOGY THERAPEUTICS. see *BIOLOGY — Biotechnology*

615.1   US   ISSN 0006-503X
BLUE AND GOLD TRIANGLE OF LAMBDA KAPPA SIGMA. 1926. 8 nos. every 2 years. $10. Lambda Kappa Sigma International Pharmaceutical Fraternity, 6250 Mountain Vista, Ste. I, Henderson, NV 89014. FAX 702-456-4309. Ed. Mary Grear. adv.; bk.rev.; illus.; circ. 12,000.

615   US
▼**BLUE BOOK: THE BUYER'S GUIDE FOR PHARMACEUTICAL PACKAGERS.** 1992. a. $50. Avalon Communications, Box 505, Southampton, PA 18966. TEL 215-357-4933. adv.; circ. 10,146.
Description: Reference source for pharmaceutical packaging equipment, materials, containers and services.

615.9 658   SP
BOLETIN INFORMATIVO A E F H.* q. 2650 ptas.($30) Asociacion Espanola de Farmaceuticos de Hospitales, C. Echegaray, 13-3o, 28014 Madrid, Spain. TEL 93-4029654. circ. 1,000.

615.1   IT   ISSN 0006-6648
CODEN: BCFAAI
BOLLETTINO CHIMICO FARMACEUTICO. (Text in French, German, Italian; summaries in English) 1861. m. $280. Societa Editoriale Farmaceutica s.r.l., Via Ausonio, 12, 20123 Milan, Italy. TEL 02-89404545. FAX 02-89401168. Ed. Aldo La Manna. adv.; bk.rev.; pat.; index; circ. 3,000. **Indexed:** Biol.Abstr., Biotech.Abstr., Chem.Abstr., Excerp.Med., I.P.A., Ind.Med.
—BLDSC shelfmark: 2236.000000.

615.19   IT
▼**BOLLETTINO DI FARMACOSORVEGLIANZA.** 1990. bi-m. free. (Societa Italiana per la Verifica e lo Sviluppo dei Farmaci Post-registrazione) Masson Italia Periodici, Via Statuto 2-4, 20121 Milan, Italy. TEL 02-6367-1. FAX 02-6367-211. Ed. Ettore Ambrosioni. circ. 80,000.

BONE AND MINERAL RESEARCH ANNUAL. see *MEDICAL SCIENCES — Orthopedics And Traumatology*

615.19   UK
BOOTS NEWS. 1970. 8/yr. free to qualified personnel. Boots Co. PLC, 1 Thane Rd. W., Nottingham NG2 3AA, England. TEL 0602-592365. FAX 0602-592727. TELEX 377811. circ. 56,000 (controlled). (back issues avail.)
Description: Staff journal for all employees of The Boots Company home and overseas.

615   GW   ISSN 0722-7159
BRAUNSCHWEIGER VEROEFFENTLICHUNGEN ZUR GESCHICHTE DER PHARMAZIE UND NATURWISSENSCHAFTEN. 1957. irreg., vol.32, 1989. price varies. Deutscher Apotheker Verlag, Postfach 101061, 7000 Stuttgart 10, Germany. TEL 0711-2582-0. FAX 0711-2582290. TELEX 723636-DAZ-D. Ed. Wolfgang Schneider.
Formerly: Technische Universitaet Braunschweig. Pharmaziegeschichtlichen Seminar. Veroeffentlichungen (ISSN 0068-0729)

615   BL
BRAZIL. CONSELHO FEDERAL DE FARMACIA. RELATORIO. irreg. Conselho Federal de Farmacia, Brasilia, Brazil. illus.

617.96   UK   ISSN 0306-5251
CODEN: BCPHBM
BRITISH JOURNAL OF CLINICAL PHARMACOLOGY. 1974. m. £195 (foreign £220). (British Pharmacological Society) Blackwell Scientific Publications Ltd., Osney Mead, Oxford OX2 0EL, England. TEL 0865-240201. FAX 0865-721205. TELEX 83355-MEDBOK-G. Ed. C.F. George. adv.; bibl.; charts; illus.; index; circ. 1,900. (also avail. in microform from UMI) **Indexed:** Abstr.Inter.Med., ASCA, Biol.Abstr., Biotech.Abstr., Chem.Abstr., Curr.Adv.Ecol.Sci., Curr.Cont., Dairy Sci.Abstr., Dent.Ind., Excerp.Med., Helminthol.Abstr., I.P.A., Ind.Med., Ind.Sci.Rev., INIS Atomind., Nutr.Abstr., Protozool.Abstr., Sci.Cit.Ind.
●Also available online.
—BLDSC shelfmark: 2307.180000.

BRITISH JOURNAL OF CLINICAL RESEARCH. see *MEDICAL SCIENCES*

615   UK   ISSN 0007-1188
CODEN: BJPCBM
BRITISH JOURNAL OF PHARMACOLOGY. 1946. m. £415. (British Pharmacological Society) Macmillan Press Ltd., Scientific & Medical Division, Houndmills, Basingstoke, Hampshire RG21 2XS, England. TEL 0256-29242. FAX 0256-810526. Ed. A.T. Birmingham. adv.; charts; illus.; index; cum.index: 1966-1973; 1974-1977; 1978-1983; 1984-1987; circ. 3,000. (also avail. in microform from UMI) **Indexed:** Biol.Abstr., Biotech.Abstr., C.I.S. Abstr., Chem.Abstr., Curr.Adv.Cancer Res., Curr.Adv.Cell & Devel.Biol., Curr.Adv.Ecol.Sci., Curr.Chem.React., Curr.Cont., Dairy Sci.Abstr., Dent.Ind., Excerp.Med., Helminthol.Abstr., High.Educ.Curr.Aware.Bull., I.P.A., Ind.Chem., Ind.Med., Ind.Sci.Rev., Ind.Vet., INIS Atomind., Nutr.Abstr., Sci.Cit.Ind., Vet.Bull.
●Also available online.
—BLDSC shelfmark: 2314.700000.
Formerly: British Journal of Pharmacology and Chemotherapy.
Description: Original papers in experimental pharmacology.

615.1   UK   ISSN 0260-535X
BRITISH NATIONAL FORMULARY. 1981. 2/yr. £9.95. Royal Pharmaceutical Society of Great Britain, 1 Lambeth High St., London SE1 7JN, England. TEL 071-735-9141. (Co-sponsor: British Medical Association) Ed. Anne B. Prasad. index.
—BLDSC shelfmark: 2331.060000.
Description: Gives information for prescribers in the National Health Service and other health care professionals about drugs and medicines available on prescriptions in the UK.

615   UK
BRITISH PHARMACOLOGICAL SOCIETY. SYMPOSIA. 1973. irreg. (1-2/yr.). price varies. British Pharmacological Society, c/o Dr. A.R. Green, Hon.Gen.Sec., British Pharmacological Society, Astra Neuroscience Research Unit, 1 Wakefield St., London WC1N 1PJ, England.

BRITISH PHARMACOPOEIA (VETERINARY). see *VETERINARY SCIENCE*

615.1   UK   ISSN 0068-2519
BRITISH SOCIETY FOR THE HISTORY OF PHARMACY. TRANSACTIONS. 1970. irreg. price varies. British Society for the History of Pharmacy, 36 York Place, Edinburgh EH1 3HU, Scotland. Ed. M.P. Earles.

615.9 615.19   PL   ISSN 0365-9445
RA1258   CODEN: BCTKAG
BROMATOLOGIA I CHEMIA TOKSYKOLOGICZNA. (Text in Polish; summaries in English and Russian) q. $66. (Polskie Towarzystwo Farmaceutyczne) Wydawnictwo Polskiego Towarzystwa Farmaceutycznego, Ul. Dluga 16, 00-238 Warsaw, Poland. TEL 31-02-41. (Dist. by: Ars Polona-Ruch, Krakowskie Przedmiescie 7, Warsaw, Poland) Ed. Henryk Mlodecki. **Indexed:** Biol.Abstr., Chem.Abstr, Dairy Sci.Abstr., Excerp.Med., Food Sci.& Tech.Abstr., Maize Abstr., Nutr.Abstr., Pig News & Info., Soils & Fert., Soyabean Abstr., Triticale Abstr., Weed Abstr.
Description: Deals with bromatology and toxicological chemistry. Contains original review papers.

PHARMACY AND PHARMACOLOGY

615.1 SP
BUTLLETI INFORMATIU DE CIRCULAR FARMACEUTICA. (Supplement to: Colegio Oficial de Farmaceuticos. Circular Farmaceutica (ISSN: 0009-7314)) 1969. m. membership. Colegio Oficial de Farmaceuticos de la Provincia de Barcelona, Pau Claris, Barcelona 10, Spain. **Indexed:** Chem.Abstr., GeoRef.

615.19 US
CODEN: CBUPEA
▼**C A S BIOTECH UPDATES. SLOW-RELEASE PHARMACEUTICALS.** 1991. s-w. $195. Chemical Abstracts Service, 2540 Olentangy River Rd., Box 3012, Columbus, OH 43210. TEL 614-447-3600. FAX 614-447-3713. TELEX 6842086.
Description: Covers slow-release pharmaceutical dosage forms, including controlled- and sustained-release systems; newer dosage forms such as osmotic-release devices, transdermal systems, polymer conjugates, and other materials giving regulated drug release rates.

615.1 US
C P F I NEWSLETTER. 1984. q. free. Christian Pharmacists Fellowship International, Box 8351, Richmond, VA 23226. TEL 804-288-7302. FAX 804-288-3631. Ed. James E. Thompson. bk.rev.; circ. 1,800. (back issues avail.)
Description: Communication link and network of Christian pharmacists around the world.

615.1 US
CALIFORNIA PHARMACIST. 1957. m. $25. California Pharmacists Association, 1112 I St., Ste. 300, Sacramento, CA 95814. TEL 916-444-7811. FAX 916-443-1915. Ed. Robert C. Johnson. adv.; bk.rev.; charts; illus.; stat.; index; circ. 7,600.
Formerly: California Pharmacy (ISSN 0008-1388)

615.321 CN
CANADIAN JOURNAL OF HERBALISM. 1979. q. Can.$25 membership. Ontario Herbalists Association, 11 Winthrop Pl., Stoney Creek, Ont. L8G 3M3, Canada. Ed. Keith Stelling. adv.; circ. 1,500.
Formerly (until 1988): Ontario Herbalists Association. Journal.
Description: Covers herbal medicine, complementary health care. Includes botanical and pharmacological profiles on specific plants, therapeutics and updates on legislation and quality control.

615.1 CN ISSN 0008-4123
CODEN: CJHPAV
CANADIAN JOURNAL OF HOSPITAL PHARMACY. (Text in English and French) 1948. bi-m. Can.$44.94. Canadian Society of Hospital Pharmacists, 1145 Hunt Club Rd., Ste. 350, Ottawa, Ont. K1V 0Y3, Canada. TEL 613-736-9733. FAX 613-736-5660. Ed. Susan Tremblay. adv.; bk.rev.; abstr.; charts; illus.; pat.; tr.lit.; index; circ. 3,300. (also avail. in microform from UMI; reprint service avail. from UMI) **Indexed:** Biol.Abstr., Biotech.Abstr., Chem.Abstr., Excerp.Med., Hosp.Lit.Ind., I.P.A.
●Also available online.
—BLDSC shelfmark: 3031.700000.
Formerly: Hospital Pharmacist.

CANADIAN JOURNAL OF PHYSIOLOGY AND PHARMACOLOGY/JOURNAL CANADIEN DE PHYSIOLOGIE ET PHARMACOLOGIE. see BIOLOGY — Physiology

615.1 CN ISSN 0828-6914
CANADIAN PHARMACEUTICAL JOURNAL/REVUE PHARMACEUTIQUE CANADIENNE. Short title: C P J - R P C. 1868. m. Can.$53.50. Canadian Pharmaceutical Association, 1785 Alta Vista Dr., Ottawa, Ont. K1G 3Y6, Canada. TEL 613-523-7877. FAX 613-523-0445. Ed. Jane Dewar. adv.; bk.rev.; circ. 12,324. **Indexed:** Biol.Abstr., Biotech.Abstr., Can.B.P.I., Excerp.Med., I.P.A.
●Also available online.
Refereed Serial

615.5 US
RM200
CARDIOLOGIST'S COMPENDIUM OF DRUG THERAPY. Spine title: Compendium of Drug Therapy. 1980. a. $40. Excerpta Medica, Inc., Core Publishing Division (Subsidiary of: Elsevier Science Publishers B.V.), 105 Raider Blvd., Belle Mead, NJ 08052.
TEL 908-874-8550. FAX 908-874-0700. Ed. Kenneth Senerth. adv.; circ. 105,000.

CARDIOVASCULAR DRUGS AND THERAPY. see MEDICAL SCIENCES — Cardiovascular Diseases

CARDIOVASCULAR PHARMACOLOGY. see MEDICAL SCIENCES — Cardiovascular Diseases

615 US ISSN 0528-1725
CAROLINA JOURNAL OF PHARMACY. 1915. m. $25. North Carolina Pharmaceutical Association, Box 151, Chapel Hill, NC 27514. TEL 919-967-2237. Ed. A.H. Mebane III. adv.; circ. 3,000. (back issues avail.) **Indexed:** I.P.A.
Description: Covers issues related to pharmacy practice with emphasis on North Carolina pharmacy.

615.19 282 US
THE CATHOLIC PHARMACIST. Short title: T.C.P. 1968. q. membership. National Catholic Pharmacists Guild of the United States, 1012 Surrey Hills Dr., St. Louis, MO 63117-1438. TEL 314-645-0085. Ed. John Paul Winkelmann. adv.; bk.rev.; circ. 375. (back issues avail.)
Description: Acquaints members with the latest developments in their church affecting their profession.

CELL CYCLE. see BIOLOGY — Cytology And Histology

CELL DIFFERENTIATION. see BIOLOGY — Cytology And Histology

CELLULAR AND MOLECULAR MECHANISMS OF INFLAMMATION; receptors of inflammatory cells: structure-function relationships. see BIOLOGY

CELLULAR SIGNALLING. see BIOLOGY — Cytology And Histology

615.9 FR ISSN 0995-3671
CENTRE NATIONAL DE DOCUMENTATION SUR LES TOXICOMANIES. BULLETIN DE LIAISON. (Supplement avail.: Cahiers Thematiques) 1983. 2/yr. (plus 2 supplements). 250 F. to individuals; institutions 500 F. Centre National de Documentation sur les Toxicomanies, 14 ave. Berthelot, 69007 Lyon, France. TEL 72-72-93-07. FAX 78-58-27-14.
Description: Devoted to the study of drug addiction, with a multidisciplinary approach.

615.19 MG
CENTRE NATIONAL DE RECHERCHES PHARMACEUTIQUES. ARCHIVES. a. FMG.8000($5) Centre National de Recherches Pharmaceutiques, Centre d'Information et de Documentation Scientifique et Technique, 27 rue Fernand Kasanga, Tsimbazaza, B.P. 6224, 101 Antananarivo, Malagasy Republic. TEL 33288. (back issues avail.)

615 CS ISSN 0009-0530
CODEN: CKFRAY
CESKOSLOVENSKA FARMACIE. (Text in Czech or Slovak; summaries in English, German, Russian) 1952. 10/yr. $62.60. (Ceskoslovenska Farmaceuticka Spolecnost) Avicenum, Czechoslovak Medical Press, Malostranske nam. 28, Mala Strana, 118 02 Prague 1, Czechoslovakia. (Dist. by: Artia, Ve Smeckach 30, 111 27 Prague 1, Czechoslovakia) (Co-sponsor: Ceskoslovenska Lekarska Spolecnost J. Ev. Purkyne) Ed. Dr. Josef Hubik. adv.; bk.rev.; index; circ. 2,400. **Indexed:** Anal.Abstr., Biol.Abstr., Biotech.Abstr., C.I.S. Abstr., Chem.Abstr., Curr.Adv.Ecol.Sci., Excerp.Med., I.P.A., Ind.Med., INIS Atomind., Protozool.Abstr.
●Also available online.
—BLDSC shelfmark: 3121.000000.

615.19 668.55 II
CHEMEXCIL MONTHLY BULLETIN. m. Basic Chemical, Pharmaceuticals and Cosmetics Export Promotion Council, Jhansi Castle 7, Cooperage Rd., Bombay 400 039, India. TEL 231288. TELEX 0114047.

CHEMICAL & PHARMACEUTICAL BULLETIN. see CHEMISTRY

CHEMICAL RESEARCH IN TOXICOLOGY. see ENVIRONMENTAL STUDIES — Toxicology And Environmental Safety

CHEMISCHE RUNDSCHAU; Wochenzeitung fuer Chemie, Pharmazie, und Lebensmitteltechnik. see CHEMISTRY

615.1 UK ISSN 0009-3033
CODEN: CHDRAJ
CHEMIST & DRUGGIST; for retailer, wholesaler, manufacturer. 1859. w. £95 (foreign £133). (Pharmaceutical Society of Northern Ireland, IE) Benn Publications Ltd., Sovereign Way, Tonbridge, Kent TN9 1RW, England. TEL 0732-364422. Ed. John Skelton. adv.; bk.rev.; charts; illus.; mkt.; pat.; tr.mk.; s-a index; circ. 15,665. (also avail. in microform from UMI) **Indexed:** Br.Tech.Ind., Chem.Abstr., I.P.A., PROMT.
●Also available online.
—BLDSC shelfmark: 3167.000000.
Incorporates: Retail Chemist (ISSN 0034-6020)

615.1 UK ISSN 0262-5881
CHEMIST & DRUGGIST DIRECTORY. 1868. a. £72 (foreign £82). Benn Business Information Services Ltd., P.O. Box 20, Sovereign Way, Tonbridge, Kent TN9 1RQ, England. TEL 0732-362666. FAX 0732-770483. TELEX 95162-BENTON-G. Ed. Sarah Walker. adv.; circ. 2,900.
—BLDSC shelfmark: 3167.500000.
Description: Directory of the pharmaceutical, drug, essential oil and cosmetic industries.

615 UK
CHEMIST & DRUGGIST PRICE LIST. 1960. m. free to subscr. of: Chemist & Druggist. Benn Publications Ltd., Sovereign Way, Tonbridge, Kent TN9 1RW, England. TEL 0732 364422. adv.; circ. 15,665.

615.1 II ISSN 0009-3041
CHEMIST & DRUGSTORE NEWS. m. Rs.20. India Publications Co., Denabank House, 2nd Fl., 31 Hamam St., Bombay 1, India. Ed. Eric Martin. bk.rev.; circ. controlled.

615.1 PK ISSN 0009-3149
CHEMISTS REVIEW. (Text in English and Urdu) 1957. m. Rs.250. P.O. Box 376, Karachi, Pakistan. Ed. M.Y. Ansari. adv.; bk.rev.; charts; illus.; circ. 5,000.

615.1 SZ ISSN 0009-3157
CODEN: CHTHBK
CHEMOTHERAPY; international journal of experimental and clinical chemotherapy. (Text in English) 1960. bi-m. 479 Fr.($320) S. Karger AG, Allschwilerstr. 10, P.O. Box, CH-4009 Basel, Switzerland. TEL 061-3061111. FAX 061-3061234. TELEX CH 962652. Ed. H. Schoenfeld. adv.; bk.rev.; bibl.; charts; illus.; circ. 1,200. (also avail. in microfilm) **Indexed:** Biodet.Abstr., Biol.Abstr., Biotech.Abstr., Chem.Abstr., Curr.Adv.Cancer Res., Curr.Cont., Dairy Sci.Abstr., Excerp.Med., Helminthol.Abstr., I.P.A., Ind.Med., Ind.Vet., Protozool.Abstr., Rev.Plant Path., Sci.Cit.Ind., Vet.Bull.
—BLDSC shelfmark: 3172.304000.
Formerly: Chemotherapia.

615.9 US
CHINA DRUG PURCHASE AUDIT. 1985. q. $17,500. ChinaMetrik, 600 New Hampshire Ave., N.W., Ste. 700, Washington, DC 20037. TEL 202-337-7327. FAX 202-337-4498. (And: c/o Mr. Zhagn Wei, Gen. Man., China Medical News Tribune, 15 Hou Hei Bei Yan, W. City, Beijin 100009, China. TEL 86-1-401-2134) Ed. A. Wolters. index. (back issues avail.)
Description: Audit of 40 major Chinese hospitals' drug purchases.

CHINESE MEDICAL SCIENCES JOURNAL. see MEDICAL SCIENCES

CHIRALITY; the pharmacological, biological, and chemical consequences of molecular asymmetry. see BIOLOGY — Microbiology

CIBA-GEIGY JOURNAL. see CHEMISTRY — Organic Chemistry

615 SP ISSN 0210-0819
CODEN: CIDFA8
CIENCIA E INDUSTRIA FARMACEUTICA. (Text in Spanish; summaries in English and French) 1969. 12/yr. 2700 ptas.($34) Universidad de Barcelona, Departamento Farmacia Galenica, Nucleo Universitario Pedralbes, Barcelona (14), Spain. adv.; bk.rev.; circ. 750. **Indexed:** Biotech.Abstr., Chem.Abstr., Curr.Adv.Ecol.Sci., Excerp.Med., I.P.A., Ind.Med.Esp., Ind.SST.
●Also available online.

PHARMACY AND PHARMACOLOGY

615.19 SP ISSN 1131-5253
CIENCIA PHARMACEUTICA. 1987. 6/yr. 5500 ptas. Alpe Editores, S.A., Pedro Rico, 27, 28029 Madrid, Spain. TEL 733 88 11. FAX 315-96-52. Pres. Dr. Jose Maria Sune Arbussa. **Indexed:** Excerp.Med.
Formerly (until 1990): Pharmaklinik (ISSN 1011-4386)

CLINICAL AND EXPERIMENTAL PHARMACOLOGY AND PHYSIOLOGY. see *BIOLOGY — Physiology*

615.9 US
CLINICAL CONSULT. 1982. m. free to members. American Society of Consultant Pharmacists, 2300 Ninth St., S., Ste. 515, Arlington, VA 22204. TEL 703-920-8492. FAX 703-486-2997. Ed. James W. Cooper. (back issues avail.)
Description: Focuses on geriatric drug therapy and, or clinical illness and offers guidance to readers on drug therapy monitoring criteria.

615 US ISSN 0362-5664
RM315 CODEN: CLNEDB
CLINICAL NEUROPHARMACOLOGY. 1976. bi-m. $113 to individuals; institutions $164. Raven Press, 1185 Ave. of the Americas, New York, NY 10036. TEL 212-950-9500. FAX 212-869-3495. TELEX 640073. Ed. Harold L. Klawans. adv.; charts; illus.; index; circ. 3,500. (back issues avail.) **Indexed:** Biol.Abstr., Chem.Abstr., Curr.Adv.Ecol.Sci., Curr.Cont., Excerp.Med., Ind.Med., Ind.Sci.Rev., Sci.Cit.Ind.
—BLDSC shelfmark: 3286.310600.
Description: Features reviews and original investigations on the pharmacology of central nervous system dysfunction.
Refereed Serial

615.19 US
CLINICAL PHARMACOKINETIC NEWSLETTER. 1984. q. $10. Rhode Island Hospital, Department of Pharmacy, 593 Eddy St., Providence, RI 02902. TEL 401-277-5050. Ed. Louis P. Jeffrey, Sc.D. bk.rev.; bibl.; charts; illus.; cum.index; circ. 1,000. (tabloid format)

615 NZ ISSN 0312-5963
CODEN: CPKNDH
CLINICAL PHARMACOKINETICS. 1976. m. NZ.$325. Adis Internatinal Ltd., 41 Centorian Dr., Private Bag, Mairangi Bay, Auckland 10, New Zealand. TEL 479-8100. Ed. Roderick H. Sayce. **Indexed:** Biol.Abstr., Biotech.Abstr., Chem.Abstr., Curr.Adv.Cancer Res., Curr.Adv.Ecol.Sci., Curr.Cont., Dairy Sci.Abstr., Dent.Ind., Excerp.Med., I.P.A., Ind.Med., Ind.Sci.Rev., Sci.Cit.Ind.
—BLDSC shelfmark: 3286.327000.

615.7 NZ ISSN 0114-0892
CLINICAL PHARMACOKINETICS DRUG DATA HANDBOOK (YEAR). a. $40. Adis International Ltd., 41 Centorian Dr., Private Bag, Mairangi Bay, Auckland 10, New Zealand. TEL 479-8100. Ed. George J. Mammen. charts.
—BLDSC shelfmark: 3286.327100.
Description: Tabular drug data reprints from monthly journal Clinical Pharmacokinetics.

615.9 378 US ISSN 0898-6398
RM108.5.U6
CLINICAL PHARMACOLOGY; a guide to training programs. 1973. triennial. $14.95. (Burroughs Wellcome Fund) Peterson's Guides, Inc., Box 2123, 202 Carnegie Center, Princeton, NJ 08543-2123. TEL 609-243-9111. FAX 609-243-9150. circ. 5,000.
Description: Covers the U.S. and Canadian postdoctoral programs devoted to training of clinical pharmacologists.

615.1 US ISSN 0009-9236
RM1 CODEN: CLPTAT
CLINICAL PHARMACOLOGY & THERAPEUTICS. 1960. m. $92 to individuals; institutions $171; students $47 (foreign $117; $196; $72). (American Society for Pharmacology and Experimental Therapeutics) Mosby - Year Book, Inc. (Subsidiary of: Times Mirror Company), 11830 Westline Industrial Dr., St. Louis, MO 63146. TEL 800-325-4117. FAX 314-432-1380. TELEX 44-2402. (Co-sponsor: American Society of Clinical Pharmacology and Therapeutics) Ed. Dr. Marcus Reidenberg. adv.; charts;illus; s-a index; circ. 5,190. (also avail. in microform from UMI; reprint service avail. from UMI) **Indexed:** Abstr.Inter.Med., ASCA, Behav.Med.Abstr., Biol.Abstr., Biotech.Abstr., Chem.Abstr., Curr.Adv.Ecol.Sci., Dairy Sci.Abstr., Dent.Ind., Excerp.Med., Helminthol.Abstr., I.P.A., Ind.Med., Ind.Sci.Rev., INIS Atomind., NRN, Nutr.Abstr., Sci.Cit.Ind.
●Also available online. Vendor(s): BRS, BRS/Saunders Colleague.
—BLDSC shelfmark: 3286.330000.
Description: Devoted to the study of the nature, action, disposition, efficacy and total evaluation of drugs as they are used in man.
Refereed Serial

615.19 US
CLINICAL PHARMACOLOGY SERIES. 1983. irreg., vol.17, 1991. price varies. Marcel Dekker, Inc., 270 Madison Ave., New York, NY 10016. TEL 212-696-9000. FAX 212-685-4540. TELEX 421419.

615 US ISSN 0278-2677
CODEN: CPHADV
CLINICAL PHARMACY. 1982. m. $80 to non-members; members $45. American Society of Hospital Pharmacists, c/o Jean Rogers, Dir., Mkt. Svcs., 4630 Montgomery Ave., Bethesda, MD 20814. TEL 301-657-3000. Ed. William A. Zellmer. circ. 8,000. (reprint service avail. from UMI) **Indexed:** Biol.Abstr., Biotech.Abstr., Chem.Abstr., Curr.Adv.Cancer Res., Curr.Adv.Ecol.Sci., Dent.Ind., Excerp.Med., Ind.Med.
—BLDSC shelfmark: 3286.330500.
Refereed Serial

615.19 US
RS122 CODEN: CRPADH
CLINICAL RESEARCH AND REGULATORY AFFAIRS; a journal devoted to documentation of the clinical research process in the pharmaceutical industry. 1983. 4/yr. $325. Marcel Dekker Journals, 270 Madison Ave., New York, NY 10016. TEL 212-696-9000. FAX 212-685-4540. TELEX 421419. (Subscr. to: Box 10018, Church St. Sta., New York, NY 10249) Ed. S.E. Rosenbaum. adv.; bk.rev.; illus.; charts; stat.; index. (also avail. in microform from RPI) **Indexed:** Biol.Abstr., Curr.Adv.Ecol.Sci., Excerp.Med.
Formerly (until 1991): Clinical Research Practices and Drug Regulatory Affairs (ISSN 0735-7915)
Refereed Serial

615.7 NE
CLINICALLY IMPORTANT ADVERSE DRUG INTERACTIONS. 1980. irreg., vol.3, 1985. price varies. Elsevier Science Publishers B.V., Books Division, P.O. Box 211, 1000 AE Amsterdam, Netherlands. TEL 020-5803911. FAX 020-5803705. TELEX 18582 ESPA NL. (Subscr. in U.S. and Canada to: Elsevier Science Publishing Co., Inc., Box 882, Madison Sq. Sta., New York, NY 10159. TEL 212-989-5800)
Refereed Serial

615.1 SP ISSN 0009-7314
COLEGIO OFICIAL DE FARMACEUTICO. CIRCULAR FARMACEUTICA. (Supplement: Butlleti Informatiu de Circular Farmaceutica) 1943. 4/yr. 1000 ptas. (non-members). Colegio Oficial de Farmaceuticos de la Provincia de Barcelona, Pau Claris, Barcelona 10, Spain. adv.; charts; illus. **Indexed:** I.P.A.
●Also available online.

615.7 IT
COLLEGAMENTO. 1957. m. L.20000. Unione Tecnica Italiana Farmacisti, Via Giuseppe Casaregis 52-8, 16129 Genova, Italy. Ed. Elio Machi. adv.; circ. 14,000. **Indexed:** I.P.A.
●Also available online.

615.1 US ISSN 0010-163X
COLORADO JOURNAL OF PHARMACY. 1958. q. $5. University of Colorado, School of Pharmacy, Box 297, Boulder, CO 80309-0297. TEL 303-492-6278. Ed. James A. Roth. illus.; circ. 1,500. **Indexed:** Biol.Abstr.
—BLDSC shelfmark: 3321.400000.

COMMENTS ON TOXICOLOGY. see *ENVIRONMENTAL STUDIES — Toxicology And Environmental Safety*

615.19 658.8 UK
COMMUNITY PHARMACY. 1980. 12/yr. £33 (foreign £40). Benn Publications, 23-27 Tudor St., London EC4, England. Eds. Anne Anstice, Liz Barnes. adv.; illus.; circ. 13,893.
Formerly (until 1986): O T C Medication (ISSN 0260-518X)
Description: Newsmonthly for those involved with pharmacies and pharmaceuticals. Product news, OTC medications and pharmacy in business.

COMPARATIVE BIOCHEMISTRY AND PHYSIOLOGY. PART C: COMPARATIVE PHARMACOLOGY & TOXICOLOGY. see *BIOLOGY — Biological Chemistry*

615 CN ISSN 0069-7966
COMPENDIUM OF PHARMACEUTICALS AND SPECIALTIES. French edition: Compendium des Produits et Specialites Pharmaceutiques (ISSN 0317-2813) (Editions in English and French) 1960. a. Can.$99 for French ed.; $87 for English ed. Canadian Pharmaceutical Association, 1785 Alta Vista Dr., Ottawa, Ont. K1G 3Y6, Canada. TEL 613-523-7877. FAX 613-523-0445. Ed. C. Gillis. bk.rev.; circ. 95,000.
—BLDSC shelfmark: 3363.971000.

610 615 621.381 US ISSN 0736-3893
COMPUTERTALK FOR THE PHARMACIST. 1981. bi-m. $45. ComputerTalk Associates, Inc., 482 Norristown Rd., Ste. 112, Blue Bell, PA 19422. TEL 215-325-7686. FAX 215-825-7641. Ed. Neil R. Bauman. adv.
Description: Offers practical advice to familiarize pharmacists with computers and computer applications. Short articles cover a broad range of topics.

610 615 US
COMPUTERTALK PHARMACY SYSTEMS BUYERS GUIDE. 1982. a. $25. ComputerTalk Associates, Inc., 482 Norristown Rd., Ste. 112, Blue Bell, PA 19422. TEL 215-825-7686. FAX 215-825-7641. Ed. Neil R. Bauman. adv.; circ. 50,000.
Formerly: ComputerTalk Directory of Pharmacy Systems (ISSN 0736-3877)
Description: A guide to available computer systems and services designed for pharmacy use. Information contained within product profiles written by vendors. Articles cover a range of topics on computers and applications.

615.329 US
CONNECTICUT PHARMACIST. 1943. bi-m. $12. Connecticut Pharmaceutical Association, 35 Cold Spring Rd., Ste. 125, Rocky Hill, CT 06067. TEL 203-563-4619. FAX 203-257-8241. Ed. Daniel C. Leone. adv.; circ. 1,949.

615.328 US ISSN 0888-5109
THE CONSULTANT PHARMACIST. 1986. m. $45 to individuals (foreign $65); institutions $75 (foreign $95). American Society of Consultant Pharmacists, 2300 Ninth St. S., Ste. 515, Arlington, VA 22204. TEL 703-920-8492. FAX 703-486-2997. Ed. L. Michael Posey. adv.; circ. 11,200. (back issues avail.) **Indexed:** Abstr.Soc.Geront.
—BLDSC shelfmark: 3423.763000.

615.9 US
CONSUMER PHARMACIST; drug information newsletter. 1982. bi-m. $48. Elba Medical Foundation, 1818 N. Turnbull Dr., Box 1403, Metairie, LA 70004-1403. TEL 504-833-3600. Ed. John F. DiMaggio. adv.; bk.rev.; circ. 6,000.

CONTROLLED RELEASE SOCIETY. INTERNATIONAL SYMPOSIUM ON CONTROLLED RELEASE OF BIOACTIVE MATERIALS. PROCEEDINGS. see *CHEMISTRY — Organic Chemistry*

615.1 IT ISSN 0010-9207
CORRIERE DEL FARMACISTA. 1945. m. L.2500.($4.) Armando Giordano, Ed. & Pub., Piazza d'Aosta 37, 80047 San Giuseppe Vesuviano, Naples, Italy. adv.; abstr. **Indexed:** Chem.Abstr., Ind.Med.

PHARMACY AND PHARMACOLOGY

CRITICAL REPORTS ON APPLIED CHEMISTRY. see *CHEMISTRY*

615.19 US ISSN 0743-4863
RS201.V43 CODEN: CRTSEO
CRITICAL REVIEWS IN THERAPEUTIC DRUG CARRIER SYSTEMS. 1985. q. $225. C R C Press, Inc., 2000 Corporate Blvd., N.W., Boca Raton, FL 33431. TEL 407-994-0555. FAX 407-998-9784. Ed. Stephen D. Bruck.
—BLDSC shelfmark: 3487.483700.

CRITICAL REVIEWS IN TOXICOLOGY. see *ENVIRONMENTAL STUDIES — Toxicology And Environmental Safety*

615.1 IT ISSN 0011-1783
CODEN: CRFMAY
CRONACHE FARMACEUTICHE. (Text in English, French and Italian) 1958. bi-m. L.50000($50) (effective 1992). Societa Italiana di Scienze Farmaceutiche, Via Giorgio Jan. 18, 20129 Milan, Italy. Ed. Piero Sensi. adv.; bk.rev.; abstr.; bibl.; illus.; index; circ. 1,800. **Indexed:** Biol.Abstr., Biotech.Abstr., Chem.Abstr., Excerp.Med., I.P.A.
●Also available online.

615 SP ISSN 0210-6566
CUADERNOS DE HISTORIA DE LA FARMACIA. 1971. irreg. price varies. Universidad de Granada, Secretariado de Publicaciones, Antiguo Colegio Maximo de Cartujo, Granada, Spain. Ed. Jose L. Valverde.

CUBA. CENTRO DE INFORMACION Y DOCUMENTACION AGROPECUARIO. BOLETIN DE RESENAS. SERIE: PLANTAS MEDICINALES. see *BIOLOGY — Botany*

CURRENT ISSUES IN TOXICOLOGY. see *ENVIRONMENTAL STUDIES — Toxicology And Environmental Safety*

615.1 AT ISSN 0311-905X
CURRENT THERAPEUTICS; journal of clinical pharmacology and therapeutics. 1960. m. Aus.$96 (effective 1992). Adis Press Australasia Pty. Ltd, 404 Sydney Rd., Balgowlah, N.S.W. 2093, Australia. FAX 02-949-5007. Ed. Jillian Sutherland. adv.; bk.rev.; abstr.; charts; circ. 22,000. **Indexed:** Excerp.Med., Rev.Plant Path.
—BLDSC shelfmark: 3504.605000.
Formerly: New Ethicals (ISSN 0028-5064)

CURRENT TOPICS IN ENVIRONMENTAL AND TOXICOLOGICAL CHEMISTRY. see *ENVIRONMENTAL STUDIES — Toxicology And Environmental Safety*

615.1 US
D C A T DIGEST. (Digest of Current Activities and Trends) 1960. m. membership only. Drug, Chemical and Allied Trades Association, Two Roosevelt Ave., 3rd Fl., Syosset, NY 11791. TEL 516-496-3317. FAX 516-496-2231. Ed. Paul B. Slawter, Jr. stat.; circ. 1,500.
Formerly: D C A T Bulletin (ISSN 0300-7340)

615.4 GW
D D F - JOURNAL. 1930. s-m. DM.65. P I B - Verlag, Truderinger Str. 2, D-8025 Unternaching, Germany. TEL 089-6127021. FAX 089-6127112. Ed. Guenther Schnepf. adv.; circ. 11,500.
Formerly: D D F - Das Drogisten Fachblatt (ISSN 0011-4804)

615.1 US ISSN 1042-9611
RM300 CODEN: DAPHEX
D I C P - THE ANNALS OF PHARMACOTHERAPY. (Text in English; summaries in French and Spanish) 1967. m. $55 to individuals; institutions $100; libraries $145. Harvey Whitney Books Company, Box 42696, Cincinnati, OH 45242. TEL 513-793-3555. FAX 513-793-3600. Ed. Harvey Whitney. adv.; bk.rev.; abstr.; bibl.; charts; illus.; index; circ. 8,000. (also avail. in microform from UMI; back issues avail.; reprint service avail.) **Indexed:** Abstr.Health Care Manage.Stud., Abstr.Hosp.Manage.Stud., Biol.Abstr., Biotech.Abstr., Chem.Abstr., CINAHL, Curr.Adv.Ecol.Sci., Curr.Cont., Dent.Ind., Excerp.Med., Helminthol.Abstr., Hosp.Lit.Ind., I.P.A., Ind.Med., Ind.Sci.Rev., Sci.Cit.Ind.
●Also available online.
—BLDSC shelfmark: 3580.280400.
Former titles (until 1988): Drug Intelligence and Clinical Pharmacy (ISSN 0012-6578); (until 1969): Drug Intelligence.
Description: For health care professionals involved in drug therapy. Provides an interdisciplinary approach to the study of pharmacotherapy.
Refereed Serial

615.1 NE
D W; drogisten weekblad. 1968. w. fl.80. Van der Weij Periodieken B.V., Post Box 285, 1200 AG Hilversum, Netherlands. TEL 035-249741. FAX 035-210951. adv.; bk.rev.; film rev.; abstr.; charts; illus.; mkt.; pat.; stat.; index; circ. 7,400. **Indexed:** Key to Econ.Sci.
Former titles: Drogisten Weekblad; Drogistenblad Vergulde Gaper (ISSN 0012-6349)

615 DK ISSN 0105-7480
DANSKE LAEGEMIDDELSTANDARDER. 1978. a. DKK 188. (Sundhedsstyrelsen, Farmaceutiske Laboratorium) Nyt Nordisk Forlag-Arnold Busck A-S, Koebmagergade 49, DK-1150 Copenhagen K, Denmark. TEL 45-33-11-11-03. FAX 45-33-93-44-90.

DE TEXTOS. see *SOCIOLOGY*

DEMENTIA. see *MEDICAL SCIENCES — Psychiatry And Neurology*

615.1 GW ISSN 0011-9849
DER DEUTSCHE APOTHEKER; die aktuelle Zeitschrift fuer pharmazeutische Berufe. 1949. m. DM.80. Verlag "Der Deutsche Apotheker", Hans-Thoma-Str. 1, Postfach 1650, 6370 Oberursel-Taunus, Germany. TEL 06171-55012. FAX 06171-55142. Ed. Siegfried Beyer-Enke. adv.; bk.rev.; bibl.; charts; illus.; index; circ. 14,000. **Indexed:** Biol.Abstr., Chem.Abstr., I.P.A.
●Also available online.
—BLDSC shelfmark: 3562.985000.

615.1 GW ISSN 0011-9857
DEUTSCHE APOTHEKER ZEITUNG; vereinigt mit Sueddeutsche Apotheker-Zeitung. Unabhaengige pharmazeutische Zeitschrift fuer Wissenschaft und Praxis. 1861. w. DM.207.60 (students DM.132). Deutscher Apotheker Verlag, Postfach 101061, 7000 Stuttgart 10, Germany. TEL 0711-2582-0. FAX 0711-2582290. TELEX 723636-DAZ-D. Ed.Bd. adv.; bk.rev.; charts; illus.; index; circ. 28,000. **Indexed:** Anal.Abstr., Biol.Abstr., Biotech.Abstr., Chem.Abstr., Excerp.Med., I.P.A.
●Also available online.
—BLDSC shelfmark: 3563.000000.

615.19 GW ISSN 0174-0164
DEUTSCHE DROGISTEN ZEITUNG; Spiel der Branche. Short title: D D Z. 1945. m. DM.60. E S Fachschriften Verlag GmbH, Paul-Gerhardt-Allee 24, 8000 Munich 60, Germany. TEL 089-8347077. FAX 089-8341962. circ. 13,000.

615.9 GW ISSN 0934-4640
DEUTSCHE GESELLSCHAFT FUER PHARMAKOLOGIE UND TOXIKOLOGIE. MITTEILUNGEN. 1988. irreg. DM.20 (free to members). (Deutsche Gesellschaft fuer Pharmakologie und Toxikologie) Wissenschaftliche Verlagsgesellschaft mbH, Postfach 105339, 7000 Stuttgart 10, Germany. Ed. W. Braun.

615 618.92 SZ ISSN 0379-8305
CODEN: DPTHDL
DEVELOPMENTAL PHARMACOLOGY AND THERAPEUTICS; international journal of perinatal-pediatric pharmacology and drug therapy. 1980. 8/yr. (2 vols. per yr.). 269 Fr.($180) per vol. S. Karger AG, Allschwilerstr. 10, P.O. Box, CH-4009 Basel, Switzerland. TEL 061-3061111. FAX 061-3061234. TELEX CH 962652. Eds. J.V. Aranda, S.J. Yaffe. adv.; illus.; index; circ. 800. (also avail. in microform from RPI) **Indexed:** Biol.Abstr., Biotech.Abstr., Chem.Abstr., Curr.Adv.Ecol.Sci., Curr.Cont., Dairy Sci.Abstr., Excerp.Med., Ind.Med., Ind.Sci.Rev., Ind.Vet., Sci.Cit.Ind., Vet.Bull.
—BLDSC shelfmark: 3579.057800.

DI CYAN BULLETIN. see *MEDICAL SCIENCES — Psychiatry And Neurology*

615.19 610 US ISSN 1054-9609
▼**DIAGNOSTICS INTELLIGENCE.** 1990. 12/yr. $357 (foreign $377). C T B International Publishing Inc., Box 218, Maplewood, NJ 07040. TEL 201-763-6855. FAX 201-763-2575. Ed. Angelo DePalma.
Description: For executives in the pharmaceutical industry. Covers company news, technical developments, regulatory changes, financial trends, market analysis, and patents.

615 MX
DICCIONARIO DE ESPECIALIDADES FARMACEUTICAS. 1944. a. $70 (effective Dec. 1991). Ediciones P L M, S.A. de C.V., San Bernardino 17, Col. del Valle, 03100 Mexico, D.F., Mexico. TEL 687-1766. FAX 536-5027. TELEX 1772912 EPLMME. Ed. Dr. Rogelio Silis. adv.; circ. 60,000.

615 BL
DICIONARIO DE ESPECIALIDADES FARMACEUTICAS. 1971. a. $70. Editora de Publicacoes Cientificas Ltda., Rua Major Suckow, 30 a 36, 20911 Rio de Janeiro RJ, Brazil. TEL 021-201-3722. FAX 021-261-3749. Ed. Jose Maria de Sousa e Melo. adv.; circ. 60,000.

615 FR ISSN 0419-1153
DICTIONNAIRE VIDAL. 1914. a. 487 F. (foreign 630 F.). O.V.P. - Editions du Vidal, 11 rue Quentin Bauchart, 75008 Paris, France. TEL 33-1-47-23-90-91. FAX 47-20-72-89. TELEX OVP 614195F. circ. 184,000.
●Also available on CD-ROM.
Supersedes: Dictionnaire des Specialites Pharmaceutiques.
Description: Directory to ethical pharmaceuticals, diagnostic products and OTC products.

615 BL ISSN 0070-6612
DIRETORIO BRASILEIRO DA INDUSTRIA FARMACEUTICA. 1968. biennial. free. Associacao Brasileira da Industria Farmaceutica, SDS Bloco L Edificio Miguel Badya-5 andar, 70300 Brasilia, DF Brazil. TEL 021-225-6703. TELEX 61-2983. adv.

615.19 NE
DISCOVERIES IN PHARMACOLOGY. 1983. irreg. vol.3, 1986. price varies. Elsevier Science Publishers B.V., Books Division, P.O. Box 211, 1000 AE Amsterdam, Netherlands. TEL 020-5803911. FAX 020-5803705. TELEX 18582 ESPA NL. (Subscr. in U.S. and Canada to: Elsevier Science Publishing Co., Inc., Box 882, Madison Sq. Sta., New York, NY 10159. TEL 212-989-5800) Eds. M.J. Parnham, J. Bruinvels. (back issues avail.)
Refereed Serial

615 TU
▼**DOGA TURKISH JOURNAL OF PHARMACY/DOGA TURK ECZACILIK DERGISI.** (Text in English, Turkish) 1991. 3/yr. $20. Scientific and Technical Research Council of Turkey - Turkiye Bilimsel ve Teknik Arastirma Kurumu, Ataturk Bulvari, No. 221, Kavaklidere, 06100 Ankara, Turkey. TEL 1673657. FAX 1277489. TELEX 43186 BTAK TR. Ed. Ekrem Sezik.

DOJIN NYUSU/DOJIN NEWS. see *CHEMISTRY — Analytical Chemistry*

DOKUMENTATION ARBEITSSCHUTZ UNFALLVERHUETUNG ARBEITSMEDIZIN. see *OCCUPATIONAL HEALTH AND SAFETY*

DR. MED. MABUSE. see *MEDICAL SCIENCES*

DROGFRITT LIV. see *DRUG ABUSE AND ALCOHOLISM*

615.1   NE   ISSN 0012-6330
DROGIST. Cover title: Nieuwe Drogist. 1902. fortn. fl.68. C. Misset B.V., Hanzestr. 1, 7006 RH Doetinchem, Netherlands. TEL 08430-49911. FAX 08430-43839. TELEX 45481. Ed. C. Theunissen. adv.: B&W page fl.2520; trim 230 x 297; adv. contact: Cor van Nek. bk.rev.; illus.; circ. 7,900. **Indexed:** Key to Econ.Sci.

615   US   ISSN 0148-0545
RA1190   CODEN: DCTODJ
DRUG AND CHEMICAL TOXICOLOGY; an international journal for rapid communication. 1978. 4/yr. $325. Marcel Dekker Journals, 270 Madison Ave., New York, NY 10016. TEL 212-696-9000. FAX 212-685-4540. TELEX 421419. (Subscr. to: Box 10018, Church St. Sta., New York, NY 10249) Ed. Gerald Fisher. (also avail. in microform from RPI) **Indexed:** Biol.Abstr., Biotech.Abstr., Chem.Abstr., Curr.Adv.Ecol.Sci., Curr.Cont., Environ.Per.Bibl., Excerp.Med., I.P.A., Ind.Med., Ind.Sci.Rev., Ind.Vet., Pig News & Info., Pollut.Abstr., Sci.Cit.Ind., Vet.Bull., Weed Abstr.
●Also available online.
—BLDSC shelfmark: 3627.985000.
 Refereed Serial

615.9   US
DRUG AND CHEMICAL TOXICOLOGY SERIES. 1984. irreg., vol.7, 1990. price varies. Marcel Dekker, Inc., 270 Madison Ave., New York, NY 10016. TEL 212-696-9000. FAX 212-685-4540. TELEX 421419. Eds. F.J. DiCarlo, F.W. Oehme.
 Refereed Serial

615 668.5   US   ISSN 0732-0760
TP200
DRUG AND COSMETIC CATALOG. 1931. a. $20. Avanstar Communications, Inc., 7500 Old Oak Blvd., Cleveland, OH 44130. TEL 216-826-2839. FAX 216-891-2726. (Subscr. to: 1 E. First St., Duluth, MN 55802) Ed. Donald A. Davis. circ. 4,743.
 Description: Annual directory of the drug and cosmetic industry.

615.1 668.5   US   ISSN 0012-6527
RS1   CODEN: DCINAQ
DRUG AND COSMETIC INDUSTRY. 1914. m. $20. Avanstar Communications, Inc., 7500 Old Oak Blvd., Cleveland, OH 44130. TEL 216-826-2839. FAX 216-891-2726. (Subscr. to: 1 E. First St., Duluth, MN 55802) Ed. Donald A. Davis. adv.; bk.rev.; abstr.; illus.; mkt.; pat.; tr.mk.; index; circ. 12,781. (also avail. in microform) **Indexed:** B.P.I, Biol.Abstr., Biotech.Abstr., Bus.Ind., Cadscan, Chem.Abstr., Curr.Cont., Curr.Pack.Abstr., Hlth.Ind., I.P.A., Int.Packag.Abstr., Lead Abstr., PROMT, Tr.& Indus.Ind., Zincscan.
●Also available online. Vendor(s): DIALOG.
—BLDSC shelfmark: 3628.000000.
 Description: Formulation, raw material procurement, production and packaging for marketers and manufacturers of personal products and health and beauty aids.

615.5   UK   ISSN 0012-6543
DRUG AND THERAPEUTICS BULLETIN. 1963. fortn. £35. Consumers' Association, 2 Marylebone Rd., London NW1 4DF, England. TEL 071-486-5544. (Subscr. to: Consumers' Association, Castlemead, Gascoyne Way, Hertford SG14 1LH, England) Ed. Dr. J.Collier. bibl.; charts; cum.index; circ. 95,000. (also avail. in microfiche from UMI; reprint service avail. from UMI) **Indexed:** Dent.Ind., Excerp.Med., FAMLI, I.P.A., Ind.Med.
●Also available online.
—BLDSC shelfmark: 3629.100000.
 Description: Provides impartial and expert information for doctors and pharmacists on the clinical use of drugs.

615   JA   ISSN 0289-9922
DRUG APPROVAL AND LICENSING PROCEDURES IN JAPAN. (Text in English) 1973. a. 56000 Yen. Yakugyo Jiho Co., Ltd., 28 Kanda Jimbo-cho, Chiyoda-ku, Tokyo 101, Japan.
 Description: Explains Japanese pharmaceutical approval procedures.

615   SP
DRUG DATA REPORT. (Text in English) 1979. m. $750. J.R. Prous, S.A. International Publishers, Apdo. de Correos 540, 08080 Barcelona, Spain. TEL (343)459-22-20. FAX 343-258-13-35. TELEX 98270 PROU E. adv.; bibl.; charts; cum.index 1985-1990. (back issues avail.)
 Formerly: Annual Drug Data Report (ISSN 0379-4121)

615.19   US   ISSN 1055-9612
RS420   CODEN: DDDIEV
DRUG DESIGN AND DISCOVERY. 1986. 4/yr. (in 1 vol., 4 nos./vol.). $155. Harwood Academic Publishers, 270 Eighth Ave., New York, NY 10011. TEL 212-206-8900. FAX 212-645-2459. TELEX 236735 GOPUB UR. (Subscr. to: Box 786, Cooper Sta., New York, NY 10276. TEL 800-545-8398; UK subscr. to: P.O. Box 90, Reading, Berkshire RG1 8JL, England. TEL 0734-560-080) Eds. G.L. Olson, J. Saunders. (also avail. in microform) **Indexed:** Excerp.Med.
—BLDSC shelfmark: 3629.115420.
 Formerly: Drug Design and Delivery (ISSN 0884-2884)
 Refereed Serial

615.19   GW   ISSN 0343-4842
           CODEN: DDEVD6
DRUG DEVELOPMENT AND EVOLUTION. 1977. irreg. price varies. Gustav Fischer Verlag, Wollgrasweg 49, Postfach 720143, 7000 Stuttgart 70, Germany. TEL 0711-458030. FAX 0711-4580334. TELEX 7111-488-FIBUCH. (U.S. address: Gustav Fischer New York Inc., 220 East 23rd St., Suite 909, New York, NY 10010) illus. **Indexed:** Chem.Abstr.
—BLDSC shelfmark: 3629.115500.

615   US   ISSN 0363-9045
RS402   CODEN: DDIPD8
DRUG DEVELOPMENT AND INDUSTRIAL PHARMACY. 1974. 20/yr. $995. Marcel Dekker Journals, 270 Madison Ave., New York, NY 10016. TEL 212-696-9000. FAX 212-685-4540. TELEX 421419. (Subscr. to: Box 10018, Church St. Sta., New York, NY 10249) Ed. Christopher T. Rhodes. (also avail. in microform from RPI) **Indexed:** Biol.Abstr., Biotech.Abstr., Chem.Abstr., Curr.Adv.Ecol.Sci., Curr.Cont., Excerp.Med., Helminthol.Abstr., I.P.A., Ind.Sci.Rev., Sci.Cit.Ind.
●Also available online.
—BLDSC shelfmark: 3629.116000.
 Formerly: Drug Development Communications (ISSN 0095-5183)
 Refereed Serial

615.19   US   ISSN 0272-4391
           CODEN: DDREDC
DRUG DEVELOPMENT RESEARCH. 1981. m. $996 (foreign $1,146). John Wiley & Sons, Inc., Journals, 605 Third Ave., New York, NY 10158. TEL 212-475-7700. FAX 212-850-6088. TELEX 12-7063. Eds. Harbans Lal, Stuart Fielding. adv.; bibl.; charts; illus.; index. **Indexed:** Biol.Abstr., Biotech.Abstr., Chem.Abstr., Curr.Adv.Cell & Devel.Biol., Curr.Adv.Ecol.Sci., Curr.Cont., Excerp.Med., Ind.Sci.Rev., Sci.Cit.Ind.
—BLDSC shelfmark: 3629.119000.
 Description: Refelects original research reports and comprehensive reviews about the systematic studies in pharmacology and toxicology, as related to the development of safe and efficacious drugs.
 Refereed Serial

615.1   US   ISSN 0277-9714
RM300
DRUG FACTS AND COMPARISONS. 1947. m. (with a. edition). $149 (a. edition $89.50). Facts and Comparisons, 111 W. Port Plaza, Ste. 423, St. Louis, MO 63146-3098. TEL 800-223-0554. FAX 314-878-5563. Ed. Bernie R. Olin. index. (looseleaf format; also avail. in microfiche)
—BLDSC shelfmark: 3629.126000.
 Formerly: Facts and Comparisons (ISSN 0014-6617)
 Description: Reference guide listing over 14,000 drugs, including Rx and OTC, arranged by therapeutic class. Facilitates comparisons of costs, brands, and drugs.

615.1   US   ISSN 0092-8615
RM1   CODEN: DGIJB9
DRUG INFORMATION JOURNAL. 1966. q. $290 (effective 1992). (Drug Information Association) Pergamon Press, Inc., Journals Division, 660 White Plains Rd., Tarrytown, NY 10591-5153. TEL 914-524-9200. FAX 914-333-2444. (And: Headington Hill Hall, Oxford OX3 0BW, England. TEL 0865-794141) Ed. Thomas Teal. index; circ. 1,500. (also avail. in microform from MIM,UMI; back issues avail.) **Indexed:** Biol.Abstr., Chem.Abstr., Curr.Adv.Ecol.Sci., Excerp.Med., I.P.A.
●Also available online.
—BLDSC shelfmark: 3629.160000.
 Formerly: Drug Information Bulletin (ISSN 0012-656X)
 Refereed Serial

615.7   US
DRUG INTERACTION FACTS. (Includes 3 quarterly updates) q. $75. Facts and Comparisons, 111 W. Port Plaza, Ste. 423, St. Louis, MO 63146-3098. TEL 800-223-0554. FAX 314-878-5563. Ed. David S. Tatro. (also avail. on diskette)
 Description: Reference for drug and food interactions of clinical significance, suspected but unsubstantiated interactions, with concise synopsis of onset, severity and documentation.

615.7   US
DRUG INTERACTIONS AND UPDATES. 1981. base vol. (plus quarterly updates). $75 (foreign $85). Applied Therapeutics, Inc., Box 5077, Vancouver, WA 98668. FAX 206-253-8475. Eds. Philip D. Hansten, John R. Horn. (looseleaf format; back issues avail.)
 Former titles: Drug Interactions (Vancouver); (until vol.8, no.11, 1989): Drug Interactions Newsletter (ISSN 0271-8707); Incorporates (in 1989): Drug Interactions (Philadelphia).

615   UK
DRUG LICENSE OPPORTUNITIES. 1978. w. IMSWORLD Publications Ltd., 11-13 Melton St., London NW1 2EH, England.
●Also available online.

615.1   CN   ISSN 0012-6586
DRUG MERCHANDISING. m. Can.$32. Maclean-Hunter Ltd., Business Publication Division, Maclean-Hunter Bldg., 777 Bay St., Toronto, Ont. M5W 1A7, Canada. TEL 416-596-5950. Ed. Polly Thompson. adv.; illus.; circ. 7,271. **Indexed:** Can.B.P.I., I.P.A.
●Also available online.
—BLDSC shelfmark: 3629.320000.
 Description: News about retail pharmacy and hospital and clinic-based pharmacists.

615   US   ISSN 0090-9556
RM301   CODEN: DMDSAI
DRUG METABOLISM AND DISPOSITION. 1973. bi-m. $75 to individuals; institutions $120. (American Society for Pharmacology and Experimental Therapeutics, Inc.) Williams & Wilkins, 428 E. Preston St., Baltimore, MD 21202. TEL 301-528-4000. FAX 301-528-4312. Ed. Dr. Vincent G. Zannoni. adv.; bk.rev.; illus.; index; circ. 1,100. (also avail. in microform; back issues avail.) **Indexed:** Biol.Abstr., Biotech.Abstr., Chem.Abstr., Curr.Adv.Ecol.Sci., Curr.Cont., Dairy Sci.Abstr., Excerp.Med., Helminthol.Abstr., Ind.Med., Ind.Sci.Rev., Ind.Vet., INIS Atomind., Mass Spectr.Bull., Nutr.Abstr., Protozool.Abstr., Sci.Cit.Ind., Vet.Bull.
—BLDSC shelfmark: 3629.325000.
 Description: Covers metabolism of pharmacological agents or drugs and environmental chemicals, reactants and preservatives for pharmacologists, toxicologists and medical chemists.
 Refereed Serial

615.19   UK
RM302   CODEN: RDMIDP
DRUG METABOLISM AND DRUG INTERACTIONS. (Text in English) 1972. q. $160. Freund Publishing House Ltd., Chesham House, Ste. 500, 150 Regent St., London W1R 5FA, England. (Alt. addr.: P.O. Box 35010, Tel Aviv, Israel. TEL 972-3-615335) Ed. N. Kingsley. adv.; bk.rev.; index. (back issues avail.) **Indexed:** Chem.Abstr., Curr.Adv.Ecol.Sci., Excerp.Med., Ind.Med.
 Former titles: Reviews on Drug Metabolism and Drug Interactions (ISSN 0334-2190); (until vol. 3): Reviews on Drug Interactions (ISSN 0048-7546)

PHARMACY AND PHARMACOLOGY

615 US ISSN 0199-7912
DRUG METABOLISM NEWSLETTER. q. $4 to non-members; members $3. American Society for Pharmacology and Experimental Therapeutics, Drug Metabolism Division, 9650 Rockville Pike, Bethesda, MD 20814.

DRUG METABOLISM REVIEWS. see *MEDICAL SCIENCES*

615.1 II ISSN 0026-8194
DRUG NEWS. 1937. m. Rs.25. India Publications Co., Denabank House, 2nd Fl., 31 Hamam St., Bombay 1, India. Ed. Eric Martin. **Indexed:** PROMT.

615.19 SP ISSN 0214-0934
CODEN: DNPEED
DRUG NEWS & PERSPECTIVES; the international drug newsmagazine. (Text in English) 1988. 10/yr. $500. J.R. Prous, S.A. International Publishers, Apdo. de Correos 540, 08080 Barcelona, Spain. TEL 343-459-22-20. FAX 343-258-15-35. TELEX 98270 PROU E. adv.; bk.rev.; illus.; cum.index 1985-1990. (back issue avail.)
—BLDSC shelfmark: 3629.340000.
Description: Covers all areas of the pharmaceutical industry, academia and regulatory agencies.

615.7 US ISSN 0731-5163
DRUG NEWSLETTER. m. $45. Facts and Comparisons, 111 W. Port Plaza, Ste.423, St. Louis, MO 63146-3098. TEL 800-223-0554. FAX 314-878-5563.
Description: Summarizes new findings and recent developments in drug therapy. Information on investigational drugs, OTCs, actions, reactions and interactions and more.

DRUG STORE MARKET GUIDE; a detailed distribution analysis of chain and wholesale drug store industry. see *BUSINESS AND ECONOMICS — Trade And Industrial Directories*

615.329 US
DRUG STORE NEWS REFERENCE FOR PHARMACY PRACTICE. 1960. a. $2. Lebhar-Friedman, Inc., 425 Park Ave., New York, NY 10022. TEL 212-756-5000. adv.; circ. 56,537.

615.19 574.192 UK ISSN 0952-0317
DRUG TARGETING. s-m. £105. Sheffield University Biomedical Information Service (SUBIS), The University, Sheffield S10 2TN, England. TEL 0742-768555. FAX 0742-739826. TELEX 547216 UGSHEF G. bk.rev. (looseleaf format; back issues avail.)
Description: Current awareness service for researchers in clinical and life sciences.

615.19 US ISSN 1058-241X
▼**DRUG TARGETING AND DELIVERY.** 1992. 2/yr. $72 (foreign $82). Academic Press, Inc., Journal Division, 1250 Sixth Ave., San Diego, CA 92101. TEL 619-230-1840. FAX 619-699-6800. TELEX 181726. Ed. Alfred Stracher.
Description: Focuses on drug delivery technology at the theoretical as well as practical level. Includes basic research, development, and application principles on the molecular, cellular, and higher levels of targeting sites, as well as physical, chemical and immunokinetic modes of delivery.
Refereed Serial

616.86 US ISSN 0001-7094
CODEN: ORTHDZ
DRUG THERAPY. 1971. m. $60 (foreign $75). Excerpta Medica, Inc., Core Publishing Division (Subsidiary of: Elsevier Science Publishers B.V.), 105 Raider Blvd., Belle Mead, NJ 08052. TEL 908-874-8550. FAX 908-874-0700. adv.; bk.rev.; circ. 110,000. (also avail. in microform from UMI; reprint service avail. from UMI) **Indexed:** Curr.Cont., Helminthol.Abstr., I.P.A., Nutr.Abstr.
●Also available online.
—BLDSC shelfmark: 3629.430000.

615.1 US ISSN 0012-6616
CODEN: DGTNA7
DRUG TOPICS. 1857. s-m. $58 (foreign $104). Medical Economics Publishing Co., Five Paragon Dr., Montvale, NJ 07645. TEL 201-358-7200. FAX 201-573-1045. Ed. Val Cardinale. adv.; bk.rev.; charts; illus.; mkt.; pat.; tr.lit.; circ. 85,000. (also avail. in microform from UMI; reprint service avail. from UMI) **Indexed:** ABI Inform, B.P.I., Bus.Ind., Hlth.Ind., I.P.A., PROMT, Tr.& Indus.Ind.
●Also available online. Vendor(s): DIALOG.
—BLDSC shelfmark: 3629.450000.
Description: Publishes current ideas, trends and developments affecting the pharmacy field. Includes merchandising, government affairs, management and clinical news.

615.1 US ISSN 0070-7376
DRUG TOPICS RED BOOK. 1897. a. $39 (foreign $75). Medical Economics Publishing Co., Five Paragon Dr., Montvale, NJ 07645. TEL 201-358-7200. FAX 201-573-1045. Ed. Valentine A. Cardinale. circ. 70,000. (also avail. in magnetic tape)
Description: Reference book for pharmacists; lists thousands of drug store products with their forms, strength, size, code numbers and price. Contains sections related to the business of retailing and merchandising.

615.1 US
DRUG TOPICS RED BOOK UPDATE. (Supplement to: Drug Topics Red Book) m. $99 (foreign $139). Medical Economics Publishing Co., Five Paragon Dr., Montvale, NJ 07645. TEL 201-358-7200. FAX 201-573-1045.
Description: Covers the changing prices of prescription and over-the-counter drugs.

615.7 US ISSN 0884-8998
DRUG UTILIZATION REVIEW. 1985. m. $279. American Health Consultants, Inc., Six Piedmont Center, Ste. 400, 3525 Piedmont Rd., N.E., Atlanta, GA 30305. TEL 404-262-7436. FAX 800-284-3291. (Subscr. to: Department L100, Box 740056, Atlanta, GA 30374-9822. TEL 800-688-2421) Ed. Julie Lindy. circ. 1,300. (back issues avail.; reprint service avail.)

615.1 NZ ISSN 0012-6667
RM1 CODEN: DRUGAY
DRUGS; international journal of current therapeutics and applied pharmacology reviews, featuring drug evaluations on drugs, review articles on drugs and drug therapy, and practical therapeutics articles. 1971. m. $460. Adis International, 41 Centorian Dr., Private Bag, Mairangi Bay, Auckland 10, New Zealand. TEL 479-8100. FAX 479-8066. Ed. Eugene M. Sorkin. adv.; abstr.; bibl.; charts; illus. **Indexed:** Biol.Abstr., Biotech.Abstr., Chem.Abstr., Curr.Adv.Cancer Res., Curr.Cont., Dent.Ind., Excerp.Med., Helminthol.Abstr., I.P.A., Ind.Med., Ind.Sci.Rev., Protozool.Abstr., Sci.Cit.Ind.
—BLDSC shelfmark: 3629.600000.

DRUGS AND BIOLOGY GUIDANCE MANUAL. see *PUBLIC HEALTH AND SAFETY*

615.9 610.73 614.8 US ISSN 8756-5935
DRUGS AND DEVICE RECALL BULLETIN. 1985. m. $45. Rx-Data-Pac Service, 8907 Terwilliger's Tr., Cincinnati, OH 45249. TEL 513-489-0943. Ed. Dr. I.H. Goodman. (looseleaf format; back issues avail.)
Description: Current data on FDA recalls.

615.7 US
DRUGS AND THE PHARMACEUTICAL SCIENCES. 1975. irreg., vol.52, 1991. price varies. Marcel Dekker, Inc., 270 Madison Ave., New York, NY 10016. TEL 212-696-9000. FAX 212-685-4540. TELEX 421419 MARDEEK. Ed. J. Swarbrick.
Refereed Serial

615 US ISSN 1051-7723
RS51
▼**DRUGS AVAILABLE ABROAD.** 1990. a. $89.95. Gale Research Inc., Box 33477, Detroit, MI 48232-9852. TEL 800-877-4253. FAX 313-961-6083. TELEX TWX 810-221-7086.
Description: Gives comprehensive and usable guide to pharmaceuticals not yet approved by the U.S. Food and Drug Administration but currently available for sale outside the United States. Offers complete information on the uses, precautions, producers, and U.S. governmental approval status of more than 1000 drugs.

615.19 US
DRUGS IN PROSPECT. 1965. bi-m. $1,295. Paul De Haen International, 2750 S. Shoshone St., Englewood, CO 80110. TEL 800-438-0296. FAX 303-789-2534. Ed. Faye N. Richendifer. index. (also avail. in microfiche; back issues avail.)
●Also available online. Vendor(s): DIALOG.
Description: Reports of newly synthesized drugs exhibiting pharmacological activity.

615.19 US
DRUGS IN RESEARCH. 1965. bi-m. $795. Paul De Haen International, 2750 S. Shoshone St., Englewood, CO 80110. TEL 800-438-0296. FAX 303-789-2534. Ed. Faye N. Richendifer. index. (also avail. in microfiche; back issues avail.)
●Also available online. Vendor(s): DIALOG.
Description: Reports of investigational drugs involved in pre-clinical studies.
Refereed Serial

615.19 US
DRUGS IN USE. 1965. bi-m. $995. Paul De Haen International, 2750 S. Shoshone St., Englewood, CO 80110. TEL 800-438-0296. FAX 303-789-2534. Ed. Faye N. Richendifer. index. (also avail. in microfiche; back issues avail.)
●Also available online. Vendor(s): DIALOG.
Description: Reports of marketed drugs involved in clinical studies.

615.1 GW ISSN 0012-6683
RS1 CODEN: DRMGAS
DRUGS MADE IN GERMANY. (Text in English) 1958. 4/yr. DM.40. Editio Cantor, Postfach 1255, 7960 Aulendorf, Germany. TEL 07525-2060. FAX 07525-20680. Ed. Viktor Schramm. adv.; bk.rev.; charts; illus.; pat.; tr.lit.; circ. 5,200. (reprint service avail. from ISI) **Indexed:** Biol.Abstr., Biotech.Abstr., Chem.Abstr., Excerp.Med., I.P.A., Ind.Med.
●Also available online.
—BLDSC shelfmark: 3629.900000.

615 619 SP ISSN 0377-8282
RM1 CODEN: DRFUD4
DRUGS OF THE FUTURE. (Text in English) 1976. m. $750. J.R. Prous, S.A. International Publishers, Apdo. de Correos 540, 08080 Barcelona, Spain. TEL 343-459-22-20. FAX 343-258-15-35. TELEX 98270 PROU E. adv.; index. cum.index: 1976-1989; circ. 3,000. (back issues avail.) **Indexed:** Biol.Abstr., Chem.Abstr., Excerp.Med.
—BLDSC shelfmark: 3629.840000.
Description: Traces drugs from the first phases of their development up to their marketing stage.

619 SZ ISSN 0378-6501
CODEN: DECRDP
DRUGS UNDER EXPERIMENTAL AND CLINICAL RESEARCH. Short title: Drugs Under Research. 1977. m. 400 SFr. Bioscience Ediprint, Inc., Rue Alexandre-Gavard 16, 1227 Carouge-Geneva, Switzerland. TEL 022-3003383. FAX 022-3002489. TELEX 423355-BIOS-CH. Ed. A. Bertelli. (also avail. in microform from UMI; reprint service avail. from UMI) **Indexed:** Biol.Abstr., Chem.Abstr., Curr.Adv.Ecol.Sci., Curr.Cont., Excerp.Med., Sci.Cit.Ind.
—BLDSC shelfmark: 3629.820000.
Description: Devoted to the study of compounds and molecules which may have possible therapeutic application. Covers animal and clinical pharmacology, medicinal chemistry, toxicology, teratology, mutagenesis, drug metabolism, pharmacokinetics, and clinical trials.

615.19 AT ISSN 0157-9509
E T C H. (Ethical Tablet and Capsule Handbook) 1980. a. Aus.$9. P V P Publications Pty. Ltd., Box 278, Balgowlah, NSW 2093, Australia. circ. 8,500.

615.19 KE
EAST AFRICAN PHARMACEUTICAL JOURNAL. q. P.O. Box 4290, Nairobi, Kenya.

615.1 II ISSN 0012-8872
EASTERN PHARMACIST. (Text in English) 1958. m. $40. 507 Ashok Bhawan, 93, Nehru Place, New Delhi 110019, India. Ed. M.C. Bazaz. adv.; bk.rev.; charts; illus.; mkt.; pat.; tr.lit.; tr.mk.; circ. 5,000. **Indexed:** Chem. Abstr., Curr.Adv.Ecol.Sci., I.P.A.
●Also available online.
—BLDSC shelfmark: 3646.800000.

PHARMACY AND PHARMACOLOGY

641.18   US
EDMUNDS PRESCRIPTION DRUG PRICES. 1981. a. $4.95 per vol. Edmund Publications Corp., 200 Baker Ave., Ste. 309, Concord, MA 01742. TEL 508-371-9788. FAX 508-371-9806.
Description: Gives difference between brand name and generic drug and vitamin prices. Includes drug and food interactions and administration recommendations.

615.1   UA   ISSN 0301-5068
RS1   CODEN: EJPSBZ
EGYPTIAN JOURNAL OF PHARMACEUTICAL SCIENCES. (Text in English; summaries in Arabic, English) 1960. 4/yr. $60. (Pharmaceutical Society of Egypt, Research Department) National Information and Documentation Centre (NIDOC), Tahrir St., Dokki, Awqaf P.O., Cairo, Egypt. Ed. S. Hilal. charts; illus.; circ. 1,750. **Indexed:** Biol.Abstr., Chem.Abstr., Food Sci.& Tech.Abstr., Hort.Abstr., I.P.A., Nutr.Abstr.
●Also available online.
Former titles (until 1972): United Arab Republic Journal of Pharmaceutical Sciences (ISSN 0301-5076); Journal of Pharmaceutical Sciences of the United Arab Republic (ISSN 0022-3557)

EISEI KAGAKU/JAPANESE JOURNAL OF TOXICOLOGY AND ENVIRONMENTAL HEALTH. see *ENVIRONMENTAL STUDIES — Toxicology And Environmental Safety*

615.9 001.64   CN
ELECTRONIC CLAIM STANDARD. irreg. Canadian Pharmaceutical Association, 1785 Alta Vista Dr., Ottawa, Ont. K1G 3Y6, Canada. TEL 613-523-7877. FAX 613-523-0445.

615.7   AT   ISSN 1034-8719
ENCAPSULATOR. 1977. q. Monash Medical Centre, Pharmacy Department, 246 Clayton Rd., Clayton, Vic. 3168, Australia. Ed. Ian Larmour. circ. 1,000. (back issues avail.)
Formerly (until 1989): Pharmacy Bulletin.

EOS; rivista di immunologia ed immunofarmacologia. see *MEDICAL SCIENCES — Allergology And Immunology*

EPILEPSY RESEARCH. see *MEDICAL SCIENCES — Psychiatry And Neurology*

615.321 635.7   IT   ISSN 0394-8196
L'ERBORISTA. q. L.30000 (foriegn L.70000)(effective 1992). Tecniche Nuove s.p.a., Via C. Menotti, 14, 20129 Milan, Italy. TEL 02-75701. FAX 02-7570205.

615   SP
ESCAPARATE FARMACEUTICO. 4/yr. 5700 ptas.($74) (effective 1992). Publica, S.A., Ecuador, 75, entlo., 08029 Barcelona, Spain. TEL 93-321-50-46. FAX 93-322-19-72.

ESPECIALIDADES ODONTOLOGICAS. see *MEDICAL SCIENCES — Dentistry*

615.1   GW   ISSN 0031-6970
                 CODEN: EJCPAS
EUROPEAN JOURNAL OF CLINICAL PHARMACOLOGY. 1968. 12/yr. DM.1,176($627) Springer-Verlag, Heidelberger Platz 3, D-1000 Berlin 33, Germany. TEL 030-8207-1. (Also Heidelberg, Tokyo, Vienna, and New York) Ed. J.K. Aronson. adv.; bk.rev.; illus. (also avail. in microform from UMI; reprint service avail. from ISI) **Indexed:** Abstr.Inter.Med., Biol.Abstr., Biotech.Abstr., C.I.S. Abstr., Chem.Abstr., Curr.Adv.Cancer Res., Curr.Adv.Ecol.Sci., Curr.Cont., Dairy Sci.Abstr., Dent.Ind., Excerp.Med., Ind.Med., Ind.Sci.Rev., INIS Atomind., Sci.Cit.Ind.
—BLDSC shelfmark: 3829.728100.
Description: Original papers, short communications, and letters to the editor on all aspects of clinical pharmacology and drug therapy in man. Focuses on clinical pharmacology and pharmacokinetics.

615.7   SZ   ISSN 0378-7966
EUROPEAN JOURNAL OF DRUG METABOLISM AND PHARMACOKINETICS. (Text in English and French) 1976. q. 220 SFr.($158) Editions Medecine et Hygiene, Case Postale 456, CH-1211 Geneva 4, Switzerland. TEL 022-469355. FAX 022-475610. Ed. A. Benakis. **Indexed:** Biol.Abstr., Biotech.Abstr., Curr.Adv.Ecol.Sci., Dent.Ind., Excerp.Med., I.P.A., Ind.Med., Ind.Sci.Rev., Sci.Cit.Ind.
●Also available online.
—BLDSC shelfmark: 3829.728300.

615   GW   ISSN 0939-9437
EUROPEAN JOURNAL OF HOSPITAL PHARMACY. 1984. q. DM.48. Medpharm GmbH Scientific Publishers, Birkenwaldstr. 44, Postfach 105339, 7000 Stuttgart 1, Germany. TEL 0711-25820. FAX 0711-2582-290. TELEX 723636-DAZ-D. Ed. Dr. Jochen Kotwas. circ. 8,000.

EUROPEAN JOURNAL OF MEDICINAL CHEMISTRY. see *BIOLOGY — Biological Chemistry*

615   GW   ISSN 0939-6411
EUROPEAN JOURNAL OF PHARMACEUTICS AND BIOPHARMACEUTICS. (Text in English, French and German) 1955. bi-m. DM.248. (Arbeitsgemeinschaft fuer Pharmazeutische Verfahrenstechnik e.V.) Wissenschaftliche Verlagsgesellschaft mbH, Postfach 105339, 7000 Stuttgart 10, Germany. TEL 0711-2582-0. FAX 0711-2582-290. TELEX 723636-DAZ-D. Ed. Peter Speiser. circ. 2,000. **Indexed:** Biotech.Abstr., Chem.Abstr., Excerp.Med., I.P.A.
●Also available online.
—BLDSC shelfmark: 3829.733900.
Formerly: Acta Pharmaceutica Technologica (ISSN 0340-3157)

615.1   NE   ISSN 0014-2999
                 CODEN: EJPHAZ
EUROPEAN JOURNAL OF PHARMACOLOGY; an international journal. 1967. 66/yr. (in 20 vols.). fl.6260($3099) (includes Environmental Toxicology and Pharmacology Section, Molecular Pharmacology Section)(effective 1992). Elsevier Science Publishers B.V., P.O. Box 211, 1000 AE Amsterdam, Netherlands. TEL 020-5803911. FAX 020-5803598. TELEX 18582 ESPA NL. (Subscr. in U.S. and Canada to: Elsevier Science Publishing Co., Inc., Box 882, Madison Sq. Sta., New York, NY 10159. TEL 212-989-5800) Ed. D. de Wied. adv.; charts; illus. (also avail. in microform from RPI; reprint service avail. from ISI) **Indexed:** Biol.Abstr., Biotech.Abstr., Chem.Abstr., Curr.Adv.Ecol.Sci., Curr.Cont., Dairy Sci.Abstr., Dent.Ind., Excerp.Med., Helminthol.Abstr., Ind.Med., Ind.Sci.Rev., Ind.Vet., INIS Atomind., Int.Abstr.Biol.Sci., Psychol.Abstr., Sci.Cit.Ind., Vet.Bull.
—BLDSC shelfmark: 3829.734000.
Description: Publishes full length papers as well as short and rapid communications on all aspects of pharmacology.
Refereed Serial

EUROPEAN JOURNAL OF PHARMACOLOGY. ENVIRONMENTAL TOXICOLOGY AND PHARMACOLOGY SECTION. see *ENVIRONMENTAL STUDIES — Toxicology And Environmental Safety*

615   NE   ISSN 0922-4106
                 CODEN: EJPPET
EUROPEAN JOURNAL OF PHARMACOLOGY. MOLECULAR PHARMACOLOGY SECTION. (Section of: European Journal of Pharmacology (ISSN 0014-2999)) (Text in English) 1989. 12/yr.(in 3 vols.; 4 nos./vol.). fl.1113 (effective 1992). Elsevier Science Publishers B.V., P.O. Box 211, 1000 AE Amsterdam, Netherlands. TEL 020-5803911. FAX 020-5803598. TELEX 18582 ESPA NL. (Subscr. in U.S. and Canada to: Elsevier Science Publishing Co., Inc., Box 882, Madison Sq., Sta., New York, NY 10159. TEL 212-989-5800) Ed.Bd. (reprint service avail. from ISI) **Indexed:** Biol.Abstr., Chem.Abstr., Curr.Cont., Ind.Med.
Description: Contains original information on interactions at the molecular level of substances in biological systems.
Refereed Serial

EUROPEAN NEUROPSYCHOPHARMACOLOGY. see *MEDICAL SCIENCES — Psychiatry And Neurology*

615.19   US
EVALUATION OF DRUG INTERACTIONS. 1988. a. (updates 6/yr.). $159 (updates $74.95). Professional Drug Systems, Inc., 330 Maryville Centre Dr., Ste. 250, St. Louis, MO 63130. TEL 800-366-4737. FAX 314-275-8819. Eds. Frederic Zucchero, Mark Hogan.

615   FR
EVOLUTION PHARMACEUTIQUE. m. 120 F. Union Nationale des Grandes Pharmacies, 57 rue Spontini, 75116 Paris, France. Dir. J. Vigan. adv.; circ. 14,000.

EXPERIMENTAL AND TOXICOLOGIC PATHOLOGY. see *MEDICAL SCIENCES — Experimental Medicine, Laboratory Technique*

F D A COMPLIANCE POLICY GUIDANCE. MANUAL. (U.S. Food and Drug Administration) see *FOOD AND FOOD INDUSTRIES*

F D A CONSUMER. (U.S. Food and Drug Administration) see *CONSUMER EDUCATION AND PROTECTION*

F D A ENFORCEMENT REPORT. (U.S. Food and Drug Administration) see *CRIMINOLOGY AND LAW ENFORCEMENT*

F D A INSPECTION OPERATIONS MANUAL. see *FOOD AND FOOD INDUSTRIES*

615.1   US
F D A MEDICAL BULLETIN. 1970. irreg. free. U.S. Food and Drug Administration, 5600 Fisher's Ln., Rockville, MD 20857. TEL 301-443-3220. Ed. Judith Willis. (back issues avail.) **Indexed:** Curr.Lit.Fam.Plan., Excerp.Med., I.P.A., Ind.Med., Ind.U.S.Gov.Per., Med. Care Rev., MEDOC, Telegen.
●Also available online. Vendor(s): BRS (DIOG), Data-Star, DIALOG.
Formerly (until 1990): F D A Drug Bulletin (ISSN 0361-4344)
Description: Reports on new drug approvals, adverse reactions, biological end-products and medical and radiological devices.

F D C CONTROL NEWSLETTER. (Food, Drug, and Cosmetics) see *FOOD AND FOOD INDUSTRIES*

615.1   US   ISSN 0276-4318
RM300
FAMILY PHYSICIAN'S COMPENDIUM OF DRUG THERAPY. Spine title: Compendium of Drug Therapy. 1980. a. $40. Excerpta Medica, Inc., Core Publishing Division (Subsidiary of: Elsevier Science Publishers B.V.), 105 Raider Blvd., Belle Mead, NJ 08052. TEL 908-874-8550. FAX 908-874-0700. Ed. Kenneth Senerth.
Formerly: Osteopathic Physician's Compendium of Drug Therapy (ISSN 0272-7064)
Refereed Serial

615.19 660   AU
FARBE AKTUELL. m. Bundesgremium des Handels Mit Drogen, Pharmazeutika, Farben, Lacken und Chemikalien, Wiedner-Hauptstr 63, Postfach 1045 Vienna, Austria. TEL 65050. TELEX 3222440.

615   YU
FARMACEUT. bi-m. Farmaceutsko Drustvo Vojvodine, Bulevar Revolucije 32, Novi Sad, Yugoslavia. Ed. Olga Stefanovic.

615.1   CS   ISSN 0014-8172
                 CODEN: FAOBAS
FARMACEUTICKY OBZOR. (Text in Czech or Slovak; summaries in English, German, Russian) 1931. m. $90. (Institut pre Dalsie Vzdelavanie Lekarov a Farmaceutov) Obzor, Ceskoslovenskej Armady 35, 815 85 Bratislava, Czechoslovakia. (Dist. by: Slovart, Gottwaldovo nam. 48, 805 32 Bratislava, Czechoslovakia) Ed.Bd. adv.; bk.rev.; abstr.; charts; illus.; stat.; index; circ. 2,500. **Indexed:** Anal.Abstr., Biol.Abstr., Chem.Abstr., Excerp.Med., I.P.A., INIS Atomind.
●Also available online.
—BLDSC shelfmark: 3881.850000.

615.1   DK   ISSN 0014-8199
FARMACEUTISK TIDENDE. (Text in Danish; summaries in English) 1890. w. DKK 300. Dansk Farmaceutforening - Danish Pharmacists' Association, Toldbbodgade 36, 1253 Copenhagen K, Denmark. Ed. Knud Soerensen. adv.; bk.rev.; abstr.; bibl.; charts; illus.; stat.; index, cum.index; circ. 3,697. **Indexed:** Chem.Abstr., I.P.A.
●Also available online.

615.1   CI   ISSN 0014-8202
                 CODEN: FAGLAI
FARMACEUTSKI GLASNIK. (Text in Croatian; summaries in English) 1907. m. 2000 din.($100) Hrvatsko Farmaceutsko Drustvo, Masarykova 2, 41000 Zagreb, Croatia. TEL 427-944. FAX 431-301. Ed. Dr. Oleg Cupahin. adv.; bk.rev.; abstr.; bibl.; charts; illus.; stat.; index; circ. 1,600. **Indexed:** Biol.Abstr., Biotech.Abstr., Chem.Abstr., I.P.A.
●Also available online.
—BLDSC shelfmark: 3884.000000.
Formerly (until 1944): Farmaceutski Vjesnik.

PHARMACY AND PHARMACOLOGY

615.1   SW   ISSN 0014-8210
FARMACEVTISK REVY. 1902. m. SEK 275. Sveriges Farmacevtfoerbund, Bryggavgatan 10, Box 750, S-10135 Stockholm, Sweden. Ed. Aake Lindfors. adv.; bk.rev.; circ. 6,932. **Indexed:** Biol.Abstr., Chem.Abstr., I.P.A.
●Also available online.
—BLDSC shelfmark: 3885.000000.

615.1   XV   ISSN 0014-8229
FARMACEVTSKI VESTNIK; strokovno glasilo slovenske farmacije. (Text in Serbo-Croatian, Slovenian; summaries English) 1950. q. $50. Slovensko Farmacevtsko Drustvo, P.O. Box 311, Masera Spasica 10, 61001 Ljubljana, Slovenia. TEL 061-221-078. Ed. Ales Krbavcic. adv.; bk.rev.; charts; illus.; tr.lit.; index; circ. 1,900. (reprint service avail. from UMI) **Indexed:** Biol.Abstr., Biotech.Abstr., Chem.Abstr., I.P.A.
●Also available online.

615.1   DK
FARMACI. (Text in Danish) 1844. m. DKK 400($27) Danmarks Apotekerforening, Bredgade 54, 1260 Copenhagen K, Denmark. Ed. Jens Povelsen. adv.; bk.rev.; abstr.; charts; illus.; index; circ. 2,500. (back issues avail.) **Indexed:** Biol.Abstr., Chem.Abstr., I.P.A., INIS Atomind.
●Also available online.
Formerly: Archiv for Pharmaci og Chemi (ISSN 0003-8938)

615.1   RM   ISSN 0014-8237
CODEN: FRMBAZ
FARMACIA/PHARMACY. (Text in Rumanian; summaries in English, French, German, Russian) 1953. 4/yr. $20. Uniunea Societatilor De Stiinte Medicale Din Republica Socialista Rumania, Str. Progresului No. 8, Bucharest, Rumania. (Subscr. to: ILEXIM, Str. 13 Decembrie Nr. 3, P.O. Box 136-137, Bucharest, Rumania) Ed.Bd. adv.; bk.rev.; abstr.; charts. **Indexed:** Abstr.Bulg.Sci.Med.Lit., Biotech.Abstr., Chem.Abstr., Excerp.Med., I.P.A.
●Also available online.

615   IT   ISSN 0394-8196
FARMACIA NATURALE. m. L.75000 (foreign L.190000)(effective 1992). Tecniche Nuove s.p.a., Via C. Menotti, 14, 20129 Milan, Italy. TEL 02-75701. FAX 02-7570205.

615.1   IT   ISSN 0014-8245
FARMACIA NUOVA; bollettino dei farmacisti Piemontesi. vol.26, 1970. m. Via Oglianico 4, 10149 Turin, Italy. Ed. Cristoforo Masino. adv. (newspaper) **Indexed:** Biol.Abstr., Chem.Abstr.

615.7   IT
FARMACISTA MODERNO. 1969. m. (10/yr.). Edifarm S.p.A., Viale Sabotino 19-2, 20135 Milan, Italy. adv.; circ. 16,000.

615   IT   ISSN 0014-8253
FARMACISTA SOCIALE; periodico indipendente dei farmacisti d'Italia. 1965. m. L.10000. (Farmacisti d'Italia) Dr. Franco Ricciardi, Ed. & Pub., Trav. D. Fontana 53-57, Naples, Italy. adv.; bibl.; illus.; stat.; tr.lit.; circ. 8,000. (tabloid format)

615.1   PL   ISSN 0014-8261
CODEN: FAPOA4
FARMACJA POLSKA. (Text in Polish; contents in English, Russian) 1945. m. 360000 Zl.($120) (effective 1992). (Polskie Towarzystwo Farmaceutyczne - Polish Pharmaceutical Society) Wydawnictwo Polskiego Towarzystwa Farmaceutycznego, Dluga 16, 00-238 Warsaw, Poland. TEL 48-22-31-02-41. (Dist. by: Ars Polona- Ruch, Krakowskie Przedmiescie 7, Warsaw, Poland) Ed. Alina Zdunska. adv.; bk.rev.; charts; illus.; tr.lit.; index; circ. 1,400. (back issues avail.) **Indexed:** Anal.Abstr., Biotech.Abstr., Chem.Abstr., Excerp.Med., I.P.A.
●Also available online.
—BLDSC shelfmark: 3887.000000.
Description: Devoted to scientific and social and professional problems of pharmacy.

615.1   IT   ISSN 0014-827X
FARMACO. (Text in English) 1945. m. L.230000 (Europe L.280000; elsewhere L.320000). Societa Chimica Italiana, Viale Liegi, 48, 00198 Rome, Italy. TEL 06-8549691. FAX 06-8548734. Ed. Giovanni Rodighiero. adv.; bk.rev.; charts; illus.; tr.lit.; index; circ. 1,500. **Indexed:** Anal.Abstr., Biol.Abstr., Biotech.Abstr., Chem.Abstr., Chem.Infd., Curr.Adv.Ecol.Sci., Curr.Chem.React., Dairy Sci.Abstr., Excerp.Med., Food Sci.& Tech.Abstr., I.P.A., Ind.Chem., Ind.Med., Mass Spectr.Bull., Nutr.Abstr., Protozool.Abstr., Sci.Cit.Ind.
●Also available online.
—BLDSC shelfmark: 3887.500000.
Description: Publishes original scientific papers and articles on various aspects of medicinal chemistry and pharmaceutical sciences.

615.19   SP   ISSN 0214-8935
FARMACOTERAPIA/JOURNAL OF PHARMACOLOGY. 1984. 18/yr. 7500 ptas. Editores Medicos, S.A., Paseo de la Castellana, 53, 28046 Madrid, Spain. TEL 442-86-56. FAX 422-80-43. circ. 12,000.

615.9   RU   ISSN 0014-8318
CODEN: FATOAO
FARMAKOLOGIYA I TOKSIKOLOGIYA/PHARMACOLOGY AND TOXICOLOGY. (Text in Russian; summaries in English) 1938. bi-m. 30.30 Rub.($10.80) (Akademiya Meditsinskikh Nauk S.S.S.R) Izdatel'stvo Meditsina, Petroverigskii pereulok 6-8, 101000 Moscow, Russia. TEL 095-120-60-44. (Co-sponsor: Vsesoyuznoe Nauchnoe Obshetstvo Farmakologov) Ed. D.A. Kharkevich. index. (tabloid format) **Indexed:** Biol.Abstr., Biotech.Abstr., Chem.Abstr., Curr.Adv.Ecol.Sci., Curr.Cont., Dent.Ind., Excerp.Med., Helminthol.Abstr., I.P.A., Ind.Med., Ind.Sci.Rev., INIS Atomind., Nutr.Abstr., Psychol.Abstr., Sci.Cit.Ind.
—BLDSC shelfmark: 0389.000000.
Description: Publishes articles devoted to the pharmacological study of medicinal preparations and of the effects produced by various poisons on animals and man.

615.1   NO   ISSN 0014-8326
CODEN: FMKTAA
FARMAKOTERAPI. (Text mainly in Norwegian; occasionally in English; summaries in English) 1945. 4/yr. free. Nycomed A-S, Nycoveien 1-2, P.O. Box 4220, Torshov 0401, Oslo 4, Norway. TEL 02-38-98-00. FAX 02-22-34-73. TELEX 77 149 NYTEX N. Eds. Ole Jacob Broch, Kamilla Dahlstroem. abstr.; bibl.; charts; illus.; index; cum.index; circ. 19,000. **Indexed:** Biotech.Abstr., Chem.Abstr.
Description: Presents articles on medicine of general nature. Directed to physicians and pharmacists.

615.1   KR   ISSN 0014-8342
FARMATSEVTYCHNYI ZHURNAL. (Text in Ukrainian; summaries in Russian) 1928-1942; resumed 1958. bi-m. $8.40. Izdatel'stvo Naukova Dumka, c/o Yu.A. Khramov, Dir, Ul. Repina, 3, Kiev 252 601, Ukraine. (Subscr. to: Mezhdunarodnaya Kniga, Moscow, G-200, Russia) charts; illus.; index; circ. 7,900. **Indexed:** Anal.Abstr., Biol.Abstr., Biotech.Abstr., Chem.Abstr., Excerp.Med., I.P.A., Ind.Med., INIS Atomind.

615   BU   ISSN 0428-0296
CODEN: FMTYA2
FARMATSIA. (Text in Bulgarian; summaries in English, Russian) 1951. bi-m. 16 lv.($10) (Ministerstvo na Narodnoto Zdrave) Izdatelstvo Meditsina i Fizkultura, 11, Pl. Slaveikov, Sofia, Bulgaria. (Dist. by: Hemus, 6, Rouski Blvd., 1000 Sofia, Bulgaria) (Co-sponsor: Nauchno Druzhestvo po Farmatsija) Ed. E. Minkov. circ. 1,133. **Indexed:** Abstr.Bulg.Sci.Med.Lit., Chem.Abstr., Excerp.Med., I.P.A., Ind.Med.
—BLDSC shelfmark: 0389.190000.

615.19   RU   ISSN 0367-3014
FARMATSIYA/PHARMACY. (Text in Russian; summaries in English) 1952. bi-m. (Vsesoyuznoe Nauchnoe Obshchestvo Farmatsevtov) Izdatel'stvo Meditsina, Petroverigskii pereulok 6-8, 101838 Moscow, Russia. (Subscr. to: Mezhdunarodnaya Kniga, Moscow, G-200, Russia) (Co-sponsor: Ministerstvo Zdravookhraneniya S.S.S.R.) Ed. A.F. Rybtsov. **Indexed:** Anal.Abstr., Biol.Abstr., Biotech.Abstr., Chem.Abstr., Curr.Cont., Excerp.Med., Hort.Abstr., I.P.A.
—BLDSC shelfmark: 0389.180000.
Description: Publishes information on scientific investigations in the field of pharmacy: training and further specialization of pharmaceutical personnel, industrial engineering, exchange of experience, rationalization and invention in pharmacy, status and development of pharmacy abroad.

615.1   SW   ISSN 0014-8520
FARMIS - REPTILEN. (Text occasionally in English) 1959. 8/yr. SEK 100($6.50) Farmaceutiska Studentkaaren, Box 8036, S-750 08 Uppsala, Sweden. Ed. Richard Gavatin. adv.; bk.rev.; circ. 1,200 (controlled).

615.1   JA   ISSN 0014-8601
CODEN: FARUAW
FARUMASHIA/PHARMACY. (Text in Japanese) 1965. m. $91 to members. Pharmaceutical Society of Japan - Nihon Yakugakkai, 12-15, Shibuya 2-chome, Shibuya-ku, Tokyo 150, Japan. Ed. Nobumasa Imura. adv.; bk.rev.; film rev.; abstr.; bibl.; charts; mkt.; stat.; tr.lit.; index; circ. 21,000 (controlled). **Indexed:** Chem.Abstr.
—BLDSC shelfmark: 3896.500000.

615   IT
FEDERFARMA NOTIZIE; organo d'informazione settimanale dei titolari di farmacia. Bound with: Farma 7. 1986. w. L.220000($150) to non-members. Editoriale Giornalidea s.r.l., Via Sebenico, 14, 20124 Milan, Italy. TEL 02-688875. FAX 02-6888780. Ed. Sossio Guarnaccia. adv.; bk.rev.; circ. 17,000. (back issues avail.)
Formerly (until 1986): Farmacia Notizie.

FITOTERAPIA; rivista di studi ed applicazioni delle piante medicinali. see BIOLOGY — Botany

615.1   US
FLORIDA PHARMACY TODAY. 1937. m. $25. Florida Pharmacy Association, 610 N. Adams St., Tallahassee, FL 32301. TEL 904-222-2400. Ed. Rod Persnell. adv.; bk.rev.; illus.; circ. 3,200.
Former titles: Florida Pharmacy Journal (ISSN 0161-746X); Florida Pharmaceutical Journal (ISSN 0015-4202); Florida Pharmacist.

615   JA   ISSN 0015-5691
CODEN: NYKZAU
FOLIA PHARMACOLOGICA JAPONICA/NIHON YAKURIGAKU ZASSHI. (Text in Japanese; summaries in English) 1925. m. 12000 Yen. Japanese Pharmacological Society, Editorial Office - Nihon Yakuri Gakkai Henshuubu, Dept. of Pharmacology, Faculty of Medicine, Kyoto University, Yoshida Konoe-cho, Sakyo-ku, Kyoto 606, Japan. TEL 075-761-8789. FAX 075-771-8972. Ed. Chikako Tanaka. adv.; illus.; index; circ. 5,100. (also avail. in microform from UMI; reprint service avail. from UMI, ISI) **Indexed:** Biol.Abstr., Biotech.Abstr., Chem.Abstr., Curr.Adv.Ecol.Sci., Curr.Cont., Dairy Sci.Abstr., Dent.Ind., Excerp.Med., Helminthol.Abstr., Ind.Med., Ind.Sci.Rev., Nutr.Abstr.
—BLDSC shelfmark: 3973.500000.

PHARMACY AND PHARMACOLOGY

615 664   UK   ISSN 0265-203X
TX553.A3   CODEN: FACOEB
FOOD ADDITIVES AND CONTAMINANTS; analysis, surveillance, evaluation, control. 1984. bi-m. £180($308) Taylor & Francis Ltd., Rankine Rd., Basingstoke, Hants RG24 0PR, England. TEL 0256-840366. FAX 0256-479438. TELEX 858540. Ed. Dr. R. Walker. **Indexed:** Anal.Abstr., Biodet.Abstr., Curr.Adv.Cancer Res., Curr.Adv.Ecol.Sci., Dairy Sci.Abstr., Environ.Abstr., Environ.Per.Bibl., Excerpt.Med., Food Sci.& Tech.Abstr., Ind.Vet., Int.Packag.Abstr., NRN, Packag.Sci.Tech., Pig News & Info., Poult.Abstr., Soyabean Abstr., Triticale Abstr., Vet.Bull.
—BLDSC shelfmark: 3977.001000.
Description: Contains original research and review articles relating to the detection, determination, occurence, persistence, safety evaluation and control of naturally occuring and man-made additives and contaminants in the food chain.
Refereed Serial

FOOD AND CHEMICAL TOXICOLOGY. see
ENVIRONMENTAL STUDIES — Toxicology And Environmental Safety

FOOD AND DRUG ADMINISTRATION. see *LAW*

FOOD AND DRUG LETTER. see *BUSINESS AND ECONOMICS — Production Of Goods And Services*

FOOD AND DRUG PACKAGING. see *PACKAGING*

615.1   SZ   ISSN 0071-786X
CODEN: FAZMAE
FORTSCHRITTE DER ARZNEIMITTELFORSCHUNG/PROGRESS IN DRUG RESEARCH/PROGRES DES RECHERCHES PHARMACEUTIQUES. (Text in English, French and German) 1959. irreg. (1-2/yr.) Birkhaeuser Verlag, P.O. Box 133, CH-4010 Basel, Switzerland. TEL 061-737740. FAX 061-737950. TELEX 963475 BIRKH CH. Ed. Ernst Jucker. **Indexed:** Biol.Abstr., Biotech.Abstr., Chem.Abstr., I.P.A., Ind.Med.
●Also available online.
—BLDSC shelfmark: 6868.200000.

615.6 610.5   CC
FUJIAN YIYAO ZAZHI/FUJIAN MEDICAL AND PHARMACOLOGICAL JOURNAL. (Text in Chinese) bi-m. Y12. Fujiansheng Yixue Kexue Yanjiusuo - Fujian Institute of Medical Sciences, 21 Mishu Xiang, Wusi Lu, Fuzhou, Fujian 350001, People's Republic of China. TEL 521704. (Dist. overseas by: Jiangsu Publications Import & Export Corp., 56 Gao Yun Ling, Nanjing, Jiangsu, P.R.C.) (Co-sponsor: Fujian Public Health Bureau - Fujiansheng Weisheng Ting) Ed. Chen Guoxi.
Description: Presents research results and developments in pharmacology and the medical sciences.

FUNDAMENTAL AND APPLIED TOXICOLOGY. see *ENVIRONMENTAL STUDIES — Toxicology And Environmental Safety*

615.19   FR   ISSN 0767-3981
CODEN: FCPHEZ
FUNDAMENTAL AND CLINICAL PHARMACOLOGY. (Text in English) 1970. 9/yr. 1395 F.($277) (foreign 1630 F.)(effective 1992). (Association des Pharmacologistes) Editions Scientifiques Elsevier, 29, rue Buffon, 75005 Paris, France. (Subscr. in U.S. and Canada to: Elsevier Science Publishing Co., Inc., Box 882, Madison Sq. Sta., New York, NY 10159. TEL 212-989-5800) Ed.Bd. adv.; bk.rev.; index. **Indexed:** Curr.Adv.Biochem., Curr.Cont., Excerp.Med., Ind.Med., INIS Atomind., Sci.Cit.Ind.
—BLDSC shelfmark: 4056.033000.
Description: Publishes full-length articles and short communications in the entire field of pharmacology from molecular studies to clinical investigations.
Refereed Serial

615   JA   ISSN 0288-349X
GAKUJUTSU ZASSHI/KYOTO COLLEGE OF PHARMACY. SCIENTIFIC JOURNAL. (Text in Japanese) 1968. a. Kyoto Yakka Daigaku, Jichikai Gakujutsubu Shokubutsu Kenkyubu - Kyoto College of Pharmacy, 5 Misasagi Nakauchi-cho, Yamashina-ku, Kyoto-shi, Kyoto-fu 607, Japan.

GASTRIC SECRETION. see *BIOLOGY — Physiology*

GASTROINTESTINAL HORMONES. see *MEDICAL SCIENCES — Gastroenterology*

615.19   GW
GELBE LISTE PHARMINDEX. 1971. q. DM.79. IMP Kommunikationsgesellschaft mbH, Die Liste Pharmindex, Am Forsthaus Gravenbruch 9, Postfach 2202, 6078 Neu-Isenburg 2, Germany. TEL 06102-5021. FAX 06102-53779. circ. 40,000.
Formerly: Liste Pharmindex (ISSN 0344-015X)

615.1   US   ISSN 0306-3623
RM1   CODEN: GEPHDP
GENERAL PHARMACOLOGY. 1970. bi-m. £555 (effective 1992). Pergamon Press, Inc., Journals Division, 660 White Plains Rd., Tarrytown, NY 10591-5153. TEL 914-524-9200. FAX 914-333-2444. (And: Headington Hill Hall, Oxford OX3 0BW, England. TEL 0865-794141) Ed. G.A. Kerkut. adv.; bk.rev.; abstr.; charts; illus.; stat.; index; circ. 1,000. (also avail. in microform from MIM,UMI; back issues avail.; reprint service avail. from UMI) **Indexed:** Biol.Abstr., Biotech.Abstr., Chem.Abstr., Curr.Adv.Biochem., Curr.Adv.Ecol.Sci., Curr.Cont., Dent.Ind., Excerp.Med., Ind.Med., Ind.Sci.Rev., Ind.Vet., Maize Abstr., Poult.Abstr., Sci.Cit.Ind., Triticale Abstr., Vet.Bull.
—BLDSC shelfmark: 4106.710000.
Formerly: Comparative and General Pharmacology (ISSN 0010-4035)
Description: Covers all aspects of pharmacology.
Refereed Serial

615.19   GW   ISSN 0939-334X
GESCHICHTE DER PHARMAZIE. (Supplement to: Deutsche Apotheker Zeitung) 1948. 4/yr. DM.21.60 free with subscr. to Deutsche Apotheker Zeitung. (Internationale Gesellschaft fuer Geschichte der Pharmazie) Deutscher Apotheker Verlag, Postfach 101061, 7000 Stuttgart 10, Germany. TEL 0711-2582-0. FAX 0711-2582290. TELEX 723636-DAZ-D. Ed. W.D. Mueller-Jahncke. bk.rev.; illus.; index.
Former titles: Beitraege zur Geschichte der Pharmazie (ISSN 0341-0099) & Zur Geschichte der Pharmazie (ISSN 0044-5509)

615.19   JA   ISSN 0434-0094
CODEN: GYDKA9
GIFU PHARMACEUTICAL UNIVERSITY. ANNUAL PROCEEDINGS. (Text in Japanese) 1951. a. free. Gifu Pharmaceutical University - Gifu Yakugaku Daigaku, 5-6-1 Mitahora-higashi, Gifu 502, Japan. FAX 0582-37-5797. Ed.Bd. **Indexed:** Chem.Abstr.
—BLDSC shelfmark: 1090.405000.

615.19   IT
GIORNALE DEL FARMACISTA. 1986. fortn. (20/yr.). L.15000 (effective 1991). (Federazione degli Ordini dei Farmacisti Italiani) Masson Italia Periodici, Via Statuto 2-4, 20121 Milan, Italy. TEL 02-6367-1. FAX 02-6367-211. Ed. Giacomo Leopardi. circ. 55,000.

GIORNALE DI NEUROPSICOFARMACOLOGIA. see *MEDICAL SCIENCES — Psychiatry And Neurology*

615   IT   ISSN 1120-3749
GIORNALE ITALIANO DI FARMACIA CLINICA; epidemiologica - informazione - ricerca. 1987. 4/yr. L.60000($110) to individuals; institutions L.100000. (Societa Italiana di Farmacia Ospedaliera - Italian Society of Hospital Pharmacy) Pensiero Scientifico Editore s.r.l., Via Panama 48, 00198 Rome, Italy. TEL 06-8553633. FAX 06-8841741. Ed. Nello Martini. adv.; bk.rev.; bibl.; circ. 2,000. **Indexed:** Excerp.Med.
—BLDSC shelfmark: 4178.215500.

THE GIST. see *FOOD AND FOOD INDUSTRIES*

615   CC
GUANGZHOU YIYAO/GUANGZHOU PHARMACY. (Text in Chinese) bi-m. Guangzhou Weisheng Ju - Guangzhou Health Bureau, No. 484, Renmin Beilu, Guangzhou, Guangdong 510180, People's Republic of China. TEL 862669. Ed. Huang Shushen.

615.1   FR
GUIDE NATIONAL DE PRESCRIPTION DES MEDICAMENTS. Abbreviated title: G N P. 1987. a. 350 F. (foreign 370 F.). O.V.P. - Editions du Vidal, 11, rue Quentin Bauchart, 75384 Paris Cedex 08, France. TEL 33-1-47-23-90-91. FAX 33-1-47-20-72-89. TELEX OVP 614 195 F. (Dist. by: EM-INTER, Allee de la Croix-Bossee, 94234 Cachan Cedex, France. TEL 33-1-45-46-15-00) circ. 10,000.
Description: Provides product category information and selection, 8,000 ethical pharmaceuticals classified.

615   CC
GUOWAI YIXUE (YAOXUE FENCE)/FOREIGN MEDICAL SCIENCES (PHARMACOLOGY). (Text in Chinese) bi-m. Junshi Yixue Kexueyuan, Duwu Yaowu Jianjiusuo - Military Academy of Medical Sciences, Institute of Poisonous and Medical Substances, 27 Taiping Lu, Beijing 100850, People's Republic of China. TEL 812343. Ed. Zhang Qikai.

615.329   CC   ISSN 1001-8751
GUOWAI YIYAO (KANGSHENGSU FENCE)/WORLD NOTES ON ANTIBIOTICS. (Text in Chinese) bi-m. $80. Sichuan Kangjunsu Gongye Yanjiusuo - Sichuan Industrial Institute of Antibiotics, 9 Shanbanqiao Lu, Chengdu, Sichuan 610051, People's Republic of China. TEL 444641. TELEX 60111 SIIA CN.

615   CC   ISSN 1001-6856
GUOWAI YIYAO - ZHIWUYAO FENCE/WORLD NOTES ON HERBAL MEDICINE. (Text in Chinese) bi-m. Guojia Yiyao Guanli-ju, Tianjin Yaowu Yanjiusuo, 308, Anshan Xidao, Tianjin 300193, People's Republic of China. TEL 711320. Ed. Liu Deyan.

615.1   HU   ISSN 0017-6036
CODEN: GYOGAI
GYOGYSZERESZET. (Text in Hungarian; summaries in English, German and Russian) 1957. m. 96 Ft.($41.50) (Magyar Gyogyszereszeti Tarsasag) Ifjusagi Lap-es Konyvkiado Vallalat, Revay u. 16, 1374 Budapest 6, Hungary. Ed. Dr. B. Lang. adv.; bk.rev.; abstr.; index; circ. 2,330. **Indexed:** Biotech.Abstr., Chem.Abstr., Excerp.Med., I.P.A., Ind.Med., INIS Atomind.
●Also available online.
—BLDSC shelfmark: 4233.900000.

615.9   NE
HANDBOOK OF ENDOTOXIN. 1984. irreg., vol.4, 1986. price varies. Elsevier Science Publishers B.V., Books Division, P.O. Box 211, 1000 AE Amsterdam, Netherlands. TEL 020-5803911. FAX 020-5803705. TELEX 18582 ESPA NL. (Subscr. in U.S. and Canada to: Elsevier Science Publishing Co., Inc., Box 882, Madison Sq. Sta., New York, NY 10159. TEL 212-989-5800) Ed. R.A. Proctor.
Refereed Serial

615.19   US   ISSN 0171-2004
CODEN: HEPHD2
HANDBOOK OF EXPERIMENTAL PHARMACOLOGY. 1950. irreg. price varies. Springer-Verlag, 175 Fifth Ave., New York, NY 10010. TEL 212-460-1500. (reprint service avail. from ISI) **Indexed:** Chem.Abstr.

HANDBOOK OF NATURAL TOXINS. see *MEDICAL SCIENCES*

615.9   US
HANDBOOK ON INJECTABLE DRUGS. irreg., latest 6th ed. $94 to non-members; members $75. American Society of Hospital Pharmacists, c/o Jean Rogers, Dir., Mkt. Svcs., 4630 Montgomery Ave., Bethesda, MD 20814. TEL 301-657-3000. Ed. Lawrence A. Trissel.
●Also available online. Vendor(s): BRS (DIFT), DIALOG (File no.229).
Also available on CD-ROM.
Description: Comprehensive coverage of injectable drugs used in admixtures including investigational drugs. Monographs are cross-referenced and arranged according to non-proprietary name.

615   CC   ISSN 1001-8131
HARBIN YIYAO/HARBIN MEDICINE. (Text in Chinese) q. Zhonghua Yixuehui, Harbin Fenhui, 34, Xi 5 Daojie, Daoli-qu, Harbin, Heilongjiang 150010, People's Republic of China. TEL 413165. Ed. Zhao Zhongwu.

PHARMACY AND PHARMACOLOGY

615 US
HARPER HOSPITAL, PHARMACY & THERAPEUTICS NEWSLETTER. 1970. bi-m. free. Harper Hospital (Detroit), 3990 John, Detroit, MI 48201. TEL 313-745-2006. FAX 313-745-1793. Ed. Margo Farber. circ. 500. (processed)
Former titles: Harper-Grace Hospitals, Pharmacy and Therapeutics Newsletter; Harper-Grace Hospital Drug Therapy Newsletter; Grace Hospital Drug Therapy Newsletter.

615.1 US ISSN 0073-1420
HAYES DRUGGIST DIRECTORY. 1912. a. $270. Edward N. Hayes, Ed. & Pub., 4229 Birch St, Newport Beach, CA 92660. TEL 714-756-9063.

615 CC
HEBEI YIYAO/JOURNAL OF HEBEI MEDICINE. (Text in Chinese) bi-m. Hebei Yixue Kexueyuan - Hebei Academy of Medical Sciences, 62 Qingyuan Jie, Shijiazhuang, Hebei 050021, People's Republic of China. Ed. Yu Zhanjiu.

HERBALGRAM. see *BIOLOGY — Botany*

615.329 II ISSN 0018-1935
RM265 CODEN: HINAAU
HINDUSTAN ANTIBIOTICS BULLETIN. 1958. q. Rs.60($15) Hindustan Antibiotics Ltd., Pimpri, Poona 411 018, India. TELEX 0146-279 IN. Ed. Dr. S.R. Naik. adv.; bk.rev.; bibl.; charts; illus.; index; circ. 400. **Indexed:** Biol.Abstr., Chem.Abstr., Excerp.Med., Ind.Med., Indian Sci.Abstr., Rev.Plant Path.
Description: Features documentation of research in and on biotechnicology and antibiotics.

641.18 CN
HOME HEALTH CARE MERCHANDISING. 1989. q. Home Health Care Publishing Inc., 26 Dorchester Ave., Toronto, Ont. M8Z 4W3, Canada. TEL 416-253-9963. FAX 416-253-4506. adv.; circ. 5,000.

615.1 US ISSN 0098-6909
CODEN: HOFOD9
HOSPITAL FORMULARY. 1966. m. $35. Avanstar Communications, Inc., 7500 Old Oak Blvd., Cleveland, OH 44130. TEL 216-826-2839. FAX 216-891-2726. (Subscr. to: 1 E. First St., Duluth, MN 55802) Ed.Bd. adv.; bk.rev.; abstr.; bibl.; charts; index; circ. 26,788. **Indexed:** Biol.Abstr., Biotech.Abstr., C.I.N.L., Curr.Cont., I.P.A.
●Also available online.
—BLDSC shelfmark: 4333.176000.
Formerly (until 1975): Hospital Formulary Management (ISSN 0018-5655)
Description: Focuses on institutional medicine: clinical tests, drug therapy, drug distribution systems, P&T Committee administration and the socio-economic aspects of health care.

615 US
HOSPITAL PHARMACIST REPORT. 1987. m. $39 (foreign $55). Medical Economics Publishing Co., Five Paragon Dr., Montvale, NJ 07645. TEL 201-358-7200. FAX 201-573-1045. Ed. Val Cardinale. adv.; circ. 14,000. (also avail. in microform from UMI; back issues avail.)
Description: Reports on early marketing and legislative trends affecting hospital pharmacy operations and management.

615.1 US ISSN 0018-5787
CODEN: HOPHAZ
HOSPITAL PHARMACY. 1966. m. $60 to individuals (foreign $80); institutions $80 (foreign $100). J.B. Lippincott Co., E. Washington Sq., Philadelphia, PA 19105. TEL 215-238-4200. Ed. Neil M. Davis. adv.; illus.; index; circ. 25,751. (also avail. in microform from UMI) **Indexed:** Abstr.Health Care Manage.Stud., Biol.Abstr., Excerp.Med., Hosp.Lit.Ind., I.P.A.
—BLDSC shelfmark: 4333.207200.

615.9 618.73 US ISSN 0739-957X
HOSPITAL PHARMACY DIRECTOR'S MONTHLY MANAGEMENT SERIES. 1979. m. $45. Rx-Data-Pac Service, 8907 Terwilliger's Tr., Cincinnati, OH 45249. TEL 513-489-0943. (looseleaf format)
Description: Contains practical management information for pharmacy managers.

615.1 CN
HOSPITAL PHARMACY IN ONTARIO. 1964. bi-m. Can.$12. Canadian Society of Hospital Pharmacists, Ontario Branch, 1145 Hunt Club Rd., Ste. 302, Ottawa, Ont. K1V 0Y3, Canada. Ed. Ming Lee. circ. 1,800. (back issues avail.)

615.19 US
HOSPITAL PHARMACY NEWS. 1983. bi-m. Academy Professional Information Services, Inc., 116 W. 32nd St., New York, NY 10001. TEL 212-736-6688. FAX 212-564-1763. Ed. Mary Chichester. adv.; circ. 21,500.

615.19 658 US ISSN 0739-9561
HOSPITAL PHARMACY SERVICE INSTANT UP-DATE. 1978. m. $65. Rx-Data-Pac Service, 8907 Terwilliger's Tr., Cincinnati, OH 45249. TEL 513-489-0943. Ed. Dr. I.H. Goodman. (looseleaf format; back issues avail.)
Description: Contains current data with "its-a-fact" quizzes, to help meet JCAHO requirements for in-service staff. Includes photocopy rights.

HUAXI YIKE DAXUE XUEBAO/WEST CHINA UNIVERSITY OF MEDICAL SCIENCES. JOURNAL. see *MEDICAL SCIENCES*

HUMAN & EXPERIMENTAL TOXICOLOGY; an international journal. see *ENVIRONMENTAL STUDIES — Toxicology And Environmental Safety*

HUMAN PSYCHOPHARMACOLOGY: CLINICAL AND EXPERIMENTAL. see *MEDICAL SCIENCES — Psychiatry And Neurology*

HUMAN REPRODUCTION. see *MEDICAL SCIENCES — Obstetrics And Gynecology*

I C R D B CANCERGRAM: ANTITUMOR AND ANTIVIRAL AGENTS - EXPERIMENTAL THERAPEUTICS, TOXICOLOGY, PHARMACOLOGY. (International Cancer Research Data Bank) see *ENVIRONMENTAL STUDIES — Toxicology And Environmental Safety*

615.1 NE ISSN 0019-039X
I P S F NEWS BULLETIN.* (Text in English, French, German and Spanish) 1958. q. $1.50. International Pharmaceutical Students Federation, Oudegracht 141 Bis, Utrecht, Netherlands. Ed. Peter J. Lindner. adv.; charts; illus.; index; circ. 1,500. **Indexed:** I.P.A.

615.1 US ISSN 0019-1221
IDAHO PHARMACIST. 1964. s-a. $15. Idaho State Pharmaceutical Association, 1365 N. Orchard, Ste. 316, Boise, ID 83706. TEL 208-376-2273. FAX 208-376-5814. Ed. Jo An Condie. adv.; stat.; circ. 500.

615.1 US ISSN 0195-2099
ILLINOIS PHARMACIST. 1909. m. $24. Illinois Pharmacists Association, 223 W. Jackson Blvd., Ste. 1000, Chicago, IL 60606-6906. TEL 312-939-7300. Ed. Dr. Conrad A. Blomquist. adv.; circ. 42,024. (also avail. in microform from UMI; reprint service avail. from UMI)
—BLDSC shelfmark: 4365.470000.
Formerly: Illinois Journal of Pharmacy (ISSN 0147-8222); Which was formed by the 1977 merger of: C R D A News; Illinois Pharmacist (ISSN 0019-2163); Which was formerly: Illinois Drug Process (ISSN 0007-9030)

IMMUNOPHARMACOLOGY. see *MEDICAL SCIENCES — Allergology And Immunology*

615 US ISSN 0892-3973
CODEN: IITOEF
IMMUNOPHARMACOLOGY AND IMMUNOTOXICOLOGY. 1979. 4/yr. $160 to individuals; institutions $320. Marcel Dekker Journals, 270 Madison Ave., New York, NY 10016. TEL 212-696-9000. FAX 212-685-4540. TELEX 421419 MARDEEK. (Subscr. to: Box 10018, Church St. Sta., New York, NY 10249) Ed. Michael A. Chirigos. (also avail. in microform from RPI) **Indexed:** Biol.Abstr., Biol.Dig., Biotech.Abstr., Chem.Abstr. Curr.Adv.Ecol.Sci., Curr.Cont., Excerp.Med., Helminthol.Abstr., Ind.Med., Ind.Sci.Rev., Sci.Cit.Ind.
—BLDSC shelfmark: 4369.760200.
Former titles: Journal of Pharmacology and Immunotoxicology; Journal of Immunopharmacology (ISSN 0163-0571)
Refereed Serial

IN VITRO TOXICOLOGY; a journal of molecular and cellular toxicology. see *ENVIRONMENTAL STUDIES — Toxicology And Environmental Safety*

615.9 FR
INCOMPATEX. 1984. a. 320 F. Societe d'Editions Medico-Pharmaceutiques (SEMP), 26 rue Lebrun, 75013 Paris, France. TEL 1-43-37-83-50. FAX 1-43-31-94-11. TELEX SEMPEX 203046 F. (looseleaf format)
Description: Contains 3,000 references to drug interactions and contra-indications.

615 GW
INDEX NOMINUM. (Text in English, French and German) 1956. biennial. DM.398. Medpharm GmbH Scientific Publishers, Birkenwaldstr. 44, 7000 Stuttgart 1, Germany. FAX 0711-2582290. TELEX 723636-DAZ-D.

615.1 II ISSN 0019-4360
INDIAN & EASTERN PHARMACY.* (Text in English) 1968. m. Rs.40. L. K. Pandeya, Ed. & Pub., Block F, 105C New Alipore, Calcutta 700053, India.

615.1 II ISSN 0019-462X
HD9672.I5 CODEN: INDRBA
INDIAN DRUGS. (Text in English) 1963. m. Rs.30($10) Indian Drug Manufacturers Association, 332 Hind Rajastan Bldg., D.S. Phalke Rd., Dadar, Bombay 400014, India. Ed. K.S. Mathew. adv.; bk.rev.; charts; tr.lit.; circ. 6,000. **Indexed:** Anal.Abstr., Biol.Abstr., Chem.Abstr.
—BLDSC shelfmark: 4396.180000.

615.1 II ISSN 0019-4638
INDIAN DRUGS AND PHARMACEUTICALS INDUSTRY. (Text in English) 1966. bi-m. Rs.20. Chary Publications, 14 Sidh Prasad, Ghatkopar Mahul Rd., Tilak Nagar, Bombay 400089, India. Ed. S.T. Chary. adv.; bk.rev.; illus.; stat.; circ. 4,000.

615.1 II ISSN 0019-526X
RA975.5.P5 CODEN: IJHPBU
INDIAN JOURNAL OF HOSPITAL PHARMACY. (Text in English) 1965. bi-m. Rs.150($20) Indian Hospital Pharmacists' Association, R-566 New Rajinder Nagar, New Delhi 110 060, India. Ed. Dr. B.D. Miglani. adv.; bk.rev.; charts; illus.; stat.; index; circ. 3,000. **Indexed:** Biol.Abstr., Chem.Abstr., Excerp.Med., I.P.A.
●Also available online.
—BLDSC shelfmark: 4415.200000.

615.1 II ISSN 0019-5464
RS119.I5 CODEN: IJPEB3
INDIAN JOURNAL OF PHARMACEUTICAL EDUCATION. 1967. q. Rs.75($20) Association of Pharmaceutical Teachers of India, c/o College of Pharmaceutical Sciences, Manipal 576 119, India. TEL 08252-20060. FAX 08252-20968. TELEX 833209 VVHC IN. Ed. P. Gundu Rao. adv.; bk.rev.; circ. 1,000. **Indexed:** Biol.Abstr., Chem.Abstr., I.P.A.

615.1 II ISSN 0250-474X
CODEN: IJSIDW
INDIAN JOURNAL OF PHARMACEUTICAL SCIENCES. (Text in English) 1939. bi-m. $40. Indian Pharmaceutical Association, Kalina Santacruz East, Bombay 400098, India. Ed. Dr. R.S. Baichwal. bk.rev.; circ. 1,500. (also avail. in microfilm from UMI; reprint service avail. from UMI) **Indexed:** Anal.Abstr., Biol.Abstr., Biotech.Abstr., Chem.Abstr., Excerp.Med., Hort.Abstr., I.P.A., Mass Spectr.Bull., Nutr.Abstr., Plant Grow.Reg.Abstr., Seed Abstr., Soils & Fert.
●Also available online.
Formerly (until 1978): Indian Journal of Pharmacy (ISSN 0019-5472)

615 II ISSN 0253-7613
CODEN: INJPD2
INDIAN JOURNAL OF PHARMACOLOGY. (Text in English) 1968. q. Rs.600($60) Indian Pharmacological Society, Department of Pharmacology, J.N. Medical College, A.M.U., Aligarh 202 002, India. TEL 0571-25684. TELEX 564 230 AMU IN. Ed. K.C. Singhal. adv.; circ. 1,100. **Indexed:** Biol.Abstr., Chem.Abstr., Curr.Adv.Ecol.Sci., Excerp.Med.

INDIAN JOURNAL OF PHYSIOLOGY AND PHARMACOLOGY. see *BIOLOGY — Physiology*

615.19 II
INDIAN PHARMACEUTICAL DIRECTORY. (Text in English) 1988. triennial. $110. Technical Press Publications, 5-1 Convent Street, Colaba, Bombay 400 039, India. TEL 2021446. TELEX 011-3479-CHEM-IN. Ed. J.P. Sousa. adv.; bk.rev.; abstr.; charts; illus.

615.1   II   ISSN 0073-6635
INDIAN PHARMACEUTICAL GUIDE. (Text in English) 1963. a. $60. Pamposh Publications, 506 Ashok Bhawan, 93 Nehru Pl., New Delhi 110019, India. Ed. Mohan C. Bazaz. adv.; circ. 5,000.

615   US
INDIANA PHARMACIST. m. Indiana Pharmacists Association, 156 E. Market St., Indianapolis, IN 46204. adv.; circ. 2,600.

615.19   SP   ISSN 0213-5574
INDUSTRIA FARMACEUTICA; investigacion y tecnologia. 1986. bi-m. 10000 ptas.($164) Editorial Alcion, S.A., Triana, 51-53, 28016 Madrid, Spain. TEL 341-457-64-00. FAX 341-457-39-45. TELEX 49236 QUMI E. Ed. Ramon R. Madrid. adv.; bk.rev.; index; circ. 2,000.

INDUSTRIAL CROPS AND PRODUCTS. see
AGRICULTURE — Crop Production And Soil

615   FR   ISSN 0154-8867
INDUSTRIE SANTE. (Supplements avail.) 1975. 10/yr. 420 F. Editions de Sante, 19, rue Louis le Grand, 75002 Paris, France. TEL 42-65-12-38. FAX 42-65-09-66. TELEX 260717. Ed. Philippe Cherel. adv.; bk.rev.; charts; illus.; stat.; circ. 3,000.
Formerly: Cadre Pharmaceutique.
Description: Information about the pharmaceutical industry in Europe such as regulatory affairs, politics, economics, companies, products, people.

616.047   NE   ISSN 0925-4692
                          CODEN: IAOAES
▼**INFLAMMOPHARMACOLOGY.** (Text in English) 1991. 4/yr. fl.328($186.50) Kluwer Academic Publishers, Postbus 17, 3300 AA Dordrecht, Netherlands. TEL 078-334911. FAX 078-334254. TELEX 29245. (Dist. by: Kluwer Academic Publishers Group, P.O. Box 322, 3300 AH Dordrecht, Netherlands; N. America dist. addr.: Box 358, Accord Station, Hingham, MA 02018-0358. TEL 617-871-6600) Ed. K.D. Rainford. **Indexed:** Excerp.Med. (1992-).
—BLDSC shelfmark: 4478.845700.
Refereed Serial

615   IT   ISSN 0073-7984
INFORMATORE FARMACEUTICO. 1940. a. L.295000 (foreign L.360000) includes Notiziario Medico Farmaceutico. Organizzazione Editoriale Medico-Farmaceutica, Via Edolo 42, Box 10434, 20125 Milan, Italy. (U.S. dist.: Drug Intelligence & Clinical Pharmacy, Box 42435, Cincinnati OH 45242) Ed. Dr. Lucio Marini.

615   IT
INFORMAZIONI SUI FARMACI. (Monographic supplements avail.) 1977. q. L.55000($43) (foreign L.80000). Servizio Informazione e Documentazione Scientifica delle Farmacie Comunali Riunite di Reggio Emilia, Via Doberdo 9, 42100 Reggio Emilia, Italy. TEL 0522-555467. FAX 0522-550146. Ed. Dino Medici. bk.rev.; charts; stat.; index; circ. 3,500. (tabloid format; back issues avail.)
Description: Covers topics in clinical pharmacology for physicians and pharmacists.

INFUSION. see *MEDICAL SCIENCES*

INHALATION TOXICOLOGY. see *ENVIRONMENTAL STUDIES — Toxicology And Environmental Safety*

615.1   NZ   ISSN 0156-2703
INPHARMA; weekly reports from the current international drug literature. 1975. w. $1095. Adis International Ltd., 41 Centorian Dr., Private Bag, Mairangi Bay, Auckland 10, New Zealand. TEL 479-8100. Ed. Peter Louisson.
●Also available online. Vendor(s): BRS.
—BLDSC shelfmark: 4515.936000.

658   UK
INSTITUTE NEWS. 1978. q. £30. Institute of Pharmacy Management International, 17 Wood View, Birkbey Park, Huddersfield, W. Yorks. HD2 2DT, England. TEL 0484-535125. Ed. Malcolm Almond. circ. 1,000. (back issues avail.)
Formerly: Journal of Management and Communication (ISSN 0958-482X)
Description: Covers management, finance and counseling in community pharmacy.

INTERKANTONALE KONTROLLSTELLE FUER HEILMITTEL. MONATSBERICHT/OFFICE INTERCANTONAL DE CONTROLE DE MEDICAMENTS. BULLETIN MENSUEL/UFFICIO INTERCANTONALE DI CONTROLLO DEI MEDICAMENTI. BOLLETTINO MENSILE. see
MEDICAL SCIENCES

INTERNATIONAL CLINICAL PSYCHOPHARMACOLOGY. see
PSYCHOLOGY

615   NE   ISSN 0074-3879
INTERNATIONAL CONGRESS OF PHARMACEUTICAL SCIENCES. PROCEEDINGS.* a., 1989, Munich. International Pharmaceutical Federation - Federation Internationale Pharmaceutique, 11 Alexanderstraat, 2514 JL The Hague, Netherlands.

INTERNATIONAL CONGRESS ON CLINICAL CHEMISTRY. ABSTRACTS. see *BIOLOGY — Biological Chemistry*

INTERNATIONAL CONGRESS ON CLINICAL CHEMISTRY. PAPERS. see *BIOLOGY — Biological Chemistry*

615   US
INTERNATIONAL DIRECTORY OF INVESTIGATORS IN PSYCHOPHARMACOLOGY.* 1973. irreg. U.S. Public Health Service, Alcohol, Drug Abuse and Mental Health Administration, 5600 Fishers Lane, Rockville, MD 20857. TEL 301-496-4000. (Co-sponsor: World Health Organization) Ed. Alice A. Leeds. circ. 6,000.

615   US
INTERNATIONAL DRUG DEVICE REGULATORY MONITOR. 1973. m. $495. Monitor Publishing Company (Washington), 1301 Pennsylvania Ave., N.W., Ste. 1000, Washington, DC 20004. TEL 202-529-5700. Ed. George Kerner. index. (back issues avail.)
Former titles: International Drug Regulatory Monitor; International Drug and Device Regulatory Monitor.

INTERNATIONAL DRUG THERAPY NEWSLETTER. see
MEDICAL SCIENCES

INTERNATIONAL FEDERATION OF CLINICAL CHEMISTRY. JOURNAL. see *BIOLOGY — Biological Chemistry*

615.328   SZ   ISSN 0300-9831
QP771   CODEN: IJVNAP
INTERNATIONAL JOURNAL FOR VITAMIN AND NUTRITION RESEARCH. (Text and summaries in English) 1930. q. 169 Fr. Verlag Hans Huber, Laenggassstr. 76, CH-3000 Berne 9, Switzerland. TEL 031-24-25-33. FAX 031-24-33-80. Ed. Dr. G. Brupbacker. adv.; bk.rev.; abstr.; circ. 800. **Indexed:** Biol.Abstr., Chem.Abstr., Curr.Adv.Ecol.Sci., Dairy Sci.Abstr., Excerp.Med., Food Sci.& Tech.Abstr., Ind.Med., Ind.Sci.Rev., Ind.Vet., Maize Abstr., Nutr.Abstr., Pig News & Info., Poult.Abstr., Sci.Cit.Ind., Soyabean Abstr., Triticale Abstr., Trop.Dis.Bull., Trop.Oil Seeds Abstr., Vet.Bull.
—BLDSC shelfmark: 4542.698000.
Formerly: Internationale Zeitschrift fuer Vitamin-Forschung (ISSN 0020-9406)

615.19   SZ   ISSN 0251-1649
                          CODEN: CPHRDE
INTERNATIONAL JOURNAL OF CLINICAL PHARMACOLOGY RESEARCH. Short title: Clinical Pharmacology Research. 1981. bi-m. 330 SFr. Bioscience Ediprint Inc., Rue Alexandre-Gavard 16, CH-1227 Carouge-Geneva, Switzerland. TEL 022-3003383. FAX 022-3002489. TELEX 423355-BIOS-CH. Ed. A. Bertell. (reprint service avail. from UMI) **Indexed:** Excerp.Med.
—BLDSC shelfmark: 4542.170800.

615.1   GW   ISSN 0174-4879
RM1
INTERNATIONAL JOURNAL OF CLINICAL PHARMACOLOGY, THERAPY AND TOXICOLOGY. (Text in English) 1967. m. DM.324($154) Dustri-Verlag Dr. Karl Feistle, Bahnhofstr. 9, 8024 Deisenhofen, Germany. TEL 089-613861-0. FAX 089-613-5412. Ed.Bd. adv.; bibl.; charts; illus.; circ. 1,200. **Indexed:** Biol.Abstr., Biotech.Abstr., Chem.Abstr., Curr.Adv.Ecol.Sci., Curr.Cont., Dairy Sci.Abstr., Dent.Ind., Excerp.Med., Helminthol.Abstr., I.P.A., Ind.Med., Ind.Sci.Rev., INIS Atomind., Psychol.Abstr., Sci.Cit.Ind., SSCI.
—BLDSC shelfmark: 4542.171000.
Former titles (until 1980): International Journal of Clinical Pharmacology and Biopharmacy (ISSN 0340-0026); Internationale Zeitschrift fuer Klinische Pharmakologie, Therapie und Toxikologie (ISSN 0020-9392)

INTERNATIONAL JOURNAL OF IMMUNOPATHOLOGY AND PHARMACOLOGY. see *MEDICAL SCIENCES — Allergology And Immunology*

615 616.97   US   ISSN 0192-0561
                          CODEN: IJIMDS
INTERNATIONAL JOURNAL OF IMMUNOPHARMACOLOGY. 1979. 8/yr. £300 (effective 1992). Pergamon Press, Inc., Journals Division, 660 White Plains Rd., Tarrytown, NY 10591-5153. TEL 914-524-9200. FAX 914-333-2444. (And: Headington Hill Hall, Oxford OX3 0BW, England. TEL 0865-794141) Ed.Bd. adv.; circ. 1,250. (also avail. in microform from MIM,UMI; reprint service avail. from UMI) **Indexed:** Biol.Abstr., Biotech.Abstr., Chem.Abstr, Curr.Adv.Ecol.Sci., Curr.Cont., Excerp.Med., Helminthol.Abstr., Ind.Med., Ind.Sci.Rev., Ind.Vet., Protozool.Abstr., Sci.Cit.Ind, Vet.Bull.
—BLDSC shelfmark: 4542.301000.
Description: Publishes contributions of clinical relevance which integrate pharmacology and immunology.
Refereed Serial

615   UK   ISSN 0260-6267
                          CODEN: IPTMDN
INTERNATIONAL JOURNAL OF PHARMACEUTICAL TECHNOLOGY & PRODUCT MANUFACTURE. 1979. 4/yr. £60($126) Childwall University Press Ltd., Box 78, London NW11 0PG, England. TEL 01-455-0011. FAX 01-458-2278. TELEX 8954242-POWDER-G. Ed. Dr. N.A. Armstrong. **Indexed:** Biol.Abstr., Biotech.Abstr., Excerp.Med.

615   NE   ISSN 0378-5173
                          CODEN: IJPHDE
INTERNATIONAL JOURNAL OF PHARMACEUTICS. (Text in English) 1978. 33/yr.(in 11 vols.; 3 nos./vol.). fl.3971 (effective 1992). Elsevier Science Publishers B.V., P.O. Box 211, 1000 AE Amsterdam, Netherlands. TEL 020-5803911. FAX 020-5803598. TELEX 18582 ESPA NL. (Subscr. in U.S. and Canada to: Elsevier Science Publishing Co., Inc., Box 882, Madison Sq. Sta., New York, NY 10159. TEL 212-989-5800) Ed. P.F. D'Arcy. adv. (also avail. in microform from RPI; back issues avail.; reprint service avail. from SWZ) **Indexed:** Biodet.Abstr., Biol.Abstr., Biotech.Abstr., Chem.Abstr., Curr.Cont., Dairy Sci.Abstr., Excerp.Med., I.P.A., Ind.Sci.Rev., INIS Atomind., Sci.Cit.Ind.
●Also available online.
—BLDSC shelfmark: 4542.454000.
Description: Publishes research results dealing with all aspects of pharmaceutics including physical, chemical, analytical, biological and engineering studies related to drug delivery.
Refereed Serial

PHARMACY AND PHARMACOLOGY

615   NE   ISSN 0925-1618
CODEN: IJPYEW
INTERNATIONAL JOURNAL OF PHARMACOGNOSY. (Text in English, French and German) 1954. q. $180 to individuals; institutions $251. Swets Publishing Service (Subsidiary of: Swets en Zeitlinger B.V.), Heereweg 347, 2161 CA Lisse, Netherlands. TEL 31-2521-35111. FAX 31-2521-15888. TELEX 41325. (Dist. in N. America by: Swets & Zeitlinger, Box 517, Berwyn, PA 19312. TEL 215-644-4944) Ed. John A. Beutler. adv.; bk.rev.; charts; illus. (also avail. in microform from SWZ; reprint service avail. from SWZ) **Indexed:** Biol.Abstr., Biotech.Abstr., Chem.Abstr., Curr.Adv.Ecol.Sci., Excerp.Med., Forest.Abstr., Forest Prod.Abstr., Hort.Abstr., Ind.Vet., Ornam.Hort., Seed Abstr.
—BLDSC shelfmark: 4542.454200.
   Former titles: Pharmacognosy; International Journal of Crude Drug Research (ISSN 0167-7314); Quarterly Journal of Crude Drug Research (ISSN 0033-5525)

615   UK
▼**INTERNATIONAL JOURNAL OF PHARMACY PRACTICE.** 1991. q. £60 (foreign £68). Royal Pharmaceutical Society, 1 Lambeth High St., London SE1 7JN, England. TEL 071-735-9141. FAX 071-735-7629. TELEX 9312131542-PS-G. Ed. Douglas Simpson. adv.; circ. 1,000.

INTERNATIONAL JOURNAL OF PSYCHOSOMATICS. see *MEDICAL SCIENCES*

INTERNATIONAL JOURNAL ON DRUG POLICY. see *POLITICAL SCIENCE* — *International Relations*

615   UN   ISSN 0257-3717
INTERNATIONAL NARCOTICS CONTROL BOARD. REPORT FOR (YEAR). French edition (ISSN 0257-3725); Spanish edition (ISSN 0257-3733) 1968. a. $12. (International Narcotics Control Board - Organe International de Controle des Stupefiants) United Nations Publications, Room DC2-0853, New York, NY 10017. TEL 212-963-8300. FAX 212-963-3489. (Or Vienna International Centre, P.O. Box 500, 1400 Vienna, Austria) **Indexed:** IIS.
   Former titles: United Nations. International Narcotics Control Board. Annual Report; United Nations. Permanent Central Opium Board. Report of the Permanent Central Opium Board on its Work; United Nations. Permanent Central Opium Board. Report to the Economic and Social Council on the Work of the Permanent Central Narcotics (Opium) Board (ISSN 0082-8343)
   Description: Focuses on the operation of the international drug control system, with an analysis of the world drug situation.

615   GW   ISSN 1010-0423
INTERNATIONAL PHARMACY JOURNAL. 1912. bi-m. DM.105. (International Pharmaceutical Federation - Federation Internationale Pharmaceutique) Medpharm GmbH Scientific Publishers, Birkenwaldstr. 44, Postfach 105339, 7000 Stuttgart 1, Germany. TEL 0711-25820. FAX 0711-2582290. TELEX 723626-DAZ-D. adv.; bk.rev. (also avail. in microform from RPI) **Indexed:** Biol.Abstr., Biotech.Abstr., Chem.Abstr., Curr.Adv.Ecol.Sci., Curr.Cont., Excerp.Med., Helminthol.Abstr., I.P.A.
—BLDSC shelfmark: 4544.924600.
   Former titles (until 1986): Pharmacy International (ISSN 0167-3157); (Until 1980): Journal Mondial de Pharmacie (ISSN 0449-2099); Bulletin del la F I P.
   Refereed Serial

INTERNATIONAL PRESS CUTTING SERVICE: CHEMICAL PROCESS ENGINEERING. DRUGS - PHARMACEUTICALS. see *ENGINEERING — Chemical Engineering*

615.19   SZ   ISSN 1013-9222
INTERNATIONAL SYMPOSIA ON THE PHARMACOLOGY OF THERMOREGULATION. (Text in English) irreg., 7th 1989, Odense. price varies. S. Karger AG, Allschwilerstr. 10, P.O. Box, CH-4009 Basel, Switzerland. TEL 061-3061111. FAX 061-3061234. TELEX CH 962652. (reprint service avail. from ISI) **Indexed:** Biol.Abstr., Curr.Cont., Ind.Med.

INTERNATIONAL SYMPOSIUM ON QUANTUM BIOLOGY AND QUANTUM PHARMACOLOGY. PROCEEDINGS. see *BIOLOGY*

615.1   GW   ISSN 0074-9729
DER INTERNATIONALEN GESELLSCHAFT FUER GESCHICHTE DER PHARMAZIE. VEROEFFENTLICHUNGEN. NEUE FOLGE. (Text in English and German) 1953; N.S. irreg., vol.58, 1990. Wissenschaftliche Verlagsgesellschaft mbH, Postfach 105339, 7000 Stuttgart 10, Germany. TEL 0711-2582-0. FAX 0711-2582-290. TELEX 723636-DAZ-D. Ed. Wolfgang-Hagen Hein.

615.5   US   ISSN 0276-4342
RM300
INTERNIST'S COMPENDIUM OF DRUG THERAPY. Spine title: Compendium of Drug Therapy. 1980. a. $40. Excerpta Medica, Inc., Core Publishing Division (Subsidiary of: Elsevier Science Publishers B.V.), 105 Raider Blvd., Belle Mead, NJ 08052. TEL 908-874-8550. FAX 908-874-0700. Ed. Kenneth Senerth.

615   US   ISSN 0167-6997
CODEN: INNDDK
INVESTIGATIONAL NEW DRUGS; the journal of anti-cancer agents. 1983. q. fl.200($105) to individuals; institutions fl.332 ($169). Kluwer Academic Publishers, 101 Philip Dr., Norwell, MA 02061. TEL 617-871-6600. FAX 617-871-6528. TELEX 200190. (Subscr. to: Box 358, Accord Sta., Hingham, MA 02018-0358) Ed. Dr. Daniel D. Von Hoff. adv.; bk.rev. (back issues avail.; reprint service avail. from SWZ,UMI) **Indexed:** ASCA, Chem.Abstr., Curr.Cont., Excerp.Med., Ind.Med., Ind.Sci.Rev., Sci.Cit.Ind., Telegen.
—BLDSC shelfmark: 4559.885000.
   Refereed Serial

615   US
IOWA PHARMACIST.* m. Iowa Pharmacist Association, 8515 Douglas No. 16, Des Moines, IA 50322. adv.; circ. 2,100.

615.1   IS   ISSN 0017-7865
ISRAEL PHARMACEUTICAL JOURNAL/HA-ROKEACH HA-IVRI/ASSOCIATION PHARMACEUTIQUE D'ISRAEL. JOURNAL. (Text in English, French and Hebrew) 1941. 6/yr. Pharmaceutical Association of Israel, P.O. Box 566, Tel Aviv 65 112, Israel. Eds. E. Menczel, Z. Tomer. adv.; charts; illus.; circ. 5,000. **Indexed:** Biol.Abstr., Chem.Abstr., Excerp.Med., I.P.A.
●Also available online.

615.9   JA
IYAKUHIN SOGO SAYO KENKYU/RESEARCH ON DRUG ACTIONS AND INTERACTIONS. (Text in Japanese) 1975. s-a. 3000 Yen. Tohoku University Hospital, Pharmaceutical Department, 1-1 Seiryo-machi, Sendai-shi, Miyagi-ken 980, Japan. Ed.Bd. bk.rev.; circ. 1,200.

615.19   JA   ISSN 0915-163X
J A P I C WEEKLY BULLETIN. (Text in Japanese) 1972. w. Japan Pharmaceutical Information Center - Nihon Iyaku Joho Senta, 3rd Fl., Nagai-Kinenkan, 2-12-15, Shibuya, Shibuya-ku, Tokyo 150, Japan. FAX 03-5466-1814. Ed. F. Kubo. bk.rev.; cum.index; circ. 600.
   Formerly: Japan Pharmaceutical Information Center. Information.

615.9   JA
JAPAN PHARMA INSIGHT; current business news, side effects of drugs, investigational drug reports. 1985. m. $1500. O.T.O. Research Corporation, Takeuchi Bldg., 1-34-12 Takatanobaba, Shinjuku-ku, Tokyo 160, Japan. Ed. Koichi Ogawa. circ. 175.

615   JA   ISSN 0917-7825
JAPAN PHARMACEUTICAL REFERENCE. (Text in English) 1989. biennial. $150. Japan Pharmaceutical, Medical & Dental Supply Exporters' Association, Ninjin Building, 7-1 Nihonbashi-Honcho 4-chome, Chuoku, Tokyo 103, Japan. TEL 81-3-3241-2106. FAX 81-3-3241-2109. Ed. Kuniichiro Ohno. charts; circ. 3,000.
   Description: Introduces pharmaceutical administration and new drugs in Japan.

JAPANESE JOURNAL OF ANTIBIOTICS. see *MEDICAL SCIENCES*

615.1   JA   ISSN 0021-5198
QP901   CODEN: JJPAAZ
JAPANESE JOURNAL OF PHARMACOLOGY. (Text in English) 1951. m. 15000 Yen. Japanese Pharmacological Society, Editorial Office - Nihon Yakuri Gakkai Henshuubu, Dept. of Pharmacology, Faculty of Medicine, Kyoto University, Yoshida Konoe-cho, Sakyo-ku, Kyoto 606, Japan. TEL 075-761-8789. FAX 075-771-8972. Ed. Chikako Tanaka. circ. 2,300. (also avail. in microform from UMI; reprint service avail. from UMI, ISI) **Indexed:** Biol.Abstr., Biotech.Abstr., Chem.Abstr., Curr.Cont., Dent.Ind., Excerp.Med., Helminthol.Abstr., Ind.Med., Ind.Sci.Rev., Ind.Vet., INIS Atomind., JTA, Nutr.Abstr., P.A.I.S., Psychol.Abstr., Sci.Cit.Ind., Vet.Bull.
—BLDSC shelfmark: 4657.000000.
   Description: Publishes original research on the interactions between chemicals and biological systems.

615.19   JA   ISSN 0021-5201
JAPANESE WEEKLY ON PHARMACY AND CHEMISTRY/YAKUGYO SHINBUN.* Alternate title: Weekly Drug News. (Text in Japanese) 1946. w. 3000 Yen. 1-13-12 Kikawa-nishino-cho, Higoshi-yodogawa-ku, Osaka, Japan. Ed. Y. Taguchi. adv.; bk.rev.; abstr.; bibl.; stat.; circ. 20,000. **Indexed:** Biol.Abstr., Chem.Abstr., I.P.A
   Formerly: Japanese Journal of Pharmacy and Chemistry.

JILIN ZHONGYIYAO/JILIN TRADITIONAL CHINESE MEDICINE. see *MEDICAL SCIENCES*

615.19   FR   ISSN 0291-1981
CODEN: JPCLDE
JOURNAL DE PHARMACIE CLINIQUE; international journal of clinical pharmacy. (Text in English or French; summaries in English, French) 1982. q. 450 F. to individuals; institutions 700 F.; students 210 F. John Libbey Eurotext, 6 rue Blanche, 92120 Montrouge, France. TEL 1-47-35-85-52. FAX 1-46-57-10-09. (Dist. by: Gauthier-Villars, Centrale des Revues, 11 rue Gossin, 92543 Montrouge Cedex, France. TEL 1-46-56-52-66) Ed. P. Sado. circ. 1,300. **Indexed:** Chem.Abstr., Excerp.Med.
—BLDSC shelfmark: 5032.050000.
   Description: Papers on all aspects of pharmaceutical sciences applied to human use.

615   FR   ISSN 0047-2166
CODEN: JPBEAJ
JOURNAL DE PHARMACIE DE BELGIQUE. (Monographic supplements accompany some nos.) 1919; N.S. 1945. bi-m. 120 ECU($140) (typically set in Jan.). (Association Pharmaceutique Belge, BE) Masson, 120 bd. Saint-Germain, 75280 Paris Cedex 06, France. TEL 1-46-34-21-60. FAX 1-45-87-29-99. TELEX 202 671 F. Ed. J. Vervaeren. adv.; illus. (reprint service avail. from ISI) **Indexed:** Biol.Abstr., Biotech.Abstr., Chem.Abstr., Curr.Adv.Biochem., Excerp.Med., Hort.Abstr., I.P.A., Ind.Med., Ind.Sci.Rev., Risk Abstr., Sci.Cit.Ind.
●Also available online.
—BLDSC shelfmark: 5032.000000.

615.1   US   ISSN 1045-6481
JOURNAL MICHIGAN PHARMACIST. 1963. m. $25. Michigan Pharmacists Association, 815 N. Washington Ave., Lansing, MI 48906. TEL 517-484-1466. FAX 517-484-4893. Ed. Debra N. McGuire. adv.: B&W page $580, color page $600; trim 7 1/4 x 9 3/4. charts; illus.; stat.; circ. 4,000. (also avail. in microform from UMI) **Indexed:** Med.Care Rev., Mich.Mag.Ind.
   Formerly: Michigan Pharmacist (ISSN 0026-2404)

JOURNAL OF ANALYTICAL TOXICOLOGY. see *ENVIRONMENTAL STUDIES — Toxicology And Environmental Safety*

JOURNAL OF ANTIBIOTICS; an international journal devoted to research on bioactive microbial products. see *MEDICAL SCIENCES*

JOURNAL OF APPLIED TOXICOLOGY. see *ENVIRONMENTAL STUDIES — Toxicology And Environmental Safety*

615 UK ISSN 0144-1795
CODEN: JAPHDU
JOURNAL OF AUTONOMIC PHARMACOLOGY. 1980. q.
£140 (foreign £155). Blackwell Scientific
Publications Ltd., Osney Mead, Oxford OX2 OEL,
England. TEL 0865-240201. FAX 0865-721205.
TELEX 83355-MEDBOK-G. Ed. Dr. K.J. Broadley.
illus. **Indexed:** Biol.Abstr., Excerp.Med., Ind.Med.,
Ind.Sci.Rev., Sci.Cit.Ind.
—BLDSC shelfmark: 4949.900000.

615.328 UK
CODEN: RCBPEJ
JOURNAL OF BASIC AND CLINICAL PHYSIOLOGY AND PHARMACOLOGY. 1980. q. $120. (Israel
Physiological and Pharmacological Society) Freund
Publishing House Ltd., Chesham House, Ste. 500,
150 Regent St., London W1R 5FA, England. (Alt.
addr.: P.O. Box 35010, Tel Aviv, Israel. TEL
972-3-615335) Eds. M. Horowitz, Y Oron. adv.;
bk.rev.; illus. (back issues avail.) **Indexed:** Biol.Abstr.,
Chem.Abstr., Curr.Adv.Ecol.Sci., Excerp.Med., I.P.A.,
Ind.Med.
Former titles (until 1989): Reviews in Clinical and
Basic Pharmacology (ISSN 0334-1534); (until
1984): Reviews in Pure and Applied
Pharmacological Sciences (ISSN 0197-2839)

615 574.192 US ISSN 1054-3406
RS57 CODEN: JBSTEL
▼**JOURNAL OF BIOPHARMACEUTICAL STATISTICS.**
1991. 2/yr. $35 to individuals; institutions $150.
Marcel Dekker Journals, 270 Madison Ave., New
York, NY 10016. TEL 212-696-9000.
FAX 212-685-4540. TELEX 421419. (Subscr. to:
Box 10018, Church St. Sta., New York, NY 10249)
Ed. K.E. Peace.
Description: Applications of statistics in
biopharmaceutical research and development and
expositions of statistical methodology with
applicability to such work.
Refereed Serial

615 616.1 US ISSN 0160-2446
RM345 CODEN: JCPCDT
JOURNAL OF CARDIOVASCULAR PHARMACOLOGY.
1979. m. $260 to individuals; institutions $460.
Raven Press, 1185 Ave. of the Americas, New York,
NY 10036. TEL 212-930-9500.
FAX 212-869-3495. TELEX 640073. Eds. Jan
Koch-Weser, Paul M. Vanhoutte. adv.; bk.rev.; index;
circ. 2,500. (back issues avail.) **Indexed:**
Biotech.Abstr., Chem.Abstr., Curr.Cont., Excerp.Med.,
Ind.Med., Ind.Sci.Rev., INIS Atomind., Sci.Cit.Ind.
—BLDSC shelfmark: 4954.868000.
Description: Publishes extensive reports on major
new drugs affecting the heart and blood vessels.
Refereed Serial

JOURNAL OF CHILD AND ADOLESCENT PSYCHOPHARMACOLOGY. see *MEDICAL SCIENCES — Psychiatry And Neurology*

JOURNAL OF CLINICAL ONCOLOGY. see *MEDICAL SCIENCES — Cancer*

615.1 US ISSN 0091-2700
CODEN: JCPCBR
JOURNAL OF CLINICAL PHARMACOLOGY. 1961. 12/yr.
$85 to individuals (foreign $160); institutions $120
(foreign $160). (American College of Clinical
Pharmacology) J.B. Lippincott Co., E. Washington
Sq., Philadelphia, PA 19105. TEL 215-238-4225.
(Subscr. to: Downville Pike, Rte. 3, Box 20-B,
Hagerstown, MD 21740) Ed. John Somberg. adv.;
bk.rev.; charts; illus.; index; circ. 5,031. (also avail.
in microform from UMI; back issues avail.) **Indexed:**
Biol.Abstr., Biotech.Abstr., Chem.Abstr., Curr.Cont.,
Dent.Ind., Excerp.Med., I.P.A., Ind.Med., Ind.Sci.Rev.,
INIS Atomind., Psychol.Abstr., Sci.Cit.Ind.
●Also available online.
—BLDSC shelfmark: 4958.680000.
Former titles: Journal of Clinical Pharmacology and
New Drugs (ISSN 0021-9754); Journal of New
Drugs (ISSN 0096-0284)
Description: Geared towards clinical
pharmacologists and physicians concerned with and
responsible for the appropriate selection,
investigation and prescribing of drugs.
Refereed Serial

615 UK ISSN 0269-4727
CODEN: JCPTED
JOURNAL OF CLINICAL PHARMACY AND THERAPEUTICS.
1976. bi-m. £116 (foreign £132). Blackwell
Scientific Publications Ltd., Osney Mead, Oxford OX2
OEL, England. TEL 0865-240201.
FAX 0865-721205. TELEX 83355-MEDBOK-G. Ed.
A. Li Wan Po. adv.; bk.rev.; index; circ. 410. (back
issues avail.; reprint service avail. from ISI) **Indexed:**
ASCA, Biol.Abstr., Biotech.Abstr., Chem.Abstr.,
Excerp.Med., I.P.A., Ind.Med., Ind.Sci.Rev., Sci.Cit.Ind.
●Also available online.
—BLDSC shelfmark: 4958.685000.
Former titles: Journal of Clinical and Hospital
Pharmacy (ISSN 0143-3180); Journal of Clinical
Pharmacy (ISSN 0308-6593)

615.19 US ISSN 0271-0749
CODEN: JCPYDR
JOURNAL OF CLINICAL PSYCHOPHARMACOLOGY. 1981.
bi-m. $63 to individuals; institutions $98. Williams
& Wilkins, 428 E. Preston St., Baltimore, MD
21202. TEL 301-528-4000. FAX 301-528-4312.
Ed. Dr. Richard I. Shader. adv.; bk.rev.; circ. 4,000.
(microfilm; back issues avail.) **Indexed:** A.D.& D.,
Adol.Ment.Hlth.Abstr., Chem.Abstr., Chic.Per.Ind.,
Curr.Cont., Dent.Ind., Excerp.Med., Ind.Med.,
Ind.Sci.Rev., Psychol.Abstr., Sci.Cit.Ind.
—BLDSC shelfmark: 4958.691000.
Description: Clinical papers for psychiatrists on
antipsychotic-, antianxiety-, antidepressant-
medications and stimulants.
Refereed Serial

615.19 US ISSN 1047-0336
JOURNAL OF CLINICAL RESEARCH AND PHARMACOEPIDEMIOLOGY. 1987. 4/yr. $140 to
institutions (foreign $162)(effective 1992).
(Associates of Clinical Pharmacology) Elsevier
Science Publishing Co., Inc. (New York), 655 Ave. of
the Americas, New York, NY 10010.
TEL 212-989-5800. FAX 212-633-3965. TELEX
420643 AEP UI. Ed. Dr. Allen Cato. **Indexed:**
Biol.Abstr., Excerp.Med.
—BLDSC shelfmark: 4958.718000.
Formerly: Journal of Clinical Research and Drug
Development (ISSN 0889-5813)
Description: Offers practical information on drug
development. Provides a forum for the exchange of
information and ideas among individuals involved in
clinical research.
Refereed Serial

JOURNAL OF CONTROLLED RELEASE. see *BIOLOGY — Biological Chemistry*

615 UK ISSN 0952-9500
RM300 CODEN: JDDVEY
JOURNAL OF DRUG DEVELOPMENT. 1988. q.
£95($185) Gardiner - Caldwell Communications
Ltd., Old Ribbon Mill, Pitt St., Macclesfield, Cheshire
SK11 7PT, England. TEL 0625-618507.
FAX 0625-610260. TELEX 665328-GCCG. Ed.
David Caldwell. bk.rev. (back issues avail.) **Indexed:**
Excerp.Med.
Description: Publishes original research papers on
subjects relevant to pharmaceutical medicine.
Refereed Serial

615.1 UA ISSN 0085-2406
JOURNAL OF DRUG RESEARCH OF EGYPT. Cover title:
Journal of Drug Research. (Text in English;
summaries in Arabic and English.) 1968. a. $12.
National Organisation for Drug Control and
Research, Drug Research and Control Center, 6,
Abou-Hazem St., Pyramids Ave., Box 29, Cairo,
Egypt. Ed.Bd. bk.rev.; illus. **Indexed:** Anal.Abstr.,
Biol.Abstr., Chem.Abstr., Excerp.Med., Food Sci.&
Tech.Abstr., I.P.A., Mass Spectr.Bull., Nutr.Abstr.
●Also available online.

615.19 IE ISSN 0378-8741
CODEN: JOETD7
JOURNAL OF ETHNOPHARMACOLOGY; an
interdisciplinary journal devoted to bioscientific
research on indigenous drugs. 1979. 12/yr.(in 4
vols.; 3 nos./vol.). $736 (effective 1992). Elsevier
Scientific Publishers Ireland Ltd., P.O. Box 85,
Limerick, Ireland. TEL 061-61944.
FAX 061-62144. TELEX 72191 ENH EI. (Subscr. in
U.S. and Canada to: Elsevier Science Publishing Co.,
Inc., Box 882, Madison Sq. Sta., New York, NY
10159. TEL 212-989-5800) Ed.Bd. bk.rev. (also
avail. in microform from RPI; reprint service avail.
from SWZ) **Indexed:** Biol.Abstr., Chem.Abstr., Cott.&
Trop.Fibr.Abstr., Curr.Cont., Excerp.Bot., Excerp.Med.,
Field Crop Abstr., Forest.Abstr., Forest Prod.Abstr.,
Hort.Abstr., I.P.A., Ind.Med., Ind.Sci.Rev., Ind.Vet.,
Protozool.Abstr., Sci.Cit.Ind., Seed Abstr., Trop.Oil
Seeds Abstr., Weed Abstr.
—BLDSC shelfmark: 4979.602400.
Description: Publishes articles concerned with the
observation and experimental investigation of the
biological activities of plant and animal substances
used in the traditional medicine of past and present
cultures.
Refereed Serial

615.7 155.67 US ISSN 8756-4629
CODEN: JGDTEF
JOURNAL OF GERIATRIC DRUG THERAPY. 1987. q. $32
to individuals; institutions $45; libraries $115.
Haworth Press, Inc., 10 Alice St., Binghamton, NY
13904. TEL 800-342-9678. FAX 607-722-1424.
Ed. James Cooper. adv.; bk.rev.; circ. 318. (also
avail. in microfiche from HAW; reprint service avail.
from HAW,ISI) **Indexed:** Abstr.Soc.Geront., Curr.Cont.,
Excerp.Med., Human Resour.Abstr., Psychol.Abstr.,
Ref.Zh., Sage Fam.Stud.Abstr., Soc.Work Res.&
Abstr., Sociol.Abstr.
—BLDSC shelfmark: 4995.073000.
Description: Covers drug therapy and related
issues in the geriatric population.
Refereed Serial

615 US ISSN 0197-1522
RB46.5 CODEN: JOUIDK
JOURNAL OF IMMUNOASSAY. 1980. 4/yr. $295.
Marcel Dekker Journals, 270 Madison Ave., New
York, NY 10016. TEL 212-696-9000.
FAX 212-685-4540. TELEX 421419. (Subscr. to:
Box 10018, Church St. Sta., New York, NY 10249)
Ed. W.H.C. Walker. (also avail. in microform from
RPI) **Indexed:** Abstr.Hyg., Biol.Abstr., Chem.Abstr.,
Curr.Adv.Ecol.Sci., Excerp.Med., Ind.Med.,
Ind.Sci.Rev., Ind.Vet., INIS Atomind., Sci.Cit.Ind.,
Telegen, Vet.Bull.
—BLDSC shelfmark: 5004.560000.
Formerly: Immunological and Molecular Probes.
Refereed Serial

615 US ISSN 0194-5106
JOURNAL OF KANSAS PHARMACY. vol.49, 1974. bi-m.
$18. Kansas Pharmacists Association, 1308 W.
10th, Topeka, KS 66604. TEL 913-232-0439. Ed.
Robert R. Williams. adv.; illus.; stat.; tr.lit.; circ.
1,200 (controlled).

615.19 US ISSN 0898-2104
RS201.L55 CODEN: JLREE7
JOURNAL OF LIPOSOME RESEARCH. 1988. 3/yr. $175.
Marcel Dekker Journals, 270 Madison Ave., New
York, NY 10016. TEL 212-696-9000.
FAX 212-685-4540. TELEX 421419 MARDEEK.
(Subscr. to: Box 10018, Church St. Sta., New York,
NY 10249) Ed. Marc J. Ostro. (also avail. in
microform from RPI) **Indexed:** Telegen.
—BLDSC shelfmark: 5010.505000.
Refereed Serial

JOURNAL OF MEDICAL AND PHARMACEUTICAL MARKETING. see *BUSINESS AND ECONOMICS — Marketing And Purchasing*

PHARMACY AND PHARMACOLOGY

615.19 610   US   ISSN 0022-2623
RS402   CODEN: JMCMAR
JOURNAL OF MEDICINAL CHEMISTRY. 1958. bi-m. $487 to non-members; members $49. American Chemical Society, 1155 16th St., N.W., Washington, DC 20036. TEL 800-333-9511. FAX 202-872-4615. TELEX 440159 ACSP UI. (Subscr. to: Box 3337, Columbus, OH 43210) Ed. Dr. Philip S. Portoghese. adv.; bk.rev.; charts; index; circ. 4,272. (also avail. in microfiche from RPI; microfilm; back issues avail.; reprint service avail. from UMI) **Indexed:** Biol.Abstr., Biotech.Abstr., Chem.Abstr., Curr.Adv.Biochem., Curr.Adv.Cancer Res., Curr.Adv.Ecol.Sci., Curr.Chem.React., Curr.Cont., Dairy Sci.Abstr., Dent.Ind., Excerp.Med., Helminthol.Abstr., Ind.Chem., Ind.Med., Ind.Sci.Rev., INIS Atomind., Mass Spectr.Bull., Nutr.Abstr., Poult.Abstr., Protozool.Abstr., Rev.Plant Path., Sci.Cit.Ind., Vet.Bull.
●Also available online. Vendor(s): STN International (CJACS).
—BLDSC shelfmark: 5017.200000.
Formerly: Journal of Medicinal and Pharmaceutical Chemistry (ISSN 0095-9065)
Description: Focuses on the relationship of chemistry to biological activity. Provides valuable research findings and comprehensive book reviews on medicinal chemistry and related areas.
Refereed Serial

616.01   UK   ISSN 0265-2048
RS201.C3   CODEN: JOMIEF
JOURNAL OF MICROENCAPSULATION. 1984. q. £122($211) Taylor & Francis Ltd., Rankine Rd., Basingstoke, Hants. RG25 0PR, England. TEL 0256-840366. FAX 0256-479438. TELEX 858540. Ed. Dr. J.R. Nixon. **Indexed:** Curr.Adv.Ecol.Sci.
—BLDSC shelfmark: 5019.530000.
Description: Devoted to the preparation, properties and uses of individually encapsulated small particles. Its scope extends beyond microcapsules to all other small particle dosage forms which involve preparative manipulating.
Refereed Serial

547.7   US   ISSN 0163-3864
QH1   CODEN: JNPRDF
JOURNAL OF NATURAL PRODUCTS. (Text mainly in English; occasionally in French or German.) 1938. m. $200 to US and Canada; elsewhere $275. American Society of Pharmacognosy, c/o David J. Slatkin, Treasurer, Chicago School of Pharmacy, 555 31st St., Downers Grove, IL 60515. TEL 708-971-6417. FAX 708-971-6097. (Co-sponsor: Lloyd Library and Museum) Ed. James E. Robbers. bk.rev.; charts; illus.; stat.; index; circ. 1,950. (back issues avail.) **Indexed:** Agroforest.Abstr., Anal.Abstr., Biol.Abstr., Biol.& Agr.Ind., Biotech.Abstr., Chem.Abstr., Chem.Infd., Curr.Adv.Biochem., Curr.Adv.Ecol.Sci., Curr.Biotech.Abstr., Curr.Chem.React., Curr.Cont., Deep Sea Res.& Oceanogr.Abstr., Excerp.Bot., Excerp.Med., Field Crop Abstr., Forest.Abstr., Forest Prod.Abstr., Helminthol.Abstr., Herb.Abstr., Hort.Abstr., I.P.A., Ind.Chem., Ind.Med., Ind.Sci.Rev., Ind.Vet., Mass Spectr.Bull., Ornam.Hort., Plant Breed.Abstr., Plant Grow.Reg.Abstr., Protozool.Abstr., Rev.Plant Path., Seed Abstr., So.Pac.Per.Ind., Soyabean Abstr., Vet.Bull., Weed Abstr.
●Also available online.
—BLDSC shelfmark: 5021.225000.
Formerly (until vol.42, 1979): Lloydia (ISSN 0024-5461)
Refereed Serial

JOURNAL OF OCULAR PHARMACOLOGY. see *MEDICAL SCIENCES — Ophthalmology And Optometry*

615.1   US   ISSN 0279-7976
                          CODEN: JPATDS
JOURNAL OF PARENTERAL SCIENCE AND TECHNOLOGY. (Supplements accompany some numbers) 1947. 6/yr. $55 (foreign $70). Parenteral Drug Association, Inc., One Penn Center, 1617 JFK Blvd., Philadelphia, PA 19103. TEL 215-564-6466. FAX 215-564-6472. (Subscr. to: Box 8500-51045, Philadelphia, PA 19178) Ed. Dr. Joseph Schwartz. adv.; charts; illus.; index; circ. 4,300. (back issues avail.) **Indexed:** Biol.Abstr., Biotech.Abstr., Curr.Adv.Ecol.Sci., Excerp.Med., I.P.A., Ind.Med.
●Also available online.
Former titles (until 1981): Parenteral Drug Association. Journal (ISSN 0161-1933); (Until vol.32, 1978): Parenteral Drug Association. Bulletin (ISSN 0048-2986)
Description: Technical articles in the field of parenteral science and sterile products.

615.19   US   ISSN 0731-7085
                          CODEN: JPBADA
JOURNAL OF PHARMACEUTICAL AND BIOMEDICAL ANALYSIS. 1983. 12/yr. £425 (effective 1992). Pergamon Press, Inc., Journals Division, 660 White Plains Rd., Tarrytown, NY 10591-5153. TEL 914-524-9200. FAX 914-333-2444. (And: Headington Hill Hall, Oxford OX3 0BW, England. TEL 0865-794141) Eds. Anthony Fell, Christopher M. Riley. (also avail. in microform from UMI,MIM) **Indexed:** Chem.Abstr., Curr.Adv.Ecol.Sci., Excerp.Med., Hort.Abstr., Mass Spectr.Bull.
—BLDSC shelfmark: 5031.600000.
Description: Publishes research reports and reviews on pharmaceutical and biomedical analysis.
Refereed Serial

615 610   NR   ISSN 0331-0604
JOURNAL OF PHARMACEUTICAL AND MEDICAL SCIENCES. 1977. bi-m. $115.20. Fred Atoki Publishing Co. Ltd., Plot 25 Kekere-Ekun St., Orile-Iganmu, Box 7313, Lagos, Nigeria. Ed. F.O. Atoki. adv.; illus.; circ. 16,000.

615   US   ISSN 1056-4950
▼**JOURNAL OF PHARMACEUTICAL CARE IN PAIN & SYMPTOM CONTROL.** 1992. q. $24 to individuals; institutions $32; libraries $48. Haworth Press, Inc., 10 Alice St., Binghamton, NY 13904. TEL 800-342-9678. FAX 607-722-1424. TELEX 4932599. Ed. Arthur Lipman. adv.; bk.rev. (also avail. in microfiche from HAW; reprint service avail. from HAW)
Refereed Serial

615.19 658   US   ISSN 0883-7597
                          CODEN: JPMMEY
JOURNAL OF PHARMACEUTICAL MARKETING AND MANAGEMENT. 1986. q. $35 to individuals; institutions $42; libraries $95. Haworth Press, Inc., 10 Alice St., Binghamton, NY 13904. TEL 800-342-9678. FAX 607-722-1424. TELEX 4932599. Ed. Mickey C. Smith. adv.; bk.rev. (also avail. in microfiche from HAW; back issues avail.; reprint service avail. from HAW) **Indexed:** Biostat., Human Resour.Abstr., Ind.Med., P.A.I.S., Sage Fam.Stud.Abstr., Tr.& Indus.Ind.
—BLDSC shelfmark: 5031.880000.
Description: Devoted to solving problems of management and the marketing of pharmaceutical products and services.
Refereed Serial

615   UK   ISSN 0958-0581
▼**JOURNAL OF PHARMACEUTICAL MEDICINE.** 1991. q. £76 (foreign £91). (Society of Pharmaceutical Medicine) Blackwell Scientific Publications Ltd., Osney Mead, Oxford OX2 0EL, England. TEL 0865-240201. FAX 0865-721205. TELEX 833355-MEDBOK-G. Eds. B. Dickson, M. Young. adv.; bk.rev.; illus.; index.
—BLDSC shelfmark: 5031.883000.

615.1   JA   ISSN 0372-7629
JOURNAL OF PHARMACEUTICAL SCIENCE AND TECHNOLOGY/YAKUZAIGAKU. (Text in English and Japanese; summaries in English) 1940. q. $55. (Academy of Pharmaceutical Science and Technology) Japan Scientific Societies Press, 6-2-10 Hongo, Bunkyo-ku, Tokyo 113, Japan. TEL 3814-2001. FAX 3814-2002. TELEX 2722268 BCJSP J. (Dist. by: Business Center for Academic Societies Japan, Koshin Bldg., 6-16-3 Hongo, Bunkyo-ku, Tokyo 113, Japan; Dist. in U.S. by: International Specialized Book Services, Inc., 5602 N.E. St., Portland, OR 97213; in Asia by: Toppan Company Pvt. Ltd., 38 Liu Fang Rd., Box 22 Jurong Town, Jurong, Singapore 2262) circ. 1,200. **Indexed:** Biol.Abstr., Chem.Abstr., I.P.A.
—BLDSC shelfmark: 5031.890000.
Formerly: Archives of Practical Pharmacy.

615.1   US   ISSN 0022-3549
RS1   CODEN: JPMSAE
JOURNAL OF PHARMACEUTICAL SCIENCES. vol.50, 1961. m. $85 to individuals; institutions $195. American Pharmaceutical Association, 2215 Constitution Ave., N.W., Washington, DC 20037. TEL 202-628-4410. FAX 202-783-2351. Ed. Edward G. Feldmann. adv.; bk.rev.; bibl.; charts; illus.; index; circ. 6,865. (also avail. in microform from UMI; reprint service avail. from UMI; back issues avail.) **Indexed:** Anal.Abstr., Biol.Abstr., Biotech.Abstr., Chem.Abstr., Chem.Infd., Curr.Adv.Cancer Res., Curr.Adv.Ecol.Sci., Curr.Chem.React., Curr.Cont., Dairy Sci.Abstr., Dent.Ind., Excerp.Med., Helminthol.Abstr., Hort.Abstr., I.P.A., Ind.Chem., Ind.Med., Ind.Sci.Rev., Ind.Vet., INIS Atomind., Mass Spectr.Bull., Nutr.Abstr., Rev.Plant Path., Vet.Bull.
●Also available online.
—BLDSC shelfmark: 5031.900000.
Description: Primary research in pharmaceutical science; graduate level and above.
Refereed Serial

615.1 574   JA   ISSN 0386-846X
                          CODEN: JOPHDQ
JOURNAL OF PHARMACOBIO-DYNAMICS. (Text in English) 1978. m. $62. Pharmaceutical Society of Japan - Nihon Yakugakkai, 12-15, Shibuya 2-chome, Shibuya-ku, Tokyo 150, Japan. Ed. Hiroshi Kaneto. adv.; charts; stat.; index; circ. 1,150. **Indexed:** Anal.Abstr., Biol.Abstr., Biotech.Abstr., Chem.Abstr., Curr.Adv.Cell & Devel.Biol., Curr.Adv.Ecol.Sci., Curr.Cont., Dent.Ind., Excerp.Med., Ind.Med., Ind.Sci.Rev., Mass Spectr.Bull.

615.19   US   ISSN 0896-6966
                          CODEN: JPHAE7
JOURNAL OF PHARMACOEPIDEMIOLOGY. 1989. q. $24 to individuals; institutions $32; libraries $48. Haworth Press, Inc., 10 Alice St., Binghamton, NY 13904. TEL 800-342-9678. FAX 607-722-1424. TELEX 4932599. Ed. Jack Fincham. adv.; bk.rev. (also avail. in microform from HAW; reprint service avail. from HAW) **Indexed:** Biostat.
—BLDSC shelfmark: 5032.500000.
Description: Facilitates the dissemination and exchange of findings, assessments, and reports of research and practice dealing with the outcomes of drug treatment.
Refereed Serial

615   US   ISSN 0090-466X
RM1   CODEN: JPBPBJ
JOURNAL OF PHARMACOKINETICS AND BIOPHARMACEUTICS. 1973. bi-m. $320 (foreign $375)(effective 1992). Plenum Publishing Corp., 233 Spring St., New York, NY 10013-1578. TEL 212-620-8000. FAX 212-463-0742. TELEX 23-421139. Eds. Leslie Z. Benet, Malcolm Rowland. adv.; index. (also avail. in microfilm from JSC; back issues avail.) **Indexed:** Biol.Abstr., Biotech.Abstr., Chem.Abstr., Curr.Adv.Ecol.Sci., Curr.Cont., Excerp.Med., I.P.A., Ind.Med., Ind.Sci.Rev., INIS Atomind.
—BLDSC shelfmark: 5032.600000.
Refereed Serial

PHARMACY AND PHARMACOLOGY

615.1   US   ISSN 0022-3565
RS1   CODEN: JPETAB
JOURNAL OF PHARMACOLOGY AND EXPERIMENTAL THERAPEUTICS. 1909. m. (4 vols. per yr.). $170 to individuals; institutions $285. (American Society of Pharmacology and Experimental Therapeutics) Williams & Wilkins, 428 Preston St., Baltimore, MD 21202. TEL 301-528-4000. FAX 301-528-4312. Ed. Eva King Killam. adv.; bibl.; charts; illus.; index; circ. 2,800. (also avail. in microform) **Indexed:** Biol.Abstr., Biotech.Abstr., Chem.Abstr., Curr.Adv.Ecol.Sci., Curr.Cont., Dairy Sci.Abstr., Dent.Ind., Excerp.Med., Helminthol.Abstr., I.P.A., Ind.Med., Ind.Sci.Rev., Ind.Vet., INIS Atomind., Nutr.Abstr., Psychol.Abstr., Vet.Bull.
●Also available online.
—BLDSC shelfmark: 5033.000000.
Description: Documents interactions of chemicals with biological systems for pharmacologists, toxicologists and biochemists.
Refereed Serial

615.1   UK   ISSN 0022-3573
CODEN: JPPMAB
JOURNAL OF PHARMACY AND PHARMACOLOGY. 1949. m. £150($315) (foreign £175). Royal Pharmaceutical Society of Great Britain, 1 Lambeth High St., London SE1 7JN, England. TEL 071-735-9141. Ed. Joseph Chamberlain. adv.; bibl.; charts; illus.; index; circ. 2,500. **Indexed:** Abstr.Hyg., Anal.Abstr., Biol.Abstr., Biotech.Abstr., Chem.Abstr., Curr.Adv.Ecol.Sci., Curr.Chem.React., Curr.Cont., Dairy Sci.Abstr., Dent.Ind., Excerp.Med., Helminthol.Abstr., I.P.A., Ind.Med., Ind.Sci.Rev., Ind.Vet., INIS Atomind., Nutr.Abstr., Protozool.Abstr., Trop.Dis.Bull., Vet.Bull.
—BLDSC shelfmark: 5034.000000.
Description: Publishes original research papers and reviews articles about the development and evaluation of medicinal substances.

615 371.3   US   ISSN 1044-0054
CODEN: JOPTET
▼**JOURNAL OF PHARMACY TEACHING.** 1990. q. $24 to individuals; institutions $32; libraries $48. Haworth Press, Inc., 10 Alice St., Binghamton, NY 13904. TEL 800-342-9678. FAX 607-722-1424. TELEX 4932599. Ed. Mickey Smith. (also avail. in microform from HAW; reprint service avail. from HAW)
—BLDSC shelfmark: 5034.025000.
Description: Focuses on the communication of information with the goal of improved teaching in pharmacy.
Refereed Serial

615.329   US   ISSN 8755-1225
CODEN: JPTEEB
JOURNAL OF PHARMACY TECHNOLOGY. 1985. bi-m. $39 to individuals; institutions $60; libraries $85. Harvey Whitney Books Company, Box 42696, Cincinnati, OH 45242. TEL 513-793-3555. FAX 513-793-3600. Ed. Harvey Whitney. adv.; bk.rev.; abstr.; bibl.; charts; illus.; index; circ. 3,000. (also avail. in microform from UMI; back issues avail.; reprint service avail.) **Indexed:** Abstr.Health Care Manage.Stud., Chem.Abstr., Curr.Adv.Ecol.Sci., Excerp.Med., I.P.A.
—BLDSC shelfmark: 5034.030000.
Description: For pharmacists and technicians. Covers therapeutic trends, current research and organizational, legal and educational activities. Includes information on new drugs and medical products and equipment.
Refereed Serial

JOURNAL OF PLANAR CHROMATOGRAPHY - MODERN T L C. see *CHEMISTRY — Analytical Chemistry*

JOURNAL OF PSYCHOACTIVE DRUGS; a multidisciplinary forum. see *DRUG ABUSE AND ALCOHOLISM*

615.7 616.8   UK
JOURNAL OF PSYCHOPHARMACOLOGY. 1987. q. £60($120) (foreign £55). Oxford University Press, Oxford Journals, Pinkhill House, Southfield Road, Eynsham, Oxford OX8 1JJ, England. TEL 0865-882283. FAX 0865-882890. TELEX 387330 OXPRES G. Ed. Malcolm H. Lader. adv.; bk.rev. **Indexed:** Excerp.Med., Psychol.Abstr.
Formerly: British Association for Psychopharmacology. Journal (ISSN 0269-8811)
Description: Presents research and review papers representing a wide range of subjects connected with psychopharmacology, from drug effects on molecular systems to epidemiological studies.

615.19 330.9   US   ISSN 0896-6621
HD9666.1   CODEN: JRPEE5
JOURNAL OF RESEARCH IN PHARMACEUTICAL ECONOMICS. 1989. q. $28 to individuals; institutions $45; libraries $85. Haworth Press, Inc., 10 Alice St., Binghamton, NY 13904. TEL 800-342-9678. FAX 067-722-1424. TELEX 4932599. Ed. Mickey Smith. adv.; bk.rev. (also avail. in microfiche from HAW; reprint service avail. from HAW) **Indexed:** Soc.Work Res.& Abstr.
—BLDSC shelfmark: 5052.026000.
Description: Devoted to the analysis of economic questions and concerns related to the use of pharmaceutical products and services.
Refereed Serial

615.9 500 610   II   ISSN 0253-7249
CODEN: JSRMDB
JOURNAL OF SCIENTIFIC RESEARCH IN PLANTS & MEDICINES. (Text in English) 1981. s-a. Rs.150 to individuals; institutions Rs.300. Yogi Pharmacy Pvt. Ltd. (Hardwar), Research & Publication Division, P.O. Gurukul Kangri, Hardwar 249404, India. TEL 6208. Ed. C.S. Trivedi. bk.rev.; circ. 5,000. (back issues avail.) **Indexed:** Biol.Abstr., Forest.Abstr., Hort.Abstr., Seed Abstr.

615.19   SW   ISSN 0281-0662
JOURNAL OF SOCIAL ADMINISTRATIVE PHARMACY. 4/yr. SEK 330($65) in Nordic countries; elsewhere SEK 400. Swedish Pharmaceutical Press, P.O. Box 1136, S-111 81 Stockholm, Sweden. TEL 46-8-24-50-80. FAX 46-8-1495-80.
—BLDSC shelfmark: 5064.714000.

JOURNAL OF TOXICOLOGY AND ENVIRONMENTAL HEALTH. see *ENVIRONMENTAL STUDIES — Toxicology And Environmental Safety*

JOURNAL OF TOXICOLOGY: CLINICAL TOXICOLOGY. see *ENVIRONMENTAL STUDIES — Toxicology And Environmental Safety*

615.9   US   ISSN 0731-3829
CODEN: JTOTDO
JOURNAL OF TOXICOLOGY: CUTANEOUS AND OCULAR TOXICOLOGY. (Second in a 3-part vol.) 1982. 4/yr. $220 to individuals; institutions $440. Marcel Dekker Journals, 270 Madison Ave., New York, NY 10016. TEL 212-696-9000. FAX 212-685-4540. TELEX 421419 MARDEEK. (Subscr. to: Box 10018, Church St. Sta., New York, NY 10249) Ed. Edward M. Jackson. (also avail. in microform from RPI) **Indexed:** Biol.Abstr., Chem.Abstr., Curr.Adv.Ecol.Sci., Energy Rev., Environ.Per.Bibl., Ind.Sci.Rev., Lab.Haz.Bull.
—BLDSC shelfmark: 5069.738500.
Refereed Serial

615.9   US   ISSN 0731-3837
RA1190   CODEN: JTTRD9
JOURNAL OF TOXICOLOGY: TOXIN REVIEWS. (Third in a 3-part vol.) 1982. 3/yr. $157.50 to individuals; institutions $315. Marcel Dekker Journals, 270 Madison Ave., New York, NY 10016. TEL 212-696-9000. FAX 212-685-4540. TELEX 421419 MARDEEK. (Subscr. to: Box 10018, Church St. Sta., New York, NY 10249) Eds. W.T. Shier, A.T. Tu. (also avail. in microform from RPI) **Indexed:** Biol.Abstr., Chem.Abstr., Curr.Adv.Ecol.Sci., Ind.Sci.Rev.
—BLDSC shelfmark: 5069.741000.
Refereed Serial

615 636.089   UK   ISSN 0140-7783
CODEN: JVPTD9
JOURNAL OF VETERINARY PHARMACOLOGY AND THERAPEUTICS. 1978. q. £112.50 (foreign £126). (Association for Veterinary Clinical Pharmacology & Therapeutics) Blackwell Scientific Publications Ltd., Osney Mead, Oxford OX2 OEL, England. TEL 0865-240201. FAX 0865-721205. TELEX 83355-MEDBOK-G. (Co-sponsors: American College of Veterinary Pharmacology and Therapeutics; European Association for Veterinary Pharmacology and Toxicology) Eds. P. Lees, J.E. Riviere. adv.; bk.rev.; circ. 550. (back issues avail.; reprint service avail. from ISI) **Indexed:** Biotech.Abstr., Chem.Abstr., Curr.Adv.Ecol.Sci., Dairy Sci.Abstr., Excerp.Med. (1992-), Ind.Med., Ind.Sci.Rev., Ind.Vet., Pig News & Info., Poult.Abstr., Protozool.Abstr., Small Anim.Abstr., Vet.Bull.
—BLDSC shelfmark: 5072.420000.

KAOHSIUNG JOURNAL OF MEDICAL SCIENCES. see *MEDICAL SCIENCES*

KEMIXON REPORTER. see *CHEMISTRY*

615   US   ISSN 0194-567X
KENTUCKY PHARMACIST. 1878. m. $30. Kentucky Pharmacists Association, Inc., 1228 U.S. Highway 127 S., Frankfort, KY 40601. TEL 502-227-2303. FAX 502-227-2258. Ed. Robert L. Barnett, Jr. adv.; bk.rev.; circ. 1,800.
—BLDSC shelfmark: 5089.654000.

615.1   RU   ISSN 0023-1134
RS402   CODEN: KHFZAN
KHIMIKO-FARMATSEVTICHESKII ZHURNAL. English translation: Pharmaceutical Chemistry Journal (US ISSN 0091-150X) 1967. m. 52.80 Rub.($28.80) (Ministerstvo Meditsinskoi Promyshlennosti) Izdatel'stvo Meditsina, Petroverigskii pereulok 6-8, 101838 Moscow, Russia. (Subscr. to: Mezhdonarodnaya Kniga, Moscow, G-200, Russia) Ed. R.G. Glushkov. bk.rev.; play rev.; charts; illus.; index. **Indexed:** Anal.Abstr., Biol.Abstr., Biotech.Abstr., Chem.Abstr., Chem.Infd., Cott.& Trop.Fibr.Abstr., Curr.Adv.Ecol.Sci., Curr.Cont., Helminthol.Abstr., Hort.Abstr., I.P.A., Ind.Chem., Ind.Sci.Rev., Plant Grow.Reg.Abstr., Soils & Fert.
●Also available online.
—BLDSC shelfmark: 0391.922000.
Description: Publishes articles on scientific-technical and production activites of chemo-pharmaceutic enterprises.

615.1   JA   ISSN 0023-1657
KINKI UNIVERSITY. BULLETIN OF PHARMACY/KINKI DAIGAKU YAKUGAKUBU KIYO. 1959. irreg. Kinki University, Faculty of Pharmaceutical Sciences, 321 Kowakae, Higashiosaka, Osaka, Japan. Ed. Shoji Takemura. circ. 1,000. **Indexed:** Biol.Abstr., Chem.Abstr., I.P.A.

615.9   JA
KOKUNAI IYAKUHIN FUKUSAYO ICHIRAN/LIST OF ADVERSE REACTIONS TO DRUGS. (Text in Japanese) 1975. s-a. 15000 Yen. Japan Pharmaceutical Information Center - Nihon Iyaku Joho Senta, 3rd Fl., Nagai-Kinenkan, 2-12-15, Shibuya, Shibuyakuu, Tokyo 150, Japan. FAX 03-5466-1814. Ed. F. Kubo. circ. 1,000.

615   KO   ISSN 0377-9459
RM1   CODEN: TYCPAQ
KOREAN JOURNAL OF PHARMACOLOGY/TAEHAN YANGNIHAK CHAPCHI. (Text in English; summaries in Korean) 1965. s-a. free. Society of Pharmacology, c/o Dept. of Pharmacology, College of Medicine, 28 Yunkun-dong, Chongro-ku, Seoul 110, S. Korea. FAX 02-1425949. Ed. Chan Woong Park. circ. 500. (back issues avail.) **Indexed:** Biol.Abstr., Chem.Abstr., Excerp.Med. Key Title: Daihan Yangrihag Jabji.
—BLDSC shelfmark: 5113.572300.

615   GW   ISSN 0173-7597
CODEN: KRANDZ
KRANKENHAUSPHARMAZIE. 1950. m. DM.162.60. (Arbeitsgemeinschaft Deutscher Krankenhausapotheker) Deutscher Apotheker Verlag, Postfach 101061, 7000 Stuttgart 10, Germany. TEL 0711-2582-0. FAX 0711-2582290. TELEX 723636-DAZ-D. Ed. P. Frank. **Indexed:** Biotech.Abstr., Chem.Abstr., I.P.A.
—BLDSC shelfmark: 5118.146200.
Formerly (until 1980): Krankenhaus-Apotheke (ISSN 0075-7071)

615   DK   ISSN 0106-1275
LAEGEFORENINGENS MEDICINFORTEGNELSE. 1963. biennial. DKK 280. Laegeforeningens Forlag, Esplanaden 8A-4, 1263 Copenhagen K, Denmark.

615   DK   ISSN 0105-287X
LAEGEMIDDELKATALOGET. 1976. s-a. DKK 333.60. Laegemiddelkataloget, Frederiksborggade 4, 1, 1360 Copenhagen K, Denmark. (Co-sponsors: Danmarks Apotekerforening, Foreningen af Danske Medicinfabrikker, Medicinimportoerforeningen)

PHARMACY AND PHARMACOLOGY

615.19   US   CODEN: LRNSEP
LAWRENCE REVIEW OF NATURAL PRODUCTS NEWSLETTER. 1980. m. $29.95. Facts and Comparisons, 111 West Port Plaza, Ste. 423, St. Louis, MO 63146-3098. FAX 314-878-5563. (looseleaf format; back issues avail.) **Indexed:** Biol.Abstr., I.P.A.
    Former titles: Lawrence Review of Natural Products Monograph System (ISSN 0734-4961) & Lawrence Review of Natural Products.
    Description: Provides referenced reviews of the history, chemistry, pharmacology and toxicity of natural products of medical, social and economic interest.
    Refereed Serial

LECTINS. see *BIOLOGY — Biological Chemistry*

LEKARSKY OBZOR. see *MEDICAL SCIENCES*

LIAONING ZHONGYI ZAZHI/LIAONING JOURNAL OF TRADITIONAL CHINESE MEDICINE. see *MEDICAL SCIENCES*

LIPOSOMES. see *BIOLOGY — Biological Chemistry*

LOOKOUT - NONFOODS. see *BEAUTY CULTURE — Perfumes And Cosmetics*

615   US   ISSN 0192-3838
LOUISIANA PHARMACIST. 1943. bi-m. $20. Louisiana Pharmacists Association, 2337 St. Claude Ave., New Orleans, LA 70117. TEL 504-949-7545. FAX 504-948-6660. Ed. Linda Foreman. adv.; illus.; circ. 2,000.

615.1   FI   ISSN 0024-8045
M D S. (Text in Finnish; summaries in English and Swedish) 1901. 6/yr. FIM 150. Yliopiston Farmasiakunta r.y. - University Pharmaceutical Association, Hallituskatu 9, 00170 Helsinki 17, Finland. Ed. Sami Paaskoski. adv.; bk.rev.; charts; illus.; pat.; stat.; tr.lit.; circ. 1,000. (looseleaf format)

615   UK   ISSN 0140-4415
M I M S AFRICA. 1961. bi-m. £22.50 (effective Jan. 1992)(free to medical profession and to hospitals in East, West and Central Africa). A.E. Morgan Publications Ltd., Stanley House, 9 West St., Epsom, Surrey KT18 7RL, England. TEL 0372-741411. FAX 0372-744493. adv.; circ. 8,300.
    Former titles: African M I M S (ISSN 0002-0079); African Medical Practitioner.
    Description: Listing of prescribable drugs for medical practitioners.

615.19   AT   ISSN 0725-4709
M I M S ANNUAL. 1977. a. Aus.$65. M I M S Australia, 48 Albany St., Crows Nest, N.S.W. 2065, Australia. Ed. Linda H. Badewitz-Dodd. adv.; charts; circ. 24,000.
    Description: Full disclosure information on all pharmaceuticals available for prescription in Australia.

615.19   AT   ISSN 1035-5723
M I M S BI-MONTHLY. 1963. bi-m. Aus.$59.95. M I M S Australia, 48 Albany St., Crows Nest, N.S.W. 2065, Australia. Ed. Linda H. Badewitz-Dodd. adv.; circ. 24,000.
    Description: Therapeutically classified prescribing information on all products available for prescription in Australia.

615   UK
M I M S CARIBBEAN. 1970. bi-m. £19.80 (effective Jan. 1992). A.E. Morgan Publications Ltd., Stanley House, 9 West St., Epsom, Surrey KT18 7RL, England. TEL 0372-741411. FAX 0372-744493. Ed. Frances Wilson. adv.; circ. 2,600.
    Description: Listing of prescribable drugs for medical practitioners.

615   SA   ISSN 0076-8847
M I M S DESK REFERENCE. 1965. a. M.I.M.S. (Subsidiary of: Times Media Ltd.), P.O. Box 2059, Pretoria 0001, South Africa. TEL 012-3485010. FAX 012-477716. Eds. Deo Botha, Dieter Brandt. adv.; index; circ. 8,300.
    Formerly: M I M S Reference Manual.
    Description: Contains details of human medicines, tablet and capsule indentification chart, and a reference section.

615   UK   ISSN 0302-4172
M I M S MIDDLE EAST. 1971. bi-m. £24.25 (effective Jan. 1992). A.E. Morgan Publications Ltd., Stanley House, 9 West St., Epsom, Surrey KT18 7RL, England. TEL 0372-741411. FAX 0372-744493. Ed. Frances Wilson. adv.; circ. 19,000.
    Description: Listing of prescribable drugs for qualified medical practitioners.

615   AG
MANUAL FARMACEUTICO. 1960. m. $150. Alfa Beta S A C I F Y S, Melian 3136, 1430 Cap. Fed., Buenos Aires, Argentina. Ed. Juan Marrari. adv.; circ. 15,000.

615   US   ISSN 0085-3100
MARIO NEGRI INSTITUTE FOR PHARMACOLOGICAL RESEARCH. MONOGRAPHS. 1970. irreg., latest 1985. price varies. Raven Press, 1185 Ave. of the Americas, New York, NY 10036. TEL 212-930-9500. FAX 212-869-3495. TELEX 640073. Ed. Silvio Garattini. **Indexed:** Biol.Abstr., Chem.Abstr., Curr.Cont.
    Description: Proceedings of international biomedical symposia covering pharmacological problems.

615   UK
MARKETLETTER. 1974. w. £440. IMSWORLD Publications Ltd., 11-13 Melton St., London NW1 2EH, England. Ed. Barbara Obstoj. index. (back issues avail.) **Indexed:** ABC.
    ●Also available online. Vendor(s): Data-Star.
    Formerly: IMS Pharmaceutical Marketletter (ISSN 0140-4288); Incorporates: IMS Monitor Report (ISSN 0262-6756); Which was formerly: IMS Monitor Report: Europe (ISSN 0140-4741)

615   UK
MARTINDALE: THE EXTRA PHARMACOPOEIA. 1883. quinquennial. £110. Royal Pharmaceutical Society of Great Britain, 1 Lambeth High St., London SE1 7JN, England. TEL 071-735-9141. (Dist. in U.S. by: Rittenhouse Book Distributors, Philadelphia, PA 19406) Ed. James E. Reynolds. index.
    ●Also available online. Vendor(s): Data-Star, DIALOG (File no.141).
    Incorporates: Squires Companion.
    Description: Provides a concise summary of the properties, actions and uses of drugs and medicines for the practising pharmacists and medical practitioners.

615.1   US   ISSN 0025-4347
MARYLAND PHARMACIST. 1925. m. $10. Maryland Pharmacists Association, 650 W. Lombard St., Baltimore, MD 21201. TEL 301-727-0746. FAX 301-725-2253. Ed. David G. Miller. adv.; bk.rev.; charts; illus.; circ. 1,400. **Indexed:** Alt.Press Ind., Chem.Abstr., I.P.A.

615.1 378   US   ISSN 0025-4789
MASSACHUSETTS COLLEGE OF PHARMACY. BULLETIN. 1911. 4/yr. free to qualified personnel. Massachusetts College of Pharmacy and Allied Health Sciences, 179 Longwood Ave., Boston, MA 02115. TEL 617-732-2800. FAX 617-732-2801. Ed. Carolyn Conaghan. illus.; circ. 8,000.
    Description: Contains organization news.

MATERIA MEDICA POLONA; the Polish journal of medicine and pharmacy. see *MEDICAL SCIENCES*

MEDICAL ADVERTISING NEWS. see *BUSINESS AND ECONOMICS — Marketing And Purchasing*

615   JA   ISSN 0289-730X
MEDICAL AND PHARMACEUTICAL SOCIETY FOR WAKAN-YAKU. JOURNAL. (Text in English and Japanese) 1984. 3/yr. 10000 Yen($70) (Medical and Pharmaceutical Society for Wakan-Yaku) Chuo Insatsu Co., 1-4-5, Shimookui, Toyama 930-01, Japan. TEL 0764-32-6572. Ed. Zenichi Ogita. circ. 1,200. (back issues avail.)
    —BLDSC shelfmark: 4824.050000.

613   SP
MEDICAL LETTER. Spanish translation of: Medical Letter on Drugs and Therapeutics (US ISSN 0025-732X) (Text in Spanish) 1979. fortn. 6500 ptas.($50) J.R. Prous, S.A. International Publishers, Apdo. de Correos 540, 08080 Barcelona, Spain. TEL 343-258-5250. FAX 343-258-1535. TELEX 98270 PROU E. index; circ. 2,600. (looseleaf format; back issues avail.)

615   US   ISSN 0025-732X
MEDICAL LETTER ON DRUGS AND THERAPEUTICS. French, Italian, Japanese and Spanish translations: Medical Letter. 1959. fortn. $18.75 for residents, interns & medical students; others $37.50. Medical Letter, Inc., 1000 Main St., New Rochelle, NY 10801. TEL 914-235-0500. FAX 914-576-3377. Ed. Dr. Mark Abramowicz. index. cum.index every 5 yrs.; circ. 150,000. (also avail. in microform from UMI; back issues avail.; reprint service avail. from UMI) **Indexed:** Curr.Cont., Dent.Ind., FAMLI, Helminthol.Abstr., I.P.A., Ind.Med., Ind.Sci.Rev.
    ●Also available online. Vendor(s): BRS.
    —BLDSC shelfmark: 5529.700000.
    Description: Provides unbiased, critical evaluations of drugs for physicians and other members of the health professions.

MEDICAL MALPRACTICE: PHARMACY LAW. see *LAW — Civil Law*

610 658.8   US   ISSN 0025-7354
HD9665.1   CODEN: MMKMB
MEDICAL MARKETING & MEDIA. Short title: M M & M. 1966. 13/yr. $75 to individuals; institutions $100. C P S Communications, Inc., 7200 W. Camino Real, Ste. 215, Boca Raton, FL 33433. TEL 407-368-9301. FAX 407-368-7870. Ed. David Gideon. adv.; bk.rev.; charts; illus.; stat.; index; circ. 11,800 (controlled). (also avail. in microfilm from UMI; back issues avail.; reprint service avail. from UMI) **Indexed:** ABI Inform, BPIA, I.P.A., PROMT.
    Formerly: Pharmaceutical Marketing and Media.
    Description: For the pharmaceutical and medical industry providing intra-industry communication and an information link with other industries and government.

615.19   US   ISSN 0199-4905
MEDICAL SCIENCES BULLETIN; focus on pharmacology: theory and practice. 1977. m. $27 to individuals (foreign $40); institutions $34. Pharmaceutical Information Associates, Ltd., 2761 Trenton Rd., Levittown, PA 19056. FAX 215-949-2594. Ed. Robert Hand. charts; illus.; index; circ. 1,800. (back issues avail.) **Indexed:** CHNI.
    —BLDSC shelfmark: 5531.893000.
    Description: Provides an account of new advances in pharmacology and therapeutics.

615.1   SP
MEDICAMENTOS DE ACTUALIDAD - DRUGS OF TODAY. (Text in English) 1965. 8/yr. $350. J.R. Prous, S.A. International Publishers, Apdo. de Correos 540, 08080 Barcelona, Spain. TEL 343-459-22-20. FAX 343-258-15-35. TELEX 98270 PROU E. adv.; bk.rev.; index; cum.index; circ. 3,000. (back issues avail.) **Indexed:** Biol.Abstr., Chem.Abstr., Excerp.Med.
    Formerly: Medicamentos de Actualidad (ISSN 0025-7656); Incorporates: Drugs of Today (ISSN 0012-6691)
    Description: Contains information on drugs being introduced in the international market.

615.19   US   ISSN 0198-6325
RM300   CODEN: MRREDD
MEDICINAL RESEARCH REVIEWS. 1981. bi-m. $260 (foreign $355). John Wiley & Sons, Inc., Journals, 605 Third Ave., New York, NY 10158-0012. TEL 212-692-6000. Ed. George de Stevens. adv.; circ. 700. (also avail. in microform from RPI) **Indexed:** Chem.Infd., Curr.Adv.Biochem., Curr.Adv.Ecol.Sci., Curr.Cont., Ind.Med., Ind.Sci.Rev., Sci.Cit.Ind.
    —BLDSC shelfmark: 5533.992000.
    Description: Embraces all aspects of research addressing the study of disease and the consequent development of therapeutic agents.

615   DK   ISSN 0900-4858
MEDICINTAKST. 1955. irreg. DKK 50. Sundhedsstyrelsen, Amaliegade 13, 1012 Copenhagen K, Denmark. (Dist. by: Staten Information, P.O. Box 1103, 1009 Copenhagen K, Denmark)

615.19   US   ISSN 0737-3139
MEDICOM DRUG INFORMATION NEWSLETTER. 1983. m. $124.95. Professional Drug Systems, Inc., 530 Maryville Centre Dr., Ste. 250, St. Louis, MO 63130. TEL 800-366-4737. FAX 314-275-8819. Eds. Frederic J. Zucchero, Mark J. Hogan. adv.; circ. 2,000. (looseleaf format; back issues avail.)
    Description: Provides information on new drug products and new interactions published in Evaluations of Drug Interactions.

MEDIKAMENT & MEINUNG; Zeitschrift fuer Arzneimittel- und Gesundheitswesen. see *MEDICAL SCIENCES*

615.19 610   NR   ISSN 0331-4782
MEDIPHARM. (Text in English) 1969. q. $130. Literamed Nigeria Ltd., Plot 45, Alausa, Oregun Village, P.M.B. 21068, Ikeja, Lagos, Nigeria. Ed. Yinka Lawal-Solarin. circ. 10,000.
    Description: Covers pharmaceutical specialties in Nigeria.

615   GW   ISSN 0939-6292
MEDIZIN OHNE NEBENWIRKUNGEN. q. DM.74. Friedr. Vieweg und Sohn Verlagsgesellschaft mbH, Postfach 5829, 6200 Wiesbaden 1, Germany. TEL 0611-160230. FAX 0611-160229. TELEX 4186928-VWV-D.

MEINE GESUNDHEIT "REISEAPOTHEKE". see *TRAVEL AND TOURISM*

615.19   SP   ISSN 0379-0355
                              CODEN: MFEPDX
METHODS AND FINDINGS IN EXPERIMENTAL AND CLINICAL PHARMACOLOGY. (Text in English) 1979. 10/yr. $350. J.R. Prous, S.A. International Publishers, Apdo. de Correos 540, 08080 Barcelona, Spain. TEL 343 459-22-20. FAX 343-258-15-35. TELEX 98270 PROU E. adv.; bk.rev.; index; circ. 3,000. (back issues avail.) **Indexed:** Biol.Abstr., Biotech.Abstr., Chem.Abstr., Curr.Adv.Cancer Res., Curr.Adv.Ecol.Sci., Curr.Cont., Dent.Ind., Excerp.Med., Ind.Med., Ind.Med.Esp., Ind.Sci.Rev., Sci.Cit.Ind.
    —BLDSC shelfmark: 5746.620000.
    Description: Forum for papers dealing with the evaluation of methodologies and the interpretation of results in the scientific assessment of drugs.

615.19   IS
MIRKACHTON. (Text in Hebrew) 1987. q. Pharmaceutical Association of Israel, Pharmacies Branch, P.O. Box 566, Tel Aviv 65 112, Israel. TEL 03-615085.

615.1   US   ISSN 0026-6663
MISSOURI PHARMACIST. 1926. m. $25. Missouri Pharmaceutical Association, 410 Madison St., Jefferson City, MO 65101. TEL 314-636-7522. FAX 314-636-7485. Ed. Deedie K. Bedosky. adv.; bk.rev.; circ. 1,200.
    Description: Includes news items, continuing education articles and professional articles of interest to Missouri pharmacists.

615   US
RS79
MODELL'S DRUGS IN CURRENT USE AND NEW DRUGS. 1955. a. price varies. Springer Publishing Company, 536 Broadway, New York, NY 10012. TEL 212-431-4370. FAX 212-941-7842. Ed. Dr. Daniel Hussar. circ. 1,880. (also avail. in microform from UMI; back issues avail.; reprint service avail. from UMI)
    Formerly: Drugs in Current Use and New Drugs (ISSN 0070-7392)

615.19   US   ISSN 0732-7218
RM301   CODEN: MMEPDE
MODERN METHODS IN PHARMACOLOGY. 1982. irreg., vol.5, 1990. price varies. Wiley-Liss, Inc., 41 E. 11th St., New York, NY 10003. TEL 212-475-7700. **Indexed:** Biol.Abstr., Chem.Abstr.
    —BLDSC shelfmark: 5890.000200.
    Refereed Serial

615   US   ISSN 0098-6925
                           CODEN: MPTOD5
MODERN PHARMACOLOGY - TOXICOLOGY SERIES. 1973. irreg., vol.21, 1982. Marcel Dekker, Inc., 270 Madison Ave., New York, NY 10016. TEL 212-696-9000. FAX 212-658-4540. TELEX 421419. Eds. W. Bousquet, R.F. Palmer. illus. **Indexed:** Chem.Abstr.
    Formerly: Modern Pharmacology (ISSN 0092-0150)
    Refereed Serial

MODERN PROBLEMS OF PHARMACOPSYCHIATRY. see *MEDICAL SCIENCES — Psychiatry And Neurology*

615   UK   ISSN 0959-5244
                            CODEN: MOLNEO
▼**MOLECULAR NEUROPHARMACOLOGY.** 1990. q. £99. (British Pharmacological Society) Macmillan Press Ltd., Scientific & Medical Division, Houndmills, Basingstoke, Hampshire RG21 2XS, England. TEL 0256-29242. FAX 0256-842754. Ed. Dr. G.N. Woodruff. adv.; abstr.; illus.; index. (also avail. in microfilm; back issues avail.) **Indexed:** Excerp.Med. (1992-).
    —BLDSC shelfmark: 5900.817990.
    Description: Provides information on molecular aspects of drug action in the central and peripheral nervous systems.

615.7   US   ISSN 0026-895X
QP901   CODEN: MOPMA3
MOLECULAR PHARMACOLOGY. m. $90 to individuals; institutions $195. (American Society for Pharmacology & Experimental Therapeutics) Williams & Wilkins, 428 E. Preston St., Baltimore, MD 21202. TEL 301-528-4000. FAX 301-528-4312. Ed. William A. Catterall. adv.; index; circ. 1,500. (also avail. in microform; back issues avail.) **Indexed:** Biotech.Abstr., Chem.Abstr., Curr.Adv.Biochem., Curr.Adv.Cancer Res., Curr.Adv.Ecol.Sci., Curr.Adv.Genetics & Molec.Biol., Curr.Cont., Dent.Ind., Helminthol.Abstr., Ind.Med., Ind.Sci.Rev., Protozool.Abstr.
    —BLDSC shelfmark: 5900.818000.
    Description: Covers research on drug action and selective toxicity at the molecular level, for pharmacologists and biochemists.
    Refereed Serial

615.1   FR   ISSN 0026-9689
MONITEUR DES PHARMACIES ET DES LABORATOIRES. 1946. w. 590 F. (foreign 850 F.). Compagnie Generale de Developpement, 15-17 rue Godefroy-Cavaignac, 75541 Paris Cedex 11, France. Ed. Alain Rabelle. adv.; illus.; circ. 35,800.

615   SP   ISSN 0463-1536
MONITOR DE LA FARMACIA Y DE LA TERAPEUTICA. 1895. m. 3000 ptas. Centros Farmaceuticos Nacional S.A., Julian Camarillo, 37, 28037 Madrid, Spain. adv.; bk.rev.; bibl.; circ. 17,000. (also avail. in cards) **Indexed:** Biol.Abstr., I.P.A.
    ●Also available online.

MONTHLY PRESCRIBING REFERENCE. see *MEDICAL SCIENCES*

615.1   US
N A B P NEWSLETTER. 1971. 10/yr. $25 to non-members. National Association of Boards of Pharmacy, 1300 Higgins Rd., No. 103, Park Ridge, IL 60068-5743. TEL 708-698-6227. Eds. Carmen Catizone, Janice Teplitz. abstr.; charts; illus.; stat.; index; circ. 1,800 (controlled). **Indexed:** I.P.A.
    ●Also available online.
    Formerly: N A B P Quarterly (ISSN 0027-5700)

615.1   US   ISSN 0027-5972
HD9666.1
N A R D JOURNAL. 1898. m. $50. National Association of Retail Druggists, 205 Daingerfield Rd., Alexandria, VA 22314. TEL 703-683-8200. FAX 703-683-3619. Ed. Todd Dankmyer. adv.; charts; illus.; tr.lit.; circ. 30,000. **Indexed:** I.P.A., Search.

615.1   US   ISSN 0162-1602
HD9666.1
N A R D NEWSLETTER. 1970. s-m. $50. National Association of Retail Druggists, 205 Daingerfield Ave., Alexandria, VA 22314. TEL 703-683-8200. FAX 703-683-3619. Ed. Bob Appel. circ. 27,000.

615.19 670
N D A PIPELINE. (New Drug Approval) a. $375. F-D-C Reports, Inc., 5550 Friendship Blvd., Ste. One, Chevy Chase, MD 20815. TEL 301-657-9830. FAX 301-656-3094.
    Description: Contains a company-by-company compilation of Rx drug development activity in the U.S. throughout the past year - from new compounds in research to those that obtained FDA marketing approval.

615   UK
N P A SUPPLEMENT. 1921. m. membership. National Pharmaceutical Association, 38-42 St. Peters St., St. Albans, Herts, England. FAX 0727-40858. Ed. Colette McCreedy. index; circ. 10,500. (looseleaf format)
    Formerly: N P U Supplement.

615   US
N W D A EXECUTIVE NEWSLETTER. 1913. bi-w. $150. National Wholesale Druggists' Association, Box 238, Alexandria, VA 22313. TEL 703-684-6400. FAX 703-548-2184. Ed. Mary Jane DeSonia-Dye. circ. 2,300.
    Description: Covers services and programs of NWDA, news of membership and industry trends. Includes some statistics on sales and growth on monthly basis.

615.1   US   ISSN 0163-1586
N Y STATE PHARMACIST. 1926. bi-m. $25 (members $10). Pharmaceutical Society of the State of New York, Pine W. Plz. IV, Washington Ave. Ext., Albany, NY 12205-5221. TEL 518-869-6595. Ed. Anthony J. Conte. adv.; bk.rev.; illus.; mkt.; circ. 2,000.
    Formerly: New York State Pharmacist (ISSN 0028-7660)

615.19   JA   ISSN 0369-5611
                            CODEN: NSDYAI
NAGOYA-SHIRITSU DAIGAKU YAKUGAKUBU KENKYU NENPO/NAGOYA CITY UNIVERSITY. FACULTY OF PHARMACEUTICAL SCIENCE. ANNUAL REPORT. (Text in English and Japanese) vol.12, 1964. a. free. Nagoya-shiritsu Daigaku, Yakugakubu - Nagoya City University, Faculty of Pharmaceutical Sciences, Tanabe-Dohri 3-1, Mizuho-ku, Nagoya 467, Japan. Ed.Bd. bibl.; circ. 400. **Indexed:** Biol.Abstr., Chem.Abstr.
    —BLDSC shelfmark: 1248.600000.

615   US   ISSN 0077-3263
NATIONAL ASSOCIATION OF BOARDS OF PHARMACY. PROCEEDINGS. 1904. a. $15. National Association of Boards of Pharmacy, 1300 Higgins Rd., No. 103, Park Ridge, IL 60068-5743. TEL 708-698-6227. Ed. Carmen Catizone. index; circ. 300. **Indexed:** I.P.A.
    ●Also available online.

NATIONAL ASSOCIATION OF CHAIN DRUG STORES. EXECUTIVE NEWSLETTER. see *BUSINESS AND ECONOMICS — Management*

615.328   US
NATIONAL ASSOCIATION OF CHAIN DRUG STORES. LEGISLATIVE NEWS LETTER. 1986. m. membership. National Association of Chain Drug Stores, Box 1417-D49, Alexandria, VA 22313. TEL 703-549-3001. Ed. Julie A. Javernick. circ. 1,200.
    Formerly (until 1971): National Association of Chain Drug Stores. Legislative News Bulletin.

615   US
NATIONAL ASSOCIATION OF PHARMACEUTICAL MANUFACTURERS. NEWS BULLETIN. 1960. m. free. National Association of Pharmaceutical Manufacturers, 747 Third Ave., New York, NY 10017. TEL 212-838-3720. FAX 212-753-6832. Ed. Robert S. Milanese. circ. 1,200. (looseleaf format)

615.1   US   ISSN 0027-9897
NATIONAL PHARMACEUTICAL ASSOCIATION. JOURNAL. vol.17, 1970. 3/yr. $15 membership. National Pharmaceutical Association, Inc., c/o Texas Southern University, College of Pharmacy, 3100 Cleburne, Houston, TX 77004. TEL 202-806-6530. Ed. Dr. Henry Lewis, III. adv.; circ. 2,000. **Indexed:** I.P.A.
    ●Also available online.

615.1   GW   ISSN 0028-1298
                           CODEN: NSAPCC
NAUNYN-SCHMIEDEBERG'S ARCHIVES OF PHARMACOLOGY. 1873. 12/yr. DM.1672($939) (Deutsche Pharmakologische Gesellschaft) Springer-Verlag, Heidelberger Platz 3, 1000 Berlin 33, Germany. TEL 030-8207-1. (And Heidelberg, Tokyo, Vienna, and New York) Ed. K. Stark. adv.; charts; illus. (also avail. in microform from UMI; back issues avail.; reprint service avail. from ISI) **Indexed:** Biol.Abstr., Chem.Abstr., Curr.Adv.Ecol.Sci., Curr.Chem.React., Curr.Cont., Dairy Sci.Abstr., Dent.Ind., Excerp.Med., Ind.Chem., Ind.Med., Ind.Sci.Rev., Mass Spectr.Bull.
    —BLDSC shelfmark: 6060.200000.
    Formerly: Naunyn-Schmiedebergs Archiv fuer Pharmakologie und Experimentelle Pathologie.
    Description: Original papers, ranging from reports on the molecular effects of drugs within the cell to observations of their effects on the whole organism. Focuses on pharmacology and toxicology.

PHARMACY AND PHARMACOLOGY

615.1   US   ISSN 0028-1891
NEBRASKA MORTAR AND PESTLE. 1937. m. $15. Nebraska Pharmacists Association, Inc., 6221 S. 58th St., Ste. A, Lincoln, NE 68516-3679. TEL 402-420-1500. FAX 402-420-1406. Ed. Tom R. Dolan. adv.; charts; illus.; circ. 1,250.

NEPAL. DEPARTMENT OF MEDICINAL PLANTS. ANNUAL REPORT. see *BIOLOGY — Botany*

615.19   NP
NEPAL PHARMACEUTICAL ASSOCIATION. JOURNAL. (Text in English and Nepali) 1974. s-a. Rs.20($5) Nepal Pharmaceutical Association, 9-382, Bhedasingh, Kathmandu, Nepal. Ed. R.R. Prasad. adv.; bk.rev.; circ. 500. **Indexed:** Chem.Abstr.
Description: Research articles on pharmacy, pharmaceuticals, medicinal plants and allied sciences.

615   GW   ISSN 0724-567X
NEUE ARZNEIMITTEL. (Suppl. to Deutsche Apotheker Zeitung) 1953. m. DM.39 or included in subscr. to Deutsche Apotheker Zeitung. Deutscher Apotheker Verlag, Postfach 101061, 7000 Stuttgart 10, Germany. TEL 0711-2582-0. FAX 0711-2582290. TELEX 723636-DAZ-D. **Indexed:** Chem.Abstr., Excerp.Med.
Formerly: Neue Arzneimittel und Spezialitaeten (ISSN 0548-2674)

NEUROHYPOPHYSIAL HORMONES. see *MEDICAL SCIENCES — Endocrinology*

615.1   UK   ISSN 0142-8233
NEUROPEPTIDES (SHEFFIELD). s-m. £110. Sheffield University Biomedical Information Service (SUBIS), The University, Sheffield S10 2TN, England. TEL 0742-768555. FAX 0742-739826. TELEX 547216-UGSHEF-G. **Indexed:** Chem.Abstr., Curr.Adv.Ecol.Sci., Excerp.Med.
Description: Current awareness service for researchers. Studies opioids, endorphins, neurotensin, cholecystokinin, TRH, VIP, neuropeptide Y and invertebrate peptides.

615.1   US   ISSN 0028-3908
RM315   CODEN: NEPHBW
NEUROPHARMACOLOGY. 1962. 12/yr. £560 (effective 1992). Pergamon Press, Inc., Journals Division, 660 White Plains Rd., Tarrytown, NY 10591-5153. TEL 914-524-9200. FAX 914-333-2444. (And: Headington Hill Hall, Oxford OX3 0BW, England. TEL 0865-794141) Eds. P.B. Bradley, Erminio Costa. adv.; bk.rev.; bibl.; charts; illus.; index; circ. 1,500. (also avail. in microform from MIM,UMI; reprint service avail. from UMI) **Indexed:** Biol.Abstr., Biotech.Abstr., Chem.Abstr., Curr.Adv.Ecol.Sci., Curr.Cont., Dent.Ind., Excerp.Med., Helminthol.Abstr., Ind.Med., Ind.Sci.Rev., Int.Aerosp.Abstr., Nutr.Abstr., Psychol.Abstr.
—BLDSC shelfmark: 6081.517500.
Formerly: International Journal of Neuropharmacology.
Description: Furthers the understanding of the mechanisms of drug actions on the nervous system. *Refereed Serial*

NEUROPSICOFARMACOLOGIA DEL COMPORTAMENTO. see *MEDICAL SCIENCES — Psychiatry And Neurology*

NEUROPSYCHOPHARMACOLOGY. see *MEDICAL SCIENCES — Psychiatry And Neurology*

615.1   NZ   ISSN 0110-9510
NEW ETHICALS CATALOGUE; the basis of a system of independent drug information. 1966. 3/yr. NZ.$68. Adis International Ltd., 41 Centorian Dr., Private Bag, Mairangi Bay, Auckland 10, New Zealand. TEL 479-8100. Ed. Jillian Sutherland. adv.; circ. 6,000.

615.1   US   ISSN 0028-5773
RS1
NEW JERSEY JOURNAL OF PHARMACY. 1928. m. $12. New Jersey Pharmaceutical Association, 120 W. State St., Trenton, NJ 08608. TEL 609-394-5596. FAX 609-394-7806. Ed. Gilbert Finkelstein. adv.; bk.rev.; illus.; circ. 4,200. (also avail. in microform from UMI; reprint service avail. from UMI)
—BLDSC shelfmark: 6084.300000.

615   UK
NEW PRODUCT LAUNCH LETTER. 1976. s-m. £2000. IMSWORLD Publications, Ltd., 11-13 Melton St., London NW1 2EH, England.
●Also available online.
Formerly (until 1990): New Product Card Index.

615.19   US
NEW PRODUCT SURVEY. 1965. m. $325. Paul De Haen International, 2750 S. Shoshone St., Englewood, CO 80110. TEL 800-438-0296. FAX 303-789-2534. Ed. Linda J. Gibson. index. (looseleaf format; back issues avail.)
Description: Reports of newly approved and newly introduced drugs.

615.7   SZ   ISSN 1011-6672
  CODEN: NTLREE
NEW TRENDS IN LIPID MEDIATORS RESEARCH. 1988. irreg. price varies. S. Karger AG, Allschwilerstr. 10, P.O. Box, CH-4009 Basel, Switzerland. TEL 061-3061111. FAX 061-3061234. TELEX CH962652. Ed. P. Braquet.
—BLDSC shelfmark: 6089.133000.

615.329   US
NEW YORK STATE PHARMACIST - CENTURY II. 1927. q. $25. Pharmaceutical Society of the State of New York, Pine W. Plz. IV, Washington Ave Ext., Albany, NY 12205-5221. TEL 518-869-6595. Ed. Anthony J. Conte. adv.; circ. 2,000.

615.4 613.7   NZ   ISSN 0111-431X
NEW ZEALAND PHARMACY. 1977. m. NZ.$58. Professional Publishers, 175 Khyber Pass, Box 37116, Auckland, New Zealand. TEL 390-914. FAX 09-377-193. Ed. Cedric Allan. charts; illust.; circ. 3,000.
—BLDSC shelfmark: 6096.495000.

616.89   JA   ISSN 0009-3165
  CODEN: NKRZAZ
NIHON KAGAKU RYOHO GAKKAI ZASSHI/CHEMOTHERAPY. (Text in English, Japanese) 1953. m. $150. Nihon Kagaku Ryoho Gakkai - Japan Society of Chemotherapy, 2-20-8 Kamiosaki, Shinagawa-ku, Tokyo 141, Japan. Ed.Bd. adv.; abstr.; index; circ. 4,500. (also avail. in microform from UMI) **Indexed:** Biol.Abstr., Biotech.Abstr., Chem.Abstr., Curr.Adv.Ecol.Sci., Curr.Cont., Excerp.Med., I.P.A., Ind.Med, Ind.Sci.Rev., Protozool.Abstr.
—BLDSC shelfmark: 3172.305000.

615.19   JA
NIPPON KAYAKU. ANNUAL REPORT. a. Nippon Kayaku Co., Tokyo Fujimi Bldg., 11-2, Fujimi 1-chome, Chiyoda-ku, Tokyo 102, Japan.

615.1   NO   ISSN 0802-8400
NORGES APOTEKERFORENINGS TIDSSKRIFT. 1893. s-m. NOK 450. Norges Apotekerforening, Box 5070, Majorstua, 0301 Oslo 3, Norway. FAX 02-608173. Ed. Tor Landsverk. adv.; bk.rev.; charts; illus.; index; circ. 1,900. **Indexed:** Biol.Abstr., Chem.Abstr., I.P.A.
—BLDSC shelfmark: 6128.000000.
Formerly (until 1985): NAT. Norges Apotekerforenings Tidsskrift (ISSN 0332-8678)

615.1   NO   ISSN 0029-1935
  CODEN: NFTDAC
NORSK FARMACEUTISK TIDSSKRIFT. 1893. 16/yr. NOK 590. Norges Farmaceutiske Forening, Stenersgt. 4, 0184 Oslo 1, Norway. FAX 02-170960. Ed. Kari Bremer. adv.; bk.rev.; abstr.; charts; illus.; tr.lit.; index; circ. 2,415 (controlled). **Indexed:** I.P.A.
—BLDSC shelfmark: 6138.000000.

615.19   IT   ISSN 0550-1156
NOTIZIARIO CHIMICO E FARMACEUTICO. 1970. m. $170. Societa Editoriale Farmaceutica s.r.l., Via Ausonio, 12, 20123 Milan, Italy. TEL 02-89404545. FAX 02-89401168. adv.; bk.rev.; bibl.; circ. 6,000. **Indexed:** I.P.A.
●Also available online.

615.1   IT   ISSN 0029-439X
NOTIZIARIO MEDICO FARMACEUTICO. (Supplements annual directory: Informatore Farmaceutico) 1950. m. included with Informatore Farmaceutico. Organizzazione Editoriale Medico-Farmaceutica, Via Edolo 42, Box 10434, 20125 Milan, Italy. (Dist. in U.S. by: Drug Intelligence & Clinical Pharmacy, Box 42435, Cincinnati, OH 45242) Ed. Dr. Lucio Marini.

615 610 382   PL   ISSN 0209-3928
NOVOSTI FARMATSII I MEDITSINY/NEWS IN PHARMACOLOGY AND MEDICINE. (Text in Russian; summaries in English) 1967. q. AGPOL - Polexportpress, Ul. Marszalkowska 124, 00-950 Warsaw, Poland. TEL 48-22-269221. Ed. Andrzej Werbeniec. adv.; bk.rev.; illus.; circ. 30,000.
Description: Covers all aspects of preparing, preserving, compounding and dispensing drugs.

NURSES' DRUG ALERT. see *MEDICAL SCIENCES — Nurses And Nursing*

OCULAR THERAPEUTICS AND PHARMACOLOGY. see *MEDICAL SCIENCES — Ophthalmology And Optometry*

615.1   AU   ISSN 0029-8859
OESTERREICHISCHE APOTHEKER-ZEITUNG. 1946. w. S.1312.04. Oesterreichische Apotheker-Verlagsgesellschaft, Spitalgasse 31, A-1094 Vienna, Austria. Ed. Gottfried Zimmermann. adv.; abstr.; index; circ. 4,500. **Indexed:** Biotech.Abstr., Chem.Abstr., I.P.A.
—BLDSC shelfmark: 6304.000000.
Description: Information and networking for Austrian pharmacists.

615   GW   ISSN 0930-2115
  CODEN: OFFIE6
DIE OFFIZIN; Pharmazie in der Praxis. 1989. q. DM.60. Georg Thieme Verlag, Ruedigerstr. 14, Postfach 104853, 7000 Stuttgart 10, Germany. TEL 0711-8931-0. FAX 0711-8931-298. TELEX 7252275-GTV-D. Ed.Bd.

615.1   US   ISSN 0030-1027
OHIO PHARMACIST. 1952. m. $20. Ohio State Pharmaceutical Association, 6037 Frantz Rd., Ste. 106, Dublin, OH 43017-3320. TEL 614-798-0037. Ed. Amy Bennett. adv.; illus.; circ. 3,400.

615   CN   ISSN 0315-1042
ON CONTINUING PRACTICE. 1973. q. Can.$28. Ontario College of Pharmacists, 483 Huron St., Toronto, Ont. M5R 2R4, Canada. TEL 416-962-4861. Eds. B. des Roches, S. Parn. bk.rev.; abstr.; charts; circ. 8,000. (also avail. in microform from UMI; back issues avail.; reprint service avail. from UMI) **Indexed:** Biotech.Abstr., Excerp.Med., I.P.A.
—BLDSC shelfmark: 6256.690000.

615   JA   ISSN 0387-480X
OSAKA UNIVERSITY. FACULTY OF PHARMACEUTICAL SCIENCES. MEMOIRS/OSAKA DAIGAKU YAKUGAKUBU KIYO. (Text in English) 1970. a. free. Osaka Daigaku, Yakugakubu - Osaka University, Faculty of Pharmaceutical Sciences, 1-6 Yamadaoka, Suita, Osaka 565, Japan. FAX 06-877-4489. Ed. Tsutomu Nishihara. abstr.; circ. 300.

615.1   JA   ISSN 0030-669X
OTSUKA PHARMACEUTICAL FACTORY. JOURNAL/OTSUKA YAKUHO. (Text in Japanese) 1950. 11/yr. 2000 Yen. Otsuka Pharmaceutical Factory - Otsuka Seiyaku Kojo, 115 Tateiwa, Muya-cho, Naruto 772, Tokushima, Japan. Ed. M. Ohsaka. illus.; circ. 61,500.

615   JA   ISSN 0300-8533
  CODEN: OYYAA2
OYO YAKURI/PHARMACOMETRICS. (Text in Japanese or English) 1967. m. 6000 Yen($100) Oyo Yakuri Kenkyukai, G.P.O. Box 180, Sendai 980-91, Japan. FAX 022-222-0515. Ed. Dr. Hikaru Ozawa. adv.; bk.rev.; index; circ. 1,200. (back issues avail.) **Indexed:** Dairy Sci.Abstr., Excerp.Med.
—BLDSC shelfmark: 6447.085000.
Description: Covers pharmacodynamics, pharmacokinetics, and toxicity tests of new drugs.

P A CER. (Pharmaceutical Advertising Council) see *ADVERTISING AND PUBLIC RELATIONS*

615.1   US   ISSN 0030-7815
P A R D BULLETIN.* 1898. bi-m. $2.50. Philadelphia Association of Retail Druggists, 630 S. 42nd St., Philadelphia, PA 19104. Ed. Raymond T. Fleisher. adv.; bk.rev.; stat.; tr.lit.; index; circ. 1,000.

PHARMACY AND PHARMACOLOGY

615   US   ISSN 1052-1372
CODEN: PPTTEK
P & T. (Pharmacy & Therapeutic); journal for formulary management. 1976. m. $60 (foreign $75). Excerpta Medica, Inc., Core Publishing Division (Subsidiary of: Elsevier Science Publishers B.V.), 105 Raider Blvd., Belle Mead, NJ 08052. TEL 908-874-8550. FAX 908-874-0700. adv. **Indexed:** I.P.A.
●Also available online.
Former titles (until Jul. 1990): Hospital Therapy (ISSN 0160-9459); Drug Therapy (Hospital Edition); Drug Therapy Hospital.
Refereed Serial

615.19   US
P D A LETTER. 1964. m. membership. Parenteral Drug Association, Inc., One Penn Center, 1617 JFK Blvd., Philadelphia, PA 19103. TEL 215-564-6466. FAX 215-564-6472. (Subscr. to: Box 8500-51045, Philadelphia, PA 19178) Ed. Frederick J. Carleton. circ. 3,400.
Description: Parenteral industry news and upcoming events, services and publications of the Parenteral Drug Association.

615.1   US   ISSN 0030-8099
P M A NEWSLETTER. 1959. w. free. Pharmaceutical Manufacturers Association, 1100 15th St. N.W., Washington, DC 20005. TEL 202-835-3400. FAX 202-835-3414. Ed. Duffy Miller. bk.rev.; circ. 4,000. (tabloid format) **Indexed:** CAD CAM Abstr., Med. Care Rev, P.N.I., PROMT, Telegen.

615.7   AT   ISSN 0156-0433
P S. (Postscript) 1979. bi-m. Aus.$25. Australian Pharmaceutical Publishing Co. Ltd., 40 Burwood Rd., Hawthorn, Vic. 3122, Australia. circ. 5,700. (back issues avail.)

615   GW   ISSN 0302-167X
CODEN: PTAHAF
P T A HEUTE. 1954. m. DM.47.40 (students DM.31.80). Deutscher Apotheker Verlag, Postfach 101061, 7000 Stuttgart 10, Germany. TEL 0711-2582-0. FAX 0711-2582290. TELEX 723636-DAZ-D. bk.rev.; circ. 33,600. **Indexed:** Chem.Abstr.
—BLDSC shelfmark: 6946.564300.
Formerly: Apothekerpraktikant und Pharmazeutisch-Technische Assistent.

615   GW   ISSN 0722-1029
P T A IN DER APOTHEKE; Fachzeitschrift fuer pharmazeutisch-technische Assistenten. (Includes supplement: P T A - Repetitorium) m. DM.99.60 (students DM.83.40). Umschau Verlag Breidenstein GmbH, Stuttgarter Str. 18-24, 6000 Frankfurt a.M. 1, Germany. TEL 069-2600-0. FAX 069-2600-609. TELEX 411964. Ed. Klaus Stutzer. adv.; circ. 9,200.
—BLDSC shelfmark: 6946.564250.
Former titles: P T A in der Praktischen Pharmazie; P T A in Apotheke und Industrie.

615.19   PK   ISSN 1011-601X
CODEN: PJPSEN
PAKISTAN JOURNAL OF PHARMACEUTICAL SCIENCES. s-a. Rs.150($25) University of Karachi, Faculty of Pharmacy, Karachi 75270, Pakistan. Ed. Dr. S. Sabir Ali.
—BLDSC shelfmark: 6341.690000.
Description: Publishes short research papers and reviews in pharmaceutical chemistry, pharmaceutics, pharmacognosy, pharmacology, and related studies in toxicology.
Refereed Serial

615   PK
PAKISTAN JOURNAL OF PHARMACOLOGY. (Text in English) 1983. s-a. $50. University of Karachi, Department of Pharmacology, Karachi 75270, Pakistan. TEL 479001. Ed. S.I. Ahmad.

615.1   PK   ISSN 0030-9850
PAKISTAN JOURNAL OF PHARMACY. vol.3, 1966. m. Rs.48. Trade and Industry Publications Limited, Trade and Industry House, West Wharf Rd., Box 4611, Karachi 2, Pakistan. Ed. Ghouse Pasha. adv.; bk.rev.; abstr.; charts; illus.; pat.; stat.; tr.lit. **Indexed:** I.P.A.
●Also available online.

615   US
PALMETTO PHARMACIST.* m. $10. State Pharmaceutical Editorial Association, 223 W. Jackson Blvd., No. 1000, Chicago, IL 60606-6906. Ed. Sharon Fennell. adv.; circ. 1,500.

615.7   IT
PANORAMA FARMACEUTICO; rivista di attualita e aggiornamento professionale del farmacista. 1978. m. L.30000 (foreign $50). Editrice Kurtis s.r.l., Via L. Zoja, 30, 20153 Milan, Italy. TEL 02-48202740. FAX 48201219. Ed. Lorenzo Verlato. adv.; circ. 20,000.
Description: Brings to every pharmacy objective data on the realistic future of the pharmaceutical field. Voices the professional's problems, provoking both a constructive exchange of views and a search for alternative solutions.

615 616.5   FR
PARAPHARMEX. a. (with 14 supplements). 354 F. (foreign 386 F.)(effective 1991). Societe d'Editions Medico-Pharmaceutiques (SEMP), 26 rue le Brun, 75013 Paris, France. TEL 1-43-37-83-50. FAX 43-31-94-11. TELEX 203046F. circ. 9,000 (controlled). (looseleaf format; also avail. in microfiche)
Description: Contains references to cosmetics, perfumary and oral hygiene.

615.19   US
PARENTERAL DRUG ASSOCIATION. TECHNICAL INFORMATION BULLETIN. irreg., latest no.4. price varies. Parenteral Drug Association, Inc., One Penn Center, 1617 JFK Blvd., Ste. 640, Philadelphia, PA 19103. TEL 215-564-6466. FAX 215-564-6472. (Subscr. to: Box 8500-51045, Philadelphia PA 19178)

615.19   US
PARENTERAL DRUG ASSOCIATION. TECHNICAL METHODS BULLETIN. irreg., latest no.3. price varies. Parenteral Drug Association, Inc., One Penn Center, 1617 JFK Blvd., Ste. 640, Philadelphia, PA 19103. TEL 215-564-6466. FAX 215-564-6472. (Subscr. to: Box 8500-51045, Philadelphia PA 19178)

615.19   US
PARENTERAL DRUG ASSOCIATION. TECHNICAL REPORTS. irreg, latest no.13. $33 to non-members (members $16.50). Parenteral Drug Association, Inc., One Penn Center, 1617 JFK Blvd., Ste. 640, Philadelphia, PA 19103. TEL 215-564-6466. FAX 215-564-6472. (Subscr. to: Box 8500-51045, Philadelphia PA 19178)

PARTICULATE SCIENCE AND TECHNOLOGY; an international journal. see *ENGINEERING — Chemical Engineering*

615.1   US   ISSN 0031-4633
PENNSYLVANIA PHARMACIST. 1926. m. $25. Pennsylvania Pharmaceutical Association, 508 N. Third St., Harrisburg, PA 17101. TEL 717-234-6151. Ed. Carmen A. DiCello. adv.; bk.rev.; illus.; tr.lit.; cum.index; circ. 2,200.
—BLDSC shelfmark: 6421.748800.

615.19   US
PERSPECTIVES IN CLINICAL PHARMACY. 1983. m. (American College of Clinical Pharmacy) Elsevier Science Publishing Co., Inc. (New York), 655 Ave. of the Americas, New York, NY 10010. TEL 212-989-5800. FAX 212-633-3965. TELEX 420643 AEP UI. Ed. Milo Gibaldi. (also avail. in microform from RPI) **Indexed:** Excerp.Med.
Formerly: Perspectives in Clinical Pharmacology (ISSN 0737-2914)
Description: Provides information on therapeutics, pharmacokinetics, and drug disposition.

615   SZ   ISSN 0378-7958
PHARMA-FLASH. 1972. 10/yr. 60 SFr.($43) Editions Medecine et Hygiene, Case Postale 456, CH-1211 Geneva 4, Switzerland. TEL 022-469355. FAX 022-475610.

615   JA   ISSN 0285-4937
CODEN: PHAREX
PHARMA JAPAN; Japan drug industry news. (Text in English) 1960. w. 180000 Yen. Yakugyo Jiho Co. Ltd., 2-36 Kanda Jimbo-cho, Chiyoda-ku, Tokyo 101, Japan. TEL 03-265-7751. (Dist. in N. America by: F-D-C Reports, Inc., 5550 Friendship Blvd., Ste. One, Chevy Chase, MD 20815) pat.; stat.
Formerly (until 1975): Pharmaceutical Daily News.
Description: Focuses on matters of importance in the Japanese pharmaceutical and medical industries.

615   JA
PHARMA JAPAN YEARBOOK. (Text in English) a. 9000 Yen($88) Yakugyo Jiho Co., Ltd., 2-36 Kanda Jimbo-Cho, Chiyoda-ku, Tokyo 101, Japan. TEL 03-265-7751. (Dist. in N. America by: F-D-C Reports, Inc., 5550 Friendship Blvd., Ste. One, Chevy Chase, MD 20815)
Former titles: Japan Drug Industry Review; (until 1976): Handbook of the Japan Drug Industry.
Description: Explains trends in Japanese pharmaceutical and medical fields.

PHARMA-MARKETING JOURNAL. see *BUSINESS AND ECONOMICS — Marketing And Purchasing*

615.1   II   ISSN 0031-6849
PHARMA TIMES. (Text in English) 1969. m. $25. Indian Pharmaceutical Association, Kalina Santacruz East, Bombay 400098, India. Ed. Dr. P.M. Naik. bk.rev.; pat.; circ. 3,500. **Indexed:** I.P.A.
●Also available online.

615.19   GW
PHARMA UND WIR. 1986. bi-m. DM.10. Werkschriften-Verlag GmbH, Bachstr. 14, Postfach 106060, 6900 Heidelberg 1, Germany. TEL 06221-49064. FAX 06221-49066. circ. 55,000.

615.7   AT
PHARMABULLETIN. 1977. m. Health Department Victoria, 555 Collins St., Melbourne, Vic. 3000, Australia. FAX 61-3-380-1789. Ed. Stuart Baker. bk.rev.; index; circ. 3,000. (back issues avail.)
Description: Technical articles on psychopharmacology and related topics.

615.1   CI   ISSN 0031-6857
CODEN: PHAMBF
PHARMACA; jugoslavenski casopis za farmakoterpiju. (Text in Serbo-Croatian and Slovenian; summaries in English) 1963. q. 300 din. Udruzenje Zdravstva SR Hrvatske, Savska 41-VII, 41000 Zagreb, Croatia. Ed. Bozidar Vrhovac. bk.rev.; circ. 3,500. **Indexed:** Biol.Abstr., Chem.Abstr.

615.1   SZ   ISSN 0031-6865
CODEN: PAHEAA
PHARMACEUTICA ACTA HELVETIAE. (Text in English, French and German) 1926. m. (10/yr.). 125 SFr. Societe Suisse de Pharmacie Stationsstr. 12, CH-3097 Berne-Liebefeld, Switzerland. TEL 031-535858. Ed. Niklaus Tueller. adv.; abstr.; bibl.; charts; illus.; index; circ. 5,000. **Indexed:** Anal.Abstr., Biol.Abstr., Biotech.Abstr., Chem.Abstr., Chem.Infd., Crop Physiol.Abstr., Curr.Adv.Ecol.Sci., Curr.Chem.React., Curr.Cont., Dairy Sci.Abstr., Dent.Ind., Excerp.Med., Helminthol.Abstr., Hort.Abstr., I.P.A., Ind.Chem., Ind.Med., Mass Spectr.Bull., Nutr.Abstr.
●Also available online.
—BLDSC shelfmark: 6442.000000.

615.19 668.5   SA   ISSN 0257-2028
PHARMACEUTICAL & COSMETIC REVIEW. 1974. 6/yr. R.55 (foreign R.110). National Publishing, P.O. Box 2271, Clareinch 7740, South Africa. TEL 021-611140. FAX 021-611389. Ed. Gill Loubser. adv.; bk.rev.; circ. 1,428. **Indexed:** Ind.S.A.Per.
—BLDSC shelfmark: 6442.750000.
Description: Keeps manufacturers, packers, and distributors of pharmaceuticals, cosmetics, detergents, soaps, and toiletries up-to-date on developing techniques. Covers all aspects of these industries, including new equipment and materials on the market, packaging trends, overseas developments, and legislation.

330 615   UK
PHARMACEUTICAL BUSINESS NEWS. 1983. 24/yr. £293 (foreign £309). Financial Times Business Information, 102 Clerkenwell Rd., London EC1M 5SA, England. TEL 071-240-9391. FAX 071-240-7946. Ed. A. Archer. adv.; circ. 2,000.
●Also available online. Vendor(s): Data-Star, DIALOG.

PHARMACY AND PHARMACOLOGY

615.19 US ISSN 0091-150X
RS402 CODEN: PCJOAU
PHARMACEUTICAL CHEMISTRY JOURNAL. English translation of: Khimiko-farmatsevticheskii Zhurnal (UR ISSN 0023-1134) 1967. m. $955 (foreign $1115)(effective 1992). (Ministerstvo Zdravookhraneniya S.S.S.R., UR) Plenum Publishing Corp., Consultants Bureau, 233 Spring St., New York, NY 10013-1578. TEL 212-620-8468. FAX 212-463-0742. TELEX 23-421139. Ed. R.G. Glushkov. (also avail. in microform from UMI; microfilm from JSC; back issues avail.) **Indexed:** Biol.Abstr., Chem.Titles, Curr.Adv.Ecol.Sci., Int.Abstr.Biol.Sci.
—BLDSC shelfmark: 0416.770000.
Refereed Serial

615 UK
PHARMACEUTICAL CODEX. 1907. quinquennial. £33. Royal Pharmaceutical Society of Great Britain, 1 Lambeth High St., London SE1 7JN, England. TEL 01-735-9141. bibl.; charts; illus.; circ. 20,000.

615.19 US
▼**PHARMACEUTICAL DIGEST.** 1991. s-a. Centcom, Ltd., 500 Post Rd. E., Box 231, Westport, CT 06881-0231. TEL 203-226-7131. FAX 203-454-9939. Ed. Joan Moynihan. adv.; circ. 30,391.
Description: Contains listings of literature and catalog descriptions.

PHARMACEUTICAL ENGINEERING. see *ENGINEERING*

615 US ISSN 0279-6570
RS1 CODEN: PHEXD2
PHARMACEUTICAL EXECUTIVE. 1981. m. $59 (foreign $117). Aster Publishing Corporation, 859 Willamette St., Box 10955, Eugene, OR 97440. TEL 503-343-1200. FAX 503-343-3641. TELEX 510-597-0365. Ed. Wayne Koberstein. adv.; illus.; circ. 15,000. **Indexed:** BPIA, Curr.Pack.Abstr., I.P.A., Telegen.
—BLDSC shelfmark: 6443.680000.
Description: Designed to meet the management and marketing needs of professionals in the pharmaceutical industry. Covers the latest marketing techniques, industry trends, sales, promotional strategies, and the legal and regulatory issues influencing product development and management.

615.1 UK ISSN 0079-1393
RS61
PHARMACEUTICAL HISTORIAN. 1967. 4/yr. £4.60 (foreign £5). British Society for the History of Pharmacy, 36 York Place, Edinburgh EH1 3HU, Scotland. Ed. Dr. J.G.L. Burnby.

615.1 UK ISSN 0031-6873
CODEN: PHJOAV
PHARMACEUTICAL JOURNAL. 1841. w. £61 (foreign £79). Royal Pharmaceutical Society of Great Britain, 1 Lambeth High St., London SE1 7JN, England. TEL 071-735-9141. Ed. D. Simpson. adv.; bk.rev.; charts; tr.lit.; index; circ. 36,400. **Indexed:** Abstr.Health Care Manage.Stud., Biol.Abstr., Biotech.Abstr., Chem.Abstr., Curr.Adv.Cancer Res., Curr.Adv.Ecol.Sci., High.Educ.Curr.Aware.Bull., I.P.A., Ind.Vet., Protozool.Abstr., Vet.Bull.
—BLDSC shelfmark: 6444.000000.

615 US
PHARMACEUTICAL: LATIN AMERICAN INDUSTRIAL REPORT. (Avail. for each of 22 Latin American countries) 1985. a. $435 per country report. Aquino Productions, Box 15760, Stamford, CT 06901. TEL 203-325-3138. Ed. Andres C. Aquino.

PHARMACEUTICAL LIBRARY BULLETIN/YAKUGAKU TOSHOKAN. see *LIBRARY AND INFORMATION SCIENCES*

PHARMACEUTICAL LITIGATION REPORTER; the national journal of record of pharmaceutical litigation. see *LAW*

PHARMACEUTICAL MANUFACTURERS OF JAPAN. see *BUSINESS AND ECONOMICS — Trade And Industrial Directories*

615 338 UK
PHARMACEUTICAL MANUFACTURING REVIEW. q. £63.90 (foreign £79.90). F M J International Publications Ltd., Queensway House, 2 Queensway, Redhill, Surrey RH1 1QS, England. TEL 0737-768611. FAX 0737-761685. TELEX 948669-TOPJNL-G. Ed. Margaret Atcheson.
Description: Covers all aspects of pharmaceutical manufacturing, from raw materials to the packagaed product, considering both management related topics and technological developments.

615 US
PHARMACEUTICAL MARKETERS DIRECTORY. 1977. a. $155. C P S Communications, Inc., Directories Division, 7200 W. Camino Real, Ste. 215, Boca Raton, FL 33433. TEL 407-368-9301. FAX 407-368-7870. adv.; circ. 3,000.
Incorporates: Medical Products Marketers Directory.
Description: Covers the entire healthcare field including names, titles, addresses, phone and FAX numbers for over 1,500 pharmaceutical and healthcare manufacturers, 300 advertising agencies, over 800 healthcare journals, as well as alternative media. Includes suppliers to the health care industry.

615 610 UK ISSN 0265-0673
CODEN: PHMDEH
PHARMACEUTICAL MEDICINE (HOUNDMILLS). 1985. q. £88. Macmillan Press Ltd., Scientific & Medical Division, Houndmills, Basingstoke, Hampshire RG21 2XS, England. TEL 0256-29242. FAX 0256-810526. Ed. Robert N. Smith. circ. 600. (also avail. in microform from UMI)
—BLDSC shelfmark: 6444.051900.
Description: Assessment of new and old methods employed to test drugs for clinical use.

PHARMACEUTICAL MEDICINE (WORTHING); symposium proceedings. see *MEDICAL SCIENCES*

615.19 US
PHARMACEUTICAL PROCESSING. 1984. 12/yr. $20 (free to qualified personnel). Gordon Publications, Inc., 301 Gibraltar Dr., Morris Plains, NJ 07950. TEL 201-292-5100. FAX 201-898-9281. Ed. Michael Averbach. adv.; tr.lit.; circ. 30,000.
Formerly: Pharmaceutical and Cosmetic Equipment (ISSN 0745-0990)

615 US ISSN 0161-8415
PHARMACEUTICAL REPRESENTATIVE. 1971. m. $23.55. McKnight Medical Communications Co., 1419 Lake Cook Rd., Deerfield, IL 60015. TEL 708-945-0345. Ed. Lisa Werner. bk.rev.; abstr.; charts; illus.; stat.; tr.lit.; circ. 18,231. (tabloid format)
Formerly: Pharmaceutical Salesman (ISSN 0048-3621)

615.19 US ISSN 0724-8741
CODEN: PHREEB
PHARMACEUTICAL RESEARCH. 1983. m. $395 (foreign $460)(effective 1992). (American Association of Pharmaceutical Scientists) Plenum Publishing Corp., 233 Spring St., New York, NY 10013-1578. TEL 212-620-8000. FAX 212-463-0742. TELEX 23-421139. Ed. Wolfgang Sadee. adv. (also avail. in microform from JSC; back issues avail.) **Indexed:** ASCA, Chem.Abstr., Curr.Adv.Ecol.Sci., Curr.Cont., Excerp.Med.
—BLDSC shelfmark: 6444.080000.
Refereed Serial

615.1 JA ISSN 0031-6903
PHARMACEUTICAL SOCIETY OF JAPAN. JOURNAL/YAKUGAKU ZASSHI. (Text in Japanese; contents page, summaries, captions in English) 1881. m. $79. Pharmaceutical Society of Japan - Nihon Yakugakkai, 12-15, Shibuya 2-chome, Shibuya-ku, Tokyo 150, Japan. Ed. Shoji Shibata. adv.; charts; illus.; index; circ. 2,800. **Indexed:** Anal.Abstr., Biol.Abstr., Biotech.Abstr., Chem.Abstr., Crop Physiol.Abstr., Curr.Adv.Biochem., Curr.Adv.Ecol.Sci., Curr.Chem.React, Curr.Cont., Dairy Sci.Abstr., Excerp.Med., Food Sci.& Tech.Abstr., Forest.Abstr., Forest Prod.Abstr., Helminthol.Abstr., Hort.Abstr., I.P.A., Ind.Chem, Ind.Med., Mass Spectr.Bull., Nutr.Abstr.
●Also available online.
—BLDSC shelfmark: 4840.000000.

615 KO ISSN 0513-4242
PHARMACEUTICAL SOCIETY OF KOREA. JOURNAL/YAKHAK HOEJI. (Text in Korean; summaries in English) 1948. bi-m. $30. Pharmaceutical Society of Korea, c/o Natural Products Research Institute, Seoul National University, Seoul 110-460, S. Korea. Ed. Eun Bang Lee. bk.rev.; circ. 1,300. (back issues avail.) **Indexed:** Biol.Abstr., Chem.Abstr., I.P.A., Ind.Med, INIS Atomind.
—BLDSC shelfmark: 4840.050000.

615 US ISSN 0147-8087
RS1 CODEN: PTECDN
PHARMACEUTICAL TECHNOLOGY. 1977. m. $59 (foreign $117). Aster Publishing Corporation, 859 Willamette St., Box 10955, Eugene, OR 97440. TEL 503-343-1200. FAX 503-343-3641. TELEX 510-597-0365. Ed. Stefan Schuber. adv.; abstr.; charts; illus.; pat.; stat.; tr.lit.; circ. 35,000. (back issues avail.) **Indexed:** Biotech.Abstr., Chem.Abstr., Curr.Pack.Abstr., Excerp.Med., I.P.A., Telegen.
Description: Offers practical hands-on information about the manufacture of pharmaceutical products, focusing on applied technology.
Refereed Serial

615 US ISSN 0164-6826
PHARMACEUTICAL TECHNOLOGY INTERNATIONAL. 1978; N.S. 1989. 10/yr. $59 (foreign $117). Aster Publishing Corporation, 859 Willamette St., Box 10955, Eugene, OR 97440. TEL 503-343-1200. FAX 503-343-3641. TELEX 510-597-0365. Ed. Martin Rosser. adv.; circ. 20,000. (back issues avail.) **Indexed:** Excerp.Med.
—BLDSC shelfmark: 6444.160000.
Description: Targets the pharmaceutical industry in Western Europe.

615.1 JA ISSN 0016-5980
PHARMACEUTICALS MONTHLY/GEKKAN YAKUJI. (Text in Japanese) 1959. m. 1200 Yen. (Pharmaceutical Research Association - Yakuji Kenkyukai) Yakugyo Jiho Co. Ltd., 2-36 Kanda Jimbo-cho, Chiyoda-ku, Tokyo 101, Japan. (Subscr. to: F-D-C Reports, Suite one, 5550 Friendship Blvd., Chevy Chase, MD 20815) Ed. Shozo Takeda. adv.; bk.rev.; abstr.; index; circ. 14,400. **Indexed:** Chem.Abstr, I.P.A.
●Also available online.
—BLDSC shelfmark: 6444.390000.
Description: Developments in medical treatment.

615.19 BE
PHARMACEUTISCH TIJDSCHRIFT. (Text in Dutch) m. 217 av. d'Huart, 1950 Kraainem, Belgium. adv.; circ. 3,200.

615.1 CN ISSN 0031-692X
LE PHARMACIEN. (Text in French) 1929. m. Can.$29. Maclean-Hunter Ltd., Business Publication Division, Maclean-Hunter Bldg., 777 Bay St., Toronto, Ont. M5W 1A7, Canada. TEL 514-845-5141. (Or: 1001 Maisonneuve Ouest, Montreal, Que. H3A 3E1) Ed. X.B. de Lusigny. adv.; illus.; circ. 4,109. **Indexed:** I.P.A.
Description: For French speaking pharmacists in retail and hospital locations.

615.1 FR ISSN 0031-6938
PHARMACIEN DE FRANCE; organe d'informations scientifiques et professionnelles. 1925. bi-m. 60 F. Federation des Syndicats Pharmaceutiques de France, 13 rue Ballu, 75009 Paris, France. circ. 17,500. **Indexed:** Biol.Abstr., Chem.Abstr., I.P.A.
●Also available online.
—BLDSC shelfmark: 6446.175000.

615.8 658 FR ISSN 0768-9179
PHARMACIEN HOSPITALIER. 1966. q. 285 F. Syndicat des Pharmaciens Gerants, 31 rue du Terrage, 75010 Paris, France. FAX 42-09-09-10. adv.; circ. 1,600.

615 UK ISSN 1053-8569
CODEN: PDSAEA
▼**PHARMACOEPIDEMIOLOGY AND DRUG SAFETY.** 1992. bi-m. $250. John Wiley & Sons Ltd., Journals, Baffins Lane, Chichester, Sussex PO19 1UD, England. TEL 0243-779777. FAX 0243-775878. TELEX 86290-WIBOOK-G. Ed. Dr. Ronald Mann.
—BLDSC shelfmark: 6446.248000.
Description: Provides an international forum for the communication and evaluation of data, methods and opinion in the emerging discipline of pharmacoepidemiology.

PHARMACOGENETICS. see *BIOLOGY — Genetics*

615.1   UK   ISSN 1043-6618
RS122   CODEN: PHMREP
PHARMACOLOGICAL RESEARCH. 1969. bi-m. $356. (Italian Pharmacological Society) Academic Press Ltd., 24-28 Oval Rd., London NW1 7DX, England. TEL 071-267-4466. Ed.Bd. **Indexed:** Biol.Abstr., Chem.Abstr., Curr.Adv.Biochem., Curr.Adv.Ecol.Sci., Curr.Cont., Dairy Sci.Abstr., Excerp.Med., Helminthol.Abstr., Ind.Med., Ind.Vet., Nutr.Abstr., Risk Abstr., Vet.Bull.
—BLDSC shelfmark: 6446.550000.
Formerly: Pharmacological Research Communications (ISSN 0031-6989)
Description: Presents papers on basic and applied pharmacological research in both animals and man for specialist whose fileds of study vary widely within the discipline of pharmacology.

615.1   US   ISSN 0031-6997
RS1   CODEN: PAREAQ
PHARMACOLOGICAL REVIEWS. 1951. q. $50 to individuals; institutions $90. (American Society for Pharmacology and Experimental Therapeutics) Williams & Wilkins, 428 E. Preston St., Baltimore, MD 21202. TEL 301-528-4000. FAX 301-528-4312. Ed. Robert E. Stitzel. adv.; bibl.; charts; circ. 2,400. (also avail. in microform) **Indexed:** Biotech.Abstr., Chem.Abstr., Curr.Adv.Ecol.Sci., Curr.Cont., Dent.Ind., Excerp.Med., I.P.A., Ind.Med., Ind.Sci.Rev., Ind.Vet., Vet.Bull.
—BLDSC shelfmark: 6447.000000.
Description: Review articles on topics of interest to pharmacologists, toxicologists and biochemists.
Refereed Serial

615.1   US   ISSN 0031-7004
RM1   CODEN: PHMCAA
PHARMACOLOGIST. 1959. q. $20 to non-members. American Society for Pharmacology and Experimental Therapeutics, 9650 Rockville Pike, Bethesda, MD 20814. Ed. Kay A. Croker. abstr.; charts; illus.; index; circ. 4,000. (also avail. in microform from UMI; back issues avail.; reprint service avail. from UMI) **Indexed:** Biol.Abstr., Biotech.Abstr., Chem.Abstr., Excerp.Med.
—BLDSC shelfmark: 6447.050000.

615.1   SZ   ISSN 0031-7012
RM1   CODEN: PHMGBN
PHARMACOLOGY; international journal of experimental and clinical pharmacology. (Text in English) 1959. m. (2 vols./yr.). 439 Fr.($293) per vol. S. Karger AG, Allschwilerstr. 10, P.O. Box, CH-4009 Basel, Switzerland. TEL 061-3061111. FAX 061-3061234. TELEX CH 962652. Eds. K.F. Sewing, E.S. Vesell. adv.; abstr.; bibl.; charts; illus.; index; circ. 1,150. (also avail. in microfilm) **Indexed:** Biol.Abstr., Biotech.Abstr., Chem.Abstr., Curr.Adv.Ecol.Sci., Curr.Cont., Dent.Ind., Excerp.Med., Helminthol.Abstr., Ind.Med., Rev.Plant Path.
—BLDSC shelfmark: 6447.060000.
Formerly: Medicina et Pharmacologia Experimentalis.

PHARMACOLOGY AND THE SKIN. see *MEDICAL SCIENCES — Dermatology And Venereology*

615   US   ISSN 0163-7258
RM1   CODEN: PHTHDT
PHARMACOLOGY AND THERAPEUTICS; journal of the International Encyclopedia of Pharmacology and Therapeutics. 1975. 12/yr. (in 4 vols.). £970 (effective 1992). (International Union of Pharmacology) Pergamon Press, Inc., Journals Division, 660 White Plains Rd., Tarrytown, NY 10591-5153. TEL 914-524-9200. FAX 914-333-2444. (And: Headington Hill Hall, Oxford OX3 0BW, England. TEL 0865-794141) Ed. A. Sartorelli. adv.; bk.rev.; charts; illus.; stat.; index. (also avail. in microform from MIM,UMI; back issues avail) **Indexed:** Biol.Abstr., Biotech.Abstr., Chem.Abstr., Curr.Adv.Biochem., Curr.Adv.Cancer Res., Curr.Adv.Ecol.Sci., Curr.Adv.Genetics & Molec.Biol., Curr.Cont., Dent.Ind., Excerp.Med., Ind.Med., Ind.Sci.Rev., Nutr.Abstr.
—BLDSC shelfmark: 6447.061800.
Formed by the Jan. 1979 merger of: Pharmacology and Therapeutics. Part A. Chemotherapy, Toxicology and Metabolic Inhibitors (ISSN 0362-5478); Pharmacology and Therapeutics. Part B. General and Systematic Pharmacology (ISSN 0306-039X); Pharmacology and Therapeutics. Part C. Clinical Pharmacology and Therapeutics (ISSN 0362-5486)
Refereed Serial

615.9   DK   ISSN 0901-9928
QP901   CODEN: PHTOEH
PHARMACOLOGY & TOXICOLOGY. (Supplements avail.) (Text in English) 1944. 12/yr. DKK 1690 includes supplements. Munksgaard International Publishers Ltd., 35 Noerre Soegade, P.O. Box 2148, DK-1016 Copenhagen K, Denmark. TEL 33-127030. FAX 33-129387. TELEX 19431-MUNKS-DK. Ed. Jens Schou. bibl.; charts; illus.; index; circ. 1,200. (also avail. in microfilm from PMC; reprint service avail. from ISI,SWZ) **Indexed:** ASCA, Biol.Abstr., Biotech.Abstr., C.I.S. Abstr., Chem.Abstr., Curr.Adv.Cell & Devel.Biol., Curr.Adv.Ecol.Sci., Curr.Cont., Dairy Sci.Abstr., Dent.Ind., Excerp.Med., Helminthol.Abstr., I.P.A., Ind.Med., Ind.Sci.Rev., Ind.Vet., Lab.Haz.Bull., NRN, Nutr.Abstr., Psychol.Abstr., Sci.Cit.Ind., Vet.Bull.
—BLDSC shelfmark: 6447.070000.
Formerly: Acta Pharmacologica et Toxicologica (ISSN 0001-6683)

PHARMACOLOGY & TOXICOLOGY. SUPPLEMENTUM. see *ENVIRONMENTAL STUDIES — Toxicology And Environmental Safety*

615   US   ISSN 0363-4655
PHARMACOPEIAL FORUM. 1975. bi-m. $195. United States Pharmacopeial Convention, Inc., 12601 Twinbrook Pkwy., Rockville, MD 20852. TEL 301-881-0666. Ed. William M. Heller. circ. 1,500. **Indexed:** Curr.Cont.
—BLDSC shelfmark: 6447.087400.

615   CC
PHARMACOPOEIA OF THE PEOPLE'S REPUBLIC OF CHINA. (Editions in Chinese, English) a. (Ministry of Public Health) People's Medical Publishing House, 10 Tianxili Lu, Beijing, People's Republic of China. (Dist. by: China Pharmaceutical Books Company, Rm. 1001-4 Champion Bldg., 287-291 Des Voeus Rd., Central, Hong Kong, Hong Kong) Ed.Bd.

PHARMACOPSYCHIATRY; clinical pharmacology, psychiatry, psychology, neurophysiology advances in theoretical and clinical research. see *MEDICAL SCIENCES — Psychiatry And Neurology*

615.19   US   ISSN 0277-0008
CODEN: PHPYDQ
PHARMACOTHERAPY; journal of human pharmacology and drug therapy. 1981. bi-m. $95. Pharmacotherapy Publications, Inc., New England Medical Center, 171 Harrison Ave., Box 806, Boston, MA 02111. TEL 617-956-5390. FAX 617-956-5318. Ed. Richard T. Scheife. adv.; bk.rev.; charts; illus.; index; circ. 3,900. (also avail. in microfilm from UMI; back issues avail.; reprint service avail. from UMI) **Indexed:** Biol.Abstr., Chem.Abstr., Curr.Cont., Dent.Ind., Excerp.Med., Ind.Med.
—BLDSC shelfmark: 6447.089000.
Refereed Serial

615.19   CN
PHARMACTUEL. (Text in French) vol.19, 1986. bi-m. Association des Pharmaciens des Etablissements de Sante du Quebec, 50 Cremazie Ouest, Bureau 505, Montreal, Que. H2P 2T2, Canada. (back issues avail.)

615.1   JA   ISSN 0044-0043
PHARMACY COMPANION/YAKKYOKU NO TOMO. (Text in Japanese) 1953. m. 50 Yen. Yamanouchi Pharmaceutical Co. Ltd. - Yamanouchi Seiyaku K. K., 2-5 Nihonbashi Hon-cho, Chuo-ku, Tokyo 103, Japan. Ed. Nobuo Yamamuro. adv.; charts; illus.; tr.lit.; circ. 20,000.

615.1   US
PHARMACY COUNSELOR.* q. free to registered pharmacists. HealthTeam Interactive Communications, Inc., 274 Madison Ave., No. PH, New York, NY 10016-0701. circ. controlled.

615.19   AT
PHARMACY GUILD OF AUSTRALIA. ANNUAL REPORT. 1975. a. Pharmacy Guild of Australia, P.O. Box 36, Deakin, A.C.T. 2600, Australia. TEL 06-281-0911. FAX 06-281-4745. circ. 5,500.
Formerly: Pharmacy Guild of Australia. National Report.

615.19   AT
PHARMACY GUILD OF AUSTRALIA. NATIONAL NEWSLETTER. 1976. irreg. free to members. Pharmacy Guild of Australia, P.O. Box 36, Deakin, A.C.T. 2600, Australia. TEL 06-281-0911. FAX 06-282-4745. Ed. Wal Williams. circ. 5,300. (back issues avail.)

615.9 610.73 614.8   US
PHARMACY HEALTH-LINE. 1982. m. $45. Rx-Data-Pac Service, 8907 Terwilliger's Trail, Cincinnati, OH 45249. TEL 513-489-0943. Ed. I.H. Goodman. (looseleaf format; back issues avail.)

615.1   US   ISSN 0031-7047
RS61   CODEN: PHHIB4
PHARMACY IN HISTORY. 1959. q. $25. American Institute of the History of Pharmacy, Pharmacy Bldg., Madison, WI 53706. TEL 608-262-5635. Ed. Gregory Higby. adv.; bk.rev.; bibl.; charts; illus.; index every 3 yrs; circ. 1,400. (also avail. in microfilm from UMI; reprint service avail. from UMI) **Indexed:** Amer.Hist.& Life, Hist.Abstr, I.P.A.
●Also available online.
—BLDSC shelfmark: 6447.350000.

615.19 340   US   ISSN 0149-1717
KF2915.P4
PHARMACY LAW DIGEST. 1965. a. (plus s-a. updates). $59.50. Facts and Comparisons, 111 W. Port Plaza, Ste. 423, St. Louis, MO 63146-3098. TEL 800-223-0554. FAX 314-878-5563. Ed. Joseph L. Fink, III. (looseleaf format)
Description: Information on controlled substances, pharmacy inspection, civil liability, pertinent court cases, business and drug control law, with emphasis on federal law.

615   SA
PHARMACY MANAGEMENT. 1980. m. R.77. Medpharm Publications, Noodhulpiga Center, 3rd Fl., 204B HF Verwoerd Dr., Randburg 2194, South Africa. TEL 011-787-4981. Ed. Joy Gasson. adv.; circ. 3,450.
Description: Contains management and clinical articles written by South African specialists.

615.1   II   ISSN 0031-7063
PHARMACY NEWS.* (Editions in English, Hindi, Punjabi, Urdu) 1962. m. Rs.8. (Punjab Pharmacists' Federation) Rajesh Publications, 1 Ansari Rd., Daryaganj, Dew Delhi 110 002, India. (Co-sponsors: All India Medical Practitioners' Association; All India Homeopathic League) Ed. Dr. Kuldip Bhatia. adv.; bk.rev.; illus.; pat.; circ. 12,000 (controlled). **Indexed:** I.P.A.
Incorporating: Modern Medical Practice.

615.1   CN
PHARMACY PRACTICE. 1985. 9/yr. $22 to individuals; students $18; foreign $40. Thomson Healthcare, 5915 Airport Rd., Ste. 700, Mississauga, Ont. L4V 1T1, Canada. TEL 416-673-2500. Ed. Ian Corks. circ. 7,000.

615   US
PHARMACY PRACTICE NEWS. m. McMahon Group, 148 W. 24th St., 8th Fl., New York, NY 10011-1916. TEL 212-620-4600. FAX 212-620-5928. Ed. Sarah Tilyou. circ. 24,577.

615.19   AT   ISSN 0314-6316
PHARMACY REVIEW. 1976. q. Aus.$40. Pharmacy Guild of Australia, P.O. Box 36, Deakin, A.C.T. 2600, Australia. TEL 06-281-0911. FAX 06-282-4745. Ed. Wal Williams. circ. 5,200.
Description: Informs members about decisions relating to pharmacy in Australia.

615 378   US   ISSN 0279-5272
PHARMACY STUDENT. vol.7, 1976. q. $25 to non-members. American Pharmaceutical Association, 2215 Constitution Ave., N.W., Washington, DC 20037. TEL 202-628-4410. Ed. Vicki Meade. circ. 11,500.
Formerly (until vol.8, 1978): S A Ph A News.

PHARMACY AND PHARMACOLOGY

615.1   US   ISSN 0003-0627
RS1
PHARMACY TIMES; devoted to professional pharmacy, pharmacy economics, and prescription practice. 1935. m. $30 registered pharmacists and students $18; foreign $75. Romaine Pierson Publishers, Inc., 80 Shore Rd., Port Washington, NY 11050. TEL 516-883-6350. FAX 516-883-6609. Ed. Raymond A. Gosselin. adv.; bk.rev.; abstr.; illus.; index; circ. 93,666. (also avail. in microform from UMI; back issues avail.; reprint service avail.) **Indexed:** Biol.Abstr., Chem.Abstr., I.P.A.
●Also available online.
—BLDSC shelfmark: 6447.530000.
    Former titles (until 1969): American Professional Pharmacist (ISSN 0096-0349); Practical Druggist; Spatula.

615   US   ISSN 1042-0991
PHARMACY TODAY. 1962. w. $50. American Pharmaceutical Association, 2215 Constitution Ave., N.W., Washington, DC 20037. TEL 202-628-4410. FAX 202-783-2351. Ed. Sara Martin. bibl.; illus.; circ. 40,000 (controlled).
    Former titles: Pharmacy Weekly; A-Ph-Armacy Weekly (ISSN 0098-2814); A Ph A Newsletter (ISSN 0567-4069)
    Description: Covers law as it is realted to pharmacy and medical sciences.

615.1   AT   ISSN 0031-7071
PHARMACY TRADE. 1967. m. Aus.$35. Reed Business Publishing Pty. Ltd., 1-5 Railway St., Chatswood, N.S.W. 2067, Australia. TEL 02-372-5222. FAX 02-419-7533. Ed. S. Kerekovic. adv.; illus.; circ. 6,785. (tabloid format)

615.19   US   ISSN 1055-9744
▼**PHARMACY UPDATE.** 1990. w. free. Valley Forge Press, 1288 Valley Forge Rd., Box 1135, Valley Forge, PA 19481. TEL 215-935-1296. FAX 215-935-3072. Ed. Eileen Moran. bk.rev.; charts; illus.; circ. 60,000 (controlled).
    Description: Items of general interest to community and hospital pharmacists, including drug recalls, legislation, and news.

615.1   US   ISSN 0191-6394
PHARMACY WEST. 1888. m. $18. Western Communications, Ltd., 333 W. Hampden Ave., Ste. 1050, Englewood, CO 80110-2340. TEL 303-761-8818. FAX 303-761-2440. Ed. Elroy FitzSenry. adv.; circ. 15,812. **Indexed:** I.P.A.
●Also available online.
    Formerly: West Coast - Rocky Mountain Druggist; Which was formed by the merger of: West Coast Druggist (ISSN 0043-3101); Rocky Mountain Druggist (ISSN 0035-757X)
    Description: News and features on the pharmaceutical industry in the 13 Western states.

PHARMALERT. see *DRUG ABUSE AND ALCOHOLISM*

615.1   US   ISSN 0048-3648
PHARMASCOPE; new products & investigational drugs. 1961. m. $525. Transpharma, Inc., 13072 Camino del Valle, Poway, CA 92064. Ed.Bd. bk.rev.; abstr.; bibl.; pat.; s-a. index.

615.1   GW   ISSN 0031-711X
    CODEN: PHINAN
DIE PHARMAZEUTISCHE INDUSTRIE. (Text in English and German) 1939. m. DM.315. Editio Cantor, Postfach 1255, 7960 Aulendorf, Germany. TEL 07525-2060. FAX 07525-20680. Ed. Viktor Schramm. adv.; bk.rev.; abstr.; bibl.; charts; illus.; mkt.; pat.; tr.lit.; index; circ. 4,000. (reprint service avail. from ISI) **Indexed:** Biotech.Abstr., Chem.Abstr., Excerp.Med., I.P.A., Int.Packag.Abstr., Key to Econ.Sci., PROMT.
●Also available online.
—BLDSC shelfmark: 6447.650000.

615.1   GW   ISSN 0031-7128
RS1   CODEN: PHMRAL
PHARMAZEUTISCHE RUNDSCHAU. 1968. m. DM.133.20 (foreign DM.152.40). (Bundesverband Deutscher Apotheker e.V.) P. Keppler Verlag GmbH und Co. KG, Industriestr. 2, 6056 Heusenstamm, Germany. TEL 06104-6060. FAX 06104-606117. TELEX 410131. Ed. Beate Fruhstorfer. adv.; bk.rev.; circ. 10,000. **Indexed:** Biol.Abstr., Excerp.Med.
    Description: Professional journal of pharmaceutical news and issues.

615.1   GW   ISSN 0031-7136
    CODEN: PHZIAP
PHARMAZEUTISCHE ZEITUNG. 1856. w. DM.176.20. (Bundesvereinigung Deutscher Apotheker) Govi-Verlag GmbH, Beethovenplatz 1-3, Postfach 970108, 6000 Frankfurt a.M. 97, Germany. Ed. Dr. Hartmut Morck. adv.; bk.rev.; bibl.; charts; illus.; index; circ. 32,000. **Indexed:** Biotech.Abstr., Chem.Abstr., Chem.Infd., I.P.A.
●Also available online.
—BLDSC shelfmark: 6447.693000.

615.19   GW   ISSN 0369-979X
    CODEN: PHZHAM
PHARMAZIE HEUTE; Beilage der Deutschen Apotheker Zeitung zur Fortbildung. (Suppl. to: Deutscher Apotheker Zeitung) 1971. irreg. Deutscher Apotheker Verlag, Postfach 101061, 7000 Stuttgart 10, Germany. TEL 0711-2582-0. FAX 0711-2582290. TELEX 723636-DAZ-D. **Indexed:** Chem.Abstr.

615   GW   ISSN 0048-3664
    CODEN: PHUZBI
PHARMAZIE IN UNSERER ZEIT. 1972. 6/yr. DM.88. (Deutsche Pharmazeutische Gesellschaft) V C H Verlagsgesellschaft mbH, Postfach 101161, 6940 Weinheim, Germany. TEL 06201-602-0. FAX 06201-602328. TELEX 465516-VCHWH-D. (US addr.: V C H Publishers Inc., 220 E. 23rd St., New York, NY, 10010-4606. TEL 212-683-8333) Ed. E. Graf. adv.; bk.rev.; circ. 7,255. (reprint service avail. from ISI) **Indexed:** Biol.Abstr., Biotech.Abstr., Chem.Abstr., Excerp.Med., Ind.Med.
—BLDSC shelfmark: 6448.600000.

615   II   ISSN 0379-556X
    CODEN: PMSDBB
PHARMSTUDENT. (Text in English) 1952. a. $8. Pharmaceutical Society, c/o Department of Pharmaceutics, Banaras Hindu University, Varanasi 221005, India. Ed. J.K. Pandit. adv.; circ. 600. **Indexed:** Chem.Abstr.

615.1   US   ISSN 0031-725X
PHILADELPHIA COLLEGE OF PHARMACY AND SCIENCE BULLETIN. 1865. m. free to alumni. Philadelphia College of Pharmacy and Science, Woodland Ave. at 43rd St., Philadelphia, PA 19104. TEL 215-596-8800. Ed. Christine L. Bailey. illus.; circ. 8,900. (reprint service avail. from UMI)

PHYSICIANS' DESK REFERENCE FOR NONPRESCRIPTION DRUGS. see *MEDICAL SCIENCES*

615.7   US
PHYSICIANS' DRUG ALERT. m. M.J. Powers & Co., 374 Millburn Ave., Millburn, NJ 07041-1343. TEL 201-467-4556. Ed. John Roche.

615.1   US   ISSN 0031-9058
RM1
PHYSICIANS' DRUG MANUAL. Short title: P D M. 1969. bi-m. $48.50. (International Congress of Pharmacology) Physicians Drug Manual, Inc., 61 E. 86th St., New York, NY 10028. Ed. Dr. Albert A. LaVerne. bk.rev.; circ. 25,000. **Indexed:** Ind.Med.

615.1   FR   ISSN 0031-8876
    CODEN: PHPHA6
PHYTIATRIE-PHYTOPHARMACIE. 4/yr. 80 F. (Societe Francaise de Phytiatrie et de Phytopharmacie) C.N.R.A., Route de St. Cyr, 78-Versailles, France. **Indexed:** Biotech.Abstr., Chem.Abstr., Field Crop Abstr., Helminthol.Abstr., Herb.Abstr., Hort.Abstr., Rev.Appl.Entomol., Rev.Plant Path., Soils & Fert.

615   GW   ISSN 0032-0943
RS164   CODEN: PLMEAA
PLANTA MEDICA; journal of medicinal plant research. (Text in English, French and German) 1935. bi-m. DM.366. (Gesellschaft fuer Arzneipflanzenforschung) Georg Thieme Verlag, Ruedigerstr. 14, Postfach 104853, 7000 Stuttgart 10, Germany. TEL 0711-8931-0. FAX 0711-8931298. Ed.Bd. adv.; bk.rev.; charts; illus.; tr.lit.; index; circ. 1,400. (also avail. in microfiche; reprint service avail. from SWZ) **Indexed:** Biol.Abstr., Biotech.Abstr., Chem.Abstr., Crop Physiol.Abstr., Curr.Adv.Ecol.Sci., Curr.Biotech.Abstr., Curr.Cont., Excerp.Med., Field Crop Abstr., Food Sci.& Tech.Abstr., Forest.Abstr., Forest Prod.Abstr., Helminthol.Abstr., Herb.Abstr., Hort.Abstr., I.P.A., Ind.Med., Ind.Vet., Mass Spectr.Bull., Ornam.Hort., Plant Grow.Reg.Abstr., Poult.Abstr., Protozool.Abstr., Seed Abstr.
●Also available online.
—BLDSC shelfmark: 6524.100000.

PLANTES MEDICINALES ET PHYTOTHERAPIE. see *BIOLOGY — Botany*

PODRAVKA; znanstveno-strucni casopis. see *AGRICULTURE*

615.9   CN
POISON MANAGEMENT MANUAL. irreg. (every 2-3 years). Can.$55. Canadian Pharmaceutical Association, 1785 Alta Vista Dr., Ottawa, Ont. K1G 3Y6, Canada. TEL 613-523-7877.

615.1   PL   ISSN 0301-0244
    CODEN: PJPPAA
POLISH JOURNAL OF PHARMACOLOGY AND PHARMACY. (Text in English; summaries in English and Polish) 1949. bi-m. $72. (Polska Akademia Nauk, Instytut Farmakologii) Ossolineum, Publishing House of the Polish Academy of Sciences, Rynek 1-9, 106 Wroclaw, Poland. TELEX 0712771 OSS PL. (Dist. by: Ars Polona-Ruch, Krakowskie Przedmiescie 7, Warsaw, Poland) bk.rev.; charts; illus.; index; circ. 725. **Indexed:** Anal.Abstr., Biol.Abstr., Biotech.Abstr., Bull Signal., Chem.Abstr., Curr.Adv.Ecol.Sci., Curr.Chem.React, Curr.Cont., Excerp.Med., Helminthol.Abstr., I.P.A., Ind.Chem., Ind.Med., Int.Abstr.Biol.Sci., Ref.Zh.
●Also available online.
—BLDSC shelfmark: 6543.671500.
    Formerly: Dissertationes Pharmaceuticae et Pharmacologicae (ISSN 0012-3870)
    Description: Covers original experimental studies in the field of pharmacology in its broadest sense.

615   FR
PORPHYRE. 1949. m. (10/yr.). 80 F. Editions du Porphyre, 1 et 3 rue du Depart, 75014 Paris, France. Ed. J. Guillon. adv.; bk.rev.; circ. 7,500.

615.7   NE   ISSN 0269-2333
    CODEN: PMSUEV
POST MARKETING SURVEILLANCE. 1986. 4/yr. fl.373 (effective 1992). Elsevier Science Publishers B.V., P.O. Box 211, 1000 AE Amsterdam, Netherlands. TEL 020-5803911. FAX 020-5803598. TELEX 18582 ESPA NL. (Subscr. in U.S. and Canada to: Elsevier Science Publishing Co., Inc., Box 882, Madison Sq. Sta., New York, NY 10159. TEL 212-989-5800) Ed. C.J. Van Boxtel. (back issues avail.) **Indexed:** Excerp.Med. (1992-).
—BLDSC shelfmark: 6558.897000.
    Description: Provides information on all aspects of pharmacoepidemiology and the study of drug efficacy and safety.
    Refereed Serial

615.1   JA   ISSN 0044-0035
PRACTICAL PHARMACY/YAKKYOKU. (Text in Japanese) 1950. m. 6000. Yen($17.) Nanzando Co., Ltd., 4-1-11 Yushima, Bunkyoku, Tokyo 113-91, Japan. Ed. Dr. Tootaroo Simizu. adv.; circ. 15,000. **Indexed:** Chem.Abstr., I.P.A.
●Also available online.

615.1   UK   ISSN 0032-7611
    CODEN: PRJOBY
PRESCRIBERS' JOURNAL. 1961. 6/yr. £10. Departments of Health and Social Security, Hannibal House, Elephant and Castle, London SE1 6TE, England. (Subscr. to: H.M.S.O., P.O. Box 276, London SW8 5DT, England) Ed. Robyn Young. **Indexed:** Curr.Adv.Ecol.Sci., I.P.A.
●Also available online.
—BLDSC shelfmark: 6609.705000.

PHARMACY AND PHARMACOLOGY

615   US
PRESCRIPTION AND O T C PHARMACEUTICALS: THE PINK SHEET. 1939. w. $640 (foreign $715). F-D-C Reports, Inc., 5550 Friendship Blvd., Ste. One, Chevy Chase, MD 20815. TEL 301-657-9830. FAX 301-656-3094. Ed. Cole Palmer Werble. charts; illus.; stat.; tr.lit. (looseleaf format; back issues avail.)
●Also available online. Vendor(s): Data-Star, DIALOG (File no.187), Mead Data Central.
    Formerly: F-D-C Reports: The Pink Sheet (ISSN 0734-6514)
    Description: Covers the pharmaceutical industry - both prescription and over-the-counter drugs.

615.7   AT   ISSN 0818-4445
PRESCRIPTION PRODUCTS GUIDE. 1959. a. Aus.$95. Australian Pharmaceutical Publishing Co. Ltd, 40 Burwood Rd., Hawthorn, Vic. 3122, Australia. Ed. J. Thomas. circ. 5,000.
    Incorporates: Non-Prescription Products Guide (ISSN 0818-4453); Formerly: Prescription Proprietaries Guide for Health Professionals.

PREVENTION OF FOOD ADULTERATION CASES. see *LAW*

PREVISIONS GLISSANTES DETAILLEES EN PERSPECTIVES SECTORIELLES (VOL.19): PARACHIMIE ET PHARMACIE. see *BUSINESS AND ECONOMICS — Economic Situation And Conditions*

PROBATUM EST; Informationen fuer den Arzt. see *MEDICAL SCIENCES*

PRODUCT MANAGEMENT TODAY. see *BUSINESS AND ECONOMICS — Marketing And Purchasing*

615.9   US
PROFESSIONAL'S GUIDE TO PATIENT DRUG FACTS. 1989. q. $59.95. Facts and Comparisons, 111 W. Port Plaza, Ste. 423, St. Louis, MO 63146-3098. TEL 800-223-0554. FAX 314-878-5563.
    Description: Drug information reference written in laymen's terms to aid healthcare professionals with the education and counseling of patients and drug therapy management.

615.7   SZ   ISSN 1011-0267
PROGRESS IN BASIC AND CLINICAL PHARMACOLOGY. (Text in English) 1988. irreg. price varies. S. Karger AG, Allschwilerstr. 10, P.O. Box, CH-4009 Basel, Switzerland. TEL 061-3061111. FAX 061-3061234. TELEX CH 962652. Eds. P. Lomax, E.S. Vesell.
    —BLDSC shelfmark: 6865.955500.

615   SZ   ISSN 0079-6085
                            CODEN: PBPHAW
PROGRESS IN BIOCHEMICAL PHARMACOLOGY. (Text in English) 1965. irreg., latest vol.24, 1990. price varies. S. Karger AG, Allschwilerstr. 10, P.O. Box, CH-4009 Basel, Switzerland. TEL 061-3061111. FAX 061-3061234. TELEX CH 962652. (US addr.: S. Karger Publishers, Inc., 26 W. Avon Rd., Box 529, Farmington, CT 06085) Ed. R. Paoletti. (reprint service avail. from ISI, back issues avail.) **Indexed:** Biol.Abstr., Chem.Abstr., Curr.Cont., Ind.Med.
    —BLDSC shelfmark: 6865.960000.
    Description: Volumes in this series consider drugs as the therapeutic agents and curative measures for dealing with various conditions of human health.

615   UK   ISSN 0278-5846
RM315   CODEN: PNPPD7
PROGRESS IN NEURO-PSYCHOPHARMACOLOGY AND BIOLOGICAL PSYCHIATRY. 1977. 6/yr. £340 (effective 1992). Pergamon Press plc, Headington Hill Hall, Oxford OX3 0BW, England. TEL 0865-794141. FAX 0865-743911. TELEX 83177 PERGAP. (And: 660 White Plains Rd., Tarrytown, NY 10591-5153. TEL 914-524-9200) Eds. Corneille Radouco-Thomas, F. Garcin. bk.rev.; index; circ. 1,000. (also avail. in microform from MIM,UMI; back issues avail.) **Indexed:** Biol.Abstr., Chem.Abstr., Curr.Adv.Ecol.Sci., Curr.Cont., Dent.Ind., Excerp.Med., Ind.Med., Ind.Sci.Rev., Psychol.Abstr.
    —BLDSC shelfmark: 6870.380000.
    Formerly: Progress in Neuro-Psychopharmacology (ISSN 0364-7722)
    Refereed Serial

615.19   UK   ISSN 0268-8654
PROPRIETARY ARTICLES TRADE ASSOCIATION. PUBLICATION. 1986. a. £10. Sterling Publications Ltd., 86-88 Edgware Rd., London W2 2YW, England. Ed. Derek Bacon. circ. 10,000.

PROTEASES AND INHIBITORS. see *BIOLOGY — Biological Chemistry*

615.9   CN
PROVINCIAL DRUG BENEFIT PROGRAMS. s-a. Can.$250. Canadian Pharmaceutical Association, 1785 Alta Vista Dr., Ottawa, Ont. K1G 3Y6, Canada. TEL 613-523-7877. FAX 613-523-0445.

615.1   GW   ISSN 0033-3158
RM315   CODEN: PSCHDL
PSYCHOPHARMACOLOGY. (Text mainly in English) 1959. 12/yr. DM.2796($1503) Springer-Verlag, Heidelberger Platz 3, D-1000 Berlin 33, Germany. TEL 030-8207-1. (Also Heidelberg, Tokyo, Vienna, and New York) Ed. H. Barry. adv.; charts; illus. (also avail. in microform from UMI; back issues avail.; reprint service avail. from ISI) **Indexed:** Biol.Abstr., Biotech.Abstr., Chem.Abstr., Curr.Adv.Ecol.Sci., Curr.Cont., Excerp.Med., Ind.Med., Psychol.Abstr.
    —BLDSC shelfmark: 6946.546500.
    Formerly (until vol.47, 1976): Psychopharmacologia.
    Description: Examines the analysis and synthesis of the effects of drugs on behavior.

615   NE
PSYCHOPHARMACOLOGY. 1983. irreg., vol.2, 1985. back issues avail. Elsevier Science Publishers B.V., Books Division, P.O. Box 211, 1000 AE Amsterdam, Netherlands. TEL 020-5803911. FAX 020-5803705. TELEX 18582 ESPA NL. (Subscr. in U.S. and Canada to: Elsevier Science Publishing Co., Inc., Box 882, Madison Sq. Sta., New York, NY 10159. TEL 212-989-5800) Ed.Bd. (back issues avail.) **Indexed:** Chem.Abstr.
    Refereed Serial

615.1 150   US   ISSN 0048-5764
                            CODEN: PSYBB9
PSYCHOPHARMACOLOGY BULLETIN. 1959. q. (plus special biennial no.). $19. U.S. Public Health Service, Alcohol, Drug Abuse and Mental Health Administration, 5600 Fishers Lane, Rockville, MD 20857. TEL 301-496-4000. (Subscr. to: Supt. of Documents, Washington, DC 20402) Ed. Allen Raskin. cum.index: 1969-1975; circ. 3,500. (also avail. in microform from MIM,UMI; reprint service avail. from UMI) **Indexed:** Biol.Abstr., Biotech.Abstr., Chem.Abstr., Curr.Adv.Ecol.Sci., Excerp.Med., I.P.A., Ind.Med., Ind.U.S.Gov.Per., MEDOC, Sci.Cit.Ind.
●Also available online. Vendor(s): National Library of Medicine.
    —BLDSC shelfmark: 6946.549000.

615   US
PSYCHOPHARMACOLOGY SUPPLEMENTA. 1984. irreg. price varies. Springer-Verlag, 175 Fifth Ave., New York, NY 10010. TEL 212-460-1500. (Also Berlin, Heidelberg, Tokyo, Vienna) (reprint service avail. from ISI)

615 616.8   FR   ISSN 0715-9684
PSYCHOTROPES; un journal d'information sur les drogues et leurs usages. 1983. 3/yr. 180 F. to individuals; institutions 270 F. Centre National de Documentation sur les Toxicomanies, 14 ave. Berthelot, 69007 Lyon, France. TEL 72-72-93-07. FAX 78-58-27-14. Ed. Ronald Verbeke.
    —BLDSC shelfmark: 6946.559530.
    Description: Publishes information on psychoactive drugs and their usage.

615   UK   ISSN 0954-3333
PULMONARY PHARMACOLOGY (SHEFFIELD). m. £65. Sheffield University Biomedical Information Service (SUBIS), The University, Sheffield S10 2TN, England. TEL 0742-768555. FAX 0742-739826.
    Description: Current awareness service for researchers.

615.1   US   ISSN 0033-4529
PURDUE PHARMACIST. 1924. 3/yr. (Sep.-Jun.). free. Purdue University, School of Pharmacy, W. Lafayette, IN 47907. TEL 317-494-1363. Ed. Frank Murphy. adv.; cum.index: 1924-1935.; circ. 6,000.
    Description: Alumni news from the Purdue University School of Pharmacy.

615.1   PK   ISSN 0033-4790
Q I M P QUARTERLY. (Quick Index of Medical Preparations) 1963. q. Rs.100($25) Salma Plaza, Mir Karam Ali Talpur Rd., Saddar, Karachi 0306, Pakistan. Ed. Dr. A.H. Qureshi. adv.; circ. 4,000.

615   US   ISSN 0163-2418
                            CODEN: QUCRB6
QUALITY CONTROL REPORTS: THE GOLD SHEET. 1967. m. $160 (foreign $170). F-D-C Reports, Inc., 5550 Friendship Blvd., Ste. One, Chevy Chase, MD 20815. TEL 301-657-9830. FAX 301-656-3094. Ed. Bill Paulson. (looseleaf format; back issues avail.)
    —BLDSC shelfmark: 7168.151500.
    Description: For executives concerned with quality assurance and quality control procedures in the prescription and over-the-counter pharmaceutical, cosmetics, and medical device industries. Covers developments in FDA regulations governing the manufacture and processing of health care products, and state-of-the-art production and quality techniques.

615.19   GW   ISSN 0722-3676
RM301.42   CODEN: QSARDI
QUANTITATIVE STRUCTURE-ACTIVITY RELATIONSHIPS; including molecular modelling and applications of computer graphics in pharmacology, chemistry and biology. (Text in English) 1982. 4/yr. DM.652($335) V C H Verlagsgesellschaft mbH, Postfach 101161, 6940 Weinheim, Germany. TEL 06201-602-0. FAX 06201-602328. TELEX 465516-VCHWH-D. (U.S. addr.: V C H Publishers Inc., 220 E. 23rd St., New York, NY, 10010-4606) Eds. J.K. Seydel, Ferenc Darvas. adv.; circ. 415. **Indexed:** Chem.Abstr, Curr.Adv.Ecol.Sci.
    —BLDSC shelfmark: 7168.343000.

615.19   UK   ISSN 0748-6111
RADIOPHARMACY AND RADIOPHARMACOLOGY YEARBOOK SERIES. 1985. irreg., vol.3, 1988. Gordon & Breach Science Publishers, P.O. Box 90, Reading, Berkshire RG1 8JL, England. TEL 0734-560-080. FAX 0734-568-211. TELEX 849870 SCIPUB G. (US addr.: Box 786, Cooper Sta., New York, NY 10276. TEL 800-545-8398) Ed. P.H. Cox. (also avail. in microform)
    —BLDSC shelfmark: 7240.017000.
    Refereed Serial

615   NZ   ISSN 0157-7271
REACTIONS; alerts to adverse drug experience. (Includes supplement: Reactions Annual (year)) 1979. w. $495. Adis International Ltd., 41 Centorian Dr., Private Bag, Mairangi Bay, Auckland 10, New Zealand. TEL 479-8100. Ed. Peter Louisson. bk.rev.; q. cum.index.
●Also available online. Vendor(s): BRS.
    Description: Clinical information on adverse drug experiences reported in international medical journals.

615.1   SP   ISSN 0034-0618
                            CODEN: ARAFAY
REAL ACADEMIA DE FARMACIA. ANALES. (Text in English, French and Spanish; summaries in English and French) 1932. q. 5000 ptas. (Latin America 5500 ptas; elsewhere 6000 ptas.). Real Academia de Farmacia, Calle de Farmacia 11, 28004 Madrid, Spain. TEL 915-31-03-07. Ed. Antonio Portoles. bk.rev.; bibl.; index; circ. 1,500. (back issues avail.) **Indexed:** Biol.Abstr., Bull.Signal., Chem.Abstr., Curr.Adv.Ecol.Sci., I.P.A., Ind.Med., Ind.SST, Ref.Zh.
    —BLDSC shelfmark: 0882.000000.

615   NE   ISSN 0048-6914
RECEPTARIUS; maanduitgave van de bedrijfsgroup gezondheidszorg. 1907. m. fl.60. Dienstenbond FNV, Houttuinlaan 3, 3447AN Woerden, Netherlands. TEL 03480-75922. (Subscr. to: Brain Communication, Postbus 1191, 1500AD Zaandam, Netherlands. TEL 075-312353) Ed. Guus van Betten. adv.; bk.rev.; circ. 4,000. (back issues avail.)

REGULATORY TOXICOLOGY AND PHARMACOLOGY. see *MEDICAL SCIENCES — Forensic Sciences*

RENIN, ANGIOTENSIN & KININS. see *BIOLOGY — Physiology*

RESEARCH COMMUNICATIONS IN CHEMICAL PATHOLOGY AND PHARMACOLOGY. see *MEDICAL SCIENCES*

PHARMACY AND PHARMACOLOGY

615.19 157.6 616.8   US   ISSN 0193-0818
RC563   CODEN: RCSADO
RESEARCH COMMUNICATIONS IN SUBSTANCES OF ABUSE. 1980. q. $75 (foreign $85). P J D Publications Ltd., Box 966, Westbury, NY 11590. TEL 516-626-0650. Ed. P.D. Sankar. adv.; bk.rev.; abstr.; charts; illus.; index. (reprint service avail.) **Indexed:** Biol.Abstr., Chem.Abstr., Curr.Adv.Ecol.Sci., Curr.Cont., Excerp.Med.
—BLDSC shelfmark: 7736.630000.
Description: Focuses on clinical and human aspects of all abused substances, including alcohol, synthetic and natural substances.
Refereed Serial

615.19   GW
RESEARCH: THE BAYER SCIENTIFIC MAGAZINE. (Text in English) 1986. a. Bayer AG, Public Relations Department, Building W4, 5090 Leverkusen, Germany. TEL 0214-3081753. Ed. Michael Schade. circ. 500,000. (back issues avail.)

RESTORATIVE NEUROLOGY AND NEUROSCIENCE. see *MEDICAL SCIENCES — Psychiatry And Neurology*

REVIEWS OF PHYSIOLOGY, BIOCHEMISTRY AND EXPERIMENTAL PHARMACOLOGY. see *BIOLOGY — Physiology*

615.1   BL   ISSN 0370-372X
             CODEN: RBFAAH
REVISTA BRASILEIRA DE FARMACIA. (Text in Portuguese; summaries in English) bi-m. Cr.$2000($40) Associacao Brasileira de Farmaceuticos, Rua do Andradas 96-10 Andar, 20.051 Rio de Janeiro, Brazil. TEL 263-0791. Ed. Nuno Alvares Pereira. charts; illus.; stat.
Description: Original papers in pharmacology and chemistry.

615   CR
REVISTA CIENCIAS FARMACEUTICAS.* (Text in Spanish; summaries in English, Spanish) 1976. a. Col.10($2) Colegio de Farmaceuticos de Costa Rica, Apdo. 396, San Jose, Costa Rica. **Indexed:** Curr.Adv.Ecol.Sci., I.P.A.

615.1   CK   ISSN 0034-7418
RS402   CODEN: RCQFAQ
REVISTA COLOMBIANA DE CIENCIAS QUIMICO FARMACEUTICAS. (Text in Spanish; summaries in English) 1969. 2/yr. free. Universidad Nacional de Colombia, Departamento de Farmacia, Apdo. Aereo 14 490, Bogota, Colombia. Ed. Lucia A. de Garcia. illus.; circ. 500. **Indexed:** Biol.Abstr., Chem.Abstr., Excerp.Med., I.P.A.
●Also available online.
—BLDSC shelfmark: 7851.401000.

615.1   CU   ISSN 0034-7515
             CODEN: RCUFAC
REVISTA CUBANA DE FARMACIA. (Text in Spanish; summaries in English, French, Spanish) 1967. s-a. $10 in N. America; S. America $12; Europe $14. Ministerio de Salud Publica, Centro Nacional de Informacion de Ciencias Medicas, Calle E No. 452, e-19 y 21, Plaza de la Revolucion, Apdo. 6520, Havana, Cuba. TEL 809-32-5338. (Dist. by: Ediciones Cubana, Obispo No. 527, Apdo. 605, Havana, Cuba) Dir. Marlene Porto. abstr.; bibl.; charts; illus.; index; circ. 1,300. **Indexed:** Chem.Abstr., Excerp.Med., Hort.Abstr., I.P.A., Ind.Med., Seed Abstr., Weed Abstr.
●Also available online.
—BLDSC shelfmark: 7852.107000.
Description: Covers the drug industry, preventive medicine, and heart defects.

615.1   BL   ISSN 0101-3793
             CODEN: RCIFDN
REVISTA DE CIENCIAS FARMACEUTICAS. 1978. a. $30 or exchange basis. Universidade Estadual Paulista, Av. Vicente Ferreira 1278, Caixa Postal 603, 17.500 Marilia SP, Brazil. TEL 0144-331844. FAX 0144-22-2504. TELEX 111-9016 UJME BR. charts; stat.; circ. controlled. **Indexed:** Anal.Abstr., Biol.Abstr., Chem.Abstr, I.P.A.
—BLDSC shelfmark: 7851.032500.
Formerly: Faculdade de Ciencias Farmaceuticas de Araraquara. Revista.
Description: Original articles, notes and technical reviews on clinical cases in all areas of pharmacology.

615.328   SP   ISSN 0213-0157
REVISTA DE FARMACOLOGIA CLINICA Y EXPERIMENTAL. (Text in English and Spanish) 1984. q. 8500 ptas.($100) (Sociedad Espanola de Farmacologia) J.R. Prous, S.A. International Publishers, Apdo. de Correos 540, 08080 Barcelona, Spain. TEL 343 459-22-20. FAX 343-258-15-35. TELEX 98270 PROU E. Ed.Bd. adv.; bk.rev.; index; circ. 2,000. (back issues avail.) **Indexed:** Curr.Adv.Ecol.Sci., Curr.Cont., Ind.Med.Esp.

615.1   AG   ISSN 0034-9496
             CODEN: RFABAN
REVISTA FARMACEUTICA. 1858. 12/yr. (in 6 double issues). $20. Academia Argentina de Farmacia y Bioquimica, Junin 956, Buenos Aires 1113, Argentina. Ed. Alfredo Jose Bandoni. adv.; bk.rev.; bibl.; charts; illus.; circ. 6,000. **Indexed:** Biol.Abstr., Biotech.Abstr., Chem.Abstr., I.P.A.
●Also available online.
—BLDSC shelfmark: 7854.550000.

615   PO
REVISTA PORTUGUESA DE FARMACIA; ordem dos farmaceuticos. (Text in Portuguese; summaries in English) 1951. q. Esc.500 per no. Sociedade Farmaceutica Lusitana, Rua da Sociedade Farmaceutica, No. 18, 1199 Lisbon Codex, Portugal. Ed.Bd. adv.; bk.rev.; bibl.; charts; stat.; cum.index; circ. 5,500. **Indexed:** Biol.Abstr., Biotech.Abstr., Chem.Abstr., I.P.A.
●Also available online.
Description: Presents original papers in pharmacology research.

615.1   FR   ISSN 0035-2349
REVUE D'HISTOIRE DE LA PHARMACIE. 1913. q. 400 F. Societe d'Histoire de la Pharmacie, 4 Av. de l'Observatoire, 75270 Paris Cedex 06, France. Eds. Louis Cotinat, Pierre Julien. adv.; bk.rev.; abstr.; illus.; index, cum.index: 1913-1963, 1964-1983; circ. 1,400. **Indexed:** Bull.Signal., I.P.A.
—BLDSC shelfmark: 7919.900000.

RICERCA & PRACTICA. see *MEDICAL SCIENCES*

RIGAKU RYOHO JANARU/JAPANESE JOURNAL OF PHYSICAL THERAPY. see *MEDICAL SCIENCES — Chiropractic, Homeopathy, Osteopathy*

615.9   IT
RIVISTA DI TOSSICOLOGIA SPERIMENTALE E CLINICA. bi-m. L.24000. (Centro Italiano Contro le Intossicazioni) Societa Editrice Universo, Via G.B. Morgagni 1, 00161 Rome, Italy. Ed. Enrico Malizia. **Indexed:** Biol.Abstr., Excerp.Med.

615.1   US
ROPE LINKS. 1925. 4/yr. membership. Rho Pi Phi Fraternity, c/o Robert M. Heyman, 9280 Hamlin, Des Plaines, IL 60016. TEL 312-635-9391. Ed. Luke Probst. adv.; bk.rev.; stat.; circ. 4,000 (controlled). (tabloid format)
Former titles: Rope Newsletter; Rope News (ISSN 0035-824X)

615   GW
ROTE LISTE. 1935. a. DM.93.50. (Bundesverband der Pharmazeutischen Industrie e.V.) Editio Cantor, Baendelstockweg 20, 7960 Aulendorf, Germany. TEL 07525-2060. FAX 07525-20680. circ. 280,000.

615   IT   ISSN 0081-0703
S.I.S.F. DOCUMENTI. 1965. irreg. price varies. Societa Italiana di Scienze Farmaceutiche, Via Giorgio Jan 18, 20129 Milan, Italy.

615.1   FR   ISSN 1157-1489
             CODEN: STSSE
S T P PHARMA SCIENCES. (Sciences Techniques Pratiques) (Text in French; summaries in English) 1953. 6/yr. 900 F. (foreign 950 F.). Editions de Sante, 19 rue Louis le Grand, 75002 Paris, France. TEL 47-42-84-30. FAX 42-65-09-66. Ed. Dominique Dupont. bk.rev.; charts; illus.; index; circ. 2,000. **Indexed:** Biotech.Abstr., Bull.Signal, Chem.Abstr., Excerp.Med., I.P.A., INIS Atomind.
●Also available online.
Supersedes in part (in 1991): S T P Pharma (ISSN 0758-6922); **Former titles:** Labo - Pharma Problems et Techniques (ISSN 0458-5747); Labo-Pharma (ISSN 0023-6470); **Incorporating:** Catalogue des Theses de Pharmacie Soutenues en France (ISSN 0069-4665)

615   FR   ISSN 1157-1497
           CODEN: SPPRE
S T P PHARMA TECHNIQUES PRATIQUES REGLEMENTATIONS. (Sciences Techniques Pratiques) (Text in French, summaries in English) 1953. 6/yr. 850 F. (foreign 890 F.). Editions de Sante, 19, rue Louis-le-Grand, 75002 Paris, France. TEL 47-42-84-30. FAX 42-65-09-66. adv.; circ. 2,000. **Indexed:** Excerp.Med.
Supersedes in part (in 1991): S T P Pharma (ISSN 0758-6922)
Description: Covers reports, symposiums proceedings, industrial, commercial and technical information, regulatory affairs articles.

615   JA
SAIKIN NO SHINYAKU/NEW DRUGS IN JAPAN. 1950. a. 4000 Yen. Yakuji Nippo, Ltd., 1-10 Kanda Izumicho, Chiyoda-ku, Tokyo 101, Japan. FAX 03-3866-8408. adv.; circ. 20,000. (back issues avail.)
Description: Description of old and new drugs marketed in Japan.

615.19   JA   ISSN 0080-6064
              CODEN: SKKNAJ
SANKYO KENKYUSHO NEMPO/SANKYO RESEARCH LABORATORIES. ANNUAL REPORT. (Text in English, Japanese; summaries in English) 1946. a. free. Sankyo Co., Ltd., Research Institute - Sankyo K.K. Sogo Kenkyujo, 1-2-58 Hiro-machi, Shinagawa-ku, Tokyo 140, Japan. TEL 03-492-3131. FAX 03-495-6734. Ed. Yoshihiko Baba. abstr.; circ. controlled. (reprint service avail. from UMI) **Indexed:** Biol.Abstr., Chem.Abstr. Key Title: Sankyo Kenkyujo Nenpo.
—BLDSC shelfmark: 1430.050000.

615 368.4   CN   ISSN 0707-0152
HD7103.5.C2
SASKATCHEWAN. PRESCRIPTION DRUG PLAN. ANNUAL REPORT. (Supplement to: Saskatchewan Health. Annual Report) 1976. a. Department of Health, Prescription Drug Plan, 3475 Albert St., Regina., Sask. S4S 6X6, Canada. TEL 306-565-3317. circ. 1,800.

615   US
SCHOOLS IN THE UNITED STATES AND CANADA OFFERING GRADUATE EDUCATION IN PHARMACOLOGY. 1963. biennial. free. American Society for Pharmacology and Experimental Therapeutics, 9650 Rockville Pike, Bethesda, MD 20814. Ed. Kay A. Croker.

615.1   SZ   ISSN 0036-7508
             CODEN: SAZTA8
SCHWEIZERISCHE APOTHEKER-ZEITUNG/JOURNAL SUISSE DE PHARMACIE/SWISS JOURNAL OF PHARMACY. 1862. s-m. 160 SFr. Societe Suisse de Pharmacie, Stationsstr. 12, CH-3097 Bern-Liebefeld, Switzerland. TEL 031-535858. Ed. Markus Kamber. circ. 5,000. **Indexed:** Biol.Abstr., Biotech.Abstr., Chem.Abstr., I.P.A.
—BLDSC shelfmark: 8113.000000.

615.1   SZ   ISSN 0036-7567
SCHWEIZERISCHE DROGISTENZEITUNG. 1900. w. 85 Fr. Schweizerischer Drogistenverband, Postfach 924, 2501 Biel, Switzerland.

615.1   AU   ISSN 0036-8709
             CODEN: SCPHA4
SCIENTIA PHARMACEUTICA. 1932. q. S.309. (Oesterreichische Apothekerkammer) Oesterreichische Apotheker-Verlagsgesellschaft, Spitalgasse 31, A-1094 Vienna, Austria. Eds. Dr. Wolfgang Kubelka, Dr. Wilhelm Fleischhacker. adv.; bk.rev.; index; circ. 800. **Indexed:** Anal.Abstr., Biol.Abstr., Biotech.Abstr., Chem.Abstr., Excerp.Med., I.P.A.
●Also available online.
—BLDSC shelfmark: 8173.000000.
Description: Covers all scientific aspects of pharmacy and related disciplines.

PHARMACY AND PHARMACOLOGY

615   UK   ISSN 0143-7690
CODEN: SCRIDK
SCRIP - WORLD PHARMACEUTICAL NEWS. 1972. s-w. £355($795) P J B Publications Ltd., 18-20 Hill Rise, Richmond, Surrey TW10 6UA, England. TEL 081-948-3262. FAX 081-948-6866. TELEX 8951042. (In U.S. subscr. to: c/o Mary Dalia, Pharmabooks Ltd., 1775 Broadway, Ste. 511, New York, NY 10019) Ed. Moira Dower. adv.; bk.rev.; q. cum.index; circ. 7,600. **Indexed:** ABC, P.N.I.
●Also available online. Vendor(s): BRS, Data-Star (PHIND), DIALOG.
—BLDSC shelfmark: 8211.859000.
Description: Worldwide coverage of company news, product development and legislation for anyone working in or for the pharmaceutical industry.

615.19   GW
SEIBT PHARMA-TECHNIK. (Text in English, French and German) 1979. a. DM.45. Seibt Verlag GmbH, Leopoldstr. 208, 8000 Munich 40, Germany. TEL 089-363067. FAX 089-364317. TELEX 521453-SEIB-D. circ. 5,300.

SELECTIVE CANCER THERAPEUTICS. see *MEDICAL SCIENCES — Cancer*

615.328   CN
SELF-MEDICATION. irreg. Can.$85 (members Can.$75). Canadian Pharmaceutical Association, 1785 Alta Vista Drive, Ottawa, Ont. K1G 3Y6, Canada. TEL 613-523-7877. Ed. C. Clarke.
Formerly: Canadian Self-Medication.

615   FI   ISSN 0049-0164
SEMINA. (Text in Finnish; summaries in Swedish) 1917. s-m. FIM 200. Suomen Farmasialiitto - Finnish Pharmacists' Association, Rautatielaisenkatu 6, 00520 Helsinki 52, Finland. FAX 0-1496354. Ed. Kirsti Bult. adv.; bk.rev.; circ. 7,500. **Indexed:** Chem.Abstr.
—BLDSC shelfmark: 8239.000000.

SEMINARS IN HEMATOLOGY. see *MEDICAL SCIENCES — Hematology*

SEMINARS IN ONCOLOGY. see *MEDICAL SCIENCES — Cancer*

SEMINARS IN ONCOLOGY NURSING. see *MEDICAL SCIENCES — Nurses And Nursing*

615   FR
SEMPEX. (Yearly revised directory with 40 supplements) 1950. w. 1144 F. (foreign 1138 F.)(effective 1991). Societe d'Editions Medico-Pharmaceutiques (SEMP), 26 rue le Brun, 75013 Paris, France. TEL 1-43-37-83-50. FAX 43-31-94-11. TELEX 203 046 F. circ. 11,000 (controlled). (looseleaf format; also avail. in microfiche)
Formerly: Sempex Pharmaceutique (ISSN 0488-2644)
Description: Contains references to human and veterinary drugs; including French equivalents to foreign patent medicines and noncommercial products in France.

SHAANXI ZHONGYI XUEYUAN XUEBAO/SHAANXI INSTITUTE OF TRADITIONAL CHINESE MEDICINE. JOURNAL. see *MEDICAL SCIENCES*

SHANDONG YIYAO/SHANDONG MEDICINE. see *MEDICAL SCIENCES*

SHANGHAI ZHONGYIYAO ZAZHI/SHANGHAI JOURNAL OF TRADITIONAL CHINESE MEDICINE. see *MEDICAL SCIENCES*

615   CC   ISSN 0253-9926
SHANXI YIYAO ZAZHI/SHANXI JOURNAL OF MEDICINE. (Text in Chinese) bi-m. Shanxi Sheng Weisheng-ting - Shanxi Provincial Bureau of Public Health, 23 Donghua Men, Taiyuan, Shanxi 030013, People's Republic of China. TEL 382791. Ed. Yang Fuhao.
—BLDSC shelfmark: 8254.601590.

615   CC
SHENYANG YAOXUEYUAN XUEBAO/SHENYANG PHARMACEUTICAL INSTITUTE. JOURNAL. (Text in Chinese) q. Shenyang Yaoxueyuan, Xuebao Bianjibu, 7, Wenhua Lu 2 Duan, Shenyang, Liaoning 110015, People's Republic of China. TEL 483706. Ed. Gu Xueqiu.

615.7   JA   ISSN 0288-1012
SHIKA YAKUBUTSU RYOHO/ORAL THERAPEUTICS AND PHARMACOLOGY. 1982. s-a. 5000 Yen($36) Japanese Society of Oral Therapeutics and Pharmacology - Shika Yakubutsu Ryoho Kenkyukai, c/o Business Center for Academic Societies Japan, 4-16, Yayoi 2-chome, Bunkyo-ku, Tokyo 113, Japan.
—BLDSC shelfmark: 6277.802000.

615.1   JA   ISSN 0037-4377
CODEN: SHZAAY
SHOYAKUGAKU ZASSHI/JAPANESE JOURNAL OF PHARMACOGNOSY. (Text in English and Japanese; summaries in English) 1947. s-a. 6400 Yen($25) Japanese Society of Pharmacognosy - Nihon Shoyaku Gakkai, c/o Japan Academic Societies Business Centre, 4-16 Yayoi 2-chome, Bunkyo-ku, Tokyo 113, Japan. Ed. Shoji Shibata. adv.; bk.rev.; charts; illus.; cum.index; circ. 700. **Indexed:** Biol.Abstr., Chem.Abstr., Excerp.Med., Hort.Abstr., I.P.A., Rice Abstr., Seed Abstr.
—BLDSC shelfmark: 4656.980000.

615.7   NE   ISSN 0583-1881
RM301
SIDE EFFECTS OF DRUGS ANNUAL. (Supplement to: Meyler's Side Effects of Drugs) 1972. a., vol.15, 1991. fl.310 (effective 1992). Elsevier Science Publishers B.V., Books Division, P.O. Box 211, 1000 AE Amsterdam, Netherlands. TEL 020-5803911. FAX 020-5803705. TELEX 18582 ESPA NL. (Subscr. in U.S. and Canada to: Elsevier Science Publishing Co., Inc., Box 882, Madison Sq. Sta., New York, NY 10159. TEL 212-989-5800) Eds. M.N.G. Dukes, L. Beeley. **Indexed:** Biol.Abstr.
●Also available online. Vendor(s): Data-Star (SEDB), DIALOG (File 70/SEDBASE).
Also available on CD-ROM. Producer(s): SilverPlatter (SEDBASE).
Refereed Serial

615.7   SZ   ISSN 1011-0283
CODEN: SKPHEU
SKIN PHARMACOLOGY. (Text in English) 1988. q. 196 SFr.($130.90) to individuals; institutions SFr. 280($187). (Skin Pharmacology Society) S. Karger AG, Allschwilerstr. 10, P.O. Box, CH-4009 Basel, Switzerland. TEL 061-3061111.
FAX 061-30161234. TELEX CH 962652. Ed. H. Schaefer. bk.rev.; charts; illus.; index. (also avail. in microform) **Indexed:** Excerp.Med.
—BLDSC shelfmark: 8295.935000.
Incorporates (1985-1990): Bioengineering and the Skin (ISSN 0266-3082)

615.1   CK   ISSN 0037-8461
SOCIEDAD COLOMBIANA DE QUIMICOS FARMACEUTICOS. BOLETIN. 1961. m. free. Sociedad Colombiana de Quimicos Farmaceuticos, Seccional del Valle del Cauca, 415 Edificio Banco de La Replica, Cali, Colombia. TEL 808336. adv.; charts; circ. 5,000.
Formerly: Colegio Colombiano de Quimicos Farmaceuticos. Boletin.

615.1   FR   ISSN 0037-9093
CODEN: BSPBAD
SOCIETE DE PHARMACIE DE BORDEAUX. BULLETIN. 1860. q. 150 F. Societe de Pharmacie de Bordeaux, c/o Faculte de Pharmacie, 3 place de la Victoire, 33076 Bordeaux Cedex, France. Ed. Jean Canellas. adv.; bk.rev.; abstr.; charts; index; circ. 900. **Indexed:** Biol.Abstr., Biotech.Abstr., Bull.Signal., Chem.Abstr., I.P.A.
—BLDSC shelfmark: 2747.500000.

615   FR
SOCIETE DE PHARMACIE DE LILLE. BULLETIN. 1946. q. 160 F. (Societe de Pharmacie) Universite de Lille, 3 rue du Professeur Laquese, Lille 1250-45, France. Ed.Bd. **Indexed:** Biol.Abstr., Biotech.Abstr., Chem.Abstr., Excerp.Med., I.P.A., Nutr.Abstr.

615.1   FR   ISSN 0037-9107
CODEN: BTSLAV
SOCIETE DE PHARMACIE DE LYON. BULLETIN DES TRAVAUX. 1957. q. 90 F. Publications Periodiques Specialisees, 11 rue d'Algerie, 69001 Lyon, France. bibl.; charts; index. **Indexed:** Chem.Abstr., I.P.A.

615.1   FR   ISSN 0037-9131
CODEN: BPMSAS
SOCIETE DE PHARMACIE DE STRASBOURG. BULLETIN. 1955. s-a. 100 F. Societe de Pharmacie de Strasbourg, Faculte de Pharmacie, B.P. 24, 67401 Illkirch Cedex, France. Ed. Dr. Boymond. adv.; bk.rev.; charts; illus.; cum.index: 1955-1964, 1965-1973, 1974-1978; circ. 600. **Indexed:** Biol.Abstr., Chem.Abstr.

SOMATOSENSORY AND MOTOR RESEARCH. see *BIOLOGY — Physiology*

SOUTH AFRICAN PHARMACEUTICAL & COSMETIC REVIEW; devoted to the manufacture & marketing of medicines, toiletries, soaps, detergents in South Africa. see *BEAUTY CULTURE — Perfumes And Cosmetics*

615.1   SA   ISSN 0038-2558
SOUTH AFRICAN PHARMACEUTICAL JOURNAL/SUID-AFRIKAANSE TYDSKRIF VIR APTEEKWESE. (Text and title in Afrikaans, English) 1934. m. R.72 (effective 1992). Pharmaceutical Society of South Africa - Aptekersvereniging van Suid-Afrika, P.O. Box 31360, Braamfontein, Johannesburg 2017, South Africa.
FAX 011-403-1309. TELEX 4-27445. Ed. Carrie R. Smith. adv.; bk.rev.; charts; illus.; circ. 5,800. **Indexed:** Biotech.Abstr., I.P.A., Ind.S.A.Per.
●Also available online.

615   SA   ISSN 0038-2639
SOUTH AFRICAN RETAIL CHEMIST. (Text in Afrikaans, English) 1951. m. R.104. George Warman Publications (Pty.) Ltd., 77 Hout St., P.O. Box 704, Cape Town 8001, South Africa. TEL 021-245320. FAX 021-261332. TELEX 521849. Ed. Anthea Barker. adv.; bk.rev.; illus.; circ. 3,300. **Indexed:** I.P.A.
Description: Retail journal circulating to all pharmacies in South Africa.

615.1   US   ISSN 0192-5792
SOUTHERN PHARMACY JOURNAL. 1908. m. $18. 3030 Peachtree Rd. N.W., Ste. 411, Atlanta, GA 30305. TEL 404-231-1267. Ed. Elroy Fitzsenry. adv.; bk.rev.; illus.; circ. 20,000. (also avail. in microform from UMI; reprint service avail. from UMI)
Formerly (until 1979): Southeastern Drug - Southern Pharmaceutical Journal (ISSN 0095-2354); Which was formed by the merger of: Southeastern Drug Journal (ISSN 0038-3651); Southern Pharmaceutical Journal (ISSN 0038-4410)
Description: Presetns news and features of pharmacy activities in the Southern United States.

615.19   US   ISSN 0896-8306
RM315   CODEN: SMGRET
SOVIET MEDICAL REVIEWS. SECTION G: NEUROPHARMACOLOGY REVIEWS. 2/yr. $118. Harwood Academic Publishers, 270 Eighth Ave., New York, NY 10011. TEL 212-206-8900.
FAX 212-645-2459. TELEX 236735 GOPUB UR. (Subscr. to: Box 786, Cooper Sta., New York, NY 10276. TEL 800-545-8398; UK subscr. to: P.O. Box 90, Reading, Berkshire RG1 8JL, England. TEL 34-560-080) (also avail. in microform)
—BLDSC shelfmark: 8359.617000.

615   CE
SRI LANKA PHARMACEUTICAL ASSOCIATION. QUARTERLY NEWSLETTER. q. Sri Lanka Pharmaceutical Association, c/o Dept. of Pharmacy, Faculty of Medicine, University of Sri Lanka, Colombo 8, Sri Lanka.

STREET PHARMACOLOGIST. see *DRUG ABUSE AND ALCOHOLISM*

615   GW   ISSN 0721-8672
STUDENT UND PRAKTIKANT; Forum fuer die Pharmazeutische Ausbildung. (Supplement to: Deutsche Apotheker Zeitung) 1982. q. Deutscher Apotheker Verlag, Postfach 101061, 7000 Stuttgart 10, Germany. TEL 0711-2582-0. FAX 0711-2582291. TELEX 723636-DAZ-D. Ed. Klaus Brauer. adv.; bk.rev.
—BLDSC shelfmark: 8480.100000.

SUBSTANCE ABUSE REPORT; twice-monthly newsletter covering all aspects of drug abuse: its prevention, detection and treatment. see *DRUG ABUSE AND ALCOHOLISM*

PHARMACY AND PHARMACOLOGY

615.9 340   US
SURVEY OF PHARMACY LAW. 1950. a. $20. National Association of Boards of Pharmacy, 1300 Higgins Rd., No. 103, Park Ridge, IL 60068-5743. TEL 708-698-6227. Ed. Carmen Catizone. stat.; charts; circ. 20,000.

615.1   SW   ISSN 0039-6524
CODEN: SFTIAE
SVENSK FARMACEUTISK TIDSKRIFT. 1897. 11/yr. SEK 300 in Nordic countries; elsewhere SEK 375. (Apotekarsocieteten) Swedish Pharmaceutical Press, P.O. Box 1136, S-11181 Stockholm, Sweden. TEL 46-8-24 50 80. FAX 46-8-14-95-80. (Affiliate: Swedish Academy of Pharmaceutical Sciences) Ed. Thony Bjoerk. adv.; bk.rev.; illus.; stat.; circ. 8,700. (also avail. in microfilm from UMI) **Indexed:** Biol.Abstr., Biotech.Abstr., Chem.Abstr., Excerp.Med., I.P.A., Ind.Med, PROMT.
●Also available online.

610   SZ   ISSN 0082-0504
SWITZERLAND. BUNDESAMT FUER SOZIALVERSICHERUNG. SPEZIALITAETENLISTE - LISTE DES SPECIALITES - ELENCO DELLE SPECIALITA. 1955. s-a. 66 Fr. Bundesamt fuer Sozialversicherung, Effingerstr. 33, CH-3003 Berne, Switzerland. TEL 031-619075. FAX 031-617880. circ. 12,000. (also avail. in microfilm)
Description: List of drugs being reimbursed by Swiss sickness funds.

TAKEDA RESEARCH LABORATORIES. JOURNAL. see *BIOLOGY*

615 613   DK   ISSN 0107-1181
TAL OG DATA, MEDICIN OG SUNDHEDSVAESEN/FACTS, MEDICINE AND HEALTH CARE, DENMARK. (Text in Danish and English) 1976. a. free. Foreningen af Danske Medicinfabrikker, Landemaerket 25, DK-1119 Copenhagen K, Denmark. FAX 32-27-00-50. illus; circ. 6,000.
Formerly: Tal og Data om Medicin.

615.9   FR
TAREX. 1969. a. 350 F. Societe d'Editions Medico-Pharmaceutiques (SEMP), 26 rue Lebrun, 75013 Paris, France. TEL 1-43-37-83-50. FAX 43-31-94-11. TELEX 203 046 F. adv.; bk.rev.; circ. 17,000 (controlled). (looseleaf format; also avail. in microfiche)

TARGET ORGAN TOXICOLOGY SERIES. see *ENVIRONMENTAL STUDIES — Toxicology And Environmental Safety*

TECHNOMARK REGISTER. CONTRACT RESEARCH ORGANISATIONS. see *MEDICAL SCIENCES*

615.1   US   ISSN 0040-2958
TEMPLE APOTHECARY. 1951. 4/yr. free to alumni. Temple University, School of Pharmacy Alumni Association, 502 Filbert Rd., Box 75, Oreland, PA 19075. TEL 215-221-4901. Ed. Irving L. Trust. adv.; illus.; circ. 4,500.

615.19   US   ISSN 1047-0166
TENNESSEE PHARMACIST. 1965. m. membership. Tennessee Pharmacists Association, 226 Capitol Blvd., Ste. 810, Nashville, TN 37219. FAX 615-255-3528. Ed. Tom C. Sharp, Jr. adv.; bk.rev.; circ. 2,500.

615   US   ISSN 0362-7926
CODEN: TXPDAE
TEXAS PHARMACY. 1879. m. $30. Texas Pharmaceutical Association, Box 14709, Austin, TX 78761-4709. FAX 512-836-0308. Ed. Luther R. Parker. adv.; bk.rev.; circ. 4,500.

THAI PHARMACEUTICAL DIRECTORY. see *BUSINESS AND ECONOMICS — Trade And Industrial Directories*

615   US   ISSN 0163-4356
RM301.5   CODEN: TDMODV
THERAPEUTIC DRUG MONITORING. 1979. bi-m. $160 to individuals; institutions $260. Raven Press, 1185 Ave. of the Americas, New York, NY 10036. TEL 212-930-9500. FAX 212-869-3495. TELEX 640073. Eds. Steven J. Soldin, Folke Sjoqvist. adv.; bk.rev.; illus.; index; circ. 2,500. (back issues avail.) **Indexed:** Anal.Abstr., ASCA, Biol.Abstr., Biotech.Abstr., Chem.Abstr., Curr.Adv.Ecol.Sci., Curr.Cont., Dent.Ind., Excerp.Med., Ind.Med.
—BLDSC shelfmark: 8814.643000.

615.6   SZ   ISSN 0040-5930
THERAPEUTISCHE UMSCHAU; Monatsschrift fuer praktische Medizin. (Text in German; summaries in English and French) 1943. m. 89 Fr. Verlag Hans Huber, Laengassstr. 76, CH-3000 Berne 9, Switzerland. TEL 031-24-25-33. FAX 031-24-33-80. Ed.Bd. adv.; bk.rev.; abstr.; bibl.; charts; illus.; index; circ. 5,000. **Indexed:** ASCA, Biol.Abstr., C.I.S. Abstr., Chem.Abstr., Curr.Cont., Dent.Ind., Excerp.Med., Helminthol.Abstr., Ind.Med.
—BLDSC shelfmark: 8814.696000.

615   DK   ISSN 0082-4003
THERIACA; samlinger til farmaciens og medicinens historie. (Text in Danish; summaries in English) 1956. irreg., no.26, 1991. price varies. Dansk Farmacihistorisk Selskab - Danish Society for the History of Pharmacy, Institut for Samfundsfarmaci, Universitetsparken 2, DK-2100 Copenhagen, Denmark.
—BLDSC shelfmark: 8814.770000.

THIRD PARTY BULLETIN. see *BUSINESS AND ECONOMICS — Marketing And Purchasing*

615.1   US
THIRD PARTY RX. 1989. m. $50. National Association of Retail Druggists, 205 Daingerfield Rd., Alexandria, VA 22314. TEL 703-683-8200. FAX 703-683-3619. Ed. Robert McCarthy. circ. 3,000.

615   CC   ISSN 0253-9896
R97.7.C5   CODEN: TIYADG
TIANJIN YIYAO/TIANJIN PHARMACY. (Text in Chinese) m. Tianjin Yixue Keji Qingbao Yanjiusuo - Tianjin Medical Science and Technology Information Institute, 131 Chengdu Dao, Tianjin 300050, People's Republic of China. TEL 311705. Ed. Zhang Yingfu.
—BLDSC shelfmark: 8820.510000.

615   JA
TOKYO TANABE QUARTERLY. (Text in Japanese) 1967. q. free. Tokyo Tanabe Co., Ltd. - Tokyo Tanabe K.K., 2-7-3 Nihonbashi Hon-cho, Chuo-ku, Tokyo 103, Japan. adv.; bk.rev.; circ. 20,000. **Indexed:** Chem.Abstr.

410   US   ISSN 0271-1206
TOPICS IN HOSPITAL PHARMACY MANAGEMENT. 1981. q. $95. Aspen Publishers, Inc., 200 Orchard Ridge Dr., Gaithersburg, MD 20878. TEL 301-417-7500. FAX 301-417-7550.
—BLDSC shelfmark: 8867.444500.

615.7   NE
TOPICS IN MOLECULAR PHARMACOLOGY. 1981. irreg., vol.4, 1987. price varies. Elsevier Science Publishers B.V., Books Division, P.O. Box 211, 1000 AE Amsterdam, Netherlands. TEL 020-5803911. FAX 020-5803705. TELEX 18582 ESPA NL. (Subscr. in U.S. and Canada to: Elsevier Science Publishing Co., Inc., Box 882, Madison Sq. Sta., New York, NY 10159. TEL 212-989-5800) (back issues avail.)
Refereed Serial

TOXICOLOGICAL AND ENVIRONMENTAL CHEMISTRY. see *ENVIRONMENTAL STUDIES — Toxicology And Environmental Safety*

TOXICOLOGY; an international journal concerned with the effects of chemicals on living systems. see *ENVIRONMENTAL STUDIES — Toxicology And Environmental Safety*

TOXICOLOGY AND APPLIED PHARMACOLOGY; for those working in the fields of toxicology, pharmacology, biochemistry, nutrition, veterinary medicine. see *ENVIRONMENTAL STUDIES — Toxicology And Environmental Safety*

TOXICOLOGY IN VITRO. see *ENVIRONMENTAL STUDIES — Toxicology And Environmental Safety*

TOXICOLOGY LETTERS; an international journal for the rapid publication of short reports on biochemical mechanisms of mammalian toxicity. see *ENVIRONMENTAL STUDIES — Toxicology And Environmental Safety*

TOXICOLOGY METHODS. see *ENVIRONMENTAL STUDIES — Toxicology And Environmental Safety*

615.9   US   ISSN 0041-0101
QP631   CODEN: TOXIA6
TOXICON; an international journal specialising in toxins. (Text in English, French, German and Spanish) 1962. 12/yr. £455 (effective 1992). (International Society on Toxinology) Pergamon Press, Inc., Journals Division, 660 White Plains Rd., Tarrytown, NY 10591-5153. TEL 914-524-9200. FAX 914-333-2444. (And: Headington Hill Hall, Oxford OX3 0BW, England. TEL 0865-794141) Ed. Alan Harvey. adv.; bk.rev.; software rev.; abstr.; charts; illus.; index; circ. 1,000. (also avail. in microform from MIM,UMI) **Indexed:** Abstr.Hyg., ASCA, Bio-Contr.News & Info., Biol.Abstr., Chem.Abstr., Crop Physiol.Abstr., Curr.Adv.Biochem., Curr.Adv.Ecol.Sci., Curr.Cont., Dairy Sci.Abstr., Deep Sea Res.& Oceanogr.Abstr., Excerp.Med., Helminthol.Abstr., Herb.Abstr., Hort.Abstr., Ind.Med., Ind.Vet., Int.Aerosp.Abstr., Ocean.Abstr., Pig News & Info., Pollut.Abstr., Poult.Abstr., Rev.Appl.Entomol., Small Anim.Abstr., Trop.Dis.Bull., Vet.Bull.
—BLDSC shelfmark: 8873.050000.
Description: Publishes original research on the chemical, pharmacological, zootoxicological and immunological proerties of naturally occurring poisons, including clinical and therapeutic observations.
Refereed Serial

615.1   UK   ISSN 0143-4241
TRANSMITTERS, RECEPTORS & SYNAPSES. 1980. s-m. £130. Sheffield University Biomedical Information Service (SUBIS), The University, Sheffield S10 2TN, England. TEL 0742-768555. FAX 0742-739826. TELEX 547216-UGSHEF-G.
Description: Current awareness service for researchers. Covers synapses, neuromuscular junction, transmitters and neuromodulators.

TRANSPLANTATION PROCEEDINGS. see *MEDICAL SCIENCES — Surgery*

615   UK   ISSN 0165-604X
TRENDS IN PHARMACOLOGICAL SCIENCES. 1979. m. £239 (effective 1992). Elsevier Science Publishers Ltd., Crown House, Linton Rd., Barking, Essex IG11 8JU, England. TEL 081-594-7272. FAX 081-594-5942. TELEX 896950 APPSCI G. (Subscr. in U.S. and Canada to: Elsevier Science Publishing Co., Inc., Box 882, Madison Sq. Sta., New York, NY 10159. TEL 212-989-5800) (Co-sponsors: International Union of Pharmacology; International Union of Toxicology) Ed. A. Abbott. adv.; bk.rev.; bibl.; index; circ. 4,000. (also avail. in microform from RPI; back issues avail.; reprint service avail. from SWZ) **Indexed:** Biol.Abstr., Chem.Abstr., Curr.Adv.Biochem., Curr.Adv.Cancer Res., Curr.Adv.Ecol.Sci., Curr.Cont., Excerp.Med., I.P.A., Ind.Sci.Rev., Sci.Cit.Ind., Telegen.
Description: Covers the sciences of pharmacology and toxicology.
Refereed Serial

615   BL   ISSN 0049-4631
TRIBUNA FARMACEUTICA. (Text in Portuguese; summaries in English, Portuguese) 1932. s-a. free or exchange basis. Universidade Federal do Parana, Faculdade de Farmacia, Rua Coronel Dulcidio 638, Caixa Postal 888, 80000 Curitiba, Parana, Brazil. FAX 041-2642243. TELEX 415100. Ed. Eduardo Augusto Moreira. adv.; bk.rev.; abstr.; bibl.; illus.; circ. 500. **Indexed:** Biol.Abstr., Chem.Abstr., I.P.A.
●Also available online.

615   US   ISSN 0090-6816
RS55
U S A N AND THE U S P DICTIONARY OF DRUG NAMES. (United States Adopted Names) 1963. a. $90. United States Pharmacopeial Convention, Inc., 12601 Twinbrook Pkwy., Rockville, MD 20852. TEL 301-881-0666. Ed. Mary C. Griffiths. circ. 3,500.
—BLDSC shelfmark: 9124.912000.

615   US   ISSN 0148-4818
RS1
U S PHARMACIST. 1976. 12/yr. $25. Jobson Publishing Corp., 352 Park Ave. S., New York, NY 10010. TEL 212-685-4848. FAX 212-696-5318. Ed. Allen Schwartz. adv.; circ. 80,000. **Indexed:** I.P.A.
●Also available online.

615   DK   ISSN 0108-948X
UNDERSOEGELSE OVER APOTEKERNES DRIFTSFORHOLD; regnskabsresultater fra apoteker. vol.9, 1944. a. DKK 75. Sundhedsstyrelsen, Amaliegade 13, 1012 Copenhagen K, Denmark. (Co-sponsor: Apotekerfonden)

615   SP
UNIFARMA. 1974. m. 780 ptas.($11) Editorial ECO, S.A., Calle de la Cruz 44, Barcelona 34, Spain. Ed. J. Mir Morato. adv.; charts; illus.; stat.; index; circ. 15,000.

615.1   US   ISSN 0077-4235
U.S. FOOD AND DRUG ADMINISTRATION. NATIONAL DRUG CODE DIRECTORY. 1969. irreg. $76 includes supplements. U.S. Food and Drug Administration, 5600 Fisher's Lane, Rockville, MD 20857. TEL 202-783-3054. (Dist. by: Supt. of Documents, Washington, DC 20402)

615.11   US   ISSN 0195-7996
RS141.2   CODEN: USPFDX
UNITED STATES PHARMACOPEIA - NATIONAL FORMULARY. 1820. every 5 yrs. $300 incl. annual supplements. United States Pharmacopeial Convention, Inc., 12601 Twinbrook Pkwy., Rockville, MD 20852.
—BLDSC shelfmark: 9100.172000.
Formed by the 1980 merger of: National Formulary (ISSN 0084-6414); United States Pharmacopeia; Which was formerly titled: Pharmacopeia of the United States of America (ISSN 0079-1407)

615.1   VE   ISSN 0041-8307
UNIVERSIDAD CENTRAL DE VENEZUELA. FACULTAD DE FARMACIA. REVISTA. 1959. q. exchange. Universidad Central de Venezuela, Facultad de Farmacia, Apto. 40109, Nueva Granada, Ciudad Universitaria, las Chaguaramos, Caracas, Venezuela. Ed. Ivonne Gomez. bk.rev.; charts; illus.; index; circ. 1,000. **Indexed:** Biol.Abstr., I.P.A.

615   SP.   ISSN 0067-4176
UNIVERSIDAD DE BARCELONA. FACULTAD DE FARMACIA. MEMORIA.* biennial. price varies. Universidad de Barcelona, Facultad de Farmacia, Av. Jose Antonio 585, Barcelona 7, Spain.

615   SP
UNIVERSIDAD DE SEVILLA. SERIE: FARMACIA. irreg., latest no.2. Universidad de Sevilla, Servicio de Publicaciones, San Fernando, 4, 41004 Seville, Spain. TEL 954-22-8071. FAX 954-22-1315.

615.19 574.192   PE
UNIVERSIDAD NACIONAL MAYOR DE SAN MARCOS. FACULTAD DE FARMACIA Y BIOQUIMICA. REVISTA. 1939. s-a. Universidad Nacional Mayor de San Marcos, Facultad de Farmacia y Bioquimica, Apdo. 1760, Lima, Peru. charts; illus.; stat.; circ. 500. **Indexed:** Biol.Abstr.

615.1   PO   ISSN 0378-9608
                              CODEN: BFFCDE
UNIVERSIDADE DE COIMBRA. FACULDADE DE FARMACIA. BOLETIM. (Text in Portuguese; summaries in English and French) 1976. s-a. Esc.2500 (foreign Esc.11000) or exchange basis (effective 1992). Universidade de Coimbra, Faculdade de Farmacia, Rua do Norte, 3000 Coimbra, Portugal. TEL 039-23681. FAX 039-27126. Ed.Bd. adv.; bibl.; charts; illus.; cum.index: 1976-1980; circ. 550. (back issues avail.) **Indexed:** Biol.Abstr., Bull.Signal., Chem.Abstr., I.P.A., Ref.Zh.
—BLDSC shelfmark: 2131.170000.
Supersedes: Universidade Coimbra. Faculdade de Farmacia. Edicao Didactica e Edicao Cientifica.
Description: Presents original papers in the pharmaceutical sciences.

615.19   BL   ISSN 0370-4726
RS1   CODEN: RFBUBI
UNIVERSIDADE DE SAO PAULO. REVISTA DE FARMACIA E BIOQUIMICA. 1939. a. exchange basis. Universidade de Sao Paulo, Faculdade de Ciencias Farmaceuticas, C.P. 66355, Sao Paulo, Brazil. FAX 8153575. bk.rev.; circ. 1,000. (back issues avail.) **Indexed:** Anal.Abstr., Chem.Abstr, Helminthol.Abstr., I.P.A., Nutr.Abstr.
●Also available online.
—BLDSC shelfmark: 7854.590000.
Formerly: Universidade de Sao Paulo. Faculdade de Farmacia e Bioquimica. Revista; Supersedes in part (in 1962): Universidade de Sao Paulo. Faculdade de Farmacia. Anais (ISSN 0365-2181)

615.329 547   BL   ISSN 0080-0228
UNIVERSIDADE FEDERAL DE PERNAMBUCO. INSTITUTO DE ANTIBIOTICOS. REVISTA. (Text in Portuguese; summaries in English and Portuguese) 1958. irreg., vol.23, 1986. exchange basis. Universidade Federal de Pernambuco, Departamento de Antibioticos, Recife, Pernambuco, Brazil. TELEX 811267. bibl.; charts; illus.; circ. 800. **Indexed:** Chem.Abstr.

615.1   BL   ISSN 0041-8846
UNIVERSIDADE FEDERAL DE SANTA MARIA. FACULDADE DE FARMACIA E BIOQUIMICA. REVISTA.* s-a. Universidade Federal de Santa Maria, Faculdade de Farmacie e Bioquimica, Caixa Postal 124, Santa Maria R.G.S., Brazil. charts; illus.

615.1   CS   ISSN 0041-9087
UNIVERSITAS COMENIANA. ACTA FACULTATIS PHARMACEUTICAE. (Text in English, German and Russian) 1958. irreg. exchange basis. Univerzita Komenskeho, Farmaceuticka Fakulta, Ustredna Kniznica, Odbojarov 10, 832 32 Bratislava, Czechoslovakia. Ed. Milan Chalabala. charts; illus.; index; circ. 500. **Indexed:** Biol.Abstr., Chem.Abstr., I.P.A.
Formerly: Acta Facultatis Pharmaceuticae Bohemoslovenicae.

615   IR
UNIVERSITY OF TEHERAN. SCHOOL OF PHARMACY. JOURNAL/DANESHGAH-E TEHERAN. DANESHKADE-YE DARUSAZI. MAJALLEH. (Text in Persian; summaries in English) 1972. s-a. Rs.120. University of Teheran, Faculty of Pharmacy, Shahreza Ave., Teheran, Iran. Ed. Iraj Lalezari. adv.

615.1   US   ISSN 0042-0441
RS1
UNLISTED DRUGS. 1949. m. $340. Pharmaco-Medical Documentation, Inc., Box 429, Chatham, NJ 07928. TEL 201-822-9200. FAX 201-765-0722. Ed. Rajka R. Anzlowar. adv.; bk.rev.; index, cum.index every 2 yrs. **Indexed:** Biol.Abstr., I.P.A.
—BLDSC shelfmark: 9120.500000.

615   US   ISSN 8755-7142
RS1
UNLISTED DRUGS INDEX - GUIDE. irreg. (every 2-3/yrs.); latest 1990. $560. Pharmaco-Medical Documentation, Inc., Box 429, Chatham, NJ 07928. TEL 201-822-9200. FAX 201-765-0722.

615.1   NO   ISSN 0042-3351
VENEFICUS; farmasistudentenes tidsskrift. 1933. 8/yr. NOK 80($6) Studentforeningen Veneficus, Universitetets Farmasoeytiske Institutt, 0371 Oslo 3, Norway. Eds. Eli Neegard, Anegedde Dane. adv.; bk.rev.; charts; illus.; index; circ. 600. **Indexed:** Chem.Abstr., I.P.A.

VETERINARY AND HUMAN TOXICOLOGY. see ENVIRONMENTAL STUDIES — Toxicology And Environmental Safety

615.1   US   ISSN 0042-6717
VIRGINIA PHARMACIST. 1917. m. $30. Virginia Pharmaceutical Association, 3119 West Clay St., Richmond, VA 23230. TEL 804-355-7941. Ed. W. Randall Wampler. adv.; bk.rev.; charts; illus.; mkt.; pat.; tr.lit.; circ. 2,000.

615.9 610.73   US   ISSN 0739-9588
VITAL SIGNS PHARMACY SERVICES NEWSLETTER. 1978. m. $70. Rx-Data-Pac Service, 8907 Terwilliger's Tr., Cincinnati, OH 45249. TEL 513-489-0943. Ed. Dr. I.H. Goodman. (looseleaf format; back issues avail.)
Description: Hospital pharmacy-nursing newsletter with photocopy rights for facility. Helps meet JCAHO requirements for hospital staff continuing education.

615.328   CN
VITAMIN SUPPLEMENT. 1985. 4/yr. Can.$1.95 per no. Abramson Publishing Ltd., 840 W. 7th Ave., Vancouver, B.C. V5Z 1C1, Canada. TEL 604-325-7311. Ed. Tracey Cochrane. circ. 284,230.

615.328   GW   ISSN 0930-4827
VITAMINE, MINERALSTOFFE, SPURENELEMENTE; in Medizin, Ernaehrung und Umwelt. 1986. q. DM.84. Hippokrates Verlag GmbH, Ruedigerstr. 14, D-7000 Stuttgart 30, Germany. TEL 0711-8931-0. Ed. K. Schmidt.

615.328 612.405   US   ISSN 0083-6729
QP801.V5   CODEN: VIHOAQ
VITAMINS AND HORMONES: ADVANCES IN RESEARCH AND APPLICATIONS. 1943. irreg., vol.45, 1989. Academic Press, Inc. (Subsidiary of: Harcourt Brace Jovanovich), 1250 Sixth Ave., San Diego, CA 92101. TEL 619-231-0926. FAX 619-699-6715. Eds. G.D. Auerbach, Donald B. McCormick. index, cum.index: vols.1-5, 1943-1947 in vol.6, 1948; vols.6-10, 1948-1952 in vol.11, 1953; vols.11-15, 1953-1957 in vol.16, 1958. (reprint service avail. from ISI) **Indexed:** Anim.Breed.Abstr., Biol.Abstr., Biotech.Abstr., Chem.Abstr., Curr.Adv.Ecol.Sci., Dairy Sci.Abstr., Excerp.Med., Ind.Med., Nutr.Abstr., Vet.Bull.
—BLDSC shelfmark: 9244.000000.
Refereed Serial

615.9   US
VOICE OF THE PHARMACIST. 1946. q. $35. American College of Apothecaries, 205 Daingerfield Rd., Alexandria, VA 22314. TEL 703-684-8603. FAX 703-683-3619. Ed. D.C. Huffman, Jr. circ. 1,000. (looseleaf format) **Indexed:** I.P.A.

VOJENSKE ZDRAVOTNICKE LISTY. see MEDICAL SCIENCES

VOJNOSANITETSKI PREGLED/MILITARY MEDICAL AND PHARMACEUTICAL REVIEW; casopis lekara i farmaceuta jugoslovenske narodne armije. see MEDICAL SCIENCES

W H O DRUG INFORMATION. (World Health Organization) see PUBLIC HEALTH AND SAFETY

615   JA   ISSN 0509-5832
WAKSMAN FOUNDATION OF JAPAN. REPORT. (Text in English) 1962. a. exchange basis. Waksman Foundation of Japan - Nihon Wakkusuman Zaidan, c/o Keio Daigaku Igakubu, 30-8 Daikyo-machi, Shinjuku-ku, Tokyo 106, Japan.

616   US   ISSN 0194-1291
KF3885.A15
WASHINGTON DRUG LETTER (WASHINGTON, 1979). 1969. w. $597. Washington Business Information, Inc., c/o Karen Harrington, 1117 N. 19th St., Arlington, VA 22209. TEL 703-247-3434. FAX 703-247-3421. Ed. Jeff Zimmer. bk.rev. (looseleaf format) **Indexed:** P.N.I., Telegen.
●Also available online. Vendor(s): BRS (DIOG), Data-Star.
Former titles: Washington Drug and Device Letter (ISSN 0162-2994); Washington Drug Letter.

615   US
WASHINGTON PHARMACIST. 1959. bi-m. $24. Washington State Pharmacists Association, 1420 Maple Ave., S.W., Ste. 101, Renton, WA 98055-3196. TEL 206-228-7171. Ed. Raymond A. Olson. adv.; bk.rev.; circ. 1,627.
Formerly: Washington-Alaska Pharmacist.

615.1   US   ISSN 0043-1893
                              CODEN: WPHRAR
WEEKLY PHARMACY REPORTS: THE GREEN SHEET. 1951. w. $40 (foreign $50). F-D-C Reports, Inc., 5550 Friendship Blvd., Ste. One, Chevy Chase, MD 20815. TEL 301-657-9830. FAX 301-656-3094. Ed. Wallace Werble, Jr.
Description: Provides pharmacists with news on the introduction and pricing of new pharmaceuticals; government regulatory activity; federal and state legislation affecting pharmacists; lawsuits of concern to pharmacists; and national and state pharmacy association meetings.

WEHRMEDIZIN UND WEHRPHARMAZIE. see MEDICAL SCIENCES

615.19   GW   ISSN 0171-4449
WER UND WAS IN DER DEUTSCHEN PHARMAZEUTISCHEN - INDUSTRIE. 1978. biennial. DM.185. B. Behr's Verlag GmbH, Averhoffstr. 10, 2000 Hamburg 76, Germany.

615.19   NR   ISSN 0303-691X
                              CODEN: WAJPAS
WEST AFRICAN JOURNAL OF PHARMACOLOGY AND DRUG RESEARCH. 1974. biennial. $10.60. (West African Society for Pharmacology) Literamed Publications Nigeria, Ltd., Oregun Village, P.M.B. 1068, Ikeja, Nigeria. **Indexed:** Biol.Abstr., Chem.Abstr., Excerp.Med., Ind.Med.

PHARMACY AND PHARMACOLOGY

615.1   CN   ISSN 0043-3829
WESTERN HORIZONS; a quarterly magazine for Western Canadian pharmacists. 1966. q. free. National Drug & Chemical Co. of Canada Ltd., Box 758, Winnipeg, Man., Canada. TEL 204-774-4511. Ed. T.H. Glenwright. adv.; circ. 3,200.

615.1   US   ISSN 0083-8969
CODEN: PWPSA8
WESTERN PHARMACOLOGY SOCIETY. PROCEEDINGS. 1958. a. $25. Western Pharmacology Society, Inc., c/o Dr. Peter Lomax, Ed., Dept. of Pharmacology, U.C.L.A. School of Medicine, Los Angeles, CA 90024. TEL 213-825-6373. FAX 310-825-6267. circ. 800. (also avail. in microform from UMI; reprint service avail. from UMI) **Indexed:** Biol.Abstr., Chem.Abstr., Curr.Adv.Ecol.Sci., Curr.Cont., Dairy Sci.Abstr., Excerp.Med., Ind.Med., Nutr.Abstr.

615.1   US
WHITE SHEET. 1967. m. free to pharmacists. Philips Roxane Laboratories, Inc., 330 Oak St., Columbus, OH 43216. TEL 614-228-5403. Ed. Richard E. Surface. bk.rev.; circ. 25,000. (tabloid format)
Formerly (until 1977): Hospital Pharmacy (ISSN 0018-5779)

615   US
WHOLESALE DRUGS MAGAZINE. 1948. 10/yr. $15. E L F Publications, 333 W. Hampden Ave., Ste. 1050, Englewood, CO 80110-2340. TEL 303-761-8818. FAX 303-761-2440. Ed. ElRoy FitzSenry. adv.; circ. 3,943.
Description: Covers news as it affects the wholesale drug industry.

615.1   US   ISSN 0043-6585
WISCONSIN PHARMACIST. vol.40, 1971. m. $30. Wisconsin Pharmacists Association, 202 Price Pl., Madison, WI 53705. TEL 608-238-5515. Ed. D. Jack Myers. adv.; circ. 1,800. **Indexed:** Chem.Abstr.
—BLDSC shelfmark: 9325.850000.

615   UK
WORLD DRUG MARKET MANUAL. 1975. a. £3685. IMSWORLD Publications Ltd., 11-13 Melton St., London NW1 2EH, England.
●Also available online.

615   US   ISSN 0276-2277
RM39
WORLD PHARMACEUTICAL DIRECTORY. irreg. (every 2-3 yrs.). $540. Pharmaco-Medical Documentation, Inc., Box 429, Chatham, NJ 07928. TEL 201-822-9200. FAX 201-765-0722.

615.19   UK
▼**WORLD PHARMACEUTICAL STANDARDS REVIEW.** 1990. m. $494. B N A International, Inc. (Subsidiary of: The Bureau of National Affairs, Inc.), 17 Dartmouth St., London SW1H 9BL, England. TEL 071-222-8831. FAX 071-222-0294. TELEX 262570 BNALDN G. (US addr.: 1231 25th St., N.W., Washington, DC 20037. TEL 202-452-4200) Ed. Bernard G. Chabel.
Description: International information and analysis service covering the pharmaceutical industry.

WORLDWIDE BIOTECH. see *BIOLOGY — Biotechnology*

615   CC   ISSN 1000-3843
XINYAO YU LINCHUANG/NEW DRUGS AND CLINICAL REMEDIES. (Text in Chinese) 1982. bi-m. $18. Shanghai Yiyao Guanli-ju, Keji Qingbao-suo - Shanghai Pharmaceutical Administration Bureau, Information Institute, No.50, Lane 532, Yuyuan Road, Shanghai 200040, People's Republic of China. TEL 2525690. (Subscr. to: China National Industry Trading Corp., Shanghai Branch, 380 Beisuzhou Road, Shanghai 200080, P.R.C.) (Co-sponsor: Chinese Pharmaceutical Association) Ed. Ding Guangsheng. circ. 30,000.

XINZHONGYI/NEW JOURNAL OF TRADITIONAL CHINESE MEDICINE. see *MEDICAL SCIENCES*

615   CC   ISSN 0254-1793
YAOWU FENXI ZAZHI/JOURNAL OF PHARMACOLOGIC ANALYSIS. (Text in Chinese) bi-m. Zhongguo Yaoxuehui - China Society of Pharmacology, Tiantan Xili, Beijing 100050, People's Republic of China. TEL 757351. Ed. Tu Guoshi. **Indexed:** Hort.Abstr.
—BLDSC shelfmark: 3180.473000.
Refereed Serial

615   CC
YAOWU YU REN/MEDICINE AND MEN. (Text in Chinese) q. Zhongguo Yaoxuehui, Beijing Fenhui, 227, Donghuashi Dajie, Congwenmenwai, Beijing 100062, People's Republic of China. TEL 7013619. Ed. Zhang Qingya.

615.19   CC
YAOXUE TONGBAO/CHINESE PHARMACEUTICAL BULLETIN. (Text in Chinese) m. $2.80 per no. Zhongguo Yaoxuehui - Chinese Pharmaceutical Association, 42 Dongsi Xidajie, Beijing 100010, People's Republic of China. (Subscr. to: China International Book Trading Corporation (Guoji Shudian), P.O. Box 2820, Beijing, P.R.C.) **Indexed:** Anal.Abstr., Chem.Abstr.

615.19   CC
YAOXUE XUEBAO/ACTA PHARMACEUTICA SINICA. (Text in Chinese) m. $3.50 per no. Guoji Shudian, Qikan Bu, Chegongzhuang Xilu 21, P.O. Box 399, Beijing 100044, People's Republic of China. **Indexed:** Abstr.Hyg., Chem.Abstr., Crop Physiol.Abstr., Curr.Adv.Ecol.Sci., Hort.Abstr., I.P.A., Ind.Med., Seed Abstr.

615.1058   US   ISSN 0084-3733
YEAR BOOK OF DRUG THERAPY. 1933. a. $57.95. Mosby - Year Book, Inc., Continuity Division, 200 N. LaSalle, Chicago, IL 60601. TEL 312-726-9733. TELEX 312-726-6075. Eds. Drs. Michael Weintraub, Louis Lasagna. illus. **Indexed:** Curr.Adv.Ecol.Sci.
●Also available online. Vendor(s): BRS.
—BLDSC shelfmark: 9411.650000.
Formerly: Year Book of General Therapeutics (ISSN 0270-3866)
Description: Presents abstracts and commentary of pertinent literature in over 900 scientific journals

615   CC
YIYAO GONGCHENG SHEJI. (Text in Chinese) bi-m. Guojia Yiyao Guanli-ju, Shanghai Yiyao Sheji-yuan - State Administration of Pharmacy, Shanghai Pharmacy Design Academy, 1856 Nanjing Donglu, Shanghai 200040, People's Republic of China. TEL 2584840. Ed. Lu Zhendong.

YOKOHAMA MEDICAL JOURNAL. see *MEDICAL SCIENCES*

YUNNAN ZHONGYI ZAZHI/YUNNAN JOURNAL OF TRADITIONAL CHINESE MEDICINE. see *MEDICAL SCIENCES*

ZHEJIANG ZHONGYI XUEYUAN XUEBAO/ZHEJIANG TRADITIONAL CHINESE MEDICAL COLLEGE. JOURNAL. see *MEDICAL SCIENCES*

ZHEJIANG ZHONGYI ZAZHI/ZHEJIANG JOURNAL OF TRADITIONAL CHINESE MEDICINE. see *MEDICAL SCIENCES*

615.328 615.89   CC
ZHONG CAO YAO/CHINESE HERBAL MEDICINE. (Text in Chinese) m. $0.80 per no. Guoji Shudian, Qikan Bu, P.O. Box 399, Beijing 100044, People's Republic of China. **Indexed:** Chem.Abstr.

615   CC   ISSN 1001-1528
ZHONG CHENG YAO/CHINESE TRADITIONAL PATENT MEDICINE. (Text in Chinese; some abstracts in English) 1978. m. Y24. Guojia Yiyao Guanli-ju, Zhong Cheng Yao Qingbao Zhongxin - State Pharmaceutical Administration, Chinese Traditional Patent Medicine Information Center, 324 Renmin Road, Shanghai 200002, People's Republic of China. TEL 3289639. (Dist. outside China by: Guoji Shudian - China International Book Trading Corp., P.O. Box 399, Beijing, P.R.C.) Ed. Zhang Yuanzhen. adv.; bk.rev.; circ. 10,000.
—BLDSC shelfmark: 3181.122320.
Description: Reports the recent research achievements in industry of Chinese patent medicine and introduces new products, dosage formulations, processes and new equipment used in this industry.

615.329   CC   ISSN 1001-8689
CODEN: KANGDS
ZHONGGUO KANGSHENGSU ZAZHI/CHINESE JOURNAL OF ANTIBIOTICS. (Text in Chinese) m. $80. Sichuan Kangjunsu Gongye Yanjiusuo - Sichuan Industrial Institute of Antibiotics, 9 Shanbanqiao Lu, Chengdu, Sichuan 610051, People's Republic of China. TEL 444641. TELEX 60111 SIIA CN.
—BLDSC shelfmark: 3180.293500.

615   CC   ISSN 1001-0408
ZHONGGUO YAOFANG. (Text in Chinese) bi-m. Chongqing Yixue Qingbaosuo - Chongqing Medical Science Information Institute, 44 Qingnian Lu, Chongqing, Sichuan 630010, People's Republic of China. TEL 41978. (Co-sponsor: Chongqing Medicine Trade Center) Ed. Chen Congyuan.

615.9 615.7   CC   ISSN 0253-9756
RM1   CODEN: CYLPDN
ZHONGGUO YAOLI XUEBAO/ACTA PHARMACOLOGICA SINICA. (Text in Chinese and English) 1980. bi-m. Y8.10($8) per no. (Chinese Society of Pharmacology) Science Press, Marketing and Sales Department, 16 Donghuangchenggen Beijie, Beijing 100707, People's Republic of China. TEL 4010642. FAX 4012180. TELEX 210247-SPBJ-CN. adv.; circ. 10,000.
—BLDSC shelfmark: 0648.100000.
Description: Contains original articles on pharmacological and toxicological research, including the therapeutic effects, toxicities, metabolism, experimental uses and mechanisms of drugs, poisons, and biologically active substances.
Refereed Serial

615   CC   ISSN 1001-1978
ZHONGGUO YAOLIXUE TONGBAO/CHINESE BULLETIN OF PHARMACOLOGY. (Text in Chinese) bi-m. Zhongguo Yaoli Xuehui - Chinese Society of Pharmacology, 21 Meishan Lu, Hefei, Anhui 230032, People's Republic of China. TEL 336600. Ed. Xu Shuyun.

615   CC
ZHONGGUO YAOLIXUE YU DULIXUE ZAZHI. (Text in Chinese). q. Junshi Yixue Kexueyuan - Military Medical Academy, 27, Taiping Lu, Beijing 100850, People's Republic of China. TEL 812343. Ed. Rong Kangtai.

615   CC
ZHONGGUO YAOXUE ZAZHI/CHINESE PHARMACEUTICAL JOURNAL. (Text in Chinese; table of contents in Chinese, English) m. Y3. Zhongguo Yaoxuehui - Chinese Pharmaceutical Association, 42 Dongsi Xidajie, Beijing 100010, People's Republic of China. (Subscr. to: China International Book Trading Corporation (Guoji Shudian), P.O. Box 2820, Beijing, P.R.C.) Ed. Zhang Tianlu.

615   CC
ZHONGGUO YIYAO/JOURNAL OF CHINESE PHARMACY. (Text in Chinese) q. Guojia Yiyao Guanli-ju - State Pharmaceutical Administration, 841 Sichuan Beilu, Shanghai 200085, People's Republic of China. TEL 3250593. Ed. Shi Heng.

615   CC   ISSN 1001-8255
CODEN: ZYGZEA
ZHONGGUO YIYAO GONGYE ZAZHI/CHINESE JOURNAL OF PHARMACEUTICAL INDUSTRY. (Text in Chinese) 1970. m. $36. Shanghai Yiyao Gongye Yanjiuyuan - Shanghai Institute of Pharmaceutical Industry, 1320 Beijing Xilu, Shanghai 200040, People's Republic of China. TEL 2479808. adv.; bk.rev.; circ. 6,200.
—BLDSC shelfmark: 3180.473500.
Formerly (until 1989): Yiyao Gongye (ISSN 0255-7223)

615   CC   ISSN 1000-4971
ZHONGGUO YIYAO XUEBAO/JOURNAL OF CHINESE PHARMACOLOGY. (Text in Chinese) bi-m. Zhonghua Quanguo Zhongyi Xuehui - All-China National Association of Chinese Medicine, A-4 Yinghualu, Hepingli Dongjie, Beijing 100029, People's Republic of China. TEL 4216650. Ed. Dong Jianhua.

615.328 615.89   CC
ZHONGYAO TONGBAO/CHINESE MEDICINE BULLETIN. (Text in Chinese) bi-m. $0.80 per no. (Association of Chinese Pharmacologists) Guoji Shudian, Qikan Bu, Chegongzhuang Xilu 21, P.O. Box 399, Beijing 100044, People's Republic of China. **Indexed:** Chem.Abstr.

615   CC   ISSN 1001-859X
ZHONGYAO YAOLI YU LINCHUANG/PHARMACOLOGY AND CLINICS OF CHINESE MATERIA MEDICA. (Text in Chinese) 1985. bi-m. $20. Sichuan Sheng Zhongyao Yanjiusuo - Sichuan Institute of Chinese Materia Medica, Huangjiaoya, Chongqingshi Nan'an, Sichuan 630065, People's Republic of China. TEL 481615.

ZHONGYI ZAZHI/JOURNAL OF TRADITIONAL CHINESE MEDICINE. see *MEDICAL SCIENCES*

PHARMACY AND PHARMACOLOGY — Abstracting, Bibliographies, Statistics

615.1 US ISSN 0065-8111
RS355
AMERICAN DRUG INDEX. 1950. a. $34.50 (effective 1992). Facts and Comparisons, 111 W. Port Plaza, Ste. 423, St. Louis, MO 63146-3098. TEL 800-223-0554. FAX 314-878-5563. Ed. Norman F. Billups.
Description: Lists over 20,000 drug entries in dictionary style with cross-indexing of brands, generic and chemical names.

C A SELECTS. ANTIARRHYTHMICS. see *MEDICAL SCIENCES — Abstracting, Bibliographies, Statistics*

350 US ISSN 0148-2459
CODEN: CSBADM
C A SELECTS. BETA-LACTAM ANTIBIOTICS. s-w. $195. Chemical Abstracts Service (Subsidiary of: American Chemical Society), 2540 Olentangy River Rd., Box 3012, Columbus, OH 43210. TEL 614-447-3600. FAX 614-447-3713. TELEX 6842086.
Description: Covers synthesis, biosynthesis, chemical reactivity, antimicrobial activity, pharmacodynamics, metabolism, toxicology, analysis, and formulation.

C A SELECTS. CALCIUM CHANNEL BLOCKERS. see *CHEMISTRY — Abstracting, Bibliographies, Statistics*

615.9 US ISSN 0162-7775
CODEN: CSDTDL
C A SELECTS. DRUG & COSMETIC TOXICITY. s-w. $195. Chemical Abstracts Service (Subsidiary of: American Chemical Society), 2540 Olentangy River Rd., Box 3012, Columbus, OH 43210. TEL 614-447-3600. FAX 614-447-3713. TELEX 6842086.
Description: Covers toxic manifestations of drugs, cosmetics, and ingredients of drug and cosmetic preparations, e.g., mutagenicity, teratogenicity, carcinogenicity, allergic potential; health hazards, side effects, and safety of drugs.

350 US ISSN 1040-7162
CODEN: CSDSEJ
C A SELECTS. DRUG DELIVERY SYSTEMS & DOSAGE FORMS. 1989. s-w. $195. Chemical Abstracts Service (Subsidiary of: American Chemical Society), 2540 Olentangy River Rd., Box 3012, Columbus, OH 43210. TEL 614-447-3600. FAX 614-447-3713. TELEX 6842086.
Description: Covers pharmaceutical dosage forms, e.g., tablets, capsules, ointments; newer delivery systems and forms such as controlled-release devices, transdermal systems, ocular inserts, osmotic devices, antibody conjugates, and liposomes; properties, formulation, bioavailability, and pharmacokinetic studies of drugs from the delivery systems and dosage forms.

C A SELECTS. DRUG INTERACTIONS. see *MEDICAL SCIENCES — Abstracting, Bibliographies, Statistics*

C A SELECTS. FOOD, DRUGS, & COSMETICS - LEGISLATIVE & REGULATORY ASPECTS. see *FOOD AND FOOD INDUSTRIES — Abstracting, Bibliographies, Statistics*

615 US ISSN 0895-5875
CODEN: CSNAEF
C A SELECTS. NEW ANTIBIOTICS. 1988. s-w. $195. Chemical Abstracts Service (Subsidiary of: American Chemical Society), 2540 Olentangy River Rd., Box 3012, Columbus, OH 43210. TEL 614-447-3600. FAX 614-447-3713. TELEX 6842086.
Description: Covers production, isolation, characterization, structure determination, and antimicrobial activity of antibiotics, both natural and synthetic.

615.19 US ISSN 0890-1902
CODEN: CPHAEW
C A SELECTS. PHARMACEUTICAL ANALYSIS. 1987. s-w. $195. Chemical Abstracts Service (Subsidiary of: American Chemical Society), 2540 Olentangy River Rd., Box 3012, Columbus, OH 43210. TEL 614-447-3600. FAX 614-447-3713. TELEX 6842086.
Description: Covers analysis of drugs in pure form or in pharmaceutical preparations.

615.19 US ISSN 0890-1910
CODEN: CAPCE7
C A SELECTS. PHARMACEUTICAL CHEMISTRY (JOURNALS). 1987. s-w. $195. Chemical Abstracts Service (Subsidiary of: American Chemical Society), 2540 Olentangy River Rd., Box 3012, Columbus, OH 43210. TEL 614-447-3600. FAX 614-447-3713. TELEX 6842086.
Description: Covers all aspects of pharmaceutical chemistry: drug standards, pharmacopeias, formulations, prosthetic materials, surgical goods, and properties of pharmaceuticals.

615.19 US ISSN 0890-1929
CODEN: CPCPEI
C A SELECTS. PHARMACEUTICAL CHEMISTRY (PATENTS). 1987. s-w. $195. Chemical Abstracts Service (Subsidiary of: American Chemical Society), 2540 Olentangy River Rd., Box 3012, Columbus, OH 43210. TEL 614-447-3600. FAX 614-447-3713. TELEX 6842086.
Description: Covers formulations, prosthetic materials, and surgical goods.

C A SELECTS. PSYCHOBIOCHEMISTRY. see *BIOLOGY — Abstracting, Bibliographies, Statistics*

615 US ISSN 0160-9173
CODEN: CSBSDB
C A SELECTS. STEROIDS (BIOCHEMICAL ASPECTS). s-w. $195. Chemical Abstracts Service (Subsidiary of: American Chemical Society), 2540 Olentangy River Rd., Box 3012, Columbus, OH 43210. TEL 614-447-3600. FAX 614-447-3713. TELEX 6842086.
Description: Covers pharmacology, toxicology, general biochemistry, and nutritional uses of steroids.

C A SELECTS. STEROIDS (CHEMICAL ASPECTS). see *CHEMISTRY — Abstracting, Bibliographies, Statistics*

615 016 US ISSN 0069-4770
CLIN-ALERT. 1962. 26/yr. $94.95 (foreign $99.95). Learned Information, Inc., 143 Old Marlton Pike, Medford, NJ 08055-8750. TEL 609-654-6266. FAX 609-654-4309. Ed. Ramona Scheible. q. cum.index. (looseleaf format; back issues avail.)
Description: Reference summaries of and conclusions about prescription drug reactions-interactions, for pharmacists, physicians, librarians, and lawyers.

CONTAMINATION CONTROL ABSTRACTS. see *ENGINEERING — Abstracting, Bibliographies, Statistics*

615 JA ISSN 0385-6747
CONTENTS. (Text in Japanese) 1973. w. 65920 Yen. Japan Pharmaceutical Information Center - Nihon Iyaku Joho Senta, 3rd Fl., Nagai-Kinenkan, 2-12-15, Shibuya, Shibuya-ku, Tokyo 150, Japan. FAX 03-5466-1818. Ed. F. Kubo. circ. 800.
Description: Lists titles of medical and pharmaceutical journals.

615 US ISSN 0965-0512
CURRENT ADVANCES IN TOXICOLOGY. 1984. m. £540 (effective 1992). Pergamon Press, Inc., Journals Division, 660 White Plains Rd., Tarrytown, NY 10591-5153. TEL 914-524-9200. FAX 914-333-2444. (And: Headington Hill Hall, Oxford OX3 0BW, England. TEL 0865-794141) Ed. H. Smith. adv. (also avail. in microfilm from MIM,UMI) *Indexed:* Curr.Cont.
●Also available online. Vendor(s): BRS (CABS).
—BLDSC shelfmark: 3494.068200.
Formerly (until 1992): Current Advances in Pharmacology and Toxicology (ISSN 0741-1685)
Description: Provides a current awareness service in the sphere of toxicology. Gives listings of titles of toxicological papers published throughout the world, classified into 127 main subject areas, and provides a comprehensive listing of review articles.
Refereed Serial

CURRENT BIBLIOGRAPHIES ON SCIENCE AND TECHNOLOGY: BIOLOGY, PHARMACY AND FOOD SCIENCE. see *BIOLOGY — Abstracting, Bibliographies, Statistics*

DRUG ABSTRACTS MONTHLY. see *DRUG ABUSE AND ALCOHOLISM — Abstracting, Bibliographies, Statistics*

615.19 US
DRUG PRODUCT INDEX - INTERNATIONAL. 1988. a. $275. Paul De Haen International, 2750 S. Shoshone St., Englewood, CO 80110. TEL 800-438-0296. FAX 303-789-2534. Ed. Faye N. Richendifer.
Description: Index of drug products introduced in major international countries during past several decades.

615.19 US
DRUG PRODUCT INDEX - U S A. 1988. a. $275. Paul De Haen International, 2750 S. Shoshone St., Englewood, CO 80110. TEL 800-438-0296. FAX 303-789-2534. Ed. Faye N. Richendifer.
Description: Index of drug products introduced in the U.S. during the past several decades.

615 016 NE ISSN 0927-2798
EXCERPTA MEDICA. SECTION 30: CLINICAL AND EXPERIMENTAL PHARMACOLOGY. 1948. 32/yr.(in 4 vols.; 8 nos./vol.). fl.2468 (effective 1992). Excerpta Medica (Subsidiary of: Elsevier Science Publishers), P.O. Box 548, 1000 AM Amsterdam, Netherlands. TEL 020-5803911. FAX 020-5803222. TELEX 18582 ESPA NL. (Dist. by: Elsevier Science Publishers Ireland Ltd., P.O. Box 85, Limerick, Ireland. TEL 061-61944; Subscr. in U.S. and Canada to: Elsevier Science Publishing Co., Inc., Box 882, Madison Sq. Sta., New York, NY 10159. TEL 212-989-5800) Ed.Bd. adv.; abstr.; index. *Indexed:* Chem.Abstr.
●Also available online. Vendor(s): BRS, DIMDI, Data-Star, DIALOG, JICST.
Also available on CD-ROM. Producer(s): SilverPlatter.
Formerly (until 1992): Excerpta Medica. Section 30: Pharmacology (ISSN 0167-9643); Supersedes: Excerpta Medica. Section 30: Pharmacology and Toxicology (ISSN 0014-4347)
Description: Covers all aspects of experimental and clinical pharmacology, including pharmacokinetics, pharmacodynamics, methodology, mathematical models, and experimental studies on human organs, tissues and cells, and on the mechanisms of action of exogenous substances.

615.9 NE ISSN 0167-8353
CODEN: TXICDD
EXCERPTA MEDICA. SECTION 52: TOXICOLOGY. 1983. 20/yr.(in 2 vols.; 10 nos./vol.). fl.1373 (effective 1992). Excerpta Medica (Subsidiary of: Elsevier Science Publishers), P.O. Box 548, 1000 AM Amsterdam, Netherlands. TEL 020-5803911. FAX 020-5803222. TELEX 18582 ESPA NL. (Dist. by: Elsevier Science Publishers Ireland Ltd., P.O. Box 85, Limerick, Ireland. TEL 061-61944; Subscr. in U.S. and Canada to: Elsevier Science Publishing Co., Inc., Box 882, Madison Sq. Sta., New York, NY 10159. TEL 212-989-5800) Ed.Bd. adv.
●Also available online. Vendor(s): BRS, DIMDI, Data-Star, DIALOG, JICST.
Also available on CD-ROM. Producer(s): SilverPlatter.
—BLDSC shelfmark: 3835.881500.
Description: Covers the toxic mechanisms and effects of both medicinal and non-medicinal substances.

615 FR
FRANCE. SERVICE D'ETUDE DES STRATEGIES ET DES STATISTIQUES INDUSTRIELLES. RESULTATS MENSUELS DES ENQUETES DE BRANCHE. INDUSTRIE PHARMACEUTIQUE. m. 260 F. (foreign 310 F.)(effective 1991). Service d'Etude des Strategies et des Statistiques Industrielles (SESSI), 85 Bd. du Montparnasse, 75270 Paris Cedex 06, France. TEL 45-56-42-34. FAX 45-56-40-71. stat.
Description: Follows developments in the pharmaceutical industry through the performance of selected indicators.

615.19 AT
GUILD DIGEST (YEAR). 1974. a. Aus.$100. Pharmacy Guild of Australia, P.O. Box 36, Deakin, A.C.T. 2600, Australia. TEL 06281-09111. FAX 06-282-4745. Ed. Vasken Demirian. index; circ. 5,500. (back issues avail.)
Former titles: Community Pharmacy in Australia; Guild Digest.
Description: Compares interfirm survey statistics on financial performance of pharmacies and some detail of drug usage and cost.

I S D D CURRENT AWARENESS BULLETIN. (Institute for the Study of Drug Dependence) see *DRUG ABUSE AND ALCOHOLISM — Abstracting, Bibliographies, Statistics*

615.19 II
INDIAN CHEMICALS AND PHARMACEUTICALS STATISTICS. (Text in English) 1967. a. free. Ministry of Chemicals and Fertilizers, Economics and Statistics Division, New Delhi, India. stat.; circ. controlled.

614 UN
INTERNATIONAL NARCOTICS CONTROL BOARD. STATISTICS ON PSYCHOTROPIC SUBSTANCES FOR (YEAR). (Text in English, French and Spanish) 1977. a. price varies. (International Narcotics Control Board - Organe International de Controle des Stupefiants) United Nations Publications, Room DC2-0853, New York, NY 10017. TEL 212-963-8300. FAX 212-963-3489. (Or: Vienna International Centre, P.O. Box 500, 1400 Vienna, Austria)
Formerly: United Nations. International Narcotics Control Board. Statistics on Psychotropic Substances Furnished by Governments in Accordance with the Convention of 1971 on Psychotropic Substances (ISSN 0253-9403)

615 016 US ISSN 0020-8264
RS1 CODEN: IPMAAH
INTERNATIONAL PHARMACEUTICAL ABSTRACTS; key to the world's literature of pharmacy. 1964. s-m. $425 to non-members; members $100. American Society of Hospital Pharmacists, c/o Jean Rogers, Dir., Mkt. Svcs., 4630 Montgomery Ave., Bethesda, MD 20814. TEL 301-657-3000. Ed. Dwight R. Tousignaut. index; circ. 1,300. (also avail. in microform from UMI; reprint service avail. from UMI) Indexed: Anal.Abstr., JAMA.
●Also available online. Vendor(s): BRS (IPAB), DIMDI, DIALOG (File no.74), European Space Agency (File no.102/IPA), Mead Data Central, National Library of Medicine, University of Tsukuba.
Also available on CD-ROM. Producer(s): SilverPlatter.
—BLDSC shelfmark: 4544.924000.

615.19 IS
M E D I C. (Monthly Ethical Drug Index Complication) (Text in English) 1971. 6/yr. $65. Shirol Publications Ltd., P.O. Box 2066, Herzlia, Israel. FAX 052-573171. Ed. S.H. Bergman. adv.; circ. 7,000.

615 JA
MEDICAL COMPANIES GUIDE TO JAPAN. (Text in English) 1987. irreg. 23,000 Yen($167) Chemical Daily Co., Ltd., International Affairs, 3-16-8, Nihonbashi Hama-cho, Chuo-ku, Tokyo 103, Japan. TEL 03-3663-7932. FAX 03-3663-2530. TELEX 2422362 NIPPO J.
Formerly (until 1992): Japan Medical and Pharmaceutical Directory.
Description: Lists pharmaceutical companies and those dealing with diagnostic agents and medical apparatuses with up-to-date information including company name, address, turnover, features, and main products.

615 US ISSN 0076-6518
MERCK INDEX: AN ENCYCLOPEDIA OF CHEMICALS AND DRUGS. 1889. irreg., 10th ed., 1983. $28.50. Merck and Co., Inc., Attn: Michele Stotz, FTA-230, Box 2000, Rahway, NJ 07065. TEL 201-855-4558. Ed. Martha Windholz.
●Also available online. Vendor(s): BRS (MRCK), BRS/Saunders Colleague, CISTI, DIALOG, Telesystemes - Questel.

NARCOTIC DRUGS: ESTIMATED WORLD REQUIREMENTS FOR (YEAR). see *PHYSICAL FITNESS AND HYGIENE* — Abstracting, Bibliographies, Statistics

615 016 FR ISSN 0761-215X
P A S C A L EXPLORE. E 63: TOXICOLOGIE. 1961. 10/yr. 865 F. Centre National de la Recherche Scientifique, Institut de l'Information Scientifique et Technique, B.P. 54, 54514 Vandoeuvre-Les-Nancy Cedex, France. TEL 83-50-46-00. index, cum.index. (also avail. in microform from MIM)
Formerly: P A S C A L Explore. Part 63: Toxicologie; Which superseded in part (in 1984): Bulletin Signaletique. Part 330: Sciences Pharmacologiques - Toxicologie (ISSN 0007-5442)

615 016 FR ISSN 0761-1943
P A S C A L FOLIO. F 70: PHARMACOLOGIE. TRAITEMENTS MEDICAMENTEUX. 1961. 10/yr. 1675 F. Centre National de la Recherche Scientifique, Institut de l'Information Scientifique et Technique, B.P. 54, 54514 Vandoeuvre-Les-Nancy Cedex, France. TEL 83-50-46-00.
Formerly: P A S C A L Folio. Part 70: Pharmacologie. Traitements Medicamenteux; Which superseded in part (in 1984): Bulletin Signaletique. Part 330: Sciences Pharmacologiques - Toxicologie (ISSN 0007-5442)

615.19 US
P M A STATISTICAL FACTBOOK; pharmaceuticals, in-vivo diagnostic. a. $21.50. Pharmaceutical Manufacturers Association, 1100 15th St., N.W., Washington, DC 20005. TEL 202-835-3400. Ed.Bd. charts; stat.; circ. 1,500. (looseleaf format)
Formerly: Prescription Drug Industry Fact Book.

615 016 US ISSN 0362-4439
P N I. (Pharmaceutical News Index) (Hard copy ceased 1984) 1975. w. University Microfilms International, Data Courier, 620 S. Third St., Louisville, KY 40202-2475. TEL 800-626-2823. FAX 502-589-5572. Ed. Paula McCoy. bibl.
●Available only online. Vendor(s): BRS, DIALOG, Orbit Information Technologies.

615 US
PHARMACEUTICAL ACTIVITIES INDEX - DIRECTORY. irreg. (every 3-4/yrs.). $530. Pharmaco-Medical Documentation, Inc., Box 429, Chatham, NJ 07928. TEL 201-822-9200. FAX 201-765-0722.

615.1 US ISSN 0031-7152
CODEN: PMDXAT
PHARMINDEX. 1958. m. $88 (effective 1992). Skyline Publishers, Inc., Box 1029 University Sta., Portland, OR 97207. TEL 503-235-0071. Ed. Frank D. Portash. adv.; mkt.; tr.lit.; index, cum.index. Indexed: Chem.Abstr., Excerp.Med., I.P.A.
—BLDSC shelfmark: 6449.100000.

PRESS DIGEST. see *DRUG ABUSE AND ALCOHOLISM* — Abstracting, Bibliographies, Statistics

615 RU ISSN 0202-5132
REFERATIVNYI ZHURNAL. FARMAKOLOGIYA EFFEKTORNYKH SISTEM. KHIMIOTERAPEVTICHESKIE SREDSTVA. 1987. m. 78.20 Rub. (90.40 Rub. with index). Vsesoyuznyi Institut Nauchno-Tekhnicheskoi Informatsii (VINITI), Baltiiskaya ul. 14, A-219 Moscow, Russia. (Subscr. to: Mezhdunarodnaya Kniga, Dimitrova ul. 39, 113095 Moscow, Russia)

615 RU ISSN 0134-580X
REFERATIVNYI ZHURNAL. FARMAKOLOGIYA. OBSHCHAYA FARMAKOLOGIYA NERVNOI SISTEMY. 1987. m. 78.20 Rub. (90.40 Rub. with index). Vsesoyuznyi Institut Nauchno-Tekhnicheskoi Informatsii (VINITI), Baltiiskaya ul. 14, A-219 Moscow, Russia. (Subscr. to: Mezhdunarodnaya Kniga, Dimitrova ul. 39, 113095 Moscow, Russia)

615 016 RU ISSN 0202-9162
REFERATIVNYI ZHURNAL. KLINICHESKAYA FARMAKOLOGIYA. 1979. m. 40 Rub. (with index 50.80 Rub.). Vsesoyuznyi Institut Nauchno-Tekhnicheskoi Informatsii (VINITI), Baltiiskaya ul. 14, Moscow A-219, Russia. (Subscr. to: Mezhdunarodnaya Kniga, Dimitrova ul. 39, 113095 Moscow, Russia)

615.9 016 RU ISSN 0202-9219
RA1190 CODEN: RZTODS
REFERATIVNYI ZHURNAL. TOKSIKOLOGIYA. 1958. m. 63 Rub. (with index 69.40 Rub.). Vsesoyuznyi Institut Nauchno-Tekhnicheskoi Informatsii (VINITI), Baltiiskaya ul. 14, Moscow A-219, Russia. (Subscr. to: Mezhdunarodnaya Kniga, Dimitrova ul. 39, 113095 Moscow, Russia) Indexed: Chem.Abstr.

615.1 016 CS ISSN 0034-2777
REFERATOVY VYBER Z LEKARENSTVI/ABSTRACTS OF PHARMACY. 1965. bi-m. 150 Kcs. Ustav Vedeckych Lekarskych Informaci, Sokolska 31, 121 32 Prague 2, Czechoslovakia. TEL 299956. Ed. Dr. Ivan Andel. bk.rev.; circ. 670.
Formerly: Referatovy Vyber z Lekarenstvi. Abstracts of Farmaci.

SELECTED CURRENT AWARENESS BULLETIN. see *DRUG ABUSE AND ALCOHOLISM* — Abstracting, Bibliographies, Statistics

615.9 016 RU ISSN 0233-6588
SIGNAL'NAYA INFORMATSIYA. TOKSIKOLOGIYA LEKARSTVENNAYA. m. 6.40 Rub. Vsesoyuznyi Institut Nauchno-Tekhnicheskoi Informatsii (VINITI), Baltiiskaya ul. 14, Moscow A-219, Russia. (Subscr. to: Mezhdunarodnaya Kniga, Dimitrova ul. 39, 113095 Moscow, Russia)
Formerly: Signal'naya Informatsiya. Toksikologiya (ISSN 0202-8514)

016 615.9 US ISSN 0140-5365
RA1190
TOXICOLOGY ABSTRACTS. 1978. m. $675 (foreign $795). Cambridge Scientific Abstracts, 7200 Wisconsin Ave., 6th Fl., Bethesda, MD 20814. TEL 301-961-6750. FAX 301-961-6720. TELEX 910 2507547 CAMB MD. Ed.Bd. adv.; bk.rev.; abstr.; index. (also avail. in magnetic tape; back issues avail.) Indexed: Cal.Tiss.Abstr., Chemorec.Abstr., Comput.& Info.Sys., Oncol.Abstr., Pollut.Abstr., World Surf.Coat.
●Also available online. Vendor(s): BRS (CSAL), DIALOG (File no.76/LIFE SCIENCES COLLECTION). Also available on CD-ROM. Producer(s): Cambridge Scientific Abstracts (Compact Cambridge Life Sciences Collection and Compact Cambridge Pol/Tox).
—BLDSC shelfmark: 8873.037600.
Description: Covers all aspects of toxicology including substance abuse, radiation, and toxicity testing.

615 CC ISSN 1003-3521
ZHONGGUO YAOXUE WENZHAI/CHINESE PHARMACEUTICAL ABSTRACTS. (Text in Chinese; a. index in English and Latin) 1982. bi-m. $100 (effective 1992). Guojia Yiyao Guanli-ju, Keji Qingbao Yanjiusuo - State Pharmaceutical Administration of China, Science and Technology Information Research Institute, A-38 Beilishilu, Beijing 100810, People's Republic of China. TEL 8313344. FAX 8311978. Ed. Liu Jingmin. adv.
Description: Published on the basis of the Traditional Chinese Medicines (TCMs) Contemporary Literature Database, as well as abstracts in modern drugs in China. Covers 260 current domestic medical journals.

PHILATELY

769.56 DK ISSN 0901-6996
A F A DANMARK FIREBLOKKE. irreg. Aarhus Frimaerkehandel, Bruunsgade 42, 8000 Aarhus C, Denmark. FAX 45-6-199281. illus.

769.56 DK ISSN 0901-7003
A F A DANMARK FRIMAERKEKATALOG. irreg. Aarhus Frimaerkehandel, Bruunsgade 42, 8000 Aarhus C, Denmark. FAX 45-6-199281. illus.

769.56 DK ISSN 0901-6643
A F A OESTEUROPA FRIMAERKEKATALOG. Title varies: Oesteuropa Frimaerkekatalog. irreg. Aarhus Frimaerkehandel, Bruunsgade 42, 8000 Aarhus C, Denmark. FAX 45-6-199281. illus.
Supersedes in part: A F A Europe Frimaerkekatalog.

769.56 DK ISSN 0901-6635
A F A SKANDINAVIEN FRIMAERKEKATALOG. irreg. Aarhus Frimaerkehandel, Bruunsgade 42, 8000 Arhus C, Denmark. FAX 45-6-199281. illus.

769.56 DK ISSN 0901-702X
A F A VESTEUROPA FRIMAERKEKATALOG. Title varies: Vesteuropa Frimaerkekatalog. 1974. irreg. Aarhus Frimaerkehandel, Bruunsgade 42, 8000 Aarhus C, Denmark. FAX 45-6-199281. illus.
Supersedes in part: A F A Europa Frimaerkekatalog.

769.56 AG ISSN 0001-1193
A F R A BOLETIN INFORMATIVO. 1939. bi-w. membership. Asociacion Filatelica de la Republica Argentina, Tucuman 672, 1 Piso, Depto. 2, 1049 Buenos Aires, Argentina. (Subscr. to: Casilla de Correo 1992, 1000 Buenos Aires, Argentina) Ed.Bd. adv.; bk.rev.
Former titles (until 1970): A F R A Boletin; Asociacion Filatelica de la Republica Argentina. Revista.

PHILATELY

769.56   GW
A G M. 1974. 3/yr. DM.30 membership. Arbeitsgemeinschaft Malta im Bund Deutscher Philatelisten e.V., Suederstr. 66B, 2398 Harrislee, Germany. TEL 0461-71109. Ed. Peter C. Hansen. bk.rev.; circ. 100. (back issues avail.)
Formerly: G M Z.
Description: Reports and studies on the postal history of Malta for advanced philatelists.

769.56   US
A.S.D.A. NEWSLETTER. 1914. m. membership. American Stamp Dealers' Association, Inc., 3 School St., Ste. 205, Glen Cove, NY 11542. TEL 516-759-7000. adv.; bk.rev.; tr.lit.; circ. 2,500.
Formerly: A.S.D.A. Bulletin.

796.56   GW   ISSN 0933-1409
A T M; der aktuelle Informationsdienst zum Thema Briefmarken-Automation. 1984. bi-w. DM.55. Verlag Brigitte Tast, Laaseweg 4, 3209 Schellerten 1, Germany. TEL 05123-4330. Ed. Hans-Juergen Tast. adv.; bk.rev. (looseleaf format; back issues avail.)

769.56   GW   ISSN 0932-5441
A T M - FORUM; die internationale Zeitschrift fuer Postwertzeichen aus Automaten und Postautomation. 1986. bi-m. DM.34. Phil-Creativ GmbH, Postfach 10, D-4056 Schwalmtal, Germany. TEL 02163-30777. FAX 02163-30003. Ed. W. Maassen. adv.; bk.rev.; circ. 3,500. (back issues avail.)

769.56   US
ACROSS THE FENCE. m. Wisconsin Federation of Stamp Clubs, 1017 Chieftain Lookout, Madison, WI 53711. Ed. Howard Sherpe.

769.56   US
AERONAUTICA AND AIR LABEL COLLECTOR. 1943. q. $10 (foreign $12). Aeronautica & Air Label Collectors Club, Box 1239, Elgin, IL 60121-1239. TEL 708-742-3328. (Affiliate: Aerophilatelic Federation of the Americas) Ed. Don Thomas. adv.; bk.rev.; circ. controlled.
Description: Air transport catalog of the world.

769.56   UK   ISSN 0142-9868
AFRICA SINCE INDEPENDENCE STAMP CATALOGUE. 1980. irreg. (in 3 parts). price varies. Stanley Gibbons Publications Ltd., Unit 5 Parkside, Christchurch Rd., Ringwood, Hamps. BH24 3SH, England. TEL 0425-472363. FAX 0425-470247.

769.56   IT
AGENZIA STAMPA FILATELICA EUROPEA. Short title: A S F E. 1977. 11/yr. L.800000. Renato Russo, Ed. & Pub., Via Mascagni 31, 80128 Naples, Italy. TEL 081-644715. FAX 081-640835. adv.; circ. 2,000.

769.56   US   ISSN 0739-0939
HE6187
AIRPOST JOURNAL. 1929. m. $12. American Air Mail Society, 102 Arbor Rd., Cinnaminson, NJ 08077. Ed. James W. Graue. adv.; bk.rev.; illus.; circ. 2,100. (tabloid format) **Indexed:** Stamp J.Ind.

ALAN SHAWN FEINSTEIN INSIDERS REPORT. see BUSINESS AND ECONOMICS — Investments

769.56   US
ALBUM PAGE. 1960. m. $15. Oregon Stamp Society, Box 02121, Portland, OR 97202. TEL 503-284-6770. Ed. Vance Terrall, M.D. adv.; circ. 400.
Description: Philatelic and related articles.

769.56   UK
ALBUM TRACKING. m. £0.25 per issue. Grassglow Ltd., 14 Rosebery Ave., London EC1R 4TD, England. adv.; circ. 35,000.

769.56   SP   ISSN 0401-3689
ALHAMBRA; revista filatelica internacional. 1950. m. 600 ptas.($10) Club International Alhambra, P.O. Box 109, Granada, Spain. Ed. F. del Darro. adv.; bk.rev.; bibl.; illus.; tr.lit.; circ. 4,000. (back issues avail.) **Indexed:** Math.R.

769.56   US
AMERICAN PHILATELIC CONGRESS. CONGRESS BOOK. 1935. a. $20 to non-members; members $17.50. American Philatelic Congress, c/o Russell V. Skavaril, 222 E. Torrence Rd., Columbus, OH 43214-3834. Ed. Barbara Mueller. adv.; charts, illus.; cum.index every 5 yrs.; circ. 1,000.

769.56   US   ISSN 0003-0473
HE6187
AMERICAN PHILATELIST. 1886. m. $27 to non-members. American Philatelic Society, Inc., Box 8000, State College, PA 16803. TEL 814-237-3803. Ed. William L. Welch, Jr. adv.; bk.rev.; illus.; index, cum.index: 1886-1986; circ. 57,000. **Indexed:** Art & Archaeol.Tech.Abstr.

769.56   US   ISSN 0163-1608
HJ5321.Z7
AMERICAN REVENUER. 1947. 10/yr. $18 to non-members. American Revenue Association, Box 56, Rockford, IA 50468. Ed. Kenneth Trettin. adv.; bk.rev.; illus.; index, cum.index; circ. 1,380. **Indexed:** Stamp J.Ind.
Description: Articles about and catalogue listings of tax stamps of the US and the world.

769.56   US
AMERICAN SOCIETY FOR NETHERLANDS PHILATELY. NEWSLETTER. 1975. q. $10 includes Journal. American Society for Netherlands Philately, 2354 Roan Lane, Walnut Creek, CA 94596. TEL 415-934-4030. Ed. Frans H.A. Rummens. circ. 400.

769.56   US
AMERICANA PHILATELIC NEWS. 1951. bi-m. $3. American Topical Association, Americana Unit, c/o June Bancroft, Sec.-Treas., Box 179, Washington, DC 20044. TEL 202-387-4649. Ed. August Mark Vaz. bk.rev.; circ. 400.
Description: News of stamps worldwide that have some relationship to the U.S. Official journal of Americana Unit.

769.56   FR
AMICALE PHILATELIQUE L'ANCRE. BULLETIN. 1976. q. Amicale Philatelique l'Ancre, 7 rue Dobre, 44100 Nantes, France. Ed.Bd. adv.; bk.rev.; circ. 350.

769.56   US
ANCHORAGE PHILATELIST. 1967. m. includes membership. Anchorage Philatelic Society, Inc., Box 10-2214, Anchorage, AK 99510. Ed. Eric Knapp. circ. 200.

APPRAISERS STANDARD; for collectors, auctioneers, dealers, etc. see ART

769.56   GW
ARBEITSGEMEINSCHAFT DEUTSCHE OSTGEBIETE. RUNDSCHREIBEN. 1959. q. DM.30. Arbeitsgemeinschaft Deutsche Ostgebiete, Tannenweg 11, 4790 Paderborn, Germany. Ed. Wolfhart Haacke.

ARCHIV FUER DEUTSCHE POSTGESCHICHTE. see COMMUNICATIONS — Postal Affairs

769.56   GW
ARGE-SAAR. MITTEILUNGSBLATT. 1969. q. membership. Arbeits und Forschungsgemeinschaft, Dorfstr. 8, 6610 Lebach, Germany.

794   US
ARIZONA PHILATELIST. 1958. m. $4. Arizona Federation of Stamp Clubs, Inc., 5063 E. North-Regency Circle, Tucson, AZ 85711. Ed. Nancy Hummel. bk.rev.; circ. 275.

ARTISTAMP NEWS. see ART

769.56   US
ASTROPHILE. 1957. bi-m. membership. Space Topic Study Unit, c/o Kerry E. Leggett, Pres., 305 S. 16th St., Ord, NE 68862. TEL 308-728-3893. Ed. Bernice Scholl. adv.; bk.rev.; circ. 1,000.

769.56   SW
ATALAYA. 1974. 2/yr. $3. Christer Brunstrom, Ed. & Pub., Kungsgatan 23, S-032 45 Halmstad, Sweden. adv.; bk.rev.

769.56   AT   ISSN 0155-8498
AUSTRALASIAN STAMP CATALOGUE. 1964. a. Aus.$19.95. Seven Seas Stamps Pty. Ltd., 62 Wingewarra St., Dubbo 2830, Australia. Ed. K. Sparks. bk.rev.; illus.; circ. 25,000.
Description: Illustrated and priced catalog of all Australian Commonwealth stamps and postal stationary. Includes Australian States and Australian Territories and Dependencies.

769.56   UK
AUSTRALIA CONCISE STAMP CATALOGUE. 1989. irreg. price varies. Stanley Gibbons Publications Ltd., Unit 5 Parkside, Christchurch Rd., Ringwood, Hamps. BH24 3SH, England. TEL 0425-472363. FAX 0425-470247. Ed. David Aggersberg.

769.56   AT
AUSTRALIAN COMMONWEALTH COLLECTORS CLUB OF NEW SOUTH WALES. BULLETIN. 1960. bi-m. Aus.$12. Australian Commonwealth Collectors Club of New South Wales, 1045 Canterbury Rd., Lakemba, N.S.W. 2195, Australia. Ed. N.J. Sheppard. bk.rev.; circ. 500.

760   AT
AUSTRALIAN STAMP BULLETIN. 1979. irreg. free. Australia Post Headquarters, Philatelic Group, G.P.O. Box 1777Q, Melbourne, Vic. 3001, Australia. TEL 03-669-7706. FAX 03-669-7744. (Subscr. to: Australian Stamp Bulletin, Locked Bag 8, S. Melbourne, Vic. 3205, Australia) Ed. John Tinney. bk.rev.; circ. 450,000.
Formerly: Philatelic Bulletin.

769.56   AT
AUSTRALIAN STAMP EXPLORER. 1977. q. free. Australia Post Headquarters, Philatelic Group, G.P.O. Box 1777Q, Melbourne, Vic. 3001, Australia. FAX 03-204-7744. Ed. Melinda Browning. circ. 170,000.
Formerly (until 1985): Junior Stamp Preview.

769.56   UK   ISSN 0142-9760
AUSTRIA & HUNGARY STAMP CATALOGUE. 1979. irreg. price varies. Stanley Gibbons Publications Ltd., Unit 5 Parkside, Christchurch Rd., Ringwood, Hamps. BH24 3SH, England. TEL 0425-472363. FAX 0425-470247.

769.56   AU   ISSN 0005-0512
AUSTRIA-PHILATELIST; Oesterreichische Briefmarken-Zeitung. 1945. q. S.120. Verlag Adolf Kosel, Postfach 55, A-1095 Vienna, Austria. Ed. Leopold Sander. adv.; bk.rev.; circ. 5,000.

769.56   UK   ISSN 0140-2889
B A P I P BULLETIN. (Former name of issuing body: British Association of Palestine - Israel Philatelists) 1952. 4/yr. £10($20) Holyland Philatelic Society, 32 St. Ronans Crescent, Woodford Green, Essex IG8 9DG, England. (Subscr. to: Mr. J.D. Shaw, 30 Buckingham Ave., London N20 9DE, England) Ed. W.Y. Loebl. adv.; bk.rev.; cum.index; circ. 400. (back issues avail.)

769.56   CN   ISSN 0045-3129
HE6187
B N A TOPICS. 1944. bi-m. Can.$20. British North America Philatelic Society Ltd., P.O. Box 10420, College Station, TX 77842. FAX 409-845-6129. Ed. V.L. Willson. adv.; bk.rev.; circ. 1,500. **Indexed:** Stamp J.Ind.
Description: Specialist philatelic journal featuring articles on stamps, postal history and related subjects of Canada and the provinces of Canada before their confederation.

769.56   UK   ISSN 0953-8720
B W I STUDY CIRCLE BULLETIN. 1954. q. £6. British West Indies Study Circle, 4 Hill Farm Close, Stafford, Staffs. ST17 9JE, England. Ed. D.G.J. Charlesworth. adv.; bk.rev.; circ. 350. **Indexed:** Stamp J.Ind.

769.56   UK
BALE CATALOGUE OF ISRAEL POSTAGE STAMPS. 1969. a. $35. Michael H. Bale, Ed. & Pub., 41 High St., Ilfracombe, England. FAX 0271-867161. adv.; circ. 2,000.
Former titles: Bale Catalogue of Palestine and Israel Stamps (ISSN 0305-4039); Bale Catalogue of Israel Stamps (ISSN 0067-3048)

769.56   UK   ISSN 0142-9779
BALKANS STAMP CATALOGUE. 1980. irreg. price varies. Stanley Gibbons Publications Ltd., Unit 5 Parkside, Christchurch Rd., Ringwood, Hamps. BH24 3SH, England. TEL 0425-472363. FAX 0425-470247.

769.56   GW   ISSN 0005-4364
BALLON KURIER. 1952. a. free. Pestalozzi Kinder- und Jugenddorf Wahlwies, 7768 Stockach 14, Germany. TEL 07771-8003-0. Ed. H.J. Scheer. adv.; bk.rev.; illus.; circ. 3,000. (looseleaf format)

PHILATELY

769.56 US ISSN 0951-9955
BATON. 1968. 3/yr. $15. Philatelic Music Circle, Box 1781, Sequim, WA 98382. TEL 206-683-6373. Ed. Irene Lawford. (back issues avail.)
Description: Provides information on music, fine art stamps and stamp auctions.

769.55 US ISSN 8756-5153
BAY PHIL. 1971. bi-m. $8. Friends of the Western Philatelic Library, Inc., Box 2219, Sunnyvale, CA 94087. Ed. Wes Nelson. bk.rev.; circ. 400.

759.56 US
BELGIOPHILE. 1983. q. $7.50. American-Belgian Philatelic Society, 25190 Canyon Dr., Carmel, CA 93923. TEL 408-624-7746. (Subscr. to: 621 Virginius Dr., Virginia Beach, VA 23452-4417) Ed. Harry W. Wilcke. adv.; cum.index: 1983-1990. (looseleaf format; back issues avail.)
Description: Covers philatelic matters of interest to persons from beginning to very advanced level.

769.56 US
BELIZE COLLECTOR. 1987. q. Belize Philatelic Society Circle, c/o Charles R. Gambill, 730 Collingswood, Corpus Christi, TX 78412.
Description: Focuses on all aspects of British Honduran and Belizean philately.

769.56 UK ISSN 0142-9787
BENELUX STAMP CATALOGUE. 1979. irreg. price varies. Stanley Gibbons Publications Ltd., Unit 5 Parkside, Christchurch Rd., Ringwood, Hamps. BH24 3SH, England. TEL 0425-472363. FAX 0425-470247.

769.56 US ISSN 1046-2813
BERMUDA POST. 1987. q. $22. Bermuda Collectors Society, c/o Thomas McMahon, 86 Nash Rd., Purdys, NY 10578. TEL 914-232-3088. FAX 203-798-9930. Ed. Reid L. Shaw. adv.; bk.rev.; cum.index; circ. 220. (back issues avail.)
Description: Covers the stamps and postal history of Bermuda.

769.56 SZ ISSN 0005-9404
BERNER BRIEFMARKEN-ZEITUNG/JOURNAL PHILATELIQUE DE BERNE. (Text in French, German) 1908. 10/yr. (including two double nos.). 37 Fr. Zumstein und Cie, P.O. Box, CH-3000 Berne 7, Switzerland. TEL 031-222215. FAX 031-212326. TELEX 912035-ZFIL-CH. Ed. Max Hertsch. bk.rev.; illus.; circ. 10,000.
Description: Stamp collectors magazine covering all countries of the world. Includes news, values, special issues, history, events and exhibitions, list of special collections, and list of new catalogs.

769.56 IT
BOLLETTINO PREFILATELICO E STORICO-POSTALE. 1977. bi-m. L.25000. (Centro Studi Internazionale di Storia Postale) Benetton Editore, Via A. Da Bassano, 31, I-35100 Padua, Italy. adv.; bk.rev.

BRIEF AUS WAHLWIES; Mitteilungen aus dem Pestalozzi Kinder- und Jugenddorf. see CHILDREN AND YOUTH — About

769.56 AU ISSN 0007-0033
BRIEFMARKE. 1954. m. S.400. Verband Oesterreichischer Philatelisten-Vereine, Getreidemarkt 1, A-1060 Vienna, Austria. TEL 0222-5876469. FAX 0222-587-7026. Ed. Karl-Heinz Wagner. adv.; bk.rev.; charts; illus.; mkt.; circ. 7,000.

769.56 GW ISSN 0933-968X
BRIEFMARKEN-MAGAZIN. 1981. 5/yr. DM.27. E M S - Verlag, Birkenhofstr. 10, 7000 Stuttgart 70, Germany. TEL 0711-454098. FAX 0711-4570666. (Subscr. to: Postfach 700140, 7000 Stuttgart 70, Germany) Ed. Wolfgang Erzinger. adv.; circ. 30,000. (back issues avail.)
Formerly: Jahrbuch der Philatelie.

769.56 GW ISSN 0007-0041
BRIEFMARKEN-SPIEGEL; internationale Filatelie. 1961. m. DM.36. Goettinger Druckerei- und Verlagsgesellschaft GmbH, Maschmuehlenweg 8-10, Postfach 206, 3400 Goettingen, Germany. Ed. H.J. Hinterthuer. adv.; bk.rev.; circ. 30,000.

769.56 GW ISSN 0171-1970
BRIEFMARKENWELT. 1978. 5/yr. DM.27.50. E M S - Verlag, Birkenhofstr. 10, 7000 Stuttgart 70, Germany. FAX 0049-711-4570666. Ed. Wolfgang Erzinger. adv.; bk.rev.; circ. 85,000. (back issues avail.)

769.56 CN ISSN 0045-2890
BRITISH CARIBBEAN PHILATELIC JOURNAL. 1961. q. $18 membership. British Caribbean Philatelic Study Group, c/o Michel Forand, Ed., Box 20145, Ottawa, Ont. K1N 9P4, Canada. adv.; bk.rev.; charts; illus.; index; circ. 500. (back issues avail.) Indexed: Stamp J.Ind.
Description: Publishes research and information about the stamps and postal history of the British West Indies, British Honduras (Belize), British Guiana (Guyana) and Bermuda.

769.56 NE ISSN 0950-575X
BRITISH JOURNAL OF RUSSIAN PHILATELY. (Text in English; summaries occasionally in transliterated Russian) 1946. s-a. £10($15) (membership). Postbus 16636, 1001 RC Amsterdam, Netherlands. Ed. I.J. Steyn. bk.rev.; index; circ. 250 (controlled). Indexed: Stamp J.Ind.
Description: Specialist articles on the philately of present and past Russian territories.

769.56 UK ISSN 0953-8119
BRITISH PHILATELIC BULLETIN. 1963. m. £10.25. British Post Office, National Postal Museum, King Edward St., London EC1A 1LP, England. (Subscr. to: British Philatelic Bureau, 20 Brandon St., Edinburgh EH3 5TT, Scotland) Ed. John Holman. bk.rev.; charts; illus.; stat.; index; circ. 65,000. (back issues avail.)
Description: Covers a wide range of philatelic topics pertaining to the British post.

769.56 UK
BRITISH PHILATELIC FEDERATION. CONGRESS HANDBOOK. a. $3. British Philatelic Federation Ltd., 107 Charterhouse St., London EC1M 6PT, England. TEL 071-251-5040. FAX 071-490-4253. Ed. Robert Seaman. adv.

769.56 UK
BRITISH POSTMARK SOCIETY. QUARTERLY BULLETIN. 1958. q. £6. British Postmark Society, c/o A.J. Howard, Secy., 21 Empress Way, Euxton, Chorley, Lancs. PR7 6QB, England. TEL 0257-2696522. Ed. B.R. Reynolds. bk.rev.; circ. 350.

769.56 FR
BULLETIN COLFRA. 1974. q. 135 F. Societe Philatelique Colfra, B.P. 628, 75367 Paris Cedex 08, France. bk.rev.; circ. 160.
Description: Postal and philatelic history of former French colonies and territories; study and research.

769.56 US
C A C NEWSLETTER. 1981. q. $6 to non-members. American Philatelic Society, Chapter Activities Committee, Box 8000, State College, PA 16803. FAX 814-237-6128. Ed. Diana Manchester. circ. 800.
Description: Keeps chapters informed of official society news, new slide programs, events and programs of interest to chapters, and serves as a forum for the exchange of information among chapters.

769.56 CN
C.A.F.I.P. BULLETIN. bi-m. Can.$25. Canadian Association for Israel Philately, 260 Adelaide St. E., York Toronto, P.O. Box 33, Toronto, Ont. M5A 1N0, Canada. TEL 416-781-9779. Ed. Joseph Berkovits. bk.rev.; abstr.; bibl.; illus.; circ. 60. (back issues avail.)

769.56 US
C O R O S CHRONICLE. 1948. bi-m. $7.50. Collectors of Religion on Stamps, 226 Robin Hood Rd., Mountainside, NJ 07092. Ed. Eileen E. Freeman. adv.; bk.rev.; circ. 750.

769.56 NZ ISSN 0112-8388
C.P. NEWSLETTER MONTHLY; for collectors of New Zealand Stamps. 1948. m. NZ.$36. Campbell Paterson Ltd., P.O. Box 5555, Auckland 1, New Zealand. TEL 793086. FAX 793087. Ed. Warwick R. Paterson. bk.rev.; circ. 2,000.
Formerly: Campbell Paterson Newsletter.

769.56 CN ISSN 0828-8755
CALGARY STAMPEDE. 1978. 5/yr. membership. Calgary Philatelic Society, P.O. Box 1478, Calgary, Alta. T2P 2L6, Canada. Ed. Dale Speirs. adv.; bk.rev.; circ. 250.
Description: General philatelic articles, with emphasis on BNA.

769.56 NZ
CAMPBELL PATERSON'S LOOSE-LEAF COLOUR CATALOGUE OF NEW ZEALAND STAMPS (SPECIALISED). 1950. a. NZ.$111.95. Campbell Paterson Ltd., P.O. Box 5555, Auckland 1, New Zealand. TEL 3793086. FAX 3793087. Ed. Campbell Paterson.
Description: Guide for collectors of New Zealand stamps from 1854 to the present day.

769.56 US
CANADA AIR MAIL NOTES. vol.15, 1973. q. $10 (foreign $12). Canadian Air Mail Collectors Club, Box 1239, Elgin, IL 60120. TEL 708-742-3328. (Co-sponsor: Aerophilatelic Federation of the Americas) Ed. Richard K. Malott. adv.; bk.rev. (processed)

769.56 CN ISSN 0045-5253
CANADIAN PHILATELIST. 1950. bi-m. membership. Royal Philatelic Society of Canada, P.O. Box 5320, Sta. "F", Ottawa, Ont. K2C 3J1, Canada. Ed. Steven Thorning. adv.; bk.rev.; index; circ. 7,000. Indexed: CMI, Stamp J.Ind.

769.56 CN
CANADIAN STAMP NEWS. 1976. bi-w. Can.$19.98. Metroland Printing, Publishing and Distributing Ltd., North York Mirror Division, 10 Tempo Ave., Willowdale, Ont. M2H 2N8, Canada. TEL 416-493-4400. Ed. Don Atanasoff. adv.; bk.rev.; illus.; stat.; circ. 16,800. Indexed: CMI.

769.56 US ISSN 0746-004X
HE6185.C24
CANAL ZONE PHILATELIST. 1952. q. $8. Canal Zone Study Group, Box 9973, College Station, TX 77840. Ed. Gilbert N. Plass. adv.; bk.rev.; circ. 1,000. Indexed: Stamp J.Ind.

769.56 JM
CARIBBEAN STAMP EXCHANGE AND PENPAL BULLETIN. 1983. bi-m. $4. Allen & Associates, P.O. Box 501, Kingston, Jamaica, W.I. Ed. Stewart Allen. tr.lit./; circ. 600. (looseleaf format; back issues avail.)

769.56 US ISSN 0891-0758
CARTO-PHILATELIST. 1955. q. 15. c/o Miklos Pinther, Pres., 206 Grayson Pl., Teaneck, NJ 07666. FAX 201-836-5602. (Co-sponsors: American Topical Association; American Philatelic Society) Ed. Mark D. Larkin. adv.; bk.rev.; circ. 210.
Description: News and articles on the science and art of map making and their depiction on postage stamps.

769.56 UK ISSN 0142-9876
CENTRAL AMERICA STAMP CATALOGUE. 1980. irreg. price varies. Stanley Gibbons Publications Ltd., Unit 5 Parkside, Christchurch Rd., Ringwood, Hamps. BH24 3SH, England. TEL 0425-472363. FAX 0425-470247.

769.56 UK ISSN 0142-9884
CENTRAL ASIA STAMP CATALOGUE. 1981. irreg. price varies. Stanley Gibbons Publications Ltd., Unit 5 Parkside, Christchurch Rd., Ringwood, Hamps. BH24 2SH, England. TEL 0425-472363. FAX 0425-470247.

769.56 CS
CESKOSLOVENSKO. Spine title: Katalog Ceskoslovenskych Znamek. irreg. 40 Kcs. (Postovni Filatelisticka Sluzba) Nakladatelstvi Dopravy a Spoju, Hybernska 5, 115 78 Prague 1, Czechoslovakia. illus.

769.56 UK ISSN 0142-5625
CHANNEL ISLANDS SPECIALISED CATALOGUE. 1979. irreg. price varies. Stanley Gibbons Publications Ltd., Unit 5 Parkside, Christchurch Rd., Ringwood, Hamps. BH24 3SH, England. TEL 0425-472363. FAX 0425-470247.

769.56 794.1 US
CHESSTAMP REVIEW.* 1978. q. $7 (foreign $11). Chess on Stamps Study Unity, Box 9789, Midland, TX 79706-2739. Ed. Russ Ott. circ. 175. (back issues avail.)

PHILATELY 3751

769.56 CL
CHILE FILATELICO. 1929. q. Almirante Simpson 75, Casilla 13245, Santiago, Chile. TEL 2-222-8036. Ed. Ricardo Boizard G.

769.56 US ISSN 0885-9779
CHINA CLIPPER; remember the old, but know the new. 1936. bi-m. $12. China Stamp Society, Inc., c/o Clarence Springstead, 1529 Hickory Lane, Bettendorf, IA 52722. Ed. Donald R. Alexander. adv.; bk.rev.; circ. 1,000. **Indexed:** Stamp J.Ind.
  Description: Devoted to all aspects of Chinese philately. Contains studies and articles of interest, brief reports of new findings, inquiries and response, and data concerning new issues.

769.56 CC
CHINA PHILATELY; the bi-monthly magazine for stamp collectors. bi-m. $11 to individuals; institutions $16. All-China Philatelic Federation, 27 Dong Chang'an Jie, Beijing, People's Republic of China. (Dist. outside China by: Guoji Shudian - China International Book Trading Corp., P.O. Box 399, Beijing, P.R.C.; Dist. in US by: China Books & Periodicals, Inc., 2929 24th San Francisco, CA 94110. TEL 415-282-2994) (back issues avail.)
  Description: News of Chinese stamps, philatelic findings, trends in China and abroad, philatelic activities, and latest market values.

769.56 UK ISSN 0142-9892
CHINA STAMP CATALOGUE. 1979. irreg. price varies. Stanley Gibbons Publications Ltd., Unit 5 Parkside, Christchurch Rd., Ringwood, Hamps. BH24 3SH, England. TEL 0425-472363. FAX 0425-470247.

769.56 US
CHINA TRADER NEWSLETTER. 1980. q. $7.50. China Trader Supply, Box 630, Millbrook, NY 12545. Ed. Gene Klein. adv.; circ. 200.
  Formerly: China.

769.56 US ISSN 0009-6008
HE6187
CHRONICLE OF U S CLASSIC POSTAL ISSUES. 1965. q. $16. U S Philatelic Classics Society, Inc., Briarwood, Lisbon, MD 21765. Ed. Susan M. McDonald. adv.; bk.rev.; illus.; tr.lit.; circ. 1,250. **Indexed:** Stamp J.Ind.

769.56 UK ISSN 0009-6911
CINDERELLA PHILATELIST. 1961. q. £10 to non-members. Cinderella Stamp Club, c/o L.N. Williams, 44 The Ridgeway, London NW11 8QS, England. adv.; bk.rev.; illus.; index; circ. 800 (controlled). **Indexed:** Stamp J.Ind.

769.56 US
CIVIL CENSORSHIP STUDY GROUP BULLETIN. 1973. q. $9. Civil Censorship Study Group, c/o L.D. Mayo, 4305 Wyandotte Dr., Indianapolis, IN 46220-5765. Eds. Regis Hoffman, A.R. Torrance. circ. 200.

769.56 VE
CLUB FILATELICO DE CARACAS. GACETA MENSUAL. 1978-1981; resumed 1986. m. exchange basis. Club Filatelico de Caracas, Apartado 61.197, Caracas 1060-A, Venezuela. FAX 782-17-31. adv.; bk.rev.; circ. 500.
  Formerly (until no.80, 1981): Fila Nova; **Supersedes** (1961-1978): Club Filatelico de Caracas. Revista (ISSN 0529-9853)

769.56 PO ISSN 0009-9651
CLUBE FILATELICO DE PORTUGAL. BOLETIM. 1943. 6/yr. $10 (effective Jan. 1991). Clube Filatelico de Portugal, Av. Almirante Reis 70, 5 Dto., 1100 Lisbon, Portugal. Ed. Silva Gama. adv.; bk.rev.; illus.; circ. 5,000.
  —BLDSC shelfmark: 2126.700000.

769.56 913 US ISSN 0896-3533
CODEX FILATELICA. 1974. bi-m. $8 (foreign $15). Meso American Archeology Study Unit, Box 1442, Riverside, CA 92502. Ed. Chris L. Moser. bk.rev.; circ. 95.
  Description: Newsletter for collectors of worldwide stamps that illustrate or relate to Pre-Columbian archeology.

769.56 UK
COLLECT BIRDS ON STAMPS. 1983. irreg. price varies. Stanley Gibbons Publications Ltd., Unit 5 Parkside, Christchurch Rd., Ringwood, Hamps. BH24 3SH, England. TEL 0425-472363. FAX 0425-470247.

769.56 UK ISSN 0069-5262
COLLECT BRITISH STAMPS. 1967. a. price varies. Stanley Gibbons Publications Ltd., Unit 5 Parkside, Christchurch Rd., Ringwood, Hamps. BH24 3SH, England. TEL 0425-472363. FAX 0425-470247.

769.56 UK
COLLECT CHANNEL ISLANDS AND ISLE OF MAN STAMPS. 1972. a. price varies. Stanley Gibbons Publications Ltd., Unit 5 Parkside, Christchurch Rd., Ringwood, Hamps. BH24 3SH, England. TEL 0425-472363. FAX 0425-470247.
  Formerly (until 1984): Collect Channel Islands Stamps (ISSN 0306-5103)

769.56 UK
COLLECT MAMMALS ON STAMPS. 1986. irreg. price varies. Stanley Gibbons Publications Ltd., Unit 5 Parkside, Christchurch Rd., Ringwood, Hamps. BH24 3SH, England. TEL 0425-472363. FAX 0425-470247. Ed. David Aggersberg.

769.56 UK
COLLECT RAILWAYS ON STAMPS. 1986. irreg. price varies. Stanley Gibbons Publications Ltd., Unit 5 Parkside, Christchurch Rd., Ringwood, Hamps. BH24 3SH, England. TEL 0425-472363. FAX 0425-470247. Ed. David Aggersberg.

769.56 UK
COLLECT SHIPS ON STAMPS. 1989. irreg. price varies. Stanley Gibbons Publications Ltd., Unit 5 Parkside, Christchurch Rd., Ringwood, Hamps. BH24 3SH, England. TEL 0425-472363. FAX 0425-470247. Ed. David Aggersberg.

769.56 990 AT ISSN 0727-4211
COLLECTION OF AUSTRALIAN STAMPS. 1981. a. Aus.$53.95. Australia Post Headquarters, Philatelic Group, G.P.O. Box 1777Q, Melbourne, Vic. 3001, Australia. FAX 03-69977432. (Subscr. to: Philatelic Bureau, GPO Box 9988, Melbourne, Vic. 3001, Australia) illus.

769.56 FR
COLLECTIONNEUR, PHILATELISTE ET MARCOPHILE. 1969. q. membership. Cercle Lyonnais d'Etudes Philateliques et Marcophiles, 17 rue Colin, 34000 Montpellier, France. Ed. A. Cambouilves. adv.; circ. 500.

769.56 US ISSN 0010-0838
HE6187
COLLECTORS CLUB PHILATELIST. 1922. bi-m. $30 to individuals; institutions $35. Collectors Club, Inc., 22 E. 35th St., New York, NY 10016-0559. Ed. E.E. Fricks. adv.; bk.rev.; abstr.; illus.; index, cum.index; circ. 1,500. **Indexed:** Stamp J.Ind.

769.56 US
COLLECTOR'S MARKETPLACE MONTHLY; including the stamp exchange. 8/yr. (every 6 w.) $8.95 for 12 nos. Box 25, Stewartsville, NJ 08886. TEL 201-479-4614.

769.56 US
COLUMBIAN (COLUMBUS). 1925. m. $8. Columbus Philatelic Club, Inc., Box 16036, Columbus, OH 43216. Ed. Jason Manchester. adv.; bk.rev.; circ. 150.
  Description: News, announcements, and articles of interest to the activities and members of the club, with lists of auction items.

769.56 US
COMMONWEALTH PHILATELY. 1980. bi-m. $7. Commonwealth International Philatelic Society, c/o Bill Scheuermann, Box 195, Minetto, NY 13115. TEL 315-343-5372. Ed. Ryan G. Lorenz. adv.; circ. 125. **Indexed:** Stamp J.Ind.

769.56 IT
CRONACA FILATELICA; mensile di filatelia e numismatica. 1970. m. L.125000. Eder s.r.l., Casella Postale 1065, 80100 Naples, Vomero, Italy. FAX 081-7611316. Ed. Carlo A. DeRosa. adv.; bk.rev.; circ. 23,000.

769.56 US
CUBAN TOPICS. 1976. q. $5. Box 52-0002, Miami, FL 33152. Ed. Agustin J. Cantens. adv.; bk.rev.; circ. 1,000.
  Description: Covers articles and news about Cuban philately and postal history, and related field of collection.

769.56 US
CZECHOSLOVAK SPECIALIST. 1939. 10/yr. $15. Society for Czechoslovak Philately, Inc., 2936 Rosemoor Lane, Fairfax, VA 22031. TEL 703-560-2972. Ed. Henry Hahn. adv.; bk.rev.; charts; illus.; index, cum.index every 10 yrs.; circ. 500. **Indexed:** Stamp J.Ind.

769.56 UK ISSN 0142-9795
CZECHOSLOVAKIA & POLAND STAMP CATALOGUE. 1980. irreg. price varies. Stanley Gibbons Publications Ltd., Unit 5 Parkside, Christchurch Rd., Ringwood, Hamps. BH24 3SH, England. TEL 0425-472363. FAX 0425-470247.

769.56 UK ISSN 0142-3525
CZECHOUT. 1975. 4/yr. £2 to non-members per issue. Czechoslovak Philatelic Society of Great Britain, 25 Weymouth Crescent, Scunthorpe, S. Humberside DN17 1TU, England. TEL 0724-842066. Ed. Alan J. Knight. bk.rev.

769.56 GW ISSN 0011-4790
D B Z. (Deutsche Zeitung fuer Briefmarkenkunde) 1925. bi-w. DM.59. Deutsche Briefmarkenzeitung GmbH & Co. KG, Postfach 1363, Feldstr. 6, 5408 Nassau, Germany. TEL 02604-70144. FAX 02604-70130. TELEX 260494. adv.; index. (back issues avail.)

769.56 DK ISSN 0109-3371
D K; frimaerkekatalog Danmark, med Groenland, Faeroeerne D V I, Island (Kongeriget). 1984. a. DKK 248. Saga, P.O. Box 82, 3520 Farum, Denmark. Ed. Tove Christensen. adv.; illus.; circ. 5,000.

769.56 US ISSN 0882-0236
D O S S U JOURNAL. 1979. q. $3 (foreign $5). American Topical Association, Dogs on Stamps Study Unit, 3208 Hana Rd., Edison, NJ 08817-2552. TEL 908-248-1865. Ed. Morris Raskin. adv.; circ. 275.
  Description: For philatelists interested in the collection and study of postal materials depicting dogs.

769.56 DK ISSN 0903-2444
DANSK FILATELISTISK TIDSSKRIFT. 1934. 9/yr. DKK 130. Danmarks Filatelist Forbund, Fuglefaengervej 8, 3400 Hillerod, Denmark. TEL 42-26 9854. Ed. Lennart Weber. adv.; circ. 9,000.

769.56 US
DAYTON STAMP CLUB. NEWSLETTER. vol.8, 1982. m. Dayton Stamp Club, Inc., Box 1574, Dayton, OH 45401. Ed. Martin Richardson.

737 769 GW ISSN 0930-858X
DEUTSCHE BRIEFMARKEN - REVUE; SD - Sammlerdienst. 1949. m. DM.57. (Fachblatt fuer Philatelie) P S B N - Verlagsgesellschaft mbH, Konkordiastr. 13, 4000 Dusseldorf 1, Germany. TEL 0211-394032. FAX 0211-3982225. Ed. Dieter Stein. adv.; bk.rev.; illus.; circ. 26,000. (back issues avail.)

769.56 US
DISPATCHER (SAN FRANCISCO, 1953). 1953. bi-m. $5. Casey Jones Railroad Unit - A T A (Subsidiary of: American Topical Association), Box 31631, San Francisco, CA 94131. Ed. Oliver C. Atchison. adv.; bk.rev.; illus.; circ. 400. (looseleaf format)
  Formerly: American Topical Association. Casey Jones Railroad Unit. Newsletter.
  Description: News and announcements pertaining to railroad-stamp collecting, with lists of recent and special issues.

769.56 FR
DOCUMENTS PHILATELIQUES. 1959. q. 200 F. Academie de Philatelie de Paris, c/o J.P. Schroeder, 7 av. Beaucour, 75008 Paris, France. bk.rev.; illus.; circ. 500. (tabloid format)

759.56 US
DUCK STAMP DATA. base vol. (plus update service). $12. U.S. Fish and Wildlife Service, Dept. of the Interior, Washington, DC 20240. TEL 703-358-1711. (Dist. by: Supt. of Documents, Washington, DC 20402)

769.56 US
E F O COLLECTOR. 1978. 6/yr. $13 (foreign $25). E F O Collectors Club, 1903 Village RD-W, Norwood, MA 02062-2516. Ed. Howard P. Gates. adv.; bk.rev.; circ. 350. (back issues avail.)

PHILATELY

769.56   FR   ISSN 0012-9240
ECHO DE LA TIMBROLOGIE; revue mensuelle de philatelie. 1887. m. 103 F. 37 rue des Jacobins, 80036 Amiens, France. Ed. Jacques Gervais. adv.; bk.rev.; bibl.; illus.; mkt.; index.

769.56   CN   ISSN 0046-1318
EDMONTON STAMP CLUB BULLETIN. 1965. m. Can.$15. Edmonton Stamp Club, P.O. Box 399, Edmonton, Alta., Canada. FAX 403-492-7196. Ed. K.R. Spencer. adv.; bk.rev.; circ. 500.

769.56   US
EESTI FILATELIST/ESTONIAN PHILATELIST. (Text in English, Estonian, German, Swedish) 1955. a. SEK 150($25) (Society of Estonian Philatelists in Sweden) Estonian Philatelic Society, c/o Rudolf Hamar, 31 Addison Terr., Old Tappan, NJ 07675. TEL 201-767-0535. FAX 212-643-1903. (Addr. in Sweden: c/o Hans Krondstrom, Sofielundsplan 40, 12231 Enskede, Sweden) Ed. Elmar Ojaste. circ. 700. (back issues avail.)

769.56   ES
EL SALVADOR FILATELICO. 1940. q. Sociedad Filatelico de El Salvador, Avda. Espana 207, Altos Vidri Panades, San Salvador, El Salvador.

769.56   US
EMERT'S STAMP QUARTERLY. q. $2. Buckingham Publications, Box 46, Buckingham, VA 23921.

769.56   GW
ERINNOPHILIE INTERNATIONAL. 1965? irreg. (3-4/yr.). DM.50. Errinophilie International im Bund Deutscher Philatelisten e.V., c/o H. Geier, Postfach 1308, 8623 Staffelstein, Germany. TEL 09573-1870. (back issues avail.)

769.56 767   US   ISSN 0014-0848
ESSAY PROOF JOURNAL; devoted to the historical and artistic background of stamps and paper money. 1944. q. $20. Essay-Proof Society, Inc., 225 S. Fischer Ave., Jefferson, WI 53549. Ed. Barbara R. Mueller. adv.; bk.rev.; bibl.; illus.; mkt.; index; circ. 500. **Indexed:** Stamp J.Ind.

769.56   US
F A P JOURNAL. 1955. q. $12. Fine Arts Philatelists, c/o Dr. Tom Ullrich, Sec., 7502 E. 80th St., Indianapolis, IN 46256. Ed. David W. Christel. bibl.; illus.; circ. 600. (looseleaf format)

769.56   GW
F G G B RUNDBRIEFE. 1970. q. DM.40. Forschungsgemeinschaft Grossbritannien, Jentgesallee 53, 4150 Krefeld 1, Germany. bk.rev.; circ. 250.

769.56   GW
F I A S-REPORT; Mitteilungsblatt der Forschungsgemeinschaft Internationale Antwortscheine, Bundesarbeitsgemeinschaft im Bund Deutscher Philatelisten. 1972. s-a. DM.24. F I A S, c/o Horst Hoffmann, Ed., Schillerstr. 3, 3110 Uelzen 1, Germany. adv.; bk.rev.; circ. 100. (back issues avail.)

769.56   US
EL FARO.* 1975. 4/yr. $8. Associated Collectors of El Salvador, c/o Robert A. Fisher, Ed., 28 Edgewood Dr., Granville, OH 43023-1076. adv.; circ. 100 (controlled). (processed) **Indexed:** Stamp J.Ind.
Formerly (until 1978): A C E S.

769.56   GW
FEUERMELDER RUNDBRIEF. (Text in English and German) 1975. q. DM.30. Motiv - Arge Feuerwehr e.V., Postfach 800427, 6230 Frankfurt a.M. 80, Germany. TEL 069-306530. Ed. Hans-Ruediger Kohn. circ. 400. (looseleaf format)

769.56   RM   ISSN 0428-3341
FILATELIA. (Text in Rumanian; summaries in English, French, German, Russian) 1958. m. $46. Federatia Filatelica Romana - Romanian Philatelic Federation, Strada Boteanu Nr.6, Bucharest 1, Rumania. (Subscr. to: Magazine "Filatelia", C.P. 1-870, 70100 Bucharest, Rumania) Ed. Aurelian Darnu. adv.; bk.rev.; bibl.; illus.; circ. 12,000. (tabloid format)

769.56   CU   ISSN 0138-631X
FILATELIA CUBANA. (Text in Spanish; summaries in English, French) 3/yr. $10 in N. and S. America; Europe $12. (Federacion Filatelica Cubano) Ediciones Cubanas, Obispo No. 527, Apdo. 605, Havana, Cuba. illus.
Description: Contains articles on stamp history; critical studies of Cuban stamps; and information on the activities carried out by the Federation and stamp clubs in Cuba and abroad; for collectors of stamps and first-day issues.

769.56   IT   ISSN 0015-0940
FILATELIA ITALIANA. 1960. m. Via della Mercede 11, 00187 Rome, Italy. Ed. Michele Picardi. adv.; bk.rev.; illus.; index; circ. 37,500.

769.56   HU   ISSN 0133-168X
FILATELIAI SZEMLE. m. $22.50. Pf. 4 H-1387, Budapest, Hungary. (Subscr. to: Kultura, Pf. 149 H-1389, Budapest, Hungary) Ed. Bela Milassin.

769.56   IT
FILATELICO. m. Casella Postale 176, 95100 Catania, Italy. Ed. Luigi Musumarra.

769.56   CS   ISSN 0015-0959
FILATELIE. (Text in Czech or Slovak; summaries in English, French, German, Russian) 1950. s-m. 72 Kcs.($63) (Svaz Ceskoslovenskych Filatelistu) Nakladatelstvi Dopravy a Spoju, Hybernska 5, 115 78 Prague 1, Czechoslovakia. (Dist. by: Artia, Ve Smeckach 30, 111 27 Prague 1, Czechoslovakia) Ed. Vitezslav Houska. adv.; bk.rev.; circ. 22,000.

769.56   CI   ISSN 0015-0967
FILATELIJA. (Text in Croatian; summary in English) 1940. irreg. (3-4/yr.). $4 per no. Hrvatski Filatelisticki Savez - Croatian Philatelic Union, Habdeliceva 2, 41000 Zagreb, Croatia. Ed. Nenad Nikolic. adv.; bk.rev.; illus.; index; circ. 4,000.

769.56   FI
FILATELISTI; stamp journal. (Text in Finnish and Swedish) 1950. m. FIM 160 (outside Scandinavia FIM 260). Suomen Filatelistiliitto r.y. - Philatelic Federation of Finland, P.O. Box 202, 00101 Helsinki 10, Finland. FAX 358-0-493900. Ed. August Leppa. adv.; bk.rev.; illus.; cum.index; circ. 6,000. (tabloid format)
Formerly: Philatelia Fennica (ISSN 0355-502X)

796.56   DK   ISSN 0108-0296
FILATELISTISK KATALOG-NOEGLE/PHILATELISTIC CATALOGUE KEY/PHILATELISTISCHER KATALOG-SCHLUESSEL. (Text in Danish, English, French and German) 1981. a. DKK 49. Kylling & Soen, Engroejel 6, DK-2670 Greve, Denmark. Preben Kylling. adv.; illus.; circ. 5,000.

769.56   RU   ISSN 0015-0983
FILATELIYA S.S.S.R.. 1966. m. 12 Rub. Vsesoyuznoe Obshchestvo Filatelistov, Moscow, Russia. Ed. B. Balashov. illus.; index.

769.56   DR
FILOTELICO. 1977. bi-m. RD.$120($15) (Sociedad Filatelica Dominicana) Artes Graficas Sordomudez, Apartado 1930, Santo Domingo, Dominican Republic. Ed. Danilo A. Mueses. adv.; bk.rev.; circ. 425. (back issues avail.)

769.56   US   ISSN 0428-4836
FIRST DAYS. 1956. 8/yr. $15. American First Day Cover Society, Box 5295, Fairlawn, OH 44333. Ed. Barry Newton. adv.; bk.rev.; illus.; index; circ. 4,000. **Indexed:** Stamp J.Ind.

769.56   UK
FORCES POSTAL HISTORY SOCIETY. NEWSLETTER. 1952. 4/yr. membership. Forces Postal History Society, 4 Springfield Court, London SW19 7AJ, England. Ed. B. Ferguson. adv.; bk.rev.; circ. 350.

769.56   GW
FORSCHUNGSGEMEINSCHAFT BERLIN. RUNDBRIEF. 1971. q. membership. Forschungsgemeinschaft Berlin, c/o Peter Koegel, Postfach 210724, 1000 Berlin 21, Germany. TEL 030-3452735. Eds. Klaus Janssen, Guenter Klein. circ. 140. (back issues avail.)
Description: Philatelic studies of Berlin.

769.56   UK   ISSN 0269-5006
FRANCE & COLONIES PHILATELIC SOCIETY OF GREAT BRITAIN. JOURNAL. q. France & Colonies Philatelic Society, 34 Traps Lane, New Malden, Surrey KT3 4SA, England. Ed. D.J. Richardson.
Former titles: France and Colonies Philatelic Society. Journal; France and Colonies Philatelic Society. Newsletter; France and Colonies Philatelic Society. Journal.

769.56   UK   ISSN 0142-9809
FRANCE STAMP CATALOGUE. 1979. irreg. price varies. Stanley Gibbons Publications Ltd., Unit 5 Parkside, Christchurch Rd., Ringwood, Hamps. BH24 3SH, England. TEL 0425-472363. FAX 0425-470247.

769   IT
FRANCOBOLLI;* rivista mensile di filatelia. 1970. m. (11/yr.). L.25000($50) Sassone Editrice s.r.l., Via A. Vera, 19, 00142 Rome, Italy. Ed. Renato Russo. adv.; circ. 10,000.

769.56   DK   ISSN 0108-4089
FRIMAERKENS VERDEN. 1982. m. DKK 37.50. Nordfrim, Kvindevadet 42, 5450 Otterup, Denmark. adv.; bk.rev.; illus.

769.56   DK   ISSN 0016-1438
FRIMAERKESAMLEREN. 1942. 7/yr. DKK 200($30) Birkemosevej 4, DK-2750 Ballerup, Denmark. FAX 42-18-90-14. Ed. Andreas Abitz. adv.; bk.rev.; circ. 3,100.

769.56   US   ISSN 0732-5517
FROM THE DRAGON'S DEN. 1969. 4/yr. membership. Ryukyu Philatelic Specialist Society, Box 172, Great Falls, VA 22066. Ed. Russ W. Carter. adv.; bk.rev.; charts; illus.; stat.; circ. 350. (back issues avail.) **Indexed:** Stamp J.Ind.

769.56   UK   ISSN 0430-8913
G B JOURNAL. 1955. 6/yr. £3.50 per issue. (Great Britain Philatelic Society) G B Philatelic Publications Ltd., Anso Corner Farm, Hempstead, Saffron Walden, Essex CB10 2NV, England. Eds. Mike Jackson, Harry Dagnall. adv.; bk.rev.; illus.; index; circ. 900. —BLDSC shelfmark: 4095.310000.

769.56   US
G I P S. bi-m. membership. Government Imprinted Penalty Stationery Society, 10926 Annette Ave., Tampa, FL 33612.

769.56   IT   ISSN 0016-3694
GABRIEL; informatore filatelico. 1962. q. L.20000($18) Gabriel Italiana, Casella Postale 7090, 00100 Rome, Italy. Ed. Nicolo Musumeci. adv.; circ. 600.

769.56   AG
GACETA FILATELICA. vol.3, 1981. m. Arg.$36000($20) G R E S Editora, Casilla de Correos 46, Sucursal 49, 1449 Buenos Aires, Argentina. Ed. Jose A. Romanelli.

769.56   IT   ISSN 0016-5654
GAZZETTA FILATELICA. 1947. m. L.15000($15) Ercole Gloria s.r.l., Piazza Pio XI, No. 1, 20123 Milan, Italy. bk.rev.; circ. 15,000.

769.56   US   ISSN 0016-8823
GERMAN POSTAL SPECIALIST; a philatelic publication for stamp collectors specializing in Germany-related stamps. (Text in English) 1950. m. $18. Germany Philatelic Society, Inc., Box 779, Arnold, MD 21012. Ed. Rudolf E. Anders. adv.; bk.rev.; charts; illus.; index, cum.index: vols.1-30; circ. 2,000. (also avail. in microfiche; back issues avail.) **Indexed:** Stamp J.Ind.
Description: Covers philately and postal history.

769.56   UK   ISSN 0142-9817
GERMANY STAMP CATALOGUE. 1979. irreg. price varies. Stanley Gibbons Publications Ltd., Unit 5 Parkside, Christchurch Rd., Ringwood, Hamps. BH24 3SH, England. TEL 0425-472363. FAX 0425-470247.

769.56   UK   ISSN 0016-9676
GIBBONS STAMP MONTHLY. (New Issue Supplement: Philatelic Discoveries) 1890. m. £17.40 (foreign £30). Stanley Gibbons Magazines Ltd., Unit 5 Parkside, Christchurch Rd., Ringwood, Hamps. BH24 3SH, England. TEL 0425-472363. FAX 0425-470247. Ed. Hugh Jefferies. adv.; bk.rev.; illus.; mkt.; index; circ. 20,000. **Indexed:** Stamp J.Ind.

PHILATELY 3753

769.56 US
▼**GLOBAL STAMP NEWS.** 1990. m. free. Brandewie Inc., 715 Johnston Dr., Box 97, Sidney, OH 45365. TEL 513-492-3183. FAX 513-492-6514. Ed. Jan Brandewie. adv.; illus.; circ. 20,000 (controlled).
Description: Covers worldwide stamp markets and collecting interests.

769.56 US
GREAT BRITAIN COLLECTORS CLUB. QUARTERLY NEWSLETTER. 1979. q. $15. Lord Byron Stamps, Box 4586, Portland, OR 97208. TEL 503-254-7093. Ed. Tom Current. adv.; bk.rev.; circ. 375.
Formerly: Great Britain Correspondence Club. Quarterly Newsletter (ISSN 0887-6819)
Description: News, articles, and announcements pertaining to this stamp collection association.

769.56 UK
GREAT BRITAIN CONCISE STAMP CATALOGUE. 1986. a. £5.95. Stanley Gibbons Publications Ltd., Unit 5 Parkside, Christchurch Rd., Ringwood, Hampshire BH24 3SH, England. TEL 0425-472363. FAX 0425-470247. Ed. David Aggersberg. circ. 20,000.
Description: Contains facts aimed at the semi-advanced collector.

769.56 UK ISSN 0072-7229
GREAT BRITAIN SPECIALISED STAMP CATALOGUE. 1963. irreg. (in 5 vols.). price varies. Stanley Gibbons Publications Ltd., Unit 5 Parkside, Christchurch Rd., Ringwood, Hamps. BH24 3SH, England. TEL 0425-472363. FAX 0425-470247. index.

769.56 GT ISSN 0046-6549
GUATEMALA FILATELICA. 1932. a. $6. Asociacion Filatelica de Guatemala, Apdo. Postal 39, 01901, Guatemala. Ed. Col. Romeo J. Routhier. adv.; bk.rev.; charts; illus.; stat.; circ. 500.

769.56 US
HAITI PHILATELY. 1975. q. $12 (foreign $15). Haitian Philatelic Society, c/o Dr. Gerald L. Boarino, 834 Pierce St., Port Townsend, WA 98363. circ. 100. Indexed: Stamp J.Ind.

383.2 US ISSN 0072-9981
HANDBOOK ON U S LUMINESCENT STAMPS. 1970. irreg. $6. Alfred G. Boerger, Ed. & Pub., Box 23822, Ft. Lauderdale, FL 33307. TEL 305-563-6590. adv.; bk.rev.; circ. 3,000.

769.56 US
HAWAIIAN PHILATELIST. 1978. irreg. (approx. 6/yr.). $9.95. Los Angeles Stamp Company, c/o Gretchen H. Mitchell, Box 1387, Los Angeles, CA 90078. TEL 213-467-2215. bk.rev.

769.56 UK
HELLENIC PHILATELIC SOCIETY OF GREAT BRITAIN. BULLETIN. 1968. 4/yr. £1.50 per no. Hellenic Philatelic Society of Great Britain, 37 Alders View Drive, East Grinstead, West Sussex RH19 2DN, England. TEL 0342-326782. Ed. W.G. Moseley. adv.; bk.rev.; circ. 220. Indexed: Stamp J.Ind.

769.56 US
HOLLYWOOD PHILATELIST. 1968. m. membership. Hollywood Stamp Club, 2030 Polk St., Hollywood, FL 33929. Ed. Ben Wishnietsky. bk.rev.; circ. 500.

383 769.56 IS ISSN 0333-6875
HOLY LAND POSTAL HISTORY. (Text in English) 1979. q. $18. Society of the Postal History of Eretz-Israel, P.O. Box 10175, Jerusalem 91101, Israel. TEL 02-711719. Eds. E. Glassman, Z. Shimony. adv.; bk.rev.; index; circ. 250. (back issues avail.)

769.56 US
I A S P EXPLORER. 1968. q. $50. International Association of Space Philatelists, Box 6655, FDR Station, New York, NY 10150-1905. TEL 212-691-1031. Eds. Roland Mantovani, Wm. P. York. adv.; bk.rev.; charts; illus.; circ. 525. (back issues avail.)
Description: For collectors of space related stamps, covers and memorabilia.

769.56 US
I C A R NEWSLETTER. 1978. bi-m. $10 membership. Interstate Cinderellans and Revenuers Educational Club, Box 9128, San Jose, CA 95157. TEL 408-996-1147. Ed. Elbert S.A. Hubbard. adv.; bk.rev.; illus.; circ. 100.
Description: Covers revenue and Cinderella stamps issued by the United States and its possessions. Promotes issuance of catalogs and listings.

769.56 US ISSN 0019-1051
ICE CAP NEWS. 1955. bi-m. $17. American Society of Polar Philatelists, c/o S.H. Jacobson, Box 945, Skokie, IL 60077. adv.; bk.rev.; illus.; index, cum.index: vols.1-16, 17-25 (1980); circ. 900. (back issues avail.)

769.56 US
ILLINOIS POSTAL HISTORIAN. 1980. q. $12 to non-members. Illinois Postal History Society, Box 1513, Des Plaines, IL 60017. Ed. Leonard Piszkiewicz. adv.; bk.rev.; circ. 225.

769.56 II
IND DAK; a journal in the English language devoted to philately & postal history. 1977. m. Rs.60($10) 190, Defence Colony, Indiranagar, Bangalore - 560 038, India. TEL 0812-542493. Ed. L.G. Shenoi. adv.; bk.rev.; circ. 2,000.

769.56 UK ISSN 0952-7729
INDIA POST. 1967. q. £12. India Study Circle for Philately, 11 Boston Court, Brownhill Rd., Chandlers Ford, Eastleigh, Hampshire SO5 2EH, England. Ed. Ron Mockford. adv.; bk.rev.; cum.index every 3 yrs.; circ. 700. Indexed: Stamp J.Ind.

769.56 US
INDO-CHINA PHILATELIST. 1970. bi-m. $15 membership. (Society of Indo-China Philatelists) Review Corporation, c/o Paul Blake, 1466 Hamilton Way, San Jose, CA 95125. TEL 213-564-0269. Ed. George E. Demeritte. adv.; bk.rev.; circ. 200. Indexed: Stamp J.Ind.

769.56 US
INFORMER (SAN RAFAEL). 1947. q. $13 membership (foreign $16)(effective 1992). Society of Australasian Specialists - Oceania, Inc., 260 Merrydale Rd., No. 15, San Rafael, CA 94903. TEL 415-472-6429. (Subscr. to: Stuart Levin, Box 24764, San Jose, CA 95154-4764) Ed. Carl L. Stieg. adv.; bk.rev.; circ. 407.
Description: Publishes original articles pertaining to Australasian stamp issues.

769.56 US ISSN 0892-9793
INTERLEAF. 1983. q. $10. Booklet Collectors Club, c/o James Natale, Box 2461, Cinnaminson, NJ 08077-5461. Ed. Gerhard G. Korn. adv.; bk.rev.; circ. 300.
Description: Devoted to the study of worldwide booklets and booklet collecting, with emphasis on United States booklets.

INTERNATIONAL ART POST. see ART

769.56 SZ ISSN 0074-7343
INTERNATIONAL PHILATELIC FEDERATION. GENERAL ASSEMBLY. PROCES-VERBAL. 1973. a. free to members. International Philatelic Federation - Federation Internationale de Philatelie, Zollikerstr. 128, CH-8008 Zurich, Switzerland. FAX 01-3831446. Ed. Ms. M.L. Heiri. circ. 180.

769.56 US
INTERNATIONAL PHILATELIC PRESS CLUB. REPORT TO MEMBERS. 1964. m. membership. International Philatelic Press Club, Inc., Box 114, Jamaica, NY 11419. Ed. Ernest A. Kehr. bk.rev.; circ. 250. (looseleaf format)

769.56 737 GW ISSN 0535-4455
INTERPHILA; international directory of philately and numismatics. (Text in English, French, German) 1963. a. DM.19.80. D B Z-Verlag, Feldstr. 6, P.O. Box 1363, 5408 Nassau, Germany. TEL 02604-701-0. circ. 6,000.

769.56 UK
IRAN PHILATELIC STUDY CIRCLE BULLETIN. 1966. 3/yr. £5. Iran Philatelic Study Circle, Flat 10, One Grand Ave., E. Sussex BN3 2LA, England. Ed. P.A. Greenway. adv.; bk.rev.; circ. 125. (looseleaf format)
Formerly: Persian Study Circle Bulletin.

769.56 IE ISSN 0332-317X
IRISH STAMP NEWS. 1978. q. £9.50($17) Ian Whyte Ltd., 27 Mount St. Upper, Dublin 2, Ireland. TEL 3531-767228. FAX 3531-767229. Ed. Ian W. Whyte. adv.; bk.rev.; illus.; circ. 1,800.

769.56 US
ISRAEL PHILATELIST. 1948. m. membership. Society of Israel Philatelists, 24355 Tunbridge Ln., Beachwood, OH 44122. TEL 216-292-3843. Ed. Oscar Stadtler. adv.; bk.rev.; circ. 2,700. Indexed: Stamp J.Ind.

769.56 UK ISSN 0142-9825
HE6185.I7
ITALY & SWITZERLAND STAMP CATALOGUE. 1980. irreg. price varies. Stanley Gibbons Publications Ltd., Unit 5 Parkside, Christchurch Rd., Ringwood, Hamps. BH24 3SH, England. TEL 0425-472363. FAX 0425-470247.

769.56 US
JACK KNIGHT AIR LOG & A F A NEWS. 1943. q. $15 (foreign $20). Aerophilatelic Federation of the Americas, Box 1239, Elgin, IL 60121-1239. TEL 708-468-0840. (Co-sponsor: Jack Knight Air Mail Society) Ed. Fred L. Wellman. adv.; bk.rev.; bibl.; charts; illus.; stat.; circ. 900. (back issues avail.)
Formerly: A F A News.

769.56 UK ISSN 0142-9906
JAPAN & KOREA STAMP CATALOGUE. 1980. irreg. price varies. Stanley Gibbons Publications Ltd., Unit 5 Parkside, Christchurch Rd., Ringwood, Hamps. BH24 3SH, England. TEL 0425-472363. FAX 0425-470247.

769.56 US ISSN 0146-0994
HE6187
JAPANESE PHILATELY. 1946. bi-m. $11.50 to non-members; members $10. International Society for Japanese Philately, Inc., c/o James E. Jacobson, Office of the Publisher, 815 Springingsguth Rd., Schaumburg, IL 60193. (Subscr. to: Kenneth Kamholz, Sec., Box 1283, Haddonfield, NJ 08033) Ed. Robert M. Spaulding, Jr. adv.; bk.rev.; charts; illus.; index, cum.index; circ. 1,500. (also avail. in microfilm; back issues avail.) Indexed: Stamp J.Ind.
Description: Covers various aspects of the postal system of Japan.

769.56 CC ISSN 0529-0325
JI YOU/CHINESE PHILATELIC MAGAZINE. (Editions in Chinese and English) m., bi-m.(English). $35. Renmin Youdian Chubanshe - People's Post and Telecommunication Publishing House, Dong Chang'an Jie 27, Beijing 100740, People's Republic of China. TEL 8138139. (Dist. in US by: China Books & Periodicals, Inc., 2929 24th St., San Francisco, CA 94110) illus.

769.56 CC
JIYOU BOLAN/PHILATELY VISION. (Text in Chinese) bi-m. $18.50. Beijing Jiyou Xiehui - Beijing Philatelic Society, 5 Nanlishilu Toutiao, Fuxingmenwai, Beijing 100045, People's Republic of China. TEL 8011108. (Dist. in US by: China Books & Periodicals, Inc., 2929 24th St., San Francisco, CA 94110. TEL 415-282-2994) Ed. Wang Lu.

769.56 CC
JIYOU YANJIU/PHILATELY RESEARCH. (Text in Chinese) 1983. q. $16.20. Zhongguo Jiyou Chubanshe, Dong Chang'an Jie 27, Beijing, People's Republic of China. (Dist. in US by: China Books & Periodicals, Inc., 2929 24th St., San Francisco, CA 94110)
Description: Covers the study and collection of Chinese stamps. Includes the theory and practice of stamp collecting, and the history of stamps, stamp collecting, and postal services.

769.56 US
▼**JOURNAL OF BRITISH COMMONWEALTH PHILATELY.** 1992. q. $25($40) Arthur C. Hamm, Inc., Box 11755, Cleveland Park Sta., Washington, DC 20008. TEL 202-362-8600.

769.56 US ISSN 0447-953X
HE6187
JOURNAL OF SPORTS PHILATELY. 1962. bi-m. $10. Sports Philatelists International, c/o Reiss, 322 Riverside Dr., Huron, OH 44839. Ed. John La Porta. adv.; bk.rev.; illus.; stat.; index; circ. 500 (controlled). Indexed: Sportsearch (1977-).

PHILATELY

769.56 US
JUDAICA PHILATELIC JOURNAL. 1963. q. $10 (foreign $13.50). Judaica Historical Philatelic Society, 80 Bruce Ave., Yonkers, NY 10705. Ed. Oscar Stadtler. adv.; bk.rev.; circ. 350.

769.56 GW ISSN 0022-6343
JUNGE SAMMLER; Zeitschrift fuer junge Briefmarkenfreunde. 1961. bi-m. DM.17. Deutsche Philatelisten Jugend e.V., Postfach 3968, 5500 Trier, Germany. Ed. Heinz Wenz. adv.; bk.rev.; illus.; circ. 13,000.

769.56 US
KANSAS PRECANCEL NEWS. 1941. bi-m. $4. Kansas Precancel Society, Box 1335, Wichita, KS 67201. Ed. Dilmond D. Postlewait. adv.; circ. 300.
    Description: Contains articles on precancelled stamps and covers activities of the society.

769.56 US
KEYSTONER. 1947. 10/yr. membership (typically set in Jan.). Western Pennsylvania Precancel Society, 119 W. Sanner St., Somerset, PA 15501. TEL 814-445-7341. (Alt. Ed. addr.: 220 Grandview Blvd., Butler, PA 16001. TEL 412-287-3532) Ed. Harold C. Bartlett. bk.rev.; circ. 175.
    Description: Describes precancelled stamps of Pennsylvania.

769.56 JA
KITTE SHUMI. vol.91, 1980. 12/yr. 42 Yen($20) Kitte Shumi-sha, 3-12-28 Mejiro, Toshima-ku, Tokyo, Japan.

769.56 NE
KOERIER; het postzegelblad voor de jeugd. 1945. m. fl.7.50($10) Drukkerij-Uitgeverij de Courier, Box 24, Putten 2950, Netherlands. Ed. G. Huisman. adv.; bk.rev.; bibl.; illus.; circ. 800.
    Formerly: Postiljon.

769.56 US
KOREAN PHILATELY. 1952. q. $15 membership. Korea Stamp Society, Inc., c/o Forrest W. Calkins, Secretary-Treasurer, Box 1057, Grand Junction, CO 81502. TEL 303-243-1179. (Editorial addr.: Box 366, Winter Park, FL, 32790) Ed. James W. Kerr. adv.; circ. 400. *Indexed:* Stamp J.Ind.

769.56 059 KN ISSN 0452-5914
KOREAN STAMPS.* (Text in English) no.62, 1974. m. Philatelists Union of the Democratic People's Republic of Korea, Pyongyang, North Korea. charts; illus.

769.56 CN
LATIN AMERICAN POST. 1976. q. $15. Latin American Philatelic Society, P.O. Box 6420, Hinton, Alta. T7V 1X7, Canada. Ed. Piet Steen. adv.; bk.rev.; circ. 250. (looseleaf format) *Indexed:* Stamp J.Ind.
    Description: Studies Latin American philately and postal history.

769.56 US
LATVIAN COLLECTOR. 1974. 3/yr. $8.50. Box 5403, San Mateo, CA 94402. Ed. Maris Tirums. circ. 200. (back issues avail.)

769.56 US
LIBERIAN PHILATELIC SOCIETY JOURNAL. 1979. q. $8. (Liberian Philatelic Society) Roy P. Mackal, Ed. & Pub., 9027 S. Oakley Ave., Chicago, IL 60620. TEL 312-238-6516. adv.; circ. 85. (back issues avail.)
    Formerly (until Fall 1988): Liberian Philatelic Society Newsletter.
    Description: Notes and articles on the activities and issues of interest to members of this stamp collector's association.

769.56 US
LILAC HINGE. m. membership. Inland Empire Philatelic Society, N. 10710 Nelson Rd., Spokane, WA 99218. Ed. Maude P. Wilson.

769.56 US ISSN 0161-6234
HE6187
LINN'S STAMP NEWS. 1928. w. $33. Amos Press Inc., Box 29, Sidney, OH 45365. TEL 513-498-0801. FAX 513-498-0814. Ed. Michael Laurence. adv.; bk.rev.; charts; illus.; stat.; circ. 75,000. (newspaper; also avail. in microform from UMI) *Indexed:* Stamp J.Ind.
    Formerly: Linn's Weekly Stamp News (ISSN 0024-4104)
    Description: Weekly news magazine for the philatelist and stamp dealer.

769.56 US ISSN 0146-6887
HE6194
LINN'S WORLD STAMP ALMANAC. 1978. irreg., 5th ed. $19.95. (Linn's Stamp News) Amos Press Inc., Box 29, Sidney, OH 45365. TEL 513-498-0801. FAX 513-498-0814.

769.56 US
LITHUANIAN PHILATELIC SOCIETY OF NEW YORK. BULLETIN. 1954. q. $9. Lithuanian Philatelic Society of New York, c/o J.J. Norton, Ed., Box 432, Syosset, NY 11791. TEL 516-364-1279. circ. 200. (back issues avail.)

769.56 UK ISSN 0024-6131
LONDON PHILATELIST. 1892. 10/yr. £35. Royal Philatelic Society, 41 Devonshire Place, London W1N 1PE, England. TEL 071-486-1044. FAX 071-486-0803. Ed. George E. Barker. adv.; bk.rev.; bibl.; illus.; index; cum.index: vols.1-77; circ. 1,700. (back issues avail.) *Indexed:* Stamp J.Ind. —BLDSC shelfmark: 5294.045000.

769.56 383 UK
LONDON POSTAL HISTORY GROUP NOTEBOOK. 1971. 5/yr. £7. London Postal History Group, 64 Gordon Road, Carshalton Beeches, Surrey SM5 3RE, England. Ed. Peter Forrestier Smith. bk.rev.; illus.; index; circ. 200. (back issues avail.)

769.56 US
LONG ISLAND POSTAL HISTORY SOCIETY JOURNAL.* 1980. s-a. $15. Long Island Postal History Society, 1 SE 3rd Ave., No. 2900, Miami, FL 33131-1718. Ed. J. Fred Rodriguez. adv.; bk.rev.; circ. 100.

769.56 US
LUNDY COLLECTORS CLUB PHILATELIC QUARTERLY. 1979. q. $10. Lundy Collectors Club, 2021 Ridge Rd., Homewood, IL 60430. Ed. Roger S. Cichorz. bk.rev.; circ. 245.

769.56 US ISSN 0739-0025
LUREN. 1969. m. $10. Scandinavian Philatelic Library of Southern California, Box 741639, Los Angeles, CA 90004-9639. TEL 714-626-1764. Ed. Paul Nelson. adv.; bk.rev.; index; circ. 250.

769.56 US
M C S C C ON COVER. 1957. m. membership. Motor City Stamp and Cover Club, 22608 Poplar Ct., Hazel Park, MI 48030. Ed. Robert Quintero. adv.; circ. 150.

769.56 US
MACHINE CANCEL FORUM.* 1974. m. free. 7 Hillside Rd., No. D, Greenbelt, MD 20770-1754. Eds. John R. McGee, John Koontz. bk.rev.; circ. 300. (back issues avail.)

769.56 NZ ISSN 0542-0997
MAIL-COACH. 1964. 6/yr. NZ.$30. Postal History Society of New Zealand, Inc., P.O. Box 99673, Newmarket, Auckland 1130, New Zealand. Ed. J. Campbell. adv.; bk.rev.; circ. 500.

769.56 US ISSN 0734-905X
HE6185.T94
MANEAPA. 1978. q. membership. Tuvalu and Kiribati Philatelic Society, Box 1209, Temple Hills, MD 20757. Ed. F. Caprio. adv.; bk.rev.; circ. 225. *Indexed:* Stamp J.Ind.
    Formerly: Tuvalu Hi-Spots.

769.56 UK ISSN 0951-5283
MAPLE LEAVES. 1946. 5/yr. £9.50 (typically set in Oct.). Canadian Philatelic Society of Great Britain, c/o D.F. Sessions, Ed., 36 The Chimes, Nailsea, Bristol BS19 2NH, England. (Subscr. to: c/o B.T. Stalker, Glaramara, Upper Bryn Coch, Mold, Clwyd CH7 1XX, England) adv.; bk.rev.; circ. 560 (controlled).
    Description: Articles concerning philately and postal history of British North America.

769.56 US
MASSACHUSETTS SPY. 1975. bi-m. $7 (effective Jan. 1992). Massachusetts Postal Research Society, Box 202, North Abington, MA 02351. TEL 617-878-4446. Ed. Robert S. Borden. adv.; bk.rev.; charts; illus.; stat.; cum.index: 1975-1991; circ. 90. (looseleaf format; back issues avail.)
    Description: Postal history research of Massachusetts.

769.56 US
MAXIMAPHILY. 1980. q. $7. Maximum Card Study Unit, c/o Edward Cramer, 4702 D Main St., Skokie, IL 60076. TEL 708-679-7356. Ed. Gary Denis. adv.; bk.rev.; illus.; circ. 150. (looseleaf format)
    Description: For both advanced and beginning collectors; covers the collecting of maximum cards, which are picture postcards with a postage stamp of the same design affixed to and cancelled on the picture side.

769.56 US ISSN 0025-8857
HE6187
MEKEEL'S STAMP NEWS. 1891. w. $15. Philatelic Communications Corp., Box 5050, White Plains, NY 10602. TEL 914-997-7261. Ed. John F. Dunn. adv.; bk.rev.; illus.mkt.; circ. 5,000. (tabloid format)
    Description: Contains news and features for serious stamp collectors.

769.56 US
MERCHANTVILLE STAMP CLUB. MONTHLY BULLETIN. 1932. m. $5. Merchantville Stamp Club, Box 2913, Cherry Hill, NJ 08034. Ed. Paul Schumacher. adv.; bk.rev.; circ. 130.

769.56 US
MIASMA PHILATELIST. 1979. q. membership. Malaria Philatelists International, Box 226, Froid, MT 59226. Ed. Mike Birrer. adv.; bk.rev.; index; circ. 200.

769.56 GW ISSN 0076-7727
MICHEL-BRIEFMARKEN-KATALOGE. 1910. a. and irreg. price varies. Schwaneberger Verlag GmbH, Muthmannstr. 4, D-8000 Munich 45, Germany.

769.56 GW ISSN 0026-198X
MICHEL-RUNDSCHAU. 1957. 12/yr. DM.35.40. Schwaneberger Verlag GmbH, Muthmannstr. 4, 8000 Munich 45, Germany. Ed. Hans Hohenester. adv.; bk.rev.; circ. 62,000.

769.56 US
MICHIANA PHILATELIST. vol.30, 1981. m. $5. Northern Indiana Philatelic Society, Box 393, Mishawaka, IN 46544. TEL 219-288-3751. Ed. Howard Wallace. bk.rev.; circ. 120.

769.56 UK ISSN 0142-9914
MIDDLE EAST STAMP CATALOGUE. 1980. irreg. price varies. Stanley Gibbons Publications Ltd., Unit 5 Parkside, Christchurch Rd., Ringwood, Hamps. BH24 3SH, England. TEL 0425-472363. FAX 0425-470247.

769.56 NE ISSN 0026-3605
MIJN STOKPAARDJE; maandblad voor filatelisten. 1945. m. fl.62.50. B.V. Uitgeverij "de Postiljon", P.O. Box 15041, 3501 BA Utrecht, Netherlands. TEL 030-717988. Ed.Bd. adv.; bk.rev.; illus.; circ. 10,000.

769.56 US
MITCHELL REPORT. m. $18.50. Los Angeles Stamp Company, c/o Gretchen H. Mitchell, Ed., Box 1387, Los Angeles, CA 90078. TEL 213-467-2215.

769.56 FR ISSN 0026-9387
MONDE DES PHILATELISTES; officiel de la philatelie. 1951. m. 215 F. Monde, 5 rue Antoine Bourdelle, 75015 Paris, France. TEL 40-65-25-25. (Subscr. to: Immeuble Sirius, 1 place Hubert-Beuve-Mery, 94852 Ivry-sur-Seine Cedex, France. TEL 49-60-32-90) Ed. M. Adalbert Vitalyos. adv.; charts; illus.; circ. 48,568.

MONEY TALKS. see *NUMISMATICS*

769.56 US
MUSEUM POST RIDER. 1959. m. $20. Cardinal Spellman Philatelic Museum, Inc., 235 Wellesey St., Weston, MA 02193. TEL 617-894-6735. FAX 617-894-8056. Ed. T.G. Kudzma. adv.; bk.rev.; charts; illus.; circ. 750. (back issues avail.)

769.56 US
N Y EESTI FILATELISTIDE SELTSI BULLETAAN. 1971. s-a. membership. Estonian Philatelic Society (New York), 243 E. 34th St., New York, NY 10016. FAX 212-643-1903. Ed. Rudolf Hamar. circ. 300. (looseleaf format; back issues avail.)

769.56 GW
NAVICULA. 1959. bi-m. S M S Navicula e.V., Fennstr. 34, 1000 Berlin 65, Germany. TEL 030-4624255. (back issues avail.)

796.56 GW
NEDERLAND ONDER DE LOEP. (Text in German) irreg. (2-3/yr.) DM.30 membership. Bund Deutscher Philatelisten e.V., Arbeitsgemeinschaft Niederlande e.V., Brunhildstr. 2, 5030 Huerth, Germany. TEL 02233-76587. FAX 02233-73728. circ. 150. (back issues avail.)
Description: Covers all aspects of Dutch philately.

769.56 US
NETHERLANDS PHILATELY JOURNAL. 1975. q. $10 includes Newsletter. American Society for Netherlands Philately, 2354 Roan Lane, Walnut Creek, CA 94596. TEL 415-934-4030. Ed. Paul E. van Reyen. adv.; bk.rev.; circ. 400. **Indexed:** Stamp J.Ind.

769.56 UK
▼**NEW ZEALAND CONCISE STAMP CATALOGUE.** 1990. irreg. price varies. Stanley Gibbon Publications Ltd., Unit 5 Parkside, Christchurch Rd., Ringwood, Hamps. BH24 3SH, England. TEL 0425-472363. FAX 0425-470247. Ed. David Aggersberg.

769.56 NZ ISSN 0112-5443
NEW ZEALAND STAMP COLLECTOR. 1919. q. NZ.$35. Royal Philatelic Society of New Zealand, Box 1269, Wellington, New Zealand. Ed. B.G. Vincent. adv.; bk.rev.; circ. 1,000.

769.56 NZ ISSN 0028-8721
NEW ZEALAND STAMP MONTHLY. 1968. m. NZ.$9. Len Jury Ltd., P.O. Box 174, New Plymouth, New Zealand. bk.rev.; circ. 2,000. (tabloid format)

769.56 US
NEWS OF HUNGARIAN PHILATELY. 1970. q. membership. Society for Hungarian Philately, Box 1162, Samp-Mortar Sta., Fairfield, CT 06430. Ed. Csaba Kohalmi. bk.rev.; circ. 250. **Indexed:** Stamp J.Ind.

769.56 US ISSN 0078-091X
NOBLE OFFICIAL CATALOG OF CANADA PRECANCELS.* 1923. irreg., 13th ed., 1981. $3. Gilbert W. Noble, Ed. & Pub., 1111 S. Lakemont Ave., Ste. 805, Winter Park, FL 32792. circ. 2,000.

769.56 US ISSN 0078-0928
NOBLE OFFICIAL CATALOG OF UNITED STATES BUREAU PRECANCELS.* 1926. irreg. $6. Gilbert W. Noble, Ed. & Pub., 1111 S. Lakemont Ave., Ste.805, Winter Park, FL 32792. circ. 1,000.

769.56 SW ISSN 0029-134X
NORDISK FILATELI. 1937. m. (10/yr.). SEK 215($35) Nordisk Filateli AB, Box 141, 182 12 Danderyd, Sweden. Ed. Sven Olof Forselius. adv.; bk.rev.; circ. 10,000.
Supersedes in part: Skandinaviska Mynt Magasinet; Which was formerly: Skandanavisk Numismatik (ISSN 0346-0479)

NORDISK FILATELI MED MYNT - MAGAZINET. see NUMISMATICS

769.56 DK ISSN 0903-3440
NORDISK FILATELISTISK TIDSSKRIFT. 1894. 4/yr. DKK 180. Koebenhavns Philatelist Klub, Postboks 3, DK-1001 Copenhagen K, Denmark. FAX 33-326632. Ed. Max Meedom. adv.; bk.rev.; circ. 1,050.

736 DK ISSN 0105-9106
NORDISK JULEMAERKE KATALOG; Nordic Christmas seal catalogue. (Text in Danish) 1977. biennial. DKK 195. Marielystvej 52, st., t.h., DK-2000 Frederiksberg, Denmark. TEL 01-88-12-78. Ed. Joergen Christoffersen.

769.56 NO
NORSK FILATELISTISK TIDSSKRIFT. Title varies: N F T. 10/yr. NOK 155($9) or membership in affiliated societies in Norway. Norsk Filatelistforbund, Postboks 2517, 7001 Trondheim, Norway. Ed. Tor Skauge. adv.; bk.rev.; illus.; stat.; index; circ. 7,600.

769.56 US
NORTH SHORE PHILATELIC SOCIETY. BULLETIN. m. membership. North Shore Philatelic Society, c/o Philip Tully, Treas., Box 11580, Chicago, IL 60611.

NOTIZIARIO STORICO NUMISMATICO FILATELICO. see NUMISMATICS

769.56 SA ISSN 1016-6734
O F S PHILATELIC MAGAZINE. 1951. m. R.1.80. Orange Free State Philatelic Society, The Secretary, P.O. Box 702, Bloemfontein 9300, South Africa. FAX 051-366727. Ed. J.A. Van Beukering. adv.; bk.rev.; circ. 250.

769.56 UK ISSN 0267-8071
O P A L JOURNAL. 1949. q. £8 (foreign £10). Oriental Philatelic Association of London, c/o Jeff Ertughrul, Ed., 62 Leopold Rd., E. Finchley, London N2 8BG, England. (Subscr. to: B. Orhan, Treas., 9 Chiltern Ave., Bushey, Herts, England) adv.; bk.rev.; circ. 300. (back issues avail.)
Description: Papers, informational articles, exchange listings, and historical sketches pertaining to stamp collectors of philately of the Ottoman Empire.

769.56 US
OHIO POSTAL HISTORY JOURNAL.* 1978. q. $2.50 per no. Ohio Postal History Society, Inc., 2848 Seaman Road, Oregon, OH 43616. Ed. George J. Ball. adv.; bk.rev.; circ. 300.

769.56 US
ORANGE COUNTY STAMP NEWS. 1931? m. membership. Orange County Philatelic Society, c/o Ron Weiner, Ed., 1020 W. Oakcrest, Brea, CA 92621-1829. adv.; circ. 150.

769.56 US ISSN 0892-5208
OREGON POSTAL HISTORY JOURNAL. 1981. q. $7.50. Oregon Postal History Society, Box 135, Lake Oswego, OR 97034. Ed. Leonard Lukens. bk.rev.; circ. 100. (back issues avail.)

769.56 IT
OSSERVATORE FILATELICO. m. Piazza Italia 5, 20093 Cologno Monzese, Italy. Ed. Rolando Gianni.

769.56 US ISSN 0737-0954
HE6185.C67
OXCART. 1960. q. $12. Society of Costa Rica Collectors, Box 8308, Wichita, KS 67208. Ed. Hal T. Edwards. adv.; bk.rev.; circ. 275. **Indexed:** Stamp J.Ind.

769.56 CN ISSN 0714-8305
P H S C JOURNAL. 1972. q. membership. Philaprint Inc., Box 203-1139 Sutnerland Ave., Kelowna, B.C. V1Y 5Y2, Canada. (Subscr. to: R.F. Narbonne, 216 Mailey Dr., Carleton Place, Ont. K7C 3X9, Canada) Ed. Robert A. Lee. adv.; bk.rev.; illus.; circ. 600. **Indexed:** Biol.Abstr., Stamp J.Ind.
Former titles: Postal History Society of Canada. Journal (ISSN 0703-5365); Postal Histo-Mine.
Description: Articles and research papers on all facets of postal history of Canada.

769.56 US ISSN 1041-4894
P M C C BULLETIN. 1947. m. (11/yr.). $12.50. Post Mark Collectors Club, c/o David H. Proulx, 7629 Homestead Dr., Baldwinsville, NY 13027. TEL 315-638-0532. (Subscr. to: c/o Robert J. Milligan, 23381 Greenleaf Blvd., Elkhart, IN 46514-4504) Ed. Kevin M. Tanzillo. adv.; illus.; circ. 950.
Description: Articles on the hobby of postmark collecting. Covers current developments and historical information to aid collectors.

796.56 US
P M C C MEMBERSHIP ROSTER. 1947. triennial. membership. Post Mark Collectors Club, c/o David H. Proulx, 7629 Homestead Dr., Baldwinville, NY 13027. TEL 315-638-0532. (Subscr. to: c/o Robert J. Milligan, 23381 Greenleaf Blvd., Elkhart, IN 46514-4504) circ. 1,500.
Description: Provides historic information on the club and its services. Lists names and addresses of members.

P S (WYNANTSKILL); a quarterly journal of postal history. see COMMUNICATIONS — Postal Affairs

769.56 UK
P T S NEWS. 1947. bi-m. membership. Philatelic Traders Society Ltd., British Philatelic Centre, 107, Charterhouse St., London EC1M 6PT, England. TEL 071-490-1005. FAX 071-253-0414. Ed. Derek J. Yardley. adv.; bk.rev.; bibl.; circ. controlled. (tabloid format)
Formerly: P T S Journal (ISSN 0048-3729)

769.56 UK ISSN 0306-0896
PACIFICA. 1962. q. £6($10) Pacific Islands Study Circle of Great Britain, 73 Neville Rd., Shirley, Solihull B90 2QN, England. Ed. B.A. Jones. adv.; bk.rev.; circ. 450. (back issues avail.) **Indexed:** Stamp J.Ind.

769.56 PK ISSN 0078-8422
PAKISTAN POSTAGE STAMPS. (Text in English) 1960. irreg., latest 1966. Rs.1.50. Post Office Department, Karachi, Pakistan. adv.; circ. 6,000.

769.56 US
PANTOGRAPH OF POSTAL STATIONERY. bi-m. $6 to non-members. United Postal Stationery Society, Box 48, Redlands, CA 92373. **Indexed:** Stamp J.Ind.

769.56 US
PASTE-UP. vol.33, 1981. m. $5 includes membership. Cedar Rapids Stamp Club, Box 2554, Cedar Rapids, IA 52406. Ed. Jon White. circ. 50 (controlled).
Description: Club meeting notices.

769.56 MY
PEMUNGUT SETEM MALAYSIA/MALAYSIAN PHILATELIST. 1970. q. membership (M.$20). Philatelic Society of Malaysia, P.O. Box 10588 GPO, 50718 Kuala Lumpur, Malaysia. Ed. C. Nagarajah. adv.; bk.rev.; circ. 800.

769.56 US
PENINSULAR PHILATELIST. 1951. q. $5. Peninsular State Philatelic Society, Box 80946, Lansing, MI 48908. Ed. William C. Allen. adv.; bk.rev.; illus.; circ. 150.
Description: Provides data on the collecting scene in Michigan. Acts as a clearinghouse for stamp exhibition dates.

769.56 US ISSN 8750-1627
PERFINS BULLETIN. 1945. m. $7. Perfins Club, c/o John F. Lyding, Ed., Box 3342, Crofton, MD 21114-3342. adv.; bk.rev.; illus.; tr.lit.; circ. 1,000. (looseleaf format) **Indexed:** Stamp J.Ind.

769.56 US
PERMIT PATTER. vol.3, 1981. bi-m. Herbert H. Harrington, Box 585, Vienna, OH 44473. Ed. Helen McGinley.

769.56 US ISSN 0279-3709
THE PETRO-PHILATELIST. 1974. q. $9 (foreign $11). Petroleum Philatelic Society International, 1740 S.W. 84 Ave., Hollywood, FL 33025-2127. Ed. Feitze Papa. adv.; circ. 225.
Description: Covers topics of interest to collectors of petroleum-related postage stamps.

769.56 US
PHAROS (NORTHVILLE). 1973. m. $10 (foreign $15). Lighthouse Study Unit, 19735 Scenic Harbour Dr., Northville, MI 48167-1979. Ed. Gary J. Kurylo. bk.rev.; charts; illus.; stat.; circ. 270. (looseleaf format; back issues avail.)
Description: Presents lighthouses on stamps: covers, cancels and postmarks.

769.56 GW
PHILA-LUPE; international advertiser for worldwide stamp exchange. (Text in English, German) 1982. 3/yr. DM.15($10) Phila-Lupe, Milkdelle 26, 4300 Essen 1, Germany. Ed. Rainer Volkenborn. adv.; circ. 1,000.
Description: Promotes exchange of stamps and information worldwide.

769.56 737 GW ISSN 0720-2245
PHILA-REPORT; die Sammlerfreundliche Briefmarkenzeitung. 1980. m. DM.12($18) Allpress-Verlagsgesellschaft mbH & Co., 5410 Hoehr-Grenzhausen, P.O. Box 1452, Rheinstr. 41, Germany. Ed. Linus Wittich. circ. 22,000. (tabloid format)

PHILATELY

769.56 US
PHILAMATH; a journal of mathematical philately. 1979. q. $5. American Topical Association, Mathematics Study Unit, c/o M. Strauss, 4209 88th St., Lubbock, TX 79423-2941. TEL 806-798-2688. (Subscr. to: 135 Witherspoon Ct., Athens, GA 30606) (Co-sponsor: American Philatelic Society) Ed. Randy Woodward. adv.; circ. 125. (looseleaf format; back issues avail.)

769.56 AT ISSN 0725-2323
PHILAS NEWS. 1972. 4/yr. Aus.$5 membership. Philatelic Association of New South Wales, P.O. Box A495, Sydney South, N.S.W. 2000, Australia. bk.rev.; circ. 500.

769.56 US ISSN 0739-6198
PHILATELI-GRAPHICS. 1976. q. $5 (foreign $8). Graphics Philately Association, Box 1513, Thousand Oaks, CA 91358. Ed. Dulcie M. Apgar. bk.rev.; illus.; index, cum.index: 1976-1982 in no.24; circ. 100. (back issues avail.)
   Description: For people interested in printing and graphic arts of and on postage stamps and other philatelic items of the world.

769.56 US ISSN 1041-2999
PHILATELIA CHIMICA ET PHYSICA. 1979. q. $8 (foreign $9). (Chemistry and Physics on Stamps Study Unit) C P O S S U, 13 Roxbury Dr., Athens, OH 45701. TEL 614-593-3729. Ed. D.G. Hendricker. bk.rev.; index; circ. 260. (back issues avail.)
   Formerly: Philatelia Chimica.

769.56 KE
PHILATELIC BULLETIN. (Text in English) 1977; N.S. 1979. q. free. Kenya Posts and Telecommunications Corporation, Kenya Stamp Bureau, P.O. Box 30368, Nairobi, Kenya. TEL 27401-2158. TELEX 22245 IJIR POSTS. circ. 3,000.

769.56 US
PHILATELIC COMMUNICATOR. 1968. q. $10. American Philatelic Society, Writers Unit No. 30, Box 3568, Jackson, MS 39207. (Subscr. to: 2501 Drexel St., Vienna, VA 22180) Ed. Ken Lawrence. adv.; bk.rev.; circ. 850.
   Formerly (until 1987): A.P.S. Writers Unit Number Thirty News Bulletin (ISSN 0147-3646)

769.56 658.048 US ISSN 0892-032X
PHILATELIC EXHIBITOR. 1986. q. membership. American Association of Philatelic Exhibitors, c/o Steven Rod, Sec., Box 432, South Orange, NJ 07079. Ed. John M. Hotchner. adv.; bk.rev.; circ. 1,300. (back issues avail.)
   Description: A forum for debate and information on philatelic exhibiting, judging, and exhibition administration. Offers encouragement to novices.

769.56 UK ISSN 0031-7381
THE PHILATELIC EXPORTER; world's greatest stamp trade journal. 1945. m. £22. Philatelic Exporter Ltd., P.O. Box 137, Hatfield, Hertfordshire AL10 9DB, England. TEL 0707-266331. FAX 0707-274782. Ed. Graham R. Phillips. adv.; bk.rev.; bibl.; charts; illus.; stat.; tr.lit.; circ. 4,000.
   Incorporating: Coin and Note Dealer; Philatelic Trader.

796.56 US ISSN 0196-5034
PHILATELIC FOUNDATION QUARTERLY. 1983. q. $30. Philatelic Foundation, 21 E. 40th St., New York, NY 10016. TEL 212-889-6483. FAX 212-447-5258. Ed. Harlan F. Stone. adv.; bk.rev.; charts; illus.; circ. 1,700. (back issues avail.)
   Formerly: Philatelic Foundation Bulletin.
   Description: Presents articles and opinions about the foundation's committee, its reference collections, research library, the educational programs, and its publications.

793 US
PHILATELIC GUILD'S INVESTMENT NEWSLETTER. 1975. m. $10. Philatelic Guild, Box 798, Lakewood, NJ 08701.

769.56 NE
PHILATELIC LITERATURE NEWS. (Text in English) 1970. 4/yr. fl.15($10) (effective Jan. 1992). P L N International, c/o C. Nieuwland, Postbus 8042, 3009 AA Rotterdam, Netherlands. bk.rev.; circ. 400.
   Formerly: Philabook International.
   Description: Information on new worldwide philatelic literature.

769.56 US ISSN 0270-1707
PHILATELIC LITERATURE REVIEW. 1942. q. $12 to individuals; institutions $30. American Philatelic Research Library, Box 8338, State College, PA 16803. TEL 814-237-3803. Ed. William L. Welch Jr. adv.; bk.rev.; cum.index 1942-1970; circ. 2,750.
   —BLDSC shelfmark: 6449.647500.

769.56 US ISSN 0273-5598
PHILATELIC OBSERVER. 1963. bi-m. $9. Junior Philatelists of America, Inc., Box 557, Boalsburg, PA 16827. Ed. Karen Weigt. adv.; bk.rev.; illus.; circ. 1,000.
   Description: Forum covering the latest news on stamp collecting and other related activities. Provides information to enhance the experience of youngsters.

769.56 US
PHILATELIC PROSPECTOR. m. Sacramento Philatelic Society, Box 13284, Sacramento, CA 95813.

769.56 UK ISSN 0265-2641
PHILATELIC QUILL. 1982. q. £10 membership. Philatelic Writers Society, 138 Chastilian Rd., Dartford, Kent DA1 3LG, England. TEL 0322-270361. (Subscr. to: A.P. Berry, 24 Irwin Rd., Guildford, Surrey GU2 5PP, England) bk.rev.; index; circ. 150. (back issues avail.)

769.56 TR
PHILATELIC SOCIETY OF T & T BULLETIN. 1946. q. $10. Philatelic Society of Trinidad & Tobago, P.O. Box 596, Port-of-Spain, Trinidad & Tobago, W.I. TEL 809-622-1673. FAX 809-632-2759. Ed. John Chay. adv.; bk.rev.; circ. 250. (processed)
   Formerly: Trinidad Philatelic Society Bulletin.

769.56 NE ISSN 0166-3437
PHILATELIE; Nederlandsch maandblad voor philatelie. 1922. m. fl.36. Stichting Nederlandsch Maandblad voor Philatelie, c/o G. van der Velden, Marshallplein 145, 2286 LL Rijswijk, Netherlands. Ed. A. Knikman. adv.; bk.rev.; illus.; index; circ. 55,000.
   Formerly: Nederlandsch Maandblad voor Philatelie (ISSN 0028-2081)

769.56 GW
PHILATELIE. 1949. bi-m. membership. Bund Deutscher Philatelisten e.V., Mainzer Landstr. 221-223, 6000 Frankfurt a.M. 1, Germany. FAX 02163-30003. Ed. Wolfgang Maassen. adv.; bk.rev.; circ. 85,000.
   Formerly: Philatelie Bundesnachrichten.

769.56 FR ISSN 0183-3634
PHILATELIE FRANCAISE. 1952. m. 155 F. Federation des Societes Philateliques Francaises, 7 rue Saint-Lazare, 75009 Paris, France. TEL 42-85-50-25. Ed. Raymond Duxin. adv.; bk.rev.; charts; illus.; index; circ. 20,000.

769.56 CN
PHILATELIE QUEBEC. (Text in French) 1969. 10/yr. Can.$28($35) (Federation Quebecoise de Philatelie) Editions Phibec Inc., 4545 Ave. Pierre de Coubertin, C.P. 1000, Succ. M, Montreal, Que. H1V 3R2, Canada. TEL 514-252-3035. FAX 514-251-8038. Ed. F. Brisse. adv.; illus.; circ. 6,500. **Indexed**: Pt.de.Rep. (1983-).
   Formerly: Philatelie au Quebec (ISSN 0381-7547)

769.56 US
PHILATELION. 1962. 10/yr. $25. Lions Philatelic Unit, 1521 Grandview Blvd., Kissimmee, FL 34744-6616. TEL 407-870-0022. Ed. Anton K. Dekom. adv.; circ. 350. (looseleaf format; back issues avail.)

769.56 UK ISSN 0260-6739
HE6187
PHILATELIST AND PHILATELIC JOURNAL OF GREAT BRITAIN. 1866. 4/yr. £12($40) (Europe £15; elsewhere £28). Premier House, Hinton Rd., Bournemouth BH1 2EF, England. TEL 0202-299277. Ed. Robson Lowe. adv.; bk.rev.; charts; illus.; mkt.; tr.lit.; index; circ. 3,500. (also avail. in microform from UMI; reprint service avail. from UMI) **Indexed**: Stamp J.Ind.
   —BLDSC shelfmark: 6449.667000.
   Formed by the 1981 merger of: Philatelist (ISSN 0031-7373); P J G B (ISSN 0030-8048)
   Description: Describes famous collections and new discoveries.

769.56 AT ISSN 0031-7403
PHILATELY FROM AUSTRALIA; a chronicle of Australasian stamps and their collectors. 1949. q. Aus.$7.50($12) Royal Philatelic Society of Victoria, Box 2071, Melbourne, Victoria 3001, Australia. Ed. H.L. Chisholm. adv.; bk.rev.; charts; illus.; index, cum.index: 1949-1958, 1959-1968; circ. 400. **Indexed**: Stamp J.Ind.

769.56 JA
PHILATELY IN JAPAN. (Text in English) 1977. q. 2000 Yen. Japan Philatelic Society Foundation, Box 1, Shinjuku, Tokyo 163-91, Japan.

769.56 US
PHILATEX.* vol.86, 1982. m. free. San Antonio Philatelic Association, c/o Patricia Cote, 3807 E. Songbird Ln., San Antonio, TX 78229-2603. circ. 220.

769.56 794.1 FR
PHILEMAT. 1986. 4/yr. $20. 10 rue A. Pluchet, 92220 Bagneux, France. Ed. Claude Geiger. bk.rev.
   Description: Devoted to the collection of chess stamps and philately.

769.56 GR ISSN 0031-8264
PHILOTELIA; bimonthly specialized philatelic magazine. (Text in English, French, Greek) 1924. bi-m. $20. Hellenic Philotelic Society, 57 Akademias St., GR-106 79 Athens, Greece. TEL 3621-125. Ed. T. Papaeliou. adv.; bk.rev.; abstr.; bibl.; charts; illus.; stat.; index, cum.index: 1924-1953; 1954-1973; 1974-1983; circ. 1,000. (also avail. in microfiche)
   ●Also available online.

769.56 US
PITCAIRN LOG. 1973. q. $10 membership. (Pitcairn Islands Study Group) Everett L. Parker, Ed. & Pub., Box 1306, Greenville, ME 04441-1306. adv.; bk.rev.; circ. 500. **Indexed**: Stamp J.Ind.

769.55 AT ISSN 0155-6215
POCKET AUSTRALIAN STAMP CATALOGUE. 1970. a. Aus.$4.95. Seven Seas Stamps Pty. Ltd., 62 Wingewarra St., Dubbo, N.S.W. 2830, Australia. Ed. D. Foster. illus.; circ. 35,000.
   Description: Simplified catalog of Australian Commonwealth stamps issued from 1913 to the present. Includes current retail values for mint and used specimens.

769.56 US
POCONO MT. NEWS.* bi-m. membership. Pocono Mt. Philatelic Society, c/o Zellers, 350 Sproat Ave., Freedom, PA 15042.

769.56 DK ISSN 0032-4418
POPULAER FILATELI. 1938. m. DKK 225($26) Aarhus Frimaerkehandel, Bruunsgade 42, 8000 Aarhus C, Denmark. Ed. Inger Andersen. adv.; bk.rev.; illus.; mkt.; circ. 4,000.

794 US ISSN 0892-5178
PORTU-INFO. 1961. q. $10 (foreign $15). International Society for Portuguese Philately, Box 1916, Philadelphia, PA 19105. TEL 215-843-2106. FAX 215-787-1532. Ed. Stephen S. Washburne. adv.; bk.rev.; illus.; tr.lit.; index; circ. 450. **Indexed**: Stamp J.Ind.

769.56 UK ISSN 0142-9833
PORTUGAL & SPAIN STAMP CATALOGUE. 1980. irreg. price varies. Stanley Gibbons Publications Ltd., Unit 5 Parkside, Christchurch Rd., Ringwood, Hamps. BH24 3SH, England. TEL 0425-472363. FAX 0425-470247.

769.56 US ISSN 0164-6184
POSSESSIONS. 1978. q. $10. United States Possessions Philatelic Society, c/o W.T. Zuehlke, Sec.-Treas., 8100 Willow Steam Dr., Sandy, UT 84093. Ed. Gilbert N. Plass. adv.; bk.rev.; circ. 600. **Indexed**: Stamp J.Ind.

LA POSTA; a journal of American postal history. see COMMUNICATIONS — Postal Affairs

769.56 NZ
POSTAGE STAMPS OF NEW ZEALAND. irreg. Royal Philatelic Society of New Zealand, Box 1269, Wellington, New Zealand.

PHILATELY

383.2   US
POSTAL SERVICE GUIDE TO U S STAMPS. 1927. a. $5.95. U.S. Postal Service, 475 L'Enfant Plaza West S.W., Washington, DC 20260-6757. TEL 202-268-2000. (Orders to: Philatelic Sales Division, Box 449997, Kansas City, MO 64144-9997. TEL 816-455-4880)
   Former titles: United States Postage Stamps; (until 1970): Postage Stamps of the United States (ISSN 0079-4244)

769.56   CN
POSTAL STATIONERY NOTES. 1981. bi-m. membership. British North American Philatelic Society, Postal Stationery Study Group, Box 549, Pinawa, Man. ROE 1L0, Canada. Ed. Robert Lemire. bk.rev.; index; circ. 75. (looseleaf format; back issues avail.)

769.56   US
POSTAL STATIONERY STUDY GROUP.* q. Germany Philatelic Society, c/o Matchinegg, Ed., 2008 Ft. Stockton Dr., San Diego, CA 92103-1512.

769.56   BO
POSTALES DE BOLIVIA. 1971. q. free. Federacion Filatelica Boliviana, Apartado 8013, La Paz, Bolivia. Dir. Eugenio von Boeck. circ. 950. (tabloid format)

769.56   US
POSTHORN; the bank of Scandinavian philatelic knowledge. 1943. q. $15. Scandinavian Collectors Club, 1214 Lakeview Dr., Fergus Falls, MN 56537-3853. TEL 901-452-8701. (Subscr. to: SCC, Exec. Sec., Box 125, Newark, DE 19715-0125) Ed. John Lindholm. adv.; bk.rev.; illus.; circ. 1,400 (controlled). **Indexed:** Stamp J.Ind.

769.56   GW
POSTILLON. 1954. 3/yr. DM.40. Bund Deutscher Philatelisten e.V., Arbeitsgemeinschaft Frankreich e.V., Tucholskyweg 5, 6500 Mainz 31, Germany. adv.; bk.rev.; circ. 500.
   Description: Covers philately of France, its French colonies and its offices abroad.

769.56   UK   ISSN 0269-1396
PRATIQUE. 1974. q. £10($16) Disinfected Mail Study Circle, 25 Sinclair Grove, London NW11 9JH, England. Ed. V. Denis Vandervelde. adv.; bk.rev.; circ. 160. (back issues avail.)

769.56   US   ISSN 0273-5415
HE6187
PRECANCEL FORUM. 1940. m. $12. Precancel Stamp Society Inc., Box 1134, Wichita, KS 67201-1134. Ed. Dilmond D. Postlewait. adv.; bk.rev.; charts; illus.; circ. 1,200. **Indexed:** Stamp J.Ind.
   Description: Covers activities of the society and its branch clubs. Includes articles on precancelled stamps and their collection.

769.56   US
PRECANCEL STAMP COLLECTOR. 1951. m. $15. National Association of Precancel Collectors, Inc., 5121 Park Blvd., Wildwood, NJ 08260-0121. Ed. Glenn W. Dye. adv.; bk.rev.; circ. 7,000.
   Description: Contains information on precanceled stamps.

769.56   UK   ISSN 0140-8003
PRIVATE POST. 1977. a. £4. Cinderella Stamp Club, c/o L.N. Williams, Ed., 44 The Ridgeway, London NW11 8QS, England. bibl.; illus.; circ. 600. (back issues avail.)

769.56   US   ISSN 0162-7902
EL QUETZAL. 1949. q. $15 membership. International Society of Guatemala Collectors, c/o Michael Barie, Box 1445, Detroit, MI 48231. TEL 313-224-7930. Ed. James C. Andrews. adv.; bk.rev.; circ. 300.
   Description: Concerned with the philatelic history of Guatemala and other portions of Central America.

769.56   UK   ISSN 0951-886X
RAILWAY PHILATELY. 1966. q. membership. Railway Philatelic Group, c/o A. Violet, Ed., 50 Roberts Rd., Prestbury, Cheltenham GL52 5DJ, England. adv.; bk.rev.; illus.; circ. 500.

769.56   629.4   US
RAPID NOTICE NEWS SERVICE. 1977. bi-m. $10. Space Philatelist International Society, Box 771, West Nyack, NY 10994. TEL 914-623-8149. FAX 914-591-6683. Ed. Scott Michaels. circ. 250. (looseleaf format; back issues avail.)

769.56   US
REPLY COUPON COLLECTOR. 1953. s-a. $10. International Society of Reply Coupon Collectors, Box 165, Somers, WI 53171-0165. Ed. Allan Hauck. adv.; bk.rev.; illus.; circ. 75. (looseleaf format)
   Description: Chronicles and studies all kinds of reply coupons issued by the various postal unions of the world.

769.56   RH
RHODESIA STAMP CATALOGUE. 1971. a. Z.$9.75. Zimbabwe Stamp Co. (Pvt.) Ltd., Box 200, Harare, Zimbabwe. Ed. D.G. Pollard. illus.; circ. 7,000.

769.56   US   ISSN 0035-8363
ROSSICA SOCIETY OF RUSSIAN PHILATELY JOURNAL. 1929. s-a. $18 per no. Rossica Society of Russian Philately, Inc., c/o Kennedy Wilson, Ed., 7415 Venice St., Falls Church, VA 22043. adv.; bk.rev.; charts; illus.; index; circ. 350. (back issues avail.) **Indexed:** Numis.Lit., Stamp J.Ind.

769.56   NZ
ROYAL PHILATELIC SOCIETY OF NEW ZEALAND. ANNUAL REPORT. a. Royal Philatelic Society of New Zealand, Box 1269, Wellington, New Zealand. Eds. D.B. Tennant, B.G. Vincent. adv.

769.56   NZ
ROYAL PHILATELIC SOCIETY OF NEW ZEALAND. MONOGRAPH SERIES. biennial. price varies. Royal Philatelic Society of New Zealand, P.O. Box 1269, Wellington, New Zealand.

769.56   UK   ISSN 0142-9841
HE6185.S652
RUSSIA STAMP CATALOGUE. 1981. irreg. price varies. Stanley Gibbons Publications Ltd., Unit 5 Parkside, Christchurch Rd., Ringwood, Hamps. BH24 3SH, England. TEL 0425-472363. FAX 0425-470247.

769.56   369.46   US
S O S S I JOURNAL. 1951. m. $12.50 membership. Scouts on Stamps Society International, 6908 Trowbridge Cove., Germantown, TN 38138. TEL 901-754-7949. Ed. Jean M. Ulmer. adv.; bk.rev.; circ. 1,600. (looseleaf format)
   Description: For those interested in collecting stamps and other philatelic material related to the Boy and Girl Scout movements.

769.56   US
ST. HELENA AND DEPENDENCIES PHILATELIC SOCIETY NEWSLETTER. 1977. q. $10. St. Helena and Dependencies Philatelic Society, 222 E. Torrence Rd., Columbus, OH 43214. TEL 614-262-3046. Ed. Russell V. Skavaril. adv.; bk.rev.; circ. 250. **Indexed:** Stamp J.Ind.

769.56   GW   ISSN 0036-3820
SAMMLER EXPRESS; Fachzeitschrift fuer Philatelie und andere Sammelgebiete. 1946. s-m. DM.60. Transpress Verlagsgesellschaft mbH, Franzoesische Str. 13-14, 1086 Berlin, Germany. TEL 203410. Ed. Alfred Peter. adv.; bk.rev.; abstr.; charts; illus.; mkt.; stat.

769.56   UK   ISSN 0261-7226
SARAWAK JOURNAL. 1947. q. £6.50 membership. Sarawak Specialists' Society, 9 Maytree Close, Sompting, Lancing, W. Sussex BN15 0ER, England. TEL 0903-762491. (Subscr. to: David Brown, 112 Hall Bower Lane, Newsome, Huddersfield, West Yorkshire HD4 6RN) Ed. Brian J. Cave. adv.; bk.rev.; circ. 300. **Indexed:** Stamp J.Ind.
   Description: Covers philately and postal history of Sarawak, Brunei, North Borneo and Labuan.

769.56   US   ISSN 0048-9255
SCALPEL AND TONGS; medical philately. 1955. bi-m. membership. American Topical Association, Medical Subjects Unit, c/o Ranes Chakravorty, Ed., 5049 Cherokee Hills Dr., Salem, VA 24153-5848. TEL 703-380-2362. adv.; bk.rev.; circ. 400. (also avail. in microform from UMI) **Indexed:** CWHM.

769.56   UK   ISSN 0142-985X
SCANDINAVIA STAMP CATALOGUE. 1980. irreg. price varies. Stanley Gibbons Publications Ltd., Unit 5 Parkside, Christchurch Rd., Ringwood, Hamps. BH24 3SH, England. TEL 0425-472363. FAX 0425-470247.

769.56   SZ
SCHWEIZER BRIEFMARKEN-ZEITUNG. 1889. 12/yr. 33 Fr. (Verband Schweizerischer Philatelistenvereine) Buri Druck AG, Eigerstr. 71, 3001 Berne, Switzerland. TEL 031-462323. FAX 031-455463. circ. 23,000.

769.56   US
SCOTT STAMP MONTHLY; with catalogue update. 1920. m. $21. Scott Publishing Company (Subsidiary of: Amos Press, Inc.), 911 Vandemark Rd., Box 828, Sidney, OH 45365. TEL 513-498-0802. Ed. Richard L. Sine. adv.; bk.rev.; illus.; tr.lit.; circ. 23,500. (back issues avail.)
   Supersedes in part (until 1982): Scott's Monthly Stamp Journal; Which was formerly: Scott's Monthly Journal (ISSN 0036-9454)

769.56   UK   ISSN 0080-8164
SCOTTISH POSTMARK GROUP. HANDBOOK.* 1962. irreg. price varies. Scottish Postmark Group, c/o David C. Jefferies, 11 Craigcrook Ave., Edinburgh EH4 3QE, Scotland.

769   UK
SCOTTISH STAMP NEWS. 1970. m. £3.50. Stanley K. Hunter, Ed. & Pub., 34, Gray Street, Glasgow G3 7TY, Scotland. adv.; bk.rev.; illus.; index; circ. 120.

769.56   US
SCOTT'S SPECIALIZED CATALOGUE OF U.S. STAMPS. 1923. a. $30. Scott Publishing Company, 911 Vandemark Rd., Box 828, Sidney, OH 45365. TEL 513-498-0802. Ed. William Cummings.

769.56   US
SCOTT'S STANDARD POSTAGE STAMP CATALOGUE. 1867. a. $30. Scott Publishing Company, 911 Vandemark Rd., Box 828, Sidney, OH 45365. TEL 513-498-0802. Ed. William Cummings.

769.56   US
SEAL NEWS. 1946. bi-m. $7. Christmas Seal & Charity Stamp Society, c/o Richard E. Roberts, Box 39696, Minneapolis, MN 55439-0696. Ed. Gerald Grigaitis. adv.; illus.; index; circ. 500. (processed)

769.56   US   ISSN 0048-9891
SEAPOSTER. 1939. bi-m. $10. Maritime Postmark Society, c/o Thomas G. Hirschinger, Ed., 141 Gordon Ave., Wadsworth, OH 44281. bk.rev.; circ. 200. (looseleaf format)

SEMPRE PRONTO; mensario escotista. see *EDUCATION*

769.56   CC
SHANGHAI JIYOU/SHANGHAI PHILATELY. (Text in Chinese) bi-m. Shanghai Shi Jiyou Xiehui - Shanghai Association of Philately, No.13, Alley 155, Julu Lu, Shanghai 200020, People's Republic of China. TEL 3270365. Ed. Le Jinxiang.

769.56   CC
SHAONIAN JIYOU/JUVENILE PHILATELY. (Text in Chinese) 1983. m. $19.70. Zhongguo Jiyou Chubanshe, Dong Chang'an Jie 27, Beijing, People's Republic of China. (Dist. in US by: China Books & Periodicals, Inc., 2929 24th St., San Francisco, CA 94110. TEL 415-282-2994)
   Description: Shows elementary and high school students the correct methods and purposes of stamp collecting, while encouraging their enthusiasm for learning and increasing their knowldge of the world.

769.56   SA
SOUTH AFRICA. PHILATELIC SERVICES AND INTERSAPA. PHILATELIC BULLETIN. (Text in Afrikaans, English) 1947. 44/yr. free. Philatelic Services and Intersapa, Private Bag X505, Pretoria 0001, South Africa. FAX 286025. circ. 67,000.
   Formerly: South Africa. Philatelic Services. Philatelic Bulletin (ISSN 0031-7349)
   Description: News of forthcoming stamp issues, with technical and historical notes.

769.56   SA   ISSN 0038-2566
SOUTH AFRICAN PHILATELIST. (Text in Afrikaans, English) 1923. bi-m. R.60($25) Philatelic Federation of Southern Africa, P.O. Box 2789, Cape Town 8000, South Africa. FAX 021-238763. Ed. Wilhelm Grutter. adv.; bk.rev.; bibl.; charts; illus.; mkt.; stat.; index; circ. 3,500. **Indexed:** Ind.S.A.Per., Stamp J.Ind.

PHILATELY

769.56 UK ISSN 0142-9922
SOUTH AMERICA STAMP CATALOGUE. 1980. irreg. price varies. Stanley Gibbons Publications Ltd., Unit 5 Parkside, Christchurch Rd., Ringwood, Hamps. BH24 3SH, England. TEL 0425-472363. FAX 0425-470247.

769.56 UK ISSN 0142-9930
SOUTH-EAST ASIA STAMP CATALOGUE. 1981. irreg. price varies. Stanley Gibbons Publications Ltd., Unit 5 Parkside, Christchurch Rd., Ringwood, Hamps. BH24 3SH, England. TEL 0425-472363. FAX 0425-470247.

769.56 US
STAMP AND COIN DIGEST. 1980. q. $1.50 per no. M & H Publications, 38 S. Madison Ave., Spring Valley, NY 10977. Ed. Martin R. Schranz.

769.56 UK
STAMP & COIN MART INTERNATIONAL. m. £14.40 (foreign £26). Maze Media Ltd., 89 East Hill, Colchester, Essex CO1 2QN, England. TEL 0206-871467. FAX 0206-871537. Ed. Sue Cook. adv.

769.56 US
STAMP AUCTION NEWS. 1980. m. $29. 85 Canisteo St., Hornell, NY 14843-1544. FAX 607-324-1753. adv.
   Description: Financial news and information relevant to the stamp market.

769.56 US
STAMP AUCTION REPORTS. 1981. q. $15. 6051 S.W. 45th St., Davie, FL 33314. Ed. J.W. Dickey.

769.56 US ISSN 0277-3899
STAMP COLLECTOR. 1931. w. $25.90. Van Dahl Publications, Box 10, Albany, OR 97321. TEL 503-928-3569. FAX 503-967-7672. Ed. Dane Claussen. adv.; bk.rev.; circ. 21,849. (tabloid format; also avail. in microform)
   Formerly: Western Stamp Collector (ISSN 0043-4213)

769.56 II ISSN 0014-5467
STAMP DIGEST. (Text in English) 1969. m. Rs.40($20) (Philatelic Research Society) Stamp Digest Publications, P-70, C.I.T. 6M, Calcutta 700054, India. Ed. Bibhash Gupta. adv.; bk.rev.; charts; illus.; tr.lit.; circ. 5,100. (tabloid format; also avail. in microfilm)

769.56 US
STAMP EXCHANGERS ANNUAL DIRECTORY. 1963. a. $7.50. Levine Publications, Box 3987, Trenton, NJ 08629. Ed. L. Jan Olssen. adv.; bk.rev.; charts; illus.; circ. 4,277.

769.56 UK ISSN 0038-9277
STAMP LOVER. 1908. 6/yr. $20 to non-members. National Philatelic Society, 107 Charterhouse St., London EC1M 6PT, England. TEL 071-251-5040. Ed. Michael Furnell. adv.; bk.rev.; illus.; index, cum.index approx. every 10 yrs.; circ. 3,000 (controlled). **Indexed:** Stamp J.Ind.

769.56 UK ISSN 0307-6679
STAMP MAGAZINE. m. £28.50. Link House Magazines Ltd., Link House, Dingwall Ave., Croydon, Surrey CR9 2TA, England. TEL 01-686-2599. FAX 01-760-0973. TELEX 947709. (Subscr. to: U M S, Stephenson House, 1st Fl., Brunel Centre, Bletchley, Milton Keynes, MK2 2EW) Ed. Richard West. adv.; bk.rev.; illus.; circ. 17,802. **Indexed:** Stamp J.Ind.
   Description: Provides information and news, technical guidance, a list of expositions, and a market catalog for the serious and avocational philatelist in the U.K.

769.56 UK ISSN 0953-5241
STAMP MAIL. 1946. m. £0.80 per issue. British Philatelic Federation Ltd., 107 Charterhouse St., London EC1M 6PT, England. TEL 071-251-5040. FAX 071-490-4253. Ed. David Sesslons. adv.; bk.rev.; circ. 2,200. **Indexed:** Stamp J.Ind.
   Former titles (until 1988): Stamp News (ISSN 0265-8216); Stamp and Postal History News (ISSN 0261-1899); Incorporates: Philately (ISSN 0031-739X); Stamp Collecting (ISSN 0038-9269); Philatelic Magazine (ISSN 0261-3107) Stamp Collecting was formerly: Stamp Collecting Weekly; Former titles of Philatelic Magazine: Philatelic Magazine and Stamp Review; Philatelic Magazine (ISSN 0031-7357).

769.56 AT
STAMP NEWS. 1954. m. Aus.$63.95. Macquarie Print, 51-59 Wheelers Lane, Dubbo, N.S.W. 2830, Australia. TEL 068-82-0813. FAX 068-859-444. Ed. B. Doherty. adv.; bk.rev.; circ. 15,000.
   Incorporates (1930-1991): Australian Stamp Monthly (ISSN 0005-0296); Former titles: Stamp News Australasia; Stamp News (ISSN 0038-9293)

769.56 US ISSN 0038-9315
HE6187
STAMP WHOLESALER; world's largest stamp dealer newspaper. 1936. 28/yr. $20. Van Dahl Publications, 520 E. First St., Albany, OR 97321. TEL 503-928-3569. Ed. Dane Claussen. adv.; bk.rev.; illus.; circ. 5,674.

769.56 US ISSN 0038-9358
HE6187
STAMPS. 1932. w. $23.50. Seneca Media, Inc., 85 Canisteo St., Hornell, NY 14843. Ed. Denise M. Axtell. adv.; bk.rev.; illus.; mkt.; q. index; circ. 18,500. (also avail. in microform from UMI; reprint service avail. from UMI) **Indexed:** Mag.Ind., Stamp J.Ind.

769.56 II ISSN 0255-8254
STAMPS WORLD. (Text in English) 1979. q. Rs.16($24) 107-2 Amherst Street, Calcutta 700 009, India. Ed. Dipok Dey. circ. 1,015. (back issues avail.)

769.56 UK ISSN 0144-249X
HE6184.P65
STANLEY GIBBONS POSTCARD CATALOGUE. 1980. irreg. £5.95. Stanley Gibbons Publications Ltd., Unit 5 Parkside, Christchurch Rd., Ringwood, Hamps. BH24 3SH, England. TEL 0425-472363. FAX 0425-470247.

769.56 UK ISSN 0081-4210
STANLEY GIBBONS SIMPLIFIED CATALOGUE. STAMPS OF THE WORLD. (In 3 Volumes: Vol.1 Foreign Countries A-J; Vol.2 Foreign Countries K-Z; Vol.3 Commonwealth Countries) 1934; N.S. 1989. a. £15 each vol.1 & 2; £13 vol.3. Stanley Gibbons Publications Ltd., Unit 5 Parkside, Christchurch Rd., Ringwood, Hamps. BH24 3SH, England. TEL 0425-472363. FAX 0425-470247. TELEX 412371 SGPUBG. illus.
   Description: For the general and thematic stamp collector. The three volumes list over 260,000 stamps with 60,000 illustrations.

737 UK ISSN 0142-9752
HE6226
STANLEY GIBBONS STAMP CATALOGUE. PART 1: BRITISH COMMONWEALTH. 1865. a. £27. Stanley Gibbons Publications Ltd., Unit 5 Parkside, Christchurch Rd., Ringwood, Hamps. BH24 3SH, England. TEL 0425-472363. FAX 0425-470247. TELEX 41271 SGPUBG.
   Description: Covers Great Britain and the British Commonwealth countries.

769.56 US ISSN 0883-6760
STATE REVENUE NEWSLETTER. 1957. bi-m. $4 includes membership. State Revenue Society, Box 505, Springfield, VA 22150. (Alt. addr.: c/o R. Bilek, Pub., 1515 S. Highland, Arlington Heights, IL 60005) Ed. Peter Martin. adv.; bk.rev.; illus.; cum.index: 1957-1976; circ. 300. (processed)
   Description: Provides current news and information on decals and stamps used by states that show payment of various taxes.

769.56 SW ISSN 0039-6532
SVENSK FILATELISTISK TIDSKRIFT. 1900. m. (10/yr.). SEK 190. Sveriges Filatelist-Foerbund, Klostergatan 15, S-532 30 Skara, Sweden. Ed. Gosta Karlsson. adv.; bk.rev.; index; circ. 18,600.

769.56 US
SWEDEN RING TYPE STAMP STUDY UNIT. NEWSLETTER.* 1980. q. $3. Sweden Ring Type Study Unit, c/o James Burgeson, Ed., 920 W. Glenoaks, Ste. A207, Glendale, CA 91202-2757. bk.rev.; circ. 75.
   Formerly: Sweden Ring Type Study Unit, Newsletter.

769.56 US
SYNCOPATED PERFS. 1930? irreg. (4-6/yr.). membership. Greater Cincinnati Philatelic Society, 3091 Riddle View Lane, Apt. 3, Cincinnati, OH 45220. TEL 513-861-4860. Eds. Virginia Fisher, Jacqueline R. Vidourek. circ. 100.

769.56 US
TELL.* 1975. bi-m. $8. American Helvetia Philatelic Society, 707 Tam O'Shanter Blvd., Williamsville, VA 23185. (Subscr. to: Richard T. Hall, Sec., Box 2425, Gaithersburg, MD 20879) Ed. Steve Turchik. adv.; bk.rev.; circ. 550.
   Formed by the merger of: Helvetia Alphorn & Helvetia Herald.

769.56 US ISSN 0893-2670
THE TEXAS PHILATELIST. 1962. bi-m. membership. Texas Philatelic Association, Inc., Rte. 2, Box 352, Leander, TX 78645-9734. TEL 512-267-4603. Ed. Jane King Fohn. adv.; bk.rev.; circ. 600.

769.56 US ISSN 0198-7992
HE6185.T45
THAI PHILATELY.* 1978. q. $12. Society for Thai Philately, 25104 Aspen Ave., Loma Linda, CA 92354-3537. Ed. Carlos Swanson. adv.; bk.rev.; index; circ. 250. (back issues avail.) **Indexed:** Stamp J.Ind.

769.56 CC
TIANJIN JIYOU/TIANJIN PHILATELY. (Text in Chinese) q. Tianjin Jiyou Xiehui - Tianjin Philately Association, 89 Jiefang Beilu, Tianjin 300041, People's Republic of China. TEL 314613. Ed. Jia Yingdong.

769.56 US
TIN CANNER. 1981. bi-m. $10. Tonga - Tin Can Mail Study Circle, Inc., 36975 S. Hwy. 213, Mt. Angel, OR 97362. Ed. Janet Klug. adv.; bk.rev.; illus.; index; circ. 180. (back issues avail.)
   Formerly: Philastannumy.
   Description: Includes stamps and stationary related to Tong; contains articles and information about club activites.

769.56 US ISSN 0049-4135
TOPICAL STAMP HANDBOOKS. 1951. irreg., no.119, 1991. price varies. American Topical Association, Inc., Box 630, Johnstown, PA 15907. TEL 814-539-6301. Ed. Donald W. Smith.

769.56 US ISSN 0040-9332
HE6187
TOPICAL TIME. 1949. bi-m. $18. American Topical Association, Inc., Box 630, Johnstown, PA 15907. TEL 814-539-6301. Ed. Donald W. Smith. adv.; bk.rev.; charts; illus.; mkt.; cum.index: 1949-1959, then every 5 yrs.; circ. 8,000. **Indexed:** Stamp J.Ind.
   Description: Deals with topical interest areas.

769.56 US
TOPICAL WOMAN. 1979. bi-m. $6. Women On Stamps Study Unit, 515 Ocean Ave., No. 6085, Santa Monica, CA 90402. (Subscr. to: Phebe Meek, 414 Falmouth Rd., Falmouth, ME 04105) Ed. Davida Kristy. index; circ. 80. (back issues avail.)
   Description: Includes biographies of women who appear on stamps; studies philatelic aspects of stamp and other elments.

769.56 US ISSN 0041-1175
HE6185.U5
TRANSIT POSTMARK COLLECTOR. 1950. 6/yr. membership. Mobile Post Office Society, c/o Warren F. Kimball, Jr., Ed., RFD 1, Box 91, Contoocook, NH 03229. TEL 603-746-3828. adv.; bk.rev.; illus.; circ. 650. (looseleaf format)
   Formerly: H.P.O. Notes.

737 769.56 IT ISSN 0393-7534
TRIBUNA DEL COLLEZIONISTA; mensile culturale di attualita e cronaca filatelica e numismatica. 1975. m. L.50000($50) Associazioni Filateliche, Via S. Nilo 4, 04024 Gaeta, Italy. TEL 0771-460305. FAX 0771-740176. Ed. Tommaso Valente. adv.; bk.rev.; illus.; circ. 10,000.

769.56 737 US
TRIDENT - VISNYK. (Text mainly in English) 6/yr. Ukrainian Philatelic and Numismatic Society, Box 3711, Silver Spring, MD 20918. Ed. Wes Capar. adv.
   Description: Ukrainian philatelic and numismatic news and events.

769.56 US ISSN 0148-673X
TRUMPETER. 1972. q. $20. Croatian Philatelic Society, 1512 Lancelot Rd., Borger, TX 79007-6341. Ed. Eck Spahich. adv.; bk.rev.; illus.; tr.lit.; index; circ. 700. (processed; back issues avail.) **Indexed:** Stamp J.Ind.

769.56 US ISSN 0279-6139
U S C S LOG. 1932. m. $16. Universal Ship Cancellation Society Log, Box 981, Healdsburg, CA 95448. TEL 707-431-1109. Ed. Robert D. Rawlins. adv.; bk.rev.; circ. 1,600.
   Description: Dedicated to the collection and study of naval and maritime postal history.

769.56 US
U S CANCELLATION CLUB NEWS.* 1951. bi-m. $2.50. U S Cancellation Club, Box 286, Bonsall, CA 92003. adv.; bk.rev.; charts; stat.; illus.; cum.index: vols. 1-10; circ. 420.

760 US ISSN 0198-6252
HE6185.U45
UKRAINIAN PHILATELIST. (Text in English, Ukrainian) 1951. s-a. $15. Ukrainian Philatelic and Numismatic Society, Box 3711, Silver Spring, MD 20918. TEL 301-593-5316. Ed. Ingert Kuzych. adv.; bk.rev.; circ. 450. (reprint service avail. from UMI, ISI)
   Formerly: Ukrains'kyi Filatelist.
   Description: Contains articles and studies on Ukrainian philately and numismatics.

794 US ISSN 0164-923X
HE6187
UNITED STATES SPECIALIST. 1930. m. $27. Bureau Issues Association, Inc., Box 3467, Crofton, MD 21114. Ed. Charles Yeager. adv.; bk.rev.; illus.; circ. 2,200.
   Description: Promotes the study of the philatelic output of the Bureau of Engraving and Printing, and of postage and revenue stamped paper produced by others for use in the United States and US administered areas.

769.56 UK ISSN 0142-9949
UNITED STATES STAMP CATALOGUE. 1981. irreg. price varies. Stanley Gibbons Publications Ltd., Unit 5 Parkside, Christchurch Rd., Ringwood, Hamps. BH24 3SH, England. TEL 0425-472363. FAX 0425-470247.

769.56 US
UNIVERSAL POSTAL UNION COLLECTORS. PUBLICATION. vol.5, 1981. q. $1.50 per no. Universal Postal Union Collectors, Box 15234, Long Beach, CA 90815. Ed. S.T. Conrad. **Indexed:** Stamp J.Ind.

769.56 UY ISSN 0042-1189
URUGUAY FILATELICO. 1928. 4/yr. $5. Club Filatelico del Uruguay, Box 518, Montevideo, Uruguay. Dir. Elias Casal Gari. illus.

769.56 US
URUGUAY PHILATELIST. 1960. q. $10 (foreign $12). Aerophilatelic Federation of the Americas, Box 1239, Elgin, IL 60121-1239. TEL 708-468-0840. Ed. Herman Kerst. circ. 1,000. (back issues avail.)

769.56 SP
VALENCIA FILATELICA; cuadernos de filatelia. m. 250 ptas.($7) c/o Jose M. Gomis Segui, Ed., Box 912, Valencia 9, Spain. adv.; illus.

769.56 US
VATICAN NOTES. 1953. bi-m. $9. Vatican Philatelic Society, 3348 Clubhouse Rd., Virginia Beach, VA 23452. TEL 804-486-3614. Ed. William M. Wickert. adv.; bk.rev.; circ. 600.

769.56 US
VERMONT PHILATELIST.* 1956. q. $5. Vermont Philatelic Society, 18 Fuller St., Montpelier, VT 05602. Ed. Morton Nash. adv.; bk.rev.; cum.index: nos.1-60; circ. controlled.

769.56 US
VIRGINIA PHILATELIC FORUM. 1974. q. $5. Virginia Philatelic Federation, Box 3486, College Station, Fredericksburg, VA 22402. Ed. James B. Gouger. adv.; bk.rev.; circ. 1,000.

769.56 US
WAR COVER CLUB BULLETIN. vol.21, 1981. q. $5. War Cover Club, c/o Chris Kulpinski, Box 464, Feasterville, PA 19047. adv.; bk.rev.; circ. 750. **Indexed:** Stamp J.Ind.

765.56 US
WATERCRAFT PHILATELY. 1954. bi-m. $6.50 (effective July 1991). Robert L. Tessier, Ed. & Pub., Box 23092, Washington, DC 20026. TEL 703-671-6484. (Subscr. to: Richard J. Howarth, 186 Butler St., Fall River, MA 02724) Ed. Robert L. Tessier. adv.; bk.rev.; circ. 350. (looseleaf format)
   Description: Features histories of watercraft depicted on stamps.

769.56 GW
WELTRAUM PHILATELIE. (Text in German; summaries in English) 1976. bi-m. DM.35($25) Weltraum Philatelie e.V., Postfach 1211, 8011 Hohenkirchen, Germany. TEL 089-60724849. Ed. P. Wilhelm. adv.; circ. 600. (back issues avail.)

769.56 US ISSN 0510-2332
HE6185.U7
WESTERN EXPRESS; early western mails. 1950. q. $15. Western Cover Society, 1615 Rose St., Berkeley, CA 94703. TEL 415-569-2817. Ed. Alan Patera. adv.; bk.rev.; cum.index: 1950-1978; circ. 350. (back issues avail.)

769.56 AU
WIENER KUNSTHANDEL. a. Landesgremium des Handels mit Gemaelden, Antiquitaeten und Kunstgegenstaenden sowie Briefmarken fuer Wien, Schwarzenbergpl. 14, A-1040 Vienna, Austria. TEL 657671.

WORLD COLLECTIONS NEWS; mensile di informazioni numismatiche e filateliche. see NUMISMATICS

769.56 US
WORLD POSTAL STATIONERY - NEW ISSUE REPORT. 1961. 3/yr. $10 (foreign $13). Classic Philatelics, Box 5637, Huntington Beach, CA 92615. TEL 714-968-1717. Ed. Pat Feiner. circ. 250.
   Former titles: New Issue Report; (until 1983): Entire Truth.
   Description: Lists of new postal stationery philatelic releases by governments of the world, with pricing in mint, first day of issue condition.

769.56 UK ISSN 0043-9061
WORLD STAMPS.* 1966. m. 22s.($3.15) Solway Publications, 4 Buccleuch St., Dumfries, Scotland. Ed. Capt. K. Jahr. adv.; bk.rev.; charts; illus.; mkt.; tr.lit.; index; circ. 8,000.

769.56 UK ISSN 0260-1265
HE6188
YEARBOOK AND PHILATELIC SOCIETIES' DIRECTORY. a. £7.50. British Philatelic Federation Ltd., 107 Charterhouse St., London EC1M 6PT, England. TEL 071-251-5040. FAX 071-490-4253.

769.56 US
YUBA - SUTTER PHILATELIC SOCIETY. NEWSLETTER. vol.4, 1980. m. Yuba - Sutter Philatelic Society, 11222 Loma Rica Rd., Marysville, CA 95901.

769.56 US ISSN 0843-7394
YULE LOG. 1969. bi-m. $10 (foreign $12). Christmas Philatelic Club, c/o Rick Norris, 5386 Roscommon Rd., Dublin, OH 43017. TEL 614-792-5451. Ed. Kathy Ward. adv.; bk.rev.; illus.; circ. 420.
   Description: Features articles on Christmas and philately for Christmas for collectors. Includes puzzles and contests.

769.56 JA
YUSHU; philatelic magazine. m. 8200 Yen. Japan Philatelic Society Foundation, Box 1, Shinjuku-ku, Tokyo 163-91, Japan. **Indexed:** Chem.Abstr.

769.56 RH
ZIMBABWE STAMP CATALOGUE. a. Zimbabwe Stamp Co. (Pvt.) Ltd., Box 200, Harare, Zimbabwe. Ed. D.G. Pollard.

769.56 US
ZIP ME NEWS. m. $5. Zippy Collectors Club, Inc., 2021 W. 9th, Emporia, KS 66801.

769.56 US
7-1-71 AFFAIR CATALOG - HANDBOOK. 1976. a. $1.95. R E M Catalog, Box 338, Newman, GA 30264-0338. TEL 404-251-5086. Ed. Roy E. Mooney. adv.; bk.rev.; circ. 300. (back issues avail.)

769.56 US
7-1-71 AFFAIR NEWSLETTER. 1976. q. free. R E M Catalog, Box 338, Newman, GA 30264-0338. TEL 404-251-5086. Ed. Roy E. Mooney. adv.; bk.rev.; circ. 300. (looseleaf format; back issues avail.)

769.56 US ISSN 0363-6542
HE6185.U5
1869 TIMES. 1975. q. membership. U S 1869 Pictorial Research Associates, Inc., c/o Jonathan Rose, Ed., 30 Golf Rd., Pleasanton, CA 94566. adv.; bk.rev.; circ. 300.

PHILATELY — Abstracting, Bibliographies, Statistics

STAMPS, COINS, POSTCARDS & RELATED MATERIALS; a directory of periodicals. see NUMISMATICS — Abstracting, Bibliographies, Statistics

PHILOSOPHY

see also Religions and Theology

A I & SOCIETY; journal of human and machine intelligence. (Artificial Intelligence) see COMPUTERS — Artificial Intelligence

182.2 BL ISSN 0001-1789
A LAMPADA. (Text in English, Portuguese and Spanish) 1931. q. free. Instituto Neo Pitagorico, P.O. Box 1047, Curitiba, Parana, Brazil. Ed.Bd. bk.rev.; abstr.; bibl.; circ. 500.

100 US
A P A NEWSLETTERS ON COMPUTER USE IN PHILOSOPHY, FEMINISM AND PHILOSOPHY, LAW AND PHILOSOPHY, MEDICINE AND PHILOSOPHY, TEACHING PHILOSOPHY, AND PHILOSOPHY AND THE BLACK EXPERIENCE. 2/yr. $15. American Philosophical Association, University of Delaware, Newark, DE 19716. TEL 302-451-1112. FAX 302-451-8690. circ. 6,000.
   Formerly: A P A Newsletter on Computer Use in Philosophy, Feminism and Philosophy, Law and Philosophy, Medicine and Philosophy, and Teaching Philosophy.

A U R A NEWSLETTER. (Association for Unity, Research and Awareness) see NEW AGE PUBLICATIONS

100 370 GW ISSN 0065-0366
ABHANDLUNGEN ZUR PHILOSOPHIE, PSYCHOLOGIE UND PAEDAGOGIK. 1954. irreg., vol.205, 1986. price varies. Bouvier Verlag Herbert Grundmann, Am Hof 32, Postfach 1268, 5300 Bonn 1, Germany.

100 340 MV ISSN 0236-3062
ACADEMIE DE STIINTE A R.S.S. MOLDOVA. FILOSOFIE SI DREPT/AKADEMIYA NAUK S.S.R. MOLDOVA. FILOSOFIYA I PRAVO. (Text in Moldavian and Russian) 1951. 3/yr. 3 Rub. Academie de Stiinte a R.S.S. Moldova, Bd. Stefan cel Mare, 1, Kishinev 277612, Moldova. bk.rev.; circ. 610.
   Supersedes in part (in 1990): Akademiya Nauk Moldavskoi S.S.R. Izvestiia. Seriya Obshchestvennykh Nauk.
   Description: Devoted to socio-philosophical, spiritual and political-legal problems relating to the Moldavian S.S.R.

ACME. see LITERATURE

100 200 IT ISSN 0065-1540
ACTA PHILOSOPHICA ET THEOLOGICA. (Text in English, French, German, Italian, Rumanian, Spanish) 1958. irreg. price varies. Societa Accademica Romena, Foro Traiano 1a, 00187 Rome, Italy.

100 SW ISSN 0283-2380
ACTA PHILOSOPHICA GOTHOBURGENSIA. irreg., no.3, 1989. price varies. Acta Universitatis Gothoburgensis, P.O. Box 5096, S-402 22 Goeteborg, Sweden. Ed. Claes Aaberg.
   —BLDSC shelfmark: 0648.330000.

PHILOSOPHY

100 370   PL   ISSN 0208-6107
ACTA UNIVERSITATIS LODZIENSIS: FOLIA PHILOSOPHICA. (Text in Polish; summaries in various languages) 1955-1974; N.S. 1981. irreg. Wydawnictwo Uniwersytetu Lodzkiego, Ul. Jaracza 34, Lodz, Poland. (Dist. by: Ars Polona-Ruch, Krakowskie Przedmiescie 7, Warsaw, Poland) Ed.Bd. **Indexed:** Math.R.
—BLDSC shelfmark: 0585.208400.
Supersedes in part: Uniwersytet Lodzki. Zeszyty Naukowe. Seria 1: Nauki Humanistyczno-Spoleczne (ISSN 0076-0358)
Description: Contains work from the members of the philosophical faculty and papers presented at symposiums and conferences organized by the faculty on the history of philosophy during the 19th and 20th centuries. Covers philosophical anthropology, the ethics of ecology and aesthetics.

100   PL   ISSN 0208-564X
ACTA UNIVERSITATIS NICOLAI COPERNICI. FILOZOFIA. 1960. irreg. price varies. Uniwersytet Mikolaja Kopernika, Fosa Staromiejska 3, Torun, Poland. (Dist.by Osrodek Rozpowszechniania Wydawnictw Naukowych PAN, Palac Kultury i Nauki, 00-901 Warsaw, Poland)
Formerly: Uniwersytet Mikolaja Kopernika, Torun. Nauki Humanistyczno-Spoleczne. Filozofia (ISSN 0083-4475)

ACTA UNIVERSITATIS SZEGEDIENSIS DE ATTILA JOZSEF NOMINATAE. DISSERTATIONES SLAVICAE. SECTIO HISTORIAE LITTERARUM. see LITERATURE

100   HU   ISSN 0231-2670
ACTA UNIVERSITATIS SZEGEDIENSIS DE ATTILA JOZSEF NOMINATAE. SECTIO PHILOSOPHICA/FILOZOFIA. (Text in Hungarian; summaries in English, German and Russian) 1922. a. exchange basis. Attila Jozsef University, c/o E. Szabo, Exchange Librarian, Dugonics ter 13, P.O.B. 393, 6701 Szeged, Hungary. (Subscr. to: Kultura, Box 149, H-1389 Budapest, Hungary) Ed. Laszlo Horuczi. circ. 500.
Supersedes (as of 1959): Acta Universitatis Szegediensis. Sectio Philosophica (ISSN 0586-3724)
Description: Treats problems of philosophy linked with the teaching and research activity of the authors.

ADVENT. see RELIGIONS AND THEOLOGY — Buddhist

212.5   GW   ISSN 0001-9011
ADYAR; theosophische Zeitschrift. 1946. 3/yr. DM.14. Theosophische Gesellschaft Adyar in Deutschland, Holbeinstr. 16, 2800 Bremen 1, Germany. Ed. Gerda Hoefer. bk.rev.; circ. 1,100.

100   ZR
AFRIQUE ET PHILOSOPHIE. (Text in French) 1976. a. 350 Fr.CFA. Faculte de Theologie Catholique de Kinshasa, Cercle Philosphique de Kinshasa, B.P. 1534, Kinshasa-Limete, Zaire. Ed. Kadioto Kabanda. adv.; bk.rev.; circ. 100.

100 301   IT
AGORA (RAVENNA). irreg., latest no.16. price varies. Angelo Longo Editore, Via Paolo Costa 33, P.O. Box 431, 48100 Ravenna, Italy. TEL 0544-217026. circ. 1,500.

100   CL   ISSN 0568-3939
AISTHESIS; revista chilena de investigaciones esteticas. 1966. a. $6.50. Pontificia Universidad Catolica de Chile, Instituto de Estetica, Diagonal Oriente 3.300, Santiago, Chile. Ed. Radoslav Ivelic. bibl.; cum.index; circ. 1,000. **Indexed:** Hisp.Amer.Per.Ind.
Description: Examines aesthetics and how it relates to art, literature, architecture and drama, with an emphasis on aesthetic criticism and research in Chile.

AKADEMIYA NAUK AZERBAIDZHANSKOI S.S.R. IZVESTIYA. SERIYA ISTORIYA, FILOSOFIYA I PRAVO. see HISTORY

100   SZ   ISSN 0149-2004
B1
ALETHEIA; an international journal of philosophy. (Text in English, German) 1977. irreg. (Internationale Akademie fuer Philosophie, LH) Verlag Peter Lang AG, Jupiterstr. 15, CH-3000 Bern 15, Switzerland. TEL 031-321122. FAX 031-321131. TELEX 912651-PELA-CH. Ed. Josef Seifert. **Indexed:** Phil.Ind.
—BLDSC shelfmark: 0786.912000.

150   NE   ISSN 0002-5275
B8.D8
ALGEMEEN NEDERLANDS TIJDSCHRIFT VOOR WIJSBEGEERTE. (Text in Dutch; summaries in English) 1907. 4/yr. fl.85 (effective 1992). Van Gorcum en Co. B.V., P.O. Box 43, 9400 AA Assen, Netherlands. TEL 05920-46846.
FAX 05920-72064. Ed. Raymond Corbey. adv.; bk.rev.; bibl.; cum.index: 1907-1958 in vols.1-50; circ. 1,000. **Indexed:** Lang.& Lang.Behav.Abstr., Phil.Ind.

100   GW   ISSN 0340-7969
ALLGEMEINE ZEITSCHRIFT FUER PHILOSOPHIE. 1976. 3/yr. DM.68. (Allgemeine Gesellschaft fuer Philosophie in Deutschland e.V.) Friedrich Frommann Verlag Guenther Holzboog, Postfach 500460, Koenig-Karl-Str. 27, 7000 Stuttgart 50, Germany. Ed. Josef Simon.
—BLDSC shelfmark: 0792.200000.

ALMAS. see RELIGIONS AND THEOLOGY

149   US   ISSN 0516-9623
BL2747.3
AMERICAN ATHEIST; a journal of Atheist news and thought. 1958. bi-m. $25. (American Atheist Library & Archives) American Atheist Press, Box 140195, Austin, TX 78714-0195. TEL 512-458-1244. FAX 512-467-9525. Ed. Robin Murray-O'Hair. adv.; bk.rev.; charts; illus.; stat.; tr.lit.; index; circ. 30,000. (back issues avail.)
Formerly: Poor Richard's Report (ISSN 0032-4310)
Description: Provides an in-depth analysis of current state-church seperation violations. Explores Atheist history and the effects of religion.

149   US
AMERICAN ATHEIST NEWSLETTER. 1959. m. membership. (American Atheist Library & Archives) American Atheist Press, Box 140195, Austin, TX 78714-0195. TEL 512-458-1244.
FAX 512-467-9525. Eds. Jon Murray, Madalyn O'Hair. circ. 70,000.
Former titles (until 1965): American Atheist Insiders' Newsletter; Poor Richard's Newsletter.
Description: Keeps the Atheist community abreast of state-church seperation violations and the latest religious financial schemes.

282 206   US   ISSN 0065-7638
B11
AMERICAN CATHOLIC PHILOSOPHICAL ASSOCIATION. PROCEEDINGS. 1926. a. $20. American Catholic Philosophical Association, The Catholic University of America, 403 Administration Bldg., Washington, DC 20064. TEL 202-635-5518. FAX 202-319-5047. Ed. Therese Anne Druart. adv.; cum.index: vols.1-63, 1926-89; circ. 2,000. (also avail. in microfilm from UMI; reprint service avail.) **Indexed:** Arts & Hum.Cit.Ind., Cath.Ind., Curr.Cont., Phil.Ind.
—BLDSC shelfmark: 6622.600000.

149.2   US
B1
AMERICAN CATHOLIC PHILOSOPHICAL QUARTERLY. 1927. q. $30. American Catholic Philosophical Association, Catholic Univ. of America, 403 Administration Bldg., Washington, DC 20064. TEL 202-635-5518. FAX 202-319-5047. Ed. Robert E. Wood. adv.; bk.rev.; cum.index: vols.1-64, 1927-1990; circ. 2,100. (also avail. in microfilm from UMI; reprint service avail.) **Indexed:** Arts & Hum.Cit.Ind., Cath.Ind., CERDIC, Curr.Cont., Mid.East: Abstr.& Ind., Phil.Ind., Psychol.Abstr.
Formerly: New Scholasticism (ISSN 0028-6621)

AMERICAN JOURNAL OF THEOLOGY & PHILOSOPHY. see RELIGIONS AND THEOLOGY

AMERICAN LIVING PRESS. see ART

106   US   ISSN 0065-972X
B11
AMERICAN PHILOSOPHICAL ASSOCIATION. PROCEEDINGS AND ADDRESSES. 1927. 7/yr. $40. American Philosophical Association, c/o University of Delaware, Newark, DE 19716. TEL 302-451-1112. FAX 302-451-8690. Ed. David A. Hoekema. adv.; circ. 8,000. (also avail. in microfilm from UMI; reprint service avail. from UMI) **Indexed:** Phil.Ind.
—BLDSC shelfmark: 6837.530000.

100   US   ISSN 0003-0481
AMERICAN PHILOSOPHICAL QUARTERLY. 1964. q. $32 to individuals; institutions $135. Bowling Green State University, Philosophy Documentation Center, Bowling Green, OH 43403-0189.
TEL 419-372-2419. FAX 419-372-6987. Ed. Nicholas Rescher. circ. 1,500. **Indexed:** Arts & Hum.Cit.Ind., Curr.Cont., Hum.Ind., Lang.& Lang.Behav.Abstr., Phil.Ind.
—BLDSC shelfmark: 0850.590000.

AMERICAN PHILOSOPHICAL SOCIETY. MEMOIRS. see SCIENCES: COMPREHENSIVE WORKS

AMERICAN PHILOSOPHICAL SOCIETY. PROCEEDINGS. see HISTORY

AMERICAN PHILOSOPHICAL SOCIETY. TRANSACTIONS. see SCIENCES: COMPREHENSIVE WORKS

106   US   ISSN 0065-9762
Q11   CODEN: YAPSAL
AMERICAN PHILOSOPHICAL SOCIETY. YEARBOOK. 1937. a. $15. American Philosophical Society, 104 S. Fifth St., Philadelphia, PA 19106. TEL 215-440-3400. Ed. Herman H. Goldstine. index. (also avail. in microform from UMI; reprint service avail. from UMI,ISI) **Indexed:** Amer.Hist.& Life, GeoRef, Hist.Abstr.

211   US   ISSN 0003-0708
BL2700
AMERICAN RATIONALIST. 1956. bi-m. $6. Rationalist Association, Inc., Box 994, St. Louis, MO 63188. Ed. Dr. Gordon Stein. adv.; bk.rev.; circ. 1,500. (also avail. in microform from UMI; back issues avail.)
Description: Concerns free thought, philosophy, critique of religion and theology, and the history of unbelief.

212.5   US   ISSN 0003-1402
AMERICAN THEOSOPHIST. 1912. bi-m. membership. Theosophical Society in America, 1926 N. Main St., Box 270, Wheaton, IL 60189-0270.
TEL 708-668-1571. FAX 708-665-8791. Ed. William Metzger. bk.rev.; circ. 5,500.

100   US   ISSN 0739-6392
AMERICAN UNIVERSITY STUDIES. SERIES 5. PHILOSOPHY. 1983. irreg. Peter Lang Publishing, Inc., 62 W. 45th St., 4th Fl., New York, NY 10036. TEL 212-302-6740. Ed. Michael Flamini.

100   NE
ANALECTA CARTESIANA. (Text in French) 1981. irreg. price varies. Quadratures, Postbus 6463, 1005 EL Amsterdam, Netherlands.
Formerly: Collectanea Cartesiana.

100   NE
ANALECTA HUSSERLIANA; yearbook of phenomenological research. (Text in English) 1971. irreg. price varies. Kluwer Academic Publishers, Spuiboulevard 50, P.O. Box 17, 3300 AA Dordrecht, Netherlands. TEL 078-334911. FAX 078-334254. TELEX 29245. (Dist. by: Kluwer Academic Publishers Group, P.O. Box 322, 3300 AH Dordrecht; U.S. address: P.O. Box 358, Accord Station, Hingham, MA 02018-0358) Ed. Anna-Teresa Tymieniecka.

100   UK   ISSN 0003-2638
B1
ANALYSIS. 1933-1940; N.S. 1947. q. £12($26) to individuals; institutions £20($43). Basil Blackwell Ltd., 108 Cowley Rd., Oxford OX4 1JF, England. TEL 0865 791100. FAX 0865-791347. TELEX 837022-OXBOOK-G. Ed. Peter Smith. adv.; index; circ. 1,350. (also avail. in microform; reprint service avail. from SWZ,UMI) **Indexed:** Arts & Hum.Cit.Ind., Br.Hum.Ind., Lang.& Lang.Behav.Abstr., Phil.Ind.
—BLDSC shelfmark: 0892.100000.

891   II
ANANDA ACHARYA UNIVERSAL SERIES. (Text in English) 1978. irreg. price varies. Vishveshvaranand Vedic Research Institute, P.O. Sadhu Ashram, Hoshiarpur 146021, Punjab, India.

ANANDA VARTA. see ORIENTAL STUDIES

PHILOSOPHY 3761

100 BE
ANCIENT AND MEDIEVAL PHILOSOPHY. SERIES 1, PUBLICATIONS OF DE WULF-MANSION CENTRE. 1978. irreg., vol.13, 1991. Leuven University Press, Krakenstraat 3, B-3000 Leuven, Belgium. TEL 016-284175. FAX 016-284176. (Dist. by: Editions Peeters s.p.r.l., Bondegenotenlaan 153, B-3000 Leuven, Belgium. TEL 016-235170)

100 BE
ANCIENT AND MEDIEVAL PHILOSOPHY. SERIES 2, HENRICI DE GANDAVO OPERA. 1979. irreg., vol.17, 1989. Leuven University Press, Krakenstraat 3, B-3000 Leuven, Belgium. TEL 016-284175. FAX 016-284176.

010 215 US ISSN 0740-2007
ANCIENT PHILOSOPHY. 1980. 2/yr. $14 to individuals; institutions $25. Mathesis Publications, Inc., Department of Philosphy, Duquesne University, Pittsburgh, PA 15282. TEL 412-434-6500. Ed. Ronald M. Polansky. adv.; bk.rev.; circ. 600. (back issues avail.) Indexed: Phil.Ind.
Description: Contains articles and reviews about classical philosophy and science.

100 SP
AL-ANDALUS; revista de las escuelas de estudios Arabes de Madrid y Granada. 1933-1978. s-a. 1600 ptas. (foreign 2400 ptas.). Consejo Superior de Investigaciones Cientificas (C.S.I.C.), Instituto de Filologia, Duque de Medinaceli, 6, 28014 Madrid, Spain.

ANFORA; revista cuatrimestral de literatura y filosofia. see *LITERATURE*

100 282 VC ISSN 0003-3081
BX800.A1
ANGELICUM; periodicum trimestre pontificae studiorum. (Text in English, French, German, Italian and Spanish) 1924. q. $30 (typically set in Apr.). Pontificia Universita S. Tommaso d'Aquino, Largo Angelicum 1, 00184 Rome, Italy. TEL 06-67021. FAX 6790407. Ed. Stephen Krasic. bk.rev.; circ. 800. Indexed: CERDIC, M.L.A., New Test.Abstr., Old Test.Abstr., Rel.& Theol.Abstr. (1979-).
—BLDSC shelfmark: 0900.930000.
Description: Scholarly articles on a variety of topics related to the Catholic religion.

ANHUI SHIDA XUEBAO (SHEHUI KEXUE BAN)/ANHUI NORMAL UNIVERSITY. JOURNAL (SOCIAL SCIENCE EDITION). see *SOCIAL SCIENCES: COMPREHENSIVE WORKS*

ANNALES D'ESTHETIQUE/CHRONIKA AISTHETIKIS. see *ART*

100 301 PL ISSN 0137-2025
ANNALES UNIVERSITATIS MARIAE CURIE-SKLODOWSKA. SECTIO I. PHILOSOPHIA-SOCIOLOGIA. (Text in English or Polish; summaries in English, French, German) 1976. a. price varies. Uniwersytet Marii Curie-Sklodowskiej, Wydawnictwo, Pl. M. Curie-Skodowskiej 5, 20-031 Lublin, Poland. TEL 48-81-375304. FAX 48-81-336699. TELEX 0643223. Ed. Z. Cackowski. circ. 500.
—BLDSC shelfmark: 0956.500000.

ANNALS OF PURE AND APPLIED LOGIC. see *MATHEMATICS*

ANNUAL EDITIONS: BUSINESS ETHICS. see *BUSINESS AND ECONOMICS*

100 IT
ANNUARIO FILOSOFICO (YEAR). 1985. a. L.50000. Ugo Mursia Editore S.p.A., Via Tadino 29, 20124 Milano, Italy. FAX 2041557. TELEX 325294. Ed. Giuseppe Riconda. bk.rev.; circ. 1,000.

ANTICHITA CLASSICA E CRISTIANA. see *HISTORY*

149.3 IT ISSN 0003-6145
ANTROPOSOFIA. 1947. 6/yr. L.32000 (effective Jan. 1992). Editrice Antroposofica S.r.l., Via Sangallo, 34, 20133 Milan, Italy. Ed.Bd. adv.; bk.rev.; circ. 700.

100 SP ISSN 0066-5215
B25 CODEN: ANFIEA
ANUARIO FILOSOFICO. 1968. s-a. 3000 ptas.($36) (Universidad de Navarra, Facultad de Filosofia y Letras) Servicio de Publicaciones de la Universidad de Navarra, S.A., Apdo. 177, 31080 Pamplona, Spain. TEL 94 25 2700. Ed. Juan J. Rodriguez Rosado. adv.; bk.rev. Indexed: Phil.Ind.

100 CN ISSN 0003-6390
APEIRON; a journal of ancient philosophy and science. 1966. 4/yr. Can.$44($48) to individuals; institutions Can.$64($67). (University of Alberta, Department of Philosophy) Academic Printing and Publishing, Box 4834, Edmonton, Alta. T6E 5G7, Canada. FAX 403-435-5852. adv.; bk.rev.; circ. 350. (processed; avail. on records) Indexed: Phil.Ind.
—BLDSC shelfmark: 1567.867200.

AQUARIAN ALCHEMIST. see *PARAPSYCHOLOGY AND OCCULTISM*

100 282 VC ISSN 0003-7362
B765.T54
AQUINAS; rivista internazionale di filosofia. 1958. 3/yr. $55. Pontificia Universita Lateranense, Piazza S. Giovanni in Laterano 4, 00120 Vatican City (Rome), State of the Vatican City. Ed. Sanchez Sorondo. bk.rev. Indexed: M.L.A., Phil.Ind.
—BLDSC shelfmark: 1583.150000.

104 US ISSN 0066-5614
AQUINAS LECTURE SERIES. 1937. a. price varies. (Marquette University, Aristotelean Society) Marquette University Press, 1324 W. Wisconsin Ave., Milwaukee, WI 53233. TEL 414-224-1564. (back issues avail.; reprint service avail. from UMI)
Description: Annual lecture originating at Marquette University.

ARABIC SCIENCES AND PHILOSOPHY; a historical journal. see *SCIENCES: COMPREHENSIVE WORKS*

100 GW ISSN 0003-8946
ARCHIV FUER BEGRIFFSGESCHICHTE; Bausteine zu einem historischen Woerterbuch der Philosophie. 1955. 2/yr. price varies. Bouvier Verlag Herbert Grundmann, Am Hof 32, Postfach 1268, 5300 Bonn 1, Germany. Ed. Karlfried Gruender. bk.rev.; circ. 600. Indexed: Phil.Ind.

109 GW ISSN 0003-9101
B3
ARCHIV FUER GESCHICHTE DER PHILOSOPHIE. vol.58, 1976. 3/yr. $105. Walter de Gruyter und Co., Genthiner Str. 13, 1000 Berlin 30, Germany. TEL 030-26005-0. FAX 030-26005251. TELEX 184027. (U.S. addr.: Walter de Gruyter, Inc., 200 Saw Mill Rd., Hawthorne, NY 10532) Ed. Hans Wagner. adv.; bk.rev.; index. Indexed: Arts & Hum.Cit.Ind., Curr.Cont., Ind.Bk.Rev.Hum., M.L.A., Phil.Ind.
—BLDSC shelfmark: 1612.060000.

170 300 340 GW ISSN 0001-2343
LAW
ARCHIV FUER RECHTS- UND SOZIALPHILOSOPHIE/ARCHIVES DE PHILOSOPHIE DU DROIT ET DE PHILOSOPHIE SOCIALE/ARCHIVES FOR PHILOSOPHY OF LAW AND SOCIAL PHILOSOPHY. Short title: A R S P. (Supplement avail.) (Text in English, French, German) 1907. q. DM.168. (Internationale Vereinigung fuer Rechts- und Sozialphilosophie) Franz Steiner Verlag Wiesbaden GmbH, Birkenwaldstr. 44, Postfach 101526, 7000 Stuttgart 1, Germany. TEL 0711-2582-0. FAX 0711-2582290. TELEX 723636-DAZD. Ed. Werner Maihofer. adv.; bk.rev.; cum.index; circ. 900. (back issues avail.; reprint services avail. from SCH) Indexed: Phil.Ind.

170 300 340 GW ISSN 0341-079X
ARCHIV FUER RECHTS- UND SOZIALPHILOSOPHIE. BEIHEFTE. (Text in English, French, German) irreg., vol.51, 1992. price varies. (Internationale Vereinigung fuer Rechts- und Sozialphilosophie) Franz Steiner Verlag Wiesbaden GmbH, Birkenwaldstr. 44, Postfach 101526, 7000 Stuttgart 1, Germany. TEL 0711-2582-0. FAX 0711-2582290. TELEX 723636-DAZD.

100 GW ISSN 0722-5679
ARCHIV FUER RECHTS UND SOZIALPHILOSOPHY. SUPPLEMENTA. irreg., vol.5, 1988. price varies. (Internationale Vereinigung fuer Rechts- und Sozialphilosophie) Franz Steiner Verlag Wiesbaden GmbH, Birkenwaldstr. 44, Postfach 101526, 7000 Stuttgart 1, Germany. TEL 0711-2582-0. FAX 0711-2582290. TELEX 723636-DAZD.

180 FR ISSN 0373-5478
B720
ARCHIVES D'HISTOIRE DOCTRINALE ET LITTERAIRE DU MOYEN AGE. (Text in English, French, German, Latin) 1926. a. price varies. Librairie Philosophique J. Vrin, 6 Place de la Sorbonne, 75005 Paris, France. FAX 43-54-48-18. Ed.Bd. index; circ. 750. Indexed: M.L.A.

100 FR ISSN 0003-9632
B1
ARCHIVES DE PHILOSOPHIE; recherches et documentation. (Summaries in English, French) 1923. 4/yr. 315 F. (foreign 400 F.). Editons Beauchesne, 72 rue des Saints Peres, 75007 Paris, France. TEL 45-48-80-28. FAX 42-22-59-79. Ed. F. Marty. adv.; bk.rev.; abstr.; charts; circ. 800. Indexed: Arts & Hum.Cit.Ind., Curr.Cont., Phil.Ind.

100 NE ISSN 0066-6610
ARCHIVES INTERNATIONALES D'HISTOIRE DES IDEES/INTERNATIONAL ARCHIVES OF THE HISTORY OF IDEAS. (Text in English and French) 1963. irreg. price varies. Kluwer Academic Publishers, Postbus 17, 3300 AA Dordrecht, Netherlands. TEL 078-334911. (Orders to: Kluwer Academic Publishers, Distribution Center, P.O. Box 322, 3300 AH Dordrecht, Netherlands) Eds. P. Dibon, R. Popkin.
—BLDSC shelfmark: 4536.110000.

100 IT ISSN 0004-0088
B4
ARCHIVIO DI FILOSOFIA. (Text in English, French, German or Italian) 1957. 3/yr. L.7500 (foreign L.100000)(effective 1991). (Universita degli Studi di Roma, Istituto di Studi Filosofici) Casa Editrice Dott. Antonio Milani, Via Jappelli 5, 35121 Padua, Italy. TEL 049-656677. FAX 049-8752900. Dir. Marco M. Olivetti. Indexed: CERDIC, Phil.Ind.
—BLDSC shelfmark: 1646.580000.

100 SP
ARCHIVUM (OVIEDO). (Text in Spanish) 1950. a. 4500 ptas. Universidad Oviedo, Arias de Velsco, No.2, Oviedo, Spain.

109 309 PL ISSN 0066-6874
ARCHIWUM HISTORII FILOZOFII I MYSLI SPOLECZNEJ. (Text in Polish; summaries in French, German, or Russian) 1954. a. price varies. (Polska Akademia Nauk, Instytut Filozofii i Socjologii) Ossolineum, Publishing House of the Polish Academy of Sciences, Rynek 9, Wroclaw, Poland. TELEX 0712771 OSS PL. Ed. Barbara Skarga.
Description: Studies the history of philosophy in Poland and throughout the world.

DAS ARGUMENT; Zeitschrift fuer Philosophie und Sozialwissenschaften. see *SOCIAL SCIENCES: COMPREHENSIVE WORKS*

100 NE ISSN 0920-427X
BC1 CODEN: ARGMEL
ARGUMENTATION; an international journal on reasoning. 1987. q. $142. (European Centre for the Study of Argumentation) Kluwer Academic Publishers, Postbus 17, 3300 AA Dordrecht, Netherlands. TEL 078-334911. FAX 078-334254. TELEX 29245. (Dist. by: Kluwer Academic Publishers Group, P.O. Box 322, 3300 AH Dordrecht, Netherlands; N. America dist. addr.: Box 358, Accord Station, Hingham, MA 02018-0358. TEL 617-871-6600) bk.rev. (reprint service avail. from SWZ)
—BLDSC shelfmark: 1664.356100.

100 UK
ARGUMENTS OF THE PHILOSOPHERS. irreg. price varies. Routledge, 11 New Fetter Lane, London EC4P 4EE, England. TEL 01-583 9855. FAX 01-585-0701. TELEX 263398 ABP LDN G. (U.S. address: Routledge, Chapman & Hall Inc., 35 W. 35th St., New York, N.Y. 10001-2291).
Description: Provides a contemporary assessment and history of the entire course of philosophical thought. Each book constitutes a detailed critical introduction to the work of a philosopher of major influence and significance.

PHILOSOPHY

100   UK   ISSN 0066-7374
ARISTOTELIAN SOCIETY. PROCEEDINGS. a. £31.50($61) (Aristotelian Society) Basil Blackwell Ltd., 108 Cowley Road, Oxford OX4 1JF, England. TEL 0865-791100. FAX 0865-791347. TELEX 837022-OXBOOK-G. (Subscr. to: Journals Department, Basil Blackwell, c/o Marston Book Services, P.O. Box 87, Oxford OX2 0DT, England) Ed. Dorothy Edgington.

100   UK   ISSN 0309-7013
ARISTOTELIAN SOCIETY. PROCEEDINGS. SUPPLEMENTARY VOLUME. a. £31.50($61) (Aristotelian Society) Basil Blackwell Ltd., 108 Cowley Road, Oxford OX4 1JF, England. TEL 0865-791100. FAX 0865-791347. TELEX 837022-OXBOOK-G. (Subscr. to: Journals Department, Basil Blackwell, c/o Marston Book Services, P.O. Box 87, Oxford OX2 0DT, England) Ed. Dorothy Edgington.

ART AND PHILOSOPHY. see *ART*

ARZT UND CHRIST; Vierteljahresschrift fuer medizinisch-ethische Grundsatzfragen. see *MEDICAL SCIENCES*

100 950   US   ISSN 0955-2367
B5000
▼**ASIAN PHILOSOPHY.** 1991. 2/yr. $100. Carfax Publishing Co., P.O. Box 25, Abingdon, Oxfordshire OX14 3UE, England. TEL 0235-555335. FAX 0235-553559. (US distr. addr.: 85 Ash St., Hopkinton, MA 01748) Eds. Indira Mahamalingam, Brian Carr. adv.; bk.rev.; index. (also avail. in microfiche; back issues avail.)
—BLDSC shelfmark: 1742.715300.
   Description: Focuses on Indian, Chinese, Japanese, Buddhist, Persian, and Islamic philosophical traditions.

144 360   FR   ISSN 0153-6133
ASSOCIATION FRANCAISE DES AMIS D'ALBERT SCHWEITZER. CAHIERS. 1955. 4/yr. 120 F. Association Francaise des Amis d'Albert Schweitzer, 1 Quai St. Thomas, 67081 Strasbourg, France. Ed. Jean Christian. bk.rev.; bibl.; illus.; circ. 2,750.

ASSOCIATION OF BRITISH THEOLOGICAL AND PHILOSOPHICAL LIBRARIES. BULLETIN. see *LIBRARY AND INFORMATION SCIENCES*

149   US   ISSN 0304-1409
BL2747.3
ATHEIST. (Issued as a supplement to the Truth Seeker) 1946. irreg. $20. (American Association for the Advancement of Atheism) Truth Seeker Co., Inc., Box 2832, San Diego, CA 92112. TEL 619-239-9043. Ed. James W. Prescott. circ. 10,000.

100 954   US
AUM NAMO NARAYANAY. 1982. bi-m. $30. Intergalactic Lovetrance Civilization Center, Aum Namo Bhagavate Vasudevay Foundation, Box 73, Harbor City, CA 90710-0073. TEL 213-831-4226. bk.rev.; bibl.; charts; illus.; stat.; circ. 25. (also avail. in audio cassette; back issues avail.)
   Description: Collection of inspirational wisdom, commentaries on Sanskrit scripture and literature, self-help and personal growth tips, bibliographies of saints and the true history of mankind.

100   US   ISSN 0733-4311
B1
AUSLEGUNG; a journal of philosophy. 1973. 2/yr. $10 to individuals; institutions $12; students $8. (Graduate Association of Students in Philosophy) University of Kansas, Department of Philosophy, Lawrence, KS 66045. TEL 913-864-2700. Ed. Albert Cinell. adv.; bk.rev.; charts; circ. 230. (back issues avail.; reprint service avail. from UMI) **Indexed:** Arts & Hum.Cit.Ind., Curr.Cont., Hum.Ind., Phil.Ind.
—BLDSC shelfmark: 1792.939000.

100   AT   ISSN 0004-8402
B1
AUSTRALASIAN JOURNAL OF PHILOSOPHY. 1923. 4/yr. Aus.$35. Australasian Association of Philosophy, Philosophy Dept., La Trobe University, Bundoora, Vic. 3083, Australia. Ed. Robert Young. adv.; bk.rev.; abstr.; bibl.; index, cum.index every 10 yrs.; circ. 1,200. (also avail. in microform from JAI,MIM) **Indexed:** Amer.Hist.& Life, Arts & Hum.Cit.Ind., Aus.P.A.I.S., Curr.Cont., Ind.Bk.Rev.Hum., Lang.& Lang.Behav.Abstr., Phil.Ind.
—BLDSC shelfmark: 1795.100000.

AUSTRALASIAN STUDIES IN HISTORY AND PHILOSOPHY OF SCIENCE. see *SOCIAL SCIENCES: COMPREHENSIVE WORKS*

211   AT   ISSN 1036-8191
AUSTRALIAN RATIONALIST. 1969. q. Aus.$25 to non-members. Rationalist Society of Australia, 42 Ruskin Ave., Croydon, Vic. 3136, Australia. TEL 03-723-2792. FAX 03-723-2792. Ed. Kate Oldaker. adv.; bk.rev.; film rev.; illus.
   Incorporates (1986-1990): News and Views; Formed by the merger of: Rationalist (ISSN 0034-0065); Australian Rationalist (ISSN 0005-0113)

100   IT   ISSN 0005-0601
B4
AUT AUT; rivista di filosofia e di cultura. 1951. bi-m. L.65000. Nuova Italia Editrice S.p.a, Via Ernesto Codignola, 50018 Scandicci (FL), Italy. Dir. Pier Aldo Rovatti. adv.; index. **Indexed:** Curr.Cont., M.L.A.

AVALOKA; a journal of traditional religion and culture. see *RELIGIONS AND THEOLOGY*

100   US   ISSN 0005-3643
BACK TO GODHEAD; magazine of the Hare Krishna movement. 1944. 6/yr. $24. Box 90946, San Diego, CA 92169-2946. TEL 818-760-8983. FAX 619-272-3673. (Subscr. to: BTG Subscriber Service Center, Box 16027, N. Hollywood, CA 91615-9900) Ed. Jayadvaita Swami. adv.; bk.rev.; illus.; index; circ. 20,000.
   Description: Promotes self-relization, spiritual culture, philosophical understanding, and devotion to Krishna, the supreme personality of godhead, as depicted in the Vedic literature of India.

BALSA DE LA MEDUSA. see *ART*

BAZMAVEP. see *HISTORY — History Of The Near East*

THE BEACON (MIAMI SHORES). see *NEW AGE PUBLICATIONS*

100   US   ISSN 0005-7339
BEACON (NEW YORK). 1922. bi-m. $15. (Lucis Trust) Lucis Publishing Co., 113 University Pl., 11th Fl., Box 722, Cooper Sta., New York, NY 10276. TEL 212-982-8770. (European and British Commonwealth countries, except Canada, subscr. to: Lucis Press Ltd., 3 Whitehall Court, Suite 54, London, SW1A 2EF, England) Ed.Bd. bk.rev.; circ. 5,000. (back issues avail.)

100 800   CN   ISSN 0832-9966
LE BEFFROI; revue philosophique et litteraire. 1986. 3/yr. Can.$50. Editions du Beffroi, 3550 du Long-Sault, Beauport, Que. G1E 1H6, Canada. TEL 418-663-3696. FAX 418-666-8602. Eds. Alexis Klimov, Jean Renaud. adv.; bk.rev.; circ. 500.

100 230   GW   ISSN 0067-5024
BEITRAEGE ZUR GESCHICHTE DER PHILOSOPHIE UND THEOLOGIE DES MITTELALTERS. NEUE FOLGE. 1894; N.S. 1970. irreg. price varies. Aschendorffsche Verlagsbuchhandlung, Soesterstr. 13, 4400 Muenster, Germany. TEL 0251-690-0. FAX 0251-690405. Eds. Ludwig Hoedl, Wolfgang Kluxen.

107 370   GW   ISSN 0005-8157
BEITRAEGE ZUR PAEDAGOGISCHEN ARBEIT. 1956. q. membership. Gemeinschaft Evangelischer Erzieher in Baden, Blumenstr. 1, 75 Karlsruhe 1, Germany. Ed. Rudolf Immig. bk.rev.; bibl.; circ. 400.

105   FR   ISSN 0339-8498
BELISANE; bulletin de philosophie et d'histoire traditionnelles. 1977. q. 24 F. Claude Boumendil, Repro 2000, 11 rue Gutenberg, 06000 Nice, France. Eds. Claude Passet, Daniel Robert.

BETTER WORLD. see *NEW AGE PUBLICATIONS*

181.4   II   ISSN 0006-0496
BHARATHA DARSHANA; the only magazine in Kannada devoted to the propagation of Mahabharatha & Ramayana. (Text in Kannada) 1957. bi-m. Rs.10. Bharatha Darshana Prakashana, 163 Manjunatha Rd., II Block, Thyagarajanagar, Bangalore 560 028, India. TEL 605381. adv.; circ. 13,000.

BHARATYA VIDYA. see *ORIENTAL STUDIES*

100 011   GW   ISSN 0173-1831
BIBLIOGRAPHIEN ZUR PHILOSOPHIE. (Text in English and German) 1979. irreg. price varies. Edition Gemini, Juelichstr. 7, 5030 Huerth-Efferen, Germany. TEL 02233-63550. Ed. Gernot Gabel. circ. 200. (back issues avail.)

BIJDRAGEN; tijdschrift voor filosofie en theologie. see *RELIGIONS AND THEOLOGY*

170 610 573.21   UK   ISSN 0269-9702
QH332
BIOETHICS. q. £29.50($59.50) to individuals; institutions £61.50($129). Basil Blackwell Ltd., 108 Cowley Road, Oxford OX4 1JF, England. TEL 0865-791100. FAX 0865-791347. TELEX 837022-OXBOOK-G. Ed.Bd.
—BLDSC shelfmark: 2072.119500.

100   NE
BOCHUMER STUDIEN ZUR PHILOSOPHIE. 1982. irreg. price varies. John Benjamins Publishing Co., Amsteldijk 44, P.O. Box 75577, 1070 AN Amsterdam, Netherlands. TEL 020-6738156. FAX 020-6739773. (In N. America: 821 Bethlehem Pike, Philadelphia, PA 19118. TEL 215-836-1200) Ed.Bd.

100 200   US
BOLLINGEN SERIES. 1941. irreg. price varies. (Bollingen Foundation) Princeton University Press, 3175 Princeton Pike, Lawrenceville, NJ 08648. TEL 609-896-1344. FAX 609-895-1081.

100   GW   ISSN 0344-1857
BONNER AKADEMISCHE REDEN. no.16, 1951. irreg., no.59, 1984. price varies. Bouvier Verlag Herbert Grundmann, Am Hof 32, Postfach 1268, 5300 Bonn 1, Germany.

BOODSCHAP. see *RELIGIONS AND THEOLOGY — Other Denominations And Sects*

100   NE   ISSN 0524-112X
BOSTON COLLEGE STUDIES IN PHILOSOPHY. (Text in English) 1966. irreg. price varies. (Boston College, US) Kluwer Academic Publishers, Postbus 17, 3300 AA Dordrecht, Netherlands. (Dist. by: Kluwer Academic Publishers Group, P.O. Box 322, 3300 AH Dordrecht; U.S. address: P.O. Box 358, Accord Station, Hingham, MA 02018-0358) Ed. J. Beinauer. **Indexed:** Phil.Ind., Rel.Ind.Two.

100 500   NE   ISSN 0068-0346
Q174   CODEN: BPSCDD
BOSTON STUDIES IN THE PHILOSOPHY OF SCIENCE; Boston colloquium for the philosophy of science. (Text in English) 1963. irreg. price varies. Kluwer Academic Publishers, Spuiboulevard 50, P.O. Box 17, 3300 AA Dordrecht, Netherlands. TEL 078-334911. FAX 078-334254. TELEX 29245. (Dist. by: Kluwer Academic Publishers Group, P.O. Box 322, 3300 AH Dordrecht; U.S. address: P.O. Box 358, Accord Station, Hingham, MA 02018-0358) Eds. Robert S. Cohen, Marx W. Wartofsky. **Indexed:** Biol.Abstr., Math.R.
—BLDSC shelfmark: 2251.830000.

BOSTON UNIVERSITY STUDIES IN PHILOSOPHY AND RELIGION. see *RELIGIONS AND THEOLOGY*

BRAHMAVADIN. see *RELIGIONS AND THEOLOGY — Buddhist*

101   GW
BRENNESSEL; Jahresschrift fuer Philosophie und verwandte Gebiete. 1974. a. Womm-Press, Mittelstr. 51, 4934 Horn - Bad Meinberg 1, Germany. Ed. H. Knauf. circ. 3,000.

100   NE
BRES'. 1965. bi-m. fl.47. Madoerastraat 10, 2585 VB The Hague, Netherlands. Eds. John P. Klautz, Alexandra Gabrielli. adv.; bk.rev.; charts; illus.; play rev.; stat.; circ. 21,000.
   Formerly: Bres-Planete (ISSN 0006-9639)

150 616.8   NE   ISSN 0924-0314
BRILL'S STUDIES IN EPISTEMOLOGY, PSYCHOLOGY AND PSYCHIATRY. 1989. irreg, vol.2, 1990. price varies. E.J. Brill, P.O. Box 9000, 2300 PA Leiden, Netherlands. TEL 071-312624. FAX 071-317532. TELEX 39296 BRILL NL. (In N. America: E.J. Brill, 24 Hudson St., Kinderhook, NY 12106. TEL 800-962-4406)

PHILOSOPHY

BRITISH JOURNAL FOR THE PHILOSOPHY OF SCIENCE. see *SCIENCES: COMPREHENSIVE WORKS*

BRITISH JOURNAL OF AESTHETICS. see *ART*

142.7   UK   ISSN 0007-1773
B829.5
BRITISH SOCIETY FOR PHENOMENOLOGY. JOURNAL. 1970. 3/yr. £31.25($50) to individuals; libraries £27.50($45). Haigh and Hochland Ltd., Precinct Centre, Oxford Rd., Manchester M13 9QA, England. TEL 061-273-4156. FAX 061-273-4340. Ed. Wolfe Mays. adv.; bk.rev.; bibl.; circ. 500. (reprint service avail. from ISI) **Indexed:** Abstr.Engl.Stud., Curr.Cont., Ind.Bk.Rev.Hum., Phil.Ind.
—BLDSC shelfmark: 4719.223000.

109   UK   ISSN 0951-5151
BRITISH SOCIETY FOR THE HISTORY OF PHILOSOPHY NEWSLETTER. 1986. irreg. (2-3/yr.). membership. British Society for the History of Philosophy, University of York, Dept. of Philosophy, Heslington, York YO1 5DD, England. TEL 0904-430000.

BROADSHEET. see *SOCIAL SCIENCES: COMPREHENSIVE WORKS*

BUDDHA WORLD. see *RELIGIONS AND THEOLOGY — Buddhist*

180   BE   ISSN 0068-4023
B721
BULLETIN DE PHILOSOPHIE MEDIEVALE. (Text mainly in French; contributions in English, German, Italian, Spanish) 1959. a. 800 Fr. Societe Internationale pour l'Etude de la Philosophie Medievale, College Thomas More, 1 Chemin d'Aristote, B-1348 Louvain-la-Neuve, Belgium. TEL 010-47-48-07. Ed. J. Hamesse. adv.; circ. 1,000. (back issues avail.) **Indexed:** Phil.Ind.
Formerly (until 1963): Societe Internationale pour l'Etude de la Philosophie Medievale. Bulletin.

100 330 620   US   ISSN 0277-2027
HF5387
BUSINESS & PROFESSIONAL ETHICS JOURNAL. 1981. q. $15 to individuals; institutions $35; foreign $45. University of Florida, Center for Applied Philosophy, 240 Dauer Hall, Gainesville, FL 32611. TEL 904-392-2084. Ed. Robert Baum. adv.; bk.rev.; circ. 650. (back issues avail.) **Indexed:** B.P.I., Eng.Ind., Phil.Ind.
—BLDSC shelfmark: 2933.219000.

100   BE   ISSN 0008-0284
BF458
CAHIERS INTERNATIONAUX DE SYMBOLISME. 1962. 3/yr. 600 Fr. to individuals (foreign 900 Fr.); institutions and libraries 1200 Fr. (foreign 1500 Fr.). Universite de Mons - Hainaut, Centre Interdisciplinaire d'Etudes Philosophiques, 20 Place du Parc, 7000 Mons, Belgium. TEL 065-37-37-36. bk.rev.; circ. 1,200. **Indexed:** Lang.& Lang.Behav.Abstr., M.L.A.

100   FR   ISSN 0241-2799
CAHIERS PHILOSOPHIQUES. 1979. 4/yr. 136 F. (foreign 152 F.)(effective 1992). (Ministere de l'Education) Centre National de Documentation Pedagogique, 29 rue de l'Ulm, 75230 Paris Cedex 05, France. (Subscr. to: CNDP-Abonnement, B.P. 107-05, 75224 Paris Cedex 5, France) bk.rev.
Description: Articles and essays on all aspects of philosophical research and thought.

100   ZR
CAHIERS PHILOSOPHIQUES AFRICAINS/AFRICAN PHILOSOPHICAL JOURNAL. (Text in French) 1972. irreg. Z.$80. (Universite Nationale du Zaire, Lubumbashi, Department de Philosophie) Presses Universitaires de Lubumbashi, B.P. 1825, Lubumbashi, Zaire. bk.rev. **Indexed:** CERDIC.

CAHIERS RATIONALISTES. see *SCIENCES: COMPREHENSIVE WORKS*

100   FR   ISSN 0763-1529
CAHIERS RAYMOND ABELLIO; recherche pour la nouvelle gnose. 1983. a. 60 F. Rencontres Litteraires et Artistiques, 16 rue de l'Arcade, 75008 Paris, France. TEL 4265-8645. Ed. Rene Chaminade. adv.; bk.rev.; circ. 1,000. (back issues avail.)

CANADIAN JOURNAL OF ITALIAN STUDIES. see *LITERATURE*

100   CN   ISSN 0045-5091
B1
CANADIAN JOURNAL OF PHILOSOPHY. (Text in English, French) 1971. q. plus a. supplement. Can.$25 to individuals (foreign US$25); institutions Can.$40 (foreign US$40); students Can.$15 (foreign US$15). (Canadian Association for Publishing in Philosophy) University of Calgary Press, 2500 University Drive N.W., Calgary, Alta. T2N 1N4, Canada. TEL 403-220-7578. FAX 403-282-0085. TELEX 03-821545. adv.; bk.rev.; index; circ. 1,200. **Indexed:** Arts & Hum.Cit.Ind., Can.Wom.Per.Ind., Curr.Cont., M.L.A., Phil.Ind.
—BLDSC shelfmark: 3033.900000.

100   CN   ISSN 0228-491X
B1
CANADIAN PHILOSOPHICAL REVIEWS/REVUE CANADIENNE DE COMPTES RENDUS EN PHILOSOPHIE. (Text in English and French) 1981. 6/yr. Can.$54($48) to individuals; institutions Can.$98($87). Academic Printing & Publishing, P.O. Box 4834, S. Edmonton, Alta. T6E 5G7, Canada. TEL 403-435-5898. FAX 403-435-5852. Ed. Roger Shiner. adv.; bk.rev.; circ. 350. **Indexed:** Bk.Rev.Ind. (1989-), Can.Wom.Per.Ind., Child.Bk.Rev.Ind. (1989-), Phil.Ind.
—BLDSC shelfmark: 3043.820000.
Description: Book review journal for recent work in philosophy.

212.5   CN   ISSN 0045-544X
CANADIAN THEOSOPHIST. 1920. bi-m. Can.$9. Theosophical Society in Canada, R.R. No.3, Burk's Falls, Ont. P0A 1C0, Canada. TEL 705-382-6012. Ed. S.L. Treloar. bk.rev.; index; circ. 500.

CARNEGIE COUNCIL NEWSLETTER. see *POLITICAL SCIENCE — International Relations*

CATHOLIC THOUGHT FROM LUBLIN. see *RELIGIONS AND THEOLOGY — Roman Catholic*

108   US
CENTER FOR PHILOSOPHIC EXCHANGE. ANNUAL PROCEEDINGS. 1969. a. $22. Center for Philosophic Exchange, State University College at Brockport, Brockport, NY 14420. TEL 716-395-2493. Ed. Jack Glickman. circ. 300.

149   US   ISSN 0360-618X
CENTER FOR PROCESS STUDIES. NEWSLETTER. 1975. 3/yr. $5. School of Theology at Claremont, Center for Process Studies, 1325 N. College Ave., Claremont, CA 91711. Ed. Laurie Huff. circ. 650. (looseleaf format; back issues avail.)
Description: For students and scholars of process philosophy and theology; covers events and developments relating to the philosophy of Alfred North Whitehead and his academic associates.

CENTRE PROTESTANT D'ETUDES DE GENEVE. BULLETIN. see *RELIGIONS AND THEOLOGY — Protestant*

100   IT   ISSN 0392-7334
B3583
CENTRO DI STUDI VICHIANI. BOLLETTINO. 1971. a. L.50000. Bibliopolis, Via Arangio Ruiz 83, 80122 Naples, Italy. TEL (081) 664606. Dirs. Giuseppe Giarrizzo, Fulvio Tessitore. **Indexed:** Lang.& Lang.Behav.Abstr., M.L.A., Phil.Ind.
Description: Focuses on Gian Battista Vico's life and works and all the studies pertinent to the Neapolitan philosopher.

160   IT
CENTRO SUPERIORE DI LOGICA E SCIENZE COMPARATE. QUADERNI. 1971. irreg., no.8, 1976. Centro Superiore di Logica e Scienze Comparate, Via Belmeloro 3, 40126 Bologna, Italy.

100   CE   ISSN 0577-4772
CEYLON RATIONALIST AMBASSADOR. (Text in English) 1967? a. Rs.5($1) Ceylon Rationalist Association, 89 Pamankada Ln., Colombo 6, Sri Lanka. Ed. Abraham T. Kovoor. circ. 3,000. (back issues avail.)

CHALCEDON REPORT. see *RELIGIONS AND THEOLOGY*

160   US   ISSN 0009-1774
B945.P44
CHARLES S. PEIRCE SOCIETY. TRANSACTIONS; a quarterly journal in American philosophy. 1965. 4/yr. $18 to individuals (foreign $23); institutions $27 (foreign $32). Charles S. Peirce Society, State University of New York at Buffalo, c/o Peter H. Hare, Dept. of Philosophy, Baldy Hall, Buffalo, NY 14260. TEL 716-636-2444. Eds. Peter H. Hare, Richard S. Robin. adv.; bk.rev.; circ. 600. **Indexed:** Arts & Hum.Cit.Ind., Ind.Bk.Rev.Hum., Phil.Ind.
—BLDSC shelfmark: 8912.377000.

100   US   ISSN 0023-8627
B1
CHINESE STUDIES IN PHILOSOPHY; a journal of translations. 1967. q. $286 to institutions. M.E. Sharpe, Inc., 80 Business Park Dr., Armonk, NY 10504. TEL 914-273-1800. FAX 914-273-2106. Ed. Chung-yeng Cheng. adv.; index. (back issues avail.) **Indexed:** Arts & Hum.Cit.Ind., Curr.Cont., Phil.Ind.
—BLDSC shelfmark: 3181.122000.
Refereed Serial

100 700   US   ISSN 0888-9384
CHRYSALIS. 1985. 3/yr. $20. Swedenborg Foundation, Inc., 139 E. 23rd St., New York, NY 10010. TEL 212-673-7310. FAX 804-983-1074. (Subscr. to: Rte. 1, Box 184, Dillwyn, VA 23936) Ed. Carol Skinner Lawson. adv.; bk.rev.; index; circ. 2,000. (back issues avail.)
Description: Draws upon diverse traditions for the purpose of exploring spiritual questions and perspectives on contemporary life, the arts and religion.

CHUNG-KUO FO CHIAO. see *RELIGIONS AND THEOLOGY — Buddhist*

CINCINNATI JOURNAL OF MAGIC. see *PARAPSYCHOLOGY AND OCCULTISM*

CLASSICS IN THE HISTORY AND PHILOSOPHY OF SCIENCE. see *SCIENCES: COMPREHENSIVE WORKS*

100   UK   ISSN 0950-8864
B1
COGITO. 3/yr. $84. (Cogito Society) Carfax Publishing Co., P.O. Box 25, Abingdon, Oxfordshire OX14 3UE, England. TEL 0235-555335. FAX 0235-553559. (Subscr. addr. in U.S.: Carfax Publishing Co., Box 2025, Dunnellon, FL 32630) Ed. Gordon Reddiford. adv.; bk.rev. (also avail. in microfiche; back issues avail.)
—BLDSC shelfmark: 3292.868500.
Description: Philosophy topics for students at the college level.

100   BL
COLECAO ECUMENISMO E HUMANISMO. vol.33, 1984. irreg. Editora Paz e Terra S.A., Rua Sao Jose, 90-18 Andar, Centro Rio de Janeiro, RJ, Brazil.

100   SP   ISSN 0069-5076
COLECCION FILOSOFICA. 1963. irreg., no.66, 1990. price varies. (Universidad de Navarra, Facultad de Filosofia y Letras) Ediciones Universidad de Navarra, S.A., Apdo. 396, 31080 Pamplona, Spain. TEL 94 825 6850.

181.45   US   ISSN 0164-1522
COLLABORATION.* 1974. q. $12. SAA-SRI Aurobundo, HCR 1 Box 98, Mt. Temper, NY 12457. TEL 914-687-9222. Ed. Jean Korstange. bk.rev.; bibl.; circ. 1,000.
Description: Explores various yoga techniques and philosophies.

100   CN
COLLECTION PHILOSOPHICA. 1972. irreg. price varies. University of Ottawa Press, 603 Cumberland, Ottawa, Ont., K1N 6N5, Canada. TEL 613-564-2270. Eds. David Carr, Theodore Geraets.
Description: Books in English and French on various subjects in the field of philosophy.

COMMENTS & CRITICISMS. see *PSYCHOLOGY*

PHILOSOPHY

100 809   US   ISSN 0961-754X
▼**COMMON KNOWLEDGE.** 1992. 3/yr. $24 to individuals; institutions $48. Oxford University Press, Journals, 200 Madison Ave., New York, NY 10016. TEL 212-679-7300. FAX 212-725-2972. TELEX 6859654. (Subscr. to: Journals Fulfillment, 2001 Evans Rd., Cary, NC 27513. TEL 919-677-0977) Ed. Jeffrey Perl. adv.; bk.rev.; circ. 500.
    Description: Addresses the restructuring of traditional debates within intellectual communities.

150   AG   ISSN 0010-4329
COMPORTAMIENTO HUMANO. vol.7, 1973. q. free. Liga pro Comportamiento Humano, Maipu 286, Buenos Aires, Argentina. Ed. Francisco A. Rizzuto. bk.rev.; circ. 10,000.

100   AU   ISSN 0010-5155
CONCEPTUS; Zeitschrift fuer Philosophie. (Text in German: summaries in English and German) 1967. 3/yr. $44.80. Verband der Wissenschaftlichen Gesellschaften Oesterreichs, Lindengasse 37, A-1070 Vienna, Austria. TEL 932166. Ed.Bd. adv.; bk.rev.; abstr.; bibl.; charts; index, cum.index; circ. 500. (reprint service avail. from KTO) **Indexed:** Math.R., Phil.Ind.

100   AU   ISSN 0259-0670
CONCEPTUS-STUDIEN. 1984. irreg., no.6, 1990. price varies. Verband der Wissenschaftlichen Gesellschaften Oesterreichs, Lindengasse 37, A-1070 Vienna, Austria. TEL 932166.

CONFERENCE ON EDITORIAL PROBLEMS: UNIVERSITY OF TORONTO. see LITERATURE

189 200   IT   ISSN 0010-6305
CONOSCENZA. 1964. bi-m. L.20000. (Centro Studi Esoterici ed Iniziatici) Carlesi Loris, Ed. & Pub. Via di San Vito 22-5, 50124 Florence, Italy. TEL 055-482422. bk.rev.; bibl.; circ. 1,000.

100   GW   ISSN 0589-4069
CONSCIENTIA. 1968. irreg., vol.12, 1984. price varies. Bouvier Verlag Herbert Grundmann, Am Hof 32, Postfach 1268, 5300 Bonn 1, Germany. Ed. Gerhard Funke.

100   US   ISSN 0895-0520
CONTEMPORARY EXISTENTIALISM. irreg. Peter Lang Publishing, Inc., 62 W. 45th St., 4th Fl., New York, NY 10036. TEL 212-302-6740. FAX 212-302-7574. Ed. Howard K. Slaatte.

100   US   ISSN 0732-4944
CONTEMPORARY PHILOSOPHY. 1966. bi-m. $30. Institute for Advanced Philosophic Research, Box 1373, Boulder, CO 80306. (Affiliate: Realia) bk.rev.; circ. controlled.
—BLDSC shelfmark: 3425.198800.
    Formerly: Philosophic Research and Analysis (ISSN 0048-3907)

100 150   US   ISSN 0889-468X
CONTINUING THE CONVERSATION; a newsletter on the ideas of Gregory Bateson. 1985. q. $8. HortIdeas Publishing, Rt. 1, Box 302, Gravel Switch, KY 40328. Ed. Gregory Williams. bk.rev.; circ. 400. (back issues avail.)

100   US   ISSN 0084-926X
CONTRIBUTIONS IN PHILOSOPHY. 1968. irreg., no.50, 1992. price varies. Greenwood Press, Inc. (Subsidiary of: Greenwood Publishing Group Inc.), 88 Post Rd. W., Box 5007, Westport, CT 06881-5007. TEL 203-226-3571. FAX 203-222-1502.
—BLDSC shelfmark: 3461.110000.

100   IT
IL CONTRIBUTO. 1976. q. L.25000($20) Editoriale B.M. Italiana, V. Piancianí 31-A4, 00185 Rome, Italy. TEL 06-6900483. Ed. Pietro Ciaravolo. adv.; bk.rev.; circ. 1,000.

CORONA. see LITERATURE

CORPUS DEI PAPIRI FILOSOFICI GRECI E LATINI. STUDI E TESTI. see CLASSICAL STUDIES

108   IT
CORPUS PHILOSOPHORUM MEDII AEVI. SERIE I. SUBSIDIA. 1980. irreg., no.8, 1991. price varies. Casa Editrice Leo S. Olschki, Casella Postale 66, 50100 Florence, Italy. TEL 055-6530684. FAX 055-6530214.

100   IT
CORPUS PHILOSOPHORUM MEDII AEVI. SERIE II. TESTI E STUDI. 1980. irreg., no.11, 1990. price varies. Casa Editrice Leo S. Olschki, Casella Postale 66, 50100 Florence, Italy. TEL 055-6530684. FAX 055-6530214.

144 360   US
COURIER (NEW YORK, 1954). 1954. s-a. membership. Albert Schweitzer Fellowship, 866 United Nations Plaza, New York, NY 10017. TEL 212-752-1760. Ed. Estelle Linzer. circ. 6,500.
    Description: Informs interested readers of the Schweitzer Fellowship's activities in support of "reverence for life".

CREATIVITY IN ACTION. see BUSINESS AND ECONOMICS — Management

100   MX   ISSN 0011-1503
B1
CRITICA; revista hispanoamericana de filosofia. (Text in English, Spanish) 1967. 3/yr. Mex.$50000($20) Universidad Nacional Autonoma de Mexico, Instituto de Investigaciones Filosoficas, Apdo. Postal 70-447, Mexico, D.F., Mexico. Ed.Bd. adv.; bk.rev.; index; circ. 1,000 (controlled). **Indexed:** Hisp.Amer.Per.Ind., Phil.Ind.
—BLDSC shelfmark: 3487.394700.

CRITICAL REVIEW. see LITERATURE

CRITIQUE (WEST VANCOUVER); the juicy embrace between information and transformation. see NEW AGE PUBLICATIONS

100   MX   ISSN 0185-2604
CUADERNOS DE CRITICA (MEXICO). 1977. irreg., no.45, 1989. Universidad Nacional Autonoma de Mexico, Instituto de Investigaciones Filosoficas, Apdo. Postal 70-447, Mexico, D.F., Mexico. (Dist. by: Direccion General de Formento Editorial, Porto Alegre No. 260, San Andres Tetepilco, 094 4, Mexico, D.F., Mexico)

100   SP   ISSN 0210-4857
CUADERNOS SALMANTINOS DE FILOSOFIA. 1974. a. 3000 ptas.($40) Universidad Pontificia, Departamento de Ediciones y Publicaciones, Apdo. de Correos 541, 37080 Salamanca, Spain. TEL 923-21-51-40. FAX 923-21-34-50. Ed. Saturnino Alvarez Turienzo.
—BLDSC shelfmark: 3490.783000.

CULTURA, HISTORIA Y FILOSOFIA. see HISTORY — History Of Europe

190   NE   ISSN 0921-3740
                              CODEN: CUDYEH
CULTURAL DYNAMICS; an international journal for the study of processes and temporality of culture. (Text in English) 1989. 4/yr. fl.128($73.36) to individuals; institutions fl.188($107.75)(effective 1992). E.J. Brill, P.O. Box 9000, 2300 PA Leiden, Netherlands. TEL 071-312624. FAX 071-317532. TELEX 39296 BRILL NL. (In N. America: E.J. Brill, 24 Hudson St., Kinderhook, NY 12106. TEL 800-962-4406) Ed. R. Pinxten.
—BLDSC shelfmark: 3491.662500.

D W D NEWSLETTER. (Death with Dignity) see LAW

101   IS   ISSN 0334-2336
DA'AT; Jewish philosophy and Kabbalah. (Text in English, French, Hebrew; summaries in English) 1978. s-a. $15 per no. (Bar-Ilan University, Department of Philosophy) Bar-Ilan University Press, Ramat-Gan 52900, Israel. FAX 03-347601. TELEX 342290-BARIL-IL. Eds. Moshe Hallamish, E. Levinas. bk.rev.; bibl.; cum.index: vols.1-20 in vol.20; circ. 600. (back issues avail.) **Indexed:** Ind.Heb.Per.
—BLDSC shelfmark: 3509.140000.

DALHOUSIE REVIEW; a Canadian quarterly of literature and opinion. see LITERARY AND POLITICAL REVIEWS

108 320   US
DANDELION. 1977. irreg., vol.20, 1987. $4.50. Michael E. Coughlin, Ed. & Pub., 1985 Selby Ave., St. Paul, MN 55104. TEL 612-646-8917. adv.; bk.rev.; circ. 400. (back issues avail.) **Indexed:** Can.Lit.Ind.
    Description: Focuses on philosophical anarchism; explores the movements through history, its philosophy and personalities.

100   DK   ISSN 0070-2749
B1
DANISH YEARBOOK OF PHILOSOPHY. (Text in English) 1964. a. DKK 150. University of Copenhagen, Museum Tusculanum Press, Njalsgade 94, DK-2300 Copenhagen S, Denmark. Ed.Bd. adv.; index; circ. 400. (reprint service avail. from ISI) **Indexed:** Curr.Cont., Phil.Ind.
—BLDSC shelfmark: 3519.900000.

181.45   US   ISSN 0892-130X
BL624
DARSHAN. 1975. 12/yr. $86. Syda Foundation, Box 600, South Fallsburg, NY 12779. FAX 914-434-3276. Ed. Patti Hayes.
    Formerly (until 1986): Siddha Path (ISSN 0278-954X)

100   II   ISSN 0011-6734
DARSHANA INTERNATIONAL; an international quarterly of philosophy, psychology, sociology, psychical research, religion and mysticism. (Text in English) 1961. q. Rs.100($40) Darashna International, Moradabad 244 001, India. TEL 28712. Ed. J.P. Atreya. adv.; bk.rev.; charts; illus.; index; circ. 1,100. **Indexed:** Curr.Cont., Phil.Ind.

DEGRES; revue de synthese a orientation semiologique. see LINGUISTICS

100   GW
DIE DEUTSCHE VOLKHOCHSCHULE. 1978. bi-m. DM.60. Postfach 1217, 3006 Burgwedel 1, Germany. Ed. Barbara Swoboda. circ. 1,000.

100   GW   ISSN 0012-1045
B3
DEUTSCHE ZEITSCHRIFT FUER PHILOSOPHIE. 1953. m. M.120.40. VEB Deutscher Verlag der Wissenschaften, Johannes-Dieckmann-Str. 10, Postfach 1216, 1080 Berlin, Germany. Ed.Bd. adv.; bk.rev.; bibl.; index. (reprint service avail. from SWZ) **Indexed:** Arts & Hum.Cit.Ind., Curr.Cont., Lang.& Lang.Behav.Abstr., Phil.Ind., SSCI.
—BLDSC shelfmark: 3575.840000.

100 378   US
DEVI-BHAGAVAT PRESENTATION. 1986. q. $20. Mani-Dwipa News Foundation, Box 73, Harbor City, CA 90710-0073. TEL 213-831-4226. Ed. Amanda Carlson. adv.
    Description: Includes English verse translations of Puranic history and philosophy, with uplighting stories and elucidations of the age-old wisdom of India.

DHARMA; a quarterly devoted to universal religion, righteousness & culture. see RELIGIONS AND THEOLOGY

DHARMA COMBAT; a magazine about spirituality, metaphysics, reality and other conspiracies. see RELIGIONS AND THEOLOGY

DIACRITICA. see LITERATURE

100   AT   ISSN 0084-9804
DIALECTIC. 1967. irreg. $3. Newcastle University Philosophy Club, c/o Department of Philosophy, Univ. of Newcastle, N.S.W. 2308, Australia. Ed.Bd. circ. 225.

120   SZ   ISSN 0012-2017
B1
DIALECTICA; international review of philosophy of knowledge. (Text in English, French and German) 1947. q. 65 Fr. (foreign 80 Fr.) Societe Dialectica, P.O. Box 5907, CH-3001 Bern, Switzerland. Ed.Bd. adv.; bk.rev.; index; circ. 700. (also avail. in microform from MIM) **Indexed:** Arts & Hum.Cit.Ind., Curr.Cont., Lang.& Lang.Behav.Abstr., Math.R., Phil.Ind., Risk Abstr., Sociol.Abstr.
—BLDSC shelfmark: 3579.700000.

100   PL
DIALECTICS AND HUMANISM; the Polish philosophical quarterly. 1973. q. $5. Polska Akademia Nauk, Palac Kultury i Nauki, 00-901 Warsaw, Poland. (Subscr. to: Ars Polona Ruch, Krakowskie Przedmiescie 7, 00-068 Warsaw, Poland) Ed. Janusz Kuczynski. bibl. **Indexed:** Mid.East: Abstr.& Ind., Phil.Ind.

PHILOSOPHY

100   NE
DIALECTICS AND REVOLUTION. 1976. irreg. price varies. John Benjamins Publishing Co., Amsteldijk 44, P.O. Box 75577, 1070 AN Amsterdam, Netherlands. TEL 020-6738156.
FAX 020-6739773. (In N. America: 821 Bethlehem Pike, Philadelphia, PA 19118. TEL 215-836-1200)
Description: Surveys the discovery and applications of dialectics.

160   IT
DIALETTICA. irreg., latest vol.4. price varies. Edizioni Studium, Via Cassiodoro 14, 00193 Rome, Italy.

100   IT   ISSN 0012-2084
DIALOGO; quaderni europei di dialogica. (Text in French, Italian and Spanish) 1957. L.1000. (Centro Studi Dialogic dell'Istituto Euromediterraneo di Scienze Umane della Citta-Studio di Urbino) A. Testa, Ed. & Pub., Via S. Isaia 67, Bologna, Italy.

100   PR   ISSN 0012-2122
B5
DIALOGOS. (Text in English or Spanish) 1964. s-a. $16 to institutions. Universidad de Puerto Rico, Departamento de Filosofia, Box 21572, U.P.R. Station, Rio Piedras, PR 00931. FAX 764-8799. Ed. Roberto Torretti. adv.; bk.rev.; bibl.; circ. 800. **Indexed:** Hisp.Amer.Per.Ind., Phil.Ind.
—BLDSC shelfmark: 3579.740000.

100   US   ISSN 0012-2246
B1
DIALOGUE (MILWAUKEE). 1956; N.S. 3/yr. $5. Phi Sigma Tau, Dept. of Philosophy, Marquette University, Milwaukee, WI 53233.
TEL 414-288-6857. Ed. Thomas L. Prendergast. adv.; bk.rev.; bibl.; index; circ. 1,500. **Indexed:** Arts & Hum.Cit.Ind., Curr.Cont., Phil.Ind.
—BLDSC shelfmark: 3579.758000.

100   CN   ISSN 0012-2173
B1
DIALOGUE: CANADIAN PHILOSOPHICAL REVIEW/REVUE CANADIENNE DE PHILOSOPHIE. (Text in English, French) 1962. q. Can.$70. (Canadian Philosophical Association) Wilfrid Laurier University Press, 75 University Ave. W., Waterloo, Ont. N2L 3C5, Canada. TEL 519-884-1970. FAX 519-884-8853. adv.; bk.rev.; cum.index: vols. 1-10; circ. 1,400. **Indexed:** Bk.Rev.Ind. (1989-), Child.Bk.Rev.Ind. (1989-), Curr.Cont., M.L.A., Phil.Ind.
—BLDSC shelfmark: 3579.755000.
Description: Covers the history of philosophy, metaphysics, epistemology, logic, philosophy of science, political philosophy, ethics, and the philosophy of religion.
Refereed Serial

100   MX   ISSN 0419-0890
DIANOIA; anuario de filosofia. 1955. a. Universidad Nacional Autonoma de Mexico, Instituto de Investigaciones Filosoficas, Circuito Maestro Mano de la Cueva, Ciudad Universitaria, Coyoacan 04510, Mexico, D.F., Mexico. circ. 1,200. (back issues avail.) **Indexed:** Hisp.Amer.Per.Ind., Phil.Ind.

100   SZ   ISSN 0070-4806
PQ1979
DIDEROT STUDIES. (Text in English and French) 1949. irreg., no.24, 1991. price varies. Librairie Droz S.A., 11, rue Massot, CH-1211 Geneva 12, Switzerland. TEL 022-466666. FAX 022-472391. Eds. Otis Fellows, Diana Guiragossian. bk.rev. **Indexed:** M.L.A.

DIJALEKTIKA/DIALECTICS; casopis za metodolosko filozofske probleme matematickih, prirodnih i tehnickih nauka. see *SCIENCES: COMPREHENSIVE WORKS*

100   GW   ISSN 0175-0135
DILTHEY-JAHRBUCH; fuer Philosophie und Geschichte der Geisteswissenschaften. (Text in English and German; summaries in German) 1983. a. DM.78. Verlag Vandenhoeck und Ruprecht, Robert-Bosch-Breite 6, Postfach 3753, 3400 Goettingen, Germany. TEL 0551-6959-22.
FAX 0551-46298. TELEX 965226-VAN-D. circ. 800. (back issues avail.)
—BLDSC shelfmark: 3588.457700.

DIOGENES (ENGLISH EDITION). see *SOCIOLOGY*

105   GR
DIOTIMA; epitheoresis philosophikes ereunes - revue de recherche philosophique - review of philosophical research. (Text in English, French, or Greek) 1973. irreg. $20. (Hellenic Society for Philosophical Studies) Grigoris Publications, 71 Solonos St., 10679 Athens, Greece. adv.; bk.rev. **Indexed:** Phil.Ind.

100   US   ISSN 0070-508X
DIRECTORY OF AMERICAN PHILOSOPHERS. 1962. biennial. $59 to individuals; institutions $99. Bowling Green State University, Philosophy Documentation Center, Bowling Green, OH 43403-0189. TEL 419-372-2419.
FAX 419-372-6987. Ed. Archie J. Bahm. circ. 1,100.
—BLDSC shelfmark: 3592.595000.

100   AG   ISSN 0327-2214
DISCURSO Y REALIDAD. 1985. 2/yr.
Arg.$250000($25) Discurso y Realidad, 25 de Mayo 950, Block C, Piso 10-B, 4000 San Miguel de Tucuman, Argentina. Dir. Rolo Maris. bk.rev.

DIVREI HA-AKADEMIA HA-LEUMIT HA-YISRAELIT LEMADAIM. see *HUMANITIES: COMPREHENSIVE WORKS*

DIVUS THOMAS; commentarium de philosophia et theologia. see *RELIGIONS AND THEOLOGY*

DONGBEI SHIDA XUEBAO (ZHEXUE SHEHUI KEXUE BAN)/NORTHEAST NORMAL UNIVERSITY. JOURNAL (PHILOSOPHY, SOCIAL SCIENCE EDITION). see *SOCIAL SCIENCES: COMPREHENSIVE WORKS*

100 301   GW
DUISBURGER STUDIEN; Geistes- und Gesellschaftswissenschaften. 1979. s-a. Gilles & Francke Verlag, Postfach 100538, 4100 Duisburg 1, Germany. TEL 0203-355097.
FAX 0203-355520. Ed.Bd. adv.; bk.rev.

E Z W - TEXTE; Arbeitstexte. (Evangelische Zentralstelle fuer Weltanschauungsfragen) see *RELIGIONS AND THEOLOGY*

EAST AND WEST SERIES; an interpreter of the life of the spirit. see *RELIGIONS AND THEOLOGY*

EASTERN BUDDHIST. see *RELIGIONS AND THEOLOGY — Buddhist*

212.5   US   ISSN 0046-1105
ECLECTIC THEOSOPHIST; following the Blavatsky and Point Loma traditions. 1971. bi-m. $5 (foreign $5.50). Point Loma Publications, Inc., 3727 Charles St., Box 6507, San Diego, CA 92106.
TEL 619-222-3291. Ed. W. Emmett Small. bk.rev.; circ. 800. (tabloid format; back issues avail.)

ECONOMIES ET SOCIETES. SERIE M. PHILOSOPHIE - SCIENCES SOCIALES ECONOMIE. see *BUSINESS AND ECONOMICS — Economic Systems And Theories, Economic History*

EDITIO; internationales Jahrbuch fuer Editionswissenschaft. see *LITERATURE*

100   UK   ISSN 0142-3371
EFRYDIAU ATHRONYDDOL. (Text in Welsh) 1938. a. £2. University of Wales Press, 6 Gwennyth St., Cathays, Cardiff CF2 4YD, Wales. TEL 0222-231919.
FAX 0222-230908. Eds. John Daniel, W.L. Gealey. bk.rev.; circ. 350.
—BLDSC shelfmark: 3664.135000.

100   CN   ISSN 0707-2287
EIDOS; the Canadian graduate journal of philosophy. (Text in English and French) 1978. s-a. Can.$8 to students; institutions Can.$28; others Can.$15. University of Waterloo, Philosophy Graduate Student Association, Dept. of Philosophy, Waterloo, Ont. N2L 3G1, Canada. TEL 519-885-1211. Eds. C. Hahn, A. Wylie. adv.; bk.rev.; circ. 160. **Indexed:** Phil.Ind.

EIGHTEENTH CENTURY: A CURRENT BIBLIOGRAPHY. see *BIBLIOGRAPHIES*

100 133.9   GW   ISSN 0178-7659
ELEMENTE; zur Metapolitik - fuer die Europaeische Wiedergeburt. 1986. a (plus 2 special issues). DM.35 (Europe DM.42). Thule-Seminar e.V., Postfach 410403, 3500 Kassel 41, Germany. Ed. Pierre Krebs. adv.; B&W page DM.600; trim 210 x 167. circ. 5,000. (back issues avail.)

100   IT   ISSN 0392-7342
B175.I7
ELENCHOS; rivista di studi sul pensiero antico. 1980. s-a. L.27000. (Centro di Studi sul Pensiero Antico) Bibliopolis, Via Arangio Ruiz 83, 80122 Naples, Italy. TEL (081) 664606. Ed. Prof. Gabriele Gionnantoni.
Description: Devoted exclusively to ancient philosophy.

EMERGING. see *NEW AGE PUBLICATIONS*

100   US   ISSN 0883-6000
EMORY VICO STUDIES. 1987. irreg. Peter Lang Publishing, Inc., 62 W. 45th St., 4th Fl., New York, NY 10036. TEL 212-302-6740. Ed. Donald Verene.

EMSHOCK LETTER. see *NEW AGE PUBLICATIONS*

100 614.7   US   ISSN 0163-4275
GF80   CODEN: ENETDD
ENVIRONMENTAL ETHICS; an interdisciplinary journal dedicated to the philosophical aspects of environmental problems. 1979. q. $18 to individuals; institutions $36. Environmental Philosophy, Inc., Department of Philosophy, University of North Texas, Box 13496, Denton, TX 76203-3496. TEL 817-565-2727.
FAX 817-565-4448. Ed. Eugene C. Hargrove. adv.; bk.rev.; cum.index: 1979-1983 in vol.5, 1984-1988 in vol.10; circ. 1,600. (also avail. in microform from UMI; reprint service avail. from UMI) **Indexed:** Curr.Cont., Ecol.Abstr., Energy Rev., Environ.Abstr., Environ.Ind., Environ.Per.Bibl., Excerp.Med., Hum.Ind., Phil.Ind., Rel.& Theol.Abstr. (1979-), Risk Abstr., Saf.Sci.Abstr., Sociol.Abstr., SSCI, Wild Life Rev.
—BLDSC shelfmark: 3791.465000.
Description: Forum for diverse interests and attitudes. Seeks to bring together the nonprofessional environmental philosophy tradition with the newly emerging professional interest in the subject.

121   IT
EPISTEMOLOGIA; an Italian journal for the philosophy of science. (Text in English and Italian; occasionally in French) 1978. s-a. (plus approx. 1 special issue/yr.) L.23000($23) Tilgher-Genova s.a.s., Via Assarotti 52, 16122 Genoa, Italy. Ed. Evandro Agazzi. adv.; bk.rev.; index. (also avail. in microform)

100   US
EPOCH (ADAIRSVILLE).* 6/yr. $10. Mandel Foundation Inc., 145 Ward Mt. Rd., Adairsville, GA 30103-9801. **Indexed:** Arts & Hum.Cit.Ind.

ERASMUS OF ROTTERDAM SOCIETY YEARBOOK. see *RELIGIONS AND THEOLOGY*

100   GW   ISSN 0179-163X
ERINNYEN; Zeitschrift fuer materialistische Ethik. 1985. a. DM.4. Hertzstr. 39, 3008 Garbsen 4, Germany. TEL 05131-1623. Ed. Bodo Gassmann. adv.; bk.rev.; circ. 700. (back issues avail.)
Description: Examines materialistic-dialectic ethics and socialistic morals.

100   NE   ISSN 0165-0106
B1   CODEN: ERKEDQ
ERKENNTNIS; an international journal of analytic philosophy. (Text in English) 1930. 6/yr. $300. Kluwer Academic Publishers, Postbus 17, 3300 AA Dordrecht, Netherlands. TEL 078-334911.
FAX 078-334254. TELEX 29245. (Dist. by: Kluwer Academic Publishers Group, P.O. Box 322, 3300 AH Dordrecht, Netherlands; N. America dist. addr.: Box 358, Accord Station, Hingham, MA 02018-0358. TEL 617-871-6600) Ed. Wolfgang Spohn. adv.; bk.rev. (reprint service avail. from SWZ) **Indexed:** Ind.Bk.Rev.Hum., Lang.& Lang.Behav.Abstr., Phil.Ind., Sociol.Abstr.

ESCRITOS. see *LITERATURE*

160   AG
ESPACIOS DE CRITICA Y PRODUCCION. s-a. Secretaria de Bienestar Estudiantil y Extension Universitaria, Facultad de Filosofia y Letra (UBA), Marcelo T. de Alvear 2230, 1 Piso, Buenos Aires, Argentina.

108   SP
ESPASA UNIVERSITARIA. FILOSOFIA Y PENSAMIENTO. irreg., no.13, 1983. Editorial Espasa-Calpe, S.A., Carretera de Irun, Madrid 34, Spain.

PHILOSOPHY

100 — SP — ISSN 0014-0716
ESPIRITU. 1952. s-a. 1200 ptas. (Instituto Filosofico de Balmesiana) Editorial Balmes, S.A., Apdo. 1382, Duran y Bas 9, 08002 Barcelona, Spain. Ed. Juan Pegueroles. bk.rev.; cum.index: 1952-1977; circ. 300. Indexed: Amer.Hist.& Life, Bull.Signal., Hist.Abstr., Phil.Ind.
—BLDSC shelfmark: 3811.658500.

100 — BE — ISSN 0071-1349
ESSAIS PHILOSOPHIQUES. no.5, 1950. irreg., no.10, 1985. price varies. (Institut Superieur de Philosophie) Editions Peeters s.p.r.l., Bondgenotenlaan 153, B-3000 Leuven, Belgium. TEL 016-235170. FAX 016-228500.
  Description: Monographs on different topics in philosophy by scholars of the institute.

100 133.91 — IT
ESSERE. 1980. s-a. L.7,500. Casa Editrice Psiche, Via Madama Cristina 70, Torino, Italy. TEL 011-6507058. Ed. Jean Klein.

100 — IT — ISSN 1121-0036
▼**ESTETICA (BOLOGNA).** 1991. a. Societa Editrice Il Mulino, Strada Maggiore 37, 40125 Bologna, Italy. TEL 051-256011. FAX 051-256034. Ed. Stefano Zecchi. circ. 2,000.

ESTETIKA/AESTHETICS. see ART

ESTUDIOS; revista trimestral publicada por los frailes de la orden de la merced. see RELIGIONS AND THEOLOGY

100 — SP — ISSN 0210-6086
B5
ESTUDIOS FILOSOFICOS; revista de investigacion y critica. 1952. 3/yr. 3500 ptas.($50) (effective 1992). Instituto Superior de Filosofia, Apdo. 586, 47080 Valladolid, Spain. TEL 35-66-99. FAX 34-34-09. Dir. D. Fernando Soria Heredia. adv.; bk.rev.; index; circ. 900. (back issues avail.) Indexed: Lang.& Lang.Behav.Abstr., Phil.Ind., Sociol.Abstr.

100 — VE
ESTUDIOS FILOSOFICOS. 1974. irreg. $4 per no. Universidad Simon Bolivar, Departamento de Filosofia, Apdo. 80659, Caracas, Venezuela. (Co-sponsor: Sociedad Venezolana de Filosofia) Ed. Alberto Rosales. bibl.

200 — UK — ISSN 0014-1690
ETHICAL RECORD. 1895. m. (except Aug. & Dec.). £10. South Place Ethical Society, 25 Red Lion Square, London WC1R 4RL, England. bk.rev.; circ. 750. (also avail. in microform from UMI; reprint service avail. from UMI)

300 320 340 — US — ISSN 0014-1704
BJ1
ETHICS: AN INTERNATIONAL JOURNAL OF SOCIAL, POLITICAL AND LEGAL PHILOSOPHY. 1890. q. $28 to individuals; institutions $54; students $20. University of Chicago Press, Journals Division, 5720 S. Woodlawn Ave., Chicago, IL 60637. TEL 312-753-3347. FAX 312-702-0694. TELEX 25-4603. (Orders to: Box 37005, Chicago, IL 60637) Ed. Russell Hardin. adv.; bk.rev.; bibl.; index, cum.index: vols.1-75; circ. 3,300. (also avail. in microform from MIM,UMI; reprint service avail. from UMI,ISI) Indexed: A.B.C.Pol.Sci., Abstr.Bk.Rev.Curr.Leg.Per., Abstr.Crim.& Pen., Arts & Hum.Cit.Ind., Bk.Rev.Ind. (1977-), C.L.I., CERDIC, Chic.Per.Ind., Child.Bk.Rev.Ind. (1977-), Commun.Abstr., Curr.Cont., G.Soc.Sci.& Rel.Per.Lit., Ind.Bk.Rev.Hum., L.R.I., Lang.& Lang.Behav.Abstr., Phil.Ind., Soc.Sci.Ind., Sociol.Abstr., SSCI.
—BLDSC shelfmark: 3814.650000.
  Refereed Serial

ETHICS AND INTERNATIONAL AFFAIRS (NEWSLETTER); a college-level curriculum development program. see POLITICAL SCIENCE — International Relations

215 — US
ETHICS AND MEDICS. 1976. m. $15 (foreign $18). Pope John XXIII Medical-Moral Research and Education Center, 186 Forbes Rd., Braintree, MA 02184. TEL 617-848-6965. Ed. Albert S. Moraczewski. cum.index: 1976-1988; circ. 22,000. (back issues avail.)
  Description: Catholic perspective on moral issues in the health and life sciences.

100 — US — ISSN 0897-0106
BJ1
ETHICS: EASIER SAID THAN DONE. 1988. q. $35 to members; institutions $40. Josephson Institute of Ethics, 310 Washington Blvd., Ste. 104, Marina del Rey, CA 90292. TEL 310-306-1868. FAX 310-827-1864. Ed. Christopher Tyner. bk.rev.; illus. (back issues avail.)

170 610 — US — ISSN 0935-7335
ETHIK IN DER MEDIZIN. 1989. 6/yr. DM.78($367) Springer-Verlag, Journals, 175 Fifth Ave., New York, NY 10010. TEL 212-460-1500. (Or: Springer-Verlag, Heidelberger Platz 3, D-1000 Berlin 33, Germany)
—BLDSC shelfmark: 3814.670000.

170 — IT
ETHOS. q. Via F. Smaldone 5, 73100 Lecce, Italy. Ed. Salvatore Borgia.

100 — AG — ISSN 0325-5387
ETHOS; revista de filosofia practica. 1973. a. $10. Instituto de Filosofia Practica, Viamonte 1596, 1055 Buenos Aires, Argentina. Ed. Julio Guido Soaje Ramos. bk.rev.; bibl.; circ. 500. Indexed: SSCI.

100 — CN — ISSN 0708-319X
ETIENNE GILSON SERIES. 1979. irreg. price varies. Pontifical Institute of Mediaeval Studies, 59 Queen's Park Crescent E., Toronto, Ont. M5S 2C4, Canada. TEL 416-926-7144. FAX 416-926-7276. circ. 600.
—BLDSC shelfmark: 3816.125000.

100 — FR — ISSN 0014-2166
ETUDES PHILOSOPHIQUES. 1926. q. 285 F. (foreign 380 F.). Presses Universitaires de France, Departement des Revues, 14 Avenue du Bois-de-l'Epine, B.P.90, 91003 Evry Cedex, France. TEL 1-60-77-82-05. FAX 1-60-79-20-45. TELEX PUF 600 474 F. Ed.Bd. adv.; bk.rev.; charts; index; circ. 1,500. (also avail. in microform from UMI; reprint service avail. from KTO,UMI) Indexed: Arts & Hum.Cit.Ind., Curr.Cont., Ind.Bk.Rev.Hum., M.L.A., Phil.Ind., SSCI.
—BLDSC shelfmark: 3821.350000.
  Description: Each issue covers the essential ideas of a great philosophical thinker.

170 — PL — ISSN 0014-2263
BJ8.P6
ETYKA. (Text in Polish; summaries in English and Russian) 1966. a. price varies. (Polska Akademia Nauk, Instytut Filozofii i Socjologii) Panstwowe Wydawnictwo Naukowe, Miodowa 10, 00-251 Warsaw, Poland. Ed. Henryk Jankowski. bk.rev.; abstr.; circ. 1,100. Indexed: Phil.Ind.

100 500 — UK — ISSN 0261-1376
EXPLORATIONS IN KNOWLEDGE; an international journal in the philosophy of science. 1984. s-a. £12 to individuals; £14 to institutions. Sombourne Press, 294 Leigh Rd., Chandlers Ford, Hants. SO5 3AU, England. TEL 0703-269687. Eds. Susan M. Easton, David Lamb. adv.; bk.rev.; circ. 500.
—BLDSC shelfmark: 3842.207100.
  Description: Covers philosophy of science, focusing on conceptual problems arising out of scientific research on the frontiers of knowledge. Subjects include the natural and human sciences as well as medical research and cognitive studies.

100 — US — ISSN 1057-1035
EXTROPY; the journal of transhumanist thought. 1988. s-a. $8 (foreign $12; institutions $18). Extropy, P.O. Box 77243, Los Angeles, CA 90007-0243. TEL 213-746-5571. Ed. Max More. adv.; bk.rev.; film rev.; bibl.; illus.; circ. 400.
  Description: Covers futurist philosophy, immortalism and cryonics, transhumanism and others.

100 200 — US — ISSN 0739-7046
FAITH AND PHILOSOPHY. 1984. q. $20 to individuals (foreign $24); institutions $35 (foreign $40). Society of Christian Philosophers, Department of Philosophy, Asbury College, Wilmore, KY 40390. TEL 606-858-3511. Ed. William P. Alston. adv.; bk.rev.; index; circ. 1,300. (also avail. in microform from UMI; back issues avail.) Indexed: Phil.Ind., Rel.& Theol.Abstr. (1987-), Rel.Ind.One.
—BLDSC shelfmark: 3865.511100.
  Formerly: Faith and Reason (Wilmore).

100 — NE — ISSN 0925-0166
▼**FICHTE-STUDIEN.** 1991. 2/yr. fl.75($37.50) Editions Rodopi B.V., Keizersgracht 302-304, 1016 EX Amsterdam, Netherlands. TEL 020-6227507. FAX 020-6380948. (In N. America: 233 Peachtree St. N.E., Ste. 404, Atlanta, GA 30303-1504. TEL 800-225-3998) bk.rev.

100 — AG
FILOSOFAR CRISTIANO. (Text in Portuguese or Spanish) 1974. s-a. $10. Asociacion Catolica Interamericana de Filosofia, Arturo M. Bas 366, 5000 Cordoba, Argentina. Ed. Alberto Caturelli. bk.rev.; circ. 1,200.
  Formerly (until 1977): Asociacion Latino-Americana de Filosofos Catolicos. Boletin.

100 500 — DK — ISSN 0106-6668
FILOSOFI OG VIDENSKABSTEORI PAA ROSKILDE UNIVERSITETSCENTER. 1979. biennial. DKK 100. Roskilde Universitetscenter, Institut for Uddannelsesforskning, Medieforskning og Videnskabsteori Institut VII, Postbox 260, 4000 Roskilde, Denmark. Ed. Arne Thing Mortensen. bk.rev.; circ. 300.

100 — IT — ISSN 0015-1823
B4
FILOSOFIA. 1950. 3/yr. L.40000. Ugo Mursia Editore, Via Tadino, 29, 20124 Milan, Italy. Eds. Vittorio Mathieu, Marzio Pinottini. adv.; bk.rev.; bibl.; index, cum.index. Indexed: Arts & Hum.Cit.Ind., Curr.Cont., Phil.Ind.

100 — IT
FILOSOFIA E SOCIETA. 1972. s-a. L.30000. Cadmo Editore s.r.l, C.P. 6225, 00100 Rome, Italy. Ed. Lido Chiusano.

294.54 — IT
FILOSOFIA E TEOLOGIA. 1987. 3/yr. L.65000 to individuals; institutions L.85000; foreign L.110000(effective 1992). Edizioni Scientifiche Italiane S.p.A., Via Chiatamone 7, 80121 Naples, Italy. TEL 081-7645768. FAX 081-7646477.

FILOSOFIA POLITICA. see POLITICAL SCIENCE

100 — IT
FILOSOFIA PUBBLICA. 1989. irreg., no.3, 1990. price varies. Liguori Editore s.r.l., Via Mezzocannone, 19, 80134 Naples, Italy. TEL 081-5227139. Eds. S. Sebastiano Maffettone, Luciano Pellicani.

100 — CS — ISSN 0015-1831
B8.C9
FILOSOFICKY CASOPIS/PHILOSOPHICAL JOURNAL. (Text in Czech; summaries in various languages; table of contents in English, French, German, Russian) 1953. bi-m. DM.173. (Czechoslovak Academy of Sciences, Institute for Philosophy and Sociology) Academia, Publishing House of the Czechoslovak Academy of Sciences, Vodickova 40, 112 29 Prague 1, Czechoslovakia. TEL 231-91-15. (Dist. in Western countries by: Kubon & Sagner, P.O. Box 34 01 08, 8000 Munich 34, Germany) Ed. Jakub Netopilik. bk.rev.; bibl.; index. Indexed: Curr.Cont., Phil.Ind., Risk Abstr., SSCI.
  Description: Examines the problems of Marxist philosophy and critiques the basic trends of present non-Marxist philosophy. Includes the history of Czechoslovak philosophy.

100 — DK — ISSN 0106-0449
FILOSOFISKE STUDIER. 1978. a. DKK 50. Koebenhavns Universitet, Filosofisk Institut - University of Copenhagen, Njalsgade 80, 2300 Copenhagen S, Denmark. FAX 45-31-53-42-32. Ed.Bd. circ. 600.

100 — BU — ISSN 0324-024X
FILOSOFSKA MISUL. 1945. m. 8.40 lv. (Bulgarska Akademiia na Naukite, Institut po Filosofiia) Publishing House of the Bulgarian Academy of Sciences, Acad. G. Bonchev St., Bldg. 6, 1113 Sofia, Bulgaria. (Dist. by: Hemus, 6, Rouski Blvd., 1000 Sofia, Bulgaria) Ed. Dobrin Spasov. bk.rev.; abstr.; stat.; index; circ. 2,300.
—BLDSC shelfmark: 0391.310000.

100 KR
FILOSOFSKAYA I SOTSIOLOGICHESKAYA MYSL'; nauchno-teoreticheskii zhurnal. Ukrainian edition: Filosofska i Sotsiologichna Dumka. (Text in Russian; summaries in English) 1927. m. 9 Rub. (Akademiya Nauk Ukrainskoi S.S.R., Institut Filosofii) Izdatel'stvo Naukova Dumka, c/o Yu.A. Khramov, Dir, Ul. Repina, 3, Kiev 252 601, Ukraine. TEL 228-48-55. (Subscr. to: Mezhdunarodnaya Kniga, Moscow, G-200, Russia) Ed. Yu.D. Prilyuk. bibl. **Indexed:** M.L.A.
Formerly (until 1989): Filosofska Dumka (ISSN 0130-5719)

197 KZ
FILOSOFSKIE NAUKI (ALMA-ATA). 1971. irreg. 0.95 Rub. Kazakhskii Gosudarstvennyi Universitet, Ul. Lenina 18, Alma-Ata, Kazakhstan. bibl.

100 RU ISSN 0015-1858
FILOSOFSKIE NAUKI (MOSCOW). 1967. bi-m. 18.90 Rub. Izdatel'stvo Vysshaya Shkola, Prospekt Marksa 18, 103009 Moscow K-9, Russia. (Co-sponsor: Ministerstvo Vysshego i Srednego Spetsial'nogo Obrazovaniya) Ed. V.S. Gott. bk.rev.; bibl.; charts; illus.; stat.; circ. 6,260. **Indexed:** Lang.& Lang.Behav.Abstr.

100 CS ISSN 0046-385X
FILOZOFIA/PHILOSOPHY. (Text in Slovak; summaries in German and Russian) 1946. bi-m. 102 Kcs.($20) (Slovenska Akademia Vied, Ustav Filozofie a Sociologie) Veda, Publishing House of the Slovak Academy of Sciences, Klemensova 19, 814 30 Bratislava, Czechoslovakia. (Dist. in Western countries by: John Benjamins B.V., Amsteldijk 44, Amsterdam (Z.), Netherlands) Ed. Vladimir Cirbes. **Indexed:** Lang.& Lang.Behav.Abstr.
Description: Offers original papers and articles from various spheres of philosophic creation.

100 PL
FILOZOFIA-LOGIKA. 1961. irreg., no.55, 1989. price varies. Adam Mickiewicz University Press, Nowowiejskiego 55, 61-734 Poznan, Poland. TEL 527-380. FAX 61-526425. TELEX 413260 UAM PL. bk.rev.
Formerly: Uniwersytet im. Adama Mickiewicza w Poznaniu. Wydzial Filozoficzno-Historyczny. Prace. Seria Filozofia-Logika (ISSN 0083-4246)
Description: Contains current research results of the university's scholars, their Ph.D. theses and monographs. Each volume contains the work of one author.

100 YU ISSN 0350-106X
FILOZOFSKE STUDIJE. 1975. a. $3 to individuals; institutions $5. Srpsko Filozofsko Drustvo - Philosophical Society of Serbia, Cika Ljubina 18-20, 11000 Belgrade, Serbia, Yugoslavia. TEL 11-638-104. Ed. Vladan Perisic.
Description: Publishes collection of descriptive, analytical and critical studies in a wide areas of philosophy: metaphysics, ethics, epistemology, logic etc.

100 150 CI ISSN 0352-6798
B1
FILOZOFSKI FAKULTET - ZADAR. RAZDIO FILOZOFIJE, PSIHOLOGIJE, SOCIOLOGIJE I PEDAGOGIJE. RADOVI. (Text in Croatian, English; summaries in English) 1985. a. $20. Filozofski Fakultet u Zadru, Obala Marsala Tita, 2, 57000 Zadar, Croatia. TEL 057-436-623. TELEX 25-882. (Co-sponsor: Samopravna Interesna Zajednica Znanosti SR Hrvatske) Ed. Katica Lackovic-Grgin. index, cum.index no.1-2; circ. 600. (back issues avail.)

FOLD ES EG. see *EARTH SCIENCES*

FOR A CHANGE; for moral re-armament. see *SOCIAL SCIENCES: COMPREHENSIVE WORKS*

100 US
FORUM TODAY. 3/yr. $10. New Forum, 4176 Greystone, Yorba Linda, CA 92686. Ed. Judith A. Christie. adv.; illus.

100 UK ISSN 0262-8228
FRANCIS BACON RESEARCH TRUST JOURNAL; studies in ancient wisdom. 1981. irreg. (typically set in Jan.). Francis Bacon Research Trust, Roses Farmhouse, Epwell Rd., Upper Tysoe, Warwickshire CV35 0TN, England. TEL 029-588-8185. FAX 0295-88-770. Ed. Peter Dawkins.
—BLDSC shelfmark: 4032.783400.
Description: Francis Bacon's life, work and teachings.

FRANCISCAN STUDIES. see *RELIGIONS AND THEOLOGY — Roman Catholic*

100 255 CK ISSN 0120-1468
BR7
FRANCISCANUM; revista de las ciencias del espiritu. 1959. 3/yr. Col.3000($15) Universidad de San Buenaventura, Calle 73 No. 10-45, Apdo. Aereo 52312, Bogota, D.E., Colombia. Ed. Luis H. Acevedo Q. adv.; bk.rev.; bibl.; index, cum.index: 1959-1983; circ. 3,000.
—BLDSC shelfmark: 4032.790000.
Description: Interdisciplinary studies of religion and philosophy.

100 US ISSN 0272-0701
BL2700
FREE INQUIRY. 1980. q. $25. Council for Democratic and Secular Humanism (CODESH Inc.), Box 664, Buffalo, NY 14226. TEL 716-636-7571. FAX 716-636-1733. Ed. Dr. Paul Kurtz. adv.; bk.rev.; film rev.; illus.; cum.index 1980-86; circ. 23,000. (also avail. in microform from UMI; back issues avail.; reprint service avail. from UMI) **Indexed:** Curr.Lit.Fam.Plan., P.A.I.S., Phil.Ind.
—BLDSC shelfmark: 4033.321930.
Description: Deals with the separation of Church and State and secular humanism.

FREE LIFE. see *POLITICAL SCIENCE*

144 US
FREE MIND. bi-m. membership. American Humanist Association, 7 Harwood Dr., Box 146, Amherst, NY 14226-0146. TEL 716-839-5080. Ed. Bette Chambers. circ. 4,600.
Description: Newsletter of the association providing membership with national, regional and chapter news.

100 US
FREE SPIRIT (BROOKLYN); a directory and journal of new realities. bi-m. $18. Paul English, Ed. & Pub., 107 Sterling Place, Brooklyn, NY 11217. TEL 718-638-3733. FAX 718-230-3459.
Description: Presents articles that illustrate the interconnection and interdependence of all things.

100 320 US
FREEDOM NETWORK NEWS. 1986. q. International Society for Individual Liberty, 1800 Market St., San Francisco, CA 94102. TEL 415-864-0952. FAX 415-864-7506. Ed. Vincent H. Miller. circ. 12,000.
Description: Dedicated to building a free and peaceful world, respect for individual rights and liberties and an open and competitive economic system based on voluntary exchange and free trade.

100 UK ISSN 0016-0687
BL2700
FREETHINKER. 1881. m. £5.60($12) G.W. Foote & Co., 702 Holloway Rd., London N19 3NL, England. TEL 01-272-1266. Ed. William McIlroy. bk.rev.; circ. 1,500. (also avail. in microform)
Description: Devoted to topics of interest to humanists and secularists.

100 200 SZ ISSN 0016-0725
BR45
FREIBURGER ZEITSCHRIFT FUER PHILOSOPHIE UND THEOLOGIE. (Text in French and German) 1914. 2/yr. 50 Fr. (Universite de Fribourg, Dominikaner-Professoren der Theologischen Fakultaet) Editions Saint Paul, Perolles 42, CH-1700 Fribourg, Switzerland. bk.rev.; bibl.; index; circ. 600. **Indexed:** CERDIC, M.L.A., New Test.Abstr., Phil.Ind.

100 301 335 GW ISSN 0067-5911
FREIE UNIVERSITAET BERLIN. OSTEUROPA-INSTITUT. PHILOSOPHISCHE UND SOZIOLOGISCHE VEROEFFENTLICHUNGEN. 1959. irreg., vol.25, 1989. price varies. (Freie Universitaet Berlin, Osteuropa-Institut) Verlag Otto Harrassowitz, Taunusstr. 14, Postfach 2929, 6200 Wiesbaden, Germany. TEL 06121-530-0. FAX 06121-530570. TELEX 4186135. Ed.Bd. circ. 500.

100 943 GW
G.W. LEIBNIZ: SAEMTLICHE SCHRIFTEN UND BRIEFE. (Text in French, German and Latin) 1950. irreg., vol.1, no.12, 1989. (Akademie der Wissenschaften der DDR) Akademie-Verlag Berlin, Leipziger Str.3-4, 1086 Berlin, Germany. TELEX 114420-AVERL-DD.
Description: Complete collection of Leibniz's work and correspondence.

GENRE HUMAN. see *HUMANITIES: COMPREHENSIVE WORKS*

GESHER. see *RELIGIONS AND THEOLOGY — Judaic*

100 IT ISSN 0017-0089
B4
GIORNALE CRITICO DELLA FILOSOFIA ITALIANA. (Text in English, French and Italian) 1920. q. L.95000. Casa Editrice G.C. Sansoni Editore Nuova S.p.A, Via Benedetto Varchi 47, 50132 Florence, Italy. Ed. Eugenio Garin. bk.rev.; bibl.; index; circ. 800. **Indexed:** Arts & Hum.Cit.Ind., Curr.Cont., M.L.A.
—BLDSC shelfmark: 4177.600000.

110 IT
GIORNALE DI METAFISICA. (Text in Italian; occasionally in English, French, German, Spanish) 1946; N.S. 1979. 3/yr. L.28500($28.50) Tilgher-Genova s.a.s, Via Assarotti 52, 16122 Genoa, Italy. Ed. Nunzio Incardona. adv.; bk.rev.; index. (also avail. in microform)

GIORNALE ITALIANO DI FILOLOGIA; rivista di cultura. see *LINGUISTICS*

GIST. see *RELIGIONS AND THEOLOGY*

GNOSIS; a journal of the Western inner traditions. see *NEW AGE PUBLICATIONS*

100 CN ISSN 0316-618X
GNOSIS; a journal of philosophic interest. (Text in English, French) 1973. a. $8 to individuals; institutions $10. Concordia University, Philosophy Department, 1455 de Maisonneuve West, Montreal, Que. H3G 1M8, Canada. TEL 514-848-2500. adv.; bk.rev.; circ. 150. **Indexed:** Phil.Ind.
—BLDSC shelfmark: 4196.576000.
Description: Purpose is to publish articles of philosophic relevance by students and occasionally, professional philosophers and scholars.
Refereed Serial

100 CI ISSN 0352-3306
GODISNJAK ZA POVIJEST FILOZOFIJE. a. Sveuciliste u Zagrebu, Institut za Povijesne Znanosti, Odjel za Povijest Filozofije, Krcka 1, 41000 Zagreb, Croatia. TEL 041-511-841. Ed.Bd. circ. 800.

100 II
GOKULDAS SANSKRIT SERIES. (Text in English and Sanskrit) no.4, 1975. irreg., no.83, 1990. price varies. Chaukhambha Orientalia, Gokul Bhawan, K 37-109 Gopal Mandir Lane, Varanasi 221001, India.

100 NE ISSN 0165-9227
B20.6
GRAZER PHILOSOPHISCHE STUDIEN; internationale Zeitschrift fuer analytische Philosophie. 1975. s-a. price varies. Editions Rodopi B.V., Keizersgracht 302-304, 1016 EX Amsterdam, Netherlands. TEL 020-6227507. FAX 020-6380948. (US and Canada subscr. to: 233 Peachtree St. N.E., Ste. 404, Atlanta GA 30303-1504. TEL 800-225-3998) Ed. Rudolf Haller. circ. 700.

GREEK ORTHODOX THEOLOGICAL REVIEW. see *RELIGIONS AND THEOLOGY — Other Denominations And Sects*

GREGORIANUM. see *RELIGIONS AND THEOLOGY — Roman Catholic*

H E C FORUM; an interdisciplinary journal on hospitals' ethical and legal issues. (Hospital Ethics Committee) see *HOSPITALS*

100 GW ISSN 0072-9604
HAMBURGER STUDIEN ZUR PHILOSOPHIE. 1970. irreg., no.7, 1979. price varies. Helmut Buske Verlag Hamburg, Friedrichsgaber Weg 138, Postfach 1249, D-2000 Norderstedt, Germany.

HANGZHOU SHIFAN XUEYUAN XUEBAO (SHEHUI KEXUE BAN)/HANGZHOU NORMAL COLLEGE. JOURNAL (SOCIAL SCIENCE EDITION). see *SOCIAL SCIENCES: COMPREHENSIVE WORKS*

HASTINGS CENTER REPORT. see *MEDICAL SCIENCES*

100 US
HEGEL SOCIETY OF AMERICA. PROCEEDINGS. 1968. biennial. price varies. State University of New York Press, State University Plaza, Albany, NY 12246.

PHILOSOPHY

100   UK
HEGEL SOCIETY OF GREAT BRITAIN. BULLETIN. 1978. 2/yr. $20. Hegel Society of Great Britain, c/o Howard Williams, Dept. of International Politics, University College of Wales, Aberystwyth SY23 3DB, Wales. TEL 0970-622707. adv.; bk.rev.; circ. 300.
Description: News and notes on the philosopher, G.W.F. Hegel.

190   GW   ISSN 0073-1587
HEGEL - STUDIEN. 1955. irreg., vol.20, 1986. price varies. (Deutsche Forschungsgemeinschaft, Hegel Kommission) Bouvier Verlag Herbert Grundmann, Am Hof 32, Postfach 1268, 5300 Bonn 1, Germany. Eds. F. Nicolin, O. Poeggeler. **Indexed:** Arts & Hum.Cit.Ind., Curr.Cont.

140   GW   ISSN 0440-5927
HEGEL - STUDIEN BEIHEFTE. 1964. irreg., latest no.29, 1986. free. Bouvier Verlag Herbert Grundmann, Am Hof 32, Postfach 1268, 5300 Bonn 1, Germany. Eds. F. Nicolini, O. Poeggeler. adv.; bk.rev.; circ. 1,000.
Formerly: Internationale Vereinigung zur Foerderung des Studiums der Hegelschen Philosophie. Veroeffentlichung.

100   GW   ISSN 0885-4580
B3279.H49
HEIDEGGER STUDIES. 1985. a. DM.68($28) Duncker und Humblot GmbH, Postfach 410329, 1000 Berlin 41, Germany. TEL 030-7900060. FAX 030-79000631. Ed.Bd. adv.; bk.rev.; bibl. (back issues avail.) **Indexed:** Phil.Ind.
—BLDSC shelfmark: 4283.885000.

HENOCH. see *LINGUISTICS*

100   US   ISSN 1043-5735
HERMENEUTIC COMMENTARIES. irreg. Peter Lang Publishing, Inc., 62 W. 45th St., 4th Fl., New York, NY 10036. TEL 212-302-6740. FAX 212-302-7574. Ed. Pietro Pucci.
Description: Presents commentaries on classical texts with a strong emphasis on the hermeneutic, rather than on the historical, grammatical or stylistic aspects of the texts.

THE HERMETIC JOURNAL. see *RELIGIONS AND THEOLOGY — Other Denominations And Sects*

100   GW
HESTIA. 1960. biennial. price varies. Bouvier Verlag Herbert Grundmann, Am Hof 32, Postfach 1268, 5300 Bonn 1, Germany.

HEYTHROP JOURNAL; a review of philosophy and theology. see *RELIGIONS AND THEOLOGY*

100 613   US   ISSN 0891-6144
HIMALAYAN INSTITUTE QUARTERLY GUIDE. 1976. q. free. (Himalayan International Institute of Yoga Science and Philosophy) Himalayan Publishers, RR 1, Box 400, Honesdale, PA 18431. TEL 800-444-5772. TELEX 510 600 1805. Ed. Lawrence Clark. adv.; illus.; circ. 35,000.
Former titles: Himalayan News; Himalayan (ISSN 0275-9802)

HISTORIOGRAPHIA LINGUISTICA; international journal for the history of the language sciences. see *LINGUISTICS*

100   UK   ISSN 0144-5340
BC1
HISTORY AND PHILOSOPHY OF LOGIC. 1980. 2/yr. £75($126) to institutions. Taylor & Francis Ltd., Rankine Rd., Basingstoke, Hants RG24 0PR, England. TEL 0256-840366. FAX 0256-479438. TELEX 858540. Ed. I. Grattan-Guinness. bk.rev. **Indexed:** Math.R.
—BLDSC shelfmark: 4317.823000.
Description: Concerned with general philosophical questions on logic: existential and ontological aspects, the relationship between classical and non-classical logics, and the connections between logic and other fields of knowledge such as mathematics, philosophy of science, epistemology, linguistics, psychology and computing.
Refereed Serial

HISTORY AND PHILOSOPHY OF THE LIFE SCIENCES. see *BIOLOGY*

HISTORY AND THEORY; studies in the philosophy of history. see *HISTORY*

100   US   ISSN 0740-0675
HISTORY OF PHILOSOPHY QUARTERLY. 1984. q. $32 to individuals; institutions $130. Bowling Green State University, Philosophy Documentation Center, Bowling Green, OH 43403-0189. TEL 419-372-2419. FAX 419-372-6987. Ed. Nicholas Rescher. circ. 500. **Indexed:** Phil.Ind.
—BLDSC shelfmark: 4318.394500.

100 330.1   NE   ISSN 0921-5891
HOBBES STUDIES. (Text in English, French, German) 1988. a. fl.70 (effective 1992). (Ben Gurion University of the Negev, IS) Van Gorcum en Co. B.V., P.O. Box 43, 9400 AA Assen, Netherlands. TEL 05920-46864. FAX 05920-72064. (Co-sponsors: Colorado College, Dartmouth College) Ed. Martin A. Bertman. adv.; bk.rev.; circ. 600.
—BLDSC shelfmark: 4319.813000.

HOSPITAL ETHICS. see *HOSPITALS*

181.11   CH   ISSN 0018-6937
HSIN JU CHIA/NEW CONFUCIANS. (Text in Chinese and English) 1967. m. $25. New Confucians Book Store, P.O. Box 22239, Taipei, Taiwan, Republic of China. Ed. Chien-Fu Chen. bk.rev.; index; circ. 1,000.
Description: Religious essays devoted to Neo-Confucianism.

HUGINN AND MUNINN; interstellar messenger. see *PARAPSYCHOLOGY AND OCCULTISM*

170 614.8 301.4   US
HUMAN LIFE ISSUES. 1975. q. $6. Human Life Center, University of Steubenville, Steubenville, OH 43952. TEL 614-282-9953. FAX 614-282-0769. Eds. Mike Marker, Rita Marker. circ. 6,000. (tabloid format; back issues avail.) **Indexed:** CERDIC.
Formerly: Love, Life, Death Issues.

100   NE   ISSN 0163-8548
B1   CODEN: HUSTDT
HUMAN STUDIES; a journal for philosophy and the social sciences. 1978. q. $62.50 to individuals; institutions $133. Kluwer Academic Publishers, Postbus 17, 3300 AA Dordrecht, Netherlands. TEL 078-334911. FAX 078-334254. TELEX 29245. (Dist. by: Kluwer Academic Publishing Group, P.O. Box 322, 3300 AH Dordrecht, Netherlands; N. America dist. addr.: Box 358, Accord Station, Hingham, MA 02018-0358. TEL 617-871-6600) Ed. George Psathas. adv.; bk.rev.; index; circ. 500. (back issues avail.; reprint service avail. from ISI,SWZ) **Indexed:** Curr.Cont., Lang.& Lang.Behav.Abstr., M.L.A., Phil.Ind., SSCI, Stud.Wom.Abstr.
—BLDSC shelfmark: 4336.467000.

100 300   US
HUMANE STUDIES REVIEW. 1980. 3/yr. $5. (Institute for Humane Studies) George Mason University, 4400 University Dr., Fairfax, VA 22030. TEL 703-323-1055. Ed. Tom G. Palmer. bk.rev.; bibl.; circ. 8,000. (back issues avail.; reprint service avail.)
Description: Covers themes relevant to the tradition of classical liberalism.

100   GW
DER HUMANIST. 1973. m. DM.26.40. (Bund Freireligioeser Gemeinden Deutschlands) Verlag Humanitas, Woerthstr. 6a, 6700 Ludwigshafen, Germany. Ed. Ortrun Lenz. adv.; bk.rev.; index; circ. 6,000. **Indexed:** Acad.Ind.
Supersedes: Freigeistige Aktion (ISSN 0016-0830)

170   NE   ISSN 0025-9489
HUMANIST. 1945. 9/yr. fl.30. Humanistische Stichting Socrates, Postbus 114, 3500 AC Utrecht, Netherlands. FAX 030-361704. Ed. Hes van Huizen. adv.; bk.rev.; film rev.; play rev.; illus.; circ. 18,000. **Indexed:** Acad.Ind., Mid.East: Abstr.& Ind.
Formerly: Mens en Wereld.

100   US   ISSN 0018-7399
B821.A1
HUMANIST. 1941. bi-m. $19.95. American Humanist Association, 7 Harwood Dr., Box 146, Amherst, NY 14226-0146. TEL 716-839-5080. Ed. Rick Szykowny. adv.; bk.rev.; illus.; index; circ. 15,000. (also avail. in microform from MIM,UMI; back issues avail.; reprint service avail. from BLH,UMI) **Indexed:** Acad.Ind., Bk.Rev.Ind. (1978-), C.I.J.E., CERDIC, Chic.Per.Ind., Child.Bk.Rev.Ind. (1978-), Except.Child.Educ.Abstr., Film Lit.Ind. (1973-), Fut.Surv., Hum.Ind., Human Resour.Abstr., Lang.& Lang.Behav.Abstr., Mag.Ind., Media Rev.Dig., P.A.I.S., Phil.Ind., PMR, R.G., SSCI.
Description: Nontheistic, secular and naturalistic approach to broad areas of personal, scientific and philosophical concern.

144   CN   ISSN 0018-7402
HUMANIST IN CANADA. 1967. q. Can.$15. Canadian Humanist Publications, P.O. Box 3769, Station "C", Ottawa, Ont. K1Y 4J8, Canada. adv.; bk.rev.; abstr.; bibl.; charts; illus.; stat.; index, cum.index; circ. 1,500. (also avail. in microfilm from UMI; reprint service avail. from UMI) **Indexed:** Alt.Press Ind., Can.Wom.Per.Ind., CMI.
—BLDSC shelfmark: 4336.524300.
Formed by the merger of: Montreal Humanist; Victoria Humanist.

144   UK
HUMANIST NEWS. 1965. bi-m. membership. British Humanist Association, 14 Lamb's Conduit Passage, London WC1R 4RH, England. TEL 071-430-0908. FAX 071-430-1271. Ed. Meredith Macardle. adv.; bk.rev.; illus.; circ. 5,000. (looseleaf format)
Former titles: Humanist Newsletter; Humanist News (ISSN 0018-7410)
Description: Examines moral issues from a non-religious viewpoint.

144   II   ISSN 0018-7429
HUMANIST OUTLOOK. (Text in English) 1966. s-a. Rs.10($6) Indian Humanist Union, H-41-D, Saket, New Delhi 110 017, India. TEL 011-686-2191. Ed. Sheila Vir Narain. adv.; bk.rev.; bibl.; circ. 400.
Description: Covers issues with the purpose of promotion of scientific attitude, ethical values, social reforms and communal harmony.

144   AT
HUMANIST POST. m. Aus.$4. Humanist Society of South Australia, Inc., 2 Almond Court, Vale Park, S.A. 5081, Australia.

144   GW   ISSN 0046-824X
HUMANISTISCHE UNION. MITTEILUNGEN. no.49, 1971. q. membership. Humanistische Union e.V., Braeuhausstr. 2, 8000 Munich 2, Germany. TEL 089-226441. FAX 089-226442. Ed. Helga Killinger. adv.; bk.rev.; circ. 3,200.

100   CN   ISSN 0319-7336
HUME STUDIES. 1975. 2/yr. Can.$15 to individuals; institutions Can.$30. University of Western Ontario, Department of Philosophy, London, Ont. N6A 3K7, Canada. TEL 519-661-3453. FAX 519-661-3922. Eds. R.G. Muehlmann, F. Wilson. bk.rev.; circ. 250. (also avail. in microfilm; back issues avail.) **Indexed:** Amer.Hist.& Life, Hist.Abstr., Phil.Ind.
—BLDSC shelfmark: 4336.650000.

100   US
HUNA WORK. 1948. q. $20. Huna Research, Inc., 126 Camellia Dr., Cape Girardeau, MO 63701. TEL 314-334-3478. (And: 1760 Anna St., Cape Girardeau, MO 63701) Ed. E. Otha Wingo. bk.rev.; circ. 1,300. (back issues avail.)

100   NE   ISSN 0167-9848
B3279.H94   CODEN: HUSTEU
HUSSERL STUDIES. (Text in English and German) 1984. 3/yr. $60 to individuals; institutions $128.50. Kluwer Academic Publishers, Postbus 17, 3300 AA Dordrecht, Netherlands. TEL 078-334911. FAX 078-334254. TELEX 29245. (Dist. by: Kluwer Academic Publishers Group, Distribution Center, Postbus 322, 3300 AH Dordrecht, Netherlands; N. America dist. addr.: Box 358, Accord Station, Hingham, MA 02018-0358. TEL 617-871-6600) Eds. J.N. Mohanty, Karl Schuhmann. adv.; bk.rev. (reprint service avail. from SWZ) **Indexed:** Phil.Ind.
—BLDSC shelfmark: 4337.854000.

100 NE ISSN 0439-9714
HUSSERLIANA. (Text in English, German) 1950. irreg., latest 1991. price varies. (Centre d'Archives Husserl, BE) Kluwer Academic Publishers, P.O. Box 17, 3300 AA Dordrecht, Netherlands. TEL 078-334911. (Dist. by: Kluwer Academic Publishers Group, P.O. Box 322, 3300 AH Dordrecht, Netherlands; N. America dist. addr.: Box 358, Accord Station, Hingham, MA 02018-0358. TEL 617-871-6600)

HYPOMNEMATA; Untersuchungen zur Antike und zu ihrem Nachleben. see CLASSICAL STUDIES

100 US ISSN 0046-8541
B823
IDEALISTIC STUDIES; international philosophical journal. 1971. 3/yr. $12 to individuals; libraries $25. c/o Walter E. Wright, Ed., Dept. of Philosophy, Clark University, Worcester, MA 01610. TEL 508-793-7414. adv.; bk.rev.; bibl.; index; circ. 600. **Indexed:** Arts & Hum.Cit.Ind., Curr.Cont., Phil.Ind.
—BLDSC shelfmark: 4362.382500.

100 US ISSN 0378-4789
B1
INDEPENDENT JOURNAL OF PHILOSOPHY/REVUE INDEPENDANTE DE PHILOSOPHIE. (Text in English, French, German) 1977. irreg. $22.50 to individuals; institutions $40.50. George Elliott Tucker, Ed. & Pub., 142 Lowell Ave., Newton, MA 02160-1505. adv.; bk.rev.; bibl.; circ. 700. (back issues avail.) **Indexed:** Phil.Ind.
—BLDSC shelfmark: 4375.885000.

100 II ISSN 0019-4271
INDIAN ACADEMY OF PHILOSOPHY. JOURNAL. (Text in English) 1962. s-a. Rs.40($12) (effective since 1988). Indian Academy of Philosophy, Belgachia-Villa, Block F, Flat 8, Calcutta 37, India. Ed.Bd. bk.rev.; bibl.

100 II ISSN 0376-4109
INDIAN PHILOSOPHICAL ANNUAL. 1967. a. Rs.10. University of Madras, Radhakrishnan Institute for Advanced Study in Philosophy, Chepauk, Triplicane P.O., Madras 600 005, Tamil Nadu, India. TELEX 6376 UNOM IN. (And: Publications Division, University of Madras, Madras 600 005, India) Ed. T.S. Devadoss. circ. 300.
Description: Publishes the proceedings of the institute's seminars and symposia. Contains a separate section for the publication of special articles.

100 II ISSN 0376-415X
B130
INDIAN PHILOSOPHICAL QUARTERLY. 1973. q. $40 to individuals; institutions $50. University of Poona, Department of Philosophy, Ganeshkhind, Poona 411 007, India. TEL 336061. (Co-sponsor: Pratap Centre of Philosophy, Amalner) Ed. M.P. Marathe. adv.; bk.rev.; circ. 800. **Indexed:** Curr.Cont., Ind.Bk.Rev.Hum., Phil.Ind.
Supersedes: Philosophical Quarterly.

181.4 NE ISSN 0924-8986
INDIAN THOUGHT. 1990. irreg., vol.2, 1992. price varies. E.J. Brill, P.O. Box 9000, 2300 PA Leiden, Netherlands. TEL 071-312624. FAX 071-317532. TELEX 39296 BRILL NL. (In N. America: E.J. Brill, 24 Hudson St., Kinderhook, NY 12106. TEL 800-962-4406) Ed. Purusottama Billimoria.

INDIVIDUAL LIBERTY. see POLITICAL SCIENCE

141.4 US ISSN 0034-0030
INDIVIDUALIST.* 1968. m. $7.50. Society for Individual Liberty, Box 1147, Warminster, PA 18974. Ed. Jarret B. Wollstein. adv.; bk.rev.; film rev.; illus.; circ. 2,000.
Formerly: Rational Individualist.

160 CN ISSN 0824-2577
CODEN: INLOEA
INFORMAL LOGIC. 1978. 3/yr. Can.$25($25) to individuals; institutions Can.$40($40)(typically set in Nov.). Department of Philosophy, University of Windsor, Windsor, Ont. N9B 3P4, Canada. TEL 519-253-4232. FAX 519-973-7050. Eds. J.A. Blair, R.H. Johnson. bk.rev.; circ. 300 (controlled).
—BLDSC shelfmark: 4481.284000.

100 GW
INFORMATION PHILOSOPHIE. 1970. bi-m. DM.51($39) Verlag Claudia Moser, Hauptstr. 42, 7850 Loeriach, Germany. Ed. Peter Moser. adv.; bk.rev.; circ. 3,200. (reprint service avail.)

100 IT
INFORMAZIONE FILOSOFICA. q. L.28000 (students L.20000). Istituto Lombardo per gli Studi Filosofici e Giuridici, Viale Monte Nero 68, 20135 Milan, Italy. TEL 02-55190714. FAX 02-5404319. (Co-sponsor: Istituto Italiano per gli Studi Filosofici) Ed. Riccardo Ruschi.

100 300 NO ISSN 0020-174X
INQUIRY; an interdisciplinary journal of philosophy. (Text in English) 1958. 4/yr. $50 to individuals; institutions $106. Universitetsforlaget, P.O. Box 2959-Toeyen, N-0608 Oslo 6, Norway. (U.S. addr.: Publications Expediting Inc., 200 Neacgan Ave., Elmont, NY 11003) Ed. Alastair Hannay. adv.; bk.rev.; index; circ. 1,000. (also avail. in microform from UMI; back issues avail.; reprint service avail. from ISI) **Indexed:** Amer.Hist.& Life, ASCA, Hist.Abstr., Ind.Bk.Rev.Hum., Lang.& Lang.Behav.Abstr., Med. Care Rev., Phil.Ind., Soc.Work Res.& Abstr.
—BLDSC shelfmark: 4516.200000.

INSTITUCION FERNAN-GONZALEZ. BOLETIN. see HISTORY

INSTITUT INTERNATIONAL J. MARITAIN. NOTES ET DOCUMENTS; pour une recherche personnaliste - for a personalist approach. see POLITICAL SCIENCE

INSTITUTE OF ASIAN STUDIES. JOURNAL. see SOCIOLOGY

100 US ISSN 0196-5603
INSTITUTE SCHOLAR. 1980. 3/yr. free. Institute for Humane Studies, c/o George Mason University, 4400 Univeristy Dr., Fairfax, VA 22030. FAX 703-764-1577. Ed. Jeremy Shearmur. (back issues avail.)
Description: News of the activities of classical liberal scholars.

100 PO
INSTITUTO NACIONAL DE INVESTIGACAO CIENTIFICA. TEXTOS CLASSICOS. irreg., no.11, 1981. (Instituto Nacional de Investigacao Cientifica, Centro de Linguistica) Universidade de Coimbra, Centro de Estudos Clasicos y Humanisticos, Faculdade de Letras, Coimbra, Portugal.

INTEGRAL. see MUSIC

100 US ISSN 0730-2355
THE INTELLECTUAL ACTIVIST; an objective review. 1979. bi-m. $24. T I A Publications, Inc., P.O. Box 262, Lincroft, NJ 07738-0262. TEL 908-842-6610. Ed. Linda Reardan. adv.; bk.rev. (back issues avail.)

INTERBEHAVIORIST; a quarterly newsletter of interbehavior psychology. see PSYCHOLOGY

100 800 MR
INTERDISCIPLINARITE ETUDES PHILOSOPHIQUES ET LITTERAIRES. N.S. 1977. s-a. DH.30 (students DH.15). Societe de Philosophie du Maroc, B.P. 25, Temara, Morocco. Ed. F. Jamai-Lahbabi. bk.rev.; circ. 4,000.
Formerly (until 1984): Etudes Philosophiques et Litteraires (ISSN 0531-1934)

212.5 IS
INTERNATIONAL ASSOCIATION FOR THE DEVELOPMENT OF CONSCIOUSNESS. INFORMATION BULLETIN. (Text in Hebrew) m. International Association for the Development of Consciousness, P.O. Box 4983, Haifa, Israel. TEL 04-642104.

100 US ISSN 0074-4603
B35
INTERNATIONAL DIRECTORY OF PHILOSOPHY AND PHILOSOPHERS. 1965. biennial. $47 to individuals; institutions $79. Bowling Green State University, Philosophy Documentation Center, Bowling Green, OH 43403-0189. TEL 419-372-2419. FAX 419-372-6987. Ed. Ramona Cormier. circ. 850.

100 CN ISSN 0925-1375
INTERNATIONAL HUMANIST. 1952. q. fl.34($15) International Humanist and Ethical Union, c/o Don Page, Ed., R.R. 1, Smith Falls, Ont. K7A 5B8, Canada. TEL 613-283-7210. FAX 613-283-9910. (Subscr. to: International Humanist and Ethical Union, Oudkerkhof 11, 3512 GH Utrecht, Netherlands)
Formerly: International Humanism (ISSN 0020-692X)

190 CN ISSN 0074-6258
INTERNATIONAL HUMANIST AND ETHICAL UNION. PROCEEDINGS OF THE CONGRESS. 1952. irreg., 8th, 1982, Amsterdam. fl.28. International Humanist and Ethical Union, Oudkerkhof 11, 3512 GH Utrecht, Netherlands. TEL (030)312155. TELEX 70104-HUMAN-NL. circ. 1,500.

INTERNATIONAL JOURNAL FOR PHILOSOPHY OF RELIGION. see RELIGIONS AND THEOLOGY

100 DK ISSN 0108-3104
INTERNATIONAL KIERKEGAARD NEWSLETTER. 1979. a. free. Julia Watkin, Ed. & Pub., Stenagervej 15, 2900 Hellerup, Denmark. adv.; bk.rev.; circ. 1,000. (back issues avail.) **Indexed:** Phil.Ind.

100 US ISSN 0019-0365
B1
INTERNATIONAL PHILOSOPHICAL QUARTERLY. 1961. q. $22 to individuals; institutions $35. Foundation for International Philosophical Exchange, Fordham University, Bronx, NY 10458. TEL 212-579-2057. Ed. Vincent G. Potter. adv.; bk.rev.; index; circ. 1,600. (also avail. in microform from KTO,UMI; reprint service avail. from ISI,UMI) **Indexed:** Amer.Bibl.Slavic & E.Eur.Stud., Arts & Hum.Cit.Ind., Bk.Rev.Ind. (1976-), Cath.Ind., Child.Bk.Rev.Ind. (1976-), Curr.Cont., Hum.Ind., Ind.Bk.Rev.Hum., Mid.East: Abstr.& Ind., Phil.Ind., SSCI.
—BLDSC shelfmark: 4544.924800.
Description: Scholarly research articles on contemporary creative, critical, and historical expression in the intercultural tradition of theistic, spiritualistic, and personalistic humanism.

INTERNATIONAL SEMIOTIC SPECTRUM. see HUMANITIES: COMPREHENSIVE WORKS

100 US ISSN 0270-5664
B1
INTERNATIONAL STUDIES IN PHILOSOPHY; an international journal of general philosophic inquiry. (Text occasionally in French, German or Italian) 1969. 3/yr. $25 to individuals; institutions $40. (State University of New York at Binghamton) Scholars Press, Box 15399, Atlanta, GA 30333-0399. TEL 404-636-4757. FAX 404-636-8301. (Subscr. to: Department of Philosophy, State University of New York at Binghamton, Binghamton, NY 13901) Ed.Bd. bk.rev.; bibl. **Indexed:** Curr.Cont., Phil.Ind.
—BLDSC shelfmark: 4549.794300.
Formerly: Studi Internazionali di Filosofia (ISSN 0039-2979)
Description: Academic journal in philosophy.

215 UK
INTERNATIONAL STUDIES IN THE PHILOSOPHY OF SCIENCE. 1987. 3/yr. $72 to individuals; institutions $168. Carfax Publishing Co., P.O. Box 25, Abingdon, Oxfordshire OX14 3UE, England. TEL 0235-555335. FAX 0235-553559. (U.S. subscr. addr.: Carfax Publishing Co., Box 2025, Dunnellon, FL 32630) Eds. Willian Newton-Smith, Kathleen Wilkes.
Formerly: International Studies in the Philosophy of Science - the Dubrovnik Papers (ISSN 0269-8595)
Description: Articles by scholars of diverse nationalities on all aspects of the philosophy of science, based on papers given at the philosophy of science seminar.

181.45 294.5 US ISSN 0277-092X
INTERNATIONAL YOGA GUIDE. m. $15 (foreign $26). Yoga Research Foundation, 6111 S.W. 74th Ave., Miami, FL 33143. TEL 305-666-2006.

160 IT
INTERPRETAZIONI; collana di filosofia. irreg., latest vol.19. price varies. Edizioni Studium, Via Cassiodoro 14, 00193 Rome, Italy. Ed. Armando Rigobello.

INTERVENTI CLASSENSI. see ART

3770 PHILOSOPHY

100   PK   ISSN 0021-0773
BP80.I6
IQBAL REVIEW. Persian and Urdu edition: Iqbaliat. (Editions in English, Persian and Urdu) 1960. s-a. Rs.20($10) to individuals; institutions $15. Iqbal Academy Pakistan, 116 McLeod Rd., Lahore, Pakistan. TEL 57214. Ed. Prof. Muhammad Munawar. adv.; bk.rev.; circ. 1,000. **Indexed:** M.L.A.

100   UK   ISSN 0266-9080
IRISH PHILOSOPHICAL JOURNAL. 1984. a. £5 to individuals; institutions £15. c/o Dr. Bernard Cullen, Dept. of Scholastic Philosophy, Queen's University, Belfast BT7 1NN, N. Ireland. TEL 0232-245133. FAX 0232-247895.
—BLDSC shelfmark: 4574.642000.
Description: Covers all areas and orientations in philosophy, including the history of philosophy.

ISLAMIC PHILOSOPHY, THEOLOGY AND SCIENCE; texts and studies. see *RELIGIONS AND THEOLOGY — Islamic*

160 510   RU   ISSN 0302-9085
QA76
ISSLEDOVANIA PO TEORII ALGORIFMOV I MATEMATICHESKOI LOGIKE. 1973. irreg. 1.12 Rub. (Akademiya Nauk S.S.S.R., Vychislitel'nyi Tsentr) Izdatel'stvo Nauka, Fizmatlit, Leninskii prospekt, 15, 117071 Moscow, Russia. TEL 234-05-84.

100   IT
ISTITUTO UNIVERSITARIO ORIENTALE. DIPARTIMENTO DI FILOSOFIA E POLITICA. QUADERNI. 1987. irreg., no.8, 1990. price varies. Liguori Editore s.r.l., Via Mezzocannone, 19, 80134 Naples, Italy. TEL 081-5227139. Ed. Biagio DeGiovanni.

294.54   IT
ITALIA FRANCESCANA; rivista di cultura. 1926. bi-m. $30. L'Italia Francescana, Via Vittorio Veneto 27, 00187 Rome RM, Italy. Ed.Bd. bk.rev.; circ. 800. (back issues avail.) **Indexed:** M.L.A.

ITINERARIUM; revista quadrimestral de cultura. see *RELIGIONS AND THEOLOGY — Roman Catholic*

100 296   IS   ISSN 0021-3306
IYYUN; Jerusalem philosophical quarterly. (2 nos. in English, 2 nos. in Hebrew) 1945. q. $23. Hebrew University of Jerusalem, S.H. Bergman Centre for Philosophical Studies, Jerusalem 91905, Israel. TEL 02-883747. FAX 02-322545. TELEX 26458. (Co-sponsor: Jerusalem Philosophical Society) Ed. Eddy M. Zemach. bk.rev.; index; circ. 700. (back issues avail.) **Indexed:** Phil.Ind.

JAG. see *POLITICAL SCIENCE*

JAPAN ASSOCIATION FOR PHILOSOPHY OF SCIENCE. ANNALS. see *SCIENCES: COMPREHENSIVE WORKS*

JERUSALEM STUDIES IN JEWISH THOUGHT. see *RELIGIONS AND THEOLOGY — Judaic*

100 300   CC   ISSN 1000-5072
AS452.C363
JINAN XUEBAO (ZHEXUE SHEHUI KEXUE BAN)/JINAN UNIVERSITY. JOURNAL (PHILOSOPHY & SOCIAL SCIENCES EDITION). (Text in Chinese; table of contents in English) 1979. q. Y6. Jinan Daxue, Xuebao Bianjibu - Jinan University, Journal Editorial Department, Rm. 216, 2nd Fl., Bldg. 75, Shipai, Guangzhou, Guangdong 510632, People's Republic of China. TEL 516511-205. (Dist. outside China by: Guoji Shudian - China International Book Trading Corp., P.O. Box 399, Beijing, P.R.C.) Eds. Jiang Shuzhuo, Yang Zengshu. adv.; bk.rev.; circ. 3,000.

JOBS FOR PHILOSOPHERS. see *OCCUPATIONS AND CAREERS*

JOURNAL FOR GENERAL PHILOSOPHY OF SCIENCE/ZEITSCHRIFT FUER ALLGEMEINE WISSENSCHAFTSTHEORIE. see *SCIENCES: COMPREHENSIVE WORKS*

212.5   US   ISSN 0090-2586
BF311   CODEN: JSCOA
JOURNAL FOR THE STUDY OF CONSCIOUSNESS. 1974. s-a. $3. Linear & Circular Permutations, 1817 De La Vina St., Santa Barbara, CA 93101. Ed. Peter Crane. charts; illus.
Formerly: Nous Letter (ISSN 0276-0290)

JOURNAL FOR THE THEORY OF SOCIAL BEHAVIOUR. see *PSYCHOLOGY*

JOURNAL OF AESTHETIC EDUCATION. see *EDUCATION*

JOURNAL OF AESTHETICS AND ART CRITICISM. see *ART*

JOURNAL OF AFRICAN RELIGION AND PHILOSOPHY; a journal of religion and philosophy in Africa. see *RELIGIONS AND THEOLOGY*

170 630   CN
BJ52.5   CODEN: JAETEC
JOURNAL OF AGRICULTURAL AND ENVIRONMENTAL ETHICS. 1988. s-a. Can.$32.10 to individuals (foreign Can.$35); institutions Can.$42.80 (foreign Can.$45); students Can.$17.12 (foreign Can.$21). University of Guelph, MacKinnon Bldg., Rm 039, Guelph, Ont., Canada. TEL 519-824-4120. Eds. Frank Hurnick, Hugh Lehman. circ. 230.
Formerly (until 1991): Journal of Agricultural Ethics (ISSN 0893-4282)
Description: Concerned with ethical issues confronting agriculture, the environment and related disciplines.
Refereed Serial

100   UK   ISSN 0264-3758
B1
JOURNAL OF APPLIED PHILOSOPHY. 1984. s-a. $80 to individuals; institutions $198. (Society of Applied Philosophy) Carfax Publishing Co., P.O. Box 25, Abingdon, Oxfordshire OX14 3UE, England. TEL 0235-555335. FAX 0235-553559. (U.S. subscr. addr.: Carfax Publishing Co., Box 2025, Dunnellon, FL 32630) Eds. Brenda Almond, Stephen Clark. adv.; bk.rev.; index. (also avail. in microfiche; back issues avail.) **Indexed:** Phil.Ind., Stud.Wom.Abstr.
—BLDSC shelfmark: 4943.800000.

100   US   ISSN 0022-0213
L11
JOURNAL OF CRITICAL ANALYSIS. 1969. irreg. membership. National Council for Critical Analysis, Box 137, Port Jefferson, NY 11777. TEL 516-928-6745. Ed. Dr. P.S. Schievella. adv.; bk.rev.; bibl.; index; circ. 500. (also avail. in microfilm from UMI; reprint service avail. from UMI) **Indexed:** Phil.Ind., Sociol.Abstr.
—BLDSC shelfmark: 4965.620000.

170   US   ISSN 1010-7304
BJ1
JOURNAL OF ETHICAL STUDIES. 1986. q. $50. International Association of Ethicists, Inc., 117 W. Harrison Bldg., Ste. I-104, 6th fl., Chicago, IL 60605. TEL 800-423-3844. adv.; bk.rev. (back issues avail.)
Description: Case studies and articles of ethical interest.

JOURNAL OF GANDHIAN STUDIES. see *POLITICAL SCIENCE*

181   NE   ISSN 0022-1791
B130
JOURNAL OF INDIAN PHILOSOPHY. 1970. q. $162.50. Kluwer Academic Publishers, Postbus 17, 3300 AA Dordrecht, Netherlands. TEL 078-334911. FAX 078-334254. TELEX 29245. (Dist. by: Kluwer Academic Publishers Group, P.O. Box 322, 3300 AH Dordrecht, Netherlands; N. America dist. addr.: Box 358, Accord Station, Hingham, MA 02018-0358. TEL 617-871-6600) Ed. B.K. Matilal. adv.; bk.rev. (reprint service avail. from SWZ) **Indexed:** Arts & Hum.Cit.Ind., Curr.Cont., M.L.A., Phil.Ind.
—BLDSC shelfmark: 5005.325000.

JOURNAL OF MEDICAL HUMANITIES. see *MEDICAL SCIENCES*

JOURNAL OF MEDICINE AND PHILOSOPHY. see *MEDICAL SCIENCES*

JOURNAL OF MIND AND BEHAVIOR; an interdisciplinary journal. see *PSYCHOLOGY*

100   UK   ISSN 0305-7240
LC268
JOURNAL OF MORAL EDUCATION. 1971. 3/yr. $44 to individuals; institutions $108. Carfax Publishing Co., P.O. Box 25, Abingdon, Oxfordshire OX14 3UE, England. TEL 0235-555335. FAX 0235-553559. (U.S. subscr. addr.: Carfax Publishing Co., Box 2025, Dunnellon, FL 32630) Ed. Monica Taylor. adv.; bk.rev.; index, cum.index. (also avail. in microfiche; back issues avail.) **Indexed:** Adol.Ment.Hlth.Abstr., ASSIA, C.I.J.E., Cont.Pg.Educ., Curr.Cont., Educ.Ind., Educ.Tech.Abstr., High.Educ.Curr.Aware.Bull., Phil.Ind., Psychol.Abstr., Sp.Ed.Needs Abstr., SSCI, Stud.Wom.Abstr.
—BLDSC shelfmark: 5020.950000.

JOURNAL OF PAN AFRICAN STUDIES; an international medium of African culture and consciousness. see *SOCIAL SCIENCES: COMPREHENSIVE WORKS*

160   NE   ISSN 0022-3611
BC51   CODEN: JPLGA7
JOURNAL OF PHILOSOPHICAL LOGIC. 1972. q. $151. (Association for Symbolic Logic) Kluwer Academic Publishers, Postbus 17, 3300 AA Dordrecht, Netherlands. TEL 078-334911. FAX 078-334254. TELEX 29245. (Dist. by: Kluwer Academic Publishers Group, P.O. Box 322, 3300 AH Dordrecht, Netherlands; N. America dist. addr.: Box 358, Accord Station, Hingham, MA 02018-0358. TEL 617-871-6600) Eds. J. Michael Dunn, Terence Parsons. adv. (reprint service avail. from SWZ) **Indexed:** Arts & Hum.Cit.Ind., Curr.Cont., Lang.& Lang.Behav.Abstr., M.L.A., Math R., Phil.Ind., Sociol.Abstr., SSCI.
—BLDSC shelfmark: 5034.400000.

100   US   ISSN 1053-8364
B1
JOURNAL OF PHILOSOPHICAL RESEARCH; a bilingual journal of philosophy. (Text and summaries in English and French) 1976. a. $21.50 to individuals; institutions $52. Bowling Green State University, Philosophy Documentation Center, Bowling Green, OH 43403-0189. TEL 419-372-2419. FAX 419-372-6987. (Co-sponsors: American Philosophical Association; Canadian Philosophical Association) Ed. Robert Audi. circ. 280. **Indexed:** Phil.Ind.
Formerly: Philosophy Research Archives (ISSN 0164-0771)

100   US   ISSN 0022-362X
B1
JOURNAL OF PHILOSOPHY. 1904. m. $30 to individuals; students $20; libraries $50. Journal of Philosophy, Inc., 709 Philosophy Hall, Columbia University, New York, NY 10027. TEL 212-666-4419. Ed.Bd. adv.; bk.rev.; bibl.; index, cum.index: 1904-1953, 1954-1963, 1964-1988; circ. 4,500. (back issues avail.) **Indexed:** Amer.Hist.& Life, Arts & Hum.Cit.Ind., Bk.Rev.Dig., Bk.Rev.Ind. (1965-), Child.Bk.Rev.Ind. (1965-), Curr.Cont., Deep Sea Res.& Oceanogr.Abstr., Hist.Abstr., Hum.Ind., Ind.Bk.Rev.Hum., M.L.A., Math.R., Mid.East: Abstr.& Ind., Phil.Ind.
—BLDSC shelfmark: 5034.500000.
Description: Encourages the interchange of ideas, explores the relation between philosophy and special interests.

100   UK   ISSN 0309-8249
LB1025.2
JOURNAL OF PHILOSOPHY OF EDUCATION. 1966. s-a. $98 to individuals; institutions $280. Carfax Publishing Co., P.O. Box 25, Abingdon, Oxfordshire OX14 3UE, England. TEL 0235-555335. FAX 0235-553559. (U.S. subscr. addr.: Carfax Publishing Co., Box 2025, Dunnellon, FL 32630) Ed. Richard Smith. adv. (also avail. in microfiche; back issues avail.) **Indexed:** C.I.J.E., Cont.Pg.Educ., Curr.Cont., Educ.Ind., Educ.Tech.Abstr., Phil.Ind., Res.High.Educ.Abstr., Sp.Ed.Needs Abstr., SSCI, Stud.Wom.Abstr.
—BLDSC shelfmark: 5034.510000.
Formerly: Philosophy of Education Society of Great Britain. Proceedings (ISSN 0048-3923)

301 100   US   ISSN 0047-2786
H1
JOURNAL OF SOCIAL PHILOSOPHY. vol.3, 1972. 3/yr.
$25 to individuals (foreign $30); libraries $50
(foreign $55). North American Society for Social
Philosophy, c/o Peter A. French, Ed., Trinity
University, San Antonio, TX 78212.
FAX 512-735-7812. bk.rev.; circ. 500. (also avail.
in microform from UMI; reprint service avail. from
UMI) Indexed: Phil.Ind., Polit.Sci.Abstr., Rel.Ind.One,
Sage Fam.Stud.Abstr.
—BLDSC shelfmark: 5064.775000.

100   US   ISSN 0891-625X
B1
JOURNAL OF SPECULATIVE PHILOSOPHY. 1987. q. $20
to individuals (foreign $27); institutions $30
(foreign $35). Pennsylvania State University Press,
Barbara Bldg., Ste. C, 820 N. University Dr.,
University Park, PA 16802-1003.
TEL 814-865-1327. FAX 814-863-1408. Eds. Carl
R. Hausman, Henry W. Johnstone, Jr. (also avail. in
microform from UMI; reprint service avail. from
UMI,KTO)
—BLDSC shelfmark: 5066.142000.
  Description: North American philosophy, offering
systematic and interpretive essays about basic
philosophical questions, and promoting constructive
interaction between continental philosophy and
American thought.

164 510   US   ISSN 0022-4812
BC1   CODEN: JSYLA6
JOURNAL OF SYMBOLIC LOGIC. (Text in English, French,
German) 1936. q. $180. Association for Symbolic
Logic, Department of Mathematics, University of
Illinois at Urbana-Champaign, 1409 W. Green St.,
Urbana, IL 61801. FAX 217-333-9576. (Subscr. to:
ASL, Journal Dept., UIP, 54 E. Gregory Dr.,
Champaign, IL 61820-6680) Ed. Herbert B.
Enderton. adv.; bk.rev.; bibl.; circ. 2,500. (also avail.
in microform from UMI) Indexed: Compumath,
Curr.Cont., Hum.Ind., Ind.Bk.Rev.Hum., Ind.Sci.Rev.,
Math.R., Phil.Ind., Sci.Abstr.
—BLDSC shelfmark: 5068.000000.

109   US   ISSN 0022-5053
B1
JOURNAL OF THE HISTORY OF PHILOSOPHY. (Text in
various languages) 1963. q. $20 to individuals;
$50 libraries. Journal of the History of Philosophy,
Inc., Emory University, Dept. of Philosophy, Atlanta,
GA 30322. TEL 404-329-6412. (Subscr. to:
Department of Philosophy, Washington University,
St. Louis, MO 63130) (Co-sponsors: Claremont
Colleges; Washington University-St. Louis; Stanford
University; University of California) Ed. Rudolf
Makkreel. adv.; bk.rev.; charts; illus.; circ. 1,600.
(also avail. in microform from UMI; reprint service
avail. from UMI) Indexed: Amer.Hist.& Life, Arts &
Hum.Cit.Ind., Curr.Cont., Hist.Abstr., Hum.Ind.,
Phil.Ind.
—BLDSC shelfmark: 5001.500000.
  Description: Articles, notes and discussions on the
history of Western philosophy.

JOURNAL OF THE PHILOSOPHY OF SPORT. see SPORTS
AND GAMES

170   NE   ISSN 0022-5363
BD232   CODEN: JVINEP
JOURNAL OF VALUE INQUIRY. 1967. q. $59 to
individuals; institutions $127.50. Kluwer Academic
Publishers, Postbus 17, 3300 AA Dordrecht,
Netherlands. TEL 078-334911. FAX 078-334254.
TELEX 29245. (Dist. by: Kluwer Academic
Publishing Group, P.O. Box 322, 3300 AH
Dordrecht, Netherlands; N. America dist. addr.: Box
358, Accord Station, Hingham, MA 02018-0358.
TEL 617-871-6600) Ed. James Wilbur. adv.; bk.rev.;
index. (back issues avail.; reprint service avail. from
SWZ) Indexed: Arts & Hum.Cit.Ind., Curr.Cont.,
Ind.Bk.Rev.Hum., Phil.Ind.
—BLDSC shelfmark: 5072.260000.

JUKIC; zbornik radova. see RELIGIONS AND THEOLOGY

KABBALAH; newsletter of current research in Jewish
mysticism. see RELIGIONS AND THEOLOGY —
Judaic

100 800   AF
KABUL MOJALA. (Text in Pashtu) 1931. m. $5.
Afghanistan Academy of Sciences, Sher Alikhan St.,
Kabul, Afghanistan. Ed. N.M. Saheem.

105   FR   ISSN 1148-9227
B2
KAIROS. 1972. a. 90 F. (effective 1992). (Universite
de Toulouse II (le Mirail)) Presses Universitaires du
Mirail, 56 rue du Taur, 31000 Toulouse, France.
TEL 61-22-58-31. FAX 61-21-84-20. Ed.
Jean-Marie Vaysse. (back issues avail.)
  Formerly (until 1990): Philosophie (Toulouse)
(ISSN 0182-7103)

142.3   GW   ISSN 0022-8877
B2750
KANT STUDIEN. (Text in English, French and German)
1896. 4/yr. $84.50. (Kant-Gesellschaft) Walter de
Gruyter und Co., Mouton Publishers, Genthiner Str.
13, 1000 Berlin 11, Germany. TEL 030-26005-0.
FAX 030-26005-251. TELEX 184027. (U.S. addr.:
Walter de Gruyter, Inc., 200 Saw Mill Rd.,
Hawthorne, NY 10532) Eds. Gerhard Funke, Rudolf
Malter. adv.; bk.rev.; abstr.; charts; index; circ.
1,000. Indexed: Arts & Hum.Cit.Ind., Curr.Cont.,
Ind.Bk.Rev.Hum., Phil.Ind.

100   PH   ISSN 0116-7073
KARUNUNGAN. (Text in English) 1985. a. P.45($6.50)
(De La Salle University, Philippine Academy of
Philosophical Research) De La Salle University Press,
2401 Taft Ave., Manila, Philippines. TEL 2-595177.
Ed. Emerita S. Quito. adv.; bk.rev.; circ. 500.
  Description: Publishes scholarly articles reflecting
significant quantitative or qualitative research.
Includes speeches, research reports, and "state of
the art" papers.

100   PL
KATOLICKI UNIWERSYTET LUBELSKI. WYDZIAL
FILOZOFICZNY. ROZPRAWY. (Text in Polish;
summaries in English, French or German) 1957.
irreg. price varies. Katolicki Uniwersytet Lubelski,
Towarzystwo Naukowe, Ul. Gliniana 21, 20-616
Lublin, Poland. index; circ. 3,150.

491.6 944   FR   ISSN 0022-9792
KELTIA; organe de recherche d'un Celtisme moderne.
(Supplement to: Bretagne Reelle) 1960. bi-m.
190 F. for 10 nos. J. Quatreboeufs, 22230
Merdrignac, Brittany, France. bk.rev.

KENNEDY INSTITUTE OF ETHICS. SCOPE NOTE. see
MEDICAL SCIENCES

100   US   ISSN 1054-6863
QH332   CODEN: KIEJEF
▼KENNEDY INSTITUTE OF ETHICS JOURNAL. 1991. q.
$45 to individuals; institutions $65; students $20.
(Kennedy Institute of Ethics) Johns Hopkins
University Press, Journals Publishing Division, 701
W. 40th St., Ste. 275, Baltimore, MD 21211.
TEL 301-338-6980. FAX 301-338-6998. Eds.
Robert M. Veatch, Renie Schapiro. adv.; circ. 1,600.

KENNIS EN METHODE; tijdschrift voor
wetenschapsfilosofie en methodologie. see
SCIENCES: COMPREHENSIVE WORKS

KEXUE JISHU YU BIANZHENGFA/SCIENCE,
TECHNOLOGY, AND DIALECTICS. see SCIENCES:
COMPREHENSIVE WORKS

100 200   DK   ISSN 0075-6032
B4377
KIERKEGAARDIANA. (Text in Danish, English, French
and German; summaries in English) 1955. biennial.
DKK 200($25) (Soren Kierkegaard Selskabet -
Soeren Kierkegaard Society) C.A. Reitzels Forlag, c/o
Birgit Bertung, Frimestervej 51, 4 tv., 2400
Copenhagen NV, Denmark. (Co-sponsor: National
Council of the Humanities) Ed.Bd. bk.rev.; circ. 500.

100   US
KIERKEGAARD'S WRITINGS. 1978. irreg., no.20, 1991.
price varies. Princeton University Press, 3175
Princeton Pike, Lawrenceville, NJ 08648.
TEL 609-896-1344. FAX 609-895-1081. (reprint
service avail. from UMI)

100   US   ISSN 0023-1568
B1
KINESIS. 1968. s-a. $10 to individuals; institutions
$15. (Graduate Students of S.I.U., Department of
Philosophy) Southern Illinois University, Carbondale,
Philosophy Dept., Carbondale, IL 62901.
TEL 618-536-6641. adv.; bk.rev.; circ. 2,000. (also
avail. in microform from UMI; reprint service avail.
from UMI) Indexed: Can.Wom.Per.Ind., Phil.Ind.
—BLDSC shelfmark: 5096.030000.
  Formerly: Kinesis Report (ISSN 0193-1911)

100   AU   ISSN 0259-0743
KLAGENFURTER BEITRAEGE ZUR PHILOSOPHIE.
(Supplement avail.) 1979. irreg. price varies.
Verband der Wissenschaftlichen Gesellschaften
Oesterreichs, Lindengasse 37, A-1070 Vienna,
Austria. TEL 932166. Eds. Thomas Macho, Christof
Subik.

KNJIZEVNA KRITIKA; casopis za umetnicku, istorijsku i
filosofsku kritiku. see LITERATURE

KNOWLEDGE AND POLICY; the international journal of
knowledge transfer. see SOCIAL SCIENCES:
COMPREHENSIVE WORKS

299.51   CC
KONGZI YANJIU/STUDIES ON CONFUCIUS. (Text in
Chinese) q. $16.50. Zhongguo Kongzi Jijinhui -
China Confucius Foundation, Qufu Shifan Daxue,
Qufu, Shandong 273165, People's Republic of
China. TEL 411831. (Dist. in US by: China Books &
Periodicals, Inc., 2929 24th St., San Francisco, CA
94110. TEL 415-282-2994) Ed. Xin Guanjie.

100 001.3   GW
KONKURSBUCH; Zeitschrift fuer Vernunftkritik. 1978.
3/yr. DM.15 per no. Konkursbuchverlag Claudia
Gehrke, Postfach 1621, Garmerstr. 29, 7400
Tuebingen 7, Germany. TEL 07071-66551.
FAX 07071-63539. Ed. Claudia Gehrke. (back
issues avail.)

100   GW   ISSN 0454-448X
KOSMOSOPHIE. irreg., vol.6, 1990. price varies.
(Paracelsus-Kommission) Franz Steiner Verlag
Wiesbaden GmbH, Birkenwaldstr. 44, Postfach
101526, 7000 Stuttgart 1, Germany.
TEL 0711-2582-0. FAX 0711-2582290. TELEX
723636-DAZD. Ed. Kurt Goldammer.

100   NE   ISSN 0168-275X
KRISIS; tijdschrift voor filosofie. 1980. q. fl.45 to
individuals; institutions fl.75 (effective Jan. 1990).
Stichting Krisis, Kleine Gartmanplantsoen 10, 1017
RR Amsterdam, Netherlands. TEL 020-6233673.
Ed.Bd. adv.; bk.rev.; circ. 1,000.

KULTURNI RADNIK. see HUMANITIES:
COMPREHENSIVE WORKS

KUNGLIGA VITTERHETS HISTORIE OCH ANTIKVITETS
AKADEMIEN. HANDLINGAR. FILOLOGISK-FILOSOFISKA
SERIEN/ROYAL ACADEMY OF LETTERS, HISTORY AND
ANTIQUITIES. PROCEEDINGS.
PHILOLOGICAL-PHILOSOPHICAL SERIES. see
LINGUISTICS

L I A S: SOURCES AND DOCUMENTS RELATING TO THE
EARLY MODERN HISTORY OF IDEAS.. see HISTORY

100   IT
▼LACOONTE. 1990. irreg. price varies. Ligouri Editore
s.r.l., Via Mezzocannone 19, 80134 Naples, Italy.
TEL 081-5227139. Ed. Umberto Carpi.

LAVAL THEOLOGIQUE ET PHILOSOPHIQUE. see
RELIGIONS AND THEOLOGY

LAW & JUSTICE. see LAW

LAW AND PHILOSOPHY; an international journal for
jurisprudence and legal philosophy. see LAW

LAW AND PHILOSOPHY LIBRARY. see LAW

100   UK   ISSN 0266-0598
LEIBNIZ NEWSLETTER. 1984. a. £2. c/o George
MacDonald Ross, Dept. of Philosophy, The University,
Leeds LS2 9JT, England. TEL 0532-333283.
  Description: Reports on research and conferences
on Leibniz, and on related 17th and 18th century
topics and philosophers.

LEICESTER LITERARY & PHILOSOPHICAL SOCIETY.
TRANSACTIONS. see LITERATURE

LENINGRADSKII UNIVERSITET. VESTNIK. SERIYA
EKONOMIKA, FILOSOFIYA I PRAVO. see BUSINESS
AND ECONOMICS

LESBIAN ETHICS. see HOMOSEXUALITY

LETRAS DE DEUSTO. see HUMANITIES:
COMPREHENSIVE WORKS

PHILOSOPHY

100　　　　　　DK　ISSN 0106-8989
LIBER ACADEMIAE KIERKEGAARDIENSIS ANNUARIUS. (Text in Danish, English, German and Italian) 1980. irreg. DKK 122. C.A. Reitzels Forlag, Norregade 20, DK-1165 Copenhagen K, Denmark.

100　　　　　　UK　ISSN 0267-7091
LIBERTARIAN ALLIANCE. PHILOSOPHICAL NOTES. 1985. irreg. £10($20) Libertarian Alliance, 1 Russell Chambers, Covent Garden, London WC2E 8AA, England. TEL 071-821-5502. FAX 071-834-2031. Ed.Bd. adv.; bk.rev.; film rev.; bibl.; circ. 1,000. (back issues avail.)

LIBERTY (PORT TOWNSEND). see *LITERARY AND POLITICAL REVIEWS*

100　　　　　　SW
LIBRARY OF THEORIA. (Text in English) 1955. irreg., no.16, 1985. price varies. Liber Forlag, S-205 10, Malmo, Sweden. Ed.Bd.

100　　　　　　SP
LIBROS DE INICIACION FILOSOFICA. 1982. irreg., no.10, 1987. price varies. (Universidad de Navarra, Facultad de Filosofia y Letras) Ediciones Universidad de Navarra, S.A., Apdo. 396, 31080 Pamplona, Spain. TEL 94 825 6850.

LICHTENBERG-JAHRBUCH. see *BIOGRAPHY*

LIER EN BOOG; international journal of aesthetics and philosophy of culture. see *ART*

100 500　　　　　US
LIFE IN ACTION MAGAZINE. 1975. bi-m. $8. (School of Natural Science Life in Action) Pioneer Press (Los Gatos), 25355 Spanish Ranch Rd., Los Gatos, CA 95030. TEL 408-353-4876. Ed. Philip Brown. bk.rev.; illus.; circ. 650.

LIGHT OF CONSCIOUSNESS. see *RELIGIONS AND THEOLOGY*

100　　　　　　US　ISSN 0075-9554
LINDLEY LECTURE. 1961. a. $1.50. University of Kansas, Department of Philosophy, Lawrence, KS 66045. TEL 913-864-2700. Ed. A.C. Genova. circ. 600.
—BLDSC shelfmark: 5221.030000.

LINGUA E STILE. see *LINGUISTICS*

100 410　　　　NE　ISSN 0165-0157
P1.A1　　　　　　　CODEN: LIPHD6
LINGUISTICS AND PHILOSOPHY; a journal of natural language syntax, semantics, logic, pragmatics, and processing. 1977. bi-m. $62 to individuals; institutions $217. Kluwer Academic Publishers, Postbus 17, 3300 AA Dordrecht, Netherlands. TEL 078-334911. FAX 078-334254. TELEX 29245. (Dist. by: Kluwer Academic Publishers Group, P.O. Box 322, 3300 AH Dordrecht, Netherlands; N. America dist. addr.: Box 358, Accord Station, Hingham, MA 02018-0358. TEL 617-871-6600) Eds. David Dowty, Jeffrey Pelletier. adv.; bk.rev.; index. (back issues avail.; reprint service avail. from SWZ) **Indexed:** Arts & Hum.Cit.Ind., Curr.Cont., Lang.& Lang.Behav.Abstr. (1977-), Lang.Teach.& Ling.Abstr., M.L.A., Phil.Ind., Sociol.Abstr.
—BLDSC shelfmark: 5221.377000.

LITERATURE AND THE SCIENCES OF MAN. see *LITERATURE*

THE LIVING LIGHT PHILOSOPHY. see *RELIGIONS AND THEOLOGY*

LIVING PRAYER. see *RELIGIONS AND THEOLOGY*

100　　　　　　UK　ISSN 0307-2606
B1250
LOCKE NEWSLETTER. (Text in English, French, German and Italian) 1970. a. £4($8) Roland Hall, Ed. & Pub., Department of Philosophy, University of York, Heslington, York YO1 5DD, England. TEL 0904-433252. adv.; bk.rev.; circ. 600. **Indexed:** Phil.Ind.
—BLDSC shelfmark: 5290.300000.

160　　　　　　BE　ISSN 0024-5836
BC1　　　　　　　CODEN: LOANAM
LOGIQUE ET ANALYSE. (Text in Dutch, English, French, German) 1958. 4/yr. Nauwelaerts Printing Cy., Begaultlaan 17, B-3010 Wilsele, Belgium. Ed. J. Dopp. bk.rev.; bibl.; circ. 1,000. **Indexed:** Lang.& Lang.Behav.Abstr., Math.R., Phil.Ind.
Description: Quarterly philosophical publication.

100　　　　　　IT　ISSN 0024-5887
B4
LOGOS;* rivista di filosofia. 1969. 3/yr. L.6000. Libreria Scientifica Editrice, Corso Umberto I N. 38 e 40, 80138 Naples, Italy. Ed. Cleto Carbonara. **Indexed:** Phil.Ind.

LOGOS (NEW YORK); the Swedenborg Foundation newsletter. see *RELIGIONS AND THEOLOGY — Other Denominations And Sects*

100 200　　　　CN　ISSN 0828-184X
LONERGAN STUDIES NEWSLETTER. 1980. q. Can.$6($5) Lonergan Research Institute, 10 St. Mary St., Ste. 500, Toronto, Ont. M4Y 1P9, Canada. TEL 416-922-8374. FAX 416-922-2898. circ. 280.

212.5　　　　　FR　ISSN 0024-6670
LOTUS BLEU; revue theosophique. vol.78, 1973. m. 240 F. Societe Theosophique de France, 4 Square Rapp, 75007 Paris, France. Ed. Francoise Caracostea. bk.rev.

100　　　　　　BE
LOUVAIN PHILOSOPHICAL STUDIES. 1987. irreg., vol.4, 1991. Leuven University Press, Krakenstraat 3, B-3000 Leuven, Belgium. TEL 016-284175. FAX 016-284176.

LOVE; the journal of the human spirit. see *NEW AGE PUBLICATIONS*

180 289.9　　　US
LOVETRANCE WORLD. q. $5 (foreign $7). Intergalactic Lovetrance Civilization Center, Aum Namo Bhagavate Vasudevay Foundation, Box 73, Harbor City, CA 90710-0073. TEL 213-831-4226.
Formerly: Lovetrance News.
Description: Includes words of wisdom, question and answer with Founder Sri Swami Prem, special events and schedules, new book and video releases.

LOVING BROTHERHOOD NEWSLETTER; a journal for personal and planetary transformation. see *HOMOSEXUALITY*

LUCA; casopis za filozofiju i sociologiju. see *SOCIOLOGY*

100　　　　　　GW
LUDWIG FEUERBACH: GESAMMELTE WERKE. 1967. irreg., vol.18, 1988. Akademie-Verlag Berlin, Leipziger Str. 3-4, 1086 Berlin, Germany. TELEX 114420-AVERL-DD. Ed. Werner Schuffenhauer.

100 410　　　　CC
LUOJI YU YUYAN XUEXI/LOGIC AND LANGUAGE STUDIES. (Text in Chinese) bi-m. Hebei Shifan Xueyuan, Zhengjiao Xi - Hebei Normal Institute, Department of Politics and Religion, Hongqi Dajie, Shijiazhuang, Hebei 050091, People's Republic of China.

MACROBIOTICS TODAY. see *NUTRITION AND DIETETICS*

MAGICAL BLEND; a transformative journey. see *NEW AGE PUBLICATIONS*

100　　　　　　HU　ISSN 0025-0090
MAGYAR FILOZOFIAI SZEMLE/HUNGARIAN PHILOSOPHICAL REVIEW. (Text in Hungarian; summaries in English, French, German and Russian) 1957. bi-m. $30. (Magyar Tudomanyos Akademia, Filozofiai Bizottsag) Akademiai Kiado, Publishing House of the Hungarian Academy of Sciences, P.O. Box 24, H-1363 Budapest, Hungary. Ed. L.F. Lendvai. adv.; bk.rev.; index. **Indexed:** Lang.& Lang.Behav.Abstr., Phil.Ind.

MAHA BODHI; international Buddhist monthly. see *RELIGIONS AND THEOLOGY — Buddhist*

181　　　　　　II　ISSN 0025-0414
MAHAJANMER LAGNA. (Text in Bengali) 1967. w. Rs.6. Sulekha Press, Arambagh, Hooghly, W. Bengal, India. Ed. Jay Krishna Mukherjee. adv.; bk.rev.; circ. 1,000. (looseleaf format)

100　　　　　　GW　ISSN 0076-2776
MAINZER PHILOSOPHISCHE FORSCHUNGEN. 1966. irreg., vol.29, 1986. price varies. Bouvier Verlag Herbert Grundmann, Am Hof 32, Postfach 1268, 5300 Bonn 1, Germany. Ed. Gerhard Funke.

MAN AND NATURE/HOMME ET LA NATURE. see *HISTORY*

100　　　　　　NE　ISSN 0025-1534
B1　　　　　　　CODEN: MWORE5
MAN AND WORLD; an international philosophical review. (Text in English, French and German) 1968. q. $133. Kluwer Academic Publishers, Postbus 17, 3300 AA Dordrecht, Netherlands. TEL 078-334911. FAX 078-334254. TELEX 29245. (Dist. by: Kluwer Academic Publishing Group, P.O. Box 322, 3300 AH Dordrecht, Netherlands; N. America dist. addr.: Box 358, Accord Station, Hingham, MA 02018-0358. TEL 617-871-6600) Ed.Bd. bk.rev.; bibl.; index. (reprint service avail. from SWZ) **Indexed:** Curr.Cont., Phil.Ind.
—BLDSC shelfmark: 5358.012500.

106 806　　　　UK
MANCHESTER MEMOIRS. 1785. a. £8. Manchester Literary and Philosophical Society, 14 Kennedy St., Manchester M2 4BY, England. FAX 061-236-9482. Ed. A.L. Smyth. bk.rev.; circ. 800. (also avail. in microfilm from BHP) **Indexed:** Amer.Hist.& Life, Br.Hum.Ind., GeoRef., Hist.Abstr.
Formerly: Manchester Literary and Philosophical Society. Memoirs and Proceedings (ISSN 0076-3721)
Description: Devoted to the stimulation of public interest and appreciation of all forms of literature, science, arts, and public affairs.

160 121　　　　BL　ISSN 0100-6045
B1
MANUSCRITO; revista internacional. (Text in English, French, Portuguese, Spanish) 1977. s-a. $12 to individuals; institutions $18. Universidade Estadual de Campinas, Centro de Logica, Epistemologia e Historia da Ciencia - State University of Campinas, Center for Logic, Epistemology and History of Science, Caixa Postal 6133, Barao Geraldo, 13801 Campinas, SP, Brazil. TEL 0192-393269. FAX 0192-394717. TELEX 0191150. Eds. Marcelo Dascal, Michael Wrigley. adv.; bk.rev.; illus.; circ. 700. **Indexed:** Phil.Ind.

100　　　　　　CC
MAO ZEDONG ZHEXUE SIXIANG YANJIU/STUDIES IN MAO ZEDONG'S PHILOSOPHICAL THOUGHT. (Text in Chinese) bi-m. Shanghai Shehui Kexueyuan, Zhexue Yanjiusuo - Shanghai Academy of Social Sciences, Institute of Philosophy, No.7, Alley 622, Huaihai Zhonglu, Shanghai 200020, People's Republic of China. TEL 3271170. Ed. Zhou Hang.

100　　　　　　CS
MASARYKOVA UNIVERZITA. FILOZOFICKA FAKULTA. SBORNIK PRACI. B: RADA FILOZOFICKA. 1953. irreg. (approx. a). price varies. Masarykova Univerzita, Filozoficka Fakulta, A. Novaka 1, 660 88 Brno, Czechoslovakia.
Formerly: Univerzita J.E. Purkyne. Filozoficka Fakulta. Sbornik Praci. B: Rada Filozoficka (ISSN 0231-7664)
Description: Articles on ethics, logic and the history of philosophy.

MASTER OF LIFE. see *NEW AGE PUBLICATIONS*

100　　　　　　US
MATERIAL FOR THOUGHT. 1970. irreg. $7.95 per no. Far West Editions, Box 27524, San Francisco, CA 94127. TEL 415-566-5145. bk.rev.; circ. 3,500.

180　　　　　　US　ISSN 0076-5856
MEDIAEVAL PHILOSOPHICAL TEXTS IN TRANSLATION. 1942. a. price varies. Marquette University Press, 1324 W. Wisconsin Ave., Milwaukee, WI 53233. TEL 414-224-1564. (reprint service avail. from UMI)

PHILOSOPHY

100   PL   ISSN 0076-5880
MEDIAEVALIA PHILOSOPHICA POLONORUM. (Text in French or German) 1957. a. price varies. (Polska Akademia Nauk, Instytut Filozofii i Socjologii) Ossolineum, Publishing House of the Polish Academy of Sciences, Rynek 9, 50-106 Wroclaw, Poland. TELEX 0712771 OSS PL. (Dist. by: Ars Polona-Ruch, Krakowskie Przedmiescie 7, Warsaw, Poland) Ed. W. Senko. **Indexed:** M.L.A.
—BLDSC shelfmark: 5525.295000.
Description: Dissertations on philosophical thought in the works of great philosophers, with commentaries.

MEDICAL ETHICS ADVISOR. see *MEDICAL SCIENCES*

MEDIEVALIA ET HUMANISTICA; studies in medieval and renaissance culture. see *HISTORY — History Of Europe*

109   IT
MEDIOEVO; rivista di storia della filosofia medievale. 1975. irreg., no.14, 1988. price varies. (Universita degli Studi di Padova, Centro per Ricerche di Filosofia Medievale) Editrice Antenore, Via Rusca 15, Padua 35100, Italy. Ed.Bd.

100   CC
MEI YU SHIDAI. (Text in Chinese) m. Zhengzhou Daxue, Meixue Yanjiusuo - Zhengzhou University, Aesthetics Research Institute, No. 75, Daxue Lu, Zhengzhou, Henan 450052, People's Republic of China. TEL 771541. Ed. Zhang Heng.

MELITA THEOLOGICA. see *RELIGIONS AND THEOLOGY*

100   AU
MENSCH UND ZIEL; Monatsschrift fuer philosophische Moral. 1970. fortn. S.310. Mag. Wilfried Josch, Ed. & Pub., Anton-Anderer-Platz 2, A-1210 Vienna, Austria. bk.rev.
Former titles (until 1977): Blaetter fuer Philosophische Ethik; Verantworten; Leben-Wirken (ISSN 0029-9936)

MERLEG; folyoiratok es konyvek szemleje. see *RELIGIONS AND THEOLOGY*

100   UK   ISSN 0026-1068
B1
METAPHILOSOPHY. 1970. q. £35($55) to individuals; institutions £67.50($133). (Metaphilosophy Foundation, US) Basil Blackwell Ltd., 108 Cowley Rd., Oxford OX4 1JF, England. TEL 0865-791100. FAX 0865-791347. TELEX 837022-OXBOOK-G. Ed. Terrell Ward Bynum. adv.; bk.rev.; index; circ. 650. (reprint service avail. from SWZ) **Indexed:** Arts & Hum.Cit.Ind., Curr.Cont., Lang.& Lang.Behav.Abstr., Phil.Ind.
—BLDSC shelfmark: 5701.600000.

110   US
METAPHYSICAL FELLOWSHIP CHURCH. NEWSLETTER. 12/yr. free. Metaphysical Fellowship Church, 10591 Flower St., Stanton, CA 90680-2326. Ed. Yvonne Goodale. adv.

018 200   US   ISSN 0736-7392
BD241
METHOD: JOURNAL OF LONERGAN STUDIES. 1983. s-a. $12 to individuals; institutions $20. Institute for Integrative Studies, Inc., Lonergan Institute at Boston College, Dept. of Philosophy, Carney Hall 216, Boston College, Chesnut Hill, MA 02167-3806. Ed.Bd. bk.rev.; circ. 250. (back issues avail.) **Indexed:** Phil.Ind.
—BLDSC shelfmark: 5745.601000.

MIDWEST QUARTERLY; a journal of contemporary thought. see *HUMANITIES: COMPREHENSIVE WORKS*

100   US   ISSN 0363-6550
MIDWEST STUDIES IN PHILOSOPHY. 1976. a. price varies. University of Notre Dame Press, Notre Dame, IN 46556. TEL 219-239-6346. TELEX 62131650. Ed.Bd. **Indexed:** Phil.Ind.
Description: Covers a single theme in philosophy reflecting a wide range of views.

MILLTOWN STUDIES. see *RELIGIONS AND THEOLOGY*

100 150   UK   ISSN 0026-4423
B1
MIND; a quarterly review of philosophy. 1876. q. £28($53) (Mind Association) Oxford University Press, Oxford Journals, Pinkhill House, Southfield Road, Eynsham, Oxford OX8 1JJ, England. TEL 0865-882283. FAX 0865-882890. TELEX 837330 OXPRES G. Ed. Mark Sainsbury. adv.; bk.rev.; index, cum.index; circ. 3,700. (also avail. in microform from UMI; reprint service avail. from KTO) **Indexed:** Amer.Hist.& Life, Arts & Hum.Cit.Ind., Br.Hum.Ind, Curr.Cont., Hist.Abstr., Hum.Ind., Ind.Bk.Rev.Hum., Lang.& Lang.Behav.Abstr., Math.R., Phil.Ind., SSCI.
—BLDSC shelfmark: 5775.500000.
Description: Expresses and gives direction to currents of thought in epistemology, the philosophy of language, metaphysics and philosophical psychology.

100   UK   ISSN 0268-1064
P37   CODEN: MILAEB
MIND & LANGUAGE. 1986. q. £28.50($50) to individuals; institutions £75($145). Basil Blackwell Ltd., 108 Cowley Rd., Oxford OX4 1JF, England. TEL 0865-791100. FAX 0865-791347. TELEX 837022-OXBOOK-G. Ed.Bd. adv.; bk.rev (also avail. in microform; reprint service avail. from SWZ)
Indexed: Art.Int.Abstr.
—BLDSC shelfmark: 5775.526400.

100 500   US   ISSN 0076-9258
Q175
MINNESOTA STUDIES IN THE PHILOSOPHY OF SCIENCE. 1956. irreg., vol.14, 1990. price varies. (Minnesota Center for Philosophy of Science) University of Minnesota Press, 2037 University Ave., S.E., Minneapolis, MN 55414. TEL 612-624-2516. FAX 612-626-7313. Ed.Bd. index. (reprint service avail. from UMI) **Indexed:** ASCA, SSCI.
—BLDSC shelfmark: 5810.465000.
Description: Essays drawn from research and conferences sponsored by the center.
Refereed Serial

MIRA; a monthly journal of Indian culture. see *LITERARY AND POLITICAL REVIEWS*

MISCELANEA COMILLAS; revista de teologia y ciencias humanas. see *RELIGIONS AND THEOLOGY*

MISCELLANEA FRANCESCANA; rivista trimestrale di scienze teologiche e di studi francescani. see *RELIGIONS AND THEOLOGY — Roman Catholic*

MITHILA INSTITUTE OF POST GRADUATE STUDIES AND RESEARCH IN SANSKRIT LEARNING. BULLETIN. see *LINGUISTICS*

MITZION TETZEH TORAH. M.T.T.. see *RELIGIONS AND THEOLOGY — Judaic*

100   GW   ISSN 0170-3013
MODERN GERMAN STUDIES. irreg., no.14, 1985. price varies. Bouvier Verlag Herbert Grundmann, Am Hof 32, Postfach 1268, 5300 Bonn 1, Germany.
—BLDSC shelfmark: 5886.720000.

100   US   ISSN 0026-8402
B1
MODERN SCHOOLMAN; a quarterly of philosophy. 1925. q. $26. St. Louis University, 221 N. Grand, St. Louis, MO 63103. TEL 314-658-3149. Ed. William C. Charron. adv.; bk.rev. **Indexed:** Arts & Hum.Cit.Ind., Cath.Ind., CERDIC, Curr.Cont., Mid.East: Abstr.& Ind., Phil.Ind.
—BLDSC shelfmark: 5896.400000.

100   US   ISSN 1051-127X
MOKSHA JOURNAL. (Text in English, Sanskrit) 1984. s-a. $8. Vajra Printing & Publishing of Yoga Anand Ashram, 49 Forrest Pl., Amityville, NY 11701. TEL 516-691-8475. circ. 500. (back issues avail.)

100   IT   ISSN 0544-7526
MOMENTO; rivista di testimonianze e di dialogo. 1965. bi-m. Via Duccio di Boninsegna 25, Milan, Italy. Ed.Bd. abstr.

100   US   ISSN 0026-9662
B1
MONIST; an international quarterly of general philosophical inquiry. 1890. q. $18 to individuals; institutions $28. Hegeler Institute, Box 600, La Salle, IL 61301. TEL 815-223-1500. FAX 815-223-4486. Ed. Barry Smith. adv.; bk.rev.; abstr.; circ. 1,600. (back issues avail.; reprint service avail. from KTO) **Indexed:** Arts & Hum.Cit.Ind., Curr.Cont., Hum.Ind., Mid.East: Abstr.& Ind., Phil.Ind., SSCI.
—BLDSC shelfmark: 5908.600000.

100 170   FR   ISSN 0026-9727
MONITEUR DU REGNE DE LA JUSTICE; journal bi-mensuel philanthropique et humanitaire, pour le relevement moral et social. (Editions in Dutch, English, French, Italian, Portuguese and Spanish) 1936. s-m. 20 F. Association les Amis de l'Homme, 22 rue David d'Angers, 75019 Paris, France. Ed. R. Cavin.

108   GW
MONOGRAPHIEN ZUR PHILOSOPHISCHEN FORSCHUNG. 1947. irreg., no.232, 1985. price varies. Verlag Anton Hain GmbH, Savignystr. 53, 6000 Frankfurt a.M. 1, Germany. Ed. Georgi Schischkoff.

MONTESSORI NEWS. see *EDUCATION*

MORGENROTE. see *RELIGIONS AND THEOLOGY*

100   RU
MOSKOVSKII UNIVERSITET. VESTNIK. SERIYA 8: FILOSOFIYA. 1946. bi-m. 13.50 Rub. Moskovskii Universitet, Ul. Gertsena 5-7, 103009 Moscow, Russia. bk.rev.; bibl.; index. **Indexed:** Rural Recreat.Tour.Abstr., World Agri.Econ.& Rural Sociol.Abstr.
Supersedes in part: Moskovskii Universitet. Vestnik. Seriya Ekonomika, Filosofiya (ISSN 0027-1365)

MOTHER EARTH NEWS; the original country magazine. see *SOCIOLOGY*

180   II   ISSN 0027-2574
MOUNTAIN PATH. 1964. q. Rs.20($20) (Sri Ramanasramam) T.N. Venkatatraman, Pub., Sri Ramanasramam, P.O., Tiruvannamali 606 603, India. TEL 2491. Ed. V. Ganesan. adv.; bk.rev.; charts; illus.; index; circ. 5,000.
Description: Spiritual articles and poems devoted to Sri Bhagavan Ramana Maharshi.

100   DR
MUSEO DEL HOMBRE DOMINICANO. SERIE CONFERENCIAS PENSAMIENTO DOMINICANO. 1974. irreg. RD.$5. Museo del Hombre Dominicano, Calle Pedro Henriquez Urena, Santo Domingo, Dominican Republic.

100   DR
MUSEO DEL HOMBRE DOMINICANO. SERIE CONFERENCIAS SOBRE EL PENSAMIENTO DE PEDRO HENRIQUEZ URENA. irreg., no.2. RD.$5. Museo del Hombre Dominicano, Calle Pedro Henriquez Urena, Santo Domingo, Dominican Republic. TEL 687-3622.

294.54   II
NANDAN KANAN. (Text in Bengali) 1975. m. Rs.66 (foreign Rs.120). Adarsha Prakashani, Ma-Mahajnana Bishwa Kalyan Trust, Kharagpur 721 305, W.B., India. TEL 03222-661. circ. 10,000.

100   UK
NATIONAL SECULAR SOCIETY. ANNUAL REPORT. 1867. a. membership. National Secular Society, 702 Holloway Rd., London N19 3NL, England. TEL 01-272-1266. Ed. T. Mullins.
Description: Contains a report of the Society's activities.

NAUCNI PODMLADAK: DRUSTVENE NAUKE I FILOZOFIJA; strucni casopis studenata Univerziteta u Nisu. see *SOCIAL SCIENCES: COMPREHENSIVE WORKS*

100 500   RU
NEKOTORYE FILOSOFSKIE VOPROSY SOVREMENNOGO ESTESTVOZNANIYA. 1973. irreg. 0.66 Rub. (Leningradskii Universitet) Lenizdat, Fontanka 59, St. Petersburg, Russia.

PHILOSOPHY

100   GW   ISSN 0085-3917
B23
NEUE HEFTE FUER PHILOSOPHIE. 1971. irreg., no.31, 1991. price varies. Vandenhoeck und Ruprecht, Theaterstr. 13, Postfach 3753, 3400 Goeitingen, Germany. TEL 0551-6959-22. FAX 0551-695917. circ. 2,200. **Indexed:** Phil.Ind.
—BLDSC shelfmark: 6077.482000.

NEW AGE EXCHANGE; a magazine of contemporary metaphysical thought. see *NEW AGE PUBLICATIONS*

NEW ATHENAEUM/NEUES ATHENAEUM. see *LITERATURE*

100   US
NEW DIRECTIONS IN PHILOSOPHY. irreg. Peter Lang Publishing, Inc., 62 W. 45th St., 4th Fl., New York, NY 10036. TEL 212-302-6740. FAX 212-302-7574. Ed. Anatole Anton.
Description: Encourages philosophers to explore certain new directions of research.

NEW FRONTIER; magazine of transformation. see *NEW AGE PUBLICATIONS*

144   UK   ISSN 0306-512X
AP4
NEW HUMANIST. 1972. q. £7($17.25) Rationalist Press Association, 88 Islington High St., London N1 8EW, England. Ed. Nicolas Walter. adv.; bk.rev. (also avail. in microform from UMI; reprint service avail. from UMI) **Indexed:** Br.Hum.Ind.
—BLDSC shelfmark: 6084.246000.
Formerly: Humanist (ISSN 0018-7380)

100   UK   ISSN 0307-0980
NEW HUMANITY JOURNAL; journal for the creative individual - the free and independent thinker. 1975. bi-m. $28. New Humanity, 51a York Mansions, Prince of Wales Drive, London SW11 4BP, England. TEL 071-622-4013. FAX 071-498-0173. Ed. Johan Henri Quanjer. adv.; bk.rev.; circ. 14,000. (back issues avail.)
—BLDSC shelfmark: 6084.246000.
Description: Integrates the disciplines of science, philosophy, politics, the arts, religion and the humanities to promote closer cooperation and understanding among them.

NEW PARADIGMS NEWSLETTER. see *SCIENCES: COMPREHENSIVE WORKS*

100   US   ISSN 1045-4500
NEW PERSPECTIVES IN PHILOSOPHICAL SCHOLARSHIP: TEXTS AND ISSUES. irreg. Peter Lang Publishing, Inc., 62 W. 45th St., 4th Fl., New York, NY 10036. TEL 212-302-6740. FAX 212-302-7574. Ed. James Duerlinger.
Description: Seeks to integrate a number of different fields in philosophy which in the past have not often been combined.

100 230.94   US   ISSN 0028-6443
BX8701
THE NEW PHILOSOPHY. 1898. q. $8 to non-members. Swedenborg Scientific Association, Box 757, Bryn Athyn, PA 19009. TEL 215-947-2577. FAX 215-438-1056. Ed. Erland J. Brock. bk.rev.; index every 3 yrs.; circ. 450.
—BLDSC shelfmark: 6084.930000.
Description: Articles address philosophical questions and topics that bear on the works of Emanuel Swedenborg.

100   US   ISSN 0093-4240
B1
NEW SCHOOL FOR SOCIAL RESEARCH. PHILOSOPHY DEPARTMENT. GRADUATE FACULTY PHILOSOPHY JOURNAL. (Text in English; contributions in French, German, Greek and Latin) 1971. s-a. $12.50 to individuals; institutions $16. New School for Social Research, Philosophy Department, 65 Fifth Ave., New York, NY 10003. TEL 212-741-5707. adv.; bk.rev.; circ. 1,000. (back issues avail.) **Indexed:** Phil.Ind.
—BLDSC shelfmark: 4206.827000.
Description: Promotes a scholarly forum exploring the diverse aspects of the history of philosophy and contemporary continental thought.

100   US   ISSN 0893-6005
NEW STUDIES IN AESTHETICS. (Text in English and other West European languages.) 1987. irreg., vol.2, 1988. Peter Lang Publishing, Inc., 62 W. 45th St., 4th Fl., New York, NY 10036. TEL 212-302-6740. Ed. Robert Ginsberg.
—BLDSC shelfmark: 6088.773000.

NEW TIMES (SEATTLE); the Northwest's monthly new age community newspaper. see *NEW AGE PUBLICATIONS*

NEW TITLES IN BIOETHICS. see *MEDICAL SCIENCES*

100   US   ISSN 0733-9542
B3580.A1
NEW VICO STUDIES. 1983. a. price varies. Humanities Press, 165 First Ave., Atlantic Highlands, NJ 07716-1289. TEL 908-872-1441. FAX 908-872-0717. Eds. Giorgio Tagliacozzo, Donald Phillip Verene. bk.rev.; circ. 750. **Indexed:** Phil.Ind.
—BLDSC shelfmark: 6089.187000.
Description: Includes articles, reviews, abstracts and notes reflecting the current state of the study of the thought of Giambattista Vico.

NEW WAVES (WASHINGTON). see *NEW AGE PUBLICATIONS*

THE NEW WORLD. see *RELIGIONS AND THEOLOGY — Roman Catholic*

140   NZ   ISSN 0028-8632
NEW ZEALAND RATIONALIST AND HUMANIST; a journal on philosophy, science, religion, literature & society. 1939. 3/yr. NZ.$10.80. New Zealand Rationalist Association Inc., 64 Symonds St., Auckland 1, New Zealand. Ed.Bd. bk.rev.; circ. 1,000.
Formerly: New Zealand Rationalist.

100   GW   ISSN 0342-1422
NIETZSCHE-STUDIEN; internationales Jahrbuch fuer die Nietzsche-Forschung. (Text in English and German) a. price varies. Walter de Gruyter und Co., Genthiner Str. 13, 1000 Berlin 30, Germany. TEL 030-26005-0. FAX 030-26005251. TELEX 184027. (U.S. addr.: Walter de Gruyter, Inc., 200 Saw Mill Rd., Hawthorne, N.Y. 10532) **Indexed:** M.L.A.
—BLDSC shelfmark: 6110.950000.

NIGHTSUN; a journal of poetry, fiction, and interviews. see *LITERATURE*

100   NE
NIJHOFF INTERNATIONAL PHILOSOPHY SERIES. (Text in English) 1976. irreg. price varies. Kluwer Academic Publishers, Postbus 17, 3300 AA Dordrecht, Netherlands. (Orders to: Kluwer Academic Publishers, Distribution Center, P.O. Box 327, 3300 AH Dordrecht, Netherlands) Ed. Jan T.J. Srzednicki. **Indexed:** Math.R.
Formerly: Melbourne International Philosophy Series.

NODE; for hackers with soul. see *MEDICAL SCIENCES — Computer Applications*

NOOR AL-ISLAM; thiqafiyyah islamiyyah - islamic cultural magazine. see *RELIGIONS AND THEOLOGY — Islamic*

100   NO   ISSN 0029-1943
CODEN: NGGTAZ
NORSK FILOSOFISK TIDSSKRIFT/NORWEGIAN JOURNAL OF PHILOSOPHY. (Text in English) 1966. q. $51. (Norwegian Geographical Society) Universitetsforlaget, P.O. Box 2959-Toeyen, N-0608 Oslo 1, Norway. (U.S. addr.: Publications Expediting Inc., 200 Meacham Ave., Elmont, NY 11003) Ed. Audun Oefsti. adv.; bk.rev.; bibl.; index; circ. 350.
—BLDSC shelfmark: 6138.130000.

NORSKE VIDENSKAPS-AKADEMI. HISTORISK-FILOSOFISK KLASSE. AVHANDLINGER. see *HISTORY*

NOTEBOOK (BARSTOW)/CUADERNO; a literary journal. see *LITERATURE*

NOTRE DAME JOURNAL OF FORMAL LOGIC. see *MATHEMATICS*

100   US   ISSN 0029-4624
B1
NOUS; nihil philosophicum a nobis alienum putamus. 1967. 5/yr. $30 to individuals; institutions $60; students and retired philosophers $23. (Indiana University, Department of Philosophy) Basil Blackwell Inc., 3 Cambridge Center, Cambridge, MA 02142. TEL 617-225-0430. Ed. Hector-Neri Castaneda. adv.; bk.rev.; index, cum.index; circ. 1,100. (also avail. in microfilm from UMI; back issues avail.) **Indexed:** Ind.Bk.Rev.Hum., Lang.& Lang.Behav.Abstr., Math.R., Phil.Ind.
—BLDSC shelfmark: 6176.310000.

100   IT   ISSN 0392-2332
AS222.N775
NOUVELLES DE LA REPUBLIQUE DES LETTRES. 1981. s-a. L.50000($47) (foreign L.80000). (Istituto Italiano per gli Studi Filosofici) Prismi, Editrice Politecnica Napoli, Via F. Caracciolo 17, 80122 Naples, Italy. TEL 081-7612884. FAX 81-668339. Eds. Paul Dibon, Tullio Gregory. adv.; bk.rev.; circ. 500. **Indexed:** M.L.A.
Description: Covers philosophy, science and art from the Renaissance and the Enlightenment periods.

NOVA MYSL. see *POLITICAL SCIENCE*

100   IT
NUOVA CIVILTA DELLE MACCHINE. 1983. q. L.50000 (foreign L.75000). E R I Edizioni R A I, Via Arsenale 41, 10121 Torin, Italy. TEL 011-8800. FAX 011-534732. Ed. Francesco Barone. bk.rev.

NUOVA CORRENTE; rivista di letteratura e filosofia. see *LITERATURE*

NUOVA UNIVERSALE STUDIUM. see *LITERATURE*

100   DK   ISSN 0107-7384
ODENSE UNIVERSITY STUDIES IN PHILOSOPHY. (Text in Danish and English) 1972. irreg. price varies. Odense University Press, Campusvej 55, DK-5230 Odense M, Denmark. TEL 66-157999. (back issues avail.)

ODGOJ I SAMOUPRAVLJANJE. see *EDUCATION*

ODRA. see *LITERATURE*

100   SA   ISSN 0256-0356
ODYSSEY; an adventure in more conscious living. 1977. bi-m. R.25 (foreign R.30). Wellstead Association, The Wellstead, 1 Wellington Avenue, Wynberg 7800, Cape Town, South Africa. TEL 021-797-8982. Ed. Rose de la Hunt. adv.; bk.rev.; tr.lit.; circ. 6,000. (back issues avail.) **Indexed:** Ind.Child.Mag.
Description: Covers self-discovery, inspiration and transformation, philosophy, holistic health and nutrition, ecology, metaphysics, personal and spiritual growth and parapsychology.

OESTERREICHISCHE AKADEMIE DER WISSENSCHAFTEN. PHILOSOPHISCH-HISTORISCHE KLASSE. ANZEIGER. see *HISTORY — History Of Europe*

100   AU
OESTERREICHISCHEN KARL-JASPERS-GESELLSCHAFT. JAHRBUCH. irreg., no.2, 1989. varies. Verband der Wissenschaftlichen Gesellschaften Oesterreichs, Lindengasse 37, A-1070 Vienna, Austria. TEL 932166.

ON COURSE; weekly perspectives on the inner journey. see *NEW AGE PUBLICATIONS*

ON WINGS. see *WOMEN'S INTERESTS*

OOMOTO. see *RELIGIONS AND THEOLOGY — Other Denominations And Sects*

100 200   US
OPINION; the way I see it. 1957. m. $10. (Gospel Truth Association) Opinion Publications, Box 254, E. Machias, ME 04630. Ed. James E. Kurtz. adv.; bk.rev.; illus.; tr.lit.; index; circ. 3,700 (controlled). (back issues avail.)
Description: Commentary on current events, with essays on philosophy, sociology, and theology.

144   US
OPOSSUM HOLLER TAROT;* an underground magazine. 1983. irreg. Larry Blazek, Ed. & Pub., RR 3 Box 109, Orleans, IN 47452-9649.

ORGANICA; a magazine of arts & activism. see *LITERATURE*

100 840 FR
ORGANOGRAPHES DU CYMBALUM PATAPHYSICUM. 1949. q. 88 F.($10) includes 2 monographs. College de Pataphysique, Courtaumont Par Sermiers, 51500 Rilly la Montagne, France. Ed. Paul Gayot. illus.
 Former titles: Subsidia Pataphysica (ISSN 0039-4386); College de Pataphysique. Dossiers.

ORIENTIERUNG; katholische Blaetter fuer weltanschauliche Information. see *RELIGIONS AND THEOLOGY*

ORIGINS (LOMA LINDA). see *SCIENCES: COMPREHENSIVE WORKS*

100 II
ORIYA-AUROVILIAN. (Text in English) 1972. q. Rs.18. Sri Aurobindo Sanskruti Sansad, Women's Wing, 39 Udyan Marg, Bhubaneswar, Orissa, India. Ed. Amar Singh. adv.; bk.rev.; illus.; circ. 1,000. (reprint service avail.)

ORPHEUS; rivista di umanita classica e cristiana. see *LITERATURE*

OSHO TIMES INTERNATIONAL. see *RELIGIONS AND THEOLOGY* — Buddhist

100 US ISSN 0030-7580
B2900
OWL OF MINERVA. 1969. s-a. $15 to individuals; institutions $25. Hegel Society of America, c/o Lawrence S. Stepelevich, Ed., Department of Philosophy, Villanova University, Villanova, PA 19085. TEL 215-645-4690. adv.; bk.rev.; bibl.; cum.index; circ. 600. (also avail. in microfilm) **Indexed:** Phil.Ind.
 —BLDSC shelfmark: 6320.540000.
 Description: Academic publication featuring articles, notes, and reports on Hegel, Hegelianism, and related subjects.

OXFORD CLASSICAL AND PHILOSOPHICAL MONOGRAPHS. see *CLASSICAL STUDIES*

OXFORD LITERARY REVIEW; critical analyses of literary, philosophical, political and psycho-analytic theory. see *LITERATURE*

P R O U T PRESS. (Progressive Utilization Theory) see *GENERAL INTEREST PERIODICALS — United States*

100 UK ISSN 0279-0750
AP2 CODEN: PPHQEJ
PACIFIC PHILOSOPHICAL QUARTERLY. 1920. q. £18.50($31) to individuals; institutions £36($52.50). (University of Southern California, School of Philosophy - US) Basil Blackwell Ltd., 108 Cowley Rd., Oxford OX4 1JF, England. TEL 0865-791100. FAX 0865-791347. TELEX 837022-OXBOOK-G. Ed.Bd. adv.; bibl.; index; circ. 850. (also avail. in microform from MIM,UMI; reprint service avail. from UMI; back issues avail.) **Indexed:** Arts & Hum.Cit.Ind., Curr.Cont., Hum.Ind., Phil.Ind., SSCI.
 —BLDSC shelfmark: 6330.700000.
 Formerly (until vol.61, Jan. 1980): Personalist (ISSN 0031-5621)

PACIFICA; Australian theological studies. see *RELIGIONS AND THEOLOGY*

100 370 US
PAIDEIA. 1972. a. $10. State University of New York at Buffalo, Department of Foundational Studies, 1300 Elmwood Ave., Buffalo, NY 14222. TEL 716-878-4303. Ed. Albert Grande. adv.; bk.rev.; circ. 1,000. **Indexed:** M.L.A.

100 CN ISSN 0838-4517
PAIDEUSIS. 1987. s-a. Can.$4 to members; non-members Can.$8; institutions Can.$12. Canadian Philosophy of Education Society, c/o Prof. Don Cochrane, Manag.Ed., University of Saskatchewan, Dept. of Educational Foundations, Saskatoon, Sask. S7N 0W0, Canada. FAX 306-966-8719. Ed. Paul O'Leary. bk.rev.; circ. 125.
 Description: Covers communication and interaction among philosophers of education in Canada.
 Refereed Serial

100 PK ISSN 0078-8406
PAKISTAN PHILOSOPHICAL CONGRESS. PROCEEDINGS. (Text in English) 1954. a. $7. Pakistan Philosophical Congress, Department of Philosophy, University of the Punjab, New Campus, Lahore 20, Pakistan. Ed. Abdul Khaliq. circ. 900.

100 PK
PAKISTAN PHILOSOPHICAL JOURNAL. (Text in English) 1962. s-a. $7. Pakistan Philosophical Congress, Department of Philosophy, University of the Punjab, New Campus, Lahore 20, Pakistan. Ed. Abdul Khaliq. adv.; bk.rev.; bibl.; circ. 1,000. **Indexed:** Phil.Ind.

100 200 II
PARMARTH; religious monthly. (Text in Gujarati) 1953. m. Jai Hind Publications, Jai Hind Press Bldg., Babubhai Shah Marg, Rajkot 360 001, India. TEL 0281-40513. Ed. Y.N. Shah. circ. 30,000.
 Description: Aims at promoting and cultivating interest for religion and philosophy to live a spiritual life.

PASHTO ACADEMY. MONTHLY JOURNAL. see *LITERATURE*

PATHWAY TO GOD. see *RELIGIONS AND THEOLOGY*

100 641.1 US
PATHWAYS TO HEALTH. 1978. 4/yr. $25 donation. A.R.E. Medical Clinic, 4018 N. 40th St., Phoenix, AZ 85018. TEL 602-955-0551. Ed. Scott Grady. adv.; circ. 3,500 (controlled).
 Description: Based on the Edgar Cayce readings, PTH includes holistic health tips, A.R.E. Clinic programs, educational activities and research projects, and Edgar Cayce insights on health.

170 US ISSN 0079-0249
PAUL ANTHONY BRICK LECTURES. 1960. irreg., no.9, 1973. price varies. University of Missouri Press, 2910 LeMone Blvd., Columbia, MO 65202. TEL 314-882-7641. FAX 314-884-4498.

104 US ISSN 0079-0257
PAUL CARUS LECTURES. 1925. irreg., no.16, 1987. price varies. (American Philosophical Association) Open Court Publishing Co., General Books (Subsidiary of: Carus Corporation), 315 Fifth St., Box 599, Peru, IL 61354. TEL 815-223-1500. index in each vol. (reprint service avail. from UMI)

100 US
PEARLS OF WISDOM. 1958. w. $40. (Church Universal and Triumphant) Summit Lighthouse, Box A, Livingston, MT 59047-1390. TEL 406-222-8300. FAX 406-222-8307. Ed. Elizabeth Clare Prophet. circ. controlled. (also avail. in microfiche; back issues avail.)
 Description: Collections of letters from Ascended Masters to their New Age disciples.

101 SP ISSN 0031-4749
B5
PENSAMIENTO; revista de investigacion e informacion filosofica. 1945. q. $41. (Administracion de Pensamiento) Casa de Escritores, S.J., Pablo Aranda 3, E-28006 Madrid, Spain. bk.rev.; bibl.; index. **Indexed:** Phil.Ind.

PERMANENCIA. see *RELIGIONS AND THEOLOGY*

PERSISTENCE OF VISION. see *MOTION PICTURES*

PERSONA Y SOCIEDAD. see *SOCIAL SCIENCES: COMPREHENSIVE WORKS*

100 US ISSN 0889-065X
B828.5.A1
PERSONALIST FORUM. 1985. s-a. $10 to individuals; institutions $15 (effective Jan. 1991). Furman University, Department of Philosophy, Poinsett Hwy., Greenville, SC 29613. TEL 803-294-3139. FAX 803-294-3001. Ed. Thomas O. Buford. circ. 150.
 ●Also available online. Vendor(s): DIALOG.
 —BLDSC shelfmark: 6428.006000.
 Description: Scholarly articles that address issues associated with being persons in this world, with reviews of philosophical works that are relevant to that theme.

PERSPECTIVE ON CONSCIOUSNESS & PSI RESEARCH. see *NEW AGE PUBLICATIONS*

100 NE
PERSPEKTIVEN DER PHILOSOPHIE. NEUES JAHRBUCH. (Text in English, German) 1975. a. fl.135. Editions Rodopi B.V., Keizersgracht 302-304, 1016 Amsterdam, Netherlands. TEL 020-6227507. FAX 020-6380948. (US and Canada subscr. to: 233 Peachtree St. N.E., Atlanta GA 30303-1504. TEL 800-225-3998) Ed.Bd. adv.; bk.rev.; circ. 500.

100 NE ISSN 0079-1350
PHAENOMENOLOGICA. (Text in English, French, German) 1958. irreg., latest 1991. price varies. (Centre d'Archives Husserl, BE) Kluwer Academic Publishers, Postbus 17, 3300 AA Dordrecht, Netherlands. TEL 078-334911. FAX 078-334254. TELEX 29245. (N. America dist. addr.: Box 358, Accord Station, Hingham, MA 02018-0358. TEL 617-871-6600) Ed. S. Ysseling. **Indexed:** Rel.Ind.Two.

142.7 GW
PHAENOMENOLOGISCHE FORSCHUNGEN/PHENOMENOLOGICAL STUDIES. 1975. s-a. (Deutsche Gesellschaft fuer Phaenomenologische Forschung) Karl Alber GmbH, Hermann Herder Str. 4, 7800 Freiburg, Germany. Ed. Ernst Wolfgang Orth. bibl.

100 US
PHENOMENA. 4/yr. $10. P O M Project Newsletter, Box 836, South Pasadena, CA 91030. Ed. Robert Stowell. illus.

PHENOMENEWS; exploring human potential, holistic health and living. see *NEW AGE PUBLICATIONS*

100 US ISSN 0885-3886
B829.5
PHENOMENOLOGICAL INQUIRY; a review of philosophical ideas and trends. (Text mainly in English; occasionally in French, German) 1976. a. $20 to individuals (foreign $25); institutions $30 (foreign $35) (effective July 1991). World Institute for Advanced Phenomenological Research and Learning, 348 Payson Rd., Belmont, MA 02178. TEL 617-489-3696. FAX 617-489-3696. Ed. A.T. Tymieniecka. adv.; bk.rev.; bibl.; circ. 1,000. (back issues avail.)
 —BLDSC shelfmark: 6449.353000.
 Formerly (until 1985): Phenomenology Information Bulletin (ISSN 0278-8322)

100 200 US
PHENOMENOLOGICAL THEOLOGY. irreg. Peter Lang Publishing, Inc., 62 W. 45th St., 4th Fl., New York, NY 10036. TEL 212-302-6740. FAX 212-302-7574. Ed. Stephen W. Laycock.

100 294.3 US
PHENOMENOLOGY AND BUDDHIST THOUGHT. irreg. Peter Lang Publishing, Inc., 62 W. 45th St., 4th Fl., New York, NY 10036. TEL 212-302-6740. FAX 212-302-7574. Ed. Steven W. Laycock.

100 CN ISSN 0820-9189
PHENOMENOLOGY & PEDAGOGY. 1983. a. Can.$27 to individuals; institutions Can.$35; students $19. University of Alberta, Publication Services, 4-116 Education North, Edmonton, Alta. T6G 2G5, Canada. TEL 403-492-4204. Ed. M. van Manen. bk.rev.; index; circ. 400. (back issues avail.)
 —BLDSC shelfmark: 6449.356000.
 Description: Interpretive and critical studies of a broad range of pedagogic relations and situations.

PHILOLOGOS. see *CLASSICAL STUDIES*

100 UK
PHILOSOPHER. 1913. 2/yr. £1.50 to non-members. Philosophical Society, 92 Worple Rd., Wimbledon, London SW19, England. adv.; bk.rev.
 Description: Covers the study of philosophy for the general public.

100 US
PHILOSOPHER OF CREATIVITY MONOGRAPH SERIES. 1984. irreg. price varies. Foundation for Philosophy of Creativity, Inc., c/o Pete A.Y. Gunter, Dept. of Philosophy, University of North Texas, Denton, TX 76203. TEL 817-565-2266. (Subscr. to: University Press of America, 4720 Boston Way, Lanham, MD) Ed. John C. Thomas. (back issues avail.)
 Description: For researchers at all levels. Explores the nature and structure of creativity.

PHILOSOPHY

100   BE   ISSN 0079-1660
PHILOSOPHES CONTEMPORAINS. no. 7, 1955. irreg. price varies. Universite Catholique de Louvain, Institut Superieur de Philosophie, 1 Chemin d'Aristote, B-1348 Louvain-La-Neuve, Belgium. TEL 016-48-81-02. FAX 016-48-14-86. TELEX 65981 PUL B. (Subscr. to: Peeters Press, B.P. 41, B-3000 Leuven, Belgium)

100   BE   ISSN 0079-1679
PHILOSOPHES MEDIEVAUX. 1948. irreg., no.27, 1986. price varies. Editions Peeters s.p.r.l., Bondgenotenlaan 153, B-3000 Leuven, Belgium. TEL 016-235170. FAX 016-228500. TELEX 65981-PULB.

100   AG   ISSN 0031-8000
PHILOSOPHIA. 1944. s-a. exchange basis. Universidad Nacional de Cuyo, Instituto de Filosofia, Facultad de Filosofia y Letras, Parque General San Martin, Mendoza, Argentina. **Indexed:** Arts & Hum.Cit.Ind.

100   IS   ISSN 0048-3893
PHILOSOPHIA; philosophical quarterly of Israel. 1971. q. $21 to individuals; institutions $28 (effective 1992). (Bar-Ilan University, Department of Philosophy) Bar-Ilan University Press, Ramat-Gan 52900, Israel. Ed. Asa Kasher. adv.; bk.rev.; bibl.; charts; circ. 600. **Indexed:** Curr.Cont., Phil.Ind.
—BLDSC shelfmark: 6461.492000.

105   GR
PHILOSOPHIA. (Text in English, French, German, or Greek) 1971. a. $40. Academy of Athens, Research Center for Greek Philosophy - Kentron Erevnis tis Hellenikes Philosophias, 14 Anagnostopoulou St., Athens 10673, Greece. TEL (01) 3600140. Ed.Bd. bk.rev.; circ. 1,000. **Indexed:** Bull.Signal., Phil.Ind.

100   DK   0108-1632
PHILOSOPHIA; tidsskrift for filosofi. (Text in Danish, English, German and Swedish) 1977. q. DKK 200 to individuals; institutions DKK 275. Filosofisk Forening i Aarhus, Institut for Filosofi, Aarhus Universitet, 8000 Aarhus C, Denmark. Ed. Lone Kalstrup. adv.; bk.rev.; circ. 500.
Formerly: Philosophia Aarhusiensis (ISSN 0556-0136)

180   NE   ISSN 0079-1687
PHILOSOPHIA ANTIQUA. 1946. irreg., vol.56, 1992. price varies. E.J. Brill, P.O. Box 9000, 2300 PA Leiden, Netherlands. TEL 071-312624. FAX 071-317532. TELEX 39296 BRILL NL. (In N. America: E.J. Brill, 24 Hudson St., Kinderhook, NY 12106. TEL 800-962-4406)
Description: Scholarly monographs on topics in ancient philosophy.

PHILOSOPHIA MATHEMATICA. see *MATHEMATICS*

530 146   GW   ISSN 0031-8027
B3
PHILOSOPHIA NATURALIS; Archiv fuer Naturphilosophie und die philosophischen Grenzgebiete der exakten Wissenschaften und Wissenschaftsgeschichte. 1950. irreg., vol.21, 1984. DM.154. Verlag Anton Hain GmbH, Savignystr. 53, 6000 Frankfurt a.M. 1, Germany. Ed. Joseph Meurers. adv.; bk.rev.; bibl.; index; circ. 1,000. **Indexed:** Math.R., Phil.Ind.

294.54   NE   ISSN 0031-8035
BX9401
PHILOSOPHIA REFORMATA. (Summaries in several languages) 1936. s-a. fl.60 to individuals. Stichting voor Reformatorische Wijsbegeerte, Postbus 368, 3500 AJ Utrecht, Netherlands. TEL 030-342030. Ed. J. van der Hoeven. bk.rev.; bibl.; circ. 800. **Indexed:** CERDIC, Phil.Ind.
Description: Addresses issues facing Calvinist philosophy.

100   NE
PHILOSOPHIA SPINOZAE PERENNIS. 1976. irreg., no.7, 1987. price varies. Van Gorcum en Co. B.V., P.O. Box 43, 9400 AA Assen, Netherlands. TEL 05920-46846. FAX 05920-72064. Eds. F. Akkerman, H. de Dijn. bibl.; index.

100 200   US
PHILOSOPHIC STUDIES IN THE UNITY OF RELIGIONS. irreg. Peter Lang Publishing, Inc., 62 E. 45th St., 4th Fl., New York, NY 10036. TEL 212-302-6740. FAX 212-302-7574. Ed. Marvin C. Sterling.
Description: Focuses on selected problems in the area of the comparative study of world religions.

100   II
PHILOSOPHICA. (Text in Bengali or English) q. Rs.10. Shankar Basu, 50b Haldarpara Rd., Calcutta 700026, India.

100   BE   ISSN 0379-8402
B63
PHILOSOPHICA. (Text in Dutch, English, French and German) 1963. s-a. 600 Fr. Rijksuniversiteit Gent, Department of Philosophy, Rozier 44, B-9000 Ghent, Belgium. Ed. Diderik Batens. adv.; bk.rev.; circ. 350. **Indexed:** Phil.Ind.
—BLDSC shelfmark: 6461.635000.
Formerly (until 1974): Studia Philosophica Gandensia (ISSN 0081-6833)

100 016   UK   ISSN 0031-8051
Z7127
PHILOSOPHICAL BOOKS. 1960. q. £22($43) to individuals; institutions £51($107). Basil Blackwell Ltd., 108 Cowley Rd., Oxford OX4 1JF, England. TEL 0865-791100. FAX 0865-791100. TELEX 837022-OXBOOK-G. Ed. Anthony Ellis. adv.; bk.rev.; circ. 850. (reprint service avail. from SWZ) **Indexed:** Arts & Hum.Cit.Ind., Curr.Cont., Ind.Bk.Rev.Hum., Phil.Ind.
—BLDSC shelfmark: 6461.640000.

100   US   ISSN 0031-806X
B1
PHILOSOPHICAL FORUM. 1942. q. $15 to individuals (foreign $19); institutions $45 (foreign $49). Philosophical Forum, Inc., c/o Baruch College, Box 239, 17 Lexington Ave., NY 10010. TEL 212-387-1682. Ed. Marx W. Wartofsky. adv.; bibl.; index; circ. 2,000. (back issues avail.) **Indexed:** Curr.Cont., Phil.Ind.
●Also available online. Vendor(s): BRS.
—BLDSC shelfmark: 6461.700000.

100   UK   ISSN 0190-0536
B1
PHILOSOPHICAL INVESTIGATIONS. 1978. q. £27.50($56) to individuals; institutions £64($137). Basil Blackwell Ltd., 108 Cowley Rd., Oxford OX4 1JF, England. TEL 0865-791100. FAX 0865-791347. TELEX 837022-OXBOOK-G. Ed. D.Z. Phillips. adv.; bk.rev.; index; circ. 650. (back issues avail.; reprint service avail. from SWZ) **Indexed:** Arts & Hum.Cit.Ind., Curr.Cont., Phil.Ind.
—BLDSC shelfmark: 6461.780000.

PHILOSOPHICAL PSYCHOLOGY. see *PSYCHOLOGY*

100   UK   ISSN 0031-8094
B1
PHILOSOPHICAL QUARTERLY. 1950. q. £17($36.50) to individuals; institutions £46($105). (University of St. Andrews, Scots Philosophical Club) Basil Blackwell Ltd., 108 Cowley Rd., Oxford OX4 1JF, England. TEL 0865 791100. FAX 0865-791347. TELEX 837022-OXBOOK-G. Ed.Bd. adv.; bk.rev.; bibl.; index; circ. 1,600. (also avail. in microform from UMI; reprint service avail. from SWZ,UMI) **Indexed:** Arts & Hum.Cit.Ind., Br.Hum.Ind., Curr.Cont., Hum.Ind., Ind.Bk.Rev.Hum., Lang.& Lang.Behav.Abstr., M.L.A., Phil.Ind, SSCI.
—BLDSC shelfmark: 6462.300000.

100   CH
PHILOSOPHICAL RESEARCH. 1982-1987; resumed 1992. a. $20 per no. Soochow University, Philosophy Department - Tung Wu Ta Hsueh Che Hsueh Hsi, Wai Shuang Hsi, Shih Lin, Taipei, Taiwan, Republic of China. FAX 8829310. bk.rev.
Formerly (until 1992): Chuanxi Lu (ISSN 1010-0725)

100   US   ISSN 0031-8108
B1
PHILOSOPHICAL REVIEW. 1892. q. $27 to individuals; institutions $46. Cornell University, Sage School of Philosophy, 327 Goldwin Smith Hall, Ithaca, NY 14853. TEL 607-255-1454. Ed. Terence Irwin. adv.; bk.rev.; bibl.; index; circ. 3,000. (also avail. in microform from MIM,UMI; reprint service avail. from UMI) **Indexed:** Arts & Hum.Cit.Ind., Bk.Rev.Ind. (1965-), Child.Bk.Rev.Ind. (1965-), Curr.Cont., Deep Sea Res.& Oceanogr.Abstr., Hum.Ind., Ind.Bk.Rev.Hum., Lang.& Lang.Behav.Abstr., M.L.A., Phil.Ind., SSCI.
—BLDSC shelfmark: 6462.700000.

100   NE   ISSN 0031-8116
B21   CODEN: PLSDA3
PHILOSOPHICAL STUDIES; an international journal for philosophy in the analytic tradition. 1950. 12/yr. $482. Kluwer Academic Publishers, Postbus 17, 3300 AA Dordrecht, Netherlands. TEL 078-334911. FAX 078-334254. TELEX 29245. (Dist. by: Kluwer Academic Publishers Group, P.O. Box 322, 3300 AH Dordrecht, Netherlands; N. America dist. addr.: Box 358, Accord Station, Hingham, MA 02018-0358. TEL 617-871-6600) Eds. Keith Lehrer, John Pollock. adv.; bk.rev. (reprint service avail. from SWZ) **Indexed:** Arts & Hum.Cit.Ind., Bull.Signal., Cath.Ind., Curr.Cont., Ind.Bk.Rev.Hum., Lang.& Lang.Behav.Abstr., M.L.A., Math.R., Phil.Ind., SSCI.
—BLDSC shelfmark: 6462.900000.

100   NE
PHILOSOPHICAL STUDIES SERIES IN PHILOSOPHY. 1974. irreg. price varies. Kluwer Academic Publishers, Spuiboulevard 50, P.O. Box 17, 3300 AA Dordrecht, Netherlands. TEL 078-334911. FAX 078-334254. TELEX 29245. (Dist. by: Kluwer Academic Publishers Group, P.O. Box 322, 3300 AH Dordrecht, Netherlands; U.S. address: P.O. Box 358, Accord Station, Hingham, MA 02018-0358) Eds. Wilfrid Sellars, Keith Lehrer. **Indexed:** Math.R.

100   US   ISSN 0276-2080
B1
PHILOSOPHICAL TOPICS. 1970. 2/yr. $25 to individuals; institutions $45. Department of Philosophy, 127 KH, University of Arkansas, Fayetteville, AR 72701. FAX 501-575-6044. Ed. Christopher Hill. circ. 750. (reprint service avail. from ISI) **Indexed:** Arts & Hum.Cit.Ind., Curr.Cont., Phil.Ind., SSCI.
—BLDSC shelfmark: 6462.947000.
Formerly: Southwestern Journal of Philosophy (ISSN 0038-481X)

100   FR   ISSN 0294-1805
PHILOSOPHIE (PARIS). 1984. q. 167 F. (foreign 192 F.). Editions de Minuit, 7, rue Bernard-Palissy, 75006 Paris, France. TEL 42-22-37-94. Eds. Didier Franck, Pierre Guenancia. bk.rev.
Description: Presents current philosophic works in the anglo-saxon world, original French works and interpretations of classical texts.

100   FR   ISSN 0760-9620
PHILOSOPHIE IMAGINAIRE. 1985. s-a. Editions de L'Eclat, Combas, F-30250 Sommieres, France. TEL 66-77-87-63.

181   GW   ISSN 0233-089X
PHILOSOPHIEHISTORISCHE TEXTE. 1955. irreg. price varies. Akademie-Verlag Berlin, Leipziger Str. 3-4, 1086 Berlin, Germany. TELEX 114420-AVERL-DD.
Formerly: Philosophische Studientexte (ISSN 0079-1717)

100   GW   ISSN 0936-7586
HQ1190
▼**DIE PHILOSOPHIN;** Forum fuer feministische Theorie und Philosophie. 1990. s-a. DM.25. Edition Diskord, Schwarzlocher Str. 104-b, 7400 Tubingen, Germany. TEL 07071-40102. FAX 07071-44710. Eds. Astrid Deuber-Mankowsky, Ursula Konnertz. adv.; bk.rev.; circ. 1,200.

100   CN   ISSN 0316-2923
B2
PHILOSOPHIQUES. 1974. s-a. $20. Editions Bellarmin, 165 Desluarier, Ville St. Laurent, Que H4N 2S4, Canada. TEL 514-745-4290. **Indexed:** Phil.Ind., Pt.de Rep. (1983-).
—BLDSC shelfmark: 6464.059500.

100   GW   ISSN 0175-6508
PHILOSOPHISCHE ABHANDLUNGEN. irreg., vol.57, 1990. price varies. Vittorio Klostermann, Frauenlobstr. 22, Postfach 900601, 6000 Frankfurt a.M. 90, Germany. TEL 069-774011. FAX 069-708038. **Indexed:** Math.R.

PHILOSOPHY

100   GW   ISSN 0031-8159
B3
PHILOSOPHISCHE RUNDSCHAU. 1953. q. DM.114 (students DM.57). Verlag J.C.B. Mohr (Paul Siebeck), Wilhelmstr 18, Postfach 2040, 7400 Tuebingen, Germany. TEL 07071-26064. FAX 07071-51104. TELEX 7262872-MOHR-D. Eds. R. Bubner, B. Waldenfels. adv.; bk.rev.; cum.index. **Indexed:** Arts & Hum.Cit.Ind., Curr.Cont., Phil.Ind.
Description: Philosophical journal that follows international philosophical publications, outlines trends, examines schools and research programs.

100   GW   ISSN 0031-8175
PHILOSOPHISCHER LITERATURANZEIGER. 1949. 4/yr. DM.138. Verlag Vittorio Klostermann GmbH, Frauenlobstr. 22, 6000 Frankfurt a.M. 90, Germany. FAX 069-708038. Ed.Bd. adv.; bk.rev.; abstr.; bibl.; index; circ. 700.
Description: Includes elaborate reports of new books in philosophy and related fields, published in German and other languages. Also includes comparative philosophical essays.

100   GW   ISSN 0031-8183
B3
PHILOSOPHISCHES JAHRBUCH. 1888. a. DM.94. (Goerres-Gesellschaft) Karl Alber GmbH, Hermann-Herder-Str.4, 7800 Freiburg, Germany. Ed.Bd. bk.rev.; abstr.; bibl.; circ. 800. (reprint service avail. from KTO). **Indexed:** Arts & Hum.Cit.Ind., Curr.Cont., Ind.Bk.Rev.Hum., Phil.Ind.
—BLDSC shelfmark: 6464.470000.

100   UK   ISSN 0031-8191
B1
PHILOSOPHY. 1925. q. $157. (Royal Institute of Philosophy) Cambridge University Press, Edinburgh Bldg., Shaftesbury Rd., Cambridge CB2 2RU, England. TEL 0223-312393. FAX 0223-315052. TELEX 851817256. (N. American addr.: Cambridge University Press, 40 W. 20th St., New York, NY 10011-4211, USA. TEL 212-924-3900) Ed. Renford Bambrough. adv.; bk.rev.; index. (also avail. in microform from UMI) **Indexed:** Br.Hum.Ind., Curr.Cont., Deep Sea Res.& Oceanogr.Abstr., Hum.Ind., Ind.Bk.Rev.Hum., Mid.East: Abstr.& Ind., Phil.Ind., Psychol.Abstr., SSCI.
—BLDSC shelfmark: 6464.500000.

PHILOSOPHY AND ARTIFICIAL INTELLIGENCE. see *COMPUTERS — Artificial Intelligence*

100 800   US   ISSN 0190-0013
PN2   CODEN: PHILEL
PHILOSOPHY AND LITERATURE. 1976. s-a. $18 to individuals (foreign $22.90); institutions $37 (foreign $40.40). (Whitman College) Johns Hopkins University Press, Journals Publishing Division, 701 W. 40th St., Ste. 275, Baltimore, MD 21211. TEL 410-516-6987. FAX 410-516-6998. Ed. Denis Dutton. adv.; bk.rev.; bibl.; circ. 1,000. (back issues avail.) **Indexed:** Abstr.Engl.Stud., Amer.Bibl.Slavic & E.Eur.Stud., Amer.Hum.Ind., Arts & Hum.Cit.Ind., Can.Rev.Comp.Lit., Curr.Cont., Ind.Bk.Rev.Hum., LCR, M.L.A., Phil.Ind.
—BLDSC shelfmark: 6464.570000.
Description: Addresses fresh perspectives to two modes on inquiry through its effective interdisciplinary approach to the study of major literary and philosophical texts.

100 610   NE
PHILOSOPHY AND MEDICINE. (Text in English) 1975. irreg. price varies. Kluwer Academic Publishers, Spuiboulevard 50, P.O. Box 17, 3300 AA Dordrecht, Netherlands. TEL 078-334911. FAX 078-334254. TELEX 29245. (Dist. by: Kluwer Academic Publishers Group, P.O. Box 322, 3300 AH Dordrecht, Netherlands; U.S. address: P.O. Box 358, Accord Station, Hingham, MA 02018-0358) Eds. H. Tristram Engelhardt Jr., Stuart F. Spicker. **Indexed:** Biol.Abstr.

100 142.7   US   ISSN 0031-8205
B1   CODEN: PPHRAI
PHILOSOPHY AND PHENOMENOLOGICAL RESEARCH. 1940. q. $15 to individuals; institutions $20. Brown University, Box 1947, Providence, RI 02912. TEL 401-863-3215. (Co-sponsor: International Phenomenological Society) Ed. Ernest Sosa. adv.; bk.rev. (also avail. in microform from MIM,UMI; reprint service avail. from KTO) **Indexed:** Amer.Bibl.Slavic & E.Eur.Stud., Arts & Hum.Cit.Ind., Curr.Cont., Hum.Ind., Ind.Bk.Rev.Hum., Lang.& Lang.Behav.Abstr., M.L.A., Mid.East: Abstr.& Ind., Phil.Ind., Psychol.Abstr., SSCI.

100 290   NE
PHILOSOPHY AND RELIGION: A COMPARATIVE YEARBOOK. (Text in English) 1989. irreg., vol.2, 1992. price varies. E.J. Brill, P.O. Box 9000, 2300 PA Leiden, Netherlands. TEL 071-312624. FAX 071-317352. TELEX 39296 BRILL NL. (In N. America: E.J. Brill, 24 Hudson St., Kinderhook, NY 12106. TEL 800-962-4406) Eds. Shlomo Biderman, Ben-Ami Scharfstein. (back issues avail.)
Description: Scholarly contributions on topics in comparative religion and philosophy.
Refereed Serial

100 808   US   ISSN 0031-8213
B1
PHILOSOPHY AND RHETORIC. 1968. q. $22.50 to individuals (foreign $30); institutions $35 (foreign $40). Pennsylvania State University Press, 820 N. University Dr., University Park, PA 16802-1003. TEL 814-865-1327. FAX 814-863-1408. Eds. Henry W. Johnstone, Jr., Gerald A. Hauser. adv.; bk.rev.; bibl.; index; circ. 750. (also avail. in microform from UMI; reprint service avail. from UMI) **Indexed:** Abstr.Engl.Stud., Arts & Hum.Cit.Ind., Curr.Cont., Ind.Bk.Rev.Hum., M.L.A., Phil.Ind.
—BLDSC shelfmark: 6464.800000.

100   US   ISSN 0031-8221
B1
PHILOSOPHY EAST AND WEST; a quarterly of comparative philosophy. 1951. q. $20 to individuals; institutions $28. University of Hawaii Press, Journals Department, 2840 Kolowalu St., Honolulu, HI 96822. TEL 808-956-8833. FAX 808-988-6052. Ed. Roger T. Ames. adv.; bk.rev.; index; circ. 1,452. (also avail. in microform from UMI; back issues avail.; reprint service avail. from ISI,SCH,UMI) **Indexed:** Arts & Hum.Cit.Ind., Curr.Cont., Hum.Ind., Ind.Bk.Rev.Hum., Lang.& Lang.Behav.Abstr., M.L.A., Mid.East: Abstr.& Ind., Phil.Ind., Rel.& Theol.Abstr. (1968-), Sociol.Abstr.
—BLDSC shelfmark: 6464.850000.
Description: Focuses on comparative and Asian philosophy.
Refereed Serial

149.2 155   US
PHILOSOPHY FOR CHILDREN NEWSLETTER. 1984. q. $8. Texas Wesleyan College, School of Education, Ft. Worth, TX 76105. TEL 817-531-4957. Ed. Ron Reed.

100   US   ISSN 0742-2733
B1
PHILOSOPHY IN CONTEXT; an examination of applied philosophy. 1972. a. $6 to individuals; institutions $10. Cleveland State University, Department of Philosophy, Euclid Ave. at E. 24th St., Cleveland, OH 44115. TEL 216-687-3900. FAX 216-687-9366. TELEX 810-421-8252. Ed.Bd. adv.; circ. 300. (back issues avail.) **Indexed:** Phil.Ind.
—BLDSC shelfmark: 6464.840000.
Description: Examines the relationship between philosophical theories and the practical contexts of policy making and professional ethics. Focus is applied philosophy; articles of interest to non-philosophers.

170   US   ISSN 0277-2434
Q174
PHILOSOPHY IN SCIENCE. 1983. a. $28. Pachart Publishing House, 1130 San Lucas Cir., Tucson, AZ 85704. TEL 602-297-4797. Eds. M. Heller, W.R. Stoeger. bk.rev.
Description: Provides a forum for the articulation of philosophical issues arising within the sciences.

100 301   NE   ISSN 0922-6001
PHILOSOPHY OF HISTORY AND CULTURE. 1988. irreg., vol.8, 1992. price varies. E.J. Brill, P.O. Box 9000, 2300 PA Leiden, Netherlands. TEL 071-312624. FAX 071-317532. TELEX 39296 BRILL NL. (In N. America: E.J. Brill, 24 Hudson St., Kinderhook, NY 12106. TEL 800-962-4406) Ed. Michael Krausz.
—BLDSC shelfmark: 6464.950500.

PHILOSOPHY OF SCIENCE. see *SCIENCES: COMPREHENSIVE WORKS*

100   US   ISSN 0163-0881
PHILOSOPHY OF SCIENCE ASSOCIATION NEWSLETTER. 1971. q. membership only. Philosophy of Science Association, Department of Philosophy, 503 S. Kedzie Hall, Michigan State University, E. Lansing, MI 48824-1032. TEL 517-353-9392. circ. 900.
Description: News items related to history and philosophy of science.

PHILOSOPHY OF THE SOCIAL SCIENCES. see *SOCIAL SCIENCES: COMPREHENSIVE WORKS*

100   US   ISSN 0031-8256
B1
PHILOSOPHY TODAY. 1957. q. $21. DePaul University, 802 W. Belden Ave., Chicago, IL 60614-3214. TEL 312-362-8767. FAX 312-362-5684. Ed. David Pellauer. adv.; bk.rev.; index; circ. 1,180. (also avail. in microform from UMI; back issues avail.; reprint service avail. from UMI) **Indexed:** Arts & Hum.Cit.Ind., Cath.Ind., Curr.Cont., Hum.Ind., Phil.Ind.
—BLDSC shelfmark: 6465.090000.

180   NE   ISSN 0031-8868
B1
PHRONESIS; a journal for ancient philosophy. (Text in English, French, German, Italian) 1956. 3/yr. fl.97.50. Van Gorcum en Co. B.V., P.O. Box 43, 9400 AA Assen, Netherlands. TEL 05920-46864. FAX 05920-72064. Ed. Malcolm Schofield. adv.; bk.rev.; index; circ. 1,100. (reprint service avail. from SWZ) **Indexed:** Arts & Hum.Cit.Ind., Curr.Cont., Ind.Bk.Rev.Hum., Phil.Ind.
—BLDSC shelfmark: 6474.530000.

POZNAN STUDIES IN THE PHILOSOPHY OF THE SCIENCES AND THE HUMANITIES. see *POLITICAL SCIENCE*

100   PL   ISSN 0079-4635
POZNANSKIE TOWARZYSTWO PRZYJACIOL NAUK. KOMISJA FILOZOFICZNA. PRACE. (Text in German, Polish; summaries in English, French, German, Russian) 1921. irreg., vol.14, 1983. price varies. Panstwowe Wydawnictwo Naukowe, Miodowa 10, 00-251 Warsaw, Poland. (Dist. by: Ars Polona, Krakowskie Przedmiescie 7, 00-068 Warsaw, Poland)

181   II   ISSN 0032-6178
BL1100
PRABUDDHA BHARATA/AWAKENED INDIA. (Text in English) 1896. m. Rs.30 in India; Sri Lanka and Bangladesh Rs.120; elsewhere $35(£25). (Ramakrishna Order) Advaita Ashrama, 5 Dehi Entally Rd., Calcutta 700 014, India. TEL 29-0898. Ed. Swami Mumukshananda. adv.; bk.rev.; charts; illus.; index; circ. 6,000.
Description: Provides Vedantas and their supporters with guidance and inspiration for daily life.

PRAGMATICS AND DISCOURSE ANALYSIS. see *LINGUISTICS*

100   PL   ISSN 0079-4872
PRAKSEOLOGIA. (Text in Polish; summaries in English) 1962. q. $46. Polska Akademia Nauk, Instytut Filozofii i Socjologii, Zaklad Prakseologii i Naukoznawstwa, Ul. Nowy Swiat 72, Palac Staszica, 00-330 Warsaw, Poland. FAX 267181. Ed. W. Gasparski. bk.rev.; bibl.; charts.
—BLDSC shelfmark: 6598.560000.
Description: International annual of practical philosophy and methodology.

181.45   US   ISSN 0149-953X
PRANA YOGA LIFE. 1977. irreg. $3. Prana Yoga Ashram, Box 1037, Berkeley, CA 94701. TEL 415-549-2911. Ed. Swami Vignanananda. adv.; bk.rev.; illus.; circ. 1,500. (back issues avail.)

100   CR
PRAXIS. 1975. q. exchange basis. Universidad Nacional, Departamento de Filosofia, c/o Jack Wilson-Pacheco, Coordinacion de Publicaciones y Canje, Centro de Documentacion e Informacion en Filosofia, Heredia, Costa Rica. Ed.Bd. bibl.; charts; illus.; stat.; circ. 1,000.

PRAXIS INTERNATIONAL. see *POLITICAL SCIENCE*

105   BL
PRESENCA FILOSOFICA. (Text in Portuguese and French; occasionally in English) 1974. irreg. $25. Sociedade Brasileira de Filosofos Catolicos, Rua Benjamin Constant 23-420, 20.241-Rio de Janeiro-RJ, Brazil. Ed. Prof. Tarcisio Meirelles Padilha. bibl.; circ. 2,000.

100   FR
PRESENCE DE GABRIEL MARCEL. a. 70 F. Association Presence de Gabriel Marcel, 85 bd. de Port-Royal, 75013 Paris, France. (Subscr. to: 9 rue Saint-Romain, 75007 Paris, France)

PHILOSOPHY

100   FR
PRESENCE DE GABRIEL MARCEL. CAHIER. 1978. a. 100 F. Presence de Gabriel Marcel, 9 ave Franklin-Roosevelt, 75008 Paris, France. Ed. Joel Bouessee. circ. 3,000.

PRESSE-INTER. see *NEW AGE PUBLICATIONS*

100   CI   ISSN 0350-2791
PRILOZI ZA ISTRAZIVANJE HRVATSKE FILOZOFSKE BASTINE. (Text in Croatian, Greek, Latin; summaries in English, French, German and Italian) 1975. s-a. 400 din.($8) Sveuciliste u Zagrebu, Institut za Povijesne Znanosti, Odjel za Povijest Filozofije, Krcka 1, 41000 Zagreb, Croatia. TEL 041 511-841. Ed. Damir Barbaric. bk.rev.; circ. 800. (back issues avail.)

100 001.3   GW
PROBLEMATA. 1971. irreg. price varies. Friedrich Frommann Verlag Guenther Holzboog, Postfach 500460, Koenig-Karl-Str. 27, 7000 Stuttgart 50, Germany. Ed. Guenther Holzboog. Indexed: Math.R.

160   RM
PROBLEME DE LOGICA. 1969. irreg., vol.9, 1986. (Academia Romana) Editura Academiei Romane, Calea Victoriei 125, 79717 Bucharest, Rumania. (Subscr. to: Artexim, Str. Piata Scinteii 1, P.O. Box 33-16, 70055 Bucharest, Rumania) Eds. Crizantema Joja, Calin Candiescu.

100   US
PROBLEMS IN CONTEMPORARY PHILOSOPHY. 1986. irreg., latest no.32. $39.95 per no. Edwin Mellen Press, 240 Portage Rd., Box 450, Lewiston, NY 14092. TEL 716-754-8566. FAX 716-754-4335.

192   US   ISSN 0360-6503
BD372
PROCESS STUDIES. 1971. q. $20 to individuals (foreign $27); institutions $30 (foreign $37). School of Theology at Claremont, Center for Process Studies, 1325 N. College Ave., Claremont, CA 91711. TEL 714-626-3521. Ed. Lewis S. Ford. adv.; bk.rev.; abstr.; circ. 1,000. (also avail. in microform from UMI; back issues avail.; reprint service avail. from ISI,UMI) Indexed: Arts & Hum.Cit.Ind., CERDIC, Curr.Cont., Phil.Ind., Rel.& Theol.Abstr. (1973-), Rel.Ind.One, Rel.Per.
—BLDSC shelfmark: 6849.990700.
    Description: Covers the process philosophy of Alfred North Whitehead, and its application to other philosophies and other fields, including aesthetics, mathematics, physics, biology, cosmology, history of religion, social science, and literary criticism.

100   NE
PROFILES; an international series on contemporary philosophers and logicians. 1979. irreg. price varies. Kluwer Academic Publishers, Spuiboulevard 50, P.O. Box 17, 3300 AA Dordrecht, Netherlands. TEL 078-334911. FAX 078-334254. TELEX 29245. (Dist. by: Kluwer Academic Publishers Group, P.O. Box 322, 3300 AH Dordrecht, Netherlands; U.S. address: P.O. Box 358, Accord Station, Hingham, MA 02018-0358) Eds. R.J. Bogdan, I. Niiniluoto. bibl.; index. (back issues avail.)

PROGRESS (MEDFORD). see *RELIGIONS AND THEOLOGY*

100   MX
PROMETEO;* revista latinoamericana de filosofia. 1984. 3/yr. Mex.$400($20) Universidad de Guadalajara, Facultad de Filosofia y Letras, Apdo. Postal 2393, Guadalajara, Jalisco, Mexico. Ed. Luis Govea.

PROPHETIC VOICES; an international literary journal. see *LITERATURE*

100   IT   ISSN 0033-1791
PROTEUS; revista di filosofia. 1970. 3/yr. L.4000. Corso Vitt. Emanuele 39, 00186 Rome, Italy. Ed. Pietro Prini. bk.rev.

100   IT
PUBBLICAZIONI DI VERIFICHE. irreg. price varies. Verifiche, Casella Postale 269, 38 100 Trento, Italy.
    Description: Focuses on philosophy.

100   US   ISSN 0887-0373
H96
PUBLIC AFFAIRS QUARTERLY. 1987. q. $30 to individuals; institutions $85. Bowling Green State University, Philosophy Documentation Center, Bowling Green, OH 43403-0189. TEL 419-372-2419. FAX 419-372-6987. Ed. Nicholas Rescher. Indexed: Phil.Ind.
—BLDSC shelfmark: 6962.765000.

PUBLICATIONS IN MEDIEVAL STUDIES. see *HISTORY — History Of Europe*

PURE LIFE SOCIETY. ANNUAL REPORT. see *SOCIAL SERVICES AND WELFARE*

QIU ZHI/SEEK KNOWLEDGE. see *POLITICAL SCIENCE*

100   IT
QUADERNI DI FILOSOFIA. 1978. irreg., no.3, 1980. price varies. (Universita degli Studi di Palermo, Istituto di Filosofia) Editrice Italo-Latino-Americana Palma, Via B. Castiglia 6, 90141 Palermo, Italy. Ed.Bd.

100   IT
QUADERNI DI VERIFICHE. irreg. price varies. Verifiche, Casella Postale 269, 38100 Trento, Italy. Ed. Franco Chiereghin. bibl.
    Description: Focuses on philosophy.

144 300   IT
QUADERNI SARDI DI FILOSOFIA E SCIENZE UMANE. vol.3, 1979. s-a. L.10000($15) Antonio Delogu, Viale Coghinas 22, 07100 Sassari, Italy. Ed.Bd.

QUAKER ENCOUNTERS. see *RELIGIONS AND THEOLOGY — Other Denominations And Sects*

100 121   FR
QUE FAIRE DE L'ECONOMIE. 1973. q. 110 F. David Kaisergruber, 77 bis rue Legendre, 75017 Paris, France.
    Formerly (until 1981): Dialectiques.

100   NE   ISSN 1011-226X
B1
QUEST; philosophical discussions. (Text in English, French) 1987. s-a. $30. (University of Zambia, Department of Philosophy, ZA) Quest, P.O. Box 9114, 9703 LC Groningen, Netherlands. TEL 31-50-636154. FAX 31-50-636160. TELEX ZA 44370. Ed.Bd. adv.; bk.rev.; circ. 500. (back issues avail.)
    Description: Endeavours to act as a channel of expression for African thinkers; reflects on the radical transformations currently taking place. Intended to serve professionals and students of philosphy, and intellectuals in other disciplines.

THE QUEST (WHEATON). see *NEW AGE PUBLICATIONS*

340   UK   ISSN 0300-211X
B1
RADICAL PHILOSOPHY. 1972. 3/yr. £8.50 to individuals; institutions £18. Radical Philosophy Group, c/o Jean Grimshaw, North View, Dundry Lane, Dundry, Bristol BS18 8JG, England. (Subscr. to: Central Books, 99 Wallis Rd., London E9 5LN, England. TEL 071-986-4854) adv.; bk.rev.; illus.; circ. 2,000. Indexed: Br.Hum.Ind., Left Ind. (1986-), Phil.Ind., Stud.Wom.Abstr.
—BLDSC shelfmark: 7228.095000.

RAINBOW RAY FOCUS. see *NEW AGE PUBLICATIONS*

211   FR   ISSN 0033-9075
RAISON PRESENTE. 1968. q. 225 F. Nouvelles Editions Rationalistes, 14 rue de l'Ecole Polytechnique, 75005 Paris, France. Ed. Victor Leduc. bk.rev.; film rev. Indexed: Lang.& Lang.Behav.Abstr.
—BLDSC shelfmark: 7253.221000.

294.54 200   IT
RASSEGNA DI LETTERATURA TOMISTICA. (Text mainly in French and Italian) 1966. a. $60. (Pontificia Universita S. Tommaso D'Aquino, VC) Herder Editrice e Libreria s.r.l., Piazza Montecitori, 120, 00186 Rome, Italy. TEL 67-94-628. FAX 678-47-51. (Co-sponsor: Domenicane Italiane) Ed. C. Vansteenkiste. bk.rev. (back issues avail.)
    Formerly: Bulletin Thomiste.
    Description: Features critical reviews and notices about the the work, thought, and influence of Thomas Aquinas.

160   IT   ISSN 0048-6779
RASSEGNA INTERNAZIONALE DI LOGICA/INTERNATIONAL LOGIC REVIEW. (Text in English, French, German and Italian) 1970. 2/yr. L.5500. Centro Superiore di Logica e Scienze Comparate, Ed. Franco Spisani, Via Belmeloro, N. 3, 40126 Bologna, Italy. circ. 6,000. Indexed: Lang.& Lang.Behav.Abstr., Math.R., Phil.Ind.

100   UK   ISSN 0034-0006
B1
RATIO. 1957. s-a. £27.50($59) to individuals; institutions £44($94). Basil Blackwell Ltd., 108 Cowley Rd., Oxford OX4 1JF, England. TEL 0865-791100. FAX 0865-791347. TELEX 837022-OXBOOK-G. Ed Edward.Craig. adv.; index; circ. 700. (reprint service avail. from SWZ) Indexed: Arts & Hum.Cit.Ind., Br.Hum.Ind., Curr.Cont., Lang.& Lang.Behav.Abstr., Math.R., Phil.Ind., SSCI.
—BLDSC shelfmark: 7295.400000.

RATIO JURIS; an international journal of jurisprudence and philosophy law. see *LAW*

211   AT   ISSN 0156-7594
THE RATIONALIST NEWS. 1966. q. $6. Rationalist Association of New South Wales, 58 Regent, Chippendale, N.S.W. 2008, Australia. Ed. Ronald Marke. bk.rev.; circ. 1,000.

100   US
RAYS FROM THE ROSE CROSS. 1915. bi-m. $15 (foreign $17). Rosicrucian Fellowship, 2222 Mission Ave., Box 713, Oceanside, CA 92054. TEL 619-757-6600. FAX 619-721-3806. Ed. Ted Sauer. bk.rev.; index; circ. 3,500.

100   US   ISSN 0882-6196
READING PLUS. 1986. irreg. Peter Lang Publishing, Inc., 62 W. 45th St., 4th Fl., New York, NY 10036. TEL 212-302-6740. Ed. Mary Ann Caws.

294.54 572   ZR
RECHERCHES PHILOSOPHIQUES AFRICAINES. (Text in English, French) 1977. a. $5. Faculte Catholique de Kinshasa, Faculte de Philosophie, B.P. 1534, Kinshasa-Limete, Zaire. Ed. Ngimbi Nseka. adv.; bk.rev.; circ. 1,500.
    Formerly (until 1977): Recherches Philosophiques Africaines. Collection.

RECONSTRUCTIONIST. see *RELIGIONS AND THEOLOGY — Judaic*

REFORMED REVIEW. see *RELIGIONS AND THEOLOGY — Protestant*

REKENSCHAP; humanistisch tijdschrift voor wetenschap en cultuur. see *LITERARY AND POLITICAL REVIEWS*

RELIGIOUS HUMANISM; a quarterly journal of religious and ethical humanism. see *RELIGIONS AND THEOLOGY — Other Denominations And Sects*

RENCONTRES INTERNATIONALES DE GENEVE. see *SOCIAL SCIENCES: COMPREHENSIVE WORKS*

REPERTORIA HEIDELBERGENSIA. see *LITERATURE*

160   PL   ISSN 0137-2904
QA9.A1   CODEN: RMLODX
REPORTS ON MATHEMATICAL LOGIC. (Text in English; summaries in Polish) 1973. irreg., no.18, 1984. price varies. (Universytet Jagiellonski) Panstwowe Wydawnictwo Naukowe, Ul.Miodowa 10, 00-251 Warsaw, Poland. (Dist. by: Ars Polona, Krakowskie Przedmiescie 7, 00-068 Warsaw, Poland) (Co-sponsor: Uniwersytet Slaski w Katowicach) Ed. W.A. Pogorzelski. circ. 700. Indexed: Math.R., Phil.Ind., Ref.Zh.
—BLDSC shelfmark: 7660.508000.
    Formerly: Uniwersytet Jagiellonski, Krakow. Zeszyty Naukowe. Prace z Logiki (ISSN 0083-4432)

100   US   ISSN 0085-5553
B829.5
RESEARCH IN PHENOMENOLOGY. 1971. a. $39.95. Humanities Press, 165 First Ave., Atlantic Highlands, NJ 07716-1289. TEL 908-872-1441. FAX 908-872-0717. Ed. John Sallis. adv.; bk.rev.; circ. 1,000. (back issues avail.) Indexed: Hum.Ind., Phil.Ind.
—BLDSC shelfmark: 7755.073000.
   Description: Dedicated to encouraging original, creative phenomenological research; to furthering the interpretative and critical study of the writings of major phenomenological philosophers; and, to providing in-depth reviews of current work in phenomenology.

100 601   US   ISSN 0161-7249
T14
RESEARCH IN PHILOSOPHY AND TECHNOLOGY. (Supplement avail.: Jacques Ellul: A Comprehensive Bibliography) 1978. a. $63.50 to institutions. (Society for Philosophy and Technology) J A I Press Inc., 55 Old Post Rd., No. 2, Box 1678, Greenwich, CT 06836-1678. TEL 203-661-7602. Eds. Paul T. Durbin, Carl Mitcham. bibl.
   Refereed Serial

100   II   ISSN 0048-7325
RESEARCH JOURNAL OF PHILOSOPHY.* (Text in English) 1966. s-a. Rs.10.($4) Ranchi University, Ranchi 1, Bihar, India. Ed. R.S. Srivastava. bk.rev.

100 300   II
RESEARCH JOURNAL OF PHILOSOPHY AND SOCIAL SCIENCES. (Text in English) 1970. s-a. Rs.20($4) Meerut University, Archana, Civil Lines, Meerut, Uttar Pradesh, India. Ed. Ram Nath Sharma. adv.; bk.rev.; bibl.

RESEARCH NOTES AND MEMORANDA OF APPLIED GEOMETRY FOR PREVENIENT NATURAL PHILOSOPHY. see *MATHEMATICS*

170   BE   ISSN 0773-1213
RESEAUX; revue interdisciplinaire de philosophie morale et politique. 1965. 3/yr. 600 Fr. to individuals (foreign 900 Fr.); institutions and libraries 1200 Fr. (foreign 1500 Fr.). Universite de Mons - Hainaut, Centre Interdisciplinaire d'Etudes Philosophiques, 20 Place du Parc, B-7000 Mons, Belgium. TEL 065-37-37-36. bk.rev.; bibl. Indexed: Lang.& Lang.Behav.Abstr.
   Formerly: Revue Universitaire de Science Morale (ISSN 0035-435X)

RESURGENCE; journal of the ecological and spiritual culture. see *POLITICAL SCIENCE*

REVELATIONS OF AWARENESS. see *NEW AGE PUBLICATIONS*

330   II   ISSN 0258-1701
H1
REVIEW JOURNAL OF PHILOSOPHY AND SOCIAL SCIENCE. (Text in English) biennial. Rs.70($10) Anu Books, Shivaji Rd, Meerut 25001, India. (Editorial office: Dr. Michael V. Belok, College of Education, Arizona State University, Tempe, AZ 85281) Ed. Michael V. Belok.

110   US   ISSN 0034-6632
B1
REVIEW OF METAPHYSICS; a philosophical quarterly. 1947. q. $25 to individuals; institutions $42; students, retirees $15. Philosophy Education Society, Inc., Catholic University of America, Washington, DC 20064. TEL 202-635-8778. FAX 202-319-5579. Ed. Jude P. Dougherty. adv.; bk.rev.; abstr.; bibl.; index. cum.index: 1947-1967; circ. 2,700. (tabloid format; also avail. in microform from UMI; reprint service avail. from UMI) Indexed: Amer.Bibl.Slavic & E.Eur.Stud., Arts & Hum.Cit.Ind., Bk.Rev.Ind. (1965-), CERDIC, Child.Bk.Rev.Ind. (1965-), Curr.Cont., Hum.Ind., Ind.Bk.Rev.Hum., Lang.& Lang.Behav.Abstr., Phil.Ind., SSCI.
—BLDSC shelfmark: 7793.070000.
   Description: Promotes technically competent, definitive contributions to philosophical knowledge.

100   US   ISSN 0899-9937
REVISIONING PHILOSOPHY. irreg. Peter Lang Publishing, Inc., 62 W. 45th St., 4th Fl., New York, NY 10036. TEL 212-302-6740. FAX 212-302-7574. Ed. David Appelbaum.
—BLDSC shelfmark: 7800.574000.

170   US
REVISIONS (NOTRE DAME). 1981. irreg., vol.11, 1992. price varies. University of Notre Dame Press, Notre Dame, IN 46556. TEL 219-239-6346. Eds. Stanley Hauerwas, Alasdair MacIntyre.

100   SP   ISSN 0212-8780
B5
REVISTA CANARIA DE FILOSOFIA Y CIENCIA SOCIAL. 1983. a. $15 to individuals; institutions $20. Universidad de La Laguna, Facultad de Filosofia y Ciencias de la Educacion. Seccion de Filosofia, Secretariado de Publicaciones, San Agustin, 30, 38201 La Laguna-Tenerife, Islas Canarias, Spain. TEL 922-25-81-27. adv.
   Description: Theoretical and empirical research in philosophy and social sicences.

100   CL   ISSN 0034-8236
REVISTA DE FILOSOFIA. 1949. s-a. $10. Universidad de Chile, Departamento de Filosofia, Facultad de Filosofia y Humanidades, Avda. Ignacio Carrera Pinto 1025, Santiago de Chile, Chile. Dir. Jorge Estrella Avila. bk.rev.; circ. 500.

100   CR   ISSN 0034-8252
B5
REVISTA DE FILOSOFIA. 1958. s-a. Col.500($20) Editorial de la Universidad de Costa Rica, Apartado 75-2060, Ciudad Universitaria Rodrigo Facio, 2050 San Pedro de Montes de Oca, San Jose, Costa Rica. TEL 506-25-3133. FAX 506-24-9367. TELEX UNICORI 2544. Dir. Rafael A. Herra. bk.rev.; index; circ. 750. (back issues avail.)
—BLDSC shelfmark: 7854.670000.

100   VE
REVISTA DE FILOSOFIA. 1974. s-a. Bs.344.10($11.63) Universidad del Zulia, Centro de Estudios Filosoficos, Facultad de Humanidades y Educacion, Edif. Viyaluz, Av. 4 esq. Calle 74, 8o piso, Maracaibo, Zulia, Venezuela. Dir. Angelo Munoz Garcia. bibl.
   Supersedes: Boletin del Centro de Estudios Filosoficos.

100   MX   ISSN 0185-3481
REVISTA DE FILOSOFIA. 1968. 3/yr. Mex.$550($20) (effective 1992). Universidad Iberoamericana, Departamento de Filosofia, Prol. Paseo de la Reforma 880, Lomas de Santa Fe, 01210 Mexico, D.F., Mexico. TEL 570-20-74. FAX 570-76-22. Ed. Jorge Aguirre Sala. bk.rev. Indexed: Phil.Ind.

100   RM   ISSN 0034-8260
B8.R8
REVISTA DE FILOSOFIE/REVUE DE PHILOSOPHIE. (Text in Rumanian; summaries in French and Russian) 1954. 6/yr. 180 lei($51) (Academia Romana) Editura Academiei Romane, Calea Victoriei 125, 79717 Bucharest, Rumania. (Dist. by: Rompresfilatelia, Calea Grivitei 64-66, P.O. Box 12-201, 78104 Bucharest, Rumania) Ed. Alexandru Surdu. bk.rev.; index. Indexed: Phil.Ind.
—BLDSC shelfmark: 7854.690000.

REVISTA DE LITERATURA. see *LITERATURE*

100   CK
REVISTA IDEAS Y VALORES. 1951. 3/yr. exchange basis. Universidad Nacional de Colombia, Departamento de Filosofia, Apdo. Aereo 14490, Ciudad Universitaria, Bogota, Colombia. TEL 2442794. Dir. Magdalena Holguin. bk.rev.; circ. 1,500.
   Formerly: Ideas y Valores (ISSN 0120-0062)
   Description: Includes articles on study and research in the field of philosophy.

100   AG   ISSN 0325-0725
B5
REVISTA LATINOAMERICANA DE FILOSOFIA. (Text in Spanish, Portuguese; summaries in English) 1975. 2/yr. $22 to individuals; institutions $32. Centro de Investigaciones Filosoficas, Casilla de Correo 5379, 1000 Buenos Aires, Argentina. TEL 5401-787-0533. (U.S. address: Box 1192, Birmingham, AL 35201) Ed.Bd. bk.rev.; circ. 500. Indexed: Phil.Ind.
—BLDSC shelfmark: 7863.430000.

100   CL
REVISTA PHILOSOPHICA. 1978. a. $33. (Universidad Catolica de Valparaiso, Instituto de Filosofia) Ediciones Universitarias de Valparaiso, Casilla 1415, Valparaiso, Chile. TEL 252900. FAX 032-212746. TELEX 230389 UCVAL CL. Ed. Juan Antonio Widow. bk.rev.; circ. 300.
   Formerly: Philosophica.

100   PO   ISSN 0870-5283
REVISTA PORTUGUESA DE FILOSOFIA. (Supplemento Bibliografico issued s-a.) 1945. q. $50. Universidade Catolica Portuguesa, Braga, Faculdade de Filosofia, Praca da Faculdade, 1, 4719 Braga Codex, Portugal. bk.rev.; bibl.; index. Indexed: M.L.A., Phil.Ind.

100 056   VE
REVISTA VENEZOLANA DE FILOSOFIA. 1973. s-a. $4 per no. (or exchange basis). Universidad Simon Bolivar, Departamento de Filosofia, Apdo. 80659, Caracas, Venezuela. (Co-sponsor: Sociedad Venezolana de Filosofia) Eds. Dinu Garber, Alberto Rosales. bk.rev. Indexed: Phil.Ind.

109   FR   ISSN 0339-6886
REVOLTES LOGIQUES; cahiers de la recherche sur les ideologies de la revolte. q. 90 F.($20) Editions Solin, 1 rue des Fosses Saint-Jacques, 75005 Paris, France.

111.85   FR   ISSN 0035-2292
REVUE D'ESTHETIQUE. 1945. 2/yr. 380 F. (foreign 500 F.). Editions Jean Michel Place, 12 rue Pierre et Marie Curie, 75005 Paris, France. (Subscr. to: Centrale des Revues (CDR), 11 rue Gossin, 92543 Montrouge Cedex, France) (Co-sponsor: Societe Francaise d'Esthetique) Ed.Bd. bk.rev.; bibl.; charts; illus.; index. Indexed: Artbibl., Artbibl.Mod., M.L.A.

110 190   FR   ISSN 0035-1571
B2
REVUE DE METAPHYSIQUE ET DE MORALE. 1893. q. 56 ECU($68) Armand Colin (Subsidiary of: Masson), 103 bd. Saint-Michel, 75005 Paris, France. TEL 1-46-34-19-12. FAX 1-43-26-96-38. TELEX 201 269 F. Ed.Bd. adv.; bk.rev.; bibl.; circ. 1,700. (reprint service avail. from KTO) Indexed: Arts & Hum.Cit.Ind., Curr.Cont., M.L.A., Phil.Ind.
—BLDSC shelfmark: 7933.200000.

100 160 300   RM
B1
REVUE DE PHILOSOPHIE. 4/yr. 140 lei($52) (Academia Romana) Editura Academiei Romane, Calea Victoriei 125, 79717 Bucharest, Rumania. (Dist. by: Rompresfilatelia, Calea Grivitei 64-66, P.O. Box 12-201, 78104 Bucharest, Rumania)
   Formerly: Revue Roumaine des Sciences Sociales. Serie de Philosophie et Logique (ISSN 0035-4031)

100   FR   ISSN 0035-1776
D1
REVUE DE SYNTHESE. 1900. q. 300 F. (Centre International de Synthese) Editions Albin Michel, 12 rue Colbert, 75002 Paris, France. TEL 1-42-97-50-68. Ed. Jean-Claude Perrot. bk.rev.; bibl.; index; circ. 1,000. Indexed: Hist.Abstr.

REVUE DE THEOLOGIE ET DE PHILOSOPHIE. see *RELIGIONS AND THEOLOGY*

REVUE DE THEOLOGIE ET DE PHILOSOPHIE. CAHIERS. see *RELIGIONS AND THEOLOGY*

215   FR   ISSN 0751-5804
AS162
REVUE DES SCIENCES MORALES ET POLITIQUES. 4/yr. 560 F. (Academie des Sciences Morales et Politiques) Gauthier-Villars, 15 rue Gossin, 92543 Montrouge Cedex, France. TEL 33-1-40-92-65-00. FAX 33-1-40-92-65-97. TELEX 270 004. (Subscr. to: Centrale des Revues, 11 rue Gossin, 92543 Montrouge Cedex, France. TEL 33-1-46-56-52-66) Ed. B. Chenot. circ. 600.
—BLDSC shelfmark: 7948.150000.
   Description: Presents the proceedings of the Academie des Sciences Morales et Politiques- an account of discussions on the major ideas which mark our present time.

PHILOSOPHY

100 200 FR ISSN 0035-2209
REVUE DES SCIENCES PHILOSOPHIQUES ET THEOLOGIQUES. 1907. q. 560 F.($112) (Faculte de Philosophie et de Theologie) Librairie Philosophique J. Vrin, 6 Place de la Sorbonne, 75005 Paris, France. TEL 1-43-54-03-47. FAX 43-54-48-18. Ed. R.P. Bernard Quelquejeu. bk.rev.; index; circ. 1,475. **Indexed:** Arts & Hum.Cit.Ind., CERDIC, M.L.A., New Test.Abstr., Old Test.Abstr., Phil.Ind., Rel.& Theol.Abstr. (1979-), Rel.Ind.One, Rel.Per.
—BLDSC shelfmark: 7948.300000.

REVUE DU M A U S S. (Mouvement Anti-Utilitariste dans les Science Sociales) see *SOCIOLOGY*

100 BE ISSN 0048-8143
B1
REVUE INTERNATIONALE DE PHILOSOPHIE. (Text in English and French) 1938. q. 2000 Fr. Universa - Wetteren, Rue Hoender 24, 9200 Wetteren, Belgium. adv.; bk.rev (reprint service avail. from ISI) **Indexed:** Arts & Hum.Cit.Ind., Curr.Cont., Ind.Bk.Rev.Hum., Lang.& Lang.Behav.Abstr., Math.R., Phil.Ind.
—BLDSC shelfmark: 7925.119000.

294.54 ZR
REVUE PHILOSOPHIQUE DE KINSHASA. (Text in French and English) 1983. a. $25. Faculte Catholique de Kinshasa, Faculte de Philosophie, B.P. 1534, Kinshasa-Limete, Zaire. Ed. Ngimbi Nseka. adv.; bk.rev.; circ. 1,500.

100 FR ISSN 0035-3833
B2
REVUE PHILOSOPHIQUE DE LA FRANCE ET DE L'ETRANGER. 1876. q. 315 F. (foreign 400 F.). Presses Universitaires de France, Departement des Revues, 14 av. du Bois-de-l'Epine, B.P.90, 91003 Evry Cedex, France. TEL 1-60-77-82-05. FAX 1-60-79-20-45. TELEX PUF 600 474 F. Dir. Yvon Bres. bk.rev.; abstr.; bibl.; index. (reprint service avail. from KTO) **Indexed:** Arts & Hum.Cit.Ind., Curr.Cont., Ind.Bk.Rev.Hum., Phil.Ind.

100 BE ISSN 0035-3841
REVUE PHILOSOPHIQUE DE LOUVAIN. (Supplement avail.: Repertoire Bibliographique de la Philosophie) (Text in French; summaries in English) 1894. q. 2000 Fr. Universite Catholique de Louvain, Institut Superieur de Philosophie, Chemin d'Aristote 1, B-1348 Louvain-la-Neuve, Belgium. TEL 016-488102. FAX 016-481486. TELEX 65981 PUL B. (Subscr. to: Editions Peeters s.p.r.l., Bondgenotenlaan 153, B-3000 Leuven, Belgium. TEL 016-235170) (Co-sponsor: Fondation Universitaire Belge) Ed. Claude Troisfontaines. adv.; bk.rev.; bibl.; index; circ. 1,400. **Indexed:** Arts & Hum.Cit.Ind., Cath.Ind., M.L.A., Phil.Ind.
Formerly: Revue Neo-Scolastique.
Description: Review of the international philosophical movement by scholars of the Institute and others as well.

REVUE THOMISTE; revue doctrinale de theologie et de philosophie. see *RELIGIONS AND THEOLOGY*

100 US ISSN 0277-3945
PN171.4
RHETORIC SOCIETY QUARTERLY. 1968. q. $10 to institutions. Rhetoric Society of America, c/o Department of Philosophy, St. Cloud State University, St. Cloud, MN 56301. TEL 612-255-2234. Ed. George E. Yoos. adv.; bk.rev.; bibl.; cum.index; circ. 700. **Indexed:** M.L.A.
Formerly: Rhetoric Society Newsletter.

100 SA ISSN 0556-8641
RHODES UNIVERSITY. DEPARTMENT OF PHILOSOPHY. PHILOSOPHICAL PAPERS. (Text in English) 1972. 3/yr. R.45($17) to individuals; institutions R.100($50); students R.20($11). Rhodes University, Department of Philosophy, P.O. Box 94, Grahamstown 6140, South Africa. TEL 716-2890. FAX 403-1926. Ed. Michael Pendlebury. adv.; circ. 450. (back issues avail.) **Indexed:** Ind.S.A.Per., Phil.Ind.
—BLDSC shelfmark: 6462.200000.
Description: An international journal of philosophy in the broad analytical tradition.

RICERCHE STORICHE SALESIANE; rivista semestrale di storia religiosa e civile. see *RELIGIONS AND THEOLOGY — Roman Catholic*

100 700 IT ISSN 0035-6212
RIVISTA DI ESTETICA. (Text in English, French and Italian) 1956-1973; N.S. 1979. 3/yr. L.60000 (Europe L.85000; elsewhere L.100000). Rosenberg & Sellier, Via Andrea Doria 14, 10123 Turin, Italy. TEL 011-561-39-07. FAX 011-532188. Ed. Gianni Vattimo. adv.; bk.rev.; abstr.; index; circ. 1,500. (back issues avail.) **Indexed:** Artbibl.Mod., M.L.A.
Description: Covers topics related to estetics, word vs. case, retoric, philosophy, poetry and anthropology.

100 IT ISSN 0035-6239
RIVISTA DI FILOSOFIA. 1909. 3/yr. L.100000. Societa Editrice Il Mulino, Strada Maggiore, 37, 40125 Bologna, Italy. TEL 051-256011. FAX 051-256034. Ed. Pietro Rossi. adv.; bk.rev.; bibl.; index; circ. 1,500. (back issues avail.; reprint service avail. from SWZ) **Indexed:** Phil.Ind.
—BLDSC shelfmark: 7985.430000.

149.2 IT ISSN 0035-6247
B4
RIVISTA DI FILOSOFIA NEOSCOLASTICA. 1909. q. L.118000($90) (effective 1992). (Universita Cattolica del Sacro Cuore) Vita e Pensiero, Largo Gemelli 1, 20123 Milan, Italy. TEL 02-8856310. FAX 02-8856260. TELEX 321033 UCATMI 1. Ed. Adriano Bausola. adv.; bk.rev.; bibl. **Indexed:** Phil.Ind.
Description: Covers various areas in philosophy.

RIVISTA DI PSICOLOGIA DELL'ARTE. see *ART*

109 IT
RIVISTA DI STORIA DELLA FILOSOFIA. 1946; N.S. q. L.70000 (foreign L.100000)(effective 1992). Franco Angeli Editore, Viale Monza 106, 20127 Milan, Italy. Ed. Mario Dal Pra. adv.; bk.rev.; abstr.; bibl.; index; circ. 1,000. (back issues avail.) **Indexed:** Arts & Hum.Cit.Ind., Curr.Cont.
Formerly: Rivista Critica di Storia della Filosofia (ISSN 0035-581X)

182 IT ISSN 0035-659X
B3614.C74
RIVISTA DI STUDI CROCIANI; dedicated to work of Benedetto Croce. (Text in English, French and Spanish; summaries in Italian) 1964. q. Maschio Angioino, 80133 Naples, Italy. adv.; bk.rev.; circ. 1,000. **Indexed:** M.L.A., Phil.Ind.

RIVISTA INTERNAZIONALE DI FILOSOFIA DEL DIRITTO. see *LAW*

100 IT ISSN 0035-7030
RIVISTA ROSMINIANA DI FILOSOFIA E DI CULTURA. (Text in English, French, Italian, Spanish) 1906; N.S. 1967. q. L.25000. (Centro Internazionale di Studi Rosminiani) Libraria Editoriale Sodalitas s.a.s, Corso Umberto 1st, 15, 28049 Stresa (Novara), Italy. Ed. P. Paolo Ottonello. adv.; bk.rev.; bibl.; index; circ. 600. **Indexed:** Lang.& Lang.Behav.Abstr.

ROCKHEAD; for rockers with brains. see *MUSIC*

100 300 PL ISSN 0035-7685
B31 CODEN: RFLZBF
ROCZNIKI FILOZOFICZNE. (In four parts: 1. Metaphysics, Logic, History of Philosophy; 2. Philosophy of Morals, Philosophy of Religion; 3. Natural Philosophy; 4. Psychology) (Text in Polish; summaries in English, French, German) 1948. irreg.? price varies. Katolicki Uniwersytet Lubelski, Towarzystwo Naukowe, Ul. Gliniana 21, 20-616 Lublin, Poland. bk.rev.; index; circ. 720. **Indexed:** Psychol.Abstr.

366.4 135.43 US ISSN 0035-8266
ROSACRUZ. (Text in Spanish) 1947. bi-m. $9. Supreme Grand Lodge of AMORC, Inc., Rosicrucian Park, San Jose, CA 95191. TEL 408-287-9171. Ed. Lisa C. Bigley. illus.; circ. controlled. (tabloid format)
Description: Explores mysticism and philosophy.

366.4 135.43 US ISSN 0035-8339
BF1623.R7
ROSICRUCIAN DIGEST. 1915. q. $10. Rosicrucian Order, AMORC, Rosicrucian Park, 1342 Naglee Ave., San Jose, CA 95191. TEL 408-287-9171. FAX 408-286-4038. Ed. Robin M. Thompson. bk.rev.; circ. 45,000.

100 PL ISSN 0035-9599
RUCH FILOZOFICZNY. (Text in Polish) 1911. q. $16. (Polish Philosophical Association) Ossolineum, Publishing House of the Polish Academy of Sciences, Rynek 9, 50-106 Wroclaw, Poland. (Dist. by: Ars Polona-Ruch, Krakowskie Przedmiescie 7, Warsaw, Poland) Ed. Leon Gumanski. bk.rev.; abstr.; bibl.; index; circ. 530.
Description: Philosophy and history of philosophy.

026 CN ISSN 0036-0163
B1649 .R94
RUSSELL: THE JOURNAL OF THE BERTRAND RUSSELL ARCHIVES. 1971. s-a. Can.$15.50 to individuals; institutions Can.$27. McMaster University Library Press, Mills Memorial Library, Hamilton, Ont. L8S 4L6, Canada. TEL 416-525-9140. FAX 416-546-0625. Ed. Kenneth Blackwell. adv.; bk.rev.; bibl.; circ. 600. **Indexed:** Arts & Hum.Cit.Ind., Curr.Cont., Ind.Bk.Rev.Hum., Phil.Ind.
—BLDSC shelfmark: 8052.660000.
Description: Articles and reviews about Bertrand Russell.

100 US
B1
RUSSIAN STUDIES IN PHILOSOPHY; a journal of translations from Soviet scholarly sources. 1962. q. $260 to institutions. M.E. Sharpe, Inc., 80 Business Park Dr., Armonk, NY 10504. TEL 914-273-1800. FAX 914-273-2106. Ed. James P. Scanlan. adv.; index. **Indexed:** Arts & Hum.Cit.Ind., ASCA, Curr.Cont., Phil.Ind., SSCI.
Formerly: Soviet Studies in Philosophy (ISSN 0038-5883)

S E R IN ACTION NEWSLETTER. (Society for Educational Reconstruction) see *EDUCATION*

100 200 US ISSN 1059-8375
▼**ST. WILLIBRORD STUDIES IN PHILOSOPHY AND RELIGION.** 1991. irreg. price varies. Borgo Press, Box 2845, San Bernardino, CA 92406. TEL 714-884-5813. Ed. Karl Prueter.
Description: Features studies on all aspects of Christianity, including histories, treatises, and manuals.

294 II ISSN 0036-3316
SAIVA SIDDHANTA. (Text in English) 1966. q. Rs.10($5) Saiva Siddhantha Peru Manram, 4, Venkatesa Agraharam Salai I Fl., Mylapore, Madras 600004, India. Eds. P. Thirngnanasambandara, C.N. Singaravelu. adv.; bk.rev.; abstr.; index; circ. 500.
Description: Siddhanta philosophy, religion, and literature.

SALESIANUM. see *RELIGIONS AND THEOLOGY — Roman Catholic*

100 920 AU ISSN 0259-0794
SALZBURGER BEITRAEGE ZUR PARACELSUSFORSCHUNG. 1960. irreg., no.27, 1990. price varies. (Internationale Paracelsus-Gesellschaft) Verband der Wissenschaftlichen Gesellschaften Oesterreichs, Lindengasse 37, A-1070 Vienna, Austria. TEL 932166.

100 AU ISSN 0080-5696
B23
SALZBURGER JAHRBUCH FUER PHILOSOPHIE. 1957. a. price varies. Universitaetsverlag Anton Pustet, Bergstr. 12, Postfach 144, A-5021 Salzburg, Austria. TEL 0662-873507. **Indexed:** Phil.Ind.

100 AU ISSN 0080-5726
SALZBURGER STUDIEN ZUR PHILOSOPHIE. 1962. irreg. price varies. Universitaetsverlag Anton Pustet, Bergstr. 12, Postschliessfach 144, 5021 Salzburg, Austria. TEL 0662-873507.

100 200 AG ISSN 0036-4703
SAPIENTIA. (Text in Spanish) 1946. q. $30. Universidad Catolica Argentina, Facultad de Filosofia y Letras, Bme. Mitre 1869, 1039 Buenos Aires, Argentina. Ed. Octavio Derisi. adv.; bk.rev.; bibl.; charts; illus.; index, cum.index: 1946-1970; circ. 1,100. (also avail. in microfilm from UMI; reprint service avail. from UMI) **Indexed:** Cath.Ind., Hisp.Amer.Per.Ind., Phil.Ind., Rel.& Theol.Abstr.

PHILOSOPHY

100 200　　　　IT　　ISSN 0036-4711
SAPIENZA; rivista internazionale di filosofia e di teologia. 1948. q. L.35000($30.50) (Dominican Fathers) Editrice Domenicana Italiana, Via Luigi Palmieri, 19, 80133 Naples, Italy. TEL (081) 459.003. Ed. Michele Miele. adv.; bk.rev.; abstr.; bibl.; index; circ. 2,500. **Indexed:** CERDIC, M.L.A., New Test.Abstr., Old Test.Abstr., Phil.Ind.

181.45　　　　US
SAT SANDESH; the message of the masters. 1968. 12/yr. $20. Sawan Kirpal Publications, RR1, Box 24, Bowling Green, VA 22427. Ed. Arthur Stein. bk.rev.; circ. 1,800.
Description: The teachings of Sant Rajinder Singh of India and earlier spiritual mentors of Sant Mat tradition, also known as Science of Spirituality.

100　　　　GW　　ISSN 0080-6935
SCHOPENHAUER-JAHRBUCH. a. DM.58. (Schopenhauer Gesellschaft e.V.) Verlag Dr. Waldemar Kramer, Bornheimer Landwehr 57a, 6000 Frankfurt a.M. 60, Germany. FAX 069-449064. bk.rev.; circ. 1,912. (reprint service avail. from KTO) **Indexed:** Phil.Ind.
Description: Articles on Schopenhauer's philosophy.

100 943　　GW　　ISSN 0138-3418
SCHRIFTEN ZUR PHILOSOPHIE UND IHRER GESCHICHTE. 1976. irreg., vol.45, 1988. (Akademie der Wissenschaften der DDR) Akademie-Verlag Berlin, Leipziger Str. 3-4, 1086 Berlin, Germany.

200　　　　NE　　ISSN 0925-2657
▼**SCHRIFTENREIHE ZUR PHILOSOPHIE KARL L. POPPERS UND DES KRITISCHEN RATIONALISMUS**. 1990. irreg. price varies. Editions Rodopi B.V., Keizersgracht 302-304, 1016 EX Amsterdam, Netherlands. TEL 020-6227507. FAX 020-6380948. (In N. America: 233 Peachtree St. N.E., Ste. 404, Atlanta GA 30303-1504. TEL 800-225-3998) Ed. Kurt Salamun.

SCIENCE AND CHRISTIAN BELIEF. see *RELIGIONS AND THEOLOGY*

200　　　　CN　　ISSN 0316-5345
BR3
SCIENCE ET ESPRIT. 1948. 3/yr. Can.$20. Editions Bellarmin, 165 Deslaurier, Ville St.-Laurent, Que. H4N 2S4, Canada. TEL 514-745-4290. bk.rev.; index; circ. 375. **Indexed:** CERDIC, M.L.A., New Test.Abstr., Old Test.Abstr., Pt.de Rep. (1983-), Rel.Ind.One, Rel.Per.

SCIENCE OF MIND MAGAZINE. see *RELIGIONS AND THEOLOGY — Other Denominations And Sects*

100　　　　PL　　ISSN 0138-0532
Q180.A1
SCIENCE OF SCIENCE; an international journal of studies on scientific reasoning and scientific enterprise. (Text in English; summaries in French, German and Russian) 1980. q. fl.191($73) per no. (Polish Academy of Science, Committee of the Science of Science) Ossolineum, Publishing House of the Polish Academy of Sciences, Rynek 9, 50-106 Wroclaw, Poland. TEL 386-25. (Dist. to: Ars Polona, Krakowskie Przedmiescie 7, 00-068 Warsaw, Poland) Ed. I. Malecki. adv.; bk.rev.; index. **Indexed:** Lang.& Lang.Behav.Abstr.
—BLDSC shelfmark: 8164.230000.
Formerly: Problems of the Science of Science.

SCUOLA NORMALE SUPERIORE DI PISA. ANNALI. CLASSE DI LETTERE E FILOSOFIA. see *HUMANITIES: COMPREHENSIVE WORKS*

SECOND OPINION (CHICAGO). see *MEDICAL SCIENCES*

100　　　　NR　　ISSN 0048-9964
SECOND ORDER; an African journal of philosophy. 1972. s-a. $17. (Obafemi Awolowo University) Obafemi Awolowo University Press, Ltd., Periodicals Dept., Ile-Ife, Nigeria. Eds. M.A. Makinde, Segun Ghadegesin. adv.; bk.rev.; bibl.; circ. 500. **Indexed:** Lang.& Lang.Behav.Abstr., Phil.Ind.

100　　　　II　　ISSN 0049-0008
SECULARIST. (Text in English) 1971. 6/yr. Rs.20($5) Indian Secular Society, 850-8A Shivajinagar, Pune 411 004, Maharashtra, India. Ed. V.K. Sinha. adv.; bk.rev.; circ. 300.
Description: Committed to secular human values and their promotion in Indian society. Seeks to combat religious obscurantism and to educate public opinion.

100　　　　IT
SEGNI E COMPRENSIONE. 1987. s-a. L.15000 (foreign L.25000). (Universita degli Studi di Lecce, Dipartimento di Filosofia) Capone Editore, s.r.l., Via Caprarica,35, 73020 Cavallino (Lecce), Italy. TEL 0832-611877. Ed. Giovanni Invitto.

SEIKYO TIMES. see *RELIGIONS AND THEOLOGY — Buddhist*

SELF & SOCIETY; European journal of humanistic psychology. see *PSYCHOLOGY*

181.45　　　　UK　　ISSN 0037-1556
SELF-KNOWLEDGE; a yoga quarterly devoted to spiritual thought and practice. 1948. q. £8. Shanti Sadan Centre of Adhyatma Yoga, 29 Chepstow Villas, London W11 3DR, England. TEL 071-727-7846. FAX 071-792-9817. Ed.Bd. bk.rev.; circ. 250.
Description: A quarterly journal devoted to spiritual thought and practice, mastery of the mind, meditation.

SELF-REALIZATION. see *RELIGIONS AND THEOLOGY*

100　　　　GW　　ISSN 0170-219X
SEMIOSIS; internationale Zeitschrift fuer Semiotik und Aesthetik. (Text in English, French, German, Italian; summaries in English) 1976. q. (Vereinigung fuer Wissenschaftliche Semiotik) Agis-Verlag GmbH, Postfach 2220, 7570 Baden-Baden, Germany. Ed. Elisabeth Walther. adv.; bk.rev.; index. (back issues avail.)

SEMIOTEXT(E). see *HUMANITIES: COMPREHENSIVE WORKS*

SEMIOTIC REVIEW OF BOOKS. see *HUMANITIES: COMPREHENSIVE WORKS*

212.5　　　　TU
SEVGI DUNYASI. 1963. m. P.T.6000($12) Sevgi Yayinlari Tic. Ltd. Sti., Aydede Cad. 4-5, Taksim, Istanbul, Turkey. (Dist. by: Sevgi Dunyasi, P.K.140, Serkeci-Istanbul, Turkey) Ed. Refet Kayserilioglu. circ. 5,000. (back issues avail.)
Description: Explores spiritualism and moral issues.

SHARE IT; a magazine to celebrate & promote awareness of our true identity. see *NEW AGE PUBLICATIONS*

SHAW ANNUAL. see *LITERATURE*

200 100　　　　II　　ISSN 0251-1746
SHREE HARI KATHA/GOSPEL OF GOD. (Text in English and Hindi) 1974. m. Rs.31. Shiksha Sansthan, B-12-223, Lodi Rd., New Delhi 110 003, India. TEL 11-611122. FAX 11-89-22592. TELEX 598214. Ed. Surendra Agrawal. circ. 1,000.

100 320　　　　BL　　ISSN 0103-4332
H8
SINTESE. (Text in Portuguese, summaries in English) 1959. q. Cr.$28000($40) (effective 1992). (Centro de Estudos Superiores da Companhia de Jesus, Faculdade de Filosofia) Edicoes Loyola, Av. Cristiano Guimaraes, 2127, 31710 Belo Horizonte (MG), Brazil. FAX 31-441-02-33. (Subscr. to: Caixa Postal 5047, 31611 Belo Horizonte MG, Brazil) Ed. Marcelo Perine. adv.; bk.rev.; abstr.; bibl.; cum.index: vols.1-17 (1974-1990); circ. 2,500. **Indexed:** CERDIC.
—BLDSC shelfmark: 8285.825000.
Formerly: Sintese Politica, Economica e Social (ISSN 0037-5772)
Description: Discusses contemporary issues in philosophy, political science, and social science. Includes editorials, papers and articles, and notes on contemporary problems.

100　　　　IT　　ISSN 0037-5888
SISTEMATICA; rivista di filosofia e di filologia. 1968. q. L.20000. Edizioni Pergamena s.a.s., Viale Ezio 7, 20149 Milan, Italy. Dir. Giovanni Giraldi. bk.rev.

SISTEMI INTELLIGENTI; rivista quadrimestrale di scienze cognitive e intelligenza artificiale. see *PSYCHOLOGY*

100 301 320　　XV　　ISSN 0353-4510
SLOVENSKA AKADEMIJA ZNANOSTI IN UMETNOSTI. FILOZOFSKI VESTNIK. (Text in English, Slovenian) 1980. s-a. 1000 SLT. Slovenska Akademija Znanosti in Umetnosti, Novi Trg 3, 61000 Ljubljana, Slovenia. TEL 61-156-068. FAX 38-61-155-253. (Subscr. to: Cankarjeba Zalozba, Trg Osvoboditve 7, 61000 Ljubljana, Slovenia) Ed. Vojislav Likar. bk.rev.; circ. 800. (back issues avail.)
Formerly: Institut za Marksisticne Studije. Vestnik (ISSN 0351-6881)

100 300　　　　UK　　ISSN 0269-1728
BD175
SOCIAL EPISTEMOLOGY; a journal of knowledge, culture and policy. 1987. q. £21($37) to individuals; institutions £77($135). Taylor & Francis Ltd., Rankine Rd., Basingstoke, Hants RG24 0PR, England. TEL 0256-840366. FAX 0256-479438. TELEX 858540. Ed. Steve Fuller. circ. 171.
—BLDSC shelfmark: 8318.087500.
Description: Devoted to research explorations in the social structure of knowledge, and the establishment of a forum for philosophical and sociological inquiry.
Refereed Serial

100　　　　US　　ISSN 0265-0525
H61
SOCIAL PHILOSOPHY AND POLICY. 1983. 2/yr. $28 to individuals; institutions $70. Cambridge University Press, Journals Dept., 40 W. 20th St., New York, NY 10011. TEL 212-924-3900. Ed. Ellen Frankel Paul. circ. 1,150. (reprint service avail. from SWZ) **Indexed:** ASCA, ASSIA, Lang.& Lang.Behav.Abstr., Phil.Ind.
—BLDSC shelfmark: 8318.129000.

170　　　　US　　ISSN 0732-9938
BJ1725
SOCIAL RESPONSIBILITY: BUSINESS, JOURNALISM, LAW, MEDICINE. 1975. a. Washington and Lee University, Social Responsibility: Business, Journalism, Law, Medicine, Lexington, VA 24450.
TEL 703-463-8786. FAX 703-463-8945. Ed. Louis W. Hodges. circ. 9,000. (also avail. in microfilm from WSH; reprint service avail. from WSH) **Indexed:** C.L.I., L.R.I., Leg.Per.
Formerly: Social Responsibility: Journalism, Law, Medicine.

SOCIAL THEORY AND PRACTICE; an international and interdisciplinary journal of social philosophy. see *SOCIOLOGY*

100　　　　CN
SOCIETE DE PHILOSOPHIE DU QUEBEC. BULLETIN. (Text in French) 1974. 3/yr. Can.$8. Societe de Philosophie du Quebec, C.P. 1370, Place Bonaventure, Montreal, Que. H5A 1H2, Canada. Ed.Bd. adv.; bibl.; circ. 350. (back issues avail.)

100　　　　FR　　ISSN 0037-9352
B12
SOCIETE FRANCAISE DE PHILOSOPHIE. BULLETIN. 1901. 4/yr. 30 ECU($38) (typically set in Jan.). Armand Colin (Subsidiary of: Masson), 103 bd. Saint-Michel, 75005 Paris, France.
TEL 1-46-34-19-12. FAX 1-43-26-96-38. TELEX 201 269 F. bk.rev.; circ. 1,000. (back issues avail.; reprint service avail. from SCH) **Indexed:** Phil.Ind.
—BLDSC shelfmark: 2739.260000.

SOCIETY FOR RENAISSANCE STUDIES. OCCASIONAL PAPERS. see *LITERATURE*

SOEKAREN. see *PARAPSYCHOLOGY AND OCCULTISM*

SOKA GAKKAI NEWS. see *RELIGIONS AND THEOLOGY — Buddhist*

SOPHIA; a journal for discussion in philosophical theology. see *RELIGIONS AND THEOLOGY*

100　　　　PH　　ISSN 0115-8988
SOPHIA; journal of philosophy. (Text in English) 1971. s-a. P.90($11) (De La Salle University, Department of Philosophy) De La Salle University Press, 2401 Taft Ave., Manila, Philippines. TEL 2-595177. Ed. Claro Ceniza. adv.; bk.rev.; circ. 300.
Description: Publishes scholarly articles reflecting significant quantitative or qualitative research in philosophy. Includes speeches, research reports, and "state of the art" papers.

PHILOSOPHY

170 330   US
SOUNDINGS (NOTRE DAME); a series of books on ethics, economics and business. 1987. irreg., vol.2, 1987. price varies. University of Notre Dame Press, Notre Dame, IN 46556. TEL 219-239-6346. Ed. Thomas Donaldson.

100   SA   ISSN 0258-0136
CODEN: SAJPEM
SOUTH AFRICAN JOURNAL OF PHILOSOPHY. (Text in Afrikaans, English) 1982. q. R.48($35) (Philosophical Society of Southern Africa) Bureau for Scientific Publications, P.O. Box 1758, Pretoria 0001, South Africa. TEL 012-322-6422. Ed. A.A. van Niekerk. circ. 450. **Indexed:** Biol.Abstr., Curr.Cont., Ind.S.A.Per., Phil.Ind.

SOUTH ASIA IN REVIEW; quarterly review of new books on South Asia. see *HISTORY — History Of Asia*

100   US   ISSN 0038-4283
B1
SOUTHERN JOURNAL OF PHILOSOPHY. 1963. q. $12 to individuals; institutions $20. Memphis State University, Department of Philosophy, Memphis, TN 38152. TEL 901-678-2535. FAX 901-678-4365. Ed. Nancy D. Simco. adv.; bk.rev.; index; circ. 1,000. (also avail. in microform from UMI; reprint service avail. from UMI) **Indexed:** Arts & Hum.Cit.Ind., Curr.Cont., Phil.Ind.
—BLDSC shelfmark: 8354.280000.

100   US
SOUTHWEST PHILOSOPHY REVIEW. JOURNAL.* 1937. s-a. membership. c/o James Swindler, 2160 Texas St., Salt Lake City, UT 84109. (Co-sponsor: Southwestern Philosophical Society) Ed. James Shelton. bk.rev.; circ. 250 (controlled). (processed)
Formerly: Southwestern Philosophical Society. Newsletter (ISSN 0038-4925)

SOUTHWESTERN JOURNAL OF THEOLOGY. see *RELIGIONS AND THEOLOGY*

SOVIET AND EAST EUROPEAN STUDIES IN AESTHETICS AND THE PHILOSOPHY OF CULTURE. irreg. Peter Lang Publishing, Inc., 62 W. 45th St., 4th Fl., New York, NY 10036. TEL 212-302-6740. FAX 212-302-7574. Ed. Willis H. Truitt.

SOVIETICA. PUBLICATIONS AND MONOGRAPHS. see *HISTORY — History Of Europe*

100   GW
SPECULA. 1978. irreg. price varies. Friedrich Frommann Verlag Guenther Holzboog, Postfach 500460, Koenig-Karl-Str. 27, 7000 Stuttgart 50, Germany. Ed. Guenther Holzboog.

SPELING. see *RELIGIONS AND THEOLOGY*

THE SPIRITUAL HEALER; journal of spiritual healing and philosophy. see *NEW AGE PUBLICATIONS*

100   IT   ISSN 0038-7649
SPIRITUALITA; rassegna di cultura varia. 1956. q. L.3000. Sodalizio Internazionale di Spiritualita Alpina, Ordine del Cardo, Eremo San Salvatore, Casorezzo, 20010 Milan, Italy. Ed. Sandro Prada. illus.

SRI AUROBINDO. ARCHIVES AND RESEARCH. see *RELIGIONS AND THEOLOGY — Buddhist*

SSU YU YEN/THOUGHT AND WORDS; journal of the humanities and social sciences. see *HUMANITIES: COMPREHENSIVE WORKS*

STARLITE TIMES; a publication for body, mind & spirit. see *NEW AGE PUBLICATIONS*

100   US
STILL WATERS NEWSLETTER. 1977. q. $5 suggested donation. Still Waters Foundation, Inc., 615 Stafford Lane, Pensacola, FL 32506. TEL 904-455-9511. Ed. John E. Pepper. bk.rev.; circ. 2,000 (controlled).
Former titles: Still Waters Presents; Still Waters Digest.

101   SW   ISSN 0491-0877
STOCKHOLM STUDIES IN PHILOSOPHY. (Subseries of Acta Universitatis Stockholmiensis) (Text in English) 1957. irreg., latest no.9, 1987. price varies. (Stockholms Universitet) Almqvist & Wiksell International, Box 638, S-101 28 Stockholm, Sweden. Eds. Harald Ofstad, Anders Wedberg. (back issues avail.)

STRATEGIES (LOS ANGELES); a journal of theory, culture and politics. see *POLITICAL SCIENCE — International Relations*

215   AG   ISSN 0049-2353
BX805
STROMATA; antigua ciencia y fe. 1944. q. (in two issues). $25 in Latin America; elsewhere $30(effective 1992). (Universidad del Salvador, Facultades de Filosofia y Teologia) Asociacion Civil Facultades Loyola, Avda. Mitre 3226, C.C. 10, 1663 San Miguel, Argentina. FAX 54-1-664-6442. Ed. Jorge R. Seibold. adv.; bk.rev.; abstr.; bibl.; cum.index 1944-1981; circ. 1,000. **Indexed:** Bull.Signal., Hisp.Amer.Per.Ind., New Test.Abstr., Old Test.Abstr., Phil.Ind.
—BLDSC shelfmark: 8475.300000.

STUDI URBINATI. SERIE B: SCIENZE UMANE E SOCIALI. see *LITERATURE*

100   IT   ISSN 0081-6310
STUDIA ARISTOTELICA. 1958. irreg., no.12, 1986. price varies. (Universita degli Studi di Padova) Editrice Antenore, Via G. Rusca 15, 35100 Padua, Italy.

100   NE
STUDIA CARTESIANA. (Text in English and French) 1979. irreg. price varies. Quadratures, Postbus 6463, 1005 EL Amsterdam, Netherlands. Ed.Bd. bk.rev.

111.85   PL   ISSN 0081-637X
STUDIA ESTETYCZNE. (Text in Polish; summaries in English and Russian) 1964. irreg., vol.17, 1981. price varies. (Polska Akademia Nauk, Instytut Filozofii i Socjologii) Panstwowe Wydawnictwo Naukowe, Ul. Miodowa 10, 00-251 Warsaw, Poland. (Dist. by: Ars Polona, Krakowskie Przedmiescie 7, 00-068 Warsaw, Poland) Ed. Slaw Krzemien-Ojak. bk.rev.; circ. 500.

100   PL   ISSN 0039-3142
B6
STUDIA FILOZOFICZNE. (Contents and summaries in English and Russian) 1957. m. $72. (Polska Akademia Nauk, Instytut Filozofii i Socjologii, Komitet Nauk Filozoficznych) Panstwowe Wydawnictwo Naukowe, Ul. Miodowa 10, 00-251 Warsaw, Poland. (Dist. by: Ars Polona, Krakowskie Przedmiescie 7, 00-068 Warsaw, Poland) Ed. D. Tanalski. bk.rev.; index; circ. 2,730. **Indexed:** Hist.Abstr.
Formerly: Mysl Filozoficzna.

100 500   GW   ISSN 0039-3185
B2550   CODEN: STLBBI
STUDIA LEIBNITIANA; Zeitschrift fuer Geschichte der Philosophie und der Wissenschaften. (Text in English and German) 1969. s-a. DM.108 (supplements individually priced). (Gottfried-Wilhelm-Leibniz Gesellschaft e.V.) Franz Steiner Verlag Wiesbaden GmbH, Birkenwaldstr. 44, Postfach 101526, 7000 Stuttgart 1, Germany. TEL 0711-2582-0. FAX 0711-2582290. TELEX 723636-DAZD. Ed.Bd. adv.; bk.rev.; circ. 450. (back issues avail.) **Indexed:** Arts & Hum.Cit.Ind., Curr.Cont., Math.R., Phil.Ind.

100   GW   ISSN 0341-0765
STUDIA LEIBNITIANA. SONDERHEFTE. (Text in English and German) irreg., vol.21, 1992. price varies. (Gottfried Wilhelm Leibniz Gesellschaft, Hannover) Franz Steiner Verlag Wiesbaden GmbH, Birkenwaldstr. 44, Postfach 101526, 7000 Stuttgart 1, Germany. TEL 0711-2582-0. FAX 0711-2582290. TELEX 723636-DAZD. Ed.Bd. **Indexed:** Math.R.

100   GW   ISSN 0303-5980
B2550
STUDIA LEIBNITIANA. SUPPLEMENTA. (Text in English, French, and German) irreg., vol.29, 1992. price varies. (Gottfried Wilhelm Leibniz Gesellschaft, Hannover) Franz Steiner Verlag Wiesbaden GmbH, Birkenwaldstr. 44, Postfach 101526, 7000 Stuttgart 1, Germany. TEL 0711-2582-0. FAX 0711-2582290. TELEX 723636-DAZD. Ed.Bd. **Indexed:** Math.R.

160   PL   ISSN 0039-3215
CODEN: SLOGAP
STUDIA LOGICA. (Text in English) 1953. q. $65.50 to individuals; institutions $160.50. (Polska Akademia Nauk - Polish Academy of Sciences, Institute of Philosophy and Sociology) Ossolineum, Publishing House of the Polish Academy of Sciences, Instytut Filozofii i Sociologii, 50-106 Wroclaw, Poland. TEL 386-25. (Dist. for socialist countries by: Ars Polona, Krakowskie Przedmiescie 7, 00-068 Warsaw, Poland; Dist. for non-socialist coutries by: Kluwer Academic Publishers Group, P.O. Box 322, 3300 AH Dordrecht, Netherlands) Ed. Ryszard Wojcicki. bk.rev.; charts; index. (reprint service avail. from SWZ) **Indexed:** Biol.Abstr., Eng.Ind., Geo.Abstr., Lang.& Lang.Behav.Abstr., Math.R., Phil.Ind.
—BLDSC shelfmark: 8482.975000.
Description: Papers on all technical issues of contemporary logic, logical systems, their semantics, methodology and application of logic in linguistics and other sciences.

189   PL   ISSN 0039-3231
STUDIA MEDIEWISTYCZNE. (Text in English, German, Latin and Polish) 1959. s-a. (Polska Akademia Nauk, Instytut Filozofii i Socjologii) Ossolineum, Publishing House of the Polish Academy of Sciences, Rynek 9, Wroclaw, Poland. TELEX 0712771 OSS PL. (Dist. by: Ars Polona-Ruch, Krakowskie Przedmiescie 7, 00-068 Warsaw, Poland) Ed. M. Markowski. **Indexed:** M.L.A.

110   PL   ISSN 0039-324X
STUDIA METODOLOGICZNE. DISSERTATIONES METHODOLOGICAE. 1965. s-a. price varies. Adam Mickiewicz University Press, Nowowiejskiego 55, 61-734 Poznan, Poland. TEL 527-380. FAX 61-526425. TELEX 413260 UAMPL. Eds. Jerzy Kmita, Jerzy Topolski. bk.rev.; bibl.; index; circ. 800.
Description: Research papers in Polish, summaries in English, prepared by sociologists, philosophers, historians, psychologists, linguists and others.

STUDIA PATAVINA; rivista di scienze religiose. see *RELIGIONS AND THEOLOGY*

100 200   SW
STUDIA PHILOSOPHIAE RELIGIONIS. (Text in English) 1975. irreg., no.15, 1989. price varies. Alqvist & Wiksell International, P.O. Box 638, S-101 28 Stockholm, Sweden. Eds. Hans Hof, Hampus Lyttkens.

100   SZ
STUDIA PHILOSOPHICA. (Text in French and German) 1981. irreg., vol.49, 1990. price varies. Paul Haupt AG, Falkenplatz 14, CH-3001 Berne, Switzerland. TEL 031-232425. Eds. Dr Helmut Holzhey, Dr. Jean-Pierre Leyvraz.

100 500   GW   ISSN 0179-3896
STUDIA SPINOZANA; an international & interdisciplinary series. (Each issue has distinctive title and theme) 1985. a. DM.48($24.80) Verlag Koenigshausen und Neumann, Postfach 6007, 8700 Wuerzburg, Germany. TEL 049-93176401. FAX 0931-83620. (Dist. in U.S. by: Dr. Douglas J. Den Uyl, Bellarmine College, Newburg Rd., Louisville, KY 40205) Ed.Bd. adv.; bk.rev.; circ. 1,000.
Description: Articles on all aspects of Spinoza's philosophy, including its cultural and intellectual background and influence.

100   RM   ISSN 0578-5480
B8.R8
STUDIA UNIVERSITATIS "BABES-BOLYAI". PHILOSOPHIA. (Text in English, French, German, Rumanian) 1958. s-a. exchange basis. Universitatea "Babes-Bolyai", Biblioteca Centrala Universitara, Str. Clinicilor 2, Cluj-Napoca, Rumania. bk.rev.; cum.index: 1956-1963, 1964-1970.
Incorporates (in 1975): Studia Universitatis Babes-Bolyai. Psychologia-Pedagogia (ISSN 0578-5502); Studia Universitatis Babes-Bolyai. Sociologia.

100 NE
STUDIEN ZUR ANTIKEN PHILOSOPHIE. 1971. irreg. price varies. John Benjamins Publishing Co., Amsteldijk 44, P.O. Box 75577, 1070 AN Amsterdam, Netherlands. TEL 020-6738156. FAX 020-6739773. (In N. America: 821 Bethlehem Pike, Philadelphia, PA 19118. TEL 215-836-1200) (back issues avail.)
— **Description:** Monographs in classical philology confined to the interpretation of ancient philosophical texts contributing to interdisciplinary discussion between philologists and philosophers.

100 GW ISSN 0340-5958
STUDIEN ZUR FRANZOESISCHEN PHILOSOPHIE DES ZWANZIGSTEN JAHRHUNDERTS. irreg., vol.12, 1986. price varies. Bouvier Verlag Herbert Grundmann, Am Hof 32, Postfach 1268, 5300 Bonn 1, Germany. Eds. V.V. Berning, H.R. Schlette.

100 NE ISSN 0167-4102
STUDIEN ZUR OESTERREICHISCHEN PHILOSOPHIE. (Text in English and German) 1979. irreg. price varies. Editions Rodopi B.V., Keizersgracht 302-304, 1016 EX Amsterdam, Netherlands. TEL 020-6227507. FAX 020-6380948. (US and Canada subscr. to: 233 Peachtree St. N.E., Ste. 404, Atlanta GA 30303-1504. TEL 800-225-3998) Ed. Rudolf Haller.

109 GW
STUDIEN ZUR PHILOSOPHIE DES 18. JAHRHUNDERTS. 1976. irreg. price varies. Verlag Peter Lang GmbH, Eschborner Landstr. 42-50, 6000 Frankfurt a.M. 90, Germany. TEL 069-7807050. FAX 069-785893.

189 940 NE ISSN 0169-9857
STUDIEN ZUR PROBLEMGESCHICHTE DER ANTIKEN UND MITTELALTERLICHEN PHILOSOPHIE. 1966. irreg., vol. 12, 1989. price varies. E.J. Brill, P.O. Box 9000, 2300 PA Leiden, Netherlands. TEL 017-312624. FAX 071-317532. TELEX 39296 BRILL NL. (In N. America: E.J. Brill, 24 Hudson St., Kinderhook, NY 12106. TEL 800-962-4406)

100 US
STUDIES IN ASIAN THOUGHT AND RELIGION. 1983. irreg., latest no.15. $39.95 per no. Edwin Mellen Press, 240 Portage Rd., Box 450, Lewiston, NY 14092. TEL 716-754-8566. FAX 716-754-4335.

170 266 UK ISSN 0953-9468
STUDIES IN CHRISTIAN ETHICS. 1988. 2/yr. £17.50($34.95) T & T Clark, 59 George St., Edinburgh EH2 2LQ, Scotland. TEL 031-225-4703. FAX 031-220-4260. TELEX 728134. Ed. Rev. R. Franklin. adv.; bk.rev.; circ. 500.
—BLDSC shelfmark: 8489.904000.
— **Description:** Each issue examines an important theme in contemporary Christian ethics with contributions from major moral theologians.

100 US ISSN 0893-6919
STUDIES IN CONTEMPORARY CONTINENTAL PHILOSOPHY. irreg. Peter Lang Publishing, Inc., 62 W. 45th St., 4th Fl., New York, NY 10036. TEL 212-302-6740. FAX 212-302-7574. Ed. Galen A. Johnson.
— **Description:** Provides a forum for English-language authors of monographs in contemporary continental philosophy.

108 US
STUDIES IN CONTEMPORARY GERMAN SOCIAL THOUGHT. irreg. (3-4/yr.). M I T Press, Book Division, 55 Hayward St., Cambridge, MA 02142. TEL 617-253-5242. Ed. Thomas McCarthy.

STUDIES IN HISTORY AND PHILOSOPHY OF SCIENCE. see *SCIENCES: COMPREHENSIVE WORKS*

STUDIES IN LANGUAGE. see *LINGUISTICS*

STUDIES IN LINGUISTICS AND PHILOSOPHY. see *PSYCHOLOGY*

STUDIES IN MARXISM. see *POLITICAL SCIENCE*

100 200 US ISSN 0899-4897
STUDIES IN MORAL PHILOSOPHY. irreg. Peter Lang Publishing, Inc., 62 W. 45th St., 4th Fl., New York, NY 10036. TEL 212-302-6740. FAX 212-302-7574. Ed. John Kekes.
—BLDSC shelfmark: 8491.126000.
— **Description:** Focuses on the nature of good lives, character and its development, virtues and vices.

100 US
STUDIES IN MORAL, POLITICAL, AND LEGAL PHILOSOPHY. irreg. price varies. Princeton University Press, 3175 Princeton Pike, Lawrenceville, NJ 08648. TEL 609-896-1344. FAX 609-895-1081. Ed. Marshall Cohen.

810 US
STUDIES IN NEW ENGLAND THOUGHT AND LITERATURE. irreg., latest no.2. $39.95 per no. Edwin Mellen Press, 240 Portage Rd., Box 450, Lewiston, NY 14092. TEL 716-754-8566. FAX 754-4335.

100 SW ISSN 1100-4290
STUDIES IN PHILOSOPHY. (Text in English, Swedish) 1989. irreg. price varies. Lund University Press, P.O. Box 141, S-221 00 Lund. TEL 46-31-20-00. FAX 46-46-30-53-38. Eds. B. Hansson, G. Hermeren.

STUDIES IN PHILOSOPHY AND EDUCATION. see *EDUCATION*

100 US ISSN 0585-6965
B21
STUDIES IN PHILOSOPHY & THE HISTORY OF PHILOSOPHY. 1961. irreg., vol.23, 1991. price varies. Catholic University of America Press, 620 Michigan Ave., N.E., Washington, DC 20064. TEL 202-319-5052. Ed. Jude P. Dougherty. (reprint service avail. from UMI) **Indexed:** Phil.Ind.
—BLDSC shelfmark: 8491.220400.

STUDIES IN SOVIET THOUGHT. see *POLITICAL SCIENCE*

100 900 US
STUDIES IN THE HISTORY OF PHILOSOPHY. vol.5, 1987. irreg., latest no.25. $39.95 per no. Edwin Mellen Press, 240 Portage Rd., Box 450, Lewiston, NY 14092. TEL 716-754-8566. FAX 716-754-4335.

STUDIES IN THE PSYCHOANALYTIC WRITINGS OF ERNEST BECKER. see *PSYCHOLOGY*

181 954 294 NE
STUDIES OF CLASSICAL INDIA. 1978. irreg. price varies. Kluwer Academic Publishers, Spuiboulevard 50, P.O. Box 17, 3300 AA Dordrecht, Netherlands. TEL 078-334911. FAX 078-334254. TELEX 29245. (Dist. by: Kluwer Academic Publishers Group, P.O. Box 322, 3300 AH Dordrecht; U.S. address: P.O. Box 358, Accord Station, Hingham, MA 02018-0358) Eds. B.K. Matilal, J.M. Masson.

100 AA ISSN 0563-5780
PG9501
STUDIME FILOLOGJIKE/ETUDES PHILOLOGIQUES. (Text in Albanian; summaries in French) vol.33, 1979. q. $24. Academies des Sciences de la RPSA, Instituti i Gjuhesise dhe i Letersise, Tirana, Albania. **Indexed:** Hist.Abstr., M.L.A.

294.54 II
SUDHI SAHITYA. (Text in Bengali and English) 1977. m. Rs.66 (foreign Rs.120). Adarsha Prakashani, Ma-Mahajnana Bishwa Kalyan Trust, Kharagpur 721 305, India. TEL 03222-661. circ. 17,000.

100 US ISSN 0562-6048
BP500
SUNRISE; Theosophic perspectives. 1951. bi-m. $9 (foreign $12). (Theosophical Society) Theosophical University Press, P.O. Bin C, Pasadena, CA 91109-7107. TEL 818-798-3378. FAX 818-798-4749. Ed. Grace F. Knoche. bk.rev.; illus. (back issues avail.)
— **Description:** Published articles on scientific, religious, and philosophic themes in the light of ancient and modern theosophy. Includes interviews and reports on significant trends.

SUPPORTIVE LIFESTYLES NEWS. see *NEW AGE PUBLICATIONS*

100 FR
SURFACES (PARIS, 1978). 1978. irreg. Editions Jean-Michel Place, 12 rue Pierre et Marie Curie, 75005 Paris, France. Dir. Peter Hoy.

SUZHOU DAXUE XUEBAO (ZHEXUE SHEHUI KEXUE BAN)/SUZHOU UNIVERSITY. JOURNAL (SOCIAL SCIENCE EDITION). see *SOCIAL SCIENCES: COMPREHENSIVE WORKS*

180 IT
SYMBOLON; studi e testi di filosofia antica e medievale. 1984. irreg., no.7, 1989. price varies. L'Erma di Bretschneider, Via Cassiodoro 19, 00193 Rome, Italy. TEL 06-687-41-27. FAX 06-687-41-29. Ed. Francesco Romano.

100 500 NE ISSN 0039-7857
AP1 CODEN: SYNTAE
SYNTHESE; an international journal for epistemology, methodology and philosophy of science. 1936. m. $600. Kluwer Academic Publishers, Postbus 17, 3300 AA Dordrecht, Netherlands. TEL 078-334911. FAX 078-334254. TELEX 29245. (Dist. by: Kluwer Academic Publishers Group, P.O. Box 322, 3300 AH Dordrecht, Netherlands; N. America dist. addr.: Box 358, Accord Station, Hingham, MA 02018-0358. TEL 617-871-6600) Ed. Jaakko Hintikka. adv.; bk.rev. (reprint service avail. from SWZ) **Indexed:** A.B.C.Pol.Sci., Arts & Hum.Cit.Ind., Curr.Cont., Ind.Bk.Rev.Hum., Lang.& Lang.Behav.Abstr., Math.R., Phil.Ind., SSCI.
—BLDSC shelfmark: 8586.750000.

109 160 NE ISSN 0082-111X
SYNTHESE HISTORICAL LIBRARY; texts and studies in the history of logic and philosophy. 1969. irreg. price varies. Kluwer Academic Publishers, Spuiboulevard 50, P.O. Box 17, 3300 AA Dordrecht, Netherlands. TEL 078-334911. FAX 078-334254. TELEX 29245. (Dist. by: Kluwer Academic Publishers Group, P.O. Box 322, 3300 AH Dordrecht, Netherlands; U.S. address: P.O. Box 358, Accord Station, Hingham, MA 02018-0358) Ed.Bd. **Indexed:** Math.R.

109 NE ISSN 0082-1128
SYNTHESE LIBRARY; monographs on epistemology, logic, methodology, philosophy of science and of knowledge, and the mathematical methods of social and behavioral sciences. 1959. irreg. price varies. Kluwer Academic Publishers, Spuiboulevard 50, P.O. Box 17, 3300 AA Dordrecht, Netherlands. TEL 078-334911. FAX 078-334254. TELEX 29245. (Dist. by: Kluwer Academic Publishers Group, P.O. Box 322, 3300 AH Dordrecht; U.S. address: P.O. Box 358, Accord Station, Hingham, MA 02018-0358) Ed. J. Hintikka. **Indexed:** Math.R.

100 US ISSN 0271-2482
T A T JOURNAL. 1977. a. T A T Foundation, Box 236, Bellaire, OH 43906. Ed. Louis Khourey. adv.; bk.rev.; illus. (back issues avail.)

TABONA; revista de prehistoria y de arqueologia y filologia clasicas. see *ARCHAEOLOGY*

TAKING SIDES: CLASHING VIEWS ON CONTROVERSIAL BIOETHICAL ISSUES. see *MEDICAL SCIENCES*

TAKING SIDES: CLASHING VIEWS ON CONTROVERSIAL ISSUES IN BUSINESS ETHICS AND SOCIETY. see *BUSINESS AND ECONOMICS*

100 US ISSN 0275-7656
BD232
TANNER LECTURES ON HUMAN VALUES. 1980. a. price varies. University of Utah Press, Salt Lake City, UT 84112. TEL 801-581-6771. Ed. Grethe B. Peterson.
—BLDSC shelfmark: 8602.573000.

TAROT NETWORK NEWS. see *NEW AGE PUBLICATIONS*

107 US ISSN 0145-5788
B52
TEACHING PHILOSOPHY. 1975. q. $22.50 to individuals; institutions $55. Bowling Green State University, Philosophy Documentation Center, Bowling Green, OH 43403-0189. TEL 419-372-2419. FAX 419-372-6987. Ed. Arnold Wilson. adv.; bk.rev.; film rev.; circ. 1,150. (back issues avail.) **Indexed:** Cont.Pg.Educ., Media Rev.Dig., Phil.Ind., RILA.
—BLDSC shelfmark: 8614.298000.

TEILHARD REVIEW AND JOURNAL OF COSMIC CONVERGENCE. see *RELIGIONS AND THEOLOGY*

TEL QUEL; litterature-philosophie-science-politique. see *SCIENCES: COMPREHENSIVE WORKS*

PHILOSOPHY

100 800   US
TELICOM. 1979. 10/yr. $27. International Society for Philosophical Enquiry, 5409 Pipers Gap Dr., Memphis, TN 38134-6417. (Subscr. to: c/o Robert J. Skinner 5409 Pipers Gap Dr., Memphis, TN 38134-6417) Ed. Robert J. Skinner. adv.; bk.rev.; circ. 480. (back issues avail.)
    Description: Expository writing by those in the 99.9 percentile of high intelligence. Restricted to authors who are members.

100   US   ISSN 0090-6514
H1
TELOS; a quarterly journal of critical thoughts. 1968. q. $28 to individuals; institutions $70. Telos Press Ltd., 431 E. 12th St., New York, NY 10009. TEL 212-228-6479. FAX 212-228-6379. Ed. Paul Piccone. adv.; bk.rev.; circ. 4,500. (also avail. in microform from UMI; back issues avail.; reprint service avail. from UMI) **Indexed:** Alt.Press Ind., Amer.Bibl.Slavic & E.Eur.Stud., HR Rep., Lang.& Lang.Behav.Abstr., Left Ind. (1982-), Mid.East: Abstr.& Ind., Phil.Ind., Sociol.Abstr.
    —BLDSC shelfmark: 8789.350000.

TEME. see SOCIOLOGY

101   SP   ISSN 0210-1602
B5
TEOREMA. 1971. q. 600($10) Universidad de Valencia, Departamento de Logica y Filosofia de Ciencic, Facultad de Filosofia y Ciencias de la Educacion, Apdo. No. 61159, 28080 Madrid, Spain. Ed.Bd. adv.; bk.rev.; bibl.; charts. **Indexed:** Math.R., Phil.Ind.

100   IT
TEORIA; rivista di filosofia. (Text in English and Italian) 1981. s-a. $15. Editrice Tecnico-Scientifica, Piazza Torricelli, 4, 56100 Pisa, Italy. Eds. Vittorio Sainati, Renzo Raggiunti. adv.; bk.rev.; circ. 1,000.

100   YU   ISSN 0351-2274
B6
TEORJA. 1957. q. $12 to individuals; institutions $18. Srpsko Filozofsko Drustvo - Philosophical Society of Serbia, Cika Ljubina 18-20, 11000 Belgrade, Serbia, Yugoslavia. TEL 11-638-104. Ed. Milorad Stupar. bk.rev.; circ. 1,750. **Indexed:** Lang.& Lang.Behav.Abstr.
    Formerly (until 1975): Filozofija (ISSN 0015-1866)
    Description: Publishes articles in all general areas of philosophy.

TEXAS TECH UNIVERSITY. GRADUATE STUDIES. see HUMANITIES: COMPREHENSIVE WORKS

THEMATA. see EDUCATION

THEOLOGIA 21. see RELIGIONS AND THEOLOGY

THEOLOGIE UND PHILOSOPHIE. see RELIGIONS AND THEOLOGY

THEORETICAL MEDICINE; an international journal for the philosophy and methodology of medical research and practice. see MEDICAL SCIENCES

100   SW   ISSN 0040-5825
B1   CODEN: THRAA5
THEORIA; a Swedish journal of philosophy. (Text in English) 1935. 3/yr. $25. Theoria, Kungshuset i Lundagaard, S-223 50 Lund, Sweden. Ed.Bd. bk.rev.; bibl. **Indexed:** Curr.Cont., Math.R., Psychol.Abstr., SSCI.
    —BLDSC shelfmark: 8814.584500.

THEORY AND DECISION; an international journal for methods and models in the social and decision sciences. see SOCIAL SCIENCES: COMPREHENSIVE WORKS

THEORY AND DECISION LIBRARY; an international series in the philosophy and methodology of the social and behavioral sciences. see SOCIAL SCIENCES: COMPREHENSIVE WORKS

212.5   NE   ISSN 0040-5868
THEOSOFIA; brotherhood, problems of society, religion and occult research. 1897. bi-m. fl.30. Theosofische Vereniging in Nederland, Tolstraat 154, NL 1074 VM Amsterdam, Netherlands. TEL 020-6765672. Ed. W.H. van Vledder. adv.; bk.rev.; index; circ. 1,200.

212.5   NE
THEOSOFISCH FORUM. 1951. m. (11/yr.). fl.17.50. Theosofische Stichting H. P. Blavatsky - H. P. Blavatsky Theosophical Society, Hortensiastr. 20, Capelle a-d IJssel, Netherlands. Ed. H.A. Kruytbosch. bk.rev.; circ. 300.
    Former titles (until 1979): Levende Gedachten (ISSN 0047-4444); Theosofisch Forum.

212.5   UK   ISSN 0040-5876
THEOSOPHICAL JOURNAL. 1960. bi-m. £4 to non-members. Theosophical Society in England, 50 Gloucester Place, London W1H 3HJ, England. adv.; bk.rev.; circ. 2,000.

212.5   II   ISSN 0040-5884
BP500
THEOSOPHICAL MOVEMENT; a magazine devoted to the living of the higher life. (Text in English) 1930. m. Rs.30($12) Theosophy Company (India) Private Ltd., 40 New Marine Lines, Bombay 400 020, India. index.

212.5   II   ISSN 0040-5892
THEOSOPHIST. 1879. m. Rs.40($10) (Theosophical Society) Theosophical Publishing House, Adyar, Madras 600 020, India. (US subscr. to: Theosophical Publishing House, P.O. Box 270. Wheaton, IL 60188) Ed. Radha Burnier. adv.; bk.rev.; s-a. index; circ. 2,500.

212.5 100   US   ISSN 0040-5906
THEOSOPHY; devoted to the theosophical movement and the brotherhood of humanity, the study of occult science and philosophy and Aryan literature. 1912. m. $10. Theosophy Co., 245 W. 33rd St., Los Angeles, CA 90007. TEL 212-535-2230. (And: 347 E. 72nd St., New York, NY 10021) Ed.Bd. bk.rev.; index; circ. 800.

100   US   ISSN 0190-3330
B105.C45
THINKING; the journal of philosophy for children. 1979. q. $22.50 to individuals; institutions $35 (effective Jan. 1991). Institute for the Advancement of Philosophy for Children, Montclair College, Upper Montclair, NJ 07043. TEL 201-893-4277. FAX 201-893-5455. Ed. Matthew Lipman. bk.rev.; charts; illus.; index; circ. 1,000. (back issues avail.) **Indexed:** ERIC, Phil.Ind.

THOMIST; a speculative quarterly review of theology and philosophy. see RELIGIONS AND THEOLOGY — Roman Catholic

THOUGHT; a review of culture and ideas. see RELIGIONS AND THEOLOGY — Roman Catholic

100   US
THOUGHTLINE. 1954. 12/yr. $20. Arcana Workshops, Box 506, Manhanttan Beach, CA 90266-0506. TEL 213-379-9990. Ed. Tom Carney. circ. 3,000.

THOUGHTS FOR ALL SEASONS; the magazine of epigrams. see LITERATURE

110   US
THRESHOLDS. 1975. 4/yr. $20. School of Metaphysics, National Headquarters, HCR 1, Box 15, Windyville, MO 65783. TEL 417-345-8411. Ed. Barbara O'Guinn. adv.; illus.; circ. 1,000. **Indexed:** Avery Ind.Archit.Per.
    Description: Reports on personal development and strategies for spiritual and material success, with interviews and features on business, health, the arts, historical subjects, and more.

100   BE   ISSN 0040-750X
TIJDSCHRIFT VOOR FILOSOFIE. (Supplement: International Philosophical Bibliography) (Text in Dutch, English, French, German) 1939. q. $100. Tijdschrift voor Filosofie V.Z.W., Kardinaal Mercierplein 2, B-3000 Leuven, Belgium. Ed. H. De Dijn. bk.rev.; bibl.; index, cum.index every 25 yrs.; circ. 1,300. **Indexed:** Arts & Hum.Cit.Ind., Curr.Cont., Lang.& Lang.Behav.Abstr., Phil.Ind., SSCI.

105   US
TOPICS IN PHILOSOPHY. 1975. irreg. price varies. University of California Press, 2120 Berkeley Way, Berkeley, CA 94720. TEL 415-642-4247. FAX 415-643-7127.
    Refereed Serial

TOPOI; an international review of philosophy. see PSYCHOLOGY

TRADITION (NEW YORK); a journal of Orthodox Jewish thought. see RELIGIONS AND THEOLOGY — Judaic

100   BL   ISSN 0101-3173
B5   CODEN: TFACDH
TRANS - FORM - ACAO; revista de filosofia. (Text in Portuguese; summaries in English and Portuguese) 1974-1975; resumed 1980. a. $30 or exchange basis. Universidade Estadual Paulista, Av. Vicente Ferreira 1278, Caixa Postal 603, 17500 Marilia SP, Brazil. TEL 0144-33-1844. FAX 0144-22-2504. TELEX 111 9016 UJME BR. bk.rev.; charts; circ. 1,000. (back issues avail.) **Indexed:** Phil.Ind.
    —BLDSC shelfmark: 8884.657000.
    Description: Interdisciplinary approach to the study of philosophy.

TRANSFORMERS NOTEBOOK. see DRUG ABUSE AND ALCOHOLISM

100 284   US
TRINITY REVIEW. 1979. bi-m. free. Trinity Foundation, Box 700, Jefferson, MD 21755. TEL 301-371-7155. Ed. John W. Robbins. bk.rev.; circ. 2,000 (controlled). (back issues avail.)
    Description: Essays in philosophy and theology.

100   US
TRUTH IN ACTION. q. Seicho-No-Ie Truth of Life Movement, 14527 S. Vermont Ave., Gardena, CA 90247. TEL 213-323-8486.

TRUTH JOURNAL. see NEW AGE PUBLICATIONS

100   US
TRUTH OF LIFE. 12/yr. $11. Seicho-No-Ie Truth of Life Movement, 14527 S. Vermont Ave., Gardena, CA 90247. TEL 313-371-2494. Ed. Masayo Tsuruta. illus.

100   US   ISSN 0041-3712
BL2700
TRUTH SEEKER. 1873. q. $20. Truth Seeker Co., Inc., Box 2832, San Diego, CA 92112. Ed. James W. Prescott. adv.; bk.rev.; circ. 10,000.
    Description: Philosophical freethought on free speech and the separation of church and state.

U.I.A.M.S. INFORMATIONS. (International Union for Moral and Social Action) see POLITICAL SCIENCE

100   CN   ISSN 0315-3002
U R A M NEWSLETTER. 1972. biennial. free to members. International Society for the Study of Human Ideas on Ultimate Reality and Meaning, Regis College, 15 St. Mary St., Toronto, Ont. M4Y 2R5, Canada. TEL 416-922-2476. FAX 416-922-2898. Ed. Tibor Horvath. (back issues avail.)
    Description: Disseminates information to members and the general public concerning the activities of the International Society for URAM.

100 200   CN   ISSN 0709-549X
BD331
ULTIMATE REALITY AND MEANING; interdisciplinary studies in the philosophy of understanding. 1978. q. Can.$30 to individuals; institutions Can.$48. University of Toronto Press, Journals Department, P.O. Box 1280, 1011 Sheppard Ave. W., Downsview, Ont. M3H 5V4, Canada. TEL 416-667-7781. FAX 416-667-7832. (U.S. Address: 340 Nagel Dr., Cheektowaga, NY 14225) Ed. Tibor Horvath. bibl.; circ. 500. **Indexed:** Amer.Bibl.Slavic & E.Eur.Stud., Arts & Hum.Cit.Ind., G.Soc.Sci.& Rel.Per.Lit., Lang.& Lang.Behav.Abstr., Phil.Ind., Rel.& Theol.Abstr. (1981-), Rel.Ind.One.
    —BLDSC shelfmark: 9082.780500.
    Supersedes: Institute for Encyclopedia of Human Ideas on Ultimate Reality and Meaning. Newsletter.

UNARIUS LIGHT MAGAZINE. see NEW AGE PUBLICATIONS

100   II   ISSN 0041-8218
UNIVERSALIST. 1968. irreg. (2-4/yr.). Rs.15.($2) (World Jnana Sadhak Society) Jnana Sadhak Publishing House, Babupara-Mishralodge, Jalpaiguri 735101, West Bengal, India. Eds. Rajkishore Mollenhauer, B. Mollenhauer. bk.rev.

UNIVERSIDAD COMPLUTENSE DE MADRID. REVISTA. see LITERATURE

PHILOSOPHY 3785

100   CK   ISSN 0120-1492
UNIVERSIDAD DE CALDAS. FACULTAD DE FILOSOFIA. REVISTA. (Text in Spanish; summaries in English) 1980. q. Col.$400($6) Universidad de Caldas, Facultad de Filosofia, Apdo. 275, Manizales, Caldas, Colombia. Ed. Luis E. Garcia. circ. 1,000.

100   SP   ISSN 0008-7750
B5
UNIVERSIDAD DE GRANADA. CATEDRA FRANCISCO SUAREZ. ANALES. 1961. a. 2500 ptas. Universidad de Granada, Dpto. de Filosofia del Derecho, Servicio de Publicaciones, Antiguo Colegio Maximo, Campus de Cartuja, 18071 Granada, Spain. TEL 281356. Dir. Nicolas M. Lopez Calera. circ. 1,000.

100   UY
UNIVERSIDAD DE LA REPUBLICA. FACULTAD DE HUMANIDADES Y CIENCIAS. REVISTA. SERIE FILOSOFIA. irreg. exchange basis. Universidad de la Republica, Facultad de Humanidades y Ciencias, Seccion Revista, Tristan Narvaja 1674, Montevideo, Uruguay. Dir. Beatriz Martinez Osorio.
     Supersedes in part: Universidad de la Republica. Facultad de Humanidades y Ciencias. Revista.

110   SP   ISSN 0580-8650
BD115
UNIVERSIDAD DE MADRID. SEMINARIO DE METAFISICA. ANALES. 1966. a. 1000 ptas. Universidad Complutense de Madrid, Departamento de Filosofia I, Metafisica y Teoria del Conocimiento, Servicio de Publicaciones, Madrid, Spain. TEL 91-499-6500. Ed. Sergio Rabade Romeo. adv.; bk.rev.; bibl.; circ. 500. **Indexed:** Phil.Ind.

100   SP   ISSN 0213-2958
UNIVERSIDAD DE MURCIA. ANALES DE FILOLOGIA FRANCESA. 1985. irreg. $600. Universidad de Murcia, Secretario de Publicaciones e Intercambio Cientifico, Santo Cristo, 1, 30001 Murcia, Spain. TEL 968 24 92 00.

100   SP   ISSN 0213-4365
UNIVERSIDAD DE MURCIA. ANALES DE FILOLOGIA HISPANICA. 1985. a. 2000 ptas. Universidad de Murcia, Secretariado de Publicaciones e Intercambio Cientifico, Santo Cristo, 1, 30001 Murcia, Spain. TEL 968-239450.

100   SP   ISSN 0212-9698
UNIVERSIDAD DE MURCIA. ANALES DE FILOSOFIA. 1955. a. 1500 ptas. Universidad de Murcia, Secretariado de Publicaciones e Intercambio Cientifico, Santo Cristo, 1, 30001 Murcia, Spain. TEL 968-239450. Ed. D. Jesus Padilla Galvez. circ. 300. (back issues avail.)
     Supersedes in part (in 1983): Universidad de Murcia. Filosofia y Letras. Anales (ISSN 0463-9863)

910   SP   ISSN 0213-5485
UNIVERSIDAD DE MURCIA. CUADERNOS DE FILOLOGIA INGLESA. 1955. a. $500. Universidad de Murcia, Secretariado de Publicaciones e Intercambio Cientifico, Santos Cristo, 1, 30001 Murcia, Spain. TEL 968-239450.
     Supersedes in part (in 1985): Universidad de Murcia. Filosofia y Letras. Anales (ISSN 0463-9863)

100 001.3   SP
UNIVERSIDAD DE SEVILLA. SERIE: FILOSOFIA Y LETRAS. 1967. irreg., latest no.121. price varies. Universidad de Sevilla, Servicio de Publicaciones, San Fernando, 4, 41004 Seville, Spain. TEL 954-22-8071. FAX 954-22-1315. **Indexed:** Amer.Hist.& Life, Biol.Abstr., Hist.Abstr.
     Former titles: Universidad Hispalensa. Anales. Serie: Filosofia y Letras (ISSN 0210-7678); (until 1969): Universidad Hispalense. Anales. Series: Filosofia y Letras, Derecho, Medicina, Ciencias y Veterinaria (ISSN 0041-8552)

100 460   MX   ISSN 0185-2558
UNIVERSIDAD NACIONAL AUTONOMA DE MEXICO. INSTITUTO DE INVESTIGACIONES FILOSOFICAS. CUADERNOS. 1959. irreg., no.50, 1989. Universidad Nacional Autonoma de Mexico, Instituto de Investigaciones Filosoficas, Apdo. Postal 70-447, Mexico, D.F., Mexico. (Dist. by: Direccion General de Fomento Editorial, Porto Alegre No. 260, San Andres Tetepilco, 09440 Mexico, D.F., Mexico) circ. 2,000.

UNIVERSIDAD PONTIFICIA COMILLAS DE MADRID. PUBLICACIONES. SERIE 1: ESTUDIOS. see *RELIGIONS AND THEOLOGY*

100   IT   ISSN 0390-0614
UNIVERSITA DEGLI STUDI DI LECCE. BOLLETTINO DI STORIA DELLA FILOSOFIA. 1973. a. free. Universita degli Studi di Lecce, Facolta di Lettere e Filosofia, Via V.M. Stampacchia, 73100 Lecce, Italy. TEL (0832) 406709. FAX 0832-4061. Ed. Giovanni Papuli.
     Description: Covers the history of philosophy. Includes lessons, seminars, reports, group studies, documents and news.

UNIVERSITA DEGLI STUDI DI PADOVA. FACOLTA DI LETTERE E FILOSOFIA. OPUSCOLI ACCADEMICI. see *LITERATURE*

UNIVERSITA DEGLI STUDI DI PADOVA. FACOLTA DI LETTERE E FILOSOFIA. PUBBLICAZIONI. see *LITERATURE*

100   IT   ISSN 0078-7779
UNIVERSITA DEGLI STUDI DI PADOVA. SCUOLA DI PERFEZIONAMENTO IN FILOSOFIA. PUBBLICAZIONI. 1963. irreg. L.1000.($1.60) Casa Editrice Dott. Antonio Milani, Via Jappelli 5, 35100 Padua, Italy.

UNIVERSITA DEGLI STUDI DI SIENA. FACOLTA DI LETTERE E FILOSOFIA. ANNALI. see *LITERATURE*

100   IT   ISSN 0394-5073
UNIVERSITA DI FIRENZE. DIPARTIMENTO DI FILOSOFIA. ANNALI. 1979. a. price varies. Casa Editrice Leo S. Olschki, Casella Postale 66, 50100 Florence, Italy. TEL 055-6530684. FAX 055-6530214. Ed. A. Zanardo. circ. 1,000. (back issues avail.)
     Formerly (until 1984): Universita degli Studi di Firenze. Istituto di Filosofia. Annali.

UNIVERSITA DI MESSINA. FACOLTA DI MAGISTERO. NUOVI ANNALI. see *HUMANITIES: COMPREHENSIVE WORKS*

UNIVERSITA DI NAPOLI. FACOLTA DI LETTERE E FILOSOFIA. ANNALI. see *HISTORY*

100   IT
▼**UNIVERSITA DI SIENA. DIPARTIMENTO DI FILOSOFIA. PUBBLICAZIONI.** 1991. irreg. price varies. Casa Editrice Leo S. Olschki, Casella Postale 66, 50100 Florence, Italy. TEL 055-6530684. FAX 055-6530214.

100   RM   ISSN 0379-7856
AS345.A1
UNIVERSITATEA "AL. I. CUZA" DIN IASI. ANALELE STIINTIFICE. SECTIUNEA 3B: FILOZOFIE. (Text in English, French, Rumanian) s-a. 35 lei. Universitatea "Al. I. Cuza" din Iasi, Calea M. Eminescu 11, Jassy, Rumania. (Subscr. to: ILEXIM, Str. 13 Decembrie Nr. 3, P.O. Box 136-137, Bucharest, Rumania) Ed. Petru Ioan. circ. 550.
     Formerly: Universitatea "Al. I. Cuza" din Iasi. Analele Stiintifice. Sectiunea 3b: Stiinte Filozofice (ISSN 0075-353X)
     Description: Works on philosophy, history of philosophy, logic and epistemology, sociology, ethics and pedagogy.

100 940 340   RM
UNIVERSITATEA BUCURESTI. ANALELE. FILOZOFIE. ISTORIE. DREPT. a. $10. Universitatea Bucuresti, Bd. Gh. Gheorghiu-Dej Nr. G4, Bucharest, Rumania.

100   BE   ISSN 0076-1273
UNIVERSITE CATHOLIQUE DE LOUVAIN. INSTITUT SUPERIEUR DE PHILOSOPHIE. COURS PUBLIES. 1964. irreg. price varies. 1 Chemin d'Aristote, B-1348 Louvain-La-Neuve, Belgium. TEL 016-48-81-02. FAX 016-48-14-86. (Subscr. to: Peeters Press, B.P. 41, B-3000 Louvain, Belgium)

084   FR
UNIVERSITE DE BESANCON. CENTRE DE DOCUMENTATION ET DE BIBLIOGRAPHIE PHILOSOPHIQUES. TRAVAUX. 1973. irreg. (Universite de Besancon, Centre de Documentation et de Bibliographie Philosophiques) Societe d'Edition Les Belles Lettres, 95, Boulevard Raspail, 75006 Paris, France. illus.

100   FR   ISSN 0771-4963
UNIVERSITE LIBRE DE BRUXELLES. INSTITUT DE PHILOSOPHIE. ANNALES. 1969. a. price varies. (Institut de Philosophie) Librairie Philosophique J. Vrin, 6 place de la Sorbonne, 75005 Paris, France. FAX 43-54-48-18. bk.rev.; bibl.; circ. 1,000.

UNIVERSITY OF KANSAS. CENTER FOR EAST ASIAN STUDIES. INTERNATIONAL STUDIES: EAST ASIAN SERIES. REFERENCE SERIES. see *HISTORY — History Of Asia*

UNIVERSITY OF KANSAS. CENTER FOR EAST ASIAN STUDIES. INTERNATIONAL STUDIES: EAST ASIAN SERIES. RESEARCH SERIES. see *HISTORY — History Of Asia*

180   II   ISSN 0076-2253
UNIVERSITY OF MADRAS. PHILOSOPHICAL SERIES.* irreg. University of Madras, Chepauk, Triplicane, Madras 600005, Tamil Nadu, India.

UNIVERSITY OF NOTRE DAME. STUDIES IN THE PHILOSOPHY OF RELIGION. see *RELIGIONS AND THEOLOGY*

105   SL
UNIVERSITY OF SIERRA LEONE. FOURAH BAY COLLEGE. PHILOSOPHICAL SOCIETY. JOURNAL. 1977. a. University of Sierra Leone, Fourah Bay College, Philosophical Society, Freetown, Sierra Leone.

501 500   NE
UNIVERSITY OF WESTERN ONTARIO SERIES IN PHILOSOPHY OF SCIENCE. Variant title: Western Ontario Series. 1972. irreg., latest 1991. price varies. Kluwer Academic Publishers, 3300 AA Dordrecht, Netherlands. TEL 078-334911. FAX 078-334254. TELEX 29245. (Dist. by: Kluwer Academic Publishers Group, P.O. Box 322, 3300 AH Dordrecht, Netherlands; N. America dist. addr.: Box 358, Accord Station, Hingham, MA 02018-0358. TEL 617-871-6600) Ed. R.E. Butts.

UNIVERZITA KOMENSKEHO. FILOZOFICKA FAKULTA. ZBORNIK: GRAECOLATINA ET ORIENTALIA. see *CLASSICAL STUDIES*

100   CS   ISSN 0083-4181
B26
UNIVERZITA KOMENSKEHO. FILOZOFICKA FAKULTA. ZBORNIK: PHILOSOPHICA. (Text in Czech or Slovak; summaries in German and Russian) 1960. a. exchange basis. Univerzita Komenskeho, Filozoficka Fakulta, c/o Ustredna Kniznica Filozofickej Fakulty, Gondova 2, 818 01 Bratislava, Czechoslovakia. Ed. M. Zigo. circ. 700.
     Incorporates: Univerzita Komeskeho. Ustav Marxismu-Leninizmu. Zbornik: Marxistiska Filozofia.

100 301   PL   ISSN 0072-0453
UNIWERSYTET GDANSKI. WYDZIAL HUMANISTYCZNY. ZESZYTY NAUKOWE. FILOZOFIA I SOCJOLOGIA. (Text in Polish; summaries in English and Russian) 1974. irreg. price varies. Uniwersytet Gdanski, Wydzial Humanistyczny, c/o Biblioteka Glowna, Ul. Armii Krajowej 110, 81-824 Sopot, Poland. TEL 51-0061. TELEX 051-2247 BMOR PL. (Dist. by: Ars Polona-Ruch, Krakowskie Przedmiescie 7, Warsaw, Poland)
     Description: Covers the history of philosophy, methodology, and philosophical anthropology. Examines the theory of knowledge, historical and dialectical materialism, and the philosophical and anxiological problems of natural science.

100   PL   ISSN 0208-5437*
H8
UNIWERSYTET SLASKI W KATOWICACH. PRACE NAUKOWE. PRACE Z NAUK SPOLECZNYCH. FOLIA PHILOSOPHICA. (Text in Polish; summaries in English and Russian) 1975. irreg. price varies. Wydawnictwo Uniwersytetu Slaskiego, Ul. Bankowa 14, 40-007 Katowice, Poland. TEL 59-69-15. FAX 48-32-599-605. TELEX 315594 USKTL. (Dist. by: CHZ Ars Polona, P.O. Box 1001, 00-950 Warsaw, Poland)
     Description: Studies on philosophy.

110   US
UPPER TRIAD. 1974. 6/yr. free. Upper Triad Association, Inc., Box 1370, Manassas, VA 22110. Ed. Peter Lunn. bk.rev.; circ. 2,000.

UTOPIA 2; commune co-operation as a global dynamic. see *NEW AGE PUBLICATIONS*

VAJRA BODHI SEA. see *RELIGIONS AND THEOLOGY — Buddhist*

PHILOSOPHY

181   II   ISSN 0042-2983
VEDANTA KESARI. (Text in English) 1914. m. Rs.30($20) (effective 1991). Sri Ramakrishna Math, 16 Ramakrishna Math Rd., Mylapore, Madras 600 004, India. Ed. Swami Smarananda. adv.; bk.rev.; charts; illus.; stat.; index, cum.index; circ. 3,500.
Description: Exposition of Vedanta philosophy.

100 200   II   ISSN 0377-6360
VEDIC LIGHT. (Text in English) vol.8, 1974. m. Rs.35 (effective 1990). International Aryan League - Sarvadishik Arya Pratinidhi Sabha, Dayanand Bhavan 3-5, Asaf Sli Road, New Delhi 110 002, India. TEL 3274771. Ed. S.C. Pathak. adv.; bk.rev.; circ. 1,000.

500 974   US   ISSN 0893-4851
K26
VERA LEX; historical & philosophical study of natural law and right. 1980. s-a. $10 to individuals; institutions $25. Pace University, Buchsbaum House, Pleasantville, NY 10570. TEL 914-773-3309. FAX 914-773-3541. (Co-sponsor: Natural Law Society) Ed. Virginia Black. adv.; bk.rev.; bibl.; illus.; cum.index; circ. 425. (back issues avail.)
Description: Attempts to strengthen the current revived interest in the discussion of natural law and advance its historical research.
Refereed Serial

100 200   SP   ISSN 0042-3718
BX3601
VERDAD Y VIDA; revista de las ciencias del espiritu. 1943. q. 2775 ptas.($50) Franciscanos Espanoles, Joaquin Costa 36, 28002 Madrid, Spain. adv.; bk.rev.; bibl.; index; circ. 550. **Indexed:** CERDIC, M.L.A.
—BLDSC shelfmark: 9155.827000.

100   IT   ISSN 0391-4186
B4
VERIFICHE; rivista trimestrale di scienze umane. 1972. q. L.30000. (Associazione Trentina di Scienze Umane) Verifiche, Casella Postale 269, 38100 Trento, Italy. Ed. Mario Rigoni. adv.; bk.rev.; bibl.; circ. 500. (back issues avail.) **Indexed:** Arts & Hum.Cit.Ind., Hist.Abstr.
Description: Focuses on literary philosophy.

100   II   ISSN 0505-7523
VISHVA JYOTI. (Text in Hindi) 1952. m. Rs.30. Vishveshvaranand Vedic Research Institute, P.O. Sadhu Ashram, Hoshiarpur 146021, Punjab, India. Ed. Veda Prakasha.
Description: Covers Hindu philosophy and Indian culture.

VISIONS (AGOURA HILLS). see *PARAPSYCHOLOGY AND OCCULTISM*

100   II   ISSN 0042-7187
VISVA - BHARATI JOURNAL OF PHILOSOPHY. (Text in Bengali, English) 1964. s-a. Rs.25($8) Visva-Bharati, Department of Philosophy and Religion, P.O. Santiniketan, Dist. Birbhum, Pin 731 235, India. TELEX 203201 RABI IN. Ed. Prof. Sushanta Sen. bk.rev.; circ. 300. **Indexed:** Ind.Per.Lit.

180   II
VITAL FORCE;* journal of T'ai Chi Chih. 1984. 6/yr. $20. Satori Resources, Inc., 108 Pasadena Ave., Oxnard, CA 93035-4576. TEL 805-687-8737. Ed. Corinn Codye. circ. 400. (back issues avail.)
Description: For students and teachers of T'ai Chi Chih. Covers T'ai Chi Chih, spiritual development, and meditation.

VIVARIUM; an international journal for the philosophy and intellectual life of the Middle Ages and Renaissance. see *HISTORY*

VLAAMSE GIDS. see *LITERARY AND POLITICAL REVIEWS*

100   RU   ISSN 0042-8744
VOPROSY FILOSOFII. (Text in Russian; summaries in English) 1947. m. 39.60 Rub. (Akademiya Nauk S.S.S.R., Institut Filosofii) Izdatel'stvo Pravda, Ul. Pravdy, 24, Moscow 125047, Russia. (Dist. by: Mezhdunarodnaya Kniga, Moscow, G-200, Russia) Ed. I.T. Frolov. adv.; bk.rev.; bibl.; index; circ. 37,000. (also avail. in microform from MIM)
Indexed: Arts & Hum.Cit.Ind., Biol.Abstr., Curr.Cont., Curr.Dig.Sov.Press, Hist.Abstr., Lang.& Lang.Behav.Abstr., Math.R., Psychol.Abstr.
—BLDSC shelfmark: 0045.130000.

WANDERER. see *RELIGIONS AND THEOLOGY*

100   AU   ISSN 0083-999X
B31
WIENER JAHRBUCH FUER PHILOSOPHIE. 1968. a. price varies. Universitaets Verlagsbuchhandlung GmbH, Servitengasse 5, A-1092 Vienna, Austria. TEL 0222-348124. FAX 0222-310-2805. Ed. Erich Heintel. bk.rev.; index; circ. 500.

181.4 954   AU   ISSN 0084-0084
DS2
WIENER ZEITSCHRIFT FUER DIE KUNDE SUEDASIENS UND ARCHIV FUER INDISCHE PHILOSPHIE. 1957. a. S.490. (Oesterreichische Akademie der Wissenschaften, Kommission fuer Sprachen und Kulturen Suedasiens) Verlag der Oesterreichischen Akademie der Wissenschaften, Dr. Ignatz-Seipel-Platz 2, A-1010 Vienna, Austria. FAX 0222-5139541. (Co-sponsor: Universitaet Wien. Indologisches Institut) Ed. G. Oberhammer. **Indexed:** Numis.Lit.
Former titles (until 1969): Wiener Zeitschrift fuer die Kunde Sued- und Ostasiens & Archiv fuer Indische Philosophie.

100 300 500   NE   ISSN 0043-5414
WIJSGERIG PERSPECTIEF OP MAATSCHAPPIJ EN WETENSCHAP/PHILOSOPHICAL PERSPECTIVES ON SOCIETY AND SCIENCE. 1960. bi-m. fl.54 (foreign fl.65)(effective 1992). Uitgeverij Boom, P.O. Box 1058, 7940 KB Meppel, Netherlands. TEL 05220-66111. FAX 05220-66198. Ed.Bd. adv.; bk.rev.; circ. 1,900.

100   NE   ISSN 0084-0106
WIJSGERIGE TEKSTEN EN STUDIES/PHILOSOPHICAL TEXTS AND STUDIES. 1956. irreg., no.23, 1975. price varies. (Rijksuniversiteit te Utrecht - University of Utrecht) Van Gorcum en Co. B.V., P.O. Box 43, 9400 AA Assen, Netherlands. TEL 05920-46864. FAX 05920-72064. (Dist. by: Londwood Publishing Group Inc., 27 S. Main Street, Wolfeboro, N.H. 03894) Eds. C.J. de Vogel, K. Kuypers.

100   GW   ISSN 0175-6486
WISSENSCHAFT UND GEGENWART. GEISTESWISSENSCHAFTLICHE REIHE. irreg., no.66, 1990. price varies. Vittorio Klostermann, Frauenlobstr. 22, Postfach 900601, 6000 Frankfurt a.M. 90, Germany. TEL 069-774011. FAX 069-708038.

574   US
WOODBRIDGE LECTURES, COLUMBIA UNIVERSITY. no.4, 1972. irreg. Columbia University Press, 562 W. 113th St., New York, NY 10025. TEL 212-678-6777.

181 891   II   ISSN 0084-1242
WOOLNER INDOLOGICAL SERIES. (Text in English, Hindi and Sanskrit) 1960. irreg., vol.21, 1976. price varies. Vishveshvaranand Vedic Research Institute, P. O. Sadhu Ashram, Hoshiarpur 146021, Punjab, India. Ed. S. Bhaskaran Nair.

100   US   ISSN 0260-4027
B1   CODEN: WOFUDM
WORLD FUTURES; the journal of general evolution. 1962. 12/yr. (in 3 vols., 4 nos./vol.). $113. Gordon and Breach Science Publishers, 270 Eighth Ave., New York, NY 10011. TEL 212-206-8900. FAX 212-645-2459. TELEX 236735 GOPUB UR. (Subscr. to: Box 786, Cooper Sta., New York, NY 10276. TEL 800-545-8398; UK subscr. to: P.O. Box 90, Reading, Berkshire RG1 8JL, England. TEL 0734-560-080) Ed. Ervin Laszlo. adv.; bk.rev.; bibl.; illus.; index. (also avail. in microform from MIM) **Indexed:** Curr.Cont., Fut.Surv., Hum.Ind., Lang.& Lang.Behav.Abstr., SSCI.
—BLDSC shelfmark: 9356.025750.
Formerly: Philosophy Forum (ISSN 0031-823X)
Refereed Serial

WORLD ORDER; a Baha'i magazine. see *RELIGIONS AND THEOLOGY — Other Denominations And Sects*

WORLD TRIBUNE. see *RELIGIONS AND THEOLOGY — Buddhist*

100   II
WORLD'S WISDOM SERIES. (Text in English) 1976. irreg. Oriental Publishers and Distributors, 1488, Pataudi House, Darya Ganj, New Delhi 110002, India.

709   PL   ISSN 0208-497X
WYDZIAL FILOLOGICZNO-FILOZOFICZNY. PRACE. (Text in Polish; summaries in English, French, German) 1948. irreg., vol.33, no.2, 1991. price varies. Towarzystwo Naukowe w Toruniu, Ul. Wysoka 16, 87-100 Torun, Poland. TEL 48-56-23941. TELEX 552388 FSBH PL. Ed. Marian Szarmach. circ. 300.

100   PL
WYZSZA SZKOLA PEDAGOGICZNA IM. KOMISJI EDUKACJI NARODOWEJ W KRAKOWIE. ROCZNIK NAUKOWO-DYDAKTYCZNY. PRACE FILOZOFICZNE. 1972. irreg., no.5, 1990. price varies. Wydawnictwo Naukowe W S P, Ul. Karmelicka 41, 31-128 Krakow, Poland. TEL 33-78-20. (Co-sponsor: Ministerstwo Edukacji Narodowej)

100   PL   ISSN 0867-3594
WYZSZA SZKOLA PEDAGOGICZNA IM. KOMISJI EDUKACJI NARODOWEJ W KRAKOWIE. ROCZNIK NAUKOWO-DYDAKTYCZNY. PRACE FIZYCZNE. 1972. irreg., no.5, 1990. price varies. Wydawnictwo Naukowe W S P, Ul. Karmelicka 41, 31-128 Krakow, Poland. TEL 33-78-20. (Co-sponsor: Ministerstwo Edukacji Narodowej)

181.45 294.54   DK   ISSN 0044-0485
YOGA; tidsskrift for universel religion. English edition: Yoga; magazine for the universal religion (ISSN 0107-7414) 1958. 3/yr. DKK 80($10) Narayanananda Universal Yoga Trust, Gylling, DK-8300 Odder, Denmark. FAX 86-551788. Ed. Swami Sagunananda. adv.; bk.rev.; index; circ. 1,000.

181.45 294.54   II   ISSN 0970-1737
YOGA AND TOTAL HEALTH. (Text in English and Sanskrit) 1933. m. Rs.60($25) Yoga Institute, Prabhat Colony, Santa Cruz East, Bombay 400 055, India. TEL 22-6122185. Ed. Jayadeva Yogendra. adv.; bk.rev.; abstr.; bibl.; charts; illus.; circ. 15,000. (back issues avail.)
Formerly: Yoga Institute. Journal (ISSN 0044-0493)

YOGA INTERNATIONAL. see *NEW AGE PUBLICATIONS*

181.45 613.7   CN
YOGA LIFE. 1961. irreg. donations. Sivananda Yoga Vedanta Centre, Headquarters, Sivananda Ashram Yoga Camp, 8th Ave., Val Morin, Que. J0T 2R0, Canada. FAX 819-322-5876. Ed. Swami Vishnu Devananda. bk.rev.; illus.; circ. 40,000.
Former titles: International Sivananda Yoga Life and Yoga Vacations (ISSN 0708-076X); International Yoga Life and Yoga Vacations (ISSN 0381-9043)

181.45 294.54   II   ISSN 0044-0507
YOGA - MIMAMSA; quarterly journal devoted to scientific-philosophico-literary research in yoga. (Text in English and Sanskrit; summaries in English) 1924. q. Rs.200. Kaivalyadhama Institution, Lonavla 410 403, District Poona, Maharashtra, India. TEL 2339. Ed. M.V. Bole. adv.; bk.rev.; charts; illus.; stat.; circ. 1,500.

YOKOHAMA KOKURITSU DAIGAKU JINBUN KIYO DAI-1-RUI, TETSUGAKU, SHAKAI KAGAKU/YOKOHAMA NATIONAL UNIVERSITY. HUMANITIES, SECTION 1: PHILOSOPHY AND SOCIAL SCIENCES. see *SOCIAL SCIENCES: COMPREHENSIVE WORKS*

100   GW   ISSN 0044-2186
N9
ZEITSCHRIFT FUER AESTHETIK UND ALLGEMEINE KUNSTWISSENSCHAFT. (Text in English, French and German) 1906. s-a. DM.65. Bouvier Verlag Herbert Grundmann, Am Hof 32, Postfach 1268, 5300 Bonn 1, Germany. Ed.Bd. bk.rev.; circ. 600. (also avail. in microfiche from BHP) **Indexed:** Artbibl.Mod., Curr.Cont., RILA.
Formerly: Jahrbuch fuer Aesthetik.

100 371.3   GW
ZEITSCHRIFT FUER DIDAKTIK DER PHILOSOPHIE. 1979. q. DM.49. Schroedel Schulbuchverlag GmbH, Postfach 810555, Hildesheimer Str. 202-206, 3000 Hannover 81, Germany. TEL 0511-8388-0. TELEX 9-23527-HSVHAD. (Subscr. to: Oeding Druck GmbH, Wilhelmstr. 1, 3300 Braunschweig, Germany) circ. 1,800.

PHILOSOPHY — ABSTRACTING, BIBLIOGRAPHIES, STATISTICS

100   AU   ISSN 0044-2763
ZEITSCHRIFT FUER GANZHEITSFORSCHUNG. 1957. q. S.200($19) Gesellschaft fuer Ganzheitsforschung, Augasse 2-6, A-1090 Vienna, Austria. TEL 0222-313364524. FAX 0222-31336727. Ed. Hanns Pichler. adv.; bk.rev.; charts; illus.; index; circ. 500.
—BLDSC shelfmark: 9462.230000.

ZEITSCHRIFT FUER KATHOLISCHE THEOLOGIE. see *RELIGIONS AND THEOLOGY — Roman Catholic*

100   GW   ISSN 0044-3301
B3
ZEITSCHRIFT FUER PHILOSOPHISCHE FORSCHUNG. 1947. 4/yr. DM.164. Verlag Anton Hain GmbH, Savignystr. 53, 6000 Frankfurt a.M.1, Germany. Eds. H.M. Baumgartner, O. Hoeffe. adv.; bk.rev.; bibl.; cum.index every 10 yrs.; circ. 1,200. **Indexed:** Arts & Hum.Cit.Ind., Curr.Cont., Ind.Bk.Rev.Hum., Phil.Ind.
—BLDSC shelfmark: 9480.500000.

101   GW   ISSN 0514-2733
ZEITSCHRIFT FUER PHILOSOPHISCHE FORSCHUNG. BEIHEFTE. 1950. irreg., no.43, 1984. price varies. Verlag Anton Hain GmbH, Savignystr. 53, 6000 Frankfurt a.M. 1, Germany. Eds. H.M. Baumgartner, O. Hoeffe.

149.946   GW   ISSN 0170-6241
P99   CODEN: ZESEE3
ZEITSCHRIFT FUER SEMIOTIK. 1979. q. DM.96. Stauffenburg Verlag, Postfach 2567, 7400 Tuebingen 1, Germany. TEL 07071-78091. FAX 07071-75288. Ed. Roland Posner. adv.; bk.rev. **Indexed:** Arts & Hum.Cit.Ind., Curr.Cont.

294.392   US
ZEN BOW NEWSLETTER. 1967. fortn. $8. Zen Center (Rochester), 7 Arnold Park, Rochester, NY 14607. TEL 716-473-9180. Ed. Dwain Wilder. circ. 1,500. (processed) **Indexed:** New Per.Ind.
Supersedes (1967-1979): Zen Bow (ISSN 0044-3956)
Description: Written by Zen Center members on Zen practice and current events at the center and its affiliates.

100   CC
ZHEXUE DONGTAI. (Text in Chinese) m. Zhongguo Shehui Kexueyuan, Zhexue Yanjiusuo - Chinese Academy of Social Sciences, Institute of Philosophy, No.5, Jianguomennei Dajie, Beijing 1000732, People's Republic of China. TEL 5137954. Ed. Ren Junming.

100   CC
ZHEXUE LUNCONG. (Text in Chinese) bi-m. Zhongguo Shehui Kexueyuan, Zhexue Yanjiusuo - Chinese Academy of Social Sciences, Institute of Philosophy, No.5, Jianguomennei Dajie, Beijing 1000732, People's Republic of China. TEL 5137954. Ed. Li Shubai.

100   CC
ZHEXUE YANJIU/PHILOSOPHY STUDIES. (Text in Chinese, table of contents in English) bi-m. Y12($33.80) China Academy of Social Sciences, Philosophy Research Institute, 5 Jianguo Mennei Dajie, Beijing 100732, People's Republic of China. TEL 513-7954. (Dist. outside China by: China International Book Trade Corp., P.O. Box 399, Beijing, P.R.C.; Dist. in US by: China Books & Periodicals, Inc., 2929 24th St., San Francisco, CA 94110. TEL 415-282-2994) Ed. Chen Junquan.

100   CC   ISSN 1001-2710
ZHEXUE YUANLI. (Subseries of: Fuyin Baokan Ziliao) (Text in Chinese) m. Y58.80. Zhongguo Renmin Daxue, Shubao Ziliao Zhongxin - China People's University, Book & Newspaper Information Center, P.O. Box 1122, Beijing 100007, People's Republic of China. TEL 441792. index.
Description: Reprints papers and articles on philosophical principles.

ZHONGGUO QINGNIAN/CHINESE YOUTH. see *CHILDREN AND YOUTH — For*

100 299.51   CC
ZHONGGUO ZHEXUESHI YANJIU. (Text in Chinese; table of contents in English) s-a. Y4.60($13.20) (Zhongguo Zhexueshi Xuehui) Shehui Kexue Zazhishe, A-158 Gulou Xidajie, Beijing 100720, People's Republic of China. (Dist. in US by: China Books & Periodicals, Inc., 2929 24th St., San Francisco, CA 94110. TEL 415-282-2994)
Description: Publishes research on the history of Chinese philosophy.

ZNAK. see *RELIGIONS AND THEOLOGY*

ZUR DEBATTE. see *RELIGIONS AND THEOLOGY — Roman Catholic*

057.8   PL   ISSN 0044-5584
BX806.P6
ZYCIE I MYSL/LIFE AND THOUGHT. (Text in Polish; summaries in French) 1950. m. 150 Zl.($8.10) Instytut Wydawniczy "Pax", Ul. Chocimska 8-10, 00-791 Warsaw, Poland. (Dist. by: Ars Polona-Ruch, Krakowskie Przedmiescie 7, Warsaw, Poland) Ed. Anna Borowska. bk.rev.; bibl.; film rev.; charts; illus.; index; circ. 8,000. **Indexed:** CERDIC, Hist.Abstr., New Test.Abstr.

PHILOSOPHY — Abstracting, Bibliographies, Statistics

ABSTRACTS OF BULGARIAN SCIENTIFIC LITERATURE. PHILOSOPHY, SOCIOLOGY, SCIENCE OF SCIENCES, PSYCHOLOGY AND PEDAGOGICS. see *EDUCATION — Abstracting, Bibliographies, Statistics*

100 200 016   SP   ISSN 0211-4143
ACTUALIDAD BIBLIOGRAFICA DE FILOSOFIA Y TEOLOGIA; selecciones de libros. 1964. s-a. 2500 ptas.($25) Instituto de Teologia Fundamental, Facultad de Teologia de Catalunya, Llaseres 30, Sant Cugat del Valles, Barcelona, Spain. TEL 93-301-23-50. (Subscr. to: Selecciones de Teologia, Roger de Lluria 13, 08010 Barcelona, Spain) Ed. Josep Boada. adv.; bk.rev.; abstr.; bibl.; index; circ. 700. **Indexed:** Amer.Hist.& Life, CERDIC, Hist.Abstr.
Formerly: Selecciones de Libros (ISSN 0037-1181)

100 016   VC   ISSN 0084-7836
BIBLIOGRAPHIA INTERNATIONALIS SPIRITUALITATIS. (Text in various languages; summaries in Latin) 1966. a. L.100000 (effective 1992). Pontificio Istituto di Spiritualita' Edizioni del Teresianum, Piazza S. Pancrazio 5-A, 00152 Rome, Italy. circ. 650.

100 016   FR   ISSN 0006-1352
Z7127
BIBLIOGRAPHIE DE LA PHILOSOPHIE/BIBLIOGRAPHY OF PHILOSOPHY. (Text in English, French, German, Italian) 1937. q. 570 F.($114) (International Institute of Philosophy) Librairie Philosophique J. Vrin, 6 Place de la Sorbonne, 75005 Paris, France. TEL 1-43-54-03-47. FAX 1-43-54-48-18. adv.; bk.rev.; bibl.; index; circ. 1,100.
—BLDSC shelfmark: 2006.500000.

100   US   ISSN 0742-6887
BIBLIOGRAPHIES AND INDEXES IN PHILOSOPHY. 1985. irreg. price varies. Greenwood Press, Inc. (Subsidiary of: Greenwood Publishing Group Inc.), 88 Post Rd. W., Box 5007, Westport, CT 06881-5007. TEL 203-226-3571. FAX 203-222-1502.

300 016   IT   ISSN 0006-6621
BOLLETTINO BIBLIOGRAFICO PER LE SCIENZE MORALI E SOCIALE.* (Supplement to de Homme) 1968. q. L.2500($5) Universita degli Studi di Roma, Istituto di Filosofia, Rome, Italy. Ed. G.G. Sansoni. adv.; bibl.

300 100 016   FR   ISSN 0007-554X
Z7127
BULLETIN SIGNALETIQUE. PART 519: PHILOSOPHIE. 1947. q. 435 F. Centre National de la Recherche Scientifique, Institut del'Information Scientifique et Technique, 54 bd. Raspail, 75270 Paris Cedex 06, France. FAX 45-48-70-15. TELEX MSH 203 104 F. cum.index.
●Also available online. Vendor(s): Telesystemes - Questel.

100   SP   ISSN 1130-9105
INDICE ESPANOL DE HUMANIDADES. SERIES D: PHILOSOPHY. 1979. a. 5000 ptas. or exchange basis. Instituto de Informacion y Documentacion en Ciencias Sociales y Humanidades, Pinar 25, 3, 28006 Madrid, Spain.
●Also available online.
Also available on CD-ROM.
Formerly: Indice Espanol de Ciencias Sociales. Series F: Philosophy; Which superseded in part (in 1982): Indice Espanol de Ciencias Sociales (ISSN 0213-019X)

100   NE
INTERNATIONAL BIBLIOGRAPHY OF AUSTRIAN PHILOSOPHY/INTERNATIONALE BIBLIOGRAPHIE ZUER OESTERREICHISCHEN PHILOSOPHIE. (Text in English, German) 1986. a. price varies. Editions Rodopi B.V., Keizersgracht 302-304, 1016 EX Amsterdam, Netherlands. TEL 020-6227507. FAX 020-6380948. (US and Canada subscr. to: 233 Peachtree St., N.E., Ste. 404, Atlanta, GA 30303-1504. TEL 800-225-3998) index.
Description: Covers philosophy, psychology, and the history of science. Includes information on libraries and other institutions of information and documentation.

100 301 011   RU   ISSN 0134-2851
NOVAYA INOSTRANNAYA LITERATURA PO OBSHCHESTVENNYM NAUKAM. FILOSOFIYA I SOTSIOLOGIYA; bibliograficheskii ukazatel' 1947. m. 7.20 Rub. Akademiya Nauk S.S.S.R., Institut Nauchnoi Informatsii po Obshchestvennym Naukam, Ul. Krasikova 28-21, 117418 Moscow V-418, Russia. Ed. A.G. Korsh.

100 011   RU   ISSN 0134-2789
NOVAYA SOVETSKAYA LITERATURA PO OBSHCHESTVENNYM NAUKAM. FILOSOFSKIE NAUKI; bibliograficheskii ukazatel' 1946. m. 7.20 Rub. Akademiya Nauk S.S.S.R., Institut Nauchnoi Informatsii po Obshchestvennym Naukam, Ul. Krasikova 28-21, 117418 Moscow V-418, Russia. Ed. E.I. Serebryanaya.
—BLDSC shelfmark: 0391.331000.

215   RU   ISSN 0202-2052
OBSHCHESTVENNYE NAUKI V S.S.S.R. FILOSOFSKIE NAUKI; referativnyi zhurnal. 1973. bi-m. 4.20 Rub. Akademiya Nauk S.S.S.R., Institut Nauchnoi Informatsii po Obshchestvennym Naukam, Ul. Krasikova 28-21, 117418 Moscow V-418, Russia. Ed. A.I. Panchenko.

100 301   RU
Z7127
OBSHCHESTVENNYE NAUKI ZA RUBEZHOM. FILOSOFIYA; referativnyi zhurnal. 1972. bi-m. 4.20 Rub. Akademiya Nauk S.S.S.R., Institut Nauchnoi Informatsii po Obshchestvennym Naukam, Ul. Krasikova 28-21, 117418 Moscow V-418, Russia. Ed. A.I. Rakitov.
Supersedes in part: Obshchestvennye Nauki za Rubezhom. Filosofiya i Sotsiologiya (ISSN 0132-7356)

100 016   US   ISSN 0031-7993
Z7127   CODEN: PHIXA
PHILOSOPHER'S INDEX; an international index to philosophical periodicals and books. (Text in English, French, German, Italian, Spanish and Portuguese) 1967. q. $42 to individuals; institutions $149. Bowling Green State University, Philosophy Documentation Center, Bowling Green, OH 43403-0189. TEL 419-372-2419. FAX 419-372-6987. Ed. Richard H. Lineback. adv.; bk.rev.; index, cum.index; circ. 1,150.
●Also available online. Vendor(s): DIALOG (File no.57).
Also available on CD-ROM.
—BLDSC shelfmark: 6461.480000.

3788 PHOTOGRAPHY

100 016   BE   ISSN 0034-4567
REPERTOIRE BIBLIOGRAPHIQUE DE LA PHILOSOPHIE/INTERNATIONAL PHILOSOPHICAL BIBLIOGRAPHY/BIBLIOGRAFISCH REPERTORIUM VAN DE WIJSBEGEERTE. (Supplement to: Revue Philosophique de Louvain) (Text in language of authors; introductions in Dutch, English, French, German, Italian, Spanish) 1949. q. 1750 Fr. Universite Catholique de Louvain, Institut Superieur de Philosophie, 1 Chemin d'Aristote, B-1348 Louvain-La-Neuve, Belgium. TEL 016-488102. FAX 016-481486. TELEX 65981 PUL B. (Subscr. to: Editions Peeters s.p.r.l., Bondgenotenlaan 153, B-3000, Leuven, Belgium. TEL 016-235170) (Co-sponsor: Institut International de Philosophie) Eds. Claude Troisfontaines, Urbain Dhondt. bk.rev.; bibl.; index; circ. 1,800. **Indexed:** Phil.Ind.
    Description: International bibliography on works, articles and reviews of philosophy.

100   FR   ISSN 0080-4789
RUDOLF STEINER PUBLICATIONS. 1963. irreg. Librairie Fischbacher, 33 Rue de Seine, 75006 Paris, France. TEL 43-26-87-84.

PHOTOGRAPHY

see also Motion Pictures

A D A MAGAZINE. (Art, Design, Architecture) see *ARCHITECTURE*

770   UK
A.F.A.E.P. AWARDS. 1984. a. £21. (Association of Photographers) Reed Information Services Ltd. (Subsidiary of: Reed International PLC), Windsor Court, E. Grinstead House, E. Grinstead, W. Sussex RH19 1XA, England. TEL 0342-326972. FAX 0342-327100. TELEX 95127 INFSER G. Ed. Valerie Lawton. adv. (back issues avail.)
    Description: Shows award winning photographers from the members of the association.

770   IT   ISSN 1120-205X
A F T; rivista di storia e fotografia. 1985. 2/yr. L.20000 (effective 1992). Archivio Fotografico Toscano, Via Ricasoli, 7, 50047 Prato, Italy. TEL 0574-452011. FAX 0574-20129. (Subscr. to: Opuslibri, Via della Torretta, No. 16, 50137 Florence, Italy. TEL 055-660833) bk.rev.; circ. 1,500.
    Description: Covers research about photography, the study of history of photography, and the preservation, restoration, and cataloguing of photographs.

778.1   SA   ISSN 0001-1932
A M NEWS - SOUTHERN AFRICA. (Text in Afrikaans & English) 1962. q. free. Addressograph-Multigraph (Pty.) Ltd., Box 282, Johannesburg 2000, South Africa. Ed. M. Power. adv.; illus.; stat.; circ. 24,000.

770   US
A P A MAGAZINE. 1989. m. free. Advertising Photographers of America, 27 W. 20th St., Rm. 601, New York, NY 10011. TEL 212-807-0399. FAX 212-727-8120. Ed. Don Heymann. adv.; circ. 7,500 (controlled). (also avail. in microfilm from KTO)
    Description: Addresses the business and aesthetic concerns of the professional photographer.

770 070.49   DK   ISSN 0109-4440
AARETS PRESSEFOTO. a. DKK 10. Pressefotografforbundet, Gammel Strand 46, 1202 Copenhagen K, Denmark.

ACOUSTICAL IMAGING. see *PHYSICS — Sound*

770   UK
▼**ACTUALITIES.** 1988. a. $17. 152 Narrow St., London E14 8BP, England.

ADVANCED IMAGING. see *COMMUNICATIONS — Computer Applications*

AERIAL ARCHAEOLOGY. see *ARCHAEOLOGY*

770   US   ISSN 0300-7472
TR640
AFTERIMAGE. 1972. m. (10/yr.). $30 to individuals (foreign $35); institutions $40 (foreign $45). Visual Studies Workshop, 31 Prince St., Rochester, NY 14607. TEL 716-442-8676. Eds. Grant H. Kester, Nadine L. McGann. bk.rev.; film rev.; illus.; index; circ. 5,000. (tabloid format; also avail. in microform from UMI; reprint service avail. from UMI) **Indexed:** Artbibl.Mod., Bk.Rev.Ind. (1984-), Child.Bk.Rev.Ind. (1984-), Film Lit.Ind. (1974-), Intl.Ind.TV, RILA.
—BLDSC shelfmark: 0735.632000.
    Description: Presents independent critical commentary on issues in media arts, including scholarly research, in-depth reviews, investigative journalism, and interviews.

AILERON; a literary journal. see *LITERATURE — Poetry*

ALLTAG; die Sensationen des Gewoehnlichen. see *LITERATURE*

770   IT
ALMANACCO DI FOTOGRAFARE. 1968. q. L.30000. Cesco Ciapanna Editore S.p.A., Via Lipari 8, 00141 Rome, Italy. Ed. Cesco Ciapanna. adv.; circ. 75,000.

770   UK   ISSN 0002-6840
AMATEUR PHOTOGRAPHER. 1884. w. I P C Magazines Ltd., Kings Reach Tower, Stamford St., London SE1 9LS, England. TEL 071-261-5849. FAX 071-261-7851. (Subscr. to: Quadrant Subscription Services, Oakfield House, Perrymount Rd., Haywards Heath, W. Sussex RH16 3DH, England) Ed. Keith Wilson. adv.; bk.rev.; illus.; s-a. index; circ. 73,704. (also avail. in microform from UMI) **Indexed:** Chem.Abstr.
    Description: Covers photo technique, equipment reviews, news and features.

770   GW
AMATEURFOTOGRAFIE. bi-m. DM.33 (foreign DM.40). Verlag fuer Technik und Handwerk, Fremersbergstr. 1, 7570 Baden - Baden, Germany. TEL 07221-2107-0. FAX 07221-2107-52.

AMERICAN CINEMATOGRAPHER; international journal of motion picture production techniques. see *MOTION PICTURES*

770   US   ISSN 1046-8986
TR1
AMERICAN PHOTO. 1978. bi-m. $19.90. Hachette Magazines, Inc., 1633 Broadway, 45th Fl., New York, NY 10009. TEL 212-767-6000. (Subscr. to: Box 52616, Boulder, CO 80322) Ed. David Schonauer. adv.; bk.rev.; circ. 261,245. **Indexed:** Access (1980-), Artbibl.Mod., Mag.Ind., P.M.I., PMR.
—BLDSC shelfmark: 0850.597000.
    Formerly (until 1990): American Photographer (ISSN 0161-6854)

770   US
AMERICAN PHOTOGRAPHERS;* an illustrated who's who among leading contemporary Americans. 1988. irreg. $39.95. American References Publishing Corp., 2210 N. Burling St., Chicago, IL 60614-3712. Ed. Les Krantz. illus.
    Description: Presents profiles of more than 1000 American photographers. Contains phone numbers, specialties, shooting situations and career overviews. Includes a list of stock photography houses, an alphabetical index with cross-references by subject and situation, and several hundred photographs.

770   US   ISSN 0361-9168
TR820
AMERICAN SOCIETY OF MAGAZINE PHOTOGRAPHERS. BULLETIN. 1944. m. membership only. American Society of Magazine Photographers, 419 Park Ave., S., Ste. 1407, New York, NY 10016. TEL 212-889-9144. adv.; bk.rev.; circ. 10,000.

ANHUI HUABAO/ANHUI PICTORIAL. see *GENERAL INTEREST PERIODICALS — China*

770   II
ANNUAL OF INDIAN PHOTOGRAPHY. 1978. a. Rs.12. Sooriya Publishing House, 52 Thaiyappa Mudali St, V.O.C. Nagar, Madras 600001, India.

770   IT
ANNUARIO FOTOGRAFICO. 1978. s-a. L.9000 per no. Editrice Progresso s.r.l., Viale Piceno 14, 20129 Milan, Italy. TEL 02-715939. FAX 02-713030. Ed. G.R. Namias. adv.; circ. 30,000.

770   BL
ANUARIO BRASILEIRO DE OTICA CINE FOTO SOM. 1971. a. Alpha Empresa de Divulgacao e Cultura Ltda., P. Don Gastao Liberal Pinto 27, CEP 04534 Sao Paulo SP, Brazil. TEL 881-1402. Ed. Sergio Salles. circ. 260,000.

770   US   ISSN 0003-6420
TR1
APERTURE. 1952. q. $40 (effective Feb. 1991). Aperture Foundation, Inc., 20 E. 23rd St., New York, NY 10010. TEL 212-505-5555. FAX 212-979-7759. TELEX 857718. Ed. Melissa Harris. adv.; bk.rev.; bibl.; illus.; cum.index: vols.1-6, 1958; circ. 17,000. (also avail. in microfilm from UMI; reprint service avail. from UMI) **Indexed:** Art Ind., Artbibl.Mod., Arts & Hum.Cit.Ind., Curr.Cont.
—BLDSC shelfmark: 1567.880000.
    Description: Devoted to photography as art, contains illustrated profiles of photographers or thematic material.

779   US   ISSN 0735-5572
TR640
ARCHIVE (TUCSON). 1976. 2/yr.? $25. University of Arizona, Center for Creative Photography, Tucson, AZ 85721. TEL 602-621-7968. FAX 602-621-9444. circ. 1,100. **Indexed:** Artbibl.Mod.
    Formerly (until 1981): Center for Creative Photography.
    Description: Presents materials from the collection of photographs, negatives and manuscripts in the center's archives.

771   GW   ISSN 0932-3333
ART BUYER'S HANDBOOK; Fotografen Journal. 1988. a. DM.120. Verlag Design und Technik GmbH, Schultheiss-Str. 27, 8000 Munich 71, Germany. TEL 089-7917045. FAX 089-7918883. circ. 12,000.
    Description: Directed to art directors and art buyers; showcases work from professional photographers.

ART CALENDAR. see *ART*

770   FR
ART ET IMAGE. 1949. q. 250 F. Musee Francais de la Photographie, 78 rue de Paris, 91570 Bievres, France. (Co-sponsor: Photo-Club du Val de Bievre) Ed. Andre Fage. adv.; bk.rev.; circ. 750.

ART NEW ZEALAND. see *ART*

ARTIBUS ET HISTORIAE; international journal for visual arts. see *ART*

770   JA   ISSN 0044-9148
ASAHI CAMERA. (Text in Japanese) 1926. m. $158.50. Asahi Shimbunsha - Asahi Shimbun Publishing Co., 3-2, Tsukiji 5-chome, Chuo-ku, Tokyo 104-11, Japan. (Subscr. to: Japan Publications Trading Co., Ltd., Box 5030, Tokyo International, Tokyo, Japan) Ed. Masami Fujisawa. adv.; bk.rev.; circ. 200,000. **Indexed:** JTA.

770   AT
AUSTRALIA CAMERA CRAFT PHOTOGRAPHER'S HANDBOOK. 1981. a. Aus.$7.95. Horwitz Grahame Pty. Ltd., 506 Miller St., Cammeray, N.S.W. 2062, Australia. TEL 02-929-6144. FAX 02-957-1814. Ed. Peter Eastway.

770   AT   ISSN 0158-2658
AUSTRALIAN CAMERA CRAFT. 1979. m. Aus.$42 (foreign Aus.$55). Horwitz Grahame Pty. Ltd., 506 Miller St., Cammeray, N.S.W. 2062, Australia. TEL 02-929-6144. FAX 02-957-1814. (Subscr. to: P.O. Box 306, Cammeray, N.S.W. 2062, Australia) Ed. Peter Eastway. circ. 16,000. (back issues avail.)
    Description: Popular magazine for photography enthusiasts.

770   AT   ISSN 0004-9964
AUSTRALIAN PHOTOGRAPHY. 1950. m. Aus.$27 (foreign Aus.$108)(effective Apr. 1992). Yaffa Publishing Group, 17-21 Bellevue St., Surry Hills, N.S.W. 2010, Australia. TEL 02-281-2333. FAX 02-281-2750. adv.: B&W page Aus.$1180, color page Aus.$1685; trim 273 x 210. bk.rev.; charts; illus.; tr.lit.; circ. 12,149. **Indexed:** Pinpointer.
—BLDSC shelfmark: 1817.700000.
    Description: Serves the enthusiast interested in cameras, craft, tools and techniques of photography.

PHOTOGRAPHY

770   AT
AUSTRALIAN PHOTOGRAPHY CAMERA TEST REPORTS.
1950. a. Aus.$3.50 (foreign Aus.$5). Yaffa Publishing Group, 17-21 Bellevue St., Surry Hills, N.S.W. 2010, Australia. TEL 02-281-2333. FAX 02-281-2750. Ed. Michael Richardson. adv.: B&W page Aus.$930, color page Aus.$1200; trim 273 x 210. circ. 7,000.
   Description: Provides information on all the top amateur cameras and related products released the previous year.

770   AT
AUSTRALIAN PHOTOGRAPHY PHOTO-DIRECTORY. 1951. a. Aus.$6.95. Yaffa Publishing Group, 17-21 Bellevue St., Surry Hills, N.S.W. 2010, Australia. TEL 02-281-2333. adv.: B&W page Aus.$1285, color page Aus.$1660; trim 273 x 210. bk.rev.; circ. 10,000.
   Formerly: Australian Photography Directory (ISSN 0067-2076)
   Description: Directory of photographic goods available on the local market.

770   UK
B A P L A JOURNAL. 1985. q. £15. British Association of Picture Libraries and Agencies, 13 Woodberry Crescent, London N10 1PJ, England. TEL 081-444-7913. FAX 081-883-9215. Ed. Brian Shuel. adv.; bk.rev.; circ. 2,200. (back issues avail.)
   Description: British photo libraries and agencies, how they work, who they are, details concerned with running libraries.

770   NE
BELICHT; foto en filmblad voor de amateurfotograaf. m. fl.47.50. Uitgeverij C P S B.V., Postbus 301, 7400 AA Deventer, Netherlands. adv.; bk.rev.; circ. 16,000.

770   AU   ISSN 0005-8947
DAS BERGMANN-ECHO. 1958. bi-m. free. (Bergmann-Kameradschaft 137. Inf. Div.) Sepp Sattelberger, Editor, Postanschrift A-3252, Petzenkirchen, Austria.

770   US
BEST OF PHOTOJOURNALISM; newspaper and magazine pictures of the year. 1975. a. $19.95. (National Press Photographers Association) Running Press Book Publishers, 125 S. 22nd St., Philadelphia, PA 19103. TEL 215-567-5080. FAX 215-567-2919. TELEX 902633. (back issues avail.)

BLITZ MAGAZINE. see ART

BLUE PITCHER; a biannual magazine of poetry and photography. see LITERATURE — Poetry

770   GW   ISSN 0932-7231
BRENNPUNKT; Magazin fuer Photographie. 1984. q. DM.18. Edition Dibue, Waghaeuseler Str. 8, 1000 Berlin 31, Germany. TEL 030-8533527. Ed. Dietmar Buehrer.

770   UK   ISSN 0007-1196
                                CODEN: BRJFAM
BRITISH JOURNAL OF PHOTOGRAPHY; technical, professional, scientific. 1854. w. £45.50. Henry Greenwood & Co. Ltd., 58 Fleet St., London EC4Y 1JU, England. TEL 01-583-0175. FAX 01-583-5183. Ed. Chris Dickie. adv.; bk.rev.; charts; illus.; stat.; index; circ. 11,500. (also avail. in microfilm from MIM) **Indexed:** Artbibl.Mod., Br.Tech.Ind., Chem.Abstr., Photo.Abstr., Print.Abstr., Sci.Abstr.
   —BLDSC shelfmark: 2317.000000.

770   UK   ISSN 0068-2217
TR1
BRITISH JOURNAL OF PHOTOGRAPHY ANNUAL. 1860. a. £19.95. Henry Greenwood & Co. Ltd., 58 Fleet St., London EC4 1JU, England. TEL 01-583-0175. FAX 01-583-5183. Ed. C. Dickie. adv.; index; circ. 4,000.

770   BU   ISSN 0007-4012
BULGARSKO FOTO; a journal of photographic art, technique, and photojournalism. (Summaries in English, French, German and Russian) 1966. 12/yr. 10 lv.($12) (Komitet za Izkustvo i Kultura) Foreign Trade Co. "Hemus", 7 Levsky St., 1000 Sofia, Bulgaria. (Dist. by: Hemus, 6, Rouski Blvd., 1000 Sofia, Bulgaria) Ed. Albert Koen. adv.; bk.rev.; abstr.; bibl.; illus.; index; circ. 10,000. (processed)
   —BLDSC shelfmark: 0018.638500.

C MAGAZINE. see ART

770   FR   ISSN 0294-4081
CAHIERS DE LA PHOTOGRAPHIE. 1981. q. 385 F. (foreign 450 F.). Association de Critique Contemporaire en Photographie, c/o Gilles Mora, Lascledes, Brax, 47310 Laplume, France. TEL 53-96-78-28. bk.rev. (back issues avail.) **Indexed:** Artbibl.Mod.
   —BLDSC shelfmark: 2951.900000.

770   US
CALIFORNIA PROFESSIONAL PHOTOGRAPHER.* 1967. bi-m. $4 to non-members. Professional Photographers of California, Inc., 1873 Market St., San Francisco, CA 94103. TEL 415-626-2525. Ed. Don Devine. adv.; bk.rev.; circ. 3,000.

770   US   ISSN 1056-8484
TR287
CAMERA & DARKROOM PHOTOGRAPHY. 1979. 12/yr. $23.95 (foreign $33.95). Larry Flynt Publications, Inc., 9171 Wilshire Blvd., Ste. 300, Beverly Hills, CA 90210. TEL 310-858-7100. FAX 310-275-3857. (Subscr. to: Box 16928, N. Hollywood, CA 91615) Ed. Ana Jones. illus.; stat.; index; circ. 75,000. (also avail. in microfilm from UMI; back issues avail.; reprint service avail. from UMI) **Indexed:** Art & Archaeol.Tech.Abstr., Graph.Arts Lit.Abstr., Ind.How.to Do It (1979-), P.M.I.
   Formerly: Darkroom Photography (ISSN 0163-9250)

770   AT
CAMERA BUYER'S GUIDE. a. P.O. Box 341, Mona Vale, N.S.W. 2103, Australia. Ed. Don Norris. circ. 23,000.

770 028.5   CN   ISSN 0008-2090
CAMERA CANADA. 1969. q. Can.$16 to non-members. National Association for Photographic Art, Inc., 22 Abbeville Rd., Scarborough, Ont. M1H 1Y3, Canada. TEL 416-438-0252. Ed. Ann Lawson. adv.; bk.rev.; circ. 4,000. **Indexed:** Artbibl.Mod., Can.Per.Ind., CMI.

770   NZ   ISSN 0114-264X
CAMERA NEW ZEALAND. 1953. bi-m. NZ.$33.75. Photographic Society of New Zealand, P.O. Box 51-365, Pakuranga Auckland, New Zealand. TEL 09-576-9239. Ed. John E.A. Reece. adv.; bk.rev.; illus.; index; circ. 2,000.
   Former titles: Camera (ISSN 0110-3989); New Zealand Camera (ISSN 0048-0118)

770   CN
CANADIAN DIRECTORY OF PROFESSIONAL PHOTOGRAPHY. 1980. a. (Professional Photographers of Canada) P.P.O.C., P.O. Box 2740, St. Marys, Ont. N4X 1A5, Canada. TEL 519-284-1388. adv.

770   CN
CANADIAN PHOTOGRAPHER. q. Can.$32($38) Canadian Photographer, Inc., 847 Sweetwater Crescent, Port Credit, Ont. L5H 4A7, Canada. TEL 416-274-5608. FAX 416-271-7908. Ed. Christie Day.

770   JA
CAPA; active camera magazine. (Text in Japanese) 1981. m. 4200 Yen. Gakken Co. Ltd., 40-5, 4-chome, Kamiikedai, Ohta-ku, Tokyo 145, Japan. Ed. Shonosuke Abe.

CAPE ROCK; a journal of poetry. see LITERATURE — Poetry

770   SA   ISSN 0008-5820
CAPE TOWN PHOTOGRAPHIC SOCIETY SYLLABUS.* 1890. m. membership. Cape Town Photographic Society, Box 2431, Cape Town, South Africa. adv.; bibl.; illus.; circ. 350. (tabloid format)

770   US   ISSN 0890-4634
CENTER QUARTERLY; journal for photography and related arts. 1979. q. $25 (Canada and Mexico $40; elsewhere $45). Center for Photography at Woodstock, 59 Tinker St., Woodstock, NY 12498. Ed. Kathleen Kenyon. adv.; bk.rev.; circ. 10,000.
   Description: Contains articles on contemporary artists and diverse aesthetic concerns.

CHAMPAIGN COUNTY HISTORICAL ARCHIVES HISTORICAL PUBLICATIONS SERIES. see HISTORY — History Of North And South America

770   FR   ISSN 0396-8235
CHASSEUR D'IMAGES. 1976. 10/yr. 250 F. Editions Jibena-G H Publications, La Petite Motte, 86100 Senille, France. TEL 49-85-49-85. FAX 49-85-49-99. TELEX 792349 F. adv.; illus.; circ. 105,000.

CHICAGO RENAISSANCE. see LITERATURE

770   SI   ISSN 0009-6954
CINE NEWS. vol.11, 1970. m. free. Singapore Cine Club, 42 Branksome Rd., Singapore 1543, Singapore. Ed. Paul Gomez. adv.; illus.; circ. 1,500.

COLOR RESEARCH AND APPLICATION. see ENGINEERING — Chemical Engineering

771   US
COLORGRAM. m. membership only. (Association of Professional Color Laboratories) Photo Marketing Association International, 3000 Picture Pl., Jackson, MI 49201. TEL 517-788-8100. FAX 517-788-8371. Ed. Charles Davenport. circ. 800. (back issues avail.)

770   US   ISSN 0145-899X
TR640
COMBINATIONS; a journal of photography. 1977. q. $12 to individuals; institutions $14. Mary Ann Lynch, Ed. & Pub., Middle Grove Rd., Greenfield Center, NY 12833. TEL 518-584-4612. adv.; bk.rev.; circ. 1,500.

770   JA
COMMERCIAL PHOTO. 12/yr. $219. Intercontinental Marketing Corp., I.P.O. Box 5056, Tokyo 100-31, Japan. FAX 81-3-667-9646.

778   AT
COMMERCIAL PHOTOGRAPHY. 1962. bi-m. Aus.$25 (foreign Aus.$63)(effective Apr. 1992). Yaffa Publishing Group, 17-21 Bellevue St., Surry Hills, N.S.W. 2010, Australia. TEL 02-281-2333. FAX 02-281-2750. adv.: B&W page Aus.$975, color Aus.$1465; trim 297 x 210. bk.rev.; illus.; circ. 3,615. (reprint service avail. from UMI)
   Former titles: Industrial and Commercial Photography (ISSN 0313-4393); Industrial Photography and Commercial Camera (ISSN 0019-8609)
   Description: Features insights into creativity, studio management, new techniques and equipment.

770   JA
COMMERCIAL PHOTOGRAPHY JOURNAL. 12/yr. Intercontinental Marketing Corp., I.P.O. Box 5056, Tokyo 100-31, Japan. FAX 81-3-667-9646.

770   US
CONTEMPORARY PHOTOGRAPHERS. 1982. quinquennial. $70. St. Martin's Press, Scholarly and Reference Division, 175 Fifth Ave., New York, NY 10010. TEL 212-674-5151. Ed.Bd.

778.315   FR   ISSN 0396-5791
COURRIER DE LA MICROCOPIE. (Text in French) 1976. m. 1050 F. Micro Journal, 11 rue de Provence, 75009 Paris, France. Ed. Jean-Jacques Maleval. adv.; bk.rev.; circ. 1,000.

CREATIVE BLACK BOOK. PORTFOLIO EDITION. see ADVERTISING AND PUBLIC RELATIONS

770   UK   ISSN 0011-0876
TR640
CREATIVE CAMERA. 1968. bi-m. $40 to individuals; institutions $60. C C Publishing, Battersea Arts Centre, The Old Town Hall, London SW11 5TF, England. TEL 01-924-3017. Ed. David Brittain. adv.; bk.rev.; illus.; circ. 7,500. **Indexed:** Artbibl.Mod.
   Formerly: Camera Owner.
   Description: Contains news about photo-based artwork with news, reviews, portfolios, and features by influential writers.

CREATIVE SOURCE. see ADVERTISING AND PUBLIC RELATIONS

CREATIVE SOURCE AUSTRALIA; the wizards of Oz. see ARTS AND HANDICRAFTS

770 700   US
D B C C PHOTOGRAPHIC SOCIETY. NEWSLETTER. 1978. q. free. Photo Society of Dayton Beach Community College, 1200 Volusia Ave., Box 1111, Dayton Beach, FL 32014. TEL 904-254-3057. Ed. Ed Davenport. adv.; bk.rev.; circ. 2,750.

3790 PHOTOGRAPHY

770   DK
DANISH PHOTOGRAPHY (YEAR). a. Selskabet for Dansk Fotografi - Society of Danish Photography, Danmarksgade 16, DK-4874 Gedser, Denmark. Ed. Niels Bjerre. adv.; circ. 1,000.

770   DK
DANSK FOTOGRAFI; kontaktblad. no.108, 1981. bi-m. DKK 70. Selskabet for Dansk Fotografi, c/o Niels Bjerre, Ed., Danmarksgade 16, 4874 Gedser, Denmark. illus.
    Formerly: Selskabet for Dansk Fotografi. Kontaktblad (ISSN 0108-2558)

770   DK
DANSK FOTOGRAFISK TIDSSKRIFT. 1879. 4/yr. DKK 150. Dansk Fotografisk Forening, Bornholmsgade 1, 1266 Copenhagen K, Denmark. FAX 33-93-26-01. Ed. Niels Elswing. adv.; bk.rev.; circ. 850. (also avail. in microform) **Indexed:** Photo.Ind.

770   US   ISSN 0195-3850
TR287
DARKROOM & CREATIVE CAMERA TECHNIQUES. 1979. bi-m. $13.95. Preston Publications, Inc., 7800 N. Merrimac Ave., Niles, IL 60648. TEL 708-965-0566. FAX 708-965-7639. TELEX 910-223-1780. (Subscr. to: Box 1079, Skokie, IL 60076-9818) Ed. David Jay. adv.; bk.rev.; charts; illus.; stat.; circ. 45,000. (back issues avail.) **Indexed:** Ind.How To Do It (1983-).
   —BLDSC shelfmark: 3533.740500.
    Description: Discusses photographic and darkroom equipment procedures and techniques for serious amateurs and professionals.

770   CC   ISSN 0494-4372
DAZHONG SHEYING/POPULAR PHOTOGRAPHY. (Text in Chinese) m. $72.80. (Zhongguo Sheyingjia Xiehui - China Photographers' Association) Dazhong Sheying Zazhishe, 61 Hongxing Hutong, Dongdan, Beijing 100705. TEL 557378. (Dist. in US by: China Books & Periodicals, Inc., 2929 24th St., San Francisco, CA 94110. TEL 415-282-2994)

DESIGN QUARTERLY. see *ARCHITECTURE*

DESIGNERS DIGEST; das umfangreiche Magazin fuer Grafik-, Industrial, Mode- und Mediendesign. see *ART*

DIRECTORY OF CONSUMER ELECTRONICS (YEAR). see *BUSINESS AND ECONOMICS — Trade And Industrial Directories*

770   FR   ISSN 0419-5361
DOCUMENTATION PHOTOGRAPHIQUE. (Includes Dossiers and Cahiers de Diapositives) 1947. 6/yr. 450 F. Documentation Francaise, 29-31 Quai Voltaire, 75340 Paris 7, France. TEL 1-40-15-70-00. bibl.; illus.; circ. 15,000.

770   US   ISSN 0896-0976
ELECTRONIC PHOTOGRAPHY NEWS. 1986. m. $90 (foreign $112). E P N Publishing, 4100 Corporate Sq., Naples, FL 33942. TEL 813-643-5666. FAX 813-643-4504. Eds. Don Franz, John Larish. bk.rev.; charts; stat.; circ. 400. (back issues avail.)

770   JA   ISSN 0011-8478
ELECTROPHOTOGRAPHY/DENSHI SHASHINGAKKAISHI. (Text in Japanese; summaries in English) 1959. q. 8000 Yen. Society of Electrophotography of Japan - Denshi Shashin Gakkai, c/o Tokyo Institute of Polytechnics, 2-9-5 Honcho, Nakano-ku, Tokyo 164, Japan. TEL 03-3373-9576. FAX 33-372-4414. Ed. Shunji Imamura. adv.; charts; illus.; circ. 1,500. **Indexed:** Chem.Abstr., JCT, JTA, Photo.Abstr., Sci.Abstr.

770 700   US   ISSN 0886-845X
ENTRY; a guide to photographic competitions and juried exhibitions. 1984. 10/yr. $22. Box 7648, Ann Arbor, MI 48107. TEL 313-663-4686. Ed. Jennifer Hill. adv.; circ. 4,000.

770   UK
EUROPEAN PHOTOGRAPHY. 1981. a. £25. D & AD European Illustration, Nash House, 12 Carlton House Terrace, London SW1Y 5AH, England. Ed. Edward Booth-Clibborn. **Indexed:** Artbibl.Mod., Artbibl.

770   GW   ISSN 0172-7028
TR640
EUROPEAN PHOTOGRAPHY. (Text in English and German) 1980. q. DM.45($30) Postfach 3043, 3400 Goettingen, Germany. TEL 0551-24820. FAX 0551-25224. Ed. Andreas Mueller-Pohle. adv.; bk.rev.; bibl.; cum.index; circ. 5,000. (back issues avail.)
    Description: International coverage of contemporary photography and media art.

770.5   US   ISSN 0098-8863
TR1
EXPOSURE (BOULDER). 1963. 3/yr. $35 to institutions. Society for Photographic Education, Campus Box 318, University of Colorado, Boulder, CO 80309. TEL 303-492-0588. Ed. Patricia Johnston. adv.; bk.rev.; illus.; circ. 1,700. **Indexed:** Artbibl.Mod., RILA.
   —BLDSC shelfmark: 3843.374500.

770 778.53   UK
EYEPIECE. bi-m. Guild of British Camera Technicians, 5-11 Taunton Rd., Metropolitan Centre, Greenford, Middlesex UB6 8UQ, England. **Indexed:** Film Lit.Ind. (1985-).

770   BE
FEDERATION NATIONALE DES PHOTOGRAPHES PROFESSIONNELS PROFESSIONNELLE. REPORT MAGAZINE. bi-m. Federation Nationale des Photographes Professionnels Professionnelle, Rue des Boers 52A, B-1040 Brussels, Belgium.

FIELD OF VISION. see *MOTION PICTURES*

770   US
FIRE PHOTOGRAPHERS JOURNAL. 1965. q. $25 (membership). International Fire Photographers Association, Box 8337, Rolling Meadows, IL 60008. TEL 708-394-5835. adv.; bk.rev.; circ. 450.
    Formerly (until 1990): I F P A Quarterly.
    Description: Provides information for fire and investigative photography. Also includes information and location of photographer's seminars and newsworthy articles by members.

770   US
FLORIDA PHOTO NEWS. 1955. w. $18. Florida Photo News Publishers, Inc., 2405 N. Dixie Hwy., Box 1583-46, W. Palm Beach, FL 33402. TEL 305-833-4511. FAX 407-833-0711. Ed. Yasmin W. Cooper. circ. 3,788. (tabloid format)
    Formerly (until 1990): Photo News (ISSN 0031-854X)

770   IE   ISSN 0790-4940
FOCUS (DUBLIN).* 1979. irreg. Irish Professional Photographers Association, c/o 74 Stringhill Ave., Blackrock, Dublin, Ireland. Ed. Edward Moss. adv.; bk.rev.; illus.; circ. 300.

770   HU   ISSN 0427-0576
FOTO. 1954. m. $30.50. Lapkiado Vallalat, Lenin korut 9-11, 1073 Budapest, Hungary. TEL 222-408. (Subscr. to: Kultura, Box 149, H-1389 Budapest, Hungary) adv.; illus.

770   DK   ISSN 0046-4775
FOTO-AVISEN.* 1962. q. DKK 12($2.) Foto-Avisen, Kallestrupvej 99, DK-9632 Moldrup, Denmark. TEL 06-69-20-41. FAX 86-69-19-21. Ed. Per Soerensen. adv.; bk.rev.

770   BL
FOTO - CINE. 1946. 6/yr. Foto - Cine Clube Bandeirante, Rua Jose Getulio 442, Caixa Postal 8861, CEP 01509 Sao Paulo SP, Brazil. Ed. Roberto B. Macedo. circ. 15,000.

770   GW
FOTO CREATIV. 1981. q. DM.69 (foreign DM.75). Vereinigte Motor-Verlage GmbH und Co. KG, Leuschnerstr. 1, 7000 Stuttgart 1, Germany. TEL 0711-18201. FAX 0711-1821756, TELEX 722036. Ed. Michael Tafelmaier. circ. 31,211.

770   DK
FOTO, FILM & VIDEO. m. (11/yr.). DKK 296. Specialbladsforlaget A-S, Finsensvej 80, 2000 Frederiksberg, Denmark. Ed. Finn Nesgaard. adv.; illus.; circ. 6,886.
    Formerly: Foto og Smalfilm.

770   SZ   ISSN 0015-8690
FOTO-FILM-VIDEO-TIP; Magazin fuer Foto, Film und Tonaufzeichnung. 1966. 10/yr. 20 Fr.($10) Alma Verlag, Postfach 1020, 8953 Dietikon, Switzerland. Ed. Albert Haeusermann. adv.; illus.
    Formerly: Foto-Film-Ton.

770   SP
FOTO GALAXIS. (Text in English & Spanish) irreg. Galaxis, S.A., Zamora 46-48, Barcelona, Spain. illus.

FOTO-KINO REVIJA; jugoslovenski casopis za fotografijui amaterski film. see *MOTION PICTURES*

770   IT
FOTO-LABORATORIO. 1974. bi-m. free. Mediaspazio, V. M. Melloni 17, 20129 Milan, Italy. Ed. Luciano Scattolin. adv.; circ. 6,000.

770   IO   ISSN 0852-596X
▼**FOTO MEDIA.** 1990. m. $34.80. PT. Elex Media Komputindo, Jalan Palmerah Selatan 22, 6th Floor, Jakarta 10270, Indonesia. TEL 021-5483008. FAX 021-5486085. TELEX 46327 KOMPAS JKT. Agus Tjahjono W. circ. 10,000.

770   IT   ISSN 0015-8720
FOTO-NOTIZIARIO. 1946. m. free. Mediaspazio, Via M. Melloni, 17, 20129 Milan, Italy. Ed. Luciano Scattolin. adv.; illus.; circ. 13,000.

770   IT
FOTO-NOTIZIARIO GIORNALE. 1980. w. free. Mediaspazio, Via M. Melloni 17, 20129 Milan, Italy. Ed. Luciano Scattolin. adv.; circ. 16,000.

770   IT
FOTO-NOTIZIARIO PROFESSIONALE. 1982. m. free. Mediaspazio, Via M. Melloni 17, 20129 Milan, Italy. TEL 02-718341. Ed. Luciano Scattolin. adv.; circ. 7,000.

770   SW
FOTO OCH FILMTEKNIK. m. (11/yr.). Specialtidningsfoerlaget AB, Sveavaegen 53, 103 64 Stockholm, Sweden. adv.; circ. 44,164.

770   NE
FOTO-VISIE. 1971. m. Blauw Media B.V., P.O. Box 1043, 3469 BA Maarsen, Netherlands. Ed. H. Louwmans. adv.; abstr.; illus.; mkt.; stat.; circ. 4,100.

770   AG   ISSN 0015-8771
FOTOCAMARA CON POPULAR PHOTOGRAPHY. 1938. m. $5. (International Federation of Photographic Art, SZ) Editora Publicitaria S.A.C.I.F., Audreas Weichselbraun, Sec. Gen., Liechtensteinstr. 13, A - 1090 Vienna, Austria. Ed. Hector Y. Faita. illus.

770   IT
FOTOCINE 80. m. L.40000 (foreign L.60000). Societa Foto Editrice s.r.l., Via Giuseppe Ricciardi 28, Naples, Italy. TEL 081-2844228. Ed. Ettore Bernabo Silorata.

770   CN   ISSN 0318-7500
FOTOFLASH. vol.14, 1981. 4/yr. membership only. National Association for Photographic Art, c/o Bruce A. Blackburn, Pub. Mgr., 23 Latham Ave., Scarborough, Ont. M1N 1M7, Canada. circ. 2,800.

770   GW   ISSN 0720-5260
TR15
FOTOGESCHICHTE; Beitraege zur Geschichte und Aesthetik der Fotografie. 1981. q. DM.110 (foreign DM.117.20). Jonas Verlag, Weidenhaeuserstr. 88, 3550 Marburg, Germany. TEL 06421-25132. Eds. Timm Starl, H. von Amelunxen. bk.rev.; index; circ. 550.

770   TU
FOTOGRAF. (Text in Turkish; contents page in English) 1978. 6/yr. TL.60000($36) Ankara Fotograf Sanatcilari Dernigli - Association of Fine Art Photographers of Ankara, PK 649 Kizilay, 06425 Ankara, Turkey. TEL 4-2300409. Ed. Tanju Akdeniz. adv.; bk.rev.; illus.; circ. 3,000.
    Description: Publishes profiles of photographers and their work, and technical articles addressing recent advances in film or equipment.

777   IT
FOTOGRAFARE. 1967. m. L.50000. Cesco Ciapanna Editore S.p.A., Via Lipari 8, 00141 Rome, Italy. Ed. Cesco Ciapanna. adv.; bk.rev.; circ. 80,000.
    Formerly: Fotografare Novita.

PHOTOGRAPHY 3791

770   PL   ISSN 0324-850X
FOTOGRAFIA. (Text in Polish; summaries in English, French, German and Russian) 1976. q. 3600 Zl.($48) Wydawnictwo Arkady, Ul. Sienkiewicza 14, 00-950 Warsaw, Poland. (Dist. by: Ars Polona-Ruch, Krakowskie Przedmiescie 7, Warsaw, Poland) Ed. Wieslaw Prazuch. bk.rev.; abstr.; illus.; index; circ. 14,000.

770   AG   ISSN 0015-881X
FOTOGRAFIA UNIVERSAL. (Includes 5 buying directories per year) 1963. m. $22. Editorial Fotografia Universal, Muniz 1327-49, Buenos Aires, Argentina. Ed. Horacio Canosa. adv.; bk.rev.; film rev.; play rev.; bibl.; charts; illus.; mkt.; index; circ. 39,500. (looseleaf format)

770   IT
FOTOGRAFIAMO. s-m. Societa Foto Editrice s.r.l., Via Giuseppe Ricciardi 28, Naples, Italy. TEL 081-284428.

770   CS
TR1
FOTOGRAFIE/PHOTOGRAPHY. (Text in Czech or Slovak; summaries in English, German, Russian) 1946. m. 60 Kcs.($61.70) Panorama, Mrstikova 23, 101 00 Prague 10, Czechoslovakia. TEL 2-781553. adv.; bk.rev.; charts; illus.; index; circ. 57,000.
Formerly: Ceskoslovenska Fotografie (ISSN 0009-0549)

770   GW   ISSN 0935-414X
FOTOGRAFIE DRAUSSEN; Erleben aus erster Hand. 1969. bi-m. DM.51 (foreign DM.56.20). Verlag Tecklenborg, Lindenstr. 4, Postfach 2465, 4430 Steinfurt, Germany. TEL 02552-3933. Ed. Hubert Tecklenborg. adv.; bk.rev.
Formerly: Tier und Naturfotografie.

770   SW   ISSN 0284-7035
FOTOGRAFISK TIDSKRIFT. (Text in Swedish; summaries in English) 1888. 6/yr. SEK 350. Svenska Fotografernas Foerbund - Swedish Professional Photographers Association, Wallingatan 38, S-111 24 Stockholm, Sweden. TEL 08-696-418472. FAX 08-696-406988. Ed. Goesta Flemming. adv.; bk.rev.; charts; illus.; tr.lit.; index; circ. 12,000.
Indexed: Chem.Abstr.
Formerly: Svensk Fotografisk Tidskrift (ISSN 0039-6540)

770   GW   ISSN 0015-8879
FOTOKINO-MAGAZIN; Fachzeitschrift fuer Foto- und Filmamateure. (Text in German; summaries in Russian) 1963. m. DM.24 (foreign DM.38.40). Fotokinoverlag Leipzig, Postfach 67, 7031 Leipzig, Germany. TEL 71370. bk.rev.; illus.
Description: Publication for amateur photographers and filmmakers, covering instruction, equipment, technique, photographs, and contests. Includes list of exhibitions, and readers' letters.

770   GW   ISSN 0015-8712
FOTOMAGAZIN. 1949. m. DM.86.40. Ringier Verlag GmbH, Gustav-Heinemann-Ring 212, 8000 Munich 83, Germany. TEL 089-638180. FAX 089-63818100. adv.; bk.rev.; illus.; index; circ. 81,572.

770 621.389   AG   ISSN 0325-7150
FOTOMUNDO. 1966. m. Ediciones Fotograficas Argentina S.A., Maipu 671, piso 5, 1006 Buenos Aires, Argentina. TEL 322-2006. Ed. Silvia Mangialardi. adv.; bk.rev.; circ. 10,000. (back issues avail.)

770   HU   ISSN 0532-3010
TR640
FOTOMUVESZET. (Text in Hungarian; summaries in English) 1966. q. $26.50. (Magyar Fotomuveszek Szovetsege) Lapkiado Vallalat, Lenin korut 9-11, 1073 Budapest, Hungary. TEL 222-408. (Subscr. to: Kultura, Box 149, H-1389 Budapest, Hungary) Ed. Tamas Fener. circ. 3,500. Indexed: Lang.& Lang.Behav.Abstr.

770 791.43   VE   ISSN 0015-8895
FOTON; fotografia, cine y sonida (photography, amateur movie and sound). 1965. m. Bs.200($30) M.G. Ediciones Especializadas, Av. Maturin, No. 15, Urb. Los Cedros, El Bosque, Caracas 1050, Venezuela. Ed. Montserrat Giol. adv.; circ. 4,500.

770   SW   ISSN 0015-8909
FOTONYHETERNA.* 1961. 10/yr. SEK 250. Kustgatan 64, 27270 Haelsingborg, Sweden. Ed. Bjoern Sandels. adv.; bk.rev.; charts; illus.; mkt.; pat.; tr.lit.; circ. 5,000.
Incorporating: Scandinavian Journal of Photography and Film.

770   IT
FOTOPRATICA. 1968. m. L.92000. Societa Editrice Fotografica, Via Ciro Menotti, 11, 20129 Milan, Italy. FAX 02-714495. TELEX 320665 GIBI. (Subscr. to: Messaggerie Internazionali s.r.l., Via Rogoredo 55, Milan, Italy) adv.; bk.rev.; circ. 22,000.
Description: Covers photography, technical aspects, cultural events and more.

770   CU
FOTOTECNICA. q. $8 in N. America; S. America $10; Europe $12; elsewhere $14. (Union de Periodistas de Cuba, Secretariado Ejecutivo) Ediciones Cubanas, Obispo No. 527, Apdo. 605, Havana, Cuba. illus.

770   GW
FOTOWIRTSCHAFT; unabhaengiges Wirtschaftsmagazin der Fotobranche fuer Industrie, Handel, Handwerk. 1950. m. DM.132. Ringier Verlag GmbH, Gustav-Heinemann-Ring 212, 8000 Munich 83, Germany. TEL 089-638180. FAX 089-63818100. adv.; charts; illus.; mkt.; pat.; stat.; index; circ. 5,602. Indexed: Photo.Abstr.
Formerly: Fotohaendler (ISSN 0015-8844)

770 301.2   US   ISSN 0895-6030
FRAME-WORK; a journal of images and culture. 3/yr. $18 to individuals (foreign $24); institutions $28 (foreign $34). Los Angeles Center for Photographic Studies, 1048 W. Sixth St., Los Angeles, CA 90017-2059. TEL 213-482-3566. Eds. Susan Kandel, Jody Zellen. adv.; circ. 2,000. (back issues avail.)
Formerly (until 1986): Obscura.

770   FR
FRANCE - PHOTOGRAPHIE. 5/yr. 140 F. Federation Photographique, 9 rue Faraday, 75017 Paris, France. FAX 47-63-65-44. adv.; bk.rev.; circ. 5,000.

FREE-LANCE WRITING & PHOTOGRAPHY. see JOURNALISM

FREELANCE WRITER'S REPORT. see JOURNALISM

FUJIAN HUABAO/FUJIAN PICTORIAL. see GENERAL INTEREST PERIODICALS — China

778.1   US   ISSN 0360-7216
TR692   CODEN: FUPHDO
FUNCTIONAL PHOTOGRAPHY (WOODBURY).* 1967. 6/yr. $7.50 (free to qualified personnel). P T N Publishing Corp., 445 Broad Hollow Rd., Ste. 21, Melville, NY 11747-4722. TEL 516-845-2700. FAX 516-845-7109. adv.; bk.rev.; abstr.; charts; illus.; circ. 35,000. Indexed: Art & Archaeol.Tech.Abstr., Biol.Abstr., Curr.Pack.Abstr., GeoRef., Graph.Arts Lit.Abstr., Sci.Abstr.
Former titles: Photographic Applications in Science, Technology and Medicine (ISSN 0098-8227); Photographic Applications in Science and Technology (ISSN 0031-871X)

GADNEY'S GUIDES TO INTERNATIONAL CONTESTS, FESTIVALS & GRANTS IN FILM & VIDEO, PHOTOGRAPHY, TV-RADIO BROADCASTING, WRITING & JOURNALISM. see COMMUNICATIONS

770   CC   ISSN 1000-3231
               CODEN: GKKHE9
GANGUANG KEXUE YU GUANGHUAXUE/PHOTOGRAPHIC SCIENCE AND PHOTOCHEMISTRY. (Text in Chinese; table of contents, summaries, and captions in English) 1983. q. $8 per no. (Chinese Academy of Sciences, Institute of Photographic Science) Science Press, Marketing and Sales Department, 16 Donghuangchenggen Beijie, Beijing 100707, People's Republic of China. TEL 4010642. FAX 4012180. TELEX 210247-SPBJ-CN. (Co-sponsor: Chinese Society of Photographic Science and Engineering (CSPSE)) Ed. Ren Xinmin. adv.; circ. 11,000.
—BLDSC shelfmark: 6471.800000.
Description: Covers photochemical imaging systems, exposure and development mechanisms, image structure and evaluation, sensitometry of photographic materials, organic photochemistry, photochemistry of polymers, photobiochemistry, photoelectrochemistry at interface, and photocatalysis.
Refereed Serial

GANSU HUABAO/GANSU PICTORIAL. see GENERAL INTEREST PERIODICALS — China

770   IT
GAZZETTA DELLA FOTOGRAFIA. m. Via Principe Granatelli 96, 90139 Palermo, Italy. Ed. Franco Randazzo.

770 659   SZ
TR690.A1
GRAPHIS PHOTO; international annual of photography. (Text in English, French, German) 1966. a. 123 Fr.($69) B. Martin Pedersen Graphis Press Corp, Dufourstr. 107, CH-8008 Zurich, Switzerland. (In US and Canada: Watson-Guptill Publications Inc., 1515 Broadway, New York, NY 10036) Ed. B. Martin Pedersen. index; circ. 12,500.
Formerly: Photographis (ISSN 0079-1830)

GRAPHIS POSTERS; international annual of poster art. see ART

770   US
GREEN BOOK (NEW YORK); the directory of natural history and general stock photography. a. price varies. A G Editions, Inc., 142 Bank St., Ste. GA, New York, NY 10014. TEL 212-929-0959. FAX 212-924-4796. Ed. Ann Guilfoyle.
Description: Directory of photo sources for editorial photo buyers. Features description of stock files and cross-referenced natural history, general stock and geographic indexes.

GUANGDONG HUABAO/GUANGDONG PICTORIAL. see GENERAL INTEREST PERIODICALS — China

770   US
GUILFOYLE REPORT. q. $68. A G Editions, Inc., 142 Bank St., Ste. GA, New York, NY 10014. TEL 212-929-0959. FAX 212-924-4796. Ed. Ann Guilfoyle.

770   GR   ISSN 1011-1638
HELLENIC PHOTOGRAPHY SELECTIONS. (Text in English, Greek) 1989. q. Dr.3200($24) (Hellenic Centre of Photography) Moressopoulos & Associates, Ltd., 19, Iperidou str., GR-105 58 Athens, Greece. TEL 1-323-4217. FAX 1-323-2082. (Subscr. to P.O. Box 30 501, GR-100 33 Athens, Greece) Ed. Stavros Moressopoulos. adv.; circ. 7,000. (back issues avail.)
Description: Photographic art magazine presenting eight contemporary Greek photographers in each issue. Includes essays and information on events.

HENAN HUABAO. see GENERAL INTEREST PERIODICALS — China

PHOTOGRAPHY

770   UK   ISSN 0308-7298
TR15
HISTORY OF PHOTOGRAPHY; an international journal. 1976. q. £76($130) Taylor and Francis Ltd., Rankine Rd., Basingstoke, Hants. RG24 0PR, England. TEL 0256-840366. FAX 0256-479438. TELEX 858540. Ed. M.L. Weaver. adv.; bk.rev. **Indexed:** Artbibl., Arts & Hum.Cit.Ind., Avery Ind.Archit.Per., Curr.Cont., RILA.
—BLDSC shelfmark: 4318.395000.
Description: Devoted to the history and early development of this graphic art form. Covers the earliest uses of photography in exploration, science and war, lives of notable practitioners and inventors; the influence of photography on painting and sculpture; history of photo-journalism; the preservation and restoration of old photographs.
Refereed Serial

HORIZONTES (PATERSON). see *LITERATURE*

770   AT   ISSN 0728-5701
IMAGE. 1964. bi-m. Aus.$24 (foreign Aus.$30). Australian Photographic Society, Inc., P.O. Box 53, Hackett, A.C.T. 2602, Australia. TEL 06-2574814. Ed. Max Leonard. adv.; bk.rev.; circ. 1,200.
Description: Contains photographs, articles about photography and society news and information.

770   UK
IMAGE (LONDON). 1969. m. £24 (foreign £40). Association of Fashion, Advertising & Editorial Photographers, 9-10 Domingo St., London EC1Y 0TA, England. TEL 071-608-1441. FAX 071-253-3007. Ed. Jackie Kelley. adv.; bk.rev.; circ. 2,500.

770   US   ISSN 0536-5465
TR1
IMAGE (ROCHESTER, 1952); journal of photography and motion pictures. 1952. q. membership. International Museum of Photography at George Eastman House, 900 East Ave., Rochester, NY 14607. TEL 716-271-3361. FAX 716-271-3970. Ed. James L. Enyeart. illus.; circ. 3,000. (back issues avail.) **Indexed:** Art.Ind., Film Lit.Ind. (1987-).

770   US   ISSN 0893-1925
IMAGING ON CAMPUS. 1987. 6/yr. Executive Business Media, Inc., 825 Old Country Rd., Box 1500, Westbury, NY 11590. TEL 516-334-3030. Ed. Barry Tenenbaum. adv.; circ. 85,000.

770   II
INDIAN JOURNAL OF MEDICAL PHOTOGRAPHY. (Text in English) 1965. q. Rs.6. Biological Photographic Association, Indian Chapter, 10-D Medical Enclave, Patiala, Punjab, India.

770   II
INDIAN JOURNAL OF PHOTOGRAPHY. (Text in English) 1966. m. 6-12-A Band Stand Area, Delhi 110009, India. Ed. Raj Monga. adv.; bk.rev.; circ. 5,000.

770   US   ISSN 0019-8595
                                    CODEN: INPHA5
INDUSTRIAL PHOTOGRAPHY.* 1952. m. $25. P T N Publishing Corp., 445 Broad Hollow Rd., Ste. 21, Melville, NY 11747-4722. TEL 516-845-2700. FAX 516-845-7109. Ed. Lynn Roher. adv.; bk.rev.; bibl.; illus.; index; circ. 45,000. **Indexed:** A.S.& T.Ind., Art & Archaeol.Tech.Abstr., Chem.Abstr., Curr.Cont., Eng.Ind., Graph.Arts Lit.Abstr., Ind.How To Do It (1970-), Ind.Sci.Rev., Ocean.Abstr., Pollut.Abstr., Sci.Abstr.
Description: Tools and techniques for image-makers in business and industry.

770   GW   ISSN 0019-0179
INPHO. 1962. fortn. DM.151.20. (Deutsche Photo-und Kinohaendler-Bund) G F W Verlag GmbH, Volmerswertherstr. 20, 4000 Duesseldorf 1, Germany. TEL 0211-39009-0. Ed. Volker Storck. adv.; bk.rev.; illus.; stat.; circ. 7,000.

770   AU   ISSN 0020-1707
INPHO OESTERREICH. 1967. m. S.308. (Oesterreichischer Fotohaendlerverband) Verlag die Galerie GmbH, Linke Wienzeile 36, A-1060 Vienna, Austria. TEL 0222-587-1078. FAX 0222-587-5524. Ed. Walter Kristof. adv.; bk.rev.; illus.; circ. 2,000.

770   GW   ISSN 0174-6944
INSTANT. 1978. irreg. DM.120 per 12 issues. Trust, Hanauer Landstr. 139-145, 6000 Frankfurt a.M. 1, Germany. FAX 069-40578599. Eds. Franz Aumueller, Thomas Feicht. adv.; bk.rev.; circ. 20,000. (back issues avail.)

771   UK   ISSN 0260-9363
INSTANT RECORD. 1980. 3/yr. free to qualified personnel. Polaroid (UK) Ltd., Ashley Rd., St. Albans, Herts. AL1 5PR, England. TEL 07072-78209. FAX 0727-69335. TELEX 263246. Ed. Pat Wallace. illus.; circ. 25,000.

770   GW   ISSN 0939-8619
INTERNATIONAL CONTACT - PHOTO, VIDEO, LAB TECHNOLOGY; independent journal for the international photographic market. 1982. bi-m. $34. C.A.T. Verlag, Freiligrathring 18-20, Postfach 1229, 4030 Ratingen 1, Germany. TEL 02102-26096. FAX 02102-21892. Ed. T. Bloemer. adv.; bk.rev.; charts; stat.; circ. 7,500. (back issues avail.)

770   US   ISSN 0020-8299
INTERNATIONAL PHOTOGRAPHER. 1929. m. $20. c/o Local 659, 7715 Sunset Blvd., Ste. 300, Hollywood, CA 90046. TEL 213-876-0160. Ed. George J. Toscas. adv.; bk.rev.; bibl.; illus.; circ. 11,500. **Indexed:** Chem.Abstr.

770   UK
INTERNATIONAL WIDESCREEN. 1964. bi-m. $35. Widescreen Association, 48 Dorset St., London W1H 3FH, England. TEL 071-935-2580. FAX 071-486-1272. Ed. Tony Shapps. adv.; bk.rev.; film rev.; circ. 5,000. (back issues avail.)
Formerly: Widescreen.
Description: Panoramic photography, 3-D, stereoscopic, multi-channel sound, multi-projector set-ups.

770 778.53   BL
IRIS. 1947. m. $80. Editora Iris Ltda, Rua Jacucaim 67, Caixa Postal 1704, Sao Paulo, S.P., Brazil. FAX 531-1627. Ed. Silvia H. de Azevedo Marques. adv.; bk.rev.; circ. 120,000.

ISLAND (LANTZVILLE). see *LITERATURE*

770   IT
ITALIA; rivista di documentazione fotografica. q. L.20000 (foreign L.24000). Istituto Poligrafico dello Stato, Piazza Verdi, 10, 00197 Rome, Italy. TEL 4745506.

771   JA   ISSN 0021-4345
JAPAN CAMERA TRADE NEWS; monthly information on cameras, optical instruments, video kits, and accessories. (Text in English) 1950. m. $85. Genyosha Publications, Inc., 18-2, Shibuya 3-chome, Shibuya-ku, Tokyo 150, Japan. TEL 03-3407-7521. FAX 03-3407-7902. Ed. K. Eda. adv.; bk.rev.; illus.; stat.; circ. 9,234. (tabloid format)

JINRI SHENGHUO/TODAY'S LIFE. see *GENERAL INTEREST PERIODICALS — China*

JOURNAL (COLUMBUS). see *LITERATURE*

JOURNAL OF BIOLOGICAL PHOTOGRAPHY. see *BIOLOGY*

614.19   US
JOURNAL OF EVIDENCE PHOTOGRAPHY. 1968. m. membership. Evidence Photographers International Council, 24 E. Main St., Norwich, NY 13815. TEL 607-334-6833. Ed. Casey Jones. adv.; circ. 500. (also avail. in microform from UMI; reprint service avail. from UMI)

770   US
JOURNAL OF IMAGING SCIENCE. 1956. bi-m. $80 (foreign $90). Society for Imaging Science & Technology (SPSE), 7003 Kilworth Ln., Springfield, VA 22151. TEL 703-642-9090. FAX 703-642-9094. Ed. Vivian K. Walworth. bk.rev.; abstr.; bibl.; charts; illus.; pat.; index; circ. 4,000. (also avail. in microform from UMI; reprint service avail. from UMI) **Indexed:** Art & Archaeol.Tech.Abstr., Cadscan, Chem.Abstr., Curr.Cont., Eng.Ind., Lead Abstr., Photo.Abstr., Print.Abstr., Sci.Abstr., Zincscan.
Formerly (until 1985): Photographic Science and Engineering (ISSN 0031-8760)

770 620   US   ISSN 0747-3583
TR1.S76   CODEN: JITEEU
JOURNAL OF IMAGING TECHNOLOGY. 1975. bi-m. $80 (foreign $90). Society for Imaging Science and Technology (SPSE), 7003 Kilworth Ln., Springfield, VA 22151. TEL 703-642-9090. FAX 703-642-9094. Ed. Harold E. Lockwood. adv.; bk.rev.; abstr.; bibl.; charts; illus.; pat.; stat.; tr.lit.; index; circ. 3,500. (also avail. in microfilm from UMI; reprint service avail. from UMI) **Indexed:** Art & Archaeol.Tech.Abstr., ASCA, Chem.Abstr., Curr.Cont., Print.Abstr., Sci.Abstr.
Formerly (until 1984): Journal of Applied Photographic Engineering (ISSN 0098-7298)

740   GW   ISSN 0863-0453
TR280   CODEN: JIRMEA
JOURNAL OF INFORMATION RECORDING MATERIALS. (Text in English and German; summaries in English, German, Russian) 1973. bi-m. DM.178.20. (Photochemisches Kombinat Wolfen) Akademie-Verlag Berlin, Leipziger Str. 3-4, 1086 Berlin, Germany. TELEX 114420-AVERL-DD. Ed. K. Stopperka. adv.; bk.rev.; charts; illus.; index. **Indexed:** Chem.Abstr., Curr.Cont., INIS Atomind., Phys.Ber., Sci.Abstr.
—BLDSC shelfmark: 5006.772500.
Formerly: Journal fuer Signalaufzeichnungsmaterialien (ISSN 0323-598X)

778.315   JA
JOURNAL OF MICROGRAPHICS/MAIKURO SHASHIN.* (Text in Japanese) 1962. m. 3600 Yen($65) Japan Microphotography Association - Nihon Maikuro Shashin Kyokai, 2nd Ohkouchi Bldg., 1-9-15 Kaji-Machi, Chiyoda-Ku, Tokyo 101, Japan. Ed. Tokuchiro Ochiai. adv.; charts; illus.; mkt.; stat.; cum.index; circ. 3,500. (also avail. in microfiche)
Formerly: Journal of Microphotography (ISSN 0026-2811)

JOURNAL OF PHOTOCHEMISTRY AND PHOTOBIOLOGY, A: CHEMISTRY; an international journal devoted to the study of the quantitative and qualitative aspects of photochemistry and energy transfer. see *CHEMISTRY — Physical Chemistry*

770   UK   ISSN 0022-3638
TR1   CODEN: JPTSAF
JOURNAL OF PHOTOGRAPHIC SCIENCE. 1953. bi-m. £80 (foreign £90)(typically set in Jan.). The Barn, Whitehall, Near Middle Marwood, Barnstaple, N. Devon EX31 4EQ, England. TEL 0271-72482. FAX 0271-72482. Ed. Michael Austin. adv.; bk.rev.; bibl.; charts; illus.; index; circ. 2,000. **Indexed:** Art & Archaeol.Tech.Abstr., Br.Tech.Ind., Cadscan, Chem.Abstr., Curr.Cont., Deep Sea Res.& Oceanogr.Abstr., Graph.Arts Lit.Abstr., Ind.Sci.Rev., INIS Atomind., Lead Abstr., Photo.Abstr., Print.Abstr., Sci.Abstr., Zincscan.
—BLDSC shelfmark: 5035.000000.
Description: Features original papers in physics and chemistry on photographic processes, and on the technology of imaging systems and their applications.
Refereed Serial

JUMP CUT; a review of contemporary media. see *MOTION PICTURES*

770   DK
KAMERA. s-a. Specialbladsforlaget A-S, Finsensvej 80, 2000 Frederiksberg, Denmark. Ed. Finn Nesgaard. adv.; circ. 54,033.

770   FI   ISSN 0022-8133
KAMERALEHTI. 1950. 11/yr. FIM 369. Kameraseura r.y., Sibeliuksenkatu 11 B 17, 00250 Helsinki, Finland. FAX 358-0-407029. Ed. Pekka Punkari. adv.; bk.rev.; index; circ. 13,906.

KARTOGRAPHISCHE NACHRICHTEN. see *GEOGRAPHY*

770   US
KODAK TECH BITS. 1963. 3/yr. free to qualified personnel. Eastman Kodak Co., 343 State St., Rochester, NY 14650-0130. TEL 716-724-4000. FAX 716-724-9624. Ed. John H. Stone. bk.rev.; illus.; circ. 43,000.
Description: Bringing imaging techniques to scientists and engineers in biology, physical sciences, engineering, industry, aerial survey, photogrammetry and remote sensing fields.

KRONIKA; casopis za Slovensko krajevno zgodovino. see *HISTORY — History Of Europe*

LAKE SUPERIOR MAGAZINE. see *HISTORY — History Of North And South America*

770   GW   ISSN 0024-0621
TR1
LEICA-FOTOGRAFIE INTERNATIONAL; Zeitschrift der Kleinbildfotografie. French edition (ISSN 0174-0261); English edition (ISSN 0174-0253) (Editions in English, French and German) 1949. 8/yr. DM.55.20. Umschau Verlag Breidenstein GmbH, Stuttgart Str. 18-24, 6000 Frankfurt a.M. 1, Germany. TEL 069-2600-0. FAX 069-2600-609. TELEX 411964. Ed. Martina Mettner. adv.; bk.rev.; bibl.; charts; illus.; index. **Indexed:** Chem.Abstr.

770   IE
LENS. 1925. bi-m. membership. Photographic Society of Ireland, 38-39 Parnell Sq., Dublin, Ireland. Ed. Joseph Webb. adv.; bk.rev.; circ. 600.

770   US
THE LENSHADE. q. Photographers Specialized Services, Inc., Box 46, Oconomowoc, WI 53066. TEL 800-558-0114. Ed. Mark Stall.

LIANHUAN HUABAO/PICTURE STORIES. see *JOURNALISM*

770   US
LIGHT AND SHADE. 1916. 9/yr. $30. Pictorial Photographers of America, 299 W. 12 St., New York, NY 10014. Ed. Sylvia Mavis. bk.rev.; circ. 100. (looseleaf format; back issues avail.)

LIGHTWORKS; illuminating thresholds of new art. see *ART*

770   US   ISSN 1049-4812
▼**LINKED RING LETTER.** 1990. q. $15 (foreign $30). Consultant Press, Ltd., 163 Amsterdam Ave., No.201, New York, NY 10023. TEL 212-838-8640. FAX 212-873-7065. Ed. Robert S. Persky. adv.; bk.rev.; circ. 25,000.
Description: For photographers who exhibit and sell fine art photography.

770   791.43   GW
M F M FOTOTECHNIK. 1953. m. DM.93.20. (Deutsches Institut fuer Normung e.V., Fachnormenausschuss Bild und Film) A.G.T. Verlag Thum GmbH, Teinacher Str. 34, Postfach 109, 7140 Ludwigsburg, Germany. TEL 07141-33046. FAX 07141-33828. TELEX 7264853. Ed. Wolfgang J. Schaezler. circ. 8,067.
Formerly: M F M - Moderne Fototechnik (ISSN 0024-8142)
Description: All fields of applied photographic, film and A V technology.

770   PL   ISSN 0324-8453
MAGAZYN FOTOGRAFICZNY FOTO. 1953. m. 1500 Zl.($33) Wydawnictwo Arkady, Sienkiewicza 14, 00-950 Warsaw, Poland. (Dist. by: Ars Polona-Ruch, Krakowskie Przedmiescie 7, Warsaw, Poland) Ed. Andrzej Jaworski. adv.; bk.rev.; abstr.; illus.; index; circ. 50,000.
—BLDSC shelfmark: 4024.440000.
Formerly: Fotografia (ISSN 0015-8801)

312 658   US   ISSN 0894-3540
MARKETS ABROAD; international marketing letter for writers and photographers. 1987. q. $25 (foreign $35). Strawberry Media, Inc., 2460 Lexington Dr., Owosso, MI 48867. TEL 517-725-9027. Ed. Michael H. Sedge. circ. 500.
Description: Provides "how-to" information on the marketing of writing and photos.

770   GW
MEDIEN AKTIV. 1962. q. DM.17.80. (Bundesgremium fuer Schulphotographie) Juenger Verlag, Shumannstr. 161, D-6050 Offenbach, Germany. TEL 06051-17758. TELEX 4152889-JUED. Ed. M. Huschner. adv.; bk.rev.; illus.; circ. 5,000.
Formerly: Kamera und Schule (ISSN 0022-8109)

770   DK
MEDLEMSAVISEN. 1981. 10/yr. DKK 240. (Medieforbundet, Fotografisk Landsforbund) Grafisk Forbundshus, Lygten 16, 2400 Copenhagen NV, Denmark. FAX 45-35821545. Ed. Jesper Bentsen. adv.; bk.rev.; illus.; circ. 2,500.
Formerly: F L's Medlevsavis (ISSN 0107-7104)

778.35   FR   ISSN 0076-6364
MEMOIRES DE PHOTO-INTERPRETATION. 1963. irreg., no.7, 1970. price varies. (Ecole Pratique des Hautes Etudes) Librairie Touzot, 38 rue Saint Sulpice, 75278 Paris Cedex 06, France. **Indexed:** GeoRef.

MICROFICHE FOUNDATION. NEWSLETTER. see *LIBRARY AND INFORMATION SCIENCES*

778.315   UK
MICROGRAPHICS AND OPTICAL STORAGE BUYER'S GUIDE. 1981. a. £10. G.G. Baker & Associates, c/o Alan Armstrong & Assoc. Ltd., 72 Park Rd., London NW1 4SH, England. adv.; illus.; circ. 1,000.
Formerly: Micrographics Year Book (ISSN 0260-7069)

778.315   US   ISSN 0883-9808
MICROGRAPHICS NEWSLETTER; monthly report for business executives who use or market microfilm services and equipment. 1969. m. $145 (foreign $160). Microfilm Publishing, Inc., Box 950, Larchmont, NY 10538-0950. TEL 914-834-3044. Eds. Mitchell M. Badler, Dorothy Miceli. (looseleaf format; also avail. in microform from UMI) **Indexed:** Info.Media & Tech., PROMT, Resour.Ctr.Ind.
Formerly: Microfilm Newsletter (ISSN 0026-2749)
Description: Summary news, stock market analysis, company profiles, and classified advertising pertaining to the industry, for executives who market or use services and equipment.

MIDLAND REVIEW. see *LITERATURE*

770   US
MINI LAB FOCUS. m. membership only. Photo Marketing Association International, 3000 Picture Pl., Jackson, MI 49201. TEL 517-788-8100. FAX 517-788-8371. Ed. Gary Pageau. circ. 3,200. (back issues avail.)

771   US
MINILAB DEVELOPMENTS. 1986. bi-m. International Minilab Association, Inc., 2627 Grimsley St., Greensboro, NC 27403. TEL 919-854-8088. FAX 919-854-8566. adv.; circ. 15,466.
Description: Focuses on how to maintain and build the success of the minilab (on-premise retail photofinishing outlet) industry.

MINZU HUABAO/NATIONALITY PICTORIAL. see *ETHNIC INTERESTS*

THE MONOCACY VALLEY REVIEW. see *LITERATURE*

770   DK   ISSN 0904-2334
MUSEET FOR FOTOKUNST. KATALOG; kvartaltidsskrift for fotografi - quarterly magazine for photography. (Text in Danish, English) 1988. q. DKK 275. Museet for Fotokunst, Brandts Passage 37 & 43, DK-5000 Odense C, Denmark. TEL 45-66137816. FAX 45-66137310. (Co-sponsor: Brandts Klaedefabrik) Eds. Henning Hansen, Finn Thrane. adv.; bk.rev.; illus.; index; circ. 1,600. (back issues avail.)
Description: Features critical and biographical essays, reviews, calendars of exhibitions and events.

771   US
N A P E T NEWS. m. membership only. (National Association of Photo Equipment Technicians) Photo Marketing Association International, 3000 Picture Pl., Jackson, MI 49201. TEL 517-788-8100. FAX 517-788-8371. Ed. Charles Davenport. circ. 600. (back issues avail.)

770   UK
NATURE PHOTOGRAPHY; animals plants landscapes. a. Fountain Press Ltd., 45 The Broadway, Tolworth, Surrey KT6 7DW, England.
Description: International coverage of nature photographers' works.

770   UK   ISSN 0143-036X
TR505
NEW MAGIC LANTERN JOURNAL. 1978. irreg. £2.50 per issue. Magic Lantern Society of Great Britain, 36 Meon Rd., London W3 8AN, England. Ed. David Henry. bk.rev.; illus.; circ. 500. **Indexed:** Film Lit.Ind. (1991-).

NEW ORLEANS REVIEW. see *LITERATURE*

NEW SPOKES. see *LITERATURE — Poetry*

NEW VIRGINIA REVIEW. see *LITERATURE*

770   US   ISSN 0199-2422
TR820
NEWS PHOTOGRAPHER; dedicated to the service and advancement of news photography. 1946. m. $28 (foreign $44). National Press Photographers Association, Inc., 1446 Conneaut Ave., Bowling Green, OH 43402-2145. FAX 419-354-5435. Ed. James Gordon. adv.; bk.rev.; illus.; circ. 12,000. (back issues avail.) **Indexed:** Graph.Arts Lit.Abstr.
Formerly (until 1974): National Press Photographer (ISSN 0027-9935)

NIHON SHASHIN SOKURYO GAKKAI. GAKUJUTSU KOENKAI HAPPYO RONBUNSHU. see *GEOGRAPHY*

770   NO
NORSK FOTOGRAFISK TIDSSKRIFT. 6/yr. NOK 180. Norges Fotografforbund, Ilebakken 24, 1670 Kraakeroy, Norway. Ed. Arne Glomdal. adv.; circ. 2,500.

770 778.5   SP
NUEVA LENTE; publicacion mensual de fotografia y cine. 1971. m. 2250 ptas. Miguel J. Goni Fernandez, Ed. & Pub., Ardemans 64, Madrid, Spain. circ. 10,000 (controlled).

770   IT
NUOVA FOTOGRAFIA.* 1970. m. L.14500. Nuova Fotografia s.r.l., Viale Bruno Buozzi, 53, 00197 Rome, Italy. Ed. Fabio Consiglio. adv.; bk.rev.; circ. 55,000.

OASIS; bimestrale di natura ecologia fotografica. see *CONSERVATION*

770   DK   ISSN 0107-6329
OBJEKTIV. 1976. 4/yr. $40. Dansk Fotohistorisk Selskab, c/o Flemming Berendt, Teglgaardsvej 308, 3050 Humlebaek, Denmark. adv.; bk.rev.; illus.; circ. 400.

770 778.53   NO
OBJEKTIVET. q. NOK 405. Oslo Kamera Klubb, Postboks 5231, Majorstua, 0303 Oslo 3, Norway. adv.; bk.rev.

770   AU   ISSN 0048-1459
OESTERREICHISCHE FOTO-ZEITUNG;* fachblatt fuer Lichtbildner. 1952. m. S.180. Zeitungsverlag Kuhn und Co., Kutschkergasse 42, A-1180 Vienna, Austria. Ed. Hans Hamann. adv.; bk.rev.; charts; illus.; tr.lit.; circ. 4,000.

686.2 778.1   GW   ISSN 0030-0594
OFFSETPRAXIS; Europaeische Fachzeitschrift fuer Offset-, Kleinoffset-Druck, Reprofotographie und Fotosatz. 1958. m. (except Aug.). DM.84 (foreign DM.96). Fachschriften Verlag GmbH, Hoehenstr. 17, Postfach 1329, 7012 Fellbach, Germany. TEL 0711-5206-1. FAX 0711-5281424. Ed. Ottmar Strebel.
Description: Industry news about printing: type and printing technology, graphics, events and meetings.

OSNOVAC. see *ART*

770   US
OUTDOOR & TRAVEL PHOTOGRAPHY. 1988. q. $3.95 per no. Harris Publications, Inc., 1115 Broadway, 8th fl., New York, NY 10010. TEL 212-807-7100. FAX 212-627-4678. circ. 62,321.
Description: For the amateur photographer whose interests include travel and the great outdoors.

770   US
OUTDOOR PHOTOGRAPHER. 1985. 10/yr. $21.95. Werner Publishing Corporation, 12121 Ventura Blvd., Ste. 1220, Los Angeles, CA 90025-1175. adv.; circ. 175,000.

770   US   ISSN 0030-8277
P S A JOURNAL. 1935. m. $35 membership. Photographic Society of America, Inc., 3000 United Founders Blvd., No. 103, Oklahoma City, OK 73112-3940. Ed. Dennis J. Ramsey. adv.; bk.rev.; abstr.; illus.; index; circ. 11,000. (also avail. in microform from UMI; reprint service avail. from UMI) **Indexed:** Bus.Ind., Chem.Abstr., Graph.Arts Lit.Abstr., Mag.Ind., Tr.& Indus.Ind.
—BLDSC shelfmark: 6945.740000.

PHOTOGRAPHY

770 US
P T N MASTER BUYING GUIDE & DIRECTORY.*
(Photographic Trade News); main entrance to the retail photographic market. 1937. a. included with subscr. to Photographic Trade News. P T N Publishing Corp., 445 Broad Hollow Rd., Ste. 21, Melville, NY 11747-4722. TEL 516-845-2700. FAX 516-845-7109. Ed. Harold Johnson. adv.; illus.; circ. 10,000 (controlled).

770 301.412 US
P W P NEWSLETTER. 1984. bi-m. $25 in NYC; outside NYC $15. Professional Women Photographers, c/o Photographics Unlimited, 17 W. 17th St., New York, NY 10011-5510. Ed. Meryl Meisler. adv.; bk.rev.; circ. 500.
Supersedes: P W P Times.

PALATINATE. see *LITERATURE*

PAN-EROTIC REVIEW. see *ART*

770 US
PENTAX LIFE. 3/yr. Pentax Corporation, 35 Inverness Drive E., Englewood, CO 80112-5404. TEL 303-799-8000. Ed. Madelaine Cassidy.

770 SA ISSN 0012-8473
PERSPECTIVE. vol.7, 1970. m. free to members. East London Photographic Society, Box 147, East London 5200, South Africa. Ed. D. Moody. adv.; bk.rev.; illus.; mkt.; circ. 50. (processed)
Formerly: East London Photographic Society Magazine.
Description: Publishes local news of the society for the benefit of members.

770 NE ISSN 0167-9104
PERSPEKTIEF; quarterly for photography. (Text in Dutch and English) 1980. q. $60. (Ministerie van W V C) Perspektief, Centrum voor Fotografie, Sint Jobsweg 30, 3024 EJ Rotterdam, Netherlands. TEL 010-4780655. FAX 010-4772072. Ed. Bas Vroege. adv.; bk.rev.; bibl.; illus.; stat.; circ. 3,000. **Indexed:** Artbibl.Mod.
Description: Contains theory concerning creative photography, portfolios, and an international bibliographical service, FOTODOK (index of 35 magazines).

770 US ISSN 0199-4913
PETERSEN'S PHOTOGRAPHIC. 1971. m. $19.94. Petersen Publishing Co., 8490 Sunset Blvd., Los Angeles, CA 90069. TEL 213-854-2222. (Subscr. to: Box 50004, Boulder, CO 80323) Ed. Bill Hurter. adv.; bk.rev.; charts; illus.; stat.; index; circ. 209,000. (also avail. in microform from UMI; back issues avail.) **Indexed:** Bk.Rev.Ind. (1978-), Child.Bk.Rev.Ind. (1978-), Consum.Ind., Ind.How To Do It (1978-), Mag.Ind., P.M.I., R.G.
●Also available online. Vendor(s): DIALOG.
Former titles (until 1979): Petersen's PhotoGraphic Magazine (ISSN 0048-3583); Photographic Quarterly.

770 FR ISSN 0151-783X
PHOT 'ARGUS (EDITION PROFESSIONNELLE). (General edition also avail.) 1965. 7/yr. 279 F. Editions V.M., 116 bd. Malesherbes, 75017 Paris, France. TEL 42-27-25-44. FAX 47-66-57-74. Ed. Robert Monnier. adv.; illus.

770 FR
PHOTO. 1960. m. 195 F. (foreign 275 F.). Daniel Filipacchi, 63 Champs-Elysees, 75306 Paris, France. TEL 42-56-75-72. TELEX 290294. (Subscr. to: 99 rue d'Amsterdam, 75008 Paris, France) Ed. Michel Decron. illus.; circ. 191,908.

770 UK
PHOTO AND ELECTRONICS MARKETING. 1985. m. £36 (free to qualified personnel). Bowman Publishing Ltd., Britania House, Leagrave Rd., Luton, Beds. LU3 1RJ, England. TEL 0582-26276. FAX 0582-411327. TELEX 825353. Ed. Christopher Wordsworth. adv.; bk.rev.; circ. 10,300. (back issues avail.)
Formerly (until 1989): Dealerama (ISSN 0268-8115)
Description: Marketing magazine serving the UK and European photo and consumer electronics retail industry.

771 778.59 AT
PHOTO & VIDEO RETAILER. 1951. m. Aus.$41 (foreign Aus.$102)(effective Apr. 1992). Yaffa Publishing Group, 17-21 Bellevue St., Surry Hills, N.S.W. 2010, Australia. TEL 02-281-2333. FAX 02-281-2750. adv.: B&W page Aus.$900, color page Aus.$1390; trim 297 x 210. illus.; circ. 2,573.
Former titles: Photo Retailer (ISSN 0816-1909); (until 1985): Photo Trade News (ISSN 0031-8590)
Description: Source of product information for the photo-finishing trade and the camcorder-video market.

770 UK
PHOTO ANSWERS. 1964. m. £20.50. Apex House, Oundle Rd., Peterborough PE2 9NP, England. TEL 0733-898100. Ed. Steve Bavister. adv.; bk.rev.; charts; illus.; index; circ. 67,694. (also avail. in microform from UMI)
Incorporates: Camera (ISSN 0144-1248); Creative Photography; Camera User; S L R Photography; Which was formerly: S L R Camera (ISSN 0036-1631)

770 US
PHOTO BUSINESS. 1956. m. $45. B P I Communications, Inc. (New York), (Subsidiary of: Affiliated Publications, Inc.), 1515 Broadway, 39th Fl., New York, NY 10036. TEL 212-764-7300. FAX 212-944-1719. Ed. Willard Clark. adv.; bk.rev.; illus.; circ. 13,000. (tabloid format; also avail. in microform from BLH)
Formerly: Photo Weekly (ISSN 0031-8647)
Description: Photo trade magazine covering industry, new products, and business news.

PHOTO CHEMICAL MACHINING INSTITUTE. JOURNAL. see *PRINTING*

770 791.43 SZ
PHOTO-CINE-EXPERT (1979); la revue suisse au service des photographes et cineastes. 1940. 9/yr. 55 Fr. Editions Jean Spinatsch SA, 13, route de Bellebouche, CH-1246 Corsier-Geneva, Switzerland. Ed. Jean Spinatsch. adv.; bk.rev.; illus.; circ. 8,500.
Former titles: Nouveau Photo-Cine-Expert; Photo-Cine-Expert (ISSN 0031-8450)

770 US ISSN 0888-5680
TR640
PHOTO DESIGN. 1984. bi-m. $42. B P I Communications, Inc. (New York) (Subsidiary of: Affiliated Publications, Inc.), 1515 Broadway, 39th Fl., New York, NY 10036. TEL 212-764-7300. FAX 212-944-1710. circ. 28,000.
Description: For creative professionals, advertising, editorial and corporate communications.

770 GW
PHOTO DESIGN UND TECHNIK. 1986. 12/yr. Verlag Design und Technik GmbH, Schultheiss Str. 27, 8000 Munich 71, Germany. TEL 089-7917045. FAX 089-791-8883. circ. 25,000. (back issues avail.)

770 CN
▼**PHOTO DIGEST.** 1990. 8/yr. Can.$19($28) (foreign $32). Editions Carni Ltee., 850 Pierre-Bertrand Blvd., Ste.440, Ville de Vanier, Que. G1M 3K8, Canada. TEL 418-687-3550. FAX 418-687-1679. Ed. Jacques Thibault. adv.

770 US
PHOTO DISTRICT NEWS. m. $36 (Canada $76; elsewhere $111). B P I Communications, Inc. (New York) (Subsidiary of: Affiliated Publications, Inc.), 1515 Broadway, 39th Fl., New York, NY 10036. TEL 212-764-7300. FAX 212-944-1719.
Description: Educates and informs the reader on all phases of professional photography.

770 686 375 US
PHOTO EDUCATOR. 1968. 2/yr. free to qualified personnel. Eastman Kodak Co., 343 State St., Rochester, NY 14650-0130. TEL 716-724-4000. Ed. Mary-Helen Maginn. charts; illus.; circ. 15,000.
Former titles: Newsletter for Photo Educators; Newsletter for Photography Instructors; Newsletter for Graphic Arts and Photography Instructors; **Supersedes:** Graphic Arts and Photography. Newsletter.
Description: Covers fields of photojournalism, commercial and portrait photography, photo illustration, industrial, biomedical and fine-art photography.

771 US ISSN 1060-4936
TR1
PHOTO ELECTRONIC IMAGING; the magazine for photographic and audio-visual professionals. 1958. m. $18. Professional Photography of America, 1090 Executive Way, Des Plaines, IL 60018. TEL 708-299-8161. FAX 708-299-2685. Ed. Kim Brody. adv.; bk.rev.; charts; illus.; tr.lit.; index; circ. 48,000. (also avail. in microform from UMI; reprint service avail.) **Indexed:** Art & Archaeol.Tech.Abstr., Graph.Arts Lit.Abstr., Ind.How To Do It (1971-), PROMT.
Former titles (until 1991): Photomethods (ISSN 0146-0153); (until 1974): Photomethods for Industry (ISSN 0030-8110)

770 AT
PHOTO FORUM. 1982. m. Aus.$44. Horwitz Grahame Pty. Ltd., 506 Miller St., Cammeray, N.S.W. 2062, Australia. TEL 02-929-6144. FAX 02-957-1814. (Subscr. to: P.O. Box 306, Cammeray, N.S.W. 2062, Australia) Ed. Margaret Brown. circ. 1,100. (back issues avail.)
Description: Publication for the world of photographic retailing and distributing.

PHOTO INTERPRETATION. see *GEOGRAPHY*

770 IT
PHOTO ITALIA. m. L.115000 in Europe; America L.160000. Publimedia Societa Editrice, Corso Venezia 18, 20121 Milan, Italy. TEL 02-77521. FAX 02-781068. Ed. Francesco Buffa di Perrero. adv.; circ. 75,000.
Formerly: Photo Italiana.

771 US
PHOTO-LAB INDEX; cumulative formulary of standard recommended photographic procedures. 1939. a. (q. updates). $65 ($30 for supplements; foreign $33). Morgan & Morgan Inc., 145 Palisade St., Dobbs Ferry, NY 10522. TEL 914-693-0023. FAX 914-693-1572. Ed. Liliane Morgan. charts; index, cum.index; circ. 8,000. (looseleaf format)

771 658 US ISSN 0164-4769
TR287
PHOTO LAB MANAGEMENT. 1979. m. $15. P L M Publishing, 1312 Lincoln Blvd., Box 1700, Santa Monica, CA 90406. TEL 213-451-1344. FAX 213-395-9058. Ed. Carolyn Ryan. bibl.; charts; illus.; stat.; tr.lit.; circ. 18,150. (back issues avail.)

770 US
PHOTO LETTER. 1980. s-a. $10. Texas Photographic Society, Box 3109, Austin, TX 78764. TEL 512-471-1976. Ed. Julie Newton. adv.; bk.rev.; circ. 2,000.

770 CN
PHOTO LIFE. 1976. 8/yr. Can.$18.64. Camar Publications Ltd., 130 Spy Court, Markham, Ont. L3R 5H6, Canada. TEL 416-485-8440. FAX 416-475-9246. Ed. Jerry Kobalenko. adv.; bk.rev.; circ. 36,000. **Indexed:** CMI.

770 IT
PHOTO MADE IN ITALY. (Text in English) 1981. 4/yr. free. Mediaspazio, Via M. Melloni 17, 20129 Milan, Italy. TEL 02-718341. Ed. Luciano Scattolin. adv.; circ. 9,000.

771 US
PHOTO MARKETING MAGAZINE. m. membership only. Photo Marketing Association International, 3000 Picture Pl., Jackson, MI 49201. TEL 517-788-8100. FAX 517-788-8371. Ed. Margaret Hooks. circ. 22,500. (back issues avail.)

771 US ISSN 0031-8531
TR1
PHOTO MARKETING NEWSLINE. 1924. bi-m. membership only. Photo Marketing Association International, 3000 Picture Pl., Jackson, MI 49201. TEL 517-788-8100. FAX 517-788-8371. Ed. Gary Pageau. illus.; circ. 12,200. (back issues avail.) **Indexed:** PROMT.

770 US
PHOTO MERCHANDISING. m. 3004 Glenview Rd., Wilmette, IL 60091. TEL 708-256-6067. FAX 708-441-2264. Ed. Saran Hirscaman.

PHOTOGRAPHY

770 UK ISSN 0956-2745
PHOTO PRO. 1966. q. £10 (foreign £14). Icon Publications Ltd., Maxwell Ln., Kelso, Roxburghshire TD5 7BB, England. TEL 0573 260326. FAX 0573-26000. Ed. David Kilpatrick. adv.; bk.rev.; illus.; circ. 10,000.
Formerly (until 1989): Master Photographer (ISSN 0047-6196)

770 US
PHOTO REVIEW. 1976. q. $25 includes Photo Review Newsletter. Photo Review, 301 Hill Ave., Langhorne, PA 19047. Ed. Stephen Perloff. adv.; bk.rev.; illus.; circ. 1,200.
Formerly: Philadelphia Photo Review (ISSN 0363-6488)
Description: Contains critical reviews of exhibitions, essays, interviews, portfolios of photography and industry news.

770 US
PHOTO REVIEW NEWSLETTER. 1976. 8/yr. $25 inlcudes Photo Review. Photo Review, 301 Hill Ave., Langhorne, PA 19047. Ed. Stephen Perloff. bk.rev.; circ. 1,200. (back issues avail.)
Formerly: Philadelphia Photo Review Newsletter.
Description: Photography exhibition listings for New York, Philadelphia, Baltimore, Washington, Pittsburgh, news and exhibition opportunities.

770 CN ISSN 0226-9708
PHOTO SELECTION. (Text in French) 1981. 8/yr. Can.$19($28) Editions Carni Ltee., 850 bd. Pierre Bertrand, Ste.440, Ville de Vanier, Que. G1M 3K8, Canada. TEL 418-687-3550. FAX 418-687-1679. Ed. Jacques Dumont. adv.; bk.rev.; cum.index: 1981-1984; circ. 18,500. (back issues avail.)

770 GW
PHOTO TECHNIK INTERNATIONAL. (Editions in English, German) 1954. bi-m. DM.72 (English edition: DM.48). Rupert-Mayer-Str. 45, 8000 Munich 70, Germany. TEL 089-7231992. FAX 089-72492250. (U.S. subscr. to: H P Marketing Corp., 16 Chapin Road, Pine Brook, NJ 07058) Ed. Hildrun Karpf-Kerkmann. adv.; bk.rev.; charts; illus.; mkt.; tr.lit.; circ. 51,500. Indexed: Photo.Abstr.
Formerly: International Photo Technik (ISSN 0020-8280)

770 GW ISSN 0342-8613
PHOTOBLAETTER. 1929. bi-m. DM.33.60. Umschau Verlag Breidenstein GmbH, Stuttgarter Str. 18-24, 6000 Frankfurt a.M. 1, Germany. TEL 069-2600-0. FAX 069-2600-609. TELEX 411964. Ed. Martina Mettner. adv.; circ. 9,500.

770 US ISSN 0885-4270
PHOTOBULLETIN. 1985. w. (d. also avail.). $510 ($625 for d. service). PhotoSource International, Pine Lake Farm, Osceola, WI 54020. TEL 715-248-3800. FAX 715-248-7394. TELEX 6511892053. Ed. Lori Johnson. circ. 227.
●Also available online. Vendor(s): NewsNet (PB26).

770 AT ISSN 0811-0859
PHOTOFILE. 1982. q. Aus.$32 to individuals; institutions Aus.$37. Australian Centre for Photography, 257 Oxford St., Paddington, N.S.W. 2021, Australia. TEL 02-331-6253. FAX 02-331-6887. Ed. Martin thomas. adv.; B&W page $375; trim 215 x 160. bk.rev.; circ. 2,500. (back issues avail.)
●Also available online.
Description: Covers photomedia including new techniques in film, video and still photography.

770 US ISSN 0889-2393
PHOTOFINISHING NEWS LETTER. 1983. bi-w. $100 (foreign $125). Photofinishing News, Inc., 4100 Corporate Sq., Naples, FL 33942. TEL 813-643-5666. FAX 813-643-4504. Ed. Don Franz. bk.rev.; stat.; circ. 500. (back issues avail.)

770 US
PHOTOFOLIO; photography collectors' newsletter. 1979. q. $20. Photocollect, 740 West End Ave., New York, NY 10025. Ed. Alan Klotz. bk.rev.; circ. 500. (back issues avail.)

PHOTOGRAMMETRIC ENGINEERING AND REMOTE SENSING. see GEOGRAPHY

PHOTOGRAMMETRIC RECORD. see GEOGRAPHY

770 US
PHOTOGRAPH COLLECTOR'S RESOURCE DIRECTORY. 1983. biennial. $24.95. Consultant Press, Ltd., 163 Amsterdam Ave., No.201, New York, NY 10023. TEL 212-838-8640. FAX 212-873-7065. Ed. Robert S. Persky. adv.
Description: Listing of galleries, museums and non-profit institutions that either exhibit, collect, or sell fine art photography. Additional sections list auction houses, photography publications, associations and organizations.

770 FR ISSN 0369-9560
PHOTOGRAPHE. m. 265 F. (foreign 440 F.). Publications Denis Jacob, 103, Bd. St. Michel, 75005 Paris, France. adv.; circ. 20,000. Indexed: Pt.de Rep.
Description: Magazine for photography professionals in France.

770 CN
PHOTOGRAPHER. vol.3, 1976. q. Can.$6. Gary Wilcox, Ed. & Pub., Box 24954, Sta. C, Vancouver, B.C. V5T 4G3, Canada. illus.

770 US
▼**PHOTOGRAPHER'S DISPATCH;** a direct communication line from photographers to editorial photo buyers. 1991. bi-m. A G Editions, Inc., 142 Bank St., Ste. GA, New York, NY 10014. TEL 212-929-0959. FAX 212-924-4796. Ed. Ann Guilfoyle.

770 US ISSN 0194-5467
TR1
PHOTOGRAPHER'S FORUM. 1978. q. $12. Serbin Communications, Inc., 511 Olive St., Santa Barbara, CA 93101. Ed. Glen R. Serbin. adv.; bk.rev.; circ. 12,000.
Formerly: Student Forum.

770 US ISSN 0147-247X
TR12
PHOTOGRAPHER'S MARKET. 1979. a. $21.95. F & W Publications, Inc., 1507 Dana Ave., Cincinnati, OH 45207. TEL 513-531-2222. Ed. Michael Willins.
—BLDSC shelfmark: 6468.870000.
Description: Lists 2500 places to sell news, publicity, product, scenic, portrait, fashion, wildlife, audiovisual, sports and travel photos.

770 GR ISSN 0259-7349
PHOTOGRAPHIA. 1977. bi-m. Dr.3000($24) Moressopoulos & Associates Ltd., 19, Iperidou str., GR-105 58 Athens, Greece. TEL 1-323-4217. FAX 1-323-2082. (Subscr. to: P.O. Box 30 564, GR-100 33 Athens, Greece) Ed. Stavros Moressopulos. adv.; bk.rev.; circ. 15,000. (back issues avail.)
Description: Photographic trade magazine for both amateurs and professionals.

770 US ISSN 1053-7031
TR6.5
PHOTOGRAPHIC ART MARKET: AUCTION PRICES (YEAR). 1981. a. $49.95. Consultant Press, Ltd., 163 Amsterdam Ave., No.201, New York, NY 10023. TEL 212-838-8640. FAX 212-873-7065. Ed. Robert S. Persky. circ. 1,000.
Formerly: Photographic Art Market Auction Price Results and Analysis.
Description: For collectors, dealers, curators, and appraisers for buying, selling, appraising, valuing a donation, insuring, or filing an insurance claim.

770 900 CN ISSN 0704-0024
PHOTOGRAPHIC CANADIANA. 1974. 5/yr. Can.$24($24) Photographic Historical Society of Canada, Box 115, Stn. S, Toronto, Ont. M5M 4L6, Canada. Ed. Everett Roseborough. bk.rev.; index; circ. 300. (back issues avail.)
Description: Provides a general history of photography and the role of Canadians.

770 UK ISSN 0031-8736
TR1
PHOTOGRAPHIC JOURNAL. 1853. m. £53 (foreign £58). Royal Photographic Society of Great Britain, Acorn House, 74-94 Cherry Orchard Dr., Croydon CR0 6BA, England. TEL 081-681-8339. FAX 081-681-1880. Ed. Roy Green. adv.; bk.rev.; bibl.; charts; illus.; circ. 10,000 (controlled). (also avail. in microform from UMI; reprint service avail. from UMI) Indexed: Artbibl.Mod., Br.Tech.Ind., Chem.Abstr., Graph.Arts Lit.Abstr., World Surf.Coat.
—BLDSC shelfmark: 6471.000000.

771 US ISSN 0031-8744
PHOTOGRAPHIC PROCESSING.* 1964. m. $10 (free to qualified personnel). P T N Publishing Corp., 445 Broad Hollow Rd., Ste. 21, Melville, NY 11747-4722. TEL 516-845-2700. FAX 516-845-7109. adv.; bk.rev.; charts; illus.; stat.; circ. 15,500. Indexed: Graph.Arts Lit.Abstr.

770 US
PHOTOGRAPHIC RESOURCE CENTER. NEWSLETTER. 1979. m. membership. Photographic Resource Center, 602 Commonwealth Ave., Boston, MA 02215-2503. TEL 617-353-0700. Ed. Tom Block. adv.; bk.rev.; circ. 2,500.

771 US ISSN 0031-8779
PHOTOGRAPHIC TRADE NEWS.* (Includes P T N Master Buying Guide and Directory) 1937. 24/yr. $6. P T N Publishing Corp., 445 Broad Hollow Rd., Ste. 21, Melville, NY 11747-4722. TEL 516-845-2700. FAX 516-845-7109. adv.; bk.rev.; illus.; tr.lit.; circ. 14,000.

770 US
PHOTOGRAPHICA.* 1969. 4/yr. $25. American Photographic Historical Society, 1150 Sixth Ave., 3rd fl., New York, NY 10036-2701. TEL 212-594-5056. Ed. George Gilbert. adv.; bk.rev.; illus.; circ. 500. (also avail. in microform from WMP)
Former titles (until 1987): Photographica Journal; Photographica (ISSN 0090-2063)
Description: News and information on early photography.

770 UK ISSN 0265-7198
TR1
PHOTOGRAPHY. 1958. m. £23.40. Argus Specialist Publications Ltd., Argus House, Boundary Way, Hemels, Hampstead, Herts HP2 7St, England. TELEX 8811 896. Ed. Stuart Cook. adv.; illus.; circ. 10,412. (also avail. in microform from UMI; reprint service avail. from UMI)
Former titles (until 1986): 35MM Photography; Photography (ISSN 0031-8809); Incorporates: Thirty-Five MM; Sub-Miniature Photography.

770 CN
PHOTOGRAPHY AT OPEN SPACE MONOGRAPHS. 1976. irreg. price varies. Photography at Open Space, P.O. Box 5207, Sta. B, Victoria, B.C. V8R 6N4, Canada. Ed. Tom Gore. bk.rev.; circ. 500.

770 JA
PHOTOGRAPHY IN JAPAN. (Text in Japanese) 1953. m. 200 Yen. Photographic Society of Japan - Nihon Shashin Kyokai, JCII Bldg., 1st Fl., 25, Ichiban-cho, Chiyoda-ku, Tokyo, Japan. FAX 03-3291-8298. Ed. Motohiko Kimura. adv.; bk.rev.; circ. 1,000.

770 US ISSN 1040-0346
PHOTOGRAPHY IN NEW YORK. 1988. bi-m. $15 (Canada $20; elsewhere $25). Photography in New York, Inc., Box 20351, Park W. Sta., New York, NY 10025. TEL 212-787-0401. FAX 212-799-3054. Ed. Bill Mindlin. adv.; bk.rev.; circ. 7,000. (back issues avail.)
Description: Presents a listing of gallery and museum exhibitions, dealers, and booksellers, as well as information about auctions, classes and workshops. Includes a calendar of events.

770 CN
PHOTOGRAPHY MONOGRAPH SERIES. 1978. irreg. Photography at Open Space, Box 5207, Sta. B, Victoria, B.C. V8R 6N4, Canada. Ed. Tom Gore. circ. 600.

770 UK ISSN 0079-1865
PHOTOGRAPHY YEAR BOOK.* 1937. a. £35. Fountain Press, 45 The Broadway, Tolworth, Surrey KT6 7DW, England. Ed. John Sanders. adv.
—BLDSC shelfmark: 6474.280000.

770 070.49 US ISSN 0893-5610
TR820
PHOTOJOURNALIST (NEWARK). 1969. a. $5.20. New Jersey Press Photographers Association, c/o New Jersey Newsphotos, Airport International Plaza, Rt. 1, Newark, NJ 07114. TEL 201-242-1111. Ed. Ray Fisk. adv.; circ. 500.

PHOTOGRAPHY

770 US ISSN 0190-1400
PHOTOLETTER. 1976. m. $90. PhotoSource International, Pine Lake Farm, Osceola, WI 54020. TEL 715-248-3800. FAX 715-248-7394. TELEX 6511892053. Ed. Lynette Layer. adv.; bk.rev.; tr.lit.; charts; index; circ. 1,850. (looseleaf format; back issues avail.)
●Also available online. Vendor(s): NewsNet.

PHOTOMAGAZINE; magazine des photographes et cineastes amateurs. see *MOTION PICTURES*

770 US ISSN 0885-4262
PHOTOMARKET; photosource international. 1984. s-m. $330. PhotoSource International, Pine Lake Farm, Osceola, WI 54020. TEL 715-248-3800. FAX 715-248-7394. TELEX 6511892053. Ed. Lori Johnson. index; circ. 595. (back issues avail.)
●Also available online. Vendor(s): NewsNet (PB17).
Description: Lists specific photographic needs of middle-range magazine and book publishers.

770 US
▼**PHOTOPRO.** 1990. bi-m. $11.97. Patch Communications, 5211 S. Washington Ave., Titusville, FL 32780. TEL 407-268-5010. FAX 407-267-7216. Ed. David Brooks. circ. 45,000.
Description: Contains technical information and creative approaches for commercial, portrait, wedding, outdoor and other working professional photographers. Includes reports on lighting tests.

770 AT ISSN 0727-3959
PHOTOWORLD. 1978. m. Australian Hi-Fi & Sepcialist Magazines Group Pty. Ltd., P.O. Box 341, Mona Vale, N.S.W. 2103, Australia. TEL 02 913-1444. FAX 913-2342. Ed. Don Norris.
Formerly: Photographic World.
Description: News about photographic equipment and technique travel plus photography.

770 AT ISSN 0813-4545
PHOTOWORLD BUYER'S DIRECTORY. a. Aus.$50. Australian Hi-Fi Publishing Services Pty. Ltd., 1 Bungan Lane, Mona Vola, N.S.W. 2103, Australia. TEL 02-997-1188. Ed. Neil Sudbury. circ. 20,000. (back issues avail.)
Description: Comparative reviews of consumer photography equipment.

770 US
PICTORIALIST. 1941. m. membership. Photo Pictorialists of Milwaukee, Inc., c/o Ed. Ronald M. Buege, 2909 S. 101 St., West Allis, WI 53227. circ. 75. (looseleaf format)

778.1 US
▼**PICTURE PERFECT.** 1990. bi-m. $20. Aquino Productions, One Bank St., Ste. 201, Box 15760, Stamford, CT 06901. TEL 203-978-0562. Ed. Andres C. Aquino. circ. 51,000.
Description: For photographers and fashion buyers, and video, TV and film producers. Covers the creative aspects of fashion and photography.

PIG IRON; the annual thematic anthology of contemporary literature. see *LITERATURE*

770 US ISSN 0032-4582
TR1
POPULAR PHOTOGRAPHY. 1937. m. $17.94 (Canada $23.94; elsewhere $25.94)(effective 1992). Hachette Magazines, Inc., 1633 Broadway, New York, NY 10009. TEL 212-767-6000. (Subscr. to: Box 54912, Boulder, CO 80322. TEL 800-876-6636) Ed. Jason Schneider. adv.; bk.rev.; charts; illus.; mkt.; index; circ. 650,000. (also avail. in microform from MIM; microfiche from UMI; reprint service avail. from UMI) **Indexed:** Acad.Ind., Art & Archaeol.Tech.Abstr., Artbibl.Mod., Bk.Rev.Ind. (1989-), Chem.Abstr., Child.Bk.Rev.Ind. (1989-), Consum.Ind., Film Lit.Ind. (1973-), Gdlns., Graph.Arts Lit.Abstr., Ind.How To Do It (1966-), Mag.Ind., P.M.I., PMR, R.G., TOM.
●Also available online. Vendor(s): DIALOG.
Formerly (until 1955): Photography.

770 UK ISSN 0032-6445
PRACTICAL PHOTOGRAPHY. m. £24.50. Frontline Ltd. (Subsidiary of: E M A P - Haymarket Ltd.), Park House, 117 Park Rd., Peterborough PE1 2TR, England. TEL 0733-555161. FAX 62788. TELEX 329292 FRONT G. Ed. Dominic Boland. adv.; bk.rev.; charts; illus.; circ. 101,116.
—BLDSC shelfmark: 6595.405000.

770 US
PRICE GUIDE TO WALLACE NUTTING PICTURES. 1980. irreg., 4th ed., 1991. $14.95. Diamond Press, Box 2458, Doylestown, PA 18901. TEL 215-345-6094. FAX 215-345-6692.

PRINTS. see *LITERATURE — Poetry*

PRINTSHOP. see *PRINTING*

770 IT ISSN 1120-4079
PRO. m. L.80000 (foreign L.150000). Editrice Reflex s.r.l., Via Di Villa Severini 54, 00191 Rome, Italy. TEL 06-3278595. FAX 06-3295648.

770 UK
PROFESSIONAL PHOTOGRAPHER. 1961. m. £31.50. E M A P Vision Ltd., 19 Scarbrook Rd., Croydon, Surrey CR9 1QH, England. TEL 081-760-9690. FAX 081-681-1672. TELEX 946665. Ed. David Warr. adv.; bk.rev.; illus.; index; circ. 7,315. (also avail. in microform from UMI; reprint service avail. from UMI) **Indexed:** Agri.Eng.Abstr.
Formerly: Industrial and Commercial Photographer (ISSN 0019-784X)

770 US ISSN 0033-0167
TR690
PROFESSIONAL PHOTOGRAPHER. 1907. m. $24.50. (Professional Photographers of America) P P A Publications and Events, Inc., 1090 Executive Way, Des Plaines, IL 60018. TEL 708-299-8161. FAX 708-299-2685. Ed. Alfred DeBat. adv.; bk.rev.; charts; illus.; index; circ. 31,000. (also avail. in microfilm from UMI; reprint service avail.) **Indexed:** Graph.Arts Lit.Abstr., Ind.How To Do It (1990-).
—BLDSC shelfmark: 6864.140000.
Formerly: National Photographer.

PROFESSIONAL PHOTOGRAPHER DIRECTORY AND BUYER'S GUIDE. see *BUSINESS AND ECONOMICS — Trade And Industrial Directories*

770 US
PROFESSIONAL PHOTOGRAPHIC EQUIPMENT DIRECTORY AND BUYING GUIDE.* 1975. a. P T N Publishing Corp., 445 Broad Hollow Rd., Ste. 21, Melville, NY 11747-4722. TEL 516-845-2700. FAX 516-845-7109. adv.; illus.

770 IT
PROFESSIONAL PHOTOGRAPHY. 1984. a. L.11000. Editrice Progresso s.r.l., Viale Piceno 14, 20129 Milan, Italy. TEL 02-715939. FAX 02-713030. bk.rev.; illus.; index; circ. 25,000.

770 AT ISSN 0159-8880
PROFESSIONAL PHOTOGRAPHY IN AUSTRALIA. 1949. m. Aus.$59 (foreign Aus.$69). Horwitz Grahame Pty. Ltd., 506 Miller St., Cammeray, N.S.W. 2062, Australia. TEL 02-929-6144. FAX 02-957-1814. Ed. Paul Burrows. adv.; bk.rev.; circ. 6,000. (back issues avail.)
Formerly: I.A.P. Professional Photography in Australia (ISSN 0046-9742)
Description: News and views for professional photographers.

770 NE
PROFESSIONELE FOTOGRAFIE.* bi-m. Vereniging van Beroepsfotografen in Nederland, Nieuwe Keizersgracht 58, 1018 DR Amsterdam, Netherlands. TEL 020-247151.

770 791.4 GW
PROFIFOTO; journal fuer professional photography. 1969. bi-m. DM.61. (Arbeitskreis Werbe-, Mode- und Industriefotographie) G F W Verlag GmbH, Volmerstr. 20, 4000 Duesseldorf 1, Germany. TEL 0211-39009-0. Ed. T. Gerwers. adv.; bk.rev.; illus.; tr.lit.; circ. 17,000.
Formerly: Fachkontakt.

770 IT ISSN 0033-0868
PROGRESSO FOTOGRAFICO; periodico culturale illustrato di fotografia. 1894. m. L.83000. Editrice Progresso s.r.l., Viale Piceno, 14, 20129 Milan, Italy. TEL 02-715939. FAX 02-713030. adv.; bk.rev.; illus.; circ. 30,000. **Indexed:** Artbibl.Mod., Chem.Abstr.

R I S D VOICE. (Rhode Island School of Design) see *ART*

770 US ISSN 0033-9202
RANGEFINDER. 1952. m. $15. Rangefinder Publishing Co., Inc., 1312 Lincoln Blvd., Box 1703, Santa Monica, CA 90406. TEL 310-451-8506. FAX 310-395-9058. Ed. Arthur Stern. adv.; bk.rev.; index; circ. 50,000. **Indexed:** Graph.Arts Lit.Abstr., Ind.How To Do It (1990-), P.M.I.

770 US ISSN 0891-5326
RE: VIEW. 1978. bi-m. membership. Friends of Photography, 250 4th St., San Francisco, CA 94103. TEL 415-495-7000. Ed. Michael Read. bk.rev.; illus.; circ. 8,000.
Formerly (until 1987): Friends of Photography. Newsletter (ISSN 0163-9552)
Description: Contains information about the field of creative photography and activities of organization.

770 IT
REFLEX. 1980. m. L.49500. Editrice Reflex s.r.l., Via di Villa Severini 54, 00191 Rome, Italy. FAX 3295648. Ed. Giulio Forti. adv.; bk.rev.; circ. 40,000.

770 CC
RENXIANG SHEYING/PORTRAIT PHOTOGRAPHY. (Text in Chinese) bi-m. (Shangye-bu, Yinshi Fuwu-ju - Ministry of Commerce, Food Service Bureau) Renxiang Sheying Zazhishe, 45 Fuxingmennei Dajie, Beijing 100801, People's Republic of China. TEL 6011012. Ed. Ji Yunbiao.

778.1 NE
REPEAT. 1972. q. (Genootschap voor Dokumentreproduktie) Drukkerij Veldwijk, Waddinxveen, Netherlands. Ed. A. Van Der Schee. bibl.; charts; illus.
Formerly: Reproduktie.

REPRO BULLETIN. see *PRINTING*

778.315 FR
REPRODUIRE. 1981. m. 730 F. C I P Publication, 40 rue St. Anne, 75002 Paris, France. Ed. Christian Tluebaut. adv.; bk.rev.; circ. 7,000.

778.1 GW
DER REPROGRAF. 1913. 5/yr. DM.70. Fachverband Reprografie e.V. Deutschland, An den Drei Steinen 23, 6000 Frankfurt a.M. 50, Germany. TEL 069-541073. FAX 069-541016. Ed. Achim Carius. adv.; bk.rev.; circ. 650.

ROCKFORD REVIEW. see *LITERATURE*

770 700 US ISSN 0883-735X
ROTKIN REVIEW. 1986. a. $25. Photography for Industry (Books), RR 4, Peekskill, NY 10566-9804. TEL 914-736-7693. FAX 914-736-7694. Ed. Charles E. Rotkin. adv.; bk.rev.; circ. 10,000. (back issues avail.)
Description: Reporting service on photography, art and communications books for libraries and book users. Includes direct marketing of reviewed books.

770 700 US
S F CAMERAWORK QUARTERLY. (San Francisco) 1984. q. $35. S F Camerawork, 70 12th St., San Francisco, CA 94103. TEL 415-621-1001. adv.; bk.rev.; circ. 2,500. (tabloid format)
Description: Presents new writing and reproductions of artists' work that reflects contemporary issues in the photographic arts.

770 US
S P F E NEWSLETTER. m. membership only. (Society of Photo Finishing Engineers) Photo Marketing Association International, 3000 Picture Pl., Jackson, MI 49201. TEL 517-788-8100. FAX 517-788-8371. Ed. Linda Tien. circ. 850. (back issues avail.)

770 620 001.644
535 US
S P S E. ANNUAL CONFERENCE. PAPER SUMMARIES (YEAR). (Former name of issuing body: Society of Photographic Scientists & Engineers) no.42, 1989. a. $35. Society for Imaging Science and Technology (SPSE), 7003 Kilworth Ln., Springfield, VA 22151. TEL 703-642-9090. FAX 703-642-9094.
Formerly: SPSE's Annual Conference. Paper Summaries.

PHOTOGRAPHY

770 330 US
SALES COUNTER. m. membership only. (Society for Photographic Counselors) Photo Marketing Association International, 3000 Picture Pl., Jackson, MI 49201. TEL 517-788-8100. FAX 517-788-8371. Ed. Lora Helou. circ. 1,000. (back issue avail.)

779 JA
SANGAKU SHASHIN NENKAN. 1974. Yama-Kei (Publishers) Co., Ltd., 1-1-33 Shiba Daimon, Minato-ku, Tokyo 105, Japan.

770 371.2 US
SCHOOL PHOTOGRAPHER. m. membership only. (Professional School Photographers of America) Photo Marketing Association International, 3000 Picture Pl., Jackson, MI 49201. TEL 517-788-8100. FAX 517-788-8371. Ed. Lora Helou. circ. 700. (back issues avail.)

770 SZ ISSN 0036-7737
SCHWEIZERISCHE PHOTORUNDSCHAU. 1938. s-m. 69 Fr. Schweizerischer Photographenverband, Postfach 17, 3930 Visp, Switzerland. (Co-sponsor: Schweizerischer Photohandlerverband) Ed. O. Ruppen. adv.; bk.rev.; illus.; circ. 2,500. **Indexed:** Chem.Abstr.

770 US ISSN 0734-1504
TR1 CODEN: SAPHES
SCIENTIFIC AND APPLIED PHOTOGRAPHY AND CINEMATOGRAPHY. English translation of: Zhurnal Nauchnoi i Prikladnoi Fotografii i Kinematografii (RU ISSN 0044-4561) 6/yr. (in 1 vol.; 6 nos./vol.). $393. Gordon & Breach Science Publishers, 270 Eighth Ave., New York, NY 10011. TEL 212-206-8900. FAX 212-645-2459. TELEX 236735 GOPUB UR. (Subscr. to: Box 786, Cooper Sta., New York, NY 10276. TEL 800-545-8398; UK subscr. to: P.O. Box 90, Reading, Berkshire RG1 8JL, England. TEL 0734-560-080) Ed. M.V. Alfimov. index. (also avail. in microform; back issues avail.)
—BLDSC shelfmark: 0420.792500.
Refereed Serial

770 UK ISSN 0269-1787
SCOTTISH PHOTOGRAPHY BULLETIN. 1986. s-a. £12 to individuals; institutions £27. Scottish Society for the History of Photography, c/o Scottish Photography Archive, Scottish National Portrait Gallery, 1 Queen St., Edinburgh EH2 1JD, Scotland. TEL 031-556-8921. adv.; bk.rev.; circ. 200.
—BLDSC shelfmark: 8211.053000.
Description: Provides a forum for critical debate on issues relating to historical and contemporary photography in Scotland.

SCREEN DIGEST. see COMMUNICATIONS — Television And Cable

770 IT
SCUOLA DI FOTOGRAFIA. 1980. m. L.30000 (free to photography stores). Curcio Periodici S.p.A., Via Corsica 4, 00198 Rome, Italy. Ed. Rosanna Falconi. adv.; circ. 143,000.

SHANGHAI PICTORIAL. see GENERAL INTEREST PERIODICALS — China

770 CC
SHEYING SHIJIE/PHOTOGRAPHY WORLD. (Text in Chinese) m. $51.20. Sheying Shijie Zazhishe, 57 Xuanwumen Xidajie, Beijing 100803, People's Republic of China. TEL 3074453. (Dist. in US by: China Books & Periodicals, Inc., 2929 24th St., San Francisco, CA 94110. TEL 415-282-2994) Ed. Liu Xinning.

770 CC
SHEYING ZHI YOU/PHOTOGRAPHY FANS. (Text in Chinese) bi-m. Zhongguo Sheyingjia Xiehui, Guangdong Fenhui, No. 23, Siheng Lu, Dongshan Xihepu, Guangzhou, Guangdong 510080, People's Republic of China. TEL 765607. Ed. Meng Shan.

770 US
SHUTTERBUG. 1971. m. $18. Patch Communications, 5211 S. Washington Ave., Titusville, FL 32780. TEL 407-268-5010. FAX 407-267-7216. Ed. Christi Ashby. adv.; bk.rev.; illus.; circ. 120,000.
Description: Photo equipment magazine for advanced amateur and professional photographers. Features articles on camera systems and techniques, including test reports, user reviews and accessory updates.

SKRIEN. see MOTION PICTURES

SLIPSTREAM (NIAGARA FALLS). see LITERATURE — Poetry

770 700 US
SOCIETY OF PHOTOGRAPHERS AND ARTIST REPRESENTATIVES. BUYERS GUIDE.* a. Society of Photographers and Artist Representatives, 60 E. 42nd St., No.1166, New York, NY 10165-0006. TEL 212-924-6023.

770 700 US
SOCIETY OF PHOTOGRAPHERS AND ARTIST REPRESENTATIVES. NEWSLETTER.* bi-m. Society of Photographers and Artist Representatives, 60 E. 42nd St., No.1166, New York, NY 10165-0006. TEL 212-924-6023.

770 700 US
SOCIETY OF PHOTOGRAPHERS AND ARTIST REPRESENTATIVES. STATEMENTS ON PHOTOGRAPHY - ART.* irreg. Society of Photographers and Artist Representatives, 60 E. 42nd St., No.1166, New York, NY 10165-0006. TEL 212-924-6023.

770 JA
SOCIETY OF PHOTOGRAPHIC SCIENCE AND TECHNOLOGY OF JAPAN. JOURNAL/NIHON SHASHIN GAKKAI EIBUNGO. vol.33, 1970. q. 1000 Yen per no. to non-members. Society of Photographic Science and Technology of Japan - Nihon Shashin Gakkai, c/o Tokyo College of Photography, 2-9-5 Honcho, Nakano-ku, Tokyo 164, Japan. FAX 03-3299-5887. Ed. Eiichi Ashikawa. adv.; bk.rev.; bibl.; charts; illus.; stat.; index; circ. 1,500.
Former titles: Society of Photographic Science and Technology of Japan. Bulletin (ISSN 0038-0059); Society of Scientific Photography in Japan. Bulletin.

SOUTHEAST ASIA MICROFILMS NEWSLETTER. see HISTORY — History Of Asia

770 US ISSN 0038-4070
SOUTHERN EXPOSURE (TALLADEGA). 1950. q. membership. Southeastern Professional Photographers Association, Inc., Box 355, Talladega, AL 35160. TEL 205-362-3485. FAX 205-362-3485. Eds. Van Blankenship, MaryLee Blankenship. adv.; bk.rev.; circ. 5,200. **Indexed:** Access.

770 RU ISSN 0038-5190
SOVETSKOE FOTO. 1926. m. 14.40 Rub. (set in Jan.). Soyuz Zhurnalistov S.S.S.R., M. Lubyanka 16, Tsentr, 101878 GSP Moscow, Russia. TEL 925-00-27. TELEX 411421 PERO SU. Ed. G. Tchudokov. adv.; bk.rev.; illus.; index; circ. 148,500. **Indexed:** Artbibl.Mod., Chem.Abstr., World Bibl.Soc.Sec.

770 US
SPECIALTY LAB UPDATE. m. membership only. Photo Marketing Association International, 3000 Picture Pl., Jackson, MI 49201. TEL 517-788-8100. FAX 517-788-8371. Ed. Linda Tien. circ. 1,700. (back issues avail.)
Description: For commercial, private and in-house photographic labs of the association.

770 CI
SPOT; casopis za fotografiju. 1972. q. $16. Galerije Grada Zagreba, Katarinin trg 2, 41000 Zagreb, Croatia. Ed. Radoslav Putar. illus.; circ. 3,000.

770 370 US
SPOT. 1983. 3/yr. $15. Houston Center for Photography, 1441 W. Alabama, Houston, TX 77006. TEL 713-529-4755. FAX 713-529-9248. adv.; bk.rev.; circ. 2,000.
Description: Serves the photographic community as a resource for educational exchange through feature articles, profiles, and exhibitions.

770 US ISSN 0191-4030
TR780
STEREO WORLD. 1974. bi-m. $22 (foreign $34)(effective 1992). National Stereoscopic Association, Inc., Box 14801, Columbus, OH 43214. Ed. John Dennis. adv.; bk.rev.; circ. 2,800.
Description: Magazine of stereophotography - everything from the study of and collecting historical stereographs to modern 3-D techniques.

770 US ISSN 0081-5586
STILL: YALE PHOTOGRAPHY ANNUAL. 1970. irreg., no.3, 1973. price varies. Yale University, School of Art and Architecture, Department of Graphic Design, 180 York St., New Haven, CT 06520. TEL 203-436-0308. (Dist. by: George Wittenborn, Inc., 1018 Madison Ave., New York, N.Y. 10021)

770 US
STUDIES IN THE PHOTOGRAPHIC ARTS. irreg., latest no.2. $39.95 per no. Edwin Mellen Press, 240 Portage Rd., Box 450, Lewiston, NY 14092. TEL 716-754-8566. FAX 716-754-4335.

770 US ISSN 0039-4122
STUDIO LIGHT. 1901. s-a. free to qualified personnel. Eastman Kodak Co., 343 State St., Rochester, NY 14650-0130. TEL 716-724-4000. Ed. Rick Allen. illus.; circ. 50,000.
Description: Showcases outstanding images and features articles on professional photographers.

771 US
STUDIO PHOTOGRAPHY.* 1964. m. $10 (free to qualified personnel). P T N Publishing Corp., 445 Broad Hollow Rd., Ste. 21, Melville, NY 11747-4722. TEL 516-845-2700. FAX 516-845-7109. adv.; bk.rev.; illus.; circ. 61,000. **Indexed:** Graph.Arts Lit.Abstr.
Formerly: Photographic Business and Product News (ISSN 0031-8728)

TAUCHEN; internationales Unterwasser-Magazin. see SPORTS AND GAMES

770 UK
TEN.8 PHOTO PAPERBACK. 1979. q. £29.95 to individuals (foreign £34.45); institutions £39.95 (foreign £44.45). Ten.8 Ltd., 9 Key Hill Drive, Hockley, Birmingham B18 5NY, England. TEL 021-554-2237. FAX 021-554-5970. Ed. Derek Bishton. adv.; bk.rev.; circ. 2,500. (back issues avail.) **Indexed:** Artbibl.Mod.
Formerly: Ten.8 International Photography Magazine (ISSN 0142-9663)
Description: Presents cultural and theoretical debate on issues involving photography, image-making and technology.

770 US
TEST PHOTOGRAPHERS IN NEW YORK CITY. 1988. a. $12.95. Peter Glenn Publications, Inc., 17 E. 48th St., New York, NY 10017. TEL 212-688-7940. Eds. Chip Brill, David Vando. circ. 2,000.
Description: Presents a working list of photographers who take pictures of aspiring models. How and where to contact these specialty photographers.

770 791.43 IT ISSN 0041-4395
TUTTI FOTOGRAFI; mensile italiano di fotografia e cinematografia. 1969. m. L.68000. Editrice Progresso s.r.l., Viale Piceno 14, 20129 Milan, Italy. TEL 02-715939. FAX 02-713030. bk.rev.; illus.; index; circ. 60,000.
—BLDSC shelfmark: 9076.178000.

770 IS
TZEILUM MIKTZOEI/PROFESSIONAL PHOTOGRAPHY. (Text in Hebrew; table of contents and summaries in English) 1985. q. $30 (outside Israel $60). Union of Professional Photographers in Israel, P.O. Box 26177, Tel Aviv 61261, Israel. TEL 3-5251470. FAX 3-5251469. Ed. Ilan Aharon. adv.; bk.rev.; circ. 5,000.
Description: Covers technical and creative aspects of visual communication with emphasis on international items of interest to the working professional photographer.

770 US
U P A A NEWSLETTER. 1961. q. membership. University Photographers' Association of America, 0004 Kastle Hall, University of Kentucky, Lexington, KY 40506-0044. TEL 409-838-8917. (Edit. address: Lamar University, Box 10079, Beaumont, TX 10079) Ed. Mark Philbrick. bk.rev.; circ. 500.

PHOTOGRAPHY — ABSTRACTING, BIBLIOGRAPHIES, STATISTICS

770　　　　　　　　US　ISSN 0163-7916
UNTITLED. 1972. 2/yr. $50 (includes subscr. to: Re:View). Friends of Photography, 250 4th St., San Francisco, CA 94103. TEL 415-495-7000. Ed. Andy Grundberg. illus.; circ. 8,000. (back issues avail.)
—BLDSC shelfmark: 9121.327400.
　Description: Individual issues are monographs on the work of specific photographers or photographic themes.

770　　　　　　　　FI　ISSN 0355-1466
VALOKUVA. (Text in English, Finnish; summaries in English) 1949. m. Fmk.300. (Suomen Valokuvajarjestojen Keskusliitto Finnfoto - Central Association of Finnish Photographic Organizations) Forssan Kustannus ky, Esko Aaltosen Katu 5, SF-30100 Forssa, Finland. TEL 90-662422. FAX 90-663433. Ed.Bd. adv.; bk.rev.; illus.; circ. 5,000.
　Formerly (until 1971): Valokuvaaja.

770　　　　　　　　FI　ISSN 0356-8075
VALOKUVAUKSEN VUOSIKIRJA/FINNISH PHOTOGRAPHIC YEARBOOK/FINSK FOTOGRAFISK ARSBOK. (Text in English, Finnish and Swedish) 1972. a. Fmk.120($30) Suomen Valokuvataiteen Museon Saatio - Foundation of the Photographic Museum of Finland, Box 596, SF-00101 Helsinki 10, Finland. FAX 90-650140. Ed. Ritva Tahtinen. adv.; illus.; circ. 4,000.

770 384.55　　　　UK
VIDEO CAMERA. 1989. m. £25($40) I P C Magazines Ltd., Kings Reach Tower, Stamford St., London SE1 9LS, England. TEL 071-261-5849. FAX 071-261-7851. (Subscr. to: 205 E. 42nd St., New York, NY 10017, USA) Ed. George Hughes. circ. 23,464. (back issues avail.)

770 700　　　　　US
VIEWFINDER JOURNAL OF FOCAL POINT GALLERY. 1982. a. $35. Focal Point Press, 321 City Island Ave., New York, NY 10464. TEL 212-885-1403. Ed. Ron Terner. circ. 3,000. (back issues avail.)
　Description: Prints of artwork from and promotional information on the gallery, located in City Island, New York.

770　　　　　　　　US　ISSN 0743-8044
VIEWS (BOSTON); the journal of photography in New England. 1977. 3/yr. $15. Photographic Resource Center, Boston University, 602 Commonwealth Ave., Boston, MA 02215. TEL 617-353-0700. FAX 617-353-1662. Ed. Dan Younger. adv.; bk.rev.; bibl.; illus.; circ. 4,000. (tabloid format)
　Description: Critical and theoretical forum addressing a broad range of issues pertaining to photography, with reviews of noteworthy exhibitions and profiles of photographers.

VISUAL RESOURCES; an international journal of documentation. see ART

VYTVARNICTVO, FOTOGRAFIA, FILM; mesacnik pre zaujmovu umelecku cinnost. see ART

770　　　　　　　　US
THE WEDDING PHOTOGRAPHER. 1978. m. membership. (Wedding Photographers International) Rangefinder Publishing, 1312 Lincoln Blvd., Box 2003, Santa Monica, CA 90406. TEL 213-451-0090. FAX 213-395-9058. Ed. Sandi Salina Messana. circ. 3,000. (back issues avail.)
　Formerly: Wedding Photographers International.
　Description: Provided information on print competitions, how-to techniques, business management, and photography conventions.

WESTWIND (LOS ANGELES); U C L A's journal of the arts. see ART

770　　　　　　　　UK　ISSN 0263-9106
WHICH CAMERA?. 1981. bi-m. Evro Publishing Co., 60 Waldgrave Rd., Teddington, Middx. TW11 8LG, England. TEL 081-943-5000. TELEX 895-2440-HAYMRT-G. illus.
　Description: Camera buyer's guide, with test results and ratings.

770　　　　　　　　US　ISSN 0084-103X
WOLFMAN REPORT ON THE PHOTOGRAPHIC INDUSTRY IN THE UNITED STATES. 1958. a. $135. Hachette Magazines, Inc., 1633 Broadway, 43th Fl., New York, NY 10009. TEL 212-767-6000. Ed. Lydia Wolfman. adv.; circ. 9,000.

770　　　　　　　　US　ISSN 0197-3444
WORKSHOP ON COLOR AERIAL PHOTOGRAPHY IN THE PLANT SCIENCES. PROCEEDINGS. biennial. $50 to non-members; members $30. American Society for Photogrammetry and Remote Sensing, 5410 Grosvenor Ln., Ste. 210, Bethesda, MD 20814-2160. TEL 301-493-0290. FAX 301-493-0208.
—BLDSC shelfmark: 3320.617000.

WRITERS' AND PHOTOGRAPHERS' MARKETING GUIDE; DIRECTORY OF AUSTRALIAN AND NEW ZEALAND LITERARY AND PHOTO MARKETS. see PUBLISHING AND BOOK TRADE

XEROX DISCLOSURE JOURNAL. see PATENTS, TRADEMARKS AND COPYRIGHTS

770　　　　　　　　CC
XIANDAI SHEYING/MODERN PHOTOGRAPHY. (Text in Chinese) q. Shenzhen Shi Wenlian, No. 13, Guiyuan Lu, 2nd Floor, Shenzhen, Guangdong 518001, People's Republic of China. TEL 236168. Ed. Yi Huiliang.

770　　　　　　　　IS
YIDIOT LETZALAM. (Text in Hebrew) bi-m. Association of Photographers and Cameramen, 16 Zemenhoff St., Tel Aviv 64 373, Israel. TEL 03-280895.

770　　　　　　　　CC　ISSN 1001-0270
YINGXIANG JISHU. (Text in Chinese) q. Quanguo Qinggong Ganguang Cailiao Keji Qingbao-zhan, 20 Dongting Lu, Hexi Qu, Tianjin 300220, People's Republic of China. TEL 840654. Ed. Wei Zhengeng.

771　　　　　　　　UK
YOU AND YOUR CAMERA. 1979. w. £0.70 per no. Eaglemoss Publications Ltd., 7 Cromwell Rd., London SW7 2HR, England. Ed. Jack Schofield. adv.; circ. 53,024.

770　　　　　　　　CC
ZHAOXIANGJI/CAMERAS. (Text in Chinese) bi-m. Hangzhou Zhaoxiangji Jixie Yanjiusuo, 94 Xixi Lu (West Brook Road), Hangzhou, Zhejiang 310013, People's Republic of China. TEL 521014. Ed. Wang Zhenkui.

770　　　　　　　　CC
ZHONGGUO SHEYING/CHINESE PHOTOGRAPHY. (Text in Chinese) bi-m. $64.40. (Zhongguo Sheyingjia Xiehui - Chinese Photographers Association) Zhongguo Sheying Zazhishe, 61 Hongxing Hutong, Dongdan, Beijing 1007 5, People's Republic of China. TEL 552277. (Dist. in US by: China Books & Periodicals, Inc., 2929 24th St., San Francisco, CA 94110. TEL 415-282-2994) Ed. Liu Bang.

770 791.43　　　　RU　ISSN 0044-4561
TR1　　　　　　　　　　CODEN: ZNPFAG
ZHURNAL NAUCHNOI I PRIKLADNOI FOTOGRAFII I KINEMATOGRAFII. 1956. bi-m. 20.70 Rub. (Akademiya Nauk S.S.S.R.) Izdatel'stvo Nauka, 90 Profsoyuznaya ul., 117864 Moscow, Russia. TEL 234-05-84. Ed. K.V. Chibisov. bibl.; charts; illus.; index; circ. 70,290. **Indexed:** Chem.Abstr., Curr.Cont., Sci.Abstr.
—BLDSC shelfmark: 0061.000000.

770　　　　　　　　IT　ISSN 0393-4330
ZOOM (ITALIAN EDITION). (Editions in English, French, Italian) 1980. bi-m. L.65000. Editrice Progresso s.r.l., Viale Piceno 14, 20129 Milan, Italy. TEL 02-715939. FAX 02-713030. bk.rev.; illus.; index; circ. 30,000.

770　　　　　　　　US
ZOOM (U S EDITION). Italian edition (ISSN 0393-4330) (Editions in French, Italian) 1980. 5/yr. $36. Box 1138, Madison Sq. Sta., New York, NY 10159. TEL 212-481-3398. Ed. Joel LaRoche. adv.; circ. 25,000.

770　　　　　　　　GW
2029 MAGAZIN. 1985. a. DM.79($44) Photogalerie The Compagnie, Poolstr. 7, 2000 Hamburg 36, Germany. TEL 040-352734. Ed. Peter Schulz Foersten. adv.; circ. 18,000. (back issues avail.)

PHOTOGRAPHY — Abstracting, Bibliographies, Statistics

BRITISH CATALOGUE OF AUDIO-VISUAL MATERIALS. see SOUND RECORDING AND REPRODUCTION — Abstracting, Bibliographies, Statistics

770　　　　　　　　FR
FRANCE. SERVICE D'ETUDE DES STRATEGIES ET DES STATISTIQUES INDUSTRIELLES. RESULTATS TRIMESTRIELS DES ENQUETES DE BRANCHE. LABOS PHOTOGRAPHIQUES ET CINEMATOGRAPHIQUES. q. 180 F. (foreign 210 F.)(effective 1991). Service d'Etude des Strategies et des Statistiques Industrielles (SESSI), 85 Bd. du Montparnasse, 75270 Paris Cedex 06, France. TEL 45-56-42-34. FAX 45-56-40-71. stat.
　Description: Provides detailed industry-wide performance statistics for comparative evaluations.

770 016　　　　　UK　ISSN 0896-100X
TR1
IMAGING ABSTRACTS. 1921. 6/yr. £240 (effective 1992). (Royal Photographic Society of Great Britain, Imaging Science and Technology Group) Pergamon Press plc, Headington Hill Hall, Oxford, OX3 0BW, England. TEL 0865-794141. FAX 0865-743911. TELEX 83177 PERGAP. (And: 660 White Plains Rd., Tarrytown, NY 10591-5153. TEL 914-524-9200) Ed. B.J. Smith. abstr.; index, cum.index; circ. 250. (also avail. in microfiche; back issues avail.)
●Also available online. Vendor(s): Orbit Information Technologies (IMABS).
　Formerly: Photographic Abstracts (ISSN 0031-8701)
　Description: Offers comprehensive coverage of the literature of imaging and photographic science and technology. Over 100 periodicals, as well as patents and other publications are scanned for relevant data on every aspect of the industry.
　Refereed Serial

770 016　　　　　RU　ISSN 0370-8063
REFERATIVNYI ZHURNAL. FOTOKINOTEKHNIKA. 1957. m. 29 Rub. (32 Rub. including index). Vsesoyuznyi Institut Nauchno-Tekhnicheskoi Informatsii (VINITI), Baltiiskaya ul., 14, Moscow A-219, Russia. (Subscr. to: Mezhdunarodnaya Kniga, Dimitrova ul. 39, 113095 Moscow, Russia)

U.S. COPYRIGHT OFFICE. CATALOG OF COPYRIGHT ENTRIES. FOURTH SERIES. PART 5: VISUAL ARTS EXCLUDING MAPS. see ART — Abstracting, Bibliographies, Statistics

PHYSICAL CHEMISTRY

see Chemistry–Physical Chemistry

PHYSICAL FITNESS AND HYGIENE

see also Medical Sciences; Nutrition and Dietetics; Public Health and Safety; Sports and Games

613　　　　　　　　US　ISSN 0002-7952
A C H A ACTION.* 1970. 6/yr. membership. American College Health Association, Box 28937, Baltimore, MD 21240-8937. TEL 301-963-1100. Ed. Joanne Hellebrand. circ. 3,200.
　Formerly: A C H Action; **Supersedes:** American College Health Association. Newsletter.

A C H P E R NATIONAL JOURNAL. (Australian Council for Health, Physical Education and Recreation) see EDUCATION

613.7 330　　　　US
A F B ACTION. bi-m. Association for Fitness in Business, 310 N. Alabama, Ste. A100, Indianapolis, IA 46204. **Indexed:** Sportsearch (1983-).

A I D S EDUCATION AND PREVENTION; an interdisciplinary journal. see MEDICAL SCIENCES — Communicable Diseases

A S H SMOKING AND HEALTH REVIEW. (Action on Smoking & Health) see LAW

A V A NEWSLETTER. (American Volkssport Association) see ETHNIC INTERESTS

ACCENT ON LIVING. see EDUCATION — Special Education And Rehabilitation

ACCENT ON LIVING BUYER'S GUIDE. see EDUCATION — Special Education And Rehabilitation

ACTA MEDICA ET SOCIOLOGICA. see SOCIOLOGY

613.7 612.67   US
▼**ACTIVE AMERICAN.** 1990. q. Russ Moore and Associates Inc., 4151 Knob Dr., St. Paul, MN 55122. TEL 612-452-0571. FAX 612-454-5791. Ed. Diane Steen. adv.; circ. 150,000.
   Description: For the mature adult who wants to take an active part in achieving and maintaining good health.

ADAPTED PHYSICAL ACTIVITY QUARTERLY. see *EDUCATION — Special Education And Rehabilitation*

613.7 612.3   US
ADVANCES. q. Box 2316, Princeton, NJ 08543-2316. TEL 609-452-8701. Ed. Amy Mone.

330 613   US   ISSN 0731-2199
RA410.A1
ADVANCES IN HEALTH ECONOMICS AND HEALTH SERVICES RESEARCH. 1979. a. $63.50 to institutions. J A I Press Inc., 55 Old Post Rd., No. 2, Box 1678, Greenwich, CT 06836-1678. TEL 203-661-7602. Eds. Richard M. Scheffler, Louis F. Rossiter. **Indexed:** Abstr.Health Care Manage.Stud.
   Formerly (until 1981): Research in Health Economics (ISSN 0197-0690)
   Refereed Serial

ADVANCES IN HEALTH EDUCATION: CURRENT RESEARCH. see *EDUCATION — Teaching Methods And Curriculum*

613.7 649   US   ISSN 0888-9287
RJ133
ADVANCES IN MOTOR DEVELOPMENT RESEARCH. 1987. a. $47.50. A M S Press, Inc., 56 E. 13th St., New York, NY 10003. TEL 212-777-4700. FAX 212-995-5413. Eds. Jane E. Clark, James H. Humphrey. bk.rev.; index. (back issues avail.)
—BLDSC shelfmark: 0709.453500.
   Description: Original research and review in the study of motor development.
   Refereed Serial

613.7   US
AEROBIC BEAT. m. $25. 7985 Santa Monica Blvd., Ste. 109, Los Angeles, CA 90046. TEL 213-937-4795. Eds. Ken Alan, Randy Sills.

613.7   US
AEROBICS NEWS. 1986. m. $20 (foreign $25). Institute for Aerobics Research, 12330 Preston Rd., Dallas, TX 75230. TEL 800-635-7050. Ed. Vicki Cason. circ. 10,000. (back issues avail.)

613   CN   ISSN 0228-586X
ALIVE; Canadian journal of health and nutrition. 1975. 8/yr. Can.$18. Canadian Health Reform Products Ltd., 4728 Byrne Rd., Burnaby, B.C. V5J 3H7, Canada. TEL 604-438-1919. FAX 604-435-4888. (Subscr. addr.: P.O. Box 80055, Burnaby, B.C. V5J 3X5, Canada) Ed. Hilda Ward. adv.; bk.rev.; circ. 150,000. **Indexed:** Mid.East: Abstr.& Ind.

613.7 790   US   ISSN 0273-8023
ALLIANCE UPDATE. 1970. 8/yr. $45 to institutions. American Alliance for Health, Physical Education, Recreation, and Dance, 1900 Association Dr., Reston, VA 22091. TEL 703-476-3400. FAX 703-476-9527. circ. 32,000. (tabloid format; reprint service avail. from UMI) **Indexed:** Sportsearch.
   Former titles: A A H P E R D Update; A A H P E R Update.
   Description: Provides comprehensive coverage of legislative developments, professional news and activities, and personalities, in the area of health, physical education, athletics, sports, dance, recreation, and leisure.

613.7   US   ISSN 1054-7711
TT950
▼**ALLURE.** 1991. m. $12. Conde Nast Publications Inc., Allure Magazine, 360 Madison Ave., New York, NY 10017. TEL 212-880-5550. Ed. Linda Wells. circ. 200,000.
   Description: Covers fitness, health, beauty and fashion.

AMENTIA; la voix des parents. see *SOCIAL SERVICES AND WELFARE*

AMERICAN BABY; for expectant and new parents. see *CHILDREN AND YOUTH — About*

613.7   US
AMERICAN FITNESS. 1983. 6/yr. $27. Aerobics and Fitness Association of America, 15250 Ventura Blvd., Ste. 310, Sherman Oaks, CA 91403. TEL 818-905-0040. Ed. Peg Jordan, R.N. adv.; bk.rev.; circ. 30,000. **Indexed:** Phys.Ed.Ind., Sportsearch (1987-).
   ●Also available online. Vendor(s): DIALOG (File no.149).
   Supersedes (in 1987): Aerobics and Fitness (ISSN 0749-8942); **Formerly** (until 1984): Aerobics and Fitness Association of America. Journal.
   Description: Provides news and information concerning health and fitness via aerobics.

613.7   US
AMERICAN FITNESS QUARTERLY. q. American Fitness Quarterly, Box 15506, Columbus, OH 43215. **Indexed:** Sportsearch (1987-).

613.7   US   ISSN 0730-7004
RA773   CODEN: AMHEEZ
AMERICAN HEALTH; fitness of body and mind. 1982. m. $14.95. Reader's Digest Association, Inc. (New York), 28 West 23rd St., New York, NY 10010. TEL 212-366-8900. FAX 212-366-8999. (Subscr. to: Box 3015, Harlan, IA 51537) Ed. Joel Gurin. adv.; bk.rev.; circ. 1,000,000. (also avail. in microform) **Indexed:** CHNI, Hlth.Ind., Phys.Ed.Ind.
—BLDSC shelfmark: 0816.575000.
   Description: Research-based news magazine on health, fitness and medicine.

AMERICAN HIKER. see *SPORTS AND GAMES — Outdoor Life*

AMERICAN HIKER NEWSLETTER. see *SPORTS AND GAMES — Outdoor Life*

AMERICAN JOURNAL OF HEALTH PROMOTION. see *PUBLIC HEALTH AND SAFETY*

AMERICAN JOURNAL OF PHYSICAL MEDICINE AND REHABILITATION. see *MEDICAL SCIENCES*

AMERICAN WANDERER. see *ETHNIC INTERESTS*

AMIS DE LA RADIESTHESIE. see *PARAPSYCHOLOGY AND OCCULTISM*

613   US   ISSN 0278-4653
RA773
ANNUAL EDITIONS: HEALTH. 1975. a. $10.95. Dushkin Publishing Group, Inc., Sluice Dock, Guilford, CT 06437-9989. TEL 203-453-4351. FAX 203-453-6000. Ed. Rick Yarian. illus.
   Former titles (1980-1981): Readings in Health (ISSN 0730-8930); Annual Editions: Readings in Health (ISSN 0360-9766)
   Refereed Serial

ANNUAL EDITIONS: NUTRITION. see *NUTRITION AND DIETETICS*

613   II   ISSN 0003-6498
APKA SWASTHYA. (Text in Hindi) 1953. m. Rs.20. Indian Medical Association, I.M.A. House, Indraprastha Marg, New Delhi 110002, India. (Subscr. to: Apka Swasthya, I.M.A. Building, C. 7-31 Chet Ganj, Varanasi 1, India) Ed.Bd. circ. 3,500.

613.7 640.73   US
AQUA INDUSTRY GUIDE. 1979. a. $40. A B Publications, 555 Anton Blvd., Ste. 820, Costa Mesa, CA 92626-7126. TEL 714-434-8989. FAX 714-434-8988. Ed. Peter Brown. adv.; circ. 15,000.
   Former titles: Aqua Buyers Guide; Spa and Sauna Buyers Guide.

613.7   US
TH6485
AQUA: THE BUSINESS MAGAZINE FOR THE SPA AND POOL INDUSTRY. 1976. m. $25. A B Publications, 555 Anton Blvd., Ste. 820, Costa Mesa, CA 92626-7126. TEL 714-434-8989. FAX 714-434-8988. Ed. Peter Brown. circ. 15,000.
   Incorporates (1972-1988): Flotation Sleep Industry (ISSN 0164-5749); **Former titles:** Spa and Sauna (ISSN 0164-4858); Spa and Sauna Trade Journal.
   Description: Contains market information, business management advice for retailers and builders.

PHYSICAL FITNESS AND HYGIENE

613.7 610   II   ISSN 0253-682X
   CODEN: AROGD8
AROGYA; a journal of health sciences. (Text in English) 1975. s-a. free. Kasturba Medical College Trust, Manipal, Department of Clinical Biochemistry, Editor - Arogyal, Manipal - 576 119, India. TEL 20060. Ed. Sudhakar S. Nayak. adv.; bk.rev.; circ. 1,000 (controlled). **Indexed:** Chem.Abstr., Food Sci.& Tech.Abstr., INIS Atomind., Rev.Med.& Vet.Mycol.

613.7   CH
ASIAN JOURNAL OF PHYSICAL EDUCATION. 1978. q. No.3, Lane 153, Section 2, Cahng An East Rd., Taipei, Taiwan, Republic of China. **Indexed:** Sportsearch (1978-).

613   GW   ISSN 0341-3403
ATEM UND MENSCH;* Zeitschrift fuer Atempflege - Massage - Entspannung - moderne Gymnastik. 1959. q. DM.14. Helfer-Verlag, E. Schuabe, Basler Str. 2, 6380 Bad Homburg, Germany. Eds. Dr. K.O. Kuppe, Guenther Braunger. bk.rev.; illus.; circ. 5,000.
   Supersedes (1962-1975): Atem (ISSN 0004-6477)

613.7   IT   ISSN 1120-3633
▼**ATTIVITA FISICA E SPORT.** 1990. q. L.20000. E S I Stampa Medica s.r.l., Casella Postale 42, Lgo. Volontari del Sangue 10, 20097 S. Donato, Milan, Italy. TEL 02-5274241. FAX 02-5274775. TELEX 324894. Ed. Bruno Pieroni. adv.; bk.rev.; circ. 8,000.

613.7   US
AUSTIN HEALTH & FITNESS. 1988. m. $20. D D J & L Publishing Inc., Box 1343, Round Rock, TX 78680. TEL 512-255-1512. Ed. Laura Burns. adv.; circ. 50,000 (controlled).

613.7 613.2   AT   ISSN 0812-8227
AUSTRALIAN WELL BEING; personal and planetary healing. 1984. q. Aus.$42. Wellspring Publishers P-L, 1-187A Avenue Rd, Mosman, N.S.W. 2088, Australia. TEL 02-969-7122. FAX 02-968-2489. Ed. Barbara McGregor. adv.; bk.rev.; circ. 30,000. (back issues avail.)

B B A - BIOENERGETICS. see *BIOLOGY — Biophysics*

BABY AGE. see *CHILDREN AND YOUTH — About*

613.7   US
BACK TO HEALTH MAGAZINE;* your guide to relief recovery and well-being. 1988. m. $17.55. Qwix Technologies Inc., 405 N.W. 44th Ter., No. 101, Deerfield Beach, FL 33442-3203. TEL 305-360-0700. Ed. Herbert Siegel. adv.; bk.rev.; circ. 200,000. (back issues avail.)
   Formerly: Backpain.
   Description: Directed towards men and women over 40 years old. Covers pain relief, proper diet, exercise and mental health.

613.194   US
BARE IN MIND.* 1972. 12/yr. $12. Leisure Publications (Perris), Box 368, Perris, CA 92370-0368. Ed. Thelma Manning. adv.; bk.rev.; circ. 2,700. (tabloid format)
   Description: Focuses on nudism.

613.7   GW   ISSN 0176-8700
BETRIFFT SPORT. 1979. 6/yr. DM.64.80. Bergmoser und Hoeller Verlag GmbH, Karl-Friedrich-Str. 76, 5100 Aachen, Germany. TEL 0241-17309-25. FAX 0241-17309-34. Ed.Bd. circ. 2,000. (looseleaf format; back issues avail.)
   Description: Magazine for exercise and dance instructors. Practical directions for rhythm and music, body movement and learning a sport.

613   LH   ISSN 0006-0429
BEWUSSTER LEBEN; Zeitschrift fuer positive Lebens- und Arbeitsgestaltung, gesunde Ernaehrung und natuerliche Lebensweise. 1935. m. 48 Fr. Leben Verlag AG, FL-9490 Vaduz, Liechtenstein. TEL 075-20977. adv.; bk.rev.; bibl.; charts; illus.; circ. 25,000.
   Formerly: Leben.

613.7   GW
BIO SPEZIAL MAGAZIN. 1984. bi-m. DM.39. Bio Verlag Ritter GmbH, Monatshauserstr. 8, 8132 Tutzing, Germany. TEL 08158-8021. Ed. Monica Ritter. circ. 60,000.

PHYSICAL FITNESS AND HYGIENE

613   GW   ISSN 0006-3487
BIONOMICA. 1950. bi-m. DM.18.
(Bionomica-Gemeinschaft e.V.) Bionomica-Verlag, Duesseldorferstr. 9-11, D-6800 Mannheim 81, Germany. Ed. Ewald Koenemann. adv.; bk.rev.

BLACK HEALTH. see *ETHNIC INTERESTS*

BODY BULLETIN NEWSLETTER. see *OCCUPATIONAL HEALTH AND SAFETY*

613.7   US
▼**BODYBUILDING LIFESTYLES.** 1990. m. $19.97. (World Bodybuilding Federation) Titan Sports, Inc., 1055 Summer St., Box 3857, Stamford, CT 06905. TEL 203-353-2894. Ed. Rochelle Larkin. circ. 200,000.
Description: Covers all aspects of bodybuilding, from getting started in the sport, to participating in advanced competitions.

613.7   US
▼**BODYWISE.** 1992. bi-m. Prestige Publications, Inc., 4151 Knob Dr., St. Paul, MN 55122-1876. TEL 800-728-3213. FAX 612-454-5791. Ed. Diane Steene. adv.; circ. 100,000.

613.7   CU
BOLETIN CIENTIFICO-TECNICO I N D E R - CUBA. 1965. q. Instituto Nacional de Deportes, Educacion Fisica y Recreacion, Centre de Documentacion e Informacion, Habana, Cuba. **Indexed:** Sportsearch (1976-).

613.194   UK   ISSN 0264-0406
BRITISH NATURISM. 1964. q. $12. Central Council for British Naturism, Assurance House, 35-41 Hazelwood Rd., Northampton NN1 1LL, England. FAX 0604-230176. adv.; illus.; circ. 11,000 (controlled).

613.7   PR
BUENA SALUD. (Text in Spanish) 1987. m. $17. (Interamerican College of Physicians and Surgeons) Casiano Communications Inc., 1700 Fernandez Juncos Ave., San Juan, PR 00909-2999. TEL 809-728-3000. FAX 809-728-7325. Ed. Dr. Renee Rodriguez. adv.; circ. 42,000.
Description: Geared towards the health needs of Hispanic Americans.

613.7 613.2   ZA
BWINO: HEALTH CARE NEWS. 1981. bi-m. free. National Food and Nutrition Commission, P.O. Box 32669, Lusaka, Zambia. circ. 6,000.

C C B C NEWSLETTER. (Council of Community Blood Centers) see *MEDICAL SCIENCES — Hematology*

613.7   CN   ISSN 0703-5624
C P H A HEALTH DIGEST. French edition: A C S P Selection Sante. (Text in English) 1977. q. free to members. Canadian Public Health Association, 1565 Carling Ave., Ste. 400, Ottawa, Ont. K1Z 8R1, Canada. TEL 613-725-3769. FAX 613-725-9826. Ed. Karen Craven. circ. 4,200 (4,000 English ed.; 200 French ed.).

C S C REPORTS. (Cooking for Survival Consciousness) see *NUTRITION AND DIETETICS*

CAHIERS DE LA PUERICULTRICE. see *CHILDREN AND YOUTH — About*

613.7   CN   ISSN 0834-1915
CANADIAN ASSOCIATION FOR HEALTH, PHYSICAL EDUCATION AND RECREATION. JOURNAL. Short title: C A H P E R Journal. (Text in English, French) 1933. q. Can.$55. Canadian Association for Health, Physical Education & Recreation, Place R. Tait McKenzie, 1600 James Naismith Dr., Gloucester, Ont. K1B 5N4, Canada. TEL 613-748-5622. FAX 613-748-5737. Ed. Lise Marie George. adv.; bk.rev.; illus.; circ. 2,000. (processed; also avail. in microfilm from MML) **Indexed:** Can.Per.Ind., CMI, Sportsearch (1952-).
—BLDSC shelfmark: 4722.300000.
   C A H P E R Journal (ISSN 0226-5478)

616.1   US   ISSN 0194-2557
CARDIAC ALERT. 1979. m. $39. Phillips Publishing, Inc., Consumer Publishing, 7811 Montrose Rd., Potomac, MD 20854. TEL 301-340-2100. FAX 301-424-7034. Ed. Dr. Jorge C. Rios. index.

CATALYST (MARIETTA); a publication resource of New Age newsletters, book reviews, personals, holistic health, and psychic connections. see *NEW AGE PUBLICATIONS*

613   CS   ISSN 0009-0573
                      CODEN: CEHYAN
CESKOSLOVENSKA HYGIENA. (Text in Czech or Slovak; summaries in English and Russian) 1955. 10/yr. $62.60. (Ceskoslovenska Spolecnost Hygieniku) Avicenum, Czechoslovak Medical Press, Malostranske nam. 28, 118 02 Prague 1, Czechoslovakia. (Dist. by: Artia, Ve Smeckach 30, 111 27 Prague 1, Czechoslovakia) (Co-sponsor: Ceskoslovenska Lekarska Spolecnost J. Ev. Purkyne) Ed. Dr. Jaroslav Lener. adv.; bk.rev.; bibl.; charts; illus.; index; circ. 1,150. **Indexed:** Abstr.Hyg., Biol.Abstr., C.I.S. Abstr., Cadscan, Chem.Abstr., Dairy Sci.Abstr., Dent.Ind., Ergon.Abstr., Excerp.Med., INIS Atomind., Lead Abstr., Protozool.Abstr., Trop.Dis.Bull., Zincscan.
—BLDSC shelfmark: 3122.250000.

CHAYIM YAFIM. see *SPORTS AND GAMES*

CHEMECOLOGY; covering health, safety and the environment. see *ENVIRONMENTAL STUDIES*

613.7 612.3   US
CHICAGO HEALTHCARE. m. Syncom, Inc., 799 Roosevelt Rd., Bldg. 6, Glen Ellyn, IL 60137-5920. TEL 708-858-1980. FAX 708-858-0440. Ed. Herb Hillabrand. circ. 15,000.

CHILD MAGAZINE'S GUIDE TO HAVING A BABY. see *CHILDREN AND YOUTH — About*

CHILDREN IN THE TROPICS. see *CHILDREN AND YOUTH — About*

613.7   US
▼**CITY FITNESS.** 1992. m. $18. City Fitness, Inc., Box 5009, No. 108, Sugar Land, TX 77487. TEL 713-265-9499. Ed. Tim Brookover. adv.; B&W page $1760. circ. 30,000. (tabloid format)
Description: For sports and fitness enthusiasts in the Houston area. Focuses on all sports, from cycling to aerobics to fitness for kids, with articles by professionals covering sports medicine and nutrition.

CLINICAL JOURNAL OF SPORT MEDICINE. see *MEDICAL SCIENCES — Sports Medicine*

CLUB BUSINESS INTERNATIONAL. see *BUSINESS AND ECONOMICS — Small Business*

613.7   US
CLUB INDUSTRY MAGAZINE. 1984. m. $68 (foreign $125). 492 Old Connecticut Path, Framingham, MA 01701-4568. TEL 508-872-2021. Ed. Margie Mararian. circ. 30,000.

613.7 616.12   FR
COEUR ET SANTE. (Includes special numbers) 1974. q. 100 F. Edicardio, 9, rue de Laborde, 75008 Paris, France. FAX 42-93-38-97. Ed. Jacques Berdah. adv.

CONDITION; die Zeitschrift fuer Lauf- und Ausdauersport. see *SPORTS AND GAMES*

613.7 155.937   US
CONNECTICUT HOSPICE NEWSLETTER; making today count. 1979. q. free. Connecticut Hospic Inc., 61 Burban Dr., Branford, CT 06405. TEL 203-481-6231. FAX 203-483-9539. circ. 50,000.
Description: Provides information related to timely medical issues as they impact hospice care; includes features about hospice services.

613   UK
CONSULTANT. q. free. Hospital Consultants and Specialists Association, No. One Kingsclere Rd., Overton, Basingstoke, Hampshire RG25 3JP, England. TEL 0265-771777. FAX 0265-770999. adv.; circ. 7,000. **Indexed:** Bus.Ind., Tr.& Indus.Ind.

613.7   US
CONSUMER REPORTS ON HEALTH. 1989. m. $24 (foreign $30). Consumers Union of United States, Inc., 101 Truman Ave., Yonkers, NY 10703-1057. TEL 914-378-2000. FAX 914-378-2906. (Subscr. to: Box 56356, Boulder, CO 80322-6356) Ed. Michael Leff. circ. 40,000.
●Also available online. Vendor(s): DIALOG (File no.646).
Formerly: Consumer Reports Health Letter (ISSN 1044-3193)
Description: Provides current information to help you make wise decisions about the health care services and products you and your family need.

CONTACT QUARTERLY; a vehicle for moving ideas. see *DANCE*

613.7   US
COORDINATOR (ST. PAUL). q. $10. National Association of Health Unit Clerks-Coordinators, 1821 University Ave., Ste. 162-S, St. Paul, MN 55104. Ed. Patricia Rohm. circ. 2,350. (looseleaf format)
Description: Information for health unit coordinators.

613.7   US
CORPORATE FITNESS DIRECTORY. 1984. a. $25. Stevens Publishing Corporation, 225 N. New Rd., Waco, TX 76710. TEL 817-776-9000. (Subscr. to: Box 2178, Santa Monica, CA 90401) Ed. Kris Kyes. adv.; tr.lit.; circ. 14,000. (back issues avail.)
Former titles: Corporate Fitness Buyer's Guide; Corporate Fitness and Recreation Buyer's Guide.

613.7   IT
CORRERE. 1981. m. L.13000. Insport Editrice S.r.l., Via Vincenzo Monti 12, Milan, Italy. Ed. Ruggero Alcanterini. adv.

613.7   US
CURRENT AWARENESS IN HEALTH EDUCATION. m. $24. U.S. Bureau of Health Education, Department of Health and Human Services, Washington, DC 20201. TEL 202-655-4000. (Subscr. to: Supt. of Documents, Washington, DC 20402)
●Also available online. Vendor(s): BRS, BRS/Saunders Colleague.

371.37 375   US   ISSN 0199-820X
CURRENT HEALTH 1; the beginning guide to health education. 1974. m. (Sep.-May). $5.25. General Learning Corporation, Curriculum Innovations Group, 60 Revere Dr., Northbrook, IL 60062-1563. TEL 800-323-5471. (Subscr. to: Box 3060, Northbrook, IL 60065-3060) Ed. Laura Ruekberg. charts; illus. (also avail. in microform from UMI; reprint service avail. from UMI) **Indexed:** Ind.Child.Mag., Jun.High.Mag.Abstr., Mag.Ind., PMR, R.G.
Description: For grades 4-7. Informational articles and essays on the physical, emotional, psychological, and nutritional health of youths, with photographs, challenges, and questions and answers.

613.7 371.3   US
CURRENT HEALTH 2; the continuing guide to health education. m. (Sep.-May). $5.60 to students; includes Human Sexuality Supplement. General Learning Corporation, Curriculum Innovations Group, 60 Revere Dr., Northbrook, IL 60062-1563. TEL 800-323-5471. (Subscr. to: Box 3060, Northbrook, IL 60065-3060) Ed. Candy Purdy. **Indexed:** Acad.Ind., Hlth.Ind., Jun.High.Mag.Abstr.
Description: For grades 7-12.

CURRENT TOPICS IN BIOENERGETICS. see *BIOLOGY — Biophysics*

613.7   US
DALLAS RECOVERY. m. 4504 Abbot, Rm. 16, Dallas, TX 75205-3936. TEL 214-521-8318. Ed. Bruce Lanahan.

613.7   CC
DAZHONG JIANKANG/ORDINARY PEOPLE'S HEALTH. (Text in Chinese) m. Jiankang Baoshe - Health Journal Publishing, 11 Shuangsi, Jiu Gulou Dajie, Beijing 100009, People's Republic of China. TEL 4015114. Ed. Li Zhimin.

DEATH. see *PSYCHOLOGY*

PHYSICAL FITNESS AND HYGIENE

613   GW   ISSN 0415-1798
DEINE GESUNDHEIT. 1955. m. DM.31.20. Verlag Gesundheit GmbH, Neue Gruenstr. 18, 1020 Berlin, Germany. TEL 030-2700516. FAX 030-2754983. TELEX 114488. Ed. U. Hertel. circ. 180,000.

DELICIOUS!; guide to natural living. see *NUTRITION AND DIETETICS*

DEMETER-BLAETTER. see *FOOD AND FOOD INDUSTRIES*

613   GW   ISSN 0343-3838
DER DEUTSCHE BADEBETRIEB. Short title: D D B. 1909. m. DM.102. (Verband Deutscher Badebetriebe e.V.) Ebert Verlag GmbH, Blankenseer Str. 6-8, 2400 Luebeck 1, Germany. Ed. Hans Juergen Ebert. circ. 14,400.
—BLDSC shelfmark: 3563.250000.
Formerly: Kurbad; Incorporates: Bad.

DIABETES DIALOGUE. see *MEDICAL SCIENCES — Endocrinology*

DIABETES SELF-MANAGEMENT. see *MEDICAL SCIENCES — Endocrinology*

613.7   US   ISSN 0899-2398
THE DIABETIC TRAVELER. 1987. q. $18.95. Box 8223 - RW, Stamford, CT 06905. TEL 203-327-5832. Ed. Mavry E. Rosenbaum. adv.; bk.rev.; index; circ. 2,500. (looseleaf format; back issues avail.)
Description: Provides hints to assist individuals with diabetes in planning safe travel.
Refereed Serial

613.7   US
DIET & HEALTH MAGAZINE. 1989. bi-m. $4.95 per no. Blockbuster Periodicals, Inc., 2131 Hollywood Blvd., Hollywood, FL 33020. TEL 305-925-5242. Ed. Barbara Newman. circ. 65,000.
Incorporates: Diet and Health Series.
Description: For adults interested in health, nutrition, weight loss, and healthy living.

613.7 610   IT
DIMENSIONE SALUTE. m. L.35000. Valentini Editore, Via Fabio Fulzi 19, 20124 Milan, Italy. TEL 02-6696471. TELEX 330299 VALEDI I. Ed. Aldo Quinto Lazzari.

DINSHAH HEALTH SOCIETY NEWSLETTER. see *MEDICAL SCIENCES — Chiropractic, Homeopathy, Osteopathy*

DIRECTORY OF U.S. BASED AGENCIES INVOLVED IN INTERNATIONAL HEALTH ASSISTANCE. see *MEDICAL SCIENCES*

613.7   DK
DIT LAEGEMAGASIN. DKK 148. Forlaget John Vaboe A-S, Hartmannsvej 47-49, DK2920 Gentofte, Denmark. TEL 39-40-80-00. FAX 39-40-82-80.

613.7   CC
DONGFANG QIGONG/ORIENTAL QIGONG. (Text in Chinese) bi-m. Beijing Qigong Yanjiuhui - Beijing Qigong Research Society, Gongren Tiyuguan-nei (Inside Beijing Workers Gym), Beijing 100027, Poeple's Republic of China. TEL 592961. Ed. Xu Yixing.

613.7   US   ISSN 0888-1375
AP2
EAST WEST: THE JOURNAL OF NATURAL HEALTH AND LIVING. 1971. bi-m. $24. East West Partners, 17 Station St., Box 1200, Brookline, MA 02147. TEL 800-666-8576. FAX 617-232-1572. (Subscr. to: Box 57320, Boulder, CO 80322-7320) Ed. Tom Rawls. adv.; bk.rev.; circ. 100,000. (also avail. in microform from UMI,MIM; back issues avail.; reprint service avail. from UMI) **Indexed:** Alt.Press Ind., CHNI, New Per.Ind.
Formerly: East West Journal (ISSN 0191-3700)
Description: Covers holistic health.

613.7   US
EATING WELL. bi-m. $2.50 per no. Telemedia Communications U S, Ferry Rd., Charlotte, VT 05445. TEL 802-425-3961. FAX 802-425-3307.

EDUCACION MEDICA Y SALUD. see *EDUCATION — Guides To Schools And Colleges*

613   IT
EDUCAZIONE SANITARIA E PROMOZIONE DELLA SALUTE. (Text in Italian; summaries in English and French) 1978. q. L.50000 to individuals; institutions L.60000($100). (Centro Sperimentale per l'Educazione Sanitaria) Pensiero Scientifico Editore s.r.l., Via Panama 48, 00198 Rome, Italy. TEL 06 855-36-33. Ed. M.A. Modolo. bk.rev.; bibl.; index; circ. 900.
Formerly: Educazione Sanitaria e Medicina Preventiva (ISSN 0391-6200); Supersedes (1956-1977): Educazione Sanitaria (ISSN 0013-2098)

613.7   HU   ISSN 0073-4004
EGESZSEGNEUELES; educatio sanitaria. 1959. bi-m. $29.50 (effective 1992). Ifsusagi Lap- es Konyvkiado Vallalat, Revay u. 16, 1374 Budapest, Hungary. (Subscr. to: Kultura, P.O.B. 149, 1398 Budapest 62, Hungary) Ed. Simon Tamas. circ. 4,300.

ELLE (CHINA); Hong Kong. see *BEAUTY CULTURE*

ELYSIUM: JOURNAL OF THE SENSES. see *NEW AGE PUBLICATIONS*

410   US   ISSN 0199-6304
EMPLOYEE HEALTH AND FITNESS; the executive update on health improvement programs. 1979. m. $238. American Health Consultants, Inc., Six Piedmont Center, Ste. 400, 3525 Piedmont Rd., N.E., Atlanta, GA 30305. TEL 404-262-7436. FAX 800-284-3291. (Subscr. to: Box 740056, Atlanta, GA 30374-9822. TEL 800-688-2421) Ed. Gail Poulton. bk.rev.; circ. 1,200. (also avail. in microfilm from UMI; back issues avail.; reprint service avail. from UMI) **Indexed:** Sportsearch (1980-).
●Also available online. Vendor(s): Mead Data Central.

613.7 368   BE   ISSN 0013-6964
EN MARCHE; journal bimensuel d'information pour les beneficiaires des soins de sante. 1948. s-m. 550 Fr. Alliance Nationale des Mutualites Chretiennes, 121 rue de la Loi, B-1040 Brussels, Belgium. TEL 02-237-46-27. FAX 02-237-33-00. Ed. H. Peemans-Poullet. adv.; bk.rev.; charts; illus.; stat.; circ. 430,000. (tabloid format)
Description: Discusses various aspects of health and relevant fields, such as insurance.

L'ENFANT. see *CHILDREN AND YOUTH — About*

ENFANT EN MILIEU TROPICAL. see *CHILDREN AND YOUTH — About*

ENVIRONMENTAL HEALTH MONTHLY. see *ENVIRONMENTAL STUDIES*

DIE ERSATZKASSE. see *SOCIAL SERVICES AND WELFARE*

613.7   MP
ERUUL MEND/HEALTH. (Text in Mongolian) 1959. bi-m. 100 tugrik($2.50) Ministry of Health, Ulan Bator, Mongolia. Ed. T. Ochirkhuu. circ. 25,000.

ESPRIT LIBRE. see *PSYCHOLOGY*

613.7   CH
EVERGREEN MONTHLY. (Text in Chinese) 1983. m. 2 Pa Teh Rd., 11th Floor, Sec.3, Taipei, Taiwan, Republic of China. TEL 02-7731665. FAX 02-7416838. circ. 140,000.
Description: Introduces health care knowledge.

613   US   ISSN 0014-4525
GV201
EXECUTIVE FITNESS NEWSLETTER. 1970. m. $36. Rodale Press, Inc., 33 E. Minor St., Emmaus, PA 18098. TEL 215-967-5171. TELEX 847338. Ed. William Gottlieb. bk.rev.; circ. 46,131. **Indexed:** Sportsearch.
Description: Offers health tips for the busy executive trying to stay in shape; with topical articles on exercise, diet and stress-reducing techniques.

613.7   HK
EXECUTIVE FITNESS NEWSLETTER. s-m. $48. Asia Letter Group, Hennessy Rd., P.O. Box 20036, Hennessy Rd. Post Office, Hong Kong.
Formerly: Executive Fitness.

613.7   UK   ISSN 0261-8230
EXECUTIVE HEALTH CLUB. 1981. m. United Health Promotion, 2 Palace Rd., London N8, England. illus.
—BLDSC shelfmark: 3836.217000.

614
EXECUTIVE HEALTH'S GOOD HEALTH REPORT. 1963. m. (plus 1 bonus issue). $34 in US; Canada, Mexico $40; elsewhere $58. Executive Health, Box 8880, Chapel Hill, NC 27515. TEL 919-929-7519. FAX 919-929-2183. Ed. A.C. Bushnell. bk.rev.; index; circ. 15,000. (also avail. in microfilm from UMI; microfiche from UMI; back issues avail.; reprint service avail. from UMI) **Indexed:** Consum.Ind., Hlth.Ind., Sportsearch.
Former titles (until June 1991): Executive Health Report (ISSN 0882-2131); Executive Health.
Description: Disseminates information on health issues, plus regular features including nutrition and exercise.

613.9   US
EXER-SAFETY NEWS. 1980. q. $25. Exer-Safety Association, Box 391466, Solon, OH 44139. TEL 216-562-8280. Ed. Sharon Foy. adv.; bk.rev.; circ. 6,000.
Description: Information on safe practices in exercise to music classes.

613.7   US
EXERCISE FOR MEN ONLY. bi-m. Chelo Publishing Inc., Empire State Bldg., 350 Fifth Ave., New York, NY 10118. TEL 212-947-4322.

613.7 641.1   US   ISSN 0748-3155
QP301
EXERCISE PHYSIOLOGY: CURRENT SELECTED RESEARCH. 1985. a. $67.50. A M S Press, Inc., 56 E. 13th St., New York, NY 10003. TEL 212-777-4700. FAX 212-995-5413. Eds. Charles O. Dotson, James H. Humphrey. index. (back issues avail.)
—BLDSC shelfmark: 3836.235900.
Description: Research articles on various topics of exercise science and sports medicine.

EXERCISE STANDARDS AND MALPRACTICE REPORTER. see *LAW*

613.7 612.3   US
EXTENDED CARE PRODUCT NEWS. q. Heath Management Publications, Inc., 550 American Rd., King of Prussia, PA 19406-1441. TEL 215-337-4466. Ed. Peter Norris. circ. 28,300.

613.7   CH
FAMILIES MONTHLY. (Text in Chinese) 1976. m. 2 Pa Teh Rd., 11th Floor, Sec.3, Taipei, Taiwan, Republic of China. TEL 02-7731665. FAX 02-7416838. circ. 155,000.
Description: Covers family life.

613.7   US
FAMILY PROGRAMMER. m. free. Bodylog Inc., 34 Maple Ave., Box 8, Armonk, NY 10504.
Formerly (until 1983): T I Source and Logo News.
Description: Information about the Step-In-Time fitness test and health and fitness awareness.

613.7   US
FEELIN' GOOD. bi-m. Ware Publishing, Inc., 400 Corporate Pointe, Rm. 580, Culver City, CA 90230-7621. TEL 213-649-3320. FAX 213-649-4057. Ed. Karen Johnson. circ. 250,000.

613.7   US
FEELING GREAT. 1984. m. $15.97. 45 W. 34th St., Rm. 407, New York, NY 10001. TEL 212-239-0855. Ed. Tim Moriarty. adv.; circ. 250,000.

613.7   US
FEMALE BODYBUILDING. bi-m. $2.95 per no. Starlog Group, Inc., 475 Park Ave., S., 8th Fl., New York, NY 10016. TEL 212-689-2830.

FIRST-TIME PARENTS. see *CHILDREN AND YOUTH — About*

FIRST YEAR OF LIFE; a guide to your baby's growth and development month by month. see *CHILDREN AND YOUTH — About*

613.7   SZ
FITNESS. 10/yr. Buechler & Co. AG, Hardeggstr. 27, 8049 Zurich, Switzerland.

PHYSICAL FITNESS AND HYGIENE

613.7   CN
FITNESS BULLETIN. 1978. m. $30. (Fitness Institute) Steen Publishing, RR 1, Cheltenham, Ont. L0P 1C0, Canada. TEL 416-838-3319. FAX 416-838-3319. Ed. David Steen. bk.rev.; circ. 4,000. (back issues avail.)
  Description: Contains health and fitness news, and instructive articles for subscribers and institute members.

613.7 658   US   ISSN 0882-0481
FITNESS MANAGEMENT. 12/yr. $45. Leisure Publications, Inc., 3923 W. 6th St., Los Angeles, CA 90020. TEL 213-385-3926. FAX 213-383-1152. Ed. Edward Pitts. circ. 21,000. (back issues avail.) **Indexed:** Sportsearch (1991-).
  Description: For owners and managers of athletic and health facilities.

613.7   US
▼**FITNESS PLUS.** 1990. m. $19.95. Focus Publishing Ltd., 300 W. 43rd St., New York, NY 10036. TEL 212-397-5200. Ed. Steve Raimondi. adv.; circ. 250,000.
  Description: Covers health, nutrition, weight training, exercise, dieting, fitness fashions. Includes celebrity profiles.

FITNESS SWIMMER. see *SPORTS AND GAMES*

613.7   US   ISSN 8750-8915
FLEX MAGAZINE. 1983. m. $27.95. I Brute Enterprises, 21100 Erwin St., Woodland Hills, CA 91367. TEL 213-884-6800. adv.; circ. 150,000.

FODOR'S HEALTHY ESCAPES. see *TRAVEL AND TOURISM*

613.7 646.7   IT
FORMA IN MODO NATURALE. m. L.50000 (foreign L.80000). Alberto Peruzzi Editore, Via E. Marelli 165, 20099 Sesto San Giovanni (MI), Italy. TEL 02-242021.

A FRIEND INDEED. see *WOMEN'S INTERESTS*

FRONTIERS OF HEALTH SERVICES MANAGEMENT. see *HOSPITALS*

613   FR
GAZETTE OFFICIELLE DU THERMALISME. bi-m. 250 F. Office des Nouvelles Internationales, Agence de Presse, 2 rue Cazaubon Norbert, 64000 Pau, France. TEL 59-30-03-28. (Subscr. to: 16 rue de l'Estrapade, 75005 Paris, France) (Co-sponsor: Federation Thermale et Climatique Francaise) Ed. Nicole Belval.

GENEESKUNDE EN SPORT. see *MEDICAL SCIENCES — Sports Medicine*

GESICHERTES LEBEN. see *SOCIAL SERVICES AND WELFARE*

613   GW   ISSN 0016-9234
GESUND LEBEN. 1952. m. DM.19.80 (foreign DM.24.80). M und H Schaper GmbH und Co. KG, Kalandstr. 4e 20, Postfach 1642, 3220 Alfeld, Germany. TEL 05181-8009-0. FAX 05181-8009-33. Ed. Arnim Sagaster. adv.; charts; illus.; circ. 60,000.

613   GW   ISSN 0016-9269
GESUNDHEIT. 1949. bi-m. DM.9. Agis Verlag GmbH, Ooser Luisenstr. 23, 7570 Baden-Baden 2220, Germany. adv.; bk.rev.; illus.; circ. 2,300,000. (also avail. in microform from UMI)
  Former titles: Gesundheit in Betrieb und Familie; Gesundheit.

613   SZ   ISSN 0016-9285
GESUNDHEITSNACHRICHTEN; vogelin utiset. (Text mainly in Dutch, Finnish and German) 1944. m. 18 Fr. Verlag A. Vogel, CH-9053 Teufen AR, Switzerland. Ed. Dr. A. Vogel. adv.; bk.rev.; circ. 50,000.

614   RU   ISSN 0016-9900
  CODEN: GISAAA
GIGIENA I SANITARIYA/HYGIENE AND SANITATION. 1922. m. 22.20 Rub.($16.20) (Vsesoyuznoe Nauchnoe Obshchestvo Gigienistov) Izdatel'stvo Meditsina, Petroverigskii pereulok 6-8, 101838 Moscow, Russia. (Co-sponsor: Ministerstvo Zdravookhraneniya S.S.S.R.) Ed. G.I. Rumyantsev. bk.rev.; bibl.; index. (tabloid format) **Indexed:** Abstr.Hyg., Anal.Abstr., Biol.Abstr., C.I.S. Abstr., Chem.Abstr., Dairy Sci.Abstr., Dent.Ind., Field Crop Abstr., Food Sci.& Tech.Abstr., Ind.Med., Ind.Vet., INIS Atomind., Int.Aerosp.Abstr., Irr.& Drain.Abstr., Nutr.Abstr., Packag.Sci.Tech., Pollut.Abstr., Potato Abstr., Soils & Fert., Soyabean Abstr., Trop.Dis.Bull., Vet.Bull., W.R.C.Inf., World Bibl.Soc.Sec.
  —BLDSC shelfmark: 0048.000000.
  Description: Publishes papers on all the branches of hygienic science and sanitary practice.

614   IT   ISSN 0017-0313
  CODEN: GIMPAP
GIORNALE DI IGIENE E MEDICINA PREVENTIVA. (Text in Italian; summaries in English) vol. 11, 1970. q. L.30000($30) Universita degli Studi di Genova, Istituto di Igiene, Via A. Pastore 1, Genova, Italy. Ed. F. L. Petrilli. charts; stat. **Indexed:** Abstr.Hyg., Biol.Abstr., C.I.S. Abstr., Chem.Abstr., Curr.Adv.Ecol.Sci., Dairy Sci.Abstr., Excerp.Med., Food Sci.& Tech.Abstr., Ind.Med., INIS Atomind., Trop.Dis.Bull.
  Description: Includes research and studies conducted in the fields of hygiene and preventive medicine.

GOOD HEALTH. see *PUBLIC HEALTH AND SAFETY*

613.7 613.2   CN
GOOD HEALTH. 1980. 6/yr. $13. 801 York Mills Rd., Ste. 201, Don Mills, Ont. M3B 1X7, Canada. TEL 416-444-4952. Ed. Ed Mounsey. adv.; circ. 35,000.

GOOD NEIGHBOR. see *SOCIAL SERVICES AND WELFARE*

613.7   US
GRANDMASTERS. a. $4.95. China Direct Publishing, Box 31578, San Francisco, CA 94131. TEL 415-824-1810. FAX 415-824-3312.

GREAT ACTIVITIES NEWSPAPER; an elementary physical education publication. see *EDUCATION*

613.7 612.3   US
GREAT BODY. 1989. bi-m. $2.95 per no. Harris Publications, Inc., 1115 Broadway, 8th fl., New York, NY 10010. TEL 212-807-7100. Ed. Mary Greenberg. adv.; circ. 30,000.
  Description: Provides information on healthy eating and dieting, as well as work-out routines and fitness programs to improve health and stamina.

613.7   US
GREAT IDEAS NEWSLETTER. m. Eymann Publications, Box 3577, Reno, NV 89505-3577. TEL 702-826-0795. Ed. Ken Eymann. circ. 1,000.

613.194   UK
GROVE. 1949. 3/yr. £10($20) Naturist Foundation, Naturist Headquarters, Orpington, Kent BR5 4ET, England. Ed. Ernest Stanley. adv.; bk.rev.; circ. 750.
  Description: Information on facilities for naturist recreation in Great Britain and elsewhere.

H V A CURRENT AWARENESS BULLETIN. (Health Visitors' Association) see *MEDICAL SCIENCES — Nurses And Nursing*

613.7   HT
HAITI SANTE. 1980. q. $7. Centre D'Hygiene Familiale, 10, 1ere Impasse Lavand, Box 430, Port-au-Prince, Haiti. Ed. Ary Bordes. circ. 4,000.

HANDBOOK OF PSYCHOLOGY AND HEALTH SERIES. see *PSYCHOLOGY*

051   US   ISSN 1052-1577
RC81.A1   CODEN: HHLEET
HARVARD HEALTH LETTER; a publication for the general readership, designed to promote accurate and timely health information. 1975. m. Can.$36($24) (foreign $39). Harvard Medical School, HMS Health Publications Group, 164 Longwood Ave., 4th Fl., Boston, MA 02115. TEL 800-333-3438. FAX 617-432-1506. (Subscr. to: Box 10944, Des Moines, IA 50340) Ed. Dr. William Ira Bennett. index; circ. 315,000. (back issues avail.) **Indexed:** Biol.Dig., CHNI, Hlth.Ind., Mag.Ind., Sportsearch. ●Also available online. Vendor(s): BRS, Information Access Company.
  Formerly: Harvard Medical School Health Letter (ISSN 0161-7486)

HEADWAY. see *SPORTS AND GAMES*

613.7   US
HEALING CURRENTS. 1976. q. $20 (foreign $24). Whole Health Institute, 4817 N. County Rd. 29, Loveland, CO 80538. TEL 303-679-4306. Ed. Kathy Bassett. bk.rev.; circ. 1,500.

613   II   ISSN 0017-8861
HEALTH; devoted to healthful living. (Text in English) 1923. m. Rs.60 (foreign Rs.360)(effective 1992). Professional Publications Ltd., P.O. Box 2, Satya Sai Nagar, Madurai 625 003, Tamil Nadu, India. adv.; circ. 11,872. (reprint service avail. from UMI)

613   US   ISSN 0279-3547
RA773   CODEN: HALTBM
HEALTH; the magazine for total well-being. 1969-1991; resumed 1992. 7/yr. $18. Health Magazine, 275 Madison Ave., Ste. 1314, New York, NY 10016. TEL 212-953-2220. (Subscr. to: Box 56892, Boulder, CO 80322. TEL 800-274-2522) Ed. Hank Herman. adv.; bk.rev.; charts; illus.; stat.; circ. 1,000,000. (also avail. in microform from UMI; reprint service avail. from UMI) **Indexed:** Acad.Ind., Biol.Abstr., Biol.Dig., C.I.N.L., Can.Per.Ind., CHNI, Curr.Lit.Fam.Plan., Gen.Sci.Ind., Hlth.Ind., Mag.Ind., Phys.Ed.Ind., PMR, R.G., Sportsearch, TOM.
  —BLDSC shelfmark: 4274.697700.
  Incorporates (in 1992): In Health (ISSN 1047-0549) Health was formerly titled: Family Health (ISSN 0014-7249); Incorporating: Today's Health (ISSN 0040-8514).
  Description: Edited for active, health-conscious women with information on the world of health-nutrition and related fields. Departments include health, beauty, food, nutrition and others.

613.7   UK
HEALTH & BEAUTY GUIDE. 1980. q. £0.65 per no. Atlas Publishing Co. Ltd., 334 Brixton Rd., London SW9 7AG, England.

613.194   UK   ISSN 0017-8888
HEALTH AND EFFICIENCY. (Text in English, French, German) 1899. 12/yr. (plus q., s-a. eds.). $45. Peenhill Ltd., 28 Charles Sq., Pitfield St., London N1 6HT, England. TEL 071-253-4037. FAX 071-253-0539. Ed. Jane Hendy-Smith. adv.; bk.rev.; illus.; circ. 130,000.
  Description: News, views and reflections on the nudist and naturist scene, including areas where nudity and naked living are accepted.

HEALTH & ENVIRONMENT DIGEST. see *ENVIRONMENTAL STUDIES*

613.7   US
HEALTH & FITNESS; magazine for healthy, sound living. Short title: H F. 1989. bi-m. Blockbuster Periodicals, Inc., 2131 Hollywood Blvd., Hollywood, FL 33020. TEL 305-925-5242. Ed. Barbara Newman. circ. 30,000.
  Incorporates: Health Series.
  Description: Probes current health and fitness issues for all ages.

613   UK   ISSN 0264-2549
HEALTH AND FITNESS (BICESTER). 1982. m. £10.80. Goodhead Publications, 27 Murdock Rd., Bicester, Oxon. OX6 7RG, England. Ed. Laura Swaffield. adv.; circ. 40,000.

613.7   UK
HEALTH AND FITNESS (LONDON). 1984. m. £20. Hudson Brothers Publishers Ltd., 40 Bowling Green Lane, London EC1R 0NE, England. TEL 071-278-0333. FAX 071-837-7612. Ed. Sharon Walker. circ. 49,000.
  Formerly: Fitness.

PHYSICAL FITNESS AND HYGIENE

613 UK
HEALTH AND HEALING. 1982. 6/yr. £1.50. Churches' Council for Health and Healing, St. Marylebone Parish Church, Marylebone Rd., London NW1 5LT, England. TEL 071-486-9644. Ed. David Goodacre. bk.rev.; circ. 3,000.
  Description: To serve Christians who care and heal, to share ideas and information, and to explore the churches' theological and spiritual role in health and healing.

613 US
▼**HEALTH & HEALING.** 1991. m. $39.95 (effective 1992). Phillips Publishing, Inc., Consumer Publishing, 7811 Montroste Rd., Potomac, MD 20854. TEL 800-777-5005. FAX 301-424-7034. Ed. Dr. Julian Whitaker. (looseleaf format)

613.7 610 US
HEALTH & MEDICAL HORIZONS. 1982. a. $21.95. Macmillan Educational Company, 881 Broadway, New York, NY 10003. Ed. Robert Famighetti. index.
  Description: Summarizes latest developments in medicine and health preservation.

HEALTH AND PHYSICAL EDUCATION/HOKEN TAIIKU KYOSHITSU. see *EDUCATION*

613.7 UK
HEALTH AND PHYSICAL EDUCATION PROJECT NEWSLETTER. q. (Health Education Authority) Physical Education Association of Great Britain and Northern Ireland, Hamilton House, Mabledon Pl., London WC1H 9TX, England. **Indexed:** Sportsearch (1986-).

613.7 US ISSN 0898-3569
HEALTH & YOU. 1985. q. $10. Health Ink Inc., 1 Executive Dr., Moorestown, NJ 08057. TEL 609-778-0011. Ed. Lou Antosh. circ. 700,000. (back issues avail.)
  Description: General health and wellness publication for consumers covering fitness, nutrition, and prevention.

HEALTH AT WORK; newsletter. see *OCCUPATIONAL HEALTH AND SAFETY*

613.7 US
HEALTH CARE ARTICLES. m. Eymann Publications, Box 3577, Reno, NV 89505-3577. TEL 702-826-0795. Ed. Ken Eymann. circ. 100,000.

HEALTH CARE STRATEGIC MANAGEMENT; the journal of planning, marketing, and resource allocation. see *HOSPITALS*

613.7 US
HEALTH CONFIDENTIAL; the leading edge preventive-curative health letter. 1987. m. $49. Box 53408, Boulder, CO 80322. FAX 212-695-7492. Ed. Lee Rath. circ. 30,000.

HEALTH CONSCIOUSNESS; an holistic magazine. see *NEW AGE PUBLICATIONS*

613 UK ISSN 0017-8969
RA421
HEALTH EDUCATION JOURNAL. 1943. q. £10. Health Education Authority, Hamilton House, Mabledon Pl., London WC1H 9TX, England. TEL 071-413-1987. FAX 071-413-0340. Ed. M. Whitehead. adv.; bk.rev.; index; circ. 5,000. (also avail. in microform from UMI; reprint service avail. from UMI) **Indexed:** Abstr.Hyg., ASSIA, Cont.Pg.Educ., Curr.Adv.Ecol.Sci., Educ.Tech.Abstr., Excerp.Med., Res.High.Educ.Abstr., SSCI, Stud.Wom.Abstr., Trop.Dis.Bull.
—BLDSC shelfmark: 4275.000000.

613 614.8 UK
HEALTH EDUCATION NEWS. bi-m. free. Health Education Authority, Hamilton House, Mabledon Place, London WC1H 9TX, England. TEL 071-413-1987. FAX 071-413-0340. Ed. Adrian Roxan. circ. 41,000.

613 US
HEALTH EXPRESS (CLEVELAND).* 1988. q. $11.70. Davis Communications, Co., 1374 W. 6th St., Cleveland, OH 44113-1308. TEL 216-662-6969. adv.; circ. 200,000.
  Description: Covers nutrition, health, fitness and psychology in short practical articles.

613.7 US
HEALTH JOURNAL; the magazine of America's leading HMOs. q. free to qualified personnel. Madison Publishing, 347 Congress St., Boston, MA 02210. TEL 617-451-1155. FAX 617-451-3320. Ed. Sandy McDowell. adv.; circ. 1,108,229 (controlled).
  Description: Combines local HMO news and information with articles on health and fitness.

HEALTH LAW DIGEST. see *LAW*

HEALTH LAW JOURNAL OF OHIO. see *LAW*

613.7 US
HEALTH OF THE REP NEWSLETTER. m. (United Association Manufacturers' Representatives) Keith Kittrell & Associates, Inc., 133 Terrace Trail W., Lake Quivira, KS 66106. TEL 913-268-9466. FAX 714-859-9131. (Subscr. to: Drawer 6266, Kansas City, KS 66106) Ed. Karen K. Mazzola.
  Description: Covers the world of manufacturing.

HEALTH PHYSICS; the radiation protection journal. see *MEDICAL SCIENCES*

613.7 US
HEALTH POLICY SERIES. 1981. a. Marcel Dekker, Inc., 270 Madison Ave., New York, NY 10016. TEL 212-696-9000. FAX 212-685-4540. TELEX 421419. (Subscr. to: Box 10018, Church St. Sta., New York, NY 10249) Ed. Milton I. Roemer. **Indexed:** Med.Care Rev.

613 US ISSN 0883-8216
HEALTH SCIENCE; living in harmony with nature. 1978. bi-m. $25 (foreign $45). American Natural Hygiene Society, Inc., Box 30630, Tampa, FL 33630. TEL 813-855-6607. Ed. James Michael Lennon. adv.; bk.rev.; charts; illus.; cum.index: 1978-1983; circ. 6,000. (back issues avail.)
  Former titles (until vol.8, no.2): Vegetarian Health Science (ISSN 8750-1643); Health Science (ISSN 0161-5874)

613.7 US
HEALTH SHOPPER. q. Swanson Health Products, 1318 39th St., N.W., Box 2803, Fargo, ND 58102. TEL 800-437-4148. adv.
  Description: Provides current health information; covers nutrition and diets.

HEALTH, SOCIETY AND CULTURE. see *SOCIOLOGY*

613.7 US
HEALTH UPDATE. bi-m. $12. 201 S. McKenny Rd., Chandler, AZ 85226. TEL 602-257-1959.
  Description: Directed towards consumers and retailers of natural foods. Includes articles on health awareness, medical research, fitness, beauty, nutrition, behavior, and parenting.

613.7 US ISSN 0147-0353
RA421 CODEN: HEVAEC
HEALTH VALUES; the journal of health behavior, education & promotion. 1977. bi-m. $55 to individuals; institutions $65. P N G Publications, Box 4593, Star City, WV 26504-4593. TEL 304-293-4699. FAX 304-293-4693. Ed. Elbert D. Glover. adv.; bk.rev.; circ. 1,500. (also avail. in microform from UMI; reprint service avail. from UMI) **Indexed:** CHNI, CINAHL, NRN, Phys.Ed.Ind.
  Description: Seeks to provide a comprehensive understanding of the relationships among personal behavior, social structure and health, and to disseminate knowledge of major behavioral science principles and strategies to assist in designing and implementing programs to prevent disease and promote health.
  Refereed Serial

HEALTH WATCH. see *NUTRITION AND DIETETICS*

613.7 US
HEALTHCARE EMPLOYMENT NEWS. fortn. Healthcare Employment News Network, Gwynedd Plaza III, Rm. 203, Spring House, PA 19477. TEL 215-653-0340. FAX 215-653-0340. Ed. Richard Barwis. circ. 34,000.

HEALTHCARE MANAGEMENT TEAM LETTER. see *BUSINESS AND ECONOMICS — Management*

613.7 US
HEALTHCARE MARKETING AND MANAGEMENT REPORT. m. Box 570217, Miami, FL 33257-0217. TEL 305-252-7757. FAX 305-252-7741. Ed. Pete Silver.

613.7 US
HEALTHCARE MARKETING REPORT. m. H M R Publication Group, Box 76002, Atlanta, GA 30358-1002. TEL 404-457-6105. FAX 404-457-0049. Ed. Beverly Seitz. circ. 1,900.

613.7 612.3 US
HEALTHCARE NEW ORLEANS. m. City Business - New Orleans Inc., 111 Veterans Blvd., Rm. 1810, Metairie, LA 70005. TEL 504-834-9292. FAX 504-837-2258. Ed. Brian Ettinger. circ. 25,000.

613 JA
HEALTHY FAMILY. (Text in Japanese) 1976. bi-m. 3420 Yen. Shufu-to-Seikatsusha Ltd., 5-7, 3-chome, Kyobashi, Chuo-ku, Tokyo 104, Japan. Ed. Kyoshi Inoue.

HEALTHY KIDS: BIRTH - 3. see *CHILDREN AND YOUTH — About*

HEALTHY KIDS: 4-10 YEARS. see *CHILDREN AND YOUTH — About*

613.7 612.3 US
HEALTHY TIMES. bi-m. Vitamin Shoppe, 4700 Westside Ave., North Bergen, NJ 07047. TEL 800-223-1216. FAX 201-866-9513. Ed. Helen Howard.

HELAN MEDICAL MAGAZINE. see *MEDICAL SCIENCES*

613 DK ISSN 0018-0149
HELSE; familiens laegemagasin. 1955. 11/yr. DKK 120. Helse - Familiens Laegemagasin, Classensgade 36, 2100 Copenhagen Oe, Denmark. TEL 31-267900. FAX 31-268760. Ed. Leif Hansgaard. adv.; circ. 340,000.

HERA; Binghamton's women's newspaper. see *WOMEN'S INTERESTS*

613 II ISSN 0018-0491
HERALD OF HEALTH. (Text in English) 1909. m. Rs.60 foreign $6 (typically set in Apr.). (Seventh-day Adventists) Oriental Watchman Publishing House, Box 35, Poona 411001, India. TELEX 145 358 SUD IN. Ed. C.B. Hammond. adv.; bk.rev.; illus.; stat.; circ. 36,000.

613.7 MX
HERCULES MODERNO. 1980. fortn. Mex.$150000($80) (Federacion Internacional de Fisioconstructores) Editormex Mexicano, S.A., Avda. Rodolfo Gaona, Edif. 82-B-203, Lomas de Sotelo, 11200 Mexico D.F., Mexico. TEL 557-07-92. FAX 525-395-65-64. Ed. Javier Barrigo. adv.; illus.; circ. 45,000.
  Description: Cover bodybuilding, nutrition, kinesiology, training, psychology and health.

613 UK ISSN 0018-0696
HERE'S HEALTH; a monthly guide to health, nutrition, natural food and natural therapy. 1956. m. £18. E M A P Elan, Victory House, 14 Leicester Pl., London WC2H 7BP, England. Ed. Simon Martin. adv.; bk.rev.; illus.
  Incorporates: Health for All (ISSN 0017-8985)
  Description: Consumer magazine covering nutrition and alternative medicine.

HIMALAYAN INSTITUTE QUARTERLY GUIDE. see *PHILOSOPHY*

HIPPOCRATES NEWS. see *NUTRITION AND DIETETICS*

HOCHSCHULSPORT. see *SPORTS AND GAMES*

613 JA ISSN 0018-3342
HOKEN NO KAGAKU/HEALTH CARE. (Text in Japanese) 1959. m. 9000 Yen. (Health Science Research Association - Hoken Kagaku Kenkyukai) Kyorin Shoin, 4-2-1 Yushima, Tokyo 113, Japan. Ed. Fusao Akiyama. index; circ. 710.
—BLDSC shelfmark: 4274.937000.

HOKKAIDO KYOIKU DAIGAKU KIYO. DAI-2-BU, C. KATEI, TAIIKU- HEN/HOKKAIDO UNIVERSITY OF EDUCATION. JOURNAL. SECTION 2 C. HOME ECONOMICS, TEACHER TRAINING FOR SCHOOL HEALTH AND PHYSICAL EDUCATION. see *HOME ECONOMICS*

PHYSICAL FITNESS AND HYGIENE

613.7 US
HOME HEALTH LINE; the home care industry's national independent newsletter. 1975. w. (48/yr.). $375. Box 250, Port Republic, MD 20676. TEL 410-535-4103. FAX 410-535-0632. Ed. Richard W.C. Falknor. adv.; index; circ. 2,800. (back issues avail.)

HOME HEALTHCARE NURSE. see MEDICAL SCIENCES

301.16 613.7 US ISSN 0891-3374
HOPE HEALTH LETTER. 1978. m. $19.95. Hope Heart Institute, Seattle, WA 98101. (Dist. by: International Health Awareness Center, 350 E. Michigan Ave., Ste. 301, Kalamazoo, MI 49007-3851. TEL 616-343-0770) Ed. Carol Garzona. illus. (looseleaf format)
  Formerly (until 1986): Hope Newsletter.
  Description: Covers many subjects on health including smoking, stress management, diet, self-care, cost-containment. Written for all levels.

613.7 790.1 PO
HORIZONTE; revista de educacao fisica e desporto. 1984. bi-m. Livros Horizonte, Lda., Rua das Chagas, 17, 1121 Lisbon Codex, Portugal. TEL 1-3466917. FAX 1-326921.

HOSPITAL REVENUE REPORT. see BUSINESS AND ECONOMICS — Marketing And Purchasing

HUMAN ECOLOGY & ENERGY BALANCING SCIENTIST. see MEDICAL SCIENCES

HUMAN MOVEMENT SCIENCE; journal devoted to pure and applied research on human movement. see MEDICAL SCIENCES

HYGIE; international journal of health education. see PUBLIC HEALTH AND SAFETY

613.7 US
HYGIENIC COMMUNITY NETWORK NEWS. 1980. bi-m. $7. Hygienic Community Network, RR 1 Box 371, Athens, NY 12015-9726. Ed. Helen Jean Story. bk.rev.; circ. 150.
  Description: For people in the Natural Hygiene movement who are interested in forming cooperative communities dedicated to healthful living.

613 UK ISSN 0018-8263
HYGIENIST. 1959. q. £8.50($17) British Natural Hygiene Society, c/o Shalimar, Harold Grove, Frinton-On-Sea, Essex, England. TEL 0255-672823. Ed. Keki R. Sidhwa. bk.rev.; circ. 300. (processed)

I A P N H NEWSLETTER. (International Association of Professional Natural Hygienists) see NUTRITION AND DIETETICS

613.7 US
I C H P E R CONGRESS PROCEEDINGS. 1958. biennial. price varies. International Council on Health, Physical Education and Recreation, 1900 Association Dr., Reston, VA 22091. TEL 202-476-3400. **Indexed:** Sportsearch.
  Formerly: I C H P E R Congress Reports (ISSN 0074-4417).
  Description: Covers physical fitness.

613.7 US
RA781.15
I D E A TODAY. 1984. 10/yr. membership. International Dance-Exercise Association, 6190 Cornerstone Court E., San Diego, CA 92121. TEL 619-535-8979. Ed. Patricia Ryan. adv.; bk.rev.; circ. 17,000. (back issues avail.) **Indexed:** Phys.Ed.Ind., Sportsearch (1988-).
  Formerly: Dance Exercise Today (ISSN 0882-1399).

613 US ISSN 1040-8282
LB2337.2
IDEA TODAY. 1982. 10/yr. $4 per no. Idea, Inc., 6190 Cornerstone Ct. E., Ste. 204, San Diego, CA 92121-3773. TEL 619-535-8979. FAX 619-535-8234. adv.; circ. 20,000 (controlled).
  Description: For fitness instructors and personal trainers. Provides how-to articles that mix theory with practical skills.

613 IT ISSN 0019-1655
CODEN: IGMPAX
IGIENE MODERNA; rivista di igiene, microbiologia, epidemiologia. (Text in English, French, Italian) 1908. m. L.150000($180) European Journal of Epidemiology Publishers, S.r.l., Via Zandonai, 11, 00194 Rome (Pratti), Italy. TEL 06-3279593. FAX 06-3290343. TELEX 611330 UCATRO. (Subscr. to: Istituto di Microbiologia, Facolta di Medicina e Chirurgia, Universita Cattolica del Sacro Cuore, Largo F. Vito, 1 00168 Rome, Italy.) Ed. Dr. Antonio Sanna. adv.; bk.rev.; abstr.; charts; illus.; index. **Indexed:** Abstr.Hyg., Biol.Abstr., C.I.S. Abstr., Chem.Abstr., Curr.Adv.Ecol.Sci., Excerp.Med., Ind.Med., Nutr.Abstr., Trop.Dis.Bull., Vet.Bull.
—BLDSC shelfmark: 4363.440000.
  Description: Covers the Italian Society of Hygiene, Preventive Medicine and Public Health; includes microbiology and epidemiology.

613 CN ISSN 0848-1733
IN TOUCH (GLOUCHESTER). (Text in English, French) 1974. 3/yr. membership. Canadian Association for Health, Physical Education, and Recreation, Place R. Tait McKenzie, 1600 James Naismith Dr., Gloucester, Ont. K1B 5N4, Canada. TEL 613-748-5622. Ed. Veronique Duvieusart. circ. 1,500. (back issues avail.)
  Former titles (until 1989): C A H P E R Keeps In Touch (ISSN 0829-1055); C A H P E R News (ISSN 0318-1960)

613.7 615.53 US
IN TOUCH FOR HEALTH.* 1982. 6/yr. $30 (includes Touch for Health Journal). Touch for Health Foundation, 1200 N. Lake Ave., No.A, Pasadena, CA 91104-3744. TEL 818-794-1181. adv.; bk.rev.; circ. 2,000.
  Description: Collection of papers on health presented at annual meeting.

613.7 FR
INFORMATIONS U F O L E P-U S E P. 1945. m. (10/yr.). 45 F. Union Francaise des Oeuvres Laiques d'Education Physique, 3 rue Recamier, 75341 Paris, France. adv.; bk.rev.; circ. 104,000.

INSTITUTE OF HEALTH EDUCATION. JOURNAL. see MEDICAL SCIENCES

INTEGRAL. see AGRICULTURE

INTERMEDICA POST. see BUSINESS AND ECONOMICS — International Development And Assistance

613.7 US
INTERNATIONAL COUNCIL FOR HEALTH, PHYSICAL EDUCATION AND RECREATION. JOURNAL. q. International Council for Health, Physical Education and Recreation - Conseil International pour l'Hygiene de l'Education et de la Recreation, 1900 Association Dr., Reston, VA 22091. TEL 202-476-3400. **Indexed:** Sportsearch (1988-).

INTERNATIONAL JOURNAL OF OBESITY. see NUTRITION AND DIETETICS

INTERNATIONAL JOURNAL OF PHYSICAL EDUCATION/INTERNATIONALE ZEITSCHRIFT FUER SPORTPAEDAGOGIK. see EDUCATION — Teaching Methods And Curriculum

613 GW ISSN 0178-7764
INTERNATIONALES SAUNA - ARCHIV. 1952. q. DM.30. (Deutscher Sauna - Bund e.V.) Sauna Matti GmbH, Kavalleriestr. 9, 4800 Bielefeld 1, Germany. TEL 0521-178134. Ed. Dr. Werner Fritzsche. adv.; bk.rev.; abstr.; charts; stat.; circ. 3,000.
—BLDSC shelfmark: 4557.057500.
  Formerly: Sauna Nachrichten mit Sauna Archiv (ISSN 0036-5033)

613 US ISSN 0047-1496
IRONMAN. 1936. m. $29.95. IronMan Publishing, Box 12009, Marina Del Ray, CA 90295. TEL 213-822-2844. FAX 213-823-2614. Ed. Peary Rader. adv.; charts; illus.; tr.lit.

ISOKINETICS AND EXERCISE SCIENCE. see MEDICAL SCIENCES — Sports Medicine

JACK HUTSLAR'S WEEKLY NEWS. see SPORTS AND GAMES

613 JA ISSN 0021-5082
CODEN: NEZAAQ
JAPANESE JOURNAL OF HYGIENE/NIHON EISEIGAKU ZASSHI. (Text mainly in Japanese) 1946. bi-m. 4500 Yen. Japanese Society for Hygiene - Nihon Eisei Gakkai, c/o Dept. of Hygiene and Preventive Medicine, Faculty of Medicine, University of Tokyo, 7-3-1 Hongo, Bunkyo-ku, Tokyo 113, Japan. FAX 81-3-5684-2297. Ed. Dr. H. Sakurai. adv.; circ. 2,700. **Indexed:** C.I.S. Abstr., Excerp.Med., Food Sci.& Tech.Abstr., Helminthol.Abstr., Ind.Med., Nutr.Abstr.
—BLDSC shelfmark: 4655.300000.

610 613.7 JA ISSN 0039-906X
JAPANESE JOURNAL OF PHYSICAL FITNESS AND SPORTS MEDICINE. (Text in English, Japanese) 1950. bi-m. $120. (Japanese Society of Physical Fitness and Sports Medicine) Japan Scientific Societies Press, 6-2-10 Hongo, Bunkyo-ku, Tokyo 113, Japan. TEL 3814-2001. FAX 3814-2002. TELEX 2722268 BCJSP J. (Dist. by: Business Center for Academic Societies Japan, Koshin Bldg., 6-16-3 Hongo, Bunkyo-ku, Tokyo 113, Japan; Dist. in U.S. by: International Specialized Book Services, Inc., 5602 N.E. Hassalo St., Portland, OR 97213; in Asia by: Toppan Company Pvt. Ltd., 38 Liu Fang Rd., Box 22 Jurong Town, Jurong, Singapore 2622) circ. 2,540. **Indexed:** Excerp.Med., Nutr.Abstr.
—BLDSC shelfmark: 4657.420000.
  Formerly: Japanese Journal of Physical Fitness.

613 II ISSN 0021-5813
JEEVAN JAUBAN. (Text mainly in Bengali; occasionally in English) 1966. m. Rs.16($2) Purabi Publishers, 85 Bepin Behari Ganguly St., Calcutta 12, India. Ed. P.K. Das. adv.; film rev.; bibl.; charts; illus.; circ. 30,000. (avail. on records)

613.7 US
▼**JENNY CRAIG'S YOUR BODY, YOUR HEALTH.** 1990. 4/yr. $2.95. Hachette Magazines, Inc., Hachette Custom Publishing, 1633 Broadway, New York, NY 10019. TEL 212-767-6797. FAX 212-921-0705. Ed. Margo Gilman. adv.; circ. 800,000.
  Formerly (until 1992): Woman's Day (Year) Guide to Your Body, Your Health.
  Description: Covers medications, nutrition, diets, exercise, cholesterol, walking and good health.

JEWISH VEGETARIAN. see NUTRITION AND DIETETICS

613.7 US
JIAN YU MEI/STRENGTH & BEAUTY. (Text in Chinese) bi-m. $20.70. China Books & Periodicals, Inc., 2929 24th St., San Francisco, CA 94110. TEL 415-282-2994. FAX 415-282-0994.

613.7 CC ISSN 1002-297X
JIANKANG/HEALTH. (Text in Chinese) 1980. m. Y12. Beijing Jiankang Jiaoyusuo - Beijing Health Education Institute, 20 Hepingli Beijie, Beijing 100013, People's Republic of China. TEL 4215827. Ed. Feng Ailan. adv.; circ. 100,000.

613 US
JIANKANG BAO/HEALTH GAZETTE. (Text in Chinese) d. $210.20. China Books & Periodicals, Inc., 2929 24th St., San Francisco, CA 94110. TEL 415-282-2994. FAX 415-282-0994. (newspaper)

613.7 CC
JIANKANG GUWEN/HEALTH CONSULTANT. (Text in Chinese) q. Renmin Tiyu Chubanshe, 8 Tiyuguan Lu, Chongwen Qu, Beijing 100061, People's Republic of China. TEL 757161. Ed. Dang Baijie.

613.7 028.5 CC
JIANKANG SHAONIAN HUABAO/HEALTHY CHILDREN'S PICTORIAL. (Text in Chinese) bi-m. Beijing Jiankang Jiaoyusuo - Beijing Health Education Institute, 20 Hepingli Beijie, Beijing 100013, People's Republic of China. TEL 4215827. Ed. Feng Ailan.

613.7 CC
JIANKANG TIANDI/HEALTHY WORLD. (Text in Chinese) bi-m. Hebei Fangyi Zhan - Hebei Epidemic Prevention Station, 18 Hongqi Lu, Baoding, Hebei 071000, People's Republic of China. TEL 24911. Ed. Zhang Furui.

PHYSICAL FITNESS AND HYGIENE

613.7   CC
JIANKANG ZHI YOU/FRIEND OF HEALTH. (Text in Chinese) bi-m. Xin Tiyu Zazhishe - New Sports Journal Publishing, 8 Tiyuguan Lu, Chongwen-qu, Beijing 100061, People's Republic of China. TEL 757161. Ed. Cao Yan.

613.7   CC
JIANKANG ZHINAN/HEALTH GUIDANCE. (Text in Chinese) q. Quanguo Laoganbu Jiankang Zhidao Weiyuanhui - National Health Committee for Senior Officials, 11 Heping Jiekou, Beijing 100029, People's Republic of China. TEL 4212731. Ed. Gao Heting.

JOSAI DAIGAKU KENKYU NENPO. SHIZEN KAGAKU HEN/JOSAI UNIVERSITY BULLETIN OF LIBERAL ARTS. NATURAL SCIENCE, HEALTH AND PHYSICAL EDUCATION. see *HUMANITIES: COMPREHENSIVE WORKS*

613   US   ISSN 0744-8481
RA564.5
JOURNAL OF AMERICAN COLLEGE HEALTH. 1952. bi-m. $39 to individuals; institutions $65. (American College Health Association) Heldref Publications, 1319 Eighteenth St., N.W., Washington, DC 20036-1802. TEL 202-296-6267. FAX 202-296-5149. (Co-sponsor: Helen Dwight Reid Educational Foundation) Ed. Martha Wedemen. adv.; bk.rev.; charts; illus.; index; circ. 2,000. (also avail. in microform; reprint service avail.) **Indexed**: ASSIA, Biol.Abstr., C.I.J.E., C.I.S. Abstr., Chem.Abstr., CINAHL, Curr.Lit.Fam.Plan., Educ.Ind., Excerp.Med., Hosp.Lit.Ind., Ind.Med., Phys.Ed.Ind., Psychol.Abstr.
Formerly (until 1982): American College Health Association. Journal (ISSN 0002-7944); Incorporates: American College Health Association. Proceedings.
Refereed Serial

JOURNAL OF BIOENERGETICS AND BIOMEMBRANES. see *BIOLOGY — Biophysics*

JOURNAL OF COMPARATIVE PHYSICAL AND EDUCATION SPORT. see *SPORTS AND GAMES*

613 610   US   ISSN 1044-2790
JOURNAL OF HEALTH & HEALING. 1975. q. $10. Wildwood Lifestyle Center & Hospital, Wildwood, GA 30757. TEL 404-820-1493. FAX 404-820-1474. Ed. Dr. Marjorie Baldwin. adv.; charts; illus.; index; circ. 10,000. (back issues avail.)

613.7 200   US   ISSN 0885-4726
BV4335
JOURNAL OF HEALTH CARE CHAPLAINCY. 1987. s-a. $24 to individuals; institutions $32; libraries $75. Haworth Press, Inc., 10 Alice St., Binghamton, NY 13904. TEL 800-342-9678. FAX 607-722-1424. Ed. Laurel Arthur Burton. adv.; bk.rev.; circ. 147. (also avail. in microfiche from HAW; reprint service avail. from HAW) **Indexed**: Curr.Cont., Ind.Med.
—BLDSC shelfmark: 4996.733000.
Description: Promotes both foundational and applied interdisciplinary research related to chaplaincy as practiced in community hospitals, medical centers, nursing homes, and other health care institutions.
Refereed Serial

JOURNAL OF HEALTH CARE MARKETING. see *BUSINESS AND ECONOMICS — Marketing And Purchasing*

JOURNAL OF HEALTH EDUCATION. see *EDUCATION — Teaching Methods And Curriculum*

JOURNAL OF HEALTH SCIENCE. see *NUTRITION AND DIETETICS*

JOURNAL OF SEX EDUCATION AND THERAPY. see *EDUCATION*

JOURNAL OF SPORTS MEDICINE AND PHYSICAL FITNESS. see *MEDICAL SCIENCES — Sports Medicine*

613.7   US   ISSN 0273-5024
GV363
JOURNAL OF TEACHING IN PHYSICAL EDUCATION. 1981. q. $36 to individuals (foreign $40); institutions $80 (foreign $84); students $24 (foreign $28). Human Kinetics Publishers, Inc., Box 5076, Champaign, IL 61825-5076. TEL 217-351-5076. FAX 217-351-2674. Eds. Drs. Judith Rink, Stephen Silverman. adv.; bk.rev.; bibl.; charts; stat.; index; circ. 870. (back issues avail.) **Indexed**: Phys.Ed.Ind., Sp.Ed.Needs Abstr., Sportsearch (1982-).
—BLDSC shelfmark: 5068.285700.
Description: Designed to stimulate and communicate research and practical applications. Offers new teaching methods and ideas to help students, teachers, teacher educators, and administrators at all levels.
Refereed Serial

K A H P E R D JOURNAL. (Kentucky Association for Health, Physical Education, Recreation and Dance) see *EDUCATION — Special Education And Rehabilitation*

613.7   GW   ISSN 0932-1055
K K H JOURNAL. 1940. q. Kaufmaennische Krankenkasse Hauptverwaltung, Hindenburgstr. 43-45, 3000 Hannover 1, Germany. TEL 0511-2802-0. FAX 0511-2802-109. TELEX 9230924. Ed.Bd. bk.rev.; circ. 1,000,000.

KENKO KYOIKU/PUBLIC HEALTH EDUCATION. see *PUBLIC HEALTH AND SAFETY*

613   JA   ISSN 0022-9946
KENKO NA KURASHI/LONGER AND HEALTHIER LIFE. (Text in Japanese) 1965. m. 1800 Yen($5) Kenko na Kurashi no Kai, 1-2, 5-chome, Hongo, Bunkyo-ku, Tokyo 113, Japan. Ed. Toshiko Yamamoto. bk.rev.; illus.; circ. 3,000.

613   GW   ISSN 0023-2254
KNEIPP BLAETTER. 1891. m. DM.34.80. Kneipp Verlag GmbH, Postfach 1451, 8939 Bad Woerishofen, Germany. adv.; bk.rev.; illus.; circ. 90,000.

613.7   GW   ISSN 0323-4916
KOERPERERZIEHUNG; Fachzeitschrift fuer Sportlehrer, Trainer und Uebungsleiter im Kinder- und Jugendsport. 1951. m. DM.36. Volk und Wissen Verlag GmbH, Lindenstr. 54A, 1086 Berlin, Germany. TEL 0372-20343-0. circ. 11,800.

613   BU   ISSN 0368-7066
                                  CODEN: KUFIAT
KURORTOLOGIJA I FIZIOTERAPIJA. (Text in Bulgarian; summaries in English, Russian) q. 10 lv. (Ministerstvo na Narodnoto Zdrave) Izdatelstvo Meditsina i Fizkultura, 11 Pl. Slaveikov, Sofia, Bulgaria. (Distr. by: Hemus, 6 Rouski Blvd., 1000 Sofia, Bulgaria) (Co-sponsor: Nauchno Druzhestvo po Kurortologija, Fizioterapija i Rehabilitacija) Ed. St. Bankov. circ. 850. **Indexed**: Abstr.Bulg.Sci.Med.Lit.
—BLDSC shelfmark: 0094.900000.

L A RESOURCES. see *NEW AGE PUBLICATIONS*

LAPIS; percorsi della reflessione femminile. see *WOMEN'S INTERESTS*

613   AU
LEBENSSCHUTZ; Der stille Weg. 1949. 4/yr. S.130 (foreign S.154). (Verein fuer Lebenskunde) Anna Pichler Verlag, Marchettigasse 6, A-1060 Vienna, Austria. TEL 0222-597-02-75. FAX 0222-597-09-84. Ed. Anna Maria Pichler. adv.; bk.rev.; illus.; circ. 5,200.
Formerly: Glueckliche Leben-der Stille Weg (ISSN 0017-1395)

LEHRHILFEN FUER DEN SPORTUNTERRICHT. see *EDUCATION — Teaching Methods And Curriculum*

613   US   ISSN 0024-1288
TX341
LET'S LIVE. 1933. m. $19.95. Hilltopper Inc., 444 N. Larchmont Blvd., Box 74908, Los Angeles, CA 90004. TEL 213-469-3901. FAX 213-469-9597. Ed. Victoria Clayton. adv.; bk.rev.; circ. 140,000. (also avail. in microform from UMI; reprint service avail. from UMI) **Indexed**: Hlth.Ind.

613.7   HK
LIFE AND HEALTH. (Text in Chinese) 1976. s-a. HK.$216($55.19) Life and Health Centre Ltd., Rm. G28, Seven Seas Shopping Centre, No. 121, King's Road, North Point, Hong Kong. TEL 5703185. FAX 8063417. Ed. Doris Lee. adv.; circ. 36,000. (back issues avail.)

613.7   CN
LIFELINES (SASKATOON). 1989. q. Can.$25. (Saskatchewan Health Educators Association) Saskatchewan Teachers' Federation, P.O. Box 1108, Saskatoon, Sask. S7K 3N3, Canada.

613.26   CN   ISSN 0834-3543
LIFELINES (TORONTO); the voice of the Toronto vegetarian community. 1954. bi-m. Can.$20. Toronto Vegetarian Association, 736 Bathurst St., Toronto, Ont. M5S 2R4, Canada. TEL 416-533-3543. Ed. Marc Coulavin. adv.: page Can.$120. bk.rev.; circ. 1,000.
Formerly: Toronto Vegetarian Association. Newsletter (ISSN 0049-4232)
Description: Information about vegetarianism.

613.7   FI   ISSN 0355-7073
LIIKUNTAKASVATUS. 1934. 5/yr. Fmk.90. Suomen Liikunnanopettajain Liitto, Rautatielaisenk 6, 00520 Helsinki, Finland. TEL 90-15021. Ed. Jussi Luukko. adv.; bk.rev.; circ. 2,200.

613   US
LIVEWELL.* 1988. m. $2.50 per no. 4353 E. 119th Way, Denver, CO 80233-1738. TEL 303-292-3343. Ed. Pam Avery. adv.; circ. 150,000.
Description: Focuses on heart attacks, cancer, lung disease, and strokes; discusses prevention and aftercare.

613.7   US
LIVING WELL. a. $1.95. Hearst Magazines, Living Well, 250 W. 55th St., New York, NY 10019. TEL 212-649-4203. FAX 212-977-9825.

613.7   US
LOOKING FIT. m. $40. Virgo Publishing, Inc., 13402 N. Scottsdale Rd., Ste. B-185, Scottsdale, AZ 85254. TEL 602-483-0014.

LOSE WEIGHT NATURALLY NEWSLETTER. see *NUTRITION AND DIETETICS*

613.7 613.2   SW
MAA BRA. 1976. 12/yr. SEK 280. Allers Specialtidningar AB, P.O. Box 27704, S-115 91 Stockholm, Sweden. FAX 08-6673439. Ed. Inger Ridstroem. adv.; circ. 65,000.

613   JA
MAINICHI LIFE. (Text in Japanese) 1970. m. 4200 Yen. Mainichi Newspapers, 1-1-1, Hitotsubashi, Chiyoda-ku, Tokyo 100-51, Japan. TEL 03-3212-0321. FAX 03-3211-8895. TELEX 22324. Ed. Yasuo Miyazawa.

613   US   ISSN 1045-4268
MASSAGE MAGAZINE; keeping those who touch - in touch. 1985. bi-m. $18. Noah Publishing Company, Box 1500, Davis, CA 95617-1500. TEL 916-757-6033. Ed. Robert Calvert. adv.; bk.rev.; film rev.; bibl.; illus.; stat.; circ. 45,000. (back issues avail.)
Former titles: Massage and Healing Arts Magazine; Massage and Bodywork Magazine.
Description: International information source covering the world of massage and bodywork with the latest touch innovations.

613   US   ISSN 0895-0814
MASSAGE THERAPY JOURNAL. 1946. q. $15. American Massage Therapy Association, 1130 W. North Shore Ave., Chicago, IL 60626. TEL 312-761-2682. FAX 815-965-2329. Ed. Rafael Tuburan. adv.; bk.rev.; circ. 14,000. (reprint service avail.)
Formerly (until 1962): Massage Journal.
Description: Covers techniques, research, case histories, anecdotes, business advice, legislative updates, philosophical reflections, poems and reviews relating to massage therapy theory and practice.

MEDECINE DU SPORT. see *MEDICAL SCIENCES — Sports Medicine*

MEDECINE ET HYGIENE. see *MEDICAL SCIENCES*

PHYSICAL FITNESS AND HYGIENE

MEDICAL AND HEALTH ANNUAL. see *MEDICAL SCIENCES*

613 US ISSN 0749-9973
R118.4.U6
MEDICAL & HEALTH INFORMATION DIRECTORY. 1978. triennial. $485 for 3 vol. set. Gale Research Inc., P.O. Box 33477, Detroit, MI 48283-9852. TEL 800-877-4253. FAX 313-961-6083. TELEX TWX 810-221-7086. Ed. Karen Backus.
Description: Guide to medical and health information in the U.S.

MEDICAL CORPS INTERNATIONAL; forum for military medicine and pharmacy. see *MEDICAL SCIENCES*

613.7 US
MEDICAL UPDATE; a monthly medical newsletter. 1976. m. $12. Benjamin Franklin Literary and Medical Society, Inc., Medical Education and Research Foundation, Box 567, 1100 Waterway Blvd., Indianapolis, IN 46202. FAX 317-637-0126. Ed.Bd. bk.rev.; circ. 15,000. **Indexed:** CHNI, Hlth.Ind.

MEDICINE, EXERCISE, NUTRITION AND HEALTH. see *MEDICAL SCIENCES*

613 GW ISSN 0179-0404
MEDIZIN HEUTE; Gesundheit fuer die ganze Familie. 1950. m. DM.36. Deutscher Aerzte-Verlag GmbH, Dieselstr. 2, Postfach 40 02 65, 5000 Cologne 40, Germany. TEL 02234-7011-0. FAX 02234-7011444. Ed. Johann Friedrich Jeurink. adv.; bk.rev.; illus.; circ. 280,000.

MELPOMENE JOURNAL; a journal for women's health research. see *WOMEN'S HEALTH*

613.7 US
MEMPHIS HEALTH CARE NEWS. fortn. Mid-South Communications, Inc., 88 Union, Rm. 200, Memphis, TN 38103-5100. TEL 901-526-2007. FAX 901-526-5240. Ed. Deborah DuBois. circ. 12,500.

613.7 790.1 US ISSN 0893-4460
GV481
MEN'S FITNESS; the healthy man's guide to living. 1985. m. $26.50. 21100 Erwin St., Woodland Hills, CA 91367. TEL 818-884-6800. Ed. Chris Weygant. adv.; bk.rev.; circ. 250,000. **Indexed:** Phys.Ed.Ind., Sports Per.Ind.
Formerly (until 1987): Sports Fitness (ISSN 0885-0763)

MEN'S HEALTH NEWSLETTER. see *MEN'S HEALTH*

613 US ISSN 0164-1336
RA440.A1
MICHIGAN HEALTH EDUCATOR. 1976. bi-m. $7.50. Michigan Health Educator Company, 2843 Hilton Rd., Ferndale, MI 48220. Ed. E. Dewey Little. adv.; bk.rev.; index; circ. 10,200. (back issues avail.)

MICHIGAN RUNNER. see *SPORTS AND GAMES — Outdoor Life*

MON BEBE. see *CHILDREN AND YOUTH — About*

MONKEYSHINES ON HEALTH AND SCIENCE. see *CHILDREN AND YOUTH — For*

MOTHERING. see *MEDICAL SCIENCES — Obstetrics And Gynecology*

613.7 GW ISSN 0170-5792
MOTORIK. q. DM.50 (students DM.44). Verlag Karl Hofmann, Steinwasenstr. 6-8, Postfach 1360, 7060 Schorndorf, Germany. TEL 07181-7811. Ed. Hans-Juergen Mueller. circ. 3,000. **Indexed:** Sportsearch (1981-).

613.7 US ISSN 0744-5105
GV481
MUSCLE & FITNESS; the best fitness and bodybuilding information available. 12/yr. $35. I Brute Enterprises, 21100 Erwin St., Woodland Hills, CA 91367. TEL 818-884-6800. Ed. Tom Deteres. adv.; circ. 600,000. **Indexed:** Hlth.Ind., Phys.Ed.Ind., Sportsearch (1981-).
Formerly: Muscle.

613 US ISSN 0047-8407
MUSCLE TRAINING ILLUSTRATED. 1965. 9/yr. $22. Muscle Man Inc., 219-10 S. Conduit Ave., Springfield Gardens, NY 11413. TEL 718-258-3900. Ed. Dan Lurie. adv.; charts; illus.; stat.; circ. 100,000. **Indexed:** Sportsearch.

613.7 CN
MUSCLEMAG INTERNATIONAL. m. $3.95 per no. Body Sculpture Barbell, 52 Bramsteele Rd., Unit 2, Brampton, Ont. L6W 3M5, Canada. TEL 416-457-3030. FAX 416-796-3563.

613 796.41 US ISSN 0047-8415
MUSCULAR DEVELOPMENT. 1964. m. $35.95. Advanced Research Press, Inc., 2120 Smithtown Ave., Ronkonkoma, NY 11779. TEL 516-467-2042. FAX 516-471-2375. Ed. Alan Paul. adv.; charts; illus.; tr.lit.; circ. 242,000. **Indexed:** Phys.Ed.Ind., Sportsearch.
Description: Comprehensive coverage of bodybuilding, sports nutrition, muscular development and strength training.

613.7 US ISSN 0272-7102
N H E L P HEALTH ADVOCATE. 1971. 4/yr. $20. National Health Law Program, 2639 S. La Cienega Blvd, Los Angeles, CA 90034. TEL 310-204-6010. FAX 310-204-0891. Ed. L.M. Lavin. bk.rev.; circ. 2,300. **Indexed:** Med. Care Rev.
Formerly: Health Law Newsletter (ISSN 0160-7227)

613.194 US
N: NUDE AND NATURAL. 1981. q. $25. Naturist Society, Box 132, Oshkosh, WI 54902. TEL 414-426-5009. FAX 414-231-9977. Ed. Lee Baxandall. adv.; bk.rev.; film rev.; play rev.; cum.index; circ. 17,000. (back issues avail.)
Formerly: Clothed with the Sun (ISSN 0883-4326)
Description: Journal of clothes-optional living.

NACHRICHTEN AUS DER AERZTLICHEN MISSION. see *RELIGIONS AND THEOLOGY*

613.7 US
NATIONAL STRENGTH & CONDITIONING ASSOCIATION BULLETIN. irreg. National Strength & Conditioning Association, Box 81410, Lincoln, NE 68501-1410. **Indexed:** Sportsearch (1986-).

613.7 US ISSN 0744-0049
NATIONAL STRENGTH & CONDITIONING ASSOCIATION JOURNAL. 1978. bi-m. membership. National Strength & Conditioning Association, Box 81410, Lincoln, NE 68501-1410. Ed. Ken Kontor. adv.; bk.rev.; circ. 14,000. **Indexed:** Phys.Ed.Ind., Sportsearch (1981-).
—BLDSC shelfmark: 6033.100560.
Description: Publishes program and practical application articles for strength and conditioning coaches. Nutrition, exercise technique and relevent research are included.

613.7 GW ISSN 0934-3407
NATUERLICH. 1988. 6/yr. DM.45. A T Fachverlag GmbH, Postfach 500180, 7000 Stuttgart 50, Germany. TEL 0711-527041. FAX 0711-5281539. Ed. J. Bopp-Herbold. illus.; circ. 25,000.

613 MX
NATURA; tu salud en la naturaleza. m. Editorial Posada, S.A., Oculistas No. 43, Col. El Sifon, 09400 Mexico, D.F., Mexico. illus.

613.7 US
NATURAL HEALING & NUTRITION ANNUAL. a. $19.95. Rodale Press, Inc., Prevention Magazine, 33 E. Minor St., Emmaus, PA 18098. TEL 800-441-7761. Eds. Mark Bricklin, Sharon Stocker Ferguson.

NATURAL HEALTH. see *NUTRITION AND DIETETICS*

613.7 US
NATURAL HEALTH AND FITNESS BULLETIN. m. Princeton Educational Publishers, Box 280, Plainsboro, NJ 08536. TEL 609-924-0319. Ed. Barry Pavelec. circ. 2,000.

613 US ISSN 0028-0704
NATURAL HEALTH WORLD.* 1961. m. $7.50. Naturopath Publishing Co., c/o Mrs. John W. Noble Jr., M.D., 3912 N.E. 44th Ave., Vancouver, WA 98661. TEL 206-695-0213. Ed. Robert W. Noble. adv.; bk.rev.; stat.; tr.lit.; circ. 3,600. (tabloid format)

613.7 US
NATURAL PHYSIQUE. 1988. bi-m. Chelo Publishing Inc., Empire State Bldg., 350 Fifth Ave., New York, NY 10118. TEL 212-947-4322.

613.194 US
NATURALLY. 1982. q. $18. Events Unlimited, Box 203, Pequannock, NJ 07440. Ed. Bernard J. Loibl. adv.; bk.rev.; circ. 5,000. (back issues avail.)
Indexed: Arts & Hum.Cit.Ind.
Formerly (until 1990): Event (Pequannock).
Description: Leisure magazine for nudists; includes information on travel, resorts, and nude beaches.

613 GW ISSN 0028-081X
DER NATURARZT; Zeitschrift fuer naturgemaesse Lebens- und Heilweise. 1861. m. DM.42. (Deutscher Naturheilbund eV.) Access Marketing GmbH, Feldbergstr. 2, 6240 Koeningstein 2, Germany. TEL 06174-7030. FAX 06174-3938. adv.; bk.rev.; charts; illus.; index; circ. 50,000.

613.194 NE ISSN 0028-0968
NATURISME. 1961. q. fl.37($19) Stichting Naturistische Uitgaven - Dutch Federation of Naturist - Organisations, Postbus 783, 3500 AT Utrecht, Netherlands. TEL 030-328810. FAX 030-332957. Ed. Bertus Boivin. adv.; bk.rev.; illus.; circ. 32,000.

613.194 IT ISSN 0392-4173
NATURISMO; rivista naturista e umanitaria. 1972. s-a. free. Egger-Lienz 1, 39100 Bolzano, Italy. Ed. Daniele Agnoli. bk.rev.; circ. 1,500.
Description: Covers nudity, nature and the unconscious being.

613 US ISSN 0028-100X
NATUROPATH.* 1961. m. $7.50. Naturopath Publishing Co., c/o Mrs. John W. Noble Jr., M.D., 3912 N.E. 44th Ave., Vancouver, WA 98661. TEL 206-695-0213. Ed. Robert W. Noble. adv.; bk.rev.; stat.; tr.lit.; circ. 3,600.

613.7 641.1 US
NAUTILUS (INDEPENDENCE). 1979-1983; resumed 1992. bi-m. $11.95. Nautilus, 709 Power House Dr., Ste. 708, Independence, VA 24348. TEL 703-773-2881. FAX 703-773-3306. adv. contact: Becky Gray. bk.rev.; circ. 150,000.
Formerly (until 1983): Nautilus Magazine (ISSN 0278-3118)

NEBRASKA JOURNAL. see *EDUCATION*

613.7 AA
NENA DHE FEMIJA. 3/yr. Ministria e Shendetesise - Ministry of Health, Tirana, Albania. TELEX 4205.

613.7 CS
NEPEGESZEG. (Text in Hungarian) m. $18. (Czechoslovak Red Cross) Obzor, Ceskoslovenskej Armady 35, 815 85 Bratislava, Czechoslovakia.

NETWORK NEWSNEWS. see *WOMEN'S HEALTH*

NEW BEGINNINGS (FRANKLIN PARK); every baby is a new beginning. see *CHILDREN AND YOUTH — About*

613.7 US
NEW BODY. 1982. bi-m. G C R Publishing Group, Inc., 1700 Broadway, 34th Fl., New York, NY 10019. TEL 212-541-7100. Ed. Nayda Rhondon. adv.; circ. 90,000.

613.7 US
NEW BODY DIET AND EXERCISE. 5/yr. G C R Publishing Group, Inc., 1700 Broadway, 34th Fl., New York, NY 10019. TEL 212-541-7100.

NEW LIFE; for those who want to make a change. see *NEW AGE PUBLICATIONS*

613.7 US
NEW LIFE NEWS. 1953. bi-m. Northwestern Mutual Life, 720 E. Wisconsin Ave., Milwaukee, WI 53202. TEL 414-299-1959. Ed. Julianne Agnew. circ. 1,700. (back issues avail.)
Description: Informational company newsletter for Northwestern Mutual Life retirees.

613.7 US
NEW LIVING. m. Box 1519, Stony Brook, NY 11790. TEL 516-981-7232. FAX 516-585-4606. Ed. Christine Lynn Harvey. circ. 20,000.

PHYSICAL FITNESS AND HYGIENE 3807

NEW OHIO JOURNAL. see *ENVIRONMENTAL STUDIES*

612.76 US
▼**NEW YORK BODIES.** 1991. bi-m. $12. New York Bodies, 105 Lexington Ave., No. 8B, New York, NY 10016. TEL 212-447-5312. Ed. Ronald L. Dobrin. adv.; circ. 50,000 (controlled). (back issues avail.)
Description: Covers topics in bodybuilding, fitness and health for the urban man and woman, including aerobics, yoga, nutrition and healing.

NEW ZEALAND PHARMACY. see *PHARMACY AND PHARMACOLOGY*

613.7 US
NEWSLETTER FOR PEOPLE WITH LACTOSE INTOLERANCE AND MILK ALLERGY. 1987. q. $15. Commercial Writing Service, Box 3074, Iowa, IA 52244. TEL 319-351-1353. Ed. Jane Zukin. bk.rev.; circ. 1,000. (reprint service avail.)
Description: Provides information, support, and recipes for those with lactose intolerance or milk protein allergy.

613 II ISSN 0029-070X
NISARG ANE AROGYA. (Text in Gujarati) 1966. m. Rs.3. S.A. Pandit, Ed. & Pub., Arya Kanya Gurukul, Rajwadi, Porbandar, India. adv.; bk.rev.; circ. 600.

NOTICIARIE A IMPRENSA FALADA E ESCRITA. see *AGRICULTURE*

NUTRITION AND HEALTH. see *NUTRITION AND DIETETICS*

OESTERREICHISCHES JUGENDROTKREUZ. ARBEITSBLAETTER. see *SOCIAL SERVICES AND WELFARE*

613.7 CN
ON THE MOVE. q. Can.$15. (Saskatchewan Physical Education Association) Saskatchewan Teachers' Federation, Box 1108, Saskatoon, Sask. S7K 3N3, Canada. TEL 306-373-1660. Ed. Janine Pratt.

ONTARIO WRESTLER MAGAZINE. see *SPORTS AND GAMES*

OREGON DISTANCE RUNNER. see *SPORTS AND GAMES*

ORTOPEDICI E SANITARI. see *MEDICAL SCIENCES — Orthopedics And Traumatology*

OSAKA JOSHI DAIGAKU KIYO. KISO RIGAKU HEN, TAIIKUGAKU HEN/OSAKA WOMEN'S UNIVERSITY. BULLETIN. SERIES OF NATURAL SCIENCE, PHYSICAL EDUCATION. see *SCIENCES: COMPREHENSIVE WORKS*

PALAESTRA; the forum of sport, physical education and recreation for the disabled. see *HANDICAPPED*

613 PL ISSN 0035-7715
 CODEN: RPZHAW
PANSTWOWY ZAKLAD HIGIENY. ROCZNIKI. (Text in Polish; summaries in English and Russian) 1950. bi-m. $132. Panstwowy Zaklad Wydawnictw Lekarskich, Dluga 38-40, Warsaw, Poland. TEL 31-42-81. (Dist. by: Ars Polona-Ruch, Krakowskie Przedmiescie 7, Warsaw, Poland) Ed. B. Urbanek - Karlowska. bk.rev.; abstr.; charts; illus.; stat.; index. **Indexed:** Biol.Abstr., Chem.Abstr., Dent.Ind., Ind.Med., Nutr.Abstr.
—BLDSC shelfmark: 8006.000000.

613 CN
▼**PATHWAYS.** 1991. 6/yr. Can.$13.48 (foreign Can.$23.48). Recovery Publications, 8 King St., E., Ste. 1000, Toronto, Ont. M5C 1B5, Canada. TEL 416-361-3500. FAX 416-361-6046. Ed. Keitha McLean. adv.; circ. 51,000.

PATHWAYS TO HEALTH. see *PHILOSOPHY*

613.7 US
PATIENT'S DIGEST. 1983. s-a. Patient's Digest, Inc., 627 Greenwich St., New York, NY 10014. TEL 212-741-2111. adv.; tr.lit. (reprint service avail.)

613.7 617.1 US ISSN 0738-7857
PERSONAL FITNESS. 1983. m. $47. (Personal Fitness Consultants) Cromwell - Sloan Publishing Company, 63 Vine St., Stamford, CT 06905-2012. TEL 203-323-6839. Ed. Paul Sloan. bk.rev.; abstr.; charts; illus.; circ. 28,000. (back issues avail.)

613.7 US
▼**PERSONAL FITNESS AND WEIGHT LOSS**; a complete guide. 1990. q. Russ Moore and Associates Inc., 4151 Knob Dr., St. Paul, MN 55122. TEL 612-452-0571. FAX 612-454-5791. Ed. Diane Steen. adv.; circ. 108,500.

613.7 UK
PHYSICAL EDUCATION ASSOCIATION OF GREAT BRITIAN AND NORTHERN IRELAND. RESEARCH SUPPLEMENT. irreg. Physical Education Association of Great Britian and Northern Ireland, Ling House, 5 Western Court, Bromley St., Digbeth, Birmingham B9 4AN, England. TEL 021-753-0909. FAX 021-753-0170. **Indexed:** Sportsearch (1987-).

PHYSICAL EDUCATION DIGEST. see *SPORTS AND GAMES*

615.8 GW ISSN 0031-9392
PHYSIOTHERAPIE. 1909. m. DM.102. (Verband Deutscher Badebetriebe e.V.) Ebert Verlag GmbH, Blankenseer Str. 6-8, 2400 Luebeck 1, Germany. Ed. Hans Juergen Ebert. adv.; bk.rev.; charts; index; circ. 9,500.
—BLDSC shelfmark: 6488.650000.
 Formerly: Fachblatt der Physikalischen Therapie.

PHYSIOTHERAPY THEORY AND PRACTICE; an international journal of physical therapy. see *MEDICAL SCIENCES*

613.7 US
▼**PILLSBURY FAST AND HEALTHY MAGAZINE.** 1992. bi-m. $14.95. Pillsbury Company, 200 S. Sixth St., Minneapolis, MN 55402. TEL 612-330-4529. FAX 612-330-4875. Ed. Diane Anderson. adv.: B&W page $3450. circ. 100,000.
Description: Food and lifestyle magazine focusing on low-fat, quick-to-make recipes and articles on well-being.

613.7 US
PLEASURE QUEST; your success guide to sensual adventures & romance. 1989. q. $12. Health & Wealth Guardian, Ltd., 462 S. Gilbert Rd., Mesa, AZ 85204. TEL 602-829-8888. FAX 602-835-5741. Ed. Phillip Fry. circ. 25,000.
Description: Promotes health methods for relieving stress, with how-to tips on leisure activities from love and romance to gourmet cooking and games.

PLENTY BULLETIN. see *AGRICULTURE — Agricultural Economics*

POOLWAYS; the magazine of outdoor living (year). see *SPORTS AND GAMES*

POWER SPORT. see *SPORTS AND GAMES*

613 US
PRESIDENT'S COUNCIL OF PHYSICAL FITNESS & SPORTS. NEWSLETTER. 1965. 6/yr. free. U.S. Department of Health and Human Services, President's Council on Physical Fitness & Sports, 450 5th St. N.W., Ste. 7103, Washington, DC 20001. TEL 202-272-3430. Ed. Diana D'Avino. circ. 10,000. **Indexed:** Sportsearch (1964-).

613 US ISSN 0032-8006
RA421 CODEN: PRVEAT
PREVENTION; the magazine for better health. 1950. m. $13.97 (foreign $47.97)(effective 1992). Rodale Press, Inc., 33 E. Minor St., Emmaus, PA 18098. TEL 800-441-7761. TELEX 847338. Ed. Mark Bricklin. adv.; bk.rev.; illus.; index; circ. 2,875,314. (also avail. in microform from UMI; reprint service avail. from UMI) **Indexed:** CHNI, Environ.Per.Bibl., Hlth.Ind., Jun.High.Mag.Abstr., Mag.Ind., PMR.
Description: Reports on new developments in nutrition, preventive medicine, fitness, natural living and drugless therapies; emphasis on practicality and self-improvement.

613.7 IT
PREVENZIONE E SALUTE;* medicina per la famiglia italiana. m. L.39000. Gedit, Gruppo Editoriale Edimedica, Via Pilo 19B, 20129 Milan, Italy. TEL 02-5512349. FAX 5512354. Ed. Cristina Kettlitz.

613 GW ISSN 0179-7360
PRIMA VITA. 1905. bi-m. DM.21. (Deutscher Verein fuer Gesundheitspflege e. V.) Saatkorn-Verlag GmbH, Grindelberg 13-17, 2000 Hamburg 13, Germany. FAX 040-418441. Eds. Dr. Ernst Schneider, Anita Sprungk. adv.; bk.rev.; index; circ. 20,000.
Formerly: Leben und Gesundheit (ISSN 0023-9895)

PROPHYGRAM. see *MEDICAL SCIENCES — Dentistry*

PSYCHOLOGY AND SOCIOLOGY OF SPORT: CURRENT SELECTED RESEARCH. see *PSYCHOLOGY*

PUERTO RICO. DEPARTMENT OF HEALTH. BOLETIN ESTADISTICO. see *PUBLIC HEALTH AND SAFETY — Abstracting, Bibliographies, Statistics*

PUERTO RICO. DEPARTMENT OF HEALTH. INFORME ANUAL DE FACILIDADES DE SALUD. see *HOSPITALS*

PUERTO RICO. DEPARTMENT OF HEALTH. INFORME DEL REGISTRO DE PROFESIONALES DE LA SALUD. see *MEDICAL SCIENCES*

PUNJAB MEDICAL JOURNAL. see *MEDICAL SCIENCES*

613.7 CC ISSN 1000-825X
QIGONG. (Text in Chinese) m. Zhejiang Sheng Zhongyiyao Yanjiusuo - Zhejiang Provincial Institute of Traditional Medicine, 26 Tianmushan Lu, Hangzhou, Zhejiang 310007, People's Republic of China. TEL 882214. Ed. Lu Zheng.

613.7 CC ISSN 1000-0895
QIGONG YU KEXUE/QIGONG AND SCIENCE. (Text in Chinese) m. Y12. (Guangdongsheng Qigong Kexue Yanjiu Xiehui - Guangdong Qigong Science Research Association) Qigong yu Kexue Zazhishe, P.O. Box 343, Guangzhou, Guangdong 510030, People's Republic of China. (Dist. overseas by: Jiangsu Publications Import & Export Corp., 56 Gao Yun Ling, Nanjing, Jiangsu, P.R.C.)
Description: Presents different theories and practice of different schools of qigong in China and abroad. Introduces the applications of this deep-breathing excercise to medical treatment, sports and education.

613.7 CC
QINGCHUN YU JIANKANG/YOUTH AND HEALTH. (Text in Chinese) 1985. m. Y7.20. (Shanghai Shi Weisheng Jiaoyu-guan - Shanghai Health Education Institute) Qingchun yu Jiankang Zazhishe, 394 Zhoushan Lu, Shanghai 200082, People's Republic of China. TEL 5460177. Ed. Hu Jinhua.

R S G RICHTING - SPORT-GERICHT; vakblad voor training, onderwijs en wetenschap. see *SPORTS AND GAMES*

RADIANCE; the magazine for large women. see *WOMEN'S INTERESTS*

613 GW
RATGEBER AUS DER APOTHEKE. 1922. s-m. free. Gebr. Storck GmbH, Bebelstr. 102, 4200 Oberhausen, Germany. bk.rev.; illus.; circ. 400,000.
Formerly: Ratgeber fuer Kranke und Gesunde (ISSN 0033-9997)

RECENT ADVANCES IN OBESITY RESEARCH. see *MEDICAL SCIENCES*

RECREATION CANADA. see *LEISURE AND RECREATION*

RECRUITMENT DIRECTIONS. see *OCCUPATIONS AND CAREERS*

PHYSICAL FITNESS AND HYGIENE

613.7 370　　　　US　ISSN 0270-1367
GV201　　　　　　CODEN: RQESD4
RESEARCH QUARTERLY FOR EXERCISE AND SPORT.
1930. q. $70 to institutions. American Alliance for Health, Physical Education, Recreation, and Dance, 1900 Association Dr., Reston, VA 22091. TEL 703-476-3400. FAX 703-476-9527. Ed. James R. Morrow, Jr. adv.; bibl.; charts; illus.; index, cum.index every 10 yrs.: 1930-1969 (in 4 vols.); circ. 10,000. (also avail. in microform (ISSN 0364-9857) from UMI; reprint service avail. from ISI,UMI) **Indexed:** Biol.Abstr., C.I.J.E., Curr.Cont., Educ.Ind., Ergon.Abstr., Excerp.Med., Phys.Ed.Ind., Psychol.Abstr., Sportsearch (1980-), SSCI.
—BLDSC shelfmark: 7759.172000.
Formerly (until 1980): American Alliance for Health, Physical Education and Recreation. Research Quarterly (ISSN 0034-5377)
Description: Includes research articles in the art and science of human movement that lead to the development of theory or the application of new techniques.

REVISTA CUBANA DE HIGIENE Y EPIDEMIOLOGIA. see *PUBLIC HEALTH AND SAFETY*

613 610　　　　RM　ISSN 0019-1620
　　　　　　　　　　CODEN: IGIBA5
REVISTA DE IGIENA, BACTERIOLOGIE, VIRUSOLOGIE, PARAZITOLOGIE, PNEUMOFTIZIOLOGIE. IGIENA. (Text in Rumanian; summaries in English, French, German, Russian) 1952. 4/yr. $20. Uniunea Societatilor de Stiinte Medicale din Republica Socialista Rumania, Str. Progresului No. 8, Bucharest, Rumania. (Subscr. to: ILEXIM, Str. 13 Decembrie Nr. 3, P.O. Box 136-137, Bucharest, Rumania) Ed.Bd. adv.; bk.rev.; abstr.; bibl.; charts; illus. **Indexed:** Biol.Abstr., Chem.Abstr., Nutr.Abstr.

613.7　　　　　　SP
REVISTA DE LA SALUD. 1985. m. Saned, Apolonia Morales 6, 28036 Madrid, Spain. TEL 91-4035014. Ed. Carmen Marino. circ. 135,000.

RIVISTA DI MEDICINA DEL LAVORO ED IGIENE INDUSTRIALE. see *OCCUPATIONAL HEALTH AND SAFETY*

613　　　　　　IT　ISSN 0035-6921
RA421　　　　　　CODEN: RIIGAV
RIVISTA ITALIANA D'IGIENE. (Text in Italian; summaries in English and Italian) vol.25, 1965. bi-m. L.80000. Nistri-Lischi Editori, P. Castelletto 7, 56100 Pisa, Italy. Ed. Prof. G. Armani. adv.; bibl.; charts; illus.; stat.; index. **Indexed:** Abstr.Hyg., Biol.Abstr., Chem.Abstr., Excerp.Med., Nutr.Abstr., Trop.Dis.Bull.

ROBERT WOOD JOHNSON FOUNDATION. ANNUAL REPORT. see *MEDICAL SCIENCES*

613.7　　　　　　US
THE RODALE REPORT. m. Rodale Press, Inc., 33 E. Minor St., Emmaus, PA 18098. TEL 215-967-5171. FAX 215-967-3044. Ed. Sid Kirchheimer.

ROYAL SOCIETY OF HEALTH JOURNAL. see *SOCIAL SERVICES AND WELFARE*

613　　　　　　UK　ISSN 0144-8560
RUNNING. 1979. m. £25.40. Stonehart Leisure Magazines Ltd., 67-71 Goswell Rd., London EC1V 7EN, England. TEL 071-410-9410. FAX 071-410-9440. Ed. Nick Troop. adv.; illus. **Indexed:** Sportsearch (1984-).
—BLDSC shelfmark: 8052.386000.
Incorporates: Jogging Magazine.

613 612.3　　　　US　ISSN 0898-5162
RUNNING & FITNEWS. 1983. m. $25 to members; health professionals $40. American Running and Fitness Association, 9310 Old Georgetown Rd., Bethesda, MD 20814. TEL 301-897-0197. FAX 301-897-0198. Ed. Susan Kalish. bk.rev.; charts; index; circ. 15,000. (back issues avail.) **Indexed:** Sportsearch (1984-).
Former titles (until 1984): Running and Fitness; Jogger (ISSN 0164-694X)
Description: Dedicated to helping athletes get the most from their exercise program by providing information and on exercise, nutrition, training, sportsmedicine, injury prevention and health.

301.4 612　　　　US　ISSN 0091-3995
HQ1
S I E C U S REPORT. 1972. bi-m. contribution. Sex Information and Education Council of the U S, 130 W. 42nd St., Ste. 2500, New York, NY 10036. TEL 212-819-9770. FAX 212-819-9776. Ed. Janet Jamar. adv.; bk.rev.; bibl.; film rev.; circ. 3,500. (also avail. in microfilm; back issues avail.; reprint service avail. from ISI,UMI) **Indexed:** Curr.Lit.Fam.Plan., Educ.Ind.
—BLDSC shelfmark: 8271.970000.
Formerly: S I E C U S Newsletter (ISSN 0036-150X)
Description: Covers all aspects of human sexuality, including AIDS.

613.7　　　　　　US
ST. RAPHAEL'S BETTER HEALTH. 1978. bi-m. $11. Institute for Better Health, 1384 Chapel St., New Haven, CT 06511. TEL 203-789-4089. Ed. Paul J. Taylor. adv.; bk.rev.; circ. 120,000.

SALUD PARA TODOS. see *CHILDREN AND YOUTH — For*

613　　　　　　IT
SALVE. m. L.36000. Rizzoli Editore-Corriere della Sera, Via A. Rizzoli 2, 20132 Milan, Italy. Ed. A. Vellani.

613.7 613.2　　　　CN　ISSN 0832-6770
SANTE. 1984. 10/yr. Can.$19.50. Editions du Feu Vert, Inc., 5148 St. Laurent Blvd., Montreal, Que. H2T 1R8, Canada. TEL 514-273-9773. FAX 514-273-9034. Ed. Lucie Desaulniers. adv.; circ. 30,044. **Indexed:** Pt.de Rep. (1989-).

SATSANG. see *AGRICULTURE*

613　　　　　　BL
SAUDE!; e vital! 1982. m. $50 for 18 nos. Editora Abril, S.A., Av. Otaviano Alves de Lima 4,400, Sao Paulo, Brazil. TEL 011-8239222. FAX 011-8643796. TELEX 011-80360 EDAB BR. (Subscr. to: Rua do Curtume, 769 CEP 05065 Lapa, Sao Paulo, Brazil) Ed. Victor Civita. adv.; illus.; circ. 174,000.
Description: Covers preventive medicine, active living, balanced diets and exercise.

613.7　　　　　　US　ISSN 0036-6382
GV561
SCHOLASTIC COACH. 1931. m. (Aug.-May). $23.95. Scholastic Inc., 730 Broadway, New York, NY 10003. TEL 212-505-3000. Ed. Herman L. Masin. adv.; bk.rev.; film rev.; illus.; index; circ. 42,000. (also avail. in microform from UMI; back issues avail.; reprint service avail. from UMI,KTO) **Indexed:** Acad.Ind., Educ.Ind., Phys.Ed.Ind., Sports Per.Ind., Sportsearch (1976-).
—BLDSC shelfmark: 8092.541000.
Incorporates (1921-198?): Athletic Journal (ISSN 0004-6655)

SCRIPPS CLINIC PERSONAL HEALTH LETTER. see *MEDICAL SCIENCES*

614.8　　　　　　US
SEARCH FOR HEALTH. m? U.S. National Institutes of Health, News Branch, Building 31, Rm. 28-10, Bethesda, MD 20892. TEL 301-496-2535. Ed. Helen Ou.

613　　　　　　FR　ISSN 0037-153X
SELF.* 1966. m. (11/yr.). 25 F. S A F P, 68 Colmar-Ingersheim, France. Ed. Marcel Rouet. adv.; bk.rev.; film rev.; illus.

SENIOR SPORTS NEWS. see *SPORTS AND GAMES*

SHAOLIN YU TAIJI. see *SPORTS AND GAMES*

613.7 301.412　　　　US　ISSN 0744-5121
SHAPE; the best information available for your body, mind, spirit and beauty. 1981. 12/yr. $20. Shape Magazine, 21100 Erwin St., Woodland Hills, CA 91367. TEL 818-884-6800. Ed. Barbara Harris. adv.; bk.rev.; circ. 700,000. **Indexed:** Hlth.Ind., Phys.Ed.Ind., Sportsearch (1983-).

SICHERHEITSBEAUFTRAGTER; Zeitschrift fuer Unfallverhuetung und Arbeitssicherheit. see *BUSINESS AND ECONOMICS — Labor And Industrial Relations*

SICHERHEITSINGENIEUR; Zeitschrift fuer Arbeitssicherheit. see *BUSINESS AND ECONOMICS — Labor And Industrial Relations*

SILENT SPORTS; Mid-America's aerobic recreational sports magazine. see *SPORTS AND GAMES*

613.7　　　　　　US
SLIM FAST MAGAZINE. q. $1.95 per no. Welsh Publishing Group, 300 Madison Ave., New York, NY 10017. TEL 212-687-0680. FAX 212-986-1849. Ed. Margot Gilman.

SLIMMING. see *NUTRITION AND DIETETICS*

613　　　　　　US
SMOKING AND HEALTH NEWSLETTER.* 1965. q. free. National Interagency Council on Smoking and Health, 7320 Greenville Ave., Dallas, TX 75231. TEL 214-750-5359. Dir. Robert E. Wallace. circ. 10,000. (processed)

SOCCER NEWS. see *SPORTS AND GAMES — Ball Games*

613.7　　　　　　JA
SOKAI. (Text in Japanese) 1974. m. Kodansha Ltd., International Division, 12-21 Otowa 2-chome, Bunkyo-ku, Tokyo 112, Japan. TEL 03-3945-1111. FAX 03-3943-7815. TELEX J34509 KODANSHA. Ed. Masaaki Kajiyama. circ. 320,000.

SOKOL POLSKI/POLISH FALCON. see *CLUBS*

613　　　　　　US　ISSN 0147-5231
SOMATICS; magazine-journal of the bodily arts and sciences. 1976. s-a. $20 to individuals; institutions $25. Novato Institute for Somatic Research and Training, 1516 Grant Avenue, Ste. 212, Novato, CA 94945. TEL 415-897-0336. Ed. Eleanor Criswell Hanna. adv.; bk.rev.; circ. 1,300. (back issues avail.) **Indexed:** Psychol.Abstr., Sociol.Abstr.
—BLDSC shelfmark: 8327.809100.
Description: Articles for professionals and laypersons in somatics.

613　　　　　　US
SORENSON HEALTH AND FITNESS BULLETIN. 1991. 6/yr. $19.95. National Institute of Fitness, 202 N. Snow Canyon Rd., Box 938, Ivins, UT 84738. TEL 800-944-3488. Ed. Marc Sorenson.
Description: Covers recent news and research in nutrition, health and fitness for a geenral audience.

613.7 910.09　　　　US
SPA FINDER. 1987. a. $4.95. Spa Finders - Travel Arrangements Ltd., 91 Fifth Ave., New York, NY 10003-3039. TEL 212-924-6800. FAX 212-924-7240. adv.; B&W page $7200, color page $8200; trim 8 1/2 x 10 3/4. maps; circ. 100,000.
Description: Contains information on the world's great spas and fitness resorts for health, fitness and beauty enthusiasts.

613.7　　　　　　US
SPA VACATIONS.* 1989. q. B W Publishing, Inc., Box 1260, Brookline, MA 02146-0010. TEL 617-782-1225. Ed. Maria Durell Stone. adv.; circ. 200,000.
Description: Showcases spas nationwide and abroad. Covers the trends in travel, fitness, and beauty.

051　　　　　　US
SPECIAL REPORT: HEALTH. (In 3 eds.: Health, Living, Sports) 1988. q. $60. Whittle Communications L.P., 333 Main Ave., Knoxville, TN 37902. TEL 615-595-5300. FAX 615-595-5670. Ed. Keith Bellows. bk.rev.; circ. 1,500,000.
Description: Covers health, lifestyle, sports, personalities and family. Each edition delves comprehensively into a single subject.

613.7　　　　　　GW　ISSN 0171-6298
SPIRIDON LAUFMAGAZIN. 1975. m. DM.60. Spiridon Verlags GmbH, Dorfstr. 18a, 4006 Erkrath, Germany. TEL 0211-726364. FAX 0211-786823. Ed. Manfred Steffny. adv.; bk.rev.; illus.; index; circ. 18,000. (back issues avail.)

SPOKANE WOMAN. see *WOMEN'S INTERESTS*

SPORDIILM. see *SPORTS AND GAMES*

PHYSICAL FITNESS AND HYGIENE 3809

613 UK ISSN 0266-8963
SPORT & FITNESS.* 1892. m. £25($45) Sport & Fitness Ltd., P.O. Box 10, Sunbury, Middlesex TW16 5PZ, England. TEL 01-891-6885. Ed. Edward Hankey. circ. 27,000. (back issues avail.) **Indexed:** Sportsearch (1984-).
  Incorporates: Health and Strength (ISSN 0017-890X)

SPORT AND RECREATION INFORMATION GROUP BULLETIN. see *SPORTS AND GAMES*

SPORT & MEDICINA. see *MEDICAL SCIENCES — Sports Medicine*

SPORT SCENE; focus on youth programs. see *SPORTS AND GAMES*

SPORTPARADE. see *EDUCATION — Special Education And Rehabilitation*

SPORTS MEDICINE BULLETIN. see *MEDICAL SCIENCES — Sports Medicine*

613.7 IT
STAR BENE. 1978. m. L.54000 (foreign L.64800). Arnoldo Mondadori Editore S.p.A., Casella Postale 1833, 20101 Milan, Italy. Ed. Gabriele Zappa. circ. 117,963.

613.7 790.1 CS
START.* w. (Czechoslovak Union of Physical Education) Sport, Vajnorska Cesta 100-a, 832-58 Bratislava, Czechoslovakia.

STRESS MASTER. see *NEW AGE PUBLICATIONS*

613.7 360 US
STUDIES IN HEALTH AND HUMAN SERVICES. 1983. irreg., latest no.20. $39.95 per no. Edwin Mellen Press, 240 Portage Rd., Box 450, Lewiston, NY 14092. TEL 716-754-8566. FAX 716-754-4335.

613.7 790.1 FI
STUDIES IN SPORT, PHYSICAL EDUCATION AND HEALTH. (Text in English and Finnish) 1971. irreg., no.9, 1976. exchange basis. Jyvaskylan Yliopisto - University of Jyvaskyla, PL 35, 40351 Jyvaskyla, Finland. Eds. Juhani Kirjonen, Harri Suominen. circ. 450.

613.7 CN
SUCCESS IN FITNESS MAGAZINE - BILLBOARD. 1986. bi-m. Can.$375($450) Success in Fitness, Inc., One rue Pacifique, Ste-Anne-de-Bellevue, Que. H9X 1C5, Canada. TEL 514-457-2340. FAX 514-457-2341. Ed. Sharon Doherty. adv.; circ. 4,500,000.

613 UK
SUCCESSFUL SLIMMING. 1976. bi-m. I P C Magazines Ltd., King's Reach Tower, Stamford St., London SE1 9LS, England. Ed. A. Usden. adv.; bk.rev.; circ. 99,214.

613.7 617.1 SA
SUID-AFRIKAANSE TYDSKRIF VIR NAVORSING IN SPORT, LIGGAAMLIKE OPVOEDKUNDE EN ONTSPANNING/SOUTH AFRICAN JOURNAL FOR RESEARCH IN SPORT, PHYSICAL EDUCATION AND RECREATION. (Text in Afrikaans, English; summaries in English) 1978. s-a. R.20($5) Southern African Federation for Movement and Leisure Sciences, P.O. Box 13206, Clubview 0014, South Africa. TEL 012-6633290. FAX 012-6633294. Ed. B.F. Thiart. circ. 600. (back issues avail.) **Indexed:** Sportsearch (1980-).
  Formerly: Suid Afrikaanse Tydskrif vir Navorsing in Sport - South African Journal for Research in Sport (ISSN 0379-9069)
  Description: Aimed at scientists involved in the areas of physical fitness, sport, sports medicine, movement education and recreation.

613 II ISSN 0039-4882
SUKH DATTA. (Text in Punjabi) 1966. m. Rs.2.($0.75) Narula Dwakhana, Maisewan, Amritsar, India. Ed. Sundersinch Narula. adv.; bk.rev.; circ. 4,000.

SUMITOMO SANGYO EISEI/SUMITOMO BULLETIN OF INDUSTRIAL HEALTH. see *OCCUPATIONAL HEALTH AND SAFETY*

613 DK ISSN 0039-5366
SUNDHEDSBLADET; hjemmets radgiver. 1881. 6/yr. DKK 126. Dansk Bogforlag, Box 770, Boerstenbindervej 4, DK-5230 Odense M, Denmark. TEL 66-158843. FAX 66-15-57-43. Ed. Aage Andersen. adv.; bk.rev.; illus.; index; circ. 40,000.

613 NO ISSN 0332-7434
SUNNHETSBLADET. 1881. m. (11/yr.). NOK 230. Norsk Bokforlag A-S, Olaf Helsets vei 8, Oslo 6, Norway. FAX 02-29-85-11. Ed. Bjoern D. Kendel. adv.; bk.rev.; circ. 15,171.

613.7 US
▼**SUPER FITNESS EXCEL.*** 1990. m. Kuliaikanuu Inc., Box 57, Placentia, CA 92670-0057. TEL 213-822-3640. Ed. George Snyder. circ. 250,000.

SWIMMING POOLS TODAY. see *SPORTS AND GAMES — Outdoor Life*

613.7 US
SYRACUSE HEALTH & FITNESS. m. Box 270, Baldwinsville, NY 13027. TEL 315-635-3921. Ed. Dave Grieves.

613.7 US ISSN 0889-0846
T A H P E R D JOURNAL. 1954. 3/yr. $32 to individuals; institutions $40. Texas Association for Health, Physical Education, Recreation and Dance, Box 7578, University Sta., Austin, TX 78713. TEL 514-471-3493. FAX 512-471-0594. Ed. Q.A. Christian. adv.; circ. 4,000. **Indexed:** Sportsearch (1983-).

613 FI ISSN 0355-1903
T H KOTILAAKARI. 1889. m. Fmk.363. Yhtyneet Kuvalehdet Oy, Maistraatinportti 1, 00240 Helsinki, Finland. TEL 0-15661. FAX 0-1566505. TELEX 121364. Ed. Irma Nikkola-Heydemann. adv.; illus.; circ. 56,186.
  Formerly: Terveydenhoitolehti (ISSN 0040-3903)

613.7 613.2 US
T O P S NEWS. 1949. m. membership. Take Off Pounds Sensibly, Inc., 4575 S. Fifth Ave., Box 07360, Milwaukee, WI 53207-0360. TEL 414-482-4620. Ed. Gail Schemberger. circ. 300,747. (back issues avail.)
  Description: News and features about weight-control and nutrition. Covers activities of the organization.

613.85 FR
TABAC ET SANTE; tabagisme. 1970. q. 50 F. (Comite National Contre le Tabagisme) Nouvelles Editions Touristiques et Artistiques, 19 rue Bergere, 75009 Paris, France. Ed. J.P. Lejard. adv.; bk.rev.; circ. 3,000.

T'AI CHI; perspectives of the way and its movement. see *ORIENTAL STUDIES*

TAIIKU NO KAGAKU/JOURNAL OF HEALTH, PHYSICAL EDUCATION AND RECREATION. see *EDUCATION — Teaching Methods And Curriculum*

TAL OG DATA, MEDICIN OG SUNDHEDSVAESEN/FACTS, MEDICINE AND HEALTH CARE, DENMARK. see *PHARMACY AND PHARMACOLOGY*

613.7 US
TAN. 1989. 9/yr. $14. 3101 Page Ave., Jackson, MI 49203. TEL 517-784-1223. Ed. Cynthia Shaw Glascock. adv.; circ. 40,000.
  Description: For tanning enthusiasts. Provides consumer-oriented information to educate those people who choose to tan. Includes features on vacation travel, fashion, hairstyles and skin care.

613.7 338 US ISSN 0885-1522
TANNING TRENDS; the magazine for the indoor tanning industry. 1985. 9/yr. $47. Tanning Trends Inc., 3101 Page Ave., Jackson, MI 49203. TEL 517-784-1772. FAX 517-787-3940. (Subscr. addr.: Box 41094, Nashville, TN 37204) Ed. Lisa C. Cellini. adv.; circ. controlled. (back issues avail.)

TEACHING ELEMENTARY PHYSICAL EDUCATION. see *EDUCATION — Teaching Methods And Curriculum*

613.7 US
TENNESSEE JOURNAL OF HEALTH, PHYSICAL EDUCATION, RECREATION AND DANCE. 1962? s-a. Tennessee Association of Health, Physical Education, Recreation and Dance, Peabody College of Vanderbilt University, Box 513, Nashville, TN 37203. **Indexed:** Phys.Ed.Ind., Sportsearch.

613 FI ISSN 0040-3911
TERVEYS. 1937. m. Fmk.240. (Suomen Adventtikirkko - Finland Union of Seventh-Day Adventists Church) Kirjatoimi Publishing House, PL 94, 33101 Tampere 10, Finland. FAX 358-31-600454. Ed. Leo Hirvonen. adv.; charts; illus.; index; circ. 26,000.

615.5 US ISSN 0040-5914
THERAPEUTIC RECREATION JOURNAL. 1967. q. $30 (foreign $35). (National Therapeutic Recreation Society) National Recreation and Park Association, 3101 Park Center Dr., Alexandria, VA 22302. TEL 703-820-4940. FAX 703-671-6772. Eds. Richard D. MacNeil, Kenneth E. Mobily. adv.; bk.rev.; circ. 4,000. (also avail. in microform from UMI; back issues avail.) **Indexed:** Phys.Ed.Ind., Sportsearch (1973-).

613.7 US
TO YOUR HEALTH!; the magazine of healing and hope. 1989. m. free. 371 Bay Ridge Parkway, Brooklyn, NY 11209. TEL 718-921-3131. Ed. Bernice Stock. adv.; illus.

613.7 US
TOPS NEWS. m. Tops Club, Inc., 4575 S. Fifth St., Milwaukee, WI 53207-5858. TEL 414-482-4620. Ed. Gail Schemberger. circ. 309,512.

613.7 US
TRAVELING HEALTHY. bi-m. 108-48 70th Rd., Forest Hills, NY 11375. TEL 718-263-2072. Ed. Karl Neumann. circ. 1,150.

613.7 GW
TRIATHLON MAGAZIN. 1985. bi-m. DM.24. Spiridon Verlags GmbH, Dorfstr. 18a, 4006 Erkrath, Germany. TEL 02104-47260. Ed. Manfred Steffny. adv.; bk.rev.; index; circ. 4,000. (back issues avail.)

U S SWIMMING NEWS. see *SPORTS AND GAMES*

613.7 612.3 US ISSN 0748-9234
RA773 CODEN: UCWLE9
UNIVERSITY OF CALIFORNIA, BERKELEY. WELLNESS LETTER; the newsletter of nutrition, fitness, and stress management. 1984. m. $20. Health Letter Associates, Box 412, Prince St. Sta., New York, NY 10012. TEL 212-505-2255. FAX 212-505-5462. (Subscr. to: Box 420148, Palm Coast, FL 32142) Ed. Rodney M. Friedman. illus.; circ. 1,000,000. (back issues avail.) **Indexed:** Hlth.Ind.

613.7 612.3 US
UNIVERSITY OF TEXAS LIFETIME HEALTH LETTER. m. 1100 Holcombe Blvd., Houston, TX 77030. TEL 713-792-4265. FAX 713-792-4216. Ed. Joe Sigler. circ. 70,000.

613.7 790.1 US ISSN 0739-4586
V A H P E R D JOURNAL. 1978. s-a. $10 (typically set in Sep.). Virginia Association for Health, Physical Education and Dance, c/o Dr. Eleanor Bobbitt, Longwood College, Farmville, VA 23901. TEL 804-395-2539. FAX 804-395-2568. Ed. Joel Vedelli. circ. 1,000. (back issues avail.) **Indexed:** Sportsearch (1979-).

V D S M - INFORMATIONSDIENST. (Internationaler Verband der Stadt-, Sport- und Mehrzwerkhallen) see *MEETINGS AND CONGRESSES*

613.7 FI
VALMENNUS & KUNTO. 8/yr. Erikoislehdet Oy, Tecnopress, P.O. Box 16, 00381 Helsinki, Finland. TEL 358-0-120-5911. FAX 358-0-120-5959. Ed. Heikki Kantola. circ. 9,061.

613.26 US ISSN 0049-5905
VEGETARIAN COURIER.* 1960. m. $2. Vegetarian Society of New York, Inc., c/o Murray Mickenberg, 87-12 Clio St., Holliswood, NY 11423. (Or: 1133 Broadway, Rm. 416, New York, NY 10010) bk.rev.; circ. 500.

PHYSICAL FITNESS AND HYGIENE

613.26   UK
TX392
VEGETARIAN LIVING. 1977. 11/yr. 1.40 per no. (effective May 1992). E S G Publishing Ltd., c/o Nicola Graimes, Ed., S. Mulgrave Chambers, 26-28 Mulgrave Rd., Sutton, Surrey SM2 6LE, England. TEL 081-770-7337. FAX 081-773-7283. adv.; bk.rev.; charts; illus.; index; circ. 52,000.
   Former titles (until 1991): Vegetarian (ISSN 0260-3233); Alive; New Vegetarian (ISSN 0309-9253); Vegetarian; British Vegetarian (ISSN 0007-1927)
   Description: Covers all aspects of vegetarianism, diet, health and ethics.

613.26 613.26   US   ISSN 0164-8497
TX392
VEGETARIAN TIMES. 1974. 12/yr. $24.95. Vegetarian Times, Inc., Box 570, Oak Park, IL 60303. TEL 708-848-8100. (Subscr. to: Box 446, Mt. Morris, IL 61054) Ed. Paul Obis, Jr. adv.; bk.rev.; illus.; tr.lit.; circ. 200,000. (also avail. in microform from UMI; reprint service avail. from UMI) **Indexed:** CHNI, Hlth.Ind., New Per.Ind.
   Incorporates: Vegetarian World.
   Description: Contains vegetarian recipes, dietary information, advice on buying whole foods and preparing foods for maximum nutritional value, and articles on nutritional approaches to disease, information for travelers and profiles of prominent vegetarians.

VEGETARIAN VOICE. see *NUTRITION AND DIETETICS*

613   US   ISSN 0749-3509
R773
VIBRANT LIFE (HAGERSTOWN); a Christian guide to total health. 1904. bi-m. $11.95. Review and Herald Publishing Association, 55 W. Oak Ridge Dr., Hagerstown, MD 21740. TEL 301-791-7000. Ed. Barbara Jackson-Hall. adv.; bk.rev.; abstr.; charts; illus.; index; circ. 37,000. (reprint service avail. from UMI) **Indexed:** C.I.N.L., CCR, Hlth.Ind.
   Former titles: Your Life and Health (ISSN 0279-2680); Life and Health (ISSN 0024-3035)

613.7   AG
VIDA FELIZ. 1899. m. $15.50. (Iglesia Adventista del Septimo Dia) Asociacion Casa Editora Sudamericana, Avda. San Martin 4555, 1602 Florida, Buenos Aires, Argentina. TEL 0541-760-2426. FAX 0541-7618455. TELEX 24646 AR (GRACES). Ed. Ricardo Bentancur. illus.; circ. 30,000.

613   FR
LA VIE CLAIRE. 1946. m. (10/yr.). 90 F. La Vie Claire, 70 Av. Republique, 94700 Maisons-Alfort, France. Ed. Marie-Pierre Vaur. adv.; bk.rev.; stat.; circ. 30,000.

613   FR   ISSN 0042-5524
VIE ET SANTE. 1890. m. 250 F. Editions Vie et Sante, 60 av. Emile Zola, 77192 Dammarie les Lys Cedex, France. FAX 64-87-00-66. Ed. Marc Geurra. adv.; bk.rev.; circ. 40,000 (controlled). **Indexed:** Pt.de Rep. (1979-).

613.7   US
VIEW (SEATTLE). 1957. bi-m. $12. Group Health Cooperative, 521 Wall St., Seattle, WA 98121. TEL 206-448-5999. FAX 206-448-4271. Ed. Jan Short. adv.: B&W page $2815, color page $4258; trim 8 1/8 x 10 7/8. circ. 187,622.
   Description: Covers health and fitness lifestyles for the Greater Seattle area.

613.7   US
VIM & VIGOR; America's family health magazine. 1985. q. $11. Vim & Vigor, Inc., 8805 N. 23rd Ave., No. 11, Phoenix, AZ 85021. FAX 602-395-5853. Ed. Fred Petrovsky. adv.; bk.rev.; tr.lit.; circ. 550,000 (controlled). (back issues avail.)
   Description: For health-conscious individuals interested in issues related to health and the environmen. Covers diagnosis, treatment, diet, fitness, exercise and health.

VISIONARY. see *MEDICAL SCIENCES — Ophthalmology And Optometry*

613.7   US
VISIONS (NASHUA). 1988. 6/yr. membership. Excellence in Exercise Association, 427-3 Amherst St., Ste. 418, Nashua, NH 03063. TEL 800-245-6766. FAX 603-595-8742. adv.; bk.rev.; circ. 7,500.
   Description: Reviews new workout videos and lists industry events. Provides current information for industry leaders in the aerobic-fitness profession. Main focus is mind-body fitness.

613   IT   ISSN 0042-7268
VITA E SALUTE; rivista mensile di medicina preventiva. 1952. m. L.45000. Edizioni A.D.V. l'Araldo della Verita, Via Chiantigiana, 30, Falciani, 50023 Impruneta, Florence, Italy. TEL 055-2020291. Ed. Bruno Rimoldi. adv.; bk.rev.; charts; illus.; index; circ. 55,000.

613   GW
VITAL; das Magazin fuer modernes Leben. 1970. m. DM.57. Jahreszeiten Verlag GmbH, Possmoorweg 5, 2000 Hamburg 60, Germany. TEL 040-27170. FAX 040-27172056. Ed. H. Hesse. circ. 510,000.
   Formerly: Vital Gesundheit, Freizeit, Lebensfreude.

613   US
VITAL SIGNS (OKLAHOMA). 1981. q. free. University of Oklahoma, O.U. Health Sciences Center, Library Rm. 162, Box 26901, Oklahoma City, OK 73190. TEL 405-271-2323. Ed. Richard Green. circ. 6,500 (controlled).
   Former titles: O U Health Sciences Magazine & People and Progress.

613   US
VITALITY. 1987. 12/yr. $12.99. Vitality, Inc., 8080 N. Central, LB 78, Dallas, TX 75206. TEL 214-691-1480. Ed. Barbara Floria. adv.; bk.rev.; circ. 750,000 (controlled).
   Description: Credible source features about diet, fitness, parenting, and personal finance.

613.7 613.2   CN   ISSN 1180-0291
VITALITY MAGAZINE; Toronto's monthly wellness journal. 1989. m. Can.$30. 320 Danforth Ave., Ste. 204, Toronto, Ont. M4K 1P3, Canada. TEL 416-463-6677. Ed. Julia Woodford. adv.; circ. 24,500 (controlled).
   Description: Presents natural methods for the healing of chronic ailments and aims to enhance overall wellness.

VITASANA. see *NUTRITION AND DIETETICS*

613   SP   ISSN 0042-7578
VIVIR; consejos para vivir con salud. 1953. bi-m. 3300 ptas.($33) Ediciones CEDEL, C. Mallorca 257, Apartado 5326, 08008 Barcelona, Spain. TEL 343-215-6039. FAX 343-215-6088. Jose Avila. adv.; bk.rev.; bibl.; illus.; tr.mk.; index. (back issues avail.)

613.7   FI
VOI HYVIN. 8/yr. Fmk.251. A-Lehdet Oy, Hitsaajankatu 7, SF-00810 Helsinki, Finland. FAX 0-786-858. Ed. Marikka Burton. circ. 73,699.
   Description: Covers health, beauty and natural way of living.

613   GW   ISSN 0042-8493
VOLKSGESUNDHEIT;* Monatzeitschrift fuer gesundes Leben und naturgemaesse Heilverfahren. 1924. m. DM.32. Helfer-Verlag E. Schwabe, PF 1645, 6380 Bad Homburg, Germany. Ed. Emil Schwabe. adv.; abstr.; illus.

WALKING! JOURNAL; the art, science and sport of walking. see *SPORTS AND GAMES — Outdoor Life*

613.7   US   ISSN 1042-2102
GV199
WALKING MAGAZINE. 1986. 6/yr. $12 (foreign $17). Walking, Inc., 9-11 Harcourt St., Boston, MA 02116. TEL 617-266-3322. FAX 617-266-7373. (Subscr. to: Box 52341, Boulder, CO 80321-2341. TEL 800-678-0881) Ed. Brad Ketchum. adv.; bk.rev.; circ. 431,000.

613.9   US
WALKWAYS.* 1985. bi-m. $17. WalkWays Center, Box 1335, Concord, NH 03302-1335. Ed. Marsha Wallen. adv.; bk.rev.; circ. 5,000.

613   JA
WATASHI NO KENKO/MY HEALTH. (Text in Japanese) 1976. m. 8520 Yen. Shufunotomo Co. Ltd., 2-9 Kanda Surugadai, Chiyoda-ku, Tokyo 101, Japan. Ed. Isao Iwasaki. adv.; bk.rev.; circ. 200,000.

WEIGHT WATCHERS MAGAZINE. see *NUTRITION AND DIETETICS*

613.7   UK
WEIGHT WATCHERS MAGAZINE. 1977. bi-m. £4.80. (Weight Watchers (U.K.) Ltd.) Gat Publishing, 141-143 Drury Lane, London WC2B 5TS, England. Ed. Harriet Cross. adv.; bk.rev.; circ. 128,443. **Indexed:** Hlth.Ind.

613.7   US
WEIGHTLIFTING U S A. 1983. bi-m. $20. U S Weightlifting Federation, 1750 E. Boulder St., Colorado Springs, CO 80909. TEL 719-578-4508. FAX 719-578-4741. Ed. Mary Ann Rinehart. adv.; bk.rev.; circ. 2,600. (back issues avail.)
   Description: Covers US weightlifting, coaching, health and fitness, sports medicine, and local, national, and international competition results.

613   US   ISSN 0740-8498
THE WELLNESS NEWSLETTER; offering a better way to better health. 1980. bi-m. $30. Carolyn Chambers Clark, Ed. & Pub., 3451 Central Ave. N, St. Petersburg, FL 33713-8522. bk.rev.; index. (back issues avail.)
   Description: Each issue focuses on a different aspect of health: self-care, nutrition, fitness, stress management, environment, or "positive" relationships.

613.7 301.4   US
WELLNESS PERSPECTIVES: RESEARCH, THEORY AND PRACTICE. 1984. q. $15 to individuals; institutions $20. University of Alabama, Box 870312, Tuscaloosa, AL 35487-0312. TEL 205-348-2956. FAX 205-348-6873. bk.rev.; circ. 1,250.
   Description: For researchers and practitioners in the professional and academic fields that relate to health promotion and wellness. Subscribes to the philosophy that health promotion and wellness include intervention, policy, corporate culture, social support and environment support components.

613   UK   ISSN 0957-1728
WHICH? WAY TO HEALTH. 1983. bi-m. £23 membership. Consumers' Association Ltd., 2 Marylebone Rd., London NW1 4DX, England. TEL 071-486 5544. FAX 071-935-1606. TELEX 918197 G. (Subscr. to: P.O. Box 44, Hertford SG14 1SH, England) Ed. David P.S. Dickinson. bk.rev.; cum.index; circ. 76,000.
   ●Also available online.
   —BLDSC shelfmark: 9310.904000.
   Formerly (until Sep. 1988): Self Health (ISSN 0265-5497)
   Description: Independent food and health magazine for the lay person. Features and information on self care and on major illnesses, health promotion and provisions in Britain; independent testing of health products and services, and information on nutrition.

WHOLE LIFE TIMES. see *NEW AGE PUBLICATIONS*

613.7   US
WILDWOOD NEWS; journal of health and healing. q. $10. Wildwood Lifestyle Center & Hospital, Wildwood, GA 30757.
   Description: Promotes the preventative medicine practiced at the Wildwood Lifestyle Center and Hospital, including hydrotherapy, hiking, and diet consciousness.

613.7   US   ISSN 0043-5856
WINGED FOOT. 1892. m. $24. New York Athletic Club, 180 Central Park South, New York, NY 10019. TEL 212-247-5100. Ed. Fred Jarvis. adv.; bk.rev.; illus.; circ. 8,400.

613   UK
WINGROVE. 1979. 12/yr. donation. Wingrove Yoga, Strawberry Cottage, 84 Maple Way, Earl Shilton, Leicester LE9 7HW, England. TEL 0455-842688. Ed. Dr. W.A. Shepherd. adv.; bk.rev.; illus.; circ. 200.
   Description: Teaching yoga for health.

WOMAN'S DAY MOTHER - CHILD. see *CHILDREN AND YOUTH — About*

WOMAN'S DAY 101 WAYS TO LOSE WEIGHT AND STAY HEALTHY. see *NUTRITION AND DIETETICS*

WOMEN & HEALTH ROUNDTABLE REPORTS. see *WOMEN'S HEALTH*

WOMENWISE. see *WOMEN'S HEALTH*

WORLD BOOK HEALTH AND MEDICAL ANNUAL. see *ENCYCLOPEDIAS AND GENERAL ALMANACS*

THE WORLD OF A S P. (American Self-Protection Association) see *SPORTS AND GAMES*

613   US   ISSN 0161-7672
RA1242.T6
WORLD SMOKING & HEALTH. 1976. 3/yr. free. American Cancer Society, Inc., 1599 Clifton Rd., N.E., Atlanta, GA 30329. TEL 404-329-7936. FAX 404-325-2217. Ed. Jerie Jordan. charts; illus.; stat.; circ. 16,000.

WUSHU JIANSHEN/HEALTH THROUGH MARTIAL ARTS. see *SPORTS AND GAMES*

WYCHOWANIE FIZYCZNE I HIGIENA SZKOLNA. see *EDUCATION — Teaching Methods And Curriculum*

WYCHOWANIE FIZYCZNE I SPORT. STUDIA I MATERIALY. see *EDUCATION — Teaching Methods And Curriculum*

613.7   CC   ISSN 1001-747X
XI'AN TIYU XUEYUAN XUEBAO/XI'AN INSTITUTE OF PHYSICAL EDUCATION. JOURNAL. (Text in Chinese) 1984. q. Y8. Xi'an Tiyu Xueyuan - Xi'an Institute of Physical Education, Lingyuan Lu, Xi'an, Shaanxi 710068, People's Republic of China. TEL 55961. (Co-sponsor: Xinwen Chubanshu) circ. 600.
 Description: Covers the latest achievement, technology and experiment of teaching, training and scientific research in physical education. Also includes news in China and abroad.

613.7 790.1   CN
Y M C A WEEKLY NEWS (VANCOUVER, BC). w. Vancouver Downtown Young Men's Christian Association, 955 Burrard St., Vancouver, B.C. V6Z 1Y2, Canada. TEL 604-681-0221. Ed. Terry Connolly. circ. 1,000.

613.7   GR
YGIA K OMORFIA/HEALTH AND BEAUTY. 1979. bi-m. Dr.3000($50) I C O International, 3A Barbanou St., Box 190.25, 117 10 Athens, Greece. TEL 01-9017806. FAX 01-9016663. Ed. Demetrios E. Tsirimocos. adv.; bk.rev.; circ. 30,000. (back issues avail.)

YOGA AND TOTAL HEALTH. see *PHILOSOPHY*

YOGA JOURNAL; for health and conscious living. see *NEW AGE PUBLICATIONS*

YOGA LIFE. see *PHILOSOPHY*

613.7   US
YOUR HEALTH & FITNESS. 1980. bi-m. General)Learning Corporation, Custom Publishing Group, 60 Revere Dr., Northbrook, IL 60062-1563. TEL 708-205-3000. FAX 708-564-8197. Ed. Laura Ruekberg.

613.7   US
YOUR HEALTH & SAFETY. 1980. bi-m. General Learning Corporation, Custom Publishing Group, 60 Revere Dr., Northbrook, IL 60062-1563. TEL 708-205-3000. FAX 708-564-8197. Ed. Laura Ruekberg.

613.7   US
YOUR PERSONAL BEST NEWSLETTER. m. $18. Rodale Press, Inc., 33 E. Minor St., Emmaus, PA 18098. TEL 215-967-5171. TELEX 847338.
 Description: Gives tips, advice and information about harnessing your mind to improve your emotions and your health.

613   CS   ISSN 0044-1953
ZDRAVIE; popularno-zdravotnicky casopis moderneho cloveka. m. $35. (Ceskoslovensky Cerveny Kriz, Slovensky Ustredni Vybor - Czechoslovak Red Cross) Obzor, Ceskoslovenskej Armady 35, 815 85 Bratislava, Czechoslovakia. (Dist. by: Slovart, Gottwaldovo nam. 48, 805 32 Bratislava, Czechoslovakia) Ed. Juraj Bogdan. adv.; bk.rev.; illus.; circ. 80,000.
 Formerly: Zdravie Ludu.

613   GW   ISSN 0044-3182
ZEITSCHRIFT FUER NATURHEILKUNDE. 1949. m. DM.48. Berufsverband der Heilpraktiker Nordrhein-Westfalen e.V., Koernerstr. 59, 5650 Solingen 11, Germany. adv.; bk.rev.; circ. 4,550.
 —BLDSC shelfmark: 9475.100000.

613.7   CC
ZHONG LAO NIAN BAOJIAN. (Text in Chinese) bi-m. Zhongri Youhao Yiyuan - Sino-Japanese Friendship Hospital, Hepingjie Beikou, Beijing 100029, People's Republic of China. TEL 4221122. Ed. Ma Xiuye.

613.7   CC   ISSN 1000-8268
ZHONGGUO QIGONG. (Text in Chinese) bi-m. Hebei Beidaihe Qigong Kangfu Yiyuan, 198 Dongjing Lu, Beidaihe-qu, Qinhuandao, Hebei 066100, People's Republic of China. TEL 441057. (Co-sponsor: Zhongguo Qigong Keyan Hui) Ed. Zhao Baofeng.

613.7   CC   ISSN 0529-5548
R97.7.C5
ZHONGJI YIKAN. (Text in Chinese) m. Renmin Weisheng Chubanshe - People's Health Publishing House, 10 Tiantan Xili, Beijing 100050, People's Republic of China. TEL 755431. Ed. Dong Mianguo.

613.7   CU   ISSN 0257-7402
16 DE ABRIL. 1961? q. $15 in N. America; S. America; Europe $25. Ministerio de Salud Publica, Instituto Superior de Ciencias Medicas de la Habana, Calle Gs-n, entre 25 y 27, Codigo Postal 10400, Havana, Cuba. TEL 30-89-42. (Dist. by: Ediciones Cubanas, Obispo No. 527, Apdo. 605, Havana, Cuba) Ed. Ricardo Moreno Pascual. circ. 40,000.

PHYSICAL FITNESS AND HYGIENE — Abstracting, Bibliographies, Statistics

016 613.85   US   ISSN 0067-7361
BIBLIOGRAPHY ON SMOKING AND HEALTH. (Subseries of: Public Health Service Bibliography Series) 1967. a. free. U.S. Office on Smoking and Health, National Center for Chronic Disease Prevention and Health Promotion, Centers for Disease Control, MS K-12, 1600 Clifton Rd., N.E., Atlanta, GA 30333. index; circ. controlled.

BRITISH JOURNAL OF PHYSICAL EDUCATION. see *EDUCATION — Teaching Methods And Curriculum*

613.7 011   GW   ISSN 0932-2884
GESUNDHEITSFOERDERUNG. (Text in English or German) 1987. irreg. DM.10 per no. Institut fuer Dokumentation und Information, Sozialmedizin und Oeffentliches Gesundheitswesen, Westerfelderstr. 35-37, Postfach 20 10 12, D-4800 Bielefeld 1, Germany. TEL 0521-86033. bk.rev.; circ. 350.

HAWAII. DEPARTMENT OF HEALTH. RESEARCH AND STATISTICS OFFICE. R & S REPORT. see *POPULATION STUDIES — Abstracting, Bibliographies, Statistics*

614   UK   ISSN 0140-3273
HEALTH EDUCATION INDEX;* a guide to voluntary social welfare organizations. 1967. 2/yr. B. Edsall & Co. Ltd., Greater London House, Hampstead Rd., London NW1 7QP, England. Ed. B. Edsall. adv.; illus.

613.7 790 370   US   ISSN 0090-5119
HEALTH, PHYSICAL EDUCATION AND RECREATION MICROFORM PUBLICATIONS BULLETIN. 1949. s-a. $10. Microform Publications, University of Oregon, 1479 Moss St., Eugene, OR 97403. TEL 503-346-4117. FAX 503-346-2814. TELEX 510-597-0354-EUG. Ed. Gwen Steigelman. cum.index: 1949-1991.; circ. 2,630. (also avail. in microfiche)
 Formerly: Health, Physical Education, and Recreation Microcard Bulletin (ISSN 0017-906X)
 Description: Lists titles and descriptions of theses and dissertations in the fields of physical education, sport sciences, health, dance, and recreational studies.

613.194   CN   ISSN 0840-6529
RA645.C34
HEALTH REPORTS. q. Can.$104($125) (foreign $146). Statistics Canada, Publications Division, Ottawa, Ont. K1A OT6, Canada.
TEL 613-951-7277. FAX 613-951-1584.

MEDICAL ABSTRACTS NEWSLETTER; your direct pipeline to the latest breakthroughs in health care. see *MEDICAL SCIENCES — Abstracting, Bibliographies, Statistics*

613 016   US
N T I S ALERTS: HEALTH CARE. w. $125 (foreign $175). U.S. National Technical Information Service, 5285 Port Royal Rd., Springfield, VA 22161. TEL 703-487-4630. FAX 703-321-8547. TELEX 64617. index. (back issues avail.)
 Former titles: Abstract Newsletter: Health Care; Abstract Newsletter: Health Planning and Health Services Research; Weekly Abstract Newsletter: Health Planning and Health Services Research; Weekly Government Abstracts. Health Planning and Health Services Research (ISSN 0199-9974); Weekly Government Abstracts. Health Planning (ISSN 0017-9086)

300 614.35   UN   ISSN 1013-3453
HV5800
NARCOTIC DRUGS: ESTIMATED WORLD REQUIREMENTS FOR (YEAR). (Text in English, French and Spanish) a. $35. (International Narcotics Control Board - Organe International de Controle des Stupefiants) United Nations Publications, Room DC2-0853, New York, NY 10017. TEL 212-963-9300.
FAX 212-963-3489. (Or Vienna International Centre, P.O. Box 500, 1400 Vienna, Austria)
—BLDSC shelfmark: 6015.348290.
 Formed by the 1989 merger of: United Nations. International Narcotics Control Board. Statistics on Narcotics Drugs for (Year); Which was formerly: United Nations. International Narcotics Control Board. Statistics on Narcotic Drugs Furnished by Governments in Accordance with the International Treaties & United Nations. International Narcotics Control Board. Comparative Statement of Estimates and Statistics on Narcotic Drugs for (Year); Which was formerly: United Nations. International Narcotics Control Board. Comparative Statement of Estimates and Statistics on Narcotics Drugs Furnished by Governments in Accordance with the International Treaties & Estimated World Requirements of Narcotic Drugs (ISSN 0082-8335) United Nations. International Narcotics Control Board. Statistics on Narcotic Drugs Furnished by Governments in Accordance with the International Treaties; Which was formerly (until 1984): United Nations. International Narcotics Control Board. Statistics on Drugs Furnished by Governments in Accordance with the International Treaties and Maximum Level of Opium Stocks (ISSN 0566-7658).

613.7 016   US   ISSN 0191-9202
GV201
PHYSICAL EDUCATION INDEX. 1978. q. $175. Ben Oak Publishing Company, Box 474, Cape Girardeau, MO 63702-0474. TEL 314-334-8789. Ed. Ronald F. Kirby. bk.rev.; index. (back issues avail.)
—BLDSC shelfmark: 6475.425000.
 Description: Subject index to health, physical education, recreation, dance, sports, and sports medicine literature in over 180 journals.

PHYSICAL FITNESS - SPORTS MEDICINE; a bibliographic service encompassing exercise physiology, sports injuries, physical conditioning and the medical aspects of exercise. see *MEDICAL SCIENCES — Abstracting, Bibliographies, Statistics*

011 613   US
SCIENCE - HEALTH ABSTRACTS. 1980. bi-m. $6. Yuchi Pines Institute, Box 319, Ft. Mitchell, AL 36856. TEL 404-288-5495. Ed. Phylis Austin. bk.rev.; index; circ. 1,000. (looseleaf format; back issues avail.)

SOZIALMEDIZIN. see *MEDICAL SCIENCES — Abstracting, Bibliographies, Statistics*

PHYSICALLY IMPAIRED

613 011   US   ISSN 0161-603X
HV5825
U.S. NATIONAL INSTITUTE ON DRUG ABUSE. STATISTICAL SERIES D. DATA FROM THE CLIENT ORIENTED DATA ACQUISITION PROCESS. QUARTERLY REPORT. PROVISIONAL DATA.* 1973. q. U.S. National Institute on Drug Abuse, 5600 Fishers Lane, Rm. 11A-55, Rockville, MD 20857. TEL 301-443-6637. charts; stat.
    Formerly: U.S. National Institute on Drug Abuse. Statistical Series D. Client Oriented Data Acquisition Process. Quarterly Report (ISSN 0145-1065)

613 016   US
WELLNESS MEDIA: AN AUDIOVISUAL SOURCEBOOK. 1986. irreg. $50. (National Information Center for Educational Media) Access Innovations, Inc., Box 40130, Albuquerque, NM 87196. TEL 505-265-3591.
    Formerly (until 1987): N I C E M Index to Health and Safety Education - Multimedia.

PHYSICALLY IMPAIRED

see Handicapped-Physically Impaired

PHYSICS

see also Physics-Computer Applications; Physics-Electricity; Physics-Heat; Physics-Mechanics; Physics-Nuclear Physics; Physics-Optics; Physics-Sound

530   US   ISSN 0275-5696
A A P T ANNOUNCER. 1971. 4/yr. $48. American Association of Physics Teachers, 5112 Berwyn Rd., College Park, MD 20740. TEL 301-345-4200. Eds. Bernard V. Khoury, Donna Willis. adv.; tr.lit.; circ. 11,000. **Indexed:** C.I.J.E.
—BLDSC shelfmark: 1053.542000.

A C O NEWSLETTER. (American College of Orgonomy) see MEDICAL SCIENCES — Psychiatry And Neurology

A I A A - A S M E JOINT FLUID MECHANICS, PLASMA DYNAMICS, AND LASER CONFERENCE. PROCEEDINGS. (American Institute of Aeronautics and Astronautics) (American Society of Mechanical Engineers) see ENGINEERING — Mechanical Engineering

530   US   ISSN 0094-243X
                                    CODEN: APCPCS
A I P CONFERENCE PROCEEDINGS. 1970. irreg., no.194, 1989. American Institute of Physics, 335 E. 45th St., New York, NY 10017. TEL 212-661-9404. FAX 516-349-9704. (Subscr. to: Member and Subscriber Service, 500 Sunnyside Blvd., Woodbury, NY 11797-2999. TEL 516-576-2270) Ed. Michael Hennelly. bibl.; charts; illus.; stat. (back issues avail.) **Indexed:** Biol.Abstr., C.P.I., Chem.Abstr., GeoRef., INIS Atomind., Math.R., Phys.Abstr., Phys.Ber., Sci.Abstr., Sci.Cit.Ind.
—BLDSC shelfmark: 0773.430000.

530   CH   ISSN 0304-5293
QC1   CODEN: RIPSD3
ACADEMIA SINICA. INSTITUTE OF PHYSICS. ANNUAL REPORT/CHUNG YANG YEN CHIU YUAN WU LI HSUEH YEN CHIU SO NIEN PAO. 1970. a. exchange basis. Academia Sinica, Institute of Physics - Chung Yang Yen Chiu Yuan Wu Li Hsueh Yen Chiu So, Nankang, Taipei Hsien, Taiwan 11529, Republic of China. FAX 02-783-4187. Ed. E.K. Lin. bk.rev.; circ. 500. **Indexed:** Biol.Abstr., Chem.Abstr., Met.Abstr., Sci.Abstr., World Alum.Abstr.

ACADEMY OF SCIENCE OF THE U S S R. LEBEDEV PHYSICS INSTITUTE. PROCEEDINGS. see PHYSICS — Optics

530   US   ISSN 0001-432X
QC1   CODEN: BUPSAA
ACADEMY OF SCIENCES OF THE U S S R. BULLETIN. PHYSICAL SERIES. English translation of: Akademiya Nauk S.S.S.R. Izvestiya. Seriya Fizicheskaya. m. $1,040. (Akademiya Nauk S.S.S.R., RU) Allerton Press, Inc., 150 Fifth Ave., New York, NY 10011. TEL 212-924-3950. **Indexed:** Sci.Abstr.
—BLDSC shelfmark: 0409.000000.

530 551.46   US
ACADEMY OF SCIENCES OF THE U S S R. INSTITUTE OF GENERAL PHYSICS. PROCEEDINGS. English translation of: Akademiya Nauk S.S.S.R. Institut Obshchei Fiziki. Trudy. 1988. irreg., no.17, 1990. price varies. (Akademiya Nauk S.S.S.R., Institut Obshchei Fiziki, RU - Academy of Sciences of the U S S R, Institute of General Physics) Nova Science Publishers, Inc., 283 Commack Rd., Ste. 300, Commack, NY 11725. TEL 516-499-3103.
    Description: Compilation of advanced physics research.
    Refereed Serial

530 510   IT   ISSN 0392-7881
AS222   CODEN: AANLAW
ACCADEMIA NAZIONALE DEI LINCEI. CLASSE DI SCIENZE FISICHE MATEMATICHE E NATURALI. RENDICONTI. (Text in English, French, Italian; summaries in English, Italian) 1847. 4/yr. L.120000($100) (foreign L.140000). Accademia Nazionale dei Lincei, Via della Lungara 10, 00165 Rome, Italy. TEL 650.831. Ed. Cesare Franco Golisano. bibl.; charts; illus.; index; circ. 1,200. **Indexed:** Appl.Mech.Rev., Biol.Abstr., Chem.Abstr., INIS Atomind., Math.R., Sci.Abstr.
    Former titles (until 1943): Reale Accademia d'Italia. Classe di Scienze Fisiche, Matematiche e Naturali (ISSN 0365-5946); (until 1939): Reale Accademia dei Lincei. Classe di Scienze Fisiche, Matematiche e Naturali (ISSN 0001-4435).
    Description: Includes articles by academy fellows or by scholars presented by fellows.

530   II   ISSN 0253-7257
                                    CODEN: JSOIDI
ACOUSTICAL SOCIETY OF INDIA. JOURNAL. 1973. q. Rs.40($25) Acoustical Society of India, Osmania University, Department of Physics, Hyderabad 500 007, India. Ed. S.K. Kor. circ. 300. **Indexed:** Chem.Abstr., Sci.Abstr.

530   PL   ISSN 0209-3316
ACTA MAGNETICA. (Text and summaries in English) 1983. a. $6. (Adam Mickiewicz University, Institute of Physics) Adam Mickiewicz University Press, Nowowiejskiego 55, 61-734 Poznan, Poland. TEL 527-380. TELEX 413260 UAM PL. Ed. Leon Kowalewski. circ. 450. (back issues avail.)
—BLDSC shelfmark: 0629.730000.
    Description: Covers all aspects of physics.

530   US   ISSN 0065-1559
                                    CODEN: APAUAV
ACTA PHYSICA AUSTRIACA. SUPPLEMENT. 1965. irreg., no.27, 1986. price varies. Springer-Verlag, Journals, 175 Fifth Ave., New York, NY 10010. TEL 212-460-1500. (Also Berlin, Heidelberg, Tokyo and Vienna) (also avail. in microform from UMI; reprint service avail. from ISI) **Indexed:** Math.R., Phys.Abstr., Sci.Abstr.

530   HU   ISSN 0231-4428
QC3   CODEN: APHUE2
ACTA PHYSICA HUNGARICA. (Text in English, French, German, Russian) 1951. 8/yr. (in 2 vols., 4 nos./vol.). $62. (Magyar Tudomanyos Akademia) Akademiai Kiado, Publishing House of the Hungarian Academy of Sciences, P.O. Box 24, H-1363 Budapest, Hungary. Ed. Istvan Kovacs. adv.; bk.rev.; bibl.; charts; illus.; index. **Indexed:** ASCA, Cadscan, Chem.Abstr., Curr.Cont., Ind.Sci.Rev., INIS Atomind., Int.Aerosp.Abstr., Lead Abstr., Math.R., Met.Abstr., Phys.Ber., Risk Abstr., Sci.Abstr., Sci.Cit.Ind., Zincscan.
—BLDSC shelfmark: 0649.075000.
    Formerly: Academia Scientiarum Hungarica. Acta Physica (ISSN 0001-6705)

530   PL   ISSN 0587-4246
QC1   CODEN: ATPLB6
ACTA PHYSICA POLONICA. SERIES A: GENERAL PHYSICS, PHYSICS OF CONDENSED MATTER, OPTICS AND QUANTUM ELECTRONICS, ATOMIC AND MOLECULAR PHYSICS, APPLIED PHYSICS. (Text in various languages) 1932. m. $132. Polska Akademia Nauk, Instytut Fizyki, Al. Lotnikiw 32-46, 02-668 Warsaw, Poland. (Dist. by: Ars Polona, Krakowskie Przedmiescie 7, 00-068 Warsaw, Poland) (Co-sponsor: Polskie Towarzystwo Fizyczne) Ed. W. Szyz. bibl.; charts; illus.; index; circ. 1,130. (also avail. in microfiche from BHP) **Indexed:** ASCA, Biwk.Pap.Rad.Chem.& Photochem., Cadscan, Ceram.Abstr., Chem.Abstr., Ind.Sci.Rev., INIS Atomind., Lead Abstr., Math.R., Met.Abstr., Sci.Abstr., Sci.Cit.Ind., World Alum.Abstr., Zincscan.
—BLDSC shelfmark: 0650.050000.
    Supersedes in part: Acta Physica Polonica (ISSN 0001-673X)

530   PL   ISSN 0587-4254
QC770   CODEN: APOBBB
ACTA PHYSICA POLONICA. SERIES B: ELEMENTARY PARTICLE PHYSICS, NUCLEAR PHYSICS, THEORY OF RELATIVITY, FIELD THEORY. (Text in English, French, German, Russian) 1932. m. $72. Polska Akademia Nauk, Instytut Fizyki, Al. Lotnikow 32-46, 02-668 Warsaw, Poland. (Dist. by: Ars Polona, Krakowskie Przedmiescie 7, 00-068 Warsaw, Poland) (Co-sponsor: Polskie Towarzystwo Fizyczne) Ed. Wieslaw Czyz. bk.rev.; index; circ. 910. (back issues avail.) **Indexed:** ASCA, Cadscan, Chem.Abstr., Ind.Sci.Rev., INIS Atomind., Lead Abstr., Math.R., Met.Abstr., Phys.Abstr., Ref.Zh., Sci.Cit.Ind., World Alum.Abstr., Zincscan.
—BLDSC shelfmark: 0650.060000.
    Supersedes in part: Acta Physica Polonica (ISSN 0001-673X)

530   CS   ISSN 0323-0465
QC1   CODEN: APSVCO
ACTA PHYSICA SLOVACA. (Text in English; summaries in English and Russian) vol.23, 1973. bi-m. 120 Kcs.($16) (Slovenska Akademia Vied, Fyzikalny Ustav) Veda, Publishing House of the Slovak Academy of Sciences, Klemensova 19, 814 30 Bratislava, Czechoslovakia. (Dist. by: Slovart, Nam. Slobody 6, 817 64 Bratislava, Czechoslovakia) Ed. Mikulas Blazek. bk.rev.; abstr.; bibl.; charts; illus. **Indexed:** ASCA, Cadscan, Chem.Abstr., Curr.Cont., Ind.Sci.Rev., INIS Atomind., Lead Abstr., Math.R., Met.Abstr., Phys.Ber., Sci.Abstr., Sci.Cit.Ind., World Alum.Abstr., Zincscan.
—BLDSC shelfmark: 0650.630000.
    Description: Publishes original scientific and special works from all areas of physics, especially physics of solid substances, nuclear and subnuclear physics, as well as borderline areas such as biophysics and physical electronics.

ACTA UNIVERSITATIS CAROLINAE: MATHEMATICA ET PHYSICA. see MATHEMATICS

530 370   PL   ISSN 0208-6190
QC1   CODEN: ALFPDG
ACTA UNIVERSITATIS LODZIENSIS: FOLIA PHYSICA. (Text in Polish; summaries in various languages) 1955-1974; N.S. 1981. s-a. Wydawnictwo Uniwersytetu Lodzkiego, Ul. Jaracza 34, Lodz, Poland. (Dist by: Ars Polona-Ruch, Krakowskie Przedmiescie 7, Warsaw, Poland)
—BLDSC shelfmark: 0585.208500.
    Supersedes in part: Uniwersytet Lodzki. Zeszyty Naukowe. Seria 2: Nauki Matematyczno-Przyrodnicze (ISSN 0076-0366)
    Description: Publishes original papers which advance the understanding of theoretical and experimental physics.

530 540   HU   ISSN 0001-6721
                                    CODEN: AUSHAF
ACTA UNIVERSITATIS SZEGEDIENSIS DE ATTILA JOZSEF NOMINATAE. ACTA PHYSICA ET CHEMICA. (Text in English, German, Russian) 1928; N.S. 1955. s-a. exchange basis. Attila Jozsef University, c/o E. Szabo, Exchange Librarian, Dugonics ter 13, P.O.B. 393, Szeged H-6701, Hungary. (Subscr. to: Kultura, Box 149, H-1389 Budapest, Hungary) Ed. Miklos I. Ban. bibl.; charts; illus.; circ. 400. **Indexed:** Biol.Abstr., Chem.Abstr., Curr.Cont., Ref.Zh., Sci.Abstr.
    Description: Journal of physics and chemistry focusing on luminescence and various problems of organic and physical chemistry.

530   SI
ADVANCED SERIES IN APPLIED PHYSICS. (Text in English) 1988. irreg., vol.2, 1990. price varies. World Scientific Publishing Co. Pte. Ltd., Farrer Rd., P.O. Box 128, Singapore 9128, Singapore. TEL 3825663. FAX 3825919. TELEX RS 28561 WSPC. (UK addr.: 73 Lynton Mead, Totteridge, London N20 8DH, England. TEL 44-81-4462461; US addr.: 1060 Main St., Ste. 1B, River Edge, NJ 07661. TEL 800-227-7562) Eds. S. Ramaseshan, Melvin Lax.

530 510   SI
ADVANCED SERIES IN MATHEMATICAL PHYSICS. (Text in English) 1987. irreg., vol.13, 1991. price varies. World Scientific Publishing Co. Pte. Ltd., Farrer Rd., P.O. Box 128, Singapore 9128, Singapore. TEL 3825663. FAX 3825919. TELEX RS 28561 WSPC. (UK addr.: 73 Lynton Mead, Totteridge, London N20 8DH, England. TEL 44-81-4462461; US addr.: 1060 Main St., Ste. 1B, River Edge, NJ 07661. TEL 800-227-7562)

530   SI
▼**ADVANCED SERIES IN NONLINEAR DYNAMICS.** (Text in English) 1991. irreg., vol.3. price varies. World Scientific Publishing Co. Pte. Ltd., Farrer Rd., P.O. Box 128, Singapore 9128, Singapore. TEL 3825663. FAX 3825919. TELEX RS 28561 WSPC. (UK addr.: 73 Lynton Mead, Totteridge, London N20 8DH, England. TEL 44-81-4463356; US addr. 1060 Main St., Ste. 1B, River Edge, NJ 07661. TEL 800-227-7562) Ed. R.S. MacKay.

530   SI
ADVANCED SERIES ON DIRECTIONS IN HIGH ENERGY PHYSICS. (Text in English) 1988. irreg., vol.10, 1992. price varies. World Scientific Publishing Co. Pte. Ltd., Farrer Rd., P.O. Box 128, Singapore 9128, Singapore. TEL 3825663. FAX 3825919. TELEX RS 28561 WSPC. (UK addr.: 73 Lynton Mead, Totteridge, London N20 8DH, England. TEL 44-81-4462461; US addr.: 1060 Main St., Ste. 1B, River Edge, NJ 07661. TEL 800-227-7562)

530   US
ADVANCES IN AEROSOL PHYSICS. irreg., vol.7, 1973. price varies. John Wiley & Sons Ltd., 605 Third Ave., New York, NY 10016. TEL 212-870-6000. Ed. V.A. Fedoseev.

530 541.3   US   ISSN 0065-2385
QD453   CODEN: ADCPAA
ADVANCES IN CHEMICAL PHYSICS. 1958. irreg., latest no.82. price varies. John Wiley & Sons, Inc., 605 Third Ave., New York, NY 10158-0012. TEL 212-850-6000. FAX 212-850-6099. TELEX 12-7063. Ed. I. Prigogine. **Indexed:** Biol.Abstr., Chem.Abstr., Deep Sea Res.& Oceanogr.Abstr., Ind.Sci.Rev., Mass Spectr.Bull., Sci.Cit.Ind.
—BLDSC shelfmark: 0703.550000.
Refereed Serial

ADVANCES IN COLLOID AND INTERFACE SCIENCE; an international journal devoted to experimental and theoretical developments in interfacial and colloidal phenomena and their implications in biology, chemistry, physics and technology. see *CHEMISTRY — Physical Chemistry*

530   SI
ADVANCES IN DISORDERED SEMICONDUCTORS. (Text in English) 1989. irreg., vol. 4, 1992. price varies. World Scientific Publishing Co. Pte. Ltd., Farrer Rd., P.O. Box 128, Singapore 9128, Singapore. TEL 3825663. FAX 3825919. TELEX RS 28561 WSPC. (UK addr.: 73 Lynton Mead, Totteridge, London N20 8DH, England. TEL 44-81-4462461; US addr.: 1060 Main St., Ste. 1B, River Edge, NJ 07661. TEL 800-227-7562) Ed. H. Fritzsche.

ADVANCES IN ELECTRONICS AND ELECTRON PHYSICS. see *ENGINEERING — Electrical Engineering*

538   US   ISSN 0065-2873
QC762   CODEN: ADMGAX
ADVANCES IN MAGNETIC RESONANCE. 1965. irreg., vol.14, 1990. Academic Press, Inc., 1250 Sixth Ave., San Diego, CA 92101. TEL 619-231-0926. FAX 619-699-6715. Ed. W. Warren. index. (reprint service avail. from ISI) **Indexed:** Ind.Sci.Rev., Sci.Cit.Ind.
Refereed Serial

ADVANCES IN MAGNETIC RESONANCE IMAGING. see *COMPUTERS — Computer Graphics*

ADVANCES IN MICROWAVES. see *ENGINEERING — Electrical Engineering*

530   UK   ISSN 0001-8732
QC1   CODEN: ADPHAH
ADVANCES IN PHYSICS. 1952. bi-m. £247($420) Taylor & Francis Ltd., Rankine Rd., Basingstoke, Hants. RG24 0PR, England. TEL 0256-840366. FAX 0256-479438. TELEX 858540. Ed. D. Sherrington. adv.; charts; circ. 1,000. (also avail. in microform from MIM) **Indexed:** Br.Tech.Ind., Chem.Abstr., Curr.Cont., GeoRef., Ind.Med., Ind.Sci.Rev., INIS Atomind., Mass Spectr.Bull., Math.R., Met.Abstr., Phys.Ber., Sci.Abstr., Sci.Cit.Ind., World Alum.Abstr.
—BLDSC shelfmark: 0710.000000.
Description: Aims to meet the need for review papers in the major branches of condensed matter physics.
Refereed Serial

530   NE
ADVANCES IN SOLID STATE TECHNOLOGY. 1985. irreg. price varies. Kluwer Academic Publishers, Spuiboulevard 50, P.O. Box 17, 3300 AA Dordrecht, Netherlands. TEL 078-334911. FAX 078-334254. TELEX 29245. (Dist. by: Kluwer Academic Publishers Group, P.O. Box 322, 3300 AH Dordrecht; U.S. address: P.O. Box 358, Accord Station, Hingham, MA 02018-0358)

530   PL   ISSN 0860-0260
AKADEMIA GORNICZO-HUTNICZA IM. STANISLAWA STASZICA. ZESZYTY NAUKOWE. FIZYKA. (Text in English and Polish; summaries in English, Polish) 1984. irreg., no.25, 1991. price varies. Wydawnictwo A G H, Al. Mickiewicza 30, paw. B-5, 31-109 Krakow, Poland. (Dist. by: Ars Polona, Krakowskie Przedmiescie 7, 00-068 Warsaw, Poland) Ed. Z. Kleczek. circ. 300.

530   PL   ISSN 0208-8940
AKADEMIA ROLNICZA, POZNAN. ROCZNIKI. FIZYKA, CHEMIA. (Text in Polish; summaries in English and Russian) 1976. irreg. price varies. Akademia Rolnicza, Poznan, Ul. Wojska Polskiego 28, 60-637 Poznan, Poland. FAX 68-414-110-22. TELEX 04-33-22. **Indexed:** Bibl.Agri.
Description: Deals with the influence of ultrasound and ultraviolet radiation on biological preparations, and spectrophotometric research on purified plant products.

AKADEMIE DER WISSENSCHAFTEN IN GOETTINGEN. ABHANDLUNGEN. MATHEMATISCH-PHYSIKALISCHE KLASSE. DRITTE FOLGE. see *MATHEMATICS*

AKADEMIE DER WISSENSCHAFTEN IN GOETTINGEN. NACHRICHTEN 2. MATHEMATISCH-PHYSIKALISCHE KLASSE. see *MATHEMATICS*

530   AI   ISSN 0002-3035
    CODEN: IAAFA3
AKADEMIYA NAUK ARMYANSKOI S.S.R. IZVESTIYA. SERIYA FIZIKA. English translation: Soviet Journal of Contemporary Physics (US ISSN 8755-4585) (Text in Russian; summaries in Armenian) 1966. bi-m. 13.20 Rub. Akademiya Nauk Armyanskoi S.S.R., Ul. Barekamutian, 24, Erevan, Armenia. Ed. G.M. Garibian. charts; illus.; index; circ. 820. **Indexed:** Chem.Abstr., INIS Atomind., Math.R., Met.Abstr., Phys.Ber., Sci.Abstr.

AKADEMIYA NAUK AZERBAIDZHANSKOI S.S.R. DOKLADY. see *MATHEMATICS*

530 510   AJ   ISSN 0002-3108
    CODEN: IAFMAF
AKADEMIYA NAUK AZERBAIDZHANSKOI S.S.R. IZVESTIYA. SERIYA FIZIKO-TEKHNICHESKIKH I MATEMATICHESKIKH NAUK. (Text in Azerbaijani and Russian) 1958. bi-m. 22.50 Rub. Izdatel'stvo Elm, Ul. Narimanova, 31, Baku 370073, Azerbaijan. (Subscr. to: Mezhdunarodnaya Kniga, Moscow, G-200, Russia) Ed. A. Guseinov. charts; illus.; index; circ. 990. **Indexed:** Chem.Abstr., INIS Atomind., Math.R., Met.Abstr., Phys.Ber., Sci.Abstr.
—BLDSC shelfmark: 0072.700000.

PHYSICS   3813

530 510   RU   ISSN 0002-3191
Q4   CODEN: IAKFBK
AKADEMIYA NAUK KAZAKHSKOI S.S.R. IZVESTIYA. SERIYA FIZIKO - MATEMATICHESKAYA. 1963. bi-m. $16.20. Izdatel'stvo Nauka, Fizmatlit, Leninskii prospekt, 15, 117071 Moscow, V-71, Russia. charts; index. **Indexed:** Chem.Abstr., INIS Atomind., Math.R.
—BLDSC shelfmark: 0073.320000.

530 600   LV   ISSN 0321-1673
TA4   CODEN: LZFTA6
AKADEMIYA NAUK LATVIISKOI S.S.R. IZVESTIYA. SERIYA FIZICHESKIKH I TEKHNICHESKIKH NAUK. (Text in Russian; summaries in English) 1964. bi-m. 14.40 Rub. Izdatel'stvo Zinatne, Turgeneva iela, 19, Riga, 226018, Latvia. Ed. A. Krogeris. illus.; index. **Indexed:** Met.Abstr., Sci.Abstr., World Alum.Abstr.

530 510 600   MV
AKADEMIYA NAUK MOLDAVSKOI S.S.R. IZVESTIYA. SERIYA FIZIKO-TEKHNICHESKIKH I MATEMATICHESKIKH NAUK. (Text in Russian) 1968. 3/yr. 6.60 Rub. Academie de Stiinte a R.S.S. Moldova - Akademiya Nauk Moldavskoi S.S.R., Bd. Stefan cel Mare, 1, Kishinev 277612, Moldova. **Indexed:** Chem.Abstr., INIS Atomind., Math.R., Met.Abstr., World Alum.Abstr.

530 551.46   RU
AKADEMIYA NAUK S.S.S.R. INSTITUT OBSHCHEI FIZIKI. TRUDY. English translation: Academy of Sciences of the U S S R. Institute of General Physics. Proceedings. 1986. irreg. 15 Rub. Izdatel'stvo Nauka, Fizmatlit, Leninskii prospekt, 15, 117071 Moscow, Russia. TEL 132-82-47. (Subscr. to: Akademkniga, B. Cherkasskij per. 2-10, 103624 Moscow, Russia) Ed. A.M. Prokhorov. adv.

AKADEMIYA NAUK TADZHIKSKOI S.S.R. DOKLADY. see *MATHEMATICS*

530 510 551   TA   ISSN 0002-3485
Q60   CODEN: IATOAN
AKADEMIYA NAUK TADZHIKSKOI S.S.R. IZVESTIYA. OTDELENIE FIZIKO-MATEMATICHESKIKH I GEOLOGO-KHIMICHESKIKH NAUK. 1966? q. 12.40 Rub. Akademiya Nauk Tadzhikskoi S.S.R., Ul. Aym, 121, Dushanbe, Tajikistan. charts; illus. **Indexed:** INIS Atomind., Math.R.
—BLDSC shelfmark: 0075.590000.

530 551   TK   ISSN 0002-3507
    CODEN: ITUFAW
AKADEMIYA NAUK TURKMENSKOI S.S.R. IZVESTIYA. SERIYA FIZIKO-TEKHNICHESKIKH, KHIMICHESKIKH I GEOLOGICHESKIKH NAUK. 1960. bi-m. $15 (effective Jan. 1992). Akademiya Nauk Turkmenskoi S.S.R., Ul. Gogolya, 15, Ashkhabad, Turkmenistan. charts; illus.; index; circ. 500. **Indexed:** Biol.Abstr., Chem.Abstr., Ind.Vet., INIS Atomind., Math.R., Met.Abstr., World Alum.Abstr.

530 510   KR   ISSN 0201-8446
AKADEMIYA NAUK UKRAINSKOI S.S.R. DOKLADY. SERIYA A. FIZIKO-MATEMATICHESKIE I TEKHNICHESKIE NAUKI; nauchnyi zhurnal. Ukrainian edition: Akademiya Nauk Ukrainskoi S.S.R. Dopovidi. Seria A. Fiziko-Matematichni ta Tekhnichni Nauki (ISSN 0002-3531) (Text in Russian; summaries in English) 1975; Ukrainian ed. 1939. m. 11.40 Rub.($16.20) Izdatel'stvo Naukova Dumka, c/o Yu.A. Khramov, Dir, Ul. Repina, 3, Kiev 252 601, Ukraine. TEL 224-40-68. (Subscr. to: Mezhdunarodnaya Kniga, Moscow, G-200, Russia) Ed. V.P. Kukhar. bk.rev.; bibl.; charts; illus.; index; circ. 252,601. (tabloid format) **Indexed:** Biol.Abstr., Chem.Abstr., Comput.Rev., Helminthol.Abstr., INIS Atomind., Met.Abstr., Phys.Ber., Sci.Abstr., World Alum.Abstr.

530 510   UZ
AKADEMIYA NAUK UZBEKSKOI S.S.R. IZVESTIYA. SERIYA FIZIKO-MATEMATICHESKIKH NAUK. (Text in Russian) bi-m. 11.10 Rub. Akademiya Nauk Uzbekskoi S.S.R., Ul. Kuibysheva 15, Tashkent, Uzbekistan. **Indexed:** Chem.Abstr., INIS Atomind., Math.R., Met.Abstr., World Alum.Abstr.

PHYSICS

530 BW ISSN 0374-4760
CODEN: VAFEAW
AKADEMIYA NAVUK BELARUSSKAI S.S.R. VESTSI. SERIYA FIZIKA-ENERGETYCHNYKH NAVUK. (Text in Russian; summaries in English) 1968. q. 13.20 Rub. Akademiya Navuk Belarusskai S.S.R. - B.S.S.R. Academy of Sciences, Leninskii prospekt 66, 220072 Minsk 72, Byelorus. TEL 39 48 15. TELEX 252277 NAUKA. Ed. A.A. Mikhalevich. bibl.; charts; illus.; index; circ. 380.
Description: Presents papers on nuclear power engineering, reactor physics, materials and technology, control and safety of nuclear power stations, heat power engineering, thermal physics, heat and mass transfer, hydrogen power engineering.

530 510 BW ISSN 0002-3574
AKADEMIYA NAVUK BELARUSSKAI S.S.R. VESTSI. SERIYA FIZIKA-MATEMATYCHNYKH NAVUK. (Text in Russian; summaries in English) 1965. bi-m. 19.80 Rub. Akademiya Navuk Belarusskai S.S.R. - B.S.S.R. Academy of Sciences, Leninskii prospekt 66, 220072 Minsk 72, Byelarus. TEL 39 48 15. TELEX 252277 NAUKA. Ed. L.N. Kuselevskii. bibl.; charts; illus.; index; circ. 540. Indexed: Math.R.
—BLDSC shelfmark: 0037.570000.
Description: Presents papers on general and theoretical physics, including optics, main branches of mathematics, computer science.

530 BW ISSN 0002-3566
AKADEMIYA NAVUK BELARUSSKAI S.S.R. VESTSI. SERIYA FIZIKA-TEKHNICHNYKH NAVUK. (Text in Russian; summaries in English) 1956. q. 13.20 Rub. Akademiya Navuk Belarusskai S.S.R. - B.S.S.R. Academy of Sciences, Leninskii prospekt 66, 220072 Minsk 72, Byelarus. TEL 39 48 15. TELEX 252277 NAUKA. Ed. S.A. Astapchik. bibl.; charts; illus.; index; circ. 530. Indexed: Chem.Abstr.
—BLDSC shelfmark: 0037.600000.
Description: Presents papers on machine-building industry, reliability and longevity of machines, physics of strength and plasticity, applied physics, pressure and thermal treatment of metals and other materials.

ALKALMAZOTT MATEMATIKAI LAPOK. see *MATHEMATICS*

AMERICAN CRYSTALLOGRAPHIC ASSOCIATION. PROGRAM & ABSTRACTS. see *CHEMISTRY — Crystallography*

530 US
AMERICAN INSTITUTE OF PHYSICS. CENTER FOR HISTORY OF PHYSICS. NEWSLETTER. 1964. s-a. free. American Institute of Physics, Center for History of Physics, 335 E. 45th St., New York, NY 10017. TEL 212-661-9404. FAX 212-949-0473. TELEX 960983-AMINSTPHYS-NYK. Ed. Spencer Weart. circ. 6,000.

530 370 US ISSN 0002-9505
CODEN: AJPIAS
AMERICAN JOURNAL OF PHYSICS. 1933. m. $205 (foreign $225). American Association of Physics Teachers, 5112 Berwyn Rd., College Park, MD 20740. TEL 301-345-4200. Ed. R. Romer. adv.; bk.rev.; illus.; index, cum.index: vols.1-20 (1933-1952), vols.21-30 (1953-1963), vols.31-40 (1963-1972). (also avail. in microform from AIP; back issues avail.) Indexed: A.S.& T.Ind., Abstr.Bull.Inst.Pap.Chem., Bibl.Ind., C.I.J.E., C.P.I., Cadscan, Chem.Abstr., Curr.Cont., Deep Sea Res.& Oceanogr.Abstr., Eng.Ind., Gen.Phys.Adv.Abstr., Gen.Sci.Ind., High.Educ.Curr.Aware.Bull., Ind.Sci.Rev., INIS Atomind., Lead Abstr., Mass Spectr.Bull., Math.R., Met.Abstr., Phys.Ber., Res.High.Educ.Abstr., Risk Abstr., Sci.Abstr., Sci.Cit.Ind., Zincscan.
—BLDSC shelfmark: 0833.000000.
Formerly (until 1940): American Physics Teacher (ISSN 0096-0322)
Refereed Serial

530 US ISSN 0003-0503
QC1 CODEN: BAPSA6
AMERICAN PHYSICAL SOCIETY. BULLETIN. 1956. 9/yr. $400 (foreign $444). (American Physical Society) American Institute of Physics, 335 E. 45th St., New York, NY 10017. TEL 212-661-9404. (Subscr. to: Member and Subscriber Service, 500 Sunnyside Blvd., NY 11797-2999. TEL 516-576-2270) Ed. N. Richard Werthamer. abstr.; index. (also avail. in microfilm from AIP) Indexed: Biol.Abstr., Chem.Abstr., Curr.Pack.Abstr., Mass Spectr.Bull., Phys.Ber.
—BLDSC shelfmark: 2391.000000.

530 GW ISSN 0003-3804
CODEN: ANPYA2
ANNALEN DER PHYSIK. 1790. 8/yr. DM.176. Johann Ambrosius Barth Verlag, Leipzig - Heidelberg, Salomonstr. 18b, 7010 Leipzig, Germany. TEL 70131. Ed. Prof. Dr. W. Walcher. adv.; charts; illus.; index. (also avail. in microfilm from PMC) Indexed: Cadscan, Chem.Abstr., Eng.Ind., INIS Atomind., Lead Abstr., Math.R., Met.Abstr., Sci.Abstr., Sci.Cit.Ind., Zincscan.
—BLDSC shelfmark: 0912.000000.

530 FI ISSN 0066-2003
CODEN: AAFPA4
ANNALES ACADEMIAE SCIENTIARUM FENNICAE. SERIES A, VI: PHYSICA. (Text in English, French, German) 1957. irreg. price varies. Suomalainen Tiedeakatemia - Academia Scientiarum Fennica, Mariankatu 5, 00170 Helsinki, Finland. (Orders to: The Bookstore Tiedekirja, Kirkkokatu 14, SF-00170 Helsinki, Finland) Ed. Matti Punkkinen. cum.index: 1957-1972 in vol. 400; circ. 600. (also avail. in microform; back issues avail.) Indexed: Appl.Mech.Rev., Bull.Signal., Chem.Abstr., GeoRef., INIS Atomind., Int.Aerosp.Abstr., Nucl.Sci.Abstr., Phys.Abstr., Phys.Ber., Ref.Zh., Sci.Abstr.
—BLDSC shelfmark: 0914.400000.

530 FR ISSN 0003-4169
QC1 CODEN: ANPHAJ
ANNALES DE PHYSIQUE. (Text and summaries in English, French) 6/yr. 1310 F. (foreign 1850 F.). Editions de Physique, Z.I. de Courtaboeuf, B.P. 112, 91944 Les Ulis Cedex, France. TEL 69073688. FAX 69288491. TELEX 602321 F. Ed. C. Boisson. bk.rev.; illus.; index; circ. 1,150. (also avail. in microfilm from PMC; reprint service avail. from ISI) Indexed: Cadscan, Chem.Abstr., Deep Sea Res.& Oceanogr.Abstr., Eng.Ind., Ind.Sci.Rev., INIS Atomind., Lead Abstr., Math.R., Met.Abstr., Sci.Abstr., World Alum.Abstr., Zincscan.
—BLDSC shelfmark: 0993.000000.
Description: Covers the basics of atomic and molecular physics, condensed matter, nuclear physics and astrophysics.

530 PL ISSN 0137-6861
QC1 CODEN: AUMADZ
ANNALES UNIVERSITATIS MARIAE CURIE-SKLODOWSKA. SECTIO AAA. PHYSICA. (Text in English, French, Polish; summaries in English, Polish) 1978. a. price varies. Uniwersytet Marii Curie-Sklodowskiej, Wydawnictwo, Pl. M. Curie-Sklodowskiej 5, 20-031 Lublin, Poland. TEL 48-81-375304. FAX 48-81-336699. TELEX 0643223. Ed. Jan Sielewiesiuk. circ. 575. Indexed: Chem.Abstr., INIS Atomind.
—BLDSC shelfmark: 0956.007000.
Supersedes in part (in 1979): Annales Universitatis Mariae Curie-Sklodowska. Section AA. Physica et Chemica (ISSN 0137-1819)

530 US ISSN 0003-4916
QC1 CODEN: APNYA6
ANNALS OF PHYSICS. 1957. 16/yr. $1152 (foreign $1335). Academic Press, Inc., Journal Division, 1250 Sixth Ave., San Diego, CA 92101. TEL 619-230-1840. FAX 619-699-6800. TELEX 181726. Ed. Herman Feshbach. adv.; charts; index. (back issues avail.) Indexed: Cadscan, Chem.Abstr., Deep Sea Res.& Oceanogr.Abstr., Eng.Ind., Ind.Sci.Rev., INIS Atomind., Int.Aerosp.Abstr., Lead Abstr., Math.R., Met. Abstr., Phys.Ber., Sci.Abstr., Sci.Cit.Ind., Zincscan.
—BLDSC shelfmark: 1043.500000.
Description: Presents original work in all areas of basic physics research. Publishes papers on particular topics spanning theory, methodology, and applications.
Refereed Serial

ANNUAL REVIEW OF ASTRONOMY AND ASTROPHYSICS. see *ASTRONOMY*

531.14 US
ANNUAL SUMMARY OF PROGRESS IN GRAVITATION SCIENCES. 1974. a. membership. (Ensanian Physicochemical Institute) Minas Ensanian Corporation, Box 98, Eldred, PA 16731. TEL 814-225-3296. Ed. Minas Ensanian. adv.; bk.rev.; abstr.; bibl.; charts; illus.; pat.; stat.; circ. 100 (controlled).

530 US
APERIODICITY AND ORDER. 1988. irreg., vol.3, 1989. Academic Press, Inc., 1250 Sixth Ave., San Diego, CA 92101. TEL 619-231-6616. FAX 619-699-6715. (back issues avail.)
Refereed Serial

530 GW ISSN 0937-9347
CODEN: APMREI
▼**APPLIED MAGNETIC RESONANCE.** 1990. 3/yr. (Russian Academy of Sciences, Kazan Physical-Technical Institute, RU) Springer-Verlag, Heidelberg Platz 3, D-1000 Berlin 33, Germany. (Also Heidelberg, Tokyo, Vienna, and New York) (Co-sponsor: Department of General Physics and Astronomy) Ed. K.M. Salikhov.
—BLDSC shelfmark: 1573.500000.
Description: Provides an international forum on the application of magnetic resonance in physics, chemistry, biology, medicine, geochemistry, ecology, engineering, and related fields. Emphasizes new applications of the technique, and new experimental methods.

621 530 GW ISSN 0721-7250
QC1 CODEN: APSFDB
APPLIED PHYSICS. A: SOLIDS AND SURFACES. (Text in English or German) 1973. 12/yr. DM.1376($683) (Deutsche Physikalische Gesellschaft - German Physical Society) Springer-Verlag, Heidelberger Platz 3, D-1000 Berlin 33, Germany. TEL 030-8207-1. (Also Heidelberg, Tokyo, Vienna, and New York) Ed. H.K.V. Lotsch. adv.; abstr.; charts; illus.; index. (also avail. in microform from UMI; reprint service avail. from ISI) Indexed: C.I.S. Abstr., Cadscan, Chem.Abstr., Curr.Cont., INIS Atomind., Int.Aerosp.Abstr., Int.Sci.Rev., Lead Abstr., Mass Spectr.Bull., Met.Abstr., Phys.Ber., Sci.Abstr, Sci.Cit.Ind., World Alum.Abstr., Zincscan.
—BLDSC shelfmark: 1576.320100.
Supersedes in part (as of 1981): Applied Physics (ISSN 0340-3793); Which superseded: Zeitschrift fuer Angewandte Physik (ISSN 0044-2283)
Description: Covers primarily the condensed state, including surface science and engineering.

621 530 GW ISSN 0721-7269
QC1 CODEN: APPCDL
APPLIED PHYSICS. B: PHOTOPHYSICS AND LASER CHEMISTRY. 12/yr. (in 2 vols., 6 nos./vol.). DM.1236($715) (Deutsche Physikalische Gesellschaft) Springer-Verlag, Heidelberger Platz 3, D-1000 Berlin 33, Germany. TEL 030-8207-1. (Also Heidelberg, Tokyo, Vienna, and New York) Ed. H.K.V. Lotsch. adv. (also avail. in microform from UMI) Indexed: Biwk.Pap.Rad.Chem.& Photochem., Chem.Abstr., Eng.Ind., Ind.Sci.Rev., INIS Atomind., Mass Spectr.Bull., Met.Abstr., Sci.Abstr., Sci.Cit.Ind., World Alum.Abstr.
—BLDSC shelfmark: 1576.320150.
Supersedes in part: Applied Physics (ISSN 0340-3793)

530 620 US ISSN 0066-5509
APPLIED PHYSICS AND ENGINEERING. (Text in English) 1967. irreg., no.12, 1976. price varies. Springer-Verlag, 175 Fifth Ave., New York, NY 10010. TEL 212-460-1500. (Also Berlin, Heidelberg, Tokyo and Vienna) (reprint service avail. from ISI)

530 US ISSN 0277-9374
TA1 CODEN: APCODQ
APPLIED PHYSICS COMMUNICATIONS. 1980. 4/yr. $310. Marcel Dekker Journals, 270 Madison Ave., New York, NY 10016. TEL 212-696-9000. FAX 212-685-4540. TELEX 421419. (Subscr. to: Box 10018, Church St. Sta., New York, NY 10249) adv.; bibl.; charts; illus. (also avail. in microform from RPI) Indexed: Chem.Abstr., Energy Info.Abstr., INIS Atomind., Met.Abstr., Sci.Abstr., World Alum.Abstr.
—BLDSC shelfmark: 1576.385000.

PHYSICS

621 530   US   ISSN 0003-6951
QC1   CODEN: APPLAB
APPLIED PHYSICS LETTERS. 1962. w. $820 (foreign $925). American Institute of Physics, 335 E. 45th St., New York, NY 10017. TEL 212-661-9404. (Subscr. to: Member and Subscriber Service, 500 Sunnyside Blvd., Woodbury, NY 11797-2999) TEL 516-576-2270) Ed. Hartmut Wiedersich. charts; illus.; index, cum.index: 1977-1981, 1982-1986. (also avail. in microfiche from AIP; back issues avail.) Indexed: Anal.Abstr., Br.Ceram.Abstr., C.P.I., Cadscan, Ceram.Abstr., Chem.Abstr., Curr.Cont., Eng.Ind., Gen.Phys.Adv.Abstr., GeoRef., Ind.Sci.Rev., INIS Atomind., Lead Abstr., Mass Spectr.Bull., Met.Abstr., Phys.Ber., Sci.Abstr., Sci.Cit.Ind., World Alum.Abstr., Zincscan.
—BLDSC shelfmark: 1576.400000.

APPLIED SOLID STATE SCIENCE; advances in materials and device research. see ENGINEERING — Electrical Engineering

ARAB GULF JOURNAL OF SCIENTIFIC RESEARCH. see SCIENCES: COMPREHENSIVE WORKS

ARKHIMEDES. see MATHEMATICS

ASTRONOMY AND ASTROPHYSICS; a European journal. see ASTRONOMY

ASTRONOMY AND ASTROPHYSICS REVIEW. see ASTRONOMY

ASTROPARTICLE PHYSICS. see ASTRONOMY

ASTROPHYSICAL JOURNAL; an international review of astronomy and astronomical physics. see ASTRONOMY

ASTROPHYSICAL JOURNAL. SUPPLEMENT SERIES. see ASTRONOMY

ASTROPHYSICAL LETTERS AND COMMUNICATIONS. see ASTRONOMY

ASTROPHYSICS. see ASTRONOMY

ASTROPHYSICS AND SPACE SCIENCE; an international journal of cosmic physics. see ASTRONOMY

ASTROPHYSICS AND SPACE SCIENCE LIBRARY; a series of books on the developments of space science and of general astronomy and astrophysics published in connection with the journal Space Science Reviews. see ASTRONOMY

ATELIERS. see CHILDREN AND YOUTH — For

AURORAL OBSERVATORY. MAGNETIC OBSERVATIONS. see ASTRONOMY

AUSTRALASIAN PHYSICAL & ENGINEERING SCIENCES IN MEDICINE. see MEDICAL SCIENCES — Experimental Medicine, Laboratory Technique

530   AT   ISSN 0004-9506
QC1   CODEN: AUJPAS
AUSTRALIAN JOURNAL OF PHYSICS. 1948. bi-m. Aus.$195($195) C.S.I.R.O., 314 Albert St., E. Melbourne, Vic. 3002, Australia. TEL 3-418-7333. FAX 3-419-4096. Ed. R.P. Robertson. adv.; bibl.; charts; illus.; index; circ. 750. (also avail. in microform from MIM,UMI,PMC; back issues avail.) Indexed: AESIS, Appl.Mech.Rev., Cadscan, Chem.Abstr., Comput.Rev., Curr.Cont., Eng.Ind., GeoRef., Ind.Sci.Rev., INIS Atomind., Lead Abstr., Mass Spectr.Bull., Math.R., Met.Abstr., Meteor.& Geoastrophys.Abstr., Phys.Abstr., Phys.Ber., Sci.Abstr., Sci.Cit.Ind., World Alum.Abstr., World Text.Abstr., Zincscan.
—BLDSC shelfmark: 1811.000000.
Description: Covers all aspects of physics ranging from elementary particles and fields to astronomy and astrophysics.

530   AT
AUSTRALIAN NATIONAL UNIVERSITY. RESEARCH SCHOOL OF PHYSICAL SCIENCES AND ENGINEERING. ANNUAL REPORT. 1972. a. Australian National University, Institute of Advanced Studies, G.P.O. Box 4, Canberra, A.C.T. 2601, Australia. FAX 62-491884. TELEX 107-19236. Ed. J.H. Carver. circ. 500.
Formerly: Australian National University. Research School of Physical Sciences. Annual Report (ISSN 0155-624X)

530   AT   ISSN 0084-7518
AUSTRALIAN NATIONAL UNIVERSITY, CANBERRA. RESEARCH SCHOOL OF PHYSICAL SCIENCES. RESEARCH PAPER. irreg. free to qualified personnel. Australian National University, Research School of Physical Sciences, G.P.O. Box 4, Canberra, A.C.T. 2601, Australia. Indexed: AESIS.

530   AT   ISSN 0004-9972
                           CODEN: AUPHBZ
AUSTRALIAN PHYSICIST. 1964. m. Aus.$44 (foreign Aus.$55). 41 Kemp St., The Junction, Newcastle N.S.W. 2291, Australia. TEL 049-613319. FAX 049-611844. adv.; bk.rev.; charts; illus.; circ. 3,000. Indexed: Aus.Educ.Ind., Aus.Sci.Ind., Chem.Abstr., INIS Atomind.
Description: Information on physics for the professional for research and teaching purposes.

B W K; Zeitschrift des Vereins Deutscher Ingenieure fuer Energietechnik und Energiewirtschaft. (Brennstoff-Waerme-Kraft) see ENERGY

BEAM MODIFICATION OF MATERIALS. see PHYSICS — Optics

BELGIUM. INSTITUT ROYAL METEOROLOGIQUE. OBSERVATIONS IONOSPHERIQUES ET DU RAYONNEMENT COSMIQUE. see METEOROLOGY

530   PL   ISSN 0137-5059
BIBLIOTEKA FIZYKI. 1974. irreg., vol.10, 1982. Panstwowe Wydawnictwo Naukowe, Ul. Miodowa 10, 00-251 Warsaw, Poland. (Dist. by: Ars Polona, Krakowskie Przedmiescie 7, 00-068 Warsaw, Poland)

BIOELECTROMAGNETICS SOCIETY NEWSLETTER. see BIOLOGY — Biophysics

538.36 574.192   US
BIOLOGICAL MAGNETIC RESONANCE. irreg., vol.10, 1992. price varies. Plenum Publishing Corp., 233 Spring St., New York, NY 10013-1578. TEL 212-620-8000. FAX 212-463-0742. TELEX 23-421139. Eds. L.J. Berliner, J. Reuben. (back issues avail.)
Refereed Serial

BIOMASS BULLETIN. see ENERGY

BIPOLAR CIRCUITS AND TECHNOLOGY MEETING. PROCEEDINGS. see ELECTRONICS

530   BU   ISSN 0323-9217
QC1   CODEN: BJPHD5
BULGARIAN JOURNAL OF PHYSICS/BOLGARSKII FIZICHESKII ZHURNAL. (Text in English; summaries in Russian) 1974. bi-m. 2.70 lv. per no. (Bulgarska Akademiia na Naukite) Publishing House of the Bulgarian Academy of Sciences, Acad. G. Bonchev St., Bldg. 6, 1113 Sofia, Bulgaria. (Dist. by: Hemus, 6, Rouski Blvd., 1000 Sofia, Bulgaria) Ed. A. Datseff. illus.; bibl.; charts; circ. 520. Indexed: BSL Math., Chem.Abstr, INIS Atomind., Int.Aerosp.Abstr., Math.R., Met.Abstr., Phys.Ber., Sci.Abstr., World Alum.Abstr.
Formed by the merger of: Bulgarska Akademiia na Naukite. Fizicheskii Institut. Izvestiia; Bulgarska Akademiia na Naukite. Institut po Elektronika. Izvestiia.

530   II   ISSN 0970-6569
BULLETIN OF PURE & APPLIED SCIENCES. SECTION D: PHYSICS. 1982. 2/yr. Rs.40($8) to individuals; institutions Rs.80($12). Dr. A.K. Sharma, Ed. & Pub., P.O. Box 38, Modinagar 201 204, India. adv.; bk.rev.; circ. 300.

530   JA   ISSN 0029-0181
BUTSURI. Variant title: Nihon Butsuri Gakkaishi. (Text in Japanese) 1946. m. 28000 Yen. Physical Society of Japan - Nihon Butsuri Gakkai, Rm. 211, Kikai Shinko Bldg., 3-5-8 Shiba Koen, Minato-ku, Tokyo 105, Japan. Ed. Y. Ichikawa. adv.; bk.rev.; abstr.; bibl.; charts; illus.; circ. 16,500. Indexed: GeoRef, JTA.
—BLDSC shelfmark: 2935.200000.
Description: Publishes original papers in all fields of physics.

C S I R O DIVISION OF MATERIALS SCIENCE & TECHNOLOGY REPORT. see CHEMISTRY — Inorganic Chemistry

530 510   UK
CAMBRIDGE MONOGRAPHS ON MATHEMATICAL PHYSICS. irreg., latest 1987. price varies. Cambridge University Press, Edinburgh Bldg., Shaftesbury Rd., Cambridge CB2 2RU, England. TEL 0223-312393. FAX 0223-315052. TELEX 851817256. Ed.Bd. Indexed: Math.R., Phys.Ber.

530   UK
CAMBRIDGE MONOGRAPHS ON PHYSICS. irreg. price varies. Cambridge University Press, Edinburgh Bldg., Shaftesbury Rd., Cambridge CB2 2RU, England. TEL 0223-312393. FAX 0223-315052. TELEX 851817256. Ed.Bd.

CAMBRIDGE PHILOSOPHICAL SOCIETY. MATHEMATICAL PROCEEDINGS. see MATHEMATICS

530   UK
CAMBRIDGE SOLID STATE SCIENCE SERIES. irreg. price varies. Cambridge University Press, Edinburgh Bldg., Shaftesbury Rd., Cambridge CB2 2RU, England. TEL 0223-312393. FAX 0223-315052. TELEX 851817256. Ed.Bd.

530   CN   ISSN 0008-4204
QC1   CODEN: CJPHAD
CANADIAN JOURNAL OF PHYSICS/JOURNAL CANADIEN DE PHYSIQUE. (Text mainly in English, occasionally in French) 1929. m. Can.$92($95) to individuals; institutions Can.$278 (effective 1992). National Research Council of Canada, Research Journals, Ottawa, Ont. K1A 0R6, Canada. TEL 613-993-9084. FAX 613-952-7656. Ed. D.D. Bettslls. adv.: B&W page Can.$550; trim 8 1/2 x 11; adv. contact: Hoda Jabbour. bibl.; illus.; index; circ. 1,550. (also avail. in microform from UMI,PMC; back issues avail.; reprint service avail. from UMI) Indexed: Abstr.Bull.Inst.Pap.Chem., Biol.Abstr., Bull.Signal., Bull.Thermodyn.& Thermochem., Cadscan, Chem.Abstr., Curr.Cont., Dairy Sci.Abstr., Deep Sea Res.& Oceanogr.Abstr., Eng.Ind., Ind.Sci.Rev., INIS Atomind., Int.Aerosp.Abstr., Lead Abstr., Mass Spectr.Bull., Math.R., Met.Abstr., Meteor.& Geoastrophys.Abstr., Nucl.Sci.Abstr., Nutr.Abstr., Petrol.Abstr., Phys.Abstr., Phys.Ber., RAPRA, Sci.Abstr., Sci.Cit.Ind., World Alum. Abstr., World Text.Abstr., Zincscan.
—BLDSC shelfmark: 3034.000000.
Refereed Serial

530   CS   ISSN 0009-0700
                           CODEN: CKCFAH
CESKOSLOVENSKY CASOPIS PRO FYZIKU. (Text and summaries in Czech or Slovak; summaries in English) 1951. bi-m. DM.241. (Czechoslovak Academy of Sciences, Institute of Physics) Academia, Publishing House of the Czechoslovak Academy of Sciences, Vodickova 40, 112 29 Prague 1, Czechoslovakia. TEL 815-27-11. (Dist. in Western countries by: Kubon & Sagner, P.O. Box 34 01 08, 8000 Munich 34, Germany) Ed. J. Dvorak. bk.rev.; charts; illus.; index; circ. 1,450. Indexed: Chem.Abstr., GeoRef., INIS Atomind., Math.R., Met.Abstr., Phys.Ber., Sci.Abstr.
Formerly (until 1971): Ceskoslovensky Casopis pro Fyziku. Sekce A.
Description: Contains review articles, theoretical papers, and short communications on experimental and applied physics. Also includes interviews with leading physicists.

530   US   ISSN 1054-1500
                           CODEN: CHAOEH
▼**CHAOS;** an interdisciplinary journal of nonlinear science. 1991. q. $160 (Canada $165; elsewhere $170). American Institute of Physics, 335 E. 45th St., New York, NY 10017-3483. TEL 212-661-9404. FAX 212-949-0473. (Subscr. to: Member and Subscriber Service, 500 Sunnyside Blvd., Woodbury, NY 11797-2999. TEL 516-576-2270) Ed. David K. Campbell.
—BLDSC shelfmark: 3129.715000.
Description: Features research articles, brief reports, and solicited technical reviews.
Refereed Serial

CHEMICAL PHYSICS; a journal devoted to the experimental and theoretical research involving problems of both a chemical and a physical nature. see CHEMISTRY — Physical Chemistry

PHYSICS

530 US ISSN 0069-3294
CHICAGO LECTURES IN PHYSICS. 1963. irreg., vol.7, 1984. price varies. University of Chicago Press, 5801 S. Ellis Ave., Chicago, IL 60637. TEL 312-702-7899. (reprint service avail. from UMI,ISI)
Refereed Serial

530 US ISSN 0273-429X
QC1 CODEN: CHPHD2
CHINESE PHYSICS; selected translations from current issues of major Chinese physics and astronomy journals. (Text in English) 1981. q. $850 (foreign $875). American Institute of Physics, 335 E. 45th St., New York, NY 10017. TEL 212-661-9404. (Subscr. to: Member and Subscriber Service, 500 Sunnyside Blvd., Woodbury, NY 11797-2999. TEL 516-576-2270) Ed. Georges Temmer. (also avail. in microform; back issues avail.) **Indexed:** Cadscan, Excerp.Med., Gen.Phys.Adv.Abstr., Ind.Sci.Rev., INIS Atomind., Int.Aerosp.Abstr., Lead Abstr., Math.R., Phys.Ber., Sci.Abstr., Sci.Cit.Ind., Zincscan.
—BLDSC shelfmark: 3181.048000.
Refereed Serial

530 US ISSN 0256-307X
CODEN: CPLEEU
CHINESE PHYSICS LETTERS/ZHONGGUO WULI KUAIBAO. 1984. m. $245. Allerton Press, Inc., 150 Fifth Ave., New York, NY 10011. TEL 212-924-3950. Ed. Huang Zujia. adv.; abstr.; bibl.; illus.; circ. 3,000. **Indexed:** INIS Atomind., Sci.Abstr.
Description: Provides information on work in progress in all areas of physics, particularly nuclear physics, fundamental areas of phenomenology, condensed matter physics, geophysics, astronomy and astrophysics.
Refereed Serial

530 UK ISSN 0264-9381
QC178 CODEN: CQGRDG
CLASSICAL AND QUANTUM GRAVITY. 1984. m. £490($980) (effective 1992). (Institute of Physics) I O P Publishing, Techno House, Redcliffe Way, Bristol BS1 6NX, England. TEL 0272-297481. FAX 0272-294318. TELEX 449149-INSTP-G. (U.S. addr.: American Institute of Physics, Member and Subscriber Services, 500 Sunnyside Blvd., Woodbury, NY 11797-2999. TEL 516-575-2270) Ed. K. Stelle. index. (also avail. in microfiche; microfilm; back issues avail.) **Indexed:** ASCA, Curr.Cont., Ind.Sci.Rev., INIS Atomind., Int.Aerosp.Abstr., Math.R., Phys.Abstr.
—BLDSC shelfmark: 3274.534200.
Description: Discusses the geometry of fluid theories, supergravity & cosmology.

CLINICAL PHYSICS AND PHYSIOLOGICAL MEASUREMENT. see *MEDICAL SCIENCES*

COLLOID JOURNAL OF THE U S S R. see *CHEMISTRY — Physical Chemistry*

530 510 FI ISSN 0788-5717
CODEN: CPHMAU
COMMENTATIONES PHYSICO-MATHEMATICAE ET CHEMICO-MEDICAE. (Text in English) 1924. irreg. price varies. Societas Scientiarum Fennica - Finnish Society of Sciences and Letters, Marieg 5, SF-00170 Helsinki, Finland. Ed. Erik Spring. charts; illus.; index; circ. 1,000. **Indexed:** Bull.Signal., Chem.Abstr., Curr.Cont., Deep Sea Res.& Oceanogr.Abstr., Ind.Sci.Rev., INIS Atomind., Phys.Ber., Ref.Zh., Sci.Abstr., Sci.Cit.Ind., Zent.Math.
Formerly: Commentationes Physico-Mathematicae (ISSN 0069-6609)

COMMENTS ON ASTROPHYSICS. see *ASTRONOMY*

530.41 US ISSN 0885-4483
CODEN: CCMPEB
COMMENTS ON CONDENSED MATTER PHYSICS. 1968. 12/yr. (in 2 vols., 6 nos./vol.) $144. Gordon and Breach Science Publishers, 270 Eighth Ave., New York, NY 10011. TEL 212-206-8900. FAX 212-645-2549. TELEX 236735 GOPUB UR. (Subscr. to: Box 786, Cooper Sta., New York, NY 10276. TEL 800-545-8398; UK subscr. to: P.O. Box 90, Reading, Berkshire RG1 8JL, England. TEL 0734-560-080) Ed. Douglas Mills. adv. (also avail. in microform from MIM) **Indexed:** Chem.Abstr., Mass Spectr.Bull., Met.Abstr., Phys.Ber., Sci.Abstr., World Alum.Abstr.
—BLDSC shelfmark: 3336.027500.
Formerly: Comments on Solid State Physics (ISSN 0308-1206)

COMMENTS ON PLASMA PHYSICS AND CONTROLLED FUSION. see *PHYSICS — Nuclear Physics*

530 510 GW ISSN 0010-3616
QC20 CODEN: CMPHAY
COMMUNICATIONS IN MATHEMATICAL PHYSICS. (Text in English, French or German) 1965. 24/yr. DM.4992($2887) (effective 1992). Springer-Verlag, Heidelberger Platz 3, D-1000 Berlin 33, Germany. TEL 030-8207-1. (Also Heidelberg, Tokyo, Vienna, and New York) Ed. A. Jaffe. adv.; bibl.; charts; illus.; index. (also avail. in microform from UMI; back issues avail.; reprint service avail. from ISI) **Indexed:** Compumath, Curr.Cont., Ind.Sci.Rev., INIS Atomind., Math.R., Phys.Ber., Sci.Abstr., Sci.Cit.Ind.
—BLDSC shelfmark: 3361.100000.
Description: Features physics papers with mathematical content. Covers a broad spectrum of topics, from classical to quantum physics.

530 CC ISSN 0253-6102
QC19.2 CODEN: CTPHDI
COMMUNICATIONS IN THEORETICAL PHYSICS/LILUN WULI. (Text in English) 1981. 8/yr (2/vols.). 436.50 Fr. per vol. (Academia Sinica, Institute of Theoretical Physics) International Academic Publishers (IAP), Xizhimenwai Dajie, Beijing Exhibition Centre, Beijing 100044, People's Republic of China. TEL 8316677. FAX 4015664. TELEX 22313 CPC CN. (Overseas dist. by: J.C. Baltzer AG, Scientific Publishing Company, Wettsteinplatz 10, CH-4058 Basel, Switzerland. TEL 61-6918925) Ed. Peng Huan-wu.
—BLDSC shelfmark: 3363.458000.
Description: Covers multifarious aspects of theoretical research in physics, such as atomic and molecular physics, condensed matter and statistical physics, plasma and fluid theory, nuclear theory, particle physics, and quantum field theory.
Refereed Serial

530 US
COMPUTATIONAL MICROELECTRONICS. 1986. irreg. price varies. Springer-Verlag, 175 Fifth Ave., New York, NY 10010. TEL 212-460-1500. (Also Berlin, Heidelberg, Tokyo, Vienna) (reprint service avail. from ISI)

530 548 US ISSN 0893-861X
QC173.4.C65 CODEN: CMTHEO
CONDENSED MATTER THEORIES. 1986. irreg., vol.5, 1990. price varies. Plenum Publishing Corp., 233 Spring St., New York, NY 10013-1578. TEL 212-620-8000. FAX 212-463-0742. TELEX 23-421139. Ed. F.B. Malik. (back issues avail.)
—BLDSC shelfmark: 3405.710000.
Description: Covers new theoretical developments in solid-state physics of condensed matter.
Refereed Serial

530 US ISSN 0272-2488
CONTEMPORARY CONCEPTS IN PHYSICS. 1981. irreg. Harwood Academic Publishers, 270 Eighth Ave., New York, NY 10011. (Subscr. to: Box 786, Cooper Sta., New York, NY 10276. TEL 800-545-8398; UK subscr. to: Box 90 Reading, Berkshire RG1 8JL, England. TEL 0734-560-080) Ed. Herman Feshbach. (microform) **Indexed:** Math.R.
—BLDSC shelfmark: 3425.177500.
Refereed Serial

530 UK ISSN 0010-7514
QC1 CODEN: CTPHAF
CONTEMPORARY PHYSICS. 1959. bi-m. £160($272) Taylor & Francis Ltd., Rankine Rd., Basingstoke, Hants. RG24 OPR, England. TEL 0256-840366. FAX 0256-479438. TELEX 858540. Ed. J.S. Dugdale. adv.; bk.rev.; bibl.; charts; illus.; index. (also avail. in microform from MIM) **Indexed:** Chem.Abstr., Curr.Cont., Excerp.Med., Gen.Sci.Ind., Ind.Sci.Rev., INIS Atomind., Int.Aerosp.Abstr., Mass Spectr.Bull., Met.Abstr., Phys.Ber., Sci.Abstr., Sci.Cit.Ind, World Alum.Abstr.
—BLDSC shelfmark: 3425.200000.
Description: Presents articles on important developments in physics that can be read and understood by anyone with an interest in and fundamental grasp of physics.
Refereed Serial

530 US
CONTEMPORARY PHYSICS. 1986. irreg. price varies. Springer-Verlag, 175 Fifth Ave., New York, NY 10010. TEL 212-460-1500. (Also Berlin, Heidelberg, Tokyo, Vienna) (reprint service avail. from ISI) **Indexed:** Gen.Sci.Ind.

530 US ISSN 1043-3996
CONTEMPORARY TOPICS IN PURE AND APPLIED CONDENSED MATTER SCIENCE. irreg., latest vol.1. Gordon and Breach Scientific Publishers, 270 Eighth Ave., New York, NY 10011. TEL 212-206-8900. FAX 212-645-2459. TELEX 236735 GOPUB UR. (Subscr. to: Box 786, Cooper Sta., New York, NY 10276. TEL 800-545-8398; UK subscr. to: P.O. Box 90, Reading, RG1 8JL, England. TEL 0734-560-080) Ed. R.R. Hasiguti.
—BLDSC shelfmark: 3425.314200.
Refereed Serial

530.44 GW ISSN 0863-1042
QC717.6 CODEN: CPPHEP
CONTRIBUTIONS TO PLASMA PHYSICS. (Text in English, French, German, Russian) 1961. bi-m. DM.226.60. Akademie-Verlag Berlin, Leipziger Str. 3-4, 1086 Berlin, Germany. TELEX 114420-AVERL-DD. Ed. J. Wilhelm. illus.; index. **Indexed:** ASCA, Chem.Abstr., Curr.Cont., Int.Aerosp.Abstr., Math.R., Phys.Ber., Sci.Abstr., Sci.Cit.Ind.
—BLDSC shelfmark: 3461.116000.
Formerly: Beitraege aus der Plasmaphysik (ISSN 0005-8025)

530 UK ISSN 0143-926X
COSMATOM. 1973. irreg., latest vol.7, 1979. £45 for 4 nos. P.O. Box 12, Worthing, Sussex BN14 7HB, England. Ed. Ian McCrimmon. bibl.; charts; circ. 1,000. **Indexed:** Chem.Abstr., Ref.Zh.

530.41 US ISSN 1040-8436
QC176.A1 CODEN: CCRSDA
CRITICAL REVIEWS IN SOLID STATE & MATERIALS SCIENCES. 1970. bi-m. $295. C R C Press, Inc., 2000 Corporate Blvd., N.W., Boca Raton, FL 33431. TEL 407-994-0555. FAX 407-998-9784. Ed. Dr. Joseph E. Greene. bibl.; charts; illus.; circ. 570. (back issues avail.) **Indexed:** Biol.Abstr., Chem.Abstr., Ind.Sci.Rev., INIS Atomind., Mass Spectr.Bull., Sci.Abstr., Sci.Cit.Ind.
—BLDSC shelfmark: 3487.482000.
Former titles: C R C Critical Reviews in Solid State and Materials Sciences (ISSN 0161-1593); C R C Critical Reviews in Solid State Sciences (ISSN 0011-085X)

CRYSTAL LATTICE DEFECTS AND AMORPHOUS MATERIALS. see *CHEMISTRY — Crystallography*

530 666 SZ
CRYSTAL PROPERTIES AND PREPARATION. 1982. 6/yr. 600 SFr. Trans Tech Publications, Hardstr. 13, P.O. Box 100, CH-4714 Aedermannsdorf, Switzerland. TEL 062-741379. FAX 011-62-741058. (back issues avail.) **Indexed:** Int.Aerosp.Abstr., Met.Abstr., World Alum.Abstr.
Former titles: Single Crystal Properties; Mechanical and Corrosion Properties. Series B. Single Crystal Properties (ISSN 0252-1067); Supersedes in part: Mechanical and Corrosion Properties (ISSN 0250-9784)

530 ISSN 0045-9348
CURRENT PHYSICS MICROFORM. 1972. m. American Institute of Physics, 335 E. 45th St., New York, NY 10017. TEL 212-661-9404. FAX 516-349-9704. (Subscr. to: Member and Subscriber Service, 500 Sunnyside Blvd., Woodbury, NY 11797-2999. TEL 516-576-2270) index, cum.index. (microfilm) **Indexed:** C.P.I.

530 UK ISSN 0732-4383
QC1
CURRENT TOPICS IN CHINESE SCIENCE. SECTION A: PHYSICS. 1982. irreg., vol.3, 1985. Gordon & Breach Science Publishers, P.O. Box 90, Reading, Berkshire RG1 8JL, England. TEL 0734-560-080. FAX 0734-568-211. TELEX 849870 SCIPUB G. (US addr.: Box 786, Cooper Sta., New York, NY 10276. TEL 800-545-8398) (also avail. in microfilm) **Indexed:** Biol.Abstr.
Refereed Serial

PHYSICS

530 NE ISSN 0165-1854
TA403 CODEN: CTMSD2
CURRENT TOPICS IN MATERIALS SCIENCE. 1977. irreg., vol.12, 1985. price varies. Elsevier Science Publishers B.V., Books Division, P.O. Box 211, 1006 AE Amsterdam, Netherlands. TEL 020-5803911. FAX 020-5803705. TELEX 18582 ESPA NL. (Subscr. in U.S. and Canada to: Elsevier Science Publishing Co., Inc., Box 882, Madison Sq. Sta., New York, NY 10159. TEL 212-989-5800) Ed. E. Kaldis. **Indexed:** Cadscan, Chem.Abstr., Lead Abstr., Zincscan.
Refereed Serial

530 US
CZECHOSLOVAK JOURNAL OF PHYSICS; europhysics journal. (Text in English, French, German; summaries in English) 1952. m. $615 (foreign $720)(effective 1992). (Czechoslovak Academy of Sciences, Institute of Physics, CS) Plenum Publishing Corp., 233 Spring St., New York, NY 10013-1578. TEL 212-620-8000. FAX 212-463-0742. TELEX 23-421139. (Co-publisher: Academia, CS) Ed. J. Kvasnica. abstr.; bibl.; charts; illus.; index; circ. 1,450. (back issues avail.) **Indexed:** Appl.Mech.Rev., Biol.Abstr., Cadscan, Chem.Abstr., Curr.Cont., Ind.Sci.Rev., INIS Atomind., Int.Aerosp.Abstr., Lead Abstr., Math.R., Met.Abstr., Phys.Ber., Ref.Zh., Sci.Abstr., Sci.Cit.Ind., World Alum.Abstr., Zincscan.
Formerly (until 1971): Czechoslovak Journal of Physics. Section B (ISSN 0011-4626)
Description: Publishes original research contributions in all branches of physics.
Refereed Serial

530 540 US
DAHLEM WORKSHOP REPORTS. PHYSICAL AND CHEMICAL SCIENCES RESEARCH REPORT. irreg. price varies. Springer-Verlag, 175 Fifth Ave., New York, NY 10010. TEL 212-460-1500. (Also Berlin, Heidelberg, Tokyo and Vienna)

530 DK ISSN 0105-0907
DANMARKS TEKNISKE HOEJSKOLE. FYSISK LABORATORIUM 1. REPORT. No. 247, 1982. irreg. Danmarks Tekniske Hoejskole, Fysisk Laboratorium I, Lundtoftvej 100, Bygn. 309, 2800 Lyngby, Denmark. illus.; circ. 100.

DEFECTS IN SOLIDS. see *CHEMISTRY — Crystallography*

DELFT PROGRESS REPORT. see *CHEMISTRY*

DELTA (WARSAW); matematyczno-fizyczny miesiecznik popularny. see *MATHEMATICS*

530 DK
DENMARK. RISOE NATIONAL LABORATORY. PHYSICS DEPARTMENT. ANNUAL PROGRESS REPORT. 1970. a. DKK 48.80. Risoe National Laboratory, Box 49, DK-4000 Roskilde, Denmark. FAX 45-46-75-56-27. TELEX 43 116. (Subscr. to: G.E.C. Gad, Vimmelskaftet 32, DK-1161 Copenhagen K, Denmark)
Formerly: Denmark. Forsoeganslaeg Risoe. Fysikafdelingen. Annual Progress Report (ISSN 0107-8348)

530 GW ISSN 0420-0195
DEUTSCHE PHYSIKALISCHE GESELLSCHAFT. VERHANDLUNGEN. (Text and summaries in English and German) 1966. irreg. (4-8/yr.). membership. (Deutsche Physikalische Gesellschaft) Physik-Verlag GmbH, Postfach 1260-1280, D-6940 Weinheim, Germany. TEL 06201-602-0. FAX 06201-602-328. (U.S. addr.: V C H Publishers, Inc., 220 E. 23rd St., New York, NY 10010-4606) Ed. U. Poerschke. adv.; circ. controlled.
—BLDSC shelfmark: 9163.360000.

530 621.3 US
DEVELOPMENTS IN NANOTECHNOLOGY. irreg. Gordon and Breach Scientific Publishers, 270 Eighth Ave., New York, NY 10011. TEL 212-206-8900. FAX 212-645-2459. TELEX 236735 GOPUB UR. (Subscr. to: Box 786, Cooper Sta., New York, NY 10276. TEL 800-545-8398; UK subscr. to: P.O. Box 90, Reading, Berkshire RG1 8JL, England. TEL 0734-056-080) Ed. D. Bowen.
Refereed Serial

DIMENSIO. see *MATHEMATICS*

530 SI
▼**DIRECTIONS IN CHAOS.** (Text in English) 1990. irreg., vol. 5, 1991. price varies. World Scientific Publishing Co. Pte. Ltd., Farrer Rd., P.O. Box 128, Singapore 9128, Singapore. TEL 3825663. FAX 3825919. TELEX RS 28561 WSPC. (UK addr.: 73 Lynton Mead, Totteridge, London N20 8DH, England. TEL 44-81-4462461; US addr.: 1060 Main St., Ste. 1B, River Edge, NJ 07661. TEL 800-227-7562)

DIRECTORY OF PHYSICS & ASTRONOMY STAFF (YEAR). see *EDUCATION — Higher Education*

530 548 NE
DISLOCATIONS IN SOLIDS. 1978. irreg., vol.8, 1989. price varies. Elsevier Science Publishers B.V., Books Division, P.O. Box 211, 1000 AE Amsterdam, Netherlands. TEL 020-5803911. FAX 020-5803705. TELEX 18582 ESPA NL. (Subscr. in U.S. and Canada to: Elsevier Science Publishing Co., Inc., Box 882, Madison Sq. Sta., New York, NY 10159. TEL 212-989-5800) Ed. F.R.N. Nabarro.
Refereed Serial

530 TU ISSN 1010-7630
DOGA TURKISH JOURNAL OF PHYSICS/DOGA TURK FIZIK DERGISI. (Text in English, Turkish) 4/yr. $20. Scientific and Technical Research Council of Turkey - Turkiye Bilimsel ve Teknik Arastirma Kurumu, Ataturk Bulvari, No. 221, Kavaklidere, 06100 Ankara, Turkey. TEL 1673657. FAX 1277489. TELEX 43186 BTAK TR. Ed. Cengiz Yalcin.
—BLDSC shelfmark: 3614.642525.
Formerly: Doga Turkish Journal of Physics and Astrophysics; Supersedes in part (in 1986): Doga Bilim Dergisi. Serie A: Basic Sciences.

DOMINION ASTROPHYSICAL OBSERVATORY, VICTORIA. PUBLICATIONS. see *ASTRONOMY*

530 IE ISSN 0070-7414
CODEN: CDIAAH
DUBLIN INSTITUTE FOR ADVANCED STUDIES. COMMUNICATIONS. SERIES A. 1943. irreg., no.28, 1984. price varies. Dublin Institute for Advanced Studies, 10 Burlington Rd., Dublin 4, Ireland. TEL 680748. FAX 680561. **Indexed:** Deep Sea Res.& Oceanogr.Abstr., Math.R., Phys.Ber., Sci.Abstr.
—BLDSC shelfmark: 3348.000000.

DYES AND PIGMENTS. see *CHEMISTRY*

ECLETICA QUIMICA; serie quimica. see *CHEMISTRY*

639.2 ER
EEST TEADUSTE AKADEEMIA. TOIMETISED. FUUSIKA. MATEMAATIKA/ESTONIAN ACADEMY OF SCIENCES. PROCEEDINGS. PHYSICS. MATHEMATICS. (Text and summaries in English, Estonian, Russian) 1956. q. $25 (effective 1992). Kirjastus Perioodika, Parnu mnt. 8, pk.107, 200090 Tallinn, Estonia. (Subscr. to: Akateeminen Kirjakauppa 128 SF, 00101 Helsinki, Finland; or to: Bibliotekstjanst AB 200, S22100 Lund, Sweden) Ed.Bd. charts; illus.; index; circ. 500. **Indexed:** Chem.Abstr., GeoRef., INIS Atomind., Met.Abstr., World Alum.Abstr.
Formerly: Akademiya Nauk Estonskoi S.S.R. Izvestiya. Fizika. Matematika (ISSN 0367-1429)

530 UA ISSN 1110-0214
EGYPTIAN JOURNAL OF PHYSICS. (Text in English; summaries in English and Arabic) 1970. s-a. $30. (Egyptian Physical Society, Research Department) National Information and Documentation Centre (NIDOC), Tahrir St., Dokki, Awqaf P.O., Cairo, Egypt. Ed. M. El-Nady. abstr.; charts; circ. 1,000. **Indexed:** Chem.Abstr, Mass Spectr.Bull., Phys.Ber.

ELEKTRONENMIKROSKOPIE. see *BIOLOGY — Microscopy*

530.44 LI
ELEKTRONY V POLUPROVODNIKAKH/ELECTRONS IN SEMICONDUCTORS. (Text in Russian; summaries in English and Lithuanian) 1978. irreg. price varies. (Lithuanian Academy of Sciences, Institute of Semiconductor Physics) Leidykla Mokslas, Zvaigzdziu 23, Vilnius 2050, Lithuania. TEL 45-85-26. TELEX 261107 LMOKSU. Ed. Y. Pozela. circ. 2,000.
Description: The physics of hot electrons and plasma phenomena in semiconductors.

ENCYCLOPEDIA OF PHYSICAL SCIENCE & TECHNOLOGY YEARBOOK. see *SCIENCES: COMPREHENSIVE WORKS*

ENERGY SOURCES; an international interdisciplinary journal of science and technology. see *ENERGY*

ENERGY SYSTEMS AND POLICY; an international interdisciplinary journal. see *ENERGY*

ENERGY TODAY. see *ENERGY*

530 NE
ENRICO FERMI INTERNATIONAL SUMMER SCHOOL OF PHYSICS. 1976. irreg., vol.112, 1992. price varies. Elsevier Science Publishers B.V., Books Division, P.O. Box 211, 1000 AE Amsterdam, Netherlands. TEL 020-5803911. FAX 020-5803705. TELEX 18582 ESPA NL. (Subscr. in U.S. and Canada to: Elsevier Science Publishing Co., Inc., Box 882, Madison Sq. Sta., New York, NY 10159. TEL 212-989-5800) (back issues avail.; reprint service avail. from ISI)
Refereed Serial

530 541.3 US ISSN 0013-8533
ENSANIAN PHYSICOCHEMICAL INSTITUTE. JOURNAL. 1969. q. membership. Ensanian Physicochemical Institute, Box 98, Eldred, PA 16731. TEL 814-225-3296. Ed. Minas Ensanian. bk.rev.; abstr.; bibl.; charts; illus.; pat.; index, cum.index; circ. 250. (processed)

530 DK ISSN 0106-407X
ENVIRONMENTAL RADIOACTIVITY IN DENMARK. 1961. a. DKK 61. Risoe National Laboratory, Box 49, DK-4000 Roskilde, Denmark. (Subscr. to: G.E.C. Gad, Vimmelskaftet 32, DK-1161 Copenhagen K, Denmark) illus.
Formerly: Environmental Radioactivity at Risoe.

530 DK ISSN 0108-0962
ENVIRONMENTAL RADIOACTIVITY IN GREENLAND. 1962. a. DKK 48.80. G.E.C. GAD, Dansk og Udenlandsk Boghandel Aktieselskab, Vimmelskaftet 32, 1161 Copenhagen K, Denmark. illus.

530 DK ISSN 0107-9069
ENVIRONMENTAL RADIOACTIVITY IN THE FAROES. 1962. a. DKK 48.80. G.E.C. GAD, Dansk og Udenlandsk Boghandel Aktieselskab, Vimmelskaftet 32, 1161 Copenhagen K, Denmark.

530 UK ISSN 0143-0807
QC1 CODEN: EJPHD4
EUROPEAN JOURNAL OF PHYSICS. 1980. 6/yr. £128($256) (effective 1992). (Institute of Physics) I O P Publishing, Techno House, Redcliffe Way, Bristol BS1 6NX, England. TEL 0272 297481. FAX 0272-294318. (U.S. addr.: American Institute of Physics, Member and Subscriber Service, 500 Sunnyside Blvd., Woodbury, NY 11797-2999. TEL 516-576-2270) (Co-sponsor: European Physical Society) Ed. B. Pippard. bk.rev.; bibl.; illus.; charts; index. (also avail. in microfiche; microfilm; back issues avail.) **Indexed:** Chem.Abstr., INIS Atomind., Math.R., Phys.Ber., Sci.Abstr.
—BLDSC shelfmark: 3829.735000.
Description: Educational and scholarly studies in physics and closely related sciences at the university level.

530 FR
EUROPHYSICS LETTERS. (Text and summaries in English, French, German, Russian) 1986. s-m. 1230 F. Editions de Physique, Zone Industrielle de Courtaboeuf, B.P. 112, 91944 Les Ulis Cedex, France. TEL 69-07-36-88. FAX 69-28-84-91. TELEX 602 321 F. Ed. W. Buckel. circ. 1,500. (back issues avail.) **Indexed:** INIS Atomind.
Description: New ideas, experimental methods, theoretical treatments and results of interest to the physics community.

530 SZ ISSN 0531-7479
CODEN: EUPNAS
EUROPHYSICS NEWS. 1969. m. 90 SFr. includes three meeting issues. European Physical Society, Box 69, CH-1213 Petit Lancy 2, Switzerland. Ed. E.N. Shaw. adv.; circ. 10,500. **Indexed:** INIS Atomind., Sci.Abstr.
—BLDSC shelfmark: 3830.420000.
Formerly: Europhysics Review.

PHYSICS

530   GW   ISSN 0014-4924
                 CODEN: EXPPAL
EXPERIMENTELLE TECHNIK DER PHYSIK/EXPERIMENTAL TECHNIQUE OF PHYSICS; zeitschrift fuer die gesamte theoretische und experimentelle physikalische Grundlagenforschung zur naturwissenschaftlichen und technischen Nutzung. 1953. bi-m. DM.130.20. VEB Deutscher Verlag der Wissenschaften, Johannes-Dieckmann-Str. 10, 1080 Berlin, Germany. Ed.Bd. adv.; bk.rev.; charts; illus.; index. **Indexed:** Appl.Mech.Rev., Chem.Abstr., INIS Atomind., Met.Abstr., Sci.Abstr.
—BLDSC shelfmark: 3841.000000.

EXPLORATORIUM QUARTERLY. see *SCIENCES: COMPREHENSIVE WORKS*

F & S. (Filtrieren und Separien) see *CHEMISTRY*

530   US   ISSN 0015-0193
QC595   CODEN: FEROA8
FERROELECTRICS. 56/yr. (in 14 vols., 4 nos./vol.). $298 includes Integrated Ferroelectrics (effective 1992). Gordon and Breach Science Publishers, 270 Eighth Ave., New York, NY 10011. TEL 212-206-8900. FAX 212-645-2459. TELEX 236735 GOPUB UR. (Subscr. to: Box 786, Cooper Sta., New York, NY 10276. TEL 800-545-8398; UK subscr. to: P.O. Box 90, Reading, Berkshire RG1 8JL, England. TEL 0734-560-080) Ed. George W. Taylor. adv.; bk.rev.; index. (also avail. in microform from MIM) **Indexed:** Cadscan, Chem.Abstr., Curr.Cont., Eng.Ind., Ind.Sci.Rev., Lead Abstr., Met.Abstr., Phys.Ber., Sci.Abstr., Sci.Cit.Ind., World Alum.Abstr., Zincscan.
—BLDSC shelfmark: 3908.400000.
Refereed Serial

530   AU   ISSN 0177-7963
QC1   CODEN: FBSYEQ
FEW-BODY SYSTEMS. ACTA PHYSICA AUSTRIACA. NEW SERIES. 1947. 8/yr. (in 2 vols., 4 nos./vol.). DM.716($434) (effective 1992). Springer-Verlag, Sachsenplatz 4-6, Postfach 89, A-1201 Vienna, Austria. TEL 212-460-1500. (Also Berlin, Heidelberg, Tokyo and New York) Eds. H. Mitter, W. Plessas. adv.; bk.rev.; charts; illus.; index. (also avail. in microform from UMI; reprint service avail. from ISI) **Indexed:** ASCA, Cadscan, Chem.Abstr., Curr.Cont., Ind.Sci.Rev., INIS Atomind., Lead Abstr., Math.R., Met.Abstr., Phys.Ber., Sci.Abstr., Sci.Cit.Ind., Zincscan.
Formerly: Acta Physica Austriaca (ISSN 0001-6713)

530   RU
FILOSOFIYA I FIZIKA. 1972. 0.75 Rub. Voronezhskii Gosudarstvennyi Universitet, Universitetskaya Ploshchad, 1, Voronezh, Russia.

530.15   AG   ISSN 0326-7512
FISICA. 1985. 2/yr. $4 per no.(effective Dec. 1991). Zagier & Urruty Publicaciones, P.O. Box 94, Sucursal 19, 1419 Buenos Aires, Argentina. TEL 541-572-1050. FAX 541-572-5766. (U.S. addr.: Box 526806, Miami, FL 33152-6806) Ed. Sergio Zagier. adv.: B&W page $400. bk.rev.; circ. 1,500.
Description: Includes articles on history, philosophy, tools and more.

530   CI   ISSN 0015-3206
QC1   CODEN: FZKAAA
FIZIKA; a journal of experimental and theoretical physics. (Supplements accompany each issue) (Text in English) 1969. q. $50. Jugoslovensko Udruzenje Matematickih i Fizickih Drustava, Komisija za Fiziku, Bijenicka C. 54, 41000 Zagreb, Croatia. FAX 38-41-425-497. Ed.Bd. circ. 700. **Indexed:** Chem.Abstr., Int.Aerosp.Abstr., Phys.Ber., Sci.Abstr.
—BLDSC shelfmark: 3949.100000.
Description: Publishes results of original experimental or theoretical research work.

530   KR   ISSN 0206-3638
FIZIKA MNOGOCHASTICHNYKH SISTEM; respublikanskii mezhvedomstvennyi sbornik nauchnykh trudov. 1975. s-a. (Akademiya Nauk Ukrainskoi S.S.R., Institut Teoreticheskoi Fiziki) Izdatel'stvo Naukova Dumka, c/o Yu.A. Khramov, Dir, Ul. Repina, 3, Kiev 252 601, Ukraine. (Subscr. to: Mezhdunarodnaya Kniga, Moscow, G-200, Russia) Ed. A.S. Dawydov. **Indexed:** Chem.Abstr.
—BLDSC shelfmark: 0389.826000.
Formerly (until 1982): Fizika Molekul (ISSN 0131-176X)

530.44   RU   ISSN 0367-2921
FIZIKA PLAZMY. English translation: Soviet Journal of Plasma Physics (US ISSN 0360-0343) 1975. m. 57.90 Rub. (Akademiya Nauk S.S.S.R) Izdatel'stvo Nauka, Fizmatlit, Leninskii prospekt, 15, 117071 Moscow, Russia. TEL 234-05-84. (Dist. by: Mezhdunarodnaya Kniga, ul. Dimitrova D.39, 113095 Moscow, Russia) Ed. M.S. Rabinovich. illus. **Indexed:** Chem.Abstr., INIS Atomind., Sci.Abstr.

530   RU   ISSN 0015-3249
FIZIKA TVERDOGO TELA. English translation: Soviet Physics - Solid State (US ISSN 0038-5654) 1959. m. 110.40 Rub. (Akademiya Nauk S.S.S.R.) Izdatel'stvo Nauka, Fizmatlit, Leninskii prospekt, 15, 117071 Moscow, V-71, Russia. Ed. S.N. Zhurkov. charts; illus.; index. (tabloid format) **Indexed:** Cadscan, Ceram.Abstr., Chem.Abstr., Curr.Cont., Ind.Sci.Rev., INIS Atomind., Lead Abstr., Met.Abstr., Sci.Abstr., Sci.Cit.Ind., World Alum.Abstr., Zincscan.

530   HU   ISSN 0015-3257
                 CODEN: FISZA6
FIZIKAI SZEMLE. 1891. m. $35.50. (Eotvos Lorand Fizikai Tarsulat) Lapkiado Vallalat, Lenin korut 9-11, 1073 Budapest 7, Hungary. (Subscr. to: Kultura, Box 149, H-1389 Budapest, Hungary) Ed. Gy. Marx. charts; index. **Indexed:** Chem.Abstr, INIS Atomind., Risk Abstr., Sci.Abstr.

530 510   BU   ISSN 0015-3265
FIZIKO-MATEMATICHESKO SPISANIE. (Contents page in English and Russian) 1959? q. 5.70 lv.($7) (Bulgarska Akademiia na Naukite, Fizicheski i Matematicheski Institut) Publishing House of the Bulgarian Academy of Sciences, Acad. G. Bonchev St., Bldg. 6, 1113 Sofia, Bulgaria. (Dist. by: Hemus, 6, Rouski Blvd., 1000 Sofia, Bulgaria) Ed. L. Iliev. bk.rev.; bibl.; illus.; index, cum.index: vols.1-10, 1968; circ. 780. **Indexed:** Chem.Abstr., Math.R., Ref.Zh.
—BLDSC shelfmark: 0389.970000.

530   PL   ISSN 0554-825X
FIZYKA. 1961. irreg., no.59, 1988. price varies. Adam Mickiewicz University Press, Nowowiejskiego 55, 61-734 Poznan, Poland. TEL 527-380. FAX 61-525425. TELEX 412360 UAMPL.
Formerly: Uniwersytet im. Adama Mickiewicza w Poznaniu. Wydzial Matematyki, Fizyki i Chemii. Seria Fizyka.
Description: Contains current physics research results, Ph.D. theses, and monographs of the university's scholars. Each volume contains the work of one author.

530   PL   ISSN 0426-3383
FIZYKA W SZKOLE. 1955. bi-m. $12. (Ministerstwo Edukacji Narodowej) Wydawnictwa Szkolne i Pedagogiczne, Pl. Dabrowskiego 8, 00-950 Warsaw, Poland. TEL 48 22 26-98-71. (Dist. by: Ars Polona-Ruch. Krakowskie Przedmiescie 7, Warsaw, Poland) circ. 13,500.
Description: Publishes articles on the theory and practice of teaching physics and astronomy, with discussions of school syllabi and research methodology in physics. Provides information on the latest developments in modern physics, astrophysics and technology, and presents new concepts in teaching physics.

530   CS
FOLIA FACULTATIS SCIENTIARUM NATURALIUM UNIVERSITATIS MASARYKIANAE BRUNENSIS: PHYSICA. vol.14, 1973. irreg. (1-2/yr.). price varies. Masarykova Universita, Prirodovedecka Fakulta - Masaryk University, Faculty of Sciences, Kotlarska 2, 611 37 Brno, Czechoslovakia. **Indexed:** Sci.Abstr.
Formerly: Folia Facultatis Scientiarum Naturalium Universitatis Purkynianae Brunensis: Physica (ISSN 0323-0287)

530   FR   ISSN 0182-4295
                 CODEN: AFLBDU
FONDATION LOUIS DE BROGLIE. ANNALES. (Text and summaries in English, French) 1975. q. 400 F. to individuals (foreign 500 F.); institutions 500 F. (foreign 600 F.). Fondation Louis de Broglie, 23 Quai de Conti, 75006 Paris, France. Eds. C. Cormier-Delanoue, D. Fargue. bk.rev.; circ. 800. (back issues avail.) **Indexed:** INIS Atomind., Phys.Abstr., Sci.Abstr.
Description: Journal of theoretical physics, primarily intended for the publication of lectures given at the foundation's seminars. Also presents articles on wave mechanics, the foundation of microphysics, wave and quantum mechanics.

530   GW   ISSN 0015-8208
QC1   CODEN: FPYKA6
FORTSCHRITTE DER PHYSIK/PROGRESS OF PHYSICS. (Text in English) 1953. m. $356.40. (Physikalische Gesellschaft der DDR) Akademie-Verlag Berlin, Leipziger Str. 3-4, Postfach 1233, 1086 Berlin, Germany. TEL 2236229. (Subscr. to: Kunst und Wissen, Erich Bieber GmbH, General Wille-Str. 4, CH-8002 Zurich, Switzerland) Ed. F. Kaschluhn. adv.; repository. illus.; index. (also avail. in microfilm from BHP) **Indexed:** Chem.Abstr., Curr.Cont., Ind.Sci.Rev., INIS Atomind., Math.R., Met.Abstr., Phys.Ber., Sci.Abstr., Sci.Cit.Ind.
—BLDSC shelfmark: 6873.458200.

530   US   ISSN 0015-9018
QC1   CODEN: FNDPA4
FOUNDATIONS OF PHYSICS; an international journal devoted to the conceptual and fundamental theories of modern physics, biophysics, and cosmology. 1970. m. $675 (foreign $790)(effective 1992). Plenum Publishing Corp., 233 Spring St., New York, NY 10013-1578. TEL 212-620-8000. FAX 212-463-0742. TELEX 23-421139. Ed. Alwyn van der Merwe. adv. (also avail. in microfilm from JSC) **Indexed:** Cadscan, Curr.Cont., Ind.Sci.Rev., INIS Atomind., Lead Abstr., Math.R., Phys.Ber., Ref.Zh., Sci.Abstr., Sci.Cit.Ind., Zincscan.
—BLDSC shelfmark: 4025.400000.
Refereed Serial

530   US   ISSN 0894-9875
QC1   CODEN: FPLEET
FOUNDATIONS OF PHYSICS LETTERS. 1988. bi-m. $205 (foreign $240)(effective 1992). Plenum Publishing Corp., 233 Spring St., New York, NY 10013-1578. TEL 212-620-8000. FAX 212-463-0742. TELEX 23-421139. Ed. Alwyn van der Merwe. adv. (also avail. in microfilm from JSC; back issues avail.)
—BLDSC shelfmark: 4025.405000.
Refereed Serial

530   NO   ISSN 0015-9247
                 CODEN: FYVDAX
FRA FYSIKKENS VERDEN. 1939. q. NOK 90. Universitetet i Oslo - Fysisk Institut, P.O. Box 1048 Blindern, N-0316 Oslo 3, Norway. FAX 2-856422. Eds. D. Holter, F. Ingebretsen. adv.; bk.rev.; charts; illus.; index; circ. 1,400. **Indexed:** Chem.Abstr., INIS Atomind., Sci.Abstr.
—BLDSC shelfmark: 4029.950000.

530   FR
FRANCE. MINISTERE DE L'INDUSTRIE ET DE LA RECHERCHE. REPERTOIRE NATIONAL DES LABORATOIRES; LA RECHERCHE UNIVERSITAIRE. TOME 1: SCIENCES DE LA MATIERE. 1964. irreg., latest 1989. 208.53 F. Documentation Francaise, 29-31 Quai Voltaire, 75340 Paris 07, France. TEL 1-40-15-70-00.
Formerly: France. Delegation Generale a la Recherche Scientifique et Technique. Repertoire National des Laboratoires; la Recherche Universitaire; Sciences Exactes et Naturelles. Tome 1: Physique (ISSN 0071-8572)

530   US   ISSN 0429-7725
                 CODEN: FRPHAY
FRONTIERS IN PHYSICS. 1961. irreg., no.79, 1989. price varies. Benjamin-Cummings Publishing Co., Inc. (Subsidiary of: Addison-Wesley Publishing Co.), 1 Jacob Way, Reading, MA 01867. TELEX 94-9416. Ed. Richard W. Mixter. **Indexed:** Math.R.

530   NE
FUNDAMENTAL THEORIES OF PHYSICS; an international series of monographs on the fundamental theories of physics: their clarification, development and application. 1982. irreg., vol.40, 1990. price varies. Kluwer Academic Publishers, Spuiboulevard 50, P.O. Box 17, 3300 AA Dordrecht, Netherlands. TEL 078-334911. FAX 078-334254. TELEX 29245. (Dist. by: Kluwer Academic Publishers Group, P.O. Box 322, 3300 AH Dordrecht; U.S. address: Box 358, Accord Sta., Hingham, MA 02018-0358. TEL 617-871-6600) Ed. Alwyn van der Merwe.

FUNDAMENTALS OF COSMIC PHYSICS. see *ASTRONOMY*

530   DK   ISSN 0109-6664
FYSIKTIPS. 1976. irreg. DKK 31.70. Danmarks Fysik og Kemilaererforening, Dyrlaege Jurgensens Gade 11, 3740 Svaneke, Denmark. TEL 01-603540. illus.
Formerly: Gode Gamle Fysiktips.

530   DK   ISSN 0016-3392
QC1   CODEN: FYTIA4
FYSISK TIDSSKRIFT. 1902. 4/yr. DKK 183. G.E.C. GAD, Dansk og Udenlandsk Boghandel Aktieselskab, Vimmelskaftet 32, 1161 Copenhagen K, Denmark. Ed.Bd. adv.; bk.rev.; cum.index: vols.1-75; circ. 800. **Indexed:** Chem.Abstr., INIS Atomind., Sci.Abstr.
—BLDSC shelfmark: 4062.000000.

530   FR   ISSN 0761-3369
G A P H Y O R. BASE DE DONNEES. (Gaz - Physique - Orsay) 1978. q. 1050 F. Centre National de la Recherche Scientifique, Institut de l'Information Scientifique et Technique, B.P. 54, 54514 Vandoeuvre-Les-Nancy Cedex, France. TEL 83-50-46-00. (Co-sponsor: Laboratoire de Physique des Gaz et des Plasmas) Ed. J.L. Delcroix. ●Also available online.
   Former titles: Bulletin Signaletique. Part 166: G A P H Y O R. Base de Donnees; Bulletin Signaletique. Part 166: G A P H Y O R. Atomes, Molecules, Gaz Neutres Et Ionises. (ISSN 0399-1571)

530   US   ISSN 1047-4811
                    CODEN: GAELEN
▼**GALILEAN ELECTRODYNAMICS.** 1990. bi-m. $25 to individuals; corporations $50; organizations $100. Petr Beckmann, Ed. & Pub., Box 251, Boulder, CO 80306. FAX 303-444-0997. bk.rev.; circ. 570.
—BLDSC shelfmark: 4067.445000.

GAUSS - GESELLSCHAFT. MITTEILUNGEN. see *ASTRONOMY*

530   US   ISSN 0001-7701
QC173.6   CODEN: GRGVA8
GENERAL RELATIVITY AND GRAVITATION. 1970. m. $545 (foreign $640)(effective 1992). (International Committee on General Relativity and Gravitation) Plenum Publishing Corp., 233 Spring St., New York, NY 10013-1578. TEL 212-620-8000. FAX 212-463-0742. TELEX 23-421139. Ed. A. Held. adv.; bk.rev.; charts. (also avail. in microfilm from JSC; back isues avail.) **Indexed:** Curr.Cont., Ind.Sci.Rev., Int.Aerosp.Abstr., Math.R., Phys.Ber., Ref.Zh., Sci.Abstr., Sci.Cit.Ind., Zent.Math.
—BLDSC shelfmark: 4109.650000.
   Refereed Serial

530   IT   ISSN 0017-0283
GIORNALE DI FISICA. 1956. q. $45 to non-members; members $40. (Societa Italiana di Fisica) Editrice Compositori s.r.l., Via Stalingrado 97-2, 40128 Bologna, Italy. TEL 51-327811. Ed. Carlo Castagnoli. circ. 1,500. (tabloid format) **Indexed:** Chem.Abstr.

GRADUATE PROGRAMS: PHYSICS, ASTRONOMY, AND RELATED FIELDS (YEAR). see *EDUCATION — Higher Education*

530   US
GRADUATE TEXTS IN CONTEMPORARY PHYSICS. 1986. irreg. price varies. Springer-Verlag, 175 Fifth Ave., New York, NY 10010. TEL 212-460-1500. (Also Berlin, Heidelberg, Tokyo, Vienna) (reprint service avail. from ISI)

530 624   GW
H E R A - BULLETIN. (Text in English, German) 1984. irreg. (3-4/yr.). free. D E S Y, Notkestr. 85, 2000 Hamburg 52, Germany. FAX 089-983282. TELEX 215124-DESY-D. Ed.Bd. circ. 3,500. **Indexed:** INIS Atomind.

538.3   JA
HANDAI KYOJIBA/OSAKA UNIVERSITY. FACULTY OF SCIENCE. REPORT ON RESEARCH AND DEVELOPMENT IN HIGH MAGNETIC FIELD LABORATORY. (Text in Japanese) 1978. 2/yr. Osaka Daigaku, Rigakubu Fuzoku Chokyojiba Jikken Shisetsu - Osaka University, Faculty of Science, High Magnetic Field Laboratory, 1-1, Machikaneyama-cho, Toyonaka-shi, Osaka-fu 560, Japan.
   Description: Contains original papers, reviews, commentary, and news.

530.44   NE
HANDBOOK OF PLASMA PHYSICS. 1983. irreg., vol.3, 1991. Elsevier Science Publishers B.V., Books Division, P.O. Box 211, 1000 AE Amsterdam, Netherlands. TEL 020-5803911. FAX 020-5803705. TELEX 18582 ESPA NL. (Subscr. in U.S. and Canada to: Elsevier Science Publishing Co., Inc., Box 882, Madison Sq. Sta., New York, NY 10159. TEL 212-989-5800) Eds. M.N. Rosenbluth, R.Z. Sagdeer.
   Refereed Serial

HANDBOOK ON FERROMAGNETIC MATERIALS. see *METALLURGY*

530 540   NE
HANDBOOK ON THE PHYSICS AND CHEMISTRY OF RARE EARTHS. 1978. irreg., vol.15, 1991. price varies. Elsevier Science Publishers B.V., Books Division, P.O. Box 211, 1000 AE Amsterdam, Netherlands. TEL 020-5803911. FAX 020-5803705. TELEX 18582 ESPA NL. (Subscr. in U.S. and Canada to: Elsevier Science Publishing CO., Inc., Box 882, Madison Sq. Sta., New York, NY 10159. TEL 212-989-5800) Eds. K.A. Gschneidner, L. Eyring.
   Refereed Serial

530 540   NE
HANDBOOK ON THE PHYSICS AND CHEMISTRY OF THE ACTINIDES. 1984. irreg., vol.6, 1991. price varies. Elsevier Science Publishers B.V., Books Division, P.O. Box 211, 1000 AE Amsterdam, Netherlands. TEL 020-5803911. FAX 020-5803705. TELEX 18582 ESPA NL. (Subscr. in U.S. and Canada to: Elsevier Science Publishing Co., Inc., Box 882, Madison Sq. Sta., New York, NY 10159. TEL 212-989-5800)
   Refereed Serial

530   SZ   ISSN 0018-0238
QC1   CODEN: HPACAK
HELVETICA PHYSICA ACTA. Short title: H P A. (Text in English, French, German and Italian) 1928. 8/yr. 598 SFr.($418) (Schweizerischen Physikalischen Gesellschaft - Swiss Society of Physics) Birkhaeuser Verlag, P.O. Box 133, CH-4010 Basel, Switzerland. TEL 061-737740. FAX 061-737950. TELEX 963475 BIRKH CH. (Dist. in N. America by: Springer-Verlag New York, Inc., Journal Fulfillment Services, Box 2485, Secaucus, NJ 07096-2491. TEL 201-348-4033) Ed. P.A. Martin. adv.; bk.rev.; charts; illus.; pat.; index. (also avail. in microfilm from UMI) **Indexed:** Chem.Abstr., Curr.Cont., Ind.Sci.Rev., INIS Atomind., Mass Spectr.Bull., Math.R., Met.Abstr., Phys.Ber., Sci.Abstr., Sci.Cit.Ind.
—BLDSC shelfmark: 4288.000000.

530 540 669   US   ISSN 1048-1141
HIGH - TC UPDATE. 1987. s-m. free. Iowa State University, Ames Laboratory, A219 Physics, Ames, IA 50011-3020. TEL 515-294-3877. FAX 515-294-1134. Ed. Dr. Ellen O. Feinberg. circ. 2,400. (back issues avail.)
   Description: Covers high-temperature superconductors. Provides analysis section, list of preprints, coming events, information resources and services.

530   GW   ISSN 0073-2850
HOCHSCHULBUECHER FUER PHYSIK. 1953. irreg. price varies. VEB Deutscher Verlag der Wissenschaften, Postfach 1216, 1080 Berlin, Germany. Eds. Robert Rompe, Ernst Schmutzer.

HOKKAIDO KYOIKU DAIGAKU KIYO. DAI-2-BU, A. SUGAKU, BUTSURI, KAGAKU, KOGAKU-HEN/HOKKAIDO UNIVERSITY OF EDUCATION. JOURNAL. SECTION 2 A. MATHEMATICS, PHYSICS, CHEMISTRY, ENGINEERING. see *MATHEMATICS*

530   NE
LES HOUCHES SUMMER SCHOOL PROCEEDINGS. (Text in English and French) 1951. irreg., vol.52, 1991. price varies. (Ecole d'Ete de Physique Theorique, Les Houches) Elsevier Science Publishers B.V., Books Division, P.O. Box 211, 1000 AE Amsterdam, Netherlands. TEL 020-5803911. FAX 020-5803705. TELEX 18582 ESPA NL. (Subscr. in U.S. and Canada to: Elsevier Science Publishing Co., Inc., Box 882, Madison Sq. Sta., New York, NY 10159. TEL 212-989-5800)
   Formerly: Ecole d'Ete de Physique Theorique. Les Houches.
   Refereed Serial

530 540   CC
HUAXUE WULI XUEBAO/JOURNAL OF CHEMICAL PHYSICS. (Text in Chinese) bi-m. Zhongguo Kexue Jishu Daxue - Chinese University of Science and Technology, 96 Jinzhai Lu, Hefei, Anhui 230026, People's Republic of China. TEL 331134. Ed. Lou Nanquan.

530   HU   ISSN 0133-5502
HUNGARIAN ACADEMY OF SCIENCES. CENTRAL RESEARCH INSTITUTE FOR PHYSICS. YEARBOOK/MAGYAR TUDOMANYOS AKADEMIA. KOZPONTI FIZIKAI KUTATO INTEZET. EVKONYV. (Text in English) 1971. s-a. avail. on exchange basis only. Magyar Tudomanyos Akademia, Kozponti Fizikai Kutato Intezet, P.O. Box 76, 1325 Budapest, Hungary. Ed. T. Dolinszky. circ. 1,400. **Indexed:** Chem.Abstr.

530   SZ   ISSN 0304-3843
QC762   CODEN: HYINDN
HYPERFINE INTERACTIONS. 1975. 24/yr. 1869 SFr. J.C. Baltzer AG, Scientific Publishing Company, Wettsteinplatz 10, CH-4058 Basel, Switzerland. TEL 061-6918925. FAX 061-6924262. Eds. B. Deutch, H. de Waard. adv. **Indexed:** Cadscan, Chem.Abstr., Curr.Cont., Ind.Sci.Rev., INIS Atomind., Lead Abstr., Phys.Ber., Sci.Abstr., Sci.Cit.Ind., Zincscan.
—BLDSC shelfmark: 4352.625000.

530   SI
I C T P SERIES IN THEORETICAL PHYSICS. (Text in English) 1984. irreg., vol. 7, 1991. price varies. World Scientific Publishing Co. Pte. Ltd., Farrer Rd., P.O. Box 128, Singapore 9128, Singapore. TEL 3825663. FAX 3825919. TELEX RS 28561 WSPC. (UK addr.: 73 Lynton Mead, Totteridge, London N20 8DH, England. TEL 44-81-4462461; US addr.: 1060 Main St., Ste. 1B, River Edge, NJ 07661. TEL 800-227-7562)

I E E E MICROWAVE AND GUIDED WAVE LETTERS. see *ENGINEERING — Electrical Engineering*

I E E E PARTICLE ACCELERATOR CONFERENCE. PROCEEDINGS. see *ENGINEERING — Electrical Engineering*

I E E E TRANSACTIONS ON APPLIED SUPERCONDUCTIVITY. see *ELECTRONICS*

530.44   US   ISSN 0093-3813
TA2001   CODEN: ITPSBD
I E E E TRANSACTIONS ON PLASMA SCIENCE. 1973. bi-m. $180 to non-members. (I E E E, Nuclear and Plasma Sciences Society) Institute of Electrical and Electronics Engineers, Inc., 345 E. 47th St., New York, NY 10017-2394. TEL 212-705-7366. FAX 212-705-7682. (Subscr. to: Box 1331, 445 Hoes Lane, Piscataway, NJ 08855-1331. TEL 908-562-3948) Ed. Steven J. Gitomer. bk.rev.; index. (also avail. in microform from UMI,EEE) **Indexed:** Chem.Abstr., Curr.Cont., Eng.Ind., Ind.Sci.Rev., INIS Atomind., Int.Aerosp.Abstr., Math.R., Phys.Ber., Sci.Abstr., Sci.Cit.Ind.
—BLDSC shelfmark: 4363.212000.

530   II   ISSN 0019-5480
Q1   CODEN: IJPYAS
INDIAN JOURNAL OF PHYSICS AND PROCEEDINGS OF THE INDIAN ASSOCIATION FOR THE CULTIVATION OF SCIENCE. (Issued in two parts: Part A: Condensed Matter, Nuclear Physics, Particle Physics; Part B: Atmospheric and Space Physics, Atomic and Molecular Physics, General Physics, Optics and Spectroscopy, Plasma Physics, Relativity and Cosmology.) (Text in English) 1926. m. Rs.500($300) to non-members; members Rs. 25. Indian Association for the Cultivation of Science, 2A & 2B Raja Subodh Chandra Mallick Road, Jadavpur, Calcutta 700 032, India. TEL 46-9371-5. TELEX 021-5501 IACS IN. Ed.Bd. adv.; bk.rev.; bibl.; charts; illus.; index; circ. 800. (back issues avail.) **Indexed:** Biol.Abstr., Cadscan, Ceram.Abstr., Chem.Abstr., INIS Atomind., Int.Aerosp.Abstr., Lead Abstr., Math.R., Met.Abstr., Phys.Abstr., Sci.Abstr., Sci.Cit.Ind., World Alum.Abstr., Zincscan.
—BLDSC shelfmark: 4419.910000.
   Description: Review articles and papers on research, as well as proceedings of national and international symposia, including annual endowment lectures.

PHYSICS

530   II   ISSN 0019-5596
QC1   CODEN: IJOPAU
INDIAN JOURNAL OF PURE & APPLIED PHYSICS. (Text in English) 1963. m. Rs.300($150) (Council of Scientific and Industrial Research, Publications & Information Directorate) Scientific Publishers, P.O. Box 91, 5A, New Pali Rd., Jodhpur 342 001, India. TEL 0291-33323. (Co-sponsor: Indian National Science Academy) Ed. K.S. Rangarajan. bibl.; charts; illus.; index; circ. 1,200. (back issues avail.) **Indexed:** Anal.Abstr., Appl.Mech.Rev., Biol.Abstr., Cadscan, Ceram.Abstr., Chem.Abstr., Curr.Cont., Ind.Sci.Rev., INIS Atomind., Lead Abstr., Mass Spectr.Bull., Math.R., Met.Abstr., Phys.Ber., Sci.Abstr., Sci.Cit.Ind., World Alum.Abstr., World Text.Abstr., Zincscan.
—BLDSC shelfmark: 4420.700000.

530   II   ISSN 0019-5693
QC1   CODEN: IJTPAL
INDIAN JOURNAL OF THEORETICAL PHYSICS. (Text in Bengali and English) 1953. q. Rs.300($25) Institute of Theoretical Physics, Bignan Kutir, 4-1 Mohan Bagan Lane, Calcutta 700004, India. Ed.Bd. bk.rev. **Indexed:** Appl.Mech.Rev., Chem.Abstr., INIS Atomind., Math.R., Phys.Ber., Sci.Abstr.
—BLDSC shelfmark: 4421.500000.

553.5   II   ISSN 0970-2334
CODEN: BIVSES
INDIAN VACUUM SOCIETY. BULLETIN. (Text in English) 1970. q. Rs.50($50) to individuals; libraries Rs.100($100). Indian Vacuum Society, c/o Technical Physics & Prototype Engineering Division, Bhabha Atomic Research Centre, Bombay 400 085, India. TEL (022)5516910. Ed. S.K. Roy. adv.; bk.rev.; circ. 500 (controlled). (back issues avail.) **Indexed:** INIS Atomind.
—BLDSC shelfmark: 2564.140000.
Formerly: V A C News (ISSN 0254-7848)

INFORMATIONSDIENST LAERM. see *ENGINEERING — Abstracting, Bibliographies, Statistics*

INSTITUT HENRI POINCARE. ANNALES: ANALYSE NON LINEAIRE. see *MATHEMATICS*

530   FR   ISSN 0020-2339
CODEN: AHPAAO
INSTITUT HENRI POINCARE. ANNALES. SECTION A: PHYSIQUE THEORIQUE. English Edition: Institut Henri Poincare. Annals. Section A: Theoretical Physics (ISSN 0246-0211) (Text in French) 1930. 8/yr. 1965 F. Gauthier-Villars, 15 rue Gossin, 92543 Montrouge Cedex, France. TEL 33-1-40-92-65-00. FAX 33-1-40-92-65-97. TELEX 270 004. (Subscr. to: Centrale des Revues, 11 rue Gossin, 92543 Montrouge Cedex, France. TEL 33-1-46-56-52-66) Ed. P. Collet. adv.; circ. 700. (also avail. in microfilm from UMI; reprint service avail. from KTO) **Indexed:** Chem.Abstr., Curr.Cont., INIS Atomind., Math.R., Sci.Abstr., Sci.Cit.Ind., Zent.Math.
Description: Covers all aspects of theoretical and mathematical physics and those areas of pure and applied mathematics that have relevance to physics.

INSTITUTE OF MATHEMATICAL SCIENCES, MADRAS. REPORTS. see *MATHEMATICS*

530 540   JA   ISSN 0020-3092
QC1   CODEN: SPIPAG
INSTITUTE OF PHYSICAL AND CHEMICAL RESEARCH. SCIENTIFIC PAPERS. (Text and summaries in English) 1922. irreg. Rikagaku Kenkyujo - Institute of Physical and Chemical Research, 2-1 Hirosawa, Wako-shi, Saitama-ken 351-01, Japan. TEL 0484-621111. FAX 0484-621554. Ed. Minoru Oda. abstr.; charts; illus.; index; circ. 1,000. **Indexed:** Appl.Mech.Rev., Chem.Abstr., Deep Sea Res.& Oceanogr.Abstr., Eng.Ind., INIS Atomind., JCT, JTA, Met.Abstr., Nucl.Sci.Abstr., Sci.Abstr., World Alum.Abstr.
—BLDSC shelfmark: 8189.500000.
Formerly: Journal of the Scientific Research Institute.

530   UK   ISSN 0305-2346
CODEN: IPHSAC
INSTITUTE OF PHYSICS, LONDON. CONFERENCE SERIES. PROCEEDINGS. 1967. irreg., no.116, 1991. price varies. (Institute of Physics) I O P Publishing, Techno House, Redcliffe Way, Bristol BS1 6NX, England. TEL 0272-297481. (U.S. addr.: American Institute of Pysics, 335 E.45th St., New York, NY 10011) **Indexed:** Chem.Abstr., Phys.Ber., Sci.Cit.Ind.

530   RM
INSTITUTUL DE SUBINGINERI ORADEA. LUCRARI STIINTIFICE: SERIA FIZICA. (Text in Rumanian, occasionally in English or French; summaries in Rumanian, French or German) 1967. a. Institutul de Subingineri Oradea, Calea Armatei Rosii Nr. 5, 3700 Oradea, Rumania.
Formerly: Institutul Pedagogic Oradea. Lucrari Stiintifice: Seria Fizica; which continues in part (in 1973): Institutul Pedagogic Oradea. Lucrari Stiintifice: Seria Matematica, Fizica, Chimie; which superseded (in 1971): Institutul Pedagogic Oradea. Lucrari Stiintifice: Seria A and Seria B; which was formerly (until 1969): Institutul Pedagogic Oradea. Lucrari Stiintifice.

INSTITUTUL POLITEHNIC "GHEORGHE ASACHI" DIN IASI. BULETINUL. SECTIA I: MECANICA MATEMATICA, FIZICA. see *MATHEMATICS*

530   UN   ISSN 0304-7091
QC1.I6285
INTERNATIONAL CENTRE FOR THEORETICAL PHYSICS. ANNUAL REPORT. 1964. a. free. International Atomic Energy Agency, International Centre for Theoretical Physics, Strada Costiera 11, Box 586, 34100 Trieste, Italy. FAX 40-224163. TELEX 460302 ICTP I. Ed. M. Farooqve. circ. 1,300.
Formerly (until 1965): International Centre for Theoretical Physics. Report (ISSN 0538-5415)

INTERNATIONAL JOURNAL OF HEAT AND MASS TRANSFER. see *ENGINEERING — Mechanical Engineering*

INTERNATIONAL JOURNAL OF HYDROGEN ENERGY. see *ENERGY*

530   US   ISSN 0899-9457
TK8315   CODEN: IJITEG
INTERNATIONAL JOURNAL OF IMAGING SYSTEMS AND TECHNOLOGY. 1989. q. $150 to institutions (foreign $200). John Wiley & Sons, Inc., Journals, 605 Third Ave., New York, NY 10158-0012. TEL 212-850-6000. FAX 212-850-6088. TELEX 12-7063. Ed.Bd.
—BLDSC shelfmark: 4542.299000.
Description: Covers current information pertinent to engineers and specialists working with imaging technology.

INTERNATIONAL JOURNAL OF MATHEMATICS AND MATHEMATICAL SCIENCES. see *MATHEMATICS*

530   SI   ISSN 0217-751X
QC793   CODEN: IMPAEF
INTERNATIONAL JOURNAL OF MODERN PHYSICS A. 1986. 30/yr. $580 to individuals and developing countries; institutions $1350. World Scientific Publishing Co. Pte. Ltd., Farrer Rd., P.O. Box 128, Singapore 9128, Singapore. TEL 3825663. FAX 3825919. TELEX RS-28561-WSPC. (UK addr.: 73 Lynton Mead, Totteridge, London N20 8DH, England. TEL 44-81-4462461; US addr.: 1060 Main St., Ste. 1B, River Edge, NJ 07661. TEL 800-227-7562) circ. 500. (back issues avail.) **Indexed:** Curr.Cont., INIS Atomind.
—BLDSC shelfmark: 4542.365200.
Description: Covers particle and field physics, nuclear physics, gravitation and cosmology.

530   SI   ISSN 0217-9792
QC173.4.C65   CODEN: IJPBEV
INTERNATIONAL JOURNAL OF MODERN PHYSICS B. (Text in English) 1987. 20/yr. $385 to individuals and developing countries; institutions $960. World Scientific Publishing Co. Pte. Ltd., Farrer Rd., P.O. Box 128, Singapore 9128, Singapore. TEL 3825663. FAX 3825919. TELEX RS-28561-WSPC. (European addr.: 73 Lynton Mead, Totteridge, London N20 8DH, England. TEL 44-81-4462461; US addr.: 1060 Main St., Ste. 1B, River Edge, NJ 07661. TEL 800-227-7562) circ. 300. (back issues avail.)
—BLDSC shelfmark: 4542.365210.
Description: Review and research articles on condensed matter, statistical and applied physics at graduate and post-graduate levels.

530 500   SI   ISSN 0129-1831
QC52   CODEN: IJMPEO
▼**INTERNATIONAL JOURNAL OF MODERN PHYSICS C: PHYSICS AND COMPUTERS.** 1990. q. $125 to individuals and developing countries; institutions $275. World Scientific Publishing Co. Pte. Ltd., Farrer Rd., P.O. Box 128, Singapore 9128, Singapore. TEL 3825663. FAX 3825919. TELEX RS-28561-WSPC. (European addr.: 73 Lynton Mead, Totteridge, London N20 8DH, England. TEL 44-81-4462461; US addr.: 1060 Main St., Ste. 1B, River Edge, NJ 07661. TEL 800-227-7562) Ed.Bd.
—BLDSC shelfmark: 4542.365220.
Description: Publishes both review and research articles on the use of computers to advance knowledge in the physical sciences and the use of physical analogies in computation.

INTERNATIONAL JOURNAL OF MULTIPHASE FLOW. see *ENGINEERING — Mechanical Engineering*

530 001.6   SI   ISSN 0129-0657
QA76.87   CODEN: IJSZEG
INTERNATIONAL JOURNAL OF NEURAL SYSTEMS. (Text in English) 1989. q. $86 to individuals and developing countries; institutions $190. World Scientific Publishing Co. Pte. Ltd., Farrer Rd., P.O. Box 128, Singapore 9128, Singapore. TEL 3825663. FAX 3825919. TELEX RS-28561-WSPC. (US addr.: 1060 Main St., Ste. 1B, River Edge, NJ 07661. TEL 800-227-7562; UK addr.: 73 Lynton Mead, totteridge, London N20 8DH, England. TEL 44-81-4462461) Eds. Benny Lautrup, S. Brunak. circ. 300. (back issues avail.)
—BLDSC shelfmark: 4542.373700.
Description: Contains original contributions on all aspects of information processing in natural and artificial neural systems.

INTERNATIONAL JOURNAL OF RADIATION BIOLOGY. see *MEDICAL SCIENCES — Cancer*

530   US   ISSN 0020-7748
QC1   CODEN: IJTPBM
INTERNATIONAL JOURNAL OF THEORETICAL PHYSICS. 1968. m. $565 (foreign $660)(effective 1992). Plenum Publishing Corp., 233 Spring St., New York, NY 10013-1578. TEL 212-620-8000. FAX 212-463-0742. TELEX 23-421139. Ed. David Finkelstein. adv.; bk.rev.; abstr.; bibl.; charts. (also avail. in microfilm from JSC; back issues avail.) **Indexed:** Chem.Abstr., Curr.Cont., Ind.Sci.Rev., INIS Atomind., Math.R., Phys.Ber., Ref.Zh., Sci.Abstr., Sci.Cit.Ind.
—BLDSC shelfmark: 4542.695000.
Refereed Serial

538   US
INTERNATIONAL MAGNETICS CONFERENCE. DIGESTS OF THE INTERMAG CONFERENCE. a. price varies. (I E E E, Magnetics Society) Institute of Electrical and Electronics Engineers, Inc., 345 E. 47th St., New York, NY 10017-2394. TEL 212-705-7900. FAX 212-705-7682. (Subscr. to: Box 1331, 445 Hoes Ln., Piscataway, NJ 08855-1331)
Former titles: Abstracts of the Intermag Conference; International Magnetics Conference. Digest (ISSN 0074-6843)
Description: Covers all areas of basic science, applied science and engineering as it pertains to magnetism.

INTERNATIONAL MONOGRAPHS ON ADVANCED MATHEMATICS AND PHYSICS. see *MATHEMATICS*

530   US
INTERNATIONAL SCHOOL OF PHYSICS "ENRICO FERMI". ITALIAN PHYSICAL SOCIETY. PROCEEDINGS. 1959-1977 (voll.57). irreg. (Societa Italiana di Fisica, IT) Academic Press, Inc., 1250 Sixth Ave., San Diego, CA 92101. TEL 619-231-0926. FAX 619-699-6715. (reprint service avail. from ISI) **Indexed:** Chem.Abstr., Math.R.
Former titles (until 1963): International School of Physics "Enrico Fermi". Proceedings (ISSN 0074-784X); International School of Physics "Ettore Majorana". Proceedings (ISSN 0074-7858)
Refereed Serial

530   US
INTERNATIONAL SERIES OF MONOGRAPHS ON PHYSICS. irreg. price varies. Oxford University Press, 200 Madison Ave., New York, NY 10016. TEL 212-679-7300. Ed.Bd. **Indexed:** Math.R.
Refereed Serial

PHYSICS 3821

533.5   US   ISSN 0020-9066
INTERNATIONAL UNION FOR VACUUM SCIENCE, TECHNIQUE AND APPLICATIONS. NEWS BULLETIN. (Text in English, French, German) 1959. q. $20. International Union for Vacuum Science Technique and Applications, c/o Dr. Theodore E. Madey, Rutgers University, P.O. Box 849, Piscataway, NJ 08855. Ed. J. Lyn Provo. adv.; bk.rev.; circ. 250.

IOWA AGRICULTURE AND HOME ECONOMICS EXPERIMENT STATION. RESEARCH BULLETIN. see *AGRICULTURE*

ISOTOPE NEWS. see *BIOLOGY — Biological Chemistry*

ISOTOPENPRAXIS. see *CHEMISTRY*

530   IS   ISSN 0309-8710
CODEN: AIPSDK
ISRAEL PHYSICAL SOCIETY. ANNALS;* conference proceedings. (Text in English) 1977. a. price varies. Israel Physical Society, c/o Racah Institute of Physics, The Hebrew University, 91904 Jerusalem, Israel. FAX 4-221581. TELEX 46406-TECON-IL. (Dist. in U.S. by: American Institute of Physics, Marketing Services, 335 E. 45 St., New York, NY 10017) (Co-sponsors: American Institute of Physics) Ed.Bd. circ. 600. (back issues avail., reprint service avail. from ISI) **Indexed:** Chem.Abstr., Math.R., Phys.Ber., Sci.Abstr.
—BLDSC shelfmark: 1028.320000.

530   RU   ISSN 0021-3411
CODEN: IVUFAC
IZVESTIYA VYSSHIKH UCHEBNYKH ZAVEDENII. SERIYA FIZIKA. English translation: Soviet Physics Journal (US ISSN 0038-5697) (Text in Russian; contents page in English) 1957. m. 54 Rub. (Vysshie Uchebnye Zavedeniya S.S.S.R.) Tomskii Universitet, Prospekt Lenina, 36, Tomsk-10, Russia. Ed. V.N. Detinko. charts; illus.; index, cum.index: 1957-1967; circ. 2,200. **Indexed:** Cadscan, Chem.Abstr., Curr.Cont., Ind.Sci.Rev., INIS Atomind., Lead Abstr., Phys.Ber., Ref.Zh., Sci.Abstr., Sci.Cit.Ind., Zincscan.
—BLDSC shelfmark: 0077.900000.

530 621.38   RU   ISSN 0021-3462
QC 661   CODEN: IVYRAY
IZVESTIYA VYSSHIKH UCHEBNYKH ZAVEDENII. SERIYA RADIOFIZIKA. English translation: Radiophysics and Quantum Electronics (US ISSN 0033-8443) (Text in Russian; summaries in English) 1958. m. 75.60 Rub. (Vysshie Uchebnye Zavedeniya S.S.S.R.) Izdatel'stvo Vysshaya Shkola, Prospekt Marksa 18, 103009 Moscow K-9, Russia. (Co-sponsor: Ministerstvo Vysshego i Srednego Spetsial'nogo Obrazovaniya) Ed. V.L. Ginzburg. charts; illus.; index. (tabloid format) **Indexed:** Chem.Abstr., Curr.Cont., INIS Atomind., Phys.Ber., Ref.Zh., Risk Abstr., Sci.Abstr., Sci.Cit.Ind.
—BLDSC shelfmark: 0077.760000.

530   US   ISSN 0021-3640
CODEN: JTPLA2
J E T P LETTERS. English translation of: Pis'ma v Zhurnal Eksperimental'noi i Teoreticheskoi Fiziki. 1965. s-m. $770 (foreign $785-$805). American Institute of Physics, 335 E. 45th St., New York, NY 10017. TEL 212-661-9404. FAX 516-349-9704. (Subscr. to: Member and Subscriber Service, 500 Subbyside Blvd., Woodbury, NY 11797-2999. TEL 516-576-2270) Ed. S.J. Amoretty. (also avail. in microfilm; back issues avail.) **Indexed:** Appl.Mech.Rev., C.P.I., Cadscan, Curr.Cont., Gen.Phys.Adv.Abstr., INIS Atomind., Int.Aerosp.Abstr., Lead Abstr., Mass Spectr.Bull., Met.Abstr., Phys.Ber., Sci.Abstr., Sci.Cit.Ind., World Alum.Abstr., Zincscan.
—BLDSC shelfmark: 0412.741000.

JAPAN SOCIETY FOR TECHNOLOGY OF PLASTICITY. JOURNAL/SOSEI TO KAKO. see *TECHNOLOGY: COMPREHENSIVE WORKS*

621 530   JA   ISSN 0021-4922
TA4   CODEN: JJAPA5
JAPANESE JOURNAL OF APPLIED PHYSICS. (Issued in 2 parts - Part 1: regular papers and short notes; Part 2: letters.) (Text in English) 1962. m. (Part 1); s-m. (Part 2). 90000 Yen. Daini Toyokaiji Bldg., 4-24-8 Shinbashi, Minato-ku, Tokyo 105, Japan. FAX 81-3-3432-0728. (Co-sponsors: Japan Society of Applied Physics, Physical Society of Japan) Eds. Ryoichi Ito, Seiichi Kagoshima. index; circ. 3,900. (also avail. in microform from MIM; reprint service avail. from UMI) **Indexed:** Art & Archaeol.Tech.Abstr., Bull.Signal., Cadscan, Ceram.Abstr., Chem.Abstr., Curr.Cont., Eng.Ind., GeoRef., Ind.Sci.Rev., INIS Atomind., Int.Aerosp.Abstr., JCT, JTA, Lead Abstr., Mass Spectr.Bull., Met.Abstr., Phys.Ber., Sci.Abstr., Sci.Cit.Ind., World Alum.Abstr., Zincscan.
—BLDSC shelfmark: 4650.880100.
Description: Research papers in the field of applied physics.

530   JA   ISSN 0913-7785
JINRUI DOTAI GAKKAI KAIHO/HUMAN ERGOLOGY SOCIETY. NEWSLETTER. (Text in Japanese) 1970. 3/yr. Human Ergology Society - Jinrui Dotai Gakkai, c/o Kyushu Geijutsu Koka Daigaku, Ningen Kogaku Kyoshitsu, 9-1 Shiobara 4-chome, Minami-ku, Fukuoka-shi, Fukuoka-ken 815, Japan.
Description: Contains news of the organization.

530 621   US   ISSN 0270-5214
TA1   CODEN: JHADDQ
JOHNS HOPKINS A P L TECHNICAL DIGEST. 1980. q. free. Johns Hopkins University, Applied Physics Laboratory, Johns Hopkins Rd., Laurel, MD 20723. TEL 301-953-5625. Ed. J.D. Shambach. bk.rev.; charts; illus.; circ. 5,000. **Indexed:** ASCA, Chem.Abstr., Curr.Cont., Deep Sea Res.& Oceanogr.Abstr., Eng.Ind., Int.Aerosp.Abstr., Meteor.& Geoastrophys.Abstr., Ocean.Abstr., Phys.Abstr.
—BLDSC shelfmark: 4671.530000.
Formerly: A P L Technical Digest (ISSN 0001-2211)
Refereed Serial

530   FR
CODEN: JOPQAG
JOURNAL DE PHYSIQUE I. (Text and summaries in English, French, German, Russian) 1872. m. 525 F. (foreign 630 F.). Editions de Physique, Zone Industrielle de Courtaboeuf, B.P. 112, 91944 Les Ulis Cedex, France. TEL 69-07-36-88. FAX 69-28-84-91. TELEX 602 321 F. Ed. D. Jerome. bk.rev.; index; circ. 1,500. (also avail. in microfiche from BHP; back issues avail.) **Indexed:** Cadscan, Chem.Abstr., Deep Sea Res.& Oceanogr.Abstr., Ind.Sci.Rev., INIS Atomind., Int.Aerosp.Abstr., Lead Abstr., Mass Spectr.Bull., Math.R., Met.Abstr., Phys.Ber., Sci.Abstr., Sci.Cit.Ind., World Alum.Abstr., Zincscan.
Formerly: Journal de Physique (ISSN 0302-0738)
Description: Original articles in theoretical and experimental research.

530   FR
JOURNAL DE PHYSIQUE II. m. 525 F. (foreign 630 F.). Editions de Physique, 7 av. du Hoggar, Z.I. de Courtaboeuf, B.P. 112, 91944 Les Ulis Cedex, France. TEL 69-07-36-88. FAX 69-28-84-91. TELEX 602 321 F.

621 530   FR
QC1
JOURNAL DE PHYSIQUE III. (Supplement to the Journal de Physique I) (Text in English, French) 1966. m. 645 F. (foreign 780 F.). Editions de Physique, Zone Industrielle de Courtaboeuf, B.P. 112, 91944 Les Ulis Cedex, France. TEL 69-07-36-88. FAX 69-28-84-91. TELEX 602 321 F. Ed. F. Rioux-Damidau. bk.rev.; charts; illus.; index; circ. 3,500. (back issues avail.) **Indexed:** Cadscan, Chem.Abstr., Curr.Cont., GeoRef., Lead Abstr., Mass Spectr.Bull., Met.Abstr., Phys.Ber., Sci.Abstr., World Alum.Abstr., Zincscan.
Formerly: Revue de Physique Appliquee (ISSN 0035-1687)
Description: Articles on original measurements relative to known phenomena or experimental methods in physics.

530   FR
JOURNAL DE PHYSIQUE IV. irreg. Editions de Physique, 7 av. du Hoggar, Z.I. de Courtaboeuf, B.P. 112, 91944 Les Ulis Cedex A, France. TEL 69-07-36-88. FAX 69-28-84-91. TELEX 602 321 F.

668.3   US   ISSN 0021-8464
QC183   CODEN: JADNAJ
JOURNAL OF ADHESION. 1969. 16/yr. (in 4 vols., 4 nos./vol.). $305. Gordon and Breach Science Publishers, 270 Eighth Ave., New York, NY 10011. TEL 212-206-8900. FAX 212-645-2459. TELEX 236735 GOPUB UR. (Subscr. to: Box 786, Cooper Sta., New York, NY 10276. TEL 800-545-8398; UK subscr. to: P.O. Box 90, Reading, Berkshire RG1 8JL, England. TEL 0734-560-080) Ed. Louis H. Sharpe. adv.; bk.rev.; charts; illus.; index. (also avail. in microform from MIM) **Indexed:** Abstr.Bull.Inst.Pap.Chem., Appl.Mech.Rev., Chem.Abstr., Curr.Cont., Ind.Sci.Rev., ISMEC, Sci.Abstr., Sci.Cit.Ind., Text.Tech.Dig., World Surf.Coat.
—BLDSC shelfmark: 4918.935000.
Refereed Serial

JOURNAL OF ALLOYS AND COMPOUNDS; an interdisciplinary journal of materials science and solid-state chemistry and physics. see *METALLURGY*

JOURNAL OF APPLIED MECHANICS AND TECHNICAL PHYSICS. see *ENGINEERING — Engineering Mechanics And Materials*

530 540   US   ISSN 0021-8979
QC1   CODEN: JAPIAU
JOURNAL OF APPLIED PHYSICS. 1931. s-m. (plus supplement). $1240 (foreign $1430). American Institute of Physics, 335 E. 45th St., New York, NY 10017. TEL 212-661-9404. FAX 516-349-9704. (Subscr. to: Member and Subscriber Service, 500 Sunnyside Blvd., Woodbury, NY 11797-2999. TEL 516-576-2270) Ed. Steve Rothman. charts; illus.; index. (also avail. in microfiche; microform; back issues avail.) **Indexed:** A.S.& T.Ind., Abstr.Bull.Inst.Pap.Chem., Appl.Mech.Rev., Br.Ceram.Abstr., C.P.I., Cadscan, Ceram.Abstr., Chem.Abstr., Curr.Cont., Deep Sea Res.& Oceanogr.Abstr., Eng.Ind., Fluidex, Gen.Phys.Adv.Abstr., Geotech.Abstr., Ind.Sci.Rev., INIS Atomind., Int.Aerosp.Abstr., Lead Abstr., Mass Spectr.Bull., Math.R., Met.Abstr., Petrol.Abstr., RAPRA, Sci.Abstr., Sci.Cit.Ind., World Alum.Abstr., World Text.Abstr., Zincscan.
—BLDSC shelfmark: 4944.000000.

530 541.3   US   ISSN 0021-9606
QD1   CODEN: JCPSA6
JOURNAL OF CHEMICAL PHYSICS. 1931. s-m. $1830 (foreign $2045). American Institute of Physics, 335 E. 45th St., New York, NY 10017. TEL 212-661-9404. Ed. J.C. Light. charts; illus.; index. (also avail. in microfiche; microform; back issues avail.) **Indexed:** Abstr.Bull.Inst.Pap.Chem., Appl.Mech.Rev., Biol.Abstr., Biwk.Pap.Rad.Chem.& Photochem., Br.Ceram.Abstr., Bull.Thermodyn.& Thermochem., C.P.I., Chem.Abstr., Chem.Eng.Abstr., Chem.Infd., Curr.Cont., Eng.Ind., Gen.Phys.Adv.Abstr., Ind.Sci.Rev., INIS Atomind., Int.Aerosp.Abstr., Mass Spectr.Bull., Math.R., Met.Abstr., Petrol.Abstr., Phys.Ber., RAPRA, Sci.Abstr., Sci.Cit.Ind., T.C.E.A.
—BLDSC shelfmark: 4957.000000.
Refereed Serial

530   NE   ISSN 0920-5071
QC660.5   CODEN: JEWAE5
JOURNAL OF ELECTROMAGNETIC WAVES AND APPLICATIONS. (Text in English) 1987. m. DM.1193. V S P, P.O. Box 346, 3700 AH Zeist, Netherlands. TEL 03404-25790. FAX 03404-32081. TELEX 40217 VSP NL. Ed. J.A. Kong. adv. (back issues avail.)
—BLDSC shelfmark: 4974.850000.
Description: Original papers and review articles on new theories, methodology, and computational results about electromagnetic wave theory and its various applications.

530   US
JOURNAL OF ELECTROTOPOGRAPHY. 1981. s-a. free. (Ensanian Physiochemical Institute) Electrotopograph Corporation, Box 98, Eldred, PA 16731. TEL 814-225-3296. Ed. Minas Ensanian. bk.rev.; bibl.; charts; illus.; circ. 1,000. (controlled).
Refereed Serial

530   US   ISSN 0737-0652
TP270.A1   CODEN: JOEMDK
JOURNAL OF ENERGETIC MATERIALS. 1983. 5/yr. $250 (foreign $260). Dowden, Brodman & Devine, Inc., Box 188, Stroudsburg, PA 18360. Ed. Paul L. Marinkas. abstr.; bibl.; charts. **Indexed:** Chem.Abstr.
—BLDSC shelfmark: 4978.240000.

PHYSICS

JOURNAL OF ENGINEERING PHYSICS. see *ENGINEERING*

JOURNAL OF FLUID MECHANICS. see *ENGINEERING — Hydraulic Engineering*

JOURNAL OF GEOMETRY AND PHYSICS. see *MATHEMATICS*

JOURNAL OF HARD MATERIALS. see *ENGINEERING — Engineering Mechanics And Materials*

530   CC   ISSN 1000-4874
JOURNAL OF HYDRODYNAMICS. Chinese Edition: Shuidong Lixue Yanjiu yu Jinzhan. (Editions in Chinese, English) q. $120. (Zhongguo Chuanbo Kexue Yanjiu Zhongxin, Shanghai Fenbu) China Ocean Press, International Cooperation Department, Haimao Dalou, 1 Fuxingmenwai Dajie, Beijing 100860, People's Republic of China. TEL 868941. FAX 862209. TELEX 22536 NBO CN. Ed.Bd.
Description: Provides up-to-date information about various aspects of hydrodynamic rsearch especially in China, including theoretical, experimental and computational techniques plus field measurement.
Refereed Serial

530   US   ISSN 0022-2348
QD380   CODEN: JMAPBR
JOURNAL OF MACROMOLECULAR SCIENCE: PART B - PHYSICS. 1967. 4/yr. $247.50 to individuals; institutions $495. Marcel Dekker Journals, 270 Madison Ave., New York, NY 10016. TEL 212-696-9000. FAX 212-685-4540. TELEX 421419 MARDEEK. (Subscr. to: Box 10018, Church St. Sta., New York, NY 10249) Ed. Phillip M. Geil. adv. (also avail. in microform from RPI) Indexed: Chem.Abstr., Curr.Cont., Ind.Sci.Rev., INIS Atomind., Sci.Abstr., Sci.Cit.Ind.
—BLDSC shelfmark: 5010.770000.
Supersedes in part: Journal of Macromolecular Chemistry (ISSN 0449-2730)
Refereed Serial

538.3   US   ISSN 0022-2364
QC762   CODEN: JOMRA4
JOURNAL OF MAGNETIC RESONANCE. 1969. 15/yr. $890 (foreign $1067). Academic Press, Inc., Journal Division, 1250 Sixth Ave., San Diego, CA 92101. TEL 619-230-1840. FAX 619-699-6800. TELEX 181726. Ed. Wallace S. Brey, Jr. adv.; abstr.; bibl.; charts; illus.; index. (back issues avail.) Indexed: Abstr.Bull.Inst.Pap.Chem., Biwk.Pap.Rad.Chem.& Photochem., Cadscan, Chem.Abstr., Curr.Cont., Ind.Sci.Rev., INIS Atomind., Lead Abstr., Sci.Abstr., Sci.Cit.Ind., Zincscan.
—BLDSC shelfmark: 5010.790000.
Description: Provides current information on the theory, techniques, methods of spectral analysis and interpretation, spectral correlations, and results of magnetic resonance pectroscopy.
Refereed Serial

JOURNAL OF MAGNETIC RESONANCE IMAGING. see *MEDICAL SCIENCES — Radiology And Nuclear Medicine*

538   NE   ISSN 0304-8853
QC750   CODEN: JMMMDC
JOURNAL OF MAGNETISM AND MAGNETIC MATERIALS. 1976. 33/yr. (in 11 vols.; 3 nos./vol.) fl.4961 (effective 1992). (European Physical Society) North-Holland (Subsidiary of: Elsevier Science Publishers B.V.), P.O. Box 211, 1000 AE Amsterdam, Netherlands. TEL 020-5803911. FAX 020-5803598. TELEX 18582 ESPA NL. (Subscr. in U.S. and Canada to: Elsevier Science Publishing Co., Inc., Box 882, Madison Sq. Sta., New York, NY 10159. TEL 212-989-5800) Ed. A.J. Freeman. adv.; charts; cum.index; circ. 800. (also avail. in microform from RPI; back issues avail.) Indexed: Cadscan, Chem.Abstr., Curr.Cont., GeoRef., Ind.Sci.Rev., INIS Atomind., Lead Abstr., Met.Abstr., Phys.Ber., Sci.Abstr., Sci.Cit.Ind., World Alum.Abstr., Zincscan.
—BLDSC shelfmark: 5010.793000.
Description: Covers the whole spectrum of topics from basic magnetism to the technology and applications of magnetic materials and magnetic recording.
Refereed Serial

530   US   ISSN 0884-2914
TA404.2   CODEN: JMREEE
JOURNAL OF MATERIALS RESEARCH. Variant title: J M R. 1986. m. $350 (foreign $375). Materials Research Society, 9800 McKnight Rd., Pittsburgh, PA 15237. TEL 412-367-3003. FAX 412-367-4373. Ed. Walter Brown. adv.; index (1986-1990). (reprint service avail. from UMI) Indexed: Appl.Mech.Rev., Ceram.Abstr., Chem.Abstr., Corros.Abstr., INIS Atomind., INSPEC, Met.Abstr., Sci.Cit.Ind., Solid St.Abstr.
—BLDSC shelfmark: 5012.240000.
Description: Provides an international forum that encompasses physical, chemical, and engineering insights on advanced materials and processing techniques.

JOURNAL OF MATHEMATICAL AND PHYSICAL SCIENCES. see *MATHEMATICS*

500   US   ISSN 0022-2488
QC20   CODEN: JMAPAQ
JOURNAL OF MATHEMATICAL PHYSICS. 1960. m. $875 (foreign $890-$905). American Institute of Physics, 335 E. 45th St., New York, NY 10017. TEL 212-661-9404. Ed. L.C. Biedenharn. abstr.; bibl.; charts. (also avail. in microfiche; microform; back issues avail.) Indexed: C.P.I., Chem.Abstr, Compumath, Curr.Cont., Eng.Ind., Gen.Phys.Adv.Abstr., Ind.Sci.Rev., INIS Atomind., Int.Aerosp.Abstr., Math.R., Phys.Ber., Sci.Abstr., Sci.Cit.Ind.
—BLDSC shelfmark: 5012.400000.
Refereed Serial

JOURNAL OF NATURAL SCIENCES AND MATHEMATICS. see *SCIENCES: COMPREHENSIVE WORKS*

530 541   NE   ISSN 0022-3093
TP845   CODEN: JNCSBJ
JOURNAL OF NON-CRYSTALLINE SOLIDS; a journal on the physical, chemical and structural properties of glasses, amorphous semiconductors and metals, including the liquid state. 1969. 36/yr. (in 12 vols.; 3 nos./vol.). fl.4752 (effective 1992). North-Holland (Subsidiary of: Elsevier Science Publishers B.V.), P.O. Box 211, 1000 AE Amsterdam, Netherlands. TEL 020-5803911. FAX 020-5803598. TELEX 18582 ESPA NL. (Subscr. in U.S. and Canada to: Elsevier Science Publishing Co., Inc., Box 882, Madison Sq. Sta., New York, NY 10159. TEL 212-989-5800) Ed. R.A. Weeks. adv.; bk.rev.; charts; illus.; stat.; cum.index; circ. controlled. (also avail. in microform from RPI; back issues avail.; reprint service avail. from ISI,SWZ) Indexed: Cadscan, Ceram.Abstr., Chem.Abstr., Curr.Cont., Ind.Sci.Rev., INIS Atomind., Int.Aerosp.Abstr., Lead Abstr., Mass Spectr.Bull., Met.Abstr., Phys.Ber., Psychol.Abstr., Sci.Abstr., World Alum.Abstr., Zincscan.
—BLDSC shelfmark: 5022.830000.
Description: Publishes review articles, research papers, on oxide and non-oxide glasses, amorphous semiconductors, non-crystalline films such as those prepared by vapor-deposition, glass ceramics and glassy composites.
Refereed Serial

530   US   ISSN 0938-8974
QC20.7.N6
▼**JOURNAL OF NONLINEAR SCIENCE.** 1991. q. $199. Springer-Verlag, 175 Fifth Ave., New York, NY 10010. TEL 212-460-1500. Eds. Eugeni A. Kuznetsov, Stephen R. Wiggins.
—BLDSC shelfmark: 5022.839000.
Description: Publishes research papers that augment the fundamental ways that humans analyze, describe, and predict aspects of the nonlinear world.

JOURNAL OF ORGONOMY. see *MEDICAL SCIENCES — Psychiatry And Neurology*

JOURNAL OF PHYSICAL AND CHEMICAL REFERENCE DATA. see *CHEMISTRY*

530   UK   ISSN 0305-4470
QC1   CODEN: JPHAC5
JOURNAL OF PHYSICS A: MATHEMATICAL AND GENERAL. 1968. 24/yr. £838($1676) (effective 1992). (Institute of Physics) I O P Publishing, Techno House, Redcliffe Way, Bristol BS1 6NX, England. TEL 0272 297481. FAX 0272-294318. (U.S. addr.: American Institute of Physics, Member and Subscriber Service, 500 Sunnyside Blvd. Woodbury, NY 11797-2999. TEL 516-576-2270) Ed. D. Sherrington. bibl.; charts; illus.; index. (also avail. in microfiche; microfilm; back issues avail.) Indexed: Appl.Mech.Rev., Br.Ceram.Abstr., Chem.Abstr., Curr.Cont., Deep Sea Res.& Oceanogr.Abstr., Eng.Ind., Ind.Sci.Rev., INIS Atomind., Int.Aerosp.Abstr., Math.R., Met.Abstr., Phys.Ber., Sci.Abstr.
—BLDSC shelfmark: 5036.237300.
Former titles: Journal of Physics A: Mathematical, Nuclear and General (ISSN 0301-0015); Journal of Physics (ISSN 0022-3689); Physical Society. Proceedings.
Description: Examines classical mechanics, chaotic systems, statistical physics and thermodynamics.

530.41   UK   ISSN 0953-4075
QC770   CODEN: JPAMA4
JOURNAL OF PHYSICS B: ATOMIC, MOLECULAR AND OPTICAL PHYSICS. 1968. 24/yr. £711($1422) (effective 1992). (Institute of Physics) I O P Publishing, Techno House, Redcliffe Way, Bristol BS1 6NX, England. TEL 0272 297481. FAX 0272-294318. (U.S. address: American Institute of Physics, Member and Subscriber Service, 500 Sunnyside Blvd., Woodbury, NY 11797-2999. TEL 516-576-2270) Ed. J.P. Connerade. bibl.; illus.; charts; index. (also avail. in microfiche; microfilm; back issues avail.) Indexed: Appl.Mech.Rev., Br.Ceram.Abstr., Bull.Thermodyn.& Thermochem., Cadscan, Chem.Abstr., Curr.Cont., Eng.Ind., Ind.Sci.Rev., INIS Atomind., Int.Aerosp.Abstr., Lead Abstr., Mass Spectr.Bull., Math.R., Met.Abstr., Phys.Ber., Sci.Abstr., Zincscan.
—BLDSC shelfmark: 5036.238400.
Former titles: Journal of Physics B: Atomic and Molecular Physics (ISSN 0022-3700); Physical Society. Proceedings.

530.41   UK   ISSN 0953-8984
QC176.A1   CODEN: JCOMEL
JOURNAL OF PHYSICS: CONDENSED MATTER. 1968. 50/yr. £1477($2894) (effective 1992). (Institute of Physics) I O P Publishing, Techno House, Redcliffe Way, Bristol BS1 6NX, England. TEL 0272-297481. FAX 0272-294318. TELEX 449149-INSTP-G. (U.S. addr.: American Institute of Physics, Member and Subscriber Service, 500 Sunnyside Blvd., Woodbury, NY 11797-2999. TEL 516-576-2270) Ed. R. Cowley. bibl.; charts; illus.; index. (also avail. in microfiche; microfilm; back issues avail.) Indexed: Appl. Mech.Rev., Br.Ceram.Abstr., Cadscan, Chem.Abstr., Curr.Cont., Eng.Ind., GeoRef., Ind.Sci.Rev., INIS Atomind., Lead Abstr., Mass Spectr.Bull., Math.R., Met.Abstr., Phys.Ber., Sci.Abstr., World Alum.Abstr., Zincscan.
—BLDSC shelfmark: 5036.800000.
Formed by the 1989 merger of: Journal of Physics F: Metal Physics (ISSN 0305-4608); Journal of Physics C: Solid State Physics (ISSN 0022-3719); Which was formerly: Physical Society. Proceedings.

530 621   UK   ISSN 0022-3727
QC1   CODEN: JPAPBE
JOURNAL OF PHYSICS D: APPLIED PHYSICS. 1968. m. £347($694) (effective 1992). (Institute of Physics) I O P Publishing, Techno House, Redcliffe Way, Bristol BS1 6NX, England. TEL 0272-297481. FAX 0272-294318. (U.S. addr.: American Institute of Physics, Member and Subscriber Service, 500 Sunnyside Blvd., Woodbury, NY 11797-2999. TEL 516-576-2270) Ed. S.B. Palmer. bibl.; charts; illus.; index. (also avail. in microfiche; microfilm; back issues avail.) Indexed: A.S.& T.Ind., Abstr.Bull.Inst.Pap.Chem., Anal.Abstr., Biol.Abstr., Br.Ceram.Abstr., Br.Tech.Ind., C.I.S. Abstr., Cadscan, Chem.Abstr., Curr.Cont., Deep Sea Res.& Oceanogr.Abstr., Eng.Ind., Fluidex, GeoRef., Ind.Sci.Rev., INIS Atomind., Int.Aerosp.Abstr., Lead Abstr., Mass Spectr.Bull., Met.Abstr., Phys.Ber., RAPRA, Sci.Abstr., World Alum.Abstr., World Text.Abstr., Zincscan.
—BLDSC shelfmark: 5036.240000.
Formerly: British Journal of Applied Physics.
Description: Theoretical and experimental aspects of physics as applied to interdisciplinary science, engineering or industry.

JOURNAL OF PHYSICS G: NUCLEAR AND PARTICLE PHYSICS. see *PHYSICS — Nuclear Physics*

530 540   US   ISSN 0022-3697
QC176.A1   CODEN: JPCSAW
JOURNAL OF PHYSICS AND CHEMISTRY OF SOLIDS. (Text in English, French and German) 1956. 12/yr. £730 (effective 1992). Pergamon Press, Inc., Journals Division, 660 White Plains Rd., Tarrytown, NY 10591-5153. TEL 914-524-9200. FAX 914-333-2444. (And: Headington Hill Hall, Oxford OX3 0BW, England. TEL 0865-794141) Ed. D.E. Cox. adv.; bk.rev.; circ. 2,300. (also avail. in microform from MIM,UMI; back issues avail.) **Indexed:** Appl.Mech.Rev., Br.Ceram.Abstr., Bull.Thermodyn.& Thermochem., Cadscan, Chem.Abstr., GeoRef., Ind.Sci.Rev., INIS Atomind., Lead Abstr., Mass Spectr.Bull., Met.Abstr., Phys.Ber., Sci.Abstr., World Alum.Abstr., Zincscan.
—BLDSC shelfmark: 5036.500000.
  Description: Covers all aspects of the fundamental physics and chemistry of the solid state.
  Refereed Serial

530 620   TU
JOURNAL OF PHYSICS ENGINEERING/FIZIK MUHENDISLIGI DERGISI. 1977. q. T M M O B Chamber of Turkish Physics Engineering, Konur Sokak 4, Kat 3, Yenisehir, 06450 Ankara, Turkey. TEL 4-188-83-96.

530.44   UK   ISSN 0022-3778
QC718   CODEN: JPLPBZ
JOURNAL OF PLASMA PHYSICS. 1967. 6/yr. (in 2 vols., 3 nos./vol.). $350 to individuals; institutions $478. Cambridge University Press, Edinburgh Bldg., Shaftesbury Rd., Cambridge CB2 2RU, England. TEL 0223-312393. FAX 0223-315052. TELEX 851817256. (North American addr.: Cambridge University Press, 40 W. 20th St., New York, NY 10011) Ed. Dr. J.P. Dougherty. adv.; bk.rev.; bibl.; charts; index. (also avail. in microform from UMI) **Indexed:** Appl.Mech.Rev., Chem.Abstr., Curr.Cont., Ind.Sci.Rev., INIS Atomind., Int.Aerosp.Abstr., Phys.Ber., Sci.Abstr., Solid St.Abstr.
—BLDSC shelfmark: 5040.550000.
  Description: Primary research articles in plasma physics, both theoretical and experimental, and its applications to fusion, laboratory plasmas and comunications devices.

JOURNAL OF SOVIET LASER RESEARCH. see *ENGINEERING*

530   US   ISSN 0022-4715
QC175   CODEN: JSTPSB
JOURNAL OF STATISTICAL PHYSICS. 1969. 24/yr. (in 3 vols.). $1295 (foreign $1515)(effective 1992). Plenum Publishing Corp., 233 Spring St., New York, NY 10013-1578. TEL 212-620-8000. FAX 212-463-0742. TELEX 23-421139. Ed. Joel L. Lebowitz. adv. (also avail. in microfilm from JSC; back issues avail.) **Indexed:** Appl.Mech.Rev., Compumath, Curr.Cont., Eng.Ind., Ind.Sci.Rev., INIS Atomind., Math.R., Nucl.Sci.Abstr., Phys.Ber., Ref.Zh., Sci.Abstr., Sci.Res.Abstr., Solid.St.Abstr.
—BLDSC shelfmark: 5066.840000.
  Refereed Serial

530   IR
JOURNAL OF THE EARTH AND SPACE PHYSICS. (Text and summaries in English, Farsi, French, German) 1972. s-a. $2.50. University of Teheran, Institute of Geophysics, Amirabad-e Shomali Ave., Teheran 14394, Iran. Ed. Bahram Akasheh. adv.; charts; stat. **Indexed:** Abstr.J.Earthq.Eng., GeoRef.

530   US   ISSN 0887-8722
TL900   CODEN: JTHTEO
JOURNAL OF THERMOPHYSICS AND HEAT TRANSFER; devoted to thermophysics and heat transfer. 1987. q. $150 to non-members (foreign $180); members $22 (foreign $35). American Institute of Aeronautics and Astronautics, Inc., 370 L'Enfant Promenade, S.W., Washington, DC 20024. TEL 202-646-7400. Ed. Alfred L. Crosbie. charts; illus.; index; circ. 1,000. (also avail. in microform; reprint service avail. from UMI) **Indexed:** Appl.Mech.Rev.
—BLDSC shelfmark: 5069.099300.
  Description: Advancement of the science and technology of thermophysics and heat transfer through the dissemination of original research papers disclosing new technical knowledge and exploratory developments and applications based on new knowledge.
  Refereed Serial

530   US   ISSN 0731-3764
JOURNAL OF UNDERGRADUATE RESEARCH IN PHYSICS. 1982. s-a. $5 to individuals; institutions $10; foreign $12. (American Institute of Physics) Guilford College, Department of Physics, Guilford, NC 27410. FAX 919-854-3606. (Co-sponsor: Society of Physics Students) Ed. Rexford E. Adelberger. bk.rev.; circ. 8,000.
—BLDSC shelfmark: 5071.518000.
  Description: Devoted to research work done by undergraduate students in physics and related fields.
  Refereed Serial

533.5   US   ISSN 0734-2101
TJ940   CODEN: JVTAD6
JOURNAL OF VACUUM SCIENCE AND TECHNOLOGY. PART A. VACUUM, SURFACES AND FILMS. 1964. 6/yr. $480 (foreign $525). (American Vacuum Society) American Institute of Physics, 335 E. 45th St., New York, NY 10017. TEL 212-661-9404. Ed. G. Lucovsky. adv.; bk.rev.; charts; illus.; index. (also avail. in microform from MIM; back issues avail.) **Indexed:** C.P.I., Cadscan, Chem.Abstr., Curr.Cont., Eng.Ind., Gen.Phys.Adv.Abstr., Ind.Sci.Rev., INIS Atomind., Int.Aerosp.Abstr., Int.Packag.Abstr., Lead Abstr., Mass Spectr.Bull., Met.Abstr., Phys.Ber., Phys.Abstr., Sci.Abstr., World Alum.Abstr., Zincscan.
—BLDSC shelfmark: 5072.210100.
  Supersedes in part: Journal of Vacuum Science and Technology (ISSN 0022-5355)
  Refereed Serial

533.5   US   ISSN 0734-211X
TJ940   CODEN: JVTBD9
JOURNAL OF VACUUM SCIENCE AND TECHNOLOGY. PART B. MICROELECTRONICS PROCESSING AND PHENOMENA. 1964. 6/yr. $385 (foreign $413). (American Vacuum Society) American Institute of Physics, 335 E. 45th St., New York, NY 10017. TEL 212-661-9404. Ed. G.E. McGuire. adv.; bk.rev.; charts; illus.; index. (also avail. in microform from MIM; back issues avail.) **Indexed:** Cadscan, INIS Atomind., Lead Abstr., Mass Spectr.Bull., Met.Abstr., Zincscan.
—BLDSC shelfmark: 5072.210150.
  Supersedes in part: Journal of Vacuum Science and Technology (ISSN 0022-5355)
  Refereed Serial

530 620   US   ISSN 0895-3996
QC480.8   CODEN: JXSTE5
JOURNAL OF X-RAY SCIENCE AND TECHNOLOGY. 1988. q. $110 (foreign $123). Academic Press, Inc., Journal Division, 1250 Sixth Ave., San Diego, CA 92101. TEL 619-230-1840. FAX 619-699-6800. TELEX 181726. Ed. Larry Knight. (back issues avail.)
—BLDSC shelfmark: 5072.705000.
  Description: Articles on recent developments in x-ray sources: synchrotons, and x-ray lasers; x-ray image formation; x-ray spectroscopy; and x-ray physics.
  Refereed Serial

530   MY   ISSN 0128-0333
JURNAL FIZIK MALAYSIA. (Text in English) 1980. q. $80 to libraries; individuals $40. Malaysian Institute of Physics, c/o Physics Department, University of Malaysia, 59100 Kuala Lumpur, Malaysia. TEL 03-7555466. FAX 3-7573661. TELEX 39845-MA-UNIMAL. Ed. S. Lee. circ. 500. (back issues avail.) **Indexed:** Chem.Abstr., INIS Atomind., Phys.Abstr.
—BLDSC shelfmark: 5075.600500.

530 540   JA
KAGAKU KOENKAI KOEN YOSHI. (Text in Japanese) 1978. a. Rikagaku Kenkyujo - Institute of Physical and Chemical Research, 2-1 Hirosawa, Wako-shi, Saitama-ken 351-01, Japan. TEL 0484-621111. FAX 0484-621554.

KAGOSHIMA DAIGAKU RIGAKUBU KIYO. SUGAKU, BUTSURIGAKU, KAGAKU/KAGOSHIMA UNIVERSITY. FACULTY OF SCIENCE. REPORTS. MATHEMATICS, PHYSICS, CHEMISTRY. see *SCIENCES: COMPREHENSIVE WORKS*

KINEMATICS AND PHYSICS OF CELESTIAL BODIES. see *ASTRONOMY*

KOLLOIDNYI ZHURNAL; journal of physico-chemistry of surface phenomenon and dispersed systems. see *CHEMISTRY — Physical Chemistry*

PHYSICS 3823

KONGELIGE DANSKE VIDENSKABERNES SELSKAB. MATEMATISK - FYSISKE MEDDELELSER. see *MATHEMATICS*

KUMAMOTO JOURNAL OF MATHEMATICS. see *MATHEMATICS*

530   JA   ISSN 0303-4070
QC1   CODEN: PRKUBN
KUMAMOTO UNIVERSITY. DEPARTMENT OF PHYSICS. PHYSICS REPORTS. 1973. biennial. free. Kumamoto Daigaku, Rigakubu Butsuri Kyoshitsu - Kumamoto University, Faculty of Science, Department of Physics, 39-1, Kurokami 2-chome, Kumamoto-shi, Kumamoto-ken 860, Japan. Ed. Tsueharu Kamiya. circ. 400. **Indexed:** GeoRef.
  Description: Presents technical research reports in physics from the university.

KVANTOVAYA ELEKTRONIKA; respublikanskii mezhvedomstvennyi sbornik nauchnykh trudov. see *ENGINEERING — Electrical Engineering*

530 548   US   ISSN 0075-787X
LANDOLT-BOERNSTEIN, ZAHLENWERTE UND FUNKTIONEN AUS NATURWISSENSCHAFTEN UND TECHNIK. NEUE SERIE. GROUP 3: CRYSTAL PHYSICS. 1966. irreg. price varies. Springer-Verlag, 175 Fifth Ave., New York, NY 10010. TEL 212-460-1500. (Also Berlin, Heidelberg, Tokyo and Vienna) Ed. K.H. Hellwege. (reprint service avail. from ISI)

LAWRENCE BERKELEY LABORATORY. CATALOG OF RESEARCH PROJECTS. see *SCIENCES: COMPREHENSIVE WORKS*

530   US   ISSN 0075-8450
            CODEN: LNPHA4
LECTURE NOTES IN PHYSICS. 1969. irreg. price varies. Springer-Verlag, 175 Fifth Ave., New York, NY 10010. TEL 212-460-1500. (also Berlin, Heidelberg, Vienna) (reprint service avail. from ISI) **Indexed:** Chem.Abstr., Ind.Sci.Rev., Phys.Ber.
—BLDSC shelfmark: 5180.350000.

530   SI
LECTURE NOTES IN PHYSICS. (Text in English) 1985. irreg., vol. 45, 1991. price varies. World Scientific Publishing Co. Pte. Ltd., Farrer Rd., P.O. Box 128, Singapore 9128, Singapore. TEL 3825663. FAX 3825919. TELEX RS 28561 WSPC. (UK addr.: 73 Lynton Mead, Totteridge, London N20 8DH, England. TEL 44-81-4462461; US addr.: 1060 Main St., Ste. 1B, River Edge, NJ 07661. TEL 800-227-7562)

530 540   RU   ISSN 0024-0826
AS262   CODEN: VLUFBI
LENINGRADSKII UNIVERSITET. VESTNIK. SERIYA FIZIKA I KHIMIYA. (Text in Russian; summaries in English) 1946. q. 18.60 Rub. Leningradskii Universitet, Universitetskaya Nab., 7-9, St. Petersburg V-164, Russia. (Subscr. to: Mezhdunarodnaya Kniga, Moscow, G-200, Russia) Ed. A.V. Storonkin. bk.rev.; charts; illus.; index; circ. 1,340. (also avail. in microfiche from BHP) **Indexed:** Chem.Abstr., Math.R.
—BLDSC shelfmark: 0031.000000.

530 510   NE   ISSN 0377-9017
QC19.2   CODEN: LMPHDY
LETTERS IN MATHEMATICAL PHYSICS; a journal for the rapid dissemination of short contributions in the field of mathematical physics. Short title: L M P. 1975. 12/yr. $471. Kluwer Academic Publishers, Postbus 17, 3300 AA Dordrecht, Netherlands. TEL 078-334911. FAX 078-334254. TELEX 29245. (Dist. by: Kluwer Academic Publishers Group, P.O. Box 322, 3300 AH Dordrecht, Netherlands; N. America dist. addr.: Box 358, Accord Sta., Hingham, MA 02018-0358. TEL 617-871-6600) Ed. M. Flato. adv. (reprint service avail. from SWZ) **Indexed:** Astron.& Astrophys.Abstr., Chem.Abstr., Compumath, Curr.Cont., Ind.Sci.Rev., INIS Atomind., Math.R., Phys.Ber., Sci.Abstr., Sci.Cit.Ind.
—BLDSC shelfmark: 5185.206400.

530   BE
LEUVEN NOTES IN MATHEMATICAL AND THEORETICAL PHYSICS. SERIES A, MATHEMATICAL PHYSICS. 1989. irreg., vol.2, 1990. Leuven University Press, Krakenstraat 3, B-3000 Leuven, Belgium. TEL 016-284175. FAX 016-284176.

PHYSICS

530   BE
▼**LEUVEN NOTES IN MATHEMATICAL AND THEORETICAL PHYSICS. SERIES B, THEORETICAL PARTICLE PHYSICS.** 1990. irreg., vol.4, 1991. Leuven University Press, Krakenstraat 3, B-3000 Leuven, Belgium. TEL 016-284175. FAX 016-284176.

LICHTENBERG-JAHRBUCH. see *BIOGRAPHY*

LIQUID CHROMATOGRAPHY MASS SPECTROMETRY ABSTRACTS. see *CHEMISTRY*

530   US   ISSN 1047-4064
QC1   CODEN: LPJOED
LITHUANIAN PHYSICS JOURNAL. English translation of: Lietuvos Fizikos Rinkinys (LI ISSN 0024-2969) 1974. bi-m. $635. (Akademiya Nauk Litvi, Institut Fiziki, LI) Allerton Press, Inc., 150 Fifth Ave., New York, NY 10011. TEL 212-924-3950. Ed. P. Brazdziunas. **Indexed:** Math.R., Phys.Ber., Sci.Abstr.
—BLDSC shelfmark: 0415.596000.
   Formerly (until 1989): Soviet Physics - Collection (ISSN 0363-7891)

530   LI   ISSN 0024-2969
QC1   CODEN: LFRMA7
LITOVSKII FIZICHESKII SBORNIK/LIETUVOS FIZIKOS RINKINYS. English translation: Lithuanian Physics Journal (US ISSN 1047-4064) (Text in Russian; summaries in English, Lithuanian) 1961. 6/yr. 1.20 Rub. per no. (Akademiya Nauk Litvi, Institut Fiziki - Lithuanian Academy of Sciences, Institute of Physics) Leidykla Mokslas, Zvaigzdziu 23, Vilnius 2050, Lithuania. TEL 45-85-26. TELEX 261107 LMOKSU. Ed. A. Sileika. bibl.; charts; illus.; circ. 1,000. **Indexed:** Chem.Abstr., INIS Atomind., Sci.Abstr., World Alum.Abstr.
—BLDSC shelfmark: 0098.200000.
   Description: Deals with semiconductor physics, spectroscopy and laser radiation.

M M I PRESS POLYMER MONOGRAPH SERIES. see *MATHEMATICS*

M M I PRESS SYMPOSIUM SERIES. see *MATHEMATICS*

538.3   US
▼**M R (SAN FRANCISCO);** the quarterly magazine of magnetic resonance. 1991. q. $35. Miller Freeman, Inc., 600 Harrison St., San Francisco, CA 94107. TEL 415-905-2200. FAX 415-905-2232. Ed. Peter Ogle. adv.; circ. 20,000.
   Description: Covers magnetic resonance imaging in detail.

530   US   ISSN 0883-7694
    CODEN: MRSBEA
M R S BULLETIN. 1976. m. $125 (foreign $140). Materials Research Society, 9800 McKnight Rd., Pittsburgh, PA 15237. TEL 412-367-3003. FAX 412-367-4373. Eds. Elizabeth Fleischer, Elton Kaufmann. adv.; bk.rev.; charts; illus.; tr.lit.; circ. 11,000. (reprint service avail. from UMI)
—BLDSC shelfmark: 5980.805700.
   Description: Serves as a forum for analysis and discussion of technical developments on a broad range of issues touching the materials community. Includes technical review articles, professional opportunities, and news on national and international materials policy and directions.

530 621.3   US   ISSN 1055-6915
TP156.M26   CODEN: MELSE3
MAGNETIC AND ELECTRICAL SEPARATION. 4/yr. (in 1 vol., 4 nos./vol.). $113. Gordon & Breach Science Publishers, 270 Eighth Ave., New York, NY 10011. TEL 212-206-8900. FAX 212-645-2459. TELEX 236735 GOPUB UR. (Subscr. to: Box 786, Cooper Sta., NY 10276. TEL 800-545-8398; UK subscr. to: P.O. Box 90, Reading, Berkshire RG1 8JL, England. TEL 0734-560-080) Eds. Jan Svoboda, F.J. Friedlander. index. (also avail. in microform) **Indexed:** Met.Abstr.
—BLDSC shelfmark: 5335.900000.
   Formerly (until vol.3): Magnetic Separation News (ISSN 0731-3632)
   Refereed Serial

MAGNETIC RESONANCE IN MEDICINE. see *MEDICAL SCIENCES — Radiology And Nuclear Medicine*

538.3   US   ISSN 0097-7330
QC762   CODEN: MRSRBL
MAGNETIC RESONANCE REVIEW. 4/yr. (in 1 vol., 4 nos./vol.). $236. Gordon and Breach Science Publishers, 270 Eighth Ave., New York, NY 10011. TEL 212-206-8900. FAX 212-645-2459. TELEX 236735 GOPUB UR. (Subscr. to: Box 786, Cooper Sta., New York, NY 10276. TEL 800-545-8398; UK subscr. to: P.O. Box 90, Reading, Berkshire RG1 8JL, England. TEL 0734-560-080) Ed. Charles P. Poole, Jr. adv.; bk.rev.; index. (also avail. in microform from MIM) **Indexed:** Chem.Abstr., Met.Abstr., Sci.Abstr.
—BLDSC shelfmark: 5337.800000.
   Refereed Serial

530   HU   ISSN 0025-0104
QC1   CODEN: MGFFAC
MAGYAR FIZIKAI FOLYOIRAT/HUNGARIAN JOURNAL OF PHYSICS. 1953. bi-m. $30.50. (Magyar Tudomanyos Akademia) Akademiai Kiado, Publishing House of the Hungarian Academy of Sciences, P.O. Box 24, H-1363 Budapest, Hungary. Ed. L. Pal. adv.; bk.rev.; charts; index. **Indexed:** Appl.Mech.Rev., Chem.Abstr, INIS Atomind., Sci.Abstr.

530 520   IR   ISSN 0254-9611
MAJALLAH-I FIZIK/IRANIAN JOURNAL OF PHYSICS. (Text in Persian; table of contents in English) 1983. q. Rs.1350 (Middle East £18; Europe £20; elsewhere £25). Iran University Press, P.O. Box 15875-4748, 85 Park Ave., Tehran, Iran. TEL 21-626031. FAX 21-4161749. TELEX 213636-8-D5300. Ed. R. Mansouri. bk.rev.; circ. 4,000. **Indexed:** INIS Atomind.
   Description: Aims to maintain personal communication among Farsi speaking physicists. Deals with educational and cultural aspects of physics. Reports on the most recent developments in fundamental and applied physics.

530   CS
MASARYK UNIVERSITY. FACULTY OF SCIENCES. SCRIPTA PHYSICA. (Text in English, French, German, Russian) 2/yr. 6.50 Kcs. per no. Masarykova Universita, Prirodovedecka Fakulta - Masaryk University, Faculty of Sciences, Kotlarska 2, 611 37 Brno, Czechoslovakia. **Indexed:** Sci.Abstr.
   Former titles: Scripta Facultatis Scientiarum Naturalium Universitatis Masarykianae Brunensis: Physica; Scripta Facultatis Scientiarum Naturalium Universitatis Purkynianae Brunensis: Physica.

MASS SPECTROMETRY. see *CHEMISTRY*

MATEMATICHESKAYA FIZIKA I FUNKTSIONAL'NYI ANALIZ. see *MATHEMATICS*

MATEMATIKA A FYZIKA VE SKOLE. see *EDUCATION*

530   NE   ISSN 0167-577X
TA401   CODEN: MLETDJ
MATERIALS LETTERS; an interdisciplinary journal affiliated with the Materials Research Society devoted to the rapid publication of short communications on the science, applications and processing of materials. (Text in English) 1982. 18/yr.(in 3 vols.; 6 nos./vol.). fl.1098 (effective 1992). (Materials Research Society) North-Holland (Subsidiary of: Elsevier Science Publishers B.V.), P.O. Box 211, 1000 AE Amsterdam, Netherlands. TEL 020-5803911. FAX 020-5803598. TELEX 18582 ESPA NL. (Subscr. in U.S. and Canada to: Elsevier Science Publishing Co., Inc., Box 882, Madison Sq. Sta., New York, NY 10159. TEL 212-989-5800) Ed.Bd. (back issues avail.) **Indexed:** Ceram.Abstr., Chem.Abstr., INIS Atomind., Int.Aerosp.Abstr., Met.Abstr., Phys.Ber., Sci.Abstr., World Alum.Abstr.
—BLDSC shelfmark: 5396.002000.
   Description: Covers the entire spectrum of materials science, from solid state physics to materials technology.
   Refereed Serial

530   NE
MATERIALS PROCESSING: THEORY AND PRACTICES. 1980. irreg., vol.9, 1991. price varies. Elsevier Science Publishers B.V., Books Division, P.O. Box 211, 1000 AE Amsterdam, Netherlands. TEL 020-5803911. FAX 020-5803705. TELEX 18582 ESPA NL. (Subscr. in U.S. and Canada to: Elsevier Science Publishing Co., Inc., Box 882, Madison Sq. Sta., New York, NY 10159. TEL 212-989-5800) Ed. F.F.Y. Wang.
   Refereed Serial

530 620 540   US   ISSN 0272-9172
    CODEN: MRSPDH
MATERIALS RESEARCH SOCIETY SYMPOSIUM PROCEEDINGS. 1981. irreg. (approx. 50/yr.). price varies. Materials Research Society, 9800 McKnight Rd., Pittsburgh, PA 15237. TEL 412-367-3012. FAX 412-367-4373. (reprint service avail. from UMI) **Indexed:** Chem.Abstr., INIS Atomind., Phys.Abstr., Phys.Ber., Sci.Abstr.
—BLDSC shelfmark: 5396.412000.

530 541.3   SZ   ISSN 0255-5476
TA401.3   CODEN: MSFOEP
MATERIALS SCIENCE FORUM. 1984. 14/yr. 1590 SFr. Trans Tech Publications, Hardstr. 13, P.O. Box 100, CH-4714 Aemannsdorf, Switzerland. FAX 62-741058. Ed.Bd. circ. 800. **Indexed:** Chem.Abstr., INIS Atomind.
—BLDSC shelfmark: 5396.435700.

530   NE   ISSN 0920-2307
TA401   CODEN: MSREEL
MATERIALS SCIENCE REPORTS; a review journal. (Text in English) 1986. 16/yr.(in 2 vols.; 8 nos./vol.). fl.712 (effective 1992). North-Holland (Subsidiary of: Elsevier Science Publishers B.V.), P.O. Box 211, 1000 AC Amsterdam, Netherlands. TEL 020-5803911. FAX 020-5803598. TELEX 18582 ESPA NL. (Subscr. in U.S. and Canada to: Elsevier Science Publishing Co., Inc., Box 882, Madison Sq. Sta., New York, NY 10159. TEL 212-989-5800) Eds. S.S. Lau, F.W. Saris. (back issues avail.)
—BLDSC shelfmark: 5396.439000.
   Description: Provides a general background of materials science and presents specialized reviews on current and significant developments in the field.
   Refereed Serial

MATHEMATICAL AND PHYSICAL SOCIETY OF EGYPT. PROCEEDINGS. see *MATHEMATICS*

MATHEMATICAL PHYSICS AND APPLIED MATHEMATICS. see *MATHEMATICS*

530 510   NE
MATHEMATICAL PHYSICS STUDIES. (Supplementary series to: Letters in Mathematical Physics) 1977. irreg. price varies. Kluwer Academic Publishers, Spuiboulevard 50, P.O. Box 17, 3300 AA Dordrecht, Netherlands. TEL 078-334911. FAX 078-334254. TELEX 29245. (Dist. by: Kluwer Academic Publishers Group, P.O. Box 322, 3300 AH Dordrecht, Netherlands; U.S. address: Box 358, Accord Sta., Hingham, MA 02018-0358. TEL 617-871-6600) Ed.Bd. **Indexed:** Math.R.

MATHEMATISCHE SEMESTERBERICHTE; zur Foerderung der Mathematik in Unterricht und Kultur. see *MATHEMATICS*

MEASUREMENT. see *METROLOGY AND STANDARDIZATION*

MEASUREMENT SCIENCE AND TECHNOLOGY. see *INSTRUMENTS*

MEDICAL PHYSICS. see *MEDICAL SCIENCES*

MEDICAL PHYSICS SERIES. see *MEDICAL SCIENCES*

530   JA   ISSN 0910-0717
MEIDAI UCHUSAN KENKYUSHITSU KIJI/NAGOYA UNIVERSITY. SOLAR-TERRESTRIAL ENVIRONMENT LABORATORY. COSMIC RAY SECTION. PROCEEDINGS. (Text in Japanese) 1947. irreg. (1-2/yr.). exchange basis. Nagoya University, Solar-Terrestrial Environment Laboratory, Cosmic Ray Section, Chikusa-ku, Nagoya-shi, Aichi-ken 464-01, Japan. cum.index: 1947-1986. **Indexed:** Chem.Abstr, JTA, Sci.Abstr.

MEISEI DAIGAKU KENKYU KIYO. RIKOGAKUBU/MEISEI UNIVERSITY. RESEARCH BULLETIN. PHYSICAL SCIENCES AND ENGINEERING. see *ENGINEERING*

MELTS. see *CHEMISTRY*

METHODEN UND VERFAHREN DER MATHEMATISCHEN PHYSIK. see *MATHEMATICS*

PHYSICS

530 US ISSN 0076-695X
CODEN: MEEPAN
METHODS OF EXPERIMENTAL PHYSICS. 1959. irreg., vol.27, 1988. Academic Press, Inc., 1250 Sixth Ave., San Diego, CA 92101. TEL 619-231-0926. FAX 619-699-6715. Eds. Robert Celotta, Juah Levine. (reprint service avail. from ISI) **Indexed:** Chem.Abstr., Phys.Ber.
Refereed Serial

MOLECULAR PHYSICS. see *CHEMISTRY — Physical Chemistry*

MONOGRAPHS IN PHYSICAL MEASUREMENT. see *ENGINEERING*

530 540 US
MONOGRAPHS ON THE PHYSICS AND CHEMISTRY OF MATERIALS. irreg. price varies. Oxford University Press, 200 Madison Ave., New York, NY 10016. TEL 212-679-7300. Ed.Bd.
Refereed Serial

530 UK ISSN 0960-0175
CODEN: JMPSEC
▼**MOSCOW PHYSICAL SOCIETY. JOURNAL**. Short title: J M P S. 1991. q. £132($264) (effective Jan. 1992). I O P Publishing, Techno House, Redcliffe Way, Bristol BS1 6NX, England. TEL 0272-297481. FAX 0272-294318. TELEX 449149-INSTP-G. (U.S. addr.: American Institute of Physics, Member and Subscriber Service, 500 Sunnyside Blvd., Woodbury, NY 11797-2999. TEL 516-576-2270) (Co-sponsor: Institute of Physics) Ed. L.V. Keldysh. (also avail. in microfiche; microform; back issues avail.)
—BLDSC shelfmark: 4828.372000.
Description: Subjects include: mathematical and general physics, classical phenomenology, non-linear phenomena, plasma physics, optics and spectroscopy, condensed matter physics, high energy physics, field theory, and general relativity.
Refereed Serial

530 US ISSN 0027-1349
Q4 CODEN: MUPBAC
MOSCOW UNIVERSITY PHYSICS BULLETIN. English translation of: Moskovskii Universitet. Vestnik. Seriya 3: Fizika, Astronomiya. 1966. bi-m. $630. (Moskovskii Universitet, RU) Allerton Press, Inc., 150 Fifth Ave., New York, NY 10011. TEL 212-924-3950. Ed. V.S. Fursov. bk.rev.; charts; illus.; index. **Indexed:** Math.R., Sci.Abstr.
—BLDSC shelfmark: 0416.240000.

530 520 RU
MOSKOVSKII UNIVERSITET. VESTNIK. SERIYA 3: FIZIKA, ASTRONOMIYA. English translation: Moscow University Physics Bulletin (US ISSN 0027-1349) (Contents page in English) bi-m. 22.80 Rub. Moskovskii Universitet, Ul. Gertsena 5-7, 103009 Moscow, Russia. bk.rev.; bibl.; index. **Indexed:** Chem.Abstr., Int.Aerosp.Abstr., Math.R., Met.Abstr., Phys.Ber., World Alum.Abstr.

MOSSBAUER EFFECT REFERENCE AND DATA JOURNAL. see *CHEMISTRY*

530 SA ISSN 0257-2109
N A C NEWS. (National Accelerator Center) irreg. Council for Scientific and Industrial Research, Division of Information Services, P.O. Box 395, Pretoria 0001, South Africa. TEL 012-86-9211.
Description: Short reports on the progress of the center.

530 US
N A T O ADVANCED SCIENCE INSTITUTES SERIES B: PHYSICS. irreg., vol.294, 1992. (North Atlantic Treaty Organization, Scientific Affairs Division, BE) Plenum Publishing Corp., 233 Spring St., New York, NY 10013. TEL 212-620-8000. FAX 212-463-0742. TELEX 23-421139. (back issues avail.)
●Also available online. Vendor(s): European Space Agency (File no.128).
Description: Proceedings of NATO sponsored conferences in physics.
Refereed Serial

533.5 NE ISSN 0169-9431
CODEN: NDVTBN
N E V A C BLAD/DUTCH VACUUM SOCIETY. JOURNAL. 1963. 4/yr. fl.50. Nederlandse Vacuumvereniging - Dutch Vacuum Society, c/o FOM - Institute for Atomic and Molecular Physics, Kruislaan 407, 1098 SJ Amsterdam, Netherlands. TEL 31-20-6081234. FAX 31-20-6684106. Ed. Elias Vlieg. adv.; bk.rev.; charts; illus.; pat.; circ. 450. **Indexed:** Chem.Abstr, Phys.Abstr.
Formerly: Nederlands Tijdschrift voor Vacuumtechniek - Dutch Journal of Vacuum Technology (ISSN 0047-9233)
Description: Studys vacuum technology and its applications.

530 NE
N I K H E F. ANNUAL REPORT. 1946. a. Nationaal Instituut voor Kernfysica en Hoge-Energiefysica, Sectie-K - National Institute for Nuclear Physics Research, Postbus 41882, 1009 AJ Amsterdam, Netherlands. TEL 020-5929444. circ. 650.
Former titles: National Instituut voor Kernfysica en Hoge-Energiefysica; Instituut voor Kernphysisch Onderzoek. Annual Report.

539.7 NE
N I K H E F. K BULLETIN. (Text in English) 1976. irreg., no.15, 1990. Nationaal Instituut voor Kernfysica en Hoge-Energiefysica, Sectie-K - Institute for Nuclear Physics Research, Postbus 41882, 1009 AJ Amsterdam, Netherlands. TEL 020-5929444. illus.; circ. 150.
Formerly: I K O Newsletter.

530 JA ISSN 0914-5613
N I P R SYMPOSIUM ON UPPER ATMOSPHERE PHYSICS. PROCEEDINGS. (Text in English) 1988. irreg., no.4, 1991. exchange basis. National Institute of Polar Research - Kokuritsu Kyokuchi Kenkyujo, Library, 9-10, Kaga 1-chome, Itabashi-ku, Tokyo 173, Japan. Ed. Takao Hoshiai. circ. 1,000. **Indexed:** Geo.Abstr., GeoRef.
—BLDSC shelfmark: 6848.270620.

530 UK ISSN 0143-1536
N P L NEWS. irreg. (1-2/yr.). National Physical Laboratory, Teddington, Middx. TW11 0LW, England. FAX 081-943-2155. Ed. J.B. Johnson.
—BLDSC shelfmark: 6180.510000.

530 II ISSN 0027-6898
N P L TECHNICAL BULLETIN. (Text in English) 1966. q. free. (National Physical Laboratory) S.K. Joshi, Ed. & Pub., Dr. K.S. Krishnan Rd., New Delhi 110012, India. TEL 581440. FAX 91-11-5721436. TELEX 031-62454 RSD IN. adv.; charts; illus.; pat.; stat.; circ. 1,000. (also avail. in record)

530.44 JA ISSN 0547-1567
QC718
NAGOYA UNIVERSITY. INSTITUTE OF PLASMA PHYSICS. ANNUAL REVIEW/NAGOYA DAIGAKU PURAZUMA KENKYUJO NENPO. (Text in English) 1960. a. exchange basis. Nagoya Daigaku, Purazuma Kenkyujo - Nagoya University, Institute of Plasma Physics, Furo-cho, Chikusa-ku, Nagoya-shi 464, Japan. **Indexed:** INIS Atomind.

530.44 JA
NAGOYA UNIVERSITY. INSTITUTE OF PLASMA PHYSICS. TECHNICAL REPORTS. (Text in English) 1969. irreg. exchange basis. Nagoya Daigaku, Purazuma Kenkyujo - Nagoya University, Institute of Plasma Physics, Furo-cho, Chikusa-ku, Nagoya-shi 464, Japan.

530 621.3 UK ISSN 0957-4484
CODEN: NNOTER
▼**NANOTECHNOLOGY**. 1990. q. £138($268) (effective Jan. 1992). (Institute of Physics) I O P Publishing, Techno House, Redcliffe Way, Bristol BS1 6NX, England. TEL 0272-297481. FAX 0272-294318. TELEX 449149-INSTP-G. (U.S. addr.: American Institute of Physics, Member and Subscriber Service, 500 Sunnyside Blvd., Woodbury, NY 11797-2999. TEL 516-576-2270) Ed. E. Clayton Teague. (also avail. in microfiche; microform; back issues avail.)
—BLDSC shelfmark: 6015.335540.
Description: Aims to promote the dissemination of research and improve understanding amongst the engineering, fabrications, optics, electronics, materials science, biological and medical communities.
Refereed Serial

NATIONAL ACADEMY OF SCIENCES, INDIA. PROCEEDINGS. SECTION A. PHYSICAL SCIENCES. see *SCIENCES: COMPREHENSIVE WORKS*

530 JA ISSN 0915-6348
NATIONAL INSTITUTE FOR FUSION SCIENCE. RESEARCH REPORT. (Text in English) irreg. National Institute for Fusion Science, Research Information Center, Nagoya 464-01, Japan.
—BLDSC shelfmark: 7762.722437.

NATIONAL INSTITUTE OF STANDARDS AND TECHNOLOGY. JOURNAL OF RESEARCH. see *METROLOGY AND STANDARDIZATION*

NATIONAL TECHNICAL REPORT. see *ENGINEERING — Electrical Engineering*

NATURWISSENSCHAFTEN IM UNTERRICHT. PHYSIK-CHEMIE. see *EDUCATION — Teaching Methods And Curriculum*

530 371 GW
NATURWISSENSCHAFTEN IM UNTERRICHT PHYSIK; Beitraege zu seinen fachlichen, methodischen und didaktischen Problemen. 1967. 5/yr. DM.65.50 (foreign DM.70.50). Erhard Friedrich Verlag GmbH, Im Brande 15, Postfach 100150, 3016 Seelze-Velber, Germany. TEL 0511-40004-0. index.; cum.index; circ. 3,000. (processed)
Formerly (until 1990): Physikunterricht (ISSN 0031-9295)

530.07 NE
NEDERLANDSE CENTRALE ORGANISATIE VOOR TOEGEPAST-NATUURWETENSCHAPPELIJK ONDERZOEK. TECHNISCH-PHYSISCHE DIENST. ANNUAL REPORT. (Text in English) 1946. a. free. Nederlandse Centrale Organisatie voor Toegepast-Natuurwetenschappelijk Onderzoek, Technisch-Physische Dienst, Stieltjesweg 1, Delft, Netherlands. Ed.Bd. circ. 2,700.

NEW TECHNOLOGY JAPAN. see *MACHINERY*

530 UN ISSN 0077-8907
NEW TRENDS IN PHYSICS TEACHING. (Text in English and French) 1968. irreg., latest no.4. price varies. Unesco, 7-9 Place de Fontenoy, 75700 Paris, France. TEL 577-16-10. (Dist. in U.S. by: Unipub, 4611-F Assembly Dr., Lanham, MD 20706-4391)
—BLDSC shelfmark: 6089.140000.

530 NE
NIELS BOHR - COLLECTED WORKS. 1972. irreg., vol.9, 1986. price varies. Elsevier Science Publishers B.V., Books Division, P.O. Box 211, 1000 AE Amsterdam, Netherlands. TEL 020-5803911. FAX 020-5803598. TELEX 18582 ESPA NL. (Subscr. in U.S. and Canada to: Elsevier Science Publishing Co., Inc., Box 882, Madison Sq. Sta., New York, NY 10159. TEL 212-989-5800) Ed. L. Rosenfeld.
Refereed Serial

540 530 JA ISSN 0287-864X
NIHON RIKAGAKU KYOKAI. KENKYU KIYO. (Text in Japanese) a. Nihon Rikagaku Kyokai - Japan Society of Physics and Chemistry Education, 11-2-217 Sugamo 1-chome, Toshima-ku, Tokyo 170, Japan.
Description: Research bulletin of the society.

539 JA
NIIGATA AIRGLOW OBSERVATORY. BULLETIN. (Text in English) 1972. a. exchange basis. Niigata Daigaku, Rigakubu, Niigata Airglow Observatory - Niigata University, Faculty of Science, 8050 Igarashi Nino-cho, Niigata-shi 950-21, Japan.

530 540 JA ISSN 0286-7125
NIIGATA RIKAGAKU/JOURNAL OF PHYSICS AND CHEMISTRY OF NIIGATA. (Text in Japanese) a. Niigata-ken Rikagaku Gijutsu Shokuin Kyogikai, Niigata-ken Eisei Kogai Kenkyujo, 314-1 Sowa, Niigata-shi, Niigata-ken 950-21, Japan. abstr. **Indexed:** Chem.Abstr.
Description: Contains original articles, reviews, commentary, and news.

530 JA
NIIGATA UNIVERSITY. FACULTY OF SCIENCE. SCIENCE REPORTS. SERIES B: PHYSICS. (Text in European languages) 1964. irreg. exchange basis. Niigata Daigaku, Rigakubu - Niigata University, Faculty of Science, 8050 Igarashi Nino-cho, Niigata-shi 950-21, Japan.

PHYSICS

NONLINEARITY. see *MATHEMATICS*

NUCLEAR FUSION/FUSION NUCLEAIRE; journal of plasma physics and thermonuclear fusion. see *PHYSICS — Nuclear Physics*

530　　　　IT　　ISSN 0393-4578
IL NUOVO SAGGIATORE. 1958. bi-m. $54 to non-members. Editrice Compositori s.r.l., Via Salingrado 97-2, 40128 Bologna, Italy. TEL 51-327811. Ed. Pio Picchi.
　Incorporates (1978-1990): Fisica e Tecnologia (ISSN 0391-9757); Formerly (until 1984): Societa Italiana di Fisica. Bollettino (ISSN 0037-8801)

530　　　　US　　ISSN 0078-6322
　　　　　　　　　　　　CODEN: SFPTDU
ORGANIZATION OF AMERICAN STATES. DEPARTMENT OF SCIENTIFIC AFFAIRS. SERIE DE FISICA: MONOGRAFIAS. (Subseries of: Coleccion de Monografias Cientificas) (Text in Spanish) 1965. irreg., no.13, 1979. $3.50 per no. Organization of American States, 1889 F St., N.W., Washington, DC 20006. TEL 703-941-1617. circ. 3,000.

ORGONOMIC FUNCTIONALISM. see *MEDICAL SCIENCES — Psychiatry And Neurology*

OTTAWA R & D REPORT. see *ENGINEERING*

P-H'ATOM; physics magazine for youth. see *CHILDREN AND YOUTH — For*

538.3　　　　RU
PARAMAGNITNYI REZONANS. irreg. 0.58 Rub. per no. Kazanskii Universitet, Ul. Lenina, 4-5, Kazan, Russia. illus. **Indexed:** Chem.Abstr.

530　　　　GW　　ISSN 0934-0866
TA418.78　　　　　　CODEN: PPCHEZ
PARTICLE & PARTICLE SYSTEMS CHARACTERIZATION; an international journal devoted to the measure and description of particle and bulk properties in dispersed systems. 1983. 4/yr. DM.398. V C H Verlagsgesellschaft mbH, Postfach 101161, 6940 Weinheim, Germany. TEL 06201-602-0. FAX 06201-602328. TELEX 465516-VCHWH-D. (U.S. addr.: V C H Publishers Inc., 220 E. 23rd St., New York, NY 10010-4606) Ed.Bd. adv.; bk.rev.; circ. 750.
　—BLDSC shelfmark: 6407.310000.
　Formerly: Particle Characterization (ISSN 0176-2265)

530　　　　US　　ISSN 1043-6790
QC793　　　　　　CODEN: PARWEG
▼**PARTICLE WORLD.** 1991. 10/yr. $173. Gordon and Breach Science Publishers, 270 Eighth Ave., New York, NY 10011. TEL 212-206-8900. FAX 212-645-2459. TELEX 236735 GOPUB UR. (Subscr. to: Box 786, Cooper Sta., New York, NY 10276. TEL 800-545-8398; UK subscr. to: P.O. Box 90, Reading, Berkshire RG1 8JL, England. TEL 0734-560-080) Ed. Robert Klapisch. (also avail. in microform)
　—BLDSC shelfmark: 6407.432000.
　Refereed Serial

PEDAGOGICKA FAKULTA V OSTRAVE. MATEMATIKA, FYZIKA. see *MATHEMATICS*

530　　　　US　　ISSN 0260-4280
QC1
PERSPECTIVE OF PHYSICS (NEW YORK). 1976. irreg., vol.4, 1980. Gordon & Breach Science Publishers, 270 Eighth Ave., New York, NY 10011. TEL 212-206-8900. FAX 212-645-2459. TELEX 236735 GOPUB UR. (Subscr. to: Box 986, Cooper Sta., New York, NY 10276. TEL 800-545-8398; UK subscr. to: P.O. Box 90, Reading, Berkshire RG1 8JL, England. TEL 34-560-080) Eds. H. Massey, R. Peierls.
　Refereed Serial

530　　　　US
PERSPECTIVES IN PHYSICS (SAN DIEGO). 1988. irreg., vol.3, 1989. Academic Press, Inc., 1250 Sixth Ave., San Diego, CA 92101. TEL 619-231-6616. FAX 619-699-6715. Ed.Bd.
　Refereed Serial

530　　　　US　　ISSN 0141-1594
QC176.8.P45　　　　CODEN: PHTRDP
PHASE TRANSITIONS. SECTIONS A & B; a multinational journal. 1979. 12/yr. (in 3 vols.; 4 nos./vol.). $168. Gordon and Breach Science Publishers, 270 Eighth Ave., New York, NY 10011. TEL 212-206-8900. FAX 212-645-2459. TELEX 236735 GOPUB UR. (Subscr. to: Box 786, Cooper Sta., New York, NY 10276. TEL 800-545-8398; UK subscr. P.O. Box 90, Reading, Berkshire RG1 8JL, England. TEL 0734-560-080) Ed. A.M. Glazer. adv.; bk.rev.; charts; illus. (also avail. in microform) **Indexed:** Cadscan, Chem.Abstr., Lead Abstr., Met.Abstr., Phys.Ber., Sci.Abstr., World Alum.Abstr., Zincscan.
　—BLDSC shelfmark: 6449.155000.
　Refereed Serial

530　　　　UK　　ISSN 0031-8086
　　　　　　　　　　　　CODEN: PHMAA4
PHILOSOPHICAL MAGAZINE. (In two parts: Part A. Defects and Mechanical Properties (ISSN 0141-8610); Part B. Electronic, Optical and Magnetic Properties (ISSN 0141-8637)) 1798. m. £695($1190) includes Philosophical Magazine Letters. Taylor & Francis Ltd., Rankine Rd., Basingstoke, Hants. RG24 0PR, England. TEL 0256-840366. FAX 0256-479438. TELEX 858540. Ed. E.A. Davis. adv.; bibl.; charts; illus.; index. **Indexed:** Appl.Mech.Rev., Br.Ceram.Abstr., Br.Tech.Ind., Cadscan, Ceram.Abstr., Chem.Abstr., Curr.Cont., Deep Sea Res.& Oceanogr.Abstr., Eng.Ind., GeoRef., Lead Abstr., Math.R., Met.Abstr., Phys.Ber., Sci.Abstr., World Alum.Abstr., Zincscan.
　—BLDSC shelfmark: 6462.060000.
　Description: Information on experimental, theoretical and applied physics of condensed matter.
　Refereed Serial

530　　　　UK　　ISSN 0950-0839
QC173.4.C65　　　　CODEN: PMLEEG
PHILOSOPHICAL MAGAZINE LETTERS. (Text and summaries in English, French and German) 1987. m. £695($1190) includes Philosophical Magazine Parts A & B. Taylor & Francis Ltd., Rankine Rd., Basingstoke, Hants RG24 0PR, England. TEL 0256-840366. FAX 0256-479438. TELEX 858540. Eds. E.A. Davis, S.R. Elliott. index; circ. 1,500. (also avail. in microfiche; back issues avail.)
　—BLDSC shelfmark: 6462.120000.
　Refereed Serial

530　　　　CN
PHYS 13 NEWS. 1971. 4/yr. Can.$5. University of Waterloo, Department of Physics, Waterloo, Ont. N2L 3G1, Canada. TEL 519-885-1211. FAX 519-746-8115. Ed. Phil Eastman. adv.; bk.rev.; circ. 4,000.

530　　　　NE　　ISSN 0378-4371
QC1　　　　　　　CODEN: PHYADX
PHYSICA A - STATISTICAL AND THEORETICAL PHYSICS. (Text in English, French and German) 1934. 40/yr.(in 10 vols.; 4 nos./vol.). fl.3710 (combined subscr. to Sections A,B,C,D fl.12943)(effective 1992). (European Physical Society) North-Holland (Subsidiary of: Elsevier Science Publishers B.V.), P.O. Box 211, 1000 AE Amsterdam, Netherlands. TEL 020-5803911. FAX 020-5803598. TELEX 18582 ESPA NL. (Subscr. in U.S. and Canada to: Elsevier Science Publishing Co., Inc., Box 882, Madison Sq. Sta., New York, NY 10159. TEL 212-989-5800) Eds. H.W. Capel, I. Oppenheim. charts; index. (also avail. in microform from RPI; back issues avail.) **Indexed:** Appl.Mech.Rev., Cadscan, Chem.Abstr., Compumath, Deep Sea Res.& Oceanogr.Abstr., Lead Abstr., Mass Spectr.Bull., Math.R., Met.Abstr., Phys.Ber., Sci.Abstr., Zincscan.
　—BLDSC shelfmark: 6475.010000.
　Supersedes in part (in 1975): Physica (ISSN 0031-8914)
　Description: Contains papers in all fields of statistical and general theoretical physics.
　Refereed Serial

531 621.3　　　NE　　ISSN 0921-4526
QC1　　　　　　　CODEN: PHYBE3
PHYSICA B - PHYSICS OF CONDENSED MATTER. (Text in English) 1934. 32/yr.(in 8 vols.; 4 nos./vol.). fl.2968 (combined subscr. to Sections A,B,C,D fl.12943)(effective 1992). (European Physical Society) North-Holland (Subsidiary of: Elsevier Science Publishers B.V.), P.O. Box 211, 1000 AE Amsterdam, Netherlands. TEL 020-5803911. FAX 020-5803598. TELEX 18582 ESPA NL. (Subscr. in U.S. and Canada to: Elsevier Science Publishing Co., Inc., Box 882, Madison Sq. Sta., New York, NY 10159. TEL 212-989-5800) Ed.Bd. (back issues avail.) **Indexed:** Eng.Ind.
　—BLDSC shelfmark: 6475.015000.
　Supersedes in part (in 1988): Physica B en C (ISSN 0378-4363); Which superseded in part (in 1975): Physica (ISSN 0031-8914)
　Description: Discusses solid state and low-temperature physics as well as fundamental research on novel materials.
　Refereed Serial

530 621.3　　　NE　　ISSN 0921-4534
QC611.9　　　　　　CODEN: PHYCE6
PHYSICA C - SUPERCONDUCTIVITY. (Text in English) 1934. 68/yr.(in 17 vols.; 4 nos./vol.). fl.6307 (combined subscr. to Sections A,B,C,D fl.12943)(effective 1992). (European Physical Society) North-Holland (Subsidiary of: Elsevier Science Publishers B.V.), P.O. Box 211, 1000 AE Amsterdam, Netherlands. TEL 020-5803911. FAX 020-5803598. TELEX 18582 ESPA NL. (Subscr. in U.S. and Canada to: Elsevier Science Publishing Co., Inc., Box 882, Madison Sq. Sta., New York, NY 10159. TEL 212-989-5800) Ed. M.B. Brodsky. illus.; tr.lit.; index. (back issues avail.)
　—BLDSC shelfmark: 6475.025000.
　Supersedes in part (in 1988): Physica B en C (ISSN 0378-4363); Which superseded in part (1975): Physica (ISSN 0031-8914)
　Description: Covers all aspects of superconductivity research: fundamental work, materials engineering and applications.
　Refereed Serial

531 621.3　　　NE　　ISSN 0167-2789
QC1　　　　　　　CODEN: PDNPDT
PHYSICA D - NONLINEAR PHENOMENA. (Text in English) 1980. 32/yr.(in 8 vols.; 4 nos./vol.). fl.2968 (combined subscr. to Sections A,B,C,D fl.12943)(effective 1992). (European Physical Society) North-Holland (Subsidiary of: Elsevier Science Publishers B.V.), P.O. Box 211, 1000 AE Amsterdam, Netherlands. TEL 020-5803911. FAX 020-5803598. TELEX 18582 ESPA NL. (Subscr. in U.S. and Canada to: Elsevier Science Publishing Co., Inc., Box 882, Madison Sq. Sta., New York, NY 10159. TEL 212-989-5800) Eds. H. Flaschka, F.H. Busse. (back issues avail.) **Indexed:** Comput.Rev., Eng.Ind., Math.R., Phys.Abstr.
　—BLDSC shelfmark: 6475.030000.
　Supersedes in part (in 1975): Physica (ISSN 0031-8914)
　Description: Explores research of theoretical physicists working in statistical mechanics, plasma physics, hydrodynamics, and solid state physics as well, as mathematics.
　Refereed Serial

530 371　　　GW　　ISSN 0340-2134
PHYSICA DIDACTICA. 1974. q. DM.48. Verlag B. Franzbecker, Mozartstr. 3, 3202 Bad Salzdetfurth, Germany. Eds. H. Mikelskis, W. Jung. adv.; bk.rev.; charts; illus.

PHYSICA MEDICA. see *MEDICAL SCIENCES*

530　　　　SW　　ISSN 0031-8949
QC1　　　　　　　CODEN: PHSTBO
PHYSICA SCRIPTA; a monthly international journal for experimental and theoretical physics. (Text in English) 1970. a. SEK 4725 (foreign $900) includes Topical issues. Kungliga Vetenskapsakademien - Royal Swedish Academy of Sciences, Box 50005, S-104 05 Stockholm, Sweden. (Co-sponsors: Academies of Sciences and Physical Societies of Denmark, Finland, Iceland, Norway and Sweden) Ed. Anders Barany. charts; stat.; index; circ. 750. (back issues avail.) **Indexed:** Appl.Mech.Rev., Cadscan, Chem.Abstr., Curr.Cont., GeoRef., Instr.Aerosp.Abstr., Lead Abstr., Mass Spectr.Bull., Math.R., Met.Abstr., Phys.Ber., Sci.Abstr., World Alum.Abstr., Zincscan.
　—BLDSC shelfmark: 6475.150000.
　Incorporates: Physica Norvegica (ISSN 0031-8930) & Physica Fennica (ISSN 0031-8922)

530　　　　　　　SW　ISSN 0281-1847
QC1　　　　　　　　　CODEN: PHSTBO
PHYSICA SCRIPTA TOPICAL ISSUES. 1982. irreg. Kungliga Vetenskapsakademien - Royal Swedish Academy of Sciences, Box 50005, S-104 05 Stockholm, Sweden. Ed. Anders Barany.
—BLDSC shelfmark: 6475.151000.

530.41　　　　　GW　ISSN 0031-8965
　　　　　　　　　　　CODEN: PSSABA
PHYSICA STATUS SOLIDI (A). APPLIED RESEARCH. (Text mainly in English; occasionally in French, German or Russian) 1970. 12/yr. (in 6 vols., 2 nos./vol.). DM.1377.60. Akademie-Verlag Berlin, Leipziger Str. 3-4, 1086 Berlin, Germany. TELEX 114420-AVERL-DD. (U.S. subscr. to: V C H Publishers, Inc., 303 N.W. 12th Ave., Deerfield Beach, FL 33442-1788) Ed. E. Gutsche. charts; illus.; index. **Indexed:** Cadscan, Chem.Abstr., Curr.Cont., Lead Abstr., Mass Spectr.Bull., Met.Abstr., Phys.Ber., Sci.Abstr., Soils & Fert., World Alum.Abstr., Zincscan.
—BLDSC shelfmark: 6475.220000.

530.41　　　　　GW　ISSN 0370-1972
　　　　　　　　　　　CODEN: PSSBBD
PHYSICA STATUS SOLIDI (B). BASIC RESEARCH. (Text mainly in English, occasionally in French, German and Russian) 1961. 12/yr. (in 6 vols., 2 nos./vol.). DM.1377.60. Akademie-Verlag Berlin, Leipziger Str. 3-4, 1080 Berlin, Germany. TELEX 114420-AVERL-DD. (U.S. subscr. to VCH Publishers Inc., 303 N.W. 12th Ave., Deerfield Beach, FL 33442-1788) Ed. E. Gutsche. abstr.; bibl.; charts; illus.; index. **Indexed:** Cadscan, Chem.Abstr., Curr.Cont., Eng.Ind., Lead Abstr., Mass Spectr.Bull., Met.Abstr., Phys.Abstr., Sci.Abstr., World Alum.Abstr., Zincscan.
—BLDSC shelfmark: 6475.230000.

530.07　　　　　　II
PHYSICAL RESEARCH LABORATORY, AHMEDABAD: ANNUAL REPORT. (Text in English) 1954. a. Physical Research Laboratory, Ahmedabad-9, India. TELEX 0121-6397 PRL IN. Ed. Dr. Purobi Chakrabarty. illus.; circ. 250.

530　　　　　　　US　ISSN 0556-2791
QC1　　　　　　　　　CODEN: PLRAAN
PHYSICAL REVIEW A (GENERAL PHYSICS). 1970. s-m. $1350 to non-members (foreign $1535). (American Physical Society) American Institute of Physics, 335 E. 45th St., New York, NY 10017. TEL 212-661-9404. Eds. B. Crasemann, I. Oppenheim. bibl.; illus.; s-a. index. (also avail. in microfiche from BHP; microform; back issues avail.) **Indexed:** Appl.Mech.Rev., C.P.I., Cadscan, Chem.Abstr., Curr.Cont., Eng.Ind., Int.Aerosp.Abstr., Lead Abstr., Mass Spectr.Bull., Math.R., Met.Abstr., Phys.Abstr., Phys.Ber., Sci.Abstr., Zincscan.
Supersedes in part (1893-1969): Physical Review (ISSN 0031-899X)
Refereed Serial

530　　　　　　　US　ISSN 0163-1829
QC176.A1　　　　　　CODEN: PRBMDO
PHYSICAL REVIEW B (CONDENSED MATTER). 1970. 48/yr. (4/m.). $2380 to non-members (foreign $2715). (American Physical Society) American Institute of Physics, 335 E. 45th St., New York, NY 10017. TEL 212-661-9404. Ed. P.D. Adams. bibl.; illus.; s-a. index. (also avail. in microfiche; microform; back issues avail.) **Indexed:** Abstr.Bull.Inst.Pap.Chem., Appl.Mech.Rev., C.P.I., Cadscan, Ceram.Abstr., Chem.Abstr., Curr.Cont., Eng.Ind., GeoRef., Int.Aerosp.Abstr., Lead Abstr., Mass Spectr.Bull., Math.R., Met.Abstr., Phys.Abstr., Phys.Ber., Sci.Abstr., World Alum.Abstr., Zincscan.
—BLDSC shelfmark: 6476.050000.
Formerly (until Jul. 1978): Physical Review B (Solid State) (ISSN 0556-2805); **Supersedes in part (1893-1969):** Physical Review (ISSN 0031-899X)
Refereed Serial

530　　　　　　　US　ISSN 0031-9007
QC1　　　　　　　　　CODEN: PRLTAO
PHYSICAL REVIEW LETTERS. 1958. w. $1000. (American Physical Society) American Institute of Physics, 335 E. 45th St., New York, NY 10017. TEL 212-661-9404. Ed.Bd. abstr.; index, cum.index: 1956-1976. (also avail. in microfiche; microform; back issues avail.) **Indexed:** Appl.Mech.Rev., C.P.I., Cadscan, Chem.Abstr., Curr.Cont., Eng.Ind., GeoRef., Int.Aerosp.Abstr., Lead Abstr., Mass Spectr.Bull., Math.R., Met.Abstr., Phys.Abstr., Phys.Ber., Sci.Abstr., World Alum.Abstr., Zincscan.
—BLDSC shelfmark: 6476.200000.
Refereed Serial

530　　　　　　　JA　ISSN 0031-9015
QC1　　　　　　　　　CODEN: JUPSAU
PHYSICAL SOCIETY OF JAPAN. JOURNAL. (Supplement avail.) (Text in English, French, German; summaries in English) 1946. m. 75000 Yen. Physical Society of Japan - Nihon Butsuri Gakkai, Kikai Shinko Bldg., 3-5-8 Shiba Koen, Minato-ku, Tokyo 105, Japan. Ed. S. Kaneko. abstr.; charts; illus.; index, cum.index; circ. 2,600. (also avail. in microfiche; back issues avail.) **Indexed:** Appl.Mech.Rev., Chem.Abstr., Curr.Cont., GeoRef., INIS Atomind., Int.Aerosp.Abstr., JCT, JTA, Mass Spectr.Bull., Math.R., Met.Abstr., Phys.Ber., Sci.Abstr., World Alum.Abstr.
—BLDSC shelfmark: 4842.000000.
Formerly: Physico-Mathematical Society of Japan. Proceedings (ISSN 0370-1239)
Description: Devoted to the publication of original papers in all fields of physics. Intended to secure prompt publication of important new discoveries in physics.

530　　　　　　　JA
PHYSICAL SOCIETY OF JAPAN. JOURNAL. SUPPLEMENT. irreg. price varies. Physical Society of Japan - Nihon Butsuri Gakkai, Rm. 211, Kikai Shinko Bldg., 3-5-8 Shiba Koen, Minato-ku, Tokyo 105, Japan.

530　　　　　　　US
PHYSICS: A SERIES OF MONOGRAPHS & TRACTS. 1981. irreg. $88. Harwood Academic Publishers, 270 Eighth Ave., New York, NY 10011. TEL 212-206-8900. FAX 212-645-2459. TELEX 236735 GOPUB UR. (Subscr. to: Box 786, Cooper Sta., New York, NY 10276. TEL 800-545-8398; UK subscr. to: Box 90, Reading, Berkshire RG1 8JL, England. TEL 0734-560-080) Ed. P.B. Burt. bk.rev. (microform)
Formerly: Quantum Mechanics and Nonlinear Waves.
Refereed Serial

530　　　　　　　CS
PHYSICS AND APPLICATIONS. (Text in English) a. price varies. (Slovenska Akademia Vied) Veda, Publishing House of the Slovak Academy of Sciences, Klemensova 19, 814 30 Bratislava, Czechoslovakia. (Dist. by: Slovart, Nam. Slobody 6, 817 64 Bratislava, Czechoslovakia) Ed. Mikulas Blazek. **Indexed:** Chem.Abstr.
Formerly: High Energy Particle Physics.

PHYSICS AND CHEMISTRY IN SPACE. see *CHEMISTRY*

PHYSICS AND CHEMISTRY OF MATERIALS TREATMENT. see *ENGINEERING — Engineering Mechanics And Materials*

530　　　　　　　US
PHYSICS AND SOCIETY. 1972. q. $10 (free to members). American Physical Society, Forum on Physics and Society, 335 E. 45th St., New York, NY 10017-3483. FAX 501-575-4580. Ed. Art Hobson. bk.rev.; circ. 4,500.
Description: Presents letters, articles, reviews, news, and comment on the relations of physics to society.

PHYSICS, CHEMISTRY AND MECHANICS OF SURFACES. see *ENGINEERING — Mechanical Engineering*

530.07 370　　　　UK　ISSN 0031-9120
QC30　　　　　　　　CODEN: PHEDA7
PHYSICS EDUCATION. 1966. 6/yr. £69($138) (effective 1992). (Institute of Physics) I O P Publishing, Techno House, Redcliffe Way, Bristol BS1 6NX, England. TEL 0272 297481. FAX 0272-294318. TELEX 449149-INSTP-G. (U.S. addr.: American Institute of Physics, Member and Subscriber Service, 500 Sunnyside Blvd., Woodbury, NY 11797-2999. TEL 516-576-2270) Ed. J. Avison. adv.; bk.rev.; charts; film rev.; illus.; index. (also avail. in microfiche; microfilm; back issues avail.) **Indexed:** C.I.J.E., Chem.Abstr., Cont.Pg.Educ., Educ.Tech.Abstr., High.Educ.Curr.Aware.Bull., Phys.Ber., Res.High.Educ.Abstr., Sci.Abstr., Stud.Wom.Abstr.
—BLDSC shelfmark: 6478.530000.

530　　　　　　　II　ISSN 0970-5953
　　　　　　　　　　　CODEN: PHEDEB
PHYSICS EDUCATION. (Text and summaries in English) 1984. q. Rs.80($20) per no. (University of Poona, Department of Physics) Wiley Eastern Ltd., Journal Division, 4835-24 Ansari Road, New Delhi 110 002, India. Ed. Arun S. Nigavekar. adv.; bk.rev.; illus.; circ. 1,000. **Indexed:** C.I.J.E., Educ.Tech.Abstr., ERIC, INSPEC, Sci.Abstr.
—BLDSC shelfmark: 6478.530500.
Description: Contains articles on physics. Aims to inform Indian audiences in academic areas of science.
Refereed Serial

530　　　　　　　CN　ISSN 0836-1398
　　　　　　　　　　　CODEN: PHESEM
PHYSICS ESSAYS. 1988. q. Can.$58 to individuals; institutions Can.$115; students Can.$32. (Advanced Laser and Fusion Technology, Inc.) University of Toronto Press, Journals Department, P.O. Box 1280, 1011 Sheppard Ave. W., Downsview, Ont. M3H 5V4, Canada. TEL 416-667-7781. (U.S. Address: 340 Nagel Dr., Cheektowaga, NY 14225) Ed. E. Panarella. circ. 200. (back issues avail.)
—BLDSC shelfmark: 6478.560000.

530　　　　　　　CN　ISSN 0031-9147
PHYSICS IN CANADA/PHYSIQUE AU CANADA. (Text in English, French) 1944. 6/yr. Can.$30. Canadian Association of Physicists, 151 Slater St., Ste. 903, Ottawa, Ont. K1P 5H3, Canada. TEL 613-237-3392. FAX 613-238-1677. Ed. J.S.C. McKee. adv.; bk.rev.; charts; illus.; index; circ. 2,000. (also avail. in microfilm from UMI; reprint service avail. from MML)
—BLDSC shelfmark: 6478.500000.
Supersedes in part: Canadian Association of Physicists. Annual Report.

530　　　　　　　US
PHYSICS - MATHEMATICS INFORMATION REVIEW. 1987. q. $63. Nova Science Publishers, Inc., 283 Commack Rd., Ste. 300, Commack, NY 11725-3401. Ed. F. Columbus. circ. 700.
Refereed Serial

530　　　　　　　US
PHYSICS NEWS. a. free. American Institute of Physics, 335 E. 45th St., New York, NY 10017. TEL 212-661-9404. (Subscr. to: Member and Subscriber Service, 500 Sunnyside Blvd., Woodbury, NY 11797-2999. TEL 516-576-2270) Ed. Philip Shewe. (back issues avail.) **Indexed:** PMR.
Formerly: Physics (ISSN 0092-8437)

530　　　　　　　II　ISSN 0253-7583
QC1　　　　　　　　　CODEN: PNEWD7
PHYSICS NEWS. (Text in English) 1970. q. Rs.40($25) Indian Physics Association, T.I.F.R., Bombay 400 005, India. FAX 2205560750. TELEX 011-71017 BARC IN. (Subscr. Address: Editor, Physics News, Tata Institute of Fundamental Research, Homi Bhabha Rd., Bombay 400005, India) Ed. S.V. Lawande. adv.; bk.rev.; charts; illus, stat.; index; circ. 3,200. (back issues avail.) **Indexed:** Chem.Abstr.
—BLDSC shelfmark: 6478.872000.

PHYSICS

530.44   US   ISSN 0899-8213
QC150   CODEN: PFADEB
PHYSICS OF FLUIDS A: FLUID DYNAMICS. 1989. m.
$1130 includes Physics of Fluids B: Plasma Physics.
American Institute of Physics, 335 E. 45th St., New
York, NY 10017-3483. TEL 212-661-9404.
(Subscr. to: Member and Subscriber Service, 500
Sunnyside Blvd., Woodbury, NY 11797-2999. TEL
516-576-2270) (Co-sponsor: American Physical
Society) Ed. Andreas Acrivos.
—BLDSC shelfmark: 6478.620000.
   Supersedes in part (1958-1989): Physics of Fluids
(ISSN 0031-9171)
   Description: Devoted to original contributions to
the physics of fluids covering kinetic theory,
statistical mechanics, structure and general physics
of gases, liquids, and other fluids, as well as certain
basic aspects of physics of fluids bordering
geophysics, astrophysics, biophysics, and other fields
of science.
Refereed Serial

530.44   US   ISSN 0899-8221
QC717.6   CODEN: PFBPEI
PHYSICS OF FLUIDS B: PLASMA PHYSICS. 1989. m.
$1130 includes Physics of Fluids A: Fluid Dynamics.
American Institute of Physics, 335 E. 45th St., New
York, NY 10017-3483. TEL 212-661-9404.
(Subscr. to: Member and Subscriber Service, 500
Sunnyside Blvd., Woodbury, NY 11797-2999. TEL
516-576-2270) (Co-sponsor: American Physical
Society) Ed. R.C. Davidson.
—BLDSC shelfmark: 6478.640000.
   Supersedes in part (1958-1989): Physics of Fluids
(ISSN 0031-9171)
   Description: Devoted to original contributions to
and reviews of the physics of plasma, including
magneto-fluid mechanics, kinetic theory and
statistical mechanics of fully and partially ionized
gases.
Refereed Serial

PHYSICS OF METALS. see *METALLURGY*

530   US   ISSN 0079-1970
QC176.A1   CODEN: PYTFA3
**PHYSICS OF THIN FILMS; ADVANCES IN RESEARCH AND
DEVELOPMENT.** 1963. irreg., vol.15, 1991.
Academic Press, Inc., 1250 Sixth Ave., San Diego,
CA 92101. TEL 619-231-0926.
FAX 619-699-6715. Ed. George Haas. index.
(reprint service avail. from ISI) **Indexed:** Chem.Abstr.
—BLDSC shelfmark: 6478.950000.
Refereed Serial

530   NE   ISSN 0370-1573
QC1   CODEN: PRPLCM
PHYSICS REPORTS; a review section of Physics Letters.
1971. 78/yr.(in 13 vols.; 6 nos./vol.). fl.4043
(combined subscr. with Physics Letters, Sections A &
B fl.12737)(effective 1992). North-Holland
(Subsidiary of: Elsevier Science Publishers B.V.), P.O.
Box 211, 1000 AE Amsterdam, Netherlands.
TEL 020-5803911. FAX 020-5803598. TELEX
18582 ESPA NL. (Subscr. in U.S. and Canada to:
Elsevier Science Publishing Co., Inc., Box 882,
Madison Sq. Sta., New York, NY 10159. TEL
212-989-5800) Ed.Bd. (also avail. in microform
from RPI; back issues avail.) **Indexed:** Chem.Abstr.,
Curr.Cont., Ind.Sci.Rev., Int.Aerosp.Abstr., Mass
Spectr.Bull., Math.R., Phys.Ber., Sci.Abstr.
—BLDSC shelfmark: 6478.885000.
   Incorporates: Case Studies in Atomic Physics (ISSN
0300-4503)
   Description: Short review articles on recent
developments in all fields of physics, including
particle and field physics, nuclear, molecular, plasma
and condensed matter physics, geophysics,
interdisciplinary papers, and applications.
Refereed Serial

530   NE
PHYSICS REPORTS REPRINTS BOOK SERIES. 1974.
irreg., vol.5, 1982. price varies. Elsevier Science
Publishers B.V., Books Division, P.O. Box 211, 1000
AE Amsterdam, Netherlands. TEL 020-5803911.
FAX 020-5803705. TELEX 18582 ESPA NL.
(Subscr. in U.S. and Canada to: Elsevier Science
Publishing Co., Inc., Box 882, Madison Sq. Sta., New
York, NY 10159. TEL 212-989-5800)
Refereed Serial

530   UK   ISSN 0959-8472
▼**PHYSICS REVIEW.** 1991. 5/yr. £17.95 (foreign
£30). Philip Allan Publishers Ltd., Deddington,
Oxfordshire OX15 OSE, England. TEL 0869-38652.
FAX 0869-38803.

530   II
PHYSICS TEACHER. (Text in English) 1958. q.
Rs.30($15) Indian Physical Society, 2-3 Raja
Subodh Mallik Rd., Calcutta 700032, India. TELEX
021-5501 IACS IN. Ed.Bd. adv.; bk.rev.; circ. 600.
Indexed: C.I.J.E., Educ.Ind.

530 370   US   ISSN 0031-921X
QC30   CODEN: PHTEAH
PHYSICS TEACHER (COLLEGE PARK). 1963. 9/yr.
$121 (foreign $133). American Association of
Physics Teachers, 5112 Berwyn Rd., College Park,
MD 20740. TEL 301-345-4200. Ed. C. Swartz.
adv.; bk.rev.; charts; film rev.; illus.; index. (also avail.
in microform; back issues avail.; reprint service avail.
from UMI) **Indexed:** C.I.J.E., C.P.I., Chem.Abstr.,
Cont.Pg.Educ., Curr.Cont., Educ.Ind., Gen.Sci.Ind.,
Phys.Ber., Sci.Abstr.
—BLDSC shelfmark: 6478.900000.

530   US   ISSN 0031-9228
QC1   CODEN: PHTOAD
PHYSICS TODAY. 1948. m. $115 (foreign $145).
American Institute of Physics, 335 E. 45th St., New
York, NY 10017. TEL 212-661-9404. (Subscr. to:
Member and Subscriber Service, 500 Sunnyside
Blvd., Woodbury, NY 11797-2999. TEL
516-576-2270) Ed. G.B. Lubkin. adv.; bk.rev.; bibl.;
charts; illus.; stat.; index; circ. 71,453. (also avail. in
microform; back issues avail.) **Indexed:** A.S.& T.Ind.,
Acad.Ind., Appl.Mech.Rev., Art &
Archaeol.Tech.Abstr., C.I.J.E., C.P.I., Cadscan,
Chem.Abstr., Curr.Cont., Curr.Pack.Abstr., Deep Sea
Res.& Oceanogr.Abstr., Energy Info.Abstr., Eng.Ind.,
Excerp.Med., Gen.Sci.Ind., GeoRef., Graph.Arts
Lit.Abstr., Int.Aerosp.Abstr., Lead Abstr., Mag.Ind.,
Mass Spectr.Bull., Phys.Ber., R.G., Sci.Abstr., TOM,
Zincscan.
—BLDSC shelfmark: 6479.000000.
Refereed Serial

530   UK   ISSN 0953-8585
QC1   CODEN: PHWOEW
PHYSICS WORLD. 1950. m. £61($120) (effective
1992). (Institute of Physics) I O P Publishing,
Techno House, Redcliffe Way, Bristol BS1 6NX,
England. TEL 0272 297481. FAX 0272-294318.
TELEX 449149-INSTP-G. (U.S. addr.: American
Institute of Physics, Member and Subscriber Service,
500 Sunnyside Blvd., Woodbury, NY 11797-2999.
TEL 516-576-2270) Ed. P. Campbell. adv.; bk.rev.;
charts; illus.; index. (also avail. in microfiche;
microfilm; back issues avail.) **Indexed:** AESIS,
Agri.Eng.Abstr., Br.Tech.Ind., Chem.Abstr.,
Excerp.Med., Phys.Ber., Res.High.Educ.Abstr.,
Sci.Abstr.
—BLDSC shelfmark: 6479.200000.
   Formerly (until 1988): Physics Bulletin (ISSN
0031-9112); **Incorporates:** Physics in Technology
(ISSN 0305-4624)

530 370   GW   ISSN 0031-9244
PHYSIK IN DER SCHULE. 1963. m. DM.40. Volk und
Wissen Verlag GmbH, Lindenstr. 54A, 1086 Berlin,
Germany. TEL 0372-20343-0. Eds. Johannes
Moehmel, Gerhard Hamann. adv.; bk.rev.; abstr,
illus, stat.; index.
—BLDSC shelfmark: 6479.850000.

530   GW   ISSN 0031-9252
QC1   CODEN: PHUZAH
PHYSIK IN UNSERER ZEIT. 1969. 6/yr. DM.88. V C H
Verlagsgesellschaft mbH, Postfach 101161,
Weinheim, Germany. TEL 06201-602-0.
FAX 06201-602328. TELEX 465516-VCHWH-D.
(US addr.: V C H Publishers Inc., 220 E. 23rd St.,
New York, NY 10010-4606. TEL 212-683-8333)
Ed. J. Fricke. adv.; bk.rev.; charts; illus.; index; circ.
7,900. (reprint service avail. from ISI) **Indexed:**
Chem.Abstr., Phys.Ber.

PHYSIK UND DIDAKTIK. see *EDUCATION — Teaching
Methods And Curriculum*

530   GW   ISSN 0079-1997
**PHYSIKALISCH-CHEMISCHE TRENN- UND
MESSMETHODEN.** 1960. irreg. price varies. VEB
Deutscher Verlag der Wissenschaften, Postfach
1216, 1080 Berlin, Germany. Ed. Erich Krell.

530   GW   ISSN 0031-9279
     CODEN: PHBLAG
PHYSIKALISCHE BLAETTER. 1944. m. DM.220.
(Deutsche Physikalische Gesellschaft) V C H
Verlagsgesellschaft mbH, Postfach 101161, 6940
Weinheim, Germany. TEL 06201-602-0.
FAX 06201-602328. TELEX 465516-VCHWH-D.
(US addr.: V C H Publishers Inc., 220 E. 23rd St.,
New York, NY 10010-4606. TEL 212-683-8333)
Ed. E. Dreisigacker. adv.; bk.rev.; abstr.; charts; illus.;
index; circ. 22,600. (also avail. in microfilm from
VCI; reprint service avail. from ISI) **Indexed:**
Chem.Abstr., Excerp.Med., Met.Abstr., Phys.Abstr.,
Phys.Ber., Sci.Abstr.
—BLDSC shelfmark: 6481.000000.

PLASMA CHEMISTRY & PLASMA PROCESSING. see
ENGINEERING — Chemical Engineering

530   US   ISSN 1051-9998
▼**PLASMA DEVICES AND OPERATIONS.** 1991. 4/yr.
$127. Gordon and Breach Science Publishers, 270
Eighth Ave., New York, NY 10011.
TEL 212-206-8900. FAX 212-645-2459. TELEX
236735 GOPUB UR. (Subscr. to: Box 786, Cooper
Sta., New York, NY 10276. TEL 800-545-8398; UK
subscr. to: P.O. Box 90, Reading, Berkshire RG1
8JL, England. TEL 0734-560-080) Ed. V.A.
Glukhikh. (also avail. in microform)
—BLDSC shelfmark: 6528.400000.
   Description: Covers plasma technology,
engineering, and applications; plasma source and
pulsed plasma devices; plasma accelerators and
pulsed plasma heating systems.
Refereed Serial

530.44   US   ISSN 0741-3335
QC770   CODEN: PPCFET
PLASMA PHYSICS AND CONTROLLED FUSION. (Contains
a section of English translations of Atomnaya
Energiya) (Text and summaries in English, French
and German) 1959. 13/yr. £455 (effective 1992).
(Institute of Physics) Pergamon Press, Inc., Journals
Division, 660 White Plains Rd., Tarrytown, NY
10591-5153. TEL 914-524-9200.
FAX 914-333-2444. (And: Headington Hill Hall,
Oxford OX3 OBW, England. TEL 0865-794141)
(Co-sponsor: European Physical Society, Plasma
Physics Division) Ed. Kurt Appert. adv.; bk.rev.; bibl.;
illus.; index; circ. 1,400. (also avail. in microform
from MIM,UMI; reprint service avail. from UMI)
Indexed: A.S.& T.Ind., Appl.Mech.Rev., ASCA,
Chem.Abstr., Curr.Cont., Eng.Ind., Sci.Abstr.
—BLDSC shelfmark: 6528.720000.
   Formerly: Plasma Physics (ISSN 0032-1028)
   Description: Research covering all aspects of
plasma physics and controlled nuclear fusion, as well
as the plasma physics of highly ionized gases, high
temperature, collective processes, and other
fusion-oriented research.
Refereed Serial

530   US   ISSN 0963-0252
▼**PLASMA SOURCES SCIENCE AND TECHNOLOGY.**
1992. q. $220. Institute of Physics, 1411 Walnut
St., Ste. 200, Philadelphia, PA 19102. Ed. Noah
Hershkowitz.
   Description: Publishes papers on nonfusion plasma
sources which operate at all ranges of pressure and
density.

**POLISH ACADEMY OF SCIENCES. BULLETIN.
MATHEMATICAL SCIENCES.** see *MATHEMATICS*

530   PL   ISSN 0072-0364
POLITECHNIKA GDANSKA. ZESZYTY NAUKOWE. FIZYKA.
(Text in English and Polish; summaries in Russian
and one Western European language) 1967. irreg.
price varies. Politechnika Gdanska, Majakowskiego
11-12, 81-952 Gdansk 6, Poland. (Dist. by:
Osrodek Rozpowszechniania Wydawnictw Naukowych
PAN, Palac Kultury i Nauki, 00-901 Warsaw,
Poland) bibl.; charts; illus.

530   PL   ISSN 0137-2564
QC1   CODEN: ZNPFDJ
POLITECHNIKA LODZKA. ZESZYTY NAUKOWE. FIZYKA.
(Text in Polish; summaries in English and Russian)
1973. irreg. price varies. Wydawnictwo Politechniki
Lodzkiej, Ul. Wolczanska 219, 93-085 Lodz, Poland.
(Dist. by: Ars Polona-Ruch, Krakowskie Przedmiescie
7, Warsaw, Poland) Ed. Cecylia
Malinowska-Adamska. circ. 186. **Indexed:**
Chem.Abstr.
   Description: Articles on technical physics.

POLITECHNIKA SLASKA. ZESZYTY NAUKOWE. MATEMATYKA - FIZYKA. see *MATHEMATICS*

530 PL
POLITECHNIKA WARSZAWSKA. INSTYTUT FIZYKI. PRACE. (Text in English, Polish and Russian) irreg., no.13, 1975. price varies. Institute of Technology and Organization of Building Production, c/o Lech Czarnecki, Dir., Warsaw Technical University, Al. Armii Ludowej 16, 00 637 Warsaw, Poland. TEL 22-25-76-37. TELEX 813307 PW PL. Ed. Wlodzimierz Scislowski. **Indexed:** Chem.Abstr.

621 PL ISSN 0137-625X
POLITECHNIKA WROCLAWSKA. INSTYTUT FIZYKI. PRACE NAUKOWE. KONFERENCJE. 1977. irreg., no.4, 1988. price varies. Politechnika Wroclawska, Wybrzeze Wyspianskiego 27, 50-370 Wroclaw, Poland. FAX 22-36-64. TELEX 712559 PWRPL. (Dist. by: Ars Polona-Ruch, Krakowskie Przedmiescie 7, Warsaw, Poland) **Indexed:** Sci.Abstr.

621 530 PL ISSN 0370-0828
QC1   CODEN: PIFWDB
POLITECHNIKA WROCLAWSKA. INSTYTUT FIZYKI. PRACE NAUKOWE. MONOGRAFIE. (Text in Polish; summaries in English and Russian) 1972. irreg., no.19, 1991. price varies. Politechnika Wroclawska, Wybrzeze Wyspianskiego 27, 50-370 Wroclaw, Poland. FAX 22-36-64. TELEX 712559 PWRPL. (Dist. by: Ars Polona-Ruch, Krakowskie Przedmiescie 7, Warsaw, Poland) **Indexed:** Sci.Abstr.

621 PL ISSN 0324-9697
QC1   CODEN: PIFWDB
POLITECHNIKA WROCLAWSKA. INSTYTUT FIZYKI. PRACE NAUKOWE. STUDIA I MATERIALY. (Text in Polish; summaries in English and Russian) 1969. irreg., no.7, 1976. price varies. Politechnika Wroclawska, Wybrzeze Wyspianskiego 27, 50-370 Wroclaw, Poland. FAX 22-26-64. TELEX 712559 PWRPL. (Dist. by: Ars Polona-Ruch, Krakowskie Przedmiescie 7, Warsaw, Poland) **Indexed:** Chem.Abstr.

POLITECHNIKA WROCLAWSKA. INSTYTUT MATEMATYKI. PRACE NAUKOWE. STUDIA I MATERIALY. see *MATHEMATICS*

530 PO ISSN 0048-4903
   CODEN: POPYA4
PORTUGALIAE PHYSICA. (Text and summaries in English and French) 1943-1975; resumed 1979. s-a. $24 to individuals; libraries $60. Sociedade Portuguesa de Fisica, Laboratorio de Fisica, Praca Gomes Teixeira, 4000 Porto, Portugal. TEL 2-325937. Ed. J.M. Machado da Silva. circ. 950. **Indexed:** Chem.Abstr., Math.R., Phys.Abstr., Phys.Ber., Sci.Abstr.

534 PL ISSN 0032-5430
QC1   CODEN: PSTFAT
POSTEPY FIZYKI. (Text in Polish; summaries in English) 1953. bi-m. $25.30. Polska Akademia Nauk, Instytut Fizyki, Ul. Lotnikow 32-46, 02-668 Warsaw, Poland. (Dist. by: Ars Polona, Krakowskie Przedmiescie 7, 00-068 Warsaw, Poland) (Co-sponsor: Polskie Towarzystwo Fizyczne) Ed. A. Sobiczewski. illus.; circ. 2,230. **Indexed:** Chem.Abstr., Phys.Ber., Sci.Abstr.

POSTEPY FIZYKI MEDYCZNEJ. see *MEDICAL SCIENCES*

POWER ENGINEERING (TULSA). see *ENGINEERING — Electrical Engineering*

530 510 PL ISSN 0137-8996
QC584   CODEN: FDRSBE
POZNANSKIE TOWARZYSTWO PRZYJACIOL NAUK. KOMISJA MATEMATYCZNO-PRZYRODNICZA. PRACE. (Text in Polish; summaries in English and French) 1921. irreg., vol.11, 1979. price varies. Panstwowe Wydawnictwo Naukowe, Ul. Miodowa 10, Warsaw, Poland. (Dist by: Ars Polona-Ruch, Krakowskie Przedmiescie 7, Warsaw, Poland) **Indexed:** Chem.Abstr.
—BLDSC shelfmark: 3949.660000.

530 II ISSN 0304-4289
QC1   CODEN: PRAMCI
PRAMANA; journal of physics. (Text in English) 1973. m. Rs.100($175) Indian Academy of Sciences, C.V. Raman Avenue, P.B. 8005, Bangalore 560 080, India. TEL 342546. FAX 91-812-346094. TELEX 0845-2178-ACAD-IN. Ed. R. Rajaraman. illus.; s-a. index; circ. 1,000. (also avail. in microform from UMI; back issues avail.; reprint service avail. from ISI,UMI) **Indexed:** Appl.Mech.Rev., Chem.Abstr., Curr.Cont., GeoRef., INSPEC, Met.Abstr., Phys.Abstr., Phys.Ber., Sci.Cit.Ind., World Alum.Abstr.
—BLDSC shelfmark: 6601.300000.

530 370 GW ISSN 0177-8374
PRAXIS DER NATURWISSENSCHAFTEN. PHYSIK; im Unterricht der Schulen. 8/yr. DM.102.40 (foreign DM.110.40). Aulis-Verlag Deubner und Co. KG, Antwerpener Str. 6-12, 5000 Cologne 1, Germany. TEL 0221-518051. FAX 0221-518443. TELEX 8883068-AVD. adv.; bk.rev.; abstr.; illus. **Indexed:** Chem.Abstr., Phys.Ber.

530 US ISSN 0079-5216
PRINCETON SERIES IN PHYSICS. 1971. irreg. price varies. Princeton University Press, 3175 Princeton Pike, Lawrenceville, NJ 08648. TEL 609-896-1344. FAX 609-895-1081. Eds. A.S. Wightman, J.J. Hopfield. (reprint service avail. from UMI) **Indexed:** Math.R.
Refereed Serial

530 551.5 RU
PROBLEMY FIZIKI ATMOSFERY.* vol.15, 1978. irreg. 1.50 Rub. per no. Leningradskii Universitet, Universitetskaya Nab. 7-9, St. Petersburg B-164, Russia. circ. 1,000. **Indexed:** Chem.Abstr., GeoRef.

530 SI
PROGRESS IN HIGH TEMPERATURE SUPERCONDUCTIVITY. (Text in English) 1987. irreg., vol. 29, 1991. price varies. World Scientific Publishing Co. Pte. Ltd., Farrer Rd., P.O. Box 128, Singapore 9128, Singapore. TEL 3825663. FAX 3825919. TELEX RS 28561 WSPC. (UK addr.: 73 Lynton Mead, Totteridge, London N20 8DH, England. TEL 44-81-4463356; US addr.: 1060 Main St., Ste. 1B, River Edge, NJ 07661. TEL 800-227-7562)

530 US ISSN 0079-6816
QD506   CODEN: PSSFBP
PROGRESS IN SURFACE SCIENCE; an international review journal. 1971. 24/yr. (in 6 vols.). £665 (effective 1992). Pergamon Press, Inc., Journals Division, 660 White Plains Rd., Tarrytown, NY 10591-5153. TEL 914-524-9200. FAX 914-333-2444. (And: Headington Hill Hall, Oxford OX3 0BW, England. TEL 0865-794141) Ed. Sydney G. Davison. (also avail. in microform from MIM,UMI) **Indexed:** Chem.Abstr., Curr.Cont., Mass Spectr.Bull., Met.Abstr., Phys.Ber., Sci.Abstr., World Alum.Abstr.
—BLDSC shelfmark: 6924.575000.
Description: Publishes review articles from all disciplines where surfaces and interfaces play an important role.
Refereed Serial

530 JA ISSN 0033-068X
QC1   CODEN: PTPKAV
PROGRESS OF THEORETICAL PHYSICS/RIRON BUTSURIGAKU NO SHINPO. (Supplements) (Text in English; summaries in European languages) 1946. m. 60000 Yen. Kyoto University, Research Institute for Fundamental Physics - Kyoto Daigaku Rigakubu Kiso Butsurigaku Kenkyujo, Riron Butsurigaku Kankokai, Publication Office, Kitashirakawa Oiwake-cho, Sakyo-ku, Kyoto 606, Japan. index, cum.index every 5 yrs.; circ. 2,300. (also avail. in microfilm; microfiche) **Indexed:** ASCA, Chem.Abstr., GeoRef., JCT, JTA, Math.R., Met.Abstr., Phys.Ber., Sci.Abstr.
—BLDSC shelfmark: 6924.600000.

PSYCHOTRONIC VIDEO. see *COMMUNICATIONS — Video*

RADIATION CHEMISTRY. see *CHEMISTRY*

RADIOISOTOPES. see *BIOLOGY — Biological Chemistry*

RAUM UND ZEIT; die neue Dimension der Wissenschaft. see *NEW AGE PUBLICATIONS*

530 SP
QC1   CODEN: AFAIDU
REAL SOCIEDAD ESPANOLA DE FISICA. ANALES DE FISICA. (Text and summaries in English, French, German, Spanish) 1903. q. $90. Real Sociedad Espanola de Fisica, Facultad de Ciencias, Ciudad Universitaria, Madrid, Spain. Ed. J. Campos Gutierrez. adv.; bk.rev.; bibl.; charts; illus.; index. **Indexed:** Chem.Abstr., Dairy Sci.Abstr., Met.Abstr., Sci.Abstr.
Former titles: Real Sociedad Espanola de Fisica y Quimica. Anales de Fisica (ISSN 0211-6243); Real Sociedad Espanola de Fisica y Quimica. Anales. Serie A: Fisica (ISSN 0034-0871)

530.1 US ISSN 0034-4877
QC19.2   CODEN: RMHPBE
REPORTS ON MATHEMATICAL PHYSICS. 1975. 6/yr. £250 (effective 1992). (Nicolaus Copernicus University, Institute of Physics, PL) Pergamon Press, Inc., Journals Division, 660 White Plains Rd., Tarrytown, NY 10591-5153. TEL 914-524-9200. FAX 914-333-2444. (And: Headington Hill Hall, Oxford OX3 0BW, England. TEL 0865-794141) (Co-publisher: Polish Scientific Publishers) Ed. Roman S. Ingarden. (also avail. in microform)
—BLDSC shelfmark: 7660.510000.
Description: Publishes papers in theoretical physics presenting a rigorous mathematical approach to problems of quantum and classical mechanics and field theories, relativity and gravitation, statistical physics and mathematical foundations of physical theories.
Refereed Serial

530 UK ISSN 0034-4885
QC3   CODEN: RPPHAG
REPORTS ON PROGRESS IN PHYSICS. 1934. m. £385($770) (effective 1992). (Institute of Physics) I O P Publishing, Techno House, Redcliffe Way, Bristol BS1 6NX, England. TEL 072 297481. FAX 0272-294318. TELEX 449149-INSTP-G. (U.S. addr.: American Institute of Physics, Member and Subscriber Service, 500 Sunnyside Blvd., Woodbury, NY 11797-2999. TEL 516-576-2270) Ed. M. Hart. bibl.; charts; illus.; cum.index. (also avail. in microfiche; microfilm) **Indexed:** Appl.Mech.Rev., Art & Archaeol.Tech.Abstr., Br.Ceram.Abstr., Cadscan, Chem.Abstr., Curr.Cont., Deep Sea Res.& Oceanogr.Abstr., GeoRef., Int.Aerosp.Abstr., Lead Abstr., Mass Spectr.Bull., Math.R., Met.Abstr., Phys.Ber., Sci.Abstr., World Alum.Abstr., Zincscan.
—BLDSC shelfmark: 7665.500000.

REPUBLIC OF CHINA. NATIONAL SCIENCE COUNCIL. PROCEEDINGS. PART A: PHYSICAL SCIENCE AND ENGINEERING. see *ENGINEERING*

530 378 UK ISSN 0308-9290
RESEARCH FIELDS IN PHYSICS AT UNITED KINGDOM UNIVERSITIES AND POLYTECHNICS. vol.7, 1984. irreg. (every 2-3 yrs.); latest vol.8, 1987. £65.50. (Institute of Physics) I O P Publishing, Techno House, Redcliffe Way, Bristol BS1 6NX, England. TEL 0272-297481. FAX 0272-294318. TELEX 449149-INSTP-G. (U.S. addr.: American Institute of Physics, 335 E. 45th St., New York, NY 10011)
—BLDSC shelfmark: 7740.600000.

RESEARCH INSTITUTE FOR MATHEMATICAL SCIENCES. PUBLICATIONS/KYOTO DAIGAKU SURI KAISEKI KENKYUJO KIYO. see *MATHEMATICS*

530 SI ISSN 0129-055X
QC19.2   CODEN: RMPHEX
REVIEWS IN MATHEMATICAL PHYSICS. (Text in English) 1989. q. $106 to individuals and developing countries; institutions $265. World Scientific Publishing Co. Pte. Ltd., Farrer Rd., P.O. Box 128, Singapore 9128, Singapore. TEL 3825663. FAX 3825919. TELEX RS-28561-WSPC. (US addr.: 1060 Main St., Ste. 1B, River Edge, NJ 07661. TEL 800-227-7562; European addr.: 73 Lynton Mead, Totteridge, London N20 8DH, England. TEL 44-81-4462461) Ed. Huzihiro Araki. circ. 150. (back issues avail.)
—BLDSC shelfmark: 7791.700000.
Description: Contains survey and expository articles in mathematical physics.

REVIEWS OF GEOPHYSICS. see *EARTH SCIENCES — Geophysics*

PHYSICS

539 US ISSN 0034-6861
QC1 CODEN: RMPHAT
REVIEWS OF MODERN PHYSICS. 1929. q. $230 (foreign $240-$250). (American Physical Society) American Institute of Physics, 335 E. 45th St., New York, NY 10017-3483. TEL 212-661-9404. Ed. David Pines. bibl.; illus.; cum.index: vols.1-27 (1929-1955); vols.28-45 (1956-1973); vols.46-53 (1974-1981). (also avail. in microfiche; microform from MIM; back issues avail.; reprint service avail.) Indexed: Appl.Mech.Rev., Biol.Abstr., C.P.I., Chem.Abstr., Deep Sea Res.& Oceanogr.Abstr., Excerp.Med., GeoRef., Ind.Med., Int.Aerosp.Abstr., Mass Spectr.Bull., Math.R., Met.Abstr., Phys.Ber., Sci.Abstr.
—BLDSC shelfmark: 7793.300000.
Refereed Serial

530.44 US ISSN 0080-2050
QC718 CODEN: RPLPAK
REVIEWS OF PLASMA PHYSICS. 1965. irreg., vol.16, 1990. price varies. Plenum Publishing Corp., Consultants Bureau, 233 Spring St., New York, NY 10013-1578. TEL 212-620-8000. FAX 212-463-0742. TELEX 23-421139. Ed. M.A. Leontovich. (back issues avail.)
Description: English translations of research originally published in Russian.
Refereed Serial

530 SI ISSN 0218-1029
QC176.A1 CODEN: RVSSE8
REVIEWS OF SOLID STATE SCIENCE. (Text in English) 1987. q. $60 to individuals and developing countries; institutions $180. World Scientific Publishing Co. Pte. Ltd., Farrer Rd., P.O. Box 128, Singapore 9128, Singapore. TEL 3825663. FAX 3825919. (UK addr.: 73 Lynton Mead, Totteridge, London N20 8DH, England. TEL 44-81-4462461; US addr.: 1060 Main St., Ste. 1B, River Edge, NJ 07661. TEL 800-227-7562) Ed. C.N.R. Rao. (back issues avail.)
—BLDSC shelfmark: 7796.917000.
Description: Covers solid state science, plasma processes, quantum mechanics.

530 BL ISSN 0374-4922
CODEN: RBFSA3
REVISTA BRASILEIRA DE FISICA. (Text in English and Portuguese) 1971. q. $50 (Cz.$100). Sociedade Brasileira de Fisica, Universidade de Sao Paulo, Instituto de Fisica, Caixa Postal 20553, 01000 Sao Paulo, Brazil. FAX 081-2710359. TELEX 2131048-PUCR-BR. Ed. Belita Koiller. charts; circ. 2,000. Indexed: Chem.Abstr., Int.Aerosp.Abstr., Phys.Abstr., Sci.Abstr.
—BLDSC shelfmark: 7844.775000.
Description: Original research work and review articles in physics.
Refereed Serial

530 CU ISSN 0253-9268
CODEN: RECFD7
REVISTA CUBANA DE FISICA. (Text in Spanish; summaries in English and Spanish) 1981. 3/yr. C.$4.50($24) in N. America; S. America $25; Europe $26. (Universidad de La Habana, Direccion de Informacion Cientifica y Tecnica) Ediciones Cubanas, Obispo No. 527, Apdo. 605, Havana, Cuba. (back issues avail.)
—BLDSC shelfmark: 7852.108000.

530 540 RM
REVISTA DE FIZICA SI CHIMIE. m. 18 lei($8) Societatea de Stiinte Fizice si Chimice din Republica Socialista Rumania, Str. Spiru Haret Nr. 12, Bucharest, Rumania. (Subscr. to: ILEXIM, Str. 13 Decembrie Nr. 3, P.O. Box 136-137, Bucharest, Rumania) Ed.Bd. illus. Indexed: Chem.Abstr.
Formed by the merger of: Revista de Fizica si Chimie. Seria A; Revista de Fizica si Chimie. Seria B.

530.15 AG ISSN 0080-2360
QA1
REVISTA DE MATEMATICA Y FISICA TEORICA. SERIE A. (Text in Spanish, French, German, Italian and English; summaries in English) 1940. a. $15. Universidad Nacional de Tucuman, Facultad de Ciencias Exactas y Tecnologia, Avda. Independencia 1800, Tucuman, Argentina. FAX 81311462. TELEX 61249-FDCET-AR. Eds. Raul Luccioni, Constantino Grosse. bk.rev.; index; circ. 250. Indexed: Math.R., Zent.Math.

REVISTA MEXICANA DE ASTRONOMIA Y ASTROFISICA. see *ASTRONOMY*

530 MX ISSN 0035-001X
QC1 CODEN: RMXFAT
REVISTA MEXICANA DE FISICA. (Supplements avail.) (Text and summaries in English and Spanish) 1952. 6/yr. Mex.$100000($100) (typically set in Dec.). Sociedad Mexicana de Fisica, A.C., Apdo. 70-348, 04510 Mexico, D.F., Mexico. TEL 525-550-5910. FAX 525-548-8186. Ed. Ana Maria Cetto. bibl.; charts; illus.; index; circ. 1,500. Indexed: Astron.& Astrophys.Abstr., Bull.Signal., Chem.Abstr., Curr.Cont., Curr.Pap.Phys., Elec.& Electron.Abstr., INIS Atomind., Math.R., Nucl.Sci.Abstr., Phys.Abstr., Phys.Ber., Sci.Abstr.
—BLDSC shelfmark: 7866.300000.
Description: Original papers in physics: research, education, instrumentation, history and philosophy; letters and review articles.

530 RM ISSN 0035-4090
QC1 CODEN: RRPQAN
REVUE ROUMAINE DE PHYSIQUE. (Text in English, French, German, Russian, Spanish) 1956. 10/yr. 400 lei($90) (Academia Romana) Editura Academiei Romane, Calea Victoriei 125, 79717 Bucharest, Rumania. (Dist. by: Rompresfilatelia, Calea Grivitei 64-66, P.O. Box 12-201, 78104 Bucharest, Rumania) Ed. Ioan Ursu. bk.rev.; charts; illus.; index. Indexed: Bull.Signal., Cadscan, Ceram.Abstr., Chem.Abstr., Curr.Cont., Lead Abstr., Math.R., Met.Abstr., Nucl.Sci.Abstr., Phys.Abstr., Phys.Ber., Ref.Zh., Sci.Abstr., Zincscan.
—BLDSC shelfmark: 7946.500000.

RIKAGAKKAISHI/JOURNAL OF PHYSICS, CHEMISTRY AND EARTH SCIENCE. see *SCIENCES: COMPREHENSIVE WORKS*

530 540 JA ISSN 0020-3084
CODEN: RKKHAO
RIKAGAKU KENKYUJO HOKOKU/INSTITUTE OF PHYSICAL AND CHEMICAL RESEARCH. REPORTS. (Text in Japanese; summaries in English) 1922. irreg. Rikagaku Kenkyujo - Institute of Physical and Chemical Research, 2-1 Hirosawa, Wako-shi, Saitama-ken 351-01, Japan. TEL 0484-621111. FAX 0484-621554. Ed. Minoru Oda. abstr.; charts; illus.; index; circ. 800. Indexed: Appl.Mech.Rev., Chem.Abstr., Eng.Ind., INIS Atomind., Jap.Per.Ind., JTA, Met.Abstr., Nucl.Sci.Abstr., Sci.Abstr., World Alum.Abstr.
—BLDSC shelfmark: 7521.400000.
Formerly: Reports of the Scientific Research Institute.

530 DK ISSN 0418-6435
RISOE-M. No.233, 1965. irreg. free. Risoe National Laboratory, P.O. Box 49, DK-4000 Roskilde, Denmark. Indexed: Chem.Abstr.

ROYAL IRISH ACADEMY. PROCEEDINGS. SECTION A: MATHEMATICAL AND PHYSICAL SCIENCES. see *MATHEMATICS*

ROYAL NETHERLANDS ACADEMY OF SCIENCES. PROCEEDINGS. see *SCIENCES: COMPREHENSIVE WORKS*

530 620 UK ISSN 0962-8428
Q41
ROYAL SOCIETY OF LONDON. PHILOSOPHICAL TRANSACTIONS. SERIES A. PHYSICAL SCIENCES AND ENGINEERING. 1665. m. £440 (foreign £471). Royal Society of London, 6 Carlton House Terrace, London SW1Y 5AG, England. TEL 071-839-5561. FAX 071-976-1837. TELEX 917876. Ed. F.T. Smith. circ. 840. (reprint service avail. from ISI,KTO) Indexed: Acid Rain Abstr., Acid Rain Ind., Appl.Mech.Rev., Biol.Abstr., Br.Archaeol.Abstr., Br.Geol.Lit., Chem.Abstr., Energy Info.Abstr., Eng.Ind., Environ.Abstr., Fluidex, Geo.Abstr., GeoRef., I D A, Mass Spectr.Bull., Math.R., Met.Abstr., Nutr.Abstr., Petrol.Abstr., Sci.Abstr., Soils & Fert., Vet.Bull.
Formerly: Royal Society of London. Philosophical Transactions. Series A. Mathematical and Physical Sciences (ISSN 0080-4614)
Refereed Serial

ROZHLEDY MATEMATICKO-FYZIKALNI. see *EDUCATION*

530 621 US ISSN 1051-8053
TJ265 CODEN: RJETER
▼**RUSSIAN JOURNAL OF ENGINEERING THERMOPHYSICS.** 1991. 4/yr. $435 (foreign $457)(effective 1992). Elsevier Science Publishing Co., Inc. (New York), 655 Ave. of Americas, New York, NY 10010. TEL 212-989-5800. FAX 212-633-3965. TELEX 420643 AEP UI. Ed. V.E. Nakoryakov.
—BLDSC shelfmark: 8052.709700.
Description: Publishes original English language articles on work conducted at major research institutions in Russia.
Refereed Serial

530 621 US ISSN 1051-8045
TA349 CODEN: RJTMED
▼**RUSSIAN JOURNAL OF THEORETICAL AND APPLIED MECHANICS.** 1991. 4/yr. $435 (foreign $457)(effective 1992). Elsevier Science Publishing Co., Inc. (New York), 655 Ave. of Americas, New York, NY 10010. TEL 212-989-5800. FAX 212-633-3965. TELEX 420643 AEP UI. Ed. V.M. Fomin.
—BLDSC shelfmark: 8052.725000.
Description: Publishes original English language articles on theoretical, analytical, experimental and applied mechanics based on research conducted at major institutions in Russia.
Refereed Serial

SAGA DAIGAKU RIKOGAKUBU SHUHO/SAGA UNIVERSITY. FACULTY OF SCIENCE AND ENGINEERING. REPORTS. see *ENGINEERING*

SAITAMA MATHEMATICAL JOURNAL. see *MATHEMATICS*

SCIEN TECH/SAGA DAIGAKU RIKOGAKUBU KOHO. see *ENGINEERING*

530 UK
SCOPE (YORK). 1951. q. membership. Institute of Physical Sciences in Medicine, P.O. Box 303, York YO1 2WR, England. TEL 0904-610821. Ed. Christine Tonge. adv.; bk.rev.; circ. 1,500.
Formerly: H P A Bulletin (Hospital Physicists Association).

SCUOLA NORMALE SUPERIORE DI PISA. ANNALI. CLASSE DI SCIENZE. see *MATHEMATICS*

SELECTA MATHEMATICA SOVIETICA. see *MATHEMATICS*

530 NE ISSN 0080-8636
SELECTED TOPICS IN SOLID STATE PHYSICS. (Text in English) 1962. irreg., vol.18, 1986. price varies. Elsevier Science Publishers B.V., Books Division, P.O. Box 211, 1000 AE Amsterdam, Netherlands. TEL 020-5803911. FAX 020-5803705. TELEX 18582 ESPA NL. (Subscr. in U.S. and Canada to: Elsevier Science Publishing Co., Inc., Box 882, Madison Sq. Sta., New York, NY 10159. TEL 212-989-5800) Ed. E.P. Wohlfarth.
Refereed Serial

530 US ISSN 0894-3923
QD571 CODEN: SELREW
SELECTIVE ELECTRODE REVIEWS; applications, theory and development of biosensors and electrochemical sensors. 1979. 2/yr. £150 (effective 1992). Pergamon Press, Inc., Journals Division, 660 White Plains Rd., Tarrytown, NY 10591-5153. TEL 914-524-9200. FAX 914-333-2444. (And: Headington Hill Hall, Oxford OX3 0BW, England. TEL 0865-794141) Ed. J.D.R. Thomas. illus. (also avail. in microform from MIM,UMI) Indexed: Agri.Eng.Abstr., Chem.Abstr., Ind.Sci.Rev., Met.Abstr., Sci.Abstr., Sci.Cit.Ind., Soils & Fert., W.R.C.Inf., World Alum.Abstr.
—BLDSC shelfmark: 8235.172500.
Formerly: Ion-Selective Electrode Reviews (ISSN 0191-5371)
Description: Publishes reviews covering all areas of science where the sensing of ions can be applied.
Refereed Serial

SENSOR TECHNOLOGY; a monthly intelligence service. see *COMPUTERS — Cybernetics*

SERIE DI MATEMATICA E FISICA. PROBLEMI.. see *MATHEMATICS*

SERIE DI MATEMATICA E FISICA. TESTI. see *MATHEMATICS*

530 SI
▼**SERIES IN MODERN CONDENSED MATTER PHYSICS.**
(Text in English) 1991. irreg., vol. 3, 1992. price varies. World Scientific Publishing Co. Pte. Ltd., Farrer Rd., P.O. Box 128, Singapore 9128, Singapore. TEL 3825663. FAX 3825919. TELEX RS 28561 WSPC. (UK addr.: 73 Lynton Mead, Totteridge, London N20 8DH, England. TEL 44-81-4462461; US addr.: 1060 Main St., Ste. 1B, River Edge, NJ 07661. TEL 800-227-7562)

530 SI
SERIES ON DIRECTIONS IN CONDENSED MATTER PHYSICS. (Text in English) 1986. irreg., vol. 11, 1991. price varies. World Scientific Publishing Co. Pte. Ltd., Farrer Rd., P.O. Box 128, Singapore 9128, Singapore. TEL 3825663. FAX 3825919. TELEX RS 28561 WSPC. (UK addr.: 73 Lynton Mead, Totteridge, London N20 8DH, England. TEL 44-81-4462461; US addr.: 1060 Main St., Ste. 1B, River Edge, NJ 07661. TEL 800-227-7562)

SEVERO-KAVKAZSKII NAUCHNYI TSENTR VYSSHEI SHKOLY. ESTESTVENNYE NAUKI. IZVESTIYA/NORTH-CAUCASUS SCIENTIFIC CENTER OF HIGH SCHOOL. NATURAL SCIENCES. NEWS. see *MATHEMATICS*

530 510 JA ISSN 0368-4571
TS1300 CODEN: JTSFAX
SHINSHU UNIVERSITY. FACULTY OF TEXTILE SCIENCE AND TECHNOLOGY. JOURNAL. SERIES F: PHYSICS AND MATHEMATICS. (Text in European languages; summaries in English) 1962. irreg. exchange basis. Shinshu University, Faculty of Textile Science and Technology - Shinshu Daigaku Sen'igakubu, 15-1 Tokida 3-chome, Ueda-shi, Nagano-ken 386, Japan.
—BLDSC shelfmark: 4751.258000.

SHUXUE WULI XUEBAO. see *MATHEMATICS*

530 US
SIGMA PI SIGMA RADIATIONS. 1930. a. American Institute of Physics, Society of Physics - Sigma Pi Sigma, 1825 Connecticut Ave., N.W., Ste. 213, Washington, DC 20009. TEL 202-232-6688. FAX 202-234-7053. Ed. Donald Kirwan. circ. 30,000.

530 IT
SOCIETA ITALIANA DI FISICA. CONGRESSO NAZIONALE.*
a. Societa Italiana di Fisica, Dipartimento di Biologia, Via L. degli Andalo 2, 40124 Bologna, Italy.

530 539.7 IT ISSN 0369-3546
CODEN: NCIAAT
SOCIETA ITALIANA DI FISICA. NUOVO CIMENTO A; nuclei, particles and fields. (Text in English, French, German; summaries in English, Italian, Russian) 1855. m. $835 to non-members; members $675. Editrice Compositori s.r.l., Via Stalingrado 97-2, 40128 Bologna, Italy. TEL 051-327811. Ed. Renato Angelo Ricci. **Indexed:** Chem.Abstr., Curr.Cont., Mass Spectr.Bull., Phys.Abstr., Phys.Ber., Sci.Abstr.
—BLDSC shelfmark: 6185.100000.
Supersedes in part in 1965: Nuovo Cimento (ISSN 0029-6341)
Description: Covers physics of elementary particles and includes articles in the field of nuclear physics.

530 520 IT ISSN 0369-3554
CODEN: NIFBAP
SOCIETA ITALIANA DI FISICA. NUOVO CIMENTO B; general physics, relativity, astronomy and mathematical physics and methods. (Text in English, French, German; summaries in English, Italian, Russian) 1855. m. $583 to non-members; members $482. Editrice Compositori s.r.l., Via Stalingrado 97-2, 40128 Bologna, Italy. TEL 051-327811. Ed. Renato Angelo Ricci. **Indexed:** Chem.Abstr., Curr.Cont., Phys.Abstr., Phys.Ber., Ref.Zh., Sci.Abstr.
—BLDSC shelfmark: 6185.200000.
Supersedes in part in 1965: Nuovo Cimento (ISSN 0029-6341)
Description: Covers general topics in classical areas of phenomenology. Includes plasma and electric discharges, fundamental astronomy and astrophysics.

530 551 IT ISSN 0390-5551
CODEN: NIFCAS
SOCIETA ITALIANA DI FISICA. NUOVO CIMENTO C; geophysics and space physics. (Text in English, French, German; summaries in English, Italian, Russian) 1978. bi-m. $295 to non-members; members $235. Editrice Compositori s.r.l., Via Stalingrado 97-2, 40128 Bologna, Italy. TEL 051-327811. Ed. Renato Angelo Ricci. **Indexed:** Chem.Abstr., Sci.Abstr.
—BLDSC shelfmark: 6185.250000.
Description: Covers geophysics and space physics

530 IT ISSN 0392-6737
CODEN: NCSDDN
SOCIETA ITALIANA DI FISICA. NUOVO CIMENTO D; condensed matter, atomic, molecular and chemical physics, fluids, plasmas, biophysics. (Text in English, French, German; summaries in English, Italian Russian) 1982. m. $505 to non-members; members $400. Editrice Compositori s.r.l., Via Stalingrado 97-2, 40128 Bologna, Italy. TEL 051-327811. Ed. Renato Angelo Ricci. index; circ. 700. (back issues avail.) **Indexed:** Chem.Abstr., Met.Abstr., Sci.Abstr.
—BLDSC shelfmark: 6185.260000.
Description: Covers atomic and molecular physics; structure, mechanical, thermal properties; electronic structure, electric, magnetical and optical properties.

530 IT ISSN 0393-697X
CODEN: RNUCAC
SOCIETA ITALIANA DI FISICA. RIVISTA DEL NUOVO CIMENTO. (Text in English) 1969. m. $318 to non-members; members $253. (Societa Italiana di Fisica) Editrice Compositori s.r.l., Via Stalingrado 97-2, 40128 Bologna, Italy. TEL 51-327811. Ed. R.A. Ricci. charts. **Indexed:** Appl.Mech.Rev., Chem.Abstr., Curr.Cont., Math.R., Phys.Abstr., Ref.Zh.
—BLDSC shelfmark: 7991.500000.
Formerly (until 1971): Rivista del Nuovo Cimento (ISSN 0035-5917)
Description: Review of original articles of general arguments in physics.

530 FR ISSN 0081-1076
SOCIETE FRANCAISE DE PHYSIQUE. ANNUAIRE. 1913. triennial. 250 F. Societe Francaise de Physique, 33 rue Croulebarbe, 75013 Paris, France.

530 FR ISSN 0037-9360
CODEN: BFPYAP
SOCIETE FRANCAISE DE PHYSIQUE. BULLETIN. (Includes supplements) 1881. q. 160 F. Societe Francaise de Physique, 33 rue Croulebarbe, 75013 Paris, France. TEL 47-07-32-98. FAX 43-31-74-26. Ed. Pierre Radvanyi. charts; illus.; stat. **Indexed:** Chem.Abstr.
Description: Lists all congresses to take place as well as all relevant information about them.

533.5 FR ISSN 0223-4335
QC166 CODEN: VCMIDS
SOCIETE FRANCAISE DU VIDE. COMPTES RENDUS DES TRAVAUX DES CONGRES ET COLLOQUES. irreg. price varies. Societe Francaise du Vide, 19 rue du Renard, 75004 Paris, France. TEL 42-78-15-82.
—BLDSC shelfmark: 9233.110000.
Description: Concerns vacuum techniques.

SOLAR-GEOPHYSICAL DATA. PART 1 - PROMPT REPORTS. see *ASTRONOMY*

SOLAR-GEOPHYSICAL DATA: PART 2 - COMPREHENSIVE REPORTS. see *ASTRONOMY*

SOLAR PHYSICS; a journal for solar and solar-stellar research and the study of solar terrestrial physics. see *ASTRONOMY*

SOLAR SYSTEM RESEARCH. see *ASTRONOMY*

SOLAR TERRESTRIAL ENVIRONMENTAL RESEARCH IN JAPAN. see *EARTH SCIENCES* — *Geophysics*

530.41 US ISSN 0038-1098
QC176.A1 CODEN: SSCOA4
SOLID STATE COMMUNICATIONS; an international journal. 1963. 48/yr. (in 4 vols., 12 nos./vol.). £915 (effective 1992). Pergamon Press, Inc., Journals Division, 660 White Plains Rd., Tarrytown, NY 10591-5153. TEL 914-524-9200. FAX 914-333-2444. (And: Headington Hill Hall, Oxford OX3 0BW, England. TEL 0865-794141) Ed. Manuel Cardona. adv.; bk.rev.; charts; illus.; index; circ. 2,000. (also avail. in microform from MIM,UMI; back issues avail.) **Indexed:** Appl.Mech.Rev., ASCA, Chem.Abstr., Curr.Cont., Eng.Ind., GeoRef., Mass Spectr.Bull., Met.Abstr., Phys.Ber., Sci.Abstr., World Alum.Abstr.
—BLDSC shelfmark: 8327.378000.
Description: Original experimental and theoretical research on the physical and chemical properties of solids and condensed systems.
Refereed Serial

530 NE ISSN 0167-2738
QC176.A1 CODEN: SSIOD3
SOLID STATE IONICS; diffusion and reactions. 1980. 32/yr.(in 8 vols.; 4 nos./vol.). fl.2528 (effective 1992). North-Holland (Subsidiary of: Elsevier Science Publishers B.V.), P.O. Box 211, 1000 AE Amsterdam, Netherlands. TEL 020-5803911. FAX 020-5803598. TELEX 18582 ESPA NL. (Subscr. in U.S. and Canada to: Elsevier Science Publishing Co., Inc., Box 882, Madison Sq. Sta., New York, NY 10159. TEL 212-989-5800) Ed. M.S. Whittingham. adv.; index. (also avail. in microform from RPI; back issues avail.) **Indexed:** ASCA, Chem.Abstr., Curr.Cont., Met.Abstr., Phys.Ber., Sci.Abstr., World Alum.Abstr.
—BLDSC shelfmark: 8327.386000.
Incorporates (1985-1989): Reactivity of Solids (ISSN 0168-7336)
Description: Devoted to the physics, chemistry and materials science of diffusion in mass transport and reactivity of solids.
Refereed Serial

530 US ISSN 0081-1947
QC173 CODEN: SSPHAE
SOLID STATE PHYSICS: ADVANCES IN RESEARCH AND APPLICATIONS. 1955. irreg., vol.44, 1991. Academic Press, Inc., 1250 Sixth Ave., San Diego, CA 92101. TEL 619-231-0926. FAX 619-699-6715. Ed.Bd. index, cum.index: vols..1-11, 1955-1960. (reprint service avail. from ISI) **Indexed:** ASCA, GeoRef.
—BLDSC shelfmark: 8327.400000.
Refereed Serial

530 SA ISSN 0379-4377
CODEN: SAPHDR
SOUTH AFRICAN JOURNAL OF PHYSICS/SUID-AFRIKAANSE TYDSKRIF VIR FISIKA. (Text and summaries in English) 1978. q. R.48($35) (South African Institute of Physics) Bureau for Scientific Publications, Box 1758, Pretoria 0001, South Africa. TEL 012-322-6422. Ed. F.J.W. Hahne. bk.rev.; charts; illus.; stat.; index; circ. 600. **Indexed:** Chem.Abstr., Ind.S.A.Per., Met.Abstr., Phys.Abstr., Phys.Ber., Sci.Abstr., World Alum.Abstr.
—BLDSC shelfmark: 8339.600000.

530 541.3 US ISSN 0733-2831
QD450 CODEN: SJCPDF
SOVIET JOURNAL OF CHEMICAL PHYSICS. English translation of: Khimicheskaya Fizika. 24/yr. (in 2 vols., 12 nos./vol.). $571. Gordon & Breach Science Publishers, 270 Eighth Ave., New York, NY 10011. TEL 212-206-8900. FAX 212-645-2459. TELEX 236735 GOPUB UR. (Subscr. to: Box 786, Cooper Sta., New York, NY 10276. TEL 800-545-8398; UK subscr. to: P.O. Box 90, Reading, Berkshire RG1 8JL, England. TEL 07734-560-080) Ed. V.I. Goldansky. index. (also avail. in microform)
—BLDSC shelfmark: 0422.853000.
Refereed Serial

530 US ISSN 8755-4585
QC1
SOVIET JOURNAL OF CONTEMPORARY PHYSICS. English translation of: Akademiya Nauk Armyanskoi S.S.R. Izvestiya. Seriya Fizika (Al ISSN 0002-3035) 1984. bi-m. $525. (Armenian Academy of Sciences, Al) Allerton Press, Inc., 150 Fifth Ave., New York, NY 10011. TEL 212-924-3950.
—BLDSC shelfmark: 0422.870000.

530.44   US   ISSN 0360-0343
QC717.6   CODEN: SJPPDC
SOVIET JOURNAL OF PLASMA PHYSICS. English translation of: Fizika Plazmy (RU ISSN 0367-2921) 1975. m. $1125 (foreign $1135-$1160). American Institute of Physics, 335 E. 45th St., New York, NY 10017. TEL 212-661-9404. (Subscr. to: Member and Subscriber Service, 500 Sunnyside Blvd., Woodbury, NY 11797-2999. TEL 516-576-2270) Ed. David L. Book. abstr.; bibl.; charts; illus.; index. (also avail. in microform; back issues avail.) **Indexed:** Gen.Phys.Adv.Abstr., Int.Aerosp.Abstr., Phys.Ber., Sci.Abstr.
—BLDSC shelfmark: 0423.600000.

SOVIET JOURNAL OF QUANTUM ELECTRONICS. see ENGINEERING — Electrical Engineering

530 548   US   ISSN 0739-8425
TA418.45
SOVIET JOURNAL OF SUPERHARD MATERIALS. English translation of: Sverkhtverdye Materialy (RU ISSN 0203-3119) 1983. bi-m. $645. Allerton Press, Inc., 150 Fifth Ave., New York, NY 10011. TEL 212-924-3950. Ed. N.V. Novikov. **Indexed:** Eng.Ind., Met.Abstr., World Alum.Abstr.
—BLDSC shelfmark: 0423.670000.

530   UK   ISSN 0960-0884
                     CODEN: SLCOER
▼**SOVIET LIGHTWAVE COMMUNICATIONS.** 1991. q. £132($264) (effective Jan. 1992). (Institute of Physics) I O P Publishing, Techno House, Redcliffe Way, Bristol BS1 6NX, England. TEL 0272-297481. FAX 0272-294318. TELEX 449149-INSTP-G. (U.S. addr.: American Institute of Physics, Member and Subscriber Service, 500 Sunnyside Blvd., Woodbury, NY 11797-2999. TEL 516-576-2270) (Co-sponsor: Russian Academy of Sciences) Ed. A.M. Prokhorov. (also avail. in microform; back issues avail.)
—BLDSC shelfmark: 8359.433000.
  Description: Offers the latest of Soviet fibre optical communications and guided wave optics research. Provides information on both fundamental physics and applications.

530   US   ISSN 0038-5689
QC1   CODEN: SPHDA9
SOVIET PHYSICS - DOKLADY. English translation of: Akademii Nauk S.S.S.R. Doklady. 1956. m. $970 (foreign $1005). American Institute of Physics, 335 E. 45th St., New York, NY 10017. TEL 212-661-9404. Ed. S.J. Amoretty. index; circ. 828. (also avail. in microform; back issues avail.) **Indexed:** Appl.Mech.Rev., C.P.I., Eng.Ind., Gen.Phys.Adv.Abstr., INSPEC, Mass Spectr.Bull., Math.R., Phys.Ber., Sci.Abstr.
—BLDSC shelfmark: 0425.100000.

530   US   ISSN 0038-5646
QC1   CODEN: SPHJAR
SOVIET PHYSICS - J E T P. English translation of: Zhurnal Eksperimental'noi i Teoreticheskoi Fiziki (RU ISSN 0044-4510) 1955. m. $1590 (foreign $1610-$1650). American Institute of Physics, 335 E. 45th St., New York, NY 10017. TEL 212-661-9404. Eds. J.G. Adashko, D.L. Book. charts; illus.; index. (also avail. in microform; back issues avail.) **Indexed:** Appl.Mech.Rev., C.P.I., Eng.Ind., Gen.Phys.Adv.Abstr., Mass Spectr.Bull., Math.R., Met.Abstr., Phys.Ber., Sci.Abstr., World Alum.Abstr.
—BLDSC shelfmark: 0425.150000.

530   US   ISSN 0038-5697
QC1   CODEN: SOPJAQ
SOVIET PHYSICS JOURNAL. English translation of: Izvestiya Vysshikh Uchebnykh Zavedenii. Seriya Fizika (RU ISSN 0021-3411) 1965. m. $1075 (foreign $1260)(effective 1992). (Vysshie Uchebnye Zavedeniya S.S.S.R., RU) Plenum Publishing Corp., Consultants Bureau, 233 Spring St., New York, NY 10013-1578. TEL 212-620-8468. FAX 212-463-0742. TELEX 23-421139. Ed. V.N. Detinko. (also avail. in microfilm from JSC; back issues avail.) **Indexed:** Appl.Mech.Rev., Chem.Titles, Eng.Ind., Math.R., Solid St.Abstr.
—BLDSC shelfmark: 0425.200000.
  Refereed Serial

530   US   ISSN 0364-2321
QC1   CODEN: SPLRD6
SOVIET PHYSICS - LEBEDEV INSTITUTE REPORTS. English translation of: Kratkie Soobshcheniya po Fizike (RU ISSN 0455-0595) 1974. m. $615. (Russian Academy of Sciences, Institute of Physics - P.N. Lebedeva, RU) Allerton Press, Inc., 150 Fifth Ave., New York, NY 10011. TEL 212-924-3950. Ed. N.G. Basov. index. **Indexed:** INSPEC, Phys.Ber., Sci.Abstr.
—BLDSC shelfmark: 0425.250000.

537.622   US   ISSN 0038-5700
QC612.S4   CODEN: SPSEBY
SOVIET PHYSICS - SEMICONDUCTORS. English translation of: Fizika i Tekhnika Poluprovodnikov (RU ISSN 0015-3222) 1967. m. $1475 (foreign $1520). American Institute of Physics, 335 E. 45th St, New York, NY 10017. TEL 212-661-9404. Ed. A. Tybulewicz. index. (also avail. in microform; back issues avail.) **Indexed:** ASCA, C.P.I., Eng.Ind., Gen.Phys.Adv.Abstr., Met.Abstr., Phys.Ber., Sci.Abstr., World Alum.Abstr.
—BLDSC shelfmark: 0425.300000.

530.41   US   ISSN 0038-5654
QC176   CODEN: SPSSA7
SOVIET PHYSICS - SOLID STATE. English translation of: Fizika Tverdogo Tela (RU ISSN 0015-3249) 1959. m. $1640 (foreign $1700). American Institute of Physics, 335 E. 45th St., New York, NY 10017. TEL 212-661-9404. Eds. L.V. Azaroff, A. Tybulewicz. bibl.; charts; illus.; index. (also avail. in microform; back issues avail.) **Indexed:** C.P.I., Eng.Ind., Gen.Phys.Adv.Abstr., Math.R., Met.Abstr., Phys.Ber., Sci.Abstr., World Alum.Abstr.
—BLDSC shelfmark: 0425.350000.

530   US   ISSN 0038-5662
QC1   CODEN: SPTPA3
SOVIET PHYSICS - TECHNICAL PHYSICS. English translation of: Zhurnal Tekhnicheskoi Fiziki (RU ISSN 0044-4642) 1956. m. $1445 (foreign $1490). American Institute of Physics, 335 E. 45th St., New York, NY 10017. TEL 212-661-9404. Ed. D.L. Book. bibl.; charts; illus.; index. (also avail. in microform; back issues avail.) **Indexed:** Appl.Mech.Rev., C.P.I., Eng.Ind., Gen.Phys.Adv.Abstr., Int.Aerosp.Abstr., Mass Spectr.Bull., Math.R., Met.Abstr., Phys.Ber., Sci.Abstr.
—BLDSC shelfmark: 0425.380000.

530   US
SOVIET PHYSICS - USPEKHI. English translation of: Uspekhi Fizicheskikh Nauk (RU ISSN 0042-1294) 1958. m. $800 (foreign $815-$835). American Institute of Physics, 335 E. 45th St., New York, NY 10017. TEL 212-661-9404. Ed. G.M. Volkoff. bibl.; charts; index. (also avail. in microform; back issues avail.) Formerly: Soviet Physics - Achievements (ISSN 0038-5670)

530   US   ISSN 0143-0394
QC1   CODEN: SSRPDH
SOVIET SCIENTIFIC REVIEWS. SECTION A: PHYSICS REVIEWS. vol.4, 1982. a. $118. Harwood Academic Publishers, 270 Eighth Ave., New York, NY 10011. TEL 212-206-8900. FAX 212-645-2459. TELEX 236735 GOPUB UR. (Subscr. to: Box 786, Cooper Sta., New York, NY 10276. TEL 800-545-8398; UK subscr. to: P.O. Box 90, Reading, Berkshire RG1 8JL, England. TEL 0734-560-080) Ed. I.M. Khalatnikov. index. (also avail. in microform; back issues avail.)
—BLDSC shelfmark: 8359.915200.
  Refereed Serial

530 510   US   ISSN 0143-0416
QC19.2   CODEN: SRCREA
SOVIET SCIENTIFIC REVIEWS. SECTION C: MATHEMATICAL PHYSICS REVIEWS. vol.2, 1981. a. $118. Harwood Academic Publishers, 270 Eighth Ave., New York, NY 10011. TEL 212-206-8900. FAX 212-645-2459. TELEX 236735 GOPUB UR. (Subscr. to: Box 786, Cooper Sta., New York, NY 10276. TEL 800-545-8398; UK subscr. to: P.O. Box 90, Reading, Berkshire RG1 8JL, England. TEL 0734-560-080) Ed. S.P. Norikov. index. (also avail. in microform; back issues avail.)
  Refereed Serial

530   US   ISSN 0275-7796
SOVIET SCIENTIFIC REVIEWS SUPPLEMENT SERIES. SECTION A: PHYSICS. irreg. Harwood Academic Publishers, 270 Eighth Ave., New York, NY 10011. TEL 212-206-8900. FAX 212-645-2459. TELEX 236735 GOPUB UR. (Subscr. to: Box 786, Cooper Sta., New York, NY 10276. TEL 800-545-8398; UK subscr. to: Box 90, Reading, Berkshire RG1 8JL, England. TEL 0734-560-080) Ed. I.M. Khalatnikov. (also avail. in microform)
—BLDSC shelfmark: 8359.915430.

530.05   US   ISSN 0360-120X
QC1   CODEN: STPLD2
SOVIET TECHNICAL PHYSICS LETTERS. English translation of: Pis'ma v Zhurnal Tekhnicheskoi Fiziki. 1975. m. $900 (foreign $915-$935). American Institute of Physics, 335 E. 45th St., New York, NY 10017. TEL 212-661-9404. Ed. J.R. Anderson. bibl.; charts; illus.; index. (also avail. in microform from MIM; back issues avail.) **Indexed:** Gen.Phys.Adv.Abstr., Int.Aerosp.Abstr., Mass Spectr.Bull., Phys.Ber., Sci.Abstr.
—BLDSC shelfmark: 0425.822000.

530   PL   ISSN 0208-8428
Z5064 .A7
SPACE PHYSICS. s-a. price varies. (Polska Akademia Nauk, Space Research Center) Panstwowe Wydawnictwo Naukowe, Miodowa 10, 00-251 Warsaw, Poland. (Dist. by: Ars Polona, Krakowskie Przedmiescie 7, 00-068 Warsaw, Poland) Ed. A. Wernik.
  Supersedes in part: Artificial Satellites (ISSN 0571-205X)

530   US   ISSN 0193-1725
SPEAKERS, TOURS AND FILMS. 1973. a. $15. American Institute of Physics, Society of Physics - Sigma Pi Sigma, 1825 Connecticut Ave., N.W., Ste. 213, Washington, DC 20009. TEL 202-232-6688. FAX 202-234-7053. Ed. Donald Kirwan. circ. 700.

530   US
SPRINGER PROCEEDINGS IN PHYSICS. 1984. irreg. price varies. Springer-Verlag, 175 Fifth Ave., New York, NY 10010. TEL 212-460-1500. (Also Berlin, Heidelberg, Tokyo, Vienna) (reprint service avail. from ISI)

530 541.3   US   ISSN 0172-6218
                     CODEN: SSCPDA
SPRINGER SERIES IN CHEMICAL PHYSICS. 1978. irreg. price varies. Springer-Verlag, 175 Fifth Ave., New York, NY 10010. TEL 212-460-1500. (Also Berlin, Heidelberg, Tokyo and Vienna) Ed.Bd. (reprint service avail. from ISI) **Indexed:** Biol.Abstr., Chem.Abstr., Phys.Ber.

530   US
SPRINGER SERIES IN MATERIALS SCIENCES. 1986. irreg. price varies. Springer-Verlag, 175 Fifth Ave., New York, NY 10010. TEL 212-460-1500. (Also Berlin, Heidelberg, Tokyo, Vienna) (reprint service avail. from ISI)

530   US   ISSN 0171-1873
                     CODEN: SSSSDV
SPRINGER SERIES IN SOLID STATE SCIENCES. 1978. irreg. price varies. Springer-Verlag, 175 Fifth Ave., New York, NY 10010. TEL 212-460-1500. (Also Berlin, Heidelberg, Tokyo and Vienna) Ed.Bd. (reprint service avail. from ISI) **Indexed:** Chem.Abstr., Phys.Ber.

530   US
SPRINGER SERIES IN SURFACE SCIENCES. 1986. irreg. price varies. Springer-Verlag, 175 Fifth Ave., New York, NY 10010. TEL 212-460-1500. (Also Berlin, Heidelberg, Tokyo, Vienna) (reprint service avail. from ISI)

539   US   ISSN 0081-3869
SPRINGER TRACTS IN MODERN PHYSICS. 1964. irreg. price varies. Springer-Verlag, 175 Fifth Ave., New York, NY 10010. TEL 212-460-1500. (Also Berlin, Heidelberg, Tokyo and Vienna) (reprint service avail. from ISI) **Indexed:** ASCA, Phys.Ber.
—BLDSC shelfmark: 8424.800000.
  Continues: Ergebnisse der Exacten Naturwissenschaften.

STAATLICHE MATHEMATISCH-PHYSIKALISCHE SALONS, DRESDEN. VEROEFFENTLICHUNGEN. see MATHEMATICS

530   RM
STUDIA UNIVERSITATIS "BABES-BOLYAI". PHYSICA. (Text in English, French, German, Rumanian) 1959. s-a. exchange basis. Universitatea "Babes-Bolyai", Biblioteca Centrala Universitara, Str. Clinicilor Nr. 2, Cluj-Napoca, Rumania. **Indexed:** Chem.Abstr., Math.R.

STUDIES IN APPLIED MATHEMATICS. see *MATHEMATICS*

530   US   ISSN 0270-4730
                          CODEN: SEPHDL
STUDIES IN HIGH ENERGY PHYSICS SERIES. irreg. Harwood Academic Publishers, 270 Eighth Ave., New York, NY 10011. TEL 212-206-8900. FAX 212-645-2459. TELEX 236735 GOPUB UR. (Subscr. to: Box 786, Cooper Sta., New York, NY 10276. TEL 800-545-8398; UK subscr. to: Box 90, Reading, Berkshire RG1 8JL, England. TEL 0734-560-080) Ed. M. Charap. (also avail. in microform)
Refereed Serial

STUDIES IN THE HISTORY OF MATHEMATICS AND PHYSICAL SCIENCES. see *MATHEMATICS*

530   RM   ISSN 0039-3940
QC1   CODEN: SCEFAB
STUDII SI CERCETARI DE FIZICA. 1950. 10/yr. 350 lei($75) (Academia Romana) Editura Academiei Romane, Calea Victoriei 125, 79717 Bucharest, Rumania. (Dist. by: Rompresfilatelia, Calea Grivitei 64-66, P.O. Box 12-201, 78104 Bucharest, Rumania) Ed. Ioan Ursu. bk.rev.; illus.; index. **Indexed:** Chem.Abstr., Int.Aerosp.Abstr., Math.R., Met.Abstr., Phys.Ber., Sci.Abstr.
—BLDSC shelfmark: 8495.700000.

530 510   KN
SUHAKKWA MULLI. (Text in Korean) q. Korean Academy of Sciences, Physics and Mathematics Committee, Pyongyang, N. Korea.

530   US
SUPER COLLIDER NEWS. m. Atlantic Information Services, Inc., 1050 17th St. N.W., Ste. 480, Washington, DC 20036. TEL 202-775-9008. FAX 202-331-9542. Ed. C. David Chaffee.

600 530   US   ISSN 0235-8964
QC611.9   CODEN: SPCUE5
SUPERCONDUCTIVITY: PHYSICS, CHEMISTRY, TECHNOLOGY. 1988. m. $920 (foreign $950). American Institute of Physics, 335 E. 45th St., New York, NY 10017-2483. TEL 212-661-9404. FAX 212-949-0473. (Subscr. to: Member and Subscriber Service, 500 Sunnyside Blvd., Woodbury, NY 11979-2999. TEL 516-576-2270)
—BLDSC shelfmark: 0425.895000.
Description: Covers Russian research in the area of superconductivity.

530 540 620   UK   ISSN 0953-2048
QC611.9   CODEN: SUSTEF
SUPERCONDUCTOR SCIENCE & TECHNOLOGY. 1988. m. £177($354) (effective Jan. 1992). (Institute of Physics) I O P Publishing, Techno House, Redcliffe Way, Bristol BS1 6NX, England. TEL 0272-297481. FAX 0272-294318. TELEX 449149-INSTP-G. (U.S. addr.: American Institute of Physics, Member and Subscriber Service, 500 Sunnyside Blvd., Woodbury, NY 11797-2999. TEL 516-576-2270) Ed. J.E. Evetts. (also avail. in microform)
—BLDSC shelfmark: 8547.075500.
Description: Provides a forum for chemists, physicists, materials scientists, and electronics and electrical engineers involved in any aspect of the science and technology of superconductors, both conventional and the new ceramic materials.

SUPERLATTICES AND MICROSTRUCTURES. see *CHEMISTRY*

530.44   JA
SUPESU PURAZUMA KENKYUKAI. (Text in English and Japanese) 1970. a. Institute of Space and Astronautical Science, Space Plasma Study Group - Uchu Kagaku Kenkyujo, Supesu Purazuma Kenkyukai, 1-1, Yoshinodai 3-chome, Sagamihara-shi, Kanagawa-ken 229, Japan.

620.1   US   ISSN 1058-093X
▼**SURFACE MODIFICATION TECHNOLOGY NEWS.** 1991. m. $275. Business Communications Co., Inc. (Norwalk), 25 Van Zant St., Ste. 13, Norwalk, CT 06855. TEL 203-426-3905. FAX 203-853-0348. TELEX 6502934929 WUI. Ed. Robert Moran. abstr.; pat. (back issues avail.)
●Also available online. Vendor(s): NewsNet.
Description: Presents news, reviews, new methods and materials used in surface treatment in electronics, optics, wear and catalysis applications.

541.345   NE   ISSN 0039-6028
QD506   CODEN: SUSCAS
SURFACE SCIENCE; a journal devoted to the physics and chemistry of interfaces. (Includes section: Surface Science Letters) (Text in English, French or German; summaries in English) 1964. 54/yr. (in 18 vols.) fl.8118 (combined subscr. with Applied Surface Science and Surface Science Reports fl.10287)(effective 1992). North-Holland (Subsidiary of: Elsevier Science Publishers B.V.), P.O. Box 211, 1000 AE Amsterdam, Netherlands. TEL 020-5803911. FAX 020-5803598. TELEX 18582 ESPA NL. (Subscr. in U.S. and Canada to: Elsevier Science Publishing Co., Inc., Box 882, Madison Sq. Sta., New York, NY 10159. TEL 212-989-5800) Ed. Harry C. Gatos. adv.; bk.rev.; bibl.; charts; illus.; index. (also avail. in microform from RPI; back issues avail.) **Indexed:** ASCA, Br.Ceram.Abstr., Chem.Abstr., Curr.Cont., INSPEC, Int.Aerosp.Abstr., Mass Spectr.Bull., Met.Abstr., Phys.Ber., Sci.Abstr., World Alum.Abstr.
—BLDSC shelfmark: 8547.950000.
Description: Deals with theoretical and experimental studies in the physics and chemistry of surfaces.
Refereed Serial

SURFACE SCIENCE LETTERS. see *PHYSICS — Abstracting, Bibliographies, Statistics*

530   NE   ISSN 0167-5729
QC173.4.S94   CODEN: SSREDI
SURFACE SCIENCE REPORTS; a review journal. (Text in English) 1981. 8/yr. fl.346 (combined subscr. with Surface Science and Applied Surface Science fl.10287)(effective 1992). North-Holland (Subsidiary of: Elsevier Science Publishers B.V.), P.O. Box 211, 1000 AE Amsterdam, Netherlands. TEL 020-5803911. FAX 020-5803598. TELEX 18582 ESPA NL. (Subscr. in U.S. and Canada to: Elsevier Science Publishing Co., Inc., Box 882, Madison Sq. Sta., New York, NY 10159. TEL 212-989-5800) Ed. A.V. Oostrom. adv. (also avail. in microform from RPI; back issues avail.) **Indexed:** Chem.Abstr., Met.Abstr., Phys.Ber., Sci.Abstr., World Alum.Abstr.
—BLDSC shelfmark: 8547.950530.
Description: Contains papers on the properties of surfaces and interfaces of metals, semiconductors and insulators with emphasis on fundamental aspects of solid and liquid interfaces, their atomic and electronic structure.
Refereed Serial

530   US   ISSN 1055-5269
                          CODEN: SSSPEN
▼**SURFACE SCIENCE SPECTRA**; an international journal devoted to archiving surface science spectra of technological and scientific interest. 1991. q. $987 (Canada $997; elsewhere $1007). (American Vacuum Society) American Institute of Physics, 335 E. 45th St., New York, NY 10017-3483. TEL 212-661-9404. FAX 212-949-0473. (Subscr. to: Member and Subscriber Service, 500 Sunnyside Blvd., Woodbury, NY 11797-2999. TEL 516-576-2270) Ed. C.B. Bryson. index.
Description: Publishes complete records of original surface spectroscopic data.

530   US   ISSN 0142-2413
QC793   CODEN: SHEPDB
SURVEYS IN HIGH ENERGY PHYSICS; an international journal. 1980. 12/yr. (in 3 vols., 4 nos./vol.). $120. Harwood Academic Publishers, 270 Eighth Ave., New York, NY 10011. TEL 212-206-8900. FAX 212-645-2459. TELEX 236735 GOPUB UR. (Subscr. to: Box 786, Cooper Sta., New York, NY 10276. TEL 800-545-8398; UK subscr. to: P.O. Box 90, Reading, Berkshire RG1 8JL, England. TEL 0734-560-080) Eds. A.B. Kaidalov, M.I. Vysotsky. bk.rev.; charts; illus. (also avail. in microfiche; microfilm; back issues avail.) **Indexed:** Chem.Abstr., Sci.Abstr.
Refereed Serial

PHYSICS   3833

530   SW
SWEDISH CENTER OF SPACE PHYSICS. UPPSALA DIVISION. TECHNICAL REPORTS. 1978. irreg. price varies. Swedish Institute of Space Physics, Uppsala Division, S-755 91 Uppsala, Sweden. TEL 46-18-40 30 00.
Formerly: Uppsala Ionospheric Observatory. Technical Reports (ISSN 0349-2680)

530   SW
SWEDISH INSTITUTE OF SPACE PHYSICS. UPPSALA DIVISION. SCIENTIFIC REPORTS. 1977. irreg. price varies. Swedish Institute of Space Physics, Uppsala Division, S-755 91 Uppsala, Sweden. TEL 46-18-40 30 00.
Formerly: Uppsala Ionospheric Observatory. Scientific Reports (ISSN 0349-2699)

SYNTHETIC METALS; an international journal integrating research and applications on intercalation compounds of graphite, transition metal compounds, and quasi one-dimensional conductors. see *CHEMISTRY*

530   US
TECHNIQUES OF PHYSICS. 1973. irreg., vol.13, 1990. Academic Press, Inc., 1250 Sixth Ave., San Diego, CA 92101. TEL 619-231-0926. FAX 619-699-6715. Eds. N.H. March, H.N. Daglish. (reprint service avail. from ISI)
Refereed Serial

530   NE
TECHNISCH FYSISCHE DIENST T N O - T H. JAARVERSLAG. (Toegepast-Natuurwetenschappelijk Onderzoek) (Text in Dutch; summaries in English) 1946. a. free. Technisch Fysische Dienst T N O - T H - T N O Institute of Applied Physics, Stieltjesweg 1, P.O. Box 155, Delft, Netherlands. Ed.Bd. illus.; circ. 2,500.

530   US   ISSN 0082-2590
TECHNISCHE PHYSIK IN EINZELDARSTELLUNGEN. 1948. irreg. price varies. Springer-Verlag, 175 Fifth Ave., New York, NY 10010. TEL 212-460-1500. (also Berlin, Heidelberg, Vienna) (reprint service avail. from ISI)

530 620   YU   ISSN 0350-0594
QC1   CODEN: TEFIDJ
TEHNICKA FIZIKA/JOURNAL OF ENGINEERING PHYSICS. (Text in English, German, Russian; summaries in Serbo-Croatian) 1964. s-a. Univerzitet u Beogradu, Tehnicki Fakultet, Zavod za Fiziku, Ruzveltova 1a, 11000 Belgrade, Serbia, Yugoslavia. Ed. Jordan Pop-Jordanov. bk.rev.; circ. 1,000. **Indexed:** Chem.Abstr., Math.R., Phys.Abstr., Ref.Zh., Sci.Abstr.
Formerly: Zavod za Fiziku. Radovi (ISSN 0522-8557)

530   IS
TEHUDA/RESONANCE; physics teacher's newsletter. (Text in Hebrew) 1972. 2/yr. $10. Weizman Institute of Science, Department of Science Teaching, Rehovot 76100, Israel. TEL 8-342981. FAX 8-466966. (Dist. by: Gestelit, P.O. Box 2088, Hayotsek St., Haifa 31020, Israel) Ed. Hanna Goldring. adv.; bk.rev.; illus.; circ. 200. (back issues avail.) **Indexed:** Ind.Heb.Per.

TEKSTER FRA I M F U F A. (Institut for Studiet af Matematik og Fysik Samt Deres Funktioner i Undervisning Forskning og Anvendelse) see *MATHEMATICS*

536   RU   ISSN 0040-3644
                          CODEN: TVYTAP
TEPLOFIZIKA VYSOKIKH TEMPERATUR. 1963. bi-m. 46.50 Rub. (Akademiya Nauk S.S.S.R., Otdelenie Fiziko-tekhnicheskikh Problem Energetiki) Izdatel'stvo Nauka, Fizmatlit, Leninskii prospekt, 15, 117071 Moscow, V-71, Russia. Ed. A.E. Sheindlin. bk.rev.; bibl.; index. (tabloid format) **Indexed:** Bull.Thermodyn.& Thermochem., Chem.Abstr., Met.Abstr., Sci.Abstr., World Alum.Abstr.
—BLDSC shelfmark: 0178.850000.

530   GW   ISSN 0233-0911
                          CODEN: TTPHE2
TEUBNER-TEXTE ZUR PHYSIK. 1984. 2/yr. B.G. Teubner Verlagsgesellschaft KG, Sternwartenstr. 8, 7010 Leipzig, Germany. TEL 293158. Ed.Bd.
—BLDSC shelfmark: 8798.289000.

530 US ISSN 0172-5998
TEXTS AND MONOGRAPHS IN PHYSICS. 1976. irreg. price varies. Springer-Verlag, 175 Fifth Ave., New York, NY 10010. TEL 212-460-1500. (And Berlin, Heidelberg, Tokyo and Vienna) Ed. W. Beiglboeck. (reprint service avail. from ISI) **Indexed:** Math.R.

530 510 US ISSN 0040-5779
QC20 CODEN: TMPHAH
THEORETICAL AND MATHEMATICAL PHYSICS. English translation of: Teoreticheskaya; Matematicheskaya Fizika. 1969. m. (3 vol./yr.). $995 (foreign $1165)(effective 1992). (Russian Academy of Sciences, RU) Plenum Publishing Corp., Consultants Bureau, 233 Spring St., New York, NY 10013-1578. TEL 212-620-8468. FAX 212-463-0742. TELEX 23-421139. Ed. A.A. Logunov. (also avail. in microfilm from JSC; back issues avail.) **Indexed:** Appl.Mech.Rev., Compumath, Curr.Cont., Math.R., Sci.Res.Abstr., Zent.Math.
—BLDSC shelfmark: 0426.250000.
Refereed Serial

530 NO
THEORETICAL PHYSICS SEMINAR IN TRONDHEIM. (Text in English) 1953. fortn. NOK 370($39) Seminar for Teoretisk Fysikk i Trondheim, N-7034 Trondheim NTH, Norway. FAX 47-7-593628. TELEX 55637. circ. 160. **Indexed:** Phys.Abstr., Ref.Zh., Sci.Abstr.
Formerly: Arkiv for det Fysiske Seminar i Trondheim (ISSN 0365-2459)

530 NE
THIN FILMS SCIENCE AND TECHNOLOGY. (Text in English) 1980. irreg. vol.7, 1990. price varies. Elsevier Science Publishers B.V., Books Division, P.O. Box 211, 1000 AE Amsterdam, Netherlands. TEL 020-5803911. FAX 020-5803705. TELEX 18582 ESPA NL. (Subscr. in U.S. and Canada to: Elsevier Science Publishing Co., Inc., Box 882, Madison Sq. Sta., New York, NY 10159. TEL 212-989-5800) Ed. G. Siddall. (back issues avail.)
Refereed Serial

541.345 SZ ISSN 0040-6090
TK7871.15.F5 CODEN: THSFAP
THIN SOLID FILMS; an international journal on the science and technology of condensed matter films. (Text in English) 1968. 32/yr. (in 16 vols., 2 nos./vol.). 5200 SFr. (effective 1992). Elsevier Sequoia S.A., P.O. Box 564, CH-1001 Lausanne, Switzerland. TEL 021-207381. FAX 021-235444. TELEX 450620 ELSA CH. (Subscr. in U.S. and Canada to: Elsevier Science Publishing Co., Inc., Box 882, Madison Sq. Sta., New York, NY 10159. TEL 212-989-5800) Ed. J.E. Greene. adv.; bk.rev.; bibl.; illus.; index. (also avail. in microform from UMI) **Indexed:** ASCA, Chem.Abstr., Curr.Cont., Eng.Ind., INSPEC, Int.Aerosp.Abstr., Mass Spectr.Bull., Met.Abstr., Phys.Abstr., Phys.Ber., Sci.Abstr., Sci.Cit.Ind., World Alum.Abstr.
—BLDSC shelfmark: 8820.120000.
Description: Serves scientists and engineers working in the fields of thin-film synthesis, characterization, and applications.
Refereed Serial

TIANTI WULI XUEBAO/ACTA ASTROPHYSICA SINICA. see *ASTRONOMY*

530 540 JA ISSN 0040-8808
Q77.T55 CODEN: SRTAA6
TOHOKU UNIVERSITY. SCIENCE REPORTS OF THE RESEARCH INSTITUTES. SERIES A: PHYSICS, CHEMISTRY, AND METALLURGY/TOHOKU DAIGAKU KENKYUJO HOKOKU. A-SHU: BUTSURIGAKU, KAGAKU, YAKINGAKU. (Text in English) 1949. s-a. exchange basis. Tohoku Daigaku, Kenkyujo Rengokai - Tohoku University, Association of the Research Institutes, 4-1 Seiryo-machi, Aoba-ku, Sendai-shi, Miyagi-ken 980, Japan. FAX 022-264-7984. Ed. Hiroyasu Fujimori. charts; illus.; index, cum.index every 10 yrs.; circ. 1,250. **Indexed:** ASCA, Cadscan, Chem.Abstr., Curr.Cont., Eng.Ind., INIS Atomind., JCT, JTA, Lead Abstr., Met.Abstr., Sci.Abstr., Sci.Cit.Ind., World Alum.Abstr., Zincscan.
—BLDSC shelfmark: 8156.545000.

530 540 520 JA ISSN 0388-5607
Q77 CODEN: SRTAD9
TOHOKU UNIVERSITY. SCIENCE REPORTS. SERIES 8: PHYSICS AND ASTRONOMY.* (Text in English, French, German) 1911. q. exchange basis. Tohoku Daigaku, Rigakubu Chishitsugaku Kenkyujo - Tohoku University, Faculty of Science, Geophysical Institute, Aoba, Aramaki, Sendai-shi, Miyagi-ken 980, Japan. Eds. M. Tanaka, K. Takakuba. charts; illus.; stat.; index; circ. 800. **Indexed:** Chem.Abstr., INIS Atomind., Math.R., Met.Abstr., Sci.Abstr., World Alum.Abstr.
—BLDSC shelfmark: 8159.501000.
Supersedes (in 1980): Tohoku University. Science Reports. Series 1: Physics, Chemistry, Astronomy (ISSN 0040-8778)

530 621 US ISSN 0303-4216
CODEN: TAPHD4
TOPICS IN APPLIED PHYSICS. 1974. irreg. price varies. Springer-Verlag, 175 Fifth Ave., New York, NY 10010. TEL 212-460-1500. (Also Berlin, Heidelberg, Tokyo and Vienna) (reprint service avail. from ISI) **Indexed:** ASCA, Biol.Abstr., Phys.Ber.

530 US ISSN 0342-6793
CODEN: TCPHDI
TOPICS IN CURRENT PHYSICS. 1976. irreg. price varies. Springer-Verlag, 175 Fifth Ave., New York, NY 10010. TEL 212-460-1500. (Also Berlin, Heidelberg, Tokyo and Vienna) (reprint service avail. from ISI) **Indexed:** Chem.Abstr, Phys.Ber.

TOPICS IN MAGNETIC RESONANCE IMAGING. see *MEDICAL SCIENCES*

530 500 US
TOTH-MAATIAN REVIEW; a journal for criticism and dissident opinion. 1982. q. $19. Toth-Maatian Press, 3101 20th St., Lubbock, TX 79410. TEL 806-797-2788. Ed. Harold Willis Milnes. bk.rev.; circ. 250. (back issues avail.)

530 540 JA ISSN 0372-039X
CODEN: TOKHA6
TOYODA KENKYU HOKOKU/TOYODA PHYSICAL AND CHEMICAL RESEARCH INSTITUTE. REPORTS. (Text in Japanese; summaries in English) 1942. a. Toyoda Rikagaku Kenkyujo - Toyoda Physical and Chemical Research Institute, 41-1, Yokomichi, Nagakute, Nagakute-cho, Aichi-gun, Aichi-ken 480-11, Japan. abstr. **Indexed:** Chem.Abstr., INIS Atomind., Jap.Per.Ind.

530 FR ISSN 0765-0019
TK5102.5
TRAITEMENT DU SIGNAL. (Text and summaries in English and French) 1964. q. (with 2 special nos.). 570 F. (outside Europe 700 F.). Groupe de Recherche et d'Etude de Traitement du Signal et des Images (GRETSI), 26 bd. Victor, 75996 Paris Armees, France. (Dist. by: Gauthier-Villars, Centrale des Revues, 11 rue Gossin, 92543 Montrouge Cedex, France. TEL 0-46-56-52-66) Ed. Maurice Bouix. bk.rev.; charts; index; circ. 800. **Indexed:** Math.R., Sci.Abstr.
Formerly: Revue du Cethedec (ISSN 0035-2535)
Description: Describes studies and finished projects in all areas of research and application of signal processing.

TRANSPORT IN POROUS MEDIA. see *CHEMISTRY*

530.13 US ISSN 0041-1450
QC175.2 CODEN: TTSPB4
TRANSPORT THEORY AND STATISTICAL PHYSICS. 1971. 6/yr. $305 to individuals; institutions $610. Marcel Dekker Journals, 270 Madison Ave., New York, NY 10016. TEL 212-696-9000. FAX 212-685-4540. TELEX 421419 MARDEEK. (Subscr. to: Box 10018, Church St. Sta., New York, NY 10249) Ed. Paul Nelson. adv. (also avail. in microform from RPI) **Indexed:** Chem.Abstr., Curr.Cont., Math.R., Phys.Ber., Sci.Abstr.
—BLDSC shelfmark: 9025.965000.
Refereed Serial

530 US
TRIESTE NOTES IN PHYSICS. 1986. irreg. price varies. Springer-Verlag, 175 Fifth Ave., New York, NY 10010. TEL 212-460-1500. (Also Berlin, Heidelberg, Tokyo and Vienna) (reprint service avail. from ISI)
Refereed Serial

U S S R COMPUTATIONAL MATHEMATICS AND MATHEMATICAL PHYSICS. see *MATHEMATICS*

530 UK ISSN 0960-6068
UKRAINIAN JOURNAL OF PHYSICS. 1956. m. £385($640) (Ukranian Academy of Sciences, KR) Riecansky Science Publishing Co., 7 Meadow Walk, Great Abington, Cambridge CB1 6AZ, England. TEL 0223-893295. FAX 0223-893295. Ed. A.G. Sitenko.
—BLDSC shelfmark: 0428.920000.

530 KR ISSN 0503-1265
CODEN: UFIZAW
UKRAINSKII FIZICHESKII ZHURNAL; nauchnyi zhurnal. 1956. m. 20.40 Rub.($37.80) (Akademiya Nauk Ukrainskoi S.S.R., Otdelenie Fiziki i Astronomii) Izdatel'stvo Naukova Dumka, c/o Yu.A. Khramov, Dir, Ul. Repina, 3, Kiev 252 601, Ukraine. TEL 265-09-11. Ed. A.A. Smirnov. charts; illus.; index; circ. 1,000. **Indexed:** Chem.Abstr., Int.Aerosp.Abstr., Math.R., Met.Abstr., Phys.Ber., Sci.Abstr.
—BLDSC shelfmark: 0384.650000.

ULTRASONIC IMAGING; an international journal. see *MEDICAL SCIENCES*

UNION MATEMATICA ARGENTINA. REVISTA. see *MATHEMATICS*

UNIVERSITA DEGLI STUDI DI MODENA. SEMINARIO MATEMATICO E FISICO. ATTI. see *MATHEMATICS*

530 RM ISSN 0041-9141
UNIVERSITATEA "AL. I. CUZA" DIN IASI. ANALELE STIINTIFICE. SECTIUNEA 1B: FIZICA. (Text in English, French, German or Russian) 1955. a. 35 lei. Universitatea "Al. I. Cuza" din Iasi, Calea M. Eminescu 11, Jassy, Rumania. (Subscr. to: ILEXIM, Str. 13 Decembrie Nr. 3, P.O. Box 136-137, Bucharest, Rumania) Ed. M. Sandulovici. bk.rev.; abstr.; charts; illus.; cir. 250. **Indexed:** Chem.Abstr., INIS Atomind., Math.R., Sci.Abstr.
Description: Review articles, original papers, short notes and book reviews on physics.

UNIVERSITATEA DIN CRAIOVA. ANALE. SERIA: MATEMATICA, FIZICA-CHIMIE. see *MATHEMATICS*

530 540 RM
UNIVERSITATEA DIN TIMISOARA. ANALELE. STIINTE FIZICE. 1963. s-a. $10. Universitatea din Timisoara, Facultatea de Stiinte ale Naturii, Bd. Vasile Pirvan Nr. 4, Timisoara, Rumania. (Dist. by: ILEXIM, Str. 13 Decembrie Nr. 3, Box 136-137, Bucharest, Rumania) Ed. Nicolae Avram.
Formerly (until vol.22, 1982): Universitatea din Timisoara. Analele. Stiinte Fizico-Chimice (ISSN 0082-4453)

UNIVERSITATEA TRANSILVANIA DIN BRASOV. BULETINUL. SERIA C. MATEMATICA, FIZICA, CHIMIE. see *MATHEMATICS*

UNIVERSITEXTS. see *MATHEMATICS*

530 520 CN
UNIVERSITY OF BRITISH COLUMBIA, PHYSICS SOCIETY. JOURNAL. 1960. a. Can.$3 to non-members. University of British Columbia, Physics Society, Dept. of Physics, 6224 Agriculture Rd., Vancouver, B.C. V6T 2A6, Canada. TEL 604-228-2211. Ed. Aaron Drake. adv.; circ. 150. (back issues avail.)
Description: Review of papers from undergraduates in physics, astronomy, and geophysics.

530 DK ISSN 0106-7222
CODEN: RCPLD8
UNIVERSITY OF COPENHAGEN. PHYSICS LABORATORY. REPORT. (Text in English) 1972. irreg. free. Koebenhavns Universitet, Physics Laboratory, H.C. Oersted Institut, Universitetsparken 5, DK-2100 Copenhagen OE, Denmark. FAX 45-31-350628. circ. 100.
—BLDSC shelfmark: 7580.454000.
Description: Preprints of papers to be published in scientific journals.

530 FI
UNIVERSITY OF JYVASKYLA. DEPARTMENT OF PHYSICS. PREPRINTS. 1969. irreg. (5-6/yr.). exchange basis. University of Jyvaskyla, Department of Physics, PL 35, SF-40351 Jyvaskyla, Finland. FAX 358-41-602351. Ed. Soili Leskinen. circ. 130. (processed)
Formerly (until 1984): Jyvaskylan Yliopisto. Department of Physics. Research Report (ISSN 0075-465X)

UNIVERSITY OF OSAKA PREFECTURE. RESEARCH INSTITUTE FOR ADVANCED SCIENCE AND TECHNOLOGY. ANNUAL REPORT/OSAKA-FURITSU-DAIGAKU FUZOKUKENKYUSHO NENPO. see *ENVIRONMENTAL STUDIES*

530   PP   ISSN 0085-4735
UNIVERSITY OF PAPUA NEW GUINEA. DEPARTMENT OF PHYSICS. TECHNICAL PAPER. 1968. irreg. free. University of Papua New Guinea, Department of Physics, P.O. Box 4820, University P.O., Papua New Guinea. circ. 75.

UNIVERSITY OF TOKYO. FACULTY OF SCIENCE. JOURNAL. SECTION 1A: MATHEMATICS/TOKYO DAIGAKU RIGAKUBU KIYO, DAI-1-RUI A, SUGAKU. see *MATHEMATICS*

530   JA   ISSN 0082-4798
UNIVERSITY OF TOKYO. INSTITUTE FOR SOLID STATE PHYSICS. TECHNICAL REPORT. SERIES A. (Text in English) 1959. irreg. University of Tokyo, Institute for Solid State Physics - Tokyo Daigaku Bussei Kenkyujo, 7-22-1 Roppongi, Minato-ku, Tokyo 106, Japan.
—BLDSC shelfmark: 8715.930000.
Description: Reprints articles published in scientific journals.

530   JA   ISSN 0082-4801
UNIVERSITY OF TOKYO. INSTITUTE FOR SOLID STATE PHYSICS. TECHNICAL REPORT. SERIES B. (Text in English) 1960. irreg., no.24, 1988. University of Tokyo, Institute for Solid State Physics - Tokyo Daigaku Bussei Kenkyujo, 7-22-1 Roppongi, Minato-ku, Tokyo 106, Japan.
Description: Original papers and other data not intended for publication elsewhere.

530 613.7   PL   ISSN 0208-4872
UNIWERSYTET GDANSKI. WYDZIAL MATEMATYKI, FIZYKI I CHEMII. ZESZYTY NAUKOWE. PROBLEMY DYDAKTYKI FIZYKI. (Text in Polish; summaries in English and Russian) 1974. irreg. price varies. Uniwersytet Gdanski, Wydzial Matematyki, Fizyki i Chemii, c/o Biblioteka Glowna, Ul. Armii Krajowej 110, 81-824 Sopot, Poland. TEL 51-0061. TELEX 051-2247 BMOR PL. (Dist. by: Ars Polona-Ruch, Krakowskie Przedmiescie 7, 00-680 Warsaw, Poland) Ed. Kazimierz Badziag. circ. 250.
—BLDSC shelfmark: 9512.436300.
Description: Reports on research work and methodology of physics didactics, proposals and discussion, school practicum, and descriptions of teaching physics in the world.

530   PL   ISSN 0083-4335
UNIWERSYTET JAGIELLONSKI. ZESZYTY NAUKOWE. PRACE FIZYCZNE. (Text in English and Polish; summaries in English and Russian) 1963. irreg., vol.23, 1984. price varies. Panstwowe Wydawnictwo Naukowe, Miodowa 10, 00-251 Warsaw, Poland. (Dist. by: Ars Polona, Krakowskie Przedmiescie 7, 00-068 Warsaw, Poland) Ed. Bronislaw Sredniawa. circ. 470. **Indexed:** Math.R.

530   RU   ISSN 0042-1294
QC1   CODEN: UFNAAG
USPEKHI FIZICHESKIKH NAUK. English translation: Soviet Physics - Uspekhi. 1918. m. 55.20 Rub. (Akademiya Nauk S.S.S.R.) Izdatel'stvo Nauka, Fizmatlit, Leninskii prospekt, 15, 117071 Moscow, Russia. bk.rev.; bibl.; charts; illus.; index; circ. 5,000. **Indexed:** Chem.Abstr., Curr.Cont., GeoRef., Ind.Med., Int.Aerosp.Abstr., Math.R., Met.Abstr., Phys.Ber., Sci.Abstr., World Alum.Abstr.
—BLDSC shelfmark: 0387.000000.

533.5 621.55   GW   ISSN 0934-9758
VAKUUM IN DER PRAXIS. (Text in German; summaries in English, French, German) 1951. 4/yr. DM.170. V C H Verlagsgesellschaft mbH, Postfach 101161, 6940 Weinheim, Germany. TEL 06201-602-0. FAX 06201-602-328. TELEX 465516-VCHWH-D. (US addr.: V C H Publishers Inc., 220 E. 23rd St., New York, NY 10010-4606. TEL 212-683-8333) Ed. J. Scherle. adv.; bk.rev.; charts; illus.; index, cum.index every 20 yrs.; circ. 4,100. **Indexed:** Chem.Abstr., Eng.Ind., Met.Abstr., Sci.Abstr., World Alum.Abstr.
—BLDSC shelfmark: 9140.900000.
Formerly: Vakuum-Technik (ISSN 0042-2266)

533.5   XV   ISSN 0351-9716
VAKUUMIST; the voice of the Slovenian Vacuum Society. (Text in Serbo-Croatian, Slovenian; occasionally in English) 1981. irreg. (2-3/yr.) $10. Drustvo za Vakuumsko Tehniko Slovenije - Slovenian Society for Vacuum Technique, Teslova 30, 61000 Ljubljana, Slovenia. TEL 061-263-461. FAX 061-263-098. TELEX 31629. Ed. Andrej Pregelj. adv.; cum.index; circ. 250. (looseleaf format; back issues avail.)

533.5   FR   ISSN 0042-5281
QC166   CODEN: VIDEAA
VIDE; les couches minces. (Text and summaries in English, French) 1946. bi-m. 715 F. (foreign 825 F.). Societe Francaise du Vide, 19 rue du Renard, 75004 Paris, France. TEL 42-78-15-82. FAX 42-78-63-20. Ed. J. Fauvet. adv.; bibl.; abstr.; charts; illus.; index; circ. 4,000. **Indexed:** Chem.Abstr., Curr.Cont., Eng.Ind., Met.Abstr., Sci.Abstr.

530   RU   ISSN 0301-6919
VOPROSY FIZIKI TVERDOGO TELA. irreg. 2.30 Rub. Chelyabinskii Gosudarstvennyi Pedagogicheskii Institut, Chelyabinsk, Russia. illus.

530   NE   ISSN 0165-2125
QA927   CODEN: WAMOD9
WAVE MOTION; an international journal reporting research on wave phenomena. (Text in English) 1979. 8/yr. (in 2 vols.; 4 nos./vol.). fl.782 (effective 1992). North-Holland (Subsidiary of: Elsevier Science Publishers B.V.), P.O. Box 211, 1000 AE Amsterdam, Netherlands. TEL 020-5803911. FAX 020-5803598. TELEX 18582 ESPA NL. (Subscr. in U.S. and Canada to: Elsevier Science Publishing Co., Inc., Box 882, Madison Sq. Sta., New York, NY 10159. TEL 212-989-5800) Ed. J.D. Achenbach. adv.; bibl.; illus.; index. cum.index. (also avail. in microform from RPI; back issues avail.) **Indexed:** Appl.Mech.Rev., Curr.Cont., Eng.Ind., Int.Aerosp.Abstr., Math.R., Phys.Ber., Sci.Abstr., Sci.Cit.Ind., Sh.& Vib.Dig.
—BLDSC shelfmark: 9280.765000.
Description: Publishes articles on analytical, numerical and experimental methods.
Refereed Serial

530   UK   ISSN 0959-7174
QC669   CODEN: WRMEEV
▼**WAVES IN RANDOM MEDIA.** 1991. q. £132($264) (effective Jan. 1992). (Institute of Physics) I O P Publishing, Techno House, Redcliffe Way, Bristol BS1 6NX, England. TEL 0272-297481. FAX 0272-294318. TELEX 449149-INSTP-G. (U.S. addr.: American Institute of Physics, Member and Subscriber Service, 500 Sunnyside Blvd., Woodbury, NY 11797-2999) Ed. A. Ishimaru. (also avail. in microform; microfiche)
—BLDSC shelfmark: 9280.775800.
Description: Provides a forum for publication of papers on new and original theoretical developments in wave propagation and scattering in random media, and new experimental or numerical studies demonstrating basic principles and theories.

WISSENSCHAFTLICHE TASCHENBUECHER. REIHE MATHEMATIK - PHYSIK. see *MATHEMATICS*

530   GW   ISSN 0138-127X
WISSENSCHAFTLICHE TASCHENBUECHER. REIHE TEXTE UND STUDIEN. 1970. irreg. price varies. Akademie-Verlag Berlin, Leipziger Str. 3-4, 1086 Berlin, Germany. TELEX 114420-AVERL-DD.

530   CC   ISSN 0379-4148
WULI/PHYSICS. (Text in Chinese) 1951. m. $6 per no. (Zhongguo Wuli Xuehui - Chinese Physical Society) Science Press, Marketing and Sales Department, 16 Donghuangchenggen Beijie, Beijing 100707, People's Republic of China. TEL 4010642. FAX 4012180. TELEX 210247-SPBJ-CN. adv.; bk.rev.; circ. 21,000.
—BLDSC shelfmark: 9365.190000.
Description: Introduces modern physics in simple language. Reports on developments in new branches of physics, new theories, phenomena, materials, experimental techniques and methods, and the application of physics in economic construction in China.
Refereed Serial

530 371.3   CC   ISSN 0509-4003
WULI JIAOXUE/PHYSICS TEACHING. (Text in Chinese) 1978. m. Y11.40($35.90) Huadong Shifan Daxue, Wuli Xi - East China Normal University, Department of Physics, Shanghai 200062, People's Republic of China. TEL 2577577. FAX 2570590. TELEX 33328 ECNU CN. (Dist. in US by: China Books & Periodicals, Inc., 2929 24th St., San Francisco, CA 94110. TEL 415-282-2994) (Co-sponsor: Zhongguo Wuli Xuehui - Chinese Physical Society) Ed. Mi Zihong. adv.; bk.rev.; index; circ. 40,000. (back issues avail.)
Description: Covers teaching material and teaching methods, and suggests physics problems and experiments. Includes information on teaching abroad, new developments in physics, and observations on physics in daily life.

530   CC
WULI SHIYAN/PHYSICS EXPERIMENTS. (Text in Chinese) bi-m. Dongbei Shifan Daxue - Northeast Normal University, 110, Stalin Street, Changchun, Jilin 130024, People's Republic of China. TEL 882320. Ed. Yu Fuchun.

530   CC   ISSN 0509-4038
WULI TONGBAO/PHYSICS BULLETIN. (Text in Chinese) 1982. m. Y11.52($18) Hebei Sheng Wuli Xuehui - Hebei Physics Society, Hebei Daxue - Hebei University, 1 Hezuo Lu, Baoding, Hebei 071002, People's Republic of China. TEL 225052. (Co-sponsor: Hebei University) Ed. Wu Zuren. circ. 10,000.

530   CC   ISSN 1000-3290
QC1   CODEN: WLHPAR
WULI XUEBAO/ACTA PHYSICA SINICA. English translation: Journal of Chinese Physics (US ISSN 1044-8357) (Text in Chinese; summaries in English) 1933. m. Y12.50($10) per no. (Zhongguo Wuli Xuehui - Chinese Physical Society) Science Press, Marketing and Sales Department, Donghuangchenggen Beijie, Beijing 100707, People's Republic of China. TEL 4010642. FAX 4012180. TELEX 210247-SPBJ-CN. adv.; circ. 11,000. **Indexed:** Corros.Abstr., INIS Atomind., Math.R., Met.Abstr., Phys.Ber., World Alum.Abstr.
—BLDSC shelfmark: 0650.500000.
Description: Covers physics research in mainland China, including surface physics, excitation, and amorphous physics.
Refereed Serial

530   PL   ISSN 0078-5385
QC1
WYZSZA SZKOLA PEDAGOGICZNA, OPOLE. ZESZYTY NAUKOWE. SERIA A. FIZYKA. (Text in Polish; summaries in English) 1963. irreg., vol.24, 1989. price varies; available on exchange. Wyzsza Szkola Pedagogiczna, Opole, Oleska 48, 45-951 Opole, Poland. TEL 48 77 383-87. (Dist. by: Ars Polona-Ruch, Krakowskie Przedmiescie 7, Warsaw, Poland) circ. 300. **Indexed:** Chem.Abstr., Math.R.
—BLDSC shelfmark: 9512.478970.

530   CC   ISSN 1001-0610
QC1   CODEN: XWZHEF
XIANDAI WULI ZHISHI/MODERN PHYSICS. (Text in Chinese) 1976. bi-m. $5 per no. Science Press, Marketing and Sales Department, 16 Donghuangchenggen Beijie, Beijing 100707, People's Republic of China. TEL 4010642. FAX 4012180. TELEX 210247-SPBJ-CN. adv.; circ. 10,000.
Formerly: Gaoneng Wuli - High Energy Physics.

ZEITSCHRIFT FUER ANGEWANDTE MATHEMATIK UND PHYSIK/JOURNAL OF APPLIED MATHEMATICS AND PHYSICS/JOURNAL DE MATHEMATIQUES ET DE PHYSIQUE APPLIQUEES. see *MATHEMATICS*

PHYSICS — Abstracting, Bibliographies, Statistics

530 541.3 523.01   GW   ISSN 0932-0784
QC1   CODEN: ZNASEI
ZEITSCHRIFT FUER NATURFORSCHUNG. SECTION A: PHYSICAL SCIENCES. (Text in English) 1946. m. DM.616. Verlag der Zeitschrift fuer Naturforschung, Postfach 2645, 7400 Tuebingen, Germany. TEL 07071-31555. FAX 06131-305388. Ed. T. Littmann. adv.; bk.rev.; charts; illus.; index; circ. 3,200. **Indexed:** Bull.Thermodyn.& Thermochem., Chem.Abstr., Chem.Infd., Curr.Cont., Deep Sea Res.& Oceanogr.Abstr., Excerpt.Med., GeoRef., Helminthol.Abstr., Int.Aerosp.Abstr., Mass Spectr.Bull., Math.R., Met.Abstr., Phys.Abstr., Phys.Ber., Sci.Abstr.
—BLDSC shelfmark: 9474.000000.
Former titles: Zeitschrift fuer Naturforschung. Section A: Physics, Physical Chemistry, Cosmic Physics (ISSN 0340-4811); Zeitschrift fuer Naturforschung. Ausgabe A (ISSN 0044-3166)

ZEITSCHRIFT FUER PHYSIK. SECTION A. ATOMIC NUCLEI. see PHYSICS — Nuclear Physics

536.44   GW   ISSN 0722-3277
CODEN: ZPCMDN
ZEITSCHRIFT FUER PHYSIK. SECTION B: CONDENSED MATTER. (Text in English, French or German; summaries in English) vols.13-14, 1971. 12/yr. DM.2196($1278) (effective 1992). Springer-Verlag, Heidelberger Platz 3, D-1000 Berlin 33, Germany. TEL 030-8207-1. (Also Heidelberg, Tokyo, Vienna, and New York) Eds. M. Campagna, H. Horner. (also avail. in microform from UMI; back issues avail.; reprint service avail. from ISI) **Indexed:** Chem.Abstr., Curr.Cont., INSPEC, Math.R., Met.Abstr., Phys.Ber., Sci.Abstr., World Alum.Abstr.
—BLDSC shelfmark: 9481.020000.
Former titles: Zeitschrift fuer Physik. Section B. Quanta and Matter (ISSN 0340-224X); Physik der Kondensierten Materie - Physique de la Matiere Condensee - Physics of Condensed Matter (ISSN 0031-9236)
Description: Papers on the physical properties of crystalline, disordered, and amorphous solids, and on classical and quantum liquids.

530   GW   ISSN 0170-9739
QC1   CODEN: ZPCFD2
ZEITSCHRIFT FUER PHYSIK. SECTION C: PARTICLES AND FIELDS. (Text in English) 1979. 16/yr. (in 4 vols., 4 nos./vol.). DM.3272($1896) (effective 1992). Springer-Verlag, Heidelberger Platz 3, D-1000 Berlin 33, Germany. TEL 030-8207-1. (Also Heidelberg, Tokyo, Vienna, and New York) Ed. G. Kramer. adv. (also avail. in microform from UMI; reprint service avail. from ISI) **Indexed:** Chem.Abstr., Curr.Cont., Math.R., Phys.Ber., Sci.Abstr.
—BLDSC shelfmark: 9481.100500.

530   GW   ISSN 0178-7683
QC170   CODEN: ZDACE2
ZEITSCHRIFT FUER PHYSIK. SECTION D: ATOMS, MOLECULES AND CLUSTERS. (Text in English) 1986. 12/yr. DM.1596($958) (effective 1992). Springer-Verlag, Heidelberger Platz 3, D-1000 Berlin 33, Germany. TEL 030-8207-1. Ed. I.V. Hertel. adv.; circ. 700. (back issues avail.) **Indexed:** Curr.Cont.
—BLDSC shelfmark: 9481.100500.

ZHONGHUA WULI YIXUE ZAZHI/CHINESE JOURNAL OF PHYSICAL MEDICINE. see MEDICAL SCIENCES

ZHONGXUESHENG SHU-LI-HUA (GAOZHONG BAN). see EDUCATION — Teaching Methods And Curriculum

530 375   CC
ZHONGXUESHENG WULI YUANDI/PHYSICS FOR MIDDLE SCHOOL STUDENTS. (Text in Chinese) bi-m. Y2.50. Fujian Society of Physics, Physics Department, Fuzhou University, Fuzhou, Fujian 350002, People's Republic of China. TEL 710845. (Dist. overseas by: Jiangsu Publications Import & Export Corp., 56 Gao Yun Ling, Nanjing, Jiangsu, P.R.C.) Ed. Qiu Jinzhang.

530   RU   ISSN 0044-4510
QC1   CODEN: ZETFA7
ZHURNAL EKSPERIMENTAL'NOI I TEORETICHESKOI FIZIKI. English translation: Soviet Physics - J E T P (US ISSN 0038-5646) (Text in Russian; summaries in English) 1931. m. 151.20 Rub. (Akademiya Nauk S.S.S.R.) Izdatel'stvo Nauka, Fizmatlit, Leninskii prospekt, 15, 117071 Moscow, Russia. TEL 234-05-84. Ed. P.L. Kapitsa. charts; illus.; index; circ. 2,700. **Indexed:** Chem.Abstr., Curr.Cont., Eng.Ind., Math.R., Met.Abstr., Phys.Ber., Sci.Abstr., World Alum.Abstr.
—BLDSC shelfmark: 0068.000000.

530   RU   ISSN 0044-4642
QC1   CODEN: ZTEFA3
ZHURNAL TEKHNICHESKOI FIZIKI. English translation: Soviet Physics - Technical Physics (US ISSN 0038-5662) 1931. m. 77.40 Rub. (Akademiya Nauk S.S.S.R.) Izdatel'stvo Nauka, Fizmatlit, Leninskii prospekt, 15, 117071 Moscow, V-71, Russia. TEL 234-05-84. Ed. B.P. Konstantinov. charts; illus.; index; circ. 4,000. **Indexed:** Appl.Mech.Rev., Chem.Abstr., Curr.Cont., Eng.Ind., Met.Abstr., Phys.Ber., Sci.Abstr., World Alum.Abstr.
—BLDSC shelfmark: 0066.000000.

ZHURNAL VYCHISLITEL'NOI MATEMATIKI I MATEMATICHESKOI FIZIKI. see MATHEMATICS

PHYSICS — Abstracting, Bibliographies, Statistics

ABSTRACTS OF BULGARIAN SCIENTIFIC LITERATURE. MATHEMATICAL AND PHYSICAL SCIENCES. see MATHEMATICS — Abstracting, Bibliographies, Statistics

534 016   UK   ISSN 0001-4974
CODEN: ACOABJ
ACOUSTICS ABSTRACTS. (In two parts: Part A (non-core journals); Part B (core journals) 1967. m. £188 for single section; both Parts A & B £255. Multi-Science Publishing Co. Ltd., 107 High St., Brentwood, Essex CM14 4RX, England. TEL 0277-224632. FAX 0277-224632. Ed. B. Hughes. abstr.; index. **Indexed:** Fluidex.
—BLDSC shelfmark: 0578.695000.
Formerly: Acoustics and Ultrasonics Abstracts.
Description: Treats all aspects of acoustics: solid, liquid and gaseous state acoustics; acoustic diagnostic techniques; acoustics measurements; ultrasonic applications, vibration, and shock noise.

539.7 614 016   UK   ISSN 0305-7615
RA569
APPLIED HEALTH PHYSICS ABSTRACTS AND NOTES. 1975. q. $295. Nuclear Technology Publishing, P.O. Box 7, Ashford, Kent TN25 4NW, England. TEL 233-641683. FAX 233-610021. TELEX 966119-NTP-UKG. Ed. E.P. Goldfinch. circ. 1,000. (back issues avail.)
Description: An international abstracts journal in applied health physics covering radiation dosimetry, measurement techniques, radiation effects, applications and transport of radioactive materials.

ASTRONOMY AND ASTROPHYSICS ABSTRACTS. see ASTRONOMY — Abstracting, Bibliographies, Statistics

539 016   CN   ISSN 0067-0405
ATOMIC ENERGY OF CANADA. LIST OF PUBLICATIONS. Title varies: Publications of A E C L 1952. irreg. free. Atomic Energy of Canada Ltd., Chalk River Nuclear Laboratories, Technical Information Branch, S.D.D.O., Sta. 14, Chalk River, Ont. K0J 1J0, Canada. TEL 613-584-3311.

539.7 016   AT
AUSTRALIA. NUCLEAR SCIENCE AND TECHNOLOGY ORGANISATION. LIST OF REPORT PUBLICATIONS. irreg. Australian Nuclear Science and Technology Organisation, Private Bag 1, Menai, N.S.W. 2234, Australia. illus.
Formerly: Australia. Atomic Energy Commission. List of Report Publications.

681 016   HU   ISSN 0231-0643
AUTOMATIZALASI, SZAMITASTECHNIKAI ES MERESTECHNIKAI SZAKIRODALMI TAJEKOZTATO/AUTOMATION, COMPUTING, COMPUTERS & MEASUREMENT ABSTRACTS. 1948. m. 9700 Ft. Orszagos Muszaki Informacios Kozpont es Konyvtar (O.M.I.K.K.) - National Technical Information Centre and Library, Muzeum u. 17, P.O. Box 12, 1428 Budapest, Hungary. (Subscr. to: Kultura, P.O. Box 149, 1389 Budapest, Hungary) Ed. Pal Konyves Toth. abstr.; index; circ. 420.
Supersedes: Muszaki Lapszemle. Fizika, Meres- es Muszertechnika, Automatika - Technical Abstracts. Physics, Measurement and Instrument Technology, Automation (ISSN 0027-500X)

BIBLIOGRAPHY ON HIGH PRESSURE RESEARCH. see CHEMISTRY — Abstracting, Bibliographies, Statistics

535   US   ISSN 0195-4911
CODEN: CAASDD
C A SELECTS. ATOMIC SPECTROSCOPY. s-w. $195. Chemical Abstracts Service (Subsidiary of: American Chemical Society), 2540 Olentangy River Rd., Box 3012, Columbus, OH 43210. TEL 614-447-3600. FAX 614-447-3713. TELEX 6842086.
Description: Covers atomic absorption, emission, and fluorescence in optical regions, i.e., infrared, visible, and ultraviolet; applications in spectrochemical analysis.

535   US   ISSN 0146-4450
CODEN: CSESDN
C A SELECTS. ELECTRON & AUGER SPECTROSCOPY. s-w. $195. Chemical Abstracts Service (Subsidiary of: American Chemical Society), 2540 Olentangy River Rd., Box 3012, Columbus, OH 43210. TEL 614-447-3600. FAX 614-447-3713. TELEX 6842086.
Description: Covers x-ray photoelectron, photoexcitation, and photoemission spectroscopy.

535   US   ISSN 0890-1872
CODEN: CSOCEQ
C A SELECTS. FIBER OPTICS AND OPTICAL COMMUNICATION. 1987. s-w. $195. Chemical Abstracts Service (Subsidiary of: American Chemical Society), 2540 Olentangy River Rd., Box 3012, Columbus, OH 43210. TEL 614-447-3600. FAX 614-447-3713. TELEX 6842086.
Description: Covers materials used for fiber optics and optical communications.

535   US   ISSN 0190-9428
CODEN: CSIADN
C A SELECTS. INFRARED SPECTROSCOPY (ORGANIC ASPECTS). s-w. $195. Chemical Abstracts Service (Subsidiary of: American Chemical Society), 2540 Olentangy River Rd., Box 3012, Columbus, OH 43210. TEL 614-337-3600. FAX 614-447-3713. TELEX 6842086.
Description: Covers organic, macromolecular, and biochemical aspects of infrared spectroscopy; spectroscopic characterization of substances.

535   US   ISSN 0190-9436
CODEN: CISAD3
C A SELECTS. INFRARED SPECTROSCOPY (PHYSICOCHEMICAL ASPECTS). s-w. $195. Chemical Abstracts Service (Subsidiary of: American Chemical Society), 2540 Olentangy River Rd., Box 3012, Columbus, OH 43210. TEL 614-447-3600. FAX 614-447-3713. TELEX 6842086.
Description: Covers applied and physicochemical aspects of infrared spectroscopy; infared lasers; infared spectroscopic determination of organic and inorganic substances.

C A SELECTS. MASS SPECTROMETRY. see CHEMISTRY — Abstracting, Bibliographies, Statistics

535   US   ISSN 0895-5867
CODEN: CSNMEH
C A SELECTS. NONLINEAR OPTICAL MATERIALS. 1988. s-w. $195. Chemical Abstracts Service (Subsidiary of: American Chemical Society), 2540 Olentangy River Rd., Box 3012, Columbus, OH 43210. TEL 614-447-3600. FAX 614-447-3713. TELEX 6842086.
Description: Covers materials with nonlinear optical properties; applications of these materials in optical communications, laser, waveguides, electrooptical devices, and photoelectric devices.

535   US   ISSN 0195-5063
CODEN: COPMDW
C A SELECTS. OPTICAL AND PHOTOSENSITIVE MATERIALS. s-w. $195. Chemical Abstracts Service (Subsidiary of: American Chemical Society), 2540 Olentangy River Rd., Box 3012, Columbus, OH 43210. TEL 614-447-3600. FAX 614-447-3713. TELEX 6842086.
Description: Covers light absorbing, transmitting, and reflective materials: films, coatings, glasses, fibers, mirrors, polarizers, solar collectors.

C A SELECTS. THERMAL ANALYSIS. see CHEMISTRY — Abstracting, Bibliographies, Statistics

C A SELECTS. ULTRAVIOLET & VISIBLE SPECTROSCOPY. see CHEMISTRY — Abstracting, Bibliographies, Statistics

PHYSICS — ABSTRACTING, BIBLIOGRAPHIES, STATISTICS

535 US ISSN 0162-7872
CODEN: CSXSDG
C A SELECTS. X-RAY ANALYSIS & SPECTROSCOPY. s-w. $195. Chemical Abstracts Service (Subsidiary of: American Chemical Society), 2540 Olentangy River Rd., Box 3012, Columbus, OH 43210. TEL 614-447-3600. FAX 614-447-3713. TELEX 6842086.
Description: Covers x-ray techniques in chemical analysis, e.g. electron microprobe.

539.7 016 UN
C I N D A; an index to the literature on microscopic neutron data. (Text in English; foreword in English, French, Russian, Spanish) 1965. a. price varies. International Atomic Energy Agency, Division of Publications, Wagramer Str. 5, P.O. Box 100, A-1400 Vienna, Austria. (Dist. by: Unipub, 4611-F Assembly Dr., Lanham, MD 20706-4391) (Co-sponsors U.S.A. National Nuclear Data Center; U.S.S.R. Nuclear Data Centre; N.E.A. Databank; IAEA Nuclear Data Section) circ. 1,500.

530 016 JA ISSN 0011-3336
CURRENT BIBLIOGRAPHY ON SCIENCE AND TECHNOLOGY: PURE AND APPLIED PHYSICS/KAGAKU GIJUTSU BUNKEN SOKUHO. BUTSURI, OYOBUTSURI-HEN. (Text in Japanese) 1959. s-m. $1742. Japan Information Center of Science and Technology - Nihon Kagaku Gijutsu Joho Senta, 5-2 Nagata-cho, 2-chome, Chiyoda-ku, Tokyo 100, Japan. TEL 03-3581-6411. FAX 03-3581-6446. TELEX 02223604 J. index; circ. 500.
●Also available online. Vendor(s): JICST.

CURRENT CONTENTS: PHYSICAL, CHEMICAL & EARTH SCIENCES. see CHEMISTRY — Abstracting, Bibliographies, Statistics

530 016 520 UK ISSN 0011-3786
QC5.5 CODEN: CPPHAL
CURRENT PAPERS IN PHYSICS; containing about 78,000 titles of research articles from the world's physics journals. 1966. fortn. £220 to non-members. INSPEC, I.E.E., Michael Faraday House, Six Hills Way, Stevenage, Herts. SG1 2AY, England. TEL 0438-313311. FAX 0438-742840. TELEX 825578-IEESTV-G. (U.S. addr.: 445 Hoes Lane, Piscataway, NJ 08854. TEL 908-562-5549) **Indexed:** Fluidex.

530 016 US ISSN 0098-9819
Z7143
CURRENT PHYSICS INDEX. 1975. q. $625. American Institute of Physics, 335 E. 45th St., New York, NY 10017. TEL 212-661-9404. (Subscr. to: Member and Subscriber Service, 500 Sunnyside Blvd., Woodbury, NY 11797-2999. TEL 516-576-2270) bibl.; cum.index. (back issues avail.)
●Also available online. Vendor(s): DIALOG.
—BLDSC shelfmark: 3501.282000.

539.7 016 UK ISSN 0301-7575
QD95
ELECTRON SPIN RESONANCE SPECTROSCOPY ABSTRACTS. 1973. q. £45. P R M Science & Technology Agency Ltd., 261a Finchley Rd., Hampstead, London NW3 6LU, England.

ENERGIAIPARI ES ENERGIAGAZDALKODASI TAJEKOZTATO/POWER ENGINEERING ABSTRACTS. see ENERGY — Abstracting, Bibliographies, Statistics

539.7 US
ENVIRONMENTAL AND SITING. (Subseries of: Nuclear Regulatory Commission Guides) irreg. price varies. (Nuclear Regulatory Commission) U.S. National Technical Information Service, 5825 Port Royal Rd., Springfield, VA 22161. TEL 703-487-4630.

539.7 015
EURO ABSTRACTS SECTION I. EURATOM AND EEC RESEARCH. (Text in English) 1962. m. $105. (European Atomic Energy Community) Office for Official Publications of the European Communities, L-2985 Luxembourg, Luxembourg. (Dist. in the U.S. by: Unipub, 4611 Assembly Dr., Lanham, MD 20706-4391) abstr.; pat.; index; circ. 2,200. (also avail. in microform from UMI) **Indexed:** Anal.Abstr., Br.Ceram.Abstr.
Former titles: Euro Abstracts (ISSN 0014-2352); EURATOM Information.

539.7 016 SZ ISSN 0304-2871
EUROPEAN ORGANIZATION FOR NUCLEAR RESEARCH. LISTE DES PUBLICATIONS SCIENTIFIQUES/LIST OF SCIENTIFIC PUBLICATIONS. (Former name of body: Conseil Europeen pour la Recherche Nucleaire) 1955. irreg. free. C E R N - European Laboratory for Particle Physics, CH-1211 Geneva 23, Switzerland.
Former titles: European Organization for Nuclear Research. Repertoire des Communications Scientifiques. Index of Scientific Publications (ISSN 0423-7781); European Organization for Nuclear Research. Repertoire des Publications Scientifiques. Index of Scientific Publications.

530 SZ
EUROPHYSICS CONFERENCE ABSTRACTS. a. 330 SFr. European Physical Society, Box 69, CH-1213 Petit-Lancy 2, Switzerland. **Indexed:** Phys.Ber.

FACHBUCHVERZEICHNIS MATHEMATIK - PHYSIK (YEAR). see MATHEMATICS — Abstracting, Bibliographies, Statistics

539.7 US
FUELS AND MATERIALS FACILITIES. (Subseries of: Nuclear Regulatory Commission Guides) irreg. price varies. (Nuclear Regulatory Commission) U.S. National Technical Information Service, 5825 Port Royal Rd., Springfield, VA 22161. TEL 703-487-4630.

GAS CHROMATOGRAPHY - MASS SPECTROMETRY ABSTRACTS. see CHEMISTRY — Abstracting, Bibliographies, Statistics

539.7 US
GENERAL. (Subseries of: Nuclear Regulatory Commission Guides) irreg. price varies. (Nuclear Regulatory Commission) U.S. National Technical Information Service, 5825 Port Royal Rd., Springfield, VA 22161. TEL 703-487-4630.

530 US ISSN 0749-4823
CODEN: GPAAE7
GENERAL PHYSICS ADVANCE ABSTRACTS. 1985. s-m. $240 (foreign $265). American Institute of Physics, 335 E. 45th St., New York, NY 10017. TEL 212-661-9404. FAX 516-349-6244. TELEX 960983 AMINSTYPHYS-NYK. (Subscr. to: Member and Subscriber Service, 500 Sunnyside Blvd., Woodbury, NY 11797-2999. TEL 516-576-2270) Ed. Lin Miller.

539.76 016 GW ISSN 0018-1447
HIGH ENERGY PHYSICS INDEX/HOCHENERGIEPHYSIK-INDEX. (Text in English; contents pages in English and German) 1963. fortn. DM.425 (subscr. includes Thesaurus). (Deutsches Elektonen-Synchrotron (DESY)) Fachinformationszentrum Karlsruhe, Gesellschaft fuer wissenschaftlich-technische Information mbH, 7514 Eggenstein-Leopoldshafen 2, Germany. TEL 07247-808-0. FAX 07247-808-666. TELEX 724710-FIZKA. adv.; bk.rev.; index; circ. 160.
Description: Index of articles, books, reports, conference proceedings on high energy physics.

016 621.48 UN ISSN 0534-7319
I A E A LIBRARY FILM CATALOG. 1962. irreg. free. International Atomic Energy Agency, Kaertner Ring 11, Wagramer Str. 5, P.O. Box 100, A-1400 Vienna, Austria. index; circ. 5,500.

539.7 016 UN ISSN 0004-7139
Z7144.N8 CODEN: INAXAC
I N I S ATOMINDEX.* (Text in English; summaries in English, French, Russian or Spanish) 1970. s-m. S.4400 incl. indexes. International Atomic Energy Agency, Lane End House, Sheenfield, Reading RG2 9BB, England. TEL 734-883-895. (Dist. in U.S. by: Unipub, 4611-F Assembly Dr., Lanham, MD 20706-4391) bibl.; s-a. index; circ. 1,650. **Indexed:** Anal.Abstr., Chem.Abstr., Mass Spectr.Bull.
●Also available online. Vendor(s): BELINDIS, CISTI, European Space Agency (File no.28/INIS), STN International (ENERGY).
Also available on CD-ROM. Producer(s): SilverPlatter (INIS).
—BLDSC shelfmark: 4513.900000.
Incorporates (as of June 1976): Nuclear Science Abstracts (United States Energy Research and Development Administration) (ISSN 0029-5612)

539.7 011 JA ISSN 0385-6437
J A E R I REPORTS ABSTRACTS/GENKEN KENKYU SEIKA SHOROKUSYU. (Text in English or Japanese) 1968. m. exchange basis. Japan Atomic Energy Research Institute, Department of Technical Information - Nihon Genshiryoku Kenkyujo, Tokai-mura, Naka-gun, Ibaraki 319-11, Japan. index.
—BLDSC shelfmark: 4616.640000.
Former titles: Kenkyuseika Yoshisyu (ISSN 0022-9954); Genken Biburio.

535.58 016 US ISSN 0022-0264
TK7871.3
JOURNAL OF CURRENT LASER ABSTRACTS. 1964. m. $410 (effective 1992). PennWell Publishing Co. (Westford), One Technology Park Dr., Box 989, Westford, MA 01886-0989. TEL 508-692-0700. bk.rev.; abstr.; bibl.; charts; illus.; pat.; index; circ. 300. (back issues avail.)
—BLDSC shelfmark: 4965.900000.
Description: Coverage of more than 1,000 source publications, concerning lasers and laser applications, including periodicals, conference proceedings, government reports, patents.

530 668.4 UK ISSN 0950-4753
KEY ABSTRACTS - ADVANCED MATERIALS. 1987. m. £78 to non-members. INSPEC, I.E.E., Michael Faraday House, Six Hills Way, Stevenage, Herts. SG1 2AY, England. TEL 0438-313311. FAX 0438-742840. TELEX 825578-IEESTV-G. (U.S. addr.: 445 Hoes Lane, Piscataway, NJ 08854. TEL 908-562-5549) index.
Description: Preparation, structure, properties and testing of ceramics, refractories, composite materials, polymers and glasses and porous materials.

536.7 UK ISSN 0953-1262
KEY ABSTRACTS - HIGH-TEMPERATURE SUPERCONDUCTORS. 1989. m. £52($88) INSPEC, I.E.E., Michael Farraday House, Six Hills Way, Stevenage, Herts SG1 2AY, England. TEL 0438-313311. FAX 0438-742-840. TELEX 825962 IEE G. (U.S. addr.: 445 Hoes Lane, Piscataway, NJ 08854) Ed. John Deave.

621.38 535 UK ISSN 0950-4826
KEY ABSTRACTS - OPTOELECTRONICS. 1987. m. £78($142) INSPEC, I.E.E., Michael Faraday House, Six Hills Way, Stevenage, Herts. SG1 2AY, England. TEL 0438-313311. FAX 0438-742840. TELEX 825578-IEESTV-G. (U.S. addr.: 445 Hoes Lane, Piscataway, NJ 08854. TEL 908-562-5549) index.
Description: Fibre optics, integrated optoelectronics, electro-optic devices, lasers and their applications, nonlinear optics and holography.

535.84 535.58 016 UK ISSN 0309-5320
LASER RAMAN & INFRARED SPECTROSCOPY ABSTRACTS. 1971. bi-m. £45. P R M Science & Technology Agency Ltd., 261a Finchley Rd., Hampstead, London NW3 6LU, England. Ed. J.N. Crosby. abstr.
Formed by the merger of: Laser Raman Spectroscopy Abstracts (ISSN 0047-410X) & Infrared Spectroscopy Abstracts.

539.7 US
MATERIALS AND PLANT PROTECTION. (Subseries of: Nuclear Regulatory Commission Guides) irreg. price varies. (Nuclear Regulatory Commission) U.S. National Technical Information Service, 5825 Port Royal Rd., Springfield, VA 22161. TEL 703-487-4630.

535.84 016 UK
MOESSBAUER SPECTROSCOPY ABSTRACTS. 1978. q. $92.56. P R M Science & Technology Agency Ltd., 261A Finchley Rd., Hampstead, London NW3 6LU, England.

539.7 US
N R C DOCKET MICROFICHE. m. $1650 per no. in US, Canada, Mexico; elsewhere $2200. (Nuclear Regulatory Commission) U.S. National Technical Information Service, 5825 Port Royal Rd., Springfield, VA 22161. TEL 703-487-4630. (microfiche)
Description: Concerns testing, licensing, and operation of nuclear power reactors.

PHYSICS — ABSTRACTING, BIBLIOGRAPHIES, STATISTICS

530 016   US
N T I S ALERTS: PHYSICS. w. $140 (foreign $195). U.S. National Technical Information Service, 5285 Port Royal Rd., Springfield, VA 22161. TEL 703-487-4630. FAX 703-321-8547. TELEX 64617. index. (back issues avail.)
    Former titles: Abstract Newsletter: Physics (ISSN 0163-1446); Weekly Abstract Newsletter: Physics; Weekly Government Abstracts. Physics.

NAGOYA UNIVERSITY. SOLAR-TERRESTRIAL ENVIRONMENT LABORATORY. COSMIC RAY SECTION. REPORT. see *ASTRONOMY — Abstracting, Bibliographies, Statistics*

539.7 016   UK   ISSN 0047-9446
NEUTRON ACTIVATION ANALYSIS ABSTRACTS. 1973. q. £45($78) P R M Science & Technology Agency Ltd., 261A Finchley Rd., Hampstead, London NW3 6LU, England. Ed. J. Silver. index.

543 539.7 016   UK   ISSN 0048-1033
QC762
NUCLEAR MAGNETIC RESONANCE SPECTROMETRY ABSTRACTS. 1971. bi-m. £60. P R M Science & Technology Agency Ltd., 261A Finchley Rd., Hampstead, London NW3 6LU, England. Ed.Bd.

539.7   US
NUCLEAR REACTORS AND TECHNOLOGY. m. $90 in US, Canada, Mexico; elsewhere $180. (Department of Energy) U.S. National Technical Information Service, 5825 Port Royal Rd., Springfield, VA 22161. TEL 703-487-4630.
    Description: Abstracts current global information on nuclear reactors and technology, including all aspects of power reactors, components and accessories, fuel elements, control systems, and materials.

539.7   US
NUCLEAR REGULATORY COMMISSION GUIDES. (Series of: Power Reactors, Research and Test Reactors, Fuels and Materials Facilities, Environmental and Siting, Materials and Plant Protection, Products, Transportation, Occupational Health, and General) irreg. price varies. (Nuclear Regulatory Commission) U.S. National Technical Information Service, 5825 Port Royal Rd., Springfield, VA 22161. TEL 703-487-4630.
    Description: Information on the methods of implementing specific parts of the Commission regulations. Describes techniques used by the NRC in evaluating specific problems and provides guidance to applicants who are involved with nuclear reactors.

539.7 614.85   US
OCCUPATIONAL HEALTH. (Subseries of: Nuclear Regulatory Commission Guides) irreg. price varies. (Nuclear Regulatory Commission) U.S. National Technical Information Service, 5825 Port Royal Rd., Springfield, VA 22161. TEL 703-487-4630.

535 011   FR   ISSN 1146-5360
P A S C A L E 27: METHODES DE FORMATION ET TRAITEMENT DES IMAGES. 1985. 10/yr. 685 F. (foreign 740 F.). Institut de l'Information Scientifique et Technique, INIST - CNRS, 2 allee du Parc de Brabois, 54514 Vandoeuvre-les-Nancy Cedex, France.
    Formerly: P A S C A L Explore. Part 27: Methodes de Formation et Traitement des Images; Supersedes in part (1961-1984): Bulletin Signaletique. Part 130: Physique Mathematique, Optique, Acoustique, Mecanique, Chaleur (ISSN 0397-7757)

530 016   FR   ISSN 0761-1951
P A S C A L EXPLORE. E 11: PHYSIQUE ATOMIQUE ET MOLECULAIRE. PLASMAS. 1984. 10/yr. 1270 F. Centre National de la Recherche Scientifique, Institut de l'Information Scientifique et Technique, B.P. 54, 54514 Vandoevre-Les-Nancy Cedex, France. TEL 83-50-46-00. abstr.; index, cum.index. (also avail. in microform from MIM)
    Former titles: P A S C A L Explore. Part 11: Physique Atomique et Moleculaire. Plasmas; Supersedes (1961-1984): Bulletin Signaletique. Part 165: Atomes et Molecules. Plasmas (ISSN 0398-9968); Bulletin Signaletique. Part 165: Atomes et Molecules. Physiques des Fluides et Plasmas (ISSN 0301-3359); Bulletin Signaletique. Part 165: Physique Atomique et Moleculaire. Physique des Fluides et des Plasmas; Supersedes in part: Bulletin Signaletique. Part 160: Structure de la Matiere I (ISSN 0007-537X)

530 016   FR   ISSN 0761-196X
P A S C A L EXPLORE. E 12: ETAT CONDENSE. 1984. 10/yr. 1325 F. Centre National de la Recherche Scientifique, Institut de l'Information Scientifique et Technique, B.P. 54, 54514 Vandoevre-Les-Nancy Cedex, France. TEL 83-50-46-00. abstr.; index, cum.index. (also avail. in microform from MIM)
    Formerly: P A S C A L Explore. Part 12: Etat Condense; Supersedes (1961-1984): Bulletin Signaletique. Part 160: Physique de l'Etat Condense (ISSN 0301-3332); Which supersedes in part: Bulletin Signaletique. Part 160: Structure de la Matiere I (ISSN 0007-537X)

P A S C A L EXPLORE. E 32: METROLOGIE ET APPAREILLAGE EN PHYSIQUE ET PHYSICOCHIMIE. see *METROLOGY AND STANDARDIZATION — Abstracting, Bibliographies, Statistics*

536 016   FR   ISSN 0761-1668
P A S C A L THEMA. T 230: ENERGIE. 1985. 10/yr. 1940 F. Centre National de la Recherche Scientifique, Institut de l'Information Scientifique et Technique, B.P. 54, 54514 Vandoeuvre-Les-Nancy Cedex, France. TEL 83-50-46-00. abstr.; index, cum.index. (also avail. in microform from MIM)
    ●Also available online. Vendor(s): European Space Agency, Telesystemes - Questel.
    Formerly: P A S C A L Thema. Part 230: Energie; Which superseded (1969-1984): Bulletin Signaletique. Part 730: Combustibles. Energie (ISSN 0007-5647)

530 016   US   ISSN 0048-4024
                                CODEN: PRVABI
PHYSICAL REVIEW ABSTRACTS. 1970. s-m. $290 (foreign $315). (American Physical Society) American Institute of Physics, 335 E. 45th St., New York, NY 10017. TEL 212-661-9404. Ed. M. Judd. abstr.
Refereed Serial

530 016   US   ISSN 0094-0003
Z7143
PHYSICAL REVIEW - INDEX. a. $60 to non-members. (American Physical Society) American Institute of Physics, 335 E. 45th St., New York, NY 10017. TEL 212-661-9404. Ed.Bd. (also avail. in microfiche)

530 016   UK   ISSN 0036-8091
QC1   CODEN: PYASAF
PHYSICS ABSTRACTS. Alternative title: INSPEC. Section A. Represents: Science Abstracts. Section A. 1898. bi-m. £1370 (foreign £1435). INSPEC, I.E.E., Michael Faraday House, Six Hills Way, Stevenage, Herts. SG1 2AY, England. TEL 0438-313311. FAX 0438-742840. TELEX 825578-IEESTV-G. (U.S. addr.: 445 Hoes Lane, Piscataway, NJ 08854. TEL 908-562-5549) adv.; abstr.; index, cum.index every 4 yrs. (also avail. in microform from MIM) **Indexed:** Br.Ceram.Abstr., Chem.Abstr., Mass Spectr.Bull.
    ●Also available online. Vendor(s): BRS (INSP), CEDOCAR, CISTI, Data-Star, DIALOG (File nos.2,3 & 4/INSPEC), European Space Agency (File no.8/INSPEC), JICST, Orbit Information Technologies (INSPEC), STN International (INSPEC), University of Tsukuba.
    —BLDSC shelfmark: 6477.000000.
    Description: Major guide to recently published research in all areas of physics, including particle, nuclear, atomic, molecular, fluid, plasma and solid-state physics, biophysics, geophysics, astrophysics, measurement and instrumentation.

530 016   GW   ISSN 0170-7434
QC1   CODEN: PHBRD3
PHYSICS BRIEFS - PHYSIKALISCHE BERICHTE; an abstracting journal covering all fields of physics. (Text in English) 1845. 24/yr. DM.4,700($2390) (Information Center for Energy, Physics, Mathematics, GW) V C H Verlagsgesellschaft mbH, Postfach 101161, 6940 Weinheim, Germany. TEL 06201-602-0. FAX 06201-602328. TELEX 465516-VCHWH-D. (US addr.: V C H Publishers Inc., 220 E. 23rd St., New York, NY 10010-4606. TEL 212-683-8333) (Co-sponsors: German Physical Society; American Institute of Physics) bk.rev.; abstr.; index; circ. 350. (also avail. in magnetic tape)
    ●Also available online. Vendor(s): STN International (PHYS).
    Supersedes: Physikalische Berichte (ISSN 0031-9260)
    Description: Covers physics, astronomy and related fields. Covers scientific and technical journals, reports, conference proceedings, books, patents, dissertations and other works - including literature from Eastern European countries.

539.7   US
POWER REACTORS. (Subseries of: Nuclear Regulatory Commission Guides) irreg. price varies. (Nuclear Regulatory Commission) U.S. National Technical Information Service, 5825 Port Royal Rd., Springfield, VA 22161. TEL 703-487-4630.

539.7   US
PRODUCTS. (Subseries of: Nuclear Regulatory Commission Guides) irreg. price varies. (Nuclear Regulatory Commission) U.S. National Technical Information Service, 5825 Port Royal Rd., Springfield, VA 22161. TEL 703-487-4630.

530 016   RU   ISSN 0034-2343
REFERATIVNYI ZHURNAL. FIZIKA. 1954. m. 551 Rub. (800 Rub. including index). Vsesoyuznyi Institut Nauchno-Tekhnicheskoi Informatsii (VINITI), Baltiiskaya ul., 14, Moscow A-219, Russia. (Subscr. to: Mezhdunarodnaya Kniga, Dimitrova ul. 39, 113095 Moscow, Russia) (also avail. in microfiche from BHP) **Indexed:** Chem.Abstr.
    —BLDSC shelfmark: 0149.000000.

535   RU   ISSN 0234-9647
REFERATIVNYI ZHURNAL. VOLOKONNO-OPTICHESKIE SYSTEMY. 1987. m. 48 Rub. Vsesoyuznyi Institut Nauchno-Tekhnicheskoi Informatsii (VINITI), Baltiiskaya ul. 14, Moscow A-219, Russia.

621.483 016   RU   ISSN 0034-2653
REFERATIVNYI ZHURNAL. YADERNYE REAKTORY. 1958. m. 32 Rub. (32.40 Rub. including index). Vsesoyuznyi Institut Nauchno-Tekhnicheskoi Informatsii (VINITI), Baltiiskaya ul., 14, Moscow A-219, Russia. (Subscr. to: Mezhdunarodnaya Kniga, Moscow G-200, Russia) **Indexed:** Chem.Abstr.

530 016   US   ISSN 0735-0791
TK7870
RELIABILITY PHYSICS. Represents: International Reliability Physics Symposium. Proceedings. a. (I E E E, Electron Devices Society and Reliability Society) Institute of Electrical and Electronics Engineers, Inc., 345 E. 47th St., New York, NY 10017-2394. TEL 212-705-7900. FAX 212-705-7682. (Subscr. to: Box 1331, 445 Hoes Ln., Piscataway, NJ 08855-1331) **Indexed:** Chem.Abstr.
    —BLDSC shelfmark: 7356.423000.
    Former titles: Reliability Physics Symposium. Proceedings; Reliability Physics Symposium. Presentation Abstracts; Reliability Physics Symposium Abstracts (ISSN 0080-0821)
    Description: Focuses on device reliability as the dominating influence in the development of new VLSI technologies and circuit designs.
Refereed Serial

539.7   US
RESEARCH AND TEST REACTORS. (Subseries of: Nuclear Regulatory Commission Guides) irreg. price varies. (Nuclear Regulatory Commission) U.S. National Technical Information Service, 5825 Port Royal Rd., Springfield, VA 22161. TEL 703-487-4630.

PHYSICS — ABSTRACTING, BIBLIOGRAPHIES, STATISTICS

532 540 016   US   ISSN 0035-452X
QC189   CODEN: RHABA3
RHEOLOGY ABSTRACTS. 1958. 4/yr. £200 (effective 1992). (British Society of Rheology) Pergamon Press, Inc., Journals Division, 660 White Plains Rd., Tarrytown, NY 10591-5153. TEL 914-524-9200. FAX 914-333-2444. (And: Headington Hill Hall, Oxford OX3 0BW, England. TEL 0865-794141) Ed. G.R. Browney. adv.; bk.rev.; abstr.; circ. 1,300. (also avail. in microform from MIM,UMI; back issues avail.) Indexed: Biol.Abstr., Br.Ceram.Abstr., RAPRA.
—BLDSC shelfmark: 7960.500000.
  Description: Covers all papers describing work within the science of rheology, the study of deformation and flow.
  Refereed Serial

530 540   JA
RIKAGAKU KENKYUJO KENKYU HAPPYO RONBUN MOKUROKU/INSTITUTE OF PHYSICAL AND CHEMICAL RESEARCH. LIST OF PAPERS. (Text in English and Japanese) 1982. a. Rikagaku Kenkyujo - Institute of Physical and Chemical Research, 2-1 Hirosawa, Wako-shi, Saitama-ken 351-01, Japan. TEL 0484-621111. FAX 0484-621554. abstr.

530 540   JA   ISSN 0557-0220
QC1
RIKAGAKU KENKYUJO KENKYU NENPO/I P C R. ANNUAL REPORTS OF RESEARCH ACTIVITIES. (Text in Japanese) 1964. a. Rikagaku Kenkyujo - Institute of Physical and Chemical Research, 2-1 Hirosawa, Wako-shi, Saitama-ken 351-01, Japan. TEL 0484-621111. FAX 0484-621554. abstr. Indexed: INIS Atomind.

530 540   JA   ISSN 0916-619X
RIKAGAKU KENKYUJO NYUSU/RIKEN NEWS. (Text in Japanese) 1968. m. Rikagaku Kenkyujo - Institute of Physical and Chemical Research, 2-1 Hirosawa, Wako-shi, Saitama-ken 351-01, Japan. TEL 0484-621111. FAX 0484-621554.
  Description: Contains information on current researches.

535.84 016   UK   ISSN 0036-1178
S D C BULLETIN. 1963. irreg. £5. Scientific Documentation Centre Ltd., Halbeath House, Dunfermline, Fife KY12 0TZ, Scotland. Ed. P.S. Davison. bk.rev.; bibl.; index.
  Formerly: Spectra Index and S D C Bulletin.

530 016   US
SEARCHABLE PHYSICS INFORMATION NOTICES. 1970. s-m. American Institute of Physics, 335 E. 45th St., New York, NY 10017. TEL 212-661-9404. (Subscr. to: Member and Subscriber Service, 500 Sunnyside Blvd., Woodbury, NY 11797-2999. TEL 516-576-2270) abstr.; bibl. (magnetic tape)
●Also available online. Vendor(s): DIALOG (File no.62/SPIN).

534 016   RU   ISSN 0320-3123
SIGNAL'NAYA INFORMATSIYA. AKUSTIKA. 1973. s-m. 27.80 Rub. Vsesoyuznyi Institut Nauchno-Tekhnicheskoi Informatsii (VINITI), Baltiiskaya ul. 14, Moscow A-219, Russia.

539.7 016   RU   ISSN 0203-5545
SIGNAL'NAYA INFORMATSIYA. ATOMNOE YADRO. 1970. s-m. 52.60 Rub. Vsesoyuznyi Institut Nauchno-Tekhnicheskoi Informatsii (VINITI), Baltiiskaya ul. 14, Moscow A-219, Russia. (Subscr. to: Mezhdunarodnaya Kniga, Dimitrova ul. 39, 113095 Moscow, Russia)

530 016   RU   ISSN 0135-0870
SIGNAL'NAYA INFORMATSIYA. ATOMY I MOLEKULY. 1973. s-m. 37.80 Rub. Vsesoyuznyi Institut Nauchno-Tekhnicheskoi Informatsii (VINITI), Baltiiskaya ul. 14, Moscow A-219, Russia. (Subscr. to: Mezhdunarodnaya Kniga, Dimitrova ul. 39, 113095 Moscow, Russia)

530 016   RU   ISSN 0320-3182
SIGNAL'NAYA INFORMATSIYA. CHASTITSY I POLYA. 1969. s-m. 52.50 Rub. Vsesoyuznyi Institut Nauchno-Tekhnicheskoi Informatsii (VINITI), Baltiiskaya ul. 14, Moscow A-219, Russia.

530 016   RU   ISSN 0320-3166
SIGNAL'NAYA INFORMATSIYA. ELEKTRICHESKIE SVOISTVA TVERDYKH TEL. 1972. s-m. 55.60 Rub. Vsesoyuznyi Institut Nauchno-Tekhnicheskoi Informatsii (VINITI), Baltiiskaya ul. 14, Moscow A-219, Russia.

539.7 016   RU   ISSN 0320-314X
SIGNAL'NAYA INFORMATSIYA. FIZIKA YADERNYKH REAKTOROV. 1970. s-m. 23.60 Rub. Vsesoyuznyi Institut Nauchno-Tekhnicheskoi Informatsii (VINITI), Baltiiskaya ul. 14, Moscow A-219, Russia.

536.7 016   RU   ISSN 0135-0889
SIGNAL'NAYA INFORMATSIYA. GAZY I ZHIDKOSTI. TERMODINAMIKA I STATISTICHESKAYA FIZIKA. 1973. s-m. 48.50 Rub. Vsesoyuznyi Institut Nauchno-Tekhnicheskoi Informatsii (VINITI), Baltiiskaya ul. 14, Moscow A-219, Russia. (Subscr. to: Mezhdunarodnaya Kniga, Dimitrova ul. 39, 113095 Moscow, Russia)

530 016   RU   ISSN 0136-0612
SIGNAL'NAYA INFORMATSIYA. MAGNITNYE SVOISTVA TVERDYKH TEL. 1972. s-m. 24 Rub. Vsesoyuznyi Institut Nauchno-Tekhnicheskoi Informatsii (VINITI), Baltiiskaya ul. 14, Moscow A-219, Russia. (Subscr. to: Mezhdunarodnaya Kniga, Dimitrova ul. 39, 113095 Moscow, Russia)

535 016   RU   ISSN 0203-5553
SIGNAL'NAYA INFORMATSIYA. NELINEINAYA OPTIKA I KVANTOVAYA ELEKTRONIKA. 1973. s-m. 46.20 Rub. Vsesoyuznyi Institut Nauchno-Tekhnicheskoi Informatsii (VINITI), Baltiiskaya ul. 14, Moscow A-219, Russia. (Subscr. to: Mezhdunarodnaya Kniga, Dimitrova ul. 39, 113095 Moscow, Russia)

535 016   RU   ISSN 0135-0897
SIGNAL'NAYA INFORMATSIYA. OPTIKA. 1973. s-m. 67.80 Rub. Vsesoyuznyi Institut Nauchno-Tekhnicheskoi Informatsii (VINITI), Baltiiskaya ul. 14, Moscow A-219, Russia. (Subscr. to: Mezhdunarodnaya Kniga, Dimitrova ul. 39, 113095 Moscow, Russia)

530 016   RU   ISSN 0208-0656
SIGNAL'NAYA INFORMATSIYA. POVERKHNOST'. 1982. s-m. 47.40 Rub. Vsesoyuznyi Institut Nauchno-Tekhnicheskoi Informatsii (VINITI), Baltiiskaya ul. 14, Moscow A-219, Russia.

530 016   RU   ISSN 0203-5561
SIGNAL'NAYA INFORMATSIYA. STRUKTURA I DINAMIKA RESHETKI TVERDYKH TEL. 1972. s-m. 50.40 Rub. Vsesoyuznyi Institut Nauchno-Tekhnicheskoi Informatsii (VINITI), Baltiiskaya ul. 14, Moscow A-219, Russia. Eds. B.B. Kadomstsev, A.M. Afanas'ev.

SOLID-LIQUID FLOW ABSTRACTS. see *ENGINEERING — Abstracting, Bibliographies, Statistics*

531 016   US   ISSN 0896-5900
TK7800   CODEN: SSABER
SOLID STATE AND SUPERCONDUCTIVITY ABSTRACTS. 1957. bi-m. $995 (foreign $1125). Cambridge Scientific Abstracts, 7200 Wisconsin Ave., 6th Fl., Bethesda, MD 20814. TEL 301-961-6750. FAX 301-961-6720. TELEX 910 2507547 CAMB MD. Ed. Evelyn Beck. adv.; bk.rev.; abstr.; bibl.; index, cum.index. (also avail. in magnetic tape; back issues avail.) Indexed: Cal.Tiss.Abstr., Chem.Abstr., Chemorec.Abstr., Oncol.Abstr.
●Also available online. Vendor(s): BRS (CSEN).
  Former titles: Solid State Abstracts Journal; Solid State Abstracts (ISSN 0038-108X) Incorporates: Science Research Abstracts Journal. Laser and Electro-Optic Reviews, Quantum Electronics, Unconventional Energy Sources; Science Research Abstracts Journal. Superconductivity, Magnetohydrodynamics and Plasma, Theoretical Physics (ISSN 0361-3321); Which was formerly: Science Research Abstracts, Part A. MHD and Plasma, Superconductivity and Research, and Theoretical Physics; Which incorporated: Theoretical Physics Journal (ISSN 0049-3678).
  Description: Covers theory, production and application of solid state materials, with emphasis on superconductivity.

SPACE ABSTRACTS ON MICROFICHE. see *AERONAUTICS AND SPACE FLIGHT — Abstracting, Bibliographies, Statistics*

530   NE
SURFACE SCIENCE LETTERS. Issued with: Surface Science (ISSN 0039-6028) 1980. 24/yr. North-Holland (Subsidiary of: Elsevier Science Publishers B.V.), P.O. Box 211, 1000 AE Amsterdam, Netherlands. TEL 020-5803911. FAX 020-5803598. TELEX 18582 ESPA NL. (N. America dist. addr.: Elsevier Science Publishing Co., Inc., Box 882, Madison Sq. Sta., New York, NY 10159. TEL 212-989-5800) Ed. Harry C. Gatos. (also avail. in microform from RPI; back issues avail.)
  Description: Current awareness service for scientists concerned with the physics and chemistry of surfaces; includes letters and abstracts of primary research papers.

530 016   UK   ISSN 0049-2639
QC157
SURFACE WAVE ABSTRACTS. 1971. q. £119 (foreign £128). Multi-Science Publishing Co. Ltd., 107 High St., Brentwood, Essex CM14 4RX, England. TEL 0277-224632. FAX 0277-224632. Ed. J.J. Aspinall. bk.rev.; abstr.; bibl.; index.
  Description: Covers the study of acoustic surface waves in applied physics and engineering.

539.7   US
TRANSPORTATION (SPRINGFIELD). (Subseries of: Nuclear Regulatory Commission Guides) irreg. price varies. (Nuclear Regulatory Commission) U.S. National Technical Information Service, 5825 Port Royal Rd., Springfield, VA 22161. TEL 703-487-4630.

530   NE   ISSN 0022-8141
UNIVERSITY OF LEIDEN. KAMERLINGH ONNES LABORATORY. COMMUNICATIONS. (Text in English; occasionally in French and German) 1885. a. free. Rijksuniversiteit te Leiden, Kamerlingh Onnes Laboratory, Nieuwsteeg 18, 2311 SB Leiden, Netherlands. TEL (071)275643. FAX 071-275819. TELEX 39058-ASTRO-NL. Ed. M. Durieux. charts, illus.; circ. 450. Indexed: Sci.Abstr.
  Description: Contains abstracts and references to the original journals of all papers published by physicists in the Kamerlingh Onnes Laboratory.

533.5 016   US   ISSN 0042-207X
QC166   CODEN: VACUAV
VACUUM; technology, applications & ion physics. 1951. 12/yr. £395 (effective 1992). (British Vacuum Council, UK) Pergamon Press, Inc., Journals Division, 660 White Plains Rd., Tarrytown, NY 10591-5153. TEL 914-524-9200. FAX 914-333-2444. (And: Headington Hill Hall, Oxford OX3 0BW, England. TEL 0865-794141) Ed. R.K. Fitch. adv.; bk.rev.; abstr.; illus.; index; circ. 1,500. (also avail. in microform from MIM,UMI) Indexed: A.S.& T.Ind., Anal.Abstr., Art & Archaeol.Tech.Abstr., Br.Tech.Ind., Chem.Abstr., Curr.Cont., Eng.Ind., Fluidex, ISMEC, Mass Spectr.Bull., Met.Abstr., Phys.Ber., Sci.Abstr., World Alum.Abstr.
—BLDSC shelfmark: 9139.000000.
  Description: Covers all theoretical, methodological, experimental and applied aspects of vacuum science and technology, including instrumentation and developments in related disciplines.
  Refereed Serial

553 016   UK   ISSN 0309-5312
X-RAY DIFFRACTION ABSTRACTS. 1973. q. £45. P R M Science and Technology Agency Ltd., 261A Finchley Rd., Hampstead, London NW3 6LU, England. abstr.; bibl.

535.84   CC
ZHONGGUO GUANGXUE YU YINGYONG GUANGXUE WENZHAI/CHINESE OPTICS AND APPLIED OPTICS ABSTRACTS. (Text in Chinese) bi-m. Chinese Academy of Science, Changchun Institute of Optical Precision Machinary, Changchun Guangxue Jingmi Jixie Yanjiusuo, 112, Stalin Street, Changchun, Jilin 130022, People's Republic of China. TEL 884692. Ed. Wang Jiaqi.

530   CC   ISSN 1000-8802
ZHONGGUO WULI WENZHAI/CHINESE PHYSICS ABSTRACTS. bi-m. Zhongguo Kexueyuan, Wenxian Qingbao Zhongxin - Chinese Academy of Sciences, Documentation Information Center, 27 Wangfujing Dajie, Beijing 100710, People's Republic of China. TEL 556180. Ed. Liu Zaili.

PHYSICS — Computer Applications

001.6 621.38 US ISSN 0894-1866
QC52 CODEN: CPHYE2
COMPUTERS IN PHYSICS. 1987. 6/yr. $195 (foreign $205-$215). American Institute of Physics, 335 E. 45th St., New York, NY 10017. TEL 212-661-9404. (Subscr. to: 500 Sunnyside Blvd., Woodbury, NY 11797. TEL 516-576-2270) Ed. Lewis M. Holmes. charts; illus.; stat.; tr.lit. (back issues avail.) **Indexed:** INIS Atomind., Oper.Res.Manage.Sci., Qual.Contr.Appl.Stat.
—BLDSC shelfmark: 3394.931350.
Description: News, features, and archival articles on computers in physics, teaching and research.

530 US ISSN 0021-9991
QC20 CODEN: JCTPAH
JOURNAL OF COMPUTATIONAL PHYSICS. 1966. m. $996 (foreign $1202). Academic Press, Inc., Journal Division, 1250 Sixth Ave., San Diego, CA 92101. TEL 619-230-1840. FAX 619-699-6800. TELEX 181726. Ed.Bd. adv.; abstr.; charts; illus.; index. (back issues avail.) **Indexed:** Appl.Mech.Rev., BMT, Chem.Abstr., Compumath, Curr.Cont., Excerp.Med., GeoRef., Ind.Sci.Rev., INIS Atomind., Int.Aerosp.Abstr., Math.R., Phys.Ber., Sci.Abstr., Sci.Cit.Ind., W.R.C.Inf.
—BLDSC shelfmark: 4963.500000.
Description: Covers the computational aspects of physical problems.
Refereed Serial

530 US ISSN 0172-5726
SPRINGER SERIES IN COMPUTATIONAL PHYSICS. 1977. irreg. price varies. Springer-Verlag, 175 Fifth Ave., New York, NY 10010. TEL 212-460-1500. (Also Berlin, Heidelberg, Tokyo and Vienna) Ed. H. Cabannes. (reprint service avail. from ISI) **Indexed:** Math.R.

PHYSICS — Electricity

RADIO SCIENCE. see *EARTH SCIENCES — Geophysics*

537 SZ ISSN 0924-4247
TK7881.2 CODEN: SAAPEB
SENSORS AND ACTUATORS: A PHYSICAL; an international journal devoted to research and development of physical and chemical transducers. (Text in English) 1981. 15/yr.(in 5 vols.; 3 nos./vol.). 960 SFr. (combined subscr. with Sensors and Actuators: B Chemical 2025 SFr.)(effective 1992). Elsevier Sequoia S.A., P.O. Box 564, CH-1001 Lausanne, Switzerland. TEL 021-207381. FAX 021-235444. TELEX 450620 ELSA CH. (Subscr. in U.S. and Canada to: Elsevier Science Publishing Co., Inc., Box 882, Madison Sq. Sta., New York, NY 10159. TEL 212-989-5800) Ed.Bd. (also avail. in microform from UMI) **Indexed:** ASCA, CAD CAM Abstr., Chem.Abstr., Cyb.Abstr., Energy Ind., Energy Info.Abstr., Fluidex, Int.Aerosp.Abstr., Robomat., Sci.Abstr., Telegen.
—BLDSC shelfmark: 8241.785200.
Supersedes in part (in 1990): Sensors and Actuators (ISSN 0250-6874)
Description: Covers all aspects of research and development of solid-state devices for transducing physical signals.
Refereed Serial

537 530 US ISSN 0172-5734
CODEN: SSELD8
SPRINGER SERIES IN ELECTROPHYSICS. 1977. irreg. price varies. Springer-Verlag, 175 Fifth Ave., New York, NY 10010. TEL 212-460-1500. (Also: Berlin, Heidelberg, Tokyo and Vienna) Ed.Bd. (reprint service avail. from ISI) **Indexed:** Chem.Abstr.

PHYSICS — Heat

536 US
A I A A - A S M E THERMOPHYSICS AND HEAT TRANSFER CONFERENCE. PROCEEDINGS. irreg., 4th, 1986, Boston. $40 to non-members; members $20. (American Institute of Aeronautics and Astronauts) American Society of Mechanical Engineers, 345 E. 47th St., New York, NY 10017. TEL 212-705-7703.

621.59 536.56 US ISSN 0065-2482
TP490 CODEN: ACYEAC
ADVANCES IN CRYOGENIC ENGINEERING. Represents: Cryogenic Engineering Conference Proceedings. Even-numbered vols. represent: International Cryogenic Materials Conferences. 1960. irreg., vol.36, 1990. price varies. Plenum Publishing Corp., 233 Spring St., New York, NY 10013-1578. TEL 212-620-8000. FAX 212-463-0742. TELEX 23-421139. Ed.Bd. **Indexed:** Chem.Abstr., INIS Atomind.
—BLDSC shelfmark: 0704.200000.
Refereed Serial

536.2 US ISSN 0065-2717
QC320.A1 CODEN: AHTRAR
ADVANCES IN HEAT TRANSFER. (Supplements avail.) 1964. irreg., vol.21, 1991. Academic Press, Inc., 1250 Sixth Ave., San Diego, CA 92101. TEL 619-231-0926. FAX 619-699-6715. Eds. James P. Hartnett, Thomas F. Irvine, Jr. index. (reprint service avail. from ISI) **Indexed:** Appl.Mech.Rev., Deep Sea Res.& Oceanogr.Abstr., GeoRef., INIS Atomind.
—BLDSC shelfmark: 0709.010000.
Refereed Serial

BOLLETTINO TERMOMECCANICA. see *ENGINEERING — Mechanical Engineering*

621.59 US
COLD FACTS. 1985. q. $50 (foreign $65). Cryogenic Society of America, c/o Huget Advertising, Inc., 1033 South Blvd., Ste. 13, Oak Park, IL 60302. TEL 708-383-6220. FAX 708-383-9337. Ed. Laurie Huget. adv.; bk.rev.; circ. 2,700. (back issues avail.)
Description: For those interested in all applications of low-temperatures (cryogenics).

COMITE INTERNATIONAL DES POIDS ET MESURES. COMITE CONSULTATIF DE THERMOMETRIE. RAPPORTS ET ANNEXES. see *METROLOGY AND STANDARDIZATION*

536.7 US ISSN 0935-1175
CODEN: CMETEJ
CONTINUUM MECHANICS AND THERMODYNAMICS. 4/yr. $179. Springer-Verlag, Journals, 175 Fifth Ave., New York, NY 10010. TEL 212-468-1500.
—BLDSC shelfmark: 3425.730000.
Description: Provides information on observed phenomena and presents models that are based upon principles of mechanics, thermodynamics and statistical thermodynamics.

536.56 US ISSN 1052-0139
CRYOGAS INTERNATIONAL; the source of timely and relevant information for the industrial gas and cryogenics industries. 1963. m. (10/yr.). $135 (foreign $165). J.R. Campbell & Associates, Inc., 5 Militia Dr., Lexington, MA 02173. TEL 617-862-0624. FAX 617-863-9411. Ed. Kay Deans. adv.: B&W page $500. bk.rev.; abstr.; pat.; index; circ. 430.
Formerly: Cryogenic Information Report (ISSN 0011-2259)
Description: Reports developments in technology, market development, and new products for the industrial gases and cryogenic equipment industries, including non-cryogenic gas production processes and specailty gases.

536.56 UK ISSN 0011-2275
TP480 CODEN: CRYOAX
CRYOGENICS; the international journal of low temperature engineering & research. 1960. 13/yr. £425 in UK and Europe; elsewhere £460. Butterworth - Heinemann Ltd. (Subsidiary of: Reed International PLC), Linacre House, Jordan Hill, Oxford OX2 8 DP, England. TEL 0865-310366. FAX 0865-310898. TELEX 83111 BHPOXF G. (Subscr. to: Turpin Transactions Ltd., Distribution Centre, Blackhorse Rd., Letchworth, Herts SG6 1HN, England. TEL 0462-672555) Ed.Bd. adv.; bk.rev.; abstr.; bibl.; illus.; index. (also avail. in microform from UMI; back issues avail.) **Indexed:** A.S.& T.Ind., Appl.Mech.Rev., Biol.Abstr., Br.Tech.Ind., Chem.Abstr., Chem.Eng.Abstr., Curr.Cont., Eng.Ind., Fuel & Energy Abstr., Gas Abstr., Ind.Sci.Rev., INIS Atomind., Met.Abstr., Phys.Abstr., Phys.Ber., Sci.Abstr., Sci.Cit.Ind., T.C.E.A., World Alum.Abstr.
—BLDSC shelfmark: 3490.150000.
Description: International coverage of cryoengineering, cryoplastics and low temperature engineering and research.
Refereed Serial

536.56 621.59 SZ
CRYOPHYSICS NEWSLETTER. 1967. s-a. 80 SFr. Cryophysics S.A., 39 rue Rothschild, CH-1202 Geneva, Switzerland. FAX 022-7385246. Ed. K.A. Geiger. circ. 7,000.

536.56 CC ISSN 1000-3258
CODEN: DWXUES
DIWEN WULI XUEBAO. (Text in Chinese; summaries in English) 1978. bi-m. $8 per no. (Zhongguo Kexue Jishu Daxue - University of Science and Technology of China) Science Press, Marketing and Sales Department, 16 Donghuangchenggen Beijie, Beijing 100707, People's Republic of China. TEL 4010642. FAX 4012180. TELEX 210247-SPBJ-CN. adv.; circ. 6,000. **Indexed:** Chem.Abstr., Sci.Abstr.
Formerly: Acta Physica Temperaturae Humilis Sinica: Cryophysics (ISSN 0253-3634)
Description: Publishes research papers in physics from China and the world. Topics include low-temperature physics and technology, and superconductors.
Refereed Serial

536 US ISSN 0891-6152
TJ260 CODEN: EXHTEV
EXPERIMENTAL HEAT TRANSFER; an international journal. q. $165. Hemisphere Publishing Corporation (Subsidiary of: Taylor & Francis Group), 1900 Frost Rd., Ste. 101, Bristol, PA 19007-1598. TEL 215-785-5800. FAX 215-785-5515. Eds. G.F. Hewitt, C.L. Tien. (also avail. in microform from UMI; back issues avail.; reprint service avail. from UMI) **Indexed:** Energy Info.Abstr.
—BLDSC shelfmark: 3839.350000.
Description: Research on measurement techniques; results of experimental studies in heat and mass transfer and related fluid flows.
Refereed Serial

536.56 KR ISSN 0132-6414
QC278 CODEN: FNTEDK
FIZIKA NIZKIKH TEMPERATUR/LOW TEMPERATURE PHYSICS; vsesoyznyi nauchnyi zhurnal. English translation: Soviet Journal of Low Temperature Physics (US ISSN 0360-0335) (Text in Russian; summaries in English) 1975. m. 15.60 Rub.($41.40) (Akademiya Nauk Ukrainskoi S.S.R., Otdelenie Fiziki i Astronomii) Izdatel'stvo Naukova Dumka, c/o Yu.A. Khramov, Dir., Ul. Repina, 3, Kiev 252 601, Ukraine. TEL 32-10-17. Ed. B.I. Verkin. illus. **Indexed:** Cadscan, Chem.Abstr., Curr.Cont., Ind.Sci.Rev., INIS Atomind., Lead Abstr., Phys.Ber., Sci.Abstr., Sci.Cit.Ind., Zincscan.
—BLDSC shelfmark: 0389.833000.

536.7 CC ISSN 0253-231X
QC310.15 CODEN: KCJPDF
GONGCHENG RE-WULI XUEBAO. English translation: Journal of Engineering Thermophysics (US ISSN 1043-8033) (Text in Chinese) 1980. q. $8 per no. (Chinese Society of Engineering Thermophysics - Zhongguo Gongcheng Re-Wuli Xuehui) Kexue Chubanshe, Qikan Bu, 16 Donghuangchenggen Beijie, Beijing 100707, People's Republic of China. TEL 4010642. FAX 4012180. TELEX 210247-SPBJ-CN. (US office: Science Press New York, 63-117 Alderton St., Rego Park, NY 11374. TEL 718-459-4638) adv.; circ. 6,000. **Indexed:** Chem.Abstr., Fluidex.
—BLDSC shelfmark: 4979.240000.
Description: Publishes original papers on engineering thermodynamics, aerothermodynamics of heat engines, heat and mass transfer, combustion, thermophysical properties of matter, and techniques related to thermophysical property measurement and experimentation.
Refereed Serial

536	US	ISSN 0890-4332
TJ260		CODEN: HRSCEQ

HEAT RECOVERY SYSTEMS & C H P. (Combined Heat & Power) 1980. bi-m. £200 (effective 1992). Pergamon Press, Inc., Journals Division, 660 White Plains Rd., Tarrytown, NY 10591-5153. TEL 914-524-9200. FAX 914-333-2444. (And: Headington Hill Hall, Oxford OX3 0BW, England. TEL 0865-794141) Ed. David Reay. (also avail. in microform from MIM,UMI; reprint service avail. from UMI) **Indexed:** Appl.Mech.Rev., Br.Tech.Ind., Chem.Abstr., Chem.Eng.Abstr., Energy Ind., Energy Info.Abstr., Environ.Abstr., Fluidex, Foul.Prev.Res.Dig., INIS Atomind., Met.Abstr., T.C.E.A., World Alum.Abstr.
—BLDSC shelfmark: 4276.090700.
Formerly (until 1983?): Journal of Heat Recovery Systems (ISSN 0198-7593)
Description: Reports developments and research in energy recovery from prime movers, overal system performance, and applications, including district heating, system viability, and economics.
Refereed Serial

HEAT TRANSFER - JAPANESE RESEARCH. see ENGINEERING — Mechanical Engineering

HEAT TRANSFER - SOVIET RESEARCH. see ENGINEERING — Mechanical Engineering

536.57	US	

HIGH TEMPERATURE. English translation of: Teplofizika Vysokikh Temperatur. 1963. bi-m. $1075 (foreign $1260)(effective 1992). (Russian Academy of Sciences, RU) Plenum Publishing Corp., Consultants Bureau, 233 Spring St., New York, NY 10013-1578. TEL 212-620-8468. FAX 212-463-0742. TELEX 23-421139. Ed. V.M. Batenin. (also avail. in microfilm from JSC; back issues avail.) **Indexed:** Appl.Mech.Rev., Chem.Eng.Abstr., Chem.Titles, Curr.Cont., Energy Res.Abstr., Eng.Ind., INIS Atomind., Sci.Res.Abstr., Solid St.Abstr., T.C.E.A.
Formerly: High Temperature Physics (ISSN 0018-151X)
Refereed Serial

536 620 540	UK	ISSN 0018-1544
QC276		CODEN: HTHPAK

HIGH TEMPERATURES - HIGH PRESSURES. (Text in English, French, German) 1969. bi-m. £200($330) Pion Ltd., 207 Brondesbury Park, London NW2 5JN, England. TEL 081-459-0069. FAX 081-451-6454. TELEX 94016265-PION-G. Ed. E. Fitzer, J. Lees. adv.; bk.rev.; index. **Indexed:** Chem.Abstr., Eng.Ind., INIS Atomind., Met.Abstr., Mineral.Abstr., Phys.Abstr., Phys.Ber., Sci.Abstr., World Alum.Abstr.
—BLDSC shelfmark: 4307.369500.
Description: Devoted primarily to experimental and theoretical study matter under extreme thermal and mechanical conditions.

I E E E SEMICONDUCTOR THERMAL AND TEMPERATURE MEASUREMENT SYMPOSIUM. PROCEEDINGS. see ENGINEERING — Electrical Engineering

536	UK	ISSN 0269-8986
		CODEN: IPSSE3

I O P SHORT MEETINGS SERIES. 1986. irreg., no.18, 1988. (Institute of Physics) I O P Publishing, Techno House, Redcliffe Way, Bristol BS1 6NX, England. TEL 0272 297481. FAX 0272-294318. TELEX 449149-INSTP-G. (back issues avail.) **Indexed:** Sci.Abstr.
—BLDSC shelfmark: 4565.249000.

536	II	ISSN 0379-0479
		CODEN: IJCRDD

INDIAN JOURNAL OF CRYOGENICS. 1976. q. $50. Indian Cryogenics Council, Jadavpur University, P.B. 17005, Calcutta 700 032, India. Ed. A. Bose. adv.; bk.rev.; circ. 300. **Indexed:** Chem.Abstr., Met.Abstr., Phys.Ber., Sci.Abstr., Sci.Cit.Ind., World Alum.Abstr.
Formerly: National Symposia on Cryogenics. Proceedings.
Description: Reviews, research papers, short communications on cryogenics and allied subjects.

536	US	ISSN 0019-8374
TH7201		CODEN: INHTAZ

INDUSTRIAL HEATING. 1934. m. $36. Business News Publishing Co., Box 2600, Troy, MI 48007. TEL 313-362-3700. FAX 313-362-0317. Ed. Stanley B. Lasday. adv.; bk.rev.; illus.; pat.; tr.lit.; circ. 22,516 (controlled). **Indexed:** B.C.I.R.A., Br.Ceram.Abstr., Cadscan, Chem.Abstr., Eng.Ind., Excerp.Med., Fuel & Energy Abstr., Gas Abstr., INIS Atomind., ISMEC, Lead Abstr., Met.Abstr., World Alum.Abstr., Zincscan.
—BLDSC shelfmark: 4455.000000.
Description: Covers manufacturing and production systems involved in primary metals producing, metals and ceramics, heat treating, brazing, forging, casting, cleaning and finishing, as well as analysis of thermal process control and heat containment.

536 535 600	JA	ISSN 0386-8044

INFRARED SOCIETY OF JAPAN. PROCEEDING. (Text and summaries in Japanese) a. 2000 Yen. Kyoto Institute of Technology, Department of Electronics, Matsugasaki, Sakyo-ku, Goshokaido-choh, Kyoto 606, Japan. Ed. Suteo Tsutsumi. circ. 1,000. **Indexed:** Sci.Abstr.
—BLDSC shelfmark: 6714.450000.

536.56	US	ISSN 0538-7051

INTERNATIONAL CRYOGENICS MONOGRAPH SERIES. 1964. irreg., latest 1989. price varies. Plenum Publishing Corp., 233 Spring St., New York, NY 10013-1578. TEL 212-620-8000. FAX 212-463-0742. TELEX 23-421139. Eds. K. Timmerhaus, A.F. Clark.
Refereed Serial

536 621	US	ISSN 0142-727X
TJ260		CODEN: IJHFD2

INTERNATIONAL JOURNAL OF HEAT AND FLUID FLOW. 1979. q. $280 (foreign $340). Butterworth - Heinemann Ltd. (Subsidiary of: Reed International PLC), 80 Montvale Ave., Stoneham, MA 02180. TEL 617-438-8464. FAX 617-438-1479. TELEX 880052. Ed.Bd. adv.; bk.rev.; abstr.; bibl.; charts; illus.; stat.; index. (also avail. in microform from UMI; back issues avail.) **Indexed:** Appl.Mech.Rev., Chem.Abstr., Chem.Eng.Abstr., Curr.Cont, Fluidex, Foul.Prev.Res.Dig., Int.Build.Serv.Abstr., ISMEC, Phys.Ber., T.C.E.A.
—BLDSC shelfmark: 4542.279000.
Description: Experimental aspects of engineering thermodynamics, heat transfer and fluid dynamics relevant to industrial applications. Includes energy use and conversion.
Refereed Serial

536	US	ISSN 0195-928X
QC192		CODEN: IJTHDY

INTERNATIONAL JOURNAL OF THERMOPHYSICS. 1980. bi-m. $425 (foreign $495)(effective 1992). Plenum Publishing Corp., 233 Spring St., New York, NY 10013-1578. TEL 212-620-8000. FAX 212-463-0742. TELEX 23-421139. Ed. Ared Cezairliyan. adv. (also avail. in microform from JSC; back issues avail.) **Indexed:** Br.Ceram.Abstr., Chem.Abstr., Curr.Cont., Eng.Ind., INIS Atomind., Met.Abstr., Phys.Ber., Sci.Abstr., World Alum.Abstr.
—BLDSC shelfmark: 4542.695200.
Refereed Serial

536.56	US	ISSN 0022-2291
QC278		CODEN: JLTPAC

JOURNAL OF LOW TEMPERATURE PHYSICS. 1969. 24/yr. (in 3 vols.). $895 (foreign $1045)(effective 1992). Plenum Publishing Corp., 233 Spring St., New York, NY 10013-1578. TEL 212-620-8000. FAX 212-463-0742. TELEX 23-421139. Ed. John P. Harrison. adv. (also avail. in microfilm from JSC; back issues avail.) **Indexed:** Appl.Mech.Rev., Bull.Thermodyn.& Thermochem., Cadscan, Chem.Abstr., Curr.Cont., Elec.& Electron.Abstr., Eng.Ind., Ind.Sci.Rev., INIS Atomind., Lead Abstr., Met.Abstr., Nucl.Sci.Abstr., Phys.Abstr., Phys.Ber., Sci.Abstr., Sci.Cit.Ind, World Alum.Abstr., Zincscan.
—BLDSC shelfmark: 5010.570000.
Description: Covers developments in the science of cryogenics.
Refereed Serial

536	GW	ISSN 0340-0204
QC318.I7		CODEN: JNETDY

JOURNAL OF NON-EQUILIBRIUM THERMODYNAMICS. (Text in English) 1976. 4/yr. $369. Walter de Gruyter und Co., Genthiner Str. 13, 1000 Berlin 30, Germany. TEL 030-26005-0. FAX 030-26005251. TELEX 184027. (U.S. addr.: Walter de Gruyter, Inc., 200 Saw Mill Rd., Hawthorne, NY 10532) **Indexed:** Appl.Mech.Rev., Chem.Abstr, Curr.Cont., Ind.Sci.Rev., INIS Atomind., Phys.Ber., Sci.Abstr.
—BLDSC shelfmark: 5022.837000.

536.7	CC	

▼**JOURNAL OF THERMAL SCIENCE/REKEXUE XUEBAO.** (Text in English) 1992. q. $120 to individuals; institutions $210. (Chinese Academy of Sciences, Institute of Engineering Thermophysics) Science Press, Marketing and Sales Department, 16 Donghuangchenggen Beijie, Beijing 100707, People's Republic of China. TEL 010642. FAX 4012180. TELEX 210247 SPBJ CN. (US office: Science Press New York, Ltd., 63-117 Alderton St., Rego Park, NY 11374. TEL 718-459-4638)
Description: Publishes original papers on experimental, numerical and theoretical investigations in the major areas of thermal and fluid sciences.
Refereed Serial

536.56	JA	ISSN 0439-3538
QC277.9		CODEN: TEKAAH

LOW TEMPERATURE SCIENCE. SERIES A. PHYSICAL SCIENCE. (Until vol.10, 1956, Series A and B issued in one vol.) (Text in Japanese; summaries in English) 1952. a. exchange basis. Hokkaido University, Institute of Low Temperature Science, North 19, West 8, Kita-ku, Sapporo 060, Japan. FAX 011-716-5698. TELEX 932261 ILTSHU J. circ. 600. **Indexed:** Deep Sea Res.& Oceanogr.Abstr., JTA, Sci.Abstr.
—BLDSC shelfmark: 5297.000000.
Formerly: Hokkaido University. Institute of Low Temperature Science. Series A. Physical Science (ISSN 0073-2931)

536	UK	ISSN 0954-0075

LUBRICATION SCIENCE; physics and chemistry of lubricants in tribological systems. 1988. q. £88($155) Leaf Coppin Publishing Co., P.O. Box 111, Deal, Kent CT14 6SX, England. TEL 0304-360241. TELEX 96118 ANZEEK G. Ed. Stephen Godfree. adv.; bk.rev.
—BLDSC shelfmark: 5302.080000.
Refereed Serial

PETROCHEMICAL EQUIPMENT. see ENGINEERING — Chemical Engineering

PHYSICA B - PHYSICS OF CONDENSED MATTER. see PHYSICS

536.56	NE	ISSN 0079-6417
QC277.9		CODEN: PLTPAA

PROGRESS IN LOW TEMPERATURE PHYSICS. 1955. irreg., vol.13, 1991. price varies. Elsevier Science Publishers B.V., Books Division, P.O. Box 211, 1000 AE Amsterdam, Netherlands. TEL 020-5803911. FAX 020-5803705. TELEX 18582 ESPA NL. (Subscr. in U.S. and Canada to: Elsevier Science Publishing Co., Inc., Box 882, Madison Sq. Sta., New York, NY 10159. TEL 212-989-5800) Ed. D.F. Brewer.
Description: Discusses various aspects of cryogenics.
Refereed Serial

REGIONAL JOURNAL OF ENERGY, HEAT AND MASS TRANSFER. see ENERGY

REVUE INTERNATIONALE DES HAUTES TEMPERATURES ET DES REFRACTAIRES. see CHEMISTRY — Physical Chemistry

536	LI	ISSN 0082-4089

SILUMINE FIZIKA/THERMOPHYSICS/TEPLOFIZIKA. (Text in Russian; summaries in English and Lithuanian) 1968. a. price varies. (Akademiya Nauk Litvi, Institut Fiziko-Tekhnicheskikh Problem Energetiki - Lithuanian Academy of Sciences, Institute of Physical and Technical Problems of Energetics) Leidykla Mokslas, Zvaigzdziu 23, Vilnius 2050, Lithuania. TEL 45-85-26. TELEX 261107 LMOKSU. Ed. A. Zukauskas.
Description: Articles on problems of heat transfer, refractory ceramics and heat exchangers.

PHYSICS — MECHANICS

536.56   US   ISSN 0360-0335
QC278   CODEN: SJLPDQ
SOVIET JOURNAL OF LOW TEMPERATURE PHYSICS.
English translation of: Fizika Nizkikh Temperatur (RU ISSN 0132-6414) 1975. m. $1200 (foreign $1210-$1235). American Institute of Physics, 335 E. 45th St., New York, NY 10017. TEL 212-661-9404. (Subscr. to: Member and Subscriber Service, 500 Sunnyside Blvd., Woodbury, NY 11797-2999. TEL 516-576-2270) Ed. R.T. Beyer. adv.; bibl.; charts; illus.; index. (also avail. in microform; back issues avail.) **Indexed:** C.P.I., Gen.Phys.Adv.Abstr., Phys.Ber., Sci.Abstr.
—BLDSC shelfmark: 0423.250000.

536.7   US   ISSN 0892-6808
QC192   CODEN: STBREJ
SOVIET TECHNOLOGY REVIEWS. SECTION B: THERMAL PHYSICS REVIEWS. a. $118. Harwood Academic Publishers, 270 Eighth Ave., New York, NY 10011. TEL 212-206-8900. FAX 212-645-2459. TELEX 236735 GOPUB UR. (Subscr. to: Box 786, Cooper Sta., New York, NY 10276. TEL 800-545-8398; UK subscr. to: P.O. Box 90, Reading, Berkshire RG1 8JL, England. TEL 0734-560-080) Eds. V.E. Fortov, A.E. Scheindlin. (also avail. in microform)
—BLDSC shelfmark: 8359.962000.
Refereed Serial

STUDIES OF HIGH TEMPERATURE SUPERCONDUCTORS. see *CHEMISTRY — Electrochemistry*

621.59   US   ISSN 0894-7635
SUPERCONDUCTOR WEEK; the newsletter of record in the field of superconductivity. 1987. w. $414. Atlantic Information Services, Inc., 1050 17th St., N.W., Ste. 480, Washington, DC 20036. FAX 202-331-9542. Ed. David Chaffee.
●Also available online. Vendor(s): Data-Star, DIALOG, NewsNet.
—BLDSC shelfmark: 8547.075550.
Description: Covers research, development and applications in high and low temperature superconductivity.

536   US   ISSN 0091-9322
QC271   CODEN: IMCIAN
TEMPERATURE: ITS MEASUREMENT AND CONTROL IN SCIENCE AND INDUSTRY. Variant title: American Institute of Physics. Symposium on Temperature. Proceedings. irreg. (approx. every 10 yrs.) price varies. American Institute of Physics, 335 E. 45th St., New York, NY 10017. TEL 212-661-9404. FAX 919-832-0237. TELEX 802540 ISA DURM. (Subscr. to: Member and Subscriber Service, 500 Sunnyside Blvd., Woodbury, NY 11797-2999. TEL 516-576-2270) (reprint service avail. from UMI, ISI and publisher)

536   LV
TEPLOPROVODNOST' I DIFFUZIYA. 1969. irreg. 0.54 Rub. Politeniskais Instituts, Riga, Ul. Lenina, 1, Riga, Latvia. illus.

THERMODYNAMICS AT TEXAS A & M. see *CHEMISTRY — Physical Chemistry*

536 537   US   ISSN 0194-6455
THERMOPHYSICS AND ELECTRONICS NEWSLETTER. 1972. q. free. Center for Information and Numerical Data Analysis and Synthesis, 2595 Yeager Rd., W. Lafayette, IN 47906. TEL 317-494-6300. Ed.Bd. bk.rev.; bibl.; charts; tr.lit.; circ. 11,000. **Indexed:** Br.Ceram.Abstr.
Formerly: Thermophysics Newsletter.

532 536   KR
VOPROSY GIDRODINAMIKI I TEPLOOBMENA V KRIOGENNYKH SISTEMAKH. 1970. irreg. 0.85 Rub. Akademiya Nauk Ukrainskoi S.S.R., Fiziko-Tekhnicheskii Institut Nizkikh Temperatur, Pr. Lenina 47, Kharkov, Ukraine. illus.

536.4 532   GW   ISSN 0042-9929
TJ260   CODEN: WASBBW
WAERME- UND STOFFUEBERTRAGUNG/THERMO- AND FLUID DYNAMICS. (Text in English or German) 1968. 6/yr. DM.534($285) Springer-Verlag, Heidelberger Platz 3, D-1000 Berlin 33, Germany. TEL 030-2807-1. (Also Heidelberg, Tokyo, Vienna, and New York) Ed. E.R.G. Eckert. adv.; bibl.; charts; illus. (also avail. in microform from UMI; back issues avail.; reprint service avail. from ISI) **Indexed:** Chem.Abstr., Eng.Ind., Petrol.Abstr., T.C.E.A.
—BLDSC shelfmark: 9261.837000.
Description: Experimental and theoretical research on the problems of heat and mass transfer.

PHYSICS — Mechanics

AIAA - ASME THERMOPHYSICS AND HEAT TRANSFER CONFERENCE. PROCEEDINGS. (American Institute of Aeronautics and Astronautics) (American Society of Mechanical Engineers) see *PHYSICS — Heat*

ACADEMY OF SCIENCE OF THE U S S R. LEBEDEV PHYSICS INSTITUTE. PROCEEDINGS. see *PHYSICS — Optics*

532.1   GW   ISSN 0065-1338
GB651   CODEN: AHPYAS
ACTA HYDROPHYSICA. 1953. 4/yr. (in 1 vol.). price varies. Akademie-Verlag Berlin, Leipziger Str. 3-4, 1086 Berlin, Germany. Ed.Bd. **Indexed:** Chem.Abstr., Deep Sea Res.& Oceanogr.Abstr., GeoRef., INIS Atomind., Ocean.Abstr., Pollut.Abstr.

ACTA MECHANICA. see *ENGINEERING — Mechanical Engineering*

531   CC   ISSN 0567-7718
QA801
ACTA MECHANICA SINICA. Chinese edition: Lixue Xuebao (ISSN 0459-1879) (Text in English) 1985. q. $275. (Chinese Society of Theoretical and Applied Mechanics) Science Press, Marketing and Sales Department, 16 Donghuangchenggen Beijie, Beijing 100707, People's Republic of China. TEL 4010642. FAX 4012180. TELEX 210247-SPBJ-CN. (US office: Science Press New York, Ltd., 63-117 Aderton St., Rego Park, NY 11374. TEL 718-459-4638; Co-publisher: Allerton Press, Inc., 150 Fifth Ave., New York, NY 10011. TEL 212-924-3950) adv.; circ. 6,000.
—BLDSC shelfmark: 0632.600000.
Description: Covers all branches of mechanics. Includes research treatises, experimental technology and methods, brief accounts of research work, studies on the history of mechanics, and academic discussions.
Refereed Serial

531   US   ISSN 0894-9166
TA349   CODEN: ASSIE8
ACTA MECHANICA SOLIDA SINICA. 1988. 4/yr. £120 (effective 1992). (Chinese Society for Theoretical and Applied Mechanics) Pergamon Press, Inc., Journals Division, 660 White Plains Rd., Tarrytown, NY 10591-5153. TEL 914-524-9200. FAX 914-333-2444. (And: Headington Hill Hall, Oxford OX3 0BW, England. TEL 0865-794141) (Co-publisher: Hunzhong Uinversity of Science and Technology) (also avail. in microform; back issues avail.)
—BLDSC shelfmark: 0632.610500.
Description: Presents research papers which reflect current advances in solid state mechanics in China.
Refereed Serial

530 620.1   US   ISSN 0065-2156
TA350   CODEN: AAMCAY
ADVANCES IN APPLIED MECHANICS. (Supplements avail.: Rarefied Gas Dynamics) 1948. irreg., vol.27, 1990. Academic Press, Inc., 1250 Sixth Ave., San Diego, CA 92101. TEL 619-231-0926. FAX 619-699-6715. Eds. Theodore Wie, John Hutchinson. index. (reprint service avail. from ISI) **Indexed:** Appl.Mech.Rev., Deep Sea Res.& Oceanogr.Abstr., Ind.Sci.Rev., Math.R., Sci.Cit.Ind.
—BLDSC shelfmark: 0699.000000.
Refereed Serial

531   US   ISSN 0272-0434
ADVANCES IN THE MECHANICS AND PHYSICS OF SURFACES SERIES. irreg. Harwood Academic Publishers, 270 Eighth Ave., New York, NY 10011. TEL 212-206-8900. FAX 212-645-2459. TELEX 236735 GOPUB UR. (Subscr. to: Box 786, Cooper Sta., New York, NY 10276. TEL 800-545-8398; UK subscr. to: Box 90, Reading, Berkshire RG1 8JL, England. TEL 0734-560-080) Eds. R.M. Latanision, T.E. Fischer. (also avail. in microform)
—BLDSC shelfmark: 0709.374500.
Refereed Serial

532   US   ISSN 0066-4189
QC145   CODEN: ARVFA3
ANNUAL REVIEW OF FLUID MECHANICS. 1969. a. $44 (foreign $49)(effective Jan. 1992). Annual Reviews Inc., 4139 El Camino Way, Box 10139, Palo Alto, CA 94303-0897. TEL 415-493-4400. FAX 415-855-9815. TELEX 910-290-0275. Eds. Milton Van Dyke, John L. Lumley. bibl.; charts; illus.; index, cum.index. (back issues avail.; reprint service avail. from ISI) **Indexed:** Appl.Mech.Rev., Biol.Abstr., Chem.Abstr., Curr.Adv.Ecol.Sci., Curr.Cont., Deep Sea Res.& Oceanogr.Abstr., Fluidex, GeoRef., Ind.Sci.Rev., Int.Aerosp.Abstr., M.M.R.I., Nucl.Sci.Abstr., Ocean.Abstr., Phys.Ber., Sci.Abstr., Sci.Cit.Ind., Sel.Water Res.Abstr., T.C.E.A.
—BLDSC shelfmark: 1522.540000.
Description: Original reviews on critical literature and current developments in fluid mechanics.

APPLIED MATHEMATICS AND MECHANICS; an international series of monographs. see *MATHEMATICS*

APPLIED MATHEMATICS AND MECHANICS. see *MATHEMATICS*

621 531   PL   ISSN 0373-2029
TA350   CODEN: AVMHBR
ARCHIVES OF MECHANICS. (Text in English; summaries in Polish, Russian) 1974? bi-m. $69. (Polska Akademia Nauk, Instytut Podstawowych Problemow Techniki) Panstwowe Wydawnictwo Naukowe, Miodowa 10, 00-251 Warsaw, Poland. (Dist. by: Ars Polona, Krakowskie Przedmiescie 7, 00-068 Warsaw, Poland) Ed. M. Sokolowski. bibl.; charts; illus.; circ. 790. **Indexed:** Appl.Mech.Rev., Chem.Abstr., Chem.Eng.Abstr., Curr.Cont., Excerp.Med., Geotech.Abstr., Ind.Sci.Rev., ISMEC, Math.R., Phys.Ber., Ref.Zh., Sci.Abstr., Sci.Cit.Ind., T.C.E.A.
—BLDSC shelfmark: 1637.470000.
Formerly: Archiwum Mechaniki Stosowanej (ISSN 0004-0800)

BAUPHYSIK. see *BUILDING AND CONSTRUCTION*

531   BU   ISSN 0204-7594
BIOMEKHANIKA/BIOMECHANICS. (Text in Bulgarian and Russian; summaries in English and Russian) 1974. irreg. 2 lv. per no. (Bulgarska Akademiia na Naukite, Tsentralna Laboratoriia po Biomekhanika) Publishing House of the Bulgarian Academy of Sciences, Acad. G. Bonchev St., Bldg. 6, 1113 Sofia, Bulgaria. (Dist. by: Hemus, 6, Rouski Blvd., 1000 Sofia, Bulgaria) Ed. G. Brankov. bibl.; illus.; circ. 470. **Indexed:** Biol.Abstr., BSL Math.
—BLDSC shelfmark: 0017.985000.

532   UK   ISSN 0045-3145
   CODEN: BBRHAO
BRITISH SOCIETY OF RHEOLOGY. BULLETIN. 1940. q. £20 (effective 1991). British Society of Rheology, c/o Mrs. C.A. Moules, Krus UK Ltd., 5-6 Carrington House, 37 Upper King St., Royston, Herts SG8 9AZ, England. TEL 0763-244280. FAX 0763-244298. Ed. Dr. P.F.G. Banfill. adv.; circ. controlled. (tabloid format) **Indexed:** Rheol.Abstr., Sci.Abstr.
—BLDSC shelfmark: 2426.000000.

531 510   UK
CAMBRIDGE MONOGRAPHS ON MECHANICS AND APPLIED MATHEMATICS. irreg. price varies. Cambridge University Press, Edinburgh Bldg., Shaftesbury Rd., Cambridge CB2 2RU, England. TEL 0223-312393. FAX 0223-315052. TELEX 851817256. Ed.Bd. **Indexed:** Math.R.

CESKOSLOVENSKA AKADEMIE VED. ACTA TECHNICA. see *ENGINEERING*

533   RU
CHISLENNYE METODY V DINAMIKE RAZREZHENNYKH GAZOV. 1973. irreg. 0.73 Rub. (Akademiya Nauk S.S.S.R., Laboratoriya Teorii Protsessov Perenosa) Izdatel'stvo Nauka, 90 Profsoyuznaya ul., 117864 Moscow, Russia. TEL 234-05-84. illus. **Indexed:** Chem.Abstr.

CLOSED LOOP; the magazine of testing and simulation technology. see *ENGINEERING — Engineering Mechanics And Materials*

CONTINUUM MECHANICS AND THERMODYNAMICS. see *PHYSICS — Heat*

PHYSICS — MECHANICS

531   PL   ISSN 0137-592X
CZASOPISMO TECHNICZNE. SERIES M: MECHANIKA. (Contents page in 4 languages) 1883. 4/yr. 12000 Zl. Politechnika Krakowska, Ul. Warszawska 24, 31-155 Krakow, Poland. TEL 48-12-374289. FAX 48-12-335773. TELEX 322468 PK PL. bk.rev.; charts; illus.; index; circ. 600.
    Supersedes in part: Czasopismo Techniczne (ISSN 0011-4561)

D C A M M REPORT. (Danish Center for Applied Mathematics and Mechanics) see *MATHEMATICS*

531   621   KR   ISSN 0419-1544
                                   CODEN: DNPRAE
DINAMIKA I PROCHNOST' MASHIN. 1965. irreg. Kharkivskyi Politekhnichnyi Instytut, Ul. Frunze, 21, Kharkov 310002, Ukraine.
  —BLDSC shelfmark: 0053.250000.

531   US   ISSN 0895-7886
TA416.5.U6
DIRECTORY OF TESTING LABORATORIES. a. $65 to non-members; members $52. American Society for Testing & Materials, 1916 Race St., Philadelphia, PA 19103. TEL 215-299-5400. FAX 215-977-9679.
  —BLDSC shelfmark: 3595.256200.

531   621   KR   ISSN 0419-8719
DVIGATELI VNUTRENNEGO SGORANIYA. 1965. irreg. Kharkivskyi Politekhnichnyi Instytut, Ul. Frunze, 21, Kharkov 310002, Ukraine.

531   NE
DYNAMICAL PROPERTIES OF SOLIDS. 1974. irreg. vol.6, 1990. price varies. Elsevier Science Publishers B.V., Books Division, P.O. Box 211, 1000 AE Amsterdam, Netherlands. TEL 020-5803911. FAX 020-5803705. TELEX 18582 ESPA NL. (Subscr. in U.S. and Canada to: Elsevier Science Publishing Co., Inc., Box 882, Madison Sq. Sta., New York, NY 10159. TEL 212-989-5800) (back issues avail.)
  Refereed Serial

533   SZ   ISSN 0084-5744
EIDGENOESSISCHE TECHNISCHE HOCHSCHULE ZUERICH. MITTEILUNGEN. AERODYNAMIK. (Text in English, French and German) no.9, 1949. irreg., no.32, 1963. price varies. E T H Zurich, Ramistr. 101, 8092 Zurich, Switzerland.

531   621   KR   ISSN 0424-9844
ENERGETICHESKOE MASHINOSTROENIE. 1966. irreg. Kharkivskyi Politekhnichnyi Instytut, Ul. Frunze, 21, Kharkov 310002, Ukraine.
  —BLDSC shelfmark: 0399.365000.

EUROPEAN JOURNAL OF MECHANICAL ENGINEERING. see *ENGINEERING — Mechanical Engineering*

531   FR   ISSN 0997-7538
QA801   CODEN: EJASEV
EUROPEAN JOURNAL OF MECHANICS A - SOLIDS. (Text in English) 1977. 6/yr. 1920 F. (A and B combined 3200 F.). Gauthier-Villars, 15 rue Gossin, 92543 Montrouge Cedex, France. TEL 33-1-40-92-65-00. FAX 33-1-40-92-65-97. TELEX 270 004. (Subscr. to: Centrale des Revues, 11 rue Gossin, 92543 Montrouge Cedex, France. TEL 33-1-46-56-52-66) Ed. J. Lemaitre. adv.; circ. 1,600. (also avail. in microform from MIM,UMI; reprint service avail. from UMI) **Indexed:** Appl.Mech.Rev., Curr.Cont., Excerp.Med., Ind.Sci.Rev., INIS Atomind., INSPEC, Int.Aerosp.Abstr., Math.R., Sci.Cit.Ind, Sh.& Vib.Dig.
  —BLDSC shelfmark: 3829.731300.
  Supersedes in part: Journal de Mecanique Theorique et Appliquee (ISSN 0750-7240); Which was formed by the merger of: Journal de Mecanique (ISSN 0021-7832); Journal de Mecanique Appliquee (ISSN 0399-0842)

531   FR   ISSN 0997-7546
QA901   CODEN: EJBFEV
EUROPEAN JOURNAL OF MECHANICS B - FLUIDS. 1977. 6/yr. 1820 F. (A and B combined 3200 F.). Gauthier-Villars, 15 rue Gossin, 92543 Montrouge Cedex, France. TEL 33-1-40-92-65-00. FAX 33-1-40-92-65-97. TELEX 270 004. (Subscr. to: Centrale des Revues, 11 rue Gossin, 92543 Montrouge Cedex, France. TEL 33-1-46-56-52-66) Eds. H.H. Fernholz, G. Iooss. adv.; circ. 1,600. **Indexed:** Appl.Mech.Rev., Curr.Cont., INSPEC, Math.R.
  —BLDSC shelfmark: 3829.731310.
  Supersedes in part: Journal de Mecanique Theorique et Appliquee (ISSN 0750-7240); Which was formed by the merger of: Journal de Mecanique (ISSN 0021-7832) & Journal de Mecanique Appliquee (ISSN 0399-0842)

531   RU
FIZICHESKAYA MEKHANIKA. 1974. irreg. vol.3, 1978. 1.80 Rub. per no. Leningradskii Universitet, Universitetskaya Nab. 7-9, St. Petersburg B-164, Russia. abstr.; bibl.; charts; circ. 2,000. **Indexed:** Chem.Abstr.

FIZIKO-KHIMICHESKA MEKHANIKA/PHYSICO-CHEMICAL MECHANICS. see *CHEMISTRY — Physical Chemistry*

532   620   US   ISSN 0015-4628
TA357   CODEN: FLDYAH
FLUID DYNAMICS. English translation of: Izvestiya Akademii Nauk SSSR. Mekhanika Zhidkosti i Gaza. 1966. bi-m. $1075 (foreign $1260)(effective 1992). (Russian Academy of Sciences, RU) Plenum Publishing Corp., Consultants Bureau, 233 Spring St., New York, NY 10013-1578. TEL 212-620-8468. FAX 212-463-0742. TELEX 23-421139. Ed. G.G. Chernyi. bk.rev. (also avail. in microfilm from JSC; back issues avail.) **Indexed:** Appl.Mech.Rev., Chem.Eng.Abstr., Energy Res.Abstr., Eng.Ind., INIS Atomind., ISMEC, Math.R., Phys.Ber., Sci.Abstr., T.C.E.A., Zent.Math.
  —BLDSC shelfmark: 4011.753000.
  Description: Focuses on rheology.
  Refereed Serial

532   PL   ISSN 0137-6462
QA911
FLUID DYNAMICS TRANSACTIONS. (Text in English) irreg., vol.14, 1989. price varies. (Polska Akademia Nauk, Instytut Podstawowych Problemow Techniki) Panstwowe Wydawnictwo Naukowe, Miodowa 10, 00-251 Warsaw, Poland. (Dist. by: Ars Polona, Krakowskie Przedmiescie 7, 00-068 Warsaw, Poland) Ed.Bd. circ. 250.

532   US   ISSN 0260-4353
                                  CODEN: FMAGDQ
FLUID MECHANICS OF ASTROPHYSICS AND GEOPHYSICS. 1981. irreg., vol.5, 1989. Gordon & Breach Science Publishers, 270 Eighth Ave., New York, NY 10011. TEL 212-206-8900. FAX 212-645-2459. TELEX 236735 GOPUB UR. (Subscr. to: Box 786, Cooper Sta., New York, NY 10276. TEL 800-545-8398; UK subscr. to: P.O. Box 90, Reading, Berkshire RG1 8JL, England. TEL 0734-560-080) Ed. P. Roberts.
  Refereed Serial

532   UK
FLUIDS HANDLING TECHNOLOGY. 1981. 6/yr. £18.50($62) Turret-Wheatland Ltd., 12 Greycaine Rd., Watford, Herts. WD2 4JP, England. Ed. Jaqui Rossi. illus. **Indexed:** Fluidex, W.R.C.Inf.
  Formerly: Fluids Handling (ISSN 0261-5878)

FONDATION LOUIS DE BROGLIE. ANNALES. see *PHYSICS*

531   621   KR   ISSN 0130-1152
GIDRAVLICHESKIE MASHINY. 1967. irreg. Kharkivskyi Politekhnichnyi Instytut, Ul. Frunze, 21, Kharkov 310002, Ukraine.
  —BLDSC shelfmark: 0048.320000.

531   KR   ISSN 0367-4088
                                  CODEN: GDMKBA
GIDROMEKHANIKA; respublikanskii mezhvedomstvennyi sbornik nauchnykh trudov. (Text in Russian) 1965. s-a. (Akademiya Nauk Ukrainskoi S.S.R, Institut Gidrodinamiki) Izdatel'stvo Naukova Dumka, c/o Yu.A. Khramov, Dir, Ul. Repina, 3, Kiev 252 601, Ukraine. (Subscr. to: Mezhdunarodnaya Kniga, Moscow, G-200, Russia) Ed. A.J. Oleynik. **Indexed:** Math.R., Sci.Abstr.
  —BLDSC shelfmark: 0048.750000.

531   CC   ISSN 0254-7805
GUTI LIXUE XUEBAO. (Editions in Chinese, English) q. Zhongguo Lixue Xuehui - China Mechanics Society, Huazhong Ligong Daxue, Yujiashan, Wuchang-qu, Wuhan, Hubei 430074, People's Republic of China. TEL 701154. Eds. Luo Zudao, Du Qinghua.
  —BLDSC shelfmark: 0632.610000.

531   US   ISSN 0895-7959
QC280   CODEN: HPRSEL
HIGH PRESSURE RESEARCH. 1988. 18/yr. (in 3 vols., 6 nos./vol.). $100. Gordon & Breach Science Publishers, 270 Eighth Ave., New York, NY 10011. TEL 212-206-8900. FAX 212-645-2459. TELEX 236735 GOPUB UR. (Subscr. to: Box 786, Cooper Sta., New York, NY 10276. TEL 800-545-8398; UK subscr. to: P.O. Box 90, Reading, Berkshire RG1 8JL, England. TEL 0734-560-080) Ed. Marvin Ross. (also avail. in microform)
  —BLDSC shelfmark: 4307.355650.
  Description: Dedicated solely to research in high pressure science and technology. Provides a forum for experimental and theoretical advances.
  Refereed Serial

INDUSTRIAL MATHEMATICS. see *MATHEMATICS*

INSTITUTUL POLITEHNIC "GHEORGHE ASACHI" DIN IASI. BULETINUL. SECTIA I: MECANICA MATEMATICA, FIZICA. see *MATHEMATICS*

531   620.1   US   ISSN 0020-7683
TA349   CODEN: IJSOAD
INTERNATIONAL JOURNAL OF SOLIDS AND STRUCTURES. 1965. 24/yr. £1035 (effective 1992). Pergamon Press, Inc., Journals Division, 660 White Plains Rd., Tarrytown, NY 10591-5153. TEL 914-524-9200. FAX 914-333-2444. (And: Headington Hill Hall, Oxford OX3 0BW, England. TEL 0865-794141) Ed. Charles Steele. adv.; charts; illus.; circ. 1,400. (also avail. in microform from MIM,UMI; reprint service avail. from UMI) **Indexed:** Abstr.J.Earthq.Eng., Appl.Mech.Rev., Chem.Abstr., Curr.Cont., Eng.Ind., Geotech.Abstr., Ind.Sci.Rev., Int.Aerosp.Abstr., Intl.Civil Eng.Abstr., ISMEC, J.of Ferroc., Math.R., Met.Abstr., Phys.Ber., Sci.Abstr., Sci.Cit.Ind., Sh.& Vib.Dig., Soft.Abstr.Eng., World Alum.Abstr.
  —BLDSC shelfmark: 4542.650000.
  Description: Original research on the mechanics of solids and structures as a field of applied science and engineering.
  Refereed Serial

681   621.38   535   CS   ISSN 0447-6441
TS500   CODEN: JMKOA5
JEMNA MECHANIKA A OPTIKA/FINE MECHANICS AND OPTICS. (Text in Czech; summaries in English, German and Russian) 1956. m. $58.30. Nakladatelstvi Technicke Literatury, Spalena 51, 113 02 Prague 1, Czechoslovakia. (Dist. by: Artia, Ve Smeckach 30, 111 27 Prague 1, Czechoslovakia) Ed. Jaroslav Nevrala. charts; illus.; circ. 1,650. **Indexed:** C.I.S. Abstr., Sci.Abstr.

JOURNAL OF ACOUSTIC EMISSION. see *PHYSICS — Sound*

JOURNAL OF FLUID CONTROL; applications and research on fluid control, hydraulics and pneumatics, instrumentation, and fluidics. see *ENGINEERING — Mechanical Engineering*

531   NE   ISSN 0377-0257
QA901   CODEN: JNFMDI
JOURNAL OF NON-NEWTONIAN FLUID MECHANICS. (Text in English) 1976. 15/yr. (in 5 vols.; 3 nos./vol.). fl.1880 (effective 1992). Elsevier Science Publishers B.V., P.O. Box 211, 1000 AE Amsterdam, Netherlands. TEL 020-5803911. FAX 020-5803598. TELEX 18582 ESPA NL. (Subscr. in U.S. and Canada to: Elsevier Science Publishing Co., Inc., Box 882, Madison Sq. Sta., New York, NY 10159. TEL 212-989-5800) Ed. K. Walters. adv.; bk.rev.; index. (also avail. in microform from RPI) **Indexed:** Appl.Ecol.Abstr., Appl.Mech.Rev., Chem.Abstr., Chem.Eng.Abstr., Curr.Cont., Eng.Ind., Eng.Mat.Abstr., Fluidex, Ind.Sci.Rev., Phys.Ber., Rheol.Abstr., Sci.Abstr., T.C.E.A.
  —BLDSC shelfmark: 5022.842000.
  Description: For those working on basic rheological science and applications.
  Refereed Serial

PHYSICS — MECHANICS

532   US   ISSN 0148-6055
QC189   CODEN: JORHD2
JOURNAL OF RHEOLOGY. 1957. 8/yr. $240 (foreign $287). (Society of Rheology) John Wiley & Sons, Inc., Journals, 605 Third Ave., New York, NY 10158-0012. TEL 212-692-6000. Ed. Arthur B. Metzner. adv.; circ. 1,900. (also avail. in microform from RPI; back issues avail.; reprint service avail. from RPI) **Indexed:** API Abstr., Appl.Mech.Rev., Chem.Abstr., Curr.Cont., Eng.Ind., Ind.Sci.Rev., INIS Atomind., Phys.Abstr., RAPRA, Sci.Cit.Ind.
—BLDSC shelfmark: 5052.051000.
Formerly: Society of Rheology. Transactions (ISSN 0038-0032)
Refereed Serial

531   US   ISSN 0896-1107
QC611.9   CODEN: JOUSEH
JOURNAL OF SUPERCONDUCTIVITY. 1988. bi-m. $215 (foreign $250)(effective 1992). Plenum Publishing Corp., 233 Spring St., New York, NY 10013-1578. TEL 212-620-8000. FAX 212-463-0742. TELEX 23-421139. Eds. D.U. Gubser, S.A. Wolf. adv. (also avail. in microform from JSC; back issues avail.)
Indexed: Energy Info.Abstr.
—BLDSC shelfmark: 5067.118000.
Description: Forum for the publication of original articles on all aspects of the science and technology of superconductivity.
Refereed Serial

531 620.1   US   ISSN 0022-5096
TA350   CODEN: JMPSA8
JOURNAL OF THE MECHANICS AND PHYSICS OF SOLIDS. 1952. 8/yr. £570 (effective 1992). Pergamon Press, Inc., Journals Division, 660 White Plains Rd., Tarrytown, NY 10591-5153. TEL 914-524-9200. FAX 914-333-2444. (And: Headington Hill Hall, Oxford OX3 0BW, England. TEL 0865-794141) Ed. J.R. Willis. adv.; bk.rev.; charts; illus.; index; circ. 1,500. (also avail. in microform from MIM,UMI; back issues avail.) **Indexed:** Agri.Eng.Abstr., Appl.Mech.Rev., Cadscan, Chem.Abstr., Eng.Ind., Geotech.Abstr., Ind.Sci.Rev., INIS Atomind., ISMEC, Lead Abstr., Math.R., Met.Abstr., Sci.Abstr., Sh.& Vib.Dig., World Alum.Abstr., Zincscan.
—BLDSC shelfmark: 5016.000000.
Description: Research, theory and practice on the properties of construction materials, from the fields of mathematics, engineering, metallurgy, and physics.
Refereed Serial

531   CC   ISSN 0258-1825
KONGQI DONGLIXUE XUEBAO. (Text in Chinese) q. Zhongguo Kongqi Dongli Yanjiu yu Fazhan Zhongxin, P.O. Box 211, Mianyang, Sichuan 621000, People's Republic of China. TEL 24012. Ed. Zhuang Fenggan.
Refereed Serial

531   JA   ISSN 0454-4544
KOTAI BUTSURI/SOLID STATE PHYSICS. m. 11000 Yen. Agne Gijutsu Center, Kitamura Bldg., 5-1-25 Minamiaoyama, Minatoku, Tokyo, Japan. **Indexed:** Chem.Abstr., INIS Atomind., JTA, Sci.Abstr.
—BLDSC shelfmark: 8327.410000.

LATIN AMERICAN APPLIED RESEARCH. see *CHEMISTRY*

531   US   ISSN 0883-623X
QA801
LENINGRAD UNIVERSITY MECHANICS BULLETIN. English translation of: Vestnik Leningradskogo Universiteta: Mekhanika. 1984. q. $395. Allerton Press, Inc., 150 Fifth Ave., New York, NY 10011. TEL 212-924-3950.
—BLDSC shelfmark: 0415.565000.

531   CC   ISSN 1000-0992
LIXUE JINZHAN/ADVANCES IN MECHANICS. (Text in Chinese) 1971. q. $18.92. Zhongguo Kexueyuan, Lixue Yanjiusuo - Chinese Academy of Sciences, Institute of Mechanics, 15 Zhongguancun Lu, Beijing 100080, People's Republic of China. TEL 2554108. FAX 86-1-2561284. TELEX 222554 MEHAS CN. (Dist. outside China by: Guoji Shudian - China International Book Trading Corp., P.O. Box 399, Beijing, P.R.C.. TEL 8413063) Ed. Tan Haosheng.
Refereed Serial

531   CC   ISSN 0459-1879
TA349   CODEN: LHHPAE
LIXUE XUEBAO. English edition: Acta Mechanica Sinica (ISSN 0567-7718) (Text in Chinese; summaries in English) 1957. bi-m. $10 per no. (Chinese Society of Theoretical and Applied Mechanics) Science Press, Marketing and Sales Department, 16 Donghuangchenggen Beijie, Beijing 100707, People's Republic of China. TEL 4010642. FAX 4012180. TELEX 210247-SPBJ-CN. adv.; circ. 11,000. **Indexed:** Chem.Abstr., Math.R., Sci.Abstr.
—BLDSC shelfmark: 0632.500000.
Description: Publishes original theses on mechanics and its branches, including research treatises, experimental technology and methodology, brief accounts of research work, studies on the history of mechanics, and academic discussions.
Refereed Serial

LIXUE YU SHIJIAN/MECHANICS AND PRACTICE. see *ENGINEERING — Mechanical Engineering*

MANUFACTURING REVIEW. see *TECHNOLOGY: COMPREHENSIVE WORKS*

MATHEMATISCHE FORSCHUNG/MATHEMATICAL RESEARCH. see *MATHEMATICS*

531   IT
MECCANICA OGGI. m. (11/yr.). L.77000 (foreign L.154000). Gruppo Editoriale Jackson S.p.A., Via Pola 9, 20124 Milan, Italy. TEL 39-2-6948289. FAX 39-2-6948238. Ed. Giuseppe Grassi. circ. 10,329 (controlled).
Description: Examines the whole metalworking production process.

531 510   US   ISSN 0076-5783
TA349
MECHANICS. 1970. 10/yr. $15. American Academy of Mechanics, c/o John Dundurs, Ed., Department of Civil Engineering, Northwestern University, Evanston, IL 60201. TEL 312-491-4034. adv.; bk.rev.; circ. 1,300.

MECHANICS AND MATHEMATICAL METHODS - SERIES OF HANDBOOKS. see *MATHEMATICS*

531   NE
MECHANICS: DYNAMICAL SYSTEMS. (Text in English) 1974. irreg. price varies. Kluwer Academic Publishers, P.O. Box 17, 3300 AA Dordrecht, Netherlands. (Dist. by: Kluwer Academic Publishers Group, P.O. Box 322, 3300 AH Dordrecht, Netherlands) bibl.

531   NE
MECHANICS OF ELASTIC AND INELASTIC SOLIDS. (Text in English) irreg. price varies. Kluwer Academic Publishers, Postbus 17, 3300 AA Dordrecht, Netherlands. (Dist. by: Kluwer Academic Publishers Group, P.O. Box 322, 3300 AH Dordrecht, Netherlands)

531   US   ISSN 0025-6544
QC176.A1   CODEN: MESOBN
MECHANICS OF SOLIDS. English translation of: Akademiya Nauk S.S.S.R. Izvestiya. Mekhanika Tverdogo Tela. 1965. bi-m. $740. (Russian Academy of Sciences, RU) Allerton Press, Inc., 150 Fifth Ave., New York, NY 10011. TEL 212-924-3950. Ed. A.Yu. Ishlinski. bk.rev.; abstr.; charts; illus.; index. **Indexed:** Appl.Mech.Rev., Math.R., Sci.Abstr.
—BLDSC shelfmark: 0415.850000.
Description: Provides reports on research being conducted at leading Soviet institutions for advanced studies in applied and theoretical mechanics.

MECHANIKA TEORETYCZNA I STOSOWANA. see *ENGINEERING — Engineering Mechanics And Materials*

531   KR   ISSN 0321-1975
MEKHANIKA TVERDOGO TELA; respublikanskii mezhvedomstvennyi sbornik nauchnykh trudov. (Text in Russian) 1969. a. (Akademiya Nauk Ukrainskoi S.S.R, Institut Prikladnoi Matematiki i Mekhaniki) Izdatel'stvo Naukova Dumka, c/o Yu.A. Khramov, Dir, Ul. Repina, 3, Kiev 252 601, Ukraine. (Subscr. to: Mezhdunarodnaya Kniga, Moscow, G-200, Russia) Ed. P.V. Kharlamov. **Indexed:** Math.R., Met.Abstr., Sci.Abstr., World Alum.Abstr.
—BLDSC shelfmark: 0114.530000.

533   GW   ISSN 0374-1257
TL507
MITTEILUNGEN AUS DEM MAX-PLANCK-INSTITUT FUER STROEMUNGSFORSCHUNG. 1950. irreg., no.101, 1991. price varies. Max-Planck-Institut fuer Stroemungsforschung, Bunsenstr. 10, 3400 Goettingen, Germany. FAX 0551-7092706. Ed. E.A. Mueller. bk.rev.; circ. 300. **Indexed:** Appl.Mech.Rev.
Formerly: Mitteilungen aus dem Max-Planck-Institut fuer Stroenmungsforschung und der Aerodynamischen Versuchsansalt (ISSN 0076-5678)

531   CC
MOCAXUE XUEBAO/JOUNAL OF FRICTION. (Text in Chinese) q. Y32. Science Press, Marketing and Sales Department, 16 Donghuangchenggen Beijie, Beijing 100707, People's Republic of China. TEL 4010642. FAX 4012180. TELEX 210247 SPBJ CN.

531   US   ISSN 0027-1330
CODEN: MUVMB8
MOSCOW UNIVERSITY MECHANICS BULLETIN. English translation of: Moscovskii Universitet. Vestnik. Mekhanika. 1966. bi-m. $590. (Moskovskii Universitet, RU) Allerton Press, Inc., 150 Fifth Ave., New York, NY 10011. TEL 212-924-3950. Ed. O.B. Lupanov. bk.rev.; abstr.; bibl.; charts; illus.; index.
Indexed: Appl.Mech.Rev.
—BLDSC shelfmark: 0416.239500.
Description: Presents articles on a variety of aspects of mechanics, with emphasis on the analytical and approximated analytical methods of current research being conducted.

MOSKOVSKII UNIVERSITET. VESTNIK. SERIYA 1: MATEMATIKA I MEKHANIKA. see *MATHEMATICS*

531   US
MOTION; guide to electronic motion control. 1985. bi-m. $36. (International Motion Control Association) Motion Corporation, 329 W. Fifth St., Carson City, NV 89701. TEL 702-885-1500. FAX 714-974-3969. Ed. Sandra Falk. adv.; circ. 33,000.
Description: Covers industrial and aerospace-related electronic motion control.

531   US   ISSN 1053-4644
▼**MOTION CONTROL.** 1990. 10/yr. $50 (foreign $90). Tower - Borner Publishing, 800 Roosevelt Rd., Bldg. C, Ste. 206, Glen Ellyn, IL 60137. TEL 708-858-1888. FAX 708-858-1957. Ed. Dan Miller. circ. 35,000.
Description: Covers new and developing techniques and the practical applications of new and existing technologies for motion control; includes sections on industry news and new products.

532 540   US   ISSN 0031-9104
QD541   CODEN: PCLQAC
PHYSICS AND CHEMISTRY OF LIQUIDS. 1968. 8/yr. (in 2 vols., 4 nos./vol.). $256. Gordon and Breach Science Publishers, 270 Eighth Ave., New York, NY 10011. TEL 212-206-8900. FAX 212-645-2459. TELEX 236735 GOPUB UR. (Subscr. to: Box 786, Cooper Sta., New York, NY 10276. TEL 800-545-8398; UK subscr. to: P.O. Box 90, Reading, Berkshire RG1 8JL, England. TEL 0734-560-080) Ed. Norman H. March. adv. (also avail. in microform from MIM) **Indexed:** Appl.Mech.Rev., Chem.Abstr., Curr.Cont., Phys.Ber., Sci.Abstr.
—BLDSC shelfmark: 6478.200000.
Refereed Serial

530 540   NE
PHYSICS AND CHEMISTRY OF MATERIALS WITH LOW-DIMENSIONAL STRUCTURES. (Text in English) 1976. irreg. price varies. Kluwer Academic Publishers, Spuiboulevard 50, P.O. Box 17, 3300 AA Dordrecht, Netherlands. TEL 078-334911. FAX 078-334254. TELEX 29245. (Dist. by: Kluwer Academic Publishers Group, P.O. Box 322, 3300 AH Dordrecht; U.S. address: Box 358, Accord Sta., Hingham, MA 02018-0358) Ed. E. Mooser. **Indexed:** Chem.Abstr.
Formerly: Physics and Chemistry of Materials with Layered Structures (ISSN 0378-1917)

531   PL   ISSN 0372-9486
POLITECHNIKA KRAKOWSKA. ZESZYTY NAUKOWE. MECHANIKA. (Text in Polish; summaries in English, French, German, Russian) 1956. irreg. price varies. Politechnika Krakowska, Ul. Warszawska 24, 31-155 Krakow, Poland. TEL 48-12-374289. TELEX 322468 PK PL. (Dist. by: Ars Polona-Ruch, Krakowskie Przedmiescie 7, 00-068 Warsaw, Poland) bibl.; charts; illus.; circ. 200. **Indexed:** Math.R.

531 621   PL   ISSN 0079-4538
POLITECHNIKA POZNANSKA. ZESZYTY NAUKOWE. MECHANIKA. (Text in Polish; summaries in English and Russian) 1958. irreg. price varies. Politechnika Poznanska, Pl. Curie-Sklodowskiej 5, Poznan, Poland. (Dist. by: Ars Polona, Krakowskie Przedmiescie 7, P.O. Box 1001, 00-068 Warsaw, Poland) Ed. Czeslaw Cempel. circ. 150.
    Description: Research notes and information covering all fields of design, manufacturing and exploitation of machinery in mechanical engineering.

POLITECHNIKA WROCLAWSKA. INSTYTUT MATERIALOZNAWSTWA I MECHANIKI TECHNICZNEJ. PRACE NAUKOWE. KONFERENCJE. see *ENGINEERING — Mechanical Engineering*

531   PL   ISSN 0324-9565
POLITECHNIKA WROCLAWSKA. INSTYTUT MATERIALOZNAWSTWA I MECHANIKI TECHNICZNEJ. PRACE NAUKOWE. MONOGRAFIE. (Text in Polish; summaries in English and Russian) 1969. irreg., no.20, 1990. price varies. Politechnika Wroclawska, Wybrzeze Wyspianskiego 27, 50-370 Wroclaw, Poland. FAX 22-36-64. TELEX 712559 PWRPL. (Dist. by: Ars Polona-Ruch, Krakowskie Przedmiescie 7, Warsaw, Poland)

531   PL   ISSN 0370-0917
TA401   CODEN: PNMMAE
POLITECHNIKA WROCLAWSKA. INSTYTUT MATERIALOZNAWSTWA I MECHANIKI TECHNICZNEJ. PRACE NAUKOWE. STUDIA I MATERIALY. (Text in Polish; summaries in English and Russian) 1970. irreg., no.28, 1991. price varies. Politechnika Wroclawska, Wybrzeze Wyspianskiego 27, 50-370 Wroclaw, Poland. FAX 22-36-64. TELEX 712559 PWRPL. (Dist. by: Ars Polona-Ruch, Krakowskie Przedmiescie 7, Warsaw, Poland) **Indexed:** Chem.Abstr.

621.3   PL   ISSN 0324-9395
POLITECHNIKA WROCLAWSKA. INSTYTUT TECHNIKI CIEPLNEJ I MECHANIKI PLYNOW. PRACE NAUKOWE. KONFERENCJE. (Text in Polish and English) 1974. irreg., no.7, 1988. price varies. Politechnika Wroclawska, Wybrzeze Wyspianskiego 27, 50-370 Wroclaw, Poland. FAX 22-36-64. TELEX 712559 PWRPL. (Dist. by: Ars Polona-Ruch, Krakowskie Przedmiescie 7, Warsaw, Poland) circ. 575.

621.3   PL   ISSN 0324-9387
POLITECHNIKA WROCLAWSKA. INSTYTUT TECHNIKI CIEPLNEJ I MECHANIKI PLYNOW. PRACE NAUKOWE. MONOGRAFIE. (Text in Polish; summaries in English and Russian) 1970. irreg., no.20, 1991. price varies. Politechnika Wroclawska, Wybrzeze Wyspianskiego 27, 50-370 Wroclaw, Poland. FAX 22-36-64. TELEX 712559 PWRPL. (Dist. by: Ars Polona-Ruch, Krakowskie Przedmiescie 7, Warsaw, Poland)

621.3   PL   ISSN 0324-9409
POLITECHNIKA WROCLAWSKA. INSTYTUT TECHNIKI CIEPLNEJ I MECHANIKI PLYNOW. PRACE NAUKOWE. STUDIA I MATERIALY. (Text in Polish; summaries in English and Russian) 1970. irreg., no.13, 1987. price varies. Politechnika Wroclawska, Wybrzeze Wyspianskiego 27, 50-370 Wroclaw, Poland. FAX 22-36-64. TELEX 712559 PWRPL. (Dist. by: Ars Polona-Ruch, Krakowskie Przedmiescie 7, Warsaw, Poland)

531 620.1   PL   ISSN 0079-3337
POLSKA AKADEMIA NAUK. KOMISJA MECHANIKI STOSOWANEJ. PRACE: MECHANIKA. (Text in English and Polish; summaries in English and Russian) 1966. irreg., no.12, 1986. price varies. Ossolineum, Publishing House of the Polish Academy of Sciences, Rynek 9, Wroclaw, Poland. TELEX 0712771 OSS PL. (Dist. by: Ars Polona-Ruch, Krakowskie Przedmiescie 7, Warsaw, Poland) Ed. Edward Maciag.
    —BLDSC shelfmark: 6587.500000.
    Formerly: Polska Akademia Nauk. Komisja Nauk Technicznych. Prace.
    Description: Presents selections from Master's theses from the Metallurgical and Mining Academy, and Technical University in Cracow.

671   RU
PRIKLADNAYA MEKHANIKA I PRIBOROSTROENIE. 1973. irreg. 1.07 Rub. (Leningradskii Universitet) Lenizdat, Fontanka, 59, Leningrad, Russia. illus.

PROBLEMY ISTORII MATEMATIKI I MEKHANIKI. see *MATHEMATICS*

531   CC   ISSN 1001-1641
QIDONG SHIYAN YU CELIANG KONGZHI. (Text in Chinese) q. Zhongguo Kongqi Dongli Yanjiu yu Fazhan Zhongxin, P.O. Box 211, Mianyang, Sichuan 621000, People's Republic of China. TEL 24012. Ed. Niu Songyong.
    Refereed Serial

531 621   KR   ISSN 0370-808X
       CODEN: RZITAJ
REZANIE I INSTRUMENT. 1970. irreg. Kharkivskyi Politekhnichnyi Instytut, Ul. Frunze, 21, Kharkov 310002, Ukraine.
    —BLDSC shelfmark: 0140.600500.

532   GW   ISSN 0035-4511
QC189   CODEN: RHEAAK
RHEOLOGICA ACTA. (Text and summaries in English, German) 1958. bi-m. DM.980. Dr. Dietrich Steinkopff Verlag, Saalbaustr. 12, Postfach 111442, 6100 Darmstadt 11, Germany. TEL 06151-26538. FAX 06151-20849. Ed. H. Winter. adv.; bk.rev.; charts; circ. 2,000. **Indexed:** API Abstr., Appl.Mech.Rev., Chem.Abstr., Chem.Eng.Abstr., Curr.Cont., Dairy Sci.Abstr., Food Sci.& Tech.Abstr., Geotech.Abstr., Math.R., Petrol.Abstr., RAPRA, T.C.E.A., World Surf.Coat.
    —BLDSC shelfmark: 7960.300000.

532   GW   ISSN 0939-5059
▼**RHEOLOGY (YEAR);** Fliessverhalten steuern. 1991. q. DM.122.20. Curt R. Vincentz Verlag, Schiffgraben 41-43, Postfach 6247, 3000 Hannover 1, Germany. TEL 0511-990980. Ed. E. Dewald.

532   US   ISSN 0035-4538
RHEOLOGY BULLETIN. 1937. irreg. membership. Society of Rheology, Center for Composite Materials, University of Delaware, Newark, DE 19716. TEL 302-451-2328. Ed. A.B. Metzner.
    —BLDSC shelfmark: 7960.525000.

531   GW
SEIBT OBERFLAECHENTECHNIK. (Text in English, French, German) 1988. a. DM.40. Siebt Verlag GmbH, Leopoldstr. 208, 8000 Munich 40, Germany. TEL 089-363067. FAX 089-364317. TELEX 5214853-SEIB-D. circ. 6,000.

531   SI
SERIES IN THEORETICAL & APPLIED MECHANICS. (Text in English) 1986. irreg., vol. 11, 1990. price varies. World Scientific Publishing Co. Pte. Ltd., Farrer Rd., P.O. Box 128, Singapore 9128, Singapore. TEL 3825663. FAX 3825919. TELEX RS 28561 WSPC. (UK addr.: 73 Lynton Mead, Totteridge, London N20, 8DH, England. TEL 44-81-4462461; US addr.: 1060 Main St., Ste. 1B, River Edge, NJ 07661. TEL 300-227-7562) Ed. R.K. T. Hsieh.

531   SI
SERIES ON ADVANCES IN STATISTICAL MECHANICS. (Text in English) 1985. irreg., vol. 7, 1991. price varies. World Scientific Publishing Co. Pte. Ltd., Farrer Rd., P.O. Box 128, Singapore 9128, Singapore. TEL 3825663. FAX 3826919. TELEX RS 28561 WSPC. (UK addr.: 73 Lynton Mead, Totteridge, London N20 8DH, England. TEL 44-81-4462461; US addr.: 1060 Main St., Ste. 1B, River Edge, NJ 07661. TEL 800-227-7562) Ed. M. Rasetti.

PHYSICS — MECHANICS   3845

531   CC   ISSN 0254-0053
SHANGHAI LIXUE/SHANGHAI JOURNAL OF MECHANICS. (Text in Chinese) 1980. q. $5.20. Shanghai Lixue Xuehui - Shanghai Mechanics Society, Tongji University, 1239 Siping Road, Shanghai 200092, People's Republic of China. TEL 5455080. FAX 5458965. Ed. Xu Zhixin. bk.rev.; circ. 1,000.

531   CC   ISSN 1001-4888
SHIYAN LIXUE/EXPERIMENTAL MECHANICS. (Text in Chinese) q. Zhongguo Lixue Xuehui - Chinese Mechanics Society, Zhongguo Keji Daxue, 96 Jinzhai Lu, Hefei, Anhui 230026, People's Republic of China. TEL 331134. Ed. Jia Youquan.

531   US   ISSN 0938-1287
       CODEN: SHWAEN
▼**SHOCK WAVES.** 1990. q. $206. Springer-Verlag, 175 Fifth Ave., New York, NY 10010. TEL 212-460-1500. Ed. I.I. Glass.
    —BLDSC shelfmark: 1570.445000.
    Description: Emphasizes both theoretical and experimental research on shock-wave phenomena in gases, liquids, solids, and two-phase media.

531   US   ISSN 0890-7358
TA349
SOVIET JOURNAL OF CONTEMPORARY ENGINEERING MECHANICS. English translation of: Akademiya Nauk Armyanskoi S.S.R. Izvestiya. Seriya Mekhanika (AI ISSN 0002-3051) 1986. bi-m. $460. Allerton Press, Inc., 150 Fifth Ave., New York, NY 10011. TEL 212-924-3950.
    —BLDSC shelfmark: 0422.854800.

531   NE
STUDIES IN APPLIED MECHANICS. 1979. irreg., vol.32, 1992. price varies. Elsevier Science Publishers B.V., Books Division, P.O. Box 211, 1000 AE Amsterdam, Netherlands. TEL 020-5803911. FAX 020-5803705. TELEX 18582 ESPA NL. (Subscr. in U.S. and Canada to: Elsevier Science Publishing Co., Inc., Box 882, Madison Sq. Sta., New York, NY 10159. TEL 212-989-5800) **Indexed:** Sci.Abstr.
    Refereed Serial

531   NE   ISSN 0081-8542
QC175   CODEN: SSTMBG
STUDIES IN STATISTICAL MECHANICS. 1962. irreg., vol.14, 1988. price varies. Elsevier Science Publishers B.V., Books Division, P.O. Box 211, 1000 AE Amsterdam, Netherlands. TEL 020-5803911. FAX 020-5803705. TELEX 18582 ESPA NL. (Subscr. in U.S. and Canada to: Elsevier Science Publishing Co., Inc., Box 882, Madison Sq. Sta., new York, NY 10159. TEL 212-989-5800) Eds. E.W. Montroll, J.L. Lebowitz.
    —BLDSC shelfmark: 8491.780000.
    Refereed Serial

531   NE
STUDIES IN SURFACE SCIENCE AND CATALYSIS. 1976. irreg., vol.72, 1992. price varies. Elsevier Science Publishers B.V., Books Division, P.O. Box 211, 1000 AE Amsterdam, Netherlands. TEL 020-5803911. FAX 020-5803705. TELEX 18582 ESPA NL. (Subscr. in U.S. and Canada to: Elsevier Science Publishing Co., Inc., Box 882, Madison Sq. Sta., New York, NY 10159. TEL 212-989-5800) (back issues avail.)
    Refereed Serial

532   US   ISSN 0082-0849
SYMPOSIUM ON NAVAL HYDRODYNAMICS. PROCEEDINGS. 1956. biennial. price varies. U.S. Department of the Navy, Office of Naval Research, 800 North Quincy, Arlington, VA 22217. TEL 202-545-6700.

T & A M REPORT. (Department of Theoretical and Applied Mechanics) see *ENGINEERING — Engineering Mechanics And Materials*

TECHNISCHE MECHANIK; Wissenschaftliche Zeitschrift fuer Grundlagen und Anwendungen der Festkoerper- und Stroemungsmechanik. see *ENGINEERING*

531   CU   ISSN 0138-8800
T4
TECNICA POPULAR. 1975. bi-m. $10 in N. America; S. America $13; Europe $15; elsewhere $21. Ministerio de la Industria Sidero Mecanica, 36 A No. 712th 7ma y 42, Playa, Havana, Cuba. TELEX 512160. (Dist. by: Ediciones Cubanas, Obispo No. 527, Apdo. 605, Havana, Cuba) circ. 5,000.

PHYSICS — NUCLEAR PHYSICS

531 621 KR ISSN 0321-4419
TEORIYA MEKHANIZMOV I MASHIN. 1966. irreg. Kharkivskyi Politekhnichnyi Instytut, Ul. Frunze, 21, Kharkov 310002, Ukraine.
—BLDSC shelfmark: 0178.250000.

TEST ENGINEERING & MANAGEMENT. see AERONAUTICS AND SPACE FLIGHT

531 NE ISSN 0167-8442
THEORETICAL AND APPLIED FRACTURE MECHANICS; an international journal devoted to research in the theoretical and experimental aspects of material damage. (In 2 parts: Fracture Mechanics Technology; Mechanics and Physics of Fracture) 1984. 6/yr. (in 2 vols.; 3 nos./vol.). fl.672 (effective 1992). Elsevier Science Publishers B.V., P.O. Box 211, 1000 AE Amsterdam, Netherlands. TEL 020-5803911. FAX 020-5803598. TELEX 18582 ESPA NL. (Subscr. in U.S. and Canada to: Elsevier Science Publishing Co., Inc., Box 882, Madison Sq. Sta., New York, NY 10159. TEL 212-989-5800) Ed. G.C. Sih. **Indexed:** Appl.Mech.Rev., Met.Abstr., Sci.Abstr.
—BLDSC shelfmark: 8814.551850.
Description: Part one emphasizes material characterization techniques and translation of specimen data to design. Part two publishes original research on material damage leading to crack growth or fracture in materials such as metal alloys, polymers, composites, rocks, ceramics and related substances.
Refereed Serial

532 US ISSN 0935-4964
QA911
THEORETICAL AND COMPUTATIONAL FLUID DYNAMICS. 1989. bi-m. DM.420($260.50) (effective 1992). Springer-Verlag, Journals, 175 Fifth Ave., New York, NY 10010. TEL 212-460-1500. Ed. M.Y. Hussaini.
—BLDSC shelfmark: 8814.552280.
Description: Presents original research in theoretical and computational fluid dynamics aimed at elucidating flow physics.

VOPROSY GIDRODINAMIKI I TEPLOOBMENA V KRIOGENNYKH SISTEMAKH. see PHYSICS — Heat

WAERME- UND STOFFUEBERTRAGUNG/THERMO- AND FLUID DYNAMICS. see PHYSICS — Heat

531 621 CC ISSN 1000-6915
YANSHI LIXUE YU GONGCHENG XUEBAO/JOURNAL OF ROCK MECHANICS AND ENGINEERING. (Text in Chinese) q. Zhongguo Yanshi Lixue yu Gongcheng Xuehui, No. A-11, Datun Lu, Dewai, Beijing 100101, People's Republic of China. Ed. Chen Yuji.
Refereed Serial

531 CC ISSN 1000-7598
YANTU LIXUE/ROCK AND SOIL MECHANICS. (Text in Chinese) q. Zhongguo Kexueyuan, Wuhan Yantu Lixue Yanjiusuo - Chinese Academy of Sciences, Wuhan Institute of Rock and Soil Mechanics, Xiaohongshan, Wuhan, Hubei 430071, People's Republic of China. TEL 813712. (Dist. outside China by: Guoji Shudian - China International Book Trading Corp., P.O. Box 399, Beijing, P.R.C.) Ed. Yuan Jianxin.
—BLDSC shelfmark: 8001.443000.
Refereed Serial

YINGYONG SHUXUE YU LIXUE/APPLIED MATHEMATICS AND MECHANICS. see MATHEMATICS

531 CC ISSN 1000-3835
ZHENDONG YU CHONGJI/VIBRATION AND SHOCK. (Text in Chinese) q. Zhongguo Zhendong Gongcheng Xuehui - Chinese Vibration Engineering Society, 121 Nanjiang Lu, Shanghai 200011, People's Republic of China. TEL 3774325. Ed. Huang Wenhu.

ZHURNAL PRIKLADNOI MEKHANIKI I TEKHNICHESKOI FIZIKI. see ENGINEERING — Mechanical Engineering

PHYSICS — Nuclear Physics

539.7 US ISSN 0272-5088
ACCELERATORS AND STORAGE RINGS SERIES. irreg. Harwood Academic Publishers, 270 Eighth Ave., New York, NY 10011. TEL 212-206-8900. FAX 212-645-2459. TELEX 236735 GOPUB UR. (Subscr. to: Box 786, Cooper Sta., New York, NY 10276. TEL 800-545-8398; UK subscr. to: Box 90, Reading, Berkshire RG1 8JL, England. TEL 0734-560-080) Eds. J.P. Blewett, F.T. Cole. (also avail. in microform)
Refereed Serial

539.7 FI ISSN 0355-2721
QC1 CODEN: APSSDG
ACTA POLYTECHNICA SCANDINAVICA. APPLIED PHYSICS SERIES. (Text and summaries in English) irreg. (4-5/yr.). FIM 300. Teknillisten Tieteiden Akatemia - Finnish Academy of Technology, Kansakoulukatu 10 A, SF-00100 Helsinki 10, Finland. Ed. Mauri Luukkala. index, cum.index: 1958-1988; circ. 250. (also avail. in microfilm from UMI; back issues avail.; reprint service avail. from UMI) **Indexed:** ASCA, Cadscan, Chem.Abstr., Curr.Cont., INIS Atomind., Intl.Civil Eng.Abstr., Lead Abstr., Met.Abstr., Sci.Abstr., Soft.Abstr.Eng., World Alum.Abstr., Zincscan.
—BLDSC shelfmark: 0661.252000.
Formerly: Acta Polytechnica Scandinavica. Physics Including Nucleonics Series (ISSN 0001-6888)
Description: Presents research results in physical engineering and technical physics.

539 US
QC173 CODEN: AAMOA2
ADVANCES IN ATOMIC, MOLECULAR AND OPTICAL PHYSICS. 1965. irreg. vol.28, 1991. Academic Press, Inc., 1250 Sixth Ave., San Diego, CA 92101. TEL 619-231-0926. FAX 619-699-6715. Eds. D.R. Bates, Immanueal Estermann. index. (reprint service avail. from ISI) **Indexed:** Chem.Abstr., Ind.Sci.Rev., INIS Atomind., Mass Spectr.Bull., Phys.Ber., Sci.Cit.Ind.
Formerly: Advances in Atomic and Molecular Physics (ISSN 0065-2199)

539 US ISSN 0065-2970
QC173 CODEN: ANUPBZ
ADVANCES IN NUCLEAR PHYSICS. 1968. irreg. vol.20, 1991. price varies. Plenum Publishing Corp., 233 Spring St., New York, NY 10013-1578. TEL 212-620-8000. FAX 212-463-0742. TELEX 23-421139. Eds. J.W. Negele, E. Vogt. **Indexed:** ASCA, Ind.Sci.Rev., INIS Atomind., Phys.Ber., Sci.Cit.Ind.
—BLDSC shelfmark: 0709.490000.
Refereed Serial

539.7 621.48 US ISSN 0065-2989
TK9001 CODEN: ANUTAC
ADVANCES IN NUCLEAR SCIENCE AND TECHNOLOGY. 1962. irreg. vol.22, 1991. Plenum Publishing Corp., 233 Spring St., New York, NY 10013-1578. TEL 212-620-8047. Eds. E.J. Henley, H. Kouts. index. **Indexed:** Chem.Abstr., INIS Atomind.
—BLDSC shelfmark: 0709.500000.
Refereed Serial

539 US ISSN 0163-8998
QC770 CODEN: ARPSDF
ANNUAL REVIEW OF NUCLEAR AND PARTICLE SCIENCE. 1952. a. $59 (foreign $64)(effective Jan. 1992). Annual Reviews Inc., 4139 El Camino Way, Box 10139, Palo Alto, CA 94303-0897. TEL 415-493-4400. FAX 415-855-9815. TELEX 910-290-0275. Ed. J.D. Jackson. bibl.; index, cum.index. (back issues avail.; reprint service avail. from ISI) **Indexed:** Biol.Abstr., Cadscan, Chem.Abstr., Curr.Cont., Energy Info.Abstr., GeoRef., Ind.Sci.Rev., INIS Atomind., Lead Abstr., M.M.R.I., Nucl.Sci.Abstr., Phys.Ber., Sci.Abstr., Sci.Cit.Ind., Zincscan.
—BLDSC shelfmark: 1523.900000.
Formerly (until 1978): Annual Review of Nuclear Science (ISSN 0066-4243)
Description: Original reviews of critical literature and current developments in nuclear and particle science.

539.7 US ISSN 0893-4908
ARCHIVES OF SOVIET SCIENCE SERIES: PHYSICAL SCIENCES SECTION. irreg. Harwood Academic Publishers, 270 Eighth Ave., New York, NY 10011. TEL 212-206-8900. FAX 212-645-2459. TELEX 236735 GOPUB UR. (Subscr. to: Box 786, Cooper Sta., New York, NY 10276. TEL 800-545-8398; UK subscr. to: Box 90, Reading, Berkshire RG1 8JL, England. TEL 0734-560-080) Eds. G.B. Abdullaev, T.D. Dzhafarov. (also avail. in microform)
Refereed Serial

539.7 JA
ATOMIC COLLISION RESEARCH IN JAPAN. PROGRESS REPORT. (Text and summaries in English) 1971. a. 3000 Yen($20) Society for Atomic Collision Research, Executive Office, Department of Physics, Sophia University, 7-1 Kioicho, Chiyoda-ku, Tokyo 102, Japan. FAX 81-3-3238-3341. Ed. Y. Awaya. circ. 500. (back issues avail.)

539 US ISSN 0092-640X
QC173 CODEN: ADNDAT
ATOMIC DATA AND NUCLEAR DATA TABLES; a journal devoted to compilations of experimental and theoretical results in atomic physics. 1969. bi-m. $321 (foreign $381). Academic Press, Inc., Journal Division, 1250 Sixth Ave., San Diego, CA 92101. TEL 619-230-1840. FAX 619-699-6800. TELEX 181726. Ed. Angela Li-Scholz. abstr.; bibl.; charts; illus.; stat.; index; circ. controlled. (back issues avail.) **Indexed:** Chem.Abstr., Excerpt.Med., Ind.Sci.Rev., INIS Atomind., Phys.Ber., Sci.Abstr. Sci.Cit.Ind.
—BLDSC shelfmark: 1769.375000.
Formed by the merger of: Atomic Data (ISSN 0004-7082) & Nuclear Data Tables (ISSN 0090-0214); Which supersedes in part: Nuclear Data (ISSN 0029-5477)
Description: Presents compilations of experimental and theoretical information in atomic physics, nuclear physics, and closely related fields.
Refereed Serial

539.7 NE
ATOMIC ENERGY LEVELS AND GROTRIAN DIAGRAMS. 1976. irreg. vol.4, 1982. price varies. Elsevier Science Publishers B.V., Books Division, P.O. Box 211, 1000 AE Amsterdam, Netherlands. TEL 020-5803911. FAX 020-5803705. TELEX 18582 ESPA NL. (Subscr. in U.S. and Canada to: Elsevier Science Publishing Co., Inc., Box 882, Madison Sq. Sta., New York, NY 10159. TEL 212-989-5800) Eds. S. Bashkin, J.O. Stoner.
Refereed Serial

539 II
BHABHA ATOMIC RESEARCH CENTRE. NUCLEAR PHYSICS DIVISION. ANNUAL REPORT. 1971. a. $5. Bhabha Atomic Research Centre, Trombay, Bombay 400085, India. circ. controlled. **Indexed:** Chem.Abstr., Nucl.Sci.Abstr.

539.7 SZ ISSN 0304-288X
QC770 CODEN: CECOA2
C E R N COURIER. French edition: Courrier C E R N (ISSN 0374-2288) (Former name of issuing body: Conseil Europeen pour la Recherche Nucleaire) (Text in English) 1959. m. (10/yr.). free. C E R N - European Laboratory for Particle Physics, CH-1211 Geneva 23, Switzerland. Ed. Gordon Fraser. adv.; bibl.; charts; illus.; circ. 25,000. **Indexed:** INIS Atomind., Phys.Abstr., Sci.Abstr.

539.7 SZ ISSN 0366-5690
C E R N - H E R A REPORTS. (Former name of issuing body: Conseil Europeen pour la Recherche Nucleaire) 1969. irreg. free. C E R N - European Laboratory for Particle Physics, CH-1211 Geneva 23, Switzerland. (also avail. in microfiche) **Indexed:** INIS Atomind, Phys.Abstr.

539.7 SZ ISSN 0007-8328
CODEN: CERNA6
C E R N REPORTS. (Former name of issuing body: Conseil Europeen pour la Recherche Nucleaire) 1955. irreg. free. C E R N - European Laboratory for Particle Physics, CH-1211 Geneva 23, Switzerland. **Indexed:** Chem.Abstr., INIS Atomind, Phys.Abstr.
—BLDSC shelfmark: 3120.110000.

539.7 SZ ISSN 0531-4283
C E R N SCHOOL OF PHYSICS. PROCEEDINGS. (Former name of issuing body: Conseil Europeen pour la Recherche Nucleaire) 1962. a. free. C E R N - European Laboratory for Particle Physics, CH-1211 Geneva 23, Switzerland. circ. 3,500. **Indexed:** INIS Atomind., Phys.Abstr.

PHYSICS — NUCLEAR PHYSICS

539.7 **CC** **ISSN 1001-6031**
CHINESE JOURNAL OF NUCLEAR PHYSICS. Chinese Edition: Yuanzihe Wuli (ISSN 0253-3790) (Text in English) q. $168. (China Institute of Atomic Energy) China Ocean Press, International Cooperation Department, Haimao Dalou, 1 Fuxingmenwai Dajie, Beijing 100860, People's Republic of China. TEL 868941. FAX 862209. TELEX 22536 NBO CN. (Co-sponsor: Chinese Nuclear Physics Society) Ed.Bd.
—BLDSC shelfmark: 3180.438200.
Description: Devoted to experimental and theoretical nuclear physics, including nuclear structure and spectroscopy, nuclear reactions of light and heavy ions, nuclear fission and fusion, and nuclear interactions. Reports developments in China and abroad.
Refereed Serial

539 **US** **ISSN 0010-2687**
QC770 **CODEN: CAMPBS**
COMMENTS ON ATOMIC AND MOLECULAR PHYSICS.
1969. 12/yr. (6/vol., 2 vol./yr.). $144. Gordon and Breach Science Publishers, 270 Eighth Ave., New York, NY 10011. TEL 212-206-8900. FAX 212-645-2459. TELEX 236735 GOPUB UR. (Subscr. to: Box 786, Cooper Sta., New York, NY 10011. TEL 800-545-8398; UK subscr. to: P.O. Box 90, Reading, Berkshire RG1 8JL, England. TEL 0734-560-080) Ed. H. Henry Stroke. adv. (also avail. in microform from MIM) **Indexed:** Chem.Abstr., Curr.Cont., INIS Atomind., Mass Spectr.Bull., Phys.Ber., Sci.Abstr.
—BLDSC shelfmark: 3336.027000.

539 **US** **ISSN 0010-2709**
  CODEN: CNPPAV
COMMENTS ON NUCLEAR AND PARTICLE PHYSICS.
1967. 12/yr. (in 2 vols., 6 nos./vol.). $131. Gordon and Breach Science Publishers, 270 Eighth Ave., New York, NY 10011. TEL 212-206-8900. FAX 212-645-2459. TELEX 236735 GO PUB UR. (Subscr. to: Box 786, Cooper Sta., New York, NY 10276. TEL 800-545-8398; UK subscr. to: P.O. Box 90, Reading, Berkshire RG1 8JL, England. TEL 0734-560-080) Ed. William Marciano. adv. (also avail. in microform from MIM) **Indexed:** Chem.Abstr., INIS Atomind., Phys.Ber., Sci.Abstr.
—BLDSC shelfmark: 3336.030000.

539.7 530.44 **US** **ISSN 0374-2806**
QC717.6 **CODEN: CPCFBJ**
COMMENTS ON PLASMA PHYSICS AND CONTROLLED FUSION. 6/yr. (in 1 vol.). $144. Gordon and Breach Science Publishers, 270 Eighth Ave., New York, NY 10011. TEL 212-206-8900. FAX 212-645-2459. TELEX 236735 GOPUB UR. (Subscr. to: Box 786, Cooper Sta., New York, NY 10276. TEL 800-545-8398; UK subscr. to: P.O. Box 90, Reading, Berkshire RG1 8JL, England. TEL 0734-560-080) Ed. Burton D. Fried. adv. (also avail. in microform from MIM) **Indexed:** Chem.Abstr., INIS Atomind., Phys.Ber., Sci.Abstr.
—BLDSC shelfmark: 3336.035000.

539.7 **US** **ISSN 0379-4229**
TK9001 **CODEN: EARRDF**
EUROPEAN APPLIED RESEARCH REPORTS: NUCLEAR SCIENCE AND TECHNOLOGY SECTION. 1979. 16/yr. $564. Harwood Academic Publishers, 270 Eighth Ave., New York, NY 10011. TEL 212-206-8900. FAX 212-645-2459. TELEX 236735 GOPUBUR. (Subscr. to: Box 786, Cooper Sta., New York, NY 10276. TEL 800-545-8398; UK subscr. to: P.O. Box 90, Reading, Berkshire RG1 8JL, England. TEL 0734-560-080) (Co-sponsor: Commission of the European Communities) Ed. K.K. Appleyard. (also avail. in microform; back issues avail.) **Indexed:** CAD CAM Abstr., Chem.Abstr., Met.Abstr., Sci.Abstr.
—BLDSC shelfmark: 3829.488500.
Refereed Serial

539.7 **US** **ISSN 0273-2998**
EUROPEAN APPLIED RESEARCH REPORTS SPECIAL TOPICS SERIES. irreg. Harwood Academic Publishers, 270 Eighth Ave., New York, NY 10011. TEL 212-206-8900. FAX 212-645-2459. TELEX 236735 GOPUB UR. (Subscr. to: Box 786, Cooper Sta., New York, NY 10276. TEL 800-545-8398; UK subscr. to: Box 90, Reading, Berkshire RG1 8JL, England. TEL 0734-560-080) (also avail. in microform)
Refereed Serial

539.764 **SZ**
EUROPEAN CONFERENCE ON CONTROLLED FUSION AND PLASMA PHYSICS. PROCEEDINGS. (Text in English) 14th, 1987. a. 260 SFr. European Physical Society, P.O. Box 69, CH-1213 Petit-Lancy 2, Switzerland. Ed.Bd.

539.7 531.64 **CC** **ISSN 0254-3052**
QC793 **CODEN: KNWLD9**
GAONENG WULI YU HE WULI. English translation: High Energy Physics and Nuclear Physics (US ISSN 0899-9996) (Text in Chinese; summaries in English) 1977. m. $8 per no. (Chinese Society of High Energy Physics - Zhongguo Gaoneng Wuli Xuehui) Science Press, Marketing and Sales Department, 16 Donghuangchenggen Beijie, Beijing 100707, People's Republic of China. TEL 4010642. FAX 4102180. TELEX 210247-SPBJ-CN. adv.; circ. 6,000. **Indexed:** Chem.Abstr., Math.R., Met.Abstr., Sci.Abstr., World Alum.Abstr.
—BLDSC shelfmark: 4307.301800.
Description: Covers physics research in China, including quantum field theory and particle physics.
Refereed Serial

539.7 **US** **ISSN 0899-9996**
QC793
HIGH ENERGY PHYSICS AND NUCLEAR PHYSICS. English translation of: Gaoneng Wuli yu He-wuli (CC ISSN 0254-3052) 1988. q. $295. (Chinese Society of High Energy Physics, CC - Zhongguo Gaoneng Wuli Xuehui) Allerton Press, Inc., 150 Fifth Ave., New York, NY 10011. TEL 212-924-3950. Ed. Xian Dingchang. (back issues avail.)
Description: Covers physics research in China, including quantum field theory, and particle physics.
Refereed Serial

530 **RM**
INSTITUTUL DE FIZICA ATOMICA. SESIUNEA STIINTIFICA ANUALA DE COMUNICARI; PROGRAM SI REZUMATE. a. Institutul de Fizica Atomica, Soseaua Magurele, Bucharest, Rumania. TELEX 11397 IFA R.

539.722 **II** **ISSN 0074-3046**
INTERNATIONAL CONFERENCE ON COSMIC RAYS. (PROCEEDINGS). 1984. biennial. 18th, 1983, India. $120. Tata Institute of Fundamental Research, c/o Prof. P.V. Ramana Murthy, Colaba, Bombay 5, India. adv.; bk.rev.

539.75 **US**
INTERNATIONAL CONFERENCE ON THE PHYSICS OF ELECTRONIC AND ATOMIC COLLISIONS. ABSTRACTS OF CONTRIBUTED PAPERS AND INVITED PAPERS. Variant titles: Electronic and Atomic Collisions. Physics of Electronic and Atomic Collisions. (Publisher varies for each conference; 7th, 10th-15th published by North-Holland) 1958. irreg., 15th, 1987, Brighton. $150. International Union of Pure and Applied Physics, Commission on Atomic and Molecular Physics and Spectroscopy, c/o Norman Bardsley, Sec., L-296, Box 800, Livermore, CA 94550. TEL 510-422-1100. (Dist. by: Elsevier Science Publishers B.V., P.O. Box 211, 1000 AE Amsterdam, Netherlands. TEL 020-5803911; Subscr. in U.S. and Canada to: Elsevier Science Publishing Co., Inc., Box 882, Madison Sq. Sta., New York, NY 10159. TEL 212-989-5800) circ. 1,500. **Indexed:** Phys.Abstr.
Formerly: International Conference on the Physics of Electronic and Atomic Collisions. Papers (ISSN 0074-333X)

539.764 **SZ**
INTERNATIONAL EUROPEAN CONFERENCE ON HIGH ENERGY PHYSICS. PROCEEDINGS. (Text in English) biennial. 130 SFr. to non-members; members 80 SFr. European Physical Society, P.O. Box 69, CH-1213 Petit-Lancy 2, Switzerland. Ed.Bd.

539.7 643 **SI** **ISSN 0129-0835**
QD96.X2
▼**INTERNATIONAL JOURNAL OF P I X E.**
(Particle-Induced X-ray Emission) (Text in English) 1990. q. $275. World Scientific Publishing Co. Pte. Ltd., Farrer Rd., P.O. Box 128, Singapore 9128, Singapore. TEL 3825663. FAX 3825919. TELEX RS-28561-WSPC. (UK addr.: 73 Lynton Mead, London N20 8DH, England. TEL 44-81-4462461; US addr.: 1060 Main St., Ste. 1B, River Edge, NJ 07661. TEL 800-227-7562) Ed. S. Morita.
—BLDSC shelfmark: 4542.467300.
Description: Publishes original papers and reviews in various aspects of particle-induced X-ray emission (PIXE).

539 616 **US** **ISSN 0883-2889**
QC770 **CODEN: ARISEF**
INTERNATIONAL JOURNAL OF RADIATION APPLICATIONS AND INSTRUMENTATION. PART A: APPLIED RADIATION AND ISOTOPES; including data, instrumentation and methods for use in agriculture, industry and medicine. (Text in English, French, German, Russian) 1956. m. £475 (combined subscr. to Parts A-E £1600)(effective 1992). Pergamon Press, Inc., Journals Division, 660 White Plains Rd., Tarrytown, NY 10591-5153. TEL 914-524-9200. FAX 914-333-2444. (And: Headington Hill Hall, Oxford OX3 0BW, England. TEL 0865-794141) Ed. H. Seligman, W.L. McLaughlin. adv.; bk.rev.; charts; illus.; index; circ. 2,000. (also avail. in microform from MIM,UMI; reprint service avail. from UMI) **Indexed:** Anal.Abstr., Biol.Abstr., Biotech.Abstr., Biwk.Pap.Rad.Chem.& Photochem., Chem.Abstr., Curr.Adv.Ecol.Sci., Curr.Cont., Dairy Sci.Abstr., Deep Sea Res.& Oceanogr.Abstr., Excerp.Med., Food Sci.& Tech.Abstr., Ind.Med., Ind.Sci.Rev., Ind.Vet., INIS Atomind., Mass Spectr.Bull., Nutr.Abstr., Ocean.Abstr., Pollut.Abstr., Sci.Abstr., Sci.Cit.Ind., Soils & Fert., Vet.Bull.
—BLDSC shelfmark: 1576.565000.
Formerly (until 1985): International Journal of Applied Radiation and Isotopes (ISSN 0020-708X)
Description: Publishes papers relating to the production, measurement and application of radionucleides and radiation in all branches of science and technology.
Refereed Serial

539 541 **US**
INTERNATIONAL JOURNAL OF RADIATION APPLICATIONS AND INSTRUMENTATION. PART C: RADIATION PHYSICS AND CHEMISTRY. (Text in English, French, German, Russian) 1969. 12/yr. (in 2 vols.) £550 (effective 1992). Pergamon Press, Inc., Journals Division, 660 White Plains Rd., Tarrytown, NY 10591. TEL 914-524-9200. FAX 914-333-2444. (And: Headington Hill Hall, Oxford OX3 0BW, England. TEL 0865-794141) Ed. A. Charlesby. adv.; bk.rev.; circ. 1,050. (also avail. in microform from MIM,UMI; back issues avail.) **Indexed:** Chem.Abstr., Curr.Cont., Excerp.Med., Mass Spectr.Bull., Rice Abstr., Sci.Abstr.
Formerly (until 1985): Radiation Physics and Chemistry (ISSN 0146-5724)
Description: Publishes papers dealing with the interaction of ionizing radiation with matter, the resultant physical and chemical changes, and the mechanisms involved, as well as papers dealing with applications and techniques.
Refereed Serial

539.7 **US**
QC787.N78
INTERNATIONAL JOURNAL OF RADIATION APPLICATIONS AND INSTRUMENTATION. PART D: NUCLEAR TRACKS AND RADIATION MEASUREMENTS. 1977. 4/yr. £240 (combined subscr. to Parts A-E £1600)(effective 1992). Pergamon Press, Inc., Journals Division, 395 Saw Mill River Rd., Elmsford, NY 10523. TEL 914-592-7700. FAX 914-592-3625. (And: Headington Hill Hall, Oxford OX3 0BW, England. TEL 0865-794141) Eds. E.V. Benton, S.A. Durrani. adv.; index; circ. 1,000. (also avail. in microform from MIM,UMI; back issues avail.) **Indexed:** ASCA, Biol.Abstr., Chem.Abstr., Curr.Cont., GeoRef., Ind.Sci.Rev., Phys.Ber., Sci.Abstr.
Former titles (until 1985): Nuclear Tracks and Radiation Measurements (ISSN 0735-245X); (until 1981): Nuclear Tracks (ISSN 0191-278X); (until 1978): Nuclear Track Detection (ISSN 0145-224X); Nuclear Tracks in Solids.
Description: Publishes the latest developments in the field of radiation measurement, emphasizing nuclear tracks, thermoluminescence and related phenomena.
Refereed Serial

PHYSICS — NUCLEAR PHYSICS

574 530 618   US   ISSN 0360-3016
RC271.R3   CODEN: IOBPD3
INTERNATIONAL JOURNAL OF RADIATION: ONCOLOGY - BIOLOGY - PHYSICS. 1976. 12/yr. $1290 (effective 1992). Pergamon Press, Inc., Journals Division, 660 White Plains Rd., Tarrytown, NY 10591-5153. TEL 914-524-9200. FAX 914-333-2444. (And: Headington Hill Hall, Oxford OX3 0BW, England. TEL 0865-794141) Ed. Dr. Philip Rubin. circ. 4,000. (also avail. in microform from MIM,UMI; reprint service avail. from UMI) **Indexed:** Abstr.Health Care Manage.Stud., Biol.Abstr., Biwk.Pap.Rad.Chem.& Photochem., Chem.Abstr., Curr.Adv.Cancer Res., Curr.Adv.Genetics & Molec.Biol., Curr.Cont., Dairy Sci.Abstr., Dent.Ind., Excerp.Med., Helminthol.Abstr., Ind.Med., Ind.Sci.Rev., INIS Atomind., Risk Abstr., Sci.Abstr., Sci.Cit.Ind.
—BLDSC shelfmark: 4542.523000.
Refereed Serial

539.7   SI
INTERNATIONAL REVIEW OF NUCLEAR PHYSICS. (Text in English) 1984. irreg., vol.7, 1991. price varies. World Scientific Publishing Co. Pte. Ltd., Farrer Rd., P.O. Box 128, Singapore 9128, Singapore. TEL 3825663. FAX 3825919. TELEX RS 28561 WSPC. (UK addr.: 73 Lynton Mead, Totteridge, London N20 8DH, England. TEL 44-81-4462461; US addr.: 1060 Main St., Ste. 1B, River Edge, NJ 07661. TEL 800-227-7562) Ed. T.T.S. Kuo.

523.01   US
J I L A DATA CENTER. REPORT. 1965. irreg. free. Joint Institute for Laboratory Astrophysics, University of Colorado, Boulder, CO 80309. TEL 303-492-7801. FAX 303-492-5235. TELEX 755842. **Indexed:** Chem.Abstr.
Formerly: J I L A Information Center. Report (ISSN 0449-1343)

621.48   NE   ISSN 0022-3115
TK9185.A1   CODEN: JNUMAM
JOURNAL OF NUCLEAR MATERIALS; materials aspects of fission and fusion. (Text in English, French, German) 1959. 30/yr. (in 10 vols.; 3 nos./vol.). fl.4510 (effective 1992). North-Holland (Subsidiary of: Elsevier Science Publishers B.V.), P.O. Box 211, 1000 AE Amsterdam, Netherlands. TEL 020-5803911. FAX 020-5803598. TELEX 18582 ESPA NL. (Subscr. in U.S. and Canada to: Elsevier Science Publishing Co., Inc., Box 882, Madison Sq. Sta., New York, NY 10159. TEL 212-989-5800) Ed. L.K. Mansur. adv.; bk.rev.; charts; illus.; cum.index. (back issues avail.) **Indexed:** Appl.Mech.Rev., Bull.Thermodyn.& Thermochem., Cadscan, Chem.Abstr., Curr.Cont., Energy Info.Abstr., Eng.Ind., Fuel & Energy Abstr., Ind.Sci.Rev., INIS Atomind., INSPEC, Lead Abstr., Met.Abstr., Phys.Ber., Sci.Abstr., World Alum.Abstr., Zincscan.
—BLDSC shelfmark: 5023.200000.
Description: Publishes papers covering the field of materials research related to nuclear science and technology.
Refereed Serial

539 621.48   JA   ISSN 0022-3131
     CODEN: JNSTAX
JOURNAL OF NUCLEAR SCIENCE AND TECHNOLOGY/NIHON GENSHIRYOKU GAKKAI OBUN RONBUNSHI. (Text in English) 1964. m. 18000 Yen($150) Atomic Energy Society of Japan - Nihon Genshiryoku Gakkai, 1-1-13, Shinbashi, Minato-ku, Tokyo 105, Japan. TEL 03-3508-1261. FAX 03-3581-6128. Ed. Kunio Higashi. adv.; abstr.; charts; illus.; index; circ. 2,000. (also avail. in microform from MIM; reprint service avail. from U.S. Dept. of Commerce) **Indexed:** Biwk.Pap.Rad.Chem.& Photochem., CAD CAM Abstr., Chem.Abstr., Crop Physiol.Abstr., Curr.Cont., Energy Info.Abstr., Environ.Abstr., Environ.Per.Bibl., Excerp.Med., Fluidex, Ind.Sci.Rev., INIS Atomind, JTA, Met.Abstr., Sci.Abstr., Sci.Cit.Ind., World Alum.Abstr.
—BLDSC shelfmark: 5023.500000.

539.7   UK   ISSN 0954-3899
QC770   CODEN: JPGPED
JOURNAL OF PHYSICS G: NUCLEAR AND PARTICLE PHYSICS. 1975. m. £489($978) (effective 1992). (Institute of Physics) I O P Publishing, Techno House, Redcliffe Way, Bristol BS1 6NX, England. TEL 072-297481. FAX 0272-294318. (U.S. addr.: American Institute of Physics, Member and Subscriber Service, 500 Sunnyside Blvd., Woodbury, NY 11797-2999. TEL 516-576-2270) Ed. A. Faessler. bibl.; charts; illus.; index. (also avail. in microfiche; microfilm; back issues avail.) **Indexed:** Cadscan, Chem.Abstr., Curr.Cont., Ind.Sci.Rev., INIS Atomind., Lead Abstr., Math.R., Phys.Ber., Sci.Abstr., Zincscan.
—BLDSC shelfmark: 5036.219000.
Formerly: Journal of Physics G: Nuclear Physics (ISSN 0305-4616)
Description: Theoretical and experimental topics in the physics of elementary particles and fluids, intermediate energy and cosmic rays.

539   US   ISSN 0075-7888
LANDOLT-BOERNSTEIN, ZAHLENWERTE UND FUNKTIONEN AUS NATURWISSENSCHAFTEN UND TECHNIK. NEUE SERIE. GROUP 1: NUCLEAR PHYSICS/LANDOLT-BOERNSTEIN NUMERICAL DATA AND FUNCTIONAL RELATIONSHIPS IN SCIENCE AND TECHNOLOGY. NEW SERIES. 1961. irreg. price varies. Springer-Verlag, 175 Fifth Ave., New York, NY 10010. TEL 212-460-1500. (Also Berlin, Heidelberg, Vienna) (reprint service avail. from ISI)

539   US   ISSN 0075-7918
LANDOLT-BOERNSTEIN, ZAHLENWERTE UND FUNKTIONEN AUS NATURWISSENSCHAFTEN UND TECHNIK. NEUE SERIE. GROUP 2: ATOMIC PHYSICS. 1965. irreg. price varies. Springer-Verlag, 175 Fifth Ave., New York, NY 10010. TEL 212-460-1500. (Also Berlin, Heidelberg, Tokyo and Vienna) (reprint service avail. from ISI)

539.7   SI   ISSN 0217-7323
QC770   CODEN: MPLAEQ
MODERN PHYSICS LETTER A. 1986. 40/yr. $430 to individuals and developing countries; institutions $860. World Scientific Publishing Co. Pte. Ltd., Farrer Rd., P.O. Box 128, Singapore 9128, Singapore. TEL 3825663. FAX 3825919. TELEX RS-28561-WSPC. (UK addr.: 73 Lynton Mead, Totteridge, London N20 8DH, England. TEL 44-81-4462461; US addr.: 1060 Main St., Ste. 1B, River Edge, NJ 07661. TEL 800-227-7562) Ed.Bd. circ. 550. (back issues avail.)
—BLDSC shelfmark: 5890.835000.
Description: Contains research papers covering current research development in particle and field physics, nuclear physics, cosmology and gravitation.

539.7   SI   ISSN 0217-9849
QC173.4.C65
MODERN PHYSICS LETTER B. (Text in English) 1987. 30/yr. $335 to individuals and developing countries; institutions $840. World Scientific Publishing Co. Pte. Ltd., Farrer Rd., P.O. Box 128, Singapore 9128, Singapore. TEL 3825663. FAX 3825919. TELEX RS-28561-WSPC. (US addr.: 1060 Main St., Ste. 1B, River Edge, NJ 07661. TEL 800-227-7562; European addr.: 73 Lynton Mead, Totteridge, London N20 8DH, England. TEL 44-81-4462461) Ed.Bd. circ. 350. (back issues avail.)
—BLDSC shelfmark: 5890.835100.
Description: Covers condensed matter physics, statistical physics and applied physics at the post-graduate level.

539.7   SZ   ISSN 0259-9805
     CODEN: MCFUEX
MUON CATALYZED FUSION. 1986. q. 356.50 SFr. J.C. Baltzer AG, Scientific Publishing Company, Wettsteinplatz 10, CH-4058 Basel, Switzerland. TEL 061-6918925. FAX 061-6924262. Eds. L.I. Ponomarev, C. Petitjean. adv.; bk.rev.
—BLDSC shelfmark: 5985.690000.
Description: Covers mesic atomic and mesic molecular physics and some aspects of nuclear physics as it examines cold fusion.

539.7   US   ISSN 0170-5989
N M R. (Nuclear Magnetic Resonance); basic principles and progress. (Text mainly in English; occasionally in German) 1969. irreg., no.28, 1992. price varies. Springer-Verlag, 175 Fifth Ave., New York, NY 10010. TEL 212-460-1500. (Subscr. to: Box 2485, Secaucus, NJ 07096-2491. TEL 201-348-4033; And Berlin, Heidelberg, Tokyo and Vienna) Ed. E. Fluck. illus. (reprint service avail. from ISI)
Supersedes: N M R Basic Principles and Progress (ISSN 0078-088X)

539.7   US   ISSN 1044-8632
QC793.5.N462   CODEN: NTNEEJ
▼**NEUTRON NEWS.** 1991. 6/yr. $157 price varies. Gordon and Breach Science Publishers, 270 Eighth Ave., New York, NY 10011. TEL 212-206-8900. FAX 212-645-2459. TELEX 236735 GOPUB UR. (Subscr. to: Box 786, Cooper Sta., New York, NY 10276. TEL 800-545-8398; UK subscr. to: P.O. Box 90, Reading, Berkshire RG1 8JL, England. TEL 0734-560-080) (also avail. in microform)
—BLDSC shelfmark: 6081.605500.
Refereed Serial

539.7 530.44   UN   ISSN 0029-5515
QC791   CODEN: NUFUAU
NUCLEAR FUSION/FUSION NUCLEAIRE; journal of plasma physics and thermonuclear fusion. (Text in English or French; summaries in English and some in French) 1960. m. S.2000($135) International Atomic Energy Agency, Wagramer Str. 5, Box 100, A-1400 Vienna, Austria. (Dist. in U.S. by: Bernan Associates-Unipub, 4611-F Assembly Dr., Lanham, MD 20706-4391) Ed. Mrs. D. Twersky. bk.rev.; abstr.; bibl.; charts; illus.; index; circ. 1,100. (also avail. in microform from UMI; reprint service avail. from UMI) **Indexed:** Appl.Mech.Rev., Chem.Abstr., Curr.Cont., Eng.Ind., Ind.Sci.Rev., INIS Atomind., Phys.Ber., Sci.Abstr.
—BLDSC shelfmark: 6180.760000.

539   NE   ISSN 0168-9002
QC785.5   CODEN: NIMAER
NUCLEAR INSTRUMENTS & METHODS IN PHYSICS RESEARCH. SECTION A. ACCELERATORS, SPECTROMETERS, DETECTORS, AND ASSOCIATED EQUIPMENT. (Text in English, French and German; summaries in English) 1957. 39/yr. (in 13 vols.; 3 nos./vol.). fl.7878 (combined subscr. to sections A & B fl.12788)(effective 1992). North-Holland (Subsidiary of: Elsevier Science Publishers B.V.), P.O. Box 211, 1000 AE Amsterdam, Netherlands. TEL 020-5803911. FAX 020-5803598. TELEX 18582 ESPA NL. (Subscr. in U.S. and Canada to: Elsevier Science Publishing Co., Inc., Box 882, Madison Sq. Sta., New York, NY 10159. TEL 212-989-5800) Ed. K. Siegbahn. adv.; bk.rev.; index. (also avail. in microform from RPI; back issues avail.) **Indexed:** Acid Rain Abstr., Acid Rain Ind., Art & Archaeol.Tech.Abstr., Cadscan, Chem.Abstr., Comput.Abstr., Energy Ind., Energy Info.Abstr., Eng.Ind., Excerp.Med., GeoRef., Ind.Sci.Rev., Int.Aerosp.Abstr., Lead Abstr., Mass Spectr.Bull., Nucl.Sci.Abstr., Phys.Ber., Sci.Abstr., Zincscan.
—BLDSC shelfmark: 6180.861300.
Supersedes in part: Nuclear Instruments and Methods in Physics Research (ISSN 0167-5087); *Formerly:* Nuclear Instruments and Methods (ISSN 0029-554X)
Description: Publishes papers on particle accelerators and other devices producing and measuring nuclear radiations.
Refereed Serial

PHYSICS — NUCLEAR PHYSICS

539.7   NE   ISSN 0168-583X
QC785.5   CODEN: NIMBEU
NUCLEAR INSTRUMENTS & METHODS IN PHYSICS RESEARCH. SECTION B. BEAM INTERACTIONS WITH MATERIALS AND ATOMS. vol.6, 1985. 40/yr. (in 10 vols.; 4 nos./vol.). fl.6060 (combined subscr. to sections A & B fl.12788)(effective 1992). North-Holland (Subsidiary of: Elsevier Science Pubishers B.V.), P.O. Box 211, 1000 AE Amsterdam, Netherlands. TEL 020-5803911. FAX 020-5803598. TELEX 18582 ESPA NL. (Subscr. in U.S. and Canada to: Elsevier Science Publishing Co., Inc., Box 882, Madison Sq. Sta., New York, NY 10159. TEL 212-989-5800) Ed. K. Siegbahn. (also avail. in microform from RPI; back issues avail.) **Indexed:** Acid Rain Abstr., Acid Rain Ind., Comput.Abstr., Mass Spectr.Bull.
—BLDSC shelfmark: 6180.861320.
Supersedes in part (after vol.233, 1984): Nuclear Instruments and Methods in Physics Research (ISSN 0167-5087); **Formerly:** Nuclear Instruments and Methods (ISSN 0029-554X)
Description: Covers all aspects of the interaction of energetic beams with atoms, molecules and aggregate forms of matter.
Refereed Serial

539.7   US
NUCLEAR PHYSICS NEWS. 4/yr. $133. (Nuclear Physics European Collaboration Committee) Gordon and Breach Science Publishers, 270 Eighth Ave., New York, NY 10011. TEL 212-206-8900. FAX 212-645-2459. TELEX 236735 GOPUB UR. (Subscr. to: Box 786, Cooper Sta., New York, NY 10276. TEL 800-545-8398; UK subscr. to: P.O. Box 90, Reading, Berkshire RG1 8JL, England. TEL 0734-560-080) (also avail. in microform)
Refereed Serial

539   NE   ISSN 0375-9474
QC173   CODEN: NUPABL
NUCLEAR PHYSICS, SECTION A; devoted to the experimental and theoretical study of the fundamental constituents of matter and their interactions. (Text in English, French and German) 1956. 60/yr. (in 15 vols.; 4 nos./vol.). fl.7740 (combined subscr. to Sections A & B fl.15336)(effective 1992). North-Holland (Subsidiary of: Elsevier Science Pubishers B.V.), P.O. Box 211, 1000 AE Amsterdam, Netherlands. TEL 020-5803911. FAX 020-5803598. TELEX 18582 ESPA NL. (Subscr. in U.S. and Canada to: Elsevier Science Publishing Co., Inc., Box 882, Madison Sq. Sta., New York, NY 10159. TEL 212-989-5800) Ed. G.E. Brown. adv.; bk.rev.; charts; index. (also avail. in microform from RPI; back issues avail.) **Indexed:** Cadscan, Chem.Abstr., Curr.Cont., Ind.Sci.Rev., Lead Abstr., Math.R., Met.Abstr., Phys.Ber., Sci.Abstr., Zincscan.
Supersedes in part (in 1967): Nuclear Physics (ISSN 0029-5582)
Description: Covers the domain of general nuclear physics together with intermediate energy and heavy-ion physics, and astrophysics.
Refereed Serial

539   NE   ISSN 0550-3213
QC173   CODEN: NUPBBO
NUCLEAR PHYSICS, SECTION B; a journal devoted to the experimental and theoretical study of the fundamental constituents of matter and their interactions. (Supplement avail.: Proceedings Supplements (ISSN 0920-5632)) 1956. 63/yr. (in 21 vols.; 3 nos./vol.). fl.10836 (combined subscr. to Sections A & B fl.15336)(effective 1992). North-Holland (Subsidiary of: Elsevier Science Publishers B.V.), P.O. Box 211, 1000 AE Amsterdam, Netherlands. TEL 020-5803911. FAX 020-5803598. TELEX 18582 ESPA NL. (Subscr. in U.S. and Canada to: Elsevier Science Publishing Co., Inc., Box 882, Madison Sq. Sta., New York, NY 10159. TEL 212-989-5800) Ed. B.G. Altarelli. index. (also avail. in microform from RPI; back issues avail.) **Indexed:** Chem.Abstr., Curr.Cont., Ind.Sci.Rev., Math.R., Phys.Ber., Sci.Abstr.
—BLDSC shelfmark: 6182.020000.
Supersedes in part (in 1967): Nuclear Physics (ISSN 0029-5582)
Description: Focuses on the domain of high energy physics and quantum field theory, and includes sections on cosmology, astrophysics and gravitation, computer simulations in physics and methods in theoretical physics.
Refereed Serial

539.7   NE   ISSN 0920-5632
     CODEN: NPBSE7
NUCLEAR PHYSICS, SECTION B, PROCEEDINGS SUPPLEMENTS. (Supplement to: Nuclear Physics, Section B (ISSN 0550-3213)) 1987. 10/yr. (in 5 vols.; 2 nos./vol.). fl.1355 (combined subscr. with Section B fl.11941)(effective 1992). North-Holland (Subsidiary of: Elsevier Science Publishers B.V.), P.O. Box 211, 1000 AE Amsterdam, Netherlands. TEL 020-5803911. FAX 020-5803598. TELEX 18582 ESPA NL. (Subscr. in U.S. and Canada to: Elsevier Science Publishing Co., Inc., Box 882, Madison Sq. Sta., New York, NY 10159. TEL 212-989-5800) Ed. B.G. Altarelli. (back issues avail.)
—BLDSC shelfmark: 6182.050000.
Description: Proceedings of large international conferences and specialized meetings in the field of high energy physics, covering developments in experimental and particle theory physics, hadronic physics, cosmology, atsrophysics and gravitation, field theory, and statistical systems.
Refereed Serial

539.7   CC
NUCLEAR SCIENCE AND TECHNIQUES. Chinese edition: He Jishu (ISSN 0253-3219) (Text in English) q. $80. (Chinese Aacademy of Sciences) Science Press, 16 Donghuangchenggen Beijie, Beijing 100707, People's Republic of China. TEL 4010642. FAX 4012180. TELEX 210247 SPBJ CN.
Description: Carries some original articles.
Refereed Serial

539.7   US
NUCLEAR SCIENCE APPLICATIONS - SECTION A: SHORT REVIEWS, RESEARCH PAPERS, AND COMMENTS. 1982. 8/yr. $182 includes Section B. Harwood Academic Publishers, 270 Eighth Ave., New York, NY 10011. TEL 212-206-8900. FAX 212-645-2459. TELEX 236735 GOPUB UR. (Subscr. to: Box 786, Cooper Sta., New York, NY 10276. TEL 800-545-8398; UK subscr. to: Box 90, Reading, Berkshire RG1 8JL, England. TEL 0734-560-080) Ed. Robert Klapisch. bk.rev. (also avail. in microfilm; microfiche; back issues avail.) **Indexed:** Sci.Abstr.
Supersedes in part: Nuclear Science Applications (ISSN 0191-1686)
Refereed Serial

539.7   US
NUCLEAR SCIENCE APPLICATIONS - SECTION B: IN DEPTH REVIEWS. (Included with section A) 1981. 8/yr. $182. Harwood Academic Publishers, 270 Eighth Ave., New York, NY 10011. TEL 212-206-8900. FAX 212-645-2459. TELEX 236735 GOPUB UR. (Subscr. to: Box 786, Cooper Sta., New York, NY 10276. TEL 800-545-8398; UK subscr. to: P.O. Box 90, Reading, Berkshire RG1 8JL, England. TEL 0734-560-080) Ed. Alexander Zucker. adv.; bk.rev. (also avail. in microfilm; microfiche; back issues avail.) **Indexed:** Sci.Abstr.
Supersedes in part: Nuclear Science Applications (ISSN 0191-1686)
Refereed Serial

539.7   JA
NUCLEAR SCIENCE INFORMATION OF JAPAN. ORAL PRESENTATION. (Text in English) 1970. s-a. exchange basis. Japan Atomic Energy Research Institute - Nihon Genshiryoku Kenkyujo, Tokai-mura, Naka-gun, Ibaraki 319-11, Japan. Ed. Akira Nakano. pat.; index; circ. 800.
Formerly (until Jan.1987): Nuclear Science Information of Japan (ISSN 0029-5620); **Supersedes:** Nuclear Science Abstracts of Japan (ISSN 0550-3248)

539   CH   ISSN 0029-5647
     CODEN: HTKHAB
NUCLEAR SCIENCE JOURNAL.* (Text in Chinese, English) 1957. q. $6. Nuclear Energy Society, 67, Lane 144, Keelung Rd., Section 4, Taipei, Taiwan 107, Republic of China. Ed. Chen-Hwa Cheng. bk.rev.; circ. 300. **Indexed:** Energy Rev., Environ.Per.Bibl., Nucl.Sci.Abstr. Key Title: Hezi Kexue.
—BLDSC shelfmark: 6183.300000.

539.7   US   ISSN 0250-4375
NUCLEAR SCIENCE RESEARCH CONFERENCE SERIES. irreg. Harwood Academic Publishers, 270 Eighth Ave., New York, NY 10011. TEL 212-260-8900. FAX 212-645-2459. TELEX 236735 GOPUB UR. (Subscr. to: Box 786, Cooper Sta., New York, NY 10276. TEL 800-545-8398; UK subscr. to: Box 90, Reading, Berkshire RG1 8JL, England. TEL 0734-560-080) Ed. A. Zucker. (also avail. in microform)
—BLDSC shelfmark: 6183.400000.
Refereed Serial

539 621.48   US   ISSN 0029-5450
TK9001   CODEN: NUTYBB
NUCLEAR TECHNOLOGY; applications for nuclear science, nuclear engineering and related arts. 1965. m. $412. American Nuclear Society, 555 N. Kensington Ave., La Grange Park, IL 60525. TEL 708-352-6611. (Co-sponsor: European Nuclear Society) Ed. William Vogelsang. bk.rev.; charts; illus.; stat.; index; circ. 1,300. (reprint service avail.) **Indexed:** A.S.& T.Ind., Art & Archaeol.Tech.Abstr., Biol.Abstr., CAD CAM Abstr., Cadscan, Chem.Abstr., Curr.Cont., Energy Info.Abstr., Eng.Ind., Environ.Abstr., Fuel & Energy Abstr., Ind.Sci.Rev., Lead Abstr., Met.Abstr., Risk Abstr., Sci.Abstr., World Alum.Abstr., Zincscan.
—BLDSC shelfmark: 6183.520000.
Formerly: Nuclear Applications and Technology.

539.7 600   US   ISSN 0048-1262
OAK RIDGE NATIONAL LABORATORY REVIEW. 1967. q. free. Oak Ridge National Laboratory, Box X, Oak Ridge, TN 37830. TEL 615-576-3000. Ed. Carolyn Krause. bk.rev.; charts; illus.; cum.index every 5 yrs.; circ. 6,000. **Indexed:** CAD CAM Abstr., Chem.Abstr., Energy Res.Abstr.
—BLDSC shelfmark: 7786.420000.

539   JA   ISSN 0473-4580
OSAKA UNIVERSITY. LABORATORY OF NUCLEAR STUDIES. ANNUAL REPORT. (Text in English) 1962. a. exchange basis. Osaka Daigaku, Laboratory of Nuclear Studies, 1-1 Machikanayama-cho, Toyonaka, Osaka 560, Japan. FAX 06-855-6664. Ed.Bd. circ. 1,200.

539.7   US   ISSN 0031-2460
QC787.P3   CODEN: PLACBD
PARTICLE ACCELERATORS. (Text in English, French and German) 1969. 16/yr. (in 4 vols., 4 nos./vol.). $232. Gordon and Breach Science Publishers, 270 Eighth Ave., New York, NY 10011. TEL 212-206-8900. FAX 212-645-2459. TELEX 236735 GOPUB UR. (Subscr. to: Box 786, Cooper Sta., New York, NY 10276. TEL 800-545-8398; UK subscr. to: P.O. Box 90, Reading, Berkshire RG1 8JL, England. TEL 0734-560-080) Ed. Eberhard Keil. adv.; bk.rev.; charts; illus.; index. (also avail. in microform from MIM) **Indexed:** Chem.Abstr., Curr.Cont., Eng.Ind., Phys.Ber., Sci.Abstr.
—BLDSC shelfmark: 6407.250000.
Refereed Serial

539   PH   ISSN 0079-1490
QC770   CODEN: PNUJAB
PHILIPPINES NUCLEAR JOURNAL. 1966. irreg. $20. Philippine Nuclear Research Institute, Don Mariano Marcos Ave., Diliman, Quezon City, Philippines. FAX 951646. TELEX 66804 PNRI PN. Ed. Alumanda de la Rosa. circ. 2,000. **Indexed:** Biol.Abstr.

539.7   US   ISSN 0556-2813
QC770   CODEN: PRVCAN
PHYSICAL REVIEW C (NUCLEAR PHYSICS). 1970. m. $620 (foreign $700). (American Physical Society) American Institute of Physics, 335 E. 45th St., New York, NY 10017. TEL 212-661-9404. Ed. S.M. Austin. bibl.; illus.; s-a. index. (also avail. in microfiche; microform; back issues avail.) **Indexed:** Appl.Mech.Rev., C.P.I., Cadscan, Chem.Abstr., Curr.Cont., Eng.Ind., Lead Abstr., Math.R., Met.Abstr., Nucl.Sci.Abstr., Phys.Abstr., Phys.Ber., Sci.Abstr., Zincscan.
—BLDSC shelfmark: 6476.060000.
Supersedes in part (1893-1969): Physical Review.
Refereed Serial

PHYSICS — NUCLEAR PHYSICS

539.7 US ISSN 0556-2821
QC721 CODEN: PRVDAQ
PHYSICAL REVIEW D (PARTICLES AND FIELDS). 1970. s-m. $890 (foreign $1000). (American Physical Society) American Institute of Physics, 335 E. 45th St., New York, NY 10017. TEL 212-661-9404. Ed.Bd. bibl.; illus.; s-a. index. (also avail. in microform; back issues avail.) **Indexed:** Appl.Mech.Rev., C.P.I., Chem.Abstr., Curr.Cont., Eng.Ind., Int.Aerosp.Abstr., Math.R., Met.Abstr., Nucl.Sci.Abstr., Phys.Abstr., Phys.Ber., Sci.Abstr.
—BLDSC shelfmark: 6476.070000.
Supersedes in part (1893-1969): Physical Review.

530 539.7 NE ISSN 0375-9601
QC1 CODEN: PYLAAG
PHYSICS LETTERS. SECTION A: GENERAL, ATOMIC AND SOLID STATE PHYSICS. 1962. 72/yr.(in 12 vols.; 6 nos./vol.) fl.3732 (combined subscr. to Sections A & B and Physics Reports fl.12737)(effective 1992). North-Holland (Subsidiary of: Elsevier Science Publishers B.V.), P.O. Box 211, 1000 AE Amsterdam, Netherlands. TEL 020-5803911. FAX 020-5803598. TELEX 18582 ESPA NL. (Subscr. in U.S. and Canada to: Elsevier Science Publishing Co., Inc., Box 882, Madison Sq. Sta., New York, NY 10159. TEL 212-989-5800) Ed.Bd. (also avail. in microform from RPI; back issues avail.) **Indexed:** Cadscan, Chem.Abstr., Curr.Cont., Deep Sea Res.& Oceanogr.Abstr., Lead Abstr., Mass Spectr.Bull., Math.R., Met.Abstr., Phys.Ber., Sci.Abstr., World Alum.Abstr., Zincscan.
—BLDSC shelfmark: 6478.761000.
Supersedes in part (in 1967): Physics Letters (ISSN 0031-9163)
Description: Covers all fields of physics excluding nuclear and particle physics.
Refereed Serial

539.7 NE ISSN 0370-2693
QC1 CODEN: PYLBAJ
PHYSICS LETTERS. SECTION B: NUCLEAR, ELEMENTARY PARTICLE AND HIGH-ENERGY PHYSICS. 1962. 88/yr. (in 22 vols.; 4 nos./vol.) fl.6842 (combined subscr. to Sections A & B and Physics Reports fl.12737)(effective 1992). North-Holland (Subsidiary of: Elsevier Science Publishers B.V.), P.O. Box 211, 1000 AE Amsterdam, Netherlands. TEL 020-5803911. FAX 020-5803598. TELEX 18582 ESPA NL. (Subscr. in U.S. and Canada to: Elsevier Science Publishing Co., Inc., Box 882, Madison Sq. Sta., New York, NY 10159. TEL 212-989-5800) Ed.Bd. (also avail. in microform from RPI; back issues avail.) **Indexed:** Cadscan, Chem.Abstr., Curr.Cont., Deep Sea Res.& Oceanogr.Abstr., Lead Abstr., Mass Spectr.Bull., Math.R., Phys.Ber., Sci.Abstr., Zincscan.
—BLDSC shelfmark: 6478.762000.
Supersedes in part (in 1967): Physics Letters (ISSN 0031-9163)
Description: Presents new results in nuclear and particle physics.
Refereed Serial

539.7 544.6 US ISSN 0079-6565
QC762 CODEN: PNMRAT
PROGRESS IN NUCLEAR MAGNETIC RESONANCE SPECTROSCOPY. 1966. 6/yr. £210 (effective 1992). Pergamon Press, Inc., Journals Division, 660 White Plains Rd., Tarrytown, NY 10591-5153. TEL 914-524-9200. FAX 914-333-2444. (And: Headington Hill Hall, Oxford OX3 0BW, England. TEL 0865-794141) Ed.Bd. index. (also avail. in microform from MIM,UMI) **Indexed:** Chem.Abstr., Curr.Cont., Met.Abstr., Sci.Abstr., World Alum.Abstr.
—BLDSC shelfmark: 6870.750000.
Description: Publishes review articles covering applications of NMR in chemistry, biochemistry and biological science, as well as fundamental theory and instrumental developments.
Refereed Serial

539.7 US ISSN 0146-6410
QC770 CODEN: PPNPDB
PROGRESS IN PARTICLE AND NUCLEAR PHYSICS. 1977. 2/yr. £270 (effective 1992). Pergamon Press, Inc., Journals Division, 660 White Plains Rd., Tarrytown, NY 10591-5153. TEL 914-524-9200. FAX 914-333-2444. (And: Headington Hill Hall, Oxford OX3 0BW, England. TEL 0865-794141) Ed. Amand Faessler. index. (also avail. in microform from MIM,UMI) **Indexed:** Chem.Abstr., Phys.Ber., Sci.Abstr.
Supersedes (1950-1976): Progress in Nuclear Physics (ISSN 0079-659X)
Description: Publishes reviews of new developments in nuclear and particle physics, with emphasis on the interface between the two fields.
Refereed Serial

539.7 JA
R C N P ANNUAL REPORT. (Text and summaries in English) 1976. a. Research Center for Nuclear Physics, Osaka University, 10-1 Mihogaoka, Ibarakishi Osaka 567, Japan. (back issues avail.)

539.7 539.7 UK ISSN 0033-7579
QD601.A1 CODEN: RAEFBL
RADIATION EFFECTS. (Includes: Radiation Effects Bulletin) 1969. 72/yr. (in 18 vols., 4 nos./vol.). $143 to individuals; academic $286; corporate $424. Gordon and Breach Science Publishers, P.O. Box 90, Reading RG1 8JL, England. TEL 0734-560080. FAX 0734-568211. TELEX 849870. (US subscr. to: Box 786, Cooper Sta., New York, NY 10276. TEL 800-545-8398) Ed. Lewis T. Chadderton. adv.; bk.rev.; abstr.; bibl.; charts; index. (also avail. in microform from MIM) **Indexed:** Biol.Abstr., Chem.Abstr., Curr.Cont., Eng.Ind., Environ.Per.Bibl., Excerp.Med., INSPEC, Mass Spectr.Bull., Met.Abstr., Sci.Abstr., World Alum.Abstr.

539.9 US ISSN 1042-0150
QD601.A1 CODEN: REDSEI
RADIATION EFFECTS AND DEFECTS IN SOLIDS. q. $226. Gordon & Breach Science Publishers, 270 Eighth Ave., New York, NY 10011. TEL 212-206-8900. FAX 212-645-2459. TELEX 236735 GOPUB UR. (Subscr. to: Box 786, Cooper Sta., New York, NY 10276. TEL 800-545-8398; UK subscr. to: P.O. Box 90, Reading, Berkshire RG1 8JL, England. TEL 0734-560-080) Ed. Jochen Biersack. (also avail. in microform)
—BLDSC shelfmark: 7227.957100.
Refereed Serial

539.9 US ISSN 1042-6493
RADIATION EFFECTS AND DEFECTS IN SOLIDS BULLETIN. q. price varies. Gordon & Breach Science Publishers, 270 Eighth Ave., New York, NY 10011. TEL 212-206-8900. FAX 212-645-2459. TELEX 236735 GOPUB UR. (Subscr. to: Box 786, Cooper Sta., New York, NY 10276. TEL 800-545-8398; UK subscr. to: P.O. Box 90, Reading, Berkshire RG1 8JL, England. TEL 0734-560-080) (also avail. in microform)

539.9 UK ISSN 1042-6485
RADIATION EFFECTS AND DEFECTS IN SOLIDS EXPRESS. q. Gordon & Breach Science Publishers, P.O. Box 90, Reading RG1 8JL, England. TEL 0734-560080. FAX 0734-568211. TELEX 849870. (US subscr. to: Box 786, Cooper Sta., New York, NY 10276. TEL 800-545-8398)

539.7 UK ISSN 0888-448X
QD625 CODEN: REBUEE
RADIATION EFFECTS BULLETIN. 6/yr. (in 1 vol.) $24 to individuals; academic $48; corporate $78; (included with subscr. to: Radiation Effects). Gordon and Breach Science Publishers, P.O. Box 90, Reading RG1 8JL, England. TEL 0734-560080. FAX 0734-568211. TELEX 849870. (US subscr. to: Box 786, Cooper Sta., New York, NY 10276. TEL 800-545-8398) Ed. Lewis T. Chadderton. **Indexed:** Biol.Abstr., Cadscan, Chem.Abstr., Environ.Per.Bibl., Excerp.Med., Lead Abstr., Mass Spectr.Bull., Met.Abstr., Sci.Abstr., World Alum.Abstr., Zincscan.
Formerly: Radiation Effects Letters (ISSN 0142-2448)

539.9 UK ISSN 0888-7322
QD625 CODEN: REFEEK
RADIATION EFFECTS EXPRESS. q. Gordon & Breach Science Publishers, P.O. Box 90, Reading RG1 8JL, England. TEL 0734-560080. FAX 0734-568211. TELEX 849870. (US subscr. to: Box 786, Cooper Sta., New York, NY 10276)

614 UK ISSN 0144-8420
R905 CODEN: RPDODE
RADIATION PROTECTION DOSIMETRY. 1981. 20/yr. (in 5 vols.). $950. Nuclear Technology Publishing, P.O. Box 7, Ashford, Kent TN25 4NW, England. TEL 233-641683. FAX 233-610021. TELEX 966119-NTP-UKG. Ed. T.F. Johns. adv.; bk.rev.; circ. 1,000. (back issues avail.) **Indexed:** ASCA, Chem.Abstr., Energy Ind., Energy Info.Abstr., Environ.Abstr., INIS Atomind, Risk Abstr., Sci.Abstr.
—BLDSC shelfmark: 7227.993000.
Description: International coverage of biological aspects, physical concepts, external and internal dosimetry and monitoring, environmental and workplace monitoring as well as dosimetry monitoring related to the protection of patients.

615.842 US ISSN 0033-7587
QC770 CODEN: RAREAE
RADIATION RESEARCH; an international journal. 1954. m. $520 (foreign $602). Academic Press, Inc., Journal Division, 1250 Sixth Ave., San Diego, CA 92101. TEL 619-230-1840. FAX 619-699-6800. TELEX 181726. Ed. R.J.M. Fry. bibl.; charts; illus.; index. (back issues avail.) **Indexed:** Biol.Abstr., Chem.Abstr., Curr.Adv.Biochem., Curr.Adv.Cancer Res., Curr.Adv.Ecol.Sci., Curr.Adv.Genetics & Molec.Biol., Curr.Cont., Dairy Sci.Abstr., Deep Sea Res.& Oceanogr.Abstr., Dent.Ind., Energy Rev., Environ.Per.Bibl., Excerp.Med., Helminthol.Abstr., Ind.Med., Ind.Vet., Mass Spectr.Bull., Nutr.Abstr., Ocean.Abstr., Pollut.Abstr., Risk Abstr., Sci.Abstr., Vet.Bull.
—BLDSC shelfmark: 7228.000000.
Description: Publishes original articles on the physical, chemical, and biological effects of radiation and on related subjects in the areas of physics, chemistry, biology, and medicine.
Refereed Serial

539 JA ISSN 0289-842X
RIKEN. ACCELERATOR PROGRESS REPORT. (Text in English) 1967. a. 5000 Yen. Rikagaku Kenkyujo, Saikurotoron Kenkyushitsu - Institute of Physical and Chemical Research, Cyclotron Laboratory, 2-1 Hirosawa, Wako-shi, Saitama-ken 351-01, Japan. FAX 0484-62-1554. TELEX 02962818-RIKEN-J.
Former titles: I P C R Accelerator Progress Report; I P C R Cyclotron Progress Report.

539 JA
RIKEN - A F - N P. (Text in English) 1970. irreg. Rikagaku Kenkyujo, Saikurotoron Kenkyushitsu - Institute of Physical and Chemical Research, Cyclotron Laboratory, 2-1 Hirosawa, Wako-shi, Saitama-ken 351-01, Japan. FAX 0484-62-1554. TELEX 02962818-RIKEN-J.
Former titles: Riken. Cyclotron Report; I P C R Cyclotron Report.

539 US ISSN 0038-5506
QC770 CODEN: SJNCAS
SOVIET JOURNAL OF NUCLEAR PHYSICS. English translation of: Yadernaya Fizika (RU ISSN 0044-0027) 1965. m. $1640 (foreign $1700). American Institute of Physics, 335 E. 45th St., New York, NY 10017. TEL 212-661-9404. (Subscr. to: Member and Subscriber Service, 500 Sunnyside Blvd., Woodbury, NY 11797-2999. TEL 516-576-2270) Ed. N.M. Queen. charts; stat. (also avail. in microform; back issues avail.) **Indexed:** ASCA, C.P.I., Curr.Cont., Gen.Phys.Adv.Abstr., Math.R., Phys.Ber., Sci.Abstr.
—BLDSC shelfmark: 0423.450000.

539.7 US ISSN 0090-4759
QC793 CODEN: SJPNA3
SOVIET JOURNAL OF PARTICLES AND NUCLEI. English translation of: Fizika Elementarnykh Chastits i Atomnogo Yadra. vol.3, 1972. bi-m. $910 (foreign $920-$935). American Institute of Physics, 335 E. 45th St., New York, NY 10017-3483. TEL 212-661-9404. (Subscr. to: Member and Subscriber Service, 500 Sunnyside Blvd., Woodbury, NY 11797-2999. TEL 516-576-2270) Ed. N.M. Queen. bibl.; charts; illus.; index. (also avail. in microform; back issues avail.) **Indexed:** C.P.I., Gen.Phys.Adv.Abstr., Math.R., Phys.Ber., Sci.Abstr.
—BLDSC shelfmark: 0423.550000.

539.7   US   ISSN 0894-0886
SYNCHROTRON RADIATION NEWS. 6/yr. $146. Gordon & Breach Science Publishers, 270 Eighth Ave., New York, NY 10011. TEL 212-206-8900.
FAX 212-645-2459. TELEX 236735 GOPUB UR. (Subscr. to: Box 786, Cooper Sta., New York, NY 10276. TEL 800-545-8398; UK subscr. to: P.O. Box 90, Reading, Berkshire RG1 8JL, England. TEL 0734-560-080) (also avail. in microform)
—BLDSC shelfmark: 8585.886500.
 Refereed Serial

539   CN
T R I U M F ANNUAL REPORT SCIENTIFIC ACTIVITIES. (Tri-University Meson Facility) 1967. a. free. T R I U M F, 4004 Wesbrook Mall, Vancouver, B.C. V6T 2A3, Canada. TEL 604-222-1047.
FAX 604-222-1047. Ed. Lorraine King. **Indexed:** Nucl.Sci.Abstr.
 Formerly (until 1980): T R I U M F Annual Report (ISSN 0082-6367)

539   CN
T R I U M F FINANCIAL AND ADMINISTRATIVE ANNUAL REPORT. (Tri-University Meson Facility) 1980. a. free. T R I U M F, 4004 Wesbrook Mall, Vancouver, B.C. V6T 2A3, Canada. TEL 604-222-1047.
FAX 604-222-1047. Ed. Michael Labrooy.

539   JA
UNIVERSITY OF TOKYO. INSTITUTE FOR NUCLEAR STUDY. ANNUAL REPORT. (Text in English) 1960. a. exchange basis. University of Tokyo, Institute for Nuclear Study - Tokyo Daigaku Genshikaku Kenkyusho, 3-2-1 Midori-cho, Tanashi-shi, Tokyo 188, Japan. abstr.

539   JA   ISSN 0495-7814
UNIVERSITY OF TOKYO. INSTITUTE FOR NUCLEAR STUDY. INS-J. (Text in English) 1957. irreg. exchange basis. University of Tokyo, Institute for Nuclear Study - Tokyo Daigaku Genshikaku Kenkyusho, 3-2-1 Midori-cho, Tanashi-shi, Tokyo 188, Japan. **Indexed:** Chem.Abstr.

539   JA
UNIVERSITY OF TOKYO. INSTITUTE FOR NUCLEAR STUDY. INS-PH. (Text in Japanese) 1969. irreg. exchange basis. University of Tokyo, Institute for Nuclear Study - Tokyo Daigaku Genshikaku Kenkyusho, 3-2-1 Midori-cho Tanashi-shi, Tokyo 188, Japan.

539   JA   ISSN 0563-7848
UNIVERSITY OF TOKYO. INSTITUTE FOR NUCLEAR STUDY. INS-PT. (Text in Japanese; summaries in English) 1957. irreg. exchange basis. University of Tokyo, Institute for Nuclear Study - Tokyo Daigaku Genshikaku Kenkyusho, 3-2-1 Midori-cho Tanashi-shi, Tokyo 188, Japan.

539   JA
UNIVERSITY OF TOKYO. INSTITUTE FOR NUCLEAR STUDY. INS-TCH. (Text in Japanese; summaries in English) 1967. irreg. exchange basis. University of Tokyo, Institute for Nuclear Study - Tokyo Daigaku Genshikaku Kenkyusho, 3-2-1 Midori-cho Tanashi-shi, Tokyo 188, Japan.

539   JA
UNIVERSITY OF TOKYO. INSTITUTE FOR NUCLEAR STUDY. INS-TEC. (Text in Japanese; summaries in English) 1971. irreg. exchange basis. University of Tokyo, Institute for Nuclear Study - Tokyo Daigaku Genshikaku Kenkyusho, 3-2-1 Midori-cho Tanashi-shi, Tokyo 188, Japan.

539   JA   ISSN 0563-7872
UNIVERSITY OF TOKYO. INSTITUTE FOR NUCLEAR STUDY. INS-TH. (Text in Japanese; summaries in English) 1954. irreg. exchange basis. University of Tokyo, Institute for Nuclear Study - Tokyo Daigaku Genshikaku Kenkyusho, 3-2-1 Midori-cho Tanashi-shi, Tokyo 188, Japan.

539   JA   ISSN 0563-7880
UNIVERSITY OF TOKYO. INSTITUTE FOR NUCLEAR STUDY. INS-TL. (Text in Japanese; summaries in English) 1954. irreg. exchange basis. University of Tokyo, Institute for Nuclear Study - Tokyo Daigaku Genshikaku Kenkyusho, 3-2-1 Midori-cho Tanashi-shi, Tokyo 188, Japan. **Indexed:** Chem.Abstr.

539   JA
UNIVERSITY OF TOKYO. INSTITUTE FOR NUCLEAR STUDY. INS-TS. (Text in Japanese; summaries in English) 1967. irreg. exchange basis. University of Tokyo, Institute for Nuclear Study - Tokyo Daigaku Genshikaku Kenkyusho, 3-2-1 Midori-cho Tanashi-shi, Tokyo 188, Japan.

539   JA   ISSN 0495-7822
UNIVERSITY OF TOKYO. INSTITUTE FOR NUCLEAR STUDY. REPORT. (Text in English) 1959. irreg. exchange basis. University of Tokyo, Institute for Nuclear Study - Tokyo Daigaku Genshikaku Kenkyusho, 3-2-1 Midori-cho Tanashi-shi, Tokyo 188, Japan. **Indexed:** INIS Atomind.

539   RU   ISSN 0044-0027
  CODEN: IDFZA7
YADERNAYA FIZIKA. English translation: Soviet Journal of Nuclear Physics (US ISSN 0038-5506) 1965. m. 118.20 Rub. (Akademiya Nauk S.S.S.R.) Izdatel'stvo Nauka, Fizmatlit, Leninskii prospekt, 15, 117071 Moscow, Russia. TEL 234-05-84. charts; index; circ. 1,000. (tabloid format) **Indexed:** Chem.Abstr., INSPEC, Phys.Ber., Sci.Abstr.
—BLDSC shelfmark: 0399.780000.

539.7   CC   ISSN 0253-3790
QC770   CODEN: YTHLDS
YUANZIHE WULI. English edition: Chinese Journal of Nuclear Physics (ISSN 1001-6031) (Editions in Chinese, English) 1979. q. $2 per no. (China Institute of Atomic Energy) China Ocean Press, International Cooperation Department, Haimao Dalou, 1 Fuxingmenwai Dajie, Beijing 100860, People's Republic of China. TEL 868941.
FAX 862209. TELEX 22536 NBO CN. (Dist. by: Guoji Shudian - China International Book Trading Corporation, P.O. Box 399, Beijing, P.R.C.) (Co-sponsor: Chinese Nuclear Physics Society) **Indexed:** Chem.Abstr., INIS Atomind., Sci.Abstr.

539.7   GW   ISSN 0930-1151
  CODEN: ZAANEE
ZEITSCHRIFT FUER PHYSIK. SECTION A. ATOMIC NUCLEI. (Text in English and German; summaries in English) 1920. 12/yr. DM.1794($1053) (effective 1992). (Deutsche Physikalische Gesellschaft) Springer-Verlag, Heidelberger Platz 3, 1000 Berlin 33, Germany. TEL 030-8207-1. (Also Heidelberg, Tokyo, Vienna, and New York) Ed. B. Povh. adv.; charts; illus. (also avail. in microform from UMI; reprint service avail. from ISI) **Indexed:** Chem.Abstr., Curr.Cont., INSPEC, Mass Spectr.Bull., Math.R., Phys.Ber., Sci.Abstr.
 Former titles: Zeitschrift fuer Physik. Section A: Atomic and Nuclei (ISSN 0340-2193); Zeitschrift fuer Physik (ISSN 0044-3328)

PHYSICS — Optics

535   US
ACADEMY OF SCIENCE OF THE U S S R. LEBEDEV PHYSICS INSTITUTE. PROCEEDINGS. 1987. irreg., no.190, 1990. price varies. (Academy of Sciences of the U S S R, Lebedev Physics Institute, RU) Nova Science Publishers, Inc., 283 Commack Rd., Ste. 300, Commack, NY 11725. TEL 516-499-3103. (back issues avail.)
 Description: Compilations of advanced physics research.
 Refereed Serial

ADVANCED MATERIALS FOR OPTICS AND ELECTRONICS.
 see CHEMISTRY — Electrochemistry

535.84   SI
ADVANCES IN MULTIPHOTON PROCESSES AND SPECTROSCOPY. (Text in English) 1984. irreg., vol. 7. price varies. World Scientific Publishing Co. Pte. Ltd., Farrer Rd., P.O. Box 128, Singapore 9128, Singapore. TEL 3825663. FAX 3825919. TELEX RS 28561 WSPC. (UK addr.: 73 Lynton Mead, Totteridge, London N20 8DH, England. TEL 44-81-4462461; US addr.: 1060 Main St., Ste. 1B, River Edge, NJ 07661. TEL 800-227-7562) Ed. S.H. Lin.

578 535   US   ISSN 0065-3012
QH201   CODEN: AOEMAK
ADVANCES IN OPTICAL AND ELECTRON MICROSCOPY. 1966. irreg., vol.12, 1991. Academic Press, Inc., 1250 Sixth Ave., San Diego, CA 92101.
TEL 619-699-6715. FAX 619-231-6616. (And: 24-28 Oval Rd., London NW1 7DX, England) Eds. V.E. Cosslett, R. Barer. (back issues avail.) **Indexed:** Biol.Abstr., Curr.Adv.Ecol.Sci., GeoRef.
—BLDSC shelfmark: 0709.553000.
 Refereed Serial

535.84 547   US   ISSN 1044-0305
QD96.M3   CODEN: JAMSEF
▼**AMERICAN SOCIETY FOR MASS SPECTROMETRY. JOURNAL.** 1990. 8/yr. $250 to institutions (foreign $284)(effective 1992). Elsevier Science Publishing Co., Inc. (New York), 655 Ave. of the Americas, New York, NY 10010. TEL 212-989-5800.
FAX 212-633-3965. TELEX 420643 AEP UI. Ed. Michael L. Gross. **Indexed:** Chem.Abstr., Curr.Cont., Eng.Mat.Abstr., Environ.Abstr., INSPEC, Sci.Cit.Ind., World Alum.Abstr.
—BLDSC shelfmark: 4692.920000.
 Description: Covers the fundamentals and applications of mass spectrometry. Principal focus is on research papers that present new and significant findings in all fields of scientific inquiry in which mass spectrometry can play a role.
 Refereed Serial

535   US
AMERICAN SOCIETY FOR PHOTOGRAMMETRY AND REMOTE SENSING FALL CONVENTION. TECHNICAL PAPERS. (Vol. for 1982 and 1983 published jointly with American Congress on Surveying and Mapping) a. $30 to non-members; members $20. American Society for Photogrammetry and Remote Sensing, 5410 Grosvenor Ln., Ste. 210, Bethesda, MD 20814-2160. TEL 301-493-0290.
FAX 301-493-0208. **Indexed:** Bibl.Cart.
 Former titles: American Society of Photogrammetry Fall Convention. Technical Papers (ISSN 0271-4043); (until 1983): American Society of Photogrammetry Fall Convention. Proceedings (ISSN 0196-674X)

535   US   ISSN 0066-4103
QC490   CODEN: NMRPAJ
ANNUAL REPORTS ON N M R SPECTROSCOPY. 1968. a. Academic Press, Inc., 1250 Sixth Ave., San Diego, CA 92101. TEL 619-231-0926.
FAX 619-699-6715. Ed. G.A. Webb. (reprint service avail. from ISI) **Indexed:** Chem.Abstr.
—BLDSC shelfmark: 1513.400000.
 Formerly: Annual Review of N M R Spectroscopy (ISSN 0066-4235)
 Refereed Serial

535   US   ISSN 0003-6935
QC350   CODEN: APOPAI
APPLIED OPTICS. (Text in English, French, German or Russian) 1962. 36/yr. (3/m.). $790. Optical Society of America, Inc., 2010 Massachusetts Ave., N.W., Washington, DC 20036-1023.
TEL 202-223-8130. Ed. William T. Rhodes. adv.; bk.rev.; charts; illus.; pat.; cum.index: vols.1-12. (also avail. in microfiche; microform) **Indexed:** A.S.& T.Ind., Abstr.Bull.Inst.Pap.Chem., Agri.Eng.Abstr., C.P.I., CAD CAM Abstr., Cadscan, Ceram.Abstr., Chem.Abstr., Comput.Abstr., Curr.Cont., Deep Sea Res.& Oceanogr.Abstr., Eng.Ind., Excerpt.Med., Fluidex, GeoRef., Graph.Arts Lit.Abstr., Ind.Sci.Rev., INIS Atomind., Lead Abstr., Met.Abstr., Phys.Abstr., Phys.Ber., Sci.Abstr., Sci.Cit.Ind., Zincscan.
—BLDSC shelfmark: 1576.250000.
 Description: Articles cover the applications of facts, principles, and methods of optics. For applied physicists, space scientists and astronomers, information processing scientists, and optical, electrical and mechanical engineers.

535 681   US   ISSN 0066-5495
  CODEN: APOSAR
APPLIED OPTICS. SUPPLEMENT. 1962. irreg., no.3, 1969. price varies. Optical Society of America, Inc., 2010 Massachusetts Ave., N.W., Washington, DC 20036-1023. TEL 202-223-8130. Eds. K.E. Shuler, W.R. Bennet, Jr. (also avail. in microfiche) **Indexed:** Phys.Abstr.
 Refereed Serial

PHYSICS — OPTICS

540 535.84   US   ISSN 0003-7028
QD71   CODEN: APSPA4
APPLIED SPECTROSCOPY. 1946. 12/yr. $165 to institutions (foreign $185). Society for Applied Spectroscopy, Box 64008, Baltimore, MD 21264. TEL 301-694-8122. Ed. William G. Fateley. adv.; bk.rev.; bibl.; charts; illus.; tr.lit.; index; circ. 7,000. (also avail. in microform from SAS; reprint service avail. from KTO) Indexed: Abstr.Bull.Inst.Pap.Chem., AESIS, Anal.Abstr., Art & Archaeol.Tech.Abstr., Biol.Abstr., Br.Ceram.Abstr., Cadscan, Chem.Abstr., Curr.Cont., Deep Sea Res.& Oceanogr.Abstr., Eng.Ind., Excerp.Med., GeoRef., Ind.Sci.Rev., INIS Atomind., Lead Abstr., Mass Spectr.Bull., Met.Abstr., Numis.Lit, Phys.Ber., Sci.Abstr., Sci.Cit.Ind., Sel.Water Res.Abstr., W.R.C.Inf., World Alum.Abstr., World Surf.Coat., Zincscan.
—BLDSC shelfmark: 1579.000000.
Refereed Serial

535.84   US   ISSN 0570-4928
QC450   CODEN: APSRBB
APPLIED SPECTROSCOPY REVIEWS; an international journal of principles, methods, and applications. 1964. 4/yr. $335. Marcel Dekker Journals, 270 Madison Ave., New York, NY 10016. TEL 212-696-9000. FAX 212-685-4540. TELEX 421419. (Subscr. to: Box 10018, Church St. Sta., New York, NY 10249) Ed. Edward G. Brame, Jr. charts; stat. (also avail. in microform from RPI) Indexed: Cadscan, Chem.Abstr., Curr.Cont., Eng.Ind., GeoRef., Ind.Sci.Rev., Ind.Sci.Rev., Lead Abstr., Phys.Abstr., Sci.Abstr., Sci.Cit.Ind., Zincscan.
Description: Provides information on principles, methods and applications of spectroscopy for the researcher and also presents discussions that relate physical concepts to chemical applications.
Refereed Serial

535   US   ISSN 0235-277X
QC974.5
ATMOSPHERIC OPTICS. English translation of: Optika Atmosfery. 1970. m. $750 (Canada $765; elsewhere $785). (Institute of Atmospheric Optics - RU) American Institute of Physics, 335 E. 45th St., New York, NY 10017. TEL 212-661-9406. (Subscr. to: Member and Subscriber Service, 500 Sunnyside Blvd., Woodbury, NY 11797-2999. TEL 516-576-2270) Ed. V.R. Zuev.
—BLDSC shelfmark: 0127.900000.

535.58   NE
BEAM MODIFICATION OF MATERIALS. 1984. irreg., vol.3, 1989. price varies. Elsevier Science Publishers B.V., Books Division, P.O. Box 211, 1000 AE Amsterdam, Netherlands. TEL 020-5803911. FAX 020-5803705. TELEX 18582 ESPA NL. (Subscr. in U.S. and Canada to: Elsevier Science Publishing Co., Inc., Box 882, Madison Sq. Sta. New York, NY 10159. TEL 212-989-5800) (reprint service avail. from ISI)
Refereed Serial

535   CC
BOPUXUE ZAZHI/JOURNAL OF SPECTRUM. (Text in Chinese) q. Zhongguo Kexueyuan, Wuhan Wuli Yanjiusuo - Chinese Academy of Sciences, Wuhan Institute of Physics, P.O. Box 7101, Xiaohongshan, Wuchang-qu, Wuhan, Hubei 430071, People's Republic of China. TEL 812541. Ed. Ye Zhaohui.

535.84 544.6   CN
QC451   CODEN: CJSPAI
CANADIAN JOURNAL OF APPLIED SPECTROSCOPY. (Text in English, French) 1963. q. Can.$115. (Spectroscopy Society of Canada) Polyscience Publications Inc., 44 Seize Arpents, P.O. Box 148, Morin Heights, Que. JOR 1HO, Canada. TEL 514-226-5870. FAX 514-226-5866. Ed. I. Butler. adv.; bk.rev.; charts; illus.; index; circ. 1,500. (reprint service avail. from UMI) Indexed: Abstr.Bull.Inst.Pap.Chem., Anal.Abstr., Biol.Abstr., Cadscan, Chem.Abstr., Curr.Cont., GeoRef, Ind.Sci.Rev., INIS Atomind., Lead Abstr., Mass Spectr.Bull., Met.Abstr., Sci.Abstr., Sci.Cit.Ind., World Alum.Abstr., Zincscan.
Formerly (until June 1990): Canadian Journal of Spectroscopy (ISSN 0045-5105); Supersedes: Canadian Spectroscopy (ISSN 0008-5057)

535   US   ISSN 0890-9903
TA1570   CODEN: CJIWER
CHINESE JOURNAL OF INFRARED AND MILLIMETER WAVES. English translation of: Hongwai Yanjiu, Ser. A (CC ISSN 0258-7114) 1987. bi-m. $345. (Optical Society of China, CC) Allerton Press, Inc., 150 Fifth Ave., New York, NY 10011. TEL 212-924-3950.
—BLDSC shelfmark: 3180.355200.

COLOURAMA; colour-light-art research. see *ART*

COMITE INTERNATIONAL DES POIDS ET MESURES. COMITE CONSULTATIF DE PHOTOMETRIE ET RADIOMETRIE. (RAPPORT ET ANNEXES). see *METROLOGY AND STANDARDIZATION*

535   DK   ISSN 0901-4632
D O P S NYT. 1986. q. DKK 230($35) Dansk Optisk Selskab, Bldg. 309, DK-2800 Lyngby, Denmark. TEL 02-883848. FAX 45-93-16-69. TELEX 37529-DTHDIA-DK. Ed. Torben Skettrup. adv.; bk.rev.; circ. 500. (back issues avail.)
—BLDSC shelfmark: 3619.501000.

535   SZ   ISSN 0084-5752
EIDGENOESSISCHE TECHNISCHE HOCHSCHULE ZUERICH. MITTEILUNGEN. PHOTOELASTIZITAET. 1943. irreg., no.18, 1990. free. E T H Zentrum, 8092 Zurich, Switzerland.

535.58 621.329   UK   ISSN 0013-4589
                                      CODEN: EOPTA4
ELECTRO OPTICS. 7/yr. £75 (foreign £80). Milton Publishing Co. Ltd., 5 Tranquil Passage, Blackheath, London SE3 0BY, England. TEL 081-297-1097. FAX 081-297-1098. Ed. David Whiffen. adv.; tr.lit.; circ. 16,000. (back issues avail.) Indexed: Ind.Sci.Rev., Sci.Abstr.
Incorporates: Laser Review.
Description: News regarding lasers, optoelectronics, fiber optics, sensors, imaging displays and optics.

535.58   UK   ISSN 0261-5657
ELECTRO OPTICS NEWSLETTER. 1981. m. £125. Milton Publishing Co. Ltd., 5 Tranquil Passage, Blackheath, London SE3 0BY, England. TEL 081-297-1097. FAX 081-297-1098. Ed. David Whiffen.

ELECTRON MICROSCOPY SOCIETY OF SOUTHERN AFRICA. PROCEEDINGS/ELEKTRONMIKROSKOPIEVERENIGING VAN SUIDELIKE AFRIKA. VERRIGTINGS. see *BIOLOGY — Microscopy*

ELECTRONIC MATERIALS AND PROCESSING. see *ELECTRONICS*

F UND M, FEINWERKTECHNIK UND MESSTECHNIK. see *ENGINEERING*

535.84   CC   ISSN 1000-7032
FAGUANG XUEBAO. (Text in Chinese) q. Changchun Wuli Yanjiusuo - Changchun Institute of Physics, 13, Xinmin Dajie, Changchun, Jilin 130021, People's Republic of China. TEL 52215. Ed. Xu Shurong.

535   GW   ISSN 0014-7680
TP890
DIE FARBE; Zeitschrift fuer alle Zweige der Farbenlehre und ihre Anwendung. (Text in English, French and German) 1952. a. DM.268. Muster-Schmidt Verlag, Gruenbergerweg 6, Postfach 2741, 3400 Goettingen, Germany. FAX 0551-7702774. TELEX 96704-GOFAFI. Ed. Dr. Manfred Richter. adv.; bk.rev.; charts; illus.; index; circ. 600. Indexed: Chem.Abstr., World Surf.Coat.
—BLDSC shelfmark: 3868.000000.

535   US   ISSN 0146-8030
TA1800   CODEN: FOIOD2
FIBER AND INTEGRATED OPTICS; a journal stressing components, systems, and future trends. 1977. q. £80($139) Taylor & Francis, 1900 Frost Rd., Ste. 101, Bristol, PA 19007. TEL 215-785-5800. FAX 215-785-5515. Ed. Henri Hodara. adv.; abstr.; index. Indexed: Chem.Abstr., Curr.Cont., Elec.& Electron.Abstr., Eng.Ind., J.Curr.Laser Abstr., Phys.Abstr., Phys.Ber., Sci.Abstr., Sci.Res.Abstr.
—BLDSC shelfmark: 3914.620000.
Description: Focuses on fiberoptic developments and in-depth surveys. Achieves a balance between scientific developments in integrated optics, systems, manufacturing and applications of optical fibers, and articles on economics and market trends.
Refereed Serial

535   US   ISSN 1051-1946
FIBER OPTIC SENSOR AND SYSTEMS; monthly newsletter on worldwide developments in fiber optic sensors and systems. Short title: F O S S. m. $480 (foreign $525). Information Gatekeepers, Inc., 214 Harvard Ave., Boston, MA 02134. TEL 617-232-3111. FAX 617-734-8562.
Description: Covers optics applications to sensors, technology, applications, markets, patents, products, and business developments.

FIBER OPTICS NEWS. see *COMMUNICATIONS*

535.58   UK   ISSN 0264-7249
FIBRE OPTICS NEWSLETTER. 1983. m. £125. Milton Publishing Co. Ltd., 5 Tranquil Passage, Blackheath, London SE3 0BY, England. TEL 081-297-1097. FAX 081-297-1098. Ed. David Whiffen.

535   IT   ISSN 0015-606X
QC350   CODEN: AFDGA2
FONDAZIONE GIORGIO RONCHI. ATTI. (Text in English, French, German, Italian) 1946. bi-m. L.225000 (foreign L.235000). Fondazione Giorgio Ronchi, Via S. Felice a Ema, 20, 50125 Florence, Italy. TEL 055-2320844. Ed. Laura Ronchi-Abbozzo. adv.; bk.rev.; charts; illus.; index, cum.index every 5 yrs: vols.1-28 (1946-1973); circ. 1,000. Indexed: Chem.Abstr., Excerp.Med., Ophthal.Lit., Psychol.Abstr., Sci.Abstr.

FOTEC FIBER OPTIC TESTING NEWS; from the fiber optic test equipment company. see *COMMUNICATIONS*

535   CC
GUANG DE SHIJIE/WORLD OF LIGHT. (Text in Chinese) bi-m. Zhongguo Guang Xuehui, Zhejiang Daxue, Zheda Lu, Hangzhou, Zhejiang 310027, People's Republic of China. TEL 572244. Ed. Tang Jinfa.

535.58   CC
GUANGDIANZI - JIGUANG/PHOTOELECTRON - LASER. (Text in Chinese) bi-m. Tianjin Daxue, Jidian Fenxiao, 47, Yingjian Lu, Yangliuqing, Tianjin 300380, People's Republic of China. TEL 792213. Ed. Zhang Guangying.

535.84   CC   ISSN 1000-0593
GUANGPUXUE YU GUANGPU FENXI/SPECTROSCOPY AND SPECTRAL ANALYSIS. (Text in Chinese) bi-m. Zhongguo Guangxue Xuehui - China Optics Society, 76 Xueyuan Nanlu, Haidian-qu, Beijing 100081, People's Republic of China. TEL 892179. Ed. Meng Guangzheng.
—BLDSC shelfmark: 8411.114400.
Refereed Serial

GUANGXIAN YU DIANLAN/OPTICAL FIBRE AND CABLE. see *ENGINEERING — Electrical Engineering*

535   CC   ISSN 0253-2239
QC350   CODEN: GUXUDC
GUANGXUE XUEBAO/ACTA OPTICA SINICA. (Text in Chinese) m. (Zhongguo Guangxue Xuehui - China Optics Society) Science Press, Marketing and Sales Department, 16 Donghuangchenggen Beijie, Beijing 100707, People's Republic of China. TEL 4010642. FAX 4012180. TELEX 210247 SPBJ CN. Ed. Wang Runwen.
—BLDSC shelfmark: 0641.790000.

GUANGXUE YIQI/OPTICAL INSTRUMENTS. see *INSTRUMENTS*

535.58   CC
GUOWAI JIGUANG/FOREIGN LASERS. (Text in Chinese) 1964. m. Y36. Zhongguo Kexueyuan - Shanghai Institute of Optics and Fine Mechanics, P.O. Box 800-211, Shanghai 201800, People's Republic of China. TEL 9534890. FAX 0086-021-9528885. TELEX 30902 SIOFM CN. (Co-sponsor: China Optics Society) Ed. Deng Ximing. circ. 1,000.

HAKIM FASHION EYEWEAR MAGAZINE. see *CLOTHING TRADE — Fashions*

535   CC
HONGWAI YANJIU/INFRARED RESEARCH. (Text in Chinese) bi-m. Zhongguo Guangxuehui - China Optics Society, 420 Zhongshan Bei 1 Lu, Shanghai 200083, People's Republic of China. TEL 5420850. Ed. Tang Dingyuan.

PHYSICS — OPTICS

535   CC
HONGWAI YU HAOMIBO XUEBAO/JOURNAL OF INFRARED AND MILLIMETRE WAVE. (Text in Chinese) bi-m. Y48. Science Press, Marketing and Sales Department, 16 Donghuangchenggen Beijie, Beijing 100707, People's Republic of China. TEL 4010642. FAX 4012180. TELEX 210247 SPBJ CN.

535.58   US
I E E E INTERNATIONAL SEMICONDUCTOR LASER CONFERENCE. CONFERENCE DIGEST. 1967. biennial. price varies. (I E E E, Laser and Electro-Optics Society) Institute of Electrical and Electronics Engineers, Inc., 345 E. 47th St., New York, NY 10017-2394. TEL 212-705-7900. FAX 212-705-6782. (Subscr. to: 445 Hoes Ln., Box 1331, Piscataway, NJ 08855-1331) **Indexed:** Sci.Abstr.
     Formerly (until 1982): I E E E Semiconductor Laser Conference.
     Description: Covers all aspects of semiconductor injection laser technology.

I E E E JOURNAL OF QUANTUM ELECTRONICS. see *ELECTRONICS*

535.58   US   ISSN 1041-1135
     CODEN: IPTLEL
I E E E PHOTONICS TECHNOLOGY LETTERS. 1989. m. $211 to non-members. Institute of Electrical and Electronics Engineers, Inc., 345 E. 47th St., New York, NY 10017-2394. TEL 212-705-7900. FAX 212-705-7682. (Subscr. to: 445 Hoes Lane, Box 1331, Piscataway, NJ 08855-1331. TEL 908-562-3948) Ed. Paul Shumate. (also avail. in microform from UMI,EEE)
     —BLDSC shelfmark: 4363.013500.
     Description: Publishes original research relevant to photonics technology; laser and electrooptic technology, laser physics and systems, and photonic - lightwave components and applications.

535 621.38   UK   ISSN 0267-3932
TA1750   CODEN: IPJOEE
I E E PROCEEDINGS PART J: OPTOELECTRONICS. 1985. bi-m. Institution of Electrical Engineers, P.O. Box 96, Stevenage, Herts SG1 2SD, England. Ed. Bernard Dunkley. circ. 2,000. (also avail. in microfiche; back issues avail.) **Indexed:** A.S.& T.Ind., Br.Tech.Ind., Sci.Abstr.
     —BLDSC shelfmark: 4362.755520.
     Description: Covers lasers and quantum electronics as they relate to optics.

535 660   US
INDUSTRIAL LASER ANNUAL HANDBOOK. a. $148 (effective 1992). Springer-Verlag, Books Division, 175 Fifth Ave., New York, NY 10010. TEL 800-777-4643. (Subscr. to: Springer-Verlag, Orders Dept., 44 Hartz Way, Secaucus, NJ 07094) (Co-publisher: PennWell Publishing Co. (Westford)) Eds. M. Levitt, D. Belforte.

621.329   US
INDUSTRIAL LASER REVIEW. 1986. m. $210 (foreign $246)(effective 1992). PennWell Publishing Co. (Westford), One Technology Park Dr., Box 989, Westford, MA 01886-0989. TEL 508-692-0700. Ed. David Belforte.
     Description: Links users, manufacturers, and suppliers of industrial lasers. Coverage includes production-line laser news, actual applications, new systems and products, technical and economic analyses, market trends, and exclusive conference reports.

535   FR   ISSN 0758-5756
INFORM'OPTIQUE; revue de liaison bimestrielle entre les professionnels de l'optique. 1971. bi-m. 440 Fr. Societe Inform' Optique, 10 rue de Buci, 75006 Paris, France. FAX 46-33-95-92. Ed. Julien Uzzan. adv.; circ. 5,500.

535   US   ISSN 0020-0891
QC457   CODEN: INFPAD
INFRARED PHYSICS. 1961. bi-m. £345 (effective 1992). Pergamon Press, Inc., Journals Division, 660 White Plains Rd., Tarrytown, NY 10591-5153. TEL 914-524-9200. FAX 914-333-2444. (And: Headington Hill Hall, Oxford OX3 0BW, England. TEL 0865-794141) Ed. T.S. Moss. adv.; bk.rev.; illus.; index; circ. 1,400. (also avail. in microform from MIM,UMI; back issues avail.; reprint service avail. from UMI) **Indexed:** Cadscan, Chem.Abstr., Curr.Cont., Eng.Ind., Ind.Sci.Rev., INIS Atomind., Int.Aerosp.Abstr., Lead Abstr., Met.Abstr., Phys.Ber., Sci.Abstr., Sci.Cit.Ind., World Alum.Abstr., Zincscan.
     —BLDSC shelfmark: 4499.400000.
     Description: Covers detectors, solid state photoconductors, multi-element and image tubes, optical materials and systems, polarizers, filters, infrared properties of solids, liquids, and gases, and all types of lasers.
     Refereed Serial

INFRARED SOCIETY OF JAPAN. PROCEEDING. see *PHYSICS — Heat*

535 621.3   US
INTERNATIONAL CONFERENCE ON INFRARED AND MILLIMETER WAVES. CONFERENCE DIGEST. (Published by other organizations when held outside of U.S.) 1974. a. price varies. (I E E E, Microwave Theory and Techniques Society) Institute of Electrical and Electronics Engineers, Inc., 345 E. 47th St., New York, NY 10017-2394. TEL 212-705-7900. FAX 212-705-7682. (Subscr. to: 445 Hoes Lane, Box 1331, Piscataway, NJ 0885-1331) Ed. Kenneth J. Button.
     Former titles: International Conference on Infrared and Millimeter Waves and Their Applications. Conference Digest; International Conference on Submillimeter Waves and Their Applications. Conference Digest.
     Description: Discusses materials measurement and techniques, submillimeter waves, free electron lasers and gyrotron.

535.58   US   ISSN 0190-4132
TA1673   CODEN: PICLDV
INTERNATIONAL CONFERENCE ON LASERS. PROCEEDINGS. Variant title: Lasers (Year). 1979. a. $125. (Society for Optical & Quantum Electronics) S T S Press, Box 245, McLean, VA 22101. TEL 703-642-5835. FAX 703-642-5838. TELEX 892320. Eds. D.G. Harris, J. Herbelin. circ. 400 (controlled). **Indexed:** Chem.Abstr.
     —BLDSC shelfmark: 6844.715000.

535   US   ISSN 0195-9271
TA1570   CODEN: IJIWDO
INTERNATIONAL JOURNAL OF INFRARED AND MILLIMETER WAVES. 1980. m. $385 (foreign $450)(effective 1992). Plenum Publishing Corp., 233 Spring St., New York, NY 10013-1578. TEL 212-620-8000. FAX 212-463-0742. TELEX 23-421139. Ed. Kenneth J. Button. adv.; illus. (also avail. in microfilm from JSC; back issues avail.) **Indexed:** Chem.Abstr., Curr.Cont., Eng.Ind., Ind.Sci.Rev., INIS Atomind., Int.Aerosp.Abstr., Phys.Ber., Sci.Abstr., Sci.Cit.Ind.
     —BLDSC shelfmark: 4542.305000.
     Refereed Serial

535.84   NE   ISSN 0168-1176
QC454   CODEN: IJMPDN
INTERNATIONAL JOURNAL OF MASS SPECTROMETRY AND ION PROCESSES. (Text in English, French and German) 1968. 30/yr.(in 10 vols.; 3 nos./vol.). fl.3410 (effective 1992). Elsevier Science Publishers B.V., P.O. Box 211, 1000 AE Amsterdam, Netherlands. TEL 212-989-5800. FAX 020-5803598. TELEX 18582 ESPA NL. (Subscr. in U.S. and Canada to: Elsevier Science Publishing Co., Inc., Box 882, Madison Sq. Sta., New York, NY 10159. TEL 212-989-5800) Ed.Bd. adv.; bk.rev.; charts; index. (also avail. in microform from RPI) **Indexed:** Anal.Abstr., Biwk.Pap.Rad.Chem.& Photochem., Chem.Abstr., Curr.Cont., Deep Sea Res.& Oceanogr.Abstr., Excerp.Med., INSPEC, Int.Aerosp.Abstr., Mass Spectr.Bull., Phys.Ber., Sci.Abstr., Sci.Cit.Ind.
     —BLDSC shelfmark: 4542.335000.
     @**Formerly:** International Journal of Mass Spectrometry and Ion Physics (ISSN 0020-7381)
     Description: Contains papers dealing with fundamental aspects of mass spectrometry and ion processes, and the application of mass spectrometric techniques to specific problems in chemistry and physics.
     Refereed Serial

535   SI   ISSN 0218-1991
QC446.15
▼**INTERNATIONAL JOURNAL OF NONLINEAR OPTICAL PHYSICS.** (Text in English) 1991. q. $75 to individuals and developing countries; institutions $275. World Scientific Publishing Co. Pte. Ltd., Farrer Rd., P.O. Box 128, Singapore 9128, Singapore. TEL 3825663. FAX 3825919. TELEX RS 28561 WSPC. (UK addr.: 73 Lynton Mead, Totteridge, London N20 8DH, England. TEL 44-81-4462461; US addr.: 1060 Main St., Ste. 1B, River Edge, NJ 07661. TEL 800-227-7562) Ed. Iam-Choon Khoo.
     —BLDSC shelfmark: 4542.395000.
     Description: Covers research and development in nonlinear interactions of light with matter, including fundamental nonlinear optical processes, novel nonlinear material properties, guided waves and solitons, intense field phenomena, and their applications in laser and coherent lightwave amplification, guiding, switching, modulation, communication and information processing.

INTERNATIONAL JOURNAL OF OPTICAL COMPUTING. see *COMPUTERS*

535   UK   ISSN 0952-5432
TA1750   CODEN: IJOOEV
INTERNATIONAL JOURNAL OF OPTOELECTRONICS. bi-m. £170($295) to institutions. Taylor & Francis Ltd., Rankine Rd., Basingstoke, Hants RG24 0PR, London, England. TEL 0256-840366. FAX 0256-479438. TELEX 858540. Ed. B. Culshaw.
     —BLDSC shelfmark: 4542.429300.
     Formerly: International Journal of Optical Sensors.
     Description: Information on optical fibers and optical sensors. Covers detectors, transmission systems, attenuators, amplifiers, couplers, and frequency and mode changers.
     Refereed Serial

535   US   ISSN 0731-2911
QC495
INTER-SOCIETY COLOR COUNCIL NEWS. 1933. bi-m. membership. Inter-Society Color Council, c/o Danny C. Rich, Sec., Datacolor Int'l, 5 Princess Rd., Lawrenceville, NJ 08648. TEL 609-895-7427. FAX 609-895-7461. (Edit. addr.: 98 Grandview Dr., Fairport, NY 14450. 27 92024. TEL 716-223-1823) Ed. Michael A. Hammel. bk.rev.; film rev.; charts; illus.; pat.; stat.; index; circ. 1,000. (processed) **Indexed:** Graph.Arts Lit.Abstr.
     Formerly: Inter-Society Color Council Newsletter (ISSN 0300-7588)

535 681.1   GW   ISSN 0075-272X
Q185
JAHRBUCH FUER OPTIK UND FEINMECHANIK. 1954. a. DM.52. Fachverlag Schiele und Schoen GmbH, Markgrafenstr. 11, 1000 Berlin 61, Germany. TEL 030-2516029. FAX 030-2517248. TELEX 181470-SUNDS-D. Ed. Horst Zarm. adv.; circ. 5,000.

JEMNA MECHANIKA A OPTIKA/FINE MECHANICS AND OPTICS. see *PHYSICS — Mechanics*

PHYSICS — OPTICS

535.84 544.6   US   ISSN 0021-9037
QD95   CODEN: JASYAP
JOURNAL OF APPLIED SPECTROSCOPY. English translation of: Zhurnal Prikladnoi Spektroskopii. 1965. m. (2 vols./yr.) $1140 (foreign $1335)(effective 1992). Plenum Publishing Corp., Consultants Bureau, 233 Spring St., New York, NY 10013-1578. TEL 212-620-8468. FAX 212-463-0742. TELEX 23-421139. Ed. V.S. Burakov. (also avail. in microfilm from JSC; back issues avail.) **Indexed:** Appl.Mech.Rev., Chem.Titles, Eng.Ind., INIS Atomind., Phys.Ber., Sci.Res.Abstr., Solid St.Abstr.
—BLDSC shelfmark: 0414.200000.
Refereed Serial

535.84   NE   ISSN 0368-2048
QC454.E4   CODEN: JESRAW
JOURNAL OF ELECTRON SPECTROSCOPY AND RELATED PHENOMENA; an international journal devoted to all aspects of electron spectroscopy - including theoretical studies and other spectroscopic measurements of relevance to the field of electron spectroscopy. (Text in English, French and German) 1972. 12/yr.(in 3 vols.; 4 nos./vol.). fl.1023 (effective 1992). Elsevier Science Publishers B.V., P.O. Box 211, 1000 AE Amsterdam, Netherlands. TEL 020-5803911. FAX 020-5803598. TELEX 18582 ESPA NL. (Subscr. in U.S. and Canada to: Elsevier Science Publishing Co., Inc., Box 882, Madison Sq. Sta. New York, NY 10159. TEL 212-989-5800) Ed.Bd. adv.; bk.rev.; charts; illus.; index. (also avail. in microform from RPI) **Indexed:** Chem.Abstr., Curr.Cont., Ind.Sci.Rev., INIS Atomind., Mass Spectr.Bull., Phys.Ber., Sci.Abstr., Sci.Cit.Ind.
—BLDSC shelfmark: 4974.900000.
Refereed Serial

535.84   US
▼**JOURNAL OF ELECTRONIC IMAGING.** 1992. q. $60 to individual non-members (foreign $80); institutions $100 (foreign $120). S P I E - the International Society for Optical Engineering, Box 10, Bellingham, WA 98227. TEL 206-676-3290. (Co-sponsor: I S & T - Society for Imaging Science and Technology) Ed. Paul G. Roetling.

621.329   US   ISSN 1042-346X
TA1671   CODEN: JLAPEN
JOURNAL OF LASER APPLICATIONS. 1976. 3/yr. $60 (foreign $85). Laser Institute of America, 12424 Research Pkwy., Ste.130, Orlando, FL 32826-3274. TEL 800-345-2737. FAX 419-380-5588. Ed. Sidney S. Charschan. adv.; bk.rev.; abstr.; bibl.; charts; illus.; index; circ. 5,000. (back issues avail.)
—BLDSC shelfmark: 5010.103000.
Formerly (until 1988): Topics of Laser Applications.
Description: Technical publication of basic and applied papers dealing with the diverse applications of laser-electro-optics.
Refereed Serial

535   JA   ISSN 0387-8805
    CODEN: JLEVDQ
JOURNAL OF LIGHT & VISUAL ENVIRONMENT. (Text in English) 1977. s-a. 3600 Yen. Illuminating Engineering Institute of Japan - Shomei Gakkai, 1-7-1 Yurako-cho, 1-chome, Chiyoda-ku, Tokyo 100, Japan. Ed. Yasuyuki Otani. **Indexed:** Chem.Abstr., Phys.Abstr.

535   US   ISSN 0733-8724
TA1501   CODEN: JLTEDG
JOURNAL OF LIGHTWAVE TECHNOLOGY. 1983. m. $350 to non-members. Institute of Electrical and Electronics Engineers, Inc., 345 E. 47th St., New York, NY 10017-2394. TEL 212-705-7366. FAX 212-705-7682. (Subscr. to: Box 1331, 445 Hoes Lane, Piscataway, NJ 08855-1331. TEL 908-562-3948) (Co-publisher: Optical Society of America) Ed. Donald Keck. (also avail. in microform from UMI) **Indexed:** ASCA, CAD CAM Abstr., Chem.Abstr., Ind.Sci.Rev., INIS Atomind., Int.Aerosp.Abstr., Sci.Cit.Ind., Tel.Abstr.
—BLDSC shelfmark: 5010.474000.
Description: Original papers reporting theoretical and-or experimental results which advance the technological base of guided-wave technology.
Refereed Serial

535   NE   ISSN 0022-2313
QC476.4   CODEN: JLUMA8
JOURNAL OF LUMINESCENCE; an interdisciplinary journal of research on excited state processes in condensed matter. (Text in English, French, German; summaries in English) 1970. 18/yr.(in 3 vols.; 6 nos./vol.). fl.1308 (effective 1992). North-Holland (Subsidiary of: Elsevier Science Publishers B.V.), P.O. Box 211, 1000 AE Amsterdam, Netherlands. TEL 020-5803911. FAX 020-5803598. TELEX 18582 ESPA NL. (Subscr. in U.S. and Canada to: Elsevier Science Publishing Co., Inc., Box 882, Madison Sq. Sta., New York, NY 10159. TEL 212-989-5800) Ed. R.S. Meltzer. adv.; bk.rev.; bibl.; charts; illus.; index, cum.index. (also avail. in microform from RPI; back issues avail.) **Indexed:** Biol.Abstr., Biwk.Pap.Rad.Chem.& Photochem., Cadscan, Chem.Abstr., Curr.Cont., Eng.Ind., GeoRef., Ind.Sci.Rev., INIS Atomind., INSPEC, Lead Abstr., Phys.Ber., Sci.Abstr., Sci.Cit.Ind., Zincscan.
—BLDSC shelfmark: 5010.650000.
Description: Provides a means of communication between scientists in different disciplines who share a common interest in the electronic excited state of molecular, ionic and covalent system, whether crystalline, amorphous, or liquid.
Refereed Serial

535   UK   ISSN 0950-0340
QC350   CODEN: JMOPEW
JOURNAL OF MODERN OPTICS. 1954. m. £588($1034) Taylor & Francis Ltd., Rankine Rd., Basingstoke, Hants. RG24 0PR, England. TEL 0256-840366. FAX 0256-479438. TELEX 858540. Ed. P.L. Knight. adv.; bk.rev.; illus.; index. (also avail. in microform from MIM) **Indexed:** Chem.Abstr., Curr.Cont., Excerp.Med., Ind.Med., Math.R., Phys.Ber., Sci.Abstr.
—BLDSC shelfmark: 5020.686000.
Formerly: Optica Acta: International Journal of Optics (ISSN 0030-3909)
Description: Aims to cover both the fundamental and applied aspects of contemporary research world-wide on such topics as: nonlinear and quantum optics; laser physics, coherence and speckle; optical fibres and thin films; integrated optics and electro-optics; optical design and testing.
Refereed Serial

535.84 544.6   US   ISSN 0022-2852
QC451   CODEN: JMOSA3
JOURNAL OF MOLECULAR SPECTROSCOPY. 1957. m. $942 (foreign $1097). Academic Press, Inc., Journal Division, 1250 Sixth Ave., San Diego, CA 92101. TEL 619-230-1840. FAX 619-699-6800. TELEX 181726. Ed. K. Narahari Rao. adv.; bibl.; charts; illus.; index. (back issues avail.) **Indexed:** Abstr.Bull.Inst.Pap.Chem., Biol.Abstr., Bull.Thermodyn.& Thermochem., Chem.Abstr., Chem.Infd., Curr.Adv.Ecol.Sci., Curr.Cont., Ind.Sci.Rev., INIS Atomind., Int.Aerosp.Abstr., Phys.Ber., Sci.Abstr., Sci.Cit.Ind.
—BLDSC shelfmark: 5020.750000.
Description: Presents experimental and theoretical articles on all subjects relevant to molecular spectroscopy and its modern applications.
Refereed Serial

535   FR   ISSN 0150-536X
QC350   CODEN: JOOPDB
JOURNAL OF OPTICS/NOUVELLE REVUE D'OPTIQUE. (Text in English, French; summaries in English, French, German) 1970. bi-m. 640 F. (foreign 830 F.). E S I Publications, 5 et 7, rue Laromiguiere, 75005 Paris, France. TEL 1-46-34-21-60. FAX 1-45-87-29-99. TELEX 202 671 F. Ed. P. Bouchareine. adv.; bk.rev.; circ. 750. (reprint service avail. from ISI) **Indexed:** Chem.Abstr., Curr.Cont., Excerp.Med., Fluidex, GeoRef., INIS Atomind., Sci.Abstr.
—BLDSC shelfmark: 5026.365000.
Former titles (1973-1976): Nouvelle Revue d'Optique (ISSN 0335-7368); **(1970-1972):** Nouvelle Revue d'Optique Appliquee (ISSN 0029-4780)

535   II   ISSN 0970-0374
JOURNAL OF OPTICS. (Text in English) 1972. q. Rs.100($50) Optical Society of India, c/o Dept. of Applied Physics, University of Calcutta, 92 Acharya Prafulla Chandra Rd., Calcutta 700 009, India. Ed. A.K. Ghosh. adv.; bk.rev.; index; circ. 350. (also avail. in microform from UMI; back issues avail. from UMI) **Indexed:** CAD CAM Abstr., Chem.Abstr., Curr.Cont., Ind.Sci.Rev., Int.Aerosp.Abstr., Sci.Abstr.

535.84   US   ISSN 0022-4073
QC451   CODEN: JQSRAE
JOURNAL OF QUANTITATIVE SPECTROSCOPY AND RADIATIVE TRANSFER. (Text in English, French, German or Russian) 1961. 12/yr (in 2 vols.). £635 (effective 1992). Pergamon Press, Inc., Journals Division, 660 White Plains Rd., Tarrytown, NY 10591-5153. TEL 914-524-9200. FAX 914-333-2444. (And: Headington Hill Hall, Oxford OX3 0BW, England. TEL 0865-794141) Ed. S.S. Penner. adv.; bk.rev.; charts; illus.; index; circ. 1,200. (also avail. in microform from MIM,UMI; back issues avail.) **Indexed:** Appl.Mech.Rev., Biol.Abstr., Cadscan, Chem.Abstr., Curr.Cont., Excerp.Med., Ind.Sci.Rev., INIS Atomind., Int.Aerosp.Abstr., Lead Abstr., Mass Spectr.Bull., Phys.Ber., Sci.Abstr., Zincscan.
—BLDSC shelfmark: 5043.700000.
Description: Covers spectral line shapes and widths, quantitative spectroscopic techniques for environmental studies, radiant energy emissions for plasmas and spectroscopic studies involving lasers.
Refereed Serial

535 770 791.4   HU   ISSN 0023-0480
TR845   CODEN: KEHTAS
KEP- ES HANGTECHNIKA. (Text in Hungarian; summaries in English, German and Russian) 1955. bi-m. $26. (Optikai, Akusztikai es Filmtechnikai Egyesulet) Lapkiado Vallalat, Lenin korut 9-11, 1073 Budapest 7, Hungary. TEL 222-408. (Subscr. to: Kultura, Box 149, H-1389 Budapest, Hungary) adv.; charts; illus.; circ. 900. **Indexed:** Photo.Abstr., Sci.Abstr.

KEY ABSTRACTS - OPTOELECTRONICS. see *PHYSICS — Abstracting, Bibliographies, Statistics*

L D & A. (Lighting Design & Application) see *ENGINEERING — Electrical Engineering*

535   UK   ISSN 0263-0346
QC689.5.L37   CODEN: LPBEDA
LASER AND PARTICLE BEAMS; pulse power & high energy densities. 1983. q. $226. Cambridge University Press, Edinburgh Bldg., Shaftesbury Rd., Cambridge CB2 2RU, England. TEL 0223-312393. FAX 0223-315052. TELEX 851817256. (N. American orders to: Cambridge University Press, 40 W. 20th St., New York, NY 10011) Eds. Heinrich Hora, George Miley. adv.; bk.rev. (reprint service avail. from SWZ) **Indexed:** Chem.Abstr., Curr.Cont., Energy Info.Abstr., INIS Atomind., Phys.Ber., Sci.Cit.Ind.
—BLDSC shelfmark: 5156.518800.
Description: Forum for physicists and engineers to pool the findings of their research on generation of high intensity beams of lasers and particle beams, and their interaction with matter.

LASER AND TECHNOLOGY; clinical and experimental. see *MEDICAL SCIENCES — Experimental Medicine, Laboratory Technique*

535.58 621.329   IT
▼**LASER APPLICAZIONI INDUSTRIALI, TECNOLOGIE, MERCATI.** 1991. 6/yr. L.30000 (foreign L.60000). Gruppo Editoriale Jackson S.p.A., Via Pola 9, 20124 Milan, Italy. TEL 39-2-69481. FAX 39-2-6948238. TELEX 316213 GEJIT 1. Ed. Giuseppe Grassi. adv.; circ. 6,000 (controlled).
Description: Covers all aspects of industrial usage, application and technology of lasers.

535.58   US   ISSN 0278-6273
QD701   CODEN: LSCHDB
LASER CHEMISTRY; a multinational journal. 4/yr. (in 1 vol., 4 nos./vol.). $177. Harwood Academic Publishers, 270 Eighth Ave., New York, NY 10011. TEL 212-206-8900. FAX 212-645-2459. TELEX 236735 GOPUB UR. (Subscr. to: Box 786, Cooper Sta., New York, NY 10276. TEL 800-545-8398; UK subscr. to: P.O. Box 90, Reading, Berkshire RG1 8JL, England. TEL 0734-560-080) Ed. R. Vetter. adv. (also avail. in microform) **Indexed:** Chem.Abstr., Mass Spectr.Bull., Sci.Abstr.
—BLDSC shelfmark: 5156.527000.
Refereed Serial

PHYSICS — OPTICS

535.58 621.329 US ISSN 1043-8092
TA1501 CODEN: LFWOE8
LASER FOCUS WORLD; the magazine of electro-optics technology. 1965. m. $90 (foreign $145). PennWell Publishing Co. (Westford), One Technology Park Dr., Box 989, Westford, MA 01886-0989. TEL 508-692-0525. Ed. Jeffrey N. Bairstow. adv.; circ. 54,000. (also avail. in microform from UMI) **Indexed**: A.S.& T.Ind., Abstr.Bull.Inst.Pap.Chem., CAD CAM Abstr., Chem.Abstr., Curr.Cont., Eng.Ind., INIS Atomind., Robomat., Sci.Abstr.
—BLDSC shelfmark: 5156.530620.
Former titles: Laser Focus (ISSN 8755-1853); Laser Focus Including Electro-Optics Magazine (ISSN 0740-2511); (1981-1983): Laser Focus with Fiberoptic Technology (ISSN 0275-1399); (until vol.17, no.3, 1981): Laser Focus with Fiberoptic Communications (ISSN 0190-1451); (until vol.14, 1978): Laser Focus (ISSN 0023-8589) Incorporates (1969-1983): Electro-Optics (ISSN 0745-5003); Which was formerly titled: Electro-Optical Systems Design (ISSN 0424-8457).
Description: Covers basic electro-optical devices and systems for OEM design engineers, technical managers, scientists, and researchers.

535 658.8 US
LASER FOCUS WORLD BUYERS' GUIDE. 1966. a. $85 (foreign $110). PennWell Publishing Co. (Westford), One Technology Park Dr., Box 991, Westford, MA 01886-0991. TEL 508-692-0525. adv.; circ. 41,000.
Former titles: Laser Focus - Electro Optics Buyers' Guide (ISSN 8755-1616); Laser Focus Buyers' Guide (ISSN 0075-8027); (until 1970): Laser Marketers' and Buyers' Guide.

535.58 US ISSN 1054-660X
CODEN: LAPHEJ
▼**LASER PHYSICS (SOVIET)**; the new international journal covering theoretical and experimental laser research and application. (English translation of Soviet title) 1991. bi-m. $140 to individuals (outside N. America $155); institutions $330 (outside N. America $345). (U S S R Academy of Sciences, Institute of General Physics, UR) New Soviet Sciences Press (USA), c/o Allen Press, Inc., Dist., Box 1897, Lawrence, KS 66044-8897. TEL 913-843-1235. FAX 913-843-1274. Ed. Alexander M. Prokhorov.
—BLDSC shelfmark: 5156.606000.
Description: Covers the whole range of questions of modern laser physics and quantum electronics, emphasizing physical effects in various media (solid, gaseous, liquid) leading to the generation of laser radiation.

535.58 621.329 US ISSN 0023-8600
LASER REPORT; the market outlook in lasers and opto-electronics. 1965. 24/yr. $295 (foreign $325). PennWell Publishing Co. (Westford), One Technology Park Dr., Box 989, Westford, MA 01886-0989. TEL 508-692-0700. Ed. David Kales. circ. 400. **Indexed**: PROMT.
Formerly: Laser Focus Mid-Month Report.
Description: Covers business news and market trends in laser equipment and systems.

535.58 US
LASER SCIENCE AND TECHNOLOGY. irreg. Harwood Academic Publishers, 270 Eighth Ave., New York, NY 10011. TEL 212-206-8900. FAX 212-645-2459. TELEX 236735 GOPUB UR. (Subscr. to: Box 786, Cooper Sta., New York, NY 10276. TEL 800-545-8398; UK subscr. to: Box 90, Reading, Berkshire RG1 8JL, England. TEL 0734-560-080) Ed. V.S. Letokhov. (also avail. in microform)
Refereed Serial

535.58 621.329 GW ISSN 0722-9003
TA1671 CODEN: LAOPD3
LASER UND OPTOELEKTRONIK. (Text in German; contents page in English) 1969. 6/yr. DM.166. A T Fachverlag GmbH, Postfach 500180, 7000 Stuttgart 50, Germany. TEL 0711-527041. FAX 0711-5281539. Ed. Uwe Brinkmann. circ. 5,000. **Indexed**: INIS Atomind., Sci.Abstr.
—BLDSC shelfmark: 5156.656000.
Former titles: Laser und Elektro-Optik; Laser (ISSN 0023-8554).

535.58 537.5 US ISSN 0733-303X
TA1671
LASERS & OPTRONICS. 1982. m. $55. Gordon Publications, Inc., 301 Gibraltar Dr., Morris Plains, NJ 07950-0650. TEL 201-292-5100. FAX 201-898-9281. Ed. Robert Clark. adv.; bk.rev.; charts; illus.; pat.; index; circ. 60,000. (tabloid format; also avail. in microform from UMI; back issues avail.) **Indexed**: Met.Abstr., Sci.Abstr., World Alum.Abstr.
Formerly: Laser and Applications.
Refereed Serial

621.329 US ISSN 0898-1507
CODEN: LAENEG
▼**LASERS IN ENGINEERING**. 1991. 4/yr. $109. Gordon and Breach Scientific Publishers, 270 Eighth Ave., New York, NY 10011. TEL 212-206-8900. FAX 212-645-2459. TELEX 236735 GOPUB UR. (Subscr. to: Box 786, Cooper Sta., New York, NY 10276. TEL 800-545-8398; UK subscr. to: P.O. Box 90, Reading, Berkshire RG1 8JL, England. TEL 0734-560-080) Ed. B.L. Mordike. (also avail. in microform)
—BLDSC shelfmark: 5156.674000.
Description: Publishes research and reviews on the use of lasers in sensors or measuring devices and as integral parts of production assemblies.
Refereed Serial

LASERS IN MEDICAL SCIENCE. see *MEDICAL SCIENCES*

LASERS IN SURGERY AND MEDICINE. see *MEDICAL SCIENCES — Surgery*

535 574 US ISSN 0886-0467
CODEN: LLSCES
LASERS IN THE LIFE SCIENCES. 1986. 4/yr. (in 1 vol., 4 nos./vol.) $111. Harwood Academic Publishers, 270 Eighth Ave., New York. TEL 212-206-8900. FAX 212-645-2459. TELEX 236735 GOPUB UR. (Subscr. to: Box 786, Cooper Sta., New York, NY 10276. TEL 800-545-8398; UK subscr. to: P.O. Box 90, Reading, Berkshire RG1 8JL, England. TEL 0734-560-080) Ed. Myron Wolbarsht. (also avail. in microform)
—BLDSC shelfmark: 5156.680500.
Refereed Serial

535 IT
▼**LIGHT DESIGN AND TECHNOLOGY**. 1990. 6/yr. L.24000 (foreign L.48000). Gruppo Editoriale Jackson S.p.A., Via Pola 9, 20124 Milan, Italy. TEL 39-2-69481. FAX 39-2-6948238. TELEX 316213 GEJIT 1. Ed. Pierantonio Palerma. adv.; circ. 14,500 (controlled).
Description: Covers all technical aspects of lighting applications, new products and new designs.

LITHUANIAN PHYSICS JOURNAL. see *PHYSICS*

LITOVSKII FIZICHESKII SBORNIK/LIETUVOS FIZIKOS RINKINYS. see *PHYSICS*

LYS; miljoe-design-teknik. see *ENGINEERING — Electrical Engineering*

535.84 US ISSN 0277-7037
QC454.M3 CODEN: MSRVD3
MASS SPECTROMETRY REVIEWS. 1982. bi-m. $280 to institutions (foreign $355). John Wiley & Sons, Inc., Journals, 605 Third Ave., New York, NY 10158-0012. TEL 212-850-6000. FAX 212-850-6088. TELEX 12-7063. Ed. Maurice M. Bursey. circ. 500. (back issues avail.) **Indexed**: AESIS, Biol.Abstr., Chem.Abstr., Ind.Sci.Rev., Mass Spectr.Bull., Sci.Cit.Ind.
—BLDSC shelfmark: 5388.250000.
Description: Current research on mass spectrometry instrumentation and application in chemistry, biology, environmental science, medicine, agriculture, engineering and physics.
Refereed Serial

535.58 610 US
MEDICAL LASER INDUSTRIAL REPORT. (Supplement avail.: Buyers' Guide) 1986. 12/yr. $295 (foreign $325)(effective 1992). PennWell Publishing Co. (Westford), One Technology Park Dr., Box 989, Westford, MA 01886-0989. Ed. Michael Moretti. circ. 700.
Description: Features news and reports about trends and developments in the medical laser business. Includes information on new technologies, market opportunites, product trends, and relevant FDA decisions.

535.38 FR
MEMOIRES OPTIQUES. 1982. m. 1300 F. Micro Journal, 11 rue de Provence, 75009 Paris, France. Ed. Jean-Jacques Maleval. bk.rev.; circ. 500. **Indexed**: Info.Media & Tech.

578 537.534 FR
QH212.E4 CODEN: JMSEDI
MICROSCOPY MICROANALYSIS MICROSTRUCURES. (Text in English, French, German) 1976. bi-m. 1200 F. (foreign 1450 F.). Societe Francaise de Microscopie Electronique, 67 rue Maurice-Gunsbourg, 94200 Ivry-sur-Seine, France. TEL 46-70-28-44. FAX 46-70-88-46. (Subscr. to: Les Editions de Physique, Av. du Hoggar, Zone Industrielle de Courtaboeuf, B.P. 112, 91944 Les Ulis Cedex, France.) (Co-sponsor: Centre National de la Recherche Scientifique) Ed. Michel Froment. adv.; bk.rev.; abstr.; bibl.; charts; illus.; index; circ. 500. **Indexed**: Biol.Abstr., Chem.Abstr., Ind.Sci.Rev., INIS Atomind., Met.Abstr., Sci.Abstr., Sci.Cit.Ind., World Alum.Abstr.
Formerly (until 1989): Journal de Microscopie et de Spectroscopie Electroniques (ISSN 0395-9279); Supersedes in part: Journal de Microscopie (ISSN 0021-7921)
Description: Presents original manuscripts dealing with developments in all aspects of microscopy and microanalysis and with their use in materials science.

535 US ISSN 1058-7268
MOLECULAR CRYSTALS AND LIQUID CRYSTALS SCIENCE AND TECHNOLOGY. SECTION B: NONLINEAR OPTICS. 1966. 8/yr. (in 2 vols., 4 nos./vol.) $111 (Sections A-D $268). Gordon and Breach Science Publishers, 270 Eighth Ave., New York, NY 10011. TEL 212-206-8900. FAX 212-645-2459. TELEX 236735 GOPUB UR. (Subscr. to: Box 786, Cooper Sta., New York, NY 10276. TEL 800-545-8398; UK subscr. to: P.O. Box 90, Reading, Berkshire RG1 8JL, England. TEL 0734-560-080) Ed. M.M. Labes. (also avail. in microform)
Supersedes in part (in 1991): Molecular Crystals and Liquid Crystals Incorporating Nonlinear Optics (ISSN 1044-1859); Which was formerly (until 1987): Molecular Crystals and Liquid Crystals (ISSN 0026-8941); Incorporates (in 1982): Nonlinear Optics; Formerly (until 1969): Molecular Crystals (ISSN 0369-1152)
Description: Covers four main areas of the development of applications of nonlinear optical materials to practical devices: principles, materials, phenomena and devices.
Refereed Serial

535 US ISSN 1058-7284
CODEN: DIMTD7
MOLECULAR CRYSTALS AND LIQUID CRYSTALS SCIENCE AND TECHNOLOGY. SECTION D: DISPLAY AND IMAGING. 1985. 6/yr. (in 1 vol., 6 nos./vol.). $175 (Sections A-D $268). Gordon & Breach Science Publishers, 270 Eighth Ave., New York, NY 10011. TEL 212-206-8900. FAX 212-645-2459. TELEX 236735 GOPUB UR. (Subscr. to: Box 786, Cooper Sta., New York, NY 10276. TEL 800-545-8398; UK subscr. to: P.O. Box 90, Reading, Berkshire RG1 8JL, England. TEL 0734-560-080) Ed. M.M. Labes. (also avail. in microform)
Formerly (until 1991): Display and Imaging Technology (ISSN 0733-2386)
Refereed Serial

535.58 US
MUSEUM OF HOLOGRAPHY. DIRECTORY & BUYERS' GUIDE. 1979. irreg. Museum of Holography, Information Services, 11 Mercer St., New York, NY 10013. TEL 212-334-8039. Eds. M. Tanko, S. Bains. adv.
Formerly: Holography Directory.

PHYSICS — OPTICS

331 US ISSN 1048-6879
TA1501
O E REPORTS. (Optical Engineering) 1984. m. $25 in N. America; elsewhere $35. S P I E - the International Society for Optical Engineering, 1000 20th St., Box 10, Bellingham, WA 98227-0010. TEL 206-676-3290. FAX 206-647-1445. TELEX 46-7053. Ed. Robert E. Fischer. adv.; circ. 30,000. (tabloid format)
Formerly: S P I E Optical Engineering Reports (ISSN 0741-5931)
Description: Contains technical articles, and interviews with recognized industry leaders in optical and optoelectronic applied science and engineering, as well as industry news, technology advances, upcoming symposia, new publications and a comprehensive employment section.

535 600 011 US
O S A ANNUAL MEETING DIGEST. a. $75. Optical Society of America, Inc., 2010 Massachusetts Ave., N.W., Washington, DC 20036. TEL 202-223-8130. FAX 202-223-1096.
Formerly: O S A Annual Meeting Proceedings.

535 PL ISSN 0078-5466
QC350 CODEN: OPAPBZ
OPTICA APPLICATA. (Text in English; summaries in Russian) 1971. q. $100. Politechnika Wroclawska, Wybrzeze Wyspianskiego 27, 50-370 Wroclaw, Poland. FAX 22-36-64. TELEX 712559 PWRPL. (Dist. by: Ars Polona-Ruch, Krakowskie Przedmiescie 7, Warsaw, Poland) Ed. Miron Gaj. circ. 350.
Indexed: Cadscan, Chem.Abstr., Lead Abstr., Phys.Abstr., Phys.Ber., Sci.Abstr., Zincscan.
—BLDSC shelfmark: 6273.050000.
Description: Papers on diffraction theory, quantum optics, holography, scientific photography and technology of manufacturing optical elements.

535 SP ISSN 0030-3917
QC350 CODEN: OPAPAY
OPTICA PURA Y APLICADA. (Text in English, French, Spanish; summaries in English, Spanish) 1968. 3/yr. 3500 ptas.($35) (effective 1992). Instituto de Optica "Daza de Valdes", Serrano 121, 28006 Madrid, Spain. TEL 91-2616800.
FAX 91-5645557. TELEX 42182. Ed. Antonio Corrons. adv.; bk.rev.; adv.; index, cum.index; circ. 1,000. (also avail. in microfilm; back issues avail.) **Indexed:** Art & Archaeol.Tech.Abstr., Chem.Abstr., Ind.SST, Phys.Ber., Sci.Abstr.

535 534 US
▼**OPTICAL AND ACOUSTICAL REVIEW.** 1990. q. $265. Nova Science Publishers, Inc., 283 Commack Rd., Ste. 300, Commack, NY 11725-3401. TEL 516-499-3103.

535 US ISSN 0091-3286
TR692.5 CODEN: OPEGAR
OPTICAL ENGINEERING. 1962. m. $150 (foreign $185). S P I E - the International Society for Optical Engineering, Box 10, 1000 20th St., Bellingham, WA 98227-0010. TEL 206-676-3290.
FAX 206-647-1445. TELEX 46-7053. Ed. Lorretta Palagi. adv.; bk.rev.; adv.; charts; illus.; tr.lit.; index, cum.index: vols.1-23 in 1985; circ. 12,900. **Indexed:** A.S.& T.Ind., Chem.Abstr., Curr.Cont., Eng.Ind., Excerp.Med., Int.Aerosp.Abstr., Phys.Ber., Risk Abstr., Sci.Abstr., Sci.Cit.Ind.
—BLDSC shelfmark: 6273.180000.
Formerly: S P I E Journal (ISSN 0036-1860)
Description: Covers engineering, design, production and applications of optical, electro-optical, fiberoptic, laser as well as photographic components and systems.

535 US
OPTICAL ENGINEERING SERIES. 1982. irreg., vol.31, 1991. price varies. Marcel Dekker, Inc., 270 Madison Ave., New York, NY 10016.
TEL 212-696-9000. FAX 212-685-4540. TELEX 421419.

535 NE ISSN 0925-3467
▼**OPTICAL MATERIALS.** 1991. 4/yr. fl.331 (effective 1992). North-Holland (Subsidiary of: Elsevier Science Publishers B.V.), P.O. Box 211, 1000 AE Amsterdam, Netherlands. TEL 020-5803911.
FAX 020-5803705. TELEX 18582 ESPA NL. (Subscr. in U.S. and Canada to: Elsevier Science Publishing Co., Inc., Box 882, Madison Sq. Sta., New York, NY 10159. TEL 212-989-5800) Ed. R.C. Powell.
—BLDSC shelfmark: 6273.328000.
Description: Publishes original papers and review articles on the design, synthesis, characterization and applications of optical materials; focuses on materials systems, optical phenomena in materials, and devices.
Refereed Serial

535 US ISSN 1045-6570
▼**OPTICAL MATERIALS AND ENGINEERING NEWS.**
1990. m. $305. Business Communications Co., Inc. (Norwalk), 25 Van Zant St., Norwalk, CT 06855. TEL 203-853-4266. FAX 203-853-0348. TELEX 6502934929 WUI. Ed. Richard Bryant.
●Also available online. Vendor(s): Data-Star, DIALOG, NewsNet.
Description: Provides information on who's doing what, developing technology, commercialization, business and economic trends, new applications, and contracts.

621.381 535 US
OPTICAL MEMORY REPORT.* a. $1995. Rothchild Consultants Inc., 2140 Shattuck Ave., Berkeley, CA 94704-1210.
Description: Covers all products and companies in the optical technology sector.
Refereed Serial

535 621 US ISSN 0078-5482
OPTICAL PHYSICS AND ENGINEERING. 1967. irreg., latest 1981. price varies. Plenum Publishing Corp., 233 Spring St., New York, NY 10013-1578. TEL 212-620-8000. FAX 212-463-0742. Ed. William L. Wolfe.
Refereed Serial

535 US ISSN 0740-3232
QC350 CODEN: JOAOD6
OPTICAL SOCIETY OF AMERICA. JOURNAL PART A.
1917. 12/yr. $350. Optical Society of America, Inc, 2010 Massachusetts Ave., N.W., Washington, DC 20036-1023. TEL 202-223-8130. Ed. B.E.A. Saleh. bk.rev.; bibl.; illus.; index; cum.index: vols.1-63, 1917-1973; circ. 9,782. (also avail. in microfiche; microform from MIM; back issues avail.) **Indexed:** A.S.& T.Ind., Abstr.Bull.Inst.Pap.Chem., Appl.Mech.Rev., Biol.Abstr., Br.Ceram.Abstr., C.P.I., Chem.Abstr, Curr.Cont., Deep Sea Res.& Oceanogr.Abstr., Eng.Ind., Ergon.Abstr., GeoRef, Graph.Arts Lit.Abstr., Ind.Med., INIS Atomind., Int.Aerosp.Abstr., Mass Spectr.Bull., Math.R., Met.Abstr., Meteor.& Geoastrophys.Abstr., Phys.Ber., Psychol.Abstr., Sci.Abstr.
—BLDSC shelfmark: 4837.010100.
Supersedes in part: Optical Society of America. Journal (ISSN 0030-3941)
Description: Basic research on optical phenomenon. Includes atmospheric, physiological and statistical optics; image processing; scattering and coherence theory, machine and color vision; design and diffraction.
Refereed Serial

535 US ISSN 0740-3224
QC392 CODEN: JOBPDE
OPTICAL SOCIETY OF AMERICA. JOURNAL PART B.
1917. 12/yr. $490. Optical Society of America, Inc., 2010 Massachusetts Ave., N.W., Washington, DC 20036-1023. TEL 202-223-8130. Ed. P.F. Liao. bk.rev.; bibl.; illus.; index; cum.index vols.1-63, 1917-1973; circ. 9,782. (also avail. in microfiche; microform from MIM; back issues avail.) **Indexed:** A.S.& T.Ind., Appl.Mech.Rev., Biol.Abstr., C.P.I., CAD CAM Abstr., Chem.Abstr., Curr.Cont., Deep Sea Res.& Oceanogr.Abstr., Eng.Ind., GeoRef., Graph.Arts Lit.Abstr., INIS Atomind., Mass Spectr.Bull., Math.R., Met.Abstr., Meteor.& Geoastrophys.Abstr., Phys.Ber., Psychol.Abstr., Sci.Abstr.
—BLDSC shelfmark: 4837.010110.
Supersedes in part: Optical Society of America. Journal (ISSN 0030-3941)
Refereed Serial

535.58 621.39 UK ISSN 0030-3992
QC350 CODEN: OLTCAS
OPTICS AND LASER TECHNOLOGY. 1968. bi-m. £170 (Europe £185). Butterworth - Heinemann Ltd. (Subsidiary of: Reed International PLC), Linacre House, Jordan Hill, Oxford OX2 8DP, England. TEL 0865-310366. FAX 0865-310898. TELEX 83111 BHPOXF G. (Subscr. to: Turpin Transactions Ltd., Distribution Center, Blackhorse Rd., Letchworth, Herts SG6 1HN, England. TEL 0462-672555) Ed. Marja Vukovojac. adv.; bk.rev.; charts; illus.; pat.; index. (also avail. in microform from UMI; back issues avail.) **Indexed:** Br.Tech.Ind., Chem.Abstr., Curr.Cont., Eng.Ind., Excerp.Med., Fluidex, ISMEC, Phys.Ber., Risk Abstr., Sci.Abstr., Sociol.Educ.Abstr.
—BLDSC shelfmark: 6273.440000.
Formerly: Optics Technology.
Refereed Serial

535.58 621.39 UK ISSN 0143-8166
CODEN: OLENDN
OPTICS AND LASERS IN ENGINEERING. 1980. 10/yr.(in 2 vols.). £269 (effective 1992). Elsevier Science Publishers Ltd., Crown House, Linton Rd., Barking, Essex IG11 8JU, England. TEL 081-594-7272. FAX 081-594-5942. TELEX 896950 APPSCI G. (Subscr. in U.S. and Canada to: Elsevier Science Publishing Co., Inc., Box 882, Madison Sq. Sta., New York, NY 10159. TEL 212-989-5800) Eds. F.-P. Chiang, G.T. Reid. adv.: B&W page #295; 140 x 200; adv. contact: Claire Coakley. bk.rev.; charts; illus.; index. (also avail. in microform from RPI; back issues avail.) **Indexed:** Appl.Mech.Rev., Curr.Cont., Eng.Ind., Int.Aerosp.Abstr., Met.Abstr., Photo.Abstr., Phys.Abstr., Phys.Ber., Sci.Abstr., Sci.Cit.Ind., World Alum.Abstr.
—BLDSC shelfmark: 6273.443000.
Description: Provides a forum for interchange of information on developments and applications of optical techniques and laser technology in engineering.
Refereed Serial

535 US ISSN 1047-6938
TA1501 CODEN: OPPHEL
OPTICS & PHOTONICS NEWS. 1975. m. $99. Optical Society of America, Inc., 2010 Massachusetts Ave. N.W., Washington, DC 20036. TEL 202-223-8130. Ed. Andrea Pendleton. circ. 13,000. **Indexed:** Abstr.Bull.Inst.Pap.Chem., Graph.Arts Lit.Abstr., Phys.Ber.
—BLDSC shelfmark: 6273.450000.
Formerly (until 1990): Optics News (ISSN 0098-907X)
Description: For scientists, engineers and business executives. Articles and papers on optics research and industry trends.

535.84 US ISSN 0030-400X
QC350 CODEN: OPSUA3
OPTICS AND SPECTROSCOPY. English translation of: Optika i Spektroskopiya (RU ISSN 0030-4034) 1959. m. $940 (foreign $958-$977). (Optical Society of America, Inc.) American Institute of Physics, 335 E. 45th St., New York, NY 10017. TEL 212-661-9404. (And: Optical Society of America, 2010 Massachusetts Ave., N.W., Washington, DC 20036-1023. TEL 202-223-8130) Ed. P.R. Wakeling. bk.rev.; bibl.; charts; illus.; tr.lit.; s-a. index. (also avail. in microform; back issues avail.) **Indexed:** Abstr.Bull.Inst.Pap.Chem., Appl.Mech.Rev., Br.Ceram.Abstr., C.P.I., Curr.Cont., Eng.Ind., Gen.Phys.Adv.Abstr., Mass Spectr.Bull., Met.Abstr., Phys.Ber., Sci.Abstr.
—BLDSC shelfmark: 0416.650000.
Description: Soviet research in optical phenomena ranging from molecular and atomic spectroscopy of gases through solid-state phenomena to physical optics.
Refereed Serial

535 US ISSN 0078-5504
OPTICS AND SPECTROSCOPY. SUPPLEMENT. (English translation of Russian language editions) 1966. irreg., no.4, 1970. $25. (Optical Society of America, Inc.) American Institute of Physics, 335 E. 45th St., New York, NY 10017. TEL 212-661-9404. (And: Optical Society of America, 2010 Massachusetts Ave., N.W., Washington, DC 20036-1023. TEL 202-223-8130)

535 NE ISSN 0030-4018
QC350 CODEN: OPCOB8
OPTICS COMMUNICATIONS; a journal devoted to the rapid publication of contributions in the field of optics and interaction of light with matter. (Text in English, French, German; summaries in English) 1969. 48/yr.(in 8 vols.; 6 nos./vol.). fl.3008 (effective 1992). North-Holland (Subsidiary of: Elsevier Science Publishers B.V.), P.O. Box 211, 1000 AE Amsterdam, Netherlands. TEL 020-5803911. FAX 020-5803598. TELEX 18582 ESPA NL. (Subscr. in U.S. and Canada to: Elsevier Science Publishing Co., Inc., Box 882, Madison Sq. Sta., New York, NY 10159. TEL 212-989-5800) Ed. F. Abeles. adv.; illus.; index. (also avail. in microform from RPI; back issues avail.; reprint service avail. from SWZ) **Indexed:** CAD CAM Abstr., Chem.Abstr., Curr.Cont., Eng.Ind., Int.Aerosp.Abstr., Phys.Ber., Sci.Abstr.
—BLDSC shelfmark: 6273.600000.
Description: Covers all fields of fundamental research in optics, both theoretical and experimental.
Refereed Serial

535 US ISSN 0146-9592
QC350 CODEN: OPLEDP
OPTICS LETTERS. 1977. s-m. $485. Optical Society of America, Inc., 2010 Massachusetts Ave., N.W., Washington, DC 20036-1023. TEL 202-223-8130. Ed. P.W.E. Smith. (also avail. in microfiche; microfilm; back issues avail.) **Indexed:** Cadscan, Chem.Abstr., Curr.Cont., Excerp.Med., Graph.Arts Lit.Abstr., Int.Aerosp.Abstr., Lead Abstr., Phys.Ber., Sci.Abstr., Zincscan.
—BLDSC shelfmark: 6273.650000.
Description: Disseminates new, important results in all branches of optics research.

535 GW ISSN 0030-4026
QC350 CODEN: OTIKAJ
OPTIK; international journal for light and electron optics. (Text in English and German) 1946. m. (3 vols./yr.). DM.354 per vol. (Deutsche Gesellschaft fuer Elektronenmikroskopie e.V.) Wissenschaftliche Verlagsgesellschaft mbH, Postfach 105339, 7000 Stuttgart 10, Germany. TEL 0711-2582-0. FAX 0711-2582-290. TELEX 723636-DAZ-D. (Co-sponsor: Deutsche Gesellschaft fuer angewandte Optik e.V.) Ed. Theo Tschudi. adv.; bk.rev.; bibl.; illus.; index; circ. 1,200. **Indexed:** Chem.Abstr., Curr.Cont., Eng.Ind., Geo.Abstr., Math.R., Met.Abstr., Phys.Ber., Sci.Abstr.
—BLDSC shelfmark: 6274.000000.

535.84 RU ISSN 0030-4034
QC476.5 CODEN: OPSPAM
OPTIKA I SPEKTROSKOPIYA. English translation: Optics and Spectroscopy (US ISSN 0030-400X) 1956. m. 84.40 Rub. (Akademiya Nauk S.S.S.R., Leningradskoe Otdelenie) Izdatel'stvo Nauka, Fizmatlit, Leninskii prospekt, 15, 117071 Moscow, Russia. (Dist. by: Mezhdunarodnaya Kniga, ul. Dimitrova D.39, 113095 Moscow, Russia) Ed. P.P. Feofilov. charts; illus.; index, cum.index every 5 yrs.; circ. 2,600. (also avail. in microfiche from BHP) **Indexed:** Chem.Abstr., GeoRef., Sci.Abstr.
—BLDSC shelfmark: 0128.000000.

621.329 UK
OPTO & LASER PRODUCTS. m. Hanover Press Ltd., 80 Highgate Rd., London NW5 1PB, England. FAX 071-485-9030. circ. 15,000.

OPTO MAGAZINE. see *MEDICAL SCIENCES — Ophthalmology And Optometry*

535.58 621.329 IT
OPTOLASER; la prima rivista italiana di laser e fibre optica. 1988. q. L.43000($64) (effective 1991). Masson Italia Periodici, Via Statuto 2-4, 20120 Milan, Italy. TEL 02-6367-1. FAX 02-6367-211. circ. 3,000.

535 US ISSN 1044-1425
TS511.U6
PHOTONICS DIRECTORY. 1954. a. $100 (foreign $115). Laurin Publishing Co., Inc., Box 4949, Berkshire Common, Pittsfield, MA 01202-4949. TEL 413-499-0514. FAX 413-442-3180. adv. *Former titles:* Photonics Industry and Systems Purchasing Directory; Optical Industry and Systems Purchasing Directory (ISSN 0191-0647); *Supersedes* (1963-1978): Optical Industry and Systems Directory (ISSN 0078-5474)
Description: Four volume buyers' guide and reference for the photonics industry.

535 544.6 US ISSN 0731-1230
TS510 CODEN: PHSAD3
PHOTONICS SPECTRA. 1967. m. $85 (foreign $100). Laurin Publishing Co., Inc., Box 4949, Berkshire Common, Pittsfield, MA 01202-4949. TEL 413-499-0514. FAX 413-442-3180. index; circ. 81,100. **Indexed:** Appl.Mech.Rev., CAD CAM Abstr., Chem.Abstr., Curr.Cont., Eng.Ind., GeoRef., Graph.Arts Lit.Abstr., Met.Abstr., PROMT, Sci.Abstr., Tel.Abstr., World Alum.Abstr.
Formerly (until 1982): Optical Spectra (ISSN 0030-395X)
Description: Presents news and information of worldwide developments in the photonics industry.

PROGRESS IN NUCLEAR MAGNETIC RESONANCE SPECTROSCOPY. see *PHYSICS — Nuclear Physics*

535 NE ISSN 0079-6638
QC351 CODEN: POPTAN
PROGRESS IN OPTICS. 1961. irreg., vol.29, 1991. price varies. Elsevier Science Publishers B.V., Books Division, P.O. Box 211, 1000 AE Amsterdam, Netherlands. TEL 020-5803911. FAX 020-5803705. TELEX 18582 ESPA NL. (Subscr. in U.S. and Canada to: Elsevier Science Publishing Co., Inc., Box 882, Madison Sq. Sta., New York, NY 10159. TEL 212-989-5800) Ed. E. Wolf. index, cum.index: vols.1-15. **Indexed:** ASCA, Deep Sea Res.& Oceanogr.Abstr., Phys.Ber.
—BLDSC shelfmark: 6871.700000.
Refereed Serial

535 UK
QC446.15 CODEN: QUOPET
QUANTUM OPTICS: JOURNAL OF EUROPEAN OPTICAL SOCIETY, PART B. 1989. bi-m. £139($278) (effective 1992). (European Optical Society) I O P Publishing, Techno House, Redcliffe Way, Bristol BS1 6NX, England. TEL 0272 287481. FAX 0272-294318. TELEX 449149-INSTP-G. (U.S. addr.: American Institute of Physics, Subscr. Services, 500 Sunnyside Blvd., Woodbury, NY 11797-2999) Ed. E.R. Pike. (also avail. in microform; microfiche; back issues avail.)
Formerly: Quantum Optics (ISSN 0954-8998)
Description: Devoted to optical phenomena that require (for descriptive purposes) the quantum theory.

535.84 301.16 UK ISSN 0951-4198
QD96.M3 CODEN: RCMSEF
RAPID COMMUNICATIONS IN MASS SPECTROMETRY. 1987. m. $545 (effective 1992). John Wiley & Sons Ltd., Journals, Baffins Ln., Chichester, Sussex PO19 1UD, England. TEL 0243-779777. FAX 0243-775878. TELEX 86290 WIBOOK G. Ed. John H. Beynon. (reprint service avail. from SWZ)
—BLDSC shelfmark: 7254.440000.
Description: Preliminary accounts of recent research in mass spectrometry.

REFERATIVNYI ZHURNAL. VOLOKONNO-OPTICHESKIE SYSTEMY. see *PHYSICS — Abstracting, Bibliographies, Statistics*

S P S E. ANNUAL CONFERENCE. PAPER SUMMARIES (YEAR). (Society for Imaging Science and Technology (SPSE)) see *PHOTOGRAPHY*

SCANNING MICROSCOPY; an international journal of scanning electron microscopy, related techniques, and applications. see *BIOLOGY — Microscopy*

535 CC ISSN 1000-8713
SE PU/CHROMATOGRAM. (Text in Chinese) bi-m. Zhongguo Kexueyuan, Dalian Huaxue Wuli Yanjiusuo - Chinese Academy of Sciences, Dalian Institute of Chemical Physics, 161 Zhongshan Lu, Dalian, Liaoning 118, People's Republic of China. TEL 331841. Ed. Lu Peizhang.
—BLDSC shelfmark: 3180.299800.

535 SI
SERIES ON OPTICS AND PHOTONICS. (Text in English) 1989. irreg., vol. 3, 1991. price varies. World Scientific Publishing Co. Pte. Ltd., Farrer Rd., P.O. Box 128, Singapore 9128, Singapore. TEL 3825663. FAX 3825919. TELEX RS 28561 WSPC. (UK addr.: 73 Lynton Mead, Totteridge, London N20 8DH, England. TEL 44-81-4462461; US addr.: 1060 Main St., Ste. 1B, River Edge, NJ 07661. TEL 800-227-7562) Ed. S.L. Chin.

535 US ISSN 0038-5514
TS510 CODEN: SJOTBH
SOVIET JOURNAL OF OPTICAL TECHNOLOGY. English translation of: Optiko-Mekhanicheskaya Promyshlennost' (RU ISSN 0030-4042) 1966. m. $895 to non-members (foreign $907-$915). (Optical Society of America, Inc.) American Institute of Physics, 335 E. 45th St., New York, NY 10017-3483. TEL 212-661-9404. (And: Optical Society of America, 2101 Massachusetts Ave., N.W., Washington, DC 20036-1023. TEL 202-223-8130) Ed. William Manthey. (also avail. in microform; back issues avail.) **Indexed:** ASCA, C.P.I., Curr.Cont., Eng.Ind., Gen.Phys.Adv.Abstr., INSPEC, Int.Aerosp.Abstr., Phys.Ber., Risk Abstr., Sci.Abstr.
—BLDSC shelfmark: 0423.500000.
Description: Reports the theoretical and experimental research concerning many phases of optical, space and astronomical engineering.

SPECTROCHIMICA ACTA. PART A: MOLECULAR SPECTROSCOPY. see *CHEMISTRY — Analytical Chemistry*

SPECTROCHIMICA ACTA. PART B: ATOMIC SPECTROSCOPY. see *CHEMISTRY — Analytical Chemistry*

SPECTROCHIMICA ACTA REVIEWS. see *CHEMISTRY — Analytical Chemistry*

SPECTROSCOPIC PROPERTIES OF INORGANIC & ORGANOMETALLIC COMPOUNDS. see *CHEMISTRY*

535.84 JA ISSN 0038-7002
CODEN: BUKKAT
SPECTROSCOPICAL SOCIETY OF JAPAN. JOURNAL/BUNKO KENKYU. (Text in English, Japanese; summaries in English) 1951. bi-m. $36. Spectroscopical Society of Japan - Nihon Bunko Gakkai, Clean Bldg., 1-13 Kanda Awajicho, Chiyoda-ku, Tokyo 101, Japan. adv.; bk.rev.; bibl.; charts; illus.; index; circ. 2,000. **Indexed:** Anal.Abstr., Chem.Abstr., INIS Atomind., JTA, Sci.Abstr.
—BLDSC shelfmark: 4902.500000.

535 543 US ISSN 0887-6703
QC450 CODEN: SPECET
SPECTROSCOPY. 1985. 9/yr. $59 (foreign $117). Aster Publishing Corporation, 859 Willamette St., Box 10955, Eugene, OR 97440. TEL 503-343-1200. FAX 503-343-3641. TELEX 510-597-0365. Ed. Linda Crabtree. adv.; charts; illus.; stat.; tr.lit.; circ. 30,000. (back issues avail.) **Indexed:** Excerp.Med., Telegen.
—BLDSC shelfmark: 8411.113900.
Description: Concise research and applications articles for users and buyers of all types of spectroscopic equipment and related accessories. Combines practical information with principles of modern science for analysts in industrial, academic, and government laboratories.

535.84 US ISSN 0038-7010
QD95 CODEN: SPLEBX
SPECTROSCOPY LETTERS; an international journal for rapid communication. 1968. 8/yr. $292.50 to individuals; institutions $585. Marcel Dekker Journals, 270 Madison Ave., New York, NY 10016. TEL 212-696-9000. FAX 212-685-4540. TELEX 421419 MARDEEK. (Subscr. to: Box 10018, Church St. Sta., New York, NY 10249) Ed. J.W. Robinson. adv.; charts. (also avail. in microform from RPI) **Indexed:** Anal.Abstr., ASCA, Ceram.Abstr., Chem.Abstr., Curr.Cont., Excerp.Med., GeoRef., Mass Spectr.Bull., Sci.Abstr.
—BLDSC shelfmark: 8411.120000.
Refereed Serial

535.84 UK ISSN 0956-9820
SPECTROSCOPY WORLD. 6/yr. £45. (Association of British Spectroscopists) Ian Michael Publications Ltd., P.O. Box 10, Selsey, Chichester, W. Sussex PO20 9HR, England. TEL 0243-603429. FAX 0243-603907. Ed. R.A.G. Carringtom.
—BLDSC shelfmark: 8411.140000.

621.39 681 IS
▼**SPECTRUM**. (Text in Hebrew) 1991. bi-m. Tzavta Publishing, P.O. Box 18287, Tel Aviv 61181, Israel. TEL 3-5622076. FAX 3-5618549. Ed. Y. Elyada. adv.; bk.rev.; circ. 4,000 (controlled).
Description: Covers advances in optical engineering, laser applications, and general photonics.

PHYSICS — SOUND

535   US   ISSN 0490-4176
CODEN: SPSKDK
SPEX SPEAKER. 1955. q. Spex Industries Inc., 3880 Park Ave., Edison, NJ 08820. TEL 201-549-7144. FAX 201-549-5125. Ed. Ray Kaminski. adv.; charts; stat.; circ. 15,000. **Indexed:** GeoRef.

535   US   ISSN 0342-4111
CODEN: SSOSDB
SPRINGER SERIES IN OPTICAL SCIENCES. 1976. irreg. price varies. Springer-Verlag, 175 Fifth Ave., New York, NY 10010. TEL 212-460-1500. (And Berlin, Heidelberg, Tokyo and Vienna) (reprint service avail. from ISI) **Indexed:** Chem.Abstr, Phys.Ber.

535   RU
USPEKHI FORONIKI. vol.6, 1977. irreg. 1.83 Rub. per no. Leningradskii Universitet, Universitetskaya Nab. 7-9, St. Petersburg B-164, Russia. abstr.; bibl.; circ. 705. **Indexed:** Chem.Abstr.

535.84   UK   ISSN 0049-8246
QC481   CODEN: XRSPAX
X R S - X-RAY SPECTROMETRY; an international journal. 1972. bi-m. £525 (effective 1992). John Wiley & Sons Ltd., Baffins Ln., Chichester, Sussex PO19 1UD, England. TEL 0243-779777. FAX 0243-775878. TELEX 86290 WIBOOK G. Ed. John V. Gilfrich. adv.; bk.rev.; bibl.; illus.; tr.lit. (also avail. in microfilm; microfiche; reprint service avail. from SWZ) **Indexed:** AESIS, Br.Ceram.Abstr., Chem.Abstr., Curr.Cont., Sci.Abstr.
—BLDSC shelfmark: 9365.780000.
Description: Covers advances in techniques, methods and equipment, news and events, and provides a platform for the discussion of more sophisticated x-ray analytical methods.

535   US
▼**X-RAY OPTICS.** 1991. irreg. price varies. Gordon and Breach Science Publishers, 270 Eighth Ave., New York, NY 10011. TEL 212-206-8900. FAX 212-645-2459. TELEX 236735 GOPUB UR. (Subscr. to: Box 786, Cooper Sta., New York, NY 10276. TEL 800-545-8393; UK subscr. to: P.O. Box 90, Reading, Berkshire RG1 8JL, England. TEL 0734-560-080) Ed. M.A. Kumakhov. (also avail. in microform)
Description: Covers the science, technology, and applications of x-ray and particle beams, including new devices made on the principle of multireflection x-ray and beam optics.

535.58   CC   ISSN 1000-372X
YINGYONG JIGUANG/APPLIED LASERS. (Text in Chinese) bi-m. Shanghai Jiguang Jishu Yanjiusuo - Shanghai Laser Technology Institute, 770 Yishan Lu, Shanghai 200233, People's Republic of China. TEL 4700560. Ed. Wang Zhijiang.
—BLDSC shelfmark: 1573.240000.

535   GW   ISSN 0044-2054
ZEISS INFORMATION. (Editions in English, German) 1953. irreg. free. Carl Zeiss, Postfach 1369-1380, 7082 Oberkochen, Germany. FAX 07364-203370. Ed. Wolfgang Pfeiffer. charts; illus.; index; circ. 80,000. **Indexed:** Biol.Abstr., Chem.Abstr., Met.Abstr., Sci.Abstr., World Alum.Abstr.

ZHONGGUO GUANGXUE YU YINGYONG GUANGXUE WENZHAI/CHINESE OPTICS AND APPLIED OPTICS ABSTRACTS. see **PHYSICS** — Abstracting, Bibliographies, Statistics

535.58   CC   ISSN 0258-7025
ZHONGGUO JIGUANG/LASER SINICA. (Text in Chinese) m. Y4.50($3) per no. (Zhongguo Guangxue Xuehui - China Optics Society) Science Press, Marketing and Sales Department, 16 Donghuangchenggen Beijie, Beijing 100707, People's Republic of China. TEL 4010642. FAX 4012180. TELEX 210247 SPBJ CN. **Indexed:** Chem.Abstr.
—BLDSC shelfmark: 3180.366000.
Formerly: Chinese Journal of Lasers.

PHYSICS — Sound

see also Sound Recording and Reproduction

534 621.3   US
A S S P WORKSHOP ON SPECTRUM ESTIMATION AND MODELING. 1981. a. price varies. (I E E E, Acoustics, Speech and Signal Processing Society) Institute of Electrical and Electronics Engineers, Inc., 345 E. 47th St., New York, NY 10017-2394. TEL 212-705-7900. FAX 212-705-7682. (Subscr. to: 445 Hoes Ln., Box 1331, Piscataway, NJ 08855-1331) **Indexed:** Sci.Abstr.
Former titles: A S S P Spectrum Estimation Workshop; A S S P Workshop on Spectral Estimation.

534 774   US
ACOUSTICAL IMAGING. Represents: International Symposium on Acoustical Imaging. Proceedings. 1969. irreg., vol.18, 1991. price varies. Plenum Publishing Corp., 233 Spring St., New York, NY 10013-1578. TEL 212-620-8000. FAX 212-463-0742. TELEX 23-421139. **Indexed:** Biol.Abstr., Chem.Abstr.
Former titles: Acoustical Imaging: Recent Advances in Visualization and Characterization (ISSN 0270-5117); (Until 1977): Acoustical Holography (ISSN 0065-0870)
Refereed Serial

534   US   ISSN 0001-4966
CODEN: JASMAN
ACOUSTICAL SOCIETY OF AMERICA. JOURNAL. 1929. m. (plus 3 supplements). $600. American Institute of Physics, 335 E. 45th St., New York, NY 10017. TEL 212-661-9404. FAX 516-349-9704. (Subscr. to: Member and Subscriber Service, 500 Sunnyside Blvd., Woodbury, NY 11797-2999. TEL 516-576-2270) Ed. Daniel W. Martin. adv.; bk.rev.; abstr.; illus.; pat.; index, cum.index: vols.1-74, 1929-1983. (also avail. in microform from AIP; back issues avail.) **Indexed:** A.S.& T.Ind., Abstr.Bull.Inst.Pap.Chem., Abstr.J.Earthq.Eng., Agri.Eng.Abstr., Appl.Mech.Rev., Biol.Abstr., C.P.I., Cadscan, Chem.Abstr., Child Devel.Abstr., Curr.Cont., Deep Sea Res.& Oceanogr.Abstr., Dent.Ind., Energy Ind., Energy Info.Abstr., Eng.Ind., Environ.Abstr., Ergon.Abstr., Excerp.Med., Fluidex, Gen.Phys.Adv.Abstr., Geo.Abstr., Geo.Ref., HRIS, Ind.Med., INIS Atomind., Int.Aerosp.Abstr., ISMEC, Lead Abstr., Math.R., Meteor.& Geoastrophys.Abstr., Noise Pollut.Publ.Abstr., Ocean.Abstr., Petrol.Abstr., Phys.Ber., Pollut.Abstr., Psychol.Abstr., Sci.Abstr., Sh.& Vib.Dig., Zincscan.
—BLDSC shelfmark: 4675.000000.
Description: Covers all phases of research and engineering of interest to acoustical scientists and engineers.
Refereed Serial

534   AT   ISSN 0814-6039
ACOUSTICS AUSTRALIA.* 1972. 3/yr. Aus.$36. Australian Acoustical Society, Science Centre, 35-43 Clarence St., Sydney, N.S.W 2000, Australia. TEL 02-528-4362. FAX 02-523-9637. Ed. H. Pollard. adv.; bk.rev.; circ. 500. **Indexed:** Acoust.Abstr., HRIS.
—BLDSC shelfmark: 0578.697100.
Formerly: Australian Acoustical Society. Bulletin (ISSN 0310-1029)
Description: Covers acoustics research, applied acoustics, hearing, noise, community and environmental acoustics, architectural and musical acoustics, vibration, underwater and physical acoustics.

534   UK   ISSN 0308-437X
ACOUSTICS BULLETIN. 1974. 6/yr. £22 (effective Jan. 1992). Institute of Acoustics, Box 320, St. Albans, Herts. AL1 1PZ, England. TEL 0727-48195. FAX 0727-50553. (Subscr. to: 11 Colwyn Close, Yaletly, Camberly, Surrey GU17 7QH, England. TEL 0252-871298) Ed. J. Tyler. adv.; bk.rev.; circ. 1,900.
—BLDSC shelfmark: 0578.697300.
Description: Written for research establishments covering all aspects of acoustics including aerodynamic noise, environmental, speech, underwater vibrations and more.

534   UK   ISSN 0140-1599
CODEN: ACLEDI
ACOUSTICS LETTERS. 1977. m. £79($150) Parjon Information Services, P.O. Box 144, Haywards Heath, Sussex RH16 2YX, England. Ed. Dr. J. Scott. bk.rev. **Indexed:** Appl.Mech.Rev., Chem.Abstr., Deep Sea Res.& Oceanogr.Abstr., Sci.Abstr.
—BLDSC shelfmark: 0578.697400.
Description: Short papers on all aspects of acoustics.

534   GW   ISSN 0001-7884
QC221   CODEN: ACUSAY
ACUSTICA; Internationale Akustische Zeitschrift - International Journal on Acoustics. (Text in English, French and German) 1936. m. (3 vols./yr.). DM.288 per vol. (Deutsche Physikalische Gesellschaft) S. Hirzel Verlag, Postfach 102237, 7000 Stuttgart 10, Germany. TEL 0711-2582-0. FAX 0711-2582290. TELEX 723636-DAZ-D. (Co-sponsor: Groupement des Acousticiens de Langue Francaise) Ed. K. Martin. adv.; bk.rev.; illus.; index; circ. 1,500. **Indexed:** Biol.Abstr., C.I.S. Abstr., Chem.Abstr., Curr.Cont., Deep Sea Res.& Oceanogr.Abstr., Energy Ind., Energy Info.Abstr., Eng.Ind., Environ.Abstr., Ergon.Abstr., Excerp.Med., Ind.Sci.Rev., Intl.Civil Eng.Abstr., Lang.& Lang.Behav.Abstr., Math.R., RILM, Sci.Abstr., Sci.Cit.Ind., Sh.& Vib.Dig., Soft.Abstr.Eng.
—BLDSC shelfmark: 0678.000000.
Formerly (until 1951): Akustische Zeitschrift.

534   RU   ISSN 0002-3914
AKUSTICHESKII ZHURNAL. (Text in Russian; contents page in English) 1955. bi-m. 39.90 Rub. (Akademiya Nauk S.S.S.R.) Izdatel'stvo Nauka, Fizmatlit, Leninskii prospekt, 15, 117071 Moscow, V-71, Russia. (Dist. by: Mezhdunarodnaya Kniga, ul. Dimitrova D.39, 113095 Moscow, Russia) Ed. V.S. Grigor'ev. bk.rev.; bibl.; charts; illus.; index; circ. 2,180. **Indexed:** Biol.Abstr., Chem.Abstr., Deep Sea Res.& Oceanogr.Abstr., Eng.Ind., INIS Atomind., Math.R., Sci.Abstr.

534   PL   ISSN 0554-8039
AKUSTYKA. 1972. irreg., latest no.9. price varies. Adam Mickiewicz University Press, Nowowiejskiego 55, 61-734 Poznan, Poland. TEL 527-380. TELEX 413260 UAMPL.
Formerly: Uniwersytet im. Adama Mickiewicza w Poznaniu. Wydzial Matematyki, Fizyki i Chemii. Prace. Seria Akustyka.

AMERICAN INSTITUTE OF ULTRASOUND IN MEDICINE. ANNUAL SCIENTIFIC CONFERENCE. PROCEEDINGS. see *MEDICAL SCIENCES*

534   UK   ISSN 0003-682X
TA365   CODEN: AACOBL
APPLIED ACOUSTICS. (Text in English, French, German) 1968. 12/yr.(in 3 vols.). £408 (effective 1992). Elsevier Science Publishers Ltd., Crown House, Linton Rd., Barking, Essex IG11 8JU, England. TEL 081-594-7272. FAX 081-594-5942. TELEX 896950 APPSCI G. (Subscr. in U.S. and Canada to: Elsevier Science Publishing Co., Inc., Box 882, Madison Sq. Sta., New York, NY 10159. TEL 212-989-5800) Ed. P. Lord. adv.; B&W page #295; 140 x 200; adv. contact: Claire Coakley. bk.rev.; illus.; index. (also avail. in microform from RPI; back issues avail.) **Indexed:** Agri.Eng.Abstr., B.C.I.R.A., BMT, C.I.S. Abstr., CAD CAM Abstr., Curr.Cont., DSH Abstr., Environ.Abstr., Excerp.Med., Fluidex, Noise Pollut.Publ.Abstr., Ocean.Abstr., Phys.Ber., Pollut.Abstr., Sci.Abstr., Sci.Cit.Ind., Sh.& Vib.Dig.
—BLDSC shelfmark: 1571.400000.
Description: For those concerned with the design of buildings, measurements and control of industrial noise and vibration, transportation noise, hearing, the understanding of the acoustics of musical instruments, the propagation of sound through the atmosphere and under water.
Refereed Serial

534   PL   ISSN 0137-5075
ARCHIVES OF ACOUSTICS. (Text in English; summaries in Polish, Russian) 1976. q. $48. (Polska Akademia Nauk, Komitet Akustyki) Panstwowe Wydawnictwo Naukowe, Miodowa 10, 00-251 Warsaw, Poland. (Dist. by: Ars Polona, Krakowskie Przedmiescie 7, 00-068 Warsaw, Poland) Ed. J. Molecki. bibl.; illus.; circ. 360. **Indexed:** Appl.Mech.Rev., Noise Pollut.Publ.Abstr., Phys.Ber., Sci.Abstr.
—BLDSC shelfmark: 1630.800000.

PHYSICS — SOUND

534   GW
AUDIO. 1978. m. DM.90 (foreign DM.102). Vereinigte Motor-Verlage GmbH und Co. KG, Leuschnerstr. 1, 7000 Stuttgart 1, Germany. TEL 0711-18201. FAX 0711-1821756. TELEX 723900. Ed. Ulrich Smyrek. adv.; bk.rev.; index; circ. 81,000. (back issues avail.) **Indexed:** A.S.& T.Ind, Consum.Ind., Ind.Sci.Rev.

534   GW   ISSN 0172-8261
                     CODEN: AUKADP
AUDIOLOGISCH AKUSTIK/AUDIOLOGICAL ACOUSTICS. (Text in English and German) 1962. bi-m. DM.48. Median Verlag, Hauptstr. 64, Postfach 103964, 6900 Heidelberg 1, Germany. TEL 06221-25731. FAX 06221-25020. Ed.Bd. adv.; bk.rev.; bibl.; charts; illus.; index; circ. 3,000. **Indexed:** Excerp.Med., Sci.Abstr.
—BLDSC shelfmark: 1789.060000.
    Formerly: Zeitschrift fuer Hoergeraete Akustik (ISSN 0044-2860)

534   UK   ISSN 0952-4622
                     CODEN: BIOAE7
BIOACOUSTICS; the international journal of animal sound and its recording. 1988. q. £89($179) (British Library National Sound Archive) A B Academic Publishers, P.O. Box 42, Bicester, Oxon OX6 7NW, England. TEL 0869-320949. Ed. Brian Lewis.
—BLDSC shelfmark: 2066.679000.
    Description: Collects research papers and articles on all aspects of wildlife recording.

534   CN   ISSN 0711-6659
                     CODEN: CAACDX
CANADIAN ACOUSTICS/ACOUSTIQUE CANADIENNE. (Text in English and French) 1973. q. Can.$35. Canadian Acoustical Association, P.O. Box 1351, Sta. F, Toronto, Ont. M4Y 2V9, Canada. TEL 613-993-0102. FAX 613-954-5984. (Subscr. to: Mr. W. Sydenborgh, 2323 Royal Windsor Dr., Mississauga, Ont. K5J 1K5, Canada) Ed. Murray Hodgson. adv.; bk.rev.; charts; circ. 500. (back issues avail.) **Indexed:** Acoust.Abstr., Sci.Abstr.
—BLDSC shelfmark: 3016.476000.
    Formerly (until Jan. 1982): Acoustics and Noise Control in Canada.

534   CC   ISSN 0217-9776
CHINESE JOURNAL OF ACOUSTICS. Chinese edition: Shengxue Xuebao. (Text in English) 1982. q. $210. (Acoustical Society of China) Science Press, Marketing and Sales Department, 16 Donghuangchenggen Beijie, Beijing 100707, People's Republic of China. TEL 4010642. FAX 4012180. TELEX 210247-SPBJ-CN. (US office: 63-117 Alderton St., Rego Park, NY 11374. TEL 718-459-4638; Also dist. by: Allerton Press, Inc., 150 Fifth Ave., New York, NY 10011. TEL 212-924-3950) Ed. Ma Dayou. adv.; circ. 6,000. (also avail. in microform; back issues avail.)
—BLDSC shelfmark: 3180.289000.
    Description: Covers acoustical research in China, including physical acoustics, underwater sound, and electroacoustics.
    Refereed Serial

534   DK   ISSN 0105-2853
DANMARKS TEKNISKE HOEJSKOLE. LABORATORIET FOR AKUSTIK. PUBLIKATION. irreg. price varies. Danmarks Tekniske Hoejskole, Laboratoriet for Akustik, Bygn 352, 2800 Lyngby, Denmark. illus.

534
EUROPEAN SOLID STATE DEVICE RESEARCH CONFERENCE. SOLID STATE DEVICES. (Published in host country: UK, France or Germany; latest UK, 1986) a. (Institute of Physics) I O P Publishing, Techno House, Redcliffe Way, Bristol BS1 6NX, England. TEL 0272-297481. (U.S. addr.: American Institute of Physics, 335 E. 45th St., New York, NY 10017)

FREQUENCY CONTROL SYMPOSIUM. see *ELECTRONICS*

534   US
HEMI-SYNC JOURNAL. 1983. q. $65. The Monroe Institute, Rt. 1, Box 175, Faber, VA 22938. TEL 804-361-1252. Ed.Bd. circ. 3,000. (back issues avail.)
    Formerly: Breakthrough (Faber).
    Description: Research in and applications of the Hemi-Sync sound technology in various professional arenas.

534   GW   ISSN 0933-1980
HOERAKUSTIK. 1965. m. DM.156. Median Verlag, Hauptstr. 64, Postfach 103964, 6900 Heidelberg 1, Germany. TEL 06221-25731. FAX 06221-25020.
    Formerly: Hoergeraete-Akustiker (ISSN 0178-4536)

534   US   ISSN 1053-5888
TK5981   CODEN: ISPRE6
I E E E - SIGNAL PROCESSING MAGAZINE. Represents: I E E E Acoustics, Speech and Signal Processing Magazine. 1984. q. $60 to non-members. (I E E E, Acoustics, Speech, and Signal Processing Society) Institute of Electrical and Electronics Engineers, Inc., 345 E. 47th St., New York, NY 10017. TEL 908-562-3948. FAX 908-961-1855. (Subscr. to: Box 1331, 445 Hoes Lane, Piscataway, NJ 08855-1331) Ed. Jack Deller. (also avail. in microform from UMI,EEE) **Indexed:** A.I.Abstr., Sci.Abstr.
—BLDSC shelfmark: 4363.066520.
    Formerly: I E E E - A S S P Magazine (ISSN 0740-7467)
    Description: Features tutorials of a light technical nature. Provides news and notes on conferences, workshops, seminars and lectures.

534   US   ISSN 0885-3010
QC244   CODEN: ITUCER
I E E E TRANSACTIONS ON ULTRASONICS, FERROELECTRICS AND FREQUENCY CONTROL. 1954. bi-m. $220 to non-members. (I E E E, Ultrasonics, Ferroelectrics and Frequency Control Society) Institute of Electrical and Electronics Engineers, Inc., 345 E. 47th St., New York, NY 10017-2394. TEL 212-705-7366. FAX 212-705-7682. (Subscr. to: Box 1331, 445 Hoes Lane, Piscataway, NJ 08855-1331. TEL 908-562-3948) Ed. William D. O'Brien. bk.rev.; abstr.; illus.; index. (also avail. in microform from MIM,UMI,EEE) **Indexed:** A.S.& T.Ind., Chem.Abstr, Comput.Lit.Ind., Curr.Cont., Deep Sea Res.& Oceanogr.Abstr., Eng.Ind., Excerp.Med., Ind.Sci.Rev., INIS Atomind., Int.Aerosp.Abstr., Math.R., Sci.Abstr., Sci.Cit.Ind.
—BLDSC shelfmark: 4363.227500.
    Former titles: I E E E Transactions on Sonics and Ultrasonics (ISSN 0018-9537); I E E E Transactions on Ultrasonics Engineering; I R E Transactions on Ultrasonics Engineering; I R E Professional Group on Ultrasonics Engineering. Transactions.
    Description: Discusses theory, design and application on generation, transmission and detection of bulk and surface mechanical waves.

534   JA   ISSN 0386-8761
INSTITUTE OF NOISE CONTROL ENGINEERING. JOURNAL. (Text in Japanese) 1972. s-m. 12000 Yen. Institute of Noise Control Engineering (INCE), c/o Kobayashi Institute of Physical Research, 3-20-41 Higashimoto-machi, Kokubunji-shi, Tokyo 185, Japan. TEL 0423-25-1652. Ed. N. Imaizumi. adv.

534   US
INTERNATIONAL AUDIO REVIEW.* 1978? q. $28 (foreign $38). Institute for Audio Research, Box 4271, Berkeley, CA 94704-0271. Ed. J. Peter Moncrieff.
    Description: Review of audio products on an international scale.

534   CN   ISSN 0074-400X
INTERNATIONAL CONFERENCE ON ACOUSTICS. REPORTS. 1953. irreg., 11th. 1983. Paris, France. International Commission on Acoustics, c/o Dr. E.A.W. Shaw, Division de Physique, Conseil National de Recherches, Ottawa, Ont. K1A 0R6, Canada. TEL 613-966-5845.

INTERNATIONAL WIDESCREEN. see *PHOTOGRAPHY*

534   FR   ISSN 0988-4319
JOURNAL D'ACOUSTIQUE. (Text in English, French, German, Russian) 6/yr. 1050 F. (foreign 1200 F.). Editions de Physique, B.P. 112, 7, Av. du Hoggar, Zone Industrielle de Courtaboeuf, 91944 Les Ulis Cedex, France. TEL 69-07-36-88. FAX 69288491. TELEX 602 321 F.
—BLDSC shelfmark: 4918.932500.
    Description: Forum for research in acoustics, including musical acoustics, hearing, physics and ultrasonics.

534   US   ISSN 0730-0050
TA418.84   CODEN: JACEDO
JOURNAL OF ACOUSTIC EMISSION. 1982. q. $90. Acoustic Emission Group, 308 Westwood Blvd., Box 364, Los Angeles, CA 90024-1647. TEL 213-825-5233. Ed. Kanji Ono. adv.; bk.rev.; circ. 300. **Indexed:** Chem.Abstr., INIS Atomind., Met.Abstr., Sci.Abstr.
—BLDSC shelfmark: 4918.922000.
    Description: Covers science and technology of acoustic emission for researchers and applications engineers.

534   US   ISSN 0091-2751
RM862.7   CODEN: JCULDD
JOURNAL OF CLINICAL ULTRASOUND. 1973. 9/yr. $175 to institutions (foreign $287.50). John Wiley & Sons, Inc., Journals, 605 Third Ave., New York, NY 10158-0012. TEL 212-850-6000. FAX 212-850-6088. TELEX 12-7063. Ed. Russell L. Deter. adv.; bk.rev.; abstr.; charts; illus.; stat.; index; circ. 5,000. (also avail. in microform from RPI; back issues avail.; reprint service avail. from RPI) **Indexed:** Bibl.Dev.Med.& Child Neur., Biol.Abstr., Curr.Adv.Cancer Res., Curr.Cont., Dent.Ind., Dok.Arbeitsmed., Excerp.Med., Helminthol.Abstr., Ind.Med., Ind.Sci.Rev., INIS Atomind., Sci.Abstr., Sci.Cit.Ind.
—BLDSC shelfmark: 4958.791000.
    Description: Covers current uses of ultrasound in evaluating disorders affecting the central nervous system, fetus and placenta, gastrointestinal system, reproductive system, urinary system.
    Refereed Serial

534   UK   ISSN 0263-0923
JOURNAL OF LOW FREQUENCY NOISE & VIBRATION. 1982. 4/yr. £91 (foreign £98). Multi-Science Publishing Co. Ltd., 107 High St., Brentwood, Essex CM14 4RX, England. TEL 0277-224632. FAX 0277-224632. Ed. H.G. Leventhall. **Indexed:** Agri.Eng.Abstr., Noise Pollut.Publ.Abstr., Sci.Abstr.
—BLDSC shelfmark: 5010.565000.
    Description: Discusses low frequency noise and vibration, their effects on man, animals, and the environment.

534 300   II   ISSN 0256-4637
JOURNAL OF PURE AND APPLIED ULTRASONICS. 1979. q. $35. Ultrasonic Society of India, c/o Ultrasonic Section, National Physical Laboratory, Hillside Rd., New Delhi 110012, India. Ed. M. Pancholy. adv.; bk.rev.; index; circ. 300. (back issues avail.) **Indexed:** Sci.Abstr.
—BLDSC shelfmark: 5043.682000.

534   UK   ISSN 0022-460X
QC221   CODEN: JSVIAG
JOURNAL OF SOUND AND VIBRATION. 1964. 24/yr. (7 vols./yr.). $1,425. Academic Press Ltd., 24-28 Oval Rd., London NW1, England. TEL 071-267-4466. FAX 071-482-2293. TELEX 25775 ACPRES G. Ed. P.E. Doak. adv.; bk.rev.; bibl.; charts; illus.; index; circ. 1,500. **Indexed:** Abstr.J.Earthq.Eng., Appl.Mech.Rev., Biol.Abstr., BMT, Br.Rail.Bd., Br.Tech.Ind., C.I.S. Abstr., Curr.Cont., Deep Sea Res.& Oceanogr.Abstr., Eng.Ind., Ergon.Abstr., Excerp.Med., Fluidex, Fuel & Energy Abstr., HRIS, Ind.Sci.Rev., INIS Atomind., Int.Aerosp.Abstr., ISMEC, Math.R., Noise Pollut.Publ.Abstr., Ocean.Abstr., Phys.Ber., Pollut.Abstr., Sci.Abstr., Sh.& Vib.Dig.
—BLDSC shelfmark: 5065.850000.
    Description: Examines experimental and theoretical work concerning all aspects of sound vibration.

530   PL   ISSN 0032-9576
                     CODEN: PVBPAO
JOURNAL OF TECHNICAL PHYSICS. (Text in English; summaries in Polish and Russian) 1959. q. $37. (Polska Akademia Nauk, Instytut Podstawowych Problemow Techniki) Panstwowe Wydawnictwo Naukowe, Miodowa 10, 00-251 Warsaw, Poland. (Dist. by: Ars Polona, Krakowskie Przedmiescie 7, 00-068 Warsaw, Poland) Ed. D. Rogula. charts; illus.; circ. 600. **Indexed:** Appl.Mech.Rev., Chem.Abstr., INIS Atomind., Math.R., Phys.Ber., Ref.Zh., Sci.Abstr.

JOURNAL OF ULTRASOUND IN MEDICINE. see *MEDICAL SCIENCES*

534   DK   ISSN 0105-614X
LYDTEKNISK INSTITUT. RAPPORT. no.31, 1982. irreg. price varies. Lydteknisk Institut, Akademiet for de Tekniske Videnskaber - Danish Acoustical Institute, Building 356, Akademivej, DK-2800 Lyngby, Denmark. TEL 45-931211. FAX 45-931990. illus.

PHYSIOLOGY

534   UK   ISSN 0950-8163
NOISE & VIBRATION IN INDUSTRY. 1986. 4/yr. £91 (foreign £98). Multi-Science Publishing Co. Ltd., 107 High St., Brentwood, Essex CM14 4RX, England. TEL 0277-224632. FAX 0277-224632.
—BLDSC shelfmark: 6115.857000.
Formerly: Noise and Vibration for Works Managers.
Description: Covers regulations governing noise at work.

OPTICAL AND ACOUSTICAL REVIEW. see *PHYSICS — Optics*

534   US   ISSN 0079-1873
PHYSICAL ACOUSTICS: PRINCIPLES AND METHODS. 1964. irreg., vol.19, 1990. Academic Press, Inc., 1250 Sixth Ave., San Diego, CA 92101. TEL 619-231-0926. FAX 619-699-6715. Eds. R. Thurston, A. Pierce. (reprint service avail. from ISI) **Indexed:** Appl.Mech.Rev., Ind.Sci.Rev.
Refereed Serial

POLITECHNIKA WROCLAWSKA. INSTYTUT TELEKOMUNIKACJI I AKUSTYKI. PRACE NAUKOWE. KONFERENCJE. see *COMMUNICATIONS — Telephone And Telegraph*

POLITECHNIKA WROCLAWSKA. INSTYTUT TELEKOMUNIKACJI I AKUSTYKI. PRACE NAUKOWE. MONOGRAFIE. see *COMMUNICATIONS — Telephone And Telegraph*

POLITECHNIKA WROCLAWSKA. INSTYTUT TELEKOMUNIKACJI I AKUSTYKI. PRACE NAUKOWE. STUDIA I MATERIALY. see *COMMUNICATIONS — Telephone And Telegraph*

534   RU
PROBLEMY DIFRAKTSII I RASPROSTRANENIYA VOLN/PROBLEMS OF DIFFRACTION AND SPREADING OF WAVES. vol.15, 1977. irreg. 1.69 Rub. per no. Leningradskii Universitet, Universitetskaya Nab. 7-9, St. Petersburg B-164, Russia. abstr.; bibl.; circ. 900.

534   KR   ISSN 0485-8972
CODEN: RTKHAJ
RADIOTEKHNIKA (KHARKOV). 1965. q. price varies. (Khar'kovskii Institut Radioelektroniki) Izdatel'stvo Vysshaya Shkola, Khar'kovskoe Otdelenie, Universitetskaya 16, 310003 Kharkov, Ukraine. Ed. A. Tereshchenko. abstr.; charts; circ. 1,000. **Indexed:** Int.Aerosp.Abstr.
—BLDSC shelfmark: 0138.200000.
Description: Presents articles dealing with the results of theoretical and experimental research in the field of radio engineering devices and systems of radio measurements, electro-dynamics and electronics of microwaves.

534.55   SP   ISSN 0210-3680
REVISTA DE ACUSTICA. (Text and summaries in English and Spanish) 1970. q. 7000 ptas.($10) Sociedad Espanola de Acustica, Serrano 144, Madrid 6, Spain. Ed. Antonio Calvo-Manzano. adv.; bk.rev.; bibl.; circ. 1,000. (tabloid format; also avail. in microfilm) **Indexed:** Ind.SST.

534.55   UK   ISSN 0048-8828
RUSSIAN ULTRASONICS. 1971. bi-m. £187 (foreign £196). Multi-Science Publishing Co. Ltd., 107 High St., Brentwood, Essex CM14 4RX, England. TEL 0277-224632. FAX 0277-224632. bibl.; charts; illus.; index.
—BLDSC shelfmark: 8053.040000.

534   CC   ISSN 1000-3630
SHENGXUE JISHU/TECHNICAL ACOUSTICS. (Text in Chinese) 1982. q. $12. Chinese Academy of Sciences, Shanghai Acoustics Lab, 456 Xiaomuqiao Road, Shanghai 200032, People's Republic of China. TEL 4311591. FAX 86-4374915. Ed. Ding Dong. adv.; bk.rev.

534   CC
QC221   CODEN: SHGHAS
SHENGXUE XUEBAO. English edition: Chinese Journal of Acoustics (ISSN 0217-9776) (Text in Chinese; summaries in English) 1964. bi-m. $8 per no. (Acoustical Society of China) Science Press, Marketing and Sales Department, 16 Donghuangchenggen Beijie, Beijing 100707, People's Republic of China. TEL 4010642. FAX 4012180. TELEX 210247-SPBJ-CN. adv.; circ. 6,000. **Indexed:** Math.R., Phys.Ber., Sci.Abstr.
Formerly: Acta Acustica (ISSN 0371-0025)
Description: Contains original papers and brief communications on acoustical research in mainland China and abroad, including physical acoustics, underwater sound, electroacoustics, and manufacture of instruments.
Refereed Serial

534   SZ
SOUND. 1978. 10/yr. A T Zeitschriftenverlag, Bahnhofstr. 39-43, 5001 Aarau, Switzerland. Ed. Fernando Palencias. circ. 11,747.
Formerly: Sound und R T E (Radio T V Electronics).

534   US   ISSN 0038-562X
QC221   CODEN: SOPAAX
SOVIET PHYSICS - ACOUSTICS. English translation of: Akusticheskii Zhurnal. 1955. bi-m. $640 (foreign $650-$665). American Institute of Physics, 335 E. 45th St., New York, NY 10017. TEL 212-661-9404. Ed. Robert T. Beyer. bibl.; charts; illus.; index. (also avail. in microform; back issues avail.) **Indexed:** Appl.Mech.Rev., ASCA, C.P.I., Curr.Cont., Deep Sea Res.& Oceanogr.Abstr., Eng.Ind., Excerp.Med., Gen.Phys.Adv.Abstr., Int.Aerosp.Abstr., Math.R., Noise Pollut.Publ.Abstr., Nucl.Sci.Abstr., Phys.Ber., Pollut.Abstr., Sci.Abstr.
—BLDSC shelfmark: 0424.850000.

534   DK   ISSN 0105-3027
TECHNICAL UNIVERSITY OF DENMARK. ACOUSTICS LABORATORY REPORT. no.34, 1982. irreg. price varies. Danmarks Tekniske Hoejskole, Laboratoriet for Akustik, Bygning 352, 2800 Lyngby, Denmark. illus. **Indexed:** Concr.Abstr.
Description: Contains research and thesis reports in acoustics.

534   LI   ISSN 0369-6367
ULTRAGARSAS/ULTRASOUND. (Text in Russian; summaries in English and Lithuanian) 1969. a. price varies. (Kaunas Technological University) Leidykla Mokslas, Zvaigzdziu 23, Vilnius 2050, Lithuania. TEL 45-85-26. TELEX 278128 LIE SU. (Co-sponsor: Lithuanian Ministry of Culture and Eudcation) Ed. V. Domarkas. circ. 500.
—BLDSC shelfmark: 0122.639000.
Description: Covers theoretical and practical problems of ultrasonic interferometry and spectroscopy, quantum and molecular acoustics and medical diagnosis.

534   UK   ISSN 0041-624X
TA367   CODEN: ULTRA3
ULTRASONICS; the world's leading journal covering the science & technology of ultrasound. 1963. bi-m. £210 (Europe £230). Butterworth - Heinemann Ltd. (Subsidiary of: Reed International PLC), Linacre House, Jordan Hill, OX2 8DP St., England. TEL 0865-310366. FAX 0865-310898. TELEX 83111 BHPOXF G. (Subscr. to: Turpin Transactions Ltd., Distribution Centre, Blackhorse Rd., Letchworth, Herts SG6 1HN, England. TEL 0462-672555) adv.; bk.rev.; abstr.; bibl.; illus.; index. (also avail. in microform from UMI; back issues avail.) **Indexed:** A.S.& T.Ind., Abstr.Bull.Inst.Pap.Chem., Appl.Mech.Rev., B.C.I.R.A., Biol.Abstr., Br.Rail.Bd., Br.Tech.Ind., C.I.S. Abstr., Chem.Abstr., Curr.Adv.Ecol.Sci., Curr.Cont., Excerp.Med., Fluidex, HRIS, Ind.Med., Int.Aerosp.Abstr., Met.Abstr., Phys.Abstr., PROMT, World Alum.Abstr.
—BLDSC shelfmark: 9082.796000.
Description: Covers the field of ultrasonics and its applications: transducers, non-destructive testing, signal processing.
Refereed Serial

620.2 534   US   ISSN 0090-5607
TA367   CODEN: ULSPDT
ULTRASONICS SYMPOSIUM. PROCEEDINGS. a. price varies. (I E E E, Ultrasonics, Ferroelectrics, and Frequency Control Society) Institute of Electrical and Electronics Engineers, Inc., 345 E. 47th St., New York, NY 10017-2394. TEL 212-705-7900. FAX 212-705-7682. (Subscr. to: Box 1331, 445 Hoes Ln., Piscataway, NJ 08855-1331) **Indexed:** Chem.Abstr. Key Title: Proceedings - Ultrasonics Symposium.
Description: Discoveries, recent advances, new devices, new techniques and application in all areas of sound.

ULTRASOUND IN MEDICINE & BIOLOGY. see *BIOLOGY*

YEAR BOOK OF ULTRASOUND. see *MEDICAL SCIENCES — Radiology And Nuclear Medicine*

534   CC   ISSN 1000-310X
YINGYONG SHENGXUE/APPLIED ACOUSTICS. (Text in Chinese) 1981. bi-m. $5 per no. (Zhongguo Shengxue Xuehui - Chinese Acoustics Society) Science Press, Marketing and Sales Department, 16 Donghuangchenggen Beijie, Beijing 100707, People's Republic of China. TEL 4010642. FAX 4012180. TELEX 210247-SPBJ-CN. adv.; circ. 11,000.
Description: Aims to present concrete applications of acoustics in various branches of China's economy. Popularizes basic knowledge of acoustics and reports on academic developments in China and other countries.
Refereed Serial

534   GW   ISSN 0174-1098
TD891
ZEITSCHRIFT FUER LAERMBEKAEMPFUNG. (Text in German) 1954. 6/yr. DM.138($74) (Deutscher Arbeitsring fuer Laermbekaempfung e.V.) Springer-Verlag, Heidelberger Platz 3, D-1000 Berlin 33, Germany. TEL 030-8207-1. (Also Heidelberg, Tokyo, Vienna, and New York) Eds. G. Jansen, M. Heckl. adv.; bk.rev.; abstr.; charts; illus.; tr.lit. (also avail. in microform from UMI; reprint service avail. from ISI) **Indexed:** Dok.Str., Excerp.Med.
—BLDSC shelfmark: 9468.750000.
Formerly: Kampf dem Laerm (ISSN 0022-8249)

PHYSIOLOGY

see *Biology-Physiology*

PLASTICS

668.44   US
A S E P NEWS AND VIEWS. 1967. q. membership. (American Society of Electroplated Plastics) International Management Group, Inc., 1101 14th St., N.W., Ste. 1100, Washington, DC 20005. TEL 202-371-1323. FAX 202-371-1090. TELEX 292046 IMGUR. Ed. David W. Barrack. adv.; circ. 500.
Formerly: A S E P Electroplater.

668.4   CK
ACOPLASTICOS. 1957. a. Asociacion Colombiana de Industrias Plasticas Acoplasticos, Carrera 10a, No. 27-27, Interior 134 Of. 901 (Edificio Bachue), Apdo. 29844, Bogota, Colombia. adv.

668.4   US   ISSN 1049-2453
ADDITIVES FOR PLASTICS D.A.T.A. DIGEST. 1987. biennial. $45. D.A.T.A. Business Publishing (Subsidiary of: Information Handling Services), 15 Inverness Way E., Box 6510, Englewood, CO 80155-6510. TEL 800-447-4666. FAX 303-799-4082. TELEX 4322083 IHS UI.
Formerly: Additives for Plastics D.A.T.A. Book.

PLASTICS

668.4 UK ISSN 0306-3747
ADDITIVES FOR POLYMERS; an international newsletter. 1971. m. £288 (effective 1992). Elsevier Science Publishers Ltd., Crown House, Linton Rd., Barking, Essex IG11 8JU, England. TEL 081-594-7272. FAX 081-594-5942. TELEX 896950 APPSCI G. (Subscr. in U.S. and Canada to: elsevier Science Publishing Co., Inc., Box 882, Madison Sq. Sta., New York, NY 10159. TEL 212-989-5800) Ed. J.A. Shelton. bk.rev.; index; circ. 60.
    Description: Summarizes information on new products and materials (including patents), new manufacturing techniques and processes, and new applications. Also industry and market news and the strategies of key players in this sector.

668.4 540 GW ISSN 0001-8198
TP967 CODEN: ADHEA2
ADHAESION; Klebstoffe, Dichtstoffe, Geraete- und Anlagentechnik, Anwendungen. 1957. 10/yr. DM.328 (foreign DM.333). Heinrich Vogel Fachzeitschriften GmbH, Neumarkter Str. 18, Postfach 802020, 8000 Munich 80, Germany. TEL 089-43180-0. Ed. Traude Wuest. adv.; bk.rev.; abstr.; bibl.; charts; illus.; mkt.; pat.; index; circ. 4,700. Indexed: Abstr.Bull.Inst.Pap.Chem., Art & Archaeol.Tech.Abstr., Chem.Abstr., Curr.Leather Lit., Eng.Ind., Excerp.Med., INIS Atomind., Int.Packag.Abstr., Packag.Sci.Tech., RAPRA, World Surf.Coat.

668.4 UK ISSN 0260-4450
TP968 CODEN: ADHED5
ADHESION. (Represents: Papers Presented at the Annual Conference on Adhesion and Adhesives, City University, London) 1977. irreg., approx a., vol.15, 1991. Elsevier Science Publishers Ltd., Books Division, Crown House, Linton Rd., Barking, Essex IG11 8JU, England, England. TEL 081-594-7272. FAX 081-594-5942. TELEX 896950 APPSCI G. (Subscr. in U.S. and Canada to: Elsevier Science Publishing Co., Inc., Box 882, Madison Sq. Sta., New York, NY 10159. TEL 212-989-5800) Ed. K.W. Allen. charts; illus.; index. Indexed: Art & Archaeol.Tech.Abstr., Chem.Abstr.
    Refereed Serial

668.4 JA ISSN 0037-0495
 CODEN: STHKAO
ADHESION AND ADHESIVES/SETCHAKU. (Text in Japanese) 1957. m. 7800 Yen. High Polymer Publishing Association - Kobunshi Kankokai, Chiekoin-Sagaru, Marutamachi, Kamikyoku, Kyoto 602, Japan. Ed. Hitoshi Okuda. adv.; charts; illus. Indexed: Chem.Abstr.
    —BLDSC shelfmark: 0680.810000.

668.3 JA ISSN 0001-8201
TP967 CODEN: NSKSAZ
ADHESION SOCIETY OF JAPAN. JOURNAL/NIHON SETCHAKU KYOKAISHI. (Text in English and Japanese) 1965. irreg. (6-8/yr.) Adhesion Society of Japan - Nihon Setchaku Kyokai, c/o Osaka-furitsu Kogyo Gijutsu Kenkyusho, Enokojima, Nishi-ku, Osaka 550, Japan. Ed. Kazumune Nakao. adv.; bk.rev.; abstr.; charts; illus.; pat.; index. Indexed: JTA.

ADHESIVE AND SEALANT COUNCIL. NEWSLETTER. see *RUBBER*

ADHESIVE AND SEALANT COUNCIL. SEMINAR PAPERS. see *RUBBER*

ADHESIVE TRENDS. see *RUBBER*

668.4 US
ADVANCED COMPOSITES. 1986. bi-m. $4 per no. Avanstar Communications, Inc., 7500 Old Oak Rd., Cleveland, OH 44130. (Subscr. to: 1 E. First St., Duluth, MN 55802) Ed. Nancy Albee. adv.; circ. 25,012.
    Description: Information for engineers and manufacturing personnel involved in planning, designing or manufacturing products made from advanced composites for an end-use market.

668.4 666 UK ISSN 0951-953X
ADVANCED COMPOSITES BULLETIN; an international newsletter. 1987. m. £219 (effective 1992). Elsevier Science Publishers Ltd., Crown House, Linton Rd., Barking, Essex IG11 8JU, England. TEL 081-594-7272. FAX 081-594-5942. TELEX 896950 APPSCI G. (Subscr. in U.S. and Canada to: Elsevier Science Publishing Co., Inc., Box 882, Madison Sq. Sta., New York, NY 10159. TEL 212-989-5800) Ed. Paul Hogg. bk.rev.; abstr.; charts; illus.; pat. (back issues avail.)
    ●Also available online. Vendor(s): Data-Star (PTBN), DIALOG (File no.636).
    —BLDSC shelfmark: 0696.838500.
    Description: Contains new materials, applications, processing and company news. Reports on technological and business opportunities in composites industry.

668.4 UK ISSN 0963-6935
▼**ADVANCED COMPOSITES LETTERS.** 1992. bi-m. £125 in Europe; America $210; elsewhere £130. Woodhead Publishing Ltd., Abington Hall, Abington, Cambridge CB1 6AH, England. TEL 0223-891358. FAX 0223-893694.
    Description: Covers the selection, design, processing and manufacture of fiber reinforced materials.
    Refereed Serial

668.4 UK ISSN 0952-9691
ADVANCED COMPOSITES MANUFACTURING CENTRE NEWSLETTER. 1987. irreg. (approx. 2/yr.). free to qualified personnel. Advanced Composites Manufacturing Centre, c/o Polytechnic South West, School of Manufacturing, Materials and Mechanical Engineering, Drake Circus, Plymouth, Devon PL4 8AA, England. TEL 0752-232650.
FAX 0752-232638. TELEX 45423 PSWAS G. Ed. John Summerscales. adv.; bk.rev.; circ. 4,600 (controlled).
    —BLDSC shelfmark: 0578.675200.
    Description: Reports progress in the manufacture of fiber reinforced composite plastics.

668.4 US ISSN 0730-6679
TP1101 CODEN: APTYD5
ADVANCES IN POLYMER TECHNOLOGY. q. $275 to institutions (foreign $319). (Polymer Processing Institute) John Wiley & Sons, Inc., Journals, 605 Third Ave., New York, NY 10158-0012. TEL 212-850-6000. FAX 212-850-6088. TELEX 12-7063. Ed. Marino Xanthos. adv.; charts; illus.; pat.; stat.; circ. 300. (also avail. in microform from RPI; back issues avail.) Indexed: Eng.Ind.
    —BLDSC shelfmark: 0710.610000.
    Formerly: Advances in Plastics Technology (ISSN 0272-9504)
    Description: Featuring articles, technical papers and the latest news on plastics technology, processing, and physics. It also focuses on materials developments, new processing techniques, and materials and processes involving new fields such as plastics in solar energy.

ADVANCES IN URETHANE SCIENCE AND TECHNOLOGY. see *CHEMISTRY — Organic Chemistry*

668.4 630 US
AGRI-PLASTICS REPORT. bi-m. $50. American Society for Plasticulture, Box 860238, St. Augustine, FL 32086. TEL 904-797-0299. Ed. H. Carl Hoefer, Jr. circ. 275.
    Description: Agricultural research on yield enhancement and earliness of vegetable crops, and flowers.

ANNUAL BOOK OF A S T M STANDARDS. VOLUME 04.09. WOOD. see *ENGINEERING — Engineering Mechanics And Materials*

ANNUAL BOOK OF A S T M STANDARDS. VOLUME 08.01. PLASTICS (1): C 177 TO D 1600. see *ENGINEERING — Engineering Mechanics And Materials*

ANNUAL BOOK OF A S T M STANDARDS. VOLUME 08.02. PLASTICS (2): D 1601 TO D 3099. see *ENGINEERING — Engineering Mechanics And Materials*

ANNUAL BOOK OF A S T M STANDARDS. VOLUME 08.04. PLASTIC PIPE AND BUILDING PRODUCTS. see *ENGINEERING — Engineering Mechanics And Materials*

668.4 BL
ANUARIO BRASILEIRO DO PLASTICO. a. Editora Quimica e Derivados Ltda., Rua Dr. Gabriel dos Santos, 55, Santa Cecilia CEP 01231, Sao Paulo, Brazil. TEL 011-826-6899. FAX 011-825-8192. TELEX 11-21801. Ed. Emanoel Fairbanks.

668.4 MX
ANUARIO LATINOAMERICANO DE LOS PLASTICOS. 1973. a. $25. Anuarios Latinoamericanos, S.A. de C.V., Colima No. 436, Piso 2, Mexico 7, DF, Mexico. Ed. Roberto J. Marquez. adv.; circ. 7,000.
    Formerly: Directorio Nacional de la Industria de los Plasticos y Proveedores (Year).

668.4 UK
ASIAN PLASTICS NEWS. 1988. q. 0($85) Reed Business Publishing Group (Subsidiary of: Reed International PLC), Quadrant House, The Quadrant, Sutton, Surrey SM2 5AS, England. TEL 081-652-8039. FAX 081-652-8986. (Subscr. to: Oakfield House, Perrymount Rd., Haywards Heath, W. Sussex RH19 3DH, England. TEL 444-445566) Ed. Philippa Hutchinson. adv.; circ. 9,877. (back issues avail.)
    Description: Focuses on the processing technology, raw materials and machinery hardware used in Asia and often sourced in Europe.

ASSOCIATION FRANCAISE DES INGENIEURS ET CADRES DU CAOUTCHOUC ET DES PLASTIQUES. ANNUAIRE. see *RUBBER*

BAUEN MIT KUNSTSTOFFEN. see *BUILDING AND CONSTRUCTION*

BIOMEDICAL MATERIALS; an international newsletter. see *MEDICAL SCIENCES*

668.4 678.2 UK ISSN 0307-6164
HD9661.G7
BRITISH PLASTICS AND RUBBER MAGAZINE. 1977. m. £80. M C M Publishing Ltd., 9 Weir Rd., London SW12 OLT, England. TEL 081-675-8043. FAX 081-675-8046. Ed. Peter Taylor. adv.; charts; illus.; tr.lit.; circ. 12,239. Indexed: Br.Tech.Ind., Cadscan, Excerp.Med., INIS Atomind., Int.Packag.Abstr., Key to Econ.Sci., Lead Abstr., PROMT, Text.Tech.Dig., Zincscan.
    —BLDSC shelfmark: 2337.300000.
    Incorporates: Polymer Age.
    Description: For managers in polymer processing companies.

668.4 CN ISSN 0008-4778
 CODEN: CNPLAJ
CANADIAN PLASTICS. (Includes annual Recycling Directory) 1943. 10/yr. Can.$48.15($55) (foreign $85). Southam Business Communications Inc. (Subsidiary of: Southam Inc.), 1450 Don Mills Rd., Don Mills, Ont. M3B 2X7, Canada. TEL 416-445-6641. FAX 416-442-2261. Ed. Edward Mason. adv.; bk.rev.; charts; illus.; stat.; tr.lit.; circ. 12,000. (also avail. in microfilm from PMC) Indexed: Can.B.P.I., Can.Per.Ind., Chem.Abstr., Key to Econ.Sci., PROMT, RAPRA.
    —BLDSC shelfmark: 3044.000000.
    Description: Covers developments in plastics markets technology in Canada.

668.4 CN ISSN 0068-9459
CANADIAN PLASTICS DIRECTORY AND BUYER'S GUIDE. 1959. a. Can.$69.55 (foreign $65). Southam Business Communications Inc. (Subsidiary of: Southam Inc.), 1450 Don Mills Rd., Don Mills, Ont. M3B 2X7, Canada. TEL 416-445-6641. FAX 416-442-2261.

CAOUTCHOUCS ET PLASTIQUES. see *RUBBER*

668.4 677 UK ISSN 0268-0491
CARBON & HIGH PERFORMANCE FIBRES DIRECTORY. 1981. biennial. £29.50($49.50) Chapman & Hall, 2-6 Boundary Row, London SE1 8HN, England. (Dist. by: International Thomson Publishing Services, Ltd., N. Way, Andover, Hampshire, SP10 5BE, England. TEL 0264-33-2424; US addr.: Chapman & Hall, 29 W. 35th St., New York, NY 10001-2291. TEL 212-244-3336) adv. (back issues avail.)

PLASTICS

668.4 660.284 UK ISSN 0262-4893
TP1183.F6 CODEN: CELPDJ
CELLULAR POLYMERS. 1982. 6/yr. £170. R A P R A Technology Ltd., Shawbury, Shrewsbury SY4 4NR, England. TEL 0939-250383. FAX 0939-251118. TELEX 35134. Ed. J.M. Buist. adv.; bk.rev.; illus. (back issues avail.) **Indexed:** Curr.Cont., Sci.Cit.Ind.
—BLDSC shelfmark: 3097.935000.
Description: Covers developments over the full range of cellular polymers, from elastomeric material to rigid plastics. Papers are included on the polymers, additives and manufacturing processes used in the industry and on the properties and applications of the finished products.

CHEMICALS & POLYMERS NEWS. see *PETROLEUM AND GAS*

668.4 HK
CHINA PLASTIC AND RUBBER JOURNAL/ZHONGGUO CUOLIAO XIANGJIAO; a plastic and rubber journal for P.R. China. (Text in Chinese; table of content in Chinese, English) 1982. q. HK.$156($40) for Asia; elsewhere $44. (Ministry of Light Industry, Institute of Plastics Processing and Application, CC) Adsale Publishing Company, Tung Wai Commercial Bldg., 21st Fl., 109-111 Gloucester Rd., Wanchai, Hong Kong. TEL 892-0511. FAX 838-4119. TELEX 63109 ADSAP. (Subscr. to: P.O. Box 20032, Hennessy Rd., Hong Kong) Ed. Josephine Cheng. adv.; circ. 15,000. (back issues avail.)
Description: Information on foreign advanced technology and market trends in the plastic and rubber industries for readers in the PRC.

668.4 UK ISSN 0952-6919
TA418.9.C6 CODEN: COPOE5
COMPOSITE POLYMERS. 1988. 6/yr. £170. R A P R A Technology Ltd., Shawbury, Shrewsbury SY4 4NR, England. TEL 0939-250383. FAX 0939-251118. TELEX 35134. Ed. P. Dickin. abstr.; bibl.; charts; illus.; stat. (back issues avail.)
—BLDSC shelfmark: 3364.966000.
Description: For engineers and designers using composite materials, particularly in the aerospace, automotive, construction and engineering industries.

668.4 US ISSN 0888-1227
COMPOSITES & ADHESIVES NEWSLETTER. 1984. bi-m. $150 (foreign $170) (effective Jan. 1992). T C Press (Subsidiary of: Technology Conferences), Box 36006, Los Angeles, CA 90036. TEL 213-938-6923. Ed. George Epstein. adv.; bk.rev.; circ. 150. (back issues avail.)
●Also available online. Vendor(s): Data-Star, DIALOG.
—BLDSC shelfmark: 3365.515000.
Description: Covers composite and adhesive materials; includes information on new applications, alerts/problems to avoid, technology developments, plus industry news about companies, schools, and professional societies.

CONFERENCE OF ELECTRICAL ENGINEERING PROBLEMS IN THE RUBBER AND PLASTICS INDUSTRIES. I E E E CONFERENCE RECORD. see *RUBBER*

668.4 GW ISSN 0936-0352
DEUTSCHEN KUNSTSTOFF-INSTITUT. MITTEILUNGEN. 1964. s-a. free. Deutsches Kunststoff-Institut, Schlossgartenstr. 6, 6100 Darmstadt, Germany.
Description: Research results and coming events at the Kunststoff-Institut.

668.4 US
DIRECTORY OF U S AND CANADIAN SCRAP PLASTICS PROCESSORS AND BUYERS. a. $40 (effective 1992). Resource Recycling, Inc., Box 10540, Portland, OR 97210. TEL 800-227-1424. FAX 503-227-6135. charts.
Description: Provides information on more than 250 plastics scrap reclaimers, with company address, contact names, and specific scrap plastic preferences.

E P E. (European Production Engineer) see *ENGINEERING — Mechanical Engineering*

668.4 UK ISSN 0952-6900
TP1101 CODEN: ENPLEB
ENGINEERING PLASTICS. 1974. 6/yr. £195. R A P R A Technology Ltd., Shawbury, Shrewsbury SY4 4NR, England. TEL 0939-250-383. FAX 0939-251118. TELEX 35134. Ed. K. Watkinson.
—BLDSC shelfmark: 3766.329000.
Description: Emphasis on practical information on the materials, properties, processing and application.

668.4 GW
EUROPAEISCHER WIRTSCHAFTSDIENST. KUNSTSTOFF-DIENST. 1926. w. DM.715. Casimir Katz Verlag, Bleichstr. 20-22, 7562 Gernsbach, Germany. TEL 07224-3091. FAX 07224-3094. TELEX 78915-DBV-D. Ed. Monika Riffel. circ. 880.

668.4 UK ISSN 0306-3534
TP1101 CODEN: EUPNBT
EUROPEAN PLASTICS NEWS. 1929. m. $170. Reed Business Publishing Group (Subsidiary of: Reed International PLC), Quadrant House, The Quadrant, Sutton, Surrey SM2 5AS, England. TEL 081-652-8986. FAX 081-652-8986. (Subscr. to: Oakfield House, Perrymount Rd., Haywards Heath, W. Sussex RH16 3DH, England. TEL 444-445566) Ed. Kevin O'Toole. adv.; bk.rev.; charts; illus.; tr.mk.; circ. 24,051 (controlled). (also avail. in microform from UMI; back issues avail. from UMI) **Indexed:** A.S.& T.Ind., BMT, Br.Ceram.Abstr., Br.Tech.Ind., C.I.S. Abstr., Cadscan, Chem.Abstr., Eng.Ind., Int.Packag.Abstr., Key to Econ.Sci., Lead Abstr., Packag.Sci.Tech., RAPRA, Zincscan.
—BLDSC shelfmark: 3829.787000.
Formerly: Europlastics; **Incorporates:** British Plastics (ISSN 0007-1625)
Description: Coverage of developments and events within Europe's plastics industry.

668.4 UK
FIBREGLASS COMPOSITES NEWS. s-a. Fibreglass Ltd., St. Helens, Merseyside WA10 3TR, England. Ed. Lynda Vaughan. circ. 5,000. (back issues avail.)

FIRE & FLAMMABILITY BULLETIN; an international newsletter. see *FIRE PREVENTION*

FOOD, COSMETICS AND DRUGS PACKAGING; an international newsletter. see *PACKAGING*

668.4 FR ISSN 0985-0503
TA418.9.C6
FRANCE COMPOSITES. (Text in English, French, German) 1988. a. 252 F. C E P P, 1 Place d'Estienne d'Orves, 75009 Paris, France. TEL 42-80-67-62. FAX 42-82-99-30. Ed.Bd. adv.; bk.rev.; circ. 10,000.

668.4 FR ISSN 0071-9056
FRANCE PLASTIQUES. 1949. a. 266 F. Creations, Editions et Productions Publicitaires, 1 Place d'Estienne d'Orves, 75009 Paris, France. TEL 42-80-67-62. FAX 42-82-99-30. Ed. Martine Clauel. adv.; circ. 5,000.

668.4 GW
GENAU. m. Bundesverband des Holz- und Kunststoffverarbeitende Industrie, Abraham-Lincoln-Str. 32, D-6200 Wiesbaden, Germany.

668.4 US
GRAFIBER NEWS. m. Composite Market Reports, Inc., 7670 Opportunity Rd., Ste.250, San Diego, CA 92111-2222. TEL 619-560-1085. FAX 619-560-0234. Ed. Steve Loud.

GREATER BATON ROUGE MANUFACTURERS DIRECTORY. see *BUSINESS AND ECONOMICS — Trade And Industrial Directories*

668.4 MX
GUIA DE LA INDUSTRIA: HULE, PLASTICOS Y RESINAS. 1964. a. Mex.$150000($50) Informatica Cosmos, S.A. de C.V., Fernandez Arrieta 5-101, Col. Los Cipreses, 04830 Mexico D.F., Mexico. TEL 677-4868. FAX 679-35-75. Ed. Cesar Macazaga. adv.
Former titles: Hule, Plasticos y Resinas (Annual) & Plasticos y Resinas (Annual).

668.4 MX
GUIA DE LA INDUSTRIA: PLASTICOS Y RESINAS. 1964. a. Editorial Cosmos, Espana No. 396, Col. Granjas Estrella, 09880 Mexico D.F., Mexico. TEL 582-99-28. circ. 5,000.

668.4 AG
GUIA DEL PLASTICO. 1952. 6/yr. Camara Argentina de la Industria Plastica, Jeronimo Salguero 1939, 1425 Buenos Aires, Argentina. TEL 826-5480. circ. 5,000.

668.4 SZ ISSN 0073-0084
HANDBUCH DER INTERNATIONALEN KUNSTSTOFFINDUSTRIE/INTERNATIONAL PLASTICS DIRECTORY/MANUEL INTERNATIONAL DES PLASTIQUES. (Text and index in English, French and German) 1958. every 10 yrs. 300 SFr. Verlag fuer Internationale Wirtschaftsliteratur GmbH, Box 30, CH-8047 Zurich, Switzerland. FAX 01-4010545. Ed. Walter Hirt. index.

668.4 UK ISSN 0264-7753
HIGH PERFORMANCE PLASTICS; an international bulletin. 1983. m. £219 (effective 1992). (Rubber and Plastics Research Association of Great Britain) Elsevier Science Publishers Ltd., Crown House, Linton Rd., Barking, Essex IG11 8JU, England. TEL 081-594-7272. FAX 081-594-5942. TELEX 896950 APPSCI G. (Subscr. in U.S. and Canada to: Elsevier Science Publishing Co., Inc., Box 882, Madison Sq. Sta., New York, NY 10159. TEL 212-989-5800) Ed. I. Guy. bk.rev.; illus.; stat. (back issues avail.)
●Also available online. Vendor(s): Data-Star, DIALOG.
—BLDSC shelfmark: 4307.338650.

668.4 II
HINDUSTAN LATEX. VARSHIKA RIPORTA/HINDUSTAN LATEX. ANNUAL REPORTS. (Text in English, Hindi) 11th ed., 1976. a. Varikkat House, TC 4-485, Kowdiar, Trivandrum 695003, India. stat.

HULE MEXICANO Y PLASTICOS; revista tecnica industrial. see *RUBBER*

668.4 UK
I A L PLASTICS YEARBOOK. 1987. irreg., latest 1990. £60. I A L Consultants Ltd., 14 Buckingham Palace Rd., London SW1W 0QP, England. TEL 01-828-5036. FAX 01-828-9318.
Formerly: Plastics Euro-Guide.
Description: Presents statistics and information about West European plastic raw materials manufacturers and markets.

668.4 UK ISSN 0261-5487
I R P I: INTERNATIONAL REINFORCED PLASTICS INDUSTRY. 1981. bi-m. £12($60) Channel Publications, Loudwater House, London Rd., Loudwater, High Wycombe HP10 9TL, England. TEL 44-494-436111. Ed. D. Pamington. adv.: B&W page $1404, color page $1854; trim 8 1/2 x 11 5/8. bk.rev.; illus.; circ. 6,442.
—BLDSC shelfmark: 4545.805000.

INDIAN RUBBER & PLASTICS AGE. see *RUBBER*

INFORMATIONS DU CAOUTCHOUC ET DES PLASTIQUES. see *RUBBER*

INTERNATIONAL BOTTLER AND PACKER. see *BEVERAGES*

668.4 UK ISSN 0143-7496
CODEN: IJAADK
INTERNATIONAL JOURNAL OF ADHESION AND ADHESIVES. 1980. q. £150 (Europe £165). Butterworth - Heinemann Ltd. (Subsidiary of: Reed International PLC), Linacre House, Jordan Hill, Oxford OX2 8DP, England. TEL 0865-310366. FAX 0865-310898. TELEX 83111 BHPOXF G. (Subscr. to: Turpin Transactions Ltd., Distribution Centre, Blackhorse Rd., Letchworth, Herts SG6 1HN, England. TEL 0462-672555) Ed. Diane Cogan. adv.; bk.rev.; abstr.; bibl.; charts; illus.; stat.; index. (back issues avail.) **Indexed:** Abstr.Bull.Inst.Pap.Chem., Appl.Mech.Rev., Chem.Abstr., Eng.Ind., HRIS, Int.Aerosp.Abstr., Int.Packag.Abstr., Met.Abstr., World Alum.Abstr., World Surf.Coat.
—BLDSC shelfmark: 4541.560000.
Description: Covers design of joints, stress analysis, surface preparation, dynamic properties, manufacturing technology, and new industrial and academic developments in sealants and adhesives.
Refereed Serial

668.4 GW ISSN 0930-777X
TP1080 CODEN: IPPREJ
INTERNATIONAL POLYMER PROCESSING. (Text in English) 1986. q. $203.40. (Polymer Processing Society) Carl Hanser Verlag, Kolbergerstr. 22, Postfach 860420, 8000 Munich 80, Germany. TEL 089-92694-0. Ed.Bd. adv.; bk.rev.; charts; illus.; circ. 2,000.
—BLDSC shelfmark: 4544.965800.
Description: Articles on the science of processing thermoplastics, thermosets, elastomers and fibers.

668.4 540 UK ISSN 0307-174X
QD380
INTERNATIONAL POLYMER SCIENCE AND TECHNOLOGY.
1974. m. £570. (British Library) R A P R A
Technology Ltd., Shawbury, Shrewsbury SY4 4NR,
England. TEL 0939-250383. FAX 0939-251118.
TELEX 35134. abstr.; circ. 350. (back issues avail.)
Indexed: Art & Archaeol.Tech.Abstr., Excerp.Med.,
Fluidex, World Surf.Coat.
—BLDSC shelfmark: 4544.965900.
Description: Contains English translations of
papers selected from twelve foreign rubber and
plastics journals.

668.4 II ISSN 0047-0899
**INTERNATIONAL PRESS CUTTING SERVICE: MODERN
PLASTICS AND ENGINEERING.** 1967. w. $65.
International Press Cutting Service, Box 63,
Allahabad 211001, India. Ed. N. Khanna. bk.rev.;
index; circ. 1,200. (processed)

668.4 547 US ISSN 0147-0671
TP1180.P8 CODEN: IPURD9
INTERNATIONAL PROGRESS IN URETHANES. 1977.
irreg. price varies. Technomic Publishing Co., Inc.,
851 New Holland Ave., Box 3535, Lancaster, PA
17604. TEL 717-291-5609. FAX 717-295-4538.
TELEX 230 753656 (TECHNOMIC UD). Ed.Bd.
Indexed: Chem.Abstr.
Refereed Serial

668.4 UK
**INTERNATIONAL STATUS REPORT ON PLASTICS
INDUSTRY WORLDWIDE.** a. £75. British Plastics
Federation, 5 Belgrave Sq., London SW1X 8PH,
England. TEL 071-2359483. FAX 071-235-8045.
TELEX 8951528.

668.4 IT ISSN 0392-3800
CODEN: INPLDK
INTERPLASTICS. 1978. bi-m. L.48000 (foreign
L.140000)(effectve 1992). Tecniche Nuove s.p.a.,
Via C. Menotti 14, 20129 Milan, Italy.
TEL 02-75701. FAX 02-7570205. circ. 5,000.
Description: Essays for those in the plastics field.

668.4 SZ
JAHRBUCH KUNSTSTOFFE: PLASTICS;
Bezugsquellenregister und Firmenverzeichnis nach
Artikelen fuer den Kunststoff-Markt. (Text in
German) 1965. a. 20 SFr. Vogt-Schild AG,
Zuchwilerstr. 21, CH-4501 Solothurn 1, Switzerland.
TEL 065-247247. FAX 065-247335. TELEX
934646. Ed. Alfred Widmer. adv.; bk.rev.; circ.
7,500. (tabloid format)

668.4 JA ISSN 0021-4582
TP986.A1 CODEN: JPLAAN
JAPAN PLASTICS AGE. (Includes Japan Plastics Industry
Annual) (Text in English) 1963. bi-m.
13000 Yen($60) Plastics Age Co. Ltd., Okochi
Bldg., 1-10-6 Kaji-cho, Chiyoda-ku, Tokyo 101,
Japan. Ed. Eiichi Asayama. circ. 23,000. (also avail.
in microform from UMI; reprint service avail. from
UMI) **Indexed:** Chem.Abstr., JTA, PROMT.

JOURNAL OF ADHESION. see PHYSICS

668.4 NE ISSN 0169-4243
TP967 CODEN: JATEE8
JOURNAL OF ADHESION SCIENCE AND TECHNOLOGY.
(Text in English) 1987. m. DM.1220 (effective
1992). V S P, P.O. Box 346, 3700 AH Zeist,
Netherlands. TEL 03404-25790.
FAX 03404-32081. TELEX 40217 VSP NL. Eds.
K.L Mittal, W.J. Van Ooij. adv.; bk.rev.; index. (back
issues avail.)
—BLDSC shelfmark: 4918.936000.
Description: Covers theoretical and basic aspects
of adhesion science and its applications in all areas
of technology.

668.4 US ISSN 0885-3282
R856.A1
JOURNAL OF BIOMATERIALS APPLICATIONS. 1986. q.
$250. Technomic Publishing Co., Inc., 851 New
Holland Ave., Box 3535, Lancaster, PA 17604.
TEL 717-291-5609. FAX 717-295-4538. TELEX
230-753565 (TECHNOMIC UD). Ed. Michael
Szycher. circ. 200. (back issues avail.)
—BLDSC shelfmark: 4953.515000.
Refereed Serial

668.44 US ISSN 0021-955X
TP1183.F6 CODEN: JCUPAM
JOURNAL OF CELLULAR PLASTICS. 1965. bi-m. $155.
Technomic Publishing Co., Inc., 851 New Holland
Ave., Box 3535, Lancaster, PA 17604.
TEL 717-291-5609. FAX 717-295-4538. TELEX
230-753565 (TECHNOMIC UD). Ed. Sidney H.
Metzger, Jr. adv.; bk.rev.; charts; illus.; pat.; stat.;
index; circ. 800. (also avail. in microform from UMI;
reprint service avail. from UMI) **Indexed:**
Appl.Mech.Rev., Chem.Abstr., Eng.Ind.,
Int.Packag.Abstr.
—BLDSC shelfmark: 4955.050000.
Refereed Serial

JOURNAL OF COATED FABRICS. see TEXTILE
INDUSTRIES AND FABRICS

668.4 US ISSN 0095-2443
TA455.P5 CODEN: JEPLAX
JOURNAL OF ELASTOMERS AND PLASTICS. 1969. q.
$180. Technomic Publishing Co. Inc., 851 New
Holland Ave., Box 3535, Lancaster, PA 17604.
TEL 717-291-5609. FAX 717-295-4538. TELEX
230 753565 (TECHNOMIC UD). Ed. Melvyn
Kohudic. adv.; bk.rev.; charts; stat.; index; circ. 500.
(also avail. in microform from UMI; reprint service
avail. from UMI) **Indexed:** Appl.Mech.Rev.,
Chem.Abstr., Curr.Cont., Eng.Ind., RAPRA.
—BLDSC shelfmark: 4973.289000.
Formerly: Journal of Elastoplastics. (ISSN
0022-071X)
Refereed Serial

668.4 US ISSN 8756-0879
CODEN: JPFSEH
JOURNAL OF PLASTIC FILM AND SHEETING. 1985. q.
$220. Technomic Publishing Co., Inc., 851 New
Holland Ave., Box 3535, Lancaster, PA 17604.
TEL 717-295-4538. TELEX 230 753565
(TECHNOMIC UD). Ed. James P. Harrington. abstr.;
bibl.; illus.; circ. 425.
—BLDSC shelfmark: 5040.695000.
Refereed Serial

JOURNAL OF REINFORCED PLASTICS & COMPOSITES.
see ENGINEERING — Engineering Mechanics And
Materials

668.4 US ISSN 0892-7057
TA418.9.C6 CODEN: JTMAEQ
JOURNAL OF THERMOPLASTIC COMPOSITE MATERIALS.
1988. q. $190. Technomic Publishing Co., Inc., 851
New Holland Ave., Box 3535, Lancaster, PA 17604.
TEL 717-291-5609. FAX 717-295-4538. TELEX
230 753565 (TECHNOMIC UD). Ed. Selcuk I.
Guceri. index; circ. 300. (back issues avail.)
—BLDSC shelfmark: 5069.099400.
Refereed Serial

668.4 US ISSN 0193-7197
TP1180.V48 CODEN: JVTEDI
JOURNAL OF VINYL TECHNOLOGY. 1979. q. $125
(foreign $140). Society of Plastics Engineers, Inc.,
14 Fairfield Dr., Brookfield, CT 06804-0403.
TEL 203-775-0471. FAX 203-775-8490. TELEX
643-712. Ed. Robert P. Braddicks, Jr. charts; illus.;
index; circ. 535. (back issues avail.)
—BLDSC shelfmark: 5072.485000.
Refereed Serial

668.4 GW ISSN 0451-1646
K MITTEILUNGEN. 1950. m. membership.
Gesamtverband Kunststoffverarbeitende Industrie
e.V., Froschpfort 16, 5430 Montabaur, Germany.
FAX 02602-4308. Ed. Reinhard Ackermann. adv.;
bk.rev.; abstr.; bibl.; stat.; circ. controlled.

668.4 GW ISSN 0177-0608
K: PLASTIC UND KAUTSCHUK ZEITUNG. 1969. fortn.
DM.103.40. Giesel Verlag fuer Publizitaet GmbH,
Stuttgarterstr. 18-24, 6000 Frankfurt a.M. 1,
Germany. Ed. H. Rupprecht. adv.; bk.rev.; illus.; stat.;
index; circ. 15,000.

668.4 RU ISSN 0023-1118
CODEN: KVLKA4
KHIMICHESKIE VOLOKNA. 1959. bi-m. 22.20 Rub.
Izdatel'stvo Khimiya, Novaya Pl. 10, Moscow K-12,
Russia. bk.rev.; bibl.; index. **Indexed:**
Abstr.Bull.Inst.Pap.Chem., Chem.Abstr., INIS
Atomind., Text.Tech.Dig., World Text.Abstr.
—BLDSC shelfmark: 0393.300000.

KLOECKNER WERKE HEUTE; Stahl, Maschinenbau,
Kunststoff. (Kloeckner-Werke AG) see METALLURGY

668.4 NE ISSN 0167-9597
CODEN: KRUBDV
KUNSTSTOF EN RUBBER; monthly review on plastics.
1948. m. 20. Kunststof en Rubber Instituut,
Schoemakerstraat 97, Postbus 6031, 2600 JA
Delft, Netherlands. Ed. J.L. Hey. adv.; bk.rev.; abstr.;
charts; illus.; tr.lit.; circ. 2,000. **Indexed:** Chem.Abstr.,
Eng.Ind., Excerp.Med., RAPRA.
—BLDSC shelfmark: 5130.795000.
Formerly: Plastica (ISSN 0032-1095)

668.4 NE
KUNSTSTOF MAGAZINE. m. fl.126 (effective 1992).
(Nederlandse Federatie voor Kunststoffen)
Uitgeversmaatschappij C. Misset B.V., Hanzestr. 1,
7006 RH Doetinchem, Netherlands.
TEL 08340-49911. FAX 08340-43839. adv.; B&W
page fl.2295; unit 187 x 257; adv. contact: Cor van
Nek. illus.; circ. 5,750.

668.4 GW ISSN 0075-7276
KUNSTSTOFF INDUSTRIE UND IHRE HELFER. a. DM.38.
Industrieschau-Verlagsgesellschaft, Berliner Allee 8,
6100 Darmstadt, Germany.

668.4 GW ISSN 0047-3766
TP1101 CODEN: KUNJD7
KUNSTSTOFF JOURNAL. 1967. m. DM.64.
Europa-Fachpresse-Verlag GmbH (Subsidiary of:
Sueddeutscher Verlag), Thomas-Dehler-Str. 27,
8000 Munich 83, Germany. TEL 089-67804-0. Ed.
Thomas Schwachulla. adv.; bk.rev.; circ. 15,000.

668.4 GW
KUNSTSTOFF- UND KAUTSCHUK-PRODUKTE. 1982. a.
DM.25. Verlag Hoppenstedt and Co., Havelstr. 9,
Postfach 4006, 6100 Darmstadt, Germany.
TEL 06151-380-0. FAX 06151-38-360. Ed. Ingrid
Bode. index; circ. 10,000.
Formerly: Kunststoff-Produkte.

668.4 GW ISSN 0172-6374
TP1101 CODEN: KUNSDY
KUNSTSTOFFBERATER. 1955. m. DM.134.40. Giesel
Verlag fuer Publizitaet GmbH, Stuttgarterstr. 18-24,
6000 Frankfurt a.M. 1, Germany. TEL 069-2600-0.
FAX 069-2600609. Ed. H. Rupprecht. adv.; bk.rev.;
illus.; mkt.; index; circ. 6,100. (also avail. in
microform from UMI; reprint service avail. from UMI)
Indexed: C.I.S. Abstr., Chem.Abstr., Excerp.Med.,
Int.Packag.Abstr., Packag.Sci.Tech., PROMT, RAPRA,
Sci.Abstr.
Formerly: Kunststoffberater, -Rundschau, -Technik
(ISSN 0340-8442); **Incorporates:** Kunststoff
Rundschau (ISSN 0023-5555) & Kunststofftechnik
(ISSN 0023-5601)

668.4 GW ISSN 0023-5563
TP986.A1 CODEN: KUNSAV
KUNSTSTOFFE; Organ deutscher
Kunststoff-Fachverbaende. English edition:
Kunststoffe - German Plastics (ISSN 0723-0192)
1911. m. DM.234. Carl Hanser Verlag, Kolbergerstr.
22, 8000 Munich 80, Germany. TEL 089-92694-0.
Ed.Bd. adv.; bk.rev.; charts; illus.; mkt.; pat.; tr.lit.;
index; circ. 11,600. **Indexed:** Anal.Abstr., C.I.S.
Abstr., Chem.Abstr., Eng.Ind., Excerp.Med., INIS
Atomind., Key to Econ.Sci., Packag.Sci.Tech., RAPRA,
World Surf.Coat.

668.4 GW ISSN 0938-9849
▼**KUNSTSTOFFE EUROPE.** 1991. q. DM.60. Carl
Hanser Verlag, Kolbergerstr. 22, 8000 Munich 80,
Germany. TEL 089-92694-0. FAX 089-984809.
Eds. Wolfgang Glenz, Diether Burkhardt. circ. 1,400.

668.4 GW ISSN 0723-0192
KUNSTSTOFFE - GERMAN PLASTICS. German edition:
Kunststoffe (ISSN 0023-5563) (Text in English,
German) m. DM.297.60. Carl Hanser Verlag,
Kolbergerstr. 22, Postfach 860420, 8000 Munich
80, Germany. TEL 089-926940. **Indexed:**
Curr.Cont., Int.Packag.Abstr., PROMT.
—BLDSC shelfmark: 5131.014000.

668.4 GW ISSN 0075-7292
KUNSTSTOFFE IM LEBENSMITTELVERKEHR. 1962.
irreg., no.40, 1991. DM.118.
(Bundesgesundheitsamt, Kunststoff-Kommission)
Carl Heymanns Verlag KG, Luxemburgerstr. 449,
5000 Cologne 41, Germany. TEL 0221-46010-0.
FAX 0221-4601069.
—BLDSC shelfmark: 5131.025000.

PLASTICS

668.4 SZ ISSN 0023-5598
TP986.A1 CODEN: KUPLAK
KUNSTSTOFFE - PLASTICS; Zeitschrift fuer die Herstellung, Verarbeitung und Anwendung von Kunststoffen. (Text in German) 1953. m. 90 SFr. Vogt-Schild AG, Zuchwilerstr. 21, CH-4501 Solothurn 1, Switzerland. TEL 065-247247. FAX 065-247335. TELEX 934646. Ed. Kurt Hermann. adv.; bk.rev.; illus.; index; circ. 5,500. (looseleaf format) **Indexed:** Chem.Abstr., Eng.Ind., Excerp.Med., Key to Econ.Sci., Met.Abstr., RAPRA, World Alum.Abstr.
—BLDSC shelfmark: 5131.050000.

LIQUID CRYSTALS; an international journal in the field of anisotropic fluids. see CHEMISTRY — Crystallography

668.4 IT ISSN 0394-3453
MACPLAS; rivista mensile per l'industria delle materie plastiche e della goma. (Includes English language supplement: Macplas International) 1976. m. L.315000 (free to qualified personnel). Promaplast S.r.l., Centro Commerciale Milanofiori, Palazzo F-2, 20090 Assago Milan, Italy. TEL 02-8241641. FAX 02-8243463. TELEX 341378 ASPLAS. Ed. Gino Delvecchio. adv.; circ. 11,000.
—BLDSC shelfmark: 5330.393750.

668.4 IT
MACPLAS INTERNATIONAL; technical magazine for the plastics and rubber industry. (Supplement to: Macplas) (Text in English) 1976. q. L.130000. Promaplast S.r.l., Centro Commerciale Milanofiori, Palazzo F-2, 20090 Assago Milan, Italy. TEL 02-8241641. FAX 02-8243463. TELEX 341378 ASPLAS. Ed. Gino Delvecchio. circ. 21,000. (back issues avail.)

668.4 RM ISSN 0025-5289
CODEN: MPLAAM
MATERIALE PLASTICE. Title varies slightly: Revista Materiale Plastice. (Text in Rumanian; summaries in English, French, German, Russian) 1964. q. 32 lei($60) Institutul Central de Cercetari Chimice, Calea Plevnei 139, 77131 Bucharest, Rumania. TELEX 10944 ICHIM. (Subscr. to: Rompresfilatelia, Export Presa, P.O. Box 12-210, Bucharest, Rumania) adv.; bk.rev.; abstr.; bibl.; charts; illus.; pat.; stat.; index; circ. 1,000. **Indexed:** C.I.S. Abstr., Chem.Abstr., Inform.Sci.Abstr.

MATERIALS AND MANUFACTURE. see ENGINEERING — Mechanical Engineering

MATERIALS AND PROCESSING REPORT; the leading edge of technology worldwide. see METALLURGY

620 666 US ISSN 0952-5211
TA401 CODEN: MAEDEV
MATERIALS EDGE. 1987. m. $476. Metal Bulletin Inc., 220 Fifth Ave., 10th Fl., New York, NY 10001. TEL 800-638-2525. FAX 212-213-6273. Ed. John Mack. bk.rev.; circ. 10,000. (back issues avail.)
—BLDSC shelfmark: 5394.265000.
Description: Covers new and improved materials in business including aerospace, ceramics, metallurgy, dentistry.

668.4 IT ISSN 0025-5459
TP1101 CODEN: MPELAK
MATERIE PLASTICHE ED ELASTOMERI.* (Text mainly in Italian; sometimes in English, French or German; summaries in Italian) 1934. m. Industria Pubblicazioni Audiovisivi, Via Monte Grappa 3, 20124 Milan, Italy. adv.; bk.rev.; abstr.; bibl.; charts; illus.; pat.; stat.; circ. 5,000. **Indexed:** Chem.Abstr., Eng.Ind., PROMT, RAPRA.
—BLDSC shelfmark: 5399.010000.

668.4 GW
MEISTERBETRIEB. q. Landesverband Holz- und Kunstoffverarbeitendend Handwerk, Leihgesterner Weg 20, D-6300 Giessen, Germany.

668.4 US ISSN 0026-8275
TP986 CODEN: MOPLAY
MODERN PLASTICS. International edition (ISSN 0026-8283) 1925. m. $41.75 (Canada $53; elsewhere $225). McGraw-Hill, Inc., 1221 Ave. of the Americas, New York, NY 10020. TEL 212-512-6267. FAX 212-512-6111. (Subscr. to: Box 601, Hightstown, NJ 08520) Ed. Robert J. Martino. adv.; bk.rev.; abstr.; illus.; pat.; tr.lit.; index; circ. 74,500 (55,000 U.S. ed., 19,500 international ed.). (also avail. in microform from UMI) **Indexed:** A.S.& T.Ind., ABI Inform., Abstr.Bull.Inst.Pap.Chem., Art & Archaeol.Tech.Abstr., Bus.Ind., Chem.Abstr., Curr.Pack.Abstr., Eng.Ind., Ind.Sci.Rev., PROMT, RAPRA, SRI, Text.Tech.Dig., Tr.& Indus.Ind.
—BLDSC shelfmark: 5891.000000.
Description: Provides analysis and assessment of significant developments in materials, processes, design and markets.

660.2 US ISSN 0085-3518
MODERN PLASTICS ENCYCLOPEDIA. (Special October issue of: Modern Plastics) 1925. a. $54 or included with subscr. to Modern Plastics. McGraw-Hill, Inc., 1221 Ave. of the Americas, New York, NY 10020. TEL 212-512-6267. FAX 212-512-6111. Ed. Rosalind Juran. adv.; circ. 48,700.
—BLDSC shelfmark: 5891.005000.

668.4 US ISSN 0026-8283
MODERN PLASTICS INTERNATIONAL. (International edition of Modern Plastics) (Text in English) 1971. m. $157 in Europe and Japan; elsewhere $110. McGraw-Hill Inc., 1221 Ave. of the Americas, New York, NY 10020. TEL 212-512-6267. FAX 212-512-6111. (Subscr. in Europe to: 50 Av. de la Gare, Lausanne, Switzerland) Ed. Dennis Brownbill. adv.; bk.rev.; index; circ. 19,500. (also avail. in microform from UMI) **Indexed:** Br.Ceram.Abstr., Cadscan, Int.Packag.Abstr., Key to Econ.Sci., Lead Abstr., Packag.Sci.Tech., PROMT, W.R.C.Inf., Zincscan.
—BLDSC shelfmark: 5892.200000.

668.4 JA
MOLDERS. 1961. m. 3600 Yen($20) Japan Plastics Journal Ltd - Nihon Parasuchikkusu Shinposha, Kimura Bldg., 38 Minami-Sumiya-cho, Minami-ku, Osaka 552, Japan. Ed. Toshiyuki Shimogaito. adv.; bk.rev.; abstr.; illus.; circ. 20,000.

668.4 HU ISSN 0027-2914
CODEN: MUGUAO
MUANYAG ES GUMI/PLASTICS AND RUBBER. (Text in Hungarian; summaries in English, French, German, Russian) 1964. m. $33. (Gepipari Tudomanyos Egyesulet) Lapkiado Vallalat, Lenin korut 9-11, 1073 Budapest 7, Hungary. TEL 222-408. (Subscr. to: Kultura, Box 149, H-1389 Budapest, Hungary) (Co-sponsor: Magyar Kemikusok Egyesulete) Eds. S. Odon Gal, Hugo Macskasy. adv.; bk.rev.; bibl.; charts; illus.; mkt.; index; circ. 1,700. **Indexed:** Chem.Abstr., Hung.Build.Bull., Intl.Polym.Sci.& Tech., RAPRA, Ref.Zh.
—BLDSC shelfmark: 5980.910000.

668.4 FI ISSN 0788-8430
MUOVI - PLAST. 10/yr. FIM 300. Muoviyhdistys - Finnish Plastics Association, Mariank 26-B, SF-00170 Helsinki, Finland. TEL 358-0-1351200. FAX 358-0-1355601. adv.; bk.rev.
Formerly (until 1989): Muoviyhdistys Tiedottaa.

668.4 US
N A P D MAGAZINE; the voice of plastics distribution. 1986. bi-m. $50 to non-members. National Association of Plastics Distributors, 6333 Long St., Ste. 340, Shawnee, KS 66216. TEL 913-268-6273. FAX 913-268-6388. Ed. Janet Thill. adv.; circ. 8,000.

668.4 678.2 NE ISSN 0165-7089
N V R - INFORMATIEF. 11/yr. fl.135. Nederlandse Vereniging van Rubber- en Kunststoffabrikanten, P.O. Box 418, 2260 AK Leidschendam, Netherlands. TEL 70-3177243. FAX 70-3177412. circ. 300.

668.4 630 US
NATIONAL AGRICULTURAL PLASTICS CONGRESS. PROCEEDINGS. 1960. irreg., 22nd, 1990. price varies. American Society for Plasticulture, c/o H. Carl Hoefer, Jr., Exec. Sec., Box 860238, St. Augustine, FL 32086. TEL 904-829-1667. circ. 350. (also avail. in microfiche)
Formerly: National Agricultural Plastics Association. Proceedings.

668.4 JA
NEW MATERIALS DEVELOPED IN JAPAN (YEAR). 1984. irreg., latest 1991. $1250. Toray Research Center, Inc., (Subsidiary of: Toray Industries, Ltd.), 3-1-8 Nihonbashi - Muromachi, Chuo-ku, Tokyo 103, Japan. TEL 81-3-3245-5895. FAX 81-3-3245-5789. TELEX J22623 TRC JA.
Description: Includes information on 379 new materials developed in Japan from April 1987 to March 1991.

NEW TECHNOLOGY JAPAN. see MACHINERY

668.4 JA ISSN 0029-0351
NIHON PURASUCHIKKUSU SHINPO/JAPAN PLASTICS JOURNAL. (Text in Japanese) 1949. 4/m. 6000 Yen($40) Japan Plastics Journal Ltd. - Nihon Purasuchikkusu Shinpo-sha, Kimura Bldg., 38 Minamisumiya-cho, Minami-ku, Osaka 552, Japan. Ed. Toshiyuki Shimogaito. adv.; bk.rev.; charts; illus.; pat.; stat.; tr.lit.; index; circ. 20,000.

668.4 NO ISSN 0332-6136
NORSK PLAST. 1968. 8/yr. NOK 185. Teknisk Presse A.S, Hovfaret 17, P.O. Box 235 Skoeyen, N-0212 Oslo 2, Norway. TEL 47-2-52-10-40. FAX 47-2-50-66-48. Ed. Ragnar Brekke. adv.; circ. 7,136.

668.4 US
NORTH CAROLINA PLASTICS PROCESSORS AND PRODUCERS. quinquennial. $15. North Carolina State University, School of Engineering, Industrial Extension Service, Box 7902, Raleigh, NC 27695-7902. TEL 919-515-2358. Ed. W. Paul Cowgill.

668.4 AG ISSN 0325-0407
NOTICIERO DEL PLASTICO - ELASTOMEROS. 1959. m. Aus.$300($300) Editorial Tecnica Siglo XXI, S.A., Talcahuano 374-1p. B, 1013 Buenos Aires, Argentina. TEL 452348. Ed. Guillermo Oliveti. adv.; bk.rev.; bibl.; stat.; circ. 6,000. (tabloid format; back issues avail.) **Indexed:** PROMT.
Description: Covers plastics and rubber, machines, technology, design, analysis of markets, tests, events and reports.

668.4 AU
OESTERREICHISCHE KUNSTSTOFF ZEITSCHRIFT. 1970. bi-m. S.504. (Gesellschaft zur Foerderung der Kunststofftechnik) Verlag Lorenz, Ebendorferstr. 10, A-1010 Vienna, Austria. TEL 0222-426695. FAX 0222-438693. Ed. Robert Hillisch. adv.; bk.rev.; illus.; pat.; stat.; circ. 1,600. **Indexed:** Chem.Abstr.
Formerly: Oesterreichische Kunststoff Zeitung (ISSN 0029-926X)

668.4 678.2 FR ISSN 0030-0462
OFFICIEL DES PLASTIQUES ET DU CAOUTCHOUC. 1954. m. (10/yr.). 200 F. S.A.D.E.P., 48 rue de la Bienfaisance, 75008 Paris, France. Ed. Marcel Roube. adv.; charts, illus.; circ. 10,000. **Indexed:** Chem.Abstr.
Formerly: Officiel des Activites des Plastiques et du Caoutchouc.

668.4 US
OXYCHEM NEWSBRIEFS. 1930. q. free. Occidental Chemical Corp., Durez Division, 528 Walck Rd., N. Tonawanda, NY 14120. TEL 716-696-6000. adv.; circ. 6,000.
Former titles: Durez Molder Newsbriefs; Durez Molder (ISSN 0012-7264)

668.4 SW
P K L PLASTER. 1969. biennial. SEK 160. Plast- och Kemikalieleverantoerers Foerening, Box 5512, S-114 85 Stockholm, Sweden. FAX 08-6678051. TELEX 19673-ALUDOR S.

668.4 MX
PANORAMA PLASTICO; la revista mexicana del plastico. 1984. m. Mex.$84000($95) Editorial Corso, S.A. de C.V., Insurgentes Sur No. 594-502, Col. del Valle, 03100 Mexico, D.F., Mexico. TEL 669-30-87. FAX 523-22-03. Ed. Carlos Moreno. bk.rev.; circ. 10,000. (back issues avail.)
Description: Provides technical information on the plastics industry in Mexico.

PAPER, FILM AND FOIL CONVERTER. see PACKAGING

668.4　　　　　　FR　　ISSN 0031-4803
PENSEZ PLASTIQUES.* (Text in English, French and German) 1954. m. (plus q. and s-a. editions). 38 F. Editions de Berne et Cie, 11 bd. des Batignolles, 75008 Paris, France. Ed. J.S. de Berne. adv.; charts; illus. **Indexed:** Chem.Abstr., RAPRA.

668.4　　　　　　IT　　ISSN 0391-7401
　　　　　　　　　　　CODEN: PLATDW
PLAST; rivista delle materie plastiche. (Text in Italian; summaries in English) 1969. m. L.64000. E R I S S.p.A., Via Tellini, 14, 20155 Milan, Italy. Ed. Aldo Rotta. adv.; bk.rev.; abstr.; bibl.; charts; illus.; pat.; stat.; circ. 8,000. **Indexed:** Chem.Abstr.

668.4　　　　　　DK　　ISSN 0106-1720
PLAST EMBALLAGE SCANDINAVIA. Issued with: Plast Panorama Scandinavia. 10/yr. DKK 550. Thomson Communications (Scandinavia) A-S, Struenseegade 7-9, DK-2200 Copenhagen N, Denmark. TEL 35-378055. FAX 35-373639. Ed. Sven Vollertzen. adv.; circ. 6,324.
—BLDSC shelfmark: 6528.791000.

668.4　　　　　　DK
PLAST PANORAMA SCANDINAVIA. 1950. 10/yr. DKK 550. (Association of Danish Plastics Industries) Thomson Communications (Scandinavia) A-S, Struenseegade 7-9, DK-2200 Copenhagen N, Denmark. TEL 45-35-37-80-55. (Co-sponsor: Plastic Industry's Employers' Association) Ed. Sven Vollertzen. adv.; circ. 6,324. **Indexed:** Int.Packag.Abstr.

668.4 678　　　　GW　　ISSN 0048-4350
TP986.A1　　　　　　　　CODEN: PLKAAM
PLASTE UND KAUTSCHUK; Zeitschrift fuer Wirtschaft, Wissenschaft und Technik der hochpolymeren Werkstoffe. (Includes: Fachteil Anstrichstoffe) 1954. m. DM.240. Deutscher Verlag fuer Grundstoffindustrie, Karl-Heine-Str. 27, 7031 Leipzig, Germany. TEL 4081011. FAX 4012571. TELEX 51451-FACHB-DD. adv.; bk.rev. **Indexed:** Anal.Abstr., Chem.Abstr., Curr.Cont., Eng.Ind., Met.Abstr., Phys.Ber., Sci.Abstr., World Alum.Abstr., World Surf.Coat.
—BLDSC shelfmark: 6528.800000.
Description: Covers the technology, research, processing, and application of plastic and rubber materials, paints. Includes reports of events.

668.4 678.2　　　SW　　ISSN 0347-8262
PLASTFORUM SCANDINAVIA. 1970. 10/yr. SEK 395 (effective Jan. 1992). Aller Specialtidningar AB, S-251 85, S-251 06 Haelsingborg, Sweden. TEL 46-42-17-35-00. FAX 46-42-17-36-00. Ed. Hans Widen. adv.; bk.rev.; circ. 6,000.
Formerly: Plastforum (ISSN 0048-4369)
Description: Focuses on plastics and rubber converting industry as well as end-uses industries.

668.4　　　　　　MX
PLASTI-NOTICIAS. 1972. m. Publi-News Latinoamericana, S.A.C.V., Colima 436, piso 2, Mexico 7 D.F., Mexico. Ed. Roberto J. Marquez. adv.; circ. controlled.

668.4　　　　　　US
THE PLASTIC BOTTLE REPORTER. 1980. q. free. Society of the Plastics Industry, Inc., Plastic Bottle Information Bureau, 1275 K St., N.W., Ste. 400, Washington, DC 20005. TEL 202-371-5244. FAX 202-408-0736. circ. 11,000. (back issues avail.)
Description: Covers new and inventive ways of collecting and recycling plastic bottles. Often includes a listing of other PBIB publications.

668.4　　　　　　US
PLASTIC BUSINESS NEWS. s-m. Washington Business Information, 1117 N. 19th St., Rm. 200, Arlington, VA 22209. TEL 703-247-3434.
Description: Covers plastics industry developments.

668.4　　　　　　UK
PLASTIC INDUSTRY DIRECTORY. irreg. E M A P Vision Ltd., Maclaren House, 19 Scarbrook Rd., Croydon CR9 1QH, England. TEL 081-760-9690. FAX 081-681-1672. TELEX 946665.
Description: Guide to the plastics industry.

PLASTIC WASTE STRATEGIES. see *PUBLIC HEALTH AND SAFETY*

PLASTICHEM. see *ENGINEERING — Chemical Engineering*

668.4　　　　　　BL　　ISSN 0102-1931
PLASTICO MODERNO. 1971. m. Cr.$50000. Editora Quimica e Derivados Ltda., Rua Dr. Gabriel dos Santos, 55, Santa Cecilia - CEP 01231, Sao Paulo, Brazil. TEL 011-826-6899. FAX 011-8258192. TELEX 11-21801. Ed. Emanoel Fairbanks. adv.; bk.rev.; charts; illus.; circ. 12,000. (back issues avail.)
Description: Deals with the Brazilian plastics industry, its producers, manufacturers and customers. Also covers the rubber industry, new materials and processing, technology and application.

668.4　　　　　　AG
PLASTICOS. 1948. bi-m. $50. Camara Argentina del Libro - Argentine Book Association, Avda. Belgrano 1580, 6 Piso, 1093 Buenos Aires, Argentina. Ed. Hugo Brik. adv.; bk.rev.; abstr.; charts; illus.; mkt.; stat.; tr.lit.; circ. 10,000. **Indexed:** Chem.Abstr.
Former titles: Sip-Plastinoticias; Plasticos (ISSN 0032-1125)

668.4　　　　　　BL　　ISSN 0032-1133
PLASTICOS EM REVISTA. 1962. m. Cr.$2700($420) Plasticos em Revista Editora Ltda., Rua Piaui 1164, Casa 8, Sao Paulo, SP, Brazil. FAX 011-66-0496. TELEX 11-24711 LRDL BR. Ed. Beatriz Helman. adv.; bk.rev.; abstr.; charts; illus.; mkt.; stat.; tr.lit.; circ. 10,700. **Indexed:** Chem.Abstr., Packag.Sci.Tech.
—BLDSC shelfmark: 6530.250000.

668.4　　　　　　GW　　ISSN 0303-4011
　　　　　　　　　　　CODEN: PLUVBY
PLASTICOS UNIVERSALES. (Text in Spanish) 1957. bi-m. 6000 ptas.($75) Carl Hanser Verlag, Kolbergerstr. 22, Postfach 860420, 8000 Munich 80, Germany. TEL 089-926940. (In Spain: Gran Via Corts Catalanes, 322-324, 08004 Barcelona, Spain. TEL 3-425-45-44) Ed. W. Glenz. adv.; charts; illus.; mkt.; pat.; tr.lit.; index; circ. 4,000. **Indexed:** Chem.Abstr, Int.Packag.Abstr.
—BLDSC shelfmark: 6530.350000.
Formerly: Kunststoffe - Plasticos (ISSN 0023-558X)

660　　　　　　　US
PLASTICS. 1974. m. $15 to qualified personnel; others $20. Western Plastics News Inc., 1704 Colorado Ave., Santa Monica, CA 90404. TEL 213-829-4876. Ed. Norry M. Hastings. adv.; bk.rev.; circ. 15,000.
Formerly: Western Plastics.

660　　　　　　　JA　　ISSN 0551-0503
　　　　　　　　　　　CODEN: PUEJDH
PLASTICS AGE/PURASUCHIKKUSU EJI. (Includes: Plastics Age Encyclopedia) (Text in Japanese; summaries in English) 1954. m. 16.000 Yen. Plastics Age Co., Ltd. - Purasuchikkuse Eji K. K., Okochi Bldg., 1-10-6 Kajicho, Chiyoda-ku, Tokyo 101, Japan. Ed. Eiichi Asayama. adv.; bk.rev.; stat.; circ. 27,000.
—BLDSC shelfmark: 6531.300000.

668.4 614.7　　　US　　ISSN 1051-0567
PLASTICS & ENVIRONMENT. fortn. $497 (foreign $547). McGraw-Hill, Inc., Chemical & Plastics Information Services, 1221 Ave. of the Americas, 43rd Fl., New York, NY 10020. TEL 800-537-9213. FAX 609-426-5905.

668.4 678.2　　　UK　　ISSN 0309-4561
TP1101　　　　　　　　　CODEN: PRUID5
PLASTICS AND RUBBER INTERNATIONAL. 1976. bi-m. £60. Plastics and Rubber Institute, 11 Hobart Pl., London SW1W OHL, England. FAX 071-823-1379. Ed. Serena Aitchison. adv.; bk.rev.; circ. 18,000. (also avail. in microfilm from UMI; reprint service avail. from ISI,UMI) **Indexed:** Art & Archaeol.Tech.Abstr., Br.Tech.Ind., Cadscan, Chem.Abstr., Curr.Cont., Curr.Pack.Abstr., Excerp.Med., High.Educ.Curr.Aware.Bull., ISMEC, Lead Abstr., Packag.Sci.Tech., Sci.Abstr., Text.Tech.Dig., Zincscan.
—BLDSC shelfmark: 6531.454000.
Former titles: Plastics and Rubber; Plastics and Polymers (ISSN 0300-3582)

668.4 678.2　　　UK　　ISSN 0032-1168
PLASTICS AND RUBBER WEEKLY. 1964. w. £73. E M A P Vision Ltd., 19 Scarbrook Rd., Croydon, Surrey CR9 1QH, England. TEL 081-760-9690. FAX 081-681-1672. TELEX 946665. Ed. G. Sommer. adv.; illus.; mkt.; pat.; stat.; tr.mk.; circ. 20,584 (controlled). (also avail. in microfilm from UMI; reprint service avail. from UMI) **Indexed:** Chem.Abstr., Fluidex, Int.Packag.Abstr., PROMT, RAPRA, World Surf.Coat., World Text.Abstr.
—BLDSC shelfmark: 6531.460000.
Description: For the plastics and rubber industries.

668.4　　　　　　CN
PLASTICS BUSINESS. 1980. 4/yr. Can.$45($55) (foreign $85). Southam Business Communications Inc. (Subsidiary of: Southam Inc.), 1450 Don Mills Rd., Don Mills, Ont. M3B 2X7, Canada. TEL 416-445-6641. FAX 416-442-2077. Ed. Edward Mason. adv.; circ. 11,070. (tabloid format)

668.4　　　　　　US　　ISSN 0734-1784
PLASTICS BUSINESS NEWS; and major market indicators report. 1982. fortn. $327 in U.S. & Canada. Washington Business Information, Inc., c/o Karen Harrington, 1117 N. 19th St., Ste. 200, Arlington, VA 22209. TEL 703-247-3422. FAX 703-247-3421. Ed. Elaine Zablocki.
●Also available online. Vendor(s): NewsNet.
—BLDSC shelfmark: 6532.010000.
Description: News and information on trends, new product development, alternate uses of plastic materials, acquisitions and mergers, as well as production and distribution processes.

668.4　　　　　　US
▼**PLASTICS - COMPOSITES MOLDING DIGEST**. 1991. m. $145 to non-members (foreign $155); members $120 (foreign $130). A S M International, Materials Information, Materials Park, OH 44073. TEL 216-338-5151. FAX 216-338-4634. TELEX 980-619. (UK addr.: Institute of Metals, Materials Information, 1 Carlton House Terr., London SW1Y 5DB, England. TEL 071-839-4071)
Description: Selection of plastics and composites molding information published in Engineered Materials Abstracts and the Materials Business Information series.

668.4　　　　　　US　　ISSN 0148-9119
TP1101　　　　　　　　　CODEN: PLCODR
PLASTICS COMPOUNDING; for resin producers, formulators and compounders. 1978. 7/yr. $40. Avanstar Communications, Inc., 7500 Old Oak Blvd., Cleveland, OH 44130. TEL 216-243-8100. FAX 216-891-2726. (Subscr. to: 1 E. First St., Duluth, MN 55802) Ed. Mary C. McMurrer. adv.; bk.rev.; circ. 13,000. (back issues avail.; reprint service avail.) **Indexed:** Chem.Abstr, Curr.Pack.Abstr., PROMT.
—BLDSC shelfmark: 6532.060000.

668.4　　　　　　US
PLASTICS COMPOUNDING REDBOOK. 1981. a. $40. Avanstar Communications, Inc., 7500 Old Oak Blvd., Cleveland, OH 44130. TEL 216-243-8100. FAX 16-891-2726. (Subscr. to: 1 E. First St., Duluth, MN 55802) Ed. Mary C. McMurrer. adv.; charts; illus.; circ. 14,000. (back issues avail.)
Description: Discusses resin production, compounding and formulating techniques, polymer materials and applications.

668.4　　　　　　US
PLASTICS CONFERENCE PROCEEDINGS (YEAR). 1976. a. $225. Business Communications Co., Inc. (Norwalk), 25 Van Zant St., Norwalk, CT 06855. TEL 203-853-4266. FAX 203-853-0348. TELEX 6502934929 WUI. Ed. Louis Naturman. circ. 1,000. (also avail. in microfilm; microfiche; back issues avail.)
Formerly: Conference on Contingency Planning for Plastics. Proceedings.

668.4　　　　　　US　　ISSN 1045-0769
TA455.P5
PLASTICS D.A.T.A. DIGEST; thermoplastics and thermosets. 8th ed., 1987. a. $224. D.A.T.A. Business Publishing (Subsidiary of: Information Handling Services), 15 Inverness Way E., Box 6510, Englewood, CO 80155-6510. TEL 800-447-4666. FAX 303-799-4082. TELEX 4322083 IHS UI.
Formerly: Plastics D.A.T.A. Book.

PLASTICS

668.4 US ISSN 0362-9376
TP1101
PLASTICS DESIGN FORUM; for designers of products and components in plastics. 1975. bi-m. $25 (free to qualified personnel). Avanstar Communications, Inc., 7500 Old Oak Blvd., Cleveland, OH 44130. TEL 216-243-8100. FAX 216-826-2726. (Subscr. to: 1 E. First St., Duluth, MN 55802) Ed. Mel Friedman. adv.; bk.rev.; index; circ. 47,471. (back issues avail.; reprint service avail.) **Indexed:** Curr.Pack.Abstr., Int.Packag.Abstr., PROMT.
—BLDSC shelfmark: 6532.250000.
Refereed Serial

668.4 US
PLASTICS DISTRIBUTOR. bi-m. P M D Publishing Inc., 2701 N. Pulaski Rd., Chicago, IL 60639-2119. TEL 312-235-3307. FAX 312-235-7204. Ed. Harry Greenwald. circ. 17,000.

668.4 US ISSN 0091-9578
TP1101 CODEN: PLEGBB
PLASTICS ENGINEERING. 1945. m. $50 (foreign $70). Society of Plastics Engineers, Inc., 14 Fairfield Dr., Brookfield Center, CT 06805. TEL 203-775-0471. FAX 203-775-8490. TELEX 743-712. Ed. Roger Ferris. adv.; bk.rev.; charts; illus.; pat.; stat.; index; circ. 25,000. (also avail. in microfilm from UMI; reprint service avail. from UMI) **Indexed:** A.S.& T.Ind., Abstr.Bull.Inst.Pap.Chem., C.I.S. Abstr., Chem.Abstr., Curr.Cont., Curr.Pack.Abstr., Eng.Ind., Excerp.Med., Int.Packag.Abstr., Packag.Sci.Tech., PROMT, RAPRA, Sci.Abstr., Text.Tech.Dig.
—BLDSC shelfmark: 6532.310000.
Formerly: S P E Journal (ISSN 0036-1844)

668.4 US
PLASTICS ENGINEERING SERIES. 1981. irreg., vol.24, 1991. price varies. Marcel Dekker, Inc., 270 Madison Ave., New York, NY 10016. TEL 212-696-9000. FAX 212-685-4540. TELEX 421419.
Refereed Serial

668.4 US ISSN 0554-2952
PLASTICS FOCUS (AMHERST). 1968. bi-w. $235. Plastics Connection, Inc., Box 814, Amherst, MA 01004. TEL 413-549-5020. FAX 413-549-9955. Ed. Michael L. Berins. (looseleaf format)
Description: Interpretive industry news report for people in the plastics and other related industries.

PLASTICS IN BUILDING CONSTRUCTION. see *BUILDING AND CONSTRUCTION*

668.4 US
PLASTICS INDUSTRY NEWS. 1979. 6/yr. $24 (foreign $42). Avanstar Communications, Inc. (Denver), 1129 E. 17th St., Denver, CO 80218. TEL 303-832-1022. FAX 303-832-1720. Ed. Mel Friedman. circ. 5,000.

668.4 JA ISSN 0032-1206
PLASTICS INDUSTRY NEWS, JAPAN. (Text in English) 1955. m. $84. Institute of Polymer Industry, Inc. - Porima Kogyo Kenkyujo, C.P.O. Box 1176, Tokyo 100-91, Japan. Ed. S. Miyamoto. adv.; bk.rev.; mkt.; pat.; tr.lit.; cum.index every 10 yrs.; circ. 10,450. (also avail. in microfilm from UMI; reprint service avail. from UMI) **Indexed:** Chem.Abstr., JTA, RAPRA.
—BLDSC shelfmark: 6532.600000.

668 US
PLASTICS: LATIN AMERICAN INDUSTRIAL REPORT. (Avail. for each of 22 Latin American countries) 1985. a. $435 per country report. Aquino Productions, Box 15760, Stamford, CT 06901. TEL 203-325-3138. Ed. Andres C. Aquino.

668.4 US ISSN 0149-4899
PLASTICS MACHINERY AND EQUIPMENT; for those who select and buy plastics processing machinery and equipment. 1972. m. $35 (free to qualified personnel). Avanstar Communications, Inc., 7500 Old Oak Blvd., Cleveland, OH 44130. TEL 216-243-8100. FAX 216-891-2726. (Subscr. to: 1 E. First St., Duluth, MN 55802) Ed. Merle Snyder. adv.; charts; illus.; tr.lit.; cum.index; circ. 25,571. (tabloid format; also avail. in microform from UMI; back issues avail.; reprint service avail. from UMI) **Indexed:** Chem.Abstr., Curr.Pack.Abstr., PROMT.

668.4 II
PLASTICS NEWS. 1960. m. Rs.250. All India Plastics Manufacturers Association, Jehangir Building, 3rd floor, 133 Mahatma Gandhi Road, Bombay 400 023, India. TEL 273989. Ed. Shri Vijay V. Merchant. adv.; circ. 3,000.
Description: Presents the latest developments in the Indian plastics industry. Includes news of relevance to those involved.

678 US
PLASTICS NEWS. 1989. w. $30. Crain Communications Inc. (Akron), 1725 Merriman Rd., Akron, OH 44313-3185. TEL 216-836-9180. FAX 216-836-1005. (Subscr. to: 965 E. Jefferson Ave., Detroit, MI 48207-3187. TEL 800-678-9595) Ed. Robert Grace. circ. 60,000.
Description: Identifies and connects the manufacturers and suppliers. Covers financial moves, plant closings, acquisitions, process developments, new machinery and price indexing.

668.4 AT
PLASTICS NEWS INTERNATIONAL. 1950. m. Aus.$40($50) (Plastics Institute of Australia) Editors Desk Pty. Ltd., P.O. Box 2131, St. Kilda W., Vic. 3182, Australia. TEL 03-512032. FAX 03-5251420. adv.; bk.rev.; circ. 4,729. **Indexed:** Aus.Rd.Ind., W.R.C.Inf.
Formerly (until May 1989): Plastics News.

668.4 UK
PLASTICS PROCESSING. 3rd ed., 1987. every 18 mos. £155 per no. Key Note Publications Ltd., Field House, Old Field Rd., Hampton TW12 2HQ, England. TEL 01 783-0755.
Description: Overview of the plastics processing industry including industry structure, market size and trends, processing techniques and related articles.

PLASTICS RECYCLING UPDATE. see *ENVIRONMENTAL STUDIES — Waste Management*

668.4 678.2 UK ISSN 0959-8111
TP1101 CODEN: PRPAEP
PLASTICS, RUBBER AND COMPOSITES PROCESSING AND APPLICATIONS. 1981. 10/yr.(in 2 vols.). £317 (effective 1992). (Plastics and Rubber Institute) Elsevier Science Publishers Ltd., Crown House, Linton Rd., Barking, Essex IG11 8JU, England. TEL 081-594-7272. FAX 081-594-5942. TELEX 896950 APPSCI G. (Subscr. in U.S. and Canada to: Elsevier Science Publishing Co., Inc., Box 882, Madison Sq. Sta., New York, NY 10159. TEL 212-989-5800) Ed. N.G. McCrum. adv.; B&W page £345; 192 x 258; adv. contact: Claire Coakley. bk.rev.; illus.; index. (also avail. in microform from RPI; back issues avail.) **Indexed:** Br.Tech.Ind., Chem.Abstr., Chem.Eng.Abstr., Curr.Cont., Curr.Pack.Abstr., Eng.Ind., Food Sci.& Tech.Abstr., HRIS, Ocean.Abstr., Pollut.Abstr., Sci.Abstr., Sci.Cit.Ind., T.C.E.A., Text.Tech.Dig., W.R.C.Inf.
—BLDSC shelfmark: 6537.187000.
Formerly: Plastics and Rubber Processing and Applications (ISSN 0144-6045)
Description: Provides an international forum for the presentation of the science and technology involved in the plastics and rubber industries.
Refereed Serial

668.4 II ISSN 0032-1249
PLASTICS, RUBBER AND LEATHER INDUSTRIES JOURNAL. (Text in English) 1962. bi-m. $30. Praveen Corp., Sayajiganj, Baroda 390005, India.

668.4 SA ISSN 0048-4385
PLASTICS SOUTHERN AFRICA. (Text in English) 1971. m. R.104. (Plastics Institute of South Africa) George Warman Publications (Pte.) Ltd., Box 3847, Cape Town 8000, South Africa. TEL 021-24-5320. FAX 021-26-1332. TELEX 5-21849 SA. Ed. Martin Wells. adv.; bk.rev.; illus.; tr.lit.; circ. 2,000. **Indexed:** Ind.S.A.Per.
Description: Technical journal of plastics.

668.4 US ISSN 0032-1257
TP1101 CODEN: PLTEAB
PLASTICS TECHNOLOGY; machinery/materials systems for maximum productivity. 1955. 13/yr. $45. Bill Communications, Inc., 633 Third Ave., New York, NY 10017. TEL 212-986-4800. Ed. Matthew H. Naitove. adv.; bk.rev.; abstr.; charts; illus.; pat.; tr.lit.; index; circ. 47,000. (reprint service avail. from UMI) **Indexed:** A.S.& T.Ind., Chem.Abstr., Excerpt.Med., Int.Packag.Abstr., Packag.Sci.Tech., PROMT, RAPRA.
—BLDSC shelfmark: 6537.300000.
Description: For plastics professionals.

668.4 US
PLASTICS TECHNOLOGY. PLASTICS MANUFACTURING HANDBOOK AND BUYERS' GUIDE. 1967. a. included in subscr. to Plastics Technology. Bill Communications, Inc., 633 Third Ave., New York, NY 10017. TEL 212-986-4800. Ed. Matthew H. Naitove. adv.; charts; illus.; tr.lit.; index; circ. 40,000. (reprint service avail. from UMI)

668.4 US ISSN 0032-1273
TP1101 CODEN: PLAWA4
PLASTICS WORLD. 1942. 13/yr. (includes Plastics World Yellow Pages). $74.95 (Canada $117.65; Mexico $109.95; elsewhere $129.95). Cahners Publishing Company (Newton) (Subsidiary of: Reed International PLC), Division of Reed Publishing (USA) Inc., 275 Washington St., Newton, MA 02158-1630. TEL 617-964-3030. FAX 617-558-4470. (Subscr. to: 44 Cook St., Denver, CO 80206. TEL 800-662-7776) Ed. Douglas Smock. adv.; bk.rev.; illus.; stat.; tr.lit.; circ. 63,500. (also avail. in microform from RPI; reprint service avail. from UMI) **Indexed:** A.S.& T.Ind., B.P.I, Bus.Ind., Chem.Abstr., Int.Packag.Abstr., Key to Econ.Sci., PROMT, Text.Tech.Dig., Tr.& Indus.Ind.
—BLDSC shelfmark: 6537.500000.
Incorporates: Plastics Industry (ISSN 0096-9168)
Description: For processors and designers involved in buying and specifying plastics materials, additives and processing equipment.

668.4 US
▼**PLASTICS WORLD MACHINERY AND EQUIPMENT YELLOW PAGES.** 1992. a. $35. Cahners Publishing Company (Newton) (Subsidiary of: Reed International PLC), Division of Reed Publishing (USA) Inc., 272 Washington St., Newton, MA 02158. TEL 617-964-3030. FAX 617-558-4417. Ed. Douglas Smock. adv.: B&W & color, B&W page $4350; trim 8 x 10 3/4. circ. 41,000.
Description: Lists equipment and machinery suppliers for the plastics processing industry.

PLASTICS WORLD YELLOW PAGES. see *BUSINESS AND ECONOMICS — Trade And Industrial Directories*

668.4 US
PLASTICSBRIEF: DESIGN & MATERIALS EDITION. w. $249. Market Search, Inc., 2727 Holland Sylvania Rd., Ste. A, Toledo, OH 43615. TEL 419-535-7899. FAX 419-535-1243. Ed. James R. Best.

668.4 US
PLASTICSBRIEF: EXTRUSION & BLOW MOLDING EDITION. w. $249. Market Search, Inc., 2727 Holland Sylvania Rd., Ste. A, Toledo, OH 43615. TEL 419-535-7899. FAX 419-535-1243. Ed. James R. Best.

668.4 US
PLASTICSBRIEF: INJECTION MOLDING EDITION. w. $249. Market Search, Inc., 2727 Holland Sylvania Rd., Ste. A, Toledo, OH 43615. TEL 419-535-7899. FAX 419-535-1243. Ed. James R. Best.

668.4 US ISSN 0744-5296
PLASTICSBRIEF: REINFORCED PLASTIC EDITION. w. $249. Market Search, Inc., 2727 Holland Sylvania Rd., Ste. A, Toledo, OH 43615. TEL 419-535-7899. FAX 419-535-1243. Ed. James R. Best.

668.4 US
PLASTICSBRIEF: THERMOPLASTICS MARKETING EDITION. 1972. w. $249. Market Search, Inc., 2727 Holland Sylvania Rd., Ste. A, Toledo, OH 43615. TEL 419-535-7899. FAX 419-535-1243. Ed. James R. Best. index; circ. 400.
Former titles: PlasticsBrief: Marketing Edition (ISSN 0745-0168); Plastics Marketing News Brief.
Description: News on sales opportunities and competitive intelligence for the industry, targeted toward executives.

PLASTICS

668.4 US ISSN 1044-9663
PLASTICSWEEK. w. $480 (foreign $530). McGraw-Hill, Inc., Chemicals & Plastics Information Services, 1220 Ave. of the Americas, 43rd Fl., New York, NY 10020. TEL 800-537-9213. FAX 609-426-5905.

668.4 678.4 YU
PLASTIKA I GUMA. (Text in Serbo-Croatian; summaries in English) 1982. q. $50. Savez Hemicara i Tehnologa Jugoslavije, Kneza Milosa 9, P.O. Box 187, 11001 Belgrade, Yugoslavia. Ed. Milenko Trbovic. adv.; bk.rev.; circ. 1,000. **Indexed:** Chem.Abstr., Ref.Zh.

668.4 NO
PLASTINDUSTRIEN. 1935. m. NOK 260. Skarland Press A-S, Sorkedalsvn 10A, Postboks 5042, Maj Oslo, Norway. Ed. Tove Gjerdrum. adv.; bk.rev.; charts; illus.; stat.; index; circ. 3,045. **Indexed:** Chem.Abstr.
Formerly: Plastnytt (ISSN 0032-1311)

668.4 FR ISSN 0180-9237
PLASTIQUES FLASH. 1965. m. 150 F. Societe Europeenne de Presse et d'Edition, 142 rue d'Aguesseau, 92100 Boulogne, France. Ed. Emmanuel Pottier. circ. 10,000.
—BLDSC shelfmark: 6537.581000.
Description: Information on state-of-the-art robotics equipment and machines used in the plastics manufacturing industry.

668.4 FR ISSN 0032-1303
TP986.A1 CODEN: PMELAW
PLASTIQUES MODERNES ET ELASTOMERES. 1948. m. 590 F. Societe de Publications Specialisees, 142 rue Montmartre, 75002 Paris, France.
FAX 45-08-55-83. TELEX 220528F. Ed. Benedite Topuz. adv.; charts; illus.; mkt.; cum.index; circ. 6,644. **Indexed:** C.I.S. Abstr., PROMT.
—BLDSC shelfmark: 6537.620000.
Incorporates: Plastiques Informations (ISSN 0032-129X); Formerly: Industrie des Plastiques Moderne et Elastomeres.

668.4 GW ISSN 0032-1338
TP986.A1 CODEN: PLARAN
PLASTVERARBEITER; kunststoffanwendung und -verarbeitung. 1950. m. DM.262.80. Zechner und Huethig Verlag GmbH, Im Weiher 10, Postfach 102869, 6900 Heidelberg 1, Germany.
TEL 06221-489-281. FAX 06221-489279. TELEX 461727-HUEHD-D. Eds. Bernhard Liesch, Fritz Vollmer. adv.; bk.rev.; illus.; index; circ. 15,728. **Indexed:** Art & Archaeol.Tech.Abstr., C.I.S. Abstr., Chem.Abstr., Eng.Ind., Excerp.Med., Int.Packag.Abstr., Packag.Sci.Tech., RAPRA.
—BLDSC shelfmark: 6537.750000.

668.4 678 CS ISSN 0322-7340
TP1101 CODEN: PLKCAS
PLASTY A KAUCUK/PLASTICS AND RUBBER. (Text in Czech or Slovak; summaries in English, German, Russian) 1963. m. $56.70. (Ceskoslovensky Zavod Gumarenskeho Prumyslu) Nakladatelstvi Technicke Literatury, Spalena 51, 113 02 Prague 1, Czechoslovakia. (Dist. by: Artia, Ve Smeckach 30, 111 27 Prague 1, Czechoslovakia) Ed. Karel Malik. adv.; bk.rev.; film rev.; abstr.; illus.; pat.; stat.; index; circ. 2,200. **Indexed:** Chem.Abstr., Farm & Garden Ind., Intl.Polym.Sci.& Tech., RAPRA.
Formerly: Plasticke Hmoty a Kaucuk (ISSN 0032-1109)
Description: Covers plastics and rubber technology, prosessing application, economic questions, testing and analysis.

668.4 678.2 CI ISSN 0351-1871
CODEN: PLMRDI
POLIMERI; Jugoslavenski casopis za plastiku i gumu. 1980. 6/yr. $100. Drustvo Plasticara i Gumaraca, Garicgradska 6, 41001 Zagreb, Croatia.
TEL 041-388-132. FAX 041-422-936. TELEX 22167. Ed. Barbara Rastovic. adv.; bk.rev.; circ. 1,000. **Indexed:** Chem.Abstr., RAPRA, Ref.Zh.
—BLDSC shelfmark: 6543.380600.

668.4 IT
POLIPLASTI; e plastici rinforzati. (Text and summaries in English, Italian) 1953. m. L.90000 (foreign L.140000). Etas s.r.l., Via Mecenate, 91, 20138 Milan, Italy. TEL 02-580841. FAX 02-5064867. Ed. Franco Barbieri Hermitte. circ. 7,023. **Indexed:** Chem.Abstr.
Former titles: Poliplasti e Materiali - Rinforzati; (until 1976): Poliplasti e Plastici Rinforzati (ISSN 0032-2768)
Description: Thermoplastics, thermoset and composite materials processing techniques.

668.4 PL ISSN 0370-0879
POLITECHNIKA WROCLAWSKA. INSTYTUT TECHNOLOGII ORGANICZNEJ I TWORZYW SZTUCZNYCH. PRACE NAUKOWE. STUDIA I MATERIALY. (Text in Polish; summaries in English and Russian) 1971. irreg., no.17, 1977. price varies. Politechnika Wroclawska, Wybrzeze Wyspianskiego 27, 50-370 Wroclaw, Poland. FAX 22-36-64. TELEX 712559 PWRPL.
(Dist. by: Ars Polona-Ruch, Krakowskie Przedmiescie 7, Warsaw, Poland) **Indexed:** Chem.Abstr.

668.4 US ISSN 0272-8397
TA418.9.C6 CODEN: PCOMDI
POLYMER COMPOSITES. 1980. 6/yr. $190 (foreign $210). Society of Plastics Engineers, Inc., 14 Fairfield Dr., Brookfield Center, CT 06776.
TEL 203-775-0471. FAX 203-775-8490. TELEX 643-712. Ed. Roger Porter. charts; illus.; index; circ. 1,000. (back issues avail.) **Indexed:** Cadscan, Chem.Abstr., Eng.Ind., Int.Aerosp.Abstr., Lead Abstr., Sci.Abstr., Zincscan.
—BLDSC shelfmark: 6547.704300.

POLYMER DEGRADATION AND STABILITY. see CHEMISTRY — Organic Chemistry

POLYMER FRIENDS FOR RUBBER, PLASTICS AND FIBER/PORIMA NO TOMO. see RUBBER

668.42 UK ISSN 0959-8103
TP1101 CODEN: PLYIEI
POLYMER INTERNATIONAL. 1969. 12/yr.(in 3 vols.). £329 (effective 1992). Elsevier Science Publishers Ltd, Crown House, Linton Rd., Barking, Essex IG11 8JU, England. TEL 081-594-7272.
FAX 081-594-5942. TELEX 896950 APPSCI G. (Subscr. in U.S. and Canada to: Elsevier Science Publishing Co., Inc., Box 882, Madison Sq. Sta., New York, NY 10159. TEL 212-989-5800) Ed. J.F. Kennedy. adv.: B&W page £345; 192 x 258; adv. contact: Claire Coakley. bk.rev.; charts; illus.; index; circ. 500. (back issues avail.) **Indexed:** Anal.Abstr., Br.Tech.Ind., Chem.Abstr., Chem.Eng.Abstr., Curr.Cont., Curr.Pack.Abstr., Dairy Sci.Abstr., Excerp.Med., Sci.Abstr., T.C.E.A., W.R.C.Inf., World Surf.Coat., World Text.Abstr.
—BLDSC shelfmark: 6547.706750.
Formerly (until 1987): British Polymer Journal (ISSN 0007-1641)
Description: Reports original research and advances in all branches of macromolecular science and technology, including polymer chemistry and physics, biopolymers and industrial polymer science.
Refereed Serial

668.4 547 UK ISSN 0142-9418
TA455.P58 CODEN: POTEDZ
POLYMER TESTING. 1980. 5/yr. £157 (effective 1992). Elsevier Science Publishers Ltd, Crown House, Linton Rd., Barking, Essex IG11 8JU, England. TEL 081-594-7272. FAX 081-594-5942. TELEX 896950 APPSCI G. (Subscr. in U.S. and Canada to: Elsevier Science Publishing Co., Inc., Box 882, Madison Sq. Sta., New York, NY 10159. TEL 212-989-5800) Ed. R. Brown. adv.: B&W page £295; 140 x 200; adv. contact: Claire Coakley. bk.rev.; illus.; index. (also avail. in microform from RPI; back issues avail.) **Indexed:** Chem.Abstr., Curr.Cont., Eng.Ind., Met.Abstr., Sci.Abstr., Sci.Cit.Ind.
—BLDSC shelfmark: 6547.740500.
Description: Provides a forum for developments in the testing of polymers and polymeric products.
Refereed Serial

POLYMERIC MATERIALS SCIENCE AND ENGINEERING. see CHEMISTRY — Organic Chemistry

668.4 678.2 UK ISSN 0268-9812
POLYMERS AND RUBBER ASIA. 1985. bi-m. £36. S K C Communication Services Ltd., Tern House, Upper West St., Reigate, Surrey RH2 9HX, England.
FAX 0737-223235. TELEX 932699-KENPUB-G. Ed. Alessandro Vitelli. adv.; bk.rev. **Indexed:** RAPRA.
—BLDSC shelfmark: 6547.742320.
Description: Technical information for the processors of plastics and rubber in the Pacific Rim area.

668.4 540 UK ISSN 1042-7147
TP1080 CODEN: PADTE5
▼**POLYMERS FOR ADVANCED TECHNOLOGIES.** 1990. 8/yr. $450 (effective 1992). John Wiley & Sons Ltd., Journals, Baffins Lane, Chichester, Sussex PO19 1UD, England. TEL 0243-779777.
FAX 0243-775878. TELEX 86290 WIBOOK G. Ed. M. Lewin.
—BLDSC shelfmark: 6547.742200.
Description: Focuses on the interst of scientists and engineers from academia and industry who are participating in new areas of polymer research and development related to advanced technologies.

668.4 US ISSN 0171-709X
POLYMERS - PROPERTIES AND APPLICATIONS. 1952. irreg. price varies. Springer-Verlag, 175 Fifth Ave., New York, NY 10010. TEL 212-460-1500. (Also Berlin, Heidelberg, Tokyo and Vienna) Ed. K.A. Wolf. (reprint service avail. from ISI)
Formerly (until vol.15, 1970): Chemie, Physik und Technologie der Kunststoffe in Einzeldarstellungen (ISSN 0069-3073)

POLYSAR PROGRESS. see RUBBER

668.4 II ISSN 0253-7303
CODEN: POPLD2
POPULAR PLASTICS. 1955. m. Rs.250($100) Colour Publications Pvt. Ltd., 126-A Dhuruwadi, Off Dr. Nariman Rd, Bombay 400 025, India.
TEL 430-9318. TELEX 71242 CEPE IN. Ed. R.V. Raghavan. adv.; bk.rev.; abstr.; charts; illus.; circ. 10,375. (also avail. in microfilm from UMI; reprint service avail. from UMI) **Indexed:** Chem.Abstr.
Former titles: Popular Plastics and Rubber; (until 1979, vol. 24): Popular Plastics (ISSN 0032-4604)

PRESSURE SENSITIVE TAPE COUNCIL. TECHNICAL SEMINAR. PROCEEDINGS. see RUBBER

PREVISIONS GLISSANTES DETAILLEES EN PERSPECTIVES SECTORIELLES (VOL.20): TRANSFORMATION DU CAOUTCHOUC ET DES MATIERES PLASTIQUES. see BUSINESS AND ECONOMICS — Economic Situation And Conditions

PROGRESS IN RUBBER AND PLASTICS TECHNOLOGY. see RUBBER

PROSPECT. see ENGINEERING — Chemical Engineering

R A P R A NEW TRADE NAMES IN THE RUBBER AND PLASTICS INDUSTRIES. (Rubber and Plastics Research Association of Great Britain) see RUBBER

668.4 678.2 658.5 UK ISSN 0140-041X
R A P R A NEWS. 1977. q. free. (Rubber and Plastics Research Association of Great Britain) R A P R A Technology Ltd., Shawbury, Shrewsbury, Shropshire SY4 4NR, England. TEL 0939-250383.
FAX 0939-25118. TELEX 35134. Ed. Sharon Lloyd. illus.; stat.; tr.lit.; circ. 7,000. (back issues avail.)

668.4 660 UK ISSN 0144-6266
RECENT ADVANCES IN CROSSLINKING & CURING. 1980. 6/yr. $300. Solihull Chemical Services, 284 Warwick Rd., Solihull, West Midlands B92 7AF, England. Ed. H. Warson. circ. 70.

668.4 UK ISSN 0034-3617
TA455.P55
REINFORCED PLASTICS. 1956. 11/yr. £59 (effective 1992). Elsevier Science Publishers Ltd, Crown House, Linton Rd., Barking, Essex IG11 8JU, England. TEL 081-594-7272. FAX 081-594-5942. TELEX 896950 APPSCI G. (N. America dist. addr.: Elsevier Science Publishing Co., Inc., Box 882, Madison Sq. Sta., New York, NY 10159. TEL 212-989-5800) Ed. Amanda Weaver. adv.; bk.rev.; charts; illus.; tr.lit.; index; circ. 3,000. **Indexed:** BMT, Br.Tech.Ind., Chem.Abstr., PROMT, RAPRA.
—BLDSC shelfmark: 7351.200000.
Description: For those involved in the polymer-based composites industry.

PLASTICS — ABSTRACTING, BIBLIOGRAPHIES, STATISTICS

668.4   UK
REINFORCED PLASTICS. COMPOSITE PAPERS. 1958. biennial. £75. British Plastics Federation, 5 Belgrave Sq., London SW1X 8PD, England. TEL 01-235-9483. FAX 01-235-8045. TELEX 8951528-PLAFED-G. circ. 1,000.
Former titles: Reinforced Plastics Congress (ISSN 0306-3607) & International Reinforced Plastics Conference. Papers and Proceedings. (ISSN 0074-7661)

668.4   SP   ISSN 0034-8708
TP986.A1   CODEN: RPMOAM
REVISTA DE PLASTICOS MODERNOS. 1950. m. $30. Instituto de Ciencia y Tecnologia de Polimeros, Juan de la Cierva 3, 28006 Madrid, Spain. FAX 91-5644853. (Co-sponsor: Consejo Superior de Investigaciones Cientificas) Ed. O. Laguna Castellanos. adv.; bk.rev.; charts; illus.; pat.; circ. 5,000. **Indexed:** Art & Archaeol.Tech.Abstr., Chem.Abstr., Ind.SST, RAPRA, World Surf.Coat. —BLDSC shelfmark: 7869.810000.

RUBBER AND PLASTICS DIGEST. see *RUBBER*

RUBBER & PLASTICS NEWS; the rubber industry's international newspaper. see *RUBBER*

RUBBER & PLASTICS NEWS II. see *RUBBER*

RUBBER RESEARCH INSTITUTE OF SRI LANKA. JOURNAL. see *RUBBER*

RUBBER SOUTHERN AFRICA. see *RUBBER*

RUBBICANA-EUROPE (YEAR). see *RUBBER*

668.4   US
S P I MEMBERSHIP DIRECTORY AND BUYER'S GUIDE. 1937. a. $180 to non-members; members $90. Society of the Plastics Industry, Inc., 1275 K St., N.W., Washington, DC 20005. TEL 202-371-5200. FAX 202-408-0736. circ. 3,000. (back issues avail.; reprint service avail.)
Description: Lists SPI member companies and their products and services.

SEALANTS; the professional's guide. see *RUBBER*

SKYLON. see *PACKAGING*

668.4   US
SOCIETY OF PLASTICS ENGINEERS. ANNUAL TECHNICAL CONFERENCE (ANTEC). PROCEEDINGS. a. $135 to non-members; members $135; institutions $160. Society of Plastics Engineers, Inc., 14 Fairfield Dr., Brookfield, CT 06804. TEL 203-775-0471. FAX 203-775-8490. TELEX 643-712.

660   US
SOCIETY OF PLASTICS ENGINEERS MONOGRAPHS. 1973. irreg., unnumbered, latest 1992. price varies. John Wiley & Sons, Inc., 605 Third Ave., New York, NY 10158-0012. TEL 212-850-6000. FAX 212-850-6088. TELEX 12-7063.

668.4   US
SOCIETY OF THE PLASTICS INDUSTRY. REINFORCED PLASTICS COMPOSITES INSTITUTE. ANNUAL TECHNICAL CONFERENCE. PREPRINT. 1946. a. $10. Society of the Plastics Industry, Composites Institute, 355 Lexington Ave., New York, NY 10017. TEL 212-351-5410. FAX 212-370-1731. Ed. J. McDermott. circ. 3,000. **Indexed:** Chem.Abstr.
Formerly: Society of the Plastics Industry. Reinforced Plastics Composites Institute. Annual Technical Conference. Proceedings.

668.4   US
SOCIETY OF THE PLASTICS INDUSTRY. URETHANE DIVISION. CONFERENCE PROCEEDINGS. 1979. irreg. price varies. Technomic Publishing Co., Inc., 851 New Holland Ave., Box 3535, Lancaster, PA 17604. TEL 717-291-5609. FAX 717-295-4538. TELEX 230 753565 (TECHNOMIC UD).
Refereed Serial

668.4   US
STRUCTURAL FOAM CONFERENCE. PROCEEDINGS. vol.3, 1975. irreg. (Society of the Plastics Industry) Technomic Publishing Co. Inc., 851 New Holland Ave., Box 3535, Lancaster, PA 17604. TEL 717-291-5609. FAX 717-295-4538. TELEX 230 753565 (TECHNOMIC UD).
Refereed Serial

668.4   CC
SUOLIAO/PLASTICS. (Text in Chinese, English) bi-m. Beijing Plastics Research Institute, 47, Jiu Gu Lou Street, Beijing 100009, People's Republic of China. TEL 441734. TELEX 22470 BFTCC CN. (Dist. overseas by: Guoji Shudian - China International Book Trading Corp., P.O. Box 339, Beijing, P.R.C.) Ed. Zhao Yiming.

TECHNICAL TEXTILES INTERNATIONAL. see *TEXTILE INDUSTRIES AND FABRICS*

668.4   US   ISSN 0120-7644
TECNOLOGIA DEL PLASTICO. 1985. bi-m. Carvajal International, Inc., 717 Ponce de Leon Blvd., Ste. 304, Coral Gables, FL 33134. TEL 305-448-6875. FAX 305-448-9942. Ed. Miguel Garzon. circ. 10,308.

TSELULOZA I KHARTIIA. see *ENGINEERING — Chemical Engineering*

UMFORMTECHNIK. see *METALLURGY*

UNION DES INDUSTRIES ET DE LA DISTRIBUTION DES PLASTIQUES ET DU CAOUTCHOUC. GUIDE. see *BUSINESS AND ECONOMICS — Trade And Industrial Directories*

668.4   US   ISSN 0149-1342
TP1180.P8   CODEN: URABB
URETHANE ABSTRACTS. 1971. m. $175. Technomic Publishing Co., Inc., 851 New Holland Ave., Box 3535, Lancaster, PA 17604. TEL 717-291-5609. FAX 717-295-4538. TELEX 230 753565 (TECHNOMIC UD). Ed. John W. DeGroot, Jr. circ. 250.
Refereed Serial

668.4 660.284   US   ISSN 0049-5700
TP1180.P8
URETHANE PLASTICS AND PRODUCTS. 1971. m. $140. Technomic Publishing Co., Inc., 851 New Holland Ave., Box 3535, Lancaster, PA 17604. TEL 717-291-5609. FAX 717-295-4538. TELEX 230 753565 (TECHNOMIC UD). Ed. Michael Margotta. bk.rev.; charts; illus.; circ. 250. (looseleaf format) **Indexed:** PROMT.

PLASTICS — Abstracting, Bibliographies, Statistics

668.4   US   ISSN 0734-869X
CODEN: CAFPEU
C A SELECTS. FIBER-REINFORCED PLASTICS. s-w. $195. Chemical Abstracts Service (Subsidiary of: American Chemical Society), 2540 Olentangy River Rd., Box 3012, Columbus, OH 43210. TEL 614-447-3600. FAX 614-447-3713. TELEX 6842086.
Description: Covers properties, processing, use of thermoplastics and thermosetting resins reinforced by natural or synthetic fibers.

668.4   US   ISSN 0734-8673
CODEN: CANPE2
C A SELECTS. NEW PLASTICS. s-w. $195. Chemical Abstracts Service (Subsidiary of: American Chemical Society), 2540 Olentangy River Rd., Box 3012, Columbus, OH 43210. TEL 614-447-3600. FAX 614-447-3713. TELEX 6842086.
Description: Covers newly synthesized or newly reported thermoplastic and thermosetting resins.

668.4   US   ISSN 0195-511X
CODEN: CSPFD5
C A SELECTS. PLASTIC FILMS. s-w. $195. Chemical Abstracts Service (Subsidiary of: American Chemical Society), 2540 Olentangy River Rd., Box 3012, Columbus, OH 43210. TEL 614-447-3600. FAX 614-447-3713. TELEX 6842086.
Description: Covers manufacture, properties, fabrication, and applications of polymeric films.

668.4   US   ISSN 0734-8681
CODEN: CAADE3
C A SELECTS. PLASTICS ADDITIVES. s-w. $195. Chemical Abstracts Service (Subsidiary of: American Chemical Society), 2540 Olentangy River Rd., Box 3012, Columbus, OH 43210. TEL 614-447-3600. FAX 614-447-3713. TELEX 6842086.
Description: Covers materials added to thermoplastic and thermosetting resins to modify properties; plasticizers, inert and reinforcing fillers, pigments, heat and light stabilizers, antioxidants, blowing agents.

668.4   US   ISSN 0275-7125
CODEN: CPFUDD
C A SELECTS. PLASTICS FABRICATION & USES. s-w. $195. Chemical Abstracts Service (Subsidiary of: American Chemical Society), 2540 Olentangy River Rd., Box 3012, Columbus, OH 43210. TEL 614-447-3600. FAX 614-447-3713. TELEX 6842086.
Description: Covers processes of chemical or chemical engineering interest for fabricating polymers or compositions containing them.

668.4   US   ISSN 0275-7133
CODEN: CSPPDZ
C A SELECTS. PLASTICS MANUFACTURE & PROCESSING. s-w. $195. Chemical Abstracts Service (Subsidiary of: American Chemical Society), 2540 Olentangy River Rd., Box 3012, Columbus, OH 43210. TEL 614-447-3600. FAX 614-447-3713. TELEX 6842086.
Description: Covers manufacture, testing, compounding, and processing of polymeric materials for use as resins or unsupported films; natural resins of industrial interest; additives for plastics and resins, e.g. crosslinking agents, plasticizers, fillers, foaming agents, pigments.

668.4   US   ISSN 0891-1886
C P I DIGEST. (Chemical Process Industries); key to world literature serving the coatings, plastics, fibers, adhesives, and related industries. 1974. m. $275. C P I Information Services, 2117 Cherokee Pkwy., Louisville, KY 40204. TEL 502-456-6288. Ed. G.S. Mattingly. abstr.; pat.; circ. 850. (back issues avail.; reprint service avail. from CPI)
Formerly: Coatings Adlibra (ISSN 0146-9290)

668.4   US   ISSN 1049-1341
▼**C2C ABSTRACTS: JAPAN - PLASTICS.** 1990. m. $200. Scan C2C, 500 E St. S.W., Ste. 800, Washington, DC 20024. TEL 800-525-3865. FAX 202-863-3855.
●Also available online. Vendor(s): Data-Star (JPTC), DIALOG (File no.582), European Space Agency (File no.241), Orbit Information Technologies (JTEC). Also available on CD-ROM. Producer(s): Dialog Information Services.
Description: Contains English abstracts of articles in Japanese scientific, business, and technical journals. Covers plastics, the plastics industry, processing, instrumentation, molding and extrusion.

011   GW   ISSN 0932-7754
D K I LITERATUR-SCHNELLDIENST KUNSTSTOFFE KAUTSCHUK FASERN. 1955. m. DM.1950. Deutsches Kunststoff-Institut, Schlossgartenstr. 6, 6100 Darmstadt, Germany. TEL 06151-162105. FAX 06151-292855. (Affiliate: Forschungesellschaft Kunststoffe e.V. Darmstadt) adv. (also avail. in microform; back issues avail.)
●Also available online. Vendor(s): FIZ Technik, STN International.
Formerly: Literatur-Schnelldienst Kunststoffeund Kautschuk (ISSN 0024-4651)
Description: Abstract journal in the field of science and technology of polymer material (plastics, rubber and fiber materials).

668.4 016   US   ISSN 0013-7154
HD9661.A1   CODEN: TEUMA
END-USE MARKETS FOR PLASTICS. Variant title: Trends in End-Use Markets for Plastics. 1968. m. $480 (effective 1992). Springborn Laboratories, Inc., 30 Springborn Center, Enfield, CT 06082. TEL 203-749-8371. FAX 203-749-8234. Ed. Cherie P. Clark. charts; stat.; index; circ. 400.
Description: Provides abstracts of articles on new plastics applications, end use market performance and growth potential, plastics penetration into market segments, and current events that may influence the plastics and allied chemicals industries.

668.4   FR
FRANCE. SERVICE D'ETUDE DES STRATEGIES ET DES STATISTIQUES INDUSTRIELLES. RESULTATS TRIMESTRIELS DES ENQUETES DE BRANCHE. TRANSFORMATION DES MATIERES PLASTIQUES. q. 180 F. (foreign 210 F.)(effective 1991). Service d'Etude des Strategies et des Statistiques Industrielles (SESSI), 85 Bd. du Montparnasse, 75270 Paris Cedex 06, France. TEL 45-56-42-34. FAX 45-56-40-71. stat.
Description: Provides detailed industry-wide performance statistics for comparative evaluations.

KEY ABSTRACTS - ADVANCED MATERIALS. see *PHYSICS — Abstracting, Bibliographies, Statistics*

668.4 330   UK   ISSN 0956-1234
NONWOVENS ABSTRACTS. 1989. m. $414.40.
(Research Association for the Paper and Board, Printing and Packaging Industries) Pira International, Randalls Rd., Leatherhead, Surrey KT22 7RU, England. TEL 0372-376161. Ed. Diana Deavin. (also avail. in microform; back issues avail.)
●Also available online. Vendor(s): Data-Star, DIALOG, European Space Agency, Orbit Information Technologies.

P A S C A L FOLIO. F 24: POLYMERES. PEINTURES. BOIS. see *CHEMISTRY — Abstracting, Bibliographies, Statistics*

PLASTICS AND RUBBERS MATERIALS DISC. see *RUBBER — Abstracting, Bibliographies, Statistics*

668.4 338   US
POLYMERS, CERAMICS, COMPOSITE ALERT. (Part of: Materials Business Information Series) 1985. m. $265 (foreign $275); Metals Abstracts subscribers $165 (foreign $175). A S M International, Materials Information, Materials Park, OH 44073. TEL 216-338-5151. FAX 216-338-4634. TELEX 980-619. (UK Addr.: Institute of Metals, Materials Information, 1 Carlton House Terr., London SW1Y 5DB, England. TEL 071-839-4071) Ed.Bd.
●Also available online. Vendor(s): CEDOCAR, CISTI, Data-Star (MBUS), DIALOG (File no.269), European Space Agency (File no.111), Orbit Information Technologies (MATERIALS/B), STN International (MATBUS).
Also available on CD-ROM. Producer(s): Dialog Information Services.
Description: International coverage of business developments for the engineered materials industries.

R A P R A ABSTRACTS. (Rubber and Plastics Research Association of Great Britain) see *RUBBER — Abstracting, Bibliographies, Statistics*

668.4 678.2   US   ISSN 0889-3144
TA455.P58   CODEN: RRVREQ
R A P R A REVIEW REPORTS; current developments in materials technology and engineering. 1988. m. £395 (effective 1992). (Rubber and Plastics Research Association of Great Britain, R A P R A Technology Ltd., UK) Pergamon Press, Inc., Journals Division, 660 White Plains Rd., Tarrytown, NY 10591-5153. TEL 914-524-9200. FAX 914-333-2444. (And: Headington Hill Hall, Oxford OX3 0BW, England. TEL 0865-794141) Ed. Rebecca Dolbey. (also avail. in microform; back issues avail.)
—BLDSC shelfmark: 7291.760000.
Description: Covers recent advances within specific fields of engineering materials technology.
Refereed Serial

URBAN WILDLIFE MANAGER'S NOTEBOOK. see *BIOLOGY*

POETRY

see *Literature–Poetry*

POLITICAL SCIENCE

see also *Political Science–Civil Rights; Political Science–International Relations; Public Administration*

322.4 947   US   ISSN 0001-0545
DK272.5
A B N CORRESPONDENCE. 1950. bi-m. $27. American Friends of the Anti-Bolshevik Bloc of Nations, 136 Second Ave., New York. Ed. Mrs. Slava Stetsko. bk.rev.; illus.; circ. 6,000. **Indexed:** Mid.East: Abstr.& Ind.
—BLDSC shelfmark: 0549.580000.

320   UY
A C F. 1983. w. Partido Nacional, A C F, Canelones 1055, Esc. 503, Montevideo, Uruguay. Dir. Horacio Muniz Durand.

329.3 330 370
531.64   US   ISSN 0896-3134
A D A TODAY; a newsletter for liberal activists. 1947. 4/yr. $20 to non-members. Americans for Democratic Action, 1625 K St. N.W., Ste. 1150, Washington, DC 20006. TEL 202-785-5980. Ed. Ron Zucker. circ. 60,000. (also avail. in microform from MIM,KTO)
Formerly: A D A World (ISSN 0001-0871)
Description: Political and governmental news and commentary from liberal viewpoint, including congressional voting records and ratings.

329.3   US
A D ACTION NEWS AND NOTES. 1989. w. $20. Americans for Democratic Action, 1625 K St. N.W., Ste. 1150, Washington, DC 20006. TEL 202-785-5980. Ed. Amy Isaacs.
Description: Reports on congressional action.

320 300   GW   ISSN 0930-8199
A F B INFO. (Text in English, German) 1986. s-a. free. Arbeitsstelle Friedensforschung Bonn - Information Unit Peace Research Bonn, Beethovenallee 4, 5300 Bonn 2, Germany. TEL 0228-356032. FAX 0228-356050. Eds. Karlheinz Koppe, Regine Mehl. circ. 3,000. (back issues avail.)

960   FR   ISSN 0754-7625
A.F.P. CAHIERS DE L'AFRIQUE OCCIDENTALE ET DE L'AFRIQUE EQUATORIALE. 1960. bi-m. 1428 F. (foreign 1680 F.). Agence France-Presse, 13 Place de la Bourse, B.P. 20, 75061 Paris Cedex 2, France. TEL 40-41-46-46. TELEX 210064 AFPA. adv.
Former titles (until 1984): Cahiers de l'Afrique Occidentale et de l'Afrique Equatoriale (ISSN 0750-0688); (until 1960): Cahiers de l'Afrique Occidentale Francaise (ISSN 0750-067X)

320   US   ISSN 0893-293X
A L F NEWSLETTER. 1976. q. $10. Association of Libertarian Feminists, Box 20252, London Terrace Post Office, New York, NY 10011. Ed. Joan Kennedy Taylor. bk.rev.; circ. 300.

320.532   CU
A N J U P E C. q. Asociacion Nacional de Jubilados y Pensionados de Comunicaciones, Oquendo No. 751, La Habana 3, Havana, Cuba.

320 920   US
A P S A BIOGRAPHICAL DIRECTORY. (Supplement: Annual Directory of Members) irreg., 7th, 1988. $35 (members $25). American Political Science Association, 1527 New Hampshire Ave, N.W., Washington, DC 20036. TEL 202-483-2512. FAX 202-483-2657.

320   US   ISSN 0094-7954
JA28
A P S A DEPARTMENTAL SERVICES PROGRAM SURVEY OF DEPARTMENTS. 1971. a. $20. American Political Science Association, 1527 New Hampshire Ave., N.W., Washington, DC 20036. TEL 202-483-2512. FAX 202-483-2657. stat.; circ. 800.

320.07   US
A P S A DIRECTORY OF DEPARTMENT CHAIRPERSONS. 1972. a. $20. American Political Science Association, 1527 New Hampshire Ave., N.W., Washington, DC 20036. TEL 202-483-2512. FAX 202-483-2657. circ. 800.
Formerly: A P S A Directory of Department Chairmen (ISSN 0092-8658)

320 350   AT
A P S A NEWSLETTER. 1980. 5/yr. Aus.$20. Australasian Political Studies Association, Dept. of Goverment, Queensland University, St. Lucia, Qld. 4067, Australia. FAX 7-365-1388. Ed. David Gow. adv.; bk.rev.; circ. 420.
Description: Aims to keep members up-to-date with what is happening in political science.

335.83   IT   ISSN 0044-5592
A - RIVISTA ANARCHICA. 1971. m. L.30000 (foreign L.40000). Editrice A Coop. a.r.l., Casella Postale 17120, 20170 Milan, Italy. TEL 02-2896627. Ed.Bd. bk.rev.; illus.; circ. 8,500. (back issues avail.)
Description: Features articles that cover poltical events and ideas concerning the anarchist movement worldwide.

A S E A N BRIEFING. (Association of Southeast Asian Nations) see *BUSINESS AND ECONOMICS — Economic Situation And Conditions*

ABHAYADUTA. see *GENERAL INTEREST PERIODICALS — India*

ABRAHAM LINCOLN ASSOCIATION. JOURNAL. see *HISTORY*

320 300   VE
ACADEMIA DE CIENCIAS POLITICAS Y SOCIALES. BOLETIN.* 1937. irreg. Academia de Ciencias Politicas y Sociales, Bolsa a San Francisco, Palacio de las Academias, Caracas 1010, Venezuela. bibl.

320   AG
ACADEMIA NACIONAL DE CIENCIAS MORALES Y POLITICAS. ANALES. 1972. a. Academia Nacional de Ciencias Morales y Politicas, Avda. Alvear 1711-P.B. (1014), Buenos Aires, Argentina.

320   US   ISSN 0065-0684
ACADEMY OF POLITICAL SCIENCE. PROCEEDINGS. 1910. irreg. (approx. 2/yr.). membership. Academy of Political Science, 475 Riverside Dr., Ste. 1274, New York, NY 10115-0012. TEL 212-870-2500. index; circ. 9,000. (also avail. in microform from UMI; reprint service avail. from KTO,UMI) **Indexed:** A.B.C.Pol.Sci., Amer.Hist.& Life, Bk.Rev.Dig., Bk.Rev.Ind., Curr.Cont., High.Educ.Curr.Aware.Bull., Hist.Abstr., Mid.East: Abstr.& Ind., P.A.I.S., R.G., Soc.Sci.Ind., Soc.Work Res.& Abstr., SSCI, Urb.Aff.Abstr.

329.9   PO
ACCAO SOCIALISTA. 1976. w. Socialist Party, Rua Sacadura Cabral 26, Dafundo, 1495 Lisbon, Portugal. TEL 01-4197705. Dir. Jose Manuel Vilaca.

ACTA FACULTATIS POLITICO-JURIDICAE UNIVERSITATIS SCIENTIARUM BUDAPESTIENSIS DE ROLANDO EOTVOS NOMINATAE. see *LAW*

320   NE   ISSN 0001-6810
ACTA POLITICA; tijdschrift voor politicologie. (Text in Dutch, English) 1966. 4/yr. fl.102.50 to individuals (foreign fl.143); institutions fl.166.50 (foreign fl.179.50)(effective 1992). (Nederlandse Kring voor Wetenschap der Politiek) Uitgeverij Boom, P.O. Box 1058, 7940 KB Meppel, Netherlands. TEL 05220-66111. FAX 05220-66198. adv.; bk.rev.; charts; circ. 750. **Indexed:** A.B.C.Pol.Sci., Amer.Hist.& Life, E.I., Hist.Abstr., Lang.& Lang.Behav.Abstr., Mid.East: Abstr.& Ind.
—BLDSC shelfmark: 0658.700000.

ACTA UNIVERSITATIS DE ATTILA JOZSEF NOMINATAE. ACTA IURIDICA ET POLITICA. see *LAW*

320   PL   ISSN 0137-6667
ACTA UNIVERSITATIS NICOLAI COPERNICI. NAUKI POLITYCZNE. 1967. irreg. price varies. Uniwersytet Mikolaja Kopernika, Fosa Staromiejska 3, Torun, Poland. (Dist. by: Osrodek Rozpowszechniania Wydawnictw Naukowych PAN, Palac Kultury i Nauki, 00-901 Warsaw, Poland)

320.531   HU   ISSN 0563-0657
ACTA UNIVERSITATIS SZEGEDIENSIS DE ATTILA JOZSEF NOMINATAE. SECTIO SCIENTIAE SOCIALISMI/TUDOMANYOS SZOCIALIZMUS. (Subseries of: Acta Universitatis Szegediensis de Attila Jozsef Nominatae. Sectio Scientiae Socialismi. ISSN 0230-3558) (Text in Hungarian, Russian; summaries in French, German and Russian) 1961. a. exchange basis. Attila Jozsef University, c/o E. Szabo, Exchange Librarian, Dugonics ter 13, P.O.B. 393, 6701 Szeged, Hungary. (Subscr. to: Kultura, Box 149, H-1389 Budapest, Hungary) Ed. Laszlo J. Nagy. circ. 300.
Description: Recent and contemporary history of Hungarian and world ideology, politics, society and economy linked with workers' and liberation movements and Marxism-Leninism.

322.4   CN   ISSN 0001-7469
ACTION NATIONALE. 1917. 10/yr. Can.$35. Ligue d'Action Nationale, 82 ouest, rue Sherbrooke, Montreal, Que. H2X 1X3, Canada. TEL 514-845-8533. FAX 514-844-6369. Ed. Gerard Turcotte. adv.; bk.rev.; index; circ. 2,000. **Indexed:** Amer.Hist.& Life, Can.Per.Ind., Hist.Abstr., Pt.de Rep. (1979-).
—BLDSC shelfmark: 0675.700000.

320.9   DM   ISSN 0044-6106
ACTION POPULAIRE. 1964. 3/wk. 2160 Fr.CFA($25.) c/o Julian Aza, Ed., Boite Postale 215, Cotonou, Benin.

POLITICAL SCIENCE

258   SZ   ISSN 0001-7507
ACTION SOCIALE. s-m. 12 Fr. Organisations Chretiennes-Sociales, Rue de l'Abbe Bovet 6, 1700 Fribourg, Switzerland.

320.531 330.1   FR
ACTUEL MARX. s-a. 190 F. (foreign 240 F.). Presses Universitaires de France, Departement des Revues, 14 av. du Bois-de-l'Epine, 91003 Evry Cedex, France. TEL 1-60-77-82-05. FAX 1-60-79-20-45. TELEX PUF 600 474 F. Dirs. Jacques Bidet, Jacques Texier.
   Description: Covers the philosophical, economic, historical, social science and literary aspects of Marxism.

320   IS   ISSN 0334-5831
HC415.25.A1
ADAM CHOFSHE/FREE MAN; free economy and society. (Text in Hebrew) 1984. bi-m. $15. P.O. Box 33180, Tel Aviv, Israel. Ed. Jacob Resler. adv.; bk.rev.; circ. 1,000.

350 338   CK   ISSN 0120-3754
JA5
ADMINISTRACION Y DESARROLLO. 1962. s-a. Col.600($8) Escuela Superior de Administracion Publica, Centro de Investigaciones en Administracion Publica, Diagonal 40 No. 46A-37, Apdo. Aereo 29745, Bogota, Colombia. Ed. Delfin Acevedo Restrepo. adv.; bk.rev.; bibl.; charts; stat.; circ. 2,000.

320 350   US   ISSN 0738-3401
ADMINISTRATION AND POLICY JOURNAL. 1981. m. $6.50. Rider College, Institute for Policy Research, Box 6400, Lawrenceville, NJ 08648. TEL 609-896-5357. Ed.Bd. bk.rev.; circ. 400.
   Indexed: Educ.Admin.Abstr.
   Formerly (until 1983): Administrative Comments and Letters.

320 350   TS
ADMINISTRATION AND POLITICAL SCIENCES REVIEW/MAJALLAT AL-ULUM AL-IDARIYYAH WAL-SIYASIYYAH.* (Text in Arabic, English) 1985. a. exchange basis. United Arab Emirates University, Faculty of Administration and Political Sciences, P.O. Box 15551, Al-Ain, United Arab Emirates. TEL 637833. TELEX 33521 JAMEAH. Ed. Abdul Hafez M. al-Kurdi. circ. 500.
   Description: Publishes research papers on topics in administration and political science.

ADMINISTRATION AND SOCIETY. see *PUBLIC ADMINISTRATION*

328 973   US
ADVANCE LOCATOR FOR CAPITOL HILL. Variant title: C.S.D. Advance Locator. 1963. a. $15. Staff Directories Ltd., Box 62, Mt. Vernon, VA 22121. TEL 703-765-3400. FAX 703-765-1300. (avail. on diskette)
   ●Also available on CD-ROM.
   Description: Update on members of Congress, staffs, titles, addresses, district offices and phone number.

322.4   US
ADVOCATE (PANHANDLE). 1986. bi-m. $5. Peace Farm, HCR2 Box 25, Panhandle, TX 79068. TEL 806-335-1715. Ed. Les Breeding. adv.; bk.rev. (back issues avail.)
   Description: Anti-nuclear and anti-war activist news and views. Aims to create an environment for peace through peaceful means, to assert that peace can exist only where there is justice, and to develop an ecological model for nonviolent social change.

320   US
ADVOCATE'S ADVOCATE. 1988. m. $25. Advocacy Institute, 1730 Rhode Island Ave., N.W., Ste. 600, Washington, DC 20036. TEL 202-659-8475. FAX 202-659-8484. Ed. Stan Cohen. bk.rev.; circ. 500. (back issues avail.)
   Formerly: GiantKilling.
   Description: Covers lobbying, using the media, and public policy advocacy.

AFRICA ANALYSIS; fortnightly bulletin on financial and political trends. see *BUSINESS AND ECONOMICS — Economic Situation And Conditions*

960   UK   ISSN 0044-6483
DT1
AFRICA CONFIDENTIAL. 1960. fortn. £125 to individuals; students £40($70); Africa £130($240); elsewhere £170($315); (effective 1990-1991). Miramoor Publications Ltd., 73 Farringdon Rd., London EC1M 3JB, England. TEL 071-831-3511. FAX 071-831-6778. (Subscr. to: Computer Posting, 120-126 Lavender Avenue, Mitcham, Surrey CR4 3HP, England) Ed. Stephen Ellis. index; circ. 3,500. (back issues avail.) **Indexed:** Curr.Cont.M.E., Key to Econ.Sci.
   —BLDSC shelfmark: 0732.153000.
   Description: Covers political and economic analysis of African countries.

320   NP   ISSN 8755-5034
AFRICA INTERNATIONAL. (Text in English) 1983. a. $100. Siveast Consultants, Inc., USA, c/o P.O. Box 1755, Kathmandu, Napal. (UK subscr. to: Dr. Ramasastry, c/o Overseas Customer Service, Midland Bank Blc., Poultry and Princes St., London EC2, England) Ed. C.V. Ramasastry. adv.; bk.rev.; circ. controlled. (looseleaf format)

960   II   ISSN 0044-6491
AFRICA LETTER. 1971. w. Rs.520($100.) K.K. Roy (Private) Ltd., 55 Gariahat Rd., P.O. Box 10210, Calcutta 700 019, India. Ed. Dr. K.K. Roy. circ. 1,180. (also avail. in microfilm)

960   US   ISSN 0191-6521
DT1
AFRICA NEWS. 1973. fortn. $48. Africa News Service, Inc., Box 3851, Durham, NC 27702. TEL 919-286-0747. FAX 919-286-2614. Ed. Reed Kramerl. adv.; bk.rev.; s-a. index; circ. 3,500. (also avail. in microform; back issues avail.; reprint service avail.) **Indexed:** Alt.Press Ind.
   ●Also available online. Vendor(s): NewsNet (IT15).
   Description: Addresses movements for improving society on the African continent. Liberation struggles, reform efforts and solidarity drives are all covered.

960   II   ISSN 0001-9828
DT1
AFRICA QUARTERLY; a journal of African affairs. (Text in English) 1961. q. Rs.20($7.) Indian Council for Cultural Relations, Azad Bhavan, Indraprastha Estate, New Delhi 110002, India. adv.; bk.rev.; index; circ. 1,900. (also avail. in microform from UMI; Reprint service avail. from UMI) **Indexed:** A.B.C.Pol.Sci., Amer.Hist.& Life, ASSIA, Curr.Cont.Africa, Hist.Abstr., Mid.East: Abstr.& Ind., P.A.I.S.

960 300 700   UK
AFRICA RESEARCH BULLETIN. SERIES A: POLITICAL. 1964. m. £185($360) combined subscr. for Series A & B £277($540). Basil Blackwell Ltd., 108 Cowley Road, Oxford OX4 1JF, England. TEL 0865-791100. FAX 0865-791347. TELEX 837022-OXBOOK-G. Ed. P. Adams. **Indexed:** Curr.Cont.Africa.
   Formerly: Africa Research Bulletin. Series A: Political, Social and Cultural (ISSN 0001-9844)

AFRICA REVIEW. see *BUSINESS AND ECONOMICS — Economic Situation And Conditions*

960 330.9   UK   ISSN 0065-3896
DT351
AFRICA SOUTH OF THE SAHARA (YEAR). 1971. a. $275. Europa Publications Ltd., 18 Bedford Sq., London WC1B 3JN, England. TEL 071-580-8236. FAX 071-636-1664. TELEX 21540 EUROPA G.
   —BLDSC shelfmark: 0732.188000.
   Description: Following a general introduction, essays on African affairs and a section covering regional organizations. Includes separate chapters on each of the countries. Also supplies the latest facts and figures and directory material.

960   US   ISSN 0001-9887
DT1
AFRICA TODAY. 1954. q. $15 to individuals; institutions $40. Africa Today Associates, c/o University of Denver, Graduate School of International Studies, Denver, CO 80208. TEL 303-871-3678. FAX 303-871-4000. Eds. George W. Shepherd, Tilden J. LeMelle. adv.; bk.rev.; bibl.; index; circ. 1,568. (also avail. in microform from UMI; back issues avail.) **Indexed:** A.B.C.Pol.Sci., Acad.Ind., Amer.Hist.& Life, Bk.Rev.Ind. (1980-), CERDIC, Child.Bk.Rev.Ind. (1980-), Curr.Cont.Africa, Curr.Cont., HR Rep., I D A, M.L.A., Mid.East: Abstr.& Ind., P.A.I.S., Soc.Sci.Ind.
   —BLDSC shelfmark: 0732.190000.
   Description: Examines issues affecting contemporary Africa, with emphasis on politics and economics.

960   UK   ISSN 0001-9909
DT1
AFRICAN AFFAIRS. 1901. q. £46($90) (Royal African Society) Oxford University Press, Oxford Journals, Pinkhill House, Southfield Road, Eynsham, Oxford OX8 1JJ, England. TEL 0865-882283. FAX 0865-882890. TELEX 837330-OXPRES-G. (U.S. address: 200 Madison Ave., New York, NY 10016) Eds. Richard Hodder-Williams, Peter Woodward. adv.; bk.rev.; bibl.; index; circ. 1,650. (also avail. in microform; reprint service avail. from KTO) **Indexed:** A.B.C.Pol.Sci., A.I.C.P., Abstr.Anthropol., Agroforest.Abstr., Amer.Hist.& Life, ASSIA, Br.Hum.Ind., Curr.Cont.Africa, Curr.Cont., Hist.Abstr., Hum.Ind., Int.Lab.Doc., Lang.& Lang.Behav.Abstr., Mid.East: Abstr.& Ind., Peace Res.Abstr., Ref.Sour., Refug.Abstr., Rural Devel.Abstr., Rural Recreat.Tour.Abstr., SSCI, World Agri.Econ.& Rural Sociol.Abstr.
   —BLDSC shelfmark: 0732.300000.
   Description: Provides a forum for the discussion of African writing by both African and non-African writers.

320   SW
AFRICAN CLARION. 1972. 6/yr. $15. Box 4037, 422 04 Hisings Backa, Sweden. Ed. T.H. Mudzingwa.
   Description: Covers African studies.

320.532 960   SA   ISSN 0001-9976
HX3
AFRICAN COMMUNIST. 1959. q. R.20($24) (South African Communist Party) Inkululeko Publications, P.O. Box 1027, Johannesburg 2000, South Africa. TEL 836-6425. FAX 836-8366. (U.S. address: Imported Publications Inc., 320 West Ohio St., Chicago, IL 60610) Ed.Bd. adv.; bk.rev.; stat.; circ. 12,500. (also avail. in microform from UMI) **Indexed:** Curr.Cont.Africa.
   —BLDSC shelfmark: 0732.390000.
   Description: Serves as a forum for Marxist-Leninist thought by the South African Communist Party.

960   II   ISSN 0002-0133
AFRICAN RECORDER; fortnightly digest of events in Africa with index. (Text in English) 1962. fortn. $99. M. S. R. Khemchand, Ed. & Pub., C-2 Gulmohar Park, PO Box 595, New Delhi 110 049, India. charts; index every 6 mos. and annually.

960   TZ   ISSN 0856-0056
AFRICAN REVIEW; a journal of African politics, development and international affairs. 1971. s-a. EAs.80($28) University of Dar es Salaam, Department of Political Science, P.O. Box 35042, Dar es Salaam, Tanzania. Ed.Bd. adv.; bk.rev.; circ. 1,000. (back issues avail.) **Indexed:** A.B.C.Pol.Sci., Amer.Hist.& Life, Hist.Abstr., Rural Recreat.Tour.Abstr., World Agri.Econ.& Rural Sociol.Abstr.
   —BLDSC shelfmark: 0732.920000.
   Formerly: African Political Review (ISSN 0002-0117)

AFRICAN STUDIES; a biannual journal devoted to the study of African anthropology, history, sociology, and languages. see *ANTHROPOLOGY*

320 350   SA   ISSN 0304-615X
AFRICANUS; journal for development administration. (Text in Afrikaans, English) 1972. a. R.7($4.50) (effective 1991). University of South Africa, Department of Development Administration, P.O. Box 392, Pretoria 0001, South Africa. FAX 429-3221. TELEX 429-3094. Ed. L. Cornwell. adv.; bk.rev.; charts; stat.; circ. 660. (also avail. in microfiche; back issues avail.) **Indexed:** Curr.Cont.Africa, Ind.S.A.Per.

POLITICAL SCIENCE

320 330.9 301   GW   ISSN 0002-0397
DT1
AFRIKA SPECTRUM; deutsche Zeitschrift fuer moderne Afrikaforschung. 1966. 3/yr. DM.80. Institut fuer Afrika Kunde, Neuer Jungfernstieg 21, 2000 Hamburg 36, Germany. TEL 040-3562523. FAX 040-3562547. Ed. Dirk Kohnert. adv.; bk.rev.; bibl.; charts; index; circ. 500. **Indexed:** Curr.Cont.Africa, I D A, Int.Lab.Doc., Key to Econ.Sci., P.A.I.S.For.Lang.Ind., P.A.I.S., Rural Devel.Abstr., Rural Ext.Educ.& Tr.Abstr., Rural Recreat.Tour.Abstr., World Agri.Econ.& Rural Sociol.Abstr.
—BLDSC shelfmark: 0735.268000.
Description: Contemporary problems and developments in Africa.

320.52   SA
DIE AFRIKANER. (Text in Afrikaans) 1970. w. R.60 (foreign R.207). (Herstigte Nasionale Party) Strydpers BPK, Pretoriusstraat 1043, P.O. Box 1888, Hatfield, Pretoria, South Africa. TEL 012-342-3410. Ed. H. Ferguson. circ. 10,000. (looseleaf format; back issues avail.)
Description: Covers political and business issues from a right-wing perspective.

327 950 960   FR   ISSN 0399-0370
DT1
AFRIQUE ET L'ASIE MODERNES; revue politique sociale et economique. 1948. q. 180 F. (foreign 250 F.). Centre des Hautes Etudes sur l'Afrique et l'Asie Modernes, Association des Anciens du C.H.E.A.M., 13 rue du Four, 75006 Paris, France. TEL 1-43-26-96-90. FAX 1-40-51-03-58. Ed. Ph. Decraene. adv.; bk.rev.; abstr.; bibl.; circ. 1,000. **Indexed:** A.I.C.P., Amer.Hist.& Life, Curr.Cont.Africa, Hist.Abstr., I D A, Int.Lab.Doc., P.A.I.S.For.Lang.Ind., Rural Recreat.Tour.Abstr., World Agri.Econ.& Rural Sociol.Abstr.
Formerly: Afrique et l'Asie (ISSN 0002-0486); Includes: Association des Anciens du C.H.E.A.M. Bulletin.

960   SG   ISSN 0002-0524
AFRIQUE MON PAYS.* no.27, 1969. m. B.P. 2469, Dakar, Senegal. Ed. Madani N'Diaya. adv.; charts; illus.

AFRIQUE NOIRE POLITIQUE ET ECONOMIQUE. see BUSINESS AND ECONOMICS — Economic Situation And Conditions

320.531   US   ISSN 0739-4853
HX1
AGAINST THE CURRENT. 1979; N.S. 1986. bi-m. $18 to individuals; institutions $25. 7012 Michigan Ave., Detroit, MI 48210. TEL 313-841-0161. FAX 313-841-8884. Center for Changes. adv.; bk.rev.; circ. 2,500. (also avail. in microform from UMI) **Indexed:** Alt.Press Ind., Chic.Per.Ind., Left Ind. (1990-).
—BLDSC shelfmark: 0735.826000.
Supersedes: Changes (Detroit) (ISSN 0746-5335); **Formerly** (until 1984): Changes Socialist Monthly.
Description: Contains discussions of movements for social and political change, and commentary from a socialist and feminist viewpoint with special emphasis on labor.

320   FR   ISSN 0242-3782
AGENCE TELEGRAPHIQUE JUIVE. BULLETIN. (Text in French) 1970. d. 250 F. Jewish Telegraph Agency, 14 rue Georges Berger, 75017 Paris, France. Ed. Adam Loss.

320   BL
AGENCIA DE NOTICIAS FIDES. NOTAS. 1972. w. $200. Agencia de Noticias Fides, Casilla 5782, La Paz, Bolivia. TEL 591-2-365152. FAX 591-2-365153. TELEX 3236 FIDES BV. Ed. Jose Gramunt. circ. 1,200.
Description: Political and economic analysis of Bolivia.

AGRICULTURAL WORKING PEOPLE OF KOREA. see AGRICULTURE

956.9   LE   ISSN 0002-3981
AHAD.* 1949. w. $50. Dar-al Kifah, Box 1462, Beirut, Lebanon. Ed. Riad Taha. adv.; circ. 5,000.

320   SA
AIDA PARKER NEWSLETTER. (Text in English) 1983. m. R.80($80) Aida Parker Newsletter Pty. Ltd., P.O. Box 91059, Auckland Park 2006, Johannesburg, South Africa. TEL 011-726-6856. FAX 011-726-5537. Ed. Aida Parker. bk.rev.; circ. 6,000.
Description: Analysis and perspectives on Southern African affairs.

320   GW   ISSN 0939-3099
AKTUELLE OSTINFORMATIONEN. 1969. s-a. DM.7.80. Gesamteuropaeisches Studienwerk Vlotho e.V., Suedfeldstr. 2-4, Postfach 1745, 4973 Vlotho, Germany. TEL 05733-2258. bk.rev.; circ. 2,000.

329.9   SW   ISSN 0345-0635
AKTUELLT I POLITIKEN. 1953. 21/yr. SEK 154. Sveriges Socialdemokratiska Arbetareparti - Swedish Social Democratic Labour Party, Torsgatan 10, 105 60 Stockholm, Sweden. Ed. Ove Andersson. adv.; illus.; circ. 75,000.
Formerly: Aktuellt Politik och Samhaelle (ISSN 0002-3884)

320.531   YU
HX365.5
AKTUELNA PITANJA SOCIJALIZMA. English edition: Socialist Thought and Practice (ISSN 0583-7200); German edition: Sozialistische Theorie und Praxis (ISSN 0350-476X); Italian edition: Questioni Attuali del Socialismo (ISSN 0351-0107); Russian edition: Sotsialisticheskaya Mysl' i Praktika (ISSN 0350-4751); Spanish edition: Cuestiones Actuales del Socialismo (ISSN 0350-8846) (Arabic edition (ISSN 0350-5413); French edition: Questions Actuelles de Socialisme (ISSN 0033-6351)) (Text in Serbo-Croatian) 1961. m. $30. Komunist, Trg Marksa i Engelsa 11, 11000 Belgrade, Yugoslavia. TEL 11-632-569. Ed. Branko Prnjat. bk.rev. **Indexed:** Key to Econ.Sci., Mid.East: Abstr.& Ind.
Description: Contains both original articles and material reprinted from other publications dealing with theoretical problems of socialist development in Yugoslavia; reviews the activities of organizations of the self-management socialist system; reviews world events and the international activity of Yugoslavia.

320.531   NO
AKTUELT PERSPEKTIV. 1964. 48/yr. NOK 200. Norske Arbeiderparti - Norwegian Labour Party, P.B. 8824, Youngstorget, N-0028 Oslo 1, Norway. Ed. Johs Skeide Larsen. bk.rev.; bibl.; circ. 17,000.
Formerly: Sosialistisk Perspektiv (ISSN 0049-1330)
Description: Traces the origins of the Norwegian Labour Party.

320   US
ALABAMA LIBERTY. 1979. bi-m. $5. Alabama Libertarian Party, Box 11514, Birmingham, AL 35202. TEL 205-322-2991. Eds. Frank and Desta Monachelli. illus.; circ. 15,000. (back issues avail.)

320   VE
ALARMA. 1977. fortn. Torre de la Prensa, Plaza del Panteon, Apdo. 2976, Caracas 101, Venezuela. Dir. Jose Campos Suarez. circ. 65,150.

949.65   US   ISSN 0002-4651
DR901
ALBANIA REPORT. 1970. irreg., no.69, 1989. contributions. (Albanian Affairs Study Group) Gamma Publishing Co., P.O. Box 206, Church Street Sta., New York, NY 10008. TEL 718-633-0530. Ed. Jack Shulman. circ. 3,000.

322.4   FR
ALBANIAN RESISTANCE. vol.25, 1978. irreg. National Democratic Committee for a Free Albania, 18 bis rue Brunel, 75017 Paris, France. (processed)
Description: Informs readers of the state of the Albanian struggle for independence.

325   FR   ISSN 0002-5313
ALGERIEN EN EUROPE. 1968. bi-m. 60 F. Centre Algerien de Documentation et d'Information, 3 rue Joseph Sansboeuf, 75008 Paris, France. Ed. G. Abdelkrim. adv.; bk.rev.; bibl.; charts. (tabloid format)

329.3 301.4157   US
ALICE REPORTS. 1972. m. $15. Alice B. Toklas Lesbian & Gay Democratic Club, Box 11316, San Francisco, CA 94101. TEL 415-621-3296. Ed. Lester Olmstead-Rose. circ. 800.

320   II
ALL INDIA CONGRESS COMMITTEE. CONGRESS BULLETIN. 1972. m. All India Congress Committee, Publications Department, 5 Dr. Rajendra Prasad Rd., New Delhi 110001, India. Ed. N. Balakrishnan.

ALLAM- ES JOGTUDOMANY/POLITICAL SCIENCE AND JURISPRUDENCE. see LAW

320   RM
ALLIANCE FOR PEACE IN RUMANIA. INFORMATION BULLETIN.. (Text in English) 1962. q. free. Alliance for Peace in Rumania, 29 Biserica Amzei St., 70172 Bucharest 29, Rumania. TEL 118948. charts; illus.
Formerly (until vol.3, 1989): National Committee for the Defence of Peace in the Socialist Republic of Rumania. Information Bulletin (ISSN 0547-5090)
Description: Discusses economic progress, industry, agricultural development, security, disarmament and human rights.

329.9   UK
ALLIANCE NEWS. 1971. m. 20p. per no. Alliance Party of Northern Ireland, 88 University St., Belfast BT7 1HE, N. Ireland. FAX 0232-333147. Ed.Bd. adv.; bk.rev.; charts; illus.; circ. 9,000.
Formerly: Alliance (ISSN 0044-734X)

320   CU
ALMA MATER. m. $20 in N. America; S. America $26; Europe $29; others $41. (Editorial Abril) Ediciones Cubanas, Obispo No. 527, Apdo. 605, Havana, Cuba.

320.531   MF
ALTERNATIVE. (Text in French) m. Mouvement Chretien pour le Socialisme, 1A, Colonel Draper, Beau Bassin, Mauritius.

967   NE   ISSN 0166-0373
AMANDLA; maandblad over zuidelijk Afrika. (Text in Dutch) 1971. m. fl.22.50 (effective 1992). Stichting Amandla, Oudezijds Achterburgwal 173, 1012 DJ Amsterdam, Netherlands. TEL 029-6232229. FAX 020-6270441. TELEX 17125. (Co-sponsors: Boycot Outspan Aktie, Komitee Zuidelijk Afrika, Werkgroep Kairos) Ed.Bd. adv.; bk.rev.; bibl.; charts; illus.; circ. 12,000.
Formerly (until 1977): Angola Bulletin (ISSN 0044-8281)
Description: Political and cultural coverage of Southern Africa.

320   AG
AMBIENTE Y RECURSOS NATURALES; revista de derecho, politica y administracion. q. (Fundacion Ambiente y Recursos Naturales) Editorial La Ley, Tucuman 1471, 1050 Buenos Aires, Argentina. TEL 49-5481-9. Ed. Pedro Tarak.

324   US   ISSN 0065-678X
JK1967
AMERICA VOTES; handbook of contemporary American election statistics. 1956. biennial. $110. Congressional Quarterly Inc., 1414 22nd St., N.W., Washington, DC 20037. TEL 202-887-8500. FAX 202-728-1863. Eds. Richard M. Scammon, Alice V. McGillivray. **Indexed:** SRI.
Description: Contents include most recent election results for senator, representative and governor by ward, county, town and congressional district; most recent state-by-state primary results; state-by-state presidential election totals since 1920; and presidential primary totals since 1972.

POLITICAL SCIENCE

320 300   US   ISSN 0002-7162
H1   CODEN: AAYPA
AMERICAN ACADEMY OF POLITICAL AND SOCIAL SCIENCE. ANNALS. 1891. bi-m. $54 hardcover, $39 soft to members; institutions $144 hardcover, $120 soft (effective 1991). Sage Publications, Inc., 2455 Teller Rd., Newbury Park, CA 91320. TEL 805-499-0721. FAX 805-499-0871. (Subscr. in Asia to: Sage Publications India Pvt. Ltd., P.O. Box 4215, New Delhi 110 048, India; in Europe, Middle East, and Africa to: Sage Publications Ltd., 28 Banner St., London EC1Y 8QE, England) Ed. Richard D. Lambert. adv.; bk.rev.; charts; cum.index every 5 yrs.; circ. 5,726. (also avail. in microfilm from KTO,PMC; back issues avail.; reprint service avail. from KTO) **Indexed:** A.B.C.Pol.Sci., Acad.Ind., Amer.Bibl.Slavic & E.Eur.Stud., Bk.Rev.Ind. (1965-), Br.Archaeol.Abstr., Child.Bk.Rev.Ind. (1965-), Commun.Abstr., Comput.Rev., Curr.Cont., Fut.Surv., Hist.Abstr., I D A, Int.Lab.Doc., Key to Econ.Sci., Lang.& Lang.Behav.Abstr., Mag.Ind., Mid.East: Abstr.& Ind., P.A.I.S., Peace Res.Abstr., Pers.Lit., R.G., Sage Fam.Stud.Abstr., Sage Urb.Stud.Abstr., Soc.Sci.Ind., SSCI.
—BLDSC shelfmark: 1018.800000.
Description: For practitioners, students and researchers. Looks at health care, social care, rehabilitation, the aging of intelligence, and the lives of older people and the changing social roles.

970   US   ISSN 0569-2245
AMERICAN ASSEMBLY. REPORT. (Title varies with topics of American Assembly programs at Columbia University) 1951. 2/yr. free. American Assembly, 412 Altschul Hall, Barnard College, Columbia University, New York, NY 10027-6598. TEL 212-854-3455. FAX 212-662-3655. circ. 50,000.
Supersedes in part: American Assembly (Background Papers and Final Report) (ISSN 0065-6976)

320   US
▼**AMERICAN CAUCUS.** 1992. fortn. $39. Congressional Quarterly Inc., 1414 22nd St., N.W., Washington, DC 20037. TEL 800-432-2250. FAX 202-728-1863. Ed. Robert Merry. adv. contact: Chuck Alston. circ. 10,000.
Description: Analysis of Capitol Hill politics.

AMERICAN COUNCIL FOR JUDAISM. SPECIAL INTEREST REPORT; a digest of news items and articles in the area of the council's interest. see *RELIGIONS AND THEOLOGY — Judaic*

320 300   US   ISSN 1047-3572
D839
AMERICAN ENTERPRISE. 1978. bi-m. $29 to individuals; corporations $56. American Enterprise Institute for Public Policy Research, 1150 17th St., N.W., Washington, DC 20036. TEL 202-862-5800. FAX 202-862-7178. TELEX 671-1239. (Subscr. to: Box 6827, Syracuse, NY 13217) Ed. Karlyn Keene. adv.; charts; stat.; circ. 15,000. (also avail. in microfiche) **Indexed:** A.B.C.Pol.Sci., Mag.Ind., Mid.East: Abstr.& Ind., P.A.I.S., Soc.Sci.Ind., SRI.
—BLDSC shelfmark: 0813.848000.
Formerly (until 1990): Public Opinion (Washington) (ISSN 0149-9157)
Description: Contains articles in economics, foreign policy, law, social policy, regulation, politics, public opinion, and media.

322.4   US
AMERICAN INDEPENDENT. 1974. m. $15 (includes California Statesman publications). William K. Shearer, Ed. & Pub., 8158 Palm St., Lemon Grove, CA 91945. TEL 619-460-4484.
Description: Current and historical information about the American Independent Party.

320   US   ISSN 0092-5853
JA1
AMERICAN JOURNAL OF POLITICAL SCIENCE. 1957. q. $25 to individuals; institutions $50. (Midwest Political Science Association) University of Texas Press, Box 7819, Austin, TX 78713. TEL 512-471-4531. Ed. David Rhode. adv.; charts; stat.; index; circ. 3,300. (also avail. in microform from KTO,UMI; reprint service avail. from KTO,UMI) **Indexed:** A.B.C.Pol.Sci., Amer.Hist.& Life, Bibl.Ind., Curr.Cont., Hist.Abstr., Int.Polit.Sci.Abstr., Lang.& Lang.Behav.Abstr., Mid.East: Abstr.& Ind., P.A.I.S., PSI, Sage Pub.Admin.Abstr., Sage Urb.Stud.Abstr., Soc.Sci.Ind., SSCI, Stud.Wom.Abstr.
—BLDSC shelfmark: 0834.300000.
Formerly: Midwest Journal of Political Science (ISSN 0026-3397)
Description: Presents academic research in American politics and international methodology.

323.4   US
AMERICAN PATRIOT (SCOTTSDALE). 1948. bi-m. $12. Harry T. Everingham, Ed. & Pub., Box A, Scottsdale, AZ 85252. TEL 602-941-0144. adv.; bk.rev.; circ. 20,000. (tabloid format)
Formerly (until 1976, vol.29, no.6): Free Enterprise (ISSN 0016-0342)

320   US
AMERICAN POLITICAL PARTIES AND ELECTION SERIES. 1980. irreg. price varies. Praeger Publishers (Subsidiary of: Greenwood Publishing Group Inc.), 88 Post Rd. W., Box 5007, Westport, CT 06881-5007. TEL 203-226-3571. FAX 203-222-1502.

320   US
AMERICAN POLITICAL REPORT. 1971. bi-w. $195. American Political Research Corp., 7316 Wisconsin Ave., Bethesda, MD 20814. TEL 301-654-4990. FAX 301-656-0822. Ed. Kevin P. Phillips. circ. 1,400.
Description: Covers American politics, polls, elections, and political economics.

320   US   ISSN 0003-0554
JA1
AMERICAN POLITICAL SCIENCE REVIEW. 1906. q. membership. American Political Science Association, 1527 New Hampshire Ave., N.W., Washington, DC 20036. TEL 202-483-2512. FAX 202-483-2657. Ed. Bingham Powell. adv.; bk.rev.; charts; illus.; index, cum.index; circ. 20,000. (also avail. in microform from MIM,PMC,UMI) **Indexed:** A.B.C.Pol.Sci., Abstr.Bk.Rev.Curr.Leg.Per., Acad.Ind., Biog.Ind., Bk.Rev.Dig., Bk.Rev.Ind. (1965-), CERDIC, Chic.Per.Ind., Child.Bk.Rev.Ind. (1965-), Commun.Abstr., Curr.Cont., Fut.Surv., Hist.Abstr., Int.Polit.Sci.Abstr., J.of Econ.Lit., Mid.East: Abstr.& Ind., Pers.Lit., R.G., Ref.Sour., Sci.Abstr., Soc.Sci.Ind., Soc.Work Res.& Abstr.
—BLDSC shelfmark: 0851.500000.

320   US   ISSN 0741-1111
JK1
AMERICAN POLITICS;* the Nation's magazine of politics. 1983. m. $23.95. American Politics, Inc., 2003 Columbia Pike, Ste. 616, Arlington, VA 22204-4531. TEL 202-347-1100. Ed. Grant Oliphant. adv.; circ. 27,000.

320.9   US   ISSN 0044-7803
JK1
AMERICAN POLITICS QUARTERLY. 1973. q. $40 to individuals; institutions $115 (effective 1991). Sage Publications, Inc., 2455 Teller Rd., Newbury Park, CA 91320. TEL 805-499-0721. FAX 805-499-0871. (And: Sage Publications, Ltd., 6 Bonhill St., London EC2A 4PU, England) Ed. Susan Welch. adv.; bk.rev.; charts; index; circ. 1,000. (back issues avail) **Indexed:** A.B.C.Pol.Sci., Amer.Hist.& Life, Commun.Abstr., Curr.Cont., Hist.Abstr., Int.Polit.Sci.Abstr., Mid.East: Abstr.& Ind., P.A.I.S., Sage Pub.Admin.Abstr., Sage Urb.Stud.Abstr., SSCI.
—BLDSC shelfmark: 0851.600000.
Description: Promotes basic research in all areas of American political behavior, including urban, state, and national policies, as well as pressing social problems requiring political solutions.

320   JA   ISSN 0387-2815
E151
AMERICAN REVIEW. (Text in Japanese; summaries in English) 1967. a. $40 (effective 1991). Japanese Association for American Studies, University of Tokyo, Center for American Studies, 8-1, 3-chome, Komaba, Meguro-ku, Tokyo 153, Japan. TEL 03-3467-1171. Ed. Takeshi Igarashi. bibl.; circ. 1,100.

320.5   US   ISSN 0278-0585
HN90.R3
AMERICAN SENTINEL. 1971. fortn. $77. Capitol Hill Publishing, Inc., 325 Pennsylvania Ave., S.E., Ste. 272, Washington, DC 20003. TEL 202-547-3622. FAX 202-543-3622. Ed. Lee Bellinger. index; circ. 10,000. (looseleaf format; also avail. in microform from UMI; reprint service avail. from UMI)
Former titles: Pink Sheet on the Left (ISSN 0048-4180); Pink Sheet on the New Left.
Description: Monitors the American political landscape, focusing on political economy, the activities of Congress and the role of the American left.

956.940 296   US   ISSN 0003-1550
DS101
AMERICAN ZIONIST. 1910. q. $5. Zionist Organization of America, 4 E. 34th St., New York, NY 10016. TEL 212-481-1500. Ed. Jordan Malmed. adv.; bk.rev.; film rev.; circ. 45,000. (also avail. in microform from UMI) **Indexed:** Ind.Jew.Per., Mid.East: Abstr.& Ind.

323   US   ISSN 0066-1236
AMERICANS FOR CONSTITUTIONAL ACTION. REPORT.* 1961. a. contributions of $15 or more. Americans for Constitutional Action, 7100 Sussex Pl., Alexandria, VA 22307. circ. 5,000.

973   US   ISSN 0003-1593
AMERICA'S FUTURE; a monthly review of news, books and public affairs. 1959. m. $10 (free to public and school libraries). Americas Future, Inc., Westfall Professional Plaza, Box 1625, PA 18337-2625. TEL 717-296-2800. FAX 717-296-2811. Eds. Allan C. Brownfeld, Philip C. Clarke. bk.rev.; index; circ. 13,500. (also avail. in microfilm; back issues avail.)

AMERICAS REVIEW. see *BUSINESS AND ECONOMICS — Economic Situation And Conditions*

322.4   CY
AMMOCHOSTOS. (Text in Greek) w. 44 Egnatias, Plati, Eylenya, Nicosia, Cyprus. TEL 02-352918. Ed. Niko Falas. circ. 2,800.
Description: Right-wing political review reflecting the voice of "Famagusta" refugees.

AMUDIM; bulletin of the religious kibbutzim. see *BUSINESS AND ECONOMICS — Cooperatives*

320 300   AG
ANALES CIENCIAS POLITICAS Y SOCIALES. 1950. s-a. free or exchange basis. Universidad Nacional de Cuyo, Facultad de Ciencias Politicas y Sociales, Biblioteca, Casilla de Correos 217, 5500 Mendoza, Argentina. bk.rev.; charts; stat.
Formerly (until 1987): Boletin de Ciencias Politicas y Sociales (ISSN 0045-2394)

320   PE
ANALISIS; cuadernos de investigacion. 1977. 2/yr. S/750($12) to individuals; institutions $20. Apdo. 11093, Correo Santa Beatriz, Lima 14, Peru. Ed. Ernesto Yepes. adv.; bk.rev.; circ. 5,000.

320   CK
ANALYSIS POLITICO. 1987. 3/yr. Universidad Nacional de Colombia, Instituto de Estudios Politicos y Relaciones Internacionales, Apdo. Aereo No. 14490, Ciudad Universitaria, Bogota, Colombia.

335.83   IT
ANARCHISMO. 1975. m. Edizioni Anarchismo, Casella Postale 61, 95100 Catania, Italy. Ed. Alfredo M. Bonanno. bk.rev.; circ. 4,000.

328 900   BE   ISSN 0066-1589
ANCIENS PAYS ET ASSEMBLEES D'ETATS. (Text in language of contributor) 1950. irreg. price varies. (International Committee of Historical Sciences, Commission for the History of State Assemblies) U. G. A., Stijn Streuvelslaan 73, B-8501 Heule-Kortrijk, Belgium. FAX 56-35-60-96. TELEX 85579.

POLITICAL SCIENCE 3873

320 301 US ISSN 1042-2471
ANCIENT CONTROVERSY; a newsletter for society's leaders. 1988. m. $96 to individuals (foreign $126); institutions $126 (foreign $168). Spencer's International Enterprises Corp., Box 43822, Los Angeles, CA 90043-0822. TEL 213-937-3099. circ. 1,000.

320 SG
ANDE SOPI. 1977. m. Mouvement Democratique Populaire, Dakar, Senegal. Ed. Mamadou Dia.

THE ANDERSON MONITOR - BUSINESS & POLITICS. see *BUSINESS AND ECONOMICS*

320 CL
ANDES; revista teorica. 1984. 3/yr. Instituto de Estudios Contemporaneos, San Antonio 378, Oficina 911, 9th Fl., Casilla 4053, Correo Central, Santiago, Chile. Dir. Patricio Quiroga Z. bk.rev.; circ. 1,000.

329 TZ
ANGOLA IN ARMS.* 1972. m. S.10($4) Departamento de Informacao e Propaganda do Comite Central, MPLA - Partido do Trabalho, Luanda, Tanzania. illus.

320 960 SG ISSN 0066-2364
ANNEE POLITIQUE AFRICAINE. 1964. a. 17.500 Fr.CFA. Societe Africaine d'Edition, B.P. 1877, Dakar, Senegal. (And 32, rue de l'Echiquier, Paris, France) Ed.Bd.
  Formed by the 1981 merger of: Annee Politique Africaine; Economie Africaine.

320 FR ISSN 0764-8138
ANNEE POLITIQUE, ECONOMIQUE ET SOCIALE. 1876; N.S. 1944. a. 475 F. Editions du Moniteur, 17 rue d'Uzes, 75002 Paris, France. FAX 40-41-94-95. TELEX UPRESSE 680876F. Ed. Jean-Marc Pilpoul.
  Formerly: Annee Politique (ISSN 0066-2356)

320 SZ ISSN 0066-2372
HC397
ANNEE POLITIQUE SUISSE/SCHWEIZERISCHE POLITIK. (Text in French, German) 1965. a. 40 Fr. Universitaet Bern, Forschungszentrum fuer Schweizerische Politik - Universite de Berne, Centre de Recherche de Politique Suisse, Neubrueckstr. 10, 3012 Bern, Switzerland. TEL 031-658331. FAX 031-658590. Ed. Hans Hirter. index; circ. 1,500.
  Description: Complete review and analysis of all political events and developments in Swiss politics.

320 CN ISSN 0706-1021
F1059.7.F83
ANNUAIRE FRANCO-ONTARIEN. 1978. a. Office des Affaires Francophones, 900 Bay St., 4th floor, Mowat Block, Toronto, Ont. M7A 1C2, Canada. TEL 416-325-4949. FAX 416-325-4980.
  Formerly: Bottin des Organismes Franco-Ontariens (ISSN 0707-3356)

320 SZ ISSN 0066-3727
JA34
ANNUAIRE SUISSE DE SCIENCE POLITIQUE/SCHWEIZERISCHES JAHRBUCH FUER POLITISCHE WISSENSCHAFT/SWISS POLITICAL SCIENCE YEARBOOK. (Text in English, French and German) 1961. a. price varies. (Forschungsstelle fuer Politische Wissenschaft) Paul Haupt AG, Falkenplatz 14, CH-3001 Berne, Switzerland. TEL 031-232425. **Indexed:** A.B.C.Pol.Sci., Amer.Hist.& Life, Hist.Abstr.
  —BLDSC shelfmark: 1073.498000.

320 327 US ISSN 1044-825X
JF37
ANNUAL DIRECTORY OF WORLD LEADERS. a. $39.95. International Academy at Santa Barbara, 800 Garden St., Ste. D, Santa Barbara, CA 93101-1552. TEL 805-965-5010. FAX 805-965-6071. Ed. Thomas S. Garrison.
  Description: Guide to leaders of national governments, political parties, international organizations, and alliances. Includes facts on more than 175 countries, addresses of embassies in the U.S., headquarters of international organizations and alliances, and extra-parliamentary, guerrilla, and illegal political movements.

320.4 US
ANNUAL EDITIONS: AMERICAN GOVERNMENT. 1971. a. $10.95. Dushkin Publishing Group, Inc., Sluice Dock, Guilford, CT 06437-9989. TEL 203-453-4351. FAX 203-453-6000. Ed. Bruce Steinbrickner. illus.
  Formerly: Annual Editions: Readings in American Government (ISSN 0090-547X)
  Refereed Serial

320 US
▼**ANNUAL EDITIONS: CANADIAN POLITICS.** 1990. a. $10.95. Dushkin Publishing Group, Inc., Sluice Dock, Guilford, CT 06437-9989. TEL 203-453-4351. FAX 203-453-6000. Eds. Gregory Mahler, Roman R. March. illus.
  Refereed Serial

320 US
ANNUAL EDITIONS: COMPARATIVE POLITICS. 1983. a. $10.95. Dushkin Publishing Group, Inc., Sluice Dock, Guilford, CT 06437-9989. TEL 203-453-4351. FAX 203-453-6000. Ed. Christian Soe. illus.
  Refereed Serial

ANNUAL EDITIONS: WORLD POLITICS. see *POLITICAL SCIENCE — International Relations*

ANNUAL POLICY REVIEW; an agenda for the future. see *ENVIRONMENTAL STUDIES*

320 UK ISSN 0066-4057
D2
ANNUAL REGISTER WORLD EVENTS. 1758. a. £84. Longman Group UK Ltd., Westgate House, The High, Harlow, Essex CM20 1YR, England. TEL 0279 442601. (Dist. in U.S. and Canada by: Gale Research Co. Ltd., Book Tower, Detroit, MI 48226) Ed. H.V. Hodson. index.

ANNUAL REPORT ON PRIVATIZATION. see *PUBLIC ADMINISTRATION*

320 US ISSN 0748-8599
JA1
ANNUAL REVIEW OF POLITICAL SCIENCE. 1986. irreg., vol.3, 1990. price varies. Ablex Publishing Corporation, 355 Chestnut St., Norwood, NJ 07648. TEL 201-767-8450. FAX 201-767-6717. TELEX 135-393. Ed. Samuel Long.
  —BLDSC shelfmark: 1528.120000.

ANNUAL THIRD WORLD CONFERENCE PROCEEDINGS. see *HISTORY*

320 AG
ANOCERO. 1985. w. Editorial Ano Cero, Libertad 936, 5-D, 1012 Buenos Aires, Argentina.

320 GR
ANTI; independent fortnightly political review. 1972. bi-w. $57. 60 Dimocharous St., 115 21 Athens, Greece. TEL 72-32-713. FAX 7226107. Ed. Christos G. Papoutsakis. adv.; bk.rev.; index; circ. 30,000. (back issues avail.)

ANUARIO DE DERECHO PUBLICO Y ESTUDIOS POLITICOS. see *LAW*

320 MX
ANUARIO POLITICO DE AMERICA LATINA. 1974. a. Universidad Nacional Autonoma de Mexico, Facultad de Ciencias Politicas y Sociales, Villa Obregon, Ciudad Universitaria, Mexico 20, D.F., Mexico.

322.4 CR
APORTES. 1980. m. Col.550($45) Editorial Aportes para la Educacion, S.A., Apdo. 103-1009 Fecosa, San Jose, Costa Rica. TEL 21-13-20. Ed. Melvin Jimenez. adv.; bk.rev.; film rev.; play rev.; illus.; cum.index 1980-1988; circ. 2,600. (back issues avail.)

320.9 FR ISSN 0003-7176
JA11
APRES - DEMAIN; journal de documentation politique. 1957. m. 150 F. (foreign 300 F.). Ligue des Droits de l'Homme, 27 rue Jean Dolent, 75014 Paris, France. Ed. Francoise Seligmann. adv.; bk.rev.; abstr.; bibl.; index, cum.index; circ. 8,000. (back issues avail.) **Indexed:** P.A.I.S.For.Lang.Ind.
  —BLDSC shelfmark: 1581.600000.

AQUI. see *SOCIOLOGY*

320 UK ISSN 0196-3538
DS63.1
ARAB-ASIAN AFFAIRS. 1975. m. (10/yr.). $175. World Reports Limited, 108 Horseferry Rd., London SWIP 2EF, England. FAX 071-233-0185. (Subscr. to: World Reports Ltd., 280 Madison Ave., Ste., 1209, New York, NY 10016-0802) Ed. Christopher Story. (back issues avail.)
  —BLDSC shelfmark: 1583.224040.
  Formerly: Afro-Asian Affairs.
  Description: Covers developments in the Middle East.

320 LE
ARAB WORLD. (Text in English) 1985. s-m. $1250. Dar Naaman lil-Thaqafah, P.O. Box 567, Jounieh, Lebanon. TEL 09-935096. Ed. Naji Naaman. index.
  Description: Covers political and economic developments in the Arab world.

ARABIAN STUDIES. see *HISTORY — History Of The Near East*

329 IS
ARACHIM/VALUES; a magazine of problems of peace and socialism. (Text in Hebrew) vol.3, 1976. bi-m. $8. Communist Party of Israel, P.O. Box 26205, Tel Aviv, Israel. Ed. Wolf Ehrlich.

320.531 GW
ARBEITERSTIMME; Zeitschrift fuer marxistische Theorie und Praxis. 1971. q. DM.20($15) Gruppe Arbeiterstimme, Postfach 910307, 8500 Nuremberg 91, Germany. Ed. Thomas Gradl. adv.; bk.rev.; circ. 3,000. (also avail. in microfilm from KTO; back issues avail.)

320 GW ISSN 0173-5403
ARBEITSHEFTE ZUR SOZIALISTISCHEN THEORIE UND PRAXIS. 1977. 5/yr. DM.20. (JUSO - Hochschulgruppen) Schueren Presseverlag GmbH, Deutschhausstr. 31, 3550 Marburg, Germany. TEL 06421-63084. circ. 1,200. (back issues avail.)

320.9 330 GW ISSN 0003-8865
ARCHIV DER GEGENWART; die weltweite Dokumentation fuer Politik und Wirtschaft. 1931. fortn. DM.460. Siegler & Co. Verlag fuer Zeitarchive GmbH, Einsteinstr. 10, 5205 St. Augustin 3, Germany. Ed.Bd. abstr.; charts; stat.; index; circ. 1,700. (also avail. in microfilm from NRP)
  Description: Detailed information on current world politics and economics; record of world events based on a variety of international sources.

320 FR
ARCHIVES PARLEMENTAIRES DE 1787 A 1860. (Text in French) irreg. Editions du C N R S, 1 Place Aristide Briand, 92195 Meudon Cedex, France. TEL 1-45-34-75-50. FAX 1-46-26-28-49. TELEX LABOBEL 204 135 F. (Subscr. to: Presses du C N R S, 20-22, rue Saint Amand, 75015 Paris, France. TEL 1-45-33-16-00) adv.; bk.rev.; index; circ. 1,500 (controlled). (also avail. in microform from BHP)

320 IT ISSN 0390-0916
DG576
ARCHIVIO TRIMESTRALE; rassegna storica di studi sul movimento republicano. 1975. q. L.25000. Istituto di Studi per la Storia del Movimento Repubblicano, Via Tomacelli 146, 00186 Rome, Italy. Ed. Graziantonio Panunzio. adv.; bk.rev.; circ. 7,500.

320 MP
ARDYN TOR/PEOPLE'S STATE. 1950. bi-m. People's Great Hural, Ulan Bator, Mongolia.

320.531 AT ISSN 0004-0932
ARENA; a Marxist journal of criticism and discussion. 1963. q. Aus.$28 to individuals; institutions Aus.$45. Arena Publications Association, P.O. Box 18, N. Carlton, Vic. 3054, Australia. TEL 03-489-9244. Ed.Bd. adv.; bk.rev.; circ. 3,000. (tabloid format) **Indexed:** Alt.Press Ind., Aus.Educ.Ind., Aus.P.A.I.S., Polit.Sci.Abstr.
  Description: Includes analyses in such areas as media and popular culture, intellectuals and society, technological change, nuclear politics, feminist theory, world economic crisis, and regional politics.

320 327 CI ISSN 0402-9283
ARENA; informativni drustveno politicki ilustrirani tjednik. 1959. w. $122. Vjesnik, Avenija Bratstva i Jedinstva 4, 41000 Zagreb, Croatia. TEL 666-666. FAX 041-3411-777. TELEX 21121 VSK ZG. Ed. Stevo Maodus. **Indexed:** E.I.

P
Q

POLITICAL SCIENCE

320   IT
ARENGO; mensile di formazione politica. 1974. m. L.10000. Centro Studi Mondialisti Arengo, Via XXIV Maggio 81-D, 87100 Cosenza, Italy. TEL (0984)76563. Dir. Pietro De Franco. adv.
Description: Looks at political issues throughout Italy as well as other countries.

ARGENTINE LETTER. see *BUSINESS AND ECONOMICS — Economic Situation And Conditions*

320.531   IT
ARGOMENTI RADICALI. 1977. bi-m. L.15000. Edizioni il Formichiere s.r.l., Via del Lauro 3, 20121 Milan, Italy. Ed. Massimo Teodori. circ. 7,000.

323.4   SW   ISSN 0004-1149
ARGUMENT FOR FRIHET OCH RAETT. 1965. q. SEK 4. Box 414, S-126 04 Haegersten 4, Sweden. Ed. Svante Hjertstrand. bk.rev.; circ. 40,000.

ARIZONA CAPITOL TIMES. see *PUBLIC ADMINISTRATION*

ARKANSAS REPORT. see *PUBLIC ADMINISTRATION*

ARMED FORCES AND SOCIETY; an interdisciplinary journal on military institutions, civil-military relations, arms control and peacekeeping, and conflict management. see *MILITARY*

320   UK   ISSN 0144-0381
JX1974
ARMS CONTROL; the journal of arms control and disarmament. 1980. 3/yr. £28($45) to individuals; £78($125) to institutions. Frank Cass & Co. Ltd., Gainsborough House, 11 Gainsborough Rd., London E11 1RS, England. TEL 081-530-4226. FAX 081-530-7795. Eds. Stuart Croft, Terry Terriff. adv.; bk.rev.; index. (also avail. in microfilm from UMI; back issues avail.) **Indexed:** A.B.C.Pol.Sci., Abstr.Mil.Bibl., P.A.I.S.
—BLDSC shelfmark: 1683.093000.
Description: Covers academic articles on arms control and disarmament and the wider area of security agreements and security.

320   US   ISSN 0196-125X
JX1974
ARMS CONTROL TODAY. 1972. m. $40 to individuals; institutions $50. Arms Control Association, 11 Dupont Circle, N.W., Washington, DC 20036. TEL 202-797-4626. FAX 202-797-4611. Ed. Matthew Bunn. adv.; bk.rev.; circ. 4,000. (also avail. in microform from UMI) **Indexed:** Abstr.Mil.Bibl., D M & T, P.A.I.S., PROMT.
—BLDSC shelfmark: 1683.097100.
Description: Covers nuclear and conventional arms control issues with timely editorials, interviews, and feature articles by experts in the field.

ASIA & PACIFIC REVIEW. see *BUSINESS AND ECONOMICS — Economic Situation And Conditions*

320 950   CH
ASIAN BULLETIN. vol.5, 1980. m. NT.$250($7) (Asian Pacific Anti-Communist League - Republic of China) A P A C L Publications, 100 Hengyang Rd., 8th Fl., Taipei, Taiwan, Republic of China. Ed. Martin L. Lasater.

ASIAN JOURNAL OF PUBLIC ADMINISTRATION. see *PUBLIC ADMINISTRATION*

950 323.2   CH   ISSN 0004-4628
DS1
ASIAN OUTLOOK. 1954. m. $15. Asian Pacific Anti-Communist League - Republic of China, P.O. Box 22992, Taipei, Taiwan, Republic of China. TEL 02-341-7027. FAX 02-397-2461. TELEX 26364. Ed. Dixon Hsu. adv.; bk.rev.; illus.; circ. 20,000. **Indexed:** HR Rep., P.A.I.S., Rehabil.Lit.
Formerly: *Free China and Asia.*

320   CH   ISSN 0571-2920
ASIAN PACIFIC ANTI-COMMUNIST LEAGUE, CHINA. PAMPHLET. (Text in English) 1955. m. Asian Pacific Anti-Communist League - Republic of China, No. 1, Tsingtao E. Rd., Sec. 1, Taipei, Taiwan, Republic of China. TEL 02-3417027. FAX 02-3972461. TELEX 26364. Ed.Bd. bibl.; circ. 20,000.

320 327   KO
ASIAN PERSPECTIVE; biannual journal of regional & international affairs. 1977. s-a. 10000 Won($16) Kyungnam University, Institute for Far Eastern Studies, 28-42 Samchung-dong, Chongro-gu, Seoul 110-230, S. Korea. FAX 02-735-4359. TELEX K26834-KIFES. Ed. Jae Kyu Park. adv.; bk.rev.; cum.index; circ. 1,500. (back issues avail.; reprint service avail.) **Indexed:** E.I.

950   US   ISSN 0004-4687
DS1
ASIAN SURVEY. 1961. m. $41 to individuals; institutions $85; students $24. University of California Press, Journals Division, 2120 Berkeley Way, Berkeley, CA 94720. TEL 510-642-4191. FAX 510-643-7127. Eds. Robert A. Scalapino, Leo E. Rose. adv.; bibl.; circ. 3,100. (also avail. in microfilm from UMI; reprint service avail. from KTO) **Indexed:** A.B.C.Pol.Sci., Abstr.Anthropol., Acad.Ind., Amer.Bibl.Slavic & E.Eur.Stud., Amer.Hist.& Life, Curr.Cont., E.I., Geo.Abstr., Hist.Abstr., Int.Lab.Doc., Key to Econ.Sci., Mid.East: Abstr.& Ind., P.A.I.S., Rural Recreat.Tour.Abstr., Sage Pub.Admin.Abstr., Sage Urb.Stud.Abstr., Soc.Sci.Ind., SSCI, World Agri.Econ.& Rural Sociol.Abstr.
—BLDSC shelfmark: 1742.750000.
Description: Provides detailed commentary on political, economic and social developments in Asia. *Refereed Serial*

320.52   FR
ASPECTS DE LA FRANCE. 1947. w. 780 F. S N I E P, 10 rue Croix des Petits Champs, 75001 Paris, France. TEL 1-40-39-92-06. Ed. Pierre Pujo. adv.; bk.rev. (tabloid format)
Incorporates: *Cahiers D'Action Francaise* (ISSN 0223-5773); **Formerly:** *Action Francaise Etudiante*; **Supersedes:** *A.F. Universite* (ISSN 0001-1231)

956   LE   ISSN 0004-5012
ASSAYAD. (Text in Arabic) 1943. w. $150. Dar Assayad S.A.L., P.O. Box 1038, Beirut, Lebanon. FAX 4529957. (UK addr.: c/o Contact Public Relations, 3 Park Pl., 12 Lawn Ln., London SW8, ENgland. TEL 071-582-2220) Ed. Issam Freiha. adv.; circ. 89,775. (tabloid format)

ASSOCIATION SENEGALAISE POUR L'ETUDE DU QUATERNAIRE AFRICAIN. BULLETIN DE LIAISON. see *HISTORY — History Of Africa*

322   IT   ISSN 0004-5985
ASSOCIAZIONE NAZIONALE EX INTERNATI. BOLLETTINO UFFICIALE. 1949. bi-m. membership. Associazione Nazionale Ex Internati, Via 20 Settembre 27-B, Rome 00187, Italy. Ed. Dr. Carlo De Luca. adv.; illus.; circ. 50,000.

320   FR
ASTROLABE; *revue de philosophie politique.* bi-m. 50 F. S E P I C, 185 rue de Solignac, 87000 Limoges, France. Ed. Philippe Liard.

320   US
AT THE POLLS SERIES. 1977. irreg. price varies. (American Enterprise Institute for Public Policy Research) Duke University Press, 6697 College Station, Durham, NC 27708. TEL 919-684-2173. FAX 919-684-8644. Ed. Howard R. Penniman.

HEATID. see *BUSINESS AND ECONOMICS — Economic Situation And Conditions*

322.4   FR   ISSN 0339-9958
AUJOURD'HUI L'AFRIQUE. 1975. q. 130 F. Association Francaise d'Amitie et de Solidarite avec les Peuples d'Afrique, 21 rue Marceau, 93100 Montreuil, France. TEL 1-48.58.72.90. Ed. Dominique Lecoq. adv.; bk.rev.
Continues: *Association Francaise d'Amitie et de Solidarite avec les Peuples d'Afrique. Bulletin d'Information* (ISSN 0335-0290)

320 350   US
AUSTIN REPORT. 1947. w. $22. Report Publications, Inc., Box 12368, Austin, TX 78711. TEL 512-478-5663. Ed. Bill Kidd. circ. 1,500.
Description: Covers Texas legislative and political activity.

329.07   AT
AUSTRALASIAN SPARTACIST. 1972. bi-m. Aus.$5 (foreign Aus.$7). Spartacist A N Z Publishing Co., G.P.O. Box 3473, Sydney, N.S.W. 2001, Australia. TEL 02-281-2181. FAX 02-281-2185.
Formerly: *Revolutionary Communist Bulletin.*

320   II
AUSTRALIA & PACIFIC ISLANDS LETTER. (Text in English) 1981. m. Rs.488($96) K.K. Roy (Private) Ltd., 55 Gariahat Rd., P.O. Box 10210, Calcutta 700 019, India. Ed. Dr. K.K. Roy.

AUSTRALIAN JOURNAL OF CHINESE AFFAIRS. see *ORIENTAL STUDIES*

320   AT   ISSN 1036-1146
JQ3995.A1
AUSTRALIAN JOURNAL OF POLITICAL SCIENCE. 1966. 3/yr. Aus.$40 to individuals (foreign Aus.$45); institutions Aus.$50 (foreign Aus.$55). Australasian Political Studies Association (Canberra), c/o University College, University of New South Wales, Australian Defence Force Academy, Canberra, A.C.T. 2600, Australia. TEL 06-268-8845. FAX 062-268-8852. Ed. Ian McAllister. adv.; bk.rev.; bibl.; charts; stat.; circ. 800. (also avail. in microfilm from UMI; reprint service avail. from UMI) **Indexed:** A.B.C.Pol.Sci., Aus.P.A.I.S., Curr.Cont., Hist.Abstr., So.Pac.Per.Ind., SSCI.
Formerly: *Politics* (ISSN 0032-3268)

320 900   AT   ISSN 0004-9522
DU80
AUSTRALIAN JOURNAL OF POLITICS AND HISTORY. 1955. 3/yr. Aus.$54($48) University of Queensland Press, P.O. Box 42, St. Lucia, Qld. 4067, Australia. TEL 07-377-2127. FAX 07-371-5896. TELEX UNIVQLD AA40315 PRESS. Ed. John Moses. adv.; bk.rev.; charts; tr.lit.; index; circ. 1,250. (also avail. in microfilm from UMI; reprint services avail. from KTO,SCH) **Indexed:** A.B.C.Pol.Sci., Amer.Hist.& Life, Arts & Hum.Cit.Ind., Aus.P.A.I.S., Br.Hum.Ind., Curr.Cont., E.I., Gdlns., Hist.Abstr., Mid.East: Abstr.& Ind., P.A.I.S., So.Pac.Per.Ind., SSCI.
—BLDSC shelfmark: 1811.150000.

320.531   AT   ISSN 0004-9638
HX9
AUSTRALIAN LEFT REVIEW; a left journal of analysis debate and information. 1966. 11/yr. Aus.$35 to individuals; libraries, institutions Aus.$45. (Australian Left Review Editorial Collective) Red Pen Publications Pte. Ltd., P.O. Box A247, S. Sydney, N.S.W. 2000, Australia. TEL 02-565-1855. Ed.Bd. adv.; bk.rev.; illus.; circ. 1,600. **Indexed:** Aus.P.A.I.S.

320.531   AT   ISSN 0310-8252
AUSTRALIAN MARXIST REVIEW. 1972. q. Aus.$12. Socialist Party of Australia, 65 Campbell St., Surry Hills, N.S.W. 2010, Australia. FAX 02-281-5795. Ed. P.D. Symon. bibl.; circ. 2,500.

320   AT
AUSTRALIAN NATIONAL UNIVERSITY, CANBERRA. RESEARCH SCHOOL OF SOCIAL SCIENCES. DEPARTMENT OF POLITICAL SCIENCE. OCCASIONAL PAPERS. 1965. irreg., no.19, 1986. price varies. Australian National University, Research School of Social Sciences, Department of Political Science, P.O. Box 4, Canberra, A.C.T. 2600, Australia. FAX 062-571893. TELEX AA 2694 SOPAC. (Dist. in U.S. by: International Scholarly Book Services, Box 4347, Portland, OR 97208) circ. 625.
Formerly: *Australian National University, Canberra. Department of Political Science. Occasional Paper.* (ISSN 0067-2033)

320   AT   ISSN 0005-0091
DU80
AUSTRALIAN QUARTERLY. 1929. q. Aus.$43. Australian Institute of Political Science, 72 Bathurst St., Sydney, N.S.W. 2000, Australia. TEL 02-264-8923. FAX 02-267-7900. Eds. Ross Barnaut, Nancy Viviani. adv.; bk.rev.; index, cum.index: 1954-1963, 1964-1968, 1969-1978; circ. 1,500. (reprint service avail. from KTO) **Indexed:** A.B.C.Pol.Sci., AESIS, Amer.Hist.& Life, ASSIA, Aus.P.A.I.S., Curr.Cont., Gdlns., Geo.Abstr., Hist.Abstr., Mid.East: Abstr.& Ind., Res.High.Educ.Abstr., SSCI.
—BLDSC shelfmark: 1818.450000.

AUTONOMIE LOCALI E SERVIZI SOCIALI; vademecum a schede. see *SOCIAL SERVICES AND WELFARE*

329.9   NQ
AVANCE. 1972. w. Partido Comunista de Nicaragua, Cuidad Jardin 0-30, Apdo. 4231, Managua JR, Nicaragua. TEL 2-43750. circ. 20,000.

POLITICAL SCIENCE 3875

329.9   PO
AVANTE. w. Communist Party, Rua Soeiro Pereira Gomes, 1699 Lisbon, Portugal. TEL 01-769725. Dir. A. Dias Lourenco da Silva.

320.9   II   ISSN 0005-2515
AZAD MAZDUR; Hindi weekly. (Text in Hindi) 1953. w. Rs.10. G.P. Koushal, Ed. & Pub., Tripti Bhavan, Station Rd., Jusalai, Jamshedpur 831006, India. adv.; bk.rev.; film rev.; play rev.; bibl.; circ. 5,000.

327 950 960   RU   ISSN 0005-2574
AZIYA I AFRIKA SEGODNYA. 1947. m. $12. (Akademiya Nauk S.S.S.R., Institut Narodov Azii) Izdatel'sto Nauka, Profsoyuznaya 90, 117864 GSP-7 Moscow, V-485, Russia. (Subscr. to: Mezhdunarodnaya Kniga, Moscow, G-200, Russia) (Co-sponsor: Institut Afriki) Ed. G.F. Kim. index. **Indexed:** Amer.Hist.& Life, Curr.Cont.Africa, E.I., Hist.Abstr.

320   LE
AZTAG SHAPATORIAG-TROSHAG. 1969. w. $24. Ste. Aztag S.A.R.L., Salim Bustany St., Beirut, Lebanon. (Dist. in U.S. by: Haig Gakavian, 9417 Curren Rd., Silver Spring, MD 20901) Ed. Sarkis Zeitlian.

320 614.7 811   US   ISSN 1043-3732
BAD HAIRCUT. 1987. irreg. (1-2/yr.) $14 (foreign $16). Ray Goforth, Ed. & Pub., 1055 Adams St., S.E., Ste. 4, Olympia, WA 98501-1443. Ed. Kim Goforth. adv.; play rev.; charts; illus.; circ. 1,000. (back issues avail.)
     Formerly: Bad Haircut Quarterly (ISSN 0893-567X)
     Description: Covers progressive political causes, such as environmental, feminist, peace, anti-nuclear, and human rights issues.

947   GW   ISSN 0005-4526
BALTISCHE BRIEFE. 1948. m. DM.69.15. Verlag Baltische Briefe Wolf J. von Kleist GmbH, Deefkamp 13, 2070 Grosshansdorf, Germany. TEL 04102-61112. FAX 04102-65388. adv.; bk.rev.; bibl.; illus.; circ. 5,900. (tabloid format)

BANGLADESH NEWS. see *ETHNIC INTERESTS*

320   BG
BANGLADESH POLITICAL STUDIES. (Text in English and Bengali) 1978. a. Tk.50($10) (£5). University of Chittagong, Department of Political Science, Chittagong, Bangladesh. TEL 414393. Ed. Muhammad A. Hakim. adv.; bk.rev.; circ. 1,000.

BARBINELLA. see *GENERAL INTEREST PERIODICALS — Italy*

322.4   NQ   ISSN 0254-802X
BARRICADA INTERNACIONAL. English edition (ISSN 1013-9567) (German edition avail.) 1981. m. $35 for English ed.; Spanish ed. $40. (Sandinista National Liberation Front) Editorial El Amanecer, Apdo. 4461, Managua, Nicaragua. TEL 75366. FAX 673941. TELEX 2017 BARR. (For English ed. subscr. to: Box 410150, San Francisco, CA 94141-0150. TEL 415-621-8981) Ed. Carlos Fernando Chamorro. adv.; bk.rev.; circ. 15,000. (also avail. in microform from UMI)
     Description: Provides news and analysis of current events in Nicaragua: the advances of the revolutionary process, political events in the Central American region, as well as information such as social services, health care, cultural activities and more.

329.9   AA
BASHKIMI. 1943. d. Fronti Demokratik i Shqiperise - Democratic Front of Albania, Bulevardi Stalin, Tirana, Albania. TEL 42-28110. Ed. Hamit Borici. circ. 30,000. (newspaper; also avail. in microfilm from NRP)

320.9   IT   ISSN 0005-6111
BASILICATA; rassegna di politica e cronache meridionali. 1954. m. L.20000. Basilicata Editrice, Via Ridola 20, Casella Postale 70, Matera 75100, Italy. Ed. Leonardo Sacco. adv.; bk.rev.; film rev.; play rev.; abstr.; bibl.; charts; illus.; stat.; circ. 10,000.(controlled).

956.940 296   US
BATNUA. 1970. bi-m. $5. Habonim Dror Labor Zionist Youth, 27 W. 20th St., 9th Fl., New York, NY 10011. TEL 212-255-1796. Ed. Charles Boxbaum. circ. 2,500. (also avail. in microfilm from AJP)
     Formerly: Bagolah (ISSN 0005-3929)
     Description: Forum for discussing relevant Zionist issues and internal Habonim Dror Labor Camp Zionist Youth issues and events.

332.4   PN
BAYANO. fortn. Partido del Pueblo de Panama, Avdas. Mexico y Justo Arosemena, Panama City, Panama. Dir. Efrain Reyes Medina.

320   GW
BAYERISCHER MONATSSPIEGEL. 1964. bi-m. DM.25. Bayerischer Monatsspiegel Verlag GmbH, Postfach 221123, 8000 Munich 22, Germany. TEL 089-167235. FAX 089-168700. Ed. Freda von Stackelberg. adv.; bk.rev.; bibl.; circ. 20,000.

320   CC
BEIJING ZHIBU SHENGHUO. (Text in Chinese) m. Zhonggong Beijing Shiwei, 53, Xibianmennei Dajie, Beijing 100053, People's Republic of China. TEL 3017333. Ed. Cheng Manzhen.

331   GW   ISSN 0005-8068
BEITRAEGE ZUR GESCHICHTE DER ARBEITERBEWEGUNG. 1959. bi-m. DM.44.20. Demokratie und Recht Zeitschriftenverlag GmbH, Postfach 203363, 2000 Hamburg 20, Germany. bk.rev.; bibl.; index. **Indexed:** Arts & Hum.Cit.Ind., Curr.Cont., Hist.Abstr.
     —BLDSC shelfmark: 1883.900000.
     Formerly: Beitraege zur Geschichte der Deutschen Arbeiterbewegung.
     Description: Includes documents, scientific information, biographies, local history of labor and business, news and information, and bibliographies.

320   GW   ISSN 0522-6643
BEITRAEGE ZUR GESCHICHTE DES PARLEMENTARISMUS UND DER POLITISCHEN PARTEIEN. 1952. irreg., vol.83, 1987. price varies. Droste-Verlag GmbH, Zuelpicher Strasse, Postfach 1135, 4000 Duesseldorf 1, Germany.

BEITRAEGE ZUR ZEITGESCHICHTE. see *HISTORY*

320   NE   ISSN 0165-1625
BELEID EN MAATSCHAPPIJ. 6/yr. fl.99 to individuals (foreign fl.130.50); institutions fl.168 (foreign fl.178)(effective 1992). Uitgeverij Boom, P.O. Box 1058, 7940 KB Meppel, Netherlands. TEL 05220-54306. FAX 05220-66198. circ. 1,000. **Indexed:** Key to Econ.Sci.
     —BLDSC shelfmark: 1887.882500.

320   BH
BELIZE TIMES. 1956. w. People's United Party, P.O. Box 506, 3 Queen St., Belize City, Belize. TEL 2-45757. Ed. Amalia Mai. circ. 5,000.

966.9   NR
BENDEL STATE GAZETTE. 1964. w. £N9.50($11) Ministry of Home Affairs and Information, Printing and Stationery Division, P.M.B. 1099, Benin City, Nigeria. charts; stat.; circ. 4,500.
     Formerly: Midwestern Nigeria Gazette (ISSN 0026-3494)

BENGAL: PAST AND PRESENT. see *HISTORY — History Of Asia*

320   US   ISSN 0067-5717
BENJAMIN F. FAIRLESS LECTURES. 1964. a. (Carnegie - Mellon University) Columbia University Press, 562 W. 113th St., New York, NY 10025. TEL 212-678-6777.

BERICHTE UND INFORMATIONEN. see *BUSINESS AND ECONOMICS*

320   HU   ISSN 0865-4093
BESZELO. 1989. w. $61 (effective 1992). Ab-Beszelo Kiado Kft., Deri Miksa u. 10, Budapest 8, Hungary. (Subscr. to: Kultura, P.O. Box 149, 1389 Budapest, Hungary) Ed. Koszeg Ferenc.

320   US
BETWEEN THE LINES (WASHINGTON). 1988. fortn. $39. Capitol Hill Publishing, Inc., 325 Pennsylvania Ave., S.E., Ste. 272, Washington, DC 20003. TEL 202-547-3622. FAX 202-543-8935. Ed. Joseph Farah. (looseleaf format)
     Description: Investigates media bias and the political activities of prominent Hollywood figures.

320   II
BHARATA VARSHA. (Text in English) 1974. q. Rs.12($4) Indian Institute for National Integration, Tulsipur, Cuttack 753008, Orissa, India. Ed. Ramahari Mishra. adv.; bk.rev.; circ. 10,000.
     Indexed: P.A.I.S.

300 011   IT   ISSN 0006-1654
BIBLIOTECA DELLA LIBERTA. 1964. q. L.55000 (foreign L.75000)(effective 1992). (Centro di Ricerca e Documentazione Luigi Einaudi) Franco Angeli Editore, Viale Monza, 106, 20127 Milan, Italy. TEL 02-2895762. FAX 11-7495796. Ed. G. Zincone. adv.; bk.rev.; film rev.; play rev.; bibl.; illus.; index; circ. 7,000. **Indexed:** Int.Polit.Sci.Abstr.

340   PE
BIBLIOTECA POPULAR. SERIE A: CAPACITACION. 1980. s-a. Centro de Estudios y Promocion del Desarrollo, Ave. Salaverry 1945, Lima 14, Peru.

320 943.8   PL   ISSN 0138-094X
BIBLIOTEKA POLONIJNA/POLONIA LIBRARY. 1960. irreg., vol.17, 1986. price varies. (Polska Akademia Nauk, Komitet Badania Polonii Zagranicznej) Ossolineum, Publishing House of the Polish Academy of Sciences, Rynek 9, Wroclaw, Poland. TELEX 0712771 OSS PL. Ed. Wiktor Szczerba.
     Formerly (until 1977): Problemy Polonii Zagranicznej (ISSN 0079-5798)

BILANS HEBDOMADAIRES. see *BUSINESS AND ECONOMICS*

BILL OF RIGHTS IN ACTION. see *LAW — Constitutional Law*

320 330.9   AG   ISSN 0326-1980
F2849.2
BIMESTRE; politico y economico. 1982. bi-m. Arg.$3000($25) Centro de Investigaciones Sociales sobre el Estado y la Administracion, Pueyrredon 510, 6 Piso, 1032 Buenos Aires, Argentina. FAX 54-1-961-8186. Ed.Bd. adv.; abstr.; charts; illus.; circ. 3,000. (also avail. in microfiche; back issues avail.)

320   GR
BIONEWS. 1987. q? membership. Biopolitics International Organisation, c/o Dr. Agni Vlavianos-Arvanitis, Ed., 10, Tim. Vassou, GR 115 21 Athens, Greece. FAX 643-4093.

320 323.4   GR   ISSN 1012-2532
BIOPOLITICS. 1988. a. $15. Biopolitics International Organisation, c/o Dr. Agni Vlavianos-Arvantis, Ed., 10, Tim. Vassou St., GR 115 21 Athens, Greece. TEL 6432419. circ. 1,000.
     Formerly: Biopolitics International Organization Report.
     Description: Essays from the International Conference on Biopolitics promoting international cooperation for the better understanding, protection and enhancement of life.

350 910.03   US   ISSN 0895-1780
BLACK CONGRESSIONAL MONITOR; a monthly report of legislative initiatives from the U.S. Congress. 1987. m. $16.95. Len Mor Publications, Box 75035, Washington, DC 20013. TEL 202-488-8879. Ed. Lenora Moragne.
     Description: Coverage of bills and resolutions introduced, sponsored hearings, congressional commentary, congressional intent language, minority set asides and other legislative initiatives by and for African Americans.

320   UK   ISSN 0045-2157
BLACK FLAG; anarchist monthly. 1970. m. £18 to individuals; institutions £30. Black Flag, BM-Hurricane, London WC1 3XX, England. Ed. L. Mitchell. bk.rev.; abstr.; bibl.; charts; illus.; pat.; stat.; tr.lit.; circ. 4,000. (back issues avail.)

POLITICAL SCIENCE

320　　　　　　US　　ISSN 0891-9631
▼BLACK POLITICAL STUDIES. 1992. irreg., no.3, 1992. Borgo Press, Box 2845, San Bernardino, CA 92406. TEL 714-884-5813. Ed. Hanes Walton, Jr.
Description: Monographs on Black politics and political figures, in North America and throughout the world.

320.57　　　　　　US
BLACK ROSE. 4/yr. $8 to individuals; institutions $16. Box 1075, Boston, MA 02103. bk.rev.; circ. 800. **Indexed:** Alt.Press. Ind.

BLACK SCHOLAR; journal of black studies and research. see *ETHNIC INTERESTS*

943 327　　　　　GW　　ISSN 0006-4416
D839
BLAETTER FUER DEUTSCHE UND INTERNATIONALE POLITIK. 1956. m. DM.97.80 to individuals; students DM.78.60. Blaetter Verlagsgesellschaft mbH, Bertha-von-Suttner-Platz 6, 5300 Bonn 1, Germany. TEL 0228-650133. FAX 0228-650251. Ed.Bd. adv.; bk.rev.; bibl.; stat.; index; circ. 18,000. **Indexed:** INIS Atomind., P.A.I.S.For.Lang.Ind.

322.4
BOLCHEVIQUE. (Text in Spanish) 1980. m. $20. October Publications, 3309 1-2 Mission St., San Francisco, CA 94110. TEL 415-695-0340. circ. 2,500.

320　　　　　　MX　　ISSN 0186-0461
BOLETIN DE POLITICA INFORMATICA. 1982. m. free or exchange basis. Instituto Nacional de Estadistica, Geografia e Informatica, Secretaria de Programacion y Presupuesto, Prol. Heroe de Nacozari 2301 Sur, Puerta 11, planta baja, Aguascalientes, 20290 Ags., Mexico. TEL 49-18-22-32. FAX 491-807-39. circ. 700.

320　　　　　　SP
BOLETIN INFORMATIVO DE CIENCIA POLITICA; publicacion de la 2a catedra de teoria del estado y derecho constitucional. 1969. q. 300 ptas.($65) Universidad Complutense de Madrid, Facultad de Ciencias Politicas y Sociologia, Seminario 18, Madrid, Spain. bk.rev.; abstr.; bibl.; cum.index.

320.532　　　　　IT　　ISSN 0392-3886
IL BOLSCEVICO. 1969. w. L.60000. Editoriale il Girasole, C.P. 477, 50100 Florence, Italy. TEL 055-2337668. Ed. Monica Martenghi.
Description: Covers the Italian Marxist-Leninist party.

320 972　　　　　US
BORDER ISSUES AND PUBLIC POLICY. RESEARCH PAPERS. 1982. irreg., no.26, 1987. $5 per no. University of Texas at El Paso, Center for Inter-American and Border Studies, Publications Program, El Paso, TX 79968-0002. FAX 915-747-5574.
Description: Examines economics, labor, politics and migration patterns.

320 972　　　　　US
BORDER PERSPECTIVES. RESEARCH PAPERS. 1983. irreg., latest no.11, 1990. $5 per no. University of Texas at El Paso, Center for Inter-American and Border Studies, Publications Program, El Paso, TX 79968-0002. FAX 915-747-5574.

320 800　　　　US　　ISSN 0278-9752
BORGO POLITICAL SCENARIOS. 1982. irreg., no.2, 1992. price varies. Borgo Press, Box 2845, San Bernardino, CA 92406. TEL 714-884-5813.
Description: Political speculations and "what if?" scenarios by writers and politicians of our time.

BORGO REFERENCE GUIDES. see *HISTORY*

320 914.706　　　　CN
BRATSTVO FRATERNITY. (Text in Serbian) 1954. m. $15. One Secroft Cres., N. York, Ont. M3N 1R5, Canada. TEL 416-769-7181. Ed. Wilaim Durovic. adv.; circ. 2,200.

329.82　　　　　US
BREAKTHROUGH (SAN FRANCISCO). 1977. 3/yr. $10 for 4 nos. to individuals (foreign $15). (Prairie Fire Organizing Committee) John Brown Education Fund, Box 14422, San Francisco, CA 94114. bk.rev.; illus.; circ. 3,500. (back issues avail.) **Indexed:** Alt.Press Ind.
Description: Provides original articles, interviews and selected reprints analyzing international and domestic issues of concern to the left and progressive movements.

320.531　　　　　SZ
BRECHE. 1969. bi-m. 55 F. Parti Socialiste Ouvrier, 11 rue de la Borde, CH-1018 Lausanne, Switzerland. FAX 021-362732. Ed. C.A. Udry. bk.rev.; bibl.; illus.; cum.index: nos.1-100; circ. 3,500. (tabloid format)

944　　　　　　FR　　ISSN 0006-9647
BRETAGNE REELLE; tribune libre-la voix du pays gallo. (Includes semi-annual supplement: An Nerzh) 1954. s-m. 650 F. J. Quatreboeufs, 22230 Merdrignac, Brittany, France. bk.rev.

320　　　　　　CN　　ISSN 0703-8968
BRIARPATCH. 1973. 10/yr. Can.$24.61 to individuals; institutions Can.$35.31. Briarpatch Society, 2138 McIntyre St., Regina, Sask. S4P 2R7, Canada. FAX 306-525-2949. Ed.Bd. adv.; bk.rev.; circ. 1,800. (also avail. in microform from MML) **Indexed:** Alt.Press Ind.
Description: Covers issues related to labor, the environment, peace, native people, and provincial and national politics, from a leftist perspective.

320 330.9　　　　TU
BRIEFING: WEEKLY INSIDE PERSPECTIVE ON TURKISH POLITICAL, ECONOMIC AND BUSINESS AFFAIRS. (Text in English) 1974. w. TL.500000($400) Ekonomik Basin Ajansi, Olgunlar Sokak 2-1, Bakanlikar, Ankara, Turkey. FAX 4-1257677. TELEX 43204 FTEB TR. Ed. Yavuz Tolun. adv.; bk.rev.; charts; stat.; circ. 1,000.

320　　　　　　UK　　ISSN 0007-1234
BRITISH JOURNAL OF POLITICAL SCIENCE. 1971. q. $75 to individuals; institutions $129. Cambridge University Press, Edinburgh Bldg., Shaftesbury Rd., Cambridge CB2 2RU, England. TEL 0223-312393. FAX 0223-315052. TELEX 851817256. (N. American addr.: Cambridge University Press, 40 W. 20th St., New York, NY 10011-4211, USA. TEL 212-924-3900) Eds. A. King, I. Crewe. adv.; charts; index; circ. 1,186. (also avail. in microform from UMI; reprint service avail. from SWZ) **Indexed:** A.B.C.Pol.Sci., Amer.Hist.& Life, ASCA, ASSIA, Curr.Cont., Hist.Abstr., Int.Polit.Sci.Abstr., Mid.East: Abstr.& Ind., P.A.I.S., Rural Recreat.Tour.Abstr., Sage Pub.Admin.Abstr., Soc.Sci.Ind., SSCI, Stud.Wom.Abstr., World Agri.Econ.& Rural Sociol.Abstr.
—BLDSC shelfmark: 2319.600000.

BUDGET AND THE REGION; a regional analysis of the President's budget request. see *PUBLIC ADMINISTRATION*

943　　　　　　GW　　ISSN 0007-3121
DER BUERGER IM STAAT. 1951. q. (Landeszentrale fuer Politische Bildung) W. Kohlhammer GmbH, Hessbruehlstr. 69, Postfach 800430, 7000 Stuttgart 80, Germany. TEL 0711-7863-1. Ed. H.G. Wehling. bk.rev.; abstr.; bibl.; stat.; index; circ. 36,000. **Indexed:** INIS Atomind.

BUERGERRECHTE & POLIZEI. see *CRIMINOLOGY AND LAW ENFORCEMENT*

322.4　　　　　　GW
BUKO KAMPAGNE STOPPT DEN RUESTUNGSEXPORT. RUNDBRIEF. 1984. irreg. Verein fuer Foerderung Entwicklungspaedagogischer Zusammenarbeit e.V., Buchstr. 14-15, 2800 Bremen 1, Germany. TEL 0421-326045. illus.

320.532　　　　　BU　　ISSN 0204-8213
BULGARO-SUVETSKA DRUZHBA. vol.26, 1970. m. 1.80 lv.($4) (Obshtonarodna Komitet za Bulgaro-Suvetska Druzhba) Foreign Trade Co. "Hemus", 7 Levsky St., 1000 Sofia, Bulgaria. circ. 65,000.

320 330 300　　　FR　　ISSN 0007-4071
Z7163
BULLETIN ANALYTIQUE DE DOCUMENTATION POLITIQUE, ECONOMIQUE ET SOCIALE CONTEMPORAINE. 1946. m. 390 F. to individuals (foreign 440 F.); institutions 755 F. (foreign 840 F.); students 275 F. (Fondation Nationale des Sciences Politiques) Presses de la Fondation Nationale des Sciences Politiques, 27 rue Saint Guillaume, 75341 Paris Cedex 07, France. TEL 1-45-49-50-50. FAX 1-45-48-04-41. TELEX 201 002 F. Ed. Nicole Richard. index; circ. 1,700. **Indexed:** P.A.I.S.For.Lang.Ind., Popul.Ind.

960　　　　　　FR　　ISSN 0045-3501
DT348
BULLETIN DE L'AFRIQUE NOIRE. (Includes special nos.) 1956. w. 5200 F. I C Publications, 10 rue Vineuse, 75116 Paris Cedex 16, France. TEL 1-45-27-30-82. FAX 1-45-20-81-74. Ed.Bd. adv.; charts; stat. **Indexed:** Curr.Cont.Africa, P.A.I.S.For.Lang.Ind., Rural Devel.Abstr., Rural Recreat.Tour.Abstr., World Agri.Econ. & Rural Sociol.Abstr.

320.531　　　　　US
BULLETIN IN DEFENSE OF MARXISM. m. $24. Fourth Internationalist Tendency, Box 1317, New York, NY 10009.
Description: Information and discussion of revolutionary theory and politics.

341.1　　　　　　UK　　ISSN 0007-5035
JX1901
BULLETIN OF PEACE PROPOSALS. 1970. q. £27($45) to individuals, institutions £67($111). (International Peace Research Association, NO) Sage Publications Ltd., 6 Bonhill St., London EC2A 4PU, England. TEL 071-374-0645. FAX 071-374-8741. Ed. Magne Barth. adv.: color page #170; trim 200 x 130; adv. contact: Bernie Folan. abstr.; bibl. (also avail. in microform from UMI) **Indexed:** Abstr.Mil.Bibl., Curr.Cont., Hist.Abstr., HR Rep., INIS Atomind., Int.Polit.Sci.Abstr., Mid.East: Abstr.& Ind., P.A.I.S., Peace Res.Abstr., Risk Abstr., Sociol.Abstr., SSCI.
—BLDSC shelfmark: 2882.480000.
Description: Discusses contemporary international and intergroup affairs, searching for solutions to conflict situations in the light of general peace research theory.

320　　　　　　FR
BULLETIN QUOTIDIEN. d. 27210 F. (effective Jan. 1992). Societe Generale de Presse et d'Editions, 13 av. de l'Opera, 75001 Paris, France. TEL 40-15-17-89. FAX 40-15-17-15. TELEX SOGPRESS230023.

DER BUND. see *ETHNIC INTERESTS*

320　　　　　　GW　　ISSN 0933-2731
BUNDESTAG REPORT. 1987. 10/yr. free. (Deutscher Bundestag) Osang Verlag GmbH Bonn, Am Roemerlager 2, 5300 Bonn 1, Germany. TEL 0228-678383. FAX 0228-679631. (Subscr. to: Deutscher Bundestag, Bundeshaus, 5300 Bonn 1, Germany) circ. 60,000. (back issues avail.)
Description: Information about German Parliament and its politics.

BUSQUEDA. see *BUSINESS AND ECONOMICS — Economic Situation And Conditions*

BYERS ELECTION LAW. see *LAW*

322.4　　　　　　UK　　ISSN 0142-7113
C A A T NEWSLETTER. 1974. bi-m. £10 to individuals; institutions £15. Campaign Against Arms Trade, 11 Goodwin St., London N4 3HQ, England. TEL 071-281-0297. FAX 071-281-0297. Eds. Janet Williamson, Ann Feltham. bk.rev.; circ. 3,500.
Description: Watchdog publication monitoring arms trade.

320　　　　　　NE
C D A ACTUEEL. 1980. w. fl.39. C D A, Dr. Kuyperstraat 5, 2514 BA The Hague, Netherlands. FAX 070-924461. TELEX 31050. Ed.Bd. adv.; illus.
Formerly: C D Actueel.

POLITICAL SCIENCE 3877

329   BE
C D - INFO. (Text in Dutch, English, French, German, Hungarian, Italian, Polish, Russian, Spanish) 1964. 4/yr. Christian Democrat International, 16 rue de la Victoire, Boite 1, B-1060 Brussels, Belgium. TEL 2-537-13-22. FAX 537-93-48. TELEX 61118 IDC.
    Former titles: Christian Democrat International. Information Bulletin; Christian Democratic World Union. Information Bulletin; (until 1972): International Christian Democratic Study and Documentation Center. Bulletin International (ISSN 0538-5520)

320   GW
C D U GERLINGEN INFORM. 1983. bi-m. (Christlich Demokratische Union) C D U Gerlingen, c/o Rainer Wieland, Ed., Vesoulerstr. 3, 7016 Gerlingen, Germany. circ. 250.

320   CU
C I A C. bi-m. free. W P C Information Center for the Americas and the Caribbean, Linea No. 556, Vedado, Havana, Cuba. TEL 809 32-0506.
    Description: Promotes materials on peace issues and against military build-up.

329.6   US
C I D. 1980. bi-m. donations. Cuba Independiente y Democratica, 10020 S.W. 37th Terr., Miami, FL 33165. TEL 305-551-7357. Ed. Mario Villar Roces. circ. 30,000. (tabloid format; back issues avail.)
    Description: For members and exiled Cubans in general.

321   SZ
C I R A BULLETIN. (Text in English, French, German, Italian, Spanish) 1957. s-a. 20 Fr. Centre International de Recherches sur l'Anarchisme, Av. de Beaumont 24, CH-1012 Lausanne, Switzerland. bk.rev.; bibl.; circ. 1,000.

C O G E L GUARDIAN. (Council on Governmental Ethics Laws) see *LAW*

320   US   ISSN 0194-0856
C P P A X NEWSLETTER. 1962. 5/yr. $5. Citizens for Participation in Political Action, 25 West St., 4th Fl., Boston, MA 02111. TEL 617-426-3040. Ed. Sarah Browning. circ. 5,000.
    Description: Covers reform oriented topics in Massachusetts such as world peace, social justice, economic democracy, and open government.

320   US
C Q ALMANAC. a. $205. Congressional Quarterly Inc., 1414 22nd St., N.W., Washington, DC 20037. TEL 800-543-7793. FAX 202-728-1863.
    Description: Key bills and amendments explained; laws passed; roll-call votes cast by every member.

320.9   US   ISSN 1056-2036
H35
C Q RESEARCHER. 1923. 4/m. $296. Congressional Quarterly Inc., 1414 22nd St., N.W., Washington, DC 20037. TEL 800-432-2250. FAX 202-728-1863. Ed. Sandra Stencil. bk.rev.; charts; index. (also avail. in microform from UMI,MIM; reprint service avail. from UMI) **Indexed:** Acad.Ind., Adol.Ment.Hlth.Abstr., INIS Atomind., Mid.East: Abstr.& Ind., Noise Pollut.Publ.Abstr., P.A.I.S., Vert.File Ind.
    —BLDSC shelfmark: 3486.410000.
    Former titles (until 1991): Congressional Quarterly's Editorial Research Reports (ISSN 1057-0926); (until 1987): Editorial Research Reports (ISSN 0013-0958)

320   US
C Q RESEARCHER BOUND VOLUME. a. $132. Congressional Quarterly Inc., 1414 22nd St., N.W., Washington, DC 20037. TEL 800-432-2250. FAX 202-728-1863. (reprint service avail.)
    Formerly: E R R Bound Volume.
    Description: Editorial research reports. Includes indexes.

320   US
C S F NOTEBOOK. 1971. q. membership. Temple University, Center for the Study of Federalism, 1616 Walnut St., Rm. 5, Philadelphia, PA 19103. TEL 215-787-1480. FAX 215-787-7784. Ed. Daniel J. Elazar. adv.; bk.rev.; circ. 1,000. (back issues avail.)
    Formerly: C F S Notebook.

C S P: CRITICAL SOCIAL POLICY; a journal of socialist theory and practice in social welfare. see *SOCIAL SERVICES AND WELFARE*

CADERNOS DO C.E.A.S.. see *SOCIOLOGY*

CAHIERS D'ETUDE ET DE RECHERCHE. see *BUSINESS AND ECONOMICS — Economic Systems And Theories, Economic History*

320.532   FR
CAHIERS D'HISTOIRE (PARIS). 1966. 4/yr. 250 F. (foreign 500 F.). Institut des Recherches Marxistes, 64 bd. Auguste Blanqui, 75013 Paris, France. Ed. Roger Bourderon. adv.; bk.rev.; circ. 3,000. **Indexed:** Hist.Abstr.
    Former titles: Institut de Recherches Marxistes. Cahiers d'Histoire (ISSN 0246-9731); Institut Maurice Thorez. Cahiers d'Histoire (ISSN 0020-2363)

CAHIERS DE L'EST. see *LITERATURE*

320.5   FR   ISSN 0007-9839
CAHIERS DE LA RECONCILIATION. 1923. q. 150 F. Mouvement International de la Reconciliation, 114 bis, rue de Vaugirard, 75006 Paris, France. TEL 1-45-44-39-42. Ed. Christian Renoux. bk.rev.; circ. 1,800. **Indexed:** CERDIC.
    —BLDSC shelfmark: 2952.140000.

320.532   FR   ISSN 0008-0136
HX5
CAHIERS DU COMMUNISME. 1924. m. (11/yr.). 300 F. (foreign 370 F.). Parti Communiste Francais, Comite Central, 2, Place du Colonel Fabien, 75019 Paris, France. TEL 40-40-13-04. Ed. A. Bocquet. bk.rev.; illus.; index. (reprint service avail. from KTO) **Indexed:** P.A.I.S.For.Lang.Ind.

CAHIERS DU MONDE RUSSE ET SOVIETIQUE. see *HISTORY — History Of Europe*

320.531   BE   ISSN 0591-0633
CAHIERS MARXISTES. 1969? m. 700 Fr. Fondation Joseph Jacquemotte, 20 Ave. de Stalingrad, 1000 Brussels, Belgium. Ed. Rosine Lewin. adv.; bk.rev.; circ. 2,000.

320   FR   ISSN 0068-5194
CAHIERS NEPALAIS. 1969. irreg. price varies. (Centre National de la Recherche Scientifique) Editions du C N R S, 1 Place Aristide Briand, 92195 Meudon Cedex, France. TEL 1-45-34-75-50. FAX 1-46-26-28-49. TELEX LABOBEL 204 135 F. (Subscr. to: Presses du C N R S, 20-22, rue Saint Amand, 75015 Paris, France. TEL 1-45-33-16-00) adv.; bk.rev.; index; circ. 1,500 (controlled).

320 300   ZR
CAHIERS ZAIROIS D'ETUDES POLITIQUES ET SOCIALES. 1973. q. Universite de Lumbashi, Faculte des Sciences Socials, Politiques et Administratives, B.P. 1825, Lumbashi, Zaire. bibl. **Indexed:** Amer.Hist.& Life, Hist.Abstr.

320 350   II
CALCUTTA JOURNAL OF POLITICAL STUDIES. (Text in English) 1980. s-a. Rps.18($3) University of Calcutta, Department of Political Science, Asutosh Bldg., Calcutta 700073, India. Ed. A. Mukherjee. adv.; bk.rev.; circ. 1,000. (back issues avail.)

327   II   ISSN 0045-3862
CALCUTTAN. (Text in English) 1960. s-a. Rs.12($8.) Indo-American Society, 2B, Mona Lisa, 17 Camac St., Calcutta 700017, India. Ed. P.N. Mookerji. adv.; illus.; circ. 550.
    Description: Cultural, scientific and economic developments in India and the U.S.A.

320.531   UK   ISSN 0262-723X
CALDER VOICE; Calderdale's socialist journal. 1977. m. £1.80. Independent Labour Publications, c/o A. Graham, 4 Upper Gaukroger, Sowerby New Rd., Sowerby Bridge, W. Yorkshire, England. illus.

320   US   ISSN 0084-8271
JK8701
CALIFORNIA GOVERNMENT & POLITICS ANNUAL. 1970. a. $7.95. California Journal Press (Subsidiary of: Information for Public Affairs, Inc.), 1714 Capitol Ave., Sacramento, CA 95814. TEL 916-444-2840. Ed. Thomas R. Hoeber, Charles Price. circ. 6,000. (also avail. in microfilm)
    Description: Reprints from California Journal. Analysis of state government and politics organized for student use.

353   US   ISSN 0008-1205
JK8701
CALIFORNIA JOURNAL; the monthly analysis of state government and politics. 1970. m. $32 to individuals; educational and governmental institutions and libraries $49 (includes index); corporations and associations $95. Information for Public Affairs, Inc., 1714 Capitol Ave., Sacramento, CA 95814. TEL 916-444-2840. Ed. Richard Zeiger. adv.; charts; stat.; index; circ. 18,000. (also avail. in microfilm) **Indexed:** Cal.Per.Ind. (1984-), P.A.I.S., Sage Pub.Admin.Abstr., Sage Urb.Stud.Abstr.
    Description: Information on events and trends in the state of California.

320 350   US
CALIFORNIA JOURNAL NEWSFILE. 1984. m. $55. Information for Public Affairs, Inc., 1714 Capitol Ave., Sacramento, CA 95814. TEL 916-444-2840. Ed. Cindy McKeeman. bk.rev.; circ. 750.
    Description: Insider information on people and organizations in California politics and government.

320 350   US   ISSN 0195-6175
CALIFORNIA POLITICAL WEEK; calpeek. 1979. w. $97. California Political Week, Inc., Box 1468, Beverly Hills, CA 90213. TEL 310-659-0205. FAX 310-657-4340. Ed. Dick Rosengarten. adv.; circ. 3,000.
    Description: California and western U.S. state and local government and political developments and trends.

322.4   US
CALIFORNIA STATESMAN. 1962. m. $15 (included in subscr. to American Independent). William K. Shearer, Ed. & Pub., 8158 Palm St., Lemon Grove, CA 91945. TEL 619-460-4480.
    Description: Contains commentary on California state and national issues.

322.4   US
CALIFORNIA STATESMAN'S FOREIGN POLICY REVIEW. 1972. m. $15 (included in subscr. to American Independent). William K. Shearer, Ed. & Pub., 8158 Palm St., Lemon Grove, CA 91945. TEL 619-460-4480.
    Description: Commentary about foreign policy issues.

322.4   US
CALIFORNIA STATESMAN'S LEGISLATIVE SURVEY. 1965. m. $15 (included in subscr. to American Independent). William K. Shearer, Ed. & Pub., 8158 Palm St., Lemon Grove, CA 91945. TEL 619-460-4480.
    Description: Newsletter covering the national and Californian political scene.

320.531   II   ISSN 0008-1728
CALL. (Text in English) vol.22, 1970-1971. m. Rs.6. Revolutionary Socialist Party, 780 Ballimaran, Delhi 6, India. Ed. Tridib Chaudhuri.

320   UK   ISSN 0575-6871
CAMBRIDGE STUDIES IN THE HISTORY AND THEORY OF POLITICS. 1967. irreg. price varies. Cambridge University Press, Edinburgh Bldg., Shaftesbury Rd., Cambridge CB2 2RU, England. TEL 0223-312393. FAX 0223-315052. TELEX 851817256. Ed.Bd.

320   US
CAMPAIGN GUIDE FOR CONGRESSIONAL CANDIDATE AND COMMITTEES. irreg. Federal Election Commission, Washington, DC 20463. TEL 202-376-3120.
    Description: Helps House and Senate candidate committees to comply with the federal campaign laws.

POLITICAL SCIENCE

320 US
CAMPAIGN GUIDE FOR CORPORATIONS AND LABOR ORGANIZATIONS. irreg. Federal Election Commission, Washington, DC 20463. TEL 202-376-3120.
Description: Helps segregated funds, political action committees, labor organizations and corporations comply with federal campaign law.

320 US
CAMPAIGN GUIDE FOR NONCONNECTED COMMITTEES. irreg. Federal Election Commission, Washington, DC 20463. TEL 202-376-3120.
Description: Helps independent political committees to comply with federal election campaign law.

320 US
CAMPAIGN GUIDE FOR POLITICAL PARTY COMMITTEES. irreg. Federal Election Commission, Washington, DC 20463. TEL 202-376-3120.
Formerly: Campaign Guide for Party Committees.
Description: Helps political parties to comply with federal election campaign law.

320 US
CAMPAIGN MAGAZINE. 1988. m. $48. Campaign Industry News, 205 Pennsylvania Ave. S.E., Washington, DC 20003. TEL 202-543-6408. adv.; circ. 10,435.
Description: For managers of political candidates and issue campaigns.

322.4 US
CAMPAIGN REPORT - JOBS WITH PEACE CAMPAIGN. 4/yr. $15. 76 Summer St., Boston, MA 02110. TEL 617-338-5783.
Description: Objective is peace conversion from weapons and military-based jobs to employment producing goods for civilian use.

320.52 UK
CAMPAIGNER. 1989. s-a. British Conservative Party, 32 Smith Sq., London SW1P 3HH, England. TEL 71-222-9000. Ed. Paul S. Gray. adv.; circ. 30,000.
Description: Examines current affairs issues of international importance.

320 US ISSN 0197-0771
JK1976
CAMPAIGNS AND ELECTIONS. 1980. bi-m. $29.95. Campaigns and Elections, 1835 K St., N.W., Ste. 403, Washington, DC 20006. TEL 202-331-3222. FAX 202-331-3218. Ed. Myron Struck. adv.; bk.rev.; charts; illus.; stat.; circ. 20,000. (also avail. in microform from UMI; back issues avail.; reprint service avail. from UMI) **Indexed:** P.A.I.S.
—BLDSC shelfmark: 3016.345000.
Description: For political professionals; includes news, views and how-to's for modern campaigns.

CANADA. PRIVACY COMMISSIONER. ANNUAL REPORT. see COMPUTERS — Computer Security

971 327 CN ISSN 0045-4257
CANADA TODAY/CANADA D'AUJOURD'HUI. 1970. irreg. (3-4/yr.). free. Canadian Embassy, Public Affairs Division, 501 Pennsylvania Ave., N.W., Washington, DC 20001. TEL 202-682-1740. FAX 202-682-7791. Ed. Judith C. Webster. bk.rev.; bibl.; illus.; circ. 80,000.
Description: News articles, commentary, graphics, and photographs focusing on the contemporary environmental, political, legislative, agricultural, geological, commercial, military, and industrial issues that affect the nation.

971 CN ISSN 0008-3402
AP5
CANADIAN DIMENSION; an independent journal of socialist opinion. 1963. 8/yr. Can.$24.50 to individuals; institutions Can.$35 (effective Jan. 1991). Dimension Publishing Inc., 228 Notre Dame Ave., Ste. 707, Winnipeg, Man. R3B 1N7, Canada. TEL 204-957-1519. FAX 204-943-4617. Ed.Bd. adv.; bk.rev.; illus.; index; circ. 5,000. (also avail. in microfiche from UMI,MML) **Indexed:** Alt.Press Ind., Amer.Hist.& Life, Can.Per.Ind., Can.Wom.Per.Ind., CMI, Hist.Abstr., Mag.Ind., Mid.East: Abstr.& Ind.
—BLDSC shelfmark: 3021.170000.

CANADIAN HUMAN RIGHTS YEARBOOK/ANNUAIRE CANADIEN DES DROITS DE LA PERSONNE. see POLITICAL SCIENCE — Civil Rights

320 301 CN ISSN 0380-9420
JA4
CANADIAN JOURNAL OF POLITICAL & SOCIAL THEORY/REVUE CANADIENNE DE THEORIE POLITIQUE ET SOCIALE. (Text in English, French) 1977. triennial. Can.$15($17) individuals; libraries Can.$30($35); students Can.$10($12). Arthur & Marilouise Kroker, Ed. & Pub., Concordia University, 1455 de Maisonneuve West, Montreal, Que. H3G 1M8, Canada. TEL 514-841-2112. FAX 514-848-3494. Eds. Arthur and Marilouise Kroker. adv.; bk.rev.; film rev.; index; circ. 2,000. (back issues avail.) **Indexed:** A.B.C.Pol.Sci., Alt.Press Ind., Can.Per.Ind., Can.Wom.Per.Ind., CMI, Film Lit.Ind. (1989-), Int.Polit.Sci.Abstr., Lang.& Lang.Behav.Abstr., Sociol.Abstr.
—BLDSC shelfmark: 3034.580000.

320 CN ISSN 0008-4239
CANADIAN JOURNAL OF POLITICAL SCIENCE/REVUE CANADIENNE DE SCIENCE POLITIQUE. (Text in English, French) 1968. q. membership. Canadian Political Science Association - Association Canadienne de Science Politique, No. 205 - 1 Stewart St., Ottawa, Ont. K1N 6H7, Canada. FAX 613-230-2746. (Dist. by: Wilfrid Laurier University Press, Waterloo, Ont. N2L 3C5, Canada) (Co-sponsor: Societe Quebecoise de Science Politique) Ed.Bd. bk.rev.; index; circ. 3,000. (also avail. in microfiche from UMI; microfilm from PMC) **Indexed:** A.B.C.Pol.Sci., Amer.Bibl.Slavic & E.Eur.Stud., ASSIA, Can.Per.Ind., Can.Wom.Per.Ind., CMI, Commun.Abstr., Curr.Cont., Geo.Abstr., Hist.Abstr., Ind.Can.L.P.L., Int.Polit.Sci.Abstr., Lang.& Lang.Behav.Abstr., Mid.East: Abstr.& Ind., P.A.I.S.For.Lang.Ind., P.A.I.S., Peace Res.Abstr., Pt.de Rep. (1979-), Soc.Sci.Ind., SSCI.
—BLDSC shelfmark: 3034.600000.
Supersedes in part (in 1967): Canadian Journal of Economics and Political Science.
Refereed Serial

328 CN ISSN 0315-6168
CANADIAN PARLIAMENTARY GUIDE (YEAR)/GUIDE PARLEMENTAIRE CANADIEN. (Text in English, French) 1867. a. Can.$59.95. Info Globe, 444 Front St. W., Toronto, Ont. M5V 2S9, Canada. TEL 416-585-5250. FAX 416-585-5249. Eds. Katherine Miller, Kathryn Flanagan. stat.
Description: Contains general, biographical and electoral information for members of the House of Commons, Senate, Prive Council and each of the provincial and territorial legislatures.

917.1 CN
CANADIAN POLITICAL NEWS & LIFE. m. 40 Bay St., Box 42, Sta. A, Toronto, Ont. M5W 1A2, Canada. TEL 416-535-8791. Ed. Joseph Zboralski.
Description: Independent, non-partisan, political broadsheet. Strategically located correspondents analyze and give new perspectives to international political events and their effect on Canada.

CAPITAL AND CLASS. see BUSINESS AND ECONOMICS

350 US
CAPITAL JOURNAL. w. during state legislative session. Business Council of New York State, Inc., 152 Washington Ave., Albany, NY 12210. TEL 518-465-7511.
Description: Newsletterr about New York State government action affecting business.

320 US
CAPITAL SOURCE. s-a. $40 per no. National Journal, Inc. (Subsidiary of: Times Mirror Company), 1730 M St., N.W., Ste. 1100, Washington, DC 20036. TEL 202-857-1400. FAX 202-833-8069. adv.
Description: Telephone directory of the Washington power structure. Includes government officials, trade associations, interest groups, political consultants and news media.

320 333.7 US ISSN 1045-5752
HD75.6
CAPITALISM, NATURE, SOCIALISM; a journal of socialist ecology. 1989. 4/yr. $20 to individuals; institutions $60. Guilford Publications, Inc., 72 Spring St., 4th Fl., New York, NY 10012. TEL 212-431-9800. FAX 212-966-6708. Ed. James O'Connor. **Indexed:** Environ.Per.Bibl., Left Ind. (1989-).
—BLDSC shelfmark: 3050.669720.

CARTHAGE; Tunisian quarterly review. see HISTORY — History Of Africa

CASOPIS MATICE MORAVSKE. see HISTORY — History Of Europe

CATHOLIC ACTIVIST. see RELIGIONS AND THEOLOGY — Roman Catholic

322.1 282 US ISSN 0008-8463
BX801
CATHOLIC WORKER. 1933. m. (bi-m; Jan.-Feb., Mar.-Apr., Jun.-Jul., Oct.-Nov.). $0.25. Catholic Worker Movement, 36 E. First St., New York, NY 10003. TEL 212-777-9617. Ed. Jo Roberts. bk.rev.; circ. 90,000. (tabloid format; also avail. in microform from UMI) **Indexed:** Alt.Press Ind., Cath.Ind., Peace Res.Abstr.

320 US ISSN 0273-3072
H1
CATO JOURNAL; an interdisciplinary journal of public policy analysis. 1981. 3/yr. $24 to individuals; institutions $50. Cato Institute, 224 Second St., S.E., Washington, DC 20003. TEL 202-546-0200. FAX 202-546-0728. Ed. James A. Dorn. adv.; circ. 3,200. (back issues avail.) **Indexed:** A.B.C.Pol.Sci., ABI Inform., Amer.Hist.& Life, C.L.I., Curr.Cont., Environ.Abstr., Hist.Abstr., INIS Atomind., J.of Econ.Lit., Leg.Per., P.A.I.S., SSCI.
—BLDSC shelfmark: 3093.272000.

320 US
CENTER FOR STRATEGIC AND INTERNATIONAL STUDIES. SIGNIFICANT ISSUES SERIES. 1979. 10/yr. $80. Center for Strategic and International Studies, 1800 K St. N.W., Ste. 400, Washington, DC 20006. TEL 202-775-3119. FAX 202-775-3199. Ed. Roberta Howard.
Formerly: Georgetown University Center for Strategic and International Studies. Significant Issues Series (ISSN 0736-7163)

320 US
CENTER FOR THE STUDY OF THE PRESIDENCY. ANNUAL REPORT. a. Center for the Study of the Presidency, 208 E. 75th St., New York, NY 10021. TEL 212-249-1200. FAX 212-628-9503. (reprint service avail. from UMI)

320 US
CENTER FOR THE STUDY OF THE PRESIDENCY. PROCEEDINGS. 1971. irreg., vol.6, 1989. membership. Center for the Study of the Presidency, 208 E. 75th St., New York, NY 10021. TEL 212-249-1200. FAX 212-628-9503. Ed. R. Gordon Hoxie. circ. 11,000. (also avail. in microform from UMI; reprint service avail. from UMI) **Indexed:** Abstr.Mil.Bibl.

956.940 296 RH ISSN 0008-9184
CENTRAL AFRICAN ZIONIST DIGEST. 1958. m. free. Central African Zionist Organisation, Box 1162, Bulawayo, Zimbabwe. Ed. Barney Katz. illus.

320 330 GT ISSN 0254-2471
HC141.A1
CENTRAL AMERICA REPORT. (Text in English) 1974. w. $205. Inforpress Centroamericana, 9 Calle A, 3-56, Zona 1, Apdo. 2823, Guatemala City, Guatemala. TEL 29432, 81997. **Indexed:** HR Rep.
Description: Contains information and analysis on the economic and political events in Belize, Guatemala, El Salvador, Honduras, Nicaragua, Costa Rica and Panama.

CENTRAL AMERICA REPORT. see RELIGIONS AND THEOLOGY

322.4 US ISSN 1054-8882
CENTRAL AMERICA UPDATE. w. $200 to individuals; institutions $300, University of New Mexico, Latin American Institute, Latin America Data Base, 801 Yale N.E., Albuquerque, NM 87131-1016. TEL 505-277-6839. FAX 505-277-5989. Ed. Barbara A. Kohl.
●Also available online. Vendor(s): DIALOG, Mead Data Central, NewsNet.
Description: Examines Central America from an alternative perspective, covering reports and analysis on human rights issues, regional security, US policy initiatives, and economic performance.

POLITICAL SCIENCE 3879

320 950   UK   ISSN 0263-4937
DS327
CENTRAL ASIAN SURVEY. 1982. q. £105 (effective 1992). (Society for Central Asian Studies) Pergamon Press plc, Headington Hill Hall, Oxford OX3 0BW, England. TEL 0865-794141. FAX 0865-743911. TELEX 83177 PERGAP. (And: 660 White Plains Rd., Tarrytown, NY 10591-5153. TEL 914-524-9200) Ed. Marie Broxup. (back issues avail.) **Indexed:** Abstr.Musl.Rel.; Amer.Hist.& Life, Curr.Cont., Hist.Abstr.
—BLDSC shelfmark: 3105.960000.
    Refereed Serial

320   BU   ISSN 0861-038X
CENTRAL COMMITTEE OF THE BULGARIAN COMMUNIST PARTY. INFORMATION BULLETIN. Bulgarian edition (ISSN 0861-0355); Russian edition (ISSN 0861-0363); Spanish edition (ISSN 0861-0371) (Text in English) 1946. m. 40.80 lv. (Bulgarian ed. 12 lv.). Central Committee of the Bulgarian Communist Party, 2, Dondoukov Blvd., 1000 Sofia, Bulgaria. (Subscr. to: RP - 2A, Klokotnitza St., 1202 Sofia, Bulgaria) Ed. Emil Markov. index; circ. 11,100 (1,800 Eng ed.; 6,300 Bulg. ed.; 1,700 Russ. ed.; 1,300 Sp. ed.).

320 330.9   US
CENTRAL INTELLIGENCE AGENCY. MONOGRAPHS. (Series avail.: Communist, Non-Communist, U.S.S.R., China, All Countries, Only Maps) irreg. price varies. U.S. National Technical Information Service, 5825 Port Royal Rd., Springfield, VA 22161. TEL 703-487-4630.
    Description: Presents the political, statistical, economic, and military conditions.

320 330.9   US
CENTRAL INTELLIGENCE AGENCY. MONOGRAPHS. ALL COMMUNIST COUNTRIES REPORTS. (Subseries of: Central Intelligence Agency. Monographs) irreg. price varies. U.S. National Technical Information Service, 5825 Port Royal Rd., Springfield, VA 22161. TEL 703-487-4630.
    Description: Presents the political, economic, statistical, and military conditions.

320 330.9   US
CENTRAL INTELLIGENCE AGENCY. MONOGRAPHS. ALL COUNTRIES REPORTS. (Subseries of: Central Intelligence Agency. Monographs) irreg. price varies. U.S. National Technical Information Service, 5825 Port Royal Rd., Springfield, VA 22161. TEL 703-487-4630.
    Description: Brings out the political, economic, statistical, and military conditions.

320 330.9   US
CENTRAL INTELLIGENCE AGENCY. MONOGRAPHS. ALL NON-COMMUNIST COUNTRY REPORTS. (Subseries of: Central Intelligence Agency. Monographs) irreg. price varies. U.S. National Technical Information Service, 5825 Port Royal Rd., Springfield, VA 22161. TEL 703-487-4630.
    Description: Reports on the political, economic, statistical, and military conditions.

320 330.9   US
CENTRAL INTELLIGENCE AGENCY. MONOGRAPHS. CHINA REPORTS. (Subseries of: Central Intelligence Agency. Monographs) irreg. price varies. U.S. National Technical Information Service, 5825 Port Royal Rd., Springfield, VA 22161. TEL 703-487-4630.
    Description: Covers the political, economic, statistical, and military conditions.

320 330.9   US
CENTRAL INTELLIGENCE AGENCY. MONOGRAPHS. MAPS ONLY. (Subseries of: Central Intelligence Agency. Monographs) irreg. price varies. U.S. National Technical Information Service, 5825 Port Royal Rd., Springfield, VA 22161. TEL 703-487-4630.
    Description: Provides visual information on political, economic, statistical, and military conditions.

327 365.64   US
CENTRAL INTELLIGENCE AGENCY. MONOGRAPHS. U.S.S.R. REPORTS. (Subseries of: Central Intelligence Agency. Monographs) irreg. price varies. U.S. National Technical Information Service, 5825 Port Royal Rd., Springfield, VA 22161. TEL 703-487-4630.
    Description: Details the political, economic, statistical, and military conditions.

CENTRE D'ETUDES ET DE DOCUMENTATION AFRICAINES. CAHIERS. see *HISTORY — History Of Africa*

CENTRE D'HISTOIRE CONTEMPORAINE DU LANGUEDOC-ROUSSILLON. BULLETIN. see *HISTORY — History Of Europe*

CENTRE FOR DEVELOPMENT RESEARCH. PUBLICATIONS. see *AGRICULTURE*

320   UK   ISSN 0577-1935
CENTREPOINT. 1974. 3/yr. free. Christian Centre Party, 157 Vicarage Rd., London E10 5DU, England. TEL 081-539-3876. Ed. Ronald King. bk.rev.; circ. controlled.
    Incorporates: London Teacher.

320   PR
CENTRO DE ESTUDIOS DE LA REALIDAD PUERTORRIQUENA. CUADERNOS. no.5, 1982. irreg. Ediciones Huracan, Inc., Avda. Gonzalez 1003, Santa Rica, Rio Piedras, PR 00925.

CENTRO DE ESTUDIOS PUBLICOS. DOCUMENTO DE TRABAJO. see *BUSINESS AND ECONOMICS — Economic Situation And Conditions*

CERCLE FUSTEC DE COULANGES. DOCUMENTS. see *HISTORY — History Of Europe*

CESKOSLOVENSKY VOJAK. see *MILITARY*

CHAIN REACTION. see *ENVIRONMENTAL STUDIES*

CHALCEDON REPORT. see *RELIGIONS AND THEOLOGY*

320.532   US   ISSN 0009-1049
E838
CHALLENGE (NEW YORK); the Revolutionary Communist newspaper. Monthly French edition: Defi. (Includes monthly supplement Desafio) (Text in English and Spanish) 1964. w. $15 to individuals; institutions $35. Progressive Labor Party, 231 W. 29th St., No. 501, New York, NY 10001. illus.; circ. 10,000. (also avail. in microform from UMI) **Indexed:** Alt.Press Ind., BPIA, Fut.Surv.

320   II
CHANDIGARH POST. (Text in English) 1972. w. Rs.12. H. No. 2017 Sector 15-C, Chandigarh 160017, India. Ed. Surrinder Khullar. adv.; illus.
    Description: News and current affairs.

329.821 052   UK   ISSN 0960-748X
▼**CHANGES (LONDON, 1990);** renewing socialist politics. 1990. fortn. £15. (Communist Party of Great Britain) James Klugmann Pictorials Ltd., 6 Cynthia St., London N1 9JF, England. TEL 071-278-4451. FAX 071-278-4427. Ed. Mike Power. adv.; bk.rev.; circ. 8,000. (tabloid format; back issues avail.)
    Formerly (until 1990): 7 Days.

320   US
CHILEAN REVIEW. 1980. m. free. Embassy of Chile, Press Office, 1732 Massachusetts Ave., N.W., Washington, DC 20036. TEL 202-785-1746. Ed.Bd. circ. 2,000.
    Formerly: Chilean Newsbrief; **Supersedes:** Chile: Summary of Recent Events.

320 951   GW   ISSN 0341-6631
DS701
CHINA AKTUELL. (English-language supplement: P R C Official Activities) 1972. m. DM.116. Institut fuer Asienkunde - Institute of Asian Affairs Hamburg, Rothenbaumchaussee 32, 2000 Hamburg 13, Germany. FAX 040-4107945. **Indexed:** Key to Econ.Sci.

951 310   US   ISSN 0190-602X
DS779.15
CHINA FACTS AND FIGURES ANNUAL. 1978. a. $71. Academic International Press, Box 1111, Gulf Breeze, FL 32562-1111. (back issues avail.)
—BLDSC shelfmark: 3180.146000.

CHINA NEWS ANALYSIS. see *GENERAL INTEREST PERIODICALS — China*

951 327   UK   ISSN 0045-6764
CHINA NOW. 1970. 4/yr. £12 to individuals (foreign £22); institutions £25 (foreign £35). Society for Anglo-Chinese Understanding Ltd., Rendezvous, 16 Portland St., Cheltenham, Glos. GL52 2PB, England. Ed. Angela Knox. adv.; bk.rev.; index.
—BLDSC shelfmark: 3180.214000.

320 301 355   US
CHINA REPORT: POLITICAL, SOCIOLOGICAL, AND MILITARY AFFAIRS. irreg. (approx. 90/yr.). $5 per no. U.S. Joint Publications Research Service, Box 12507, Arlington, VA 22209. TEL 703-487-4630. (Dist. by: NTIS, Springfield, VA 22161)

CHINESE LAW AND GOVERNMENT; a journal of translations. see *LAW*

320   NE
CHRISTEN DEMOCRATISCHE VERKENNINGEN. 1981. m. fl.60 (students fl.37.50). C D A, Wetenschappelijk Instituut, Dr. Kuyperstraat 5, 2514 BA The Hague, Netherlands. TEL 070-3424870. Ed. Th. B.F.M. Brinkel. bk.rev.; circ. 3,000.
    Supersedes: Socialisme en Democratie (ISSN 0037-8135)

320.5   US   ISSN 0195-9387
CHRISTIAN ANTI-COMMUNISM CRUSADE. NEWSLETTER. Variant title: C.A.C.C. Newsletter. 1954. bi-w. contributions. Christian Anti-Communism Crusade, 227 E. 6th St., Box 890, Long Beach, CA 90801-0890. TEL 213-437-0941. FAX 213-432-2074. Ed. Fred Schwarz. bk.rev.; rec.rev.; circ. 50,000. (also avail. in microform from UMI)

CHRISTIAN BEACON. see *RELIGIONS AND THEOLOGY — Protestant*

CHRISTIAN JEWISH RELATIONS. see *RELIGIONS AND THEOLOGY*

CHRISTIAN PRISONERS IN THE U.S.S.R.. see *RELIGIONS AND THEOLOGY*

320.531   UK   ISSN 0009-5648
HX51
CHRISTIAN SOCIALIST. 1960. q. £1.60. Christian Socialist Movement, 47 Fyfield Rd., London E17 3RE, England. Ed.Bd. adv.; bk.rev.; circ. 1,300. (also avail. in microform from KTO)
    Formerly: C S M News.

CHRISTIAN STATESMAN. see *RELIGIONS AND THEOLOGY*

329   BE
CHRISTIANSKAYA DEMOCRATIA. (Text in English, French, Spanish) m. Christian Democrat International, 16 rue de la Victoire, Boite 1, B-1060 Brussels, Belgium. TEL 02-5371322. FAX 02-5379348. TELEX 61118 IDC B.

CHRISTLICHE DEMOKRATIE; Vierteljahresschrift fuer Zeitgeschichte, Sozial-, Kultur- und Wirtschaftsgeschichte. see *HISTORY — History Of Europe*

CHRONICLE OF LATIN AMERICAN ECONOMIC AFFAIRS. see *BUSINESS AND ECONOMICS — Economic Situation And Conditions*

320   SZ
CHRONICLE OF PARLIAMENTARY ELECTIONS AND DEVELOPMENTS. (Editions in English, French) 1967. a. 30 Fr. Inter-Parliamentary Union, International Center for Parliamentary Documentation - Union Interparlementaire, Place du Petit-Saconnex, B.P. 438, 1211 Geneva 19, Switzerland. TEL 022-7344150. FAX 022-7333141. TELEX 414217-IPU-CH.
    Formerly (until vol.12, 1978): Chronicle of Parliamentary Elections (ISSN 0074-1043)

CHRONIQUE JUDICIAIRE D'HAITI; revue juridique et culturelle Haitienne. see *LAW*

320.532 951   CH   ISSN 1015-9355
CHUNG KUNG YEN CHIU/STUDIES ON CHINESE COMMUNISM. (Text in Chinese; contents page in English) 1967. m. $27. Institute for the Study of Chinese Communist Problems, P.O. Box 351, Taipei, Taiwan, Republic of China. Ed.Bd. index; circ. 1,800. Key Title: Zhonggong Yanjiu.
    Formerly: Fei Ch'ing Yen Chiu (ISSN 0014-9667)

POLITICAL SCIENCE

320.532 951   CH   ISSN 1013-2716
CHUNG-KUO TA-LU YEN-CHIU/MAINLAND CHINA STUDIES. (Text in Chinese) 1958. m. $53. Institute of International Relations, 64 Wan Shou Rd., Mucha, Taipei, Taiwan, Republic of China.
TEL 02-939-4921. Ed. Chao Chun-shan. index; circ. 5,000. (also avail. in microform from UMI; reprint service avail. from ISI,UMI) Key Title: Zhongguo Dalu Yanjiu.
    Formerly (until 1985): Fei Ch'ing Yueh Pao - Chinese Communist Affairs Monthly (ISSN 0014-9675)

CHURCH & STATE. see *RELIGIONS AND THEOLOGY*

CINEMA POLITIQUE; dans la perspective d'une vie passionnante. see *MOTION PICTURES*

CIRCLE (JAMAICA PLAIN); a paper for Native American People. see *ETHNIC INTERESTS*

CIRCOLO ROSSELLI. QUADERNI. see *CLUBS*

320   FR   ISSN 0756-3205
CITE; revue de la nouvelle citoyennete. 1982. 4/yr. 150 F. Societe Nationale Presse Francaise, 17 rue des Petits Champs, 75001 Paris, France.
TEL 42-97-42-57. Ed. Bertrand Renouvin. circ. 3,000. (back issues avail.)
—BLDSC shelfmark: 3267.769200.

320.531 284   FR
CITE NOUVELLE. 1945. m. 50 F. 46 rue de Vaugirard, 75006 Paris, France.

320   CN
CITOYEN.* 1941. w. Can.$13. Groupe Hebcor, Inc., 4545 Frontenad St., Quebec, Que. H2H 2R7, Canada. TEL 819-879-5409. Ed. Roger Laliberte. adv.; circ. 4,600. (tabloid format)

355   US   ISSN 0045-7035
CIVIL AFFAIRS JOURNAL & NEWSLETTER. 1949. bi-m. $10. Civil Affairs Association, 1903 N. Quintana St., Arlington, VA 22205. TEL 717-249-3843. Ed. James O. Lloyd. bk.rev.; illus.; circ. 2,600.
    Formerly: Military Government Journal and Newsletter (ISSN 0026-3990)

CIVILIAN CONGRESS; includes a directory of persons holding executive branch-military office in Congress contrary to constitutional prohibition (Art.1, Sec.6, Cl.2) of concurrent office-holding. see *LAW*

327   NE   ISSN 0030-3283
AP15
CIVIS MUNDI. 1962. q. fl.42.50. Stichting Civis Mundi, Akkerwindestraat 23, 3051 LA Rotterdam, Netherlands. TEL 010-4182580.
FAX 010-4525332. Ed. S.W. Couwenberg. adv.; bk.rev.; bibl.; index; circ. 1,000. **Indexed:** Key To Econ.Sci.
    Formerly: Oost-West.
    Description: Covers political culture and philosophy.

320   IT   ISSN 0009-8191
H7
CIVITAS; periodico di studi politici. (Text in Italian; summaries in English, French, German, Serbo-Croatian, Spanish) 1919. m. L.25000. Edizioni Civitas, Via Tirso 92, 00198 Rome, Italy. TEL 06-8555651. Ed. Paolo E. Taviani. adv.; bk.rev.; charts; stat; index; circ. 8,580. **Indexed:** Amer.Hist.& Life, Hist.Abstr.
—BLDSC shelfmark: 3274.250000.

320   II
CLARITY; newsman's newsweekly. (Text in English) 1974. w. Rs.100. Writers Foundation Charitable Trust, Barrack No. 3,2-3, Adarsh Nagar, Prabhadevi, Bombay 400 025, India. Ed. S.B. Kolpe. adv.; bk.rev.; illus.; circ. 5,000.

320.531   NO
CLASS STRUGGLE. (Text in English) 1969. d. NOK 150. Workers Communist Party (Marxist-Leninist) of Norway, P.O. Box 83 Bryn, 0611 Oslo 6, Norway. Ed. S. Allern. adv.; bk.rev.; circ. 8,000. (back issues avail.)

320   SZ   ISSN 0069-4533
CLASSIQUES DE LA PENSEE POLITIQUE. 1965. irreg., no.14, 1990. price varies. Librairie Droz S.A., 11, rue Massot, CH-1211 Geneva 12, Switzerland. TEL 022-466666. FAX 022-472391. circ. 1,000.

320   CU
CLAVE. q. $7 in N. America; S. America and Europe $8; others $9. (Ministerio de Cultura) Ediciones Cubanas, Obispo No. 527, Apdo. 605, Havana, Cuba.

320   AG
CLAVES PARA INTERPRETAR LOS HECHOS. 1984. m. Editorial Claves, Riombamba 212, Buenos Aires, Argentina. Ed. Juan Carlos Cerutti.

320.531   GW
COCHISE; Zeitung des sozialistischen Schuelerbundes Berlin. 1986. q. Sozialistischen Schuelerbundes Berlin, Muellerstr. 163, 1000 Berlin 65, Germany. TEL 030-4792132.

320   GW   ISSN 0932-3473
CODE; Exclusives aus Politik und Wirtschaft. 1974. m. DM.93. Verlag Diagnosen, Untere Burghalde 51, 7250 Leonberg, Germany. TEL 07152-26011. Ed. Ekkehard Franke-Gricksch. adv.; circ. 30,000.

COEXISTENCE; a review of East-West and development issues. see *SOCIAL SCIENCES: COMPREHENSIVE WORKS*

COGITATIONS ON LAW AND GOVERNMENT. see *LAW*

320   BL
COLECAO CAMINHOS BRASILEIROS. irreg. Edicoes Tiempo Brasileiro Ltda, Rua Gago Coutinho 61, C.P. 16099, ZC-01 Laranjeiras, Rio de Janeiro, Brazil. Dir. Carlos Chagas Filho.

320   BL
COLECAO TENDENCIAS. irreg., vol.3, 1982. Edicoes Graal Ltda., Rua Hermenegildo de Barroa, 31-A, 20241 Gloria, Rio de Janeiro RJ, Brazil.

320 330   PO
COLECCAO HORIZONTE UNIVERSITARIO. no.30, 1982. irreg., no.53, 1990. Livros Horizonte, Lda., Rua das Chagas, 17, 1121 Lisbon Codex, Portugal.
TEL 1-34666917.

320   UY
COLECCION CIEN TEMAS BASICOS.* no.18, 1976. irreg. Editorial Medina s.r.l., Tristan Naruaja 1547, Montevideo, Uruguay.

320   CR
COLECCION CUADERNOS C E D A L. 1974. irreg. Centro de Estudios C E D A L, Apdo. 874, San Jose, Costa Rica. Ed. Alberto Baeza Flores.

320   ES
COLECCION DEBATE. 1983. irreg. (Universidad Centroamericana Jose Simeon Canas) U C A Editores, Autopista Sur, Jardines de Guadalupe, Apdo. Postal 01-575, San Salvador, El Salvador. Ed. Rodolfo Cardenal. circ. 1,300.

320   DR
COLECCION ESTUDIOS POLITICOS. irreg. Publicaciones O N A P, Edif. de Oficinas Gubernamentales, Av. Mexico esq. Leopoldo Navarro, Santo Domingo, Dominican Republic. circ. 750.

320   SP
COLECCION IBERICA. 1976. irreg. Editorial Anagrama, S.A., Calle Pedro de la Creu, 58, 08034 Barcelona, Spain.

320   VE
COLECCION MONOGRAFIAS POLITICAS.* 1978. irreg. Editorial Juridica Venezolana, Edif. Galipan, Av. Francisco de Miranda, Piso 3, Apdo. 17598, Caracas 1015-A, Venezuela.

320   SP
COLECCION VIERA Y CLAVIJO. 1982. a. Universidad de la Laguna, Cabildo Insular de Gran Canaria, Secretariado de Publicaciones, San Agustin, 30, 38201 La Laguna-Tenerife, Islas Canarias, Spain. TEL 922-25-81-27.

320   US
▼**COLLECTIVE VOICE**; a multi-issue magazine of politics and culture. 1990. 6/yr. $15 to individuals; institutions $30; students $10. 3255 Hennepin Ave., Ste. 254, Minneapolis, MN 55408-3470. Ed. Meleah Maynard. adv.; film rev.illus.; circ. 300.
    Description: Publishes pieces by people working at the grass roots level for everything from farmers' rights to women's rights.

320 378.83   US
COLLEGE REPUBLICAN. 1980. q. free. College Republican National Committee, 310 First St., S.E., Washington, DC 20003. TEL 202-662-1330. Ed. Steve Satran. circ. 35,000.
    Formerly: C R Report.

320   US
COLONIE QUARTERLY. 1976. q. Town of Colonie, 747 Downing St., Schenectady, NY 12309.
TEL 518-783-2700. Ed. Robert E. Keating. circ. 33,000.

320   US
COLORADO STATESMAN. 1898. w. $39. Box 18129, Denver, CO 80218. TEL 303-827-8600. Ed. Jody Strogoff. (newspaper)
    Description: Covers all levels of Colorado politics.

320.9   PK   ISSN 0010-2121
COMBAT; an independent news weekly. (Text in English) 1969. w. Rs.24. 81-82 Farid Chambers, Abdullah Haroon Rd., Karachi 3, Pakistan. Ed. Yunus Said. adv.

320.531   FR
COMBAT CULTUREL.* 1975. irreg. price varies. Editions Syros, 6, rue Montmarte, 75001 Paris, France. illus.

320.531   FR
COMBAT POUR LA DIASPORA.* 1980. 5/yr. 70 F. Editions Syros, 6 rue Montmartre, 75001 Paris, France. Ed. Francoise Chaonat.

322.4   CK
COMITE DE ACCION INTERAMERICANA DE COLOMBIA. BOLETIN. irreg. Comite de Accion Interamericana de Colombia, Cra. 7 No.32-33, Of. 1601, Apdo. Aereo 10598, Bogota, Colombia.

320   US
COMMITTEE TO RESTORE THE CONSTITUTION. BULLETIN. 1965. m. $25. Committee to Restore the Constitution, Box 986, Ft. Collins, CO 80522.
TEL 303-484-2575.
    Description: Reveals hidden facts behind national crisis. Explains constitutional authority to halt economic-political exploitation. Incorporates model procedures for county and state action to restore interest-free money, defend - preserve freedom of person and property.

320   US   ISSN 0271-9592
JK1
COMMON CAUSE MAGAZINE; people, power and politics in Washington. 1980. bi-m. $20. Common Cause, 2030 M St., N.W., Washington, DC 20036.
TEL 202-833-1200. FAX 202-659-3716. Ed. Deborah Baldwin. bk.rev.; circ. 270,000. **Indexed:** Acad.Ind., Environ.Abstr., P.A.I.S., PSI.
    Supersedes: Frontline (Washington) & In Common (ISSN 0196-6677)
    Description: Articles advocating government accountability and ethics.

341.1 100   UK   ISSN 0010-3276
COMMON LIFE;* a newsletter on reconciliation, non-violence, peace and spiritual communism. 1951. q. free. Vedanta Movement, Batheaston Villa, Batheaston, Bath, England. Ed. Swami Avyaktanananda.

322.4   US
COMMON SENSE; the newsletter for libertarians and other friends of liberty. 1971. 5/yr. $10. Libertarian Information Services, Box 520191, Miami, FL 33152-0191. FAX 305-471-0113. Ed. T. Paine. adv.; tr.lit.; circ. 600.
    Formerly: Florida Libertarian.
    Description: Digest of news and commentary of interest to friends of liberty.

320 330   AT
COMMON SENSE. 1981. irreg. Common Sense Publications, 1 Schneider Rd., Rosevale, Qld. 4340, Australia. TEL 074-640-533. Ed. Mr. Viv Forbes. circ. 800.
    Description: Political and economic commentary from free market perspective.

POLITICAL SCIENCE 3881

320   US
COMMON SENSE IN JEFFERSON COUNTY. 1987. m. $5.
Alabama Libertarian Party, Box 11514, Birmingham, AL 35202. TEL 205-322-2991. Eds. Frank Monachelli, Steve Smith. illus.; circ. 20,000. (back issues avail.)
  Description: Editorials and commentary on libertarian activities to promote governmental responsibility and restraint in the community of Birmingham, Alabama.

320.5   UK
COMMON WEALTH JOURNAL. 1966. 4/yr. 50p.
Common Wealth, c/o W.J. Taylor, 107 Pilton St., Pilton, Barnstaple, Devon, England. Ed. J.C. Banks. bk.rev.; circ. 1,000. (processed)
  Former titles: Common Wealth; Libertarian (ISSN 0024-2004)

COMMONWEALTH. see *LITERARY AND POLITICAL REVIEWS*

320   SW   ISSN 0283-2925
COMMUNIDAD. (Text in Spanish) 1977. q.
SEK 130($25) Centrum foer Kooperativa Studier och Verkamhetet, P.O. Box 15128, S-10465 Stockholm, Sweden. FAX 46-8-6445985. Ed. Ruben G. Prieto. bk.rev.; circ. 2,500. (back issues avail.)

329.9   FR   ISSN 2209-7007
COMMUNISME; revue d'histoire, de sociologie et de science politique. (Summaries in English, French) 1982. 3/yr. 220 F. Editions l'Age d'Homme, 5 rue Ferou, 75006 Paris, France. Ed. Stephane Courtois. bk.rev.; circ. 700.

COMMUNIST ECONOMIES AND ECONOMIC TRANSFORMATION. see *BUSINESS AND ECONOMICS — Economic Systems And Theories, Economic History*

320.532   FR
COMMUNISTES FRANCAIS ET L'EUROPE. 1978. irreg.
Parti Communiste Francais, 2 Place du Colonel Fabien, 75019 Paris, France.

320.3   US   ISSN 0010-4140
JA3
COMPARATIVE POLITICAL STUDIES. 1968. q. $40 to individuals; institutions $120. Sage Publications, Inc., 2455 Teller Rd., Newbury Park, CA 91320. TEL 805-499-0721. FAX 805-499-0871. (And: Sage Publications, Ltd., 6 Bonhill St., London EC2A 4PU, England) Ed. James A. Caporaso. adv.; bk.rev.; bibl.; charts; stat.; index; circ. 1,500. (also avail. in microform from UMI; back issues avail.) Indexed: A.B.C.Pol.Sci., Amer.Bibl.Slavic & E.Eur.Stud., Amer.Hist.& Life, ASSIA, Commun.Abstr., Curr.Cont., Geo.Abstr., Hist.Abstr., Int.Polit.Sci.Abstr., Mid.East: Abstr.& Ind., P.A.I.S., Rural Recreat.Tour.Abstr., Soc.Sci.Ind., Sociol.Abstr., SSCI, Stud.Wom.Abstr., World Agri.Econ.& Rural Sociol.Abstr.
  —BLDSC shelfmark: 3363.795000.

320   US   ISSN 1047-1006
JK2403
COMPARATIVE STATE POLITICS. vol.9, 1988. bi-m. $12.50. Illinois Legislative Studies Center, Sangamon State University, Springfield, IL 62794-9243. TEL 217-786-6574. Ed. David H. Everson. bk.rev.; index; circ. 375. Indexed: P.A.I.S.
  Formerly (until 1989): Comparative State Politics Newsletter (ISSN 0273-1347)
  Description: Covers political events nationwide, focusing on state governments. Analyzes election results, and provides highlights of legislative works.

320   US   ISSN 0149-5933
JX1   CODEN: COSTDY
COMPARATIVE STRATEGY; an international journal. 1978. q. $110. Taylor & Francis, 1900 Frost Rd., Ste. 101, Bristol, PA 19007. TEL 215-785-5800. FAX 215-785-5515. Ed. Richard B. Foster. adv.; bk.rev.; abstr.; index. Indexed: Abstr.Mil.Bibl., Amer.Bibl.Slavic & E.Eur.Stud., Curr.Cont., Int.Polit.Sci.Abstr., P.A.I.S., Peace Res.Abstr., SSCI.
  —BLDSC shelfmark: 3363.830000.
  Description: Focus is on American strategic thought and the influence of history and ideas on the strategic interactions between the West and the Soviet Union.
  Refereed Serial

320   AG
COMPROMISO POLITICO Y SOCIAL. 1984. m. Ediciones Compromiso, Mendes de Andes 33-35, Buenos Aires, Argentina. Ed. Miguel Angel Marcos.

COMUNI D'EUROPA. see *PUBLIC ADMINISTRATION — Municipal Government*

320.532   IT   ISSN 0393-6740
COMUNISMO. 1979. q. L.10000($13) Partito Comunista Internazionale, Casella Postale 1157, 50100 Florence, Italy. Ed. Lazzaro Guadagni. circ. 1,000. (back issues avail.)

320   DR
CONCERTACION. m. Presidencia de la Republica de Guatemala, Secretaria de Relaciones Publicas, Guatemala City, Guatemala.

320   US   ISSN 0738-8942
JX1291
CONFLICT MANAGEMENT AND PEACE SCIENCE. 1974. irreg., vol.12, no.1, 1992. $12 per no. Peace Science Society (International), Department of Political Science, Box 6000, State University of New York at Binghamton, Binghamton, NY 13902-6000. Ed. Stuart A. Bremer. bk.rev.; circ. 1,000. (back issues avail.; reprint service avail. from SCH) Indexed: A.B.C.Pol.Sci., Amer.Hist.& Life, Curr.Cont., Hist.Abstr., Mid.East: Abstr.& Ind., P.A.I.S., SSCI.
  —BLDSC shelfmark: 3410.654000.
  Formerly (until 1981): Journal of Peace Science (ISSN 0094-3738)

322.4   AG
CONFRONTACION; de ideas para una nueva sociedad. 1986. q. Avda. Belgrano 1787, piso 2, 1093 Buenos Aires, Argentina. TEL 45-4756. Dir. Julian Lemoine.

CONGRESS. see *PUBLIC ADMINISTRATION*

320 350   US
CONGRESS AND THE NATION. 1965. every 4 yrs. $168. Congressional Quarterly Inc., 1414 22nd St., N.W., Washington, DC 20037. TEL 202-887-8500. FAX 202-728-1863.
  Description: Covers summary of Reagan's first term and important congressional decisions between 1981 and 1984. Description of legislative issues summarize key activities for each year.

320 970   US   ISSN 0734-3469
JK1041
CONGRESS AND THE PRESIDENCY. 1972. s-a. $12 individuals; institutions $15. American University, Center for Congressional and Presidential Studies, Washington, DC 20016. TEL 202-686-6250. FAX 202-885-2967. Eds. Jeff Fishel, Susan Hammond. adv.; bk.rev.; abstr.; bibl.; illus.; circ. 650. (also avail. in microform from UMI) Indexed: A.B.C.Pol.Sci., Amer.Hist.& Life, Hist.Abstr., Int.Polit.Sci.Abstr., P.A.I.S., SSCI.
  —BLDSC shelfmark: 3415.828000.
  Former titles (until 1981): Congressional Studies (ISSN 0194-4053); (until 1978): Capitol Studies (ISSN 0045-5687)

320   US
CONGRESS IN PRINT; the weekly catalog of congressional documents. 1969. 48/yr. $198. Congressional Quarterly Inc., 1414 22 St., N.W., Washington, DC 20037. TEL 800-432-2250. FAX 202-728-1863. Ed. David Masci. (looseleaf format)
  ●Also available online.
  Incorporates (in Sept. 1985): Checklist of Congressional Hearings and Committee Prints (ISSN 0195-3761); **Formerly (1954-19??):** Checklist of Congressional Hearings (ISSN 0009-2096)
  Description: Notification of hearings, committee reports, prints and staff studies released by the Government Printing Office.

329.9   II   ISSN 0376-5776
JQ298.I5
CONGRESS MARCHES AHEAD. (Text in English) 1970. irreg. price varies. All India Congress Committee, Publications Department, 5 Dr. Rajendra Prasad Rd., New Delhi 110001, India.

320 323.4   SA
CONGRESS RESISTER. (Text in English) 1983. bi-m. Transvaal Indian Congress, P.O. Box 658, Crown Mines 2025, South Africa. circ. 20,000. (back issues avail.)

973 328   US   ISSN 0010-5899
JK1
CONGRESSIONAL DIGEST. 1921. 10/yr. $32. Congressional Digest Corp., 3231 P St., N.W., Washington, DC 20007. TEL 202-333-7332. FAX 202-625-6670. index. (also avail. in microform from UMI) Indexed: Acad.Ind., Adol.Ment.Hlth.Abstr., Curr.Cont., Energy Rev., Mag.Ind., Mid.East: Abstr.& Ind., P.A.I.S., PMR, PSI, R.G., Soc.Sci.Ind., TOM.
  —BLDSC shelfmark: 3415.950000.
  Description: Features major controversies in the Congress, pro and con.

320   US   ISSN 0196-0784
CONGRESSIONAL INSIGHT; the weekly newsletter analyzing the pressures, people and politics that shape Capitol Hill decisions. 1976. w. $299. Congressional Quarterly Inc., 1414 22nd St., N.W., Washington, DC 20037. TEL 800-432-2250. FAX 202-728-1863. Ed. Brian Nutting.
  ●Also available online.
  Description: Coverage devoted exclusively to the U.S. Congress including its priorities, power struggles and personalities.

973 328   US   ISSN 0010-5902
CONGRESSIONAL MONITOR; daily listing of all scheduled Congressional committee hearings, with witnesses. Variant titles: Congressional Daily Monitor. Daily Congressional Monitor. 1965. d. (plus w. supplements). $1258. Congressional Quarterly Inc., 1414 22nd St., N.W., Washington, DC 20037. TEL 800-432-2250. FAX 202-728-1863. Ed. Brian Nutting.
  ●Also available online.
  Incorporating: Congress Daily.
  Description: Provides schedule of congressional action, including the agenda for congressional hearings and witness lists.

973 328   US   ISSN 0010-5910
JK1
CONGRESSIONAL QUARTERLY SERVICE. WEEKLY REPORT. (Includes annual almanac) 1945. w. $1220. Congressional Quarterly Inc., 1414 22nd St., N.W., Washington, DC 20037. TEL 800-432-2250. FAX 202-728-1863. Ed. Robert W. Merry. charts; index every 90 days and annually; circ. 11,000. (also avail. in microform from UMI,MIM; reprint service avail. from UMI) Indexed: Acad.Ind., Bank.Lit.Ind., Mid.East: Abstr.& Ind., Noise Pollut.Publ.Abstr., P.A.I.S.
  ●Also available online.
  —BLDSC shelfmark: 3415.960000.
  Description: Provides detailed reports on all major legislative action, the president's legislative proposals, statements and major speeches and analyses of the Supreme Court's decisions. Includes coverage of political and lobbying activities.

320   US
CONGRESSIONAL ROLL CALL (YEAR); a chronology and analysis of votes in the House and Senate. 1972. a. $19.95 (paperback). Congressional Quarterly Inc., 1414 22nd St., N.W., Washington, DC 20037. TEL 202-887-8500. FAX 202-728-1863. charts. (back issues avail.; reprint service avail. from UMI)
  Description: Shows every roll-call vote for all members of Congress for that year. Also shows votes on critical issues, each member's party unity, presidential support and voting record.

973 350   US   ISSN 0069-8938
CONGRESSIONAL STAFF DIRECTORY. 1959. s-a. $59. Staff Directories Ltd., Box 62, Mount Vernon, VA 22121. TEL 703-739-0900. FAX 703-739-0234. Ed. Ann L. Brownson. (avail. on diskette)
  ●Also available on CD-ROM.
  Description: Lists 16,00 congressional staff with updated biographical briefs of over 3,300 congressional members, their staffs and their districts. Includes voting stats of cities and counties, including names, titles, addresses, telephone numbers in Washington and home offices.

320 370 574   US
CONNECTIONS (DAYTON). 1961. a. free. Charles F. Kettering Foundation, 200 Commons Rd., Dayton, OH 45459-2799. circ. 10,000.
  Former titles: Kettering Report; Charles F. Kettering Foundation. Annual Report (ISSN 0069-2735)

POLITICAL SCIENCE

320   CN   ISSN 0708-9422
CONNEXIONS DIGEST; a social change sourcebook. 1976. q. Can.$25($25) Connexions Information Sharing Services, 427 Bloor St. W., Toronto, Ont. M5S 1X7, Canada. TEL 416-960-3903. Ed. Ulli Diemer. adv.; bk.rev.; abstr.; bibl.; illus.; index; circ. 1,200. (back issues avail.) **Indexed:** HR Rep.
 Description: Acts as a networking medium, improving the exchange of ideas, strategies and resources among grass roots groups in Canada.

322.4   HO
CONSEJO CENTRAL EJECUTIVO DEL PARTIDO LIBERAL DE HONDURAS. MEMORIA. irreg. Partido Liberal, Consejo Central Ejecutivo, Tegucigalpa, Honduras.

CONSERVATION VOTER. see *ENVIRONMENTAL STUDIES*

329   UK
CONSERVATIVE NEWS LINE. 1946. m. £8. Conservative & Unionist Central Office, 32 Smith Sq., Westminster, London SW1P 3HH, England. adv.; bk.rev.; circ. 100,000. (tabloid format)
 Formerly: Conservative and Unionist Central Office. Monthly News (ISSN 0010-6518)

320 301   US   ISSN 1047-5990
H53.U5   CODEN: CORWE5
▼**CONSERVATIVE REVIEW.** 1990. bi-m. $28 to individuals; institutions $56. Council for Social and Economic Studies, 6861 Elm St., Ste. 4H, McLean, VA 22101. TEL 703-442-8010. FAX 703-847-9524. Ed. Roger Pearson. bk.rev.

320 929   US   ISSN 0270-532X
CONSTANTIAN. 1970. 4/yr. $12 to non-members (foreign $15). Constantian Society, 123 Orr Rd., Pittsburgh, PA 15241-2219. TEL 412-831-8750. Ed. Randall J. Dicks. adv.; bk.rev.; charts; illus.; stat.; circ. 400.
 Description: Features articles and essays on current and historical topics regarding royalty and monarchy throughout the world, biographical sketches, analysis, genealogical information, and reports on current developments and trends.

320   US   ISSN 1046-0896
K3
CONSTITUTION (NEW YORK). 1988. q. $25. Foundation for the United States Constitution, 1271 Ave. of the Americas, New York, NY 10020. Ed. John A. Meyers. circ. 50,000.
 Description: Devoted to the US Constitution and how it influences history and our lives.

328   FR   ISSN 0010-6623
CONSTITUTIONAL AND PARLIAMENTARY INFORMATION. (Editions in English, French) 1948. s-a. 35 Fr. (Interparliamentary Union, SZ) Association of Secretaries General of Parliaments, c/o Vincent Tocanne, Assemble Nationale, 75355 Paris, France. adv.; index; circ. 1,500. **Indexed:** P.A.I.S.

CONSTITUTIONAL POLITICAL ECONOMY. see *LAW — Constitutional Law*

CONSUMING INTEREST. see *CONSUMER EDUCATION AND PROTECTION*

324.271   CN
CONTACT (OTTAWA). 1981. q. Progressive Conservative Party of Canada, P C Canada Fund, 161 Laurier Ave. W., Ste. 200, Ottawa, Ont. K1P 5J2, Canada. TEL 613-238-6111.

CONTEMPORARY CHINA PAPERS. see *HISTORY — History Of Asia*

320   US   ISSN 0955-3843
HC241.2
CONTEMPORARY EUROPEAN AFFAIRS. (Editions in English, French, German) 1988. q. £120 (effective 1992). Pergamon Press, Inc., Journals Division, 660 White Plains Rd., Tarrytown, NY 10591-5153. TEL 914-524-9200. FAX 914-333-2444. (And: Headington Hill Hall, Oxford OX3 0BW, England. TEL 0865-794141) Eds. Edgard Pisani, Sami Nair. (also avail. in microform; back issues avail.)
 —BLDSC shelfmark: 3425.181750.
 Description: Stimulates research into the economic, monetary, political, social, strategic and cultural aspects of European integration.
 Refereed Serial

943.8   PL   ISSN 0010-7522
CONTEMPORARY POLAND. German edition: Polens Gegenwart. French edition: Pologne Contemporaine. (Text in English) 1967. s-m. $15. Polska Agencja Interpress, Ul. Bagatela 12, 00-585 Warsaw, Poland. **Indexed:** Key to Econ.Sci.

CONTEMPORARY RECORD; the journal of contemporary British history. see *HISTORY — History Of Europe*

320   UK   ISSN 0958-4935
▼**CONTEMPORARY SOUTH ASIA.** 1992. 3/yr. $70 to individuals; institutions $150. Carfax Publishing Co., P.O. Box 25, Abingdon, Oxfordshire OX14 3UE, England. TEL 0235-555335. FAX 0235-553559. (U.S. subscr. addr.: Carfax Publishing Co., Box 2025, Dunnellon, FL 32630) Ed. Gowher Rizvi. (also avail. in microfiche; back issues avail.)
 Description: Presents research and analysis of contemporary policy issues as well as historical articles on South Asia.

320 959   SI   ISSN 0129-797X
DS520
CONTEMPORARY SOUTHEAST ASIA. (Text in English) 1979. 4/yr. S.$40($24) to individuals; institutions S.$48 ($30). Institute of Southeast Asian Studies, Heng Mui Keng Terrace, Off Pasir Panjang Rd., Singapore 0511, Singapore. TEL 7780955. FAX 7781735. TELEX RS 37068 ISEAS. Ed.Bd. bk.rev.; bibl.; index, cum.index. (back issues avail.; reprint service avail. from SCH) **Indexed:** E.I., Mid.East: Abstr.& Ind., P.A.I.S., Rural Recreat.Tour.Abstr., World Agri.Econ.& Rural Sociol.Abstr.
 —BLDSC shelfmark: 3425.305500.
 Description: Specializes in the politics, international relations, and security-related issues of Southeast Asia and its wider geostrategic environment.

CONTINENTAL NEWSTIME. see *BUSINESS AND ECONOMICS — Economic Situation And Conditions*

320   US
CONTINUING INQUIRY. 1976. m. $24. Penn Jones Publications, Inc., Rt. 6, Box 356, Watahachie, TX 75165. Ed. Penn Jones. bk.rev.; circ. 300.

320.531   IT
LA CONTRADDIZIONE; bimestrale di marxismo. 1987. bi-m. L.30000. Associazione Cultura Marxista Contraddizione, 11-188 Montesacro, 00141 Rome, Italy. FAX 39-6-8553197. bk.rev.; circ. 550.
 Description: Forum on Marxism that looks at theoretical problems in the structure of economics, society and history, from an analytical rather than an ideological point of view.

CONTREPOINT. see *LITERARY AND POLITICAL REVIEWS*

320   US   ISSN 0147-1066
CONTRIBUTIONS IN POLITICAL SCIENCE. 1978. irreg., no.306. 1992. price varies. Greenwood Press, Inc. (Subsidiary of: Greenwood Publishing Group Inc.), 88 Post Rd. W., Box 5007, Westport, CT 06881-5007. TEL 203-226-3571. FAX 203-222-1502. Ed. Bernard K. Johnpoll.
 —BLDSC shelfmark: 3461.120000.

CONTRIBUTIONS TO POLITICAL ECONOMY. see *BUSINESS AND ECONOMICS — Economic Situation And Conditions*

320   CK   ISSN 0120-4165
CONTROVERSIA. 1972. irreg. Col.$8000($50) Centro de Investigacion y Educacion Popular, Carrera 5, No.33A-08, Apdo. Aereo 25916, Bogota, Colombia. TEL 2858977. Ed. Alejandro Angulo. stat.; circ. 2,000. (also avail. in microfiche)
 Formerly (until 1975): Anali C I A S.

320   BL   ISSN 0102-2636
CONVIVIUM; investigacao e cultura. 1961. bi-m. $30. Sociedade Brasileira de Cultura, Alameda Eduardo Prado 705, C.P. 30004, 01218 Sao Paulo, Brazil. Ed. Gumercindo Rocha Dorea. adv.; bk.rev.; bibl.; circ. 3,500. **Indexed:** Hisp.Amer.Per.Ind, Phil.Ind.
 Description: Political philosophy and cultural problems of Brazil.

320   US
COOK POLITICAL REPORT. 1984. 12/yr. $295. Cook and Company, 900 Second St., N.E., Ste. 107, Washington, DC 20002. TEL 202-289-1625. FAX 202-289-0454. Ed. Charles E. Cook, Jr. circ. 800.
 ●Also available online.
 Formerly: National Political Review.
 Description: Bi-partisan analysis of congressional, gubernatorial and presidential elections as well as political trends.

320 910.09   IT
CORRIERE DEL MEZZOGIORNO; Giornale indipendente di informazioni. (Text in English, French, German, Spanish) 1967. w. L.300000($215) Via Ascoli, 43-M (Villa Cotti), Casella Postale 33, 71100 Foggia, Italy. TEL 0881-618009. Ed. Conte Lorenzo Vittorio Vasco. adv.; illus.; charts; circ. 7,000.

329.9   IT
CORRIERE DELL'ADDA. 1860. fortn. L.10000($10) Partito Liberale Italiano, Sezione di Lodi, Corso V. Emanuele 21, 20075 Lodi, Italy. Ed. Vitaliano Peduzzi. adv.; bk.rev.; film rev.; play rev.; circ. 4,000. (tabloid format; back issues avail.)

320.531   IT   ISSN 0010-9304
CORRISPONDENZA SOCIALISTA. vol.8, 1967. m. Via Virgilio 1-L, 00193 Rome, Italy. Ed. Giorgio Verdecchi. adv.; illus.

322.4   IT
COSCIENZA DEL CITTADINO. w. Via Madonna di Loreto 4, 00015 Monterotondo, Rome, Italy. Ed. Domenico Moreschi.

251 320 301   IT
COSTAROSSA; rivista subalpina di studi politici e sociali. 1973. q. L.4000. Circulo Culturale Costa Rossa, Via Roma 55, Cuneo, Italy. Ed. Sergio Fenoglio. adv.; bk.rev.; illus.; circ. 2,500.

338   FR   ISSN 0252-0958
D1050
COUNCIL OF EUROPE FORUM. French edition (ISSN 0251-320X); German edition (ISSN 0252-0966) (Editions in English, French, German, Italian) 1959-19??; N.S. 1990. 4/yr. 80 F. Council of Europe, Publications Section, B.P. 431 R6, F-67006 Strasbourg Cedex, France. TEL 88-41-20-00. FAX 88-41-27-81. TELEX 870 943 EUR F. (Subscr. to: Societe Mereau, 27 rue de Rome, 75008 Paris, France; Dist. in U.S. by: Manhattan Publishing Co., Box 650, Croton-on-Hudson, N.Y. 10520) Ed. Gustaves Berntgen. bk.rev.; circ. 120,000. **Indexed:** Excerp.Med.
 —BLDSC shelfmark: 4024.083600.
 Supersedes (since 1977, no. 32): Education and Culture (ISSN 0013-1229); Forward in Europe (ISSN 0015-8631)
 Description: Provides detailed information on the Council of Europe's activities.

320   US   ISSN 0196-2809
G1
COUNTRIES OF THE WORLD AND THEIR LEADERS YEARBOOK. (In 2 vols.) 1974. irreg., latest 1991. $155 (supplement $75). Gale Research Inc., 835 Penobscot Bldg., Detroit, MI 48226. TEL 313-961-2242. FAX 313-961-6083. TELEX 810-221-7086. Ed. Frank E. Bair.
 —BLDSC shelfmark: 3481.520000.
 Formerly: Countries of the World.
 Description: Annual reference on countries worldwide with a guide to their leadership.

POLITICAL SCIENCE 3883

332 382   US   ISSN 1041-3553
HC10
COUNTRY FORECASTS. 1985. s-a. $495. Political Risk Services (Subsidiary of: I B C USA (Publications), Inc.), Box 6482, Syracuse, NY 13217-6482. TEL 315-472-1224. FAX 315-472-1235. Eds. William D. Coplin, Michael K. O'Leary. (also avail. on diskette)
●Also available online. Vendor(s): Data-Star, DIALOG, NewsNet.
   Incorporates (1981-1988): Political Climate for International Business (ISSN 0887-7637); (1986-1988): Political Risk Database (ISSN 0890-4928); (1986-1988): Country Database (ISSN 0890-4952) Former titles (until 1988): Country Facts (ISSN 0889-5007); Country Data Quarterly.
   Description: Contains rankings and data for 85 countries on political, economic, and social variables; methods of data-gathering and forecasting; and assumptions underlying the forecasts.

320 330.9   UK   ISSN 0269-6053
COUNTRY PROFILE. ALGERIA; annual survey of political and economic background. 1952. a. £50($95) (Economist Intelligence Unit) Business International Ltd., 40 Duke St., London W1A 1DW, England. TEL 71-493-6711. FAX 71-449-9767. TELEX 266353 EIUG. (US addr.: Business International Corp., 215 Park Ave. S., New York, NY 10003. TEL 212-460-0600)
—BLDSC shelfmark: 3481.893010.

320 330.9   UK   ISSN 0269-7092
COUNTRY PROFILE. ANGOLA, SAO TOME & PRINCIPE; annual survey of political and economic background. 1952. a. £50($95) (Economist Intelligence Unit) Business International Ltd., 40 Duke St., London W1A 1DW, England. TEL 71-493-6711. FAX 71-449-9767. TELEX 266353 EIUG. (US addr.: Business International Corp., 215 Park Ave. S., New York, NY 10003. TEL 212-460-0600)

320 330.9   UK   ISSN 0269-4468
COUNTRY PROFILE. ARGENTINA; annual survey of political and economic background. 1952. a. £50($95) (Economist Intelligence Unit) Business International Ltd., 40 Duke St., London W1A 1DW, England. TEL 71-493-6711. FAX 71-449-9767. TELEX 266353 EIUG. (US addr.: Business International Corp., 215 Park Ave. S., New York, NY 10003. TEL 212-460-0600)

320 330.9   UK   ISSN 0269-4476
COUNTRY PROFILE. AUSTRALIA; annual survey of political and economic background. 1952. a. £50($95) (Economist Intelligence Unit) Business International Ltd., 40 Duke St., London W1A 1DW, England. TEL 71-493-6711. FAX 71-449-9767. TELEX 266353 EIUG. (US addr.: Business International Corp., 215 Park Ave. S., New York, NY 10003. TEL 212-460-0600)

320 330.9   UK   ISSN 0269-4484
HC261
COUNTRY PROFILE. AUSTRIA; annual survey of political and economic background. 1952. a. £50($95) (Economist Intelligence Unit) Business International Ltd., 40 Duke St., London W1A 1DW, England. TEL 71-493-6711. FAX 71-449-9767. TELEX 266353 EIUG. (US addr.: Business International Corp., 215 Park Ave. S., New York, NY 10003. TEL 212-460-0600)

320 330.9   UK   ISSN 0269-7335
COUNTRY PROFILE. BAHRAIN, QATAR; annual survey of political and economic background. 1952. a. £50($95) (Economist Intelligence Unit) Business International Ltd., 40 Duke St., London W1A 1DW, England. TEL 71-493-6711. FAX 71-449-9767. TELEX 266353 EIUG. (US addr.: Business International Corp., 215 Park Ave. S., New York, NY 10003. TEL 212-460-0600)

320 330.9   UK   ISSN 0269-8145
COUNTRY PROFILE. BANGLADESH; annual survey of political and economic background. 1952. a. £50($95) (Economist Intelligence Unit) Business International Ltd., 40 Duke St., London W1A 1DW, England. TEL 71-493-6711. FAX 71-449-9767. TELEX 266353 EIUG. (US addr.: Business International Ltd., 215 Park Ave. S., New York, NY 10003. TEL 212-460-0600)

320 330.9   UK   ISSN 0269-4352
HC311
COUNTRY PROFILE. BELGIUM, LUXEMBOURG; annual survey of political and economic background. 1952. a. £50($95) (Economist Intelligence Unit) Business International Ltd., 40 Duke St., London W1A 1DW, England. TEL 71-493-6711. FAX 71-449-9767. TELEX 266353 EIUG. (US addr.: Business International Corp., 215 Park Ave. S., New York, NY 10003. TEL 212-460-0600)
—BLDSC shelfmark: 3481.893290.

320 330.9   UK   ISSN 0269-4514
COUNTRY PROFILE. BELIZE, BAHAMAS, BERMUDA; annual survey of political and economic background. 1952. a. £50($95) (Economist Intelligence Unit) Business International Ltd., 40 Duke St., London W1A 1DW, England. TEL 71-493-6711. FAX 71-449-9767. TELEX 266353 EIUG. (US addr.: Business International Corp., 215 Park Ave. S., New York, NY 10003. TEL 212-460-0600)

320 330.9   UK   ISSN 0269-5952
COUNTRY PROFILE. BOLIVIA; annual survey of political and economic background. 1952. a. £50($95) (Economist Intelligence Unit) Business International Ltd., 40 Duke St., London W1A 1DW, England. TEL 71-493-6711. FAX 71-449-9767. TELEX 266353 EIUG. (US addr.: Business International Corp., 215 Park Ave. S., New York, NY 10003. TEL 212-460-0600)
—BLDSC shelfmark: 3481.893315.

320 330.9   UK   ISSN 0269-7394
COUNTRY PROFILE. BOTSWANA, LESOTHO, SWAZILAND; annual survey of political and economic background. 1952. a. £50($95) (Economist Intelligence Unit) Business International Ltd., 40 Duke St., London W1A 1DW, England. TEL 71-493-6711. FAX 71-449-9767. TELEX 266353 EIUG. (US addr.: Business International Corp., 215 Park Ave. S., New York, NY 10003. TEL 212-460-0600)
—BLDSC shelfmark: 3481.893320.

320 330.9   UK   ISSN 0269-4492
COUNTRY PROFILE. BRAZIL; annual survey of political and economic background. 1952. a. £50($95) (Economist Intelligence Unit) Business International Ltd., 40 Duke St., London W1A 1DW, England. TEL 71-493-6711. FAX 71-449-9767. TELEX 266353 EIUG. (US addr.: Business International Corp., 215 Park Ave. S., New York, NY 10003. TEL 212-460-0600)
—BLDSC shelfmark: 3481.893330.

320 330.9   UK   ISSN 0269-6398
HC403.A1
COUNTRY PROFILE. BULGARIA, ALBANIA; annual survey of political and economic background. 1952. a. £50($95) (Economist Intelligence Unit) Business International Ltd., 40 Duke St., London W1A 1DW, England. TEL 71-493-6711. FAX 71-449-9767. TELEX 266353 EIUG. (US addr.: Business International Corp., 215 Park Ave. S., New York, NY 10003. TEL 212-460-0600)

320 330.9   UK   ISSN 0269-7963
COUNTRY PROFILE. CAMEROON, CENTRAL AFRICAN REPUBLIC, CHAD; annual survey of political and economic background. 1952. a. £50($95) (Economist Intelligence Unit) Business International Ltd., 40 Duke St., London W1A 1DW, England. TEL 71-493-6711. FAX 71-449-9767. TELEX 266353 EIUG. (US addr.: Business International Corp., 215 Park Ave. S., New York, NY 10003. TEL 212-460-0600)
—BLDSC shelfmark: 3481.893370.

320 330.9   UK   ISSN 0269-4379
COUNTRY PROFILE. CANADA; annual survey of political and economic background. 1952. a. £50($95) (Economist Intelligence Unit) Business International Ltd., 40 Duke St., London W1A 1DW, England. TEL 71-493-6711. FAX 71-449-9767. TELEX 266353 EIUG. (US addr.: Business International Corp., 215 Park Ave. S., New York, NY 10003. TEL 212-460-0600)
—BLDSC shelfmark: 3481.893410.

320 330.9   UK   ISSN 0269-5081
COUNTRY PROFILE. CHILE; annual survey of political and economic background. 1952. a. £50($95) (Economist Intelligence Unit) Business International Ltd., 40 Duke St., London W1A 1DW, England. TEL 71-493-6711. FAX 71-449-9767. TELEX 266353 EIUG. (US addr.: Business International Corp., 215 Park Ave. S., New York, NY 10003. TEL 212-460-0600)

320 330.9   UK   ISSN 0269-509X
COUNTRY PROFILE. CHINA, NORTH KOREA; annual survey of political and economic background. 1952. a. £50($95) (Economist Intelligence Unit) Business International Ltd., 40 Duke St., London W1A 1DW, England. TEL 71-493-6711. FAX 71-449-9767. TELEX 266353 EIUG. (US addr.: Business International Corp., 215 Park Ave. S., New York, NY 10003. TEL 212-460-0600)

320 330.9   UK   ISSN 0269-5103
HC196
COUNTRY PROFILE. COLOMBIA; annual survey of political and economic background. 1952. a. £50($95) (Economist Intelligence Unit) Business International Ltd., 40 Duke St., London W1A 1DW, England. TEL 71-493-6711. FAX 71-449-9767. TELEX 266353 EIUG. (US addr.: Business International Corp., 215 Park Ave. S., New York, NY 10003. TEL 212-460-0600)

320 330.9   UK
COUNTRY PROFILE. COMMONWEALTH OF INDEPENDENT STATES; annual survey of political and economic background. 1952. a. £50($95) (Economist Intelligence Unit) Business International Ltd., 40 Duke St., London W1A 1DW, England. TEL 71-493-6711. FAX 71-449-9767. TELEX 266353 EIUG. (US addr.: Business International Corp., 215 Park Ave. S., New York, NY 10003. TEL 212-460-0600)
   Formerly (until 1991): Country Profile. U S S R.

320 330.9   UK   ISSN 0269-6363
HC980.A1
COUNTRY PROFILE. CONGO; annual survey of political and economic background. 1952. a. £50($95) (Economist Intelligence Unit) Business International Ltd., 40 Duke St., London W1A 1DW, England. TEL 71-493-6711. FAX 71-449-9767. TELEX 266353 EIUG. (US addr.: Business International Corp., 215 Park Ave. S., New York, NY 10003. TEL 212-460-0600)

320 330.9   UK   ISSN 0269-7068
COUNTRY PROFILE. COTE D'IVOIRE; annual survey of political and economic background. 1952. a. £50($95) (Economist Intelligence Unit) Business International Ltd., 40 Duke St., London W1A 1DW, England. TEL 71-493-6711. FAX 71-449-9767. TELEX 266353 EIUG. (US addr.: Business International Corp., 215 Park Ave. S., New York, NY 10003. TEL 212-460-0600)

320 330.9   UK   ISSN 0269-5111
HC152.5.A1
COUNTRY PROFILE. CUBA; annual survey of political and economic background. 1952. a. £50($95) (Economist Intelligence Unit) Business International Ltd., 40 Duke St., London W1A 1DW, England. TEL 71-493-6711. FAX 71-449-9767. TELEX 266353 EIUG. (US addr.: Business International Corp., 215 Park Ave. S., New York, NY 10003. TEL 212-460-0600)
—BLDSC shelfmark: 3481.893610.

320 330.9   UK   ISSN 0269-8048
COUNTRY PROFILE. CZECHOSLOVAKIA; annual survey of political and economic background. 1952. a. £50($95) (Economist Intelligence Unit) Business International Ltd., 40 Duke St., London W1A 1DW, England. TEL 71-493-6711. FAX 71-449-9767. TELEX 266353 EIUG. (US addr.: Business International Corp., 215 Park Ave. S., New York, NY 10003. TEL 212-460-0600)

320 330.9   UK   ISSN 0269-5138
COUNTRY PROFILE. DENMARK, ICELAND; annual survey of political and economic background. 1952. a. £50($95) (Economist Intelligence Unit) Business International Ltd., 40 Duke St., London W1A 1DW, England. TEL 71-493-6711. FAX 71-449-9767. TELEX 266353 EIUG. (US addr.: Business International Corp., 215 Park Ave. S., New York, NY 10003. TEL 212-460-0600)

POLITICAL SCIENCE

320 330.9   UK   ISSN 0269-512X
HC153.5.A1
COUNTRY PROFILE. DOMINICAN REPUBLIC, HAITI, PUERTO RICO; annual survey of political and economic background. 1952. a. £50($95) (Economist Intelligence Unit) Business International Ltd., 40 Duke St., London W1A 1DW, England. TEL 71-493-6711. FAX 71-449-9767. TELEX 266353 EIUG. (US addr.: Business International Corp., 215 Park Ave. S., New York, NY 10003. TEL 212-460-0600)
—BLDSC shelfmark: 3481.893710.

320 330.9   UK   ISSN 0269-7971
COUNTRY PROFILE. ECUADOR; annual survey of political and economic background. 1952. a. £50($95) (Economist Intelligence Unit) Business International Ltd., 40 Duke St., London W1A 1DW, England. TEL 71-493-6711. FAX 71-449-9767. TELEX 266353 EIUG. (US addr.: Business International Corp., 215 Park Ave. S., New York, NY 10003. TEL 212-460-0600)

320 330.9   UK   ISSN 0269-5227
HC830.A1
COUNTRY PROFILE. EGYPT; annual survey of political and economic background. 1952. a. £50($95) (Economist Intelligence Unit) Business International Ltd., 40 Duke St., London W1A 1DW, England. TEL 71-493-6711. FAX 71-449-9767. TELEX 266353 EIUG. (US addr.: Business International Corp., 215 Park Ave. S., New York, NY 10003. TEL 212-460-0600)
—BLDSC shelfmark: 3481.893810.

320 330.9   UK   ISSN 0269-7084
COUNTRY PROFILE. ETHIOPIA, SOMALIA, DJIBOUTI; annual survey of political and economic background. 1952. a. £50($95) (Economist Intelligence Unit) Business International Ltd., 40 Duke St., London W1A 1DW, England. TEL 71-493-6711. FAX 71-449-9767. TELEX 266353 EIUG. (US addr.: Business International Corp., 215 Park Ave. S., New York, NY 10003. TEL 212-460-0600)
—BLDSC shelfmark: 3481.893830.

320 330.9   UK   ISSN 0269-5332
HC340.2.A1
COUNTRY PROFILE. FINLAND; annual survey of political and economic background. 1952. a. £50($95) (Economist Intelligence Unit) Business International Ltd., 40 Duke St., London W1A 1DW, England. TEL 71-493-6711. FAX 71-449-9767. TELEX 266353 EIUG. (US addr.: Business International Corp., 215 Park Ave. S., New York, NY 10003. TEL 212-460-0600)
—BLDSC shelfmark: 3481.893850.

320 330.9   UK   ISSN 0269-5340
HC271
COUNTRY PROFILE. FRANCE; annual survey of political and economic background. 1952. a. £50($95) (Economist Intelligence Unit) Business International Ltd., 40 Duke St., London W1A 1DW, England. TEL 71-493-6711. FAX 71-449-9767. TELEX 266353 EIUG. (US addr.: Business International Corp., 215 Park Ave. S., New York, NY 10003. TEL 212-460-0600)

320 330.9   UK   ISSN 0269-6371
HC975.A1
COUNTRY PROFILE. GABON, EQUATORIAL GUINEA; annual survey of political and economic background. 1952. a. £50($95) (Economist Intelligence Unit) Business International Ltd., 40 Duke St., London W1A 1DW, England. TEL 71-493-6711. FAX 71-449-9767. TELEX 266353 EIUG. (US addr.: Business International Corp., 215 Park Ave. S., New York, NY 10003. TEL 212-460-0600)

320 330.9   UK   ISSN 0264-4495
COUNTRY PROFILE. GERMANY; annual survey of political and economic background. 1952. q. £50($95) (Economist Intelligence Unit) Business International Ltd., 40 Duke St., London W1A 1DW, England. TEL 71-493-6711. FAX 71-449-9767. TELEX 266353 EIUG. (US addr.: Business International Corp., 215 Park Ave. S., New York, NY 10003. TEL 212-460-0600)

320 330.9   UK   ISSN 0269-4549
COUNTRY PROFILE. GHANA; annual survey of political and economic background. 1952. a. £50($95) (Economist Intelligence Unit) Business International Ltd., 40 Duke St., London W1A 1DW, England. TEL 71-493-6711. FAX 71-449-9767. TELEX 266353 EIUG. (US addr.: Business International Corp., 215 Park Ave. S., New York, NY 10003. TEL 212-460-0600)

320 330.9   UK   ISSN 0269-5367
COUNTRY PROFILE. GREECE; annual survey of political and economic background. 1952. a. £50($95) (Economist Intelligence Unit) Business International Ltd., 40 Duke St., London W1A 1DW, England. TEL 71-493-6711. FAX 71-449-9767. TELEX 266353 EIUG. (US addr.: Business International Corp., 215 Park Ave. S., New York, NY 10003. TEL 212-460-0600)
—BLDSC shelfmark: 3481.893970.

320 330.9   UK   ISSN 0269-4387
COUNTRY PROFILE. GUATEMALA, EL SALVADOR, HONDURAS; annual survey of political and economic background. 1952. a. £50($95) (Economist Intelligence Unit) Business International Ltd., 40 Duke St., London W1A 1DW, England. TEL 71-493-6711. FAX 71-449-9767. TELEX 266353 EIUG. (US addr.: Business International Corp., 215 Park Ave. S., New York, NY 10003. TEL 212-460-0600)
—BLDSC shelfmark: 3481.894010.

320 330.9   UK   ISSN 0269-4417
COUNTRY PROFILE. GUINEA, MALI, MAURITANIA; annual survey of political and economic background. 1952. a. £50($95) (Economist Intelligence Unit) Business International Ltd., 40 Duke St., London W1A 1DW, England. TEL 71-493-6711. FAX 71-449-9767. TELEX 266353 EIUG. (US addr.: Business International Corp., 215 Park Ave. S., New York, NY 10003. TEL 212-460-0600)

320 330.9   UK   ISSN 0269-8110
HC206
COUNTRY PROFILE. GUYANA, BARBADOS, WINDWARD & LEEWARD ISLANDS; annual survey of political and economic background. 1952. a. £50($95) (Economist Intelligence Unit) Business International Ltd., 40 Duke St., London W1A 1DW, England. TEL 71-493-6711. FAX 71-449-9767. TELEX 266353 EIUG. (US addr.: Business International Corp., 215 Park Ave. S., New York, NY 10003. TEL 212-460-0600)

320 330.9   UK   ISSN 0269-7319
COUNTRY PROFILE. HONG KONG, MACAU; annual survey of political and economic background. 1952. a. £50($95) (Economist Intelligence Unit) Business International Ltd., 40 Duke St., London W1A 1DW, England. TEL 71-493-6711. FAX 71-449-9767. TELEX 266353 EIUG. (US addr.: Business International Corp., 215 Park Ave. S., New York, NY 10003. TEL 212-460-0600)
—BLDSC shelfmark: 3481.894090.

320 330.9   UK
COUNTRY PROFILE. HUNGARY; annual survey of political and economic background. 1952. a. £50($95) (Economist Intelligence Unit) Business International Ltd., 40 Duke St., London W1A 1DW, England. TEL 71-493-6711. FAX 71-449-9767. TELEX 266353 EIUG. (US addr.: Business International Corp., 215 Park Ave. S., New York, NY 10003. TEL 212-460-0600)

320 330.9   UK   ISSN 0269-5359
HC435.2.A1
COUNTRY PROFILE. INDIA, NEPAL; annual survey of political and economic background. 1952. a. £50($95) (Economist Intelligence Unit) Business International Ltd., 40 Duke St., London W1A 1DW, England. TEL 71-493-6711. FAX 71-449-9767. TELEX 266353 EIUG. (US addr.: Business International Corp., 215 Park Ave. S., New York, NY 10003. TEL 212-460-0600)
—BLDSC shelfmark: 3481.894170.

320 330.9   UK   ISSN 0269-6622
COUNTRY PROFILE. INDOCHINA: VIETNAM, LAOS, CAMBODIA; annual survey of political and economic background. 1952. a. £50($95) (Economist Intelligence Unit) Business International Ltd., 40 Duke St., London W1A 1DW, England. TEL 71-493-6711. FAX 71-449-9767. TELEX 266353 EIUG. (US addr.: Business International Corp., 215 Park Ave. S., New York, NY 10003. TEL 212-460-0600)
—BLDSC shelfmark: 3481.894190.

320 330.9   UK   ISSN 0269-5375
COUNTRY PROFILE. INDONESIA; annual survey of political and economic background. 1952. a. £50($95) (Economist Intelligence Unit) Business International Ltd., 40 Duke St., London W1A 1DW, England. TEL 71-493-6711. FAX 71-449-9767. TELEX 266353 EIUG. (US addr.: Business International Corp., 215 Park Ave. S., New York, NY 10003. TEL 212-460-0600)
—BLDSC shelfmark: 3481.894210.

320 330.9   UK   ISSN 0269-5960
COUNTRY PROFILE. IRAN; annual survey of political and economic background. 1952. a. £50($95) (Economist Intelligence Unit) Business International Ltd., 40 Duke St., London W1A 1DW, England. TEL 71-493-6711. FAX 71-499-9767. TELEX 266353 EIUG. (US addr.: Business International Corp., 215 Park Ave. S., New York, NY 10003. TEL 212-460-0600)

320 330.9   UK   ISSN 0269-4395
COUNTRY PROFILE. IRAQ; annual survey of political and economic background. 1952. a. £50($95) (Economist Intelligence Unit) Business International Ltd., 40 Duke St., London W1A 1DW, England. TEL 71-493-6711. FAX 71-449-9767. TELEX 266353 EIUG. (US addr.: Business International Corp., 215 Park Ave. S., New York, NY 10003. TEL 212-460-0600)

320 330.9   UK   ISSN 0269-5324
COUNTRY PROFILE. IRELAND; annual survey of political and economic background. 1952. a. £50($95) (Economist Intelligence Unit) Business International Ltd., 40 Duke St., London W1A 1DW, England. TEL 71-493-6711. FAX 71-449-9767. TELEX 266353 EIUG. (US addr.: Business International Corp., 215 Park Ave. S., New York, NY 10003. TEL 212-460-0600)

320 330.9   UK   ISSN 0269-5383
COUNTRY PROFILE. ISRAEL; annual survey of political and economic background. 1952. a. £50($95) (Economist Intelligence Unit) Business International Ltd., 40 Duke St., London W1A 1DW, England. TEL 71-493-6711. FAX 71-449-9767. TELEX 266353 EIUG. (US addr.: Business International Corp., 215 Park Ave. S., New York, NY 10003. TEL 212-460-0600)

320 330.9   UK   ISSN 0269-5391
HC301
COUNTRY PROFILE. ITALY; annual survey of political and economic background. 1952. a. £50($95) (Economist Intelligence Unit) Business International Ltd., 40 Duke St., London W1A 1DW, England. TEL 71-493-6711. FAX 71-449-9767. TELEX 266353 EIUG. (US addr.: Business International Corp., 215 Park Ave. S., New York, NY 10003. TEL 212-460-0600)
—BLDSC shelfmark: 3481.894410.

320 330.9   UK   ISSN 0269-4506
COUNTRY PROFILE. JAMAICA; annual survey of political and economic background. 1952. a. £50($95) (Economist Intelligence Unit) Business International Ltd., 40 Duke St., London W1A 1DW, England. TEL 71-493-6711. FAX 71-449-9767. TELEX 266353 EIUG. (US addr.: Business International Corp., 215 Park Ave. S., New York, NY 100003. TEL 212-460-0600)

320 330.9   UK   ISSN 0269-5405
COUNTRY PROFILE. JAPAN; annual survey of political and economic background. 1952. a. £50($95) (Economist Intelligence Unit) Business International Ltd., 40 Duke St., London W1A 1DW, England. TEL 71-493-6711. FAX 71-449-9767. TELEX 266353 EIUG. (US addr.: Business International Corp., 215 Park Ave. S., New York, NY 10003. TEL 212-460-0600)

POLITICAL SCIENCE 3885

320 330.9 UK ISSN 0269-8072
COUNTRY PROFILE. JORDAN; annual survey of political and economic background. 1952. a. £50($95) (Economist Intelligence Unit) Business International Ltd., 40 Duke St., London W1A 1DW, England. TEL 71-493-6711. FAX 71-449-9767. TELEX 266353 EIUG. (US addr.: Business International Corp., 215 Park Ave. S., New York, NY 10003. TEL 212-460-0600)
—BLDSC shelfmark: 3481.894570.

320 330.9 UK ISSN 0269-4530
HC865.A1
COUNTRY PROFILE. KENYA; annual survey of political and economic background. 1952. q. £50($95) (Economist Intelligence Unit) Business International Ltd., 40 Duke St., London W1A 1DW, England. TEL 71-493-6711. FAX 71-449-9767. TELEX 266353 EIUG. (US addr.: Business International Corp., 215 Park Ave. S., New York, NY 10003. TEL 212-460-0600)

320 330.9 UK ISSN 0269-7327
COUNTRY PROFILE. KUWAIT; annual survey of political and economic background. 1952. a. £50($95) (Economist Intelligence Unit) Business International Ltd., 40 Duke St., London W1A 1DW, England. TEL 71-493-6711. FAX 71-449-9767. TELEX 266353 EIUG. (US addr.: Business International Corp., 215 Park Ave. S., New York, NY 10003. TEL 212-460-0600)
—BLDSC shelfmark: 3481.894690.

320 330.9 UK ISSN 0269-7351
COUNTRY PROFILE. LEBANON, CYPRUS; annual survey of political and economic background. 1952. a. £50($95) (Economist Intelligence Unit) Business International Ltd., 40 Duke St., London W1A 1DW, England. TEL 71-493-6711. FAX 71-449-9767. TELEX 266353 EIUG. (US addr.: Business International Corp., 215 Park Ave. S., New York, NY 10003. TEL 212-460-0600)

320 330.9 UK ISSN 0269-6347
COUNTRY PROFILE. LIBYA; annual survey of political and economic background. 1952. a. £50($95) (Economist Intelligence Unit) Business International Ltd., 40 Duke St., London W1A 1DW, England. TEL 71-493-6711. FAX 71-449-9767. TELEX 266353 EIUG. (US addr.: Business International Corp., 215 Park Ave. S., New York, NY 10003. TEL 212-460-0600)

320 330.9 UK ISSN 0269-736X
COUNTRY PROFILE. MADAGASCAR, COMOROS; annual survey of political and economic background. 1952. a. £50($95) (Economist Intelligence Unit) Business International Ltd., 40 Duke St., London W1A 1DW, England. TEL 71-493-6711. FAX 71-449-9767. TELEX 266353 EIUG. (US addr.: Business International Corp., 215 Park Ave. S., New York, NY 10003. TEL 212-460-0600)
—BLDSC shelfmark: 3481.894810.

320 330.9 UK ISSN 0269-4522
HC935.A1
COUNTRY PROFILE. MALAWI; annual survey of political and economic background. 1952. a. £50($95) (Economist Intelligence Unit) Business International Ltd., 40 Duke St., London W1A 1DW, England. TEL 71-493-6711. FAX 71-449-9767. TELEX 66353 EIUG. (US addr.: Business International Corp., 215 Park Ave. S., New York, NY 10003. TEL 212-460-0600)
—BLDSC shelfmark: 3481.894830.

320 330.9 UK ISSN 0269-5588
HC445.5.A1
COUNTRY PROFILE. MALAYSIA, BRUNEI; annual survey of political and economic background. 1952. a. £50($95) (Economist Intelligence Unit) Business International Ltd., 40 Duke St., London W1A 1DW, England. TEL 71-493-6711. FAX 71-449-9767. TELEX 266353 EIUG. (US addr.: Business International Corp., 215 Park Ave. S., New York, NY 10003. TEL 212-460-0600)
—BLDSC shelfmark: 3481.894850.

320 330.9 UK ISSN 0269-8137
COUNTRY PROFILE. MALTA; annual survey of political and economic background. 1952. a. £50($95) (Economist Intelligence Unit) Business International Ltd., 40 Duke St., London W1A 1DW, England. TEL 71-493-6711. FAX 71-449-9767. TELEX 266353 EIUG. (US addr.: Business International Corp., 215 Park Ave. S., New York, NY 10003. TEL 212-460-0600)
—BLDSC shelfmark: 3481.894860.

320 330.9 UK ISSN 0269-7378
COUNTRY PROFILE. MAURITIUS, SEYCHELLES; annual survey of political and economic background. 1952. a. £50($95) (Economist Intelligence Unit) Business International Ltd., 40 Duke St., London W1A 1DW, England. TEL 71-493-6711. FAX 71-449-9767. TELEX 266353 EIUG. (US addr.: Business International Corp., 215 Park Ave. S., New York, NY 10003. TEL 212-460-0600)
—BLDSC shelfmark: 3481.894870.

320 330.9 UK ISSN 0269-5596
COUNTRY PROFILE. MEXICO; annual survey of political and economic background. 1952. a. £50($95) (Economist Intelligence Unit) Business International Ltd., 40 Duke St., London W1A 1DW, England. TEL 71-493-6711. FAX 71-449-9767. TELEX 266353 EIUG. (US addr.: Business International Corp., 215 Park Ave. S., New York, NY 10003. TEL 212-460-0600)

320 330.9 UK ISSN 0269-6614
COUNTRY PROFILE. MOROCCO; annual survey of political and economic background. 1952. a. £50($95) (Economist Intelligence Unit) Business International Ltd., 40 Duke St., London W1A 1DW, England. TEL 71-493-6711. FAX 71-449-9767. TELEX 266353 EIUG. (US addr.: Business International Corp., 215 Park Ave. S., New York, NY 10003. TEL 212-460-0600)

320 330.9 UK ISSN 0269-7017
COUNTRY PROFILE. MOZAMBIQUE; annual survey of political and economic background. 1952. a. £50($95) (Economist Intelligence Unit) Business International Ltd., 40 Duke St., London W1A 1DW, England. TEL 71-493-6711. FAX 71-449-9767. TELEX 266353 EIUG. (US addr.: Business International Corp., 215 Park Ave. S., New York, NY 10003. TEL 212-460-0600)

320 330.9 UK ISSN 0269-7386
COUNTRY PROFILE. NAMIBIA; annual survey of political and economic background. 1952. a. £50($95) (Economist Intelligence Unit) Business International Ltd., 40 Duke St., London W1A 1DW, England. TEL 71-493-6711. FAX 71-449-9767. TELEX 266353 EIUG. (US addr.: Business International Corp., 215 Park Ave. S., New York, NY 10003. TEL 212-460-0600)

320 330.9 UK ISSN 0264-4886
COUNTRY PROFILE. NETHERLANDS; annual survey of political and economic background. 1952. a. £50($95) (Economist Intelligence Unit) Business International Ltd., 40 Duke St., London W1A 1DW, England. TEL 71-493-6711. FAX 71-449-9767. TELEX 266353 EIUG. (US addr.: Business International Corp., 215 Park Ave. S., New York, NY 10003. TEL 212-460-0600)

320 330.9 UK ISSN 0269-5618
COUNTRY PROFILE. NEW ZEALAND; annual survey of political and economic background. 1952. a. £50($95) (Economist Intelligence Unit) Business International Ltd., 40 Duke St., London W1A 1DW, England. TEL 71-493-6711. FAX 71-449-9767. TELEX 266353 EIUG. (US addr.: Business International Corp., 215 Park Ave. S., New York, NY 10003. TEL 212-460-0600)

320 330.9 UK ISSN 0269-4409
COUNTRY PROFILE. NICARAGUA, COSTA RICA, PANAMA; annual survey of political and economic background. 1952. a. £50($95) (Economist Intelligence Unit) Business International Ltd., 40 Duke St., London W1A 1DW, England. TEL 71-493-6711. FAX 71-449-9767. TELEX 266353 EIUG. (US addr.: Business International Corp., 215 Park Ave. S., New York, NY 10003. TEL 212-460-0600)

320 330.9 UK ISSN 0269-8064
HC1020.A1
COUNTRY PROFILE. NIGER, BURKINA FASO; annual survey of political and economic background. 1952. a. £50($95) (Economist Intelligence Unit) Business International Ltd., 40 Duke St., London W1A 1DW, England. TEL 71-493-6711. FAX 71-449-9767. TELEX 266353 EIUG. (US addr.: Business International Corp., 215 Park Ave. S., New York, NY 10003. TEL 212-460-0600)
—BLDSC shelfmark: 3481.895110.

320 330.9 UK ISSN 0269-6339
HC1055.A1
COUNTRY PROFILE. NIGERIA; annual survey of political and economic background. 1952. a. £50($95) (Economist Intelligence Unit) Business International Ltd., 40 Duke St., London W1A 1DW, England. TEL 71-493-6711. FAX 71-449-9767. TELEX 266353 EIUG. (US addr.: Business International Corp., 215 Park Ave. S., New York, NY 10003. TEL 212-460-0600)

320 330.9 UK ISSN 0269-5626
COUNTRY PROFILE. NORWAY; annual survey of political and economic background. 1952. a. £50($95) (Economist Intelligence Unit) Business International Ltd., 40 Duke St., London W1A 1DW, England. TEL 71-493-6711. FAX 71-449-9767. TELEX 266353 EIUG. (US addr.: Business International Corp., 215 Park Ave. S., New York, NY 10003. TEL 212-460-0600)

320 330.9 UK ISSN 0269-7343
COUNTRY PROFILE. OMAN, YEMEN; annual survey of political and economic background. 1952. a. £50($95) (Economist Intelligence Unit) Business International Ltd., 40 Duke St., London W1A 1DW, England. TEL 71-493-6711. FAX 71-449-9767. TELEX 266353 EIUG. (US addr.: Business International Corp., 215 Park Ave. S., New York, NY 10003. TEL 212-460-0600)

320 330.9 UK ISSN 0269-8080
COUNTRY PROFILE. PACIFIC ISLANDS: FIJI, SOLOMON ISLANDS, WESTERN SAMOA, VANUATU, TONGA; annual survey of political and economic background. 1952. a. £50($95) (Economist Intelligence Unit) Business International Ltd., 40 Duke St., London W1A 1DW, England. TEL 71-493-6711. FAX 71-449-9767. TELEX 266353 EIUG. (US addr.: Business International Corp., 215 Park Ave. S., New York, NY 10003. TEL 212-460-0600)

320 330.9 UK ISSN 0269-5634
COUNTRY PROFILE. PAKISTAN, AFGHANISTAN; annual survey of political and economic background. 1952. a. £50($95) (Economist Intelligence Unit) Business International Ltd., 40 Duke St., London W1A 1DW, England. TEL 71-493-6711. FAX 71-449-9767. TELEX 266353 EIUG. (US addr.: Business International Corp., 215 Park Ave. S., New York, NY 10003. TEL 212-460-0600)
—BLDSC shelfmark: 3481.895250.

320 330.9 UK ISSN 0269-8099
HC683.5.A1
COUNTRY PROFILE. PAPUA NEW GUINEA; annual survey of political and economic background. 1952. a. £50($95) (Economist Intelligence Unit) Business International Ltd., 40 Duke St., London W1A 1DW, England. TEL 71-493-6711. FAX 71-449-9767. TELEX 266353 EIUG. (US addr.: Business International Corp., 215 Park Ave. S., New York, NY 10003. TEL 212-460-0600)
—BLDSC shelfmark: 3481.895270.

320 330.9 UK ISSN 0269-5944
COUNTRY PROFILE. PERU; annual survey of political and economic background. 1952. a. £50($95) (Economist Intelligence Unit) Business International Ltd., 40 Duke St., London W1A 1DW, England. TEL 71-493-6711. FAX 71-449-9767. TELEX 266353 EIUG. (US addr.: Business International Corp., 215 Park Ave. S., New York, NY 10003. TEL 212-460-0600)
—BLDSC shelfmark: 3481.895290.

POLITICAL SCIENCE

320 330.9   UK   ISSN 0269-5979
COUNTRY PROFILE. PHILIPPINES; annual survey of political and economic background. 1952. a. £50($95) (Economist Intelligence Unit) Business International Ltd., 40 Duke St., London W1A 1DW, England. TEL 71-493-6711. FAX 71-449-9767. TELEX 266353 EIUG. (US addr.: Business International Corp., 215 Park Ave. S., New York, NY 10003. TEL 212-460-0600)
—BLDSC shelfmark: 3481.895330.

320 330.1   UK   ISSN 0269-5219
COUNTRY PROFILE. POLAND; annual survey of political and economic background. 1952. a. £50($95) (Economist Intelligence Unit) Business International Ltd., 40 Duke St., London W1A 1DW, England. TEL 71-493-6711. FAX 71-449-9767. TELEX 266353 EIUG. (US addr.: Business International Corp., 215 Park Ave. S., New York, NY 10003. TEL 212-460-0600)
—BLDSC shelfmark: 3481.895370.

320 330.9   UK   ISSN 0269-5987
HC391
COUNTRY PROFILE. PORTUGAL; annual survey of political and economic background. 1952. a. £50($95) (Economist Intelligence Unit) Business International Ltd., 40 Duke St., London W1A 1DW, England. TEL 71-493-6711. FAX 71-449-9767. TELEX 266353 EIUG. (US addr.: Business International Corp., 215 Park Ave. S., New York, NY 10003. TEL 212-460-0600)

320 330.9   UK   ISSN 0269-638X
COUNTRY PROFILE. ROMANIA; annual survey of political and economic background. 1952. a. £50($95) (Economist Intelligence Unit) Business International Ltd., 40 Duke St., London W1A 1DW, England. TEL 71-493-6711. FAX 71-449-9767. TELEX 266353 EIUG. (US addr.: Business International Corp., 215 Park Ave. S., New York, NY 10003. TEL 212-460-0600)

320 330.9   UK   ISSN 0269-6355
HC415.33.A1C67
COUNTRY PROFILE. SAUDI ARABIA; annual survey of political and economic background. 1952. a. £50($95) (Economist Intelligence Unit) Business International Ltd., 40 Duke St., London W1A 1DW, England. TEL 71-493-6711. FAX 71-449-9767. TELEX 266353 EIUG. (US addr.: Business International Corp., 215 Park Ave. S., New York, NY 10003. TEL 212-460-0600)
—BLDSC shelfmark: 3481.895490.

320 330.9   UK   ISSN 0269-6037
HC1045.A1
COUNTRY PROFILE. SENEGAL; annual survey of political and economic background. 1952. a. £50($95) (Economist Intelligence Unit) Business International Ltd., 40 Duke St., London W1A 1DW, England. TEL 71-493-6711. FAX 71-449-9767. TELEX 266353 EIUG. (US addr.: Business International Corp., 215 Park Ave. S., New York, NY 10003. TEL 212-460-0600)

320 330.9   UK   ISSN 0269-5057
HC1065.A1
COUNTRY PROFILE. SIERRA LEONE, LIBERIA; annual survey of political and economic background. 1952. a. £50($95) (Economist Intelligence Unit) Business International Ltd., 40 Duke St., London W1A 1DW, England. TEL 71-493-6711. FAX 71-449-9767. TELEX 266353 EIUG. (US addr.: Business International Corp., 215 Park Ave. S., New York, NY 10003. TEL 212-460-0600)

320 330.9   UK   ISSN 0269-7041
COUNTRY PROFILE. SINGAPORE; annual survey of political and economic background. 1952. a. £50($95) (Economist Intelligence Unit) Business International Ltd., 40 Duke St., London W1A 1DW, England. TEL 71-493-6711. FAX 71-449-9767. TELEX 266353 EIUG. (US addr.: Business International Corp., 215 Park Ave. S., New York, NY 10003. TEL 212-460-0600)

320 330.9   UK   ISSN 0269-8153
HC905.A1
COUNTRY PROFILE. SOUTH AFRICA; annual survey of political and economic background. 1952. a. £50($95) (Economist Intelligence Unit) Business International Ltd., 40 Duke St., London W1A 1DW, England. TEL 71-493-6711. FAX 71-449-9767. TELEX 266353 EIUG. (US addr.: Business International Corp., 215 Park Ave. S., New York, NY 10003. TEL 212-460-0600)

320 330.9   UK   ISSN 0269-7955
COUNTRY PROFILE. SOUTH KOREA; annual survey of political and economic background. 1952. a. £50($95) (Economist Intelligence Unit) Business International Ltd., 40 Duke St., London W1A 1DW, England. TEL 71-493-6711. FAX 71-449-9767. TELEX 266353 EIUG. (US addr.: Business International Corp., 215 Park Ave. S., New York, NY 10003. TEL 212-460-0600)

320 330.9   UK   ISSN 0269-5995
HC381
COUNTRY PROFILE. SPAIN; annual survey of political and economic background. 1952. a. £50($95) (Economist Intelligence Unit) Business International Ltd., 40 Duke St., London W1A 1DW, England. TEL 71-493-6711. FAX 71-449-9767. TELEX 266353 EIUG. (US addr.: Business International Corp., 215 Park Ave. S., New York, NY 10003. TEL 212-460-0600)

320 330.9   UK   ISSN 0269-5073
HC424.A1
COUNTRY PROFILE. SRI LANKA; annual survey of political and economic background. 1952. a. £50($95) (Economist Intelligence Unit) Business International Ltd., 40 Duke St., London W1A 1DW, England. TEL 71-493-6711. FAX 71-449-9767. TELEX 266353 EIUG. (US addr.: Business International Corp., 215 Park Ave. S., New York, NY 10003. TEL 212-460-0600)

320 330.9   UK   ISSN 0269-705X
COUNTRY PROFILE. SUDAN; annual survey of political and economic background. 1952. a. £50($95) (Economist Intelligence Unit) Business International Ltd., 40 Duke St., London W1A 1DW, England. TEL 71-493-6711. FAX 71-449-9767. TELEX 266353 EIUG. (US addr.: Business International Corp., 215 Park Ave. S., New York, NY 10003. TEL 212-460-0600)

320 330.9   UK   ISSN 0269-6002
COUNTRY PROFILE. SWEDEN; annual survey of political and economic background. 1952. a. £50($95) (Economist Intelligence Unit) Business International Ltd., 40 Duke St., London W1A 1DW, England. TEL 71-493-6711. FAX 71-499-9767. TELEX 266353 EIUG. (US addr.: Business International Corp., 215 Park Ave. S., New York, NY 10003. TEL 212-460-0600)

320 330.9   UK   ISSN 0269-6010
HC395
COUNTRY PROFILE. SWITZERLAND; annual survey of political and economic background. 1952. a. £50($95) (Economist Intelligence Unit) Business International Ltd., 40 Duke St., London W1A 1DW, England. TEL 71-493-6711. FAX 71-449-9767. TELEX 266353 EIUG. (US addr.: Business International Corp., 215 Park Ave. S., New York, NY 10003. TEL 212-460-0600)

320 330.9   UK   ISSN 0269-6045
HC415.23.A1
COUNTRY PROFILE. SYRIA; annual survey of political and economic background. 1952. a. £50($95) (Economist Intelligence Unit) Business International Ltd., 40 Duke St., London W1A 1DW, England. TEL 71-493-6711. FAX 71-449-9767. TELEX 266353 EIUG. (US addr.: Business International Corp., 215 Park Ave. S., New York, NY 10003. TEL 212-460-0600)

320 330.9   UK   ISSN 0269-7025
COUNTRY PROFILE. TAIWAN; annual survey of political and economic background. 1952. a. £50($95) (Economist Intelligence Unit) Business International Ltd., 40 Duke St., London W1A 1DW, England. TEL 71-493-6711. FAX 71-449-9767. TELEX 266353 EIUG. (US addr.: Business International Corp., 215 Park Ave. S., New York, NY 10003. TEL 212-460-0600)

320 330.9   UK   ISSN 0269-6630
HC885.A1
COUNTRY PROFILE. TANZANIA; annual survey of political and economic background. 1952. a. £50($95) (Economist Intelligence Unit) Business International Ltd., 40 Duke St., London W1A 1DW, England. TEL 71-493-6711. FAX 71-449-9767. TELEX 266353 EIUG. (US addr.: Business International Corp., 215 Park Ave. S., New York, NY 10003. TEL 212-460-0600)

320 330.9   UK   ISSN 0269-5065
HC445.A1
COUNTRY PROFILE. THAILAND, BURMA; annual survey of political and economic background. 1952. a. £50($95) (Economist Intelligence Unit) Business International Ltd., 40 Duke St., London W1A 1DW, England. TEL 71-493-6711. FAX 71-449-9767. TELEX 266353 EIUG. (US addr.: Business International Corp., 215 Park Ave. S., New York, NY 10003. TEL 212-460-0600)
—BLDSC shelfmark: 3481.896010.

320 330.9   UK
COUNTRY PROFILE. THE GAMBIA, GUINEA-BISSAU, CAPE VERDE; annual survey of political and economic background. 1952. a. £50($95) (Economist Intelligence Unit) Business International Ltd., 40 Duke St., London W1A 1DW, England. TEL 71-493-6711. FAX 71-449-9767. TELEX 266353 EIUG. (US addr.: Business International Corp., 215 Park Ave. S., New York, NY 10003. TEL 212-460-0600)

320 330.9   UK   ISSN 0269-8056
HC1015.A1
COUNTRY PROFILE. TOGO, BENIN; annual survey of political and economic background. 1952. a. £50($95) (Economist Intelligence Unit) Business International Ltd., 40 Duke St., London W1A 1DW, England. TEL 71-493-6711. FAX 71-449-9767. TELEX 266353 EIUG. (US addr.: Business International Corp., 215 Park Ave. S., New York, NY 10003. TEL 212-460-0600)
—BLDSC shelfmark: 3481.896050.

320 330.9   UK   ISSN 0269-8102
HC157.3
COUNTRY PROFILE. TRINIDAD & TOBAGO; annual survey of political and economic background. 1952. a. £50($95) (Economist Intelligence Unit) Business International Ltd., 40 Duke St., London W1A 1DW, England. TEL 71-493-6711. FAX 71-449-9767. TELEX 266353 EIUG. (US addr.: Business International Corp., 215 Park Ave. S., New York, NY 10003. TEL 212-460-0600)

320 330.9   UK   ISSN 0269-8129
COUNTRY PROFILE. TUNISIA; annual survey of political and economic background. 1952. a. £50($95) (Economist Intelligence Unit) Business International Ltd., 40 Duke St., London W1A 1DW, England. TEL 71-493-6711. FAX 71-449-9767. TELEX 266353 EIUG. (US addr.: Business International Corp., 215 Park Ave. S., New York, NY 10003. TEL 212-460-0600)
—BLDSC shelfmark: 3481.896130.

320 330.9   UK
COUNTRY PROFILE. TURKEY; annual survey of political and economic background. 1952. a. £50($95) (Economist Intelligence Unit) Business International Ltd., 40 Duke St., London W1A 1DW, England. TEL 71-493-6711. FAX 71-449-9767. TELEX 266353 EIUG. (US addr.: Business International Corp., 215 Park Ave. S., New York, NY 10003. TEL 212-460-0600)

320 330.9   UK   ISSN 0269-7076
COUNTRY PROFILE. UGANDA; annual survey of political and economic background. 1952. a. £50($95) (Economist Intelligence Unit) Business International Ltd., 40 Duke St., London W1A 1DW, England. TEL 71-493-6711. FAX 71-449-9767. TELEX 266353 EIUG. (US addr.: Business International Corp., 215 Park Ave. S., New York, NY 10003. TEL 212-460-0600)

320 330.9   UK   ISSN 0269-6606
HC415.36.A1
COUNTRY PROFILE. UNITED ARAB EMIRATES; annual survey of political and economic background. 1952. a. £50($95) (Economist Intelligence Unit) Business International Ltd., 40 Duke St., London W1A 1DW, England. TEL 71-493-6711. FAX 71-449-9767. TELEX 266353 EIUG. (US addr.: Business International Corp., 215 Park Ave. S., New York, NY 10003. TEL 212-460-0600)
—BLDSC shelfmark: 3481.896250.

POLITICAL SCIENCE

320 330.9   UK   ISSN 0269-798X
HC251
COUNTRY PROFILE. UNITED KINGDOM; annual survey of political and economic background. 1952. a. £50($95) (Economist Intelligence Unit) Business International Ltd., 40 Duke St., London W1A 1DW, England. TEL 71-493-6711. FAX 71-449-9767. TELEX 266353 EIUG. (US addr.: Business International Corp., 215 Park Ave. S., New York, NY 10003. TEL 212-460-0600)
—BLDSC shelfmark: 3481.896290.

320 330.9   UK   ISSN 0269-8005
COUNTRY PROFILE. UNITED STATES OF AMERICA; annual survey of political and economic background. 1952. a. £50($95) (Economist Intelligence Unit) Business International Ltd., 40 Duke St., London W1A 1DW, England. TEL 71-493-6711. FAX 71-449-9767. TELEX 266353 EIUG. (US addr.: Business International Corp., 215 Park Ave. S., New York, NY 10003. TEL 212-460-0600)
—BLDSC shelfmark: 3481.896370.

320 330.9   UK   ISSN 0269-7998
COUNTRY PROFILE. URUGUAY, PARAGUAY; annual survey of political and economic background. 1952. a. £50($95) (Economist Intelligence Unit) Business International Ltd., 40 Duke St., London W1A 1DW, England. TEL 71-493-6711. FAX 71-449-9767. TELEX 266353 EIUG. (US addr.: Business International Corp., 215 Park Ave. S., New York, NY 10003. TEL 212-460-0600)

320 330.9   UK   ISSN 0269-607X
COUNTRY PROFILE. VENEZUELA, SURINAME, NETHERLANDS ANTILLES; annual survey of political and economic background. 1952. a. £50($95) (Economist Intelligence Unit) Business International Ltd., 40 Duke St., London W1A 1DW, England. TEL 71-493-6711. FAX 71-449-9767. TELEX 266353 EIUG. (US addr.: Business International Corp., 215 Park Ave. S., New York, NY 10003. TEL 212-460-0600)

320 330.9   UK   ISSN 0269-803X
COUNTRY PROFILE. YUGOSLAVIA; annual survey of political and economic background. 1952. a. £50($95) (Economist Intelligence Unit) Business International Ltd., 40 Duke St., London W1A 1DW, England. TEL 71-493-6711. FAX 71-449-9767. TELEX 266353 EIUG. (US addr.: Business International Corp., 215 Park Ave. S., New York, NY 10003. TEL 212-460-0600)

320 330.9   UK   ISSN 0269-6320
COUNTRY PROFILE. ZAIRE, RWANDA, BURUNDI; annual survey of political and economic background. 1952. a. £50($95) (Economist Intelligence Unit) Business International Ltd., 40 Duke St., London W1A 1DW, England. TEL 71-493-6711. FAX 71-449-9767. TELEX 266353 EIUG. (US addr.: Business International Corp., 215 Park Ave. S., New York, NY 10003. TEL 212-460-0600)

320 330.9   UK   ISSN 0269-7300
COUNTRY PROFILE. ZAMBIA; annual survey of political and economic background. 1952. a. £50($95) (Economist Intelligence Unit) Business International Ltd., 40 Duke St., London W1A 1DW, England. TEL 71-493-6711. FAX 71-449-9767. TELEX 266353 EIUG. (US addr.: Business International Corp., 215 Park Ave. S., New York, NY 10003. TEL 212-460-0600)
—BLDSC shelfmark: 3481.896610.

320 301.9   UK   ISSN 0269-4360
COUNTRY PROFILE. ZIMBABWE; annual survey of political and economic background. 1952. a. £50($95) (Economist Intelligence Unit) Business International Ltd., 40 Duke St., London W1A 1DW, England. TEL 71-493-6711. FAX 71-449-9767. TELEX 266353 EIUG. (US addr.: Business International Corp., 215 Park Ave. S., New York, NY 10003. TEL 212-460-0600)
—BLDSC shelfmark: 3481.896650.

332 330.9   UK   ISSN 0161-5475
COUNTRY PROFILES; annual survey of political and economic background. (Series consists of 108 vols. covering developments in 165 countries) 1952. a. £3780($7182) for 108 vols. (per vol. £50($95)). (Economist Intelligence Unit) Business International Ltd., 40 Duke St., London W1A 1DW, England. TEL 71-493-6711. FAX 71-449-9767. TELEX 266353 EIUG. (US addr.: Business International Corp., 215 Park Ave. S., New York, NY 10003. TEL 212-460-0600)
●Also available online. Vendor(s): DIALOG.

COUNTRY REPORT. ALGERIA; analysis of economic and political trends every quarter. see *BUSINESS AND ECONOMICS — Economic Situation And Conditions*

COUNTRY REPORT. ANGOLA, SAO TOME & PRINCIPE; analysis of economic and political trends every quarter. see *BUSINESS AND ECONOMICS — Economic Situation And Conditions*

COUNTRY REPORT. ARGENTINA; analysis of economic and political trends every quarter. see *BUSINESS AND ECONOMICS — Economic Situation And Conditions*

COUNTRY REPORT. AUSTRALIA; analysis of economic and political trends every quarter. see *BUSINESS AND ECONOMICS — Economic Situation And Conditions*

COUNTRY REPORT. AUSTRIA; analysis of economic and political trends every quarter. see *BUSINESS AND ECONOMICS — Economic Situation And Conditions*

COUNTRY REPORT. BAHRAIN, QATAR; analysis of economic and political trends every quarter. see *BUSINESS AND ECONOMICS — Economic Situation And Conditions*

COUNTRY REPORT. BANGLADESH; analysis of economic and political trends every quarter. see *BUSINESS AND ECONOMICS — Economic Situation And Conditions*

COUNTRY REPORT. BELGIUM, LUXEMBOURG; analysis of economic and political trends every quarter. see *BUSINESS AND ECONOMICS — Economic Situation And Conditions*

COUNTRY REPORT. BRAZIL; analysis of economic and political trends every quarter. see *BUSINESS AND ECONOMICS — Economic Situation And Conditions*

COUNTRY REPORT. CAMEROON, CENTRAL AFRICAN REPUBLIC, CHAD; analysis of economic and political trends every quarter. see *BUSINESS AND ECONOMICS — Economic Situation And Conditions*

COUNTRY REPORT. CANADA; analysis of economic and political trends every quarter. see *BUSINESS AND ECONOMICS — Economic Situation And Conditions*

COUNTRY REPORT. CHILE; analysis of economic and political trends every quarter. see *BUSINESS AND ECONOMICS — Economic Situation And Conditions*

COUNTRY REPORT. CHINA, NORTH KOREA; analysis of economic and political trends every quarter. see *BUSINESS AND ECONOMICS — Economic Situation And Conditions*

COUNTRY REPORT. COLOMBIA; analysis of economic and political trends every quarter. see *BUSINESS AND ECONOMICS — Economic Situation And Conditions*

COUNTRY REPORT. COMMONWEALTH OF INDEPENDENT STATES; analysis of economic and political trends every quarter. see *BUSINESS AND ECONOMICS — Economic Situation And Conditions*

COUNTRY REPORT. CONGO, GABON, EQUATORIAL GUINEA; analysis of economic and political trends every quarter. see *BUSINESS AND ECONOMICS — Economic Situation And Conditions*

COUNTRY REPORT. COTE D'IVOIRE; analysis of economic and political trends every quarter. see *BUSINESS AND ECONOMICS — Economic Situation And Conditions*

COUNTRY REPORT. CUBA, DOMINICAN REPUBLIC, HAITI, PUERTO RICO; analysis of economic and political trends every quarter. see *BUSINESS AND ECONOMICS — Economic Situation And Conditions*

COUNTRY REPORT. CZECHOSLOVAKIA; analysis of economic and political trends every quarter. see *BUSINESS AND ECONOMICS — Economic Situation And Conditions*

COUNTRY REPORT. DENMARK, ICELAND; analysis of economic and political trends every quarter. see *BUSINESS AND ECONOMICS — Economic Situation And Conditions*

COUNTRY REPORT. ECUADOR; analysis of economic and political trends every quarter. see *BUSINESS AND ECONOMICS — Economic Situation And Conditions*

COUNTRY REPORT. EGYPT; analysis of economic and political trends every quarter. see *BUSINESS AND ECONOMICS — Economic Situation And Conditions*

COUNTRY REPORT. FINLAND; analysis of economic and political trends every quarter. see *BUSINESS AND ECONOMICS — Economic Situation And Conditions*

COUNTRY REPORT. FRANCE; analysis of economic and political trends every quarter. see *BUSINESS AND ECONOMICS — Economic Situation And Conditions*

COUNTRY REPORT. GERMANY; analysis of economic and political trends every quarter. see *BUSINESS AND ECONOMICS — Economic Situation And Conditions*

COUNTRY REPORT. GHANA, SIERRA LEONE, LIBERIA; analysis of economic and political trends every quarter. see *BUSINESS AND ECONOMICS — Economic Situation And Conditions*

COUNTRY REPORT. GREECE; analysis of economic and political trends every quarter. see *BUSINESS AND ECONOMICS — Economic Situation And Conditions*

COUNTRY REPORT. GUATEMALA, EL SALVADOR, HONDURAS; analysis of economic and political trends every quarter. see *BUSINESS AND ECONOMICS — Economic Situation And Conditions*

COUNTRY REPORT. GUINEA, MALI, MAURITANIA; analysis of economic and political trends every quarter. see *BUSINESS AND ECONOMICS — Economic Situation And Conditions*

COUNTRY REPORT. HONG KONG, MACAU; analysis of economic and political trends every quarter. see *BUSINESS AND ECONOMICS — Economic Situation And Conditions*

COUNTRY REPORT. HUNGARY; analysis of economic and political trends every quarter. see *BUSINESS AND ECONOMICS — Economic Situation And Conditions*

COUNTRY REPORT. INDIA, NEPAL. see *BUSINESS AND ECONOMICS — Economic Situation And Conditions*

COUNTRY REPORT. INDOCHINA: VIETNAM, LAOS, CAMBODIA; analysis of economic and political trends every quarter. see *BUSINESS AND ECONOMICS — Economic Situation And Conditions*

COUNTRY REPORT. INDONESIA; analysis of economic and political trends every quarter. see *BUSINESS AND ECONOMICS — Economic Situation And Conditions*

COUNTRY REPORT. IRAN; analysis of economic and political trends every quarter. see *BUSINESS AND ECONOMICS — Economic Situation And Conditions*

COUNTRY REPORT. IRAQ; analysis of economic and political trends every quarter. see *BUSINESS AND ECONOMICS — Economic Situation And Conditions*

COUNTRY REPORT. IRELAND; analysis of economic and political trends every quarter. see *BUSINESS AND ECONOMICS — Economic Situation And Conditions*

COUNTRY REPORT. ISRAEL; analysis of economic and political trends every quarter. see *BUSINESS AND ECONOMICS — Economic Situation And Conditions*

COUNTRY REPORT. ITALY; analysis of economic and political trends every quarter. see *BUSINESS AND ECONOMICS — Economic Situation And Conditions*

COUNTRY REPORT. JAMAICA, BELIZE, BAHAMAS, BERMUDA; analysis of economic and political trends every quarter. see *BUSINESS AND ECONOMICS — Economic Situation And Conditions*

POLITICAL SCIENCE

COUNTRY REPORT. JAPAN; analysis of economic and political trends every quarter. see BUSINESS AND ECONOMICS — Economic Situation And Conditions

COUNTRY REPORT. JORDAN; analysis of economic and political trends every quarter. see BUSINESS AND ECONOMICS — Economic Situation And Conditions

COUNTRY REPORT. KENYA; analysis of economic and political trends every quarter. see BUSINESS AND ECONOMICS — Economic Situation And Conditions

COUNTRY REPORT. KUWAIT; analysis of economic and political trends every quarter. see BUSINESS AND ECONOMICS — Economic Situation And Conditions

COUNTRY REPORT. LEBANON, CYPRUS; analysis of economic and political trends every quarter. see BUSINESS AND ECONOMICS — Economic Situation And Conditions

COUNTRY REPORT. LIBYA; analysis of economic and political trends every quarter. see BUSINESS AND ECONOMICS — Economic Situation And Conditions

COUNTRY REPORT. MADAGASCAR, MAURITIUS, SEYCHELLES, COMOROS; analysis of economic and political trends every quarter. see BUSINESS AND ECONOMICS — Economic Situation And Conditions

COUNTRY REPORT. MALAYSIA, BRUNEI; analysis of economic and political trends every quarter. see BUSINESS AND ECONOMICS — Economic Situation And Conditions

COUNTRY REPORT. MEXICO; analysis of economic and political trends every quarter. see BUSINESS AND ECONOMICS — Economic Situation And Conditions

COUNTRY REPORT. MOROCCO; analysis of economic and political trends every quarter. see BUSINESS AND ECONOMICS — Economic Situation And Conditions

COUNTRY REPORT. NAMIBIA, BOTSWANA, LESOTHO, SWAZILAND; analysis of economic and political trends every quarter. see BUSINESS AND ECONOMICS — Economic Situation And Conditions

COUNTRY REPORT. NETHERLANDS; analysis of economic and political trends every quarter. see BUSINESS AND ECONOMICS — Economic Situation And Conditions

COUNTRY REPORT. NEW ZEALAND; analysis of economic and political trends every quarter. see BUSINESS AND ECONOMICS — Economic Situation And Conditions

COUNTRY REPORT. NICARAGUA, COSTA RICA, PANAMA; analysis of economic and political trends every quarter. see BUSINESS AND ECONOMICS — Economic Situation And Conditions

COUNTRY REPORT. NIGERIA; analysis of economic and political trends every quarter. see BUSINESS AND ECONOMICS — Economic Situation And Conditions

COUNTRY REPORT. NORWAY; analysis of economic and political trends every quarter. see BUSINESS AND ECONOMICS — Economic Situation And Conditions

COUNTRY REPORT. OMAN, YEMEN; analysis of economical and political trends every quarter. see BUSINESS AND ECONOMICS — Economic Situation And Conditions

COUNTRY REPORT. PACIFIC ISLANDS: PAPUA NEW GUINEA, FIJI, SOLOMON ISLANDS, WESTERN SAMOA, VANUATU, TONGA; analysis of economic and political trends every quarter. see BUSINESS AND ECONOMICS — Economic Situation And Conditions

COUNTRY REPORT. PAKISTAN, AFGHANISTAN; analysis of economic and political trends every quarter. see BUSINESS AND ECONOMICS — Economic Situation And Conditions

COUNTRY REPORT. PERU, BOLIVIA; analysis of economic and political trends every quarter. see BUSINESS AND ECONOMICS — Economic Situation And Conditions

COUNTRY REPORT. PHILIPPINES; analysis of economic and political trends every quarter. see BUSINESS AND ECONOMICS — Economic Situation And Conditions

COUNTRY REPORT. POLAND; analysis of economic and political trends every quarter. see BUSINESS AND ECONOMICS — Economic Situation And Conditions

COUNTRY REPORT. PORTUGAL; analysis of economic and political trends every quarter. see BUSINESS AND ECONOMICS — Economic Situation And Conditions

COUNTRY REPORT. ROMANIA, BULGARIA, ALBANIA; analysis of economic and political trends every quarter. see BUSINESS AND ECONOMICS — Economic Situation And Conditions

COUNTRY REPORT. SAUDI ARABIA; analysis of economic and political trends every quarter. see BUSINESS AND ECONOMICS — Economic Situation And Conditions

COUNTRY REPORT. SENEGAL, THE GAMBIA, GUINEA-BASSAU, CAPE VERDE; analysis of economic and political trends every quarter. see BUSINESS AND ECONOMICS — Economic Situation And Conditions

COUNTRY REPORT. SINGAPORE; analysis of economic and political trends every quarter. see BUSINESS AND ECONOMICS — Economic Situation And Conditions

COUNTRY REPORT. SOUTH AFRICA; analysis of economic and political trends every quarter. see BUSINESS AND ECONOMICS — Economic Situation And Conditions

COUNTRY REPORT. SOUTH KOREA; analysis of economic and political trends every quarter. see BUSINESS AND ECONOMICS — Economic Situation And Conditions

COUNTRY REPORT. SPAIN; analysis of economic and political trends every quarter. see BUSINESS AND ECONOMICS — Economic Situation And Conditions

COUNTRY REPORT. SRI LANKA; analysis of economic and political trends every quarter. see BUSINESS AND ECONOMICS — Economic Situation And Conditions

COUNTRY REPORT. SUDAN; analysis of economic and political trends every quarter. see BUSINESS AND ECONOMICS — Economic Situation And Conditions

COUNTRY REPORT. SWEDEN; analysis of economic and political trends every quarter. see BUSINESS AND ECONOMICS — Economic Situation And Conditions

COUNTRY REPORT. SWITZERLAND; analysis of economic and political trends every quarter. see BUSINESS AND ECONOMICS — Economic Situation And Conditions

COUNTRY REPORT. SYRIA; analysis of economic and political trends every quarter. see BUSINESS AND ECONOMICS — Economic Situation And Conditions

COUNTRY REPORT. TAIWAN; analysis of economic and political trends every quarter. see BUSINESS AND ECONOMICS — Economic Situation And Conditions

COUNTRY REPORT. TANZANIA, MOZAMBIQUE; analysis of economic and political trends every quarter. see BUSINESS AND ECONOMICS — Economic Situation And Conditions

COUNTRY REPORT. THAILAND, BURMA; analysis of economic and political trends every quarter. see BUSINESS AND ECONOMICS — Economic Situation And Conditions

COUNTRY REPORT. TOGO, NIGER, BENIN, BURKINA FASO; analysis of economic and political trends every quarter. see BUSINESS AND ECONOMICS — Economic Situation And Conditions

COUNTRY REPORT. TRINIDAD & TOBAGO, GUYANA, BARBADOS, WINDWARD & LEEWARD ISLANDS; analysis of economic and political trends every quarter. see BUSINESS AND ECONOMICS — Economic Situation And Conditions

COUNTRY REPORT. TUNISIA, MALTA; analysis of economic and political trends every quarter. see BUSINESS AND ECONOMICS — Economic Situation And Conditions

COUNTRY REPORT. TURKEY; analysis of economic and political trends every quarter. see BUSINESS AND ECONOMICS — Economic Situation And Conditions

COUNTRY REPORT. U S A; analysis of economic and political trends every quarter. see BUSINESS AND ECONOMICS — Economic Situation And Conditions

COUNTRY REPORT. UGANDA, ETHIOPIA, SOMALIA, DJIBOUTI; analysis of economic and political trends every quarter. see BUSINESS AND ECONOMICS — Economic Situation And Conditions

COUNTRY REPORT. UNITED ARAB EMIRATES; analysis of economic and political trends every quarter. see BUSINESS AND ECONOMICS — Economic Situation And Conditions

COUNTRY REPORT. UNITED KINGDOM; analysis of economic and political trends every quarter. see BUSINESS AND ECONOMICS — Economic Situation And Conditions

COUNTRY REPORT. URUGUAY, PARAGUAY; analysis of economic and political trends every quarter. see BUSINESS AND ECONOMICS — Economic Situation And Conditions

COUNTRY REPORT. VENEZUELA, SURINAME, NETHERLANDS ANTILLES; analysis of economic and political trends every quarter. see BUSINESS AND ECONOMICS — Economic Situation And Conditions

COUNTRY REPORT. YUGOSLAVIA; analysis of economic and political trends every quarter. see BUSINESS AND ECONOMICS — Economic Situation And Conditions

COUNTRY REPORT. ZAIRE, RWANDA, BURUNDI; analysis of economic and political trends every quarter. see BUSINESS AND ECONOMICS — Economic Situation And Conditions

COUNTRY REPORT. ZAMBIA; analysis of economic and political trends every quarter. see BUSINESS AND ECONOMICS — Economic Situation And Conditions

COUNTRY REPORT. ZIMBABWE, MALAWI; analysis of economic and political trends every quarter. see BUSINESS AND ECONOMICS — Economic Situation And Conditions

COUNTRY REPORTS; analysis of economic and political trends every quarter. see BUSINESS AND ECONOMICS — Economic Situation And Conditions

COURRIER DES PAYS DE L'EST. see BUSINESS AND ECONOMICS

959.7 VN ISSN 0045-8902
COURRIER DU VIETNAM. (Editions in English, French, Russian) 1964. m. $10.70. 46 Tran Hung Dao, Hanoi, Socialist Republic of Vietnam. Ed.Bd. adv.; bk.rev.; charts; illus. (tabloid format)

341.1 FR ISSN 0011-0574
COURRIER EUROPEEN.* 1952. m. 4 F. Organisation Francaise du Mouvement Europeen, 24 rue Feydeau, 75 Paris (2e), France. Dir. Raymond Andrieu.

320 BE
COURRIER HEBDOMADAIRE. 1959. w. 9500 Fr. (effective 1992). Centre de Recherche et d'Information Socio-Politiques (CRISP), Rue du Congres 35, B-1000 Brussels, Belgium. **Indexed:** Int.Lab.Doc.

320 US ISSN 0275-309X
JK468.I6
COVERT ACTION INFORMATION BULLETIN. 1978. q. $17 to individuals; institutions $22. Covert Action Publications, Inc., 1500 Massachusetts Ave. NW, No. 732, Washington, DC 20005. Ed.Bd. bk.rev.; cum.index: 1978-1982; 1982-1986; circ. 10,000. (also avail. in microform from UMI; reprint service avail. from UMI; back issues avail.) **Indexed:** Alt.Press Ind., HR Rep.
—BLDSC shelfmark: 3486.109000.
Description: In-depth international coverage, investigating wherever the hands of Western intelligence service can be found and exposed.

320 CU
CRITERIOS; teoria literaria, estetica y cultural. q. $4 in N. America; S. America $12; Europe $17. (Ministerio de Cultura) Ediciones Cubanas, Obispo No. 527, Apdo. 605, Havana, Cuba.

POLITICAL SCIENCE

320   IT
CRITICA DEL DIRITTO; stato e conflitto de classe. 1974. 3/yr. L.80000. Sapere 2000 S.r.l., Via Filippo Turati 48, 00185 Romeo, Italy. TEL 06-730 776. Ed. Angelo Ruggieri. bk.rev.; bibl.

320.532   IT   ISSN 0011-152X
CRITICA MARXISTA/MARXIST CRITICISM. 1963. bi-m. L.50000 (L.71000 foreign). Editori Riuniti, Via Serchio 9-11, 00198 Rome, Italy. TEL 06-866383. FAX 06-8416096. TELEX EDIRIU I 625292. Ed. A. Zanardo. adv.; bibl.; charts; index; circ. 12,000.

320   IT
CRITICA UMBRA.* no.16, 1976. m. L.2000. Piazza Fanti, 1, Citta di Castello (Pg), Italy. bk.rev.

614   US   ISSN 0194-1909
CRITICAL ISSUES. 1979. irreg. price varies. Heritage Foundation, 214 Massachusetts Ave., N.E., Washington, DC 20002. TEL 202-546-4400. FAX 202-546-8328.
●Also available online. Vendor(s): Mead Data Central.

320.531   UK   ISSN 0301-7605
DK246
CRITIQUE; a journal of Soviet studies & socialist theory. 1973. s-a. £7($14) to individuals; institutions £20($40). Glasgow Polytechnic, Department of Economics, Cowcaddens Rd., Glasgow G4 0BA, Scotland. TEL 041-331-3312. Ed. Dr. R. Arnot. adv.; bk.rev.; cum.index: vols.1-6, 7-12, 13-21; circ. 5,000. (back issues avail.) **Indexed:** Alt.Press Ind., Amer.Hist.& Life (until 1990), Arts & Hum.Cit.Ind., Hist.Abstr. (until 1990).
—BLDSC shelfmark: 3487.489200.

320.531   FR   ISSN 0045-9089
CRITIQUE SOCIALISTE.* 1970. bi-m. 100 F. (Parti Socialiste Unifie) Editions Syros, 6 rue Montmarte, 75001 Paris, France. Ed. Roger Cerat.

340   AG
CRONICA DOCUMENTAL DE LAS MALVINAS. w. Editorial Redaccion S.A., Bartolome Mitre 1970, Buenos Aires, Argentina. Eds. Hugo Gambini, Emiliana Lopez Saavedra.

CROSSCURRENTS. see *SOCIOLOGY*

320   AT   ISSN 0334-4649
HM1   CODEN: CSRDD9
CROSSROADS; an international socio-political journal. 1978. q. $60 to individuals; institutions $120. James Nicholas Publishers, P.O. Box 244, Albert Park, Vic. 3206, Australia. TEL 03-696-5545. FAX 613-699-2040. Eds. Ilya Zemtsov, Genady Osipov. adv.; bk.rev. (also avail. in microfilm from UMI; back issues avail.) **Indexed:** Int.Polit.Sci.Abstr., Sociol.Abstr.
Description: Examines international and comparative aspects of political theory, international relations and socio-economic and cultural factors as reflected in political, economic and administrative organizations, patterns of power, leadership, ideology and culture, with special focus on the USA, USSR and the Middle East.

320.5   MX   ISSN 0011-2208
CRUZADO; si lo leyo en el cruzado es veridico. 1961. d. Mex.$500($24) Roberto Murillo Rocha, Ed. & Pub., Manuel Ocaranza 13 B., Uruapan, Michoacan, Mexico. adv.; circ. 9,500.

322.4   UY
CUADERNOS DE ALTERNATIVA. 1985. bi-m. $12. Ediciones de la Alianza, Casilla 5009, San Felipe y Santiago de Montevideo, Uruguay. Ed. Horacio Labandera Suarez. circ. 2,000.

320   AG
CUADERNOS DE ESTUDIOS LATINOAMERICANOS. no.2, 1974. irreg. Universidad Nacional del Nordeste, Instituto de Letras, Resistencia, Chaco, Argentina. Dir. Alfredo Veirave.

CUADERNOS DE NUESTRA AMERICA. see *LITERARY AND POLITICAL REVIEWS*

320   UY
CUADERNOS DEL 26. bi-m. Movimiento 26 de Marzo, Rivera 2572 bis, Montevideo, Uruguay.

320   MX
CUADERNOS POLITECNICAS; ciencia y cultura. 1973. bi-m. Mex.$60($5) Instituto Politecnico Nacional, Comision de Operacion y Fomento de Actividades Academicas, Tolsa y Tresquerras 27, Mexico 1 D.F., Mexico. circ. 6,000.

320   CU
CUBA. MINISTERIO DE CULTURA. CARTELERA. w. Ministerio de Cultura, 4 No. 251 esq. a 11, Vedado, Havana, Cuba.

972.91   CU   ISSN 0011-2593
CUBA INTERNACIONAL. (Editions in Russian, Spanish) 1969. m. $20 in N. America; S. America $22; Europe $24; elsewhere $26. Ediciones Cubanas, Obispo No. 527, Aptdo. 605, Havana, Cuba. TEL 7-32-9353. Dir. Jesus Hernandez. charts; illus.; circ. 30,000.

320 016   US   ISSN 0361-4441
F1751
CUBAN STUDIES/ESTUDIOS CUBANOS; scholarly multidisciplinary annual book publication devoted entirely to Cuba. (As of 1986, subseries of Pitt Latin American Series) (Text in English or Spanish) 1970. a. price varies. University of Pittsburgh Press, 127 N. Bellefield Ave., Pittsburgh, PA 15260. TEL 412-624-4111. FAX 412-624-7380. Ed. Carmelo Mesa-Lago. adv.; bk.rev.; abstr.; bibl.; circ. 750. (back issues avail.) **Indexed:** A.B.C.Pol.Sci., Amer.Bibl.Slavic & E.Eur.Stud, Amer.Hist.& Life, Hisp.Amer.Per.Ind., Hist.Abstr., I D A.
—BLDSC shelfmark: 3490.858000.
Formerly: Cuban Studies Newsletter - Boletin de Estudios Cubanos (ISSN 0011-2631)

972.91   US
CUBATIMES.* 1974. 6/yr. $12 to individuals; $24 to institutions. Cuba Resource Center, 11-A Seventh Ave., Brooklyn, NY 11200. Ed.Bd. adv.; bk.rev.; bibl.; charts; circ. 450. (back issues avail.) **Indexed:** Alt.Press Ind., Left Ind.
Former titles: Cuba Review (ISSN 0147-8869); C R C Newsletter.

320 300   AG
CULTURA NACIONAL; revista bimestrale de politica y ciencias sociales. bi-m. Cnel. Zelaya 1438, Lanus Oeste, Provincia de Buenos Aires, Argentina. Ed. Eduardo Varela.

CULTURAL POLICY. see *POLITICAL SCIENCE — International Relations*

322   AG
▼**CUMPA.** 1986. s-m. Hechos S.A., Florida 716 3, Buenos Aires, Argentina. TEL 392-8529.

320   PK
CURRENT. (Text in English) 1975. w. Rs.65. Sheika Bldg., Faiz Mohd Fatehali Rd., P.O. Box 789, Karachi, Pakistan. Ed. M.T. Bokhari. illus. **Indexed:** G.Soc.Sci.& Rel.Per.Lit.

CURRENT (WASHINGTON, 1960); significant new material from all sources on the frontier problems of today. see *EDUCATION*

351   US   ISSN 0196-612X
JK1
CURRENT AMERICAN GOVERNMENT; a survey of recent significant developments in national government and politics. s-a. $11.95. Congressional Quarterly Inc., 1414 22nd St., N.W., Washington, DC 20037. TEL 202-887-8500. FAX 202-728-1863. index.
Formerly (until 1970): C Q Guide to Current American Government (ISSN 0007-8956)
Description: Topics and articles of current political, legislative or judicial interest.

320   SX
CURRENT EVENTS IN NAMIBIA. (Text in English) 1974. q. South West Africa People's Organization, P.O. Box 1071, Windhoek, Namibia. TEL 38364. FAX 32368. TELEX 724.

320.9 909   US   ISSN 0011-3530
D410
CURRENT HISTORY; the monthly magazine of world affairs. 1914. m. (9/yr.). $31. Current History, Inc., 4225 Main St., Philadelphia, PA 19127. TEL 215-482-4464. FAX 215-482-9197. Ed. William W. Finan, Jr. bk.rev.; index; circ. 24,560. (also avail. in microform from UMI) **Indexed:** A.B.C.Pol.Sci., Acad.Ind., Amer.Bibl.Slavic & E.Eur.Stud., Amer.Hist.& Life (until 1992), Bk.Rev.Ind. (1965-), Child.Bk.Rev.Ind. (1965-), Curr.Cont., Hist.Abstr. (until 1992), I D A, Mag.Ind., Mid.East: Abstr.& Ind., P.A.I.S., PMR, R.G., Rural Ext.Educ.& Tr.Abstr., Rural Recreat.Tour.Abstr., SSCI, TOM, World Agri.Econ.& Rural Sociol.Abstr.
●Also available online. Vendor(s): BRS, DIALOG.
—BLDSC shelfmark: 3497.500000.

320 330.9   US   ISSN 1057-2309
D2009
▼**CURRENT POLITICS AND ECONOMICS OF EUROPE.** 1991. q. $95. Nova Science Publishers, Inc., 238 Commack Rd., Ste. 300, Commack, NY 11725-3401. TEL 516-499-3103.
Description: Focuses on the momentous changes in Europe, spanning the entire spectrum of contemporary politics and economics.

320 330.9   US   ISSN 1056-7593
CURRENT POLITICS AND ECONOMICS OF JAPAN. 1991. q. $95. Nova Science Publishers, Inc., 238 Commack Rd., Ste. 300, Commack, NY 11725-3401. TEL 516-499-3109.

320.531   US
CURRENT SOVIET POLICIES. 1953. irreg., vol.11, 1991 (28th CPSU Congress). $25 for vol.10; vol.11 $27. Current Digest of the Soviet Press, 3857 N. High St., Columbus, OH 43214-3747. TEL 614-292-4234. FAX 614-267-6310. Eds. Ann C. Bigelow, Robert S. Ehlers.
Description: Contains documents from the Congresses and conferences of the Communist Party of the Soviet Union; Congress volumes (except vol.11) include a who's who of the Central Committee and all contain an index.

327   US   ISSN 0192-6802
D839   CODEN: CWOLED
CURRENT WORLD LEADERS; almanac & biography & news-speeches & reports. (Issued in two parts: The Almanac, 3/yr., and Biography & News-Speeches & Reports, 3/yr.) 1957. 6/yr. $150 to individuals and public libraries; others $185. International Academy at Santa Barbara, 800 Garden St., Ste. D, Santa Barbara, CA 93101. TEL 805-965-5010. Ed. Thomas S. Garrison. bibl.; illus.; charts; stat.; index; cum.index; circ. 2,000. (also avail. in microform from UMI,MIM; back issues avail.; reprint service avail. from UMI)
Formed by the merger of: Almanac of Current World Leaders (ISSN 0002-6255) & Current World Leaders - Biography and News (ISSN 0002-6263) & Current World Leaders - Speeches, Reports and Position Papers (ISSN 0092-1386)
Description: Lists current key officials of independent states, international organizations and alliances. It also lists current population, area, major cities, religions and ethnic groups, languages, form of currency and membership in international organizations and alliances for each country. Includes speeches and reports from government officials and other experts.

D D R STUDIEN/EAST GERMAN STUDIES. see *HISTORY*

D E; I U S magazine on the democratization and reform of education. see *EDUCATION*

320   IS
D I A.* (Decisions, Issues and Alternatives) (Text in English) 1975. m. $12. University Publishing Projects Ltd., 28 Hanatziv St., Tel Aviv, Israel. Ed. Shlomo Einstein. illus.

320   DK   ISSN 0905-5525
D S U'EREN. 1983. 10/yr. membership. Danmarks Socialdemokratiske Ungdom, Landsforbundet, Torveporten 2-5, 2500 Valby, Denmark. FAX 36-44-14-90. adv.; bk.rev.; illus.; circ. 12,000.
Former titles (until 1989): En Tern. Informations og Debatblad (ISSN 0109-6397) & D S U -Nyt (ISSN 0109-6389)
Description: Focuses on Danish and international politics as seen through the eyes of young Danish Social Democrats.

POLITICAL SCIENCE

320   VN
DAI DOAN KET/GREAT UNITY. 1977. w. Viet-Nam Fatherland Front, 66 Ba Trieu, Hanoi, Socialist Republic of Vietnam. TEL 62420. (Alt. addr.: 176 Vo Thi Sau St., Ho Chi Minh City, Hanoi, Vietnam) Ed. Nguyen Ngoc Thach.

DANCERS FOR DISARMAMENT NEWSLETTER. see *DANCE*

DANDELION. see *PHILOSOPHY*

320   CC
DANG JIAN/PARTY CONSTRUCTION. (Text in Chinese) m. Xuanchuan Bu - Ministry of Propaganda, 5 Xichang'an Jie, Beijing 100031, People's Republic of China. TEL 651485. Ed. Song Shixiong.

329.9 378   US
DANGXIAO LUNTAN/C C P PARTY SCHOOL MAGAZINE. (Text in Chinese) m. $41.30. (Zhongguo Gongchandang, CC - Chinese Communist Party) China Books & Periodicals, Inc., 2929 24th St., San Francisco, CA 94110. TEL 415-282-2994. FAX 415-282-0994.

320   CC
DAODE YU WENMING/MORALITY AND CIVILIZATION. (Text in Chinese) bi-m. Tianjin Shi Shehui Kexueyuan, 7 Yingshui Dao, Nankai-qu, Tianjin 300191, People's Republic of China. TEL 344047. Ed. Li Qi.

DAWN TRAIN. see *LITERARY AND POLITICAL REVIEWS*

320   UK
DDRAIG GOCH. (Text in Welsh) 1925. bi-m. £2.50. Plaid Cymru (Welsh Nationalist Party), 21 Penllyn, Caernarfon, Gwynedd, Wales. FAX 0286-5159. Ed. A.F. Jones. adv.; bk.rev.; circ. 5,000. (also avail. in microfilm)

320   JO
DEBATE/HIWAR.* (Text in Arabic) 1973. m. Jordan University, Public Administration and Political Sciences Society, Amman, Jordan.

320   PE
DEBATE SOCIALISTA. 1977. irreg. Mosca Azul Editores, Conquistadores 1130, Lima 27, Peru. Ed. Mirko Lauer. circ. 2,000.

320   US
DECENTRALIZE!; non-violent radical decentralist strategy. 1986. q. $4. Carol Moore, Ed. & Pub., Box 1608, Washington, DC 20013-1608. circ. 500. (back issues avail.)
    Description: Covers decentralist strategy and networking.

320   US
DEFENSE & DISARMAMENT ALTERNATIVES.* 1985. m. $25. Institute for Defense and Disarmament Studies, 675 Massachusetts Ave., Ste. 8, Cambridge, MA 02139-3396. TEL 617-354-4337. Ed. Ken White. circ. 3,000.
    Formerly (until Feb., 1988): Defense and Disarmament News.
    Description: Covers issues on disarmament and arms control.

320   US   ISSN 0277-4933
UA10
DEFENSE & FOREIGN AFFAIRS; the international journal of national management and national security management. 1972. m. $99. International Media Corporation, 110 N. Royal St., Ste. 307, Alexandria, VA 22314. TEL 703-684-8455. FAX 703-684-2207. Ed. Gregory R. Copley. adv.; bk.rev.; circ. 9,400. (back issues avail.) **Indexed:** Air Un.Lib.Ind., DM & T, PROMT.
    ●Also available online. Vendor(s): Mead Data Central.
    Description: Contains reports of U.S. and Soviet policies, arms transfer and price tables and in-depth strategic analysis.

320   UY
DEMOCRACIA. 1981. w. (Partido Nacional) Editorial por la Patria S.A., Colonia 1308, Montevideo, Uruguay. Ed. Alberto Zumaran.

329.3   US
DEMOCRACY IN THE WORLD. 1986. irreg. price varies. Praeger Publishers (Subsidiary of: Greenwood Publishing Group Inc.), 88 Post Rd. W., Box 5007, Westport, CT 06881-5007. TEL 203-226-3571. FAX 203-222-1502.

329.9   SA
DEMOCRAT. (Text in Afrikaans, English) 1971. 5/yr. R.3. Democratic Party, 501 Ruskin House, 2 Roeland St., Cape Town 8001, South Africa. FAX 021-461-5276. Ed.Bd. adv.; bk.rev.; illus.; circ. 38,000. (tabloid format)
    Former titles (until Mar. 1989): Progress & Newsline & Deurbraak (ISSN 0033-0582); Which was formed by the merger of: Party's Afrikaans Magazine; (1967-1970): Progress.

329   CN   ISSN 0070-3346
DEMOCRAT.* 1933. 10/yr. Can.$5. Democrat Publications, Ltd., 3665 Kingsway, Vancouver, B.C. V5R 5W2, Canada. Ed. Stephen Brewer. adv.; bk.rev.; film rev.; circ. 30,000. (tabloid format; also avail. in microfilm)

329.9   SG
LE DEMOCRATE. 1974. m. 4500 Fr.CFA. Parti Democratique Senegalais, 10 rue de Thiong, Dakar, Senegal. illus.

320   US   ISSN 0164-3207
DEMOCRATIC LEFT. 1972. bi-m. $8 to individuals; institutions $15. Democratic Socialists of America, 15 Dutch St., Ste. 500, New York, NY 10038-3705. TEL 212-962-0390. Ed. Barbara Ehrenreich. adv.; bk.rev.; bibl.; illus.; circ. 5,500. (also avail. in microform; back issues avail.) **Indexed:** Alt.Press Ind.
    Formerly: Newsletter of the Democratic Left.
    Description: Features organizational affairs, views of rank-and-file activists are also heard in this effective alliance of grassroots and national organizers.

320   II   ISSN 0301-9047
DEMOCRATIC WORLD; political and economic analysis. (Text in English) 1972. w. Rs.16($6) M. Gulab Singh & Sons (P). Ltd., 6 Bahadur Shah Zafar Marg, New Delhi 1, India. Ed. Thomas P. Matthai. adv.; bk.rev.; circ. 3,000.
    Formerly: Parliamentary Studies (ISSN 0048-3001)

321.8   FR   ISSN 0011-8222
DEMOCRATIE MODERNE; l'hebdomadaire des democrates sociaux. 1967. w. 200 F. (Centre des Democrates Sociaux) Societe Editions et Publicite France-Etranger, 133 bis, rue de l'Universite, 75007 Paris, France. FAX 45-55-94-62. Ed. Stephane Lafertey.

329.9   SA   ISSN 0011-829X
DEMOKRAAT. (Text in Afrikaans and English) 1968. m. R.1.00($1.50) Democratic National Party of S.A., P.O. Box 2931, Pretoria, South Africa. Ed. Dr. C.J. Du Preez. adv.; bk.rev.; illus.; circ. 7,000(controlled). (looseleaf format)

329.3   RU
▼**DEMOKRATICHESKAYA GAZETA.** 1990. m. 0.50 Rub. per issue. Demokraticheskaya Partiya Rossii, Ul. Koroleva 8, Korpus 2, pod'ezd 3, 129515 Moscow, Russia. Ed. Ivan Podshivalov. circ. 50,000. (newspaper)

DERECHO PENAL Y CIENCIAS PENALES. ANUARIO. see *LAW*

943   GW   ISSN 0012-0510
DEUTSCHE NATIONAL-ZEITUNG. 1951. w. DM.1.80 per no. D S Z Druckschriften- und Zeitungs- Verlag GmbH, Paosostr. 2, 8000 Munich 60, Germany. FAX 089-8341534. TELEX 524685. Ed. Dr. Gerhard Frey. adv.; bk.rev.; circ. 100,000. (also avail. in microfilm from NRP)
    Formerly: Soldaten-Zeitung.

943   GW   ISSN 0723-4295
DEUTSCHE UMSCHAU; Zeitung fuer Gesamtdeutsche und europaeische Politik, Wirtschaft und Kultur. 1954. m. DM.8. (Bund der Vertriebene) Osmipress Gesellschaft zur Foerderung der Ost und Mitteldeutschen Heimatpresse mbH, St. Augustiner-Strasse 19, D-5300 Bonn 3, Germany. TEL 0228-466466. adv.; bk.rev.; illus.; stat.
    Formerly: Heimatwacht.

943   GW   ISSN 0012-1428
DD261
DEUTSCHLAND ARCHIV; Zeitschrift fuer das vereinigte Deutschland. 1968. m. DM.70. Verlag Wissenschaft und Politik Berend von Nottbeck, Salierring 14, 5000 Cologne 1, Germany. Ed. Ilse Spittmann. adv.; bk.rev.; charts; index; circ. 6,000. **Indexed:** Amer.Hist.& Life, CERDIC, Hist.Abstr., P.A.I.S.For.Lang.Ind.

943   GW   ISSN 0012-1436
DEUTSCHLAND-BERICHTE.* (Text in English, German and Hebrew) 1965. m. free. Birkemweg 14, 5300 Bonn 1, Germany. Ed. Rolf Vogel. bk.rev.; index; circ. 6,000.

320   GW   ISSN 0012-141X
DEUTSCHLAND-MAGAZIN. 1969. m. DM.50. (Deutschland Stiftung e.V.) Verlag Deutschland Magazin, Koenigstr. 42, 8211 Breitbrunn, Germany. TEL 08051-3041. FAX 08051-62497. Ed. Hans-Juergen Mahlitz. adv.; bk.rev.; charts; illus.; circ. 100,000.

DIALECTICAL ANTHROPOLOGY. see *ANTHROPOLOGY*

320   IT
DIALOGO (JESI). m. Piazza Indipendenza 2, 60035 Jesi, Italy. Ed. Bruno Bravetti.

DIALOGO SOCIAL. see *SOCIOLOGY*

320   GO
DIALOGUE. 1969. m. Parti Democratique Gabonais, B.P. 213, Libreville, Gabon. Ed. Eloie Chambrien. circ. 3,000.

322.4   US
DIALOGUE ON LIBERTY.* 1974. 8/yr. $1. Young Americans for Freedom, Inc., 14018 Sullyfield Cir., Ste. A, Chantilly, VA 22021-1617. Ed. Hon. Gerry O'Brien. illus.; circ. 30,000. (back issues avail.)

DIANA (MARCIANISE); rassegna di politica e di cultura. see *LITERARY AND POLITICAL REVIEWS*

322.4   IT
IL DIBATTITO FEDERALISTA. 1972. m. L.20000. Sezione Gioventu Federalista Europea, Vicolo Tre Re 1, 27100 Pavia, Italy. Ed. Luigi V. Majocchi. bk.rev.; circ. 1,000.
    Supersedes (as of 1984): Federalismo Militante.

320   UK
A DICTIONARY OF MODERN POLITICS. 1985. irreg. $70. Europa Publications Ltd., 18 Bedford Sq., London WC1B 3JN, England. TEL 071-580-8236. FAX 071-636-1664. TELEX 21540-EUROPA-G.
    Description: A comprehensive guide to the ideology and terminology of the world of politics.

320   GW   ISSN 0932-6162
DIESSEITS; Zeitschrift fur Aufklaerung und Humanismus. 1987. q. DM.3.50. Deutscher Freidenker-Verband, Hobrechtstr. 8, 1000 Berlin 44, Germany. TEL 030-623-70-34. circ. 3,000. (back issues avail.)

322.4   FR   ISSN 0247-9095
DIFFERENCES; magazine contre le racisme pour l'amitie entre les peuple. 1981. m. 240 F. (foreign 300 F.) Mouvement contre le Racisme et pour l'Amitie entre les Peuples (MRAP), 89 rue Oberkampf, 75543 Paris Cedex 11, France. TEL 1-48-06-88-00. FAX 1-48-06-88-01. Eds. Isabelle Avran, Cherifa Benabdessadok. adv.; B&W page 10000 F.; adv. contact: Melina Gazsi. bk.rev.; circ. 15,000. **Indexed:** HR Rep.
    Description: Current information and comments on racial-ethnic conflicts and various forms of action to suppress racism (law, education, mutual understanding).

320   KO
DIPLOMACY; international magazine. (Text in English) 1975. m. $60. Diplomacy Co., Rm. 906, Samduck Bldg., 131 Da-dong, Choong-ku, Seoul, S. Korea. TEL 777-3370-4906. FAX 773-8862. Ed. Kim Suk-won. adv.; circ. 30,000. (reprint service avail.)
    Description: Promotes diplomatic relations through non-governmental diplomacy.

POLITICAL SCIENCE 3891

320   LE   ISSN 0417-5190
DS41
DIRASAT ARABIYAT/ARAB STUDIES; majallat fikriyat iqtisidyat ijtimaiyat. (Text in Arabic) 1964. m. $75. Dar at-Tali'at, P.O. Box 111813, Beirut, Lebanon. TELEX INTCO 20376 LE. Ed. J. Safir. adv.; bk.rev.; circ. 6,500.

972.9   CU   ISSN 0046-0338
DIRECT FROM CUBA. (Text in English) 1969. s-m. $108. Prensa Latina Agencia Informativa Latinoamericana, Calle 23 No. 201, Havana 4, Cuba. illus.; circ. controlled. (also avail. in microform from UMI; reprint service avail. from UMI) **Indexed:** Alt.Press Ind.

354   BU
DIRECTORY OF KEY BULGARIAN GOVERNMENT AND PARTY OFFICIALS. (Monthly supplement avail.) a. 42 lv. American Embassy (in Bulgaria), 1, Aleksandur Stamboliiski Blvd., Sofia, Bulgaria.
Description: Includes state agencies, institutions, organizations.

320   US
DIRECTORY OF UNDERGRADUATE POLITICAL SCIENCE FACULTY (YEAR). 1984. triennial. $25 to non-members; members $15. American Political Science Association, 1527 New Hampshire Ave., N.W., Washington, DC 20036. TEL 202-483-2512. FAX 202-483-2657. Ed. Patricia Spellman.

322.4   FR   ISSN 0294-8281
HD28
DIRIGEANT; magazine trimestriel du centre des jeunes dirigeants d'entreprise. 1968. q. 350 F. 13 rue Duroc, 75007 Paris, France. TEL 1-47-83-42-28. FAX 1-42-73-32-90. TELEX 200 298 F CJDETAP. Ed. Jacques Chaize. adv.; bk.rev.; illus.; circ. 5,000.

322.4   UN   ISSN 0257-1897
DISARMAMENT NEWSLETTER. (Editions in English, French, Russian, Spanish) 1983. q. free. United Nations, Department of Disarmament Affairs, Room S-3150 F, New York, NY 10017. TEL 212-963-5597. circ. 28,000 English and Russian eds., 15,000 French and Spanish eds.

322.4   UN   ISSN 0259-3629
JX1974
DISARMAMENT TIMES. 1978. 6/yr. $15. United Nations, Non-Govermental Organizations Committee on Disarmament, 777 United Nations Plaza, New York, NY 10017. TEL 212-304-0222. Ed. Jim Wurst. bk.rev.; circ. 5,000. (tabloid format)

320   IT   ISSN 0416-0371
DISCUSSIONE. 1953. w. L.28000. Discussione s.r.l., Piazza Luigi Sturzo 31, 00144 Rome, Italy. TEL 06-5901353. Ed.Bd. adv.; circ. 50,000.

320.9 051   US   ISSN 0012-3846
HX1
DISSENT (NEW YORK). 1954. q. $22 to individuals; institutions $30. Foundation for the Study of Independent Social Ideas, Inc., 521 Fifth Ave., New York, NY 10017. TEL 212-687-0890. Ed. Irving Howe. adv.; bk.rev.; cum.index every 2 yrs.; circ. 9,000. (also avail. in microform from UMI,MIM; reprint service avail. from KTO) **Indexed:** A.B.C.Pol.Sci., Acad.Ind., Alt.Press Ind., Amer.Hist.& Life, Bk.Rev.Ind. (1965-), Child.Bk.Rev.Ind. (1965-), Film Lit.Ind. (1973-), Fut.Surv., Hist.Abstr., Lang.& Lang.Behav.Abstr., Left Ind. (1982-), P.A.I.S., Soc.Sci.Ind.
—BLDSC shelfmark: 3598.900000.
Description: Scholarly but effective social democratic journal.

AL-DJEICH; revue de l'Armee Nationale Populare. see *MILITARY*

340   PO
DOCUMENTACO E DIREITO COMPARADO. (Supplement to: Portugal. Ministerio da Justica. Boletin) (Text in French and Portuguese) 1980. q. Esc.4000($26) Ministerio da Justica, Gabinete de Gestao Financeira, Praca do Comercio, 1100 Lisbon, Portugal. circ. 6,000.
Description: Deals with common market law, international organizations and legal developments concerning human rights.

320   FR
DOCUMENTS ET INFORMATIONS PARLEMENTAIRES; revue hebdomadaire d'information et de documentation sur la vie politique et parlementaire en France. w. 4360 F. (effective Jan. 1992). Societe Generale de Presse et d'Editions, 13 av. de l'Opera, 75001 Paris, France. TEL 40-15-17-89. FAX 40-15-17-15. TELEX SOGPRES 230023.

320   UK   ISSN 0070-7007
DOD'S PARLIAMENTARY COMPANION. 1832. a. £75. Dod's Parliamentary Companion Ltd., Hurst Green, E. Sussex TN19 7PX, England. TEL 071-828-7256. FAX 071-828-7269. Ed. Michael Bedford. adv.; bk.rev.; index; circ. 5,000.
Description: Complete guide to who's who in UK politics and government. Includes over 7,000 contacts and information.

052   PK   ISSN 0012-4907
DOGAR'S GENERAL KNOWLEDGE DIGEST. Variant title: General Knowledge Digest. (Text in English) vol.4, 1970. m. Rs.70. Dogar Bros., Santnagar, Lahore, Pakistan. Ed. Haji Wali Muhammad Dogar.

320 940   GW   ISSN 0070-7031
DD257.4
DOKUMENTE ZUR DEUTSCHLANDPOLITIK. (In five series) 1961. irreg., vol.5, no.2, 1987. price varies. Bundesminister des Inneren, Postfach 170290, 5300 Bonn 1, Germany. Eds. Karl Dietrich Bracher, Hans-Adolf Jacobsen.

320 940   GW   ISSN 0341-3276
DOKUMENTE ZUR DEUTSCHLANDPOLITIK. BEIHEFTE. 1975. irreg., vol.7, 1985. price varies. Bundesminister des Inneren, Postfach 170290, 5300 Bonn 1, Germany. Eds. K.D. Bracher, H.A. Jacobsen.

320   US   ISSN 1060-0655
▼**DOMESTIC AFFAIRS**. 1991. q. $39. Domestic Affairs Press, 1545 New York Ave., N.E., Washington, DC 20002. Ed. Mark Goldberg.

320   DQ
DOMINICA OFFICIAL GAZETTE. 1877. w. EC$18 (foreign EC$45). (House of Assembly) Government Printery, Roseau, Dominica, W.I. adv.; circ. 600.

320   DR
DOMINICAN REPUBLIC. SECRETARIADO TECNICO DE LA PRESIDENCIA. BOLETIN.* 4/yr. Secretariado Tecnico de la Presidencia, Edif. de Oficinas Publicas, Ave. Mexico esq. Leopoldo Navarro, Santo Domingo, Dominican Republic, W.I. Ed. Victor Grimaldi.

DOMOVA POKLADNICA. see *LITERATURE*

338   EI
DOSSIER EUROPA. 1955. s-a. free. Commissione delle Comunita Europee, Ufficio per l'Italia, Via Poli 29, 00187 Rome, Italy. TEL 06-699-1160. FAX 06-472-2163. TELEX 610184. Ed. Luciano Angelino. adv.; bk.rev.; charts; illus.; stat.; index; circ. 5,000 (controlled).
Formerly (until 1987): Comunita Europee (ISSN 0010-5058)

DROIT/AL-HAQQ. see *LAW*

DRUM; black literary experience. see *LITERATURE*

320 614.7   US
DUKE PRESS GLOBAL ISSUES SERIES. 1983. irreg. price varies. Duke University Press, 6697 College Station, Durham, NC 27708. TEL 919-684-2173. FAX 919-684-8644. Eds. James E. Harf, B. Thomas Trout.

320   US
DUKE PRESS POLICY STUDIES. 1981. irreg. Duke University Press, 6697 College Station, Durham, NC 27708. TEL 919-684-2173. FAX 919-684-8644.

322.4   RU
▼**DUMA**; nezavisimaya gazeta Ural'skogo gornozavodskogo regiona. 1990. m. 0.25 Rub. per issue. Ul. K. Marksa 19, 624170 Nev'yansk, Sverdlovskaya Oblast', Russia. Ed. Aleksandr Sustavov. circ. 7,000. (newspaper)

320.531   US
DYNAMIC. 1983. q. $4 to individuals; institutions $10 (for 6 issues). Young Communist League USA, 235 W. 23rd St., 5th Fl., New York, NY 10011. FAX 212-645-5436. Ed. Jason Rabinowitz. adv.; bk.rev.; circ. 15,000.
Formerly (until May 1983): Young Worker.
Description: Covers current events, student rights, culture, international affairs, etc. - from a left perspective.

320   IT
E C U NEWSLETTER. 1981. q. free. (Istitut Bancario San Paolo di Torino) Direzione Studi e Pianificazione, Via Santa Teresa 3-C, 10121 Turin, Italy. FAX 553383. (Or: Research Dept., Schillerstr. 26, D-6000 Frankfurt am Main 1, Germany) Ed. Roberto Di Pietro. bk.rev.; circ. 15,000. **Indexed:** World Agri.Econ.& Rural Sociol.Abstr.

300   FR   ISSN 0421-4226
E S O P E. (Etudes Sociales-Politiques, Economiques) 1953. bi-m. 230 F. Societe d'Editions Generales et de Documentation (SEGEDO), 6 Villa Bosquet, 75007 Paris, France. circ. 3,000.

320 301   US
EAST EUROPE REPORT. irreg. (approx. 200/yr.). $7 per no. (foreign $14 per no.). U.S. Joint Publications Research Service, Box 10257, Arlington, VA 22209. TEL 703-487-4630. (Orders to: NTIS, Springfield, VA 22161)

EAST EUROPEAN NEWS. see *BUSINESS AND ECONOMICS — Labor And Industrial Relations*

320 947   US   ISSN 0888-3254
JN96.A2
EAST EUROPEAN POLITICS & SOCIETIES. Abbreviated title: E E P S. 1987. 3/yr. $27 to individuals (foreign $32); institutions $46 (foreign $51); students $21 (foreign $26). (Joint Committee on Eastern Europe) University of California Press, Journals Division, 2120 Berkeley Way, Berkeley, CA 94720. TEL 510-642-4191. FAX 510-643-7127. Ed. Ivo Banac. adv.; circ. 650. **Indexed:** A.B.C.Pol.Sci., Curr.Cont., Soc.Sci.Ind.
—BLDSC shelfmark: 3646.597500.
Description: Examines the social, political, and economic issues in Eastern Europe.
Refereed Serial

320 330.9   UK
▼**EASTERN EUROPE AND THE COMMONWEALTH OF INDEPENDENT STATES (YEAR)**. 1991. biennial. $375. Europa Publications Ltd., 18 Bedford Sq., London WC1B 3JN, England. TEL 071-580-8236. FAX 071-636-1664. TELEX 21540-EUROPA-G.
Formerly (until 1991): Eastern Europe and the U S S R (Year) (ISSN 0962-1040)
Description: Information on the region as a whole is followed by separate chapters on the countries and states in the area.

960   UV   ISSN 0046-1032
ECCLAIRE.* no.28, 1972. bi-m. Mouvement de Liberation Nationale, B.P. 606, Ouagadougou, Burkina Faso. Ed. Hyacinthe Sandwidi.

ECOLE ET LA NATION-ACTUALITES. see *EDUCATION*

320.57   CN
ECOMEDIA BULLETIN. 1984. fortn. Can.$18 to individuals; institutions $50. Ecomedia - Toronto, P.O. Box 915, Sta. F, Toronto, Ont. M4Y 2N9, Canada. circ. 2,500.
Description: Covers controversial local and international issues from an anarchist perspective.

ECONEWS. see *ENVIRONMENTAL STUDIES*

ECONOMIC AFFAIRS. see *BUSINESS AND ECONOMICS*

POLITICAL SCIENCE

320 330   UK   ISSN 0143-831X
HD5650
ECONOMIC AND INDUSTRIAL DEMOCRACY; an international journal. 1980. 4/yr. £37($61) to individuals; institutions £95($157). (Arbetslivscentrum, SW - The Swedish Center for Working Life) Sage Publications Ltd., 6 Bonhill St., London EC2A 4PU, England. TEL 071-374-0645. FAX 071-374-8741. Ed. Rudolf Meidner. adv.: color page #130; trim 177 x 101; adv. contact: Bernie Folan. bk.rev. **Indexed:** ABI Inform, BPIA, Bus.Ind., Cont.Pg.Manage., Curr.Cont., Int.Lab.Doc., Manage.Cont., Pers.Manage.Abstr., Sociol.Abstr., SSCI, Stud.Wom.Abstr.
—BLDSC shelfmark: 3651.466000.
   Description: Covers all aspects of industrial democracy, from practical problems of industrial democracy to analysis of broad social, political and economic issues.

ECONOMIC AND POLITICAL WEEKLY; a journal of current economic and political affairs. see *BUSINESS AND ECONOMICS*

320.532   UK   ISSN 0309-7854
ECONOMIC BULLETIN (LONDON). no.7, 1980. s-a. £2. Communist Party of Great Britain, 16 St. John St., London EC1M 4AL, England. Ed. J. Grahl.

ECONOMICS & POLITICS. see *BUSINESS AND ECONOMICS — Economic Systems And Theories, Economic History*

320.531   FR
ECONOMIE ET POLITIQUE;* revue Marxiste d'economie. 1954. m. 120 F. 2 place du Colonel Fabiene, 75019 Paris, France. Ed.Bd. bibl. **Indexed:** P.A.I.S.For.Lang.Ind.

ECONOMY AND SOCIETY. see *SOCIAL SCIENCES: COMPREHENSIVE WORKS*

320 330   AG
ECOS DE A L A D I. m. Asociacion Latinoamericana de Integracion, Cangallo 1515, 10 Piso, Buenos Aires, Argentina.

EDUCATION AND URBAN SOCIETY. see *EDUCATION*

EDUCATION LINKS. see *EDUCATION*

335.83   UK
THE EGOIST; an individualist review. 1963. irreg., no.8, 1986. £1.70($4) for four nos. S.E. Parker, Ed. & Pub., 19 St. Stephen's Gardens, London W2 5QU, England. adv.; bk.rev.; circ. 175. (also avail. in microform from BHP; reprint service avail. from KTO)
   Formerly: Ego; Incorporating: Minus One (ISSN 0026-5721)

320   GW   ISSN 0013-2497
EICHHOLZBRIEF. 1964. q. DM.12. (Konrad-Adenauer-Stiftung fuer Politische Bildung und Studienfoerderung e.V.) Ernst Knoth GmbH, Postfach 226, 452 Melle 1, Germany. TEL 05422-2895. Ed. Guenther Ruether. bk.rev.

324.2   II
ELECTION ARCHIVES AND INTERNATIONAL POLITICS. (Text in English) 1970. bi-m. $120. Institute for Electoral Studies, Aptt. 201-202, 22-75, West Punjabi Bagh, New Delhi 110 026, India. TEL 594160. Ed. Shiv Lal. adv.; bk.rev.; circ. 1,000. (also avail. in microfilm from UMI; reprint service avail. from UMI)
   Former titles: Election Archives Updating International Encyclopedia of Politics and Laws; Election Archives and International Electoral Politics and Law; Which was formed by the merger of: Election Archives (ISSN 0046-1644); International Electoral Politics and Law.

320   UK   ISSN 0261-3794
JF1001
ELECTORAL STUDIES. 1982. 4/yr. £135 in UK & Europe; elsewhere £150. Butterworth - Heinemann Ltd. (Subsidiary of: Reed International PLC), Linacre House, Jordan Hill, Oxford OX2 8DP, England. TEL 0865-310366. FAX 0865-310898. TELEX 83111 BHPOXF G. (Subscr. to: Turpin Transactions Ltd., Distribution Centre, Blackhorse Rd., Letchworth, Herts SG6 1HN, England. TEL 0462-672555) Eds. David Butler, Bo Sarlvik. bk.rev.; index. (also avail. in microform from UMI; back issues avail) **Indexed:** A.B.C.Pol.Sci., Amer.Hist.& Life, Hist.Abstr., P.A.I.S., SSCI.
—BLDSC shelfmark: 3670.890000.
   Description: Focuses on the behavior of voters, the impact of electoral systems, and on the rules pertaining to elections. For historians, sociologists, political scientists, economists, geographers, lawyers, game theorists, and statisticians.
   Refereed Serial

EMBASSY OF SWITZERLAND BULLETIN. see *SCIENCES: COMPREHENSIVE WORKS*

320 350   US   ISSN 0747-0711
JK3401
EMPIRE STATE REPORT; the magazine of politics and public policy in New York State. 1982. m. $35. Empire State Report Magazine, Inc., 545 8th Ave., 16th Fl., New York, NY 10018. TEL 212-239-9797. FAX 212-564-0196. Ed. Alex Storozynski. adv.; bk.rev.; bibl.; circ. 11,750. (also avail. in microfilm) **Indexed:** P.A.I.S.
   Former titles: Empire State Report Weekly; Empire State Report (ISSN 0363-7190)

329.3   NQ
EN MARCHA. m. C.$2. Partido Conservador Democrata de Nicaragua, Cine Cabrera 2, Apdo. 725, Managua, Nicaragua.

320   US
ENCYCLOPEDIC DICTIONARY OF AMERICAN GOVERNMENT. irreg., 3rd ed., 1985. $12.95. Dushkin Publishing Group, Inc., Sluice Dock, Guilford, CT 06437-9989. TEL 203-453-4351. FAX 203-453-6000. illus.

956 960   UA   ISSN 0013-7146
DT107.83
ENCYCLOPEDIE POLITIQUE ARABE. DOCUMENTS ET NOTES.* s-a. P.T.100. Centre de Documentation et de Recherches, Administration de l'Information, 22 rue Talaat Harb, Cairo, Egypt.

320 972   MX
ENFOPRENSA. (Text in English, Dutch, French, Spanish) 1982. w. $50. Agencia Centroamericana de Noticias Enfoprensa, Insurgentes Centro no. 125, B-304, Mexico, D.F. 06470, Mexico. TEL 5927398. circ. 2,000.

ENIGMA; revista de literatura policiaca. see *LITERARY AND POLITICAL REVIEWS*

ENLIGHTENMENT AND DISSENT. see *HISTORY*

320.9   II   ISSN 0013-8517
ENQUIRY. (Text in English) vol.3, 1969. 3/yr. Rs.6. (Enquiry Association) New Age Press, 15C University Rd., Delhi 7, India. Ed. Bipan Chandra. adv.; bk.rev.; bibl

ENSAIOS F E E. (Fundacao de Economia e Estatistica) see *BUSINESS AND ECONOMICS — Economic Systems And Theories, Economic History*

ENVIO. see *HISTORY — History Of North And South America*

329.3   RU
EPOKHA. 1989. w.? Sotsial Demokraticheskaya Partiya R.S.F.S.R., Pr. Suslova, d.36, Korpus 7, kv.25, 198215 St. Petersburg, Russia. TEL 255-84-95. Ed. Vadim Lifshitz. (newspaper)
   Formerly (until 1990): E S D E K.

320   RM
ERA SOCIALISTA.* 1920. s-m. 120 lei($46) Partidul Comunist Roman, Comitetul Central, c/o Rompresfilatelia, Calea Grivitei 64-66, P.O. Box 12-201, Bucharest, Rumania. Ed.Bd. illus.; circ. 50,000.
   Formerly (until 1972): Lupta de Clasa.

300   IT   ISSN 0014-0260
ERRE U. 1961. bi-m. L.6000. Centro Italiano Relazioni Umane, Via Magenta, 5, Rome, Italy. Ed. Corrado Felici. adv.; bk.rev.; film rev.; charts; illus.; circ. 10,000.

320.531   SZ   ISSN 0014-0732
L'ESPOIR DU MONDE. 1908. q. 10 SFr. Socialistes Chretiens de Langue Francaise, c/o Georges Cuendet, Gd-Vennes 3c, CH-1010 Lausanne, Switzerland. Ed. J.-F. Martin. circ. 400.
   Formerly: Socialiste Chretien.

320   GW
ESPRESSO. 1985. q. Junge Union Main-Taunus, Hattersheimerstr. 46, 6238 Hofheim, Germany. TEL 06195-25093. FAX 06195-8715. Ed. Joerg Wiederhold. film rev.; play rev.; circ. 1,200. (back issues avail.)

320   GW
ESPRIT;* the German political and society magazine. 1969. m. DM.54($24) Heinz Moeller-Verlag, c/o S P S, Karl-Maud-Str. 2, 5400 Koblenz, Germany. Ed. Heinz Moeller. adv.; bk.rev.; bibl.; illus.; circ. 60,000. **Indexed:** Arts & Hum.Cit.Ind.
   Formerly: Bonn Journal.

320   US
ESSAYS FOR THE THIRD CENTURY. 1978. irreg., latest 1983. price varies. University Press of Kentucky, 663 S. Limestone St., Lexington, KY 40508-4008. TEL 606-257-2951. Ed. Vincent Davis. (reprint service avail. from UMI)
   Description: Deals with the major issues and challenges confronting the United States and their consequences for the immediate future.
   Refereed Serial

320   FR   ISSN 0014-1062
ESSOR DU COMMINGES. 1966. q. 5 F. Association pour l'Avenir du Comminges et du Saint Gaudinois, La Serre d'Estadens, 31160 Aspet Cedex 1361, France. Dir. Jean-Paul Buffelan.

ESTANQUERO 11. see *BUSINESS AND ECONOMICS — Economic Situation And Conditions*

320   BO   ISSN 0014-1429
HC161
ESTUDIOS ANDINOS. 1970. 3/yr. $9. Instituto Boliviano de Estudio y Accion Social, Casilla 3277, La Paz, Bolivia. bk.rev.; bibl. **Indexed:** Amer.Hist.& Life, Hist.Abstr.

320   AG   ISSN 0302-2420
ESTUDIOS INTERDISCIPLINARIOS.* 1973. q. Centro de Estudios Politicos, San Nicolas 66, Cordoba, Argentina. Ed. Bd.

320   CL   ISSN 0716-1468
ESTUDIOS NORTEAMERICANOS. 1984. q. Esc.1000($10) Universidad de Chile, Instituto de Ciencia Politica, Belgrado 11, Casilla 258, Santiago, Chile. Ed. Hernan Rodriquez Fisse.

327.05   MX   ISSN 0185-1616
JA5
ESTUDIOS POLITICOS. (Subseries of: Mexico (City). Universidad Nacional. Centro de Relaciones Internacionales. Cuadernos) 1975. q? $7. Universidad Nacional Autonoma de Mexico, Facultad de Ciencias Politicas y Sociales, Villa Obregon, Ciudad Universitaria, Mexico 20, D.F., Mexico. Ed. Juan Molinar Horcasitas. circ. 2,000. **Indexed:** Amer.Hist.& Life, Hist.Abstr., P.A.I.S.For.Lang.Ind.
   Formerly: Estudios Internacionales (ISSN 0421-5370)

320   SP
ESTUDIOS POLITICOS. 4/yr. $44. (Centro de Estudios Constitucionales) Edisa, Lopez de Hoyos, 141, 28002 Madrid, Spain. TEL 415-97-12.

ESTUDIOS PUBLICOS. see *BUSINESS AND ECONOMICS — Economic Situation And Conditions*

320.532   CL   ISSN 0014-1550
ESTUDIOS SOBRE EL COMMUNISMO.* 1953. q. Esc.20($8) Miguel Poradowski, Casilla 261, Santiago, Chile. adv.; bk.rev.; abstr.; charts; index.

POLITICAL SCIENCE 3893

320   BL   ISSN 0101-546X
ESTUDOS AFRO-ASIATICOS. 1978. 2/yr. Cr.$210($30) for 3 nos.; or exchange basis. Sociedade Brasileira de Instrucao, Centro de Estudos Afro-Asiaticos, Rua da Assembleia, 10 Conj. 501, 20011 Rio de Janeiro, Brazil. TEL 021-221-3536. Ed. Jose Pereira. adv.; bk.rev.; circ. 2,000.

320 300   PO   ISSN 0014-1623
ESTUDOS POLITICOS E SOCIAIS. (Text in English, French and Portuguese) 1963. q. $3.60. Instituto Superior de Ciencias Sociais e Politicas, Rua da Junqueira 86, 1399 Lisbon, Portugal. Ed. Dir. Prof. Adriano Moreira. adv.; bk.rev.; bibl.; charts; illus.; index; circ. 1,500. (tabloid format) **Indexed:** Lang.& Lang.Behav.Abstr.

320 200   US
ETHICS AND PUBLIC POLICY CENTER NEWSLETTER. 1982. q. membership. Ethics and Public Policy Center, 1015 15th St., N.W., Ste. 900, Washington, DC 20005. TEL 202-682-1200. FAX 202-408-0632. Ed. Jacqui Stark. circ. 15,000.
Description: Reports on activities of the Center, a non-partisan organization that conducts a program of research, writing, publications, and conferences to encourage debate on domestic and foreign policy issues among religious, academic, political, and other leaders. Special interest in positions of religious bodies on public policy questions.

329.3   SG
ETHIOPIQUE. 1974. m. Parti Democratique Senegalais, B.P. 260, Dakar, Senegal.

ETHIOPIQUES. see *HISTORY — History Of Africa*

ETHNIC GROUPS. see *ETHNIC INTERESTS*

329.9   GP
ETINCELLE. w. 119 rue Vatable, 97110 Pointe-a-Pitre, Guadeloupe. TELEX 919419. Ed. Raymond Baron. circ. 5,000.

320   SZ
ETUDES POLITIQUES. 1969. m. 35 Fr. Schweizerisches Ost-Institut - Swiss Eastern Institute, Jubilaeumsstr. 41, CH-3000 Berne 6, Switzerland. Eds. Peter Sager, Claude Rieser. adv.; bk.rev.; circ. 2,500.
Formerly: Bulletin d'Etudes Politiques.

320   VN   ISSN 0531-206X
ETUDES VIETNAMIENNES.* English Edition: Vietnamese Studies (ISSN 0085-7823) (Text in French) 1964. q. 46 Tran Hung Dao, Hanoi, Socialist Republic of Vietnam. Ed. Mai Ly Quang. charts; illus.

916.75   ZR
ETUDES ZAIROISES. 1961. q. K.85 per no. Institut National d'Etudes Politiques, B.P. 2307, Kinshasa, Zaire. bibl.
Supersedes: Etudes Congolaises.

EUROPA ETHNICA; Vierteljahresschrift fuer Nationalitaetenfragen. see *ETHNIC INTERESTS*

940   AU   ISSN 0014-2522
EUROPA-KORRESPONDENZ; Monatsinformationen. 1954. m. S.70($6) Gesellschaft zur Foerderung der Unabhaengigen Presse, Favoritenstr. 56, A-1040 Vienna, Austria. Ed. Wilhelm Landig. bk.rev.; circ. 1,500. (processed)

320   EI
EUROPAEISCHE INTEGRATION. MITTEILUNGEN. 1981. s-a. Arbeitskreis Europaeische Integration, Zitelmannstr. 22, 5300 Bonn 1, Germany. FAX 0228-53900-50. circ. 1,800. (back issues avail.)
Formerly: Europaeische Intervention.

320.531   UK   ISSN 0046-2705
EUROPE LEFT. 1970. m. free to members. Labour Movement in Europe, Europe House, 1 Whitehall Place, London SW1A 2DA, England. Ed.Bd. bk.rev.; charts; illus.; circ. 2,500. (also avail. in microform from HPL)
Description: News of the European Labor Movement.

EUROPE-MAGAZINE. see *LITERARY AND POLITICAL REVIEWS*

320   GR
EUROPE SUD-EST; la revue d'Athenes. (Text in French) 1950. q. Dr.200($15) Editions Europe Sud-Est, 18 Anagnostopoulou, Athens 136, Greece. Ed. Marc Marceau. bk.rev.; film rev.; play rev.; abstr.; stat.; circ. 3,000 (controlled).

329.9   UK   ISSN 0309-474X
EUROPEAN BULLETIN AND PRESS. (Text in English, French, German and Polish) 1963. s-a. $3.60. Central European Federalists, 39 Stanwick Mansions, Stanwick Rd., London W.14, England. Ed. A.J. Jez-Cydzik. adv.; bk.rev.; charts; illus.; circ. 5,000.

THE EUROPEAN COMMUNITY; annual five-year forecast for international business. see *BUSINESS AND ECONOMICS — International Commerce*

EUROPEAN JOURNAL OF DEVELOPMENT RESEARCH. see *BUSINESS AND ECONOMICS — International Development And Assistance*

EUROPEAN JOURNAL OF POLITICAL ECONOMY. see *BUSINESS AND ECONOMICS — Macroeconomics*

320   NE   ISSN 0304-4130
JA88.E9   CODEN: EJPRDY
EUROPEAN JOURNAL OF POLITICAL RESEARCH. 1973. 8/yr. $282. (European Consortium for Political Research) Kluwer Academic Publishers, Postbus 17, 3300 AA Dordrecht, Netherlands. TEL 078-334911. FAX 078-334254. TELEX 29245. (Dist by: Kluwer Academic Publishers Group, P.O. Box 322, 3300 AH Dordrecht, Netherlands; N. America dist. addr.: Box 358, Accord Sta., Hingham, MA 02018-0358. TEL 617-871-6600) Eds. Mogens Pederson, Derek Urwin. adv.; bk.rev.; index. (reprint service avail. from SWZ) **Indexed:** A.B.C.Pol.Sci., ASSIA, Commun.Abstr., Curr.Cont., Int.Polit.Sci.Abstr., Lang.& Lang.Behav.Abstr., Mid.East: Abstr.& Ind., Risk Abstr., Sociol.Educ.Abstr., SSCI, Stud.Wom.Abstr.
—BLDSC shelfmark: 3829.737000.

329.3   EI
EUROPEAN PARLIAMENT. CHRISTIAN-DEMOCRATIC GROUP. REPORT ON THE ACTIVITIES; group of the European People's Party. a. European Parliament, Secretariat, L-2929 Luxembourg, Luxembourg. FAX 43-70-09.

320   EI   ISSN 0259-2290
D1058
EUROPEAN POLITICAL COOPERATION DOCUMENTATION BULLETIN. s-a. $32. Office for Official Publications of the European Communities, L-2985 Luxembourg, Luxembourg. (Dist. in the U.S. by: Unipub, 4611-F Assembly Dr., Lanham, MD 20706-4391)
—BLDSC shelfmark: 3829.788400.

EUROPEAN UNIVERSITY NEWS. see *EDUCATION*

329.9   US   ISSN 0014-3650
EVANS-NOVAK POLITICAL REPORT; what's happening...who's ahead...in politics today. (Includes special reports.) 1967. fortn. $175. Evans-Novak Political Report Company, 1750 Pennsylvania Ave., N.W., Rm. 1312, Washington, DC 20006. TEL 202-393-4340. FAX 202-393-5588. Ed. Robert A. Gutwillig. circ. 2,000.
Description: Covers fast-breaking political and economic developments.

320   MX
EXAMEN; una publicacion por la democracia. 1972. m. Mex.$60000($40) Partido Revolucionario Institucional, Insurgentes Norte, No.59, Col. Buenavista, 06359 Mexico, D.F., Mexico. TEL 535-82-31. adv.; bk.rev.; bibl.; illus.; stat.; circ. 15,000.
Formerly (until 1989): Linea.

322.4   US
EXCELLENCE EDUCATION JOURNAL. 1983. m. $24. Gloria J. Hunt Keith, Box 333, Panama City, FL 32402. TEL 904-769-3745. adv.; bk.rev.
Formerly: Action Speaks.
Description: Examines issues facing Black Americans, other people of color, and other underserved persons, particularly in the USA.

320   US   ISSN 0273-6314
HF1410
EXECUTIVE INTELLIGENCE REVIEW. Short title: E I R. 1974. w. $396. E I R News Service, Box 65178, Washington, DC 20035. TEL 202-544-7022. FAX 703-771-3099. (Subscr. to: Box 17390, Washington, DC 20041-0390) Ed. Nora Hamerman. adv.; bk.rev.; circ. 14,000.
—BLDSC shelfmark: 3836.219500.
Description: Review of economics, science, politics and culture.

320   US   ISSN 0046-2926
JA1
EXPERIMENTAL STUDY OF POLITICS.* 1971. 3/yr. $12. c/o Marilyn Dantico, Ed., Arizona State University West, Office of Vice Probos for Academic Affairs, 4701 W. Thunderbird, Box 37100, Phoenix, AZ 85069-7100. TEL 602-543-4504. bk.rev. (also avail. in microform from UMI; reprint service avail. from UMI)

329.9   GW   ISSN 0343-5121
EXPRESS; Zeitung fuer sozialistische Betriebs-und Gewerkschaftsarbeit. 1962. m. DM.54. (Sozialistiches Buero) Verlag 2000 GmbH, Bleichstr. 5-7, Postfach 102062, 6050 Offenbach 1, Germany. TEL 069-885006. adv.; bk.rev.; illus.

320 055.1   IT
EXPRESSION; trimestrale di attualita cultura e politica. q. Rusconi Editori Associati S.p.A., Via Vitruvio, 43, 20124 Milan, Italy. TEL 02-67561.

320   US
EXTENSIONS. 4/yr. free. University of Oklahoma, Carl Albert Center, 630 Parrington Oval, Norman, OK 73019-0375. TEL 405-325-6372. FAX 405-325-6419. Ed. Danney Goble.

F C I B COUNTRY CREDIT REPORT. (Finance, Credit and International Business - National Association of Credit Management) see *BUSINESS AND ECONOMICS — Banking And Finance*

F C I B - N A C M. MINUTES OF ROUND TABLE CONFERENCE. (Finance, Credit and International Business - National Association of Credit Management) see *BUSINESS AND ECONOMICS — Banking And Finance*

328 364 360   US   ISSN 0071-9560
F C L ACTION ALERTS. 1955. irreg. price varies. Friends Committee on Legislation of California, 926 J St., Rm. 707, Sacramento, CA 95814. TEL 916-443-3734. Ed.Bd. circ. 750.
Formerly: F C L Action.
Description: Urges contact of legislators to express opinions on bills relating to criminal justice, human services, and peace.

320   US   ISSN 0532-7091
F C L NEWSLETTER. 1952. 10/yr. $18. Friends Committee on Legislation of California, 926 J St., Rm. 707, Sacramento, CA 95814. TEL 916-443-3734. Ed. Doug Thompson. circ. 4,000.
Description: Informs readers of legislation and related matters regarding social issues, including criminal justice, human services, and peace.

322.1 200   US   ISSN 0014-5734
F C N L WASHINGTON NEWSLETTER. 1943. m. (11/yr.). $25. Friends Committee on National Legislation, 245 Second St., N.E., Washington, DC 20002. TEL 202-547-6000. FAX 202-547-6019. circ. 10,000. (also avail. in microform from UMI; reprint service avail. from UMI) **Indexed:** HR Rep.
Description: Public policy and issues of interest to Quakers and others.

320.531   UK
HX3
FABIAN NEWS. 1891. q. £3. Fabian Society, 11 Dartmouth St., London SW1H 9BN, England. TEL 01-222 8877. FAX 01-976-7153. Ed. Lois Sparling. adv.; bk.rev.; circ. 4,000. (reprint service avail. from KTO)
Former titles: Fabian Review; Fabian News (ISSN 0014-6196)
Description: Explores issues that pertain to Britain's Labour movement, working with the unions and trade unionists.

POLITICAL SCIENCE

320 330   AT
FABIAN NEWSLETTER. 1960. bi-m. Aus.$45($25) Australian Fabian Society, P.O. Box 2707X, Melbourne, Vic. 3001, Australia. TEL 03 568 6008. bk.rev.; circ. 1,500.

320   UK
FABIAN PAMPHLET. 1884. 6/yr. £19($35) Fabian Society, 11 Dartmouth St., London SW1H 9BN, England. TEL 01-222 8877. FAX 01-976-7153. circ. 5,500. (reprint service avail. from KTO)
Formerly: Fabian Tract (ISSN 0307-7535)

320   UK   ISSN 0071-3570
FABIAN SOCIETY. ANNUAL REPORT. 1891. a. £3.50. Fabian Society, 11 Dartmouth St., London, SW1H 9BN, England. TEL 01-222 8877. FAX 01-976-7153. (reprint service avail. from KTO)
Formerly: Annual Report on Work of Fabian Society.

320.9   US   ISSN 0014-651X
FACT FINDER. 1942. fortn. $27. Harry T. Everingham, Ed. & Pub., Box A, Scottsdale, AZ 85252. TEL 602-947-4466. circ. 12,000.

320   SA
FACT PAPER ON SOUTHERN AFRICA. 1976. irreg. £1. (International Defense and Aid Fund for Southern Africa (IDAFSA)) I D A F Publications Ltd., University of the Cape, Private Bag X17, Bellville 7535, South Africa.

320   EI
FACT SHEETS ON THE EUROPEAN PARLIAMENT. every 30 mos. European Parliament, Directorate General for Research, L-2929 Luxembourg, Luxembourg.

FACTS ON FILE WORLD NEWS DIGEST WITH INDEX. see HISTORY

320   BL
FACULDADE DE FILOSOFIA, CIENCIAS E LETRAS DE ARARAQUARA. CADEIRA DE POLITICA. BOLETIM. 1968. m. Faculdade de Filosofia, Ciencias e Letras de Araraquara, Cadeira de Politica, Praca Santos Dumont, Caixa Postal 174, Araraquara, Brazil. bk.rev.; bibl.

340   PE
FAENA. q. S/200. Instituto de Promocion y Educacion Popular, Av. Pardo 130, Chimbote, Peru. Ed. Roberto Lopez Linares.

320 330.9   UK   ISSN 0071-3791
DS1
FAR EAST AND AUSTRALASIA (YEAR). 1969. a. $295. Europa Publications Ltd., 18 Bedford Sq., London WC1B 3JN, England. TEL 071-580-8236. FAX 071-636-1664. TELEX 21540 EUROPA G.
—BLDSC shelfmark: 3865.785000.
Description: Information on the region as a whole is followed by separate chapters on each of the countries and territories. These include general and statistical surveys, and directories of the government, diplomatic corps, political parties, communications, finance, trade and industry, tourism and atomic energy.

FAR EASTERN AFFAIRS. see HISTORY — History Of Europe

320   IT   ISSN 0393-4195
LA FAVILLA. 1984. m. free. Gruppo Aziendale Repubblicano Ferrovieri, Via Generale Baldissera, 42-8, 33100 Udine, Italy. TEL 0432-505320. FAX 0432-505320. Ed. Giorgio Bellini. bk.rev.; circ. 4,500.

320   US
FEDERAL ELECTION COMMISSION RECORD. Variant title: F E C Record. 1975. m. free. U.S. Federal Election Commission, Washington, DC 20463. TEL 202-219-3420. Ed. Louise D. Wides. abstr.; charts; index; circ. 12,000. (looseleaf format; also avail. in microfilm) **Indexed:** Ind.U.S.Gov.Per.
Description: Reports on all FEC actions; summarizing advisory opinions, litigation and compliance and providing data on reporting requirements.

320   US   ISSN 0195-749X
KF5406.A15
FEDERAL REGULATORY DIRECTORY. quadrennial, 6th ed. $85. Congressional Quarterly Inc., 1414 22nd St. N.W., Washington, DC 20037. TEL 202-887-8500. FAX 202-728-1863.
Description: Describes over 100 federal regulatory bodies, including the laws and regulations they enforce. Includes names, addresses and phone numbers of key personnel; organization charts; appendix with texts of major regulatory laws.

FEDERAL STAFF DIRECTORY. see PUBLIC ADMINISTRATION

320.9   IT   ISSN 0393-1358
FEDERALIST; a political review. French edition: Federaliste (ISSN 0393-344X); Italian edition: Federalista (ISSN 0392-1042) (Text in English) 1959. q. $40. E D I F, Via Porta Pertusi 6, 27100 Pavia, Italy. Ed. Mario Albertini. adv.; bk.rev.; index; circ. 3,000.
—BLDSC shelfmark: 3901.948530.

329.9   CC
FENDOU/STRUGGLE. (Text in Chinese) m. Y1 per no. (Zhongguo Gongchandang, Heilongjiang Sheng-Wei - Chinese Communist Party, Heilongjiang Provincial Committee) Fendou Zazhishe, 62 Huayuan Jie, Nangang Qu, Harbin, Heilongjiang 150001, People's Republic of China. TEL 37784. illus.

335.83   FR   ISSN 0015-041X
FEUILLE ANARCHISTE.* no.12, 1970. q. 5 F. 122 Ave. de Choisy, Paris (13e), France. bk.rev.

320   UK   ISSN 0143-5426
FIGHT RACISM! FIGHT IMPERIALISM!. 1979. s-m. £8 (foreign £13). Larkin Publications, B.C.M. Box 5909, London WC1N 3XX, England. Ed.Bd. adv.; bk.rev.; circ. 7,000.

322.4   US
FIGHTING BACK. 1983. bi-m. $5. People's Anti-War Mobilization, Box 1819, Madison Sq. Sta., New York, NY 10159. TEL 212-741-0633. (Co-sponsor: All-Peoples Congress) Ed. Naomi Cohen. circ. 8,000. (tabloid format; back issues avail.)

320   NE
FILIPPIJNENBULLETIN. 1975. bi-m. fl.20. Filippijnengroep Nederland, Korte Janstraat 2A, 3512 GN Utrecht, Netherlands. TEL 030-319323. Ed.Bd. adv.; bk.rev.; circ. 1,000.

332.4   BL
FILOSOFIA POLITICA. 1985. 2/yr. L & P M Editores Ltda., Rua Nova Iorque, 306, 90.000 Porto Alegre, Rio Grande do Sul, Brazil. Ed. Bd.

320 901   IT   ISSN 0394-7297
FILOSOFIA POLITICA. 1987. 3/yr. L.80000. Societa Editrice Il Mulino, Strada Maggiore, 37, 40125 Bologna, Italy. TEL 051-256011. FAX 051-256034. Ed. Nicola Matteucci. adv.; index; circ. 1,000. (back issues avail.)

FIN DE SIGLO. see GENERAL INTEREST PERIODICALS — Argentina

320 052   IE
FINE GAEL NEWS. 1978. 6/yr. £5. Fine Gael Party, Fine Gael Press Rooms, Leinster House, Dublin 2, Ireland. Ed. Peter White. adv.; bk.rev.; illus.; circ. 20,000.
Former titles (until 1984): New Democrat (Dublin) (ISSN 0790-1267); (until 1983): National Democrat.

FINLAND; books and publications in politics, political history and international relations. see HISTORY — History Of Europe

320 011   FI   ISSN 0355-2195
FINLAND. TILASTOKESKUS. VALTIOLLISET VAALIT. TASAVALLAN PRESIDENTIN VAALIT VALISIJAMIESTEN. (Text in English, Finnish, Swedish) 1926. every 6 yrs. FIM 35. Tilastokeskus - Central Statistical Office of Finland, Annankatu 44, SF-00101 Helsinki 10, Finland.

322.4   US   ISSN 0015-2722
FIRING LINE. 1952. m. $7. American Legion, National Americanism Commission, Box 1055, Indianapolis, IN 46204. TEL 317-635-8411. Ed.Bd. index; circ. 8,500. (also avail. in microfiche from KTO)

329.6   US   ISSN 0145-1677
JK2351
FIRST MONDAY. 1970. q. donation. Republican National Committee, Communications Division, 310 First St., S.E., Washington, DC 20003. TEL 202-863-8610. FAX 202-863-8820. Ed. Chuck Jenkins. illus.; circ. 450,000. **Indexed:** Mid.East: Abstr.& Ind.
Former titles: Monday (ISSN 0093-318X); Battle Line (ISSN 0045-1576); Republican Battle Line (ISSN 0034-5067)
Description: Features articles and personality profiles of the Republican Party. Covers the party's impact on policy, politics and society.

320.9   FR   ISSN 0015-3516
FLASH ACTUALITE. 1961. w. 6000 F. Agence Transcontinentale de Presse, 28 rue Navarin, 75009 Paris, France. TEL 45-26-02-75. FAX 33-1-40-16-09-51. TELEX 642 717. adv.; circ. 260.
Incorporating: Politique Interieure & Coulisse Diplomatique (ISSN 0010-986X)

320.531   FR
FLASH ALTERNATIVE. 1969. w. 80 F. (Parti Pour une Alternative Communiste) Presse d'Aujourd'hui, B.P. 90, 75962 Paris Cedex 20, France. Ed. M. Cuisinier. bk.rev.
Former titles (until 1982): Pont Flash; P C M L-Flash (ISSN 0754-2143)

320   BD
FLASH-INFOR;* bulletin quotidien d'information. (Text in French) no.539, 1972. m. Departement de la Presse, 6 Ave. de la Poste, B. P. 1400, Bujumbura, Burundi.

FLINDERS JOURNAL OF HISTORY AND POLITICS. see HISTORY — History Of Australasia And Other Areas

320.532   UK
FOCUS (LONDON, 1982); a Communist monthly. 1982. m. Communist Party of Great Britain, 16 St. John St., London EC1M 4AL, England. (Subscr. to: Central Books Ltd., 14 the Leathermarket, London SE1, England) adv.; bk.rev.; illus.; index; circ. 3,500. (also avail. in microfilm)
Supersedes: Comment (London) (ISSN 0010-2547); World News.

FOCUS ON POLITICS. see HISTORY

320 301.412   SW
FOKUS. 1910. m. SEK 60. Centerpartiets Riksorganisation, Bergsgatan 7 B, P.O. Box 22107, 104 22 Stockholm, Sweden. FAX 46-6-526440. Ed. Lennart Svensson. adv.; circ. 140,000.

320   NO
FOLKETS FRAMTID. 1948. s-w. NOK 300. Oevre Vollgatan 13, Postbus 453, 0158 Oslo 1, Norway. TEL 02-208005. FAX 02-336250. Ed. Odd Hagen. adv.; bk.rev.; circ. 12,000.

320 910   IT
FONDAZIONE GUARASCI. BOLLETTINO MENSILE D'INFORMAZIONE. 1986? m. Fondazione Guarasci, Via Idria, No.26, 87100 Cosenza, Italy. TEL 0984-25145. Ed. Antonlivio Perfetti.
Description: Forum covering regional social and political issues.

320   US   ISSN 0749-9825
FOOD FIRST NEWS. 1978. 4/yr. $30 (effective 1992). Institute for Food & Development Policy, 145 Ninth St., San Francisco, CA 94103. FAX 415-864-3909. bk.rev.; circ. 20,000.

320   US
FOOT PRINTS. Citizen Network for Common Security, Anabel Taylor Hall, Cornell University, Ithaca, NY 14853.

320 320   UK
FOREIGN REPORT; the private intelligence behind the news. 1946. w. $265. Economist Newspaper, 25 St. James St., London SW1A 1HG, England. TEL 071-839-7000. FAX 071-839-2968. TELEX 919555. (U.S. addr.: 11 W. 57th St., New York, NY 10019)
Description: Reports on political and business developments around the world.

320.532 054.1   **FR**
LA FORGE. 1979. s-m. 200 F. Parti Communiste des Ouvriers de France, c/o Pierrel Christian, 15 Cite Popincourt, 75011 Paris, France. TEL 805-30-14. adv.; bk.rev.; circ. 3,000.
  Description: Marxist-leninist perspective on national and international political situation, with special emphasis on French colonies.

320   **DK**   **ISSN 0108-3279**
FORUM; et aabent venstresocialistik debatblad. 1982. irreg. (5-6/yr.). DKK 85. Aurikelvej 18, 2500 Valby, Denmark. illus. Indexed: Abstr.Engl.Stud.
  Formerly: V S R Kommunikation (ISSN 0108-4232)

320   **GW**
FORUM LIBERAL; liberale Zeitung. 1972. 8/yr. DM.4. Wirtschafts- und Sozialpolitik Verlag, Sternstr. 44, 4000 Duesseldorf, Germany. TEL 0211-4981106. Ed. Klaus Golombek. adv.; bk.rev.; circ. 50,000. (back issues avail.)

330 370 614.7 320   **GW**   **ISSN 0724-9780**
FORUM LOCCUM. 1982. 3/yr. DM.20. Evangelische Akademie Loccum, c/o Beate Blatz, 3056 Rehburg-Loccum 2, Germany. TEL 05766-810. FAX 05766-81188. TELEX 17576610. bibl.; illus.; cum.index: 1982-1984; circ. 2,000. (back issues avail.)
  Description: Protestant publication discussing religion, Church, human ethics, humanities and social science. Includes activities of the Protestant Academies.

FORUM POLITISCHE BILDUNG. see *EDUCATION — Teaching Methods And Curriculum*

320.531   **US**
FORWARD MOTION MAGAZINE. 1982. bi-m. Box 1884, Jamaica Plain, MA 02130.

323.4   **GW**   **ISSN 0015-928X**
FRAGEN DER FREIHEIT; Schriftenreihe fuer Ordnungsfragen der Wirtschaft des Staates und des kulturellen Lebens. 1957. bi-m. DM.48. Seminar fuer Freiheitliche Ordnung e.V., Badstrasse 35, 7325 Boll-Eckwaelden 35, Germany. TEL 07164-3573. circ. 1,500.

FRAMEWORK. see *CHILDREN AND YOUTH — For*

320.531   **FR**
FRANCE DES POINTS CHAUDS.* Short title: Points Chauds. irreg. price varies. Editions Syros, 6 rue Montmarte, 75001 Paris, France.

320.9   **FR**   **ISSN 0046-4910**
FRANCE FORUM.* 8/yr. 30 F. 133 bis, rue de l'Universite, 75007 Paris, France. Eds. Etienne Borne, Henri Bourbon. adv.; bk.rev.; film rev.; illus. **Indexed:** P.A.I.S.For.Lang.Ind.

327   **FR**   **ISSN 0082-5409**
FRANCE - IBERIE RECHERCHE. ETUDES ET DOCUMENTS. 1970. irreg. price varies. Presses Universitaires du Mirail, 56, rue du Taur, 31069 Toulouse, France.

329.3   **IV**
FRATERNITE - HEBDO. w. Parti Democratique de la Cote d'Ivoire, 01 B.P. 1212, Abidjan 01, Ivory Coast. TEL 21-29-15. Ed. Guy Pierre Nouama.

329.3   **IV**
FRATERNITE - MATIN. 1964. d. Parti Democratique de la Cote d'Ivoire, Blvd. du General de Gaulle, 01 B.P. 1807, Abidjan 01, Ivory Coast. TEL 21-27-27. TELEX 23718. Ed. Auguste Miremont. circ. 80,000.
  Description: Official journal of record for government activities.

320   **GW**   **ISSN 0016-0202**
FRAU UND POLITIK. 1954. m. DM.20. (Christlich-Demokratische Union (CDU), Frauenvereinigung) Union-Betriebs-Gesellschaft mbH, Friedrich-Ebert-Allee 73-75, 5300 Bonn 1, Germany. TEL 0228-234091. adv.; bk.rev.; charts; illus.; stat.; index; circ. 2,700.

FREE ASSOCIATIONS; psychoanalysis, groups, politics, culture. see *PSYCHOLOGY*

320 301.412   **SA**
FREE AZANIA. (Text in English) 1982. bi-m. R.2.00. Free Azania, P.O. Box 49, Southfield, Capetown 7880, South Africa. Eds. Ashley Duplooy, Na-lem Dollie. bk.rev.; circ. 400.

322.4 100 301   **UK**   **ISSN 0260-5112**
FREE LIFE. 1979. q. £10($20) Libertarian Alliance, 1 Russell Chambers, The Piazza, Covent Garden, London WC2E 8AA, England. TEL 071-821-5502. FAX 071-834-2031. Ed.Bd. adv.; bk.rev.; film rev.; bibl.; circ. 1,000. (also avail. in microfiche; back issues avail.)
  —BLDSC shelfmark: 4033.324500.

052   **UK**
FREE RADICAL. 1991. 6/yr. £5 to non-members. Young Liberal Democrats and Student Liberal Democrats of England, 4 Cowley St., London SW1P 3NB, England. Ed. Richard Grayson. circ. 2,000.
  Former titles (until 1991): Young Liberal News; Y L Newsletter.

950 322.4   **JA**   **ISSN 0021-6984**
FREE WORLD/JIYU SEKAI;* liberty & responsibility. 1964. m. 1300. Yen($3.30) Free Asia Association, Rm. 323, Yaesu Bldg., 2-6 Marunouchi, Chiyoda-ku, Tokyo, Japan. Ed. Kattsundo Jono. circ. 10,000.

323.4   **UK**   **ISSN 0016-0504**
HX821
FREEDOM. 1886. fortn. £14 to individuals (foreign £18); institutions £22 (foreign £25). Freedom Press, 84b Whitechapel High St. (in Angel Alley), London E1 7QX, England. Ed.Bd. bk.rev.; circ. 2,000. (also avail. in microform from RPI)

322.4   **PK**
FREEDOM. (Text in English) m. Rs.15. c/o Mohammed Arif, Tabbani Market, Nazimabad No. 3, Karachi 18, Pakistan. (Subscr. to: al Qamar, V-B Nazimabad, Karachi 18, Pakistan) Ed. Mohammed Salman Usmani. adv.; illus.

322.4   **KO**
FREEDOM DIGEST. (Text in English) 1967. q. $20. (World League for Freedom and Democracy) World Freedom Center Press, World Freedom Center, Changchung-dong San 5-19, Chung-gu, Seoul, S. Korea. TEL 02-235-0823. FAX 02-236-7059. TELEX TOWER-K28246. Ed. Dr. Woo Jae-Seung. adv.; bk.rev.; abstr.; charts; illus.; stat.; circ. 2,000.
  Formerly (until 1982): W A C L Bulletin (ISSN 0042-9449)
  Description: Covers political philosophy: problems of communism and global military strategy.

323.4   **II**   **ISSN 0016-0547**
FREEDOM FIRST; journal of liberal ideas. (Text in English) 1952. q. Rs.30($20) Democratic Research Service, 127 Maneckjee Wadia Bldg., Mahatma Gandhi Rd., 4th Fl., Bombay 400 001, India. TEL 273914. Eds. S.V. Raju, R. Srinivasan. adv.; bk.rev.; circ. 2,000. (also avail. in microfilm from UMI; reprint service avail. from UMI)

FREEDOM NETWORK NEWS. see *PHILOSOPHY*

FREEDOM SOCIALIST; voice of revolutionary feminism. see *WOMEN'S INTERESTS*

FREEDOMWAYS; a quarterly review of the Freedom Movement. see *ETHNIC INTERESTS*

323.4   **US**   **ISSN 0016-0652**
AP2
FREEMAN; ideas on liberty. 1950. m. $15. Foundation for Economic Education, Inc., 30 S. Broadway, Irvington-on-Hudson, NY 10533. TEL 914-591-7230. Eds. Brian Summers, Beth Hoffman. bk.rev.; index; circ. 32,000. (also avail. in microform from UMI; back issues avail.; reprint service avail. from UMI) **Indexed:** Amer.Hist.& Life, Hist.Abstr., Ind.Free Per., P.A.I.S.

FREIE LEHRERSTIMME. see *EDUCATION*

323.4   **GW**   **ISSN 0016-0768**
FREIE PRESSE-KORRESPONDENZ. 1953. m DM.24. Verband der Freien Presse e.V., Postfach 440208, 8000 Munich 44, Germany. Ed. Stefan Marinoff. adv.; bk.rev.; circ. 2,000.

FREIE UNIVERSITAET BERLIN. OSTEUROPA-INSTITUT. BERICHTE. see *HUMANITIES: COMPREHENSIVE WORKS*

FREIE UNIVERSITAET BERLIN. OSTEUROPA-INSTITUT. ERZIEHUNGSWISSENSCHAFTLICHE VEROEFFENTLICHUNGEN. see *EDUCATION*

POLITICAL SCIENCE   3895

FREIE UNIVERSITAET BERLIN. OSTEUROPA-INSTITUT. PHILOSOPHISCHE UND SOZIOLOGISCHE VEROEFFENTLICHUNGEN. see *PHILOSOPHY*

320   **AU**
FREIHEITLICHER PRESSEDIENST. 1953. s-w. Freiheitliche Partei Oesterreichs, Kaerntnerstr. 28-l, A-1010 Vienna, Austria. TEL 523535. TELEX 113610. circ. 180. (looseleaf format)

320   **US**   **ISSN 0882-1267**
DC417
FRENCH POLITICS & SOCIETY. 4/yr. $20 to individuals (foreign $25); institutions $30 (foreign $35). Harvard University, Minda de Gunzburg Center for European Studies, 27 Kirkland St., Cambridge, MA 02138-2043. TEL 617-495-4303. FAX 617-495-8509. Eds. Stanley Hoffmann, George Ross. bk.rev. (back issues avail.)
  Description: Provides current information on developments in contemporary France.

322.4   **GW**
FRIEDEN. 1981. a. Lamuv Verlag GmbH, Duestere Str. 3, 3400 Goettingen, Germany. Eds. A. Meyer, K. Rabe. circ. 15,000. (back issues avail.)

320   **GW**
FRIEDEN UND ABRUESTUNG. 1982. q. DM.30. Initiative fuer Frieden e.V., Stralsunder Weg 50, 5300 Bonn 1, Germany. TEL 0228-664442. FAX 0228-665843. Ed. Wolfgang Biermann. adv.; bk.rev.; circ. 2,000.

370 355 320   **GW**   **ISSN 0930-830X**
FRIEDENSFORSCHUNG AKTUELL. 1981. q. free. Peace Research Institute Frankfurt (PRIF), Leimenrode 29, 6000 Frankfurt a.M. 1, Germany. TEL 069-550191. FAX 069-558481. (Co-sponsor: Hessische Stiftung Friedens- und Konfliktforschung (HSFK)) Ed. Ruediger Schlaga. circ. 4,000. (back issues avail.)
  Description: Articles and essays on current topics of peace and foreign policy, as well as peace research and peace movements.

322.4   **GW**
FRIEDENSFORUM; Rundbrief der Friedensbewegung. 1983. bi-m. DM.20. Foerderverein Frieden, Romerstr. 88, 5300 Bonn 1, Germany. TEL 0228-692904. circ. 4,000.

323.4   **SW**   **ISSN 0016-142X**
FRIHET. 1917. 9/yr. SEK 140($17) Sveriges Socialdemokratiska Ungdomsfoerbund, P.O. Box 115 44, 100 61 Stockholm, Sweden. FAX 08-7149508. TELEX 15547-SSU-S. Ed. Carina Persson. adv.; bk.rev.; illus.; play rev.; index; circ. 50,000.

320.9   **II**   **ISSN 0016-2094**
FRONTIER. (Text in English) 1968. w. $50. Germinal Publications Pvt. Ltd., 61 Mott Lane, Calcutta 700 013, India. Ed. Timir Basu. adv.; bk.rev.; circ. 3,000.

320   **SA**   **ISSN 0256-0240**
FRONTLINE. (Text in English) 1979. 12/yr. R.35 (foreign R.120). Saga Press, P.O. Box 32219, Braamfontein 2017, South Africa. TEL 011-836-0904. FAX 011-834-1542. Ed. Denis Beckett. adv.; bk.rev.; circ. 10,000. (back issues avail.)

320   **CC**   **ISSN 0427-7112**
FUDAO YUAN. (Text in Chinese) m. Zhongguo Qingnian Chubanshe, Qikan Bu, No. 21, Dongsi 12 Tiao, Beijing 100708, People's Republic of China. TEL 442125. Ed. Miu Li.

320.9   **SP**   **ISSN 0016-2477**
AP60
FUERZA NUEVA. 1967. w. 2200 ptas. Nunez de Balboa, 31, Madrid 1, Spain. Dir. Pedro Rodrigo Martinez. adv.; bk.rev.

320   **AG**
FUNDACION ECUMENICA DE CUYO. BOLETIN DE DOCUMENTACION. 1979. bi-m. Arg.$70($10) Fundacion Ecumenica de Cuyo, Pedernera 1291, Guaymallen, Mendoza, Argentina. (Subscr. to: Libros Dialogo, 9 de Julio 718, 5500 Mendoza, Argentina) Dir. Maria Teresa Brachetta.

FUTURIFIC; foundation for optimism. see *TECHNOLOGY: COMPREHENSIVE WORKS*

POLITICAL SCIENCE

G A N P A C BRIEF. (German-American National Political Action Committee) see *ETHNIC INTERESTS*

320.9 US ISSN 1051-2616
HM261.A1
GALLUP POLL MONTHLY. 1965. m. $65 to non-profit institutions; others $95; foreign $110. Gallup Poll News Service, 100 Palmer Sq., Box 628, Princeton, NJ 08542. TEL 609-924-9600. FAX 609-924-2584. Ed. Leslie C. McAneny. adv.; charts; illus.; stat.; index; circ. 1,300. (processed) **Indexed:** P.A.I.S., PROMT, SRI.
●Also available online.
—BLDSC shelfmark: 4067.549500.
Former titles (until Dec. 1989): Gallup Report (ISSN 0731-6143); Gallup Opinion Index (ISSN 0016-4194); Gallup Political Index.

GARIBALDI. see *LITERARY AND POLITICAL REVIEWS*

320 US
GARTH ANALYSIS; research by Penn & Schoen Associates. 1982. bi-m. $295. Penn and Schoen Associates, Inc., 245 E. 92nd St., New York, NY 10028. TEL 212-534-4000. Ed. Jeffrey Toobin. stat.; circ. 200. (also avail. in microform from UMI)

320.531 CN ISSN 1183-2053
LA GAUCHE. (Text in French) 1983. 10/yr. Can.$10($10) to individuals; institutions Can.$25($25). C.P. 5152 Succ. N, Montreal, Que. H2X 3N2, Canada. TEL 514-845-6797. Ed. Francois Moreau. bk.rev.; circ. 3,000. (back issues avail.)
Formerly (until 1991): Gauche Socialiste.

GAY LEFT; a socialist journal produced by gay people. see *HOMOSEXUALITY*

GAY VOTE. see *HOMOSEXUALITY*

320 IT
GAZZETTA DEL LUNEDI. 1945. w. Via Varese 2, Genoa, Italy. TEL 010-517851. Dir. Mimmo Angeli. circ. 150,000. (newspaper)

320.531 JA ISSN 0435-1754
GEKKAN SHAKAITO. m. 600 Yen per month. Social Democratic Party of Japan - Nihon Shakaito, 1-8-1 Nagata-cho, Chiyoda-ku, Tokyo, Japan. FAX 81-03-3580-0691. illus.

320 296 AU ISSN 0021-2334
DIE GEMEINDE. 1958. m. S.300. Israelitische Kultusgemeinde Wien, Seitenstetteng. 4, A-1010 Vienna, Austria. FAX 0222-5334516. TELEX 136298-ISKUL-A. Ed. Karl Pfeifer. adv.; bk.rev.; illus.; circ. 6,000.

GENTE MESE; mensile di politica, attualia, cultura. see *GENERAL INTEREST PERIODICALS — Italy*

320 US
GEORGIA BEAT. 1986. 22/yr. $90. Joe Sports Associates, Inc., 21 Finch Trail, Atlanta, GA 30308. TEL 404-873-3728. FAX 404-874-8512. Ed. Joe Sports. circ. 1,000.
Description: Inside report of people and politics of Georgia.

320 US ISSN 0882-7079
DD1
GERMAN POLITICS & SOCIETY. 3/yr. $18 to individuals (foreign $23); institutions $28 (foreign $33). Harvard University, Minda de Gunzburg Center for European Studies, 27 Kirkland St., Cambridge, MA 02138-2043. TEL 617-495-4303. FAX 617-495-8509. Ed.Bd. (back issues avail.)
—BLDSC shelfmark: 4162.150700.
Description: Focuses on developments in contemporary Germany.

GERMAN STUDIES REVIEW. see *HISTORY — History Of Europe*

GESCHICHTE, POLITIK UND IHRE DIDAKTIK. see *HISTORY — History Of Europe*

322 AU ISSN 0016-9099
HN401
GESELLSCHAFT UND POLITIK; Zeitschrift fuer soziales und wirtschafliches Engagement. 1965. q. S.200. Institut fuer Sozialpolitik und Sozialreform (Dr. Karl Kummer-Institut), Ebendorferstr. 6-4, A-1010 Vienna, Austria. Ed. Josef Steurer. adv.; bk.rev.; charts; stat.; circ. 1,500. (tabloid format)

322 GW ISSN 0016-9102
GESELLSCHAFTSPOLITISCHE KOMMENTARE. 1954. s-m. DM.36. c/o Leo Schuetze, Ed. & Pub., Postfach 64, 5544 Schoenekken, Germany. TEL 06553-866. FAX 06553-1290. bk.rev.; index; circ. 5,500. (looseleaf format)

GHANA DIGEST. see *GENERAL INTEREST PERIODICALS — Ghana*

966.7 US ISSN 0016-9579
GHANA NEWS. 1970. m. free. Embassy of Ghana, Information Section, 3512 International Dr. N.W., Washington, DC 20003-3035. TEL 202-686-4520. illus.; circ. 8,000.

320.9 IT ISSN 0017-0186
GIORNALE DEL MEZZOGIORNO; economico-politico. 1947. w. L.45000. Vito Bianco, Ed. & Pub., Via Messina, 31, 00198 Rome, Italy. TEL 06-8443151. FAX 8417595. adv.; bk.rev.; charts; illus.; mkt.; tr.lit.
Description: An economic, political, independent weekly newspaper.

GIUSTIZIA NUOVA. see *LAW*

320 330.9 US
GLOBAL OPTIONS DATALINE; research & advocacy on world affairs. q. $5. Global Options, Box 40601, San Francisco, CA 94140-0601. TEL 415-550-1703.
Formerly: Institute for the Study of Labor and Economic Crisis. Occasional Papers.

320 SW
GOETEBORG STUDIES IN POLITICS. irreg. price varies. Goeteborgs Universitet, Statsvetenskapliga Institutionen, Spraengskullsgatan 19, S-41123 Goeteborg, Sweden. Eds. Bo Saerlvik, Lars Stroemberg.
Formerly: Studier i Politik - Studies in Politics.

300 II ISSN 0436-1326
GOKHALE INSTITUTE MIMEOGRAPH SERIES. 1967. irreg. price varies. Gokhale Institute of Politics and Economics, Pune 411 004, India. TEL (0212)54287.

320 330 II ISSN 0072-4912
GOKHALE INSTITUTE OF POLITICS AND ECONOMICS. STUDIES. (Text in English) 1931. irreg., no.68, 1983. price varies. Gokhale Institute of Politics and Economics, Pune 411004, India. TEL (0212)54287. (Dist. by: Orient Longman Ltd., Nicol Rd., Ballard Estate, Bombay 400 038, India)

GOLDEN STATE REPORT. see *PUBLIC ADMINISTRATION*

GOOD GOVERNMENT; a journal of political, social & economic content. see *BUSINESS AND ECONOMICS — Economic Systems And Theories, Economic History*

GOSPEL TRUTH. see *RELIGIONS AND THEOLOGY — Other Denominations And Sects*

320 330.9 RU
▼**GOSPODIN NAROD;** Rossiiskaya respublikanskaya gazeta. (Text in Russian) 1990. w.? Ul. Lobachevskogo 66, A, 117454 Moscow, Russia. TEL 432-96-66. (newspaper)

320 US ISSN 0952-1895
JA1.A1
GOVERNANCE. 1987. 4/yr. $54 to individuals in N.America (rest of world $61); institutions $101 in N.America (rest of world $112). Basil Blackwell Inc., 3 Cambridge Center, Cambridge, MA 02142. TEL 617-225-0430. circ. 800.
—BLDSC shelfmark: 4203.819600.

320 350 UK ISSN 0017-257X
JA8
GOVERNMENT AND OPPOSITION. 1965. q. $70 to individuals; institutions $99. London School of Economics and Political Science, Houghton St., London W.C.2, England. FAX 071-242-0392. Ed. Ghita Ionescu. adv.; bk.rev.; abstr.; cum.index: vols.1-5, 6-10; circ. 1,500. **Indexed:** A.B.C.Pol.Sci., Amer.Hist.& Life, Br.Hum.Ind., Hist.Abstr., Int.Polit.Sci.Abstr., Mid.East: Abstr.& Ind., P.A.I.S., Soc.Sci.Ind., SSCI.
—BLDSC shelfmark: 4203.900000.

GOVERNMENT AND POLITICS ALERT. see *PUBLIC ADMINISTRATION*

320 IT
GOVERNO. m. Governo, Via dei Benci 4, 50122 Florence, Italy. TEL (055) 244781. Dir. Gianni Conti.

320 US ISSN 0888-8647
GOVERNORS' WEEKLY BULLETIN. 1967. w. $50 for state personnel; others $75. National Governors' Association, 444 North Capitol St., N.W., Ste. 250, Washington, DC 20001. TEL 202-624-5330. Ed. Alan Janesch. circ. 3,400.
Former titles: Capital Ideas; Governors' Bulletin.
Description: Features latest information on Governors' initiatives and policies, giving readers an insider's perspective on opportunities and problems faced by state governors.

320.532 CU ISSN 0864-4632
GRANMA INTERNACIONAL (PORTUGUESE EDITION). 1984. w. $40. Comite Central del Partido Comunista de Cuba - Central Committee of the Communist Party of Cuba, Ave. General Suarez y Territorial, Plaza de la Revolucion, 10699 Habana 6, Cuba. TEL 70-8218. TELEX 0511-355. Ed. Gabriel Molina Franchossi. circ. 5,000.

320.532 CU ISSN 0864-4616
GRANMA INTERNACIONAL (SPANISH EDITION); resumen semanal. 1966. w. $40. Comite Central del Partido Comunista de Cuba - Central Committee of the Communist Party of Cuba, Ave. General Suarez y Territorial, Plaza de la Revolucion, 10699 Havana 6, Cuba. TEL 70-8218. TELEX 0511-355. Ed. Gabriel Molina Franchossi. circ. 25,000.

320.532 CU ISSN 0864-4624
GRANMA INTERNATIONAL (ENGLISH EDITION); weekly review. 1966. w. $40. Comite Central del Partido Comunista de Cuba - Central Committee of the Communist Party of Cuba, Av. Suarez y Territorial, Plaza de la Revolucion, 10699 Havana 6, Cuba. TEL 70-8218. TELEX 511221. (Subscr. to: Granma, Apdo. 6260, Havana 6, Cuba. TEL 70-771-432) Ed. Gabriel Molina Franchossi. adv.; bk.rev.; charts; illus.; circ. 23,000. (newspaper; also avail. in microform from BLH) **Indexed:** Alt.Press Ind.

320.532 CU ISSN 0864-4640
GRANMA INTERNATIONAL (FRENCH EDITION); resume hebdomaire. 1966. w. $40. Comite Central del Partido Comunista de Cuba - Central Committee of the Communist Party of Cuba, Ave. General Suarez y Territorial, Plaza de la Revolucion, 10699 Havana 6, Cuba. TEL 70-8218. TELEX 0511-355. Ed. Gabriel Molina Franchossi. circ. 10,000.

320 US
GRASS ROOTS CAMPAIGNING. 1979. m. $36. Campaign Consultants, Box 7281, Little Rock, AR 72217. TEL 501-225-3996. FAX 501-225-5167. Ed. Jerry L. Russell. circ. 200. (looseleaf format; back issues avail.)
Description: Covers political campaign techniques, philosophy, and psychology.

320 800 301 US ISSN 0270-7497
GREAT ISSUES OF THE DAY. 1981. irreg., no.7, 1992 (approx. 2/yr.). price varies. Borgo Press, Box 2845, San Bernardino, CA 92406. TEL 714-884-5813. Ed. Jeffery M. Elliot.
Description: Discussion on vital topics of the day, by leading academics, professionals, writers, and government officials.

327 US
GREECE; the week in review. 1974? 6/yr. free. Embassy of Greece, Press and Information Office, 2211 Massachusetts Ave. N.W., Washington, DC 20008. TEL 202-332-2727. FAX 202-265-4931. illus.; circ. 8,000.

322.4 614.7 UK ISSN 0957-5170
GREEN ANARCHIST; global anarchist 'zine. 1980. irreg. (approx. 4/yr.). £5.50. Box H, 34 Cowley Rd., Oxford OX4 1HZ, England. adv.; bk.rev.; illus.; circ. 2,200.

322.4 UK
GREENPEACE NEWSLETTER. 1971. q. free to supporters. Greenpeace (London), 5 Caledonian Rd., London N1, England. Ed.Bd. bk.rev.; circ. 750. (processed)

POLITICAL SCIENCE

320 — US
GREENWOOD HISTORICAL ENCYCLOPEDIA OF THE WORLD'S POLITICAL PARTIES. 1982. irreg. price varies. Greenwood Press, Inc. (Subsidiary of: Greenwood Publishing Group Inc.), 88 Post Rd., W., Box 5007, Westport, CT 06881-5007. TEL 203-226-3571. FAX 203-222-1502.
   Formerly: Greenwood Encyclopedia of the World's Political Parties.

320 — US
GREYZONE;* newsletter of Twin Cities anarchists. bi-m. Back Room Anarchist Books, Box 10854, Minneapolis, MN 55458-3854. TEL 612-870-7008.

320.5 — IE — ISSN 0017-4254
GRILLE;* Irish Christian left. 1969. bi-m. 10s. 14 Kinvara Rd., Dublin 7, Ireland. Eds. John Feeney, William Ledwich. bk.rev.; bibl.

322 — US — ISSN 0017-4742
E838
GROUP RESEARCH REPORT. 1962. m. $40. Group Research, Inc., 527 Woodward Bldg., 733 15th St., N.W., Washington, DC 20005. Ed. Wesley McCune. bk.rev.; illus.; index.
   Description: News and announcements pertaining to the political bloc of right-wing activists and intellectuals.

322.44 — GP
GUADELOUPE 2000. fortn. Residence Massabielle, 97110 Pointe-a-Pitre, Guadeloupe. Ed. Edouard Boulogne. circ. 4,000.

320.5 — US — ISSN 0017-5021
AP2
GUARDIAN; independent radical newsweekly. 1948. 46/yr. $33.50. Institute for Independent Social Journalism, 24 W. 25th St., New York, NY 10010-2704. TEL 212-691-0404. Ed. Karen Gellen. adv.; bk.rev.; film rev.; play rev.; bibl.; illus.; cum.index for yrs.:1951, 1970, 1971; 1974 to present; circ. 20,000. (tabloid format; also avail. in microform from UMI; back issues avail.; reprint service avail. from UMI) **Indexed:** Alt.Press Ind., Chic.Per.Ind., Child.Lit.Abstr., High.Educ.Curr.Aware.Bull., Int.Packag.Abstr., Key to Econ.Sci., Paper & Bd.Abstr., World Text.Abstr.
   Formerly: National Guardian.
   Description: Contains national and international news, focusing on struggles for peace, justice, economic equality and efforts to fight racism, sexism and environmental destruction.

320.531 — AT
GUARDIAN. w. Aus.$48. Socialist Party of Australia, 65 Campbell St., Surry Hills, N.S.W. 2010, Australia. FAX 02-281-5795.
   Formerly: Socialist.

320.5 — US — ISSN 8756-0208
GUIDE TO THE AMERICAN LEFT; directory and bibliography. 1979. a. $24.95. Laird Wilcox, Box 2047, Olathe, KS 66061. TEL 913-829-0609. FAX 913-829-0609. bibl.; circ. 700. **Indexed:** P.A.I.S., Vert.File Ind.
   Former titles: Directory of the American Left; (until 1970): Guide to the American Left (ISSN 0017-5315)
   Description: Directory of 1200 left-wing organizations and serials. Includes a bibliography.

320 — US — ISSN 8756-0216
HS2321
GUIDE TO THE AMERICAN RIGHT; directory and bibliography. 1978. a. $24.95. Laird Wilcox, Box 2047, Olathe, KS 66061. TEL 913-829-0609. FAX 913-829-0609. circ. 1,800. **Indexed:** P.A.I.S., Vert.File Ind.
   Formerly: Directory of the American Right.
   Description: Directory of 1200 right-wing organizations and serials. Includes a bibliography.

988 — GY
GUYANA INFORMATION BULLETIN. 1964. m. free. People's Progressive Party, Freedom House, 41 Robb St., Georgetown, Guyana. Ed. Janet Jagan. circ. 1,000. (processed) **Indexed:** HR Rep.
   Former titles (until 1979): Overseas Mirror; (until 1978): Guyana Information Bulletin (ISSN 0017-5862)

988.1 — GY — ISSN 0046-6654
GUYANA JOURNAL.* 1970. q. Ministry of External Affairs, Carmichael St., Georgetown, Guyana. Ed. L. Searwar. illus.

327 — SI
HAMMER.* (Text in English) 1972. m. $2.60. Workers' Party, Suite 602, Colombo Court, Singapore 0617. illus.

320 — MY
AL-HARAKAH; parti Islam se-Malaysia. 1973. w. M.26. Islamic Party of Malaysia, 28A Jalan Pahang Barat off Jalan Pah., Kuala Lumpur 53000, Malaysia. TEL 03-4233343. Ed.Bd. adv.; bk.rev.; circ. 50,000.
   Formerly (until 1987): Berita Pas.

320 — US — ISSN 0090-1032
JK1
HARVARD POLITICAL REVIEW. 1972. q. $15 in U.S. and Canada; Europe $25; elsewhere $30. Institute of Politics, Student Advisory Committee, 79 John F. Kennedy St., Cambridge, MA 02138. TEL 617-495-1360. FAX 617-495-1364. Ed. David Weller. adv.; bk.rev.; illus.; circ. 12,000.

320.532 — II
HAYAT.* (Text in Urdu) 1970. w. Ajoy Bhavan, Kutla Road, New Delhi, India. illus.

320 — IS
HEBETIM; aspects of kibbutz in research themes. 1986. irreg. IS.20. Federation of Kibbutz Movements, Inter-Kibbutz Educational Committee, P.O. Box 303, Tel Aviv 61 002, Israel. Ed. Dov Vardi.
   Description: Papers by secondary school graduates on various aspects of kibbutz.

327 — UK
HER MAJESTY'S CONSULS LIST. 1903. bi-m. £45. Southern Magazines Ltd., Jewson Complex, Eccelson Rd., Tovil, Maidstone, Kent ME15 6ST, England. TEL 0622-677014. FAX 0622-759818. Ed. Roderick Cooper. adv.; bk.rev.; circ. 3,500. (controlled)

320 — CK
HERALDO DE CALDAS. w. Col.2 per no. Editorial Sigma - Pereira, Carrera 23, no. 20-59, Manizales, Colombia. Ed. Alberto Trujillo Escobar. adv.; illus. (tabloid format)

320 — US
HERITAGE FOUNDATION. ISSUE BULLETINS. irreg., latest 1989. $125 includes Backgrounder and Backgrounder Update. Heritage Foundation, 214 Massachusetts Ave., N.E., Washington, DC 20002. TEL 202-546-4400. FAX 202-546-8328.
   ●Also available online. Vendor(s): Mead Data Central.

323.44 — US
▼**HETERODOXY;** articles and animadversions on political correctness and other follies. 1992. 11/yr. $25. 12400 Ventura Blvd., Ste. 304, Studio City, CA 91604. TEL 916-265-9306. Eds. Peter Collier, David Horowitz. adv. contact: David Horowitz. (back issues avail.)
   Description: Covers freedom of speech issues in academia.

950 — II — ISSN 0018-1900
HIMMAT/COURAGE; Asia's new voice. (Text in English) 1964. w. Rs.30($25) Himmat Publications Trust, 501 Arun Chambers, Tardeo Road, Bombay 400034, India. Ed. Kalpana Sharma. adv.; bk.rev.; charts; illus.; circ. 10,000.

322.4 — GW — ISSN 0722-8252
HIMMEL & ERDE; international revue. 1981. irreg. Verlag Roter Funke, Goethestr. 22, D-2800 Bremen 1, Germany. Ed. Klaus Mecking. (back issues avail.)

HISPO. see HISTORY — History Of Europe

HISTORIA ECONOMICA. see BUSINESS AND ECONOMICS — Economic Situation And Conditions

HISTORIC DOCUMENTS. see HISTORY — History Of North And South America

HISTORICAL METHODS. see HISTORY

HISTORICAL SOCIAL RESEARCH/HISTORISCHE SOZIALFORSCHUNG. see HISTORY — History Of Europe

DAS HISTORISCH-POLITISCHE BUCH; Ein Wegweiser durch das Schrifttum. see HISTORY

320 900 — UK — ISSN 0143-781X
JA8
HISTORY OF POLITICAL THOUGHT. 1980. q. £29($52) to individuals; institutions £62.50($112.50); (effective Jan. 1991). Imprint Academic, 32 Haldon Rd., Exeter, Devon EX4 4DZ, England. TEL 0392-438104. FAX 0392-425877. Eds. Janet Coleman, Iain Hampshire-Monk. adv.; bk.rev.; circ. 700. (back issues avail.) **Indexed:** A.B.C.Pol.Sci., Amer.Hist.& Life, Arts & Hum.Cit.Ind., Curr.Cont., Hist.Abstr., Int.Polit.Sci.Abstr., Phil.Ind. —BLDSC shelfmark: 4318.405000.

HISTORY WORKSHOP; a journal of socialist historians. see HISTORY

HITOTSUBASHI JOURNAL OF LAW AND POLITICS. see LAW

HOGAKU/JOURNAL OF LAW AND POLITICAL SCIENCE. see LAW

HOGAKU KENKYU/JOURNAL OF LAW, POLITICS, AND SOCIOLOGY. see LAW

HOKOUK. see LAW

HOMME LIBRE; fils de la terre. see PSYCHOLOGY

320 350 — US
HOTLINE (FALLS CHURCH). 1987. d. price varies. American Political Network, Inc., 282 N. Washington St., Falls Church, VA 22046. TEL 703-237-5130. Ed. Will Salatin.
   Description: Coverage of American politics, focusing on gubernatorial, Senate and House races.

057.8 — CN — ISSN 0702-3855
F1035.C7
HRVATSKI PUT/CROATIAN WAY. (Text occasionally in English) 1962. m. Can.$36. Croatian-Canadian Society, Postal Station "M", Box 78, Toronto, Ont. M6S 4T2, Canada. TEL 416-979-5341. Ed. Rudi Tomic. adv.; bk.rev.; illus.; circ. 3,000.
   Formerly: Nas Put - Our Way (ISSN 0027-8092)
   Description: Covers world affairs and Croatian national culture and political activity throughout the world.

320 342 — CH
HSIEN CHENG SSU CH'AO. (Text in Chinese) q. (Kuo Min Ta Hui, Hsien Cheng Yen T'ao Wei Yuan Hui - National People's Council, Committee for the Discussion of Constitutional Government) Hsien Cheng Ssu Ch'ao Magazine House, No. 1, Hsiushan St., Taipei, Taiwan, Republic of China. TEL 02-311-4066.
   Description: Investigates systems of government and political theories, centering on the concept and reality of Constitutional rule. Includes translations.

320 — UK — ISSN 0142-7377
HULL PAPERS IN POLITICS. 1978. irreg. price varies. University of Hull, Department of Politics, Hull HU6 7RX, England. Ed. Philip Norton.

320.9 — US — ISSN 0018-7194
D410
HUMAN EVENTS; the national conservative weekly. 1944. w. $40. Human Events, Inc., 422 First St., S.E., Washington, DC 20003. TEL 202-546-0856. Ed. Thomas S. Winter. adv.; bk.rev.; illus.; index.; circ. 30,000. (tabloid format; also avail. in microform from UMI; microfiche from BHP,KTO; back issues avail.; reprint service avail. from UMI) **Indexed:** Bk.Rev.Ind. (1977-), Child.Bk.Rev.Ind. (1977-).

HUMAN RESOURCES ABSTRACTS; an international information service. see SOCIOLOGY — Abstracting, Bibliographies, Statistics

320 — GW
HUMANE GESELLSCHAFT. 1972. q. Junge Union Baden-Wuerttemberg, Hohenheimerstr. 9, 7000 Stuttgart 1, Germany. TEL 0711-2104353. adv.; bk.rev.; bibl.; film rev.; illus.; play rev.; stats.; circ. 20,000.

320 — DK — ISSN 0106-4177
HVEM, HVAD, HVOR. 1934. a. DKK 99. Politikens Forlag A-S, Vestergade 24, DK-1456 Copenhagen K, Denmark. FAX 45-33-93-21-52.

I C P S R BULLETIN. (Inter-University Consortium for Political and Social Research) see *SOCIAL SCIENCES: COMPREHENSIVE WORKS*

I F M - S E I BULLETIN. (International Falcon Movement - Socialist Educational International) see *EDUCATION*

320.531　　　　UK　　ISSN 0951-2187
HD4805
I L P MAGAZINE. 1987. m. £3.50. (Independent Labour Publications) Labour Leader Publications Ltd., 49 Top Moor Side, Leeds, W. Yorkshire LS11 9LW, England. TEL 0532-430613. Ed. Barry Winter. adv.; bk.rev.; illus.; circ. 4,000. (tabloid format; also avail. in microfilm from BHP)
　　Incorporates (1922-1975): Labour Leader (ISSN 0305-0297); Formerly: Socialist Leader (ISSN 0037-8224)

I LAISVE/TOWARD FREEDOM; Lithuanian magazine of politics. see *ETHNIC INTERESTS*

320　　　　　GW　　ISSN 0177-6657
I N P R E K O R R. (Internationale Pressekorrespondenz) 1970. m. DM.35. I S P-Verlag, Postfach 111017, 6000 Frankfurt, Main 1, Germany. adv.; bk.rev.; index; circ. 1,200. (back issues avail.)

300 320　　　　II　　ISSN 0019-0403
I P S S BULLETIN. (Text in English) vol.4, 1969. Rs.10. Institute of Political and Social Studies, 357-1C Prince Anwar Shah Rd., Calcutta 31, India. Ed. K.K. Sinha.

327 330.1　　　GW　　ISSN 0046-970X
HF1410
I P W BERICHTE. (Internationale Politik und Wirtschaft) 1972. m. DM.72. Demokratie und Recht Zeitschriftenverlag GmbH, Postfach 203363, 2000 Hamburg 20, Germany. Ed.Bd. bk.rev.; abstr.; bibl.; charts; stat. Indexed: P.A.I.S.For.Lang.Ind., SSCI.
—BLDSC shelfmark: 4567.490000.

320　　　　　SZ
I P Z INFORMATION. REIHE S: SUBVERSION. 1971. irreg., no. 19, 1987. price varies. Institut fuer Politologische Zeitfragen, Postfach 6934, CH-8023 Zurich, Switzerland. TEL 01-2117776. bk.rev.; circ. 1,500.

I S H I OCCASIONAL PAPERS IN SOCIAL CHANGE. (Institute for the Study of Human Issues) see *SOCIOLOGY*

320.531　　　　AU
I U S Y NEWSLETTER. 1971. irreg. free. International Union of Socialist Youth, Neustiftgasse, A-1070 Vienna, Austria. TEL 431-931267. FAX 431-523124385. TELEX 75312469 SJOE. Ed. Ricard Torrell. bk.rev.; illus.; circ. 1,500.
　　Former titles (until 1985): I U S Y Bulletin; I U S Y Survey (ISSN 0019-0888)

I W K. (Internationale Wissenschaftliche Korrespondenz zur Geschichte der Deutschen Arbeiterbewegung) see *LABOR UNIONS*

IBYKUS; Zeitschrift fuer Poesie, Wissenschaft und Staatskunst. see *LITERATURE* — *Poetry*

320.9　　　　　NO　　ISSN 0046-8517
IDE. 1967. q. NOK 100 prices typically set in January. Valo Forlag A-S, Postboks 478, Sentrum, 0105 Oslo 1, Norway. Ed. Johannes Morken. bk.rev.; bibl.; illus.; circ. 1,500.

320　　　　　IT
IDEA LIBERALE. 1959. bi-m. L.20000. Edizioni Pergamena s.a.s., Viale Ezio 7, 20149 Milan, Italy. Dir. Giovanni Giraldi.

320　　　　　PE
IDEOLOGIA Y POLITICA. 1973. irreg., no.7, 1990. price varies. (Instituto de Estudios Peruanos) I E P Ediciones, Horacio Urteaga 694 (Campo de Marte), Lima 11, Peru. TEL 323070. FAX 324981.

329　　　　　US
ILLINOIS LIBERTARIAN. 1975. m. $15. Libertarian Party of Illinois, Box 313, Chicago, IL 60690. TEL 312-475-0391. FAX 708-475-3776. Ed. Ken Prazak. adv.; bk.rev.; circ. 1,000.
　　Description: Newsletter of articles, letters, book reviews, editorials, announcements, and directories of interest to support the platform of the Libertarian Party.

374 320　　　　GW　　ISSN 0721-2097
IM GESPRAECH. 1971. q. DM.16. (Institut fuer Begabtenfoerderung) Ernst Knoth GmbH, Postfach 226, 4520 Melle 1, Germany. TEL 05422-2895. FAX 05422-43038. Ed. Julius Becker. circ. 5,000.

IMMIGRATION REPORT. see *LAW — Civil Law*

IMPACT; Asian magazine for human transformation. see *SOCIAL SCIENCES: COMPREHENSIVE WORKS*

IN DE WAAGSCHAAL. see *RELIGIONS AND THEOLOGY*

320.531　　　　US　　ISSN 0160-5992
AP2
IN THESE TIMES. 1976. 41/yr. (bi-w. during summer). $34.95. Institute for Public Affairs, 2040 N. Milwaukee Ave., 2nd Fl., Chicago, IL 60647-4002. TEL 312-472-5700. FAX 312-772-4180. Ed. James Weinstein. adv.; bk.rev.; illus.; circ. 35,000. (tabloid format; also avail. in microfilm from UMI; back issues avail.; reprint service avail. from UMI)
Indexed: Alt.Press Ind., Chic.Per.Ind., HR Rep., Left Ind. (1982-).
　　Description: Presents a leftist viewpoint; however, with frequent discussions of strategies for working within the Democratic Party. It is strong on its labor and women's movement coverage; less strong on the international front.

INCHIESTA; ricerca e pratica sociale. see *SOCIAL SERVICES AND WELFARE*

L'INCONTRO DELLE GENTI; rivista di scienze lettere ed arte. see *ART*

320 301 800　　　　IT
INDAGINI E PROSPETTIVE. irreg., latest no.14. price varies. Angelo Longo Editore, Via Paolo Costa 33, P.O. Box 431, 48100 Ravenna, Italy. TEL 0544-217026.

INDEPENDENT NATIONAL EDITION; a monthly journal for thoughtful Canadians. see *ENVIRONMENTAL STUDIES*

954　　　　　US　　ISSN 0019-4212
INDIA NEWS. 1962. fortn. 15. India Information Service, Embassy of India, 2107 Massachusetts Ave., N.W., Washington, DC 20008. TEL 202-265-5050. FAX 202-939-7027. Ed. Dayakar Ratakonda. bk.rev.; illus.; circ. 15,000. (newspaper; also avail. in microform from MIM) Indexed: P.A.I.S.

320 320　　　　II
INDIAN INSTITUTE OF PUBLIC OPINION. MONTHLY PUBLIC OPINION SURVEYS. (Text in English) 1955. m. Rs.400($80) Indian National Institute of Public Opinion Private Ltd., 2-A National Insurance Bldg., Parliament St., Box 288, New Delhi 110001, India. Ed. E.P.W. da Costa. charts; stat.
　　Description: Highlights survey results on socio-economic and political affairs by a variety of demographic variables.

320　　　　　II　　ISSN 0019-5510
JA26
INDIAN JOURNAL OF POLITICAL SCIENCE. (Text in English) 1937. q. $65. Indian Political Science Association, Anna Centre for Public Affairs, University of Madras, Madras 600 005, India. TEL 566693. TELEX 416376 UNOM IN. Ed. R. Thandavan. adv.; bk.rev.; circ. 2,000. (also avail. in microform from UMI; reprint service avail. from UMI) Indexed: A.B.C.Pol.Sci., ASSIA, Hist.Abstr., Int.Polit.Sci.Abstr.

320　　　　　II　　ISSN 0303-9951
JA26
INDIAN JOURNAL OF POLITICS. 1967. q. Rs.100($35) (effective 1991). Aligarh Muslim University, Department of Political Science, Aligarh 202 002, Uttar Pradesh, India. Ed. A.S. Usmani. adv.; bk.rev.; circ. 1,000. (also avail. in microform; reprint service avail. from ISI) Indexed: A.B.C.Pol.Sci., Amer.Hist.& Life, Curr.Cont., Hist.Abstr., Ind.Per.Lit., Int.Polit.Sci.Abstr., Sociol.Abstr.

320 990　　　　AT　　ISSN 1037-7131
INDIAN OCEAN CENTRE FOR PEACE STUDIES. BRIEFING PAPERS. irreg? price varies. Indian Ocean Centre for Peace Studies, University of Western Australia, Nedlands, W.A. 6009, Australia. FAX 09-380-1074.

320 990　　　　AT
INDIAN OCEAN CENTRE FOR PEACE STUDIES. MONOGRAPHS. irreg? Aus.$25 per issue. Indian Ocean Centre for Peace Studies, University of Western Australia, Nedlands, W.A. 6009, Australia. FAX 09-380-1074. Ed.Bd.

320 990　　　　AT　　ISSN 1037-7123
INDIAN OCEAN CENTRE FOR PEACE STUDIES. OCCASIONAL PAPERS. irreg? price varies. Indian Ocean Centre for Peace Studies, University of Western Australia, Nedlands, W.A. 6009, Australia. FAX 09-380-1074.

320 990　　　　AT　　ISSN 1031-2331
DS331
INDIAN OCEAN REVIEW. (Text in English and French) 1980. q. Aus.$30 to individuals; institutions Aus.$40. Indian Ocean Centre for Peace Studies, University of Western Australia, Nedlands, W.A. 6009, Australia. FAX 09-380-1074. Ed. Kenneth McPherson. bk.rev.; illus.; charts; circ. 900. (back issues avail.)
　　Formerly: Indian Ocean Newsletter (ISSN 0728-4330)
　　Description: Multi-disciplinary publication centered upon issues concerning the Indian Ocean region.

323.4 100　　　　US
INDIVIDUAL LIBERTY. 1970. m. $10. Society for Individual Liberty, Box 1147, Warminster, PA 18974. TEL 215-365-7389. Eds. David Walter, Donald Ernsberger. adv.; bk.rev.; circ. 1,700. (processed)
　　Formerly: S I L News (ISSN 0036-1550)
　　Description: Monthly newsletter of the Society for Individual Liberty, a Pennsylvania-based group of the Libertarian Party. Addresses Constitutional concerns and news of the Libertarian Party.

INDIVIDUALIST. see *PHILOSOPHY*

954　　　　　GW　　ISSN 0019-719X
DS401
INDO-ASIA; fuer Politik, Kultur und Wirtschaft Indiens und Suedost Asiens. (Text in German; occasionally in English) 1959. 4/yr. DM.61.50. (Deutsch-Indische Gesellschaft) Burg-Verlag, 7123 Sachsenheim-Hohenhaslach, Germany. adv.; bk.rev.; charts; illus.; index; circ. 2,500. Indexed: P.A.I.S.For.Lang.Ind.

327　　　　　II　　ISSN 0042-9740
INDO-IRAN JOURNAL. (Text in English and Persian) 1969. q. Rs.7($1) Indo-Iran Society, Tilak Marg, New Delhi 110001, India. Ed. H. Kardoosh. illus.

INDONESIA LETTER. see *BUSINESS AND ECONOMICS — Economic Situation And Conditions*

959.8　　　　　IO　　ISSN 0304-2170
INDONESIAN QUARTERLY. (Text in English) 1972. 3/m. $35. Centre for Strategic and International Studies, Jalan Tanah Abang III-27, Jakarta 10160, Indonesia. TEL 356532-35. FAX 021-375317. TELEX 45164-CENTRE-IA. Ed. Daniel Setyawan. adv.; bk.rev.; bibl.; charts; circ. 3,000. Indexed: Abstr.Mil.Bibl., E.I., Rice Abstr.

INFORMACION POLITICA Y ECONOMICA. see *BUSINESS AND ECONOMICS — Economic Situation And Conditions*

INFORMATION FUER ORMESHEIM. see *PUBLIC ADMINISTRATION — Municipal Government*

300　　　　　AU　　ISSN 0083-6125
INFORMATIONEN ZU AKTUELLEN FRAGEN DER SOZIAL- UND WIRTSCHAFTPOLITIK. 1962. irreg. price varies. Verein fuer Sozial- und Wirtschaftsforschung, Renngasse 12, A-1010 Vienna, Austria. Ed.Bd. circ. 1,000.

320 371.3　　　GW　　ISSN 0046-9408
INFORMATIONEN ZUR POLITISCHEN BILDUNG/INFORMATION FOR CIVIC EDUCATION. 1952. 4/yr. free. Bundeszentrale fuer Politische Bildung, Berliner Freiheit 7, 5300 Bonn 1, Germany. FAX 0228-515113. Ed. Horst Poetzsch. bk.rev.; circ. 1,300,000. Indexed: Hist.Abstr.
　　Description: Devoted to the study and teaching of political science in Germany. Includes bibliography and list of educational materials.

INFORME LATINOAMERICANO. see *BUSINESS AND ECONOMICS — Economic Situation And Conditions*

POLITICAL SCIENCE 3899

340   PE
INFORMES. no.8, 1982. irreg. Instituto de Promocion y Educacion Popular, Av. Pardo 130, Chimbote, Peru.

320 332   GT   ISSN 0252-8754
INFORPRESS CENTROAMERICANA. 1972. w. $410. Inforpress Centroamericana, 9 Calle A, 3-56, Zona 1, Guatemala City, Guatemala. TEL 29432, 81997. charts. (back issues avail.)
   Description: Contains information and analysis on the economic and political events in Belize, Guatemala, El Salvador, Honduras, Nicaragua, Costa Rica and Panama.

INK W E L (Women's Electoral Lobby A.C.T.) see *WOMEN'S INTERESTS*

INSIDE ALABAMA POLITICS. see *PUBLIC ADMINISTRATION*

994   AT   ISSN 0046-9629
INSIDE CANBERRA. 1948. w. Aus.$297. Australian Press Services Pty., Ltd., P.O. Box E 160, Queen Victoria Terrace, A.C.T. 2600, Australia. Ed. R. D. Chalmers.

INSIDE MICHIGAN POLITICS. see *PUBLIC ADMINISTRATION*

320   SP
INSTITUCIONES EUROPEAS. 3/yr. $40. (Centro de Estudios Constitucionales) Edisa, Lopez Hoyos, 141, 28002 Madrid, Spain. TEL 415-97-12.

INSTITUT DES HAUTES ETUDES DE L'AMERIQUE LATINE. COLLECTION DES TRAVAUX ET MEMOIRES. see *HISTORY — History Of North And South America*

INSTITUT DES RECHERCHES MARXISTES. ISSUES. see *BUSINESS AND ECONOMICS*

INSTITUT DES RECHERCHES MARXISTES. RECHERCHES INTERNATIONALES. see *POLITICAL SCIENCE — International Relations*

320 100   IT   ISSN 0393-6503
INSTITUT INTERNATIONAL J. MARITAIN. NOTES ET DOCUMENTS; pour une recherche personnaliste - for a personalist approach. 1975. q. $30. (Institut International Jacques Maritain) Notes et Documents, Via Quintino Sella, 33, 00187 Rome, Italy. TEL 06-4874336. FAX 06-4825188. adv.; bk.rev.; circ. 4,000 (controlled).

INSTITUT PO ISTORIIA NA B K P. IZVESTIIA. see *HISTORY — History Of Europe*

330 301   US   ISSN 0364-0779
HV95   CODEN: JISSDW
INSTITUTE FOR SOCIOECONOMIC STUDIES. JOURNAL. 1976. q. Institute for Socioeconomic Studies, Airport Rd., White Plains, NY 10604. TEL 914-428-7400. Ed. B.A. Rittersporn, Jr. circ. 17,500. (also avail. in microfiche from WSH; microfilm from WSH) **Indexed:** ASSIA, BPIA, CLOA, Fut.Surv., Med.Care Rev., Mid.East: Abstr.& Ind., P.A.I.S., Sage Pub.Admin.Abstr. Key Title: Journal of the Institute for Socioeconomic Studies.

INSTITUTE OF DEVELOPING ECONOMIES. LIBRARY BULLETIN/AJIA KEIZAI SHIRYO-GEPPO. see *LIBRARY AND INFORMATION SCIENCES*

INSTITUTE OF URBAN STUDIES NEWSLETTER. see *HOUSING AND URBAN PLANNING*

320   US
INSTITUTION ANALYSIS. 1977. irreg., latest 1988. $3 per no. Heritage Foundation, 214 Massachusetts Ave., N.E., Washington, DC 20002. TEL 202-546-4400. FAX 202-546-8328.
  ●Also available online. Vendor(s): Mead Data Central.

320   AG   ISSN 0074-0063
INSTITUTO DE CIENCIA POLITICA RAFAEL BIELSA. ANUARIO. 1968. a. Arg.$75($8) Universidad Nacional de Rosario, Instituto de Ciencia Politica Rafael Bielsa, Facultad de Ciencia Politica y Relaciones Internacionales, Division Publicaciones, Cordoba 2020, Rosario, Argentina. Ed. Alberto Dominguez.

INSTITUTO DE ESTUDIOS PERUANOS. DOCUMENTOS DE TRABAJO. see *ANTHROPOLOGY*

320   SP   ISSN 0020-3866
INSTITUTO DE ESTUDIOS POLITICOS. BOLETIN.* no.7, 1966. bi-m. membership. (Centro de Estudios Constitucionales) Libreria Europa, Plaza de la Marina Espanola 9, Madrid 13, Spain. adv.; charts; stat. **Indexed:** Hist.Abstr.

320   PE
INSTITUTO PERUANO DE POLEMOLOGIA. 1986. s-a. free. Instituto Peruano de Polemologia, Apdo. Postal 2284, Lima 1, Peru. Ed. Luis Callegari Botteri. circ. 2,000.

320   GT
INTEGRACION EN CIFRAS. no.31, Mar. 1976. q. Q.6($25) (Mercado Comun Centroamericano, Secretaria Permanente del Tratado General de Integracion Economica Centroamericana - Central American Common Market, Permanent Secretariat of the General Treaty of Central American Economic Integration) S I E C A, Apdo. 1237, 4 Avenida No. 10-25, Zona 14, Guatemala C.A., Guatemala. TEL 682151. FAX 502-681071. TELEX 6203 SIECA GU. Ed. Eduardo Bolanos. charts; stat.

320   UK   ISSN 0268-4527
INTELLIGENCE AND NATIONAL SECURITY. 1986. 4/yr. £32($45) to individuals; institutions £80($125). Frank Cass & Co. Ltd., Gainsborough House, 11 Gainsborough Rd., London E11 1RS, England. TEL 081-530 4226. FAX 081-530-7795. Eds. Christopher Andrew, Michael Handel. adv.; bk.rev.; index. (also avail. in microfilm from UMI; back issues avail.)
  —BLDSC shelfmark: 4531.827000.
   Description: Scholarly journal covering the history of intelligence and counter-intelligence work by the major powers.

320.9   UK
INTELLIGENCE DIGEST - A REVIEW OF WORLD AFFAIRS; international political, economic and strategic intelligence. 1938. w. $197 includes: Intelligence Digest Strategic Briefing Paper. Intelligence International Ltd., 17 Rodney Rd., Cheltenham, Glos. GL50 1HX, England. bk.rev
  Former titles: Intelligence Digest (Cheltenham); Intelligence Digest Political and Strategic Review; Intelligence Digest World Report; Intelligence Digest (ISSN 0020-4900) Intelligence Digest Weekly Review (ISSN 0307-188X); Weekly Review (ISSN 0043-1915).

320.9   UK
INTELLIGENCE DIGEST STRATEGIC BRIEFING PAPER. 6/yr. $197 (includes Intelligence Digest - A Review of World Affairs). Intelligence International Ltd., 17 Rodney Rd., Cheltenham, Glos. GL50 1HX, England.
  Former titles: Intelligence Digest Briefing Paper; Intelligence Digest Political Brief; Intelligence Digest Special Brief.

320.5   AT   ISSN 0047-0406
INTELLIGENCE SURVEY. 1953. m. Aus.$6. Australian League of Rights, 273 Little Collins St., Melbourne, Victoria 3001, Australia. Ed. Eric D. Butler. circ. 2,000. (tabloid format)

322.44   IS
INTER; review of international terrorism in (year). (Text in English) a. IS.35($22.50) (Tel Aviv University, Jaffee Center for Strategic Studies) Jerusalem Post, P.O. Box 81, Jerusalem 91000, Israel. TEL 02-551616. FAX 02-537527. (U.S. addr.: Westview Press, 5500 Central Ave., Boulder, CO 80301) circ. 2,000. (back issues avail.)
   Description: Contains in-depth survey of events and trends in world terrorism, including analysis and extensive tables.

323.44   US   ISSN 0579-6695
INTER AMERICAN PRESS ASSOCIATION. COMMITTEE ON FREEDOM ON THE PRESS. REPORT. Vol. for 1973- issued under a variant name of the committee: Committee on Freedom of the Press and Information. s-a. membership. Inter American Press Association, 2911 N.W. 39th St., Miami, FL 33142. TEL 305-634-2465. TELEX 522873.

INTERESSE; soziale Information. see *SOCIAL SERVICES AND WELFARE*

320   US   ISSN 0362-8507
JK325
INTERGOVERNMENTAL PERSPECTIVE. 1975. q. free. U.S. Advisory Commission on Intergovernmental Relations, 800 K St., N.W., Ste. 450-South, Washington, DC 20575. bk.rev.; charts; illus.; circ. 20,000. (also avail. in microform from UMI; reprint service avail. from UMI) **Indexed:** Amer.Stat.Ind., Ind.U.S.Gov.Per.
   Description: Current issues in federal and state local relations.

320   US
INTERNATIONAL CORRESPONDENCE. (Editions in English, French, Spanish) bi-m. $10. New International Distributors, Box 471, Ansonia Sta., New York, NY 10023.
   Description: Examines the international struggle of workers and oppressed masses from a socialist perspective.

INTERNATIONAL JOURNAL OF CONFLICT MANAGEMENT. see *BUSINESS AND ECONOMICS — Management*

INTERNATIONAL JOURNAL OF GAME THEORY. see *MATHEMATICS*

INTERNATIONAL JOURNAL OF GROUP TENSIONS. see *PSYCHOLOGY*

320   US   ISSN 0885-0607
UB250
INTERNATIONAL JOURNAL OF INTELLIGENCE AND COUNTERINTELLIGENCE. 1986. q. $75. Intel Publishing Group, Inc., Box 188, Stroudsburg, PA 18360. Ed. F. Reese Brown.
  —BLDSC shelfmark: 4542.310300.

341   US   ISSN 0891-1916
JA1.A1
INTERNATIONAL JOURNAL OF POLITICAL ECONOMY; a journal of translations. 1971. q. $260 to institutions. M. E. Sharpe, Inc., 80 Business Park Dr., Armonk, NY 10504. TEL 914-273-1800. FAX 914-273-2106. Ed. Paul Mattick, Jr. adv.; index. (back issues avail.) **Indexed:** Amer.Hist.& Life, Curr.Cont., Hist.Abstr., Mid.East: Abstr.& Ind., SSCI.
  —BLDSC shelfmark: 4542.470900.
  Former titles (until 1987): International Journal of Politics (ISSN 0012-8783); Eastern European Studies in Law and Government.
  Refereed Serial

INTERNATIONAL JOURNAL OF PUBLIC OPINION RESEARCH. see *SOCIAL SCIENCES: COMPREHENSIVE WORKS*

320 338.91   US
INTERNATIONAL POLITICAL ECONOMY YEARBOOK. 1985. a. price varies. Lynne Rienner Publishers, 1800 30th St., Ste. 314, Boulder, CO 80301. TEL 303-444-6684. FAX 303-444-0824.

320   NO
INTERNATIONAL POLITICAL SCIENCE ASSOCIATION. WORLD CONGRESS. 1951. triennial, 12th, 1982 Rio de Janeiro; 13th, 1985 Paris; 14th, 1988 Washington; 15th, 1991, Buenos Aires. price varies. International Political Science Association, c/o University of Oslo, Institute of Political Science, Box 1097 Blindern, 0317 Oslo 3, Norway. TEL 02-455168. (also avail. in microfiche)
  Formerly: International Political Science Association. World Conference. Proceedings (ISSN 0074-7467)

320   AT   ISSN 0312-0627
INTERNATIONAL RESEARCH AND INFORMATION ASSOCIATION. SURVEY. 1975. m. Aus.$20. International Research and Information Association, P.O. Box K535, Haymarket, 2000, Australia. Ed. W.J. Brown. circ. 8,000.
   Description: Covers social, political and economic aspects of life in the USSR and other socialist countries.

INTERNATIONAL SOCIALISM. see *LITERARY AND POLITICAL REVIEWS*

320 327   IT   ISSN 0393-2729
D839
INTERNATIONAL SPECTATOR. (Text in English) 1966. q. L.48000. (Istituto Affari Internazionali) Casa Editrice Fratelli Palombi, Via dei Gracchi 181-185, 00192 Rome, Italy. TEL 06-354456. FAX 06-319806. Ed. Gianni Bonvicini. adv.; circ. 1,500. **Indexed:** E.I.
   Description: Forum covering internal politics.

POLITICAL SCIENCE

320.53   CS
INTERNATIONAL UNION OF STUDENTS. SECRETARIAT REPORTS. French edition: Union Internationale des Etudiants. Secretariat au Fil du Mois. Spanish edition: Union Internacional de Estudiantes. El Secretariado Informa. (Editions in Arabic, English, French, Spanish) m. free. International Union of Students, 17 November St., P.O. Box 58, 110 01 Prague 01, Czechoslovakia.

320   FR   ISSN 0294-2925
INTERNATIONAL VIEWPOINT. French edition: Imprecor. (Text in English) 1982. fortn. 280 Fr.($48) (N. America 340 F.($57)). Presse-Edition-Communication (PEC), 2 rue Richard Lenoir, 93108 Montreuil, France. FAX 43-79-21-06. Ed. Gerry Foley. bk.rev.; charts, illus, stat.; index; circ. 5,000. (back issues avail.) Indexed: Alt.Press Ind.
Description: News and analysis under the auspices of the United Secretariat of the Fourth International. Likely to be of interest to activists in socialist and worker's movement.

INTERNATIONAL YEAR BOOK AND STATESMEN'S WHO'S WHO. see *BIOGRAPHY*

320   GW   ISSN 0936-5184
INTERNATIONALE BEZIEHUNGEN. 1989. irreg., vol.3, 1990. price varies. Franz Steiner Verlag Wiesbaden GmbH, Birkenwaldstr. 44, Postfach 101526, 7000 Stuttgart 1, Germany. TEL 0711-2582-0. FAX 0711-2582290.

329.9   AU   ISSN 0020-9473
INTERNATIONALES FREIES WORT. 1964. q. S.20 (foreign S.30). Bund Demokratischer Sozialisten, Gussriegelstr. 50, 1100 Vienna, Austria. (U.S. subscr. to: World Socialist Party, 259 Huntington Ave., Boston, MA 02115) Ed. F. Vogt. adv.; bk.rev.; circ. 2,000.
Formerly: Wiener Freie Wort - W F W.

320   SZ   ISSN 0579-8337
INTER-PARLIAMENTARY UNION. SERIES: "REPORTS AND DOCUMENTS". 1965. irreg., no.19, 1991. price varies. Inter-Parliamentary Union, Place du Petit-Saconnex, B.P. 438, 1211 Geneva 19, Switzerland. TEL 022-7344150. FAX 022-7333141. TELEX 414217-IPU-CH.

320   US   ISSN 0020-9635
JA26
INTERPRETATION (FLUSHING); a journal of political philosophy. 1970. 3/yr. $21 to individuals; institutions $34; students $12. Queens College, Flushing, NY 11367-0904. TEL 718-520-7099. Ed. Hilail Gildin. bk.rev.; circ. 950. **Indexed:** Biol.Abstr., Bk.Rev.Ind., CERDIC, Chr.Per.Ind., Curr.Cont., G.Soc.Sci.& Rel.Per.Lit., M.L.A., Mid.East: Abstr.& Ind., New Test.Abstr., Old Test.Abstr., Phil.Ind., Rel.Ind.One.
—BLDSC shelfmark: 4557.347200.

320   US   ISSN 0074-1078
INTER-UNIVERSITY CONSORTIUM FOR POLITICAL AND SOCIAL RESEARCH. ANNUAL REPORT. 1963. a. free. Inter-University Consortium for Political and Social Research, Box 1248, Ann Arbor, MI 48106. TEL 313-764-2570. FAX 313-764-8041.
Description: Report of finances, data collections released, major activities, funding, member organizations, council, and staff of computerized social science data archives.

329.81   US
IOWA IDEA. 1978. q. $5 donation. Iowa Socialist Party, State Committee, Box 924, Iowa City, IA 52244. TEL 515-243-3577. Ed. Aric West. bk.rev.; circ. 2,000. (tabloid format; back issues avail.)

320   IR
IRAN PRESS DIGEST (POLITICAL). w. Iran Press Digest Establishment, Hafiz Ave., 4 Kucheh Hurtab, P.O. Box 11365-5551, Teheran, Iran. TEL 016-668114. TELEX 212300.

320   CE
IRANAMA. 1964. w. 5 Gunasena Mawatha, Colombo 12, Sri Lanka. TEL 1-23864.

IRISH AMERICA MAGAZINE. see *ETHNIC INTERESTS*

320   IE
IRISH PEOPLE. 1973. w. £20. (Sinn Fein the Workers' Party) Repsol Publications, 30 Gardiner Pl., Dublin 1, Ireland. Ed. John Gallagher. adv.; circ. 26,000.

329.9   UK
IRISH POLITICAL REVIEW. 1965. m. £8. Comment Group, 28 Elm Castle Drive, Kilnamanagh, Dublin 28, Ireland. circ. 500.
Supersedes: Irish Communist.
Description: Covers Irish current affairs.

320   IE   ISSN 0790-7184
JN1400
IRISH POLITICAL STUDIES. 1986. a. £10($21) Political Studies Association of Ireland, Social Sciences Research Centre, University College Galway, Ireland. FAX 091-25700. Eds. M. Gallagher, M. Marsh. bk.rev.; circ. 500.
—BLDSC shelfmark: 4574.650700.

IRISH VOICE. see *ETHNIC INTERESTS*

IRODALOM - SZOCIALIZMUS. see *LITERATURE*

ISLAM ET SOCIETES AU SUD DU SAHARA. see *HISTORY — History Of Africa*

320 297   NP   ISSN 8755-8912
ISLAM INTERNATIONAL. 1986. s-a. $50. Siveast Consultants, Inc., USA, c/o P.O. Box 1755, Kathmandu, Nepal. (UK subscr. to: Dr. Ramasastry, c/o Overseas Customer Service, Midland Bank Blc., Poultry and Princes St., London EC 2, England) Ed. C.V. Ramasastry. adv.; bk.rev.; circ. 20(controlled). (looseleaf format; reprint service avail.)

956.940 296   DK   ISSN 0021-194X
ISRAEL. 1948. q. DKK 90. Dansk Zionist Forbund, Ny Kongensgade 6, 1472 Copenhagen K, Denmark. FAX 45-33-91-00-91. Ed. Hans Henrik Fafner. adv.; bk.rev.; illus.; circ. 3,000.
Description: Covers events in Israel and the Middle East as well as events of interest to Jews elsewhere.

956.94 328   IS   ISSN 0012-4249
ISRAEL. KNESSET. DIVREI HA-KNESSET. (Text in Hebrew) 1948. w. Knesset, Jerusalem, Israel. Ed. Gideon Greif.

956.940 327   US   ISSN 0021-2083
DS101
ISRAEL HORIZONS; the socialist Zionist journal. 1952. q. $15. Americans for Progressive Israel, 224 W. 35th St., Ste. 403, New York, NY 10001. Ed. Ralph Seliger. adv.; bk.rev.; film rev.; charts; illus.; index; circ. 2,000. **Indexed:** HR Rep., Left Ind. (1986-), Mid.East: Abstr.& Ind., P.A.I.S.
—BLDSC shelfmark: 4583.790000.
Description: Deals with the Israeli left and the peace camp in Israel, Israeli culture and life, the world Jewish community, and questions confronting socialism.

ISRAEL STUDIES. see *SOCIAL SCIENCES: COMPREHENSIVE WORKS*

320   GW   ISSN 0175-7024
ISRAEL UND PALAESTINA; Zeitschrift fuer Dialog. 1984. bi-m. (plus special issues). DM.40. (Deutsch-Israelischer Arbeitskreis fuer Frieden im Nahen Osten) Haag & Herchen GmbH, Fichardstr. 30, D-6000 Frankfurt, Main 1, Germany. TEL 069-550911. FAX 06323-2195. circ. 500. (back issues avail.)

320   IS
ISRAELI DEMOCRACY (HEBREW EDITION). q. free. Israel Democracy Institute, P.O. Box 4702, Jerusalem 91040, Israel. FAX 02-635319.

320   IT
ISTITUTO GRAMSCI PIEMONTESE. MATERIALI.* vol.2, 1976. irreg. (Istituto Gramsci Piemontese) T. Musolini Editore, Via Rubiana 47, 10139 Turin, Italy.

ISTORIYA I OBSHTESTVOZNANIE. see *HISTORY — History Of Europe*

ITALIA CONTEMPORANEA. see *HISTORY — History Of Europe*

322.4   IT
ITALIA DEL POPOLO. 1981. w. L.15000. Via del Corso 504, Rome, Italy. Ed. Mauro Mita. bk.rev.; circ. 10,000.

320 055.1   IT
ITALIA VIVA; mensile politico. 1971. m. L.10000($6) (effective Jan. 1991). Via Milano 37 (UD), 33037 Pasian di Prato, Italy. TEL 0432-699055. Ed. Antonio Bottega. bk.rev.; circ. 1,500.

320.532   IT
ITALIAN COMMUNISTS; foreign bulletin of the P C I. (Text in English, French, German, Spanish) q. free. Partito Comunista Italiano, Foreign Section, Via delle Botteghe Oscure, 4, Rome 00186, Italy. TEL 06-6711. Dir. Bernardino Bernardini. bk.rev.; circ. 4,500.
Description: Compares the philosophy of the Italian communist party with Italy's other political parties. Reviews the politics of Italy and the problems that face its foreign policies, and outlines the international activities of the PCI.

ITALIAN POLITICS; a review. see *BUSINESS AND ECONOMICS*

945   IT   ISSN 0021-3063
ITALY - DOCUMENTS AND NOTES. (Editions in English, French, German, Italian and Spanish) 1952. bi-m. L.5000. Presidenza del Consiglio dei Ministri, Via Po 14, 00198 Rome, Italy. Ed. Renato Giomcole. adv.; charts; illus.; stat.; index, cum.index; circ. 15,000. **Indexed:** Amer.Hist.& Life, Geo.Abstr., Hist.Abstr., P.A.I.S., Rural Recreat.Tour.Abstr., World Agri.Econ.& Rural Sociol.Abstr.
Formerly: Italian Affairs.

320   IS
IYUNIM B'BIKORET HAMEDINA. (Text in Hebrew) 1962. a. State Comptrollers Office, P.O. Box 1081, Jerusalem 91 010, Israel. FAX 02-384978. Ed. B. Geist. bk.rev.; circ. 1,000.

IZVESTIYA NA DARZHAVNITE ARKHIVI. see *HISTORY — History Of Europe*

320 350   US   ISSN 0888-8957
JK1342
J C P S CONGRESSIONAL DISTRICT FACT BOOK. a. Joint Center for Political Studies, Inc., 1301 Pennsylvania Ave., N.W., Ste. 400, Washington, DC 20004. TEL 202-626-3500.

355   IS
J C S S STUDIES. (Text in English) a. price varies. (Tel Aviv University, Jaffee Center for Strategic Studies) Jerusalem Post, P.O. Box 81, Jerusalem 91000, Israel. TEL 03-420200. FAX 02-537527. (U.S. subscr. to: 211 E. 43rd St., Ste 601, New York, NY 10017) Ed. Joseph Alpher. circ. 1,500.
Formerly (until 1985): J C S S Papers.
Description: Covers strategic subjects in Middle East politics, military, economy, and international relations.

J P I - JUGEND PRESSE INFORMATIONEN. see *CHILDREN AND YOUTH — For*

J T A COMMUNITY NEWS REPORTER. (Jewish Telegraphic Agency) see *ETHNIC INTERESTS*

296   US   ISSN 0021-6763
J T A WEEKLY NEWS DIGEST. 1935. w. $70. Jewish Telegraphic Agency, 330 Seventh Ave., 11th Fl., New York, NY 10001. TEL 212-643-1890. FAX 212-643-8498. TELEX 126978. Ed. Mark Joffe. circ. 7,000. (also avail. in microfilm from AJP).
Description: Weekly summary of international events of concern to and affecting Jews and Jewish communities.

051   US   ISSN 0021-390X
JAG. 1962. irreg. (9-10/yr.). free. Jag, Inc., 10 E. Charles, Oelwein, IA 50662. TEL 319-283-3491. FAX 319-283-3926. Ed. Dr. R.S. Jaggard. bk.rev.; circ. 1,000. (processed; back issues avail.) **Indexed:** C.L.I., Leg.Per.
Description: Covers politics as it relates to medicine.

320   LE
JAMHOUR - AL-JADID.* 1936. w. £L150($50) c/o Farid Abu Shahla, P.O. Box 1834, Beirut, Lebanon.

328.54   II   ISSN 0448-2433
JQ620.K35
JAMMU AND KASHMIR. LEGISLATIVE COUNCIL. COMMITTEE ON PRIVILEGES. REPORT. (Text in English) irreg. Legislative Council, Committee on Privileges, Srinagar, Jammu and Kashmir, India.

059.94 II ISSN 0021-4205
JANA SANGH PATRIKA.* (Text in Malayalam) 1967. s-m. Rs.6. Bharatiya Janasangh Kerala Pradesh, M.G. Road, Cochin 11, India. Ed. P. Narayanan. circ. controlled.

320 CE
JANAKAVI. (Text in Sinhala) fortn. 47 Jayantha Weerasekera Mawatha, Colombo 10, Sri Lanka. Ed. Karunaratne Amerasinghe.

320.531 II ISSN 0021-4213
JANAMAN; a spokesman for democratic socialism. (Text and summaries in Hindi) 1969. w. Rs.15. U. Shukla, Ed. & Pub., 107 Gopalganj, Sagar, Madhya Pradesh, India. adv.; bk.rev.

320.531 II ISSN 0021-4221
DS401
JANATA. (Text in English) 1946. w. $40. Janata Trust, c/o G.G. Parikh, National House, 6 Tulloch Rd., Bombay 1, India. Ed. H.K. Paranjape. adv.; circ. 6,000.

952 US
JAPAN POLITICAL RESEARCH; an annual review. 1969. a. $6 (foreign $7). Brigham Young University, Asian Studies Program, 745 SWKT, Provo, UT 84602. TEL 801-378-3303. FAX 801-378-5730. Ed. Lee W. Farnsworth. bk.rev.; bibl.; circ. 200. (tabloid format; back issues avail.)
  Formerly: Newsletter of Research on Japanese Politics.

JAPAN REPORT (ARLINGTON). see BUSINESS AND ECONOMICS — Economic Situation And Conditions

320.532 JA ISSN 0007-4683
JAPANESE COMMUNIST PARTY. CENTRAL COMMITTEE. BULLETIN: INFORMATION FOR ABROAD. (Text in English and Spanish) 1961. irreg. $60. Japanese Communist Party, Sendagaya 4-26-7, Shibuya-ku, Tokyo, Japan. FAX 03-3746-0767. TELEX J34652. adv.; illus.

320 330.9 CK ISSN 0021-5562
JAVERIANA. no.438, 1977. m. (Feb.-Nov.) Col.15000($50) (effective 1992). Compania de Jesus de Colombia, Carrera 23 no. 39-69, Apdo. Aereo 24773, Bogota, Colombia. Ed. Javier Sanin. adv.; bk.rev.; bibl.; index; circ. 8,000. (also avail. in microform from UMI)
  Description: Studies important current themes of national and international interest in Latin America.

320 JA ISSN 0385-0749
JEIWA KENKYU/PEACE STUDIES. (Text in Japanese) 1976. a. 2,800 Yen. (Nihon Heiwa Gakkai - Peace Studies Association of Japan) Waseda Daigaku Shuppanbu - Wasedu University Press, 1-1-3 Totsuka-machi, Shinjuku-ku, Tokyo 169, Japan. circ. 1,500.

320.532 296 US ISSN 0021-6305
DS101
JEWISH AFFAIRS. 1970. bi-m. $7.50. Communist Party, U S A, 235 W. 23rd St., 7th Fl., New York, NY 10011. TEL 212-989-4994. Ed. Herbert Aptheker. adv.; bk.rev.; bibl.; circ. 1,500. (also avail. in microfilm from AJP)

JEWISH DEFENSE LEAGUE ITON. see ETHNIC INTERESTS

JEWISH FRONTIER. see ETHNIC INTERESTS

323.1 US ISSN 0047-200X
JEWISH RADICAL. 1969. 3/yr. $5 to individuals; $10 to organizations. Radical Jewish Union, 300 Eshleman Hall, University of Calif., Berkeley, CA 94720. TEL 415-642-6000. Ed.Bd. circ. 6,000. (also avail. in microfilm from AJP)

323.1 947 296 IS ISSN 0021-6895
JEWS AND THE JEWISH PEOPLE; excerpts from the Soviet press. 1961. irreg. (2-4/yr.) $20 per vol. Hebrew University, Center for Research and Documentation of East-European Jewry, Givat Ram, 91904 Jerusalem, Israel. TEL 02-584271. Ed. S. Yitzikas. bk.rev.
  Description: Collects material from the Soviet Press on Jews.

JIHOCESKY SBORNIK HISTORICKY. see HISTORY — History Of Europe

320 US ISSN 0747-5659
E839.5
JOE SCOTT'S THE POLITICAL ANIMAL. 1973. bi-w. $175. Political Animal, Ltd., 990 W. 190th St., Ste. 201, Torrance, CA 90502-1001. TEL 213-515-1511. FAX 213-515-2901. Ed. Joe Scott. (back issues avail.)
  Formerly: Political Animal (ISSN 0195-9670)
  Description: Covers national politics.

JOHNS HOPKINS UNIVERSITY STUDIES IN HISTORICAL AND POLITICAL SCIENCE. see HISTORY

320 US
JOINT CENTER FOR POLITICAL STUDIES. NEW AND RECENT BOOKS. s-a. (Joint Center for Political Studies, Inc.) University Press of America, 4720-A Boston Way, Lanham, MD 20706. TEL 301-459-3366.

320 KN
JOKOOK TONGIL. (Text in Korean) 1961. m. Committee for the Peaceful Unification of Korea, Kangan 1 Dong, Youth Avenue, Sonkyo District, Pyongyang, N. Korea. Ed. Li Myong Gyu. circ. 70,000.

JOURNAL OF CHURCH AND STATE. see RELIGIONS AND THEOLOGY

338 UK ISSN 0021-9886
HC241
JOURNAL OF COMMON MARKET STUDIES. 1962. q. £42.50($87) to individuals; institutions £73.50($150). Basil Blackwell Ltd., 108 Cowley Rd., Oxford OX4 1JF, England. TEL 0865-791100. FAX 0865-791347. TELEX 837022-OXBOOK-G. Ed. Peter Robson. adv.; bk.rev.; circ. 1,400. (also avail. in microfilm from RRI; reprint service avail. from RRI,UMI) Indexed: A.B.C.Pol.Sci, ABI Inform, ASSIA, B.P.I, BPIA, Br.Hum.Ind., Bus.Ind., C.L.I., C.R.E.J., Cont.Pg.Manage., Curr.Cont., Hist.Abstr., Int.Lab.Doc., J.of Econ.Lit., Key to Econ.Sci., Leg.Per., Manage.Cont., Mgmt.& Market.Abstr., P.A.I.S., Rural Recreat.Tour.Abstr., SCIMP (1978-), Soc.Sci.Ind., SSCI, Tr.& Indus.Ind., World Agri.Econ.& Rural Sociol.Abstr., World Bank.Abstr.
  —BLDSC shelfmark: 4961.200000.

320.532 UK ISSN 0268-4535
HX3
JOURNAL OF COMMUNIST STUDIES. 1985. 4/yr. £30($45) to individuals; institutions £80($120). Frank Cass & Co. Ltd., Gainsborough House, 11 Gainsborough Rd., London E11 1RS, England. TEL 081-530-4226. FAX 081-530-7795. Eds. Michael Waller, Richard Gillespie. adv.; bk.rev.; index. (also avail. in microform from UMI; back issues avail.) Indexed: A.B.C.Pol.Sci.
  —BLDSC shelfmark: 4961.665000.
  Description: Covers the study of communism and the process of transformation and change it is currently undergoing.

328 II ISSN 0022-0043
JQ201
JOURNAL OF CONSTITUTIONAL & PARLIAMENTARY STUDIES. (Text in English) 1967. q. Rs.100($20) Institute of Constitutional and Parliamentary Studies, 18-21 Vithalbhai Patel House, Rafi Marg, New Delhi 110001, India. Ed. Phul Chand. circ. 1,000. (also avail. in microfilm from UMI; reprint service avail. from UMI) Indexed: A.B.C.Pol.Sci., Ind.Per.Lit., Int.Polit.Sci.Abstr.
  —BLDSC shelfmark: 4965.180000.

JOURNAL OF CONTEMPORARY HISTORY. see HISTORY

329.3 US ISSN 1045-5736
JF1051
▼**JOURNAL OF DEMOCRACY.** 1990. q. $24 to individuals; institutions $45. (National Endowment for Democracy) Johns Hopkins University Press, Journals Publishing Division, 701 W. 40th St., Ste. 275, Baltimore, MD 21211. TEL 410-516-6980. FAX 410-516-6998. Eds. Larry Diamond, Marc F. Plattner. adv.; bk.rev.; circ. 819. Indexed: A.B.C.Pol.Sci.
  —BLDSC shelfmark: 4968.250000.
  Description: Scholarly journal devoted to the study of democracy and democratic institutions worldwide.

JOURNAL OF DEVELOPING AREAS. see BUSINESS AND ECONOMICS — International Development And Assistance

JOURNAL OF DEVELOPMENT STUDIES. see BUSINESS AND ECONOMICS — International Development And Assistance

320 KO
JOURNAL OF EAST AND WEST STUDIES/TONGSO YONGU. (Text in English) 1973. s-a. $20. Yonsei University, Institute of East and West Studies, 134 Shinchon-Dong, Seodaemoon-gu, Seoul, S. Korea. FAX 02-393-9027. TELEX K29127. Ed. Dalchoong Kim. adv.; bk.rev.; circ. 700.
  Description: Publishes articles in all disciplines pertinent to East-West and North-South problems in the field of social sciences.

JOURNAL OF ECONOMIC AND INTERNATIONAL RELATIONS. see BUSINESS AND ECONOMICS — Economic Situation And Conditions

320 100 II
JOURNAL OF GANDHIAN STUDIES. (Text in English) 1973. q. $30. Institute of Gandhian Thought and Peace Studies, University of Allahabad, Gandhi Bhawan, Allahabad, India. TEL 54900. Ed. J.S. Mathur. adv.; bk.rev.; bibl.; circ. 500. Indexed: Amer.Hist.& Life, Hist.Abstr.
  Description: Encourages objective study of Gandhi's non-violent methods.

320 II ISSN 0251-3056
JOURNAL OF GOVERNMENT AND POLITICAL STUDIES. (Text in English) 1977. s-a. Rs.10($3) Punjabi University, Department of Political Science, Patiala 147002, India. bk.rev.

JOURNAL OF HEALTH POLITICS, POLICY AND LAW. see MEDICAL SCIENCES

JOURNAL OF HISPANIC POLICY. see ETHNIC INTERESTS

320 340 GW ISSN 0932-4569
H5
JOURNAL OF INSTITUTIONAL AND THEORETICAL ECONOMICS. 1844. q. DM.278. Verlag J.C.B. Mohr (Paul Siebeck), Wilhelmstr 18, Postfach 2040, 7400 Tuebingen, Germany. TEL 07071-26064. FAX 07071-51104. TELEX 7262872-MOHR-D. Ed. Rudolf Richter. adv.; bk.rev.; charts; index. Indexed: C.R.E.J., J.of Econ.Lit., Key to Econ.Sci., P.A.I.S.For.Lang.Ind., P.A.I.S., SCIMP (1991-).
  —BLDSC shelfmark: 5007.506000.
  Formerly: Zeitschrift fuer die Gesamte Staatswissenschaft.
  Description: Covers political economy and modern institutional economics.

JOURNAL OF INTERNATIONAL DEVELOPMENT: POLICY, ECONOMICS, & INTERNATIONAL RELATIONS. see SOCIAL SCIENCES: COMPREHENSIVE WORKS

JOURNAL OF LATIN AMERICAN STUDIES. see HISTORY — History Of North And South America

JOURNAL OF LAW AND POLITICS/HO-SEI KENKYU. see LAW

JOURNAL OF MANAGEMENT INFORMATION SYSTEMS. see BUSINESS AND ECONOMICS — Management

320 960 UK ISSN 0022-278X
DT1
JOURNAL OF MODERN AFRICAN STUDIES. 1963. q. $52 to individuals; institutions $119. Cambridge University Press, Edinburgh Bldg., Shaftesbury Rd., Cambridge CB2 2RU, England. FAX 0223-315052. TELEX 851817256. (U.S. addr.: 40 W. 20th St., New York, NY 10011; And: 32 E. 57th St., New York NY 10022) Ed. David Kimble. adv.; bk.rev.; bibl.; index. (also avail. in microform from UMI; reprint service avail. from SWZ) Indexed: A.B.C.Pol.Sci., Abstr.Anthropol., Acad.Ind., Amer.Hist.& Life, Br.Hum.Ind., C.R.E.J., CERDIC, Curr.Cont., Curr.Cont.Africa, G.Soc.Sci.& Rel.Per.Lit., Geo.Abstr., Hist.Abstr., I D A, Int.Lab.Doc., Lang.& Lang.Behav.Abstr., M.L.A., Mid.East: Abstr.& Ind., Numis.Lit., P.A.I.S., Rice Abstr., Rural Devel.Abstr., Rural Recreat.Tour.Abstr., Sage Fam.Stud.Abstr., Soc.Sci.Ind., SSCI, World Agri.Econ.& Rural Sociol.Abstr.
  —BLDSC shelfmark: 5020.600000.
  Description: Covers the politics, economics and related aspects of contemporary Africa.

JOURNAL OF PAN AFRICAN STUDIES; an international medium of African culture and consciousness. see SOCIAL SCIENCES: COMPREHENSIVE WORKS

POLITICAL SCIENCE

320   US
JOURNAL OF PEACE & JUSTICE STUDIES. 1989. s-a. $15 to individuals (foreign $25); institutions $30 (foreign $40). Villanova University, Center for Peace and Justice Education, Villanova, PA 19085. Eds. Joseph Des Jardins, Barbara Wall. adv.
Description: Covers a variety of disciplines, including but not limited to philosophy, theology, social and political theory, and public policy, all from a primarily Judeo-Christian intellectual perspective.

JOURNAL OF POLICY ANALYSIS AND MANAGEMENT. see *PUBLIC ADMINISTRATION*

320   US   ISSN 0161-8938
H1   CODEN: JPMOD5
JOURNAL OF POLICY MODELING; a social science forum of world issues. 1979. 5/yr. $192 to institutions (foreign $218)(effective 1992). (Society for Policy Modeling) Elsevier Science Publishing Co., Inc. (New York), 655 Ave. of the Americas, New York, NY 10010. TEL 212-989-5800. FAX 212-633-3965. TELEX 420643 AEP UI. Ed. Antonio Maria Costa. (also avail. in microform from RPI; reprint service avail.) **Indexed:** ABI Inform, ASSIA, BPIA, Bus.Ind., C.R.E.J., Curr.Cont., Deep Sea Res.& Oceanogr.Abstr., Fut.Surv., J. of Econ.Lit., Sociol.Abstr., SSCI, Tr.& Indus.Ind., World Agri.Econ.& Rural Sociol.Abstr.
—BLDSC shelfmark: 5040.843000.
Description: Focuses upon the economic, social and political interdependencies between national and regional systems.
Refereed Serial

JOURNAL OF POLITICAL ECONOMY. see *BUSINESS AND ECONOMICS*

954.9 320   PK
JOURNAL OF POLITICAL SCIENCE. (Text in English) 1971. a. Rs.80($4) Government College, Department of Political Science, Lahore, Pakistan. (Subscr. to: No. C-40, G O R III, Shadman, Lahore, Pakistan. TEL 412592) Eds. Hameed A.K. Rai, Ahmed Husain. adv.; bk.rev.; bibl.; charts; stat.; circ. 200. **Indexed:** A.B.C.Pol.Sci., Hist.Abstr.
Formerly: Journal of History and Political Science.

320   US   ISSN 0098-4612
JA1
JOURNAL OF POLITICAL SCIENCE (CLEMSON). 1973. s-a. $11.95. (South Carolina Political Science Association) Clemson University, Department of Political Science, Clemson, SC 29631. TEL 803-656-3233. FAX 803-656-0258. Ed. Martin Slann. adv.; bk.rev.; circ. 300. **Indexed:** A.B.C.Pol.Sci., Amer.Hist.& Life, Hist.Abstr.

320   II   ISSN 0047-2700
JQ201
JOURNAL OF POLITICAL STUDIES. (Text in English) 1968. s-a. Rs.30($5) D.A.V. College, Post-Graduate Department of Political Science, Jullundur, Punjab, India. Ed. K.C. Mahendru. adv.; bk.rev.; bibl.; circ. 500. (also avail. in microfilm) **Indexed:** Int.Polit.Sci.Abstr.

320   US   ISSN 0022-3816
JA1
JOURNAL OF POLITICS. 1939. q. $20 to individuals (foreign $28.25); institutions $40 (foreign $48.25); students $10 (foreign $18.25). (Southern Political Science Association) University of Texas Press, Box 7819, Austin, TX 78713. TEL 512-471-7233. FAX 512-320-0668. TELEX 776453-UTEXPRES-AUS. Ed. Cecil Eubanks. adv.; bk.rev.; bibl.; charts; index; circ. 3,500. (also avail. in microform from MIM,UMI) **Indexed:** A.B.C.Pol.Sci., Acad.Ind., Amer.Bibl.Slavic & E.Eur.Stud., Amer.Hist.& Life, Bk.Rev.Ind. (1965-), Child.Bk.Rev.Ind. (1965-), Commun.Abstr., Curr.Cont., Hist.Abstr., Int.Polit.Sci.Abstr., Lang.& Lang.Behav.Abstr., P.A.I.S., Pers.Lit., Res.High.Educ.Abstr., Soc.Sci.Ind., SSCI.
—BLDSC shelfmark: 5040.900000.
Description: Covers American, comparative, and international political science. Includes various methodological approaches.

JOURNAL OF PROGRESSIVE HUMAN SERVICES. see *SOCIAL SERVICES AND WELFARE*

300 150 301   II   ISSN 0970-3357
JOURNAL OF RURAL DEVELOPMENT. (Text in English) 1967. bi-m. Rs.100($50) Ministry of Agriculture and Rural Development, National Institute of Rural Development, Rajendranagar, Hyderabad 500 030, India. TEL 245001. FAX 245-277. TELEX 0425-6510. Ed. T.L. Sankar. bk.rev.; charts; illus.; circ. 1,000. **Indexed:** ASSIA, Curr.Cont., Dairy Sci.Abstr., Energy Ind., Energy Info.Abstr., Forest.Abstr., Geo.Abstr., I D A, Int.Polit.Sci.Abstr., Lang.& Lang.Behav.Abstr., Rice Abstr., Rural Devel.Abstr., Rural Ext.Educ.& Tr.Abstr., Sociol.Abstr., World Agri.Econ.& Rural Sociol.Abstr.
—BLDSC shelfmark: 5052.127400.
Formed by the 1982 merger of: Rural Development Digest; Behavioural Sciences and Rural Development (ISSN 0379-797X); Which was formerly (until 1977): Behavioural Sciences and Community Development (ISSN 0005-7843)
Description: Studies research in rural development with emphasis on social science aspects.

JOURNAL OF SEXUAL LIBERTY. see *LAW — Civil Law*

320   US   ISSN 0278-839X
H1
JOURNAL OF SOCIAL, POLITICAL AND ECONOMIC STUDIES. 1976. q. $35 to individuals; libraries and institutions $70. Council for Social and Economic Studies, 6861 Elm St., Ste. 4H, McLean, VA 22101. TEL 703-442-8010. FAX 703-847-9524. Ed. Roger Pearson. bk.rev.; index; circ. 1,300. **Indexed:** A.B.C.Pol.Sci., Amer.Bibl.Slavic & E.Eur.Stud., Amer.Hist.& Life, Arts & Hum.Cit.Ind., ASSIA, Chic.Per.Ind., Curr.Cont., Energy Ind., Energy Info.Abstr., Hist.Abstr., Lang.& Lang.Behav.Abstr., Mag.Ind., Mid.East: Abstr.& Ind., P.A.I.S., Sociol.Abstr., SSCI.
Former titles: Journal of Social and Political Studies (ISSN 0193-5941); Journal of Social and Political Affairs (ISSN 0362-580X)
Description: An academic level publication providing in-depth data relating to contemporary events and issues of international interest and significance.

320   US   ISSN 0895-724X
JOURNAL OF SOCIAL, POLITICAL AND ECONOMIC STUDIES MONOGRAPH SERIES. 1975. irreg. Council for Social and Economic Studies, 6861 Elm St., Ste. 4H, McLean, VA 22101. TEL 703-442-8010. FAX 703-847-9524.
Description: Deals with contemporary issues of national and world interest in historical perspectives. Emphasis is on data rather than theory.

JOURNAL OF SOUTHEAST ASIAN STUDIES. see *HISTORY — History Of Asia*

320   US   ISSN 1043-7916
DK33
▼**JOURNAL OF SOVIET NATIONALITIES.** 1990. q. $45. Center on East - West Trade, Investment, and Communications, 2114 Campus Dr., Duke University, NC 27706. Ed. Jerry F. Hough.
—BLDSC shelfmark: 5066.082000.
Description: Focuses on nationalities questions and regional issues facing the Soviet Union.

320 350.6   II
JOURNAL OF STATE AND ADMINISTRATION. (Text in English) 1978. s-a. Rs.35($10) Sambalpur University, Department of Political Science and Public Administration, Jyoti Vihar, Burla, Sambalpur, Orissa 768017, India. Eds. Drs. A.P. Padhi & Kvrao. adv.; bk.rev.; circ. 600.

352   US   ISSN 0039-0097
JK2403
JOURNAL OF STATE GOVERNMENT; the in-depth journal of state affairs. 1930. q. $45. Council of State Governments, Iron Works Pike, Box 11910, Lexington, KY 40578-9989. TEL 606-231-1939. bk.rev.; index; circ. 9,000. **Indexed:** A.B.C.Pol.Sci., ASCA, BPIA, Bus.Ind., Curr.Cont., Fut.Surv., Hist.Abstr., Manage.Cont., P.A.I.S., Sage Pub.Admin.Abstr., Soc.Sci.Ind., SSCI, Tr.& Indus.Ind.
—BLDSC shelfmark: 5066.700000.
Description: Provides a forum for the discussion of state governments. Articles highlight innovations, trends, and issues.

320   UK   ISSN 0951-6298
JA1.A1   CODEN: JTPOEF
JOURNAL OF THEORETICAL POLITICS. q. £26($43) to individuals; institutions £77($127). Sage Publications Ltd., 6 Bonhill St., London EC2A 4PU, England. TEL 071-374-0645. FAX 071-374-8741. Ed.Bd. adv.: color page #150; trim 193 x 114; adv. contact: Bernie Folan. bk.rev.; charts. **Indexed:** A.B.C.Pol.Sci., Int.Polit.Sci.Abstr.
—BLDSC shelfmark: 5069.075600.
Description: An international journal fostering the development of theory in the study of political processes.

956.940   SZ
JUEDISCHE RUNDSCHAU MACCABI; la gazette Juive. (Text in French, German) 1941. w. 65 Fr. Juedische Rundschau Maccabi GmbH, P.O. Box 298, CH-4009 Basel, Switzerland. TEL 061-238589. FAX 061-238804. Ed. Peter Bollag. adv.; bk.rev.; circ. 5,000.
Description: Newspaper of interest to Jews in Switzerland and abroad. Covers religion, politics, economics, news about Israel, culture, etc.

320   GW
JUNGE LIBERALE BAYERN. FORUM. 1983. q. DM.20. Junge Liberale Bayern e.V., Agnesstr. 47, 8000 Munich 40, Germany. TEL 089-12600960. FAX 089-1294149. Ed. Florian Reichl. adv.; circ. 1,000.

JUNGES FORUM. see *HISTORY — History Of Europe*

954   II
JUNIOR STATESMAN. (Text in English) 1969. w. Rs.35. Statesman House, 4 Chowringhee Square, Calcutta 700001, India.
Description: Discusses current affairs.

JURIDICAL REVIEW; law journal of Scottish universities. see *LAW*

320   MQ
JUSTICE. w. Parti Progressiste Martiniquais, Rue E. Zola, Fort-de-France, Martinique. Ed. G. Thimotee. circ. 8,000.

KAILASH; journal of Himalayan studies. see *HISTORY — History Of Asia*

KANSAI UNIVERSITY REVIEW OF LAW AND POLITICS. see *LAW*

328   US   ISSN 0270-4331
KFK20
KANSAS. LEGISLATIVE RESEARCH DEPARTMENT. REPORT ON KANSAS LEGISLATIVE INTERIM STUDIES. 1971. a. free. Legislative Research Department, Topeka, KS 66612. TEL 913-296-3181. circ. controlled.

KENTUCKY JOURNAL. see *PUBLIC ADMINISTRATION*

967.62   KE   ISSN 0023-0472
Newspaper
KENYA WEEKLY NEWS.* no.2256, 1968. w. 60s. D. A. Hawkins Ltd., P.O. Box 2768, Nairobi, Kenya. Ed. Jack Ensoll. adv.; bk.rev.; charts; film rev.; illus.; play rev.; circ. 7,000.

320   II
KERALASABDAM; independent political Malayalam weekly. (Text in Malayalam) w. R. Krishnaswamy Memorial Building, Lekshminada, Kollam 691 013, Kerala, India. TEL 3377. TELEX 0886-296 RKY.

320 052   UK   ISSN 0140-7562
KEVREN. (Text in Cornish and English) 1970. s-a. £3. Cowethas Flamank, 101 Haytor Ave., Seacrest, Paignton, Devon TQ4 7TB, England. TEL 0803-529944. Ed. A.M. Casey. bk.rev.; circ. 100. (processed)
Description: Discusses the political, cultural and environmental state of Cornwall.

320   UK   ISSN 0338-0181
DS63.1
KHAMSIN; journal of revolutionary socialists of the Middle East. no.6, 1978. q. £3.50 to individuals; £12 to institutions. Zed Books, 57 Caledonian Rd., London N1, England. Ed.Bd. adv.; bk.rev.; bibl.; circ. 2,000. **Indexed:** Left Ind. (1983-1990).

POLITICAL SCIENCE 3903

320 614.7   CN   ISSN 0823-6526
KICK IT OVER. 1981. q. Can.$9. P.O. Box 5811, Sta. A, Toronto, Ont. M5W 1P2, Canada. adv.; bk.rev.; film rev.; rec.rev.; circ. 3,500. (back issues avail.) **Indexed:** Alt.Press Ind.
    Description: Explores political, social and personal issues from an anarchist, feminist and ecological perspective.

320.531   DK   ISSN 0023-2025
KLASSEKAMPEN; socialistisk ugeavis. 1971. w. DKK 150 to individuals; institutions DKK 250. Socialistisk Arbejderparti, Noerre Alle 11 A, 2200 Copenhagen N, Denmark. TEL 31-373217. Ed. Soeren Soendergaard. adv.; bk.rev.; bibl.; illus.; circ. 2,500.

KOBLENZER GEOGRAPHISCHES KOLLOQUIUM. see *GEOGRAPHY*

320   DK   ISSN 0900-274X
KOEBENHAVNS UNIVERSITET. INSTITUT FOR SAMFUNDSFAG OG FORVALTNING. FORSKNINGRAPPORT. 1974. irreg. DKK 15 per issue. University of Copenhagen, Institute of Political Studies, Rosenborggade 15, DK-1130 Copenhagen K, Denmark. illus.

349 320   JA   ISSN 0454-1723
KOKUGAKUIN UNIVERSITY. FACULTY OF LAW AND POLITICS. JOURNAL/KOKUGAKUIN HOGAKU. 1963. 2000 Yen. Kokugakuin University, Faculty of Law and Politics, 4-10-28 Higashi, Shibuya-ku, Tokyo 150, Japan. TEL 03-3409-0111.
—BLDSC shelfmark: 5101.776000.

320 301   NE
KOMMA;* tijdschrift voor politiek en sociaal onderzoek. 1980. q. fl.52. (Stichting Instituut voor Politiek en Sociaal Onderzoek) Leeuwenbergh B.V., Postbus 139, 2170 AC Sassenheim, Netherlands. (Dist. by: I P S O, c/o Pegasus, Leidsestraat 25, 1017 NT, Amsterdam, Netherlands) Ed. Paul Streumer. adv.; bk.rev.; circ. 1,200.

320.532   GW   ISSN 0723-7669
KOMMUNE; Forum fuer Politik - Oekonomie - Kultur. 1973. m. DM.87. Kuehl Verwaltung GmbH & Co. Verlags KG, 11 11 62 Mainzer Landstr. 147, 6000 Frankfurt 11, Germany. FAX 069-732605. Ed.Bd. adv.; bk.rev.; circ. 4,000.
    Formerly: Kommunismus und Klassenkampf.

320.532   RU   ISSN 0023-3099
KOMMUNIST; teoreticheskii i politicheskii zhurnal. 1924. 18/yr. 10.80 Rub. (Kommunisticheskaya Partiya Sovetskogo Soyuza, Tsentral'nyi Komitet) Izdatel'stvo Pravda, Ul. Pravdy, 24, Moscow 125047, Russia. Ed. V.G. Afanasiev. bk.rev.; index; circ. 976,000. (also avail. in microform from MIM; microfilm from KTO) **Indexed:** Curr.Dig.Sov.Press, Lang.& Lang.Behav.Abstr.

320.532   BW   ISSN 0023-3102
KOMMUNIST BELORUSSII. (Editions in Belorussian, Russian) 1959. m. 6 Rub. (Kommunisticheskaya Partiya Belorussii, Tsentral'nyi Komitet) Izdatel'stvo Zvyazda, Leninskii prospekt, 77, Minsk, Byelarus. (Dist. by: Mezhdunarodnaya Kniga, Moscow, G-200, Russia) Ed. Ya.I. Kachan. bk.rev.; bibl.

320.532   KR   ISSN 0023-3110
HX8
KOMMUNIST UKRAINY. (Editions in Russian and Ukrainian) 1925. m. 7.20 Rub. Vul. Ordzkonikidze 8, 254025 Kiev, Ukraine. TEL 044-291-5752. Ed. Ya E. Pashko. bk.rev.; bibl.; circ. 21,700 (Rus.ed.); 11,200 (Ukr.ed.). (also avail. in microfilm from KTO)

320.532   TK   ISSN 0023-3129
KOMMUNISTI TOCHIKISTON. 1936. m. 3 Rub. Kommunisticheskaya Partiya Tadzhikskoi S.S.R., Tsentral'nyi Komitet, Pr. Lenina, 34, 734610 Dushanbe, Tadzhikistan. (Dist. by: Mezhdunarodnaya Kniga, ul. Dimitrova D.39, 113095 Moscow, Russia) Ed. S. Goibnazarov. bk.rev.; illus.; circ. 11,000.

320.532   RU
KOMMUNISTICHESKAYA PARTIYA SOVETSKOGO SOYUZA. VYSSHAYA PARTIINAYA SHKOLA. UCHENYE ZAPISKI. 1973. irreg. 1.14 Rub. Izdatel'stvo Mysl', Leninskii Prospekt 15, 117071 Moscow B-71, Russia.

320.532   YU   ISSN 0023-320X
KOMUNIST. (Editions in Albanian, Macedonian, Serbo-Croatian, Slovenian; shortened editions in Bulgarian, Hungarian, Italian, Romanian, Ruthenian, Slovakian) 1925. w. $25. (Savez Komunista Jugoslavije) Komunist, Trg Marksa i Engelsa 11, 11000 Belgrade, Yugoslavia. Ed. Vlajko Krivokapic.

320   IS
KONGRES HA-TSIYONI. HAHLATOT/WORLD ZIONIST ORGANIZATION. ZIONIST CONGRESS.* (Text in Hebrew) irreg. World Zionist Organization - Kongres ha-Tsiyoni, P.O. Box 92, Jerusalem 91920, Israel. TEL 02-527156. FAX 02-533542.

950 960 980   PL   ISSN 0023-3765
G464
KONTYNENTY. m. $7.70. Warszawskie Wydawnictwo Prasowe R S W "Prasa-Ksiazka-Ruch", Al. Jerozolimskie 125-127, 02-017 Warsaw, Poland. (Dist. by: Ars Polona-Ruch, Krakowskie Przedmiescie 7, Warsaw, Poland)
    Description: Devoted to African, Asian and South American problems.

320 330   KO
KOREA POLICY SERIES.* no.16, 1973. irreg. Korean Overseas Information Service, Seoul, S. Korea.

320.531   KN
KOREA TODAY. (Edtions in Arabic, Chinese, English, French, Russian, Spanish) m. Foreign Languages Publishing House, Pyongyang, N. Korea.

KOREAN AFFAIRS REPORT. see *BUSINESS AND ECONOMICS — Economic Situation And Conditions*

327   KO   ISSN 0377-0451
JX1
KOREAN JOURNAL OF INTERNATIONAL STUDIES. (Text in English) 1970. q. $35 to individuals; $40 to institutions. Korean Institute of International Studies, K.P.O. Box 426, Seoul 110-604, S. Korea. TEL 02-752-7727. FAX 02-752-7710. TELEX K-26439. Ed. Chong-Ki Choi. adv.; bk.rev.; bibl.; circ. 1,200. (back issues avail.) **Indexed:** Abstr.Mil.Bibl., Geo.Abstr., Met.Abstr.
—BLDSC shelfmark: 5113.562000.
    Description: Aims to act as a forum for discussion on peace research and international relations, with emphasis on the East Asian region.

320   US
KOREAN RESEARCH BULLETIN. vol.6, 1976. s-a. free. Korean Research Council, 1565 Miramar Ave., Seaside, CA 93955. Ed. Sae Woon Chang.

320 301.412   KN
HQ1765.6
KOREAN WOMEN.* (Editions in English, French) q. Korean Democratic Women's Union, Central Committee, Pyongyang, N. Korea. illus.

951.9   KO
DS901
KOREANA; a quarterly on Korean culture. (Editions in English, Japanese, Spanish) 1987. q. $29. International Cultural Society of Korea, 526, 5-ga, Namdaemunno, Chung-gu, C.P.O. Box 2147, Seoul, S. Korea. TEL 02-753-6464. FAX 02-757-2049. (US office: P.O. Box 312, Hartsdale, NY 10530. TEL 914-472-4587) S. Chang. adv.; stat. **Indexed:** M.L.A.

KRIEGSOPFER- UND BEHINDERTEN. RUNDSCHAU; Zeitschrift fuer Kriegsopfer und Behindertenfragen, Sozialpolitik Versorgungsbrecht und Gesellschaftspolitik. see *SOCIOLOGY*

320.531   GW   ISSN 0178-7691
KRISIS; Zeitschrift fuer revolutionaere Theorie. 1986. irreg. DM.16 per no. Krisis Verlag, Kleinreutherweg 47, 8500 Nuremburg 10, Germany. TEL 0911-341113. Ed. Bernd Suffert. (back issues avail.)

329.9   SW   ISSN 0284-9941
KRISTDEMOKRATEN. 1965. w. SEK 345. Samhaellsgemenskaps Foerlags AB, P.O. Box 19098, S-10432 Stockholm, Sweden. FAX 08-6127953. Ed. Andres Tiger. adv.; bk.rev.; illus.; circ. 10,000 (controlled). (tabloid format)
    Formerly: Samhaellsgemenskap (ISSN 0036-3782)

KRONIKA WIELKOPOLSKI. see *HISTORY — History Of Europe*

320 328   KO   ISSN 0027-8580
KUKHOEBO/NATIONAL ASSEMBLY REVIEW. (Text in Korean) 1949. m. National Assembly, c/o Secretary-General, 1-1 Yeoidodong, Yeongdungpo-ku, Seoul, S. Korea. TEL 788-2058. FAX 788-3348. Ed. Sok Doo Soo. charts; illus.; stat.; circ. 5,500 (controlled).

940   GW   ISSN 0342-1716
KULTUR VORSCHAU EUROPA/CULTURAL PREVIEW. 1925. q. DM.27.50 per no. Verlag Horst Deike KG, Robert-Bosch-Str. 18, Postfach 100452, 7750 Konstanz, Germany. adv.; bk.rev.; charts; film rev.; play rev.; tr.lit.; tr.mk.; circ. 5,400.
    Formerly: Vorschau Europa (ISSN 0042-8892)

322.4   GW
KULTURREVOLUTION. 3/yr. DM.27. Klartext Verlag, Viehofer Platz 1, 4300 Essen 1, Germany. TEL 0201-234538. FAX 0201-238502.

DER KURIER (LIESBORN); der christlichen mitte. see *RELIGIONS AND THEOLOGY*

960   BS   ISSN 0023-5733
DT790
KUTLWANO/MUTUAL UNDERSTANDING. (Text in English and Setswana) 1961. m. P.40. Information and Broadcasting, Private Bag 0060, Gaborone, Botswana. Ed. Keboeletse Nkarabang. adv.; charts; illus.; circ. 12,000.

320   PE   ISSN 0360-3350
BX1425.A1
L A D O C. (Text in English) 1970. bi-m. $18. Latin American Documentation, Apdo. 5594, Lima 100, Peru. Ed. Lucy Giacchetti. circ. 850. (also avail. in microform) **Indexed:** Cath.Ind., CERDIC, HR Rep.
—BLDSC shelfmark: 5143.617000.

320   AT
LABOR COLLEGE REVIEW. 1959-1984; N.S. 1987. q. Aus.$10 (foreign Aus.$20). Victorian Labor College, P.O. Box 39, Trades Hall, Carlton South, Vic. 3053, Australia. TEL 03-499-2386. Ed. Chris Gaffney. adv.; bk.rev.; circ. 1,300.
    Description: Includes articles on politics, economics and history from a Marxist viewpoint.

329   AT   ISSN 0819-9825
LABOR TIMES. 1966. m. $50. Australian Labor Party, New South Wales Branch, c/o J. Della Bosca, 377 Sussex St., Sydney, N.S.W. 2000, Australia. TEL 02-264-2732. FAX 02-264-2574. Ed. Jarka Sipka. adv.; bk.rev.; circ. 16,000.
    Formerly (until 1987): Australian Labor Party. A.L.P. (ISSN 0045-0669)

329.9   AT
LABOR VOICE. 1959. bi-m. Aus.$12. Australian Labor Party, Western Australia Branch, 2nd Fl., Labor Centre, 82 Beaufort St., Perth, W.A. 6000, Australia. FAX 09-2279585. Ed. John A Cowdell. adv.; bk.rev.; illus.; circ. 10,000 (controlled). (tabloid format)
    Formerly (until 1979): Western Sun (ISSN 0043-423X)

320   UK   ISSN 0260-6615
LABOUR & IRELAND. 1980. 5/yr. £4.50. Labour Committee on Ireland, c/o L.C.I. BM Box 5355, London WC1N 3XX, England. (Dist. in U.S. by: Qunlan Publishing Co., Inc., Box 657, Boston, MA 02134) Ed. Martin Collins. adv.; bk.rev.; illus.; circ. 5,000.
    Description: News and opinion within British labor movement, advocating withdrawal from Ireland.

LABOUR & TRADE UNION REVIEW. see *LABOR UNIONS*

320.532   IE   ISSN 0790-1712
LABOUR COMMENT (CORK). 1968. fortn. $30. Labour Comment (Cork) Ireland, 26 Church Ave., Roman St., Cork, Ireland. FAX 021-506360. (Co-sponsor: Brotherhood of Irish Compositors) Ed. Patrick Noel Maloney. adv.; bk.rev.; circ. 1,000.
    Former titles (until 1984): Comment (Dublin); Communist Comment.

320   UK   ISSN 0260-3810
LABOUR PARTY. CAMPAIGN BRIEFING. 1980. m. £7. Labour Party, Policy Directorate, 150 Walworth Rd., London SE17 1JT, England. FAX 01-701-6363. Ed. Nick Sigler. s-a. index; circ. 3,000. (back issues avail.)
    Description: Review of main items of political interest to Labour Party members and supporters.

POLITICAL SCIENCE

329.9 UK
LABOUR STUDENT. 1980. 3/yr. £3. Labour Students, 150 Walnorth Rd., London SE17 1JT, England. adv.; bk.rev.; illus.; circ. 12,000.
Formerly: Socialist Youth (ISSN 0260-7336)

320 US
LAISSEZ FAIRE BOOKS FREE MARKET CATALOG. 1973. m. free. Laissez Faire Books, 942 Howard St., San Francisco, CA 94103. TEL 415-541-9780. FAX 415-541-0597. Ed. Roy Childs. adv.; bk.rev.; tr.lit.; circ. 50,000.
Former titles: Laissez Faire Free Market Catalog; Laissez Faire Libertarian Catalog.

943 GW ISSN 0340-7837
LAND AKTUELL. s-m. DM.7.80. Rheinischer Landwiertschafrs Verlag, Roshusstrasse 18, D-5300 Bonn 1, Germany. Ed. H. Schruefer. bk.rev.
Formerly: Dorf Aktuell (ISSN 0012-5547)

320 410 US
▼**LANGUAGE AND IDEOLOGY.** 1991. irreg. price varies. Praeger Publishers (Subsidiary of: Greenwood Publishing Group Inc.), 88 Post Rd. W., Box 5007, Westport, CT 06881-5007. TEL 203-226-3571. FAX 203-222-1502.

320 II
LATIN AMERICA LETTER. (Text in English) 1981. m. Rs.500($100) K.K. Roy (Private) Ltd., 55 Gariahat Rd., P.O. Box 10210, Calcutta 700 019, India. Ed. K.K. Roy.

LATIN AMERICA REGIONAL REPORTS - BRAZIL. see BUSINESS AND ECONOMICS — Economic Situation And Conditions

LATIN AMERICA REGIONAL REPORTS - CARIBBEAN. see BUSINESS AND ECONOMICS — Economic Situation And Conditions

LATIN AMERICA REGIONAL REPORTS - MEXICO & CENTRAL AMERICA. see BUSINESS AND ECONOMICS — Economic Situation And Conditions

LATIN AMERICA REPORT. see BUSINESS AND ECONOMICS — Economic Situation And Conditions

LATIN AMERICA WEEKLY REPORT. see BUSINESS AND ECONOMICS — Economic Situation And Conditions

LATIN AMERICAN PERSPECTIVES; a journal on Capitalism and Socialism. see SOCIAL SCIENCES: COMPREHENSIVE WORKS

LATIN AMERICAN REGIONAL REPORTS - ANDEAN GROUP. see BUSINESS AND ECONOMICS — Economic Situation And Conditions

LATIN AMERICAN REGIONAL REPORTS - SOUTHERN CONE. see BUSINESS AND ECONOMICS — Economic Situation And Conditions

320 US
LATVIAN NEWS DIGEST. 1976. q. $15. American Latvian Association in the United States, Inc., 400 Hurley Ave., Box 4578, Rockville, MD 20850. Ed. Martins Zvaners. bk.rev.; circ. 6,000.

LAVORO E SOCIETA; economia-cultura-politica-sociologia. see BUSINESS AND ECONOMICS

LAW AND LEGISLATION IN THE GERMAN DEMOCRATIC REPUBLIC. see LAW

LAW & POLICY. see LAW

LAW AND POLITICAL REVIEW. see LAW

LAW AND STATE; a biannual collection of recent German contributions to these fields. see LAW — International Law

055.1 IT ISSN 0023-9526
LAZIO. q. Via dei Frentani 4, Rome, Italy. (tabloid format)

LEADER IN ACTION. see EDUCATION

LEADERSHIP QUARTERLY; an international journal of political, social and behavioral science. see BUSINESS AND ECONOMICS — Management

320 LE
LEBANESE JOURNAL OF POLITICAL SCIENCE. (Text in Arabic, English, French) s-a. P.O. Box 3865, Beirut, Lebanon. Ed. Bechir Aridi. bibl.

320 IS
LEBNS FRAGN. (Text in Yiddish) 1951. q. $15. Brith Haavoda, 48 Kalisher St., Tel Aviv 65165, Israel. TEL 03-656764. Ed. Yitzak Luden. bk.rev.; circ. 2,500.

LECTURE ET TRADITION; bulletin litteraire, contrerevolutionnaire. see LITERATURE

944 FR ISSN 0024-0133
LECTURES FRANCAISES; revue de la politique francaise. 1957. m. 180 F. (foreign 210 F.). Diffusion de la Pensee Francaise, Chire-en-Montreuil, 86190 Vouille, France. TEL 49-51-83-04. Ed. Jean Auguy. adv.; bk.rev.; bibl.; circ. 7,500.
—BLDSC shelfmark: 5179.910000.

320 IE
LEFT. 1980. 6/yr. donations. Irish Democratic Youth Movement, 30 Gardiner Place, Dublin 1, Ireland. TEL 01-740716. FAX 01-787921. TELEX WP-EI-31490. Ed.Bd. illus.; circ. 25,000.
Former titles: Socialist Youth; Challenge (Dublin).

320.531 US
LEFT COURT. 1983. irreg. $10 (foreign $20). Socialist Party of Illinois, 6452 N. Bosworth Ave., No.1, Chicago, IL 60626. TEL 312-764-1851. adv.; bk.rev.; circ. 600. (also avail. in microform; back issues avail.)

322.4 US
K1
LEGAL REFORMER. Short title: A L R. 1979. q. membership. (Organization of Americans for Legal Reform) Halt, Inc., 1319 F St., N.W., Ste. 300, Washington, DC 20004. FAX 202-347-9606. Ed. Richard Hebert. bk.rev.; circ. 110,000.
Formerly (until vol.8, no.4, 1988): Americans for Legal Reform (ISSN 0739-6813)

320.531 CU
LEGALIDAD SOCIALISTA. q. $15 in N. and S. America; Europe $16; elsewhere $18. (Fiscalia General de la Republica) Ediciones Cubanas, Obispo No. 527, Apdo. 605, Havana, Cuba. (Alt. addr.: San Rafael No.·3, Havana, 2, Cuba)

350 US ISSN 0362-9805
JF501
LEGISLATIVE STUDIES QUARTERLY. 1976. q. $30 to individuals; institutions $60. University of Iowa, Comparative Legislative Research Center, 349 Schaeffer Hall, Iowa City, IA 52242. TEL 319-335-2361. FAX 319-335-3755. Ed.Bd. adv.; bk.rev.; bibl.; charts; index; circ. 1,000. (also avail. in microform from UMI; reprint service avail. from UMI) Indexed: A.B.C.Pol.Sci., Amer.Bibl.Slavic & E.Eur.Stud, Curr.Cont., Int.Polit.Sci.Abstr., SSCI.
—BLDSC shelfmark: 5181.461000.

320 US
LEGISLATIVE UPDATE (DALLAS); opinion ballot, national poll & voting records. 1958. m. $99.50. National "Write Your Congressman" Inc., 12115 Self Plaza, Dallas, TX 75218. FAX 214-324-5245. Ed. David N. Adamson. circ. 60,000.
Description: Excerpts from Congressmen's speeches, opinion polls and letters to the editor on major national issues including SDI, abortion, gun control, taxation and government spending.

328 II ISSN 0024-0508
LEGISLATOR. (Text in English) 1969. m. Rs.12. D-32 Kirti Nagar, New Delhi 15, India. Ed. Raj Sauldie. adv.; illus.; stat.

329.9 GW
LEHEL AKTUELL. 1973. q. (Sozialdemokratische Partei Deutschland) S P D - Ortsverein Lehel, c/o Dr. Thomas Lange, Knobelstr. 30, 8000 Munich 22, Germany. TEL 89-222918. adv.; circ. 7,200. (back issues avail.)

320.532 AI ISSN 0130-8114
LENINYAN UGIOV. Russian edition: Po Leninskomu Puti (ISSN 0235-0033) 1923. m. 3 Rub. Kommunisticheskaya Partiya Armyanskoi S.S.R, Tsentral'nyi Komitet, Pr. Ordzhonikidze 2, 375023 Erevan, Armenia. TEL 52-89-93. Ed. Aram S. Simonyan. bk.rev.; abstr.; bibl.; charts; illus.; stat.; circ. 12,000.

320.51 DK ISSN 0047-4460
LIBERAL. 1970. 4/yr. DKK 120. Venstres Landsorganisation, Soelleroedvej 30, 2840 Holte, Denmark. Ed. Claus Hjort Frederiksen. circ. 3,500.

329.3 RU
▼**LIBERAL.** 1990. m? Liberal'no-demokraticheskaya Partiya Sovetskogo Soyuza, c/o A.Kh. Khalitov, Ed., Sovkhoz im. Lenina, d.13, kv.126, Leninskii r-on, Moskovskaya obl., Russia.

320.51 UK ISSN 0954-5735
LIBERAL DEMOCRAT NEWS. 1946. w. £25. Liberal Democrats, 4 Cowley St., Westminster, London SW1P 3NB, England. TEL 071-222-4422. FAX 071-222-7904. Ed. Mike Harskin. adv.; bk.rev.; illus.; circ. 11,000. (back issues avail.)
Former titles: Liberal Party Organisation. Liberal News (ISSN 0024-1849); Liberal News Commentary.
Description: Newspaper of the Liberal Democrat political party, reporting on current affairs, social issues, and internal Party news.

320 UK ISSN 0954-5735
LIBERAL DEMOCRAT NEWS. 1982. w. £26. Liberal Democrats, 4 Cowley St., London SW1P 3NB, England. TEL 071-222-7999. FAX 071-222-7904. Ed. Mike Harskin. adv.; bk.rev.; circ. 11,000. (tabloid format)
Former titles: Social and Liberal Democrats News; (until 1988): Social Democrat.
Description: Covers the platform and activities of this political party in Great Britain.

332.4 329.3 CE
LIBERAL REVIEW. 1986. m. Rs.150($50) Liberal Party, 88-1 Rosmead Place, Colombo 7, Sri Lanka. TEL 582779. FAX 588875. TELEX 22658-GLAXY-CE. Eds. Chanaka Amaratunga, Rajiva Wijesinha. adv.; bk.rev.; circ. 1,000 (controlled).
Description: Covers Sri Lankan political events from a liberal perspective.

329.3 JA
LIBERAL STAR. (Text in English) 1972. m. $10. Liberal Democratic Party, 1-11-23 Nagata-Cho, Chiyoda-ku, Tokyo 100, Japan. TEL 03-3581-6211. Ed. Koichi Yamaguchi. circ. 500,000.

320.51 SW ISSN 0024-1857
LIBERAL UNGDOM. 1909. bi-m. SEK 50. Folkpartiets Ungdomsfoerbund - Youth Organization of the Swedish Liberal Party, Box 6508, 113 83 Stockholm, Sweden. FAX 8-349591. Ed. David Nystrom. adv.; illus.; circ. 15,000.

320.531 US ISSN 1051-7871
HX1
LIBERATION AND MARXISM. 1989. bi-m. $10 to individuals; institutions $15. W W Publishers Inc., 46 W. 21st St., New York, NY 10010. TEL 212-255-0352. FAX 212-929-3153. Ed. Sharon Ayling. bk.rev.; circ. 2,000. (back issues avail.)
Formerly: Liberation! (ISSN 1047-594X)

322.4 UK ISSN 0267-7121
LIBERTARIAN ALLIANCE. BACKGROUND BRIEFINGS. 1985. irreg. £10($20) Libertarian Alliance, 1 Russell Court, Covent Garden, London WC2E 8AA, England. TEL 071-821-5502. FAX 071-834-2031. Ed.Bd. adv.; bk.rev.; film rev.; bibl.; circ. 1,000. (back issues avail.)

323.4 UK ISSN 0267-677X
LIBERTARIAN ALLIANCE. CULTURAL NOTES. 1983. irreg. £10($20) Libertarian Alliance, 1 Russell Court, Covent Garden, London WC2E 8AA, England. TEL 071-821-5502. FAX 071-834-2031. Ed.Bd. adv.; bk.rev.; film rev.; bibl.; circ. 1,000. (back issues avail.)

332.4 UK ISSN 0267-6761
LIBERTARIAN ALLIANCE. FOREIGN POLICY PERSPECTIVES. 1983. irreg. £10($20) Libertarian Alliance, 1 Russell Chambers, Covent Garden, London WC2E 8AA, England. TEL 071-821-5502. FAX 071-843-2031. Ed.Bd. adv.; bk.rev.; film rev.; bibl.; circ. 1,000. (back issues avail.)

POLITICAL SCIENCE

332.4 UK ISSN 0267-7156
LIBERTARIAN ALLIANCE. PERSONAL PERSPECTIVES. 1984. irreg. £10($20) Libertarian Alliance, 1 Russell Chambers, Covent Garden, London WC2E 8AA, England. TEL 071-821-5502. FAX 071-834-2031. Ed.Bd. adv.; bk.rev.; film rev.; bibl.; circ. 1,000. (back issues avail.)

322.4 UK ISSN 0267-7059
LIBERTARIAN ALLIANCE. POLITICAL NOTES. 1979. irreg. £10($20) Libertarian Alliance, 1 Russell Chambers, Covent Garden, London WC2E 8AA, England. TEL 071-821-5502. FAX 071-834-2031. Ed.Bd. adv.; bk.rev.; film rev.; bibl.; circ. 1,000. (back issues avail.)

300 320 UK ISSN 0267-7067
LIBERTARIAN ALLIANCE. SCIENTIFIC NOTES. 1985. irreg. £10($20) Libertarian Alliance, 1 Russell Chambers, Covent Garden, London WC2E 8AA, England. TEL 071-836-6913. Ed.Bd. adv.; bk.rev.; film rev.; bibl.; circ. 1,000. (back issues avail.)

320 UK ISSN 0267-7180
LIBERTARIAN ALLIANCE. STUDY GUIDES. 1985. irreg. £10($20) Libertarian Alliance, 1 Russell Chambers, Covent Garden, London WC2E 8AA, England. TEL 071-821-5502. FAX 071-834-2031.

322.4 UK
LIBERTARIAN ALLIANCE. TACTICAL NOTES. 1985. irreg. £10($20) Libertarian Alliance, 1 Russell Chambers, Covent Garden, London WC2E 8AA, England. TEL 071-821-55-0. FAX 071-834-2031. Ed.Bd. adv.; bk.rev.; film rev.; bibl.; circ. 1,000. (back issues avail.)

322.4 UK
LIBERTARIAN ALLIANCE. WORLD REPORTS. 1985. irreg. £10($20) Libertarian Alliance, 1 Russell Chambers, Covent Garden, London WC2E 8AA, England. TEL 071-821-5502. FAX 071-843-2031. Ed.Bd. adv.; bk.rev.; film rev.; bibl.; circ. 1,000. (back issues avail.)
Formerly (until 1985): Liberation Alliance. International Reports.

320.5 US ISSN 0047-4517
LIBERTARIAN FORUM.* 1969. m. $15. 3916 Waterford Ln., Las Vegas, NV 89119-5149. Ed. Murray N. Rothbard. adv.; bk.rev.; bibl.; cum.index every 2 yrs; circ. 750. (looseleaf format; also avail. in microform from UMI; reprint service avail. from UMI)
Formerly: Libertarian.

322.4 UK ISSN 0267-6788
LIBERTARIAN NEWS. 1982. irreg. £10($20) Libertarian Alliance, 1 Russell Chambers, Covent Garden, London WC2E 8AA, England. TEL 071-821-5502. FAX 071-834-2031. Ed.Bd. adv.; bk.rev.; film rev.; bibl.; circ. 1,000. (back issues avail.)

322.4 US
LIBERTARIAN PARTY NEWS. 1972. m. $25. (Libertarian National Committee) Solstice, Inc., Box 780, Winchester, VA 22601. TEL 703-662-3691. Ed. Burton R. Langhenry. adv.; circ. 12,000.

322.4 UK ISSN 0267-6796
LIBERTARIAN REPRINTS. 1979. irreg. £10($20) Libertarian Alliance, 1 Russell Chambers, Covent Garden, London WC2E 8AA, England. TEL 071-821-5502. FAX 071-834-2031. Ed.Bd. adv.; bk.rev.; film rev.; bibl.; circ. 1,000. (back issues avail.)

320 UK ISSN 0267-7199
LIBERTARIAN STUDENT. 1985. q. £10($20) Libertarian Alliance, 1 Russell Chambers, Covent Garden, London WC2E 9JY, England. TEL 071-821-5502. FAX 071-834-2031.

LIBERTY (PORT TOWNSEND). see *LITERARY AND POLITICAL REVIEWS*

322.7 US ISSN 0145-7667
LIBERTY BELL. 1973. m. $40. Liberty Bell Publications, Reedy, WV 25270. TEL 304-927-4486. Ed. George P. Dietz. adv.; bk.rev.; circ. 9,500. (back issues avail.)

320 LH
LIECHTENSTEIN POLITISCHE SCHRIFTEN. 1972. irreg. $30. Verlag der Liechtensteinischen Akademischen Gesellschaft, Am Schraegen Weg 2, Postfach 44, FL-9490 Vaduz, Liechtenstein. TEL 011-41-75-22424. FAX 011-41-75-22837. TELEX 889246. circ. 1,000.

322.4 US
LIMIT. 1974. m. $5. Libertarian Republican Alliance, 1149 E. 32nd St., Brooklyn, NY 11210. Ed. Elliott Capon. adv.; bk.rev.; circ. 500.

320.531 IT
LINEAMENTI; quale marxismo oggi. 1985. q. L.1100. Edizioni GB, Via Curzola 9, 35135 Padova, Italy. TEL 604102. circ. 2,000.

320.531 GW ISSN 0024-404X HX6
LINKS; Sozialistische Zeitung. 1969. m. DM.62. (Sozialistisches Buero) Verlag 2000 GmbH, Bleichstr. 5-7, Postfach 102062, 6050 Offenbach 1, Germany. TEL 069-885006. Ed.Bd. adv.; bk.rev.; illus. (tabloid format) **Indexed:** Rehabil.Lit.

320.531 NE ISSN 0167-093X
LINKSAF. 1974. 10/yr. fl.17.50. Jonge Socialisten in de Partij van de Arbeid, Nicolaas Witsenkade 30, 1017 ZT Amsterdam, Netherlands. FAX 020-5512330. Ed.Bd. adv.; bk.rev.; illus.; stat.; circ. 13,000.
Supersedes: Opinie (ISSN 0030-3771); Former titles: Kapitalist; Paraat.

LITIGATION UNDER THE FEDERAL OPEN GOVERNMENT LAWS. see *LAW*

320.5 UK ISSN 0047-4827
LIVERPOOL NEWSLETTER. 1960. m. £3($10) Gild of Saint George, Rose Cottage, 17 Hadassah Grove, Larke Lane, Liverpool L17 8XH, England. Ed. Anthony Cooney. adv.; bk.rev.; circ. 200.

329 AT
LOBBY. 1973. q. Aus.$10 to non-members. Australian Labor Party, Australian Capital Territory Branch, Labor Club, Chandler St., Belconnen, A.C.T. 2617, Australia. Ed. Lembit Suur. adv.; bk.rev.; circ. 1,500.
Former titles: Australian Labor Party. A.C.T. Branch. Magazine; Australian Labor Party. A.C.T. Branch. Newsletter.

320 UK
LOBSTER. 1983. irreg. (2-3/yr.) price varies. 214 Westbourne Ave., Hull HU5 3JB, England. Eds. Stephen Dorril, Robin Ramsay. adv.; illus.

322.4 GW
LOKALES; aus Babenhausen und Umgebung. 1981. 4/yr. free. Die Gruenen - Babenhausen, Neugasse 1, 6113 Babenhausen, Germany. TEL 06073-62452. circ. 6,000.

328 II ISSN 0024-595X
LOKTANTRA SAMIKSHA. (Text in Hindi) 1969. q. Rs.30($10) Institute of Constitutional and Parliamentary Studies, 18-21 Vithalbhai Patel House, Rafi Marg, New Delhi 110001, India. Ed. O.P. Khadasia.

LOOK JAPAN. see *BUSINESS AND ECONOMICS — International Development And Assistance*

059.95 HK
LOOK MAGAZINE. (Text in Chinese) 1958. m. $20. Chih Luen Press, B1, Carnarvon Mansion, 10th Fl., 12, Carnarvon Rd., Kowloon, Hong Kong. Ed. Smarlo Ma. bk.rev. **Indexed:** Mag.Ind.
Formerly: Look Fortnightly (ISSN 0024-6387)

320 US
LOYOLA LECTURE SERIES IN POLITICAL ANALYSIS. 1977. irreg. price varies. University of Notre Dame Press, Notre Dame, IN 46556. TEL 219-239-6346. Ed. Richard Shelly Hartigan.

LUA NOVA; cultura e politica. see *SOCIOLOGY*

320 GW
LUEGINSLAND; Monatszeitschrift fuer Augsburg. 1979. m. DM.1500. (Verein zur Foerderung und Wahrung des Augsburger Kulturgutes e.V.) Mueller-Doldi, Postfach 112326, 8900 Augsburg, Germany. Ed.Bd.

320 SG
LUTTE. 1977. q. Parti Africain de l'Independance, B.P. 820, Dakar, Senegal. Ed. Bara Goudiaby. circ. 1,000.

320 FR ISSN 0458-5143
LUTTE DE CLASSE; pour la reconstruction de la quatrieme internationale. 1956. m. 80 F. (foreign 95 F.). Lutte Ouvriere, B.P. 233, 75865 Paris Cedex 18, France. Ed. Michel Rodinson.

322.4 FR ISSN 0150-4428
LYS ROUGE; revue trimestrielle d'etudes royalistes. 1976. q. 90 F. Societe Nationale Presse Francaise, 17 rue des Petits Champs, 75001 Paris, France. TEL 42-97-48-57. Ed. Yvam Aumont. circ. 1,000.

320 MR
M A P ACTUALITE; daily national and international political news bulletin. 1976. d. DH.1401.56($173.89) Maghreb Arab Press, 122 Av. Allal Ben Abdellah, B.P. 1049, Rabat, Morocco. TEL 76-40-83. FAX 670-97. TELEX 310-44. Ed. Abdeljalil Fenjiro.

M I R S LEGISLATIVE REPORT. (Michigan Information and Research Service, Inc.) see *PUBLIC ADMINISTRATION*

320 US ISSN 0076-1729
M L SEIDMAN MEMORIAL TOWN HALL LECTURE SERIES. 1967. a. $5. Rhodes College, 2000 N. Pkwy., Memphis, TN 38112. TEL 901-274-1800. circ. 600.

320 FR ISSN 0243-6450 JA11
M O T S: MOTS, ORDINATEURS, TEXTES, SOCIETES. (Text in French, summaries in English, French, Spanish) 1980. q. 235 F. to individuals; (foreign 280 F.); institutions 315 F. (foreign 380 F.); students 170 F. Presses de la Fondation Nationale des Sciences Politiques, 27, rue Saint-Guillaume, 75341 Paris Cedex 07, France. TEL 1-45-49-50-50. FAX 1-45-48-04-41. TELEX 201 002 F. Ed. Maurice Tournier. adv.; bk.rev.; abstr.; bibl.; circ. 800.
—BLDSC shelfmark: 5978.718300.

320 US ISSN 0464-1973
M P S A NEWSLETTER. 1957. s-a. $5. Missouri Political Science Association, c/o George Connor, Sect.-Treas., Dept. of Political Science, Southwest Missouri State University, Springfield, MO 65804. TEL 417-836-6956. bibl.; circ. 200 (controlled).

956.940 296 US ISSN 0017-6850
HA-MAAPIL. 1962. m. membership. Habonim Dror Labor Zionist Youth, 27 W. 20th St., 9th Fl., New York, NY 10011. TEL 212-255-1796. Ed. Charles Boxbaum. circ. 1,650. (processed)
Description: University students' progressive Zionist journal.

MCCARVILLE - HILL REPORT. see *PUBLIC ADMINISTRATION*

MACEDONIAN TRIBUNE. see *CLUBS*

320 US ISSN 1049-9776 PQ4627.M2
MACHIAVELLI STUDIES. 1987. a. $15 to individuals; institutions $25. University of New Orleans, Foreign Language Department, New Orleans, LA 70148. TEL 504-286-6657. Eds. Edmund Jacobitti, Victor A. Santi. bk.rev.; bibl.

320.531 GW ISSN 0024-967X
MAERKISCHE ZEITUNG. 1957. m. DM.60. Landsmannschaft Berlin-Mark Brandenburg, Landesverband Berlin, Stresemannstr. 90, 1000 Berlin 61, Germany. TEL 2611046. Ed Herbert Willmann. adv.; bk.rev.; abstr.; illus.; circ. 8,500 (controlled). (newspaper)

960 FR ISSN 0336-6324
MAGHREB, MACHREK, MONDE ARABE. 1964. q. 190 F. (Fondation Nationale des Politiques et Direction de la Documentation) Documentation Francaise, 29-31 Quai Voltaire, 75340 Paris cedex 07, France. TEL 1-40-15-70-00. bk.rev.; bibl.; cum.index; circ. 2,000. (also avail. in microfiche) **Indexed:** Curr.Cont.Africa, Curr.Cont.M.E., Rural Recreat.Tour.Abstr., World Agri.Econ.& Rural Sociol.Abstr.
—BLDSC shelfmark: 5334.754000.
Formerly: Maghreb (ISSN 0024-9890)

MAGHREB REVIEW; a quarterly journal on all aspects of North African or Islamic studies from AD 600 to the present day. see HISTORY — History Of Africa

320   GP
MAGWA. 1981. m. $30. Media Press Gwadloup, Residence Vatable, Batiment F, B.P. 1286, 97178 Point-a-Pitre, Guadeloupe. Ed. Dannick Zandronis. adv.; bk.rev.; circ. 4,000.
  Formerly: Magazine Guadeloupeen.

614.7 323.4   US
MAINE PROGRESSIVE. 1986. m. $10. Invert, P.O. Box 776, Monroe, ME 04951. TEL 207-525-7776. FAX 207-725-6546. (Subscr. to: 387 Gorham Rd., Scarborough, ME 04074) Ed. Selma Sternlieb. adv.; bk.rev.; circ. 4,500. (tabloid format; back issues avail.)
  Description: Contains information on political and social change activities in Maine.

320   US   ISSN 1059-3535
MAJOR CONCEPTS IN POLITICS AND POLITICAL THEORY. irreg. price varies. Peter Lang Publishing, Inc., 62 W. 45th St., 4th Fl., New York, NY 10036. TEL 212-302-6740. Ed. Garrett Ward Sheldon.
  Description: Focuses on major concepts in politics and political theory in prominent traditions, periods, and thinkers.

320   UG
MAKERERE POLITICAL REVIEW.* 1971. irreg. Makerere Political Society, Political Science Department, Makerere University, Kampala, Uganda. Ed. Amos Danson Twino. bibl.

320.531   CE
MAKSVADAYA. (Text in Singhalese) 1970. irreg. Nava Sama Samaja Party, 17 Barracks Lane, Colombo 2, Sri Lanka. Ed. Vickamabahu Karanarathne. adv.; bk.rev.; circ. 500.

320   MW   ISSN 0076-3225
MALAWI. MINISTRY OF LOCAL GOVERNMENT. ANNUAL REPORT. a. K.0.50. Government Printer, Box 37, Zomba, Malawi.

959.5   MY   ISSN 0047-5629
MALAYSIAN DIGEST. 1969. m. free. Ministry of Foreign Affairs, External Information Division - Kementerian Luar Negeri, Wisma Putra, 50602 Kuala Lumpur, Malaysia. TEL 03-2488088. Ed. Sulochana K. Indran. charts; illus.; circ. 25,000. (tabloid format)
  Description: Discusses current political, economic, social and cultural affairs.

320 914   UK   ISSN 0542-4550
DG987
MALTA YEARBOOK. a. $10. New Product Newsletter Co. Ltd., 1A Chesterfield St., London W.1., England.

320   MP
▼**MANAY INDER/OUR PLATFORM.** (Text in Mongolian) 1990. m. Mongolian People's Revolutionary Party, Ulan Bator, Mongolia.
  Formerly: Namyn Am'dral.

322.4   US
MANTOOTH REPORT. 1979. m. $12. RR 1, Box 387, Salem, IN 47167. TEL 812-883-2435. Ed. Don Mantooth. adv.; bk.rev.; circ. 2,000. (tabloid format; back issues avail.)
  Description: Contains political and economic news of the real world and the new world order.

956.940   IS
MAPAM; direct line from Israel. 1982. m. Department of International Affairs, P.O. Box 1777, Tel Aviv 61016, Israel. circ. 1,000.

329.3 350   US
MARK SIEGEL AND ASSOCIATES WASHINGTON INSIDER. 1987. fortn. $125. Mark Siegel Publications, 1030 15th St., N.W., Ste. 408, Washington, DC 20005. TEL 202-371-5600. Eds. Mark Siegel, Steven Money.
  Description: Report on national politics and government from Democratic Party's perspective.

320   GW
MARKTGEFLUESTER. 1986. irreg. (1-2/yr.). Sozialdemokratische Partei Deutschland, Ortsvereine im Markt Maroldsweisach, Meininger Str. 4, D-8617 Maroldsweisach, Germany. TEL 09532-325.

322.4   FR
MAROC REPRESSION. 1978. bi-m. 25 Fr. per no. Association de Soutien aux Comite's de Lutte Contre la Repression au Maroc, 14 rue de Nanteuil, 75015 Paris, France. TEL 45-32-01-89. Ed. Francis Della Sudda. adv.; bk.rev.

320.531   IT
MARX CENTOUNO; rivista internazionale di dibattito teorico e politico. N.S. 1990. 3/yr. L.35000. Edizioni Associate s.r.l., Festa del Perdono 6, 20122 Milan, Italy. TEL 02-58303958.

MARX MEMORIAL LIBRARY BULLETIN. see LIBRARY AND INFORMATION SCIENCES

MARXISM AND THE MASS MEDIA; towards a basic bibliography. see COMMUNICATIONS

320.531   IT
MARXISMO OGGI. 1987. bi-m. L.4000 per no. Marxismo Oggi, Via Alberto da Giussano 15, 20145 Milan, Italy. TEL 02-434224. Ed. Gian Mario Cazzaniga. adv.

320.532   GW   ISSN 0934-649X
MARXISMUS HEUTE. 1969. m. DM.20. Edition Wissenschaft Kultur und Politik, Postfach 510618, 1000 Berlin 51, Germany. Ed. Paul Schulz.
  Formerly: Arbeiterstimme.

320.531   II   ISSN 0025-4134
MARXIST VEEKSHANAM; theoretical discussion forum. (Text in Malayalam; summaries in English) 1970. m. Rs.20. Kerala Institute of Marxist Studies, 6-589 P.T.P. Nagar, Trivandrum, India. Ed. K.V. Surendranath. adv.; bk.rev.; bibl.; circ. 2,000. (tabloid format; also avail. in cards)

320   GW   ISSN 0542-7770
HX6
MARXISTISCHE BLAETTER; fuer Probleme der Gesellschaft, Wirtschaft und Politik. 1963. bi-m. DM.39. V V G Verlags- und Vertriebsgesellschaft mbH, P.O.B. 10 15 55, D-4040 Neuss 1, Germany. TEL 02101-59800. FAX 02101-589100. TELEX 85517506. Ed. Kurt Steinhaus. adv.; bk.rev.; index; circ. 8,000. (back issues avail.) Indexed: INIS Atomind., P.A.I.S.For.Lang.Ind.

MARXISTISCHE STUDIEN. see SOCIAL SCIENCES: COMPREHENSIVE WORKS

MARXISTISK ANTROPOLOGI. see ANTHROPOLOGY

320.531   SW   ISSN 0047-6072
HX9.S9
MARXISTISKT FORUM.* vol.6, 1970. bi-m. Kommunistiska Foerbundet, Kvrkkullen Vaksala, c/o Frycklund, 755 90 Uppsala, Sweden. Ed. Bo Gustafsson. illus.

MARYLAND REPORT. see PUBLIC ADMINISTRATION

320   UK
AL-MASSAR. 1983. w. £50. At-Tayar Press Ltd., P.O. Box 36, Great Missenden, Bucks HP16 OHS, England. TEL 02406-6288. Ed. Sami Farag Ali. circ. 10,000.

320   US
MATCH; an anarchist journal. 1969. 4/yr. $10. Fred Woodworth, Ed. & Pub., Box 3488, Tucson, AZ 85722. bk.rev.; circ. 1,500.

320   UY
MATE AMARGO. 1986. 2/yr. Movimiento de Liberacion Nacional, Bartolome Mitre 1431-Of. 203, Montevideo, Uruguay. TEL 91 56 08. Dir. Emundo Canalda. circ. 22,500.

070 320   US   ISSN 0177-5332
MATERIALY SAMIZDATA. (Text in Russian) 1975. bi-m. $160. (Radio Free Europe - Radio Liberty - GW) Ohio State University, Foreign Language Publications, 83 Pressey Hall, 1070 Carmack Rd., Columbus, OH 43210-1002. TEL 614-292-3838. FAX 614-292-2682. Ed.Bd. circ. 70. (back issues avail.)
  Description: Writings from inside the Soviet Union which have not been or could not be published there.

MATERIAUX POUR L'HISTOIRE DE NOTRE TEMPS. see HISTORY — History Of Europe

320   UK   ISSN 0265-444X
DT469.M4
MAURITIAN INTERNATIONAL. 1964. q. £18 for 3 yrs. Nautilus Publishing Co., 2A Vant Rd., London SW17 8TJ, England. TEL 081-767-2439. FAX 081-767-5265. Ed. Jacques K. Lee. adv.; bk.rev.; circ. 18,000.
  Formerly: Voice of Mauritians.
  Description: News items and editorials pertaining to Mauritius, the southern Indian Ocean region, and Mauritians living overseas.

329.9   CE
MAVBIMA. (Text in Singhalese) w. Rs.0.35 per no. Ceylon Communist Party, 91 Cotta Rd., Colombo 8, Sri Lanka.

058.7   SW   ISSN 0025-665X
MEDBORGAREN. 1915. 6/yr. SEK 100. Moderata Samlingspartiets Riksorganisation - Swedish Moderate Party, P.O. Box 1243, 111 82 Stockholm, Sweden. FAX 46-8-216123. Ed. Folke Schoett. adv.; bk.rev.; abstr.; charts; illus.; circ. 100,000.

MEDIA MONITOR (WASHINGTON). see COMMUNICATIONS

MEDIAWATCH. see JOURNALISM

MEDICINE AND WAR. see MEDICAL SCIENCES

MEI-KUO HSIN WEN YU SHIH CHIEH PAO TAO. see GENERAL INTEREST PERIODICALS — United States

320   AT   ISSN 0085-3224
MELBOURNE JOURNAL OF POLITICS. 1968. a. Aus.$7. University of Melbourne, Political Science Society, Parkville, Vic. 3052, Australia. TEL 03-344-4000. TELEX AA35185 UNIMEL. Ed.Bd. adv.; bk.rev.; circ. 1,000. (back issues avail.) Indexed: Aus.P.A.I.S. —BLDSC shelfmark: 5536.815000.
  Refereed Serial

320   AT
MELBOURNE POLITICS MONOGRAPHS. 1973. a. Aus.$8.95. University of Melbourne, Department of Political Science, Parkville, Vic. 3052, Australia. FAX 344-7894. Ed.Bd. adv.; bk.rev.; bibl.; circ. 1,000.

949.3   BE   ISSN 0025-908X
DH403
MEMO FROM BELGIUM. (Editions in Dutch, English, French, German, Italian, Spanish) 1960. irreg. free. Ministere des Affaires Etrangeres, 2 rue Quatre Bras, 1000 Brussels, Belgium. (For English edition inquire: Consulat General de Belgique, Information Officer, 50 Rockefeller Plaza, Ste. 1104, New York, NY 10020, U.S.A.) charts; illus.; circ. 3,000. Indexed: P.A.I.S.

320   US
MENSAJE. (Text in Spanish) 1980. w. free. Latin American News and Book Inc., 614 Franklin St., Elizabeth, NJ 07206. TEL 908-355-8835. FAX 908-527-9160. Ed. Jose Tenreiro Napoles. circ. 52,000.
  Description: Focuses on international, national, state and local political issues and news.

320   US
MERSHON MEMO. 1975. q. free. Mershon Center, c/o Ohio State University, 199 W. 10th Ave., Columbus, OH 43201. TEL 614-292-1681. FAX 614-292-2407. TELEX MERSHCCTR. bibl.; circ. 2,000.
  Former titles (until vol.13, no.3, 1988): Mershon Center Communique; (until vol.13, no.2, 1988): Mershon Center Report Quarterly.
  Description: Activities and works-in-progress related to national and international security studies by faculty associates of the center.

MESOAMERICA. see HISTORY — History Of North And South America

320   US
MICHIGAN: AROUND AND ABOUT. 1985. m. $10. George Wahr Publishing Company, 304 1-2 South State St., Ann Arbor, MI 48104. TEL 313-668-6097. Ed. George Wahr Sallade. circ. 1,000.
  Description: Commentary and analysis on international events and issues.

POLITICAL SCIENCE 3907

320   US
MICHIGAN JOURNAL OF POLITICAL SCIENCE. 1980. 2/yr. $8 (typically set in Mar.). University of Michigan, Michigan Journal of Political Science, 5620 Haven Hall, Ann Arbor, MI 48109-1045. TEL 313-764-6386. Ed. Peter Harbage. adv.; bk.rev.; circ. 1,000 (controlled). **Indexed:** Amer.Hist.& Life, Hist.Abstr., Int.Polit.Sci.Abstr.
   Description: Covers all aspects of political science, including, but not limited to, political theory, methodology, world politics, comparative politics, American government, public policy, economics, sociology and political economy. All papers written by graduate students, undergraduates and professors.

320 330.9   UK   ISSN 0076-8502
MIDDLE EAST AND NORTH AFRICA (YEAR); survey and directory of lands of Middle East and North Africa. 1948. a. $265. Europa Publications Ltd., 18 Bedford Sq., London WC1B 3JN, England. TEL 071-580-8236. FAX 071-636-1664. TELEX 21540 EUROPA G.
   —BLDSC shelfmark: 5761.350000.
   Description: Covers economic, social, cultural and political affairs.

320   CN   ISSN 0705-8594
DS63.1
MIDDLE EAST FOCUS; Canada's magazine on the contemporary Middle East. 1978. q. Can.$15. Canadian Academic Foundation for Peace in the Middle East, P.O. Box 81509, 1057 Steeles Ave. W., North York, Ont. M2R 3X1, Canada. TEL 416-963-9477. Ed. Irving Abella. bk.rev.; circ. 4,000. **Indexed:** Curr.Cont.M.E., Mid.East: Abstr.& Ind.
   —BLDSC shelfmark: 5761.374600.

327   US
MIDDLE EAST INSTITUTE NEWSLETTER. q. membership. Middle East Institute, 1761 N St. N.W., Washington, DC 20036. TEL 202-785-1141. Ed. Kristina Palmer. bibl.

956   US   ISSN 0047-7249
MIDDLE EAST INTERNATIONAL. 1971. fortn. $59 to individuals; libraries $79; institutions $120. Middle East International (Publishers) Ltd., 1700 17th St. NW, Washington, DC 20009. FAX 202-232-8376. Ed. Michael Wall. bk.rev.; circ. 10,000. (also avail. in microform from UMI; reprint service avail. from UMI) **Indexed:** Curr.Cont.M.E., Mid.East: Abstr.& Ind.
   —BLDSC shelfmark: 5761.378000.
   Description: Political and social developments in the Middle East and Arab world.

320   US   ISSN 0026-315X
MIDDLE EAST MONITOR. 1971. m. $90. Middle East Monitor, Box 236, Ridgewood, NJ 07451-0236. FAX 808-545-1058. Ed. Amir N. Ghazaii. (also avail. in microfiche; back issues avail.)

320 915.602   US
MIDDLE EAST POLICY SURVEY. 1980. bi-w. $150. Middle East Policy Group, 3405 Rodman St. N. W., Washington, DC 20008. TEL 202-363-3495. FAX 202-352-4513. Ed. Richard Straus. circ. 500. (back issues avail.)
   Description: Insider's guide to Middle East events, issues, and personalities.

MIDDLE EAST STUDIES ASSOCIATION BULLETIN. see SOCIAL SCIENCES: COMPREHENSIVE WORKS

956   UK   ISSN 0026-3206
DS41
MIDDLE EASTERN STUDIES. 1964. q. £38($55) to individuals; institutions £98($155). Frank Cass & Co. Ltd., Gainsborough House, 11 Gainsborough Rd., London E11 1RS, England. TEL 081-530-4226. FAX 081-530-7795. Eds. Elie Kedourie, Sylvia G. Haim. adv.; bk.rev.; index. (also avail. in microfilm from UMI; back issues avail.) **Indexed:** A.B.C.Pol.Sci., Abstr.Anthropol., Amer.Hist.& Life, Br.Hum.Ind., Curr.Cont.Africa, Curr.Cont.M.E., Hist.Abstr., Lang.& Lang.Behav.Abstr., Mid.East: Abstr.& Ind., Soc.Sci.Ind., SSCI.
   —BLDSC shelfmark: 5761.406000.
   Description: Timely articles cover academic research on the history and politics of the Arabic-speaking countries and Israel.

MIDEAST MARKETS; survey of business, finance, law and political risk in the Middle East and North Africa. see BUSINESS AND ECONOMICS

MIDEAST MONITOR. see HISTORY — History Of The Near East

320   US
MIDSOUTH POLITICAL SCIENCE JOURNAL. 1980. 4/yr. $15. (University of Central Arkansas, Department of Political Science) University of Central Arkansas Press, Conway, AR 72032. TEL 501-450-5686. Ed. Gary Wekkin. circ. 200.

MIDSTREAM; a monthly Jewish review. see LITERARY AND POLITICAL REVIEWS

320   US
MIDWEST POLITICAL CONSULTANT. 1987. m. $50. Christian Schock and Associates, 361 S. Commonwealth Ave., Elgin, IL 60123. TEL 708-741-1753. Ed. Christian Schock. bk.rev.
   Description: Focuses on politics and political compaigning.

325   IT   ISSN 0391-5492
MIGRANTI-PRESS. (Supplement to: Servizio Migranti) 1979. w. L.45000. Fondazione Migrantes, Via Aurelia 481, 00165 Rome, Italy. FAX 06-662-0530. TELEX 623328 UCEI I.

320 628   US   ISSN 0887-378X
RA418.3.U6   CODEN: MIQUES
MILBANK QUARTERLY. 1923. q. with 2 supplements. $31 to individuals; institutions $62. (Milbank Memorial Fund) Cambridge University Press, 40 W. 20th St., New York, NY 10011. TEL 212-924-3900. FAX 212-691-3239. Ed. David P. Willis. charts; illus.; stat.; circ. 3,000. (also avail. in microform from UMI; microfiche; reprint service avail. from UMI) **Indexed:** Abstr.Health Care Manage.Stud., Abstr.Hyg., Abstr.Soc.Geront., Acad.Ind., Arts & Hum.Cit.Ind., B.P.I, Biol.Abstr., BPIA, Chem.Abstr., Curr.Cont., Curr.Lit.Fam.Plan., Fut.Surv., Hlth.Ind., Hosp.Lit.Ind., Ind.Med., Med. Care Rev., Mid.East: Abstr.& Ind., Nutr.Abstr., P.A.I.S., Psychol.Abstr., Risk Abstr., Sage Fam.Stud.Abstr., Sage Pub.Admin.Abstr., Soc.Work Res.& Abstr., Soc.Work Res.& Abstr., Sociol.Abstr., SSCI, Tr.& Indus.Ind.
   —BLDSC shelfmark: 5766.040000.
   Former titles: Health and Society (ISSN 0160-1997); Milbank Memorial Fund Quarterly (ISSN 0026-3745)
   Description: Scholarly articles on research and policy analysis in health care focusing on economic, social, demographic, ethical and philosophical aspects.

320   AG
MILITANCIA (BUENOS AIRES, 1973);* Peronista para la liberacion. 1973. s-m. Arg.$3 per no. c/o Arturo Apicella e Hijo, 319 Esmera Ida, Buenos Aires, Argentina. Ed. Carlos Maria Duhalde. illus.

320   AG
MILITANCIA (BUENOS AIRES, 1986). 1986. m. Nestor Vicente, Parana 761 1 A, Buenos Aires, Argentina.

320   MX
MILITANCIA: TEMAS DEL SOCIALISMO.* 1974. bi-m. Mex.$15 per copy. Milan 28-104, Mexico 6, D.F., Mexico. Ed. Rodolfo F. Pena. bk.rev.; film rev.

320.531   US   ISSN 0026-3885
MILITANT; a socialist newsweekly published in the interests of the working people. (Supplement avail.: International Socialist Review) 1928. w. $45 to individuals; institutions $80. Militant, Inc., 410 West St., New York, NY 10014. TEL 212-243-6392. FAX 212-727-0150. Ed. Greg McCartan. adv.; bk.rev.; circ. 10,000. (tabloid format; also avail. in microform from UMI; back issues avail.; reprint service avail. from UMI)
   Description: Covers developments in the labor movement, women's rights issues and racial issues. Coverage is international.

320.532   CU   ISSN 0864-2362
MILITANTE COMUNISTA. 1967. m. $3. Partido Comunista, Calle 11, No. 160, Vedado, Havana, Cuba. TEL 7-32-7581. Dir. Manuel Menendez. circ. 200,000.

320   PK
MILLAT. (Text in Urdu) 1978. w. Rs.4. Islamabad Publications, 9 Hamid Chambers, Aab Parah, Islamabad, Pakistan.

320.9   US   ISSN 0026-4474
MINDSZENTY REPORT. 1958. m. $12. Cardinal Mindszenty Foundation, Inc., Box 11321, St. Louis, MO 63105. TEL 314-991-2939. FAX 314-991-5128. circ. 9,000. (also avail. in microform from UMI)
   Formerly: Release (St. Louis).

320.5   FR   ISSN 0996-9640
MINUTE. 1962. w. 430 F. Societe Editions Parisiennes Associees, Ave. d'le'na, 75016 Paris, France. TEL 1-42-85-54-54. FAX 1-48-74-23-64. Ed. Jean Claude Goudeau. adv.; bk.rev.; film rev.; play rev.; bibl.; illus.; circ. 220,000. (tabloid format)
   Formerly (until 1989): Minute, le Chardon (ISSN 0987-903X); Which was formed by the 1987 merger of: Minute (ISSN 0026-573X) & Chardon (ISSN 0982-7757)

320   CC
MINZHU/DEMOCRACY. (Text in Chinese) m. Minjin Zhongyang Weiyuanhui, No. 98, Gulou Xin'anli, Beijing 100009, People's Republic of China. TEL 447673. Ed. Mao Qifen.

320 340   CC
MINZHU YU FAZHI/DEMOCRACY & LEGAL SYSTEMS. (Text in Chinese) m. $41.30. (Zhongguo Faxuehui - China Jurisprudence Society) Minzhu yu Fazhi Bianjibu, No.100, Dongsi 10 Tiao, Beijing 100007, People's Republic of China. TEL 4016660-115. (Dist. in US by: China Books & Periodicals, Inc., 2929 24th St., San Francisco, CA 94110. TEL 415-282-2994) Wang Shuren.

320   CC
MINZHU YU KEXUE/DEMOCRACY AND SCIENCE. (Text in Chinese) bi-m. Jiusan Xueshe Zhongyang Weiyuanhui, No. 4, Banshang Hutong, Xisi, Beijing 100034, People's Republic of China. TEL 6011627. Ed. Li Fengming.

320   FR
MINZHU ZHONGGUO. (Text in Chinese; table of contents in Chinese and English) 1989. bi-m. 26 F. in France; Hong Kong HK.$20; Taiwan NT.$100; elsewhere $3.50 per no. (Federation for a Democratic China - Minzhu Zhongguo Zhenxian) SARL Minzhu Zhongguo, 12, rue de la Grange-Bateliere, 75009 Paris, France. TEL 48-01-01-03. FAX 48-01-01-04. (US orders to: 733 15th St. N.W., Ste. 525, Washington, DC 20005. TEL 202-347-5912; Taiwan orders to: 561 Chung Hsiao E. Rd. Sec. 4, Taipei, Taiwan, R.O.C.) Ed. Yuan Zhiming. illus.
   Description: Covers the activities of the federation, and of the Chinese democracy movement.

320   US
MISSOURI ANNUAL CAMPAIGN FINANCE REPORT. 1979. a. free. Office of the Secretary of State, Campaign Reporting Division, Box 1370, Jefferson City, MO 65102. TEL 314-751-3077. FAX 314-526-3242. Ed. Gayla Thomas. circ. 2,500.

322   US
MOBILIZER. 1978. q. $15. Mobilization for Survival, 45 John St., No. 811, New York, NY 10038. TEL 212-385-2222. Ed. John Miller. adv.; bk.rev.; charts; illus.; circ. 15,000. (tabloid format; back issues avail.) **Indexed:** Alt.Press Ind., HR Rep.
   Description: Covers grassroots political activities and concerns on disarmament, non-intervention, and nuclear issues.

320.5   SW   ISSN 0026-7449
MODERAT DEBATT. 1934. 4/yr. SEK 100($5) Moderata Ungdomsfoerbundet - Young Conservatives, P.O. Box 1243, 111 82 Stockholm, Sweden. FAX 8-203449. Ed. Anders Hultin. adv.; bk.rev.; circ. 30,000.
   Formerly: Ung Hoeger.

MODERN AGE. see LITERARY AND POLITICAL REVIEWS

MODERN ASIAN STUDIES. see ORIENTAL STUDIES

320   SG
MOMSAREEW. 1958. m. Parti Africain de l'Independance, B.P. 820, Dakar, Senegal. Ed. Malamine Badji. circ. 2,000.

POLITICAL SCIENCE

321.6   UK
MONARCHIST LEAGUE NEWSLETTER. 1948. q. £20($30) Monarchist League, International Headquarters, BM Monarchist, London WC1N 3XX, England. TEL 071-823-4476. Ed. Gregory Lauder-Frost. adv.; bk.rev.; bibl.; illus.; circ. 2,000.
    Former titles: Monarchist Newsletter; Monarchist (ISSN 0047-7834)

321   CN   ISSN 0319-4019
MONARCHY CANADA. 1970. q. Can.$15. (Monarchist League of Canada) Loyalty Publications, 3050 Yonge St., Ste. 206, Toronto, Ont. M4N 2K4, Canada. TEL 416-482-4157. (Subscr. addr.: P.O. Box 1057, Oakville, Ont. L6J 5E9) Ed. Arthur Bousfield. adv.; bk.rev.; charts; illus.; circ. 8,000.
    Formerly: Canadian Monarchist.
    Description: Looks at monarchy from a Canadian perspective and at Canada from a monarchist one. Offers current and historical articles on constitutional, social and political affairs, as well as personality profiles and reviews of books and the arts.

MONASH PAPERS ON SOUTHEAST ASIA. see HISTORY — History Of Asia

LE MONDE. see LITERARY AND POLITICAL REVIEWS

335.83   FR   ISSN 0026-9433
MONDE LIBERTAIRE.* 1954. w. 180 F. Federation Anarchiste, 145 rue Amelot, 75011 Paris, France. bk.rev.; film rev.; tele.rev.; bibl.; circ. 17,500.

320   IT
MONDO; settimanale di economia e politica del Corriere della Sera. 1949. w. L.156000. Rizzoli Editore-Corriere della Sera, Via A. Rizzoli 2, 20132 Milan, Italy. Ed. R. Mori. **Indexed:** P.A.I.S.For.Lang.Ind.

329.9   IT
MONDO OPERAIO. Variant title: Mondoperaio. 1948. m. L.50000. (Partito Socialista Italiano) Mondo Operaio Edizioni Avanti S.p.A., Via Tomacelli 146, 00186 Rome, Italy. Ed. Luciano Vasconi. adv.; bk.rev.; film rev.; play rev.; circ. 15,000.

MONDO PADANO. see BUSINESS AND ECONOMICS — Chamber Of Commerce Publications

MONGOLIA REPORT. see BUSINESS AND ECONOMICS — Economic Situation And Conditions

320.531   US   ISSN 0027-0520
HX1
MONTHLY REVIEW; an independent socialist magazine. 1949. m. (bi-m. Jul.-Aug.). $25 to individuals; institutions $45. Monthly Review Press, 122 W. 27th St., 10th fl., New York, NY 10001. TEL 212-691-2555. Eds. Paul M. Sweezy, Harry Magdoff. adv.; bk.rev.; index; circ. 6,000. (also avail. in microform from UMI; reprint service avail. from UMI) **Indexed:** Acad.Ind., Alt.Press Ind., Amer.Bibl.Slavic & E.Eur.Stud., Amer.Hist.& Life, Bus.Ind., Hist.Abstr., Lang.& Lang.Behav.Abstr., Left Ind. (1982-), Mag.Ind., Mid.East: Abstr.& Ind., P.A.I.S., PROMT, R.G., Rural Recreat.Tour.Abstr., Soc.Sci.Ind., SSCI, Tr.& Indus.Ind., World Agri.Econ.& Rural Sociol.Abstr.
    —BLDSC shelfmark: 5947.800000.
    Description: Uses Marxist thought to critique contempory conditions.

MOSCA NEWS. see BUSINESS AND ECONOMICS

947   RU   ISSN 0027-1306
MOSCOW NEWS. (Editions in English, French, German, Greek, Hungarian, Italian, Russian) 1939. w. 16-2 Gorky St., Moscow, Russia. TEL 7095-200-02-78. FAX 7095-209-02-78. Eds. Egor Yakovlev (Russian ed.), Vladimir Pichugin (Eng.ed.). (newspaper)
    Description: Covers local and international news plus the full text of all major political speeches.

MOSHE DAYAN CENTER FOR MIDDLE EASTERN AND AFRICAN STUDIES. BULLETIN. see GENERAL INTEREST PERIODICALS — Israel

335   RU
MOSKOVSKII UNIVERSITET. VESTNIK. SERIYA 13: TEORIYA NAUCHNOGO KOMMUNIZMA. (Text in Russian; contents page in English) bi-m. 12.90 Rub. Moskovskii Universitet, Ul. Gertsena 5-7, 103009 Moscow, Russia. bk.rev.; bibl.; index.

320   GP
MOUN/PEOPLE; a cultural review from Guadeloupe. 1985. bi-m. 180 F. Media Press Gwadloup, B.P. 128, 97184 Pointe-a-Pitre, Guadeloupe. Ed. Danik A. Zandwonis. adv.; circ. 3,500.

320   DK   ISSN 0109-4599
MULDVARPEN; blad for undergravende virksomhed. 1984. bi-m. DKK 5. Venstresocialisternes Ungdom, Noerrebrogade 14 B-3, 2200 Copenhagen N, Denmark. illus.

320   RM
MUNCA DE PARTID.* m. 30 lei($25) Partidul Comunist Roman, Comitetul Central, c/o Rompresfilatelia, Calea Grivitei 64-66, P.O. Box 12-201, Bucharest, Rumania. Ed.Bd. illus.

320   AG
MUNDO ARABE.* 1981. m. Camara de Comercio, 25 de Mayo, 67, 1002 Buenos Aires, Argentina.

MUNDO ISRAELITA; actualidad de la semana en Israel y en el mundo judio. see GENERAL INTEREST PERIODICALS — Israel

320 200   PK
MUSLIM WORLD; weekly review of the Motamar. (Includes: World Muslim Conference Proceedings) (Text in English) 1963. w. Rs.60($30) World Muslim Congress - Motamar Al-Alam al-Islami, Box 5030, Karachi 74000, Pakistan. FAX 92-21-466878. Ed. Inamullah Khan. adv.; charts. **Indexed:** Abstr.Musl.Rel., Arts & Hum.Cit.Ind., Curr.Cont., Hist.Abstr., Rel.& Theol.Abstr.

329   GW   ISSN 0027-5093
MUT. 1965. m. DM.108. Mut-Verlag, Bahnhofstr. 1, Postfach 1, 2811 Asendorf, Germany. TEL 04253-566. Ed. Bernhard C. Wintzek. bk.rev.; illus.
    Description: Non-political publication promoting unity, justice, freedom, and world peace.

341.2   BE   ISSN 0255-3813
UA646.3
N A T O REVIEW. Norwegian edition: N A T O Nytt. French edition: Revue de l'OTAN. Danish edition: N A T O Nyt. Dutch edition: N A V O Kroniek. German edition: N A T O Brief. Greek edition: Deltio N A T O. Italian edition: Notizie N A T O. Portuguese edition: Noticias da O T A N. Spanish edition: Revista de la O T A N. Turkish edition: N A T O Dergisi. (Text in English) 1953. bi-m. (Norwegian, Danish, Portuguese, Turkish eds. q.; Icelandic ed., a.). free. North Atlantic Treaty Organization, Information and Press Service, B-1110 Brussels, Belgium. TEL 32-2-728-41-11. FAX 32-2-728-45-79. (U.S. address: Distribution Services Staff, Bureau of Public Affairs, Dept. of State, Rm 5815A, Washington, DC 20520) Ed. Peter Jenner. bk.rev.; bibl.; circ. 260,000. (also avail. in microform from UMI; reprint service avail. from UMI) **Indexed:** A.B.C.Pol.Sci., Abstr.Mil.Bibl., DM & T, Ind.Free Per., Key to Econ.Sci., Mid.East: Abstr.& Ind., PMR, Pt.de Rep.
    Formerly: N A T O Letter (ISSN 0027-6057)
    Description: International information on political and defense subjects, as well as some economic and scientific topics relevant to NATO. Contributions from leading experts, politicians, academics, and NATO officials.

320   AU
N F Z; NEUE FREIE ZEITUNG. 1973. w. S.9 per no. Freiheitliche Partei Oesterreichs, Kaerntner Str. 28, A-1010 Vienna, Austria. TEL 5129452. FAX 5138858. Ed. Christian Wehrschuetz. adv.; bk.rev.; illus.
    Supersedes: Neue Front: Zeitung der Freiheitlichen.

335   FR   ISSN 0222-4275
N R S. (Nouvelle Revue Socialiste) 1974. 4/yr. 285 F. Nouvelles Editions de l'An 2000, 10 rue de Solferino, 75333 Paris Cedex 07, France. TEL 45-50-34-35. adv.; bk.rev.
    Former titles (until 1978): Nouvelle Revue Socialiste; Revue Socialiste.

335   US
▼**N Y: THE CITY JOURNAL.** 1990. q. $25. Manhattan Institute, 42 E. 71st St., New York, NY 10021. TEL 212-988-7300. Ed. Richard Vigilante. circ. 5,000 (controlled).
    Description: Covers politics and culture.

320.531   GW
NACHRICHTEN FUER SCHOENBERG. 1975. 4/yr. Sozialdemokratische Partei Deutschland (SPD), Ortsverein, Krummbeker Weg 8a, 1306 Schoenberg, Germany. TEL 04344-9941. adv.

972   MX   ISSN 0027-7509
NACION; organo de accion nacional. 1941. fortn. Mex.$60000($45) Estudios y Publicaciones Economicas y Sociales, S.A., Cerrada de Eugenia, 25, Col. del Valle, Delegacion Benito Juarez, Apartado Postal 32-470, CP 03100 Mexico DF, Mexico. TEL 536-18-31. FAX 525-687-2922. adv.; charts; illus.; circ. 15,000 (controlled).

NAMIBIA. see ETHNIC INTERESTS

320   PK
NAQIB-I MILLAT. (Text in Urdu) vol.2, 1978. w. Rs.3. Maulvi Hidayatullah, Kucha Chen Teliyan, Bazar Wachchuwali, Shah Alam Market, Lahore, Pakistan.

323.4   US   ISSN 0888-1391
NATIONAL ALLIANCE (NEW YORK). 1979. w. $15. (New Alliance Productions, Inc.) Castillo Publications, 500 Greenwich St., Ste. 210, New York, NY 10013. TEL 212-941-5800. Ed. Jacqueline Salit. adv.; bk.rev.; circ. 100,000.
    Formerly: New York Alliance; Supersedes (1977-1979): Don't Mourn, Organize.
    Description: Political and cultural newsweekly aimed at a black, gay, women's and progressive readership.

808.8   UK
NATIONAL AWAMI PARTY OF BANGLADESH (IN GREAT BRITAIN). BULLETIN.* irreg., no.5, 1973. National Awami Party of Bangla Desh, 86 Oakleigh Road, London N.11, England. Ed. Fazlul Huq.

NATIONAL DIRECTORY OF CORPORATE PUBLIC AFFAIRS. see BUSINESS AND ECONOMICS

320
NATIONAL GUARD. (Text in English) m. Rs.20($12) Ashok Walia, 103-a, Kamla Nagar, Delhi 110007, India. Ed. R.P. Ahluwalia. adv.; illus. **Indexed:** Air Un.Lib.Ind.

320 327   US   ISSN 0884-9382
E840
NATIONAL INTEREST. 1985. q. $21 (foreign $31). National Affairs, Inc., 1112 16th St., N.W., Ste. 540., Washington, Washington, DC 20036. TEL 202-467-4884. FAX 202-467-0006. (Subscr. to: Box 3000, Dept. NI, Denville, NJ 07834) Ed. Owen Harries. adv.; bk.rev.; circ. 6,000. (also avail. in microform from UMI; back issues avail.) **Indexed:** Amer.Hist.& Life, Hist.Abstr., Int.Polit.Sci.Abstr., P.A.I.S., Polit.Sci.Abstr.
    —BLDSC shelfmark: 6025.934000.
    Description: Presents analyses of American foreign policy and of issues which confront the United States.

320   US   ISSN 0360-4217
JK1
NATIONAL JOURNAL; the weekly on politics and government. (Includes s-a supplement: Capital Source) 1969. w. $767. National Journal, Inc. (Subsidiary of: Times Mirror Company), 1730 M St., N.W., Ste. 1100, Washington, DC 20036. TEL 202-857-1400. FAX 202-833-8069. Ed. Richard S. Frank. adv.; bk.rev.; charts; illus.; s-a. index; circ. 6,000. (also avail. in microfilm from UMI) **Indexed:** Bank.Lit.Ind., CAD CAM Abstr., Energy Ind., Energy Info.Abstr., Environ.Abstr., Med.Care Rev., P.A.I.S., Pers.Lit., Sel.Water Res.Abstr., Tel.Abstr., Telegen.
    ●Also available online. Vendor(s): Mead Data Central.
    —BLDSC shelfmark: 6026.150000.
    Incorporates: National Issues Outlook (ISSN 0092-9778); **Former titles:** National Journal Reports (ISSN 0091-3685); National Journal (ISSN 0027-9560)
    Description: Provides policymakers with non-partisan analysis of major national policy issues.

320   AT
NATIONAL LEADER. 1948. q. Aus.$8. National Party of Australia, 3rd Fl., 34 Hunter St., Sydney, N.S.W. 2000, Australia. TEL 02 231-4377. FAX 02-221-6151. Ed. John Hunter. adv.
    Description: Discusses matters affecting rural and metropolitan electorates.

322.4   AT
NATIONAL MESSAGE. vol.2, 1975. q. Aus.$0.20 per no. Australian Citizens for Freedom, P.O. Box 1881, Brisbane, Qld. 4001, Australia. Ed. Harold J. Wright. circ. 1,000.

329   US   ISSN 0077-5282
NATIONAL PARTY PLATFORMS. SUPPLEMENT. (Sixth edition covers 1840-1976; supplement in 1982 covers 1980) 1961. irreg. latest 1982. price varies. University of Illinois Press, 54 E. Gregory Dr., Champaign, IL 61820. TEL 217-333-0950. FAX 217-244-8082. Ed. Donald B. Johnson.

320   US   ISSN 0896-629X
JK1
NATIONAL POLITICAL SCIENCE REVIEW. a. $19.95. (National Conference of Black Political Scientists) Transaction Publishers, Dept. 3091, Rutgers University, New Brunswick, NJ 08903. TEL 908-932-2280. FAX 908-932-3138. Ed. Mathew Holden.
   Description: Examines the theoretical and empirical aspects of politics and policies that advantage or disadvantage groups by reasons of race, ethnicity, sex, and other factors.

353   US   ISSN 0027-9943
NATIONAL PROGRAM LETTER. 1942. m. $10. National Education Program, c/o Guy Rose, Box 11000, Oklahoma City, OK 73136-1100. TEL 405-425-5040. FAX 405-425-5316. Ed. Pendleton Woods. bk.rev.; circ. 26,000. (also avail. in microform from UMI; reprint service avail. from UMI)
   Formerly: Harding College Letter.
   Description: Presents editorials representing conservative viewpoints.

320.52   US   ISSN 0028-0038
AP2
NATIONAL REVIEW; a journal of fact and opinion. 1955. fortn. $57. National Review, Inc., 150 E. 35th St., New York, NY 10016. TEL 212-679-7330. FAX 212-696-0309. Ed. John O'Sullivan. adv.; bk.rev.; illus.; index; circ. 150,000. (also avail. in microform from UMI,MIM; reprint service avail. from UMI) **Indexed:** Acad.Ind., Amer.Bibl.Slavic & E.Eur.Stud., Bk.Rev.Dig., Bk.Rev.Ind. (1965-), Child.Bk.Rev.Ind. (1965-), Curr.Lit.Fam.Plan., Film Lit.Ind. (1973-), Fut.Surv., Mag.Ind., Media Rev.Dig., Mid.East: Abstr.& Ind., Pers.Lit., PMR, PSI, R.G., TOM.
●Also available online. Vendor(s): DIALOG.
Also available on CD-ROM. .
—BLDSC shelfmark: 6031.050000.
   Description: Discusses national and international issues from a rightwing viewpoint; includes books, arts, and manners.

320 355   PH
NATIONAL SECURITY REVIEW. 1973. q. free. National Defense College of the Philippines, Fort Bonifacio, Rizal, Philippines. Ed.Bd. bibl.; charts; circ. 2,000. **Indexed:** Artbibl.

324.24   US   ISSN 0028-0372
E740
NATIONAL VOTER. 1951. 6/yr. $8 to non-members. League of Women Voters of the U S, 1730 M St., N.W., 10th, Washington, DC 20036. TEL 202-429-1965. FAX 202-429-0854. Ed. Karen Everhart Bedford. adv.; bk.rev.; index; circ. 130,000. (also avail. in microfilm from UMI)
   Description: Nonpartisan articles on public policy and campaign issues of interest to the American electorate.

960 338   CX   ISSN 0028-050X
NATIONS NOUVELLES. (Text in French) N.S. 1966. irreg. 3500 Fr.CFA. Organisation Commune Africaine et Mauricienne (OCAM), B.P. 965, Bangui, Central African Republic. Ed. Pierre Debato. adv.; bibl.; charts; illus.; stat.; circ. 700.

320.351   US   ISSN 0890-6130
B809.8
NATURE, SOCIETY, AND THOUGHT; a journal of dialectical and historical materialism. 1987. q. $15 to individuals; institutions $28. (Marxist Educational Press) M E P Publications, University of Minnesota, 116 Church St., S.E., Minneapolis, MN 55455. TEL 612-647-9748. (Orders to: Nature, Society, and Thought, University of Minnesota, 116 Church St., S.E., Minneapolis, MN 55455) Ed. Erwin Marquit. adv.; bk.rev. **Indexed:** Left Ind. (1987-).
—BLDSC shelfmark: 6047.357000.
   Description: Devoted to applications of Marxist methods to various fields of study.

329   PL   ISSN 0137-141X
NAUKI POLITYCZNE. Issue titles vary. 1974. irreg., 10, 1988. price varies. Adam Mickiewicz University Press, Nowowiejskiego 55, 61-734 Poznan, Poland. TEL 527-380. FAX 61-526425. TELEX 413260 UAMPL.
—BLDSC shelfmark: 9120.471000.
   Description: Contains current research results on one author in the field of political science including Ph.D. works and other monographs.

322.4   CE
NAVA SAMA SAMAJA BULLETINE. (Text in English) 1985. irreg. Nava Sama Samaja Party, 17 Barracks Lane, Colombo 2, Sri Lanka. Ed. Vickamabahu Karanarathne. adv.; bk.rev.

329.9   CE
NAVALOKAYA. (Text in Sinhala) 1941. m. Communist Party of Sri Lanka, Gampaha, WP, Sri Lanka.
   Description: Covers literature, art, politics, education and science.

NAVE PARVA. see *TRAVEL AND TOURISM*

320   UK   ISSN 0307-0832
NAVIN WEEKLY. 1975. w. £32. 59-61 Broughton Rd., Fulham, London SW6 2LA, England. Ed. Ramesh Kumar. adv.; bk.rev.; film rev.; tr.lit.; circ. 55,000.

NEAR EAST - SOUTH ASIA REPORT. see *BUSINESS AND ECONOMICS — Economic Situation And Conditions*

NEPAL - ANTIQUARY; journal of social-historical research and digest. see *ORIENTAL STUDIES*

320   NP
NEPALESE JOURNAL OF POLITICAL SCIENCE. 1979. s-a. Tribhuvan University, Political Science Instruction Committee, Kirtipur Multiple Campus, Kathmandu, Nepal.

320   US
NETWORKER: INTERNATIONAL PEACE. 2/yr. price varies. Interfaith Impact for Justice and Peace, 110 Maryland Ave., NE, Washington, DC 20002. TEL 202-543-2800.

320.531   GW
NEUE ARBEITERPRESSE. 1976. w. DM.65 (foreign DM.95). Bund Sozialistischer Arbeiter, Postfach 100105, 4300 Essen 1, Germany. TEL 0201-733556. Ed. Bettina Rippert. bk.rev.

320.5   GW   ISSN 0177-6738
DIE NEUE GESELLSCHAFT - FRANKFURTER HEFTE. 1954. m. DM.90. Verlag J.H.W. Dietz Nachf. GmbH, In der Raste 2, 5300 Bonn 1, Germany. Ed. Peter Glotz. adv.; bk.rev.; index; circ. 6,500. **Indexed:** CERDIC, P.A.I.S.For.Lang.Ind.
   Formerly (until 1985): Neue Gesellschaft (ISSN 0028-3177); **Incorporates (since 1984):** Frankfurter Hefte.

320.9   GW   ISSN 0028-3258
NEUE KOMMENTARE. 1958. m. DM.60. Georg Herde, Mauerweg 20, 6000 Frankfurt, Germany. index. (looseleaf format)

320.5   AU   ISSN 0028-3274
DER NEUE MAHNRUF; Zeitschrift fuer Freiheit, Recht und Demokratie. 1948. m. S.70. Bundesverband Oesterreichischer Widerstandskaempfer und Opfer des Faschismus, Lassallestr. 40, A-1020 Vienna, Austria. TEL 265389. Ed. Oskar Wiesflecker. adv.; bk.rev.; charts; illus.; circ. 4,500.

POLITICAL SCIENCE   3909

320.9   GW   ISSN 0028-3320
H5
NEUE POLITISCHE LITERATUR; Berichte ueber das internationale Schrifttum. (Supplement avail.: Neue Politische Literatur. Beihefte. (ISSN 0176-604X)) 1956. 3/yr. DM.88. Verlag Peter Lang GmbH, Eschborner Landstr. 42-50, 6000 Frankfurt a.M. 90, Germany. TEL 069-7807050. FAX 069-785893. Ed.Bd. adv.; bk.rev.; bibl.; index, cum.index: 1966-1975 (vols.11-20); circ. 1,450. (back issues avail.) **Indexed:** Amer.Hist.& Life, Hist.Abstr., P.A.I.S.For.Lang.Ind.

320   GW   ISSN 0176-604X
NEUE POLITISCHE LITERATUR. BEIHEFTE.; Forschungsberichte zur internationalen Literatur. irreg., vol.5, 1988. price varies. Franz Steiner Verlag Wiesbaden GmbH, Birkenwaldstr. 44, Postfach 101526, 7000 Stuttgart 1, Germany. TEL 0711-2582-0. FAX 0711-2582290. TELEX 723636-DADZ.

320   AU
DAS NEUE WORT. 1972. m. S.150. Volkssozialistische Bewegung Oesterreichs, Apfelgasse 1-7, 1040 Vienna, Austria. Ed. Alfred Warton. bk.rev.; circ. 5,000.
   Description: Newsletter of Socialist analysis and opinion.

320   GW
NEUIGKEIDNBLAEDDLE. 1988. q. free. Sozialdemokratische Partei Deutschlands (SPD), Ortsverein Gartenstadt-Theuerbruennlein-Eselhoehe, Kornmarkt 17, D-8720 Schweinfurt, Germany. TEL 049-9721-21429. (Subscr. to: c/o Traudl Steinmueller, Wilhelm-Zinn-Str. 20, D-8720 Schweinfurt, Germany) circ. 2,200. (back issues avail.)

350   US   ISSN 0196-7355
JK8501
NEVADA PUBLIC AFFAIRS REVIEW. 1960. irreg. $8. University of Nevada, Reno, Senator Alan Bible Center for Applied Research, Reno, NV 89557. TEL 702-784-6718. Ed. J.M. Winter. circ. 2,000.
   Former titles (until 1979): Nevada Public Affairs Report (ISSN 0364-3921); Governmental Research Newsletter (ISSN 0017-2677)
   Description: Each issue features in-depth report and analysis of a current policy issue relevant to Nevada.

320 363.35   US
NEW ABOLITIONIST. 1982. q. $15. Nuclear Free America, 325 E. 25th St., Baltimore, MD 21218. TEL 301-235-3575. FAX 301-462-1039. Ed. Chuck Johnson. bk.rev.; circ. 6,000. (tabloid format; back issues avail.)
   Description: Covers the international Nuclear Free Zone movement, with information about campaigns and related topics.

320 330   UK   ISSN 0140-1378
DT1
NEW AFRICAN YEARBOOK. a. £34.95($54.95) I.C. Publications Ltd., P.O. Box 261, Carlton House, 69 Gt. Queen St., London WC2B 5BN, England. TEL 071-404-4333. FAX 071-404-5336. TELEX 8811757 ARABY G. Ed. Linda van Buren. adv.; circ. 10,000.
—BLDSC shelfmark: 6081.752500.
   Formed by the merger of: New African Yearbook: West and Central; New African Yearbook: East and South.
   Description: Provides information on Africa including the major facts and figures on 48 countries.

320.532   II   ISSN 0047-9500
NEW AGE. 1953; N.S. 1964. w. $55. Communist Party of India, 15 Kotla Rd., New Delhi 110002, India. TELEX 3165982 CNS IN. Ed. Pauly V. Parakal. adv.; bk.rev.; film rev.; play rev.; charts; illus.; circ. 15,000. (tabloid format) **Indexed:** Child.Bk.Rev.Ind.

POLITICAL SCIENCE

320 051   US
NEW AMERICAN (APPLETON). 1965. bi-w. $39. Review of the News Inc., Box 8040, Appleton, WI 54913. TEL 414-749-3784. FAX 414-749-3785. Ed. Gary Benoit. adv.; bk.rev.; circ. 30,000. (also avail. in microform from UMI; reprint service avail. from UMI) **Indexed:** G.Soc.Sci.& Rel.Per.Lit.
    Formed by the 1985 merger of: American Opinion (ISSN 0003-0236); Review of the News (ISSN 0034-6802)
    Description: For constitutional conservatives and economic libertarians. Focuses on political science, social opinion and economic theory, while rejecting an accidental view of history and exposing the behind-the-scences forces shaping American politics and culture.

320.532   II
NEW DEMOCRACY.* 1972. m. Rs.12. Committee of Communist Revolutionaries, 129-A Circular Garden Reach Rd., Calcutta 23, India. Ed. Ranajit Samaddar. bibl.

320 330   UK
NEW DEMOCRAT INTERNATIONAL; magazine of radical politics and the future. 1983. 5/yr. £7.50 (foreign £15). Letterhurst Ltd., Box ND1, London WC1 3XX, England. Ed. David Boyle. adv.; bk.rev.; circ. 5,000. (back issues avail.)
    Formerly: New Democrat (London).

NEW DIRECTIONS IN PUBLIC ADMINISTRATION RESEARCH. see *PUBLIC ADMINISTRATION*

320   US
NEW FEDERALIST. w. $20. Box 889, Leesburg, VA 22075. TEL 703-777-9451. Ed. Nancy Spannaus.

320.531 331   UK   ISSN 0266-7835
NEW GROUND. 1983. q. £12($18) Socialist Environment and Resources Association, 11 Goodwin St., London N4 3HQ, England. TEL 071-263-7424. Ed. Tina Cox. adv.; bk.rev.; charts; illus.; stat.; circ. 2,500.
    Formerly: S E R A News.
    Description: Covers environmental issues from a socialist point of view and provides theoretical articles on Green Socialism.

322.4   US   ISSN 0028-5137
AP2
NEW GUARD.* 1961. q. $10. Young Americans for Freedom, Inc., 14018 Sullyfield Cir, Ste. A, Chantilly, VA 22021-1617. Ed. R. Cort Kirkwood. bk.rev.; illus.; circ. 25,000. (processed; also avail. in microform from UMI; back issues avail.)

320   NR   ISSN 0794-439X
NEW HORIZON; Nigeria's Marxist monthly. 1975. m. £N48($24) I F & W O G Enterprises, P.O. Box 2165, Mushin, Lagos, Nigeria. Ed. Ikpe Etokudo. circ. 25,000.

320.531   US   ISSN 0737-3724
HX1
NEW INTERNATIONAL; a magazine of Marxist politics and theory. 1983. irreg. price varies. 408 Printing & Publishing Co., 410 West St., New York, NY 10014. TEL 212-243-6392. Ed.Bd. adv.; bk.rev.; circ. 2,500. (back issues avail.) **Indexed:** Alt.Press Ind.

320.531   IS
NEW INTERNATIONAL REVIEW. (Text in English) 1977. q. $6. P.O. Box 2126, Afula, Israel. Ed. Eric Lee. adv.; bk.rev.; circ. 2,000.

NEW LEFT REVIEW. see *LITERARY AND POLITICAL REVIEWS*

320   US
NEW LIBERTARIAN; the magazine of record of the libertarian movement. 1971. bi-m. $25. New Libertarian Company of Free Traders, 17220 Newhope, Ste. 201, Fountain Valley, CA 92708. FAX 714-979-5739. Ed. Samuel Edward Konkin, III. adv.; bk.rev.; circ. 2,000. (also avail. in microfiche)
    Description: Covers news of the movement and analysis of the world.

NEW OPTIONS; new values, new politics. see *LITERARY AND POLITICAL REVIEWS*

956.94   IS   ISSN 0028-6427
DS41
NEW OUTLOOK; Middle East magazine. (Text in English) 1957. 6/yr. $42 to institutions; students $27. (Israel Peace Research Society) Hashkafah Hadashah, 9 Gordon St., Tel Aviv 63458, Israel. TEL 03-236496. FAX 03-232252. (U.S. subscr. to: Friends of New Outlook, 295 Seventh Ave., New York, NY 10001) Ed. Chaim Shur. adv.; bk.rev.; film rev.; play rev.; charts; illus.; stat.; index; circ. 7,000. (also avail. in microform from MIM,UMI; reprint service avail. from UMI) **Indexed:** Alt.Press Ind., HR Rep., P.A.I.S.
    —BLDSC shelfmark: 6084.850000.

322.4   TZ
NEW OUTLOOK TANZANIA. Variant title: New Outlook. 1976. m. EAs.90($30) P.O. Box 165, Dar es Salaam, Tanzania. Ed. Joe Kamuzora.

321.8   US   ISSN 0893-7850
E839.5
NEW PERSPECTIVES QUARTERLY. Short title: N P Q. 1967. q. $35 (Canada and Mexico $42.50; elsewhere $55). Center for the Study of Democratic Institutions, 10951 W. Pico Blvd., Ste. 202, Los Angeles, CA 90064. TEL 213-474-0011. FAX 213-474-8061. (Subscr. to: Box 319, Mt. Morris, IL 61054) Ed. Nathan Gardels. bk.rev.; illus.; circ. 15,000. (also avail. in microform from UMI; back issues avail., reprint service avail. from UMI) **Indexed:** Acad.Ind., P.A.I.S., PSI, Soc.Sci.Ind.
    —BLDSC shelfmark: 6084.924200.
    Formerly (until 1988): Center for the Study of Democratic Institutions. Center Magazine (ISSN 0008-9125)
    Description: Examines social and political thought on economics, environment, politics, culture, and the critical issues of our common future.

320   US   ISSN 0739-3148
JA1
NEW POLITICAL SCIENCE. 1979. q. $30 to individuals (foreign $35); institutions $60 (foreign $65). Caucus for a New Political Science, c/o John C. Berg, Treas., Dept. of Government, Suffolk University, Boston, MA 02108-2770. Ed.Bd. adv.; bk.rev.; circ. 400. **Indexed:** Alt.Press Ind., Left Ind. (1982-).
    —BLDSC shelfmark: 6085.750000.
    Description: Political science scholarship from a radical perspective.

320   UK   ISSN 0261-6912
HX3
NEW SOCIALIST. 1981. 6/yr. £1.20 per issue. Labour Party, 11 Dartmouth St., London SW1H 9BN, England. TEL 071-976-7129. FAX 071-976-7153. Ed. Gordon Marsden. adv.; bk.rev.; circ. 12,000. **Indexed:** HRIS.
    Description: All aspects of politics and culture from a "left-of-centre" perspective.

320   US
NEW UNIONIST. 1973. m. $3. New Union Party, 621 W. Lake St., Ste. 210, Minneapolis, MN 55408. TEL 612-823-2593. Ed. Jeff Miller. bk.rev.; circ. 9,000.
    Description: Analyzes contemporary political-economic developments from a revolutionary viewpoint; promotes programs for socially-owned, democratic economies and workplace governments.

320   DK   ISSN 0108-1829
NEW UNITED NATIONS PUBLICATIONS. 1982. irreg. (5-6/yr.) free. F N S Informationskontor for de Nordiske Lande - United Nations Information Centre for the Nordic Countries, H.C. Andersens Boulevard 37, 1553 Copenhagen V, Denmark. **Indexed:** Soils & Fert.
    Formerly: United Nations Publications.

320.9   II   ISSN 0047-9969
NEW WAVE; India's national newsweekly. (Text in English) 1971. w. Rs.70($70) New Wave Society, c/o Ganesh Shukla, Ed., 285 Defence Colony Flyover, New Delhi 110024, India. adv.; bk.rev.; illus.; circ. 10,000. (tabloid format; also avail. in microfilm from UMI; reprint service avail. from UMI)

320 330   US   ISSN 0895-8505
NEW WEST NOTES. 1987. m. $150. Box 221364, Sacramento, CA 95822. TEL 916-395-0709. Ed. Bill Bradley.
    Formerly: Larkspur Report.
    Description: Reports on national political and economic issues from a California perspective.

988.1   GY   ISSN 0028-7008
NEW WORLD. 1963. fortn. New World Associates, 215 King St., Georgetown, Guyana. Ed. David De Caires. adv.; bk.rev.; illus.; circ. 800. (processed)

NEW ZEALAND SLAVONIC JOURNAL. see *HUMANITIES: COMPREHENSIVE WORKS*

320.531   NZ
NEW ZEALAND TRIBUNE. 1966. 24/yr. NZ.$21.60 (foreign NZ.$20). (Socialist Unity Party of New Zealand) Socialist Publishing & Distributing Co., P.O. Box 11478, Manners St., Wellington, New Zealand. adv.; illus. (tabloid format)
    Description: Includes discussion on political, economic and social development.

320.9   US   ISSN 0028-8969
HX1
NEWS & LETTERS. 1955. 10/yr. $2.50. News & Letters Committees, 59 E. Van Buren St., Ste. 707, Chicago, IL 60605-1216. TEL 312-663-0839. Eds. Eugene Walker, Felix Martin. bk.rev.; film rev.; illus.; circ. 6,000. (tabloid format; also avail. in microform from UMI; back issues avail.; reprint service avail. from UMI) **Indexed:** Alt.Press Ind.
    Description: Journal of labor, civil rights, women's liberation, and anti-war struggles nationally and internationally with an emphasis on Marxist-Humanist theory.

320.532   US
NEWS BEHIND THE NEWS; an independent research report. 1979. bi-m. $5 contribution. News Behind the News, 5909 E. 26th St., Tulsa, OK 74114. TEL 918-836-4431. Ed. Julian Williams. circ. 150.
    Description: Newsletter concerning communist mind warfare operations against the U.S.

329.6   US
NEWS CUBA. 1983. m. free. Cuba Independiente y Democratica, 10020 S.W. 37th Terr., Miami, FL 33165. TEL 305-551-7357. Ed. Huber Matos, Jr. circ. 15,000. (back issues avail.)
    Description: To inform politicians, academicians, newsmen, and university students about Cuba.

320.9   AT   ISSN 0159-7345
NEWS DIGEST - INTERNATIONAL. 1963. q. Aus.$6($7) International Information Centre, Box 535, Parramatta, N.S.W. 2150, Australia. TEL 02-630-2309. Ed. J.P. Kedys. adv.; bk.rev.; bibl.; charts; illus.; stat.; index; cum.index; circ. 7,000. (back issues avail.)
    Description: Covers international politics, communism, history, defense and economy.

322.4   US
NEWS NOTES (WASHINGTON). 1975. bi-m. $10 (effective Apr. 1991). Maryknoll Fathers and Brothers, Justice and Peace Office, 3700 Oak View Terr., NE, Washington, DC 20017. TEL 202-832-1780. FAX 202-832-5195. adv.; bk.rev.; circ. 1,200. **Indexed:** HR Rep.
    Description: Covers international justice and peace issues.

NEWS OF THE WORLD. see *GENERAL INTEREST PERIODICALS — Great Britain*

NEWSCOPE - ELEMENTARY EDITION; weekly news summary and teaching quiz. see *EDUCATION — Teaching Methods And Curriculum*

NEWSCOPE - HIGH SCHOOL-COLLEGE EDITION; a weekly news summary and teaching quiz. see *EDUCATION — Teaching Methods And Curriculum*

NEWSCOPE - MIDDLE-INTERMEDIATE-JUNIOR HIGH SCHOOL EDITION; a weekly news summary and teaching quiz. see *EDUCATION — Teaching Methods And Curriculum*

NEWSNAMES - CURRENT EVENTS. see *EDUCATION — Teaching Methods And Curriculum*

NEWSPUZZLER: CURRENT EVENTS. see *EDUCATION — Teaching Methods And Curriculum*

NEWSQUESTIONNAIRE: CURRENT EVENTS. see *EDUCATION — Teaching Methods And Curriculum*

POLITICAL SCIENCE

320.531   VN
NGUOI DAI BIEU NHAN DAN/PEOPLE'S DEPUTY. 1988. bi-m. 35 Ngo Quyen, Hanoi, Socialist Republic of Vietnam. TEL 52861. Ed. Nguyen Ngoc Tho.
Description: Disseminates resolutions of the National Assembly and Council of State.

320 972   US
NICARAGUA UPDATE. 1979. q. $15. Nicaragua Interfaith Committee for Action (NICA), 942 Market, No. 706, San Francisco, CA 94102. Ed. Janine Chagoya.
Description: In-depth newsletter with information on Nicaragua and U.S. policy, gathered through research, interviews and media reports in Nicaragua and the U.S.

320   US   ISSN 0885-5706
F1521
NICARAGUAN PERSPECTIVES. 1981. q. $18 to institutions. Nicaragua Information Center, Box 2929, Oakland, CA 94618-0129. adv.; bk.rev.; circ. 3,000. (back issues avail.) **Indexed:** Alt.Press Ind., HR Rep., Left Ind. (1983-).

NIEUW GELUID. see *RELIGIONS AND THEOLOGY — Judaic*

320   NG   ISSN 0545-9532
NIGER: FRATERNITE - TRAVAIL - PROGRES. w. Ministere de l'Information, B.P. 368, Niamey, Niger. Ed. Sahidou Alou. illus.

322.4   US
NO K K K, NO FASCIST U S A!. 1982. q. $6 for 2 yrs. John Brown Anti-Klan Committee, 220 Ninth St., No. 443, San Francisco, CA 94103. TEL 415-330-5363. Ed.Bd. bk.rev.; illus.; circ. 5,000.
Formerly (until winter 1987): Death to the Klan!

320   US   ISSN 0078-0979
NOMOS. 1958. a. price varies. (American Society for Political and Legal Philosophy) New York University Press, 70 Washington Square S., New York, NY 10012. TEL 212-998-2575. FAX 212-995-3833. TELEX 235128 NYU UR. Eds. Alan Wertheimer, John W. Chapman. **Indexed:** A.I.C.P.

322.4   US   ISSN 8755-7428
JX1901
NONVIOLENT ACTIVIST. 1984. 6/yr. $15 to individuals; institutions $25. War Resisters League, 339 Lafayette St., New York, NY 10012. TEL 212-228-0450. FAX 212-228-6193. Ed. Ruth Benn. adv.; bk.rev.; film rev.; illus.; cum.index; circ. 15,000. (back issues avail.) **Indexed:** Alt.Press Ind.
Description: Political analysis from a pacifist perspective.

322.44   US
NONVIOLENT ANARCHIST NEWSLETTER. 1983. a. $3. Slough Press, Box 1385, Austin, TX 78767. Ed. Chuck Taylor. adv.; bk.rev.; circ. 500. (looseleaf format)

NONVIOLENT SANCTIONS; news from the Albert Einstein Institute. see *SOCIOLOGY*

945   IT   ISSN 0029-1188
DG401
NORD E SUD. 1954. q. L.70000 to individuals; institutions L.100000; foreign L.120000(effective 1992). Edizioni Scientifiche Italiane S.p.A., Via Chiatamone 7, 80121 Naples, Italy. TEL 081-7645768. FAX 081-7646477. Ed. Antonio Aurigemma. adv.; bk.rev.; charts; illus.; index; circ. 1,100.

320   NO   ISSN 0801-1745
NORSK STATSVITENSKAPELIG TIDSSKRIFT/NORWEGIAN POLITICAL SCIENCE JOURNAL. 1985. q. $46 to individuals; institutions $58. (Norwegian Association for Political Science) Universitetsforlaget, P.O. Box 2959-Toeyen, N-0608 Oslo 1, Norway. (U.S. addr.: Publications Expediting Inc., 200 Meacham Ave., Elmont, NY 11003) Eds. Oddbjoern Knutsen, Bjoern Erik Rasch. adv.; bk.rev.; index; circ. 600. (back issues avail.)

NORTH AMERICAN FARMER. see *AGRICULTURE*

320   US
NORTH CAROLINA INSIGHT. 1978. q. $36 to individuals; libraries $50. North Carolina Center for Public Policy Research, Inc., Box 430, Raleigh, NC 27602. Ed. Jack Betts. adv.; circ. 2,000.
Description: Covers North Carolina state and local government.

320   KO
NORTH KOREA NEWS. (Text in English) w. Naewoe Press, 42-2 Chuja-dong, P.O. Box 9708, Chung-gu, Seoul 100-240, S. Korea. Ed. One Hoe Kim.

320   GW
NORTH KOREA QUARTERLY. (Text in English) 1974. q. DM.50($20) Institut fuer Asienkunde - Institute of Asian Affairs, Rothenbaumchaussee 32, 2000 Hamburg 13, Germany. TEL 040-443001. FAX 040-4107945. illus.

320 301.2   II   ISSN 0970-7913
NORTH-EAST INDIA COUNCIL FOR SOCIAL SCIENCE RESEARCH. JOURNAL. (Text in English) 1977. s-a. Rs.50($18) (£6). North-East India Council for Social Science Research, B.T. Hostel, Laitumkhrah, Shillong 793 003, Meghalaya, India. Ed.Bd. adv.; bk.rev.; circ. 500.

320   II   ISSN 0301-6404
DS401
NORTH-EASTERN AFFAIRS. (Text in English) 1972. q. Rs.10.($14) c/o S. Sarin, Ed., Jowai Rd., Shillong 3, India. adv.; bk.rev.; charts; illus.

320 341   US   ISSN 1040-8614
NORTHERN IRELAND NEWS SERVICE; NINS NewsBreak. 1985. w. $44. Box 57, Albany, NY 12211-0057. TEL 518-329-3003. Ed. Rev. Francis G. McCloskey. circ. 266. (back issues avail.)
•Also available online. Vendor(s): NewsNet.
Description: Irish republican, nationalist and loyalist news sources and spokespersons, also British and Irish governments' Northern Ireland Office. Covers Anglo-Irish relations, public demonstrations, street and border disputes, business openings and closings, application of MacBride Principles, employment and unemployment, and the churches.

NORTHERN SUN NEWS; alternatives for the North Country in energy and politics. see *ENERGY*

320   US   ISSN 0890-9776
NORTHWESTLETTER. 1981. fortn. $167. East Oregonian Publishing Company, Box 210, Astoria, OR 97103. TEL 503-325-3211. FAX 503-325-6573. Ed. Larry Swisher.
Description: Focuses on politics and issues of Pacific Nothwest--Idaho, Oregon and Washington--in the nation's capitol.

NOTAS. see *BUSINESS AND ECONOMICS*

320.351   NE   ISSN 0298-7902
NOTEBOOKS FOR STUDY AND RESEARCH. French edition: Cahiers d'etude et de Recherche (ISSN 0298-7899) (Text in English) 1986. 4/yr. £10($16) for five nos. International Institute for Research and Education - Institut International de Recherche et de Formation, Postbus 53290, 1007 RG Amsterdam, Netherlands. TEL 020-6717263. FAX 020-6732106. adv.; circ. 1,000.
Description: Educational tool for students, trade unionists and social activities, covering Europe, both east and west, the Americas, Africa and the major issues of socialist theory.

960   SG   ISSN 0029-3954
DT1
NOTES AFRICAINES. 1939. q. 60 F. Institut Fondamental d'Afrique Noire - Cheikh Anta Diop, B.P. 206, Dakar, Senegal. Ed. Abdoulaye Bara Diop. charts; illus.; maps; cum.index: 1939-1948, 1949-1963, 1964-1976; circ. 1,500. (reprint service avail. from SWZ) **Indexed:** A.I.C.P.

329.6   US
NOTI CUBA. (Text in Spanish) 1983. m. free. Cuba Independiente y Democratica, 10020 S.W. 37th Terr., Miami, FL 33165. TEL 305-551-7357. Ed. Huber Matus, Jr. circ. 3,500. (back issues avail.)
Description: To inform politicians, academicians, and newsmen about Cuba in Spanish-language areas.

320 296   FR
NOTRE VOIX.* (Text in Yiddish) vol.37, 1974. bi-m. 50 F. B. Goutmann, Ed. & Pub., 52 rue Rene Boulanger, 75010 Paris, France.

320.532   FR
NOUVEAU CLARTE.* 6/yr. Union des Etudiants Communistes de France, 19 rue Victor Hugo, 93170 Bagnolet, France. adv.; illus.

320   MF
NOUVEAU MILITANT. (Text in French) w. Mouvement Militant Mauricien, 21, rue Poudriere, Port Louis, Mauritius.
Former titles: Peuple; Militant.

322.4   IV
▼**NOUVEL HORIZON.** 1990. Front Populaire Ivoirien, Abidjan, Ivory Coast. circ. 15,000.

320.5   FR   ISSN 0244-7878
LE NOUVEL HUMANISME. 1970. q. 12 F. (foreign 15 F.) Georges Krassovsky, Ed. & Pub., B.P. 164, 75664 Paris Cedex 14, France. illus. (tabloid format)
Formerly (until 1981): Combat pour l'Homme (ISSN 0045-7469)
Description: Dedicated to ecology, disarmament and human rights.

320   UK   ISSN 0143-3563
DB361
NOVA HRVATSKA. (Text in Croatian) 1958. s-m. $85. Nova Hrvatska Ltd., P.O. Box 190, London SW19 8DL, England. FAX 081-947-0498. Ed. J. Kusan. adv.; bk.rev.; circ. 15,000.

320.5315 335.4   CS
NOVA MYSL. 1947. m. $18.50. Rude Pravo, Na Porici 30, 112 86 Prague 1, Czechoslovakia. (Subscr. to: Artia, Ve Smeckach 30, 111 27 Prague 1, Czechoslvakia) bibl.; index. **Indexed:** CERDIC.

320   BL   ISSN 0100-7025
NOVOS ESTUDOS C E B R A P. 1981. 3/yr. $40. (Centro Brasileiro de Analise e Planejamento) Editora Brasileira de Ciencias, Ltda., Rua Morgado de Mateus 615, 04015 Sao Paulo, SP, Brazil. Ed. Francisco de Oliveira. bk.rev.; circ. 3,000. **Indexed:** Curr.Cont., Sociol.Abstr., SSCI.
Supersedes (1971-1980): Estudos C E B R A P (ISSN 0101-3300)

322.4 900   US   ISSN 0883-9875
NUCLEAR RESISTER; a chronicle of hope. 1980. every 6 weeks. $18. National No-Nukes Prison Support Collective, Box 43383, Tucson, AZ 85733. TEL 602-323-8697. Eds. Jack Cohen-Joppa, Felice Cohen-Joppa. stat.; circ. 1,000. (tabloid format; also avail. in microfiche from UMI; back issues avai.)
Formerly (until 1982): National No-Nukes Prison Support Collective. Newsletter.
Description: Dedicated to jailed and imprisoned anti-nuclear activists in the United States and Canada. Provides comprehensive reporting on arrests and jailings of civil disobediences, while encouraging support for those behind bars.

322.4   US   ISSN 0734-5836
JX1974.7
NUCLEAR TIMES; issues & activism for global survival. 1982-1989 (May); resumed 1990-1991 (Aug., vol.10, no.2-3). 4/yr. $18 to individuals; institutions $20. Winston Foundation for World Peace, 401 Commonwealth Ave., Boston, MA 02215. TEL 617-266-1193. FAX 617-266-2364. (Subscr. to: Box 351, Kenmore Sta., Boston, MA 02215) Eds. John Tirman, Sonia Shah. adv.; bk.rev.; film rev.; illus.; stat.; tr.lit.; circ. 30,000. (back issues avail.) **Indexed:** Alt.Press Ind., HR Rep.
Description: Examines the economic, environmental and political impacts of military and foreign policies.

322 614.8 531.64   US   ISSN 0888-5729
NUCLEUS (CAMBRIDGE). 1976. q. donation; libraries $15. Union of Concerned Scientists, 26 Church St., Cambridge, MA 02238. TEL 617-547-5552. FAX 617-864-9405. Ed. Janet S. Wager. bk.rev.; circ. 130,000. (tabloid format; back issues avail.)
Description: Examines energy policy, national security, and nuclear power safety.

POLITICAL SCIENCE

320   AG
NUESTRA PALABRA.* 1973. w. $2 per no. Partido Comunista, Entre Rios 1031, Buenos Aires, Argentina. Ed. Fernando Nadra. bk.rev. (tabloid format)

320   EC
NUEVA. 1974. m. Apdo. 3224, Quito, Ecuador. Dir. Magdalena Jaramillo de Adoum. adv.; illus.

320   VE   ISSN 0251-3552
NUEVA SOCIEDAD; revista Latinoamerica bimestral. 1972. bi-m. $30 in Latin America; elsewhere $50. Editorial Nueva Sociedad Ltda., Apdo. 61712-Chacao, Caracas 1060-A, Venezuela. TEL 31-31-89-329975. FAX 313397. TELEX 25163 ILDIS VC. Ed. Alberto Koschuetzke. adv.; bk.rev.; index; circ. 6,500.
Description: Covers political, economic and cultural reviews of Latin America. Includes topics such as International relations, trade unions and various social movements.

320.1   IT
NUOVI STUDI POLITICI. 1971. q. L.38000. Bulzoni Editore, Via dei Liburni 14, 00185 Rome, Italy. TEL 06-4455207. FAX 06-4450355. Ed. Salvatore Valitutti.

320.9   IT   ISSN 0029-6384
NUOVO OSSERVATORE. 1961. m. (11/yr.). L.50000($12) (foreign L.80000). Nuovo Osservatore S.R.L., Via IV Novembre, 114, 00187 Rome, Italy.

320.531   NO
NY TID; sosialistisk ukeavis. 1975. w. NOK 410. A S Ny Tid, Schweigaardsgt. 34, Oslo 1, Norway. FAX 02-172260. Ed. Bernt Eggen. adv.; bk.rev.; illus.; circ. 10,000. (tabloid format)
Incorporates: Orientering (ISSN 0030-5480)

320   NO   ISSN 0800-336X
JA26
NYTT NORSK TIDSSKRIFT; a Norwegian journal of politics, research and culture. q. $46 to individuals; institutions $77. Universitetsforlaget, P.O. Box 2959-Toeyen, N-0608 Oslo 6, Norway. (U.S. addr.: Publications Expediting Inc., 200 Meacham Ave., Elmont, NY 11003) Ed. Rune Slagstad. adv.; bk.rev.; index; circ. 2,600. **Indexed:** Hist.Abstr. (until 1991).

320   FR
O F C E OBSERVATIONS ET DIAGNOSTICS ECONOMIQUES. LETTRE. 1982. 10/yr. 70 F. to individuals; institutions 140 F. (Observatoire Francais des Conjonctures Economiques) Presses de la Fondation Nationale des Sciences Politiques, 27 rue Saint-Guillaume, 75341 Paris Cedex 07, France. TEL 1-45-49-50-50. FAX 1-45-48-04-41. TELEX 201 002 F. (Subscr. to: OFCE, 69 quai d'Orsay, 75007 Paris, France. TEL 1-45-55-95-12) **Indexed:** P.A.I.S.For.Lang.Ind.
—BLDSC shelfmark: 6200.658000.

O I O C NEWSLETTER. (Oriental and India Office Collections) see *ORIENTAL STUDIES*

323.4   AU   ISSN 0029-7534
OBEROESTERREICHISCHE F P O - NACHRICHTEN FUER FREIHEIT UND RECHT. 1956. m. S.180($10.50) Freiheitliche Partei Oesterreichs, Landesgruppe Oberoesterreich, Bluetenstr. 21-1, Postfach 3, A-4041 Linz, Austria. Ed. Hannes Lackner. adv.; bk.rev.; tr.lit.; index; circ. 15,000.

OBJECTIF. see *BUSINESS AND ECONOMICS — Economic Situation And Conditions*

322.4   US   ISSN 0279-103X
UB343
OBJECTOR; journal of draft and military counseling. 1979. every 6 weeks. $15 to individuals and high school libraries; institutions and foreign $20. Central Committee for Conscientious Objectors, Western Region, Box 42249, San Francisco, CA 94142-2249. FAX 415-474-2311. adv.; bk.rev.; index; circ. 3,000. (back issues avail.)
Description: News articles and information on the military and the draft, focusing on community-organizational, legislative, and legal issues pertaining to conscientious objection, harassment in the military, and the need for combat and other military services counseling.

OBLASTNI MUZEUM JIHOVYCHODNI MORAVY. ACTA MUSEALIA. see *HISTORY — History Of Europe*

320   AU
OBSERVER; Zeitschrift fuer Politik und Wirtschaft. fortn. S.500. H. Schnurr Zeitungen- und Nachrichtengesellschaft mbH, Postfach 39, A-5023 Salzburg, Austria. TEL 066232-4071. FAX 06323-4073. adv.; bk.rev.
Formerly (until 1984): Zyklus.

320.532   RU   ISSN 0202-2036
H8
OBSHCHESTVENNYE NAUKI V S.S.S.R. SERIYA 1: PROBLEMY NAUCHNOGO KOMMUNIZMA. 1973. bi-m. 17.70 Rub. Akademiya Nauk S.S.S.R., Institut Nauchnoi Informatsii po Obshchestvennym Naukam, Ul. Krasikova 28-21, Moscow 117418, Russia. Ed. M.I. Kulichenko.

320.532   RU   ISSN 0202-2125
OBSHCHESTVENNYE NAUKI ZA RUBEZHOM. PROBLEMY NAUCHNOGO KOMMUNIZMA. 1972. bi-m. 17.70 Rub. Akademiya Nauk S.S.S.R., Institut Nauchnoi Informatsii po Obshchestvennym Naukam, Ul. Krasikova 28-21, Moscow 117418, Russia. Ed. V.S. Semenov.

320 301 940   FR
OCCITANIA PASSAT E PRESENT.* (Text in Occitan) 1974. bi-m. 24 F. 11 Av. du Mas Ensoleille, 06600 Antibes, France. Ed. Francoise Bernard. bk.rev.; charts; illus.

320.531   HK
OCTOBER REVIEW/SHIH YUEH P'ING LUN. (Text mainly in Chinese; table of contents and some articles in English) bi-m. HK.$12. G.P.O. Box 10144, Hong Kong. TEL 3-862780. illus.
Description: Covers world news, events, and politics from a socialist perspective.

DIE OEFFENTLICHE VERWALTUNG; Zeitschrift fuer oeffentliches Recht und Verwaltungswissenschaft. see *PUBLIC ADMINISTRATION*

OEKOLOGIEPOLITIK. see *CONSERVATION*

329.9   AU   ISSN 0029-9308
DB99.1
OESTERREICHISCHE MONATSHEFTE; Zeitschrift fuer Politik. 1945. m. S.200. Oesterreichische Volkspartei, Bundesparteileitung, Kaerntnerstr. 51, A-1010 Vienna, Austria. TEL (0222)51521-0. Ed. Alfred Grinschgl. adv.; bk.rev.; charts; illus.; stat.; index; circ. 3,000. **Indexed:** P.A.I.S.For.Lang.Ind.
Description: Publication of the Bundespartei covering Austrian and foreign politics, economics, and ecology. Includes list of events.

943.6   AU   ISSN 0029-9375
DR1
OESTERREICHISCHE OSTHEFTE. (Text in German; occasionally in English) 1959. q. S.660. Oesterreichisches Ost und Suedosteuropa Institut, Josefsplatz 6, A-1010 Vienna, Austria. Ed. Walter Lukan. adv.; bk.rev.; charts; stat.; index; circ. 800. **Indexed:** Hist.Abstr.
—BLDSC shelfmark: 6308.200000.

320   AU
OESTERREICHISCHE ZEITSCHRIFT FUER POLITIKWISSENSCHAFT. 1972. q. S.350. (Oesterreichische Gesellschaft fuer Politikwissenschaft) Verlag fuer Gesellschaftskritik, Kaiserstr. 91, A-1070 Vienna, Austria. (Subscr. to: Institut fuer Staats- und Politikwissenschaft, Hoehenstaufengasse 9, A-1010 Vienna, Austria) Eds. Wolfgang Mueller, Karl Ucakar. adv.; circ. 2,500. **Indexed:** P.A.I.S.For.Lang.Ind.
Description: Studies political science with special emphasis on Austrian politics.

320   AU   ISSN 0170-0847
JN2012.3
OESTERREICHISCHES JAHRBUCH FUER POLITIK. a. price varies. Verlag fuer Geschichte und Politik, Neulinggasse 26, A-1030 Vienna, Austria. Ed.Bd.
Indexed: A.B.C.Pol.Sci.

956.94   IS   ISSN 0017-8926
OFAKIM. (Text in Hebrew) 1970. 8/yr. $90. Am Oved Ltd. Publishers, Box 470, Tel Aviv, Israel. circ. 3,000.

OFARI'S BI-MONTHLY. see *ETHNIC INTERESTS*

335   FR   ISSN 0078-3803
OFFICE UNIVERSITAIRE DE RECHERCHE SOCIALISTE. CAHIERS. 1969. m. 325 F. (foreign 430 F.). Office Universitaire de Recherche Socialiste (OURS), 86 rue de Lille, Paris 7e, France. Ed. Henri Cerclier. adv.; bk.rev.; circ. 1,500.

OGGI E DOMANI. see *PARAPSYCHOLOGY AND OCCULTISM*

320.9   PE   ISSN 0030-1280
AP63
OIGA; semanario de actualidades. castellano. 1962. w. S/2000($47.) Av. Salaverry 674, Lima, Peru. TEL 14-475851. Ed. Francisco Igartua. adv.; illus.; circ. 60,000.

353   US   ISSN 0030-1795
OKLAHOMA OBSERVER. 1969. s-m. $25. Troy Enterprises, Co., 500 N.E., 39 Terrace, Box 53371, Oklahoma City, OK 73152. TEL 405-525-5582. Ed. Frosty Troy. adv.; bk.rev.; film rev.; circ. 8,000. (tabloid format; also avail. in microform from UMI; report service avail. from UMI) **Indexed:** Access (1975-).
Description: Commentary on politics, government, education and social issues.

320 330.9   US
ON PRINICIPLE.* 1982. fortn. $43. Apriori Publishing, 278 Gorwin Dr., Holliston, MA 01746-1533. Ed. Donald A. Feder. bk.rev.; illus.; index; circ. 1,700.
Formerly: First Priniciple.

320.531   UK   ISSN 0308-1230
ON TARGET. 1970. 4/yr. £1.20($3.50) Middle East Research and Action Group, 5 Caledonian Rd., London N.1., England. Eds. Stephen Vines, Edward Rosen. adv.; bk.rev.; illus. (also avail. in microfilm from UMI)
Incorporates: Flashpoint (ISSN 0046-4058)

320.971   CN
ON TARGET. 1967. w. Can.$40. Canadian Intelligence Publications, Box 78, High River, Alta. TOL 1BO, Canada. Ed. Ron Gostick. bk.rev.; circ. 2,000.

329.9   NE
ONS BURGERSCHAP. 1948. m. fl.30. Gereformeerd Politiek Verbond - National Reformed Political Association, P.O. Box 439, 3800 AK Amersfoort, Netherlands. FAX 610132. Ed.Bd. adv.; bk.rev.; index; circ. 13,600.
Formerly: Ons Politeuma (ISSN 0030-2740)

329.3   CN   ISSN 0028-4564
ONTARIO NEW DEMOCRAT. 1961. 8/yr. Can.$5. New Democratic Party of Ontario, 184 Main St., Toronto, Ont. M4E 2W1, Canada. TEL 416-699-6637. Ed. Mike Foster. adv.; bk.rev.; circ. 30,000.

OPEN MAGAZINE PAMPHLET SERIES. see *POLITICAL SCIENCE — International Relations*

322.48   CR
OPINION POPULAR. 1982? m. $5 or exchange basis. Movimiento Nacional Revolucionario de El Salvador, Apdo. 230 (2050), San Pedro de Montes de Oca, Costa Rica. **Indexed:** HR Rep.

322.4　　　　IT
OPINIONE. w. L.50000. Societa Editoriale Attivita Culturali, Via Leccosa 58, 00186 Rome, Italy. TEL 6861172. FAX 6547612. adv.; bk.rev.

320　　　　JA
OPINIONS/SEIRON.* (Text in Japanese) 1973. m. 4800 Yen. Sankei Publishing Ltd., Sankei-Honsha Bldg., 1-7-2 Otemachi, Chiyoda-ku, Tokyo, 100, Japan. Ed. Masashi Onoda.

329　　　　XN
OPSTESTVENO POLITICKITE ORGANIZACII NA SR MAKEDONIJA. BILTEN. 1956. m. 1 din. per no. Opstestveno Politikite Organizacii na SR Makedonija, llinldenska 66, Skopje, Macedonia. Ed. Zoge Grguevski.

059.91　　　　YU　　ISSN 0030-3895
OPSTINA; casopis za teoriju i praksu razvoja opstine. (Text in Serbo-Croatian) 1948. m. 800 din. Zavod za Javnu Upravu, Belgrade, Nemanjina 22, Belgrade, Yugoslavia. Ed. Miodrag Visnjic. adv.; bk.rev.; bibl.; circ. 1,200.

320.532 330　　　　IT
ORIENTAMENTI NUOVI PER LA PICCOLA E MEDIA INDUSTRIA. 1978. m. L.12000. Partito Comunista Italiano, Via delle Botteghe Oscure 4, 00186 Rome, Italy. Ed. Federico Brini. adv.; circ. 10,000.

OSSERVATORE POLITICO LETTERARIO. see LITERARY AND POLITICAL REVIEWS

940 947　　　　GW　　ISSN 0030-6428
DR1
OSTEUROPA; Zeitschrift fuer Gegenwartsfragen des Ostens. 1950. m. DM.114 (students DM.76.80). (Deutsche Gesellschaft fuer Osteuropakunde) Deutsche Verlags-Anstalt GmbH, Neckarstr. 121, Postfach 106012, 7000 Stuttgart 10, Germany. TEL 0711-7200591. FAX 0711-2631-292. Ed. A. Steininger. adv.; bk.rev.; bibl.; charts; index; circ. 2,400. (reprint service avail. from SCH) **Indexed:** A.B.C.Pol.Sci., CERDIC, Geo.Abstr., Hist.Abstr., Key to Econ.sci., Lang.& Lang.Behav.Abstr.., P.A.I.S.For.Lang.Ind., SCIMP (1991-), SSCI.
—BLDSC shelfmark: 6312.190000.

320.53　　　　CS　　ISSN 0030-655X
OTAZKY MIRU A SOCIALISMU; teoreticky a informacni casopis komunistickych a delnickych stran. (Czechoslovak edition of Problems of Peace and Socialism) 1958. m. 36 Kcs.($12.30) Rude Pravo, Na Porici 30, 112 86 Prague 1, Czechoslovakia. (Subscr. to: Artia, Ve Smeckach 30, 111 27 Prague 1, Czechoslovakia) Ed.Bd. bk.rev.; stat.

OTECHESTVO; Izdanie na Natsionalniia Suvet na Otechestveniia. see HISTORY — History Of Europe

320　　　　IS　　ISSN 0792-4615
THE OTHER ISRAEL. (Text in English) 1983. bi-m. $30 to individuals; institutions $50. Israeli Council for Israeli - Palestinian Peace, P.O. Box 956, Tel Aviv 61008, Israel. TEL 03-5565804. (U.S. address: America - Israel Council for Israeli - Palestinian Peace, 4186 Cornell Ave., Downers Grove, IL, 60515) Ed. Adam Keller. circ. 4,000.
Description: Covers the Israeli peace movement; comments on events in Israel and the Middle East.

OUR GENERATION. see SOCIOLOGY

320.532　　　　UK
OUR HISTORY. 1956-19??; resumed 19?? q. £5. Socialist History Society, 6 Cynthia St., London N1 9JF, England. Eds. John Foster, Willie Thompson. bibl.; circ. 1,000.

OVERVIEW. see BUSINESS AND ECONOMICS — Economic Situation And Conditions

320　　　　US
P A CS & LOBBIES. (Political Action Committees) 1980. s-m. $287. Amward Publications, Inc., 2000 National Press Bldg., Washington, DC 20045. TEL 202-488-7227. FAX 301-251-9058. Ed. Edward P. Zuckerman. bk.rev. (looseleaf format; back issues avail.)
●Also available online. Vendor(s): NewsNet (PO02).
Formerly: Political Finance - Lobby Reporter (ISSN 0270-353X)
Description: Covers campaign finance and lobbying developments.

320.9　　　　US
P A R ANALYSIS. 1951. irreg. Public Affairs Research Council of Louisiana, Inc., Box 14776, Baton Rouge, LA 70898-4776. TEL 504-926-8414. FAX 504-926-8417. Ed. Jan Carlock. charts; stat.; circ. 7,000. **Indexed:** ERIC, P.A.I.S.
Formerly: P.A.R. News Analysis (ISSN 0030-7807)

320　　　　GW
P & A. (Preiswert & Attraktiv) 1977. q. DM.5. P & A, Schuelerzeitung am Gymnasium Pegnitz, Wilhelm-von-Humboldt Str. 7, 857 Pegnitz, Germany. circ. 600.

P & M. (Politics & Money) see BUSINESS AND ECONOMICS — Banking And Finance

320.52　　　　CN
P.C. TALK. irreg. (4-5/yr.). membership. Progressive Conservative Association of Alberta, 9919 106th St., Edmonton, Alta. T5K 1E2, Canada. adv.; circ. 80,000.
Former titles: P.C. Action (Year); Progressive Conservative Association of Alberta. Progress Bulletin.

320.531 301 327　　GW　　ISSN 0176-0750
P D S. (Perspektiven des Demokratishen Sozialismus) 1984. q. DM.30 (foreign DM.40). (Hochschulinitiative Demokratischer Sozialismus) Schueren Presseverlag GmbH, Deutschhausstr. 31, 3550 Marburg, Germany. TEL 06421-63084. Ed.Bd. adv.; bk.rev.; circ. 1,200.

320　　　　UK　　ISSN 0955-6281
P S A NEWS. 1975. 3/yr. £28. Political Studies Association of the United Kingdom, Department of Public Administration, University of Ulster, Derry BT48 7JL, N. Ireland. TEL 0504-265261. FAX 0504-267261. Ed. Neil Collins. adv.; bk.rev.; circ. 2,000.
Formerly (until 1988): Political Studies Association of the United Kingdom. Newsletter (ISSN 0144-7440)
Description: Contains articles, news, listings on contemporary political studies.

320 338　　　　UK
P S I: REPORT SERIES. 1933. irreg. £130 (includes Discussion Papers; Studies in European Politics; Policy Studies. Policy Studies Institute, 100 Park Village East, London NW1, England.
Formerly: P E P (ISSN 0030-7947)

320　　　　US　　ISSN 1049-0965
JA28
P S: POLITICAL SCIENCE & POLITICS. 1968. q. membership. American Political Science Association, 1527 New Hampshire Ave., N.W., Washington, DC 20036. TEL 202-483-2512. FAX 202-483-2657. Ed. Robert J.P. Hauck. adv.; circ. 16,000. (also avail. in microform from UMI; reprint service avail. from UMI) **Indexed:** A.B.C.Pol.Sci., Chic.Per.Ind., Curr.Cont., Int.Polit.Sci.Abstr., Pers.Lit., Soc.Sci.Ind.
Incorporates (1974-1990): Political Science Teacher (ISSN 0896-0828)

320　　　　CU
PABLO. 16/yr. Union de Periodistas y Escritores de Cuba, Calle 28, No. 112, entre 1ra y 3ra, Mirimar, Havana, Cuba. TEL 7-22-5892. circ. 53,000.

990　　　　CN　　ISSN 0030-851X
DU1
PACIFIC AFFAIRS; an international review of Asia and the Pacific. 1927. q. Can.$35 to individuals; institutions Can.$50. Pacific Affairs, University of British Columbia, 2029 West Mall, Vancouver, B.C. V6T 1W5, Canada. TEL 604-822-6508. FAX 604-822-5207. TELEX 04-51233. Ed. Ian Slater. adv.; bk.rev.; index; circ. 3,000. (also avail. in microform from UMI; microfiche; back issues avail.; reprint service avail. from UMI) **Indexed:** A.B.C.Pol.Sci., Abstr.Anthropol., Abstr.Mil.Bibl., Acad.Ind., Amer.Bibl.Slavic & E.Eur.Stud., Bk.Rev.Dig., Bk.Rev.Ind. (1965-), Child.Bk.Rev.Ind. (1965-), CMI, Curr.Cont., E.I., Hist.Abstr., Hum.Ind., Int.Lab.Doc., Key to Econ.Sci., Mid.East: Abstr.& Ind., P.A.I.S., Rural Devel.Abstr., Rural Recreat.Tour.Abstr., So.Pac.Per.Ind., Soc.Sci.Ind., SSCI, World Agri.Econ.& Rural Sociol.Abstr.
Description: Scholarly journal dealing with Asia and the Pacific.

PACIFIC ISLANDS MONTHLY. see BUSINESS AND ECONOMICS — Economic Situation And Conditions

POLITICAL SCIENCE   3913

PAKISTAN. NATIONAL ASSEMBLY. DEBATES. OFFICIAL REPORT. see PUBLIC ADMINISTRATION

322.4　　　　SZ
LA PALESTINE. (Text in French) 1988. bi-m. 18 Fr. Association Suisse - Palestine, Section Geneve, Case Postale 247, CH-1211 Geneva 3, Switzerland. Ed.Bd. illus.

PAMIETNIKARSTWO POLSKIE. see HISTORY — History Of Europe

PANSTWO I PRAWO. see LAW

335.83　　　　IT
PANTAGRUEL;* rivista anarchica di analisi sociale, economica, filosofica e metodologica. (Supplement to: Anarchismo) 1981. 3/yr. Edizioni Anarchismo, Casella Postale 61, 95100 Catania, Italy.

PARAMETERS (CARLISLE BARRACKS); United States Army War College. see MILITARY

328　　　　GW　　ISSN 0031-2258
DAS PARLAMENT; die Woche im bundeshaus. (Supplement avail.: Aus Politik und Zeitgeschichte (ISSN: 0479-611X)) 1950. w. DM.52.80. Bundeszentrale fuer Politische Bildung, Berliner Freiheit 7, 5300 Bonn, Germany. TEL 0228-515229. bk.rev.; index; circ. 125,000. (newspaper; also avail. in microform from NRP)

320　　　　GW　　ISSN 0933-6958
PARLAMENTS- UND PARTEISTIFTUNGSARCHIVARE BERICHTEN. 1977. a. Parlaments- und Parteiarchivare im Verein Deutscher Archivare, Konrad-Adenauerstr. 3, 7000 Stuttgart 1, Germany. TEL 0711-2063551. FAX 0711-2063521. Ed. Guenther Bradler.

328　　　　UK　　ISSN 0031-2282
PARLIAMENTARIAN. 1920. q. £23 to non-members. Commonwealth Parliamentary Association, Headquarters, 7 Old Palace Yard, Westminster, London SW1P 3JY, England. TEL 01-799 1460. FAX 01-222-6073. Ed. Andrew Imlach. adv.; bk.rev.; illus.; index, cum.index: 1966-1980, 1981-1985; circ. 9,500. (also avail. in microform from UMI; reprint service avail. from UMI) **Indexed:** A.B.C.Pol.Sci., Br.Hum.Ind., Curr.Cont., Mid.East: Abstr.& Ind., P.A.I.S., So.Pac.Per.Ind., SSCI.
—BLDSC shelfmark: 6406.830000.
Formerly: Journal of the Parliaments of the Commonwealth.

328　　　　UK　　ISSN 0031-2290
JN101
PARLIAMENTARY AFFAIRS; devoted to all aspects of parliamentary democracy. 1947. q. £44($85) (Hansard Society for Parliamentary Government) Oxford University Press, Oxford Journals, Pinkhill House, Southfield Road, Enysham, Oxford Ox8 1JJ, England. TEL 0865-882283. FAX 0865-882890. TELEX 837330-OXPRES-G. Ed. F.F. Ridley. adv.; bk.rev.; charts; illus.; index, cum.index; circ. 1,700. (also avail. in microform from UMI) **Indexed:** A.B.C.Pol.Sci., Br.Hum.Ind., Curr.Cont., Hist.Abstr., Lang.& Lang.Behav.Abstr., Mid.East: Abstr.& Ind., P.A.I.S., Soc.Sci.Ind., SSCI, SSCI.
—BLDSC shelfmark: 6406.840000.
Description: Covers all aspects of government and politics directly or indirectly connected with Parliament and parliamentary systems in Britain and throughout the world.

322　　　　AT
PARLIAMENTARY HANDBOOK OF THE COMMONWEALTH OF AUSTRALIA. 1915. irreg. (approx every 3 yrs.). price varies. Australian Government Publishing Service, G.P.O. Box 84, Canberra, A.C.T. 2601, Australia. illus.; circ. 2,000.
Former titles: Australian Parliamentary Handbook; Parliamentary Handbook of the Commonwealth of Australia.

328　　　　US　　ISSN 0048-2994
JF515
PARLIAMENTARY JOURNAL. 1960. q. $15 (effective Jan.1991). American Institute of Parliamentarians, 203 W. Wayne, Ste. 312, Box 12452, Fort Wayne, IN 46863. TEL 219-422-3680. Ed. Hy Farwell. bk.rev.; circ. 1,500. (also avail. in microform from UMI; reprint service avail. from UMI) **Indexed:** Mid.East: Abstr.& Ind.

POLITICAL SCIENCE

320 NO ISSN 0709-6941
PARTICIPATION. (Text in English and French) 1977. 3/yr. (plus annual supplement). $35 non-members. International Political Science Association, c/o University of Oslo, Institute of Political Science, Box 1097 Blindern, 0317 Oslo 3, Norway. TEL 02-455168. circ. controlled.
—BLDSC shelfmark: 6407.230000.
Formerly: International Political Science Association. Circular (ISSN 0074-7459)

329.9 SP
PARTIDO SOCIALISTA POPULAR. CONGRESO. (ACTAS).* no.3, 1976. irreg. Tucar Ediciones S.A., Eduardo Dato 21, Madrid 10, Spain.

320 PE
PARTIDO SOCIALISTA REVOLUCIONARIO. INFORMES.* 1977. irreg. Partido Socialista Revolucionario, Jiron Azangaro 105, Lima 1, Peru. Ed. Francisco Moncloa.

320.532 RU ISSN 0031-2509
PARTIINAYA ZHIZN'. 1919. 24/yr. 10.20 Rub. (Kommunisticheskaya Partiya Sovetskogo Soyuza, Tsentral'nyi Komitet) Izdatel'stvo Pravda, Ul. Pravdy, 24, Moscow 125047, Russia. Ed. M.I. Chaldeev. bk.rev.; bibl.; circ. 1,142,000. **Indexed:** Curr.Dig.Sov.Press.

329.9 II
PARTY LIFE; journal of the Communist Party of India. (Text in English) 1964. m. Rs.10($3) People's Publishing House Private Ltd., 5E Rani Jhansi Road, New Delhi 110055, India. Ed. M. Farooqi. circ. 2,500.

320 CU
PATRIA. m. Antiguos Alumnos del Seminario Martiano, Fragua Martiana, Principe y Hospital, Havana, Cuba.

320 AG
PATRIA Y PUEBLO. 1986. m. Arg.$20. Juan Bautista Alberdi 1878 Dpto. 2, C.P. 1406, Buenos Aires, Argentina. Ed. Carlos A. D'Aprile.

320.9 SW ISSN 0048-3087
PAX; tidning for fred. 1972. 8/yr. SEK 90. Svenska Freds- och Skiljedomsfoereningen, Brannkyrkagatan 76, 117 23 Stockholm, Sweden. FAX 46-8-668-1870. Ed.Bd. adv.; bk.rev.; bibl.; illus.; circ. 10,000.
Description: Extensive peace magazine.

320 AG
PAZ Y JUSTICIA. 1973. q. $20. Paz y Justicia SRL, Piedras 730, 1070 Buenos Aires, Argentina. bk.rev.; bibl.; circ. 1,500. (tabloid format)

322.4 US
PEACE & JUSTICE NEWS.* 6/yr. Peace & Justice Associates, 1200 S. Shelby St., Louisville, KY 40203-2627. TEL 502-451-5451. Ed. Pat McCollough.

320 US
PEACE CHRONICLE. 1975. bi-m. $45 includes Peace Change. (Consortium on Peace Research, Education and Development) Sage Publications, Inc., 2455 Teller Rd., Newbury Park, CA 91320. TEL 805-499-0721. circ. 1,000.

322.4 US
PEACE CURRENTS. 6/yr. $10. Sacramento Peace Center, 1917A 16th St., Sacramento, CA 95814. TEL 916-446-0787. adv.; illus.; circ. 1,000.

PEACE DEVELOPMENTS. see *HUMANITIES: COMPREHENSIVE WORKS*

322.4 US
PEACE EDUCATION CENTER MONTHLY OF PEACE AND JUSTICE ACTION. 1981. 11/yr. $5. Peace Education Center, 1118 S. Harrison, East Lansing, MI 48823. TEL 517-351-4648. Ed. Mary Catharine Knightwright. bk.rev.; circ. 800.
Formerly: Peace Education Center Newsletter.

322.4 327 374 US
PEACE GAZETTE. 1969. 11/yr. $15. Mount Diablo Peace Center, 65 Eckley Lane, Walnut Creek, CA 94596. Ed. Sasha Futran. bk.rev.; illus.; circ. 2,500 (controlled). (reprint service avail.)
Description: Features articles on current peace and justice issues and highlights urgent political actions and activities.

341.1 UK ISSN 0031-3548
JX1901
PEACE NEWS; for nonviolent revolution. 1936. m. £7.50 (foreign £9). Peace News Ltd., 55 Dawes St., London SE17 1EL, England. TEL 071-703-7189. FAX 071-708-2545. Ed.Bd. adv.; bk.rev.; bibl.rev.; play rev.; illus.; circ. 3,000. (also avail. in microform from UMI,HPL; back issues avail.; reprint service avail. from UMI) **Indexed:** Alt.Press Ind.
●Also available online.
Incorporates: W R I Newsletter (ISSN 0085-7882)

322.4 US ISSN 0735-4134
PEACE NEWSLETTER; central New York's voice for peace and social justice. 1936. m. $12 to individuals; institutions $15. Syracuse Peace Council, 924 Burnet Ave., Syracuse, NY 13203. TEL 315-472-5478. adv.; bk.rev.; circ. 4,500. (also avail. in microform from UMI; back issues avail.)
Indexed: HR Rep.
Description: Provides a forum for articles which discuss issues of concern to the peace movement, and to facilitate community interaction.

320 CN ISSN 0553-4283
JX1901
PEACE RESEARCH REVIEWS. 1967. irreg. (approx. 3/yr.). $48 for 6 nos. Peace Research Institute-Dundas, 25 Dundana Ave., Dundas, Ont. L9H 4E5, Canada. TEL 416-628-2356. Ed. Hanna Newcombe. circ. 400. **Indexed:** A.B.C.Pol.Sci., Abstr.Mil.Bibl., Hist.Abstr., Mid.East.: Abstr.& Ind.
—BLDSC shelfmark: 6413.795000.
Description: Monograph series usually with several hundred references.

320 US ISSN 1040-2659
JX1901 CODEN: PEAREC
PEACE REVIEW; the international quarterly of world peace. 1989. q. $24. Peace Review Publications Inc., 2439 Birch St., Ste. 8, Palo Alto, CA 94306. FAX 415-328-7518. TELEX 1542205417. Ed. John L. Harris. adv.; bk.rev.; circ. 1,000.
Description: Multi-disciplinary study of world peace.

322.4 US
PEACELETTER. 1983. 4/yr. $27 membership. Peace Resource Center of Santa Barbara, 13 W. Figueroa St., Santa Barbara, CA 93101-3103. TEL 805-965-8583. FAX 805-965-6227. adv.; bk.rev.; circ. 3,000.
Description: Covers local and global peace issues, and news of the Center's activities.

322.4 US
PEACELINES. bi-m. $10 to non-members. Women Strike for Peace, 1930 Chestnut St., Ste. 1500, Philadelphia, PA 19103. TEL 215-563-2269. Eds. Libby Frank, Ethel Taylor. adv.; bk.rev.; charts; illus.; stat.; circ. 2,500. (back issues avail.)

341.1 200 NZ
PEACEMAKER. 1936. q. NZ.$5 (foreign NZ$10). New Zealand Christian Pacifist Society, 3 Muir Ave., Christchurch 3, Aotearoa, New Zealand. Ed. Richard Thompson. bk.rev.; circ. 450. (tabloid format)
Indexed: CERDIC.
Former titles: C.P.S. Bulletin; Peace Bulletin; New Zealand Christian Pacifist (ISSN 0028-7997)

320 US ISSN 0748-0725
PEACEWORK; New England peace movement newsletter. 1972. m. $10. American Friends Service Committee, Inc., New England Regional Office, 2161 Massachusetts Ave., Cambridge, MA 02140. TEL 617-661-6130. FAX 617-354-2832. Ed. Pat Farren. bk.rev.; circ. 2,500. (also avail. in microform) **Indexed:** Alt.Press Ind.

320 AG
PENSAMIENTO Y NACION;* revista de doctrina politica y de cultura. 1981. bi-m. Pensamiento y Nacion Editora S.R.L., c/o Leopoldo Frenkel, Ed., Juncal 2101, Buenos Aires, Argentina.

320.531 FR
PENSEE (PARIS). (Text in French; summaries in English) 1939. 6/yr. 400 F. (foreign 700 F.). Institut des Recherches Marxistes, 64 bd. Auguste Blanqui, 75013 Paris, France. Ed. Antoine Casanova. adv.; bk.rev.; cum.index; circ. 5,000. **Indexed:** CERDIC, Hist.Abstr.

320.5 IT ISSN 0031-482X
PENSIERO MAZZINIANO. 1946. m. L.2000($1.60) Associazione Mazziniana Italiana, Via S. Francesco da Paola 10 Bis, 10123 Turin, Italy. Ed. Vittorio Parmentola. bk.rev.; film rev.; play rev.; rec.rev.; illus.; index; circ. 2,600.

320.5 IT ISSN 0031-4846
JA18
PENSIERO POLITICO; rivista di storia delle idee politiche e sociali. 1968. 3/yr. L.68000 (foreign L.85000). Casa Editrice Leo S. Olschki, Casella Postale 66, 50100 Florence, Italy. TEL 055-6530684. FAX 055-6530214. Ed.Bd. adv.; bk.rev.; bibl.; circ. 1,000. **Indexed:** Hist.Abstr., M.L.A.
—BLDSC shelfmark: 6422.640000.

320.5 IT
PENSIERO POLITICO. BIBLIOTECA. 1969. irreg., no.15, 1989. price varies. Casa Editrice Leo S. Olschki, Casella Postale 66, 50100 Florence, Italy. TEL 055-6530684. FAX 055-6530214.

320.531 US ISSN 0199-350X
HX1
PEOPLE (PALO ALTO). 1891. fortn. $4. Socialist Labor Party of America, Box 50218, Palo Alto, CA 94303. TEL 415-494-1532. (Subscr. to: 914 Industrial Ave., Palo Alto, CA 94303) Ed.Bd. bk.rev.; illus.; circ. 9,300. (tabloid format; also avail. in microform from UMI,BHP; microfilm from KTO; reprint service avail. from UMI) **Indexed:** Alt.Press Ind.
Formerly (until 1979): Weekly People (ISSN 0043-1885)

951.9 JA ISSN 0031-5036
Newspaper
PEOPLE'S KOREA. (Text in English, French, Spanish) 1961. w. 12000 Yen($100) Choson Shinbo Co., Inc., 2-4 Tsukudo, Hachiman-cho, Shinjuku-ku, Tokyo, Japan. FAX 03-3268-8583. Ed. Song Jae Ryong. adv.; bk.rev.; illus.; circ. 30,000. (newspaper)

954 II ISSN 0377-2713
HX3
PEOPLE'S POWER. (Text in English) 1972. m. per no. Unity Compound, Juhu, Bombay 54, India. Ed.Bd. bibl.

329.3 BH
PEOPLE'S PULSE. 1988. w. $40 (typically set in Jan.). (United Democratic Party) People's Pulse Ltd., 7 Tanoomah St., Box 1104, Belize City, Belize. TEL 501-2-77035. FAX 501-2-76012. Ed. Floyd Neal. adv.; bk.rev.; circ. 2,000.

PEOPLE'S REPUBLIC OF CHINA YEAR BOOK. see *ENCYCLOPEDIAS AND GENERAL ALMANACS*

320.532 US
PEOPLE'S TRIBUNE. Spanish edition: Tribuno del Pueblo. 1974. fortn. $10 to individuals; institutions $15. Peoples Tribune, Box 3524, Chicago, IL 60654. Ed.Bd. bk.rev.; illus.; circ. 15,000.
Description: Provides communist commentary on the issues of the day.

322.4 SJ
PEOPLE'S VOICE. (Text in English) irreg., vol.2, no.7, 1980. Tigray People's Liberation Front, Foreign Relations Bureau, Box 8177, Khartoum, Sudan.

341.1 UK ISSN 0268-2419
PEP TALK. 1984. 3/yr. £10. Peace Pledge Union, 6 Endsleigh St., London WC1H 0DX, England. TEL 01-387-5501.
Description: Covers peace education, world studies, conflict resolution, curriculum development, teaching methods, co-operative play.

PERIPHERIE; Zeitschrift fuer Politik und Oekonomie in der dritten Welt. see *BUSINESS AND ECONOMICS — International Development And Assistance*

300 FR ISSN 0031-5478
PERMANENCES; organe de formation civique. 1963. 10/yr. 350 F. price varies. (Office International Oeuvres Formation Civique) Montalza, 49 rue des Renaudes, 75017 Paris, France. bk.rev.; circ. 5,000.

320 AG
PERONISTA; para la liberacion nacional. m. Ayolas 2251, 2000 Rosario, Argentina. Dir. Hugo A. Bagli. adv.; bk.rev. (tabloid format)
Formerly: Reflexion.

POLITICAL SCIENCE

320   US   ISSN 0164-3169
AP62
PERSPECTIVA MUNDIAL; una revista socialista destinada a defender los intereses del pueblo trabajador. (Text and summaries in Spanish) 1977. m. (except Aug.). $17. 408 Printing & Publishing Co., 410 West St., New York, NY 10014. TEL 212-929-3486. FAX 212-727-0150. Ed. Luis Madrid. adv.; bk.rev.; charts; illus.; stat.; circ. 3,100. (also avail. in microform from UMI; back issues avail.) **Indexed:** Alt.Press Ind.

320   II
PERSPECTIVE ON CURRENT AFFAIRS. 1976. s-a. Rs.56($20) Natraj Publishers, 17 Rajpur Rd., Dehra Dun, Uttar Pradesh, India. Ed. Sohan Lall. adv.; bk.rev.; circ. 9,000.

028.1   US   ISSN 1045-7097
JA1
PERSPECTIVES ON POLITICAL SCIENCE. 1972. q. $39 to individuals; institutions $78. (Helen Dwight Reid Educational Foundation) Heldref Publications, 1319 Eighteenth St., N.W., Washington, DC 20036-1802. TEL 202-296-6267. FAX 202-296-5149. Ed. Lorraine Brinka. adv.; bk.rev.; circ. 700. (also avail. in microform; reprint service avail.) **Indexed:** A.B.C.Pol.Sci., Bk.Rev.Ind. (1981-), Child.Bk.Rev.Ind. (1981-), Hist.Abstr.
—BLDSC shelfmark: 6428.149950.
    Formerly (until 1990): Perspective (Washington) (ISSN 0048-3494); Incorporates (1973-1990): Teaching Political Science (ISSN 0092-2013)
Refereed Serial

001.45 960   US
PERSPECTIVES ON SOUTHERN AFRICA. irreg., no.42, 1987. price varies. University of California Press, 2120 Berkeley Way, Berkeley, CA 94720. TEL 415-642-4247. FAX 415-643-7127.
Refereed Serial

320.532   RU
PERSPEKTIVY. 1918. m. 12 Rub.($24) (Vsesoyuznyi Leninskii Kommunisticheskii Soyuz Molodezhi, Tsentral'nyi Komitet) Izdatel'stvo Molodaya Gvardiya, Novodmitrovskaya ul. 5A, 125015 Moscow, Russia. TEL 972-0546. FAX 972-0582. TELEX 411261 FAKEL. (Dist. by: Mezhdunarodnaya Kniga, Ul. Dimitrova D.39, 113095 Moscow, Russia) Ed. Z.G. Apresian. adv.; bk.rev.; bibl.; illus.; tr.lit.; index; circ. 125,000. **Indexed:** Curr.Dig.Sov.Press.
    Formerly (until 1991): Molodoi Kommunist (ISSN 0026-9077)

320   PH
PHILIPPINE POLITICAL SCIENCE JOURNAL. 1974. s-a. P.11($6) (Philippine Political Science Association) Philippine Social Science Council, Central Subscription Service, P.O. Box 655, Greenhills, Metro Manila 3113, Philippines. Ed. Loretta Makasiar Sicat. circ. 300. **Indexed:** Ind.Phil.Per.

320   US   ISSN 0048-3915
H1
PHILOSOPHY AND PUBLIC AFFAIRS. 1971. q. $24 to individuals; institutions $40; students $12. Johns Hopkins University Press, Journals Publishing Division, 701 W. 40th St., Ste. 275, Baltimore, MD 21211. TEL 410-516-6980. FAX 410-516-6998. Ed. Marshall Cohen. index; circ. 2,790. (also avail. in microform from UMI; back issues avail.; reprint service avail. from UMI) **Indexed:** A.B.C.Pol.Sci., Arts & Hum.Cit.Ind., Crim.Just.Abstr., Curr.Cont., Fut.Surv., Hum.Ind., Lang.& Lang.Behav.Abstr., Leg.Cont., Mid.East: Abstr.& Ind., Phil.Ind, SSCI.
—BLDSC shelfmark: 6464.650000.

954.9   PK   ISSN 0031-9651
PICTORIAL NEWS REVIEW. (Text in English) 1970. m. Rs.300($30) Pictorial News Review Publications, 1 Victoria Chambers, Hajji Abdullah Haroon Rd., Karachi 74400, Pakistan. TEL 5682694. FAX 21-735276. TELEX 23035 PCOKR PK 284. Ed. Mahmudul Aziz. adv.; bk.rev.; charts; illus.; circ. 5,000. (also avail. in microform)
    Description: Highlights political developments in Pakistan and abroad. Includes activities of the diplomatic and consular corps and features on other countries. For executives, parliamentarians, Pakistanis abroad, and foreigners in Pakistan.

320   US
PITTSBURGH SERIES IN POLICY & INSTITUTIONAL STUDIES. 1983. irreg. price varies. University of Pittsburgh Press, 127 N. Bellefield Ave., Pittsburgh, PA 15260. TEL 412-624-4111. FAX 412-624-7380. Ed. Bert A. Rockman.

329.9   UK   ISSN 0032-1370
JN1129.C8
PLATFORM (MANCHESTER). 1965. bi-m. £6. Co-operative Union Ltd., Holyoake House, Hanover St., Manchester M60 0AS, England. TEL 061-832-4300. FAX 061-831-7684. Ed.Bd. bk.rev.; charts; illus.; stat.; circ. 24,000. (tabloid format)

320   CN   ISSN 0703-1866
PLOUGHSHARES MONITOR. 1977. q. Can.$25($25) (Canadian Council of Churches) Project Ploughshares, Waterloo, Ont. N2L 3G6, Canada. TEL 519-888-6541. FAX 519-885-0014. Ed.Bd. bk.rev.; circ. 9,000. **Indexed:** HR Rep.
    Description: Provides information on disarmament, militarism, global security, Canadian military production and exports, regional conflicts and alternatives to Canadian security policies.

322.4   US
PLOWSHARES NEWS. 1979. 10/yr. donation. Plowshare Peace Center, Box 1623, Roanoke, VA 24008. TEL 703-985-0808. Eds. Polly Branch, Pat Pratali. bk.rev.; illus.; circ. 900.

PLURAL. see *SOCIOLOGY*

PLURAL SOCIETIES. see *SOCIOLOGY*

320   PL
PO PROSTU. 1947-1957; resumed 1990. w. Ul. Krucza 36, 00-921 Warsaw, Poland. TEL 48-22-280281. Ed. Ryszard Turski. circ. 40,000.

329   FR
LE POING ET LA ROSE. 1970. irreg. Parti Socialiste, 10 rue de Solferino, 75333 Paris Cedex 07, France. Ed. Lionel Jospin.
    Formerly: Bulletin Socialiste (ISSN 0068-4155)

320   CR
POLEMICA. 1981. 3/yr. Instituto Centroamericano de Documentacion e Investigaciones Sociales, Paseo de los Estudiantes, Apdo. 1006, San Jose, Costa Rica. TEL 33-3964. Ed. Gabriel Aguilera Peralta. **Indexed:** HR Rep.

320   US   ISSN 0160-2675
H62.5.U5
POLICY GRANTS DIRECTORY. 1977. irreg. $4 to individuals; institutions $8. Policy Studies Organization, University of Illinois, 361 Lincoln Hall, Urbana, IL 61801. TEL 217-359-8541. Eds. Stuart Nagel, Marian Neef. bibl.; charts; stat.; index; circ. 2,400. (reprint service avail. from UMI)
    Description: Covers governmental and private funding sources for policy studies research. Also contains suggestions for applicants and for funding sources.

POLICY OPTIONS/OPTIONS POLITIQUES. see *PUBLIC ADMINISTRATION*

320 070.5   US   ISSN 0272-0671
H61
POLICY PUBLISHERS AND ASSOCIATIONS DIRECTORY. 1980. irreg. $4 to individuals; institutions $8. Policy Studies Organization, University of Illinois at Urbana-Champaign, 361 Lincoln Hall, Urbana, IL 61801. TEL 217-359-8541. Eds. Stuart Nagel, Kathleen Burkholder. (reprint service avail. from UMI)
    Description: Covers activities, procedures, and other information for policy-relevant journals, book publishers, scholarly associations, and interest groups.

320   US   ISSN 0270-1200
H62.5.U5
POLICY RESEARCH CENTERS DIRECTORY. 1978. irreg. $4 to individuals; institutions $8. Policy Studies Organization, University of Illinois, 361 Lincoln Hall, Urbana, IL 61801. TEL 217-359-8541. Eds. Stuart Nagel, Marian Neef. bibl.; charts; stat.; index; circ. 2,400. (reprint service avail. from UMI)
    Description: Covers university and non-university centers, institutes, and organizations that conduct policy studies research. Also contains generalizations for understanding and improving such centers.

320   US   ISSN 0146-5945
H1
POLICY REVIEW. 1977. q. $18. Heritage Foundation, 214 Massachusetts Ave., N.E., Washington, DC 20002. TEL 202-546-4400. FAX 202-546-8328. Ed. Adam Meyerson. adv.; bk.rev.; bibl.; charts; index; circ. 13,500. (back issues avail.) **Indexed:** A.B.C.Pol.Sci., Bk.Rev.Ind. (1980-), Child.Bk.Rev.Ind. (1980-), Curr.Cont., Environ.Abstr., Fut.Surv., HR Rep., Human Resour.Abstr., Int.Polit.Sci.Abstr., Key to Econ.Sci., Mag.Ind., Mid.East: Abstr.& Ind., P.A.I.S., PROMT, Sage Pub.Admin.Abstr., Sage Urb.Stud.Abstr., Soc.Sci.Ind., Sociol.Abstr., SSCI, Urb.Aff.Abstr.
●Also available online. Vendor(s): Mead Data Central.
—BLDSC shelfmark: 6543.327850.

320 330 301   NE   ISSN 0032-2687
H1
POLICY SCIENCES; an international journal devoted to the improvement of policy making. 1970. q. $148. Kluwer Academic Publishers, Postbus 17, 3300 AA Dordrecht, Netherlands. TEL 078-334911. FAX 078-334254. TELEX 29245. (Dist. by: Kluwer Academic Publishing Group, P.O. Box 322, 3300 AH Dordrecht, Netherlands; N. America dist. addr.: Box 358, Accord Sta., Hingham, MA 02018-0358. TEL 617-871-6600) Ed. Peter de Leon. adv.; bk.rev.; illus. (reprint service avail. from SWZ) **Indexed:** A.B.C.Pol.Sci., ASSIA, Commun.Abstr., Cont.Pg.Manage., Curr.Cont., E.I., Educ.Admin.Abstr., Energy Ind., Energy Info.Abstr., Fut.Surv., Human Resour.Abstr., Inform.Sci.Abstr., Int.Abstr.Oper.Res., Int.Polit.Sci.Abstr., J.of Econ.Lit., Lang.& Lang.Behav.Abstr., Med.Care Rev., Mid.East: Abstr.& Ind., P.A.I.S., Risk Abstr., Sage Pub.Admin.Abstr., Sage Urb.Stud.Abstr., SCIMP, Sociol.Abstr., SSCI, Urb.Aff.Abstr.
—BLDSC shelfmark: 6543.328000.

320 338   UK   ISSN 0144-2872
POLICY STUDIES. 1976. q. $72. (Policy Studies Institute) Carfax Publishing Ltd., P.O. Box 25, Abingdon, Oxfordshire OX14 3UE, England. TEL 0235-555335. FAX 0235-553559. (U.S. distr. addr.: 85 Ash St., Hopkinton, MA 01748) **Indexed:** Cont.Pg.Manage., Int.Lab.Doc., Key to Econ.Sci., Mid.East: Abstr.& Ind., P.A.I.S.
—BLDSC shelfmark: 6543.328900.

309.2   US   ISSN 0362-6016
H62.5.U5
POLICY STUDIES DIRECTORY. 1972. irreg. $4 to individuals; institutions $8. Policy Studies Organization, University of Illinois at Urbana-Champaign, 361 Lincoln Hall, Urbana, IL 61801. TEL 217-359-8541. Eds. Stuart Nagel, Marian Neef. bibl.; charts; stat.; index; circ. 2,400. (reprint service avail. from UMI)
    Description: Covers policy studies activities in American political science departments and interdisciplinary policy studies programs at the Ph.D., M.A., and B.A. levels.

POLITICAL SCIENCE

320   US   ISSN 0190-292X
H1
POLICY STUDIES JOURNAL. 1972. q. (and special issues). $18 to individuals; institutions $68. Policy Studies Organization, University of Illinois, 361 Lincoln Hall, Urbana, IL 61801. TEL 217-359-8541. Ed. Stuart S. Nagel. adv.; bk.rev.; circ. 2,400. (also avail. in microform from MIM; reprint service avail. from UMI) **Indexed:** A.B.C.Pol.Sci., Amer.Bibl.Slavic & E.Eur.Stud., Amer.Hist.& Life, ASSIA, Curr.Cont., E.I., Educ.Admin.Abstr., Environ.Abstr., Fut.Surv., Hist.Abstr., Human Resour.Abstr., Inform.Sci.Abstr., Int.Polit.Sci.Abstr., Lang.& Lang.Behav.Abstr., Mid.East: Abstr.& Ind., P.A.I.S., Pers.Lit., Risk Abstr., Sage Pub.Admin.Abstr., Sage Urb.Stud.Abstr., Sociol.Abstr., SSCI, Tel.Abstr.
—BLDSC shelfmark: 6543.329100.
Description: Covers the application of political science and social science to important public policy problems.

309.2   US   ISSN 0275-4002
H62.5.U5
POLICY STUDIES PERSONNEL DIRECTORY. 1979. irreg. $4 to individuals; institutions $8. Policy Studies Organization, 361 Lincoln Hall, University of Illinois, Urbana, IL 61801. TEL 217-359-8541. Eds. Stuart Nagel, Nancy Munshaw. bibl.; charts; stat.; index; circ. 2,400. (reprint service avail. from UMI)
Description: Contains descriptions of individuals interested in policy studies with regard to their interests, affiliations, backgrounds, publications, and research activities.

320   US   ISSN 0278-4416
H97
POLICY STUDIES REVIEW. 1981. q. $18 to individuals; students $12; institutions $68. Policy Studies Organization, University of Illinois, 361 Lincoln Hall, 702 S. Wright, Urbana, IL 61801. TEL 217-359-8541. Ed.Bd. (also avail. in microform from UMI; microfiche from UMI,KTO; reprint service avail. from UMI) Indexed: A.B.C.Pol.Sci., Amer.Hist.& Life, ASSIA, Curr.Cont., E.I., Educ.Admin.Abstr., Energy Info.Abstr., Environ.Abstr., Fut.Surv., Hist.Abstr., Human Resour.Abstr., I D A, Inform.Sci.Abstr., Int.Polit.Sci.Abstr., Lang.& Lang.Behav.Abstr., P.A.I.S., Pers.Lit., Sage Pub.Admin.Abstr., Sage Urb.Stud.Abstr., Sociol.Abstr., SSCI.
Description: Covers the application of political and social science to important public policy problems.

320 301   IT   ISSN 1120-9488
POLIS; ricerche e studi su societa e politica in italia. 1987. 3/yr. L.90000. Societa Editrice Il Mulino, Strada Maggiore, 37, 40125 Bologna, Italy. TEL 051-256011. FAX 051-256034. Eds. Marzio Barbagli, Arturo Parisi, Gianfranco Pasquino. adv.; circ. 1,300. (back issues avail.)

943.8   UK   ISSN 0032-2784
POLISH AFFAIRS. 1952. q. £4($12.50) Polish Government in Exile, London, Editorial Committee, 43 Eaton Place, London SW1X 8BX, England. adv.; bk.rev.; circ. 2,300.

POLISH PERSPECTIVES. see *LITERARY AND POLITICAL REVIEWS*

320   PL   ISSN 0208-7375
HM7
POLISH POLITICAL SCIENCE. (Text in English) 1967. a. price varies. (Polskie Towarzystwo Nauk Politycznych) Ossolineum, Publishing House of the Polish Academy of Sciences, Rynek 9, Wroclaw, Poland. TELEX 0712771 OSS PL. (Dist. by: Ars Polona-Ruch, Krakowskie Przedmiescie 7, Warsaw, Poland) Ed. Longin Pastusiak. circ. 700.
—BLDSC shelfmark: 6543.722000.
Formerly (until 1981): Polish Round Table (ISSN 0079-3000)
Description: Basic problems of political theory, political organization and functioning of society.

943.8 327   US   ISSN 0032-3047
POLISH WESTERN ASSOCIATION OF AMERICA. QUARTERLY.* 1960. q. free. Polish Western Association of America, 2952 N. Milwaukee Ave., Rm. 210, Chicago, IL 60618. Ed. Stefan Marcinkowski. bk.rev.; stat.; index, cum.index; circ. 800. **Indexed:** Amer.Bibl.Slavic & E.Eur.Stud.

POLIT; a journal of literature and politics. see *LITERATURE*

POLITECHNIKA CZESTOCHOWSKA. ZESZYTY NAUKOWE. NAUKI SPOLECZNO-EKONOMICZNE. see *SOCIAL SCIENCES: COMPREHENSIVE WORKS*

320   VE
POLITEIA. 1972. irreg., no.13, 1990. price varies. Universidad Central de Venezuela, Instituto de Estudios Politicos, Facultad de Ciencias Juridicas y Politicas, Caracas, Venezuela. FAX 6621913. (Subscr. to: Servicio de Distribucion y Venta, Biblioteca Central, Universidad Central, Caracas, Venezuela) bk.rev.; circ. 2,000.

320   SI   ISSN 0217-7587
POLITEIA. (Text in English) 1971. a. S.$2.50. National University of Singapore, Political Science Society, c/o Department of Political Science, Kent Ridge, Singapore 0511, Singapore. Ed. Leong Sook Mei. adv.; bk.rev.; circ. 2,000.
Formerly: University of Singapore Political Science Society. Journal.

320   SA
POLITEIA. s-a. R.8.80($7) University of South Africa, P.O. Box 392, Pretoria 0001, South Africa. FAX 012-429-3221. TELEX 350068. (reprint service avail. from UMI)
Description: Articles on political science, public administration, municipal government and administration, international politics and strategic studies.

320   BE
POLITICA; sociale wetenschappen en beleid. 1950. q. 400 Fr. Katholieke Universiteit te Leuven, Faculty of Social Science, Van Evenstraat 2 B, B-3000 Louvain, Belgium. Ed.Bd. adv.; bk.rev.; bibl.; circ. 1,000.
Formerly: Politika Berichten.

320   BL
POLITICA. 1976. q. Cr.$50. Fundacao Milton Campos para Pesquisas e Estudos Politicos, Camara dos Deputados, Edificio do Congresso Nacional, 70160 Brasilia, D.F., Brazil. Dir. Walter Costa Porto. bk.rev.; circ. 5,000.

320   UY   ISSN 0079-3027
POLITICA.* irreg. Editorial Arca, Colonia 1263, Montevideo, Uruguay.

320   CL
POLITICA. 1982. s-a. Esc.300($11) Universidad de Chile, Instituto de Ciencia Politica, Calle Belgrado No. 10, Santiago, Chile. Ed. Bernardino Bravo Lira. bk.rev.; circ. 500. **Indexed:** P.A.I.S.For.Lang.Ind.

320   IT
POLITICA E SOCIETA. 1976. m. L.10000. Partito Comunista Italiano, Comitato Regionale Toscano, Via Alamanni 41, 50123 Florence, Italy. Dir. Renzo Cassigoli.

320 330   IT   ISSN 1120-9496
POLITICA ECONOMICA. 1985. 3/yr. L.100000. Societa Editrice Il Mulino, Strada Maggiore, 37, 40125 Bologna, Italy. TEL 051-256011. FAX 051-256034. Ed. Paolo Bosi. adv.; index; circ. 1,000. (back issues avail.) **Indexed:** J.of Econ.Lit.

320 330   IT
POLITICA ED ECONOMIA/POLITICS AND ECONOMICS. 1970. m. L.60000 (foreign L.89000). Editori Riuniti, Via Serchio 9-11, 00198 Rome, Italy. TEL 06-866383. FAX 06-8416096. TELEX EDIRIU I 625292. Ed. Eugenio Peggio. circ. 15,000. **Indexed:** Rural Recreat.Tour.Abstr., World Agri.Econ.& Rural Sociol.Abstr.

320   SP   ISSN 0213-6856
DP85.8
POLITICA EXTERIOR. 1987. q. (plus suppl.). 5000 ptas. (foreign 10000 ptas.). Estudios de Politica Exterior, S.A., Padilla, 28006 Madrid, Spain. TEL 5777251. FAX 5777252. TELEX 22555. Ed. Dario Valcarcel. adv.; bk.rev.; charts; illus.; circ. 10,000.
Description: Covers international political affairs.

320   FR
POLITICA HERMETICA. 1987. a. 100 F. L'Age d'Homme S.a.r.l., 5, rue Ferou, 75006 Paris, France. TEL 46-34-18-51. FAX 40-51-71-02. bk.rev.

320   IT   ISSN 1120-950X
POLITICA IN ITALIA; i fatti dell'anno e le interpretazioni. 1986. a. (Istituto Carlo Cattaneo) Societa Editrice Il Mulino, Strada Maggiore 37, 40125 Bologna, Italy. TEL 051-256011. FAX 051-256034. circ. 1,500. (back issues avail.)

322.4   VE
POLITICA INTERNACIONAL; revista Venezolana de asuntos mundiales y politica exterior. q. Bs.160($25) Politica Internacional, Apdo. 6475, Caracas 1010, Venezuela. bk.rev.

POLITICA INTERNAZIONALE (FLORENCE). see *POLITICAL SCIENCE — International Relations*

320   AG
POLITICA OBRERA. bi-m. $4. Partido Obrero, Avda. Belgrano 2608, Buenos Aires, Argentina. TEL 953-3824. FAX 953-8433. bk.rev.; circ. 5,000.

320   SP
POLITICA SOCIAL. q. 2200 ptas.($24) Centro de Estudios Constitucionales, Plaza de la Marina Espanola, 9, Apdo. 50.877, Madrid 13, Spain.

330 320   AG
POLITICA Y ECONOMIA.* m. Arg.$120. 25 de Mayo 486, Buenos Aires, Argentina. illus.; stat.

320.532   US   ISSN 0032-3128
HX1
POLITICAL AFFAIRS; journal of Marxist thought. 1922. m. $18 to individuals; institutions $27. (Communist Party, U.S.A.) Political Affairs Publishers, Inc., 235 W. 23rd St., New York, NY 10011. TEL 212-989-4994. Ed. Leonard Levenson. adv.; bk.rev.; index; circ. 5,000. (also avail. in microfilm from UMI; reprint service avail. from KTO,UMI) **Indexed:** Alt.Press Ind., Amer.Bibl.Slavic & E.Eur.Stud., Chic.Per.Ind., Mid.East: Abstr.& Ind., P.A.I.S.
Supersedes (1928-1944): Communist.

320 330.9   US   ISSN 1057-2295
DK285
▼**POLITICAL AND ECONOMIC SPECTRUM OF RUSSIA.** 1991. q. $95. Nova Science Publishers, Inc., 238 Commack Rd., Ste. 300, Commack, NY 11725-3401. TEL 615-499-3103.
Formerly: Political and Economic Spectrum of the Soviet Union.

POLITICAL AND LEGAL ANTHROPOLOGY. see *SOCIOLOGY*

320   US   ISSN 0190-9320
JA74.5
POLITICAL BEHAVIOR. 1979. 4/yr. $105 (foreign $125)(effective 1992). Plenum Publishing Corp., 233 Spring St., New York, NY 10013-1578. TEL 212-620-8000. FAX 212-463-0742. TELEX 23-421139. Eds. R.A.Brody, P.M. Sniderman. adv.; index. (also avail. in microform from UMI; microfilm from JSC; back issues avail; reprint service avail. from UMI) **Indexed:** A.B.C.Pol.Sci., Int.Polit.Sci.Abstr., Mid.East: Abstr.& Ind., Polit.Sci.Abstr., Psychol.Abstr., Sociol.Abstr.
—BLDSC shelfmark: 6543.873000.
Description: Interdisciplinary studies, both theoretical and empirical, of groups and individuals as they interact with the political process.
Refereed Serial

320   US   ISSN 0195-7473
JF1525.P8   CODEN: PCPEDX
POLITICAL COMMUNICATION AND PERSUASION; an international journal. 1980. q. $100. Taylor & Francis, 1900 Frost Rd., Ste. 101, Bristol, PA 19007. TEL 215-785-5800. FAX 215-785-5515. Ed. Yonah Alexander. adv.; bk.rev.; abstr. **Indexed:** A.B.C.Pol.Sci., Commun.Abstr., Int.Polit.Sci.Abstr., Lang.& Lang.Behav.Abstr., P.A.I.S., Sociol. Abstr.
Description: Examines the roles of governmental, intergovernmental and nongovernmental organizations as political communicators.
Refereed Serial

POLITICAL SCIENCE

320 309 US ISSN 0193-175X
JF37
POLITICAL HANDBOOK OF THE WORLD. 1928. a. $49.95. (State University of New York at Binghamton, Center for Social Analysis) McGraw-Hill, Inc., 1221 Ave. of the Americas, New York, NY 10020. TEL 212-512-2000. Ed. Arthur S. Banks. circ. 7,000. (reprint service avail. from KTO)
—BLDSC shelfmark: 6543.886000.
Formerly: Political Handbook and Atlas of the World (ISSN 0079-3035)

320 UK
POLITICAL PARTIES OF THE WORLD. 1980. triennial. £85. Longman Group UK Ltd., Westgate House, The Highl, Harlow, Essex CM20 1YR, England. TEL 0279-442601. Ed. Alan J. Day.

320 301 US ISSN 0198-8719
JA1
POLITICAL POWER AND SOCIAL THEORY; a research annual. 1980. a. $63.50 to institutions. J A I Press Inc., 55 Old Post Rd., No. 2, Box 1678, Greenwich, CT 06836-1678. TEL 203-661-7602. Ed. Maurice Zeitlin. **Indexed:** Amer.Bibl.Slavic & E.Eur.Stud, Lang.& Lang.Behav.Abstr., Sociol.Abstr. (1980-).
—BLDSC shelfmark: 6543.888000.

320 US ISSN 0162-895X
JA74.5 CODEN: POPSEO
POLITICAL PSYCHOLOGY. 1979. q. $235 (foreign $275)(effective 1992). (International Society of Political Psychology) Plenum Publishing Corp., 233 Spring St., New York, NY 10013-1578. TEL 212-620-8000. FAX 212-463-0742. TELEX 23-421139. Eds. Stanley A. Renshon, Alfred M. Freedman. adv.; bk.rev. (also avail. in microfilm from JSC; back issues avail.; reprint service avail. from UMI) **Indexed:** Curr.Cont., Psychol.Abstr., Risk Abstr.
—BLDSC shelfmark: 6543.888500.
Refereed Serial

320 UK ISSN 0032-3179
JA8
POLITICAL QUARTERLY. 1930. q. £50($95.50) Basil Blackwell Ltd., 108 Cowley Rd., Oxford OX4 1JF, England. TEL 0865 791100. FAX 0865 791347. TELEX 937022-OXBOOK-G. Eds. Colin Cranch, David Marquand. adv.; bk.rev.; index. (also avail. in microfilm from RPI) **Indexed:** A.B.C.Pol.Sci., ASSIA, Br.Hum.Ind., Commun.Abstr., Curr.Cont., Hum.Ind., Mid.East: Abstr.& Ind., P.A.I.S., Soc.Sci.Ind., SSCI, World Agri.Econ.& Rural Sociol.Abstr.
—BLDSC shelfmark: 6543.890000.

320 US ISSN 1051-4287
POLITICAL REPORT. 1978. fortn. $197. 717 Second St., N.E., Washington, DC 20002. Ed. Stuart Rothenberg.
Description: Reports on congressional campaigns and elections and provides analysis on national political trends and developments.

320 US ISSN 0898-4271
JK2283
POLITICAL RESOURCE DIRECTOR. 1987. a. $95. Political Resources, Inc., Box 363, Rye, NY 10580. Ed. Carol Hess. adv.

POLITICAL RISK LETTER. see *BUSINESS AND ECONOMICS — International Commerce*

320 NZ ISSN 0032-3187
JA1
POLITICAL SCIENCE. 1948. s-a. $36 to individuals; institutions $40. (Victoria University of Wellington, School of Political Science & Public Administration) Victoria University Press, P.O. Box 600, Wellington, New Zealand. Eds. G. Debnan, R. Vasil. adv.; bk.rev.; bibl, charts, illus.; cum.index every 2 yrs.; circ. 600. (back issues avail.; reprint service avail. from KTO) **Indexed:** A.B.C.Pol.Sci., Br.Hum.Ind, Curr.Cont., E.I., Hist.Abstr., Int.Polit.Sci.Abstr., Mid.East: Abstr.& Ind., SSCI.
—BLDSC shelfmark: 6543.908000.

320 US ISSN 0032-3195
H1
POLITICAL SCIENCE QUARTERLY. 1886. q. membership. Academy of Political Science, 475 Riverside Dr., Ste. 1274, New York, NY 10115-0012. TEL 212-870-2500. Ed. Demetrios Caraley. adv.; bk.rev.; circ. 9,000. (also avail. in microfilm from UMI; reprint service avail. from KTO,UMI) **Indexed:** A.B.C.Pol.Sci., Abstr.Bk.Rev.Curr.Leg.Per., Acad.Ind., Amer.Bibl.Slavic & E.Eur.Stud., Amer.Hist.& Life, Bk.Rev.Dig., Bk.Rev.Ind. (1965-), CERDIC, Chic.Per.Ind., Child.Bk.Rev.Ind. (1965-), Curr.Cont., Curr.Cont.M.E., E.I., Fut.Surv., Hist.Abstr., Int.Polit.Sci.Abstr., Mid.East: Abstr.& Ind., P.A.I.S., Refug.Abstr., Rural Recreat.Tour.Abstr., Sage Urb.Stud.Abstr., Soc.Sci.Ind., Soc.Work Res.& Abstr., SSCI, World Agri.Econ. & Rural Sociol.Abstr.

320 II ISSN 0554-5196
JA26
POLITICAL SCIENCE REVIEW. 1961. q. Rs.70($50) (typically set in Dec.). University of Rajasthan, Department of Political Science, Bapunagar, Jaipur 302 004, India. TEL 60271-267. Ed. Dr. S.L. Verma. adv.; bk.rev.; bibl.; index; circ. 500. (also avail. in microfilm from UMI; back issues avail; reprint service avail. from UMI) **Indexed:** A.B.C.Pol.Sci., Hist.Abstr., Int.Polit.Sci.Abstr.

320 US ISSN 0091-3715
JA1
POLITICAL SCIENCE REVIEWER;* an annual review of books. 1971. a. $10. Young America's Foundation, 110 Elden St., Herndon, VA 22070. TEL 703-318-9608. Ed. George W. Carey. adv.; bk.rev.; circ. 2,000. (also avail. in microfilm from UMI; back issues avail.) **Indexed:** Bk.Rev.Ind. (1980-), Child.Bk.Rev.Ind. (1980-).
—BLDSC shelfmark: 6543.918000.
Description: Features articles on classic and contemporary studies in law and politics.

320 II ISSN 0032-3209
POLITICAL SCIENTIST. (Text in English) 1964. s-a. Rs.10.($3.) Ranchi University, Department of Political Science, Ranchi 834008, Bihar, India. Ed. Ram Naresh Trivedi. adv.; bk.rev.; charts; circ. 500. **Indexed:** Int.Polit.Sci.Abstr.

320 UK ISSN 0306-6061
POLITICAL SOCIAL ECONOMIC REVIEW. no.5, 1976. bi-m. £50 (foreign £60). N O P Market Research Ltd., Tower House, Southampton St., London WC2E 7HN, England. TEL 01-836-1511. FAX 01-836-2052. Ed. D. Marshall. charts; illus.; stat.; circ. 175.
—BLDSC shelfmark: 6543.921000.
Supersedes: N O P Political Bulletin.
Description: Studies by NOP Market Research on political, social and economic topics.

320 UK ISSN 0032-3217
JA1
POLITICAL STUDIES. 1953. 5/yr. £63.50($123.50) (Political Studies Association of the United Kingdom) Basil Blackwell Ltd., 108 Cowley Road, Oxford OX4 1JF, England. TEL 0865-791100. FAX 0865-791347. TELEX 837022-OXBOOK-G. Ed. Jack Hayward. adv.; bk.rev.; index, cum.index every 10 yrs. (also avail. in microfilm from UMI; back issues avail.) **Indexed:** A.B.C.Pol.Sci., ASSIA, Br.Hum.Ind., Curr.Cont., Hist.Abstr., Lang.& Lang.Behav.Abstr., Mid.East: Abstr.& Ind., P.A.I.S., Soc.Sci.Ind., Sociol.Abstr., SSCI.
—BLDSC shelfmark: 6543.924000.

320 US ISSN 0090-5917
JA1.A1
POLITICAL THEORY; an international journal of political philosophy. 1973. q. $42 to individuals; institutions $122. Sage Publications, Inc., 2455 Teller Rd., Newbury Park, CA 91320. TEL 805-499-0721. FAX 805-499-0871. (And: Sage Publications, Ltd., 6 Bonhill Rd., London EC2A 4PU, England) Ed. Tracy B. Strong. adv.; bk.rev.; bibl.; index; circ. 2,000. (also avail. in microfilm from UMI; back issues avail.; reprint service avail. from UMI) **Indexed:** A.B.C.Pol.Sci., Amer.Bibl.Slavic & E.Eur.Stud., ASSIA, CERDIC, Curr.Cont., Hist.Abstr., Int.Polit.Sci.Abstr., Mid.East: Abstr.& Ind., P.A.I.S., Phil.Ind., Sage Urb.Stud.Abstr., SSCI.
—BLDSC shelfmark: 6543.926000.

POLITICHE DEL LAVORO. see *BUSINESS AND ECONOMICS — Labor And Industrial Relations*

320 IT
POLITICHE DEL TERRITORIO. 1981. bi-m. Editrice Sindacale Italiana s.r.l., Corso d'Italia 25, 00198 Rome, Italy. Ed. Lionello Bignami.

329.9 RU ISSN 0032-3225
POLITICHESKOE SAMOOBRAZOVANIE. 1957. m. 9 Rub. (Kommunisticheskaya Partiya Sovetskogo Soyuza, Tsentral'nyi Komitet) Izdatel'stvo Pravda, Ul. Pravdy, 24, Moscow 125047, Russia. Ed. A.S. Vishnyakov. (also avail. in microform from MIM) **Indexed:** Curr.Dig.Sov.Press.

320 CI ISSN 0032-3241
POLITICKA MISAO/POLITICAL THOUGHT; casopis za politicke nauke. (Text in Croatian; summaries in English) 1964. q. $15. Sveuciliste u Zagrebu, Fakultet Politickih Nauka, Lepusiceva 6, 41000 Zagreb, Croatia. FAX 412-283. Ed. Davor Rodin. bk.rev.; abstr.; bibl.; circ. 1,200. (tabloid format) **Indexed:** Hist.Abstr.
—BLDSC shelfmark: 6543.934000.

320 IT ISSN 0032-325X
POLITICO; rivista italiana di scienze politiche. (Text and summaries in English, French, and Italian) 1950. q. L.70000 (foreign L.105000). (Universita degli Studi di Pavia, Istituto di Scienze Politiche) Casa Editrice Dott. A. Giuffre, Via Busto Arsizio 40, 20151 Milan, Italy. TEL 02-38000905. FAX 02-3809582. Ed. Pasquale Scaramozzino. adv.; bk.rev.; bibl.; upd. 27 92017; circ. 1,100. **Indexed:** A.B.C.Pol.Sci., Hist.Abstr., Lang.& Lang.Behav.Abstr., Mid.East: Abstr.& Ind., P.A.I.S.For.Lang.Ind.

322.4 US ISSN 0032-3276
POLITICS. 1964. q. $30. Business-Industry Political Action Committee, Political Education Council, 1747 Pennsylvania Ave., N.W., Washington, DC 20006. TEL 202-833-1880. FAX 202-833-2338. Ed. Don R. Kendall. bk.rev.; circ. 23,000. **Indexed:** A.B.C.Pol.Sci.
Description: Digest of political trends and developments of interest to the business community.

320 UK ISSN 0263-3957
POLITICS. 1981. s-a. £11($25) (Political Studies Association of the United Kingdom) Whiting & Birch Ltd., P.O. Box 872, Forest Hill, London SE23 3HZ, England. TEL 081-699-0914. FAX 081-699-3685. Ed. Andrew Taylor. adv.; bk.rev.; circ. 1,200. (back issues avail.) **Indexed:** ASSIA
—BLDSC shelfmark: 6543.937500.

320 US
POLITICS AND PUBLIC AFFAIRS.* 1987. q. free. Market Opinion Research, 31700 Middlebelt Rd., Ste. 220, Farmington Hills, MI 48334-2373. TEL 313-963-2414. Ed. Susan McKee.
Former titles: Political Trends and Perspectives; Public Affairs.
Description: Reports on Market Opinion Research activities and current policy issues.

320 US ISSN 0032-3292
H1 CODEN: PSOCEX
POLITICS AND SOCIETY. 1970. q. $105 (foreign $140). Sage Publications, Inc., 2455 Teller Rd., Newbury Park, CA 91320. TEL 805-499-0721. FAX 805-499-0871. (UK addr.: Sage Publications Ltd., 6 Bonhill St., London EC2A 4PU, England. TEL 071-374-0645) Ed.Bd. adv.; bk.rev. (also avail. in microform from UMI; back issues avail.; reprint service avil. from SCH) **Indexed:** A.B.C.Pol.Sci., Amer.Bibl.Slavic & E.Eur.Stud., ASSIA, Curr.Cont., E.I., Hist.Abstr., Left Ind. (1982-), Left Ind., Mid.East: Abstr.& Ind., Soc.Sci.Ind., SSCI.
—BLDSC shelfmark: 6543.944000.
Description: Analysis of politics, its social roots and consequences.
Refereed Serial

320 GW ISSN 0939-6071
▼**POLITICS AND THE INDIVIDUAL;** international journal of political socialization and political psychology. 1991. s-a. DM.64. Verlag Dr. R. Kraemer, Postfach 130584, 2000 Hamburg 13, Germany. TEL 040-4101429. Ed.Bd.

POLITICAL SCIENCE

320 US
POLITICS IN AMERICA. 1981. biennial. $69.95 hardcover; softcover $39.95. Congressional Quarterly Inc., 1414 22nd St., N.W., Washington, DC 20037. TEL 202-887-8500. FAX 202-728-1863. Ed. Phil Duncan.
●Also available online.
 Description: Profiles of every member of Congress, both in Washington and at home. Describes their backgrounds, districts, key votes, committee seats, and campaign funds. Covers election races.

320 US
POLITICS IN LATIN AMERICA. 1982. irreg. price varies. Praeger Publishers (Subsidiary of: Greenwood Publishing Group Inc.), 88 Post Rd. W., Box 5007, Westport, CT 06881-5007. TEL 203-226-3571. FAX 203-222-1502.

320 US
POLITICS IN MINNESOTA. 1983. 22/yr. $48. Political Communications, Inc., 525 Park St., Ste. 211, St. Paul, MN 55103. TEL 612-293-3911. Eds. Wy Spano, D.J. Leary.
 Description: Reports on Minnesota politics.

320 UK ISSN 0959-8480
▼**POLITICS REVIEW.** 1991. q. £15.50 (foreign £24.50). Philip Allan Publishers Ltd., Deddington, Oxfordshire OX15 0SE, England. TEL 0869-38652. FAX 0869-38803.

320.52 UK ISSN 0307-7039
POLITICS TODAY. 1946. fortn. £21. Conservative and Unionist Central Office, 32 Smith Square, London SW1P 3HH, England. Ed.Bd. index. **Indexed:** Mag.Ind., Mid.East: Abstr.& Ind.
 —BLDSC shelfmark: 6543.950000.
 Supersedes: Notes on Current Politics (ISSN 0029-4055) & Overseas Review (ISSN 0030-7491)

320 BE ISSN 0048-475X
POLITIEKE DOKUMENTATIE. 1969. q. 500 Fr. to individuals; institutions 750 Fr. Instituut voor Europese Vorming V.Z.M., P-A Lenoirstraat 13, B-1090 Brussels, Belgium. Ed. J.D. Peeters. adv.; bk.rev.; bibl.; index every 3 yrs; circ. 350. (reprint service avail. from UMI)

320 FI ISSN 0032-3365
JN6701.A1
POLITIIKKA. (Text in Finnish or Swedish; summaries in English) 1959. q. Fmk.110 (outside Scandinavia Fmk.120). Finnish Political Science Association, Department of Political Sciences, University of Turku, SF 20500 Turku, Finland. TEL 21-6335386. FAX 21-6335090. Ed. Heikki Paloheimo. adv.; bk.rev.; charts; illus.; index; circ. 1,400. **Indexed:** A.B.C.Pol.Sci., Hist.Abstr., Int.Polit.Sci.Abstr., Sociol.Abstr.
 —BLDSC shelfmark: 6543.958000.

320 GW ISSN 0342-5746
POLITIK - AKTUELL FUER DEN UNTERRICHT. 1975. w. DM.80. Madog Verlag GmbH, Broicher Dorfstr. 28, 4044 Kaarst 1, Germany. TEL 02131-64053. Ed. E. Bizer. circ. 2,500.

320 GR
POLITIKA THEMATA. w. J. Chron, Ed. & Pub., Odos Ipsilantou 25, 106 75 Athens, Greece. TEL 721-8421. circ. 2,544.

320 SA ISSN 0258-9346
JA26
POLITIKON; South African journal of political science. (Text and summaries in Afrikaans, English) 1974. s-a. $35 (effective 1992). Staatkundige Vereniging van Suid Afrika - Political Science Association of South Africa, P.O. Box 1041, Florida 1710, South Africa. Ed. Mervyn Frost. adv.; bk.rev.; circ. 1,300. (also avail. in microfilm from UMI; reprint service avail. from UMI) **Indexed:** A.B.C.Pol.Sci., Ind.S.A.Per, Int.Polit.Sci.Abstr.
 —BLDSC shelfmark: 6544.040000.
 Description: Advances the study of political science, international politics and related topics through scholarly discourse and dissemination of research results.
 Refereed Serial

320 BW
POLITINFORMATOR I AGITATOR. 1932. s-m. 0.06 Rub. Kommunisticheskaya Partiya Belorussii, Tsentral'nyi Komitet, Leninskii Prospekt, 77, 220041, Minsk, Byelaru. illus.

320 FR ISSN 0244-7827
JQ1872
POLITIQUE AFRICAINE. 1981. q. 295 F. (foreign 480 F.). (Association des Chercheurs de Politique Africaine) Karthala Editions, 22-24 Bd. Arago, 75013 Paris, France. TEL 43-31-15-59. FAX 45-35-27-05. TELEX 250303 PUBLICXPARIS. Ed.Bd. adv.; bk.rev.; bibl.; circ. 3,500. **Indexed:** Rural Devel.Abstr., World Agri.Econ.& Rural Sociol.Abstr.
 —BLDSC shelfmark: 6544.093000.

320 327 FR
POLITIQUE ETRANGERE. q. (Institut Francais des Relations Internationales) Armand Colin (Subsidiary of: Masson), 103 bd. St-Michel, 75005 Paris, France. TEL 1-46-34-19-12. FAX 1-43-26-96-38. TELEX 201 269 F. Ed. Dominique Moisi. circ. 4,500.

327 FR
POLITIQUE ETRANGERE DE LA FRANCE. 1935. 6/yr. 445 F. (Minstere des Relations Exterieures) Documentation Francaise, 29-31 Quai Voltaire, 75340 Paris Cedex 07, France. TEL 1-40-15-70-00. (Co-sponsor: Institut Francais de Relations Internationales) bk.rev.; bibl.; index; circ. 1,500. (also avail. in microfiche) **Indexed:** A.B.C.Pol.Sci., Abstr.Mil.Bibl., E.I., Hist.Abstr., Key to Econ.Sci., P.A.I.S.For.Lang.Ind., Pt.de Rep. (1979-), Rural Recreat.Tour.Abstr., World Agri.Econ.& Rural Sociol.Abstr.
 Formerly: Politique Etrangere (ISSN 0032-342X)

320 FR ISSN 0221-2781
D839
POLITIQUE INTERNATIONALE. (Text in French; summaries in English and Spanish) 1978. q. 240 F. to individuals (foreign 295 F.); institutions 290 F. (foriegn 340 F.). 11 rue du Bois de Boulogne, 75116 Paris, France. TEL 45-00-15-26. FAX 45-00-38-79. Ed. Patrick Wajsman. adv.; bk.rev. (back issues avail.)
 —BLDSC shelfmark: 6544.112000.

320 AU
POLITISCHE BILDUNG. irreg. price varies. (Bundesministerium fuer Unterricht und Kunst) Verlag fuer Geschichte und Politik, Neulinggasse 26, A-1030 Vienna, Austria. Ed.Bd.

320 GW ISSN 0032-3446
H5
DIE POLITISCHE MEINUNG; Monatsschrift zu Fragen der Zeit. 1956. m. DM.98. Verlag A. Fromm, Postfach 1948, 4500 Osnabrueck, Germany. FAX 0541-310315. Ed. Peter Hopen. adv.; bk.rev.; charts; upd. 27 91351; circ. 5,000. **Indexed:** P.A.I.S.For.Lang.Ind.
 —BLDSC shelfmark: 6544.115000.

320 AU ISSN 0032-3454
POLITISCHE PERSPEKTIVEN;* Blaetter zur Zeitkritik. 1965. 6/yr. S.150. (Oesterreichischer Akademikerbund GmbH und Co. KG) Signum Verlag, Boesendorfer Str. 2, 1010 Vienna, Austria. TEL 0222-505-7215. Ed. Dr. Heinz Wittmann. adv.; bk.rev.; play rev.; circ. 11,000.
 Supersedes: Akademiker.

320 SZ
POLITISCHE RUNDSCHAU/REVUE POLITIQUE; Zeitschrift fuer Kultur, Politik und Wirtschaft. (Text in German and French) 1921. q. 12 Fr.($3) Freisinnig-Demokratische Partei der Schweiz, Postfach 6136, Bahnhofplatz 10, CH-3001 Berne, Switzerland. TEL 031-1223438. Ed. Anna-Marie Kappeler. bk.rev.; bibl.; stat. (tabloid format)

320 GW ISSN 0032-3470
JA14
POLITISCHE VIERTELJAHRESSCHRIFT. 1960. q. DM.108 (students DM.76). (Deutsche Vereinigung fuer Politische Wissenschaft) Westdeutscher Verlag GmbH, Postfach 5829, 6200 Wiesbaden 1, Germany. TEL 0611-160230. FAX 0611-160229. TELEX 4186928-VWV-D. Ed.Bd. adv.; bk.rev.; circ. 2,000. **Indexed:** A.B.C.Pol.Sci., Hist.Abstr., P.A.I.S.For.Lang.Ind., Peace Res.Abstr.

320 FR ISSN 0295-2319
POLITIX; travaux de science politique. 1988. q. 240 F. to individuals (foreign 290 F.); institutions 340 F. (foreign 420 F.); students 200 F. (Centre National des Lettres) Presses de la Fondation Nationale des Sciences Politiques, 27 rue Saint-Guillaume, 75341 Paris Cedex 07, France. TEL 1-45-49-50-50. FAX 1-45-48-04-41. TELEX 201 002 F. Ed.Bd.
 Description: Forum for political scientists, sociologists, historians, geographers, economists, and anthropologists.

320 US ISSN 0032-3497
JA3
POLITY. 1968. q. $20 to individuals; institutions $35. Northeastern Political Science Association, Thompson Hall, University of Massachusetts, Amherst, MA 01003. TEL 413-545-1354. Ed. Jerome M. Mileur. adv.; bk.rev.; index, cum.index every 3 vols.; circ. 1,300. (also avail. in microform from MIM,UMI; back issues avail., reprint service avail. from UMI) **Indexed:** A.B.C.Pol.Sci., Amer.Bibl.Slavic & E.Eur.Stud, Amer.Hist.& Life, Curr.Cont., E.I., Fut.Surv., Human Resour.Abstr., Int.Polit.Sci.Abstr., Mid.East: Abstr.& Ind., Sage Pub.Admin.Abstr., Sage Urb.Stud.Abstr., SSCI.
 —BLDSC shelfmark: 6544.155000.
 Description: Covers American politics, comparative politics, political theory and international relations.

320 PL ISSN 0032-3500
AP54
POLITYKA. (Supplement avail.: Polityka - Import - Export) 1957. w. 110 Zl. per no. Ul. Dubois 9, 00-958 Warsaw, Poland. TEL 48-22-6353491. TELEX 812546. (Subscr. to: RSW "Prasa-Ksiazka-Ruch" Centrala Kolportazu Prasy i Wydawnictw, ul. Towarowa 28, 00-958 Warsaw, Poland) Ed. Jan Bijak. bk.rev.; charts; illus.; stat.; circ. 400,000. **Indexed:** M.L.A.

320 PL
POLITYKA POLSKA. 1982. m. Ul. Marchlewskiego 32-11, 00-141 Warsaw, Poland. TEL 48-22-241931. Ed. Marek Gadzala. circ. 400,000.

POLSKA MYSL POLITYCZNA XIX I XX WIEKU. see HISTORY — History Of Europe

945 IT ISSN 0032-437X
POPOLO DEL FRIULI-VENEZIA GIULIA. 1963. 10/yr. L.100 per no. Comitato Regionale della Democrazia Cristiana, Piazza S. Giovanni 5, 34122 Trieste, Italy. Ed.Bd. circ. 10,500.

320 IT
POPOLO E LIBERTA. 1976. w. L.15000. Partito Popolare Italiano, Piazzetta Matilde Serao 7, 80132 Naples, Italy. Ed. Morani Volturno. adv.; bk.rev.

950 US ISSN 0032-4515
JK4101
POPULAR GOVERNMENT. 1931. q. $12. University of North Carolina at Chapel Hill, Institute of Government, CB No. 3330, Knapp Bldg., Chapel Hill, NC 27599-3330. TEL 919-966-4119. FAX 919-962-0654. Ed. Charles D. Liner. adv.; bk.rev.; charts; illus.; index, cum.index every 3 yrs; circ. 5,050. (also avail. in microform from UMI; reprint service avail. from UMI) **Indexed:** HRIS, P.A.I.S.
 —BLDSC shelfmark: 6550.550000.
 Description: Includes articles on North Carolina state and local government.

320 910 900 GW ISSN 0932-2272
PORTUGAL - MAGAZIN. 1979. q. DM.48. Deutsch-Portugiesische Gesellschaft e.V., Weyerstr. 48-52, 5000 Cologne 1, Germany. TEL 0221-2070312. FAX 0221-236464. TELEX 8881828-PNEUD. Ed. Peter Neufert. adv.; bk.rev.; charts; illus.; circ. 950. (looseleaf format)
 Formerly: Portugal - Nachrichten (ISSN 0722-6713)

329.9 PO
PORTUGAL SOCIALISTA. 1967. q. Socialist Party, Rua da Emenda 46, 1200 Lisbon, Portugal. TEL 01-3464375. Dir. Antonio Reis. circ. 5,000.

PORTUGUESE TIMES. see ETHNIC INTERESTS

329.9 DR
POSICION SOCIALISTA. 3/yr. Editora Nuevo Rumbo, Apdo. Postal 2298, Santo Domingo, Dominican Republic.

POLITICAL SCIENCE

322.4 600   US
POSITIVE ALTERNATIVES. 1975. 4/yr. $35. Center for Economic Conversion, 222C View St., Ste. C, Mountain View, CA 94041. TEL 415-968-8798. FAX 415-968-1126. Ed. Beth Delson. bk.rev.; circ. 7,500.
Formerly (until vol.15, no.3, 1990): Plowshare Press.
Description: International newsletter on economic conversion, which promotes the orderly redirection of resources from the military economy to more socially useful and peaceful economic activity.

322.4   NR   ISSN 0331-9911
POSITIVE REVIEW. 1978. q. $18. University of Ife, Department of African Languages & Literatures, Ile-Ife, Nigeria. (Subscr. outside of Africa to: Hans Zell, Box 56, Oxford OX1 3EI, England) Ed.Bd. bk.rev.

320   GW   ISSN 0032-5201
POSSEV; obchshestvenno-politicheskii zhurnal. (Text in Russian) 1945. 6/yr. DM.60. Possev-Verlag, Flurscheideweg 15, 6230 Frankfurt a.M. 80, Germany. TEL 069-341265. FAX 069-341265. Ed. A. Jugov. adv.; bk.rev.; bibl.; illus.; index; circ. 2,000. (also avail. in microform)

329.9   US
POST-AMERIKAN. 1972. 6/yr. $4. Box 3452, Bloomington, IL 61701. TEL 309-828-7232. adv.; bk.rev.; film rev.; play rev.; charts; illus.; circ. 3,500. (tabloid format; also avail. in microfiche; back issues avail.) **Indexed:** Alt.Press Ind.

320   US
POSTCONTEMPORARY INTERVENTIONS. 1989. irreg. Duke University Press, 6697 College Station, Durham, NC 27708. TEL 919-684-2173. FAX 919-684-8644. Eds. Stanley Fish, Fredric Jameson.

320   FR   ISSN 0152-0768
POUVOIRS. 1977. q. 295 F. (foreign 400 F.). Presses Universitaires de France, Departement des Revues, 14 Avenue du Bois-de-l'Epine, B.P.90, 91003 Evry Cedex, France. TEL 1-60-77-82-05. FAX 1-60-79-20-45. TELEX PUF 600 474 F. Dirs. Philippe Ardant, Olivier Duhamel. bk.rev.; bibl. (reprint service avail. from KTO) **Indexed:** A.B.C.Pol.Sci.
—BLDSC shelfmark: 6571.420000.
Description: Covers the political aspects of the economy, social life and culture.

329.3   PO
POVO LIBRE. w. Social Democratic Party, Rua S. Caetano 9, 1200 Lisbon, Portugal. TEL 01-602140. TELEX 13528. Dir. Duarte Lima.

320   US
POWER (NIAGARA FALLS). 1978. m. $20 donation. Samisdat Publishers Ltd., Box 791, Niagara Falls, NY 14302. TEL 416-922-9850. Ed. Ernst Zundel. circ. 50,000.

320.532   RU
▼**POZITSIYA.** 1991. w. 0.15 Rub. per issue. Ul. Krasnoznamenskaya 21-33, 180007 Pskov, Russia. TEL 3-83-50. Ed. A.Ya. Kirsanov. circ. 3,000. (newspaper)

320.531   NE   ISSN 0303-8157
POZNAN STUDIES IN THE PHILOSOPHY OF THE SCIENCES AND THE HUMANITIES. (Text in English) 1975. irreg. price varies. (Adam Mickiewics University, PL) Editions Rodopi B.V., Keizersgracht 302-304, 1016 EX Amsterdam, Netherlands. TEL 020-6227507. FAX 020-6380948. (US and Canada subscr. to: 233 Peachtree St. N.E., Ste. 404, Atlanta GA 30303-1504. TEL 800-225-3998) Ed. Jerzy Brzezinski. adv.; bk.rev. (back issues avail.) **Indexed:** Phil.Ind.
—BLDSC shelfmark: 6579.127000.

320   PL   ISSN 0032-6186
PRACA I ZABEZPIECZENIA SPOLECZNE. (Text in Polish; summaries in English and Russian) 1959. m. $81. Panstwowe Wydawnictwo Ekonomiczne, Niecala 4a, Warsaw, Poland. TEL 48-22-278001. (Dist. by: Ars Polona-Ruch, Krakowskie Przedmiescie 7, Warsaw, Poland) Ed. Wieslaw Krencik. bk.rev.; bibl.; charts; index; circ. 6,000.
—BLDSC shelfmark: 6579.260000.

320 330   US
HX1
PRACTICE (NEW YORK); the magazine of psychology and political economy. 1983. 3/yr. $15 to individuals, institutions $30. Castillo Publications, 500 Greenwich St., Ste. 201, New York, NY 10013. TEL 212-941-5800. FAX 212-941-8340. Ed. Lois Holzman. adv.; bk.rev.; film rev.; circ. 2,000. (back issues avail.) **Indexed:** Alt.Press Ind., Sociol.Abstr.
Former titles: Practice, the journal of politics, economics, psychology, sociology and culture (ISSN 0742-9940) & Struggle (ISSN 0146-8006)
Description: An international forum for dialogue on psychology, ideology, education and politics.

320 301.16   US
▼**PRAEGER SERIES IN POLITICAL COMMUNICATIONS.** 1990. irreg. price varies. Praeger Publishers (Subsidiary of: Greenwood Publishing Group Inc.), 88 Post Rd. W., Box 5007, Westport, CT 06881-5007. TEL 203-226-3571. FAX 203-222-1502.

320 330   US
PRAEGER SERIES IN POLITICAL ECONOMY. 1988. irreg. price varies. Praeger Publishers (Subsidiary of: Greenwood Publishing Group Inc.), 88 Post Rd. W., Box 5007, Westport, CT 06881-5007. TEL 203-226-3571. FAX 203-222-1502.

320   US   ISSN 1062-0931
▼**PRAEGER SERIES IN PRESIDENTIAL STUDIES.** 1992. irreg. price varies. Praeger Publishers (Subsidiary of: Greenwood Publishing Group Inc.), 88 Post Rd. W., Box 5007, Westport, CT 06881-5007. TEL 203-226-3571. FAX 203-222-1502.

320   US
▼**PRAEGER SERIES IN TRANSFORMATIONAL POLITICS AND POLITICAL SCIENCE.** 1992. irreg. price varies. Praeger Publsihers (Subsidiary of: Greenwood Publishing Group Inc.), 88 Post Rd. W., Box 5007, Westport, CT 06881-5007. TEL 203-226-3571. FAX 203-222-1502.

322.4   IT
PRAXIS; una rivista per una nuova sinistra. 1976. m. L.10000. Edizioni Praxis, Via Segesta 9, Palermo, Italy. Ed. Gabriella Emiliani. adv.; bk.rev. **Indexed:** Artbibl.

320   PH   ISSN 0116-709X
PRAXIS; journal of political science. (Text in English) 1987. s-a. P.140($15) (De La Salle University, Political Science Department) De La Salle University Press, 2401 Taft Ave., Manila, Philippines. TEL 2-595177. Ed. Socorro Reyes. adv.; bk.rev.; circ. 300.
Description: Publishes scholarly articles reflecting significant quantitative or qualitative research. Includes speeches, research reports, and "state of the art" papers.

320 100   UK   ISSN 0260-8448
B809.8
PRAXIS INTERNATIONAL. 1981. q. £28($57) to individuals; institutions £82($173). Basil Blackwell Ltd., 108 Cowley Rd., Oxford OX4 1JF, England. TEL 0865 791100. FAX 0865-791347. TELEX 837022-OXBOOK-G. Eds. Seyla Benhabib, Svetozar Stojanovic. adv.; bk.rev. (reprint service avail. from SWZ,UMI) **Indexed:** Alt.Press Ind., Lang.& Lang.Behav.Abstr., Left Ind. (1986-), Phil.Ind.
—BLDSC shelfmark: 6603.171350.

320   AG
PRENSA OBRERA. 1982. w. $100. (Partido Obrero) Editorial Rumbos, S.R.L., Ayacucho 444, Buenos Aires, Argentina. TEL 953-8433. Ed. Eduardo Salas. bk.rev.; circ. 16,000.

PRESIDENTIAL MUSEUM. NEWS AND VIEWS. see *MUSEUMS AND ART GALLERIES*

321.804   US   ISSN 0360-4918
JK501
PRESIDENTIAL STUDIES QUARTERLY. 1972. q. $40. Center for the Study of the Presidency, 208 E. 75th St., New York, NY 10021. TEL 212-249-1200. FAX 212-628-9503. Ed. R. Gordon Hoxie. adv.; bk.rev.; bibl.; circ. 13,500. (also avail. in microform from UMI; reprint service avail. from UMI) **Indexed:** A.B.C.Pol.Sci., Amer.Hist.& Life, Bk.Rev.Ind. (1989-), Child.Bk.Rev.Ind. (1989-), Commun.Abstr., Hist.Abstr., Human Resour.Abstr., Int.Polit.Sci.Abstr., Mid.East: Abstr.& Ind., P.A.I.S., Pers.Lit., Sage Fam.Stud.Abstr., Sage Pub.Admin.Abstr., Sage Urb.Stud.Abstr.
—BLDSC shelfmark: 6609.880000.
Formerly: Center for the Study of the Presidency. Center House Bulletin (ISSN 0098-809X)
Refereed Serial

PREZENTACJE; miesiecznik teoretyczno-polityczny materialy z prasy zagranicznej. see *SOCIOLOGY*

320 301   IT
PRIMO MAGGIO;* saggi e documenti per una storia di classe. 1974. 3/yr. Colletivo Editoriale Calusca, Via Isonzo 44, 52100 Arezzo, Italy.

325   CN
PRINCE EDWARD ISLAND. CIVIL SERVICE COMMISSION. ANNUAL REPORT. 1963. a. free. Civil Service Commission, P.O. Box 2000, Charlottetown, P.E.I. C1A 7N8, Canada. TEL 902-368-4185. FAX 902-368-5544. circ. 125.

320 900   US
PRINCETON STUDIES IN INTERNATIONAL HISTORY AND POLITICS. 1991. irreg. price varies. Princeton University Press, 3175 Princeton Pike, Lawrenceville, NJ 08648. TEL 609-895-1344. FAX 609-895-1081.

320 352   US
PRIVATIZATION WATCH.* 1976. m. $95. Local Government Center, 3415 S. Sepulveda Blvd., Ste. 400, Los Angeles, CA 90034-6060. TEL 213-392-0443. FAX 213-392-0942. Ed. Philip E. Fixler, Jr. circ. 1,000. (back issues avail.)
Formerly: Fiscal Watchdog.

320   SZ
PRO UND KONTRA. 1982. irreg. 8 Fr. Schweizerische Arbeitsgemeinschaft fuer Demokratie, Feldeggstr. 65, Postfach 387, 8034 Zurich, Switzerland. circ. 3,000. (back issues avail.)

320   US
PROBE (NEW YORK); intelligence magazine of the working left. q. $12 to individuals; institutions $24. Castillo Publications, 500 Greenwich St., Ste. 201, New York, NY 10013. TEL 212-941-5800.
Description: Provides news coverage from a radical perspective.

320.532   US   ISSN 0032-941X
HX1
PROBLEMS OF COMMUNISM. 1952. bi-m. $9. U.S. Information Agency, 301 4th St., S.W., Washington, DC 20547. TEL 202-485-2230. (Dist. by: Supt. of Documents, Washington, DC 20402) Ed. Wayne Hall. bk.rev.; illus.; index; circ. 34,000. (also avail. in microform from UMI,MIM; reprint service avail. from UMI,ISI) **Indexed:** A.B.C.Pol.Sci., Amer.Bibl.Slavic & E.Eur.Stud., CERDIC, Curr.Cont., Econ.Abstr., Hist.Abstr., HR Rep., Ind.U.S.Gov.Per., P.A.I.S., Peace Res.Abstr., Rural Devel.Abstr., Soc.Sci.Ind., SSCI.
—BLDSC shelfmark: 6617.878100.

329.9   UK
PROBLEMS OF COMMUNISM. 1974. irreg. £12 for 4 nos. Problems of Communism Committee, 10 Athol St., Belfast BT12 4GX, N. Ireland. Ed. Jack Lane. circ. 750. Indexed: A.B.C.Pol.Sci., Acad.Ind., Curr.Cont., Ind.U.S.Gov.Per., Mid.East: Abstr.& Ind., P.A.I.S., Soc.Sci.Ind., SSCI, World Agri.Econ.& Rural Sociol.Abstr.

335   II
PROBLEMS OF NATIONAL LIBERATION. (Text in English) 1974. irreg. Rs.3. Ranadhir Dasgupta, 10 Bondel Rd., Calcutta 700019, India. Eds. Satyendra Narayan Mazumdar, Narahari Kaviraj. adv.; bk.rev.; circ. 1,000.

POLITICAL SCIENCE

332.4 ES ISSN 0259-9864
PROCESO; informativo semanal. 1980. w. Col.60($35) Universidad Centroamericana, Center for Information, Documentation and Research Support, Apdo. 01-16B, San Salvador, El Salvador. TEL 503-240011. FAX 503-240288. (Subscr. to: Apdo. 01-575, San Salvador, El Salvador) index; circ. 1,200. (looseleaf format)
   Description: Analyzes the current political, economic, military, labor and human rights situation of El Salvador.

320 US
PROFILES (ARLINGTON);* a non-partisan view of politics, people and issues. Variant title: Political Profiles. 1985. bi-m. $30. Political Profiles Inc., 240 S. Reynolds St., No. 401, Alexandria, VA 22304.

320 MQ
PROGRESSISTE. w. Parti Progressiste Martiniquais, Rue de Tallis Clariere, Fort-de-France, Martinique. Ed. Paul Gabourg. circ. 13,000.

320.5 US ISSN 0033-0736
AP2
PROGRESSIVE (MADISON). 1909. m. $30 to individuals; institutions $50. Progressive, Inc., 409 E. Main St., Madison, WI 53703. TEL 608-257-4626. FAX 608-257-3373. (Subscr. to: Cable Publishers, Box 421, Mt. Morris, IL 61054) Ed. Erwin Knoll. adv.; bk.rev.; film rev.; index; circ. 50,000. (also avail. in microform from UMI; back issues avail.; reprint service avail. from UMI) **Indexed:** Acad.Ind., Alt.Press Ind., Amer.Bibl.Slavic & E.Eur.Stud., Bk.Rev.Ind. (1979-), Chic.Per.Ind., Child.Bk.Rev.Ind. (1979-), Environ.Per.Bibl., Fut.Surv., Mag.Ind., Media Rev.Dig., Mid.East: Abstr.& Ind., P.A.I.S., Peace Res.Abstr., PMR, R.G., Sage Pub.Admin.Abstr.
   —BLDSC shelfmark: 6924.640000.
   Description: Investigative reporting, analysis, and commentary on political, economic and social issues, culture, and the arts.

320 US
PROJECT; ruling class conspiracy analysis for investors & political activists. 1974. m. $25. (A-albionic Society) A-albionic Research, Box 20273, Ferndale, MI 48220. Ed. Lloyd Miller. adv.; bk.rev.; circ. 1,000. (looseleaf format; back issues avail.)
   Formerly: Conspiracy Digest.

320 II
PROLETARIAN PATH. (Text in English) bi-m. Rs.12. 25-1 Jyotish Roy Rd., Calcutta 53, India. Eds. D.V. Rao, Muni Guha. bibl.; charts.

320.531 US ISSN 0894-0754
PROLETARIAN REVOLUTION. 1976. q. $5 for 8 issues. (League for the Revolutionary Party) Socialist Voice Publishing Co., 170 Broadway, Rm. 201, New York, NY 10038. TEL 212-962-6464. Ed. Walter Dahl. circ. 1,000. (back issues avail.)
   Formerly: Socialist Voice.

320 IT
PROMETHEUS (MILAN); rivista internazionale di politica della scienza. 4/yr. L.89000 (foreign L.110000)(effective 1992). Franco Angeli Editore, Viale Monza, 106, Casella Postale 17175, 20100 Milan, Italy. TEL 02-2895762.

320 US
PROPAGANDA REVIEW. 1987. q. $20. Media Alliance, Ft. Mason, Bldg. D, San Francisco, CA 94123. Ed. Johan Carlisle.

320 CN
PROSPECTUS.* (Text in French and English) 1968. q. free. Progressive Conservative Youth Federation, 161 Laurier Ave. W., Ste. 200, Ottawa, Ont. K1P 5J2, Canada. Ed. Debbie Collinson. circ. 15,000. (tabloid format)

320 IT
PROSPETTIVE NEL MONDO. 1976. m. Via delle Carrozze 16, Rome, Italy.

320 330 IT
PROVINCIA IBLEA. s-m. L.3000. c/o Giovanni Gurrieri, Viale N. Colaianni 41, 97100 Ragusta, Italy. adv.; circ. 1,500.

320 IT
PROVO RADICALE.* 1971. q. L.3000. Via Baccina 90, 00184 Rome, Italy. Ed. Massimo Teodori. bk.rev.

PRZEGLAD LUBUSKI. see HISTORY — History Of Europe

PUBLIC ADMINISTRATION AND DEVELOPMENT; an international journal of training, research and practice. see BUSINESS AND ECONOMICS — International Development And Assistance

PUBLIC ADMINISTRATION SURVEY. see PUBLIC ADMINISTRATION

320 US ISSN 0555-5914
JK6501
PUBLIC AFFAIRS. 1960. irreg. (approx. 3/yr). free. University of South Dakota, Governmental Research Bureau, Vermillion, SD 57069. TEL 605-677-5242. Ed. Steve Feimer. charts; illus.; circ. 1,800. **Indexed:** P.A.I.S.
   Description: Each issue focuses on a different public policy issue.

PUBLIC AFFAIRS COMMENT. see SOCIAL SCIENCES: COMPREHENSIVE WORKS

320.9 350 US ISSN 0033-3417
JK8701
PUBLIC AFFAIRS REPORT. 1960. bi-m. free. University of California, Berkeley, Institute of Governmental Studies, 119 Bernard Moses Hall, Berkeley, CA 94720. Ed. Maria Wolf. charts; stat.; circ. 4,000. (reprint service avail. from UMI) **Indexed:** Med.Care Rev., P.A.I.S., Sage Fam.Stud.Abstr.

320 US ISSN 0275-9322
PUBLIC EYE (BOSTON);* a journal of social and political issues concerning repression in America. 1977. irreg. (approx. 4/yr.). $8 to individuals; institutions $15. (N L G Foundation) National Lawyers Guild (Boston), Civil Liberties Committee, 14 Beacon St., Ste. 407, Boston, MA 02108. Ed. Chip Berlet. bk.rev.; illus.; circ. 7,000. (also avail. in microfilm; back issues avail.) **Indexed:** Alt.Press Ind., HR Rep.

PUBLIC INTEREST. see SOCIAL SCIENCES: COMPREHENSIVE WORKS

320 US ISSN 1054-6626
▼**PUBLIC OPINION IN THE SOVIET UNION: STATISTICS AND ANALYSIS**. (English translation of Soviet title) 1991. bi-m. $100 to individuals (outside N. America $115); institutions $200 (outside N. America $215). (Soviet Center for Public Opinion and Market Research, UR) New Soviet Sciences Press (USA), c/o Allen Press, Inc., Dist., Box 1897, Lawrence, KS 66044-8897. TEL 913-843-1235. FAX 913-843-1274. Ed. Tatyana Zaslavskaya.
   Description: Current analysis of the changing attitudes and economic needs of the Soviet people in the democratic restructuring of Soviet society.

320.9 US ISSN 0033-362X
HM261.A1 CODEN: POPQAE
PUBLIC OPINION QUARTERLY. 1937. 4/yr. $20 to individuals; institutions $40; students $18. (American Association for Public Opinion Research) University of Chicago Press, Journals Division, 5720 S. Woodlawn Ave., Chicago, IL 60637. TEL 312-753-3347. FAX 312-702-0694. TELEX 25-4603. (Subscr. to: Box 37005, Chicago, IL 60637) Ed. Howard Schuman. adv.; bk.rev.; charts; index, cum.index: vols. 1-46. (also avail. in microform from UMI; reprint service avail. from UMI,SCH) **Indexed:** A.B.C.Pol.Sci., ABI Inform, Acad.Ind., Account.Ind. (1974-), Amer.Bibl.Slavic & E.Eur.Stud., ASSIA, Bk.Rev.Ind. (1980-), Bus.Ind., Child.Bk.Rev.Ind. (1980-), Commun.Abstr., Cont.Pg.Manage., Crim.Just.Abstr., Curr.Cont., Hist.Abstr., Lang.& Lang.Behav.Abstr., Mag.Ind., Mid.East: Abstr.& Ind., P.A.I.S., Psychol.Abstr., Res.High.Educ.Abstr., Soc.Sci.Ind., Sociol.Abstr. (1952-), SRI, SSCI.
   —BLDSC shelfmark: 6967.850000.
   Refereed Serial

320 070 US
PUBLIC OPINION REPORT. vol.5, 1992. q. $50. Brown University, A. Alfred Taubman Center for Public Policy and American Institutions, Public Opinion Laboratory, Box 1977, Providence, RI 02912. circ. 500.
   Description: Reports of public opinion surveys in Rhode Island.

321 US ISSN 0048-5950
JK1
PUBLIUS; the journal of federalism. 1971. q. $25 to individuals (foreign $30); institutions $35 (foreign $40). Center for the Study of Federalism, c/o Editors, Department of Political Science, University of North Texas, Denton, TX 76203-5338. TEL 817-565-2313. FAX 817-565-2599. Eds. Daniel J. Elazar, John Kincaid. adv.; bk.rev.; bibl.; charts; stat.; index; circ. 1,000. (also avail. in microform from UMI; reprint service avail. from UMI) **Indexed:** A.B.C.Pol.Sci., Curr.Cont., Hist.Abstr., Int.Polit.Sci.Abstr., Lang.& Lang.Behav.Abstr., Mid.East: Abstr.& Ind., P.A.I.S., Sage Pub.Admin.Abstr., Sage Urb.Stud.Abstr., Sociol.Abstr., SSCI.
   —BLDSC shelfmark: 7156.095000.

329.6 US
PUEBLO UNIDO. (Text in Spanish.) 1986. bi-m. free. Cuba Independiente y Democratica, 10020 S.W. 37th Terr., Miami, FL 33165. TEL 305-551-7357. Ed. Huber Matos, Jr. circ. 10,000. (looseleaf format; back issues avail.)
   Description: Sent to Cuba via underground ways to inform Cubans about democracy.

320 MX
PUNTO FINAL INTERNACIONAL. m. Mex.$80($60) Centro Latinoamericano de Comunicaciones, San Lorenzo 173, Interior 101, Colonia del Valle, Mexico.

320 BO
PUNTOS DE VISTA. 1982. q. Banco Central de Bolivia, Division Tecnica, Casilla de Correo No. 3118, La Paz, Bolivia. **Indexed:** P.A.I.S.For.Lang.Ind.

320 UY
PURIFICACION. 1977. irreg. Instituto Nacional de Investigaciones Historicas y Geopoliticas, Avda. 18 de Julio 2226, Montevideo, Uruguay. Ed. J.J. Scapusio.

320 KN
THE PYONGYANG TIMES. (Editions in English, French, Spanish) w. Sochon-dong, Sosong District, Pyongyang, N. Korea.

320 DK ISSN 0109-887X
Q - AVISEN; Kristeligt Folkepartis medlemsavis. 1984. bi-m. membership. Kristeligt Folkeparti, Bernhard Bangs Alle 23, 2000 Frederiksberg, Denmark. TEL 00945-38885152. FAX 00945-38883115. Ed. Bent Dahl Jensen. adv.; illus.

320 US
QATAR NEWS. 1974. bi-m. free. Embassy of the State of Qatar, 600 New Hampshire Ave., Washington, DC 20037. TEL 202-338-0111. FAX 202-337-2686. circ. 6,000.

329.9 CC
QIU ZHI/SEEK KNOWLEDGE. (Text in Chinese) m. Y1.20 per no. (Zhongguo Gongchandang, Tianjin Shi-Wei Dangxiao - Chinese Communist Party, Tianjin City Committee Party School) Qiu Zhi Bianjibu, 4, Yuliang Dao, Nankai Qu, Tianjin 300191, People's Republic of China. TEL 342087. (Dist. by: China Publications Foreign Trade Corp., Tianjin Branch, 27 Hubei Lu, Tianjin, P.R.C.) Ed. Gao Xiaokun. adv.; circ. 30,000.

329.9 IT
QUADERNI DI AZIONE SOCIALE. 1970. bi-m. L.45000. Via G. Marocora, 18-20, Rome, Italy. FAX 5840462. Ed. D. Rosati. adv.; bk.rev.; circ. 2,500.

QUADERNI FIORENTINI PER LA STORIA DEL PENSIERO GIURIDICO MODERNO. see LAW

320 301 IT
QUALESOCIETA; rivista bimestrale di dialogo. 1972. bi-m. Via Antonio Chinotto 16, 00195 Rome, Italy. Ed. Alceste Santini. bk.rev.; film rev.; illus.

QUE FAIRE DE L'ECONOMIE. see PHILOSOPHY

320 PE ISSN 0250-9806
QUEHACER; realidad nacional-problemas y alternativas. 1979. bi-m. $12. Centro de Estudios y Promocion del Desarrollo (DESCO), Leon de la Fuente 110, Magdalena del Mar, Lima 17, Peru. TEL 14-627193. FAX 14-617309. (Subscr. to: PUBLIREC S.A., Jr. Guillermo Dansey 084, Lima 1, Peru) adv.; circ. 15,000. (back issues avail.) **Indexed:** P.A.I.S.For.Lang.Ind.

340   AG
QUEHACER NACIONAL. 1982. m. Hipolito Yrigoyen 1394, Buenos Aires, Argentina. Ed. Antonio Canales.

322 327   IT
QUESTE ISTITUZIONI; cronache del sistema politica. 1973. q. L.50000($40) (Gruppo di Studio Societa e Istituzioni) Quest Istituzioni Ricerche S.R.L., Corso Trieste, 62, 00198 Rome, Italy. TEL 06-8419608. Ed. Sergio Ristuccia. adv.; bk.rev.; illus.; circ. 2,000. (tabloid format)

320.531   YU   ISSN 0033-6351
HX365.5
QUESTIONS ACTUELLES DU SOCIALISME. English edition: Socialist Thought and Practice (ISSN 0583-7200); German edition: Sozialistische Theorie und Praxis (ISSN 0350-476X); Italian edition: Questioni Attuali del Socialismo (ISSN 0351-0107); Russian edition: Sotsialisticheskaya Mysl' i Praktika (ISSN 0350-4751); Serbo-Croatian edition: Aktuelna Pitanja Socijalizma. (Spanish edition: Cuestiones Actuales del Socialismo (ISSN 0350-8846); Arabic edition (ISSN 0350-5413)) (Text in French) 1951. m. $30. Komunist, Trg Marksa i Engelsa 11, 11000 Belgrade, Yugoslavia. Ed. Branko Prnjat.
—BLDSC shelfmark: 7216.230000.

945   IT   ISSN 0033-6378
QUESTITALIA. vol.13, 1970. m. S. Croce 598, Venice, Italy. Ed. Wladimiro Dorigo. bk.rev.; bibl.

320   US   ISSN 0033-6629
QUIXOTE;* the anti-capitalist renegade Marxist wordslingers collective. 1965. m. $20. (Marxist Renegade Collective) Quixote Press, Inc., 2407 Watts St., Houston, TX 77030-1829. TEL 713-667-6639. Eds. Morris Edelson, Melissa Bondy. adv.; bk.rev.; film rev.; play rev.; circ. 300. (processed)
Formerly: Quickoats.

320 320   US   ISSN 0882-3456
QUORUM REPORT. 1982. s-m. $140. Texas Analyst, Inc., Box 8, Austin, TX 78768. TEL 512-444-4574. FAX 512-326-2126. Ed. Harvey Kronberg. bk.rev.
Description: Reports on Texas government and politics.

320 330   II
R.B.R.R. KALE MEMORIAL LECTURES. 1937. a; none published 1947 or 1970. price varies. Gokhale Institute of Politics and Economics, Pune 411004, India. TEL (0212)54287. (Dist. by: Orient Longman, Ltd., Nicol Rd., Ballard Estate, Bombay 400 038, India)

329.3   KR
▼**RABOCHAYA SOLIDARNOST**. 1990. m? c/o Sergei V. Bilyk, Ed., Glavpochtamt, 252000 Kiev, Ukraine. circ. 1,000.

320   US   ISSN 0033-7617
HD4802
RADICAL AMERICA. 1967. bi-m. $20 to individuals; institutions $38. Alternative Education Project, Inc., One Summer St., Somerville, MA 02143. TEL 617-628-6585. Ed.Bd. adv.; bk.rev.; index; circ. 5,000. (also avail. in microform from UMI; back issues avail.; reprint service avail. from UMI) Indexed: Alt.Press Ind., Amer.Bibl.Slavic & E.Eur.Stud., Amer.Hist.& Life, Film Lit.Ind. (1990-), Hist.Abstr., Lang.& Lang.Behav.Abstr., Left Ind. (1982-), Mid.East: Abstr.& Ind., Sociol.Abstr., Wom.Stud.Abstr.
Description: Independent journal exerting much influence on the Democratic left with its articles, properly balanced between historical perspective and topical strategy.

320.5   DK
RADIKAL POLITIK. 1964. fortn. DKK 60. Radikale Venstre - Danish Social-Liberal Party, Christiansborg, 1240 Copenhagen K, Denmark. TEL 33-374747. FAX 33-137251. adv.; bk.rev.; circ. 10,000.
Formerly: Fremsyn (ISSN 0016-1012)

320 327   US   ISSN 0079-9491
RADNER LECTURES. irreg., no.7, 1976. Columbia University Press, 562 W. 113th St., New York, NY 10025. TEL 212-678-6777.

RAIN. see ENVIRONMENTAL STUDIES

320.532   DK   ISSN 0109-1700
RAMBUKKEN. 1983. s-a. free. (Danmarks Kommunistiske Parti-Marxister-Leninister i Aarhus Amt) Arbejderens Bogbutik, Munkegade 2, 8000 Aarhus C, Denmark. illus.

320 053.1   GW   ISSN 0004-7899
RAN; ein politisches Jugendmagazin. 1948. m. DM.24. (Deutscher Gewerkschaftsbund) Bund-Verlag GmbH, Hansestr. 63a, Postfach 900840, 5000 Cologne 90, Germany. Ed. Gustav Wilden. adv.; bk.rev.; illus.; circ. 50,000.
Formerly: Aufwaerts.

320   US
RAND RESEARCH REVIEW. 1977. 3/yr. free. Rand Corporation, Publications Department, 1700 Main St., Box 2138, Santa Monica, CA 90407-2138. TEL 213-393-0411. FAX 213-393-4818. TELEX 9103436878. Ed. Ann M. Shoben. charts; illus.; circ. 8,000.
Description: Reports on Rand Corporation's research programs of matters affecting the nation's security and domestic welfare.

320.531   CE
RATULANKA. (Text in Sinhalese) 1978. m. Rs.0.50. Janatha Vimukthi Peramuna - People's Liberation Front, 149-6 Devanam Piyatissa Mawatha, Colombo 10, Sri Lanka.

320   UK   ISSN 0951-4066
RAVEN. 1987. q. £11 to individuals (foreign £12); institutions £13 (foreign £15). Freedom Press, 84b Whitechapel High St. (in Angel Alley), London E1 7QX, England. circ. 2,000.

320 301   US
READINGS IN SOCIAL AND POLITICAL THEORY. 1984. irreg. price varies. New York University Press, 70 Washington Square S., New York, NY 10012. TEL 212-998-2575. FAX 212-995-3833. TELEX 235128 NYU UR.

320   GO   ISSN 0486-106X
REALITES GABONAISES. (Text in French) 1960. irreg. (3-4/yr.). 1000 Fr.CFA($44.12) Institut Pedagogique National, B.P. 813, Libreville, Gabon. Ed. M.A. Bouanga. illus. Indexed: Curr.Cont.Africa.

320.532   CN
REBEL YOUTH. 1970. irreg. Can.$5. Socialist Perspectives for Youth, 24 Cecil St., Toronto, Ont., Canada. Ed. Olga Lazavidis. adv.; bk.rev.; circ. 3,000.
Former titles: Young Worker (ISSN 0382-4047) & Young Communist (ISSN 0382-4039)

RECHTS- UND STAATSWISSENSCHAFTEN. see LAW

RECHTSWISSENSCHAFT UND SOZIALPOLITIK. see LAW

RED LETTERS; a review of cultural politics. see LITERARY AND POLITICAL REVIEWS

RED MENACE; a libertarian socialist newsletter. see LITERARY AND POLITICAL REVIEWS

320.531   CE
RED POWER. (Text in English) bi-m. Rs.12($3) Janatha Vimukthi Peramuna - People's Liberation Front, 149-6 Devanam Piyatissa Mawatha, Colombo 10, Sri Lanka.

320.9   GW   ISSN 0034-2092
REDAKTIONS-ARCHIV; Zahlenbilder aus Gesellschaft, Wirtschaft, Politik und Recht. 1955. m. DM.148. Erich Schmidt Verlag GmbH & Co. (Berlin), Genthiner Str. 30 G, 1000 Berlin 30, Germany. Ed. G. Huck. charts; illus.; stat.; index; circ. 1,200. (looseleaf format)

056.940   CN   ISSN 0384-9120
REGARDS SUR ISRAEL. (Text in French) 1973. m. free. Canada Israel Committee, 1310 Avenue Green, Suite 710, Montreal, Que. H3Z 2B2, Canada. TEL 514-934-0771. Ed. Michel M. Solomon. adv.; bk.rev.; illus.; circ. 4,000.

320   UK   ISSN 0959-230X
▼**REGIONAL POLITICS AND POLICY**; an international journal. 1991. 3/yr. £30($40) to individuals; institutions £55($90). Frank Cass & Co. Ltd., Gainsborough House, 11 Gainsborough Rd., London E11 1RS, England. TEL 081-530-4226. FAX 081-530-7795. Eds. John Loughlin, Paul Hainsworth. adv.; bk.rev.; index. (back issues avail.)

320   UK   ISSN 0264-522X
THE REGIONALIST SEMINAR. 1982. 2/yr. £1.50 to individuals; institutions £5. c/o D. Robins, Ed., 16 Adolphus St. West, Seaham Harbour, Co. Durham, England. bk.rev.; circ. 500. (processed)

RELEASE. see ETHNIC INTERESTS

967.571   RW
RELEVE. 1976. m. $27. Office Rwandais d'Information, B.P. 83, Kigali, Rwanda. TEL 75-665. TELEX 557. Ed. Christophe Mfizi. adv.; bk.rev.; illus.; circ. 1,000. Incorporates: Rwanda-Carrefour d'Afrique (ISSN 0036-0481)
Description: Covers politics, economics and culture.

320   US
RENDON REPORT. 1982. q. $25. Rendon Group, Inc., 116 Newbury St., 5th Fl., Boston, MA 01116. TEL 617-536-6033. FAX 617-536-6409. Ed. Erin Callanan.
Description: Reports on Massachusetts politics.

322.4   US
RENEWAL.* 16/yr. $15. New World Alliance, 3129 Ninth Rd., Arlington, VA 22201. TEL 703-667-6895. Ed. Mark Satin. bk.rev.

320   MX
RENGLON. 1986. q. Mex.$2500. Editorial Terra Firme, Priv. de la Providencia 38, Sn. Jeronimo Lidice, Mexico 20, D.F., Mexico. Ed. Ulises Canchola Gutierrez. bk.rev.; circ. 2,000.

RENMIN ZHENGXIE BAO/JOURNAL OF THE C P P C C. (Zhongguo Renmin Zhengzhi Xieshang Huiyi) see PUBLIC ADMINISTRATION

972.93   DR   ISSN 0034-446X
RENOVACION. 1936. fortn. RD.$6. Puerta del Sol, Calle Jose Reyes esq. El Conde, Santo Domingo, Dominican Republic. Ed. Olga Quisqueya Viuda Martinez. adv.; charts; illus.; circ. 15,000. (back issues avail.)

329.3   SG
RENOVATEUR. m. Parti Democratique Senegalais - Renovation, B.P. 12172, Dakar, Senegal.

REPORT FROM THE CAPITAL. see RELIGIONS AND THEOLOGY — Protestant

REPORT FROM THE HILL. see LAW

320.9   UK   ISSN 0034-4737
D410
REPORT ON WORLD AFFAIRS. vol.52, 1971. q. £5.($14.) Fitzken Publishers, 3 Alma Square, London NW8 6QD, England. (also avail. in microform from MIM,UMI; reprint service avail. from UMI)

324.21   UK   ISSN 0034-4893
REPRESENTATION. N.S. 1960. q. $30. The Arthur McDougall Fund, 6 Chancel St., London SE1 0UU, England. TEL 071-928-1622. FAX 071-928-4366. Ed. Paul Wilder. adv.; bk.rev.; circ. 2,000. Indexed: Amer.Hum.Ind.
—BLDSC shelfmark: 7690.700000.
Representation: Journal of Electoral Record and Comment.

320   IE
REPSOL PAMPHLETS. irreg, no.7, 1971. Republican Educational Department, 30 Gardiner Place, Dublin 1, Ireland. Ed.Bd. charts.

329   US   ISSN 0363-9290
JK1967
REPUBLICAN ALMANAC. biennial. $40. Republican National Committee, Computer Services Division, 310 First St., S.E., Washington, DC 20003. TEL 202-863-8670. Ed. Clark H. Bensen. illus.

REPUBLICAN CHINA. see HISTORY — History Of Asia

320   UK   ISSN 0144-7548
REPUBLICAN ENGLISHMAN. 1979. irreg. Republican Party of England, 44 Water St., Accrington, Lancs. BB5 6QZ, England. Ed. Thomas Smith. bk.rev.; circ. 50.

POLITICAL SCIENCE

329.6   US
REPUBLICAN WOMAN. 1972. q. $15. National Federation of Republican Women, 310 First St. S.E., Washington, DC 20003. TEL 202-547-9341. FAX 202-547-8485. Ed. Karen Johnson. bk.rev.; illus.; circ. 130,000.
    Former titles (until Oct.-Nov. 1987): New Challenge (Washington); Challenge (Washington) (ISSN 0045-6233)

320   BE   ISSN 0486-4700
JA1.A1
RES PUBLICA. 1959. 4/yr. 850 Fr. Politologisch Instituut, Van Evenstraat 2B, B-3000 Louvain, Belgium. FAX 016-28-32-53. Ed. Wilfried Dewachter. circ. 1,000. **Indexed:** A.B.C.Pol.Sci., Int.Bibl.Soc.Sci., Lang.& Lang.Behav.Abstr., M.L.A., Sociol.Abstr., SSCI.

RESEARCH IN POLITICAL ECONOMY; an annual compilation of research. see BUSINESS AND ECONOMICS — Economic Systems And Theories, Economic History

RESEARCH IN SOCIAL PROBLEMS AND PUBLIC POLICY; a research annual. see SOCIOLOGY

RESEAUX; revue interdisciplinaire de philosophie morale et politique. see PHILOSOPHY

322.4   US
RESOURCE CENTER FOR NON VIOLENCE. NEWSLETTER. 1979. 2/yr. donations. Resource Center for Non Violence, 515 Broadway, Santa Cruz, CA 95060-4621. TEL 408-423-1626. Ed. Jim Wake. circ. 4,000. (tabloid format)

320   US   ISSN 1053-0754
JC330.15   CODEN: RECOEZ
▼**RESPONSIVE COMMUNITY;** rights and responsibilities. 1990. q. $24. Center for Policy Research, 2020 Pennsylvania Ave., Ste. 282, Washington, DC 20006. TEL 202-994-8194. FAX 202-994-1639. Ed. Amitai Etzioni. adv.; bk.rev.; circ. 1,500.
    Description: Explores the relationships between individual rights and community responsibilities, and the foundations of a new moral-social order.

320   PE   ISSN 0250-9792
RESUMEN SEMANAL. Running title: D E S C O Resumen Semanal. 1978. w. $100. Centro de Estudios y Promocion del (DESCO), Av. Salaverry 1945, Lima 14, Peru. (Subscr. to: PUBLIREC S.A., Jr. Guillermo Dansey 084, Lima 1, Peru) adv.; circ. 3,000.

320.5 100   UK   ISSN 0034-5970
JX1901
RESURGENCE; journal of the ecological and spiritual culture. 1966. bi-m. £20($36) Resurgence Limited, Salem Cottage, Trelill, Bodmin, Cornwall PL30 3HZ, United Kingdom. TEL 0237-441293. FAX 0237-441203. Ed. Satish Kumar. adv.; bk.rev.; index; circ. 8,500. **Indexed:** Environ.Per.Bibl., Fut.Surv.
    —BLDSC shelfmark: 7785.410000.
    Incorporates: Undercurrents (ISSN 0306-2392)

RETHINKING MARXISM. see BUSINESS AND ECONOMICS — Economic Systems And Theories, Economic History

320   IT
RETI - PRATICHE E SAPERI DI DONNE. 1987. bi-m. L.41000 (L.61000 foreign). Editori Riuniti, Via Serchio 9-11, 00198 Rome, Italy. TEL 06-866383. FAX 06-8416096. TELEX EDIRIU I 625292. Ed. Maria Luisa Boccia. bk.rev.; bibl.; illus.; circ. 12,000. (back issues avail.)
    Supersedes (1970?-1987): Donne e Politica - Women and Politics (ISSN 0393-6775)

RETORNO DEL PUEBLO. see GENERAL INTEREST PERIODICALS — Argentina

320   AT   ISSN 0310-9143
RETRIEVAL. (Text in English and French) 1971. m. Aus.$4. P.O. Box 51, Fitzroy, Vic. 3065, Australia.

320.531   FR   ISSN 0034-6292
REVEIL SOCIALISTE DE LANNEMEZAN.* 1966. m. 10 F.($2) Federation des Hautes Pyrenees du Parti Socialiste Unifie, 6 rue du 4 Septembre, Lannemezan, France. Ed. Leopold Dasque. bk.rev.; circ. 2,500.

320 330.9   UK   ISSN 0953-8259
HB1
REVIEW OF POLITICAL ECONOMY. 1989. 4/yr. £33($59) to individuals; institutions £66($125). Edward Arnold (Subsidiary of: Hodder & Stoughton), Mill Rd., Dunton Green, Sevenoaks, Kent TN13 2YA, England. TEL 0732-450111. FAX 0732-461321. (Dist. in U.S. and Canada by: Cambridge University Press, 40 W. 20th St., New York, NY 10011) Ed. John Pheby.
    —BLDSC shelfmark: 7794.119000.

920   US   ISSN 0034-6705
JA1
REVIEW OF POLITICS. 1939. q. $25 to individuals (foreign $29); institutions $30 (foreign $34). University of Notre Dame, Review of Politics, Box B, Notre Dame, IN 46556. TEL 219-239-6623. Ed. Donald P. Kommers. adv.; bk.rev.; index; circ. 1,700. (also avail. in microform from MIM,UMI; reprint service avail. from KTO,UMI) **Indexed:** A.B.C.Pol.Sci., Acad.Ind., Amer.Bibl.Slavic & E.Eur.Stud., Bk.Rev.Ind. (1980-), Cath.Ind., Child.Bk.Rev.Ind. (1980-), Curr.Cont., Hist.Abstr., Mid.East: Abstr.& Ind., P.A.I.S., Polit.Sci.Abstr., Sage Pub.Admin.Abstr., Soc.Sci.Ind., SSCI.

REVIEW OF SOCIALIST LAW. see LAW

320   AG   ISSN 0034-7019
REVISTA ARGENTINA DE CIENCIA POLITICA.* vol.2, 1961. irreg. Asociacion Argentina de Ciencia Politica, Solis 443, Buenos Aires, Argentina. bk.rev.

320   AG   ISSN 0326-6427
U4
REVISTA ARGENTINA DE ESTUDIOS ESTRATEGICOS. 1984. q. $30. (Centro Argentino de Estudios Estrategicos) Olcese Editores, Viamonte 494, Segundo Piso, Of. 8, 1053 Buenos Aires, Argentina. Ed. Haroldo Olcese. circ. 5,000.

320   AG
REVISTA ARGENTINA DE ESTUDIOS POLITICOS. 1945. 3/yr. Instituto Argentino de Estudios Politicos, Mansilla 2698, Buenos Aires, Argentina. bk.rev.; bibl.

320   AG
REVISTA ARGENTINA DE POLITICA.* 1958. irreg. Editorial Norte, Tucuman 1438, 1050 Buenos Aires, Argentina. Ed. S. W. Medraho.

320   DR
REVISTA ATENEO DOMINICANO. 1976. m. RD.$10. Calle Felix Mariano Lluberes 18, Apdo. Postal 263-2, Santo Domingo, Dominican Republic. Ed. Julio J. Julia. bk.rev.; bibl.

320   BL   ISSN 0034-7191
JA5
REVISTA BRASILEIRA DE ESTUDOS POLITICOS. (Text in Portuguese) 1956. s-a. $30. Universidade Federal de Minas Gerais, Av. A. Cabral 211, 30170 Belo Horizonte (MG), Brazil. Eds. Orlando M. Carvalho, Raul Machado Horta. adv.; bk.rev.; bibl.; charts; cum.index; circ. 3,500. **Indexed:** A.B.C.Pol.Sci., Amer.Hist.& Life, Hisp.Amer.Per.Ind., Hist.Abstr., P.A.I.S.For.Lang.Ind.
    —BLDSC shelfmark: 7844.700000.

REVISTA DE DERECHO Y CIENCIAS POLITICAS. see LAW

320   SP   ISSN 0048-7694
H8
REVISTA DE ESTUDIOS POLITICOS. (Text in Spanish; summaries in English and French) 1940. q. 900 ptas.($17) (Centro de Estudios Constitucionales) Libreria Europa, Valverde 32, 1o, 28004 Madrid, Spain. TEL 91-5325069. Ed. Pedro de Vega. bk.rev.; bibl.; circ. 1,500. **Indexed:** A.B.C.Pol.Sci., CERDIC, Hist.Abstr.
    —BLDSC shelfmark: 7854.510000.

972.8   CR   ISSN 0378-3340
F1421
REVISTA DEL PENSAMIENTO CENTROAMERICANO. 1960. q. $18 in Central America; Latin America $24; USA $24; Europe $28. Asociacion Libro Libre, Apdo. 1154-1250, Escazu, Costa Rica. FAX 286028. Ed. Xavier Zavala Cuadra. adv.; bk.rev.; bibl.; illus.; stat.; index; circ. 3,000. (also avail. in microform from UMI; reprint service avail. from UMI) **Indexed:** Amer.Hist.& Life, Hisp.Amer.Per.Ind., Hist.Abstr.
    —BLDSC shelfmark: 7869.574100.
    Formerly (1960-1972): Revista Conservadora del Pensamiento Centroamericano (ISSN 0034-7477)

320 330.9   BL   ISSN 0101-3157
HC186
REVISTA ECONOMIA POLITICA. q. $40. Editora Brasiliense S.A., Rua da Consolacao, 2697, 01416 Sao Paulo, Brazil. TEL 011-02801222.

320   DR
REVISTA ESTUDIOS DOMINICANOS. 1984. 3/yr. $8. (Instituto de Estudios Dominicanos) Liberia America, Apdo. Postal 20693, Calle Ciriaco Ramirez No. 49, 3 Piso, Santo Domingo, Dominican Republic. circ. 300.

320   SP   ISSN 0210-7716
D1
REVISTA HISTORIA, INSTITUCIONES, DOCUMENTOS. (Text in Greek, Latin, Spanish) 1974. a. price varies. Universidad de Sevilla, Departamentos de Historia Medieval, Historia del Derecho, Paleografia y Diplomatica, Servicio de Publicaciones, San Fernando, 4, 41004 Seville, Spain.
TEL 954-22-8071. FAX 954-22-1315.

320   MX   ISSN 0185-1918
JA5
REVISTA MEXICANA DE CIENCIAS POLITICAS Y SOCIALES. 1955. q. $12. Universidad Nacional Autonoma de Mexico, Facultad de Ciencias Politicas y Sociales, Villa Obregon, Ciudad Universitaria, Mexico 20, D.F., Mexico. Ed. Rosa Maria Velasco. adv.; bk.rev.; bibl.; charts; index; circ. 2,000. **Indexed:** A.B.C.Pol.Sci., Hisp.Amer.Per.Ind., Hist.Abstr., Lang.& Lang.Behav.Abstr.
    Former titles: Revista Mexicana de Ciencia Politica (ISSN 0034-9976); Ciencias Politicas y Sociales.

320 342   SP   ISSN 0211-5581
JA26
REVISTA POLITICA COMPARADA. 1980. q. 1500 ptas. Universidad Internacional Menendez Pelayo, Palacio de la Magdalena, Santander, Spain. (Dist. by: Distribuciones Oficiales Reunidas, S.A., C. Plaza 15, 2o piso, 28043 Madrid, Spain. TEL 759-70-49) circ. 2,500.

320.531   US   ISSN 0193-3612
REVOLUTION. Spanish edition: Revolucion (ISSN 0193-3493) 1973. irreg., approx. 2/yr. $14 to individuals; libraries $20. (Revolutionary Communist Party, Central Committee) R C P Publications, Inc., Box 3486, Merchandise Mart, Chicago, IL 60654. TEL 312-663-5920. bk.rev.; index; circ. 5,000. (also avail. in microfilm from UMI; reprint service avail. from UMI) **Indexed:** Alt.Press Ind.

960 322.4   AE   ISSN 0035-0621
REVOLUTION AFRICAINE. (Text in French) 1963. w. $126. Front de Liberation Nationale, 7 rue du Stade, Hydra, Algiers, Algeria. (Dist. in US by: African Imprint Library Service, Box 350, West Falmouth, MA 02574. TEL 508-540-5378) Ed. Zoubir Zemzoum. adv.; bk.rev.; film rev.; play rev.; charts; illus.; circ. 5,000.

331.88   AE   ISSN 0484-8365
REVOLUTION ET TRAVAIL. (Editions in Arabic, French) m. Union General des Travailleurs Algeriens, 1 rue Abdelkader Benbarek, Pl. du 1er Mai, Algiers, Algeria. TEL 2-66-73-53. TELEX 65051. (Dist. in US by: African Imprint Library Service, Box 350, West Falmouth, MA 02574. TEL 508-540-5378) Ed. Lakhdari Mohamed Lakhdar.

320   MG
REVOLUTION MALAGASY; international d'information et d'analyse. 1982. q. Ministere de l'Information de l'Animation Ideologique et de la Cooperativisation, P.O. Box 271, Antananarivo 101, Malagasy Republic. Ed. Adolphe Randriakoto.

329.82 US ISSN 0193-3485
REVOLUTIONARY WORKER. Spanish edition: Obrero Revolucunario. 1979. w. $40 to individuals; institutions $52. (Revolutionary Communist Party) R C P Publications, Inc., Box 3486, Merchandise Mart, Chicago, IL 60654. TEL 312-663-5920. bk.rev.; charts; illus.; stat.; tr.lit.; index; circ. 50,000. (tabloid format; back issues avail.)

REVUE ALGERIENNE DES SCIENCES JURIDIQUES. see *LAW*

341 327 SZ ISSN 0035-1091
JX3
REVUE DE DROIT INTERNATIONAL DE SCIENCES DIPLOMATIQUES ET POLITIQUES. (Text in English, French, German, Italian) 1923. q. 180 Fr. Case Postale 138, CH-1211 Geneva 12, Switzerland. FAX 022-29-22-06. TELEX 427-019 CH. Ed. C.L. Heinbach. index. (reprint service avail. SWZ)
—BLDSC shelfmark: 7898.520000.

956 960 SY ISSN 0035-1245
REVUE DE LA PRESSE ARABE. (Text in French) 1948. s-w. £S4500($700) Office Arabe de Presse et de Documentation, P.O. Box 3550, 67 Place Chahbandar, Damascus, Syria. Ed. A. Khani.
 Formerly: Bulletin de la Presse Arabe.

REVUE DU DROIT PUBLIC ET DE LA SCIENCE POLITIQUE EN FRANCE ET A L'ETRANGER. see *LAW*

960 SG ISSN 0035-3027
DT1
REVUE FRANCAISE D'ETUDES POLITIQUES AFRICAINES. 1966. m. 12000 Fr.CFA. Societe Africaine d'Edition, B.P. 1877, Dakar, Senegal. (And 32 rue de l'Echiquier, Paris, France) adv.; bk.rev.; bibl.; charts; index; circ. 4,000. **Indexed:** Curr.Cont.Africa, Int.Lab.Doc., Rural Recreat.Tour.Abstr., World Agri.Econ.& Rural Sociol.Abstr.

320 SG ISSN 0338-2060
DE100
REVUE FRANCAISE D'ETUDES POLITIQUES MEDITERRANEENNES. 1975. m. (10/yr.). 10000 Fr.CFA. Societe Africaine d'Edition, B.P. 1877, Dakar, Senegal. (And 32 rue de l'Echiquier, Paris, France) Ed. Paulette Decraene. **Indexed:** Rural Recreat.Tour.Abstr., World Agri.Econ.& Rural Sociol.Abstr.

320 FR ISSN 0035-2950
JA11
REVUE FRANCAISE DE SCIENCE POLITIQUE. (Text in French, summaries in English, French) 1951. bi-m. 350 F. to individuals (foreign 390 F.); institutions 600 F. (foreign 650 F.); students 245 F. (Fondation Nationale des Sciences Politiques) Presses de la Fondation Nationale des Sciences Politiques, 27 rue Saint Guillaume, 75341 Paris Cedex 07, France. TEL 1-45-49-50-50. FAX 1-45-48-04-41. TELEX 201 002 F. (Co-sponsor: Association Francaise de Science Politique) Ed. Georges Lavau. bk.rev.; abstr.; bibl.; index; circ. 3,500. **Indexed:** A.B.C.Pol.Sci., E.I., Hist.Abstr., Int.Lab.Doc., P.A.I.S.For.Lang.Ind., Pt.de Rep. (1979-), SSCI.
—BLDSC shelfmark: 7904.420000.
 Description: Scientific presentation of research, ideas and methodological criticism of politics.

320 CN ISSN 0702-8571
F1053.2
REVUE INDEPENDANTISTE; la voix du Canada reel. (Text in French) 1977. irreg. Can.$36 for 12 nos. Editions du Franc-Canada, 1849 rue Amherst, Montreal, Que. H2L 3L7, Canada. Ed. Raoul Roy. bk.rev.; circ. 1,000. (back issues avail.) **Indexed:** Pt.de Rep.

320.532 FR
REVUE INTERNATIONALE DU MOUVEMENT COMMUNISTE. Portuguese edition: Comunismo ou Civilizacao. 1976. s-a. $7. B.P. 88, 75722 Paris Cedex 15, France. Ed. D. Cotte. circ. 500.
 Formerly: Communisme ou Civilisation.

320 328 FR ISSN 0035-385X
REVUE POLITIQUE ET PARLEMENTAIRE; economie, finance, urbanisme. 1894. bi-m. 610 F. (effective 1991). 110 rue de Rivoli, 75001 Paris, France. adv.; bk.rev.; charts; illus.; stat.; index; circ. 10,000. (also avail. in microform) **Indexed:** P.A.I.S.For.Lang.Ind.
—BLDSC shelfmark: 7942.550000.

320.531 FR ISSN 0035-4139
REVUE SOCIALISTE; revue de culture politique et sociale. 1885. m. 77 F.($15.50) Parti Socialiste et Cercle d'Etudes Socialistes Jean Jaures, 16 rue Vigee Le Brun, 75015 Paris, France. Ed. R. Pagosse. adv.; bk.rev.; index.

968.9 RH ISSN 0035-4694
RHODESIA AND WORLD REPORT. 1966. m. I.G. Anderson, Ed. & Pub., 52 Baines Ave., Harare, Zimbabwe. adv.; bk.rev.; circ. 6,000. (back issues avail.)

RIGHT TO KNOW AND THE FREEDOM TO ACT. see *POLITICAL SCIENCE — Civil Rights*

320.9 IT ISSN 0035-5380
RINASCITA; rassegna politica di attualita, economia, e cultura. (Supplement to: Contemporaneo) 1944. w. L.16000. Unita S.p.A., Via d' Aracoeli 13, 00186 Rome, Italy. TEL 06-4951251. Ed. Luciano Barca. adv.; bk.rev.; abstr.; bibl.; charts; illus.; index; circ. 80,000.

320.5 US ISSN 0035-5526
JK2351
RIPON FORUM. 1965-1980; resumed 1981. bi-m $30 to individuals; students $17.50. Ripon Society, 709 Second St., N.E., Ste. 100, Washington, DC 20002. TEL 202-546-1292. Ed. Bradley Kendall. adv.; bk.rev.; cum.index; circ. 3,500. (also avail. in microfilm from UMI; reprint service avail. from UMI)
 Formerly: Ripon Society Newsletter.

322 PO ISSN 0870-9912
RISCO. 1985. 4/yr. $15. Editorial Fragmentos, Av. Infante Santo, 21-1o Dto., 1300 Lisbon, Portugal. Dir. Joao Carlos Espada. adv.; bk.rev.; circ. 2,000.

320 II
RISING SUN. (Text in English) 1971. w. Rs.15. 52-A Kodam Bakkam, High Road, Madras 600034, India. Ed. Murasoli Maran. adv.; bk.rev.; illus.

320 GW
RISSENER JAHRBUCH. 1956. a. DM.25. Rissener Landstr. 193, 2000 Hamburg 56, Germany. TEL 040-81-80-21. Ed. Hans Rissen. index; circ. 2,000. (back issues avail.)

320 GW
RISSENER RUNDBRIEF. 1956. m. DM.40. Rissener Landstr. 193, 2000 Hamburg 56, Germany. TEL 040-818021. Ed. Hans Rissen. circ. 2,500. (back issues avail.)

RIVISTA AMMINISTRATIVA DELLA REPUBBLICA ITALIANA. see *LAW*

320 IT
RIVISTA D'EUROPA.* 1978. q. L.25000. Cadmo Editore s.r.l., C.P. 6225, 00100 Rome, Italy. Ed. Lido Chiusano.

320 IT ISSN 0048-8402
JA18
RIVISTA ITALIANA DI SCIENZA POLITICA. (Text in Italian; summaries in English) 1971. 3/yr. L.100000. Societa Editrice Il Mulino, Strada Maggiore, 37, 40125 Bologna, Italy. TEL 051-256011. FAX 051-256034. Eds. Giovanni Sartori, Leonardo Morlino. adv.; bk.rev.; bibl.; index; circ. 1,700. (tabloid format; back issues avail.) **Indexed:** A.B.C.Pol.Sci., Hist.Abstr., Lang.& Lang.Behav.Abstr., SSCI.
—BLDSC shelfmark: 7987.605000.

320.5 IC ISSN 0034-6195
RJETTUR. 1916. q. $20. Sidumula 6, Reykjavik, Iceland. Ed. Einar Olgeirsson. adv.; bk.rev.; index; circ. 2,500.

320.532 CN ISSN 0047-6110
ROAD OF THE PARTY. 1970. irreg. Can.$20. Communist Party of Canada (Marxist - Leninist), Central Committee, Box 666, Station C, Montreal, Que., Canada. TEL 416-252-3658. (Dist. by: National Publications Centre, Box 727, Adelaide Station, Toronto, Ont. M5C 2J8, Canada) Ed. Hardial S. Bains. charts; illus.
 Formerly (until 1980): Mass Line.

335 UK ISSN 0483-2027
ROBOTNIK. (Text in Polish; summaries in English) vol.81, 1975. q. Polish Socialist Party in Exile, 84 Fordhook Ave., London W. 5, England. Ed. Leszek Talko. bk.rev.; circ. 2,000.

329.9 MY ISSN 0048-8461
ROCKET. vol.6, 1971. bi-m. M.$3.20. Democratic Action Party of Malaysia, 77 Jalan, 20-9 Paramount Garden, Petaling Jaya, Selangor, Malaysia. FAX 04-361909. Ed.Bd. bk.rev.; charts; illus.; circ. 35,000. (tabloid format)

320 350 II
ROLE OF STATE LEGISLATURES IN THE FREEDOM STRUGGLE. 1976. irreg. Rs.30. Indian Council of Historical Research, 35 Ferozeshah Rd., New Delhi 110001, India. (Distributed by: People's Publishing House Ltd., Rani Jhansi Rd., New Delhi 110 005, India)

ROTE BAUSTEINE. see *CHILDREN AND YOUTH — For*

320.532 GW ISSN 0936-1421
ROTE FAHNE; Wochenzeitung der M L P D. 1970. w. DM.45. (Marxistisch-Leninistische Partei Deutschland) Neuer Weg Verlag & Druck GmbH, Kaninenberghoehe 2, 4300 Essen 1, Germany. TEL 0201-25914. bk.rev.; illus.

320.531 SZ
ROTE REVUE;* Sozialdemokratische Zeitschrift fuer Politik, Wirtschaft und Kultur. 1921. m. 38 Fr. Sozialdemokratische Partei der Schweiz, Genossenschaftsdruckerei, CH-4600 Olten, Switzerland. Ed. Toya Maissen. adv.; bk.rev.; index; circ. 3,000.
 Former titles: Rote Revue - Profil; Profil; Rote Revue (ISSN 0035-8428)

320.532 GW ISSN 0939-2947
ROTER MORGEN. 1967. m. DM.15. (Kommunistischen Partei Deutschlands) Zeitungsverlag Roter Morgen, Postfach 401051, 7000 Stuttgart 40, Germany. TEL 069-6314378. FAX 069-6314379. (Subscr. to: Postfach 1942, 6380 Bad Homburg, Germany) circ. 800. (looseleaf format; back issues avail.)

320 FR
ROUGE. 1969. 2 rue Richard Lenoir, 93100 Montreuil, France. TEL 48-59-00-80. circ. 10,000.

322.4 FR ISSN 0151-5772
ROYALISTE; bi-mensuel de l'action Royaliste. 1971. bi-m. 270 F. Societe Nationale Presse Francaise, 17 rue des Petits Champs, 75001 Paris, France. TEL 42-97-42-47. Ed. Bertrand Renouvin. bk.rev.; film rev.; circ. 15,000. (back issues avail.)
 Formerly: N.A.F.

320 US
ROYALTON REVIEW. 1966. q. $10. Royalton College Press, Box 218, South Royalton, VT 05068. TEL 802-763-7766. Ed. Edwin G. Dolan. **Indexed:** P.A.I.S.

320 AA
RRUGA E PARTISE. m. $9.24. Parti du Travail d'Albanie, Tirana, Albania.

LA RUE; revue culturelle et litteraire d'expression anarchiste. see *LITERARY AND POLITICAL REVIEWS*

320 US ISSN 1055-3908
RURAL SOUTHERN VOICE FOR PEACE. 1981. bi-m. $25. (Fellowship for Reconciliation) Rural Southern Voice for Peace, 1898 Hannah Branch Rd., Burnsville, NC 28714. TEL 704-675-5933. Ed. Clare Hanrahan. bk.rev.; circ. 2,500. (also avail. in microform from UMI; back issues avail.)
 Description: Promotes grassroots organizing to build a network of nonviolent activism to foster peace, ecological awareness, and political, spiritual and social alternatives in the rural communities and small cities of the southeastern US.

RUSSIAN POLITICS; a journal of translations. see *LAW*

947 US
AS261
RUSSIAN SOCIAL SCIENCE REVIEW; a journal of translations. 1960. bi-m. $80. M.E. Sharpe, Inc., 80 Business Park Dr., Armonk, NY 10504. TEL 914-273-1800. FAX 914-273-2106. Ed. Patricia A. Kolb. adv.; index. (also avail. in microform from UMI) **Indexed:** Mid.East: Abstr.& Ind., P.A.I.S., Soc.Sci.Ind.
 Formerly: Soviet Review.
 Refereed Serial

S A I P A; journal of public administration-tydskrif vir publieke administrasie. (South African Institute of Public Administration) see *PUBLIC ADMINISTRATION*

POLITICAL SCIENCE

320 **US**
S C A FREE SPEECH YEARBOOK. 1960. a. price varies. (Speech Communication Association) Southern Illinois University Press, Box 3697, Carbondale, IL 62901. TEL 618-453-2281. FAX 618-453-1221. Ed. Dale Herbeck. bk.rev.; circ. 700.
Formerly: Freedom of Speech Yearbook (ISSN 0071-9366)

329.9 **DK** **ISSN 0902-1612**
S F. STATUS. 1975. a. DKK 95. Socialistiske Perspektiver Forlag, Silkeborgvej 13, DK-8000 Aarhus C, Denmark. TEL 45 86 19 79 82. Eds. Dorete Dandanell, Lars Kjargaard. adv.; bk.rev.; circ. 800.
Former titles: Socialistisk Folkeparti. Status (ISSN 0108-7908); S F Status.

329.9 **SZ**
S O I-BILANZ. 1975. m. 150 Fr. Schweizerisches Ost-Institut - Swiss Eastern Institute, Jubilaeumsstr. 41, CH-3000 Berne 6, Switzerland. Eds. Peter Sager, Jacques Baumgartner. circ. 2,500.

320 301 **GW** **ISSN 0170-4613**
S P W. (Sozialistische Politik und Wirtschaft) 1978. bi-m. DM.51. S P W Verlag, Kielerstr. 13, 5000 Cologne 80, Germany. TEL 0221-623271. FAX 0221-612815. Ed.Bd. adv.; bk.rev.; circ. 3,000. (back issues avail.)

320 **AU** **ISSN 0036-1585**
S Z.* (Sozialwirtschaftliche Korrespondenz) (Text in German) vol.22, 1973. m. S.220. Ed. Magdalena Troestler, Christian-Coulin Str. 13, Postfach 324, A-4021 Linz, Austria. adv.; bk.rev.; bibl.

320 340 **US** **ISSN 0486-8161**
SACRAMENTO NEWSLETTER. 1947. w. $60. Susan Wilson, Ed. & Pub., Box 214651, Sacramento, CA 95821-0651. TEL 916-483-0760. FAX 916-961-5570. circ. 750. (back issues avail.)
Description: Overview of state legislation, government and politics.

320 **US**
SAGE YEARBOOKS IN POLITICS AND PUBLIC POLICY. 1975. a. $17.95 softcover; hardcover $36. (Policy Studies Organization) Sage Publications, Inc., 2455 Teller Rd., Newbury Park, CA 91320. TEL 805-499-0721. FAX 805-499-0871. (And Sage Publications, Ltd., 6 Bonhill St., London EC2A 4PU, England) Ed. Stuart S. Nagel. bibl.; charts; illus.; stat. (back issues avail.)

965 **FR** **ISSN 0036-2638**
SAHARA; bulletin d'information. 1957. bi-m. 1296 F. (foreign 1560 F.). Agence France-Presse, 13 Place de la Bourse, B.P. 20, 75061 Paris Cedex 2, France. TEL 40-41-46-46. TELEX 210064 AFPA. bk.rev.; bibl.; stat.
Description: Economic and political problems concerning Sahara (Algeria) and neighboring countries.

320 **MG**
SAHY. (Text in Malagasy) 1957. Lot VD 42, Ambanidia, 101 Antananarivo, Malagasy Republic. TEL 22715. Ed. Aline Rakoto. circ. 9,000.

ST. VINCENT GOVERNMENT INFORMATION SERVICE NEWS BULLETIN. see *PUBLIC ADMINISTRATION*

320.532 **CE**
SAMAJAWADHAYA. (Text in Sinhala) m. Communist Party of Sri Lanka, 91 Dr. N.M. Perera Mawatha, Colombo 8, Sri Lanka. TEL 1-595328.

SAMISDAT; Stimmen aus den "anderen Russland". see *HISTORY — History Of Europe*

320 **US**
SAN DIEGO LIBERTARIAN. 1973. m. $12. San Diego Libertarian Party, Box 16449, San Diego, CA 92176. TEL 619-276-1776. FAX 619-274-1776. Ed. Betsy Mill. adv.; bk.rev.; circ. 900. (back issues avail.)
Description: Newsletter with events and articles of interest to people with a distaste for big government at every level.

SAN DIEGO POLITICAL WATCH. see *PUBLIC ADMINISTRATION — Municipal Government*

320 **SZ**
ST. GALLER STUDIEN ZUR POLITIKWISSENSCHAFT. 1975. irreg., no.13, 1989. price varies. Paul Haupt AG, Falkenplatz 14, CH-3001 Berne, Switzerland. TEL 031-232425.

320 297 **II**
SANT SIPAHI. (Text in Punjabi) vol.27, 1972. m. Rs.10. Lal Haveli, Gate Mahan Singh, Amritsar 24, India. adv.
Description: Covers Sikh politics and religion.

954.9 **BG**
SAPTAHIKA THIKANA. Variant title: Thikana. (Text in Bengali) 1976. w. Tk.0.50 per no. Abul Hossain Mir, Ed. & Pub., Press Club Bhavan, Mujib Sarak, Jessore, Bangladesh.
Description: Covers political news and views.

954 **II**
SATYACHAR. (Text in Gujarati) 1947. fortn. Rs.5. Shukla Hariprasad, Ed. & Pub., Halvad 363330, Gujarat, India. adv.; circ. 500.
Former titles: Red Light; Sahakar (ISSN 0036-2603)

322.4 **US**
SATYAGRAHA;* truth force. 1969. 5/yr. $30. Clergy and Laity Concerned, Metro Chicago Chapter, 59 E. Van Buren St., Ste. 1400, Chicago, IL 60605-1218. Ed. John Montgomery. adv.; bk.rev.; illus.; circ. 1,500. (tabloid format)
Description: News articles, essays, and announcements pertaining to the members and activities of the Chicago Clergy and Laity Concerned, which espouses positive social change through educational and political action promoting peace and equality.

945 **IT** **ISSN 0036-5157**
SAVOIA. 1962. bi-m. free. Gruppo Savoia, Casella Postale 1233, 20101 Milan, Italy. Ed.Bd. bk.rev.; illus.; circ. 1,600.

SCALA; a periodical from the Federal Republic of Germany. see *GENERAL INTEREST PERIODICALS — Germany*

320 **NO** **ISSN 0080-6757**
JN7001
SCANDINAVIAN POLITICAL STUDIES. (Text in English) 1965; N.S. 1978. 4/yr. $78. (Nordic Political Science Association) Universitetsforlaget, P.O. Box 2959-Toeyen, N-0608 Oslo 1, Norway. (U.S. addr.: Publications Expediting Inc., 200 Meacham Ave., Elmont, NY 11003) Eds. Lawrence Rose, Knut Heidar. adv.; bk.rev.; bibl.; index; circ. 600. (also avail. in microform from UMI; back issues avail.; reprint service avail. from ISI) Indexed: A.B.C.Pol.Sci., Hist.Abstr., Stud.Wom.Abstr.
—BLDSC shelfmark: 8087.572000.
Supersedes (1968-1977): Scandinavian Political Studies Yearbook.

SCARLET WOMAN; socialist feminist magazine. see *WOMEN'S INTERESTS*

943 **GW** **ISSN 0036-6250**
LAW
SCHOEFFE; Zeitschrift fuer Schoeffen und Schiedskommissionen. 1954. m. DM.24. (Ministerium fuer Justiz) Staatsverlag der DDR, Otto-Grotewohl-Str. 17, 1086 Berlin, Germany. adv.; bk.rev.; charts; index; circ. 52,000.

320 **US**
SCHOOL OF INTERNATIONAL STUDIES. PUBLICATIONS ON RUSSIA AND EASTERN EUROPE. 1969. irreg., no.12, 1983. price varies. (University of Washington, School of International Studies) University of Washington Press, Box 50096, Seattle, WA 98105. TEL 206-543-4050.
Formerly: Publications on Russia and Eastern Europe (ISSN 0079-7790)
Refereed Serial

SCHULER LECTURES IN HISTORY AND POLITICAL SCIENCE. see *HISTORY*

322.4 801 792 **GW** **ISSN 0722-8988**
SCHWARZER FADEN; Vierteljahresschrift fuer Lust und Freiheit. 1980. q. DM.20. Trotzdem Verlag, Postfach 1159, 7043 Grafenau 1, Germany. TEL 07033-45273. FAX 07033-44264. Ed. Wolfgang Haug. adv.; bk.rev.; bibl.; illus.; film rev.; play rev.; cum.index; circ. 3,000.

320 358 290 **US** **ISSN 0048-9581**
Q127.U6
SCIENCE AND GOVERNMENT REPORT. 1971. s-m. $325. Science and Government Reports, Inc., Box 6226A, Northwest Sta., Washington, DC 20015. TEL 800-522-1970. Ed. Daniel S. Greenberg. bk.rev.; circ. 1,500. (also avail. in microform from UMI; reprint service avail. from UMI)
Description: Provides news and analysis of policy and political developments that affect research and development.

300 500 **US** **ISSN 0036-8237**
H1
SCIENCE AND SOCIETY; an independent journal of Marxism. 1936. q. $20 to individuals; institutions $60. Guilford Publications, Inc., 72 Spring St., 4th Fl., New York, NY 10012. TEL 212-431-9800. FAX 212-966-6708. Ed. David Laibman. adv.; bk.rev.; index, cum.index every 25 yrs.; circ. 2,300. (also avail. in microform from MIM,UMI,KTO; reprint service avail. from UMI,ISI,SCH) Indexed: A.B.C.Pol.Sci., Acad.Ind., Alt.Press Ind., Amer.Bibl.Slavic & E.Eur.Stud., Amer.Hist.& Life, ASCA, ASSIA, Bk.Rev.Ind. (1965-), Child.Bk.Rev.Ind. (1965-), Curr.Cont., Energy Ind., Energy Info.Abstr., Hist.Abstr., Int.Lab.Doc., J.of Econ.Lit., Lang.& Lang.Behav.Abstr., Left Ind. (1982-), Mid.East: Abstr.& Ind., P.A.I.S., So.Pac.Per.Ind., Soc.Sci.Ind., SSCI.
—BLDSC shelfmark: 8134.190000.
Description: Examines new ideas in economic and social thought.
Refereed Serial

SCIENCE AS CULTURE. see *SCIENCES: COMPREHENSIVE WORKS*

SCIENCE, TECHNOLOGY & DEVELOPMENT. see *BUSINESS AND ECONOMICS — International Development And Assistance*

322.4 280 **US**
SCOREBOARD ALERT; grassroots citizens working an agenda for the preservation of American values. 1989. bi-m. $14. National Citizens Action Network, Box 10459, Costa Mesa, CA 92627. TEL 714-850-0349. FAX 714-662-3952. Ed. David W. Balsiger. adv.; bk.rev.; film rev.; circ. 100,000. (back issues avail.)
Description: Covers legislative and governmental issues from a conservative Christian viewpoint.

941 **UK** **ISSN 0036-9071**
SCOTS INDEPENDENT. 1926. m. £6.50. Scots Independent (Newspapers) Ltd., 51 Cowane St., Stirling FK8 1JW, Scotland. Ed. Kenneth Fee. adv.; bk.rev.; play rev.; stat.; circ. 9,000. (tabloid format)

320 **UK**
SCOTTISH GOVERNMENT YEARBOOK. 1976. a. price varies. Unit for the Study of Government in Scotland, 31 Buccleuch Place, Edinburgh EH8 9JT, Scotland. FAX 031-667-7938. Ed. Lindsay Patterson. adv.; bk.rev.; bibl.; stat.; circ. 900. (back issues avail.)

320 **UK** **ISSN 0262-4591**
SEARCHLIGHT. 1975. m. £25 to individuals; institutions £30. Searchlight Publishing Ltd., 37B New Cavendish St., London W1M 8JR, England. TEL 01-928 9801. Ed. Gerry Gable. adv.; bk.rev.; illus.; index; circ. 8,000. (back issues avail.)

320 355 **US**
HV6432
SECURITY INTELLIGENCE REPORT. 1986. bi-w. $350. Interests, Ltd., 8512 Cedar St., Silver Spring, MD 20910. TEL 301-588-7916. FAX 301-588-2085. Ed. Frank G. McGuire. adv.; bk.rev.
●Also available online. Vendor(s): NewsNet.
Former titles: Counter-Terrorism and Security Intelligence; Counter-Terrorism (ISSN 0887-6398)
Description: Focuses on security intelligence, aviation security and terrorism.

909 **JA** **ISSN 0582-4532**
AP95.J2
SEKAI/WORLD. (Text in Japanese) 1946. m. 8100 Yen. Iwanami Shoten Publishers, 2-5-5 Hitotsubashi, Chiyoda-ku, Tokyo 101-02, Japan. FAX 03-3239-9618. (Dist. overseas by: Japan Publications Trading Co., Ltd., Box 5030, Tokyo International, Tokyo 100-31, Japan; Or: 1255 Howard St., San Francisco, CA 94103) circ. 100,000.

| 320 | US |

▼**SELF-GOVERNANCE.** 1990. biennial. free. Institute for Contemporary Studies, 243 Kearny St., San Francisco, CA 94108. TEL 415-981-5353. FAX 415-986-4878. Ed. Elise Bylan. bk.rev.; circ. 12,000.
  Description: Explores the theory and practice of self-government world-wide, through past and present experimentation and evolving literature.

| 320 | IS | ISSN 0334-889X |

SEMANA. (Text in Spanish) 1973. w. $112. Semana Publishing Co. Ltd., P.O. Box 2427, Jerusalem 91023, Israel. FAX 2-290774. TELEX 26174-BXJM-IL-7644. Ed. Salomon Lewinsky. adv.; bk.rev.; circ. 12,000. (back issues avail.)

| 329.9 | CU |

SEMANARIO INFANTIL PIONERO. w. $50 in N. America; S. America $72; Europe $82; elsewhere $85. (Union de Jovenes Comunistas (UJC), Organizacion de Pioneros "Jose Marti") Ediciones Cubanas, Obispo No. 527, Apdo. 605, Havana, Cuba. TEL 32-5556-60. Dir. Pedro Gonzalez. illus.; circ. 210,000.

| 320 | CR |

SEMANARIO LIBERTAD. 1962. w. Partido del Pueblo Costarricense, Apdo. 10138, Calle 4, Avda. 8 y 10, 1000 San Jose, Costa Rica. TEL 23-7651. Ed. Jose A. Zuniga. circ. 10,000.

SEMINARIA PA'LANTE. see *LITERARY AND POLITICAL REVIEWS*

| 320 | US |

SENATE REPORT. 19791. q. $35. Conservative Caucus Research Analysis and Evaluation Foundation, 450 Maple Ave. E., Vienna, VA 22180. TEL 703-281-6782. Ed. Howard Phillips.
  Description: Covers selected U.S. Senate votes.

SENNACHIE. see *HISTORY*

SEQUOIA (SAN FRANCISCO); news of religion & society. see *RELIGIONS AND THEOLOGY*

| 320 | FR | ISSN 0080-8938 |

SERIE AFRIQUE NOIRE. 1970. irreg. price varies. (Institut d'Etudes Politiques de Bordeaux) Editions A. Pedone, 13 rue Soufflot, 75005 Paris, France.

SERIE NOVAS PERSPECTIVAS. see *HISTORY — History Of North And South America*

| 320 | FR | ISSN 0586-9889 |

SERIE VIE LOCALE. 1969. irreg. price varies. (Institut d'Etudes Politiques de Bordeaux, Centre d'Etude et de Recherche sur la Vie Locale) Editions A. Pedone, 13 rue Soufflot, 75005 Paris, France.

| 325 | IT | ISSN 0037-2803 |

SERVIZIO MIGRANTI. 1965. bi-m. L.45000. Fondazione Migrantes, Via Aurelia, 481, 00165 Rome, Italy. FAX 06-662-0530. TELEX 623328 UCEI I. adv.; bk.rev.; stat.; index; circ. 2,700.
  Formerly: Ufficio Centrale per l'Emigrazione Italiana, Bollettino.

SEVERNI MORAVA. see *HISTORY — History Of Europe*

| 329.9 | JA |

SHAKAI SHINPO. s-w. 800 Yen per month. Social Democratic Party of Japan - Nihon Shakaito, 1-8-1 Nagato-cho, Chiyoda-ku, Tokyo, Japan. FAX 81-03-3580-0691.

| 320 | UK | ISSN 0262-9860 |

SHAKTI. 1978. m. £12. (National Association for Asian Youth) Catbird Productions Ltd., 46 High St., Southall, Middx. UB1 3DB, England. Ed. Ravi Jain. adv.; bk.rev.; film rev.; circ. 8,500. (back issues avail.)
  Formerly: N A A Y Information Bulletin.

HA-SHAVUA. see *BUSINESS AND ECONOMICS — Cooperatives*

SHIMANE LAW REVIEW. see *LAW*

| 320 | MP |

SHINE UYE/NEW GENERATION. (Text in English, Mongolian) w. 120 tugrik($1) Mongolian Newspaper Company, Erkhuu Street - 5, Ulan Bator, Mongolia. TEL 55208. Ed. S. Amarsanaa. circ. 15,000. (tabloid format)

SHVUT; Jewish problems in the USSR and Eastern Europe. see *ETHNIC INTERESTS*

SIMMONS POLITICAL REPORT. see *PUBLIC ADMINISTRATION*

| 320 954.9 | PK |

SIND JOURNAL OF POLITICAL SCIENCE AND MODERN HISTORY; an international publication. (Text in English) 1975. s-a. Rs.25($10) University of Sind, Department of Political Science & Modern History, Jamshoro, Sind, Pakistan. (Subscr. in U.S., Canada, and other Western countries to: Edinboro State College, Office of International Education, Box 318, Edinboro, PA 16412) (Co-sponsor: Edinboro State College, Department of History) Ed.Bd. adv.

SINSEMILLA TIPS; domestic marijuana journal. see *GARDENING AND HORTICULTURE*

SINTESE. see *PHILOSOPHY*

SIR GEORGE EARLE MEMORIAL LECTURE ON INDUSTRY AND GOVERNMENT. see *BUSINESS AND ECONOMICS*

| 954 | NP | ISSN 0049-0628 |
| HC497.N5 | | |

SIRJANA; an English journal of Nepal's economic, social and political developments, reviews and excerpts. 1971. m. Rs.1. per no. 1-202 Dilli Bazar, Kathmandu, Nepal. Ed. Hari Dhoj Pant. adv.; bk.rev.; charts; illus.

| 320.532 | CC |

SIXIANG ZHENGZHI GONGZUO YANJIU/STUDY IN IDEOLOGY AND POLITICS. (Text in Chinese) m. Zhongguo Zhigong Sixiang Zhengzhi Gongzuo Yanjiuhui, Dong Yuan, 9 Xihuangchenggen Nanjie, Dong Cheng Qu, Beijing 100032, People's Republic of China. TEL 66-6982. Ed. Yang Wenshang.

| 320 | LE |

SIYASSA WAS STRATEGIA/POLITICS AND STRATEGY/POLITIQUE ET STRATEGIE. (Text in Arabic) 1981. 36/yr. $1,250. Dar Naaman lil-Thaqafah, P.O. Box 567, Jounieh, Lebanon. TEL 09-935096. Ed. Naji Naaman. index.
  Description: Covers regional political, economic, and strategic issues affecting the Middle East.

SKUPNOST; glasilo Slovenske skupnosti. see *ETHNIC INTERESTS*

SLEZSKE MUZEUM. CASOPIS. SERIE B. VEDY HISTORICKE. see *HISTORY — History Of Europe*

SLOVAK PRESS DIGEST. see *ETHNIC INTERESTS*

SLOVANSKE STUDIE. see *HISTORY — History Of Europe*

| 943.7 947 | CS | ISSN 0037-6922 |

SLOVANSKY PREHLED/SLAVONIC REVIEW. (Text in Czech; summaries in English, German, Russian) 1898. bi-m. DM.141. (Czechoslovak Academy of Sciences, Czechoslovak - Soviet Institute) Academia, Publishing House of the Czechoslovak Academy of Sciences, Vodickova 40, 112 29 Prague 1, Czechoslovakia. TEL 53-15-45. (Dist. in Western countries by: Kubon & Sagner, P.O. Box 34 01 08, 8000 Munich 34, Germany) Ed. Antonin Dolejsi. bk.rev.; abstr.; illus.; index, cum.index; circ. 1,750. **Indexed:** Hist.Abstr.
  —BLDSC shelfmark: 8309.600000.
  Description: Scholarly articles on the history and culture of the central, southeast and east European nations, their mutual relations and their relations to the West.

SLOVENSKA AKADEMIJA ZNANOSTI IN UMETNOSTI. FILOZOFSKI VESTNIK. see *PHILOSOPHY*

SLOVENSKA ARCHIVISTIKA. see *HISTORY — History Of Europe*

| 943.7 322.4 | CN | ISSN 0037-6957 |

SLOVENSKA DRZAVA; for a free Slovenia. (Text in Slovenian; summaries in English and Slovenian) 1949. m. Can.$12. (Slovenian National Federation of Canada) Weller Publishing Co. Ltd., 412 Bloor St. W., Toronto, Ont., Canada. TEL 416-924-2502. Ed. Vladimir Mauko. adv.; bk.rev.; play rev.; bibl.; illus.; circ. 3,560.

| 322.4 | RU |

▼**SLOVO;** chastnaya svobodnaya gazeta. 1990. w. 0.10 per issue. Ul. Lenina 33, 184200 Apatity, Murmanskaya Oblast', Russia. TEL 3-17-20. Ed. N.V. Dobrotvor. circ. 5,000. (newspaper)

| 320 355 | UK | ISSN 0959-2318 |
| JC328.5 | | |

▼**SMALL WARS AND INSURGENCIES.** 1990. 3/yr. £28($39) to individuals; institutions £60($95). Frank Cass & Co. Ltd., Gainsborough House, 11 Gainsborough Rd., London E11 1RS, England. TEL 081-530-4226. FAX 081-530-7795. Eds. Ian Beckett, Thomas Durell-Young. adv.; bk.rev.; index. (back issues avail.)
  —BLDSC shelfmark: 8310.169100.
  Description: Provides a forum for the discussion of the historical, political, social, economic and psychological aspects of conflict.

| 320 | IS | ISSN 0334-7621 |

SMOL. 1979. m. IS.40($20) Israeli Socialist Left, P.O. Box 33076, Tel Aviv 61 330, Israel. TEL 03-663154. FAX 03-450917. Ed. Nimrod Oved. adv.; bk.rev.; circ. 3,700.
  Description: Provides news on the Israeli-Palestinian struggle for peace. Covers Marxist views on workers' struggle, Israel, the Middle East and the Third World.

SOCIAL ALTERNATIVES. see *SOCIOLOGY*

| 320.5 | SW | ISSN 0349-9375 |

SOCIAL DEBATT. 1964. 5/yr. SEK 150. Svenska Ekumeniska Naemnden - Swedish Ecumenical Council, Stortorget 3, 111 29 Stockholm, Sweden. FAX 08-7230414. Ed. Anne-Marie Thunberg. adv.; bk.rev.; abstr.; cum.index: 1969-1970; circ. 1,600.
  Formerly: Social Debatt i Tidningar och Tidskrifter (ISSN 0037-7708)

| 320.531 | US |

SOCIAL DEMOCRAT.* 1972. irreg. $2. Young Social Democrats, 815 Fifteenth St., N.W., No. 511, Washington, DC 20005-2201. TEL 202-638-1515. FAX 202-347-5585. adv.; bk.rev.; circ. 1,500.

SOCIAL RESEARCH; an international journal of political and social science. see *SOCIAL SCIENCES: COMPREHENSIVE WORKS*

SOCIAL THEORY AND PRACTICE; an international and interdisciplinary journal of social philosophy. see *SOCIOLOGY*

| 320 | US | ISSN 0885-4300 |
| HX1 | | |

SOCIALISM AND DEMOCRACY. 1985. 3/yr. $15 to individuals; libraries $24. City University of New York, Graduate School, Research Group on Socialism and Democracy, Box 375, Graduate Center, 33 W. 42nd St., New York, NY 10036-8099. TEL 212-642-2445. Ed. Bd. adv.; bk.rev.; circ. 1,000. (also avail. in microform from UMI) **Indexed:** Alt.Press Ind., Amer.Hist.& Life, Hist.Abstr., IBR, IBZ, Int.Polit.Sci.Abstr., Left Ind. (1985-), P.A.I.S., Polit.Sci.Abstr., Sociol.Abstr. (1987-).
  —BLDSC shelfmark: 8318.243730.

| 335.43 | RU |

SOCIALISM: THEORY AND PRACTICE. (Editions in English, French, German, Spanish) m. $5. Novosti Press Agency, 4 Zubovsky Boulevard, Moscow, Russia. (Subscr. to: Eastern News Distributors, Inc. 55 W. 15th St., New York, NY 10011) illus.

| 320.531 | BE | ISSN 0037-8127 |
| HX5 | | |

SOCIALISME. 1954. bi-m. 800 Fr. Institut Emile Vandervelde, 13 Bd. de l'Empereur, 1000 Brussels, Belgium. TEL 02-5132019. Ed. Andre Flahaut. adv.; bk.rev.; film rev.; abstr.; circ. 2,000. **Indexed:** ASCA, P.A.I.S.For.Lang.Ind., SSCI.
  —BLDSC shelfmark: 8318.244500.

| 320 | BL |

SOCIALISMO & DEMOCRACIA. 1984. 4/yr. Editora Alfa-Omega, Ltda., 05413 Rua Lisboa 500, Sao Paulo, Brazil. Eds. Daniel Fresnot, Jacob Bazarian.

| 320 | PO |

SOCIALISMO & POLITICA. 3/yr. c/o F. Marcelo Curto, Av. da Republica, 36, Lado A 3rd Fl. Esq., 1000 Lisbon, Portugal. Ed. Herdeiros de Jose Trigo de Morais.

POLITICAL SCIENCE

320.531   PE
SOCIALISMO Y PARTICIPACION. 1977. q. $55 (foreign $60). (Centro de Estudios para el Desarrollo y la Participacion (CEDEP) Ediciones Socialismo y Participacion, Av. Jose Faustino Sanchez Carrion 790-798, Magdalena del Mar, Lima 17, Peru. TEL 62-98-33. FAX 616446. TELEX 933524 GEONET G. Ed. Luis Cueva Sanchez. adv.; bk.rev.; charts; stat.; cum.index: 1977-1979; circ. 1,500.
    Description: Dedicated to the study and analysis of the economic, social, political and cultural reality of Peru. Also looks at the rest of Latin America and the Third World.

329.81   US   ISSN 0884-6154
SOCIALIST. 1972. m. $8. Socialist Party, U.S.A., 5502 W. Adams Blvd., Los Angeles, CA 90016. TEL 213-939-8287. Ed. Charles Curtiss. adv.; bk.rev.; film rev.; circ. 2,000.
    Formerly: Socialist Tribune.
    Description: Provides news and editorials of interest to democratic socialists.

320.531   UK   ISSN 0049-0946
SOCIALIST AFFAIRS. 1951. q. £12($25) (Socialist International) Longman Group UK Ltd., Fourth Ave., Harlow, Essex CM19 5AA, England. TEL 0279-442601. (Subscr. to: 8 Flowers Mews, Archway Close, London N19 3TB England) Ed. Harry Drost. adv.; bk.rev.; bibl.; circ. 10,000.
    —BLDSC shelfmark: 8318.245500.
    Formerly: S I I - Socialist International Information (ISSN 0036-1534)

320.531   CN
SOCIALIST CHALLENGE. 1980. 6/yr. Can.$5($5) Box 12082, Edmonton, Alta. T5J 3L2, Canada. Ed. Harold Cavender. (back issues avail.)
    Description: Keeps reader up-to-date on socialist and feminist action in Canada. Reports on conventions and protests.

320.531   US   ISSN 0037-8194
SOCIALIST FORUM. 1969. irreg., no.7, 1985. $10. Institute for Democratic Socialism, 15 Dutch St., Ste. 500, New York, NY 10038. TEL 212-962-0390. Ed. Sherri Levine. bk.rev.; bibl.; illus.; circ. 1,000. (also avail. in microform from UMI)

320.531   II   ISSN 0037-8208
SOCIALIST INDIA. (Text in English) 1970. w. Rs.25. All India Congress Committee, Publications Department, 5 Dr. Rajendra Prasad Rd., New Delhi 110001, India. Ed. P.V. Narasimha Rao. adv.; bk.rev.; illus.; circ. 5,000.

335.4   CE
SOCIALIST NATION. (Text in English) w. Rs.3.75 per no. Lanka Sama Samaja Party, 42 Jayakantha Lane, Colombo 5, Sri Lanka.
    Description: Focuses on Trotskyism.

320.351   II   ISSN 0970-8863
SOCIALIST PERSPECTIVE; a quarterly journal of social sciences. (Text in English) 1973. q. Rs.30($10) (typically set in July). Council for Political Studies, 140-20E, South Sinthee Rd., 1st Fl., Calcutta 700 050, India. Ed. A.K. Mukhopadhyay. adv.; bk.rev.; index; circ. 1,000 (controlled).

320.531   NZ
SOCIALIST POLITICS. 1971. 4/yr. NZ.$18 (foreign $20) plus postage. (Socialist Unity Party of New Zealand) Socialist Publishing & Distributing Co., P.O. Box 11478, Manners St., Wellington, New Zealand. Ed. Marilyn Tucker. adv.
    Description: Discussion journal of political and social development.

335   UK   ISSN 0081-0606
HX15
SOCIALIST REGISTER; a survey of movements and ideas. 1964. a. price varies. Merlin Press Ltd., 10 Malden Road, London NW5 3HR, England. FAX 071-284-3092. Ed.Bd. bk.rev.; circ. 6,000.

320.531   US   ISSN 0161-1801
HX1
SOCIALIST REVIEW (SAN FRANCISCO). 1970. 4/yr. $24 to individuals(foreign $29); institutions $48(foreign $53). Center for Social Research and Education, 2940 16th St., Ste. 102, San Francisco, CA 94103. TEL 415-255-2296. FAX 415-255-2298. Ed. L.A. Kauffman. adv.; bk.rev.; circ. 5,500. (also avail. in microform from UMI; back issues avail.; reprint service avail. from UMI) **Indexed:** Acad.Ind., Alt.Press Ind., Int.Polit.Sci.Abstr., Lang.& Lang.Behav.Abstr., Left Ind. (1982-), Mid.East: Abstr.& Ind., Sociol.Abstr., SSCI.
    Former titles: Socialist Revolution (ISSN 0037-8240); (1959-1967): Studies on the Left (ISSN 0585-7449)
    Description: Operates within the broad consensus that there is no contradiction between democracy and socialism. Feminism, culture and labor groups are the focus of this investigative magazine.

320.531   UK   ISSN 0037-8259
HX3
SOCIALIST STANDARD. 1904. m. £8 (foreign £15). Socialist Party of Great Britain, 52 Clapham High St., London SW4 7UN, England. TEL 071-622-3811. Ed.Bd. bk.rev.; illus.; index; circ. 4,000. (also avail. in microfilm from HPL; back issues avail.)
    Description: Presents the case for socialism, with Marxist analysis of world capitalism.

320.531   CN   ISSN 0836-7094
SOCIALIST WORKER. 1975. 10/yr. Can.$10($12) International Socialist, P.O. Box 339, Sta. E, Toronto, Ont. M6H 4E3, Canada. bk.rev. **Indexed:** Alt.Press Ind.
    Description: Marxist analysis of Canadian, American and international social and political issues. Anti-Stalinist and non-dogmatic.

320   II
SOCIALIST WORLD. (Text in English) 1973. fortn. Rs.20($12) 4126 Urdu Bazar, Delhi, India. Ed. Shamim Faroogi.

320 360 301   CS   ISSN 0049-0962
SOCIALNI POLITIKA. (Editions in English and Slovak) 1950. m. 36 Kcs.($9) Federalni Ministerstvo Prace a Socialnich Veci, Palackeho nam. 4, 128 01 Prague, Czechoslovakia. TEL 2-21181111. FAX 2-297731. (Dist. by: Artia, Ve Smeckach 30, 111 27 Prague 1, Czechoslovakia) Ed. Jaroslav Havelka. bk.rev.; charts; illus.; stat.; circ. 6,000. **Indexed:** SSCI.
    Formerly: Socialni Zabezpeceni.

SOCIETE FRANCAISE. see SOCIOLOGY

SOCIETE SAINT-JEAN-BAPTISTE DE MONTREAL. INFORMATION NATIONALE. see SOCIOLOGY

320   YU   ISSN 0489-5967
SOCIJALIZAM; casopis Saveza komunista Jugoslavije. 1958. m. 2160 din.($26) (Savez Komunista Jugoslavije) Komunist, Trg Marksa i Engelsa 11, 11000 Belgrade, Yugoslavia. Ed. Stipe Suvar. bk.rev.

SOCIOLOGIE ET SOCIETES. see SOCIOLOGY

320 914.7   BU
SOFIA NEWS; weekly for politics, economics, culture, tourism and sport. (Editions in English, French, German and Russian) 1969. w. $20. Sofia Press, 113 Lenin Blvd., Sofia, Bulgaria. (Dist. by: Hemus, 6, Rouski Blvd., 1000 Sofia, Bulgaria) charts; illus.; circ. 30,000. (looseleaf format)

320.531   BU   ISSN 0204-9619
HX8
SOFIISKI UNIVERSITET. KATEDRA PO NAUCHEN KOMUNIZM. GODISHNIK. (Text in Bulgarian) irreg., vol.72, 1979. 2.36 lv. Sofiiski Universitet, Katedra po Nauchen Komunizm., Sofia, Bulgaria. Ed. S. Petrov. circ. 550.
    Formerly: Sofiiski Universitet. Ideologicheski Katedri. Godishnik.

SOFIYA. see HISTORY — History Of Europe

972   MX   ISSN 0038-0857
SOL DE URUAPAN.* w. Mex.$30. Asociacion Periodistica Uruapense, Av. Cupatitzio 175, Uruapan, Michoacan, Mexico. Ed. Prof. Sabas Tolentino. adv.; illus. (tabloid format)

320.5   FR   ISSN 0038-1012
SOLEIL;* journal de la droite nationale et populaire. (Supplement avail.) 1966. w. 50 F.($10.) 4 Bis rue Caillaux, 75013 Paris, France. Eds. Andre Cantelaube, Pierre Sedos. bk.rev.; charts; circ. 20,000.

320.531   IT   ISSN 0392-9043
IL SOLIDALE. 1979. q. L.5000($3.75) Movimento Solidale, Box 1215, 50100 Florence, Italy. Ed. Alessandro Mazzerelli. adv.; bk.rev.; circ. 2,500. (back issues avail.)
    Description: Political forum featuring articles on the Christian solidarity movement. Includes informative and historical news on this topic.

320.531   UK
SOLIDARITY; a libertarian socialist journal. 1960. q. £6. London Solidarity, 123 Lathom Rd., London E6, England. TEL 01-552-3985. Ed.Bd. circ. 2,000.

SOOCHOW JOURNAL OF POLITICAL SCIENCE & SOCIOLOGY. see SOCIAL SCIENCES: COMPREHENSIVE WORKS

329.3   SG
SOPI. 1988. w. Parti Democratique Senegalais, Dakar, Senegal. Ed. Cheikh Koureyssi Ba.

320.531   FI   ISSN 0038-1616
HX9
SOSIALISTINEN AIKAKAUSLEHTI. 1905. 4/yr. Fmk.55. Osoite Saariniemenkatu 6, 00530 Helsinki 53, Finland. Ed. Matti Linnanahde. adv.; bk.rev.; illus.; circ. 6,000. **Indexed:** World Bibl.Soc.Sec.

320 330.9   UK   ISSN 0260-6976
HC59.69
SOUTH. 1980. m. £14($29) South Media and Communications Ltd., 525-527 Fulham Rd., London SW6 1HF, England. TEL 071-381-1555. FAX 071-610-1495. (U.S. dist. addr.: 230 Park Ave., Ste. 932, New York, NY 10169) Ed. Mushtak Parker. adv.; bk.rev.; film rev.; play rev.; abstr.; charts; index; circ. 79,365. (back issues avail.) **Indexed:** HR Rep., Key to Econ.Sci., P.A.I.S., Rural Recreat.Tour.Abstr., World Agri.Econ.& Rural Sociol.Abstr., World Bank.Abstr.
    —BLDSC shelfmark: 8330.820000.

SOUTH AFRICA FOUNDATION REVIEW. see BUSINESS AND ECONOMICS — Economic Situation And Conditions

070   SA   ISSN 0015-5055
DT751
SOUTH AFRICA INTERNATIONAL. 1970. q. R.35. South Africa Foundation, P.O. Box 7006, Johannesburg 2000, South Africa. TEL 012-726-6105. FAX 012-726-4705. Ed. Gavin Lewis. adv.; bk.rev.; bibl.; charts; stat.; circ. 12,000. **Indexed:** Amer.Hist.& Life, Curr.Cont.Africa, Ind.S.A.Per., Int.Polit.Sci.Abstr., Mid.East: Abstr.& Ind.
    —BLDSC shelfmark: 8330.830000.
    Supersedes: South African Press Review (ISSN 0038-2574)
    Description: Covers current affairs in South Africa, with emphasis on its relation to decision-making. Provides a forum for debate on domestic and international affairs affecting South Africa.

322   SA
SOUTH AFRICAN INSTITUTE OF RACE RELATIONS. TOPICAL BRIEFINGS. irreg. (approx. 10/yr.). South African Institute of Race Relations, P.O. Box 31044, Braamfontein 2017, South Africa. TEL 403-3600. FAX 011-403-3671.

968   SA   ISSN 0038-2523
SOUTH AFRICAN OBSERVER; a journal for realists. 1955. m. R.20($18) S.E.D. Brown, Ed. & Pub., Box 2401, Pretoria, South Africa. TEL 012-322-2950. FAX 012-322-0215. bk.rev.; circ. 6,000.

320 330.9   UK   ISSN 0268-0661
F1401
SOUTH AMERICA, CENTRAL AMERICA AND THE CARIBBEAN (YEAR). 1985. biennial. $220. Europa Publications Ltd., 18 Bedford Sq., London WC1B 3JN, England. TEL 071-580-8236. FAX 071-636-1664. TELEX 21540 EUROPA G. bibl.; stat.
    Description: Contains essays on important aspects of economic and political life in Latin America and a general essay on the Caribbean. Provides up-to-date statistical survey on each of the major countries and a directory of essential names and addresses.

POLITICAL SCIENCE

320   II   ISSN 0970-4868
SOUTH ASIA JOURNAL. (Text in English) 1987. q. $32 to individuals; institutions $68. Sage Publications India (Pvt) Ltd., M-32 Market, Greater Kailash - 1, P.O. Box 4215, New Delhi 110 048, India. TEL 11-6419884. (Dist. in US by: Sage Publications, Inc., 2455 Teller Rd., Newbury Park, CA 91320; in Europe by: Sage Publications Ltd., 6 Bonhill St., London EC2A 4PU, England. TEL 805-499-0721) Ed. Bimal Prasad. adv.; bk.rev.
—BLDSC shelfmark: 8348.570000.
Description: Journal of the Indian Council for South Asian Co-operation

SOUTH ASIAN STUDIES. see *HISTORY — History Of Asia*

SOUTH CAROLINA FORUM. see *PUBLIC ADMINISTRATION*

SOUTHEAST ASIA REPORT. see *BUSINESS AND ECONOMICS — Economic Situation And Conditions*

320   SI   ISSN 0377-5437
DS502
SOUTHEAST ASIAN AFFAIRS. (Text in English) 1974. a. S.$24($14) Institute of Southeast Asian Studies, Heng Mui Keng Terrace, Pasir Panjang Rd., Singapore 0511, Singapore. TEL 7780955. FAX 7781735. TELEX RS 37068 ISEAS.
Formerly: Institute of Southeast Asian Studies. Annual Review.
Description: Review of the major political, economic and social issues of each country in Southeast Asia.

320 900   AT   ISSN 0158-6041
SOUTH EAST ASIAN MONOGRAPH SERIES. 1976. irreg. price varies. James Cook University of North Queensland, Centre for South East Asian Studies Committee, Townsville, Qld. 4811, Australia. adv.; bk.rev.; circ. 350.

320.05   US   ISSN 0730-2177
JA1
SOUTHEASTERN POLITICAL REVIEW. 1973. s-a. $10 to individuals; institutions $12 (typically set in Jan.). (Georgia Political Science Association) Georgia Southern University, Department of Political Science, Landrum Box 8101, Statesboro, GA 30460-8101. TEL 912-681-5698. FAX 912-681-5348. Ed. Roger N. Pajari. adv.; bk.rev.; stat.; circ. 425. **Indexed:** Amer.Bibl.Slavic & E.Eur.Stud, Int.Polit.Sci.Abstr.
Formerly: G P S A Journal (ISSN 0092-9395)

322.4   US
SOUTHERN LIBERTARIAN MESSENGER. 1972. m. $6. Quality Education, Inc., Rte. 10, Box 52A, Florence, SC 29501. Ed. John T. Harllee. adv.; bk.rev.; charts; illus.; stat.; circ. 800. (also avail. in microform from UMI; back issues avail.) **Indexed:** Alt.Press Ind.

SOUTHERN PARTISAN. see *GENERAL INTEREST PERIODICALS — United States*

320   US   ISSN 0739-3938
SOUTHERN POLITICAL REPORT. 1978. fortn. $157. Southern Political Report, Box 15507, Washington, DC 20003-5507. TEL 202-547-8098. Ed. Hastings Wyman, Jr. circ. 650. (back issues avail.)
Description: Focuses on the politics and politicians of the 12 Southern states.

916   UK   ISSN 0952-7524
SOUTHSCAN; a bulletin of southern African affairs. 1986. w. $220 institutions. P.O. Box 724, London N16 5RZ, England. TEL 071-359-2328. FAX 071-359-2443. bk.rev.
●Also available online. Vendor(s): NewsNet.
Description: News and analysis of current situation in southern Africa.

947   RU
SOVETY NARODNYKH DEPUTATOV. 1957. m. 8.40 Rub. Izdatel'stvo Izvestiya, Pl. Pushkina, 5, 103798 Moscow, Russia. Ed. M.F. Strepukhov. bibl.; illus.; circ. 271,400.
Formerly: Sovety Deputatov Trudyashchikhsya (ISSN 0038-5247)

320   UK   ISSN 0049-1713
DK274
SOVIET ANALYST. 1972. 10/yr. £150($300) (effective Nov. 1991). World Reports Ltd., 108 Horseferry Rd., Westminster, London SW1P 2EF, England. TEL 071-222-3836. FAX 071-233-0185. Ed. Barry Holland. (back issues avail.)
Description: Analyzes political and economic developments in the USSR, with special emphasis on strategic deception intelligence.

323.1 947 296   UK   ISSN 0038-545X
DS135.R92
SOVIET JEWISH AFFAIRS; a journal on Jewish problems in the USSR and Eastern Europe. 1971. s-a. £18($30) to individuals; institutions £25($40). Institute of Jewish Affairs, 11 Hertford St., London W1Y 7DX, England. TEL 01-491 3517. FAX 01-493-5838. (Co-sponsor: World Jewish Congress) Ed. Dr. L. Hirszowicz. adv.; bk.rev.; bibl.; index; circ. 1,500. (also avail. in microform from UMI; reprint service avail. from UMI) **Indexed:** Hist.Abstr., HR Rep., Mid.East: Abstr.& Ind.
—BLDSC shelfmark: 8359.330000.
Description: Studies relevant to the understanding of the position and prospects of Jews in communist-governed countries.

947   II   ISSN 0038-5522
SOVIET LAND. (Text in English) vol.23, 1970. s-m. Rs.7. U.S.S.R. Embassy in India, Information Department, 25 Barakhamba Rd., New Delhi 110001, India. Ed. G.L. Kolokolov.

SOVIET STUDIES. see *BUSINESS AND ECONOMICS*

SOVIET STUDIES. see *SOCIOLOGY*

329.9   GW   ISSN 0038-6030
DER SOZIALDEMOKRAT. 1955. m. DM.1955. (Sozialdemokratische Partei Deutschlands) Presse und Bildung GmbH, Fischerfelderstr. 7, 6000 Frankfurt, Germany. adv.; charts; illus. (tabloid format)

320.531   GW   ISSN 0722-7353
SOZIALIST; Zeitschrift Marxistische Sozialdemokratenlinnen. 1975. bi-m. DM.21. Verein fuer Soziale Verstaendigung und Internationale Cooperation, Im Koerbchen 10, D-3400 Goettingen, Germany. TEL 0551-631216. Ed. Uwe Rueger. adv.; bk.rev.; film rev.; circ. 2,000. (back issues avail.)

SOZIALISTISCHE ERZIEHUNG; Zeitschrift fuer die Bildungsarbeit der sozialistischen Bewegung Oesterreichs. see *EDUCATION*

320.531 323.4   GW   ISSN 0176-0947
SOZIALISTISCHE PRAXIS. 1977. m. DM.36. Schueren Presseverlag GmbH, Deutschhausstr. 31, 3550 Marburg, Germany. TEL 06421-63084. FAX 06421-681190. Ed. Norbert Schueren. adv.; bk.rev.; circ. 3,000. (back issues avail.)

320   GW   ISSN 0341-1117
SOZIALPOLITISCHE INFORMATIONEN. 1967. irreg. Bundesminister fuer Arbeit und Sozialordung, Postfach 14 02 80, 5300 Bonn 1, Germany. TEL 0228-527-1. Ed. Ludger Reuber.

SPAK-FORUM. see *SOCIAL SCIENCES: COMPREHENSIVE WORKS*

320.531   US   ISSN 0038-6596
SPARTACIST. (Supplement to: Workers Vanguard) 1964. irreg. $0.50 per no.; included in subscr. to Workers Vanguard. (Spartacist League) Spartacist Publishing Co., Box 1377, New York, NY 10116. TEL 212-732-7861. Ed.Bd. **Indexed:** Alt.Press Ind.

329.82 331   IT
SPARTACO. 1980. q. L.6000. (Lega Trotskista d'Italia) Luigi Candreva Ed. & Pub., c/o Fidacaro, C.P. 1591, 20101 Milan, Italy. circ. 2,000.

SPOLECENSKE VEDY VE SKOLE; casopis provyucovani dejepisu a obcanske nauce. see *HISTORY — History Of Europe*

320   GR
SPOTLIGHT. m. (Institute of Political Studies) George Nicolopoulos, Ed. & Pub., 13, Kerkyras St., GR - 16342 Athens, Greece.

323.4   US
SPOTLIGHT (WASHINGTON). 1960. w. $32. Cordite Fidelity Inc., 300 Independence Ave. S.E., Washington, DC 20003. TEL 202-544-1794. Ed. Vincent J. Ryan. adv.; bk.rev.; circ. 100,000. (also avail. in microform from UMI)
Supersedes: Liberty Lowdown; Former titles: National Spotlight; Liberty Letter (ISSN 0024-2098)

320   US   ISSN 0584-9365
DT1
SPOTLIGHT ON AFRICA. 1966. a. $10. American-African Affairs Association, 1001 Connecticut Ave., N.W., Ste. 1135, Washington, DC 20036. TEL 202-223-5110. Ed. J.A. Parker. bk.rev.; circ. 1,500.

320   GW   ISSN 0038-884X
LAW
DER STAAT; Zeitschrift fuer Staatslehre, Oeffentliches Recht und Verfassungsgeschichte. 1962. q. DM.148. Duncker und Humblot GmbH, Postfach 410329, 1000 Berlin 41, Germany. TEL 030-7900060. FAX 030-79000631. Ed.Bd. adv.; bk.rev.; index. **Indexed:** CERDIC, P.A.I.S.For.Lang.Ind.
—BLDSC shelfmark: 8425.530000.

320   SZ   ISSN 0081-4105
STAAT UND POLITIK. 1966. irreg., vol.37, 1989. price varies. Paul Haupt AG, Falkenplatz 14, 3001 Berne, Switzerland. TEL 031-232425. Ed. Richard Reich.

320   GW   ISSN 0038-8858
K23
STAAT UND RECHT. 1952. m. DM.96. (Akademie fuer Staats- und Rechtswissenschaft der DDR) Staatsverlag der DDR, Otto Grotewohl Str. 17, 1086 Berlin, Germany. **Indexed:** Rural Recreat.Tour.Abstr., World Agri.Econ.& Rural Sociol.Abstr.

320   SZ   ISSN 0038-8874
DER STAATSBUERGER; Magazin fuer Wirtschaft und Politik. vol.57, 1973. 6/yr. 57 Fr. Verlag Keller und Co. AG, Baselstr. 11, CH-6003 Luzern, Switzerland. TEL 041-281111. adv.; bk.rev.; bibl.; circ. 1,200.

322.4   GW
STACHLIGE ARGUMENTE. 1985. bi-m. DM.40 for 10 nos. Die Gruenen - Alternative Liste, Badensche Str. 29, 1000 Berlin 31, Germany. TEL 030-863-0030. FAX 030-861-9204. circ. 4,000. (back issues avail.)
Description: Presents discussion of topics concerning the issues and politics of the Green Party.

320   GW
STAFFEL AKTUELL; Buergerinformation der SPD. 1984. q. Sozialdemokratische Partei Deutschlands (SPD), Ortsbezirk Staffel, c/o Frank Schmidt, Ed., Koblenzer 23a, 6250 Limburg 3, Germany. TEL 06431-22130.

STANFORD LAWYER. see *LAW*

322.4   US
STANISLAUS CONNECTIONS. 1970. m. $15 donation. Modesto Peace - Life Center - Stanislaus Safe Energy Committee, Box 134, Modesto, CA 95353. TEL 209-529-5750. adv.; bk.rev.; circ. 5,000. (newspaper; back issues avail.)
Formerly: Modesto Peace - Life Center - Stanislaus Safe Energy Committee. Newsletter.

STAT A PRAVO. see *LAW*

320   CE
STATE; a Marxist quarterly. (Text in English) 1975. q. Lanka Sama Samaja Party, Colombo, Sri Lanka.

STATE GOVERNMENT (WASHINGTON); guide to current issues and activities. see *PUBLIC ADMINISTRATION*

352   US   ISSN 0039-0119
JK2403
STATE GOVERNMENT NEWS; the monthly magazine covering all facets of state government. 1958. m. $39. Council of State Governments, Iron Works Pike, Box 11910, Lexington, KY 40578-9989. TEL 606-231-1939. adv.; index; circ. 17,000. (also avail. in microfiche from WSH) **Indexed:** Acid Pre.Dig., Energy Ind., Energy Info.Abstr., Manage.Cont., P.A.I.S., Sage Urb.Stud.Abstr.
Description: Covers events and developments in the administrative, legislative and judicial branches of state government.

POLITICAL SCIENCE

STATE GOVERNMENT RESEARCH CHECKLIST. see *PUBLIC ADMINISTRATION*

353   US   ISSN 0147-6041
JK2403
STATE LEGISLATURES. 1975. m. $49 (Canada $51.50). National Conference of State Legislatures, 1560 Broadway, Ste. 700, Denver, CO 80202-5140. TEL 303-830-2200. FAX 303-863-8003. Ed. Karen Hansen. adv.; index; circ. 14,957. **Indexed:** Sage Urb.Stud.Abstr.
    Description: Articles on state tax reform, education, child welfare, criminal justice, health care and other public policy issues.

STATESMAN; week-end review. see *GENERAL INTEREST PERIODICALS — Pakistan*

320   NR
STATESMAN. 1973. a. £N1($3.40) Political Science Student Association, Political Science Students Association, University of Ibadan, Department of Political Science, Ibadan, Nigeria. Ed. Doji Ajayi. adv.; bk.rev.; bibl.; circ. 500.

954   II   ISSN 0039-0321
STATESMAN WEEKLY; news and comments from "The Statesman" of New Delhi and Calcutta. 1924. w. Statesman Ltd., Statesman House, 4 Chowringhee Square, Calcutta 700 001, India. Ed. Sunanda Kumar Datta-Ray. adv.; bk.rev.; illus.; mkt.; circ. 1,000.

320   US   ISSN 0081-4601
JA51
THE STATESMAN'S YEAR - BOOK; statistical and historical annual of the states of the world. 1864. a. $75. St. Martin's Press, 175 Fifth Ave., New York, NY 10010. TEL 800-221-7945. TELEX TWX 710-581-6459. Ed. John Paxton. index; circ. 35,000.
    Description: Listing of political, social, and economic institutions and strcutures by country worldwide.

320   IT   ISSN 0392-9701
HF19
STATO E MERCATO. 1981. 3/yr. L.90000. Societa Editrice Il Mulino, Strada Maggiore, 37, 40125 Bologna, Italy. TEL 051-256011. FAX 051-256034. Eds. Arnaldo Bagnasco, Carlo Trigilia. adv.; index; circ. 1,500. (back issues avail.) **Indexed:** P.A.I.S.For.Lang.Ind.

948.5   SW   ISSN 0039-0747
H8
STATSVETENSKAPLIG TIDSKRIFT. 1897. 4/yr. SEK 150 (effective 1991). Fahlbeckska Stiftelsen, Box 52, S-221 00 Lund, Sweden. Ed. Lennart Lundquist. adv.; bk.rev.; charts; index; circ. 900. **Indexed:** A.B.C.Pol.Sci., Hist.Abstr.

320   SW   ISSN 0346-6620
STOCKHOLM STUDIES IN POLITICS. (Text in Swedish or English; summaries in English) 1971. irreg. price varies. University of Stockholm, Department of Political Science - Stockholms Universitet. Statsvetenskapliga Institutionen, S-106 91, Stockholm, Sweden. FAX 46-8-15-25-29. TELEX 8105199 UNIVERS.

STOKVIS STUDIES IN HISTORICAL CHRONOLOGY & THOUGHT. see *HISTORY*

320   US
STONO; an international journal of culture and politics. q. $18 to individuals; institutions $30. Castillo Publications, 500 Greenwich St., Ste. 201, New York, NY 10013. TEL 212-941-5800.
    Description: Presents coverage of the arts from a radical perspective.

320 355   AT
STRATEGIC AND DEFENCE STUDIES CENTRE NEWSLETTER. 1981. q. Strategic and Defence Studies Centre, Australian National University, G.P.O. Box 4, Canberra, A.C.T. 2601, Australia. TEL 062-493-690. FAX 062-571893. TELEX AA62694 SOPAC. Ed. Desmond Ball. bk.rev.; circ. 1,000.

STRATEGIC REVIEW FOR SOUTHERN AFRICA. see *CIVIL DEFENSE*

STRATEGIQUE. see *MILITARY*

320.531   322   US
STRUGGLE; a magazine of proletarian revolutionary literature. (Text in English; occasionally in Spanish) 1985. q. $6. Marxist-Leninist Party, U S A, Detroit Branch, Box 13261, Harper Sta., Detroit, MI 48213-0261. Ed. Tim Hall. film rev.; play rev. (back issues avail.)
    Description: Creative literature on the rebellion of the working class and oppressed people of all races and nationalities in the US and abroad against the capitalist ruling class.

STUDI PARLAMENTARI E DI POLITICA; costituzionale. see *ENVIRONMENTAL STUDIES*

320   PL
STUDIA POLITYCZNE. 1968-1990; resumed 1992. q. $42. Polska Akademia Nauk, Instytut Studiow Politycznych, Palac Kultury i Nauki, Pietro XVII, pok.17-10, 00-901 Warsaw. (Dist. by: Ars Polona, Krakowskie Przedmiescie 7, 00-068 Warsaw, Poland) Ed. A. Bodnar. bk.rev.; circ. 1,260. **Indexed:** Amer.Hist.& Life, Hist.Abstr.
    Formerly (until 1990): Studia Nauk Politycznych.

STUDIA UNIVERSITATIS "BABES-BOLYAI". SOCIOLOGIA - POLITOLOGIA. see *SOCIOLOGY*

STUDIEN ZU POLITIK UND VERWALTUNG. see *LAW*

320   US
STUDIES IN AMERICAN POLITICAL DEVELOPMENT. 1986. s-a. $29 individuals; institutions $55. Cambridge University Press, Journals Dept., 40 W. 20th St., New York, NY 10011. TEL 212-924-3900. Eds. Karen Orren, Stephen Skowronek.

STUDIES IN CHURCH AND STATE. see *RELIGIONS AND THEOLOGY*

320.532   UK   ISSN 0039-3592
HX1
STUDIES IN COMPARATIVE COMMUNISM. 1968. 4/yr. £62 (foreign £69). Butterworth - Heinemann Ltd. (Subsidiary of: Reed International PLC), Linacre House, Jordan Hill, Oxford OX2 8DP, England. TEL 0865-310366. FAX 0865-310898. TELEX 83111 BHPOXF G. (Subscr. to: Turpin Transactions Ltd., Distribution Centre, Blackhorse Rd., Letchworth, Herts SG6 1HN, England. TEL 0462-672555) Ed. D. Cattell. adv.; bk.rev.; index, cum.index: vols. 1-10, 1968-1977. (also avail. in microform from UMI; back issues avail.) **Indexed:** A.B.C.Pol.Sci., Amer.Bibl.Slavic & E.Eur.Stud., ASCA, Curr.Cont., Hist.Abstr., Int.Polit.Sci.Abstr., Mid.East: Abstr.& Ind., P.A.I.S., Soc.Sci.Ind., SSCI.
    —BLDSC shelfmark: 8490.230000.
    Description: Provides research, probes the origins of the malaise and evaluates the reforms and likelihood of their success.
    Refereed Serial

STUDIES IN DEFENSE POLICY. see *MILITARY*

320   II
STUDIES IN ELECTORAL POLITICS IN THE INDIAN STATES. (Text in English) irreg. Manohar Book Service, 2 Daryaganj, Ansari Rd., Panna Bhawan, Delhi 110006, India. Eds. Myron Weiner, John Osgood Field. charts, stat.

320 338   UK
STUDIES IN EUROPEAN POLITICS. 1979. irreg. £55 includes P S I Report Series; Discussion Papers; Policy Studies. Policy Studies Institute, 100 Park Village East, London NW1, England.

320   US   ISSN 0273-1231
STUDIES IN FREEDOM. 1981. irreg. price varies. (Freedom House) Greenwood Press, Inc. (Subsidiary of: Greenwood Publishing Group Inc.), 88 Post Rd. W., Box 5007, Westport, CT 06881-5007. TEL 203-226-3571. FAX 203-222-1502.
    —BLDSC shelfmark: 8490.574000.

320   US   ISSN 0081-7996
STUDIES IN HISTORICAL AND POLITICAL SCIENCE. EXTRA VOLUMES. irreg., vol.15, 1968. (Johns Hopkins University) Bergman Publishers, Inc., 224 W. 20th St., New York, NY 10011. TEL 212-685-9074.

STUDIES IN HISTORY AND POLITICS/ETUDES D'HISTOIRE ET DE POLITIQUE. see *HISTORY*

320   US   ISSN 0081-802X
STUDIES IN INTERNATIONAL AFFAIRS (BALTIMORE). 1967. irreg, no.26, 1975. price varies. (Washington Center of Foreign Policy Research) Johns Hopkins University Press, 710 W. 40th St., Ste. 275, Baltimore, MD 21211. TEL 410-516-6900. FAX 410-516-6998. (reprint service avail. from UMI)

320.531   US
STUDIES IN MARXISM. 1977. irreg. (Marxist Educational Press) M E P Publications, University of Minnesota, 116 Church St., S.E., Minneapolis, MN 55455-0112. TEL 612-647-9748. Ed. Harold Schwartz. adv.; circ. 1,500.
    Description: Devoted to application of Marxist methods of analysis to various fields of study.

320.531   US
STUDIES IN MARXIST HISTORY AND THEORY. irreg. $39.95. Edwin Mellen Press, 240 Portage Rd., Box 450, Lewiston, NY 14092. TEL 716-754-8566. FAX 716-754-4335.

320 330.1   CN   ISSN 0707-8552
STUDIES IN POLITICAL ECONOMY. SOCIALIST REVIEW.. 1979. 3/yr. $24 to individuals; institutions $48; students $15. (Social Sciences and Humanities Research Council of Canada) Politecon, Box 4729, Station E, Ottawa, Ont. K1S 5H9, Canada. TEL 613-788-6625. bk.rev.; circ. 1,000. (back issues avail.) **Indexed:** Alt.Press Ind., Can.Per.Ind., Lang.& Lang.Behav.Abstr., Left Ind. (1984-), P.A.I.S. —BLDSC shelfmark: 8491.223720.
    Description: Scholarly journal providing detailed analyses of current issues and informed commentary on topics in Canadian and international political economy.
    Refereed Serial

320   US
STUDIES IN SOCIAL AND POLITICAL THEORY. 1986. irreg. (3-4/yr.), latest no.14. $39.95 per no. Edwin Mellen Press, 240 Portage Rd., Box 450, Lewiston, NY 14092. TEL 716-754-8566. FAX 716-754-4335.

947   NE   ISSN 0039-3797
B809.8   CODEN: SSVTBD
STUDIES IN SOVIET THOUGHT. (Text in English, French and German) 1961. 6/yr. $259. Kluwer Academic Publishers, Spuiboulevard 50, Postbus 17, 3300 AA Dordrecht, Netherlands. TEL 078-334911. FAX 078-334254. TELEX 29245. (Dist. by: Kluwer Academic Publishers Group, P.O. Box 322, 3300 AH Dordrecht, Netherlands; N. America dist. addr.: Box 358, Accord Sta., Hingham, MA 02018-0358. TEL 617-871-6600) Ed. Edward M. Swiderski. adv.; bk.rev.; bibl.; index. (reprint service avail. from SWZ) **Indexed:** A.B.C.Pol.Sci., Arts & Hum.Cit.Ind., Bull.Signal., Curr.Cont., Hist.Abstr., SSCI.
    —BLDSC shelfmark: 8491.720000.

320 330   CN
STUDIES IN THE POLITICAL ECONOMY OF CANADA. 1970. irreg. price varies. University of Toronto Press, 5201 Dufferin St., Downsview, Ont. M3H 5T8, Canada. TEL 416-667-7791. FAX 416-667-7832. (U.S. address: 340 Nagel Drive, Cheektowaga, NY 14225)

320 355   CN   ISSN 0081-8690
STUDIES IN THE STRUCTURE OF POWER: DECISION MAKING IN CANADA. 1964. irreg. price varies. (Social Science Research Council of Canada) University of Toronto Press, 5201 Dufferin St., Downsview, Ont. M3H 5T8, Canada. TEL 416-667-7791. FAX 416-667-7832. (U.S. address: 340 Nagel Drive, Cheektowaga, NY 14225)

956.94 296 UK ISSN 0334-1771
DS149.A1
STUDIES IN ZIONISM; a journal of Israel studies. (Text in English) 1980. 2/yr. £28($28) to individuals; institutions £35($55). (Tel Aviv University, Institute for Zionist Research, IS) Frank Cass & Co. Ltd., Gainsborough House, 11 Gainsborough Rd., London E11 1RS, England. TEL 081-530-4226. FAX 081-530-7795. Eds. Ronald Zweig, Sarah Koclav. adv.; circ. 300. (also avail. in microfiche; back issues avail.) **Indexed:** Hist.Abstr., Ind.Jew.Per., Rel.& Theol.Abstr. (1988-).
 Supersedes (in 1982): Zionism: Studies in the History of the Zionist Movement and of the Jews in Palestine - Ha-Tsiyonut (ISSN 0084-5523)
 Description: Covers Zionism and the State of Israel's social, political, and intellectual history.

STUDIES ON FASCISM AND HITLERITE CRIMES. see HISTORY — History Of Europe

SUB-SAHARAN AFRICA REPORT. see BUSINESS AND ECONOMICS — Economic Situation And Conditions

940 GW ISSN 0722-480X
SUEDOST-EUROPA. ZEITSCHRIFT FUER GEGENWARTSFORSCHUNG; Quellen und Berichte ueber Staat, Verwaltung, Recht, Bevoelkerung, Wirtschaft, Wissenschaft und Veroeffentlichungen in Suedosteuropa. 1952. m. DM.72. (Suedost-Institut) R. Oldenbourg Verlag, Postfach 801360, 8000 Munich 80, Germany. Ed.Bd. bibl.; charts; stat.; index.
 —BLDSC shelfmark: 8509.285000.
 Formerly: Wissenschaftlicher Dienst Suedosteuropa (ISSN 0043-695X)

320 GW ISSN 0722-8821
SUEDOSTASIEN AKTUELL. bi-m. DM.96. Institut fuer Asienkunde, Rothenbaumchaussee 32, 2000 Hamburg 13, Germany. TEL 040-443001. FAX 040-4107945.

320 US ISSN 0146-2156
SUMMARY OF CONGRESS. Variant title: Congressional Summary. 1976. biennial. $585 includes Taylor's Encyclopedia of Government Officials. Political Research, Inc., Tegoland at Bent Tree, 16850 Dallas Pkwy., Dallas, TX 75248. TEL 214-931-8827. FAX 214-248-7159.
 Description: Chronological list of all bills passed by both sessions of Congress with section on major legislation.

SURMACH. see MILITARY

320.532 AT
SURVEY (SYDNEY); a monthly digest of trends in the Soviet Union and other socialist countries. 1975. m. Aus.$20. International Research and Information Association, P.O. Box K 535, Haymarket, N.S.W. 2000, Australia. Ed. W.J. Brown. adv.; bk.rev.; circ. 5,000.
 Description: Social, political and economic aspects of life in the USSR and other socialist countries.

320 IS
SURVEY OF ARAB AFFAIRS. (Text in English) 1985. q. IS.18($18) to individuals; institutions IS.42($25). Jerusalem Center for Public Affairs, 21 Arlozorov St., Jerusalem 92 181, Israel. TEL 2-639281. FAX 2-639286. (U.S. subscr. to: c/o Georges Buzaglo, Center for Jewish Community Studies, 1017 Gladfelter Hall, Temple University, Philadelphia, PA 19122)
 Description: Analysis of the political attitudes of Israeli and Palestinian Arabs.

320.9 UK ISSN 0039-6214
DA20
SURVEY OF CURRENT AFFAIRS. 1955. m. free. H.M.S.O., P.O. Box 276, London SW8 5DT, England. abstr.; charts; stat.; index. (also avail. in microform from UMI; reprint service avail. from UMI) **Indexed:** Key to Econ.Sci., So.Pac.Per.Ind.
 —BLDSC shelfmark: 8549.090000.
 Formerly: Survey of British and Commonwealth Affairs.

320.531 BN ISSN 0350-0144
H1
SURVEY SARAJEVO; periodical for social studies. Cover title: Survey. (Text in English) 1974. s-a. 10000 din.($15) Univerzitet u Sarajevu - University of Sarajevo, Obala 7-III, Room 202, P.O. Box 265, 71000 Sarajevo, Bosnia Hercegovina. TEL 071 213-296. Ed. Radovan Milanovic. bk.rev.; bibl.
 —BLDSC shelfmark: 8548.401000.
 Description: Discusses current social matters, mostly in the fields of sociology, history, economy, philosophy and literature.

320.531 CS
SVET SOCIALISMU. vol.27, 1965. w. $94. (Svaz Ceskoslovensko-Sovetskeho Pratelstvi - Union of the Czechoslovak-Soviet Friendship) Obzor, Ceskoslovenskej Armady 35, 815 85 Bratislava, Czechoslovakia. (Subscr. to: Artia, Ve Smeckach 30, 111 27 Prague 1, Czechoslovakia) Ed. Josef Masin. illus.; circ. 105,000.
 Formerly: Svet Sovetu (ISSN 0039-7024)

328 SW
SWEDEN. RIKSDAGEN. FOERTECKNING OEVER RIKSDAGENS LEDAMOETER. a. SEK 15. Riksdagen Foervaltningskontor, Informationsenheten, Riksdagens Tryckeriexpedition, S-100 12 Stockholm, Sweden. FAX 08-218878. circ. 10,000.

320 SW
SWEDEN. RIKSDAGEN. RIKSDAGEN AARSBOK. a. Fritzes Bokhandel, PO Box 16356, S-103 27 Stockholm, Sweden.
 Formerly: Sweden. Riksdagen. Riksdag.

320 UK ISSN 0049-271X
SWINTON JOURNAL.* vol.16, 1971. q. 10s. Swinton Conservative College, Mealhouse Lane, Bolton, Lancs. BL1 1DE, England. Ed. Stephen Eyres. adv.; bk.rev.; bibl.

320.5 UK
T P S BULLETIN. 1964. s-a. $16 (includes newsletter). Thomas Paine Society, 43 Wellington Gardens, Selsey, W. Surrey PO20 0RF, England. TEL 0243-605730. Ed. A.C. Goodwin. adv.; bk.rev.; bibl.; illus.; circ. 670. **Indexed:** Abstr.Engl.Stud.
 Former titles (until 1985): Journal of Radical History; T P S Bulletin (ISSN 0049-3813)

967 TZ ISSN 0049-2817
JQ2945.A1
TAAMULI; a political science forum. (Text in English) 1970. s-a. $15. University of Dar es Salaam, Department of Political Science, P.O. Box 35042, Dar es Salaam, Tanzania. Ed.Bd. adv.; bk.rev.; circ. 1,000. (also avail. in microform from UMI) **Indexed:** Curr.Cont.Africa, Hist.Abstr.

320 300 LU
TAGEBLATT. (Text and summaries in French, German) 6/w. 4260 Fr. Editpress, 44 rue du Canal, P.O. Box 147, L-4050 Esch - Alzette, Luxembourg. TEL 00352-547131. FAX 00352-547130. TELEX 3478. Ed. Alvin Sold. film rev.; play rev.; stat.; circ. 24,908. (back issues avail.)

320.531 322.4
614.7 GW ISSN 0931-9085
TAGESZEITUNG. Short title: T A Z. 1978. 6/wk. DM.390. Freunde der Alternativen Tageszeitung e.V., Postfach 610229, 1000 Berlin 61, Germany. TEL 030-25902-239. FAX 030-2518095. adv.; bk.rev.; circ. 84,000. (also avail. in microfilm; back issues avail.)

TAIWAN YANJIU/TAIWAN STUDY. see SOCIAL SCIENCES: COMPREHENSIVE WORKS

320 US
TAKING SIDES: CLASHING VIEWS ON CONTROVERSIAL POLITICAL ISSUES. irreg., 7th ed., 1990. $11.95. Dushkin Publishing Group, Inc., Sluice Dock, Guilford, CT 06437-9989. TEL 203-453-4351. FAX 203-453-6000. Eds. Stanley Feingold, George McKenna. illus.

320 CH
TAMKANG JOURNAL: AREA STUDIES. (Text in Chinese and English) NT.$120($4) Tamkang University, Area Studies Publication Association, Chin-hua St. Lane 199, No. 5, Taipei, Taiwan 10610, Republic of China. Ed. Stephan Hsu.

POLITICAL SCIENCE 3929

320 AU
TANGENTE. bi-m. S.45. Ring Freiheitlicher Jugend, Kaerntnerstrasse 28, Mezzanin, A-1010 Vienna, Austria. Ed. Karl Sevelda. adv.

320.532 VN
TAP CHI CONG SAN/COMMUNIST REVIEW. 1955. m. 1 Nguyen Thuong Hien, Hanoi, Socialist Republic of Vietnam. TEL 52061. Ed. Ha Xuan Truong. circ. 55,000.
 Formerly: Hoc Tap.

TAYLOR'S ENCYCLOPEDIA OF GOVERNMENT OFFICIALS. FEDERAL AND STATE. see ENCYCLOPEDIAS AND GENERAL ALMANACS

320 MX
TEMAS NACIONALES. 1975. irreg. Mex.$25($2.50) Instituto de Estudios Politicos Economicos y Sociales, Insurgentes Norte, 59, Mexico, D.F., Mexico. charts.

TEME. see SOCIOLOGY

320 IE
TEOIRIC. 1971. q. 40p. (Sinn Fein the Workers' Party) Repsol Publications, 30 Gardiner Pl., Dublin 1, Ireland. Ed.Bd. bk.rev.; circ. 1,500.

320 IT
TEORIA POLITICA. 1983. 3/yr. L.66000 (foreign L.80000)(effective 1992). Franco Angeli Editore, Viale Monza, 106, Casella Postale 17175, 20100 Milan, Italy. TEL 02-2895762. Ed. Luigi Bonanate.

320 IT ISSN 0392-2154
TEORIE E OGGETTI. 1978. irreg., no.46, 1991. price varies. Liguori Editore s.r.l., Via Mezzocannone 19, 80134 Naples, Italy. TEL 081-5227139. Eds. Roberto Esposito, Giancarlo Mazzacurati.

320 XV ISSN 0040-3598
TEORIJA IN PRAKSA; revija za druzbena vprasanja. (Text in Slovenian) 1964. m. 1000 din. Univerza Edvarda Kardelja v Ljubljani, Fakulteta za Sociologijo, Politicne Vede in Novinarstvo, Kardeljeva ploscad 5, 61000 Ljubljana, Slovenia. TEL 341-461. (Co-sponsor: Kulturna Skupnost Slovenije) Ed. Andrej Kirn. bk.rev.; index; circ. 4,500. (back issues avail.)
 —BLDSC shelfmark: 8791.830000.

630 FR ISSN 0040-3814
TERRE; hebdomadaire paysan du parti communiste Francais. 1933. w. 83 F. 29 rue des Recollets, 75481 Paris Cedex 10, France. Ed. Andre Lajoinie. adv.; bk.rev.; film rev.; play rev.; illus.; stat.; circ. 193,469. (newspaper)

960 CX ISSN 0049-3473
TERRE AFRICAINE. vol.4, 1966. w. 1000 Fr.CFA. B.P. 373, Bangui, Central African Republic. adv.; charts; illus.

320 355 UK ISSN 0954-6553
TERRORISM AND POLITICAL VIOLENCE. 1989. 4/yr. £35($45) to individuals; institutions £85($125). Frank Cass & Co. Ltd., Gainsborough House, 11 Gainsborough Rd., London E11 1RS, England. TEL 081-530-4226. FAX 081-530-7795. Eds. David C. Rapoport, Paul Wilkinson. adv.; bk.rev. **Indexed:** A.B.C.Pol.Sci., Br.Hum.Ind., Int.Polit.Sci.Abstr., Polit.Sci.Abstr.
 —BLDSC shelfmark: 8796.127000.
 Description: Offers academic study of all aspects of terrorism and political violence.

TESINSKO. see HISTORY — History Of Europe

320 VE
TESTIMONIOS VIOLENTOS. irreg., no.6, 1982. Universidad Central de Venezuela, Facultad de Ciencias Economicas y Sociales, Division de Publicaciones, Caracas, Venezuela.

TEXAS AGENDA. see PUBLIC ADMINISTRATION

350 320 US ISSN 0164-9221
TEXAS GOVERNMENT NEWSLETTER. 1973. 40/yr. $26. Box 13274, Austin, TX 78711. TEL 512-416-9394. Ed. Tom Whatley. bk.rev.; circ. 1,400.
 Description: Contains information about Texas state government and politics; includes reviews of news and in-depth analysis of single topics.

POLITICAL SCIENCE

320   US   ISSN 0191-0930
JK4801
TEXAS JOURNAL OF POLITICAL STUDIES. 1978. s-a. $7.95 individual; institutions $10. Sam Houston State University, Department of Political Science, Huntsville, TX 77341. TEL 409-294-1462. Ed. Edwin S. Davis. adv.; bk.rev.; circ. 150.
    Description: Publishes a wide spectrum of social science research which relates to international, national, state and local political systems.

320.5   US   ISSN 0040-4519
TEXAS OBSERVER; a journal of free voices. 1954. fortn. $27. Texas Observer Publishing Co., 307 W. 7th St., Austin, TX 78701-2917. TEL 512-477-0746. Ed. Louis Dubose. adv.; bk.rev.; film rev.; play rev.; charts; illus.; index, cum.index: 1954-1981; circ. 12,400. (also avail. in microfilm from UMI; back issues avail.) **Indexed:** Access (1975-).
    Description: Covers Texas government and politics.

320.52   US
TEXAS TRIBUNE. s-a. Box 15405, Austin, TX 78761. TEL 512-836-1316.

TEXAS WEEKLY. see *PUBLIC ADMINISTRATION*

320 940 330   GW   ISSN 0179-3063
THAT'S YUGOSLAVIA. Croatian edition: Hrvatska Domovina (ISSN 0179-3055) (Text in English) 1982. m. DM.24($15) Ost-Dienst, Hudtwalckerstr. 26, 2000 Hamburg 60, Germany. TEL 040-462702. FAX 040-462769. Ed. Hans Peter Rullmann. adv.; bk.rev.; circ. 3,000. **Indexed:** HR Rep.

322.4   UK   ISSN 0959-5031
THIRD WAY - BEYOND CAPITALISM AND COMMUNISM. 1980. bi-m. £10 (foreign £14). Third Way Publications Ltd., P.O. Box 1243, London SW7 3PB, England. TEL 071-373-3432. Ed. Patrick Harrington. adv.; bk.rev.; illus.; circ. 3,000.
    Former titles (until 1990): Third Way (London, 1980) & Nationalism Today (ISSN 0260-2407)
    Description: A voice of opposition to all forms of authoritarianism, promoting popular democracy and preservation of the European cultural identity.

320   US   ISSN 0885-2200
D880
▼**THIRD WORLD IN PERSPECTIVE;** an interdisciplinary journal. 1991. q. $120. Third World Conference Foundation Publications, 22334 Governors Hwy., Richton Park, IL 60471-1909. Ed. Roger K. Oden.
    Description: Focuses on research and policies related to the globalization of social and economic problems and the corresponding marginalization of Third World societies.

320   CN   ISSN 0381-3746
L11
THIS MAGAZINE. 1966. 8/yr. Can.$20.87($22.50) Red Maple Foundation, 16 Skey La., Toronto, Ont. M6J 3S4, Canada. TEL 416-588-6580. Ed. Judy MacDonald. adv.; bk.rev.; circ. 8,000. (also avail. in microfilm from UMI,MML; reprint service avail. from UMI, MML) **Indexed:** Abstr.Pop.Cult., Alt.Press Ind., Can.Educ.Ind., Can.Per.Ind., Mid.East: Abstr.& Ind., New Per.Ind.
    Former titles: This Magazine: Education, Culture, Politics; This Magazine Is About Schools (ISSN 0040-6228)

329.9   GY   ISSN 0040-6635
JL689.A8
THUNDER. (Text in English) 1950. q. G.$20. People's Progressive Party, Freedom House, 41 Robb St., Georgetown, Guyana. Ed. Clinton Collymore. bk.rev.; circ. 7,000. (tabloid format)

951   II   ISSN 0040-6708
DS785.A1
TIBETAN REVIEW. (Text in English) 1968. m. Rs.48($20) c/o Tibetan SOS Youth Hostel, Sector 14 Ext. Rohini, Delhi 110 085, India. Ed. Tsering Wangyal. adv.; bk.rev.; index; circ. 2,500. **Indexed:** HR Rep.
    Formerly: Voice of Tibet.

320   SW   ISSN 0040-6759
HX8
TIDEN. 1908. 10/yr. SEK 135. Sveriges Socialdemokratiska Arbetareparti - Swedish Social Democratic Labour Party, Torsgatan 10, 105 60 Stockholm, Sweden. Ed. Bjoern von Sydow. adv.; bk.rev.; illus.; index; circ. 8,000.

948.5   SW   ISSN 0040-6988
TIDSKRIFTEN HEIMDAL. 1962. 8/yr. SEK 20($4) Foereningen Heimdal, Box 2043, S-750 02 Uppsala, Sweden. Ed. Ritva Roennberg. adv.; bk.rev.; illus.; circ. 1,500.

TIEN PHONG/VANGUARD. see *CHILDREN AND YOUTH — For*

335   NE
TIJDSCHRIFT VOOR SOCIALE GESCHIEDENIS. 1975. q. fl.32. (Nederlandse Vereniging tot Beoefening van de Sociale Geschiedenis - Dutch Association for Social History) Uitgeverij S.M. Ontwikkeling, Box 33, 2300 AA Leiden, Netherlands. Ed.Bd. adv.; bk.rev.; circ. 1,450.

329.3   RU
▼**TIKHVIISKAYA PLOSHCHAD'.** 1990. 6/yr. 2 Rub. per issue. Irkutskaya Organizatsiya "Demokraticheskii Soyuz", Mikroraion Pervomaiskii, d.42, kv.80, 664058 Irkutsk, Russia. Ed. Irina Shishkina. circ. 3,000.

320 920   UK   ISSN 0082-4399
TIMES GUIDE TO THE HOUSE OF COMMONS; complete survey of Parliament after a General Election. 1880. irreg., latest Jun. 1987. £20. Times Books Ltd., 77-85 Fulham Palace Rd., Hammersmith, London W6 8JB, England. TEL 081-741-7070. FAX 081-307-4440. Ed. Alan Wood. index; circ. 7,500.

TOUCHSTONE (CHICAGO); the touchstone of the pilgrim Church's self-understanding is dialogue. see *RELIGIONS AND THEOLOGY — Roman Catholic*

320.531   RU
▼**TOVARISHCH.** 1991. w. Novokuznetskaya Gorodskaya Organizatsiya K.P.S.S., Ul. Sverdlova 20, 654083 Novokuznetsk, Kemerovksaya Oblast', Russia. TEL 46-27-22. Ed. N.N. Tkachenko. circ. 5,000. (newspaper)

320   CU
TRABAJO POLITICO. s-m. Ministerio de las Fuerzas Armadas Revolucionarias, Plaza de la Revolucion, Apdo. Postal 7034, Havana, Cuba.

320 327 360 600   IT
TRANSIZIONE. 1985. bi-m. L.40000. (Istituto Gramsci Emilia-Romagna) Nuova Casa Editrice Cappelli, Via Marsili 9, I-40121 Bologna, Italy. circ. 1,500. (back issues avail.)
    Formerly: Problemi della Transizione.

329.9   MF
TRAVAILLEUR. (Text in English and French) 1968. fortn. Rs.26($6) Mauritius People's Progressive Party, Box 545, Port Louis, Mauritius. Ed. Teekaran Sibsurun. adv.; bk.rev.; bibl.; illus.; circ. 15,000.

320.531   FR   ISSN 0754-281X
TRAVAILLEURS. 1982. m. 200 F. (Parti pour une Alternative Communiste) Presse d'Aujourd'hui, B.P. 90, 75962 Paris Cedex 20, France. Ed. M. Cuisinier.
    Supersedes in part: Humanite Rouge (ISSN 0018-750X)

329.9   CK
TRIBUNA ROJA. 1971. q. Pro-Maoist Communist Party (MOIR), Apdo. Aereo 19042, Bogota, Colombia. TEL 243-0371. Dir. Carlos Naranjo. circ. 300,000.

TRIBUNE. see *LABOR UNIONS*

320.531   TR
TRIBUNE; a journal of socialist thought. m. Commonwealth Publishers International Ltd., Box 1016, Port-of-Spain, Trinidad.

320.5   FR
TRIBUNE GAULLISTE. 1976. bi-m. 40 F. (Union des Jeunes pour le Progres) T G Presse, 91 rue du Faubourg Saint Denis, 75010 Paris, France. Ed. Gilbert Trompas. adv.; charts; illus. (tabloid format)
    Supersedes: Renaissance Deux-Mille (ISSN 0034-4311)

320.531   FR
TRIBUNE INTERNATIONALE. 1970. 12/yr. 150 F.($14) 87 rue du Faubourg Saint Denis, 75010 Paris, France. Ed. Luis Favre. bibl.
    Formerly (until 1980): Nouvelles Etudes Marxistes (ISSN 0029-4918)

059.91   YU   ISSN 0041-302X
TRINAESTI MAJ; casopis saveznog sekretarijata za unutresnje poslove. 1948. bi-m. 40 din. Savezni Sekretarijat za Unutresnje Poslove, Kneza Milosa 92, Box 870, Belgrade, Yugoslavia. Ed. Radoman Zarkovic.

320.531   AU   ISSN 0041-3356
TROTZDEM; das sozialistische Jugendmagazin. 1948. m. S.15. Sozialistische Jugend Oesterreichs - Socialist Youth of Austria, Neustiftgasse 3, A-1070 Vienna, Austria. FAX 931243-85. TELEX 75312469-SJOE-A. Ed. M. Winkler. adv.; bk.rev.; film rev.; illus.; circ. 40,000.

320 327   GW
TUDUV-STUDIE. REIHE POLITIKWISSENSCHAFTEN. 1983. irreg. price varies. Tuduv Verlagsgesellschaft mbH, Gabelsbergerstr. 15, 8000 Munich 2, Germany.

320   US   ISSN 0082-6774
TULANE STUDIES IN POLITICAL SCIENCE. 1954. irreg., vol.15, 1975. price varies per vol. Tulane University, Department of Political Science, New Orleans, LA 70118. TEL 504-865-5166. FAX 504-862-8745. circ. 500.
    —BLDSC shelfmark: 9070.397500.

320   GW
TUTZINGER STUDIEN; Texte und Dokumente zur politischen Bildung. 1971-1981; N.S. 1985. s-a. DM.8.40. Evangelische Akademie Tutzing, Schloss, 8132 Tutzing, Germany. TEL 08158-251-112. FAX 08158-251133. Ed. Klaus Honigschnabel. bk.rev.; bibl.

329.3   PL
TYGODNIK DEMOKRATYCZNY. 1953. w. Stronnictwo Demokratyczne (SD), Ul. Hibnera 11, 00-950 Warsaw, Poland. TEL 48-22-272493. Ed. Lidia Smyczynska. circ. 38,500.

THE TYNDALL REPORT. see *COMMUNICATIONS — Television And Cable*

327   GW   ISSN 0041-5103
U.I.A.M.S. INFORMATIONS. (Text in English, French, German) 1952. q. 250 Fr. International Union for Moral and Social Action, Jaegerallee 5, 4700 Hamm 1, Germany. Ed.Bd. bk.rev.; circ. 1,000.
    Formerly: Renovation (ISSN 0034-4494)

U R P E NEWSLETTER. (Union for Radical Political Economics) see *BUSINESS AND ECONOMICS*

320 330.9   UK   ISSN 0956-0904
THE U S A AND CANADA (YEAR). 1989. triennial. $375. Europa Publications Ltd., 18 Bedford Sq., London WC1B 3JN, England. TEL 071-631-3361. FAX 071-636-1664. TELEX 21540-EUROPA-G.
    Description: Provides a detailed analytical survey of these neighboring North American nations and of their constituent states, provinces and territories.

320   US   ISSN 0161-7389
L11
U S A TODAY. 1915. m. $24.95. Society for the Advancement of Education, 99 W. Hawthorne Ave., Ste. 518, Valley Stream, NY 11580-6101. Ed. Stanley Lehrer. adv.; bk.rev.; bibl.; index; circ. 249,000. (also avail. in microform from UMI,MIM; reprint service avail. from UMI) **Indexed:** Acad.Ind., Amer.Bibl.Slavic & E.Eur.Stud., Bk.Rev.Ind. (1984-1987), C.I.J.E., Child.Bk.Rev.Ind. (1984-1987), Coll.Stud.Pers.Abstr., Curr.Cont., Educ.Admin.Abstr., Educ.Ind., Film Lit.Ind. (1978-), Hlth.Ind., Ind.Per.Art.Relat.Law, Mag.Ind., PMR, R.G., SSCI, TOM, Wom.Stud.Abstr.
    ●Also available online. Vendor(s): DIALOG, Mead Data Central, VU/TEXT Information Services, Inc..
    —BLDSC shelfmark: 9124.840000.
    Former titles (until 1978): Intellect; School and Society (ISSN 0036-6455)

U S NEWS & WORLD REPORT. see *GENERAL INTEREST PERIODICALS — United States*

320.531   US
U S S R CALENDAR OF EVENTS. 1988. a. $71. Academic International Press, Box 1111, Gulf Breeze, FL 32562-1111. Ed. J.P. Mastro.

POLITICAL SCIENCE

320.531   US
U S S R DOCUMENTS. 1988. a. $71. Academic International Press, Box 1111, Gulf Breeze, FL 32562-1111. Ed. J.L. Black.
   Description: Covers record of principal events across the entire spectrum of Soviet national life.

320.532   IS
U S S R OVERVIEW. (Text in English) 1985. m. $20 (foreign $40). International Research Center on Contemporary Society, P.O. Box 687, Jerusalem 91006, Israel. TEL 02-636126. FAX 02-664069. Ed. Ilya Zemtsov.
   Description: Reports and analyses of Soviet domestic developments, foreign policy and military activities.

320.253   US
U S S R REPORT: KOMMUNIST. 1966. irreg. (approx. 20/yr.). $7 per no. (foreign $14 per no.). U.S. Joint Publications Research Service, Box 12507, Arlington, VA 22209. TEL 703-487-4630. (Subscr. to: NTIS, Springfield, VA 22161)
   Former titles: U S S R Report: Translations from "Kommunist; Translations from "Kommunist".

320.253 301   US
U S S R REPORT: POLITICAL AND SOCIOLOGICAL AFFAIRS. 1969. irreg. (approx. 60/yr.). $7 per no. (foreign $14 per no.). U.S. Joint Publications Research Service, Box 12507, Arlington, VA 22209. TEL 703-487-4630. (Orders to: NTIS, Springfield, VA 22161)
   Formerly: Translations on U S S R Political and Sociological Affairs.

U S S R REPORT: PROBLEMS OF THE FAR EAST. see POLITICAL SCIENCE — International Relations

U S S R REPORT: U S A: ECONOMICS, POLITICS, IDEOLOGY. see BUSINESS AND ECONOMICS — Economic Situation And Conditions

320.531   US
U S S R TODAY. 1981. irreg., 8th ed., 1991. $28. Current Digest of the Soviet Press, 3857 N. High St., Columbus, OH 43214-3747. TEL 614-292-4234. FAX 614-267-6310. Ed. Fred Schulze.

320   US
UGANDA NEWSLETTER. 1988. m. free. Embassy of the Republic of Uganda, 5909 16th St. N.W., Washington, DC 20011. TEL 202-726-7100. circ. 3,000.

947   US   ISSN 0041-6010
DK508.A2
UKRAINIAN QUARTERLY; a journal of East European and Asian affairs. (Text in English) 1944. q. $25. Ukrainian Congress Committee of America, Inc., 203 Second Ave., New York, NY 10003. TEL 212-228-6840. FAX 212-254-4721. Ed. Nicholas Chirovsky. adv.; bk.rev.; abstr.; cum.index; circ. 5,000. (also avail. in microform from UMI) **Indexed:** Amer.Bibl.Slavic & E.Eur.Stud, Hist.Abstr., M.L.A., P.A.I.S.
—BLDSC shelfmark: 9082.709000.

UKRAINIAN REVIEW. see ETHNIC INTERESTS

320   UK
ULSTER NATION. 1988. q. £7. Ulster Nation the Third Way, P.O. Box 140, Belfast, Ulster BT15 2HY, N. Ireland. TEL 0232-755182. Ed. George Walker. adv.; bk.rev.; illus.; circ. 1,000.
   Description: Promotes the identity and culture of the Ulster nation and advocates political independence for Northern Ireland.

320.531   IT
UMANITA. 1969. w. L.7500. (Italian Socialist Democratic Party) Edizioni Popolari, Via S. Nicolo da Tolentino, 18, 00187 Rome, Italy. Ed. Giovanni Baldari. bk.rev.; illus.; stat.
   Supersedes: Socialismo Democratico (ISSN 0037-8143)

UMEAA STUDIES IN POLITICS AND PUBLIC ADMINISTRATION. see PUBLIC ADMINISTRATION

322.4   AU   ISSN 1015-8529
UMFELD. 1983. m. S.100. Schulg. 46, A-1180 Vienna, Austria. TEL 0222-4248623. Ed. Guenter Ofner. adv.; bk.rev.; circ. 4,000.
   Formerly: Gruene Demokraten.

320   SA
UMSEBENZI. 6/yr. (South African Communist Party) Inkululeko Publications, P.O, Box 1027, Johannesburg 2000, South Africa. TEL 836-6425. FAX 836-8366. Ed.Bd. circ. 30,000.
   Description: News journal of the South African Communist Party.

332.4   PN
UNIDAD. fortn. Partido del Pueblo de Panama, Calle 1a, Perejil, Panama City, Panama. Dir. Carlos F. Changmarin.

320   KO
UNIFICATION POLICY QUARTERLY. (Text in English) vol.2, 1976. q. $100. Research Center for Peace and Unification, 8 Ye Chang-dong, Chung-ku, Seoul, S. Korea. Ed.Bd.

320   GW
UNION. 1948. bi-m. DM.29.50. (Christlich-Demokratische Union (CDU)) Union GmbH und Co., Schanneustr. 82, D-4000 Dusseldorf 11, Germany. TEL 0211-5502-0. circ. 800,000.

320   MQ
UNION. w. Union Departmentaliste Martiniquaise, Fort-de-France, Martinique. Ed. Jean Maran.

UNION DEMOCRACY REVIEW. see LABOR UNIONS

329.9   IT
UNITA. 1924. d. L.46500. (Partito Comunista Italiano) Unita S.p.A., Via d'Aracoeli 13, 20162 Milan, Italy. Eds. Luca Pavolini, Claudio Petruccioli. adv.; bk.rev.; film rev.; play rev.; bibl.; charts; illus.; tr.lit.; circ. 400,000 (controlled). (newspaper; also avail. in microfilm)

320.532   IT
UNITA PROLETARIA. 1975. m. L.6000. Via Tomacelli 146, 00186 Rome, Italy.

329.9   SG
UNITE AFRICAINE. 1974. m. Parti Socialiste Senegalais, B.P. 22010, Dakar, Senegal.

UNITED KINGDOM - COMMONWEALTH OF NATIONS - DIRECTORY OF GOVERNMENTS. see BUSINESS AND ECONOMICS — Trade And Industrial Directories

320   MY
UNITED MALAYS NATIONAL ORGANISATION. ANNUAL REPORT. 1949. a. free to party delegates. United Malays National Organisation, Tingkat 38, Menara Dato Oun, Jalan Tun Ismail, 50480 Kuala Lumpur, Malaysia. TEL 03-2939511. circ. 3,000.
   Formerly: United Malays National Organisation. Penvata.

UNITED NATIONS. GENERAL ASSEMBLY. ANNEXES. see BUSINESS AND ECONOMICS

UNITED NATIONS. GENERAL ASSEMBLY. OFFICIAL RECORDS. see BUSINESS AND ECONOMICS

UNITED NATIONS. GENERAL ASSEMBLY. PROVISIONAL RECORDS. see BUSINESS AND ECONOMICS

UNITED NATIONS ASSOCIATION OF THE REPUBLIC OF CHINA NEWS LETTER. see POLITICAL SCIENCE — International Relations

UNITED NATIONS DISARMAMENT YEARBOOK. see MILITARY

UNITED NATIONS ECONOMIC AND SOCIAL COUNCIL. DISARMAMENT STUDY SERIES. see MILITARY

328   US   ISSN 0363-7239
KF35   CODEN: CGLRB3
U.S. CONGRESS. CONGRESSIONAL RECORD; proceedings and debates of the Congress. 1873. d. (when Congress is in session). $225 (foreign $281.25). U.S. Congress, Washington, DC 20515. TEL 202-275-2051. FAX 202-275-0019. TELEX 710-822-8413 USGPO WSH. (Subscr. to: Supt. of Documents, Government Printing Office, Washington, DC 20402) (also avail. in microfilm from UMI; magnetic tape; microfiche ed. avail. from Supt. Docs.)
●Also available online.
Also available on CD-ROM.
   Description: Verbatim report of congressional debates and other proceedings, including daily summaries.

U.S. DEPARTMENT OF STATE. OFFICE OF THE GEOGRAPHER. GEOGRAPHIC NOTES. see GEOGRAPHY

320   US
U.S. FEDERAL ELECTION COMMISSION. ANNUAL REPORT. 1975. a. price varies. Federal Election Commission, Washington, DC 20463. TEL 202-376-3120. Ed. Louise D. Wides. charts; illus.; stat.; circ. 1,800. (also avail. in microfilm; back issues avail.)
   Description: Describes FEC programs, internal operations and efforts to administer federal election law.

320 980   US
U.S. FOREIGN BROADCAST INFORMATION SERVICE. DAILY REPORTS: LATIN AMERICA. (Vol. VI) 1979. d. (microfiche w.). $525 in N. America; microfiche $230 (foreign $1050). U.S. National Technical Information Service, 5285 Port Royal Rd., Springfield, VA 22161. TEL 703-487-4600. FAX 703-321-8547. TELEX 64617. (also avail. in microfiche)
   Description: Features news accounts, commentaries, and government statements from Latin American broadcasts, press agency transmissions, newspapers and periodicals published in the previous 48 to 72 hours.

320 956   US
U.S. FOREIGN BROADCAST INFORMATION SERVICE. DAILY REPORTS: NEAR EAST & SOUTH ASIA. (Vol. V ; includes the Arabian Peninsula & Iraq, and South Asia) d. $525 in N. America; microfiche $230 (foreign $1050). U.S. National Technical Information Service, 5285 Port Royal Rd., Springfield, VA 22161. TEL 703-487-4600. (also avail. in microfiche) **Indexed:** Mid.East: Abstr.& Ind.
   Formed by the merger of: U.S. Foreign Broadcast Information Service. Daily Reports: South Asia; U.S. Foreign Broadcast Information Service. Daily Reports: Middle East abd Africa; Which was formerly: U.S. Foreign Broadcast Information Service. Daily Reports: Middle East and North Africa (ISSN 0270-9384)

320 951   US
U.S. FOREIGN BROADCAST INFORMATION SERVICE. DAILY REPORTS: PEOPLE'S REPUBLIC OF CHINA. (Vol. I) d. (microfiche w.). $525 in N. America; microfiche $230 (foreign $1050). U.S. National Technical Information Service, 5285 Port Royal Rd., Springfield, VA 22161. TEL 703-487-4600. FAX 703-321-8547. TELEX 64617. (also avail. in microfiche)

320 960   US
U.S. FOREIGN BROADCAST INFORMATION SERVICE. DAILY REPORTS: SUB-SAHARAN AFRICA. (Vol. VIII) d. (microfiche w.). $525 in N. America; microfiche $230 (foreign $1050). U.S. National Technical Information Service, 5285 Port Royal Rd., Springfield, VA 22161. TEL 703-487-4600. FAX 702-321-8547. TELEX 64617. (also avail. in microfiche)

320 947   US   ISSN 0565-5560
U.S. FOREIGN BROADCAST INFORMATION SERVICE. DAILY REPORTS: SOVIET UNION. (Vol. III) d. (microfiche w.). $525 in N. America; microfiche $230 (foreign $1050). U.S. National Technical Information Service, 5285 Port Royal Rd., Springfield, VA 22161. TEL 703-487-4600. FAX 703-321-8547. TELEX 64617. (also avail. in microfiche)

320 950   US
U.S. FOREIGN BROADCAST INFORMATION SERVICE. DAILY REPORTS (FBIS). (In 8 Vols.: Vol.I: People's Republic of China; Vol.II: Eastern Europe; Vol.III: Central Eurasia; Vol.IV: East Asia; Vol.V: Near East & South Asia; Vol.VI: Latin America; Vol.VII: Western Europe; Vol.V: III Sub-Saharan Africa) 1978. d. $525 in N. America; microfiche $230 (elsewhere $1050). U.S. National Technical Information Service, 5285 Port Royal Rd., Springfield, VA 22161. TEL 703-487-4600. FAX 703-321-8547. TELEX 64617. (also avail. in microfiche)
   Description: Features news accounts, commentaries, and government statements from foreign broadcasts, press agency transmissions, newspapers and periodicals published in the previous 48 to 72 hours.

POLITICAL SCIENCE

320 940   **US**   ISSN 0271-0269
D1065.U5
U.S. FOREIGN BROADCAST INFORMATION SERVICE. DAILY REPORTS: WESTERN EUROPE. (Vol. VII) d. (microfiche w.). $525 in N. America; microfiche $230 (foreign $1050). U.S. National Technical Information Service, 5285 Port Royal Rd., Springfield, VA 22161. TEL 703-487-4600. FAX 703-321-8547. TELEX 64617. (also avail. in microfiche)

U.S. OFFICE OF THE FEDERAL REGISTER. WEEKLY COMPILATION OF PRESIDENTIAL DOCUMENTS. see *PUBLIC ADMINISTRATION*

327.73   **US**   ISSN 0270-370X
E840
UNITED STATES FOREIGN POLICY; a report of the Secretary of State. 1969. a. U.S. Department of State, 2201 C St. N.W., Washington, DC 20520. TEL 202-634-3600.

UNITED STATES GOVERNMENT MANUAL. see *PUBLIC ADMINISTRATION*

320   **US**
UNITED STATES POLITICAL SCIENCE DOCUMENTS. 1975. a. $395. University of Pittsburgh, Mid-Atlantic Technology Applications Center (MTAC), 823 William Pitt Union, Pittsburgh, PA 15260. TEL 412-648-7000. FAX 412-648-7003. Ed. Jan P. Miller. circ. 300.
● Also available online. Vendor(s): DIALOG (File no.93).
    Description: Directed to scholars and educators conducting research in the political, social, and policy sciences. Contains in-depth abstracts of all articles found in approximately 150 major journals published in the U.S. within a given year. Subject areas covered are domestic and foreign policy, international politics, behavioral sciences, public administration, economics and all areas of political science.

UNIVERSIDAD DE LOS ANDES. FACULTAD DE CIENCIAS JURIDICAS Y POLITICAS. ANUARIO. see *LAW*

320   **IT**
UNIVERSITA DEGLI STUDI DI TRIESTE. FACOLTA DI SCIENZE POLITICHE. PUBBLICAZIONI. 1975. irreg., no.20, 1981. price varies. Casa Editrice Dott. A. Giuffre, Via Busto Arsizio 40, 20151 Milan, Italy. TEL 02-38000905. FAX 02-38009582. bibl.

UNIVERSITA KARLOVA. ACTA UNIVERSITATIS CAROLINAE. PHILOSOPHICA ET HISTORICA. see *HISTORY — History Of Europe*

UNIVERSITY OF BRIDGEPORT LAW REVIEW. see *LAW*

327 301   **US**   ISSN 0068-6093
UNIVERSITY OF CALIFORNIA, BERKELEY. INSTITUTE OF INTERNATIONAL STUDIES. RESEARCH SERIES. 1961. irreg. (2-3/yr.). price varies. University of California, Berkeley, Institute of International Studies, 215 Moses Hall, Berkeley, CA 94720. TEL 415-642-7189. FAX 415-643-5045. Ed. Paul M. Gilchrist. Indexed: GeoRef.
    —BLDSC shelfmark: 7769.970000.
    Description: Monographs based on scholarly research in comparative and international studies in social sciences.

UNIVERSITY OF DENVER NEWS. see *COLLEGE AND ALUMNI*

320   **UK**   ISSN 0305-8646
UNIVERSITY OF GLASGOW. INSTITUTE OF LATIN AMERICAN STUDIES. OCCASIONAL PAPERS. (Text in English) 1971. irreg. University of Glasgow, Institute of Latin American Studies, Glasgow GL2 8QH, Scotland. Ed.Bd. bibl.

320   **US**
UNIVERSITY OF TEXAS, AUSTIN. LYNDON B. JOHNSON SCHOOL OF PUBLIC AFFAIRS. POLICY RESEARCH PROJECT REPORT SERIES. 1971. irreg., no.90, 1989. University of Texas at Austin, Lyndon B. Johnson School of Public Affairs, Drawer Y, Austin, TX 78713-7450. TEL 512-471-4962. charts; stat.
    Former titles: University of Texas, Austin. Lyndon B. Johnson School of Public Affairs. Policy Research Project Report & University of Texas, Austin. Lyndon B. Johnson School of Public Affairs. Seminar Research Report.

320   **PL**   ISSN 0208-4732
UNIWERSYTET GDANSKI. WYDZIAL HUMANISTYCZNY. ZESZYTY NAUKOWE. NAUKI POLITYCZNE. (Text in Polish; summaries in English and Russian) 1972. irreg. price varies. Uniwersytet Gdanski, Wydzial Humanistyczny, c/o Biblioteka Glowna, Ul. Armii Krajowej 110, 81-824 Sopot, Poland. TEL 51-0061. TELEX 051 2247 BMOR PL. (Dist. by: Ars Polona-Ruch, Krakowskie Przedmiescie 7, 00-680 Warsaw, Poland) Ed. Romuald Stanczyk.
    —BLDSC shelfmark: 9512.434200.
    Description: Covers political sciences and theory of politics, political organization of society, social policy, educational policy, and problems of economics of education.

320   **PL**   ISSN 0137-2378
JA49
UNIWERSYTET JAGIELLONSKI. ZESZYTY NAUKOWE. PRACE Z NAUK POLITYCZNYCH. (Text in Polish; summaries English or Russian) 1971. irreg., vol.21, 1984. price varies. Panstwowe Wydawnictwo Naukowe, Miodowa 10, 00-251 Warsaw, Poland. (Dist. by: Ars Polona, Krakowskie Przedmiescie 7, 00-068 Warsaw, Poland) Ed. P. Sarnecki. circ. 420.

UNIWERSYTET SLASKI W KATOWICACH. PRACE NAUKOWE. Z PROBLEMATYKI PRAWA PRACY I POLITYKI SOCJALNEJ. see *LAW*

320   **PL**   ISSN 0137-5822
UNIWERSYTET WARSZAWSKI. INSTYTUT NAUK POLITYCZNYCH. ZESZYTY NAUKOWE. 1974. irreg., vol.15, 1987. price varies. Wydawnictwa Uniwersytetu Warszawskiego, Ul. Obozna 8, 00-032 Warsaw, Poland. (Dist. by: Ars Polona, Krakowskie Przedmiescie 7, 00-068 Warsaw, Poland) circ. 500.

320   **GW**
UNSER BREMERHAVEN; sozialdemokratische Zeitung fuer die Seestadt. 1980. q. (Sozialdemokratische Partei Deutschlands, Unterbezirk Bremerhaven) Verlag fuer Neue Wissenschaft GmbH, Am Alten Hafen 113-115, 2850 Bremerhaven, Germany. TEL 0471-46093. circ. 40,000.

320   **GW**
UNSER DORFBLAETTCHEN. 1984. 7/yr. S P D Ortsverein Erkeln, Gelle Breite 2, 3492 Brakel - Erkeln, Germany. TEL 05272-8290. circ. 300.

320   **GW**
UNSERE STADT. 1975. q. S P D Landau, Karl-Sauer-Str. 8, 6740 Landau, Germany. TEL 06341-86230. Ed. Elisabeth Morawietz. adv.

320 972   **US**
UPDATE ON GUATEMALA.* 1980. m. $10. Committee in Solidarity with the People of Guatemala (CSPG), 494 Broadway, New York, NY 10012. TEL 212-219-2704.

320   **UK**   ISSN 0958-0336
VACHER'S EUROPEAN COMPANION. 1972. q. £35.50. Vacher's Publications, 113 High St., Berkhamsted, Herts HP4 2DJ, England. TEL 0442-876135. FAX 0442-870148. Ed. Elizabeth Gunn. adv. (also avail. in microform from UMI) Indexed: Br.Ceram.Abstr.
    —BLDSC shelfmark: 9138.696000.
    Description: A diplomatic, political and commercial reference book for West Europe.

327   **SW**   ISSN 0042-2134
VAERLDSHORISONT. 1947. bi-m. SEK 100. Svenska FN-Foerbundet - United Nations Association of Sweden, Box 15115, S-104 65 Stockholm 15, Sweden. TEL 46-8-6449835. FAX 08-6418876. Ed. Anneli Dahlbam. adv.; bk.rev.; illus.; index; circ. 9,000.
    Description: Directed to inform and be a forum for debate about the UN and UN-related questions.

320   **IV**
VAILLANTE AFRIQUE.* (Text in French) 1973. bi-m. Centre National CV-AV, B.P. 1287, Abidjan, Ivory Coast. Ed.Bd. adv.; bk.rev.

320   **LS**
VALASAN PATHET LAO. (Text in Lao) q. 80 rue Sethathirath, BP 989, Vientiane, Laos. TEL 2405. illus.; circ. 2,000.

320.532 330.9   **KO**
VANTAGE POINT; developments in North Korea. (Text in English) 1978. m. free. Naewoe Press, 42-2 Chuja-dong, Box 9708, Chung-gu, Seoul 100-240, S. Korea. Ed. Li Ik-Sang. index; circ. 3,000. Indexed: Bk.Rev.Ind.

320   **NP**
VASHUDHA. (Text in English) m. T.L. Shrestha, Ed. & Pub., Makhan, Kathmandu, Nepal.
    Description: Covers social, political and economic affairs.

329.9   **IS**
DER VEG. (Text in Yiddish) 1965. w. $17. Communist Party of Israel, Box 26205, Tel-Aviv, Israel. Ed. Meir Vilner.

VEKOVE. see *HISTORY — History Of Europe*

329.9   **FR**   ISSN 0995-0583
VENDREDI; l'hebdomadaire des Socialistes. (Supplement avail.: Paris Vendredi (ISSN 1146-0296)) 1989. w. (42/yr.). 250 F. (EEC 400 F.; elsewhere 600 F.). Parti Socialiste, 10 rue de Solferino, 75333 Paris Cedex 07, France. TEL 1-45-56-78-47. FAX 1-47-05-15-78. TELEX 200 174 F. Ed. Lyne Cohen-Solal. adv.; bk.rev.; illus.; circ. 215,500.

VENTO DEL SUD; periodico di lotta meridionale. see *ETHNIC INTERESTS*

320   **NO**
VERDEN OG VI. 1965. bi-m. NOK 150. Communist Party of Norway, Postboks 3715, Gamlebyen, 0135 Oslo 1, Norway. FAX 2-671796. Ed. Hans Petter Hansen. adv.; bk.rev.; bibl.; circ. 1,200.

320 340   **GW**   ISSN 0083-5676
LAW
VERFASSUNG UND VERFASSUNGSWIRKLICHKEIT. 1966. irreg., vol.12, 1978. price varies. Duncker und Humblot GmbH, Postfach 410329, 1000 Berlin 41, Germany. TEL 030-7900060. FAX 030-79000631. Eds. Ferdinand A. Hermens, Werner Kaltefleiter. adv.; bk.rev.

947   **RU**   ISSN 0042-3017
VERKHOVNYI SOVET S.S.S.R. VEDOMOSTI. (Text in Russian; editions in all languages of the U.S.S.R.) 1938. w. 7.80 Rub. Verkhovnyi Sovet, Prospekt Kalinina 4-22, Moscow, Russia.

LA VETTA D'ITALIA; mensile di politica e di cultura dell'Alto Adige. see *BIOGRAPHY*

945   **IT**   ISSN 0042-4986
VIA LIBERA. 1954. m. L.1000. Via Volturno 33, Milan, Italy. Ed. Livio Casati. adv.; bk.rev.; film rev.; charts; illus.; circ. 16,000. (tabloid format)

320   **CH**   ISSN 0582-9860
AP95.C4
VICTORIOUS. (Text mainly in Chinese; occasionally in English) 1953. m. NT.$600 039505788; Hong Kong $67; Asia-Pacific region $75; elsewhere $83. New China Publication Service - Hsin Chung-kuo Ch'u Pan She, 7F, 3 Hsinyi Rd. Sec. 1, Taipei, Taiwan, Republic of China. TEL 02-396-9856. Ed. Kao Chuan-hsi. adv.; bk.rev.; illus.; circ. 30,000. Key Title: Shengli zhi Guang.
    Formerly (until 1984): Torch of Victory.

320.531   **GW**   ISSN 0259-5818
VIERTE INTERNATIONALE; Zeitschrift fuer internationalen Marxismus. 1986. s-a. DM.45. Arbeiterpresse Verlag, Postfach 100105, Alfredstr. 71, 4300 Essen 1, Germany. TEL 0201-733556. Ed. David North. (back issues avail.)

959.7   **AT**   ISSN 0049-6340
VIETNAM DIGEST.* 1970. 5/yr. Aus.$2. Friends of Vietnam (Australia), Box E-137, Canberra 2600, Australia. Ed. Peter Samuel. bk.rev.; bibl.; illus.

320.9   **UK**   ISSN 0042-5834
VIEWPOINT (LONDON, 1965). 1965. q. Delane Press, 157 Vicarage Rd., London E10 5DU, England. TEL 081-539-3876. Ed. Ronald King. bk.rev.; illus.; circ. controlled.
    Description: Political review with particular emphasis on corporatism, freemasonry, and subversion of the social order.

POLITICAL SCIENCE

956.940 296   CN   ISSN 0042-5818
DS101
VIEWPOINTS. (Supplement to: Canadian Jewish News) 1970. 6/yr. c/o Canadian Jewish Congress, 1590 Avenue Docteur Penfield, Montreal, Que. H3G 1C5, Canada. FAX 514-931-0548. Ed. William Abrams. bk.rev.; circ. 48,000.
    Description: Highlights Canadian-Jewish writers.

980   US   ISSN 0042-6962
F1401
VISION LETTER;* a political and economic report on Latin America. 1952. s-m. $49. Vision, Inc., 310 Madison Ave., No. 1412, New York, NY 10017-6000. Ed. Richard Schroeder.

973   US   ISSN 0042-739X
AP2
VITAL ISSUES; the journal of African American Speeches. 1950-1984; N.S. 1991. q. $35. (Center for Information on America) Bethune - Dubois Publications, 600 New Hampshire Ave., N.W., Ste. 330, Washington, DC 20037. Ed. Teta V. Banks. bibl.; charts; index; circ. 5,000. (also avail. in microform from UMI; reprint service avail. from UMI) **Indexed:** P.A.I.S., Vert.File Ind.

VIVA. see LITERARY AND POLITICAL REVIEWS

VLASTIVEDNE MUZEUM V OLOMOUCI. ZPRAVY. see HISTORY — History Of Europe

VLASTIVEDNY CASOPIS PAMIATKY A MUZEA. see HISTORY — History Of Europe

VOCE DELL'EMIGRANTE. see ETHNIC INTERESTS

320   IT
VOCE DELLA CAMPANIA. m. L.20000. Cinqueprint S.r.l., Via Catullo 64, 80122 Naples, Italy. TEL 081-669339. Ed. Andrea Cinquegrani.
    Description: Covers politics for political leaders.

VOICE OF THE UNIONS. see BUSINESS AND ECONOMICS — Labor And Industrial Relations

320   IT
VOLKSBOTE. (Text in German) m. Sudtiroler Volkpartei, Via del Vigneto 7, 39100 Bolzano, Italy. TEL 0471-925111.

329.9   SA
VOLKSTEM; voice of the New Republic. (Text in Afrikaans and English) 1873. m. R.6.50. (New Republic Party) Inspan Publishers (Pty) Ltd., Box 1539, Cape Town 8001, South Africa. Ed. C.P. van Wyk. adv.; circ. 5,000. (also avail. in microform from PSL)
    Former titles: Onward-Voorwaarts (ISSN 0030-3186); Advance-Voorwaarts.

320   IT   ISSN 0392-5013
VOLONTA; laboratorio di ricerche anarchiche. 1946. q. L.25000. Editrice A Coop. a.r.l., Via Rovetta 27, 20127 Milan, Italy. TEL 2846923. Ed. Luciano Lanza. index; circ. 1,500. (back issues avail.)
    Description: Theories and ideas concerning anarchist and libertarian movements.

320   US
VOLUNTARYIST. 1982. bi-m. $18. Voluntaryists, Box 1275, Gramling, SC 29348. TEL 803-472-2750. Ed. Carl Watner. adv.; bk.rev.; circ. 300. (back issues avail.)
    Description: Advocates a non-state, pro-free market, anti-electoral and non-violent position on social change.

329.9 947   RU   ISSN 0320-8907
JN6598.K4
VOPROSY ISTORII K.P.S.S.. (Text in Russian; table of contents in English, French, German and Japanese) 1957. m. 31.20 Rub. (Institut Marksizma-Leninizma pri Ts.K. K.P.S.S.) Izdatel'stvo Pravda, Ul. Pravdy 24, 125047 Moscow, Russia. (Subscr. to: Ul. Vil'gel'ma Pika 4, 129256 Moscow 1-256, Russia) bk.rev.; bibl.; index. **Indexed:** Curr.Dig.Sov.Press, Hist.Abstr., Int.Bibl.Soc.Sci.

    LV
VOPROSY KRITIKI BURZHUAZNOI POLITIKI I IDEOLOGII. SBORNIK NAUCHNYKH TRUDOV. (Text in Russian) vol.3, 1977. a. 0.42 Rub. per issue. Latviiskii Gosudarstvennyi Universitet, Kafedra Nauchnogo Kommunizma, Bulvar Raynisa, 19, Riga, Latvia. **Indexed:** Nutr.Abstr.

320   GW   ISSN 0507-4150
AP30
VORGAENGE; Zeitschrift fuer Buergerrechte und Gesellschaftspolitik. 1962. bi-m. DM.65. Leske und Budrich GmbH, Gerhart-Hauptmann-Str. 27, Postfach 300406, 5090 Leverkusen, Germany. TEL 02171-2079. Ed. Dieter Hoffmann. adv.; bk.rev.; bibl.; circ. 4,500. **Indexed:** CERDIC.

943   GW   ISSN 0042-8949
VORWAERTS; sozialdemokratische Wochenzeitung fuer Politik, Wirtschaft und Kultur. 1876. w. DM.108. Vorwaerts-Verlag GmbH, Am Michaelshof 8-10, Postfach 20 13 64, 5300 Bonn 2, Germany. Ed. Gunter Verheugen. adv.; bk.rev.; illus.

VORWAERTS/FORWARD; democratic monthly. see ETHNIC INTERESTS

320 360   US
VOTE AND SURVEY; magazine of political, social and economic issues. 1986. m. $24. Gibbs Publishing Company, Box 600927, N. Miami Beach, FL 33160. Ed. James Calvin Gibbs. adv.; bk.rev.; circ. 5,000.

320 301.412   US
W C P S QUARTERLY. 1982. q. $25. Women's Caucus for Political Science, c/o American Political Science Association, Dept. of Political Science, Texas A & M University, College Station, TX 77843. Ed. Judy Baer. circ. 900.
    Description: Information on WCPS events, networking, job openings, communications.

W F D Y NEWS. (World Federation of Democratic Youth) see CHILDREN AND YOUTH — For

320   US
W R I NEWSLETTER. 1985. irreg., no.7, 1987. $20. Western Review Institute, Box 806, Chino, CA 91708. Ed. Robert E. Sagehorm. bk.rev.; circ. 500. (also avail. in microfilm)

W Z B - MITTEILUNGEN. (Wissenschaftszentrum Berlin fuer Sozialforschung) see SOCIAL SCIENCES: COMPREHENSIVE WORKS

WAGNER LATIN AMERICAN NEWSLETTER. see HISTORY — History Of North And South America

320.531   AU   ISSN 0042-9996
DIE WAHRHEIT; Betriebszeitung der Voest-Alpine. 1950. m. S.2 per no. Sozialistische Partei Oesterreichs, Bezirksorganisation Linz-Stadt, Landstr. 36, A-4020 Linz, Austria. (Betriebsektion Voest Alpine) adv.; bk.rev.; play rev.; charts; illus.; stat.; circ. 16,000. (newspaper)

967.3 322.4   TZ   ISSN 0043-020X
WAR COMMUNIQUES.* 1975, no.15, 1969. free. Departamento de Informacao e Propaganda do Commite Central, MPLA - Partido do Trabalho, Luanda, Tanzania. (processed)

320   GW   ISSN 0043-0404
WAS TUN.* 1968. w. DM.39. (Gruppe Internationaler Marxisten) Internationale Sozialistische Publikationen GmbH, Mainzer Landstr. 147, Postfach 111107, 6000 Frankfurt a.M. 1, Germany. (Affiliate: Fourth Socialist International) Ed. Winfried Wolf. bk.rev.; charts; illus.; circ. 5,000. (tabloid format)

320   JA   ISSN 0511-196X
WASEDA POLITICAL STUDIES. (Text in English) 1957. irreg. free. Waseda University, Graduate School of Political Science, 1-6-1 Nishi-Waseda, Shinjuku-ku, Tokyo 169, Japan. TEL 03-203-4141 ext.71-4140.

320 330   JA   ISSN 0287-7007
WASEDA SEIJI KEIZAIGAKU ZASSHI/WASEDA JOURNAL OF POLITICAL SCIENCE AND ECONOMICS. (Text in Japanese) 1925. bi-m. Waseda Daigaku, Seiji Keizai Gakkai - Waseda University, Society of Political Science and Economics, 6-1 Nishi-Waseda 1-chome, Shinjuku-ku, Tokyo 160, Japan. Ed. Seiichi Iwakura. bk.rev.; circ. 3,000.
—BLDSC shelfmark: 9263.080000.

320   US   ISSN 0887-8064
F192.3
WASHINGTON INFORMATION DIRECTORY (YEAR). 1976. a. $69.95. Congressional Quarterly Inc., 1414 22nd St., N.W., DC 20037. TEL 202-887-8500. FAX 202-728-1863.
—BLDSC shelfmark: 9263.155000.
    Description: Organizes thousands of names, addresses, and phone numbers for the federal government and the many private groups in its orbit. Includes name and subject indexes; organized by area of activity.

320   US
WASHINGTON INQUIRER. 1981. w. $33. Council for the Defense of Freedom, 1275 K St., N.W., Ste. 1150, Washington, DC 20005. TEL 202-789-4294. FAX 202-371-9054. Ed. Arthur D. Randall. adv.; bk.rev.; circ. 6,000.

917.202   US
WASHINGTON LETTER ON PUERTO RICO. 1974. 24/yr. $119. Caribbean Publications, 1545 New York Ave., N.E., Washington, DC 20002. TEL 202-529-5700. Ed. Ed Konstant.
    Description: Analysis of Washington, D.C. governmental action, as well as business trends, affecting Puerto Rico.

973 328   US   ISSN 0043-0633
E838
WASHINGTON MONTHLY. 1969. m. (10/yr.). $33. Washington Monthly Co., 1611 Connecticut Ave., N.W., Washington, DC 20009. TEL 202-462-0128. Ed. Charles Peters. adv.; bk.rev.; illus.; circ. 33,000. (also avail. in microform from UMI; back issues avail.) **Indexed:** Acad.Ind., Bk.Rev.Ind. (1978-), Child.Bk.Rev.Ind. (1978-), Fut.Surv., Hist.Abstr., Mag.Ind., Mid.East: Abstr.& Ind., P.A.I.S., Pers.Lit., R.G., Rehabil.Lit., Soc.Sci.Ind.
●Also available online. Vendor(s): DIALOG.
—BLDSC shelfmark: 9263.170000.

322.4   US   ISSN 1050-2823
WASHINGTON PEACE LETTER. 1963. 11/yr. $25. Washington Peace Center, 2111 Florida Ave., N.W., Washington, DC 20008. TEL 202-234-2000. FAX 202-265-5233. adv.; bk.rev.; circ. 5,000. (tabloid format)
    Formerly: Washington Peace Center. Newsletter.

320   US
WASHINGTON POST: NATIONAL WEEKLY EDITION. 1983. w. $48. Washington Post Co., 1150 15th St., N.W., Washington, DC 20071. FAX 202-334-5669. TELEX 248334-RCA. (Subscr. to: Box 37262, Washington, DC 20013) Ed. Lawrence Meyer. adv.; bk.rev.; circ. 85,000. (also avail. in microform from RPI,UMI) **Indexed:** Telegen.

320   US
WASHINGTON REPORT (ST. PETERSBURG); dedicated to exposing the Washington standards of greed, corruption, self-indulgence and the Great American Dream of profit at all cost! 1979. m. $25. Editors Release Service, Box 10309, St. Petersburg, FL 33733. TEL 813-866-1598. Ed. William A. Leavell. circ. 17,000. **Indexed:** Rehabil.Lit.
    Formerly: Washington C.R.A.P. Report.
    Description: Alternative reports of the Washington political scene not generally covered by the media.

320 330.9   US   ISSN 0733-8104
HC800.A1
WASHINGTON REPORT ON AFRICA. 1982. s-m. $249. Welt Publishing Co., 1413 K St., N.W., Ste. 800, Washington, DC 20005. TEL 202-371-0555. Ed. Steve McDonald. bk.rev.; bibl.; charts; stat. (looseleaf format; back issues avail.)
    Formerly: African Business and Trade.
    Description: Covers news and economic and legislative developments affecting Africa.

POLITICAL SCIENCE

320   US   ISSN 0887-428X
E839.5
WASHINGTON SPECTATOR. 1975. s-m. $10. Public Concern Foundation, Box 20065, London Terrace Sta., NY 10011. TEL 212-741-2365. FAX 212-366-6585. Ed. Tristram Coffin. bk.rev.; circ. 60,000. (tabloid format; also avail. in microform from UMI; back issues avail.; reprint service avail. from UMI)
   Formerly: Washington Spectator - Between the Lines (ISSN 0145-160X); Formed by the 1976 merger of: Washington Spectator (ISSN 0162-3133); Between the Lines (ISSN 0006-0305)
   Description: Provides information on major news developments, including arms control, economy and politics.

320   PK
WEEKLY AL-FATAH. (Editions in English and Urdu) 1974. w. Rs.36. 87-D, Nursery Commercial Area, P.E.C.H.S., Karachi 29, Pakistan. Ed. Wahab Siddiqf. adv.; illus. (tabloid format)

320   US
WEEKLY CONGRESSIONAL MONITOR; weekly listing of all scheduled Congressional committee hearings, with witnesses. 1969. w. $598. Congressional Quarterly Inc., 1414 22nd St., N.W., Washington, DC 20037. TEL 800-432-2250. FAX 728-1863. Ed. Brian Nutting. (looseleaf format)
   ●Also available online.
   Formerly: Monday Monitor.
   Description: Provides schedule of congressional action, including the agenda for committee and subcommittee hearings and witness lists.

320 301   NR   ISSN 0795-896X
WEEKLY PROBES. 1988. w. £N52($40) Crier Communications Ltd., P.O. Box 681, Surulere, Lagos, Nigeria. TEL 01-921198. Ed. Bosun Adewunmi. circ. 50,000.

WEEKLY REVIEW. see *PUBLIC ADMINISTRATION*

320.532   GW
WEG DER PARTEI; Theoretisches Organ der K P D. 1985. irreg. DM.30 per 6 issues. (Kommunistische Partei Deutschlands) Zeitungsverlag Roter Morgen, Postfach 401051, 7000 Stuttgart 40, Germany. TEL 069-6314378. FAX 069-6314379. (Subscr. to: Postfach 1942, 6380 Bad Homburg, Germany) circ. 500. (back issues avail.)

320.531   AU   ISSN 0043-2024
WEG UND ZIEL; Monatsschrift fuer Theorie und Praxis des Marxismus-Leninismus. (Supplement) 1936. m. S.200. Globus-Verlag, Hoechstaedtplatz 3, A-1200 Vienna, Austria. Ed. Erwin Scharf. adv.; bk.rev.; charts; illus.; index; circ. 5,000.

943   GW   ISSN 0043-2202
WEISS - BLAUE RUNDSCHAU; Bayerische Zeitschrift fuer Politik, Wirtschaft und Kultur. 1958. m. DM.10($4) Bayernbund e.V., Falkenstr. 4, 8000 Munich 90, Germany. Ed. Philipp Baude. adv.; bk.rev.; circ. 5,000. (looseleaf format)

942   UK   ISSN 0043-2458
WELSH NATION. 1932. m. £3. (Plaid Cymru - Welsh Nationalist Party) Welsh Nation Office, 51 Cathedral Dr., Cardiff CF1 9HD, Wales. Ed. Dafydd Williams. adv.; bk.rev.; illus.; circ. 10,000. (tabloid format)

320   GW
WENTORFER COURIER. 1974. q. Sozialdemokratische Partei Deutschlands, Ortsverein Wentorf bei Hamburg, Sandweg 22, 2057 Wentorf, Germany. TEL 040-7201143. circ. 3,500. (looseleaf format; back issues avail.)

966   UK   ISSN 0043-2962
DT491
WEST AFRICA. 1917. w. $150. West Africa Publishing Co. Ltd., 43-45 Coldharbour Lane, Camberwell, London SE5 9NR, England. TEL 01-737-2946. FAX 01-978-8334. TELEX 892420-WESTAF-G. Ed. Kaye Whiteman. adv.; bk.rev.; illus.; index; circ. 30,000. (also avail. in microform from MIM)
   Indexed: Child.Lit.Abstr., Curr.Cont.Africa, HR Rep., Key to Econ.Sci., M.L.A., PROMT, Rural Ext.Educ.& Tr.Abstr., Rural Recreat.Tour.Abstr., World Agri.Econ.& Rural Sociol.Abstr.
   —BLDSC shelfmark: 9298.674000.

WEST AFRICAN JOURNAL OF SOCIOLOGY AND POLITICAL SCIENCE. see *SOCIOLOGY*

WEST BENGAL. see *PUBLIC ADMINISTRATION*

WEST EUROPE REPORT. see *BUSINESS AND ECONOMICS — Economic Situation And Conditions*

320   UK   ISSN 0140-2382
JN94.A1
WEST EUROPEAN POLITICS. 1978. 4/yr. £36($55) to individuals; institutions £98($150). Frank Cass & Co. Ltd., Gainsborough House, 11 Gainsborough Rd., London E11 1RS, England. TEL 081-530-4226. FAX 081-530-7795. Eds. Vincent Wright, Gordon Smith. adv.; bk.rev.; index. (also avail. in microfilm from UMI; back issues avail.) Indexed: A.B.C.Pol.Sci, Hist.Abstr., Lang.& Lang.Behav.Abstr., P.A.I.S., Stud.Wom.Abstr.
   —BLDSC shelfmark: 9298.917000.
   Description: Covers all major political and social developments in Western European countries.

320 330.9   UK   ISSN 0953-6906
HC240
WESTERN EUROPE (YEAR); a political and economic survey. 1988. biennial. $190. Europa Publications Ltd., 18 Bedford Sq., London WC1B 3JN, England. TEL 071-580-8236. FAX 071-636-1664. TELEX 21540. bibl.; charts; stat.
   Description: Covers recent history and politics, economy, geography, social affairs, media and communications, transport, tourism.

320 341.37   NP
WESTERN POLICIES. (Text in English) 1985. a. $100. Siveast Consultants, Inc., USA, c/o P.O. Box 1755, Kathmandu, Nepal. (UK subscr. to: Dr. Ramasastry, c/o Overseas Customer Service, Midland Bank Blc., Poultry and Princes St., London EC2, England) Ed. C.V. Ramasastry. adv.; bk.rev.; circ. 10 (controlled). (looseleaf format)
   Formerly: N A T O - Warsaw and Strategies (ISSN 0749-0674)
   Description: Provides a forum for objective analysis of various issues that confront the Western nations due to their policies.

320   GW
WEYHER WECKER. 1985. s-a. Sozialdemokratische Partei Deutschlands, c/o H. Kessels, Bachstr. 3, 2803 Weyhe, Germany. circ. 7,000.

051   US   ISSN 0512-5804
D410
WHAT THEY SAID; the yearbook of world opinion. 1969. a. $41. Monitor Book Co., Inc., 610 N. Ave. Caballeros, Box 9078, Palm Springs, CA 92263. TEL 619-323-2270. Eds. Alan F. Pater, Jason R. Pater.
   Description: Standard source for contemporary quotations derived from speeches, news conferences, interviews, TV and radio broadcast, forums, symposia, lectures, and congressional hearings.

320   CH   ISSN 0512-5278
WHAT'S HAPPENING ON THE CHINESE MAINLAND. 1974. fortn. free. Chung Hwa Information Service, PO Box 337, Taipei, Taiwan, Republic of China. (U.S. subscr. to: Chinese Information Service, 159 Lexington Ave., New York, NY 10016) Ed.Bd. circ. 3,200.

320   US
WHAT'S NEWS IN FLORIDA POLITICS; a monthly Florida political newsletter. 1975. m. $250 (to lobbysts only). Editors Release Service, Box 10309, St. Petersburg, FL 33733. TEL 813-866-1598. Ed. William A. Leavell. circ. 4,500.
   Formerly: Pinellas C.R.A.P. Report.
   Description: Reports on Florida politics.

WHITE HOUSE WEEKLY. see *PUBLIC ADMINISTRATION*

WHO'S WHO IN AMERICAN POLITICS. see *BIOGRAPHY*

WHO'S WHO IN ASIAN AND AUSTRALASIAN POLITICS. see *BIOGRAPHY*

WHO'S WHO IN EUROPEAN POLITICS. see *BIOGRAPHY*

WHO'S WHO IN SOUTH AFRICAN POLITICS. see *BIOGRAPHY*

WHO'S WHO OF WOMEN IN WORLD POLITICS; biographies of women currently in government legislatures. see *BIOGRAPHY*

320   GW
WINDESHEIMER RUNDSCHAU. 1982. s-a. free. Sozialdemokratische Partei Deutschlands (SPD), Ortsverein Windesheim, Waldstr. 13, 6531 Windesheim, Germany. TEL 06707-564. circ. 750. (tabloid format)

320   GW   ISSN 0175-9485
WIR SELBST; Zeitschrift fuer nationale Identitaet. 1979. bi-m. DM.33. Verlag Siegfried Bublies, Postfach 168, 5400 Koblenz, Germany. TEL 0261-32337. Ed. Siegfried Bublies.

320 330   US
WOLFE'S VERSION; a socio-political-economic analysis. 1975. m. $15. Box 99, Blue Springs, MO 64015. TEL 314-635-3154. Ed. James F. Wolfe. bk.rev. (back issues avail.)
   Description: Discusses economics and how they affect Missouri and national politics.

WOLNOSC I LUD. see *HISTORY — History Of Europe*

320 305.4   US   ISSN 0195-7732
HQ1236
WOMEN & POLITICS. 1980. q. $32 to individuals; institutions $75; libraries $150. Haworth Press, Inc., 10 Alice St., Binghamton, NY 13904. TEL 800-342-9678. FAX 607-722-1424. TELEX 4932759. Ed. Rita Mae Kelly. adv.; bk.rev.; charts; illus.; circ. 322. (also avail. in microfiche from HAW; back issues avail.; reprint service avail. from HAW)
   Indexed: A.B.C.Pol.Sci., Alt.Press Ind., Amer.Bibl.Slavic & E.Eur.Stud., Amer.Hist.& Life, Chic.Per.Ind., Excerp.Med., Hist.Abstr., Int.Polit.Sci.Abstr., Lang.& Lang.Behav.Abstr., P.A.I.S., Sociol.Abstr., Stud.Wom.Abstr., Urb.Aff.Abstr., Wom.Stud.Abstr. (1980-).
   —BLDSC shelfmark: 9343.275000.
   Description: Dedicated to uniting the field of women's studies with political science, sociology, and psychology.
   Refereed Serial

320 305.4   US
WOMEN AND POLITICS (WESTPORT). 1985. irreg. price varies. Praeger Publishers (Subsidiary of: Greenwood Publishing Group Inc.), 88 Post Rd. W., Box 5007, Westport, CT 06881-5007. TEL 203-226-3571. FAX 203-222-1502.

322.4   US
WOMEN'S INTERNATIONAL LEAGUE FOR PEACE AND FREEDOM. PROGRAM AND LEGISLATIVE ACTION. bi-m. $12. Women's International League for Peace and Freedom, 1213 Race St., Philadelphia, PA 19107-1691. TEL 215-563-7110. FAX 215-864-2022. circ. 1,000.

320 301.412   US   ISSN 0195-1688
WOMEN'S POLITICAL TIMES. 1971. 4/yr. $20. National Women's Political Caucus, 1275 K St., N.W., Ste. 750, Washington, DC 20005. TEL 202-898-1100. Ed. Pat Reilly. adv.; bk.rev.; circ. 30,000. (tabloid format)

956.940 296   SA
WOMEN'S ZIONIST ORGANIZATION OF SOUTH AFRICA. NEWS AND VIEWS. 1949. 2/yr. membership. Women's Zionist Organization of South Africa, Zionist Centre, P.O. Box 18, Johannesburg 2000, South Africa. TEL 337-3000. FAX 299-596. Ed. Sonia Benjamin. adv.; bk.rev.; play rev.; charts; illus.; circ. 12,500.
   Formerly: Women's Zionist Council of South Africa. News and Views (ISSN 0043-7603)

320   US
THE WOODLANDS FORUM. 1984. 2/yr. free. Center for Global Studies, 2001 Timberloch Pl., Box 4000, The Woodlands, TX 77380. FAX 713-377-5802. Ed. Jeff Awalt. bk.rev.; circ. 10,000.

320.531   US   ISSN 0276-363X
WORKERS' ADVOCATE. 1969. m. $11. (Marxist-Leninist Party of the U.S.A.) Marxist-Leninist Publications, Box 11972, Ontario St. Sta., Chicago, IL 60611. (tabloid format)

320   US   ISSN 0882-6366
WORKERS' ADVOCATE SUPPLEMENT. 1985. m. $12. (Marxist-Leninist Party of the U.S.A) Marxist-Leninist Publications, Box 11972, Ontario St. Stn., Chicago, IL 60611.

POLITICAL SCIENCE

329.9 331.8   US
WORKER'S DEMOCRACY. 1981. q. $6 to individuals; institutions $12. Worker's Democracy Press, Box 24115, St. Louis, MO 63130. Ed. Don Fitz. adv.; illus.; circ. 400.

320   IE
WORKERS LIFE. 1980. m. $18. (Workers' Party, Ireland) Repsol Publishing, 30 Gardiner Place, Dublin-1, Ireland. Ed. Des O'Hagan. adv.; bk.rev.; bibl.; charts; illus.; circ. 12,000. (tabloid format)
Formerly (until May 1980): United Irishman.

320   JM
WORKERS TIME. 1976. m. $6. Social Action Centre Ltd., 9 Central Ave, Kingston 10, Jamaica. Ed. Hopeton Dunn. bk.rev.; circ. 3,000.

320   US
WORKERS VANGUARD. 1971. fortn. $7 includes subscr. to Spartacist. (Spartacist League) Spartacist Publishing Co., Box 1377, New York, NY 10116. TEL 212-732-7861. Ed. Jan Norden. bibl.; illus. (tabloid format) **Indexed:** Alt.Press Ind.

320.531   US   ISSN 0043-809X
WORKERS WORLD. 1959. w. $15. (Workers World Party) W W Publishers Inc., 46 W. 21st St., New York, NY 10010. TEL 212-966-8222. FAX 212-463-7952. TELEX 6503925801. Ed. Deirdre Griswold. bk.rev.; circ. 12,500. (tabloid format; also avail. in microform from UMI) **Indexed:** Alt.Press Ind.

322.4   US
WORKING CLASS OPPOSITION/OPOSICION OBRERA. (Text in English, Spanish) 1981. m. $20. (Internationalist Workers Party (Fourth International)) October Publications, 3309 1-2 Mission St., Ste. 135, San Francisco, CA 94110. TEL 415-695-0340. (Co-sponsor: International Workers League) Eds. Ted Baker, Claudia Mejia. bk.rev.; illus.; circ. 3,500.
Description: Covers political events throughout the world from a Socialist and Communist perspective.

327   NZ   ISSN 0043-8189
WORLD AFFAIRS. 1945. 3/yr. NZ.$5.50. United Nations Association of New Zealand, P.O. Box 11-750, Wellington, New Zealand. Ed. Joan Morrell. bk.rev.; illus.; maps; circ. 2,200. (also avail. in microform from UMI; reprint service avail. from UMI) **Indexed:** SSCI.

WORLD CHRONOLOGY SERIES. see *HISTORY*

320   US
WORLD COUNTRY REPORTS SERVICE. m. Frost & Sullivan, Inc., 106 Fulton St., New York, NY 10038. TEL 212-233-1080.

WORLD ECONOMIC REVIEW. see *BUSINESS AND ECONOMICS — International Development And Assistance*

320.9   II
WORLD FOCUS. (Text in English) 1980. m. Rs.40($12) H. S. Chhabra, F-15 Bhagat Singh Market, New Delhi-110001, India.

320.531   UK   ISSN 0266-867X
WORLD MARXIST REVIEW. 1960. m. £8.50. Problems of Peace & Socialism, 16 St. John St., London EC1M 4AY, England. bk.rev.; index; circ. 20,000. (back issues avail.) **Indexed:** Mid.East: Abstr.& Ind.

320   SU
WORLD NEWS DIGEST.* 1979. 2/yr. $34 s.R.120. Muslim World League, P.O. Box 538, Mecca, Saudi Arabia. Ed. Dr. Hasan Zaman. adv.; circ. 1,500. (back issues avail.)

320   US   ISSN 0094-2316
JK1
WORLD OF POLITICS. 1971. m. $585 includes Taylor's Encyclopedia of Government Officials. Federal and State. Political Research, Inc., Tegoland at Bent Tree, 16850 Dallas Parkway, Dallas, TX 75248. TEL 214-931-8827. FAX 214-248-7159. Ed. John Clements. charts; illus.; s-a index.
Description: Covers current events and developments in the U.S. government.

322.4   US
WORLD PEACEMAKERS QUARTERLY. 1979. q. $5. World Peacemakers Inc., 2025 Massachussetts Ave., N.W., Washington, DC 20036. TEL 202-265-7582. Ed. William J. Price. circ. 1,000.
Description: Presents alternatives for U.S. foreign policy and action based on religious faith.

320.531   UK   ISSN 0269-9141
A WORLD TO WIN. (Editions in English, Farsi, Spanish and Turkish) 1985. q. £10($20) A World to Win, 27 Old Gloucester St., London WC1N 3XX, England. FAX 071-831-9489. TELEX 262433 W6787. (Dist. in U.S. by: Revolution Books, 13 E. 16th St., New York, NY 10003) Ed. Don Horne. adv.; bk.rev.; circ. 5,000.
Description: International journal examing the main events and issues throughout the political arena.

WORLD YOUTH/JEUNESSE DU MONDE/JUVENTUD DEL MUNDO; international youth magazine. see *CHILDREN AND YOUTH — For*

956.940 296   IS   ISSN 0084-2516
WORLD ZIONIST ORGANIZATION. GENERAL COUNCIL. ADDRESSES, DEBATES, RESOLUTIONS.* (Text in English) a. World Zionist Organization, P.O. Box 92, Jerusalem 91920, Israel. TEL 02-527156. FAX 02-533542.

296 059   IS
WORLD ZIONIST PRESS SERVICE. (Text mainly in English and Russian; occasionally in various languages) m. World Zionist Organization, Department of Information, P.O. Box 92, Jerusalem 91920, Israel. TEL 02-527156. FAX 02-513542. Ed. June Spitzer.
Formerly: World Zionist Organization Press Service.

320   SG
XARELI. fortn. And Jef - Mouvement Revolutionnaire Pour la Democratie Nouvelle, B.P. 12136, Dakar, Senegal. TEL 22-54-63. circ. 7,000.

320   CC   ISSN 1000-4513
XIANDAI LINGDAO/MODERN LEADER. (Text in Chinese) 1986. bi-m. Y6.60. (Shanghai Kexue Yanjiusuo - Shanghai Scientific Research Institute) Xiandai Lingdao Bianjibo, 52 Yongfu Road, Shanghai 200031, People's Republic of China. TEL 4332558. Ed. Feng Zhijun. adv.; B&W page Y5,000; adv. contact: Hengxin Chen. bk.rev.; circ. 40,000.
Description: Explores the science and the art of leadership in China.

320   CC
XUANCHUAN SHOUCE/PROPAGANDA HANDBOOK. s-m. Beijing Ribao She, 34, Xibaobei Hutong, Dongdan, Beijing 100734, People's Republic of China. Ed. Wang Minying.

329.9   CC
XUEXI YU YANJIU. (Text in Chinese) m. Y1 per no. (Zhonggong Beijing Shiwei) Xuexi yu Janjiu Zazhishe, No. 6, Chegongzhuang Dajie, Beijing 100044, People's Republic of China. TEL 896061. (Dist. outside China by: China International Book Trading Corp., P.O. Box 399, Beijing, P.R.C.) Ed. Tao Yifan.

320   IS   ISSN 0792-2337
DS150.L3
YA'AD. (Text in Hebrew) 1971. 3/yr. Documentation & Research Center of Hashomer Hatzair, Givat Haviva, M.P. Menashe 37 850, Israel. TEL 063-78944. Ed. David Zait.
Formerly (until 1988): Ma'asef (ISSN 0334-3952)
Description: Studies in the history of the Israeli labor movement and socialism.

320   IS   ISSN 0334-1003
HX9.H4
YALKUT LEMACHSHAVA SOTZIALISTIT. 1984. q. IS.15. Yad Tabenkin, Efal 52 960, Israel. TEL 3-343311. FAX 3-346376. Ed. Dan Karmon. bk.rev.; circ. 650.

320   CC
YAN - ZHAO XIANGYIN. (Text in Chinese) bi-m. Hebei Sheng Zhengzhi Xieshang Weiyuanhui, 34, Weiming Jie, Shijiazhuang, Hebei 050051, People's Republic of China. TEL 23477. Ed. Wang Xin.

YE OLDE BASTARDS BULLETIN. see *BIOGRAPHY*

320 350   US
YEARBOOK OF MARYLAND LEGISLATORS. quadrennial. $135. Bancroft Information Group, Inc., Box 65360, Baltimore, MD 21209. TEL 301-358-0658. FAX 301-358-0658. Ed. Bruce Bortz.

YELLOW SHEET REPORT. see *PUBLIC ADMINISTRATION*

YOUNG AGE; social and cultural fortnightly. see *SOCIOLOGY*

369.4   UK   ISSN 0513-5982
YOUNG FABIAN PAMPHLET. 1961. irreg., no.51, 1988. £19($35) Fabian Society, 11 Dartmouth St., London SW1H 9BN, England. TEL 01-222 8877. FAX 01-976-7153. Ed.Bd. charts, stat.; circ. 5,500. (reprint service avail. from KTO)

320.531   US   ISSN 0360-0157
HX1
YOUNG SOCIALIST.* 1959. bi-m. $3. Young Socialist Alliance, Box 211, New York, NY 10011. Ed. Marea Himelgrin. adv.; bk.rev.; charts; illus.; circ. 6,000.
Formerly: Young Socialist - The Organizer (ISSN 0044-0892)

956.940 296   US   ISSN 0044-1171
YOUTH AND NATION; magazine for radical Jewish youth. 1934. q. $2.50. Hashomer Hatzair Zionist Youth Movement, 150 Fifth Ave., New York, NY 10011. TEL 212-929-4955. Ed. Allan Lutzker. bk.rev.; film rev.; play rev.; circ. 1,500.
Incorporates: Neged Hazerem.

YOUTH & SOCIETY. see *CHILDREN AND YOUTH — About*

320.532   YU   ISSN 0350-9508
YUGOSLAV INFORMATION BULLETIN; of the League of Communists of Yugoslavia & the Socialist Alliance of Working People of Yugoslavia. French edition: Bulletin d'Information Yougoslave (ISSN 0407-825X); Spanish edition: Boletin de Informacion Yugoslavo (ISSN 0350-7777) (Text in English) 1974. m. free. Komunist, Trg Marksa i Engelsa 11, 11000 Belgrade, Yugoslavia. Ed. Jovan Lakicevic. bk.rev.

322.4 323.4   US   ISSN 1056-5507
Z MAGAZINE. 1988. m. $25 to individuals; institutions $35 (foreign $50). Institute for Social and Cultural Communications, 150 W. Canton, Boston, MA 02118. TEL 617-236-5878. FAX 617-247-3179. Eds. Michael Albert, Lydia Sargent. bk.rev.; film rev.; illus.; circ. 26,000. (back issues avail.)
Formerly: Zeta Magazine (ISSN 0896-1328)
Description: Covers U.S. politics, feminism, ecology, foreign news, racism, economics and political activism.

960   ZR   ISSN 0049-8513
ZAIRE - AFRIQUE; economie-culture-vie sociale. 1961. m. 5000 Fr.CFA($60) Centre d'Etudes pour l'Action Sociale, 9, ave Pere Boka, B.P. 3375, Kinshasa-Gombe, Zaire. TEL 30066. Eds. Rene Beeckmans, Kikassa Mwanalessa. adv.; bk.rev.; bibl.; index; circ. 4,500. (tabloid format) **Indexed:** CERDIC, Curr.Cont.Africa, Rural Recreat.Tour.Abstr., World Agri.Econ.& Rural Sociol.Abstr.
Formerly: Congo-Afrique (ISSN 0010-5767)

057.8   XN   ISSN 0044-1872
ZASTITA. (Text in Macedonian) vol.6, 1966. m. $2.60. Sojuzot na Trudovite Invalidi na Makedonija, Marsala Tita, Box 437, Skopje, Macedonia.

ZEITSCHRIFT FUER AUSLAENDERRECHT UND AUSLAENDERPOLITIK. see *LAW*

ZEITSCHRIFT FUER LATEINAMERIKA WIEN. see *HISTORY — History Of North And South America*

320 350   GW   ISSN 0340-1758
JN3971.A7
ZEITSCHRIFT FUER PARLAMENTSFRAGEN. 1970. q. DM.43 (students DM.29.80). (Deutsche Vereinigung fuer Parlamentsfragen) Westdeutscher Verlag GmbH, Postfach 5829, 6200 Wiesbaden 1, Germany. TEL 0611-160230. FAX 0611-160229. TELEX 4186928-VWV-D. Ed.Bd. adv.; bk.rev.; bibl.; index; circ. 1,900.
—BLDSC shelfmark: 9476.500000.

320   GW   ISSN 0044-3360
JA14
ZEITSCHRIFT FUER POLITIK. 1907; N.S. 1954. q. DM.98. (Hochschule fuer Politik) Carl Heymanns Verlag KG, Luxemburgerstr. 449, 5000 Cologne 41, Germany. TEL 0221-46010-0. FAX 0221-4601069. Ed.Bd. adv.; bk.rev.; bibl.; index; circ. 1,350. **Indexed:** A.B.C.Pol.Sci, P.A.I.S.For.Lang.Ind., P.A.I.S., SSCI.
—BLDSC shelfmark: 9484.300000.

POLITICAL SCIENCE — ABSTRACTING, BIBLIOGRAPHIES, STATISTICS

320   GW   ISSN 0514-2776
ZEITSCHRIFT FUER SOZIALREFORM. 1954. m. DM.816. Verlag Chmielorz GmbH, Wilhelmstr. 42, Postfach 2229, 6200 Wiesbaden, Germany. TEL 0611-36098-0. Ed.Bd. (back issues avail.)

320.531   SW   ISSN 0044-3980
ZENIT; nordisk socialistisk tidskrift. 1956. q. SEK 130($9) Tidskriftsfoereningen Zenit, Box 1156, S-221 05 Lund 1, Sweden. Ed.Bd. adv.; bk.rev.; abstr.; circ. 2,000.

320.531   GW   ISSN 0044-4278
ZENTRALBLATT FUER SOZIALVERSICHERUNG, SOZIALHILFE UND VERSORGUNG; Zeitschrift fuer das Recht der Sozialen Sicherheit. (Text in German; summaries in English and French) 1947. m. DM.177.60. Asgard-Verlag Dr. Werner Hippe KG, Einsteinstr. 10, Postfach 1465, 5205 St. Augustin, Germany. TEL 02241-3164-0. Ed. Horst Straesser. adv.; bk.rev.; bibl.; circ. 1,000. **Indexed:** World Bibl.Soc.Sec.

329.9   AA
ZERI I POPULLIT. 1942. d. (except Mon.). Partia e Punes e Shqiperise - Party of Labour of Albania, Bulevardi Stalin, Tirana, Albania. TEL 42-27808. FAX 42-26713. TELEX 4151. Ed. Spiro Dede. circ. 120,000. (newspaper)

322   PL   ISSN 0514-342X
ZESZYTY "ARGUMENTOW". (Text in Polish; table of contents in French and Russian) 1964. bi-m. price varies. Wydawnictwo Wspolczesne R S W "Prasa-Ksiazk-Ruch", Ul. Wiejska 12, 00-420 Warsaw, Poland. TEL 48-22-285330.

ZHENGFA LUNTAN/POLITICAL SCIENCE & LAW TRIBUNE; zhongguo zhengfa daxue xuebao. see *LAW*

ZHENGZHI JIAOYU/POLITICAL EDUCATION. see *EDUCATION*

ZHENGZHI YU FALU/POLITICS AND LAW. see *LAW*

324   CC   ISSN 1000-3355
JA26
ZHENGZHIXUE YANJIU/POLITICAL SCIENCE RESEARCH. (Text in Chinese) 1985. bi-m. $25.20. (Zhongguo Shehui Kexueyuan, Zhengzhixue Yanjiusuo - Chinese Academy of Social Sciences, Institute of Political Science) Zhongguo Shehui Kexueyuan Chubanshe, Gulou Xidajie A 158, Beijing, People's Republic of China. (Dist. in US by: China Books & Periodicals, Inc., 2929 24th St., San Francisco, CA 94110. TEL 415-282-2994)

329.9 951   CC
ZHONG GONG DANGSHI YANJIU/JOURNAL OF CHINESE COMMUNIST PARTY HISTORY. (Text in Chinese) bi-m. $36. Zhonggong Zhongyang Dangshi Yanjiushi - Central Committee of Chinese Communist Party, Party History Research Center, P.O. Box 1924, Beijing 100091, People's Republic of China. TEL 2581534. (Dist. in US by: China Books & Periodicals, Inc., 2929 24th St., San Francisco, CA 94110. TEL 415-282-2994) Ed. Li Chuanhua.

320 951   CC
ZHONGGONG DANGSHI/HISTORY OF THE CHINESE COMMUNIST PARTY. (Text in Chinese) s-m. Zhongguo Zhonggong Dangshi Xuehui, Zhongyang Dangxiao, Nanyuan Nei, Beijing 100091, People's Republic of China. TEL 2581534. Ed. Wang Zhixin.

320   CC
ZHONGGUO MINZHENG. (Text in Chinese) m. Shehui Baozhang Baoshe, No. A-12, Shifangyuan, Beijing 100636, People's Republic of China. TEL 8652657. Ed. Zhou Juncheng.

320   CC
ZHONGGUO QINGYUN/CHINESE YOUTH MOVEMENT. (Text in Chinese) bi-m. Gongqingtuan Zhongyang, Qingyunshi Yanjiushi, 25, Xisanhuan Beilu, Beijing 100081, People's Republic of China. TEL 8021144. Ed. Zhang Xiuxue.

322.4   PL
ZIELONY SZTANDAR. 1931. w. Polskie Stronnictwo Ludowe (PSL) - Polish Peasant Party, Ul. Grzybowska 4, 00-950 Warsaw, Poland. TEL 48-22-207554. Ed. Pawel Popiak. circ. 195.800.

320   GW
DIE ZIGARRE. 1970. s-a. Sozialdemokratische Partei Deutschlands (SPD), Ortsverein Hatzenbuehl, c/o Dieter Boehm, Schubertstr. 7, 6729 Hatzenbuehl, Germany. TEL 07275-4803.

329   IS
ZO HA-DEREKH. (Text in Hebrew) vol.3, 1976. w. $21. Communist Party of Israel, P.O. Box 3063, Tel Aviv, Israel. Ed. Meir Willner.

ZSHURNALIST. see *JOURNALISM*

327   NE   ISSN 0044-5428
ZUID - AFRIKA; onafhankelijk maandblad, uitgegeven door Z A S M in Amsterdam. Short title: Z - A. 1924. 10/yr. fl.27.50. Zuid - Afrikaansche Stichting Moederland, Keizersgracht 141, 1015 CK Amsterdam, Netherlands. TEL 020-249318. Ed.Bd. adv.; bk.rev.; abstr.; bibl.; illus.; index; circ. 1,250.
Description: Covers political developments in South Africa, with commentary from a Dutch point of view.

057.8   II   ISSN 0044-5479
ZULQARNAIN. (Text in Urdu) 1903. w. Rs.30. Nizami Press, Badaun, Uttar Pradesh, India. Ed. Moonis Nizami. adv.; bk.rev.; abstr.; bibl.; tr.lit.; circ. 20,000. (also avail. in microfilm)

322.4   GW   ISSN 0044-5487
ZUM NACHDENKEN. 1963. irreg., vol.35, 1992. free. Hessische Landeszentrale fuer Politische Bildung, Rheinbahnstr. 2, 6200 Wiebaden, Germany. FAX 0611-3682653. Ed. Herbert Lilge. adv.; circ. 7,000.

ZUR POLITIK UND ZEITGESCHICHTE. see *HISTORY*

320   CR
15 DIAS EN COSTA RICA.* 1971. m. Casa Presidencial, San Jose, Costa Rica. illus.

320 350   US   ISSN 0164-0356
50 STATE LEGISLATIVE REVIEW. 1977. biennial. $585 includes Taylor's Encyclopedia of Government Officials, Federal and State. Political Research, Inc., Tegoland at Bent Tree, 16850 Dallas Parkway, Dallas, TX 75248. TEL 214-931-8827. FAX 214-248-7159.
Description: Summary of laws dealing with topics of national concern passed in each state.

320   AG
84;* semanario politico independiente. 1982. w. Montevideo 373, Buenos Aires, Argentina. Ed. Carlos Garramuno.

POLITICAL SCIENCE — Abstracting, Bibliographies, Statistics

320 016   US   ISSN 0001-0456
Z7161   CODEN: ABPSC
A B C POL SCI; a bibliography of contents: political science and government. 1969. 6/yr. (including indexes). price varies. A B C-Clio, 130 Cremona, Box 1911, Santa Barbara, CA 93116-1911. TEL 805-968-1911. FAX 805-685-9685. Ed. Lloyd W. Garrison. index.

321   US   ISSN 0066-1228
A C A INDEX;* analysis of voting records of members of U.S. Congress. 1960. a. contributions of $15 or more. Americans for Constitutional Action, 7100 Sussex Pl., Alexandria, VA 22307. cum.index: 1955 (Senate); 1957 (House of Representatives); circ. 5,000.

ALTERNATIVE PRESS INDEX; an index to alternative and radical publications. see *LITERARY AND POLITICAL REVIEWS — Abstracting, Bibliographies, Statistics*

320   AG   ISSN 0325-3147
ARGENTINA. CONGRESO DE LA NACION. BIBLIOTECA. SERIE BIBLIOGRAFICA. irreg., no.3, 1982. Congreso de la Nacion, Biblioteca, Subdireccion de Referencia Legislativa, Rivadavia 1850, 1033 Buenos Aires, Argentina.

950 015   SI   ISSN 0004-4520
DS1
ASIAN ALMANAC; weekly abstracts of Asian affairs. (Text in English) 1963. w. S.$300($150) P.O. Box 2737, Singapore 9047, Singapore. Ed. Vedagiri T. Sambandan. index; circ. 600. (looseleaf format; back issues avail.)

BIBLIOGRAFIA DE POLITICA INDUSTRIAL. see *BUSINESS AND ECONOMICS — Abstracting, Bibliographies, Statistics*

BIBLIOGRAPHIES AND INDEXES IN LAW AND POLITICAL SCIENCE. see *LAW — Abstracting, Bibliographies, Statistics*

320.531   US   ISSN 1056-5515
BIBLIOGRAPHIES OF BRITISH STATESMEN. 1988. irreg. price varies. Greenwood Press, Inc. (Subsidiary of: Greenwood Publishing Group Inc.), 88 Post Rd. W., Box 5007, Westport, CT 06881-5007. TEL 203-226-3571. FAX 203-222-1502.

320 973   US   ISSN 1061-6500
BIBLIOGRAPHIES OF THE PRESIDENTS OF THE UNITED STATES. 1988. irreg. price varies. Greenwood Press, Inc. (Subsidiary of: Greenwood Publishing Group Inc.), 88 Post Rd. W., Box 5007, Westport, CT 06881-5007. TEL 203-226-3571. FAX 203-222-1502.

320 900   US   ISSN 1056-5523
BIBLIOGRAPHIES OF WORLD LEADERS. 1989. irreg. price varies. Greenwood Press, Inc. (Subsidiary of: Greenwood Publishing Group Inc.), 88 Post Rd. W., Box 5007, Westport, CT 06881-5007. TEL 203-226-3571. FAX 203-222-1502.

320 016   GW   ISSN 0067-8015
BIBLIOTHECA IBERO-AMERICANA. 1959. irreg. price varies. (Ibero-Amerikanisches Institut, Berlin) Colloquium Verlag, Luetzowstr. 105, 1000 Berlin 30, Germany. Ed. Dietrich Briesemeister. circ. 1,000.

320   GW
BOCHUM. AMT FUER STATISTIK, STADTFORSCHUNG UND WAHLEN. REIHE "WAHLEN IN BOCHUM". 1946. irreg. DM.20. Amt fuer Statistik, Stadtforschung und Wahlen, Postfach 102270, 4630 Bochum 1, Germany. TEL 0234-9102330. FAX 0234-9103307. charts; stat.
Description: Report and survey of general elections.

011 320   EI
COMMISSION OF THE EUROPEAN COMMUNITIES. DOCUMENTATION BULLETIN.. (Text in Danish, Dutch, English, French, German, Italian) no.8, 1975. s-m. Commission of the European Communities, Central Archives and Documentation Service, 200 rue de la Loi, B-1049 Brussels, Belgium. Ed. Carel Martens.

320   US
CONGRESSIONAL RECORD SCANNER. 180/yr. $555. Congressional Quarterly Inc., 1414 22nd St., N.W., Washington, DC 20037. TEL 800-432-2250. FAX 202-728-1863. Ed. Evelyn Russell.
●Also available online.
Description: Abstracts to each day's Congressional Record.

CONNEXIONS DIGEST; a social change sourcebook. see *POLITICAL SCIENCE*

327   US   ISSN 0882-2743
Z1605
CONTENTS OF PERIODICALS ON LATIN AMERICA. 1983. q. $24. University of Miami, North - South Center Publications, Graduate School of International Studies, c/o Mercy F. Vega, Box 284123, Coral Gables, FL 33124-3010. TEL 305-284-6868. FAX 305-284-6370. Ed. Jaime Suchlicki. circ. 500.

320   DK   ISSN 0107-0452
COPENHAGEN POLITICAL STUDIES ABSTRACTS. 1982. irreg. free. University of Copenhagen, Institute of Political Studies - Koebenhavns Universitet, Rosenborggade 15-2, 1130 Copenhagen K, Denmark. Ed.Bd. bk.rev.; circ. 500.
Formerly: C P S A.

POLITICAL SCIENCE — ABSTRACTING, BIBLIOGRAPHIES, STATISTICS

327   FR
COUNCIL OF EUROPE. DOCUMENTATION SECTION. BIBLIO BULLETIN. SERIES: EAST - WEST RELATIONS. 1990. m. free. Council of Europe, Documentation Section, BP 431 R6, 67006 Strasbourg, France. TEL 88-41-20-00. FAX 88-36-70-57. TELEX EUR 870 943F. (Dist. in U.S. by: Manhattan Publishing Co., 225 Lafayette St., New York, NY 10012) circ. 300.
   Description: Bibliographic references to periodical articles and books available in the Library and Documentation Centers on subjects relevant to the Council of Europe in the field of East-West relations. Includes a topical section giving extracts, facts and figures, or news on a particular country or event.

320 016 330
COUNCIL OF EUROPE. DOCUMENTATION SECTION. BIBLIO BULLETIN. SERIES: POLITICAL, ECONOMIC AND SOCIAL AFFAIRS. 1972. m. free. Council of Europe, Documentation Section, BP 431 R6, 67006 Strasbourg, France. TEL 88-44-20-00. FAX 88-36-70-57. TELEX EUR 870 943F. (Dist. in U.S. by: Manhattan Publishing Co., 225 Lafayette St., New York, NY 10012) circ. 300.
   Former titles: Council of Europe. Central Library. Biblio Bulletin. Series: Political and Social Affairs; Council of Europe. Documentation Section and Library. Bibliographical Bulletin. Series: Political, Economic and Social Affairs; Council of Europe. Documentation Section and Library. Bibliographical Bulletin. Series: Political and Economic Affairs.
   Description: Index of periodical articles on international relations, politics, economic and social affairs.

960 016   US   ISSN 0011-3255
Z3501
CURRENT BIBLIOGRAPHY ON AFRICAN AFFAIRS. 1968. q. $110. Baywood Publishing Co., Inc., 26 Austin Ave., Box 337, Amityville, NY 11701. TEL 516-691-1270. FAX 516-691-1770. Ed. Paula Boesch. bk.rev.; bibl.; author index. (back issues avail.) **Indexed:** CERDIC, Curr.Cont.Africa, M.L.A. —BLDSC shelfmark: 3494.450000.
   Description: Features commentary and bibliographic section.

015   US
D839
CURRENT DIGEST OF THE POST-SOVIET PRESS. 1949. w. $755 to institutions. Current Digest of the Soviet Press, 3857 N. High St., Columbus, OH 43214-3747. TEL 614-292-4234. FAX 614-267-6310. Ed. Fred C. Schulze. bk.rev.; abstr.; charts; illus.; q. index; circ. 1,200. (also avail. in microfiche; microfilm; back issues avail.) **Indexed:** Int.Polit.Sci.Abstr., Mid.East: Abstr.& Ind., P.A.I.S.
●Also available online. Vendor(s): DIALOG (File no.645), Mead Data Central.
   Formerly (until 1991): Current Digest of the Soviet Press (ISSN 0011-3425); Incorporates: Current Abstracts of the Soviet Press (ISSN 0011-3166)
   Description: Translations or abstracts of materials selected from approximately 90 periodicals from countries in the former Soviet Union.

320.531   US
CURRENT DIGEST OF THE POST-SOVIET PRESS. ANNUAL INDEX. 1976. a. price varies. Current Digest of the Soviet Press, 3857 N. High St., Columbus, OH 43214-3747. TEL 614-292-4234. FAX 614-267-6310. Ed. Robert S. Ehlers.
   Formerly (until 1991): Current Digest of the Soviet Press. Annual Index.

CURRENT MILITARY AND POLITICAL LITERATURE. see POLITICAL SCIENCE — International Relations

011   US   ISSN 1046-4239
Z1223.Z9
DECLASSIFIED DOCUMENTS CATALOG. 1975. 6/yr. $845. Research Publications, Inc. (Woodbridge), 12 Lunar Dr., Drawer AB, Woodbridge, CT 06525. TEL 203-397-2600. FAX 203-397-3893. Ed. Evelyn Hatkin. (also avail. in microfiche from RPI; back issues avail.)
   Formerly: Declassified Documents Quarterly Catalog (ISSN 0099-0957)
   Description: Includes information regarding United States' post-World War II international relations from the Cold War through the Vietnam era. Provides a comprehensive compilation of documents microfilmed, abstracted, and indexed as they are released by government agencies or obtained from the National Archives and Presidential Libraries.

DEUTSCHE BUECHER. see LITERATURE — Abstracting, Bibliographies, Statistics

DIRECTORY OF POLITICAL PERIODICALS; a guide to newsletters, journals and newspapers. see BUSINESS AND ECONOMICS — Trade And Industrial Directories

DOCUMENTATIEBLAD: THE ABSTRACTS JOURNAL OF THE AFRICAN STUDIES CENTRE LEIDEN. see SOCIAL SCIENCES: COMPREHENSIVE WORKS — Abstracting, Bibliographies, Statistics

015 327   II   ISSN 0419-5345
Z3001
DOCUMENTATION ON ASIA. 1960. a. Rs.100($30) Indian Council of World Affairs, Library, Sapru House, Barakhamba Rd., New Delhi 110001, India. Eds. V. Machwe, Ashok Jambhakar.

EDITORIALS ON FILE; newspaper editorial reference service with index. see HISTORY — Abstracting, Bibliographies, Statistics

328   PN
ESTADISTICA PANAMENA. SITUACION POLITICA, ADMINISTRATIVA Y JUSTICIA. SECCION 611. ESTADISTICA ELECTORAL. 1960. irreg. BI.0.75. Direccion de Estadistica y Censo, Contraloria General, Apartado 5213, Panama 5, Panama. FAX 63-9322. circ. 2,000.
   Formerly: Estadistica Panamena. Estadistica Electoral (ISSN 0078-897X)

314 320   FI
FINLAND. TILASTOKESKUS. VALTIOLLISET VAALIT. KANSANEDUSTAJAIN VAALIT/FINLAND. STATISTIKCENTRALEN. STATLIGA VAL. RIDSDAGSMANNAVALEN/FINLAND. CENTRAL STATISTICAL OFFICE. NATIONAL ELECTIONS. PARLIAMENTARY ELECTIONS. (Section XXIX A of Official Statistics of Finland) (Text in Finnish, Swedish and English) 1909. irreg. FIM 32. Tilastokeskus, Annankatu 44, SF-00100 Helsinki 10, Finland.
   Formerly: Finland. Tilastokeskus. Kansanedustajain Vaalit (ISSN 0355-2209)

FINLAND. TILASTOKESKUS. VALTIOLLISET VAALIT. TASAVALLAN PRESIDENTIN VAALIT VALISIJAMIESTEN. see POLITICAL SCIENCE

HISTORICAL ABSTRACTS. PART A: MODERN HISTORY ABSTRACTS, 1450-1914. see HISTORY — Abstracting, Bibliographies, Statistics

HISTORICAL ABSTRACTS. PART B: TWENTIETH CENTURY ABSTRACTS, 1914 TO THE PRESENT. see HISTORY — Abstracting, Bibliographies, Statistics

HUMAN RIGHTS ORGANIZATIONS & PERIODICALS DIRECTORY. see BUSINESS AND ECONOMICS — Trade And Industrial Directories

320   II   ISSN 0250-9660
JA26
I C S S R JOURNAL OF ABSTRACTS AND REVIEWS: POLITICAL SCIENCE. (Text in English) 1973. s-a. Rs.30 to individuals; institutions Rs.50($10). Indian Council of Social Science Research, 35 Ferozshah Rd., New Delhi 110 001, India. TEL 381571. TELEX 31-61083-ISSR-IN. Ed. Kuldeep Mathur. adv.; bk.rev.; bibl.; circ. 550. (back issues avail.)
   Description: Abstracts of articles in political science published in Indian journals.

320 011   US   ISSN 0191-1058
Z1223.5.I3
ILLINOIS. STATE LIBRARY, SPRINGFIELD. PUBLICATIONS OF THE STATE OF ILLINOIS.. a. free. State Library, 300 S. Second St., Springfield, IL 62701. TEL 217-782-4887. (also avail. in microform)

327 011   US
INDEX: FOREIGN BROADCAST INFORMATION SERVICE DAILY REPORTS: AFRICA SUB-SAHARA. 1980. m. (plus annual cum.). $195. NewsBank, Inc., 58 Pine St., New Canaan, CT 06840-5426. TEL 203-966-1100. FAX 203-966-6254. Ed. Jean Austin. (also avail. in microfiche; back issues avail.)
●Also available on CD-ROM.
   Former titles: Index: Foreign Broadcast Information Service Daily Reports: South Asia (ISSN 0731-3233); Index: Foreign Broadcast Information Service Daily Reports: Sub-Saharan Africa.

327 011   US   ISSN 0271-1761
DS701
INDEX: FOREIGN BROADCAST INFORMATION SERVICE DAILY REPORTS: CHINA. 1975. m. (plus annual cum.) $195. NewsBank, Inc., 58 Pine St., New Canaan, CT 06840-5426. TEL 203-966-1100. FAX 203-966-6254. Ed. Jean Austin. (also avail. in microfiche; back issues avail.)
●Also available on CD-ROM.
   Formerly: Index: Foreign Broadcast Information Service Daily Reports: People's Republic of China.

327 011   US
INDEX: FOREIGN BROADCAST INFORMATION SERVICE DAILY REPORTS: EAST ASIA. 1978. m. (plus annual cum.) $195. NewsBank, Inc., 58 Pine St., New Canaan, CT 06840-5426. TEL 203-966-1100. FAX 203-966-6254. Ed. Jean Austin. (also avail. in microfiche; back issues avail.)
●Also available on CD-ROM.
   Formerly: Index: Foreign Broadcast Information Service Daily Reports: Asia and Pacific (ISSN 0272-3875)

327 011   US   ISSN 0731-4116
DJK1
INDEX: FOREIGN BROADCAST INFORMATION SERVICE DAILY REPORTS: EASTERN EUROPE. 1978. m. (plus annual cum.). $195. NewsBank, Inc., 58 Pine St., New Canaan, CT 06840-5426.
TEL 203-966-1100. FAX 203-966-6254. Ed. Jean Austin. (also avail. in microfiche; back issues avail.)
●Also available on CD-ROM.

327 011   US   ISSN 0278-1360
F1401
INDEX: FOREIGN BROADCAST INFORMATION SERVICE DAILY REPORTS: LATIN AMERICA. 1978. m. (plus annual cum.). $195. NewsBank, Inc., 58 Pine St., New Canaan, CT 06840-5426.
TEL 203-966-1100. FAX 203-966-6254. Ed. Jean Austin. (also avail. in microfiche; back issues avail.)
●Also available on CD-ROM.

327 011   US
INDEX: FOREIGN BROADCAST INFORMATION SERVICE DAILY REPORTS: NEAR EAST AND SOUTH ASIA. 1980. m. (plus annual cum.). $195. NewsBank, Inc., 58 Pine St., New Canaan, CT 06840-5426. TEL 203-966-1100. FAX 203-966-6254. Ed. Jean Austin. (also avail. in microfiche; back issues avail.)
●Also available on CD-ROM.
   Former titles: Index: Foreign Broadcast Information Service Daily Reports: Middle East and Africa; Index: Foreign Broadcast Information Service Daily Reports: Middle East and North Africa (ISSN 0736-3427)

327 011   US   ISSN 0731-3276
DK1
INDEX: FOREIGN BROADCAST INFORMATION SERVICE DAILY REPORTS: SOVIET UNION. 1977. m. (plus annual cum.). $195. NewsBank, Inc., 58 Pine St., New Canaan, CT 06840-5426.
TEL 203-966-1100. FAX 203-966-6254. Ed. Jean Austin. (also avail. in microfiche; back issues avail.)
●Also available on CD-ROM.

327 011   US
INDEX: FOREIGN BROADCAST INFORMATION SERVICE DAILY REPORTS: WESTERN EUROPE. 1978. m. (plus annual cum.). $195. NewsBank, Inc., 58 Pine St., New Canaan, CT 06840-5426.
TEL 203-966-1100. FAX 203-966-6254. Ed. Jean Austin. (also avail. in microfiche; back issues avail.)
●Also available on CD-ROM.

INDIA AND WORLD AFFAIRS: AN ANNUAL BIBLIOGRAPHY. see HISTORY — Abstracting, Bibliographies, Statistics

INDICE ESPANOL DE CIENCIAS SOCIALES. SERIES B: ECONOMICS, SOCIOLOGY AND POLITICAL SCIENCE. see BUSINESS AND ECONOMICS — Abstracting, Bibliographies, Statistics

327 016   YU
INSTITUT ZA MEDUNARODNU POLITIKU I PRIVREDU. BILTEN DOKUMENTACIJE. 1972. s-a. Institut za Medjunarodnu Politiku i Privredu - Institute of International Politics and Economics, Makedonska 25, Box 750, Belgrade, Yugoslavia. Ed. Vera Sekulic. bibl.

POLITICAL SCIENCE — ABSTRACTING, BIBLIOGRAPHIES, STATISTICS

320 016.32   UK   ISSN 0085-2058
Z7163
INTERNATIONAL BIBLIOGRAPHY OF THE SOCIAL SCIENCES. POLITICAL SCIENCE. Title page also reads: International Bibliography of Political Science. (Text in English, French) 1953. a. £95($170) in U.K. and Europe. British Library of Political and Economic Science, Lionel Robbins Building, 10 Portugal St., London WC2A 2HD, England. TEL 071-955-7144. (Co-sponsor: Routledge, 11 New Fetter Lane, London EC4P 4EE) (reprint service avail. from KTO)
    Description: Indexes monographs and the contents of over 2000 journals in the social sciences from a selective bibliography by subject, geographical terms, and author.

320 016   US   ISSN 0960-1538
▼**INTERNATIONAL CURRENT AWARENESS SERVICES. POLITICAL SCIENCE.*** 1990. m. £150 in U.K. and Europe; U.S. $295; elsewhere £175. British Library of Political and Economic Science, Lionel Robbins Building, 10 Portugal St., London WC2A 2HD, England. TEL 071-955-7144. (Co Sponsor: Routledge, 11 New Fetter Lane, London EC4P 4EE)
    Description: Lists tables of contents of political science journals, book reviews and contents of selected multi-authored monographs. Indexed by subject keywords, and geographical placenames.

320   NO   ISSN 0020-8345
JA36
INTERNATIONAL POLITICAL SCIENCE ABSTRACTS/DOCUMENTATION POLITIQUE INTERNATIONALE. (Summaries in English, French) 1951. bi-m. $65 to individuals; institutions $220 (1480 F.). International Political Science Association, c/o University of Oslo, Institute of Political Science, Box 1097 Blindern, 0317 Oslo 3, Norway. Ed. Serge Hurtig. adv.; index. cum.index; circ. 1,500. (back issues avail.) **Indexed:** E.I.
    —BLDSC shelfmark: 4544.960000.
    Description: Abstracts of political science articles in periodicals and yearbooks worldwide.

320 352 310   US
IOWA OFFICIAL REGISTER. 1892. biennial. free. Secretary of State of Iowa, Statehouse, Des Moines, IA 50319. TEL 515-281-8796. FAX 515-242-6307. (Subscr. to: State Printing Office, Grimes State Office Building, Des Moines, IA 50319) Ed. Mark John Conley. illus.; circ. 13,000.

JOINT ACQUISITIONS LIST OF AFRICANA. see ANTHROPOLOGY — Abstracting, Bibliographies, Statistics

JOURNALS OF DISSENT AND SOCIAL CHANGE; a bibliography of titles in the California State University, Sacramento, library. see SOCIOLOGY — Abstracting, Bibliographies, Statistics

327 011   UK   ISSN 0950-6128
D410
KEESING'S RECORD OF WORLD EVENTS. 1931. 12/yr. £150($299) Longman Group UK Ltd., Westgate House, The High, Harlow, Essex CM20 1YR, England. TEL 0279 442601. (Dist. in U.S. and Canada by: Keesing's Contemporary Archives, Box 1584, Birmingham, AL 35201) Ed. Roger East. charts; quarterly index; circ. 5,000. (also avail. in microfiche from HPL)
    ●Also available online.
    —BLDSC shelfmark: 5088.350500.
    Formerly: Keesing's Contemporary Archives (ISSN 0022-9679)

KUKHOE HOEUIROK SAEGIN/INDEX TO THE NATIONAL ASSEMBLY DEBATES. see PUBLIC ADMINISTRATION — Abstracting, Bibliographies, Statistics

980   US   ISSN 0090-9416
F1401
LATIN AMERICAN INDEX. 1973. s-m. $249. Welt Publishing Co., 1413 K St. N.W., Ste. 800, Washington, DC 20005. TEL 202-371-0555. Ed. Barbara Annis. bk.rev.; bibl.; charts; stat.; tr.lit.; index, s-a. index. (looseleaf format; back issues avail.; reprint service avail. from KTO)

320 016   US   ISSN 0733-2998
Z7164.S67
LEFT INDEX; a quarterly index to periodicals of the left. 1982. q. $30 to individuals; institutions $60. Reference and Research Services, 511 Lincoln St., Santa Cruz, CA 95060. TEL 408-426-4479. Ed. Joan Nordquist. (back issues avail.)
    —BLDSC shelfmark: 5181.307850.
    Description: Provides a subject author index to the contents of periodicals with a leftist perspective.

N T I S TITLE INDEX. (U.S. National Technical Information Service) see TECHNOLOGY: COMPREHENSIVE WORKS — Abstracting, Bibliographies, Statistics

920   US
NAMES IN THE NEWS. 1978. m. (q. and a. cums.). price varies. NewsBank, Inc., 58 Pine St., New Canaan, CT 06840-5426. TEL 203-966-1100. FAX 203-966-6254. (paper index; articles on microfiche; CD ROM index)

324   NE   ISSN 0168-4884
NETHERLANDS. CENTRAAL BUREAU VOOR DE STATISTIEK. STATISTIEK DER VERKIEZINGEN. GEMEENTERADEN/ELECTION STATISTICS. MUNICIPAL COUNCILS. (Text in Dutch and English) 1946. irreg. Centraal Bureau voor de Statistiek, Prinses Beatrixlaan 428, Voorburg, Netherlands. (Subscr. to: SDU - Publishers, Christoffel Plantijnstraat, The Hague, Netherlands)

324   NE   ISSN 0168-5686
NETHERLANDS. CENTRAAL BUREAU VOOR DE STATISTIEK. STATISTIEK DER VERKIEZINGEN. TWEEDE KAMER DER STATEN-GENERAAL/ELECTION STATISTICS. SECOND CHAMBER OF THE STATES-GENERAL. (Text in Dutch and English) 1946. irreg. Centraal Bureau voor de Statistiek, Prinses Beatrixlaan 428, Voorburg, Netherlands. (Subscr. to: SDU - Plantijnstraat, The Hague, Netherlands)

NEW YORK TIMES INDEX HIGHLIGHTS. see JOURNALISM — Abstracting, Bibliographies, Statistics

971 011   CN   ISSN 0704-6839
NORTHERN TITLES: K W I C INDEX. (Key Word in Context) m. (with a. cum.). Can.$55. Canadian Circumpolar Library, University of Alberta, Edmonton, Alta. T6G 2E9, Canada. TEL 403-492-4409. circ. 60. (looseleaf format; back issues avail.)

320   RU   ISSN 0134-2800
NOVAYA INOSTRANNAYA LITERATURA PO OBSHCHESTVENNYM NAUKAM. NAUKOVEDENIE. 1947. m. 7.20 Rub. Akademiya Nauk S.S.S.R., Institut Nauchnoi Informatsii po Obshchestvennym Naukam, Ul. Krasikova 28-21, 117418 Moscow V-418, Russia. (Dist. by: Mezhdunarodnaya Kniga, ul. Dimitrova 39, Moscow G-200, Russia) Ed. N.I. Makeshin.

320.532 011   RU   ISSN 0134-2940
NOVAYA SOVETSKAYA I INOSTRANNAYA LITERATURA PO OBSHCHESTVENNYM NAUKAM. MEZHDUNARODNOE RABOCHEE DVIZHENIE; bibliograficheskii ukazatel' 1966. m. 7.20 Rub. Akademiya Nauk S.S.S.R., Institut Nauchnoi Informatsii po Obshchestvennym Naukam, Ul. Krasikova 28-21, 117418 Moscow V-418, Russia. Ed. D.Kh. Gol'skaya.

320   RU   ISSN 0208-0052
NOVAYA SOVETSKAYA LITERATURA PO OBSHCHESTVENNYM NAUKAM. NAUCHNYI KOMMUNIZM. 1982. bi-m. 10.40 Rub. Akademiya Nauk S.S.S.R., Institut Nauchnoi Informatsii po Obshchestvennym Naukam, Ul. Krasikova 28-21, Moscow 117418, Russia. (Subscr. to: Mezhdunarodnaya Kniga, Moscow 113095, Russia) Ed. G.L. Man'kovskaya.

341.1 016   CN   ISSN 0031-3599
JX1901
PEACE RESEARCH ABSTRACTS JOURNAL. 1964. m. Can.$240. Peace Research Institute-Dundas, 25 Dundana Ave., Dundas, Ont. L9H 4E5, Canada. TEL 416-628-2356. Ed. Dr. Hanna Newcombe. abstr.; index; circ. 400. **Indexed:** Abstr.Mil.Bibl.
    —BLDSC shelfmark: 6413.780000.
    Description: Abstracts of papers, articles and books dealing with questions of war and peace.

320 920   UK
PEOPLE IN POWER. 1987. bi-m. £142($222) Longman Group UK Ltd., Westgate House, The High, Harlow, Essex CM20 1YR, England. TEL 0279 442601. Ed. Ian Gorvin. (looseleaf format)

475   US
POLITICAL SCIENCE ABSTRACTS. 1967. a. price varies. I F I - Plenum (Subsidiary of: Plenum Publishing Corp.), 233 Spring St., New York, NY 10013. TEL 212-620-8000. FAX 212-463-0742. TELEX 23-421139.
    Formerly: Universal Reference System: Political Science, Government, and Public Policy Series. Annual Supplement.
    Description: Covers all aspects of political science and related fields.

029 320 016   GW   ISSN 0032-3438
JA14
POLITISCHE DOKUMENTATION; Referatedienst. Short title: Pol-Dok. 1966. 3/yr. DM.298. (Freie Universitaet Berlin, Leitstelle Politische Dokumentation) K.G. Saur Verlag KG, Ortlerstr. 8, Postfach 701620, 8000 Munich 70, Germany. TEL 089-76902-0. FAX 089-76902150. Ed. O. Kruss. circ. 1,000. **Indexed:** P.A.I.S.For.Lang.Ind.

907   US   ISSN 0887-171X
POLLING REPORT. 1985. fortn (w. in fall of even numbered yrs.). $195 (students & teachers $78). Polling Report, Inc., 509 Capitol Ct., N.E., No.100, Washington, DC 20002. TEL 202-544-5455. FAX 202-544-1695. Ed. Thomas H. Silver. bk.rev.; circ. 1,000.
    Description: Reports results of public opinion surveys on political, public affairs and business issues. Provides analytical articles by pollsters, academics and other opinion experts.

320 011   UK   ISSN 0307-9201
HT1501
SAGE RACE RELATIONS ABSTRACTS. 1976. q. £48($79) to individuals; institutions £120($198). (Institute of Race Relations) Sage Publications Ltd., 6 Bonhill St., London EC2A 4PU, England. TEL 071-374-0645. FAX 071-374-8741. Ed. Louis Kushnick. adv.: color page #130; trim 177 x 101; adv. contact: Bernie Folan. bibl.; index. (back issues avail.)
    —BLDSC shelfmark: 8069.253500.
    Description: Discusses discrimination, education, employment, health, politics and law.

015   SI
SINGAPORE NATIONAL PRINTERS. PUBLICATIONS CATALOGUE. (Text in English) 1973. irreg. free. Singapore National Printers Ltd., 303 Upper Serangoon Road, P.O. Box 485, Singapore 1334, Singapore. TEL 2820611. FAX 2854894. TELEX SNP-RS-24462. circ. 600.
    Supersedes: Singapore. Catalogue of Government Publications.

327 011   SA
SOUTH AFRICAN INSTITUTE OF INTERNATIONAL AFFAIRS. BIBLIOGRAPHICAL SERIES/SUID-AFRIKAANSE INSTITUUT VAN INTERNASIONALE AANGELEENTHEDE. BIBLIOGRAFIESE REEKS. 1976. a. price varies. South African Institute of International Affairs, P.O. Box 31596, Braamfontein 2017, South Africa. TEL 011-339-2021. FAX 011-339-2154. TELEX 4-27291 SA.

STUDIES IN PSEPHOLOGY. see POPULATION STUDIES — Abstracting, Bibliographies, Statistics

327 016   UN   ISSN 0250-5584
Z6481
U N D O C: CURRENT INDEX. (United Nations Documents) (Text in English) 1950. q. (plus annual cummulation on microfiche). $150 for complete series. United Nations Publications, Room DC2-853, New York, NY 10017. TEL 212-963-8302. FAX 212-963-3489. (Or: Distribution and Sales Section, Palais des Nations, CH-1211 Geneva 10, Switzerland) (also avail. in microfiche; reprint service avail. from KTO)
    Formerly (until 1979): U N D E X (ISSN 0041-7351)
    Description: Gives a comprehensive coverage of UN documentation including full bibliographic description, subject, author, and title indexes, and a check-list of UN documents received at Headquarters.

U S AND FOREIGN DIPLOMATIC CONTACTS. see
BUSINESS AND ECONOMICS — Trade And Industrial Directories

320 310   US   ISSN 0148-7760
HA1446
U S S R FACTS & FIGURES ANNUAL. 1977. a. $71. Academic International Press, Box 1111, Gulf Breeze, FL 32562-1111. (back issues avail.)
—BLDSC shelfmark: 9135.103400.

327 016   UN   ISSN 0041-7343
Z733
UNITED NATIONS. DAG HAMMARSKJOLD LIBRARY. CURRENT BIBLIOGRAPHICAL INFORMATION. (Text in English and French) 1971. m. $75. United Nations Publications, Rm. DC2-853, New York, NY 10017. TEL 212-963-8300. FAX 212-963-3489. (Or: Distribution and Sales Section, Palais des Nations, CH-1211 Geneva 10, Switzerland) (reprint service avail. from KTO) **Indexed:** Popul.Ind.
—BLDSC shelfmark: 3494.430000.
Formed by the merger of: Current Issues; New Publications in the Dag Hammarskjold Library.

341.13   UN   ISSN 0082-8084
Z7161
UNITED NATIONS. ECONOMIC AND SOCIAL COUNCIL. INDEX TO PROCEEDINGS. Chinese edition (ISSN 0252-547X) 1946. a. price varies. United Nations Publications, Rm. DC2-853, New York, NY 10017. TEL 212-963-8300. FAX 212-963-3489. (Or: Distribution and Sales Section, Palais des Nations, CH-1211 Geneva 10, Switzerland) (also avail. in microfiche; reprint service avail. from KTO)
—BLDSC shelfmark: 1973.980000.

341.13   UN   ISSN 0082-8157
UNITED NATIONS. GENERAL ASSEMBLY. INDEX TO PROCEEDINGS. Arabic edition (ISSN 0251-7655); Chinese edition (ISSN 0251-7647); French edition: Nations Unies. Assemblee Generale. Index des Actes (ISSN 0258-3682) (Issued as subseries of Official Records. Supplements) 1946. a. price varies. United Nations Publications, Rm. DC2-853, New York, NY 10017. TEL 212-963-8302. FAX 212-963-3489. (Or: Distribution and Sales Section, Palais des Nations, CH-1211 Geneva 10, Switzerland) (reprint service avail. from KTO)
Formerly: Resolutions of the General Assembly of the United Nations (ISSN 0082-8211)

341.13   UN   ISSN 0082-8408
JX1977
UNITED NATIONS. SECURITY COUNCIL. INDEX TO PROCEEDINGS. Chinese edition (ISSN 0251-3994) 1946. a. price varies. United Nations Publications, Rm. DC2-853, New York, NY 10017. TEL 212-963-8300. FAX 212-96303489. (Or: Distribution and Sales Section, Palais des Nations, CH-1211 Geneva 10, Switzerland) (also avail. in microfiche; reprint service avail. from KTO)

341.13   UN   ISSN 0082-8491
UNITED NATIONS. TRUSTEESHIP COUNCIL. INDEX TO PROCEEDINGS. 1953. a. $4. United Nations Publications, Room DC2-853, New York, NY 10017. TEL 212-963-8302. FAX 212-963-3489. (Or: Distribution and Sales Section, Palais des Nations, CH-1211 Geneva 10, Switzerland) (also avail. in microfiche; reprint service avail. from KTO)

327 016   UN   ISSN 0251-6616
Z949
UNITED NATIONS LIBRARY. MONTHLY BIBLIOGRAPHY. PART 1: BOOKS, OFFICIAL DOCUMENTS, SERIALS. (Text in English and French) 1971. bi-m. $60. United Nations Publications, Rm. DC2-853, New York, NY 10017. TEL 212-963-8300. FAX 212-963-3489. (Or: Distribution and Sales Section, Palais des Nations, CH-1211 Geneva 10, Switzerland) **Indexed:** Popul.Ind.
—BLDSC shelfmark: 5930.711000.
Formerly (until 1977): United Nations Library. Monthly List of Books Catalogued in the Library of the United Nations. (ISSN 0041-7394)
Description: A subject compilation of newly acquired books, official documents and periodicals received in the UN Library in Geneva.

327 016   UN   ISSN 0251-6624
UNITED NATIONS LIBRARY. MONTHLY BIBLIOGRAPHY. PART 2: SELECTED ARTICLES. (Text in English and French) 1971. m. $60. United Nations Publications, Rm. DC2-853, New York, NY 10017. TEL 212-963-8300. FAX 212-963-3489. (Or: Distribution and Sales Section, Palais des Nations, CH-1211 Geneva 10, Switzerland) circ. 1,610.
—BLDSC shelfmark: 5930.712000.
Formerly (until 1977): United Nations Library. Monthly List of Selected Articles (ISSN 0041-7408)
Description: A worldwide list of selected journal articles on political, legal, economic, financial and other topics of current United Nations interest.

320   US
U.S. BUREAU OF THE CENSUS. CONGRESSIONAL DISTRICTS. (Series PHC80-4) 1961. irreg. price varies. U.S. Bureau of the Census, Data User Services Division, Washington, DC 20233. TEL 301-763-4100. (Dist. by: Supt. of Documents, Washington, DC 20402) (also avail. in microfiche)

U.S. DEPARTMENT OF STATE. LIBRARY. COMMERCIAL LIBRARY PROGRAM. PUBLICATIONS LIST. see *LIBRARY AND INFORMATION SCIENCES — Abstracting, Bibliographies, Statistics*

WASHINGTON SUMMARY. see *LAW — Abstracting, Bibliographies, Statistics*

ZIONIST LITERATURE. see *PUBLISHING AND BOOK TRADE — Abstracting, Bibliographies, Statistics*

POLITICAL SCIENCE — Civil Rights

323.9   US   ISSN 0896-8217
A A A A NEWS. q. $15. American Association for Affirmative Action, 11 E. Hubbard St., Ste. 200, Chicago, IL 60611. TEL 312-329-2512. FAX 312-329-9131. Ed. Patricia O'Keefe. adv.; bk.rev.; circ. 1,500.

323.4   UK
▼ **A A M BRIEFINGS SERIES.** 1990. 4/yr. £3. Anti-Apartheid Movement, 13 Mandela St., London NW1 0DW, England. TEL 071-387-7966. FAX 071-388-0173.

323.4   US
A C L U NEWS. 1936. 8/yr. $20 includes membership. American Civil Liberties Union of Northern California, 1663 Mission, San Francisco, CA 94103. TEL 415-621-2488. FAX 415-255-1478. Ed. Elaine Elinson. bk.rev.; circ. 20,000. (tabloid format)

323.4   AT   ISSN 1032-2205
A C S J C OCCASIONAL PAPERS. 1988. q. Australian Catholic Social Justice Council, Leo XIII House, 19 Mackenzie St., N. Sydney, N.S.W. 2060, Australia. TEL 02-956-5811. FAX 02-956-5782.

323.4   US
E184.A1
A D L ON THE FRONT LINE. 1943. m. $12. Anti-Defamation League of B'nai B'rith, 823 United Nations Plaza, New York, NY 10017. TEL 212-490-2525. Ed. Jane R. Ornauer. illus.; circ. 110,000. (also avail. in microform from UMI; reprint service avail. from UMI) **Indexed:** HR Rep., Ind.Jew.Per.
Formerly (until 1991): A D L Bulletin (ISSN 0001-0936)

323.4   SA
A F R A ADVICE SHEET. (Text in English and Zulu) 1989. irreg. R.1. Association for Rural Advancement, P.O. Box 2517, Pietermaritzburg 3200, South Africa. TEL 0331-57607. FAX 0331-455106. circ. 900. (tabloid format)

323.4   SA
A F R A NEWSLETTER. (Text in English) 1988. irreg. R.1. Association for Rural Advancement, P.O. Box 2517, Pietermaritzburg 3200, South Africa. TEL 0331-57607. FAX 0331-455106. circ. 900. (tabloid format; back issues avail.)
Description: Aims to publicize rural removals and farm worker conditions, and encourage rural African development in Natal, South Africa.

323.4   SA
A F R A SPECIAL REPORTS. 1980. irreg. Association for Rural Advancement, P.O. Box 2517, Pietermaritzburg 3200, South Africa. TEL 0331-57607. FAX 0331-455106. Ed. Marie Dyer. circ. 1,400. (looseleaf format; back issues avail.)

ACTING OUT. see *SOCIAL SERVICES AND WELFARE*

323.4 340   US
THE ADVOCATE (INDIANAPOLIS). 1983. q. $10. Indiana Civil Liberties Union, 445 N. Pennsylvania, Ste. 911, Indianapolis, IN 46204-1882. TEL 317-635-4059. FAX 317-635-4105. Ed. Donna L. Dean. illus.; circ. 7,000. (tabloid format; back issues avail.) **Indexed:** C.L.I.

AFFIRMATIVE ACTION REGISTER; the E E O recruitment publication. see *OCCUPATIONS AND CAREERS*

323.4   US
AFRICA WATCH. Variant title: News from Africa Watch. irreg. $40. Human Rights Watch, Africa Watch, 485 Fifth Ave., New York, NY 10017-6104. TEL 212-972-8400. FAX 212-972-0905. TELEX 910240 1007.
Description: Monitors and promotes observance of internationally recognized human rights in Africa.

323.4   US
AFRICA WATCH REPORT. irreg. Human Rights Watch, Africa Watch, 485 Fifth Ave., New York, NY 10017-6104. TEL 212-972-8400. FAX 212-972-0905. TELEX 910240 1007.
Description: In-depth coverage of human rights violations in Africa.

AFRICAN COMMUNIST. see *POLITICAL SCIENCE*

323.4 301.45   US
AGE DISCRIMINATION. 1981. 4 base vols. (plus a. suppl.). $240. Shepard's - McGraw-Hill, Inc., Box 35300, Colorado Springs, CO 80935-3530. TEL 800-525-2474. (looseleaf format)
Description: Contains annotations to more than 3,200 cases and hundreds of statutory and regulatory provisions.

AIM MAGAZINE (CHICAGO). see *ETHNIC INTERESTS*

323.4   US
AMERICAS WATCH. Variant title: News from Americas Watch. irreg. $40. Human Rights Watch, Americas Watch, 485 Fifth Ave., New York, NY 10017-6104. TEL 212-972-8400. FAX 212-972-0905. TELEX 910240 1007.
Description: Monitors and promotes observance of internationally recognized human rights in the Americas.

323.4   US
AMERICAS WATCH REPORT. irreg. Human Rights Watch, Americas Watch, 485 Fifth Ave., New York, NY 10017-6104. TEL 212-972-8400. FAX 212-972-9050. TELEX 910240 1007.
Description: In-depth coverage of human rights abuses, primarily in Central and South America.

355.224   US   ISSN 0003-1933
AMNESTY ACTION. 1967. bi-m. $25. Amnesty International U S A, 322 Eighth Ave., New York, NY 10001. TEL 212-807-8400. Ed. Ron LaJoie. bk.rev.; illus.; circ. 300,000. **Indexed:** Alt.Press Ind., HR Rep.

323.4   CN   ISSN 0831-9227
AMNESTY INTERNATIONAL. CANADIAN SECTION (ENGLISH SPEAKING). BULLETIN. 1974. 6/yr. Can.$15 to individuals; institutions Can.$25. Amnesty International, Canadian Section (English Speaking), 900-130 Slater Street, Ottawa, Ont. K1P 6E2, Canada. TEL 613-563-1891. FAX 613-563-7214. TELEX 053-3295. Ed. Patricia Acheson. bk.rev.; tr.lit.; circ. 12,000. (back issues avail.)
Description: Information about Amnesty International's work to release prisoners of conscience.

370 323.4   AT   ISSN 0256-0771
AMNESTY INTERNATIONAL AUSTRALIAN NEWSLETTER. 1983. m. Aus.$25. Amnesty International Australia, Private Bag 23, Broadway, N.S.W. 2007, Australia. FAX 211-3608. TELEX AA123206. Ed. June McGowan. bk.rev.; circ. 16,000.

POLITICAL SCIENCE — CIVIL RIGHTS

355.224 UK ISSN 0308-6887
AMNESTY INTERNATIONAL NEWSLETTER. (Editions in Arabic, English, French and Spanish) 1963. m. £7($12) for Newsletter; with Amnesty International Report £18($30). Amnesty International, 1 Easton St., London WC1X 8DJ, England. TEL 071-413-5500. FAX 071-956-1157. TELEX 28502. bk.rev.; circ. 35,000. **Indexed:** HR Rep.
  Former titles: Amnesty International Monthly (ISSN 0003-1941); Amnesty International Review.

AMNESTY INTERNATIONAL REPORT. see POLITICAL SCIENCE — International Relations

323.4 IE
AN REABHLOID/REVOLUTION. 1969. q. £4.50 to individuals; institutions £11. Peoples Democracy, 38 Clanawley Rd., Killester, Dublin 5, Ireland. Ed.Bd. adv.; bk.rev.; circ. 5,000.
  Formerly (until 1986): Socialist Republic; Incorporates: Unfree Citizen; Which was formerly: Free Citizen.
  Description: Organ of the Peoples Democracy, Irish Section, Fourth International.

ANGLES; the monthly magazine for Vancouver's lesbian and gay community. see HOMOSEXUALITY

ANNEE AFRICAINE. see LAW — International Law

323.4 UK
ANTI-APARTHEID MOVEMENT. ANNUAL REPORT OF ACTIVITIES AND DEVELOPMENTS. a. £10($30) Anti-Apartheid Movement, 13 Mandela St., London NW1 0DW, England. TEL 071-387-7966. FAX 071-388-0173. circ. 40,000.

323.4 UK ISSN 0003-5580
ANTI-APARTHEID NEWS. 1965. 10/yr. £10($30) (foreign £12) to individuals; institutions £13.50 (foreign £17). Anti-Apartheid Movement, 13 Mandela St., London NW1 0DW, England. TEL 071-387-7966. FAX 071-388-0173. Ed.Bd. adv.; bk.rev.; charts; illus.; circ. 20,000. (newspaper)
  Description: News and analysis on events in South Africa and campaigning information on the Anti-apartheid struggle.

ANTI-CENSORSHIP NEWSLETTER. see SOCIOLOGY

323.4 UK
ANTI-SLAVERY REPORTER. 1840. a. £4.95. Anti-Slavery International, 180 Brixton Rd., London, SW9 6AT, England. TEL 071-582-4040. FAX 071-587-0573. Ed. Alan Whittaker. adv.; bk.rev.; circ. 1,500.

323.4 US ISSN 0044-8931
ARMED CITIZEN NEWS. no.52, 1975. bi-m. $10. National Association to Keep and Bear Arms, Box 78336, Seattle, WA 98178. TEL 206-226-0467. Ed. Bill Pike. adv.; bk.rev.; illus.; circ. 20,000.

323.4 US
ASIA WATCH REPORT. irreg. Human Rights Watch, Asia Watch, 485 Fifth Ave., New York, NY 10017-6104. TEL 212-972-8400. FAX 212-972-9050. TELEX 910240 1007.
  Description: Covers human rights violations in Asia.

323.4 AT
AUSTCARE NEWS. 1976. 3/yr. Aus.$5. Australians Care for Refugees, 69-71 Parrmatta Rd., Camperdown, Sydney, N.S.W. 2050, Australia. TEL 02-565-9111. Ed. Margaret Piper. bk.rev.; circ. 11,000.
  Description: Covers refugee issues and policy.

323.4 GW
B M D - BERATUNGSDIENST. 1973. q. free. Bund der Mitteldeutschen e.V., Poppelsdorfer Allee 82, 5300 Bonn 1, Germany. TEL 0228-657071. (back issues avail.)

BACKLASH TIMES. see WOMEN'S INTERESTS

323.4 US ISSN 1043-6898
BALLOT ACCESS NEWS. 1985. 13/yr. $6. Coalition for Free and Open Elections, 3201 Baker St., San Francisco, CA 94123. TEL 415-922-9779. Ed. Richard Winger. bk.rev.; circ. 520.
  Description: Focuses on the rights of voters to support minor political parties and describes the progress being made against restrictive ballot access laws.

BATTERED WOMEN'S DIRECTORY. see WOMEN'S INTERESTS

323.4 US
BILL OF RIGHTS JOURNAL. 1952. a. $15. National Emergency Civil Liberties Committee, 175 Fifth Ave., Rm. 814, New York, NY 10010. TEL 212-673-2040. FAX 212-460-8359. Ed. Jeff Kisseloff. (also avail. in microform from UMI; reprint service avail. from UMI) **Indexed:** Alt.Press Ind., C.L.I., L.R.I., Leg.Per.

BIOPOLITICS. see POLITICAL SCIENCE

BLACK HERITAGE UNVEILED NEWSLETTER. see ETHNIC INTERESTS

322.4 US
BLACK LIBERATION JOURNAL. 1976. q. $4. (Communist Party, U.S.A.) Black Liberation Journal, Inc., 235 W. 23rd St., New York, NY 10011. TEL 212-989-4994. Ed. Charlene Mitchell. adv.; bk.rev.; illus.; circ. 2,000.

323.4 300 US ISSN 0895-5786
BLUEPRINT FOR SOCIAL JUSTICE. 1948. 10/yr. $10. Twomey Center for Peace through Justice, Loyola University, P.O. Box 12, New Orleans, LA 70118. TEL 504-861-5830. FAX 504-861-5833. Ed. Richard McCarthy. circ. 3,500. (back issues avail.)

323.4 IE
BOTTOM DOG. 1976. m. £2($5) 109 O'Malley Park, Limerick, Ireland. Ed. Joe Harrington. bk.rev.; film rev.; circ. 1,000. (back issues avail.)

323.4 SA ISSN 0262-3781
BRIEFING PAPER ON SOUTHERN AFRICA. (Supplement to: Focus on Political Repression in Southern Africa) 1981. irreg. (International Defence and Aid Fund for Southern Africa (IDAFSA), I D A F Research, Information and Publications Department) University of the Wester Cape, Private Bag X17, Bellville 7535, South Africa. Ed.Bd. **Indexed:** HR Rep.

323.4 CN
BRITISH COLUMBIA. COUNCIL OF HUMAN RIGHTS. ANNUAL REPORT. a. free. Council of Human Rights, Victoria, B.C. V8X 5Z8, Canada. TEL 604-387-3710. FAX 604-387-3643.

054.1 FR ISSN 0007-2672
BRULOT. 1936. m. 30 F. (foreign 35 F.) Gustave Arthur Dassonville, Ed. & Pub., 30b rue Moliere, 93170 Bagnolet, France. bk.rev.; abstr.; bibl.; circ. 3,500.

BUERGERRECHTE & POLIZEI. see CRIMINOLOGY AND LAW ENFORCEMENT

C A A NEWSLETTER (SAN FRANCISCO). (Chinese for Affirmative Action) see ETHNIC INTERESTS

C A A T NEWSLETTER. (Campaign Against Arms Trade) see POLITICAL SCIENCE

C A B NEWS. (National Association of Citizens Advice Bureaux) see LAW

C A R E NEWSLETTER. (Campaign Against Racial Exploitation (Australia) Inc.) see ETHNIC INTERESTS

355.224 US ISSN 0008-5952
UB342.U5
C C C O NEWS NOTES; covering war, peace and conscience. 1949. 4/yr. $6 to libraries; free to others. Central Committee for Conscientious Objectors, 2208 South St., Philadelphia, PA 19146. TEL 215-545-4626. Ed. Robert A. Seeley. adv.; bk.rev.; bibl.; circ. 40,000. (tabloid format; also avail. in microform from UMI; reprint service avail. from UMI) **Indexed:** Alt.Press Ind.
  Description: News items on contemporary issues pertaining to peace activism and conscientious objection.

323.4 AT
C C H R NEWSLETTER. 1972. irreg., latest Nov. 1985. Aus.$12($15) Citizens Committee on Human Rights, 24 Waymouth St., Adelaide, S.A. 5000, Australia. Ed. Colin Harris. circ. 350. (back issues avail.)

323.4 371.9 US
C D R REPORTS. 1983. m. $10. Council for Disability Rights, 208 S. La Salle St., Ste. 1330, Chicago, IL 60604-1102. TEL 312-444-9484. FAX 312-444-1977. Ed. Josephine E. Holzer. circ. 3,500. (also avail. in magnetic tape)

C L G R O NEWSLETTER. (Coalition for Lesbian and Gay Rights in Ontario) see HOMOSEXUALITY

323.4 910.03 US ISSN 0300-743X
E185.5
C O R E MAGAZINE.* vol.3, 1973. q. $10. (Congress of Racial Equality) C O R E Publications, 30 Cooper Sq., No. 9, New York, NY 10003-7151. TEL 212-598-4000. FAX 212-982-0184. Ed. George Holmes. adv.; bk.rev.; film rev.; charts; illus.; circ. 50,000.

CAHIERS DE FEMINISME. see WOMEN'S INTERESTS

CAHIERS DE L'AVENIR DE LA BRETAGNE. see HISTORY

CAMPUS WATCH. see EDUCATION — Higher Education

CANADA. INFORMATION COMMISSIONER. ANNUAL REPORT. see LAW — International Law

323.4 CN
CANADIAN HUMAN RIGHTS YEARBOOK/ANNUAIRE CANADIEN DES DROITS DE LA PERSONNE. 1983. a. Can.$50. (Human Rights Research and Education Centre) University of Ottawa Press, 603 Cumberland, Ottawa, Ont. K1N 6N5, Canada. TEL 613-564-2270. bibl. (back issues avail.)

CATACOMBES; messager supraconfessionel de l'Eglise du silence. see RELIGIONS AND THEOLOGY

323.4 309 CN ISSN 0824-2062
CATALYST (TORONTO). 1978. 8/yr. Can.$15 to non-members. C J L Foundation, Citizens for Public Justice, 229 College St., Ste. 311, Toronto, Ont. M5T 1R4, Canada. TEL 416-979-2443. Ed. Andrew Brouwer. adv.; bk.rev.; illus.; circ. 4,000. **Indexed:** Lang.& Lang.Behav.Abstr., Telegen.
  Former titles: Committee for Justice and Liberty. Newsletter (ISSN 0705-2103); C J L Foundation. Newsletter.
  Description: Forum for discussion of varied political views from a Christian justice perspective.

282 US ISSN 0164-0674
BX1617
CATHOLIC NEAR EAST MAGAZINE. 1974. q. $10. Catholic Near East Welfare Association, 1011 First Ave., New York, NY 10022-4195. TEL 212-826-1480. FAX 212-838-1344. TELEX 910 250 1440 NYK UQ. Ed. Michael L. Civita. bk.rev.; illus.; circ. 170,000. (controlled).
  Description: Articles and essays on human rights issues in Middle East, Eastern Europe and the former Soviet Union, India and Ethiopia. Includes articles on Eastern Christianity, both Catholic and Orthodox.

CENSORSHIP NEWS. see JOURNALISM

327 US ISSN 0735-8237
DS779.20
CHINA SPRING. (Text in Chinese) 1982. m. $28 to individuals; institutions $60. (Zhongguo Minzhu Tuanjie Lianmeng) China Spring Research Inc., 74-14 Woodside Ave., Elmhurst, NY 11373. TEL 718-429-6777. (Subscr. to: Box 701400, Trainsmeadow Sta., Flushing, NY 11370-9998) adv.; circ. 6,000. (back issues avail.) Key Title: Zhongguo zhi Chun.
  Description: Covers human rights, economics, and the politics of China.

CHRISTIANS IN CRISIS. see RELIGIONS AND THEOLOGY

323.4 360 US
CIVIL LIBERTARIAN; journal of civil, social and sexual liberty. 1983. bi-m. $15. L G L C, 1800 Market St., San Francisco, CA 94102. TEL 415-864-0952. Ed. Jim Peron. adv.; bk.rev. (back issues avail.)

323.4 US ISSN 0009-790X
JC599.U5
CIVIL LIBERTIES (NEW YORK). 1931. 3/yr. $20 membership. American Civil Liberties Union, 132 W. 43rd St., New York, NY 10036. FAX 212-869-9065. Ed. Jean Carey Bond. bk.rev.; illus.; circ. 275,000. (tabloid format) **Indexed:** HR Rep.

CIVIL LIBERTIES ALERT. see MEETINGS AND CONGRESSES

POLITICAL SCIENCE — CIVIL RIGHTS

323.4 US
CIVIL LIBERTIES OF WASHINGTON. 1969. irreg. (5-6/yr.). $25. American Civil Liberties Union of Washington, 705 Second Ave., Ste. 300, Seattle, WA 98104. TEL 206-624-8124. Ed. Doug Hinig. adv.; bk.rev.; illus.; circ. 9,500. (tabloid format)
Formerly: Civil Liberties (Seattle) (ISSN 0045-7051)
Description: Reports the activities and concerns of ACLU of Washington.

CIVIL LIBERTIES REPORTER. see *LAW — Civil Law*

323.4 US ISSN 0888-0417
CIVIL LIBERTIES REVIEW. 1988. 10/yr. $15. Box 2047, Olathe, KS 66061. TEL 913-829-0609.
Description: Reports on civil liberties and First Amendment issues, including due process, government surveillance, censorship and freedom of worship.

320 AT
CIVIL LIBERTY. 1968. q. Aus.$20. New South Wales Council for Civil Liberties, P.O. Box 201, Glebe, N.S.W. 2037, Australia. TEL 02-660 7582. FAX 02-660-5979. Ed. Beverley Schurr. adv.; bk.rev.; illus.; circ. 1,000.

323.4 UK
JC571
CIVIL LIBERTY AGENDA. 1976. q. £6 (foreign £8). National Council for Civil Liberties, 21 Tabard St., London SE1 4LA, England. TEL 071-403-3888. FAX 071-407-5354. Ed. Renee Harris. adv.; bk.rev.; circ. 8,000. **Indexed:** HR Rep.
Former titles (until 1991): Civil Liberty (ISSN 0267-5153); (until 1985): Rights (ISSN 0308-8227)

CIVIL RIGHTS AND CIVIL LIBERTIES LITIGATION: THE LAW OF SECTION 1983, 3-E. see *LAW — Civil Law*

323.4 SA ISSN 0045-706X
CIVIL RIGHTS NEWSLETTER. 1954. irreg. R.15($30) Civil Rights League, P.O. Box 23394, Claremont 7735, South Africa. Ed.Bd. adv.; bk.rev.; circ. 500.

323.4 AT ISSN 0155-2899
CLEAN AIR CLARION. 1978. q. Aus.$30. Non-smokers' Movement of Australia, Box 6 Trades Hall, 4 Goulburn St., Sydney, N.S.W. 2000, Australia. TEL 61-2-264-6243. FAX 61-2-267-4393. Ed. Arthur Chesterfield-Evans. adv.; bk.rev.; circ. 2,000. (back issues avail.)

323.4 NQ
COMISION NACIONAL DE PROMOCION Y PROTECCION DE LOS DERECHOS HUMANOS. BOLETIN. 4/yr. Comision Nacional de Promocion y Proteccion de los Derechos Humanos, Apdo. Postal 2595, Reparto Las Palmas, Casa 802, Managua, Nicaragua. Ed. Mario Ruiz Calderon. **Indexed:** HR Rep.

323.4 PY
COMITE DE IGLESIAS PARA AYUDAS DE EMERGENCIA. CUADERNOS. 1987. irreg., no.11, 1991. Comite de Iglesias para Ayudas de Emergencia, Gral Diaz 429, Asuncion, Paraguay.

323.4 PY
COMITE DE IGLESIAS PARA AYUDAS DE EMERGENCIA. ESTUDIOS. irreg., no.17, 1990. Comite de Iglesias para Ayudas de Emergencia, Gral Diaz 429, Asuncion, Paraguay.

323.4 PY
COMITE DE IGLESIAS PARA AYUDAS DE EMERGENCIA. NOTAS TRIMESTRALES. no. 20, 1991. q. Comite de Iglesias para Ayudas de Emergencia, Gral Diaz 429, Asuncion, Paraguay.

323.4 054.1 FR
COMITE SOLIDARITE PHILIPPINES. BULLETIN. q. Comite Solidarite Philippines, 68 rue de Babylone, 75007 Paris, France.

323.4 US
COMMUNICATOR (DES MOINES). 1975. q. Iowa Civil Rights Commission, c/o Grimes State Office Bldg., 211 E. Maple St., 2nd Fl., Des Moines, IA 50309-1858. TEL 515-281-4121. FAX 515-242-5840. illus.; circ. 2,000.
Formerly (until 1980): Challenger.
Description: News of agency's work, civil rights events in Iowa, and articles on civil rights issues.

COMPARATIVA. see *LAW*

COMPORTAMIENTO HUMANO. see *PHILOSOPHY*

CONGRESS RESISTER. see *POLITICAL SCIENCE*

325.4 US
CONSCIENCE; a magazine for war tax resisters. Variant title: Conscience and Military Tax Campaign. 1979. q. $10. Conscience & Military Tax Campaign, 4534 1-2 University Way N.E., Ste. 205, Seattle, WA 98105. TEL 206-547-0952. bk.rev.; charts; illus.; stat.; circ. 2,000. (back issues avail.)
Formerly (until 1987): C M T C Newsletter.
Description: Addresses issues of war tax resistance, military spending, non-violent action and the peace movement.

323.4 333.7 CN ISSN 0823-8669
CONSCIENCE CANADA NEWSLETTER. 1979. 4/yr. Can.$15. Conscience Canada Inc., Box 8601, Vic. Cent. PO, Victoria, BC V8W 3S2, Canada. TEL 604-384-5532. FAX 604-386-4453. Ed.Bd. bk.rev.; illus.; circ. 1,400. (back issues avail.)
Description: Supports the exercise of freedom of conscience and religion, especially the direction of taxes to peace instead of the military.

261 SZ ISSN 0259-0360
CONSCIENCE ET LIBERTE. 1948; N.S. 1971. 2/yr. 33 Fr.($24) International Association for the Defense of Religious Liberty - Association Internationale pour la Defense de la Liberte Religieuse, Schosshaldenstr. 17, CH-3006 Berne, Switzerland. FAX 031-446266. Ed. G. Rossi. bk.rev.; bibl.; circ. 10,750. **Indexed:** CERDIC.

323.4 US ISSN 0742-7115
K3
CONSTITUTIONAL COMMENTARY. 1984. s-a. $15. (University of Minnesota, Law School) Constitutional Commentary Inc., 229 19th Ave. S., Minneapolis, MN 55455. TEL 612-376-7235. FAX 612-625-2011. Eds. Dan Farber, Suzanna Sherry. adv.; bk.rev.; circ. 600. (also avail. in microfiche from WSH; back issues avail.; reprint service avail. from WSH) **Indexed:** Abstr.Bk.Rev.Curr.Leg.Per., C.L.I., Leg.Per.
●Also available online. Vendor(s): WESTLAW.
Description: Topical, inter-disciplinary journal on constitutional law.

341.48 FR
COUNCIL OF EUROPE. STANDING COMMITTEE ON THE EUROPEAN CONVENTION ON ESTABLISHMENT (INDIVIDUALS). PERIODICAL REPORT. 1971. irreg. Council of Europe, Publishing and Documentation Service, 67006 Strasbourg, France. (Dist. in U.S. by: Manhattan Publishing Co., One Croton Point Ave., Box 650, Croton-on-Hudson, NY 10520)

323.4 US ISSN 0010-9991
COUNCILOR.* 1959. s-m. $8. Councilor of LA, Inc., c/o June A. Touchstone, 7616 England Dr., Plano, TX 75025-3115. Ed. Ned Touchstone. adv.; bk.rev.; illus.; circ. 21,850. (tabloid format)

CRISIS (NEW YORK, 1910); a record of the darker races. see *ETHNIC INTERESTS*

323.4 US
CUBA: POLITICAL EXECUTIONS AND HUMAN RIGHTS. a. (Cuban Committee for Human Rights, CU) Georgetown University Press, Box 1260, Hoya Sta., Washington, DC 20054.

323.4 US
CUBAN AMERICAN NATIONAL FOUNDATION. PUBLICATION. irreg. no.28, 1988. Cuban American National Foundation, 1000 Thomas Jefferson St., N.W., Ste. 601, Washington, DC 20007. TEL 202-265-2822.

323.4 US
CUBAN UPDATE. irreg. Cuban American National Foundation, 1000 Thomas Jefferson St., N.W., Ste. 601, Washington, DC 20007.

323.4 ZA
DAWN. 1978. bi-m. $25. African National Congress of South Africa, Department of Information and Publicity, Box 31791, Lusaka, Zambia. Ed. Umkhonto Wesize. bk.rev.

DEMOCRAT. see *ADVERTISING AND PUBLIC RELATIONS*

323.4 SP ISSN 0210-301X
DERECHO CIVIL. ANUARIO. a. (plus q. updates). 6400 ptas. (foreign 7200 ptas.). Ministerio de Justicia, Centro de Publicaciones, Secretaria General Tecnica, Gran Via, 76-8, 28013 Madrid, Spain. TEL 247 54 22.
—BLDSC shelfmark: 1563.450000.

DIRECTORY OF CENTRAL AMERICA ORGANIZATIONS. see *BUSINESS AND ECONOMICS — Trade And Industrial Directories*

DISABILITY RAG. see *HANDICAPPED*

DOCUMENTACO E DIREITO COMPARADO. see *POLITICAL SCIENCE*

DZIENNIK POLSKI I DZIENNIK ZOLNIERZA/POLISH DAILY AND THE SOLDIERS DAILY. see *ETHNIC INTERESTS*

323.4 FR ISSN 0012-9224
ECHO DE LA LIBERTE DE L'OUEST; organe mensuel independant de Defense des Libertes Scolaires et Familiales. no.212, 1969. m. 35 F. Defense des Libertes Scolaires et Familiales, 10 rue Jules-Dauban, Angers, France. Ed. J. Bouyer. bk.rev.

EDUCATING IN FAITH. see *RELIGIONS AND THEOLOGY — Roman Catholic*

341.1 UK ISSN 0262-7922
JX1974.7
END PAPERS. 1967. 2/yr. £20($35) (Bertrand Russell Peace Foundation) Spokesman, Bertrand Russell House, 45 Gamble St., Nottingham NG7 4ET, England. TEL 0602-708318. FAX 0602-420433. Ed. K. Coates. adv.; bk.rev.; circ. 2,000. (back issues avail.) **Indexed:** HR Rep.
—BLDSC shelfmark: 3739.200000.
Incorporates: Spokesman (ISSN 0024-5992); London Bulletin.
Description: Forum for the discussion of international affairs with a particular focus on nuclear disarmament issues.

323.4 US
EQUAL EMPLOYMENT OPPORTUNITY. ANNUAL PROGRAM. a. (Office of Equal Employment Opportunity and Contract Compliance) Prentice Hall Law & Business, 270 Sylvan Ave., Englewood Cliffs, NJ 07632-2513. TEL 201-894-8484. FAX 201-894-8666.

EQUAL OPPORTUNITIES INTERNATIONAL. see *WOMEN'S STUDIES*

EQUAL RIGHTS. see *WOMEN'S INTERESTS*

ETHIOPIAN JEWRY REPORT. see *RELIGIONS AND THEOLOGY — Judaic*

ETHNIC AND RACIAL STUDIES. see *ETHNIC INTERESTS*

EUROPE LEFT. see *POLITICAL SCIENCE*

323.4 FR ISSN 0379-8461
EUROPEAN COMMISSION OF HUMAN RIGHTS. DECISIONS AND REPORTS. (Text in English, French) 1975. q. $12. Council of Europe, Publishing and Documentation Service, 67006 Strasbourg, France. (Dist. in U.S. by: Manhattan Publishing Co., One Croton Point Ave., Box 650, Croton, NY 10520)

323.4 NE ISSN 0071-2701
EUROPEAN CONVENTION ON HUMAN RIGHTS. YEARBOOK. (Not issued in 1964) 1959. a. price varies. (Council of Europe, FR) Kluwer Academic Publishers, Postbus 17, 3300 AA Dordrecht, Netherlands. TEL 078-334911. FAX 078-334254. TELEX 29245. (Dist. by: Kluwer Academic Publishers Group, P.O. Box 322, 3300 AH Dordrecht, Netherlands; N. America dist. addr.: Box 358, Accord Sta., Hingham, MA 02018-0358. TEL 617-871-6600)

323.4 GW ISSN 0073-3903
EUROPEAN COURT OF HUMAN RIGHTS. PUBLICATIONS. SERIES A: JUDGMENTS AND DECISIONS/COUR EUROPEENNE DES DROITS DE L'HOMME. PUBLICATIONS. SERIE A: ARRETS ET DECISIONS. (Text in English and French) 1961. irreg., vol.189, 1991. Carl Heymanns Verlag KG, Luxemburgerstr. 449, 5000 Cologne 41, Germany. TEL 0221-46010-0. FAX 0221-4601069.
—BLDSC shelfmark: 7059.767000.

POLITICAL SCIENCE — CIVIL RIGHTS

323 GW ISSN 0073-3911
EUROPEAN COURT OF HUMAN RIGHTS. PUBLICATIONS. SERIES B: PLEADINGS, ORAL ARGUMENTS AND DOCUMENTS/COUR EUROPEENNE DES DROITS DE L'HOMME. PUBLICATIONS. SERIE B: MEMOIRES, PLAIDOIRIES ET DOCUMENTS. (Text in English and French) 1961. irreg., vol.86, 1991. price varies. Carl Heymanns Verlag KG, Luxemburgerstr. 449, 5000 Cologne 41, Germany. TEL 0221-46010-0. FAX 0221-4601069.
—BLDSC shelfmark: 7059.767500.

EUROPEAN HUMAN RIGHTS REPORTS. see *LAW*

EVERYONE'S BACKYARD. see *ENVIRONMENTAL STUDIES — Waste Management*

EXILFORSCHUNG; ein internationales Jahrbuch. see *SOCIOLOGY*

EXPONENT II; a quarterly newspaper concerning Mormon women, published by Mormon women, and of interest to Mormon women and others. see *WOMEN'S INTERESTS*

F E W'S NEWS AND VIEWS. (Federally Employed Women Inc.) see *WOMEN'S INTERESTS*

F O I A UPDATE. (Freedom of Information Act) see *JOURNALISM*

323.4 US
FACT SHEETS ON INSTITUTIONAL RACISM; minority outlook on current issues. 1973. irreg., latest Nov. 1984. $2.95 per no. Council on Interracial Books for Children, Inc., 1841 Broadway, Rm. 500, New York, NY 10023. TEL 212-757-5339. bibl.; illus.
Supersedes: Viewpoint; Minority Outlook on Current Issues.

323.4 US
FACT SHEETS ON INSTITUTIONAL SEXISM. 1973. irreg., latest Apr. 1986. $2.95 per no. Council on Interracial Books for Children, Inc., 1841 Broadway, Rm. 500, New York, NY 10023. TEL 212-757-5339.

FAIR HOUSING: DISCRIMINATION IN REAL ESTATE, COMMUNITY DEVELOPMENT AND REVITALIZATION. see *HOUSING AND URBAN PLANNING*

FATHERS' JOURNAL. see *MEN'S INTERESTS*

FEDERAL STAFFING DIGEST. see *PUBLIC ADMINISTRATION*

FEMMES D'ICI. see *WOMEN'S INTERESTS*

323.4 US ISSN 0363-0447
KF4742
FIRST PRINCIPLES. 1975. 4/yr. $15. (Center for National Security Studies, Washington Legislative Office) American Civil Liberties Union (Washington, D.C.), 122 Maryland Ave., N.E., Washington, DC 20002. TEL 202-544-1681. FAX 202-546-0738. (National Headquarters addr.: 132 W. 43rd St., New York, NY 10036) Ed. Gary Stern. bk.rev.; circ. 3,500. **Indexed:** HR Rep.

323.4 US ISSN 0740-0195
E185.5
FOCUS (WASHINGTON, 1970). 1986. m. $15. Joint Center for Political Studies, Inc., 1301 Pennsylvania Ave., N.W., Ste. 400, Washington, DC 20004. TEL 202-626-3500. Ed. Sherille Ismail. charts; stat.; cum.index: 1972-1985; circ. 12,000. (back issues avail.) **Indexed:** P.A.I.S.
—BLDSC shelfmark: 3964.203000.

323.4 SA ISSN 0308-3586
DT737
FOCUS ON POLITICAL REPRESSION IN SOUTHERN AFRICA. Short title: Focus (London). (Supplement avail.: Briefing Papers) 1977. bi-m. £10($20) (International Defence and Aid Fund for Southern Africa (IDAFSA), I D A F Research, Information and Publications Department) University of the Western Cape, Private Bag X17, Bellville 7535, South Africa. TEL 071-359 9181. FAX 071-359-9690. TELEX 28110. (U.S. subscr. addr.: International Defence and Aid Fund for Southern Africa, U.S. Committee, Box 17, Cambridge, MA 02138) Ed.Bd. circ. 3,500. (back issues avail.) **Indexed:** HR Rep.
Description: Covers events in South Africa and Namibia. It focuses on repression by the apartheid regime and its illegal occupation of Namibia and on resistance to its rule.

323.4 IS
FOCUS SOVIET JEWRY. (Text in English) 1986. m. free. Israel Public Council for Soviet Jewry, Rehov Bak 1, Tel Aviv 67019, Israel. TEL 03-338267. FAX 3-334950. (Co-sponsor: World Zionist Organization) Ed. Deborah Lipson. circ. 6,000.
Description: Reports on the situation of Jews in the Soviet Union.

FORWARD (KAMPALA). see *SOCIAL SCIENCES: COMPREHENSIVE WORKS*

320 360 US ISSN 0882-3723
FOURTH WORLD JOURNAL. 1972. m. $7. Fourth World Movement, 7600 Willow Hill Dr., Landover, MD 20785-4658. TEL 301-336-9489. FAX 301-336-0092. Ed. Susan M. Devins. circ. 8,500. **Indexed:** HR Rep.

323.4 956 AT ISSN 0157-3845
FREE PALESTINE. 1979. bi-m. Aus.$10($20) P L O Office, c/o A. Kazak, P.O. Box 4646, Kingston, A.C.T. 2604, Australia. TEL 61-62-733711. FAX 61-62-733903. TELEX AA61367. Ed.Bd. bk.rev.; circ. 4,500.
Description: Covers developments in the Israel-Palestinian conflict.

FREE PRESS NETWORK. see *JOURNALISM*

323.4 US
FREE SPEECH NEWSLETTER. 1966. 3/yr. free. Speech Communication Association, 5105 Backlick Rd., Bldg. E., Annandale, VA 22003. TEL 703-750-0533. Ed. John Llewelyn. circ. 225.
Formerly: Free Speech.

323.4 US
FREEDOM MONITOR. 1985. bi-m. $25. Freedom House, 48 E. 21st St., New York, NY 10010. TEL 212-473-9691. Eds. Jonathan Karl, George Zarycky. circ. 3,000. (back issues avail.)

323.4 UK
FREEDOM TODAY. 1976. bi-m. £6. (Freedom Association Ltd.) Far and Wide Publishers Ltd., 35 Westminster Bridge Rd., London SE1 7JB, England. TEL 01-928-9925. FAX 01-928-9925. Ed. Philip Vander Elst. adv.; bk.rev.; circ. 10,000.
Formerly: Free Nation (ISSN 0309-3980)

323.4 US ISSN 1059-6372
FREEDOM WRITER; the national newsletter that defends separation of church and state. 1984. 10/yr. membership. Institute for First Amendment Studies, Inc., Box 589, Great Barrington, MA 01230. TEL 413-274-3786. FAX 413-274-3786. Ed. Skipp Porteous. bk.rev.; cum.index; circ. 7,000 (controlled). (looseleaf format; also avail. in microfiche; back issues avail.)
Description: Promotes human rights and the preservation of traditional American freedoms as guaranteed by the Constitution's Bill of Rights, with emphasis on seperation of church and state issues.

323.4 GW ISSN 0016-0911
DIE FREIHEITSGLOCKE/BELL OF FREEDOM. 1950. 11/yr. DM.30($15) Gemeinschaft Ehemaliger Politischer Haeftlinge (VOS), Borsigallee 6, 5300 Bonn 1, Germany. TEL 0228-257496. Ed. E. Reese. bk.rev.; index; circ. 2,500.

323.4 US ISSN 0741-353X
FROM THE STATE CAPITALS. CIVIL RIGHTS. 1946. w. $215 (foreign $235)(effective Dec. 1990). Wakeman-Walworth, Inc., 300 N. Washington St., Alexandria, VA 22314. TEL 703-549-8606. FAX 703-549-1372. (processed)
●Also available online. Vendor(s): WESTLAW.
Former titles: From the State Capitals. Racial Relations and Civil Rights; From the State Capitals. Racial Relations (ISSN 0016-1896)
Description: State and local governmental action in the US on ethnic, race and sex discrimination, desegregation, affirmative action, discrimination compensation, gay rights, the civil rights of the disabled.

FULL DISCLOSURE; for truth, justice, and the American way. see *CRIMINOLOGY AND LAW ENFORCEMENT — Security*

323.4 US
FUND FOR FREE EXPRESSION. irreg. $40. Human Rights Watch, Fund for Free Expression, 485 Fifth Ave., New York, NY 10017-6104. TEL 212-972-8400. FAX 212-972-9050. TELEX 910240 1007.
Description: Aims to monitor and combat censorship in the US and around the world.

G L B AMES NEWSLETTER. (Gays, Lesbians and Bisexuals of Ames) see *HOMOSEXUALITY*

323.4 301.4157 US ISSN 0890-7951
G L C VOICE; news and opinion for gays, lesbians and civilized others. 1979. s-m. $25. G L C Media, Inc., 1624 Harmon Pl., Ste. 206, Minneapolis, MN 55403-1916. TEL 612-338-1411. Ed. Tim Campbell. adv.; bk.rev.; circ. 16,000.

GAY SCOTLAND; for lesbians, gays & bisexuals. see *HOMOSEXUALITY*

GLAUBE IN DER 2. WELT; Zeitschrift fuer Religionsfreiheit und Menschenrechte. see *RELIGIONS AND THEOLOGY*

DIE GLOCKE VOM ETTERSBERG. see *HISTORY — History Of Europe*

GRACE AND TRUTH. see *RELIGIONS AND THEOLOGY — Roman Catholic*

GRAUER PANTHER. see *GERONTOLOGY AND GERIATRICS*

THE GUIDE: GAY TRAVEL, ENTERTAINMENT, POLITICS, AND SEX. see *HOMOSEXUALITY*

GUIDE MAGAZINE (SEATTLE). see *HOMOSEXUALITY*

H M K KURIER; aktuelle Berichte, Mitteilungen und Meinungen von und ueber Christen, die heute nicht in Freiheit leben. (Hilfsaktion Maertyrerkirche e.V.) see *RELIGIONS AND THEOLOGY*

323.4 200 US ISSN 0896-243X
HARMONY (SAN FRANCISCO); voices for a just future. 1987. bi-m. $12 (foreign $16). Sea Fog Press, Inc., Box 210056, San Francisco, CA 94121-0056. TEL 415-221-8527. Ed. Rose Evans. adv.; bk.rev.; circ. 670.
Description: Covers ethics, the opposition of the death penalty, war, abortion, euthanasia and economic injustice.

HARVARD BLACKLETTER JOURNAL. see *LAW*

HARVARD CIVIL RIGHTS - CIVIL LIBERTIES LAW REVIEW. see *LAW — Civil Law*

323.4 US
HARVARD HUMAN RIGHTS JOURNAL. 1988. a. $15 (foreign $17). Harvard University, Law School, Publications Center, Hastings Hall, Cambridge, MA 02138. TEL 617-495-3694. circ. 500. (reprint service avail. from WSH)
Description: Explores issues in human rights studies.

323 340.5 US
HARVARD HUMAN RIGHTS YEARBOOK. a. $10 (foreign $15). Harvard Law School, Cambridge, MA 02138. TEL 617-495-9362. bk.rev.
Refereed Serial

323.4 US
HELSINKI WATCH. Variant title: News from Helsinki Watch. irreg. $40. Human Rights Watch, Helsinki Watch, 485 Fifth Ave., New York, NY 10017-6104. TEL 212-972-8400. FAX 212-972-0905. TELEX 910240 1007.
Description: Monitors and promotes observance of internationally recognized human rights in Croatia.

323.4 US
HELSINKI WATCH REPORT. irreg. Human Rights Watch, Helsinki Watch, 485 Fifth Ave., New York, NY 10017-6104. TEL 212-972-8400. FAX 212-972-0905. TELEX 910240 1007.
Description: Covers human rights violations in Croatia.

POLITICAL SCIENCE — CIVIL RIGHTS 3943

323.4 AT ISSN 0815-9904
HERALD; South Australia's labor voice. 1894. q. Aus.$4.50($3.60) (Australian Labor Party, South Australian Branch) Workers Weekly Herald Pty. Ltd., A.L.P. Office, Trades Hall, 11 South Terrace, Adelaide, S.A. 5000, Australia. TEL 618-211-8744. FAX 231-4095. Ed. Philip Robins. adv.; bk.rev.; circ. 6,000. (tabloid format; back issues avail.)
Description: Political publication serving the Australian Labor Party and the United Trades and Labor Council in South Australia.

HERTHA. see *WOMEN'S INTERESTS*

HOLOCAUST STUDIES ANNUAL. see *HISTORY — History Of Europe*

323.4 NE
HOMOBEVRIJDING. q. fl.17.50. P S P-Homogroep, Postbus 700, 1000 AS Amsterdam, Netherlands. Ed. Paul van Ettekoven. bk.rev.; circ. 800.

HOMOSEXUAL INFORMATION CENTER. NEWSLETTER. see *HOMOSEXUALITY*

323.4 AT ISSN 0818-0954
HRVATSKA SLOBODA. (Text in Croatian and English) 1985. bi-m. Aus.$40($30) Croatian Cultural & Welfare Association, 10 Volga St., Glenroy, Vic. 3046, Australia. TEL (03)306-3153. Ed. Anton Babic. circ. 3,000. (tabloid format)
Description: Promotes the establishment of a free and democratic state of Croatia.

323.4 US ISSN 0046-8185
K8
HUMAN RIGHTS. 1970. 4/yr. $17 to non-members. American Bar Association, Individual Rights and Responsibilities Section, 750 N. Lake Shore Dr., Chicago, IL 60611. TEL 312-988-6047. FAX 312-988-6281. Ed. Vicki Quade. adv.; bk.rev.; bibl.; circ. 7,000. (also avail. in microfilm from RRI; reprint service avail. from RRI) **Indexed:** C.L.I., HR Rep., L.R.I., Leg.Per., Soc.Sci.Ind., SSCI.
●Also available online. Vendor(s): WESTLAW (HUMRT).
—BLDSC shelfmark: 4336.437000.
Description: News articles, features, and commentary on human rights and individual rights and responsibilities.

323.4 CN
HUMAN RIGHTS ACT OF BRITISH COLUMBIA. 1976. a. free. Council of Human Rights, Parliament Bldgs., Victoria, B.C. V8X 5Z8, Canada. TEL 604-387-3710. FAX 604-387-3643.
Supersedes: British Columbia. Human Rights Commission. Annual Report (ISSN 0706-5426)

323.4 UN ISSN 0251-7019
HUMAN RIGHTS BULLETIN. French edition: Bulletin des Droits de l'Homme (ISSN 0251-6993) (Text in English) 1969-1982; resumed 1986. q. free. United Nations Centre for Human Rights, Palais des Nations, 8-14 avenue de la Paix, 1211 Geneva 10, Switzerland. circ. 3,500.
Description: Examines the Declaration's impact on international law.

323.4 US
HUMAN RIGHTS BULLETIN (NEW YORK). 1945. s-a. $20 (subscr. includes International League for Human Rights. Annual Report). International League for Human Rights, 432 Park Ave. S., Ste. 1103, New York, NY 10016-8013. TEL 212-972-9554. Ed. Felice Gaer. circ. 3,600. **Indexed:** HR Rep.
Formerly: Rights of Man.

323.4 CN
HUMAN RIGHTS COUNCIL DECISIONS. irreg (36-40/yr.). Can.$122. Council of Human Rights, Victoria, B.C., Canada. TEL 604-387-3710. FAX 604-387-3643. (Subscr. to: Crown Publications, 546 Yates St., Victoria, B.C. V8W 1K8, Canada. TEL 604-386-4636)

323.4 CN ISSN 0275-049X
JC571
HUMAN RIGHTS INTERNET REPORTER. 1976. 4/yr. $50 to individuals; institutions $75. Human Rights Internet, c/o Human Rights Centre, University of Ottawa, 57 Louis Pasteur, Ottawa, Ont. K1N 6N5, Canada. TEL 613-564-3492. FAX 613-564-4054. TELEX 5106014536. Ed. Laurie S. Wiseberg. adv.; bk.rev.; bibl.; index; circ. 2,000. (also avail. in microform; back issues avail.) **Indexed:** Alt.Press Ind., Amer.Bibl.Slavic & E.Eur.Stud.
Formerly: Human Rights Internet Newsletter (ISSN 0163-9048)

HUMAN RIGHTS LAW JOURNAL. see *LAW — Constitutional Law*

323.4 UN ISSN 1014-4986
HUMAN RIGHTS NEWSLETTER. French edition: Courrier des Droits de l'Homme (ISSN 1014-4978) 4/yr. United Nations Centre for Human Rights, Palais des Nations, 8-14 avenue de la Paix, 1211 Geneva 10, Switzerland. TEL 4122-7346011. FAX 4122-7339879. TELEX 289696.

HUMAN RIGHTS ORGANIZATIONS & PERIODICALS DIRECTORY. see *BUSINESS AND ECONOMICS — Trade And Industrial Directories*

323.4 US
HUMAN RIGHTS RESOURCES. 1985. bi-m. $20. Human Rights Resource Center, 615 B St., San Rafael, CA 94901-3805. Ed. Patrisha Tulloch. circ. 1,500.
Description: Provides brief news reports and information for community groups, law enforcement agencies, and schools to deal with tensions resulting from intolerance and discrimination.

323.4 US
HUMAN RIGHTS WATCH. 1982. 4/yr. $20. Human Rights Watch, 485 Fifth Ave. 3rd Fl., New York, NY 10017-6104. TEL 212-972-8400. FAX 212-972-0905. TELEX 9102401007. Ed. Gara LaMarche. illus.; circ. 3,000. **Indexed:** HR Rep.
Description: Covers human rights issues and news. Includes a country-by-country summary of recent organization activites.

323.4 US ISSN 1054-948X
JC571
▼**HUMAN RIGHTS WATCH WORLD REPORT**. 1990. a. $20. Human Rights Watch, 485 Fifth Ave., New York, NY 10017-6104. TEL 212-972-8400. FAX 212-972-0905. TELEX 910240 1007. Ed. Kenneth Roth.
Description: Monitors and promotes human rights throughout the world.

323.4 GW ISSN 1015-5945
▼**HUMAN RIGHTS WORLDWIDE**. (Text in English) 1990. bi-m. $10. Internationale Gesellschaft fuer Menschenrechte, Kaiserstr. 72, 6000 Frankfurt a.M., Germany. TEL 069-236971. FAX 069-234100. Eds. Robert Chambers, Sylvia Waehling. circ. 5,000.

HUMAN SERVE CAMPAIGN NEWSLETTER. see *SOCIAL SERVICES AND WELFARE*

323.4 MP
HUNIY ERH/HUMAN RIGHTS. (Text in Mongolian) m. Voluntary Committee for Defence of Human Rights, P.O. Box 107, Ulan Bator, Mongolia. (Co-sponsor: Mongolian Section of Amnesty International)

I J A. RESEARCH REPORTS. (Institute of Jewish Affairs) see *ETHNIC INTERESTS*

I L G A BULLETIN. (International Lesbian and Gay Association) see *HOMOSEXUALITY*

I W G I A DOCUMENTS; documentation of oppression of ethnic groups in various countries. (International Work Group for Indigenous Affairs) see *ANTHROPOLOGY*

I W G I A NEWSLETTER. (International Work Group for Indigenous Affairs) see *ANTHROPOLOGY*

I W G I A YEARBOOK. (International Work Group for Indigenous Affairs) see *ANTHROPOLOGY*

347 US ISSN 0093-8939
KFI1725.5.A6
ILLINOIS. JUDICIAL INQUIRY BOARD. REPORT. 1973. irreg. free. Judicial Inquiry Board, 100 W. Randolph St., Ste. 14-500, Chicago, IL 60601. TEL 312-917-5554. FAX 312-814-5719. circ. 1,000. Key Title: Report - Judicial Inquiry Board (Chicago).

IMAGE (FORT WORTH). see *BUILDING AND CONSTRUCTION*

IMPARTIAL CITIZEN. see *ETHNIC INTERESTS*

323.4 US ISSN 0888-9724
IN THE MAINSTREAM. 1975. bi-m. $60. Mainstream, Inc., 3 Bethesda Metro Center, Ste. 830, Bethesda, MD 20814. TEL 301-654-2400. FAX 301-654-2403. Ed. Fritz Rumpel. bk.rev.; circ. 700. (magnetic tape; back issues avail.)
Description: Reports on the practical and legal issues of bringing persons with disabilities into the workplace.

323.4 US
INDEPENDENT TAIWAN. (Text in Chinese) 1972. m. $18. World United Formosans for Independence, Box 503, Kearny, NJ 07032. Ed. T.T. Huang. bibl.; index; circ. 10,000.

323.1 US ISSN 0046-8967
INDIAN AFFAIRS. 1949. q. $10. Association on American Indian Affairs, Inc., 245 Fifth Ave.., Ste. 1801, New York, NY 10016. FAX 212-685-4692. Dir. Gary Kimble. bk.rev.; circ. 40,000. (also avail. in microform from UMI; reprint service avail. from UMI)

INFOCUS NEWSLETTER. see *ETHNIC INTERESTS*

INFORMATIVO LEGAL RODRIGO. see *LAW*

323 US ISSN 0074-0764
INTER-AMERICAN COMMISSION OF WOMEN. SPECIAL ASSEMBLY. FINAL ACT/COMISION INTERAMERICANA DE MUJERES. ASAMBLEA EXTRAORDINARIA. ACTA FINAL. 3rd, 1963. biennial. price varies. Organization of American States, 1889 F St., N.W., Washington, DC 20006. TEL 703-941-1617. circ. 3,000.

323.4 CN ISSN 0226-661X
JC599.L3
INTER-CHURCH COMMITTEE ON HUMAN RIGHTS IN LATIN AMERICA. NEWSLETTER. 1977. 6/yr. Can.$20 to individuals; institutions Can.$35. Inter-Church Committee on Human Rights in Latin America, Ste. 201, 40 St. Clair Ave. E., Toronto, Ont. M4T 1M9, Canada. FAX 416-921-7478. Ed. Anne Beretta. circ. 1,200.
Description: Issues and information regarding human rights in Latin America.

INTER-HEMISPHERIC EDUCATION RESOURCE CENTER. BULLETIN. see *POLITICAL SCIENCE — International Relations*

323.4 SZ ISSN 0259-3696
INTERNATIONAL CHILDREN'S RIGHTS MONITOR. French edition: Tribune Internationale des Droits de l'Enfant. Spanish edition: Tribuna International de los Derechos del Nino. (Text in English) 1983. q. 30 Fr. to individuals; institutions 50 Fr. Defence for Children International, P.O. Box 88, CH-1211 Geneva 20, Switzerland. TEL 022-734-05-58. TELEX 414128 DCICH. bk.rev.; circ. 5,500. (also avail. in microfiche)
—BLDSC shelfmark: 4538.622000.
Description: Attempts to foster awareness about, and efforts in favor of, children and their rights throughout the world, by informing its readers about the needs and initiatives in this area.

323.4 SZ
INTERNATIONAL DOCUMENTATION ON MACEDONIA. (Text in English and French) 1979. irreg., vol.13, 1982. 120 Fr.($60) Case Postale 37, 1292 Chambesy, Geneva, Switzerland. Ed. Theodore D. Dimitrov. bibl.; charts; illus.; index. (back issues avail.)

INTERNATIONAL JOURNAL OF REFUGEE LAW. see *POLITICAL SCIENCE — International Relations*

POLITICAL SCIENCE — CIVIL RIGHTS

301.45 968   UN   ISSN 0538-8333
DT763
INTERNATIONAL LABOUR OFFICE. SPECIAL REPORT OF THE DIRECTOR-GENERAL ON THE APPLICATION OF THE DECLARATION CONCERNING THE POLICY OF APARTHEID OF THE REPUBLIC OF SOUTH AFRICA. 1965. a. price varies. (International Labour Office) I L O Publications, CH-1211 Geneva 22, Switzerland. TEL 022-796111. FAX 022-798-6358. TELEX 415-647-ILO-CH. (Dist. in U.S. by: I L O Publications Center, 49 Sheridan Ave., Albany, NY 12210) (also avail. in microform from WMP)

323.4   US   ISSN 0363-9347
JC571
INTERNATIONAL LEAGUE FOR HUMAN RIGHTS. ANNUAL REPORT. 1950. a. $20 includes subscription to Human Rights Bulletin. International League for Human Rights, 432 Park Ave. S., Ste. 1103, New York, NY 10016-8013. TEL 212-972-9554. Ed. Felice Gaer. circ. controlled. (also avail. in microform)
Formerly: International League for the Rights of Man. Annual Report.

INTERNATIONAL STUDIES. NORDIC SEMINAR ON HUMAN RIGHTS. PROCEEDINGS. see *LAW*

323.4   NE
INTERNATIONAL STUDIES ON HUMAN RIGHTS. (Text in English) a. Kluwer Academic Publishers, P.O. Box 17, 3300 AA Dordrecht, Netherlands. TEL 31-78-334267. (Dist. by: Kluwer Academic Publishers, P.O. Box 322, 3300 AH Dordrecht, Netherlands)

INTO THE COURTS. see *HOMOSEXUALITY*

320   US
IOWA CIVIL RIGHTS COMMISSION. ANNUAL REPORT. no.8, 1975. a. Iowa Civil Rights Commission, c/o Grimes State Office Bldg., 2nd Fl., 211 E. Maple St., 2nd Fl., Des Moines, IA 50319-1858. TEL 515-281-4121. FAX 515-242-5840. circ. 1,000.

323.4   US
IOWA CIVIL RIGHTS COMMISSION. CASE REPORTS. 1977. a. free. Iowa Civil Rights Commission, c/o Grimes State Office Bldg., 211 E. Maple St., 2nd Fl., Des Moines, IA 50319-1858. TEL 515-281-4121. FAX 515-242-5840. circ. 1,000.
Description: Decisions from the Hearings, Iowa District Court of Appeals and Iowa Supreme Court on Commision cases.

323 341   IS   ISSN 0333-5925
LAW
ISRAEL YEARBOOK ON HUMAN RIGHTS. (Text in English) 1971. a. $12. Tel Aviv University, Faculty of Law, Ramat Aviv, Tel Aviv, Israel. Ed. Dr. Yoram Dinstein. bk.rev.; circ. 1,500. *Indexed:* A.B.C.Pol.Sci., HR Rep.
—BLDSC shelfmark: 4583.960000.

323.4 340   JM
J.C.H.R. NEWS LETTER. 1974. q. $20. Jamaica Council of Human Rights, 131 Tower St., Kingston, Jamaica, W.I. TEL 809-92-25012. Ed. Florizelle A. O'Connor. bk.rev.; circ. 2,000. (also avail. in microfiche)
Indexed: HR Rep.

JACKSONVILLE FREE PRESS. see *ETHNIC INTERESTS*

323.4   IS
DS101
JEWS AND JEWISH TOPICS IN THE SOVIET UNION AND EASTERN EUROPE. 1985. 3/yr. IS.20($20) Hebrew University, Center for Research and Documentation of East European Jewry, Givat Ram, 91904 Jerusalem, Israel. TEL 02-584271. FAX 02-666804. bk.rev.; circ. 500.
Formerly: Jews and Jewish Topics in Soviet and East European Publications (ISSN 0334-6641)
Description: Includes a survey of trends and attitudes of publications produced in the USSR concerning Jews and Israel and a bibliography of relevant publications.

JEWS OF THE SOVIET UNION; immigration and struggle in the 1980's. see *RELIGIONS AND THEOLOGY — Judaic*

323. 918.103   BL
JORNAL DA F U N A I. 1986. m. free. Fundacao Nacional do Indio, Assessoria de Comunicacao Social, Quadra 702 Sul, Projecao "A" Ed. Lex, Sala 301, Brasilia, D.F., Brazil. illus.

323.4   IV
JOURNAL DES AMIS DU PROGRES DE L'AFRIQUE NOIRE. 5/wk. Abidjan, Ivory Coast.

338.91   UK   ISSN 0951-6328
HV640
JOURNAL OF REFUGEE STUDIES. 1988. q. £45($94) (Refugee Studies Programme) Oxford University Press, Oxford Journals, Pinkhill House, Southfield Road, Eynsham, Oxford OX8 1JJ, England. TEL 0865-882283. FAX 0865-882890. TELEX 837330-OXPRES-G. (U.S. addr.: 200 Madison Ave., New York, NY 10016) Ed. Roger Zetter. circ. 700.
—BLDSC shelfmark: 5048.550000.
Description: Academic exploration of the complex problems of forced migration and national and international responses. Includes anthropology, economics, health and education, international relations, law, politics, psychology and sociology.

323.4 296   SW
JUDARNA I SOVJET. 1973. irreg., (4-6/yr.). free. Svenska Kommitten foer Sovjets Judar - Swedish Committee for Soviet Jewry, Box 7427, S-103 91 Stockholm, Sweden. FAX 8-6118125. Ed.Bd. charts; circ. 2,600. *Indexed:* Inform.Sci.Abstr.

JULI-MAGAZIN. see *MEETINGS AND CONGRESSES*

JURISPRUDENTIE VOOR GEMEENTEN. see *LAW*

323.4   AT   ISSN 0157-6011
JUSTICE TRENDS. 1977. q. free. Australian Catholic Social Justice Council, Leo XIII House, 19 Mackenzie St., N. Sydney, N.S.W. 2060, Australia. TEL 02-956-5811. FAX 02-956-5782. circ. 5,000.
Indexed: HR Rep.

KATALLAGETE. see *RELIGIONS AND THEOLOGY*

KENTUCKY DIRECTORY OF BLACK ELECTED OFFICIALS. see *PUBLIC ADMINISTRATION*

323.4   JA   ISSN 0910-0156
H8.J3
KOKUSAI KENKYU/INTERNATIONAL STUDIES. (Text in Japanese and various languages) 1984. irreg. (approx. 1/yr.). exchange basis. Chubu University, Institute for International Studies - Chubu Daigaku, Kokusai Chiiki Kenkyujo, Matsumoto-machi 1200, Kasugai-shi, Aichi-ken 487, Japan. TEL 0568-51-1111.

KOLA. see *LITERATURE*

323.4 327 951.9   US
KOREA UPDATE. 1981. m. $20. Korea Church Coalition for Peace, Justice & Reunification, 475 Riverside Dr., Rm. 902, New York, NY 10115. bk.rev.; bibl.; stat.; circ. 1,700. (back issues avail.)
Description: Analysis of the human rights situation and U.S. policy relating to peace and justice in the Korean Penninsula.

323.4   GW   ISSN 0023-4834
K11
KRITISCHE JUSTIZ. 1968. q. DM.38 to individuals; students DM.28. Europaeische Verlagsanstalt GmbH, Savignystr. 61-63, 6000 Frankfurt 1, Germany. Ed.Bd. adv.; bk.rev.; index; circ. 5,000. (reprint service avail. from SCH) *Indexed:* INIS Atomind.
—BLDSC shelfmark: 5118.340000.

L I P NEWSLETTER. (Lesbian Interest Press) see *HOMOSEXUALITY*

323.4 350   AT
LAND RIGHTS NEWS; a newspaper for Aboriginals people and their supporters. no.6, 1976. 4/yr. Northern Territory Land Councils, P.O. Box 39843, Winnellie, N.T. 0821, Australia. TEL 089-817011. FAX 089-816899. TELEX AA85042. bk.rev.; circ. 4,000. (newspaper)

LAW & INEQUALITY; a journal of theory and practice. see *LAW*

323.4   US
LAW GROUP DOCKET. 1981. irreg. (2-3/yr.). $15 (foreign $20). International Human Rights Law Group, 1601 Connecticut Ave., N.W., Ste. 700, Washington, DC 20009. bk.rev.; circ. 2,200.
Indexed: HR Rep.
Description: Newsletter monitoring human rights violations.

LEFT. see *POLITICAL SCIENCE*

323.4 326.7   US
LEGAL RIGHTS OF CHILDREN. base vol. (plus a. suppl.). Shepard's - McGraw-Hill, Inc., Box 35300, Colorado Springs, CO 80935-3530. TEL 800-525-2474.
Description: Covers every issue concerning children's rights, including economic interests, children as litigants, public benefit programs, custody disputes, rights of adolescents, and protection of children from exploitation.

LESBIAN CONNECTION. see *HOMOSEXUALITY*

323.4   US
LET'S BE HUMAN. 1953. q. $10. Harry Fleischman, Ed. & Pub., 11 Wedgewood Lane, Wantagh, NY 11793. TEL 516-731-3069. bk.rev.; circ. 1,200.
Description: Advocates civil rights and social, labor-market, educational, and cultural equality in the United States.

323.4   UK   ISSN 0024-1873
D839
LIBERATION. 1958. bi-m. $6.50. 490 Kingsland Rd., London E8 4AE, England. TEL 01 254 6223. Ed. Kay Beauchamp. adv.; bk.rev.; bibl.; circ. 1,500.
Formerly: Colonial Freedom News.

LIBERTARIAN ALLIANCE. CULTURAL NOTES. see *POLITICAL SCIENCE*

LINK (LONDON, 1973). see *WOMEN'S INTERESTS*

323.4   US   ISSN 0894-3036
LINKS: HEALTH AND DEVELOPMENT REPORT. 1983. q. $12 to individuals; institutions $25; free to members. National Central American Health Rights Network, Box 202, Cooper Sq. Sta., New York, NY 10003. TEL 212-420-9635. Ed. Tom Frieden. adv.; bk.rev.
Formerly: Links.
Description: Promotes health in the Third World and works to keep the American public informed of health and human rights issues in the area.

LOK RAJYA. see *EDUCATION*

M A L D E F NEWSLETTER. (Mexican American Legal Defense and Educational Fund) see *ETHNIC INTERESTS*

323.4 323   US
M O H R NEWS. 1978. q. $25. Michigan Organization for Human Rights, 835 Louisa, Ste. 103, Lansing, MI 48911. TEL 517-887-2605. adv.; circ. 2,500.
Former titles: M O H R News & Notes; M O H R Information.

323.4   FR   ISSN 0292-7934
MAGYAR FUZETEK. 1978. q. 200 Ft.($50) Dialogues Europeens, 12 rue Drouet-Peupion, 92240 Malakoff, France. Ed. Peter Kende. bk.rev.; circ. 2,000. (back issues avail.)
Description: Samizdat essays.

323.4   GW   ISSN 0025-0511
DIE MAHNUNG. 1953. m. DM.24. Bund der Verfolgten des Naziregimes Berlin e.V., Mommsenstr. 27, 1000 Berlin 12, Germany. TEL 030-3242632. Ed.Bd. adv.; bk.rev.

323.4   CN   ISSN 0383-5588
JC599.C2
MANITOBA. HUMAN RIGHTS COMMISSION. ANNUAL REPORT. 1974. a. free. Human Rights Commission, 301-259 Portage Ave., Winnipeg, Man. R3B 2A9, Canada. TEL 204-945-3007. illus.; circ. 3,500.

323.4   US
MARTIN LUTHER KING, JR. CENTER FOR NON-VIOLENT SOCIAL CHANGE NEWSLETTER. 1973. irreg. donations. Martin Luther King, Jr. Center for Non-Violent Social Change, 449 Auburn Ave., N.E., Atlanta, GA 30312. TEL 404-524-1956. Ed. Hilda R. Tompkins. illus.; circ. 30,000.
Formerly: Martin Luther King, Jr. Center for Social Change Newsletter.

POLITICAL SCIENCE — CIVIL RIGHTS

MARTYRDOM AND RESISTANCE. see *ETHNIC INTERESTS*

323.4   ZA   ISSN 0025-6188
MAYIBUYE. N.S. 1975. m. $12. African National Congress of South Africa, Department of Information and Publicity, Box 31791, Lusaka, Zambia. circ. 8,000.

323.4   AU   ISSN 0025-9616
DAS MENSCHENRECHT. 1946. q. S.200($6) Oesterreichische Liga fuer Menschenrechte, Hermanngasse 9-14, A-1070 Vienna, Austria. Ed. J. Bister. adv.; bk.rev.; charts; illus.; cum.index; circ. 3,000.
—BLDSC shelfmark: 5678.495500.

323.4   GW   ISSN 0171-5976
MENSCHENRECHTE; Dokumente-Schicksale-Informationen. 1976. 5/yr. DM.26. Internationale Gesellschaft fuer Menschenrechte, Kaiserstr. 72, 6000 Frankfurt a.M., Germany. TEL 069-236971. FAX 069-234100. TELEX 4185181-IGFM-D. Ed. Christa v. Koeller. bk.rev.; circ. 6,000. (back issues avail.)

323.4   US
MICHIGAN. CIVIL RIGHTS COMMISSION. ANNUAL REPORT. 1964. a. free. Department of Civil Rights, 303 W. Kalamazoo, 4th Fl., Lansing, MI 48913. TEL 517-373-1189. Ed. James H. Horn II. circ. 1,000.
Former titles (until 1972): Civil Rights in Michigan; (until 1970): Michigan. Civil Rights Commission. Report (ISSN 0076-7875)
Description: Activities and accomplishments of the Michigan Civil Rights Commission. Describes the Commission's and Department's on-going efforts to obtain access and protection for individuals who have been denied equal opportunity in areas of jurisdiction.

323.4   US   ISSN 0047-7087
MICHIGAN CIVIL RIGHTS COMMISSION NEWSLETTER. 1971. q. free. Department of Civil Rights, 303 W. Kalamazoo, 4th Fl., Lansing, MI 48913. TEL 517-373-1189. Ed.Bd. charts; illus.; stat.; circ. 7,000.
Description: Activities and accomplishments of the Michigan Civil Rights Commission.

323.4   US
MIDDLE EAST WATCH. Variant title: News from Middle East Watch. irreg. $40. Human Rights Watch, Middle East Watch, 485 Fifth Ave., New York, NY 10017-6104. TEL 212-972-8400. FAX 212-972-0905. TELEX 910240 1007.
Description: Monitors and promotes observance of internationally recognized human rights in the Middle East.

323.4   US
MIDDLE EAST WATCH REPORT. irreg. Human Rights Watch, Middle East Watch, 485 Fifth Ave., New York, NY 10017-6104. TEL 212-972-8400. FAX 212-972-0905. TELEX 910240 1007.
Description: Presents in-depth research on human rights violations in the Middle East.

323   US   ISSN 0076-9118
JC599.U52
MINNESOTA. DEPARTMENT OF HUMAN RIGHTS. BIENNIAL REPORT. 1967. biennial. free. Department of Human Rights, 500 Bremer Tower, 7th & Minnesota, St. Paul, MN 55101. TEL 612-296-5663. circ. 1,000.

301.45 910.03   UK   ISSN 0305-6252
MINORITY RIGHTS GROUP. REPORTS. 1970. 6/yr. £30($55) Minority Rights Group, 379 Brixton Rd., London SW9 7DE, England. TEL 071-930-6659. bibl.; illus.; stat.; circ. 1,500. Indexed: HR Rep., I D A, Int.Lab.Doc.

MORGONBRIS. see *WOMEN'S INTERESTS*

323.4   FI
MY LIFE DEPENDS ON YOU. 1981. a. free. Martti Koski, Ed. & Pub., Kanervakummuntie 5, 21290 Rusko, Finland. TEL 921-788482. bk.rev.; circ. 5,000.
Description: Examines electrical brain manipulation and the issue of human experimentation.

N O W NEWS (BOSTON). (National Organization for Women) see *WOMEN'S INTERESTS*

323.4   US   ISSN 0746-0201
N.Y. CIVIL LIBERTIES. 1953. q. membership. New York Civil Liberties Union, 132 W. 43rd St., New York, NY 10036-6503. Ed. Norman Siegel. bk.rev.; circ. 25,000. (tabloid format; also avail. in microform from UMI; reprint service avail. from UMI) Indexed: Alt.Press Ind.
Formerly: Civil Liberties in New York (ISSN 0009-7926)

323.4   XV
NAS DELAVEC. (Includes supplements: Manuals about Employment, Health and Insurance Security) (Text in Slovenian) 1978. m. 2750 din.($13) T.O.Z.D. Delavska Enotnost, N.sol.o. Celovska 43, N.sub.o. CGP Delo, Box 313-VI, 61001 Ljubljana, Slovenia. Ed. Matjaz Vizjak.

323.4   AT   ISSN 0047-8792
NATIONAL COUNCIL OF WOMEN OF AUSTRALIA. QUARTERLY BULLETIN. 1969. q. Aus.$3. National Council of Women of Australia, P.O. Box 693, Turramurra, N.S.W. 2074, Australia. TEL 489-2252. Ed.Bd. illus.; circ. 760.

NATIONAL GAY AND LESBIAN TASK FORCE. TASK FORCE REPORTS. see *HOMOSEXUALITY*

NATIONAL PRISON PROJECT JOURNAL. see *CRIMINOLOGY AND LAW ENFORCEMENT*

NATIONAL PRISON PROJECT STATUS REPORT. see *CRIMINOLOGY AND LAW ENFORCEMENT*

323.1   US   ISSN 0047-9314
NEIGHBORS - INTERRACIAL LIVING.* 1971. bi-m. $25. National Neighbors, 3552 Cumberland St., N.W., Washington, DC 20008. TEL 202-785-4836. Ed. Lisa Gitlin. bk.rev.; illus.; circ. 3,000.

NETHERLANDS QUARTERLY OF HUMAN RIGHTS. NEWSLETTER. see *LAW*

NETWORK CONNECTION; national Catholic social justice lobby. see *RELIGIONS AND THEOLOGY — Roman Catholic*

NETWORK NEWS (CLEVELAND). see *PSYCHOLOGY*

323.4   US
NETWORKER: CIVIL, HUMAN AND VOTING RIGHTS. 2/yr. price varies. Interfaith Impact for Justice and Peace, 110 Maryland Ave., NE, Washington, DC 20002. TEL 202-543-2800.

323.4   US
NEW PARTY. 1978. a. Sophia Circle, 8319 Fulham Ct., Richmond, VA 23227. TEL 804-266-7400. Ed. Jerome Gorman.
Description: Advocates the nationalization of health insurance and the abolishment of the death penalty and military conscription.

NEW YORK (CITY). COMMISSION ON THE STATUS OF WOMEN. STATUS REPORT. see *WOMEN'S INTERESTS*

323.4   US
NEW YORK (STATE). DIVISION OF HUMAN RIGHTS. ANNUAL REPORT. 1946. a. free. Division of Human Rights, 55 W. 125th St., New York, NY 10027. TEL 212-870-8400. FAX 212-870-8552. Ed. Don Zirkel. circ. 3,000.
Former titles: State of Human Rights in New York; New York (State). Division of Human Rights. Annual Report.

323.4   US   ISSN 8756-8926
K14
NEW YORK LAW SCHOOL JOURNAL OF HUMAN RIGHTS. 1982. s-a. $22 (foreign $27). New York Law School, 57 Worth St., New York, NY 10013-2960. TEL 212-431-2112. circ. 1,000. (back issues avail.; reprint service avail. from RRI) Indexed: C.L.I., Leg.Per.
—BLDSC shelfmark: 6089.340800.

NEW ZEALAND TRIBUNE. see *POLITICAL SCIENCE*

NEWS NETWORK INTERNATIONAL. see *RELIGIONS AND THEOLOGY*

322 301.45   US
NEWSBREAK (NEW YORK). no.69, 1975. fortn. $36. National Conference on Soviet Jewry, Soviet Jewry Research Bureau, 10 E. 40th St., Ste. 701, New York, NY 10016. TEL 212-679-6122. FAX 212-686-1193. circ. 1,500. Indexed: HR Rep.
Former titles: National Conference on Soviet Jewry. Press Service; National Conference on Soviet Jewry. News Bulletin.

NO K K K, NO FASCIST U S A!. see *POLITICAL SCIENCE*

341.1   UN   ISSN 0029-7593
HT1521
OBJECTIVE: JUSTICE. French edition: Objectif: Justice (ISSN 0378-9934) 1971. s-a. $12. United Nations Publications, Room DC2-853, New York, NY 10017. TEL 212-963-8300. FAX 212-963-3489. (And: Distribution and Sales Section, Palais des Nations, CH-1211 Geneva, Switzerland) Ed. Hosni Khalifa. bibl.; charts; illus. (also avail. in microform from UMI; reprint service avail. from UMI) Indexed: P.A.I.S., So.Pac.Per.Ind.
—BLDSC shelfmark: 6197.100000.
Description: Dedicated to the promotion of justice through the self-determination of peoples, the elimination of apartheid and racial discrimination, and the advancement of human rights.

320.532 919.7   US
OF HUMAN RIGHTS. 1977. a. free. Of Human Rights, Inc., Box 2160-Hoya Sta., Georgetown University, Washington, DC 20057. TEL 202-342-1586. circ. 10,000. (back issues avail.)

ON GUARD. see *MILITARY*

323.4   CN   ISSN 0702-0538
JC599.C2
ONTARIO. HUMAN RIGHTS COMMISSION. ANNUAL REPORT. Title varies slightly. (Text in English and French) 1962. a. free. Human Rights Commission, 400 University Ave., Toronto, Ont. M7A 2R9, Canada. TEL 416-314-4528. FAX 416-314-4533. circ. 10,000.

OPEN FORUM. see *LAW*

THE OTHER SIDE (PHILADELPHIA); justice rooted in discipleship. see *RELIGIONS AND THEOLOGY*

323.4   US
OUR STRUGGLE/NUESTRA LUCHA. 1981. irreg. (4-5/yr.). $15. 2827 Cantania Way, Sacramento, CA 95826. TEL 916-361-9072. bk.rev.; circ. 250.
Description: Conveys common concerns of the Latino rights movement and democratic socialism. Demands economic democracy, equality and self-determination in Latin America and in the barrios of the US.

OUTLINES; the voice of the gay and lesbian community. see *HOMOSEXUALITY*

323.4   UK   ISSN 0260-6402
OUTSIDER. 1978. 3/yr. Minority Rights Group, 379 Brixton Rd., London SW9 7DE, England. TEL 071-930-6659.
Formerly: Minority Rights Group. Newsletter.

323.4   SZ
P C R INFORMATION; reports and background papers. 1979. 2/yr. free. World Council of Churches, Programme to Combat Racism, 150 Rte. de Ferney, Box 2100, CH-1211 Geneva 2, Switzerland. TEL 022-7916111. FAX 022-791-0361. TELEX 415730-OIK-CH. Ed. Bob Scott. bk.rev.; circ. 5,000.

323.4   US
PALESTINE HUMAN RIGHTS CAMPAIGN NEWSLETTER. 1981. bi-m. $25. Palestine Human Rights Campaign, 4753 N. Broadway St., Ste. 930, Chicago, IL 60640-4907. TEL 312-334-4019. circ. 5,500. (back issues avail.)

320   PY
PARAGUAY NOTICIAS. 1982. m. $48. Espana 596, Asuncion, Paraguay. TEL 24-845. Ed. Rafaela Guanes.
Description: Covers politics, human rights, indian matters, and trade unions in Paraguay.

POLITICAL SCIENCE — CIVIL RIGHTS

322.4   IT   ISSN 0031-3130
PATRIA INDIPENDENTE; quindicinale della Resistenza e degli ex-combattenti. 1951. fortn. L.20000 (foreign L.30000). Associazione Nazionale Partigiani d'Italia, Comitato Nazionale, Via degli Scipioni 271, 00192 Rome, Italy. TEL 06-3211309. FAX 06-3218495. Dir. A. Bartolini. adv.; bk.rev.; film rev.; bibl.; illus.; circ. 20,000.

PATTERNS OF PREJUDICE. see *SOCIOLOGY*

323.4   UY
PAZ Y JUSTICIA: SUMARIO DE DERECHOS HUMANOS. 1985. 3/yr. $12. Servicio Paz y Justicia, Joaquin Requeno 1642, Montevideo, Uruguay. bk.rev.
    Formerly: Sumario de Derechos Humanos.

323.4 327   US   ISSN 0749-5900
PEACE & DEMOCRACY NEWS. 1984. s-a. $10 to individuals; institutions $20. Campaign for Peace and Democracy, Box 1640, Cathedral Sta., New York, NY 10025. TEL 212-666-5924. FAX 212-662-5892. Eds. Joanne Landy, Jennifer Scarlott. adv.; bk.rev.; circ. 5,500. (back issues avail.) **Indexed:** Alt.Press Ind., HR Rep., Left Ind. (1985-).
    Description: Promotes international dialogue and common action from below by linking members of the peace movement, environmentalists, trade unionists, feminists, and gay and minority rights activists with democratic movements throughout the world.

323.4   US
PEACE LAW DOCKET. biennial. $40. Meiklejohn Civil Liberties Institute, 1715 Francisco St., Berkeley, CA 94703. TEL 415-848-0599. (Subscr. to: Box 673, Berkeley, CA 94701) Eds. Ann Fagan Ginger, David Christiano.
    Formerly: Studies in Law and Social Change.

323.4 336   US
PEACE TAX FUND NEWSLETTER. q. $25 to non-members. National Campaign for a Peace Tax Fund, 2121 Decatur Pl., N.W., Washington, DC 20008. TEL 202-483-3751. circ. 5,000. (back issues avail.)
    Description: Covers the status of legislation establishing conscientious objection to military taxes.

323.4 200   US
PHILIPPINE WITNESS. 1985. bi-m. $10 donation. Church Coalition for Human Rights in the Philippines, 110 Maryland Ave., N.E., Box 70, Washington, DC 20002. TEL 202-543-1094. FAX 202-546-0090. Ed. Katheryn Johnson. bk.rev.; bibl.; charts; illus.; circ. 3,000. (looseleaf format)
    Description: Ecumenical coalition of churches and church-related organizations addressing the issue of human rights.

301.412   FR   ISSN 0048-4229
BX1680.3
PIROGUE; revue Africaine realisee par des Africains. 1971. q. 36 F. Editions Saint Paul, 184 av. de Verdun, 92130 Issy-les-Moulineaux, France. illus.; circ. 15,000. **Indexed:** CERDIC.

PLAEDOYER; das Magazin fuer Recht und Politik. see *LAW*

PLUS. see *HISTORY — History Of The Near East*

323.4 914   GW
POGROM. 1970. bi-m. DM.40. Gesellschaft fuer Bedrohte Voelker, Gemeinnuetziger Verein e.V. - Association for Threatened Peoples, Postfach 2024, 3400 Goettingen, Germany. TEL 551-55822. FAX 551-58028. Ed. Tilman Zuelch. adv.; bk.rev.; illus.; circ. 6,000. **Indexed:** HR Rep.

320   US
POINT BLANK. 1971. m. $15. Citizens Committee for the Right to Keep and Bear Arms, 12500 N.E. 10th Pl., Bellevue, WA 98005. TEL 206-454-4911. FAX 206-451-3959. (Alt. addr.: 600 Pennsylvania Ave., S.E., Ste. 205, Washington, DC 20003) Ed. John M. Snyder. adv.; bk.rev.; circ. 110,000.

320.5   US   ISSN 0032-2318
POINT OF VIEW. 1968. fortn. $35 to individuals; institutions $50. Box 99530, Cleveland, OH 44199. TEL 216-321-2527. Ed. Roldo S. Bartimole. illus.; circ. 825. (also avail. in microform from UMI; reprint service avail. from UMI) **Indexed:** CINAHL.

323.4   GW
PRESSESPIEGEL ZUR RECHTSENTWICKLUNG. 1989. q. DM.20. Aktion Suhnezeichen Friedensdienste e.V., Jebensstr. 1, 1000 Berlin 12, Germany. TEL 030-310261. FAX 030-3126541. Ed.Bd. circ. 600. (back issues avail.)

301.45   SA
PRISMA. (Text in Afrikaans and English) 1963. m. free. House of Representatives, Administration, Private Bag 9008, Cape Town 8000, South Africa. Ed. C.W. Jonker. bk.rev.; abstr.; illus.; stat.; index; circ. 22,000. **Indexed:** Ind.S.A.Per.
    Formerly: Alpha (ISSN 0002-6379)

PRISONERS ASSISTANCE DIRECTORY. see *CRIMINOLOGY AND LAW ENFORCEMENT*

323.4   US   ISSN 0145-7659
KF1262.A15
PRIVACY JOURNAL; an independent monthly on privacy in a computer age. 1974. m. $109. Robert Ellis Smith, Ed. & Pub., Box 28577, Providence, RI 02908. TEL 401-274-7861. bk.rev.; tr.lit.; index, cum.index; circ. 2,100. (looseleaf format; also avail. in microform from UMI; back issues avail.; reprint service avail. from UMI) **Indexed:** Bank.Lit.Ind., Comput.Lit.Ind.
    Description: Reports on legislation, legal trends, new technology, and public attitudes affecting the confidentiality of information and the individual's right to privacy.

PRIVACY LAW AND PRACTICE. see *LAW*

323.4 340   US
PRIVACY TIMES. 1981. fortn. $250. Privacy Times Inc., Box 21501, Washington, DC 20009. TEL 202-829-3660. FAX 202-829-3653. Ed. Evan Hendricks.

322.4   US
PRO-LIFE REPORTER. 1973. q. $10. United States Coalition for Life, Box 315, Export, PA 15632. Ed. Randy Engel. bk.rev.; bibl.; illus.; circ. 2,750.

323.4   US   ISSN 0032-9177
PROBE (SANTA BARBARA). 1968. irreg. donations. Box 13390 UCSB, Santa Barbara, CA 93107. Ed. Perry Adams. adv.; bk.rev.; illus.; circ. 15,000. (tabloid format)
    Formerly: Argo.

323.4 289.6   CN   ISSN 0229-1916
QUAKER CONCERN. 1977. q. donations. Canadian Friends Service Committee, 60 Lowther Ave., Toronto, Ont. M5R 1C7, Canada. TEL 416-920-5213. Ed. Richard McCutcheon. bk.rev.; illus.; circ. 3,500. (tabloid format; back issues avail.)

QUAKER SERVICE BULLETIN. see *RELIGIONS AND THEOLOGY*

323.4   SA   ISSN 1011-5536
DT763
QUARTERLY COUNTDOWN. q. South African Institute of Race Relations, P.O. Box 31044, Braamfontein 2017, South Africa. TEL 403 3600. FAX 403-3671.

301.45   SA   ISSN 0033-734X
DT763
RACE RELATIONS NEWS. 1938. q. R.1 per no. South African Institute of Race Relations, P.O. Box 31044, Braamfontein 2017, South Africa. TEL 403 3600. FAX 403-3671. Ed. T. Coggin. adv.; bk.rev.; index; circ. 3,000. (newspaper) **Indexed:** A.I.C.P., HR Rep.

301.45   SA   ISSN 0258-7246
DT763
RACE RELATIONS SURVEY. 1948. a. South African Institute of Race Relations, P.O. Box 31044, Braamfontein 2017, South Africa. TEL 403.3600. circ. 6,000. **Indexed:** HR Rep.
    Former titles: Survey of Race Relations in South Africa (ISSN 0081-9778); Race Relations Survey.

RECONCILIATION INTERNATIONAL. see *RELIGIONS AND THEOLOGY*

323.4   SZ
REFUGEES. (Text mainly in English; occasionally in French and Spanish) m. free. World Council of Churches, Refugee Service, 150 Rte. de Ferney, Box 2100, CH-1211 Geneva 2, Switzerland. TEL 022-791-6111. FAX 022-791-0361. TELEX 415730-OIK-CH. circ. 3,000. (back issues avail.)

340 200   US   ISSN 0275-3529
KF4783.A59
RELIGIOUS FREEDOM REPORTER. 1981. m. $95. (Church - State Resource Center) Campbell University, R F R, Attn.: Marta Bowser, Box 505, Buies Creek, NC 27506. TEL 919-893-4111. FAX 919-893-5462. Ed. Donna Simmons. index; circ. 350. (back issues avail.)
    Description: Comprehensive coverage of pending and decided cases, Attorney General opinions, new legislation, and law review articles related to religious freedom and social-ethical issues.

REPORT ON SCIENCE AND HUMAN RIGHTS. see *SCIENCES: COMPREHENSIVE WORKS*

323.4   US
REPRODUCTIVE FREEDOM. a. $10. American Civil Liberties Union, Reproductive Freedom Project, 132 W. 43rd St., New York, NY 10036. TEL 212-869-9068. (looseleaf format)
    Description: National compendium of reproductive rights cases designed to inform laypersons on the litigation and legal status of reproductive rights issues, to enable lawyers to keep abreast of recent developments in this area of law, and to identify successful and unsuccessful legal strategies.

323.4   US
REPRODUCTIVE RIGHTS UPDATE. fortn. American Civil Liberties Union, Reproductive Freedom Project, 132 W. 43rd St., New York, NY 10036. TEL 212-869-9068.
    Description: Reports on current issues concerning reproductive freedom. Includes legislative issues, and recent cases concerning reproductive rights.

323.4 327   US
RESIST NEWSLETTER. 1967. m. (10/yr.). $15. One Summer St., Sommerville, MA 02143. TEL 617-623-5110. Ed. Tatiana Schreiber. bk.rev.; circ. 5,000. (back issues avail.)
    Description: Articles on topics of interest to all those concerned with peace and social justice. Covers AIDS, reproductive rights, homelessness, ecology movements, Middle East and Third World organizing efforts.

323.4 355 028.5   US
RESISTANCE NEWS. 1980. q. $15. National Resistance Committee, Box 42488, San Francisco, CA 94142. TEL 415-824-0214. Ed. Edward Hasbrouck. bk.rev.; abstr.; illus.; circ. 5,000. (tabloid format; also avail. in magnetic tape; Braille; back issues avail.)

323.4   UK
REVOLUTIONARY ZIMBABWE. 4/yr. £1.50. Zimbabwe Solidarity Front, 66a Etherley Rd., London N15, England.

323.4   FR
REVUE ABOLITIONNISTE. (Text in English and French) q. 40 F. International Abolitionist Federation, 47 rue de Rivoli, 75001 Paris, France. Ed. Francois Pignier.

323.4   US
RIGHT TO KNOW AND THE FREEDOM TO ACT. 1987. irreg. (2-3/yr.). $15. National Committee Against Repressive Legislation, 3321 12th St., N.E., Washington, DC 20017. TEL 202-529-4225. Ed. Kit Gage. bk.rev.; charts; illus.; circ. 4,000. (looseleaf format; back issues avail.)
    Incorporates (in 1992): F B I News; Former titles: N C A R L - D C Memo; Abolition News (ISSN 0001-3234)
    Description: Monitors developments related to protection of First Amendment rights, with particular focus on the activities of the FBI and CIA.

323.4   US   ISSN 0035-5283
JC599.U5
RIGHTS. 1953. q. $15. National Emergency Civil Liberties Committee, 175 Fifth Ave., Rm. 814, New York, NY 10010. TEL 212-673-2040. FAX 212-460-8359. Ed. Jeff Kisseloff. adv.; bk.rev.; illus.; circ. 10,000. **Indexed:** Alt.Press Ind., HR Rep., PMR.

POLITICAL SCIENCE — CIVIL RIGHTS

323.4   CN
RIGHTS AND FREEDOMS. q. R.R. 1, Maniwaki, Que. J9E 3A8, Canada. TEL 819-449-6072. Ed. Charles Walden.

323.4   CN   ISSN 1187-3272
RIGHTS AND LIBERTIES. 1978. q. membership. Manitoba Association for Rights and Liberties, 435 Elgin Ave., Winnipeg, Man. R3A 1P2, Canada. TEL 204-947-0213. FAX 204-956-0976. Ed. L.K. Harris. bk.rev.; circ. 300. (back issues avail.)
     Formerly: M A R L Newsletter.

RIGHTS OF PHYSICALLY HANDICAPPED PERSONS. see LAW — *Civil Law*

RITES; for lesbian and gay liberation. see *HOMOSEXUALITY*

RIVISTA INTERNAZIONALE DEI DIRITTI DELL' UOMO. see *LAW*

301.45   UK
RUNNYMEDE BULLETIN. 1969. 10/yr. £12 to individuals; voluntary organizations £14; institutions £16. Runnymede Trust, 11 Princelet St., London E1 6QH, England. TEL 071-375-1496. Eds. Kaushika Amin, Paul Gordon. adv.; bk.rev.; bibl.; circ. 3,000. (looseleaf format)
     Former titles: Race and Immigration: Runnymede Trust Bulletin (ISSN 0262-9925); Runnymede Trust Bulletin (ISSN 0142-971X); Race Relations Bulletin (ISSN 0033-7323)

323.4 331   SA   ISSN 1018-3493
S A BAROMETER; fortnightly journal of current affairs statistics. (Text in English) 1987. fortn. R.200 (in Europe; N. America R.275; Far East R.325). Hoopoe Publications, P.O. Box 261303, Excom 2023, South Africa. TEL 011-331-3321. FAX 011-331-7540. Ed. Stephen Heyns. index; circ. 300. (looseleaf format; back issues avail.)
     Description: Provides a daily chronology of events in South Africa, with document texts, and statistics.

323.4   SA
S A F POSITION PAPER. 1977-1990 (Dec.). m. South African Forum - Suider-Afrikaanse Forum, P.O. Box 3763, Randburg 2125, South Africa. TEL 011-787-1058. FAX 011-787-8371. (looseleaf format)
     Formerly (until 1980): S A F F Position Paper.

323.4   US   ISSN 0891-608X
S P S C LETTER. 1979. q. $5 donation. Saharan Peoples Support Committee, 217 E. Lehr, Ada, OH 45810. TEL 419-634-3666. Ed. Anne Lippert. bk.rev.; charts; circ. 750. **Indexed:** HR Rep.

SAGE: A SCHOLARLY JOURNAL ON BLACK WOMEN. see *WOMEN'S STUDIES*

323.4   US
SAHARAN PEOPLE'S SUPPORT COMMITTEE. MONOGRAPH SERIES. irreg. Saharan People's Support Committee, 217 E. Lehr, Ada, OH 45810. TEL 419-634-3666.

320.5   SA   ISSN 0036-4843
DT751
SASH. (Text in English) 1956. q. R.20 (overseas R.60). Black Sash, 5 Long St., Mowbray 7700, South Africa. TEL 021-685-3513. FAX 021-685-7510. Ed.Bd. bk.rev.; charts; illus.; circ. 2,000. **Indexed:** HR Rep.
     Formerly: Black Sash.

323.4   IT
SAVONA A C L I. 1985. m. L.5000($10) Associazioni Cristiane Lavoratori Italy, P.zza Marconi 2, 17100 Savona, Italy. TEL 019 21075.

SCENE OUT. see *HOMOSEXUALITY*

SCHIEDSMANNS ZEITUNG. see *LAW*

323.4   ZA   ISSN 0037-0509
DT763
SECHABA. 1967. m. $12. African National Congress of South Africa, Department of Information and Publicity, Box 31791, Lusaka, Zambia. Ed. F. Meli. adv.; bk.rev.; play rev.; abstr.; bibl.; charts; illus.; stat.; circ. 30,000. (also avail. in microfilm from UMI; reprint service avail. from UMI) **Indexed:** Alt.Press Ind., HR Rep., M.L.A.

323.4 370   US
SEX EQUITY IN EDUCATION UPDATE. q. Department of Education, Bureau of Publications, 721 Capitol Mall, Box 944272, Sacramento, CA 94244-2720. TEL 916-322-7388.

341.1   US   ISSN 0080-9160
SHALOM; Jewish peace letter. 1941. q. $5. Jewish Peace Fellowship, Box 271, Nyack, NY 10960. TEL 914-358-4601. FAX 914-358-4924. Ed. Murray Polner. bk.rev.; circ. 3,000 (controlled). (back issues avail.)
     Formerly: Jewish Peace Fellowship Newsletter (ISSN 0021-664X)
     Description: Addresses the question of peace.

301.4   US
SISTERLIFE JOURNAL. 1973. q. $15. Feminists for Life of America, Inc., 811 E. 47th St., Kansas City, MO 64110. TEL 816-753-2130. Ed. Frederica Mathewes-Green. adv.; bk.rev.; circ. 5,000.
     Description: Publication devoted to the philosophy of "pro-life feminism," which holds that abortion is detrimental to women and contrary to the tenets of feminism.

SKUPNOST; glasilo Slovenske skupnosti. see *ETHNIC INTERESTS*

SLAVERY & ABOLITION; a journal of comparative studies. see *SOCIOLOGY*

323.4   SA
SOUTH AFRICAN INSTITUTE OF RACE RELATIONS. SPECIAL REPORTS. irreg. (approx. 6/yr.). South African Institute of Race Relations, P.O. Box 31044, Braamfontein 2017, South Africa. TEL 403-3600. FAX 011-403-3671.

323.4   SA   ISSN 1011-5544
HN801
SOUTH AFRICAN INSTITUTE OF RACE RELATIONS. UPDATE. q. South African Institute of Race Relations, P.O. Box 31044, Braamfontein 2017, South Africa. TEL 403-3600. FAX 011-403-3671.
     Formerly: Social and Economic Update.

323.4 340   SA   ISSN 0258-7203
K23
SOUTH AFRICAN JOURNAL ON HUMAN RIGHTS. (Text in English) 1985. 3/yr. R.90($48) (University of the Witwatersrand, Centre for Applied Legal Studies) Juta & Co. Ltd., P.O. Box 14373, Kenywn 7790, South Africa. TEL 021-797-5101. FAX 021-761-5010. Ed.Bd. adv.; bk.rev.; index; circ. 1,000. (back issues avail.) **Indexed:** Polit.Sci.Abstr. —BLDSC shelfmark: 8338.869000.
     Description: For lawyers and human rights activists on human rights issues from a legal perspective.

323.4 910.03   CN   ISSN 0820-5582
SOUTHERN AFRICA REPORT. 1985. 5/yr. Can.$18 to individuals; institutions Can.$40. Toronto Committee for the Liberation of Southern Africa, 427 Bloor St. W., Toronto, Ont. M5S 1X7, Canada. TEL 416-967-5562. adv.; bk.rev.; film rev.; illus.; circ. 800. (reprint service avail.)
     Description: Serves the anti-apartheid movement by providing in-depth articles analyzing political events and trends in Southern Africa, Canada and the United States.

323.4   US   ISSN 0193-2446
JC599.U5
SOUTHERN CHANGES. 1978. 6/yr. $30 to individuals; institutions $75. Southern Regional Council, Inc., 134 Peachtree St., N.W., Ste. 1900, Atlanta, GA 30303-1825. TEL 404-522-8764. FAX 404-522-8791. Ed. Allen Tullos. adv.; bk.rev.; index; circ. 6,000. (also avail. in microform from UMI; back issues avail.; reprint service avail. from UMI) **Indexed:** Hist.Abstr.
     Former titles: New South; South Today; Southern Voices.
     Description: Reports on regional politics, civil, worker's and women's rights, literature and the arts. Provides a forum for opinion about issues affecting the South.

SOUTHERN COMMUNITIES. see *HOUSING AND URBAN PLANNING*

SOZIALISTISCHE PRAXIS. see *POLITICAL SCIENCE*

SPARTACIST CANADA. see *POLITICAL SCIENCE — International Relations*

SPARTACUS INTERNATIONAL GAY GUIDE. see *HOMOSEXUALITY*

323.4   US   ISSN 0012-4427
LAW
THE SPECTRUM (TOPEKA); newsletter of the Kansas commission on civil rights. 1969. s-a. free. Kansas Human Rights Commission, 900 S.W. Jackson St., Ste. 851 S., Topeka, KS 66612-1258. TEL 913-296-3206. FAX 913-296-6729. Ed. Steven J. Ramirez. bk.rev.; charts; illus.; circ. 6,700.
     Formerly (until 1983): Docket.

STANFORD GAY AND LESBIAN AWARENESS WEEK PROGRAM. see *HOMOSEXUALITY*

323   US   ISSN 0148-6985
E185.5
STATE OF BLACK AMERICA. 1975. a. $18. (National Urban League) Transaction Publishers, Transaction Periodicals Consortium, Department 3092, Rutgers University, New Brunswick, NJ 08903. TEL 908-932-2280. FAX 908-932-3138. Ed. Janet Dewart. **Indexed:** SRI.
     Description: Record of trends and events in black America. Educators, public officials, and community leaders analyze recent developments in economics, education, housing, legislation, politics, and race relations as they affect and are affected by blacks.

323.4   US
STATISTICAL PROOF OF DISCRIMINATION. 1980. base vol. (plus a. suppl.). $95. Shepard's - McGraw-Hill, Inc., Box 35300, Colorado Springs, CO 80935-3530. TEL 800-525-2474.
     Description: Introduces many substantive requirements of proof under disparate treatment and disparate impact theories of discrimination.

323.4   GW
STREIT; feministische Rechtszeitschrift. 1983. q. DM.64. Verein Frauen Streiten fuer ihr Recht, c/o Barbara Becker-Rojczyk, Hedderichstr. 102, 6000 Frankfurt a.M. 90, Germany. TEL 0421-490079. FAX 0421-440914. (Subscr. to: Sabine Heinke, Hamburgerstr. 181, 2800 Bremen 1) bk.rev.; index; circ. 1,000. (back issues avail.)
     Description: German feminist law journal.

STUDIES IN HUMAN RIGHTS. see *POLITICAL SCIENCE — International Relations*

SUBVERSIVE AGENT. see *LITERATURE — Poetry*

323.4 572   UK
SURVIVAL (LONDON, 1983). 1983. biennial. £1 per no. Survival International, 310 Edgware Rd., London W2 1DY, England. TEL 071-723-5535. FAX 071-723-4059. Ed. Charlotte Sankey. bk.rev.; film rev.; circ. 8,000. (also avail. in microfiche) **Indexed:** A.I.C.P.
     Formerly: Survival International News (ISSN 0265-1327)
     Description: Reports on worldwide movement to support tribal peoples and their right to decide their own future.

323.4 572   UK
SURVIVAL INTERNATIONAL ANNUAL REVIEW. 1988. a. Survival International, 310 Edgware Rd., London W2 1DY, England. TEL 071-723-5535. FAX 071-723-4059.
     Description: Covers the field projects and violations cases handled by the organization in the past year.

323.4 950   US
TAIWAN COMMUNIQUE. 1980. 6/yr. $12. International Committee for Human Rights in Taiwan, Box 45205, Seattle, WA 98105. circ. 1,500. **Indexed:** HR Rep.

323.4   US
TEXAS BILL OF RIGHTS; a commentary and litigation manual. 1987. base vol. (plus a. suppl.). $90. Butterworth Legal Publishers (Salem) (Subsidiary of: Reed International PLC), 90 Stiles Rd., Salem, NH 03079. TEL 800-548-4001. FAX 603-898-9858. Ed. James C. Harrington.
     Description: Analysis of Texas courts' protection of individual freedom in such areas as equal protection, due process, free speech and assembly, privacy and criminal procedure.

THIS WEEK IN TEXAS. see *HOMOSEXUALITY*

TRENDS IN HOUSING. see *HOUSING AND URBAN PLANNING*

POLITICAL SCIENCE — INTERNATIONAL RELATIONS

323.4   US
JK2391.N35
THE TRUTH AT LAST. 1963. m. $15. (American Segregation Party) Truth at Last, Inc., Box 1211, Marietta, GA 30061. TEL 404-422-1180. Ed. Edward R. Fields. bk.rev.; circ. 30,000. (tabloid format; also avail. in microfilm from UMI)
   Formerly: Thunderbolt (ISSN 0040-6643)

323.4   UK   ISSN 0960-3069
TURKEY BRIEFING. 1987. bi-m. £20($35) Turkey Briefing Group, 87 Glebe St., London W4 2BB, England. bk.rev.; circ. 500. (looseleaf format)

TYGODNIK SOLIDARNOSC/SOLIDARITY WEEKLY. see BUSINESS AND ECONOMICS — Economic Situation And Conditions

323.4   US   ISSN 0897-9669
DJK50
UNCAPTIVE MINDS. 1988. bi-m. $20 (Canada $25, elsewhere $30). Institute for Democracy in Eastern Europe, 48 E. 21st St., 3rd Fl., New York, NY 10010. TEL 212-677-5801. FAX 212-475-5829. Eds. Eric Chenoweth, Irena Lasota. adv.; circ. 2,000. (back issues avail.)
   Description: Covers Eastern European opposition movements, political developments, and human rights reporting.

323.4   US   ISSN 0082-9641
U.S. COMMISSION ON CIVIL RIGHTS. CLEARINGHOUSE PUBLICATIONS. 1965. irreg. U.S. Commission on Civil Rights, 1121 Vermont Ave. N.W., Washington, DC 20425. TEL 202-376-8110. (Subscr. to: U.S. Commission on Civil Rights, 1121 Vermont Ave. N.W., attn. Publications Unit, Washington, DC 20425)

U.S. EQUAL EMPLOYMENT OPPORTUNITY COMMISSION. ANNUAL REPORT. see BUSINESS AND ECONOMICS — Labor And Industrial Relations

323.4   US
UNITED STATES ANTI-APARTHEID NEWSLETTER. 1988. q. $10. American Friends Service Committee, Inc., Peace Education Division, 1501 Cherry St., Philadelphia, PA 19102. TEL 215-241-7501. FAX 215-864-0104.
   Description: Promotes communication among organizations that educate, campaign, and organize against apartheid in South Africa.

323.4   US
URBAN LEAGUE NEWS. 1970. q. free. National Urban League, 500 E. 62nd St., New York, NY 10021. TEL 212-310-9000. bk.rev.; circ. 10,000. (tabloid format)

URBAN LEAGUE REVIEW. see ETHNIC INTERESTS

323.4 572   UK
URGENT ACTION BULLETIN. (Editions in English, French, Italian, Portuguese and Spanish) 1982. irreg. (10/yr.). Survival International, 310 Edgware Rd., London W2 1DY, England. TEL 071-723-5535. FAX 071-723-4059.
   Description: Covers events affecting the rights and treatment of indigenous groups.

323.4   GW
V I A MAGAZIN; Fachzeitschrift fuer Praktiker. 1986. bi-m. DM.2.50. Verband der Initiativgruppen in der Auslaenderarbeit e.V., Theaterstr. 10, D-5300 Bonn 1, Germany. TEL 0228-655553. circ. 800.

V O W: VOICE OF WOMEN. see WOMEN'S INTERESTS

323.4   AT   ISSN 1036-9538
VICTORIA. OFFICE OF THE COMMISSIONER FOR EQUAL OPPORTUNITY. ANNUAL REPORT. 1979. a. Aus.$7.50 (effective Sep. 1990). Office of the Commissioner for Equal Opportunity, 4th Fl., 356 Collins St., Melbourne, Vic. 3000, Australia. TEL 03-602-3338. FAX 03-670-2922. circ. 500.
   Former titles: Victoria. Office of the Commissioner for Equal Opportunity and the Victorian Equal Opportunity Board. Annual Report; Victoria. Equal Opportunity Board. Annual Report.

323.4   US   ISSN 0042-8183
VOICE OF THE BLACK COMMUNITY. 1968. w. $24. (Black Marble Inc., N N P A) Voice Newspaper, 625 E. Wood St., Decatur, IL 62522.
TEL 217-423-5043. Ed. Horace G. Livingston Jr. adv.; illus.; circ. 20,000.

323.4   US
VOTING RIGHTS NETWORKER. irreg. $25 contribution. Interfaith Action for Economic Justice, Churches' Committee for Voter Registration - Education, 110 Maryland Ave., N.E., Washington, DC 20002. TEL 202-543-2800.

323.4 365.64   RU   ISSN 0868-9520
▼VYZOV. 1990. 6/yr. 3.20 Rub. per no. Permskii Gorispolkom, Upravlenie Vnutrennikh Del, Ul. Druzhby 34, 614600 Perm, Russia. TEL 48-39-24. FAX 32-52-19. Ed. D.E. Krasik. circ. 50,000 (controlled).

W D L NEWS. (Workers Defense League, Inc.) see BUSINESS AND ECONOMICS — Labor And Industrial Relations

323.4   US
W I D BULLETIN. 3/yr. $12 or exchange basis. Michigan State University, Women and International Development Program, 202 International Center, E. Lansing, MI 48824-1035. TEL 517-353-5040. FAX 517-353-7254. TELEX 650 277 3148 ISP. Ed. Rita S. Gallin. circ. 2,000.
   Formerly: W I D Newsletter.

338.91   US   ISSN 0888-7772
W I D FORUM. 1984. irreg., no.22, 1991. Michigan State University, Women and International Development Program, 202 International Center, E. Lansing, MI 48824-1035. TEL 517-353-5040. FAX 517-353-7254. TELEX 650 277 3148 ISP. Ed. Rita S. Gallin. circ. 250.

323.4   US   ISSN 0892-3116
W R E E - VIEW OF WOMEN. (Text mainly in English; occasionally in Spanish) 1976. q. $6. Women for Racial and Economic Equality, 198 Broadway, Rm. 606, New York, NY 10038. TEL 212-385-1103. Ed. Jan C. Jamshidi. adv.; bk.rev.; circ. 15,000.
   Former titles: W R E E - View; (until 1983): W R E E - View of Women.
   Description: Covers racism, affirmative action, women's economic security and equality.

323.4 284   GW   ISSN 0936-6520
WAS UNS BETRIFFT; Zeitschrift fuer Kriegsdienstverweigerer und Zivildienstleistende. Short title: W U B. 1970. q. DM.10($5) Evangelische Arbeitsgemeinschaft zur Betreuung der Kriegsdienstverweigerer (EAK), Carl-Schurz-Str. 17, 2800 Bremen 1, Germany. FAX 0421-3491961. (Subscr. to: Buero Pfarrer Schlueter, Barbarossaplatz 4, 5000 Cologne 1, Germany) circ. 45,000. (back issues avail.)

323.4   US   ISSN 0083-8594
JC599.U52
WEST VIRGINIA. HUMAN RIGHTS COMMISSION. REPORT.* 1961. a. free. Human Rights Commission, 1321 Plaza E., Ste. 104, Charleston, WV 25301-1405. TEL 304-348-2616. circ. 1,000.

323.4 960   US   ISSN 0895-8491
WESTERN SAHARA CAMPAIGN NEWS.* 1985. q. $15 to individuals; institutions $50. Western Sahara Campaign for Human Rights & Humanitarian Relief, 4406 48th St., N.W., Washington, DC 20016. TEL 202-387-0412. Ed. Teresa K. Smith. circ. 500. (back issues avail.)
   Description: Discusses human rights, conflict resolution and development in Northwest Africa, with emphasis on the Western Sahara conflict.

323.1 301.412   US   ISSN 0049-7770
WOMAN ACTIVIST; an action bulletin for women's rights from the courthouse to the White House. 1971. m. (10/yr.). $17. Woman Activist, Inc., 2310 Barbour Rd., Falls Church, VA 22043. Ed. Flora Crater. adv.; bk.rev.; charts; stat.; circ. 600 (controlled). (processed; also avail. in microform)

323.4   US
WOMEN STRIKE FOR PEACE. LEGISLATIVE ALERT. 10/yr. $25. Women Strike for Peace (Washington), 110 Maryland Ave., N.E., Ste.302, Washington, DC 20002. TEL 202-543-2660. Eds. Edith Villastrigo, Karen Hoehn. circ. 3,300. (looseleaf format; back issues avail.)
   Description: Legislative update on peace and human rights issues.

323.4 331.8   SA
WORK IN PROGRESS. (Text in English) 1977. 8/yr. R.44($66) to individuals; institutions R.120($132)(effective 1992). Southern African Research Service, P.O. Box 32716, Braamfontein, Johannesburg 2017, South Africa.
TEL 011-403-1912. FAX 011-403-2534. adv.; bk.rev.; circ. 15,000. (back issues avail.)
   Description: Contemporary anti-apartheid magazine covering politics and labor.

323.4 572   CN
WORLD COUNCIL OF INDIGENOUS PEOPLES. NEWSLETTER. 1987. irreg. (4-6/yr.). World Council of Indigenous Peoples, 555 King Edward Ave., 2nd Fl., Ottowa K1N 6N5 Ontario, Canada.
TEL 613-230-9030. Ed. Donald Rojoas Marota.
   Description: Contains news and events of the organization, whose purpose is to advance the self-sufficiency and autonomy of indigenous peoples.

WORLD DIRECTORY OF HUMAN RIGHTS TEACHING AND RESEARCH. see BUSINESS AND ECONOMICS — Trade And Industrial Directories

WORLD NEWS DIGEST. see POLITICAL SCIENCE

(YEAR) PEACE CALENDAR. see LITERATURE — Poetry

323.4   UN   ISSN 0084-4098
YEARBOOK ON HUMAN RIGHTS. (Editions in English and French) 1946. irreg., latest 1985. price varies. United Nations Publications, Rm. DC2-853, New York, NY 10017. TEL 212-963-8302.
FAX 212-963-3489. (Or: Distribution and Sales Section, CH-1211 Geneva 10, Switzerland) (also avail. in microfiche; reprint service avail. from KTO)
—BLDSC shelfmark: 9413.300000.

ZEICHEN. see RELIGIONS AND THEOLOGY — Protestant

323.4   GW   ISSN 0342-5851
ZEITLUPE. 1975. s-a. free. Bundeszentrale fuer Politische Bildung, Referat IV-2, Berliner Freiheit 7, 5300 Bonn, Germany. TEL 0228-515224.
FAX 0228-515113. Eds. Franz Kiefer, Hannegret Homberg. circ. 800,000. (back issues avail.)

323.4   GW   ISSN 0170-0413
ZEITSCHRIFT FUER DEUTSCHES UND INTERNATIONALES BAURECHT. 1978. bi-m. DM.203 (foreign DM.222). (Deutsche Gesellschaft fuer Baurecht e.V., Institut fuer Deutsches und Internationales Baurecht) Bauverlag GmbH, Postfach 1460, 6200 Wiesbaden, Germany. TEL 0611-791-0. FAX 0611-791-285. TELEX 4186792. Ed.Bd. adv.; circ. 2,000.
—BLDSC shelfmark: 9457.670000.

323.4   GW
4-3 FACHZEITSCHRIFT ZU KRIEGSDIENSTVERWEIGERUNG, WEHRDIENST UND ZIVILDIENST. 1982. q. DM.26. D F G - V K, Schwanenstr. 16, 5620 Velbert, Germany. TEL 02051-4217. FAX 02051-4210. circ. 1,000.
   Description: Provides information about conscientious objection to military service and alternative civilian service.

POLITICAL SCIENCE — International Relations

see also Law–International Law

327   US
A C O A ACTION NEWS. s-a. $15 to individuals; institutions $25. American Committee on Africa, 198 Broadway, New York, NY 10038.
TEL 212-962-1210. FAX 212-964-8570. Ed. Richard Knight. bibl.; tr.lit.

320   FR
A D U K. (Adresar Ukraintsiv u Vilnomu Sviti) 1973. irreg. Premiere Imprimerie Ukrainienne en France, 3, rue du Sabot, 75006 Paris, France. illus.

A F L - C I O. DEPARTMENT OF INTERNATIONAL AFFAIRS. BULLETIN. (American Federation of Labor - Congress of Industrial Organizations) see LABOR UNIONS

A.I.D. HIGHLIGHTS. (U.S. Agency for International Development) see BUSINESS AND ECONOMICS — International Development And Assistance

POLITICAL SCIENCE — INTERNATIONAL RELATIONS 3949

A J M E NEWS. (Americans for Justice in the Middle East) see HISTORY — History Of The Near East

325.21   US
A N E R A NEWSLETTER. 1969. q. free. American Near East Refugee Aid, Inc., 1522 K St., N.W., No. 22, Washington, DC 20005. TEL 202-347-2558. FAX 202-682-1637. Ed. Paula Stinson. bk.rev.; illus.; circ. 34,000. **Indexed:** HR Rep.
   Description: Information about ANERA activities: economic development and relief in the West Bank, Gaza Strip and Lebanon.

327   NR
A P R I JOURNAL. 1986. bi-m. £N48($40) African Peace Research Institute, P.O. Box 51757, Falomo, Ikoyi, Lagos, Nigeria. TEL 633437. Ed. Temitope Oguntayo. bk.rev.; stat.; cum.index; circ. 250. (back issues avail.)
   Formerly: A P R I Newsletter.
   Description: Carries and analyzes information on current peace research issues, i.e. environment, violence conflict, disarmament, and foreign debt.

A S A E INTERNATIONAL NEWS. (American Society of Association Executives) see BUSINESS AND ECONOMICS — Management

325   AU   ISSN 0001-2947
HV640
A W R BULLETIN; quarterly on refugee problems. (Text in English, French, German, Italian) 1963. q. S.370. (Association for the Study of the World Refugee Problems) Wilhelm Braumueller, Universitaets-Verlagsbuchhandlung GmbH, Servitengasse 5, A-1092 Vienna, Austria. TEL 0222-348124. FAX 0222-310-2805. adv.; bk.rev.; index; circ. 1,000. **Indexed:** HR Rep., Refug.Abstr.
   —BLDSC shelfmark: 1840.700000.

327   US   ISSN 0890-118X
ACROSS FRONTIERS. 1983. q. $10 to individuals; institutions $25. Box 2382, Berkeley, CA 94702. Ed. A. Winton Jackson. bk.rev.; illus.; circ. 2,000. (back issues avail.) **Indexed:** Alt.Press Ind., Left Ind.

327   UK   ISSN 0567-932X
U162
ADELPHI PAPERS.* 1964. 12/yr. $120. (International Institute for Strategic Studies) Brassey's, 50 Fetter Ln., London EC4A 1AA, England. TEL 071-377-4881. FAX 071-377-4888. (Subscr. to: Turpin Transactions, Distribution Centre, Blackhorse Rd., Letchworth, Herts. SG6 1HN, England. TEL 0462-672555) bibl.; charts; stat.; circ. 7,000. (also avail. in microform from UMI; reprint service avail. from UMI) **Indexed:** Abstr.Mil.Bibl., PROMT.
   Description: Monographs analyzing current and future problems of international security concerns.

AFFARI SOCIALI INTERNAZIONALI. see SOCIOLOGY

AFRICA; rivista trimestrale di studi e documentazione. see HISTORY — History Of Africa

AFRICA. see HISTORY — History Of Africa

327   US   ISSN 0950-0650
DT30.5
AFRICA AND THE WORLD. 1988. q. $60. 200 Meacham Ave., Elmont, NY 11003. Ed. Chuba Okadigbo.
   —BLDSC shelfmark: 0732.150600.
   Description: Treats world events from an Afrocentric perspective.

960   II   ISSN 0001-978X
DT1
AFRICA DIARY. 1961. w. $38. Africa Publications (India), F-15 Bhagat Singh Market, Box 702, New Delhi 1, India. Ed. Hari Sharan Chhabra. index.

327   US   ISSN 0748-4356
AFRICA INSIDER; an exclusive bi-weekly report on U.S.-Africa affairs from Washington, D.C. 1984. fortn. $75 to individuals; institutions $150. Matthews Associates, Box 53398, Temple Heights Sta., Washington, DC 20009. TEL 202-332-1622. Ed. Dan Matthews.
   Description: Covers political and foreign affairs analysis in relations between Africa and the United States.

327   US   ISSN 0001-9836
DT1
AFRICA REPORT. 1957. bi-m. $30 to individuals; institutions $37. African-American Institute, 833 United Nations Plaza, New York, NY 10017. TEL 212-949-5666. FAX 212-682-6174. TELEX 666565 AFRAM. (Subscr. to: Box 3000, Denville, NJ 07834) Ed. Margaret A. Novicki. adv.; bk.rev.; charts; illus.; index; circ. 14,000. (also avail. in microform from UMI; back issues avail.; reprint service avail. from SWZ,UMI) **Indexed:** A.B.C.Pol.Sci., Abstr.Mil.Bibl., Acad.Ind., Amer.Hist.& Life, Bibl.Ind., Curr.Cont.Africa, Curr.Cont.M.E., Hist.Abstr., HR Rep., Hum.Ind., M.L.A., Mid.East: Abstr.& Ind., P.A.I.S., Rural Recreat.Tour.Abstr., Soc.Sci.Ind., World Agri.Econ.& Rural Sociol.Abstr.
   —BLDSC shelfmark: 0732.180000.
   Description: Covers African political and economic developments.

327   GW   ISSN 0340-5796
AFRIKA; review of German-African relations. (Editions in English and French) 1960. 6/yr. DM.15. Afrika-Verlag, Tueritorstr. 14, Postfach 86, 8068 Pfaffenhofen, Germany. Ed. Inga Krugmann. adv.; bk.rev.; charts; illus.; circ. 15,700. **Indexed:** Curr.Cont.Africa.

968   SW   ISSN 0346-9158
AFRIKABULLETINEN. 1964. 6/yr. SEK 170 to individuals; institutions SEK 190. Afrikagrupperna i Sverige - Africa Groups of Sweden, Barnaengsgat 23, 116 41 Stockholm, Sweden. FAX 08-411135. Ed. Birgit Joedahl. adv.; bk.rev.; illus.; cum.index: 1968-1980 (vols.1-55); circ. 4,500.
   Former titles (until no.27, 1975): Soedra Afrika. Informations Bulletin (ISSN 0038-0490); Syd- och Sydvaestrafrika Bulletinen.

960   FR   ISSN 0002-0478
DT348
AFRIQUE CONTEMPORAINE; documents d'Afrique noire et de Madagascar. 1962. q. 175 F. Documentation Francaise, 29-31 Quai Voltaire, 75340 Paris cedex 07, France. TEL 1-4015-7000. Ed. Mrs. Porges. bk.rev.; bibl.; charts; stat.; circ. 2,000. (also avail. in microfiche) **Indexed:** Curr.Cont.Africa, I D A.
   —BLDSC shelfmark: 0735.320000.

940   BE   ISSN 0002-080X
AGENOR. (Text in English) 1967. q. 1800 Fr. Agenor Societe Cooperative, 22 rue Toulouse, B-1040 Brussels, Belgium. FAX 2-230-5957. Ed. John Lambert. adv.; illus.; circ. 1,000. (also avail. in microfilm from HPL; back issues avail.) **Indexed:** Mid.East: Abstr.& Ind.
   —BLDSC shelfmark: 0736.252000.

AHFAD JOURNAL; women and change. see WOMEN'S STUDIES

AKTUELLER INFORMATIONSDIENST MODERNER ORIENT/ORIGINAL NEWS AND COMMENTS FROM MIDDLE EASTERN NEWSPAPERS. see ORIENTAL STUDIES

949.65   AA   ISSN 0002-4643
ALBANIA OGGI. vol.3, 1970. bi-m. Associazione Nazionale Italia Albania, c/o Ndermarrja e Librit, Tirana, Albania. Ed. Giorgio Puglisi. adv.; charts; illus.

327   IT
ALBANIA SOCIALISTA.* vol.9, 1976. 3/yr. L.3000. Associazione Nazionale Italia Albania, Via Torino 122, 00184 Rome, Italy. Ed. Corrado Corghi. illus.

327
ALERT!: FOCUS ON CENTRAL AMERICA. 1982. bi-m. $15. Committee in Solidarity with the People of El Salvador (CISPES), Box 12156, Washington, DC 20005. TEL 202-265-0890. FAX 202-265-8137. Ed. Kate Thompson. adv.; bk.rev.; circ. 7,000.
   Description: Covers Central American politics, particularly El Salvador, and U.S. foreign policy. Also covers Belize to Nicaragua from the front line.

341.1   FR   ISSN 0002-5186
ALERTE ATOMIQUE; contre toutes les bombes. bi-m. 8 F.($6) Mouvement pour le Desarmement, la Paix et la Liberte, 25 rue de la Reynie, 75 Paris (1er), France. Ed. Jean Seiler. bibl.; illus.

327 954 942   II   ISSN 0002-5585
ALL-INDIA ANGLO-INDIAN ASSOCIATION. REVIEW. vol.39, 1968. m. All India Anglo-Indian Association, Bombay Life Bldg., Connaught Circus, New Delhi 110001, India. Ed. Frank Anthony. bk.rev.; charts; illus.

ALTERNATIVE TRADING NEWS. see BUSINESS AND ECONOMICS — International Development And Assistance

327   US   ISSN 0304-3754
HC59.7
ALTERNATIVES; social transformation and humane governance. 1974. q. $28 to individuals; institutions $60. (World Order Models Project, Centre for the Study of Developing Societies, International Peace Research Institute Meigaku) Lynne Rienner Publishers, 1800 30th St., Ste. 314, Boulder, CO 80301-1032. TEL 303-444-6684. FAX 303-444-0824. Ed.Bd. adv.; circ. 1,000. (also avail. in microfilm from UMI,WSH; microfiche from UMI; reprint service avail. from UMI,WSH) **Indexed:** A.B.C.Pol.Sci., Amer.Hist.& Life, Art Ind., Biog.Ind., C.L.I., Environ.Abstr., Fut.Surv., Hist.Abstr., Leg.Per., Mag.Ind., P.A.I.S., R.G.
   —BLDSC shelfmark: 0803.670000.
   Description: Analyzes the structure of current world problems, presenting alternative scenarios and policies, to promote discussion of ways to achieve a more equitable future.

327 973   US
AMERICAN FOREIGN POLICY LIBRARY. irreg. price varies. Harvard University Press, 79 Garden St., Cambridge, MA 02138. TEL 617-495-2600. FAX 617-495-5898.
   Refereed Serial

327   GW
AMERICAN-GERMAN STUDIES/DEUTSCH-AMERIKANISCHE STUDIEN. (Text and summaries in English, German) 1985. irreg. price varies. Verlag Hans-Dieter Heinz, Steiermaerkerstr. 132, 7000 Stuttgart 30, Germany. Ed.Bd. bk.rev.; circ. 400. (back issues avail.) **Indexed:** M.L.A.

327 296   US
AMERICAN JEWISH ALTERNATIVES TO ZIONISM. REPORT. 1968. irreg. (2-3/yr.). contribution. American Jewish Alternatives to Zionism, Inc., 347 Fifth Ave., Ste. 900, New York, NY 10016-5010. TEL 212-213-9125. FAX 212-213-9142. bk.rev.; circ. 1,500.

AMERICAN O R T FEDERATION. YEARBOOK. see ETHNIC INTERESTS

327   US   ISSN 0272-2011
F1008
AMERICAN REVIEW OF CANADIAN STUDIES. 1971. 4/yr. $45 to individuals; institutions $90. Association for Canadian Studies in the U S, One Dupont Circle, Ste. 620, Washington, DC 20036. TEL 202-887-6375. FAX 202-296-8379. Ed. Lee Briscoe Thompson. adv.; bk.rev.; bibl.; circ. 1,200. (also avail. in microfilm from MML,UMI; reprint service avail. from UMI) **Indexed:** Amer.Bibl.Slavic & E.Eur.Stud, Amer.Hist.& Life, Can.Lit.Ind., Can.Per.Ind., Can.Wom.Per.Ind., CMI, Hist.Abstr.
   Formerly: A C S U S Newsletter (ISSN 0193-6093)

327 370.196 500   US
AMERICANS FOR THE UNIVERSALITY OF UNESCO NEWSLETTER. 1985. q. (with occasional supplement issues). $25. Americans for the Universality of Unesco, Box 18418, Asheville, NC 28814. TEL 704-253-5383. FAX 704-252-9728. Ed. John E. Fobes. bk.rev.; circ. 3,000. (back issues avail.)
   Description: Contains news and commentary on UNESCO including multilateral cooperation in education, science, culture, communication as well as the U.S. role in these matters.

AMERICAS. see HUMANITIES: COMPREHENSIVE WORKS

AMITIES CATHOLIQUES FRANCAISES. see RELIGIONS AND THEOLOGY — Roman Catholic

POLITICAL SCIENCE — INTERNATIONAL RELATIONS

323   UK
AMNESTY INTERNATIONAL REPORT. (Editions in English, French, Arabic and Spanish) 1962. a. £18($30) (with Amnesty International Newsletter only). Amnesty International, 1 Easton St., London WC1X 8DJ, England. TEL 071-413-5500. FAX 071-956-1157. TELEX 28502. **Indexed:** HR Rep.
Formerly: Amnesty International Annual Report (ISSN 0569-9495)

980   BO   ISSN 0003-2948
ANDES;* revista interamericana. 1967. $1.50 per no. Casilla 4171, La Paz, Bolivia.
Description: Explores politics and government in Latin America.

327 942 943   UK   ISSN 0003-3340
ANGLO-GERMAN REVIEW. 1954. q. £1 per no. to non-members. Anglo-German Association, 17 Bloomsbury Sq., London WC1A 2LP, England. TEL 081-6586466. Ed. Peter B. Johnson. adv.; bk.rev.; circ. 800.
Description: Discusses relations between Britain and Germany, activities of the Association.

327   UK   ISSN 0044-8265
DK1
ANGLO-SOVIET JOURNAL. 1937. 3/yr. £7.50 (foreign £15). Society for Cultural Relations with the U.S.S.R., 320 Brixton Rd., London SW9 6AB, England. TEL 071-274-2282. FAX 071-489-0391. TELEX 888941-LCCI-G. adv.; bk.rev.; illus.; circ. 2,000.
Description: Discusses Britain's relations with Russia.

327 942 946   UK   ISSN 0003-3383
ANGLO-SPANISH QUARTERLY REVIEW. 1951. q. £8 (foreign £17). Anglo-Spanish Society, 61 Pont St., London SW1X 0GB, England. TEL 0279-724024. Ed. A.T. Wright. adv.; bk.rev.; illus.; index every 5 yrs.; circ. 950.
Description: Publishes articles on matters of Anglo-Spanish interest, Spanish culture, civilization and history.

327 382   US   ISSN 1045-0513
ANGOLA PEACE MONITOR; promoting national reconciliation in Angola. 1989. m. $105. International Freedom Foundation, 200 G St., N.E., Ste. 300, Washington, DC 20002. TEL 202-546-5788. FAX 202-546-5488. TELEX 9102408891. Ed. Margaret Calhoun. circ. 1,000 (controlled).
●Also available online. Vendor(s): NewsNet.
Description: Provides current information on international political and economic developments with regard to the domestic situation in Angola.

327   FR   ISSN 0066-295X
ANNUAIRE DIPLOMATIQUE ET CONSULAIRE DE LA REPUBLIQUE FRANCAISE. 1858. a. 500 F. Ministere des Affaires Etrangeres, Direction du Personnel et de l'Administration Generale, 23 rue La Perouse, 75016 Paris, France. (Subscr. to: L'Imprimerie Nationale, 27, rue de la Convention, 75015 Paris, France) adv.; circ. 3,000.

ANNUAL DIRECTORY OF WORLD LEADERS. see POLITICAL SCIENCE

327 320   US
ANNUAL EDITIONS: WORLD POLITICS. 1977. a. $10.95. Dushkin Publishing Group, Inc., Sluice Dock, Guilford, CT 06437-9989. TEL 203-453-4351. FAX 203-453-6000. Ed. Suzanne Ogden. illus.
Refereed Serial

ANNUAL ON TERRORISM (YEAR). see CRIMINOLOGY AND LAW ENFORCEMENT

ANNUAL POLICY REVIEW; an agenda for the future. see ENVIRONMENTAL STUDIES

327 900   US
ANNUAL REGISTER. a. $147. Gale Research Inc., 835 Penobscot Bldg., Detroit, MI 48226. TEL 800-877-4253. FAX 313-877-4253. TELEX 810-221-7086. Ed. H.V. Hodson. (back issues avail.)
Description: Historical reference book.

327   BE
▼**ANNUAL REVIEW OF EUROPEAN COMMUNITY AFFAIRS (YEAR).** (Text in English) 1990. a. 2000 Fr. Centre for European Policy Studies, 33 rue Ducale, B-1000 Brussels, Belgium. TEL 2-513-40-88. FAX 2-511-59-60. TELEX 62818-CEPS-B. Ed. Peter Lomas.

ANNUAL REVIEW OF PROJECT PERFORMANCE RESULTS. see BUSINESS AND ECONOMICS — International Development And Assistance

341.13 327   US   ISSN 0066-4340
JX1977.A1
ANNUAL REVIEW OF UNITED NATIONS AFFAIRS. 1949. a. price varies. Oceana Publications, Inc., Dobbs Ferry, NY 10522. TEL 914-693-1320. FAX 914-693-0402. Ed. William A. Landskron. circ. 500.
—BLDSC shelfmark: 1529.500000.
Description: Reviews activities of the United Nations.

327   IT
ANNUARIO DIPLOMATICO DELLA REPUBBLICA ITALIANA. 1963. a. Ministero degli Affari Esteri, Rome, Italy. circ. 1,500.
Formerly: Annuario Diplomatico del Regno d'Italia.
Description: Covers areas of diplomatic and administrative personnel.

ANTI-DRAFT. see MILITARY

956 960   UK   ISSN 0003-7389
ARAB.* 1967. m. League of Arab States, 52 Green St., London W1Y 3RH, England. bk.rev.; charts; illus.; stat.

ARAB AFFAIRS. see BUSINESS AND ECONOMICS — International Commerce

ARAB BOOK WORLD. see HISTORY — History Of The Near East

956   KE
ARAB WORLD. (Text in English and Kiswahili) 1972. bi-m. League of Arab States, Uchumi House, 10th Fl., Box 30770, Nairobi, Kenya. illus.
Formerly: Voice of Egypt.

327   SY
ARD. 1973. fortn. Al-Ard Institute of Palestine Studies - Muassasat al-Ard Lil-Dirasat al-Filastiniyah, Box 3392, Damascus, Syria. illus.

ARENA; informativni drustveno politicki ilustrirani tjednik. see POLITICAL SCIENCE

355   AG   ISSN 0325-0792
ARGENTINA. ESCUELA DE DEFENSA NACIONAL. REVISTA. 1973. s-a. exchange basis. Escuela de Defensa Nacional, Maipu 262, Buenos Aires 1084, Argentina. TEL 45-1315. adv.; charts; illus.; index; circ. 1,600. **Indexed:** Abstr.Mil.Bibl.
Formerly: Argentina. Escuela Superior de Guerra. Revista (ISSN 0014-0430)
Description: Articles cover politics, foreign affairs, national defense and geopolitics.

327   AG
ARGENTINA. MINISTERIO DE RELACIONES EXTERIORES Y CULTO. REVISTA. 1974. q. free. Ministerio de Relaciones Exteriores y Culto, Buenos Aires, Argentina.

947   AI   ISSN 0004-2293
ARMENYA SEGODNIA. English edition: Armenia Today. (Editions in English, French, German and Russian) 1966. bi-m. free. Armenian Society for Friendship and Cultural Relations with Foreign Countries, Ul. Abovian, 3, Erevan, Armenia. TEL 56-45-14. Ed. Arsen Kakossian. charts; illus.; circ. 60,000. **Indexed:** Numis.Lit.

341.37   US   ISSN 0886-3490
ARMS CONTROL REPORTER. 1982. m. $160 to students (foreign $170); institutions $365 (foreign $375); businesses and government $550 (foreign $560). Institute for Defense and Disarmament Studies, 675 Massachusettes Ave., 8th Fl., Cambridge, MA 02130-3396. TEL 617-354-4337. FAX 617-354-1450. TELEX 403618 IDDS USA UD. Ed. Chalmers Hardenbergh. abstr.; charts; stat.; circ. 450. (looseleaf format; back issues avail.)
Description: Comprehensive compilation of all public information on all international arms control negotiations and relevant weapons. Non-partisan chronologies, texts, and analysis.

ARMS CONTROL TODAY. see POLITICAL SCIENCE

327   US
ARROW (BROOKLYN)/FLECHA. (Text in English, Spanish) 1977. bi-m. $2 to individuals; libraries $5. International Committee Against Racism, Inc., Box 904, G.P.O., Brooklyn, NY 11202. TEL 212-629-0003. bk.rev.; circ. 10,000. (back issues avail.)
Description: Covers racism, includes segregation, social issues and anti-racist movements.

327   US
ASIA SERIAL REPORTS: KOREA: KULLOJA. irreg. $150 in US, Canada, Mexico; elsewhere $300. (Joint Publications Research Service) U.S. National Technical Information Service, 5825 Port Royal Rd., Springfield, VA 22161. TEL 703-487-4630.

327   US
ASIA SERIAL REPORTS: VIET NAM: TOP CHI CHONG SAN. irreg. $125 in US, Canada, Mexico; elsewhere $250. (Joint Publications Research Service) U.S. National Technical Information Service, 5825 Port Royal Rd., Springfield, VA 22161. TEL 703-487-4630.

327   US
ASIA WATCH. Variant title: News from Asia Watch. 1985. irreg. $40. Human Rights Watch, Asia Watch, 485 Fifth Ave., New York, NY 10017-6104. TEL 212-972-8400. FAX 212-972-0905. (Also: 1522 K St. N.W., Ste. 910, Washington, D.C. 20005-1202. TEL 202-371-6592)
Description: Frequent newsletter of Asia Watch.

327   US   ISSN 0092-7678
DS33.4.U6
ASIAN AFFAIRS: AN AMERICAN REVIEW. 1973. q. $29 to individuals; institutions $57. (American-Asian Educational Exchange, Inc.) Heldref Publications, 1319 Eighteenth St., N.W., Washington, DC 20036-1802. TEL 202-296-6267. FAX 202-296-5149. (Co-sponsor: Helen Dwight Reid Educational Foundation) Ed. Sandy Grimm. adv.; circ. 360. (also avail. in microform; reprint service avail.) **Indexed:** A.B.C.Pol.Sci., Amer.Bibl.Slavic & E.Eur.Stud, Amer.Hist.& Life, ASSIA, Hist.Abstr., Int.Polit.Sci.Abstr., Mid.East: Abstr.& Ind., P.A.I.S. Key Title: Asian Affairs (New York).
—BLDSC shelfmark: 1742.270500.
Formerly: Southeast Asian Perspectives.
Description: Focuses on US policy in Asia, as well as on the domestic politics, economics, and international relations of the Asian countries.
Refereed Serial

320.9   JA
ASIAN PARLIAMENTARIANS' UNION. CENTRAL SECRETARIAT. REPORT ON MEETING OF APU SECRETARIES-GENERAL IN TOKYO.* 1972. a. Asian Parliamentarians' Union, TBR Bldg., Room 807, 2-10-2 Nagata-cho, Chiyoda-ku, Tokyo, Japan.

ASIAN PERSPECTIVE; biannual journal of regional & international affairs. see POLITICAL SCIENCE

327   JA
ASIAN SECURITY.* 1984. a. $35.95. Research Institute for Peace and Security, Roppongi Denki Bldg., 6-1-20 Roppongi, Minato-ku, Tokyo 106, Japan. FAX 81-3-3478-3105. Ed. Masataka Kosaka. circ. 3,000. (back issues avail.)

327   US
ASIAN STUDIES CENTER BACKGROUNDER. 1983. irreg. no.119, 1992. Heritage Foundation, 214 Massachusetts Ave., N.E., Washington, DC 20002. TEL 202-546-4400. FAX 202-546-8328. Ed. Burton Yale Pines. (looseleaf format)
●Also available online. Vendor(s): Mead Data Central.

POLITICAL SCIENCE — INTERNATIONAL RELATIONS 3951

327 382   FR   ISSN 0153-3657
ASSOCIATION POUR L'ETUDE DES PROBLEMES D'OUTRE MER. DOCUMENTATION-DEVELOPPEMENT. 1947. 8/yr. 1000 F. Association pour l'Etude des Problemes d'Outre Mer, 190 Bd. Haussmann, 75008 Paris, France. Ed. J. Alibert. charts; stat.

327   NE   ISSN 0167-1847
ATLANTISCH PERSPEKTIEF. 1963. 10/yr. fl.3.50. Stichting Atlantische Commissie, Laan van Meerdervoort 96, 2517 AR The Hague, Netherlands. TEL 070-3639495. FAX 070-3646309. Ed. Mrs. L.F.M. Sprangers. adv.; bk.rev.; circ. 3,000. **Indexed:** Key to Econ.Sci.
     Formerly: Atlantische Tijdingen (ISSN 0067-0235)

327   GW
AUSBLICK (LUEBECK); Zeitschrift fuer deutsch-skandinavische Beziehungen. 1949. s-a. DM.20. Deutsche Auslandsgesellschaft, Holstenstr. 17, 2400 Luebeck 1, Germany. Ed. Karsten Jessen. adv.; bk.rev.; circ. 1,500.

327   GW   ISSN 0004-8194
D839
AUSSENPOLITIK; Zeitschrift fuer internationale Fragen. (Editions in English and German) 1950. q. DM.50 (English ed.). Interpress Verlag GmbH, Hartwicusstr. 3-4, 2000 Hamburg 76, Germany. FAX 040-2285260. TELEX 2-14733. adv.; bk.rev.; index; circ. 7,100 (English ed.); 2,500 (German ed.). (also avail. in microfiche; reprint service avail. from KTO) **Indexed:** A.B.C.Pol.Sci., Amer.Hist.& Life, Curr.Cont., Hist.Abstr., P.A.I.S.For.Lang.Ind., Peace Res.Abstr., Rural Recreat.Tour.Abstr., SCIMP (1991-), So.Pac.Per.Ind., SSCI, World Agri.Econ.& Rural Sociol.Abstr.
     —BLDSC shelfmark: 1792.960000.

327   AT   ISSN 0727-2987
J905
AUSTRALIA. CHINA COUNCIL ANNUAL REPORT. a. (China Council) Australian Government Publishing Service, G.P.O. Box 84, Canberra, A.C.T. 2601, Australia.

327   AT
AUSTRALIA. DEPARTMENT OF FOREIGN AFFAIRS AND TRADE. SELECT DOCUMENTS ON INTERNATIONAL AFFAIRS; international treaties and conventions. irreg. price varies. Department of Foreign Affairs and Trade, Treaties Section, Administration Bldg., Parkes, A.C.T. 2600, Australia, Australia. FAX 062-613455. TELEX 62007.
     Formerly: Australia. Department of Foreign Affairs. Select Documents on International Affairs (ISSN 0519-5950); Incorporates: Australia. Department of Foreign Affairs. International Treaties and Conventions (ISSN 0084-7135)

361   AT   ISSN 0810-0055
AUSTRALIA NEW ZEALAND FOUNDATION. ANNUAL REPORT (YEAR); promoting friendship across the Tasman. a. price varies. (Australia New Zealand Foundation) Australian Government Publishing Service, P.O. Box 70E, Queen Victoria Terrace, Canberra, A.C.T. 2600, Australia.

327   AT
AUSTRALIAN-AMERICAN NEWS N.S.W. ANNUAL EDITION. irreg. Aus.$50 per no. Australian-American Association, N.S.W. Division, 39-41 Lower Fort St., Sydney, N.S.W. 2000, Australia. Ed. T. Padley. adv.; illus.

327   AT
JX1162
AUSTRALIAN FOREIGN AFFAIRS AND TRADE: THE MONTHLY RECORD. 1936. m. Aus.$40 to individuals; free to qualified personnel. Department of Foreign Affairs and Trade, Publications Unit, OIB Edmund Barton Bldg., Barton, A.C.T. 2600, Australia. FAX 062-733577. TELEX 62007. charts; illus.; maps; index; circ. 9,500. **Indexed:** Abstr.Mil.Bibl., Amer.Hist.& Life, Aus.P.A.I.S., E.I., Gdlns., Gdlns, Hist.Abstr., INIS Atomind., P.A.I.S., So.Pac.Per.Ind.
     Former titles: Australian Foreign Affairs Record (ISSN 0311-7995) & Current Notes on International Affairs (ISSN 0011-3751)
     Description: Informs Australian and overseas readers on a regular basis of developments in the Australian Government's foreign policy.

994 327   AT   ISSN 1035-7718
DU80
AUSTRALIAN JOURNAL OF INTERNATIONAL AFFAIRS. 1947. 2/yr. Aus.$30 (foreign Aus.$40)(effective 1991). Australian Institute of International Affairs, Australian Capital Territory Branch, P.O. Box E181, Canberra, A.C.T. 2600, Australia. Ed. J. Cotton. adv.; bk.rev.; charts; circ. 2,600. (also avail. in microfilm; reprint service avail. from UMI) **Indexed:** A.B.C.Pol.Sci., Abstr.Mil.Bibl., Amer.Hist.& Life, Aus.P.A.I.S., Br.Hum.Ind, Curr.Cont., E.I., Gdlns., Hist.Abstr., Int.Polit.Sci.Abstr., Mid.East: Abstr.& Ind., P.A.I.S., PROMT, So.Pac.Per.Ind.
     Formerly: Australian Outlook (ISSN 0004-9913)

327   AT
AUSTRALIA'S OVERSEAS DEVELOPMENT ASSISTANCE. BUDGET PAPER. 1973. a. price varies. (Department of the Treasury) Australian Government Publishing Service, G.P.O. Box 84, Canberra, A.C.T. 2601, Australia.
     Former titles: Australia's Overseas Development Assistance (ISSN 0312-9217); Australia's External Aid (ISSN 0310-6152)

943.6   US   ISSN 0005-0520
DB1
AUSTRIAN INFORMATION. 1947? m. (except summer months). free. Austrian Information Service, 31 E. 69th St., New York, NY 10021. TEL 212-288-1727. FAX 212-772-8926. TELEX 147285. Ed. Wolfgang Petritsch. bk.rev.; illus.; circ. 13,000. (also avail. in microform from UMI)

AYIN L'TZION. see ETHNIC INTERESTS

327   CN   ISSN 0708-0859
B.C. PEACE NEWS. 1978. irreg. membership. B.C. Peace Council, 712-207 West Hastings St., Vancouver, B.C. V6B 1H7, Canada. TEL 604-685-9958. Ed.Bd. bk.rev.; circ. 500.
     Formerly: B.C. News (ISSN 0708-0840)
     Description: Explores the peace movement in British Columbia, news about upcoming events.

B.C. VOICE. see WOMEN'S INTERESTS

327 355   GW   ISSN 0302-9468
AP30
B G S. (Bundesgrenzschutz) 1974. m. DM.48. (Bundesministerium des Innern) A. Bernecker Verlag, Unter dem Schoeneberg 1, 3508 Melsungen, Germany. Ed. Otto Wiegand. bk.rev.; circ. 16,200.

327   US   ISSN 0382-8352
BACKGROUNDER. 1977. irreg., no.815, 1992. $125 includes Issue Bulletins and Backgrounder Update. Heritage Foundation, 214 Massachusetts Ave., N.E., Washington, DC 20002. TEL 202-546-4400. FAX 202-546-8328. Ed. Burton Y. Pines. **Indexed:** INIS Atomind.
     ●Also available online. Vendor(s): Mead Data Central.

327 341   UK
BAILRIGG PAPERS ON INTERNATIONAL SECURITY. 1980. irreg. University of Lancaster, Centre for the Study of Arms Control and International Security, Bailrigg, Lancaster LA1 4YR, England.

327 949   US
BALTIC BULLETIN. 1981. bi-m. $25. Baltic-American Freedom League, Box 29657, Los Angeles, CA 90029. Ed. William Hough, III. circ. 10,000.

327   ER   ISSN 1018-7286
▼**THE BALTIC INDEPENDENT.** (Text in English) 1990. w. £24($45) Estonian News Agency (ETA), P.O. Box 100, Rm. 802, Parnu Rd. 67a, Tallinn 200090, Estonia. TEL 0142-683074. FAX 0142-691537. TELEX 173193 ETA SU. (Subscr. in UK to: Wyvern House, 150 Cranbrook Rd., Poole, Dorset BH12 3JB, England) Ed. Tarmu Tammerk. adv.; circ. 7,000. (newspaper)
     Formerly (until June 1990): Estonian Independent.
     Description: Presents news from an independent viewpoint on Estonian politics, business, and culture in the Baltic States.

327   CN
BAROMETER. 1989. q. Can.$45($45) Canadian Centre for Arms Control and Disarmament - Centre Candien pour le Controle des Armements et le Desarrement, 151 Slater St., Ste. 710, Ottawa, Ont. K1P 5H3, Canada. TEL 613-230-7755. FAX 613-230-7910. Ed. Tariq Rauf. bk.rev.; circ. 3,000. (back issues avail.)
     Supersedes: Arms Control; Formerly (until 1989): Arms Control Chronicle (ISSN 0825-1908)
     Description: Focuses on international and Canadian arms control developments.

341.13   UN   ISSN 0067-4419
JX1977.A37
BASIC FACTS ABOUT THE UNITED NATIONS. irreg. $5. United Nations Publications, Room DC2-853, New York, NY 10017. TEL 212-963-8300. FAX 212-963-3489. (Or: Distribution and Sales Section, Palais des Nations, CH-1211 Geneva 10, Switzerland)

327 200   US
BASTA!. (Text in English) 1984. 3/yr. $18 to individuals; institutions $30. Chicago Religious Task Force on Central America, 59 E. Van Buren, Ste. 1400, Chicago, IL 60605. TEL 312-663-4398. FAX 312-427-4171. (And: 8th Day Center for Justice, 1020 S. Wabash, Rm. 680, Chicago, IL 60605-2214) bk.rev.; circ. 1,500.
     Description: Provides news and information from Central America, including social and political analysis, and theological reflections.

327   GW
BEGEGNUNG UND AUSTAUSCH MIT FRANZOSEN. 1973. a. free. Deutsch-Franzoesisches Jugendwerk, Rhoendorferstr. 23, 5340 Bad Honnef 1, Germany. TEL 02224-1808-0. FAX 02224-1808-52. circ. 60,000.

971 327   CN   ISSN 0005-7983
F1034
BEHIND THE HEADLINES. 1940. 4/yr. Can.$12. Canadian Institute of International Affairs, 15 King's College Circle, Toronto, Ont. M5S 2V9, Canada. TEL 416-979-1851. FAX 416-979-8575. Ed. David Stafford. circ. 2,800. (also avail. in microfilm from UMI; reprint service avail. from UMI) **Indexed:** Amer.Hist.& Life, Can.Per.Ind., CMI, Hist.Abstr., Vert.File Ind.
     —BLDSC shelfmark: 1878.102000.
     Description: A series of pamphlets for the general reader on current affairs.

327 956   LE
▼**BEIRUT REVIEW.** 1991. s-a. $24 to individuals; institutions $48. Lebanese Center for Policy Studies, Tayyar Bldg., Mkalles, Sin al-Fil, Beirut, Lebanon. TEL 01-490561. FAX 01-490375. TELEX 40543 LE. (Subscr. outside Lebanon: Box 53365, Washington, DC 20009 USA. TEL 202-232-8350) Ed. Paul E. Salem. bk.rev.; bibl.
     Description: Contains articles on political and economic affairs in Lebanon and the Middle East, and a chronology of events.

327   GR
BLUELINE; Greek and Mediterranean report. (Supplement avail.: Blueline Documents) (Text in English) m. (Institute of Political Studies) Dimitris Dimopolous, 28 Pericleous St., GR 143, 43, Nea Halkidona, Athens, Greece.

BRAZIL WATCH. see BUSINESS AND ECONOMICS — Economic Situation And Conditions

237   UK
BRITAIN AND EUROPE DURING (YEAR). 1973. a. $30. Research Publications Ltd., P.O. Box 45, Reading RG1 8HF, England. TEL 0734-583247. FAX 0734-591325. (Dist. in U.S. by: Research Publications Inc., 12 Lunar Dr., Drawer AB, Woodbridge, CT 06525) (back issues avail.)
     Description: Guide to microfilm collection.

BRITISH COUNCIL ANNUAL REPORT AND ACCOUNTS (YEAR). see EDUCATION — Higher Education

327 947 942   UK   ISSN 0007-1803
BRITISH-SOVIET FRIENDSHIP. 1955. m. £7 (foreign £12). British Soviet Friendship Society, 36 St. Johns Square, London EC1 4JH, England. Ed. T. Foley. adv.; bk.rev.; illus.; circ. 3,000.

POLITICAL SCIENCE — INTERNATIONAL RELATIONS

950 322.4   US   ISSN 0007-4810
DS1
BULLETIN OF CONCERNED ASIAN SCHOLARS. 1968. q. $22 to individuals (foreign $23); institutions $55 (foreign $56). Bulletin of Concerned Asian Scholars, Inc., 3239 9th St., Boulder, CO 80304-2112. TEL 303-449-7439. FAX 303-449-8870. Ed.Bd. adv.; bk.rev.; bibl.; charts; illus.; circ. 1,600. (also avail. in microform from UMI; reprint service avail. from UMI,ISI; back issues avail.) **Indexed:** Alt.Press Ind., Curr.Cont., E.I., Hist.Abstr., HR Rep., I D A, Int.Lab.Doc., Int.Polit.Sci.Abstr., Left Ind. (1982-), Mid.East: Abstr.& Ind., SSCI.
—BLDSC shelfmark: 2458.145000.
Formerly: C C A S Newsletter.
Refereed Serial

327   US   ISSN 0096-3402
TK9145   CODEN: BASIAP
BULLETIN OF THE ATOMIC SCIENTISTS; magazine of science and world affairs. 1945. 10/yr. $30. Educational Foundation for Nuclear Science, 6042 S. Kimbark Ave., Chicago, IL 60637. TEL 312-702-2555. FAX 312-702-0725. adv.; bk.rev.; illus.; index; circ. 18,000. (also avail. in microform from UMI,MIM; reprint service avail. from UMI) **Indexed:** A.B.C.Pol.Sci., Acad.Ind., Amer.Bibl.Slavic & E.Eur.Stud., Amer.Hist.& Life, Biog.Ind., Biol.Abstr., Biol.Dig., Bk.Rev.Dig., Bk.Rev.Ind. (1965-), C.I.J.E., Chem.Abstr., Child.Bk.Rev.Ind. (1965-), Curr.Adv.Ecol.Sci., Curr.Cont., Energy Info.Abstr., Energy Rev., Environ.Abstr., Environ.Per.Bibl., Excerp.Med., Fut.Surv., Gen.Sci.Ind., GeoRef, Hist.Abstr., Ind.Sci.Rev., INIS Atomind., Mag.Ind., Media Rev.Dig., Met.Abstr., Mid.East: Abstr.& Ind., Nucl.Sci.Abstr., PMR, Pollut.Abstr., R.G., Risk Abstr., Sci.Cit.Ind., So.Pac.Per.Ind., Sociol.Abstr., SSCI, Telegen, World Alum.Abstr.
●Also available on CD-ROM.
—BLDSC shelfmark: 2408.000000.
Formerly: Science and Public Affairs Bulletin of the Atomic Scientists (ISSN 0007-5094)
Description: Helps to redefine international security in terms that embrace economic, environmental, cultural, and military factors.

327   GW   ISSN 0435-7183
D839
BUNDESINSTITUT FUER OSTWISSENSCHAFTLICHE UND INTERNATIONALE STUDIEN. BERICHTE. 1967. irreg. DM.30. Bundesinstitut fuer Ostwissenschaftliche und Internationale Studien, Lindenbornstr. 22, 5000 Cologne 30, Germany. TEL 0221-5747-0. bibl.; circ. 1,100.

327 338.91   US
BUSINESS COUNCIL FOR THE U N BRIEFING. Variant title: B C U N Briefing. 1987. q. Business Council for the U N, 60 E. 42nd St., Rm. 2925, New York, NY 10165. TEL 212-661-1772. Ed. Evelyn Wilkens. circ. 4,500. (tabloid format; back issues avail.)
Formerly (until 1984): F Y I to C E O's.

327   US   ISSN 0739-9189
C A L C REPORT. 1975. bi-m. $30. National Clergy and Laity Concerned, 340 Mead Rd., Decatur, GA 30030. TEL 404-377-1983. FAX 404-377-5367. Ed. Mark Reeve. adv.; bk.rev.; illus.; circ. 10,000. (back issues avail.) **Indexed:** HR Rep.
Incorporates: T W C Bulletin (Third World Caucus); **Formerly:** American Report.

C C I A BACKGROUND INFORMATION. (World Council of Churches, Commission of the Churches on International Affairs) see *RELIGIONS AND THEOLOGY*

327   BE
C E P S PAPERS. (Text in English) 1983. irreg. 500 Fr. free to members. Centre for European Policy Studies, 33 rue Ducale, 1000 Brussels, Belgium. Ed. Peter Lomas. (back issues avail.)

327 330.1   BE
C E P S WORKING DOCUMENTS. (Text in English) 1983. irreg. 220 Fr. Centre for European Policy Studies, 33 rue Ducale, 1000 Brussels, Belgium. Ed. Peter Lomas. (back issues avail.)
Formed by the merger of: C E P S Working Documents (Economic) & C E P S Working Documents (Political).

327   SW   ISSN 1100-4177
C E S I C STUDIES IN INTERNATIONAL CONFLICT. (Text in English, Swedish) 1989. irreg. price varies. Lund University Press, P. O. Box 141, S-221 00 Lund, Sweden. TEL 46-46-31-20-00. FAX 46-46-30-53-38. Eds. G. Rystad, S. Taegil.

327   EI
C O M DOCUMENTS. (Text in Danish, Dutch, English, French, German, Greek, Italian, Portuguese, Spanish) 1983. s-m. $1380. Office for Official Publications of the European Communities, L-2985 Luxembourg, Luxembourg. FAX 301-923-0056. (Dist. in the U.S. by: Unipub, 4611-F Assembly Dr., Lanham, MD 20706-4391) (also avail. in microfiche)

C S I CONGRESSIONAL RECORD ABSTRACTS: FOREIGN AFFAIRS EDITION. see *PUBLIC ADMINISTRATION — Abstracting, Bibliographies, Statistics*

327   YU   ISSN 0353-0353
C S S PAPERS. (Text in English) 1987-1988 (no.4); suspended. 2/yr. $15. Center for Strategic Studies, Makedonska 25, P.O. Box 750, 11000 Belgrade, Yugoslavia. FAX 011-322-864. Ed.Bd.
—BLDSC shelfmark: 3490.325000.

327   US
CALIFORNIA STATE UNIVERSITY, LOS ANGELES. CENTER FOR THE STUDY OF ARMAMENT AND DISARMAMENT. OCCASIONAL PAPERS SERIES. 1972. irreg., no.19, 1990. price varies. California State University, Los Angeles, Center for the Study of Armament and Disarmament, 5151 State University Dr., Los Angeles, CA 90032. (Dist. by: Regina Books, Box 280, Claremont, CA 91711) Ed. Udo Heyn. circ. 300. **Indexed:** Vert.File Ind.

327   CN
CANADA. DEPARTMENT OF EXTERNAL AFFAIRS. REFERENCE PAPERS. irreg. Department of External Affairs, External Information Programs Division, 125 Sussex Dr., Ottawa, Ont. K1A 0G2, Canada. TEL 613-996-9134.

327   CN
CANADA. DEPARTMENT OF EXTERNAL AFFAIRS. STATEMENTS AND SPEECHES. 1945. irreg. free. Department of External Affairs, External Communications Division (BFE), 125 Sussex Dr., Ottawa, Ont. K1A 0G2, Canada. TEL 613-992-9280. circ. 4,000.

327   US   ISSN 1047-1073
▼**CANADIAN - AMERICA PUBLIC POLICY.** 1990. q. $20 (foreign $25; typically set in Jan.). (University of Maine, Canadian - American Center) Canadian - American Center, 154 College Ave., Orono, ME 04469-1050. TEL 207-581-4220. FAX 207-581-4223. Ed. Robert H. Babcock. adv.; circ. 200.
—BLDSC shelfmark: 3017.039000.
Description: Focuses on contemporary issues in United States-Canada relations.

327   CN   ISSN 0317-5693
AS4.U825
CANADIAN COMMISSION FOR UNESCO. ANNUAL REPORT. (Text in English, French) 1958. a. free. Canadian Commission for Unesco, Box 1047, Ottawa, Ont. K1P 5V8, Canada. TEL 613-598-4325. circ. 4,000.

CANADIAN COMMISSION FOR UNESCO. BULLETIN/COMMISSION CANADIENNE POUR UNESCO. BULLETIN. see *EDUCATION*

327   CN
CANADIAN FOREIGN RELATIONS.* Cover title: Annual Review. (Text in English and French) a. Canadian Institute of International Affairs, 15 King's College Circle, Toronto, Ont. M5S 2V9, Canada. TEL 613-996-9134. illus.
●Also available online. Vendor(s): QL Systems Ltd..

CANADIAN JEWISH HERALD. see *ETHNIC INTERESTS*

CANADIAN WORLD FEDERALIST/FEDERALISTE MONDIAL DU CANADA. see *LAW — International Law*

CANADO-AMERICAIN. see *ETHNIC INTERESTS*

327 330.9   US   ISSN 0894-0223
CARIBBEAN NEWSLETTER. 1980. bi-m. $13 to individuals; institutions $15 (effective Jan. 1992). Friends for Jamaica Collective, Box 20392, Park West Sta., New York, NY 10025. Ed.Bd. bk.rev.; film rev.; illus.; tr.lit.; circ. 500. (also avail. in microfiche; back issues avail.) **Indexed:** HR Rep.
Formerly: Friends for Jamaica Newsletter.

327 382   US   ISSN 0271-6577
CARIBBEAN STUDIES NEWSLETTER. 1974. q. $30. (Caribbean Studies Association) City College of New York, Department of Political Science, Convent Ave. & 138th St., New York, NY 10031. TEL 212-690-5470. Ed. J.A. Braveboy-Wagner. adv.; circ. 1,000. (back issues avail.)
Description: News of academic and general interest on Caribbean politics and government, teaching and research.

327   CN   ISSN 0383-2848
CARLETON UNIVERSITY, OTTAWA. NORMAN PATERSON SCHOOL OF INTERNATIONAL AFFAIRS. BIBLIOGRAPHY SERIES. 1975. irreg. (1-2/yr). Can.$6 per no. Carleton University, Norman Paterson School of International Affairs, Ottawa, Ont. K1S 5B6, Canada. TEL 613-788-6667. Ed. Vivian Cummins. circ. 600.

942   UK
CARN. 1973. q. $20. Celtic League, c/o Bernard Moffat, 11 Hilltop View, Farmhill, Braddan, Isle of Man, England. Ed. Patricia Bridson. adv.; bk.rev.; circ. 2,000.
Formed by the merger of: Breton News (ISSN 0006-9671) & Celtic League Annual & Celtic News (ISSN 0008-8773)

327 100   US
CARNEGIE COUNCIL NEWSLETTER. 1984. q. Carnegie Council on Ethics and International Affairs, c/o Olivia Wakeman, Dir., Public Relations, Merrill House, 170 E. 64th St., New York, NY 10021. TEL 212-838-4120. FAX 212-752-2432.
Description: Contains information regarding Carnegie Council activities.

327.172   US   ISSN 0094-3029
JX1906
CARNEGIE ENDOWMENT FOR INTERNATIONAL PEACE. FINANCIAL REPORT. irreg. Carnegie Endowment for International Peace, 2400 N St., N.W., Ste. 700, Washington, DC 20037. TEL 202-862-7900. (reprint service avail. from UMI) Key Title: Financial Report - Carnegie Endowment for International Peace.

CATHOLIC NEAR EAST MAGAZINE. see *POLITICAL SCIENCE — Civil Rights*

327   SZ
CAUX INFORMATION; Informationsdienst Moralische Aufruestung. 1949. m. 32 Fr. (foreign 37 Fr.). Caux Verlag AG, Postfach 4419, CH-6002 Lucerne, Switzerland. TEL 041-422213. FAX 041-422214. Ed. Konrad von Orelli. bk.rev.; charts; illus.; circ. 1,900.
Description: Offers ideas about resolution of conflicts through social and economic change.

327   AG
CEINAR. 1975. 3/yr. Arg.$1200($16) Centro de Estudios Internacionales Argentinos, Defensa 251, 1B, 1065 Buenos Aires, Argentina. Ed. Luis Dallanegra Pedraza. adv.; bk.rev.; circ. 1,500. **Indexed:** Abstr.Mil.Bibl.
Formerly: Revista Argentina de Relaciones Internacionales (ISSN 0325-1888)

327   US
▼**CENTER FOR INTELLIGENCE STUDIES. REPRINT SERIES.** 1990. irreg. $50 membership. Center for Intelligence Studies, 301 S. Columbus St., Alexandria, VA 22314. TEL 703-684-0625. FAX 703-836-8429. Ed. Charles S. Via, Jr. circ. 25,000. (tabloid format)
Description: Reprints of particularly important non-classified or de-classified intelligence studies.

327   US   ISSN 0732-0078
CENTER FOR PEACE AND CONFLICT STUDIES. OCCASIONAL PAPERS. 1981. irreg. price varies. Wayne State University, Center for Peace and Conflict Studies, 2319 Faculty Administration Bldg., Detroit, MI 48202. TEL 313-577-3453.
Description: Articles on the peacemaking process.

POLITICAL SCIENCE — INTERNATIONAL RELATIONS 3953

341.1 US
CENTER FOR PEACE AND CONFLICT STUDIES - DETROIT COUNCIL FOR WORLD AFFAIRS. NEWSLETTER. 1965. 4/yr. membership. Wayne State University, Center for Peace and Conflict Studies, 2319 Faculty Administration Bldg., Detroit, MI 48202. TEL 313-577-3453. (Co-sponsor: Detroit Council for World Affairs) bibl.; circ. 1,000. (processed)
Formerly: Center for Teaching About Peace and War. Newsletter (ISSN 0008-9133)
Description: News and articles on the peacemaking process.

CENTERVIEWS. see *BUSINESS AND ECONOMICS — International Commerce*

327 338.91 CN ISSN 0823-7689
CENTRAL AMERICA UPDATE. 1979. bi-m. Can.$30 to institutions; individuals Can.$25. Latin American Working Group, P.O. Box 2207, Sta. P, Toronto, Ont. M5S 2T2, Canada. TEL 416-533-4221. FAX 416-533-4579. (Co-sponsor: Jesuit Centre for Social Faith and Justice) circ. 1,200. **Indexed:** HR Rep.
● Also available online. Vendor(s): DIALOG, NewsNet.
Description: Provides analysis of events in Central America; highlights Canada's relations to the region.

CENTRAL AND INNER ASIAN STUDIES. see *HISTORY — History Of Asia*

327 BE
CENTRE FOR EUROPEAN POLICY STUDIES. NEWSLETTER. q. membership. Centre for European Policy Studies, 33 rue Ducale, B-1000 Brussels, Belgium. TEL 2-513-40-88. FAX 2-511-59-60. TELEX 62818-CEPS-B. Ed. Peter Lomas.

327 CN
CENTRE QUEBECOIS DE RELATIONS INTERNATIONALES. COLLECTION DOSSIERS. 3/yr. Centre Quebecois de Relations Internationales, Faculte des Sciences Sociales, Pavillon de Koninck, Universite Laval, Quebec, Que. G1K 7P4, Canada. TEL 418-656-2462. Ed. Claude Basset.

CHALLENGE (LONDON, 1961). see *RELIGIONS AND THEOLOGY — Protestant*

341.1 SZ ISSN 1017-2874
CHANGER. 1964. m. 33 Fr. (foreign 35 Fr.). Caux Edition S.A., Rue du Panorama, CH-1824 Caux, Switzerland. FAX 21-9635260. Ed. Jean-Jacques Odier. adv.; bk.rev.; circ. 2,500.
Former titles: Changer - Tribune de Caux; (until 1979): Tribune de Caux; Which incorporates: Courrier d'Information-Rearmement Moral (ISSN 0011-0523)

327 365.64 US
CHIEFS OF STATE AND CABINET MEMBERS OF FOREIGN GOVERNMENTS. m. $80 in US, Canada, Mexico; elsewhere $160. (Central Intelligence Agency) U.S. National Technical Information Service, 5825 Port Royal Rd., Springfield, VA 22161. TEL 703-487-4630.
Description: Lists approximately 155 governments.

CHILDREN AND WAR NEWSLETTER; a newsletter for adults. see *CHILDREN AND YOUTH — About*

327 UK
CHILEAN NEWS. 1942. 2/yr. £13. Anglo Chilean Society, 12 Devonshire St., London W1N 2DS, England. TEL 01-580-1271. Ed. M.C. Cannon. bk.rev.; bibl.; illus.; circ. 600 (controlled).

327 CC
CHINA AND AFRICA/ZHONGGUO YU FEIZHOU. (Editions in English, French) m. Ministry of Culture, Foreign Language Bureau, 24 Baiwanzhuang Lu, Fuwai, Beijing 100037, People's Republic of China. TEL 8315599. Ed. Zhang Lifang.

327 US ISSN 1044-890X
CHINA AND PACIFIC RIM LETTER. 1977. bi-m. $25 to members; non-members $100. U S Global Strategy Council, 1800 K St., N.W., Ste. 1102, Washington, DC 20006. TEL 202-466-6029. FAX 202-331-0109. (Co-sponsor: Committee for a Free China) circ. 1,000. (back issues avail.)
Formerly (until 1988): China Letter.
Description: Covers China's realtionship with the Pacific Rim.

327 JA
CHINA DIRECTORY (YEAR)/ZHONGGUO ZUZHIBIE RENMINGBU/CHUGOKU SOSHIKIBETSU JINMEIBO. (Text in Chinese and English) 1971. a. 16000 Yen($98) Radiopress, Inc., R-Bldg. Shinjuku 5F, 33-8, Wakamatsu-cho, Shinjuku-ku, Tokyo 162, Japan. TEL 03-5273-2171. FAX 03-5273-2180. bk.rev.; index; circ. 2,500. (back issues avail.)
Description: Organization-based directory of 7,000 Chinese leaders and 2,000 organizations. Covers state council structural reforms, new cabinet members and other changes of past year; names listed in Chinese and Pinyin romanization.

951 US ISSN 0009-4455
DS777.55
CHINA REPORT. (Text in English) 1964. q. $32 to individuals, institutions $62. (Centre for the Study of Developing Societies, II) Sage Publications, Inc., 2455 Teller Rd., Newbury Park, CA 91320. TEL 805-499-0721. FAX 805-499-0871. (And: Sage Publications India Pvt. Ltd., P.O. Box 4215, New Delhi 110 048, India) Ed. C.R.M. Rao. bk.rev.; stat.; index. **Indexed:** Amer.Hist.& Life, Hist.Abstr., Key to Econ.Sci., Rural Devel.Abstr., World Agri.Econ.& Rural Sociol.Abstr.
—BLDSC shelfmark: 3180.233000.
Description: Encourages the increased understanding of contemporary China and its East Asian neighbors, their cultures and ways of development, and their impact on India and other South Asian countries.

CHINA SPRING. see *POLITICAL SCIENCE — Civil Rights*

327 FR ISSN 0529-8016
CITES UNIES. 1957. q. 100 F. United Towns Organization, 22, rue d'Alsace, 92300 Levallois, France. adv.; bk.rev.; circ. 7,000.

327 355 900 US ISSN 0886-6015
CIVILIAN - BASED DEFENSE: NEWS AND OPINION. 1982. 6/yr. $15. Civilian - Based Defense Association, 154 Auburn St., Cambridge, MA 02139-3969. TEL 617-868-6058. Ed.Bd. bk.rev.; circ. 850. (looseleaf format; back issues avail.)
Description: Explores civilian-based defense, a defense in which well prepared but unarmed civilians resist invasions on coups d'itat through noncorporation, strikes, demonstrations, sanctions.

CIVIS MUNDI. see *POLITICAL SCIENCE*

CLARION CALL; the voice of transcendence. see *NEW AGE PUBLICATIONS*

327 US ISSN 0145-9678
JF37
CLEMENTS' ENCYCLOPEDIA OF WORLD GOVERNMENTS. 1974. biennial. $435 (includes Clements' International Report, Updates and Matching Supplement Organizer). Political Research, Inc., Tegoland at Bent Tree, 16850 Dallas Pkwy., Dallas, TX 75248. TEL 214-931-8827. FAX 214-248-7159. Ed. John Clements.
Description: Directory of current information on the economy, people, climate, government, officials and foreign affairs of each independent nation.

327 US ISSN 0145-9678
CLEMENTS' INTERNATIONAL REPORT. 1976. m. included in subscription to Clements' Encyclopedia of World Governments. Political Research, Inc., Tegoland at Bent Tree, 16850 Dallas Pkwy., Dallas, TX 75248. TEL 214-931-8827. FAX 214-248-7159. Ed. John Clements.
Description: Covers current events and developments throughout the world.

327 CN ISSN 0709-874X
COLLECTION CHOIX. 1971. a. Can.$20. Centre Quebecois de Relations Internationales, Faculte de Sciences Sociales, Pavillon de Koninck, Universite de Laval, Quebec, Que. G1K 7P4, Canada. TEL 418-656-2462. FAX 418-656-3634. Ed. Claude Basset-Hervouet. circ. 600. **Indexed:** Pt.de Rep. (1983-).

327 UK ISSN 0141-8513
COMMONWEALTH CURRENTS. 1978. bi-m. free. Commonwealth Secretariat, Publications Division, Marlborough House, Pall Mall, London SW1Y 5HX, England. Ed. Dale Gunthorp. bk.rev.; circ. 29,700. (tabloid format) **Indexed:** Apic.Abstr, So.Pac.Per.Ind.
Supersedes: Commonwealth Diary of Coming Events (ISSN 0309-0388); Commonwealth Record of Recent Events.

COMMONWEALTH INSTITUTE, LONDON. ANNUAL REPORT. see *GEOGRAPHY*

COMPARE NOTES SERIES. see *ETHNIC INTERESTS*

327 IT ISSN 0010-5066
JX1903
COMUNITA INTERNAZIONALE. (Text in English, French and Italian) 1946. q. L.50000 (foreign L.75000)(effective 1991). (Societa Italiana per l'Organizzazione Internazionale) Casa Editrice Dott. Antonio Milani, Via Japelli 5, 35121 Padua, Italy. TEL 049-656677. FAX 049-8752900. Ed. Luigi Ferrari Bravo. adv.; bk.rev.; index; circ. 3,000. **Indexed:** A.B.C.Pol.Sci., Amer.Hist.& Life, Hist.Abstr., P.A.I.S.For.Lang.Ind.
—BLDSC shelfmark: 3399.200000.

327 IT ISSN 0045-7981
COMUNITA MEDITERRANEA; rivista di diritto e relazioni internazionali, politica economica e finanziari. (Text in English, French and Italian) vol.2, 1969. q. L.6000. Lungotevere Flaminio 34, 00196 Rome, Italy. Ed. Enrico Noune. bk.rev.; bibl.

327 UK
CONFLICT BULLETIN. 1970. q. Research Institute for the Study of Conflict and Terrorism, 136 Baker St., London W1M 1FH, England. TEL 071-224-2659. FAX 071-486-3064. TELEX 8954734. adv.; bk.rev.; circ. 1,000.

327 UK ISSN 0069-8792
D839
CONFLICT STUDIES. 1969. m. £65($120) Research Institute for the Study of Conflict and Terrorism, 136 Baker St., London W1M 1FH, England. TEL 071-224-2659. FAX 071-486-3064. TELEX 8954734. Ed. Josephine O'Connor Howe. bk.rev. **Indexed:** Abstr.Mil.Bibl., Mid.East: Abstr.& Ind.
—BLDSC shelfmark: 3410.660000.

CONTENTS OF PERIODICALS ON LATIN AMERICA. see *POLITICAL SCIENCE — Abstracting, Bibliographies, Statistics*

327 948 UK ISSN 0010-8367
JX1
COOPERATION AND CONFLICT; Nordic journal of international studies. 1965. q. £24($40) to individuals; institutions £58($96). (Nordic Cooperation Committee for International Studies, NO) Sage Publications Ltd., 6 Bonhill St., London EC2A 4PU, England. TEL 071-374-0645. FAX 071-374-8741. (U.S. address: Publications Expediting Inc., 200 Meacham Ave., Elmont, NY 11003) Ed. Christian Thune. adv.: color page £150; trim 175 x 112; adv. contact: Bernie Folan. bk.rev.; charts; index; circ. 600. (also avail. in microform from UMI; back issues avail.; reprint services also avail. from ISI) **Indexed:** A.B.C.Pol.Sci., Abstr.Mil.Bibl., Amer.Hist.& Life, Hist.Abstr., Int.Polit.Sci.Abstr., Mid.East: Abstr.& Ind., P.A.I.S.
—BLDSC shelfmark: 3464.120000.
Description: Devoted to studies of the foreign policies of the Nordic countries and to studies of international politics by Nordic scholars.

327 CL
COSAS. 1976. fortn. Almirante Pastene 329, Providencia, Santiago, Chile. TEL 2-225-8630. FAX 2-225-7799. TELEX 340905. Ed. Monica Comandari Kaiser. circ. 25,000.

341.1 US ISSN 0010-955X
COSMOPOLITAN CONTACT. (Text in various languages) 1962. irreg. $4. (Planetary Legion for Peace - PLP) Pantheon Press - General Enterprises, Box 89300, Honolulu, HI 96830-9300. Ed. Romulus Rexner. adv.; bk.rev.; illus.; circ. 1,500. (processed; back issues avail.)

COUNCIL OF EUROPE. COMMITTEE OF INDEPENDENT EXPERTS ON THE EUROPEAN SOCIAL CHARTER. CONCLUSIONS. see *SOCIAL SERVICES AND WELFARE*

327.73 US ISSN 0192-236X
JX27.C6
COUNCIL ON FOREIGN RELATIONS. ANNUAL REPORT. a. Council on Foreign Relations, Inc., 58 E. 68th St., New York, NY 10021. TEL 212-734-0400.
Formerly: Council on Foreign Relations. President's Report (ISSN 0093-4615)

POLITICAL SCIENCE — INTERNATIONAL RELATIONS

COUNCIL ON HEMISPHERIC AFFAIRS NEWS AND ANALYSIS. see *BUSINESS AND ECONOMICS — International Development And Assistance*

COUNCIL SPOTLIGHT BOOKNOTES. see *BIBLIOGRAPHIES*

327 330.9 US
COUNTRIES IN CRISIS. 1989. irreg. $25. St. James Press, 845 Penobscot Bldg., 645 Griswold St., Detroit, MI 48226-4232. TEL 800-345-0392.
Description: Focuses on nations facing a period of turmoil in their domestic affairs, international affairs or both. Includes background information and detailed analyses.

500 UN
COURIER (PARIS). (Supplement avail. in Braille) (Editions in Arabic, Basque, Bulgarian, Catalan, Chinese, Dutch, English, Finnish, French, German, Greek, Hausa, Hindi, Italian, Korean, Macedonian, Malaysian, Pushto, Persian, Portuguese, Russian, Serbo-Croatian, Sinhala, Slovene, Spanish, Swahili, Swedish, Tamil, Thai, Turkish, Urdu and Vietnamese; Braille supplements in English, French, Korean, Spanish) 1948. m. $50. Unesco, 7-9 Place de Fontenoy, 75700 Paris, France. TEL 577-16-10. (Dist. in U.S. by: Unipub, 4611-F Assembly Dr., Lanham, MD 20706-4391. TEL 800-274-4888) Ed. adel Rifaat. bibl.; illus.; circ. 37,300 (English ed. only). (also avail. in microfilm from UMI; microfiche from UMI; microform from BLH) **Indexed:** Acad.Ind., Arts & Hum.Cit.Ind., Curr.Cont., Excerp.Med., Gdlns, Mag.Ind., Peace Res.Abstr, R.G., So.Pac.Per.Ind.
●Also available online. Vendor(s): DIALOG.
Formerly: Unesco Courier (ISSN 0041-5278)

COVERT INTELLIGENCE LETTER. see *MILITARY*

327 FR
HC59.7
CROISSANCE - LE MONDE EN DEVELOPPEMENT. 1961. m. (11/yr.). 330 F. (foreign 360 F.). Malesherbes Publications, 163 bd. Malesherbes, 75017 Paris, France. TEL 1-48-88-46-00. FAX 1-47-64-04-53. TELEX 649 333. adv.; bk.rev.; bibl.; charts; illus.; circ. 30,000. **Indexed:** Int.Lab.Doc., Pt.de Rep. (1990-).
Formerly (until 1991): Croissance des Jeunes Nations (ISSN 0011-1686)
Description: Information on developing nations.

CROSSROADS; an international socio-political journal. see *POLITICAL SCIENCE*

341.1 US ISSN 0011-2054
CROSSROADS (PITTSBURGH).* 1970. m. $1.50. Youth Institute for Peace in the Middle East, Box 81865, Pittsburgh, PA 15217. Ed. Kristeen Bruun. illus.; tr.lit.; circ. 10,000. (also avail. in microfilm from UMI; reprint service avail. from UMI)

327 US
CROSSROADS COMMUNIQUE.* 1962. q. Operation Crossroads Africa, Inc., 475 Riverside Dr., No.916, New York, NY 10027. TEL 212-242-8550. Ed. Michael John Weber. adv.; bk.rev.; circ. 8,000.

327 UK
CROWN AGENTS REVIEW. 1976. 3/yr. free. Crown Agents for Oversea Governments and Administrations, St. Nicholas House, Sutton, Surrey SM1 1EL, England. TEL 081-643-3311. FAX 081-643-8232. TELEX 916205 CALOND G. Ed. S. Adamson. illus.; circ. 7,000. (also avail. in microfiche) **Indexed:** P.A.I.S.
Formerly: Crown Agents Quarterly Review.
Description: Development-related topics likely to be of interest to developing nations and practitioners.

327 US ISSN 0196-0830
F1751
CUBA UPDATE. 1977. q. $25 to non-members. Center for Cuban Studies, Inc., 124 W. 23rd St., New York, NY 10011. TEL 212-242-0559. Ed. Sandra Levinson. adv.; bk.rev.; illus.; circ. 2,000. **Indexed:** HR Rep.
Description: Progress of the advancement of Cuban society and relations between Cuba and other nations are featured. Perspectives of Cuban barrios, workplaces and culture find space here.

327 320 FR ISSN 0252-0869
CULTURAL POLICY. French edition: Politiques Culturelles. (Editions in English, French) 1977. q. free. Council of Europe, Publishing and Documentation Service B.P. 431R6, 67007 Strasbourg Cedex, France. Ed. Sezen Germen. bk.rev.; bibl.; stat. (back issues avail.)
—BLDSC shelfmark: 3491.668240.

CURRENT BIBLIOGRAPHY ON AFRICAN AFFAIRS. see *POLITICAL SCIENCE — Abstracting, Bibliographies, Statistics*

327 US ISSN 0161-6641
JK1
CURRENT ISSUES (ALEXANDRIA); critical issues confronting the nation and the world. 1977. a. $11.95. Close Up Foundation, 44 Canal Center Plaza, Ste. 6501, Alexandria, VA 22314-1592. TEL 800-765-3131. FAX 703-706-0002. Ed. Lynn Page Whittaker. charts; illus.; stat.; index; circ. 63,000.
Description: Covers ten foreign and ten domestic policy issues. Contains an introduction to the issue, key questions, background and history, current issues (what's happening now), and outlook (what to expect in the future).

327 355 015 UK ISSN 0954-3589
CURRENT MILITARY AND POLITICAL LITERATURE. 1983. bi-m. $324. Military Press Ltd., 92A Church Way, Iffley, Oxford OX4 4EF, England.
TEL 0865-770144. FAX 0256-479438. Ed.Bd. index.
—BLDSC shelfmark: 3500.430000.
Formerly: Current Military Literature (ISSN 0264-1674)
Description: Presents abstracts and citations, with comment, of articles from journals and monographs about strategic and defence studies, military science, political science and international affairs.

327 US
▼**CURRENT POLITICS OF RUSSIA.** 1990. q. $95. Nova Science Publishers, Inc., 283 Commack Rd., Ste. 300, Commack, NY 11725-3401.
TEL 516-499-3103.
Formerly (until 1991): Current Politics of the Soviet Union (ISSN 1048-7387)
Description: Presents current information concerning the changing political situation in Russia.

CURRENT WORLD LEADERS; almanac & biography & news-speeches & reports. see *POLITICAL SCIENCE*

327 CY
CYPRUS DIPLOMATIST. 1989. bi-m. 16-18 Halkokondyli St., POB 660, Nicosia, Cyprus. TEL 02-366866. Ed. George Lantis. circ. 2,000.

CZECHOSLOVAK HISTORY NEWSLETTER. see *ETHNIC INTERESTS*

327 917.306 US
CZECHOSLOVAK NEWSLETTER. 1976. m. $8. Council of Free Czechoslovakia, 420 E. 71st St., New York, NY 10021. circ. 650.

327 364.4 US
D I S A M JOURNAL. 1982. q. $12. Defense Institute of Security Assistance Management, c/o Mr. John Lindbloom, DISAM-DIRP, Wright-Patterson Air Force Base, OH 45433-5000. TEL 513-255-2994. FAX 513-255-4319. Ed. Lou Samelson. circ. 2,800. **Indexed:** Air Un.Lib.Ind.

327 943 947 GW ISSN 0011-5142
D S F - JOURNAL.* (Text in German and Russian) 1961. q. DM.8. (Gesellschaft fuer Deutsch-Sowjetische Freundschaft Berlin West) Aktiv Werben und Reisen GmbH, Wilhelmsane 133, 1000 Berlin 31, Germany. Ed. Heinz W. Pahlke. adv.; bk.rev.; illus.
Description: Publication aiming to strengthen relations between West Berlin and the USSR, and to encourage peace between East and West. Covers Soviet politics, culture, science, social issues, news, and history.

327 DK ISSN 0107-6396
DANSK JAPANSK VENSKABSFORENINGS BLAD. Variant title: Fureai. 1981. q. DKK 60. Dansk Japansk Venskabsforening, Postboks 1126, 8200 Aarhus N, Denmark. Ed. Jacqueline Ann Houtved. adv.; bk.rev.; circ. 300.

327 GW ISSN 0340-6296
DARMSTAEDTER BLAETTER FUER KULTURELLE EVOLUTION. 1956. m. DM.30. Darmstaedter Blaetter Veralg, Haubachweg 5, 6100 Darmstadt, Germany. TEL 06151-48106. Ed. Gunther Schwarz. circ. 3,000.

327 UK ISSN 0070-2900
DAVID DAVIES MEMORIAL INSTITUTE OF INTERNATIONAL STUDIES, LONDON. ANNUAL MEMORIAL LECTURE. 1954. a. £4 (included with subscr. to International Relations). David Davies Memorial Institute of International Studies, 2 Chadwick St., London SW1P 2EP, England. Ed. Sheila Harden.

327 DK ISSN 0108-8580
DAYANISMA/SOLIDARITET. (Text in Danish and Turkish) 1983. bi-m. DKK 30. Tyrkisk-Dansk Forening, Klostergade 37, 8000 Aarhus C, Denmark. illus.

DEADLINE. see *JOURNALISM*

DECLASSIFIED DOCUMENTS CATALOG. see *POLITICAL SCIENCE — Abstracting, Bibliographies, Statistics*

DEFENSE AND FOREIGN AFFAIRS STRATEGIC POLICY. see *MILITARY*

DEFENSE AND FOREIGN AFFAIRS WEEKLY; the weekly report on the Middle East, Africa, Asia, the Pacific and Latin America. see *MILITARY*

DEFENSE FOREIGN AFFAIRS HANDBOOK; political, economic & defense data on every country in the world. see *MILITARY*

DESTINY. see *ETHNIC INTERESTS*

DEVELOPMENT. see *BUSINESS AND ECONOMICS — International Development And Assistance*

DEVELOPMENT AND CHANGE. see *SOCIAL SCIENCES: COMPREHENSIVE WORKS*

DEVELOPMENT BUSINESS. see *BUSINESS AND ECONOMICS — International Development And Assistance*

327 338.9 SW ISSN 0345-2328
HD82
DEVELOPMENT DIALOGUE. 1972. s-a. Dag Hammarskjold Foundation, Dag Hammarskjold Centre, Oevre Slottsgatan 2, S-753 10 Uppsala, Sweden. FAX 018-122072. TELEX 76234 DHCENT. Eds. S. Hamrell, O. Nordberg. bk.rev.; circ. 12,000. **Indexed:** Commun.Abstr., E.I., HR Rep., I D A, Mid.East: Abstr.& Ind., Rural Devel.Abstr., Rural Recreat.Tour.Abstr., World Agri.Econ.& Rural Sociol.Abstr.

DEVELOPMENT HOTLINE; news for policy leaders. see *BUSINESS AND ECONOMICS — International Development And Assistance*

327 331 UK ISSN 0950-8473
AL DIA. (Text in Spanish) m. £118($165) Lettres (UK) Ltd., 61 Old St., London EC1V 9HX, England. TEL 071-251-0012. FAX 071-253-8193. Ed. Miguel Angel Diez. (back issues avail.)

327 AU
DIALOGO; Austria-America Latina. (Text in Portuguese, Spanish) 1982. a. free. Oesterreichisches Lateinamerika-Institut, Schmerlingplatz 8, A-1010 Vienna, Austria. Ed.Bd. adv.; circ. 3,000. (back issues avail.)

327 US ISSN 0012-2262
DIALOGUE (WASHINGTON)/FACETAS. Czech translation: Spektrum (Prague). (Distribution by U.S embassies; not distributed within continental United States) (Text in various languages) 1968. q. U.S. Information Agency, 301 4th St., S.W., Washington, DC 20547. TEL 202-485-2185. Ed. Peter J. Laine. bk.rev.; circ. 200,000.
Description: Magazine of ideas, trends and developments in American society and culture, edited for a foreign audience of the leadership and intellectual elites.

POLITICAL SCIENCE — INTERNATIONAL RELATIONS

327   **TS**
AL-DIBLOMASI/DIPLOMAT. (Text in Arabic) 1980. q. exchange basis. Ministry of Foreign Affairs, Department of Legal Affairs and Studies - Wizarat al-Kharijiyyah, Idarat al-Shu'un al-Qanuniyyah wal-Dirasat, P.O. Box 1, Abu Dhabi, United Arab Emirates. TEL 652200. FAX 668015. TELEX 22217 KHARJIYA EM. circ. 500 (controlled).
  Description: Publishes studies and research in diplomatic affairs and international relations, as well as news of conferences, official reports and documents pertaining to international matters.

DICKINSON JOURNAL OF INTERNATIONAL LAW. see *LAW — International Law*

DIGEST OF WORLD EVENTS. see *HISTORY*

327   **UK**   **ISSN 0959-2296**
▼**DIPLOMACY & STATECRAFT.** 1990. 3/yr. £28($38) to individuals; institutions £55($90). Frank Cass & Co. Ltd., Gainsborough House, 11 Gainsborough Rd., London E11 1RS, England. TEL 081-530-4226. FAX 081-530-7795. Eds. David Armstrong, Erik Goldstein. adv.; bk.rev.
  —BLDSC shelfmark: 3589.290000.
  Description: Covers diplomatic history as well as the contemporary conduct of international affairs.

327   **PK**
DIPLOMAT. (Text in English) 1972. m. Rs.75. 442-2 Jauharabad, Karachi 38, Pakistan. Ed. Mohammed Ali Jilani. adv.; charts; illus.

327   **UK**   **ISSN 0951-032X**
DIPLOMAT. 1947. bi-m. £32($90) Diplomatist Associates, 58 Theobalds Rd., London WC1X 8SF, England. TEL 44-1-405-4874. FAX 071-831-0667. Ed. Wendy Holden. adv.; bk.rev.; circ. 3,000 (controlled). (back issues avail.)
  —BLDSC shelfmark: 3589.330000.
  Description: Occupations and career news in the London diplomatic community.

327   **GW**
▼**DIPLOMATEN SPIEGEL.** 1992. a. DM.5. ProPress Verlag GmbH, Am Buschhof 8, 5300 Bonn 3, Germany. TEL 0228-449090. FAX 0228-444296. circ. 30,000.

327   **UK**
DIPLOMATIC & CONSULAR YEAR BOOK. 1978. a. £14.95($25) Blakes (Corporate) Ltd., 12-14 High Rd., London N2 9JP, England. Ed. Gina Senko. adv.; bk.rev.; circ. 5,000.

327   **CN**   **ISSN 0486-4514**
JX1729.A2
DIPLOMATIC CORPS AND CONSULAR AND OTHER REPRESENTATIVES IN CANADA/CORPS DIPLOMATIQUE ET REPRESENTANTS CONSULAIRES ET AUTRES AU CANADA. (Text in English and French) 1969. irreg. Can.$2.75. Department of External Affairs, Ottawa, Ont. K1A 0G2, Canada. TEL 613-996-9134.

DIPLOMATIC HISTORY. see *HISTORY*

327   **NP**
DIPLOMATIC LIST AND LIST OF REPRESENTATIVES OF UNITED NATIONS AND ITS SPECIALIZED AGENCIES AND OTHER MISSIONS. (Text in English) a. Protocol Division, Ministry of Foreign Affairs, Kathmandu, Nepal.

327.2   **NZ**
DIPLOMATIC LIST - DIPLOMATIC AND CONSULAR REPRESENTATIVES IN NEW ZEALAND. 1943. s-a. NZ.$24.95 per issue. Ministry of External Relations and Trade, Private Bag, Wellington 1, New Zealand. TEL 04-4728-877. (Dist. by: New House Publishers Ltd., P.O. Box 33-376, Takapuna, Auckland, New Zealand. TEL 09-410-6517) circ. 2,100.
  Former titles: New Zealand Diplomatic Corps and Consular and Other Representatives (ISSN 0111-6142) & Overseas Representatives in New Zealand and New Zealand Representatives Overseas.
  Description: Provides a comprehensive list of heads of foreign diplomatic missions in New Zealand given in order of precedence.

341.7 327   **GW**   **ISSN 0172-3227**
DIPLOMATIC OBSERVER/OBSERVATEUR DIPLOMATIQUE/INTERNATIONALES DIPLOMATISCHES MAGAZIN.* (Text in English, French, German) 1972. m. DM.55($16.50) (Institute for International Sociological Research) Ellenberg Publishers Ltd., Wiener Weg 6, 5000 Cologne 40, Germany. (Co-sponsor: Akademie fuer Diplomatie und Internationale Beziehungen) Ed. E. Ellenberg. adv.; bk.rev.; circ. 11,000.

327   **UK**
DIPLOMATIC SERVICE LIST. a. price varies. H.M.S.O., P.O. Box 276, London SW8 5DT, England. circ. 3,000.

327   **US**   **ISSN 0363-8200**
JX1977.A1
DIPLOMATIC WORLD BULLETIN AND DELEGATES WORLD BULLETIN;* dedicated to serving the United Nations and the international community. vol.12, 1982. fortn. $45. Diplomatic World Bulletin Publications, Inc., 763 UN Plaza, New York, NY 10017. TEL 212-747-9500. Ed. Richard A. Holman. adv.; illus.; tr.lit. (tabloid format)
  Formerly: Delegates World Bulletin.

327   **UK**   **ISSN 0012-3110**
DIPLOMATIST; the review of the diplomatic and consular world. (Quarterly and semi-Annual supplements) 1947. 6/yr. £28($70) Diplomatist Associates Ltd., Bedfort Row House, 58 Theobalds Rd., London, England. TEL 01 405-4874. Ed. Vanessa Peet. adv.; bk.rev.; illus.; stat.; circ. 23,000. (also avail. in microform from UMI; reprint service avail. from UMI)

DIRECTORY OF WORLD LEADERS & FACTBOOK (YEAR). see *BUSINESS AND ECONOMICS — International Commerce*

DISMANTLER. see *MILITARY*

327   **US**
E840
▼**DISPATCH (WASHINGTON).** 1991. w. $75 (foreign $93.75). U.S. Department of State, Bureau of Public Affairs, Office of Public Communication, 2201 C St. N.W., Washington, DC 20520. (Subscr. to: Superintendent of Documents, Government Printing Office, Washington, DC 20402-9371) s-a. index.
  Incorporates (in 1991): U.S. Department of State. Bureau of Public Affairs. Current Policy (ISSN 0196-8939) & Gist.
  Description: Contains information about U.S. foreign policy.

327   **SP**   **ISSN 0584-7109**
F1414.2
DOCUMENTACION IBEROAMERICANA. 1971. m. Instituto de Cooperacion Iberoamericana, Centro de Documentacion, Avda. de los Reyes Catolicos, 4, Madrid 28040, Spain.
  Supersedes (since 1975): Sintesis Informativa Iberoamericana.

DOCUMENTS D'ACTUALITE INTERNATIONALE. see *LAW — International Law*

DOKUMENTE; Zeitschrift fuer den deutsch-franzoesischen Dialog. see *GENERAL INTEREST PERIODICALS — Germany*

DRITTE WELT MATERIALIEN. see *HISTORY*

323.4   **FR**   **ISSN 0012-6373**
DROIT DE VIVRE. vol.34, 1967. m. 80 F. 40 Rue de Paradis, 75010 Paris, France. Ed. Bernard Lecache. adv.; film rev.; illus.; play rev.

327 943 949.2   **NE**   **ISSN 0012-7051**
DUITSE KRONIEK; orgaan voor culturele betrekkingen met Duitsland. (Text in Dutch and German) 1948. q. DM.55 to individuals; students fl.36. Prof. J. Aler, Ed. & Pub., Jan Luykenstr. 4, HS Amsterdam, Netherlands. bk.rev.
  —BLDSC shelfmark: 3630.945000.

327   **US**
DUKE UNIVERSITY. CENTER FOR INTERNATIONAL STUDIES. PUBLICATIONS. 1956. irreg. price varies. Duke University Press, Center for International Studies, 6697 College Sta., Durham, NC 27708. TEL 919-684-2173. FAX 919-684-8644. TELEX 802829.
  Formerly: Duke University. Commonwealth-Studies Center. Publications (ISSN 0070-7473)

327   **US**
DUKE UNIVERSITY CENTER FOR INTERNATIONAL STUDIES PUBLICATIONS. 1983. irreg. Duke University Press, 6697 College Station, Durham, NC 27708. TEL 919-684-2173. FAX 919-684-8644.

327   **FR**   **ISSN 0423-6645**
E A A S NEWSLETTER. (Text in English) 1955. biennial. (European Association for American Studies) Presses Universitaires de Nancy, 25 rue Baron Loius, 54000 Nancy, France. Ed. Jean-Marie Bonnet. adv.; circ. 3,000. **Indexed:** Amer.Hist.& Life, Hist.Abstr.

327   **GW**
E G INFORMATIONEN. 1989. m. Kommission der Europaeischen Gemeinschaft, Vertretung in der Bundesrepublik Deutschland, Zitelmannstr. 22, 5300 Bonn 1, Germany. circ. 40,000.

327   **UK**
▼**E I A NEWS.** 1991. m. European Information Association, European Documentation Centre, Wales Euro Info Centre, UWCC, P.O. Box 430, Cardiff, Wales CF1 3XT, England. TEL 0222-874262. FAX 0222-229740.

327   **EI**   **ISSN 0960-5398**
E L F. (European Labour Forum) 1990. 4/yr. £10 (foreign £12). (European Parliament, Socialist Group) Spokesman, Bertrand Russell House, 45 Gamble St., Nottingham NG7 4ET, England. TEL 0602-708318. FAX 0602-420433. Ed. Ken Coates. adv.; bk.rev.; circ. 5,000.
  —BLDSC shelfmark: 3829.747900.
  Description: Covers and analyzes developments in Europe and beyond from the perspective of members of the Socialist Group of the European Parliament.

327   **UK**
E L T S A NEWSLETTER. 1974. irreg. (3-4/yr.). £2.50. End Loans to South Africa, c/o Methodist Church, 56 Camberwell Rd., London SE5 OEN, England. TEL 071-708-4702. FAX 071-708-5751. bk.rev.; circ. 1,000. (looseleaf format) **Indexed:** HR Rep.

EAST ASIA; international review of economic, political and social development. see *BUSINESS AND ECONOMICS — Economic Situation And Conditions*

327   **US**   **ISSN 0070-8100**
EAST EUROPE MONOGRAPHS. 1969. irreg., no.4, 1974. price varies. (Studiengesellschaft fuer Fragen Mittel- und Osteuropaeischer Partnerschaft, GW) Park College, Governmental Research Bureau, Kansas City, MO 64152. TEL 816-741-2000. Eds. Jerzy Hauptmann, Gotthold Rhode.

327   **US**   **ISSN 1055-9795**
▼**EAST-WEST CENTER. VIEWS.** 1991. bi-m. free. East-West Center Public Education, Public Affairs Office, 1777 East-West Road, Honolulu, HI 96848. TEL 808-944-7194. Grady Timmons.

327 940 950   **UK**   **ISSN 0012-8627**
D839
EAST-WEST DIGEST. 1965. fortn. £10($24) Foreign Affairs Publishing Co., 139 Petersham, Nr. Richmond, Surrey, England. Ed. D.G. Stewart-Smith. adv.; bk.rev.; index; circ. 5,000. (also avail. in microfilm from UMI; reprint service avail. from UMI)

327 330.9   **US**
ECONOMIC AND ENERGY INDICATORS. s-m. $90 per issue in US, Canada, Mexico; elsewhere $180. (Central Intelligence Agency) U.S. National Technical Information Service, 5825 Port Royal Rd., Springfield, VA 22161. TEL 703-487-4630.
  Description: Information on changes in domestic and external economic activities of major non-communist developed countries. Updated from press ticker and Embassy reporting.

327 330   **CN**
ECONOMIC JUSTICE REPORT; global issues of economic justice. 1973. 4/yr. Can.$35 to individuals; institutions Can.$45. Ecumenical Coalition for Economic Justice, 11 Madison Ave., Toronto, Ont. M5R 2S2, Canada. TEL 416-921-4615. FAX 416-942-5356. bk.rev.; illus.; circ. 1,000.
  Former titles: GATT-Fly Report (ISSN 0228-359X); GATT-Fly.

POLITICAL SCIENCE — INTERNATIONAL RELATIONS

327   II
EGYPT NEWS. (Text in English) 1954. w. free. Embassy of the Arab Republic of Egypt, Press Bureau, 1-50M, Niti Marge, Chanakyapuri, New Delhi 110021, India. TEL 6876653. TELEX 72245EGND IN. Ed. Fathi Ahmed Osman. bk.rev.; circ. 2,000.
    Formerly: Cairo Bulletin; Cairo Information Bulletin.

ELDERS; een kroniek van zaken buiten de grenzen. see *POPULATION STUDIES*

327   US   ISSN 0501-9664
JX1705
EMPLOYEES OF DIPLOMATIC MISSIONS. q. $9.50. U.S. Department of State, Bureau of Public Affairs, 2201 C St., N.W., Washington, DC 20520. (Orders to: Supt. of Documents, Washington, DC 20402)

327 301   GW
AS2.5
ENCYCLOPEDIA OF WORLD PROBLEMS AND HUMAN POTENTIAL. (In 2 vols.) 1976. irreg., 3rd. ed., 1991. 2300 Fr.($415) (Union of International Associations, BE) K.G. Saur Verlag KG, Ortlerstr. 8, Postfach 701620, 8000 Munich 70, Germany. TEL 089-76902-0. FAX 089-76902150. (US addr.: K.G. Saur, A Reed Reference Publishing Company, 121 Chanlon Rd., New Providence, NJ 07974. TEL 908-665-3576) bibl.
    Formerly: Yearbook of World Problems and Human Potential (ISSN 0304-0089)
    Description: Focuses on more than 13,000 issues of global concern.

END PAPERS. see *POLITICAL SCIENCE — Civil Rights*

ENFANTS DU MONDE. see *SOCIAL SERVICES AND WELFARE*

327   US
ENGLISH SPEAKING UNION TODAY. 1953. 4/yr. membership. English-Speaking Union of the United States, 16 E. 69th St., New York, NY 10021. TEL 212-879-6800. FAX 212-772-2886. Ed. Claire Wyckoff. adv.; circ. 18,000.
    Former titles: English Speaking: The E-S U News; English-Speaking Union News (ISSN 0013-8371)

327   GW
ENTWICKLUNGSPOLITISCHE KORRESPONDENZ. 1970. 4/yr. DM.24 to individuals; institutions DM.40. Gesellschaft fuer Entwicklungspolitische Bildungsarbeit e.V., Nernstweg 32, 2000 Hamburg 50, Germany. TEL 040-3905221. Ed.Bd. adv.; bk.rev.; bibl.; circ. 3,000.

327   UK   ISSN 0964-4016
▼**ENVIRONMENTAL POLITICS.** 1992. q. £35($50) to individuals; institutions £70($105). Frank Cass & Co. Ltd., Gainsborough House, 11 Gainsborough Rd., London E11 1RS, England. TEL 081-530-4226. FAX 081-530-7795. Eds. Michael Waller, Stephen Young. adv.; bk.rev.; index.
    Description: Presents academic study of environmental politics with a focus on the industrialized countries.

327   GW   ISSN 0939-7507
ERZIEHERBRIEF. 1952. 5/yr. DM.36($27) Arbeitsgemeinschaft Sudetendeutscher Lehrer und Erzieher e.V., Hochstr. 8, 8000 Munich 80, Germany. TEL 089-480003-28. (Co-sponsor: Gesamtdeutsches Institut) circ. 1,400.
    Formerly: Sudetendeutscher Erzieherbrief.

ESPERANTO. see *LINGUISTICS*

ESPERANTO-DOKUMENTOJ. NOVA SERIO. see *LINGUISTICS*

327 940 950   FR   ISSN 0014-1267
D839
EST ET OUEST. 1949; N.S. 1984. m. 430 F. Association d'Etudes Politiques Internationales, 15, av. Raymond-Poincare, 75116 Paris, France. (Co-sponsor: Institut d'Histoire Sociale) Ed. Morvan Duhamel. bk.rev.; stat.; circ. 500.
    —BLDSC shelfmark: 3812.506000.

EST - OVEST. see *BUSINESS AND ECONOMICS — Economic Situation And Conditions*

327   MX
ESTADOS UNIDOS: PERSPECTIVA LATINOAMERICANA. CUADERNOS SEMESTRALES. 1976. s-a. Centro de Investigacion y Docencia Economicas, Difusion de Publicaciones, Apdo. Postal 116-114, 01130 Mexico, D.F., Mexico. adv.; circ. 4,000.

THE ESTIMATE; political and security intelligence analysis of North Africa, the Middle East, South Asia, East Asia, & the Pacific. see *MILITARY*

327   US
THE ESTIMATES. 1989. fortn. $295 (foreign $330). International Estimates, 1514 17th St., N.W., Ste. 315, Washington, DC 20036. TEL 202-332-0849.

ESTUDIOS HISTORICOS. see *HISTORY — History Of North And South America*

327   CL   ISSN 0716-0240
F1414.2
ESTUDIOS INTERNACIONALES. 1967. q. $35 to individuals; institutions $40. Instituto de Estudios Internacionales, Universidad de Chile, Casilla 14187, Suc. 21, Santiago, Chile. Ed. Pilar Alamos Varas. adv.; index; circ. 500. **Indexed:** A.B.C.Pol.Sci.
    —BLDSC shelfmark: 3812.773000.

327   SP
ESTUDIOS INTERNACIONALES. q. 2200 ptas.($24) Centro de Estudios Constitucionales, Plaza de la Marina Espanola, 9, Apartado 50.877, Madrid 13, Spain. **Indexed:** A.B.C.Pol.Sci.

327   US
ETHICS & INTERNATIONAL AFFAIRS (JOURNAL). 1987. a. $10. Carnegie Council on Ethics and International Affairs, c/o Olivia Wakeman, Dir., Public Relations, Merrill House, 170 E. 64th St., New York, NY 10021. TEL 212-838-4120. FAX 212-752-2432. Ed. Joel Rosenthal.
    Description: Presents applications of ethics to various international problems from a variety of perspectives.

327 170   US   ISSN 0892-6794
JX1255
ETHICS AND INTERNATIONAL AFFAIRS (NEWSLETTER); a college-level curriculum development program. 1987. s-a. Carnegie Council on Ethics and International Affairs, c/o Olivia Wakeman, Dir., Public Relations, Merrill House, 170 E. 64th St., New York, NY 10021. TEL 212-838-4120. FAX 212-752-2432. Ed. Joel Rosenthal.
    —BLDSC shelfmark: 3814.656700.
    Description: College level curriculum development program for teaching ethics and international affairs.

327   CN   ISSN 0014-2123
D849
ETUDES INTERNATIONALES. (Text in French) 1970. q. Can.$45. Centre Quebecois de Relations Internationales, Faculte des Sciences Sociales, Universite Laval, Quebec, Que. G1K 7P4, Canada. TEL 418-656-2462. Ed. Gerard Hervouet. adv.; bk.rev.; index, cum.index; circ. 1,700. **Indexed:** A.B.C.Pol.Sci., Amer.Hist.& Life (until 1991), Can.Per.Ind., Curr.Cont., Hist.Abstr. (until 1991), Int.Polit.Sci.Abstr., P.A.I.S.For.Lang.Ind., Peace Res.Abstr., Periodex, Pt.de Rep. (1979-), SSCI.
    —BLDSC shelfmark: 3820.720000.
    Description: Articles and reviews cover important international political affairs.

327 016   EI   ISSN 0071-2213
ETUDES UNIVERSITAIRES SUR L'INTEGRATION EUROPEENNE/UNIVERSITY STUDIES ON EUROPEAN INTEGRATION. (Editions in English and French) 1963. irreg. price varies. (European Community Institute for University Studies) Commission of the European Communities, 200, rue de la Loi, B-1049 Brussels, Belgium. Ed. Anne-Marie Nantermoz. circ. 4,000.

940 327   GW   ISSN 0014-2476
D839
EUROPA-ARCHIV; Zeitschrift fuer internationale Politik. 1946. s-m. DM.190. (Deutsche Gesellschaft fuer Auswaertige Politik e.V.) Verlag fuer Internationale Politik GmbH, Bachstr. 32, Postfach 1529, 5300 Bonn, Germany. TEL 0228-7290010. FAX 0228-695734. TELEX 8-86822. Ed. Wolfgang Wagner. adv.; bk.rev.; bibl.; charts; index. cum.index: 1946-1965, 1966-1970, 1971-1975, 1976-1980, 1981-1985; circ. 4,800. (reprint service avail. from ISI) **Indexed:** A.B.C.Pol.Sci., Abstr.Mil.Bibl., Amer.Hist.& Life, Curr.Cont., Geo.Abstr., Hist.Abstr., Key to Econ.Sci., P.A.I.S.For.Lang.Ind., Peace Res.Abstr, SSCI.
    —BLDSC shelfmark: 3829.292000.

320 330   AU
EUROPAEISCHE RUNDSCHAU. 1973. q. S.250. Europaverlag AG, Altmannsderferstr. 154-156, A-1232 Vienna 23, Austria. Ed. Paul Lendvai. adv.; bk.rev.; bibl.; circ. 2,750. **Indexed:** P.A.I.S.For.Lang.Ind.

327 341   GW   ISSN 0071-2329
EUROPAEISCHE SCHRIFTEN. 1963. irreg. (Institut fuer Europaeische Politik, Bonn) Europa Union Verlag GmbH, Bachstr. 32, 5300 Bonn 1, Germany. TEL 0228-7290010. FAX 0228-695734. TELEX 8-86822. Ed. Wolfgang Wessels.

940 327   GW
EUROPAEISCHE ZEITUNG. 1949. m. DM.36. (Europa-Union Deutschland e.V.) Europa Union Verlag GmbH, Bachstr. 32, 5300 Bonn 1, Germany. TEL 0228-7290010. FAX 0228-695734. TELEX 8-86822. Ed. Walter Bohm. adv.; bk.rev.; illus.; circ. 40,000.
    Former titles: Europaeische Zeitung Europa-Union; Europa-Union (ISSN 0014-2611)

940 943   GW
EUROPAEISCHES FORUM. (Supplement to: Europaeische Zeitung) 1949. m. DM.36. Europa Union Verlag GmbH, Bachstr. 32, 5300 Bonn 1, Germany. TEL 0228-7290010. FAX 0228-695734. TELEX 8-86822. Ed. Walter Boehm. bk.rev.; circ. 40,000.
    Formerly: Informationsdienst des Deutschen Rates der Europaeischen Bewegung (ISSN 0020-0549)

320.5   AU   ISSN 0014-2727
EUROPASTIMME. 1960. bi-m. Europaeische Foederalistische Bewegung, Postfach 228, A-8011 Graz, Austria. Ed. Wolfgang Wratschgo. bk.rev.; illus.; stat.; circ. 10,000.

EUROPE. see *BUSINESS AND ECONOMICS — Economic Situation And Conditions*

EUROPE MAGAZINE. see *BUSINESS AND ECONOMICS — International Commerce*

944 327   FR
EUROPE OUTREMER. 1923. m. 750 F. Societe Nouvelle des Editions France Outre-Mer, 178 Quai L. Bleriot, 75016 Paris, France. TEL 1-46-47-78-44. Ed. Robert Taton. adv.; charts; illus.; stat.; circ. 17,800. **Indexed:** Cott.& Trop.Fibr.Abstr., Curr.Cont.Africa, Int.Lab.Doc., Key to Econ.Sci., World Agri.Econ.& Rural Sociol.Abstr.
    Formerly: Europe France Outremer (ISSN 0014-2816)

EUROPEAN COMMUNITIES. ECONOMIC AND SOCIAL COMMITTEE. ANNUAL REPORT (YEAR). see *BUSINESS AND ECONOMICS*

THE EUROPEAN COMMUNITIES ENCYCLOPEDIA AND DIRECTORY (YEAR). see *ENCYCLOPEDIAS AND GENERAL ALMANACS*

327 382   IT   ISSN 0394-6444
D1050
EUROPEAN JOURNAL OF INTERNATIONAL AFFAIRS. (Text in English) q. L.70000 to individuals (foreign $54); institutions L.100000 (foreign $77). Erasmus Press, Via dei Giubbonari, 30, 00186 Rome, Italy. TEL 687-31-96. FAX 687-25-49. Ed. Giuseppe Sacco. bk.rev.; illus.
    —BLDSC shelfmark: 3829.730800.

328.3   EI   ISSN 0423-7846
JN32
EUROPEAN PARLIAMENT. BULLETIN. (Supplements with title Annex accompany some issues) w. European Parliament, Secretariat, L-2929 Luxembourg, Luxembourg. FAX 43-70-09.

POLITICAL SCIENCE — INTERNATIONAL RELATIONS

940   IT   ISSN 0014-3235
EUROSUD. 1966. w. L.60000($75) Centro Studi Comunita Europee, c/o Eurocampus, Strata Prov. Bitonto, Km. 2.200, S. Spirito, 70032 Bitonto, Italy. index; circ. 1,800 (controlled). (looseleaf format)

327 338.91   US
EUROWATCH. 1989. fortn. $747 (foreign $769). Buraff Publications (Subsidiary of: Millin Publications, Inc.), 1350 Connecticut Ave. N.W., Ste. 1000, Washington, DC 20036. TEL 202-862-0990. FAX 202-862-0999. Ed. Graeme Littler. index. (back issues avail.)
    Formerly (until 1991): 1992: The External Impact of European Unification.

341.13   UN   ISSN 0251-690X
JX1977.A37
EVERYONE'S UNITED NATIONS. French edition: Ce Qu'il Faut Savoir des Nations Unies (ISSN 0251-6896); Spanish edition: Naciones Unidas. Origenes, Organizacion, Actividades (ISSN 0251-6918) 1948. irreg., latest no.10. $14.95 per no. United Nations Publications, Room DC2-853, New York, NY 10017. TEL 212-963-8300. FAX 212-963-3489. (Or: Distribution and Sales Section, Palais des Nations, CH-1211 Geneva 10, Switzerland.)
    Formerly (until 1979): Everyman's United Nations (ISSN 0071-3244)

327   US
EXECUTIVE MEMORANDUM. 1982. irreg., latest 1989. $1.50 per no. Heritage Foundation, 214 Massachusetts Ave., N.E., Washington, DC 20002. TEL 202-546-4400. FAX 202-546-8328. (looseleaf format; back issues avail.)
●Also available online. Vendor(s): Mead Data Central.

327   US
EYES; the newsmagazine for the new generation. 1989. m. $15. Ten-Fifty Publications, W. Tower, Ste. 1050, 11845 W. Olympic Blvd., Los Angeles, CA 90064. TEL 213-312-8245. Ed. Sarah Pritzkar. circ. 100,000 (controlled).
    Description: Covers domestic and international news stories and features, as seen through the eyes of the nation's youths.

327   DK   ISSN 0014-5998
F.N. ORIENTERING. 1969. 6/yr. DKK 165($8) Danish United Nations Association - F N -Forbundet, Skindergade 26, 1, DK-1159 Copenhagen K, Denmark. FAX 45-33-12-10-58. (Co-sponsor: Ministry of Foreign Affairs) Ed. Uffe Torm. adv.; bk.rev.; illus.; circ. 2,000.
    Supersedes: Verden og Vi.

327   UK   ISSN 0306-0772
FACTS. 1973. m. £2. European Movement, 158 Buckingham Palace Rd., London SW1 9TRA, England. charts; illus. Indexed: Met.Abstr.

327   US
AL-FAJR JERUSALEM PALESTINIAN WEEKLY. (English edition of Al-Fajr (E. Jerusalem)) 1980. w. $50 to individuals and libraries; students $40. 16 Crowell St., Hempstead, NY 11550. TEL 516-485-5905. FAX 516-564-8850. TELEX 967701 OMAR HEM. Ed. Hanna Siniora. bk.rev.; circ. 5,000. (also avail. in microfilm)
    Formerly: Jerusalem al-Fajr.
    Description: Provides news coverage of Palestinians under Israeli occupation.

320.5   LU   ISSN 0014-9268
FEDERALISTE EUROPEEN. vol.16, 1968. s-a. $2.50. Conseil Luxembourgeois du Mouvement Europeen, 20 B, rue Louvigny, B.P. 105, Luxembourg, Luxembourg. bk.rev.; bibl.

320.5   US   ISSN 0014-9810
JX1901
FELLOWSHIP. 1934. m. $15. Fellowship of Reconciliation, 523 N. Broadway, Box 271, Nyack, NY 10960. TEL 914-358-4601. FAX 914-358-4924. Ed. Murray Polner. adv.; bk.rev.; film rev.; illus.; index; circ. 8,000. (also avail. in microform from UMI; reprint service avail. from UMI) Indexed: HR Rep., P.A.I.S, Peace Res.Abstr., Rehabil.Lit.
    —BLDSC shelfmark: 3905.130000.

FILMOTECA ULTRAMARINA PORTUGUESA. BOLETIM. see HISTORY

327   FI   ISSN 0071-528X
FINLAND. ULKOASIAINMINISTERIO. ULKOPOLIITTISIA LAUSUNTOJA JA ASIAKIRJOJA. (Text in Finnish; occasionally in English, French, German and Swedish) 1959. s-a. Ulkoasiainministerio - Ministry for Foreign Affairs, PL 176, 00160 Helsinki, Finland. circ. 2,000.

327   US   ISSN 1046-1868
D839
FLETCHER FORUM OF WORLD AFFAIRS. 1977. s-a. $15 to individuals (foreign $29); institutions $25 (foreign $39). Fletcher School of Law and Diplomacy, Tufts University, Medford, MA 02155. TEL 617-628-7010. FAX 617-381-3508. Ed.Bd. adv.; bk.rev.; charts; illus.; circ. 1,000. Indexed: A.B.C.Pol.Sci., Amer.Bibl.Slavic & E.Eur.Stud, C.C.L.P., C.L.I., L.R.I., Leg.Cont., P.A.I.S.
●Also available online. Vendor(s): WESTLAW.
    —BLDSC shelfmark: 3950.532000.
    Formerly (until vol.12, no.2, 1988): Fletcher Forum (ISSN 0147-0981)

FOOD FIRST NEWS. see POLITICAL SCIENCE

327   US   ISSN 0015-7120
D410   CODEN: FRNAA3
FOREIGN AFFAIRS. 1922. 5/yr. $38. Council on Foreign Relations, Inc., 58 E. 68th St., New York, NY 10021. TEL 212-734-0400. Ed. William G. Hyland. adv.; bk.rev.; index; circ. 115,000. (also avail. in microform from UMI,MIM,WSH; reprint service avail. from KTO) Indexed: A.B.C.Pol.Sci., ABI Inform, Abstr.Mil.Bibl., Acad.Ind., Amer.Hist.& Life, Bk.Rev.Ind. (1984-), BPIA, C.R.E.J., Chic.Per.Ind., Child.Bk.Rev.Ind. (1984-), Curr.Cont.M.E., Deep Sea Res.& Oceanogr.Abstr., E.I., Fut.Surv., Hist.Abstr., HR Rep., INIS Atomind., Int.Lab.Doc., J.of Econ.Lit., Key to Econ.Sci., Mag.Ind., Mgmt.& Market.Abstr., Mid.East: Abstr.& Ind., P.A.I.S., Peace Res.Abstr., PROMT, R.G., Soc.Sci.Ind., SSCI, Tr.& Indus.Ind., World Bank.Abstr.
●Also available online. Vendor(s): Mead Data Central.
    Description: Magazine on international politics and economic thought.

327   NP
FOREIGN AFFAIRS JOURNAL. (Text in English) 1976. 3/yr. Rs.25. Bhola Bikrum Rana, Ed. & Pub., 5-287 Lagon, Kathmandu, Nepal.

959.5 327   MY   ISSN 0126-690X
FOREIGN AFFAIRS MALAYSIA. 1966. q. free. Ministry of Foreign Affairs - Kementerian Luar Negeri, Jalan Wisma Putra, Kuala Lumpur, Malaysia. illus.; circ. 6,000. Indexed: Abstr.Mil.Bibl.
    —BLDSC shelfmark: 3986.810000.

327   II
FOREIGN AFFAIRS RECORD. 1955. m. Ministry of External Affairs, External Publicity Division, New Delhi, India. (U.S. address: Consulate General of India, 3 E. 64th St., New York, NY 10021) index; circ. 1,600.

327   II   ISSN 0015-7155
FOREIGN AFFAIRS REPORTS. (Text in English) 1952. m. $45. Indian Council of World Affairs, Sapru House, Barakhamba Rd., New Delhi 110001, India. Ed. S.C. Parasher. index; circ. 800. Indexed: Abstr.Mil.Bibl.

327   US   ISSN 0071-7320
JX1705
FOREIGN CONSULAR OFFICES IN THE UNITED STATES. (Subseries of: U.S. Department of State. Department and Foreign Service Series) 1932. a. U.S. Department of State, 2201 C St. N.W., Washington, DC 20520. TEL 202-655-4000. (Dist. by: Supt. of Documents, Washington, DC 20402)

FOREIGN GOVERNMENT OFFICES IN CALIFORNIA; a directory. see PUBLIC ADMINISTRATION

327 977 338.91   US   ISSN 0748-2841
E840
FOREIGN POLICY (SAN DIEGO); opposing viewpoints sources. 1984. a. $10.95 (sourcebook $39.95). Greenhaven Press, Inc., Box 289009, San Diego, CA 92198-0009. TEL 619-485-7424. FAX 619-485-9549. Ed. Bruno Leone. (back issues avail.)
    Description: Covers US foreign policy towards other countries.

327   US   ISSN 0015-7228
E744
FOREIGN POLICY (WASHINGTON). 1970. q. $28 to individuals; institutions $35. Carnegie Endowment for International Peace, 2400 N St., N.W., Ste. 700, Washington, DC 20037. TEL 202-862-7900. (Subscr. to: Foreign Policy, Box 2104, Knoxville, IA 50197-2104. TEL 800-678-0916) Ed. Charles William Maynes. bk.rev.; s-a index; circ. 28,000. (also avail. in microform from UMI; reprint service avail. from UMI) Indexed: A.B.C.Pol.Sci., Abstr.Mil.Bibl., Acad.Ind., Access, Amer.Bibl.Slavic & E.Eur.Stud, Amer.Hist.& Life, C.L.I., Curr.Cont., Curr.Cont.M.E., Deep Sea Res.& Oceanogr.Abstr., Fut.Surv., Hist.Abstr., HR Rep., INIS Atomind., Leg.Per., Mag.Ind., Mar.Aff.Bibl., P.A.I.S., PMR, PROMT, R.G., Rural Recreat.Tour.Abstr., Soc.Sci.Ind., SSCI, World Agri.Econ.& Rural Sociol.Abstr.
●Also available on CD-ROM.
    —BLDSC shelfmark: 3987.105000.

327   US   ISSN 0017-8780
E744
FOREIGN POLICY ASSOCIATION. HEADLINE SERIES. 1935. 4/yr. $15. Foreign Policy Association, 729 Seventh Ave., New York, NY 10019. TEL 212-764-4050. FAX 212-302-6123. Ed. Nancy Hoepli. bibl.; charts; illus.; circ. 15,000. (also avail. in microfilm from UMI; back issues avail.; reprint service avail. from UMI,KTO) Indexed: Hum.Ind., P.A.I.S., Soc.Sci.Ind.
    —BLDSC shelfmark: 4274.655000.

327   US
FOREIGN POLICY NEWS CLIPS. q. Institute on Global Conflict and Cooperation, University of California, San Diego, Q-068, La Jolla, CA 92093. TEL 619-534-3352.

320 330.9 338.91   US   ISSN 0015-7244
FOREIGN PROJECTS NEWSLETTER; a biweekly advance summary of significant capital expansion projects and economic development programs outside U.S.A. 1958. fortn. $300. Richards, Lawrence & Company, Box 1826, Santa Monica, CA 90406. TEL 213-395-3977. Ed. L.R. Chase. (back issues avail.) Indexed: Key to Econ.Sci.

327   US   ISSN 0071-7355
JX233
FOREIGN RELATIONS OF THE UNITED STATES. 1861. irreg. price varies. U.S. Department of State, Bureau of Public Affairs, Office of the Historian, Washington, DC 20520. TEL 202-655-4000. (Dist. by: Supt. of Documents, Washington, DC 20402)

327   US   ISSN 0015-7279
FOREIGN SERVICE JOURNAL. 1924. 11/yr. $40 (foreign $50). American Foreign Service Association, 2101 E St., N.W., Washington, DC 20037. TEL 202-338-4045. FAX 202-338-6820. Ed. Anne Stevenson-Yang. adv.; bk.rev.; illus.; index; circ. 11,500. (also avail. in microform from UMI; reprint service avail. from UMI) Indexed: Amer.Bibl.Slavic & E.Eur.Stud, Amer.Hist.& Life, Hist.Abstr., Mid.East: Abstr.& Ind., P.A.I.S., Pers.Lit.
    —BLDSC shelfmark: 3987.170000.
    Former titles (until 1951): American Foreign Service Journal (ISSN 0360-8425); American Consular Bulletin.

327   MX   ISSN 0185-013X
D839
FORO INTERNACIONAL. 1960. 4/yr. Mex.$2500($32) to individuals (foreign $42); institutions $50 (foreign $60). Colegio de Mexico, A.C., Departamento de Publicaciones, Camino al Ajusco 20, Codigo Postal 01000, Mexico, D.F., Mexico. TEL 568 6033. FAX 6526233. TELEX 1777585 COLME. Ed. Rafael Segovia. adv.; bk.rev.; bibl.; charts; index, cum.index; circ. 2,000. (back issues avail.; reprint service avail. from Swets & Zeitlinger) Indexed: A.B.C.Pol.Sci., Amer.Hist.& Life, Hisp.Amer.Per.Ind., Hist.Abstr., P.A.I.S.For.Lang.Ind.
    —BLDSC shelfmark: 4008.950000.

327   GW
FORSCHUNGEN ZU OSTEUROPA. 1986. irreg. Edition Temmen, Hohenlohestr. 21, 2800 Bremen 1, Germany. TEL 0421-344280. FAX 0421-348094. Ed.Bd.

POLITICAL SCIENCE — INTERNATIONAL RELATIONS

329   NO
D880
FORUM FOR DEVELOPMENT STUDIES. 2/yr. NOK 125. Norsk Utenrikspolitisk Institutt - Norwegian Institute of International Affairs, P.O. Box 8159 Dep., 0033 Oslo 1, Norway. TEL 02-177050. FAX 02-177015. Ed. Olav Stokke. **Indexed:** I D A.
    Formerly (until 1992): Forum for Utviklingsstudier (ISSN 0332-8244)

354   FR
FRANCE. MEDIATEUR. RAPPORT ANNUEL DU MEDIATEUR. 1973. a. Direction des Journaux Officiels, 26 rue Desaix, 75727 Paris Cedex 15, France. TEL 1-45-78-61-44.

327   FR
FRANCE. MINISTERE DES RELATIONS EXTERIEURES. SOUS-DIRECTIONS DES ETUDES ET DEVELOPPEMENT. ETUDES ET DOCUMENTS. irreg. Ministere des Relations Exterieures, Sous-Direction des Etudes du Developpement, Service de la Cooperation et du Developpement, 20 rue Monsieur, 75700 Paris, France. circ. 500.
    Former titles: France. Ministere de la Cooperation. Sous-Direction des Etudes de Developpement. Etudes et Documents; France. Ministere de la Cooperation. Services des Etudes et Questions Internationales. Etudes et Documents (ISSN 0247-4468)

327   FR   ISSN 0071-8181
FRANCE - ALLEMAGNE. 1967. irreg. (approx. 3/yr.). free. Internationale Union of Mayors, Mairie de Paris, 75196 Paris, France.

944   FR   ISSN 0015-959X
FRANCE INFORMATIONS.* (Text in English, French and Spanish) 1967. m. free. Secretariat d'Etat aux Affaires Etrangeres Charge de la Cooperation, Direction de l'Aide au Developpement, 37 Quai d'Orsay, 75007 Paris, France. Ed. Janine Landau.

FRANCE - PAYS ARABES. see HISTORY — History Of The Near East

327   FR   ISSN 0399-9505
FRANCE U.R.S.S. MAGAZINE. 1945. m. (10/yr.). 180 F. Association France-U.R.S.S., 61 rue Boissiere, 75116 Paris, France. TEL 45-01-59-00. FAX 45-53-28-76. TELEX FRANURS 612950F. adv.; bk.rev.; circ. 54,000.

327 944 970   FR   ISSN 0015-9751
FRANCE - U.S.A; journal des relations Franco-Americaines. 1945. q. 10 F. Association France Etats Unis, 6 bd. de Grenelle, 75015 Paris, France. TEL 45-77-48-92. Ed. A. Singer. adv.; bk.rev.; illus.; circ. 25,000. (tabloid format)

327   US
D839
FREEDOM REVIEW; documenting the universal struggle for freedom. 1970. bi-m. $20. Freedom House, 48 E. 21st St., New York, NY 10010. TEL 212-473-9691. FAX 212-477-4126. Ed. James Finn. adv.; bk.rev.; index; circ. 1,493. (also avail. in microform from UMI; back issues avail.; reprint service avail. from UMI) **Indexed:** Amer.Bibl.Slavic & E.Eur.Stud, Amer.Hist.& Life, Hist.Abstr., HR Rep., P.A.I.S.
    Formerly: Freedom at Issue; Which incorporated: Freedom Appeals (ISSN 0016-0520)

DIE FRIEDENS - WARTE; Blaetter fuer internationale Verstaendigung und zwischenstaatliche Organisation. see LAW — International Law

341.1   GW   ISSN 0016-3481
G D R PEACE COUNCIL. INFORMATION. (Editions in English, French, German, Italian, Spanish) 1959. m. Peace Council, Clara-Zetkin-Str. 103, P.O. Box 1364, 1086 Berlin, Germany.
    Description: Devoted to peace and nuclear disarmament. Covers meetings and speeches of the peace movement, reports of events.

327   US   ISSN 0077-0582
G S I S MONOGRAPH SERIES IN WORLD AFFAIRS. 1963. irreg., latest 1990. price varies. (University of Denver, Graduate School of International Studies) Lynne Rienner Publishers, 1800 30th St., Ste. 314, Boulder, CO 80301. TEL 303-444-4684. FAX 303-444-0824. Ed. Karen A. Feste. adv.; circ. 1,000. **Indexed:** SSCI.

327   II
GANDHI PEACE FOUNDATION LECTURES. irreg. Radakrishna Indraprastha Estate, Nehru House, 221-3 Deen Royal Upadhyaya Marg, New Delhi 110002, India.

327   GW   ISSN 0930-8571
GEHEIM. English edition: Top Secret (ISSN 0935-3909) 1985. 3/yr. DM.45($45) Geheim Verlag, Postfach 270324, 5000 Cologne 1, Germany. TEL 0221-513751. FAX 0221-529552. TELEX 8886391-MP-D. Ed. Michael Opperskalski. circ. 3,500. (back issues avail.)

327 614.7   UK
GEM POLITICS ONE. a. Edinburgh University Press, 22 George Sq., Edinburgh EH8 9LF, Scotland. Ed. Wolfgang Rudig.

227 960   SZ   ISSN 0016-6774
DT1
GENEVA - AFRICA/GENEVE - AFRIQUE. (Text in English, French) 1962-1976; resumed. 2/yr. 32 Fr. Institut Universitaire d'Etudes du Developpement, 24 rue Rothschild, Case Postale 136, CH-1211 Geneva 21, Switzerland. FAX 22-7384416. TELEX 412584-IUED-CH. Ed. Laurent Monnier. adv.; bk.rev.; abstr.; bibl.; illus.; circ. 700. (reprint service avail. from SWZ) **Indexed:** A.B.C.Pol.Sci., A.I.C.P., CERDIC, Curr.Cont.Africa, Geo.Abstr., Hist.Abstr., HR Rep., I D A, M.L.A., Rice Abstr., World Agri.Econ.& Rural.Sociol.Abstr.
    —BLDSC shelfmark: 4115.560000.

GENEVA NEWS AND INTERNATIONAL REPORT. see BUSINESS AND ECONOMICS — Economic Situation And Conditions

320.3 918.903   UY   ISSN 0250-7609
GEOSUR. (Includes monographic supplements) 1979. 6/yr. $70. Asociacion Sudamericana de Estudios Geopoliticos e Internacionales, Casilla de Correos 5006, Montevideo, Uruguay. TEL 592953. FAX 598-2-961923. Ed. Bernardo Quagliotti de Bellis. adv.; bk.rev.; circ. 1,500. **Indexed:** Abstr.Mil.Bibl.
    —BLDSC shelfmark: 4158.897500.

327   UK   ISSN 0964-4008
▼**GERMAN POLITICS.** 1992. 3/yr. £28($35) to individuals; institutions £45($75). Frank Cass & Co. Ltd., Gainsborough House, 11 Gainsborough Rd., London E11 1RS, England. TEL 081-530-4226. FAX 081-530-7795. Ed.Bd.
    Description: Presents the academic study of domestic German politics together with treatment of international European Community and security issues from a German perspective.

GERMANY (FEDERAL REPUBLIC, 1949-). DEUTSCHER BUNDESTAG. WISSENSCHAFTLICHE DIENSTE. MATERIALIEN. see BIBLIOGRAPHIES

327   GW   ISSN 0016-9390
GEWALTFREIE AKTION; Vierteljahreshefte fuer Frieden und Gerechtigkeit. 1969. q. DM.12. Versoehnungsbund e.V., Kuehlenstr. 5a-7, 2082 Uetersen, Germany. Ed. Gernot Jochheim. adv.; bk.rev.; bibl.; circ. 6,000.

327   US   ISSN 0886-6198
D839
GLOBAL AFFAIRS. 1986. q. $24 (foreign $45). International Security Council, 1155 15th St. NW, Ste. 502, Washington, DC 20005. TEL 212-828-0802. FAX 202-429-2563. Ed. Charles M. Lichenstein. adv.; bk.rev.; circ. 8,700. **Indexed:** A.B.C.Pol.Sci.
    —BLDSC shelfmark: 4195.337000.
    Description: A forum for responsible and expert views on international security affairs.

GLOBAL LINKS. see BUSINESS AND ECONOMICS — International Development And Assistance

327   US   ISSN 0730-9112
GLOBAL REPORT; progress toward a world of peace with justice. 1977. irreg. (approx. 4/yr.). $20. Center for War - Peace Studies, 218 E. 18th St., New York, NY 10003. TEL 212-475-1077. FAX 212-260-6384. Ed. Richard Hudson. circ. 3,500.
    Description: Chronicles events at the United Nations, with a perspective of improving the effectiveness of the organization.

GLOBAL RISK ASSESSMENTS; issues, concepts and applications. see BUSINESS AND ECONOMICS — International Commerce

327   US
GLOBAL STUDIES: AFRICA. irreg., 4th ed., 1991. $11.95. Dushkin Publishing Group, Inc., Sluice Dock, Guilford, CT 06437-9989. TEL 203-453-4351. FAX 203-453-6000. Ed. Jeff Ramsey. illus.

327   US
GLOBAL STUDIES: CHINA. irreg., 4th ed., 1991. $11.95. Dushkin Publishing Group, Inc., Sluice Dock, Guilford, CT 06437-9989. TEL 203-453-4351. FAX 203-453-6000. Ed. Suzanne Ogden. illus.

327   US
▼**GLOBAL STUDIES: JAPAN AND THE PACIFIC RIM.** 1991. irreg. $11.95. Dushkin Publishing Group, Inc., Sluice Dock, Guilford, CT 06437-9989. TEL 203-453-4351. FAX 203-453-6000. Ed. Dean Collingwood. illus.

327   US
GLOBAL STUDIES: LATIN AMERICA. irreg., 4th ed., 1990. $11.95. Dushkin Publishing Group, Inc., Sluice Dock, Guilford, CT 06437-9989. TEL 203-453-4351. FAX 203-453-6000. Ed. Paul Goodwin. illus.

327   US   ISSN 1056-6848
GLOBAL STUDIES: MIDDLE EAST. irreg., 3rd ed., 1990. $11.95. Dushkin Publishing Group, Inc., Sluice Dock, Guilford, CT 06437-9989. TEL 203-453-4351. FAX 203-453-6000. Ed. William Spencer. illus.

327   US
GLOBAL STUDIES: SOVIET UNION & EASTERN EUROPE. irreg., 3rd ed., 1990. $11.95. Dushkin Publishing Group, Inc., Sluice Dock, Guilford, CT 06437-9989. TEL 203-453-4351. FAX 203-453-6000. Ed. Minton F. Goldman. illus.

327   US
GLOBAL STUDIES: WESTERN EUROPE. 1989. irreg., 2nd ed., 1991. $11.95. Dushkin Publishing Group, Inc., Sluice Dock, Guilford, CT 06437-9989. TEL 203-453-4351. FAX 203-453-6000. Ed. Henri J. Warmenhoven. illus.

327   US   ISSN 0194-8660
JX1293.U6
GOVERNMENT-SPONSORED RESEARCH ON FOREIGN AFFAIRS; a quarterly report of project information. 1975. q. $7.50. U.S. Department of State, Office of Public Services, Bureau of Public Affairs, 2201 C St., N.W., Washington, DC 20520. TEL 202-634-3600. (Dist. by: Supt. of Documents, Washington, DC 20402)
    Formerly: Government-Supported Research on Foreign Affairs (ISSN 0147-4529)

327   UK   ISSN 0072-6397
GREAT BRITAIN. FOREIGN AND COMMONWEALTH OFFICE. TREATY SERIES. 1892. irreg. H.M.S.O., P.O. Box 276, London SW8 5DT, England. (reprint service avail. from UMI)

327.73   US   ISSN 0072-727X
E744
GREAT DECISIONS. 1955. a. $11 (effective Jan. 1992). Foreign Policy Association, 729 Seventh Ave., New York, NY 10019. TEL 212-764-4050. FAX 212-302-6123. Ed. Nancy Hoepli. circ. 80,000. (reprint service avail. from UMI) **Indexed:** Abstr.Mil.Bibl., SRI.
    Description: Focuses on key foreign policy issues with background, current data and alternative options for the US.

327   SP
GRUPO ESPANOL DE LA UNION INTERPARLAMENTARIA. BOLETIN DE INFORMACION. 1968. q. free. Cortes Espanolas, Grupo Espanol de la Union Interparlamentaria, Madrid, Spain.

327   KN
GUKJESAENGHWAL/INTERNATIONAL LIFE. (Text in English and Korean) 1986. m. Pyongyang, N. Korea.
    Description: Covers North Korea's foreign policy and international events.

POLITICAL SCIENCE — INTERNATIONAL RELATIONS

327 330 UK ISSN 0953-5411
GULF STATES NEWSLETTER. 1975. fortn. $520 (effective Jan. 1992). Middle East Newsletters, P.O. Box 124, Crawley, Sussex RH10 3YT, England. TEL 0342-712929. FAX 0342-712829. Ed. John Christie. bk.rev.
Description: Covers political, economic and defense issues in the Gulf Region.

327 CC
GUOJI GONGYUNSHI YANJIU/RESEARCH IN THE HISTORY OF THE INTERNATIONAL COMMUNIST MOVEMENT. (Text in Chinese) q. Zhongyang Malie Zuzuo Bianyi-ju, Guoji Gongyunshi Yanjiusuo, 36, Xixie Jie, Xidan, Beijing 100032, People's Republic of China. Ed. Hu Wenjian.

327 382 CC ISSN 0452-8832
GUOJI WENTI YANJIU/INTERNATIONAL STUDIES. (Text in Chinese; summaries and table of contents in English) q. $12.95. (Zhongguo Guoji Wenti Yanjiusuo - China Institute of International Studies) Shijie Zhishi Chubanshe - World Affairs Press, 31-A, Waijiaobu Jie, Beijing 100005, People's Republic of China. (Dist. outside China by: China International Book Trading Corp., P.O. Box 2820, Beijing, P.R.C.; Dist. in US by: China Books & Periodicals, Inc., 2929 24th St., San Francisco, CA 94110. TEL 415-282-2994) Ed. Ma Yaohui.
Formerly: Journal of International Studies.

327 CC ISSN 0452-8778
GUOJI ZHANWANG/INTERNATIONAL PROSPECT. (Text in Chinese) s-m. Shanghai Guoji Wenti Yanjiusuo - Shanghai Research Institute of International Issues, No.1, Alley 845, Julu Lu, Shanghai 200040, People's Republic of China. TEL 4334263.

327 658 CY ISSN 0256-5935
H C J COMMUNICATIONS REPORT. 1984. m. $395. H C J Communications Ltd., P.O. Box 5704, Nicosia, Cyprus. Ed. Christian Doumit. adv.; bk.rev. (back issues avail.)
Description: Covers educational trends in the Middle East.

HAITI NEWS. see BUSINESS AND ECONOMICS — International Development And Assistance

327 UK
HALIFAX NUCLEAR DISARMAMENT GROUP NEWSLETTER. 1980. 6/yr. £1($15) c/o Julian Harber, Ed., 17 Bankhouse Lane, Salterhebble, Halifax, England. circ. 400. (back issues avail.)
Formerly: Halifax Nuclear Disarmament Group. Bulletin.
Description: Covers events and current issues of the Halifax Disarmament Group.

327 GW
HAMBURGER BEITRAEGE ZUR FRIEDENSFORSCHUNG UND SICHERHEITSPOLITIK. (Text in English, German) 1986. irreg. (8-12/yr.) Institut fuer Friedensforschung und Sicherheitspolitik, An der Universitaet Hamburg, Falkenstein 1, 2000 Hamburg 55, Germany. TEL 040-869054. FAX 866-3615. adv.; circ. 500.
Description: Covers research in peace and national security. Each volume devoted to a single topic.

327 US ISSN 1049-3999
HANDBOOK OF ORGANIZATIONS INVOLVED IN SOVIET-AMERICAN RELATIONS. a. $25. Institute for Soviet-American Relations, 1601 Connecticut Ave. N.W., Ste. 301, Washington, DC 20009. TEL 202-387-3034. FAX 202-667-3291.
Description: Profiles 313 nonprofit groups involved in Soviet-American relations, also listed by: environment, trade and economics, education, health and world security.

327 US ISSN 0194-3790
G122
HANDBOOK OF THE NATIONS. 1979. irreg., 10th ed., 1990. $95. Gale Research Inc., 835 Penobscot Bldg., Detroit, MI 48226. TEL 313-961-2242. FAX 313-961-6083. TELEX 810-221-7086.
Description: Reprint of the CIA's World Factbook.

HARRIMAN INSTITUTE FORUM. see LITERARY AND POLITICAL REVIEWS

327 382 US ISSN 0739-1854
D839
HARVARD INTERNATIONAL REVIEW. 1979. bi-m. $14 to individuals; institutions $29. Harvard International Relations Council, Inc., Box 401, Cambridge, MA 02238. adv.; bk.rev.; circ. 8,000. (back issues avail.) Indexed: Curr.Cont., P.A.I.S.
—BLDSC shelfmark: 4267.210000.

341 327 US ISSN 0073-0734
JX1295.H45
HARVARD UNIVERSITY. CENTER FOR INTERNATIONAL AFFAIRS. ANNUAL REPORT. 1961. a. free. Harvard University, Center for International Affairs, 1737 Cambridge St., Cambridge, MA 02138. TEL 617-495-4420. FAX 617-495-8292. Ed. Elizabeth Hurwit. circ. 3,000.

HELLENIC JOURNAL. see ETHNIC INTERESTS

327 US ISSN 0898-3038
F1401
HEMISPHERE; a magazine of Latin American and Caribbean affairs. 1988. 3/yr. $20 (foreign $27). Latin American and Caribbean Center, Florida International University, University Park, Miami, FL 33199. TEL 305-348-2894. FAX 305-348-3593. Ed. Anthony P. Maingot. adv.; bk.rev.; circ. 3,000.

327 GW
HESSISCHE STIFTUNG FRIEDENS- UND KONFLIKTFORSCHUNG. MITTEILUNGEN; Bericht ueber Organisation und laufende Forschung. 1971. a. DM.5. Hessische Stiftung Friedens- und Konfliktforschung, Leimenrode 29, 6000 Frankfurt a.M. 1, Germany. TEL 069-550191. FAX 069-558481. Ed. Ruediger Schlaga. circ. 180.
Description: Review of progress of the Institute's research programs.

HISTORIC PALESTINE SERIES. see ETHNIC INTERESTS

327 382 HK ISSN 0257-3636
HONG KONG COUNTDOWN: PERSPECTIVES ON CHANGE. (Text in English) 1984. 18/yr. HK.$1150($147) N & N International (Hong Kong) Ltd., GPO Box 8926, Hong Kong. FAX 852-856-5648. Ed. R.B. Cunningham.
Description: Newsletter that focuses on news and analyses leading up to the return of Hong Kong from the British to Chinese rule in 1997.

327 GW ISSN 0724-0279
HORIZONT (COLOGNE); Magazin fuer internationale Beziehungen. 1979. bi-m. DM.30. Horizont Verlag GmbH, Eifelstr. 8, Postfach 10 13 04, 5000 Cologne 1, Germany. Ed. Ferenc Pal Balazs. adv.

327 CC
HUAN QIU/GLOBE. (Text in Chinese) m. $33.20. (Xinhua News Agency) Huan Qiu Zazhishe, 57 Xuanwumen Xidajie, Beijing 100803, People's Republic of China. TEL 3073511. (Dist. in US by: China Books & Periodicals, Inc., 2929 24th St., San Francisco, CA 94110. TEL 415-282-2994) Ed. Ye Jin.

327 US
HUDSON INSTITUTE BRIEFING PAPER. irreg. Hudson Institute, Herman Kahn Center, 5395 Emerson Way, Box 26-919, Indianapolis, IN 46226-0919. TEL 317-545-1000. FAX 317-545-9639. TELEX 855477.

327 US
Q180.U5
HUDSON INSTITUTE REPORT. 1962. a. free. Hudson Institute, Herman Kahn Center, 5359 Emerson Way, Box 26-919, Indianapolis, IN 46226. TEL 317-545-1000. FAX 317-545-9639. TELEX 855477. circ. 4,500.
Formerly: Hudson Institute. Report to the Members (ISSN 0073-3776)

327 FR ISSN 0242-3502
HUDSON LETTER; letter of international forecast. (Supplements avail. 4/yr.) (Text in English) 1975. 22/yr. $550 (effective 1991). H R I, 1, rue Favart, 75002 Paris, France. TEL 43-07-34-10. FAX 43-07-34-10. Ed. Duncan H. James. adv.; bk.rev.; charts; stat.
Description: Reports on research conducted by the organization on economic and political events worldwide.

327 US ISSN 0882-2751
I A S NEWS. 1983. 2/yr. University of Miami, North-South Center Publications, Box 248123, Coral Cables, FL 33124-3010. Ed. Gina Bryson. circ. 10,000.

327 UK
I C A B A. 1984. 3/yr. free. End Loans to South Africa, c/o Methodist Church, 56 Camberwell Rd., London SE5 OFN, England. TEL 071-708-4702. FAX 071-708-5751. Ed. Hugo Burdick.

327 338.91 UN ISSN 0254-3036
I F D A DOSSIER. (Text in English, French, Spanish) 1978. bi-m. $32 to individuals; libraries $64. International Foundation for Development Alternatives, 4 place du Marche, 1260 Nyon, Switzerland. Ed. Marc Nerfin. bk.rev.; circ. 22,000. (also avail. in microfiche) Indexed: Forest.Abstr., HR Rep., I D A, Int.Lab.Doc., Rural Devel.Abstr., Rural Ext.Educ.& Tr.Abstr.
—BLDSC shelfmark: 4363.279500.

327 US
I G C C NEWSLETTER. 3/yr. Institute on Global Conflict and Cooperation, University of California, San Diego, Q-068, La Jolla, CA 92093. TEL 619-534-3352.

327 JA ISSN 0285-2608
I H J BULLETIN. (Text in English) 1981. q. 1000 Yen($10) International House of Japan, Inc., 11-16 Roppongi 5-chome, Minato-ku, Tokyo 106, Japan. FAX 03-3490-3170. Ed.Bd. bk.rev.; circ. 7,400. (back issues avail.)

327 AU ISSN 1017-6861
I I P MONITOR. (Text in English) irreg. S.120 per no. International Institute for Peace, Moellwaldplatz 5, A-1040 Vienna, Austria. TEL 0431-6564370. FAX 0431-65643722. Eds. Peter Stania, Lev Voronkov.

327 AU
I I P OCCASIONAL PAPER. (Text in English) irreg. S.60 per no. International Institute for Peace, Moellwaldplatz 5, A-1040 Vienna, Austria. TEL 0431-6564370. FAX 0431-65643722.

341.1 US
I P R A NEWSLETTER. 1963. q. $24 to non-members. International Peace Research Association, c/o Antioch College, YELLOW Springs, OH 45387. TEL 513-767-7331. FAX 513-767-1891. Ed. Paul Smoker. adv.; bk.rev.; abstr.; bibl.; circ. 1,350. (also avail. in microform from UMI; reprint service avail. from UMI) Indexed: HR Rep., Mid.East: Abstr.& Ind.
Formerly: International Peace Research Newsletter (ISSN 0020-8213)

IDEAS AND INFORMATION ABOUT DEVELOPMENT EDUCATION. see EDUCATION — International Education Programs

IMPARTIAL CITIZEN. see ETHNIC INTERESTS

320 US ISSN 1055-9809
▼**IN DEPTH (WASHINGTON).** 1991. 3/yr. $12. Washington Institute for Values in Public Policy, 1015 18th St., N.W., Ste. 300, Washington, DC 20036. Ed. Richard Rubenstein.
Description: Covers a wide range of foreign and public policy issues confronting the American polity.

341.1 IT ISSN 0019-3496
L'INCONTRO; pacifist periodical independent. 1949. m. L.15000($15) Via Consolata N. 11, 10122 Torino, Italy. TEL 51-90-82. Ed. Dr. Bruno Segre. adv.; bk.rev.; illus.; circ. 8,000. (newspaper)

327 016 US ISSN 0193-905X
HM261
INDEX TO INTERNATIONAL PUBLIC OPINION. 1980. a. price varies. (Survey Research Consultants International, Inc.) Greenwood Press, Inc. (Subsidiary of: Greenwood Publishing Group Inc.), 88 Post Rd. W., Box 5007, Westport, CT 06881-5007. TEL 203-226-3511. FAX 203-222-1502. Eds. Elizabeth Hann Hastings, Philip K. Hastings.

327 II ISSN 0376-9771
DS401
INDIA INTERNATIONAL CENTRE QUARTERLY. (Text in English) 1974. q. Rs.60($16.50) India International Centre, 40 Lodi Estate, New Delhi 110003, India. Ed.Bd. bk.rev.; bibl.; circ. 2,400. Indexed: Ind.India.

POLITICAL SCIENCE — INTERNATIONAL RELATIONS

954   II   ISSN 0019-4220
INDIA QUARTERLY. (Text in English) 1945. q. $40. Indian Council of World Affairs, Sapru House, Barakhamba Rd., New Delhi 110001, India. Ed. S.C. Parashar. adv.; bk.rev.; bibl.; index; circ. 2,000.
Indexed: A.B.C.Pol.Sci., Abstr.Mil.Bibl., Amer.Hist.& Life, Hist.Abstr., Mid.East: Abstr.& Ind., P.A.I.S.

327 330.9   FR   ISSN 0294-6475
DT365
INDIAN OCEAN NEWSLETTER. French edition: Lettre de l'Ocean Indien (ISSN 0294-6467) (Editions in English, French) 1981. w. 3450 F.($639) Indigo Publications, 10, rue de Sentier, 75002 Paris, France. TEL 45-08-14-80. FAX 45-08-59-83. TELEX 215405 F. Ed. Maurice Botbol. bk.rev.; index; circ. 1,500. (looseleaf format; back issues avail.) **Indexed:** HR Rep.
Description: Covers newsworthy, diplomatic, political and economic events in African countries of the Indian Ocean region.

327 954   II   ISSN 0537-2704
JX21
INDIAN YEARBOOK OF INTERNATIONAL AFFAIRS. 1952-1968; N.S. 1973. a. Indian Study Group of International Affairs, University of Madras, Chepauk, Triplicane P.O., Madras 600005, Tamil Nadu, India. bk.rev.; index.
Description: Looks at law and international relations.

327 330.9   GW   ISSN 0046-9149
INDIEN. 1972. q. Indische Botschaft in Deutschland, Adenauerallee 262-264, 5300 Bonn, Germany. bk.rev.; charts; illus.; stat.; circ. 5,500.

INDO-BRITISH REVIEW; a journal of history. see HISTORY — History Of Asia

INDO-IRANICA. see LITERATURE

327   II
INDO-ISRAEL. (Text in English) vol.16, 1973. bi-m. Rs.1 per no. Bombay Zionist Association, 41 Hamam St., Bombay 400 023, India. Ed. E.M. Jacob. illus.

327   II
INDO-KOREAN FRIENDSHIP. 1970. m. R.0.60 per no. All India Indo-Korean Friendship Association, F60 Bhagat Singh Market, New Delhi 1, India. Ed. Amar Nath Vidyalankar. adv.; bk.rev.; circ. 2,000.

327   US
INDOCHINA DIGEST. 1987. w. $35 to individuals (foreign $45); corporations $100 (foreign $150). Indochina Project, 2001 S St., N.W., Ste. 700, Washington, DC 20009. TEL 202-483-9222. FAX 202-483-9214. TELEX 6503397753 MCI UW. circ. 1,000.
Description: Tracks develoments in or related to Indochina, with emphasis on business, economics, and politics.

327   US   ISSN 0738-4548
DS531
INDOCHINA ISSUES. 1979. irreg. (10/yr.). $20 (foreign $30). Indochina Project, 2001 S St. NW, Ste. 740, Washington, DC 20009. TEL 202-483-9222. FAX 202-483-9314. TELEX 6503397753 MCI UW. circ. 2,500. (looseleaf format) **Indexed:** Alt.Press Ind., HR Rep.
Description: Publication concerned with furthering understanding and relations between the U.S. and the Indochina states, with an emphasis on human rights and humanitarian affairs.

327   US
INDOCHINA NEWSLETTER. 1980. bi-m. $15. Asia Resource Center, 2161 Massachusetts Ave., Cambridge, MA 02140. TEL 617-497-5273. FAX 617-354-2832. cum.index: 1980-89; circ. 1,000. (back issues avail.)
Incorporates: Asia Insights.
Description: Examines the legacy of the Vietnam war in an attempt to counter attempts by those who support U.S. intervention to rewrite the history and lessons of the Vietnam experience. Focuses on developments inside Indochina and U.S. policy toward the region.

INDONESIAN QUARTERLY. see POLITICAL SCIENCE

327   IO   ISSN 0046-9173
DS638
INDONESIAN REVIEW OF INTERNATIONAL AFFAIRS. 1970. q. $1.50 per no. Indonesian Institute of International Affairs, 82 Jalan Tjikini Raya, Jakarta 4, Indonesia. Eds. A. Subardjo Djovoadisuryo, S. Suryodpuro. adv.; circ. 2,000.

327 959   AT   ISSN 0813-4820
INDONESIAN STUDIES. (Text in English and Indonesian) 1984. s-a. Aus.$8 to individuals; institutions Aus.$12. Indonesian Cultural and Educational Institute (ICEI), P.O. Box 73, Clayton, Vic. 3168, Australia. TEL (03) 4792303. Ed. Abe L. Kelabora. adv.; bk.rev.; circ. 250. (back issues avail.)
Description: Publishes articles, notes, reviews and announcements on Indonesia and Indonesia's international relations.

341.1   GW   ISSN 0020-0085
INFORMATION FROM THE PEACE MOVEMENT OF THE GERMAN DEMOCRATIC REPUBLIC. (Editions in English, French, German, Italian, Spanish) 1960. m. Peace Council, Invalidenstr. 120-121, 1040 Berlin, Germany. illus.
Description: Covers international peace movement organizations and events.

INFORMATION PROCHE-ORIENT. see LITERARY AND POLITICAL REVIEWS

327   GW
INFORMATIONEN. 1978. q. Ohne Rustung Leben, Furtbachstr. 10, 7000 Stuttgart 1, Germany. TEL 0711-6409620. FAX 0711-6407980. Ed. Gerhard Voss. circ. 6,000.

INFORMATIONSDIENST SUEDLICHES AFRIKA. see BUSINESS AND ECONOMICS — International Development And Assistance

327   CH   ISSN 0250-961X
INSIDE CHINA MAINLAND. (Text in English) 1979. m. $17 in Asia; elsewhere $20. Institute of Current China Studies, P.O. Box 14-19, Taipei, Taiwan, Republic of China. Ed. T.L. Wang. index; circ. 8,000. (back issues avail.)
—BLDSC shelfmark: 4518.151800.
Description: Presents translations of reprinted and original articles concerning issues of policy and politics in mainland China.

327 338.91   AT   ISSN 0814-1185
INSIDE INDONESIA. 1983. q. $26 to individuals; institutions $36. Indonesia Resources & Information Programme, P.O. Box 190, Northcote, Vic. 3070, Australia. TEL 03-417-7505. Ed.Bd. adv.; bk.rev.; circ. 2,000. (back issues avail.)
—BLDSC shelfmark: 4518.152130.
Description: Reports on Indonesian culture, politics, economy and human rights.

320   FR   ISSN 0294-3069
INSTITUT DES RECHERCHES MARXISTES. RECHERCHES INTERNATIONALES. 1957. q. 250 F. (foreign 500 F.). Institut des Recherches Marxistes, 64 bd. Auguste Blanqui, 75013 Paris, France. adv.; bk.rev.; cum.index; circ. 2,500.
Formerly (until 1981): Recherches Internationales a la Lumiere du Marxisme (ISSN 0486-1345); **Supersedes:** Recherches Sovietiques.

INSTITUT ZUR ERFORSCHUNG DER EUROPAEISCHEN ARBEITERBEWEGUNG. MITTEILUNGSBLATT. see LABOR UNIONS

327   US
INSTITUTE FOR EAST - WEST SECURITY STUDIES. ANNUAL REPORT. a. Institute for East - West Security Studies, 360 Lexington Ave., New York, NY 10017. TEL 212-557-2570. FAX 212-949-8043. TELEX 760-8127 EWS.

327   BL
INSTITUTO CULTURAL ITALO-BRASILEIRO. CADERNO. no.8, 1972. irreg. Instituto Cultural Italo-Brasileiro, Rua Frei Caneca 1071, Sao Paulo, Brazil.

327   GW   ISSN 0720-5120
INTEGRATION. 1978. q. DM.36. (Institut fuer Europaeische Politik, Bonn) Europa Union Verlag GmbH, Bachstr. 32, 5300 Bonn 1, Germany. TEL 0228-7290010. FAX 0228-6957348. TELEX 8-86822. circ. 6,300.
—BLDSC shelfmark: 4531.816290.
Description: European integration in science and research.

327   US
▼**INTELLIGENCE BRIEFS (IRREGULAR).** 1990. irreg. $50 includes membership. Center for Intelligence Studies, 301 S. Columbus St., Alexandria, VA 22314. TEL 703-684-0625. FAX 703-836-8429. Ed. K. Leigh Dyer. circ. 25,000.
Description: In-depth analysis of particular aspects of intelligence, counterintelligence, security, and related issues.

327   US
▼**INTELLIGENCE BRIEFS (MONTHLY).** 1991. m. $50 membership. Center for Intelligence Studies, 301 S. Columbus St., Alexandria, VA 22314. TEL 703-684-0625. FAX 703-836-8429. circ. 25,000.
Description: Provides overview of current security and intelligence issues.

INTERAMERICAN OPPORTUNITIES BRIEFING; a guide to economic reform and business activities in Latin America and the Caribbean. see BUSINESS AND ECONOMICS — International Development And Assistance

341.1   US   ISSN 0094-5072
D839
INTERDEPENDENT. 1974. 6/yr. $10. United Nations Association of the U.S.A., 485 Fifth Ave., 2nd Fl., New York, NY 10017-6104. Ed. John Tessitore. adv.; bk.rev.; illus.; circ. 22,000. (newspaper)
Formerly: Vista (ISSN 0042-711X)
Description: Covers world affairs and features news and analysis of global issues shaping international politics.

327 323.4   US   ISSN 0891-2688
INTER-HEMISPHERIC EDUCATION RESOURCE CENTER. BULLETIN. (Text in English and Spanish) 1985. q. $5. Inter-hemispheric Education Research Center, Box 4506, Albuquerque, NM 87196. TEL 505-842-8288. FAX 505-246-1601. Ed. John Hawley. circ. 3,500. (tabloid format; back issues avail.)
Description: Covers research and analysis of current international issues including US policy in third world countries.

327   NO   ISSN 0020-577X
D839
INTERNASJONAL POLITIKK. (Text in Norwegian; summaries in English) 1938. q. NOK 215 in Scandinavia; elsewhere NOK 285. Norsk Utenrikspolitisk Institutt – Norwegian Institute of International Affairs, Postboks 8159, Dep., 0033 Oslo 1, Norway. TEL 02-177050. FAX 02-177015. Ed. Olav Fagelund Knudsen. adv.; bk.rev.; charts; stat.; cum.index; circ. 2,750. (also avail. in microform from UMI; reprint service avail. from UMI)
Indexed: A.B.C.Pol.Sci., Abstr.Mil.Bibl., Amer.Hist.& Life, Hist.Abstr., INIS Atomind., SSCI.
—BLDSC shelfmark: 4534.925000.

327   UK   ISSN 0020-5850
JX1
INTERNATIONAL AFFAIRS. 1922. q. $49 to individuals; institutions $63. (Royal Institute of International Affairs) Cambridge University Press, Edinburgh Bldg., Shaftesbury Rd., Cambridge CB2 2RU, England. TEL 0223-312393. FAX 0223-315052. TELEX 851817256. (N. American addr.: Cambridge University Press, 40 W. 20th St., New York, NY 10011-4211, USA. TEL 212-924-3900) Ed. Lucy Seton-Watson. adv.; bk.rev.; index; cum.index. (also avail. in microform from MIM; reprints & back issues avail.) **Indexed:** A.B.C.Pol.Sci., Abstr.Mil.Bibl., Acad.Ind., Amer.Hist.& Life, Br.Hum.Ind., C.R.E.J., Curr.Cont., Curr.Cont.M.E., E.I., Geo.Abstr., Hist.Abstr., I D A, Key to Econ.Sci., Lang.& Lang.Behav.Abstr., Mid.East: Abstr.& Ind., P.A.I.S., Risk Abstr., Rural Recreat.Tour.Abstr., Soc.Sci.Ind., SSCI, World Agri.Econ.& Rural Sociol.Abstr.
—BLDSC shelfmark: 4535.630000.
Description: Promotes the flow of information and ideas on international political, economic, legal and related questions.

POLITICAL SCIENCE — INTERNATIONAL RELATIONS

327   RU   ISSN 0130-9641
D839
INTERNATIONAL AFFAIRS; a monthly journal of world politics, diplomacy and international relations. Russian edition: Mezhdunarodnaya Zhizn' (ISSN 0020-5869) (Editions in English, French, Russian) 1955 (Eng.ed.); 1954 (Russ.ed.). m. $5.50. Vsesoyuznoe Obshchestvo "Znanie", 14 Gorokhovskii Pereulok, Moscow K-16, Russia. Ed. Boris D. Piadyshev. bk.rev.; charts; maps; index. (also avail. in microform from MIM) **Indexed:** A.B.C.Pol.Sci., Amer.Hist.& Life, Hist.Abstr., Mar.Aff.Bibl., Mid.East: Abstr.& Ind., P.A.I.S.
—BLDSC shelfmark: 4535.633000.
  Description: Features articles on the Soviet Union's stand at various international forums. Presents an analysis of the world economic situation and the activity of the main financial groupings and transnational corporations. Also covers some aspects of international law.

327   SA   ISSN 0258-7270
INTERNATIONAL AFFAIRS BULLETIN. (Text mainly in English) 1977. 3/yr. R.25 (foreign R.35). South African Institute of International Affairs, P.O. Box 31596, Braamfontein 2017, South Africa. TEL 011-339-2021. FAX 011-339-2154. TELEX 4-27291 SA. circ. 3,500. **Indexed:** Ind.S.A.Per.
—BLDSC shelfmark: 4535.641000.
  Supersedes (in Dec. 1976): South African Institute of International Affairs. Newsletter.

INTERNATIONAL COUNTERTERRORISM & SECURITY. see CRIMINOLOGY AND LAW ENFORCEMENT — Security

327   US
INTERNATIONAL ESTIMATE SERIES. 1988. irreg. price varies. International Estimates, 1514 17th St., N.W., Ste. 315, Washington, DC 20036. TEL 202-332-0849.

INTERNATIONAL FRIENDSHIP AND GOOD WILL BULLETIN. see SOCIAL SERVICES AND WELFARE

327   SZ
INTERNATIONAL GENEVA YEARBOOK. 1985. a. Verlag Peter Lang AG, Jupiterstr. 15, CH-3000 Bern 15, Switzerland. TEL 031-321122. FAX 031-321131. TELEX 912651-PELA-CH.

341.1   US   ISSN 0305-0629
JX1   CODEN: INIAAH
INTERNATIONAL INTERACTIONS; empirical research in industrial relations. 1974. 4/yr. (in 1 vol., 4 nos./vol.). $91. Gordon and Breach Science Publishers, 270 Eighth Ave., New York, NY 10011. TEL 212-206-8900. FAX 212-645-2459. TELEX 236735 GOPUB UR. (Subscr. to: Box 786, Cooper Sta., New York, NY 10276. TEL 800-545-8398; UK subscr. to: P.O. Box 90, Reading, Berkshire RG1 8JL, England. TEL 0734-560-080) Ed. Harvey Starr. adv.; bk.rev.; abstr.; bibl.; charts; illus.; index. cum.index. (also avail. in microform from MIM) **Indexed:** Mid.East: Abstr.& Ind., P.A.I.S., Peace Res.Abstr., Soc.Sci.Ind.
—BLDSC shelfmark: 4541.431000.
  Formerly: War - Peace Report (ISSN 0043-0277); **Incorporating:** New Priorities (ISSN 0047-9837) Refereed Serial

327   CN   ISSN 0020-7020
D839
INTERNATIONAL JOURNAL. (Text in English, French) 1946. q. Can.$32.10($31) to individuals; institutions Can.$37.45 ($35). Canadian Institute of International Affairs, 15 King's College Circle, Toronto, Ont. M5S 2V9, Canada. TEL 416-979-1851. FAX 416-979-8575. Eds. Kim Richard Nossal, Stephen J. Randall. adv.; bk.rev.; index; circ. 2,100. (also avail. in microform from UMI; back issues avail.; reprint service avail. from KTO,UMI) **Indexed:** A.B.C.Pol.Sci., Abstr.Mil.Bibl., Amer.Bibl.Slavic & E.Eur.Stud., Amer.Hist.& Life, Bus.Ind., Can.Per.Ind., CMI, Hist.Abstr., Int.Lab.Doc., Int.Polit.Sci.Abstr., Mar.Aff.Bibl., Mid.East: Abstr.& Ind., P.A.I.S., SSCI, World Agri.Econ.& Rural Sociol.Abstr.
—BLDSC shelfmark: 4541.450000.
  Description: Devoted to scholarly articles on post 1945 international affairs; often publishes several articles on a single theme. Refereed Serial

327   US   ISSN 0891-4486
JA76   CODEN: ICSOE2
INTERNATIONAL JOURNAL OF POLITICS, CULTURE, AND SOCIETY. 1987. q. $140 (foreign $165). (Florida Atlantic University) Human Sciences Press, Inc. (Subsidiary of: Plenum Publishing Corp.), 233 Spring St., New York, NY 10013. TEL 212-620-8000. FAX 212-463-0742. TELEX 23-421139. Ed.Bd. adv.; bk.rev.; circ. 500. (also avail. in microform from UMI) **Indexed:** Curr.Cont., Lang.& Lang.Behav.Abstr., Soc.Sci.Ind., Soc.Work Res.& Abstr., Sociol.Abstr.
—BLDSC shelfmark: 4542.473000.
  Formerly: International Journal of Politics, Culture, and State.
  Description: Forum for discussion, dialogue and debate on points of tension between state and civil society, between nations and global institutions. Refereed Serial

325.21 340.5   UK   ISSN 0953-8186
K9
INTERNATIONAL JOURNAL OF REFUGEE LAW. 1989. 4/yr. £55($115) Oxford University Press, Oxford Journals, Pinkhill House, Southfield Road, Eynsham, Oxford OX8 1JJ, England. TEL 0965-882283. FAX 0865-882890. TELEX 837330-OXPRES-G. Ed. Guy S. Goodwin-Gill. adv.; bk.rev.; index; circ. 950.
—BLDSC shelfmark: 4542.525600.
  Description: Aims to stimulate research and thinking on refugee law and its development.

327 157.63   UK
INTERNATIONAL JOURNAL ON DRUG POLICY. 1989. 5/yr. £35($60) to individuals; institutions £70($120). 10 Maryland St., Liverpool L1 9BX, England. TEL 051-709-3511. FAX 051-709-4916. Ed. Alan J. Matthews. adv.; bk.rev.; circ. 500.

327   US   ISSN 0742-3640
INTERNATIONAL JOURNAL ON WORLD PEACE. 1984. q. $15 to individuals; institutions $30; students $10. Professors World Peace Academy, University of Toledo, Toledo, OH 43606. Ed. Panos D. Bardis. adv.; bk.rev.; index; circ. 10,000. (back issues avail.) **Indexed:** Curr.Cont., Geo.Abstr., Int.Polit.Sci.Abstr., Key to Econ.Sci., Lang.& Lang.Behav.Abstr., P.A.I.S., Peace Res.Abstr., Psychol.Abstr., S.S.C.I., Soc.Work Res.& Abstr., Soc.Work Res.& Abstr., Sociol.Abstr., Sociol.Educ.Abstr.
—BLDSC shelfmark: 4542.701900.
  Description: All aspects of peace are discussed; theory and practice, qualitative and quantitative, past, present and future. International debate is emphasized.

INTERNATIONAL LAW NEWS. see LAW — International Law

INTERNATIONAL LAW REPORTS. see LAW — International Law

327   US
INTERNATIONAL LEADERSHIP.* 1987. q. free. American Center for International Leadership, 401 E. Pratt St., Ste. 2415, Baltimore, MD 21202-3003. TEL 812-376-3456. FAX 812-378-8608. TELEX 4900009526 ACL UI (TCN-ITT NETWORK). Ed. Tom Henry. circ. 10,000.

INTERNATIONAL LEADS. see LIBRARY AND INFORMATION SCIENCES

341.1   US   ISSN 0020-8183
JX1901
INTERNATIONAL ORGANIZATION. 1947. q. $30 to individuals (foreign $44); institutions $70 (foreign $84); students $20 (foreign $34). (World Peace Foundation) M I T Press, 55 Hayward St., Cambridge, MA 02142. TEL 617-253-2889. FAX 617-258-6779. TELEX 921473. (Editorial addr.: Dept. of Political Science, Stanford University, Stanford, CA 94305-2044) Ed. Stephen D. Krasner. adv.; bk.rev.; bibl.; charts; index; circ. 2,760. (also avail. in microform from MIM,UMI; back issues avail.; reprint service avail. from KTO,UMI) **Indexed:** A.B.C.Pol.Sci., Amer.Hist.& Life, ASSIA, C.L.I., Commun.Abstr., Curr.Cont., Deep Sea Res.& Oceanogr.Abstr., Fut.Surv., Hist.Abstr., HR Rep., INIS Atomind., Int.Bibl.Soc.Sci., Int.Lab.Doc., Int.Polit.Sci.Abstr., J.of Econ.Lit., Key to Econ.Sci., L.R.I., Mid.East: Abstr.& Ind., P.A.I.S., Rural Recreat.Tour.Abstr., SCIMP (1982-), Soc.Sci.Ind., SSCI, World Agri.Econ.& Rural Sociol.Abstr.
—BLDSC shelfmark: 4544.850000.
  Description: Covers political and economic affairs affecting foreign policy and history.

327   CN   ISSN 0381-4874
INTERNATIONAL PERSPECTIVES. 1972. bi-m. $25. Baxter Publishing, 310 Dupont Street, Toronto, Ont. M5R 1V9, Canada. TEL 613-238-2628. FAX 613-234-2452. Ed. Gordon Cullingham. adv.; bk.rev.; bibl.; illus.; circ. 3,000. (also avail. in microform from MIM) **Indexed:** A.B.C.Pol.Sci., Abstr.Mil.Bibl., Amer.Bibl.Slavic & E.Eur.Stud, Amer.Hist.& Life, Can.Per.Ind., CMI, Curr.Cont., Hist.Abstr., Mid.East: Abstr.& Ind., P.A.I.S., Pt.de Rep.
  Incorporates: International Canada (ISSN 0027-0512); **Supersedes:** External Affairs (ISSN 0014-5432)

327   US   ISSN 0738-6508
INTERNATIONAL POLICY REPORT. 1975. 5/yr. $9. Center for International Policy, 1755 Massachusetts Ave., N.W., Ste. 324, Washington, DC 20036. TEL 202-232-3317. FAX 202-232-3440. Ed. Jim Morrell. circ. 1,500. (looseleaf format) **Indexed:** HR Rep.
—BLDSC shelfmark: 4544.957000.
  Description: Reports on US policy towards the Third World and its impact on human rights and human needs.

327   UK   ISSN 0192-5121
JA1.A1
INTERNATIONAL POLITICAL SCIENCE REVIEW/REVUE INTERNATIONALE DE SCIENCE POLITIQUE. Short title: I P S R - R I S P. (Text in English and French) 1980. q. £70. (International Political Science Association) Butterworth - Heinemann Ltd. (Subsidiary of: Reed International PLC), Linacre House, Jordan Hill, Oxford OX2 8DP, England. TEL 0865-310366. FAX 0865-310898. TELEX 83111 BHPOXF G. (Subscr. to: Turpin Transactions Ltd., Distribution Centre, Blackhorse Rd., Letchworth, Herts SG6 1HN, England. TEL 0462-672555) Ed. John Meisel. adv.; abstr.; index. (also avail. in microform from WSH; microform from UMI; back issues avail.) **Indexed:** A.B.C.Pol.Sci., Int.Polit.Sci.Abstr, Mid.East: Abstr.& Ind., Peace Res.Abstr.
—BLDSC shelfmark: 4544.965200.
  Description: For political scientists throughout the world who are interested in the advancement of their discipline and in escaping the parochialism threatening the pursuit of knowledge within the confines of a single culture.

327   II
INTERNATIONAL POST. (Text in English) q. Rs.15. R.N.S. Anil, Ed. & Pub., B-146 East of Kailash, New Delhi 110024, India. adv.; bk.rev.; charts; illus.

327   IS   ISSN 0020-840X
INTERNATIONAL PROBLEMS; society and politics. (Text in English, French, Hebrew) 1963. s-a. IS.35($30) Israel Institute of International Affairs, Israel Graduates Social Sciences & Humanities, 21 Hess St., Tel Aviv 63324, Israel. TEL 03-296482. Ed. Marian Mushkat. adv.; bk.rev.; index; cum.index; circ. 5,000. (tabloid format; also avail. in microform from MIM,UMI; reprint service avail. from UMI) **Indexed:** Abstr.Mil.Bibl., Amer.Hist.& Life, Hist.Abstr., Ind.Heb.Per., Mid.East: Abstr.& Ind., P.A.I.S., Peace Res.Abstr.
—BLDSC shelfmark: 4544.978500.

INTERNATIONAL PUBLIC RELATIONS REVIEW. see ADVERTISING AND PUBLIC RELATIONS

327   UK   ISSN 0047-1178
JX1
INTERNATIONAL RELATIONS. 1954. 3/yr. £20($40) membership (includes Annual Memorial Lecture). David Davies Memorial Institute of International Studies, 2 Chadwick St., London SW1P 2EP, England. Ed. Sheila Harden. adv.; bk.rev.; circ. controlled. **Indexed:** A.B.C.Pol.Sci., Amer.Hist.& Life, Hist.Abstr., Mar.Aff.Bibl., Rural Recreat.Tour.Abstr., World Agri.Econ.& Rural Sociol.Abstr.

327   PL
INTERNATIONAL RELATIONS: STUDIES OF THE P I S M. q. $32. Polski Instytut Spraw Miedzynarodowych, Warecka 1a, 00-950 Warsaw, Poland. (Distr. by: Ars Polona, Krakowskie Przedmiescie 7, 00-068 Warsaw, Poland) Ed. Janusz Symonides. bk.rev.; bibl.; circ. 1,000.

POLITICAL SCIENCE — INTERNATIONAL RELATIONS

327　　　　　　US　　ISSN 0740-669X
D839
INTERNATIONAL REPORT (IRVINE). 1983. 3/yr. $6 to individuals; libraries $15; institutions $50. Box 4882, Irvine, CA 92716. FAX 714-856-8441. Ed. Raul Fernandez. adv.; circ. 500. **Indexed:** HR Rep.
Formerly: Colombia Report.
Description: Analyzes world news.

327　　　　　　US　　ISSN 0162-2889
JX1901
INTERNATIONAL SECURITY. 1976. q. $30 to individuals (foreign $44); institutions $75 (foreign $89); students $20 (foreign $34). (Harvard University, Center for Science and International Affairs) M I T Press, 55 Hayward St., Cambridge, MA 02142. TEL 617-253-2889. FAX 617-258-6779. TELEX 921473. Ed. Steven E. Miller. adv.; circ. 5,530. (also avail. in microform from UMI; back issues avail.; reprint service avail. from UMI) **Indexed:** A.B.C.Pol.Sci., Abstr.Mil.Bibl., Air Un.Lib.Ind., Amer.Bibl.Slavic & E.Eur.Stud., Amer.Hist.& Life, DM& T, Fut.Surv., Hist.Abstr., INIS Atomind., Int.Bibl.Soc.Sci., Int.Polit.Sci.Abstr., Mid.East: Abstr.& Ind., P.A.I.S., Polit.Sci.Abstr., PROMT, Risk Abstr., SSCI.
—BLDSC shelfmark: 4548.895500.
Description: Essays on all aspects of the control and use of force from all political viewpoints. Articles cover contemporary policy issues, probing the historical and theoretical and questions behind them.

INTERNATIONAL SKYLINE. see *COMMUNICATIONS*

INTERNATIONAL SPECTATOR. see *POLITICAL SCIENCE*

327 900　　　　NE
INTERNATIONAL STRAITS OF THE WORLD. 1978. irreg. price varies. Kluwer Academic Publishers, Postbus 17, 3300 AA Dordrecht, Netherlands. TEL 078-334911. (U.S. address: P.O. Box 358, Accord Station, Hingham, MA 02018-0358)

327　　　　　　US　　ISSN 0020-8817
JX18
INTERNATIONAL STUDIES. 1961. q. $36 to individuals; institutions $74. (Jawaharlal Nehru University, School of International Studies, II) Sage Publications, Inc., 2455 Teller Rd., Newbury Park, CA 91320. TEL 805-499-0721. FAX 805-499-0871. (And: Sage Publications Pvt. Ltd., P.O. Box 4215, New Delhi 110 048, India) Ed. Anirudha Gupta. adv.; bibl.; index; circ. 900. **Indexed:** A.B.C.Pol.Sci., Abstr.Mil.Bibl., Amer.Hist.& Life, E.I., Hist.Abstr., Mid.East: Abstr.& Ind., Rural Recreat.Tour.Abstr., World Agri.Econ.& Rural Sociol.Abstr.
—BLDSC shelfmark: 4549.750000.
Formerly: International Studies Newsletter (ISSN 0097-8965)

327　　　　　　US　　ISSN 0094-7768
JX1291
INTERNATIONAL STUDIES NOTES. 1974. q. $20. c/o Bemidji State University, Bemidji, MN 56601. Eds. Joan Wadlow, Leslie Duly. adv.; circ. 3,500. (also avail. in microfilm from UMI) **Indexed:** A.B.C.Pol.Sci., Amer.Hist.& Life, Hist.Abstr.

327　　　　　　US　　ISSN 0020-8833
D839　　　　　　　　　　CODEN: ISTQEN
INTERNATIONAL STUDIES QUARTERLY. 1957. q. $100 (foreign $145). (International Studies Association) Basil Blackwell Inc., 3 Cambridge Center, Cambridge, MA 02142. TEL 617-225-0430. Ed.Bd. adv.; charts; index. (also avail. in microform from UMI; back issues avail.; reprint service avail.) **Indexed:** A.B.C.Pol.Sci., Amer.Bibl.Slavic & E.Eur.Stud, Amer.Hist.& Life, Curr.Cont., Deep Sea Res.& Oceanogr.Abstr., Hist.Abstr., Human Resour.Abstr., Int.Polit.Sci.Abstr., Mid.East: Abstr.& Ind., P.A.I.S., Peace Res.Abstr, PROMT, Risk Abstr., Sage Urb.Stud.Abstr., Soc.Sci.Ind., SSCI, Stud.Wom.Abstr.
—BLDSC shelfmark: 4549.800000.
Formerly: Background.
Description: Presents theoretical and practical papers addressing the various political, economic, social, or cultural forces affecting more than one society and supporting diverse outlooks and practices.
Refereed Serial

327　　　　　　US　　ISSN 0738-9191
INTERNATIONAL TERRORISM NEWSLETTER. 1978. m. Box 22425, Louisville, KY 40222. Ed. Charles Merle Hellebusch. bk.rev.; circ. 1,703. (also avail. in looseleaf format) **Indexed:** Abstr.Mil.Bibl.

327 011　　　　US
INTERNATIONAL THIRD WORLD STUDIES - JOURNAL AND REVIEW. 1989. s-a. $30 to individuals; institutions $55. Oasis Publishing Co., Box 30242, Lincoln, NE 68502-0242. TEL 402-466-9665. Ed. Peter Suzuki. circ. 300. (back issues avail.)
Description: Explores Third World issues within the disciplines of literature, linguistics, education, and political science.

330　　　　　　II
INTERNATIONAL UNDERSTANDING. vol.2, 1966. m. Rs.60($26) Indian Institute of International Understanding, G-36, Connaught Circus, P.O. Box 618, New Delhi 110001, India. (Subscr. to: Central News Agency, 23-90 Connaught Circus, New Delhi, 110 001) Ed. S.S. Bhatia. adv.; bk.rev.; charts; illus.; circ. 25,000.
Supersedes: Economic Review and Report (ISSN 0013-0311)

327　　　　　　GW
INTERNATIONALE POLITIK UND WIRTSCHAFT. irreg., vol.50, 1987. price varies. (Deutsche Gesellschaft fuer Auswaertige Politik) R. Oldenbourg Verlag GmbH, Rosenheimerstr. 145, 8000 Munich 80, Germany.

960 327　　　　GW　　ISSN 0020-9430
DT1
INTERNATIONALES AFRIKAFORUM. 1965. q. DM.118. (Europaeisches Institut fuer Politische, Wirtschaftliche und Soziale Fragen e.V.) Weltforum Verlag, Marienburgerstr. 22, 5000 Cologne 51, Germany. Eds. Hans-Gert Braun, Alois Graf von Waldburg-Zeil. adv.; bk.rev. **Indexed:** Curr.Cont.Africa, Key to Econ.Sci., P.A.I.S.For.Lang.Ind., World Agri.Econ.& Rural Sociol.Abstr.
—BLDSC shelfmark: 4556.760000.

960 327　　　　GW　　ISSN 0020-9449
INTERNATIONALES ASIENFORUM. 1970. q. DM.110. (Europaeisches Institut fuer Politische, Wirtschaftliche und Soziale Fragen e.V.) Weltforum Verlag, Marienburgerstr. 22, 5000 Cologne 51, Germany. Eds. Detlef Kantowsky, Alois Graf von Waldburg-Zeil. adv.; bk.rev. **Indexed:** Amer.Hist.& Life, E.I., Hist.Abstr., Int.Lab.Doc., Key to Econ.Sci., Mid.East: Abstr.& Ind., P.A.I.S.For.Lang.Ind., SSCI.
—BLDSC shelfmark: 4557.003000.

327　　　　　　GW
INTERNATIONALES HANDBUCH - LAENDER AKTUELL. 1936. w. DM.92.10 per quarter. Munzinger-Archiv GmbH, Hans-Zuericher-Weg 7, 7980 Ravensburg, Germany. TEL 0751-31916. FAX 0751-17261. Ed. Dr. Ludwig Munzinger. circ. 1,500.
●Also available online.
Formerly: Internationales Handbuch (ISSN 0020-949X)

327　　　　　　SW　　ISSN 0020-952X
INTERNATIONELLA STUDIER. 1968. irreg. (4/yr.) latest Sep. 1991. SEK 188. Utrikespolitiska Institutet - Swedish Institute of International Affairs, Box 1253, 111 82 Stockholm, Sweden. FAX 8-201049. Ed. Erland Jansson. adv.; bk.rev.; charts; circ. 3,000.

327　　　　　　US
INTERNEWSLETTER AFRIQUE; la seule revue de presse Americaine en Francais sur l'Afrique. (Text in French) 1977. s-m. $598 to individuals; libraries $498. Internews Media Services Inc., 499 National Press Bldg., N.W., Washington, DC 20045. TEL 202-347-4575. FAX 703-734-6956. Ed. Marie-Benoite Allizon. adv. (looseleaf format; back issues avail.)

328　　　　　　SZ　　ISSN 0020-5079
JX1930
INTER-PARLIAMENTARY BULLETIN. (Editions in English, French) 1921. q. 16 SFr. Inter-Parliamentary Union, Place du Petit-Saconnex, 1211 Geneva 19, Switzerland. TEL 022-7344150. FAX 022-7333141. TELEX 414217-IPU-CH. adv.; bk.rev.; circ. 1,950 (French ed.) 1,500 (English ed.) **Indexed:** Mid.East: Abstr.& Ind., P.A.I.S.
—BLDSC shelfmark: 4557.280000.

320　　　　　　SZ
INTER-PARLIAMENTARY UNION. SUMMARY RECORDS OF THE INTER-PARLIAMENTARY CONFERENCES. (Text in English and French) 1897. s-a. 25 SFr. Inter-Parliamentary Union - Union Interparlementaire, Place du Petit Saconnex, B.P. 438, 1211 Geneva 19, Switzerland. TEL 022-7344150. FAX 022-7333141. TELEX 414217-IPU-CH. circ. 800.
Formerly: Inter-Parliamentary Union. Conference Proceedings (ISSN 0074-1051)

INTRIGUE. see *CRIMINOLOGY AND LAW ENFORCEMENT — Security*

327 338.91　　　IE　　ISSN 0332-1460
DA964.A2
IRISH STUDIES IN INTERNATIONAL AFFAIRS. 1979. a. I£6 to individuals; institutions I£10. Royal Irish Academy, 19 Dawson St., Dublin 2, Ireland. TEL 01-762570. FAX 01-762346. Ed. J. Bradley. (back issues avail.)
—BLDSC shelfmark: 4574.830000.

ISRAEL HORIZONS; the socialist Zionist journal. see *POLITICAL SCIENCE*

ISRAEL UND PALAESTINA; Zeitschrift fuer Dialog. see *POLITICAL SCIENCE*

327　　　　　　DK　　ISSN 0108-3783
ISRAELSKE AMBASSADE. INFORMATION. 1980. irreg. free. Israelske Ambassade, Trondhjems Plads 4, 2100 Copenhagen OE, Denmark.

327　　　　　　CH　　ISSN 1013-2511
ISSUES & STUDIES. (Text in English) 1964. m. $44 to individuals, institutions $64. Institute of International Relations, 64 Wan Shou Rd., Mucha, Taiwan, Republic of China. Ed.Bd. adv.; stat.; index. (also avail. in microform from UMI; reprint service avail. from ISI, UMI) **Indexed:** A.B.C.Pol.Sci., Amer.Hist.& Life, Curr.Cont., Geo.Abstr., Hist.Abstr., Int.Polit.Sci.Abstr., Risk Abstr., Rural Devel.Abstr., SSCI, World Agri.Econ.& Rural Sociol.Abstr.
—BLDSC shelfmark: 4584.120000.
Description: Highlights world affairs and communist problems.

327　　　　　　SI
ISSUES IN SOUTHEAST ASIAN SECURITY. 1984. irreg., latest no.13, 1991. price varies. Institute of Southeast Asian Studies, Heng Mui Keng Terrace, Pasir Panjang, Singapore 0511, Singapore. TEL 7780955. FAX 7781735. TELEX RS 37068 ISEAS.
Description: International relations and strategic studies pertaining to the Asian-Pacific region.

327 382 338.91　　　IT
ITALIA AFRICA MEDIO ORIENTE; mensuel d'informations economiques, techniques et commerciales. (Text in French, Italian) m. L.100000 (foreign L.130000). Editore B I E P s.r.l. (Business International Economic Promotion), Via Chiossetto 5, 20122 Milan, Italy. Ed. Ferdinando Capecchi. adv.; charts; illus.
Description: Covers Italian-African relations. Includes articles on Italians working in Africa, banking in Africa and various Italian-African organizations.

327　　　　　　US　　ISSN 0075-2142
JACOB BLAUSTEIN LECTURES IN INTERNATIONAL AFFAIRS. 1967. irreg., no.2, 1971. Columbia University Press, 562 W. 113th St., New York, NY 10025. TEL 212-678-6777.

327 952 970　　　US　　ISSN 0021-4299
JAPAN-AMERICA SOCIETY OF WASHINGTON. BULLETIN. 1957. 10/yr. $35. Japan-America Society of Washington Inc., 606 18th St., N.W., Washington, DC 20006. TEL 202-289-8290. FAX 202-789-8265. Ed. Patricia R. Kearns. adv.; bk.rev.; illus.; circ. 3,000.

327　　　　　　UK　　ISSN 0960-1473
▼**JAPAN DIGEST.** 1990. q. Japan Library Ltd., Knoll House, 35 The Crescent, Sandgate Folkestone, Kent CT20 3EE, England. TEL 0303-220277. FAX 0303-43087. Ed. Paul Norbury.
—BLDSC shelfmark: 4648.233000.

POLITICAL SCIENCE — INTERNATIONAL RELATIONS

327   UK   ISSN 0955-5803
JAPAN FORUM. 1989. 2/yr. £46($90) Oxford University Press, Oxford Journals, Pinkhill House, Southfield Road, Eynsham, Oxford OX8 1JJ, England. TEL 0865-882283. FAX 0865-882890. TELEX 837330 OXPRES G. Ed. John Chapman.
—BLDSC shelfmark: 4648.271000.
Description: Provides scholarly articles on Japanese culture, both historical and contemporary.

327 952 942   UK
JAPAN SOCIETY. REVIEW. 1950. 2/yr. £10 (foreign £12). Japan Society, Rm. 331, 162-168 Regent St., London W1R 5TB, England. Ed. R. Douglas. adv.; bk.rev.; circ. 1,500. **Indexed:** Amer.Hist.& Life, Hist.Abstr.
Formerly (until 1985): Japan Society of London. Bulletin (ISSN 0021-4701)

327   US   ISSN 0363-2865
JX18
JERUSALEM JOURNAL OF INTERNATIONAL RELATIONS. (Text and summaries in English) 1975. q. $26 to individuals (foreign $33); institutions $44 (foreign $50). (Hebrew University of Jerusalem, Leonard Davis Institute of International Relations, Jerusalem, IS) Johns Hopkins University Press, Journals Publishing Division, 701 W. 40th St., Ste. 275, Baltimore, MD 21211. TEL 410-516-6987. FAX 410-516-6998. Ed. Gabriel Sheffer. adv.; bk.rev.; index; circ. 409. (back issues avail.) **Indexed:** A.B.C.Pol.Sci., Amer.Hist.& Life, Curr.Cont.M.E., Hist.Abstr., Mid.East: Abstr.& Ind., Peace Res.Abstr.
—BLDSC shelfmark: 4667.512000.
Description: Examines the politics of small and medium-sized countries, reflecting primarily on the economic aspects of politics, problems of war and peace, the global significance of the Middle East conflict, and Israel's foreign policy.

960   FR   ISSN 0021-6089
AP27
JEUNE AFRIQUE; le devoir d'informer - la liberte d'ecrire. (Includes supplements) 1960. w. 16 F. per no. J A Press, 57 bis rue D'Auteuil, 75016 Paris, France. TEL 44-30-19-60. FAX 45-20-09-69. Ed. Bechir Ben Yahmed. adv.; bk.rev.; charts; illus.; circ. 100,000. (also avail. in microfilm; reprint service avail. from KTO) **Indexed:** Curr.Cont.Africa, Curr.Cont.M.E., Key to Econ.Sci., Pt.de Rep. (1991-).
—BLDSC shelfmark: 4668.220000.
Formerly: J A.
Description: Features articles about events taking place in Africa and important figures of African descent.

327   US   ISSN 0449-0754
E740.J6
JOHN BIRCH SOCIETY. BULLETIN. 1959. m. $20. John Birch Society, Box 8040, Appleton, WI 54913. FAX 414-749-3785. Ed. Gary Benoit. adv.; bk.rev.; circ. 30,000. (back issues avail.)

327 900   SA   ISSN 0258-2422
JOURNAL FOR CONTEMPORARY HISTORY/JOERNAAL VIR EIETYDSE GESKIEDENIS. 2/yr. $16. University of the Orange Free State, Institute for Contemporary History - Universiteit van die Oranje-Vrystaat, Instituut vir Eietydse Geskiedenis, P.O. Box 2320, Bloemfontein 9300, South Africa. FAX 051-473416. **Indexed:** Ind.S.A.Per.
—BLDSC shelfmark: 4965.229000.
Formerly: Journal for Contemporary History and International Relations.

327   US   ISSN 0275-3588
DS36
JOURNAL OF ARAB AFFAIRS. 1981. s-a. $25. M E R G Analytica, 2611 N. Fresno St., Fresno, CA 93703-1897. FAX 209-226-2789. (Subscr. to: 7872 Fairview Rd., Boulder, CO 80303) Ed. Tawfic E. Farah. adv.; circ. 1,300. (also avail. in microform from UMI) **Indexed:** A.B.C.Pol.Sci., Curr.Cont., P.A.I.S., SSCI.
—BLDSC shelfmark: 4947.162000.

JOURNAL OF ASIAN AND AFRICAN AFFAIRS. see ORIENTAL STUDIES

320 330   US   ISSN 0886-5655
JOURNAL OF BORDERLAND STUDIES. 1986. 2/yr. $25 membership; libraries $20. Association for Borderlands Scholars, Department of Economics, Box 30001, New Mexico State University, Las Cruces, NM 88003. TEL 505-646-3113. FAX 505-646-1915. (Co-sponsor: New Mexico State University) Eds. Jim Peach, Anthony Popp. cum.index 1986-1990; circ. 425. (back issues avail.)
Description: Multidisciplinary journal focusing on international borders.

942   UK   ISSN 0306-3631
JN248
JOURNAL OF COMMONWEALTH & COMPARATIVE POLITICS. 1973. 3/yr. £30($45) to individuals; institutions £70($115). Frank Cass & Co. Ltd., Gainsborough House, 11 Gainsborough Rd., London E11 1RS, England. TEL 081-530-4226. FAX 081-530-7795. Eds. Arnold Hughes, David Potter. adv.; bk.rev.; index. (also avail. in microfilm from UMI; back issues avail.; reprint service avail. from SWZ) **Indexed:** A.B.C.Pol.Sci., Amer.Hist.& Life, Curr.Cont., Hist.Abstr., Lang.& Lang.Behav.Abstr., Mid.East: Abstr.& Ind., P.A.I.S., Rural Devel.Abstr., Rural Recreat.Tour.Abstr., So.Pac.Per.Ind., SSCI, World Agri.Econ.& Rural Sociol.Abstr.
—BLDSC shelfmark: 4961.250000.
Formerly: Journal of Commonwealth Political Studies (ISSN 0021-9908)
Description: Features articles on the comparative politics of Commonwealth countries.

JOURNAL OF CONFLICT RESOLUTION; research on war and peace between and within nations. see SOCIAL SCIENCES: COMPREHENSIVE WORKS

327   UK
JOURNAL OF EUROPEAN SOCIAL POLICY. q. £64($108) to institutions; individuals £32($54). Longman Group UK Ltd., Westgate House, The High, Harlow, Essex CM20 1YR, England. TEL 0279-442601. FAX 0279-444501. (Subscr. to: Longman Group UK, Subscr. Dept., Fourth Ave., Harlow, Essex, CM19 5AA, England) Ed. Graham Room.
Description: Provides a source of independent information and analysis covering a broad range of social policy issues across Europe.

327   US
JOURNAL OF INTELLIGENCE STUDIES. 1986. q. $50 membership. Center for Intelligence Studies, 301 S. Columbus St., Alexandria, VA 22314. TEL 703-684-0625. FAX 703-836-8429. Ed. K. Leigh Dyer. circ. 25,000. (tabloid format; back issues avail.)
Formerly (until 1990): Security and Intelligence Foundation. Special Report.
Description: Addresses important current issues related to the U.S. intelligence, counterintelligence services, and U.S. national security.

327   US   ISSN 0022-1937
F1401
JOURNAL OF INTERAMERICAN STUDIES AND WORLD AFFAIRS. 1959. q. $34 to individuals (foreign $44); institutions $68 (foreign $88); students $17. University of Miami, North - South Center Publications Studies, c/o Jaime Suchlicki, Ed., Box 248123, Coral Gables, FL 33124-3010. TEL 305-284-6869. FAX 305-284-6370. bk.rev.; charts; index; circ. 305-284-6,370. (also avail. in microfilm from UMI; back issues avail.; reprint service avail. from SWZ,UMI) **Indexed:** A.B.C.Pol.Sci., Abstr.Mil.Bibl., Amer.Bibl.Slavic & E.Eur.Stud, Amer.Hist.& Life, CERDIC, Curr.Cont., Hisp.Amer.Per.Ind., Hist.Abstr., Hum.Ind., Mid.East: Abstr.& Ind., P.A.I.S., Soc.Sci.Ind., SSCI.

327   US   ISSN 0022-197X
JX1
JOURNAL OF INTERNATIONAL AFFAIRS. 1947. s-a. $14 to individuals (foreign $18); institutions $28 (foreign $32). Columbia University, Journal of International Affairs, Box 4, International Affairs Bldg., New York, NY 10027. TEL 212-854-4775. FAX 212-864-4847. Ed. Matthew Tiedemann. adv.; bk.rev.; index every 5 yrs; circ. 4,000. (also avail. in microform from UMI; reprint service avail. from UMI) **Indexed:** A.B.C.Pol.Sci., Amer.Bibl.Slavic & E.Eur.Stud, Amer.Hist.& Life, C.L.I., Hist.Abstr., Hum.Ind., Int.Polit.Sci.Abstr., L.R.I., Mid.East: Abstr.& Ind., P.A.I.S., Soc.Sci.Ind.
—BLDSC shelfmark: 5007.550000.
Description: Scholarly analysis of international affairs issues.

300   KO
JOURNAL OF INTERNATIONAL AFFAIRS. (Text in Korean) 1970. m. 6000 Won($12) Kukje Munje-Sa, 95 Yeunji-Dong, Chongro-ku, Seoul, S. Korea. Ed. Ho Jik Hwang. adv.; bk.rev.; index. **Indexed:** A.B.C.Pol.Sci., Abstr.Mil.Bibl., L.R.I., Mar.Aff.Bibl., Soc.Sci.Ind, SSCI.

327   JA   ISSN 0910-5476
JOURNAL OF INTERNATIONAL STUDIES. 1978. 2/yr. 1456 Yen per no. Sophia University, Institute of International Relations - Jochi Daigaku, 7-1 Kioi-cho, Chiyoda-ku, Tokyo 102, Japan. TEL 03-3238-3561. FAX 03-3238-3885. bk.rev.; circ. 500.
Description: Offers a unique perspective on world-wide subjects to specialists in international relations and international comparative studies from a Japanese perspective.

341.1   UK   ISSN 0022-3433
AS9
JOURNAL OF PEACE RESEARCH; an interdisciplinary and international quarterly of scholarly work in peace research. 1964. q. £31($45) to individuals; institutions £72($116). (International Peace Research Association) Sage Publications Ltd., 6 Bonhill St., London EC2A 4PU, England. TEL 071-374-0645. FAX 071-374-8741. Eds. Nils Petter Gleditsch, I. Steintonnesson. adv.: color page £190; trim 200 x 130; adv. contact: Bernie Folan. bk.rev.; charts; illus.; stat.; index. (also avail. in microform from UMI) **Indexed:** A.B.C.Pol.Sci., Amer.Hist.& Life, Curr.Cont., Fut.Surv., Hist.Abstr., Int.Lab.Doc., Lang.& Lang.Behav.Abstr., Mid.East: Abstr.& Ind., P.A.I.S., Peace Res.Abstr, Polit.Sci.Abstr., Risk Abstr., Sage Pub.Admin.Abstr., Soc.Sci.Ind., Soc.Work.Res.Abstr., Sociol.Abstr., SSCI.
—BLDSC shelfmark: 5030.100000.
Description: Provides a global focus on conflict and peacemaking. Encourages a wide conception of peace but focuses on the causes of violence and conflict resolution.

JOURNAL OF THIRD WORLD STUDIES. see HISTORY

JUS GENTIUM; diritto delle relazioni internazionali. see LAW — International Law

JUSTPEACE. see RELIGIONS AND THEOLOGY

327   AT   ISSN 0311-0419
KABAR. 1969. 10/yr. Aus.$12. Australia Indonesia Association of New South Wales, G.P.O. Box 802, Sydney, N.S.W. 2001, Australia. Ed. Megan Lavender. adv.; bk.rev.; circ. 150.
Formerly: Australia Indonesia Association of New South Wales. Bulletin.

338   US
KALEIDOSCOPE: CURRENT WORLD DATA. 1956. w. A B C-Clio, 130 Cremona, Box 1911, Santa Barbara, CA 93116-1911. TEL 805-968-1911. FAX 805-685-9685. Ed. Timothy O'Donnell. stat.; index. (cards)
●Also available online. Vendor(s): DIALOG, Mead Data Central.
Former titles: Deadline Data on World Affairs (ISSN 0011-5061); D M S I Market Intelligence Reports.

341.1   AU   ISSN 0022-8230
KAMPF DEM KRIEG; Blaetter fuer internationale Verstaendigung. 1967. 4/yr. S.30.($3) Suttner-Gesellschaft, Oesterreichische Friedensgesellschaft, Landstr. Hauptstr. 14-5, A-1030 Vienna, Austria. circ. 1,000.

327 614.7 301   NE   ISSN 0925-5893
KAN ANDERS. vol. 4, 1981. 4/yr. fl.5.50 per no. Kan Anders, Werkgemeenschap voor Pacifisme, Ekologie en Socialisme, Vlamingstraat 82, 2611 LA Delft, Netherlands. TEL 015-121694. Ed.Bd. adv.; bk.rev.; illus.; circ. 900.

327 956.94   LE
KATIB AL-FILASTINI. (Text in Arabic) 1978. irreg. £L150. Ittihad al-Amm lil-Kuttab wa-al-Sahafiyin al-Filastiniyin, Box 3075, Beirut, Lebanon.

327 330.9   US
KEESING'S SPECIAL REPORTS. 1987. irreg. $45. St. James Press, 845 Penobscot Bldg., 645 Griswold St., Detroit, MI 48226-4232. TEL 800-345-0392.
Description: Selects major areas of topical concern and provides factual accounts of recent events as well as analytical essays on issues facing these areas.

POLITICAL SCIENCE — INTERNATIONAL RELATIONS

KERK EN VREDE. see *RELIGIONS AND THEOLOGY*

327   JA   ISSN 0285-7928
KOKUSAI KYORYOKU/INTERNATIONAL COOPERATION.
(Text in Japanese) 1953. m. 400 Yen per no. Japan International Cooperation Agency, Box 216, Mitsui Bldg., Shinjuku-ku, Tokyo 163, Japan. Ed. Akira Sugino. bk.rev.; circ. 17,000.
Continues: Kaigai Gijutsu Kyoryoku.

KOLEINU. see *RELIGIONS AND THEOLOGY — Judaic*

327   DK   ISSN 0105-0982
KONTAKT (COPENHAGEN, 1948). 1949. 8/yr. DKK 205($33) Mellemfolkeligt Samvirke, Borgergade 14, 1300 Copenhagen K, Denmark. TEL 33-326244. FAX 33-156243. Ed. Arne Skadhede. circ. 7,000.
Description: Third World magazine which presents an introduction to development questions.

327   KO
KOREA & WORLD AFFAIRS. (Text in English) 1977. q. $12. Research Center for Peace and Unification, 541, 5-ka, Namdaemun-no, Chung-ku, Seoul, S. Korea. TEL 777-2628. Ed. Chang Dong-Hoon. bk.rev. Indexed: Amer.Hist.& Life, Hist.Abstr., P.A.I.S., Sage Pub.Admin.Abstr.

327   DK   ISSN 0108-8467
KOREA BULLETIN.* (Text in Danish) 1983. 4/yr. free. Venskabsforeningen Danmark Den Demokratiske Folkerepublik Korea, Noerre Soegade 31B, DK-1370 Copenhagen K, Denmark. TEL 45-1-129553. FAX 01-936011. Ed. Gert Poder. bk.rev.; circ. 1,000.
Formerly: Ny Korea (ISSN 0106-1356)
Description: Articles, news and essays concerning the economical, social, political and cultural development on the Korean peninsula (North and South) with special regard to unification.

327 382   HK   ISSN 1016-2658
▼**THE KOREA LETTER.** (Text in English) 1991. m. $495. N & N International (Hong Kong) Ltd., P.O. Box 54332, North Point Post Office, Hong Kong. FAX 852-856-5648. Ed. R.B. Cunningham.

KOREA UPDATE. see *POLITICAL SCIENCE — Civil Rights*

327   KO
KOREAN JOURNAL OF INTERNATIONAL RELATIONS. 1963. irreg. Korean Association of International Relations, c/o Graduate School of Public Administration, Seoul National University, 119 Tongsung-Dong, Chongno-Ku, Seoul, S. Korea.

327   US   ISSN 0163-0229
DS922
KOREAN REVIEW. 1978. bi-m. $10 to individuals; institutions $15. Korean Review, Box 32, Knickerbocker Sta., New York, NY 10002. Ed. S.J. Noumoff.

951.9   SW   ISSN 0023-4079
KOREANSK JOURNAL. (Text in Swedish; summaries in English) 1950. irreg. (4-6/yr.). SEK 25($5) Swedish-Korean Society, Box 3259, S-103 65 Stockholm 3, Sweden. Eds. Aake J. Ek, Lennart V. Toernqvist. adv.; bk.rev.; abstr.; art rev.; film rev.; illus.; play rev.; stat.; tr.lit.; circ. 4,500.

327   HU   ISSN 0133-0616
KULPOLITIKA/FOREIGN AFFAIRS. (Text in Hungarian; summaries in English and Russian) 1974. q. $23.50. (Magyar Kulugyi Intezet) Lapkiado Vallalat, Lenin korut 9-11, 1073 Budapest 7, Hungary. TEL 222-408. (Subscr. to: Kultura, Box 149, H-1389 Budapest, Hungary) Ed. Gyula Bognar. bk.rev.; bibl.

947 327   RU   ISSN 0023-5199
KUL'TURA I ZHIZN/CULTURE AND LIFE. (Editions in English, French, German, Russian, Spanish) 1957. m. $4.50. (Soyuz Sovetskikh Obshchestv Druzhby i Kul'turnoi Svyazi s Zarubezhnymi Stranami) Izdatel'stvo Sovetskaya Rossiya, Proezd Sapunova 13-15, Moscow K-12, Russia. Ed. B.S. Rzhanov. bk.rev.; circ. 100,000. (also avail. in microform from MIM) Indexed: Mid.East: Abstr.& Ind.

KULTUUR JA ELU/CULTURE AND LIFE. see *ETHNIC INTERESTS*

327 338.91   CN   ISSN 0316-3393
L A W G LETTER. 1967. irreg. Can.$6 per no. Latin American Working Group, Box 2207, Sta. P, Toronto, Ont. M5S 2T2, Canada. TEL 416-533-4221. FAX 416-533-4579. Ed.Bd. bk.rev.; illus.; circ. 7,000. Indexed: HR Rep. —BLDSC shelfmark: 5161.476000.
Description: Focuses on Canada'a trade, aid and investment links to South and Central America.

327   US
LACSA'S WORLD. (Text in English, Spanish) 1985. bi-m. $25. E.R. Publishing, Co., 1911 N.W. 114th Avenue, Pembroke Lakes, FL 33026. TEL 305-431-4661. FAX 305-431-4661. Ed. Manoa R. Ppen. circ. 20,000.

327   GW
LAGEBERICHT AUS AUSTRALIEN. 1976. m. free. Australian Embassy, Public Affairs Section, Godesberger Allee 107, 5300 Bonn 2, Germany. TEL 0228-8130169. FAX 0228-376268. Eds. Peter Woodforde, Guenter Schlothauer. circ. 1,000.
Description: News about Australia and its affairs in German.

327   UK   ISSN 0963-6633
▼**LAISSEZ - FAIRE**; a quarterly journal of European free market thought. 1991. q. £15($30) International Freedom Foundation, Chesham House, Regent St., Ste. 500, London W1R 5FA, England. TEL 071-729-5664. Ed. Andrew Hubback. adv.; bk.rev. (back issues avail.)
—BLDSC shelfmark: 5143.792000.
Description: Features articles from prominent European politicians, economists, academics and specialists.

327   AU
LATEINAMERIKA ANDERS; Report. 1976. m. S.100. Informationsgruppe Lateinamerika, Muenzwardeingasse 2, A-1060 Vienna, Austria. Ed. Werner Hoertner. adv.; bk.rev.; circ. 1,500. (back issues avail.)
Description: News and background information on Latin America.

LATEINAMERIKA NACHRICHTEN. see *BUSINESS AND ECONOMICS — International Development And Assistance*

327   US   ISSN 0736-4148
LATIN AMERICA AND CARIBBEAN CONTEMPORARY RECORD. 1981. a. $380. Holmes & Meier Publishers, Inc., 30 Irving Pl., New York, NY 10003. TEL 212-254-4100. FAX 212-254-4104. (U.K. addr.: Book Representation & Distribution, Ltd., P.O. Box 17, Canvey Island, Essex SS8 8HZ, England. TEL 0268-696280) Eds. James Malloy, Eduardo Gamarra. adv.; bk.rev.; bibl.; charts; illus.; stat.; index. (back issues avail.)
Description: Comprehensive analysis of events and trends by scholars, journalists and area experts.

327   US   ISSN 0738-601X
LATIN AMERICA UPDATE. 1975. q. $18 to individuals; institutions $30; foreign $20. Washington Office on Latin America, 110 Maryland Ave., N.E., Ste. 404, Washington, DC 20002. TEL 202-544-8045. FAX 202-546-5288. Ed. Rachel Neild. charts; illus.; index, cum.index; circ. 2,000. (looseleaf format; back issues avail.)

LATIN AMERICAN TIMES. see *BUSINESS AND ECONOMICS — International Commerce*

327   US
▼**LATINO STUDIES JOURNAL.** 1990. 3/yr. $30. Center for Latino Research, DePaul University, 2323 N. Seminary, Chicago, IL 60614. Ed. Felix Padilla.

LAWYER'S COMMITTEE ON NUCLEAR POLICY NEWSLETTER. see *LAW*

LEADERS. see *BUSINESS AND ECONOMICS — International Commerce*

327   UK
LEAGUE SENTINEL. 1989. bi-m. £4 (foreign £5). (League of St. George) League Enterprises, 27 Old Gloucester St., London WC1N 3XX, England. Ed. E. Shepherd. circ. 500. (looseleaf format; back issues avail.)
Description: British and European nationalist political newsletter combining fascist and national socialist ideas.

327   US   ISSN 1043-5913
DS80.A2
LEBANON NEWS (ARABIC EDITION). 1981. w. $50. Lebanese Information and Research Center, 1730 M St., N.W., Ste. 807, Washington, DC 20036. TEL 202-785-6666. FAX 202-785-6628. TELEX 64427-LEBANON WSH. Ed. Robert Farah. bk.rev.; circ. 6,000.
Description: Political publication reporting events and their impact on Lebanese political and daily life.

327   US   ISSN 0742-9665
LEBANON NEWS (ENGLISH EDITION). 1978. m. $30. Lebanese Information and Research Center, 1730 M St., N.W., Ste. 807, Washington, DC 20036. TEL 202-785-6666. FAX 202-785-6628. TELEX 64427-LEBANON WSH. Ed. Joseph G. Bou-Saada. circ. 10,000.
Description: Political articles, editorials and a daily progress report about events and their effect on Lebanese daily life.

327 956   LE
▼**LEBANON REPORT.** 1990. m. $37.50 to individuals; institutions $75. Lebanese Center for Policy Studies, Tayyar Bldg., Mkalles, Sin al-Fil, Beirut, Lebanon. TEL 01-490-561. FAX 01-490375. TELEX 40543 LE. (Subscr. outside Lebanon: Box 53365, Washington, DC 20009 USA. TEL 202-232-8350) Ed. Paul E. Salem. (back issues avail.)
Description: Analyzes political, diplomatic, military and economic trends in Lebanon, and developments in the Middle East affecting the Lebanese situation.

LEONARD HORWIN COLLECTION. see *ETHNIC INTERESTS*

327   LO   ISSN 0460-2099
LESOTHO. MINISTRY OF FOREIGN AFFAIRS. DIPLOMATIC AND CONSULAR LIST. 1976. a. $1. Ministry of Foreign Affairs, Maseru, Lesotho. circ. 500.

320   FR
LETTRE DU CONTINENT. 1985. 23/yr. 2900 F.($537) Indigo Publications, 10, rue du Sentier, 75002 Paris, France. TEL 45-08-14-80. FAX 45-08-59-83. TELEX LOI 215405F. Dir. Antoine Glaser.

327 956 945   IT   ISSN 0024-1504
DS63.2.I8
LEVANTE. (Text in Arabic and Italian) 1953. q. L.35000 (foreign L.55000). Centro per le Relazioni Italo-Arabe, Via Caroncini 19, 00197 Rome, Italy. TEL 06-877291. Ed. Antonio de Bonis. adv.; bk.rev.; bibl.; charts; illus.; stat.; cum.index: 1953-1968.
Description: Includes articles written on Italian-Arab relations, with emphasis on Arab culture.

327   CC
LIANHEGUO JISHI/UNITED NATIONS CHRONICLE. (Text in Chinese) q. Zhongguo Duiwai Fanyi Chuban Gongsi, No. 4, Taipingqiao Dajie, Beijing 100810, People's Republic of China. TEL 662134. Ed. Zheng Yuzhi.

LIBERATION. see *POLITICAL SCIENCE — Civil Rights*

327.666   LB   ISSN 0300-2241
JX1122
LIBERIA. DEPARTMENT OF STATE. NEWSLETTER.* 1974. w. free. Department of State, Monrovia, Liberia. circ. 500.

354   LB
LIBERIA. MINISTRY OF FOREIGN AFFAIRS. ANNUAL REPORT.* a. Ministry of Foreign Affairs, Monrovia, Liberia.

327   GW   ISSN 0341-9762
LIBERTAS; European review. (Text in English and German) 1976. q. DM.40. Libertas Verlag, Hintere Gasse 35-1, 7032 Sindelfingen, Germany. TEL 07031-81855. FAX 07031-83693. TELEX 7265320-HJZD. Eds. Ladislaus Barlay, Hans-Juergen Zahorka. adv.; bk.rev.; circ. 1,400. Indexed: CERDIC, Sociol.Abstr.
Description: Quarterly on European and international politics, economics, philosophy, social science and legal issues in favor of European integration and Atlantic alliance.

LIBERTY AT BAY; issues impacting on freedom in our time. see *BUSINESS AND ECONOMICS — Economic Situation And Conditions*

| 327 | DK | ISSN 0108-3236 |

LIBYEN BULLETIN. 1982. 3/yr. DKK 30. Dansk Libysk Arabisk Venskabsforening, Vermundsgade 16-st. tv., 2100 Copenhagen OE, Denmark. illus.

| 956 | US | ISSN 0024-4007 |
| DS119.7 | | |

LINK (NEW YORK). 1967. bi-m. $25. Americans for Middle East Understanding, Inc., 475 Riverside Dr., Rm. 241, New York, NY 10115. TEL 212-870-2336. FAX 212-870-2050. Ed. J. Mahoney. bk.rev.; bk.rev.; abstr.; bibl.; illus.; circ. 50,000. Indexed: High.Educ.Curr.Aware.Bull., HR Rep.

| 327 350 | NE | ISSN 0927-202X |

▼**LOKAAL & MONDIAL - VAKMATIG.** 1992. 3/yr. fl.35. V N G Uitgeverij, P.O. Box 30435, 2500 GK The Hague, Netherlands. TEL 070-3738888. FAX 070-3651826. Eds. P. Knip, E.J. Hertogs. adv.; bk.rev.; circ. 1,000. (back issues avail.)
  Description: For specialists in the field of international cooperation and development assistance.

LONDON DEFENCE STUDIES. see *MILITARY*

LUCHA - STRUGGLE; a journal of Christian reflection on struggles for liberation. see *RELIGIONS AND THEOLOGY — Roman Catholic*

| 327 | RM | |

LUMEA. (Text in English, French, German, Rumanian, Russian, Spanish) 1963. w. 104 lei($18) (Uniunea Ziaristilor din Republica Socialista Romania) Agerpres the Romanian News Agency, Piata Presei Libere 1, 71341 Bucharest, Rumania. TEL 185081. (Subscr. to: ILEXIM, P.O. Box 136-137, 13 Decembrie St., No. 3, 11226 Bucharest, Rumania) Ed. Darie Novaceanu. circ. 110,000.

| 327 | PH | |

M F A REVIEW.* 1974. m. (Ministry of Foreign Affairs) Office of Press and Public Affairs, Dept. of Foreign Affairs, PICC Bldg., Agrifina Circle, Manila, Philippines.

| 329 | DK | ISSN 0900-5072 |

M S BIBLIOTEKSNYT. 1968. 12/yr. DKK 195 to individuals; institutions DKK 380. Mellemfolkeligt Samvirke - Danish Association for International Co-operation, Borgergade 14, 1300 Copenhagen K, Denmark. TEL 33-32-62-44. bk.rev.; circ. 600.
  Description: Registers and annotates 1,800 books and 3,000 articles on Third World affairs.

| 327 | FR | ISSN 1150-4447 |

▼**MAGHREB CONFIDENTIEL.** 1990. w. (46/yr.). 2500 F.($440) Indigo Publications, 10 rue du Sentier, 75002 Paris, France. TEL 33-1-45-08-14-80. FAX 33-1-45-08-59-83. Ed. Antoine Glaser. circ. 1,000. (back issues avail.)
  Description: Insight into the politics and economy of North African countries.

| 327 | HU | ISSN 0541-9220 |
| DB956 | | |

MAGYAR KULPOLITIKAI EVKONYV. 1968. a. $7.20. Magyar Kulugyminiszterium, Doumentacios Foosztaly, Hungary. (Dist. by: Kultura, I. Fo utca 32, 1011 Budapest, Hungary)

| 327 | IT | |

MANUALI DI POLITICA INTERNAZIONALE. irreg. price varies. Istituto per gli Studi di Politica Internazionale (I S P I), Via Clerici, 5, 20121 Milan, Italy.

| 327 | IS | |

MARJORIE MAYROCK CENTER FOR SOVIET AND EAST EUROPEAN RESEARCH. OCCASIONAL PAPERS. (Text in English) irreg. price varies. Hebrew University, Marjorie Mayrock Center for Soviet and East European Research, c/o Faculty of Social Sciences, Mount Scopus, Jerusalem 91905, Israel. TEL 02-883180. FAX 02-322545. TELEX 26458.

MASADA. see *ETHNIC INTERESTS*

| 327 | GW | |

MATERIALIEN ZUM INTERNATIONALEN KULTURAUSTAUSCH/STUDIES IN INTERNATIONAL CULTURAL RELATIONS. 1972. irreg. Institut fuer Auslandsbeziehungen, Charlottenplatz 17, 7000 Stuttgart 1, Germany. TEL 0711-542138. (back issues avail.)

MAURITIUS DIRECTORY OF THE DIPLOMATIC CORPS. see *BUSINESS AND ECONOMICS — Trade And Industrial Directories*

MEDIAGUIDE; a critical review of the news media's recent coverage of the world political economy. see *BUSINESS AND ECONOMICS — Economic Situation And Conditions*

| 327 | GW | ISSN 0176-5116 |

MEDIATUS; Zeitschrift fuer handlungsrientierte Friedensforschung. 1981. m. DM.48. Forschungsinstitut fuer Friedenspolitik, Lohgasse 3, Postfach, 8120 Weilheim, Germany. TEL 0811-4586. FAX 0811-2080. adv.; bk.rev.; circ. 4,000. (back issues avail.)
  Description: Information on current research results, developments and activities relevant to questions of peace research.

| 327 | US | ISSN 1047-4552 |
| D839 | | |

MEDITERRANEAN QUARTERLY; a journal of global issues. 1989. q. $24 to individuals; institutions $44. Duke University Press, 6697 College Station, Durham, NC 27708. TEL 919-684-2173. FAX 919-684-8644. Ed. Nikolaos A. Stavrou.
  —BLDSC shelfmark: 5534.743000.
  Refereed Serial

| 327 | YU | ISSN 0025-8555 |
| D839 | | |

MEDJUNARODNI PROBLEMI. (Text in Serbo-Croatian; summaries in English and Russian) 1959. q. 520 din. Institut za Medjunarodnu Politiku i Privredu - Institute of International Politics and Economics, Makedonska 25, P.O. Box 750, Belgrade, Yugoslavia. Ed. Brana Markovic. Indexed: Amer.Hist.& Life, Hist.Abstr.

| 327 | DK | |

MELLEMOEST INFORMATION. MAANEDSOVERSIGT. 1984. m. DKK 915. Odense Universitet, Mellemoest Information, Campusvej 55, 5230 Odense M, Denmark. FAX 09-158928. TELEX 59918. Ed. Dernille Bramming.
  Former titles: Arabisk Verden. Maanedsoversigt (ISSN 0901-1374) & Odense Universitet. Arabisk Informationscenter. Nyhedsbrev (ISSN 0109-582X)

MERIDIAN; development news for youth. see *BUSINESS AND ECONOMICS — International Development And Assistance*

MEXICO UPDATE. see *BUSINESS AND ECONOMICS — Chamber Of Commerce Publications*

| 327 330 | CS | |

MEZINARODNI VZTAHY; ceskoslovenska revue pro mezinarodni politiku a ekonomiku. (Text in Czech or Slovak; summaries in English, French, German, Russian) vol.7, 1972. bi-m. $40.50. (Ustav Mezinarodnich Vztahu) Panorama, Halkova 1, 120 72 Prague 2, Czechoslovakia. Ed. Jaroslava Krylova. bk.rev.; bibl.; charts; circ. 1,600.

MIDDLE EAST CONTEMPORARY SURVEY. see *HISTORY — History Of The Near East*

| 327 | US | ISSN 0731-9371 |
| D839 | | |

MIDDLE EAST INSIGHT. 1980. q. $37 to individuals; institutions and corporations $52. International Insight, Inc., 2029 Q St., N.W., Washington, DC 20009. TEL 202-667-9004. FAX 202-861-0621. TELEX 201962 NEIN UR. Ed. George A. Nader. adv.; bk.rev.; circ. 2,000. (back issues avail.) Indexed: P.A.I.S., Polit.Sci.Abstr.
  —BLDSC shelfmark: 5761.376800.
  Description: Contemporary Middle East developments for businessmen, diplomats and observers.

| 327 | US | ISSN 0026-3141 |
| DS1 | | |

MIDDLE EAST JOURNAL. 1947. q. $30 to individuals; institutions $40. (Middle East Institute) Indiana University Press, Journals Division, 601 N. Morton St., Bloomington, IN 47404. TEL 812-855-9449. Ed. Christopher Van Hollen. adv.; bk.rev.; bibl.; charts; index, cum.index: 1947-1966, 1967-1977; circ. 4,500. (also avail. in microform from UMI; reprint service avail. from UMI) Indexed: A.B.C.Pol.Sci., A.I.C.P., Acad.Ind., Amer.Bibl.Slavic & E.Eur.Stud., Amer.Hist.& Life, Bk.Rev.Ind. (1965-), Child.Bk.Rev.Ind. (1965-), Curr.Cont., Curr.Cont.M.E., G.Soc.Sci.& Rel.Per.Lit., Geo.Abstr., Hist.Abstr., Hum.Ind., I D A, Int.Lab.Doc., Int.Polit.Sci.Abstr., Key to Econ.Sci., Mid.East: Abstr.& Ind., P.A.I.S., Popul.Ind., Ref.Sour., Rural Recreat.Tour.Abstr., Soc.Sci.Ind., SSCI, World Agri.Econ.& Rural Sociol.Abstr.
  —BLDSC shelfmark: 5761.380000.

| 382 327 | US | |
| DS63.1 | | |

MIDDLE EAST POLICY. 1982. q. $25 (typically set in Sep.). Middle East Policy Council, 1730 M St., N.W., Ste. 512, Washington, DC 20036. TEL 202-296-6767. FAX 202-296-5791. TELEX 440506-AMARA-UI. Ed. Anne Joyce. adv.; bk.rev.; cum.index: 1982-1991 in vol.38; circ. 15,000 (controlled). (also avail. in microform from UMI; reprint service avail. from WSH) Indexed: A.B.C.Pol.Sci., Bk.Rev.Ind. (1983-), Child.Bk.Rev.Ind. (1983-), Curr.Cont.M.E., HR Rep., Ind.Islam., Int.Polit.Sci.Abstr., Mid.East: Abstr.& Ind., P.A.I.S., Polit.Sci.Abstr.
  Formerly (until 1992): American Arab Affairs (ISSN 0731-6763)
  Description: Provides viewpoints on recent developments that affect US - Middle East policy.

MIDDLE EAST STRATEGIC STUDIES QUARTERLY. see *MILITARY*

| 956 | US | ISSN 0026-3230 |

MIDEAST REPORT.* 1967. s-m. $385 (foreign $410). MidEast Report, Inc., 292 5th Ave., Ste. 602, New York, NY 10001-4513. TEL 212-714-3530. FAX 212-983-0039. TELEX 236328 MIDE UR. (Subscr. to: Box 2460 Grand Central Sta., New York, NY 10163-2460) Ed. Jocelyne Mizrahi. (processed)

| 320.9 | UK | ISSN 0026-3737 |

MILAP WEEKLY. 1965. w. £44. 59-61 Broughton Rd., Fulham, London SW6 2LA, England. Ed. Ramesh Kumar Soni. adv.; bk.rev.; film rev.; tr.lit.; circ. 70,000. (avail. on records)

| 320.5 | FR | ISSN 0026-3877 |

MILITANT; revue nationaliste pour la defense de l'identite francaise et europeenne. 1967. s-m. 250 F. (foreign 400 F.)(effective Dec. 1989). 44 Quai de Jemmapes, B.P. 154, 75010 Paris, France. TEL 42-49-03-23. Ed. M. Pauty. adv.; bk.rev.; illus.; circ. 2,000.
  Description: Covers world news of a political or nationalistic nature.

| 327 | UK | ISSN 0305-8298 |
| JX1 | | |

MILLENNIUM; journal of international studies. 1971. 3/yr. £14($28) to individuals; institutions £30($60). (London School of Economics & Political Science) Millenium Publishing Group, Houghton St., London WC2A 2AE, England. TEL 071-405-7686. FAX 071-242-0392. Eds. Malory Greene, Ian Rowlands. adv.; bk.rev.; index; circ. 900. (also avail. in microfilm from UMI) Indexed: A.B.C.Pol.Sci., A.I.C.P., Abstr.Mil.Bibl., Amer.Hist.& Life, Br.Hum.Ind., Hist.Abstr., Int.Polit.Sci.Abstr., Intl.Ind.TV, P.A.I.S.
  —BLDSC shelfmark: 5773.945000.

MIROVAYA EKONOMIKA I MEZHDUNARODNYE OTNOSHENIYA. see *BUSINESS AND ECONOMICS*

| 327 | NE | ISSN 0165-6546 |
| DS611 | | |

MOESSON; onafhankelijk Indisch tijdschrift. 1958. s-m. fl.90. Tjalie Robinson B.V., Pr. Mauritslaan 36, 2582 LS The Hague, Netherlands. Ed. R.F.G. Boekholt. adv.; bk.rev.; bibl.; charts; illus.; circ. 7,500.
  Formerly: Tong-Tong (ISSN 0040-9189)

MONDE ARABE ECONOMIQUE ET LES AFFAIRES INTERNATIONALES. see *BUSINESS AND ECONOMICS — Economic Situation And Conditions*

POLITICAL SCIENCE — INTERNATIONAL RELATIONS

327   FR   ISSN 0026-9395
JX3
MONDE DIPLOMATIQUE. 1954. m. 190 F. Monde, 5 rue Antoine Bourdelle, 75015 Paris, France. TEL 1-40-65-25-25. FAX 1-45-48-23-96. TELEX 650 572. (Subscr. to: Immeuble Sirius, 1 place Hubert-Beuve-Mery, 94852 Ivry-sur-Seine Cedex, France. TEL 49-60-32-90) Ed. Micheline Paunet. illus.; index; circ. 165,000. (also avail. in microform from RPI) **Indexed:** HR Rep., Int.Lab.Doc., Pt.de Rep. (1979-).

327 614   US   ISSN 1042-3249
MONTHLY PLANET. 1985. m. $15. Nuclear Weapons Freeze of Santa Cruz County, Box 8463, Santa Cruz, CA 95061-8463. TEL 408-429-8755. Ed. John Govsky. adv.; bk.rev.; illus.; index; circ. 15,000. (tabloid format; back issues avail.)
●Also available online.
Description: Covers the peace movement and disarmament worldwide, with a focus on local grassroots activism.

N A F S A GOVERNMENT AFFAIRS BULLETIN. (National Association for Foreign Student Affairs) see EDUCATION — International Education Programs

N A F S A NEWSLETTER. (National Association for Foreign Student Affairs) see EDUCATION

355   BE
N A T O BASIC DOCUMENTS/O T A N DOCUMENTS FONDAMENTAUX. 1975. irreg. North Atlantic Treaty Organization, Information and Press Service, B-1110 Brussels, Belgium. (U.S. address: Distribution Officer, Bureau of Public Affairs, Dept. of State, Washington, DC 20520)

355   BE
N A T O FINAL COMMUNIQUES/O T A N COMMUNIQUES FINALS. (Annual supplements avail.) 1970. quinquennial. North Atlantic Treaty Organization, Information and Press Service, 1110 Brussels, Belgium. (U.S. Address: Distribution Officer, Bureau of Public Affairs, Dept. of State, Washington, DC 20520)

355   BE   ISSN 0549-7175
JX1393
N A T O HANDBOOK. French ed.: Manuel de l' O T A N. (Editions in various languages) 1952. irreg. free. North Atlantic Treaty Organization, Information and Press Service, B-1110 Brussels, Belgium. TEL 32-2-728-41-11. FAX 32-2-728-45-79. TELEX 23-867. (U.S. address: Distribution Office, Bureau of Public Affairs, Dept. of State, Washington, DC 20520)

327 355   GW
N A T O'S SIXTEEN NATIONS. (North Atlantic Treaty Organization) 1955. 8/yr. DM.90($60) Moench Publishing Group, P.O. Box 14 02 61, 5300 Bonn 1, Germany. TEL 0228-6483-0. FAX 0228-6483-109. TELEX 8869-429-MVB-D. adv.; circ. 26,110. **Indexed:** Abstr.Mil.Bibl., Air Un.Lib.Ind., DM & T, Mid.East: Abstr.& Ind.
Formerly: N A T O's Nations.

327   NO   ISSN 0800-0018
D839
N U P I NOTAT. (Text in English, Norwegian) irreg. no.440, 1991. NOK 35. Norsk Utenrikspolitisk Institutt - Norwegian Institute of International Affairs, Postboks 8159, Dep., 0033 Oslo 1, Norway. TEL 02-177050. FAX 02-177015. **Indexed:** Abstr.Mil.Bibl.
—BLDSC shelfmark: 6187.026200.

327   NO   ISSN 0800-000X
N U P I RAPPORT. (Text in English, Norwegian) irreg. no.154, 1991. price varies. Norsk Utenrikspolitisk Institutt - Norwegian Institute of International Affairs, Postboks 8159, Dep., 0033 Oslo 1, Norway. TEL 02-177050. FAX 02-177015.
—BLDSC shelfmark: 6187.026400.

NAJDA NEWSLETTER. see WOMEN'S INTERESTS

327   US
NATIONAL COMMITTEE ON U.S.-CHINA RELATIONS. NOTES FROM THE NATIONAL COMMITTEE. 1969. 3/yr. $5. National Committee on U.S.-China Relations, Inc., 777 U.N. Plaza, New York, NY 10017. TEL 212-922-1385. FAX 212-557-8258. Ed.Bd. bk.rev.; charts; circ. 3,000.
Formerly: National Committee on U.S. China Relations. Highlights of Notes.
Description: Reports on committee activities and current trends in China.

NATIONAL INTEREST. see POLITICAL SCIENCE

NEAR EAST FOUNDATION. ANNUAL REPORT. see BUSINESS AND ECONOMICS — International Development And Assistance

956   US   ISSN 0028-176X
DS41
NEAR EAST REPORT; a Washington newsletter on American policy in the Middle East. 1957. w. $30. Near East Research, Inc., 440 First St., N.W., Ste. 607, Washington, DC 20001. TEL 202-638-1225. FAX 202-347-4916. Ed. Mitchell Bard. adv.; bk.rev.; index; circ. 40,000. (also avail. in microfilm from UMI; reprint service avail. from UMI) **Indexed:** HR Rep., Ind.Jew.Per.

327   US   ISSN 0748-4526
HD42   CODEN: NEJOEQ
NEGOTIATION JOURNAL; on the process of dispute settlement. 1985. q. $145 (foreign $170)(effective 1992). (Program on Negotiation) Plenum Publishing Corp., 233 Spring St., New York, NY 10013-1578. TEL 212-620-8000. FAX 212-463-0742. TELEX 23-421139. Ed. Jeffrey Z. Rubin. adv.; bibl. (also avail. in microfilm from JSC; back issues avail.) **Indexed:** Crim.Just.Abstr., Curr.Cont.
—BLDSC shelfmark: 6075.154000.
Refereed Serial

327   GW
NETZ. 1979. q. DM.30($20) (Entwicklung und Gerechtigkeit e.V.) Netz, c/o Elisabeth Dissinger, Van Wingenastr. 5, 2974 Groothusen, Germany. TEL 06645-8590. FAX 06645-1540. (Subscr. to: An der Kirche 4, 6324 Feldatal 4, Germany) Ed. Peter Dietzel. bk.rev.; circ. 1,100. (back issues avail.)

327   GW   ISSN 0548-2801
NEUE HEIMAT. 1973. bi-m. (Vereinigung fuer Verbindungen mit Buergern deutscher Herkunft in Ausland) Verlag Zeit im Bild, Julian Grimau-Allee 10, 8010 Dresden, Germany. Ed. Heinz Vierich. charts; illus.; circ. 12,000.
—BLDSC shelfmark: 8426.235000.

NEW HAVEN STUDIES IN INTERNATIONAL LAW AND WORLD PUBLIC ORDER. see LAW — International Law

327   UK   ISSN 0305-9529
D839
NEW INTERNATIONALIST. 1971. m. £18.40($36) to individuals; institutions £35($50). New Internationalist Publications Ltd., 55 Rectory Rd., Oxford OX4 1BW, England. TEL 0865-728181. FAX 0865-793152. (U.S. addr.: Box 1143, Lewiston, NY 14092; Canada addr.: 1057 McNicoll Ave., Ste. 108, Scarborough, Ont. M1W 3W6, Canada) Ed.Bd. adv.; bk.rev.; charts; film rev.; illus.; stat.; index; circ. 70,000. (also avail. in microform; back issues avail.) **Indexed:** Alt.Press Ind., GdIns., Geo.Abstr., Int.Lab.Doc., Mid.East: Abstr.& Ind., Peace Res.Abstr, Rural Recreat.Tour.Abstr., World Agri.Econ.& Rural Sociol.Abstr.
—BLDSC shelfmark: 6084.255000.
Description: World issues and the relationships between the world's rich and poor nations.

NEW MUSES. see LITERATURE — Poetry

341.1   UK   ISSN 0028-6990
NEW WORLD. 1958. bi-m. £3. United Nations Association of Great Britain & Northern Ireland, 3 Whitehall Court, London SW1A 2EL, England. TEL 01-930 2931. FAX 071-930-5893. TELEX 837883-SPEND-G. Ed. Malcolm Harper. adv.; bk.rev.; illus.; circ. 5,500.
—BLDSC shelfmark: 6089.208000.

327.931   NZ
NEW ZEALAND. MINISTRY OF EXTERNAL RELATIONS AND TRADE. ANNUAL REPORT. (Subseries of: New Zealand. Ministry of External Relations and Trade) a. price varies. Ministry of External Relations and Trade, Wellington, New Zealand. (Dist. by: Government Bookshop, Private Bag, Wellington, New Zealand)
Formerly: New Zealand. Ministry of Foreign Affairs. Report.

327   NZ   ISSN 0110-4802
NEW ZEALAND. MINISTRY OF FOREIGN AFFAIRS. DEVELOPMENT; New Zealand's co-operation with developing countries. q. free. Ministry of Foreign Affairs, External Aid Division, c/o Information Officer, Private Bag, Wellington, New Zealand. circ. 6,500.

327   NZ   ISSN 0111-5251
HC60
NEW ZEALAND. MINISTRY OF FOREIGN AFFAIRS. PROJECT PROFILES; New Zealand bilateral aid programme. 1980. a. free. Ministry of Foreign Affairs, External Aid Division, c/o Information Officer, Private Bag, Wellington, New Zealand. circ. 3,000.

327   NZ   ISSN 0114-3999
JX1591
NEW ZEALAND EXTERNAL RELATIONS REVIEW. 1951. q. free. Ministry of External Relations and Trade, Wellington, New Zealand. charts; illus.; maps; index; circ. 3,000. **Indexed:** Abstr.Mil.Bibl., Key to Econ.Sci., Mid.East: Abstr.& Ind., P.A.I.S., So.Pac.Per.Ind.
—BLDSC shelfmark: 6091.360000.
Former titles: New Zealand Foreign Affairs Review (ISSN 0014-5440) & External Affairs Review.
Description: Reviews New Zealand activity in the area of external relations and trade for the preceeding quarter.

327   NZ   ISSN 0110-0262
D839
NEW ZEALAND INTERNATIONAL REVIEW. 1976. bi-m. NZ.$37 (foreign NZ$43). New Zealand Institute of International Affairs, Box 600, Wellington 2, New Zealand. TEL 04-4727-430. FAX 04-4731-261. Ed. Ian McGibbon. adv.; bk.rev.; circ. 1,500. **Indexed:** Abstr.Mil.Bibl., So.Pac.Per.Ind.
—BLDSC shelfmark: 6092.480000.

355   II
NEWS REVIEW ON EAST ASIA. (Text in English) 1968. m. Rs.66. Institute for Defence Studies & Analyses, Sapru House, Barakhamba Rd., New Delhi 110001, India. Ed. Jasjit Singh. circ. 250.
Former titles: News Review on China, Mongolia and the Koreas; News Review on China.

327   II
NEWS REVIEW ON SOUTH ASIA AND INDIAN OCEAN. (Text in English) 1967. m. Rs.66. Institute for Defence Studies and Analyses, Sapru House, Barakhamba Rd., New Delhi 110001, India. Ed. Jasjit Singh. circ. 200.
Former titles (1972-1977): News Review on South Asia; (1968-1971): News Review on Pakistan.

355.03   II
NEWS REVIEW ON SOUTH EAST ASIA, AND AUSTRALASIA. (Text in English) 1972. m. Rs.66. Institute for Defence Studies and Analyses, Sapru House, Barakhamba Rd., New Delhi 110001, India. Ed. Jasjit Singh. circ. 250.
Former titles: News Review on Japan, South East Asia, and Australia; (1969-1972): New Review on Countries Bordering India.

327   II
NEWS REVIEW ON U.S.S.R. & EUROPE. (Text in English) 1972. m. Rs.66. Institute for Defence Studies and Analyses, Sapru House, Barakhamba Rd., New Delhi 110001, India. Ed. Jasjit Singh. circ. 250.
Formerly: News Review on North America & Europe; Supersedes in part: News Review on East Asia, Australasia and West Asia.

327 382   RU
▼**NEZAVISIMAYA GAZETA.** 1991. 5/w. Nezavisimaya Gazeta, Myasnitskaya, 13, 101000 Moscow, Russia. Ed. Vitalii Tretyakov. adv.; circ. 225,000. (newspaper)
Description: Provides political and business communications between the U.S. and Russia.

POLITICAL SCIENCE — INTERNATIONAL RELATIONS 3967

327   NE   ISSN 0028-9876
NIEUW WERELD NIEUWS. 1968. m. fl.25 (students fl.12.50). (Nieuwsdienst Morele Herbewapening - Moral Rearmament News Service) Nederlandse Stichting voor Morele Herbewapening, Amaliastr. 10, 2514 JC The Hague, Netherlands. FAX 070-617209. Eds. A.R. Burger, P. Hintzen. adv.; bk.rev.; illus.; circ. 2,250.
  Description: News and reports of events concerning moral rearmament.

327   NR   ISSN 0331-2151
NIGERIA BULLETIN ON FOREIGN AFFAIRS. 1971-1983; resumed 1987. m. £N20. (Nigerian Institute of International Affairs) N I I A Press, Kofo Abayomi Rd., G.P.O. Box 1727, Lagos, Nigeria. Ed. D. Nworah. bibl. **Indexed:** Mid.East: Abstr.& Ind.
  —BLDSC shelfmark: 6111.716000.
  Description: Contains a collection of documents, papers and commentaries about Nigerian foreign policy, edited by the Library Department of the Nigerian Institute of International Affairs.

327 338.91   NR   ISSN 0189-0816
DT30.5
NIGERIA FORUM. 1981. m. £N25($20) (Nigerian Institute of International Affairs) N I I A Press, Kofo Aboyomi Rd., Victoria Island, G.P.O. Box 1727, Lagos, Nigeria. (Dist. in U.S. by: First Western Corp., 6323 Beachway Dr., Falls Church, VA 22044) adv.; bk.rev.; bibl.; charts; stat.; index; circ. 3,000. (back issues avail.)
  —BLDSC shelfmark: 6112.050000.
  Description: Provides factual and authoritative information about current world issues by scholars statesmen, soldiers, and university students.

916.69   NR   ISSN 0078-0685
DT515
NIGERIA YEAR BOOK. (Text in English) 1952. a. price varies. Daily Time of Nigeria, P.O. Box 139, Lagos, Nigeria. TEL 900850-9. Ed. Gbenga Odusanya. adv.

327   NR   ISSN 0331-6262
JX1
NIGERIAN INSTITUTE OF INTERNATIONAL AFFAIRS. LECTURE SERIES. (Text in English) 1969. irreg. £N5($3.50) N I I A Press, G.P.O. Box 1727, Lagos, Nigeria.
  —BLDSC shelfmark: 5180.568000.

327   NR   ISSN 0331-6254
NIGERIAN INSTITUTE OF INTERNATIONAL AFFAIRS. MONOGRAPH SERIES. (Text in English) 1979. irreg. £N15($10) (Nigerian Institute of International Affairs) N I I A Press, G.P.O. Box 1727, Kofo Aboyomi Rd., Victoria Island, Lagos, Nigeria. (Dist. in U.S. by: First Western Corp., 6323 Beachway Dr., Falls Church, VA 22044) charts; stat. (back issues avail.)
  —BLDSC shelfmark: 6113.166030.

327.05   NR   ISSN 0331-3646
JX18
NIGERIAN JOURNAL OF INTERNATIONAL AFFAIRS. 1975. s-a. £N30($20) (Nigerian Institute of International Affairs) N I I A Press, P.O. Box 1727, Kofo Abayomi Rd., Victoria Island, Lagos, Nigeria. (Dist. in U.S. by: First Western Corp., 6323 Beachway Dr., Falls Church, VA 22044) bk.rev.; bibl.; charts; stat.; index. (back issues avail.)
  —BLDSC shelfmark: 6112.125600.
  Description: Written as a collection of scholarly articles about international affairs; devotes special sections to book reviews and official documents.

327   NR
NIGERIAN JOURNAL OF INTERNATIONAL STUDIES. 1975. s-a. £N12($24) Nigerian Society of International Affairs, Box 1727, Lagos, Nigeria. (Dist. in U.S. by: First Western Corp., 6323 Beachway Dr., Falls Church, VA 22044) Ed. A. Bolaji Akinyemi. adv.; bk.rev.; circ. 1,000.

327   NR   ISSN 0331-8524
NIGERIAN JOURNAL OF POLITICAL SCIENCE. (Text in English) 1979. s-a. £N7.50($12) Ahmadu Bello University, Department of Political Science, Zaire, Nigeria. Ed. Ibrahim Gambari. circ. 3,000. (back issues avail.)

301.29   NO
NORGE-AMERIKA FORENINGEN. YEARBOOK. 1945. a. free. Norway-America Association, Drammensvn. 20C, 0255 Oslo 2, Norway. Ed. Bjorn Heimar. adv.; bk.rev.; illus.; circ. 2,000.
  Supersedes: Norge-Amerika Foreningen. Report.

225   NO   ISSN 0332-7299
NORSK UTENRIKSPOLITISK AARBOK. (Subseries of: Utenrikspolitiske Skrifter) 1974. a. NOK 225. Norsk Utenrikspolitisk Institutt - Norwegian Institute of International Affairs, Postboks 8159, Dep., 0033 Oslo 1, Norway. TEL 02-177050. FAX 02-177015. stat.; circ. 1,300.

NORTE; revista hispanoamericano. see *LITERATURE*

355   BE
NORTH ATLANTIC TREATY ORGANIZATION. FACTS AND FIGURES/ALLIANCE ATLANTIQUE. STRUCTURE, FAITS ET CHIFFRES. 1957. irreg. North Atlantic Treaty Organization, Information and Press Service, B-1110 Brussels, Belgium. (U.S. Address: Distribution Officer, Bureau of Public Affairs, Dept. of State, Washington, DC 20520)

327   JA
NORTH KOREA DIRECTORY (YEAR). (Text in English and Chinese characters) 1988. a. 5500 Yen($50) (effective Oct. 1990). Radiopress, Inc., 5th Fl., R-Bldg. Shinjuku, 33-8 Wakamatsu-cho, Shinjuku-ku, Tokyo 162, Japan. TEL 03-5273-2171. FAX 03-5273-2180.
  Description: Lists personnel and structural changes in North Korea's government, state organs, political parties, and mass organizations. Lists names in Chinese characters, Roman letters, and Japanese hiragana.

327   IT   ISSN 0048-0916
NOTIZIE DALL'ALBANIA. 1971. m. L.150. Associazione Nazionale Italia Albania, Via Torino 122, 00184 Rome, Italy. Ed. Antonello Satta. circ. 5,000.

327   FR   ISSN 0754-3786
NOUVELLES DU VIETNAM. N.S. 1976. q. Ambassade de la Republique Socialiste du Vietnam en France, 62 rue Boileau, 75016 Paris, France. Dir. M. Aquettaz. illus.; circ. 500.
  Formerly: Bulletin du Vietnam.

947   RU   ISSN 0029-5280
NOVOE VREMYA. English edition: New Times (ISSN 0206-1473) (Editions in Czech, English, French, German, Greek, Italian, Polish, Portuguese, Russian, Spanish) 1943. w. $5.50. Izdatel'stvo Trud, Pl. Pushkina, Moscow 103782 GSP, Russia. TEL 229-88-72. TELEX 411164A NEWT SU. Eds. Aleksandr Pumpyanskii (Rus.ed.), Vasilii Korolev (Eng.ed.). adv.; bk.rev.; bibl.; charts; illus.; index. (also avail. in microform from UMI,MIM,BHP) **Indexed:** P.A.I.S.

327.1 355.8   US   ISSN 0748-2876
U264
NUCLEAR ARMS; opposing viewpoints sources. (In 2 vols.) 1983. a. $10.95 (sourcebook $39.95). Greenhaven Press, Inc., Box 289009, San Diego, CA 92198-0009. TEL 619-485-7424. FAX 619-485-9549. Ed. Bruno Leone. (back issues avail.)
  Description: Covers arms race and control, defense spending.

320.531   IT   ISSN 0029-621X
NUOVA RIVISTA INTERNAZIONALE/NEW INTERNATIONAL REVIEW; problemi della pace e del socialismo. m. L.65000 (L.89000 foreign). (Partito Comunista Italiano) Editori Riuniti, Via Serchio 9-11, 00198 Rome, Italy. TEL 06-866383. FAX 06-8416096. TELEX EDIRIU I 625292. Ed. Bernardino Bernardini. bk.rev.; circ. 5,000.
  —BLDSC shelfmark: 6184.908800.

327 960   ET
O A U ECHO. (Text in Arabic, English or French) 1980. m. free. Organization of African Unity, General Secretariat, Press and Information Division, Box 2343, Addis Ababa, Ethiopia. TELEX 21046 OAU. Ed. I. Dagash. circ. 7,500.

327   US
ODYSSEY (BRATTLEBORO). 1972. q. free. Experiment in International Living, Box 676, Brattleboro, VT 05302. TEL 802-257-7751. FAX 802-254-6674. Ed. Gayle Rountree. illus.; circ. 84,000.
  Former titles: Odyssey International; Odyssey.

OESTERREICH - POLEN, AUSTRIA - POLSKA. see *ETHNIC INTERESTS*

327   AU
OESTERREICHISCHES JAHRBUCH FUER INTERNATIONALE POLITIK. a. S.180. (Oesterreichisches Institut fuer Internationale Politik) Boehlau Verlag GmbH & Co. KG, Sachsenplatz 4-6, Postfach 87, A-1201 Vienna, Austria. TEL 0222-3302427. FAX 0222-3302432. TELEX 114506-SPRIW-A.

327   EI
OFFICIAL JOURNAL OF THE EUROPEAN COMMUNITIES. C SERIES: INFORMATION AND NOTICES; notifications of open competitions. (Editions in Danish, Dutch, English, French, German, Italian) d. $30. (Commission of the European Communities) Office for Official Publications of the European Communities, L-2985 Luxembourg, Luxembourg. (Dist. in the U.S. by: Unipub, 4611-F Assembly Dr., Lanham, MD 20706-4391) **Indexed:** Dairy Sci.Abstr., EC Ind., Fuel & Energy Abstr., World Surf.Coat., World Text.Abstr.

327   EI
OFFICIAL JOURNAL OF THE EUROPEAN COMMUNITIES. L & C: LEGISLATION AND COMPETITION. (Editions in Danish, Dutch, English, French, German, Italian) d. $460. Office for Official Publications of the European Communities, L-2985 Luxembourg, Luxembourg. (Dist. in the U.S. by: Unipub, 4611-F, Assembly Dr., Lanham, MD 20706-4391) (also avail. in microfiche) **Indexed:** Cadscan, EC Ind., Lead Abstr., Rural Recreat.Tour.Abstr., World Agri.Econ.& Rural Sociol.Abstr., Zincscan.
  ●Also available on CD-ROM.
  Formerly: Official Journal of the European Communities. L Series: Legislation.

341.1 338   NE   ISSN 0030-3232
ONZE WERELD. 1957. m. fl.67.50. Nederlandse Organisatie voor Internationale Ontwikkelingssamenwerking - Netherlands Organization for International Development Cooperation, Editorial Room, Kloveniersburgwal 23, 1011 JV Amsterdam, Netherlands. FAX 20-6251288. Ed. Kees Waagmeester. adv.; bk.rev.; bibl.; charts; illus.; stat.; index; circ. 39,000.

327 983   CL   ISSN 0716-4513
OPCIONES. 1983. 3/yr. Esc.1000($40) Academia de Humanismo Cristiano, Centro de Estudios de la Realidad Contemporanea, Catedral 1063, 5 piso, Santiago, Chile. TEL 6980864. FAX 716804. Ed. Carlos Bascunan. adv.; bk.rev.; circ. 1,500. (back issues avail.)
  Formerly: Alternativas.

327   US
▼**OPEN MAGAZINE PAMPHLET SERIES.** 1991. every 6 weeks. $35 for 10 nos. to individuals; institutions $40; students $30. Open Media, Box 2726, Westfield, NJ 07091. TEL 908-789-6908. Ed. Greg Ruggiero. circ. 10,000. (back issues avail.)
  Description: Publishes lecture transcripts, interviews and articles critical of U.S. foreign and domestic policy, presenting scholarly analyses and radical perspectives on the media, the Middle East and the Gulf War and ecological issues.

OPPORTUNITIES BRIEFING; news and analysis of political and economic reform in East-Central Europe. see *BUSINESS AND ECONOMICS — International Commerce*

327   US   ISSN 0030-4387
D839
ORBIS (PHILADELPHIA); a journal of world affairs. 1957. q. $25 to individuals; institutions $50; students $20. Foreign Policy Research Institute, 3615 Chestnut St., Philadelphia, PA 19104. TEL 215-382-0685. FAX 215-382-0131. Ed. Patrick L. Clawson. adv.; bk.rev.; charts; illus.; index; circ. 3,500. (also avail. in microform from KTO,UMI; back issues avail.; reprint service avail. from KTO) **Indexed:** A.B.C.Pol.Sci., Abstr.Mil.Bibl., Acad.Ind., Amer.Hist. & Life., ASSIA, Curr.Cont., Fut.Surv., Hist.Abstr., HR Rep., Int.Polit.Sci.Abstr., Key to Econ.Sci., Mid.East: Abstr.& Ind., P.A.I.S., Peace Res.Abstr., Risk Abstr., Soc.Sci.Ind.
  —BLDSC shelfmark: 6277.850000.
  Description: Contains articles on contemporary international affairs.

ORGANIZATION OF AMERICAN STATES. DIRECTORY. see *BUSINESS AND ECONOMICS — Trade And Industrial Directories*

POLITICAL SCIENCE — INTERNATIONAL RELATIONS

341.18   US
ORGANIZATION OF AMERICAN STATES. GENERAL ASSEMBLY. ACTAS Y DOCUMENTOS. irreg. price varies. Organization of American States, Department of Publications, 1889 F St., N.W., Washington, DC 20006. TEL 703-941-1617. circ. 2,000.

327   US
OUTPOST. 1972. m. membership. Americans for a Safe Israel, 147 E. 76th St., No. 5, New York, NY 10021-2824. TEL 212-628-9400. Ed. Ruth King. bk.rev.; illus.; circ. 10,000. (back issues avail.) **Indexed:** So.Pac.Per.Ind.

OVERSEAS LIVING. see *TRAVEL AND TOURISM*

P D S. (Perspektiven des Demokratischen Sozialismus) see *POLITICAL SCIENCE*

P S R MONITOR. (Physicians for Social Responsibility) see *PUBLIC HEALTH AND SAFETY*

P S R QUARTERLY. (Physicians for Social Responsibility) see *PUBLIC HEALTH AND SAFETY*

P S R REPORTS. (Physicians for Social Responsibility) see *PUBLIC HEALTH AND SAFETY*

323.1   NO
PAA FLUKT/NEW FUTURE. (Text in Norwegian; summaries in English) 1960. 5/yr. NOK 100. Norske Flyktningeraad - Norwegian Refugee Council, P.O. Box 5856, Hegdehaugen, 0308 Oslo 3, Norway. FAX 02-600272. Ed. Odd Iglebaek. adv.; bk.rev.; abstr.; illus.; circ. 25,000.
Formerly: Ny Fremtid (ISSN 0029-6732)
Description: News about the world's refugee situation.

327   FI   ISSN 0355-1849
PAASIKIVI - SOCIETY. MIMEOGRAPH SERIES. (Text in Finnish) irreg., no.68, 1987. Ulkopoliittinen Instituutti, Pursimiehenkatu 8, SF-00150 Helsinki, Finland. TEL 358-0-170434. FAX 358-0-669375. (processed)
Description: Consists of speeches at the Paasikivi Society.

327 355   AT   ISSN 1031-9379
PACIFIC RESEARCH. 1986. q. Aus.$20. Peace Research Centre, Research School of Pacific Studies, Australian National University, G.P.O. Box 4, Canberra, A.C.T. 2601, Australia. TEL 062-49-3098. FAX 61-6-149-0174. TELEX A62694. Ed. Trevor Findlay. adv.; bk.rev.; circ. 2,200. **Indexed:** Aus.P.A.I.S.
Formerly (until May 1988): Peace Research Centre Newsletter (ISSN 0818-2469)
Description: Critical analysis of defense and foreign policy of all goverments in Asia-Pacific region. Includes arms control, disarmament.

057 327   UK   ISSN 0951-2748
DU29
PACIFIC REVIEW. 1988. 4/yr. £64($115) Oxford University Press, Oxford Journals, Pinkhill House, Southfield Road, Eynsham, Oxford OX8 1JJ, England. TEL 0865-882283. FAX 0865-882890. TELEX 837330 OXPRES G. (U.S. addr.: 200 Madison Ave., New York, NY 10016) Ed. Gerald Segal. adv.; bk.rev.; circ. 1,500.
—BLDSC shelfmark: 6330.877000.
Description: Interdisciplinary forum for the exchange of ideas and trends in Pacific politics, history, military strategy, economics and culture.

327   SI   ISSN 0218-1924
PACIFIC STRATEGIC PAPERS. (Text in English) 1990. irreg., no.5, 1991. price varies. Institute of Southeast Asian Studies, Heng Mui Keng Terrace, Off Pasir Panjang Rd., Singapore 0511, Singapore. TEL 778-0955. FAX 778-1735. TELEX RS 37068 ISEAS.
Description: Monograph series on regional issues of current interest in the Asian-Pacific region.

327   UK   ISSN 0048-265X
JX1901
PACIFIST. 1961. 6/yr. £6. Peace Pledge Union, 6 Endsleigh St., London, W.C.1, England. Ed. Jan Melichar. bk.rev.; illus.; circ. 1,600. (microfilm)
Incorporating: Peace Pledge Union Newsletter
Description: Theory, practice and history of pacifism and non-violence.

327   PK   ISSN 0030-980X
DS376
PAKISTAN HORIZON. (Text in English) 1948. q. Rs.120($24) Pakistan Institute of International Affairs, P.O. Box 1447, Aiwan-i-Sadar Rd., Karachi 74200, Pakistan. Ed. Hafeez R. Khan. adv.; bk.rev.; index; circ. 800. (also avail. in microform from UMI; reprint service avail. from UMI) **Indexed:** A.B.C.Pol.Sci., A.B.C.Pol.Sci, Abstr.Mil.Bibl., Hist.Abstr., Int.Lab.Doc., Int.Polit.Sci.Abstr, Mid.East: Abstr.& Ind.
—BLDSC shelfmark: 6340.850000.
Description: Facilitates understanding of international affairs and promotes the scientific study of international issues.

954.91   PK
PAKISTAN JOURNAL OF SOCIAL SCIENCE. (Text in English) 1974. s-a. Rs.15($8) Quaid-i-Azam University, Faculty of Science, c/o Bookshop, Bookbank and Publication Cell, Islamabad, Pakistan.
Formerly: Scrutiny.
Description: International and Pakistan studies.

327   US   ISSN 0883-8577
PALESTINE FOCUS. 1983. bi-m. $10 to individuals (foreign $15); institutions $20. Palestine Solidarity Committee, Box 372, Peck Slip Sta., NY 10272. TEL 415-861-1552. FAX 415-861-7966. TELEX 6503177279-SF. Ed.Bd. bk.rev.; circ. 20,000. **Indexed:** Alt.Press Ind.
Description: Reports on activities not only of its committee but also of other Palestine solidarity groups. Provides commentary and analysis of events in the Middle East, especially in Palestine and Israel.

PALESTINE REFUGEES TODAY. see *SOCIAL SERVICES AND WELFARE*

PAN-EUROPEAN ASSOCIATIONS; a directory of multi-national organisations in Europe. see *BUSINESS AND ECONOMICS — Trade And Industrial Directories*

330.9   GW
PANEUROPA DEUTSCHLAND. 1977. q. DM.20. (Paneuropa Union und Paneuropa-Jugend) Paneuropa-Verlag, Karlstr. 57, 8000 Munich 2, Germany. TEL 089-554683. FAX 089-594768. Eds. W. Stock, D. Phil. adv.; bk.rev.; circ. 35,000. (back issues avail.)
Formerly: Paneuropa-Jugend in Paneuropa Deutschland (ISSN 0932-7592)

341.1   US   ISSN 0031-2568
PARTNERS. (Text in English and Spanish) 1967. bi-m. free. Partners of the Americas, 1424 "K" St., N.W., Washington, DC 20005. TEL 202-628-3300. Ed. Cynthia Kenny. charts; illus.; circ. 15,000.

327   GW
PARTNERSCHAFT MIT DER ARABISCHEN WELT; Berichte und Meinungen ueber die Deutsch-Arabische Zusammenarbeit. Arabic edition: Al-Ta'awun Ma'a al Alam al Arabi. (Editions in Arabic and German) 1957. m. free. Inter Nationes e.V., Kennedyallee 91-103, Postfach 200349, 5300 Bonn 2, Germany. TEL 0228-880-1. FAX 0228-880457. TELEX 17228308. Ed. Hassan Suliak. circ. 200 (German ed.); 1,000 (Arabic ed.).
Description: Covers German-Arabic political and economic relations.

341.1   SZ   ISSN 0031-3327
JX1901
PAX ET LIBERTAS. (Text in English, occasional articles in French and German) 1925. q. $12. Women's International League for Peace and Freedom, 1 rue Varembe, CH-1211 Geneva 20, Switzerland. FAX 022-7401063. TELEX 427993-WILDE-CH. Ed. Janet Bruin. adv.; bk.rev.; circ. 2,000. (processed)

327   CU
PAZ Y SOBERANIA. q. free. Cuban Movement for Peace and Sovereignty of Peoples, Linea No. 556, Vedado, Havana, Cuba. TEL 809 32-0506. Ed. Miguel Sosa Herrera.
Description: Promotes materials on the struggle for peace and freedom and the sovereignty of all cultures.

327   US   ISSN 0149-0508
JX1901   CODEN: PCHAEG
PEACE & CHANGE; a journal of peace research. 1972. q. $39 to individuals; institutions $85. (Consortium on Peace Research, Education, and Development) Sage Publications, Inc., 2455 Teller Rd., Newbury Park, CA 91320. TEL 216-672-3143. (Alt. addr.: c/o Abigail Fuller, Mang. Ed., Dept. of Sociology, Campus Box 327, University of Colorado, Boulder, CO 80309-0327) (Co-sponsor: Council on Peace Research in History) Eds. Robert D. Schulzinger, Paul Wehr. adv.; bk.rev.; circ. 1,300. **Indexed:** Abstr.Mil.Bibl., Hist.Abstr., HR Rep., Int.Polit.Sci.Abstr., Mid.East: Abstr.& Ind., P.A.I.S., Peace Res.Abstr., Sage Pub.Admin.Abstr., Sage Urb.Stud.Abstr.
—BLDSC shelfmark: 6413.757000.
Description: Publishes scholarly and interpretive articles related to the achieving of a peaceful, just and humane society. Articles relate to peace and war, social change, conflict resolution, and appropriate justice.

PEACE & DEMOCRACY NEWS. see *POLITICAL SCIENCE — Civil Rights*

341.1   US   ISSN 0015-9093
JX1965
PEACE AND FREEDOM. 1941. 6/yr. $12. Women's International League for Peace and Freedom, 1213 Race St., Philadelphia, PA 19107. TEL 215-563-7110. (Affiliate: Jane Addams Peace Association) Ed. Roberta Spivek. adv.; bk.rev.; charts; circ. 11,000. (also avail. in microform from UMI; reprint service avail. from UMI)
Formerly: Four Lights.
Description: Devoted to the women's peace movement in the U.S. and other countries. Covers the empowerment of women, racism, the redirection of U.S. budget priorities, women's history, feminism and peace.

341.1   UK   ISSN 0031-3491
PEACE AND FREEDOM. N.S. 1952. q. £10. Women's International League for Peace and Freedom, 157 Lyndhurst Road, Worthing, Sussex BN11 2DG, England. TEL 903-205161. Ed.Bd. bk.rev.; circ. 500.

327   CN   ISSN 0831-1846
PEACE & SECURITY/PAIX ET SECURITE. (Text in English and French) 1986. q. Canadian Institute for International Peace and Security, 360 Albert St., Ste. 900, Ottawa, Ont. K1R 7X7, Canada. TEL 613-990-1593. FAX 613-563-0894. Ed. Micheal Bryans. bk.rev.; illus.; circ. 9,000 (controlled). (also avail. in microfiche; back issues avail.) **Indexed:** Can.Per.Ind.
Description: Covers issues of international peace and security from a Canadian perspective.

341.1   AU   ISSN 0031-3513
PEACE AND THE SCIENCES. (Text in English) 1970. q. S.300. International Institute for Peace, Moellwaldplatz 5, A-1040 Vienna, Austria. TEL 431-6564370. FAX 431-65643722. Ed. Peter Stania. bk.rev.; circ. 800. (processed)
—BLDSC shelfmark: 6413.765000.
Supersedes: Nuclear Energy.

327   US
PEACE CONVERSION TIMES. 1981. bi-m. $25 to members; low income students $15. Alliance for Survival, 200 N. Main St., Ste. M-2, Santa Ana, CA 92701-4851. FAX 714-547-6322. Ed. Kim Madison. adv.; bk.rev.; circ. 8,000. (also avail. in microform)
Description: Devoted to peace, social justice and safe energy. Features action alerts, children's items and a southern California events calendar.

PEACE CORPS TIMES. see *BUSINESS AND ECONOMICS — International Development And Assistance*

341.1   FI   ISSN 0031-594X
PEACE COURIER. (Editions in English, Arabic) 1966. m. $12 to individuals; institutions $30. World Peace Council, Lonnrotinkatu 25A, 5th fl., 00180 Helsinki 18, Finland. TEL 6931542. FAX 6933703. TELEX 121680 WOPAX SF. Ed. Sadhan Mukherjee. adv.; bk.rev.; bibl.; cum.index; circ. 17,000.
Description: Reports news of activities fostering peace throughout the world, and discusses problem areas where human rights violations occur. Also provides extensive coverage on worldwide ecological issues and nuclear weapons testing.

PEACE GAZETTE. see POLITICAL SCIENCE

327 355   CN   ISSN 0826-9521
PEACE MAGAZINE. 1985. 6/yr. Can.$15($20) Canadian Disarmament Information Service (CANDIS), 736 Bathurst St., Toronto, Ont. M5S 2R4, Canada. TEL 416-533-7581. FAX 416-531-6214. Ed. Metta Spencer. adv.; bk.rev.; circ. 8,000. **Indexed:** Can.Per.Ind.

341.1   AT   ISSN 0031-3564
PEACE PLANS. (Text in English and German) 1964. irreg. Aus.$1 per microfiche. Libertarian Microfiche Publishing, 7 Oxley St, Berrima, N.S.W. 2577, Australia. TEL 048-771-436. Ed. John M. Zube. adv.; bk.rev.; bibl.; index, cum.index. (microfiche)
   Description: Emphasis on individual secessionism, monetary freedom and minority autonomy.

327   US   ISSN 1049-0779
PEACE REPORTER. 1986. q. membership. National Peace Foundation, 1835 K St. N.W., Ste. 610, Washington, DC 20006-1203. TEL 202-223-1770. FAX 202-223-1718. Ed. Kathleen J. Lansing. circ. 15,000. (looseleaf format; back issues avail.)
   Formerly (until 1990): Peace Institute Reporter (ISSN 0890-8702)
   Description: Provides information on peace education and developments of other peace programs. Informs members of growth and development of the foundation and of the US Institute of Peace.

327   CN   ISSN 0008-4697
JX1904.5
PEACE RESEARCH. 1969. 4/yr. Can.$24($27) to individuals; institutions Can.$36($39). M.V. Naidu, Ed. & Pub., Brandon University, Brandon, Man. R7A 6A9, Canada. FAX 204-726-4573. TELEX 07-502721. adv.; bk.rev.; index; circ. 1,000. (also avail. in microfiche from UMI; reprint service avail.)
   Description: Scientific and scholarly work on world peace, focusing on the problems of violence, war, armaments, peace movements and human rights.

PEACELINES. see POLITICAL SCIENCE

341.1   US   ISSN 0031-3602
JX1901
PEACEMAKER. 1948. m. $10. Peacemaker Movement, Box 627, Garberville, CA 95440. Eds. Kathy Epling, Paul Encimer. bk.rev.; circ. 1,200. (also avail. in microfilm from UMI; reprint service avail. from UMI) **Indexed:** Alt.Press Ind.

PEOPLE (KANSAS CITY). see EDUCATION — International Education Programs

327   UN
PERMANENT MISSIONS TO THE UNITED NATIONS/MISSIONS PERMANENTES AUPRES DES NATIONS UNIES A GENEVE ET ORGA PRINCIPAUX DES NATIONS UNIES. (Subseries of: United Nations. Document) 1966. s-a. $25. United Nations, Protocol Section, Geneva Office - Section du Protocole des Nations Unies a Geneve, Bureau 143, Palais des Nations, CH-1211 Geneva 10, Switzerland. circ. 3,000.

327   BO
PERU. 1972. m. Embajada del Peru en Bolivia, Avda. 6 de Agosto 2190, La Paz, Bolivia. charts; illus.

327   PE
PERU. MINISTERIO DE RELACIONES EXTERIORES. BOLETIN TRIMESTRAL. q. Ministerio de Relaciones Exteriores, Lima, Peru.

PHILIPPINES CHINESE HISTORICAL ASSOCIATION. ANNALS. see HISTORY — History Of Asia

PITT LATIN AMERICAN SERIES. see SOCIAL SCIENCES: COMPREHENSIVE WORKS

PLAIN TRUTH; a magazine of understanding. see RELIGIONS AND THEOLOGY — Other Denominations And Sects

POLEMICAL DOCUMENTS SERIES. see ETHNIC INTERESTS

327   GW   ISSN 0930-4584
POLEN UND WIR; Zeitschrift fuer Deutsch-Polnische Verstaendigung. 1984. q. DM.18($15) Deutsche-Polnische Gesellschaft der Bundesrepublik Deutschland e.V., Beethoven Str. 5, 4800 Bielefeld 1, Germany. TEL 0521-176728. Ed. Karl Forster. adv.; bk.rev.; bibl.; illus.; film rev.; circ. 2,600.

POLISH-ANGLOSAXON STUDIES. see HISTORY

943.8 327   PL   ISSN 0032-3039
DK443
POLISH WESTERN AFFAIRS. (Editions in English) 1960. s-a. $14. Instytut Zachodni, Stary Rynek 78-79, 61-772 Poznan, Poland. (Dist. by: Ars Polona- Ruch, Krakowskie Przedmiescie 7, Warsaw, Poland) bk.rev.; bibl.; charts; maps; stat.; index; circ. 20,000. **Indexed:** Hist.Abstr.
   —BLDSC shelfmark: 6543.830000.
   Description: For scholars interested in present-day ecomonic, social and political problems of Germany and Central Europe.

320 355   BL
POLITICA E ESTRATEGIA. 1983. q. $30. Sociedade Brasileira de Cultura, Alameda Eduardo Prado, 705, C.P. 30004, 01218 Sao Paulo, Brazil. Ed. Antonio Carlos Pereira. adv.; circ. 6,000.

327 320   IT   ISSN 0032-3101
POLITICA INTERNAZIONALE (FLORENCE). 1969. bi-m. L.80000. Institute for Relations with Africa, Latin America and the Middle East (IPALMO), Via del Tritone 62, 00187 Rome, Italy. TEL 55 579 751. FAX 06-6797849. (Subscr. to: Licosa, Via Lamarmora 45, 50121 Florence, Italy) adv.; bk.rev.; index; circ. 5,000. (back issues avail.) **Indexed:** Abstr.Mil.Bibl.
   Description: Covers relations with developing countries in Africa, Latin America and Middle East.

327 947   US
▼**POLITICAL ARCHIVES OF THE SOVIET UNION.** 1990. q. $95. Nova Science Publishers, Inc., 283 Commack Rd., Ste. 300, Commack, NY 11725-3401. TEL 516-499-3103.

POLITICAL DIGEST SERIES. see ETHNIC INTERESTS

POLITICAL SCIENTIST. see POLITICAL SCIENCE

POLITICS AND THE LIFE SCIENCES. see MEDICAL SCIENCES

POLITICS OF LIBERATION SERIES. see HISTORY — History Of Europe

POLITIQUE ETRANGERE. see POLITICAL SCIENCE

947 327   CS   ISSN 0032-6593
PRAHA - MOSKVA; revue pro ceskoslovensko-sovetskou kulturni, vedeckou a technickou spolupraci. 1936. bi-m. 15 Kcs.($13.20) Svaz Ceskoslovensko-Sovetskeho Pratelstvi, Smetanovo nabr. 18, 115 65 Prague 1, Czechoslovakia. (Dist. by: Artia, Ve Smeckach 30, 111 27 Prague 1, Czechoslovakia) Ed. Marta Mackova.

341 327   US
PRINCETON UNIVERSITY. CENTER OF INTERNATIONAL STUDIES. MONOGRAPH SERIES. 1990. irreg., no.3, 1991. price varies. Princeton University, Center of International Studies, Bendheim Hall, Princeton University, Princeton, NJ 08544. TEL 609-258-4851. FAX 609-258-3988. (back issues avail.; reprint service avail. from UMI)

341 327   US
PRINCETON UNIVERSITY. CENTER OF INTERNATIONAL STUDIES. PROGRAM ON U S - JAPAN RELATIONS. MONOGRAPH SERIES. 1991. irreg., no.2, 1991. price varies. Princeton University, Center of International Studies, Bendheim Hall, Princeton University, Princeton, NJ 08544. TEL 609-258-4851. FAX 609-258-3988. (back issues avail.; reprint service avail. from UMI)

327   US
PRINCETON UNIVERSITY. CENTER OF INTERNATIONAL STUDIES. WORLD ORDER STUDIES PROGRAM: OCCASIONAL PAPER. 1975. irreg., no.21, 1991. price varies. Princeton University, Center of International Studies, Bendheim Hall, Princeton University, Princeton, NJ 08544. TEL 609-258-4851. FAX 609-258-3988. (reprint service avail. from UMI)

320 300   FR   ISSN 0015-9743
H3
PROBLEMES POLITIQUES ET SOCIAUX; articles et documents d'actualites mondiale. (Supplements avail.: Extreme Orient; U.S.S.R.) 1970. fortn. 450 F. Documentation Francaise, 29-31 Quai Voltaire, 75340 Paris Cedex 07, France. TEL 1-40-15-70-00. index; circ. 4,000. (also avail. in microfiche) **Indexed:** Geo.Abstr., Int.Lab.Doc., Pt.de Rep. (1989-).
   —BLDSC shelfmark: 6617.871900.
   Formerly: France. Direction de la Documentation Articles et Documents.

PROFILE OF JEWISH DISSIDENTS SERIES. see ETHNIC INTERESTS

IHR PROGRAMM. see HISTORY — History Of Europe

900 327   PL   ISSN 0033-2437
DK4010
PRZEGLAD ZACHODNI. (Text in Polish, German; summaries in English) 1945. bi-m. $26.40. Instytut Zachodni, Stary Rynek 78-79, 61-772 Poznan, Poland. Ed. Hanka Dmochowska. bk.rev.; bibl.; charts; stat.; index; circ. 1,420. **Indexed:** Hist.Abstr.
   —BLDSC shelfmark: 6944.930000.

327 960   BS
PULA; Botswana journal of African studies. (Text in English) q. $12 per copy. University of Botswana, c/o Library, Private Bag 0022, Gaborone, Botswana. (Subscr. to: Botswana Book Centre, P.O. Box 91, Gaborone, Botswana) Ed. L.D. Ngconaco. (back issues avail.)

PURA VERDAD; noticiario de comprension. see RELIGIONS AND THEOLOGY — Other Denominations And Sects

PURE VERITE; revue de bonne comprehension. see RELIGIONS AND THEOLOGY — Other Denominations And Sects

QUAKER SERVICE BULLETIN. see RELIGIONS AND THEOLOGY

QUESTE ISTITUZIONI; cronache del sistema politica. see POLITICAL SCIENCE

327   FR
QUINZAINE AFRICAINE. fortn. 3000 F. Agence Transcontinentale de Presse, 28 rue de Navarin, 75009 Paris, France. TEL 45-26-02-75. FAX 33-1-40-16-09-51. TELEX 642 717.

R C D A. (Religion in Communist Dominated Areas) see RELIGIONS AND THEOLOGY

327   GW
▼**R F E - R L DAILY REPORT.** 1990. 240/yr. $350. Radio Free Europe - Radio Liberty Inc., Publications Department, Oettingenstr. 67, 8000 Munich 22, Germany. TEL 089-21022631. FAX 089-497205. TELEX 523228. Ed. Sallie Wise. circ. 400.

991 959   AT
R I M A: REVIEW OF INDONESIAN AND MALAYSIAN AFFAIRS; a semi-annual survey of political, economic, social and cultural aspects of Indonesia and Malaysia. 1967. s-a. Aus.$22 (foreign Aus.$30). University of Sydney, Department of Indonesian & Malayan Studies, Sydney, N.S.W. 2006, Australia. (Co-sponsor: Royal Institute for Anthropology and Linguistics) Ed.Bd. adv.; bk.rev.; circ. 400. **Indexed:** Aus.P.A.I.S., E.I., M.L.A.
   Former titles: Review of Indonesian and Malayan Affairs (ISSN 0034-6594); R I M A: Review of Indonesian and Malayan Affairs.

R U S I NEWSBRIEF. (Royal United Services Institute for Defence Studies) see MILITARY

RADNER LECTURES. see POLITICAL SCIENCE

327   US
RANGEL'S REPORTS. 1977. q. $10. (Second Republic Research Center (SRRC)) Bravado Feature Service, Box 2498, Rockefeller Ctr. Sta., New York, NY 10185. Ed. Marc Rangel. illus.; circ. 2,000.
   Formerly (until 1984): Second Republic Newsletter (ISSN 0146-2547); Supersedes: Bravado.

327   IT
RASSEGNA DEL MONDO ARABO. N.S. vol.16, 1976. m. Lega degli Stati Arabi a Roma, Piazzale delle Belle Arti 6, Rome, Italy. Ed. Kris Mancuso. charts; illus.

POLITICAL SCIENCE — INTERNATIONAL RELATIONS

RAZVOJ/DEVELOPMENT; casopis za probleme drustveno-ekonomskog razvoja, zemalja u razvoju i medunarodnih odnosa. see *BUSINESS AND ECONOMICS — International Development And Assistance*

327   FR   ISSN 0080-0333
RECUEIL DES INSTRUCTIONS DONNEES AUX AMBASSADEURS ET MINISTRES DE FRANCE. irreg. price varies. (Centre National de la Recherche Scientifique) Editions du C N R S, 1 Place Aristide Briand, 92195 Meudon Cedex, France. TEL 1-45-34-75-50. FAX 1-46-26-28-49. TELEX LABOBEL 204 135 F. (Subscr. to: Presses du C N R S, 20-22, rue Saint Amand, 75015 Paris, France. TEL 1-45-33-16-00) adv.; bk.rev.; index; circ. 1,500 (controlled).

327 325.1   US
REFUGEE AND IMMIGRANT RESOURCE DIRECTORY (YEAR). 1987. triennial. $47.50. Denali Press, Box 021535, Juneau, AK 99802-1535. TEL 907-586-6014. FAX 907-463-6780.
    Description: Includes information on over 1,000 local, regional and national organizations, associations, agencies, academic programs, research centers, museums and other groups in the United States that offer services to provide information and policy analysis about refugees and immigrants.

341.1 323.1   UN   ISSN 0252-791X
REFUGEES. (Editions in English, French, German, Italian, Japanese, Spanish) 1972. q. free. United Nations High Commissioner for Refugees, P.O. Box 2500, CH-1211 Geneva 2, Switzerland. TEL 022-739-81-11. FAX 022-739-84-49. Ed. Sylvana Foa. illus.; circ. 200,000. **Indexed:** HR Rep., Refug.Abstr.
    —BLDSC shelfmark: 7336.350000.
    Former titles: U N H C R; H C R Bulletin (ISSN 0017-615X)
    Description: Describes the problems and plight of refugees around the world.

REFUGEES. see *POLITICAL SCIENCE — Civil Rights*

323.1   UN   ISSN 1014-1235
REFUGEES MAGAZINE. (Supplement to: Refugees) (Editions in English, French, German, Italian, Japanese, Spanish) 1968. q. United Nations High Commissioner for Refugees, P.O. Box 2500, 1211 Geneva 2, Switzerland. TEL 22-739-81-11. FAX 22-739-8449. TELEX 412972 PIHC CH. Ed. Sylvana Foa. circ. 200,000. **Indexed:** Refug.Abstr.
    Formerly (until 1982): U N H C R Report (ISSN 0041-5308)
    Description: Publishes articles, interviews and dossiers describing the problems and plight of refugees around the world, as well as human rights, development, environment, political and social matters related to population movements.

327   GW   ISSN 0936-8965
REIHE DER VILLA VIGONI. 1989. irreg. (Verein der Villa Vigoni e.V.) Max Niemeyer Verlag, Postfach 2140, 7400 Tuebingen 1, Germany. TEL 07071-81104. FAX 07071-87419.
    Description: Reports on political, historical and cultural relations between Germany and Italy.

327   MX   ISSN 0185-0814
JX9
RELACIONES INTERNACIONALES. 1973. q. $8. Universidad Nacional Autonoma de Mexico, Facultad de Ciencias Politicas y Sociales, Centro de Relaciones Internacionales, Villa Obregon, Ciudad Universitaria, Mexico 20, D.F., Mexico. (Subscr. to: c/o Lic. Rosa Maria Lince Campillo, Jefe del Depto. de Publicaciones, Edif. "C" Planta Baja, Cubiculo No. 24, Ciudad Universitaria, Mexico 20, D.F., Mexico) Ed. Rosa Maria Velasco. bk.rev.; bibl.; circ. 2,000. **Indexed:** Hisp.Amer.Per.Ind.
    Formerly: Revista de Relaciones Internacionales.

327   FR   ISSN 0335-2013
D410
RELATIONS INTERNATIONALES. 1974. q. 180 F.($30) (Universite de Paris I (Pantheon-Sorbonne), Institut d'Histoire des Relations Internationales Contemporaines) Societe d'Etudes Historiques des Relations Internationales Contemporaines (S.E.H.R.I.C.), 17 rue de la Sorbonne, 75005 Paris, France. (Co-sponsor: Institut Universitaire de Hautes Etudes Internationales, Geneva) Eds. Jean B. Duroselle, Jacques Freymond. bk.rev.; bibl.
    —BLDSC shelfmark: 7352.077000.

327   IT   ISSN 0034-3846
D410
RELAZIONI INTERNAZIONALI; trimestrale dell'Istituto per gli Studi di Politica Internazionale. (Text in English and Italian) 1936. q. L.60000($85) (Istituto per gli Studi di Politica Internazionale (ISPI)) Electa, Via Clerici 5, 00121 Milan, Italy. TEL 02-878266. FAX 02-8692055. Ed. Dr. Gerolamo Fiori. adv.; bk.rev.; charts; illus.; index; circ. 5,000.

327   US   ISSN 0748-0571
JX1932
REPORT OF A VANTAGE CONFERENCE. 1973. irreg., no.15, 1989. free. Stanley Foundation, 216 Sycamore St., Ste. 500, Muscatine, IA 52761. TEL 319-264-1500. FAX 319-264-0864. circ. 10,000.
    Formerly: Vantage Conference Report (ISSN 0145-8833)
    Description: Discusses the evolving world situation and addresses timely, emerging issues.

327 947   GW   ISSN 0937-7441
DJK51
REPORT ON EASTERN EUROPE. (Text in English) 1956. w. DM.270($150) Radio Free Europe - Radio Liberty, Inc., Oettingenstr. 67, 8000 Munich 22, Germany. TEL 089-2102-0. FAX 089-2285188. (Orders to: RFERL, Inc., 1775 Broadway, New York, N.Y. 10019) Ed. Ronald Linden. circ. 2,000. (back issues avail.) **Indexed:** HR Rep.
    —BLDSC shelfmark: 7643.436000.
    Former titles: Radio Free Europe Research Reports on Eastern Europe; Radio Free Europe Research Reports (ISSN 0744-1339)

327 330.9   US   ISSN 1043-3856
REPORT ON GUATEMALA. 1978. q. $10 to individuals; institutions $15. Guatemala News and Information Bureau, Box 28594, Oakland, CA 94604. TEL 415-835-0810. FAX 510-835-3017. Ed. David Loeb. adv.; bk.rev.; bibl.; charts; illus.; stat.; circ. 1,200. (back issues avail.) **Indexed:** HR Rep.
    Formerly (until 1987): Guatemala!
    Description: Articles, news briefs, interviews, and resource listings on the politics and domestic and foreign policy of this Central American country.

REPORT ON SCIENCE AND HUMAN RIGHTS. see *SCIENCES: COMPREHENSIVE WORKS*

980   US   ISSN 1058-5397
F1401
REPORT ON THE AMERICAS. 1967. 5/yr. $22 to individuals; institutions $40. North American Congress on Latin America, Inc., 475 Riverside Dr., Rm. 454, New York, NY 10115. TEL 212-870-3146. Ed. Mark Fried. adv.; bk.rev.; abstr.; charts; circ. 11,000. (also avail. in microfilm from UMI; back issues avail.; reprint service avail. from UMI) **Indexed:** Alt.Press Ind., Hisp.Amer.Per.Ind., HR Rep., Left Ind. (1982-), PAIS, Peace Res.Abstr.
    Former titles: N A C L A Report on the Americas (ISSN 0149-1598); N A C L A's Latin America and Empire Report (ISSN 0095-5930); N A C L A News (ISSN 0048-0630)

327   US
REPORT ON THE SITUATION ON HUMAN RIGHTS IN THE REPUBLIC OF GUATEMALA. 1962. irreg., latest 1983. $6. Inter-American Commission on Human Rights, 1889 F. St. N.W., Ste. 820E, Washington, DC 20006. TEL 202-789-6000. (Subscr. to: General Secretatiat, Organization of American States, Office of Publications, Washington, DC 20006)

327 914.7   GW
REPORT ON THE U S S R. (Text in English) 1956. w. $150. Radio Free Europe - Radio Liberty, Inc., Oettingenstr. 67, 8000 Munich 22, Germany. TEL 089-2102-0. FAX 089-2285188. (Orders to: RFERL, Inc., 1775 Broadway, New York, N.Y. 10019) Ed. Elizabeth Teague. circ. 2,000. (back issues avail.) **Indexed:** HR Rep.
    Former titles: Radio Liberty Research Bulletins on the Soviet Union; Radio Liberty Research Bulletins (ISSN 0148-2548)

327   US   ISSN 0034-4931
DK266.A2
REPRINTS FROM THE SOVIET PRESS. (Supplements) (Texts in English) 1965. s-m. $35 to individuals (Canada and Mexico $45; elsewhere $55); institutions $60 (Canada and Mexico $70; elsewhere $80) (effective 1991). Compass Point Publications, Inc., Box 20673, Cathedral Financial Sta., New York, NY 10025. Ed. Jean Karsavina. index; circ. 1,500. (also avail. in microform from UMI; reprint service avail. from UMI) **Indexed:** Int.Polit.Sci.Abstr., Mid.East: Abstr.& Ind.
    Description: Contains articles, speeches, documents and reports from the original sources, providing Soviet points-of-view on various topics including: unfolding process of Perestroika and Glasnost, economics, politics, foreign affairs, law, labor, agriculture, industry, and science.

RESIST NEWSLETTER. see *POLITICAL SCIENCE — Civil Rights*

327   UK   ISSN 0305-6244
HC501
REVIEW OF AFRICAN POLITICAL ECONOMY. 1974. 3/yr. $40 to individuals; institutions $90. R.O.A.P.E. Publications Ltd., Box 678, Sheffield S1 1BF, England. TEL 0742-752671. FAX 0742-738214. Ed. Jan Burgess. adv.; bk.rev.; circ. 1,500. **Indexed:** Alt.Press Ind., Curr.Cont.Africa, I D A, P.A.I.S., Rice Abstr., Rural Devel.Abstr., Stud.Wom.Abstr., World Agri.Econ.& Rural Sociol.Abstr.
    —BLDSC shelfmark: 7786.769000.

327   YU   ISSN 0486-6096
REVIEW OF INTERNATIONAL AFFAIRS; politics, economics, law, science, culture. French edition: Revue de Politique Internationale (ISSN 0035-1695); German edition: International Politik (ISSN 0535-4129); Russian edition: Mezhdunarodnaya Politika (ISSN 0350-2511); Serbian edition: Medunarodna Politika (ISSN 0543-3657); Spanish edition: Politica International (ISSN 0352-1958) (Text in English) 1950. fortn. $34. (Assembly of the SFRY) Medjunarodna Politika, Nemanjina 34, 11000 Belgrade, Yugoslavia. TEL 641-546. Dir. Ranko Petkovic. bk.rev.; index; circ. 18,000. (reprint service avail. from JRC) **Indexed:** P.A.I.S., Rural Recreat.Tour.Abstr., World Agri.Econ.& Rural Sociol.Abstr.
    —BLDSC shelfmark: 7790.800000.
    Description: Focuses on foreign policy, military treaties and strategies, economic developments and disarmament.

341.1   SZ   ISSN 0034-6608
REVIEW OF INTERNATIONAL COOPERATION. (Text in English) 1908. q. 60 Fr. International Co-operative Alliance, 15, rte. des Morillons, 1218 Grand Saconnex, Switzerland. TEL 022-798-4121. FAX 022-798-4122. TELEX 415620-ICA-CH. adv.; bk.rev.; illus.; stat.; index; circ. 4,500. (also avail. in microform from UMI; reprint service avail. from UMI) **Indexed:** P.A.I.S., Rural Recreat.Tour.Abstr., World Agri.Econ.& Rural Sociol.Abstr.
    —BLDSC shelfmark: 7851.750000.

327   UK   ISSN 0260-2105
JX1
REVIEW OF INTERNATIONAL STUDIES. 1975. 4/yr. $42 individuals; institutions $69. (British International Studies Association) Cambridge University Press, Edinburgh Bldg., Shaftesbury Rd., Cambridge CB2 2RU, England. TEL 0223-312393. (U.S. addr.: 40 West 20th St., New York, NY 10011) Ed. Richard Little. bk.rev.; index. (back issues avail.) **Indexed:** A.B.C.Pol.Sci., Abstr.Mil.Bibl., Hist.Abstr., P.A.I.S.
    —BLDSC shelfmark: 7790.940000.
    Description: Review of politics, law, history and other areas of social science in the international arena.

327   BL   ISSN 0034-7329
D839
REVISTA BRASILEIRA DE POLITICA INTERNACIONAL. (Text in Portuguese; summaries in English, Portuguese) 1958. s-a. Cr.$1000($25) Instituto Brasileiro de Relacoes Internacionais, Praia de Botafogo 186, 22250 Rio de Janeiro, Brazil. TEL 021-551-0598. Ed. Cleantho de Paiva Leite. adv.; bk.rev.; bibl.; charts; cum.index; circ. 1,000. (also avail. in microform from UMI; reprint service avail. from UMI) **Indexed:** Abstr.Mil.Bibl.

REVISTA DE DERECHO INTERNACIONAL Y CIENCIAS DIPLOMATICAS. see *LAW — International Law*

POLITICAL SCIENCE — INTERNATIONAL RELATIONS

327   BO   ISSN 0034-9194
REVISTA DIPLOMATICA E INTERNACIONAL. 1966. m. $1.50. Casilla 1598, La Paz, Bolivia. Ed. Cesar La Faye. adv.; bk.rev.; illus.

327   CU   ISSN 0049-4682
REVISTA TRICONTINENTAL. French edition: Revue Tricontinental (ISSN 0864-1587); English edition: Tricontinental Magazine (ISSN 0864-1595) 1967. bi-m. $10. Organization of Solidarity of the Peoples of Asia, Africa, and Latin America, Apdo. Postal 4224 y 6130, Calle C No. 668 e-27 y 29 Vedado, Havana, Cuba. TEL 809-30-5510. TELEX 512259. (Dist. by: Ediciones Cubanas, Obispo No. 527, Aptdo. 605, Havana, Cuba) Ed. Jose M. Ortiz. bk.rev.; charts; illus.; circ. 12,000 (other eds. 10,000 ea.). (back issues avail.) **Indexed:** HR Rep.

943   FR
REVUE D'ALLEMAGNE ET DES PAYS DE LANGUE ALLEMANDE. 1969. q. 240 F. (foreign 290 F.)(typically set in Jan.). (Centre d'Etudes Germaniques) Societe d'Etudes Allemandes, 8 rue des Ecrivains, 67081 Strasbourg Cedex, France. TEL 88-36-45-14. FAX 88-35-64-42. Ed. Mme. Falbisaner. adv.; bk.rev.; bibl.; charts. **Indexed:** Hist.Abstr.
Formerly: Revue d'Allemagne (ISSN 0035-0974)

327   CN   ISSN 0703-6337
REVUE D'INTEGRATION EUROPEENNE/JOURNAL OF EUROPEAN INTEGRATION. 1977. s-a. Can.$35. Canadian Council for European Affairs - Conseil Canadien des Affaires Europeennes, c/o Department of Political Studies, University of Saskatchewan, Saskatoon, Sask. S7N 0W0, Canada. TEL 306-966-5231. FAX 306-966-5250. TELEX 0742659. Eds. H.J. Michelmann, Panayotis Soldatos. adv.; bk.rev.; circ. 400. **Indexed:** Pt.de Rep. (1983-).
—BLDSC shelfmark: 4979.606000.
Formerly (until 1980): Centre d'Etudes et de Documentation Europeennes. Bulletin d'Information Documentaire.
Description: Focuses on political, economic, legal and social integration in Western Europe and worldwide.

327   MG
REVUE DIPLOMATIQUE DE L'OCEAN INDIEN. (Text in French) 1982. q. $29. Communication et Media Ocean Indien, Rue H. Rabesahala, B.P. 46, Antsakaviro, 101 Antananarivo, Malagasy Republic. TEL 22536. FAX 34534. TELEX 22225. Ed. Georges Ranaivosoa. adv.; bk.rev.; circ. 3,000.

327   FR
REVUE FRANCO-UKRAINIENNE ECHANGES. 1972. bi-m. 100 F. Association Franco Ukrainienne, 26 villa Auguste Blanqui, 75013 Paris, France. Ed. M. Musianowycz. adv.; bibl.; illus.; circ. 1,200.

327   US
REVUE OF INTERNATIONAL AFFAIRS. 1972. m. $300. (International Foundation for Theoretical Research, Institute for Economic & Political World Strategic Studies) American Classical College, Box 4526, Albuquerque, NM 87106. TEL 505-843-7749. Ed. C.M. Flumiani. circ. 37.
Description: World political history viewed from the criteria of the philosophy of history.

327.4   RM   ISSN 0048-8178
DR201
REVUE ROUMAINE D'ETUDES INTERNATIONALES. Rumanian edition: Revista Romana de Studii Internationale. (Text in English, French, Russian) 1967. 6/yr. 180 lei($56) (Asociatia de Drept International si Relatii Internationale "N. Titulescu" - Romanian Association for International Law and International Relations) Editura Academiei Romane, Calea Victoriei 125, 79717 Bucharest, Rumania. (Dist. by: Rompresfilatelia, Calea Grivitei 64-66, P.O. Box 12-201, 78104 Bucharest, Rumania) Ed. A. Pop. bk.rev.; bibl.; circ. 1,500. (tabloid format) **Indexed:** Abstr.Mil.Bibl, Hist.Abstr.
—BLDSC shelfmark: 7870.515000.

RISK MANAGEMENT REVIEW. see *BUSINESS AND ECONOMICS — International Commerce*

327   UK
RIVISTA; the journal of the British-Italian Society. 1941. bi-m. free to members. British-Italian Society, 24 Rutland Gate, London SW7 1BB, England. Ed. M.K. Grindrod. adv.; bk.rev.; circ. 600.

327   IT   ISSN 0035-6611
JX7
RIVISTA DI STUDI POLITICI INTERNAZIONALI. 1934. q. L.60000. Giuseppe Vedovato, Ed. & Pub., Lungarno del Tempio 40, 50121 Florence, Italy. adv.; bk.rev.; bibl.; index, cum.index: 1934-1983; circ. 1,200. **Indexed:** A.B.C.Pol.Sci., Hist.Abstr.

327   UK   ISSN 0035-8533
AP4
THE ROUND TABLE; the commonwealth journal of international affairs. 1910. 4/yr. $66 to individuals; institutions $205. Carfax Publishing Co., P.O. Box 25, Abingdon, Oxfordshire OX14 3UE, England. TEL 0235-555335. FAX 0235-553559. (U.S. subscr. addr.: Carfax Publishing Co., Box 2025, Dunnellon, FL 32630) Ed. P. Lyon. adv.; bk.rev.; index. (also avail. in microform from UMI; back issues avail.) **Indexed:** A.B.C.Pol.Sci., Hist.Abstr., I D A, Mid.East: Abstr.& Ind., P.A.I.S., Rural Recreat.Tour.Abstr., So.Pac.Per.Ind., Soc.Sci.Ind., SSCI, World Agri.Econ.& Rural Sociol.Abstr.
—BLDSC shelfmark: 8025.800000.
Refereed Serial

ROYAL UNITED SERVICES INSTITUTE OF AUSTRALIA. JOURNAL. see *MILITARY*

940   GW   ISSN 0036-0414
RUSSLAND UND WIR; ein Forum. 1961. q. DM.16. (Deutsch-Russlaendische Gesellschaft e.V.) Russland und Wir - Verlag und Handlung, Sindlinger Weg 1, 6380 Bad Homburg 1, Germany. TEL 06172-35191. Ed. Siegfried Keiling. adv.; bk.rev.; circ. 1,350.
Description: Covers political, social and economic news and developments affecting relations between Germany and Russia.

327   US   ISSN 0036-0775
D839
S A I S REVIEW; a journal of international affairs. 1956-1975; resumed 1981. s-a. $14 to individuals; institutions $28; students $12. Johns Hopkins Foreign Policy Institute, Paul H. Nitze School of Advanced International Studies, 1740 Massachusetts Ave., N.W., Washington, DC 20036. TEL 202-663-5766. FAX 202-663-5782. (Subscr. to: 1619 Massachusetts Ave., N.W., Washington, DC 20036) Ed. Bartolomeo Magone. adv.; bk.rev.; index; circ. 2,000. **Indexed:** A.B.C.Pol.Sci., Abstr.Mil.Bibl., Amer.Bibl.Slavic & E.Eur.Stud., Hist.Abstr., P.A.I.S., SSCI.
—BLDSC shelfmark: 8070.270000.
Description: Analyses contemporary international issues and recent publications on foreign affairs.

327   SW   ISSN 0348-2626
S A R E C REPORT. (Text in English) 1976. irreg. (2-5/yr.). Swedish Agency for Research Cooperation with Developing Countries - Styrelsen foer U-Landsforskning, P.O. Box 16140, S-103 23 Stockholm, Sweden. bibl.; illus.; circ. 4,000.
—BLDSC shelfmark: 8076.033800.
Formerly: S I D A Development Studies.

327 614.7   JA   ISSN 0288-2930
BQ8400
S G I. (Text in English) q. (Soka Gakkai International) Nichiren Shoshu International Center, 1-33-11 Sendagaya, Shibuya-ku, Tokyo 151, Japan. TEL 03-3356-7141. Ed. Yukio Yamaguchi. adv.
Description: News of SGI - a non-governmental international organization which advocates peace, environmental protection, human rights, and cultural and educational exchange.

327   UK
S I N. (Studies in Nonviolence) 3/yr. £3. Peace Pledge Union, Dick Sheppard House, 6 Endsleigh Street, London WC1H 0DX, England. TEL 01-387-5501.
Description: Explores theoretical and practical aspects of nonviolence.

327 341.37   UK   ISSN 0267-2537
S I P R I CHEMICAL & BIOLOGICAL WARFARE STUDIES. irreg. (Stockholm International Peace Research Institute, SW) Oxford University Press, Walton St., Oxford OX2 6DP, England. TEL 0865-56767. FAX 0865-56646. TELEX 837330 OXPRES G.
—BLDSC shelfmark: 8286.040000.

327   UK
S I P R I YEARBOOK: WORLD ARMAMENTS AND DISARMAMENT. 1969. a. varies. (Stockholm International Peace Research Institute, SW) Oxford University Press, Walton St., Oxford OX2 6DP, England. TEL 0865-56767. FAX 0865-56646. TELEX 837330 OXPRES G. Ed. Tim Barton. circ. 3,500.
Formerly: World Armaments and Disarmament: S I P R I Yearbook (ISSN 0347-2205)

SAN MARINO (REPUBBLICA). DIPARTIMENTO AFFARI ESTERI. NOTIZIA. see *PUBLIC ADMINISTRATION*

341.1   US
JX1974.7
SANE - FREEZE NEWS; campaign for global security. 1961. 3/yr. $25 to libraries (effective Oct. 1991). SANE - Freeze, Inc., Campaign for Global Security, 1819 H St., N.W., Ste. 640, Washington, DC 20006-3603. TEL 202-862-9740. FAX 202-862-9762. Ed. Monica Green. bk.rev.; charts; illus.; circ. 77,000. (looseleaf format; also avail. in microfilm from UMI; reprint service avail. from UMI)
Formerly (until 1990): SANE World - Freeze Focus (ISSN 0036-4304)

SARVODAYA. see *SOCIAL SERVICES AND WELFARE*

327   SZ
SCHWEIZERISCHE GESELLSCHAFT FUER AUSSENPOLITIK. SCHRIFTENREIHE. 1972. irreg., no.10, 1984. price varies. Paul Haupt AG, Falkenplatz 14, CH-3001 Berne, Switzerland. TEL 031-232425.

327 500   US   ISSN 1048-7042
SCIENCE AND GLOBAL SECURITY MONOGRAPH SERIES. irreg., latest vol.1. Gordon and Breach Scientific Publishers, 270 Eighth Ave., New York, NY 10011. TEL 212-206-8900. FAX 212-645-2459. TELEX 236735 GOPUB UR. (Subscr. to: Box 786, Cooper Sta., New York, NY 10276. TEL 800-545-8398; UK subscr. to: P.O. Box 90, Reading, Berkshire RG1 8JL, England. TEL 0734-560-080) Ed. H.A. Feiveson.
Refereed Serial

SEA POWER. see *MILITARY*

327   US   ISSN 0272-5827
DS36
SEARCH (BRATTLEBORO); journal for Arab-Islamic studies. 1980. a. $15 to individuals; institutions 25; students $12. Center for Arab & Islamic Studies, Inc., Box 543, Brattleboro, VT 05301. TEL 802-257-0872. FAX 802-254-5123. Ed. Samir A. Rabbo. adv.; bk.rev.; cum.index 1980-1984; circ. 4,000. (back issues avail.) **Indexed:** Hist.Abstr.
—BLDSC shelfmark: 8213.809900.

327 956   UK
SEMINAR FOR ARABIAN STUDIES. PROCEEDINGS. 1971. a. price varies. Seminar for Arabian Studies, 15 Crathie Rd., London SE12 8BT, England. bk.rev.; circ. 200.

351   SG
SENEGAL. LISTE DU CORPS DIPLOMATIQUE. irreg. Imprimerie Nationale, Rufisque, Senegal.
Supersedes: Senegal. Service du Protocole. Liste Diplomatique et Consulaire.

327   FR   ISSN 0080-8903
SENNACIECA REVUO. (Text in Esperanto) 1952. a. $8. Sennacieca Asocio Tutmonda, 67 av. Gambetta, 75020 Paris, France. TEL 47-97-87-05. bk.rev.

327   FR
SENNACIULO. (Text in Esperanto) m. $50. Sennacieca Asocio Tutmonda, 67 av. Gambetta, 75020 Paris, France. TEL 47-97-87-05.

327   BL
SERIE CAPISTRANO DE ABREU. 1982. a. Colegio Pedro II, Secretaria de Ensino, Campo de Sao Cristovao, 177 CEP 20291, Rio de Janeiro, Brazil.

SHALOM. see *ETHNIC INTERESTS*

POLITICAL SCIENCE — INTERNATIONAL RELATIONS

327 CC ISSN 0583-0176
SHIJIE ZHISHI/WORLD AFFAIRS. (Text in Chinese) 1934. s-m. $48.70. Shijie Zhishi Chubanshe - World Affairs Press, 31-A Waijiaobu Jie, Dongcheng Qu, Beijing 100005, People's Republic of China. TEL 5125544. (Dist. in US by: China Books & Periodicals, Inc., 2929 24th St., San Francisco, CA 94110. TEL 415-282-2994) Ed. Yao Dongqiao.

327 UA ISSN 0583-4597
AL-SIASSA AL-DAWLYA. (Text in English) 1965. q. Mu'assasat al-Ahram, Sharia al-Galaa, Cairo, Egypt. TEL 02-758333. FAX 02-745888. TELEX 92001. Ed. Butrus Ghali. **Indexed:** Curr.Cont.M.E.

327 GW ISSN 0175-274X
JX1903
SICHERHEIT UND FRIEDEN. Short title: S und F. q. DM.49. Nomos Verlagsgesellschaft mbh und Co. KG, Waldseestr. 3-5, 7570 Baden-Baden, Germany. TEL 07221-21040. FAX 07221-210427. TELEX 051-933524. circ. 5,000.
—BLDSC shelfmark: 8053.653600.

327 915.3 TS
AL-SIJIL AL-SHAHRI LI-AHDATH AL-ALAM/MONTHLY RECORD OF WORLD EVENTS. (Text in Arabic) 1981. m. Ministry of Information and Culture, Information Department, P.O. Box 17, Abu Dhabi, United Arab Emirates. TEL 453000. circ. 1,000 (controlled).
Description: Reviews international events and their impact on the U.A.E.

940 IT
SINISTRA EUROPEA. 1959. bi-m. L.20000 (foreign L.30000). Piazza Augusto Imperatore 32, 00186 Rome, Italy. TEL 06-68-78-689. Ed. Luciano Fraschetti. adv.; bk.rev.; illus. (back issues avail.)
Formerly: Iniziativa Europea (ISSN 0020-1340)
Description: Political forum that covers socialism and other left wing movements throughout Europe as well as the United States.

327 CH
SINO-AMERICAN RELATIONS. 1975. q. $30. Chinese Culture University Press, Chinese Culture University, Hwa Kang, Taiwan 11114, Republic of China. FAX 02-861-5487. Ed. Yu-Tang Daniel Lew. adv.; bk.rev.; circ. 1,500. **Indexed:** C.L.I., Leg.Per.

327 US ISSN 0740-6169
E183.7
SOCIETY FOR HISTORIANS OF AMERICAN FOREIGN RELATIONS. NEWSLETTER. 1970. q. $10. Society for Historians of American Foreign Relations (S.H.A.F.R.), c/o Tennessee Technological University, Department of History, Cookeville, TN 38505. TEL 615-372-3336. FAX 615-372-3898. Ed. William Brinker. adv.; bibl.; circ. 1,100. **Indexed:** Hist.Abstr.

327 FR ISSN 0296-4333
SOLIDARITE ATLANTIQUE. 1984. bi-m. 150 F.($30) Union Nationale Inter-Universitaire (UNI), 8, rue de Musset, 75016 Paris, France. TEL 45-25-34-65. FAX 45-25-51-33. Ed. Dominique Ansery. adv.; bk.rev.; circ. 20,000.

327 US
SOUNDINGS FROM AROUND THE WORLD; an idea exchange in rural development communications. 1970. s-a. $5 to industrialized countries; developing countries free. World Neighbors, Inc., 4127 N.W. 122nd St., Oklahoma City, OK 73120-8869. TEL 405-752-9700. FAX 405-752-9393. TELEX 5106002674. Ed.Bd. bk.rev.; film rev.; charts; illus.; circ. 1,700 (controlled).

327 UN
SOURCE (NEW YORK, 1989). 1989. q. United Nations Development Programme, Division of Information, One UN Plaza, New York, NY 10017. Ed. Lloyd Garrison.

327 SA
DT770
SOUTH AFRICAN INSTITUTE OF INTERNATIONAL AFFAIRS. BIENNIAL REPORT OF THE NATIONAL CHAIRMAN. 1978. biennial. R.5. South African Institute of International Affairs, P.O. Box 31596, Braamfontein 2017, South Africa. TEL 011-339-2021. FAX 011-339-2154. TELEX 4-27291 SA.
Former titles (until 1984): South African Institute of International Affairs. Report of the National Chairman; South African Institute of International Affairs. Biennial Council Report; Supersedes (1966-1977): South African Institute of International Affairs. Annual Report (ISSN 0081-2439)

327 SA
SOUTH AFRICAN INSTITUTE OF INTERNATIONAL AFFAIRS. OCCASIONAL PAPERS. irreg. price varies. South African Institute of International Affairs, P.O. Box 31596, Braamfontein 2017, South Africa. TEL 011-339-2021. FAX 011-339-2154. TELEX 4-27291 SA.

327 SA
SOUTH AFRICAN INSTITUTE OF INTERNATIONAL AFFAIRS. SPECIAL STUDIES. 1977. irreg. price varies. South African Institute of International Affairs, P.O. Box 31596, Braamfontein 2017, South Africa. TEL 011-339-2021. FAX 011-339-2154. TELEX 4-27291 SA.

320.9 KO
SOUTH-NORTH DIALOGUE IN KOREA. 1973. q. free. International Cultural Society of Korea, C.P.O. Box 2147, Seoul, S. Korea. circ. 50,000.

327 NL ISSN 1017-9267
SOUTH PACIFIC CONFERENCE. REPORT. (Text in English or French) 1950. a. South Pacific Commission, B.P. D5, Noumea, Cedex, New Caledonia. TEL 26-2000. FAX 687-263818. TELEX 3139 NM SOPACOM.

327 US ISSN 1011-1980
SOUTHERN AFRICA FREEDOM BULLETIN. bi-m. International Freedom Foundation, 200 G St., N.E., Ste. 300, Washington, DC 20002. TEL 202-546-5788. FAX 202-546-5488. TELEX 9102408891. (And: I F F (Southern African Office), P.O. Box 67926, 2021 Bryanston, South Africa. TEL 339-2621) Ed. Warwick Davies-Webb.
●Also available online.
Description: Describes and analyses South-African and international issues of importance to sub-Saharan Africa.

327.68 SA ISSN 0377-5445
SOUTHERN AFRICA RECORD. (Text in Afrikaans or English) 1975. 4/yr. R.32 (foreign R.45). South African Institute of International Affairs, P.O. Box 31596, Braamfontein 2017, South Africa. TEL 011-339-2021. FAX 011-339-2154. TELEX 4-27291 SA. circ. 650.
—BLDSC shelfmark: 8352.570000.

SOVIET-AMERICAN DEBATE; opposing viewpoints sources. see BUSINESS AND ECONOMICS — International Commerce

327 US
SOVIET FOREIGN POLICY TODAY; reports and commentaries from the Soviet press. 1983. irreg., 4th ed., 1990. $28. Current Digest of the Soviet Press, 3857 N. High St., Columbus, OH 43214-3747. TEL 614-292-4234. FAX 614-267-6310. Ed. Gordon Livermore.

SOVIET PERSPECTIVES; a monthly guide to economic reform and business activity in the Soviet Union. see BUSINESS AND ECONOMICS — International Commerce

327 301 AT ISSN 1034-7437
▼**SOVIET SOCIETY;** international review of Soviet studies. 1990. s-a. Aus.$90. James Nicholas Publishers, P.O. Box 244, Albert Park, Vic. 3206, Australia. TEL 03-696-5545. FAX 613-699-2040. Ed. Joseph Zajda. adv.; bk.rev.; index.
Formerly: Soviet Review (ISSN 1033-6257)
Description: Concerned with all aspects of contemporary Soviet society, including Soviet economy, labor and management, Soviet foreign policy, political culture and leadership, minorities in the USSR, religion, women studies, youth organizations, vocational training, schools and higher education.

327 IS ISSN 0334-4142
DS63.2.S65
SOVIET UNION AND THE MIDDLE EAST. (Text in English) 1976. m. $35 (effective 1992). Hebrew University, Marjorie Mayrock Center for Soviet and East European Research, c/o Faculty of Social Sciences, Mount Scopus, Jerusalem 91905, Israel. TEL 02-883180. FAX 02-322545. TELEX 26458. Ed. Stefani Hoffman. circ. 300. **Indexed:** HR Rep.

SPACE NEWS (SPRINGFIELD). see AERONAUTICS AND SPACE FLIGHT

320 331 CN ISSN 0229-5415
SPARTACIST CANADA. 1975. q. Can.$2 (foreign Can.$5). (Trotskyist League of Canada) Spartacist Canada Publishing Association, Box 6867, Sta. A, Toronto, Ont. M5W 1X6, Canada. TEL 416-593-4138. FAX 416-593-1529. Ed. John Masters. (back issues avail.)

327 CS
SPEKTRUM. Czech translation of: Dialogue (Washington) (US ISSN 0012-2262) 1972. q. free. Americke Velvyslanectvi - American Embassy (Prague), Trziste 15, 125 48 Prague 1, Czechoslovakia. FAX 011-431-408-8288. adv.; bk.rev.; illus.; circ. 7,000.
Formed by the merger of: Americka Kultura; Americka Veda.

327 330.9 GW ISSN 0342-0388
F1414.2
SPIEGEL DER LATEINAMERIKANISCHEN PRESSE/BOLETIN DE PRENSA LATINOAMERICANA. (Text in English, Portuguese, Spanish) 1976. m. DM.115. Institut fuer Iberoamerika-Kunde, Alsterglacis 8, 2000 Hamburg 36, Germany. TEL 040-414782-01. FAX 040-457960. Eds. Guilherme de Almeida, Wolfgang Grenz. circ. 350.

327 PL ISSN 0038-853X
SPRAWY MIEDZYNARODOWE. (Text in Polish; contents page in English, French, Polish and Russian; summaries in English) 1948. m. $51. Polski Instytut Spraw Miedzynarodowych, Ul. Warecka 1a, 00-871 Warsaw, Poland. TEL 048-22-278888. FAX 48-22-274738. (Dist. by: Ars Polona-Ruch, Krakowskie Przedmiescie 7, Warsaw, Poland) Ed. Michal Dobroczynski. bk.rev.; bibl.; circ. 3,400. (also avail. in microform from UMI; reprint service avail. from UMI)

327 US ISSN 0278-1859
JX1
STATE (WASHINGTON). 1961. m. (except Aug.). $22. U.S. Department of State, Washington, DC 20520. TEL 202-655-4000. (Orders to: Supt. of Documents, Washington, DC 20402) illus. (also avail. in microform from MIM,UMI; reprint service avail. from UMI) **Indexed:** Amer.Bibl.Slavic & E.Eur.Stud, Ind.U.S.Gov.Per., P.A.I.S., Pers.Lit.
Formerly: U.S. Department of State. Newsletter (ISSN 0041-7629)

327 301 IS ISSN 0334-2514
JQ1825.P3
STATE, GOVERNMENT AND INTERNATIONAL RELATIONS. 1971. s-a. IS.14. Hebrew University of Jerusalem, Leonard Davis Institute for International Relations, Jerusalem 91 905, Israel. FAX 826-249. (Co-sponsor: Bialik Institute) Ed. Gabriel Sheffer. adv.; bk.rev.; cum.index; circ. 1,000. (back issues avail.)

STEIRISCHE KRIEGSOPFER ZEITUNG. see MILITARY

327 IT ISSN 1120-0677
STORIA DELLE RELAZIONI INTERNAZIONALI. 1985. s-a. L.63000 (foreign L.80000). Casa Editrice Leo S. Olschki, Casella Postale 66, 50100 Florence, Italy. TEL 055-5630684. FAX 055-6530214. Ed. Ennio Di Nolfo.
—BLDSC shelfmark: 8466.492700.

327 PL ISSN 0209-0961
D839
STOSUNKI MIEDZYNARODOWE. 1982. irreg., vol.9, 1989. (Uniwersytet Warszawski, Instytut Stosunkow Miedzynarodowych) Wydawnictwa Uniwersytetu Warszawskiego, Ul. Obozna 8, 00-032 Warsaw, Poland. (Dist. by: Ars Polona, Krakowskie Przedmiescie 7, 00-068 Warsaw, Poland) Ed. Jozef Kukulka. circ. 500.

STRATEGIC REVIEW. see MILITARY

POLITICAL SCIENCE — INTERNATIONAL RELATIONS

327　　　　　　UK　ISSN 0459-7230
U162
STRATEGIC SURVEY.* 1967. a. $25. (International Institute for Strategic Studies) Brassey's, 50 Fetter Ln., London EC4A 1AA, England. TEL 071-377-4881. FAX 071-377-4888. (Subscr. to: Turpin Transactions, Distribution Centre, Blackhorse Rd., Letchworth, Herts. SG6 1HN, England. TEL 0462-672555) Ed. Sidney Bearman. charts; circ. 13,000.
　Description: An examination of the year's significant events and their importance for international security.

327 001.3　　　US　ISSN 1040-2136
JA1
STRATEGIES (LOS ANGELES); a journal of theory, culture and politics. 1988. 2/yr. $12 to individuals; institutions $20 (foreign $16). University of California, Los Angeles, Strategies Collective, 4289 Bunche Hall, Los Angeles, CA 90024. TEL 310-599-5006. Ed.Bd. adv.; circ. 250. **Indexed:** Film Lit.Ind. (1989-).
　—BLDSC shelfmark: 8474.034195.
　Description: Interdisciplinary examination of theory, culture and politics.

327　　　　　　US　ISSN 0748-9641
JX1932
STRATEGY FOR PEACE U.S. FOREIGN POLICY CONFERENCE. REPORT. 1960. a. free. Stanley Foundation, 216 Sycamore St., Ste. 500, Muscatine, IA 52761. TEL 319-264-1500. FAX 319-264-0864. circ. 22,000.
　—BLDSC shelfmark: 8474.041000.
　Formerly: Strategy for Peace Conference. Report (ISSN 0081-5942)
　Description: Recommendations as developed through conference discussions among policy shapers in the U.S. government, academia and private sector.

STUDENT ACTION. see *COLLEGE AND ALUMNI*

327　　　　　　BE
STUDIA DIPLOMATICA. (Text occasionally in English) 1948. bi-m. 1700 Fr. Institut Royal des Relations Internationales, 88 Av. de la Couronne, 1050 Brussels, Belgium. Ed. E. Coppieters. adv.; bk.rev.; index. cum.index; circ. 2,500. **Indexed:** A.B.C.Pol.Sci., Abstr.Mil.Bibl, P.A.I.S.
　Formerly: Chronique de Politique Etrangere (ISSN 0009-6059)

327　　　　　　US
JA1　　　　　　　　　　CODEN: CONFDZ
STUDIES IN CONFLICT AND TERRORISM. 1978. q. $115. Taylor & Francis, 1900 Frost Rd., Ste. 101, Bristol, PA 19007. TEL 215-785-5800. FAX 215-785-5515. Ed. George K. Tanham. adv.; bk.rev.; index. **Indexed:** A.B.C.Pol.Sci., Abstr.Mil.Bibl., Air Un.Lib.Ind., Curr.Cont., Hist.Abstr. (until 1991), Int.Polit.Sci.Abstr., Mid.East: Abstr.& Ind., Pub.Admin.Abstr., SSCI.
　Formed by the merger of (1978-1992): Conflict (ISSN 0149-5941); (1977-1992): Terrorism (Bristol) (ISSN 0149-0389)
　Description: Focuses on conflicts short of formal war such as guerilla warfare, revolution, unconventional warfare, and terrorism, and on non-physical conflicts of an economic, social, and political nature.
　Refereed Serial

323.4　　　　　US　ISSN 0146-3586
STUDIES IN HUMAN RIGHTS. 1975. irreg., latest 1992. price varies. Greenwood Press, Inc. (Subsidiary of: Greenwood Publishing Group Inc.), 88 Post Rd. W., Box 5007, Westport, CT 06881-5007. TEL 203-226-3571. FAX 203-222-1502. Ed. George W. Shepherd.
　—BLDSC shelfmark: 8490.688000.

327　　　　　　US
STUDIES IN INTERNATIONAL AFFAIRS (COLUMBIA). 1961. irreg., latest 1979. University of South Carolina, Institute of International Studies, Columbia, SC 29208. TEL 803-777-8180. Ed. Donald J. Puchala. (back issues avail.)

327　　　　　　BE
STUDIES IN INTERNATIONAL RELATIONS. 1973. irreg., no.5, 1986. Leuven University Press, Krakenstraat 3, B-3000 Leuven, Belgium. TEL 016-284175. FAX 016-284176.

327　　　　　　US
STUDIES IN WORLD PEACE. irreg., latest no.6. $39.95 per no. Edwin Mellen Press, 240 Portage Rd., Box 450, Lewiston, NY 14092. TEL 716-754-8566. FAX 716-754-4335.

327 382　　　　US　ISSN 1018-1520
▼**SUB-SAHARAN MONITOR.** 1991. bi-m. $105. International Freedom Foundation, 200 G St., N.E., Ste. 300, Washington, DC 20002. TEL 202-546-5788. FAX 202-546-5488. TELEX 9102408891. Ed. Richard Sincere. bk.rev.
　●Also available online.
　Description: Examines political and economic issues, with periodic country reports, aid and trade briefs, and investment analysis for African countries below latitude 15 degrees North.

SURVEILLANT; acquisitions for the intelligence professional. see *BIBLIOGRAPHIES*

327　　　　　　US
SURVEY OF INTERNATIONAL AFFAIRS. irreg. price varies. (Royal Institute of International Affairs, UK) Oxford University Press, 200 Madison Ave., New York, NY 10016. TEL 212-679-7300.

SURVEY OF PRESS FREEDOM IN LATIN AMERICA. see *JOURNALISM*

341.1　　　　　UK　ISSN 0039-6338
U162
SURVIVAL.* 1959. bi-m. $40. (International Institute for Strategic Studies) Brassey's, 50 Fetter Ln., London EC4A 1AA, England. TEL 071-377-4881. FAX 071-377-4888. (Subscr. to: Turpin Transactions, Distribution Centre, Blackhorse Rd., Letchworth, Herts. SG6 1HN, England. TEL 0462-672555) Ed. Hans Binnendijk. adv.; bk.rev.; index; circ. 6,500. (also avail. in microform from UMI; reprint service avail. from SWZ,UMI) **Indexed:** Abstr.Mil.Bibl., Air Un.Lib.Ind., Curr.Cont.M.E., Hist.Abstr.
　—BLDSC shelfmark: 8553.050000.
　Description: Original documents, articles and book reviews providing a forum for both policy debate and academic discussion.

327　　　　　　US
SURVIVING TOGETHER: A JOURNAL ON RELATIONS WITH THE FORMER SOVIET UNION. 1983. 4/yr. $25 to individuals; institutions $30; students $15. Institute for Soviet-American Relations, 1601 Connecticut Ave. N.W., Ste. 301, Washington, DC 20009. TEL 202-387-3034. FAX 202-667-3291. Ed.Bd. adv.; bk.rev.; circ. 5,000. (back issues avail.)
　Formerly: Surviving Together: A Journal on Soviet-American Relations (ISSN 0895-6286)
　Description: Chronicles the multi-faceted relationship between Americans and the peoples of the former Soviet Union. Covers sustainable economics and agriculture, technical assistance and aid, and the development of civil society and cultural pride.

SWISS-AMERICAN HISTORICAL SOCIETY. REVIEW. see *HISTORY*

956.91　　　　SY　ISSN 0039-7962
HC497.S8
SYRIE ET MONDE ARABE; etude mensuelle economique, politique et statistique. (Text in French) 1951. m. £S2000($250) Office Arabe de Presse et de Documentation, P.O. Box 3550, 67 Place Chahbandar, Damascus, Syria. Ed. A. Khani. charts; stat. **Indexed:** Curr.Cont.M.E., Key to Econ.Sci., P.A.I.S.For.Lang.Ind.
　—BLDSC shelfmark: 8589.070000.

327　　　　　　US
TAKING SIDES: CLASHING VIEWS ON CONTROVERSIAL ISSUES IN WORLD POLITICS. irreg., 3rd ed., 1991. $11.95. Dushkin Publishing Group, Inc., Sluice Dock, Guilford, CT 06437-9989. TEL 203-453-4351. FAX 203-453-6000. Ed. John Rourke.

327　　　　　　UK
TAPOL. 1973. bi-m. £12 to individuals; institutions £18. (Indonesia Human Rights Campaign) Tapol, 111 Northwood Rd., Thornton Heath, Surrey CR7 8HW, England. TEL 081-771-2904. FAX 081-653-0322. Eds. C Budiardjo, S.L. Liem. bk.rev.; circ. 1,100. (also avail. in microform)
　Indexed: HR Rep.

327　　　　　　IS
TEL AVIV UNIVERSITY. DAVID HOROWITZ INSTITUTE FOR THE RESEARCH OF DEVELOPING COUNTRIES. ANNUAL REPORT. (Text in English) a. Tel Aviv University, David Horowitz Institute for the Research of Developing Countries, Tel Aviv, Israel.

327　　　　　　IS
TEL AVIV UNIVERSITY. DAVID HOROWITZ INSTITUTE FOR THE RESEARCH OF DEVELOPING COUNTRIES. RESEARCH REPORTS AND PAPERS. (Text in English, Hebrew) 1972. irreg. Tel Aviv University, David Horowitz Institute for the Research of Developing Countries, Tel Aviv, Israel. circ. 250. (looseleaf format)

327　　　　　　US　ISSN 1056-8018
D860
TERRA NOVA. q. $16 (Canada, Central America and the Caribbean $20; elsewhere $25). International Freedom Foundation, 200 G St., N.E., Ste. 300, Washington, DC 20002. TEL 202-546-5788. FAX 202-546-5488. TELEX 9102408891. Eds. Mark A. Franz, Joseph J. Gimenez, III. adv.; bk.rev.; circ. 7,500.
　—BLDSC shelfmark: 8794.761200.
　Incorporates (in 1991): International Freedom Review (ISSN 0897-506X) & European Freedom Review & South African Freedom Review.
　Description: Presents free market economic and political thought, with articles from editors in IFF offices around the world.

327　　　　　　TH　ISSN 0125-6459
DS586
THAILAND. MINISTRY OF FOREIGN AFFAIRS. FOREIGN AFFAIRS NEWSLETTER. no.9, 1977. m. free. Ministry of Foreign Affairs, Department of Information, Bangkok, Thailand. TEL 2226875. FAX 222-1941. circ. 8,000.
　Formerly: Thailand. Ministry of Foreign Affairs. News Bulletin.

THIRD WORLD IN PERSPECTIVE; an interdisciplinary journal. see *POLITICAL SCIENCE*

327 341　　　　US　ISSN 1046-2066
HF1413
THIRD WORLD WITHOUT SUPERPOWERS: COLLECTED DOCUMENTS OF THE GROUP OF 77. 1981. irreg., vol.15, 1991. price varies. Oceana Publications, Inc., 75 Main St., Dobbs Ferry, NY 10522. TEL 914-693-1320. FAX 914-693-0402. Ed. Karl P. Sauvant. circ. 400. (back issues avail.)
　Description: Contains reports issued by ad hoc committees as well as declarations adopted by ministerial-level meetings and conferences.

327 341　　　　US　ISSN 1046-2074
JX1393.N54
THIRD WORLD WITHOUT SUPERPOWERS: COLLECTED DOCUMENTS OF THE NON-ALIGNED COUNTRIES. 1978. irreg., vol.10, 1989. price varies. Oceana Publications, Inc., 75 Main St., Dobbs Ferry, NY 10522. TEL 914-693-1320. FAX 914-693-0402. Eds. Odette Jankowitsch, Karl P. Sauvant. circ. 450. (back issues avail.)
　Description: Provides the documents of the non-aligned countries since the inception of the non-aligned movement and the political organization of the Third World.

327　　　　　　KO
THIS MONTH IN KOREA. (Text in English) m. Korea International Relations Institute, 37-2, 2-ka, Namsan-dong, Chung-ku, Seoul, S. Korea. TEL 752-6310. Ed. Suh Myung-Suk.

DER TIROLER; Zeitung fuer ein einiges und freies Tirol. see *HISTORY — History Of Europe*

327　　　　　　US　ISSN 0040-9898
D839
TOWARD FREEDOM; a progressive perspective on Europe, the Third World and the Non-Aligned movement. 1952. 8/yr. $20. Toward Freedom, Inc., 209 College St., Burlington, VT 05401. TEL 802-658-2523. FAX 802-658-3738. Ed. Kevin J. Kelley. adv.; bk.rev.; maps; index; circ. 3,000. (tabloid format)

POLITICAL SCIENCE — INTERNATIONAL RELATIONS

327   US   ISSN 0041-0063
JX1
TOWSON STATE JOURNAL OF INTERNATIONAL AFFAIRS.
1967. s-a. $2. Towson State University, Department of Political Science, Towson, MD 21204. TEL 301-321-2149. FAX 301-830-3829. Ed. Christina Sprecher. adv.; bk.rev.; bibl.; circ. 750. **Indexed:** A.B.C.Pol.Sci., Amer.Bibl.Slavic & E.Eur.Stud, Hist.Abstr., Mid.East: Abstr.& Ind.
—BLDSC shelfmark: 8873.007000.
Description: Gives all students an opportunity to publish their ideas and findings in the the field of International Affairs and related subjects.

949.2   NE   ISSN 0023-3412
TRACTATENBLAD VAN HET KONINKRIJK DER NEDERLANDEN. (Text mainly in Dutch; occasionally in English, French) 1951. 200/yr. (Ministerie van Buitenlandse Zaken) Staatsuitgeverij, Chr. Plantijnstraat 2, 2515 TZ The Hague, Netherlands. index; circ. 500. **Indexed:** Key to Econ.Sci.

327   US   ISSN 0192-477X
HC101
TRANSATLANTIC PERSPECTIVES. 1979. 4/yr. free. German Marshall Fund of the United States, 11 Dupont Circle, N.W., Washington, DC 20036. TEL 202-745-3950. FAX 202-265-1662. TELEX 197533 GMFUS. Ed. Nick Allen. bk.rev.; circ. 9,000 (controlled). **Indexed:** Ind.Free Per., Sage Pub.Admin.Abstr., Sage Urb.Stud.Abstr.
—BLDSC shelfmark: 9020.567700.
Description: Contains articles on U.S.-European relations and projects supported by the Fund.

TRANSIZIONE. see POLITICAL SCIENCE

327   GW   ISSN 0344-9823
TRANSNATIONAL. irregg. price varies. Europa Union Verlag GmbH, Bachstr. 32, Postfach 15 29, 5300 Bonn 1, Germany. TEL 0228-7290010. FAX 0228-695734. TELEX 8-86822. Ed. Walter Boehm.

060 327   BE   ISSN 0250-4928
AS1
TRANSNATIONAL ASSOCIATIONS/ASSOCIATIONS TRANSNATIONALES. (Text in English and French) 1949. bi-m. 1100 Fr.($30) Union of International Associations - Union des Associations Internationales, 40 rue Washington, 1050 Brussels, Belgium. adv.; bk.rev.; bibl.; charts; illus.; stat.; index. **Indexed:** Rural Devel.Abstr.
Formerly (until vol.29, 1977): International Associations (ISSN 0020-6059)

320.5   SZ   ISSN 0252-9505
TRANSNATIONAL PERSPECTIVES; an independent journal of world concerns. 1974. 3/yr. $10. Case Postale 161, 1211 Geneva 16, Switzerland. Ed. Rene Wadlow. adv.; bk.rev.; illus.; circ. 6,000. (also avail. in microfiche) **Indexed:** HR Rep., P.A.I.S., Refug.Abstr.
—BLDSC shelfmark: 9024.978000.
Formerly: World Federalist (ISSN 0043-843X)

327   SI   ISSN 0082-6316
TRENDS IN SOUTHEAST ASIA. (Text in English) 1971. irreg., no.9, 1986. price varies. Institute of Southeast Asian Studies, Heng Mui Keng Terrace, Pasir Panjang, Singapore 0511, Singapore. TEL 7780955. FAX 7781735. TELEX RS 37068 ISEAS.
Description: Political trends in Southeast Asia.

327   US   ISSN 0275-5351
D839
TRIALOGUE; report of the annual plenary meeting. 1973. a. $12 includes Task Force Reports, Triangle Papers. Trilateral Commission, 345 E. 46 St., New York, NY 10017. TEL 212-661-1180. FAX 212-949-7268. Ed. Andrew V. Frankel. circ. 5,500. **Indexed:** P.A.I.S.

327   US
TRIANGLE PAPERS. 1973. irreg. (approx. a.). price varies. Trilateral Commission, 345 E. 46th St., New York, NY 10017. TEL 212-661-1180. FAX 212-949-7268. TELEX 235128 NYU UR. Ed.Bd. circ. 3,000. (back issues avail.)

TRIBUNE. see WOMEN'S INTERESTS

TUDUV-STUDIE. REIHE POLITIKWISSENSCHAFTEN. see POLITICAL SCIENCE

TURKEY BRIEFING. see POLITICAL SCIENCE — Civil Rights

327   RU   ISSN 0320-7986
TWENTIETH CENTURY AND PEACE; bulletin of the Soviet Peace Committee. Russian edition: Vek 20 i Mir. French edition: Vingtieme Siecle et la Paix. German edition: 20 Jahrhundert und der Frieden. Spanish edition: Siglo 20 y la Paz. (Editions in English, French, German, Russian, Spanish) 1958. m. 1.20 Rub. Sovetskii Komitet Zashchity Mira - Soviet Peace Committee, 16-2 Gorky St., 103009 Moscow, Russia. TEL 200-38-07. Ed. Anatoly Belyaev. adv.; bk.rev. **Indexed:** Curr.Dig.Sov.Press.
Description: Includes controversial topical themes like Chernobyl, perestroika and glasnost. Retrospective material on the Stalin years, Russian involvement in World War II and the 1917 Revolution add historical perspective to current events.

366   US
TWENTIETH CENTURY FUND. NEWSLETTER. 1949. irreg. (approx. 3/yr.). free. Twentieth Century Fund, 41 E. 70th St., New York, NY 10021. TEL 212-535-4441. FAX 212-535-7534. Ed. Beverly Goldberg. circ. 10,000. (reprint service avail. from KTO) **Indexed:** Vert.File Ind.
Former titles: Twentieth Century Fund. Bulletin; Twentieth Century Fund. Newsletter (ISSN 0041-4611)

U N C H S HABITAT NEWS. (United Nations Centre for Human Settlements) see HOUSING AND URBAN PLANNING

341.1   UN   ISSN 0251-7329
JX1977.A1
U N CHRONICLE. (Editions in English, French and Spanish) 1964. 11/yr. $20. United Nations Publications, Room DC2-853, New York, NY 10017. TEL 212-963-8302. FAX 212-963-3489. (Or: Distribution and Sales Section, Palais des Nations, CH-1211 Geneva 10, Switzerland) bk.rev.; bibl.; charts; illus.; index; circ. 7,000. (also avail. in microfiche from UMI) **Indexed:** Acad.Ind., C.L.I., Deep Sea Res.& Oceanogr.Abstr., Hlth.Ind., HR Rep., Leg.Per., Mag.Ind., PMR, R.G., Soc.Sci.Ind.
Formerly: U N Monthly Chronicle (ISSN 0041-5367); Which superseded: United Nations Review.
Description: Contains reports on the wide-ranging activities of the entire UN system as it deals with problems ranging from food and health to nuclear disarmament and the world economy.

327 355   UN   ISSN 1012-4934
JX1974
U N I D I R NEWSLETTER/LETTRE DE L'U N I D I R. (Text in English and French) 1988. q. $25. United Nations Institute for Disarmament Research, Palais des Nations, 1211 Geneva 10, Switzerland. TEL 04122-7346011. FAX 04122-7339879. Ed. Chantal de Jonge Oudraat. bk.rev.; bibl.; circ. 3,000.
Description: Focuses and provides detailed information on recent and on-going research on a specific subject in the field of disarmament and international security. Also includes conference announcements and news from institutes.

327   US
U N REFORM CAMPAIGNER; dedicated to building a more effective United Nations systems. 1976. s-a. $10. Campaign for U N Reform, Box 15270, Washington, DC 20003-0270. TEL 202-546-3956. Ed. Eric Cox. circ. 2,000.

327   UN
U N STUDIES. 1982. irreg. Heritage Foundation, 214 Massachusetts Ave., N.E., Washington, DC 20002. TEL 202-546-4400. (looseleaf format; also avail. in microfiche; back issues avail.)

327   BE
U P INFORMATIONS. 1976. q. 120 Fr. Universite de Paix - University of Peace, Bd. du Nord 4, 5000 Namur, Belgium. FAX 32-81-231882. Ed. Dominique de Crombrugghe. bk.rev.; circ. 4,000.

327   MX
U R S S EMBAJADA. BOLETIN DE INFORMACION.* vol. 30, 1974. m. Embajada de U R S S, Calzada de Tacubaya 204, Zona 11, Apdo. 11-379, Admon de Correos No. 11, Mexico D.F., Mexico. charts; illus.

U S AND FOREIGN DIPLOMATIC CONTACTS. see BUSINESS AND ECONOMICS — Trade And Industrial Directories

327 333.7   US
U S ASSOCIATION FOR THE CLUB OF ROME NEWSLETTER. 1977. irreg. (6-8/yr.). $35. U S Association for the Club of Rome, Four Linden Square, Wellesley, MA 02181. TEL 617-235-5320. Ed. David Dodson Gray. bk.rev.; circ. 350. (tabloid format)

327   US
U S - CHINA REVIEW. 1975. 4/yr. $15 to individuals; institutions $18 (foreign $20). U S - China Peoples Friendship Association, 306 W. 38th St., Rm. 603, New York, NY 10018-2903. TEL 212-736-7355. Ed. Hugh Deane. adv.; bk.rev.; circ. 17,000. **Indexed:** Mid.East: Abstr.& Ind., New Per.Ind.
Incorporates: New China.
Description: Features articles on Chinese politics, economics, social trends and culture, as well as on US-China relations.

327 330.9 320   US
U S S R REPORT: PROBLEMS OF THE FAR EAST. irreg. (approx. 5/yr.). $5 per no. U.S. Joint Publications Research Service, Box 12507, Arlington, VA 22209. TEL 703-487-4630. (Orders to: NTIS, Springfield, VA 22161)
Formerly: Problems of the Far East.
Description: Translations of articles by Soviet writers on Soviet relations with China and other Asian countries, and on economic and political conditions in China and Asia.

U S S R REPORT: WORLD ECONOMY AND INTERNATIONAL RELATIONS. see BUSINESS AND ECONOMICS

327 629.1   US
U S S R SERIAL REPORTS: AVIATION AND COSMONAUTICS. irreg. $100 in US, Canada, Mexico; elsewhere $200. (Joint Publications Research Service) U.S. National Technical Information Service, 5825 Port Royal Rd., Springfield, VA 22161. TEL 703-487-4630.

327   US
U S S R SERIAL REPORTS: ECONOMIC AFFAIRS. irreg. $150 in US, Canada, Mexico; elsewhere $300. (Joint Publications Research Service) U.S. National Technical Information Service, 5825 Port Royal Rd., Springfield, VA 22161. TEL 703-487-4630.

327 355   US
U S S R SERIAL REPORTS: FOREIGN MILITARY REVIEW. irreg. $200 in US, Canada, Mexico; elsewhere $400. (Joint Publications Research Service) U.S. National Technical Information Service, 5825 Port Royal Rd., Springfield, VA 22161. TEL 703-487-4630.

327   US
U S S R SERIAL REPORTS: INTERNATIONAL AFFAIRS. irreg. $275 in US, Canada, Mexico; elsewhere $550. (Joint Publications Research Service) U.S. National Technical Information Service, 5825 Port Royal Rd., Springfield, VA 22161. TEL 703-487-4630.

327 355   US
U S S R SERIAL REPORTS: MILITARY HISTORY JOURNAL. irreg. $150 in US, Canada, Mexico; elsewhere $300. (Joint Publications Research Service) U.S. National Technical Information Service, 5825 Port Royal Rd., Springfield, VA 22161. TEL 703-487-4630.

327 301   US
U S S R SERIAL REPORTS: SOCIOLOGICAL STUDIES. irreg. $150 in US, Canada, Mexico; elsewhere $300. (Joint Publications Research Service) U.S. National Technical Information Service, 5825 Port Royal Rd., Springfield, VA 22161. TEL 703-487-4630.

U S - THIRD WORLD POLICY PERSPECTIVES. see HISTORY

POLITICAL SCIENCE — INTERNATIONAL RELATIONS 3975

327 DK ISSN 0903-7845
UDENRIGS; det udenrigspolitiske magasin. 1945. q. DKK 250 (typically set in Mar.). Udenrigspolitiske Selskab - Foreign Policy Society, Amaliegade 40 A, DK-1256 Copenhagen K, Denmark.
TEL 33-14-88-86. FAX 33-14-85-20. Ed.Bd. adv.; bk.rev.; charts; illus.; stat.; index; circ. 1,800. (back issues avail.)
Formerly: Fremtiden (ISSN 0016-1020)

327 DK ISSN 0041-5693
UDENRIGSPOLITISKE SKRIFTER. 1953. q. DKK 119. Udenrigspolitiske Selskab, Amaliegade 40 A, 1256 Copenhagen K, Denmark. Ed.Bd. circ. 2,000.

327 DK
UDVIKLING DANMARK OG U-LANDENE. 8/yr. DKK 85. Danida, Ministry of Foreign Affairs - Danish International Development Assistance, Asiatisk Plads 2, DK-1448 Copenhagen K, Denmark.
TEL 33-92-08-48. FAX 33-92-07-10. TELEX 31292-ETR-DK. Ed. Jesper Soe. illus.

327 GW ISSN 0343-0553
UEBERBLICK; Zeitschrift fuer oekumenische Begegnung und internationale Zusammenarbeit. 1965. q. DM.25. Verlag Dienste in Uebersee, Esplanade 14, 2000 Hamburg 36, Germany. TEL 040-341444. FAX 040-353800. Eds. Renate Wilke-Launer, Cord Aschenbrenner. bk.rev.; film rev.; charts; illus.; circ. 18,000. (back issues avail.)

327 FI ISSN 0501-0659
ULKOPOLITIIKKA/FINNISH JOURNAL OF FOREIGN AFFAIRS/UTRIKESPOLITIK. (Text in Finnish, Swedish; Summary and contents page in English) 1972. q. Ulkopoliittinen Instituutti - Finnish Institute of International Affairs, Pursimiehenkatu 8, SF-00150 Helsinki, Finland. TEL 358-0-170434.
FAX 358-0-669375. Ed. Jyrko Livonen. circ. 4,500.
Description: Specializes in foreign policy questions.

ULTIMATE ISSUES. see RELIGIONS AND THEOLOGY — Judaic

327 UN ISSN 0082-7509
UNESCO. RECORDS OF THE GENERAL CONFERENCE. PROCEEDINGS. (Text in English, French, Russian and Spanish) irreg., 25th session, 1989. price varies. Unesco, 7-9 Place de Fontenoy, 75700 Paris, France.

327 UN ISSN 0082-7517
UNESCO. RECORDS OF THE GENERAL CONFERENCE. RESOLUTIONS. (Text in Arabic, English, French, Spanish and Russian) irreg., 25th session, 1989. price varies. Unesco, 7-9 Place de Fontenoy, 75700 Paris, France. TEL 577-16-10.

327 UN ISSN 0082-7525
UNESCO. REPORT OF THE DIRECTOR-GENERAL ON THE ACTIVITIES OF THE ORGANIZATION. (Text in Arabic, English, French, Russian and Spanish) 1959. biennial. price varies. Unesco, 7-9 Place de Fontenoy, 75700 Paris, France.
—BLDSC shelfmark: 7448.080000.

327 US ISSN 0250-779X
JX1904.5
UNESCO YEARBOOK ON PEACE AND CONFLICT STUDIES. 1981. a. price varies. (United Nations Educational, Scientific and Cultural Organization) Greenwood Press, Inc. (Subsidiary of: Greenwood Publishing Group Inc.), 88 Post Rd. W., Box 5007, Westport, CT 06881-5007. TEL 203-226-3571.
FAX 203-222-1502. Ed. Hylke Tromp. Indexed: GeoRef.

UNITED KINGDOM - COMMONWEALTH OF NATIONS - DIRECTORY OF GOVERNMENTS. see BUSINESS AND ECONOMICS — Trade And Industrial Directories

327 US ISSN 0954-075X
UNITED KINGDOM FREEDOM BULLETIN. bi-m. $30. International Freedom Foundation, 200 G St., N.E., Ste. 300, Washington, DC 20002.
TEL 202-546-5788. FAX 202-546-5488. TELEX 9102408891. (And: I F F (UK), Chesham House, 150 Regent St., Ste. 500, London W1R 5FA, England. TEL 071-729-5664) circ. 1,500 (controlled).
Description: Describes and analyses issues regarding the United Kingdom, the Commonwealth, Europe and the European Community.

341.13 UN
UNITED NATIONS. CONFERENCE ON TRADE AND DEVELOPMENT. TRADE AND DEVELOPMENT BOARD. OFFICIAL RECORDS. SUPPLEMENTS. 1965. irreg. price varies. United Nations Publications, Rm. DC2-853, New York, NY 10017.
TEL 212-963-8302. FAX 212-963-3489. TELEX 28-96-96. (Or: Palais des Nations, 1211 Geneva 10, Switzerland. TEL 800-253-9646) circ. 3,500. (also avail. in microfiche)
Formerly: United Nations. Trade and Development Board. Official Records. Supplements (ISSN 0082-8483)
Description: Includes numbered supplements which contain the resolutions and decisions of the Trade and Development Board; reports and resolutions and decisions of its main subsidiary bodies.

341.13 UN ISSN 0082-8092
UNITED NATIONS. ECONOMIC AND SOCIAL COUNCIL. OFFICIAL RECORDS. irreg. price varies. United Nations Publications, Rm. DC2-853, New York, NY 10017. TEL 212-963-8302. FAX 212-963-3489. (Or: Distribution and Sales Section, Palais des Nations, CH-1211 Geneva 10, Switzerland. TEL 800-253-9646) (also avail. in microfiche)

341.13 UN ISSN 0082-8416
UNITED NATIONS. SECURITY COUNCIL. OFFICIAL RECORDS. (Supplement avail.) irreg. price varies. United Nations Publications, Rm. DC2-853, New York, NY 10017. TEL 212-963-8302.
FAX 212-963-3489. (Or: Distribution and Sales Section, Palais des Nations, CH-1211 Geneva 10, Switzerland. TEL 800-253-9646) (also avail. in microfiche)
—BLDSC shelfmark: 6242.487000.

341.13 UN ISSN 0257-067X
UNITED NATIONS. SECURITY COUNCIL. OFFICIAL RECORDS. SUPPLEMENT. French edition: Nations Unies. Conseil de Securite. Documents Officials. Supplement (ISSN 0257-0769); Russian edition: Organizatsiya Ob'edinennykh Natsii. Sovet Bezopasnosti. Ofitsial'nye Otchety. Dopolnenie (ISSN 0257-1250); Spanish edition: Naciones Unidas. Consejo de Seguridad. Documentos Oficiales. Suplemento (ISSN 0257-0971) 1950. a. United Nations Publications, Room DC2-853, New York, NY 10017. TEL 212-963-8302. FAX 212-963-3489. (Or: Distribution and Sales Section, Palais des Nations, CH-1211 Geneva 10, Switzerland)

327 330 UN
UNITED NATIONS. TRUSTEESHIP COUNCIL. OFFCIAL RECORDS. VERBATIM RECORDS OF PLENARY MEETINGS. (Text in English, French) 1946? a. United Nations Publications, Rm. DC2-0853, New York, NY 10017. TEL 212-963-8302.
FAX 212-963-3489.

341.13 UN ISSN 0082-8505
UNITED NATIONS. TRUSTEESHIP COUNCIL. OFFICIAL RECORDS. irreg., 39th session, 1972. price varies. United Nations Publications, Rm. DC2-853, New York, NY 10017. TEL 212-963-8302.
FAX 212-963-3489. (Or: Distribution and Sales Section, Palais des Nations, CH-1211 Geneva 10, Switzerland. TEL 800-253-9646) (also avail. in microfiche)
—BLDSC shelfmark: 6242.493000.

327 330 UN
UNITED NATIONS. TRUSTEESHIP COUNCIL. OFFICIAL RECORDS. ANNEXES - SESSIONAL FASCICLE. 1946. a. United Nations Publications, Rm. DC2-0853, New York, NY 10017. TEL 212-963-8302.
FAX 212-3489. Text in English, French.

327 330 UN
UNITED NATIONS. TRUSTEESHIP COUNCIL. OFFICIAL RECORDS. RESOLUTIONS. (Text in English, French) 1946? a. United Nations Publications, Rm. DC2-0853, New York, NY 10017.
TEL 212-963-8302. FAX 212-963-3489.

341.13 UN ISSN 0082-8513
UNITED NATIONS. TRUSTEESHIP COUNCIL. OFFICIAL RECORDS. SUPPLEMENTS. irreg. price varies. United Nations Publications, Rm. DC2-853, New York, NY 10017. TEL 212-963-8302. FAX 212-963-3489. (Or: Distribution and Sales Section, Palais des Nations, CH-1211 Geneva 10, Switzerland) (also avail. in microfiche)

341.13 UN ISSN 0082-8521
JX1977.A37
UNITED NATIONS. YEARBOOK. 1946. a. price varies. (United Nations, Department of Public Information) United Nations Publications, Rm. DC2-853, New York, NY 10017. TEL 212-963-8902.
FAX 212-963-3489. (Or: Distribution and Sales Section, Palais des Nations, CH-1200 Geneva 10, Switzerland) index. (also avail. in microfiche; reprint service avail. from KTO)
—BLDSC shelfmark: 9406.400000.

327 370.196 CN
UNITED NATIONS ASSOCIATION IN CANADA. QUARTERLY BULLETIN. (Text in English, French) 1975. q. Can.$20. United Nations Association in Canada, 808-63 Sparks St., Ottawa, Ont. K1P 5A6, Canada. TEL 613-232-5751. FAX 613-563-2455. Ed. Angus Archer. bk.rev.; circ. 3,500.

327 CH
UNITED NATIONS ASSOCIATION OF THE REPUBLIC OF CHINA NEWS LETTER. (Text in English) 1950. m. free. United Nations Association of the Republic of China, 101 Ning Po West St., Taipei, Taiwan, Republic of China. TEL 02-301-2654. Ed. Lei Pao-chung. circ. 1,400.
Description: Discusses political reform, trade policy, economics, foreign relations, and news about mainland China and Taiwan.

327 AT
UNITED NATIONS GENERAL ASSEMBLY: REPORT OF THE AUSTRALIAN DELEGATION. 1946. a. price varies. Australian Government Publishing Service, G.P.O. Box 84, Canberra, A.C.T. 2601, Australia.
Formerly: Australian Mission to the United Nations. United Nations General Assembly. Australian Delegation. Report.

341.23 NZ ISSN 0110-1951
DU400
UNITED NATIONS HANDBOOK. a. $15. Ministry of External Relations and Trade, Wellington, New Zealand.
Supersedes: United Nations and Related Agencies Handbook.
Description: Guide to the membership and structure of organizations in the U.N. family.

341.13 US ISSN 0743-9180
UNITED NATIONS ISSUES CONFERENCE. REPORT. 1970. a. free. Stanley Foundation, 216 Sycamore St., Ste. 500, Muscatine, IA 52761. TEL 319-264-1500. FAX 319-264-0864. circ. 12,000.
—BLDSC shelfmark: 7673.780000.
Former titles: Conference on United Nations Procedures. Report (ISSN 0069-8601); Conference on Organization and Procedures of the United Nations Report.
Description: Reports discussion of current concern or organizational procedure by groups of officials and academic specialists.

341.13 US ISSN 0748-433X
UNITED NATIONS OF THE NEXT DECADE CONFERENCE. REPORT. 1965. a. free. Stanley Foundation, 216 Sycamore St., Ste. 500, Muscatine, IA 52761. TEL 319-264-1500. FAX 319-264-0864. circ. 15,000.
Description: Discussion of a major issue and its future implications by groups of officials and international experts.

327 341 UN ISSN 0817-9751
UNITED NATIONS REVIEW. 1971. bi-m. free. United Nations Information Centre, G.P.O. Box 4045, Sydney, N.S.W. 2001, Australia. TEL 02-283-1144. FAX 02-283-1319. circ. 1,800. (back issues avail.)
Indexed: Mag.Ind.
Description: Covers United Nation matters of general interest.

327 382 338.91 US
UNITED NATIONS WEEKLY REPORT. 1982. w. $93. Renate B. McCarter, Ed. & Pub., 823 Park Ave., New York, NY 10021. TEL 212-288-8505. circ. 1,400. (back issues avail.)

354.47 US
U.S. CENTRAL INTELLIGENCE AGENCY. APPEARANCES OF SOVIET LEADERS. s-a. U.S. Central Intelligence Agency, Washington, DC 20505. (Dist. to non-U.S. Government users by: Document Expediting (DOCEX) Project, Library of Congress, Washington, DC 20540)

POLITICAL SCIENCE — INTERNATIONAL RELATIONS

327   US   ISSN 0012-3099
JX1705
U.S. DEPARTMENT OF STATE. DIPLOMATIC LIST. q. price varies. U.S. Department of State, Office of Information Services, Washington, DC 20520. TEL 202-655-4000. (Orders to: Supt. of Documents, Washington, DC 20402)
Description: Lists foreign diplomats in and around Washington, D.C.

327   US   ISSN 0023-0790
JX1705
U.S. DEPARTMENT OF STATE. KEY OFFICERS OF FOREIGN SERVICE POSTS; guide for business representatives. 2/yr. $10. U.S. Department of State, Office of Information Services, Washington, DC 20520. TEL 202-655-4000. (Orders to: Supt. of Documents, Washington, DC 20402-9371)
●Also available online. Vendor(s): DIALOG.

327   US
U.S. FOREIGN BROADCAST INFORMATION SERVICE. TRENDS. w. $240 in N. America (foreign $480). U.S. National Technical Information Service, 5285 Port Royal Rd., Springfield, VA 22161. TEL 703-487-4600. FAX 703-321-8547. TELEX 64617. (also avail. in microfiche).
Formerly: Trends in Communist Media.
Description: Offers expert analysis of international political events.

327   US   ISSN 0083-3088
U.S. PEACE CORPS. ANNUAL REPORT. 1962. irreg. free. U.S. Peace Corps, 1990 K St., N.W., Washington, DC 20526. TEL 202-254-5010. Ed. James C. Flanigan.

327   US
UNITED STATES IN THE WORLD: FOREIGN PERSPECTIVES. 1975. irreg., no.4, 1985. price varies. University of Chicago Press, 5801 S. Ellis Ave., Chicago, IL 60637. TEL 312-702-7899. Ed. Akira Iriye. adv.; bk.rev. (reprint service avail. from UMI,ISI)
Refereed Serial

327   US   ISSN 0083-0208
UNITED STATES PARTICIPATION IN THE UNITED NATIONS; report by the President to Congress. (Subseries of its International Organization and Conference Series) 1947. a. U.S. Department of State, Bureau of International Organization Affairs, 2201 C St., N.W., Washington, DC 20520. (Subscr. to: Supt. of Documents, Washington, D.C. 20520)

327.2   CL
UNIVERSIDAD DE GUAYAQUIL. ESCUELA DE DIPLOMACIA. REVISTA. 1973. irreg. Universidad de Guayaquil, Escuela de Diplomacia, Calle Chile 900, Apdo. 471, Guayaquil, Chile.

UNIVERSIDAD DE PANAMA. FACULTAD DE DERECHO Y CIENCIAS POLITICAS. CUADERNOS. see *LAW*

327   GW   ISSN 0341-3233
UNIVERSITAET HAMBURG. INSTITUT FUER INTERNATIONALE ANGELEGENHEITEN. VEROEFFENTLICHUNGEN. 1975. irreg., vol. 11, 1983. price varies. Nomos Verlagsgesellschaft mbH und Co. KG, Waldseestr. 3-5, Postfach 610, 7570 Baden-Baden, Germany. Indexed: Rural Recreat.Tour.Abstr., World Agri.Econ.& Rural Sociol.Abstr.

UNIVERSITAET HAMBURG. INSTITUT FUER INTERNATIONALE ANGELEGENHEITEN. WERKHEFTE. see *LAW — International Law*

327.73   BE   ISSN 0076-1206
UNIVERSITE CATHOLIQUE DE LOUVAIN. CENTRE D'ETUDES POLITIQUES. WORKING GROUP "AMERICAN FOREIGN POLICY." CAHIER.* 1969. irreg. Universite Catholique de Louvain, Centre d'Etudes Politiques, 1348 Louvain-la-Neuve, Belgium. (Dist. in U.S. by: Humanities Press, Inc., 171 First Ave., Atlantic Highlands, NJ 07716, U.S.A.)

320   US   ISSN 0731-6321
UNIVERSITY OF CALIFORNIA, BERKELEY. INSTITUTE OF INTERNATIONAL STUDIES. POLICY PAPERS IN INTERNATIONAL AFFAIRS. 1977. irreg. (2-3/yr.). price varies. University of California, Berkeley, Institute of International Studies, 215 Moses Hall, Berkeley, CA 94720. TEL 415-642-7189. FAX 415-643-5045. Ed. Paul M. Gilchrist.
—BLDSC shelfmark: 6543.327200.
Description: Essays on important current policy issues related to international affairs.

327   US   ISSN 0085-6452
UNIVERSITY OF SOUTH CAROLINA. INSTITUTE OF INTERNATIONAL STUDIES. ESSAY SERIES. 1967. irreg., no.9, 1979. $5 per no. University of South Carolina, Institute of International Studies, Columbia, SC 29208. TEL 803-777-8180. circ. 200. (back issues avail.)

327   US
UPDATE CENTRAL AMERICA. 1981. 10/yr. $15. Inter-Religious Task Force on Central America, 475 Riverside Dr., Rm. 563, New York, NY 10115. TEL 212-870-3383. circ. 2,000. (tabloid format; back issues avail.)
Description: Mobilize U.S. religious and solidarity activities toward a more just U.S. policy towards Central America.

327   US   ISSN 0884-6227
DK266.A2
UPDATE U S S R.* 1932. 10/yr. $7.50. New World Review Publications, Inc., 239 W. 23rd St., New York, NY 10011-2302. Ed. Marilyn Bechtel. adv.; bk.rev.; index; circ. 5,000. (also avail. in microfilm from UMI; reprint service avail. from UMI) Indexed: Amer.Hist.& Life, Hist.Abstr., Mid.East: Abstr.& Ind.
Former titles (1951-1985): New World Review (ISSN 0028-7067); (1932-1951): Soviet Russia Today.

327   NO
UTENRIKSPOLITISKE SKRIFTER/NORWEGIAN FOREIGN POLICY STUDIES. (Text in English, Norwegian) irreg. Norsk Utenrikspolitisk Institutt - Norwegian Institute of International Affairs, Postboks 8159, Dep., 0033 Oslo 1, Norway. TEL 02-177050. FAX 02-177015.

VAART FOERSVAR. see *MILITARY*

327   SW   ISSN 0042-2754
VAERLDSPOLITIKENS DAGSFRAGOR. 1940. 12/yr. SEK 197. Utrikespolitiska Institutet - Swedish Institute of International Affairs, Box 1253, 111 82 Stockholm, Sweden. Ed. Ulla Nordloef. charts; circ. 8,000.

VENTO DEL SUD; periodico di lotta meridionale. see *ETHNIC INTERESTS*

327   GW   ISSN 0042-384X
VEREINTE NATIONEN. 1962. bi-m. DM.45($28) (Deutsche Gesellschaft fuer die Vereinten Nationen) N.P. Englel Verlag, P.O. Box 1670, D-7640 Kehl am Rhein, Germany. TEL 7851-2463. FAX 7851-4234. TELEX 753560. Ed. Volker Weyel. adv.; bk.rev.; charts; stat.; illus.; circ. 3,600. Indexed: P.A.I.S.For.Lang.Ind.
—BLDSC shelfmark: 9155.852000.
Description: Presents articles, reports and documentation concerning the procedures and actions of the UN

327   AU
VERZEICHNIS DER KONSULARISCHEN VERTRETUNGEN IN OESTERREICH. 1973. bi-m. Bundesministerium fuer Auswaertige Angelegenheiten, Ballhausplatz 2, A-1014 Vienna, Austria. circ. controlled.

327 338.9   GW
VIERTELJAHRESBERICHTE - PROBLEME DER INTERNATIONALEN ZUSAMMENARBEIT. (Text in German; summaries in English, French) 1960. q. DM.54. (Friedrich-Ebert-Stiftung, Forschung Institut) Verlag H.J.W. Dietz Nachf. GmbH, In der Raste 2, 5300 Bonn 1, Germany. TEL 0228-238083. adv.; bk.rev.; abstr.; bibl.; index; circ. 1,500. Indexed: P.A.I.S.For.Lang.Ind., Rural Recreat.Tour.Abstr., World Agri.Econ. & Rural Sociol.Abstr.
Formerly: Vierteljahresberichte - Probleme der Entwicklungslaender (ISSN 0015-7910)

VIGIL/HA-MISHMAR. see *ETHNIC INTERESTS*

327   GW   ISSN 0938-863X
▼**VILLA VIGONI. JAHRBUCH.** 1990. a. (Verein der Villa Vigoni e.V.) Max Niemeyer Verlag, Postfach 2140, 7400 Tuebingen 1, Germany. TEL 07071-81104. FAX 07071-87419. circ. 2,000.

327   FR
VINGTIEME SIECLE FEDERALISTE. no.396, 1968. q. 160 F. La Federation, 244 rue de Rivoli, 75001 Paris, France. Ed. Jacques Bassot. bk.rev.; bibl.

266 276   BE   ISSN 0042-7527
G1
VIVANT UNIVERS; revue de la promotion humaine et chretienne en Afrique et dans le monde. 1934. bi-m. 1168 Fr.($30) ASBL "Grands Lacs", 115 Chaussee de Dinant, B-5000 Namur, Belgium. Ed. R.P. Boom. adv.; bk.rev.; abstr.; bibl.; charts; illus.; stat.; circ. 20,000. Indexed: World Agri.Econ.& Rural Sociol.Abstr.
Formerly: Vivante Afrique.

327 943 947   GW   ISSN 0042-8337
VOLK AUF DEM WEG. 1971. m. DM.48. Landsmannschaft der Deutschen aus Russland e.V., Raitelsbergstr. 49, D-7000 Stuttgart 1, Germany. TEL (0711)2623417. Ed. Frau Braun. bk.rev.; illus.; circ. 4,000.

327   NE
VREDE; maandblad voor vredesvraagstukken. 1964. m. fl.37.50. Stichting Vredesopbouw, Oosterkade 13, 3582 AT Utrecht, Netherlands. Ed.Bd. bk.rev.; circ. 1,500.
Former titles: Vredesopbouw (ISSN 0042-9120); Stichting Vredesopbouw. Maandschrift.

327 330   PL   ISSN 0860-7591
WARSAW VOICE. (Text in English) 1988. w. $98 (Europe $78). Polska Agencja Interpress, Ul. Bagatela 12, 00-585 Warsaw, Poland. TEL 48-22-282221. FAX 48-22-284651. TELEX 814775. Ed. Andrzej Jonas. adv.; circ. 20,000.
Description: Provides information on current Polish affairs.

332.6   US   ISSN 0278-937X
WASHINGTON PAPERS. 1972. irreg. (Center for Strategic and International Studies) Praeger Publishers (Subsidiary of: Greenwood Publishing Group Inc.), 88 Post Rd., W., Box 5007, Westport, CT 06881. TEL 203-226-3571. FAX 203-222-1502. Ed. Walter Laqueur. (back issues avail.) Indexed: A.B.C.Pol.Sci.
—BLDSC shelfmark: 9263.240000.

327   US   ISSN 0163-660X
D839
WASHINGTON QUARTERLY. 1978. q. $30 to individuals (foreign $44); institutions $65 (foreign $79); students $20 (foreign $34). (Center for Strategic and International Studies) M I T Press, 55 Hayward St., Cambridge, MA 02142. TEL 617-253-2889. FAX 617-258-6779. TELEX 921473. (Editorial addr.: Center for Strategic and International Studies, 1800 K St. N.W., Ste. 400, Washington, DC 20006) Ed. Brad Roberts. adv.; index; circ. 3,000. (also avail. in microform from UMI; back issues avail.; reprint service avail. from UMI) Indexed: A.B.C.Pol.Sci., Abstr.Mil.Bibl., Amer.Bibl.Slavic & E.Eur.Stud, Amer.Hist.& Life, Curr.Cont., Hist.Abstr., Mid.East: Abstr.& Ind., P.A.I.S., Risk Abstr., SSCI.
●Also available online. Vendor(s): Mead Data Central.
Formerly: Washington Review of Strategic and International Studies (ISSN 0147-1465)
Description: Essays on foreign and defense policy, international economics, as well as emerging international issues.

327   US   ISSN 8755-4917
WASHINGTON REPORT ON MIDDLE EAST AFFAIRS; a survey of United States relations with Middle East countries. 1982. 12/yr. $19 to individuals; institutions $50. American Educational Trust (A E T), Box 53062, Washington, DC 20009. TEL 202-939-6052. FAX 202-265-4574. Ed. Richard H. Curtiss. adv. contact: Greg Noakes. bk.rev.; circ. 30,000.

327 330.9   US   ISSN 0275-5599
WASHINGTON REPORT ON THE HEMISPHERE. 1980. fortn. $165 to individuals; institutions $268. Council on Hemispheric Affairs, 724 9th St., N.W., Ste. 401, Washington, DC 20001. TEL 202-393-3322. FAX 202-393-3423. Ed. Laurence R. Birns. bk.rev.; index; circ. 1,500. Indexed: HR Rep.
Description: Organization that monitors US, Canadian and Latin-American relations as well as political, economic and social issues in the western hemisphere.

POLITICAL SCIENCE — INTERNATIONAL RELATIONS

940 327   GW   ISSN 0049-7134
WELTGESCHEHEN. 1964. q. DM.40. Siegler & Co. Verlag fuer Zeitarchive GmbH, Einsteinstr. 10, 5205 St. Augustin 3, Germany. adv.; abstr.; stat.; index.; cum.index; circ. 800. **Indexed:** E.I.
Formerly: Internationales Europaforum (ISSN 0020-9465)
Description: Articles on contemporary history, documentary style, information on foreign countries, their politics and economy.

327 200   BE
WERELDBRIEF. 1982. m. 400 BEF. V.Z.W. Wereldwijd, Arthur Goemaerelei 69, 2018 Antwerp, Belgium. Ed. Marc van Laere. circ. 1,400.

WERELDWIJD; tijdschrift over evangelizatie en ontwikkeling. see RELIGIONS AND THEOLOGY

327   GW
WERKSTATT 3 - PROGRAMM. 1979. m. free. Verein Werkstatt 3, Nernstweg 32-34, 2000 Hamburg 50, Germany. TEL 040-392191. FAX 040-3909866. circ. 10,000.
Description: Information about the problems of the relations between industrialized countries and developing countries.

327 950 970   CH   ISSN 0043-3047
DS895.F7
WEST & EAST/CHUNG-MEI YUEH-K'AN; an independent monthly. (Text in Chinese and English) 1956. m. NT.$300($10) (Sino-American Cultural and Economic Association) Chang Chao Wen-yi, No. 23 Hungchow S. Rd., Sec. 1, 11th Floor, Taipei, Taiwan, Republic of China. TEL 02-3914200. Ed. Yih-hsien Yu. adv.; charts; stat.; circ. 2,400.
Description: Sino-American exchange of cultural and economic news.

WESTERN POLICIES. see POLITICAL SCIENCE

WHY; challenging hunger and poverty. see SOCIAL SERVICES AND WELFARE

327   AU
WIENER BLAETTER ZUR FRIEDENSFORSCHUNG. 1974. 4/yr. S.260($22) Universitaetszentrum fuer Friedenforschung, Schottenring 21, A-1010 Vienna, Austria. TEL 0222-31-25-44. Eds. Rudolf Weiler, Sigrid Poellinger. adv.; bk.rev.; circ. 500.

320.9   ISSN 0274-5852
WILLIAM WINTER COMMENTS; a twice monthly personal newsletter on current world affairs. 1961. s-m. $33.50. William Winter, Ed. & Pub., 6025 El Escorpion Rd., Woodland Hills, CA 91367-1199. TEL 818-347-7417. FAX 818-347-7417. TELEX 299374-WINT-UR. maps; circ. 10,000. (also avail. in microfilm from UMI; reprint service avail. from UMI)
Formerly: Comments on Current World Affairs (ISSN 0043-5619)

WOMEN STRIKE FOR PEACE. LEGISLATIVE ALERT. see POLITICAL SCIENCE — Civil Rights

327   BE
WORKING - PARTY REPORTS. (Text in English) 1989. irreg. 2250 Fr. Centre for European Policy Studies, 33 rue Ducale, B-1000 Brussels, Belgium. TEL 2-513-40-88. FAX 2-511-59-60. TELEX 62818-CEPS-B. Ed. Peter Lomas.

341.1   US   ISSN 0043-8200
JX1901
WORLD AFFAIRS. 1837. q. $30 to individuals; institutions $45. (American Peace Society) Heldref Publications, 1319 Eighteenth St., N.W., Washington, DC 20036-1802. TEL 202-296-6267. FAX 202-296-5149. (Co-sponsor: Helen Dwight Reid Educational Foundation) Eds. Joyce Horn, Evron M. Kirkpatrick. adv.; bk.rev.; circ. 700. (also avail. in microfilm; reprint service avail.) **Indexed:** A.B.C.Pol.Sci., Amer.Bibl.Slavic & E.Eur.Stud, Arts & Hum.Cit.Ind., Bk.Rev.Ind, Curr.Cont., Hist.Abstr. (until 1991), Mid.East: Abstr.& Ind., P.A.I.S., Soc.Sci.Ind., SSCI.
—BLDSC shelfmark: 9352.430000.
Refereed Serial

327   US   ISSN 0090-7103
D839
WORLD AFFAIRS REPORT. (Print ed. ceased vol.20, 1991) 1970. q. $16 to individuals; institutions $25. California Institute of International Studies, 766 Santa Ynez, Stanford, CA 94305. TEL 415-322-2026. Ed. Ronald Hilton. adv.; bk.rev.; bibl.; illus.; circ. 400. (also avail. in microfilm from UMI; reprint service avail. from UMI) **Indexed:** A.B.C.Pol.Sci., Abstr.Mil.Bibl, Hist.Abstr., Mid.East: Abstr.& Ind.
●Available only online. Vendor(s): DIALOG (File no. 167).
—BLDSC shelfmark: 9352.435000.
Formerly: California Institute of International Studies. Report (ISSN 0068-564X)
Description: Commentaries, book reviews, and bibliographies pertaining to Soviet activities and declared intentions throughout the world, with analysis broken down by subject and country.

WORLD CITIZEN NEWS. see LAW — International Law

327   UN
WORLD DIRECTORY OF PEACE RESEARCH AND TRAINING INSTITUTIONS. irreg., 6th ed., 1988. Unesco, 7 Place de Fontenoy, 75700 Paris, France.

327   US   ISSN 0277-1527
G122
WORLD FACTBOOK. a. U.S. Central Intelligence Agency, Washington, DC 20505. (Avail. from: Document Expediting (DOCEX) Project, Library of Congress, Washington, DC 20540; Supt. of Documents, Government Printing Office (GPO), Washington, DC 10402; National Technical Information Office (NTIS), 5285 Port Royal Rd., Springfield, VA 22161)
●Also available on CD-ROM.
Formerly: National Basic Intelligence Factbook (ISSN 0098-2091)

327   US
WORLD FEDERALIST NEWSLETTER. 1976. q. $5. World Federalist Association, 418 7th St., S.E., Washington, DC 20003-0250. Ed. Eric Cox. bk.rev.; illus.; circ. 10,000. (also avail. in microform from UMI)
Description: Discusses options for world peace, economic progress and a liveable environment.

341.1   II   ISSN 0043-8448
WORLD FEDERATION. (Text in English) 1929. m. Rs.3. Shiva Kumar, Ed. & Pub., P.M.V. Keshighat, Vrindaban, Uttar Pradesh, India.

327   US
WORLD GOODWILL COMMENTARY; a bulletin on current trends in world affairs. 1968. irreg. donations. (Lucis Trust) Lucis Publishing Co., 113 University Place, 11th Fl., Box 722, Cooper Sta., New York, NY 10276. TEL 212-982-8770. (Or: 1 rue de Varembe (3e), C.P. 31, 1211 Geneva 20, Switzerland; Or: 3 Whitehall Ct., Suite 54, London SW1A 2EF, England) Ed.Bd. bibl.; circ. 12,000.

327   II   ISSN 0043-857X
WORLD INFORMO; current events of national and international importance and matters connected with the United Nations and its specialized agencies. (Text in English) 1953. m. Rs.5. United Schools Organisation of India, U S O House, 6 Special Institutional Area, New Delhi 110 067, India. FAX 09111-6862042. Ed. J.L. Jain. adv.; circ. 6,000.

WORLD LINK. see BUSINESS AND ECONOMICS — Macroeconomics

327   US
WORLD NEIGHBORS IN ACTION; a newsletter for overseas project personnel. French edition: Voisins Mondiaux en Action. Spanish edition: Vecinos Mundiales en Accion. 1965. q. $10 to industrialized countries; developing countries free. World Neighbors, Inc., 4127 N.W. 122nd St., Oklahoma City, OK 73120-8869. TEL 405-752-9700. FAX 405-752-9393. Ed. Debra Johnson. bibl.; charts; illus.; cum.index; circ. 2,166. (back issues avail.)

327 338.91   US   ISSN 1042-1572
G1 /b .W67
WORLD NEWS DIGEST.* 1988. q. $99 softcover; hardcover $128.95. World News Digest, Inc., Box 3443, Littleton, CO 80161-3443. FAX 303-295-2331. (Subscr. to: Box 46035, Denver CO 80201) Ed. William J. Sims. charts; illus.; stat.; circ. 5,000. (looseleaf format; back issues avail.)
Description: Provides concise historical, geographic, socio-economic and political information on world affairs on an individual country basis. Covers current news of over 125 countries.

WORLD NEWSMAP OF THE WEEK - HEADLINE FOCUS; world news and world geography. see GEOGRAPHY

327   US   ISSN 0193-3329
D839
WORLD OPINION UPDATE. 1977. m. $60 to individuals; educational institutions $45. Survey Research Consultants International, Inc., Box 25, Williamstown, MA 01267. TEL 413-458-4414. Eds. Elizabeth Hann Hastings, Philip K. Hastings. index; circ. 1,000.

327   US   ISSN 0895-7452
D839
WORLD OUTLOOK; a journal of international affairs. 1985. s-a. $8. Dartmouth College, Trustees, Hinman Box 6025, Hanover, NH 03755. TEL 603-646-2023. FAX 603-640-2168. Eds. Sarah A. Carlson, Eric Zandvliet. bk.rev.; circ. 1,000. **Indexed:** P.A.I.S.
—BLDSC shelfmark: 9356.959800.
Description: Provides a non-partisan forum for original thinking on international affairs.

327   NR   ISSN 0300-225X
WORLD PEACE.* q. International Society of United Modern Enterprise, 60 A Campbell St., P.O. Box 1944, Lagos, Nigeria. illus.

327   CE
WORLD PEACE JOURNAL. (Text in English and Sinhalese) 1974. bi-m. Rs.12. World Government Movement, c/o Bandula Sri Gunawardhana, Ed., 270 Park Rd., Colombo 5, Sri Lanka. adv.; bk.rev.; illus.; index; circ. 10,000. (back issues avail.)
Formerly: World Government Journal.

327   US   ISSN 0049-8130
WORLD PEACE NEWS; a world government report. 1970. 6/yr. $20 for 3 yrs. World Peace News, 777 United Nations Plaza, 11th Fl., New York, NY 10017. TEL 212-686-1069. Ed. Thomas Liggett. bk.rev.; illus.; circ. 2,000. (tabloid format; back issues avail.)
Description: World government report with emphasis on what is and what is not going on at the U.N., in the news media and with non-governmental organizations.

327   US   ISSN 1058-1022
WORLD PERSPECTIVES; alternative news and analysis from shortwave sources. m. $19 to individuals; institutions $23; impoverished and incarcerated $9; foreign $32. People's News Service, Box 3074, Madison, WI 53704-0074. TEL 608-241-4812. Ed. Esty Dinur. adv.
Description: Monitors shortwave broadcasts worldwide, presents news and analysis from the perspectives of the world outside the United States to broaden that of those dependent on the American media.

327   US   ISSN 0740-2775
D839
WORLD POLICY JOURNAL. 1983. q. $23 to individuals; institutions $30. World Policy Institute, 777 United Nations Plaza, New York, NY 10017. TEL 212-490-0010. FAX 212-986-1482. Ed. Richard Caplan. adv.; bk.rev.; charts; circ. 7,000. (also avail. in microform from UMI; back issues avail.) **Indexed:** A.B.C.Pol.Sci., Alt.Press Ind., Amer.Hist.& Life, Curr.Cont., Fut.Surv., Hist.Abstr., Int.Polit.Sci.Abstr., Lang.& Lang.Behav.Abstr., Left Ind. (1983-), P.A.I.S., Sociol.Abstr., SSCI.
—BLDSC shelfmark: 9358.073000.
Description: Covers progressive international affairs including global security issues, trade and economic policy, environmental concerns and developments in Europe, Latin America, Asia and Africa.

POLITICAL SCIENCE — INTERNATIONAL RELATIONS

327   US   ISSN 0043-8871
D839
WORLD POLITICS (BALTIMORE); a quarterly journal of international relations. 1948. q. $21 to individuals; institutions $44. (Princeton University, Center of International Studies) Johns Hopkins University Press, Journals Publishing Division, 701 W. 40th St., Ste. 275, Baltimore, MD 21211. TEL 410-516-6980. FAX 410-516-6998. Ed. Henry S. Bienen. adv.; bk.rev.; index; circ. 3,851. (also avail. in microform from MIM,UMI; back issues avail.; reprint service avail. from SCH,UMI) **Indexed:** A.B.C.Pol.Sci., Abstr.Mil.Bibl., Acad.Ind., Amer.Bibl.Slavic & E.Eur.Stud., Bk.Rev.Dig., Bk.Rev.Ind. (1965-), Child.Bk.Rev.Ind. (1965-), Curr.Cont., E.I., Fut.Surv., Hist.Abstr., Int.Polit.Sci.Abstr., Mag.Ind., Mid.East: Abstr.& Ind., P.A.I.S., Rural Recreat.Tour.Abstr., Sage Pub.Admin.Abstr., Soc.Sci.Ind., SSCI, World Agri.Econ.& Rural Sociol.Abstr.
—BLDSC shelfmark: 9358.080000.

327   AT
WORLD REVIEW; a journal of contemporary relevance. 1962. 4/yr. Aus.$36. Australian Institute of International Affairs, Queensland Branch, P.O. Box 279, Indooroopilly, Brisbane, Qld. 4068, Australia. Ed.Bd. adv.; bk.rev.; circ. 1,000. **Indexed:** Aus.P.A.I.S., Curr.Cont., Gdlns.

327   UK   ISSN 0043-9134
D410
WORLD TODAY. 1945. m. $48 to individuals; institutions $68; students $35. Royal Institute of International Affairs, Chatham House, 10 St. James's Sq., London SW1Y 4LE, England. TEL 071-957-5700. FAX 071-957-5710. Ed. C. Cviic. adv.; bk.rev.; index; circ. 4,000. (also avail. in microform from UMI) **Indexed:** A.B.C.Pol.Sci., Abstr.Mil.Bibl, ASSIA, Curr.Cont., Int.Lab.Doc., Key to Econ.Sci., Mar.Aff.Bibl., Mid.East: Abstr.& Ind., P.A.I.S., Rural Recreat.Tour.Abstr., Soc.Sci.Ind., SSCI, World Agri.Econ.& Rural Sociol.Abstr.
—BLDSC shelfmark: 9360.150000.

341.37   US
WORLD TREATY INDEX. 1975. irreg., 2nd, 1984. A B C-Clio, 130 Cremona, Box 1911, Santa Barbara, CA 93116-1911. TEL 805-968-1911. FAX 805-685-9685. Ed. Peter H. Rohn.

327   II   ISSN 0043-9185
WORLD UNION. (Text in English) 1961. q. Rs.20($8) World Union International Centre, Pondicherry 605002, India. Ed. M.P. Pandit. adv.; bk.rev.; charts; illus.; circ. 1,200.

WORLD VISION. see *SOCIAL SERVICES AND WELFARE*

327   US
THE WORLDPAPER; international news and views. (Text in Chinese, English, Icelandic, Polish, Russian, Spanish) 1978. m. $18 (foreign $28). World Times, Inc., 210 World Trade Center, Boston, MA 02210. TEL 617-439-5400. FAX 617-439-5415. TELEX 6817273 WORLDP. Ed. Daniel Passent. adv.; bk.rev.; circ. 890,100. (tabloid format; back issues avail.)
•Also available online. Vendor(s): Mead Data Central.
Description: International news and views on political, social and economic issues of global importance, featuring writers indigenous to the regions they write about.

WORLDVIEW MAGAZINE. see *BUSINESS AND ECONOMICS — International Development And Assistance*

327 355   US
WORLDWIDE REPORT: ARMS CONTROL. irreg. (approx. 100/yr.). $7 per no. (foreign $14 per no.). U.S. Joint Publications Research Service, Box 12507, Arlington, VA 22209. TEL 703-487-4630. (Orders to: NTIS, Springfield, VA 22161)

327   CC   ISSN 1000-6192
XIANDAI GUOJI GUANXI/MODERN INTERNATIONAL RELATIONS. (Text in Chinese) q. Xiandai Guoji Guanxi Yanjiusuo - Modern International Relations Institute, No. A-2, Wanshousi, Haidian-qu, Beijing 100081, People's Republic of China. TEL 8412266. Ed. Liu Biqing.

327   NE
YEARBOOK OF EUROPEAN STUDIES/ANNUAIRE D'ETUDES EUROPEENNES. (Text mainly in English; occasionally in French) 1988. a. price varies. (University of Amsterdam, Department of European Studies) Editions Rodopi B.V., Keizersgracht 302-304, 1016 EX Amsterdam, Netherlands. TEL 020-6227507. FAX 020-6380948. (US and Canada subscr. to: 233 Peachtree St., N.E., Ste. 404, Atlanta, GA 30303-1504. TEL 800-225-3998) Ed. J.Th. Leerssen.
Description: Interdisciplinary studies involving literature, history, law, and economics to assess topics within the field of European relations.

327.471   FI   ISSN 0355-0079
DK451.7
YEARBOOK OF FINNISH FOREIGN POLICY. (Text in English) 1973. a. Fmk.60($12) Ulkopoliittinen Instituutti - Finnish Institute of International Affairs, Pursimiehenkatu 8, SF-00150 Helsinki, Finland. TEL 358-0-170434. FAX 358-0-669375. Ed. Jyrki Livonen. **Indexed:** A.B.C.Pol.Sci., Int.Polit.Sci.Abstr.
—BLDSC shelfmark: 9411.850000.
Description: Deals with domestic and international questions impinged relating to Finland's foreign policy.

327   BE   ISSN 0084-3806
YEARBOOK OF INTERNATIONAL CONGRESS PROCEEDINGS. (Text in English; index in French) 1969. irreg. 960 Fr. Union of International Associations, Rue Washington 40, 1050 Brussels, Belgium.

327   GW   ISSN 0084-3814
JX1904
YEARBOOK OF INTERNATIONAL ORGANIZATIONS/ANNUAIRE DES ORGANISATIONS INTERNATIONALES. (In 3 vols.: Vol. 1: Organization Descriptions and Index; Vol. 2: International Organization Participation; Vol. 3: Global Action Networks) (Text in English; index in English and French) 1910. a. DM.1498($825) (Union of International Associations, BE) K.G. Saur Verlag KG, Ortlerstr. 8, Postfach 701620, 8000 Munich 70, Germany. TEL 089-76902-0. FAX 089-76902150. (N. America subscr. to: K.G. Saur, A Reed Reference Publishing Company, 121 Chanlon Rd., New Providence, NJ 07974. TEL 908-665-3576)
—BLDSC shelfmark: 9414.010000.
Description: Provides detailed information for organizations in every field of human endeavor. Lists organizations, administrators, embassies and government agencies concerned with international affairs.

327   BE   ISSN 0771-7962
YEARBOOK OF THE EUROPEAN COMMUNITIES AND OF THE OTHER EUROPEAN ORGANIZATIONS. (Text in English, French, German) a. 3500 Fr. (effective 1992). Editions Delta, Rue Scailquin 55, B-1030 Brussels, Belgium. TEL 02-217-55-55. FAX 02-217-93-93. (Dist. by: Unipub, 4611-F Assemby Dr., Lanham MD, 20706-4391) Ed. G.F. Seingry. adv.; index; circ. 8,000.
—BLDSC shelfmark: 9384.371000.
Description: Provides information on the structure and operation of the European Communities and on all other European organizations, whether public or private, which contribute to European integration: political, economic, scientific, technical, and military.

327   FI   ISSN 0781-2442
YHDISTYNEIDEN KANSAKUNTIEN YLEISKOKOUS (YEAR). (Text in Finnish; occasionally in English) 1957. a. Ulkoasiainministerio - Ministry for Foreign Affairs, PL 176, SF-00161 Helsinki, Finland. TEL 90-134151. FAX 629840. TELEX 1000306. circ. 650.
Formerly: Suomen Osallistuminen Yhdistyneiden Kansakuntien Toimintaan (ISSN 0081-9441)

327   CC
YOU SHENG. English edition: Friendly Voice. (Text in Chinese) bi-m. Zhongguo Renmin Duiwai Youhao Xiehui, No. 1, Taijichang, Beijing 100740, People's Republic of China. TEL 5122782. Ed. Gu Zixin.

327   UK   ISSN 0958-4234
YOUNG INDIA. 1989. q. £15 for 2 yrs. N R I Forum (UK), P.O. Box 42, Wellingborough NN8 3HL, England. Ed. Bharat Ratna Kurukshetra.
Description: Devoted to politics and ideology in India and to the re-unification of India in its borders as in 1947.

YOUR UNITED NATIONS; official guidebook. see *HISTORY*

327 338.9   US   ISSN 0427-8968
YUGOSLAV FACTS AND VIEWS. Title varies: Facts & Views. (Text in English) 1948. irreg. free. Yugoslav Press and Cultural Center, 767 Third Ave., New York, NY 10017. TEL 212-838-2306. circ. 2,000. (back issues avail.)

227   YU
YUGOSLAVIA. FEDERAL SECRETARIAT FOR FOREIGN AFFAIRS. DIPLOMATIC LIST. (Text in French) 1946. a. free. Savezni Sekretarijat za Inostrane Poslove - Federal Secretariat for Foreign Affairs, Belgrade, Yugoslavia. circ. 1,000.
Formerly (until Mar. 1991): Liste des Membres du Corps Diplomatique a Beograd.

327   RU   ISSN 0044-1554
ZA RUBEZHOM; weekly review of foreign press. (Text in Russian) 1960. w. $18. Izdatel'stvo Pravda, Ul. Pravdy, 24, Moscow 125865, Russia. TEL 095-257-2387. FAX 095-200-2296. Ed. S. Morozov. illus.; circ. 650,000. (also avail. in microform from MIM) **Indexed:** Curr.Dig.Sov.Press.

327   PL   ISSN 0044-1929
ZBIOR DOKUMENTOW/RECUEIL DE DOCUMENTS. (Text in original language of documents with Polish translation) 1945. m. $51. Polski Instytut Spraw Miedzynarodowych - Institut Polonais des Affaires Internationales, Warecka 1a, 00-950 Warsaw, Poland. (Dist. by: Ars Polona-Ruch, Krakowskie Przedmiescie 7, Warsaw, Poland) cum.index: 1945-1954, 1955-1964; circ. 1,000.

327   SZ   ISSN 0044-2100
ZEITBILD. 1960. fortn. 63 Fr. Schweizerisches Ost-Institut - Swiss Eastern Institute, Jubilaeumsstrasse 41, CH-3000 Berne 6, Switzerland. Eds. Peter Sager, Christian Bruegger. adv.; bk.rev.; charts; illus.; circ. 11,500.
Formerly: Klare Blick.

327   GW   ISSN 0044-2976
DD68
ZEITSCHRIFT FUER KULTURAUSTAUSCH. 1962. q. DM.40($18) Institut fuer Auslandsbeziehungen, Charlottenplatz 17, 7000 Stuttgart 1, Germany. TEL 0711-542138. Ed. Nikolaus Klein. adv.; bk.rev.; bibl.; illus.; record rev.; index; circ. 6,000. **Indexed:** P.A.I.S.For.Lang.Ind.
Formerly: Institut fuer Auslandsbeziehungen. Mitteilungen.

327   CC
ZHONGGUO - LIAODONG BANDAO GUOJI JIAOLIU/CHINA - LIAODONG PENINSULA INTERNATIONAL EXCHANGE. (Text in Chinese) q. Liaoning Sheng Duiwai Wenhua Jiaoliu Xiehui, Liaoning Tiyuguan 1 Lou, 2, Qingnan Dajie 1 Duan, Heping-qu, Shenyang, Liaoning 110003, People's Republic of China. TEL 394664. Ed. Liu Mingde.

327   CC
ZHONGGUO ZHI YOU/FRIENDS OF CHINA. (Text in Chinese) bi-m. Zhongguo zhi You Zazhishe, No. A-3, Fucheng Lu, Beijing 100037, People's Republic of China. TEL 894831. Ed. Shen Deyi.

341.1   GW
ZIVILCOURAGE; antimilitaristische Zeitschrift. 1964; N.S. 1975. q. DM.12. Deutsche Friedensgesellschaft-Vereinigte Kriegsdienstgegner (DFG-VK), Schwanenstr. 16, 5620 Velbert 1, Germany. FAX 0228-665843. adv.; bk.rev.; film rev.; illus.; circ. 12,000.
Formerly: Courage.

1066 TIDSSKRIFT FOR HISTORISK FORSKNING. see *HISTORY — History Of Europe*

POLLUTION

see Environmental Studies–Pollution

POPULATION STUDIES

see also Birth Control

325.1   US
A C I M NEWSLETTER. 1952. 4/yr. free. American Committee on Italian Migration, 352 W. 44th St., New York, NY 10036. TEL 212-247-7373. Ed. Rev. Joseph A. Cogo, C.S. circ. 10,000.
Formerly: A C I M Dispatch.

A F R A NEWSLETTER. (Association for Rural Advancement) see *POLITICAL SCIENCE — Civil Rights*

A L L NEWS. (American Life Lobby) see *BIRTH CONTROL*

A P D U NEWSLETTER. (Association of Public Data Users) see *STATISTICS*

A P L I C COMMUNICATOR. (Association for Population - Family Planning Library & Information Center International) see *LIBRARY AND INFORMATION SCIENCES*

312   GW   ISSN 0937-907X
▼**ACTA DEMOGRAPHICA.** 1990. a. DM.68. (Deutsche Gesellschaft fuer Bevoelkerungswissenschaft) Physica-Verlag GmbH & Co., Tiergartenstr. 17, Postfach 10 52 80, 6900 Heidelberg 1, Germany. TEL 06221-487492. FAX 06221-413982. TELEX 461723 SPHDB D. (Subscr. to: Springer GmbH, Auslieferungs-Gesellschaft, Haberstr. 7, 6900 Heidelberg-Rohrbach, Germany; In N. America: Springer Verlag New York Inc., 175 Fifth Ave., New York, NY 10010. TEL 212-460-1500) Ed.Bd.
Description: Covers empirical and theoretical topics in population research.

312   UN
AFRICAN POPULATION NEWSLETTER. (Text in English and French) 1970. s-a. free. United Nations Economic Commission for Africa, Population Division, P.O. Box 3001, Addis Ababa, Ethiopia. TELEX 21029. Ed.Bd. bk.rev.; circ. 1,500.

312
ALABAMA STATE DATA CENTER NEWSLETTER. 1985. q. free. University of Alabama, Alabama State Data Center, Box 870221, Tuscaloosa, AL 35487. TEL 205-348-6191. FAX 205-348-2951. Ed. Annette Watters. illus. (back issues avail.)

312   CN
ALBERTA - EDMONTON SERIES REPORT. 1977. irreg. free. Population Research Laboratory, Department of Sociology, University of Alberta, Edmonton, Alta. T6G 2H4, Canada. TEL 403-492-4659. (reprint service avail. from MML)
Formerly: Edmonton Area Series Report (ISSN 0703-8763)
Description: Data gathered from the annual All Alberta Study.

ALL ABOUT ISSUES. see *BIRTH CONTROL*

ALLEES ALL AROUND; includes Alley, Ally, Allie, Alyea. see *GENEALOGY AND HERALDRY*

312   US   ISSN 0163-4089
HB3505   CODEN: AMDEEF
AMERICAN DEMOGRAPHICS; consumer trends for business leaders. 1979. m. $62. American Demographics, Inc., Box 68, Ithaca, NY 14851-0068. TEL 607-273-6343. FAX 607-273-3196. (Subscr. to: Box 58184, Boulder, CO 80322-8184) Ed. Brad Edmondson. adv.; bk.rev.; charts; illus.; stat.; index, cum.index: 1981-1988; circ. 35,000. (also avail. in microform from UMI; back issues avail.; reprint service avail. from UMI) **Indexed:** ABI Inform., B.P.I., BPIA, Bus.Ind., Chic.Per.Ind., CLOA, Curr.Lit.Fam.Plan., Environ.Abstr., Fut.Surv., Hlth.Ind., Manage.Cont., P.A.I.S., Popul.Ind., PROMT, Tr.& Indus.Ind.
●Also available online. Vendor(s): DIALOG, Dow Jones/News Retrieval, Mead Data Central.
—BLDSC shelfmark: 0812.737000.

312   US
AMERICAN MARKETPLACE. 1980. fortn. $300.04 (effective Sep. 1992). Business Publishers, Inc., 951 Pershing Dr., Silver Spring, MD 20910-4464. TEL 301-587-6300. FAX 301-585-9075. Ed. David Speights. bk.rev.; charts; stat. (looseleaf format)
●Also available online. Vendor(s): NewsNet.
Formerly: U S Census Report (ISSN 0276-2900)
Description: Prepared for marketing professionals and business planners. Includes news on consumer trends, population shifts, employment gains and losses.

304   US   ISSN 0741-2150
AMERICAN UNIVERSITY STUDIES. SERIES 16. ECONOMICS. 1984. irreg. Peter Lang Publishing, Inc., 62 W. 45th St., 4th Fl., New York, NY 10036. TEL 212-302-6740. Ed. Michael Flamini.

312   FR   ISSN 0066-2062
HB848
ANNALES DE DEMOGRAPHIE HISTORIQUE. (Text in English, French) 1970. a. $35. (Societe de Demographie Historique) Editions de l' Ecole des Hautes Etudes en Sciences Sociales, 131 bd. St-Michel, 75005 Paris, France. TEL 43-54-47-15. FAX 43-54-80-73. (Dist. by: Centre Interinstitutionnel pour la Diffusion de Publications en Sciences Humaines, 131 bd. St-Michel, 75005 Paris, France) (reprint service avail. from SWZ) **Indexed:** Amer.Hist.& Life, Hist.Abstr., Popul.Ind.
—BLDSC shelfmark: 0971.450000.

312   FR
ANNUAIRE DES CENTRES DE RECHERCHE DEMOGRAPHIQUE/DIRECTORY OF DEMOGRAPHIC RESEARCH CENTERS. 1974. irreg., 2nd, 1980. free. Committee for International Cooperation in National Research in Demography, 27 rue du Commandeur, 75675 Paris Cedex 14, France.

312   UK   ISSN 0066-3964
ANNUAL ESTIMATES OF THE POPULATION OF SCOTLAND. 1958. a. £1.25. H.M.S.O. (Scotland), 13a Castle St., Edinburgh EH2 3AR, Scotland. (Co-sponsor: General Register Office, Scotland) circ. 600.

312   MX
ANUARIO ESTADISTICO DE PUEBLA. (In 2 vols.) a. $43. Instituto Nacional de Estadistica, Geografia e Informatica, Secretaria de Programacion y Presupuesto, Prol. Heroe de Nacozari, 2301, Acceso 10, C.P. 20290, Aguascalientes Ags., Mexico. TEL 91-491-81968. FAX 91-491-80739.

ARKANSAS VITAL STATISTICS. see *POPULATION STUDIES — Abstracting, Bibliographies, Statistics*

325   US   ISSN 0891-6683
ASIA - PACIFIC POPULATION & POLICY. 1987. q. free. (East-West Population Institute) Center for Cultural and Technical Interchange Between East and West, Inc., 1777 East-West Rd., Honolulu, HI 96848. TEL 808-944-7401. FAX 808-944-7490. TELEX 989171 EWC UD. Ed. Sandra E. Ward. circ. 3,000.

301.426   UN   ISSN 0259-238X
HA4551
ASIA - PACIFIC POPULATION JOURNAL. 1986. q. United Nations Economic and Social Commission for Asia and the Pacific (ESCAP), Population Division, United Nations Bldg., Rajdamnern Ave., Bangkok 10200, Thailand. Ed. Nibhon Debavalya. bk.rev.; abstr.; bibl.; charts; illus.; circ. 2,000. (back issues avail.) **Indexed:** IIS.
—BLDSC shelfmark: 1742.261300.

312   US   ISSN 0891-2823
HB3633.A3
ASIAN AND PACIFIC POPULATION FORUM. 1974. q. $12 (free to qualified personnel). (East-West Population Institute) Center for Cultural and Technical Interchange Between East and West, Inc., 1777 East-West Rd., Honolulu, HI 96848. TEL 808-944-7401. FAX 808-944-7490. TELEX 989171 EWC UD. Ed. Sandra E. Ward. bk.rev.; charts; illus.; stat.; cum.index: 1974-1983; circ. 1,850. **Indexed:** I D A, Popul.Ind.
—BLDSC shelfmark: 1742.354800.

Former titles (until 1986): Asian and Pacific Census Forum (ISSN 0732-0515); (until 1978): Asian and Pacific Census Newsletter.

312   AT
AUSTRALIAN INSTITUTE OF FAMILY STUDIES. ANNUAL REPORT. 1981. a. free. Australian Institute of Family Studies, 300 Queen St., Melbourne, Vic. 3000, Australia. TEL 03-608-6888. TELEX 03-600-0886. circ. 1,000.

AUSTRIA. STATISTISCHES ZENTRALAMT. DEMOGRAPHISCHES JAHRBUCH OESTERREICHES. see *POPULATION STUDIES — Abstracting, Bibliographies, Statistics*

312   GW   ISSN 0722-1509
HB848
B I B MITTEILUNGEN. 1980. 6/yr. Bundesinstitut fuer Bevoelkerungsforschung, Gustav-Stresemann-Ring 6, Postfach 5528, 6200 Wiesbaden 1, Germany. TEL 0611-752235. FAX 0611-39544. TELEX 4186511-STB-D. Ed. Charlotte Hoehn. circ. 600.

300   US
BALANCE REPORT. 1973. q. membership. Population-Environment Balance, Inc., 1325 G St., N.W., Ste. 1003, Washington, DC 20005. TEL 202-879-3000. FAX 202-879-3019. Ed. D. Petete. circ. 10,000.
Former titles: Balance; (until May 1986): Other Side (Washington).
Description: Covers a variety of U.S. population issues including family planning, local growth control, immigration, and environmental carrying capacity.

BANGLADESH DEVELOPMENT STUDIES. see *BUSINESS AND ECONOMICS — Economic Situation And Conditions*

312   II
BARODA REPORTER. (Text in English) 1960. a. free. Population Research Centre, Maharajah Sayajirao University of Baroda, Faculty of Science, Baroda 390 002, India. Ed. M.M. Gandotra. adv.; bk.rev.; abstr.; bibl.; charts; illus.; stat.; circ. 500. (record)
Description: Newsletter of the center, describing research projects and findings.

312   BE
BELGIUM. CENTRE D'ETUDE DE LA POPULATION ET DE LA FAMILLE. DOSSIERS. (Text in French) irreg. (Ministere de la Sante Publique et de la Famille, Centre d'Etude de la Population et de la Famille) Editions Labor, Chaussee de Haecht 156-158, 1030 Brussels, Belgium.

312   BE
BELGIUM. CENTRE D'ETUDE DE LA POPULATION ET DE LA FAMILLE. POPULATION ET FAMILLE. 3/yr. (Ministere de la Sante Publique et de la Famille, Centre d'Etude de la Population et de la Famille) Editions Labor, Chaussee de Haecht 156-158, 1030 Brussels, Belgium.

312   SZ
BEVOELKERUNGSBEWEGUNG IN DER SCHWEIZ/MOUVEMENT DE LA POPULATION EN SUISSE. (Text in French and German) 1867. a. 17 Fr. Bundesamt fuer Statistik, Hallwylstr. 15, CH-3003 Bern, Switzerland. TEL 031-618836. FAX 031-617856.

312   BE   ISSN 0523-1159
HB848
BEVOLKING EN GEZIN. (Text in Dutch; summaries in English) 1962. 3/yr. 440 Fr. (Nederlands Interuniversitair Demografisch Instituut, NE) Uitgeverij Pelckmans, Kapelsestraat 222, B-2080 Kapellen, Belgium. FAX 03-665-0263. (Co-sponsor: Ministere de la Sante Publique et de la Famille, Centrum voor Bevolkings- en Gezinsstudien) bk.rev.; circ. 1,200. **Indexed:** Lang.& Lang.Behav.Abstr., Popul.Ind.

BOLETIN MEDICO. see *BIRTH CONTROL*

325.1   US
BORDER WATCH. 1983. m. $48. American Immigration Control Foundation, Main St., Box 525, Monterey, VA 24465. TEL 703-468-2022. Ed.Bd. bk.rev.; circ. 100,000.
Formerly: A I C F Report.
Description: Covers immigration to the United States from a restrictionist point of view.

POPULATION STUDIES

325.2 SW ISSN 0345-1798
BRIDGE. Swedish edition: Bryggan (ISSN 0345-178X) (Text in English) 1972. q. SEK 50($10) Samfundet Emigrantforskningens Fraemjande - Society for the Promotion of Emigration Research, Box 331, S-651 08 Karlstad, Sweden. Ed. Erik Gustavson. adv.; bk.rev.; illus.; index; circ. 1,500.

312 333.33 CN ISSN 0828-2919
BRITISH COLUMBIA POPULATION FORECAST. a. Can.$10.40. Ministry of Finance and Corporate Relations, Parliament Bldgs., Victoria, B.C. V8V 1X4, Canada. (Subscr. to: Crown Publications, 546 Yates St., Victoria, B.C. V8W 1K8, Canada. TEL 604-386-4636) charts; stat.
  Description: Reflects the population growth, demographics and the housing market.

325.2 948 SW ISSN 0345-178X
BRYGGAN. English edition: Bridge (ISSN 0345-1798) 1969. 4/yr. SEK 50($10) Samfundet Emigrantforskningens Fraemjande, Postbox 331, 651 08 Karlstad, Sweden. Ed. Erik Gustavson. adv.; bk.rev.; circ. 1,500.
  Formerly (until 1972): Emigranten.

BULLETIN ON AGEING. see *GERONTOLOGY AND GERIATRICS*

C E D P A WORLD WIDE. (Centre for Development and Population Activities) see *WOMEN'S INTERESTS*

C M J S CENTERPIECES. (Cohen Center for Modern Jewish Studies) see *ETHNIC INTERESTS*

362 FR ISSN 0007-9995
CAHIERS DE SOCIOLOGIE ET DE DEMOGRAPHIE MEDICALES. 1961. q. 290 F. (foreign 320 F.). Centre de Sociologie et Demographie Medicales, 60 bvd. de Latour-Maubourg, 75007 Paris, France. Ed.Bd. bk.rev.; charts; stat.; index. **Indexed:** Abstr.Hyg., Biol.Abstr., Excerp.Med., Ind.Med., Trop.Dis.Bull.
  —BLDSC shelfmark: 2952.240000.

301.32 CN ISSN 0380-1721
CAHIERS QUEBECOIS DE DEMOGRAPHIE.* 1975. 4/yr. Can.$5. Association des Demographes du Quebec, C.P. 403, succ. Cote-des-Neiges, Montreal, Que. H3S 2S7, Canada. **Indexed:** P.A.I.S.For.Lang.Ind., Popul.Ind., Pt.de Rep. (1982-).

CANADA. IMMIGRATION AND DEMOGRAPHIC POLICY GROUP. IMMIGRATION STATISTICS. see *POPULATION STUDIES — Abstracting, Bibliographies, Statistics*

325.1 CN
CANADIAN IMMIGRATION HOTLINE. m. Can.$15. Willian C. Hopkinson League, P.O. Box 278, Stn. K, Toronto, Ont. M4P 2G5, Canada.
  Description: Deals with the results of current immigration policies in Canada and other countries.

312 CN ISSN 0380-1489
HB848
CANADIAN STUDIES IN POPULATION. (Text in English, French) 1974. s-a. price varies. University of Alberta, Department of Sociology, Population Research Laboratory, Edmonton, Alta. T6G 2H4, Canada. TEL 403-492-4659. FAX 403-432-7196. Ed. Wayne W. McVey. bk.rev.; index: 1974-1983; circ. 300. (back issues avail.) **Indexed:** Popul.Ind.
  Description: Articles on population studies, both methodological and substantive.

312 US
▼**CENSUS HIGHLIGHTS.** (Supplement to: University of Virginia. Center for Public Service. Reports) 1991. m. $12. University of Virginia, Center for Public Service, 2015 Ivy Rd., 4th Fl., Charlottesville, VA 22903-1795. TEL 804-924-3396. FAX 804-924-4538.
  Description: Identifies trends emerging from the 1990 Census.

325.1 US ISSN 8756-4467
CENTER FOR MIGRATION STUDIES NEWSLETTER. 1974. s-a. free. Center for Migration Studies, 209 Flagg Pl., Staten Island, NY 10304-1199. TEL 718-351-8800. FAX 718-667-4598. Ed. Lydio F. Tomasi. adv.; bk.rev.; circ. 1,000. (tabloid format; back issues avail.; reprint service avail. from UMI)
  Description: Reports on research publications, conferences and documentation activities of the Center for Migration Studies.

CENTRE FOR URBAN AND COMMUNITY STUDIES. MAJOR REPORT SERIES. see *HOUSING AND URBAN PLANNING*

CENTRE FOR URBAN AND COMMUNITY STUDIES. RESEARCH PAPERS. see *HOUSING AND URBAN PLANNING*

312 PY ISSN 1017-6047
CENTRO DE DOCUMENTACION Y ESTUDIOS. INFORMATIVO CAMPESINO. 1988. m. $35. Centro de Documentacion y Estudios, Pai Perez 737, Asuncion, Paraguay. (Dist. by: D.I.P.P., Box 2507, Asuncion, Paraguay) Ed. Quintin Riquelme. circ. 900.

312 UN ISSN 0378-5386
HB3530.5.A3
CENTRO LATINOAMERICANO DE DEMOGRAFIA. BOLETIN DEMOGRAFICO. (Text in English and Spanish) 1968. 2/yr. $10. United Nations, Centro Latinoamericano de Demografia - United Nations, Regional Center for Demographic Training and Research in Latin America, Casilla 91, Santiago, Chile. TEL 485051. bibl.; charts; stat.; circ. 1,000. (back issues avail.) **Indexed:** P.A.I.S.For.Lang.Ind., Popul.Ind.
  Description: Contains population projections and estimates, birth and death rates for the Latin American and Caribbean countries.

312 UN ISSN 0303-1829
HB3530.5.A3
CENTRO LATINOAMERICANO DE DEMOGRAFIA. NOTAS DE POBLACION; revista latinoamericana de demografia. (Text in Spanish; summaries in English) 1973. 3/yr. $20. United Nations, Centro Latinoamericano de Demografia - United Nations, Regional Center for Demographic Training and Research in Latin America, Casilla 91, Santiago, Chile. TEL 485051. bk.rev.; index; circ. 1,000. (back issues avail.) **Indexed:** P.A.I.S.For.Lang.Ind.
  —BLDSC shelfmark: 6153.900000.
  Description: Recent studies on population dynamics in Latin America and the Caribbean, information on work in the field of demographics.

312 UN
CENTRO LATINOAMERICANO DE DEMOGRAFIA. SERIE OI: PUBLICACIONES CONJUNTAS CON INSTITUCIONES NACIONALES DE PAISES DE AMERICA LATINA. 1967. irreg. $6 per no. United Nations, Centro Latinoamericano de Demografia - United Nations, Regional Centre, Casilla 91, Santiago, Chile. stat.

312 CL
CHILE. INSTITUTO NACIONAL DE ESTADISTICAS. BOLETIN ESTADISTICO MENSUAL. 1967. m. Instituto Nacional de Estadisticas, Avda. Bulnes 418, Santiago, Chile.

312 US ISSN 1044-8403
HB3654.A3
CHINESE JOURNAL OF POPULATION SCIENCE. Chinese edition: Zhongguo Renkou Kexue (ISSN 1000-7881) (Text in English) 1989. q. $260. (Zhongguo Shehui Kexueyuan, Renkou Yanjiusuo, CC - Chinese Academy of Social Sciences, Institute of Population Research) Allerton Press, Inc., 150 Fifth Ave., New York, NY 10011. TEL 212-924-3950. Ed. Tian Xueyuan. (back issues avail.)
  —BLDSC shelfmark: 3180.559500.
  Description: Covers population research in China, including population theories, and population age and sex structures.

COLOMBIA. DEPARTAMENTO ADMINISTRATIVO NACIONAL DE ESTADISTICA. ANUARIO DEMOGRAFICO. see *POPULATION STUDIES — Abstracting, Bibliographies, Statistics*

312 FR
COMITE INTERNATIONAL DE COOPERATION DANS LES RECHERCHES NATIONALES EN DEMOGRAPHIE. ACTES DES SEMINAIRES. 1973. irreg. Committee for International Cooperation in National Research in Demography, 27 rue du Commandeur, 75675 Paris Cedex 14, France.

383 914.2 301 UK ISSN 0268-4160
HM104
CONTINUITY AND CHANGE; a journal of social structure, law and demography in past societies. 1986. 3/yr. $38 to individuals; institutions $75. Cambridge University Press, Edinburgh Building, Shaftesbury Rd., Cambridge CB2 2RU, England. TEL 0223-312393. FAX 0223-315052. TELEX 851817256. (North American orders to: Cambridge University Press, 40 W. 20th St., New York, NY 10011) Eds. Lloyd Bonfield, Richard Wall. adv.; bk.rev. (also avail. in microform from UMI; back issues avail.) **Indexed:** PSI.
  —BLDSC shelfmark: 3425.688700.
  Description: Covers historical sociology concerned with long-term continuities and discontinuity in the structures of past societies, with emphasis on studies methodology; combines elements from history, sociology, law, demography, economics or anthropology.

312 US ISSN 0082-9471
CURRENT POPULATION REPORTS. (In 8 major series) 1947. irreg. price varies. U.S. Bureau of the Census, Data User Services Division, Washington, DC 20233. TEL 301-763-4100. (Subscr. to: Supt. of Documents, Washington, DC 20402) **Indexed:** Curr.Lit.Fam.Plan.

312 US
CURRENT POPULATION REPORTS: LOCAL POPULATION ESTIMATES. (Series P-26) 1969. irreg. U.S. Bureau of the Census, Data User Services Division, Washington, DC 20233. TEL 301-763-4100. (Dist. by: Supt. of Documents, Washington, DC 20402)
●Also available online. Vendor(s): CompuServe Consumer Information Service, DIALOG.
  Formerly: Current Population Reports: Federal-State Cooperative Program for Population Estimates (ISSN 0565-0917)

301 US ISSN 0363-6836
HA195 CODEN: CPCSI
CURRENT POPULATION REPORTS: POPULATION CHARACTERISTICS. (Series P-20; 3 titles in series. Includes P-23 and P-60) 1946. irreg. $65. U.S. Bureau of the Census, Data User Services Division, Washington, DC 20233. TEL 202-783-3238. (Dist. by: Supt. of Documents, Washington, DC 20402)

312 US
CURRENT POPULATION REPORTS: POPULATION CHARACTERISTICS. GEOGRAPHICAL MOBILITY. (Series P-20) 1948. a. $65 (includes series P-20, P-23 and P-60). U.S. Bureau of the Census, Data User Services Division, Washington, DC 20233. TEL 301-763-4100. (Dist. by: Supt. of Documents, Washington, DC 20402)
●Also available online. Vendor(s): CompuServe Consumer Information Service, DIALOG.
  Formerly: Current Population Reports: Population Characteristics. Mobility of the Population of the United States (ISSN 0076-986X)

312 US
CURRENT POPULATION REPORTS: POPULATION CHARACTERISTICS. HOUSEHOLD AND FAMILY CHARACTERISTICS. (Series P-20) a. $65 (includes series P-20, P-23, and P-60). U.S. Bureau of the Census, Data User Services Division, Washington, DC 20233. TEL 301-763-4100. (Dist. by: Supt. of Documents, Washington, DC 20402)

312 US
CURRENT POPULATION REPORTS: POPULATION CHARACTERISTICS. MARITAL STATUS AND LIVING ARRANGEMENTS. (Series P-20). a. $65 (includes series P-20, P-23 and P-60). U.S. Bureau of the Census, Data User Services Division, Washington, DC 20233. TEL 301-763-4100. (Dist. by: Supt. of Documents, Washington, DC 20402)
●Also available online. Vendor(s): CompuServe Consumer Information Service, DIALOG.
  Formerly: Current Population Reports: Population Characteristics. Marital Status and Family Status (ISSN 0082-9501)

312　　　　　US
CURRENT POPULATION REPORTS: POPULATION CHARACTERISTICS. RESIDENTS OF FARMS AND RURAL AREAS. (Series P-20) 1945. a. $65 (includes series P-20, P-23 and P-60). U.S. Bureau of the Census, Data User Services Division, Washington, DC 20233. TEL 301-763-4100. (Dist. by: Supt. of Documents, Washington, DC 20402)
Formerly: Current Population Reports: Population Characteristics. Rural and Rural Farm Population; Incorporates (in 1987): Current Population Reports: Rural and Rural Farm Population; Which was formerly (until 1986): Current Population Reports: Farm Population.

312　　　　　US
CURRENT POPULATION REPORTS: POPULATION CHARACTERISTICS. SCHOOL ENROLLMENT: SOCIAL AND ECONOMIC CHARACTERISTICS OF STUDENTS. (Series P-20) a. $65 (includes series P-20, P-23 and P-60). U.S. Bureau of the Census, Data User Services Division, Washington, DC 20233. TEL 301-763-4100. (Dist. by: Supt. of Documents, Washington, DC 20402)
●Also available online. Vendor(s): CompuServe Consumer Information Service, DIALOG.
Formerly: U.S. Bureau of the Census. Current Population Reports: School Enrollment: October (Year) (ISSN 0082-9528)

CURRENT POPULATION REPORTS: POPULATION CHARACTERISTICS, SPECIAL STUDIES, CONSUMER INCOME. see *BUSINESS AND ECONOMICS — Macroeconomics*

312　　　　　US
CURRENT POPULATION REPORTS: POPULATION ESTIMATES AND PROJECTIONS. (Series P-25) 1947. m. (plus a. issue). $20. U.S. Bureau of the Census, Data User Services Division, Washington, DC 20233. TEL 301-763-4100. (Subscr. to: Supt. of Documents, Washington, DC 20402)
●Also available online. Vendor(s): CompuServe Consumer Information Service, DIALOG.

312　　　　　US
CURRENT POPULATION REPORTS: POPULATION ESTIMATES AND PROJECTIONS. UNITED STATES POPULATION ESTIMATES AND COMPONENTS OF CHANGE.. (Series P-25) a. $20. U.S. Bureau of the Census, Data User Services Division, Washington, DC 20233. TEL 301-763-4100. (Dist. by: Supt. of Documents, Washington, DC 20402)
Formerly: Current Population Reports: Population Estimates and Projections. Estimates of the Population of the United States and Components of Population Change (ISSN 0071-1616)

312　　　　　US
CURRENT POPULATION REPORTS: POPULATION ESTIMATES AND PROJECTIONS. UNITED STATES POPULATION ESTIMATES BY AGE, SEX, RACE AND HISPANIC ORIGIN. (Series P-25) a. $20. U.S. Bureau of the Census, Data User Services Division, Washington, DC 20233. TEL 301-763-4100. (Dist. by: Supt. of Documents, Washington, DC 20402) Indexed: Rehabil.Lit.
●Also available online. Vendor(s): CompuServe Consumer Information Service, DIALOG.
Former titles: Current Population Reports: Population Estimates and Projections. United States Population Estimates by Age, Sex and Race; Current Population Reports: Population Estimates and Projections. Estimates of the Population of the United States by Age, Race and Sex; Current Population Reports, P-25: Population Estimates and Projections. Estimates of the Population of the United States by Age, Color and Sex (ISSN 0071-1624)

312　　　　　US
CURRENT POPULATION REPORTS: SPECIAL CENSUSES. (Series P-28) irreg. U.S. Bureau of the Census, Data User Services Division, Washington, DC 20233. TEL 301-763-4100. (Dist. by: Supt. of Documents, Washington, DC 20402)

312　　　　　US　　ISSN 0498-8485
HA203
CURRENT POPULATION REPORTS: SPECIAL STUDIES. (Series P-23) 1949. irreg. $65 (includes series P-20, P-60). U.S. Bureau of the Census, Data User Services Division, Washington, DC 20233. TEL 301-763-4100. (Dist. by: Supt. of Documents, Washington, DC 20402)

312　　301.2　　HU　　ISSN 0011-8249
HB3592.H8
DEMOGRAFIA; review of population sciences. (Text in Hungarian; summaries and contents page in English and Russian) 1958. q. 264 Ft.($28) (Magyar Tudomanyos Akademia, Demografiai Bizottsag) Statisztikai Kiado Vallalat, Kaszasdulo u. 2, P.O. Box 99, 1300 Budapest 3, Hungary. TEL 803-311. TELEX 22-6699. (Subscr. to: Kultura, Box 149, 1389 Budapest, Hungary) (Co-sponsor: Kozponti Statisztikai Hivatal) Ed. Andras Klinger. bk.rev.; bibl.; charts; stat.; index; circ. 1,000. Indexed: Amer.Hist.& Life, Curr.Cont., Hist.Abstr., Lang.& Lang.Behav.Abstr., Popul.Ind.

312　　　　　KR　　ISSN 0207-0383
HB3608.U5
DEMOGRAFICHESKIE ISSLEDOVANIYA; respublikanskii mezhvedomstvennyi sbornik nauchnykh trudov. 1970. a. (Akademiya Nauk Ukrainskoi S.S.R., Institut Ekonomiki) Izdatel'stvo Naukova Dumka, c/o Yu.A. Khramov, Dir., Ul. Repina 3, Kiev 252601, Ukraine. TEL 224-40-68. (Subscr. to: Mezhdunarodnaya Kniga, Moscow G-200, Russia) Ed. V.S. Steshenko.
—BLDSC shelfmark: 0052.675000.

312
DEMOGRAPHIC GUIDE TO ARIZONA (YEAR). 1967. a. free. Department of Economic Security, Population Statistics Unit, Box 6123, Site Code 0452, Phoenix, AZ 85005. TEL 602-542-5984. circ. 2,000.
Formerly: Population Estimates of Arizona (ISSN 0079-3906)

312　　　　　UN
DEMOGRAPHIC HANDBOOK FOR AFRICA/GUIDE DEMOGRAPHIE DE L'AFRIQUE. (Text in English and French) irreg., latest 1978. United Nations Economic Commission for Africa, P.O. Box 3001, Addis Ababa, Ethiopia.

910　　　　　US　　ISSN 0275-9594
DEMOGRAPHIC MONOGRAPHS. 1968. irreg., vol.9, 1970. price varies. Gordon & Breach Science Publishers, 270 Eighth Ave., New York, NY 10011. TEL 212-206-8900. FAX 212-645-2459. TELEX 236735 GOPUB UR. (Subscr. to: Box 786, Cooper Sta., New York, NY 10276. TEL 800-545-8398; UK subscr. to: P.O. Box 90, Reading, Berkshire RG1 8JL, England. TEL 0734-560-080) Ed.Bd.
Refereed Serial

312　　　　　UN　　ISSN 0082-8041
HA17
DEMOGRAPHIC YEARBOOK. (Text in English and French) 1949. a. price varies. (United Nations, Department of Economic and Social Affairs) United Nations Publications, Room DC2-853, New York, NY 10017. TEL 212-963-8300. FAX 212-963-3489. (Dist. by: United Nations Sales Section, Room DC2-0853, New York, NY; or Palais des Nations, CH-1211 Geneva 10, Switzerland) Indexed: IIS.
—BLDSC shelfmark: 3550.605000.

312　　　　　CM　　ISSN 0151-1408
DEMOGRAPHIE AFRICAINE: BULLETIN DE LIAISON. (Supplement avail.: Groupe de Demographie Africaine. Etudes et Documents) 1979. 3/yr. free. Institut de Formation et de Recherche Demographiques (I F O R D), B.P. 1556, Yaounde, Cameroon. TEL 22-24-71. adv.; circ. 1,000. Indexed: Popul.Ind.
Formerly: Demographie en Afrique d'Expression Francaise: Bulletin de Liaison.

312　　　　　FR　　ISSN 0070-3362
DEMOGRAPHIE ET SOCIETES. 1960. irreg. price varies. (Ecole Pratique des Hautes Etudes, Centre de Recherches Historiques) Librairie Touzot, 38 rue Saint Sulpice, 75278 Paris Cedex 06, France.

312　　　　　US　　ISSN 0070-3370
HB881.A1
DEMOGRAPHY. 1964. q. $85. Population Association of America, 1722 N St., N.W., Washington, DC 20036-2983. TEL 202-429-0891. FAX 202-785-0146. circ. 4,000. (also avail. in microform from MIM,UMI; reprint service avail. from UMI) Indexed: ABI Inform., Abstr.Hyg., ASSIA, Biostat., Chic.Per.Ind., Curr.Lit.Fam.Plan., Environ.Abstr., I D A, Ind.Med., Int.Lab.Doc., J.of Econ.Lit., Mid.East: Abstr.& Ind., P.A.I.S., Popul.Ind., Soc.Sci.Ind., SSCI, Trop.Dis.Bull.
—BLDSC shelfmark: 3550.610000.

312　　　　　II　　ISSN 0970-454X
DEMOGRAPHY INDIA; population-society-economy-environment-interactions. (Text in English) 1972. s-a. $40. (Indian Association for the Study of Population) Hindustan Publishing Corp., 6-U.B. Jawahar Nagar, Delhi 110007, India. TEL 2915059. FAX 6863511. Ed. M.E. Khan. bk.rev.; charts; stat.; circ. 950. Indexed: I D A, Popul.Ind., Trop.Dis.Bull.

312　　　　　NE　　ISSN 0169-1473
HB848
DEMOS. 1972. 10/yr. free. Nederlands Interdisciplinair Demografisch Instituut - Netherlands Interdisciplinary Demographic Institute, Lange Houtstraat 19, 2511 CV The Hague, Netherlands. TEL 070-3565200. FAX 070-3647187. TELEX 31138 NIDI NL. circ. 5,000. Indexed: Popul.Ind.
Formerly (until 1985): Demografie (ISSN 0166-574X)

DENMARK. DANMARKS STATISTIK. BEFOLKNINGENS BEVAEGELSER. see *POPULATION STUDIES — Abstracting, Bibliographies, Statistics*

DIALOGO. see *SOCIOLOGY*

DIASPORA: A JOURNAL OF TRANSNATIONAL STUDIES. see *SOCIAL SCIENCES: COMPREHENSIVE WORKS*

325.1　　　　　US　　ISSN 0277-724X
HV89
DIRECTORY OF NONPROFIT IMMIGRATION COUNSELING AGENCIES. a. U.S. Immigration and Naturalization Service, 425 I St. N.W., Washington, DC 20536. TEL 202-724-7796.

325　　　　　IT　　ISSN 0391-3457
DOSSIER EUROPA - EMIGRAZIONE. 1964. m. L.30000 (foreign L.35000). Centro Studi Emigrazione, Via Dandolo 58, 00153 Rome, Italy. TEL 58-09-764. adv.; bk.rev.; charts; stat.; index; circ. 1,000. (processed; back issues avail.)
Formerly: C.S.E.R. Selezione (ISSN 0007-9081)
Description: Discusses the sociological and pastoral aspects of migration, with an emphasis on Europe.

312　　　　　BE
DOSSIERS DE DEMOGRAPHIE DE LA BELGIQUE. 1975. irreg. 325 Fr. (Societe Belge de Demographie) Editions Derouaux, 10, Place St.-Jacques, Liege, Belgium. (looseleaf format)

301.32　　　　　UN　　ISSN 0258-1914
E S C W A POPULATION BULLETIN. (Text in Arabic, English) 1970. s-a. price varies. (Economic and Social Commission for Western Asia, Social Development and Population Division) United Nations Publications, Room DC2-853, New York, NY 10017. Ed. Walid Halil. bk.rev.; circ. 1,800. (back issues avail.) Indexed: Trop.Dis.Bull.
—BLDSC shelfmark: 6552.203000.
Former titles: E C W A Population Bulletin; U N Economic and Social Office. Population Bulletin.
Description: Presents articles on population and related issues relevant to Arab countries and theoretical and methodological subjects of relevance to population training in the Arab world.
Refereed Serial

325　　　　　US
EAST-WEST POPULATION INSTITUTE. PAPERS. 1970. irreg., no.113, 1989. $12 (free to qualified personnel). (East-West Population Institute) Center for Cultural and Technical Interchange Between East and West, Inc., 1777 East-West Rd., Honolulu, HI 96848. TEL 808-944-7401. FAX 808-944-7490. TELEX 989171 EWC UD. Ed. Sandra E. Ward. circ. 900. Indexed: I D A, SRI.
Former titles: East-West Center. Papers; East-West Population Institute. Working Papers (ISSN 0732-0531)

325　　　　　US
EAST-WEST POPULATION INSTITUTE. WORKING PAPERS. irreg., no.59, 1989. price varies. (East-West Population Institute) Center for Cultural and Technical Interchange Between East and West, Inc., 1777 East-West Rd., Honolulu, HI 96848. TEL 808-944-7401. FAX 808-944-7490. TELEX 989171 EWC UD.

POPULATION STUDIES

301.426   UA
EGYPT. POPULATION STUDIES. QUARTERLY REVIEW.* (Supplement avail.: Research Monographs) (Text in English) 1973. q. free. (National Population Council) Cairo Demographic Centre, No. 78, St.4, Hadhaba el-Olya, Mokattam 11571, Cairo, Egypt. Ed. M.S. Abd El-Hakim. adv.; bk.rev.; circ. 2,000. **Indexed:** Popul.Ind.
 Formerly: Egypt. Population and Family Planning Board. Population Studies Quarterly Review.

325   NE   ISSN 0013-4082
ELDERS; een kroniek van zaken buiten de grenzen. 1964. m. free. Netherlands Emigration Service, Muzenstraat 30, 2511 VW The Hague, Netherlands. TEL 070-624611. Ed. J.W. van Eyk. bk.rev.; illus.; stat.; circ. 3,500.

325   US
ESCOGE LA VIDA!. (Text in Spanish) 1984. bi-m. $10 donation. Vida Humana Internacional, 4345 S.W. 72nd Ave., Ste. E, Miami, FL 33155. TEL 305-662-1497. FAX 305-662-1499. Ed. Magaly Llaguno. bk.rev.; circ. 6,000.
 Description: features news stories from the United States and other parts of the world, as well as articles on current affairs and family health.

312 910   FR   ISSN 0755-7809
ESPACES - POPULATIONS - SOCIETES. (Text and summaries in English, French) 1983. 3/yr. 320 F. Universite des Sciences et Technologies de Lille, UFR de Geographie, 59655 Villeneuve d'Ascq Cedex, France. TEL 20-43-65-52. FAX 20-43-44-41. TELEX USTL 136 339 F. adv.; bk.rev.; index. (back issues avail.)
 —BLDSC shelfmark: 3811.327000.
 Description: Explores the links between space, population and societies.

312   CK
ESTUDIOS DE POBLACION. 1976. m. Asociacion Colombiana para el Estudio de la Poblacion, Departamento de Publicaciones, Carrera 23 no. 39-82, Bogota, D.E. 1, Colombia. (Co-sponsor: Consejo de Poblacion) Ed. Rafael Salazar Santos.

312   MX   ISSN 0186-7210
HB3531
ESTUDIOS DEMOGRAFICOS Y URBANOS. 1986. 3/yr. Mex.$48000($35) Colegio de Mexico, A.C., Centro de Estudios Demograficos y de Desarrollo Urbano, Camino al Ajusco 20, Codigo Postal 01000, Mexico, D.F., Mexico. TEL 568 6033. TELEX 1777585 COLME. Ed. Martha Schteingart. adv.; bk.rev.; circ. 1,000.
 —BLDSC shelfmark: 3812.739300.

325   AG   ISSN 0326-7458
JV7398
ESTUDIOS MIGRATORIOS LATINOAMERICANOS. 1985. 3/yr. Arg.$300000($33) in N. America; elsewhere $36. Centro de Estudios Migratorios Latinoamericanos (CEMLA), Independencia 20, 1099 Buenos Aires C.F., Argentina. TEL 331-0832. Dir. Luigi Favero. adv.; bk.rev.; circ. 800. **Indexed:** Hist.Abstr., Sociol.Abstr.
 —BLDSC shelfmark: 3812.775800.

EUGENICS SPECIAL INTEREST GROUP BULLETIN. see BIOLOGY — Genetics

312   IS   ISSN 0333-9041
FAMILIES IN ISRAEL. (Text in English and Hebrew) a. $12. Central Bureau of Statistics, P.O. Box 13015, Jerusalem 91 130, Israel. TEL 02-553400.

FAMILY HISTORY NEWS AND DIGEST. see HISTORY — History Of Europe

325.2   GW
FLUECHTLINGS FORUM. 1985. s-a. German Red Cross, General Secretariat, Friedrich-Ebert-Allee 71, 5300 Bonn 1, Germany. TEL 02281541-298. circ. 3,000.

310   FR   ISSN 0071-8823
FRANCE. INSTITUT NATIONAL D'ETUDES DEMOGRAPHIQUES. CAHIERS DE TRAVAUX ET DOCUMENTS. 1946. irreg., no.131, 1991. price varies. Institut National d'Etudes Demographiques, 27 rue du Commandeur, 75675 Paris Cedex 14, France. Ed. G. Calot.

301.32   IT   ISSN 0016-6987
HB881   CODEN: GNUSA7
GENUS. (Summaries in English and French) 1934. s-a. L.80000 (foreign 100 S.Fr.). (Italian Committee for the Study of Population Problems) E S I A Books and Journals, Via Palestro, 30, 00185 Rome, Italy. FAX 00396-4747743. Ed. Nora Federici. adv.; bk.rev.; bibl.; circ. 2,000. **Indexed:** A.I.C.P., Abstr.Hyg., Amer.Hist.& Life, Biol.Abstr., Curr.Adv.Ecol.Sci., Curr.Cont., Hist.Abstr., Popul.Ind.
 —BLDSC shelfmark: 4116.700000.
 Description: International journal devoted to various aspects of demography: demographical analysis, historical demography, economic demography, social demography, theory of population policy.

GEOGRAPHICAL VIEW POINT. see GEOGRAPHY

GERONTOLOSKO DRUSTVO S R SRBIJE. see GERONTOLOGY AND GERIATRICS

312   GH
GHANA POPULATION STUDIES. 1969. irreg., no.8, 1977. price varies. University of Ghana, Institute of Statistical, Social and Economic Research, Legon, Ghana.

301.426   SW
GOETEBORGS UNIVERSITET. DEMOGRAPHIC RESEARCH INSTITUTE. REPORTS. no.14, 1974. irreg. Goeteborgs Universitet, Demographic Research Institute, Viktoriagatan 13, S-411 25 Goeteborg, Sweden. (Dist. by: Almqvist & Wiksell International, 26 Gamla Brogatan, S-111 20 Stockholm, Sweden)

312 610   UK   ISSN 0072-6400
GREAT BRITAIN. GENERAL REGISTER OFFICE. STUDIES ON MEDICAL AND POPULATION SUBJECTS. 1948. irreg. price varies. H.M.S.O., P.O. Box 276, London SW8 5DT, England. (reprint service avail. from UMI)

312   UK
GREAT BRITAIN. OFFICE OF POPULATION CENSUSES AND SURVEYS. POPULATION ESTIMATES: ENGLAND AND WALES. a. H.M.S.O., P.O. Box 276, London SW8 5DT, England.

314   DK   ISSN 0105-0885
HB1946.A3
GROENLANDS BEFOLKNING/KALATDLIT NUNANE INUIT. (Text in Danish and Greenlandic) 1976. a. free. Statsministeriet, Groenlandsdepartmentet, Hausergade 3, 1128 Copenhagen K, Denmark. circ. 600.

312   UN
GUIDE TO SOURCES OF INTERNATIONAL POPULATION ASSISTANCE. (Text in English, French, Spanish) 1976. triennial. $20 per issue. United Nations Population Fund, 220 E. 42nd St., Rm. 2306, New York, NY 10017. circ. 3,000. (also avail. in microfilm)
 Description: Contains information on the types of assistance international and other agencies and organizations provide in the population field.

325   CN
H L I CANADIAN REPORT. (Text in French) m. Can.$35($20) Human Life International in Canada Inc., P.O. Box 7400, Sta. V, Vanier, Ont. K1L 8E4, Canada. TEL 613-745-9405. FAX 613-745-9868.
 Formerly: H L I Sister Lucille's Special Canadian Report.

325   US   ISSN 0899-2673
H L I REPORTS. 1983. m. $25 donation. Human Life International, 7845-E Airpark Rd., Gaithersburg, MD 20879. TEL 301-670-7884. FAX 301-869-7363. Ed. William Marshner. charts; illus.; stat.; tr.lit; circ. 21,000. (looseleaf format; back issues avail.)
 Former titles (until 1984): H L I Report; Loveline.
 Description: Provides international reservoir of pro-life and pro-family information and perspectives.

325   CN
H L I REPORTS. m. $35. Human Life International in Canada Inc., P.O. Box 7400, Sta. V, Vanier, Ont. K1L 8E4, Canada. TEL 613-745-9405. FAX 613-745-9868.
 Formerly: H L I Reports - Canada.

312   TU
HACETTEPE UNIVERSITY. INSTITUTE OF POPULATION STUDIES. TURKISH POPULATION AND HEALTH SURVEY. 1968. quinquennial. Hacettepe University, Institute of Population Studies - Hacettepe Universitesi, Nufus Etutleri Enstituti, Ankara, Turkey. FAX 4-311-8141. TELEX 42237 HTK TR. Ed. Dr. Ergul Tuncbilek.

300   US
HAVE YOU HEARD. 1986. q. membership. Population - Environment Balance, Inc., 1325 G. St., N.W., Ste. 1003, Washington, DC 20005. TEL 202-879-3000. FAX 202-879-3019. Ed. K. Owens.
 Description: Provides updates and information on U.S. population issues.

HISTORICKA DEMOGRAFIE. see HISTORY — History Of Europe

312   HU   ISSN 0134-0050
HB849
HISTORISCH-DEMOGRAPHISCHE MITTEILUNGEN/COMMUNICATIONS DE DEMOGRAPHIE HISTORIQUE/REVIEW OF HISTORICAL DEMOGRAPHY. (Text in French and German) 1971. irreg. DM.6($4) Eotvos Lorand Tudomanyegyetem, Allam es Jogtudomanyi Kar, Statisztikai Tanszek - University Eotvus Lorand, Faculty of Law, Department of Statistics, Egyetem ter 1-3, H-1364 Budapest, Hungary. FAX 1-1174-114. TELEX 225467. Ed. Jozsef Kovacsics. bk.rev.; stat. **Indexed:** Popul.Ind.

HOMMES ET MIGRATIONS. see SOCIOLOGY

HOUSING AND POPULATION CENSUS OF MAURITIUS. see HOUSING AND URBAN PLANNING

HUMAN GEOGRAPHY/JIMBUN-CHIRI. see GEOGRAPHY

325   US   ISSN 0899-420X
HUMAN LIFE INTERNATIONAL. SPECIAL REPORT. 1981. m. $20 donation. Human Life International, 7845-E Airpark Rd., Gaithersburg, MD 20879. TEL 301-670-7884. FAX 301-869-7363. Ed. Rev. Paul Marx. stat.; cum.index: 1981-1988; circ. 23,500. (looseleaf format; back issues avail.)
 Formerly: Human Life International. Letter Dr. Report.
 Description: Accounts of Rev. Marx's pro-life missionary travels.

HUNGARY. KOZPONTI STATISZTIKAI HIVATAL. DEMOGRAFIAI EVKONYV. see POPULATION STUDIES — Abstracting, Bibliographies, Statistics

325   US   ISSN 0018-8514
KF4819.A15
I AND N REPORTER. (Immigration and Naturalization) Variant title: I N S Reporter. 1943. q. $9. U.S. Immigration and Naturalization Service, 425 I St. N.W., Washington, DC 20536. TEL 202-724-7796. (Subscr. to: Supt. of Documents, Washington, DC 20402) Ed. Janet R. Graham. charts; illus.; stat.; index; circ. 3,200. **Indexed:** Amer.Hist.& Life, Hist.Abstr.

301.426   II
I I P S NEWSLETTER. (Text in English) 1960. q. free. International Institute for Population Sciences, Govandi Station Rd., Deonar, Bombay 400 088, India. TEL 22-5511347. Ed. Ravi K. Verma. bibl.; charts; illus.; circ. 1,500.
 Formerly: International Institute for Population Studies. Newsletter (ISSN 0047-0716)
 Description: Contains organization news as well as summaries of new dissertations.

I M C H NEWSLETTER. (Institute of Maternal and Child Health) see CHILDREN AND YOUTH — About

325   SZ
I O M MONTHLY DISPATCH. (Editions in English, French, Spanish) 1979. m. free. International Organization for Migration, 17 route des Morillons, Case Postale 71, CH-1211 Geneva 19, Switzerland. TEL 022-717-9111. circ. controlled. **Indexed:** IIS.
 Former titles: I C M Monthly Dispatch; Intergovernmental Committee for European Migration. Monthly Dispatch.
 Description: Covers current activities of the organization on refugee and migration movements and programs.

312　　　　　　BE　　ISSN 0771-2022
HB848
I U S S P NEWSLETTER/U I E S P BULLETIN DE LIAISON.
(Text in English, French) 3/yr. $10 per no.
International Union for the Scientific Study of
Population, 34 rue des Augustins, B-4000 Liege,
Belgium. FAX 041-223847. TELEX 42648 POPUN.
charts; stat.; circ. 2,000. (back issues avail.)

312　　　　　　BE
I U S S P PAPERS/U I E S P DOCUMENTS DE L'UNION.
1974. irreg. price varies. International Union for the
Scientific Study of Population, 34 rue des Augustins,
B-4000 Liege, Belgium. FAX 041-223847. TELEX
42648 POPUN. bibl.; charts; illus.; stat. (back issues
avail.)

325.1　　　　　US　　ISSN 0749-5951
**IMMIGRANT COMMUNITIES & ETHNIC MINORITIES IN
THE UNITED STATES & CANADA.** 1984. irreg., no.67,
1990. price varies. A M S Press, Inc., 56 E. 13th
St., New York, NY 10003. TEL 212-777-4700.
FAX 212-995-5413. (back issues avail.)
—BLDSC shelfmark: 4369.637150.
Description: Monographs on ethnic enclaves and
communities within the United States and Canada.

325.1　　　　　UK　　ISSN 0261-9288
JV1.A2
IMMIGRANTS & MINORITIES. 1982. 3/yr. £30($45) to
individuals; institutions £70($110). Frank Cass &
Co. Ltd., Gainsborough House, 11 Gainsborough Rd.,
London E11 1RS, England. TEL 081-530-4226.
FAX 081-530-7795. Eds. Colin Holmes, Kenneth
Lunn. adv.; bk.rev.; bibl.; index. (also avail. in
microform from UMI; back issues avail.) **Indexed:**
Amer.Hist.& Life, ASSIA, E.I., Hist.Abstr.
—BLDSC shelfmark: 4369.637500.
Description: Covers study of immigration, racial
and ethnic minorities; the response of receiving
societies towards newcomers.

IMMIGRATION AND NATIONALITY LAW REVIEW. see
LAW — Civil Law

235.1　　　　　US　　ISSN 0897-6708
KF4802
IMMIGRATION BRIEFINGS; practical, tight-knit analysis
of U.S. immigration and nationality law. m. $280.
Federal Publications, Inc., 1120 20th St., N.W., Ste.
500 S., Washington, DC 20036.
TEL 202-337-7000. FAX 202-223-0755. Ed. Bruce
A. Hake.

325.1　　　　　US　　ISSN 0899-5400
IMMIGRATION DIGEST. 1987. irreg. (2-3/yr.). $10 per
no. Family History World, Box 22045, Salt Lake City,
UT 84122. TEL 801-257-6174. Ed. Arlene H.
Eakle. bk.rev.; circ. 400.
Description: Provides current information on new
resources to link your immigrant ancestors with their
origins: naming patterns and changed name forms,
exit documents and where to find them, passenger
lists and naturalizations, administrative boundary
maps.

325.1　　　　　US　　ISSN 0579-4374
E184.A1
IMMIGRATION HISTORY NEWSLETTER. 1969. s-a. $17
to individuals; institutions $32 (includes journal).
Immigration History Society, c/o Balch Institute, 18
S. 7th St., Philadelphia, PA 19106.
TEL 215-925-8090. Ed. M. Mark Stolarik. bk.rev.;
bibl.; circ. 750. **Indexed:** Amer.Hist.& Life (until
1990), Hist.Abstr. (until 1990).

IMMIGRATION LAW REPORT. see LAW — Civil Law

325.1　　　　　CN　　ISSN 0835-3808
KE4454.A45
IMMIGRATION LAW REPORTER. SECOND SERIES. N.S.
1988. 12/yr. (in 3 vols.). Can.$130. Carswell
Publications, Corporate Plaza, 2075 Kennedy Rd.,
Scarborough, Ont. M1T 3V4, Canada.
TEL 416-609-8000. FAX 416-298-5094. Ed. Cecil
L. Rotenberg.

325.1　　　　　US　　ISSN 0892-547X
KF4802
IMMIGRATION POLICY & LAW. 1987. bi-w. $497
(foreign $517). Buraff Publications (Subsidiary of:
The Bureau of National Affairs, Inc.), 1350
Connecticut Ave., N.W., Ste. 1000, Washington, DC
20036. TEL 202-862-0990. FAX 202-822-8092.
TELEX 285656 BNAI WSH. Ed. Corby Anderson.
(back issues avail.)
●Also available online. Vendor(s): Human Resources
Information Network (CDD, HDD).
Description: Covers the Immigration Reform and
Control Act of 1986. Reports on requirements and
procedures, litigation, enforcement action, activities
of the Immigration and Naturalization Service and
the Congress.

IMMIGRATION REPORT. see LAW — Civil Law

325　　　　　US　　ISSN 0275-634X
IN DEFENSE OF THE ALIEN; proceedings of the Annual
National Legal Conference on Immigration &
Refugee Policy. 1978. a. $14.95. Center for
Migration Studies of New York, Inc., 209 Flagg Pl.,
Staten Island, NY 10304-1199.
TEL 718-351-8800. FAX 718-667-4598. Ed.Bd.
circ. 850. (back issues avail.) **Indexed:** Refug.Abstr.
Description: Legal, legislative and socio-economic
developments in migration and refugee policy. For
students, lawyers and social workers interested in
the current legal and policy issues on migration and
refugees.

INDIAN HEALTH TRENDS AND SERVICES. see PUBLIC
HEALTH AND SAFETY

613.9　　　　　US
INDUCED ABORTION: A WORLD REVIEW. 1973. irreg.,
6th ed. 1986; supplement 1990. $10. Alan
Guttmacher Institute, 111 Fifth Ave., New York, NY
10003. TEL 212-254-5656. Ed. Stanley K.
Henshaw. charts; circ. 17,000. (reprint service avail.
from UMI)

312　　　　　BL　　ISSN 0100-7173
INFORME DEMOGRAFICO. 1980. irreg. $41.50.
Fundacao Sistema Estadual de Analise de Dados, Av.
Casper Libero, 464, 01033 Sao Paulo, Brazil. circ.
500.
Description: Devoted to specific topics such as:
mortality rates, migration and the fertility rate in the
state of Sao Paulo.

301.32　　　　　US　　ISSN 0277-2302
AP2
INSTAURATION. 1975. m. $30. Howard Allen
Enterprises, Inc., Box 76, Cape Canaveral, FL
32920. Ed. Wilmot Robertson. adv.; bk.rev.; film rev.
Description: Explores the effects of population
group dynamics on contemporary political, economic
and social issues.

312　　　　　CM
**INSTITUT DE FORMATION ET DE RECHERCHE
DEMOGRAPHIQUES. ANNALES.** 1975. 2/yr. free.
Institut de Formation et de Recherche
Demographiques (I F O R D), B.P. 1556, Yaounde,
Cameroon. TEL 22-24-71. circ. 500.

312　　　　　II　　ISSN 0070-3311
**INSTITUTE OF ECONOMIC GROWTH, DELHI. CENSUS
STUDIES.** (Text in English) 1969. irreg. Rs.30.
Institute of Economic Growth, Delhi, Univeristy of
Delhi, Delhi 110007, India.

312　　　　　II
**INSTITUTE OF ECONOMIC RESEARCH. PUBLICATIONS ON
DEMOGRAPHY.** (Text in English) irreg. price varies.
Institute of Economic Research, Director, Vidyagiri,
Dharwar 580004, Karnataka, India.
FAX 836-41001.

312　　　　　IS　　ISSN 0333-9874
INTEGRATED RURAL DEVELOPMENT. PUBLICATIONS.
(Text in English) irreg., latest 1991. price varies.
Development Study Center, P.O. Box 2355, Rehovot
76122, Israel. TEL 08-474111. FAX 08-475884.

POPULATION STUDIES　　3983

301.32　　　　　II
**INTERNATIONAL INSTITUTE FOR POPULATION SCIENCES.
DIRECTOR'S REPORT.** (Text in English) 1956. a. free.
International Institute for Population Sciences,
Govandi Station Rd., Deonar, Bombay 400 088,
India. TEL 5511347. Dir. K. Srinivasan. circ. 800.
Former titles: International Institute for Population
Studies. Annual Report; Demographic Training and
Research Centre. Annual Report; International
Institute for Population Studies. Director's Report.

312　　　　　SZ　　ISSN 0020-7985
JV6001.A1
INTERNATIONAL MIGRATION. (Text mainly in English;
occasionally French or Spanish) 1961. q. $20 to
individuals; institutions $25. International
Organization for Migration, 17 Route des Morillons,
Case Postale 71, 1211 Geneva 19, Switzerland.
TEL 022-717-9111. Ed. R.T. Appleyard. bk.rev.;
bibl.; charts; stat.; index; circ. 3,800. **Indexed:**
Amer.Hist.& Life, Chic.Per.Ind., Geo.Abstr.,
Hist.Abstr., I D A, IIS, Int.Lab.Doc., Key to Econ.Sci.,
Lang.& Lang.Behav.Abstr., Popul.Ind., Refug.Abstr.,
SSCI.
—BLDSC shelfmark: 4544.230000.
Formed by the merger of: Migration; R E M P
Bulletin.
Description: Covers current migration issues as
analyzed by demographers, economists and
sociologists all over the world. Includes reports and
announcements of events and new publications.

325 300　　　　　US　　ISSN 0197-9183
JV6001
INTERNATIONAL MIGRATION REVIEW; a quarterly
studying sociological, demographic, economic,
historical, and legislative aspects of human migration
movements and ethnic group relations. 1966. q.
$27.50 to individuals; institutions $44. Center for
Migration Studies, 209 Flagg Place, Staten Island,
NY 10304-1199. TEL 718-351-8800.
FAX 718-667-4598. Ed. Silvano M. Tomasi. adv.;
bk.rev.; abstr.; bibl.; charts; stat.; index, cum.index;
circ. 2,500. (also avail. in microform from UMI; back
issues avail.; reprint service avail. from UMI) **Indexed:**
A.I.C.P., Abstr.Anthropol., Amer.Bibl.Slavic &
E.Eur.Stud., Amer.Hist.& Life, ASSIA, C.I.J.E.,
Chic.Per.Ind., Curr.Cont., E.I., Hisp.Amer.Per.Ind.,
Hist.Abstr., I D A, Lang.& Lang.Behav.Abstr.,
Mid.East: Abstr.& Ind., P.A.I.S., Popul.Ind.,
Refug.Abstr., Rural Recreat.Tour.Abstr., Sage
Fam.Stud.Abstr., So.Pac.Per.Ind., Soc.Sci.Ind.,
Soc.Work Res.& Abstr., Sociol.Abstr., SSCI,
Stud.Wom.Abstr., World Agri.Econ.& Rural
Sociol.Abstr.
Formerly: International Migration Digest.
Description: Articles and research notes on
migration and refugee issues.

325　　　　　CN　　ISSN 0383-2767
INTERNATIONAL NEWSLETTER ON MIGRATION. 1971.
irreg. University of Waterloo, Waterloo, Ont. N2L
3GI, Canada. TEL 519-885-1211.
Formerly: International Migration Newsletter (ISSN
0383-2759)

325　　　　　SZ
**INTERNATIONAL ORGANIZATION FOR MIGRATION.
ANNUAL REPORT.** (Editions in English, French and
Spanish) 1969. a. free. International Organization
for Migration, 17 Route des Morillons, Case Postale
71, CH-1211 Geneva 19, Switzerland.
TEL 022-717-9111. circ. 5,000. **Indexed:** IIS.
Former titles: International Organization for
Migration. Annual Review; Intergovernmental
Committee for Migration. Annual Review;
Intergovernmental Committee for Migration. Review
of Achievements; Intergovernmental Committee for
European Migration. Review of Achievements.
Description: Report of the organization covering
migration activities, migration for development
programs, migration planning, cooperation and
research, administration, management, finance,
information and publications.

312　　　　　BE　　ISSN 0074-9338
**INTERNATIONAL POPULATION CONFERENCE.
PROCEEDINGS.** French edition: Congres International
de la Population. Proceedings (ISSN 0254-5217)
quadrennial. price varies. International Union for the
Scientific Study of Population, 34 rue des Augustins,
B-4000 Liege, Belgium. FAX 041-223847. TELEX
42648 POPUN. **Indexed:** Popul.Ind.

P
Q

POPULATION STUDIES

312   US
INTERNATIONAL POPULATION DATA. irreg. U.S. Bureau of the Census, Data User Services Division, Washington, DC 20233. TEL 301-763-4100. (Dist. by: Supt. of Documents, Washington, DC 20402) ●Also available online. Vendor(s): CompuServe Consumer Information Service, DIALOG.
Former titles: Current Population Reports: International Population Data; Current Population Reports: International Population Reports (ISSN 0082-9498)

325   US   ISSN 0020-9686
JK1751
INTERPRETER RELEASES; report and analysis of immigration and nationality law. 1926. w. $320 to non-profit organizations and government; other institutions $385. Federal Publications, Inc., 1120 20th St., N.W., Ste. 500 S., Washington, DC 20036. TEL 202-337-7000. FAX 202-223-0755. (Subscr. to: Box 41094, Nashville, TN 37204) Ed. Maurice A. Roberts. bk.rev.; index. (processed) **Indexed:** P.A.I.S., Vert.File Ind.

325.1 948   SW   ISSN 0345-5505
INVANDRARRAPPORT; Invandrarnas debatt- och kulturtidskrift. 1973. q. SEK 160. Immigrant Institutet, Kvarngatan 16, S-502 33 Boras, Sweden. FAX 46-33-136075. Ed. Miguel Benito. adv.; bk.rev.; bibl.
Description: Covers all aspects of immigration in Sweden: refugees, bilingual education, immigrant authors and organizations, and immigration law and legislation.

301.32   UN   ISSN 0363-5155
HQ763
INVENTORY OF POPULATION PROJECTS IN DEVELOPING COUNTRIES AROUND THE WORLD. (Text in English, French) 1975. a. $20. United Nations Population Fund, 220 E. 42 St., Rm.2306, New York, NY 10017. circ. 3,000. (also avail. in microfilm) **Indexed:** IIS.
Description: Contains information on population projects, listed by country and geographic region, and supported by both national and international agencies and organizations.

ITALIA NOSTRA. SEZIONE DI TRENTO. BOLLETTINO. see ENVIRONMENTAL STUDIES

JAHRBUCH FUER FRAENKISCHE LANDESFORSCHUNG. see HISTORY — History Of Europe

312   JA
JAPAN. INSTITUTE OF POPULATION PROBLEMS. ANNUAL REPORT. 1977. a. free. Ministry of Health and Welfare, Institute of Population Problems - Jinko Mondai Kenkyusho, 2-2, 1-chome, Kasumigaseki, Chiyoda-ku, Tokyo 100, Japan.

312   IS
JEWISH POPULATION SERIES. irreg. Magnes Press, Hebrew University, P.O. Box 7695, Jerusalem 91 076, Israel.

312   JA   ISSN 0387-2793
JINKO MONDAI KENKYU/JOURNAL OF POPULATION PROBLEMS. (Text in Japanese; summaries in English) 1940. q. free. Ministry of Health and Welfare, Institute of Population Problems - Kosei-sho Jinko Mondai Kenkyujo, 1-2-2 Kasumigaseki, Chiyoda-ku, Tokyo 100, Japan. bk.rev.; stat. **Indexed:** Popul.Ind.
—BLDSC shelfmark: 5041.145000.

325   US   ISSN 0887-0241
JOHNS HOPKINS UNIVERSITY. POPULATION INFORMATION PROGRAM. POPULATION REPORTS. ENGLISH EDITION.. 1973. 5/yr. free to qualified personnel. Johns Hopkins University, Population Information Program, 527 St. Paul Place, Baltimore, MD 21202. TEL 301-659-6300. TELEX 240430. Ed. Ward Rinehart. bibl.; charts; illus.; stat.; circ. 77,500. (looseleaf format; back issues avail.) **Indexed:** Popul.Ind.
Formerly: George Washington University. Population Information Program. Population Reports.

325   US   ISSN 0887-025X
JOHNS HOPKINS UNIVERSITY. POPULATION INFORMATION PROGRAM. POPULATION REPORTS. FRENCH EDITION. 1973. 5/yr. free to qualified personnel. Johns Hopkins University, Population Information Program, 527 St. Paul Place, Baltimore, MD 21202. TEL 301-659-6300. TELEX 240430. Ed. Ward Rinehart. bibl.; charts; illus.; stat.; circ. 11,000. (looseleaf format; back issues avail.) **Indexed:** Popul.Ind.
Formerly: George Washington University. Population Information Program. Population Reports.

325   US   ISSN 0887-0276
JOHNS HOPKINS UNIVERSITY. POPULATION INFORMATION PROGRAM. POPULATION REPORTS. PORTUGUESE EDITION. 1973. 5/yr. free to qualified personnel. Johns Hopkins University, Population Information Program, 527 St. Paul Place, Baltimore, MD 21202. TEL 301-659-6300. TELEX 240430. Ed. Ward Rinehart. bibl.; charts; illus.; stat.; circ. 14,000. (looseleaf format; back issues avail.) **Indexed:** Popul.Ind.
Formerly: George Washington University. Population Information Program. Population Reports.

325   US   ISSN 0887-0268
JOHNS HOPKINS UNIVERSITY. POPULATION INFORMATION PROGRAM. POPULATION REPORTS. SPANISH EDITION. 1973. 5/yr. free to qualified personnel. Johns Hopkins University, Population Information Program, 527 St. Paul Place, Baltimore, MD 21202. TEL 301-659-6300. TELEX 240430. Ed. Ward Rinehart. bibl.; charts; illus.; stat.; circ. 39,200. (looseleaf format; back issues avail.) **Indexed:** Popul.Ind.
Formerly: George Washington University. Population Information Program. Population Reports.

JOURNAL OF BIOSOCIAL SCIENCE. see BIOLOGY — Genetics

312   TH   ISSN 0857-2143
HB848
JOURNAL OF DEMOGRAPHY/WARASARN PRACHAKORNSATR. 1985. s-a. $5. Chulalongkorn University, Institute of Population Studies, Phyathai Rd., Bangkokd, Thailand. TEL 2511133. circ. 500.

312   IO   ISSN 0126-0251
HA1815
JOURNAL OF INDONESIAN DEMOGRAPHY/MAJALAH DEMOGRAFI INDONESIA. (Text in English or Indonesian) 1974. s-a. Rps.15000($35) Universitas Indonesia, Lembaga Demografi, Jalan Salemba 4, Jakarta 10430, Indonesia. TEL 336539. FAX 62-21-310-2457. Eds. Prijono Tjiptoherijanto, Rozy Munir. adv.; circ. 1,000. **Indexed:** E.I., Popul.Ind.

JOURNAL OF ONE-NAME STUDIES. see GENEALOGY AND HERALDRY

330   US   ISSN 0933-1433
HB849.41   CODEN: JPECEW
JOURNAL OF POPULATION ECONOMICS. 1988. q. $97. (European Society for Population Economics) Springer-Verlag, Journals, 175 Fifth Ave., New York, NY 10010. TEL 212-460-1500. (Subscr. to: Service Center Secaucus, 44 Hartz Way, Secaucus, NJ 07094) Ed.Bd.
—BLDSC shelfmark: 5041.144000.
Description: Focuses on the relation between economics and demographics, and addresses diverse topics in this area.

JOURNAL OF REFUGEE STUDIES. see POLITICAL SCIENCE — Civil Rights

312   US
KANSAS. DEPARTMENT OF HEALTH AND ENVIRONMENT. ANNUAL SUMMARY OF VITAL STATISTICS. a. Department of Health and Environment, 900 S.W. Jackson, Topeka, KS 66612-1290. TEL 913-296-5640. stat. **Indexed:** SRI.

KIBBUTZ STUDIES. see BUSINESS AND ECONOMICS — Labor And Industrial Relations

LANDSCAPE. see GEOGRAPHY

LIBYA. CENSUS AND STATISTICS DEPARTMENT. GENERAL POPULATION CENSUS. see POPULATION STUDIES — Abstracting, Bibliographies, Statistics

312   UK   ISSN 0143-2974
HB3583
LOCAL POPULATION STUDIES. (Occasional supplements) 1968. s-a. £6 (foreign £7). Tawney House, Matlock, Derbyshire DE4 3BT, England. (Subscr. to: Mrs. M.H. Charlton, 27 St. Margarets Rd., St. Marychurch, Torquay, Devon, England) Ed.Bd. adv.; bk.rev.; bibl.; charts; stat.; circ. 1,500. (also avail. in microform from UMI; back issues avail.; reprint service avail. from UMI) **Indexed:** Amer.Hist.& Life, Br.Hum.Ind., Hist.Abstr., Popul.Ind.
—BLDSC shelfmark: 5290.044700.

312   US
MAINE. DEPARTMENT OF HUMAN SERVICES. POPULATION ESTIMATES FOR MINOR CIVIL DIVISIONS BY COUNTY. 1981. a. $4.40. Department of Human Services, Office of Data, Research, and Vital Statistics, State House Sta. No.11, Augusta, ME 04333. TEL 207-624-5445. Ed. Ellen M. Naor. circ. 500.
Description: Population estimates of MCD's by age group.

301.32   MY   ISSN 0126-8104
MALAYSIA. NATIONAL POPULATION AND FAMILY DEVELOPMENT BOARD. BULETIN KELUARGA. 1969. q. free. National Population and Family Development Board, Box 10416, Jalan Raja Laut, 50712 Kuala Lumpur, Malaysia. TEL 2937555. TELEX POPMAL MA 31911. Ed. Yusuff Yunus. abstr.; stat.; circ. 35,000.
Description: Discusses family development, population and family planning.

301.32   MY   ISSN 0128-1232
MALAYSIAN JOURNAL OF FAMILY STUDIES. (Text in English) 1989. a. $10. National Population and Family Development Board, P.O. Box 10416, Jalan Raja Laut, 50712 Kuala Lumpur, Malaysia. TEL 2937555. FAX 03-2921357. Ed. Ang Eng Suan. circ. 500.
Description: Provides various results of research in the area of family development in Malaysia.

MALTA. CENTRAL OFFICE OF STATISTICS. DEMOGRAPHIC REVIEW. see POPULATION STUDIES — Abstracting, Bibliographies, Statistics

MARYLAND TOMORROW. see HOUSING AND URBAN PLANNING

312   US   ISSN 0889-8480
HB849.51   CODEN: MPSTEG
MATHEMATICAL POPULATION STUDIES; an international journal of mathematical demography. 4/yr. $126. Gordon & Breach Science Publishers, 270 Eighth Ave., New York, NY 10011. TEL 212-206-8900. FAX 212-645-2459. TELEX 236735 GOPUB UR. (Subscr. to: Box 786, Cooper Sta., New York, NY 10276. TEL 800-545-8398; UK subscr. to: P.O. Box 90, Reading, Berkshire RG1 8JL, England. TEL 0734-560-080) Ed. Marc Artzrouni. (also avail. in microform)
—BLDSC shelfmark: 5402.576570.
Refereed Serial

325   FR   ISSN 0335-0894
MIGRANTS FORMATION. 1973. q. 78 F. (foreign 101 F.). Centre National de Documentation Pedagogique, 29 rue de l'Ulm, 75230 Paris Cedex 05, France. (Subscr. to: CNDP - Abonnements, B.P. 107 - 05, 75224 Paris Cedex 05, France) Ed.Bd. bk.rev.; bibl. **Indexed:** Abstr.Musl.Rel.
—BLDSC shelfmark: 5761.528000.
Description: Offers information and discussion on education, immigration and educational development of children, young adults and adults.

325   FR   ISSN 0397-944X
Z7164.I3
MIGRANTS NOUVELLES. 1974. 10/yr. 52 F. (foreign 74 F.). Centre National de Documentation Pedagogique, 29 rue de l'Ulm, 75230 Paris Cedex 05, France. (Subscr. to: CNDP - Abonnements, B.P. 107 - 05, 75224 Paris Cedex 05, France) Ed. Pierre Trincal. charts; stat.
Description: Provides information briefs on all aspects of immigration.

POPULATION STUDIES

325   FI
MIGRATION INSTITUTE. MIGRATION STUDIES. (Includes three series: A (Finnish); B (Swedish); C (English)) 1974. irreg. price varies. Migration Institute, Piispankatu 3, 20500 Turku 50, Finland. Dir. Olavi Koivukangas. bk.rev.; charts; stat.; circ. 1,000.
Formerly: Institute for Migration, Turku. Migration Studies (ISSN 0356-780X)

301.3   SZ   ISSN 0544-1188
MIGRATION TODAY. (Editions in English, French and Spanish) 1963. 2/yr. free. World Council of Churches, Commission on Sharing and Service, Migration Secretariat, P.O. Box 2100, CH-1211 Geneva 2, Switzerland. TEL 022-7916323. FAX 022-7910361. TELEX 415730 OIK CH. bk.rev.; circ. 4,000. **Indexed:** Abstr.Musl.Rel., C.I.J.E., CERDIC, HR Rep., P.A.I.S., Stud.Wom.Abstr.

301.32 300   US
JV6001
MIGRATION WORLD; a bi-monthly magazine focusing on the newest immigrant and refugee groups; policy and legislation; resources. 1973. 5/yr. $19 to individuals; institutions $25. Center for Migration Studies, 209 Flagg Place, Staten Island, NY 10304-1199. TEL 718-351-8800. FAX 718-667-4598. Ed. Lydio Tomasi. adv.; bk.rev.; abstr.; illus.; circ. 1,800. (tabloid format; also avail. in microfilm; back issues avail.) **Indexed:** Amer.Hist.& Life, C.I.J.E., Chic.Per.Ind., Hist.Abstr., HR Rep., Mid.East: Abstr.& Ind., P.A.I.S., Refug.Abstr., Sociol.Abstr.
Formerly: Migration Today (ISSN 0197-9175)
Description: Articles, legal analyses, dateline updates on recent immigrants and refugees.

312   US   ISSN 0734-032X
MISSOURI POPULATION ESTIMATES; by county, by age, by sex. a. $10. Department of Health, Center for Health Statistics, Box 570, Jefferson City, MO 65102. TEL 314-751-6272. Ed. Garland Land.

312   US   ISSN 0077-0930
CODEN: MPOBA6
MONOGRAPHS IN POPULATION BIOLOGY. 1967. irreg., no.27, 1989. price varies. Princeton University Press, 3175 Princeton Pike, Lawrenceville, NJ 08648. TEL 609-896-1344. FAX 609-895-1081. (reprint service avail. from UMI) **Indexed:** Biol.Abstr., Ind.Med.
—BLDSC shelfmark: 5915.960000.

312   US
MONTHLY PRODUCT ANNOUNCEMENT. 1980. m. free. U.S. Bureau of the Census, Data User Services Division (DAUS), Washington, DC 20233. TEL 301-763-4100. FAX 301-763-4794. Ed. Mary Kilbride. circ. 6,500. (also avail. in microform) **Indexed:** Amer.Stat.Ind., MEDOC.

MOSELLA. see *GEOGRAPHY*

MOUVEMENT NATUREL DE LA POPULATION DE LA GRECE. see *POPULATION STUDIES — Abstracting, Bibliographies, Statistics*

MOVIMIENTO NATURAL DE LA POBLACION DE ESPANA. see *POPULATION STUDIES — Abstracting, Bibliographies, Statistics*

N A T O ADVANCED SCIENCE INSTITUTES SERIES D: BEHAVIOURAL AND SOCIAL SCIENCES. (North Atlantic Treaty Organization) see *SOCIAL SCIENCES: COMPREHENSIVE WORKS*

312   NE   ISSN 0922-7210
N I D I. RAPPORT - REPORT - BERICHT - RAPPORTO. 1988. irreg. free. Nederlands Interdisciplinair Demografisch Instituut - Netherlands Interdisciplinary Demographic Institute, Lange Houtstraat 19, 2511 CV The Hague, Netherlands. TEL 070-3565200. FAX 070-3647187. TELEX 31138 NIDI NL. Ed.Bd. (back issues avail.)

312   BU   ISSN 0205-0617
HB3627
NASELENIE. 1983. q. 1.62 lv. per issue. (Bulgarska Akademiia na Naukite) Publishing House of the Bulgarian Academy of Sciences, 7 Noemvri St. 1, 1040 Sofia, Bulgaria. (Dist. by: Hemus, 6 Rouski Blvd., 1000 Sofia, Bulgaria) circ. 800. **Indexed:** Bibl.Ind., BSL Econ.
—BLDSC shelfmark: 0119.255000.

312   NE
NEDERLANDS INTERUNIVERSITAIR DEMOGRAFISCH INSTITUUT. PUBLICATIONS. (Text in English) 1976. irreg. price varies. (Nederlands Interuniversitair Demografisch Instituut - Netherlands Interuniversity Demographic Institute) Kluwer Academic Publishers, Postbus 17, 3300 AA Dordrecht, Netherlands. TEL 078-334911. FAX 078-334254. TELEX 29245. (Dist. by: Kluwer Academic Publishers Group, P.O. Box 322, 3300 AH Dordrecht, Netherlands) (Co-sponsor: Population and Family Study Centre)

NEW ZEALAND. HEALTH STATISTICAL SERVICES. HOSPITAL AND SELECTED MORBIDITY DATA. see *HOSPITALS — Abstracting, Bibliographies, Statistics*

312   NQ
NICARAGUA. INSTITUTO NACIONAL DE ESTADISTICAS Y CENSOS. BOLETIN DEMOGRAFICO. no.2, 1978. irreg. C.$15($4) per no. Instituto Nacional de Estadisticos y Census, Apdo. Postal 4031, Managua, Nicaragua. stat.
Formerly: Nicaragua. Oficina Ejecutiva de Encuestos y Censos. Boletin Demografico.

312   CN   ISSN 0714-0541
F1056.5
NORTHERN ONTARIO DIRECTORY; information guide to unincorporated communities & Indian reserves. 1979. biennial. Ministry of Northern Development and Mines, Communications Services, 159 Cedar St., 6th Fl., Sudbury, Ont. P3E 6A5, Canada. TEL 705-670-7117. FAX 705-670-7108. circ. 1,000.

312   US   ISSN 0732-1597
NUMBERS NEWS. 1983. m. $149. American Demographics, Inc., Box 68, Ithaca, NY 14851-0068. TEL 607-273-6343. FAX 607-273-3196. Ed. Diane Crispell. stat.; circ. 1,300. (reprint service avail. from UMI)

325   US
NUOVA VIA. 1968. 4/yr. free. American Committee on Italian Migration, 352 W. 44th St., New York, NY 10026-5419. TEL 212-247-7373. circ. 5,000.

325.1   SW   ISSN 0345-8660
NY I SVERIGE. 1971. 6/yr. SEK 75. Statens Invandrarverk - Swedish Immigration Board, Box 6113, 600 06 Norrkoeping, Sweden. bk.rev.; circ. 11,000.

301.32   MG
NY MPONIN'I MADAGASIKARA. (Text in French or Malagasy) 1975. irreg. Direction de la Recherche Scientifique et Technique, Section de Demographie, B.P. 4096, Antananarivo, Malagasy Republic.

312 614   US
OKLAHOMA. DEPARTMENT OF HEALTH. MONTHLY VITAL STATISTICS REPORT. 1974. m. Department of Health, N.E. Tenth and Stonewall, Box 53551, Oklahoma City, OK 73105. TEL 405-271-5600. circ. 400.

301.412 312   US
OPTIONS (WASHINGTON). q. Center for Population Options, 1025 Vermont Ave., N.W., Ste. 210, Washington, DC 20005. TEL 202-347-5700. FAX 202-347-2263. Ed. Robin K. Lewis. bk.rev.; circ. 5,000. (back issues avail.)
Incorporates: Issues: Action; Population Options.

OWNER OCCUPIED HOUSING STATISTICS FROM HOMESTEAD REBATE AND INCOME TAX DATA MATCH. see *HOUSING AND URBAN PLANNING — Abstracting, Bibliographies, Statistics*

312   US   ISSN 0300-6816
HB848
P A A AFFAIRS. 1968. q. $5. Population Association of America, 1722 N St., N.W., Washington, DC 20036-2983. TEL 202-429-0891. FAX 202-785-0146. circ. 2,600. **Indexed:** Curr.Lit.Fam.Plan.
Description: General items of interest to members.

PACIFIC VIEWPOINT; specialises in the study of development, change and underdevelopment. see *GEOGRAPHY*

PENNSYLVANIA VITAL STATISTICS. see *POPULATION STUDIES — Abstracting, Bibliographies, Statistics*

301.32   MY   ISSN 0127-9068
POFAM. (Text in English) 1986. s-a. free. National Population and Family Development Board, P.O. Box 10416, Jalan Raja Laut, 50712 Kuala Lumpur, Malaysia. TEL 2937555. FAX 03-2921357. TELEX POP MAL MA 31911. Ed. Annuar Maaruf. circ. 3,000.
Description: Discusses various aspects of family development and population issues in Malaysia.

312   ET
POPINDEX AFRICA. (Text in English and French) 1985. s-a. Population Information Network for Africa, Coordinating Unit, P.O. Box 3001, Addis-Ababa, Ethiopia. Ed. Petrina Amooni.

312   US
POPLINE. 1979. 6/yr. $25. Population Institute, 110 Maryland Ave., N.E., Washington, DC 20002. TEL 202-544-3300. FAX 202-544-0068. Ed. Harold N. Burdett. circ. 70,000. (tabloid format)
Description: News and feature service provided to more than 2,100 daily newspapers worldwide. Explores, analyzes, and evaluates facts and public policies relating to the problems of world over-population.

312   UN
POPULATION. (Editions in Arabic, English, French, Spanish) 1975. m. free. United Nations Population Fund, 220 E. 42nd St., Rm.2307, New York, NY 10017. Ed. Alex Marshall. bk.rev.; illus. **Indexed:** Curr.Lit.Fam.Plan., Trop.Dis.Bull.
Formerly: Population Newsletter (ISSN 0048-4849)
Description: Focuses on the organization's programs, policies and strategies as they relate to population activities worldwide.

312   FR   ISSN 0032-4663
POPULATION. 1946. irreg. (5-6/yr.). 360 F. Institut National d'Etudes Demographiques, 27 rue du Commandeur, 75675 Paris Cedex 14, France. circ. 4,500. (reprint service avail. from KTO)
—BLDSC shelfmark: 6552.000000.
Incorporates: Demographie et Sciences Humaines (ISSN 0070-3354)

312   US
POPULATION (WASHINGTON); briefing papers on issues of national and international importance in the population field. 1976. irreg. price varies. Population Crisis Committee, 1120 Nineteenth St., N.W., Ste. 550, Washington, DC 20036. TEL 202-659-1833. FAX 202-293-1795. TELEX 440450. charts; stat.; circ. 55,000. **Indexed:** Curr.Lit.Fam.Plan.

312 301.32   US   ISSN 0098-7921
HB848
POPULATION AND DEVELOPMENT REVIEW. (Text in English; summaries in English, French, Spanish) 1975. q. $24. Population Council, One Dag Hammarskjold Plaza, New York, NY 10017. FAX 212-755-6052. Ed. Paul Demeny. bk.rev.; abstr.; charts; index, cum.index: vols. 1-10 in 1985; circ. 5,000. (also avail. in microfilm from UMI; reprint service avail from UMI) **Indexed:** A.B.C.Pol.Sci., Abstr.Hyg., Amer.Bibl.Slavic & E.Eur.Stud., Amer.Hist.& Life, ASSIA, Curr.Cont., Curr.Lit.Fam.Plan., E.I., Environ.Abstr., Geo.Abstr., I D A, Int.Lab.Doc., J.of Econ.Lit., Lang.& Lang.Behav.Abstr., Mid.East: Abstr.& Ind., P.A.I.S., Popul.Ind., Ref.Sour., Rural Recreat.Tour.Abstr., Sage Fam.Stud.Abstr., Sage Urb.Stud.Abstr., Sociol.Abstr., SSCI, Trop.Dis.Bull., Urb.Aff.Abstr., World Agri.Econ. & Rural Sociol.Abstr.

POPULATION AND ENVIRONMENTAL PSYCHOLOGY NEWSLETTER. see *PSYCHOLOGY*

312   NE   ISSN 0169-1422
POPULATION AND FAMILY IN THE LOW COUNTRIES. (Text in English) 1976. irreg. fl.30 per vol. Nederlands Interdisciplinair Demografisch Instituut - Netherlands Interdisciplinary Demographic Institute, Lange Houtstr. 19, 2511 CV The Hague, Netherlands. TEL 070-3565200. FAX 070-3647187. TELEX 31138 NIDI NL. (Co-sponsor: Centrum voor Bevolkings- en Gezinsstudien - Population and Family Study Centre) Ed.Bd.

POPULATION STUDIES

312   BE
POPULATION AND FAMILY STUDY CENTRE. PROGRESS REPORT. a. Centrum voor Bevolkings- en Gesinsstudien - Population and Family Study Centre, Markiesstraat 1, 1000 Brussels, Belgium. FAX 507-34-19.
Formerly: Centre d'Etude de la Population et Centre d'Etude de la Population et de la Famille. Annual Report.

312   US   ISSN 0032-468X
HB881.A1   CODEN: POPBA3
POPULATION BULLETIN. 1945. 4/yr. $7. Population Reference Bureau, Inc., 1875 Connecticut Ave., N.W., Ste. 520, Washington, DC 20009. TEL 202-483-1100. Ed. Mary Kent. charts; stat.; circ. 6,000. (also avail. in microform from UMI) **Indexed:** Acad.Ind., ASSIA, Biol.Abstr., Curr.Cont., Curr.Lit.Fam.Plan., E.I., Environ.Abstr., Fut.Surv., Geo.Abstr., I D A, Mid.East: Abstr.& Ind., P.A.I.S., Popul.Ind., PROMT, Sci.Cit.Ind., Soc.Sci.Ind., SRI, SSCI.
—BLDSC shelfmark: 6552.200000.
Description: Focuses on national and world issues in the field by recognized authorities.

325   UN   ISSN 0251-7604
HB848
POPULATION BULLETIN OF THE UNITED NATIONS. French edition: Bulletin Demographique des Nations Unies (ISSN 0251-7612); Spanish edition: Boletin de Poblacion de las Naciones Unidas (ISSN 0251-7590) (Text in English, French, Spanish) 1948. irreg. price varies. United Nations Publications, Sales Section, Rm. DC2-0853, New York, NY 10017. TEL 212-963-8302. FAX 212-963-3489.

312   PP   ISSN 0079-3868
POPULATION CENSUS OF PAPUA NEW GUINEA. POPULATION CHARACTERISTICS BULLETIN SERIES. 1966. irreg., latest 1980. K.5. National Statistical Office, P.O. Wards Strip, Papua New Guinea. FAX 657-255057. TELEX FINANCE NE 22312. Ed. Nick Suvulo. circ. 842.

312   US   ISSN 0361-7858
HB849   CODEN: POPCA6
POPULATION COUNCIL ANNUAL REPORT. 1952. a. free. Population Council, One Dag Hammarskjold Plaza, New York, NY 10017. TEL 212-644-1300. FAX 212-755-6052. Ed. Robert Heidel. **Indexed:** Biol.Abstr.

312 370   UN
POPULATION EDUCATION IN ASIA AND THE PACIFIC NEWSLETTER AND FORUM. 1974. s-a. free or on exchange basis. Unesco, Principal Regional Office for Asia and the Pacific, Population Education Programme Service, P.O. Box 1425, Bangkok 10500, Thailand. TEL 391-0703. FAX 391-0866. TELEX 20591 TH. Ed. C.L. Villanueva. bk.rev.; charts; illus.; circ. 3,000. **Indexed:** ERIC.
Former titles: Population Education in Asia and the Pacific Newsletter; Population Education in Asia Newsletter; Which superseded: Unesco. Regional Office for Education in Asia. Regional Conference Reports (ISSN 0503-4469)
Description: Examines regional and international news as well as innovation in population education.

312 300   FR   ISSN 0184-7783
HB848
POPULATION ET SOCIETES; bulletin mensuel d'informations demographiques, economiques, sociales. 1968. m. 75 F. Institut National d'Etudes Demographiques, 27 rue du Commandeur, 75675 Paris Cedex 14, France. Ed. M. Levy. charts; stat.; cum.index: 1968-1975, 1976-1981; circ. 40,000. **Indexed:** Popul.Ind.
—BLDSC shelfmark: 6552.270000.

301.32   UN   ISSN 0252-3639
POPULATION HEADLINERS. (Text in English) 1971. m. free upon request. United Nations Economic and Social Commission for Asia and the Pacific (ESCAP), Population Division, United Nations Bldg., Rajadamnern Ave, Bangkok 10200, Thailand. charts; illus.; circ. 5,500. **Indexed:** So.Pac.Per.Ind., Trop.Dis.Bull.
Formerly: Asian Population Programme News (ISSN 0084-6821)

301.32   TH   ISSN 0125-6440
POPULATION NEWSLETTER. 1969. irreg. (3-4/yr.). free. Chulalongkorn University, Institute of Population Studies, Phyathai Rd., Bangkok 10330, Thailand. TEL 2511133-34. bk.rev.; circ. 2,500. (tabloid format) **Indexed:** Abstr.Hyg.

POPULATION OF THE MUNICIPALITIES OF THE NETHERLANDS. see *POPULATION STUDIES — Abstracting, Bibliographies, Statistics*

POPULATION REPORTS. see *POPULATION STUDIES — Abstracting, Bibliographies, Statistics*

312 330.9   NE   ISSN 0167-5923
HB848
POPULATION RESEARCH AND POLICY REVIEW. 1980. 3/yr. $142. Kluwer Academic Publishers, Postbus 17, 3300 AA Dordrecht, Netherlands. TEL 078-334911. FAX 078-334254. TELEX 29245. (Dist. by: Kluwer Academic Publishers Group, P.O. Box 322, 3300 AH Dordrecht, Netherlands; N. America dist. addr.: Box 358, Accord Station, Hingham, MA 02018-0358. TEL 617-871-6600) Ed. Larry Barnett. (reprint service avail. from SWZ) **Indexed:** Curr.Cont., Geo.Abstr., Ind.Per.Art.Relat.Law, Int.Polit.Sci.Abstr., J.of Econ.Lit., P.A.I.S., Popul.Ind., Sage Pub.Admin.Abstr., Sage Urb.Stud.Abstr., Soc.Work.Res.Abstr., SSCI.
—BLDSC shelfmark: 6552.482000.

312   US
POPULATION RESEARCH CENTER NEWSLETTER. vol.3, no.1, 1991. irreg. University of Texas at Austin, Population Research Center, Main Bldg. 1800, Austin, TX 78712-1088. TEL 512-471-5514. FAX 512-471-4886. Ed. Debra Haden.
Description: Research and administrative news of the center's activities.

312 917.602   US   ISSN 0191-913X
POPULATION RESEARCH CENTER PAPERS. 1979. irreg., vol.10, no.12. $4 per no. University of Texas at Austin, Population Research Center, Main Bldg. 1800, Austin, TX 78712-1088. TEL 512-471-5514. FAX 512-471-4886.

312   CN   ISSN 0317-3100
POPULATION RESEARCH LABORATORY. POPULATION REPRINT SERIES. 1972. irreg. free. Population Research Laboratory, Department of Sociology, University of Alberta, Edmonton, Alta. T6G 2H4, Canada. TEL 403-492-4659.
Description: Reprints of articles in the area of population studies published in academic journals.

312   CN
POPULATION RESEARCH LABORATORY. RESEARCH DISCUSSION PAPER SERIES. 1973. irreg. free. Population Research Laboratory, Department of Sociology, University of Alberta, Edmonton, Alta. T6G 2H4, Canada. TEL 403-492-4659. (reprint service avail. from MML)
Formerly: Population Research Laboratory. Discussion Paper Series (ISSN 0317-2473)
Description: Research papers in the field of population studies, survey research and methodology.

301.3   UK   ISSN 0032-4728
HB848   CODEN: POSTA4
POPULATION STUDIES. 1947. 3/yr. £42($92) Population Investigation Committee, London School of Economics, Houghton St., Aldwych, London WC2A 2AE, England. TEL 071-955-7666. FAX 071-242-0392. TELEX 24655-BLPES-G. Ed.Bd. adv.; bk.rev.; index; circ. 3,000. (also avail. in microform from MIM; reprint service avail. from UMI) **Indexed:** A.I.C.P., Abstr.Hyg., Amer.Hist.& Life, ASSIA, Biol.Abstr., Br.Hum.Ind., Curr.Cont., Curr.Lit.Fam.Plan., E.I., Environ.Per.Bibl., Excerp.Med., Geo.Abstr., I D A, Key to Econ.Sci., Lang.& Lang.Behav.Abstr., Mid.East: Abstr.& Ind., P.A.I.S., Popul.Ind., Rural Recreat.Tour.Abstr., Sociol.Abstr. (1952-), SSCI, Trop.Dis.Bull., World Agri.Econ.& Rural Sociol.Abstr.
—BLDSC shelfmark: 6553.000000.
Description: Covers the field of demography: population movements, the effectiveness of birth control programs, fertility and economic and social implications of demographic trends.

312   UN   ISSN 0082-805X
JX1977
POPULATION STUDIES. (Editions in English, French, Spanish) 1948. irreg., no.110, 1988. price varies. (United Nations, Department of Economic and Social Affairs) United Nations Publications, Room DC2-853, New York, NY 10017. TEL 212-963-8302. FAX 212-963-3489. **Indexed:** Geo.Abstr., I D A, J.of Econ.Lit., Nutr.Abstr., World Bank.Abstr.
—BLDSC shelfmark: 6553.105000.

312   CN   ISSN 0712-5828
POPULATION STUDIES CENTRE. HIGHLIGHTS. 1982. s-a. free. Population Studies Centre, Rm. 3227 SSC, University of Western Ontario, London, Ont. N6A 5C2, Canada. TEL 519-661-3819. FAX 519-661-3200. Ed. Suzanne Shiel. circ. 300. (looseleaf format)
Description: Presents current projects and publications of the Centre and its associates.

301.426   US   ISSN 0749-2448
POPULATION TODAY. 1973. 11/yr. membership. Population Reference Bureau, Inc., 1875 Connecticut Ave., N.W., Ste. 520, Washington, DC 20009. TEL 202-483-1100. Ed. Susan Kalish. bk.rev.; charts; illus.; stat.; circ. 6,000. (also avail. in microfilm; reprint service avail. from UMI) **Indexed:** Curr.Lit.Fam.Plan., Environ.Abstr., Popul.Ind., Sage Fam.Stud.Abstr., Sage Urb.Stud.Abstr., SRI.
—BLDSC shelfmark: 6553.230000.
Formerly (until 1984): Intercom (Washington) (ISSN 0092-444X)

312   UK   ISSN 0307-4463
HB3583
POPULATION TRENDS. 1975. q. £8.56. Office of Population Services and Surveys, P.O. Box 276, London SW8 5DT, England. (Avail. from: H.M.S.O., c/o Liaison Officer, Atlantic House, Holborn Viaduct, London EC1P 1BN, England) charts; illus.; stat.; circ. 1,700. **Indexed:** Abstr.Hyg., ASSIA, Curr.Adv.Ecol.Sci., Lang.& Lang.Behav.Abstr., Nutr.Abstr., Popul.Ind., Trop.Dis.Bull.
—BLDSC shelfmark: 6553.250000.

312   US   ISSN 0736-7716
POPULATION TRENDS AND PUBLIC POLICY. 1980. irreg. $5. Population Reference Bureau, Inc., 1875 Connecticut Ave., N.W., Ste. 520, Washington, DC 20009. TEL 202-483-1100. circ. 6,000. **Indexed:** Popul.Ind., SRI.
Description: Discusses policy implications of current demographic trends.

301.32   UN   ISSN 0251-6861
HB848
POPULI. 1974. q. $14. United Nations Population Fund, 220 E. 42 St., Rm. DN 2305, New York, NY 10017. bk.rev.; illus. **Indexed:** Curr.Lit.Fam.Plan., Environ.Abstr., Geo.Abstr., IIS, P.A.I.S., Popul.Ind.
Description: Covers a broad range of topics such as development, media and population, and individual decision-making on childbearing and child spacing.

301.3   FR   ISSN 0032-583X
POUR LA VIE;* revue d'etudes familiales. 1945. q. 15 F. 28 Place Saint-Georges, Paris (9e), France. Ed. E. Videcoq. index. cum.index: 1945-1968.

301.4   PL   ISSN 0552-2234
PROBLEMY RODZINY. 1961. bi-m. $30. Panstwowy Zaklad Wydawnictw Lekarskich, Dluga 38-40, Warsaw, Poland. TEL 31-42-81. Ed. B. Caban-Dabrowska. bk.rev.; abstr.; bibl.; stat.; circ. 4,000 (controlled).
—BLDSC shelfmark: 6617.957500.
Description: Presents papers on demography, legislation, sociology and sexology.

312 301.32   PL   ISSN 0079-7189
HB3608.7
PRZESZLOSC DEMOGRAFICZNA POLSKI; materialy i studia. (Text in Polish; summaries in English) 1967. irreg., no.14, 1983. price varies. (Polska Akademia Nauk, Komitet Nauk Demograficznych) Panstwowe Wydawnictwo Naukowe, Ul. Miodowa 10, 00-251 Warsaw, Poland. (Dist. by: Ars Polona, Krakowskie Przedmiescie 7, 00-068 Warsaw, Poland) Ed. E. Vidrose. bibl.; circ. 300. **Indexed:** Popul.Ind.

POPULATION STUDIES 3987

312   FR
RAPPORT SUR LA SITUATION DEMOGRAPHIQUE DE LA FRANCE. 1970. a. 30 Fr. Institut National d'Etudes Demographiques, 27 rue du Commandeur, 75675 Paris Cedex 14, France. Ed. G. Calot. bk.rev.; stat.; circ. 2,000.

325   CN   ISSN 0229-5113
REFUGE; Canada's periodical on refugees. French edition (ISSN 0229-5121) 1981. q. Can.$25 (foreign $30). (York University, Centre for Refugee Studies) York Lanes Press, 351 York Lanes, 4700 Keele St., North York, Ont. M3J 1P3, Canada. FAX 416-736-5837. circ. 1,200. **Indexed:** HR Rep., Refug.Abstr.

REFUGEE AND IMMIGRANT RESOURCE DIRECTORY (YEAR). see POLITICAL SCIENCE — International Relations

325   US   ISSN 0884-3554
REFUGEE REPORTS. 1979. m. $37.50. American Council for Nationalities Service, 1025 Vermont Ave., N.W., Ste. 920, Washington, DC 20005. TEL 202-347-3507. Eds. Virginia Hamilton, Bill Frelick. bk.rev.; circ. 2,000. **Indexed:** HR Rep., Refug.Abstr., SRI.

312   CC
RENKOU DONGTAI. (Text in Chinese) bi-m. Y7.20. Zhongguo Renkou Qingbao Yanjiu Zhongxin - China Population Research Center, P.O. Box 2444, Beijing 100081, People's Republic of China.
   Description: Contains papers on China's population problem, applications of population theory, and the interrelationship between population and development.

304.6   CC   ISSN 1000-6087
HB3654.A3
RENKOU YANJIU/POPULATION STUDIES. (Text in Chinese; table of contents in English) 1977. bi-m. Y9($24.30) Zhongguo Renmin Daxue, Renkou Lilun Yanjiusuo - People's University, Institute of Population Theory, 39 Haidian Lu, Haidian Qu, Beijing 100872, People's Republic of China. TEL 285431-2895. (Dist. outside China by: China International Book Trading Corp., P.O. Box 399, Beijing, P.R.C.; Dist. in US by: China Books & Periodicals, Inc., 2929 24th St., San Francisco, CA 94110. TEL 415-282-2994) Ed. Liu Zheng.
   Description: Contains papers on population studies and demographics, as well as news of meetings and academic activities.

301.32 312   CC
RENKOU YU FAZHAN/POPULATION AND DEVELOPMENT. (Text in Chinese) q. Sichuan University, Renkou Yanjiusuo - Population Studies Institute, Jiugenqiao, Sichuan Daxue Xiaonei, Chengdu, Sichuan 610064, People's Republic of China. TEL 583875-416.

304.6 339   CC   ISSN 1000-4149
HB3654.A3
RENKOU YU JINGJI/POPULATION & ECONOMICS. (Text in Chinese; table of contents in English) 1980. bi-m. Y11.40($24.30) Beijing Jingji Xueyuan, Renkou Jingji Yanjiusuo - Beijing Institute of Economics, Hongmiao, Chaoyangmenwai, Beijing 100026, People's Republic of China. TEL 5005511. (Dist. outside China by: China International Book Trading Corp., P.O. Box 399, Beijing, P.R.C.; Or: China Publications Export Corp., P.O. Box 782, Beijing, P.R.C.; Dist. in US by: China Books & Periodicals, Inc., 2929 24th St., San Francisco, CA 94110. TEL 415-282-2994) Ed. Feng Litian.
   Description: Publishes papers interrelating population studies and economics. Also includes publication news and software reviews.

312   CC
RENKOU YU YOUSHENG. (Text in Chinese) q. Zhejiang Yike Daxue, Renkou Yanjiusuo - Zhejiang University of Medical Sciences, Population Research Institute, 157 Yan'an Lu, Hangzhou, Zhejiang 310006, People's Republic of China. TEL 722700. Ed. Ding Deyun.

301.32   CC
RENKOU ZHANXIAN/POPULATION FRONT. (Text in Chinese) q. Hebei Sheng Jihua Shengyu Weiyuanhui, Renkou Xuehui - Hebei Provincial Family Planning Committee, Population Association, 1 Yuhua Lu, Shijiazhuang, Hebei 050016, People's Republic of China. TEL 49941. Ed. Wang Mingyuan.

REPRODUCTIONS. see BIOLOGY

325   NE   ISSN 0080-1623
RESEARCH GROUP FOR EUROPEAN MIGRATION PROBLEMS. PUBLICATIONS. 1951. irreg. price varies. Kluwer Academic Publishers, Postbus 17, 3300 AA Dordrecht, Netherlands. (Dist. by: Kluwer Academic Publishers Group, Postbus 322, 3300 AH Dordrecht, Netherlands) Ed. G. Beyer.

301.32 330   US   ISSN 0163-7878
HB848
RESEARCH IN POPULATION ECONOMICS; an annual compilation of research. 1978. a. $63.50 to institutions. J A I Press Inc., 55 Old Post Rd., No. 2, Box 1678, Greenwich, CT 06836-1678. TEL 203-661-7602. Ed. Paul Schultz. **Indexed:** Curr.Cont., Popul.Ind.
—BLDSC shelfmark: 7755.077600.

301.426   US
RESEARCH MONOGRAPHS ON HUMAN POPULATION. irreg. price varies. Oxford University Press, 200 Madison Ave., New York, NY 10016. TEL 212-679-7300. Ed. G. Ainsworth Harrison.

595.7   JA   ISSN 0034-5466
RESEARCHES ON POPULATION ECOLOGY/KOTAIGUN SEITAIGAKU NO KENKYU. (Text in English) 1952. s-a. $70. Society of Population Ecology - Kotaigun Seitaigakkai, Shimotachiuri, Ogawa-Higashi, Kamikyoku, Kyoto 602, Japan. Ed.Bd. circ. 700. **Indexed:** Bio-Contr.News & Info., Biol.Abstr., Curr.Adv.Ecol.Sci., Curr.Cont., Deep Sea Res.& Oceanogr.Abstr., Environ.Per.Bibl., Environ.Per.Bibl., Forest.Abstr., Geo.Abstr., Helminthol.Abstr., Maize Abstr., Rev.Appl.Entomol., Rice Abstr., Soils & Fert., Triticale Abstr.
—BLDSC shelfmark: 7777.050000.

325.2   UK
RESIDENT ABROAD; the magazine for expatriates. 1979. m. £30. Financial Times Business Information Ltd., Tower House, Southampton St., London WC2E 7HA, England. TEL 071-240-9391. FAX 071-240-7946. TELEX 296926-BUSINF-G. Ed. David Phillips. adv.; bk.rev.; circ. 19,500.

325 301.4   DR
RESUMENES SOBRE POBLACION DOMINICANA. 1984. s-a. $9. Asociacion Dominicana Pro-Bienestar de la Familia, Socorro Sanchez, No. 64, Zona 1, Apdo. Postal 1053, Santo Domingo, D.N., Dominican Republic. (Co-sponsor: Federacion Internacional de Planificacion de la Familia) (Affiliate: International Planned Parenthood Federation)

312   FR   ISSN 0377-8967
HB848
REVIEW OF POPULATION REVIEWS. French edition: Revue des Revues Demographiques (ISSN 0377-8959) 1976. q. free. Committee for International Cooperation in National Research in Demography, 27 rue du Commandeur, 75675 Paris Cedex 14, France. Ed. Jean Bourgeois-Pichat. bk.rev. (back issues avail.) **Indexed:** Popul.Ind.

REVISTA DE ADMINISTRACAO MUNICIPAL. see PUBLIC ADMINISTRATION — Municipal Government

312   BL   ISSN 0101-7217
REVISTA DOCPOP; resumos sobre populacao no Brasil. 1982. 2/yr. $52.10. Fundacao Sistema Estadual de Analise de Dados, Av. Casper Libero, 464, 01033 Sao Paulo, CP 8223, Brazil. TEL 011-2292433. bibl.; circ. 500. (back issues avail.) **Indexed:** P.A.I.S.For.Lang.Ind.
   Description: Discusses general population, mortality, fertility, migration, spatial distribution, nuptiality and family, characteristics and needs of the population.

312   BG   ISSN 1010-3783
HB850.5.B3
RURAL DEMOGRAPHY. (Text in English) 1974. s-a. $6. University of Dhaka, Institute of Statistical Research and Training, Ramna, Dhaka 1000, Bangladesh. Ed.Bd. charts; stat. **Indexed:** Popul.Ind.
—BLDSC shelfmark: 8052.422000.

312   RW
RWANDA. OFFICE NATIONAL DE LA POPULATION. FAMILLE, SANTE, DEVELOPPEMENT.. q. 550 Fr. Office National de la Population, Service de l'Information, B.P. 1055, Kigali, Rwanda.

312   US
S D A NEWSLETTER. 1971. q. $10. Southern Demographic Association, c/o John Marcum, Box 70192, Louisville, KY 40270. TEL 502-569-5161. circ. 300. (tabloid format)
   Formerly: S R D G Newsletter.

301.32   NL
S P C - I L O REPORTS ON MIGRATION, EMPLOYMENT AND DEVELOPMENT IN THE SOUTH PACIFIC. 1983. irreg., no.23b, 1986. South Pacific Commission, B.P. D5, Noumea, Cedex, New Caledonia. TEL 26-2000. FAX 687-263818. TELEX 3139 NM SOPACOM.

312 325   KO
SEOUL NATIONAL UNIVERSITY. POPULATION AND DEVELOPMENT STUDIES CENTER. BULLETIN. (Text in English; summaries in Korean) 1972. a. 3200 Won($6) Seoul National University, Population and Development Studies Center, Gwan-ak Gu, Seoul 151 742, S. Korea. FAX 82-01-885-5272. TELEX SNUROK K29664. Ed. Tai Hwan Kwon. bk.rev.; bibl.; circ. 500. **Indexed:** Rural Devel.Abstr.

325.1   US
SERIE INMIGRACION AL CONO SUR DE AMERICA. (Text in Spanish) 1985. irreg., vol.5, 1989. price varies. Organization of American States, Instituto Panamericano de Geografia e Historia - Organizacion de los Estados Americanos, 1889 F St., N.W., Washington, DC 20006-4499. TEL 202-458-3527. FAX 202-458-3534. (Distr. by: Center for Promotion and Distribution of Publications, Box 66398, Washington, DC 20035)

SERVICE DE CENTRALISATION DES ETUDES GENEALOGIQUES ET DEMOGRAPHIQUES DE BELGIQUE. NOUVELLES BREVES. see GENEALOGY AND HERALDRY

312   IT
SERVIZI DEMOGRAFICI; rivista mensile dei servizi di anagrafe, stato civile, elettorale, statistica, e leva dei comuni. 1982. m. (11/yr.) L.168000 (effective 1992). Maggioli Editore, Via Crimea, 1, Casella Postale 290, 47037 Rimini, Italy. TEL 0541-626777. FAX 0541-622020. Ed.Bd.

325   FI   ISSN 0355-3779
SIIRTOLAISUUS/MIGRATION. 1974. q. 4. Migration Institute, Piispankatu 3, 20500 Turku 50, Finland.

SOCIAL BIOLOGY. see BIOLOGY — Genetics

312   FR
SOCIO-ECONOMIC DIFFERENTIAL MORTALITY IN INDUSTRIALIZED SOCIETIES. 1980. a. free. Committee for International Cooperation in National Research in Demography (CICRED), 27 rue du Commandeur, 75675 Paris Cedex 14, France. circ. 500.

312   AT
SOUTH AUSTRALIA. DEPARTMENT OF ENVIRONMENT AND PLANNING. POPULATION PROJECTION FOR THE ADELAIDE STATISTICAL DIVISION. irreg. Aus.$15. Department of Environment and Planning, G.P.O. Box 667, Adelaide, S.A. 5001, Australia. TEL 618-216-7777. FAX 618-212-3962.

312   AT   ISSN 1032-8793
SOUTH AUSTRALIA. DEPARTMENT OF ENVIRONMENT AND PLANNING. STATE AND REGIONAL PROJECTIONS. BULLETIN. 1989. irreg. Aus.$2 per no. Department of Environment and Planning, G.P.O. Box 667, Adelaide, S.A. 5001, Australia. TEL 618-216-7777. FAX 618-212-3962.

312   AT
SOUTH AUSTRALIA. DEPARTMENT OF EVIRONMENT AND PLANNING. POPULATION PROJECTION FOR SOUTH AUSTRALIA. irreg. Aus.$15 per issue. Department of Environment and Planning, G.P.O. Box 667, Adelaide, S.A. 5001, Australia. TEL 618-216-7777. FAX 618-212-3962.

312   US
SOUTH CAROLINA. STATE DATA CENTER. NEWSLETTER. q. Budget and Control Board, Division of Research & Statistical Services, Rembert C. Dennis Bldg., 1000 Assembly St., Rm. 442, Columbia, SC 29201. TEL 803-734-3788. FAX 803-734-3619.

POPULATION STUDIES

325 US
SPECTRUM (ST. PAUL). 1975. irreg., latest 1988. $5 to individuals; institutions $8. University of Minnesota, Immigration History Research Center, 826 Berry St., St. Paul, MN 55114. TEL 612-627-4208. bk.rev.; illus.; circ. 500. (back issues avail.)

301.3 YU ISSN 0038-982X
HB848
STANOVNISTVO. (Text in Serbian; summaries and contents page in English, French and Russian) 1963. q. $14.20. Institut Drustvenih Nauka u Beogradu, Centar za Demografska Istrazivanja, Narodnog Fronta 45, Belgrade, Yugoslavia. Ed. Miladin Kovacevic. adv.; bk.rev.; charts; illus.; stat.; index; circ. 800. **Indexed:** Popul.Ind.

325 IT ISSN 0039-2936
STUDI EMIGRAZIONE/ETUDES MIGRATIONS. (Text and summaries in English, French, Italian, Spanish) 1964. 4/yr. L.48000 (foreign L.55000). Centro Studi Emigrazione, Via Dandolo 58, 00153 Rome, Italy. TEL 58 09 764. Ed.Bd. adv.; bk.rev.; abstr.; bibl.; charts; stat.; index; circ. 1,500. (back issues avail.) **Indexed:** Lang.& Lang.Behav.Abstr., P.A.I.S.For.Lang.Ind., Popul.Ind., Refug.Abstr.
—BLDSC shelfmark: 8481.820000.
Description: Explores the phenomenon of massive population displacement.

312 PL ISSN 0039-3134
HB881.A1
STUDIA DEMOGRAFICZNE. (Text in English, Polish, Russian; summaries in English and Russian) 1963. q. $30. (Polska Akademia Nauk, Komitet Nauk Demograficznych) D T P Akapit, Spolka z o.o., Ul. Skolimowska 4 m. 11, 00-795 Warsaw, Poland. (Dist. by: Ars Polona, Krakowskie Przedmiescie 7, 00-068 Warsaw, Poland) Ed. Marek Okolski. bk.rev.; abstr.; charts; stat.; circ. 650. **Indexed:** Popul.Ind.

301.3 PL
STUDIA POLONIJNE. (Text in Polish; summaries in English) 1976. irreg. price varies. Katolicki Uniwersytet Lubelski, Towarzystwo Naukowe, Ul. Gliniana 21, 20-616 Lublin, Poland. index; circ. 3,125.

STUDIEN ZUR BEVOELKERUNGSOEKONOMIE. see *BUSINESS AND ECONOMICS*

301.426 US ISSN 0039-3665
HQ763 CODEN: SFPLA3
STUDIES IN FAMILY PLANNING. 1963. bi-m. $18. Population Council, One Dag Hammarskjold Plaza, New York, NY 10017. TEL 212-644-1300. FAX 212-755-6052. Ed. Valeda Slade. charts; abstr.; index; circ. 6,000. (also avail. in microform from KTO; reprint service avail. from UMI) **Indexed:** Abstr.Hyg., Adol.Ment.Hlth.Abstr., ASCA, ASSIA, Biol.Abstr., CINAHL, Curr.Cont., Curr.Lit.Fam.Plan., Environ.Abstr., Environ.Ind., Excerp.Med., Geo.Abstr., I D A, I.P.A., Ind.Med., Mid.East: Abstr.& Ind., Nutr.Abstr., P.A.I.S., Popul.Ind., Rural Ext.Educ.& Tr.Abstr., Rural Recreat.Tour.Abstr., So.Pac.Per.Ind., Sp.Ed.Needs Abstr., SSCI, Stud.Wom.Abstr., Trop.Dis.Bull., World Agri.Econ.& Rural Sociol.Abstr.
—BLDSC shelfmark: 8490.545000.
Incorporates: Current Publications in Family Planning (ISSN 0011-3867)

312 301.32 US
STUDIES IN POPULATION. 1974. irreg., latest 1990. Academic Press, Inc., 1250 Sixth Ave., San Diego, CA 92101. TEL 619-231-0926. FAX 619-699-6715. Ed. H.H. Winsborough. (reprint service avail. from ISI) **Indexed:** Math.R.

312 US ISSN 0147-1104
STUDIES IN POPULATION AND URBAN DEMOGRAPHY. 1975. irreg. price varies. Greenwood Press, Inc. (Subsidiary of: Greenwood Publishing Group Inc.), 88 Post Rd. W., Box 5007, Westport, CT 06881-5007. TEL 203-226-3571. FAX 203-222-1502. Ed. Kingsley Davis.

312 US
STUDIES IN SOCIAL AND ECONOMIC DEMOGRAPHY. 1978. irreg. Duke University Press, 6697 College Station, Durham, NC 27708. TEL 919-684-2173. FAX 919-684-8644.

614 312 PY
TEMAS DE POBLACION. 1968. bi-m. free or exchange basis. Centro Paraguayo de Estudios de Poblacion, Edif. El Dorado, piso 8, Manduvira y O'Leary, Asuncion, Paraguay. TEL 447334. Ed. Helio Vera. bk.rev.; circ. 3,500.
Formerly: Temas Medicos.

THEORETICAL POPULATION BIOLOGY; an international journal. see *BIOLOGY*

312 JA
TOCHIGI-KEN NO JINKO/POPULATION IN TOCHIGI PREFECTURE. 1970. a. free. Tochigi-ken Kikaku-bu - Tochigi Prefecture, Department of Planning, 1-20 Hanawada 1-chome, Utsunomiya-shi 320, Japan. FAX 0286-23-2247. Ed. Mashamitsu Sakakibara. circ. 500. (back issues avail.)

312 US
TOWARD THE 21ST CENTURY. 8/yr. $28. Population Institute, 110 Maryland Ave., N.E., Washington, DC 20002. TEL 202-544-3300. FAX 202-544-0068. Ed. Harold N. Burdett. circ. 3,000.

312 TU
TURKISH JOURNAL OF POPULATION STUDIES/NUFUSBILIM DERGISI. 1979. a. TL.12000($7) Hacettepe University, Institute of Population Studies - Hacettepe Universitesi, Nufus Etutleri Enstituti, Ankara, Turkey. FAX 4-311-8141. TELEX 42237 HTK TR. Ed. Dr. Ergul Tuncbilek. circ. 1,000.
Description: Features applied and theoretical articles in the field of population studies.

301.3 UN ISSN 0066-8451
JX1977
UNITED NATIONS. ECONOMIC AND SOCIAL COMMISSION FOR ASIA AND THE PACIFIC. ASIAN POPULATION STUDIES SERIES. (Text in English) 1967. irreg. free. United Nations Economic and Social Commission for Asia and the Pacific (ESCAP), Population Division, United Nations Bldg., Rajadamnern Ave., Bangkok 10200, Thailand. (Dist. by: United Nations Publications, Room LX-2300, New York, NY 10017; Or: Distribution and Sales Section, Palais des Nations, CH-1211 Geneva 10, Switzerland) **Indexed:** Popul.Ind.

312 UN ISSN 0503-3934
HA755
UNITED NATIONS. REGIONAL CENTRE FOR DEMOGRAPHIC TRAINING AND RESEARCH IN LATIN AMERICA. SERIE A/CENTRO LATINOAMERICANO DE DEMOGRAFIA. SERIE A. (1989 Catalog avail.) 1962. irreg. $6 per no. United Nations, Centro Latinoamericano de Demografia - United Nations, Regional Center for Demographic Training and Research in Latin America, Casilla 91, Santiago, Chile. stat.; circ. 400.

312 UN ISSN 0503-3942
UNITED NATIONS. REGIONAL CENTRE FOR DEMOGRAPHIC TRAINING AND RESEARCH IN LATIN AMERICA. SERIE C/CENTRO LATINOAMERICANO DE DEMOGRAFIA. SERIE C. (1987 Catalog available) 1963. irreg. $6 per no. United Nations, Centro Latinoamericano de Demografia, Casilla 91, Santiago, Chile. stat.; circ. 400.

312 UN ISSN 0503-3950
UNITED NATIONS. REGIONAL CENTRE FOR DEMOGRAPHIC TRAINING AND RESEARCH IN LATIN AMERICA. SERIE D/CENTRO LATINOAMERICANO DE DEMOGRAFIA. SERIE D. (1989 Catalog available) 1962. irreg. $6 per no. United Nations, Centro Latinoamericano de Demografia, Casilla 91, Santiago, Chile. circ. 400.

312 UN
UNITED NATIONS. REGIONAL CENTRE FOR DEMOGRAPHIC TRAINING AND RESEARCH IN LATIN AMERICA. SERIE E/CENTRO LATINOAMERICANO DE DEMOGRAFIA. SERIE E. (1989 Catalog avail.) 1967. irreg. price varies. United Nations, Centro Latinoamericano de Demografia - United Nations, Regional Centre for Demographic Training and Research in Latin America, Casilla 91 Santiago, Chile. stat.; circ. 400.

312 340 UN
UNITED NATIONS POPULATION FUND. ANNUAL REVIEW OF POPULATION LAW. a. $45. United Nations Population Fund, Pound Hall, Rm. 402, Cambridge, MA 02138. (Harvard Law School) Ed. Reed Boland. bibl.
Description: Compendium of national, regional and international legal developments in population and related fields.

U.S. CENTERS FOR DISEASE CONTROL. MORBIDITY AND MORTALITY WEEKLY REPORT. see *PUBLIC HEALTH AND SAFETY*

325 US ISSN 0083-1220
U.S. IMMIGRATION AND NATURALIZATION SERVICE. ADMINISTRATIVE DECISIONS UNDER IMMIGRATION AND NATIONALITY LAWS. 1940. irreg. price varies. U.S. Immigration and Naturalization Service, Board of Immigration Appeals, Washington, DC 20530. TEL 202-724-7796. (Orders to: Supt. of Documents, Washington, DC 20402)

325 US ISSN 0083-1239
U.S. IMMIGRATION AND NATURALIZATION SERVICE. ADMINISTRATIVE DECISIONS UNDER IMMIGRATION AND NATIONALITY LAWS. INTERIM DECISIONS OF THE DEPARTMENT OF JUSTICE. irreg. $63. U.S. Immigration and Naturalization Service, Department of Justice, Office of Information, 425 I St., N.W., Washington, DC 20536. TEL 202-724-7796. (Orders to: Supt. of Documents, Washington, DC 20402)

325 US ISSN 0083-1247
JV6414
U.S. IMMIGRATION AND NATURALIZATION SERVICE. ANNUAL REPORT. 1892. a. price varies. U.S. Immigration and Naturalization Service, 425 I St. N.W., Washington, DC 20536. TEL 202-724-7796. (Orders to: Supt. of Documents, Washington, DC 20402)

301.32 US
U.S. INTERAGENCY COMMITTEE ON POPULATION RESEARCH. INVENTORY AND ANALYSIS OF FEDERAL POPULATION RESEARCH. 1970. a. free. U.S. Department of Health and Human Services, NICHD, NIH, Bldg. 31, Rm. 2A47, Bethesda, MD 20892. TEL 301-496-1971. FAX 301-496-4757. Ed. George Lewerenz. circ. 3,000.
Former titles: U.S. Center for Population Research. Inventory of Federal Population Research; U.S. National Institute of Child Health and Human Development. Center for Population Research. Federal Program in Population Research.

312 US ISSN 0896-4416
UNITED STATES POPULATION DATA SHEET. 1981. a. $3. Population Reference Bureau, Inc., 1875 Connecticut Ave., N.W., Ste. 520, Washington, DC 20009. TEL 202-483-1100. Ed. Carl Haub. charts; stat.; circ. 15,000. (back issues avail.)
Description: Provides population, demographic and social indicators by state.

UNIVERSITY OF DAR ES SALAAM. BUREAU OF RESOURCE ASSESSMENT AND LAND USE PLANNING. ANNUAL REPORT. see *ENVIRONMENTAL STUDIES*

UNIVERSITY OF DAR ES SALAAM. BUREAU OF RESOURCE ASSESSMENT AND LAND USE PLANNING. RESEARCH PAPER. see *ENVIRONMENTAL STUDIES*

UNIVERSITY OF DAR ES SALAAM. BUREAU OF RESOURCE ASSESSMENT AND LAND USE PLANNING. RESEARCH REPORT. see *ENVIRONMENTAL STUDIES*

312 US ISSN 0071-6030
HB3525.F6
UNIVERSITY OF FLORIDA. BUREAU OF ECONOMIC AND BUSINESS RESEARCH. POPULATION STUDIES. 1955. 4/yr. $24. University of Florida, College of Business Administration, Bureau of Economic and Business Research, 221 Matherly Hall, Gainesville, FL 32611-2017. TEL 904-392-0171. Ed. Stanley K. Smith. circ. 1,250.

312 301.2 NR
UNIVERSITY OF LAGOS. HUMAN RESOURCES RESEARCH UNIT. MONOGRAPH. 1974. irreg. (University of Lagos, Human Resources Research Unit) Lagos University Press, P.O. Box 12003, Lagos, Nigeria.

POPULATION STUDIES — ABSTRACTING, BIBLIOGRAPHIES, STATISTICS

301.32 US
UNIVERSITY OF MICHIGAN. POPULATION STUDIES CENTER. REPORT. 1961. irreg., latest 1989-91. University of Michigan, Population Studies Center, Ann Arbor, MI 48104. TEL 313-998-7275. FAX 313-998-7415. Ed. Cynthia Housh. circ. 600.
Formerly: University of Michigan. Population Studies Center. Annual Report.

312
▼**UNIVERSITY OF VIRGINIA. CENTER FOR PUBLIC SERVICE. REPORTS.** (Supplement avail.: Census Highlights) 1991. a. University of Virginia, Center for Public Service, 2015 Ivy Rd., 4th Fl., Charlottesville, VA 22903-1795. TEL 804-924-3396. FAX 804-924-4538.
Description: Analyzes specific areas of census data. Discusses how emerging demographic trends are shaping the Commonwealth's character and its public policy choice at the state, regional, and local levels.

301.3 US ISSN 0084-0734
UNIVERSITY OF WISCONSIN, MADISON. APPLIED POPULATION LABORATORY. POPULATION NOTES. 1961. irreg., no.19, 1989. free. University of Wisconsin-Madison, Applied Population Laboratory, Department of Rural Sociology, 316 Agricultural Hall, Madison, WI 53706. TEL 608-262-1515. circ. 800.
Description: Overview of specific topics concerning Wisconsin's population.

301.3 US ISSN 0084-0742
UNIVERSITY OF WISCONSIN, MADISON. APPLIED POPULATION LABORATORY. POPULATION SERIES. 1961. irreg., no.80-7, 1988. price varies. University of Wisconsin-Madison, Applied Population Laboratory, Department of Rural Sociology, 316 Agricultural Hall, Madison, WI 53706. TEL 608-262-1515. circ. 500.

312 US
UNIVERSITY OF WISCONSIN, MADISON. APPLIED POPULATION LABORATORY. TECHNICAL SERIES. 1977. irreg., no.70-6, 1981. University of Wisconsin-Madison, Applied Population Laboratory, Department of Rural Sociology, 316 Agricultural Hall, Madison, WI 53706. TEL 608-262-1515.

V I A MAGAZIN; Fachzeitschrift fuer Praktiker. (Verband der Initiativgruppen in der Auslaenderarbeit e.V.) see POLITICAL SCIENCE — Civil Rights

VOCE DI FIUME. see HISTORY

312 IO ISSN 0125-9679
WARTA DEMOGRAFI. (Text in Indonesian) 1971. m. Rps.12000($30) University of Indonesia, Faculty of Economics, Demographic Institute, Jalan Salemba Raya 4, Jakarta 10430, Indonesia. FAX 06221-3102457. Ed. Aris Ananta. circ. 600.
Indexed: E.I.
Description: Covers current issues on demographic topics in Indonesia.

312 US
WASHINGTON (STATE) OFFICE OF FINANCIAL MANAGEMENT FORECASTING. POPULATION TRENDS. 1968. a. free. State Office of Financial Management, Forecasting Division, Insurance Bldg., Olympia, WA 98504. TEL 206-753-4549. FAX 206-586-8380. (Dist. by: State Library, Olympia WA 98504) circ. 2,000. (also avail. in microfiche) Indexed: SRI.
Former titles: Washington (State) Office of Financial Management, Policy Analysis and Forecasting. Population Trends; Washington (State) Office of Financial Management. Forecasting and Support Division. Population Trends & Washington (State) Office of Program Planning and Fiscal Management. Population and Enrollment Section. Population Trends (ISSN 0083-7482); (until 1970): Washington (State) Planning and Community Affairs Agency. Population Series.

312 US ISSN 0091-5254
HA711
WISCONSIN POPULATION PROJECTIONS. 1969. irreg., 3rd ed., 1975. $5. Department of Administration, Bureau of Program Management, Madision, WI 53702. TEL 608-266-1694. (Subscr. to: Document Sales Unit, 202 S. Thornton Ave., Madison, WI 53702) stat.

312 NE
WORLD FERTILITY SURVEY. BASIC DOCUMENTATION. (Editions in Arabic, English, French and Spanish) irreg., vol. 12, 1984. free. International Statistical Institute, Prinses Beatrixlaan 428, Postbus 950, 2270 AZ Voorburg, Netherlands. TEL 070-3375737. TELEX 32260 ISI NL.

321 NE
WORLD FERTILITY SURVEY. COUNTRY REPORTS. (Editions in Arabic, English, French, and Spanish) 1976. irreg. free. International Statistical Institute, Prinses Beatrixlaan 428, Postbus 950, 2270 AZ Voorburg, Netherlands. TEL 070-3375737. TELEX 32260 ISI NL. stat. Indexed: Biol.Abstr.

312 NE
WORLD FERTILITY SURVEY. OCCASIONAL PAPERS. 1973. irreg., vol.25, 1982. free. International Statistical Institute, Prinses Beatrixlaan 428, Postbus 950, 2270 AZ Voorburg, Netherlands. TEL 070-3375737. TELEX 32260 ISI NL.

312 NE
WORLD FERTILITY SURVEY. SCIENTIFIC REPORTS. 1977. irreg., vol.84, 1987. free. International Statistical Institute, Prinses Beatrixlaan 428, Postbus 950, 2270 AZ Voorburg, Netherlands. TEL 070-3375737. TELEX 32260 ISI NL. Indexed: Biol.Abstr., Popul.Ind.

312 NE
WORLD FERTILITY SURVEY. SUMMARIES OF COUNTRY REPORTS. (Editions in Arabic, English and French) 1977. irreg., vol.51, 1984. International Statistical Institute, Prinses Beatrixlaan 428, Postbus 950, 2270 AZ Voorburg, Netherlands. TEL 070-3375737. TELEX 32260 ISI NL. Indexed: Popul.Ind.
Formerly: World Fertility Survey. Summaries.

312 NE
WORLD FERTILITY SURVEY. TECHNICAL BULLETINS. 1977. irreg., vol.11, 1982. free. International Statistical Institute, Prinses Beatrixlaan 428, Postbus 950, 2270 AZ Voorburg, Netherlands. TEL 070-3375737. TELEX 32260 ISI NL. stat. Indexed: Popul.Ind.

312 US ISSN 0085-8315
WORLD POPULATION DATA SHEET. 1962. a. $3. Population Reference Bureau, Inc., 1875 Connecticut Ave., N.W., Ste. 520, Washington, DC 20009. TEL 202-483-1100. FAX 202-328-3937. Eds. Carl Haub, Machiko Yanagishita. stat.; circ. 130,000. (wall chart format; also avail. on diskette) Indexed: Energy Ind., Energy Info.Abstr., SRI.

312 FI ISSN 0506-3590
HB848
YEARBOOK OF POPULATION RESEARCH IN FINLAND/VAESTOENTUTKIMUKSEN VUOSIKIRJA. (Text in English) 1946. a. Fmk.100. Vaestontutkimuslaitos - Population Research Institute, Kalevankatu 16, 00100 Helsinki 10, Finland. TEL 0-640235. FAX 0-6121211. Ed. Jarl Lindgren. adv.; bk.rev.; bibl.; circ. 700. Indexed: Popul.Ind.
—BLDSC shelfmark: 9415.570000.
Description: Includes articles on questions of current interest in demography in Finland. Also population data compiled at the institute, and a bibliography of the Finnish population research every other year.

312 IS
YIDIOT HAMERCAZ LEDEMOGRAFIA. 1979. s-a. Ministry of Employment and Welfare, Demography Center, P.O. Box 915, Jerusalem 91 008, Israel. Ed. Simon Yair. circ. 1,500.

304.8 914.3 929 US
YORKER PALATINE NEWSLETTER. 1982. q. $19. Palatines to America, New York State Chapter, RD 1, Box 128, Camden, NY 13316. TEL 315-245-0990. Ed. Eila Schiffer. (looseleaf format; back issues avail.)
Description: Promotes German immigration to North America. Covers Columbia, Dutchess, Herkimer, Montgomery, Resselaer, Schoharie and Ulster Counties.

YUGOSLAVIA. SAVAZNI ZAVOD ZA STATISTIKU. DEMOGRAFSKA STATISTIKA. see POPULATION STUDIES — Abstracting, Bibliographies, Statistics

312 US ISSN 0199-0071
Z P G REPORTER. 1969. 6/yr. $10 to non-members. Zero Population Growth, Inc., 1400 16th St., N.W., Ste. 320, Washington, DC 20036. TEL 202-332-2200. FAX 202-332-2302. Ed. Dianne Sherman. adv.; bk.rev.; charts; stat.; circ. 40,000. (tabloid format) Indexed: Curr.Lit.Fam.Plan., Environ.Abstr.
Formerly: Z P G National Reporter (ISSN 0049-8718)

325 ZA ISSN 0084-4802
ZAMBIA. IMMIGRATION DEPARTMENT. REPORT. 1964. a. 20 n. Government Printer, Box 136, Lusaka, Zambia.
Description: Paper on immigration control and the issuance of employment permits in Zambia.

ZEITLUPE. see POLITICAL SCIENCE — Civil Rights

312 GW ISSN 0340-2398
HB848
ZEITSCHRIFT FUER BEVOELKERUNGSWISSENSCHAFT: DEMOGRAPHIE. (Text in German; summaries in English, French and German) 1975. q. DM.96. (Bundesinstitut fuer Bevoelkerungsforschung) Harald Boldt Verlag GmbH, Postfach 1110, 5407 Boppard am Rhein 1, Germany. TEL 06742-2511.

POPULATION STUDIES — Abstracting, Bibliographies, Statistics

312 US ISSN 0066-0752
HA1
AMERICAN STATISTICAL ASSOCIATION. SOCIAL STATISTICS SECTION. PROCEEDINGS. 1958. a. $49 to non-members; members $33. American Statistical Association, 1429 Duke St., Alexandria, VA 22314-3402. TEL 703-684-1221. FAX 703-684-2037. (also avail. in microform from UMI)
—BLDSC shelfmark: 6636.205000.

318 AG
ARGENTINA. INSTITUTO NACIONAL DE ESTADISTICA Y CENSOS. ANUARIO ESTADISTICO. 1973. a. $60. Instituto Nacional de Estadistica y Censos, Hipolito Yrigoyen 250, piso 12 of. 1209, 1310 Buenos Aires, Argentina.

312 US ISSN 0094-3576
HA251
ARKANSAS. BUREAU OF VITAL STATISTICS. ANNUAL REPORT OF BIRTHS, DEATHS, MARRIAGES AND DIVORCES AS REPORTED TO THE BUREAU OF VITAL STATISTICS. Variant title: Arkansas Vital Statistics Report. a. free. Bureau of Vital Statistics, Little Rock, AR 72201. TEL 501-661-2336. illus.; stat. Key Title: Annual Report of Births, Deaths, Marriages and Divorces as Reported to the Bureau of Vital Statistics (Little Rock).

312.097 US ISSN 0364-0728
HA251
ARKANSAS VITAL STATISTICS. 1970. a. free. Division of Health Statistics and Epidemiology, 4815 W. Markham St., Little Rock, AR 72201. TEL 501-661-2368. circ. 750. Indexed: SRI.

312 319.4 AT ISSN 1031-0150
AUSTRALIA. BUREAU OF STATISTICS. BIRTHS, AUSTRALIA. 1968. a. Aus.$11.50 (foreign Aus.$13.75)(effective 1991). Australian Bureau of Statistics, P.O. Box 10, Belconnen, A.C.T. 2616, Australia. TEL 062-527911. FAX 062-516009. circ. 422.
Description: Provides detailed statistics on confinements and live births presented in 24 tables.

312 AT ISSN 1031-2005
RA407.5.A8
AUSTRALIA. BUREAU OF STATISTICS. CAUSES OF DEATH, AUSTRALIA. 1962. a. Aus.$16.50 (foreign Aus.$20.10)(effective 1991). Australian Bureau of Statistics, P.O. Box 10, Belconnen, A.C.T. 2616, Australia. TEL 062-527911. FAX 062-516009. circ. 476.
Formerly (until 1978): Australia. Bureau of Statistics. Causes of Death (Canberra) (ISSN 0067-0766)
Description: Number of deaths by sex and selected age groups classified according to the World Health Organization's International Classification of Diseases.

POPULATION STUDIES — ABSTRACTING, BIBLIOGRAPHIES, STATISTICS

350 312.2   AT   ISSN 1031-0223
AUSTRALIA. BUREAU OF STATISTICS. DEATHS, AUSTRALIA. a. Aus.$16.50 (foreign Aus.$20.10)(effective 1991). Australian Bureau of Statistics, P.O. Box 10, Belconnen, A.C.T. 2616, Australia. TEL 062-527911. FAX 062-516009. illus.; circ. 427.
Description: Numbers of deaths classified by age, sex, birthplace, marital status; occupation, month of death, cause of death and usual residence of deceased by State or Territory.

312.5 319.4   AT   ISSN 1031-2188
AUSTRALIA. BUREAU OF STATISTICS. DIVORCES, AUSTRALIA. 1960. a. Aus.$11 (foreign Aus.$12.80)(effective 1991). Australian Bureau of Statistics, P.O. Box 10, Belconnen, A.C.T. 2616, Australia. TEL 062-527911. FAX 062-516009.
Formerly (until 1976): Australia. Bureau of Statistics. Divorces (Canberra) (ISSN 0587-5757)
Description: Number of petitions filed and decrees granted for dissolution of marriage.

312 319.4   AT   ISSN 0810-0039
AUSTRALIA. BUREAU OF STATISTICS. ESTIMATED RESIDENT POPULATION BY SEX AND AGE: STATES AND TERRITORIES OF AUSTRALIA. 1968. a. Aus.$11.50 (foreign Aus.$13.60)(effective 1991). Australian Bureau of Statistics, P.O. Box 10, Belconnen, A.C.T. 2616, Australia. TEL 062-527911. FAX 062-516009. circ. 838.
Description: Estimates of population for each State and Territory classified by sex and single years of age (0 to 84); also grouped ages, sex ratios, median and mean ages and dependency ratios of the population; age-sex pyramid for Australia only.

312.5 312   AT   ISSN 1031-0452
AUSTRALIA. BUREAU OF STATISTICS. MARRIAGES, AUSTRALIA. 1967. a. Aus.$11.50 (foreign Aus.$13.75)(effective 1991). Australian Bureau of Statistics, P.O. Box 10, Belconnen, A.C.T. 2616, Australia. circ. 320.
Description: Registrations of marriages classified according to state or territory of registration, age, previous marital status and country of birth of brides and bridegrooms; type of celebrant and month of celebration of marriage.

312 332   AT
AUSTRALIA. BUREAU OF STATISTICS. NEW SOUTH WALES OFFICE. MONTHLY SUMMARY OF STATISTICS. 1931. m. Aus.$90. Australian Bureau of Statistics, New South Wales Office, 3rd Fl., St. Andrew's House, Sydney Square, Sydney, N.S.W. 2000, Australia. stat.
Description: Monthly and quarterly data (including year-to-date totals) of a wide range of items classified in varying degrees of detail for the following topics; population and vital statistics; employment and unemployment; wages and prices; production; building; finance; trade; and transport.

312.2   AT   ISSN 1031-0053
AUSTRALIA. BUREAU OF STATISTICS. PERINATAL DEATHS, AUSTRALIA. 1973. a. Aus.$14 (foreign Aus.$17.60)(effective 1991). Australian Bureau of Statistics, P.O. Box 10, Belconnen, A.C.T. 2616, Australia. TEL 062-527911. FAX 062-516009. circ. 229.
Formerly (until 1978): Australia. Bureau of Statistics. Perinatal Deaths (Canberra) (ISSN 0312-4428)
Description: Number of stillbirths and deaths at ages under 4 weeks classified by sex, age, age and usual residence of mother, weight at birth, period of gestation, time of cessation of heartbeat and causes in the child and causes in the mother selected from the World Health Organizations' International Classification of Diseases.

312   AT   ISSN 0814-3951
AUSTRALIA. BUREAU OF STATISTICS. POPULATION ESTIMATES, AUSTRALIA. 1983. irreg., latest 1986. free. Australian Bureau of Statistics, P.O. Box 10, Belconnen, A.C.T. 2616, Australia. TEL 062-527911. FAX 062-516009. circ. 539.
Description: Shows quarterly estimates of resident population and components of population growth for States, Territories and Australia.

312   AT   ISSN 0816-3391
AUSTRALIA. BUREAU OF STATISTICS. PROJECTIONS OF THE POPULATIONS OF AUSTRALIA, STATES AND TERRITORIES. 1955. irreg. Aus.$25 (foreign Aus.$36)(effective 1991). Australian Bureau of Statistics, P.O. Box 10, Belconnen, A.C.T. 2616, Australia. TEL 062-527911. FAX 062-516009. circ. 429.
Formerly (until 1984): Australia. Bureau of Statistics. Projections of the Population.

312   AT   ISSN 1037-3594
AUSTRALIA. BUREAU OF STATISTICS. QUEENSLAND OFFICE. AGE AND SEX DISTRIBUTION OF THE ESTIMATED RESIDENT POPULATION, QUEENSLAND. 1981. a. Aus.$25 (foreign Aus.$36). Australian Bureau of Statistics, Queensland Office, 313 Adelaide St., Brisbane, Qld. 4000, Australia. TEL 07-222-6022. FAX 07-229-6171. TELEX AA 40271. (also avail. on floppy disk (ISSN 1032-7274))
Formerly (until 1986): Australia. Bureau of Statistics. Queensland Office. Age and Sex Distribution of the Estimated Resident Population in Local Authority Areas.
Description: Estimated resident population by sex and five-year age groups for each statistical local area, statistical division, statistical subdivision, statistical district and local government area.

312   AT   ISSN 0816-0465
AUSTRALIA. BUREAU OF STATISTICS. QUEENSLAND OFFICE. DEATHS, QUEENSLAND. 1983. a. Aus.$14. Australian Bureau of Statistics, Queensland Office, 313 Adelaide St., Brisbane, Qld. 4000, Australia. TEL 07-222-6022. FAX 07-229-6171. TELEX AA 40271.
Incorporates (1973-1990): Australia. Bureau of Statistics. Queensland Office. Causes of Death, Queensland (ISSN 0811-8655)
Description: Lists data on causes of death by sex, age and statistical division.

312   AT   ISSN 1036-2649
AUSTRALIA. BUREAU OF STATISTICS. QUEENSLAND OFFICE. DEMOGRAPHY, QUEENSLAND. 1983. a. Aus.$25. Australian Bureau of Statistics, Queensland Office, 313 Adelaide St., Brisbane, Qld. 4000, Australia. TEL 07-222-6022. FAX 07-229-6171. TELEX AA 40271.
Formed by the 1990 merger of: Australia. Bureau of Statistics. Queensland Office. Demographic Summary, Queensland (ISSN 0816-3537); Australia. Bureau of Statistics. Queensland Office. Demography: Small Area Summary, Queensland (ISSN 1031-217X) & Australia. Bureau of Statistics. Queensland Office. Births, Queensland (ISSN 0815-8681) & Australia. Bureau of Statistics. Queensland Office. Divorces, Queensland (ISSN 0816-0783) & Australia. Bureau of Statistics. Queensland Office. Marriages, Queensland (ISSN 1030-2638)
Description: Population counts at Census dates, estimated resident population and sex, summary statistics of births, deaths, marriages, divorces, overseas arrivals and departures, interstate and intrastate migration and historical summary.

312   AT   ISSN 1031-8100
AUSTRALIA. BUREAU OF STATISTICS. QUEENSLAND OFFICE. ESTIMATED RESIDENT POPULATION AND AREA, QUEENSLAND. 1972. a. Aus.$10 (foreign Aus.$15). Australian Bureau of Statistics, Queensland Office, 313 Adelaide St., Brisbane, Qld. 4000, Australia. stat.; circ. 1,100. (processed)
Former titles (until 1987): Estimated Resident Population and Area for Local Authority Areas, Queensland (ISSN 1032-903X); Australia. Bureau of Statistics. Queensland Office. Population Estimates and Areas for Local Authority Areas.

312   AT   ISSN 1030-911X
AUSTRALIA. BUREAU OF STATISTICS. QUEENSLAND OFFICE. ESTIMATED RESIDENT POPULATION AND AREA, QUEENSLAND, PRELIMINARY. 1983. a. Aus.$10 (foreign Aus.$15). Australian Bureau of Statistics, Queensland Office, 313 Adelaide St., Brisbane, Qld. 4000, Australia. TEL 07-222-6022. FAX 07-229-6171. TELEX AA 40271.
Formerly (until 1986): Australia. Bureau of Statistics. Queensland Office. Estimated Resident Population and Area for Local Authority Areas, Queensland, Preliminary (ISSN 0814-3609)

312   AT   ISSN 1031-6264
AUSTRALIA. BUREAU OF STATISTICS. QUEENSLAND OFFICE. ESTIMATED RESIDENT POPULATION: COMPONENTS OF CHANGE, QUEENSLAND. 1966. irreg., latest 1986. Aus.$3. Australian Bureau of Statistics, Queensland Office, 313 Adelaide St., Brisbane, Qld. 4000, Australia. TEL 07-222-6022. FAX 07-222-6022. TELEX AA 40271.
Formerly: Australia. Bureau of Statistics. Queensland Office. Population Growth and Growth Rates in the Intercensal Period in Statistical Divisions and Local Authority Areas.

312   AT
AUSTRALIA. BUREAU OF STATISTICS. QUEENSLAND OFFICE. ESTIMATED RESIDENT POPULATION, QUEENSLAND. 1976. irreg. Aus.$5. Australian Bureau of Statistics, Queensland Office, 313 Adelaide St., Brisbane, Qld. 4000, Australia. TEL 07-222-6022. FAX 07-229-6171. TELEX AA 40271.
Formerly: Australia. Bureau of Statistics. Queensland Office. Estimated Resident Population in Local Authority Areas.
Description: Estimated resident population of each local goverment area, statistical division and statistical district at Census dates with revised intercensal estimates.

312   AT
AUSTRALIA. BUREAU OF STATISTICS. QUEENSLAND OFFICE. FERTILITY TRENDS IN QUEENSLAND. 1984. irreg. Aus.$1.80. Australian Bureau of Statistics, Queensland Office, 313 Adelaide St., Brisbane, Qld. 4000, Australia. TEL 07-222-6022. FAX 07-229-6171. TELEX AA 40271.

312   AT   ISSN 0725-4857
AUSTRALIA. BUREAU OF STATISTICS. QUEENSLAND OFFICE. HOSPITAL MORBIDITY, QUEENSLAND. 1959. a. Aus.$12 (foreign Aus.$17). Australian Bureau of Statistics, Queensland Office, 313 Adelaide St., Brisbane, Qld. 4000, Australia. TEL 07-222-6022. FAX 07-229-6171. TELEX AA 40271.
Formerly (until 1978): Australia. Bureau of Statistics. Queenslnad Office. Patients Treated in Hospitals.
Description: Patients discharged: principal condition treated by numbers and rates, age group and sex, total and average stay (public and private hospitals), selected durations of stay; external cause (type of accident) by age group and sex; principal operation performed by age group and sex.

301.32   AT
AUSTRALIA. BUREAU OF STATISTICS. QUEENSLAND OFFICE. MIGRATION PATTERNS IN QUEENSLAND. 1986. irreg. Aus.$15 (foreign Aus.$24). Australian Bureau of Statistics, Queensland Office, 313 Adelaide St., Brisbane, Qld. 4000, Australia. TEL 07-222-6022. FAX 07-229-6171. TELEX AA 40271.
Description: Includes data by sex, age, urban and non-urban population, mobility rates, income levels and reasons for moving for overseas and interstate migration to and from Queensland as well as internal migration within the state.

312   AT   ISSN 0067-0898
AUSTRALIA. BUREAU OF STATISTICS. SOUTH AUSTRALIAN OFFICE. DEATHS, SOUTH AUSTRALIA. 1969. a. Aus.$14 (foreign Aus.$17.60). Australian Bureau of Statistics, South Australian Office, Box 2272, G.P.O., Adelaide, S.A. 5001, Australia. FAX 08-237-7566.

312   AT
HB1095
AUSTRALIA. BUREAU OF STATISTICS. SOUTH AUSTRALIAN OFFICE. DEMOGRAPHY, SOUTH AUSTRALIA. 1969. a. Aus.$25. Australian Bureau of Statistics, South Australian Office, Box 2272, G.P.O., Adelaide, S.A. 5001, Australia. FAX 08-237-7566.
Formerly: Australia. Bureau of Statistics. South Australian Office. Births, South Australia (ISSN 0067-088X)

312   AT   ISSN 0067-0901
AUSTRALIA. BUREAU OF STATISTICS. SOUTH AUSTRALIAN OFFICE. DIVORCES, SOUTH AUSTRALIA. 1947. a. Aus.$9. Australian Bureau of Statistics, South Australian Office, Box 2272, G.P.O., Adelaide, S.A. 5001, Australia. FAX 08-237-7566.

POPULATION STUDIES — ABSTRACTING, BIBLIOGRAPHIES, STATISTICS 3991

301   AT   ISSN 0705-5773
AUSTRALIA. BUREAU OF STATISTICS. TASMANIAN OFFICE. DIVORCES TASMANIA. 1979. a. Aus.$5. Australian Bureau of Statistics, Tasmanian Office, G.P.O. Box 66 A, Hobart, Tas. 7001, Australia.
Description: Record of divorces in Tasmania.

312 310   AT   ISSN 0819-6575
AUSTRALIA. BUREAU OF STATISTICS. VICTORIAN OFFICE. ESTIMATED RESIDENT POPULATION IN STATISTICAL LOCAL AREAS, VICTORIA. 1955. a. Aus.$10.50. Australian Bureau of Statistics, Victorian Office, Box 2796Y, G.P.O., Melbourne, Vic. 3001, Australia. circ. 3,000.
Former titles (until 1983): Australia. Bureau of Statistics. Victorian Office. Estimated Resident Population in Local Government Areas, Victoria; Australia. Bureau of Statistics. Victorian Office. Estimated Population in Local Government Areas, Victoria (ISSN 0705-6257); Australia. Bureau of Statistics. Victorian Office. Estimated Population and Dwellings by Local Government Areas.
Description: Preliminary estimated resident population for statistical local areas, statistical districts, and statistical divisions.

312   AT   ISSN 1031-055X
AUSTRALIAN DEMOGRAPHIC STATISTICS. 1979. q. Aus.$46 (foreign Aus.$60.40)(effective 1991). Australian Bureau of Statistics, P.O. Box 10, Belconnen, A.C.T. 2616, Australia. stat.; circ. 1,072.
Description: Summary data including rates of birth, deaths, infant deaths, marriages, divorces, interstate and overseas movements and latest population estimates for Australia, States and Territories.

AUSTRALIAN FAMILY AND SOCIETY ABSTRACTS. see *SOCIOLOGY — Abstracting, Bibliographies, Statistics*

312   AU
AUSTRIA. STATISTISCHES ZENTRALAMT. DEMOGRAPHISCHES JAHRBUCH OESTERREICHES. (Subseries of: Beitraege zur Oesterreichischen Statistik) 1951. a. S.350. Oesterreichisches Statistisches Zentralamt, Hintere Zollamtsstr. 2b, 1003 Vienna, Austria. circ. 500.
Formerly: Austria. Statistisches Zentralamt. Die Natuerliche Bevoelkerungsbewegung (ISSN 0067-2335)
Description: Demographic yearbook for Austria.

BARBADOS. REGISTRATION OFFICE. REPORT ON VITAL STATISTICS & REGISTRATIONS. see *PUBLIC ADMINISTRATION — Abstracting, Bibliographies, Statistics*

312   DK   ISSN 0108-8076
HA1471
BEFOLKNINGEN I KOMMUNERNE/POPULATIONS OF MUNICIPALITIES. 1971. a. DKK 83.61. Danmarks Statistik, Sejroegade 11, 2100 Copenhagen OE, Denmark. TEL 31-298222. FAX 31-184801. TELEX 16236. stat. (back issues avail.)
Formerly: Denmark. Danmarks Statistik. Befolkningen i de Enkelte Kommuner.

309   BE
BELGIUM. INSTITUT NATIONAL DE STATISTIQUE. BEVOLKINGSSTATISTIEKEN. irreg. 290 Fr. (foreign 590 Fr.). Institut National de Statistique - Nationaal Instituut voor de Statistiek, Leuvenseweg 44, B-1000 Brussels, Belgium.

312   BE   ISSN 0067-5490
BELGIUM. INSTITUT NATIONAL DE STATISTIQUE. STATISTIQUES DEMOGRAPHIQUES. (Text in Dutch, French) 1969. irreg. 290 Fr. (foreign 590 Fr.). Institut National de Statistique, 44 rue de Louvain, B-1000 Brussels, Belgium. **Indexed:** P.A.I.S.For.Lang.Ind.
Incorporates: Belgium. Institut National de Statistique. Mouvement de la Population des Communes.

312.2   BE
BELGIUM. INSTITUT NATIONAL DE STATISTIQUE. STATISTIQUES DES CAUSES DE DECES. irreg., latest 1978. 430 Fr. (foreign 530 Fr.). Institut National de Statistique, 44 rue de Louvain, B-1000 Brussels, Belgium.

312   PL   ISSN 0067-7795
BIBLIOTEKA WIADOMOSCI STATYSTYCZNYCH. 1967. irreg., vol.8, 1990. Glowny Urzad Statystyczny, Al. Niepodleglosci 208, 00-925 Warsaw, Poland. TEL 48 22 35-03-45.

BOCHUM. AMT FUER STATISTIK, STADTFORSCHUNG UND WAHLEN. STATISTICAL YEARBOOK. see *HOUSING AND URBAN PLANNING — Abstracting, Bibliographies, Statistics*

BRITISH COLUMBIA REGIONAL INDEX. see *BUSINESS AND ECONOMICS — Abstracting, Bibliographies, Statistics*

312   UA
C D C MONOGRAPHS. STUDIES IN AFRICAN AND ASIAN DEMOGRAPHY. 1970. a. $40. Cairo Demographic Centre, No. 78, St. 4, Hadhaba el-Olya, Mokattam 11571, Cairo, Egypt. TEL 929797. TELEX 92034 DP UN. Ed. M. Sobhi Abdel-Hakim. circ. 200. (back issues avail.)
Description: Studies in demography and related fields.

312   UA
C D C OCCASIONAL PAPERS. 1972. irreg., no.6, 1991. $5 per no. Cairo Demographic Centre, No. 78, St. 4, Hadhaba el-Olya, Mokattam 11571, Cairo, Egypt. TEL 929797. TELEX 92034 DP UN. (Co-Sponsors: United Nations and Egyptian Government) Ed. M. Sobhi Abdel-Hakim. circ. 200. (back issues avail.)
Description: Studies in demography and related fields.

312   UA
C D C WORKING PAPERS. 1981. irreg., no.21, 1991. $5 per no. Cairo Demographic Centre, No. 78, St. 4, Hadhaba el-Olya, Mokattam 11571, Cairo, Egypt. TEL 929797. TELEX 92034 DP UN. (Co-Sponsors: United Nations and Egyptian Government) Ed. M. Sobhi Abdel-Hakim. circ. 200. (back issues avail.)
Description: Studies in demography and related fields.

312   CN
CANADA. IMMIGRATION AND DEMOGRAPHIC POLICY GROUP. IMMIGRATION STATISTICS. (Text in English and French) a. Department of Employment and Immigration, Regional Library, P.O. Box 7500, Station A, Montreal, Que. H3C 3L4, Canada. TEL 514-283-4695.
Formerly: Canada. Immigration Division. Immigration Statistics (ISSN 0576-2286)

CANADA. STATISTICS CANADA. FAMILY INCOMES, CENSUS FAMILIES. see *BUSINESS AND ECONOMICS — Abstracting, Bibliographies, Statistics*

317   CU
CENSO DE POBLACION Y VIVIENDAS. (Issued from 1972 as a number of Anuario Estadistico de Cuba) a. free. Comite Estatal de Estadisticas, Centro de Informacion Cientifico-Tecnica, Direccion de Informacion y Relaciones Internacionales, Almendares No. 156, esq. a Desague, Gaveta Postal 6016, Havana, Cuba. charts; stat.

312   CK
COLOMBIA. DEPARTAMENTO ADMINISTRATIVO NACIONAL DE ESTADISTICA. ANUARIO DEMOGRAFICO. a. Departamento Administrativo Nacional de Estadistica, Banco Nacional de Datos, Apdo Nacional 80043, Bogota D.E., Colombia.

314   IT   ISSN 0010-4965
COMUNE DI ROMA. UFFICIO DI STATISTICA E CENSIMENTO. NOTIZIARIO STATISTICO MENSILE. 1948. m. L.3750 per no. Comune di Roma, Ufficio di Statistica - Censimento e Toponomastica, Via della Greca 5, 00186 Rome, Italy. circ. 650.

312.8   CY   ISSN 0590-4846
CYPRUS. DEPARTMENT OF STATISTICS AND RESEARCH. DEMOGRAPHIC REPORT. (Text in English, Greek) 1963. a. £C4. Ministry of Finance, Department of Statistics and Research, Nicosia, Cyprus.
Description: Population estimates by month: births and fertility statistics, death and mortality statistics.

310   CY
CYPRUS. DEPARTMENT OF STATISTICS AND RESEARCH. DEMOGRAPHIC SURVEY. (YEAR). (Text in English) 1980. irreg. £C5. Ministry of Finance, Department of Statistics and Research, Nicosia, Cyprus.
Formerly: Cyprus. Department of Statistics and Research. Multi-Round Demographic Survey. Main Report.
Description: Data on the socio-economic structure of the population, fertility and internal migration.

310   CY
CYPRUS. DEPARTMENT OF STATISTICS AND RESEARCH. MULTI-ROUND DEMOGRAPHIC SURVEY. MIGRATION IN CYPRUS. (Text in English) 1980. irreg. £C1.50. Ministry of Finance, Department of Statistics and Research, Nicosia, Cyprus.
Description: Analysis of recent and lifetime migration in Cyprus with an examination of variables such as sex, age, present and previous place of residence, place of birth, type of movement and reasons for moving.

CYPRUS. DEPARTMENT OF STATISTICS AND RESEARCH. TOURISM, MIGRATION AND TRAVEL STATISTICS. see *TRAVEL AND TOURISM — Abstracting, Bibliographies, Statistics*

312 012   UN   ISSN 0378-5378
HB3530.5
D O C P A L RESUMENES SOBRE POBLACION EN AMERICA LATINA/D O C P A L LATIN AMERICAN POPULATION ABSTRACTS. (Text in English and Spanish) 1977. 2/yr. $20. United Nations, Centro Latinoamericano de Demografia - United Nations, Regional Center for Demographic Training and Research in Latin America, Casilla 91, Santiago, Chile. TEL 485051. circ. 1,000. (back issues avail.) **Indexed:** P.A.I.S.For.Lang.Ind., Popul.Ind.
Description: Abstracts of published and non-published literature on population written in or about Latin America and the Caribbean.

DATEN UND INFORMATION. see *PUBLIC ADMINISTRATION — Abstracting, Bibliographies, Statistics*

312   CS   ISSN 0011-8265
DEMOGRAFIE. (Text in Czech; summaries in English and Russian) 1959. q. 40 Kcs.($39.80) (Federalni Statisticky Urad) Panorama, Halkova 1, 120 72 Prague 2, Czechoslovakia. Ed. Jerina Ruzickova. bk.rev.; stat.; index; circ. 1,800. **Indexed:** Popul.Ind.
Supersedes in part: Statistika a Demografie.

312   DK   ISSN 0070-3478
HA1473
DENMARK. DANMARKS STATISTIK. BEFOLKNINGENS BEVAEGELSER. (Text in Danish; notes in English) 1931. a. DKK 95.10. Danmarks Statistik, Sejroegade 11, 2100 Copenhagen OE, Denmark. TEL 31-298222. FAX 31-184801. TELEX 16236.

614 388.312 314   DK   ISSN 0070-3516
DENMARK. DANMARKS STATISTIK. FAERDSELSUHELD. (Text in Danish, notes in English) 1930. a. DKK 46.72. Danmarks Statistik, Sejroegade 11, 2100 Copenhagen OE, Denmark. TEL 31-298222. FAX 31-184801. TELEX 16236.

312   DK   ISSN 0108-5646
DOEDSAARSAGERNE/CAUSES OF DEATH IN DENMARK. (Included in the series: Vitalstatistik) (Text in Danish and English) 1980. a. DKK 75. Sundhedsstyrelsen, Amaliegade 13, 1012 Copenhagen K, Denmark. (Orders to: Statens Information, P.O. Box 1103, 1009 Copenhagen K, Denmark)
Formerly: Doedsaarsagerne i Kongeriget Danmark.

312 310   PN   ISSN 0379-4237
ESTADISTICA PANAMENA. SITUACION DEMOGRAFICA. SECCION 221. ESTADISTICAS VITALES. (In 3 vols.; vol.1: Matrimonios y Divorcios; vol.2: Nacimientos Vivos y Defunciones Fetales; vol.3: Defunciones) 1957. a. Bl.2.50. Direccion de Estadistica y Censo, Contraloria General, Apartado 5213, Panama 5, Panama. FAX 63-9322. circ. 1,800.

325.7287   PN   ISSN 0378-4975
JV7429
ESTADISTICA PANAMENA. SITUACION DEMOGRAFICA. SECCION 231. MIGRACION INTERNACIONAL. 1957. a. Bl.0.75. Direccion de Estadistica y Censo, Contraloria General, Apdo. Postal 5213, Panama 5, Panama. FAX 63-9322. circ. 1,000.

312 310   AT
ESTIMATED RESIDENT POPULATIONS BY AGE AND SEX IN STATISTICAL LOCAL AREAS, VICTORIA. 1988. a. Aus.$12.50. Australian Bureau of Statistics, Victorian Office, G.O.P. Box 2796Y, Melbourne, Vic. 3001, Australia.
Description: Gives extensive data on Victoria's estimated resident population.

POPULATION STUDIES — ABSTRACTING, BIBLIOGRAPHIES, STATISTICS

312 015   NE   ISSN 0168-6577
EUROPEAN JOURNAL OF POPULATION/REVUE EUROPEENNE DE DEMOGRAPHIE. (Text and summaries in English, French) 1970-1983; resumed 1985. q. fl.301 (effective 1992). (European Association for Population Studies) North-Holland (Subsidiary of: Elsevier Science Publishers B.V.), P.O. Box 211, 1000 AE Amsterdam, Netherlands. TEL 020-5803911. FAX 020-5803598. TELEX 18582 ESPA NL. (Subscr. in U.S. and Canada to: Elsevier Science Publishing Co., Inc., Box 882, Madison Sq. Sta., New York, NY 10159. TEL 212-989-5800) Eds. Daniel Courgeau, John Simons. adv.; bk.rev.; index; circ. 400. (tabloid format; back issues avail.) **Indexed:** Curr.Cont., Geo.Abstr., P.A.I.S., Popul.Ind., Sage Fam.Stud.Abstr., Sociol.Abstr.
—BLDSC shelfmark: 3829.737500.
Formerly (until 1983): European Demographic Information Bulletin (ISSN 0046-2756)
Description: Reports and analyzes demographic experiences, including theoretical explanations, research strategies and policy implications.
Refereed Serial

312   FJ
FIJI. BUREAU OF STATISTICS. FIJI FERTILITY SURVEY. 1974. irreg. $2.50 (effective Jan. 1991). Bureau of Statistics, P.O. Box 2221, Suva, Fiji.

312   FJ
FIJI. BUREAU OF STATISTICS. POPULATION OF FIJI; monograph for the U N World population. 1974. irreg. free. Bureau of Statistics, Box 2221, Suva, Fiji.

FIJI. BUREAU OF STATISTICS. TOURISM AND MIGRATION STATISTICS. see *TRAVEL AND TOURISM — Abstracting, Bibliographies, Statistics*

312   FI
FINLAND. TILASTOKESKUS. KUOLLEISUUS. KUOLLEISUUS- JA ELOONJAAMISTAULUJA/FINLAND. STATISTIKCENTRALEN. DOEDLIGHET. DOEDLIGHETSOCH LIVSLAENGDSTABELLER/FINLAND. CENTRAL STATISTICAL OFFICE. MORTALITY. LIFE TABLES. (Text in English, Finnish and Swedish) 1924. irreg. Tilastokeskus, Annankatu 44, SF-00100 Helsinki 10, Finland.
Formerly: Finland. Tilastokeskus. Kuolleisuus- Ja Eloonjaamistauluja (ISSN 0355-2128)

312   FI
FINLAND. TILASTOKESKUS. VAESTOE/FINLAND. STATISTIKCENTRALEN. BEFOLKNING/FINLAND. CENTRAL STATISTICAL OFFICE. POPULATION. (Section VIA of Official Statistics of Finland) (Text in English, Finnish and Swedish) 1871. a. FIM 145. Tilastokeskus, Annankatu 44, SF-00100 Helsinki 10, Finland. (Subscr. to: Government Printing Centre, Box 516, SF-00100 Helsinki 10, Finland)
Formerly: Finland. Tilastokeskus. Vaestonmuutokset (ISSN 0430-5612)

312   FI
FINLAND. TILASTOKESKUS. VAESTOE- JA ASUNTOLASKENTA/FINLAND. STATISTIKCENTRALEN. FOLK- OCH BOSTADSRAEKNINGEN/FINLAND. CENTRAL STATISTICAL OFFICE. POPULATION AND HOUSING CENSUS. (Section VI C of Official Statistics of Finland) (Text in English, Finnish and Swedish) 1950. irreg. (every 5 years), latest 1985. price varies. Tilastokeskus, Annankatu 44, SF-00100 Helsinki 10, Finland.
Formerly: Finland. Tilastokeskus. Vaestolaskenta (ISSN 0355-2136)

312   US
FLORIDA. DEPARTMENT OF HEALTH AND REHABILITATIVE SERVICES. VITAL NEWS AND QUARTERLY VITAL STATISTICS REPORT. q. Department of Health and Rehabilitative Services, Public Health Statistics Section, Office of Vital Statistics, Box 210, Jacksonville, FL 32231. TEL 904-359-6960. FAX 904-359-6697. charts; stat.; circ. 1,500.
Formerly: Florida. Department of Health and Rehabilitative Services. Quarterly Vital Statistics Report.

310   US
FLORIDA VITAL STATISTICS. 1935. a. Department of Health & Rehabilitative Services, Office of Vital Statistics, Public Health Statistics & Records Registration, Box 210, Jacksonville, FL 32231. TEL 904-354-3961. FAX 904-359-6697. charts; circ. 1,000.

325   FR
FRANCE. OFFICE DES MIGRATIONS INTERNATIONALES. OMISTATS. 1967. a. 190 F. Office des Migrations Internationales, Service de la Communication, 44 rue Bargue, 75732 Paris Cedex 15, France. TEL 45-66-27-22. FAX 47-34-88-57. TELEX 250 677 OFMIDEX. circ. 500.
Formerly: France. Office National d'Immigration. Statistiques de l'Immigration (ISSN 0071-903X)

312   US
GEORGIA DESCRIPTIONS IN DATA. 1982. a. $10 hardcopy; computer diskettes $10. Demographic & Statistical Services Division, Office of Planning and Budget, 254 Washington St., S.W., Rm. 640, Atlanta, GA 30334-8501. FAX 414-656-3828. Ed. Robin Kirkpatrick. circ. 1,000. **Indexed:** SRI.
Supersedes: Georgia. State Data Center. City Population Estimates (ISSN 0362-3904)

312   US
GEORGIA VITAL STATISTICS REPORT. 1947. a. price varies. Department of Human Resources, Division of Public Health, 878 Peachtree St., N.E., Ste. 200, Atlanta, GA 30309. TEL 404-894-6482. circ. 600 (controlled).
Former titles (until 1983): Georgia Vital Statistics Data Book; Georgia Vital and Health Statistics (ISSN 0362-0662); Georgia Vital Morbidity Statistics (ISSN 0072-1379)
Description: Disseminates selected information by race and age on births, deaths, marriages, divorces, abortions and projected populations for the calendar year.

016   BE
GEZINSWETENSCHAPPELIJKE DOCUMENTATIE; Jaarboek. 1976. a. 1750 BEF. Leuven University Press, Krakenstraat 3, B-3000 Leuven, Belgium. TEL 016-284175. FAX 016-284176. Ed.Bd. circ. 800.
Formerly (until 1983): Gezinssociologische Documentatie.

312   LU
GRAND-DUCHE DE LUXEMBOURG EN CHIFFRES (YEAR). (Editions in Dutch, English, French, German, Spanish) a. free. Service Central de la Statistique et des Etudes Economiques, 19-21 Bvd. Royal, B.P. 304, 2013 Luxembourg, Luxembourg. TEL 4794-292.

325   US
H I A S STATISTICAL ABSTRACT. vol.14, 1973. a. free. H I A S Inc., 333 Seventh Ave., New York, NY 10001-5004. charts; stat.; circ. 1,000. (processed)

312   US   ISSN 0093-3481
HB3525.H3
HAWAII. DEPARTMENT OF HEALTH. RESEARCH AND STATISTICS OFFICE. R & S REPORT. 1973. irreg. free. Department of Health, Research and Statistics Office, Box 3378, Honolulu, HI 96801. TEL 808-548-6454. stat. Key Title: R & S Report (Honolulu).

312   HU   ISSN 0073-4020
HA1201
HUNGARY. KOZPONTI STATISZTIKAI HIVATAL. DEMOGRAFIAI EVKONYV. 1965. a. 495 Ft. Statisztikai Kiado Vallalat, Kaszasdulo u. 2, P.O.B.99, 1300 Budapest 3, Hungary. TEL 688-635. TELEX 22-6699. circ. 1,200.

312   BE
I P D WORKING PAPERS. (Text in English) 1975. irreg. price varies. Vrije Universiteit Brussel, Interuniversity Programme in Demography, Pleinlaan 2, B-1050 Brussels, Belgium. FAX 02-6413645. Ed. R. Lesthaeghe. bibl.; charts; stat.; circ. 200. **Indexed:** Popul.Ind.
Formerly (until 1983): Demografie.

325.1   CN
IMMIGRATION HIGHLIGHTS. 4/yr. Can.$25. Ministry of Finance and Corporate Relations, 1405 Douglas St., 2nd Fl., Victoria, B.C. V8V 1X4, Canada. TEL 604-387-0327. FAX 604-387-0329.
Description: Features immigrant landings to British Columbia and Canada by place of origin, destination and immigration status: independent or dependent, entrepreneur and investor.

312   II
INDIA. MINISTRY OF HOME AFFAIRS. VITAL STATISTICS DIVISION. SAMPLE REGISTRATION BULLETIN. (Text in English) 1964. biennial. Ministry of Home Affairs, Vital Statistics Division, Registrar General, West Block No. 1, R. K. Puram, New Delhi 110066, India. charts; stat. (processed)
Incorporates: India. Office of the Registrar General. Newsletter (ISSN 0537-0035)

312.2   II
INDIA. MINISTRY OF HOME AFFAIRS. VITAL STATISTICS DIVISION. SURVEY OF CAUSES OF DEATH (RURAL). (Text in English) a. Ministry of Home Affairs, Vital Statistics Division, Registrar General, West Block No. 1, R. K. Puram, New Delhi 110066, India. stat.
Formerly: India. Ministry of Home Affairs. Vital Statistics Division. Causes of Death: a Survey.

312   BE   ISSN 0255-0849
Z7164.D3
INTERNATIONAL BIBLIOGRAPHY OF HISTORICAL DEMOGRAPHY/BIBLIOGRAPHIE INTERNATIONALE DE LA DEMOGRAPHIE HISTORIQUE. (Text in English, French) 1978. a. $10. International Union for the Scientific Study of Population, 34 rue des Augustins, B-4000 Liege, Belgium. FAX 041-223847. TELEX 42648 POPUN. Ed.Bd. bibl.; index; circ. 4,000. (back issues avail.) **Indexed:** Popul.Ind.

312   IE
IRELAND. CENTRAL STATISTICS OFFICE. QUARTERLY REPORT ON VITAL STATISTICS. q. £10. Government Publications Office, Trade and Postal Sales, Bishop Street, Dublin 8, Ireland. TEL 01-781-666.
Formerly: Ireland. Central Statistics Office. Quarterly Report on Births, Deaths and Marriages and on Certain Infectious Diseases.

312   IS   ISSN 0075-0999
ISRAEL. CENTRAL BUREAU OF STATISTICS. CAUSES OF DEATH. (Subseries of its Special Series) (Text in Hebrew and English) 1950. irreg. price varies. Central Bureau of Statistics, Box 13015, Jerusalem 91 130, Israel. TEL 02-21 12 11.

325.1   IS   ISSN 0302-816X
HA1931
ISRAEL. CENTRAL BUREAU OF STATISTICS. IMMIGRATION TO ISRAEL. (Text in English and Hebrew) a. Central Bureau of Statistics, P.O. Box 13015, Jerusalem 91 130, Israel. TEL 02-211211.

325.1   IS   ISSN 0334-9721
ISRAEL. CENTRAL BUREAU OF STATISTICS. PROJECTIONS OF POPULATION IN JUDEA, SAMARIA AND GAZA AREA UP TO 2002. (Text in English and Hebrew) irreg. $6. Central Bureau of Statistics, P.O. Box 13015, Jerusalem 91 130, Israel. TEL 02-553400.

312   IS
ISRAEL. CENTRAL BUREAU OF STATISTICS. SUICIDES AND ATTEMPTED SUICIDES. (Text in Hebrew and English) 1968? irreg., latest 1976. price varies. Central Bureau of Statistics, Box 13015, Jerusalem 91 130, Israel. TEL 02-21 12 11.

310   IS   ISSN 0075-1111
ISRAEL. CENTRAL BUREAU OF STATISTICS. VITAL STATISTICS. (Subseries of its Special Series) (Text in English and Hebrew) 1960. irreg., no.745, 1981. price varies. Central Bureau of Statistics, Box 13015, Jerusalem 91 130, Israel. TEL 02-21 12 11.

325 331   IT
HD8477
ITALY. ISTITUTO CENTRALE DI STATISTICA. STATISTICHE DEL LAVORO. 1959. a. L.12000. Istituto Centrale di Statistica, Via Cesare Balbo 16, 00100 Rome, Italy. circ. 1,350.
Former titles: Italy. Istituto Centrale di Statistica. Annuario di Statistiche del Lavoro (ISSN 0390-6450); Italy. Istituto Centrale di Statistica. Annuario di Statistiche del Lavoro e dell'Emigrazione (ISSN 0075-1693)

312   IT
HA1363
ITALY. ISTITUTO CENTRALE DI STATISTICA. STATISTICHE DEMOGRAFICHE. (In 2 vols.) 1951. a. L.18900 per vol. Istituto Centrale di Statistica, Via Cesare Balbo 16, 00100 Rome, Italy. circ. 1,200.
Formerly: Italy. Istituto Centrale di Statistica. Annuario di Statistiche Demografiche (ISSN 0075-1685)

POPULATION STUDIES — ABSTRACTING, BIBLIOGRAPHIES, STATISTICS

312   JA   ISSN 0286-1410
JAPAN STATISTICAL ASSOCIATION. ANNUAL REPORT ON THE INTERNAL MIGRATION IN JAPAN DERIVED FROM THE BASIC RESIDENT REGISTERS. (Text in English, Japanese) a. Nihon Tokei Kyokai - Japan Statistical Asssociation, Crest 21, 6-21, Yocho-machi, Shinjuku-ku, Tokyo 162, Japan. TEL 03-5269-3051. FAX 03-5269-3058. (Subscr. to: Government Publications Service Center, 2-1 Kasumigaseki 1-chome, Chiyoda-ku, Tokyo 100, Japan)

312   KO
KOREA (REPUBLIC). NATIONAL STATISTICAL OFFICE. ANNUAL REPORT ON THE INTERNAL MIGRATION STATISTICS. (Text in English and Korean) 1970. a. 7000 Won. National Statistical Office, 90, Gyongun-dong, Jongro-gu, Seoul 110-310, S. Korea. TEL 02-720-2788. (Subscr. to: the Korean Statistical Association, Room 302, Chungok Building, 561-30, Sinsa-dong, Gangnam-gu, Seoul 135-120, S. Korea) circ. 300.
    Formerly: Korea (Republic). Economic Planning Board. Yearbook of Migration Statistics.

315 312   KO
KOREA (REPUBLIC). NATIONAL STATISTICAL OFFICE. POPULATION & HOUSING CENSUS REPORT. (Text in English and Korean) 1925. quinquennial. 68850 Won. National Statistical Office, 90, Gyongun-dong, Jongro-gu, Seoul 110-310, S. Korea. TEL 02-720-2788. (Subscr. to: the Korean Statistical Association, Room 302, Chungok Building, 516-30, Sinsa-dong, Gangnam-gu, Seoul 135-120, S. Korea) circ. 1,500.
    Formerly: Korea (Republic). National Bureau of Statistics. Population and Housing Census Report.

301.32 310   CY
LABOUR FORCE AND MIGRATION SURVEY. irreg. EC$6 per no. Ministry of Finance, Department of Statistics and Research, 13, Lord Byron Ave., Nicosia, Cyprus. TEL 30-3208. FAX 456712.
    Description: Provides complete set of tables on the demographic characteristics of the population in its various dissections, potential labor force and migration.

312   LY   ISSN 0075-9236
LIBYA. CENSUS AND STATISTICS DEPARTMENT. GENERAL POPULATION CENSUS. (Text in Arabic and English) 1954. decennial. free. Secretariat of Planning, Census and Statistics Department, P.O. Box 600, Tripoli, Libya.

016 312   NE
LITERATUUR- EN DOKUMENTATIEOVERZICHT N I D I-BIBLOTHEEK. 1978. q. free. Nederlands Interdisciplinair Demografisch Instituut - Netherlands Interdisciplinary Demographic Institute, Lange Houtstraat 19, 2511 CV The Hague, Netherlands. TEL 070-3647187. TELEX 31138 NISI NL. Ed. T.J. Augenbroe-Siebenga. circ. 225. **Indexed:** Popul.Ind.

312   LU
LUXEMBOURG. SERVICE CENTRAL DE LA STATISTIQUE ET DES ETUDES ECONOMIQUES. COLLECTION RP: RECENSEMENT DE LA POPULATION ET MOUVEMENT DE LA POPULATION. 1962. irreg. 250 Fr. per no. Service Central de la Statistique et des Etudes Economiques, 19-21 Boulevard Royal, B.P. 304, 2013 Luxembourg, Luxembourg. TEL 4794-292.
    Formerly: Luxembourg. Service Central de la Statistique et des Etudes Economiques. Collection RP: Recensement de la Population (ISSN 0076-1613)

312   MH
MACAO. DIRECCAO DOS SERVICOS DE ESTATISTICA E CENSOS. CENSOS DA POPULACAO/MACAO. CENSUS AND STATISTICS DEPARTMENT. POPULATION CENSUS. (Text in Chinese, Portuguese) 1950. every 10 yrs. free. Direccao dos Servicos de Estatistica e Censos, P.O. Box 3022, Macao.

312   MH
MACAO. DIRECCAO DOS SERVICOS DE ESTATISTICA E CENSOS. ESTATISTICAS DEMOGRAFICAS/MACAO. CENSUS AND STATISTICS DEPARTMENT. DEMOGRAPHIC STATISTICS. (Text in Chinese, Portuguese) 1984. m. free. Direccao dos Servicos de Estatistica e Censos, Rua Inacio Baptista, No.4D-6, P.O. Box 3022, Macao. TEL 550935. FAX 561884.
    Description: Presents the latest figures for movement of population, births, deaths, marriages, divorces and immigration.

312   MH
MACAO. DIRECCAO DOS SERVICOS DE ESTATISTICA E CENSOS. ESTIMATIVAS DA POPULACAO RESIDENTE EM MACAU/MACAO. CENSUS AND STATISTICS DEPARTMENT. ESTIMATION OF RESIDENT POPULATION IN MACAO. (Text in Portuguese) 1980. irreg. free. Direccao dos Servicos de Estatistica e Censos, P.O. Box 3022, Macao.

325.1   MH
MACAO. DIRECCAO DOS SERVICOS DE ESTATISTICA E CENSOS. IMPORTACAO DE MAO-DE-OBRA E RENOVACAO DE CONTRATOS DE TRABALHADORES NAO RESIDNETES/MACAO. CENSUS AND STATISTICS DEPARTMENT. STATISTICS OF NON RESIDENT WORKERS IMPORTATION. (Text in Chinese, Portuguese) 1988. m. free. Direccao dos Servicos de Estatistica e Censos, Rua Inacio Baptista, No.4D-6, P.O. Box 3022, Macao. TEL 550935. FAX 561884.

312   MH
MACAO. DIRECCAO DOS SERVICOS DE ESTATISTICA E CENSOS. RECENSEAMENTO DOS ALOJAMENTOS INFORMAIS/MACAO. CENSUS AND STATISTICS DEPARTMENT. CENSUS OF INFORMAL ACCOMODATION. (Text in Portuguese) 1988. irreg. free. Direccao dos Servicos de Estatistica e Censos, P.O. Box 3022, Macao.

312   US
MAINE. DEPARTMENT OF HUMAN SERVICES. VITAL STATISTICS. 1892. a. $10.50. Department of Human Services, Office of Data, Research, and Vital Statistics, State House Sta. 11, Augusta, ME 04333. TEL 207-624-5445. Ed. Ellen M. Naor. circ. 500. **Indexed:** SRI.
    Former titles: Maine. Department of Human Services. Bureau of Health Planning and Development. Vital Statistics; Maine. Division of Research and Vital Records. Annual Statistical Report.

310 312   MW   ISSN 0076-3276
MALAWI. NATIONAL STATISTICAL OFFICE. HOUSEHOLD INCOME AND EXPENDITURE SURVEY. 1968. irreg. K.10($9.50) National Statistical Office, Box 333, Zomba, Malawi.

312   MW   ISSN 0076-3306
MALAWI. NATIONAL STATISTICAL OFFICE. POPULATION CENSUS FINAL REPORT. 1966. irreg. (approx. every 10 yrs.). K.7($10.20) National Statistical Office, Box 333, Zomba, Malawi.

312   MY
MALAYSIA. DEPARTMENT OF STATISTICS. QUARTERLY REVIEW OF MALAYSIAN POPULATION STATISTICS. (Text in English) 1986. q. M.$5 per no. Department of Statistics, Wisma Statistik, Block E, Jalan Cenderasari, 50514 Kuala Lumpur, Malaysia. TEL 03-2922133.

312   MY   ISSN 0127-466X
MALAYSIA. DEPARTMENT OF STATISTICS. VITAL STATISTICS, PENINSULAR MALAYSIA. (Text in English & Malay) 1963. a. M.$8. Department of Statistics - Jabatan Perangkaan, Wisma Statistik, Block E, Jalan Cenderasari, 50514 Kuala Lumpur, Malaysia. TEL 03-2922133. circ. 800.

312   MY   ISSN 0126-9267
MALAYSIA. DEPARTMENT OF STATISTICS. VITAL STATISTICS SARAWAK. (Text in English) 1966. a. M.$5. Department of Statistics, Wisma Statistik, Block E, Jalan Cenderasari, 50514 Kuala Lumpur, Malaysia. (Orders to: Department of Statistics, Malaysia (Sarawak Branch), 5th Fl., Bangunan Tun Datuk, Patinggi Tuanku Hj. Bujang, 93514 Kuching, Sarawak, Malaysia)

312   MM   ISSN 0076-3470
MALTA. CENTRAL OFFICE OF STATISTICS. DEMOGRAPHIC REVIEW. a. L.1. Central Office of Statistics, Auberge d'Italie, Valletta, Malta. (Subscr. to: Publications Bookshop, Auberge de Castille, Valletta, Malta)

312   MF
MAURITIUS. CENTRAL STATISTICAL OFFICE. DIGEST OF DEMOGRAPHIC STATISTICS. 1985. a. Rs.100. Central Statistical Office, Port-Louis, Mauritius. (Subscr. to: G P O, La Tour Koenig, Port-Louis, Mauritius)

312   MF
MAURITIUS. CENTRAL STATISTICAL OFFICE. HOUSING AND POPULATION CENSUS. ANALYSIS REPORT. Rs.75 per no. Central Statistical Office, Port-Louis, Mauritius. (Subscr. to: G.P.O., La Tour Koenig, Port-Louis, Mauritius)

325.2   CN
MIGRATION HIGHLIGHTS. 4/yr. Can.$25. Ministry of Finance and Corporate Relations, 1405 Douglas St., 2nd.Fl., Victoria, B.C. V8V 1X4, Canada. TEL 604-387-0327. FAX 604-387-0329.
    Description: Provides detailed current information on the flow of people between B.C. and other provinces and territories. Contains components of population change.

312   US
MISSOURI MONTHLY VITAL STATISTICS. 1967. m. free. Department of Health, Center for Health Statistics, Box 570, Jefferson City, MO 65102. TEL 314-751-6272. Ed. Garland Land. charts; stat.; circ. 800.
    Description: Contains vital statistics data and short analytical article concerning public health issues.

312   MR   ISSN 0851-092X
HD5838.3
MOROCCO. DIRECTION DE LA STATISTIQUE. POPULATION ACTIVE URBAINE, RAPPORT DE SYNTHESE. (Editions in Arabic, French) a. DH.33. Direction de la Statistique, B.P. 178, Rabat, Morocco.

312   MR   ISSN 0851-6804
MOROCCO. DIRECTION DE LA STATISTIQUE. POPULATION ACTIVE URBAINE, RESULTATS DETAILLES. (Editions in Arabic, French) a. DH.99. Direction de la Statistique, B.P. 178, Rabat, Morocco.

312   GR   ISSN 0077-6114
MOUVEMENT NATUREL DE LA POPULATION DE LA GRECE. (Text in Greek and French) 1956. a., latest 1983. $10. National Statistical Service of Greece, Statistical Information and Publications Division, 14-16 Lycourgou St., 10166 Athens, Greece. TEL 3244-748. FAX 3222205. TELEX 216734 ESYE GR.

325   SP   ISSN 0077-1767
MOVIMIENTO NATURAL DE LA POBLACION DE ESPANA. 1961. a. Instituto Nacional de Estadistica, P. de la Castellana, 183, 28071 Madrid, Spain.

312 614   NE   ISSN 0168-4000
HA1381
NETHERLANDS. CENTRAAL BUREAU VOOR DE STATISTIEK. JAARSTATISTIEK VAN DE BEVOLKING/POPULATION STATISTICS. (Supplement to: Maandstatistiek van Bevolking en Volksgezonheid) 1971. a. Centraal Bureau voor de Statistiek, Prinses Beatrixlaan 428, Voorburg, Netherlands. (Orders to: SDU - Publishers, Christoffel Plantijnstraat, The Hague) circ. 1,000.
    Formerly: Netherlands. Centraal Bureau voor de Statistiek. Jaaroverzicht Bevolking en Bevolking en Volksgezondheid.

312   NE   ISSN 0024-8711
HA1381
NETHERLANDS. CENTRAAL BUREAU VOOR DE STATISTIEK. MAANDSTATISTIEK VAN DE BEVOLKING. 1953. m. fl.82. Centraal Bureau voor de Statistiek, Prinses Beatrixlaan 428, Voorburg, Netherlands. (Dist. by: SDU - Publishers, Christoffel Plantijnstraat, The Hague, Netherlands) stat.; index; circ. 785.

312   US   ISSN 0095-5523
HA511
NEW HAMPSHIRE VITAL STATISTICS. 1880. a. Bureau of Vital Records and Health Statistics, Division of Public Health Services, Concord, NH 03301. TEL 603-271-4651. Ed. Charles Sirc. circ. 350.

POPULATION STUDIES — ABSTRACTING, BIBLIOGRAPHIES, STATISTICS

312.097 — US
NEW JERSEY. DIVISION OF LABOR MARKET AND DEMOGRAPHIC RESEARCH. POPULATION ESTIMATES FOR NEW JERSEY. (Report year ends July 1) a. Department of Labor, Division of Labor Market and Demographic Research, CN-388, Trenton, NJ 08625-0388. TEL 609-292-0076.
Formerly: New Jersey. Office of Demographic and Economic Analysis. Population Estimates for New Jersey (ISSN 0091-9187)
Description: Presents provisional estimates of total population for New Jersey, and its 21 counties and 567 municipalities. Includes revised estimates and notes on data and methods.

312 — NZ — ISSN 0113-3667
HA3171
NEW ZEALAND. DEPARTMENT OF STATISTICS. DEMOGRAPHIC TRENDS. a. NZ.$49.95. Department of Statistics, P.O. Box 2922, Wellington, New Zealand. TEL 04-495-4600. FAX 04-472-9135.
Former titles: New Zealand. Department of Statistics. Demographic Trends Bulletin (ISSN 0112-9155); New Zealand. Department of Statistics. Population and Migration. Part A: Population (ISSN 0110-375X); Supersedes in part: New Zealand. Department of Statistics. Population and Migration; New Zealand. Department of Statistics. Statistical Report of Population, Migration and Building. (ISSN 0077-9903)

312 — NZ
NEW ZEALAND. DEPARTMENT OF STATISTICS. POPULATION CENSUS: AGES, MARITAL STATUS AND FERTILITY. quinquennial, 1986, issued 1988. NZ.$29.95. Department of Statistics, P.O. Box 2922, Wellington, New Zealand.
Formerly: New Zealand. Department of Statistics. Population Census: Ages and Marital Status (ISSN 0077-9687)

312 — NZ
NEW ZEALAND. DEPARTMENT OF STATISTICS. POPULATION CENSUS: BIRTHPLACES AND ETHNIC ORIGIN. quinquennial, 1986, issued 1988. NZ.$25.50. Department of Statistics, P.O. Box 2922, Wellington, New Zealand.
Formerly: New Zealand. Department of Statistics. Population Census: Race (ISSN 0077-9776)

312 — NZ — ISSN 0077-9695
NEW ZEALAND. DEPARTMENT OF STATISTICS. POPULATION CENSUS: DWELLINGS. quinquennial, 1986, issued 1987. NZ.$19.95. Department of Statistics, P.O. Box 2922, Wellington, New Zealand.

312 — NZ
NEW ZEALAND. DEPARTMENT OF STATISTICS. POPULATION CENSUS: EDUCATION AND TRAINING. quinquennial, 1986 issued 1988. NZ.$20.50. Department of Statistics, P.O. Box 2922, Wellington, New Zealand.
Formerly: New Zealand. Department of Statistics. Population Census: Education (ISSN 0077-9709)

312 — NZ
NEW ZEALAND. DEPARTMENT OF STATISTICS. POPULATION CENSUS: FAMILIES. quinquennial, 1986, issued 1988. NZ.$20.50. Department of Statistics, P.O. Box 2922, Wellington, New Zealand.
Former titles: New Zealand. Department of Statistics. Population Census: Households and Families; New Zealand. Department of Statistics. Population Census: Households (ISSN 0077-9725)

312 — NZ — ISSN 0110-8700
NEW ZEALAND. DEPARTMENT OF STATISTICS. POPULATION CENSUS: GENERAL INFORMATION. quinquennial, 1986 issued 1988. NZ.$30.65. Department of Statistics, P.O. Box 2922, Wellington, New Zealand.
Formerly: New Zealand. Department of Statistics. Population Census: General Report (ISSN 0077-9717)

312 — NZ
NEW ZEALAND. DEPARTMENT OF STATISTICS. POPULATION CENSUS: INCOMES AND WELFARE PAYMENTS. quinquennial, 1986, issued 1988. NZ.$20.50. Department of Statistics, P.O. Box 2922, Wellington, New Zealand.
Former titles: New Zealand. Department of Statistics. Population Census: Incomes and Social Security Benefits; New Zealand. Department of Statistics. Population Census: Incomes (ISSN 0077-9733)

310 312 — NZ
NEW ZEALAND. DEPARTMENT OF STATISTICS. POPULATION CENSUS: INTERNAL MIGRATION. 1971. quinquennial, 1986, issued 1988. NZ.$25.50. Department of Statistics, P.O. Box 2922, Wellington, New Zealand.

312 — NZ
NEW ZEALAND. DEPARTMENT OF STATISTICS. POPULATION CENSUS: LABOUR FORCE. quinquennial, 1986, issued 1988. NZ.$30.65. Department of Statistics, P.O. Box 2922, Wellington, New Zealand. (Subscr. to: Government Printing Office, Publications, Private Bag, Wellington, New Zealand)
Formerly: New Zealand. Department of Statistics. Population Census: Industries and Occupations (ISSN 0077-9741)

312 — NZ
NEW ZEALAND. DEPARTMENT OF STATISTICS. POPULATION CENSUS: MAORI POPULATION AND DWELLINGS. quinquennial, 1986, issued 1988. NZ.$30.65. Department of Statistics, P.O. Box 2922, Wellington, New Zealand.

312 — NZ — ISSN 0077-9784
NEW ZEALAND. DEPARTMENT OF STATISTICS. POPULATION CENSUS: RELIGIOUS PROFESSIONS. quinquennial, 1986, issued 1988. NZ.$20.50. Department of Statistics, P.O. Box 2922, Wellington, New Zealand.

312 — NZ
NEW ZEALAND. DEPARTMENT OF STATISTICS. POPULATION CENSUS: TOTAL POPULATION STATISTICS. quinquennial, 1986. NZ.$20.50. Department of Statistics, P.O. Box 2922, Wellington, New Zealand.
Formerly: New Zealand. Department of Statistics. Population Census. Location and Increase of Population. Part A: Population Size and Distribution; Which supersedes in part: New Zealand. Department of Statistics. Population Census. Increase and Location of Population (ISSN 0077-9792)

312.2 — NZ — ISSN 0548-9911
RA407.5.N4
NEW ZEALAND. HEALTH STATISTICAL SERVICES. MORTALITY AND DEMOGRAPHIC DATA. a. NZ.$30. Health Statistical Services, c/o Josephine Ryan, 133 Molesworth St., P.O. Box 5013, Wellington, New Zealand. TEL 04-469-2000. FAX 04-496-2050. circ. controlled.

312 — NQ
NICARAGUA. INSTITUTO NACIONAL DE ESTADISTICAS Y CENSOS. ESTADISTICAS VITALES. q. Instituto Nacional de Estadisticas y Censos, Apdo. Postal 4031, Managua, Nicaragua.

312 — US
NORTH CAROLINA. DEPARTMENT OF ENVIRONMENT, HEALTH AND NATURAL RESOURCES. STATE CENTER FOR HEALTH AND ENVIRONMENTAL STATISTICS. NORTH CAROLINA VITAL STATISTICS. 1916. a. free. Department of Environment, Health and Natural Resources, State Center for Health and Environmental Statistics, Box 27687, Raleigh, NC 27611-7687. TEL 919-733-4728.
Former titles: North Carolina. Division of Health Services. State Center for Health Statistics. North Carolina Vital Statistics; North Carolina. Division of Health Services. Public Health Statistics Branch. North Carolina Vital Statistics (ISSN 0078-1371)

312 — NO — ISSN 0801-6690
NORWAY. STATISTISK SENTRALBYRAA. BEFOLKNINGS STATISTISK HEFTE 2/NORWAY. CENTRAL BUREAU OF STATISTICS. POPULATION STATISTICS VOL.2. (Subseries of its Norges Offisielle Statistikk) (Text in English and Norwegian) a. NOK 70. Statistisk Sentralbyraa, Box 8131 Dep., 0033 Oslo 1, Norway. TEL 02-864500. FAX 02-864973. circ. 1,750.
Formerly: Norway. Statistisk Sentralbyraa. Folkmengde Etter Alder og Ekteskapelig Status - Norway. Central Bureau of Statistics. Population by Age and Marital Status (ISSN 0550-7170)

312 — US
OKLAHOMA POPULATION ESTIMATES. 1967. a. free. Employment Security Commission, Office of Economic Analysis, 213 Will Rogers Bldg., Oklahoma City, OK 73105. Ed. Roger Jacks. charts; stat.; circ. 850.

312 — US
OMAHA - COUNCIL BLUFFS METROPOLITAN AREA PLANNING AGENCY. POPULATION AND HOUSING UNIT ESTIMATES. irreg. $10. Omaha - Council Bluffs Metropolitan Area Planning Agency, 2222 Cuming St., Omaha, NE 68102-4328. TEL 402-444-6866. FAX 402-342-0949. circ. 500.
Description: Intercensal estimates by census tract of population and housing units in Douglas and Sarpy counties in Nebraska and Pottawattamie county in Iowa.

312 325 — PP — ISSN 1017-6551
PAPUA NEW GUINEA INTERNATIONAL ARRIVALS AND DEPARTURES. 1957. q. K.5 (foreign K.7). National Statistical Office, P.O. Wards Strip, Papua New Guinea. FAX 675-255057. TELEX FINANCE NE 22312. Ed. Nick Suvulo. circ. 520.
Former titles: Papua New Guinea International Migration; Papua New Guinea Overseas Migration (ISSN 0031-1510); Papua New Guinea Territory. Quarterly Migration Bulletin.
Description: Contains statistics compiled from Passenger Arrival and Departure Cards; provides a breakdown of persons arriving in Papua New Guinea, by purpose of journey, age, nationality and occupation, overseas address and length of stay in Papua.

312 — US
PENNSYLVANIA VITAL STATISTICS. 1951. a. free. Department of Health, State Health Data Center, Box 90, Harrisburg, PA 17108. TEL 717-783-2548. circ. 1,000. (also avail. in microfiche) Indexed: SRI.
Formerly: Pennsylvania Natality and Mortality Statistics.

315 312 — PH — ISSN 0116-1520
PHILIPPINE YEARBOOK. (Text in English) 1940. biennial, lastest 1989. $80. National Statistics Office, Ramon Magsaysay Blvd., Box 779, Manila, Philippines. FAX 610794. circ. 2,000.

315 — PH — ISSN 0116-2675
HA1821
PHILIPPINES. NATIONAL STATISTICS OFFICE. VITAL STATISTICS REPORT. a, latest 1988. National Statistics Office, Ramon Magsaysay Blvd., Box 779, Manila, Philippines. FAX 610794.
Formerly: Philippines. National Census and Statistics Office. Vital Statistical Report.

312 — PL — ISSN 0079-2616
HB3608.7
POLAND. GLOWNY URZAD STATYSTYCZNY. ROCZNIK DEMOGRAFICZNY. (Subseries of its: Statystyka Polski) (Text in Polish; summaries in English and Russian) 1968. a. 85 Zl. Glowny Urzad Statystyczny, Al. Niepodleglosci 208, 00-925 Warsaw, Poland. TEL 48 22 25-03-45.

312 — GR
POPULATION DE LA GRECE AU RECENSEMENT. (Text in Greek; summaries in French) 1940. decennial. price varies. National Statistical Service of Greece, Statistical Information and Publications Division, 14-16 Lycourgou St., 10166 Athens, Greece. TEL 3244-748. FAX 3222205. TELEX 216734 ESYE GR.

301.42 — US — ISSN 0032-4701
Z7164.D3
POPULATION INDEX. 1935. q. $85. (Population Association of America) Princeton University, Office of Population Research, 21 Prospect Ave., Princeton, NJ 08544-2091. TEL 609-258-4949. FAX 609-258-1039. Ed. Richard Hankinson. adv.; abstr.; bibl.; charts; index, cum.index; circ. 4,600. (also avail. in microfilm from UMI; reprint service avail. from UMI) Indexed: Curr.Cont., Curr.Lit.Fam.Plan., E.I., P.A.I.S., SSCI.
●Also available online. Vendor(s): National Library of Medicine.
Also available on CD-ROM. Producer(s): SilverPlatter.

312 — NE — ISSN 0168-3853
POPULATION OF THE MUNICIPALITIES OF THE NETHERLANDS. (Text in Dutch and English) 1944. a. Centraal Bureau voor de Statistiek, Prinses Beatrixlaan 428, Voorburg, Netherlands. (Orders to: SDU - Publishers, Christoffel Plantijnstraat, The Hague, Netherlands)

POPULATION STUDIES — ABSTRACTING, BIBLIOGRAPHIES, STATISTICS

301.32   US   ISSN 0145-9643
POPULATION REPORTS. 1973. irreg. free. Department of Health, Research and Statistics Office, Box 3378, Honolulu, HI 96801. TEL 808-548-6454. **Indexed:** Curr.Adv.Ecol.Sci., Curr.Lit.Fam.Plan., Environ.Abstr., Hlth.Ind., So.Pac.Per.Ind., SRI.
Supersedes (in 1973): Population Mobility in Hawaii (ISSN 0094-0348)

312   PO   ISSN 0379-7007
PORTUGAL. INSTITUTO NACIONAL DE ESTATISTICA. CENTRO DE ESTUDOS DEMOGRAFICOS. CADERNO. 1976. irreg., no.9, 1988. Instituto Nacional de Estatistica, 1078 Lisbon Codex, Portugal. (Orders to: Imprensa Nacional, Casa da Moeda, Direccao Comercial, rua D. Francisco Manuel de Melo 5, 1000 Lisbon, Portugal) charts.

312   PO
PORTUGAL. INSTITUTO NACIONAL DE ESTATISTICA. ESTATISTICAS DEMOGRAFICAS. CONTINENTE, ACORES E MADEIRA. 1887. a. Esc.5000. Instituto Nacional de Estatistica, Av. Antonio Jose de Almeida, 1078 Lisbon Codex, Portugal. (Orders to: Imprensa Nacional, Casa da Moeda, Direccao Comercial, rua D. Francisco Manuel de Melo 5, 1000 Lisbon, Portugal)
Former titles: Portugal. Instituto Nacional de Estatistica. Estatisticas Demograficas Continente e Ilhas Adjacentes (ISSN 0377-2284); Portugal. Instituto Nacional de Estatistica. Estatisticas Demograficas; Portugal. Instituto Nacional de Estatistica. Anuario Demografico. (ISSN 0079-4104)

312   PO   ISSN 0871-875X
HB3621
PORTUGAL. INSTITUTO NACIONAL DE ESTATISTICA. GABINETE DE ESTUDOS DEMOGRAFICOS. ESTUDOS DEMOGRAFICOS. 1945. irreg. Instituto Nacional de Estatistica, 1078 Lisbon Codex, Portugal. (Orders to: Imprensa Nacional, Casa da Moeda, Direccao Comercial, rua D. Francisco Manuel de Melo 5, 1000 Lisbon, Portugal) **Indexed:** Popul.Ind.
Formerly: Portugal. Instituto Nacional de Estatistica. Centro de Estudos Demograficos. Revista (ISSN 0079-4082)

312   PR
PUERTO RICO. DEPARTMENT OF HEALTH. OFFICE OF PLANNING, EVALUATION AND REPORTS. DIVISION OF STATISTICS AND REPORTS. ANNUAL VITAL STATISTICS REPORT. Cover title: Estadisticas Vitales. (Text in English and Spanish) 1970. a. Department of Health, Health Facilities and Services Administration, Office of Health Statistics, PO Box 9342, Santurce, PR 00901.
Formerly: Puerto Rico. Division of Demographic Registry and Vital Statistics. Annual Vital Statistics Report (ISSN 0555-6511)
Description: Information on population, deaths, births, marriages and divorces by municipality and regions.

325.2   UN   ISSN 0253-1445
HV640
REFUGEE ABSTRACTS. (Text in English, French, Spanish) 1982. q. $20 to individuals and organizations; libraries $30. United Nations High Commissioner for Refugees, Centre for Documentation on Refugees (CDR), Case Postale 2500, 1211 Geneva 2, Switzerland. TEL 022-739-8458. FAX 022-739-8682. TELEX 415740 HCR CH. Ed. Hans Thoolen. bk.rev.; circ. 1,150. (back issues avail.) **Indexed:** HR Rep.
—BLDSC shelfmark: 7336.320000.
Description: Collection of abstracted literature concerning refugees, references to bibliographies, reviews of recent books, basic texts and announcements of new publications, meetings and conferences.

312   CN
REGIONAL POPULATION ESTIMATES AND PROJECTIONS. a. Can.$80. Ministry of Finance and Corporate Relations, 1405 Douglas St., 2nd Fl., Victoria, B.C. V8V 1X4, Canada. TEL 604-387-0327. FAX 604-387-0329.
Description: Provides historical and forecast population by age and sex, including components of change for regional districts or local health areas.

312   IE   ISSN 0790-7710
REPORT ON VITAL STATISTICS. q. £10. Stationery Office, Dublin, Ireland. TEL 781666. (Subscr. to: Government Publications Sales Office, Bishop St., Dublin 8, Ireland)
Description: Contains summaries of births, deaths and marriages registered in each county.

312   CF
REPUBLIQUE DE CONGO EN QUELQUES CHIFFRES. 1980. a. 3500 Fr.CFA. Centre National de la Statistique et des Etudes Economiques, B.P. 2031, Brazzaville, Congo. TEL 83-36-94.

312   GR
RESULTATS DU RECENSEMENT DE LA POPULATION ET DES HABITATIONS. (In 5 Vols.: Vol.1: Population; Vol.2: Caracteristiques Demographiques et Sociales; Vol.3: Caracteristiques Economiques; Vol.4: Habitations, Conditions de Logement des Menages; Vol.5: Caracteristiques Demographiques, Sociales et Economiques de la Population des Departements d'Attique, Salonique, Le Reste de Grece Central et Euubee, Peloponese et Iles Ioniennes.) (Text in French and Greek) 1951. decennial. price varies. National Statistical Service of Greece, Statistical Information and Publications Division, 14-16 Lycourgou St., 10166 Athens, Greece. TEL 3244-748. FAX 3222205. TELEX 216734 ESYE GR.

312   US
RHODE ISLAND. DEPARTMENT OF HEALTH. VITAL STATISTICS. a. free. Department of Health, 101 Health Bldg., Three Capitol Hill, Providence, RI 02908. TEL 401-277-2812. **Indexed:** SRI.

312 330   IT   ISSN 0035-6832
HB3599
RIVISTA ITALIANA DI ECONOMIA DEMOGRAFIA E STATISTICA. 1947. 4/yr. L.30000. Societa Italiana di Economia Demografia e Statistica, Casella Postale 12003, 00136 Rome-Belsito, Italy. Dir. Giovanni Somogyi. bk.rev.; bibl.; circ. 1,000.

325.2 910.09   XK
ST. LUCIA. STATISTICAL DEPARTMENT. ANNUAL MIGRATION AND TOURISM STATISTICS. 1980. a. EC$6. Statistical Department, New Government Bldg., 2nd Fl., Castries, St. Lucia, W.I. TEL 809-45-22697. FAX 809-45-31648. TELEX 6394 FORAFF. Ed. Bryan Boxill.

325.2   XK
ST. LUCIA. STATISTICAL DEPARTMENT. QUARTERLY MIGRATION & TOURISM STATISTICS. 1980. q. EC$6 per no. Statistical Department, New Government Bldg., 2nd Fl., Castries, St. Lucia, W.I. TEL 809-45-22697. FAX 809-92-31648. TELEX 6394 FORAFF. Ed. Bryan Boxill.

312   XK
ST. LUCIA. STATISTICAL DEPARTMENT. VITAL STATISTICS REPORT. 1984. a. EC$15. Statistical Department, New Government Bldg., 2nd Fl., Castries, St. Lucia, W.I. TEL 809-45-22697. FAX 809-45-31648. TELEX 6394 FORAFF. Ed. Bryan Boxill.

312   SW   ISSN 1100-6722
SALARIES OF SALARIED EMPLOYEES (YEAR). 1986. a. SEK 40. Svenska Arbetsgivarefoereningen - Swedish Employers' Confederation, S-103 30 Stockholm, Sweden. TEL 8-7626000. FAX 8-762-6290. Ed. Kjell Frykhammar. circ. 1,500.

312   UK   ISSN 0080-7869
SCOTLAND. REGISTRAR GENERAL. ANNUAL REPORT. 1855. a. price varies. H.M.S.O., P.O. Box 276, London SW8 5DT, England. (reprint service avail. from UMI)

016 312   NE   ISSN 0167-4757
Z7164.D3
SELECTED ANNOTATED BIBLIOGRAPHY OF POPULATION STUDIES IN THE NETHERLANDS. (Text in English) 1975. a. fl.6.50 in the Netherlands; elsewhere free. Nederlands Interdisciplinair Demografisch Instituut - Netherlands Interdisciplinary Demographic Institute, Lange Houtstraat 19, 2511 CV The Hague, Netherlands. TEL 070-3565200. FAX 070-3647187. TELEX 31138 NIDI NL. (Co-sponsor: Netherlands Demographic Society) Ed. T.J. Augenbroe-Siebenga. circ. 750. **Indexed:** Popul.Ind.
Supersedes (1970-1973): Bibliografie van in Nederland Verschenen Demografische Studies.

310   CN   ISSN 1188-3642
HA39.C23
SELECTED VITAL STATISTICS AND HEALTH STATISTICS INDICATORS. ANNUAL REPORT. 1944. a. Can.$6.95. Ministry of Health, Division of Vital Statistics, 818 Fort St., Victoria, B.C. V8W 1H8, Canada. TEL 604-387-4832. FAX 604-387-5708. (Dist. by: Crown Publications Inc., 546 Yates St., Victoria, B.C. V8W 1K8, Canada. TEL 604-386-4636) Ed. R.J. Danderfer. circ. 700.
Formerly (until 1990): Vital Statistics of the Province of British Columbia (ISSN 0702-9446)
Description: Presents comprehensive information pertaining to the births, deaths and marriages of British Columbians.

319   SE
SEYCHELLES. PRESIDENT'S OFFICE. STATISTICS DIVISION. CENSUS. irreg., latest 1977. Rs.80. President's Office, Department of Finance, Statistics Division, Box 206, Mahe, Seychelles.

312 310   SE
SEYCHELLES. PRESIDENT'S OFFICE. STATISTICS DIVISION. POPULATION AND VITAL STATISTICS. 1982. s-a. Rs.5. President's Office, Department of Finance, Statistics Division, Box 206, Mahe, Seychelles.

312   SA
SOUTH AFRICA. CENTRAL STATISTICAL SERVICE. BIRTHS - WHITES, COLOUREDS AND ASIANS. (Report No. 03-05-01) a., latest 1988. Central Statistical Service, Private Bag X44, Pretoria 0001, South Africa. TEL 012-310-8911. FAX 012-3108500. (Orders to: Government Printing Works, Private Bag X85, Pretoria 0001, South Africa)
Former titles: South Africa. Central Statistical Service. Report on Births: White, Coloured and Asian; South Africa. Department of Statistics. Report on Births: Whites, Coloureds, Asians; South Africa. Department of Statistics. Report on Births.

312 316   SA
SOUTH AFRICA. CENTRAL STATISTICAL SERVICE. DEATHS OF BLACKS. (Text in Afrikaans, English) a., latest 1988. Central Statistical Service, Private Bag X44, Pretoria 0001, South Africa. TEL 012-310-8911. FAX 012-3108500. stat.
Formerly: South Africa. Department of Statistics. Report on Bantu Deaths in Selected Magisterial Districts - Verslag oor Bantoesterfgevalle in Uitgesoekte Landdrosdistrikte.

312.5   SA
SOUTH AFRICA. CENTRAL STATISTICAL SERVICE. REPORT ON MARRIAGES AND DIVORCES: SOUTH AFRICA. (Report No. 03-07) 1972. a., latest 1986. Central Statistical Service, Private Bag X44, Pretoria 0001, South Africa. TEL 012-310-8911. FAX 012-322-6325. (Orders to: Government Printer, Bosman St., Private Bag X85, Pretoria 0001, South Africa)
Formerly: South Africa. Department of Statistics. Report on Marriages and Divorces: South Africa.

301.32 916.804   SA
SOUTH AFRICA. CENTRAL STATISTICAL SERVICE. TOURISM AND MIGRATION. (Report No. 03-51-01) a., latest 1988. Central Statistical Service, Private Bag X44, Pretoria 0001, South Africa. TEL 012-310-8911. FAX 012-3108500. (Orders to: Government Printing Works, Private Bag X85, Pretoria 0001, South Africa)
Formerly: South Africa. Department of Statistics. Tourism and Migration.

312   US   ISSN 0094-6338
HA621
SOUTH CAROLINA VITAL AND MORBIDITY STATISTICS. 1972. a. Department of Health and Environmental Control, Office of Vital Records and Public Health Statistics, 2600 Bull St., Columbia, SC 29201. TEL 803-734-4860. FAX 803-734-5131. circ. 650. (also avail. in microfiche) **Indexed:** SRI.

STATECO. see *BUSINESS AND ECONOMICS — Abstracting, Bibliographies, Statistics*

317 312   JM
STATISTICAL INSTITUTE OF JAMAICA. DEMOGRAPHIC STATISTICS. 1971. a. Jam.$18. Statistical Institute of Jamaica, 9 Swallowfield Rd., Kingston 5, Jamaica, W.I. stat. (back issues avail.)
Formerly: Jamaica. Department of Statistics. Demographic Statistics.

POPULATION STUDIES — ABSTRACTING, BIBLIOGRAPHIES, STATISTICS

312 630   IO   ISSN 0126-2912
HA1811
STATISTICAL YEAR BOOK OF INDONESIA. (Text in English, Indonesian) 1976. a. Rps.25000($15.50) Central Bureau of Statistics - Biro Pusat Statistik, Jalan Dr. Sutomo No. 8, Box 3, Jakarta Pusat, Indonesia. TEL 21-372808. circ. 1,500.

312   GW
STATISTISCHER JAHRESBERICHT DER STADT MUENSTER. 1948. a. DM.20. Statistischer Amt, Postfach 5909, D-4400 Muenster, Germany. TEL 0251-492-2150.

324.6   II
▼**STUDIES IN PSEPHOLOGY.** 1990. 3/yr. Rs.550($200) K.K. Roy (Private) Ltd., 55 Gariahat Road, P.O. Box 10210, Calcutta 700 019, India. Ed. K.K. Roy. adv.; abstr.; bibl.; index; circ. 2,100.
Description: Provides an international forum for all psephologists to discuss and analyze elections and patterns of voting behavior in their respective areas of interest.

315 312   TH   ISSN 0858-0391
SURVEY OF MIGRATION IN BANGKOK METROPOLIS. (Text in English and Thai) 1974. irreg. National Statistical Office, Statistical Information Division, Larn Luang Rd., Bangkok 10100, Thailand. FAX 2813814. charts; stat.
Description: Reports on a survey concerning migration to the Bangkok Metropolis.

312   SW   ISSN 0082-0156
SWEDEN. STATISTISKA CENTRALBYRAAN. BEFOLKNINGSFOERAENDRINGAR. (In 3 parts: Part 1 (ISSN 0347-6707); Part 2 (ISSN 0347-6715); Part 3 (ISSN 0347-6723)) (Text in Swedish; summaries in English) 1911. a. SEK 620 for 3 vols. Publishing Unit, S-701 89 Oerebro, Sweden. circ. 1,600.

312   SW
SWEDEN. STATISTISKA CENTRALBYRAAN. FOLKMAENGD. (In 3 parts: Part 1-2 (ISSN 0347-6677); Part 3 (ISSN 0347-6693)) (Text in English; summaries in English) 1910. a. SEK 330 for 2 vols. Statistiska Centralbyraan, Publishing Unit, S-701 89 Oerebro, Sweden. circ. 2,700.

312   SW   ISSN 0082-0245
HB2077
SWEDEN. STATISTISKA CENTRALBYRAAN. STATISTISKA MEDDELANDEN. SUBGROUP BE (POPULATION & LIVING CONDITIONS). (Text in Swedish; table heads and summaries in English) 1963 N.S. irreg. SEK 500. Statistiska Centralbyraan, Publishing Unit, S-701 89 Oerebro, Sweden. circ. 1,700. **Indexed:** Popul.Ind.

312.5   SZ
SWITZERLAND. BUNDESAMT FUER STATISTIK. BILANZ DER WOHNBEVOELKERUNG IN DEN GEMEINDEN DER SCHWEIZ - BILAN DEMOGRAPHIQUE DES COMMUNES SUISSES. 1971. a. 36 Fr. Bundesamt fuer Statistik, Hallwylstr. 15, CH-3003 Berne, Switzerland. FAX 031-617856. TELEX 912871. stat.; circ. 750.
Formerly: Switzerland. Bundesamt fuer Statistik. Heiraten, Lebendgeborene und Gestorbene in den Gemeinden - Marriages, Naissances et Deces dans les Communes.

312 315   CH
TAIWAN DEMOGRAPHY QUARTERLY. (Text in Chinese, English) 1965. q. free to qualified personnel. Ministry of the Interior, Department of Population, Population, Statistics and Census Division, Taipei, Taiwan, Republic of China. Ed.Bd. charts; stat.
Formerly (until Jan. 1975): Taiwan Demography Monthly.

301.32   TZ
TANZANIA. BUREAU OF STATISTICS. MIGRATION STATISTICS. 1968. irreg. Bureau of Statistics, Box 796, Dar es Salaam, Tanzania. (Dist. by: Government Publications Agency, Box 1801, Dar es Salaam, Tanzania)

312   US   ISSN 0495-257X
HA651
TEXAS VITAL STATISTICS. 1973. a. Department of Health, Bureau of Vital Statistics, 1100 W. 49th St., Austin, TX 78756. TEL 512-458-7111. circ. 3,000. **Indexed:** SRI.

312 317.29   TR   ISSN 0564-2612
HA867
TRINIDAD AND TOBAGO. CENTRAL STATISTICAL OFFICE. CONTINUOUS SAMPLE SURVEY OF POPULATION. 1964. biennial. T.T.$3. Central Statistical Office, 23 Park St., P.O. Box 98, Port-of-Spain, Trinidad & Tobago, W.I. TEL 809-62-53705. (Dist. by: Government Printing Office, 110 Henry St., Port-of-Spain, Trinidad & Tobago, W.I.)

301.32   TR
TRINIDAD AND TOBAGO. CENTRAL STATISTICAL OFFICE. ESTIMATED INTERNAL MIGRATION. BULLETIN.. 1974. irreg. Central Statistical Office, 23 Park St., P.O. Box 98, Port-of-Spain, Trinidad & Tobago, W.I. TEL 809-62-53705. (Dist. by: Government Printing Office, 110 Henry St., Port-of-Spain, Trinidad & Tobago, W.I.)

312   TR   ISSN 0082-6553
HA867
TRINIDAD AND TOBAGO. CENTRAL STATISTICAL OFFICE. POPULATION AND VITAL STATISTICS; REPORT. 1953. a. T.T.$4. Central Statistical Office, 23 Park St., P.O. Box 98, Port-of-Spain, Trinidad & Tobago, W.I. TEL 809-62-53705. (Dist. by: Government Printer, 110 Henry St., Port-of-Spain, Trinidad & Tobago, W.I.)

314   UN   ISSN 0041-7416
UNITED NATIONS. POPULATION AND VITAL STATISTICS REPORT. 1949. q. $30. (United Nations, Department of International Economic and Social Affairs) United Nations Publications, Room DC2-0853, New York, NY 10017. TEL 212-963-9302. FAX 212-963-3489. **Indexed:** IIS.
Description: Provides latest census data, plus worldwide demographic statistics on birth and mortality.

312 016   US
U.S. BUREAU OF THE CENSUS. CENSUS CATALOG AND GUIDE. 1946. a. price varies. U.S. Bureau of the Census, Data User Services Division, Washington, DC 20233. TEL 301-763-4100. (Dist. by: Supt. of Documents, Washington, DC 20402) Ed. Gary M.Young. circ. 8,000. (also avail. in microfiche)
Formerly: U.S. Bureau of the Census. Bureau of the Census Catalog (ISSN 0007-618X)

312   US   ISSN 0082-9390
U.S. BUREAU OF THE CENSUS. CENSUS OF POPULATION. (Issued in several series) 1790. decennial. price varies. U.S. Bureau of the Census, Data User Services Division, Washington, DC 20233. TEL 301-763-4100. (Dist. by: Supt. of Documents, Washington, DC 20402)

U.S. NATIONAL CENTER FOR HEALTH STATISTICS. CATALOG OF PUBLICATIONS. see PUBLIC HEALTH AND SAFETY — Abstracting, Bibliographies, Statistics

312   US   ISSN 0364-0396
HA203
U.S. NATIONAL CENTER FOR HEALTH STATISTICS. MONTHLY VITAL STATISTICS REPORT. (Supplements accompany some numbers) 1952. m., no. 13 of each vol. is annual summary. free. U.S. National Center for Health Statistics, 6525 Belcrest Road, Hyattsville, MD 20782. TEL 301-436-8500. **Indexed:** Abstr.Health Care Manage.Stud., Abstr.Hyg., Curr.Lit.Fam.Plan., MEDOC, Nutr.Abstr., Popul.Ind., PROMT, Rehabil.Lit., Trop.Dis.Bull. Key Title: Monthly Vital Statistics Report.

U.S. NATIONAL CENTER FOR HEALTH STATISTICS. VITAL AND HEALTH STATISTICS. SERIES 1. PROGRAMS AND COLLECTION PROCEDURES. see PUBLIC HEALTH AND SAFETY — Abstracting, Bibliographies, Statistics

U.S. NATIONAL CENTER FOR HEALTH STATISTICS. VITAL AND HEALTH STATISTICS. SERIES 2. DATA EVALUATION AND METHODS RESEARCH. see PUBLIC HEALTH AND SAFETY — Abstracting, Bibliographies, Statistics

U.S. NATIONAL CENTER FOR HEALTH STATISTICS. VITAL AND HEALTH STATISTICS. SERIES 3. ANALYTICAL STUDIES. see PUBLIC HEALTH AND SAFETY — Abstracting, Bibliographies, Statistics

U.S. NATIONAL CENTER FOR HEALTH STATISTICS. VITAL AND HEALTH STATISTICS. SERIES 4. DOCUMENTS AND COMMITTEE REPORT. see PUBLIC HEALTH AND SAFETY — Abstracting, Bibliographies, Statistics

U.S. NATIONAL CENTER FOR HEALTH STATISTICS. VITAL AND HEALTH STATISTICS. SERIES 20. DATA ON MORTALITY. see PUBLIC HEALTH AND SAFETY — Abstracting, Bibliographies, Statistics

U.S. NATIONAL CENTER FOR HEALTH STATISTICS. VITAL AND HEALTH STATISTICS. SERIES 21. DATA ON NATALITY, MARRIAGE, AND DIVORCE. see PUBLIC HEALTH AND SAFETY — Abstracting, Bibliographies, Statistics

312   US
U.S. NATIONAL CENTER FOR HEALTH STATISTICS. VITAL AND HEALTH STATISTICS. SERIES 23: DATA FROM THE NATIONAL SURVEY OF FAMILY GROWTH. 1976. irreg., latest no.15. U.S. National Center for Health Statistics, 6525 Belcrest Road, Hyattsville, MD 20782. TEL 301-436-8500. **Indexed:** Popul.Ind.

314 312   IT
UNIVERSITA DEGLI STUDI DI PADOVA. FACOLTA DI SCIENZE STATISTICHE, DEMOGRAFICHE ED ATTUARIALI. SERIE ESTRATTI. 1969. irreg., no.204, 1980. (Universita degli Studi di Padova, Facolta di Scienze Statistiche, Demografiche ed Attuariali) C L E U P, Via G. Prati, 19, 35100 Padua, Italy. bibl.

314 312   IT
UNIVERSITA DEGLI STUDI DI PADOVA. FACOLTA DI SCIENZE STATISTICHE, DEMOGRAFICHE ED ATTUARIALI. SERIE PUBBLICAZIONI. 1971. irreg., no.16, 1981. (Universita degli Studi di Padova, Facolta di Scienze Statistiche, Demografiche ed Attuariali) C L E U P, Via G. Prati, 19, 35100 Padua, Italy.

312   UY
URUGUAY. DIRECCION GENERAL DE ESTADISTICA Y CENSOS. ESTADISTICAS VITALES. (Vol. from 1978 contains 1975 statistics) 1961-1974; N.S. 1978. irreg. Direccion General de Estadistica y Censos, Montevideo, Uruguay.

312.5   US
UTAH MARRIAGE AND DIVORCE ANNUAL REPORT. a. $10. Department of Health, Bureau of Vital Records and Health Statistics, Box 16700, Salt Lake City, UT 84116-0700. TEL 801-538-6186. **Indexed:** SRI.

614   US   ISSN 0500-7720
HA664
UTAH VITAL STATISTICS ANNUAL REPORT. a. $10. Department of Health, Bureau of Vital Records and Health Statistics, Box 16700, Salt Lake City, UT 84116-0700. TEL 801-538-6186. stat.

312   NN
VANUATU. STATISTICS OFFICE. OVERSEAS MIGRATION. (Text in English, French) 1972. a. $5. Statistics Office, Private Mail Bag 19, Port-Vila, Vanuatu. stat.; circ. 300. (processed)
Former titles: Vanuatu. National Planning and Statistics Office. Overseas Migration; Vanuatu. Bureau of Statistics. Overseas Migration.

312   NN
VANUATU. STATISTICS OFFICES. CENSUS OF POPULATION (YEAR). BASIC TABLES. (Text in English and French) 1972. irreg. $25. Statistics Office, Private Mail Bag 19, Port-Vila, Vanuatu. stat.; circ. 300.
Former titles: Vanuatu. National Planning and Statistics Office. Census of Population (Year). Base Tables; (until 1983): Vanuatu. Condominium Bureau of Statistics. Census of Population and Housing, Vila and Santo, Preliminary Results.

312   US   ISSN 0161-8695
HA375
VITAL STATISTICS OF IOWA. 1975. a. $5. Department of Public Health, Bureau of Vital Statistics, Des Moines, IA 50319. TEL 515-281-4945. Ed. Michael Dare. stat.; circ. 400. (also avail. in microfiche)
Formed by the merger of: Iowa Summary of Vital Statistics (ISSN 0090-5143) & Iowa Detailed Report of Vital Statistics (ISSN 0362-9473)

VITAL STATISTICS OF THE UNITED STATES. see PUBLIC HEALTH AND SAFETY — Abstracting, Bibliographies, Statistics

312　　　　　YU　ISSN 0084-4357
HA1631
YUGOSLAVIA. SAVAZNI ZAVOD ZA STATISTIKU. DEMOGRAFSKA STATISTIKA. 1956. a. 100 din.($11.11) Savezni Zavod za Statistiku, Kneza Milosa 20, Belgrade, Yugoslavia. TEL 681-999. circ. 600.
 Formerly: Yugoslavia. Savezni Zavod za Statistiku. Vitalna Statistika.

316 325　　　ZA　ISSN 0084-4543
ZAMBIA. CENTRAL STATISTICAL OFFICE. MIGRATION STATISTICS. Title varies: Zambia. Central Statistical Office. Migration Statistics: Immigrants and Visitors. 1965. a. $4. Central Statistical Office, P.O. Box 31908, Lusaka, Zambia. TEL 211-231.

316 312　　　ZA　ISSN 0084-456X
HA1977.R48
ZAMBIA. CENTRAL STATISTICAL OFFICE. VITAL STATISTICS. Variant title: Zambia. Central Statistical Office. Registered Births, Marriages and Deaths (Vital Statistics). 1965. a. $1. Central Statistical Office, P.O. Box 31908, Lusaka, Zambia. TEL 211-231.

ZIMBABWE. CENTRAL STATISTICAL OFFICE. MONTHLY MIGRATION AND TOURIST STATISTICS. see *TRAVEL AND TOURISM — Abstracting, Bibliographies, Statistics*

POSTAL AFFAIRS

see *Communications–Postal Affairs*

POULTRY AND LIVESTOCK

see *Agriculture–Poultry and Livestock*

PRINTING

760　　　　　US　ISSN 0275-9470
NC998.5.A1
A I G A GRAPHIC DESIGN U S A. 1980. a. $65. (American Institute of Graphic Arts) Watson-Guptill Publications, 1515 Broadway, New York, NY 10036. TEL 201-363-5679.
 Supersedes: A I G A Best Books Show; Communication Graphics; Covers; Insides.

760　　　　　US
A I G A JOURNAL OF GRAPHIC DESIGN. 1982. q. $20. American Institute of Graphic Arts, 1059 Third Ave., New York, NY 10021. TEL 212-752-0183. FAX 212-755-6749. Ed. Steven Heller. bk.rev.; bibl.; illus.; circ. 6,000. (tabloid format)
 Formerly: American Institute of Graphic Arts. Journal.
 Description: Focuses on criticism, professional practice, review, debate and the history of graphic design.

686.2　　　　US
A P H A LETTER. Variant title: A P H A Newsletter. 1974. bi-m. membership. American Printing History Association, Box 4922, Grand Central Sta., New York, NY 10163. Ed. Edward Colker. circ. 1,200.

686.2　　　　US
A T F NEWSLETTER. 1978. a. $2 (foreign $4). American Typecasting Fellowship, Box 263, Terra Alta, WV 26764. TEL 304-789-2455. Ed. Richard L. Hopkins. adv.; bk.rev.; circ. 400.
 Description: Articles on the preservation and promotion of hot-metal typecasting equipment and technology.

655 370　　　UK　ISSN 0308-6895
A T P A S PRINTING EDUCATION & TRAINING JOURNAL. 1952. 3/yr. £1. Association of Teachers of Printing and Allied Subjects, c/o Frank Chapple, Ed., 15 Sandy Lane, Westerham, Kent, England. adv.; bk.rev.; illus.; circ. 1,000.
 Formerly: A T P A S Bulletin (ISSN 0001-2769)

760　　　　　US
ABRACADABRA. 1988. a. $25 includes membership. (Alliance for Contemporary Book Arts) U S C Fine Arts Press, c/o U S C - R A N, 3716 S. Hope St., Los Angeles, CA 90007. TEL 213-743-3939. Ed. Gerald Lange. bk.rev.; circ. 500.
 Description: Provides a medium for studying and promoting the arts of the book, including printing, typography, papermaking, calligraphy, bookbinding, and illustration.

760　　　　　DK
AKTUEL GRAFISK INFORMATION. Swedish edition: Aktuell Grafisk Information. 1970. m. DKK 395 (Swedish ed. DKK 345). Forlaget Aktuel Viden A-S, Fuglsevej 54, DK-4960 Holeby, Denmark. TEL 53907055. FAX 45-53-90-64-77. Eds. Mogens Staffe (Danish ed.); Eric Saxell (Swedish ed.). adv.; circ. 22,436 (11,291 Danish ed.; 10,500 Swedish ed.).

686.2　　　　US　ISSN 0002-8916
TP949　　　　　CODEN: AMIKAK
AMERICAN INKMAKER;* for manufacturers of printing inks and related graphic arts specialty colors. 1923. m. $18. MacNair Publications, 445 Broadhollow RD., Melville, NY 11747-3601. Ed. Francine Del Vescoro. adv.; bk.rev.; charts; illus.; pat.; tr.lit.; tr.mk.; index; circ. 4,000. **Indexed:** Abstr.Bull.Inst.Pap.Chem., Chem.Abstr., Graph.Arts Lit.Abstr., Key to Econ.Sci., PROMT, World Surf.Coat. —BLDSC shelfmark: 0820.500000.

655　　　　　US　ISSN 0744-6616
Z119
AMERICAN PRINTER (CHICAGO, 1982). 1883. m. $50. Maclean Hunter Publishing Company, 29 N. Wacker Dr., Chicago, IL 60606. TEL 312-726-2802. FAX 312-726-2574. TELEX 270258 EXP. Ed. Jill Roth. adv.; bk.rev.; illus.; tr.lit.; circ. 94,839 (controlled). (also avail. in microfilm from UMI) **Indexed:** A.S.& T.Ind., ABI Inform., B.P.I., Bus.Ind., Chem.Abstr., Graph.Arts Lit.Abstr., Photo.Abstr., Print.Abstr., PROMT, PSI, Tr.& Indus.Ind.
 Former titles (until 1982): American Printer and Lithographer (ISSN 0192-9933); (until 1979): Inland Printer - American Lithographer (ISSN 0020-1502)
 Description: Covers the printing and lithographic industry including its allied manufacturing and service segments.

686.2　　　　IT　ISSN 0003-5165
ANNUNCIATORE POLIGRAFICO; periodico mensile d'informazione tecnica per i settori poligrafico cartotecnico e legatoria. 1954. m. L.75000 (foreign L.125000). Gruppo Editoriale Fabbri S.p.A., Divisione Periodici, Via Mecenate, 91, 20138 Milan, Italy. TEL 02 50951. FAX 02-55400388. Ed. Enrico Parisini. adv.; charts; illus.; circ. 4,876. (back issues avail.) **Indexed:** Graph.Arts Lit.Abstr.

760　　　　　AG　ISSN 0004-105X
ARGENTINA GRAFICA. 1935. 4/yr. $7 per no. to non-members. Camara de Industriales Graficos de la Argentina, Av. Belgrano 4299, 1210 Buenos Aires, Argentina. Ed. Alberto Mahmud. adv.; charts; illus.; tr.lit.; circ. 2,500.

686.2 331　　　US
AROUND THE BARGAINING LOOP. m. $250 to non-members; members $125. Graphic Arts Employers of America, 100 Daingerfield Rd., Alexandria, VA 22314. TEL 703-841-8150. FAX 703-841-8178. Ed. William Solomon. circ. 325.
 Description: Contract language from negotiated collective bargaining agreements.

760　　　　　MX　ISSN 0004-3508
ARTES GRAFICAS EN MEXICO.* 1949. bi-m. Mex.$40($8) Sociedad de Industriales de las Artes Graficas, Dr Arce 88, Mexico City, Mexico. Dir. Pablo Martinez Malpica. adv.

ARTIKEL 5; das Wirtschaftsmagazin der Printmedien. see *PUBLISHING AND BOOK TRADE*

686.2　　　　US
ASCENDERS. q. Autologic Incorporated, 1050 Rancho Conejo Blvd., Newbury Park, CA 91320. TEL 805-498-9611. Ed. Peter Jedrzejek.

686.2　　　　HK　ISSN 1012-8662
ASIAN PRINTING; the magazine for the graphic arts industry. (Text in Chinese and English) 1989. m. HK.$260($69) Travel & Trade Publishing (Asia) Ltd., 16-F, Capitol Centre, 5-19 Jardine's Bazaar, Causeway Bay, Hong Kong. TEL 890-3067. FAX 895-2378. TELEX 76591-TPAL-HX. Ed. Chris Hunter. circ. 5,358.
 Description: For those who buy and sell printing in Asia and between Asia and the rest of the world.

686.2 380.1　　HK　ISSN 0258-218X
ASIAN PRINTING DIRECTORY. a. $25. Travel & Trade Publishing (Asia) Ltd., 16-F, Capitol Centre, 5-19 Jardine's Bazaar, Causeway Bay, Hong Kong. TEL 890-3067. FAX 895-2375. TELEX 76591-TPAL-HX. Ed. Chris Hunter.
 Description: Gives expanded detail on major suppliers of export quality print products in 10 Asian countries.

760　　　　　GW
ASSOCIATION EUROPEENNE DES GRAVEURS ET DES FLEXOGRAPHES. BULLETIN PROFESSIONAL. 3/yr. Association Europeene des Graveurs et des Flexographes, Biebricher Allee 79, Postfach 1869, 6200 Wiesbaden, Germany. TEL 0611-803115. FAX 0611-803113. TELEX 4186888.

763　　　　　AT　ISSN 0159-2319
AUSTRALIAN LITHOGRAPHER, PRINTER, AND PACKAGER. 1964. bi-m. Aus.$35. (Australian Institute of Packaging) Prestige Publishing Pty. Ltd., G.P.O. Box 5158, Sydney, N.S.W. 2001, Australia. Ed. F. Stern. adv.; bk.rev.; index; circ. 8,936. (reprint service avail.) **Indexed:** Graph.Arts Abstr., Graph.Arts Lit.Abstr., Print.Abstr.
 Formerly: Australian Lithographer (ISSN 0004-9700); Incorporates: Printer and Packager.

686.2　　　　AT　ISSN 1033-1522
AUSTRALIAN PRINTER MAGAZINE. 1950. m. Aus.$70. Calmor & Associates Pty. Ltd., P.O. Box 1316, North Sydney, N.S.W. 2059, Australia. TEL 02-922-6133. FAX 02-922-4734. Ed. Patrick Howard. adv.; bk.rev.; illus.; index; circ. 9,746. **Indexed:** C.I.S. Abstr., Graph.Arts Lit.Abstr., Print.Abstr.
 —BLDSC shelfmark: 1818.315000.
 Formerly: Australasian Printer Magazine (ISSN 0004-8453)
 Description: Journal of graphic industry management and production. For printers, trade shops, typesetters, art studios, publishers and packaging companies.

686.2　　　　US
BEFORE & AFTER. bi-m. PageLab, Inc., 331 J St., No.150, Sacramento, CA 95814-2214. TEL 916-443-4890. FAX 916-443-7431. Ed. Gaye McWade.

BIBLIOGRAPHY NEWSLETTER. see *LIBRARY AND INFORMATION SCIENCES*

BIBLIOPHILIA. see *HISTORY — History Of Europe*

BIBLIOTHECA HUNGARICA ANTIQUA. see *PUBLISHING AND BOOK TRADE*

BOARD REPORT FOR GRAPHIC ARTISTS. see *ADVERTISING AND PUBLIC RELATIONS*

686.2　　　　DK
BOGTRYKKERNE - DISTRIKTSBLADENE. m. Dansk Bogtrykker- og Presseforening, City Vest, P.O. Box 1559, DK-8220 Brabrand, Denmark. adv.; circ. 1,600.

BOGVENNEN. see *PUBLISHING AND BOOK TRADE*

760　　　　　FR
BON A TIRER. 1978. m. Presse-Edition-Communication, 28 rue du Chateau Landon, 75010 Paris, France. Ed. Michele Goldstein.
 Description: Focuses on the graphic arts.

686.2　　　　US　ISSN 0739-7895
Z116.A3
BOOK ARTS REVIEW. 1982. q. $35. Center for Book Arts, 626 Broadway, New York, NY 10012. TEL 212-460-9768. adv.; bk.rev.; illus.; circ. 1,000. (tabloid format; back issues avail.)

PRINTING

686.2 070.172   AT
BORDER WATCH. 1861. 4/w. Aus.$75. Border Watch Pty. Ltd., P.O. Box 309, Mount Gambler, S.A. 5290, Australia. TEL (087) 25 73 33. Ed. Gary Trotter. adv.; circ. 9,101.

686.2   AT   ISSN 0811-3971
BRANDYWINE DOCUMENTS ON THE HISTORY OF BOOKS & PRINTING. (Text in Dutch, English, French and Russian) 1980. irreg. (1-2/yr.). price varies. Brandywine Press & Archive, 20 Murray Rd., Beecroft, N.S.W. 2119, Australia. TEL (02)863627. Ed. J.P. Wegner. (back issues avail.)
  Formerly: Brandywine Documents on Printing and Printing History.

686.2   AT   ISSN 0157-5619
BRANDYWINE KEEPSAKE. (Text in English, German and Russian) 1979. a. price varies. Brandywine Press & Archive, 20 Murray Rd., Beecroft, N.S.W. 2119, Australia. TEL (02)86-3627. (back issues avail.)

BRITAIN'S TOP 300 PRINTERS. see *BUSINESS AND ECONOMICS — Trade And Industrial Directories*

760   UK
BRITISH DESIGN & ART DIRECTION ANNUAL. 1962. a. £56. (Designers & Art Directors Association) Polygon Editions S.A.R.L., 12 Carlton House Terrace, London SW1Y 5AH, England. Ed. Edward Booth-Clibborn. **Indexed:** Mgmt.& Market.Abstr.
  Formerly: Design and Art Direction Annual.

686.2   UK   ISSN 0007-1684
Z119
BRITISH PRINTER; leading technical journal of the printing industry. 1888. m. £75. Maclean Hunter Ltd., Maclean Hunter House, Chalk Lane, Cockfosters Rd., Barnet, Herts EN4 OBU, England. TEL 081-975-9759. FAX 081-440-1796. TELEX 299072 MACHUN G. Ed. Sian Griffiths. adv.; bk.rev.; illus.; index; circ. 13,960. **Indexed:** Abstr.Bull.Inst.Pap.Chem., Br.Tech.Ind., Graph.Arts Lit.Abstr., Print.Abstr.
  —BLDSC shelfmark: 2340.000000.

686.2   SZ   ISSN 0007-5736
BULLETIN TECHNIQUE; industrie graphique et technique de communication. 1966. 5/yr. 40 Fr. (Schweizerische Lithografenbund) Conzett & Huber AG, Baslerstr. 30, Postfach, 8048 Zurich, Switzerland. (Co-sponsor: Verband der Schweizer Druckindustrie) Ed.Bd. adv.; bk.rev.; bibl.; charts; illus.; index. **Indexed:** Chem.Abstr.

686.2   FR   ISSN 0572-7529
BUREAU INTERNATIONAL DES SOCIETES GERANT LES DROITS D'ENREGISTREMENT ET DE REPRODUCTION MECANIQUE. BULLETIN. 1959. irreg. International Bureau of the Societies Administering the Rights of Mechanical Recording and Reproduction, 56, Av. Kleber, 75116 Paris, France. FAX 47-55-11-53. TELEX 643124F.

655   US
BUSINESS DOCUMENTS. 4/yr. $36 (foreign $56). North American Publishing Co., 401 N. Broad St., Philadelphia, PA 19108. TEL 215-238-5300. FAX 215-238-5457. Ed. William Drennan. circ. 15,000.
  Former titles: Forms and Label Purchasing; Forms and Systems Professional; Incorporates: Forms Professional.
  Description: Serves the needs and interests of business document managers, buyers and users. Covers forms and systems design, application and management.

655   US
BUSINESS FORMS, LABELS AND SYSTEMS. 1963. s-m. $49 (foreign $89). North American Publishing Co., 401 N. Broad St., Philadelphia, PA 19108. TEL 215-238-5300. FAX 215-238-5457. Ed. William Drennan. adv.; bk.rev.; tr.lit. (also avail. in microform from UMI; reprint service avail. from UMI) **Indexed:** Graph.Arts Lit.Abstr., Print.Abstr., Sci.Abstr.
  Former titles: Business Forms and Systems; Business Forms Reporter (ISSN 0007-6767)
  Description: Reports on trends, product developments, design techniques and new information on marketing and manufacturing.

686.2 338   US
BUSINESS INDICATOR REPORT. 1979. q. $150. National Association of Printers and Lithographers, 780 Palisade Ave., Teaneck, NJ 07666. TEL 201-342-0707. Ed. Andrew D. Paparozzi. circ. 4,000. (looseleaf format; back issues avail.)
  Formerly: Quarterly Printing Industry Business Indicator Report.

CAMBRIDGE AUTHORS' AND PUBLISHERS' GUIDES. see *PUBLISHING AND BOOK TRADE*

686.2   CN   ISSN 0849-0767
CANADIAN PRINTER. (Directory number avail.) 1892. m. Can.$45 (foreign Can.$90) includes Printing Product Guide. Maclean-Hunter Ltd., Business Publication Division, Maclean-Hunter Bldg., 777 Bay St., Toronto, Ont. M5W 1A7, Canada. TEL 416-596-5884. FAX 416-596-3189. Ed. Martti Kangas. adv.; bk.rev.; abstr.; charts; illus.; stat.; tr.lit.; index; circ. 7,547. (also avail. in microform from UMI) **Indexed:** Abstr.Bull.Inst.Pap.Chem., Can.B.P.I., Graph.Arts Lit.Abstr., Print.Abstr.
  Formerly (until 1989): Canadian Printer and Publisher (ISSN 0008-4816)
  Description: Deals with shifting markets and economic conditions, changing technology and evolving management techniques.

686.2   FR   ISSN 0008-6126
Z119
CARACTERE; magazine des professionnels de l'imprime. 1949. 24/yr. 530 F. (foreign 734 F.)(effective Jan. 1992). Groupe Usine Nouvelle, 1 cite Bergere, 75009 Paris, France. TEL 48-24-23-24. FAX 40-22-02-70. TELEX 650702. Eds. Caroline Aubry, Yvon Guemard. adv.; bk.rev.; abstr.; bibl.; charts; illus.; index; circ. 8,000. **Indexed:** Photo.Abstr., Print.Abstr.

CATALOGO DELLA GRAFICA ITALIANA. see *ART*

760   US
CHICAGO TALENT SOURCEBOOK (NO.). 1980. a. $50. Alexander Communications, Inc., 212 W. Superior, Ste. 203, Chicago, IL 60610. TEL 312-944-5115. FAX 312-944-7865. circ. 12,000 (controlled).
  Description: For Chicago's graphic arts community. More than 60 talent and supplier categories, ranging from photographers to typographers, are featured along with business service categories and city information.

COLOR PUBLISHING. see *PUBLISHING AND BOOK TRADE*

COLOUR. see *PUBLISHING AND BOOK TRADE*

686.2   SA
COMMERCIAL PRINTING. fortn. Lord Doddinghurst Publications, 170 Hendrick Verwoerd Dr., Randburg, Box 70352, Bryanston, Johannesburg, South Africa. adv.

COMMUNICATION ARTS. see *ADVERTISING AND PUBLIC RELATIONS*

COMMUNICATIONS CONCEPTS; the best ideas in print for professional communicators. see *ADVERTISING AND PUBLIC RELATIONS*

CONNOISSEURS GUIDE TO CALIFORNIA WINE. see *BEVERAGES*

CONTEMPORARY GRAPHIC ARTISTS; a biographical, bibliographical, and critical guide to current illustrators, animators, cartoonists, designers, and other graphic artists. see *BIOGRAPHY*

686.2   US
COPY MAGAZINE. 1981. bi-m. $25. Coast Publishing, Inc., 1680 S.W. Bayshore Blvd., Port St. Lucie, FL 34984-3598. TEL 407-879-6666. FAX 407-879-7388. (Co-publisher: Quion Communications, Inc.) Ed. Dan Witte. adv.; circ. 35,234.

686.2   US
CRAFTSMEN REVIEW. q. I A P H C, Inc., 7042 Brooklyn Blvd., Minneapolis, MN 55429-1370. TEL 612-560-1620. FAX 612-560-1350. Ed. Cheryl Sunness. circ. 12,000.

760   DK   ISSN 0107-7112
DANSK GRAFIA. Short title: Grafia. 1975. w. (48/yr.). DKK 200. Dansk Typograf-Forbund, Grafisk Kartel, Lygten 16, 2400 Copenhagen NV, Denmark. FAX 01-822422. Ed. Kjeld Jacobsen. adv.; bk.rev.; illus.; circ. 15,000.

686.2   US
DEALER COMMUNICATOR; a nationwide link between dealers and their suppliers in the graphics industry. 1980. m. $24. Fichera Publications, 777 S. State Rd. 7, Margate, FL 33068. TEL 800-327-8999. FAX 305-971-4362. adv.; bk.rev.; circ. 9,110. (tabloid format)
  Description: Presents news about products and graphic arts dealers.

760   NE   ISSN 0923-9790
DELINEAVIT ET SCULPSIT. 1989. irreg. (2-3/yr.). $37. Redactiesecretatiaat, c/o Print Room of the University, Rapenburg 65, NL 2311 GJ Leiden, Netherlands.
  Description: Deals with the graphic arts of the Netherlands.

DIE DEUTSCHE SCHRIFT; Zeitschrift zur Foerderung von Gotisch, Schwabacher und Fraktur. see *ART*

686.2   GW   ISSN 0012-1096
DEUTSCHER DRUCKER. 1965. 42/yr. DM.159.60 (foreign DM.183.60). Deutscher Drucker Verlagsgesellschaft mbH und Co. KG, Riedstr. 25, Postfach 4124, 7302 Ostfildern 1, Germany. TEL 0711-44817-0. FAX 0711-442099. TELEX 7111490. Ed. Theodor J. Anton. adv.; bk.rev.; abstr.; bibl.; charts; illus.; stat.; cum.index; circ. 13,500. **Indexed:** Graph.Arts Lit.Abstr., Print.Abstr.

686.2   GW
DRUCK - A B C. bi-m. Zentral-Fachausschuss fuer die Druckindustrie, Kurfuerstenanlage 69, D-6900 Heidelberg 1, Germany.

686.2   GW
DRUCK INTERN. m. Verband der Druckindustrie Westen-Lippe e.V., Schwanenwall 23, Postfach 822, D-4600 Dortmund 1, Germany. TEL 0231-579765. TELEX 22264.

686.2   GW   ISSN 0012-6462
Z119
DRUCK-PRINT. (Text in English and German) 1863. m. DM.121.80 (foreign DM.184.20). P. Keppler Verlag GmbH und Co. KG, Industriestr. 2, 6056 Heusenstamm, Germany. TEL 06104-6060. FAX 06104-606144. Ed. H. Schloesser. adv.; bk.rev.; abstr.; charts; illus.; stat.; circ. 9,250. **Indexed:** Excerp.Med., Graph.Arts Lit.Abstr.

686.2   GW
DRUCK-SACHEN; Informationsdienst der deutschen Druckindustrie. a. Bundesverband Druck E.V., Biebricher Allee 79, 6200 Wiesbaden, Germany. FAX 0611-803113. Ed. Peter Klemm.

686.2   SZ   ISSN 0046-0737
DRUCKINDUSTRIE. 1971. 22/yr. 71 Fr. (foreign 90 Fr.). Zollikofer AG, Fuerstenlandstr. 122, CH-9001 St. Gallen, Switzerland. TEL 071-297777. FAX 071257487. Ed. Franz Wick. adv.; charts; illus.; circ. 13,000. **Indexed:** Print.Abstr.
  —BLDSC shelfmark: 3627.670000.
  Description: Articles by Swiss members of the Euro Graphic Press Association.

686.2   GW   ISSN 0012-6500
Z119
DER DRUCKSPIEGEL; Zeitschrift fuer Deutsche und internationale Drucktechnik. 1946. m. DM.108. Druckspiegel Verlagsgesellschaft mbH & Co., Borsigstr. 1-3, 6056 Heusenstamm, Germany. TEL 06104-6060. FAX 06104-606444. TELEX 410131. Ed.Bd. adv.; bk.rev.; charts; illus.; index; circ. 12,795. **Indexed:** Graph.Arts Lit.Abstr., Print.Abstr.

686.2   GW   ISSN 0012-6519
Z119
DRUCKWELT; Journal der Unternehmer und Fuehrungskraefte. 1951. s-m. DM.166. Schluetersche Verlagsanstalt GmbH und Co., Georgswall 4, Postfach 5440, 3000 Hannover 1, Germany. TEL 0511-1236-0. Eds. K. Helms, F. Krakowitzky. adv.; bk.rev.; bibl.; charts; illus.; index; circ. 8,022. **Indexed:** Print.Abstr., PROMT.
  —BLDSC shelfmark: 3627.850000.
  Formerly: Graphische Woche.

PRINTING

686.2 UK
DUNOON OBSERVER & ARGYLLSHIRE STANDARD. 1871. w. £28.10 (foreign £39.50). E. & R. Inglis, 219 Argyll Street, Dunoon, Argyll PA23 7QT, Scotland. FAX 3458. Ed. Bill Millarichael. circ. 6,500.

686.2 CN
E & B GUIDE. (Estimators & Buyers') 1984. a. $18. North Island South Ltd., 1606 Sedlescomb Dr., Unit 8, Mississauga, Ont. L4X 1M6, Canada. TEL 416-625-7070. FAX 416-625-4856. adv.

686.2 070.5 US
ELECTRONIC PRINTING SYSTEMS: PROFESSIONAL ELECTRONIC PUBLISHING CONFERENCE PROCEEDINGS. (In 2 vols.) 1984. a. $95 per vol. Dunn Technology, Inc., 1855 E. Vista Way, No.1, Vista, CA 92084. FAX 619-758-5401. Ed. Patrice M. Dunn. (back issues avail.)
  Formerly: Electronic Printing Systems: Directions in Digital Imaging. Conference Proceedings.
  Description: Focus on the markets and technology for professional electronic publishing.

686.2 331 US
EMPLOYER RESOURCES NEWSLETTER. bi-m. $350 to non-members; members $175. Graphic Arts Employers of America, 100 Daingerfield Rd., Alexandria, VA 22314. TEL 703-841-8150. FAX 703-841-8178. Ed. William Solomon. circ. 325.
  Description: Discusses current events in industrial relations.

760 SZ
EUROPRO. CONGRESS SUMMARIES. a. Europro, Schosshaldenstr. 20, CH-3000 Bern 32, Switzerland. TEL 031-431511.
  Formerly: Union Internationales des Industries Graphiques de Reproduction. Congress Summaries.

760 BE
F E B E L G R A TIJDSCHRIFT. bi-w. Federatie van de Belgische Industrie, Dambruggestraat 60, Postbus 1, D-2008 Antwerpen, Belgium. TEL 2317118.

760 NE
F N V MAGAZINE (AMSTERDAM). 1955. fortn. fl.225. Box 9354, 1006 AJ Amsterdam, Netherlands. TEL 020-6143105. FAX 020-6151091. Ed. R.U. Tilborg. adv.; bk.rev.; film rev.; charts; illus.; circ. 48,500 (controlled).
  Former titles: Drukwerk; Grafia; Druk en Papier (ISSN 0017-2871)

686.2 GW ISSN 0014-6293
FACHBERATER; Fachtechnische Beratungen und Anregungen fuer das Gesamtgebiet des Offsetdruckes. 1948. 4/yr. free. Hanns Eggen GmbH und Co. KG, Postfach 1746, 3000 Hannover, Germany. index; circ. 7,000. (processed)

686.2 SZ
FACHHEFTE BULLETIN TECHNIQUE; grafische Industrie und Kommunikationstechnik. French edition: Bulletin Technique (ISSN 0007-5736) (Editions in French and German) 1954. 5/yr. 44 Fr. (Schweizerischer Lithographenbund) Conzett & Huber AG, Baslerstr. 30, Postfach, 8048 Zurich, Switzerland. TEL 01-522500. FAX 01-4912922. (Co-sponsor: Verband der Schweizer Druckindustrie) Ed.Bd. adv.; bk.rev.; bibl.; charts; illus.; index. Indexed: Abstr.Bull.Inst.Pap.Chem., Chem.Abstr., Print.Abstr.
  Formerly: Fachhefte fuer Chemigraphie, Lithographie und Tiefdruck (ISSN 0014-6374)

FACTOTUM. see *LIBRARY AND INFORMATION SCIENCES*

686.2 US ISSN 0361-3801
Z119
FINE PRINT; the review for the arts of the book. 1975. 4/yr. $45 membership. Pro Arte Libri, Box 193394, San Francisco, CA 94119. TEL 415-543-4455. Ed. Sandra Kirshenbaum. adv.; bk.rev.; circ. 3,500. Indexed: Artbibl., Artbibl.Mod., Bk.Rev.Ind. (1981-), Child.Bk.Rev.Ind. (1981-).
  —BLDSC shelfmark: 3927.760000.
  Description: Articles about type design, printing, typography, bookbinding, calligraphy and the history of the book. Descriptions and reviews of limited editions and artists' books.

686.2 US ISSN 1051-7324
FLEXO. 1976. m. $33. Foundation of Flexographic Technical Association, 900 Marconi Ave., Ronkonkoma, NY 11779-7212. TEL 516-737-6020. FAX 516-737-6813. TELEX 221213. Ed. Douglas Finlay. adv.; circ. 9,300. Indexed: Curr.Pack.Abstr., Graph.Arts Lit.Abstr., Print.Abstr.
  Formerly (until 1984): Flexographic Technical Journal (ISSN 0734-6980)

686.2 US ISSN 1051-6352
FLEXO ESPANOL. (Text in Spanish) 1986. q. $12. Foundation of Flexographic Technical Association, 900 Marconi Ave., Ronkonkoma, NY 11779-7212. TEL 516-737-6020. FAX 516-737-6813. TELEX 221213. Ed. Douglas Finlay. index; circ. 6,000. (back issues avail.)

760 US
FLORIDA CREATIVE DIRECTORY. a. $45. Alexander Communications, Inc., 212 W. Superior, Ste. 203, Chicago, IL 60610. TEL 312-944-5115. FAX 312-944-7865. circ. 6,000 (controlled).

686.2 GW
FOGRA-LITERATUR-PROFIL. 1975. irreg. (4-6/yr.). DM.420 to non-members; members DM.315. Deutsche Forschungsgesellschaft fuer Druck- und Reproduktionstechnik e.V. (FOGRA), Postfach 800469, Streitfeldstr. 19, 8000 Munich 80, Germany.

686.2 GW ISSN 0015-5322
FOGRA-LITERATURDIENST. 1955. m. DM.420 to non-members; members DM.315. Deutsche Forschungsgesellschaft fuer Druck- und Reproduktionstechnik e.V. (FOGRA), Streitfeldstr. 19, 8000 Munich 80, Germany. Ed. W. Probst. bk.rev.; circ. 550. Indexed: Graph.Arts Lit.Abstr., Print.Abstr.

686.2 GW ISSN 0015-5330
FOGRA-MITTEILUNGEN. 1953. q. network. Deutsche Forschungsgesellschaft fuer Druck- und Reproduktionstechnik e.V. (FOGRA), Streitfeldstr. 19, 8000 Munich 80, Germany. Ed. W. Probst. adv.; circ. 2,500. Indexed: Graph.Arts Lit.Abstr., Print.Abstr.
  —BLDSC shelfmark: 3964.350000.

686.2 608.7 GW
FOGRA-PATENTSCHAU. m. DM.640 to non-members; members DM.480. Deutsche Forschungsgesellschaft fuer Druck- und Reproduktionstechnik e.V. (F O G R A), Postfach 800469, Streitfeldstr. 19, 8000 Munich 80, Germany. pat.; stat.
  Formerly: Fogra-Patentkurzberichte.

686.2 US ISSN 0532-1700
FORM. 1963. m. $36 to non-members; members $24. National Business Forms Association, 433 E. Monroe Ave., Alexandria, VA 22301. TEL 703-836-6232. FAX 703-836-2241. Ed. Brad Holt. adv.; bk.rev.; illus.; index; circ. 10,000. Indexed: Graph.Arts Lit.Abstr.

FORMAT; Zeitschrift fuer verbale und visuelle Kommunikation. see *ART*

686.2 US
FORMSMFG. 1987. m. $62. International Business Forms Industries, Inc., 2111 Wilson Blvd., Ste. 350, Arlington, VA 22201-3008. TEL 703-841-9191. FAX 703-522-5750. TELEX 440172 IBFI UI. Ed. Judith Polas. adv.; circ. 3,297.
  Description: For manufacturers of business forms, labels, direct mail and information systems.

760 US
FOSSIL; historians of amateur journalism. 1904. q. $16. Fossils, Inc., 112 E. Burnett St., Stayton, OR 97383. FAX 503-769-4520. bk.rev.; circ. 200.

686.2 US
Z252.5.F6
FOUNDATION OF FLEXOGRAPHIC TECHNICAL ASSOCIATION. REPORT OF THE PROCEEDINGS: ANNUAL MEETING AND TECHNICAL FORUM. 1959. a. $26 to non-members. Foundation of Flexographic Technical Association, 900 Marconi Ave., Ronkonkoma, NY 11779-7212. TEL 516-737-6020. FAX 516-737-6813. TELEX 221213. illus.; circ. 1,500. Key Title: Report of the Proceedings. Annual Meeting and Technical Forum.
  Formerly: Flexographic Technical Association. Report of the Proceedings: Annual Meeting and Technical Forum (ISSN 0428-5670)

760 FR ISSN 0015-9565
FRANCE GRAPHIQUE. 1947. m. 600 F.($85) Edipresse, 16 rue Guillaume Tell, 75017 Paris, France. TEL 1-47 66 00 05. Ed. George Pecontal. adv.; bk.rev.; charts; illus.; index; circ. 5,000.

686.2 FR
FRANCE MECANOGRAPHIQUE. m. 80 F. Societe d'Organisation Professionnelle, 136, Cours Lafayette, 69-Lyon (3e), France. Ed. Bernadette Grua. adv.; circ. 2,000.

760 600 US
G A T F WORLD. 1989. bi-m. $90 to non-members. Graphic Arts Technical Foundation, 4615 Forbes Ave., Pittsburgh, PA 15213-3796. TEL 412-621-6941. FAX 412-621-3049. TELEX 9103509221. Dir. Frank S. Benevento.
  Incorporates (1971-1989): E C B Newsletter (ISSN 0895-6928); (1947-1989): Graphic Arts Abstracts (ISSN 0017-3282); (1970-1989): G A T F Environmental Control Report (ISSN 0046-2241); (1970-1989): G A T F (Year).
  Description: Dedicated to the advancement of the graphic communications industries worldwide.

760 AU ISSN 0016-3562
G L V MITTEILUNGEN. (Graphische Lehr- und Versuchsanstalt) 1959. irreg. (1-2/yr.). free. Hoehere Graphische Bundes Lehr und Versuchsanstalt, Leyserstr. 6, A-1140 Vienna, Austria. Ed. Dr. Wilhelm Mutschlechner. bk.rev.; charts; illus.; index; circ. 500.

686.2 US
GOVERNMENT AFFAIRS. m. Association of the Graphic Arts, 5 Penn Plaza, New York, NY 10001. TEL 212-760-1729.

686.2 070.5 US
GOVERNMENT PUBLISHER. 1981. a. $66. G P, Inc., Box 170, Salem, NH 03079. TEL 603-898-2822. FAX 603-898-3393. Ed. W. Bunnell. adv.; bk.rev.; circ. 11,000.
  Description: Applications of electronic publishing by federal and state governments.

760 SW ISSN 0017-288X
GRAFIA. 1895. s-m. (m. June-Aug.). SEK 180. Grafiska Fackfoerbundet - Graphic Workers Union, Box 1101, S-111 81 Stockholm, Sweden. Ed. Bjoern Burell. adv.; bk.rev.; illus.; index; circ. 46,592.
  Incorporates: Grafisk Revy (ISSN 0017-2987)

686.2 GW
GRAFICAS MUNDIALES. (Text in Spanish) 1908. 4/yr. $53. World Wide Printer, P.O. Box 4124, 7302 Ostfildern 1, Germany. TEL 0711-444005. FAX 0711-442099. TELEX 177111490. Ed. Theodor J. Anton. adv.; charts; illus.; stat.; tr.lit.; circ. 10,000.
  Formerly: Arte Tipografico (ISSN 0004-346X)

760 PO ISSN 0017-2928
GRAFICO.* 1962. 4/yr. $2. Federacao Nacional dos Sindicatos dos Tipografos, Litografos e Oficios Correlativos, Rua da Barroca 107, Lisbon, Portugal. illus.; circ. 50,000.

760 NE ISSN 0017-2936
GRAFICUS; onafhankelijk weekblad voor de grafische en communicatie- industrie. 1917. w. fl.115. Wegener Tijl Tijdschriften Groep B.V., J. Veltmanstr. 29, 1065 EG Amsterdam, Netherlands. TEL 020-5182828. FAX 020-5182843. Ed. Rien Berends. adv.; bk.rev.; abstr.; charts; illus.; pat.; stat.; circ. 10,000. Indexed: Key to Econ.Sci.

686.2 NE
GRAFICUS MAGAZINE. 1987. q. fl.75. Wegener Tijl Tijdschriften Groep B.V., P.B. 43, 1006 AP Amsterdam, Netherlands. TEL 020-5182828. FAX 020-5182843. Ed. R. Berends.

760 BE ISSN 0017-2944
GRAFIEK. 1936. 5/yr. 1125 Fr. V Z W Grafiek, Industrieweg 226, B-9910 Mariakerke-Gent, Belgium. FAX 091-279202. Ed. A. van Huffel. adv.; bk.rev.; charts; illus.; circ. 5,500.
  —BLDSC shelfmark: 4208.053800.

PRINTING

686.2   NE   ISSN 0922-1328
GRAFISCH NEDERLAND; informatie voor en over grafisch management. 1970. w. fl.120. Koninklijk Verbond van Grafische Ondernemingen, Postbus 220, 1180 AE Amstelveen, Netherlands. TEL 020-5475678. FAX 020-5475475. Ed. Alwin van Steijn. adv.; bk.rev.; charts; illus.; index; circ. 6,000. **Indexed:** Abstr.Bull.Inst.Pap.Chem., Excerp.Med., Key to Econ.Sci.
    Former titles: Repro en Druk; Drukkerswereld (ISSN 0012-6713)

686.2   NO
GRAFISK. 1973. m. NOK 290. Grafisk Litteratur A-S, Gamle Torggt. Bad 4-26, 0181 Oslo 1, Norway. Ed. Fred Mathisen. adv.; circ. 1,733.

760   SW   ISSN 0017-2979
GRAFISK FAKTORSTIDNING. 1914. 10/yr. SEK 175. Grafiska Faktors- och Tjaenstemannafoerbundet - Graphical Managers and Overseers Association, Sankt Eriksgatan 26 III, Box 12069, 102 22 Stockholm, Sweden. Ed. Ove Moezzer. adv.; circ. 3,800.

760   DK
GRAFISK LEVERANDOERHAANDBOG; produktion udstyr til den grafiske branche. a. Forlaget de Grafiske Haandboeger, Finsensvej 80, 2000 Frekeriksberg, Denmark. adv.; circ. 4,188.
    Formerly: Leverandoerhaandbogen (Hellerup).

686.2   DK   ISSN 0017-2995
DE GRAFISKE FAG. 1921. 11/yr. DKK 400. Grafisk Arbejdsgiverforening, Helgavej 26, 5230 Odense M, Denmark. TEL 66-130-601. FAX 66-136115. Ed. Eivind S. Johansen. adv.; bk.rev.; illus.; circ. 70,000.
    Formerly (until 1991): Bogtrykkerbladet (ISSN 0006-5730)

760   SW   ISSN 0017-3002
GRAFISKT FORUM. 1895. m. SEK 400. Grafiska Industriefoerbundet, Blasieholmsgatan 4 A, S-111 48 Stockholm, Sweden. TEL 468-762-6800. FAX 468-611-6102. Ed. Gunnar Svensson. adv.; bk.rev.; abstr.; charts; illus.; index; circ. 5,861.

655   US   ISSN 1044-7970
Z244.6.U5
GRAPHIC ARTS BLUE BOOK. DELAWARE VALLEY-OHIO EDITION; directory of graphic arts operating firms and suppliers in Ohio, Pennsylvania, Delaware, Maryland, District of Columbia, and its Virginia suburbs. 1910. biennial. $82.95. A.F. Lewis Co., Inc. (New York), 79 Madison Ave., New York, NY 10016. TEL 212-679-0770. FAX 212-545-7963. adv.; index; circ. 7,000.
    Formerly: Printing Trades Blue Book. Delaware Valley-Ohio Edition (ISSN 0193-3949)

655   US   ISSN 1044-8527
Z475
GRAPHIC ARTS BLUE BOOK. METRO NEW YORK - NEW JERSEY EDITION; directory of graphic arts operating firms and suppliers in metropolitan New York and New Jersey. 1910. a. $82.95. A.F. Lewis Co., Inc. (New York), 79 Madison Ave., New York, NY 10016. TEL 212-679-0770. FAX 212-545-7963. adv.; index; circ. 6,000.
    Formerly: Printing Trades Blue Book. New York Edition (ISSN 0079-5348)

655   US   ISSN 1044-8535
Z475
GRAPHIC ARTS BLUE BOOK. MIDWESTERN EDITION; directory of graphic arts operating firms and suppliers in Illinois, Indiana, Michigan, Wisconsin, Missouri, Iowa, Minnesota. 1970. a. $82.95. A.F. Lewis Co. Inc., 15 Spinning Wheel Rd., Hinsdale, IL 60521. TEL 708-323-9777. FAX 708-323-9379. (And: 79 Madison Ave., New York, NY 10016) Eds. Bill Curran, Linda Kubista. adv.; index; circ. 12,000.
    Former titles: Graphic Arts Green Book (ISSN 0147-1651); Graphic Arts Trade Directory and Register (ISSN 0072-5498)

655   US   ISSN 1044-646X
Z475
GRAPHIC ARTS BLUE BOOK. NORTHEASTERN EDITION; directory of graphic arts operating firms and suppliers in New England and upstate New York. 1910. biennial. $82.95. A.F. Lewis Co., Inc. (New York), 79 Madison Ave., New York, NY 10016. TEL 212-679-0770. FAX 212-545-7963. adv.; index; circ. 6,000.
    Formerly: Printing Trades Blue Book. Northeastern Edition (ISSN 0079-5356)

655   US   ISSN 1044-7989
Z475
GRAPHIC ARTS BLUE BOOK. SOUTHEASTERN EDITION; directory of graphic arts operating firms and suppliers in Virginia (except D.C. suburbs), W. Virginia, North Carolina, South Carolina, Georgia, Florida, Kentucky, Tennessee, Alabama, Mississippi, and Louisiana. 1910. biennial. $82.95. A.F. Lewis Co., Inc. (New York), 79 Madison Ave., New York, NY 10016. TEL 212-679-0770. FAX 212-545-7963. adv.; index; circ. 7,000.
    Formerly: Printing Trades Blue Book. Southeastern Edition (ISSN 0079-5364)

655   US
GRAPHIC ARTS BLUE BOOK. WEST COAST EDITION; directory of graphic arts operating firms and suppliers in California, Oregon, Washington, Nevada, and Arizona. biennial. $82.95. A.F. Lewis Co., Inc. (New York), 79 Madison Ave., New York, NY 10016. TEL 212-679-0770. FAX 212-545-7963. circ. 11,000.

760   US   ISSN 1047-9325
    CODEN: GAMOE4
GRAPHIC ARTS MONTHLY. 1929. m. $84.95 (Canada $164.95; Mexico $153.95; elsewhere $169.95). Cahners Publishing Company (New York) (Subsidiary of: Reed International PLC), Division of Reed Publishing (USA) Inc., 249 W. 17th St., New York, NY 10011. TEL 212-463-6834. FAX 212-463-6733. (Subscr. to: 44 Cook St., Denver, CO 80206-5800. TEL 800-662-7776) Ed. Rodger Ynostroza. adv.; illus.; tr.lit.; index; circ. 94,015 (controlled). (also avail. in microform from RPI; back issues avail.) **Indexed:** Abstr.Bull.Inst.Pap.Chem., B.P.I. Bus.Ind., Chem.Abstr., Graph.Arts Lit.Abstr., Photo.Abstr., Print.Abstr., Resour.Ctr.Ind., Tr.& Indus.Ind.
●Also available online. Vendor(s): DIALOG.
    —BLDSC shelfmark: 4211.950000.
    Formerly: Graphic Arts Monthly and the Printing Industry (ISSN 0017-3312)
    Description: For corporate management, production management, production operations in the printing industries. Highlights cost and time saving methods of combining ink, paper and type into a quality finished product.

760   US   ISSN 0274-5976
GRAPHIC ARTS PRODUCT NEWS (CHICAGO). 1980. 6/yr. $40. Maclean Hunter Publishing Company, 29 N. Wacker Dr., Chicago, IL 60606. TEL 312-726-2802. FAX 312-726-2574. TELEX 270258 EXP. Ed. Jill Roth. adv.; illus.; tr.lit.; circ. 94,524 (controlled).
    Description: Serves the printing industry and allied graphic arts industries.

686.2 070.5   US
GRAPHIC COMMUNICATIONS WORLD. 1968. bi-w. $195. Green Sheet Communications, Inc., Box 727, Hartsdale, NY 10530-0727. TEL 914-472-3051. Ed. John R. Werner. bk.rev.; circ. 4,000. (back issues avail.) **Indexed:** Abstr.Bull.Inst.Pap.Chem., Graph.Arts Lit.Abstr.
    Description: For senior management in the printing and publishing industry.

GRAPHIC DESIGN: U S A. see *ADVERTISING AND PUBLIC RELATIONS*

686.2 760   CN   ISSN 0227-2806
GRAPHIC MONTHLY. 1980. 6/yr. $18. North Island Publishing, 1606 Sedlescomb Dr., Unit 8, Mississauga, Ont. I4X 1M6, Canada. TEL 416-625-7070. Ed. Alexander Donald. adv.; circ. 6,711.

760   US
GRAPHIC NETWORK. 1984. m. $45. 729 Washington Rd., Pittsburgh, PA 15228. TEL 412-341-3722. FAX 412-341-6344. Ed. Jack Gove. adv.; circ. 30,000. (back issues avail.)
    Description: For graphic consumers and producers in Mid-Atlantic area.

GRAPHICOMMUNICATOR. see *LABOR UNIONS*

760   US
GRAPHICS UPDATE. m. Printing Industry of South Florida, Box 170010, Hialeah, FL 33017-0010. TEL 305-558-4855. FAX 305-823-8965. Ed. Gene Strul. circ. 9,000.

760   IT   ISSN 0017-3436
GRAPHICUS. 1911. 10/yr. L.120000. Associazione Culturale Progresso Grafico, Via Morgari 36/B, Castello del Valentino, 10125 Turin, Italy. TEL 39-650-96-59. Ed. Luciano Lovera. adv.; bk.rev.; bibl.; charts; illus.; index; circ. 5,500 (controlled). **Indexed:** Chem.Abstr., Graph.Arts Lit.Abstr., Print.Abstr.
    —BLDSC shelfmark: 4212.520000.

GRAPHIS; international journal of visual communication. see *ART*

GRAPHIS DESIGN; international annual of design and illustration. see *ART*

760   NE
GRAPHISCH ORGAAN. 22/yr. Grafische Bond C.N.V., Valeriusplein 30, 1075 BJ Amsterdam, Netherlands. TEL 020-713279.

760   AU   ISSN 0017-3479
GRAPHISCHE REVUE OESTERREICHS; Fachzeitschrift fuer das gesamte graphische Gewerbe. 1899. bi-m. S.500. Gewerkschaft Druck und Papier, Seidengasse 15, A-1070 Vienna, Austria. Ed. Josef Keller. adv.; bk.rev.; charts; illus.; tr.lit.; index; circ. 4,800. **Indexed:** Print.Abstr.
    —BLDSC shelfmark: 4212.545000.

763   AU   ISSN 0075-2266
Z119
GRAPHISCHE UNTERNEHMUNGEN OESTERREICHS. JAHRBUCH. 1930. a. S.400. Hauptverband der Graphischen Unternehmungen Oesterreichs, Gruenangergasse 4, A-1010 Vienna, Austria. adv.; circ. 950.

686.2   SA
GRAPHIX; the monthly journal for the graphic communications industry. 1973. m. R.80. Graphix Publications (Pty) Ltd., P.O. Box 751119, Gardenview 2047, South Africa. Ed. B. Stickland. adv.; bk.rev.; circ. 4,000. **Indexed:** Ind.S.A.Per.
    Description: South African journal for the printing and graphic arts industries.

760   AT
GRAPHIX. m. Aus.$40. Peter Isaacson Publications Pty. Ltd., 45-50 Porter St., Prahran, Vic. 3181, Australia. TEL 03-520-5555. FAX 03-521-3647. Ed. Michael Atkin. adv.; circ. 5,000. (also avail. in microform from UMI; reprint service avail. from UMI)

686.2   GW   ISSN 0015-7775
GRAVEUR FLEXOGRAF; Fachzeitung fuer Formenbauer, Formgestalter und Fertigungstechniker, Graveure, Gurtler. (Supplements avail.) 1875. m. DM.115.80. Ruehle-Diebener Verlag GmbH und Co. KG, Wolfschlugener Str. 5a, Postfach 700450, 7000 Stuttgart 70, Germany. TEL 0711-765075. FAX 0711-766551. adv.; abstr.; charts; illus.; circ. 4,910.

686.2   US   ISSN 0271-1699
TD195.P7
GRAVURE ENVIRONMENTAL NEWSLETTER. 1972. s-a. membership. Gravure Association of America, Inc., Gravure Environmental Council, 1200A Scottsville Rd., Rochester, NY 14624-5703. TEL 716-436-2150. FAX 716-436-7689. Ed. John Sippel. bk.rev.; charts; illus.; pat.; stat.; circ. 1,000 (controlled). (back issues avail.) **Indexed:** Graph.Arts Lit.Abstr.
    Formerly: Gravure Environmental and O S H A Newsletter (ISSN 0091-5203)

760   US
GRAVURE MAGAZINE. 1950. q. $42 (effective Jan. 1990). Gravure Association of America, Inc., 1200A Scottsville Rd., Rochester, NY 14624-5703. TEL 716-436-2150. FAX 716-436-7689. Ed. John Sippel. adv.; bk.rev.; charts; illus.; circ. 2,500. **Indexed:** Graph.Arts Lit.Abstr., Print.Abstr.
    Former titles: Gravure Bulletin; Gravure Technical Association Bulletin (ISSN 0017-3576)

GUILD OF BOOK WORKERS JOURNAL. see *PUBLISHING AND BOOK TRADE*

LE GUTENBERG; relieur et cartonnier. see *LABOR UNIONS*

686.2   GW   ISSN 0933-6230
GUTENBERG - GESELLSCHAFT. KLEINE DRUCKE. 1926. irreg. membership. Gutenberg-Gesellschaft, Internationale Vereinigung fuer Geschichte und Gegenwart der Druckkunst e.V., Liebfrauenplatz 5, 6500 Mainz, Germany. TEL 06131-226420. circ. 2,000. (back issues avail.)
 Description: Results of research on the history of printing; activities of the Gutenberg-Gesellschaft.

943 655   GW   ISSN 0072-9094
Z1008
GUTENBERG - JAHRBUCH. 1926. a. DM.115. (International Association for Past and Present History of the Art of Printing) Gutenberg Gesellschaft, Liebfrauenplatz 5, 6500 Mainz, Germany. TEL 06131-226420. Ed. Hans-Joachim Koppitz. adv.; bk.rev.; circ. 2,200. **Indexed:** M.L.A.
 Description: Research results in the history of printing worldwide.

686.2   GW   ISSN 0073-0173
HANDBUCH FUER DIE DRUCKINDUSTRIE BERLIN. 1946. a. DM.10. Kupijai und Prochnow, Verlag und Druckerei, Bluecherstr. 22, 1000 Berlin 61, Germany.

686.2   GW
HANDSATZLETTER; Monografien der modernen Typographie. 1967. irreg. free. Johannes Wagner Schriftgiesserei und Messinglinienfabrik, Theodor-Heuss-Str. 49, Postfach 101027, 8070 Ingolstadt, Germany. TEL 0841-58047. FAX 0841-58048. TELEX 55757-LSI-D. Ed. M. Droese. circ. 7,000.
 Description: Publication of modern typography. Includes many samples of print which can be used by all printers. Each issue devoted to a single topic.

760   GW   ISSN 0177-2945
HIGH QUALITY; Zeitschrift ueber das Gestalten, das Drucken und das Gedruckte. Short title: H Q. (Text in German; summaries in English) 1985. 3/yr. DM.69($61) (Heidelberger Druckmaschinen Aktiengesellschaft) High Quality GmbH, Zaehringerstr. 2, D-6900 Heidelberg, Germany. TEL 06221-14020. FAX 06221-15024. Eds. Guenter Braus, Rolf Mueller. circ. 15,000.
 Description: Magazine about design and printing.

686.2   US   ISSN 0737-1020
Z119
HIGH VOLUME PRINTING. bi-m. $39. Innes Publishing Company, 425 Huehl Rd., Box 368, Northbrook, IL 60062. TEL 708-564-5940. Ed. Catherine Stanulis. circ. 38,000. **Indexed:** Graph.Arts Lit.Abstr., Phys.Abstr., Print.Abstr., PROMT.

HOW; the magazine of ideas and techniques in graphic design. see HOW-TO AND DO-IT-YOURSELF

HOW'S BUSINESS ANNUAL. see ADVERTISING AND PUBLIC RELATIONS

686.2   BE   ISSN 0018-9782
I G F - JOURNAL; journal of the printing, bookbinding and paper workers in all countries. (Editions in English, French, German, Spanish and Swedish) 1950. s-a. free. International Graphical Federation, Rue des Fripiers 17, Bloc 2, Galerie du Centre, 1000 Brussels, Belgium. TEL 02-223-18-14. FAX 02-223-02-20. circ. 2,500. **Indexed:** Print.Abstr.
 Incorporates (in 1973): International Graphical Federation. Conference. Proceedings (ISSN 0074-6169)

I G MEDIEN FORUM. see PUBLISHING AND BOOK TRADE

I T U REVIEW. (International Typographical Union) see LABOR UNIONS

IMAGE WORLD; careers in graphic communications. see OCCUPATIONS AND CAREERS

070 686.2   MX
IMPRESOR; al servicio de las artes graficas. (Text in English, Spanish) 1977. m. Mex.$100000($175) (effective Nov. 1991). Imprentas Menra, S.A., Sta. Ma. la Rivera 9-103, 06400 Mexico D.F., Mexico. TEL 525-546-8725. FAX 525-566-1038. Ed. Joaquin Menendez. adv.; bk.rev.; illus.; stat.; tr.lit.; circ. 10,000. (tabloid format)
 Formerly: Impresor Internacional.
 Description: Covers the graphic arts industry. Includes industry news, new techniques and machinery, politics and cultural notes.

760   FR
IMPRESSIONS. 1976. q. Imprimerie Nationale, 27-39 rue de la Convention, 75015 Paris, France. Ed. Gabin Caillard.

760   VE
IMPRIMASE. 1958. 6/yr. free. Asociacion de Industrialse de Artes Graficas de Venezuela, Edificio Camara de Industriales, Piso 2, Esq. Puente Anauco, Apdo. 14.405, Caracas 1011A, Venezuela. adv.; bk.rev.; circ. 2,000.

760   GW
IMPRIMATUR. NEUE FOLGE; ein Jahrbuch fuer Buecherfreunde. irreg., vol.14, 1991. price varies. Verlag Otto Harrassowitz, Taunusstr. 14, Postfach 2929, 6200 Wiesbaden 1, Germany. TEL 0611-530-0. FAX 0611-530570. TELEX 4186135. Ed. Eva Hanebutt-Benz. **Indexed:** M.L.A.
 Formerly: Imprimatur. Jahrbuch fuer Buecherfreunde. Neue Folge (ISSN 0073-5620)

686.2   FR
IMPRIMERIE FRANCAISE.* m. Federation Francaise des Travailleurs du Livre, 263 rue de Paris, 93100 Montrenil, France. adv.

IMPRINT. see LABOR UNIONS

760 974   US   ISSN 0277-7061
NE505
IMPRINT (BROOKLYN HEIGHTS). 1976. s-a. $30 (foreign $40). American Historical Print Collectors Society, 12 Monroe Pl., Brooklyn Heights, NY 11201. FAX 718-875-5121. Ed. Rona Schneider. bk.rev.; illus.; circ. 500. (back issues avail.) **Indexed:** Amer.Hist.& Life, Hist.Abstr., RILA.
 Description: Scholarly articles concerning history, meanings, and techniques of prints made in America or about American subjects before 1900.

760   US   ISSN 0883-6973
IN HOUSE GRAPHICS. 1984. m. $117. United Communications Group, 11300 Rockville Pike, Ste. 1100, Rockville, MD 20852-3030. TEL 301-816-8950. FAX 301-816-8945. Ed. Ronnie Lipton. bk.rev.; charts; illus.; index. (back issues avail.)
 Description: Gives news and how-to design tips for copy and editing, photography, printing and production to help communicators produce high-quality ads, brochures and publications.

686.2   US
IN-PLANT PRINTER & ELECTRONIC PUBLISHER. 1961. bi-m. $39. Innes Publishing Company, 425 Huehl Rd., Box 368, Northbrook, IL 60062. TEL 708-564-5940. Ed. Andrea Cody. adv.; bk.rev.; abstr.; charts; illus.; tr.lit.; index; circ. 42,000. (also avail. in microform from UMI; reprint service avail. from UMI) **Indexed:** Graph.Arts Lit.Abstr., Print.Abstr., Resour.Ctr.Ind.
 Former titles: In-Plant Printer (ISSN 0019-3232); In-Plant Offset Printer.

PRINTING 4001

655   US
IN-PLANT REPRODUCTIONS. 1951. m. $65 (foreign $87). North American Publishing Co., 401 N. Broad St., Philadelphia, PA 19108. TEL 215-238-5300. FAX 215-238-5457. Ed. Judy Bocklage. adv.; bk.rev.; charts; illus.; stat.; circ. 41,000. (also avail. in microform from UMI; reprint service avail. from UMI) **Indexed:** Abstr.Bull.Inst.Pap.Chem., Graph.Arts Lit.Abstr., Print.Abstr., Resour.Ctr.Ind.
 Former titles: In-Plant Reproductions and Electronic Publishing. In-Plant Productions (ISSN 0198-9065); Reproductions Review and Methods (ISSN 0164-4327); Graphic Arts Supplier News (ISSN 0017-3355); Reproductions Methods; Reproductions Review (ISSN 0034-4974).
 Description: Written for management and technical personnel connected with basic printing and production processes and techniques. Examines in-plant and electronic publishing concerns for business, industry and government.

686.2 658.7   US
IN-REGISTER NEWSLETTER.* 1982. bi-m. $36. In-Register, Inc., 111 Pine St, K No. 1410, San Francisco, CA 94111-5616. TEL 415-467-8760. FAX 415-467-8762. Ed. Richard Michaels. bk.rev.; charts; stat.; tr.lit.; circ. 500. (back issues avail.)
 Description: Information for wide range of print buyers or suppliers, industry trends, libraries and research.

INDIAN & EASTERN NEWSPAPER SOCIETY PRESS HANDBOOK. see JOURNALISM

INDIAN PRESS. see JOURNALISM

655   II   ISSN 0019-6185
INDIAN PRINT & PAPER;* a journal for printers, papermakers and the allied industries. 1934. q. Rs.8($2) Commercial Products Ltd., 95 Park Street, Calcutta 700 016, India. Ed. Bimal Bose. adv.; bk.rev.; abstr.; bibl.; charts; illus.; stat.; index. **Indexed:** Chem.Abstr.

760 676.3   US   ISSN 1054-2434
INDUSTRIA GRAFICA Y ARTES GRAFICAS. (Text in Spanish) 1967. 6/yr. $40 (foreign $60). C C International Publishing, Inc., 1680 S.W. Bayshore Blvd., Port St. Lucia, FL 34984. TEL 407-879-6666. FAX 407-879-7388. Ed. Miguel Garzon. adv.; bk.rev.; circ. 20,000. **Indexed:** Graph.Arts Lit.Abstr., Packag.Sci.Tech.
 Formed by the merger of: Industria Grafica (ISSN 0120-7601) & Artes Graficas U S A (ISSN 0164-1905); Incorporates: Export Graficas U S A (ISSN 0741-7160); **Formerly:** Artes Graficas (ISSN 0004-3494)
 Description: International trade publication with technical articles covering the printing, packaging and converting industries.

INDUSTRIEGEWERKSCHAFT MEDIEN. SCHRIFTENREIHE FUER BETRIEBSRATE. see PUBLISHING AND BOOK TRADE

INK & GALL; the marbling journal. see ARTS AND HANDICRAFTS

686.2   UK
INK & PRINT INTERNATIONAL. 1958. q. £18 (foreign £22). (Society of British Printing Ink Manufacturers) Batiste Publications Ltd., Pembroke House, Campsbourne Rd., Hornsey, London N8 7PE, England. TEL 081-340-3291. FAX 081-341-4840. TELEX 267727 BATGRP. Ed. Dr. R.H. Leach. adv.; illus.; tr.lit.; circ. 2,500. **Indexed:** Abstr.Bull.Inst.Pap.Chem., Br.Tech.Ind., Chem.Abstr., Graph.Arts Lit.Abstr., Key to Econ.Sci., Print.Abstr., PROMT, World Surf.Coat.
 Formerly: Ink and Print (ISSN 0263-497X); **Supersedes:** British Ink Maker (ISSN 0007-0831)

686.2   UK   ISSN 0143-9871
INKLINGS. 1948. 3/yr. Coates Lorilleux, Cray Avenue, St. Mary Cray, Orpington, Kent BR5 3PP, England. TEL 0689-75800. Ed. C. Armstrong. circ. 10,000. **Indexed:** Print.Abstr.

686.2   JA   ISSN 0020-1766
INSATSUKAI/PRINTING WORLD. (Text in Japanese) 1950. m. 20400 Yen (foreign $150). Japan Printing News Co. Ltd. - Nippon Insatsu Shinbunsha, 16-8, 1-chome, Shintomi, Chuo-ku, Tokyo 104, Japan. TEL 03-3553-5681. FAX 03-3553-5684. (US subscr. to: North American Publishing Co., 134 N. 13th St., Philadelphia, PA 19107) Ed. Hideo Arai. adv.; illus.; circ. 8,500. **Indexed:** Chem.Abstr.

PRINTING

686.2 US
INSTANT & SMALL COMMERCIAL PRINTER. 1982. 10/yr. $39. Innes Publishing Company, 425 Huehl Rd., Box 368, Northbrook, IL 60062. TEL 708-564-5940. Ed. Stephanie Riefe. circ. 55,000. **Indexed:** Graph.Arts Lit.Abstr.
Formerly: Instant Printer (ISSN 0744-3854)

INTERNATIONAL DIRECTORY OF PRIVATE PRESSES. see BUSINESS AND ECONOMICS — Trade And Industrial Directories

655 CS
INTERPRESSGRAPHIC; international quarterly for visual culture and communication. Russian edition (ISSN 0209-7494) 1970. q. $34. International Organization of Journalists, Parizska 9, 110-10 Prague, Czechoslovakia. TELEX 122631. (Subscr. to: Interpress Editorial Office, Pal u.204, Budapest VIII, Hungary) Ed. Andras Szekely. adv.; bk.rev.; circ. 4,500. **Indexed:** Artbibl.Mod.
Formerly (until 1986): Interpressgrafik (ISSN 0020-9619)
Description: Devoted to questions of visual art, layout of newspapers, magazines, books, advertising materials and posters.

686.2 IE ISSN 0790-2026
IRISH PRINTER. 1969. m. £20. Jemma Publications Ltd., Marino House, 52-53 Glasthule Rd., Sandycove, Dun Laoghaire, Co. Dublin, Ireland. TEL 01-800000. FAX 01-844041. (Subscr. to: P.O. Box 1973, Rathmines, Dublin 6, Ireland) Ed. Frank Corr. adv.; bk.rev.; illus.; circ. 1,722. **Indexed:** Print.Abstr.
Formerly: Modern Irish Printer.

686.2 760 IS
ISRAEL BIBLIOPHILES NEWSLETTER. (Text in English and Hebrew) 1980. a. $5. Israel Bibliophiles, P.O. Box 4368, 91043 Jerusalem, Israel. Ed. Leila Avrin.

ISRAEL BOOK TRADE DIRECTORY; a guide to publishers, printers and ancillary book trade services in Israel. see PUBLISHING AND BOOK TRADE

686.2 IT
L'ITALIA GRAFICA. 1946. 8/yr. L.60000. (National Association of the Italian Graphics Industry) Editing S.p.A., Piazza Conciliazione 1, 20123 Milano, Italy. TEL 02-4980268. FAX 02-4816947. Ed. Silvano Boroli. adv.: B&W page L.2548000; trim 210 x 297; adv. contact: Roberta Reineke. bk.rev.; circ. 12,000. **Indexed:** Graph.Arts Lit.Abstr., Print.Abstr.

686.221 JA
JAPAN TYPOGRAPHY ANNUAL/NIHON TAIPOGURAFI NENKAN. (Text in Japanese; title and captions for plates in English) 1974. a. $30. (Japan Typography Association - Nihon Taipogurafi Kyokai) Gurafikku Sha, Box 102, 1-9-12 Kudan Kita, Chiyoda-ku, Tokyo, Japan. (Overseas Distributor: Orion Books, Export Dept., 1-58 Kanda Jimbocho, Chiyoda-ku, Tokyo 101, Japan) illus.
Formerly: Nihon Retaringu Nenkan.

760 JA
JAPANESE SOCIETY OF PRINTING SCIENCE AND TECHNOLOGY. BULLETIN. (Text in Japanese; summaries in English) vol.15, 1975. q. Japanese Society of Printing Science and Technology - Insatsu Gakkai Shuppanbu, 1-16-8 Shinlomi, Chuo-ku, Tokyo 104, Japan. adv.; bk.rev.; abstr.; charts; illus. **Indexed:** Graph.Arts Lit.Abstr., JTA.
Formerly: Technical Association of Graphic Arts of Japan. Bulletin (ISSN 0040-0874)

760 JA
JAPANESE SOCIETY OF PRINTING SCIENCE AND TECHNOLOGY. BULLETIN (OVERSEAS EDITION). (Text in English) 1969. q. $20. Japanese Society of Printing Science and Technology - Insatsu Gakkai Shuppanbu, 1-16-8 Shinlomi, Chuo-ku, Tokyo 104, Japan. Ed. Masakazu Kawamata. **Indexed:** Graph.Arts Lit.Abstr., Print.Abstr.
Formerly: Technical Association of Graphic Arts of Japan. Bulletin (Overseas Edition).

KANSAS PUBLISHER. see JOURNALISM

610 FI ISSN 0017-2731
KIRJAPAINOTAITO - GRAAFIKKO. 1906. 8/yr. FIM 350. Osuuskunta Kirjapainotaito, Loennrotinkatu 11 A, 00120 Helsinki, Finland. FAX 358-0-603914. Ed. Mirja Mantynen. adv.; bk.rev.; circ. 4,313 (controlled).
—BLDSC shelfmark: 5097.505000.
Formerly: Graafikko.

686.2 US
LASERJET JOURNAL. 1987. 6/yr. $49. 1945 Techny Rd., Northbrook, IL 60062-5306. TEL 800-323-2686. (reprint service avail.)

686.2 US
LASERS IN GRAPHICS: ELECTRONIC PUBLISHING IN THE 90'S. CONFERENCE PROCEEDINGS. (In 2 vols.) 1979. a. $95 per vol. Dunn Technology, Inc., 1855 E. Vista Way, No. 1, Vista, CA 92084. FAX 619-758-5401. Ed. Patrice M. Dunn. (back issues avail.) **Indexed:** Graph.Arts Lit.Abstr.
Formerly: Lasers in Graphics: Electronic Publishing in the 80's. Conference Proceedings.
Description: Focus on the markets and the technology for commercial electronic design, pre-press and publishing.

LETOPIS' PECHATNYKH PROIZVEDENII IZOBRAZITEL'NOGO ISKUSSTVA. see ART

686.2 US ISSN 0738-9302
Z250
LIGATURE. vol.2, 1983. 2/yr. $1.50. World Typeface Center, Inc., 303 Park Ave. S., 2nd Fl., New York, NY 10010-3601. Ed. Tom Carnase. adv.; circ. 40,000. **Indexed:** Graph.Arts Lit.Abstr., Print.Abstr.

760 IT ISSN 0024-3744
LINEAGRAFICA. 1983. bi-m. L.130000. Azzura Editrice s.r.l., Via della Moscova 49, 20121 Milan, Italy. TEL 02-6552498. FAX 02-29002192. Ed. Giusi Brivio. adv.; bk.rev.; circ. 21,000. (back issues avail.)
Formerly: Nuova Linea Grafica.
Description: Covers the world of graphics and visual communication. Includes articles on calligraphy, computer images and technology.

763 UK ISSN 0264-732X
LITHO WEEK. 1979. w. £136. Haymarket Magazines Ltd., 38-42 Hampton Rd., Teddington, Middx. TW11 0JE, England. TEL 081-943-5000. TELEX 895-2440-HAYMRT-G. Ed. Simon Kanter. adv.; bk.rev.; illus.; circ. 12,832 (controlled). **Indexed:** Br.Tech.Ind., Chem.Abstr., Fluidex, Graph.Arts Lit.Abstr., Print.Abstr.
—BLDSC shelfmark: 5277.385000.
Formerly: Lithoprinter Week (ISSN 0024-4929)

686.2 070.5 US ISSN 0882-049X
Z253.5
MAGAZINE DESIGN AND PRODUCTION. 1985. 10/yr. $48 (foreign $150). South Wind Publishing Co., 8340 Mission Rd., Ste. 106, Prairie Village, KS 66206. TEL 913-642-6611. FAX 913-642-6676. (Subscr. to: Box 970, Floral Park, NY 11001) Ed. Michael Scheibach. adv.; bk.rev.; illus.; circ. 15,000. (also avail. in microfilm; back issues avail.)
Description: Covers trends, techniques, and technologies in publication design, production, and printing.

760 HU ISSN 0479-480X
Z119
MAGYAR GRAFIKA/HUNGARIAN GRAPHIC ARTS. (Text in Hungarian; summaries in German and Russian) 1957. bi-m. $29.50. Papir- es Nyomdaipari Mueszaki Egyesuelet, Kossuth Lajos ter 6-8, 1055 Budapest 5, Hungary. (Subscr. to: Kultura, Box 149, 1389 Budapest, Hungary) Ed. M. Gara. adv.; bk.rev.; abstr.; bibl.; charts; illus.; index; circ. 3,000. **Indexed:** Chem.Abstr., Graph.Arts Lit.Abstr.

655 CN ISSN 0025-0996
LE MAITRE IMPRIMEUR. (Text in French) 1937. m. Can.$25. Association des Arts Graphiques du Quebec, Inc., 65, rue de Castelnau Ouest, Bureau 101, Montreal, Que. H2R 2W3, Canada. TEL 514-274-7440. FAX 514-274-7482. adv.; charts; illus.; circ. 4,555. **Indexed:** Pt.de Rep.

686.2 658 US
MANAGING PRINT SALES; a monthly publication for the sales executive. m. $90 (members $60). Printing Industries of America, Inc., 100 Daingerfield Rd., Alexandria, VA 22314. TEL 703-519-8146. Ed. Cliff Weiss. (back issues avail.)

760 MX
MERCADO DE LAS ARTES GRAFICAS. 1974. 6/yr. Publi-Representaciones, Tlacotalpan No. 109-204, Mexico 7, DF, Mexico. Ed. Armando Ramirez. adv.; circ. 4,000.

686.2 LU
METIERS GRAPHIQUES. BULLETIN. (Text in Dutch and French) q. 1 rue Montee de la Petruisse, Luxembourg. adv.; circ. 600.

686.2 CH
MODERN PRINTING.* (Text in Chinese) 1973. bi-m. Jeng-yih Lin, 12, Lane 28, Tunghwa St., Taipei, Taiwan, Republic of China. adv.; illus.

MOROCCO BOUND. see HOBBIES

686.2 GW ISSN 0178-0522
MYOSOTIS; Zeitschrift fuer Buchwesen. 1985. 3/yr. DM.20. Andreasstr. 8, 6250 Worms, Germany. Ed. Ralf Reinhold. bibl.; circ. 1,000. (back issues avail.)
Description: History of printing, publishing, and book trade.

NATIONAL AMATEUR. see JOURNALISM

763 US
NATIONAL ASSOCIATION OF PRINTERS AND LITHOGRAPHERS. SPECIAL REPORTS. bi-w. National Association of Printers and Lithographers, 780 Palisade Ave., Teaneck, NJ 07666. TEL 201-342-0700.

NEW COLLAGE MAGAZINE. see LITERATURE

655 US ISSN 0162-8771
Z119
NEW ENGLAND PRINTER AND PUBLISHER. 1938. m. $11. New England Printer & Publisher Inc., 12 Carleton Dr., Box 810, Newburyport, MA 01950. TEL 508-462-9461. FAX 508-462-9160. Ed. Jean Hansen. adv.; bk.rev.; illus.; tr.lit.; circ. 4,400. **Indexed:** Graph.Arts.Abstr., Graph.Arts Lit.Abstr.
Formerly: New England Printer and Lithographer (ISSN 0028-484X)
Description: Information on regional and national industry and trade association news. Calendar of regional and national events, supplier product-services, and new literature.

NEW YORK TYPOGRAPHICAL UNION NUMBER SIX. BULLETIN. see LABOR UNIONS

686.2 AT
NEW ZEALAND PRINTER. 6/yr. Aus.$50. Calmor & Associates Pty. Ltd., P.O. Box 1316, North Sydney, N.S.W. 2059, Australia. TEL 02-922-6133. FAX 02-922-4734. Ed. Ann Callahan. circ. 3,481.
Description: Technical journal circulates to managers of print shops, trade shops, typesetters, art studios, publishers and packaging companies.

NEWS & VIEWS (PORTLAND). see BUSINESS AND ECONOMICS — Marketing And Purchasing

760 GR
NEWS OF GRAPHIC ARTS. 1982. m. Dr.1500($30) Fakinov, 157 Sokratous St., 176 73 Kallithea, Athens, Greece. Ed. D. Fakinov. circ. 5,200. (back issues avail.)

686.2 GW
NEWSPAPER TECHNIQUES. French edition: Techniques de Presse. German edition: Zeitungstechnik. 1962. m. DM.180 to non-members. I N C A - F I E J Research Association (IFRA), Washingtonplatz 1, 6100 Darmstadt, Germany. TEL 6151-7005-0. FAX 6151-784542. TELEX 04-19273. Ed. G.B. Smith. adv.; bk.rev.; circ. 2,500. **Indexed:** Print.Abstr.
Formerly: Monthly Newspaper Techniques (ISSN 0019-333X)

646.2 NR
NIGERIAN PRINTER. 1980. q. $25. Nigerian Printer Publications, P.O. Box 632, Yaba, Nigeria. TEL 082-221782. Ed. Austin Odiadi. circ. 3,000.
Description: Technological articles and current technology and applications.

PRINTING 4003

655 JA ISSN 0546-0719
NIHON INSATSU NENKAN/JAPAN PRINTING ART ANNUAL. (Text in Japanese) 1957. a. 9000 Yen. Japan Printing News Co., Ltd. - Nippon Insatsu Shinbunsha, 16-8, 1-chome, Shintomi, Chuo-ku, Tokyo 104, Japan. TEL 03-3553-5681. FAX 03-3553-5684. Ed. Hiroshi Kurihara. adv.; circ. 4,500.

686.2 JA
NIPPON INSATSU SHINBUN/JAPAN PRINTING NEWS. (Text in Japanese) 1943. s-w. 21600 Yen (foreign $160). Japan Printing News Co., Ltd. - Nippon Insatsu Shinbunsha, 16-8, 1-chome, Shintomi, Chuo-ku, Tokyo 104, Japan. TEL 03-3553-5681. FAX 03-3553-5684. Ed. Hideo Murata. adv.; circ. 15,000.

760 NO ISSN 0029-1978
NORSK GRAFISK TIDSSKRIFT. 1892. m. NOK 250. Grafiske Bedrifters Landsforening, Akersgt. 16, 0158 Oslo 1, Norway. Ed. Tom Prent. adv.; bk.rev.; stat.; tr.lit.; circ. 2,100.

NORTHERN ADVOCATE. see *ADVERTISING AND PUBLIC RELATIONS*

655 FR ISSN 0029-4888
NE1
NOUVELLES DE L'ESTAMPE. 1963. 5/yr. 330 F. (foreign 410 F.). Comite National de la Gravure Francaise, 58 rue de Richelieu, 75084 Paris Cedex 02, France. TEL 47-03-83-88. Ed.Bd. adv.; bk.rev. (processed) **Indexed:** Artbibl.Mod., Artbibl., RILA.
—BLDSC shelfmark: 6176.773000.

760 BE ISSN 0029-4926
NOUVELLES GRAPHIQUES/GRAFISCH NIEUWS. (Editions in Dutch and French) 1950. s-m. 1500 Fr. Internationale Drukkerij en Uitgeverij Keesing N.V., 2-20 Keesinglaan, B-2100 Deurne, Belgium. TEL 03-324-38-90. FAX 03-324-38-98. TELEX 32507 KEESNG B. Eds. Alain Vermeire, Steven Van De Rijt. adv.; bk.rev.; charts; illus.; tr.lit.; circ. 7,300 (4,200 Dutch ed.; 3,100 French ed.). (back issues avail.) **Indexed:** Print.Abstr.
—BLDSC shelfmark: 6176.782800.

NOVUM GEBRAUCHSGRAPHIK/INTERNATIONAL JOURNAL FOR COMMUNICATION DESIGN. see *ADVERTISING AND PUBLIC RELATIONS*

760 AU ISSN 0029-9170
DAS OESTERREICHISCHE GRAPHISCHE GEWERBE. 1949. m. S.650. Landesinnung Druck, Gruenangergasse 4, A-1010 Vienna, Austria. adv.; bk.rev.; charts; illus.; tr.lit.; index; circ. 1,900.

686.2 UK ISSN 0263-4384
OFFSET PRINTING & REPRODUCTION. 1969. m. £65. Maclean Hunter Ltd., Maclean Hunter House, Chalk Lane, Cockfosters Rd., Barnet, Herts EN4 0BU, England. TEL 081-975-9759. FAX 081-440-1796. TELEX 299072-MACHUN-G. illus.; stat.; circ. 14,523. **Indexed:** Br.Tech.Ind., Build.Manage.Abstr., Graph.Arts Lit.Abstr.
Former titles: Offset Printer; Offset Printing; Small Offset Printing (ISSN 0037-7201)

686.2 GW
OFFSET-TECHNIK; Fachzeitschriften fuer Druck- und Kommunikationstechniken. 1968. m. DM.83.20. Support GmbH, Grethenweg 21, 6000 Frankfurt a.M. 70, Germany. TEL 069-615469. FAX 069-624937. adv.; bk.rev.; circ. 8,000. (back issues avail.)

OFFSETPRAXIS; Europaeische Fachzeitschrift fuer Offset-, Kleinoffset-Druck, Reprofotographie und Fotosatz. see *PHOTOGRAPHY*

760 US
▼**OHIO SOURCEBOOK (YEAR).** 1991. a. $45. Alexander Communications, Inc., 212 W. Superior, Ste. 203, Chicago, IL 60610. TEL 312-944-5115. FAX 312-944-7865. circ. 6,200 (controlled).

686.2 676.2 AT ISSN 0158-6319
P A T E F A NEWS BULLETIN. 1985. m. membership. Printing & Allied Trades Employers Federation of Australia, 77 Lithgow Street, St. Leonards, N.S.W. 2065, Australia. TEL 02-438 2777. FAX 02-439-2405. circ. 2,500.
Description: Informs members about industry events, technology, government action, marketing trends.

P I R A ANNUAL REVIEW OF RESEARCH & SERVICES. (Paper, Printing & Packaging Industries Research Association) see *PAPER AND PULP*

686.2 US
TS196.7
PACKAGE PRINTING & CONVERTING; diemaking and diecutting, flexography, gravure and offset. 1974. m. $49 (foreign $73). North American Publishing Co., 401 N. Broad St., Philadelphia, PA 19108. TEL 215-238-5300. FAX 215-238-5457. Ed. David Luttenberger. adv.; bk.rev.; charts; illus.; stat.; index; circ. 24,000. (reprint service avail. from UMI) **Indexed:** Abstr.Bull.Inst.Pap.Chem., Curr.Pack.Abstr., Graph.Arts Lit.Abstr., Int.Packag.Abstr., Packag.Sci.Tech.
Former titles: Package Printing (ISSN 0163-9234); (until Mar. 1978): Package Printing and Diecutting (ISSN 0098-7778); Which was formed by the merger of: Diemaking, Diecutting and Converting (ISSN 0012-2556); Gravure (ISSN 0017-3568); Flexography Printing and Converting.
Description: Focuses on new machinery and new methods in the specialized field of printing and converting packages, boxes, cartons, bags and cellophane.

PAINT AND INK INTERNATIONAL. see *PAINTS AND PROTECTIVE COATINGS*

PAPIER UND DRUCK; Fachzeitschrift fuer Typografie, polygrafische Technik und Papierverarbeitung. see *PAPER AND PULP*

PERSPECTIVES (LIBERTY). see *BUSINESS AND ECONOMICS — Management*

771 US
PHOTO CHEMICAL MACHINING INSTITUTE. JOURNAL. 1980. q. membership only. Photo Chemical Machining Institute, 4113 Barberry Dr., Lafayette Hill, PA 19444. TEL 215-825-2506. FAX 215-941-6773. Ed. Judith Ginsberg. adv.; bibl.; charts; illus.; pat.; circ. 1,200. (back issues avail.)

PHOTO EDUCATOR. see *PHOTOGRAPHY*

686.2 US ISSN 0032-0595
TR921.A1
PLAN & PRINT; the magazine of methods and technology for design reproduction. 1928. m. $36 (free to qualified personnel; Canada $42; foreign $60). International Reprographic Association, 2000 York Rd., Ste. 125, Oak Brook, IL 60521-8820. TEL 708-571-4685. FAX 708-571-4731. Ed. Mercedes Vance. adv.; bk.rev.; charts; illus.; index; circ. 30,000 (controlled). (also avail. in microfilm from UMI; microfiche; reprint service avail. from UMI) **Indexed:** Graph.Arts Lit.Abstr., Resour.Ctr.Ind.
—BLDSC shelfmark: 6508.120000.
Formerly: International Blue Printer.

686.2 IT ISSN 0032-2709
POLIGRAFICO ITALIANO. 1960. m. $125. Zeta's s.r.l., Via Kolbe 8, 20137 Milan, Italy. TEL 76110075. FAX 02-7387371. Ed. Ruggero Zuliani. adv.; bk.rev.; abstr.; charts; illus.; pat.; tr.lit.; index; circ. 10,000.
Description: Concerns the polygraphic field: publishers, trade printers, phototypesetters, bindery plants, and paper industry.

686.2 PL ISSN 0373-9864
CODEN: POLGDZ
POLIGRAFIKA. 1947. m. $171. (Stowarzyszenie Inzynierow i Technikow Mechanikow Polskich, Sekcja Poligrafow) Oficyna Wydawnicza SIMP Press, Ltd., Ul. Zurawia 22, 00-515 Warsaw, Poland. (Dist. by: Ars Polona-Ruch, Krakowskie Przedmiescie 7, Warsaw, Poland) Ed. Apolinary Brodecki. circ. 2,400. **Indexed:** Chem.Abstr.

665 RU ISSN 0032-2717
CODEN: PLGFAH
POLIGRAFIYA. 1924. m. 8.40 Rub. (Komitet po Pechati Soveta Ministrov) Izdatel'stvo Kniga, 50, Gorky St., 125047 Moscow, Russia. Ed. A.I. Ovsyannikav. bk.rev.; bibl.; charts; illus.; index; circ. 27,000. (tabloid format) **Indexed:** Abstr.Bull.Inst.Pap.Chem., Chem.Abstr., Graph.Arts Lit.Abstr.
—BLDSC shelfmark: 0130.050000.

686.2 US
POLITICAL ADVISOR. q. National Association of Printers and Lithographers, 780 Palisade Ave., Teaneck, NJ 07666-3129. TEL 201-342-0707. FAX 201-692-0286. Ed. Patrick Henry. circ. 6,000.

POLONIA TYPOGRAPHICA SAECULI SEDECIMI. see *ART*

686.2 GW ISSN 0032-3845
Z119
DER POLYGRAPH; trade magazine for the printing industry and communications technology. 1947. s-m. DM.165.60. Polygraph Verlag GmbH, Schaumainkai 85, 6000 Frankfurt a.M. 70, Germany. TEL 069-639066. FAX 069-6313502. TELEX 413562. Ed. Walter Mikolasch. adv.; bk.rev.; charts; illus.; mkt.; pat.; tr.lit.; index; circ. 13,000. **Indexed:** Bibl.Cart., C.I.S. Abstr., Excerp.Med., Graph.Arts Lit.Abstr.
Description: Trade news of the graphic arts industry.

655 GW ISSN 0343-5199
POLYGRAPH INTERNATIONAL; magazine for the printing industry and communication technology. (Text in English; summaries in French, Spanish) 1952. 6/yr. DM.75. Polygraph Verlag GmbH, Postfach 700854, Schaumainkai 85, 6000 Frankfurt a.M. 70, Germany. TEL 069-639066. FAX 069-6313502. TELEX 413562. Ed. Walter Mikolasch. adv.; charts; illus.; mkt.; tr.lit.; circ. 9,000. **Indexed:** Graph.Arts Lit.Abstr., Print.Abstr.
Formerly: Export Polygraph International (E P I) (ISSN 0014-5173)

760 US ISSN 1040-6301
POST GUTENBERG; bi-weekly graphic arts newspaper serving the East Coast. 1986. fortn. free. Lee Publications, Inc., Box 121, Grand St. W., Palatine Bridge, NY 13428. TEL 518-673-3237. FAX 518-673-2699. Ed. Sally-Jean Taylor. adv.; bk.rev.; illus.; circ. 21,000 (controlled). (tabloid format)
Description: Newsletter of articles and announcements of interest to graphic artists located in the northeastern United States.

686.2 658 US
PRACTICAL MARKETING FOR PRINTERS. m. $79. Printing Industries of America, Inc., 100 Daingerfield Rd., Alexandria, VA 22314. TEL 703-519-8146. Ed. Cliff Weiss. circ. 150. (back issues avail.)
Description: Provides information on how to market a graphic arts company and its services.

760 NE ISSN 0032-7476
PRENT 190; new circle of collectors of modern graphic art. 1965. a. fl.725. Gerlach en Co. B. V., Art Section, Schiphol-Center, Amsterdam, Netherlands. Ed. L. Gans. circ. 1,500.

686.2 US ISSN 8750-2224
PREPRESS BULLETIN. 1911. bi-m. $15. International Prepress Association, 552 W. 167 St., South Holland, IL 60473. TEL 312-596-5110. FAX 312-596-5112. Ed. Bessie Halfacre. adv.; bk.rev.; charts; illus.; stat.; circ. 2,000. **Indexed:** Graph.Arts Lit.Abstr., Photo.Abstr.
Former titles (until 1984): Photoplatemakers Bulletin (ISSN 0031-8841); (until 1968): Photoengravers Bulletin (ISSN 0097-5877)
Description: Provides management and technical information on the graphic arts prepress industry.

PRESSTIME. see *JOURNALISM*

686.2 UK ISSN 0032-8529
PRINT. 1968. 10/yr. £10. National Graphical Association (N G A), Graphic House, 63-67 Bromham Rd., Bedford MK40 2AG, England. FAX 0234-218640. Ed. A.D. Dubbins. adv.; bk.rev.; illus.; index. (tabloid format)
Former titles: Graphical Journal; Incorporates: S L A D E Journal; Which was formerly: Process Journal (ISSN 0032-9614)

PRINT; America's graphic design magazine. see *COMPUTERS — Computer Graphics*

PRINT. see *PUBLISHING AND BOOK TRADE*

628.2 UK
PRINT & CONVERTING MONTHLY. 1984. m. £18 (Europe £27.50; elsewhere £45). A.E. Morgan Publications Ltd., Stanley House, 9 West St., Epson, Surrey KT18 7RL, England. TEL 0206-766756. FAX 0206-768558. Ed. David Andrews. adv.; circ. 12,500. (back issues avail.; reprint service avail.)
Former titles: Print Monthly; (until 1988): Print Advertiser.
Description: Covers all printing industry and allied trades with exception of screen printers.

PRINTING

760 US ISSN 0273-9550
PRINT & GRAPHICS. 1980. m. $39 (free to qualified personnel). East-West Communications, 911 N. Fillmore St., Arlington, VA 22201-2127. TEL 703-525-4800. FAX 703-525-4805. Ed. Charles Kerwin. adv.; bk.rev.; software rev.; circ. 20,000 (controlled). (also avail. on diskette)
  Description: Trade publication for the Mid-Atlantic graphic arts industry. Features include technology and industry segment focus, product news, business briefs, installations, and people.

686.2 UK
PRINT AND PRODUCTION MANUAL. 1986. a. £65. Chapman & Hall, 2-6 Boundary Row, London SE1 8HN, England. TEL 071-865-0066. FAX 071-522-9623. TELEX 290164-CHAPMAG. (Dist. by: International Thomson Publishing Services, Ltd., N. Way, Andover, Hampshire SP10 5BE, England. TEL 0264-33-2424; US addr.: Chapman & Hall, 29 W. 35th St., New York, NY 10001-2291. TEL 212-244-3336) Ed.Bd.

686.2 US
PRINT BUSINESS REGISTER. fortn. Quoin Research, 800 W. Huron, No.4-S, Chicago, IL 60622-5973. TEL 312-226-5600. FAX 312-226-4640. Ed. Rod Piechowski. circ. 650.

686.2 US
PRINT BUYERS REVIEW. 1989. bi-m. $9.95. Successful Media, Box 36, S. Weymouth, MA 02190. TEL 617-340-2066. FAX 617-426-1456. Ed. Robert F. Dixon. adv.; circ. 15,000.
  Description: Covers the process of buying materials for printing and book publishing.

686.2 UK
PRINT BUYING. 1967. 12/yr. £45 (foreign £75). Macro Publishing, Conbar House, Mead Lane, Hertford, Herts SG13 7AS, England. TEL 0992-584233. FAX 0992-500717. Ed. Harry Attrill. adv.; bk.rev.; stat.; circ. 7,500.
  Former titles (until 1988): Print Buyer (ISSN 0262-6101); Print and Promotion; Print Buyer.

655 US ISSN 0048-5314
PRINT-EQUIP NEWS.* 1965. m. $10. P - E N Publications Inc., 215 Allen Ave., Box 5540, Glendale, CA 91201-5540. Ed. Paul B. Kissel. adv.; illus.; circ. 24,800. (tabloid format) **Indexed:** Graph.Arts Lit.Abstr.

686.2 CN
PRINTACTION. (Text in English, French) 1962. 12/yr. Can.$29($39.95) Youngblood Publishing Co. Ltd., 505 Consumers Rd., Ste.102, Willowdale, Ont. M2J 4V8, Canada. TEL 416-492-5777. FAX 416-492-7595. Ed. David Bosworth. adv.; bk.rev.; stat.; tr.lit.; circ. 15,000.
  Description: Covers the graphic arts and printing industries in Canada.

760 070.5 US
PRINTER'S DEVIL; graphic arts for the small press. 1986. 3/yr. $6.25. Mother of Ashes Press, Box 66, Harrison, ID 83833-0066. adv.; circ. 300.
  Description: Focuses on providing accurate and timely information on all phases of the graphic arts and on providing art and craft in contemporary printing.

686.2 US ISSN 0192-6314
PRINTERS HOT LINE. w. $89. Heartland Communications Group, Inc., 900 Central Ave., Box 916, Fort Dodge, IA 50501. TEL 515-955-1600. FAX 800-247-2000. circ. 16,000.
  Description: Designed to stimulate business between buyers and sellers of new and used equipment, and providers and users of related services and supplies.

686.2 US
PRINTER'S INK. 1984. q. free. Thomson-Shore, Inc., 7300 W. Joy Rd., Box 305, Dexter, MI 48130-0305. TEL 313-426-3939. Ed. Ned Thomson. circ. 14,000.

655 NZ ISSN 0048-5330
Z119
PRINTERS NEWS. 1942. m. NZ.$37.50. Printing Industries Federation of New Zealand (Inc.), Box 1422, Wellington, New Zealand. TEL 04-723 497. FAX 04-723-534. Ed. W.R. Johnson. adv.; bk.rev.; circ. 1,100.
  —BLDSC shelfmark: 6613.530000.

686.2 UK
PRINTERS YEARBOOK. 1982. a. £40. British Printing Industries Federation, 11 Bedford Row, London, WC1R 4DX, England. TEL 071-242-6904. FAX 071-405-7784. adv.; index; circ. 3,700.
  Former titles: Printing Industries Annual (ISSN 0308-1443); British Federation of Master Printers. Master Printers Annual (ISSN 0068-1989)
  Description: Buyer's guide to UK printing industry: technical information, economic and law issues, and company addresses.

686.2 UK
PRINTING AND BOOKBINDING TRADE REVIEW; equipment-materials-production. 1958. m. £3. George L. Howe Press Service Ltd., 85 Elmhurst Dr., Hornchurch, Essex RM11 1PB, England. Ed. George L. Howe. adv.; bk.rev.; charts; illus.; tr.lit.

PRINTING & PACKAGING; with Arabian food and packaging. see *PACKAGING*

PRINTING & PUBLISHING: LATIN AMERICAN INDUSTRIAL REPORT. see *PUBLISHING AND BOOK TRADE*

PRINTING AND PUBLISHING NEWSLETTER. see *OCCUPATIONAL HEALTH AND SAFETY*

665.1 UK ISSN 0079-5321
Z119
PRINTING HISTORICAL SOCIETY. JOURNAL. 1965. a. £20($35) to non-members. Printing Historical Society, St. Bride Institute, Bride Lane, Fleet St, London EC4Y 8EE, England. Ed. James Mosley. circ. 1,000. **Indexed:** Artbibl.Mod., Br.Hum.Ind.
  —BLDSC shelfmark: 4843.250000.

686.2 UK ISSN 0144-7505
PRINTING HISTORICAL SOCIETY BULLETIN. 1980. 2/yr. £20($35) membership. Printing Historical Society, St. Bride Institute, Bride Lane, Fleet St., London EC4Y 8EE, England. Ed. Steven Tuohy. bibl.
  —BLDSC shelfmark: 2685.040000.
  Supersedes: Printing Historical Society Newsletter (ISSN 0556-1515)

686.2 US ISSN 0192-9275
Z124.A2
PRINTING HISTORY. s-a. $30 to individuals (foreign $35); institutions $35 (foreign $40). American Printing History Association, Box 4922, Grand Central Sta., New York, NY 10163. Ed. David Pankow. **Indexed:** Lib.Lit.
  —BLDSC shelfmark: 6614.050000.

655 US ISSN 0032-860X
PRINTING IMPRESSIONS. 1958. 24/yr. $75 (foreign $130). North American Publishing Co., 401 N. Broad St., Philadelphia, PA 19108. TEL 215-238-5300. FAX 215-238-5457. Ed. Mark Michelson. adv.; bk.rev.; circ. 94,046. (also avail. in microform from UMI; reprint service avail. from UMI) **Indexed:** Abstr.Bull.Inst.Pap.Chem., Curr.Pack.Abstr., Graph.Arts Lit.Abstr.
  —BLDSC shelfmark: 6614.100000.
  Incorporates: Printing Management (ISSN 0032-8650)
  Description: Features marketing studies, equipment reviews and coverage of international exhibits and conferences.

686.2 UK ISSN 0307-7195
Z120
PRINTING INDUSTRIES. 1901. m. £45 to non-members. British Printing Industries Federation, 11 Bedford Row, London WC1R 4DX, England. adv.; bk.rev.; illus.; index; circ. 5,100. **Indexed:** Graph.Arts Lit.Abstr.
  —BLDSC shelfmark: 6614.130000.
  Formerly: British Federation of Master Printers. Members Circular (ISSN 0007-0696)
  Description: Management journal for the printing industry.

686.2 US ISSN 0191-8273
PRINTING JOURNAL. 1974. m. free to qualified personnel. East-West Communications, 911 N. Fillmore St., Arlington, VA 22201-2127. TEL 703-525-4800. FAX 703-525-4805. Ed. Geoff Lindsay. adv.; bk.rev.; illus.; circ. 19,000 (controlled). (tabloid format) **Indexed:** Graph.Arts Abstr., Graph.Arts Lit.Abstr.
  Description: Covers marketplace trends, issues and technology affecting the graphics arts industry in the Pacific and Mountain States, including Alaska and Hawaii.

686.2 658 US
PRINTING MANAGER. 1979. bi-m. National Association of Printers and Lithographers, 780 Palisade Ave., Teaneck, NJ 07666. TEL 201-342-0700. Ed. Don Lupo. bk.rev.; circ. 5,000. (back issues avail.)

686.2 US ISSN 1046-8595
Z119
PRINTING NEWS - EAST. 1928. 51/yr. $24.95 (Canada $30.95; elsewhere $39.95). Cahners Publishing Company (New York), Publishing & Printing Group (Subsidiary of: Reed International PLC), Division of Reed Publishing (USA) Inc., 249 W. 17th St., New York, NY 10011. TEL 212-463-6727. FAX 212-463-6733. (Subscr. to: Box 336, Brewster, NY 10509) Ed. Joann Strashun. adv.; bk.rev.; illus.; tr.lit.; circ. 9,000. (tabloid format) **Indexed:** Abstr.Bull.Inst.Pap.Chem., Graph.Arts Lit.Abstr.
  Formerly (until Oct. 1989): Printing News (ISSN 0032-8626)
  Description: Devoted primarily to the Greater New York and Philadelphia Metropolitan Areas. Contains news, economic forecasts, upcoming trade shows, services to the trade, technical updates and industry leader profiles.

655 US
PRINTING NEWS - MIDWEST; for the Midwest printer. 1934. m. $20. Cahners Publishing Company (Des Plaines) (Subsidiary of: Reed International PLC), Division of Reed Publishing (USA) Inc., 1350 E. Touhy Ave., Box 5080, Des Plaines, IL 60017-5080. TEL 708-635-8800. FAX 708-299-8622. (Subscr. to: Box 336, Brewster, NY 10509) Ed. Edwin G. Schwenn. adv.; bk.rev.; illus.; stat.; tr.lit.; circ. 14,941. (also avail. in microform from UMI; reprint service avail. from UMI) **Indexed:** Graph.Arts Abstr., Graph.Arts Lit.Abstr.
  Formerly (until 1990): Printing Views (ISSN 0030-8439)
  Description: For owners, managers, and production executives in commercial, newspaper and private printing plants. Directed towards the regional interest of the Midwest printing producer.

655 UK ISSN 0032-8642
PRINTING PRODUCT INFORMATION CARDS. 1969. 3/yr. free. Maclean Hunter Ltd., Maclean Hunter House, Chalk Lane, Cockfosters Rd., Barnet, Herts EN4 0BU, England. TEL 081-975-9759. FAX 081-440-1796. TELEX 299072 MACHUN G. adv.; tr.lit.; circ. 13,321.

686.2 676.3 US
PRINTING PRODUCT INTERNATIONAL. (Text in English) 1968. 4/yr. $30 (foreign $50). Coast Publishing, Inc., 1680 S.W. Bayshore Blvd., Port St. Lucia, FL 34984. TEL 407-879-6666. FAX 407-879-7388. Ed. Jeff Macharyas. adv.; circ. 10,000. **Indexed:** Graph.Arts Lit.Abstr.
  Formerly: Export Grafics U S A (ISSN 0147-409X)
  Description: Trade publication with special-feature editorial sections covering the printing, packaging and converting industries.

686.2 338 US
PRINTING SALES INDEX. 1989. bi-m. $75 to non-members. National Association of Printers and Lithographers, 780 Palisade Ave., Teaneck, NJ 07666. TEL 201-342-0700. stat.
  Description: Provides analysis of industry performance for comparative purposes.

686.2 II ISSN 0401-3956
PRINTING TIMES. (Text in English) 1955. bi-m. Rs.210($3.37) All India Federation of Master Printers, E-14, 3rd Fl., South Extn. Market Part II, New Delhi 110 049, India. TEL 11-6449855. Ed. V.N. Chhabra. adv.; bk.rev.; illus.; circ. 2,000. (back issues avail.)

655 UK ISSN 0079-5372
PRINTING TRADES DIRECTORY. 1960. a. £79 (foreign £89). Benn Business Information Services Ltd., P.O. Box 20, Sovereign Way, Tonbridge, Kent TN9 1RQ, England. TEL 0732-362666. FAX 0732-770483. TELEX 95162-BENTON-G. Ed. Caroline Miles. adv.; index; circ. 2,950.
  —BLDSC shelfmark: 6615.091000.
  Description: List of printers, suppliers of equipment material and services.

PRINTING

686.2 331   AT   ISSN 1030-9160
PRINTING TRADES JOURNAL. 1917. m. free. Printing and Kindred Industries Union, 596 Crown Street, Surry Hills, N.S.W. 2010, Australia. FAX 02-699-1061. Ed. J.P. Cahill. adv.; bk.rev.; circ. 48,000. (back issues avail.)
  Description: Information for trade unionists in printing, newspaper and paper making industries.

686.2   UK   ISSN 0032-8715
PRINTING WORLD. 1878. w. £65 (foreign £95). Benn Publications Ltd., Sovereign Way, Tonbridge, Kent TN9 1RW, England. TEL 0732-364422. Ed. Gareth Ward. adv.; bk.rev.; illus.; pat.; index; circ. 11,300. (also avail. in microform from UMI; reprint service avail. from UMI) **Indexed:** Br.Tech.Ind., Graph.Arts Lit.Abstr., Key to Econ.Sci.
  —BLDSC shelfmark: 6615.105000.
  Incorporates: Printing Today; Which was formerly: Printing Equipment and Materials (ISSN 0032-8596)

686.2   UK   ISSN 0960-9253
▼**PRINTMAKING TODAY.** 1990. q. £14. 14B Elsworthy Terr., London NW3 3DR, England.

686.2 681.65   UK
PRINTSHOP. no.6, May 1981. q. £6.50. Franchise Publications, James House, 37 Nottingham Rd., London SW17 7EA, England. Ed. Robert Riding. adv.; illus.

686.2   UK   ISSN 0032-9878
PRODUCTION JOURNAL. 1958. 10/yr. £20. Newspaper Society, Bloomsbury House, Bloomsbury Sq., 74-77 Great Russell St., London WC1B 3DA, England. TEL 071-636-7014. Ed. Rex Winsbury. adv.; charts; illus.; stat.; index; circ. 3,000 (controlled). (tabloid format) **Indexed:** Abstr.Bull.Inst.Pap.Chem., Graph.Arts Lit.Abstr., Phys.Abstr.
  —BLDSC shelfmark: 6853.150000.

760 659.1   DK
PRODUKTIONSHAANDBOGEN; virksomheder med grafisk produktion - reklamevirksomhed. a. Forlaget de Grafiske Haandboeger, Finsensvej 80, 2000 Frederiksberg, Denmark. adv.; circ. 4,958.
  Description: Directory of prepress, printing, and printfinishing companies in Denmark.

686.2   UK   ISSN 0308-4205
Z120
PROFESSIONAL PRINTER. 1957. bi-m. £18 (foreign £20). Institute of Printing, 8 Lonsdale Gardens, Tunbridge Wells, Kent TN1 1NU, England. TEL 0892-38118. FAX 0582-471334. Ed. Dennis Griffith. adv.; bk.rev.; illus.; index; circ. 2,800. (also avail. in microform from UMI; reprint service avail. from UMI) **Indexed:** Abstr.Bull.Inst.Pap.Chem., Br.Tech.Ind., Graph.Arts Lit.Abstr., P.I.R.A.
  —BLDSC shelfmark: 6864.206000.
  Incorporates: Printing Technology (ISSN 0032-8685)

PUBLISHING & PRODUCTION EXECUTIVE. see *PUBLISHING AND BOOK TRADE*

QUAERENDO; a quarterly journal from the Low Countries devoted to manuscripts and printed books. see *PUBLISHING AND BOOK TRADE*

686.2   US   ISSN 0739-6732
Z119
QUALITY CONTROL SCANNER. 1981. m. $100. Graphic Arts Publishing Co., 3100 Bronson Hill Rd., Livonia, NY 14487. TEL 716-346-2776. FAX 716-346-2276. Eds. Miles & Donna Southworth. bk.rev.; bibl.; adv.; illus.; index; circ. 600. (looseleaf format; back issues avail.)
  —BLDSC shelfmark: 7168.151600.
  Description: Practical ideas for improving quality and productivity in color reproduction by the printing process.

686.2   US   ISSN 0191-4588
QUICK PRINTING; the information source for commercial copyshops and printshops. 1977. m. $22. Coast Publishing, Inc., 1680 S.W. Bayshore Blvd., Port St. Lucie, FL 34984. TEL 407-879-6660. FAX 407-879-7388. Ed. Bob Hall. adv.; charts; illus.; stat.; circ. 60,000. (back issues avail.) **Indexed:** Graph.Arts Lit.Abstr.

R S V P: THE DIRECTORY OF ILLUSTRATION AND DESIGN. see *BUSINESS AND ECONOMICS — Trade And Industrial Directories*

760   IT   ISSN 0033-9687
RASSEGNA GRAFICA. 1950. fortn. L.2400 (foreign L.200000). Editrice Arti Poligrafiche Europee, Via Casella, 16, 20156 Milan, Italy. TEL 02-330221. FAX 02-39214341. Ed. Antonio Ghiorzo. adv.; charts; illus.; circ. 13,000 (controlled).

760   BL   ISSN 0034-4168
REMAG; revista metodos de artes graficas. 1963. m. $30. Editora Metodos Ltda., Caixa Postal 15085, Rua Cardoso Marinho, 42, 20220 Rio de Janeiro RJ, Brazil. Ed. J.M. Lopez Barreto. adv.; bk.rev.; circ. 3,000. **Indexed:** Graph.Arts Lit.Abstr.

686.2   SZ
REPRO BULLETIN.* q. Verband Schweizerische Lichtpaus- und Reprografie-Betriebe - Association Suisses des Ateliers d'Heliographie et de Reprographie Zurich, Postfach 319, CH-8034 Zurich, Switzerland. TEL 01-2117390.

686.2   UK   ISSN 0034-4958
REPRODUCTION; for the printing department and drawing office. 1964. m. £24 (foreign £30). Maclean Hunter Ltd., Maclean Hunter House, Chalk Lane, Cockfosters Rd., Barnet, Herts EN4 0BU, England. TEL 081-975-9759. FAX 081-440-1796. adv.; bk.rev.; charts; illus.; mkt.; stat.; index; circ. 14,500. **Indexed:** Br.Tech.Ind., Build.Manage.Abstr., Info.Media & Tech., World Surf.Coat.

676.2 686.2   US
REPRODUCTION BULLETIN. 1954. q. free. Andrews Paper & Chemical Co., Inc., 1 Channel Dr., Box 509, Port Washington, NY 11050. TEL 516-767-2800. FAX 516-767-1632. Ed. Peter Muller. bk.rev.; pat.; cum.index: nos.1-84 (1954-1974); circ. 2,500. **Indexed:** Abstr.Bull.Inst.Pap.Chem., Chem.Abstr.
  Formerly: Reproduction Paper News Bulletin (ISSN 0034-4966)
  Description: Contains items of interest on Diazotpe reproduction processes.

RESPONSE. see *BUSINESS AND ECONOMICS — Marketing And Purchasing*

686.2   PO
REVISTA DE IMPRENSA. 1987. m. free. Secretaria de Estado da Cultura, Divisao de Relacoes Publicas, Ava. da Republica, 16, 1094 Lisbon, Portugal. TEL 579037. FAX 579592. circ. 540.
  Description: Collection of printing formats as shown by selections from various periodicals.

686.2   GW
S I P - SIEBDRUCK INFOPOST; Kennziffer-Fachzeitschrift fuer grafischen/industriellen Siebdruck und Werbetechnik. 1985. 10/yr. DM.48. S I P - Siebdruck Infopost, Postfach 246, 6553 Sobernheim, Germany. TEL 06751-6150. FAX 06751-4014. Eds. Karl Kahlstatt, Eberhard Lendle. circ. 4,500.

764.8   UK
S P A NEWS. q. membership. Screen Printing Association (UK) Ltd., Association House, 7A West St., Reigate, Surrey RH2 9BL, England. TEL 0737-240792. FAX 0737-240770. circ. 250.
  Formerly: Display Producers and Screen Printers Association. Monthly.

686.2   UK
SCOTTISH DECORATORS' YEAR BOOK AND REVIEW. a. £7.50. Scottish Decorators Federation, 41 York Place, Edinburgh EH1 3HT, Scotland. TEL 031-557-9345. Ed. C.W. Aitken. adv.; circ. 500.
  Formerly: Scottish Decorators' Review.

764.8   US   ISSN 0036-9594
TT273
SCREEN PRINTING. 1953. m. $30. S T Publications Inc., 407 Gilbert Ave., Cincinnati, OH 45202. TEL 513-421-2050. FAX 513-421-5144. Ed. Steve Duccilli. adv.; bk.rev.; stat.; tr.lit.; circ. 12,000 (paid); 3,000 (controlled). (back issues avail.) **Indexed:** Abstr.Bull.Inst.Pap.Chem., Art & Archaeol.Tech.Abstr., Graph.Arts Lit.Abstr., Photo.Abstr.
  —BLDSC shelfmark: 8211.759700.
  Description: Aimed at all types of screen printers. Features how-to tips, new products, technology updates, industry news.

764.8   US
SCREEN PRINTING ASSOCIATION, INTERNATIONAL. TABLOID. m. membership. Screen Printing Association, International, 10015 Main St., Fairfax, VA 22031. TEL 703-385-1335.

764.8   US
SCREEN PRINTING NETWORK. 13/yr. Virgo Publishing Inc., 4141 N. Scottsdale Rd., No.316, Scottsdale, AZ 85251. TEL 602-483-0014. FAX 602-483-1247. Ed. Marcia Flint.

655.316   UK
SCREEN PROCESS. 1952. m. £32 (foreign £38). Batiste Publications Ltd., Pembroke House, Campsbourne Rd., Hornsey, London N8 7PE, England. TEL 081-340-3291. FAX 081-341-4840. TELEX 267727 BATGRP. Ed. Geoff Ellis. adv.; illus.; tr.lit. **Indexed:** Graph.Arts Lit.Abstr., Int.Packag.Abstr.
  Formerly: Point of Sale and Screenprinting (ISSN 0036-9586); **Incorporates:** Screenprinting (ISSN 0261-1309)

764.8   US
SCREENPLAY. m. Windsor Communications, Inc., 9723 Hillview Dr., Dallas, TX 75231-3813. TEL 214-361-2200. FAX 214-361-1904. Ed. Michelle Welch. circ. 15,000.

686.2   CN
SECOND IMPRESSIONS. 1985. 6/yr. Can.$18 (foreign Can.$22)(effective Apr. 1991). 344401 Alberta Inc., Box 6540-Station C, Edmonton, Alta. T5B 4L8, Canada. TEL 403-455-1718. FAX 403-451-4758. Ed. Roy McFadyen. adv.; circ. 6,189.

760   IT   ISSN 0394-5901
SERIGRAFIA. 1956. bi-m. $67. Zeta's s.r.l., Via P.M. Kolbe 8, 20137 Milan, Italy. TEL 02-716332. FAX 02-7387371. Ed. Ruggero Zuliani. adv.; circ. 2,800.
  Description: Concerns the screen printing field.

SERIGRAFIA (RIO DE JANEIRO). see *ART*

764.8   GW   ISSN 0178-2835
SIEBDRUCK; die Europaeische Fachzeitschrift fuer graphischen und industriellen Siebdruck. 1955. m. DM.97. Graphische Werkstaetten GmbH, Schwertfegerstr. 7, 2400 Luebeck, Germany. TEL 0451-87999-0. FAX 0451-87999-99. Ed. Michael Ringelsiep. circ. 4,600. (back issues avail.)
  —BLDSC shelfmark: 8271.930000.

SIGN BUSINESS. see *ADVERTISING AND PUBLIC RELATIONS*

764.8   NE   ISSN 0037-5268
SILK SCREEN; Nederlands vaktijdschrift voor zeefdruk. 1952. m. fl.150. Eisma B.V. Publishers, Celsiusweg 37, B012062299, 8901 BC Leeuwarden, Netherlands. TEL 058-152545. FAX 058-154000. adv.; illus.; circ. 1,400. **Indexed:** Excerpt.Med.
  —BLDSC shelfmark: 8280.258000.

760   UK
SOCIETY OF GRAPHIC ARTISTS. PUBLICATION. a. Society of Graphic Artists, 17 Carlton House Terrace, London SW1Y 5BD, England.

SOUTH AFRICAN TYPOGRAPHICAL JOURNAL/SUID-AFRIKAANSE TIPOGRAFIESE JOERNAAL. see *LABOR UNIONS*

686.2   AT   ISSN 0129-1262
SOUTH EAST ASIAN PRINTER MAGAZINE. 1988. 6/yr. Aus.$60. Calmor & Associates Pty. Ltd., P.O. Box 1315, N. Sydney, N.S.W. 2059, Australia. TEL 02-922-6133. FAX 02-922-4734. Ed. Brian Moore. adv.; bk.rev.; illus.; index; circ. 10,556. (back issues avail.) **Indexed:** Print.Abstr.
  Description: Technical journal for graphic industry management and production, for managers of print shops, trade shops, typesetters, art studios, publishers and packaging companies.

PRINTING — ABSTRACTING, BIBLIOGRAPHIES, STATISTICS

686.2 760 US ISSN 0274-774X
SOUTHERN GRAPHICS; covering the graphic arts in the South. 1924. m. $15. Coast Publishing, Inc., 1680 S.W. Bayshore Blvd., Pt. St. Lucie, FL 34984. TEL 305-879-6660. FAX 407-879-7388. Ed. Kenneth Moran. adv.; bk.rev.; illus.; circ. 20,000. **Indexed:** Graph.Arts Lit.Abstr.
Formed by the merger of: Southern Printer and Lithographer & Graphics (Kissimmee) (ISSN 0192-7256); Graphic Communications.
Description: Covers entire graphic arts industry in 14 Southern states.

760 301.16 770 US ISSN 0886-7682
STEP-BY-STEP GRAPHICS; the how-to reference magazine for the visual communicator. 1985. bi-m. $42. Step-by-Step Publishing (Subsidiary of: Dynamic Graphics), 6000 N. Forest Park Dr., Peoria, IL 61614-3592. TEL 309-688-2300. FAX 309-698-0831. Ed. Nancy Aldrich-Ruenzel. adv.; bk.rev.; illus.; tr.lit.; cum.index; circ. 46,000. (back issues avail.)
—BLDSC shelfmark: 8464.213500.

686.2 658
SUCCESSFUL PRINT SALES; a monthly publication for the graphic arts company sales team. m. $79. Printing Industries of America, Inc., 100 Daingerfield Rd., Alexandria, VA 22314. TEL 703-519-8146. Ed. Cliff Weiss.

760 US
T A G A NEWSLETTER. q. $60. Technical Association of the Graphic Arts, One Lomb Memorial Dr., Box 9887, Rochester, NY 14623-0887. TEL 716-272-0557. FAX 716-475-2250. Ed. Karen Lawrence.

760 US ISSN 0082-2299
CODEN: TAPRAV
T A G A PROCEEDINGS; technical papers presented at annual meeting. 1949. a. $70 (foreign $95). Technical Association of the Graphic Arts, One Lomb Memorial Dr., Box 9887, Rochester, NY 14623-0887. TEL 716-272-0557. FAX 716-475-2250. Ed. Richard S. Fisch. index, cum.index: 1949-1985; circ. 1,000. (back issues avail.) **Indexed:** Abstr.Bull.Inst.Pap.Chem., Graph.Arts Lit.Abstr.

760 US ISSN 0895-6529
T & E NEWS. 1973. 9/yr. free. Rochester Institute of Technology, Technical and Education Center of the Graphic Arts, Box 9887, One Lomb Memorial Dr., Rochester, NY 14623. TEL 716-475-2737. FAX 716-475-7052. Ed. Sandy Richolson. bk.rev.; charts; illus.; circ. 70,000. **Indexed:** Abstr.Bull.Inst.Pap.Chem.
Former titles: T and E Center Newsletter (ISSN 0276-9611); Graphic Arts Research Center. G A R C Newsletter (ISSN 0271-9479)
Description: Provides information on training, seminars and research for the graphic arts industry.

686.2 GW
TAG FUER TAG. bi-m. Berufsgenossenschaft Druck und Papierverarbeitung, Rheinstr. 6-8, Postfach 1549, D-6200 Wiesbaden 1, Germany.

TECHNICAL COMMUNICATION. see COMMUNICATIONS

764.8 US
TECHNICAL GUIDE BOOK OF SCREEN PRINTING. a. (plus s-a. supplements). membership. Screen Printing Association, International, 10015 Main St., Fairfax, VA 22031. TEL 703-385-1335.

760 CU
TECNICA GRAFICA. q. $22 in N. America; S. America $24; Europe $28. (Ministerio de Cultura, Departamento de Informacion Cientifico-Tecnica, CEDE Poligrafico) Ediciones Cubanas, Obispo No. 527, Apdo. 605, Havana, Cuba.

760 CU
TECNICA GRAFICA. SUPLEMENTO. 3/yr. (Ministerio de Cultura, Departamento de Informacion Cientifico-Tecnica, CEDE Poligrafico) Ediciones Cubanas, Obispo No. 527, Apdo. 605, Havana, Cuba.

686.2 US
TEXAS PRINTER. 1988. q. (Printing Industry of America) Branch-Smith Inc., 120 St. Louis, Box 1868, Ft. Worth, TX 76104. TEL 817-332-8236. FAX 817-877-1862. Ed. Nolan Moore. circ. 4,000.

760 US
TEXAS SOURCEBOOK (NO.). 1989. a. $45. Alexander Communications, Inc., 212 W. Superior, Ste. 203, Chicago, IL 60610. TEL 312-944-5115. FAX 312-944-7865. circ. 7,000 (controlled).
Description: Comprehensive guide to the leading graphic arts professionals in Texas. More than 20 categories feature design firms, photographers, illustrators, and printers. Contains over 60 categories of business service listings, Texas facts and figures, and maps.

686.2 SW ISSN 0347-4135
TIDNINGSTEKNIK. 1967. q. SEK 120. (Nordisk Avis-Teknisk Samarbetsnaemnd - Scandinavian Newspapers Technical Cooperation Council) TU: S Foerlags AB, Box 22500, 104 22 Stockholm, Sweden. Ed. Erik Joensson. adv.; circ. 1,600.

686.2 GR ISSN 0257-4292
TIPOGRAFIA. (Text in Greek) 1957. fortn. Dr.1500($400) Athens Typographic Organization Ltd., 13 Agion Anargyron Str., 105 54 Athens, Greece. FAX 3213408. Ed. Fotis Landas. adv.; bk.rev.; circ. 3,000. (tabloid format) Key Title: E Tipografia.

TOKYO ART DIRECTORS ANNUAL/A D C NENKAN. see ADVERTISING AND PUBLIC RELATIONS

686.2 SP ISSN 0212-9280
TOPOGRAFIA Y CARTOGRAFIA. Abbreviated title: TopCart. bi-m. 4500 ptas. (foreign 6500 ptas.)(effective 1992). Colegio Oficial de Ingenieros Tecnicos en Topografia, Junta de Gobierno, Paseo de la Castellana, 210, 9o - 11, 28046 Madrid, Spain. TEL 457-26-77. FAX 345-9026.

686.2 FR
TRANSACTION. 1946. 33/yr. Societe Transaction, 78 av. Andre-Morizet, 92100 Boulogne-Billancourt, France. circ. 20,000.

686.2 US
TYPESETTERS OF CHARLESTON.* w. 54 John Street, Charleston, SC 29403.

686.2 US ISSN 0194-4851
TYPEWORLD; the newspaper for page processing, electronic publishing, typesetting, & graphic communications. 1977. 18/yr. $30 (foreign $165). Pennwell Publishing Co. (Westford), One Technology Park Dr., Westford, MA 01886. TEL 508-392-2157. FAX 508-692-0525. (Subscr. to: Box 2709, Tulsa, OK 74101) Ed. Frank Romano. adv.; bk.rev.; charts; illus.; circ. 50,100. (tabloid format) **Indexed:** Graph.Arts Lit.Abstr., PROMT, Resour.Ctr.Ind.
—BLDSC shelfmark: 9077.565000.

686.2 CS
TYPOGRAFIA. m. (General Management of Printing Industry) Nakladatelstvi Technicke Literatury, Spalena 51, 113 02 Prague 1, Czechoslovakia. (Dist. by: Artia, Ve Smeckach 30, 111 00 Prague 1, Czechoslovakia) Ed. V. Marad.

686.2 SZ ISSN 0041-4840
TYPOGRAFISCHE MONATSBLAETTER; Schweizer Graphische Mitteilungen-revue suisse de l'imprimerie. (Text in English, French and German) 1882. bi-m. 100 Fr. (foreign 125 Fr.). (Gewerkschaft Druck und Papier) Zollikofer AG, Fuerstenlandstr. 122, CH-9001 St. Gallen, Switzerland. TEL 071-297777. FAX 071-297487. TELEX 77537. adv.; bk.rev.; bibl.; charts; illus.; mkt.; circ. 3,000.
—BLDSC shelfmark: 7953.370000.

686.2 US ISSN 0279-0327
TYPOGRAPHER. 1975. m. $24 (Canada $30; elsewhere $36). Typographers International Association, 2233 Wisconsin Ave., N.W., Ste. 235, Washington, DC 20007. TEL 202-965-3400. FAX 202-965-3522. Ed. Xenia Jowyk. adv.; bk.rev.; circ. 10,000.
Description: Contains typesetting industry news, profiles of industry suppliers and end-users, management, production, and legislative trends affecting the commercial typesetting industry.

686.2 US ISSN 0275-6870
Z243.A2
TYPOGRAPHY. 1980. a. $45. (Type Directors Club of New York) Watson-Guptill Publications, 1515 Broadway, New York, NY 10036. TEL 201-363-5679. circ. 20,000.

686 US ISSN 0362-6245
Z119 CODEN: ULCCDC
U & L C. (Upper and Lower Case); the international journal of type and graphic design. 1974. q. $30 for 3 yrs.(free to qualified personnel). International Typeface Corp., 866 Second Ave., New York, NY 10017. TEL 212-371-0699. FAX 212-752-4752. Ed. Margaret Richardson. adv.; bk.rev.; illus.; circ. 180,000. (tabloid format; also avail. in microfiche from UMI; back issues avail.) **Indexed:** Artbibl.Mod., Graph.Arts Lit.Abstr.

686.2 SZ
U G R A MITTEILUNGEN. 1963. 3/yr. 20 Fr. Verein zur Foerderung Wissenschaftlicher Untersuchungen im der Graphischen Industrie, c/o E M P A, Postfach 977, CH-9001 St. Gallen, Switzerland. FAX 071-227220. TELEX 71278 EMPA CH. Ed. Walter Steiger. bk.rev.; bibl.; charts; illus.; circ. 3,500. **Indexed:** Abstr.Bull.Inst.Pap.Chem.
Description: Provides professional information for and of the graphics industry.

686.2
UNITED STATES TRADE SHOW TIMES. (Separate editions for each trade show) 1965. irreg. free. Fichera Publications, 777 S. State Rd. 7, Margate, FL 33068. TEL 305-971-4360. FAX 305-971-4362. adv.; circ. 10,000.
Description: Printing industry trade show journal.

686.2 SZ
V S D - MITTEILUNGEN. bi-w. 67 Fr. (foreign 85 Fr.). Verband der Schweizer Druckindustrie, Schosshaldenstr. 20, CH-3000 Bern 32, Switzerland. TEL 031-431511. FAX 031-443738. adv.; bk.rev.

686.2 SZ
V S F - BULLETIN. irreg. Vereinigung Schweizerischer Formular-Hersteller, Schosshaldenstr. 20, CH-3000 Bern 32, Switzerland. TEL 031-431511.

686.2 US
WASHINGTON INDUSTRY AND ASSOCIATION NEWS.* 1960. q. free. Acropolis Books Ltd., 13950 Park Center Rd., Herndon, VA 22071-3222. Ed. A.J. Hackl. adv.; bk.rev.; circ. 3,500 (controlled).

686.2 GW ISSN 0724-9586
WOLFENBUETTLER SCHRIFTEN ZUR GESCHICHTE DES BUCHWESENS. 1977. irreg., vol.16, 1989. price varies. Verlag Otto Harrassowitz, Taunusstr. 14, Postfach 2929, 6200 Wiesbaden 1, Germany. TEL 0611-530-0. FAX 0611-530570. TELEX 4186135. Ed. Paul Raabe.

686.2 GW ISSN 0147-4804
Z119
WORLD WIDE PRINTER. 1977. bi-m. $60. World-Wide Printer, P.O. Box 4124, 7302 Ostfildern 1, Germany. TEL 0711-444005. FAX 0711-442099. TELEX 177111490. Ed. Theodor J. Anton. adv.; charts; illus.; stat.; circ. 25,500. **Indexed:** Graph.Arts Lit.Abstr.

686.2 CC
YINSHUA ZAZHI/PRINTING MAGAZINE. (Text in Chinese) bi-m. Shanghai Yinshua Jishu Yanjiusuo - Shanghai Printing Technology Institute, No.60, Lane 1209, Xinzha Lu, Shanghai 200041, People's Republic of China. TEL 2562064. Ed. Che Maofeng.

ZUGAKU KENKYU/JOURNAL OF GRAPHIC SCIENCE OF JAPAN. see ART

PRINTING — Abstracting, Bibliographies, Statistics

016 686.2 NE
ANNUAL BIBLIOGRAPHY OF THE HISTORY OF THE PRINTED BOOK AND LIBRARY. Variant title: A B H B. (Text in English) 1973. a. price varies. Kluwer Academic Publishers, Postbus 17, 3300 AA Dordrecht, Netherlands. TEL 078-334911. (Dist. by: Kluwer Academic Publishers Group, P.O. Box 322, 3300 AH Dordrecht, Netherlands; U.S. address: P.O. Box 358, Accord Station, Hingham, MA 02018-0358) Ed. H.D.L. Vervliet.

686.2 AT ISSN 0811-3963
BRANDYWINE BIBLIOGRAPHY. 1981. irreg. price varies. Brandywine Press & Archive, 20 Murray Rd., Beecroft, N.S.W. 2119, Australia. TEL (02)863627. Ed. J.P. Wegner. (back issues avail.)

PSYCHOLOGY 4007

686.2 070   CN   ISSN 0575-9412
Z487
CANADA. STATISTICS CANADA. PRINTING, PUBLISHING AND ALLIED INDUSTRIES. (Catalogue 36-251) (Text in English and French) 1920. a. Can.$35($42) (foreign $49). Statistics Canada, Publications Sales and Services, Ottawa, Ont. K1A 0T6, Canada. TEL 613-951-7277. FAX 613-951-1584.
Description: Annual census of manufactures.

DESIGN AND APPLIED ARTS INDEX. see *ART — Abstracting, Bibliographies, Statistics*

686.2   AT   ISSN 0729-6568
DIRECTORY OF COMPANY HISTORIES OF THE BOOK INDUSTRIES/VERZEICHNIS VON JUBILAEUMSSCHRIFTEN DER GRAPHISCHEN INDUSTRIE. (Text in English and German) 1981. irreg., approx. a. Aus.$10($7.15) Brandywine Press and Archive, 20 Murray Road, Beecroft, N.S.W. 2119, Australia. TEL (02)863627. Ed. Juergen P. Wegner. circ. 100. (back issues avail.)

760   UK
HOT GRAPHICS; for those in the creative design & graphics businesses. 1979. q. £15. Creative Magazines Ltd., 35 Britannia Row, London N1 8QH, England. TEL 071-226-1739. FAX 071-226-1540. TELEX 268279 BRITRO G. (U.S. distr. addr.: 10 E. 21 St., Ste.1710, New York, NY 10010) Ed. Robert T. Prior. adv.; bk.rev.; illus.; circ. 11,000. **Indexed:** Br.Ceram.Abstr.
Description: Presents innovative corporate identity, packaging, graphic design, illustration and computer graphics work from the international circuit.

760   US
Z119
INSTITUTE OF PAPER SCIENCE AND TECHNOLOGY. GRAPHIC ARTS BULLETIN. 1954. m. $400. Institute of Paper Science and Technology, Information Services Division, 575 14th St. N.W., Atlanta, GA 30318. TEL 404-853-9500. FAX 404-853-9510. Ed. Rosanna M. Bechtel. bk.rev.; circ. 350. **Indexed:** Abstr.Bull.Inst.Pap.Chem., Graph.Arts Lit.Abstr., Print.Abstr.
Former titles: Graphic Arts Literature Abstracts (ISSN 0090-8207); Graphic Arts Progress (ISSN 0017-3347); Which incorporates (1951-1953): Graphic Arts Index; Which supersedes: P I A Management Reports.

686 016   RU
NOVOSTI TEKHNICHESKOI LITERATURY. POLIGRAFICHESKAYA PROMYSHLENNOST'. 1969. m. $4. (Komitet po Pechati Soveta Ministrov) Izdatel'stvo Kniga, 50, Gorky St., 125047 Moscow, Russia.

665 016   UK   ISSN 0031-109X
Z118.A3
PRINTING ABSTRACTS.* 1946. m. $935. (Research Association for the Paper and Board, Printing and Packaging Industries) Pira International, Randalls Rd., Leatherhead, Surrey KT22 7RU, England. Ed. Elizabeth Wilce. bk.rev.; abstr.; index. (also avail. in microfilm from UMI) **Indexed:** Curr.Cont., Graph.Arts Lit.Abstr., World Surf.Coat., World Text.Abstr.
●Also available online. Vendor(s): Orbit Information Technologies (PIRA).
—BLDSC shelfmark: 6613.620000.

686.2 016   RU   ISSN 0235-2222
Z119
REFERATIVNYI ZHURNAL. IZDATEL'SKOE DELO I POLIGRAFIYA. 1975. m. 48.60 Rub. Vsesoyuznyi Institut Nauchno-Tekhnicheskoi Informatsii (VINITI), Baltiiskaya ul. 14, Moscow A-219, Russia. (Subscr. to: Mezhdunarodnaya Kniga, Dimitrova ul. 39, 113095 Moscow, Russia)
Formerly: Referativnyi Zhurnal. Ekonimika, Organizatsiya, Tekhnologiya i Oborudovanie Poligraficheskogo Proizvodstva (ISSN 0320-5223)

PRINTING — Computer Applications

see also Computers–Computer Graphics

686.2   US   ISSN 1050-6993
DATEK IMAGING SUPPLIES MONTHLY; the newsletter of the imaging supplies industries, covering consumables for electronic printers, copiers, and other imaging equipment for the office, industry and home. 1987. m. $275 (foreign $305). BIS Strategic Decisions (Subsidiary of: NYNEX), Box 68, Newtonville, MA 02160. TEL 617-893-9130. FAX 617-894-5093. Ed. Bob Leahey.

DUNN REPORT; electronic publishing & prepress systems news & views. see *PUBLISHING AND BOOK TRADE*

686.2   US
ELECTRIC PAGES; the future of print in the information age. m. Interactive Features, 405 Fourth St., Brooklyn, NY 11215. TEL 718-499-1884. Ed. Jack Powers.
Description: Devoted to the new publishing and media technologies including fax publishing, CD-ROM, electronic photography and other tools for the new decade.

686.2 659.1 070.3   US
G C A REVIEW. 1988. m. membership. Graphic Communications Association, 100 Daingerfield Rd., Alexandria, VA 22314. TEL 703-519-8160. FAX 703-548-2867. Ed. Vivian Sanchez. circ. 400.
Formerly (until 1991): Perspectives (Alexandria).

GOVERNMENT PUBLISHER. see *PRINTING*

686.2   US   ISSN 1050-7019
▼**IMAGING BUSINESS REPORT.** 1990. m. $395 (foreign $495). BIS Strategic Decisions (Subsidiary of: NYNEX), Box 68, Newtonville, MA 02160. TEL 617-893-9130. FAX 617-894-5093. Ed. Donna Amrhein.
Description: Covers latest applications, technology, and product news for imaging users and vendors. Includes strategies for evaluating, implementing, and managing an imaging system.

686.2
IMAGING SUPPLIES ANNUAL; product overview and supplies market directory. a. $125 (foreign $140). BIS Strategic Decisions (Subsidiary of: NYNEX), Box 68, Newtonville, MA 02160. TEL 617-893-9130. FAX 617-894-5093. Ed. Robert Leahey.
Formerly: Datek Imaging Supplies Annual; Incorporates: Annual Guide to Ribbons and Toner.
Description: Editorial, product directories and supplies market articles of ribbons, toner, ink-jet ink, technology specific media, and printwheel industries.

686.2   US   ISSN 1042-0304
Z286.E43
PRE-. 1989. 7/yr. $30. South Wind Publishing Co., 8340 Mission Rd., Ste. 106, Prairie Village, KS 66206. TEL 913-642-6611. FAX 913-642-6676. Ed. Michael Scheibach. adv.; bk.rev.; circ. 32,000.
Description: Aimed at users, buyers, and specifiers of electronic design and pre-press products and services. Covers news, trends, and products in the field.

686.2 640.73   US
PRINTERS BUYER'S GUIDE AND HANDBOOK. 2/yr. Bedford Communications, Inc., 150 Fifth Ave., New York, NY 10011. TEL 212-807-8220. FAX 212-807-8737.

686.21   US   ISSN 0887-7556
PRINTOUT. 1977. m. $325 (foreign $355). BIS Strategic Decisions (Subsidiary of: NYNEX), Box 68, Newtonville, MA 02160. TEL 617-893-9130. FAX 617-894-5093. Ed. Adina Levin.
Incorporates (1981-1987): Printout Magazine (ISSN 0738-6613)
Description: Covers company, product and market developments in the computer printer and printer-related industries.

PRODUCTION OF GOODS AND SERVICES

see Business and Economics–Production of Goods and Services

PROTESTANTISM

see Religions and Theology–Protestant

PSYCHIATRY AND NEUROLOGY

see Medical Sciences–Psychiatry and Neurology

PSYCHOLOGY

see also Medical Sciences–Psychiatry and Neurology

301.1   US
A A - B A NEWSLETTER. 1978. q. $50 includes membership. American Anorexia - Bulimia Association, Inc., 418 E. 76th St., New York, NY 10021-3130. TEL 212-734-1114. Ed. Phyllis Ehrenfeld. bk.rev.; bibl.; circ. 7,000.
Description: For professionals and lay persons; includes ongoing updates on clinical and research information on eating disorders; recognition and inspirational support for sufferers, the recovered, families and caregivers; and information and outreach on prevention.

155.4   US
A A C R C NEWSLETTER. 1986. bi-m. $50. American Association of Children's Residential Centers, 440 First St., N.W., Ste. 310, Washington, DC 20001. TEL 202-638-1604. Ed. Claudia C. Waller. circ. 350.

155   US
A B A NEWSLETTER. 1977. 4/yr. $15 to individuals; institutions $25. Association for Behavior Analysis, Western Michigan University, Kalamazoo, MI 49008-5052. TEL 616-387-4494. FAX 616-387-4457. Ed. Stephen Graf. adv.; circ. 2,000.
Description: Covers association activities, news and conference announcements.

157   US
▼**A D A A REPORTER.** 1990. q. $6. Anxiety Disorders Association of America, 6000 Executive Blvd., Ste. 513, Rockville, MD 20852. TEL 301-231-9350. Ed. Dr. Norman Klombers. circ. 6,000. (tabloid format)
Description: Includes scientific articles, self-help information, and association news items.

A D A M H A NEWS. (Alcohol, Drug Abuse, and Mental Health Administration) see *DRUG ABUSE AND ALCOHOLISM*

A H A F JOURNAL. (American Handwriting Analysis Foundation) see *EDUCATION*

158   US
A H P PERSPECTIVE. 1962. m. $59 to individuals; students $39. Association for Humanistic Psychology, 1772 Vallejo St., Ste. 3, San Francisco, CA 94123. TEL 415-346-7929. FAX 415-346-7993. Ed. Mary King. adv.; bk.rev.; circ. 6,000. (back issues avail.)
Formerly: A H P Newsletter.

A M S STUDIES IN MODERN SOCIETY. see *PUBLIC HEALTH AND SAFETY*

301.1 610 155.4   US
A N A D: WORKING TOGETHER. 1979. q. $25 membership. National Association of Anorexia Nervosa and Associated Disorders, Box 7, Highland Park, IL 60035. TEL 708-831-3438. Ed.Bd. bk.rev.; circ. 15,000.
Description: Discusses issues and challenges facing persons suffering from eating disorders and related afflictions.

PSYCHOLOGY

301.19 167   US
A N R E D ALERT. 1979. 10/yr. $10. Anorexia Nervosa & Related Eating Disorders, Inc., Box 5102, Eugene, OR 97405. TEL 503-344-1144. Ed. Dr. J. Bradley Rubel. bk.rev.; circ. 15,000. (back issues avail.)
Description: Causes, consequences, symptoms and treatment of anorexia nervosa and bulimia nervosa.
Refereed Serial

150   US   ISSN 0001-2114
BF1
A P A MONITOR. 1970. 12/yr. $25 to non-members (foreign $37) and institutions (foreign $49). American Psychological Association, 750 First St., N.E., Washington, DC 20002-4242. TEL 202-336-5563. FAX 202-336-5568. Ed. Laurie Denton. adv.; charts; illus.; tr.lit.; circ. 85,000. (also avail. in microform from UMI)
Incorporates: American Psychological Association. Employment Bulletin.
Description: Reports on the science, practice, and social responsibility activities of psychology, including latest legislative developments affecting mental health, education, and research support.

152   II
A P R C JOURNAL OF EXPERIMENTAL PSYCHOLOGY. (Text in English) 1978. 2/yr. Rs.50($22.75) Agra Psychological Research Cell, Tiwari Kothi, Belanganj, Agra 282004, India. Ed. Govind Tiwari. (reprint service avail. from ISI)

155   US   ISSN 0001-2300
A R G R JOURNAL. 1959. s-a. $1. Association for Research in Growth Relationships, c/o Thomas P. Nally, University of Rhode Island, Dept. of Education, Kingston, RI 02881. TEL 401-792-2564. Eds. Richard Clark, Gerald Wohlfred. bk.rev.; charts; stat.; circ. 200. (processed)

152   US
A S D NEWSLETTER. 1984. q. membership. Association for the Study of Dreams, Box 1600, Vienna, VA 22183. TEL 703-242-8888. Ed. Sarah Lillre. bk.rev.; abstr.; bibl.; charts; illus.; circ. 500. (back issues avail.)
Description: International, multidisciplinary, basic and applied dream research.

301.1 150   VE
A V E P S O FASCICULO. 1983. a. Bs.45($6) Asociacion Venezolana de Psicologia Social, Apdo. 47101, Los Chaguaramos, Caracas 1041-A, Venezuela. TEL 6624751; 619811-30, Ext. 2643, 3043. Ed. Beatriz Rodriguez. circ. 500. (back issues avail.)
Indexed: Psychol.Abstr.

ABHIGYAN. see *SOCIAL SCIENCES: COMPREHENSIVE WORKS*

150   US
ACADEMIC PRESS SERIES IN COGNITION AND PERCEPTION. 1973. irreg., latest 1988. Academic Press, Inc., 1250 Sixth Ave., San Diego, CA 92101. TEL 619-231-0926. FAX 619-699-6715. Eds. Edward C. Carterette, Morton P. Friedman. (reprint service avail. from ISI)
Refereed Serial

370.15 150   US   ISSN 0193-1709
BF1
ACADEMIC PSYCHOLOGY BULLETIN. 1979. 3/yr. $15 to non-members; institutions $20. Michigan Psychological Association, University of Detroit, Institute of Gerontology, 4001 West McNichols, Detroit, MI 48221. TEL 517-355-9564. bk.rev.; bibl.; charts; illus.; stat.; circ. 850. (back issues avail.) **Indexed:** Psychol.Abstr.
Description: Details advances in the mental health fields.

ACTA PAEDOLOGICA; an international journal of child development. see *CHILDREN AND YOUTH — About*

150   NE   ISSN 0001-6918
BF1   CODEN: APSOAZ
ACTA PSYCHOLOGICA; international journal of psychonomics. (Text in English) 1941. 9/yr.(in 3 vols.; 3 nos./vol.) fl.672 (effective 1992). North-Holland (Subsidiary of: Elsevier Science Publishers B.V.), P.O. Box 211, 1000 AE Amsterdam, Netherlands. TEL 020-5803911. FAX 020-5803598. TELEX 18582 ESPA NL. (Subscr. in U.S. and Canada to: Elsevier Science Publishing Co., Inc., Box 882, Madison Sq. Sta., New York, NY 10159. TEL 212-989-5800) Ed. J.G.W. Raaijmakers. adv.; bibl.; illus.; index. (also avail. in microform from RPI; back issues avail.; reprint service avail. SWZ) **Indexed:** ASCA, ASSIA, Bibl.Ind., Biol.Abstr., Commun.Abstr., Curr.Cont., Ind.Med., Lang.& Lang.Behav.Abstr., Mid.East: Abstr.& Ind., Psychol.Abstr., Res.High.Educ.Abstr., Sociol.Abstr., SSCI.
—BLDSC shelfmark: 0661.490000.
Description: Publishes original papers reporting on experimental studies, as well as theoretical and review articles, in human experimental psychology.
Refereed Serial

152   FI
ACTA PSYCHOLOGICA FENNICA. (Text in Finnish) 1951. irreg. FIM 40. Finnish Psychological Society, Mariankatu 7 C, 00170 Helsinki, Finland. TEL 90-608586. Ed. Helena Hurne. circ. 500.

370.15 150   PL   ISSN 0208-6093
L51
ACTA UNIVERSITATIS LODZIENSIS: FOLIA PAEDAGOGICA ET PSYCHOLOGICA. (Text in German and Polish; summaries in English and German) 1955-1974; N.S. 1980. irreg. (Uniwersytet Lodzki, Wydzial Pedagogiki i Psychologii) Wydawnictwo Uniwersytetu Lodzkiego, Ul. Jaracza 34, Lodz, Poland. charts.
—BLDSC shelfmark: 0585.208000.
Supersedes in part: Uniwersytet Lodzki. Zeszyty Naukowe. Seria 1: Nauki Humanistyczno-Spoleczne (ISSN 0076-0358)
Description: Contains articles from the fields of history, theory of social education, didactics, social pedagogics and psychology, as well as reports and proceedings of scientific conferences organized by Department of Pedagogics and Psychology in the University of Lodz.

370.15 150   HU   ISSN 0324-7260
LA682
ACTA UNIVERSITATIS SZEGEDIENSIS DE ATTILA JOZSEF NOMINATAE. SECTIO PAEDAGOGICA ET PSYCHOLOGICA. (Text in English or Hungarian) 1956. a. exchange basis. Attila Jozsef University, c/o E. Szabo, Exchange Librarian, Dugonics ter 13, P.O.B. 393, Szeged H-6701, Hungary. (Subscr. to: Kultura, Box 149, H-1389 Budapest, Hungary) Ed. Gyorgy Agoston. circ. 300. **Indexed:** M.L.A.
Description: Journal of Hungarian education with the use of psychology as an auxiliary science for education.

ADOLESCENCE; an international quarterly devoted to the physiological, psychological, psychiatric, sociological, and educational aspects of the second decade of human life. see *CHILDREN AND YOUTH — About*

155   US   ISSN 0748-8572
BF712
ADVANCES IN APPLIED DEVELOPMENTAL PSYCHOLOGY. 1985. irreg., vol.4, 1990. price varies. Ablex Publishing Corporation, 355 Chestnut St., Norwood, NJ 07648. TEL 201-767-8450. FAX 201-767-6717. TELEX 135-393. Ed. Irving Sigel. **Indexed:** Psychol.Abstr.

150 301.1   US
ADVANCES IN APPLIED SOCIAL PSYCHOLOGY. 1980. irreg., vol.3, 1986. $49.95 cloth. Lawrence Erlbaum Associates, Inc., 365 Broadway, Hillsdale, NJ 07642. TEL 201-666-4110. FAX 201-666-2394. Eds. M.J. Saks, L. Saxe. (back issues avail.) **Indexed:** Curr.Cont., Psychol.Abstr.
Refereed Serial

155   US
ADVANCES IN BEHAVIORAL BIOLOGY. irreg., vol.38B, 1990. price varies. Plenum Publishing Corp., 233 Spring St., New York, NY 10013-1578. TEL 212-620-8000. FAX 212-463-0742. TELEX 23-421139. (back issues avail.)
Refereed Serial

152.8 330.9   US   ISSN 0890-0159
HB1
ADVANCES IN BEHAVIORAL ECONOMICS. 1987. irreg., vol.2, 1990. price varies. Ablex Publishing Corporation, 355 Chestnut St., Norwood, NJ 07648. TEL 201-767-8450. FAX 201-767-6717. TELEX 135-393. Eds. Leonard Green, John Kagel.

150   US   ISSN 0146-6402
RC489.B4   CODEN: ABRTDI
ADVANCES IN BEHAVIOUR RESEARCH AND THERAPY; an international journal for reviews and reports of original research. 1978. 4/yr. £145 (effective 1992). Pergamon Press, Inc., Journals Division, 660 White Plains Rd., Tarrytown, NY 10591-5153. TEL 914-524-9200. FAX 914-333-2444. (And: Headington Hill Hall, Oxford OX3 0BW, England. TEL 0865-794141) Ed. S. Rachman. (also avail. in microform from MIM,UMI) **Indexed:** Adol.Ment.Hlth.Abstr., ASSIA, Biol.Abstr., Excerp.Med., Ind.Sci.Rev., Psychol.Abstr., SSCI.
—BLDSC shelfmark: 0699.916000.
Refereed Serial

155 618.92   US   ISSN 0065-2407
BF721   CODEN: ADCDA8
ADVANCES IN CHILD DEVELOPMENT AND BEHAVIOR. 1963. irreg., vol.22, 1989. Academic Press, Inc., 1250 Sixth Ave., San Diego, CA 92101. TEL 619-231-0926. FAX 619-699-6715. Eds. L.P. Lipsitt, Charles C. Spiegel. index. (reprint service avail. from ISI) **Indexed:** Biol.Abstr., Ind.Med., SSCI.
—BLDSC shelfmark: 0703.800000.
Refereed Serial

155.4   US   ISSN 0149-4732
RJ503.3
ADVANCES IN CLINICAL CHILD PSYCHOLOGY. 1977. irreg., vol.13, 1990. price varies. Plenum Publishing Corp., 233 Spring St., New York, NY 10013-1578. TEL 212-620-8000. FAX 212-463-0742. TELEX 23-421139. Eds. Benjamin Lahey, Alan Kazdin. **Indexed:** Psychol.Abstr., SSCI.
—BLDSC shelfmark: 0703.910000.
Refereed Serial

150   US
▼**ADVANCES IN COMPARATIVE PSYCHOLOGY.** 1991. irreg. price varies. Praeger Publishers (Subsidiary of: Greenwood Publishing Group Inc.), 88 Post Rd. W., Box 5007, Westport, CT 06881-5007. TEL 203-226-3571. FAX 203-222-1502.

155   US   ISSN 0276-9913
BF1
ADVANCES IN DESCRIPTIVE PSYCHOLOGY. 1981. a. $58.50 to institutions. (Society for Descriptive Psychology) J A I Press Inc., 55 Old Post Rd., No. 2, Box 1678, Greenwich, CT 06836-1678. TEL 203-661-7602. Eds. Keith E. Davis, Thomas O. Mitchell. **Indexed:** Psychol.Abstr.
Refereed Serial

155   US   ISSN 0275-3049
BF712
ADVANCES IN DEVELOPMENTAL PSYCHOLOGY. 1981. irreg., vol.4, 1986. $49.95. Lawrence Erlbaum Associates, Inc., 365 Broadway, Hillsdale, NJ 07642. TEL 201-666-4110. FAX 201-666-2394. Ed. Michael E. Lamb. bibl.; charts; illus. (back issues avail.) **Indexed:** Curr.Cont., Psychol.Abstr.
—BLDSC shelfmark: 0704.244000.
Refereed Serial

150 614.7   US
ADVANCES IN ENVIRONMENTAL PSYCHOLOGY. 1978. irreg., vol.6, 1986. $24.95. Lawrence Erlbaum Associates, Inc., 365 Broadway, Hillsdale, NJ 07642. TEL 201-666-4110. FAX 201-666-2394. Ed.Bd. (back issues avail.) **Indexed:** Curr.Cont., Psychol.Abstr.
Refereed Serial

ADVANCES IN EXPERIMENTAL SOCIAL PSYCHOLOGY. see *SOCIOLOGY*

PSYCHOLOGY

301.1   UK   ISSN 0270-9228
RC488.5   CODEN: AFITE2
ADVANCES IN FAMILY INTERVENTION, ASSESSMENT AND THEORY; a research annual. 1980. a? $85. Jessica Kingsley Publishers, 118 Pentonville Rd., London N1 9JN, England. TEL 071-833-2307. FAX 071-837-2917. (Dist. in U.S. by: Taylor & Francis, 1900 Frost Rd., Ste. 101, Bristol PA 19007-1598. TEL 215-785-5800) Ed. John P. Vincent. **Indexed**: Psychol.Abstr.
—BLDSC shelfmark: 0706.470000.
    Description: Provides an arena for clinical family researchers to share their work and grapple with the complicated issues involved in conceptualizing, assessing, and intervening with problem families.

ADVANCES IN HEALTH EDUCATION: CURRENT RESEARCH. see *EDUCATION — Teaching Methods And Curriculum*

156   NE
ADVANCES IN HUMAN FACTORS - ERGONOMICS. 1984. irreg., vol.18B, 1990. price varies. Elsevier Science Publishers B.V., Books Division, P.O. Box 211, 1000 AE Amsterdam, Netherlands. TEL 020-5803911. FAX 020-5803705. TELEX 18582 ESPA NL. (Subscr. in U.S. and Canada to: Elsevier Science Publishing Co., Inc., Box 882, Madison Sq. Sta., New York, NY 10159. TEL 212-989-5800)
Refereed Serial

ADVANCES IN INFANCY RESEARCH. see *MEDICAL SCIENCES — Pediatrics*

150   US   ISSN 0163-5379
LB1051
ADVANCES IN INSTRUCTIONAL PSYCHOLOGY. 1978. irreg., vol.3, 1989. $59.95 cloth. Lawrence Erlbaum Associates, Inc., 365 Broadway, Hillsdale, NJ 07642. TEL 201-666-4110. FAX 201-666-2394. Ed. Robert Glaser. illus. (back issues avail.) **Indexed**: Curr.Cont., Psychol.Abstr.
Refereed Serial

ADVANCES IN LEARNING AND BEHAVIORAL DISABILITIES. see *CHILDREN AND YOUTH — About*

614.58   US
ADVANCES IN MOTIVATION AND ACHIEVEMENT. 1984. a. $63.50 to institutions. J A I Press Inc., 55 Old Post Rd., No. 2, Box 1678, Greenwich, CT 06836-1678. TEL 203-661-7602. Ed. Martin L. Maehr.

155   US   ISSN 8755-0032
QP363.5
ADVANCES IN NEURAL AND BEHAVIORAL DEVELOPMENT. 1985. irreg., vol.4, 1992. price varies. Ablex Publishing Corporation, 355 Chestnut St., Norwood, NJ 07648. TEL 201-767-8450. FAX 201-767-6717. TELEX 135-393. Ed. Paul Shinkman.
—BLDSC shelfmark: 0709.475000.
Refereed Serial

150 616.8   US   ISSN 0278-2367
BF698.4
ADVANCES IN PERSONALITY ASSESSMENT. 1982. irreg., vol.8, 1990. $49.95 cloth. Lawrence Erlbaum Associates, Inc., 365 Broadway, Hillsdale, NJ 07642. TEL 201-666-4110. FAX 201-666-2394. Eds. Charles D. Spielberger, James N. Butcher. (back issues avail.) **Indexed**: Curr.Cont., Psychol.Abstr.
—BLDSC shelfmark: 0709.599000.
Refereed Serial

370.15 150   NE
ADVANCES IN PSYCHOLOGY. 1980. irreg., vol.86, 1992. price varies. Elsevier Science Publishers B.V., Books Division, P.O. Box 211, 1000 AE Amsterdam, Netherlands. TEL 020-5803911. FAX 020-5803705. TELEX 18582 ESPA NL. (Subscr. in U.S. and Canada to: Elsevier Science Publishing Co., Inc., Box 882, Madison Sq. Sta., New York, NY 10159. TEL 212-989-5800)
Refereed Serial

370.15   US   ISSN 0270-3920
ADVANCES IN SCHOOL PSYCHOLOGY. 1981. irreg., vol.7, 1990. $39.95 cloth. Lawrence Erlbaum Associates, Inc., 365 Broadway, Hillsdale, NJ 07642. TEL 201-666-4110. FAX 201-666-2394. Ed. Thomas R. Kratochwill. (back issues avail.) **Indexed**: Curr.Cont., Psychol.Abstr.
—BLDSC shelfmark: 0711.382000.
Refereed Serial

157   NE
ADVANCES IN TEST ANXIETY RESEARCH. 1982. irreg., vol. 7, 1992. Swets Publishing Service (Subsidiary of: Swets en Zeitlinger B.V.), Heereweg 347, 2161 CA Lisse, Netherlands. TEL 31-2521-35111. FAX 31-2521-15888. TELEX 41325. (Dist. in N. America by: Swets & Zeitlinger, Box 517, Berwyn, PA 19312. TEL 215-644-4944) Ed.Bd. (back issues avail.)

155.937   US   ISSN 0196-1934
BD444
ADVANCES IN THANATOLOGY. q. $66.50. Foundation of Thanatology, Foundation Book & Periodical Division, Box 1191, Brooklyn, NY 11202-1202. TEL 718-858-3026. Ed. David Peretz. adv. (also avail. in microform from UMI; back issues avail.)
—BLDSC shelfmark: 0711.605000.
    Formerly: Journal of Thanatology (ISSN 0046-4813)
    Description: Articles cover life threatening disease, dying, death, bereavement, hospice care, and widowhood.

152.8 371.3   US   ISSN 0278-2359
BF431
ADVANCES IN THE PSYCHOLOGY OF HUMAN INTELLIGENCE. 1982. irreg., vol.5, 1989. $49.95 cloth. Lawrence Erlbaum Associates, Inc., 365 Broadway, Hillsdale, NJ 07642. TEL 201-666-4110. FAX 201-666-2394. Ed. Robert J. Sternberg. (back issues avail.) **Indexed**: Curr.Cont., Psychol.Abstr.
—BLDSC shelfmark: 0711.068000.
Refereed Serial

150   US
ADVANCES IN THE STUDY OF AGGRESSION. 1984. irreg., vol.2, 1986. Academic Press, Inc., 1250 Sixth Ave., San Diego, CA 92101. TEL 619-231-6616. FAX 619-699-6715. Eds. J. Robert, Caroline Blanchard. (back issues avail.)
Refereed Serial

150   US   ISSN 0065-3454
QL750   CODEN: ADSBBF
ADVANCES IN THE STUDY OF BEHAVIOR. 1965. irreg., vol.20, 1991. Academic Press, Inc., 1250 Sixth Ave., San Diego, CA 92101. TEL 619-231-0926. FAX 619-699-6715. Ed.Bd. index. (reprint service avail. from ISI) **Indexed**: Biol.Abstr., Curr.Adv.Ecol.Sci., Dairy Sci.Abstr., Ind.Sci.Rev., Sci.Cit.Ind.
—BLDSC shelfmark: 0711.590000.
Refereed Serial

150 301.16   US
ADVANCES IN THE STUDY OF COMMUNICATION AND AFFECT.. 1974. irreg., vol.11, 1986. price varies. Plenum Publishing Corp., 233 Spring St., New York, NY 10013-1578. TEL 212-620-8000. FAX 212-463-0742. TELEX 23-421139.
Refereed Serial

614.58 302 616.8   US   ISSN 8756-3010
AFTERWORDS; suicide: the busy professionals newsletter. 1984. q. $35 (Canada $45; elsewhere $55). Adina Wrobleski, Ed. & Pub., 5124 Grove St., Minneapolis, MN 55436-2481. TEL 612-929-6448. circ. 2,000.

350   US   ISSN 0096-140X
BF575.A3   CODEN: AGBEDU
AGGRESSIVE BEHAVIOR; a multidisciplinary journal devoted to the experimental and observational analysis of conflict in humans and animals. 1975. bi-m. $205 (foreign $425). (International Society for Research on Agression) John Wiley & Sons, Inc., Journals, 605 Third Ave., New York, NY 10158. TEL 212-850-6000. FAX 212-850-6088. TELEX 12-7063. Ed. Ronald Baenninger. adv.; bk.rev.; bibl.; charts; illus.; index. (back issues avail.; reprint service avail. from ISI) **Indexed**: Adol.Ment.Hlth.Abstr., Biol.Abstr., Chem.Abstr., Commun.Abstr., Curr.Adv.Ecol.Sci., Curr.Cont., Excerp.Med., Ind.Sci.Rev., Ind.Vet., Mid.East: Abstr.& Ind., Peace Res.Abstr., Pig News & Info., Psychol.Abstr., Sci.Cit.Ind., SSCI, Vet.Bull.
●Also available online.
—BLDSC shelfmark: 0736.285000.
    Description: Devoted to the empirical and theoretical analysis of conflict and the scientific understanding of agression in human and animals.
Refereed Serial

AMERICAN ACADEMY OF PSYCHIATRY AND THE LAW. NEWSLETTER. see *LAW*

150.19   US   ISSN 0090-3604
RC500   CODEN: JAAPCC
AMERICAN ACADEMY OF PSYCHOANALYSIS. JOURNAL. 1973. 4/yr. $45 to individuals; institutions $105. (American Academy of Psychoanalysis) Guilford Publications, Inc., 72 Spring St., 4th Fl., New York, NY 10012. TEL 212-431-9800. FAX 212-966-6708. Ed. Jules Bemporad. adv.; bk.rev.; index; circ. 1,500. (also avail. in microform from RPI; back issues avail.; reprint service avail. from RPI) **Indexed**: Adol.Ment.Hlth.Abstr., Biol.Abstr., Curr.Cont., Excerp.Med., Ind.Med., PSI, Psychoanal.Abstr., Psychol.Abstr., Psychol.R.G., Soc.Work Res.& Abstr., SSCI.
—BLDSC shelfmark: 4683.735000.
Refereed Serial

AMERICAN ART THERAPY ASSOCIATION NEWSLETTER. see *EDUCATION — Special Education And Rehabilitation*

157   US
AMERICAN ASSOCIATION OF SUICIDOLOGY. PROCEEDINGS OF THE ANNUAL MEETING. 8th., 1975. a. price varies. American Association of Suicidology, 2459 S. Ash, Denver, CO 80222. TEL 303-692-0985. Ed. Dr. David Lester. circ. 1,000. (looseleaf format; back issues avail.)

614.58 614.58   US   ISSN 0895-8009
                         CODEN: MAMREB
AMERICAN ASSOCIATION ON MENTAL RETARDATION. MONOGRAPHS. 1973. irreg. price varies. American Association on Mental Retardation, 1719 Kalorama Rd., N.W., Washington, DC 20009-2683. TEL 202-387-1968. FAX 202-387-2193. Ed. Michael J. Begab.
—BLDSC shelfmark: 5914.216600.
    Formerly (until 1987): American Association on Mental Deficiency. Monographs (ISSN 0730-7128)

AMERICAN BEHAVIORAL SCIENTIST. see *SOCIAL SCIENCES: COMPREHENSIVE WORKS*

155.3 301   US
▼**AMERICAN CROSSDRESSER.** 1990. q. $10 (effective 1990). Chevalier Publications, Box 194, Tulare, CA 93275. Ed. Carol Beecroft. circ. 1,500. (back issues avail.)
    Description: Covers heterosexual crossdressing.

301.4   US
AMERICAN FAMILY THERAPY ASSOCIATION NEWSLETTER. 1980. q. $16. American Family Therapy Association, Inc., 2020 Pennsylvania Ave., N.W., Ste. 273, Washington, DC 20006. adv.; bk.rev.; circ. 1,000. (back issues avail.)

616.89   US
AMERICAN GROUP PSYCHOTHERAPY MONOGRAPH SERIES. 1984. irreg., no.7. price varies. International Universities Press, Inc., 59 Boston Post Rd., Box 1524, Madison, CT 06443-1524. TEL 203-245-4000. Ed. Dr. Howard Kibel.
Refereed Serial

AMERICAN IMAGO; a psychoanalytic journal for culture, science and the arts. see *MEDICAL SCIENCES — Psychiatry And Neurology*

AMERICAN JOURNAL OF ART THERAPY; art in psychotherapy, education, and rehabilitation. see *EDUCATION — Special Education And Rehabilitation*

AMERICAN JOURNAL OF COMMUNITY PSYCHOLOGY. see *SOCIOLOGY*

AMERICAN JOURNAL OF DANCE THERAPY. see *DANCE*

PSYCHOLOGY

150 301 US ISSN 0192-6187
RC488.5 CODEN: IJFPDM
AMERICAN JOURNAL OF FAMILY THERAPY. 1973. q. $38 to individuals (foreign $46); institutions $75 (foreign $83). Brunner-Mazel Publishing Co., 19 Union Sq. W., New York, NY 10003. TEL 212-924-3344. Ed. S. Richard Sauber. bk.rev.; index; circ. 2,000. (also avail. in microform from UMI; reprint service avail. from UMI) **Indexed:** Adol.Ment.Hlth.Abstr., C.I.J.E., Curr.Cont., Lang.& Lang.Behav.Abstr., Mid.East: Abstr.& Ind., Psychol.Abstr., Sage Fam.Stud.Abstr., Soc.Work Res.& Abstr., Sp.Ed.Needs Abstr., SSCI.
—BLDSC shelfmark: 0824.620000.
Former titles (until 1979): International Journal of Family Counseling (ISSN 0147-1775); (until 1976): Journal of Family Counseling (ISSN 0093-3171)
Description: Interdisciplinary forum for innovation, theory, research and clinical practice in family therapy.

301.1 340 US ISSN 0733-1290
K1
AMERICAN JOURNAL OF FORENSIC PSYCHOLOGY; interfacing issues of psychology and law. 1983. q. $50 to individuals (foreign $65); institutions $55 (foreign $70). (American College of Forensic Psychology) Edward Miller, Ed. & Pub., 26701 Quail Creek, No. 295, Laguna Hills, CA 92656. TEL 714-831-0236. Ed. Debra Miller. bk.rev.; circ. 500. (also avail. in microfilm from WSH,PMC; microfiche; back issues avail.; reprint services avail. from WSH) **Indexed:** Psychol.Abstr.
—BLDSC shelfmark: 0824.645000.
Description: For psychologists used as expert witnesses in civil and criminal court cases.
Refereed Serial

616.89 US ISSN 0002-9432
RA790.A1 CODEN: AJORAG
AMERICAN JOURNAL OF ORTHOPSYCHIATRY. 1930. q. $30 to individuals; institutions $45. American Orthopsychiatric Association, Inc., 19 W. 44th St., New York, NY 10036. TEL 212-354-5770. FAX 212-302-9463. (Subscr. to: 49 Sheridan Ave., Albany, NY 12201-1413) Ed. Milton F. Shore. adv.; bibl.; charts; illus.; index, cum.index; circ. 13,000. (also avail. in microform from UMI,MIM; reprint service avail. from UMI) **Indexed:** Acad.Ind., Adol.Ment.Hlth.Abstr., ASSIA, Bibl.Dev.Med.& Child Neur., Bibl.Ind., Biol.Abstr., Chem.Abstr., Child.Devel.Abstr., CINAHL, Crim.Just.Abstr., Curr.Adv.Ecol.Sci., Curr.Cont., Curr.Lit.Fam.Plan., Educ.Ind., Except.Child.Educ.Abstr., Excerp.Med., Hosp.Lit.Ind., Ind.Med., Ind.Sci.Rev., Int.Nurs.Ind., Lang.& Lang.Behav.Abstr., Ment.Retard.Abstr., Nutr.Abstr., Psychol.Abstr., Psycscan C.P., Psycscan D.P., Risk Abstr., Sage Fam.Stud.Abstr., Sci.Cit.Ind., Soc.Sci.Ind., Soc.Work Res.& Abstr., Sp.Ed.Needs Abstr., SSCI, Stud.Wom.Abstr.
—BLDSC shelfmark: 0829.250000.
Refereed Serial

616.891 US ISSN 0002-9548
RC321 CODEN: AJPYA8
AMERICAN JOURNAL OF PSYCHOANALYSIS. 1941. q. $95 (foreign $110). (Association for the Advancement of Psychoanalysis) Human Sciences Press, Inc. (Subsidiary of: Plenum Publishing Corp.), 233 Spring St., New York, NY 10013. TEL 212-620-8000. FAX 212-463-0742. TELEX 23-421139. Ed. Dr. Mario Rendon. adv.; bk.rev.; bibl.; index, cum.index: 1941-1965. (also avail. in microform from UMI; reprint service avail. from UMI) **Indexed:** Abstr.Soc.Work., Biol.Abstr., Chem.Abstr., Chicago Psychoanal.Lit.Ind., Curr.Cont., Educ.Ind., Excerp.Med., Ind.Med., Ind.Med., Mid.East: Abstr.& Ind., Psychoanal.Abstr., Psychol.Abstr., Soc.Work Res.& Abstr., SSCI.
—BLDSC shelfmark: 0835.300000.
Description: Intended to communicate modern concepts of psychoanalytic theory and practice, plus related investigations in allied fields.
Refereed Serial

150 US ISSN 0002-9556
BF1 CODEN: AJPCAA
AMERICAN JOURNAL OF PSYCHOLOGY. 1887. q. $24 to individuals; institutions $48. (University of Illinois at Urbana-Champaign) University of Illinois Press, 54 E. Gregory Dr., Champaign, IL 61820. TEL 217-333-0950. FAX 217-244-8082. Ed. Don Dulany. adv.; bk.rev.; bibl.; charts; stat.; index, cum.index every 25 vols.; circ. 2,600. (also avail. in microform from MIM,UMI,PMC; reprint service avail. from KTO,UMI) **Indexed:** Acad.Ind., Adol.Ment.Hlth.Abstr., ASSIA, Biol.Abstr., Bk.Rev.Ind. (1980-), C.I.S. Abstr., Chem.Abstr., Child.Bk.Rev.Ind. (1980-), Commun.Abstr., Curr.Cont., Ergon.Abstr., Ind.Med., Lang.& Lang.Behav.Abstr., Mid.East: Abstr.& Ind., Pers.Lit., Psychol.Abstr., Soc.Sci.Ind., SSCI.
—BLDSC shelfmark: 0835.500000.
Refereed Serial

AMERICAN POLYGRAPH ASSOCIATION NEWSLETTER. see *CRIMINOLOGY AND LAW ENFORCEMENT*

370.15 US ISSN 1052-7958
AMERICAN PSYCHOANALYST. 1967. q. $25 to individuals (foreign $45); institutions $50 (foreign $70). (American Psychoanalytic Association) Analytic Press, Inc., 365 Broadway, Hillsdale, NJ 07642. TEL 800-926-6579. FAX 201-666-2394. Ed. Dr. Arnold Richards. circ. 4,000. (back issues avail.)
Formerly: American Psychoanalytic Association. Newsletter.
Description: Information and news of the association.

616.891 US ISSN 0003-0651
BF173.A2 CODEN: JAPOAE
AMERICAN PSYCHOANALYTIC ASSOCIATION. JOURNAL. (Supplements avail.) 1953. q. $82.50 to individuals (foreign $92.50); institutions $102.50 (foreign $112.50). International Universities Press, Inc., Journal Department, 59 Boston Post Rd., Box 1524, Madison, CT 06443-1524. TEL 203-245-4000. FAX 203-245-0775. Ed. Dr. Theodore Shapiro. adv.; bk.rev.; abstr.; bibl.; charts; index, cum.index: vols.1-22, vols.23-33; circ. 7,500. (back issues avail.) **Indexed:** Adol.Ment.Hlth.Abstr., ASSIA, Biol.Abstr., Curr.Cont., Excerp.Med., Ind.Med., Mid.East: Abstr.& Ind., Psychoanal.Abstr., Psychol.Abstr., SSCI.
—BLDSC shelfmark: 4692.070000.
Description: Covers articles in clinical and theoretical applied psychoanalytic studies.
Refereed Serial

150 US ISSN 0065-9843
AMERICAN PSYCHOANALYTIC ASSOCIATION. JOURNAL. MONOGRAPH. 1953. irreg., no.4, 1971. International Universities Press, Inc., 59 Boston Post Rd., Box 1524, Madison, CT 06443-1524. TEL 203-245-4000. **Indexed:** Biol.Abstr., SSCI.
Refereed Serial

150.19 US
AMERICAN PSYCHOANALYTIC ASSOCIATION. WORKSHOP SERIES. 1985. irreg., no.7. price varies. International Universities Press, Inc., 59 Boston Post Rd., Box 1524, Madison, CT 06443-1524. TEL 203-245-4000. Ed. Scott Dowling.
Refereed Serial

AMERICAN PSYCHOLOGICAL ASSOCIATION. DIRECTORY. see *BIOGRAPHY*

150 US ISSN 0003-066X
BF1 CODEN: AMPSAB
AMERICAN PSYCHOLOGIST. 1946. m. $100 to non-members (foreign $112); institutions $200 (foreign $224). American Psychological Association, 750 First St., N.E., Washington, DC 20002-4242. TEL 202-336-5563. FAX 202-336-5568. Ed. Raymond D. Fowler. adv.; illus.; index; circ. 95,200. (also avail. in microform from MIM,UMI,PMC; back issues avail.; reprint service avail. from KTO) **Indexed:** Acad.Ind., Adol.Ment.Hlth.Abstr., Amer.Bibl.Slavic & E.Eur.Stud., ASSIA, Biol.Abstr., C.I.J.E., CERDIC, Chem.Abstr., Child Devel.Abstr., Commun.Abstr., Crim.Just.Abstr., Curr.Adv.Ecol.Sci., Curr.Cont., Fut.Surv., Ind.Med., Int.Nurs.Ind., Lang.& Lang.Behav.Abstr., M.L.A., Mid.East: Abstr.& Ind., Pers.Lit., PSI, Psychol.Abstr., Res.High.Educ.Abstr., Risk Abstr., Sage Fam.Stud.Abstr., Sage Pub.Admin.Abstr., Soc.Sci.Ind., Soc.Work Res.& Abstr., SSCI, Stud.Wom.Abstr.
—BLDSC shelfmark: 0853.400000.
Description: Publishes empirical, theoretical and practical articles.
Refereed Serial

362.29 US ISSN 0740-0454
AMERICAN UNIVERSITY STUDIES. SERIES 8. PSYCHOLOGY. 1983. irreg. Peter Lang Publishing, Inc., 62 W. 45th St., 4th Fl., New York, NY 10036. TEL 212-302-6740. Ed. Michael Flamini.
—BLDSC shelfmark: 0858.078200.
Refereed Serial

AMSTERDAM STUDIES IN THE THEORY AND HISTORY OF LINGUISTIC SCIENCE. SERIES 2: CLASSICS IN PSYCHOLINGUISTICS. see *LINGUISTICS*

158 PO ISSN 0870-8231
RC500
ANALISE PSICOLOGICA. 1977. q. $45. Instituto Superior de Psicologia Aplicada, Rua Jardim do Tabaco, 44, 1100 Lisbon, Portugal. TEL 86-31-84. FAX 86-09-54. Ed. Frederico Pereira. adv.; bk.rev.
—BLDSC shelfmark: 0890.525000.

150.19 808.8 US
ANALYTICAL PSYCHOLOGY CLUB OF NEW YORK. BULLETIN. 1938. 8/yr. membership. Analytical Psychology Club of New York, 28 E. 39th St., New York, NY 10016. TEL 212-697-7877. Ed.Bd. bk.rev.; film rev.; circ. 300.
Description: Covers club business, programs and brief accounts of talks.

150 SZ ISSN 0301-3006
RC500 CODEN: ANAPC4
ANALYTISCHE PSYCHOLOGIE; Zeitschrift fuer analytische Psychologie und ihre Grenzgebiete. (Text in German; summaries in English and German) 1970. q. 108 Fr.($72) per vol. S. Karger AG, Allschwilerstr. 10, P.O. Box, CH-4009 Basel, Switzerland. TEL 061-3061111. FAX 061-3061234. TELEX CH 962652. Eds. H. Dieckmann, C.A. Meier. adv.; bk.rev.; bibl.; circ. 1,700. **Indexed:** Biol.Abstr., Curr.Cont., Psychoanal.Abstr., Psychol.Abstr., SSCI.
—BLDSC shelfmark: 0897.170000.
Supersedes: Zeitschrift fuer Analytische Psychologie und ihre Grenzgebiete (ISSN 0049-8580)

301.1 150 IO
ANDA; majalah psikologi populer. irreg. Yayasan Bina Psikologi, c/o Mulyono & Associates, Gedung Pant Trisula, Jalan Menteng Raya 35, Box 3216, Jakarta, Indonesia.

150 US
ANDROS DIGEST.* 1982. 17/yr. $39. PeopleScience, Inc., 1015 S. Park Ave., Highland Park, NJ 08904-2910. TEL 908-572-3120. Ed. Fred Streit.

150 001.3 IT
ANIMA. 1988. a. L.40000 (foreign L.60000) for 2 yrs. S.U.Fl., Casella Postale 18.265, Florence, Italy. TEL 698185. Ed. Francesco Donfrancesco. circ. 450. **Indexed:** Bull.Signal.
Description: Multidisciplinary forum featuring readings on archetypical psychology, religion, art and humanities.

ANIMAL BEHAVIOUR. see *BIOLOGY — Zoology*

PSYCHOLOGY

591.5   US   ISSN 0090-4996
QL785   CODEN: ALBVAB
ANIMAL LEARNING & BEHAVIOR. 1973. q. $74 (foreign $80). Psychonomic Society, Inc., 1710 Fortview Rd., Austin, TX 78704. TEL 512-462-2442. Ed. Vincent Lolordo. adv.; illus.; circ. 1,300. (also avail. in microform from KTO,UMI; back issues avail.; reprint service avail. from UMI) **Indexed:** Biol.Abstr., Curr.Adv.Ecol.Sci., Excerp.Med., Gen.Sci.Ind., Ind.Sci.Rev., Nutr.Abstr., Psychol.Abstr., Risk Abstr., Sci.Cit.Ind., SSCI.
—BLDSC shelfmark: 0905.002000.
Description: Includes articles on animal learning, motivation, emotion and comparative behavior.

616.8   FR   ISSN 0003-4487
CODEN: AMPYAT
ANNALES MEDICO-PSYCHOLOGIQUES. 1843. 10/yr. 190 ECU($235) (typically set in Jan.). (Societe Medico-Psychologique) Masson, 120 bd. Saint-Germain, 75280 Paris Cedex 06, France. TEL 1-46-34-21-60. FAX 1-45-87-29-99. TELEX 202 671 F. Ed. L. Vidart. bk.rev.; abstr.; illus.; index; circ. 1,900. (reprint service avail. from ISI) **Indexed:** Biol.Abstr., Biotech.Abstr., C.I.S. Abstr., Curr.Cont., Excerp.Med., Ind.Med., Psychol.Abstr.
—BLDSC shelfmark: 0984.150000.

ANNALES UNIVERSITATIS MARIAE CURIE-SKLODOWSKA. SECTIO J. PAEDAGOGIA - PSYCHOLOGIA. see *EDUCATION*

155.4   UK
ANNALS OF CHILD DEVELOPMENT. 1984. a. $75. Jessica Kingsley Publishers, 118 Pentonville Rd., London N1 9JN, England. TEL 071-833-2307. FAX 071-837-2917. (Dist in U.S. by: Taylor & Francis, 1900 Frost Rd., Ste. 101, Bristol PA 19007-1598. TEL 215-785-5800) Ed. Ross Vasta.
Description: Presents an array of topics by scholars in their respective specialties.
Refereed Serial

152.8   US
ANNALS OF THEORETICAL PSYCHOLOGY. 1984. irreg., vol.7, 1991. Plenum Publishing Corp., 233 Spring St., New York, NY 10013-1578. TEL 212-670-8000. FAX 212-463-0742. TELEX 23-421139. Ed. L.P. Mos.
Refereed Serial

150   FR   ISSN 0003-5033
BF2
ANNEE PSYCHOLOGIQUE. (Text in French; summaries in English, French) 1884. q. 500 F. (foreign 610 F.). Presses Universitaires de France, Departement des Revues, 14 Avenue du Bois-de-l'Epine, B.P.90, 91003 Evry Cedex, France. TEL 1-60-77-82-05. FAX 1-60-79-20-45. TELEX PUF 600 474 F. Ed. Maire-France Ehrlich. bk.rev.; charts; index; circ. 1,500. (also avail. in microform from MIM; reprint service avail. from KTO) **Indexed:** Curr.Cont., Ind.Med., Lang.& Lang.Behav.Abstr., Psychol.Abstr., SSCI.
—BLDSC shelfmark: 1049.250000.
Description: Presents original research, critical reviews, bibliographic analyses.

370.15   US
ANNUAL EDITIONS: EDUCATIONAL PSYCHOLOGY. 1981. a. $10.95. Dushkin Publishing Group, Inc., Sluice Dock, Guilford, CT 06437-9989. TEL 203-453-4351. FAX 203-453-6000. Ed.Bd. illus.
Refereed Serial

ANNUAL EDITIONS: HUMAN DEVELOPMENT. see *BIOLOGY — Physiology*

ANNUAL EDITIONS: HUMAN SEXUALITY. see *BIOLOGY*

158.105   US   ISSN 0198-912X
BF698.A1
ANNUAL EDITIONS: PERSONAL GROWTH AND BEHAVIOR. 1975. a. $10.95. Dushkin Publishing Group, Inc., Sluice Dock, Guilford, CT 06437-9989. TEL 203-453-4351. FAX 203-453-6000. Ed. Karen G. Duffy. illus.; index. (back issues avail.)
Formerly: Annual Editions: Readings in Personality and Adjustment (ISSN 0361-3836)
Refereed Serial

150   US   ISSN 0272-3794
BF149
ANNUAL EDITIONS: PSYCHOLOGY. 1971. a. $10.95. Dushkin Publishing Group, Inc., Sluice Dock, Guilford, CT 06437-9989. TEL 203-453-4351. FAX 203-453-6000. Eds. Hiram Fitzgerald, Michael G. Walraven. illus.
Formerly: Annual Editions: Readings in Psychology (ISSN 0197-0542)
Refereed Serial

636.089   JA   ISSN 0003-5130
ANNUAL OF ANIMAL PSYCHOLOGY. (Text in English or Japanese; summaries in English) 1947. s-a. 2400 Yen. Japanese Society for Animal Psychology, c/o Dept. of Psychology, University of Tokyo, Bunkyo-ku 113, Tokyo, Japan. (Subscr. to: Japan Publishing Trading Co. Ltd., P.O. Box 5030, Tokyo International, Tokyo, Japan) Ed. Osamu Fujita. adv.; index; circ. 500. (back issues avail.) **Indexed:** Psychol.Abstr.

150   US   ISSN 0066-4308
BF30   CODEN: ARPSAC
ANNUAL REVIEW OF PSYCHOLOGY. 1950. a. $43 (foreign $48)(effective Jan. 1992). Annual Reviews Inc., 4139 El Camino Way, Box 10139, Palo Alto, CA 94303-0897. TEL 415-493-4400. FAX 415-855-9815. TELEX 910-290-0275. Eds. Lyman W. Porter, Mark R. Rosenzweig. bibl.; index, cum.index. (also avail. in microfilm from PMC; back issues avail.; reprint service avail. from ISI) **Indexed:** Adol.Ment.Hlth.Abstr., Biol.Abstr., Chem.Abstr., Child Devel.Abstr., Curr.Adv.Ecol.Sci., Curr.Cont., DSH Abstr., Excerp.Med., Ind.Med., Ind.Sci.Rev., Lang.& Lang.Behav.Abstr., M.M.R.I., Psychol.Abstr., Psycscan D.P., Sci.Cit.Ind., Soc.Sci.Ind., SSCI.
—BLDSC shelfmark: 1528.400000.
Description: Original reviews of critical literature and current developments in psychology.
Refereed Serial

150   SP   ISSN 0066-5126
ANUARIO DE PSICOLOGIA. (Text in Spanish; summaries in English and French) 1969. 2/yr. 2500 ptas.($6) Universidad de Barcelona, Facultad de Psicologia, Avenida de Chile, S-N, 08028 Barcelona, Spain. TEL 334-61-00. Ed. Miguel Siguan. bk.rev.; circ. 1,000. **Indexed:** Psychol.Abstr.
—BLDSC shelfmark: 1565.132000.

157   US   ISSN 0891-7779
BF575.A6   CODEN: ANRSEW
ANXIETY RESEARCH; an international journal. 1988. 4/yr. (in 1 vol., 4 nos./vol.). $91. Harwood Academic Publishers, 270 Eighth Ave., New York, NY 10011. TEL 212-206-8900. FAX 212-645-2459. TELEX 236735 GOPUB UR. (Subscr. to: Box 786, Cooper Sta., New York, NY 10276. TEL 800-545-8398; UK subscr. to: P.O. Box 90, Reading, Berkshire RG1 8JL, England. TEL 0734-560-080) Ed. J.B. Davies. (also avail. in microform) **Indexed:** Psychol.Abstr.
—BLDSC shelfmark: 1566.610000.
Description: Emphasizes research reports, theoretical papers, and interpretive reviews or meta-analysis of the literature.
Refereed Serial

150.19   US   ISSN 0962-1849
▼**APPLIED AND PREVENTIVE PSYCHOLOGY.** 1992. q. $85. (American Association of Applied and Preventive Psychology) Cambridge University Press, Edinburgh Bldg., Shaftesbury Rd., Cambridge CB2 2RU, England. TEL 0223-312393. FAX 0223-315052. TELEX 851917256. Ed. Logan Wright.
Description: Focuses on the scientific, epidemiological, or public health approach to psychological problems.

370.15 150   UK   ISSN 0888-4080
BF311   CODEN: ACPSED
APPLIED COGNITIVE PSYCHOLOGY. 1982. 8/yr. $265 (effective 1992). John Wiley & Sons Ltd., Journals, Baffins Lane, Chichester, Sussex PO19 1UD, England. TEL 0243 779777. FAX 0243-775878. TELEX 86290 WIBOOK G. Eds. G. Davies, M. Pressley. adv.; bk.rev.; charts; illus.; index. (also avail. in microform from SWZ,UMI; reprint service avail. from SWZ,UMI) **Indexed:** ASSIA, Cont.Pg.Educ., Curr.Cont., Psychol.Abstr., SSCI.
—BLDSC shelfmark: 1571.936500.
Formerly (until 1987): Human Learning (ISSN 0277-6707)
Description: Reviews and reports papers dealing with psychological analyses of problems of memory, learning, thinking, language, and consciousness as they are reflected in the real world.

APPLIED ERGONOMICS; human factors in technology and society. see *ENGINEERING*

APPLIED PSYCHOLINGUISTICS; psychological studies of language processes. see *LINGUISTICS*

APPLIED PSYCHOLINGUISTICS AND COMMUNICATION DISORDERS. see *LINGUISTICS*

150   US   ISSN 0146-6216
BF39
APPLIED PSYCHOLOGICAL MEASUREMENT. 1976. q. $55 (foreign $66). Applied Psychological Measurement, Inc., N660 Elliott Hall, University of Minnesota, 75 E. River Rd., Minneapolis, MN 55455. TEL 612-625-0862. FAX 612-626-2079. Ed. David J. Weiss. adv.; charts; illus.; circ. 975. (also avail. in microfiche from UMI) **Indexed:** Biol.Abstr., Child Devel.Abstr., Psychol.Abstr., Psycscan, SSCI.
—BLDSC shelfmark: 1576.550000.
Description: Presents empirical research on the application of techniques of psychological measurement to substantive problems in all areas of psychology and related disciplines.

158   UK   ISSN 0269-994X
BF636.A1   CODEN: ADPYE4
APPLIED PSYCHOLOGY; an international review. (Text in English; abstracts in French) 1951. 4/yr. £33($63) to individuals; institutions £82.50($157). (International Association of Applied Psychology) Lawrence Erlbaum Associates Ltd., 27 Palmeira Mansions, Church Rd., Hove, East Sussex BN3 2FA, England. TEL 0273-207411. FAX 0273-205612. Ed. Michael Frese. adv.; bk.rev.; circ. 2,000. **Indexed:** Adol.Ment.Hlth.Abstr., Cont.Pg.Manage., Curr.Cont., Ergon.Abstr., Psychol.Abstr., Psycscan, SSCI.
—BLDSC shelfmark: 1576.555000.
Formerly: International Review of Applied Psychology.
Description: Serves as a forum for the scholarly exchange of research findings and professional standards, and promotes awareness of important professional issues.
Refereed Serial

155.4   FR   ISSN 0999-792X
APPROCHE NEUROPSYCHOLOGIQUE DES APPRENTISSAGES CHEZ L'ENFANT. Short title: A N A E. (Text in English, French) 4/yr. 450 F. to individuals (foreign 600 F.); institutions 580 F.(foreign 720 F.); students 300 F.(foreign 390 F.). John Libbey Eurotext, 6 rue Blanche, 92120 Montrouge, France. TEL 1-47-35-85-52. FAX 1-46-57-10-09. (Dist. by: Gauthier-Villars, Centrale des Revues, 11 rue Gossin, 92543 Montrouge Cedex, France. TEL 1-46-56-52-66) —BLDSC shelfmark: 1580.615000.
Description: For researchers and clinicians.

301.1 150   GW
ARBEITEN ZUR SOZIALWISSENSCHAFTLICHEN PSYCHOLOGIE. 1972. irreg. price varies. Aschendorffsche Verlagsbuchhandlung, Soesterstr. 13, 4400 Muenster, Germany. TEL 0251-690-0. FAX 0251-690405.

150.19   GW   ISSN 0721-9628
ARBEITSHEFTE KINDERPSYCHOANALYSE. 1982. a. DM.36. Gesamthochschule Kassel, Wissenschaftliches Zentrum II, Gottschalkstr. 26, 3500 Kassel, Germany. TEL 0561-8042807. Ed. Hilde Kipp. circ. 700. (back issues avail.)

ARCHAEUS. see *PARAPSYCHOLOGY AND OCCULTISM*

PSYCHOLOGY

301.1 150   UK   ISSN 0260-4523
ARCHITECTURAL PSYCHOLOGY NEWSLETTER. 1969. 4/yr. £8. Architectural Psychology Research Unit, Kingston Polytechnic, Knights Park, Kingston-upon-Thames, Surrey KT1 2QJ, England. TEL 01-549-6151.
  Description: Research concerned with the interrelationship between people and their physical surroundings.

ARCHITECTURE & BEHAVIOUR/ARCHITECTURE ET COMPORTEMENT. see *ARCHITECTURE*

150   GW   ISSN 0066-6475
                                                        CODEN: APSYCX
ARCHIV FUER PSYCHOLOGIE. (Text in English and German) 1903. q. DM.124. Bouvier Verlag Herbert Grundmann, Am Hof 32, Postfach 1268, 5300 Bonn, Germany. Ed. W.D. Froehlich. adv.; illus.; circ. 600. (also avail. in microfilm from PMC; back issues avail.) **Indexed:** Ger.J.Psych., Ind.Med., Psychol.Abstr., SSCI.
  Supersedes: Archiv fuer die Gesamate Psychologie.

ARCHIV FUER RELIGIONSPSYCHOLOGIE. see *RELIGIONS AND THEOLOGY*

150   SZ   ISSN 0003-9640
BF2
ARCHIVES DE PSYCHOLOGIE. (Text in English and French) 1901. q. 68 SFr.($48.50) (Universite de Geneve, Faculte de Psychologie et des Sciences de l'Education, Section de Psychologie) Editions Medecine et Hygiene, Case Postale 456, CH-1211 Geneva 4, Switzerland. TEL 022-469355. FAX 022-475610. Ed.Bd. charts; cum.index irreg.; circ. 600. **Indexed:** Psychol.Abstr.
  —BLDSC shelfmark: 1640.450000.

ARCHIVES OF CLINICAL NEUROPSYCHOLOGY. see *MEDICAL SCIENCES — Psychiatry And Neurology*

ARCHIVIO DI PSICOLOGIA, NEUROLOGIA E PSICHIATRIA. see *MEDICAL SCIENCES — Psychiatry And Neurology*

ART THERAPY. see *EDUCATION — Special Education And Rehabilitation*

ARTIFEX; journal of cyberbiology. see *PARAPSYCHOLOGY AND OCCULTISM*

616.89   US   ISSN 0197-4556
RC489.A7   CODEN: APCYAJ
THE ARTS IN PSYCHOTHERAPY; an international journal. 1973. 5/yr. £130 (effective 1992). Pergamon Press, Inc., Journals Division, 660 White Plains Rd., Tarrytown, NY 10591-5153. TEL 914-524-9200. FAX 914-333-2444. (And: Headington Hill Hall, Oxford OX3 0BW, England. TEL 0865-794141) Ed. Robert J. Landy. adv.; bk.rev. (also avail. in microform from MIM; reprint service avail. from ISI,UMI) **Indexed:** Artbibl.Mod., Biol.Abstr., Curr.Cont., Except.Child.Educ.Abstr., Excerp.Med., Psychol.Abstr., SSCI.
  —BLDSC shelfmark: 1736.825000.
  Formerly: Art Psychotherapy (ISSN 0090-9092)
  Description: Innovative research in artistic inquiry and expression and its use in the treatment of mental disorders.
  Refereed Serial

370   II
ASIAN JOURNAL OF PSYCHOLOGY AND EDUCATION. (Text in English) 1976. 6/yr. Rs.140($39.50) Agra Psychological Research Cell, Tiwari Kothi, Belanganj, Agra 282004, India. Eds. B.V. Patel, N.S. Chauhan. adv.; bk.rev. (reprint services avail. from ISI) **Indexed:** Psychol.Abstr.

301.1 150   VE   ISSN 1011-6273
ASOCIACION VENEZOLANA DE PSICOLOGIA SOCIAL. BOLETIN. 1978. q. Bs.60($20) to individuals; institutions $25. Asociacion Venezolana de Psicologia Social (AVEPSO), Apdo. 47101, Los Chaguaramos, Caracas 1041-A, Venezuela. TEL 619811-30 Ext. 2643. Ed. Lucia Azuaje. adv.; bk.rev.; circ. 500. (back issues avail.)
  Description: Features theoretical and methodological papers and information about social psychology in Latin America.

150 610   US
BF319.5.B5
ASSOCIATION FOR APPLIED PSYCHOPHYSIOLOGY AND BIOFEEDBACK. PROCEEDINGS OF THE ANNUAL MEETING. 1972. a. $35 to non-members; members $17. Association for Applied Psychophysiology and Biofeedback, 10200 W. 44th Ave., Ste. 304, Wheat Ridge, CO 80033. TEL 303-422-8436. FAX 303-422-8894. Ed. Francine Butler. adv.; circ. 2,000.
  Formerly: Biofeedback Society of America. Proceedings of the Annual Meeting (ISSN 0094-0895)

ASSOCIATION FOR CHILD PSYCHOANALYSIS. NEWSLETTER. see *CHILDREN AND YOUTH — About*

370.15   US   ISSN 1054-0792
ASSOCIATION FOR PAST-LIFE RESEARCH AND THERAPY. NEWSLETTER. Running title: A P R T Newsletter. 1980. a. $10. Association for Past-Life Research and Therapies, Inc., Box 20151, Riverside, CA 92516. TEL 714-784-1570. Ed. Terry Nash. adv.; bk.rev.; circ. 800.
  Description: Articles by past-life regression therapists and researchers, includes case histories and techniques, alternative therapies.

616.891   US   ISSN 0004-542X
RC500
ASSOCIATION FOR PSYCHOANALYTIC MEDICINE. BULLETIN. 1961. q. $10. Association for Psychoanalytic Medicine, 4560 Delafield Ave., Bronx, NY 10471. TEL 212-874-0070. Ed. Dr. Elizabeth Auchincloss. bk.rev.; cum.index: 1961-1967; circ. 1,500 (controlled).

155.4 572 790.1   US
ASSOCIATION FOR THE STUDY OF PLAY NEWSLETTER. 1974. 3/yr. $15. Association for the Study of Play, Box 6375, Georgetown, TX 78626. (Subscr. to: c/o E.P. Jonnsen, Dept. of Educational Psychology, University of Kansas, Lawrence, KS 66945-2338) Ed. Dan Hilliard. circ. 200. (back issues avail.)
  Description: Covers social science and humanistic study of play behavior.

158.2   US
ASSOCIATION FOR TRANSPERSONAL PSYCHOLOGY. NEWSLETTER. q. Transpersonal Institute, 345 California Ave., Palo Alto, CA 94306. TEL 415-327-2066. Ed.Bd. adv.; illus.
  Formerly: Association for Transpersonal Development. Newsletter.
  Description: News and information for and about members of the association.

ATTI DELLO PSICODRAMMA. see *THEATER*

AUSTRALIAN AND NEW ZEALAND JOURNAL OF FAMILY THERAPY. see *SOCIOLOGY*

AUSTRALIAN EARLY CHILDHOOD RESOURCE BOOKLETS. see *CHILDREN AND YOUTH — About*

AUSTRALIAN JOURNAL OF MARRIAGE AND FAMILY. see *MATRIMONY*

616.89   AT
AUSTRALIAN JOURNAL OF PSYCHOTHERAPY. 1982. s-a. Aus.$40 to individuals; libraries and institutions Aus.$50. Psychotherapy Association of Australia, c/o Secretary, 25 Marchall Ave., St. Leonards, N.S.W. 2065, Australia. TEL 02 436-3031. Ed. L. Rumiz. adv.; bk.rev.; circ. 400. (back issues avail.)

AUSTRALIAN PARAPSYCHOLOGICAL REVIEW. see *PARAPSYCHOLOGY AND OCCULTISM*

150   AT   ISSN 0005-0067
                                                      CODEN: AUPCBK
AUSTRALIAN PSYCHOLOGIST. 1966. 3/yr. Aus.$55 to individuals; institutions Aus.$60 (foreign Aus.$65). Australian Psychological Society, c/o Prof. Graham Davidson, School of Humanities and Social Sciences, University of Central Queensland, Rockhampton M.C., Qld. 4702, Australia. FAX 079-269501. (Subscr. to: Australian Psychological Society, Clunies Ross House, 191 Royal Parade, Parkville, Vic. 3052, Australia) adv.; bk.rev.; abstr.; charts; illus.; index; circ. 5,000. **Indexed:** ASSIA, Aus.Educ.Ind., Aus.P.A.I.S., Biol.Abstr., Child Devel.Abstr., Curr.Cont., Psychol.Abstr., Res.High.Educ.Abstr., SSCI.
  —BLDSC shelfmark: 1818.350000.
  Description: Publishes articles of relevance to professional and applied psychology.

152   CK   ISSN 0120-3797
AVANCES EN PSICOLOGIA CLINICA LATINOAMERICANA. 1982. a. $7 to individuals; institutions $14. Foundation for the Advancement of Psychology, Apdo. 92621, Bogota, Colombia. Ed. Ruben Ardila. adv.; bk.rev.; bibl.; illus.; stat.; circ. 2,500. **Indexed:** Biol.Abstr., Curr.Cont., Psychol.Abstr.
  —BLDSC shelfmark: 1837.110500.
  Description: Articles on all areas of clinical psychology: diagnosis, psychotherapy, research and prevention programs.

B A S H MAGAZINE. (Bulimia Anorexia Self-Help) see *MEDICAL SCIENCES — Psychiatry And Neurology*

150   BG
BANGLADESH JOURNAL OF PSYCHOLOGY. (Text in English) 1968. a. $5. Bangladesh Psychological Association, Dept. of Psychology, University of Dhaka, Dhaka 1000, Bangladesh.
  Description: Contains research and review articles on all branches of psychology.

301.1 150   US   ISSN 0197-3533
HM251   CODEN: BASPEG
BASIC AND APPLIED SOCIAL PSYCHOLOGY. 1980. q. $45 to individuals (foreign $70); institutions $165 (foreign $190). Lawrence Erlbaum Associates, Inc., 365 Broadway, Hillsdale, NJ 07642. TEL 201-666-4110. FAX 201-666-2394. Ed. Paul Paulus. adv.; bk.rev.; abstr.; bibl.; charts; illus.; stat.; circ. 1,000. **Indexed:** Curr.Cont., Psychol.Abstr., Psycscan, SSCI.
  —BLDSC shelfmark: 1863.913300.
  Description: Presents material relevant to basic and applied research in all areas of social psychology in order to bring relevant social psychological studies from other specialties and disciplines to the attention of social psychologists.
  Refereed Serial

150   US   ISSN 0738-6729
BF199
THE BEHAVIOR ANALYST. 1978. 2/yr. (in 1 vol., 2 nos./vol.). $42.35 in U.S. & Canada; elsewhere $62.35. Society for the Advancement of Behavior Analysis, 260 Wood Hall, Western Michigan Univ., Kalamazoo, MI 49008-5052. TEL 616-387-4495. FAX 616-387-4457. Ed. Jay Moore. adv.; bk.rev.; cum.index; circ. 2,300. (also avail. in audio cassette; back issues avail.) **Indexed:** Behav.Abstr., Curr.Cont., Psychol.Abstr., SSCI, SSCI.
  —BLDSC shelfmark: 1876.652500.
  Description: Devoted to trend issues, policies, and developments in behavior anaylsis.

301.1 150   UK   ISSN 0144-929X
QA75.5   CODEN: BEITD5
BEHAVIOR AND INFORMATION TECHNOLOGY. 1982. bi-m. £133($231) Taylor & Francis Ltd., Rankine Rd., Basingstoke, Hants RG24 0PR, England. TEL 0256-840366. FAX 0256-479438. TELEX 858540. Ed. T.F.M. Stewart. adv.; bk.rev. **Indexed:** ASSIA, Commun.Abstr., Compumath, Comput.Abstr., Ergon.Abstr., Psychol.Abstr., Robomat., Sci.Abstr.
  —BLDSC shelfmark: 1876.660000.
  Description: All aspects of human-computer interaction.
  Refereed Serial

150   US
BF199
BEHAVIOR AND PHILOSOPHY. 1972. s-a. $16 to individuals; institutions $28. Cambridge Center for Behavioral Studies, 11 Waterhouse St., Cambridge, MA 02138. TEL 617-491-9020. FAX 617-491-1072. (Subscr. to: 49 Sheridan Ave., Albany, NY 12210) Ed. Max Hocutt. adv.; bk.rev.; illus.; circ. 600. **Indexed:** Adol.Ment.Hlth.Abstr., Biol.Abstr., Curr.Cont., Excerp.Med., Mid.East: Abstr.& Ind., Phil.Ind., Psychol.Abstr., SSCI.
  Formerly: (until vol.12, no.2, 1982): Behaviorism (ISSN 0090-4155)
  Refereed Serial

150 658   US
BEHAVIOR IMPROVEMENT NEWS; the behavior modification newsletter. 1977. m. $36. Behavior Improvement Associates, Box 296, New Paltz, NY 12561. (Subscr. to: Research Press, 2612 N. Mattis, Champaign, IL 61820) Ed. Marlene Casley. bk.rev.; bibl.; index. (looseleaf format; back issues avail.)

PSYCHOLOGY 4013

150 US ISSN 0145-4455
BF637.B4
BEHAVIOR MODIFICATION. 1977. q. $45 to individuals; institutions $125. Sage Publications, Inc., 2455 Teller Rd., Newbury Park, CA 91320. TEL 805-499-0721. FAX 805-499-0871. Eds. Michel Hersen, Alan S. Bellack. adv.; bk.rev.; index; circ. 1,300. (back issues avail.) **Indexed:** Adol.Ment.Hlth.Abstr., Curr.Cont., Excerp.Med., Human Resour.Abstr., Ind.Med., Mid.East: Abstr.& Ind., Psychol.Abstr., Psychol.R.G., Sage Fam.Stud.Abstr., Sage Urb.Stud.Abstr., Soc.Sci.Ind., SSCI.
—BLDSC shelfmark: 1876.720000.
Description: Describes assessment and modification techniques for problems in psychiatric, clinical, educational, and rehabilitational settings.

572 US ISSN 0743-3808
BF180 CODEN: BRMCEW
BEHAVIOR RESEARCH METHODS, INSTRUMENTS, AND COMPUTERS. 1968. bi-m. $94 (foreign $101). Psychonomic Society, Inc., 1710 Fortview Rd., Austin, TX 78704. TEL 512-462-2442. Ed. N. John Castellan, Jr. adv.; circ. 1,250. (also avail. in microform from KTO,UMI; back issues avail.; reprint service avail. from UMI) **Indexed:** Biol.Abstr., Curr.Adv.Ecol.Sci., Curr.Cont., Ergon.Abstr., Geo.Abstr., Lang.& Lang.Behav.Abstr., Mid.East: Abstr.& Ind., Psychol.Abstr., Sci.Abstr., SSCI.
—BLDSC shelfmark: 1876.832000.
Formerly (until 1984): Behavior Research Methods and Instrumentation (ISSN 0005-7878)
Description: Contains articles in the areas of methods, techniques and instrumentation of research in experimental psychology.
Refereed Serial

301.1 US
BEHAVIOR THERAPIST. 1978. 10/yr. $30. Association for Advancement of Behavior Therapy, 15 W. 36th St., New York, NY 10018. TEL 212-279-7970. Ed. Arthur Freeman. adv.; bk.rev.; film rev.; circ. 4,500. **Indexed:** Psychol.Abstr., Yrbk.Assoc.Educ.& Rehab.Blind.
Formerly: Association for Advancement of Behavior Therapy. Newsletter.

150 US ISSN 0005-7894
RC489.B4 CODEN: BHVTAK
BEHAVIOR THERAPY. 1970. 4/yr. $55 to individuals; institutions $110. Association for Advancement of Behavior Therapy, 15 W. 36th St., New York, NY 10018. TEL 212-279-7970. Ed. W. Edward Craighead. adv.; circ. 3,500. **Indexed:** Adol.Ment.Hlth.Abstr., Behav.Med.Abstr., Biol.Abstr., Curr.Cont., Except.Child.Educ.Abstr., Excerp.Med., Mid.East: Abstr.& Ind., Psychol.Abstr., Psycscan C.P., Sp.Ed.Needs Abstr., SSCI, Stud.Wom.Abstr.
—BLDSC shelfmark: 1876.930000.
Description: Interdisciplinary journal which presents treatment research covering theory, methodology, clinical and ethical issues.
Refereed Serial

150 US ISSN 0005-7924
BF636.A1
BEHAVIOR TODAY; the weekly newsletter for mental health & family relations professionals. 1969. w. $129 to individuals; institutions $180. Atcom, Inc., Atcom Bldg., 2315 Broadway, New York, NY 10024-4397. TEL 212-873-5900. FAX 212-799-1728. Ed. Ira Rosofsky. adv.; circ. 1,800. (reprint service avail. from UMI) **Indexed:** Except.Child.Educ.Abstr., Pers.Lit.
Incorporates: Sexuality Today (ISSN 0148-883X) & Marriage and Divorce Today (ISSN 0148-8821)
Description: Geared towards the mental health, marriage and family, and sexuality professionals.

150 574 616.8 UK ISSN 0140-525X
QP360 CODEN: BBSCDH
BEHAVIORAL AND BRAIN SCIENCES; an international journal of current research and theory with open peer commentary. 1978. q. $73 to individuals; institutions $174. Cambridge University Press, Edinburgh Bldg., Shaftesbury Rd., Cambridge CB2 2RU, England. TEL 0223-312393. FAX 0223-315052. TELEX 851817256. (N. America addr.: Cambridge University Press, 40 W. 20th St., New York, NY 10011) Ed. Stevan Harnad. adv.; bk.rev.; charts; illus.; index. (also avail. in microform from UMI; back issues avail.) **Indexed:** Art.Int.Abstr., Biol.Abstr., Curr.Adv.Ecol.Sci., Curr.Cont., Excerp.Med., Ind.Sci.Rev., Lang.& Lang.Behav.Abstr., Psychol. Abstr., Sci.Cit.Ind., Sociol.Abstr., SSCI, Telegen.
—BLDSC shelfmark: 1877.293000.
Description: Covers psychology, neuroscience, behavioural biology, or cognitive science.

BEHAVIORAL AND NEURAL BIOLOGY. see *BIOLOGY*

150 US ISSN 0191-5401
RC489.B4 CODEN: BEHSDV
BEHAVIORAL ASSESSMENT. 1979. q. £110 (effective 1992). (Association for Advancement of Behavior Therapy) Pergamon Press, Inc., Journals Division, 660 White Plains Rd., Tarrytown, NY 10591-5153. TEL 914-524-9200. FAX 914-333-2444. (And: Headington Hill Hall, Oxford OX3 0BW, England. TEL 0865-794141) Ed. John D. Cone. adv.; bk.rev.; stat.; index; circ. 2,500. (also avail. in microform from MIM,UMI) **Indexed:** Biol.Abstr., Curr.Adv.Ecol.Sci., Curr.Cont., Excerp.Med., Psychol.Abstr., SSCI.
—BLDSC shelfmark: 1877.298000.
Description: Interdisciplinary journal publishing original contributions in the areas of assessment, design, methodology, statistics, measurement and program evaluation.
Refereed Serial

BEHAVIORAL ECOLOGY AND SOCIOBIOLOGY. see *ENVIRONMENTAL STUDIES*

BEHAVIORAL EDUCATOR. see *EDUCATION — Teaching Methods And Curriculum*

616.8 US
RB152
BEHAVIORAL MEDICINE; investigations of environmental influences on health and behavior. 1975. q. $40 to individuals; institutions $72. (Helen Dwight Reid Educational Foundation) Heldref Publications, 1319 Eighteenth St., N.W., Washington, DC 20036-1802. TEL 202-396-6267. FAX 202-296-5149. Ed. Martha Wedeman. adv.; bk.rev.; charts; stat.; index; circ. 1,000. (also avail. in microform; back issues avail.; reprint service avail.) **Indexed:** Abstr.Anthropol., Adol.Ment.Hlth.Abstr., ASSIA, Biol.Abstr., Curr.Cont., Excerp.Med., Ind.Med., Mid.East: Abstr.& Ind., Psychol.Abstr., Psycscan, SSCI.
Formerly: Journal of Human Stress (ISSN 0097-840X)
Refereed Serial

BEHAVIORAL NEUROPSYCHIATRY. see *MEDICAL SCIENCES — Psychiatry And Neurology*

156 616.8 US ISSN 0735-7044
BF1 CODEN: BENEDJ
BEHAVIORAL NEUROSCIENCE. 1983. bi-m. $120 to non-members (foreign $126); members $60; institutions $240 (foreign $252). American Psychological Association, 750 First St., N.E., Washington, DC 20002-4242. TEL 202-336-5500. FAX 202-336-5568. Ed. Richard F. Thompson. adv.; charts; illus.; index; circ. 2,000. (also avail. in microform from MIM,UMI) **Indexed:** Abstr.Anthropol., Anim.Breed.Abstr., Biol.Abstr., Biol.& Agr.Ind., Chem.Abstr., Curr.Adv.Ecol.Sci., Dairy Sci.Abstr., Dent.Ind., Excerp.Med., Ind.Med., Ind.Sci.Rev., INIS Atomind., NRN, Nutr.Abstr., Poult.Abstr., Psychol.Abstr., Sci.Cit.Ind., Soc.Sci.Ind.
—BLDSC shelfmark: 1877.610000.
Supersedes in part (1947-1982): Journal of Comparative and Physiological Psychology (ISSN 0021-9940)
Description: Covers research in the broad field of the biological bases of behavior; includes occasional review and theoretical articles that make original contributions to the field.
Refereed Serial

150 340 UK ISSN 0735-3936
K2 CODEN: BSLADR
BEHAVIORAL SCIENCES AND THE LAW. 1983. q. $175 (effective 1992). John Wiley & Sons Ltd., Journals, Baffins Lane, Chichester, Sussex PO19 1UD, England. TEL 0243-779777. FAX 0243-775878. TELEX 86290-WIBOOK-G. Ed. R. Wettstein. (also avail. in microform from RPI; reprint service avail. from SWZ) **Indexed:** C.L.I., Excerp.Med., Psychol.Abstr.
—BLDSC shelfmark: 1877.905000.
Description: Explores the dynamics between mental health and the law.

150 658 US ISSN 0361-4646
BEHAVIORAL SCIENCES NEWSLETTER. 1972. fortn. $97. Roy W. Walters & Associates, Inc., 45 Whitney Rd., Mahwah, NJ 07430. TEL 201-891-5757. FAX 201-891-4112. Ed. Clem Russo. bk.rev.; index; circ. 3,500.

150 US ISSN 0005-7967
RC321 CODEN: BRTHAA
BEHAVIOUR RESEARCH AND THERAPY; an international multi-disciplinary journal. 1963. bi-m. £210 (effective 1992). Pergamon Press, Inc., Journals Division, 660 White Plains Rd., Tarrytown, NY 10591-5153. TEL 914-524-9200. FAX 914-333-2444. (And: Headington Hill Hall, Oxford OX3 0BW, England. TEL 0865-794141) Ed. S. Rachman. adv.; bk.rev.; charts; illus.; index; circ. 4,300. (also avail. in microform from MIM,UMI; back issues avail.) **Indexed:** Adol.Ment.Hlth.Abstr., Behav.Med.Abstr., Bibl.Dev.Med.& Child Neur., Biol.Abstr., Child Devel.Abstr., CINAHL, Curr.Adv.Ecol.Sci., Curr.Cont., Dent.Ind., Excerp.Med., Ind.Med., M.L.A., Psychol.Abstr., Psycscan C.P., Soc.Work Res.& Abstr., SSCI.
—BLDSC shelfmark: 1876.810000.
Description: Focuses on the application of existing modern learning theory to psychiatric and social problems, relating learning to maladaptive behavior.
Refereed Serial

BEHAVIOURAL PHARMACOLOGY. see *PHARMACY AND PHARMACOLOGY*

150 UK
BEHAVIOURAL PSYCHOTHERAPIST. 1981. 3/yr. £15 to non-members. British Association for Behavioural Psychotherapy, c/o Dr. Peck, Dept. of Psychology, Craig Phadrig Hospital, Iverness 1V3 6PJx, Scotland. adv.; bk.rev.; circ. 1,500.
Formerly: British Association for Behavioural Psychotherapy. Newsletter (ISSN 0262-3110)

150 UK ISSN 0141-3473
RC489.B4 CODEN: BEPSD3
BEHAVIOURAL PSYCHOTHERAPY.* 1972. q. £51($99) British Association for Behavioural Psychotherapy (London), 59 Revelstoke Rd., Wimbledon Park, London SW18 5NJ, England. Eds. D. Clark, P. Salkovskis. **Indexed:** ASSIA, Psychol.Abstr., Sp.Ed.Needs Abstr., SSCI.
—BLDSC shelfmark: 1877.750000.
Description: Multidisciplinary original research, of an experimental or clinical nature, that contributes to the theory, practice, and evaluation of behavior therapy.

157 GW
BEITRAEGE ZUR INDIVIDUALPSYCHOLOGIE. 1978. irreg., no.14, 1990. price varies. Ernst Reinhardt GmbH und Co., Verlag, Kemnatenstr. 46, 8000 Munich 19, Germany. TEL 089-1783005.

155.4 GW ISSN 0340-0123
BEITRAEGE ZUR PSYCHODIAGNOSTIK DES KINDES. 1972. irreg., no.7, 1984. price varies. Ernst Reinhardt GmbH und Co., Verlag, Kemnatenstr. 46, 8000 Munich 19, Germany. TEL 089-1783005. Eds. G. Biermann, M. Kos.

614.58 GW ISSN 0173-0967
BEITRAEGE ZUR PSYCHOLOGIE UND SOZIOLOGIE DES KRANKEN MENSCHEN. 1974. irreg., no.6, 1986. price varies. Ernst Reinhardt GmbH und Co., Verlag, Kemnatenstr. 46, 8000 Munich 19, Germany. TEL 089-1783005. Eds. G. Biermann, J. von Troschke.

150 US ISSN 0175-5943
BEITRAEGE ZUR PSYCHOPATHOLOGIE. irreg., vol.5, 1987. DM.40. Springer-Verlag, 175 Fifth Ave., New York, NY 10010. TEL 212-460-1500. (And Berlin, Heidelberg, Tokyo and Vienna)

PSYCHOLOGY

155.2　　　　GW　ISSN 0067-5210
　　　　　　　　　CODEN: BSXFAV
BEITRAEGE ZUR SEXUALFORSCHUNG. 1952. irreg., vol.66, 1990. price varies. (Deutsche Gesellschaft fuer Sexualforschung) Ferdinand Enke Verlag, Postfach 101254, 7000 Stuttgart 10, Germany. TEL 0711-8931-0. FAX 0711-8931-419. TELEX 07252275-GTV-D. Ed.Bd. **Indexed:** Biol.Abstr., Excerp.Med., Ind.Med.

BETHLEM AND MAUDSLEY GAZETTE. see *MEDICAL SCIENCES — Psychiatry And Neurology*

150　610　　　　　US
BIOFEEDBACK. a. Association for Applied Psychophysiology and Biofeedback, 10200 W. 44th Ave., Ste. 304, Wheat Ridge, CO 80033. TEL 303-422-8436. FAX 303-422-8894.

613　　　　　US　ISSN 0363-3586
BF319.5.B5　　　　CODEN: BSELDP
BIOFEEDBACK & SELF REGULATION. 1975. q. $195 (foreign $230)(effective 1992). Plenum Publishing Corp., 233 Spring St., New York, NY 10013-1578. TEL 212-620-8000. FAX 212-463-0742. TELEX 23-421139. Eds. Edward B. Blanchard, Mary R. Cook. adv. (also avail. in microfilm from JSC; back issues avail.) **Indexed:** Adol.Ment.Hlth.Abstr., Biol.Abstr., Curr.Adv.Ecol.Sci., Curr.Cont., Dent.Ind., Excerp.Med., Ind.Med., Psychol.Abstr., Sci.Abstr.
—BLDSC shelfmark: 2072.140000.
Refereed Serial

574　150　　　　NE　ISSN 0301-0511
　　　　　　　　　CODEN: BLPYAX
BIOLOGICAL PSYCHOLOGY. 1973. 6/yr.(in 2 vols.; 3 nos./vol.). fl.646 (effective 1992). North-Holland (Subsidiary of: Elsevier Science Publishers B.V.), P.O. Box 211, 1000 AE Amsterdam, Netherlands. TEL 020-5803911. FAX 020-5803598. TELEX 18582 ESPA NL. (Subscr. in U.S. and Canada to: Elsevier Science Publishing Co., Inc., Box 882, Madison Sq. Sta., New York, NY 10159. TEL 212-989-5800) Ed. R.E. Jennings. adv.; bk.rev.; charts; index; circ. 375. (also avail. in microfilm from RPI; back issues avail.; reprint service avail. from ISI) **Indexed:** Chem.Abstr., Commun.Abstr., Curr.Adv.Ecol.Sci., Curr.Cont., Dent.Ind., Excerp.Med., Ind.Med., Psychol.Abstr., SSCI.
—BLDSC shelfmark: 2077.560000.
Description: Publishes original scientific papers on the biological aspects of psychological states and processes.
Refereed Serial

150　370　610　　　IT
BIOPSYCHE; rivista di scienze antropologiche. 1970. q. L.15000. Ispasa Societa Cooperativa, Corso Italia, 104, 95129 Catania, Italy. TEL 095-532181. bk.rev. (back issues avail.)

BIRD BEHAVIOUR; an international and multidisciplinary journal. see *BIOLOGY — Ornithology*

BIRTH PSYCHOLOGY BULLETIN. see *MEDICAL SCIENCES — Obstetrics And Gynecology*

270.15　　　　　CU
BOLETIN DE PSICOLOGIA. 1971. irreg. free. Ministerio de Salud Publica, Hospital Psiquiatrico de la Habana, Avenida de Independencia No. 26520, Mazorra, Havana, Cuba. TEL 5683-2465. Dr. Noemi Perez. adv.; circ. 6,000. **Indexed:** Psychol.Abstr.

158　　　　　IT　ISSN 0006-6761
BOLLETTINO DI PSICOLOGIA APPLICATA. 1954. bi-m. L.60000($15) Organizzazioni Speciali, Via Scipione Ammiroto 37, 50136 Florence, Italy. Dir. Francesca Morino Abbele. bk.rev.; bibl.; charts; circ. 1,000. (also avail. in microform from UMI; reprint service avail. from UMI) **Indexed:** Biol.Abstr., Lang.& Lang.Behav.Abstr., Psychol.Abstr., SSCI.
—BLDSC shelfmark: 2240.700000.

150　　　　　US　ISSN 0278-2626
QP376
BRAIN AND COGNITION. 1982. bi-m. $150 (foreign $181). Academic Press, Inc., Journal Division, 1250 Sixth Ave., San Diego, CA 92101. TEL 619-230-1840. FAX 619-699-6800. TELEX 181726. Ed. Harry A. Whitaker. adv. (back issues avail.) **Indexed:** Child Devel.Abstr., Curr.Adv.Ecol.Sci., Ind.Sci.Rev., Psychol.Abstr., Sci.Cit.Ind., SSCI.
—BLDSC shelfmark: 2268.032000.
Description: Presents clinical case histories, original research papers, reviews, notes, and commentaries on neuropsychology.
Refereed Serial

150　410　　　US　ISSN 0093-934X
RC423.A1　　　　CODEN: BRLGA
BRAIN AND LANGUAGE. 1974. 8/yr. $270 (foreign $338). Academic Press, Inc., Journal Division, 1250 Sixth Ave., San Diego, CA 92101. TEL 619-230-1840. FAX 619-699-6800. TELEX 181726. Ed. Harry A. Whitaker. (back issues avail.) **Indexed:** Abstr.Anthropol., Bibl.Dev.Med.& Child Neur., Curr.Adv.Ecol.Sci., Curr.Cont., Dent.Ind., Excerp.Med., Ind.Med., Ind.Sci.Rev., INIS Atomind., Lang.& Lang.Behav.Abstr. (1974-), M.L.A., Psychol.Abstr., Sci.Cit.Ind., SSCI.
—BLDSC shelfmark: 2268.040000.
Description: Original theoretical, clinical, and experimental papers on human language and communication: speech, hearing, reading, writing, and higher language functions, as they relate to brain structure and function.
Refereed Serial

301.1　150　　　　US
BREAKTHROUGH (NASHVILLE). 1973. q. free. Department of Mental Health & Mental Retardation, 706 Church St., Nashville, TN 37243-0675. TEL 615-741-2167. Ed. Patricia Latham. circ. 10,000.

616.89　　　　UK　ISSN 0954-0350
BRITISH ASSOCIATION OF PSYCHOTHERAPISTS. JOURNAL. 1968. a. £6. British Association of Psychotherapists, c/o Mary Stumpfl, Cantelowes Rd., London NW1 9XR, England. TEL 071-267-1954. adv.; bk.rev.; circ. 600.
—BLDSC shelfmark: 4712.930000.
Formerly: British Association of Psychotherapists. Bulletin (ISSN 0268-6643)
Description: Covers topics related to Freudian or Jungian psycho-dynamic psychotherapy.

301.1　150　　　UK　ISSN 0144-6657
BF1　　　　　　CODEN: BJCPDW
BRITISH JOURNAL OF CLINICAL PSYCHOLOGY. 1981. q. $171. British Psychological Society, St. Andrew's House, 48 Princess Rd East, Leicester LE1 7DR, England. TEL 0533-549568. FAX 0533-470787. Ed. Chris Brewin. adv.; bk.rev.; charts; illus.; index; circ. 3,000. (also avail. in microform; reprint service avail. from ISI,SWZ) **Indexed:** Adol.Ment.Hlth.Abstr., ASSIA, Bibl.Dev.Med.& Child Neur., Biol.Abstr., CINAHL, Curr.Adv.Ecol.Sci., Curr.Cont., Dent.Ind., Excerp.Med., Ind.Med., Lang.& Lang.Behav.Abstr., Psychol.Abstr., Psycscan C.P., Sociol.Educ.Abstr., SSCI.
—BLDSC shelfmark: 2307.230000.
Supersedes in part: British Journal of Social and Clinical Psychology (ISSN 0007-1293)
Description: New findings, theoretical, methodological and review papers on all aspects of clinical and health psychology.

155　　　　　UK　ISSN 0261-510X
BF712
BRITISH JOURNAL OF DEVELOPMENTAL PSYCHOLOGY. 1983. q. $156. British Psychological Society, St. Andrew's House, 48 Princess Rd East, Leicester LE1 7DR, England. TEL 0533 549568. FAX 0533-470787. Ed. George Butterworth. adv.; bk.rev.; charts; illus.; index; circ. 1,300. (also avail. in microform from SWZ; reprint service avail. from ISI,SWZ) **Indexed:** ASSIA, Bibl.Dev.Med.& Child Neur., Lang.& Lang.Behav.Abstr., Psychol.Abstr., Psycscan D.P., Yrbk.Assoc.Educ.& Rehab.Blind.
—BLDSC shelfmark: 2307.480000.
Description: Empirical, conceptual and review articles on all aspects of development.

152.8　　　　UK　ISSN 0007-1102
BF1
BRITISH JOURNAL OF MATHEMATICAL AND STATISTICAL PSYCHOLOGY. 1948. s-a. $152. British Psychological Society, St. Andrew's House, 48 Princess Rd. East, Leicester LE1 7DR, England. TEL 0533-549568. FAX 0533-470787. Ed. Philip T. Smith. adv.; bk.rev.; charts; illus.; index; circ. 750. (also avail. in microform from SWZ; reprint service avail. from ISI) **Indexed:** Compumath, Comput.Abstr., Curr.Cont., Curr.Ind.Stat., Ind.Med., J.Cont.Quant.Meth., Math.R., Psychol.Abstr., Psyscan, SSCI, Trop.Dis.Bull.
—BLDSC shelfmark: 2311.300000.

616.89　150　　　UK　ISSN 0007-1129
RC321　　　　　　CODEN: BJMPAB
BRITISH JOURNAL OF MEDICAL PSYCHOLOGY. 1920. q. $177. British Psychological Society, St. Andrew's House, 48 Princess Rd. East, Leicester LE1 7DR, England. TEL 0533 549568. FAX 0533-470787. Ed. Dr.J. Birtchnell. adv.; bk.rev.; charts; illus.; index; circ. 2,300. (also avail. in microform from SWZ; reprint service avail. from ISI,SWZ) **Indexed:** Adol.Ment.Hlth.Abstr., Bibl.Dev.Med.& Child Neur., Biol.Abstr., Chem.Abstr., CINAHL, Curr.Adv.Ecol.Sci., Curr.Cont., Dent.Ind., Excerp.Med., Ind.Med., Ind.Sci.Rev., Lang.& Lang.Behav.Abstr., Mid.East: Abstr.& Ind., Nutr.Abstr., Psychol.Abstr., Sci.Cit.Ind., SSCI.
—BLDSC shelfmark: 2311.850000.

BRITISH JOURNAL OF MENTAL SUBNORMALITY. see *EDUCATION — Special Education And Rehabilitation*

616.89　　　　UK　ISSN 0309-7757
　　　　　　　　　CODEN: BJPSD4
BRITISH JOURNAL OF PROJECTIVE PSYCHOLOGY. 1955. a. £18. British Society for Projective Psychology, Dept. of Psychology, 155 Crail St., Glasgow G31 5RB, Scotland. Ed. Zahid Mahmood. adv.; bk.rev.; circ. 200. (back issues avail.) **Indexed:** Psychol.Abstr.
Formerly: British Journal of Projective Psychology and Personality Study.

150　　　　　UK　ISSN 0007-1269
BF1　　　　　　CODEN: BJSGAE
BRITISH JOURNAL OF PSYCHOLOGY. 1904. 4/yr. $228. British Psychological Society, St. Andrew's House, 48 Princess Rd. East, Leicester LE1 7DR, England. TEL 0533 549568. FAX 0533-470787. Ed. A.J. Chapman. adv.; bk.rev.; bibl.; charts; index; circ. 3,300. (also avail. in microform from SWZ; reprint service avail. from ISI,SWZ) **Indexed:** Adol.Ment.Hlth.Abstr., ASSIA, Bibl.Dev.Med.& Child Neur., Biol.Abstr., Br.Educ.Ind., Br.Hum.Ind., C.I.J.E., Commun.Abstr., Curr.Adv.Ecol.Sci., Curr.Cont., Ergon.Abstr., Ind.Med., Lang.& Lang.Behav.Abstr., M.L.A., Mid.East: Abstr.& Ind., Psychol.Abstr., Res.High.Educ.Abstr., Risk Abstr., Sci.Abstr., So.Pac.Per.Ind., Soc.Sci.Ind., SSCI.
—BLDSC shelfmark: 2321.000000.
Description: Empirical studies, critical reviews of the literature and theoretical contributions on psychology.

301.1　150　　　UK　ISSN 0144-6665
BF1　　　　　　CODEN: BJSPDA
BRITISH JOURNAL OF SOCIAL PSYCHOLOGY. 1981. q. $152. British Psychological Society, St. Andrew's House, 48 Princess Rd. East, Leicester LE1 7DR, England. TEL 0533 549568. FAX 0533-470787. Ed. Dr.M. Hewstone. adv.; bk.rev.; charts; illus.; index; circ. 2,200. (also avail. in microform from SWZ; reprint service avail. from ISI,SWZ) **Indexed:** Adol.Ment.Hlth.Abstr., ASSIA, Bibl.Dev.Med.& Child Neur., Biol.Abstr., Br.Hum.Ind., Commun.Abstr., Curr.Adv.Ecol.Sci., Curr.Cont., Excerp.Med., High.Educ.Curr.Aware.Bull., Ind.Med., Lang.& Lang.Behav.Abstr., Mid.East: Abstr.& Ind., Psychol.Abstr., Res.High.Educ.Abstr., Sociol.Educ.Abstr., SSCI, Stud.Wom.Abstr.
—BLDSC shelfmark: 2324.784000.
Supersedes in part: British Journal of Social and Clinical Psychology (ISSN 0007-1293)
Description: Describes applications of social psychology. Includes research and review papers.

150　　　　　UK　ISSN 0309-7773
BF11
BRITISH PSYCHOLOGICAL SOCIETY. ANNUAL REPORT. a. free. British Psychological Society, St. Andrew's House, 48 Princess Rd., E., Leicester LE1 7DR, England. TEL 0533-549568. circ. 12,950.
—BLDSC shelfmark: 1127.250000.

PSYCHOLOGY 4015

364 UK
BRITISH PSYCHOLOGICAL SOCIETY. DIVISION OF CRIMINOLOGICAL & LEGAL PSYCHOLOGY. OCCASIONAL PAPERS. 1981. irreg. £7 per no. British Psychological Society, Division of Criminological and Legal Psychology, St. Andrew's House, 48 Princess Rd. E., Leicester LE1 7DR, England.
TEL 0533-549568. FAX 0533-470787. Eds. Mary McMurray, Cynthia McDougal. circ. 250.

157 301.1 UK ISSN 0950-3005
BRITISH REVIEW OF BULIMIA AND ANOREXIA NERVOSA. 1986. s-a. £15 (foreign £30). Eating Disorders Association, 44 Magdalen St., Norwich, Norfolk NR3 1JE, England. TEL 0603-621414.
FAX 0603-664915. TELEX 975660-SVILLE-G. Ed. Alan Cockett. adv.; bk.rev.; circ. 300. (back issues avail.) **Indexed:** Excerp.Med., Psychol.Abstr.
—BLDSC shelfmark: 2342.185000.
Description: Journal that covers all aspects of bulimia and anorexia nervosa for the complete range of professionals who deal with patients suffering from these eating disorders.

BRITISH SOCIETY FOR MUSIC THERAPY. BULLETIN. see *MUSIC*

155.4 US ISSN 0885-7261
HQ767.8
BROWN UNIVERSITY CHILD AND ADOLESCENT BEHAVIOR LETTER; monthly reports on the problems of children and adolescents growing up. 1984. m. $67 to individuals (foreign $87); institutions $97 (foreign $117). Manisses Communications Group, Inc., 205 Governor St., Box 3357, Providence, RI 02906-0757. TEL 401-831-6020.
FAX 401-861-6370. Ed. Lewis P. Lippsitt. bk.rev.; abstr.; bibl.; stat.
Formerly (until 1991): Brown University Child Behavior and Development Letter (ISSN 0898-2562)
Description: Updates on research and theories on the problems of children and adolescents growing up.

616.89 CN ISSN 0832-7475
BULLETIN I R P. 1986. irreg. price varies. Institute of Psychological Research, Inc., 34 Fleury St. W., Montreal, Que. H3L 1S9, Canada.
TEL 514-382-3000. FAX 514-382-3007. Eds. Jean-Marc Chevrier, Malko von Osten.

370.15 150 US
C A C D JOURNAL. vol.9, 1989. a. $8. California Association for Counseling and Development, 2555 E. Chapman Ave., Ste. 201, Fullerton, CA 92631-3617. TEL 714-871-6460. Ed. Dr. Patricia Wickwire. adv.; charts; stats.; circ. 3,000.
Description: Presents articles in the field of counseling and guidance for professionals.

150 BL
CADERNOS DE PSICOLOGIA APLICADA.* s-a. Centro de Orientacao e Selecao Psicotencia, Rua Jacinto Gomes 540, Porto Algre (R.S.), Brazil. bibl. **Indexed:** Psychol.Abstr.

616.89 301.4 FR ISSN 0241-5453
CAHIERS CRITIQUES DE THERAPIE FAMILIALE ET DE PRATIQUES DE RESEAUX. 2/yr. 290 F. Editions Edouard Privat, 14 rue des Arts, 31000 Toulouse, France. (Subscr. to: Dunod, Centrule des Revues (CDR), 11 rue Gossin, 92543 Montrouge Cedex, France. TEL 1-46-56-52-66)
Description: Proposes a systematic analysis of social change on both a small and large scale.

150 FR ISSN 0249-9185
CAHIERS DE PSYCHOLOGIE COGNITIVE/EUROPEAN BULLETIN OF COGNITIVE PSYCHOLOGY. (Text in English, French) 1981. bi-m. 685.60 F. A D R S C, Traverse Charles Susini, 13388 Marseille cedex 13, France. FAX 33-91-61-14-20. Ed. Jean Pailhous. adv.; circ. 700. (reprint service avail. from ISI) **Indexed:** ASCA, Curr.Cont., Psychol.Abstr., Psychol.R.G., SSCI, Yrbk.Assoc.Educ.& Rehab.Blind.
—BLDSC shelfmark: 2952.120800.

301.1 150 BE
CAHIERS INTERNATIONAUX DE PSYCHOLOGIE SOCIALE. (Text in French) 1989. q. 2900 Fr. De Boeck Wesmael, Serials Department, Av. Louise 203, Boite 1, B-1050 Brussels, Belgium. TEL 2-627-35-37. FAX 2-627-36-50. TELEX 65701 DBWES B. (Dist. by: Acces Plus, Rue Fonds Jean Paques, 4, B-1348 Louvain-la-Neuve, Belgium)
Description: Discusses various aspects of social psychology.

CANADA'S MENTAL HEALTH. see *MEDICAL SCIENCES*

150 CN ISSN 0008-400X
CODEN: CJBSAA
CANADIAN JOURNAL OF BEHAVIOURAL SCIENCE/REVUE CANADIENNE DES SCIENCES DU COMPORTEMENT. (Text in English, French) 1969. q. Can.$65($67) Canadian Psychological Association, Rue Vincent Road, Old Chelsea, Que. JOX 2N0, Canada. Ed. Prem Fry. adv.; bk.rev.; charts; tr.lit.; index; circ. 2,800. (also avail. in microform from UMI) **Indexed:** Adol.Ment.Hlth.Abstr., Biol.Abstr., Can.Wom.Per.Ind., Curr.Adv.Ecol.Sci., Curr.Cont., Excerp.Med., Ind.Sci.Rev., Lang.& Lang.Behav.Abstr., Mid.East: Abstr.& Ind., Psychol.Abstr., Sci.Cit.Ind., Sp.Ed.Needs Abstr., SSCI, Stud.Wom.Abstr.
—BLDSC shelfmark: 3028.700000.

150 301.1 CN ISSN 0713-3936
CANADIAN JOURNAL OF COMMUNITY MENTAL HEALTH/REVUE CANADIENNE DE SANTE MENTALE COMMUNAUTAIRE. 2/yr. Can.$25 to individuals; institutions Can.$40. (Canadian Periodical for Community Studies Inc.) Wilfrid Laurier University Press, Waterloo, Ont. N2L 3C5, Canada. **Indexed:** Soc.Work Res.& Abstr.
—BLDSC shelfmark: 3031.046000.
Description: Devoted to the sharing of information and valid knowledge about phenomena pertinent to the mental well-being of Canadians and their communities.

150 CN ISSN 0008-4255
BF1 CODEN: CJPSAC
CANADIAN JOURNAL OF PSYCHOLOGY/REVUE CANADIENNE DE PSYCHOLOGIE. (Text in English and French) 1947. q. Can.$65($67) Canadian Psychological Association, Rue Vincent Rd., Old Chelsea, Que. JOX 2N0, Canada.
TEL 819-827-3927. FAX 819-827-4639. Ed. Gordon Winocur. adv.; bibl.; charts; illus.; index, cum.index: 1947-1961; circ. 2,600. (also avail. in microform from JAI,MIM,UMI; reprint service avail. from SWZ,UMI) **Indexed:** Adol.Ment.Hlth.Abstr., ASCA, ASSIA, Biol.Abstr., Child Devel.Abstr., Curr.Adv.Ecol.Sci., Curr.Cont., Ergon.Abstr., Ind.Med., Lang.& Lang.Behav.Abstr., Psychol.Abstr., RADAR, Soc.Sci.Ind., Sp.Ed.Needs Abstr., SSCI, Yrbk.Assoc.Educ.& Rehab.Blind.
—BLDSC shelfmark: 3034.900000.

150 CN ISSN 0068-9211
CANADIAN MENTAL HEALTH ASSOCIATION. ANNUAL REPORT/ASSOCIATION CANADIENNE POUR LA SANTE MENTALE. RAPPORT ANNUEL. 1926. a. free. Canadian Mental Health Association, 2160 Yonge St., Toronto, Ont. M4S 2Z3, Canada.
TEL 416-484-7750. **Indexed:** Curr.Cont.

150 CN ISSN 0708-5591
BF1 CODEN: CPSGD2
CANADIAN PSYCHOLOGY. (Text in English, French) 1959. q. Can.$65($67) Canadian Psychological Association, Chemin Vincent Road, Old Chelsea, Que. JOX 2N0, Canada. TEL 819-827-3927.
FAX 819-827-4639. Ed. John Conway. adv.; bk.rev.; circ. 4,600. (also avail. in microform from MIM; back issues avail.) **Indexed:** ASSIA, Biol.Abstr., Can.Per.Ind., Can.Wom.Per.Ind., CMI, Curr.Cont., Lang.& Lang.Behav.Abstr., Mid.East: Abstr.& Ind., Psychol.Abstr., SSCI.
—BLDSC shelfmark: 3044.105000.
Former titles: Canadian Psychological Review (ISSN 0318-2096); Canadian Psychologist.

CAREER PLANNING & ADULT DEVELOPMENT JOURNAL. see *EDUCATION — Adult Education*

CAREER PLANNING AND ADULT DEVELOPMENT NETWORK NEWSLETTER; a newsletter for career counselors, educators, and human resource specialists. see *EDUCATION — Adult Education*

150.19 155.4 US
CARNEGIE-MELLON SYMPOSIA ON COGNITION SERIES. Also known as: Carnegie Symposium on Cognition. 1974. irreg., vol.23, 1992. Lawrence Erlbaum Associates, Inc., 365 Broadway, Box 237, Hillsdale, NJ 07642. TEL 201-666-4110.
FAX 201-666-2394. **Indexed:** Curr.Cont., Psychol.Abstr.

CASE ANALYSIS; in social science and social therapy. see *SOCIAL SCIENCES: COMPREHENSIVE WORKS*

150 US
CENTENNIAL PSYCHOLOGY SERIES. 1982. irreg. price varies. Praeger Publishers (Subsidiary of: Greenwood Publishing Group Inc.), 88 Post Rd. W., Box 5007, Westport, CT 06881-5007. TEL 203-226-3571. FAX 203-222-1502.

616.89 IT ISSN 0392-3398
CENTRO RICERCHE BIOPSICHICHE. (Text in Italian; summaries in English) 1957. irreg. free. Centro Ricerche Biopsichiche, Via Dante 60, 35139 Padua, Italy. bk.rev.; circ. 600. **Indexed:** Psychol.Abstr.

150 CS ISSN 0009-062X
BF8.C9 CODEN: CEPSBC
CESKOSLOVENSKA PSYCHOLOGIE/CZECHOSLOVAK PSYCHOLOGY. (Text mainly in Czech or Slovak; occasionally in English, German, Russian; summaries in English and Russian) 1957. bi-m. DM.141. (Czechoslovak Academy of Sciences, Institute of Psychology) Academia, Publishing House of the Czechoslovak Academy of Sciences, Vodickova 40, 112 29 Prague 1, Czechoslovakia. TEL 231-91-15. (Dist. in Western countries by: Kubon & Sagner, P.O. Box 34 01 08, 8000 Munich 34, Germany) Ed. J. Linhart. adv.; bk.rev.; charts; illus.; stat.; index; circ. 2,800. **Indexed:** Biol.Abstr., C.I.S. Abstr., Child Devel.Abstr., Curr.Cont., Ergon.Abstr., Psychol.Abstr., SSCI.
—BLDSC shelfmark: 3122.500000.
Description: Covers all fields of psychology, theoretical and applied. Includes basic research into general and social psychology, survey studies which have been given preference and reports on important conferences and institutes.

CHALLENGE ADVOCATE. see *SOCIAL SERVICES AND WELFARE*

CHANGES; an international journal of psychology and psychotherapy. see *SOCIAL SERVICES AND WELFARE*

CHEIRON NEWSLETTER. see *SOCIAL SCIENCES: COMPREHENSIVE WORKS*

CHILD ABUSE REVIEW. see *SOCIAL SERVICES AND WELFARE*

155.4 157 US ISSN 0731-7107
RJ504
CHILD & FAMILY BEHAVIOR THERAPY. 1978. q. $45 to individuals; institutions $95; libraries $200. Haworth Press, Inc., 10 Alice St., Binghamton, NY 13904. TEL 800-342-9678. FAX 607-722-1424. Ed. Cyril M. Franks. adv.; bk.rev.; film rev.; bibl.; charts; stat.; circ. 514. (also avail. in microfiche from HAW; back issues avail.; reprint service avail. from HAW) **Indexed:** Adol.Ment.Hlth.Abstr., Behav.Abstr., Bull.Signal., C.I.J.E., Child Devel.Abstr., Curr.Cont., Educ.Ind., Except.Child Educ.Abstr., Lang.& Lang.Behav.Abstr., Psychol.Abstr., Rehabil.Lit., Sage Fam.Stud.Abstr., Soc.Work Res.& Abstr., Sociol.Abstr., Sociol.Educ.Abstr., Sp.Ed.Needs Abstr., SSCI, Stud.Wom.Abstr.
—BLDSC shelfmark: 3172.915100.
Formerly (until 1982): Child Behavior Therapy (ISSN 0162-1416)
Description: Scholarly and interdisciplinary journal devoted to research and clinical applications in behavior therapy with children and adolescents, as well as the enhancement of parenting.
Refereed Serial

CHILD AND YOUTH CARE FORUM; an independent journal of day and residential child and youth care practice. see *CHILDREN AND YOUTH — About*

CHILD ASSESSMENT NEWS. see *CHILDREN AND YOUTH — About*

CHILD BEHAVIOR AND DEVELOPMENT. see *MEDICAL SCIENCES — Pediatrics*

PSYCHOLOGY

CHILD DEVELOPMENT. see *CHILDREN AND YOUTH — About*

CHILD STUDY JOURNAL. see *EDUCATION*

150 130   CH   ISSN 1013-9656
CHINESE JOURNAL OF PSYCHOLOGY. (Text in Chinese and English) 1958. s-a. $25 to individuals; institutions $40 (effective 1992). Chinese Psychological Association, c/o Department of Psychology, National Taiwan University, Taipei 10764, Taiwan, Republic of China. FAX 886-2-3629909. Ed. Chia-Hung Hsu. adv.; circ. 500. (back issues avail.) **Indexed:** ASCA, Biol.Abstr., Curr.Cont., Psychol.Abstr., SSCI.
    Formerly: Acta Psychologica Taiwanica (ISSN 0065-1613)

CLAUSTROPHOBIA; life expansion news. see *MEDICAL SCIENCES*

150.19   SP   ISSN 0210-0657
RC475
CLINICA Y ANALISIS GRUPAL; revista de psicoterapia, psicoanalisis y grupo. (Text in Spanish; summaries in English, French) 1976. 3/yr. 4500 ptas.($70) (effective 1992). Grupo Quipu de Psicoterapia Sociedad Cooperativa Ltda., Principe de Vergara 35, 28001 Madrid, Spain. TEL 577-60-39. Ed.Bd. adv.; bk.rev.; index; circ. 1,500. (back issues avail.) **Indexed:** Psychol.Abstr.

157   US   ISSN 0009-9244
BF1
CLINICAL PSYCHOLOGIST. Bound with: Clinical Psychology Review (ISSN 0272-7358) 1946. 6/yr. (American Psychological Association) Pergamon Press, Inc., Journals Division, 660 White Plains Rd., Tarrytown, NY 10591-5153. TEL 914-524-9200. FAX 914-333-2444. (And: Headington Hill Hall, Oxford OX3 0BW, England. TEL 0865-794141) Ed. Gerald P. Koocher. circ. 6,000. **Indexed:** Psychol.Abstr., Psycscan C.P., Rehabil.Lit.
    Refereed Serial

157   UK   ISSN 0269-0144
CLINICAL PSYCHOLOGY FORUM. 6/yr. British Psychological Society, St. Andrews House, 48 Princess Rd., E., Leicester LE1 7DR, England. TEL 0533 549568. Eds. Jenny West, Penny Spinks. (reprint service avail. from ISI)
    —BLDSC shelfmark: 3286.344000.

157.9   US   ISSN 0272-7358
RC467   CODEN: CPSRDZ
CLINICAL PSYCHOLOGY REVIEW. 1981. 8/yr. $375 (effective 1992). (American Psychological Association, Division of Clinical Psychology) Pergamon Press, Inc., Journals Division, 660 White Plains Rd., Tarrytown, NY 10591-5153. TEL 914-524-9200. FAX 914-333-2444. (And: Headington Hill Hall, Oxford OX3 0BW, England. TEL 0865-794141) Eds. Alan S. Bellack, Michel Hersen. (also avail. in microform) **Indexed:** Curr.Cont., Dok.Arbeitsmed., Excerp.Med., Psychol.Abstr., Psycscan C.P., SSCI.
    —BLDSC shelfmark: 3286.345500.
    Refereed Serial

152   US   ISSN 8756-3207
CLINICIAN'S RESEARCH DIGEST. 1983. m. $63 to non-members (foreign $99); members $34; institutions $84 (foreign $156). American Psychological Association, 750 First St., N.E., Washington, DC 20002-4242. TEL 202-336-5500. FAX 202-336-5568. Ed. Gary R. VandenBos.
    Description: Highlights current information on clinical research and professional practice in a concise manner.

153.4   NE   ISSN 0010-0277
BF311   CODEN: CGTNAU
COGNITION; international journal of cognitive psychology. (Text in English; summaries in French) 1972. 12/yr.(in 4 vols.; 3 nos./vol.). fl.1120 (effective 1992). Elsevier Science Publishers B.V., P.O. Box 211, 1000 AE Amsterdam, Netherlands. TEL 020-5803911. FAX 020-5803598. TELEX 18582 ESPA NL. (Subscr. in U.S. and Canada to: Elsevier Science Publishing Co., Inc., Box 882, Madison Sq. Sta., New York, NY 10159. TEL 212-989-5800) Ed. Jacques Mehler. adv.; bibl.; charts; illus.; index. (also avail. in microform from UMI; back issues avail.; reprint service avail. from SWZ) **Indexed:** A.I.Abstr., Adol.Ment.Hlth.Abstr., Biol.Abstr., CAD CAM Abstr., Child Devel.Abstr., Curr.Cont., Lang.& Lang.Behav.Abstr., Lang.Teach.& Ling.Abstr., M.L.A., Phil.Ind., Psychol.Abstr., Sci.Cit.Ind., SSCI.
    —BLDSC shelfmark: 3292.870000.
    Description: Publishes theoretical and experimental papers covering all aspects of the study of the mind. Includes research papers in the fields of psychology, linguistics, neuroscience, ethology, philosophy and epistemology.
    Refereed Serial

301.1 150   UK   ISSN 0269-9931
BF309   CODEN: COEMEC
COGNITION AND EMOTION. 1987. 6/yr. £40($76) to individuals; institutions £82.50($154). Lawrence Erlbaum Associates Ltd., 27 Palmeira Mansions, Church Rd., Hove, E. Sussex BN3 2FA, England. TEL 0273-207411. FAX 0273-205612. Ed. Fraser N. Watts. adv.; bk.rev.; circ. 1,000. **Indexed:** Psychol.Abstr., Sociol.Abstr.
    —BLDSC shelfmark: 3292.871500.
    Description: Explores the interrelationship of cognition and emotion.
    Refereed Serial

370.15   US   ISSN 0737-0008
LB1060
COGNITION AND INSTRUCTION. 1984. q. $39 to individuals (foreign $64); institutions $135 (foreign $160). Lawrence Erlbaum Associates, Inc., 365 Broadway, Hillsdale, NJ 07642. TEL 201-666-4110. FAX 201-666-2394. Ed. Lauren B. Resnick. **Indexed:** Psychol.Abstr.
    —BLDSC shelfmark: 3292.872000.
    Description: Interdisciplinary journal devoted to cognitive investigations of instruction and learning.
    Refereed Serial

COGNITION AND LANGUAGE; a series in psycholinguistics. see *LINGUISTICS*

COGNITION AND LITERACY. see *EDUCATION*

370.15 150   US   ISSN 0885-2014
BF1
COGNITIVE DEVELOPMENT. 1986. q. $40 to individuals; institutions $85. Ablex Publishing Corporation, 355 Chestnut St., Norwood, NJ 07648. TEL 201-767-8450. FAX 201-767-6717. TELEX 135-393. Ed. Katherine Nelson. index; circ. 500. (back issues avail.; reprint service avail. from ISI) **Indexed:** Psychol.Abstr.
    —BLDSC shelfmark: 3292.876600.

157 616.89   UK   ISSN 0264-3294
    CODEN: COGNEP
COGNITIVE NEUROPSYCHOLOGY. 1984. 6/yr. £40($76) to individuals; institutions £105($198). Lawrence Erlbaum Associates Ltd., 27 Palmeira Mansions, Church Rd., Hove, E. Sussex BN3 2FA, England. TEL 0273-207411. FAX 0273-205612. Ed. Max Coltheart. adv.; bk.rev.; circ. 1,000. **Indexed:** Bibl.Dev.Med.& Child Neur., Excerp.Med., Psychol.Abstr.
    —BLDSC shelfmark: 3292.879000.
    Description: Studies cognitive processes from a neuropsychological perspective.
    Refereed Serial

153.4   US   ISSN 0010-0285
BF309   CODEN: CGPSBQ
COGNITIVE PSYCHOLOGY. 1970. q. $149 (foreign $184). Academic Press, Inc., Journal Division, 1250 Sixth Ave., San Diego, CA 92101. TEL 619-230-1840. FAX 619-699-6800. TELEX 181726. Ed. Douglas L. Medin. adv.; abstr.; bibl.; charts; stat. (back issues avail.) **Indexed:** Adol.Ment.Hlth.Abstr., C.I.J.E., Child Devel.Abstr., Commun.Abstr., Curr.Cont., Lang.& Lang.Behav.Abstr., M.L.A., Mid.East: Abstr.& Ind., Psychol.Abstr., Psycscan D.P., Sci.Abstr., Soc.Sci.Ind., SSCI.
    —BLDSC shelfmark: 3292.880000.
    Description: Concerned with advances in the study of memory, language processing, perception, problem solving, and thinking. Presents original empirical, theoretical, and tutorial papers, methodological articles, and critical reviews.
    Refereed Serial

020 410   US   ISSN 0364-0213
BF311   CODEN: COGSD5
COGNITIVE SCIENCE; a multidisciplinary journal of artificial intelligence, psychology, and language. 1977. q. $50 to individuals; institutions $125. Ablex Publishing Corporation, 355 Chestnut St., Norwood, NJ 07648. TEL 201-767-8450. FAX 201-767-6717. TELEX 135-393. Ed. Martin Ringle. index; circ. 2,400. (back issues avail.; reprint service avail. from ISI) **Indexed:** A.I.Abstr., Art.Int.Abstr., C.I.J.E., CAD CAM Abstr., Curr.Cont., Excerp.Med., Lang.& Lang.Behav.Abstr., M.L.A., Psychol.Abstr., Sociol.Abstr., SSCI.
    —BLDSC shelfmark: 3292.885000.

301.1   US   ISSN 0732-1295
COGNITIVE SCIENCE SERIES (CAMBRIDGE). irreg., vol.9, 1989. Harvard University Press, 79 Garden St., Cambridge, MA 02138. TEL 617-495-2600. FAX 617-495-5898.
    Refereed Serial

150   US
COGNITIVE SCIENCE SERIES: TECHNICAL MONOGRAPHS AND EDITED COLLECTIONS. 1981. irreg., vol.13, 1991. $99.95. Lawrence Erlbaum Associates, Inc., 365 Broadway, Hillsdale, NJ 07642. TEL 201-666-4110. FAX 201-666-2394. Ed. Andrew Ortony. bibl.; charts; illus. **Indexed:** Curr.Cont., Psychol.Abstr.
    Refereed Serial

152   NE   ISSN 0256-663X
COGNITIVE SYSTEMS. 1985. q. fl.120. European Society for the Study of Cognitive Systems, c/o Dept. for Psychology, University of Groningen, P.O. Box 72, 9700 AB Groningen, Netherlands. FAX 50-636304. Ed. G.J. Dalenoort. bk.rev.; circ. 60. (back issues avail.)
    —BLDSC shelfmark: 3292.892500.

150   US   ISSN 0147-5916
BF311   CODEN: CTHRD8
COGNITIVE THERAPY AND RESEARCH. 1977. 6/yr. $210 (foreign $245)(effective 1992). Plenum Publishing Corp., 233 Spring St., New York, NY 10013-1578. TEL 212-620-8000. FAX 212-463-0742. TELEX 23-421139. Ed. Philip C. Kendall. adv. (also avail. in microfilm from JSC; back issues avail.) **Indexed:** Adol.Ment.Hlth.Abstr., Behav.Abstr., Biol.Abstr., Curr.Cont., Excerp.Med., Psychol.Abstr., Psycscan C.P., Ref.Zh., SSCI.
    —BLDSC shelfmark: 3292.895000.
    Refereed Serial

155.4 370   FR
COLLECTION ORIENTATIONS. irreg. price varies. Editions Scientifiques et Psychologiques, 6 bis, rue Andre Chenier, 92130 Issy-les-Moulineaux, France. TEL 46-45-38-12. FAX 40-95-73-32. TELEX 270 105 F. Ed. G. Pihouee.

156   FR
COLLECTION PSYCHOLOGIE. irreg. price varies. Editions Scientifiques et Psychologiques, 6 bis, rue Andre Chenier, 92130 Issy-les-Moulineaux, France. TEL 46-45-38-12. FAX 40-95-73-32. TELEX 270 105 F. Ed. T. Ego.

COLLECTION PSYCHOLOGIE ET PEDAGOGIE DE LA MUSIQUE. see *MUSIC*

PSYCHOLOGY

152 790.1 FR
COLLECTION PSYCHOLOGIE ET PEDAGOGIE DU SPORT. irreg. price varies. Editions Scientifiques et Psychologiques, 6 bis, rue Andre Chenier, 92130 Issy-les-Moulineaux, France. TEL 46-45-38-12. FAX 40-95-73-32. TELEX 270 105 F. Ed. A. Vom Hofe.

158.7 FR
COLLECTION PSYCHOLOGIE ET PEDAGOGIE DU TRAVAIL. irreg. price varies. Editions Scientifiques et Psychologiques, 6 bis, rue Andre Chenier, 92130 Issy-les-Moulineaux, France. TEL 46-45-38-12. FAX 40-95-73-32. TELEX 270 105 F. Ed. B. Gillet.

156 FR
COLLECTION TESTS PSYCHOLOGIQUES. irreg. price varies. Editions Scientifiques et Psychologiques, 6 bis, rue Andre Chenier, 92130 Issy-les-Moulineaux, France. TEL 46-45-38-12. FAX 40-95-73-32. TELEX 270 104 F. Ed. R. Simonnet.

156 109 US ISSN 0267-9469
COMMENTS & CRITICISMS. 1983. irreg. Prytaneum Press, 1015 Bryan, Amarillo, TX 79102. TEL 806-372-7888. Ed. Don D. Davis. bk.rev.; circ. 500.

616.89 200 US ISSN 0885-8500
COMMON BOUNDARY; between spirituality and psychotherapy. 1980. bi-m. $22. Common Boundary, Inc., 4304 East-West Hwy., Bethesda, MD 20814. TEL 301-652-9495. FAX 301-652-0579. Ed. Anne A. Simpkinson. adv.; bk.rev.; circ. 21,000. (back issues avail.)
Description: Articles, news and research for psychotherapists and pastoral counselors interested in the interface with spirituality.

301.1 US
COMMON GROUND (SAN ANSELMO); resources for personal transformation. 1973. 4/yr. $10. 305 San Anselmo Ave., Ste. 313, San Anselmo, CA 94960. TEL 415-459-4900. FAX 415-459-4974. TELEX 428701. Ed. Baha-Uddin Alpine. adv.; bk.rev.; circ. 85,000.
Description: Directory of resources for personal transformation.

301.1 US
COMMON GROUND HAWAII.* 4/yr. $4. 571 Kaimalino St., Kailua, HI 96734-1611. TEL 808-239-7190. adv.

370 US ISSN 0164-775X
COMMUNIQUE (SILVER SPRING). 8/yr. $30. National Association of School Psychologists, 8455 Colesville Rd., Ste. 1000, Silver Spring, MD 20910. TEL 301-608-0500. FAX 301-608-2514. Ed. Alex Thomas. adv.; circ. 15,600. (tabloid format)
Description: Newsletter with practical professional articles to help school psychologists. Includes job listings, convention information, organizational news, and other newsworthy items.

COMMUNITY MENTAL HEALTH JOURNAL. see *SOCIAL SERVICES AND WELFARE*

COMMUNITY PSYCHIATRY JOURNAL. see *MEDICAL SCIENCES — Psychiatry And Neurology*

370.15 150 IS
COMMUNITY STRESS PREVENTION. (Text in English and Hebrew) 1985. q. free. Community Stress Prevention Centre, Merkaz Habriut, Kiryat Shmona 10200, Israel. TEL 06-948827. FAX 06-950740. Eds. Mooli Lahad, Alan Cohen. bk.rev.; circ. 100.
Formerly: School Psychology Emergency Centre. Newsletter.
Description: Covers the work and activities of the Centre.

614.58 US ISSN 1051-7782
▼**COMPREHENSIVE MENTAL HEALTH CARE.** 1991. 3/yr. $70. Springer-Verlag, 175 Fifth Ave., New York, NY 10010. TEL 212-460-1500. Ed. Steve Pfeiffer.
—BLDSC shelfmark: 3366.384300.
Description: Contains original articles on the diagnosis, treatment, and habilitation of children, adolescents, and adults with developmental disabilities, psychiatric disorders, or multiple handicaps.

COMPREHENSIVE PSYCHIATRY. see *MEDICAL SCIENCES — Psychiatry And Neurology*

616.89 UK ISSN 0275-7222
RC475
COMPREHENSIVE PSYCHOTHERAPY. 1980. irreg., vol.4, 1984. Gordon & Breach Science Publishers, P.O. Box 90, Reading, Berkshire RG1 8JL, England. TEL 0734-560-080. FAX 0734-568-211. TELEX 849870 SCIPUB G. (US addr.: Box 786, Cooper Sta., New York, NY 10276) Ed. P. Olsen. (also avail. in microfilm; microfiche)
Refereed Serial

COMPUTERS IN HUMAN BEHAVIOR. see *SOCIOLOGY — Computer Applications*

301.1 150 IT
COMUNICAZIONI SCIENTIFICHE DI PSICOLOGIA GENERALE. 1976. s-a. L.56000 to individuals; institutions L.66000; foreign L.80000(effective 1992). Edizioni Scientifiche Italiane S.p.A., Via Chiatamone, 7, 80121 Naples, Italy. TEL 081-7645768. FAX 081-7646477. Ed. Marta Olivetti Belardinelli.

CONCEPTS IN NEUROSCIENCE. see *BIOLOGY — Biophysics*

150.9 FR
CONFLUENTS PSYCHANALYTIQUES. 1980. irreg. Societe d'Edition les Belles Lettres, 95 bd. Raspail, 75006 Paris, France.

CONNECTICUT HOSPICE NEWSLETTER; making today count. see *PHYSICAL FITNESS AND HYGIENE*

370.15 US ISSN 1053-8100
▼**CONSCIOUSNESS AND COGNITION;** an international journal. 1992. 4/yr. $122 (foreign $143). Academic Press, Inc., Journal Division, 1250 Sixth Ave., San Diego, CA 92101. TEL 619-230-1840. FAX 619-699-6800. TELEX 181726. Eds. Bernard Baars, William Banks. bk.rev.
Description: Provides a forum for a natural-science approach to the issues of consciousness, voluntary control, and self. Features two types of articles: empirical research (in the form of regular articles and short reports) and theoretical articles.
Refereed Serial

152 US
CONSCIOUSNESS AND SELF-REGULATION: ADVANCES IN RESEARCH AND THEORY. 1976. irreg., vol.4, 1986. price varies. Plenum Publishing Corp., 233 Spring St., New York, NY 10013-1578. TEL 212-620-8000. FAX 212-463-0742. TELEX 23-421139. Eds. Gary Schwartz, David Shapiro.
Formerly: Consciousness and Self-Regulation: Advances in Research.
Refereed Serial

CONTEMPORARY EDUCATIONAL PSYCHOLOGY. see *EDUCATION*

301.4 US ISSN 0892-2764
CONTEMPORARY FAMILY THERAPY; an international journal. 1979. bi-m. $195 (foreign $230). Human Sciences Press, Inc. (Subsidiary of: Plenum Publishing Corp.), 233 Spring St., New York, NY 10013-1578. TEL 212-620-8000. FAX 212-463-0742. Ed. William C. Nichols. adv.; bk.rev. (reprint service avail. from ISI,UMI) **Indexed:** Adol.Ment.Hlth.Abstr., ASSIA, Biol.Abstr., C.I.J.E., Curr.Cont., Past.Care & Couns.Abstr., Psychol.Abstr., Soc.Work Res.& Abstr., Sp.Ed.Needs Abstr., SSCI, Stud.Wom.Abstr.
Formerly (until 1986): International Journal of Family Therapy (ISSN 0148-8384)
Description: Presents latest theory, research, and practice with an emphasis on examination of the family within the socioeconomic matrix of which it is an integral part.
Refereed Serial

616.89 UK ISSN 0960-5290
CODEN: COHYET
CONTEMPORARY HYPNOSIS. 1983. 3/yr. $49 to individuals; institutions $74. (British Society of Experimental and Clinical Hypnosis) Whurr Publishers Ltd., 19b Compton Terrace, London N1 2UN, England. TEL 071-359-5979. FAX 071-226-5290. Ed. Brian Fellows. adv.; bk.rev.; index; circ. 400. (back issues avail.) **Indexed:** Psychol.Abstr.
—BLDSC shelfmark: 3425.182900.
Formerly: British Journal of Experimental and Clinical Hypnosis (ISSN 0265-1033)
Description: Covers all aspects of theory, research and practice of hypnosis.

616.89 US ISSN 0010-7530
RC500 CODEN: CPPSBL
CONTEMPORARY PSYCHOANALYSIS. 1964. q. $45 to individuals (foreign $49); institutions $67.50 (foreign $71.50). William Alanson White Psychoanalytic Institute, 20 W. 74th St., New York, NY 10023. TEL 212-873-0725. FAX 212-362-6967. Ed. Arthur H. Feiner. bk.rev.; index; circ. 1,650. (back issues avail.) **Indexed:** Biol.Abstr., Curr.Cont., Mid.East: Abstr.& Ind., Psychoanal.Abstr., Psychol.Abstr., Soc.Work Res.& Abstr., Sociol.Abstr., SSCI.
Description: Presents a scholarly approach to the contemporary psychoanalytic scene. Covers a wide range of subjects, from schizophrenia and the neuroses, to group processes and community psychiatry, from a clinical perspective.
Refereed Serial

155 US ISSN 0010-7549
BF1
CONTEMPORARY PSYCHOLOGY; a journal of reviews. 1956. m. $100 to non-members; members $42; institutions $200. American Psychological Association, 750 First St., N.E., Washington, DC 20002-4646. TEL 202-336-5500. FAX 202-336-5568. adv.; bk.rev.; film rev.; illus.; index; circ. 5,500. (also avail. in microform from MIM) **Indexed:** Adol.Ment.Hlth.Abstr., Biol.Abstr., Bk.Rev.Ind. (1975-), Chic.Per.Ind., Child.Bk.Rev.Ind. (1975-), Curr.Cont., Risk Abstr., SSCI.
—BLDSC shelfmark: 3425.250000.
Refereed Serial

CONTINUING THE CONVERSATION; a newsletter on the ideas of Gregory Bateson. see *PHILOSOPHY*

616.89 BL
CONTRIBUICOES EM PSICOLOGIA, PSIQUIATRIA E PSICANALISE. irreg. Editora Campus Ltda. (Subsidiary of: Elsevier Science Publishers B.V.), Rua Barao de Itapagipe 55, Rio Comprido, 20261 Rio de Janeiro RJ, Brazil.

150 US ISSN 0736-2714
CONTRIBUTIONS IN PSYCHOLOGY. 1983. irreg. price varies. Greenwood Press, Inc. (Subsidiary of: Greenwood Publishing Group Inc.), 88 Post Rd. W., Box 5007, Westport, CT 06881-5007. TEL 203-226-3571. FAX 203-222-1502. bibl.; index.
—BLDSC shelfmark: 3461.153000.

155.4 US
CONTRIBUTIONS TO RESIDENTIAL TREATMENT. 1957. a. $15. American Association of Children's Residential Centers, 440 First St., N.W., Ste. 310, Washington, DC 20001. TEL 202-638-1604. Ed. Claudia C. Waller. circ. 200. (back issues avail.)

616.8 US ISSN 0093-1551
RC321
CORRECTIVE AND SOCIAL PSYCHIATRY AND JOURNAL OF BEHAVIORAL TECHNOLOGY METHODS AND THERAPY. 1954. q. $60 (foreign $65). Martin Psychiatric Research Foundation, Box 3365, Fairfield, CA 94533-0587. FAX 7078640910. Ed. Clyde V. Martin, M.D. adv.; bk.rev.; film rev.; charts; illus.; circ. 1,200. (also avail. in microform from UMI; back issues avail.; reprint service avail. from KTO) **Indexed:** Adol.Ment.Hlth.Abstr., Chic.Per.Ind., Crim.Just.Abstr., Curr.Cont., Excerpt.Med., Mid.East: Abstr.& Ind., Psychol.Abstr., SSCI.
—BLDSC shelfmark: 3472.172000.
Formerly: Corrective and Social Psychiatry and Journal of Applied Behavior Therapy (ISSN 0091-2611); Supersedes: Corrective Psychiatry and Journal of Social Therapy (ISSN 0010-9053)
Refereed Serial

157.9 US ISSN 0011-0000
BF637.C6 CODEN: CPSYB
THE COUNSELING PSYCHOLOGIST. 1973. q. $40 to individuals; institutions $112. Sage Publications, Inc., 2455 Teller Rd., Newbury Park, CA 91320. TEL 805-499-0721. FAX 805-499-0871. Ed. Gerald L. Stone. adv.; circ. 5,300. (also avail. in microform from MIM,UMI; reprint service avail. from UMI; back issues avail.) **Indexed:** Adol.Ment.Hlth.Abstr., C.I.J.E., Curr.Cont., Educ.Ind., Mid.East: Abstr.& Ind., Psychol.Abstr., Soc.Sci.Ind., SSCI.
—BLDSC shelfmark: 3481.330000.

PSYCHOLOGY

150 616.8   UK   ISSN 0951-5070
CODEN: CPQUEZ
COUNSELLING PSYCHOLOGY QUARTERLY. 1988. q. $88 to individuals; institutions $220. Carfax Publishing Co., P.O. Box 25, Abingdon, Oxfordshire OX14 3UE, England. TEL 0235-555335. FAX 0235-553559. (Subscr. addr. in U.S.: Carfax Publishing Co., Box 2025, Dunnellon, FL 32630) Ed. W.J. Alladin. adv.; bk.rev. (also avail. in microfiche) **Indexed:** Sp.Ed.Needs Abstr.
—BLDSC shelfmark: 3481.338300.

COUNSELOR EDUCATION AND SUPERVISION. see *EDUCATION*

CREATIVE CHILD AND ADULT QUARTERLY. see *CHILDREN AND YOUTH — About*

CREATIVE INTELLIGENCE ENHANCEMENT. see *SOCIOLOGY*

301.1 150   US
CREATIVITY RESEARCH JOURNAL. 1988. q. $45 to individuals; institutions $95. Ablex Publishing Corporation, 355 Chestnut St., Norwood, NJ 07648. TEL 201-767-8450. FAX 201-767-6717. TELEX 135-393. Ed. Mark Runco. adv.; abstr.; bibl.; circ. 400. (back issues avail.; reprint service avail.)

157 364   UK   ISSN 0957-9664
▼**CRIMINAL BEHAVIOUR AND MENTAL HEALTH.** 1991. 4/yr. $84 to individuals; institutions $126. Whurr Publishers Ltd., 19b Compton Terrace, London N1 2UN, England. TEL 071-359-5979. Ed.Bd. adv.; bk.rev.; charts; illus.; stats.; index.
—BLDSC shelfmark: 3487.346200.

CRIMINAL JUSTICE & BEHAVIOR; an international journal. see *CRIMINOLOGY AND LAW ENFORCEMENT*

157.744   CN   ISSN 0227-5910
CRISIS; international journal of suicide and crisis studies. (Text and summaries in English, French and German) 1980. s-a. Can.$29.50 to individuals; institutions $42. (International Association for Suicide Prevention) Hogrefe & Huber Publishers, 14 Bruce Park Ave., Toronto, Ont. M4P 2S3, Canada. TEL 416-482-6339. FAX 416-484-4200. Ed. R. Battegay. adv. **Indexed:** Psychol.Abstr., Soc.Sci.Ind.
—BLDSC shelfmark: 3487.382350.
Description: International research into the prevention of suicidal behavior.

618.92   US
CRITICAL ISSUES IN DEVELOPMENTAL & BEHAVIORAL PEDIATRICS. 1987. irreg., vol.3, 1991. price varies. Plenum Publishing Corp., 233 Spring St., New York, NY 10013-1578. TEL 212-620-8000. FAX 212-463-0742. TELEX 23-421139. Ed. Martin Gottlieb. (back issues avail.)
Formerly: Developmental and Behavioral Pediatrics: Selected Topics.
Refereed Serial

156   US   ISSN 0710-068X
CROSS-CULTURAL PSYCHOLOGY BULLETIN. (Text in English) 1967. q. $20. International Association for Cross-Cultural Psychology, c/o Dr. John Adamopoulos, Ed., Department of Psychology, Box 7111, South Bend, IN 46634. bk.rev.; abstr.; bibl.; circ. 600. (looseleaf format)
—BLDSC shelfmark: 3488.810000.
Formerly (until vol.15, 1981): International Association for Cross-Cultural Psychology. Newsletter.

150   CL
CUADERNOS DE PSICOLOGIA. 1972. irreg. Universidad de Chile, Departamento de Psicologia, Av. Bernardo O'Higgins 1058, Casilla 10-D, Santiago, Chile. illus.

150   CK
CUADERNOS DE PSICOLOGIA. 1976. 2/yr. $8. Universidad del Valle, Departamento de Psicologia, Apdo. Aereo 25360, Cali, Colombia. FAX 923-398484. adv.; bk.rev.; circ. 1,000. **Indexed:** Psychol.Abstr.

157   US
CULT AWARENESS NETWORK NEWS. 1980. m. $30 (foreign $40). Cult Awareness Network, 2421 W. Pratt Blvd., Ste. 1173, Chicago, IL 60645. TEL 312-267-7777. Ed. Cynthia S. Kisser. bk.rev.; circ. 2,000. (tabloid format; back issues avail.)
Description: News briefs and feature articles on destructive cults, indoctrination and conversion techniques, and legal and social issues concerning cult activity.

155.4   US
CULTURAL CONTEXT OF INFANCY. 1989. irreg., vol.2, 1991. price varies. Ablex Publishing Corporation, 355 Chestnut St., Norwood, NJ 07648. TEL 201-767-8450. FAX 201-767-6717. TELEX 135-393. Ed. J. Kevin Nugent.

150.19   UK   ISSN 0963-7214
▼**CURRENT DIRECTIONS IN PSYCHOLOGICAL SCIENCE.** 1992. bi-m. $120. (American Psychological Association) Cambridge University Press, 40 W. 20th St., New York, NY 10011-4211. TEL 212-924-3900. FAX 212-691-3232. Eds. Sandra Scarr, Charles R. Gallistel.

616.89   US
CODEN: CIPPEY
CURRENT ISSUES IN PSYCHOANALYTIC PRACTICE. MONOGRAPHS. 1984. irreg. price varies. Brunner-Mazel Publishing Co., 19 Union Sq. W., New York, NY 10003. TEL 212-924-3344. Ed. Herbert S. Strean. (back issues avail.) **Indexed:** Excerp.Med., Psychol.Abstr.
Formerly: Current Issues in Psychoanalytic Practice. Journal (ISSN 0737-7851)

150   US
CURRENT PSYCHOLOGY (HENDERSONVILLE). 1979. m. $25. Psychological Press, Box 309, Hendersonville, TN 37075. (also avail. in microform from UMI) **Indexed:** Psychol.Abstr.

150
BF1   US   ISSN 1046-1310
CURRENT PSYCHOLOGY (NEW BRUNSWICK); research & reviews. 1981. q. $40 to individuals (foreign $60); institutions $76 (foreign $96). Transaction Publishers, Transaction Periodicals Consortium, Department 3092, Rutgers University, New Brunswick, NJ 08903. TEL 908-932-2280. FAX 908-932-3138. Eds. Noel P. Sheehy, Nathaniel Pallone. circ. 500. **Indexed:** HRIS, Psychol.Abstr., Sage Fam.Stud.Abstr.
Former titles: Current Psychological Research and Reviews (ISSN 0737-8262) & Current Psychological Research; Current Psychological Reviews.
Description: International forum for rapid dissemination of psychological information.
Refereed Serial

150   US   ISSN 8755-0040
BF431
CURRENT TOPICS IN HUMAN INTELLIGENCE. 1985. irreg., vol.2, 1991. price varies. Ablex Publishing Corporation, 355 Chestnut St., Norwood, NJ 07648. TEL 201-767-8450. FAX 201-767-6717. TELEX 135-393. Ed. Douglas Detterman. **Indexed:** Psychol.Abstr.

370.15 150   US
CURRENT TOPICS IN LEARNING DISABILITIES. 1984. irreg. price varies. Ablex Publishing Corporation, 355 Chestnut St., Norwood, NJ 07648. TEL 201-767-8450. FAX 201-767-6717. TELEX 135-393. Eds. James McKinney, Lynne Feagans.

150 301   PL   ISSN 0239-3271
CZLOWIEK I SPOLECZENSTWO. (Text in Polish, occasionally in English) 1984. a. $6. (Adam Mickiewicz University, Institute of Sociology) Adam Mickiewicz University Press, Nowowiejskiego 55, 61-734 Poznan, Poland. TEL 527-380. TELEX 413260 UAM PL. Ed. Maria Tyszka. bk.rev.; circ. 500. (back issues avail.)
—BLDSC shelfmark: 3508.529000.
Description: Covers psychology, sociology and education.

616.89   GW   ISSN 0935-2066
D G I P - INTERN. 1982. q. membership. Deutsche Gesellschaft fuer Indivualpsychologie e.V., Ruffinstr. 10, 8000 Munich 19, Germany. TEL 089-1688068. FAX 089-168138. Ed. Horst Groener. adv.; bk.rev.; circ. 1,800.

301.1 150   US
DAILY DEVELOPMENT. m. 12755 State Hwy. 55, Minneapolis, MN 55441. TEL 612-559-2322. Ed. Barbara Winter.

DANMARKS LAERERHOESKOLE. INSTITUT FOR PAEDAGOGIK OG PSYKOLOGI. TESTSAMLING. see *EDUCATION*

DARSHANA INTERNATIONAL; an international quarterly of philosophy, psychology, sociology, psychical research, religion and mysticism. see *PHILOSOPHY*

DAY CARE AND EARLY EDUCATION. see *SOCIAL SERVICES AND WELFARE*

150   CC
DAZHONG XINLIXUE/POPULAR PSYCHOLOGY. (Text in Chinese) bi-m. Huadong Shifan Daxue, Jiaoyu Kexue Xueyuan - East China Normal University, School of Education, 3663 Zhongshan Beilu, Shanghai 200062, People's Republic of China. TEL 2518532. (Co-sponsor: Shanghai Society of Psychology) Ed. Zeng Xingchu.

613   US   ISSN 0161-4835
DEATH. 1978. m. $9.95. Bad Seed, Inc., 116 W. 14th St., New York, NY 10011. TEL 212-898-8001. adv.; circ. 250,000. (tabloid format)

150   US   ISSN 0748-1187
BF789.D4   CODEN: DESTEA
DEATH STUDIES; education-counseling-care-law-ethics. 1977. bi-m. $132. Hemisphere Publishing Corporation (Subsidiary of: Taylor & Francis Group), 1900 Frost Rd., Ste. 101, Bristol, PA 19007-1598. TEL 215-785-5800. FAX 215-785-5515. Ed. Hannelore Wass. adv.; bk.rev.; abstr.; bibl.; charts; illus.; index; circ. 800. (also avail. in microform from UMI; back issues avail.; reprint service avail. from UMI) **Indexed:** Abstr.Soc.Geront., C.I.J.E., CERDIC, CINAHL, Cont.Pg.Educ., Curr.Cont., Excerp.Med., Past.Care & Couns.Abstr., Psychol.Abstr., Res.High.Educ.Abstr., Risk Abstr., Sage Fam.Stud.Abstr., Soc.Work Res.& Abstr., Sociol.Abstr., Sp.Ed.Needs Abstr., SSCI.
—BLDSC shelfmark: 3535.960460.
Formerly (until 1985): Death Education (ISSN 0145-7624)
Description: International and interdisciplinary forum in the field of death studies. Refereed papers cover education, counseling, bioethics, and psychosocial research.
Refereed Serial

150.19   FR
DECOUVERTE FREUDIENNE. (Supplement to: Pas Tant) 3/yr. 230 F. (effective 1992). (Universite de Toulouse II (le Mirail)) Presses Universitaires du Mirail, 56 rue du Taur, 31000 Toulouse, France. TEL 61-22-58-31. FAX 61-21-84-20. (back issues avail.)

157   UK   ISSN 0957-4573
DEPRESSION BRIEFING. q. £20($35) to individuals; institutions £40($70). Lawrence Erlbaum Associates Ltd., 27 Palmeira Mansions, Church Rd., Hove, E. Sussex BN3 2FA, England. Ed. F. Neil Johnson. bk.rev.
—BLDSC shelfmark: 3554.590500.
Description: Directed to health care professionals; covers depressive illness and related conditins for up-to-date information about research results and developments in therapy.

150   UK   ISSN 0954-5794
DEVELOPMENT AND PSYCHOPATHOLOGY. 1989. q. $35 to individuals; institutions $75. Cambridge University Press, Edinburgh Building, Shaftesbury Rd., Cambridge CB2 2RU, England. TEL 0223-312393. (North American orders to: Cambridge University Press, 40 W. 20th St., New York, NY 10011) Eds. Dante Cicchetti, Barry Nurcombe.
—BLDSC shelfmark: 3578.855000.
Description: Devoted to the publication of original empirical, theoretical and review papers which address the interrelationship of normal and pathological development in adults and children.

PSYCHOLOGY 4019

155 US
DEVELOPMENTAL DISABILITIES; special interest section newsletter. (Consists of 7 sections: Administration and Management; Developmental Disabilities; Gerontology; Mental Health; Physical Disabilities; Sensory Integration; Work Programs) vol.12, no.2, 1989. q. $15. American Occupational Therapy Association, Inc., 1383 Piccard Dr., Box 1725, Rockville, MD 20850-0822. TEL 301-948-9626. FAX 301-948-5512.

370.15 US ISSN 8756-5641
CODEN: DENEE8
DEVELOPMENTAL NEUROPSYCHOLOGY; an international journal of life-span issues in neuropsychology. 1985. q. $45 to individuals (foreign $70); institutions $150 (foreign $175). Lawrence Erlbaum Associates, Inc., 365 Broadway, Hillsdale, NJ 07642. TEL 201-666-4100. FAX 201-666-2394. Ed. Francis J. Pirozzolo. adv.; circ. 750. (back volumes avail.) Indexed: Psychol.Abstr.
—BLDSC shelfmark: 3579.057300.
  Description: Covers issues concerning the structure and function of both the developing and the aging brain.
  Refereed Serial

DEVELOPMENTAL PSYCHOBIOLOGY. see *BIOLOGY*

155 US ISSN 0012-1649
BF699 CODEN: DEVPA9
DEVELOPMENTAL PSYCHOLOGY. 1969. bi-m. $110 to non-members (foreign $128); members $40; institutions $220 (foreign $212) (effective 1992). American Psychological Association, 750 First St., N.E., Washington, DC 20002-4242.
TEL 202-336-5500. FAX 202-336-5568. Ed. Ross D. Parke. adv.; bibl.; charts; stat.; circ. 4,300. (also avail. in microform from MIM,UMI; reprint service avail. from UMI; back issues avail.) Indexed: Adol.Ment.Hlth.Abstr., ASSIA, Bibl.Dev.Med.& Child Neur., Biol.Abstr., C.I.J.E., Child Devel.Abstr., Commun.Abstr., Crim.Just.Abstr., Curr.Adv.Ecol.Sci., Curr.Cont., Energy Ind., Energy Info.Abstr., M.L.A., Mid.East: Abstr.& Ind., Psychol.Abstr., Psycscan D.P., Sage Fam.Stud.Abstr., Soc.Sci.Ind., Soc.Work Res.& Abstr., Sp.Ed.Needs Abstr., SSCI, Stud.Wom.Abstr.
—BLDSC shelfmark: 3579.059000.
  Description: Empirical contributions that advance knowledge and theory about human psychological growth and development from infancy to old age.
  Refereed Serial

150 US ISSN 0273-2297
BF721
DEVELOPMENTAL REVIEW; perspectives in behavior and cognition. 1981. q. $82 (foreign $104). Academic Press, Inc., Journal Division, 1250 Sixth Ave., San Diego, CA 92101. TEL 619-230-1840.
FAX 619-699-6800. TELEX 181726. Ed. Grover J. Whitehurst. adv.; index. (back issues avail.) Indexed: Child Devel.Abstr., Psychol.Abstr., Psycscan D.P., SSCI.
—BLDSC shelfmark: 3579.059780.
  Description: Provides child and developmental, child clinical, and educational psychologists with articles that reflect current thinking and covers scientific developments.
  Refereed Serial

157 US
DEVELOPMENTS IN CLINICAL PSYCHOLOGY. 1984. irreg. price varies. Ablex Publishing Corporation, 355 Chestnut Ln., Norwood, NJ 07648.
TEL 201-767-8450. FAX 201-767-6717. TELEX 135-393. Ed. Glenn R. Caddy.

DEVIANCE ET SOCIETE. see *SOCIOLOGY*

DEVIANT BEHAVIOR; an interdisciplinary journal. see *SOCIOLOGY*

DI CYAN BULLETIN. see *MEDICAL SCIENCES — Psychiatry And Neurology*

155.28 GW ISSN 0012-1924
CODEN: DGNSAQ
DIAGNOSTICA; Zeitschrift fuer psychologische Diagnostik, zugleich Informationsorgan ueber psychologische Tests und Untersuchungsmethoden. (Text in German; summaries in English) 1955. q. DM.74. Verlag fuer Psychologie Dr. C.J. Hogrefe, Rohnsweg 25, Postfach 3751, 3400 Goettingen, Germany. TEL 0551-54044. Ed. H. Westmeyer. adv.; bk.rev.; bibl.; charts; circ. 1,000. (also avail. in microfiche from BLH; reprint service avail. from SWZ) Indexed: Biol.Abstr., Ger.J.Psych., Psychol.Abstr.
—BLDSC shelfmark: 3579.670000.

150 US
DIALOGUES IN CONTEMPORARY PSYCHOLOGY SERIES. 1981. irreg. price varies. Praeger Publishers (Subsidiary of: Greenwood Publishing Group Inc.), 88 Post Rd. W., Box 5007, Westport, CT 06881-5007. TEL 203-226-3571.
FAX 203-222-1502.

370.15 150 SW ISSN 0346-5020
DIDAKOMETRY AND SOCIOMETRY. (Text in English) 1969. s-a. Laerarhoeghskolan i Malmoe, Inst. foer Pedagogik och Specialmetodik - Malmoe School of Education, box 23501, S-200 45 Malmoe, Sweden. Ed. Aake Bjerstedt. Indexed: Educ.Tech.Abstr., Psychol.Abstr., Sociol.Abstr.

DIMENSIONS (RIMROCK). see *PARAPSYCHOLOGY AND OCCULTISM*

DIRECTORY FOR EXCEPTIONAL CHILDREN; a listing of educational and training facilities. see *EDUCATION — Special Education And Rehabilitation*

DIRECTORY OF GRADUATE TRAINING IN BEHAVIOR THERAPY. see *EDUCATION — Guides To Schools And Colleges*

DIRECTORY OF PSYCHOLOGY INTERNSHIPS: PROGRAMS OFFERING BEHAVIORAL TRAINING. see *EDUCATION — Guides To Schools And Colleges*

157.744 US
DIRECTORY OF SUICIDE PREVENTION AND CRISIS INTERVENTION CENTERS. a. $15. American Association of Suicidology, 2459 S. Ash, Denver, CO 80222. TEL 303-692-0985.

150 301 370 US ISSN 0731-8081
BF431 CODEN: DUEMEV
DIRECTORY OF UNPUBLISHED EXPERIMENTAL MENTAL MEASURES. 1974. irreg., vol.4, 1985. Human Sciences Press, Inc. (Subsidiary of: Plenum Publishing Corp.), 233 Spring St., New York, NY 10013-1578. TEL 212-620-8000.
FAX 212-463-0742. Ed. Bert A. Goldman. (reprint service avail. from ISI,UMI)
  Refereed Serial

156 FR ISSN 0766-5350
DIRES. 2/yr. 70 F. Universite de Montpellier (Universite Paul Valery), Centre d'Etudes Freudiennes de Montpellier, B.P. 5043, 34032 Montpellier Cedex 1, France. TEL 67-14-20-00. bk.rev.
  Description: Presents poetical and analytical research.

150 301 UK ISSN 0957-9265
P302 CODEN: DISOEN
▼**DISCOURSE & SOCIETY.** 1990. q. £26($43) to individuals; institutions £60($99). Sage Publications Ltd., 6 Bonhill St., London EC2A 4PU, England. TEL 071-374-0645. FAX 071-374-8741. Ed. Teun A. van Dijk. adv.; color page £190; trim 193 x 114; adv. contact: Bernie Folan.
—BLDSC shelfmark: 3595.810000.
  Description: Explores the relevance of discourse analysis to the social sciences, with a particular focus on the political implications of discourse and communication.

616.891 FR ISSN 0012-477X
DOCUMENTS ET DEBATS.* 1970. irreg. (4-5/yr.). membership. Association Psychoanalytique de France, 24 Place Dauphine, 75006 Paris, France. Ed. Dr. G. Rosolato. bk.rev.; abstr.; bibl.; circ. 200. (processed)
  Description: Explores psychoanalytic techniques.

155.3 236 367 US
DOMINANT NEWSLETTER. 1975. 10/yr. $20. Skye Publishing, Box 324, Riverside, IL 60546. Ed. Jonathan Lee. adv.; bk.rev.; circ. 300. (looseleaf format; back issues avail.)

DREAM NETWORK; a quarterly journal exploring dreams and myth. see *NEW AGE PUBLICATIONS*

150 US
DREAM SWITCHBOARD. 1988. q. $5. (Community Dreamsharing Network) Dream Switchboard, Box 8032, Hicksville, NY 11802-8032.
TEL 516-796-9455. FAX 516-731-2395. Ed. Harold R. Ellis. adv.; bk.rev.; film rev.; play rev. (also avail. on diskette)
  Description: Self-help medium that links people interested in understanding dreams with free neighborhood clubs facilitated by experienced dream-workers, not necessarily professionals.
  Refereed Serial

DREAMING. see *BIOLOGY — Physiology*

E R I C CLEARINGHOUSE ON TESTS, MEASUREMENT, AND EVALUATION. T M E REPORT SERIES. (Educational Resources Informational Center) see *EDUCATION*

155.4 UK ISSN 1057-3593
▼**EARLY DEVELOPMENT AND PARENTING**; an international journal of research and practice. 1992. q. $165. John Wiley & Sons Ltd., Journals, Baffins Lane, Chichester, Sussex PO19 1UD, England. TEL 0243-779777. FAX 0243-775878. TELEX 86290-WIBOOK-G. Ed.Bd.
  Description: Contains theoretical, empirical and methodological papers covering all aspects related to psychological development during infancy and early childhood.

EARLY EDUCATION AND DEVELOPMENT. see *EDUCATION*

EATING DISORDERS REVIEW; current clinical information for the professional treating eating disorders. see *NUTRITION AND DIETETICS*

370.1 US ISSN 1040-7413
BF353 CODEN: ECPSEN
ECOLOGICAL PSYCHOLOGY. 1989. q. $29.50 to individuals (foreign $54); institutions $110 (foreign $135). (International Society for Ecological Psychology) Lawrence Erlbaum Associates, Inc., 365 Broadway, Hillsdale, NJ 07642.
TEL 201-666-4110. FAX 201-666-2394. Ed. William Mace. bk.rev.
—BLDSC shelfmark: 3649.050000.
  Description: Presents empirical, theoretical, and methodological papers in the form of research reports, target articles and commentary.
  Refereed Serial

EDUCATION AND PSYCHOLOGY REVIEW. see *EDUCATION*

370.15 150 155.4 UK
EDUCATIONAL & CHILD PSYCHOLOGY. 1984. q. £21. British Psychological Society, Division of Educational and Child Psychology, St. Andrews House, 48 Princess Rd. E., Leicester LE1 7DR, England. Ed. Peter Graves. circ. 1,000.
  Formerly: British Psychological Society. Division of Educational and Child Psychology. Papers (ISSN 0267-1611)

370 150 SW ISSN 0070-9263
CODEN: EPINDT
EDUCATIONAL AND PSYCHOLOGICAL INTERACTIONS. (Text in English) 1964. irreg. Malmoe School of Education, Inst. foer Pedagogik och Specialmetodik, Box 23501, S-200 45 Malmoe, Sweden. Ed. Aake Bjerstedt. (back issues avail.) Indexed: Child Devel.Abstr., Cont.Pg.Educ., Educ.Tech.Abstr., Psychol.Abstr., Sociol.Abstr., Sp.Ed.Needs Abstr.
—BLDSC shelfmark: 3661.365000.

PSYCHOLOGY

155.28 370.15   US   ISSN 0013-1644
BF1   CODEN: EPMEAJ
EDUCATIONAL AND PSYCHOLOGICAL MEASUREMENT; devoted to the development and application of measures of individual differences. 1941. q. $58 (foreign $62). Educational and Psychological Measurement, Inc., Box 6856, College Sta., Durham, NC 27708. TEL 919-688-3227. FAX 919-286-0794. Ed. William B. Michael. bk.rev.; bibl.; charts; index; circ. 2,700. (also avail. in microform from UMI,MIM; back issues avail.; reprint service avail. from UMI) **Indexed:** Acad.Ind., Adol.Ment.Hlth.Abstr., C.I.J.E., Chem.Abstr., CINAHL, Compumath, Cont.Pg.Educ., Educ.Ind., Except.Child.Educ.Abstr., High.Educ.Curr.Aware.Bull., Mid.East: Abstr.& Ind., Pers.Lit., Psychol.Abstr., Psycscan, Res.High.Educ.Abstr., Sp.Ed.Needs Abstr., SSCI.
—BLDSC shelfmark: 3661.366000.
Description: Discusses problems in the field of measuring individual differences and reports research on the development and use of tests and measurements in education.

370.15   US   ISSN 0046-1520
LB1051   CODEN: EDPSDT
EDUCATIONAL PSYCHOLOGIST. 1963. q. $37.50 to individuals (foreign $62.50); institutions $135 (foreign $160). (American Psychological Association, Division of Educational Psychology) Lawrence Erlbaum Associates, Inc., 365 Broadway, Hillsdale, NJ 07642. TEL 201-666-4110. FAX 201-666-2394. Ed. Claire E. Weinstein. adv.; index; circ. 3,700. (also avail. in microform from UMI; reprint service avail. from UMI) **Indexed:** Educ.Ind., Psychol.Abstr.
—BLDSC shelfmark: 3661.530000.
Description: Provides detailed explorations of new educational concepts and accepted educational practices.
Refereed Serial

370.15 180   UK   ISSN 0144-3410
LB1051
EDUCATIONAL PSYCHOLOGY; an international journal of experimental educational psychology. 1981. q. $120 to individuals; institutions $298. Carfax Publishing Co., P.O. Box 25, Abingdon, Oxfordshire OX14 3UE, England. TEL 0235-555335. FAX 0235-553559. (U.S. subscr. addr.: Carfax Publishing Co., Box 2025, Dunnellon, FL 32630) Eds. Kevin Wheldall, Richard Riding. adv.; bk.rev.; stat.; index; circ. 1,000. (also avail. in microfiche) **Indexed:** Child Devel.Abstr., Cont.Pg.Educ., Psychol.Abstr., Sp.Ed.Needs Abstr., Stud.Wom.Abstr.
—BLDSC shelfmark: 3661.535000.

370.15 150   UK   ISSN 0266-7363
EDUCATIONAL PSYCHOLOGY IN PRACTICE. 4/yr. £37($66) (Association of Educational Psychologists) Longman Group UK Ltd., Westgate House, The Highl, Harlow, Essex CM20 1YR, England. TEL 0279-442601. **Indexed:** Cont.Pg.Educ., Psychol.Abstr.
—BLDSC shelfmark: 3661.540000.
Formerly: A E P Journal (ISSN 0309-3573)

EDUCATIONAL PSYCHOLOGY REVIEW. see *EDUCATION*

158   RU
EKSPERIMENTAL'NAYA I PRIKLADNAYA PSIKHOLOGIYA. irreg., vol.8, 1977. 0.80 Rub. per issue. Leningradskii Universitet, Universitetskaya Nab. 7-9, St. Petersburg B-164, Russia. circ. 5,150.

150   RU
EKSPERIMENTAL'NOE ISSLEDOVANIE LICHNOSTI I TEMPERAMENTA. (Subseries of: Permskii Gosudarstvennyi Pedagogicheskii Institut. Uchenye Zapiski) irreg. 0.50 Rub. Permskii Gosudarstvennyi Pedagogicheskii Institut, Perm, Russia. Ed. Bronislaw Aleksandrovich Vyatkin. illus.

ELEMENTARY SCHOOL GUIDANCE & COUNSELING. see *EDUCATION*

155.937   US
ELISABETH KUBLER ROSS CENTER NEWSLETTER. 1979. 4/yr. membership. Elisabeth Kubler Ross Center, S. Rt. 616, Headwaters, VA 24442. adv.; circ. 25,000.
Formerly: Shanti Nilaya Newsletter.
Description: Promotes the concept of unconditional love as an attainable ideal.

ELTERNBLATT. see *CHILDREN AND YOUTH — About*

150   US
EMOTION; theory, research and experience. 1980. irreg., vol.5, 1990. Academic Press, Inc., 1250 Sixth Ave., San Diego, CA 92101. TEL 619-231-0926. FAX 619-699-6715. (reprint service avail. from ISI)
Refereed Serial

EMOTION; Wilhelm-Reich-Zeitschrift ueber Triebenergie, Charakterstruktur, Krankheit, Natur und Gesellschaft. see *ENERGY*

616.89 361   US   ISSN 0739-828X
RC480.6
EMOTIONAL FIRST AID; a journal of crisis intervention. 1984. q. $30 to individuals; institutions $55. American Academy of Crisis Interveners, c/o James L. Greenstone, Ed., Box 670292, Dallas, TX 75367-0292. (Co-sponsor: Southwestern Academy of Crisis Interveners) adv.; bk.rev.; index; circ. 400. (also avail. in microform from UMI; back issues avail.) **Indexed:** Psychol.Abstr.
—BLDSC shelfmark: 3733.568000.

EMPLOYEE TESTING & THE LAW; reporting legal, technical, and business developments in employee testing. see *BUSINESS AND ECONOMICS — Personnel Management*

EMPORIA STATE RESEARCH STUDIES. see *HISTORY — History Of North And South America*

616.89   US
ENCOUNTERER. 1971. irreg. $5 for 20 nos. Golden Gate Foundation for Group Treatment, Box 1141, Vallejo, CA 94590. Ed. Dr. F.H. Ernst.

370.15   US
ENCYCLOPEDIC DICTIONARY OF PSYCHOLOGY. irreg., 3rd ed., 1985. $12.95. Dushkin Publishing Group, Inc., Sluice Dock, Guilford, CT 06437-9989. TEL 203-453-4351. FAX 203-453-6000. Ed. Terry F. Pettijohn. illus.

152   FR   ISSN 0982-6238
ENERGIE ET CREATION. q. 17 rue Racine, 84000 Avignon, France. TEL 90-86-10-09. Ed. Dominique Moiselet. (back issues avail.)
Formerly: Energie et Creativite (ISSN 0766-0863)

ENFANCE; psychologie, pedagogie, neuro-psychiatrie, sociologie. see *CHILDREN AND YOUTH — About*

ENGRAMI. see *MEDICAL SCIENCES — Psychiatry And Neurology*

158   MX   ISSN 0185-1594
ENSENANZA E INVESTIGACION EN PSICOLOGIA.* 1975. s-a. Mex.$290($12) Consejo Nacional para la Ensenanza e Investigacion en Psicologia, c/o Universidad Iberoamericana, Prol. Paseo de la Reforma 880, Col. Lomas de Santa Fe, 01210 Mexico DF, Mexico. Ed. Juan Lafarga. adv.; bk.rev.; abstr.; bibl.; index; circ. 2,500. (also avail. in microfilm from UMI; reprint service avail. from UMI) **Indexed:** Biol.Abstr., Psychol.Abstr.
—BLDSC shelfmark: 3776.330000.

150   AG
ENTREDICHOS. 1983. m. La Rioja 718, Buenos Aires, Argentina.

ENVIRONMENT AND BEHAVIOR. see *SOCIOLOGY*

ENVOY (PITTSBURGH). see *RELIGIONS AND THEOLOGY*

ERGONOMICS; an international journal of research and practice in human factors and ergonomics. see *ENGINEERING*

150   US
ESALEN CATALOG. 1961. 3/yr. $12. Esalen Institute, Big Sur, CA 93920. Ed Susan Stone. circ. 25,000.

150   FR   ISSN 0014-0783
ESPRIT LIBRE. 1958. q. 12 F. (foreign 15 F.). Georges Krassovsky, Ed. & Pub., B.P. 164, 75664 Paris Cedex 14, France. circ. 1,000. (processed)
Description: How-to style journal helps the reader get free from obstinate opinions, prejudices, fixed convictions, social conditioning and political and religious phantasms.

150   US
ESSENTIALS OF ADOLESCENCE.* 1975. m. (11/yr.). $25. PeopleScience, Inc., 1015 S. Park Ave., Highland Park, NJ 08904-2910. TEL 908-572-3120. Ed. Fred Streit. circ. 2,200. (back issues avail.)
Formerly: Essence of Adolescence.

301.1 150   IT   ISSN 0392-0658
RJ131
ETA EVOLUTIVA; rivista di scienze dello sviluppo. 1978. q. L.35000. Giunti Gruppo Editoriale S.p.A., Via Vincenzo Gioberti, 34, 50121 Florence, Italy. TEL 055-66791. FAX 055-268312. Ed.Bd. circ. 2,000. (back issues avail.) **Indexed:** Psychol.Abstr.
—BLDSC shelfmark: 3814.194000.

370.15 150   US   ISSN 1050-8422
BJ1725
▼**ETHICS & BEHAVIOR**. 1991. q. $25 to individuals (foreign $50); institutions $90 (foreign $115). Lawrence Erlbaum Associates, Inc., 365 Broadway, Hillsdale, NJ 07642. TEL 201-666-4110. FAX 201-666-2394. Ed. Gerald P. Koocher.
—BLDSC shelfmark: 3814.655500.
Description: Publishes articles on an array of topics pertaining to various moral issues and conduct.
Refereed Serial

ETHOLOGY. see *BIOLOGY — Zoology*

ETOLOGIA. see *BIOLOGY — Zoology*

616.891   FR   ISSN 0014-2107
ETUDES FREUDIENNES. 1969. 3/yr. price varies. Editions Denoel, 19 rue de l'Universite, Paris (7e), France. Dir. Conrad Stein. circ. 3,500.
Description: Discusses methods of psychoanalysis.

616.89   FR
ETUDES PSYCHOTHERAPIQUES. 1970. q. 150 F. (students 100 F.). Editions du Centurion, 22 cours Albert 1e, 75008 Paris, France. (Subscr. to: Centrale des Revues (CDR), 11 rue Gossin, 92543 Montrouge Cedex, France) Ed. Daniele Gilbert. **Indexed:** Biol.Abstr., Psychoanal.Abstr., Psychol.Abstr.

155   UK
EUROPEAN JOURNAL OF COGNITIVE PSYCHOLOGY. 1989. 4/yr. £27.50($52) to individuals; institutions £55($105). (European Society for Cognitive Psychology) Lawrence Erlbaum Associates Ltd., 27 Palmeira Mansions, Church Rd., Hove, E. Sussex BN3 2FA, England. TEL 0273-207411. FAX 0273-205612. Ed. Lars-Goran Nilsson. adv. **Indexed:** Sociol.Abstr.
Formerly: European Cognitive Psychology (ISSN 0954-1446)
Description: Focuses on articles of either a theoretical or a review nature in order to provide an integrated rather than empirical approach.
Refereed Serial

156   UK   ISSN 0890-2070
BF698.A1
EUROPEAN JOURNAL OF PERSONALITY. (Text in English; summaries in English, French and German) 1987. 5/yr. $265 (effective 1992). (European Association of Personality Psychology) John Wiley & Sons Ltd., Journals, Baffins Lane, Chichester, W. Sussex PO19 1UD, England. TEL 0243 779777. FAX 0243-775878. TELEX 86290 WIBOOK G. Ed. G. Van Heck. bk.rev. **Indexed:** Curr.Cont., Psychol.Abstr.
—BLDSC shelfmark: 3829.733800.
Description: Reflects all areas of current personality psychology with emphasis on human individuality.

EUROPEAN JOURNAL OF PSYCHOLOGY OF EDUCATION. see *EDUCATION*

PSYCHOLOGY

301.1 UK ISSN 0046-2772
HM251 CODEN: EJSPA6
EUROPEAN JOURNAL OF SOCIAL PSYCHOLOGY. 1971. bi-m. $265 (effective 1992). John Wiley & Sons Ltd., Baffins Lane, Chichester, Sussex PO19 1UD, England. TEL 0243 779777. FAX 0243-775878. TELEX 86290-WIBOOK-G. Ed. Guus Van Heck. adv.; bk.rev.; charts. (reprint service avail. from ISI,SWZ,UMI) **Indexed:** Adol.Ment.Hlth.Abstr., ASSIA, Commun.Abstr., Curr.Cont., Excerp.Med., Lang.& Lang.Behav.Abstr., Mid.East: Abstr.& Ind., Psychol.Abstr., Sp.Ed.Needs Abstr., SSCI, Stud.Wom.Abstr.
—BLDSC shelfmark: 3829.739000.
Description: Reflects all areas of current personality psychology emphasizing human individuality as manifested in cognitive processes, emotional and motivational functioning, and personal ways of interacting with the environment.

301.15 US
EUROPEAN MONOGRAPHS IN SOCIAL PSYCHOLOGY. 1971. irreg., no.35, 1985. (European Association of Experimental Social Psychology) Academic Press, Inc., 1250 Sixth Ave., San Diego, CA 92101. TEL 619-231-0926. FAX 619-699-6715. Ed. H. Tajfel. (reprint service avail. from ISI) **Indexed:** Psychol.Abstr.

301.1 150 UK ISSN 1046-3283
HM251 CODEN: ERSPEW
▼**EUROPEAN REVIEW OF SOCIAL PSYCHOLOGY.** 1990. a. $110 (effective 1992). John Wiley & Sons Ltd., Journals, Baffins Lane, Chichester, Sussex PO19 1UD, England. TEL 0243-779777. FAX 0243-775878. Eds. W. Stroebe, M. Hewstone.
—BLDSC shelfmark: 3829.953300.
Description: Reflects the dynamism of social psychology in Europe and the attention now paid to European ideas and research.

158.7 UK ISSN 0960-2003
CODEN: EWOPED
▼**EUROPEAN WORK AND ORGANIZATIONAL PSYCHOLOGIST.** 1991. q. £25($47.50) to individuals; institutions £50($95). (International Association of Applied Psychology) Lawrence Erlbaum Associates Ltd., 27 Palmeira Mansions, Church Rd., Hove, E. Sussex BN3 2FA, England. TEL 0273-207411. FAX 0273-205612. Ed. Charles De Wolff. bk.rev.
—BLDSC shelfmark: 3830.370850.
Description: Provides a bridge between academies who enlarge the knowledge base of work psychology, and practitioners who apply this knowledge to clients and organizations.

155 AU ISSN 0938-2623
▼**EVOLUTION AND COGNITION.** 1991. biennial. S.800. Springer-Verlag, Sachsenplatz 4-6, Postfach 89, A-1201 Vienna, Austria. TEL 0222-3302415-0. Ed. F.M. Wuketits.
—BLDSC shelfmark: 3834.210000.
Description: Interdisciplinary forum devoted to all aspects of cognition, at both the animal and human level.

EXCEPTIONAL CHILDREN. see *CHILDREN AND YOUTH — About*

612.67 US ISSN 0361-073X
QP86 CODEN: EAGRDS
EXPERIMENTAL AGING RESEARCH. 1975. q. $25 to individuals; institutions $110 (foreign $135). Beech Hill Enterprises, Inc., Box 40, Mt. Desert, ME 04660-0040. TEL 207-667-2431. Ed. M.F. Elias. adv.; bk.rev.; illus.; index; circ. 1,500. (also avail. in microform from UMI; back issues avail.; reprint service avail. from UMI) **Indexed:** Abstr.Soc.Geront., Biol.Abstr., Chem.Abstr., CINAHL, CLOA, Curr.Cont., Excerp.Med., Helminthol.Abstr., Ind.Med., Ind.Sci.Rev., INIS Atomind., NRN, Psychol.Abstr., Sci.Cit.Ind.
—BLDSC shelfmark: 3838.570000.
Description: Multidisciplinary, scientific journal dealing with all areas of scientific inquiry, human and animal, involving aging and the elderly.

152 GW ISSN 0933-1093
EXPERIMENTELLE UND KLINISCHE HYPNOSE. (Text in German; summaries in English, German) 1983. s-a. DM.22. (Deutsche Gesellschaft fuer Hypnose) Verlag Dr. Dieter Winkler, Katharinastr. 37, 4630 Bochum 1, Germany. TEL 0234-17508. Ed. Hans-Christian Kossak. adv.; bk.rev.; circ. 700. (back issues avail.) **Indexed:** Psychol.Abstr.
Description: For medical or psychiatric professionals interested in using hypnosis as a therapeutic method.

301.1 150 FR
FACTUELLES.* 1977. irreg. Editions Copernic, 21 rue Cassette, 75006 Paris, France. Dir. Alain de Benoist.

FALLING LEAF. see *MILITARY*

392 301 GW ISSN 0342-2747
FAMILIENDYNAMIK; interdisziplinaere Zeitschrift fuer systemorientierte Praxis und Forschung. 1976. q. DM.98. Verlag Klett-Cotta, Rotebuehlstr. 77, Postfach 10 60 16, 7000 Stuttgart 10, Germany. FAX 0711-6672505. circ. 3,400.

370.15 150 US ISSN 1054-8726
CODEN: FDAQES
▼**FAMILY DYNAMICS OF ADDICTION QUARTERLY.** 1991. q. $55. Aspen Publishers, Inc., 200 Orchard Ridge Dr., Gaithersburg, MD 20878. TEL 301-417-7500. FAX 301-417-7550. Eds. Gary Lawson, Ann Lawson.
Refereed Serial

370.15 150 US ISSN 1041-9985
FAMILY LETTER. 1980. 8/yr. $25. National Academy of Counselors and Family Therapists, 55 Morris Ave., Springfield, NJ 07081-1422. TEL 201-379-7496. Eds. Anthony T. Palisi, Mary Kelly Blakeslee. adv.; bk.rev.; circ. 400.
Description: Covers family, family-life, education and psychology.

150 370 US ISSN 0732-9962
HQ10
FAMILY LIFE EDUCATOR. 1982. 4/yr. $35 to individuals; institutions $55. Network Publications (Subsidiary of: E T R Associates), Box 1830, Santa Cruz, CA 95061-1830. TEL 408-438-4060. FAX 408-438-4284. Ed. Kay Clark. bk.rev.; abstr.; bibl.; circ. 3,500.
Description: For educators in the field of family life education at the middle school and high school levels, including relevant news and teaching tools.

FAMILY PERSPECTIVE. see *SOCIOLOGY*

158 US ISSN 0014-7370
RC488.5.A1 CODEN: FAPRA
FAMILY PROCESS. 1962. q. $27 to individuals; institutions $44. Family Process, Inc., 29 Walter Hammond Pl., Ste.A, Waldwick, NJ 07463. TEL 201-612-9868. FAX 201-612-9892. (Subscr. to: Box 6889, Syracuse, NY 13217) Ed. Peter Steinglass. adv.; bk.rev.; abstr.; bibl.; charts; index; circ. 12,000. (also avail. in microform from UMI; back issues avail.; reprint service avail. from SWZ,UMI) **Indexed:** Adol.Ment.Hlth.Abstr., ASSIA, CINAHL, Commun.Abstr., Curr.Cont., Excerp.Med., Ind.Med., Lang.& Lang.Behav.Abstr., Mid.East: Abstr.& Ind., Past.Care & Couns.Abstr., Psychol.Abstr., Sage Fam.Stud.Abstr., Soc.Work.Res.& Abstr., SSCI, Stud.Wom.Abstr.
—BLDSC shelfmark: 3865.576000.
Description: Covers family mental health and psychotherapy.

157.61 US ISSN 0739-0882
RC488.5
FAMILY THERAPY NETWORKER. 1982. bi-m. $20. Family Therapy Network, Inc., 7705 13th St., N.W., Washington, DC 20012. TEL 202-829-2452. FAX 202-726-7983. (Subscr. to: 8528 Bradford Rd., Silver Spring, MD 20901. TEL 301-589-6536) Ed. Richard Simon. adv.; bk.rev.; circ. 50,000. (back issues avail.) **Indexed:** Soc.Work Res.& Abstr.
—BLDSC shelfmark: 3865.576390.
Description: Professional journal for social workers, psychologists, therapists and educators.

301.4 US ISSN 0277-6464
FAMILY THERAPY NEWS. 1969. bi-m. $25 to individuals; institutions $40. American Association for Marriage and Family Therapy, 1100 17th St. N.W., 10th fl., Washington, DC 20036. Ed. William C. Nichols. adv.; circ. 17,500. (reprint service avail. from UMI)
Formerly: American Association for Marriage and Family Therapy Newsletter.

150 301.412 UK ISSN 0959-3535
HQ1206
▼**FEMINISM & PSYCHOLOGY.** 1991. 3/yr. £21($35) to individuals; institutions £45($74). Sage Publications Ltd., 6 Bonhill St., London EC2A 4PU, England. TEL 071-374-0645. FAX 071-374-8741. Ed. Sue Wilkinson. adv.; color page £190; trim 193 x 114; adv. contact: Bernie Folan. bk.rev.
—BLDSC shelfmark: 3905.195980.
Description: Fosters the development of feminist theory and practice in psychology.

FILOZOFSKI FAKULTET - ZADAR. RAZDIO FILOZOFIJE, PSIHOLOGIJE, SOCIOLOGIJE I PEDAGOGIJE. RADOVI. see *PHILOSOPHY*

150 US
FLORIDA PSYCHOLOGIST. 1950. bi-m. $60 to non-members. Florida Psychological Association, 408 Office Plaza, Tallahassee, FL 32301-2757. TEL 904-656-2222. Ed. Robert A. Hall. adv.; bk.rev.; bibl.; circ. 1,700.
Formerly: F P (ISSN 0046-4171)

614.58 US
FOCUS (ALEXANDRIA). 1980. q. $15. National Mental Health Association, 1021 Prince St., Alexandria, VA 22314-2971. TEL 703-684-7722. FAX 703-684-5963. Ed. J. David Gallagher. bk.rev.; circ. 4,500. (tabloid format; back issues avail.)

301.1 150 IT ISSN 0393-5418
FOGLI DI INFORMAZIONE. (Text in Italian; summaries in English) 1972. m. L.100000($30) Cooperativa Centro di Documentazione, Via Orafi 29, Casella Postale 347, 51100 Pistoia, Italy. TEL 0573-367144.

138 SZ ISSN 0015-7694
FORM UND GEIST; illustrierte Blaetter fuer angewandte Menschenkenntnis und Sozialreform. 1941. bi-m. 22 Fr.($10.50) Helioda-Verlag, Hardturmstr. 284, CH-8005 Zurich, Switzerland. Ed. W. Alisbach. bk.rev.; illus.; circ. 4,000.

150 UK ISSN 0015-833X
FORUM (LONDON, 1967); the journal of human relations and psycho-sexual studies. 1967. 13/yr. £27. (Forum International) Northern & Shell Publications, Northern & Shell Bldg., P.O. Box 381, Mill Harbour, London E14 9TW, England. (U.S. addr.: Penthouse-Forum, 21st Fl., 909 Third Ave., New York, NY 10022) Ed. Isabel Koprowski. adv.; bk.rev.; illus.; index; circ. 1,500,000. **Indexed:** Res.High.Educ.Abstr.

150.19 GW ISSN 0178-7667
FORUM DER PSYCHOANALYSE; Zeitschrift fuer klinische Theorie und Praxis. 1985. 4/yr. DM.124($80) Springer-Verlag, Heidelberger Platz 3, D-1000 Berlin 33, Germany. TEL 030-8207-1. (Subscr. to: 44 Hartz Way, Secaucus, NJ 07094) Ed. Friedrich Beese. adv. (also avail. in microform from UMI; back issues avail.; reprint service avail. from ISI) **Indexed:** Excerp.Med.
—BLDSC shelfmark: 4024.098000.

155.937 US
FORUM FOR DEATH EDUCATION & COUNSELING NEWSLETTER.* 10/yr. $25. Department of Human Development & Family Studies, Justice Hall, Kansas State University, Manhattan, KS 66506. TEL 913-532-5510. Ed. Joan N. McNeil.

156 GW ISSN 0720-0447
FORUM KRITISCHE PSYCHOLOGIE. 1978. s-a. DM.33 to individuals; students DM.27. Argument-Verlag GmbH, Rentzelstr. 1, 2000 Hamburg 13, Germany. TEL 040-456018. Ed. Klaus Holzkamp. (back issues avail.)

PSYCHOLOGY

155.937   US   ISSN 0160-7081
FOUNDATION OF THANATOLOGY. ARCHIVES. q. $66.50. Foundation of Thanatology, Foundation Book & Periodical Division, Box 1191, Brooklyn, NY 11202-1202. TEL 718-858-3026. Ed. Austin H. Kutscher. (also avail. in microform from UMI; back issues avail.)
Description: Contains abstracts of conference proceedings on aging, dying, death, bereavement, and grief.

155.937   US
FOUNDATION OF THANATOLOGY SERIES. irreg. price varies. 2600 South First St., Springfield, IL 62794-9265. TEL 217-789-8980. FAX 217-789-9130.

616.89 300   UK   ISSN 0267-0887
FREE ASSOCIATIONS; psychoanalysis, groups, politics, culture. 1984. q. £20 to individuals; institutions £40. Free Associations Books, 26 Freegrove Rd., London N7 9RQ, England. TEL 01 609-5646. (And: Guilford Publications, Inc., 72 Spring St., 4th Fl., New York, NY 10012. TEL 212-431-9800) (Co-publisher: Guilford Publications, Inc.) Ed. Robert M. Young. adv.; bk.rev.; bibl.; index; circ. 2,000. (back issues avail.) **Indexed:** Alt.Press Ind., ASSIA, Chicago Psychoanal.Lit.Ind., Left Ind. (1985-), Sociol.Abstr.
—BLDSC shelfmark: 4033.310000.

155.937 393   CN
FRONTIERES; les vivants et les morts. 1988. 3/yr. Can.$18($20) Universite de Quebec a Montreal, Service des Publications, Centre d'Etudes sur la Mort, Box 8888, Succ. A, Montreal, Que H3C 3P8, Canada. TEL 514-987-4581. FAX 514-987-7856. Ed. Eric Volant. adv.; bk.rev.; film rev.; bibl.; illus.; stat.; circ. 1,500 (controlled). (back issues avail.)
Description: Discusses death and grieving for professionals and volunteers in the health services.

370.15 150   US
▼**FRONTIERS IN PSYCHOTHERAPY.** 1990. irreg. price varies. Ablex Publishing Corporation, 355 Chestnut St., Norwood, NJ 07648. TEL 201-767-8450. FAX 201-767-6717. TELEX 135-393. Ed. Edward Tick.

155.937   US
G E I NEWSLETTER.* 1979. q. $5. Grief Education Institute, 1780 S. Bellaire St., Ste. 132, Denver, CO 80222. Ed. Carole Rawland. bk.rev.; circ. 2,000.

370.15 371.3   US   ISSN 8756-7865
BF1
G. STANLEY HALL LECTURE SERIES. 1981. a. price varies. American Psychological Association, 750 First St., N.E., Washington, DC 20002-4242. TEL 202-336-5500. FAX 202-336-5568. (back issues avail.)

301.1 150 510   US   ISSN 0899-8256
QA269   CODEN: GEBEEF
GAMES AND ECONOMIC BEHAVIOR. 1989. q. $122 (foreign $147). Academic Press, Inc., Journal Division, 1250 Sixth Ave., San Diego, CA 92101. TEL 619-230-1840. FAX 619-699-6800. TELEX 181726. Ed. Ehud Kalai. (back issues avail.) **Indexed:** J.of Econ.Lit.
—BLDSC shelfmark: 4069.168000.
Description: Deals with game-theoretic modeling in the social, biological and mathematical sciences. Addresses the beliefs in the importance of interchange of game-theoretic ideas leading to a mathematical science of games and economic behavior.

150   NE
GEDRAG & GEZONDHEID/BEHAVIOUR & HEALTH; tijdschrift voor psychologie - journal of psychology. (Text in Dutch, English) 1952. 6/yr. fl.83.50. Vuga Uitgeverij B.V., P.O. Box 16400, 2500 BK The Hague, Netherlands. TEL 070-3614011. Ed. G.J.J. Calis. adv.; bk.rev.; bibl.; charts; illus.; index; circ. 1,000. **Indexed:** Biol.Abstr., Curr.Cont., Psychol.Abstr., Risk Abstr., SSCI.
Former titles: Gedrag (ISSN 0377-7308); Gawein (ISSN 0016-5271)

GEISTIGE BEHINDERUNG; Fachzeitschrift der Lebenshilfe fuer geistig Behinderte. see EDUCATION — Special Education And Rehabilitation

GENESIS OF BEHAVIOR. see MEDICAL SCIENCES — Psychiatry And Neurology

155   US   ISSN 0740-9583
BF712
GENETIC EPISTEMOLOGIST. q. $45 to members; students $25. Jean Piaget Society, Department of Psychology, Pennsylvania State University, University Park, PA 16802. TEL 302-451-2311. (Subscr. to: Ann Renninger, Tres., Jean Piaget Society, Swarthmore College, Swarthmore, PA 19081) Ed. David S. Palermo. adv.; bk.rev.; circ. 550.
—BLDSC shelfmark: 4111.849000.
Description: Interdisciplinary approach to the study of knowledge and its development.

156 155   US   ISSN 8756-7547
LB1101   CODEN: GSGMEQ
GENETIC, SOCIAL, AND GENERAL PSYCHOLOGY MONOGRAPHS. 1926. q. $78. (Helen Dwight Reid Educational Foundation) Heldref Publications, 1319 Eighteenth St., N.W., Washington, DC 20036-1802. TEL 202-296-6267. FAX 202-296-5149. Ed. Doris Chalfin. bibl.; charts; s-a. index; circ. 880. (back issues avail.; reprint service avail. from SWZ) **Indexed:** Abstr.Soc.Work, Biol.Abstr., Child Devel.Abstr., Child.Devel.Abstr., Curr.Adv.Ecol.Sci., Curr.Cont., DSH Abstr., Except.Child.Educ.Abstr., Excerp.Med., Ind.Med., Lang.& Lang.Behav.Abstr., Psychol.Abstr., Psycscan D.P., Risk Abstr., Soc.Work Res.& Abstr., SSCI, Stud.Wom.Abstr.
Formerly: Genetic Psychology Monographs (ISSN 0016-6677)
Refereed Serial

150 616.89   US   ISSN 0190-0412
GESTALT JOURNAL. 1978. s-a. $30 to individuals; institutions $45. Center for Gestalt Development, Inc., Box 990, Highland, NY 12528. Ed. Joe Wysong. adv.; bk.rev.; circ. 2,000. (back issues avail.) **Indexed:** Psychol.Abstr.
—BLDSC shelfmark: 4163.350000.
Description: Articles and reviews relating to the theory and practice of Gestalt therapy.

150.19   GW   ISSN 0170-057X
BF203
GESTALT THEORY; an international multidisciplinary journal. (Text in English, German) 1979. q. DM.148 (students DM.85). (Society for Gestalt Theory and Its Applications (GTA)) Westdeutscher Verlag GmbH, Postfach 5829, 6200 Wiesbaden 1, Germany. TEL 0611-160230. FAX 0611-160229. TELEX 4186928-VWV-D. Ed. A.C. Zimmer. adv.; bk.rev.; circ. 2,000. **Indexed:** Ger.J.Psych., Psychol.Abstr.
—BLDSC shelfmark: 4163.400000.

GIFTED CHILD QUARTERLY. see CHILDREN AND YOUTH — About

GIFTED INTERNATIONAL. 'see EDUCATION — Special Education And Rehabilitation

GIORNALE DI NEUROPSICHIATRIA DELL'ETA EVOLUTIVA. see MEDICAL SCIENCES — Psychiatry And Neurology

150.5   IT   ISSN 0390-5349
GIORNALE ITALIANO DI PSICOLOGIA/ITALIAN JOURNAL OF PSYCHOLOGY. 1974. 5/yr. L.120000. Societa Editrice il Mulino, Strada Maggiore, 37, 40125 Bologna, Italy. TEL 051-256011. FAX 051-256034. Ed. Gaetano Kanizsa. adv.; index; circ. 1,300. (back issues avail.) **Indexed:** Child Devel.Abstr., Psychol.Abstr.

150   IT   ISSN 0391-2515
BF84
GIORNALE STORICO DI PSICOLOGIA DINAMICA. 1977. s-a. L.27000 per no. Liguori Editore s.r.l., Via Mezzocannone 19, 80134 Naples, Italy. TEL 081-5227139. Ed. Aldo Carotenuto. **Indexed:** Psychoanal.Abstr., Psychol.Abstr.

150 016   SW   ISSN 0301-0996
     CODEN: GPSRDB
GOETEBORG PSYCHOLOGICAL REPORTS. (Text in English) 1971. 15/yr. SEK 25($5) per no. Goeteborgs Universitet, Department of Psychology, Box 14158, S-400 20 Goeteborg, Sweden. TEL 031-631000. FAX 046-31-632648. Ed. Dr. Carl Martin Allwood. circ. 400. **Indexed:** Psychol.Abstr.

150 591   US
GORILLA. 1976. s-a. $30. Gorilla Foundation, Box 620-530, Woodside, CA 94062. TEL 415-851-8505. Ed. Dr. Francine Patterson. bk.rev.; circ. 30,000. (tabloid format; back issues avail.)
Description: Reports of the results and progress of ongoing study of gorilla behavior and interspecies communication, with other topics relating to the preservation and captive maintenance of gorillas.

150 378   US
GRADUATE STUDY IN PSYCHOLOGY AND ASSOCIATED FIELDS. 17th ed., 1984. a. $19.50 to non-members; members $15.50. American Psychological Association, Education Programs Office, 750 First St., N.E., Washington, DC 20002. TEL 202-336-5500. FAX 202-336-5568. Ed. Cynthia G. Baum. circ. 15,000. **Indexed:** Psychol.Abstr.
Formerly (until 1983): Graduate Study in Psychology (ISSN 0072-5277)

370.15   US
GRADUATE TRAINING IN BEHAVIOR THERAPY AND EXPERIMENTAL-CLINICAL PSYCHOLOGY. 1988. biennial. $17. Association for Advancement of Behavior Therapy, 15 W. 36th St., New York, NY 10018. TEL 212-279-7970. circ. 1,000.
Description: Lists 390 programs which emphasize behavior therapy on graduate level.

616.89   US   ISSN 0362-4021
RC488.A1   CODEN: GROUDE
GROUP (NEW YORK). 1977. q. $34 to individuals (foreign $42); institutions $62 (foreign $70). (Eastern Group Psychotherapy Society) Brunner-Mazel Publishing Co., 19 Union Sq. W., New York, NY 10003. TEL 212-924-3344. Ed. Peter J. Schlachet. bk.rev.; index; circ. 1,200. (also avail. in microform from UMI; reprint service avail. from ISI,UMI) **Indexed:** Biol.Abstr., Curr.Cont., Excerp.Med., Psychol.Abstr.
Description: Advances, theoretical and clinical contributions, and research in dynamic group psychotherapy.

616.8   UK
GROUP ANALYSIS; journal of group-analytic psychotherapy. 1967. q. £33($54) to individuals; institutions £78($129). Sage Publications Ltd., 6 Bonhill St., London EC2A 4PU, England. TEL 071-374-0645. FAX 071-374-8741. Ed. Malcolm Pines. adv.: color page #150; trim 177 x 101; adv. contact: Bernie Folan. bk.rev. **Indexed:** Excerp.Med., Psychol.Abstr.
Formerly: Group Analysis: International Panel and Correspondence (ISSN 0533-3164)
Description: Concerned with all approaches to the theory, practice and experience of analytic group psychotherapy.

150   US   ISSN 1059-6011
HM134   CODEN: GOSTDA
GROUP & ORGANIZATION MANAGEMENT; international journal for group facilitators. 1976. q. $48 to individuals; institutions $120. Sage Publications, Inc., 2455 Teller Rd., Newbury Park, CA 91320. TEL 805-499-0721. FAX 805-499-0871. Ed. Michael S. Kavanaugh. bk.rev.; index; circ. 1,100. (also avail. in microform from UMI; back issues avail.; reprint service avail. from UMI) **Indexed:** ABI Inform., BPIA, Bus.Ind., C.I.J.E., CINAHL, Human Resour.Abstr., Lang.& Lang.Behav.Abstr., Manage.Cont., Pers.Lit., Psychol.Abstr., Psycscan, Sage Fam.Stud.Abstr., Sage Pub.Admin.Abstr., Stud.Wom.Abstr.
—BLDSC shelfmark: 4220.173900.
Formerly (until Mar. 1992): Group and Organization Studies (ISSN 0364-1082)

GROUPWORK. see SOCIAL SERVICES AND WELFARE

155 301   GW   ISSN 0046-6514
     CODEN: GRUPDT
GRUPPENDYNAMIK; Zeitschrift fuer angewandte Sozialpsychologie. 1970. q. DM.67 to individuals; students DM.56. Leske Verlag und Budrich GmbH, Gerhart-Hauptmann-Str. 27, Postfach 300551, 5090 Leverkusen 3, Germany. Ed.Bd. bk.rev.; circ. 1,800. (back issues avail.) **Indexed:** Ger.J.Psych., Psychol.Abstr.
—BLDSC shelfmark: 4223.458000.

PSYCHOLOGY

150   GW   ISSN 0085-1302
GRUPPENPSYCHOTHERAPIE UND GRUPPENDYNAMIK. BEIHEFTE. 1972. irreg., no.22, 1986. price varies. Vandenhoeck und Ruprecht, Robert-Bosch-Breite 6, Postfach 37 53, 3400 Goettingen, Germany. TEL 0551-6959-0. FAX 0551-695917. Ed. A. Heigl-Evers. circ. 1,900. **Indexed:** Excerp.Med.

616.89   US   ISSN 0884-5808
HAKOMI FORUM. 1984. a. $7.50. Hakomi Institute, Box 1873, Boulder, CO 80306. TEL 303-443-6209. FAX 303-443-8613. Ed. Gregory J. Johanson. bk.rev.; cum.index; circ. 1,000. (back issues avail.) **Indexed:** Psychol.Abstr.
   Description: Journal for therapists with an emphasis on transpersonal, body-centered, cognitive aspects of therapy. Aims to foster the principles of unity, organicity, mind-body holism, mindfulness, and non-violence.

155.4 613.7   US
HANDBOOK OF PSYCHOLOGY AND HEALTH SERIES. 1982. irreg., vol.5, 1987. Lawrence Erlbaum Associates, Inc., 365 Broadway, Hillsdale, NJ 07642. TEL 201-666-4110. FAX 201-666-2394. Eds. Andrew Baum, Jerome E. Singer. (back issues avail.) **Indexed:** Curr.Cont., Psychol.Abstr.
   Refereed Serial

150   UK   ISSN 0266-4771
HARVEST. 1954. a. £12.50($25) Analytical Psychology Club, 37 York Street Chambers, York St., London W1H 1DE, England. TEL 071-724-5661. Ed. Joel Ryce-Menuhin. adv.; bk.rev.; circ. 600.
   Description: Concerned with the depth psychology of C.G. Jung.

150   US   ISSN 0278-6133
R726.5
HEALTH PSYCHOLOGY. 1982. bi-m. $55 to individuals (foreign $85); institutions $195 (foreign $240). (American Psychological Association, Division of Health Psychology) Lawrence Erlbaum Associates, Inc., 365 Broadway, Hillsdale, NJ 07642. TEL 201-666-4110. FAX 201-666-2394. Ed. Karen Matthews. adv.; bk.rev.; abstr.; bibl.; charts; illus.; stat.; circ. 4,500. **Indexed:** ASCA, Behav.Med.Abstr., Curr.Cont., NRN, Psychol.Abstr., Risk Abstr.
   —BLDSC shelfmark: 4275.105200.
   Description: Addresses the relationship between behavior and health.
   Refereed Serial

150   CN   ISSN 0085-1493
HERE AND NOW; a brief of news from the IPR. (Text and summaries in French) 1969. irreg. free. Institute of Psychological Research, Inc., 34 Fleury St. W., Montreal, Que. H3L 1S9, Canada. TEL 514-382-3000. FAX 514-382-3007. Ed. Jean-Marc Chevrier. adv.; bk.rev.; circ. 2,000 (controlled).

370.15 150   US
HIGH SCHOOL PSYCHOLOGY TEACHER. 1970. bi-m. $20. American Psychological Association, 750 First St., N.E., Washington, DC 20002-4242. TEL 202-336-5500. FAX 202-336-5568. Ed. Chi Chi Sileo. film rev.; cum.index; circ. 1,300.
   Description: For teachers of psychology in secondary schools. Provides news, announcements, classroom and lecture ideas, and reviews of educational materials.

150 301.1   US   ISSN 0739-9863
RC451.5.H57   CODEN: HJBSEZ
HISPANIC JOURNAL OF BEHAVIORAL SCIENCES. (Text in English, Spanish) 1979. q. $38 to individuals; institutions $83. (University of California, Los Angeles) Sage Publications, Inc., 2455 Teller Rd., Newbury Park, CA 91320. TEL 805-499-0721. FAX 805-499-0871. Ed. Dr. Amado M. Padilla. adv.; bk.rev.; film rev.; index; circ. 900. (also avail. in microform from UMI; back issues avail.; reprint service avail. from UMI) **Indexed:** C.I.J.E., Chic.Per.Ind., Curr.Cont., High.Educ.Abstr., Psychol.Abstr., Sp.Ed.Needs Abstr., SSCI.
   —BLDSC shelfmark: 4315.772700.
   Description: Contains empirical articles, case study reports, and scholarly notes of theoretical or methodological interest pertaining to Hispanics. Focus on the fields of anthropology, linguistics, psychology, public health, and sociology.

HOLOS PRACTICE REPORT. see *MEDICAL SCIENCES*

150   FR   ISSN 0018-4314
HOMME LIBRE; fils de la terre. 1960. q. 50 F. (foreign 64 F.). Cercle d'Etudes Psychologiques, B.P. 205, 42005 St. Etienne Cedex 1, France. Ed. Marcel Renoulet. bk.rev.; bibl.

616.89   HK   ISSN 0379-4490
HONG KONG PSYCHOLOGICAL SOCIETY. BULLETIN. 1978. s-a. HK.$100. Hong Kong Psychological Society Ltd., c/o Department of Psychology, Chinese University of Hong Kong, Shatin, N.T., Hong Kong. FAX 852-6035019. Ed. Hing Keung Ma. bk.rev.; circ. 300. (back issues avail.) **Indexed:** Human Resour.Abstr., Psychol.Abstr., Sage Fam.Stud.Abstr., Sage Urb.Stud.Abstr.
   —BLDSC shelfmark: 2555.320300.

155   US
HUMAN BEHAVIOR AND ENVIRONMENT. 1976. irreg., vol.11, 199C. price varies. Plenum Publishing Corp., 233 Spring St., New York, NY 10013-1578. TEL 212-620-8000. FAX 212-463-0742. TELEX 23-421139. Eds. Irwin Altman, J.F. Wohlwill. (back issues avail.) **Indexed:** Psychol.Abstr.
   Refereed Serial

HUMAN - COMPUTER INTERACTION (HILLSDALE); a journal of theoretical, empirical, and methodological issues of user psychology and of system design. see *COMPUTERS*

574.1   SZ   ISSN 0018-716X
     CODEN: HUDEA8
HUMAN DEVELOPMENT. (Text in English) 1958. bi-m. 280 Fr.($187) per vol. S. Karger AG, Allschwilerstr. 10, P.O. Box, CH-4009 Basel, Switzerland. TEL 061-3061111. FAX 061-3061234. TELEX CH 962652. Ed. D. Kuhn. adv.; bk.rev.; bibl.; charts; illus.; index; circ. 1,900. (also avail. in microform from RPI; reprint service avail. from SWZ) **Indexed:** Adol.Ment.Hlth.Abstr., Biol.Abstr., CLOA, Curr.Adv.Ecol.Sci., Curr.Cont., Educ.Ind., Excerp.Med., Ind.Med., M.L.A., Mid.East: Abstr.& Ind., Psychol.Abstr., Psycscan D.P., Rehabil.Lit., SSCI.
   —BLDSC shelfmark: 4336.050000.
   Formerly: Vita Humana.
   Description: Scholarly articles on psychological development over an entire lifespan, from infancy through aging.

150 284   US   ISSN 0197-3096
BV4012
HUMAN DEVELOPMENT (HARTFORD). 1980. q. $20. Jesuit Educational Center for Human Development, 400 Washington St., Hartford, CT 06106. Ed. Dr. James J. Gill. bk.rev.; circ. 13,000. (back issues avail.) **Indexed:** C.I.J.E., Cath.Ind., Educ.Ind., Lang.& Lang.Behav.Abstr.
   —BLDSC shelfmark: 4336.052000.

155   US
HUMAN DEVELOPMENT (NORWOOD). 1986. irreg., vol.4, 1991. price varies. Ablex Publishing Corporation, 355 Chestnut St., Norwood, NJ 07648. TEL 201-767-8450. FAX 201-767-6717. TELEX 135-393. Ed. Sidney Strauss.
   Refereed Serial

155.3   US
HUMAN DIGEST; the sexual behavior journal. 1977. 10/yr. $10. Thomaston Publications, 535 Fifth Ave., 2nd Fl., New York, NY 10017. TEL 212-490-0172. Ed. Angela Snow.

HUMAN EVOLUTION, BEHAVIOR, AND INTELLIGENCE. see *BIOLOGY — Genetics*

HUMAN FACTORS. see *ENGINEERING*

301.1   US   ISSN 0163-5182
TA166   CODEN: PHFSDQ
HUMAN FACTORS SOCIETY ANNUAL MEETING. PROCEEDINGS. 1972. a. $65 to non-members. Human Factors Society, Box 1369, Santa Monica, CA 90406. TEL 310-394-1811. FAX 310-394-2410. (also avail. in microform from UMI; reprint service avail. from UMI) **Indexed:** Int.Aerosp.Abstr.
   —BLDSC shelfmark: 6844.113800.
   Formerly: Human Factors Society. Proceedings of the Annual Meeting (ISSN 0363-9797)

HUMAN FACTORS SOCIETY BULLETIN. see *ENGINEERING*

HUMAN MOVEMENT SCIENCE; journal devoted to pure and applied research on human movement. see *MEDICAL SCIENCES*

HUMAN NATURE; an interdisciplinary biosocial perspective. see *SOCIAL SCIENCES: COMPREHENSIVE WORKS*

152   US   ISSN 0895-9285
HUMAN PERFORMANCE. 1988. q. $40 to individuals (foreign $65); institutions $135 (foreign $160). Lawrence Erlbaum Associates, Inc., 365 Broadway, Hillsdale, NJ 07642. TEL 201-666-4110. FAX 201-666-2394. Eds. Frank J. Landy, Sheldon Zedeck. **Indexed:** Psychol.Abstr.
   —BLDSC shelfmark: 4336.265000.
   Description: For behavioral scientists interested in the factors that motivate and influence excellence in human behavior, publishes research and theory that investigates the nature of goal-directed human activity.
   Refereed Serial

150 301   US
HUMAN POTENTIAL.* 1984. bi-m. $18. Human Potential Publishing Company, 2224 NW 102nd Way, Gainesville, FL 32606-5563. adv.
   Description: Covers personal growth and change, decision making and problem solving.

370.15 150   UK   ISSN 0955-4815
HUMAN POTENTIAL MAGAZINE. 1977. q. £5 (subscr. includes "Resource Directory"). Human Potential, 5 Layton Rd., London N1 0PX, England. TEL 01-354-5792. Ed. Aron Gersh. adv.; bk.rev.; circ. 5,000.
   —BLDSC shelfmark: 4336.359000.
   Formerly (until 1988): Human Potential Resources (ISSN 0263-5100)
   Description: Intended as a service to those who are searching for new directions to take in their personal development and growth.

370.15 574   US   ISSN 0883-1289
HQ1
HUMAN SEXUALITY; opposing viewpoints sources. 1985. a. $10.95. Greenhaven Press, Inc., Box 289009, San Diego, CA 92198-0009. TEL 619-485-7424. FAX 619-485-9549. Ed. Bruno Leone. (back issues avail.)

370.15 155.5 301   US   ISSN 0885-1174
BF575.S75
HUMAN STRESS: CURRENT SELECTED RESEARCH. 1986. a. $57.50. A M S Press, Inc., 56 E. 13th St., New York, NY 10003. TEL 212-777-4700. FAX 212-995-5413. Ed. James H. Humphrey. bk.rev.; index. (back issues avail.)
   —BLDSC shelfmark: 4336.466800.
   Formerly: Human Stress Current Advances in Research.
   Description: Articles on biological and behavioral problems related to stress.

150   US   ISSN 0887-3267
THE HUMANISTIC PSYCHOLOGIST. 1973. 3/yr. $20 to individuals (foreign $24); institutions $40 (foreign $44). American Psychological Association, Division of Humanistic Psychology, c/o Christopher M. Anastoos, Ed., Psychology Department, W. Georgia College, Carrollton, GA 30118. FAX 404-836-6720. adv.; bk.rev.; circ. 1,200. (back issues avail.) **Indexed:** Psychol.Abstr.
   —BLDSC shelfmark: 4336.530800.

HUMOR; international journal of humor research. see *SOCIAL SCIENCES: COMPREHENSIVE WORKS*

HYMAN BLUMBERG SYMPOSIUM SERIES. see *EDUCATION*

HYPNOTHERAPY TODAY. see *MEDICAL SCIENCES — Hypnosis*

301.1   FR   ISSN 0046-9688
I F E P P INFORMATIONS. 1970. q. 20 F. Institut de Formation et d'Etudes Psycho-Sociologiques et Pedagogiques, 140 bis rue de Rennes, Paris 6, France. Ed. B. Honore. bk.rev.

PSYCHOLOGY

150   BE
I L S M H NEWS. (Text in English, French, German, Spanish) a. 50 Fr.($35) International League of Societies for Persons with Mental Handicap, 248 Av. Louise, Bte. 17, B-1050 Brussels, Belgium. TEL 02-647-61-80. FAX 02-647-29-69. Ed. P.J. Renoir. bk.rev.; circ. 15,000 (7,000 English ed.; 4,000 French ed.; 2,000 German ed.; 2,000 Spanish ed.).
    Former titles: International League of Societies for Persons with Mental Handicap. News; International League of Societies for the Mentally Handicapped. World Congress Proceedings. (ISSN 0074-6754)
    Description: Publishes various pamphlets, position papers, reports of seminars, conferences and more.

156   US
I P A BULLETIN. a. (included in subscr. to Journal of Psychohistory). International Psychohistorical Association, Box 314, New York, NY 10024. Ed. J. Lee Shneidman.

I P O ANNUAL PROGRESS REPORT. (Institute for Perception Research) see LINGUISTICS

I S P T JOURNAL OF RESEARCH IN EDUCATIONAL & PSYCHOLOGICAL MEASUREMENT. (Institute for Studies in Psychological Testing) see EDUCATION

152.8   II
I S P T QUARTERLY BULLETIN. q. Institute for Studies in Psychological Testing, 101 Doon Vihar, Jakhan, Dehradun 248009, India.
    Description: Provides information regarding Institute members, news, awards, honors and its publication. Occasionally, an article is also published on psychological testing.

614.58   IT   ISSN 0019-1647
IGIENE MENTALE. 1957. q. L.10000. Lega Italiana di Igiene e Profilassi Mentale, Ospedale Psichiatrico Provinciale di Trapani, Trapani, Italy. Ed.Bd. adv.; bk.rev.; abstr.; charts; illus.; stat.; index, cum.index; circ. 250. **Indexed:** Excerp.Med.

370.15 150   US   ISSN 1041-8377
IMAGERY TODAY. 1983. s-a. $10. (International Imagery Association) Brandon House, Inc., Box 240, Bronx, NY 10471. circ. 13,427.

133 152   US   ISSN 0276-2366
BF311
IMAGINATION, COGNITION AND PERSONALITY. 1981. q. $36 to individuals; institutions $102. Baywood Publishing Co., Inc., 26 Austin Ave., Box 337, Amityville, NY 11701. TEL 516-691-1270. FAX 516-691-1770. Eds. Dr. Kenneth S. Pope, Dr. Jerome L. Singer. bk.rev. (back issues avail.) **Indexed:** Biol.Abstr., Excerp.Med., Psychol.Abstr.
    —BLDSC shelfmark: 4368.996200.
    Supersedes (1973-1980): Journal of Altered States of Consciousness (ISSN 0094-5498); Formerly: International Journal of Altered States of Consciousness.
    Description: Authoritative articles examine the diverse uses of imagery, fantasy, consciousness in psychotherapy, behavior modification, and related areas of study.

IMAGO; revista de psicoanalisis, psiquiatria y psicologia. see MEDICAL SCIENCES — Psychiatry And Neurology

IMPACT (AUSTIN). see MEDICAL SCIENCES — Psychiatry And Neurology

150   IT   ISSN 0391-3198
INCONSCIO E CULTURA. 1978. irreg., no.17, 1990 (numbers not published consecutively). price varies. Liguori Editore s.r.l., Via Mezzocannone 19, 80134 Naples, Italy. TEL 081-5227139. Ed. Aldo Carotenuto.

158   II   ISSN 0019-4247
INDIAN ACADEMY OF APPLIED PSYCHOLOGY. JOURNAL. (Text in English) vol.17, 1974. 2/yr. Rs.40($12) to institutions; individuals Rs.20($6). Indian Academy of Applied Psychology, University of Madras, Department of Psychology, Madras 5, India. charts; stat.; index. **Indexed:** Psychol.Abstr.

158   II   ISSN 0019-5073
BF636.A1   CODEN: IJAPBI
INDIAN JOURNAL OF APPLIED PSYCHOLOGY. (Text in English) 1964. s-a. Rs.90($28) University of Madras, Department of Psychology, Chepauk, Triplicane P.O., Madras 600005, Tamil Nadu, India. Ed.Bd. adv.; bk.rev.; charts; index; circ. 200. (also avail. in microfilm from UMI; reprint service avail. from UMI) **Indexed:** Biol.Abstr., Psychol.Abstr., Sp.Ed.Needs Abstr.

301.1 150   II   ISSN 0970-0897
BF1
INDIAN JOURNAL OF BEHAVIOUR. (Text in English) 1976. q. $50 to individuals; institutions Rs.$100($100). Institute of Psychological Research, 780, First Cross Rd., Mahalakshmi Layout, Bangalore 560 086, India. Ed. Dr. T.R. Rao. adv.; bk.rev.; circ. 500. (reprint service avail.) **Indexed:** Biol.Abstr., Indian Psychol.Abstr., Psychol.Abstr.
    —BLDSC shelfmark: 4410.368000.

152   II   ISSN 0303-2582
RC467
INDIAN JOURNAL OF CLINICAL PSYCHOLOGY. (Text in English) 1974. s-a. Rs.150($50) Indian Association of Clinical Psychologists, I.J.C.P. Department of Psychiatry, Postgraduate Institute of Medical Education and Research, Chandigarh 160 011, India. Ed. S.K. Verma. adv.; bk.rev.; abstr.; bibl.; index; circ. 700. **Indexed:** Indian Psychol.Abstr., Lang.& Lang.Behav.Abstr., Psychol.Abstr., Psychol.R.G., Sociol.Abstr.

150   II
▼**INDIAN JOURNAL OF PSYCHOLOGICAL DEVELOPMENT**. (Text in English) 1992. q. $50 to individuals; institutions Rs.$100($100). Institute of Psychological Research, 780, First Cross Rd., Mahalakshmi Layout, Bangalore 560 086, India. Ed. K. Sreenivasan. adv.

370.15 150   II   ISSN 0046-9009
INDIAN JOURNAL OF PSYCHOMETRY AND EDUCATION. (Text in English) 1970. s-a. Rs.30($10) Indian Psychometric and Educational Research Association, University of Patna, Dept. of Education, Patna 800 004, India. (Dist. by: Nandini Enterprises, 23-451 Wazirpura, Agra-282 003, India.) Ed. R.P. Singh. adv.; bk.rev.; bibl.; charts; circ. 500. **Indexed:** Lang.& Lang.Behav.Abstr., Psychol.Abstr.

156   II
INDIAN PSYCHOLOGICAL REVIEW. (Text in English) 1954. 6/yr. Rs.165($51.50) Agra Psychological Research Cell, Tiwari Kothi, Belanganj, Agra 282004, India. Eds. S. Jalota, M.C. Joshi. adv.; bk.rev. (reprint service avail. from ISI) **Indexed:** Psychol.Abstr.

150   US   ISSN 0277-7010
BF1
INDIVIDUAL PSYCHOLOGY; the journal of Adlerian research, theory & practice. 1940. q. $40 to individuals; institutions $40. (North American Society of Adlerian Psychology) University of Texas Press, Box 7819, Austin, TX 78713. TEL 512-471-4531. Ed. Guy J. Manaster. adv.; bk.rev.; bibl.; charts; stat.; index; circ. 700. (reprint service avail. from UMI,KTO) **Indexed:** Adol.Ment.Hlth.Abstr., Biol.Abstr., Curr.Cont., Curr.Lit.Fam.Plan., Ind.Med., Lang.& Lang.Behav.Abstr., Mid.East: Abstr.& Ind., Psychoanal.Abstr., Psychol.Abstr., Res.High.Educ.Abstr., Soc.Work Res.& Abstr., SSCI.
    —BLDSC shelfmark: 4437.505000.
    Former titles (until 1981): Journal of Individual Psychology (ISSN 0022-1805); Individual Psychologist; American Journal of Individual Psychology; Individual Psychology Bulletin; Individual Psychology News.
    Description: Presents current scholarly and professional research dealing with all aspects of the theories founded by Alfred Adler.

150   GW   ISSN 0019-7157
INDIVIDUAL PSYCHOLOGY NEWS LETTER. (Text in English, German) 1950. q. DM.14($14) International Association of Individual Psychology, Ruffinistr. 10, 8000 Munich 19, Germany. TEL 089-1688068. Ed. Horst Groener. adv.; bk.rev.; index; circ. 800. (back issues avail.) **Indexed:** Abstr.Anthropol.

370.15 616.8   US   ISSN 0888-4595
INDIVIDUAL PSYCHOLOGY REPORTER. 1982. q. $15 (foreign $17). Americas Institute of Adlerian Studies, 600 N. McClurg Court, Ste. 2502A, Chicago, IL 60611-3027. TEL 312-337-5066. Ed. Jane Griffith. bk.rev.; circ. 1,500. (back issues avail.)
    Description: Covers the individual psychology of Alfred Adler, with applications in the clinic, school, workplace, and home.

618.92   US   ISSN 0163-6383
BF719   CODEN: IBDEDP
INFANT BEHAVIOR AND DEVELOPMENT; an international & interdisciplinary journal. 1978. q. $45 to individuals; institutions $105. Ablex Publishing Corporation, 355 Chestnut St., Norwood, NJ 07648. TEL 201-767-8450. FAX 201-767-6717. TELEX 135-393. Ed. Carolyn Rovee-Collier. bk.rev.; index; circ. 1,200. (back issues avail.; reprint service avail. from ISI) **Indexed:** Bibl.Dev.Med.& Child Neur., Biol.Abstr., Chicago Psychoanal.Lit.Ind., Child Devel.Abstr., Curr.Cont., Excerp.Med., Lang.& Lang.Behav.Abstr., M.L.A., Psychol.Abstr., Psycscan D.P., Sociol.Abstr., Sp.Ed.Needs Abstr., SSCI.
    —BLDSC shelfmark: 4478.270000.
    Refereed Serial

INFANT MENTAL HEALTH JOURNAL. see MEDICAL SCIENCES — Pediatrics

INFANZIA. see CHILDREN AND YOUTH — About

155.4 157   IT
INFANZIA PSICOANALISI E ISTITUZIONI. 1981. irreg., no.6, 1990. price varies. Liguori Editore s.r.l., Via Mezzocannone, 19, 80134 Naples, Italy. TEL 081-5227139. Ed. Bianca Iaccarino.

150   UK   ISSN 0073-9561
INSTITUTE OF PSYCHOPHYSICAL RESEARCH. PROCEEDINGS. 1968. irreg. £14.95($24.95) per vol. Institute of Psychophysical Research, 118 Banbury Rd., Oxford OX2 6JU, England. TEL 865-58787. (Dist. in U.S. by: State Mutual Book & Periodical Service Ltd., 521 Fifth Ave., New York, NY 10017) Ed.Bd. circ. 2,500. (back issues avail.)

370 150   RM
INSTITUTUL DE SUBINGINERI ORADEA. LUCRARI STIINTIFICE: SERIA PEDAGOGIE, PSIHOLOGIE, METODICA. (Text in Rumanian, occasionally in English or French; summaries in English, French, German or Rumanian) 1967. irreg. Institutul de Subingineri Oradea, Calea Armatei Rosii Nr. 5, 3700 Oradea, Rumania.
    Formerly: Institutul Pedagogic Oradea. Lucrari Stiintifice: Seria Pedagogie, Psihologie, Metodica; which continues in part (in 1973): Institutul Pedagogica Oradea. Lucrari Stiintifice: Seria Istorie, Stiinte Sociale, Pedagogie; which superseded in part (in 1971): Institutul Pedagogica Oradea. Lucrari Stiintifice: Seria A and Seria B; which was formerly (until 1969): Institutul Pedagogic Oradea. Lucrari Stiintifice.

INSTRUCTIONAL SCIENCE; an international journal. see EDUCATION

150   RU
INTEGRAL'NOE ISSLEDOVANIE INDIVIUDAL'NOSTI. 1977. irreg. 1 Rub. Permskii Gosudarstvennyi Pedagogicheskii Institut, Perm, Russia. TEL 32-85-90. Ed. Bronislaw Aleksandrovich Vyatkin. circ. 700.

152   US
BF1   CODEN: PJBSAH
INTEGRATIVE PHYSIOLOGICAL AND BEHAVIORAL SCIENCE. 1966. q. $80 to individuals (foreign $100); institutions $120 (foreign $140). (Pavlovian Society) Transaction Publishers, Transaction Periodicals Consortium, Department 3092, Rutgers University, New Brunswick, NJ 08903. TEL 908-932-2280. FAX 908-932-3138. Ed. Dr. F.J. McGuigan. index; circ. 500. (also avail. in microform from UMI) **Indexed:** Biol.Abstr., Chem.Abstr., Curr.Adv.Ecol.Sci., Curr.Cont., Dent.Ind., Excerp.Med., Hosp.Lit.Ind., Ind.Med., Psychol.Abstr., Sci.Cit.Ind., SSCI.
    Former titles: Pavlovian Journal of Biological Science (ISSN 0093-2213); Conditional Reflex (ISSN 0010-5392)
    Description: Contains articles pertaining to empirical, theoretical, review, apparatus, and historical topics.

155.4 GW ISSN 0342-6831
INTEGRATIVE THERAPIE; Zeitschrift fuer Verfahren Humanistischer Psychologie und Paedagogik. (Text in German; summaries in English) 1975. q. DM.56 (students DM.46). (Fritz Perls Institut) Junfermann-Verlag, Imadadstr. 40, Postfach 1840, 4790 Paderborn, Germany. TEL 05251-34034. FAX 05251-36371. Ed. Hilarion Petzold. adv.; bk.rev.; index; circ. 2,000.

370.15 150 US ISSN 0160-2896
BF431 CODEN: NTLLDT
INTELLIGENCE (NORWOOD); a multidisciplinary journal. 1977. q. $40 to individuals; institutions $100. Ablex Publishing Corporation, 355 Chestnut St., Norwood, NJ 07648. TEL 201-767-8450. FAX 201-767-6717. TELEX 135-393. Ed. Douglas Detterman. bk.rev.; index; circ. 650. (back issues avail.; reprint service avail. from ISI) **Indexed**: A.I.Abstr., ASSIA, Biol.Abstr., C.I.J.E., Child Devel.Abstr., Curr.Cont., Lang.& Lang.Behav.Abstr., Psychol.Abstr., Sociol.Abstr.
—BLDSC shelfmark: 4531.826500.
Refereed Serial

INTERACTION (NEW YORK); the management psychology letter. see BUSINESS AND ECONOMICS — Management

370.15 150 100 US ISSN 8755-612X
INTERBEHAVIORIST; a quarterly newsletter of interbehavior psychology. 1970. q. $7 to individuals (foreign $8); institutions $12; students $5. c/o Linda Hayes, Ed., Dept. of Psychology, University of Nevada, Reno, NV 89557. TEL 913-864-4840. adv.; bk.rev.; circ. 125. (back issues avail.)
Description: Includes news, information, discussions, comments and brief articles pertaining to interbehavioral psychology. Provides a contextualistic, integrated-field approach to the natural science of behavior.

150 300 AG ISSN 0325-8203
BF5
INTERDISCIPLINARIA; revista de psicologia y ciencias afines/journal of psychology and related sciences. (Text in English and Spanish) 1980. s-a. $21 (foreign $26) to individuals; institutions $16 (foreign $21). (National Research Council of Argentina) Centro Interamericano de Investigaciones Psicologicas y Ciencias Afines, Tte. Gral. Juan D. Peron 2158, 1040 Buenos Aires, Argentina. TEL 953-1477. FAX 953-3541. Eds. Dr. Horacio J.A. Rimoldi, Dr. Maria Cristina Richaud de Minzi. bk.rev.; circ. 600. **Indexed**: Psychol.Abstr.
—BLDSC shelfmark: 4533.356240.

155 AG ISSN 0326-1913
INTERDISCIPLINARIA MONOGRAPHS. 1982. irreg. price varies. (National Research Council of Argentina) Centro Interamericano de Investigaciones Psicologicas y Ciencias Afines, Tte. Gral. Juan D. Peron 2158, 1040 Buenos Aires, Argentina. TEL 953-1477. FAX 953-3541. Eds. Horacio J.A. Rimoldi, Dr. Maria Cristina Richaud de Minzi. circ. 500.
—BLDSC shelfmark: 5915.468000.
Description: Covers a study of some perceptual and personality correlates of problem solving solutions.

INTERFACES: LINGUISTICS, PSYCHOLOGY AND HEALTH THERAPEUTICS; an international journal of research, notes and commentary. see LINGUISTICS

150 NE
INTERNATIONAL ASSOCIATION FOR CROSS-CULTURAL PSYCHOLOGY. INTERNATIONAL CONFERENCE. SELECTED PAPERS. irreg., 9th, 1990, Newcastle, Australia. Swets Publishing Service (Subsidiary of: Swets en Zeitlinger B.V.), Heereweg 347, 2161 CA Lisse, Netherlands. TEL 31-2521-35111. FAX 31-2521-15888. TELEX 41325. (Dist. in N. America by: Swets & Zeitlinger, Box 517, Berwyn, PA 19312. TEL 215-644-4944)

572 II ISSN 0020-613X
H1
INTERNATIONAL BEHAVIOURAL SCIENTIST. (Text in English) 1969. q. Rs.25($6.50) Sadhna Prakashan, Rastogi St., Subhash Bazar, Meerut 2, India. Ed. D.P. Rastogi. adv.; bk.rev.; abstr.; bibl.; charts; illus.; circ. 500. (also avail. in microfilm from UMI; reprint service avail. from UMI) **Indexed**: Curr.Cont., Int.Polit.Sci.Abstr., Lang.& Lang.Behav.Abstr., Ref.Zh., Sociol.Abstr.

157 615.7 UK
INTERNATIONAL CLINICAL PSYCHOPHARMACOLOGY. 1986. q. £64($114) to individuals; institutions £115($207). Rapid Communications of Oxford Ltd., The Old Malthouse, Paradise St., Oxford OX1 1LD, England. TEL 0865-790447. FAX 0865-244012. Eds. Trevor Silverstone, S.A. Montgomery. **Indexed**: Psychol.Abstr.
Description: Bridges the gap between research and clinical practice in psychopharmacology.

150 GW ISSN 0085-2112
INTERNATIONAL CONGRESS OF PSYCHOLOGY. PROCEEDINGS.* (Published by host national organization: Great Britain, 1969; Japan, 1972; France, 1976; German Democratic Republic, 1980; Mexico, 1984) quadrennial; 1988, 24th, Australia. International Union of Psychological Science, c/o Prof. Kurt Pawlik, Universitaet Hamburg, Psychologisches Institut, Von Melle Park 11, D-2000 Hamburg 13, Germany.

INTERNATIONAL JOURNAL FOR THE PSYCHOLOGY OF RELIGION. see RELIGIONS AND THEOLOGY

INTERNATIONAL JOURNAL OF AVIATION PSYCHOLOGY. see AERONAUTICS AND SPACE FLIGHT

155 UK ISSN 0165-0254
BF712 CODEN: IJBDDY
INTERNATIONAL JOURNAL OF BEHAVIORAL DEVELOPMENT. 1978. q. £33($63) to individuals; institutions £82($157). (International Society for the Study of Behavioral Development) Lawrence Erlbaum Associates Ltd., 27 Palmeira Mansions, Church Rd., Hove, E. Sussex BN3 2FA, England. TEL 0273-207411. FAX 0273-205612. Ed. Linda Seigel. adv.; bk.rev. (also avail. in microform from RPI) **Indexed**: ASSIA, Biol.Abstr., C.I.J.E., Child Devel.Abstr., CINAHL, Curr.Cont., PSI, Psychol.Abstr., Psycscan D.P., Sociol.Abstr., SSCI, Stud.Wom.Abstr.
—BLDSC shelfmark: 4542.128000.
Description: Promotes the discovery and application of knowledge about developmental processes at all stages of the lifespan, from infancy through old age.
Refereed Serial

INTERNATIONAL JOURNAL OF BIOSOCIAL AND MEDICAL RESEARCH; bridging the gap between the natural and social sciences to better understand human behavior. see NUTRITION AND DIETETICS

INTERNATIONAL JOURNAL OF CLINICAL NEUROPSYCHOLOGY. see MEDICAL SCIENCES — Psychiatry And Neurology

156 US ISSN 0889-3667
CODEN: IJCPE8
INTERNATIONAL JOURNAL OF COMPARATIVE PSYCHOLOGY. 1987. q. $125 (foreign $145). (International Society for Comparative Psychology) Human Sciences Press, Inc. (Subsidiary of: Plenum Publishing Corp.), 233 Spring St., New York, NY 10013-1578. TEL 212-620-8000. FAX 212-463-0742. Ed. Ethel Tobach. adv. (reprint service avail. from UMI) **Indexed**: Psychol.Abstr., Soc.Work Res.& Abstr.
—BLDSC shelfmark: 4542.172950.
Description: Explores how the study of the development and evolution of behavior elucidates behavior, and investigates relationship of scientific research and theory to fundamental concepts about the evolutionary history and nature of humanity.
Refereed Serial

INTERNATIONAL JOURNAL OF EATING DISORDERS. see NUTRITION AND DIETETICS

616.8 US ISSN 0020-7284
RC488 CODEN: IJGPAO
INTERNATIONAL JOURNAL OF GROUP PSYCHOTHERAPY. 1951. q. $60 to individuals (foreign $80); institutions $110 (foreign $130). (American Group Psychotherapy Association) Guilford Publications, Inc., 72 Spring St., 4th Fl., New York, NY 10012. TEL 212-431-9800. FAX 212-966-6708. Ed. Dr. Robert Dies. adv.; bk.rev.; abstr.; bibl.; charts; stat.; index. (back issues avail.) **Indexed**: Adol.Ment.Hlth.Abstr., ASSIA, Biol.Abstr., Curr.Cont., Excerp.Med., Ind.Med., Int.Nurs.Ind., Lang.& Lang.Behav.Abstr., Mid.East: Abstr.& Ind., Psychol.Abstr., Soc.Work Res.& Abstr., SSCI.
—BLDSC shelfmark: 4542.270000.
Description: Devoted to reporting and interpreting the research and practice of group psychotherapy.
Refereed Serial

301.1 320 US ISSN 0047-0732
HN1 CODEN: IJGTB3
INTERNATIONAL JOURNAL OF GROUP TENSIONS. 1971. q. $125 (foreign $145). (International Organization for the Study of Group Tensions) Human Sciences Press, Inc. (Subsidiary of: Plenum Publishing Corp.), 233 Spring St., New York, NY 10013-1578. TEL 212-620-8000. FAX 212-463-0742. Ed. Benjamin B. Wolman, Joseph B. Gittler. adv.; bk.rev.; bibl.; index. (also avail. in microform from UMI; reprint service avail. from UMI) **Indexed**: Mid.East: Abstr.& Ind., Psychol.Abstr., SSCI.
—BLDSC shelfmark: 4542.272000.
Description: Publishes research findings and theoretical analyses pertaining to bias, prejudice, discrimination, hostility, and violence - and methods of resolving these conflicts.
Refereed Serial

INTERNATIONAL JOURNAL OF HUMAN FACTORS IN MANUFACTURING. see COMPUTERS — Automation

614.58 US ISSN 0020-7411
RA790.A1 CODEN: IJMHBV
INTERNATIONAL JOURNAL OF MENTAL HEALTH. 1972. q. $232 to institutions. M.E. Sharpe, Inc., 80 Business Park Dr., Armonk, NY 10504. TEL 914-273-1800. FAX 913-273-2106. Ed. Dr. Martin Gittelman. adv.; bk.rev. **Indexed**: Adol.Ment.Hlth.Abstr., ASSIA, Biol.Abstr., Child Devel.Abstr., Curr.Cont., Excerp.Med., Mid.East: Abstr.& Ind., Psychol.Abstr., Soc.Sci.Ind., SSCI, Stud.Wom.Abstr.
—BLDSC shelfmark: 4542.352000.
Refereed Serial

155 US ISSN 0893-603X
BF698.9.P47 CODEN: IPCPEG
INTERNATIONAL JOURNAL OF PERSONAL CONSTRUCT PSYCHOLOGY. q. $75. Hemisphere Publishing Corporation (Subsidiary of: Taylor & Francis Group), 1900 Frost Rd., Ste. 101, Bristol, PA 19007-1598. TEL 215-785-5800. FAX 215-785-5515. Ed. Robert A. Neimeyer. (also avail. in microform from UMI; reprint service avail. from UMI)
—BLDSC shelfmark: 4542.452700.
Description: Empirical research, conceptual analyses, critical reviews, case studies on personal construct theory and related approaches to psychology.
Refereed Serial

INTERNATIONAL JOURNAL OF PSYCHIATRY IN MEDICINE; an international journal of medical psychology and psychiatry in the general hospital. see MEDICAL SCIENCES — Psychiatry And Neurology

150.19 UK ISSN 0020-7578
BF173.A2 CODEN: IJPSAA
INTERNATIONAL JOURNAL OF PSYCHO-ANALYSIS. Issued with: International Psycho-Analytical Association. Bulletin (ISSN 0074-753X) (Printed in International Journal of Psycho-Analysis) (Text in English; summaries in French, German, Spanish) 1920. q. £62($120) (Institute of Psychoanalysis) Routledge, 11, New Fetter Lane, London EC4P 4EE, England. TEL 01-583-9855. (Subscr. to: ABP Journals Subscription Dept., North Way, Andover Hants SP10 5BE, England) Eds. David Tucket, Tom Hayley. adv.; bk.rev.; index. (back issues avail.) **Indexed**: Biol.Abstr., Curr.Cont., Excerp.Med., Ind.Med., Mid.East: Abstr.& Ind., Psychoanal.Abstr., Psychol.Abstr., SSCI.
—BLDSC shelfmark: 4542.498000.

150 UK ISSN 0020-7594
BF1 CODEN: IJPSBB
INTERNATIONAL JOURNAL OF PSYCHOLOGY/JOURNAL INTERNATIONAL DE PSYCHOLOGIE. (Text in English, French) 1966. 6/yr. £29.50. (International Union of Psychological Science) Lawrence Erlbaum Associates Ltd., 27 Palmeira Mansions, Church Rd., Hove, East Sussex BN3 2FA, England. TEL 0273-207411. FAX 0273-205612. Ed. M. Sabourin. adv.; bk.rev.; abstr.; charts; illus.; stat.; circ. 1,500. (also avail. in microform from RPI; reprint service avail. from ISI,SWZ) **Indexed**: Adol.Ment.Hlth.Abstr., ASSIA, Biol.Abstr., Curr.Cont., Mid.East: Abstr.& Ind., Psychol.Abstr., SSCI, Stud.Wom.Abstr.
—BLDSC shelfmark: 4542.506000.

PSYCHOLOGY

150   **NE**   ISSN 0167-8760
CODEN: IJPSEE
INTERNATIONAL JOURNAL OF PSYCHOPHYSIOLOGY.
(Text in English) 1983. 6/yr.(in 2 vols.; 3 nos./vol.)
fl.918 (effective 1992). (International Organization of Psychophysiology) Elsevier Science Publishers B.V., P.O. Box 211, 1000 AE Amsterdam, Netherlands. TEL 020-5803911.
FAX 020-5803598. TELEX 18582 ESPA NL. (N. America dist. addr.: Elsevier Science Publishing Co., Inc., Box 882, Madison Sq. Sta., New York, NY 10159. TEL 212-989-5800) Ed.Bd. adv.; bk.rev.; circ. 750. (also avail. in microfiche; back issues avail.) **Indexed:** Curr.Cont., Excerp.Med., Ind.Med., Psychol.Abstr.
— BLDSC shelfmark: 4542.506500.
Description: Covers all aspects of psychophysiology.

INTERNATIONAL JOURNAL OF PSYCHOSOMATICS. see *MEDICAL SCIENCES*

616.89   **UK**
INTERNATIONAL JOURNAL OF SHORT TERM PSYCHOTHERAPY. q. $165 (effective 1992). John Wiley & Sons Ltd., Journals, Baffins Lane, Chichester, Sussex PO19 1UD, England.
TEL 0243-779777. FAX 0243-775878. TELEX 86290 WIBOOK G. Ed. Paul Fink. (reprint service avail. from SWZ)
Description: Offers the researcher and the practitioner access to ongoing systematic research and developments in the spectrum of short-term psychotherapies.

INTERNATIONAL JOURNAL OF SPORT PSYCHOLOGY. see *SPORTS AND GAMES*

150   **US**   ISSN 0047-116X
BF1
INTERNATIONAL PSYCHOLOGIST. 1959. q. $24 to non-members. International Council of Psychologists, Inc., c/o Dr. Carleton Shay, Ed., 2261 Talmadge St., Los Angeles, CA 90027. (Subscr. to: Box 62, Hopkinton, RI 02833-0062. TEL 401-377-3092) Ed. Carleton Shay. adv.; bk.rev.; abstr.; circ. 1,700. (looseleaf format)
— BLDSC shelfmark: 4545.350000.

INTERNATIONAL REGISTRY OF ORGANIZATION DEVELOPMENT PROFESSIONALS AND ORGANIZATION DEVELOPMENT HANDBOOK. see *BUSINESS AND ECONOMICS — Personnel Management*

158.7   **UK**   ISSN 0886-1528
HF5548.7
INTERNATIONAL REVIEW OF INDUSTRIAL AND ORGANIZATIONAL PSYCHOLOGY. 1986. a. $110.
John Wiley & Sons Ltd., Journals, Baffins Lane, Chichester, Sussex PO19 1UD, England.
TEL 0243-779777. FAX 0243-775878. TELEX 86290-WIBOOK-G. Eds. Cary Cooper, Ivan Robertson.
— BLDSC shelfmark: 4547.325000.
Description: Provides reviews in the field of industrial and organizational psychology.

616.89   **UK**   ISSN 0306-2643
BF173.A2   CODEN: IRPADF
INTERNATIONAL REVIEW OF PSYCHO-ANALYSIS. (Text in English; summaries French, German, Spanish) 1974. q. £58($115) (Institute of Psychoanalysis) Routledge, 11, New Fetter Lane, London EC4P 4EE, England. TEL 01-583-9855. (Subscr. to: Routledge Journals Subscription Dept., North Way, Andover, Hants SP10 5BE) Eds. T.T.S. Hayley, David Tuckett. adv.; bibl.; charts; index. (back issues avail.) **Indexed:** Ind.Med., Mid.East: Abstr.& Ind., Psychoanal.Abstr., Psychol.Abstr., SSCI.
— BLDSC shelfmark: 4547.520000.

152.8   **UK**   ISSN 0379-2439
INTERNATIONAL TEST COMMISSION. BULLETIN. (Text and summaries in English, French) s-a. International Test Commission, Psychological Service Unit, c/o Mr. J. Toplis, Post Office Headquarters, Freeling House 23, Glasshill St., London SE1 OBQ, England. Ed. J. Schegel. circ. 300. (back issues avail.)
— BLDSC shelfmark: 2589.100000.

INTERVENTION IN SCHOOL AND CLINIC; an interdisciplinary journal directed to an international audience of teachers and specialists working with capable but underachieving children and youth. see *EDUCATION — Special Education And Rehabilitation*

IRISH JOURNAL OF PSYCHOLOGICAL MEDICINE. see *MEDICAL SCIENCES — Psychiatry And Neurology*

150   **IE**   ISSN 0303-3910
CODEN: IRJPAR
IRISH JOURNAL OF PSYCHOLOGY. 1971. q. I£40($80) Psychological Society of Ireland, c/o Trinity College, Department of Psychology, 25 Westland Row, Dublin 2, Ireland. TEL 01-772941. FAX 01-772694. Ed. Howard Smith. adv.; bk.rev.; bibl.; charts; circ. 900.
Indexed: Biol.Abstr., Br.Educ.Ind., Curr.Cont., Psychol.Abstr., Ref.Zh., SSCI.
— BLDSC shelfmark: 4572.200000.

616.89 156   **IS**   ISSN 0334-6080
BF8.H4
ISRAEL QUARTERLY OF PSYCHOLOGY. (Text in Hebrew) q. IS.30. Histadrut Hapsikologim B'yisrael, Rehov Haniviim 2, Tel Aviv 65 456, Israel.
TEL 03-288844.

616.89   **US**   ISSN 0097-6555
RC475
ISSUES IN EGO PSYCHOLOGY. 1978. s-a. $15.
Washington Square Institute, 41 E. 11th St., New York, NY 10003. Ed. Alison Harrison. bk.rev.; circ. 300. (back issues avail.) **Indexed:** Psychol.Abstr.
— BLDSC shelfmark: 4584.241000.

ISSUES IN MENTAL HEALTH NURSING. see *MEDICAL SCIENCES — Nurses And Nursing*

150   **GW**   ISSN 0075-2363
JAHRBUCH DER PSYCHOANALYSE; Beitraege zur Theorie und Praxis. 1964. irreg., vol.28, 1991. price varies. Friedrich Frommann Verlag Guenther Holzboog, Postfach 500460, Koenig-Karl-Str. 27, 7000 Stuttgart 50, Germany. Ed.Bd. adv.; circ. 1,000. (reprint service avail. from KTO) **Indexed:** Psychoanal.Abstr., Psychol.Abstr.
— BLDSC shelfmark: 4632.050000.

JAPANESE BULLETIN OF ART THERAPY. see *ART*

157   **JA**   ISSN 0017-7547
JAPANESE JOURNAL OF CRIMINAL PSYCHOLOGY/HANZAI SHINRIGAKU KENKYU. (Text in Japanese; summaries in English) 1963. 3/yr. 1500 Yen($4.) Japanese Association of Criminal Psychology, 2-11-7 Hikawadai, Nerima-ku, Tokyo, Japan. Ed. Toshimitsu Fukutomi. **Indexed:** Psychol.Abstr.

370.15 150   **JA**   ISSN 0021-5015
CODEN: JJEPAP
JAPANESE JOURNAL OF EDUCATIONAL PSYCHOLOGY.
(Text in Japanese; contents page in English) 1953. q. 8000 Yen. Japanese Association of Educational Psychology - Nihon Kyoiku Shinri Gakkai, c/o Faculty of Education, University of Tokyo, 7-3-1 Hongo, Bunkyo-ku, Tokyo 113, Japan. Ed.Bd. adv.; bk.rev.; charts; circ. controlled. **Indexed:** Psychol.Abstr., SSCI.
— BLDSC shelfmark: 4651.750000.

150   **JA**   ISSN 0021-5368
BF76.5   CODEN: JPREAV
JAPANESE PSYCHOLOGICAL RESEARCH. (Text in English, French, German) 1954. q. $65. (Japanese Psychological Association) Japan Scientific Societies Press, 6-2-10 Hongo, Bunkyo-ku, Tokyo 113, Japan. TEL 3814-2001. FAX 3814-2002. TELEX 2722268 BCJSP J. (Dist. by: Business Center for Academic Societies Japan, Koshin Bldg., 6-16-3 Hongo, Tokyo 113, Japan; Dist. in U.S. by: International Specialized Book Services, Inc., 5602 N.E. Hassalo St., Portland, OR 97213) adv.; bk.rev.; abstr.; charts; illus.; index; circ. 4,000. **Indexed:** Biol.Abstr., Curr.Cont., Ergon.Abstr., Psychol.Abstr., SSCI.
— BLDSC shelfmark: 4661.100000.

JEDNOTNA SKOLA; journal for pedagogical theory and praxis and psychology. see *EDUCATION*

155   **PO**   ISSN 0870-4783
JORNAL DE PSICOLOGIA. (Text in Portuguese; summaries in English) 1982. q. Esc.1000 to individuals (foreign $25); institutions Esc.2500 (foreign $30). Grupo de Estudos e Reflexao em Psicologia, R. das Taipas, 76, 4000 Porto, Portugal. Ed. Rui Abrunhosa Goncalves. adv.; bk.rev.; bibl.; charts; stat.; circ. 1,000. (back issues avail.) **Indexed:** Psychol.Abstr.
Description: Presents discussions and research in the field of psychology and other related sciences. Includes theoretical and research articles, brief reports and interviews.

150 200   **US**
JOURNAL FOR CREATIVE CHANGE. 1979. 3/yr. $15. Association for Creative Change, Box 1022, Clemson, SC 29633-1022. FAX 803-654-8416. Ed. Judith Guttman. bk.rev.; charts; stat.; circ. 600.
Formerly: Journal of Religion and the Applied Behavioral Sciences.

158   **US**   ISSN 0193-3922
BF637.C6
JOURNAL FOR SPECIALISTS IN GROUP WORK. 1978. 4/yr. $12. (Association for Specialists in Group Work) American Association for Counseling and Development, 5999 Stevenson Ave., Alexandria, VA 22304. TEL 703-823-9800. FAX 703-823-0252. Ed. Samuel T. Gladding. circ. 6,000. (also avail. in microfiche; reprint service avail. from UMI) **Indexed:** C.I.J.E., Lang.& Lang.Behav.Abstr., Psychol.Abstr., Soc.Work Res.& Abstr., Sp.Ed.Needs Abstr.
— BLDSC shelfmark: 5066.138000.
Formerly: Together (Washington, 1975) (ISSN 0161-0333)
Description: Includes empirical research, history of group work, work with groups, theoretical discussions and current group literature reviews.

155 300   **UK**   ISSN 0021-8308
JOURNAL FOR THE THEORY OF SOCIAL BEHAVIOUR. 1971. 4/yr. £33($49.90) to individuals; institutions £79.50($129.90). Basil Blackwell Ltd., 108 Cowley Rd, Oxford OX4 1JF, England. TEL 0865-791100. FAX 0865-791347. TELEX 837022-OXBOOK-G. Ed. Charles W. Smith. adv.; circ. 800. (reprint service avail. from SWZ,UMI) **Indexed:** Adol.Ment.Hlth.Abstr., ASSIA, Mid.East: Abstr.& Ind., Phil.Ind., Psychol.Abstr., Res.High.Educ.Abstr., SSCI.
— BLDSC shelfmark: 5069.076000.

155.4   **US**   ISSN 0091-0627
RJ499.A1   CODEN: JABCAA
JOURNAL OF ABNORMAL CHILD PSYCHOLOGY. 1973. bi-m. $250 (foreign $295)(effective 1992). Plenum Publishing Corp., 233 Spring St., New York, NY 10013-1578. TEL 212-620-8000.
FAX 212-463-0742. TELEX 23-421139. Ed. Herbert C. Quay. adv.; bibl.; charts. (also avail. in microfilm from JSC; back issues avail.) **Indexed:** Adol.Ment.Hlth.Abstr., ASSIA, Bibl.Dev.Med.& Child Neur., Biol.Abstr., C.I.J.E., Child Devel.Abstr., Curr.Cont., Except.Child.Educ.Abstr., Excerp.Med., Ind.Med., Mid.East: Abstr.& Ind., Psychol.Abstr., Psycscan D.P., Ref.Zh, Sp.Ed.Needs Abstr., SSCI.
— BLDSC shelfmark: 4918.820000.
Refereed Serial

157   **US**   ISSN 0021-843X
RC321   CODEN: JAPCAC
JOURNAL OF ABNORMAL PSYCHOLOGY. 1906. q. $63 to non-members (foreign $75); members $26; institutions $100 (foreign $108) (effective 1992). American Psychological Association, 750 First St., N.E., Washington, DC 20002-4242.
TEL 202-336-5500. FAX 202-336-5568. Ed. Don C. Fowles. adv.; charts; index; circ. 5,400. (also avail. in microform from MIM,UMI; back issues avail.; reprint service avail. from KTO,UMI) **Indexed:** Abstr.Health Care Manage.Stud., Acad.Ind., ASSIA, Biol.Abstr., Biol.Dig., Crim.Just.Abstr., Curr.Cont., Dok.Arbeitsmed., Except.Child.Educ.Abstr., Excerp.Med., Hlth.Ind., Ind.Med., M.L.A., Mid.East: Abstr.& Ind., Psychol.Abstr., Psycscan C.P., Sage Fam.Stud.Abstr., Soc.Sci.Ind., Soc.Work Res.& Abstr., Sp.Ed.Needs Abstr., SSCI, Stud.Wom.Abstr.
— BLDSC shelfmark: 4918.840000.
Description: Provides articles on basic research and theory in the broad field of abnormal behavior.
Refereed Serial

JOURNAL OF ADOLESCENT RESEARCH. see *CHILDREN AND YOUTH — About*

157 616.8   **UK**   ISSN 0887-6185
RC531   CODEN: JADIE8
JOURNAL OF ANXIETY DISORDERS. 1987. q. £85 (effective 1992). Pergamon Press plc, Headington Hill Hall, Oxford OX3 0BW, England.
TEL 0865-794141. FAX 0865-743911. TELEX 83177 PERGAP. (And: 660 White Plains Rd., Tarrytown, NY 10591-5153. TEL 914-524-9200) Eds. Cynthia G. Last, Michel Hersen. index; circ. 1,500. (also avail. in microform; back issues avail.) **Indexed:** Excerp.Med., Psychol.Abstr.
— BLDSC shelfmark: 4939.300000.
Refereed Serial

155   US   ISSN 0021-8855
BF636.A1   CODEN: JOABAW
JOURNAL OF APPLIED BEHAVIOR ANALYSIS. 1968. q. $54. Society for the Experimental Analysis of Behavior, Inc. (Lawrence), c/o Department of Human Development, University of Kansas, Lawrence, KS 66045. Ed. Scott Geller. adv.; bk.rev.; charts; illus.; index; circ. 5,500. (also avail. in microfilm; back issues avail.) **Indexed:** Adol.Ment.Hlth.Abstr., ASSIA, Biol.Abstr., C.I.J.E., Child Devel.Abstr., Commun.Abstr., Cont.Pg.Manage., Curr.Cont., Except.Child.Educ.Abstr., Ind.Med., INIS Atomind., Mid.East: Abstr.& Ind., Psychol.Abstr., Psyscan, Soc.Sci.Ind., SSCI, Yrbk.Assoc.Educ.& Rehab.Blind.
—BLDSC shelfmark: 4940.450000.
Refereed Serial

158   US   ISSN 0021-8863
H1   CODEN: JABHAP
JOURNAL OF APPLIED BEHAVIORAL SCIENCE. 1965. q. $45 to individuals; institutions $90. Sage Publications, Inc., 2455 Teller Rd., Newbury Park, CA 91320. TEL 805-499-0721. FAX 805-499-0871. Ed. Louis A. Zurcher, Jr. adv.; bk.rev.; abstr.; charts; index. (back issues avail.) **Indexed:** A.B.C.Pol.Sci., ABI Inform., ASSIA, BPIA, Cont.Pg.Manage., Curr.Cont., Educ.Admin.Abstr., Educ.Ind., Lang.& Lang.Behav.Abstr., Manage.Cont., Pers.Lit., Psychol.Abstr., Psyscan, Sage Fam.Stud.Abstr., Sage Pub.Admin.Abstr., SCIMP, Soc.Sci.Ind., SSCI, Stud.Wom.Abstr.

155   US   ISSN 0193-3973
BF636.A1
JOURNAL OF APPLIED DEVELOPMENTAL PSYCHOLOGY. 1980. q. $40 to individuals; institutions $90. Ablex Publishing Corporation, 355 Chestnut St., Norwood, NJ 07648. TEL 201-767-8450. FAX 201-767-6717. TELEX 135-393. Ed. Irving E. Sigel. circ. 450. (back issues avail.; reprint service avail. from ISI) **Indexed:** Biol.Abstr., Child Devel.Abstr., Psychol.Abstr., Psyscan D.P., Sociol.Abstr.
—BLDSC shelfmark: 4942.450000.
Refereed Serial

158   US   ISSN 0021-9010
BF1   CODEN: JAPGBP
JOURNAL OF APPLIED PSYCHOLOGY. 1917. bi-m. $100 to non-members (foreign $106); members $50; institutions $200 (foreign $212). American Psychological Association, 750 First St., N.E., Washington, DC 20002-4242. TEL 202-336-5500. FAX 202-336-5568. Ed. Neal Schmitt. adv.; bibl.; charts; index; circ. 5,600. (also avail. in microform from MIM,UMI; reprint service avail. from KTO,UMI) **Indexed:** ABI Inform., Acad.Ind., Adol.Ment.Hlth.Abstr., ASSIA, Biol.Abstr., BPIA, CINAHL, Commun.Abstr., Cont.Pg.Manage., Crim.Just.Abstr., Curr.Cont., Dok.Arbeitsmed., Educ.Admin.Abstr., Educ.Ind., Ergon.Abstr., Excerp.Med., Hlth.Ind., Ind.Med., Int.Aerosp.Abstr., Int.Lab.Doc., Int.Nurs.Ind., Mid.East: Abstr.& Ind., Pers.Lit., Psychol.Abstr., Psyscan, Res.High.Educ.Abstr., Risk Abstr., SCIMP, Soc.Sci.Ind., Sp.Ed.Needs Abstr., SSCI, Stud.Wom.Abstr.
—BLDSC shelfmark: 4947.000000.
Description: Research on applications of psychology in work settings such as industry, correction systems, government, and educational institutions.
Refereed Serial

158   US   ISSN 0021-9029
HM251   CODEN: JASPBX
JOURNAL OF APPLIED SOCIAL PSYCHOLOGY. 1971. 24/yr. $398 (foreign $458). V.H. Winston & Son, Inc., 7961 Eastern Ave., Ste. 202A, Silver Spring, MD 20910. TEL 301-587-3356. Ed. Andrew Baum. abstr.; charts; illus.; stat.; index; circ. 1,100. (back issues avail.) **Indexed:** ASSIA, Crim.Just.Abstr., Curr.Cont., Curr.Lit.Fam.Plan., Excerp.Med., Mid.East: Abstr.& Ind., Psychol.Abstr., Psyscan, Soc.Sci.Ind., Sportsearch, SSCI, Stud.Wom.Abstr.
—BLDSC shelfmark: 4947.080000.
Refereed Serial

JOURNAL OF APPLIED SPORT PSYCHOLOGY. see *MEDICAL SCIENCES — Sports Medicine*

JOURNAL OF AUTISM AND DEVELOPMENTAL DISORDERS. see *MEDICAL SCIENCES — Psychiatry And Neurology*

JOURNAL OF BEHAVIOR THERAPY AND EXPERIMENTAL PSYCHIATRY; an interdisciplinary journal. see *MEDICAL SCIENCES — Psychiatry And Neurology*

150.194   US   ISSN 1053-0819
LB1060.2   CODEN: JBEDE5
▼**JOURNAL OF BEHAVIORAL EDUCATION.** 1991. q. $85 (foreign $100). Human Sciences Press, Inc. (Subsidiary of: Plenum Publishing Corp.), 233 Spring St., New York, NY 10013. TEL 212-620-8000. FAX 212-463-0742. TELEX 23-421139. Ed. Nirbhay N. Singh. adv.
—BLDSC shelfmark: 4951.260000.
Description: Intended as a forum for research on the application of behavioral principles and technology to education.
Refereed Serial

JOURNAL OF BEHAVIORAL MEDICINE. see *MEDICAL SCIENCES — Psychiatry And Neurology*

150   UK   ISSN 0143-1218
JOURNAL OF BIODYNAMIC PSYCHOLOGY. 1980. a. £3. Biodynamic Psychology Publications, Boyesen Institute for Biodynamic Psychology, Centre Ave., Acton, London W. 3, England. Ed. Courtney Young. adv.; bk.rev.; circ. 1,000.

155.84   US   ISSN 0095-7984
E185.625
JOURNAL OF BLACK PSYCHOLOGY. 1974. s-a. $30 to members; institutions $50. Association of Black Psychologists, Box 55999, Washington, DC 20040-5999. TEL 202-722-0808. FAX 202-722-5941. Ed. Dr. Kathleen Burlew. adv.; bk.rev.; circ. 1,000. (also avail. in microform from UMI; reprint service avail. from UMI) **Indexed:** Adol.Ment.Hlth.Abstr., Psychol.Abstr.
—BLDSC shelfmark: 4954.180000.

JOURNAL OF BRITISH MUSIC THERAPY. see *EDUCATION — Special Education And Rehabilitation*

158.7 330   US   ISSN 0889-3268
JOURNAL OF BUSINESS & PSYCHOLOGY. 1986. q. $155 (foreign $180). (Business Psychology Research Institute) Human Sciences Press, Inc. (Subsidiary of: Plenum Publishing Corp.), 233 Spring St., New York, NY 10013-1578. TEL 212-620-8000. FAX 212-463-0742. Ed. John W. Jones. adv. (reprint service avail. from UMI) **Indexed:** B.P.I., Psychol.Abstr.
—BLDSC shelfmark: 4954.661070.
Description: Highlights empirical research, case studies, and literature reviews dealing with psychological programs implemented in business settings.
Refereed Serial

150   US
▼**JOURNAL OF CHILD AND FAMILY STUDIES.** 1992. q. $85 (foreign $100). Human Sciences Press, Inc. (Subsidiary of: Plenum Publishing Corp.), 233 Spring St., New York, NY 10013-1578. TEL 212-620-8000. FAX 212-463-0742. Ed. Nirbhay N. Singh. adv.
Refereed Serial

155.4   US   ISSN 0021-9630
RJ499.A1   CODEN: JPPDAI
JOURNAL OF CHILD PSYCHOLOGY & PSYCHIATRY & ALLIED DISCIPLINES. 1960. 8/yr. £195 (effective 1992). (Association of Child Psychology and Psychiatry) Pergamon Press, Inc., Journals Division, 660 White Plains Rd., Tarrytown, NY 10591-5153. TEL 914-524-9200. FAX 914-333-2444. (And: Headington Hill Hall, Oxford OX3 0BW, England. TEL 0865-794141) Eds. Eric Taylor, Dorothy Bishop. adv.; bk.rev.; charts; illus.; index; circ. 4,700. (also avail. in microform from MIM,UMI; back issues avail.; reprint service avail. from UMI) **Indexed:** Adol.Ment.Hlth.Abstr., ASSIA, Bibl.Dev.Med.& Child Neur., Biol.Abstr., C.I.J.E., Child Devel.Abstr., CINAHL, Curr.Cont., Educ.Ind., Except.Child.Educ.Abstr., Excerp.Med., Ind.Med., Mid.East: Abstr.& Ind., Nutr.Abstr., Psychol.Abstr., Psyscan D.P., Risk Abstr., Sp.Ed.Needs Abstr., SSCI.
—BLDSC shelfmark: 4957.800000.
Description: Primarily concerned with child and adolescent psychology and psychiatry, including experimental and developmental studies and especially developmental psychopathology.
Refereed Serial

155.4 616.89   UK   ISSN 0075-417X
JOURNAL OF CHILD PSYCHOTHERAPY. 1963. s-a. £18($35) Association of Child Psychotherapists, Burgh House, New End Sq., London NW3 1LT, England. Ed. Susan Kegerreis. adv.; bk.rev.; circ. 950. **Indexed:** Abstr.Soc.Work, Child Devel.Abstr., Mid.East: Abstr.& Ind., Psychol.Abstr.
—BLDSC shelfmark: 4957.900000.

JOURNAL OF CLASSIFICATION. see *MATHEMATICS*

JOURNAL OF CLINICAL AND EXPERIMENTAL NEUROPSYCHOLOGY. see *MEDICAL SCIENCES — Psychiatry And Neurology*

155.4   US   ISSN 0047-228X
BF721   CODEN: JCCPD3
JOURNAL OF CLINICAL CHILD PSYCHOLOGY. 1972. q. $45 to individuals (foreign $70); institutions $145 (foreign $170). (American Psychological Association, Clinical Child Psychology) Lawrence Erlbaum Associates, Inc., 365 Broadway, Hillsdale, NJ 07642. TEL 504-388-3202. FAX 201-666-2394. Ed. Donald K. Routh. adv.; bk.rev.; illus.; circ. 1,700. (also avail. in microform from MIM; reprint service avail. from UMI) **Indexed:** ASSIA, Bibl.Dev.Med.& Child Neur., Child Devel.Abstr., Curr.Cont., Except.Child.Educ.Abstr., Mid.East: Abstr.& Ind., Psychol.Abstr., Psyscan C.P., Psyscan D.P., SSCI.
—BLDSC shelfmark: 4958.384000.
Description: Features the research and viewpoints of child advocates in all disciplines.
Refereed Serial

616.891   US
▼**JOURNAL OF CLINICAL PSYCHOANALYSIS.** 1992. q. $45 to individuals (foreign $60); institutions $65 (foreign $80). International Universities Press, Inc., 59 Boston Post Rd., Box 1524, Madison, CT 06443-1524. TEL 203-245-4000. FAX 203-245-0775. TELEX 282986 IUP BK. Eds. Drs. Herbert Wyman, Stephen Rittenberg. bk.rev.
Description: Explains, in jargon-free language, what actually happens in an analysis.
Refereed Serial

157   US   ISSN 0021-9762
RC321   CODEN: JCPYAO
JOURNAL OF CLINICAL PSYCHOLOGY. 1945. bi-m. $45 to individuals; libraries $140. Clinical Psychology Publishing Co., Inc., 4 Conant Sq., Brandon, VT 05733. TEL 802-247-6871. FAX 802-247-6853. Ed. Dr. Vladimir Pishkin. adv.; charts; index; circ. 2,529. (also avail. in microform from UMI; back issues avail.) **Indexed:** Abstr.Health Care Manage.Stud., Adol.Ment.Hlth.Abstr., ASSIA, Biol.Abstr., C.I.J.E., Chem.Abstr., Chic.Per.Ind., CINAHL, Commun.Abstr., Crim.Just.Abstr., Curr.Cont., Dent.Ind., Excerp.Med., Hosp.Lit.Ind., Ind.Med., Ind.Sci.Rev., Int.Nurs.Ind., Lang.& Lang.Behav.Abstr., Mid.East: Abstr.& Ind., Nutr.Abstr., Psychol.Abstr., Psyscan C.P., Sage Fam.Stud.Abstr., Sci.Cit.Ind., Soc.Sci.Ind., Soc.Work Res.& Abstr., SSCI.
—BLDSC shelfmark: 4958.690000.
Refereed Serial

JOURNAL OF COGNITIVE NEUROSCIENCE. see *MEDICAL SCIENCES — Psychiatry And Neurology*

616.89   US   ISSN 0889-8391
JOURNAL OF COGNITIVE PSYCHOTHERAPY. 1987. q. $34 to individuals; institutions $60. Springer Publishing Company, 536 Broadway, New York, NY 10012. TEL 212-431-4370. FAX 212-941-7842. Ed. Thomas Dowd. adv.; abstr. **Indexed:** Excerp.Med., Psychol.Abstr.
—BLDSC shelfmark: 4958.799200.
Refereed Serial

PSYCHOLOGY

616.89 US ISSN 8756-8225
JOURNAL OF COLLEGE STUDENT PSYCHOTHERAPY.
1986. q. $32 to individuals; institutions $45; libraries $105. Haworth Press, Inc., 10 Alice St., Binghamton, NY 13904. TEL 800-342-9678. FAX 607-722-1424. Ed. Leighton C. Whitaker. adv.; bk.rev.; circ. 113. (also avail. in microfiche from HAW; back issues avail.; reprint service avail. from HAW) **Indexed:** C.I.J.E., High.Educ.Abstr., Psychol.Abstr., Sage Fam.Stud.Abstr., Sage Pub.Admin.Abstr., Soc.Work Res.& Abstr., Sociol.Abstr., Sociol.Educ.Abstr., Sp.Ed.Needs Abstr., Stud.Wom.Abstr.
—BLDSC shelfmark: 4958.830000.
Description: Enhances the lives of college and university students by stimulating high quality practice theory, and research in mental and personal development.
Refereed Serial

JOURNAL OF COMMUNICATION. see *COMMUNICATIONS*

617.8 US ISSN 0021-9924
RC423.A1 CODEN: JCDIAI
JOURNAL OF COMMUNICATION DISORDERS. 1968. 4/yr. $204 to institutions (foreign $226)(effective 1992). Elsevier Science Publishing Co., Inc. (New York), 655 Ave. of the Americas, New York, NY 10010. TEL 212-989-5800. FAX 212-633-3965. TELEX 420643 AEP UI. Ed. R.W. Rieber. adv.; bk.rev.; charts; illus. (also avail. in microform from RPI; reprint service avail. from SWZ) **Indexed:** ASSIA, Bibl.Dev.Med.& Child Neur., Biol.Abstr., C.I.J.E., Curr.Cont., Dent.Ind., DSH Abstr., Except.Child.Educ.Abstr., Excerp.Med., Ind.Med., Lang.& Lang.Behav.Abstr. (1977-), Mid.East: Abstr.& Ind., Psychol.Abstr., Rehabil.Lit., Sociol.Abstr., SSCI, Yrbk.Assoc.Educ.& Rehab.Blind.
—BLDSC shelfmark: 4961.600000.
Description: Provides up-to-date information on clinical and research advances in a wide range of hearing and speech disorders.
Refereed Serial

301.1 150 UK ISSN 1052-9284
HM251. CODEN: JLCPEX
JOURNAL OF COMMUNITY AND APPLIED SOCIAL PSYCHOLOGY; an international journal of applied social psychology. 1986. q. $125 (effective 1992). John Wiley & Sons Ltd., Journals, Baffins Lane, Chichester, Sussex PO19 1UD, England. TEL 0243-779777. FAX 0243-775878. TELEX 86290 WIBOOK G. Eds. Geoffrey M. Stephenson, Jim Orford. **Indexed:** ASSIA, Curr.Cont.
—BLDSC shelfmark: 4961.693000.
Formerly (until 1990): Social Behaviour (ISSN 0885-6249)
Description: Fosters international communication among those concerned with the social psychological analysis and critical understanding of community issues and problems and to develop this understanding in the context of proposals for intervention and social policy.

132 301.15 US ISSN 0090-4392
RC467 CODEN: JCPSD9
JOURNAL OF COMMUNITY PSYCHOLOGY. 1973. q. $45 to individuals; libraries $140. Clinical Psychology Publishing Co., Inc., 4 Conant Sq., Brandon, VT 05733. TEL 802-247-6871. FAX 802-247-6853. Ed. Dr. Raymond P. Lorion. adv.; index; circ. 820. (also avail. in microform from UMI; back issues avail.) **Indexed:** Adol.Ment.Hlth.Abstr., Commun.Abstr., Curr.Cont., Lang.& Lang.Behav.Abstr., Mid.East: Abstr.& Ind., PSI, Psychol.Abstr., Sage Pub.Admin.Abstr., SSCI.
—BLDSC shelfmark: 4961.750000.
Refereed Serial

156 US ISSN 0735-7036
BF1 CODEN: JCOPDT
JOURNAL OF COMPARATIVE PSYCHOLOGY. 1983. q. $50 to non-members (foreign $62); members $21; institutions $100 (foreign $124). American Psychological Association, 750 First St., N.E., Washington, DC 20002-4242. TEL 202-336-5500. FAX 202-336-5568. Ed. Gordon G. Gallup, Jr. adv.; charts; illus.; index; circ. 2,000. (also avail. in microform from UMI; reprint service avail. from UMI) **Indexed:** Adol.Ment.Hlth.Abstr., Anim.Breed.Abstr., Biol.Abstr., Biol.& Agr.Ind., Chem.Abstr., Ind.Med., Ind.Sci.Rev., INIS Atomind., Psychol.Abstr., Sci.Cit.Ind., Soc.Sci.Ind.
—BLDSC shelfmark: 4963.300000.
Supersedes in part (1947-1982): Journal of Comparative and Physiological Psychology (ISSN 0021-9940)
Description: Laboratory and field studies of the behavioral patterns of various species as they relate to evolution, development, ecology, control and functional significance.
Refereed Serial

157 616.8 US ISSN 0022-006X
BF1 CODEN: JCLPBC
JOURNAL OF CONSULTING AND CLINICAL PSYCHOLOGY. 1968. bi-m. $125 to non-members (foreign $143); members $50; institutions $250 (foreign $286). American Psychological Association, 750 First St., N.E., Washington, DC 20002-4242. TEL 202-336-5500. FAX 202-336-5568. Ed. Alan E. Kazdin. adv.; bibl.; charts; illus.; index; circ. 12,000. (also avail. in microform from MIM,UMI; reprint service avail. from KTO,UMI) **Indexed:** Acad.Ind., Adol.Ment.Hlth.Abstr., ASSIA, Biol.Abstr., C.I.J.E., Commun.Abstr., Crim.Just.Abstr., Curr.Cont., Dok.Arbeitsmed., Except.Child.Educ.Abstr., Excerp.Med., Hlth.Ind., Ind.Med., Mid.East: Abstr.& Ind., Psychol.Abstr., Psycscan C.P., Risk Abstr., Sage Fam.Stud.Abstr., Soc.Sci.Ind., Soc.Work Res.& Abstr., Sp.Ed.Needs Abstr., SSCI.
—BLDSC shelfmark: 4965.195000.
Formerly: Journal of Consulting Psychology (ISSN 0095-8891)
Description: Research on techniques of diagnosis and treatment in disordered behavior as well as studies of populations of clinical interest.
Refereed Serial

150 US ISSN 0894-8577
RC489.E93
JOURNAL OF CONTEMPLATIVE PSYCHOTHERAPY. 1980. a. $10. Naropa Institute, 2130 Arapahoe Ave., Boulder, CO 80302. TEL 303-444-0202. Ed. Tim Stokes. bk.rev.; circ. 3,000. (back issues avail.) **Indexed:** Psychol.Abstr.
Formerly: Naropa Institute Journal of Psychology (ISSN 0271-7557)
Description: Articles explore the clinical application of contemplative disciplines in the practice of psychotherapy. Includes scholarly articles.

616.89 US ISSN 0022-0116
RC475 CODEN: JCPTBA
JOURNAL OF CONTEMPORARY PSYCHOTHERAPY. 1970. q. $150 (foreign $175). Human Sciences Press, Inc. (Subsidiary of: Plenum Publishing Corp.), 233 Spring St., New York, NY 10013-1578. TEL 212-620-8000. FAX 212-463-0742. Ed. Erwin Parson. adv.; bk.rev.; bibl.; charts. (also avail. in microfilm from UMI; reprint service avail. from ISI,UMI) **Indexed:** Abstr.Soc.Work., Excerp.Med., Mid.East: Abstr.& Ind., Psychol.Abstr., Rehabil.Lit., Soc.Work Res.& Abstr., SSCI.
—BLDSC shelfmark: 4965.240000.
Description: Presents progressive research and clinical papers covering advances in psychotherapeutic concepts and methodology. Offers an eclectic approach to the promotion of emotional health and maturity.
Refereed Serial

150 371.4 US ISSN 0022-0167
BF637.C6
JOURNAL OF COUNSELING PSYCHOLOGY. 1954. q. $65 to non-members (foreign $77); members $26; institutions $130 (effective 1992). American Psychological Association, 750 First St., N.E., Washington, DC 20002-4242. TEL 202-336-5500. FAX 202-336-5568. Ed. Lenore W. Harmon. adv.; bk.rev.; bibl.; charts; index; circ. 6,000. (also avail. in microform from MIM,UMI; reprint service avail. from UMI) **Indexed:** Adol.Ment.Hlth.Abstr., ASSIA, Bk.Rev.Ind. (1965-1979), C.I.J.E., Child.Bk.Rev.Ind. (1965-1979), Child Devel.Abstr., Curr.Cont., Educ.Ind., Mid.East: Abstr.& Ind., Psychol.Abstr., Psycscan C.P., Rehabil.Lit., Res.High.Educ.Abstr., Sage Fam.Stud.Abstr., Soc.Sci.Ind., Soc.Work Res.& Abstr., Sp.Ed.Needs Abstr., SSCI, Stud.Wom.Abstr.
—BLDSC shelfmark: 4965.450000.
Description: Empirical studies about counseling processes and interventions, theoretical articles about counseling, and studies dealing with evaluation of counseling applications and programs.
Refereed Serial

616.89 US ISSN 0897-4446
RC488.5 CODEN: JCTHEV
JOURNAL OF COUPLES THERAPY. 1989. q. $24 to individuals; institutions $32; libraries $75. Haworth Press, Inc., 10 Alice St., Binghamton, NY 13904. TEL 800-342-9678. FAX 607-722-1424. Ed. Barbara Jo Brothers. adv.; bk.rev. (also avail. in microfiche from HAW; reprint service avail. from HAW) **Indexed:** Soc.Work Res.& Abstr.
—BLDSC shelfmark: 4965.455000.
Description: Devoted entirely to the study of human bonding and intimacy. For couples therapists, marriage, family and clinical practitioners who deal with couples and intimacy and bonding issues as a focus in their practice.
Refereed Serial

JOURNAL OF CREATIVE BEHAVIOR. see *EDUCATION*

155 US ISSN 0022-0221
BF728 CODEN: JCPGB5
JOURNAL OF CROSS-CULTURAL PSYCHOLOGY. 1970. q. $42 to individuals; institutions $112. (International Association for Cross-Cultural Psychology) Sage Publications, Inc., 2455 Teller Rd., Newbury Park, CA 91320. TEL 805-499-0721. FAX 805-499-0871. (And Sage Publications, Ltd., 6 Bonhill St., London EC2A 4PU, England) (Co-sponsor: Center for Cross-Cultural Research) Eds. Walter Lonner, John E. Williams. adv.; bk.rev.; charts; illus.; cum.index; circ. 1,700. (also avail. in microfilm from UMI; back issues avail.; reprint service avail. from UMI) **Indexed:** Abstr.Anthropol., Adol.Ment.Hlth.Abstr., ASSIA, C.I.J.E., Chic.Per.Ind., Child Devel.Abstr., Commun.Abstr., Curr.Cont., Lang.& Lang.Behav.Abstr., Mid.East: Abstr.& Ind., PHRA, Psychol.Abstr., Psychol.R.G., Sage Fam.Stud.Abstr., SSCI, Stud.Wom.Abstr.
—BLDSC shelfmark: 4965.670000.

JOURNAL OF EARLY ADOLESCENCE. see *CHILDREN AND YOUTH — About*

JOURNAL OF ECONOMIC PSYCHOLOGY. see *BUSINESS AND ECONOMICS — Marketing And Purchasing*

JOURNAL OF EDUCATION AND PSYCHOLOGY. see *EDUCATION*

JOURNAL OF EDUCATIONAL AND PSYCHOLOGICAL CONSULTATION. see *EDUCATION*

370.15 150   US   ISSN 0022-0663
LB1051.A2
JOURNAL OF EDUCATIONAL PSYCHOLOGY. 1910. q. $65 to non-members (foreign $77); members $26; institutions $130 (foreign $154) (effective 1992). American Psychological Association, 750 First St., N.E., Washington, DC 20002-4242. TEL 202-336-5500. FAX 202-336-5568. Ed. Robert C. Calfee. adv.; bibl.; charts; index; circ. 4,400. (also avail. in microform from MIM,UMI; reprint service avail. from UMI) **Indexed:** Acad.Ind., Adol.Ment.Hlth.Abstr., ASSIA, Bibl.Dev.Med.& Child Neur., Biol.Abstr., C.I.J.E., Child Devel.Abstr., Commun.Abstr., Cont.Pg.Educ., Educ.Admin.Abstr., Educ.Ind., Educ.Tech.Abstr., Except.Child.Educ.Abstr., High.Educ.Curr.Aware.Bull., Ind.Med., Lang.Teach.& Ling.Abstr., Mid.East: Abstr.& Ind., Psychol.Abstr., Psycscan D.P., Res.High.Educ.Abstr., Sage Fam.Stud.Abstr., Sp.Ed.Needs Abstr., SSCI, Stud.Wom.Abstr.
—BLDSC shelfmark: 4973.200000.
Description: Deals with learning and cognition, psychological development, relationships, and adjustment of the individual, especially as related to the problems of instruction. Articles pertain to all levels of education and to all age groups.
Refereed Serial

150   UK   ISSN 0272-4944
BF353   CODEN: JEPSEO
JOURNAL OF ENVIRONMENTAL PSYCHOLOGY. 1980. q. $136. Academic Press Ltd., 24-28 Oval Rd., London NW1 7DX, England. TEL 071-267-4466. FAX 071-482-2293. TELEX 25775 ACPRES G. Ed. David V. Canter. **Indexed:** ASSIA, Br.Tech.Ind., Ergon.Abstr., Psychol.Abstr., Psycscan, Sage Fam.Stud.Abstr., Sage Urb.Stud.Abstr.
—BLDSC shelfmark: 4979.389000.
Description: Directed toward individuals in a wide range of disciplines who have an interest in the study of the transactions and interrelationships between people and their sociophysical surroundings (including man-made and natural environments) and the relation of this field to other social and biological sciences and to the environmental professions.

150   US   ISSN 0737-4828
PN56.P93
JOURNAL OF EVOLUTIONARY PSYCHOLOGY. 1979. 2/yr. $12 to non-members; membership $20. Institute for Evolutionary Psychology, 5117 Forbes Ave., Pittsburgh, PA 15213. TEL 412-621-7057. Ed. Paul Neumarkt. bk.rev.; film rev.; play rev.; circ. 300. **Indexed:** M.L.A.
●Also available on CD-ROM.
—BLDSC shelfmark: 4979.643000.
Description: Presents psychological interpretation of literature. Also includes poetry.

155.4 152   US   ISSN 0022-0965
BF721   CODEN: JECPAE
JOURNAL OF EXPERIMENTAL CHILD PSYCHOLOGY. 1964. m. $274 (foreign $333). Academic Press, Inc., Journal Division, 1250 Sixth Ave., San Diego, CA 92101. TEL 619-230-1840. FAX 619-699-6800. TELEX 181726. Ed. Hayne Reese. adv.; charts; index. (back issues avail.) **Indexed:** Adol.Ment.Hlth.Abstr., ASSIA, Bibl.Dev.Med.& Child Neur., Biol.Abstr., C.I.J.E., Child Devel.Abstr., Curr.Cont., Educ.Ind., Ind.Med., Mid.East: Abstr.& Ind., Psychol.Abstr., Psycscan D.P., Sci.Cit.Ind., Soc.Sci.Ind., SSCI.
—BLDSC shelfmark: 4981.300000.
Description: Covers all aspects of the behavior of children.
Refereed Serial

152   US   ISSN 0097-7403
QL750   CODEN: JPAPDG
JOURNAL OF EXPERIMENTAL PSYCHOLOGY: ANIMAL BEHAVIOR PROCESSES. Short title: J E P: A B P. 1975. q. $50 to non-members (foreign $62); members $21; institutions $100 (foreign $124) (effective 1992). American Psychological Association, 750 First St., N.E., Washington, DC 20002-4242. TEL 202-336-5500. FAX 202-336-5568. Ed. Michael Domjan. circ. 2,400. (also avail. in microform from MIM,UMI; reprint service avail. from UMI) **Indexed:** Biol.Abstr., Child Devel.Abstr., Curr.Cont., Ind.Med., Ind.Sci.Rev., Psychol.Abstr., Sci.Cit.Ind., Soc.Sci.Ind.
—BLDSC shelfmark: 4982.501000.
Supersedes in part: Journal of Experimental Psychology (ISSN 0022-1015)
Description: Experimental studies on the basic mechanisms of perception, learning, motivation and performance, especially in nonhuman animals.
Refereed Serial

152   US   ISSN 0096-3445
BF180   CODEN: JPGEDD
JOURNAL OF EXPERIMENTAL PSYCHOLOGY: GENERAL. Short title: J E P: GEN. 1975. q. $50 to non-members (foreign $62); members $21; institutions $100 (foreign $124) (effective 1992). American Psychological Association, 750 First St., N.E., Washington, DC 20002-4242. TEL 202-336-5500. FAX 202-336-5568. Ed. Sam Glucksberg. adv.; charts; illus.; stat.; index; circ. 3,200. (also avail. in microform from MIM,UMI; back issues avail.; reprint service avail. from UMI,KTO) **Indexed:** Biol.Abstr., Child Devel.Abstr., Curr.Cont., Ergon.Abstr., Ind.Med., Mid.East: Abstr.& Ind., Psychol.Abstr., Risk Abstr., Soc.Sci.Ind., SSCI, Yrbk.Assoc.Educ.& Rehab.Blind.
—BLDSC shelfmark: 4982.503000.
Supersedes in part: Journal of Experimental Psychology (ISSN 0022-1015)
Description: Presents reports of interest to all experimental psychologists.
Refereed Serial

152.05   US   ISSN 0096-1523
BF311   CODEN: JPHPDH
JOURNAL OF EXPERIMENTAL PSYCHOLOGY: HUMAN PERCEPTION AND PERFORMANCE. Short title: J E P: H P P. 1975. q. $100 to non-members; members $40; institutions $200. American Psychological Association, 750 First St., N.E., Washington, DC 20002-4242. TEL 202-336-5500. FAX 202-336-5568. Ed. James E. Cutting. circ. 3,000. (also avail. in microform from MIM,UMI; reprint service avail. from UMI) **Indexed:** ASSIA, Biol.Abstr., C.I.J.E., Child Devel.Abstr., Commun.Abstr., Curr.Cont., Dent.Ind., Ergon.Abstr., Ind.Med., Psychol.Abstr., Soc.Sci.Ind., SSCI.
—BLDSC shelfmark: 4982.507000.
Supersedes in part: Journal of Experimental Psychology (ISSN 0022-1015)
Refereed Serial

152   US   ISSN 0278-7393
LB1051
JOURNAL OF EXPERIMENTAL PSYCHOLOGY: LEARNING, MEMORY, AND COGNITION. Short title: J E P: L M C. 1975. bi-m. $115 to non-members (foreign $133); members $46; institutions $230 (foreign $266) (effective 1992). American Psychological Association, 750 First St., N.E., Washington, DC 20002-4242. TEL 202-336-5500. FAX 202-336-5568. Ed. Henry L. Roediger. circ. 3,600. (also avail. in microform from MIM,UMI; reprint service avail. from UMI) **Indexed:** Biol.Abstr., C.I.J.E., Child Devel.Abstr., Curr.Cont., Ergon.Abstr., Ind.Med., Psychol.Abstr., Soc.Sci.Ind., SSCI.
—BLDSC shelfmark: 4982.509000.
Formerly (until Jan. 1982): Journal of Experimental Psychology: Human Learning and Memory (ISSN 0096-1515); Which supersedes in part: Journal of Experimental Psychology (ISSN 0022-1015)
Description: Experimental studies on fundamental encoding, transfer, memory, and cognitive processes in human behavior.
Refereed Serial

152 301.1   US   ISSN 0022-1031
HM251   CODEN: JESPAQ
JOURNAL OF EXPERIMENTAL SOCIAL PSYCHOLOGY. 1965. bi-m. $155 (foreign $196). Academic Press, Inc., Journal Division, 1250 Sixth Ave., San Diego, CA 92101. TEL 619-230-1840. FAX 619-699-6800. TELEX 181726. Ed. Charles Judd. (back issues avail.) **Indexed:** ASSIA, Biol.Abstr., Commun.Abstr., Crim.Just.Abstr., Curr.Cont., Mid.East: Abstr.& Ind., Psychol.Abstr., Soc.Sci.Ind., SSCI.
—BLDSC shelfmark: 4982.700000.
Description: Publishes original research and theory on human social behavior and related phenomena.
Refereed Serial

150   US
HQ1
JOURNAL OF FAMILY AND ECONOMIC ISSUES. 1978. q. $130 (foreign $150). Human Sciences Press, Inc. (Subsidiary of: Plenum Publishing Corp.), 233 Spring St., New York, NY 10013-1578. TEL 212-620-8000. FAX 212-463-0742. Ed. Charles B. Hennon. adv.; bk.rev.; film rev.; bibl.; charts; stat.; index. (back issues avail.; reprint service avail. from UMI) **Indexed:** Abstr.Soc.Work., Curr.Cont., Educ.Ind., Mid.East: Abstr.& Ind., Psychol.Abstr., Sage Fam.Stud.Abstr., SSCI.
Former titles (until 1991): Lifestyles: Family and Economic Issues (ISSN 0882-3391); Alternative Lifestyles (ISSN 0161-570X)
Description: Covers family consumer behavior, household division of labor and productivity, the relationship between economic and non-economic decisions, and interrelationships between work life and family life.
Refereed Serial

155   US   ISSN 0893-3200
JOURNAL OF FAMILY PSYCHOLOGY. 1987. q. $39 to individuals; institutions $90. American Psychological Association, Division of Family Psychology, 750 First St., N.E., Washington, DC 20002-4242. TEL 202-336-5500. FAX 202-336-5568. Ed. Howard A. Liddle. **Indexed:** Psychol.Abstr.
—BLDSC shelfmark: 4983.733000.

616.89   US   ISSN 0897-5353
CODEN: JFAPEF
JOURNAL OF FAMILY PSYCHOTHERAPY; the quarterly journal of case studies, treatment reports, and strategies in clinical practice. 1985. q. $32 to individuals; institutions $42; libraries $75. Haworth Press, Inc., 10 Alice St., Binghamton, NY 13904. TEL 800-342-9678. FAX 607-722-1424. TELEX 4932599 HAWORTH. Ed. Terry Trepper. adv.: page $300. bk.rev.; circ. 316. (also avail. in microfiche from HAW; back issues avail.; reprint service avail. from HAW) **Indexed:** Biol.Dig., DNP, Excerp.Med., Ind.Med., Ind.Per.Art.Relat.Law, Past.Care & Couns.Abstr., Ref.Zh., Sage Fam.Stud.Abstr., Soc.Work Res.Abstr., Soc.Work Res.& Abstr., Sociol.Abstr., Sp.Ed.Needs Abstr., Sp.Ed.Needs Abstr., Stud.Wom.Abstr.
—BLDSC shelfmark: 4983.735000.
Formerly (until 1988): Journal of Psychotherapy and the Family (ISSN 0742-9703)
Description: Provides an exchange for clinicians across the disciplines to share solutions to difficult family problems. Offers detailed clinical case studies, descriptions of successful treatment programs, innovative strategies in clinical practice.
Refereed Serial

JOURNAL OF FAMILY THERAPY. see *MEDICAL SCIENCES — Psychiatry And Neurology*

JOURNAL OF FEMINIST FAMILY THERAPY. see *WOMEN'S STUDIES*

PSYCHOLOGY

150 301   US   ISSN 0094-730X
RC423.A1   CODEN: JFDID8
JOURNAL OF FLUENCY DISORDERS. 1974. 4/yr. $174 to institutions (foreign $196)(effective 1992). Elsevier Science Publishing Co., Inc. (New York), 655 Ave. of the Americas, New York, NY 10010. TEL 212-989-5800. FAX 212-633-3965. TELEX 420643 AEP UI. Ed. Gene J. Brutten. adv.; bk.rev. (also avail. in microform from RPI) **Indexed:** Biol.Abstr., Curr.Cont., DSH Abstr., Excerp.Med., Lang.& Lang.Behav.Abstr. (1978-), Psychol.Abstr., Rehabil.Lit., Sociol.Abstr., Sp.Ed.Needs Abstr., SSCI.
—BLDSC shelfmark: 4984.450000.
Description: Provides comprehensive coverage of clinical, experimental, and theoretical aspects of stuttering, including the latest remediation techniques.
Refereed Serial

JOURNAL OF GAY & LESBIAN PSYCHOTHERAPY. see *HOMOSEXUALITY*

150   US   ISSN 0022-1309
BF1   CODEN: JGPSAY
JOURNAL OF GENERAL PSYCHOLOGY; experimental, physiological, and comparative psychology. 1927. q. $75. (Helen Dwight Reid Educational Foundation) Heldref Publications, 1319 Eighteenth St., N.W., Washington, DC 20036. TEL 202-296-6267. FAX 202-296-5149. Ed. Marcie Kanakis. bibl.; charts; index; circ. 1,550. (also avail. in microform; back issues avail.; reprint service avail. from SWZ) **Indexed:** Abstr.Soc.Work., ASSIA, Biol.Abstr., Biol.& Agr.Ind., C.I.J.E., Chem.Abstr., Child Devel.Abstr., Commun.Abstr., Curr.Adv.Ecol.Sci., Curr.Cont., Dent.Ind., Ergon.Abstr., Except.Child Educ.Abstr., Excerp.Med., Ind.Med., Indian Psychol.Abstr., Lang.& Lang.Behav.Abstr., Psychol.Abstr., Soc.Sci.Ind., Soc.Work Res.& Abstr., SSCI.
—BLDSC shelfmark: 4989.200000.
Refereed Serial

150   US
▼**JOURNAL OF GENETIC COUNSELING.** 1992. q. $85 (foreign $100). (National Society of Genetic Counselors, Inc.) Human Sciences Press, Inc. (Subsidiary of: Plenum Publishing Corp.) 233 Spring St., New York, NY 10013-1578. TEL 212-620-8432. FAX 212-463-0742. Ed. Deborah L. Eunpu. adv.
Description: Covers psychosocial issues, educational and counseling techniques, legislation and regulations affecting genetic counseling, and other issues related to the provision of counseling services.
Refereed Serial

155 156   US   ISSN 0022-1325
L11   CODEN: JGPYAI
JOURNAL OF GENETIC PSYCHOLOGY; developmental and clinical psychology. 1891. q. $65. (Helen Dwight Reid Educational Foundation) Heldref Publications, 1319 Eighteenth St., N.W., Washington, DC 20036-1802. TEL 202-296-6267. FAX 202-296-5149. Ed. Marcie Kanakis. bibl.; charts; index; circ. 1,450. (also avail. in microfilm; reprint service avail. from SWZ) **Indexed:** Abstr.Soc.Work, Adol.Ment.Hlth.Abstr., Bibl.Dev.Med.& Child Neur., Biol.Abstr., C.I.J.E., Child Devel.Abstr., Curr.Adv.Ecol.Sci., Curr.Cont., DSH Abstr., Except.Child Educ.Abstr., Excerp.Med., Ind.Med., Indian Psychol.Abstr., Lang.& Lang.Behav.Abstr., Mid.East: Abstr.& Ind., Psychol.Abstr., Psycscan D.P., Soc.Sci.Ind., Soc.Work Res.& Abstr., Sociol.Educ.Abstr., SSCI, Stud.Wom.Abstr.
—BLDSC shelfmark: 4989.900000.
Refereed Serial

130   US   ISSN 0022-1449
JOURNAL OF GRAPHOANALYSIS. 1929. m. International Graphoanalysis Society, 111 N. Canal St., Chicago, IL 60606. TEL 312-930-9440. Ed. S.A. Ferrara. bk.rev.; abstr.; bibl.; charts; illus.; tr.lit.; circ. 35,000.

150.19   US   ISSN 0731-1273
RC488.A1
JOURNAL OF GROUP PSYCHOTHERAPY, PSYCHODRAMA & SOCIOMETRY. 1947. q. $55 (foreign $64). (American Society of Group Psychotherapy and Psychodrama) Heldref Publications, 1319 Eighteenth St., N.W., Washington, DC 20036-1802. TEL 202-296-6267. FAX 202-296-5149. (Co-sponsor: Helen Dwight Reid Educational Foundation) Eds. Helen Kress, Martha Wedeman. adv.; bk.rev.; circ. 1,200. (also avail. in microform; reprint service avail.) **Indexed:** ASSIA, Curr.Cont., Psychol.Abstr., Sociol.Abstr., SSCI.
—BLDSC shelfmark: 4996.522000.
Former titles (until 1982): Group Psychotherapy, Psychodrama and Sociometry (ISSN 0146-6178); Handbook of International Sociometry (ISSN 0160-4635); (until 1975): Group Psychotherapy and Psychodrama (ISSN 0096-0586); Group Psychotherapy (ISSN 0017-4734); Sociometry, a Journal of Interpersonal Relations.
Description: Articles on the application of action methods to psychotherapy, consulting, and education.
Refereed Serial

152.4 610   UK   ISSN 0306-7297
QP303   CODEN: JHMSDT
JOURNAL OF HUMAN MOVEMENT STUDIES. 1975. bi-m. $35. Teviot Scientific Publications, 31 Montpelier Park, Edinburgh EH10 4LX, Scotland. Ed. W.J. Irvine. bk.rev.; cum.index. **Indexed:** Biol.Abstr., Curr.Cont., Ergon.Abstr., Excerp.Med., Lang.& Lang.Behav.Abstr., Phys.Ed.Ind., Sportsearch (1975-), SSCI.
—BLDSC shelfmark: 5003.418000.

150 170   US   ISSN 0022-1678
BF1
JOURNAL OF HUMANISTIC PSYCHOLOGY. 1961. q. $40 to individuals; institutions $110. (Association for Humanistic Psychology) Sage Publications, Inc., 2455 Teller Rd., Newbury Park, CA 91320. TEL 805-499-0721. FAX 805-499-0871. Ed. Thomas C. Greening. adv.; bk.rev.; stat.; index, cum.index: 1961-1979; circ. 3,100. (also avail. in microfilm from UMI; reprint service avail. from UMI; back issues avail.) **Indexed:** ASSIA, C.I.J.E., Commun.Abstr., Curr.Cont., Lang.& Lang.Behav.Abstr., Mid.East: Abstr.& Ind., Psychol.Abstr., Soc.Sci.Ind., SSCI.
—BLDSC shelfmark: 5003.450000.

301.1 150   II   ISSN 0379-3885
BF1
JOURNAL OF INDIAN PSYCHOLOGY. 1977. s-a. $6 to individuals; institutions $9. (Andhra University, Department of Psychology & Parapsychology) Andhra University Press and Publications, Waltair, Visakhapatnam 530 003, Andhra Pradesh, India. **Indexed:** Psychol.Abstr.
Formerly: Indian Psychology.

JOURNAL OF INSTRUCTIONAL PSYCHOLOGY. see *EDUCATION*

616.89   MX
JOURNAL OF INTEGRATIVE AND ECLECTIC PSYCHOTHERAPY. 1982. 4/yr. $34 to individuals (foreign $39); institutions $65 (foreign $70). International Academy of Eclectic Psychotherapists, c/o Emmanuel O. Olukotun, Apdo. 51042, 45080 Guadalajara, Jalisco, Mexico. FAX 36-21-00-61. adv.; bk.rev.; circ. 500. **Indexed:** Psychol.Abstr.
Formerly (until 1986): International Journal of Eclectic Psychotherapy (ISSN 0729-8579)
Description: Forum for the exploration and advancement of integrative psycho-social treatments and the synthesis of therapy methods, theories and formats.

JOURNAL OF INTERPERSONAL VIOLENCE; concerned with the study and treatment of victims and perpetrators of physical and sexual violence. see *CRIMINOLOGY AND LAW ENFORCEMENT*

301.1 150   UK   ISSN 0261-927X
JOURNAL OF LANGUAGE AND SOCIAL PSYCHOLOGY. 1982. 4/yr. £68($143) Multilingual Matters Ltd., Bank House, 8a Hill Rd., Clevedon, Avon BS21 7HH, England. TEL 0272-876519. FAX 0272-343096. Ed. Howard Giles. adv.; bk.rev.; index; circ. 500. (back issues avail.) **Indexed:** Lang.& Lang.Behav.Abstr. (1985-), Lang.Teach.& Ling.Abstr., Psychol.Abstr.
—BLDSC shelfmark: 5010.096000.

JOURNAL OF LEARNING DISABILITIES. see *EDUCATION — Special Education And Rehabilitation*

JOURNAL OF MANAGERIAL PSYCHOLOGY. see *BUSINESS AND ECONOMICS — Management*

301.4   US   ISSN 0194-472X
HQ1   CODEN: JMFTA
JOURNAL OF MARITAL AND FAMILY THERAPY. 1975. q. $45 to individuals; institutions $75. American Association for Marriage and Family Therapy, 1100 17th St., N.W., 10th fl., Washington, DC 20036. Ed. Douglas Sprenkle. adv.; bk.rev.; circ. 18,000. (also avail. in microform from UMI; reprint service avail. from UMI,KTO) **Indexed:** Abstr.Soc.Work., Adol.Ment.Hlth.Abstr., Biol.Abstr., C.I.J.E., CERDIC, Curr.Cont., Excerp.Med., Lang.& Lang.Behav.Abstr., Past.Care & Couns.Abstr., Psychol.Abstr., Sage Fam.Stud.Abstr., Soc.Work Res.& Abstr., Sociol.Abstr., SSCI, Stud.Wom.Abstr.
—BLDSC shelfmark: 5012.060000.
Formerly (until 1979): Journal of Marriage and Family Counseling (ISSN 0094-5102)

JOURNAL OF MASS MEDIA ETHICS. see *COMMUNICATIONS*

150   US   ISSN 0022-2496
BF1   CODEN: JMTPAJ
JOURNAL OF MATHEMATICAL PSYCHOLOGY. 1964. q. $200 (foreign $246). Academic Press, Inc., Journal Division, 1250 Sixth Ave., San Diego, CA 92101. TEL 619-230-1840. FAX 619-699-6800. TELEX 181726. Ed. Thomas S. Wallsten. adv.; bibl.; charts. (back issues avail.) **Indexed:** Biol.Abstr., Child Devel.Abstr., Compumath, Curr.Cont., J.Cont.Quant.Meth., Math.R., Psychol.Abstr., SSCI.
—BLDSC shelfmark: 5012.420000.
Description: Presents theoretical and empirical research in all areas of mathematical psychology.
Refereed Serial

362.2   US   ISSN 1040-2861
BF637.C6
JOURNAL OF MENTAL HEALTH COUNSELING. 1979. q. $38 to individuals; institutions $82. (American Mental Health Counselors Association) Sage Publications, Inc., 2455 Teller Rd., Newbury Park, CA 91320. TEL 805-499-0721. FAX 805-499-0871. (And: Sage Publications Ltd., 6 Bonhill St., London EC2A 4PU, England) Ed. Lawrence H. Gerstein. circ. 13,500. **Indexed:** C.I.J.E., Psychol.Abstr., Soc.Work Res.& Abstr.
Formerly: A M H C A Journal (ISSN 0193-1830)

150   US   ISSN 0364-5541
BF367
JOURNAL OF MENTAL IMAGERY. 1977. 4/yr. $40 to individuals; institutions $75. (International Imagery Association) Brandon House, Inc., Box 240, Bronx, NY 10471. Ed. Dr. Akhter Ahsen. adv.; bk.rev.; charts. (back issues avail.) **Indexed:** Curr.Cont., Psychol.Abstr., Soc.Sci.Ind.
—BLDSC shelfmark: 5017.690000.

150 121   US   ISSN 0271-0137
BF1
JOURNAL OF MIND AND BEHAVIOR; an interdisciplinary journal. 1980. q. $42 to individuals; institutions $73. Institute of Mind & Behavior, Box 522, Village Sta., New York, NY 10014. TEL 212-595-4853. Ed. Dr. Raymond Russ. adv.; bk.rev.; abstr.; charts; illus.; stat.; index; circ. 1,089 (controlled). **Indexed:** Curr.Cont., Lang.& Lang.Behav.Abstr., Phil.Ind., Phys.Abstr., Psychol.Abstr., Soc.Work Res.& Abstr., Sociol.Abstr., SSCI.
—BLDSC shelfmark: 5020.140000.
Description: Publishes articles pertaining to mind and body epistemology in the social sciences, theory of consciousness and ideation, and historical investigations of science.

152.3   US   ISSN 0022-2895
QP303   CODEN: JMTBAB
JOURNAL OF MOTOR BEHAVIOR. Short title: J M B. 1969. q. $40 to individuals; institutions $79. (Helen Dwight Reid Educational Foundation) Heldref Publications, 1319 Eighteenth St., N.W., Washington, DC 20036-1802. TEL 202-296-5149. FAX 202-296-5149. Ed. Betty Adelman. abstr.; bibl.; charts; illus.; circ. 1,300. (also avail. in microform; reprint service avail.) Indexed: Biol.Abstr., Child Devel.Abstr., Curr.Cont., Ergon.Abstr., Excerp.Med., Lang.& Lang.Behav.Abstr., Phys.Ed.Ind., Psychol.Abstr., Sp.Ed.Needs Abstr., Sportsearch (1974-), SSCI.
—BLDSC shelfmark: 5021.050000.
Refereed Serial

371.9   US   ISSN 0883-8534
LC3701
JOURNAL OF MULTICULTURAL COUNSELING AND DEVELOPMENT. 1972. 4/yr. $10. (Association for Multicultural Counseling and Development) American Association for Counseling and Development, 5999 Stevenson Ave., Alexandria, VA 22304. TEL 703-823-9800. FAX 703-823-0252. Ed. Frederick Harper. adv.; circ. 4,000. (also avail. in microform from UMI; reprint service avail. from UMI) Indexed: C.I.J.E., Educ.Ind., Psychol.Abstr., Soc.Work Res.& Abstr.
Formerly: Journal of Non-White Concerns in Personnel and Guidance (ISSN 0090-5461)
Description: Issues include state-of-the-art multicultural counseling research and reports on applications of the latest theoretical ideas and concepts.

155.937   US   ISSN 0891-4494
BF789.D4   CODEN: JNDAE7
JOURNAL OF NEAR-DEATH STUDIES. 1981. q. $125 (foreign $145). (International Association for Near-Death Studies) Human Sciences Press, Inc. (Subsidiary of: Plenum Publishing Corp.), 233 Spring St., New York, NY 10013-1578. TEL 212-620-8000. FAX 212-463-0742. Ed. Dr. Bruce Greyson. adv.; bk.rev. (reprint service avail. from UMI) Indexed: Psychol.Abstr., Soc.Work Res.& Abstr.
—BLDSC shelfmark: 5021.392000.
Formerly (until 1986): Anabiosis: The Journal for Near-Death Studies (ISSN 0743-6238)
Description: Publishes articles on the empirical effects and theoretical implications of near-dearth experiences.
Refereed Serial

301.3 150   US   ISSN 0191-5886
BF353   CODEN: JNVBDV
JOURNAL OF NONVERBAL BEHAVIOR. 1976. q. $165 (foreign $195). Human Sciences Press, Inc. (Subsidiary of: Plenum Publishing Corp.), 233 Spring St., New York, NY 10013-1578. TEL 212-620-8000. FAX 212-463-0742. Ed. Miles Patterson. adv. (also avail. in microform from UMI; reprint service avail. from ISI,UMI) Indexed: Biol.Abstr., C.I.J.E., Child Devel.Abstr., Commun.Abstr., Curr.Adv.Ecol.Sci., Curr.Cont., Human Resour.Abstr., M.L.A., Psychol.Abstr., Psychol.R.G., Saf.Sci.Abstr., Sage Fam.Stud.Abstr., Soc.Work Res.& Abstr., Sp.Ed.Needs Abstr., SSCI.
—BLDSC shelfmark: 5022.843000.
Formerly (until 1979): Environmental Psychology and Nonverbal Behavior (ISSN 0361-3496)
Description: Presents theoretical and empirical research on nonverbal communications including paralanguage, proxemics, facial expressions, eye contact, face-to-face interaction, and nonverbal emotive expression.
Refereed Serial

158   UK   ISSN 0963-1798
HF5548.8   CODEN: JOCCEF
JOURNAL OF OCCUPATIONAL AND ORGANIZATIONAL PSYCHOLOGY. 1922. q. $148. British Psychological Society, St. Andrews House, 48 Princess Rd. East, Leicester LE1 7DR, England. TEL 0533-549568. FAX 0533-470787. Ed. Dr. M. West. adv.; bk.rev.; charts; illus.; index; circ. 2,200. (also avail. in microform from SWZ; reprint service avail. from ISI,SWZ) Indexed: ABI Inform., Account.& Data Proc.Abstr., Anbar., ASSIA, Biol.Abstr., BMT, BPIA, Br.Educ.Ind., Br.Hum.Ind., Bus.Ind., C.I.S. Abstr., Cont.Pg.Manage., Curr.Cont., Ergon.Abstr., Hlth.Ind., Ind.Med., Int.Lab.Doc., Lang.& Lang.Behav.Abstr., Manage.Cont., Noise Pollut.Publ.Abstr., Pers.Lit., Psychol.Abstr., Psycscan, Res.High.Educ.Abstr., Sci.Abstr., SCIMP, Sp.Ed.Needs Abstr., SSCI, Stud.Wom.Abstr., Tr.& Indus.Ind.
—BLDSC shelfmark: 5026.082000.
Former titles: Journal of Occupational Psychology (ISSN 0305-8107); Occupational Psychology (ISSN 0029-7976)
Description: Examines industrial and organizational psychology, describes and interprets new research about people at work.

150   US   ISSN 0160-8061
HD58.7
JOURNAL OF ORGANIZATIONAL BEHAVIOR MANAGEMENT. 1977. s-a. $40 to individuals; institutions $90; libraries $150. Haworth Press, Inc., 10 Alice St., Binghamton, NY 13904. TEL 800-342-9678. FAX 607-722-1424. TELEX 4932599. Ed. Thomas C. Mawhinney. adv.; bk.rev.; circ. 545. (also avail. in microfiche from HAW; reprint service avail. from HAW) Indexed: ABI Inform., Abstr.Health Care Manage.Stud., Behav.Abstr., BPIA, Bull.Signal., Bus.Ind., Human Resour.Abstr., Manage.Cont., Oper.Res.Manage.Sci., Pers.Lit., Pers.Manage.Abstr., Psychol.Abstr., Psycscan, Qual.Contr.Appl.Stat., Sage Pub.Admin.Abstr., Tr.& Indus.Ind.
—BLDSC shelfmark: 5027.068000.
Description: Devoted to behavior management in organizations; provides systematic and effective approaches to behavior management.
Refereed Serial

301.1 150   UK   ISSN 0894-3796
HD6951   CODEN: JORBEJ
JOURNAL OF ORGANIZATIONAL BEHAVIOUR. 1979. 7/yr. $315 (effective 1992). John Wiley & Sons Ltd., Baffins Lane, Chichester, Sussex PO19 1UD, England. TEL 0243-779777. FAX 0243-775878. TELEX 86290 WIBOOK G. Ed. Cary L. Cooper. (reprint service avail. from ISI,SWZ,UMI) Indexed: ABI Inform., ASSIA, BPIA, Bus.Ind., Cont.Pg.Manage., Curr.Cont., Ergon.Abstr., Int.Lab.Doc., Lang.& Lang.Behav.Abstr., Noise Pollut.Publ.Abstr., Psychol.Abstr., Psycscan, Sage Fam.Stud.Abstr., SCIMP (1982-), SSCI, Tr.& Indus.Ind.
—BLDSC shelfmark: 5027.066000.
Formerly (until 1988): Journal of Occupational Behaviour (ISSN 0142-2774)
Description: Aims to report and review the growing research in the industry - organizational behavior fields, and in all topics associated with occupational - organizational behavior.

JOURNAL OF PASTORAL CARE. see *RELIGIONS AND THEOLOGY*

155.4   US   ISSN 0146-8693
RJ503.3   CODEN: JPPSDW
JOURNAL OF PEDIATRIC PSYCHOLOGY. 1976. bi-m. $275 (foreign $320)(effective 1992). (Society of Pediatric Psychology) Plenum Publishing Corp., 233 Spring St., New York, NY 10013-1578. TEL 212-620-8000. FAX 212-463-0742. TELEX 23-421139. Ed. Michael C. Roberts. adv. (also avail. in microfilm from JSC; back issues avail.) Indexed: Bibl.Dev.Med.& Child Neur., Biol.Abstr., Child Devel.Abstr., CINAHL, Curr.Cont., Excerp.Med., Ind.Med., Psychol.Abstr., Psycscan D.P., Risk Abstr., Soc.Work Res.& Abstr., Sociol.Abstr., Sp.Ed.Needs Abstr.
—BLDSC shelfmark: 5030.260000.
Formerly: Pediatric Psychology.
Refereed Serial

155.2   US   ISSN 0022-3506
BF1   CODEN: JOPEAE
JOURNAL OF PERSONALITY. 1932. q. $36 to individuals (foreign $44); institutions $72 (foreign $80); students $18 (foreign $26). Duke University Press, 6697 College Station, Durham, NC 27708. TEL 919-684-2173. FAX 919-684-8644. Ed. Stephen G. West. adv.; bibl.; charts; illus.; index; circ. 2,000. (also avail. in microform from MIM,UMI; reprint service avail. from ISI,UMI) Indexed: Acad.Ind., Adol.Ment.Hlth.Abstr., ASSIA, Biol.Abstr., Commun.Abstr., Curr.Cont., Educ.Ind., Ind.Med., Lang.& Lang.Behav.Abstr., Mid.East: Abstr.& Ind., Past.Care & Couns.Abstr., Psychol.Abstr., Risk Abstr., Soc.Sci.Ind., SSCI.
—BLDSC shelfmark: 5030.900000.
Refereed Serial

152 158.3   II   ISSN 0970-1206
JOURNAL OF PERSONALITY AND CLINICAL STUDIES. (Text in English) bi-m. (Association of Clinical Psychologists) Habib Ahmad, c/o Samar Offset Printers, 1788 Kalan Mahal Daryaganj, New Dehli 110 002, India. Ed.Bd. Indexed: Psychol.Abstr.
—BLDSC shelfmark: 5030.900500.

155.2   US   ISSN 0022-3514
HM251   CODEN: JPSPB2
JOURNAL OF PERSONALITY AND SOCIAL PSYCHOLOGY. (Contains material formerly covered by the Journal of Abnormal and Social Psychology) 1965. m. $247 to non-members (foreign $283); members $99; institutions $495 (foreign $567) (effective 1992). American Psychological Association, 750 First St., N.E., Washington, DC 20002-4242. TEL 202-336-5500. FAX 202-336-5568. Ed.Bd. adv.; charts; stat.; index; circ. 5,500. (also avail. in microform from MIM,UMI; reprint service avail. from UMI) Indexed: Acad.Ind., Adol.Ment.Hlth.Abstr., ASSIA, Biol.Abstr., C.I.J.E., Chic.Per.Ind., Child Devel.Abstr., Commun.Abstr., Crim.Just.Abstr., Curr.Cont., Educ.Admin.Abstr., Ind.Med., INIS Atomind., M.L.A., Mid.East: Abstr.& Ind., PSI, Psychol.Abstr., Psycscan D.P., Sage Fam.Stud.Abstr., Sage Urb.Stud.Abstr., Soc.Sci.Ind., Soc.Work Res.& Abstr., Sp.Ed.Needs Abstr., Sportsearch, SSCI, Stud.Wom.Abstr.
—BLDSC shelfmark: 5030.901000.
Description: Research in three major areas: attitudes and social cognition; interpersonal relations and group processes; and personality processes and individual differences.
Refereed Serial

155.2   US   ISSN 0022-3891
BF698.4
JOURNAL OF PERSONALITY ASSESSMENT. vol.34, 1970. 6/yr, 2 vols. $65 to individuals (foreign $95); institutions $200 (foreign $245). (Society for Personality Assessment) Lawrence Erlbaum Associates, Inc., 365 Broadway, Hillsdale, NJ 07642. TEL 201-666-4110. FAX 201-666-2394. (Alt. addr.: c/o Ann O'Rourk, 866 Amelia Ct., N.E., St. Petersburg, FL 33702-2784) Ed. Dr. Irving B. Weiner. adv.; bk.rev.; abstr.; bibl.; charts; illus.; index; circ. 2,700. (also avail. in microform from UMI; reprint service avail. from UMI,SCH) Indexed: Adol.Ment.Hlth.Abstr., ASSIA, Biol.Abstr., C.I.S. Abstr., Child Devel.Abstr., Curr.Cont., Except.Child.Educ.Abstr., Excerp.Med., Ind.Med., Lang.& Lang.Behav.Abstr., Mid.East: Abstr.& Ind., Psychol.Abstr., Psycscan C.P., SSCI.
—BLDSC shelfmark: 5030.950000.
Formerly: Journal of Projective Techniques and Personality Assessment.
Description: Presents commentaries, case reports, and research studies dealing with the application of methods of personality assessment.
Refereed Serial

370.15   US   ISSN 0885-579X
RC554
JOURNAL OF PERSONALITY DISORDERS. 1986. 4/yr. $32 to individuals; institutions $77. (International Society for the Study of Personality Disorders) Guilford Publications, Inc., 72 Spring St., 4th Fl., New York, NY 10012. TEL 212-431-9800. FAX 212-966-6708. Eds. Theodore Millon, Allen J. Frances. adv.; bk.rev.; index. (reprint service avail.) Indexed: Biol.Abstr., Excerp.Med., Psychol.Abstr., Soc.Work Res.& Abstr.
—BLDSC shelfmark: 5030.955000.
Description: Presents new research, and clinical techniques for assessing, diagnosing and treating personality disorders.
Refereed Serial

PSYCHOLOGY

150 US ISSN 0047-2662
BF204.5 CODEN: JPHPAE
JOURNAL OF PHENOMENOLOGICAL PSYCHOLOGY; studies in the science of human experience and behavior. (Text in English, French and German; summaries in English) 1970. 2/yr. $39.95 to individuals; libraries $50. Humanities Press, 165 First Ave., Atlantic Highlands, NJ 07716-1289. TEL 908-872-1441. FAX 908-872-0717. Ed. A. Giorgi. adv.; bk.rev.; index. (also avail. in microform from UMI; reprint service avail. from UMI) **Indexed:** Curr.Cont., Psychol.Abstr., SSCI.
—BLDSC shelfmark: 5034.100000.
Description: For the application of phenomenological research to the problems of psychology.

JOURNAL OF POETRY THERAPY; the interdisciplinary journal of practice, theory, research, and education. see LITERATURE — Poetry

150 616.8 US ISSN 0737-1195
JOURNAL OF POLYMORPHOUS PERVERSITY. 1984. s-a. $14 to individuals; institutions $20; foreign $21.75. Wry-Bred Press, Inc., Box 1454 Madison Sq. Sta., New York, NY 10159-1454. TEL 212-689-5473. Ed. Glenn C. Ellenbogen. bk.rev.; circ. 4,125. (back issues avail.)
Description: Humorous and satirical look at the fields of psychology, psychiatry, medicine and education.

613 US ISSN 0278-095X
RA790.A1 CODEN: JPPRDT
JOURNAL OF PRIMARY PREVENTION. 1980. q. $155 (foreign $180). (Vermont Conference on Primary Prevention of Psychopathology) Human Sciences Press, Inc. (Subsidiary of: Plenum Publishing Corp.), 233 Spring St., New York, NY 10013-1578. TEL 212-620-8000. FAX 212-463-0742. Ed. Thomas P. Gullotta. adv. (reprint service avail. from ISI,UMI) **Indexed:** Adol.Ment.Hlth.Abstr., Biol.Abstr., Excerp.Med., Psychol.Abstr., Sociol.Abstr.
—BLDSC shelfmark: 5042.370000.
Formerly (until vol.2): Journal of Prevention (ISSN 0163-514X)
Description: Presents theoretical, empirical, and methodological research on preventative intervention in human services and discusses innovative programs and concepts.
Refereed Serial

JOURNAL OF PSYCHOACTIVE DRUGS; a multidisciplinary forum. see DRUG ABUSE AND ALCOHOLISM

370.15 150 US ISSN 0734-2829
LB1131 CODEN: JPSAES
JOURNAL OF PSYCHOEDUCATIONAL ASSESSMENT. 1982. q. $45 to individuals; institutions $120. Clinical Psychology Publishing Co., Inc., 4 Conant Sq., Brandon, VT 05733. TEL 802-247-6871. FAX 802-247-6853. Ed. Dr. Bruce Bracken. adv.; bk.rev.; bibl.; charts; illus.; index; circ. 1,700. (back issues avail.) **Indexed:** Psychol.Abstr.
—BLDSC shelfmark: 5043.275000.
Refereed Serial

900 150 US ISSN 0145-3378
HQ768 CODEN: JOPSDP
JOURNAL OF PSYCHOHISTORY. 1973. q. $52 to individuals; institutions $99. Association for Psychohistory, Inc., Atcom Bldg., 2315 Broadway, New York, NY 10024-4397. TEL 212-873-3760. FAX 212-799-1728. Ed. Lloyd deMause. adv.; bk.rev.; illus.; circ. 1,500. (also avail. in microform from UMI; reprint service avail. from UMI) **Indexed:** Amer.Hist.& Life, Child Devel.Abstr., Curr.Lit.Fam.Plan., Hist.Abstr., Lang.& Lang.Behav.Abstr., Mid.East: Abstr.& Ind., Psychol.Abstr., Sociol.Abstr.
—BLDSC shelfmark: 5043.280000.
Incorporates (1978-1988): Journal of Psychoanalytic Anthropology (ISSN 0278-2944); **Formerly (until 1976):** History of Childhood Quarterly (ISSN 0091-4266)

JOURNAL OF PSYCHOLINGUISTIC RESEARCH. see LINGUISTICS

150 II ISSN 0022-3972
BF1 CODEN: JPSRB8
JOURNAL OF PSYCHOLOGICAL RESEARCHES. (Text in English) 1957. 3/yr. Rs.60($21) Madras Psychology Society, University of Madras, Department of Psychology, Madras 600005, India. Ed. Dr. T.E. Shanmugam. adv.; bk.rev.; charts; index; circ. 400. (also avail. in microform from UMI; reprint service avail. from UMI) **Indexed:** Biol.Abstr., Psychol.Abstr.

150 US ISSN 0022-3980
BF1
JOURNAL OF PSYCHOLOGY; the general field of psychology. 1936. bi-m. $88. (Helen Dwight Reid Educational Foundation) Heldref Publications, 1319 Eighteenth St., N.W., Washington, DC 20036-1802. TEL 202-296-6267. FAX 202-296-5149. Ed. Doris Chalfin. bibl.; index; circ. 1,650. (reprint service avail. from SWZ) **Indexed:** Abstr.Soc.Work., Acad.Ind., Biol.Abstr., C.I.J.E., CERDIC, Chem.Abstr., Chic.Per.Ind., Child Devel.Abstr., Commun.Abstr., Crim.Just.Abstr., DSH Abstr., Ergon.Abstr., Except.Child.Educ.Abstr., Excerp.Med., Ind.Med., Indian Psychol.Abstr., Lang.& Lang.Behav.Abstr., Mid.East: Abstr.& Ind., Psychol.Abstr., SSCI, Stud.Wom.Abstr.
—BLDSC shelfmark: 5043.400000.
Refereed Serial

150 US ISSN 0733-4273
BR110
JOURNAL OF PSYCHOLOGY AND CHRISTIANITY. 1982. q. $35 to individuals; libraries $50. Christian Association for Psychological Studies International, c/o Robert R. King, Jr., Box 890279, Temecula, CA 92589. TEL 714-695-2277. FAX 714-695-3431. Ed. Peter C. Hill. adv.; bk.rev.; circ. 2,300. (also avail. in microfilm from UMI; back issues avail.; reprint service avail. from UMI) **Indexed:** A.S.& T.Ind., Educ.Ind., PSI, Psychol.Abstr., R.G., Rel.& Theol.Abstr. (1986-), Rel.Ind.One, Soc.Sci.Ind.
Supersedes (1974-1981): Christian Association for Psychological Studies. Bulletin; **Incorporates:** Christian Association for Psychological Studies. Proceedings (ISSN 0092-072X)
Description: Investigation of theoretical and applied issues in the relationship of Christianity and the psychological and pastoral professions.

155.3 US ISSN 0890-7064
BF692 CODEN: JPSXET
JOURNAL OF PSYCHOLOGY & HUMAN SEXUALITY. 1988. q. $24 to individuals; institutions $35; libraries $95. Haworth Press, Inc., 10 Alice St., Binghamton, NY 13904. TEL 800-342-8678. FAX 607-722-1424. TELEX 4932599. Ed. Eli Coleman. adv.; bk.rev.; circ. 207. (also avail. in microform from HAW; reprint service avail. from HAW) **Indexed:** Soc.Work Res.& Abstr.
—BLDSC shelfmark: 5043.408000.
Description: Publishes original articles and reviews about human sexuality.
Refereed Serial

156 296 US ISSN 0700-9801
BF51 CODEN: JPJUD8
JOURNAL OF PSYCHOLOGY AND JUDAISM. 1976. q. $135 (foreign $150). Human Sciences Press, Inc. (Subsidiary of: Plenum Publishing Corp.), 233 Spring St., New York, NY 10013-1578. TEL 212-620-8000. FAX 212-463-0742. Ed. Dr. Reuben P. Bulka. adv.; bk.rev.; circ. 1,000. (also avail. in microform from UMI; reprint service avail. from ISI,UMI) **Indexed:** Curr.Cont., Excerp.Med., G.Soc.Sci.& Rel.Per.Lit., Ind.Jew.Per., Mid.East: Abstr.& Ind., MLA, Past.Care & Couns.Abstr., Psychol.Abstr., Rel.& Theol.Abstr. (1979-), Rel.Ind.One, SSCI.
—BLDSC shelfmark: 5043.410000.
Incorporates (1986-1991): Journal of Aging and Judaism (ISSN 0884-8688)
Description: Explores the relationship between modern psychology and Judaism on philosophical and clinical levels.
Refereed Serial

150 200 US ISSN 0091-6471
BF1 CODEN: JPSTDG
JOURNAL OF PSYCHOLOGY AND THEOLOGY; an evangelical forum for the integration of psychology and theology. 1973. q. $32 (foreign $35). Biola University, Rosemead School of Psychology, 13800 Biola Ave., La Mirada, CA 90639. TEL 213-903-6000. Ed. William F. Hunter. adv.; bk.rev.; circ. 1,700. (also avail. in microform from UMI; back issues avail.; reprint service avail. from UMI) **Indexed:** Arts & Hum.Cit.Ind., CERDIC, Chr.Per.Ind., Curr.Cont., G.Soc.Sci.& Rel.Per.Lit., Old Test.Abstr., Psychol.Abstr., Psychol.R.G., Rel.& Theol.Abstr. (1973-), Rel.Ind.One, SSCI.
●Also available online. Vendor(s): BRS, DIALOG.
—BLDSC shelfmark: 5043.420000.
Description: Communicates recent scholarly thinking on the interrelationships of psychological and theological concepts and considers the application of these concepts to a variety of professional settings.

150 US ISSN 0882-2689
BF698.4 CODEN: JPBAEB
JOURNAL OF PSYCHOPATHOLOGY AND BEHAVIORAL ASSESSMENT. 1979. q. $190 (foreign $220)(effective 1992). Plenum Publishing Corp., 233 Spring St., New York, NY 10013-1578. TEL 212-620-8000. FAX 212-463-0742. TELEX 23-421139. Eds. Henry E. Adams, Samuel M. Turner. adv.; bk.rev. (also avail. in microfilm from JSC; back issues avail.) **Indexed:** Adol.Ment.Hlth.Abstr., Biol.Abstr., Curr.Cont., Excerp.Med., Psychol.Abstr., Ref.Zh., Soc.Work Res.& Abstr., SSCI.
—BLDSC shelfmark: 5043.430000.
Formerly (until 1986): Journal of Behavioral Assessment (ISSN 0164-0305)
Refereed Serial

JOURNAL OF PSYCHOPHARMACOLOGY. see PHARMACY AND PHARMACOLOGY

616.8 GW ISSN 0269-8803
JOURNAL OF PSYCHOPHYSIOLOGY. 1987. q. Verlag fuer Psychologie Dr. C.J. Hogrefe, Rihnsweg 25, Postfach 3751, 3400 Goettingen, Germany. TEL 0551-54044. Eds. G. Sartory, I. Martin. adv.; bk.rev. **Indexed:** Excerp.Med., Psychol.Abstr.
—BLDSC shelfmark: 5043.465000.
Description: Outlet for original research in all areas employing psychophysiological techniques.

158 US ISSN 0894-9085
RC489.R3
JOURNAL OF RATIONAL-EMOTIVE AND COGNITIVE-BEHAVIOR THERAPY. 1983. q. $150 (foreign $175). (Institute for Rational-Emotive Therapy) Human Sciences Press, Inc. (Subsidiary of: Plenum Publishing Corp.), 233 Spring St., New York, NY 10013-1578. TEL 212-620-8000. FAX 212-463-0742. Eds. Russel Grieger, Paul J. Woods. adv.; bk.rev.; illus. (also avail. in microform from UMI; reprint service avail. from UMI) **Indexed:** Adol.Ment.Hlth.Abstr., Lang.& Lang.Behav.Abstr., Psychol.Abstr.
—BLDSC shelfmark: 5046.800000.
Formerly (until 1987): Journal of Rational-Emotive Therapy (ISSN 0748-1985); **Supersedes (1966-1983):** Rational Living (ISSN 0034-0049)
Description: Provides a forum for the stimulation and maintenance of rational-emotive therapy and other forms of cognitive-behavior therapy.
Refereed Serial

370.1 US ISSN 1054-0830
JOURNAL OF REGRESSION THERAPY. 1986. a. $8 to individuals; libraries $15. Association for Past-Life Research and Therapy, Inc., Box 20151, Riverside, CA 92516. TEL 714-784-1570. bk.rev.; circ. 800.

PSYCHOLOGY 4033

152 US ISSN 0092-6566
BF1 CODEN: JRPRA6
JOURNAL OF RESEARCH IN PERSONALITY. 1965. q. $151 (foreign $187). Academic Press, Inc., Journal Division, 1250 Sixth Ave., San Diego, CA 92101. TEL 619-230-1840. FAX 619-699-6800. TELEX 181726. Ed. William Griffitt. adv.; charts. (back issues avail.) **Indexed:** Adol.Ment.Hlth.Abstr., ASSIA, Biol.Abstr., Commun.Abstr., Crim.Just.Abstr., Curr.Adv.Ecol.Sci., Curr.Cont., Excerp.Med., Mid.East: Abstr.& Ind., Psychol.Abstr., Soc.Work Res.& Abstr., SSCI.
—BLDSC shelfmark: 5052.025000.
Formerly: Journal of Experimental Research in Personality (ISSN 0022-1023)
Description: Examines issues in the field of personality and in related fields basic to the understanding of personality.
Refereed Serial

JOURNAL OF RESEARCH ON ADOLESCENCE. see *CHILDREN AND YOUTH — About*

JOURNAL OF RISK AND UNCERTAINTY. see *BUSINESS AND ECONOMICS*

150 US ISSN 0276-2285
RA790.A1
JOURNAL OF RURAL COMMUNITY PSYCHOLOGY. 1980. s-a. $20 to individuals; institutions $30. California School of Professional Psychology - Fresno, 1350 M St., Fresno, CA 93721. TEL 209-486-8420. FAX 209-486-0734. Eds. Mary Beth Kenkel, I.M. Abou-Ghorra. adv.; bk.rev.; bibl.; circ. 160. (reprint service avail. from UMI) **Indexed:** Psychol.Abstr.
—BLDSC shelfmark: 5052.126000.

150 US
BF1
JOURNAL OF RUSSIAN AND EAST EUROPEAN PSYCHOLOGY; a journal of translations. 1962. bi-m. $330 to institutions. M.E. Sharpe, Inc., 80 Business Park Dr., Armonk, NY 10504. TEL 914-273-1800. FAX 914-273-2106. Ed. Michael Cole. adv.; charts; index. **Indexed:** Adol.Ment.Hlth.Abstr., Biol.Abstr., Psychol.Abstr.
Formerly: Soviet Psychology (ISSN 0038-5751)
Refereed Serial

370.15 US ISSN 0022-4405
LB3013.6 CODEN: JSCPAA
JOURNAL OF SCHOOL PSYCHOLOGY. 1963. q. $130 (effective 1992). Pergamon Press, Inc., Journals Division, 660 White Plains Rd., Tarrytown, NY 10591-5153. TEL 914-524-9200. FAX 914-333-2444. (And: Headington Hill Hall, Oxford, OX3 0BW, England. TEL 0865-794141) Ed. Raymond S. Dean. adv.; bk.rev.; abstr.; bibl.; index; circ. 2,000. (also avail. in microform from MIM,UMI; reprint service avail. from ISI,UMI) **Indexed:** Adol.Ment.Hlth.Abstr., ASCA, C.I.J.E., Cont.Pg.Educ., Curr.Cont., Educ.Ind., Except.Child Educ.Abstr., Lang.& Lang.Behav.Abstr., Psychol.Abstr., Sp.Ed.Needs Abstr., SSCI.
—BLDSC shelfmark: 5052.670000.
Description: Publishes original articles on research and practice relevant to the development of school psychology as both a scientific and an applied specialty.
Refereed Serial

155.3 US ISSN 0092-623X
RC556 CODEN: JSMTB
JOURNAL OF SEX & MARITAL THERAPY. 1974. q. $38 to individuals (foreign $42); institutions $75 (foreign $83). Brunner-Mazel Publishing Co., 19 Union Sq. W., New York, NY 10003. TEL 212-924-3344. Ed.Bd. adv.; bk.rev.; index; circ. 2,000. (also avail. in microform from UMI; reprint service avail. from ISI,UMI) **Indexed:** Adol.Ment.Hlth.Abstr., Biol.Abstr., Curr.Cont., Excerp.Med., Ind.Med., Lang.& Lang.Behav.Abstr., Mid.East: Abstr.& Ind., Psychol.Abstr., Sage Fam.Stud.Abstr., SSCI, Stud.Wom.Abstr.
—BLDSC shelfmark: 5064.017000.
Description: Contemporary forum for new clinical techniques and conceptualizations and research in sex and marital therapy.

JOURNAL OF SEX EDUCATION AND THERAPY. see *EDUCATION*

155.3 US ISSN 0022-4499
HQ5 CODEN: JSXRAJ
JOURNAL OF SEX RESEARCH. 1965. 4/yr. $47 to individuals; institutions $74. Society for the Scientific Study of Sex, Box 208, Mount Vernon, IA 52314. TEL 319-895-8407. Ed. Paul Abramson. adv.; bk.rev.; charts; illus.; stat.; circ. 1,600. (also avail. in microfilm from UMI; back issues avail.; reprint service avail. from SWZ,UMI) **Indexed:** Abstr.Anthropol., Adol.Ment.Hlth.Abstr., ASSIA, Commun.Abstr., Curr.Cont., Curr.Lit.Fam.Plan., Excerp.Med., Lang.& Lang.Behav.Abstr., Mid.East: Abstr.& Ind., Psychol.Abstr., Sociol.Abstr., SSCI, Stud.Wom.Abstr.
—BLDSC shelfmark: 5064.020000.

301.1 US ISSN 0736-7236
RC467
JOURNAL OF SOCIAL AND CLINICAL PSYCHOLOGY. 1983. q. $35 to individuals; institutions $95. Guilford Publications, Inc., 72 Spring St., 4th Fl., New York, NY 10012. TEL 212-431-9800. FAX 212-966-6708. Ed. C.R. Snyder. adv.; bk.rev.; index; circ. 500. (back issues avail.) **Indexed:** Curr.Cont., Psychol.Abstr., Soc.Work Res.& Abstr., Sp.Ed.Needs Abstr., Stud.Wom.Abstr.
—BLDSC shelfmark: 5064.718000.
Description: Covers theory, research and practice in the growing interface of social and clinical psychology.
Refereed Serial

150 UK ISSN 0265-4075
CODEN: JSRLE9
JOURNAL OF SOCIAL AND PERSONAL RELATIONSHIPS. 1984. q. £33($54) to individuals; institutions £85($140). Sage Publications Ltd., 6 Bonhill St., London EC2A 4PU, England. TEL 071-374-0645. FAX 071-374-8741. Ed. Steve Duck. adv.: color page #170; trim 177 x 101; adv. contact: Bernie Folan. bk.rev. **Indexed:** ASSIA, Curr.Cont., Sociol.Educ.Abstr., Stud.Wom.Abstr.
—BLDSC shelfmark: 5064.740000.
Description: Multidisciplinary examination of personal relationships, drawing on materials from the fields of social, clinical and developmental psychology, communications, and sociology.

150 300 US ISSN 0886-1641
BF698.A1 CODEN: JSBPE9
JOURNAL OF SOCIAL BEHAVIOR AND PERSONALITY. 1986. q. $30 to individuals; libraries $65. Select Press, Box 37, Corte Madera, CA 94925. TEL 415-924-1612. (back issues avail.) **Indexed:** Psychol.Abstr.
—BLDSC shelfmark: 5064.751500.
Description: Academic approach to the study of psychology, sociology, speech, management and other social sciences.

301.1 150 US ISSN 0022-4537
HN51 CODEN: JSISAF
JOURNAL OF SOCIAL ISSUES. 1944. q. $170 (foreign $200)(effective 1992). (Society for the Psychological Study of Social Issues) Plenum Publishing Corp., 233 Spring St., New York, NY 10013-1578. TEL 212-620-8000. FAX 212-463-0742. TELEX 23-421139. Ed. Stuart Oskamp. adv.; abstr.; bibl.; charts; index, cum.index. (also avail. in microfilm from UMI; reprint service avail. from KTO,UMI) **Indexed:** A.B.C.Pol.Sci., Abstr.Anthropol., Adol.Ment.Hlth.Abstr., Amer.Hist.& Life, ASSIA, Bus.Ind., C.I.J.E., Commun.Abstr., Crim.Just.Abstr., Curr.Cont., Curr.Lit.Fam.Plan., Educ.Admin.Abstr., Geo.Abstr., Hist.Abstr., Lang.& Lang.Behav.Abstr., Mid.East: Abstr.& Ind., P.A.I.S., Peace Res.Abstr., Psychol.Abstr., Psycscan, Sage Fam.Stud.Abstr., Sage Urb.Stud.Abstr., Soc.Sci.Ind., Soc.Work Res.& Abstr., Sp.Ed.Needs Abstr., SSCI, Stud.Wom.Abstr.
—BLDSC shelfmark: 5064.755000.
Refereed Serial

301.1 150 US ISSN 0022-4545
HM251.A1 CODEN: JSPSAG
JOURNAL OF SOCIAL PSYCHOLOGY. 1929. bi-m. $88. (Helen Dwight Reid Educational Foundation) Heldref Publications, 1319 Eighteenth St., N.W., Washington, DC 20036-1802. TEL 202-296-6267. FAX 202-296-5149. Ed. Juanita Ruffin. bibl.; charts; index; circ. 2,350. (reprint service avail. from SWZ) **Indexed:** Abstr.Soc.Work, Adol.Ment.Hlth.Abstr., ASSIA, Biol.Abstr., Child Devel.Abstr., Commun.Abstr., Crim.Just.Abstr., Curr.Cont., DSH Abstr., Except.Child Educ.Abstr., Excerp.Med., Ind.Med., Indian Psychol.Abstr., Lang.& Lang Behav.Abstr., Mid.East: Abstr.& Ind., Pers.Lit., PSI, Psychol.Abstr., Res.High.Educ.Abstr., Soc.Sci.Ind., Soc.Work Res.& Abstr., Sociol.Educ.Abstr., SSCI, Stud.Wom.Abstr.
—BLDSC shelfmark: 5064.800000.
Refereed Serial

150 US ISSN 0895-2779
GV706.4
JOURNAL OF SPORT AND EXERCISE PSYCHOLOGY. Short title: J S E P. 1979. q. $36 to individuals (foreign $40); institutions $80 (foreign $84); students $24 (foreign $28). Human Kinetics Publishers, Inc., Box 5076, Champaign, IL 61825-5076. TEL 217-351-5076. FAX 217-351-2674. Ed. Dr. W. Jack Rejeski. adv.; bk.rev.; bibl.; charts; illus.; stat.; index; circ. 1,700. (back issues avail.) **Indexed:** Biol.Abstr., Child Devel.Abstr., Curr.Cont., Educ.Ind., Ergon.Abstr., Phys.Ed.Ind., Psychol.Abstr., Sportsearch (1988-), SSCI.
—BLDSC shelfmark: 5066.183500.
Formerly: Journal of Sport Psychology (ISSN 0163-433X)
Description: Multidisciplinary journal designed to stimulate and communicate research and theory. Examines the influence of psychological variables on sport performance and the influence of sport participation on psychological phenomena.
Refereed Serial

JOURNAL OF SPORT BEHAVIOR. see *SPORTS AND GAMES*

616.89 CN ISSN 0711-5075
JOURNAL OF STRATEGIC AND SYSTEMIC THERAPIES. 1981. q. Can.$33. Box 2484, Station "B", London, Ont. N6A 4G7, Canada. TEL 519-433-3101. Ed. Don Efron. adv.; bk.rev.; circ. 1,200. (back issues avail.) **Indexed:** Psychol.Abstr.
—BLDSC shelfmark: 5066.872800.

370.15 150 US ISSN 0022-4774
L11 CODEN: JSTLAF
JOURNAL OF STRUCTURAL LEARNING. 4/yr. (in 1 vol., 4 nos./vol.). $98. (International Study Group for Mathematics Learning) Gordon & Breach Science Publishers, 270 Eighth Ave., New York, NY 10011. TEL 212-206-8900. FAX 212-645-2459. TELEX 236735 GOPUB UR. (Subscr. to: Box 786, Cooper Sta., New York, NY 10276. TEL 800-545-8398; UK subscr. to: P.O. Box 90, Reading, Berkshire RG1 8JL, England. TEL 0734-560-080) (Co-sponsor: Structural Learning Society) Ed. Joseph M. Scandura. adv.; index. (also avail. in microform from MIM) **Indexed:** Curr.Cont., Educ.Tech.Abstr., Psychol.Abstr., SSCI, Stud.Wom.Abstr.
—BLDSC shelfmark: 5066.880000.
Description: Presents study and teaching methods.
Refereed Serial

152 US ISSN 0022-5002
BF1 CODEN: JEABAU
JOURNAL OF THE EXPERIMENTAL ANALYSIS OF BEHAVIOR. 1958. 6/yr. $86. Society for the Experimental Analysis of Behavior, Inc., c/o Psychology Department, Indiana University, Bloomington, IN 47405. TEL 812-339-4718. Ed. Marc Branch. adv.; bk.rev.; bibl.; charts; index, cum.index: vols.1-40; circ. 2,600. (back vols. avail.) **Indexed:** ASSIA, Biol.Abstr., Chem.Abstr., Curr.Cont., Excerp.Med., Ind.Med., INIS Atomind., Mid.East: Abstr.& Ind., Psychol.Abstr., Psychol.R.G., Soc.Sci.Ind., SSCI.
—BLDSC shelfmark: 4979.700000.
Description: Presents original experiments relevant to the behavior of individual organisms.

PSYCHOLOGY

150   US   ISSN 0022-5061
BF1   CODEN: JHBSA5
JOURNAL OF THE HISTORY OF THE BEHAVIORAL SCIENCES. 1965. q. $45 to individuals; libraries $115. Clinical Psychology Publishing Co., Inc., 4 Conant Sq., Brandon, VT 05733. TEL 802-247-6871. FAX 802-247-6853. Ed. Dr. Barbara Ross. adv.; bk.rev.; index; circ. 800. (also avail. in microform from MIM,UMI; back issues avail.; reprint service avail. from UMI) **Indexed:** Abstr.Anthropol., Amer.Bibl.Slavic & E.Eur.Stud., Amer.Hist.& Life, ASCA, ASSIA, Curr.Cont., Hist.Abstr., Ind.Med., Lang.& Lang.Behav.Abstr., Mid.East: Abstr.& Ind., Psychol.Abstr., Psychol.R.G., Sociol.Abstr., SSCI.
—BLDSC shelfmark: 5000.600000.
Refereed Serial

JOURNAL OF THE LEARNING SCIENCES; a journal of ideas and their applications. see *EDUCATION*

150   US   ISSN 0887-252X
JOURNAL OF THEORETICAL PSYCHOLOGY. 1986. irreg. $5 per no. Harbor Publishing, 80 N. Moore St., Ste. 4J, New York, NY 10013. TEL 212-349-1818. Ed. Laura M. Morrison. adv.; bk.rev.; bibl.; charts; illus.; circ. 5,000. (back issues avail.)

370.15 150   US   ISSN 0895-7673
JOURNAL OF TRAINING & PRACTICE IN PROFESSIONAL PSYCHOLOGY. 1987. s-a. free to qualified personnel. Forest Institute of Professional Psychology, 2611 Leeman Fery Rd., Huntsville, AL 35801-5611. TEL 205-536-9088. FAX 205-533-7405. Ed. Edwin Wagner. adv.; abstr.; bibl.; charts; illus.; circ. 1,600 (controlled). **Indexed:** Psychol.Abstr.
Description: Dedicated to the advancement of knowledge in the field of professional clinical psychology. Covers diagnostic, therapeutic and administrative issues.

158   US   ISSN 0022-524X
BF1   CODEN: JTPSAN
JOURNAL OF TRANSPERSONAL PSYCHOLOGY. 1969. s-a. $24 to individuals; institutions $32. Transpersonal Institute, 345 California Ave., Palo Alto, CA 94306. TEL 415-327-2066. Ed. Miles A. Vich. bk.rev.; circ. 3,800. (also avail. in microform from UMI) **Indexed:** Curr.Cont., Psychol.Abstr., Psychol.R.G., Soc.Sci.Ind., SSCI.
—BLDSC shelfmark: 5069.870000.
Description: Focus on psychological and spiritual states, experiences, practices and concepts.

370.15 150   US   ISSN 0894-9867
RC552.P67   CODEN: JTSTEB
JOURNAL OF TRAUMATIC STRESS. 1988. q. $120 (foreign $140)(effective 1992). Plenum Publishing Corp., 233 Spring St., New York, NY 10013-1578. TEL 212-620-8000. FAX 212-463-0742. TELEX 23-421139. Ed. Charles R. Figley. adv. (also avail. in microfilm from JSC; back issues avail.) **Indexed:** Psychol.Abstr.
—BLDSC shelfmark: 5070.520000.
Refereed Serial

158   US   ISSN 0001-8791
HF5381.A1   CODEN: JVBHA2
JOURNAL OF VOCATIONAL BEHAVIOR. 1971. bi-m. $214 (foreign $265). Academic Press, Inc., Journal Division, 1250 Sixth Ave., San Diego, CA 92101. TEL 619-230-1840. FAX 619-699-6800. TELEX 181726. Ed. Howard E.A. Tinsley. index. (back issues avail.) **Indexed:** ASSIA, C.I.J.E., Chic.Per.Ind., CINAHL, Curr.Cont., Lang.& Lang.Behav.Abstr., Mid.East: Abstr.& Ind., Pers.Lit., Psychol.Abstr., Psycscan, SSCI, Stud.Wom.Abstr.
—BLDSC shelfmark: 5072.510000.
Description: Publishes empirical and theoretical articles that expand knowledge of vocational behavior and career development across the life span.

155 301.1   MY   ISSN 0127-8029
JURNAL PSIKOLOGI MALAYSIA. (Text in English and Malay) 1972. a. $15. Penerbit Universiti Kebangsaan Malaysia, 43600 UKM Bangi, Selangor, Malaysia.
Description: Discusses various fields of psychology such as social, developmental, physiological, industrial, counseling, and others particularly relevant to Malaysia.

JYVASKYLA STUDIES IN EDUCATION, PSYCHOLOGY AND SOCIAL RESEARCH. see *EDUCATION*

KANSAS ACADEMY OF SCIENCE. TRANSACTIONS. see *SCIENCES: COMPREHENSIVE WORKS*

KAYA TAO. see *SOCIOLOGY*

DAS KIND. see *CHILDREN AND YOUTH — About*

KINDHEIT; Zeitschrift zur Erforschung der psychischen Entwicklung. see *CHILDREN AND YOUTH — About*

616.89   GW   ISSN 0343-9429
KLINISCHE PSYCHOLOGIE UND PSYCHOPATHOLOGIE. 1978. irreg., no.56, 1991. price varies. Ferdinand Enke Verlag, Postfach 101254, 7000 Stuttgart 10, Germany. TEL 0711-8931-0. FAX 0711-8931-419. TELEX 07252275-GTV-D. Ed. H. Remschmidt.

310   JA   ISSN 0385-5481
KODO KEIRYOGAKU/JAPANESE JOURNAL OF BEHAVIORMETRICS. (Text in Japanese; summaries in English) 1974. a. Nihon Kodo Keiryo Gakkai - Behaviormetric Society of Japan, 6-7, Minami-Azabu 4-chome, Minato-ku, Tokyo 106, Japan. **Indexed:** Psychol.Abstr.

616.89   JA   ISSN 0910-6529
KODO RYOHO KENKYU/JAPANESE JOURNAL OF BEHAVIOR THERAPY. (Text in English or Japanese; summaries in English) 1974. s-a. 5000 Yen. Kodo Ryoho Gakkai - Japanese Association of Behavior Therapy, c/o Yuji Sakano, Sec.-Gen., Dept. of Health Sciences, School of Human Sciences, Waseda University, Mikajima 2-579-15, Tokorozawa, Saitama 359, Japan. TEL 03-3203-4141. FAX 03-3203-4141-764413. (Subscr. to: Iwasaki Gakujutsu Shuppansha Inc., 1-4-8 Kohinata, Bunkyo-ku, Tokyo 112, Japan) Ed. Kotaro Harano. adv.; bk.rev.; index; circ. 1,200. (back issues avail.) **Indexed:** Psychol.Abstr.
—BLDSC shelfmark: 4651.010000.
Description: Covers experimental and clinical research in behavior therapy.
Refereed Serial

156   GW
▼**KOGNITIONSWISSENSCHAFT.** 1990. q. DM.198. Springer-Verlag, Heidelberger Platz 3, 1000 Berlin 33, Germany. TEL 030-8207-0. FAX 030-8214091. Ed.Bd. adv. contact: E. Lueckermann.

616.8   JA   ISSN 0023-2807
KOKORO TO SHAKAI/MIND AND SOCIETY. (Text in Japanese) 1969. q. 1500 Yen($5) Nihon Seishin Eiseikai - Japan Mental Health Society, 91 Benten-cho, Shinjuku-ku, Tokyo 162, Japan. Ed. Dr. Haruo Akimoto.

157   GW   ISSN 0937-289X
▼**KRANKENHAUSPSYCHIATRIE.** 1990. q. DM.98. Ferdinand Enke Verlag, Postfach 101254, 7000 Stuttgart 10, Germany. TEL 0711-8931-0. FAX 0711-8931-419. TELEX 07252275-GTV-D. Eds. F. Reimer, V. Faust.
—BLDSC shelfmark: 5118.146300.

616.89   NE   ISSN 0167-238X
KWARTAALSCHRIFT VOOR DIRECTIEVE THERAPIE EN HYPNOSE. 4/yr. fl.105 (effective 1992). Bohn Stafleu Van Loghum B.V., P.O. Box 246, 3990 GA Houten, Netherlands. TEL 3403-95711. FAX 3403-50903. adv.; bk.rev.; circ. 2,000.

370   JA   ISSN 0452-9650
KYOIKU SHINRIGAKU NENPO/ANNUAL REPORT OF EDUCATIONAL PSYCHOLOGY IN JAPAN. 1961. a. 2000 Yen. Japanese Association of Educational Psychology - Nihon Kyoiku Shinri Gakkai, c/o Faculty of Education, University of Tokyo, 7-3-1 Hongo, Bunkyo-ku, Tokyo 113, Japan.

LANGUAGE ACQUISITION; a journal of developmental linguistics. see *LINGUISTICS*

LANGUAGE AND COGNITIVE PROCESSES. see *LINGUISTICS*

LANGUAGE SCIENCES; a world journal of the sciences of language. see *LINGUISTICS*

808.87   US   ISSN 0731-1788
LAUGHING MATTERS. 1981. q. $15. Saratoga Institute, Humor Project, 110 Spring St., Saratoga Springs, NY 12866. TEL 518-587-8770. Ed. Dr. Joel Goodman. bk.rev.; illus.; cum.index; circ. 10,000. (back issues avail.)

LAW AND HUMAN BEHAVIOR. see *LAW*

LAW AND PSYCHOLOGY REVIEW. see *LAW*

LEADERSHIP QUARTERLY; an international journal of political, social and behavioral science. see *BUSINESS AND ECONOMICS — Management*

370.15 150   US   ISSN 1041-6080
LB1051   CODEN: LIDIEI
LEARNING AND INDIVIDUAL DIFFERENCES; a multidisciplinary journal in education. 1989. q. $45 to individuals; institutions $90 (effective 1990). J A I Press Inc., 55 Old Post Rd., No. 2, Box 1678, Greenwich, CT 06836-1678. TEL 203-661-7602. Ed. H. Lee Swanson.
—BLDSC shelfmark: 5179.325880.

LEARNING AND MOTIVATION. see *EDUCATION*

616.89   GW
LEBENDIGE SEELSORGE; Zeitschrift fuer alle Fragen der Seelsorge. 1949. s-m. DM.42. Seelsorge Verlag Echter, Juliuspromenade 64, D-8700 Wuerzburg, Germany.

150   US
LEHR- UND FORSCHUNGSTEXTE PSYCHOLOGIE/LECTURE NOTES IN PSYCHOLOGY. (Text in German) 1981. irreg. price varies. Springer-Verlag, 175 Fifth Ave., New York, NY 10010. TEL 212-460-1500. (And Berlin, Heidelberg, Tokyo and Vienna) Ed.Bd.

LESBIAN AND GAY COUNSELLING NEWS. see *HOMOSEXUALITY*

301.1 150   UK   ISSN 0267-7172
LIBERTARIAN ALLIANCE. PSYCHOLOGICAL NOTES. 1985. irreg. £10($20) Libertarian Alliance, 1 Russell Chambers, Covent Garden, London WC2E 8AA, England. TEL 071-821-5502. FAX 071-834-2031.

156   US
LIBRARY OF ANALYTICAL PSYCHOLOGY SERIES. 1973. irreg., vol.7, 1986. (Society of Analytical Psychology) Brunner-Mazel Publishing Co., 19 Union Sq. W., New York, NY 10003. TEL 212-924-3344. Ed. K. Lambert. (reprint service avail. from ISI)
Refereed Serial

LITERATURE AND PSYCHOLOGY; a quarterly journal of literary criticism as informed by depth psychology. see *LITERATURE*

LIVING HEALTHY; learning to live with digestive disease. see *MEDICAL SCIENCES — Gastroenterology*

370.15 150   US   ISSN 8756-4610
LOSS, GRIEF & CARE; a journal of professional practice. 1986. q. $32 to individuals; institutions $45; libraries $75. Haworth Press, Inc., 10 Alice St., Binghamton, NY 13904. TEL 800-342-8678. FAX 607-722-1424. TELEX 4932599. Ed. Austin H. Kutscher. adv.; bk.rev.; circ. 138. (also avail. in microfiche from HAW; reprint service avail. from HAW) **Indexed:** ASSIA, Int.Polit.Sci.Abstr., LISA, Past.Care & Couns.Abstr., Psychol.Abstr., Ref.Zh., Soc.Work Res.Abstr., Sociol.Abstr.
—BLDSC shelfmark: 5294.735000.
Description: Explores the critical issues of psychosocial care for chronically, critically, and terminally ill patients and their family members.
Refereed Serial

LOVING BROTHERHOOD NEWSLETTER; a journal for personal and planetary transformation. see *HOMOSEXUALITY*

150   GW   ISSN 0933-3347
BF173.A2
LUZIFER-AMOR; Zeitschrift zur Geschichte der Psychoanalyse. 1988. s-a. DM.48. Edition Diskord, Schwarzlocher Str. 104-b, 7400 Tubingen, Germany. TEL 07071-40102. FAX 07071-44710. Eds. Gerd Kimmerle, Hanna Gekle. adv.; bk.rev.; circ. 1,000. (back issues avail.)

M I D S NEWSLETTER. (Miscarriage, Infant Death, and Stillbirth) see *MEDICAL SCIENCES — Obstetrics And Gynecology*

150   HU   ISSN 0025-0279
BF8.H8
MAGYAR PSZICHOLOGIAI SZEMLE/HUNGARIAN PSYCHOLOGICAL REVIEW. (Text in Hungarian; summaries in English, Russian) 1928. q. $35. (Magyar Tudomanyos Akademia) Akademiai Kiado, Publishing House of the Hungarian Academy of Sciences, P.O. Box 24, H-1363 Budapest, Hungary. (Co-sponsor: Magyar Pszichologiai Tarsasag) Ed. P. Popper. adv.; bk.rev.; index. **Indexed:** C.I.S. Abstr., Curr.Cont., Lang.& Lang.Behav.Abstr., Psychol.Abstr.

150 301 574   II   ISSN 0025-1615
MANAB MON; a journal depicting the modern trends in psychology, biology, and sociology. (Text in English) 1972. q. Rs.8($1) Pavlov Institute, 132-1A Bidhan Sarani, Calcutta 4, India. Ed. Dr. D.N. Ganguly. adv.; bk.rev.; circ. 1,000.

150   II   ISSN 0025-1984
MANAS; a journal of scientific psychology. (Text in English) 1954. s-a. Rs.25($6) (Behavioural Sciences Centre) Manasayan, 32 Netaji Subhash Marg, New Delhi 110002, India. Ed.Bd. adv.; bk.rev.; circ. 300. (back issues avail.) **Indexed:** Psychol.Abstr.

MANKIND QUARTERLY; an international quarterly journal dealing with both physical and cultural anthropology including related subjects such as psychology, demography, genetics, linguistics and mythology. see *ANTHROPOLOGY*

370.15   CS
                  CODEN: SPFFB6
MASARYKOVA UNIVERZITA. FILOZOFICKA FAKULTA. SBORNIK PRACI. I: RADA PEDAGOGICKA - PSYCHOLOGICKA. 1966. irreg. (approx. a). price varies. Masarykova Univerzita, Filozoficka Fakulta, A. Novaka 1, 660 88 Brno, Czechoslovakia. **Indexed:** Psychol.Abstr.
Formerly: Univerzita J.E. Purkyne. Filozoficka Fakulta. Sbornik Praci. I: Rada Pedagogicka - Psychologicka (ISSN 0068-2705)
Description: Covers all aspects of pedagogics and psychology.

MATHEMATICS EDUCATION LIBRARY. see *EDUCATION*

301.1 150 340   US   ISSN 0739-4098
KF9084.A15
MEDIATION QUARTERLY. 1983. q. $48 to individuals; institutions $82. (Academy of Family Mediators) Jossey-Bass Inc., Publishers, 350 Sansome St., 5th Fl., San Francisco, CA 94104. TEL 415-433-1767. FAX 415-433-0499. Ed. Peter R. Maida. bk.rev.; circ. 1,900. (back issues avail.) **Indexed:** Psychol.Abstr., Sage Fam.Stud.Abstr., Sage Urb.Stud.Abstr., Sociol.Abstr.
—BLDSC shelfmark: 5525.380000.
Description: Covers the latest developments in the theory and practice of mediation, an alternative to traditional means of resolving conflicts such as those involving family members, labor and management, landlords and tenants, neighbors, and others.
Refereed Serial

MEDICAL HYPNOANALYSIS JOURNAL. see *MEDICAL SCIENCES — Hypnosis*

616.89   CN   ISSN 0835-3069
RC321
MEDICAL PSYCHOTHERAPY; an international journal. a. Can.$45($39) (American Board of Medical Psychotherapists) Hogrefe & Huber Publishers, 14 Bruce Park Ave., Toronto, Ont. M4P 2S3, Canada. TEL 416-482-6339. FAX 416-484-4200. (Subscr. to: 9536 N.E. 141st Pl., Bothell, WA 98011, USA or Box 51, Lewiston, NY 14092, USA) Ed. C.L. Sheridan. adv.; bk.rev.; circ. 3,500. (back issues avail.)
Description: A scholarly forum for the dissemination of research and clinical findings that integrate the areas of physical health and disease with the psychotherapies.
Refereed Serial

150.19   US
MEDICAL PSYCHOTHERAPY IN INTERNATIONAL JOURNAL. a. American Board of Medical Psychotherapists, 9536 N.E. 141st Pl., Bothell, WA 98011. TEL 416-482-6339.

MEDICINA E PSYCHE/MEDICINE AND MIND; semestrale di psicologia medica e di filosofia della medicina - semi-annual journal of philosophy of medicine and medical psychology. see *MEDICAL SCIENCES — Psychiatry And Neurology*

301.1 150   GW   ISSN 0936-7780
P96.P75
MEDIENPSYCHOLOGIE; Zeitschrift fuer Individual- und Massenkommunikation. (Text in German and English) 1989. q. DM.84. Westdeutscher Verlag GmbH, Postfach 5829, 6200 Wiesbaden 1, Germany. TEL 0611-160230. FAX 0611-160229. Ed.Bd. adv.; bk.rev.; index; circ. 500. (back issues avail.)

MEGAMOT; behavioural sciences quarterly. see *SOCIOLOGY*

152   US   ISSN 0090-502X
BF371   CODEN: MYCGAO
MEMORY AND COGNITION. 1973. bi-m. $100 (foreign $109). Psychonomic Society, Inc., 1710 Fortview Rd., Austin, TX 78704. TEL 512-462-2442. Ed. Margaret Jean Intons-Peterson. adv.; bibl.; illus.; circ. 2,300. (also avail. in microform from KTO,UMI; back issues avail.; reprint service avail. from UMI) **Indexed:** Biol.Abstr., Child Devel.Abstr., Commun.Abstr., Curr.Adv.Ecol.Sci., Curr.Cont., Ergon.Abstr., Excerp.Med., Lang.& Lang.Behav.Abstr., M.L.A., Mid.East: Abstr.& Ind., Psychol.Abstr., SSCI.
—BLDSC shelfmark: 5678.300000.
Description: Covers human memory, learning, conceptual processes, psycholinguistics, and problem solving, along with reports of work in computer simulation and experimental social psychology.

MENNINGER CLINIC. BULLETIN; a journal for the mental health professions. see *MEDICAL SCIENCES — Psychiatry And Neurology*

MENNINGER PERSPECTIVE. see *MEDICAL SCIENCES — Psychiatry And Neurology*

MENSA RESEARCH JOURNAL. see *EDUCATION*

150 340.5   US
MENTAL CAPACITY: MEDICAL AND LEGAL ASPECTS OF THE AGING. 1977. base vol. (plus a. suppl.). Shepard's - McGraw-Hill, Inc., Box 35300, Colorado Springs, CO 80935-3530. TEL 800-525-2474.
Description: Covers the physiological and legal aspects of mental incompetence, including symptoms, causes and treatments of senility.

370.15 150   US
MENTAL HEALTH; special interest section newsletter. (Consists of 7 sections: Administration and Management; Developmental Disabilities; Gerontology; Mental Health; Physical Disabilities; Sensory Integration; Work Programs) vol.12, no.4, 1989. q. $15. American Occupational Therapy Association, Inc., 1383 Piccard Dr., Box 1725, Rockville, MD 20850-0822. TEL 301-948-9626. FAX 301-948-5512.

155.4 362.7 616.8   US
MENTAL HEALTH IN CHILDREN. 1975. irreg. $69.95. P J D Publications Ltd., Box 966, Westbury, NY 11590. TEL 516-626-0650. Ed. Dr. D.V. Siva Sankar. (back issues avail.)
Description: Articles for professionals in the area of child mental health.

MENTAL HEALTH LAW NEWS. see *LAW — Civil Law*

MENTAL HEALTH LAW REPORTER. see *LAW — Civil Law*

616.89   UK
MENTAL HEALTH MATTERS. 1962. q. membership. Northern Ireland Association for Mental Health, 80 University St., Belfast BT7 1HE, N. Ireland. FAX 0232-234940. Ed. Margery Magee. bk.rev.; circ. controlled.
Former titles (until 1991): Beacon House Bulletin (ISSN 0144-2368); Northern Ireland Association for Mental Health. Newsletter; Beacon House News.

301.1 150   US   ISSN 1058-1103
MENTAL HEALTH WEEKLY; news for policy and program decision-makers. w. $295 to individuals (foreign $335); institutions $395 (foreign $435). Manisses Communications Group, Inc., 205 Governor St., Box 3357, Providence, RI 02906-0757. TEL 800-333-7771. FAX 401-861-6370. Ed. Robert Curley.
Description: Reports on state and federal legislative and administrative developments; news of the mental health field across the country; coverage of both public and private policy issues.

151.22 371.26   US   ISSN 0076-6461
Z5814.P8
MENTAL MEASUREMENTS YEARBOOK. 1938. biennial. price varies. Buros Institute of Mental Measurements, 135 Bancroft, University of Nebraska-Lincoln, Lincoln, NE 68588-0348. TEL 402-472-6203. FAX 402-472-6207. (Dist. by: University of Nebraska Press, 901 N. 17th St., Lincoln, NE 68588-0520)
●Also available online. Vendor(s): BRS (MMYD).

301.1 150   IT
MENTE E SOCIETA. 1985. irreg. no.5, 1988. price varies. Liguori Editore s.r.l., Via Mezzocannone, 19, 80134 Naples, Italy. TEL 081-5227139. Ed. Guglielmo Bellelli.

MERIDIAN; Zeitschrift fuer Kosmobiologie, Astrologie und angewandte Psychologie. see *NEW AGE PUBLICATIONS*

150 301   US   ISSN 0026-0150
HQ1   CODEN: MPQUA5
MERRILL - PALMER QUARTERLY. 1954. q. $33 to individuals; institutions $66; students $24. (Merrill - Palmer Institute) Wayne State University Press, Leonard N. Simons Bldg., 5959 Woodward Ave., Detroit, MI 48202. TEL 313-577-6120. FAX 313-577-6131. Ed. Carolyn U. Shantz. bk.rev.; charts; illus.; index; circ. 1,290. (also avail. in microform from UMI) **Indexed:** Abstr.Soc.Work., Adol.Ment.Hlth.Abstr., Bibl.Dev.Med.& Child Neur., Biol.Abstr., C.I.J.E., Child.Devel.Abstr., Curr.Cont., DSH Abstr., Educ.Ind., Except.Child.Educ.Abstr., Lang.& Lang.Behav.Abstr., Mid.East: Abstr.& Ind., PSI, Psychol.Abstr., Psyscan D.P., Sage Fam.Stud.Abstr., Soc.Work Res.& Abstr., Sociol.Abstr., Sp.Ed.Needs Abstr., SSCI.
—BLDSC shelfmark: 5682.280000.
Description: Theoretical and empirical papers in the areas of human development and family-child relationships.

METAPHOR AND SYMBOLIC ACTIVITY. see *LINGUISTICS*

301.1 150   CN   ISSN 0932-6510
H61
METHODIKA. 1987. a. Can.$29($24) Huber & Hogrefe International, Inc., 12-14 Bruce Park Ave., Toronto, Ont. M4P 2S3, Canada. TEL 416-482-6339. FAX 416-484-4200. (back issues avail.)
—BLDSC shelfmark: 5746.320000.
Description: Includes articles from psychological statistics, observational methods, data analysis, psychometrics, mathematical psychology, educational statistics, and educational measurement.

301.1   GW
METHODIKA. 1985. a. DM.68. Verlag fuer Psychologie Dr. C.J. Hogrefe, Rohnsweg 25, Postfach 3751, 3400 Goettingen 1, Germany. TEL 0551-54044.

METHODOLOGIA; pensiero linguaggio modelli - thought language models. see *LINGUISTICS*

301.1 355   US   ISSN 0899-5605
U22.3
MILITARY PSYCHOLOGY. 1989. q. $35 to individuals (foreign $57.50); institutions $125 (foreign $150). (American Psychological Association, Division 19) Lawrence Erlbaum Associates, Inc., 365 Broadway, Hillsdale, NJ 07642. TEL 201-666-4110. FAX 201-666-2394. Ed. Martin F. Wiskoff. **Indexed:** Psychol.Abstr.
—BLDSC shelfmark: 5768.167000.
Description: Presents behavioral science research papers having military applications in clinical and health psychology, cognition and training, human factors, manpower and personnel, social and organizational systems, and testing and measurement.
Refereed Serial

330 614.7   US
MIND MATTERS REVIEW. 1988. q. 20 F.($15) 2040 Polk St., Box 234, San Francisco, CA 94109. Ed. Carrie L. Drake. adv.; bk.rev.; circ. 1,000. (back issues avail.)
Description: Forum for discussion on the politics of mind, encompassing politics of religion, psychiatry, science, ideology.

PSYCHOLOGY

155.4 US ISSN 0076-9266
BF721 CODEN: MSCRBG
MINNESOTA SYMPOSIA ON CHILD PSYCHOLOGY SERIES. 1966. irreg., vol.24, 1991. $49.95. (University of Minnesota, Institute of Child Development) Lawrence Erlbaum Associates, Inc., 365 Broadway, Hillsdale, NJ 07642. TEL 201-666-4110.
FAX 201-666-2394. (back issues avail.) **Indexed:** Biol.Abstr., Curr.Cont., Psychol.Abstr., SSCI.
—BLDSC shelfmark: 5810.490000.

MISCELANEA COMILLAS; revista de teologia y ciencias humanas. see *RELIGIONS AND THEOLOGY*

150 CE
MNANSA. (Text in Sinhala) 1978. m. 150 Dutugemunu St., Dehiwala, Sri Lanka. TEL 1-553994. Ed. Sumanadasa Samarasinghe. circ. 6,000.

150 US ISSN 0361-5227
RC500
MODERN PSYCHOANALYSIS. 1976. s-a. $15. Center for Modern Psychoanalytic Studies, 16 W. 10th St., New York, NY 10011. TEL 212-260-7050. Ed. Phyllis W. Meadow. bk.rev.; index; circ. 1,100. **Indexed:** Chicago Psychoanal.Lit.Ind., CINAHL, Mid.East: Abstr.& Ind., Psychoanal.Abstr., Psychol.Abstr.
—BLDSC shelfmark: 5894.420000.
Description: Dedicated to extending the theory and practice of psychoanalysis to the full range of emotional disorders.
Refereed Serial

150 130 SP ISSN 0077-0469
MONOGRAFIAS DE PSICOLOGIA, NORMAL Y PATOLOGICA. 1945. irreg. price varies. Espasa-Calpe, S.A., Carretera de Irun, km. 12,200, Apdo. 547, 28049 Madrid, Spain. Ed. Jose Germain.

150 PL ISSN 0077-0515
MONOGRAFIE PSYCHOLOGICZNE. (Text in Polish; summaries in English and Russian) 1968. irreg., vol.55, 1987. price varies. (Polska Akademia Nauk, Komitet Nauk Psychologicznych) Ossolineum, Publishing House of the Polish Academy of Sciences, Rynek 9, 50-106 Wroclaw, Poland. TELEX 0712771 OSS PL. (Dist. by: Ars Polona-Ruch, Krakowskie Przedmiescie 7, Warsaw, Poland) Ed. Tadeusz Tomaszewski. **Indexed:** Math.R.

155 US ISSN 0749-1190
CODEN: MPSYEV
MONOGRAPHS IN PSYCHOBIOLOGY. 1985. irreg., vol.6, 1989. Gordon & Breach Science Publishers, 270 Eighth Ave., New York, NY 10011.
TEL 212-206-8900. FAX 212-645-2459. TELEX 236735 GOPUB UR. (Subscr. to: Box 786, Cooper Sta., New York, NY 10276. TEL 800-545-8398; UK subscr. to: P.O. Box 90, Reading, Berkshire RG1 8JL, England. TEL 0734-560-080) Ed. S.A. Corson.
—BLDSC shelfmark: 5915.972000.
Refereed Serial

MONOGRAPHS ON INFANCY. see *MEDICAL SCIENCES — Pediatrics*

155.3 US ISSN 0027-1004
MORALITY IN MEDIA NEWSLETTER. 1962. bi-m. $20. Morality in Media, Inc., 475 Riverside Dr., New York, NY 10115. TEL 212-870-3222.
FAX 212-870-2765. Ed. Betty Wein. bk.rev.; illus.; circ. 20,000.
Formerly: Morality in Media.
Description: News and profiles pertaining to activities to combat obscenity in the media.

150 US ISSN 0146-7239
BF683 CODEN: MOEMDJ
MOTIVATION AND EMOTION. 1977. q. $175 (foreign $205)(effective 1992). Plenum Publishing Corp., 233 Spring St., New York, NY 10013-1578.
TEL 212-620-8000. FAX 212-463-0742. TELEX 23-421139. Ed. Alice M. Isen. adv. (also avail. in microfilm from JSC; back issues avail.) **Indexed:** Biol.Abstr., Child Devel.Abstr., Curr.Cont., Psychol.Abstr., SSCI.
—BLDSC shelfmark: 5969.060000.
Refereed Serial

152 US ISSN 0027-3171
BF39 CODEN: MVBRAV
MULTIVARIATE BEHAVIORAL RESEARCH. 1966. q. $37.50 to individuals (foreign $62.50); institutions $145 (foreign $170). Lawrence Erlbaum Associates, Inc., 365 Broadway, Hillsdale, NJ 07642. TEL 201-666-4110. FAX 201-666-2394. adv.; index; circ. 905. (also avail. in microform from UMI; back issues avail.) **Indexed:** Biol.Abstr., Biostat., C.I.J.E., Commun.Abstr., Compumath, Curr.Cont., J.Cont.Quant.Meth., Lang.& Lang.Behav.Abstr., Mid.East: Abstr.& Ind., Psychol.Abstr., Psycscan, Sci.Cit.Ind., SSCI.
Description: Reports results of behavioral research employing multivariate methods.
Refereed Serial

157 US ISSN 0147-3964
BF698.A1 CODEN: MCREDA
MULTIVARIATE EXPERIMENTAL CLINICAL RESEARCH; a journal for basic behavioral research into personality dynamics and clinical psychology. 1973. q. $29 (foreign $35). Psychology Press, c/o Dr. Charles Burdsal, Ed., Department of Psychology, No.34, Wichita State University, Wichita, KS 67208. TEL 316-689-3170. adv.; bk.rev.; circ. 200. (processed) **Indexed:** Biol.Abstr., Curr.Cont., Excerp.Med., Psychol.Abstr., Sci.Cit.Ind., SSCI.
Formerly: Journal of Multivariate Experimental Personality and Clinical Psychology (ISSN 0149-9688)
Description: Outlet for clinical and personality researches using sophisticated, multivariate experimental methods. Both manipulative and non-manipulative research is accepted.

MUSIKPSYCHOLOGIE. see *MUSIC*

616.89 GW ISSN 0172-5505
ML3920
MUSIKTHERAPEUTISCHE UMSCHAU. (Text in German; summaries in English) 4/yr. DM.93. Gustav Fischer Verlag, Wollgrasweg 49, Postfach 720143, 7000 Stuttgart 70, Germany. TEL 0711-458030.
FAX 0711-4580334. TELEX 7111488-FIBUCH. (U.S. subscr. to: Gustav Fischer New York Inc., 220 E. 23rd St., Ste. 909, New York, NY 10010) Ed. V. Bernius. **Indexed:** Dok.Arbeitsmed., Excerp.Med., Psychol.Abstr., RILM.
—BLDSC shelfmark: 5991.114320.
Description: Publication containing studies in music oriented therapy, and its application in medicine, psychotherapy, and psychology.

658.3 SA
N I P R NEWS. (Text in Afrikaans, English) 1974. 3/yr. free. National Institute for Personnel Research, Box 32410, Braamfontein 2017, South Africa.
FAX 011-403-2353. Eds. J. Duckitt, C. Marais. circ. 7,000.

NAGOYA DAIGAKU KYOYOBU KIYO B. SHIZEN KAGAKU, SHINRIGAKU/NAGOYA UNIVERSITY. COLLEGE OF GENERAL EDUCATION. RESEARCH BULLETIN B. NATURAL SCIENCE AND PSYCHOLOGY. see *SCIENCES: COMPREHENSIVE WORKS*

NANNY TIMES. see *CHILDREN AND YOUTH — About*

370.15 150 US
NATIONAL CHARACTER LABORATORY NEWSLETTER. 1971. q. $5. National Character Laboratory, 4635 Leeds Ave., El Paso, TX 79903.
TEL 915-562-5046. Ed. A.J. Stuart, Jr. bk.rev.; abstr.; bibl.; stat.; circ. 150.
Description: Reports research results on character, and encourages and coordinates further research.

150.19 US ISSN 0077-5339
NATIONAL PSYCHOLOGICAL ASSOCIATION FOR PSYCHOANALYSIS. BULLETIN. 1950. s-a. National Psychological Association for Psychoanalysis, Inc., 150 W. 13th St., New York, NY 10011.
TEL 212-924-7440. circ. 7,000.

150.19 US
NATIONAL PSYCHOLOGICAL ASSOCIATION FOR PSYCHOANALYSIS. NEWS AND REVIEWS. 1970. 3/yr. $10. National Psychological Association for Psychoanalysis, Inc., 150 W. 13th St., New York, NY 10011. TEL 212-924-7440. Ed. Harvey A. Kaplan. circ. 1,000.

150 US
NATIONAL SOCIETY FOR GRAPHOLOGY NEWSLETTER. 1972. 6/yr. $20 (foreign $30). National Society for Graphology, 250 W. 57th St., Ste. 2032, New York, NY 10107. TEL 212-265-1148.
FAX 212-307-5671. Ed. Louise Erpelding. circ. 300. (back issues avail.)
Description: Handwriting analysis for all levels of expertise.

159 US ISSN 0070-2099
BF683
NEBRASKA SYMPOSIUM ON MOTIVATION (PUBLICATION). (Subseries of: Research in Motivation Series) 1953. a. price varies. (University of Nebraska, Department of Psychology) University of Nebraska Press, 901 N. 17th St., Lincoln, NE 68588-0520. TEL 402-472-3581.
FAX 402-472-6214. index, cum.index. (back issues avail.) **Indexed:** Ind.Med., Psychol.Abstr., SSCI.
Description: Includes timely paper topics for the Nebraska Symposium which deal with all aspects of motivation.

155 658 CN ISSN 1188-2921
▼**NEIL MUSCOTT'S SUCCESS NEWSLETTER;** strategies and stories for successful people. 1991. bi-m. free. Neil Muscott Seminars, 529 Manning Ave., Toronto, Ont. M6G 2V8, Canada. TEL 416-532-1433.
FAX 416-537-7361. Ed. Neil Muscott. adv.; bk.rev.; circ. 2,000. (looseleaf format)

370.15 374 US
NETWORK NEWS (CLEVELAND). 1966. s-a. $20. Center for Nonviolent Communication, 3326 E. Overlook Rd., Cleveland, OH 44118-2116.
TEL 216-371-1123. Ed. Rita Herzog. circ. 5,000. (back issues avail.)
Formerly: Newsletter for Soulmates.

NEUROPSYCHOLOGICAL REHABILITATION; an international journal. see *MEDICAL SCIENCES — Psychiatry And Neurology*

NEUROPSYCHOLOGY. see *MEDICAL SCIENCES — Psychiatry And Neurology*

NEUROPSYCHOLOGY REVIEW. see *MEDICAL SCIENCES — Psychiatry And Neurology*

155.4 US ISSN 0195-2269
BF721 CODEN: NDCDDI
NEW DIRECTIONS FOR CHILD DEVELOPMENT. 1978. q. $52 to individuals; institutions $70. Jossey-Bass Inc., Publishers, 350 Sansome St., 5th Fl., San Francisco, CA 94104. TEL 415-433-1767.
FAX 415-433-0499. Ed. William Damon. bibl.; circ. 550. (back issues avail.; reprint service avail. from UMI) **Indexed:** Biol.Abstr., Child Devel.Abstr., Educ.Ind., Psychol.Abstr.
—BLDSC shelfmark: 6083.326000.
Description: Covers the latest findings in developmental psychology; addresses children's cognitive, social, moral, and emotional growth.

NEW DIRECTIONS FOR MENTAL HEALTH SERVICES. see *MEDICAL SCIENCES — Psychiatry And Neurology*

150 US ISSN 0732-118X
BF1
NEW IDEAS IN PSYCHOLOGY; international journal of innovative theory in psychology. 1983. 3/yr. £115 (effective 1992). Pergamon Press, Inc., Journals Division, 660 White Plains Rd., Tarrytown, NY 10591-5153. TEL 914-524-9200.
FAX 914-333-2444. (And: Headington Hill Hall, Oxford, OX3 0BW, England. TEL 0865-794141) Ed. Pierre Moessinger. (also avail. in microform from UMI,MIM) **Indexed:** ASCA, Curr.Adv.Ecol.Sci., Psychol.Abstr.
—BLDSC shelfmark: 6084.249500.
Refereed Serial

370.15 150 US ISSN 0896-3126
NEW JERSEY JOURNAL OF SCHOOL PSYCHOLOGY. 1982. irreg. $7 to non-members; libraries $10. New Jersey Association of School Psychologists, c/o Valerie Hill, 25 Round Top Rd., Warren, NJ 07059-5521. bk.rev.; circ. 700. **Indexed:** Psychol.Abstr.

NEW SENSE BULLETIN; news from the leading edge. see *MEDICAL SCIENCES — Psychiatry And Neurology*

150   US   ISSN 0077-9008
BF173.A2
NEW YORK PSYCHOANALYTIC INSTITUTE. KRIS STUDY GROUP. MONOGRAPHS. 1965. irreg., no.7, 1984. price varies. International Universities Press, Inc., 59 Boston Post Rd., Box 1524, Madison, CT 06443-1524. TEL 203-245-4000. Ed. Dr. Edward Joseph. **Indexed:** Biol.Abstr.
Refereed Serial

150   US
NEW YORK SOCIETY OF ETHICAL HYPNOSIS. NEWSLETTER.* 4/yr. $10. New York Society of Ethical Hypnosis, c/o Carol Styron-Gore, Ed., Box 2843, Sedona, AZ 86336.

150   US   ISSN 0028-7687
NEW YORK STATE PSYCHOLOGIST.* 1948. m. $20. Foundation of New York State Psychological Association, Inc., 1529 Western Ave., Albany, NY 12203-3513. TEL 212-787-6487. FAX 914-683-5223. Ed. Laurence S. Baker. adv.; bk.rev.; charts; illus.; stat.; tr.lit.; circ. 4,000. (back issues avail.) **Indexed:** Psychol.Abstr.

150   NZ   ISSN 0112-109X
NEW ZEALAND JOURNAL OF PSYCHOLOGY. 1972. s-a. NZ.$25. New Zealand Psychological Society, c/o Dr. G. Rhodes, Ed., Canterbury University, Dept. of Psychology, Private Bag, Christchurch, New Zealand. FAX 03-642-181. adv.; bk.rev.; circ. 900. (back issues avail.) **Indexed:** Curr.Cont., Psychol.Abstr., Risk Abstr., SSCI.
—BLDSC shelfmark: 6094.655000.
Formerly (until 1983): New Zealand Psychologist.

370.15   US   ISSN 0894-1750
NEWSLETTER OF THE FREUDIAN FIELD. 1987. s-a. $10 to individuals; institutions $20. Foundation Freudian Field, c/o Ellie Ragland-Sullivan, Ed., Department of English, 107 Tate Hall, University of Missouri, Columbia, MO 65211. bk.rev.; circ. 900.
—BLDSC shelfmark: 6108.648500.
Description: Dedicated to discussion of Jacques Lacan's teachings in psychoanalysis, as well as in literary, film and art theory.

157.744   US
NEWSLINK (DENVER). q. membership. American Association of Suicidology, 2459 S. Ash, Denver, CO 80222. TEL 303-692-0985. circ. 1,500.
Description: Provides suicide prevention information.

NINTH STREET CENTER JOURNAL. see *HOMOSEXUALITY*

NODE; for hackers with soul. see *MEDICAL SCIENCES — Computer Applications*

150   DK   ISSN 0029-1463
BF8.D3   CODEN: NOPSAW
NORDISK PSYKOLOGI. (Text mainly in Danish, Norwegian, Swedish; occasionally in English; summaries in English) 1949. 4/yr. DKK 401. Akademisk Forlag, Store Kannikestraede 8, P.O. Box 54, 1002 Copenhagen K, Denmark. Ed. Per Schultz Joergensen. adv.; bk.rev.; bibl.; charts; illus.; stat.; index; circ. 7,000. **Indexed:** Biol.Abstr., Chem.Abstr., Psychol.Abstr., SSCI.

370.15 150   DK   ISSN 0900-8772
NORDISK PSYKOLOGISK LITTERATUR. a. DKK 150. Akademisk Forlag, Store Kannikestraede 8, P.O. Box 54, DK-1002 Copenhagen K, Denmark.

NORDISK TIDSSKRIFT FOR SPESIALPEDAGOGIKK; Scandinavian journal for special education and rehabilitation. see *EDUCATION — Special Education And Rehabilitation*

159   US   ISSN 0889-9428
NORTH AMERICAN SOCIETY OF ADLERIAN PSYCHOLOGY. NEWSLETTER.* m. $5. North American Society of Adlerian Psychology, 65 E. Wacker Pl., Ste. 400, Chicago, IL 60601-3703. Ed. Don C. Dinkmeyer, Jr. circ. 1,000.
Description: Information on news and activities of the Society. Covers recent conventions in the field.

616.89   FR
NOUVELLE REVUE DE PSYCHANALYSE. no.10, 1974. 2/yr. 375 F. for two yrs. Editions Gallimard, 5 rue Sebastien-Bottin, 75007 Paris, France. TEL 33-1-46-59-89-00. Ed. J.B. Pontalis. **Indexed:** Psychoanal.Abstr., Psychol.Abstr.

NUTRITION HEALTH REVIEW. see *NUTRITION AND DIETETICS*

ODENSE UNIVERSITY STUDIES IN PSYCHIATRY AND MEDICAL PSYCHOLOGY. see *MEDICAL SCIENCES — Psychiatry And Neurology*

ODGOJ I SAMOUPRAVLJANJE. see *EDUCATION*

614.58   US
OKLAHOMA. DEPARTMENT OF MENTAL HEALTH AND SUBSTANCE ABUSE SERVICES. ANNUAL REPORT. a. free. Department of Mental Health and Substance Abuse Services, Box 53277, Oklahoma City, OK 73152. TEL 405-271-7474. Ed. Rosemary Brown. circ. 1,000.
Former titles: Oklahoma. Department of Mental Health. Annual Report; Mental Health Care in Oklahoma. Annual Report.

150 616   US   ISSN 0030-2228
BF789.D4   CODEN: OMGABX
OMEGA (AMITYVILLE); journal of death and dying. 1970. 8/yr. (in 2 vols., 4 nos./vol.). $54 to individuals; institutions $145. Baywood Publishing Co., Inc., 26 Austin Ave., Box 337, Amityville, NY 11701. TEL 516-691-1270. FAX 516-691-1770. Ed. Dr. Robert J. Kastenbaum. bk.rev.; abstr.; bibl.; charts. (back issues avail.) **Indexed:** ASSIA, Biol.Abstr., C.I.J.E., CINAHL, Compumath, Excerp.Med., Lang.& Lang.Behav.Abstr., Psychol.Abstr., Soc.Sci.Ind.
—BLDSC shelfmark: 6256.425000.
Description: Guide for clinicians, social workers, and health professionals dealing with problems in crisis management, such as terminal illness, fatal accidents, catastrophes, suicide and bereavement.

ON COURSE; weekly perspectives on the inner journey. see *NEW AGE PUBLICATIONS*

150   CN   ISSN 0030-3054
RC467
ONTARIO PSYCHOLOGIST. 1969. 8/yr. Can.$50. Ontario Psychological Association, 730 Yonge St., Suite 221, Toronto, Ont. M4Y 2B7, Canada. TEL 416-961-5552. FAX 416-961-5516. Ed. E. Blackstock. adv.; bk.rev.; bibl.; charts; illus.; stat.; circ. 1,400. (also avail. in microform from UMI; reprint service avail. from UMI) **Indexed:** Psychol.Abstr.
—BLDSC shelfmark: 6262.090000.

301.1 309   US
ONTARIO SYMPOSIA ON PERSONALITY AND SOCIAL COGNITION SERIES. 1981. irreg., vol.6, 1990. $49.95. Lawrence Erlbaum Associates, Inc., 365 Broadway, Hillsdale, NJ 07642. TEL 201-666-4110. FAX 201-666-2394. Ed.Bd. index. **Indexed:** Curr.Cont., Psychol.Abstr.

150   US
OREGON PSYCHOLOGY.* 1959. 3/yr. $15 to non-members. Oregon Psychological Association, 1750 S.W. Skyline Blvd., No. 12, Portland, OR 97221. Ed. Richard S. Colman. adv.; bk.rev.; circ. 700 (controlled). (tabloid format)
Formerly: Oregon Psychological Association. Newsletter (ISSN 0471-9336)

150   US
ORGANIZATIONAL AND OCCUPATIONAL PSYCHOLOGY. 1979. irreg., vol.18, 1987. Academic Press, Inc., 1250 Sixth Ave., San Diego, CA 92101. TEL 619-231-0926. FAX 619-699-6715. Ed. P. Warr. (reprint service avail. from ISI)

158   US   ISSN 0749-5978
BF636.A1
ORGANIZATIONAL BEHAVIOR AND HUMAN DECISION PROCESSES; a journal of fundamental research and theory in applied psychology. 1966. 9/yr. $303 (foreign $358). Academic Press, Inc., Journal Division, 1250 Sixth Ave., San Diego, CA 92101. TEL 619-230-1840. FAX 619-699-6800. TELEX 181726. Ed. James C. Naylor. adv.; bibl.; charts; stat. (back issues avail.) **Indexed:** ASSIA, B.P.I, BPIA, Bus.Ind., CINAHL, Commun.Abstr., Curr.Cont., Int.Lab.Doc., Mid.East: Abstr.& Ind., Psychol.Abstr., Psyscan, Risk Abstr., SCIMP, SSCI, Tr.& Indus.Ind.
—BLDSC shelfmark: 6290.749000.
Formerly (until 1985): Organizational Behavior and Human Performance (ISSN 0030-5073)
Description: Features articles that describe original empirical research and theoretical developments in all areas of human decision processes and organizational psychology.

150 158.7   FR   ISSN 0249-6739
ORIENTATION SCOLAIRE ET PROFESSIONNELLE. 1972. q. 210 F. (foreign 250 F.). Institut National d'Etude du Travail et d'Orientation Professionnelle, 41 rue Gay Lussac, 75005 Paris, France. TEL 44-10-78-33. Ed. M. Huteau. adv.; bk.rev.; abstr.; bibl.; charts; stat.; index; circ. 2,000. (back issues avail.) **Indexed:** Bull.Signal., Psychol.Abstr.
Formerly: B I N O P Bulletin (ISSN 0005-3147)

150   II
OSMANIA UNIVERSITY. DEPARTMENT OF PSYCHOLOGY. RESEARCH BULLETIN. (Text in English) 1965. irreg. Osmania University, Department of Psychology, Hyderabad 500007, Andhra Pradesh, India. Ed. Shalini Bhogle. bk.rev.; bibl.; charts; stat.; circ. controlled. **Indexed:** Psychol.Abstr.

OUR GIFTED CHILDREN. see *CHILDREN AND YOUTH — About*

P E P S Y. (Pedagogisk och Psykologisk Litteratur i Norden) see *EDUCATION*

150   US
P S C P TIMES.* 1971. irreg. (6-8/yr.). $5. Philadelphia Society of Clinical Psychologists, Cedarbrook Hill Apts, E. Mall Bld. 1, Wyncote, PA 19095-2601. Eds. Lita L. Schwartz, Frank A. Melone. circ. 200.

155.3   NE   ISSN 0167-4749
PAEDO ALERT NEWS MAGAZINE. Short title: P A N Magazine. 1979. 5/yr. fl.40($20) Spartacus International Ltd., Box 3496, 1001 AG Amsterdam, Netherlands. Ed. Roger Hunt. adv.; bk.rev.; illus.; circ. 4,000.

PAIDIKA; the journal of paedophilia. see *HOMOSEXUALITY*

301.1 301.4   US   ISSN 0737-5123
PARENTING STUDIES. 1984. q. Eterna International, Inc., 27 W. 560 Warrenville Rd., Warrenville, IL 60555. TEL 708-393-2930. Ed. Sedahlia Jasper Crase. abstr.; charts; illus.; index. **Indexed:** Psychol.Abstr.

150.19   FR   ISSN 0769-4679
PAS TANT. (Supplement avail.: Decouverte Freudienne) q. 200 F. to individuals; students 170 F. (effective 1992). (Universite de Toulouse II (le Mirail)) Presses Universitaires du Mirail, 56 rue du Taur, 31000 Toulouse, France. TEL 61-22-58-31. FAX 61-21-84-20. Dir. Michel Lapeyre. (back issues avail.)

150 200   US   ISSN 0031-2789
PASTORAL PSYCHOLOGY. 1952. bi-m. $195 (foreign $230). Human Sciences Press, Inc., 233 Spring St., New York, NY 10013-1578. TEL 212-620-8000. FAX 212-463-0742. Ed. Lewis R. Rambo. adv.; bk.rev. (also avail. in microfilm from UMI; reprint service avail. from ISI,UMI) **Indexed:** Rel.& Theol.Abstr. (1969-).
—BLDSC shelfmark: 6409.300000.
Description: Examines pastoral counseling, and brings psychological and behavioral science into relation and dialogue with the work of the ministry.
Refereed Serial

301.1   US
PATHWAYS (TAKOMA PARK). 1978. 4/yr. $5. Yes Educational Society, Box 5719, Takoma Park, MD 20912-0719. Ed. Ollie Popenoe. adv.; bk.rev.; circ. 40,000.

370.5 155.4   SW   ISSN 0346-5004
PEDAGOGISK-PSYKOLOGISKA PROBLEM. 1964. irreg. Malmoe School of Education, Inst. foer Pedagogik och Specialmetodik, Box 23501, S-20045 Malmoe, Sweden. Ed. Aake Bjerstedt. (back issues avail.) **Indexed:** Psychol.Abstr.

155.4 618.92   US   ISSN 0278-4998
PEDIATRIC MENTAL HEALTH. 1982. bi-m. $32 (foreign $36). Pediatric Projects, Inc., Box 571555, Tarzana, CA 91357-1555. TEL 818-705-3660. FAX 818-705-3660. Ed. Pat Azarnoff. bk.rev.; bibl.; tr.lit.; index; circ. 2,000. (back issues avail.)
Description: Covers research and practice about supported parenting, therapeutic play and psychological preparation of ill, disabled or hospitalized children.

PSYCHOLOGY

150 617.7 **UK** **ISSN 0301-0066**
BF311 **CODEN: PCTNBA**
PERCEPTION. (Text in English, French and German) 1972. bi-m. £135($220) Pion Ltd., 207 Brondesbury Park, London NW2 5JN, England. TEL 081-459-0066. FAX 081-451-6454. TELEX 94016265-PION-G. Ed. R.L. Gregory. adv.; bk.rev.; index. **Indexed:** ASSIA, Commun.Abstr., Dent.Ind., Excerp.Med., Ind.Med., Mid.East: Abstr.& Ind., Psychol.Abstr.
—BLDSC shelfmark: 6423.150000.
Description: Reports experimental results and theoretical ideas in the fields of animal, human and machine perception.

152 **US** **ISSN 0031-5117**
BF233 **CODEN: PEPSBJ**
PERCEPTION & PSYCHOPHYSICS. 1966. m. $140 (foreign $154). Psychonomic Society, Inc., 1710 Fortview Rd., Austin, TX 78704. TEL 512-462-2442. Ed. Charles W. Eriksen. adv.; charts; illus.; index; circ. 1,800. (also avail. in microform from KTO,UMI; back issues avail.; reprint service avail. from UMI) **Indexed:** Biol.Abstr., Commun.Abstr., Curr.Adv.Ecol.Sci., Curr.Cont., Dent.Ind., Ergon.Abstr., Excerp.Med., Int.Aerosp.Abstr., Lang.& Lang.Behav.Abstr., M.L.A., Psychol.Abstr., Sp.Ed.Needs Abstr., SSCI.
—BLDSC shelfmark: 6423.200000.
Description: Contains articles that deal with sensory processes, perception and psychophysics. Some theoretical and evaluative reviews are published.
Refereed Serial

152 **US** **ISSN 0031-5125**
BF311 **CODEN: PMOSAZ**
PERCEPTUAL AND MOTOR SKILLS. 1949. bi-m. (2 vols./yr.). $210. Dr. C.H. Ammons & Dr. R.B. Ammons, Eds. & Pubs., Box 9229, Missoula, MT 59807. adv.; bk.rev.; bibl.; charts; illus.; index; circ. 2,000. (also avail. in microform) **Indexed:** Abstr.Anthropol., Bibl.Dev.Med.& Child Neur., Biol.Abstr., C.I.J.E., Child Devel.Abstr., Commun.Abstr., Curr.Cont., Dent.Ind., DSH Abstr., Ergon.Abstr., Except.Child.Educ.Abstr., Excerp.Med., HRIS, Ind.Med., Lang.& Lang.Behav.Abstr., M.L.A., Mid.East: Abstr.& Ind., Nutr.Abstr., Phys.Ed.Ind., Psychol.Abstr., Risk Abstr., Sci.Cit.Ind., Soc.Sci.Ind., Sp.Ed.Needs Abstr., Sportsearch (1974-), SSCI, Stud.Wom.Abstr.
—BLDSC shelfmark: 6423.300000.
Description: Encourages scientific originality and creativity. Includes experimental or theoretical articles dealing with perception or motor skills, especially as affected by experience.

150 **US** **ISSN 0191-8869**
BF698.A1 **CODEN: PEIDD9**
PERSONALITY AND INDIVIDUAL DIFFERENCES; an international journal of research into the structure and development of personality and the causation of individual differences. 1980. 12/yr. £290 (effective 1992). (International Society for the Study of Individual Differences) Pergamon Press, Inc., Journals Division, 660 White Plains Rd., Tarrytown, NY 10591-5153. TEL 914-524-9200. FAX 914-333-2444. (And: Headington Hill Hall, Oxford OX3 0BW, England. TEL 0865-794141) Ed. H.J. Eysenck. adv.; circ. 1,500. (also avail. in microform from MIM,UMI) **Indexed:** ASSIA, Biol.Abstr., Curr.Cont., PSI, Psychol.Abstr., SSCI.
—BLDSC shelfmark: 6428.010500.
Refereed Serial

150 **US** **ISSN 0146-1672**
BF698.A1
PERSONALITY AND SOCIAL PSYCHOLOGY BULLETIN. 1975. bi-m. $52 to non-members; institutions $160. (Society for Personality and Social Psychology) Sage Publications, Inc., 2455 Teller Rd., Newbury Park, CA 91320. TEL 805-499-0721. FAX 805-499-0871. Ed. Richard E. Petty. adv.; circ. 3,000. (also avail. in microform from MIM,UMI; reprint service avail. from UMI) **Indexed:** A.B.C.Pol.Sci., Adol.Ment.Hlth.Abstr., ASSIA, Commun.Abstr., Curr.Cont., PSI, Psychol.Abstr., Sage Fam.Stud.Abstr., Sage Urb.Stud.Abstr., Soc.Sci.Ind., SSCI, Stud.Wom.Abstr.
Formerly: American Psychological Association. Division of Personality and Social Psychology. Proceedings.

150 **US** **ISSN 0079-0931**
CODEN: PEPSDL
PERSONALITY, PSYCHOPATHOLOGY AND PSYCHOTHERAPY; a series of texts, monographs and treatises. 1967. irreg., vol.39, 1989. Academic Press, Inc., 1250 Sixth Ave., San Diego, CA 92101. TEL 619-231-0926. FAX 619-699-6715. Eds. David T. Lykken, Philip C. Kendall. (reprint service avail. from ISI) **Indexed:** Chem.Abstr.
Formerly: Personality and Psychopathology.
Refereed Serial

156 **II** **ISSN 0970-8111**
PERSONALITY STUDY AND GROUP BEHAVIOUR. (Text in English) 1981. s-a. Rs.60 to individuals; institutions Rs.80 (foreign $30). Guru Nanak Dev University, Publication Office, Amritsar 143 005, India. Ed. Rita Agrawal. circ. 500. **Indexed:** Psychol.Abstr.
Description: Examines research reports and other related scholarly endeavors which have a theoretical, empirical orientation.

158 **US** **ISSN 0031-5826**
HF5549.A2 **CODEN: PPSYAQ**
PERSONNEL PSYCHOLOGY. 1948. q. $50 (foreign $55). Personnel Psychology, Inc., 745 Haskins Rd., Ste. A, Bowling Green, OH 43402-1600. TEL 419-352-1562. FAX 419-352-2645. Ed. Michael A. Campion. adv.; bk.rev.; charts; index; circ. 3,400. (also avail. in microform from UMI) **Indexed:** ABI Inform., B.P.I., Bk.Rev.Ind. (1980-), BPIA, Bus.Ind., C.I.J.E., Child.Bk.Rev.Ind. (1980-), Commun.Abstr., Cont.Pg.Manage., Curr.Cont., Educ.Admin.Abstr., Manage.Cont., Pers.Lit., Pers.Manage.Abstr., Psychol.Abstr., Psycscan, SCIMP, SSCI, Work Rel.Abstr.
●Also available online. Vendor(s): BRS, Information Access Company.
—BLDSC shelfmark: 6428.095000.
Description: Research articles on industrial psychology, employees and the workplace.
Refereed Serial

301.1 150 **CK** **ISSN 0120-3878**
BF5
PERSPECTIVAS EN PSICOLOGIA. (Editions in English and Spanish) 1982. a. Col.$400($6) Fundacion Universidad de Manizales, Facultad de Psicologia, Apdo. Aereo 868, Manizales, Colombia. Ed.Bd. bk.rev.; circ. 1,000. **Indexed:** Psychol.Abstr.

PERSPECTIVES IN LAW AND PSYCHOLOGY. see *LAW*

370.15 150 **II** **ISSN 0971-1562**
PERSPECTIVES IN PSYCHOLOGICAL RESEARCHES. (Text in English and Hindi) 1978. s-a. free. 410 Opposite Gupta Medical, Asifgani, Purani Kotwali, Azamgarh 276 001, India. TEL 0546-222006. Ed. Dr. Ramji Srivastava. adv.; bk.rev.; stat.; circ. 1,000.

616.89 **US** **ISSN 0735-4037**
PERSPECTIVES IN PSYCHOTHERAPY. 1983. irreg., vol.1, 1983. Gordon & Breach Science Publishers, 270 Eighth Ave., New York, NY 10011. TEL 212-206-8900. FAX 212-645-2459. TELEX 236735 GOPUB UR. (Subscr. to: Box 786, Cooper Sta., New York, NY 10276. TEL 800-545-8398; UK subscr. to: P.O. Box 90, Reading, Berkshire RG1 8JL, England. TEL 0734-560-080) Ed. P. Olsen.
Refereed Serial

616.89 **PH**
PHILIPPINE JOURNAL OF COUNSELING PSYCHOLOGY. (Text in English) 1987. s-a. P.65($7) (De La Salle University, Department of Psychology, Guidance and Counseling) De La Salle University Press, 2401 Taft Ave., Manila, Philippines. TEL 2-595177. (Co-sponsor: Philippine Association for Counselor Education, Research & Supervision (PACERS)) Ed. Rose Marie Salazar-Clemena. adv.; bk.rev.; circ. 500.
Description: Publishes original contributions on counseling in different populations. Emphasizes empirical studies on counseling techniques and intervention strategies; the development and validation of assessment instruments; group treatment programs; and counselor education and supervision. Also accepts reviews, concept papers, and research notes.

150 **PH**
PHILIPPINE JOURNAL OF PSYCHOLOGY. 1968. s-a. P.40($5) Psychological Association of the Philippines, Philippine Social Science Council (PSSC) Bldg., Commonwealth Ave., Diliman, Quezon City, Philippines. Ed. Allen L. Tan. adv.; charts; illus.; circ. 175. (tabloid format) **Indexed:** Ind.Phil.Per., Psychol.Abstr.

156 **UK** **ISSN 0951-5089**
PHILOSOPHICAL PSYCHOLOGY. 1988. 4/yr. Carfax Publishing Co., P.O. Box 25, Abingdon, Oxfordshire OX14 3UE, England. TEL 0235-555335. FAX 0235-553559. (U.S. subscr. addr.: Carfax Publishing Co., Box 2025, Dunnellon, FL 32630) Eds. John Rust, Bill Bechtel.
—BLDSC shelfmark: 6462.260000.
Description: Deals with the application of philosophical psychology to the cognitive and brain sciences, and to areas of applied psychology. Of interest to advanced students in philosophy, psychology, computer science, linguistics and the neurosciences.

150 **PL** **ISSN 0079-2993**
BF1 **CODEN: PPBUDY**
POLISH PSYCHOLOGICAL BULLETIN. (Text in English) 1970. q. $40. Polskie Towarzystwo Psychologiczne, Ul. Stawki 5-7, 00-183 Warsaw, Poland. (Dist. by: Ars Polona-Ruch, Krakowskie Przedmiescie 7, 00-068 Warsaw, Poland) Ed. Jan Strelau. bibl.; circ. 500. **Indexed:** Curr.Cont., Psychol.Abstr., Sage Fam.Stud.Abstr., Sp.Ed.Needs Abstr., SSCI.
—BLDSC shelfmark: 6543.723000.

POLITICAL PSYCHOLOGY. see *POLITICAL SCIENCE*

POLYGRAPH (SEVERNA PARK). see *CRIMINOLOGY AND LAW ENFORCEMENT*

158 **US** **ISSN 0199-0039**
HB848 **CODEN: PENVDK**
POPULATION AND ENVIRONMENT; a journal of interdisciplinary studies. 1978. bi-m. $185 (foreign $215). (American Psychological Association, Division of Population and Environmental Psychology) Human Sciences Press, Inc. (Subsidiary of: Plenum Publishing Corp.) 233 Spring St., New York, NY 10013-1578. TEL 212-620-8000. FAX 212-463-0742. Ed. Virginia Abernethy. adv.; bk.rev.; charts; index. (also avail. in microfilm from UMI; reprint service avail. from ISI,UMI) **Indexed:** Abstr.Hyg., Biol.Abstr., C.I.J.E., Coll.Stud.Pers.Abstr., Curr.Adv.Ecol.Sci., Curr.Cont., Curr.Lit.Fam.Plan., Environ.Abstr., Environ.Per.Bibl., Excerp.Med., G.Soc.Sci.& Rel.Per.Lit., Lang.& Lang.Behav.Abstr., P.A.I.S., Popul.Ind., Psychol.Abstr., Psycscan, Saf.Sci.Abstr., Soc.Work Res.& Abstr., Sociol.Abstr., SSCI.
—BLDSC shelfmark: 6552.022000.
Former titles (until vol.4, 1981): Journal of Population (ISSN 0146-1052); Population (New York).
Description: Explores relationships between population and societal, cultural, and physical environments. Covers demographic variables linked to lifestyle, law, health, business, economics, and international relations.
Refereed Serial

150 **US**
POPULATION AND ENVIRONMENTAL PSYCHOLOGY NEWSLETTER. 1974. 3/yr. $5. American Psychological Association, 750 First St., N.E., Washington, DC 20002-4242. TEL 202-336-5500. FAX 202-336-5568. Ed. Patricia Parmelee. bk.rev.; bibl.; circ. 700.
Formerly: Population Psychology Newsletter.

370.15 **UK** **ISSN 0959-6828**
▼**POSITIVE TEACHING;** a journal for teachers, educational psychologists and other educationists. 1990. 2/yr. £10. (Institute for Positive Teaching) Positive Products, P.O. Box 45, Cheltenham, Glos. GL52 3BX, England. TEL 021-459-6559. Eds. Frank Merrett, K. Wheldall. bk.rev.; circ. 100.
—BLDSC shelfmark: 6558.848200.

PRACTICE (NEW YORK); the magazine of psychology and political economy. see *POLITICAL SCIENCE*

PRAGMATICS AND DISCOURSE ANALYSIS. see *LINGUISTICS*

PRAXIS DER KINDERPSYCHOLOGIE UND KINDERPSYCHIATRIE. see *MEDICAL SCIENCES — Psychiatry And Neurology*

150 616.89 **GW** **ISSN 0085-5073**
PRAXIS DER KINDERPSYCHOLOGIE UND KINDERPSYCHIATRIE. BEIHEFTE. 1958. irreg. price varies. Vandenhoeck und Ruprecht, Theaterstr. 13, Postfach 3753, 3400 Goettingen, Germany. TEL 0551-6959-22. FAX 0551-695917. Ed. Annemarie Duehrssen. **Indexed:** Ind.Med., Lang.& Lang.Behav.Abstr., Psychol.Abstr., SSCI.

PRAXIS DER PSYCHOTHERAPIE UND PSYCHOSOMATIK; Zeitschrift fuer Fort- und Weiterbildung. see *MEDICAL SCIENCES — Psychiatry And Neurology*

PRAXIS SPIEL UND GRUPPE. see *EDUCATION*

157 370 US ISSN 0886-6694
PREVENTING SEXUAL ABUSE. 1986. 4/yr. $32. S A F E Institute, c/o Molly Davis, Ed., 1225 NW Murray Rd., Ste. 214, Portland, OR 97229. TEL 503-644-6600. FAX 503-643-3798. bk.rev.; circ. 2,800.

150 US ISSN 0164-5056
PRIMAL INSTITUTE NEWSLETTER. 1978. bi-m. $11 (foreign $15). Primal Institute, 1950 Cotner Ave., Los Angeles, CA 90025-5602. TEL 213-478-0167. Ed. Victoria Hillen. bk.rev.; index; circ. 1,600. (back issues avail.)
Supersedes (1973-1978): Journal of Primal Therapy (ISSN 0091-9772)

PRIMATES; journal of primatology. see *BIOLOGY — Zoology*

152.182 US ISSN 0032-8448
PRINCETON UNIVERSITY CUTANEOUS RESEARCH PROJECT REPORTS. 1962. s-a. free. Princeton University, Department of Psychology, Green Hall, Princeton, NJ 08544. TEL 609-258-5277. FAX 609-258-1113. Ed.Bd. bibl.; charts; illus.; circ. 120 (controlled). (processed)
Description: Covers progress in research on the sensory processes of the skin.

370.15 150 US
PROBLEM BEHAVIOR MANAGEMENT. 1982. base vol. (plus s-a. updates), 2nd ed., 1992. $125 for base vol.; s-a updates $45 per no. Aspen Publishers, Inc., 200 Orchard Ridge Dr., Gaithersburg, MD 20878. TEL 301-417-7500. FAX 301-417-7550.

158.7 US ISSN 0277-4178
PROBLEMS OF INDUSTRIAL PSYCHIATRIC MEDICINE SERIES. irreg., vol.11, 1985. prices varies. Human Sciences Press, Inc. (Subsidiary of: Plenum Publishing Corp.), 233 Spring St., New York, NY 10013-1578. TEL 212-620-8000. FAX 212-463-0742. Ed. Sherman N. Keiffer. (reprint service avail. from UMI)
Refereed Serial

150 371.4 US
PROFESSIONAL CHRISTIAN COUNSELOR. 1983. q. $20 to non-members. United Association of Christian Counselors International, 41 Short St., Harrisburg, PA 17109-3731. TEL 717-652-7688. Ed. Arthur L. Sprunger. adv.; bk.rev.; film rev.; circ. 1,000. (tabloid format)
Former titles: Paracletic Counselor; Christian Communique.
Description: Covers all areas of professional counseling and counselor education that is based on a Christian worldview.

150 US ISSN 0735-7028
RC467
PROFESSIONAL PSYCHOLOGY: RESEARCH AND PRACTICE. 1969. bi-m. $72 to non-members (foreign $90); members $29; institutions $144 (foreign $180) (effective 1992). American Psychological Association, 750 First St., N.E., Washington, DC 20002-4242. TEL 202-336-7500. FAX 202-336-5568. Ed. Ursula Delworth. adv.; index; circ. 4,100. (also avail. in microform from MIM,UMI; back issues avail.; reprint service avail. from UMI) **Indexed:** Abstr.Health Care Manage.Stud., Adol.Ment.Hlth.Abstr., Crim.Just.Abstr., Curr.Cont., Mid.East: Abstr.& Ind., Psychol.Abstr., Psyscan C.P., Sage Fam.Stud.Abstr., SSCI.
—BLDSC shelfmark: 6864.211000.
Formerly (until 1982): Professional Psychology (ISSN 0033-0175)
Description: Articles on techniques and practices used in the application of psychology, including applications of research, standards of practice, interprofessional relations, delivery of services, and training.
Refereed Serial

616.8 US ISSN 0099-037X
BF637.B4 CODEN: PBMOE8
PROGRESS IN BEHAVIOR MODIFICATION. 1975. irreg., vol.20, 1986. Academic Press, Inc., 1250 Sixth Ave., San Diego, CA 92101. TEL 619-231-0926. FAX 619-699-6715. Ed. M. Hersen. (reprint service avail. from ISI) **Indexed:** Adol.Ment.Hlth.Abstr., Ind.Med., SSCI.

131 US
PROGRESS IN PSYCHOBIOLOGY AND PHYSIOLOGICAL PSYCHOLOGY. 1967. irreg., vol.14, 1990. Academic Press, Inc., 1250 Sixth Ave., San Diego, CA 92101. TEL 619-231-0926. FAX 619-699-6715. Ed. Alan N. Epstein. (reprint service avail. from ISI) **Indexed:** Curr.Adv.Ecol.Sci.
Former titles: Psychobiology and Physiological Psychology; (until vol.6): Progress in Physiological Psychology (ISSN 0079-6670)
Refereed Serial

616.89 US ISSN 0893-5483
BF697
PROGRESS IN SELF PSYCHOLOGY. 1985. a. price varies. Guilford Publications, Inc., 72 Spring St., 4th Fl., New York, NY 10012. TEL 212-431-9800. FAX 212-966-6708. Ed. Arnold Goldberg. bibl. (back issues avail.; reprint service avail.)
—BLDSC shelfmark: 6924.539000.
Description: Presents new concepts and controversies in the field of self psychology.
Refereed Serial

155.4 US
PROGRESS NOTES. 1976. 3/yr. membership. Society of Pediatric Psychology, Ferkauf Graduate School of Psychology, Yeshiva University, Mazer Hall, 1300 Morris Park Ave., Bronx, NY 10461. TEL 212-430-4201. FAX 212-430-3252. (Subscr. to: Debra Bendelt Estroff, 887 Praderia Circle, Fremont, CA 94539) Ed. Lawrence J. Siegel. adv.; circ. 1,000.
Formerly: Society of Pediatric Psychology. Newsletter.

150 PL ISSN 0048-5675
BF26 CODEN: PRZPBF
PRZEGLAD PSYCHOLOGICZNY/PSYCHOLOGICAL REVIEW. (Text in Polish; summaries in English and Russian) 1952. q. $54. (Polskie Towarzystwo Psychologiczne) Ossolineum, Publishing House of the Polish Academy of Sciences, Rynek 9, Wroclaw, Poland. TELEX 0712771 OSS PL. (Dist. by: Ars Polona-Ruch, Krakowskie Przedmiescie 7, Warsaw, Poland) Ed. R. Stachowski. bk.rev.; index; circ. 2,200. (also avail. in microform from UMI; reprint service avail. from UMI) **Indexed:** Acad.Ind., C.I.J.E., Curr.Adv.Ecol.Sci., Lang.& Lang.Behav.Abstr., Psychol.Abstr.

150 US ISSN 0033-2569
LJ121
PSI CHI NEWSLETTER. 1934. q. $6.25 (foreign $8.50). Psi Chi National Office, 201 Frazier Ave., Ste. F, Chattanooga, TN 37405. TEL 615-756-2044. FAX 615-265-1529. Ed. Kay Wilson. circ. 20,000.

PSICHIATRIA E PSICOTERAPIA ANALITICA/ANALYTIC PSYCHOTHERAPY AND PSYCHOPATHOLOGY. see *MEDICAL SCIENCES — Psychiatry And Neurology*

150 SP ISSN 0377-8320
BF5
PSICODEIA; revista de psicologia. 1975. m. 1200 ptas. (Instituto de Aplicaciones Psicologicas y Parapsicologicas) Ediciones I N A P P, Habana 66, Madrid 16, Spain. Ed. Carlos Gil Munoz. adv.; bk.rev.; illus.; circ. 15,000.

150 PO
PSICOLOGIA. irreg., vol.8 no.1, 1991. price varies. (Associacao Portuguesa de Psicologia) Edicioes Afrontamento, Lda., Rua de Costa Cabral, 859, Apdo. 2009, 4201 Porto Codex, Portugal. TEL 489271. FAX 491777. **Indexed:** Psychol.Abstr.

150 IT ISSN 0390-346X
PSICOLOGIA CONTEMPORANEA. bi-m. L.24000 (foreign L.31000). Giunti Gruppo Editoriale S.p.A., Via Vincenzo Gioberti, 34, 50121 Florence, Italy. TEL 055-66791. FAX 055-268312.

158.7 IT ISSN 0048-5691
PSICOLOGIA E LAVORO. 1968. 3/mo. L.70000($27) Patron Editore, Via Badini 12, 40127 Bologna, Italy. adv.; bk.rev.; bibl.; stat.; circ. 1,000. **Indexed:** Psychol.Abstr.
—BLDSC shelfmark: 6945.857000.

PSICOLOGIA MEDICA; revista argentina de psicologia medica, psicoterapia y ciencias afines. see *MEDICAL SCIENCES — Psychiatry And Neurology*

370.15 150 BL ISSN 0102-3772
PSICOLOGIA: TEORIA E PESQUISA/PSYCHOLOGY: THEORY AND RESEARCH. (Text and summaries in English, Portuguese) 1985. q. $15. Universidade de Brasilia, Instituto de Psicologia, Campus Universitario, Brasilia-70910, Brazil. TEL 348-2426. FAX 55-061-272-1053. Ed. Dr. Joao Claudio Todorov. bk.rev.; circ. 500. (back issues avail.) **Indexed:** Psychol.Abstr.

616.89 SP ISSN 0211-5549
PSICOPATOLOGIA. q. 4300 ptas.($65) Editorial Garsi, S.A., Londres, 17, 28028 Madrid, Spain. TEL 256-08-00. FAX 361-10-07. Dir. Dr. Alonso Fernandez. circ. 700. **Indexed:** Psychol.Abstr.
—BLDSC shelfmark: 6945.864000.

PSIHIJATRIJA DANAS/PSYCHIATRY TODAY. see *MEDICAL SCIENCES — Psychiatry And Neurology*

150 RM
▼**PSIHOLOGIA.** 1991. q. Piata Presei Libere 1, 79781 Bucharest, Rumania. Ed. Adina Chelcea. circ. 30,000.

158 RU
PSIKHOLOGICHESKIE ISSLEDOVANIYA. no.6, 1976. irreg. Moskovskii Universitet, Ul. Gertsena 5-7, 103009 Moscow, Russia. circ. 5,500.

150 BU
PSIKHOLOGIIA.* 1973. q. 1.60 lv. Druzhestvo na Psikholozite, c/o Kathedre of Psychology, Sofia University, Blvd. Rusky 15, Sofia, Bulgaria. (Dist. by: Hemus, 6, Rouski Blvd., 1000 Sofia, Bulgaria) Ed. S. Ganovski. circ. 500. **Indexed:** Psychol.Abstr.

PSIQUIS; revista de psiquiatria, psicologia y psicosomatica. see *MEDICAL SCIENCES — Psychiatry And Neurology*

370.15 150 US ISSN 1044-1514
Z7201
PSYCBOOKS. 1987. irreg., latest 1990. $399 for 5-vol. set. American Psychological Association, PsycINFO User Service, 750 First St., N.E., Washington, DC 20002-4242. TEL 800-374-2722. FAX 202-336-5633.
Description: Contains information about 1,441 books and 6,836 separately authored chapters. Arranged by subject in four volumes; a fifth volume contains subject, author, title, and publisher indexes.

370.15 150 US
PSYCH DISCOURSE. 1970. bi-m. $95. Association of Black Psychologists, Box 55999, Washington, DC 20040-5999. TEL 202-722-0808. Ed. Dr. Halford Fairchild. circ. 1,500. (back issues avail.)
Formerly: Association of Black Psychologists Newsletter.
Description: Covers news of member and chapter activities.

PSYCH IT; the sophisticated newsletter for everyone. see *NEW AGE PUBLICATIONS*

150 FR ISSN 0338-2397
PSYCHANALYSE A L'UNIVERSITE. 1975. q. 385 F. (foreign 460 F.). Presses Universitaires de France, Departement des Revues, 14 av. du Bois-de-l'Epine, B.P. 90, 91003 Evry Cedex, France. TEL 1-60-77-82-05. FAX 1-60-79-20-45. TELEX PUF 600 474 F. Dir. Jean Laplanche. bk.rev.; bibl.; cum.index every 2 yrs.; circ. 2,000. **Indexed:** Psychol.Abstr.
—BLDSC shelfmark: 6945.993000.
Description: Examines the universality of schools of thought.

PSYCHOLOGY

150.19 GW ISSN 0033-2623
BF173.A2 CODEN: PSYEDK
PSYCHE; Zeitschrift fuer Psychoanalyse und ihre Anwendungen. 1947. m. DM.142. Verlag Klett-Cotta, Rotebuehlstr. 77, Postfach 10 60 16, 7000 Stuttgart 10, Germany. Ed.Bd. adv.; bk.rev.; abstr.; bibl.; charts; index; circ. 7,500. (reprint service avail.) **Indexed:** Excerp.Med., Ger.J.Psych., Ind.Med., Psychol.Abstr., SSCI.
—BLDSC shelfmark: 6946.115000.

PSYCHIATRIC & PSYCHOLOGICAL EVIDENCE. see *LAW*

PSYCHO GERIATRIE. see *GERONTOLOGY AND GERIATRICS*

PSYCHO-LINGUA; a biannual research journal devoted to communicative behavior. see *LINGUISTICS*

PSYCHOANALYSIS AND PSYCHOTHERAPY. see *MEDICAL SCIENCES — Psychiatry And Neurology*

150.19 616.891 US
PSYCHOANALYTIC CROSSCURRENTS. 1985. irreg. price varies. New York University Press, 70 Washington Square S., New York, NY 10012. TEL 212-998-2575. FAX 212-995-3833. TELEX 235128 NYU UR. Ed. Leo Goldberger.

616.89 US ISSN 1048-1885
RC500
▼**PSYCHOANALYTIC DIALOGUES;** a journal of relational perspectives. 1991. q. $37.50 to individuals (foreign $62.50); institutions $90 (foreign $115). Analytic Press, Inc., 365 Broadway, Hillsdale, NJ 07642. TEL 800-926-6579. FAX 201-666-2394. Ed. Stephen A. Mitchell. (back issues avail.)
—BLDSC shelfmark: 6946.267000.
Description: Psychoanalytic contributions on interpersonal psychoanalysis, object relations theory, self psychology, infant research and child development.

150 US ISSN 0735-1690
RC500
PSYCHOANALYTIC INQUIRY; a topical journal for mental health professionals. 1980. q. $49.50 to individuals (foreign $74.50); institutions $120 (foreign $145). Analytic Press, Inc., 365 Broadway, Hillsdale, NJ 07642. TEL 800-926-6579. FAX 201-666-2394. Ed. Dr. Joseph D. Lichtenberg. circ. 1,100. **Indexed:** Psychoanal.Abstr., Psychol.Abstr.
—BLDSC shelfmark: 6946.269000.

150 616.8 US ISSN 0736-9735
PSYCHOANALYTIC PSYCHOLOGY. 1984. q. $50 to individuals (foreign $75); institutions $135 (foreign $160). (American Psychological Association, Division of Psychoanalysis) Lawrence Erlbaum Associates, Inc., 365 Broadway, Hillsdale, NJ 07642. TEL 201-666-4110. FAX 201-666-2394. Ed. Bertram J. Cohler. bk.rev.; abstr.; bibl. **Indexed:** Psychoanal.Abstr., Psychol.Abstr.
—BLDSC shelfmark: 6946.269600.
Description: Forum for the study of psychoanalytic issues in psychology and psychological issues in psychoanalysis.
Refereed Serial

616.89 US ISSN 0033-2828
BF173.A2 CODEN: PSQAAX
PSYCHOANALYTIC QUARTERLY. 1932. q. $65. Psychoanalytic Quarterly, Inc, 175 Fifth Ave., Rm. 517, New York, NY 10010. TEL 212-982-9358. Ed. Dr. Sander M. Abend. bk.rev.; abstr.; bibl.; index, cum.index: vols.1-35, 36-45, 46-55; circ. 3,800. **Indexed:** Abstr.Soc.Work, Chicago Psychoanal.Lit.Ind., Curr.Cont., Ind.Med., Lang.& Lang.Behav.Abstr., Mid.East: Abstr.& Ind., Psychoanal.Abstr., Psychol.Abstr., Soc.Work Res.& Abstr., SSCI.
—BLDSC shelfmark: 6946.270000.

150 616.89 US ISSN 0033-2836
BF1 CODEN: PSREAG
PSYCHOANALYTIC REVIEW. 1913. q. $33 to individuals; institutions $105. (National Psychological Association for Psychoanalysis, Inc.) Guilford Publications, Inc., 72 Spring St., 4th Fl., New York, NY 10012. TEL 212-431-9800. FAX 212-966-6708. Ed. Martin Schulman. adv.; bk.rev.; film rev.; play rev.; bibl.; index; circ. 2,100. (also avail. in microform from MIM,UMI; back issues avail.; reprint service avail. from ISI,UMI) **Indexed:** Abstr.Anthropol., Abstr.Engl.Stud., Biol.Abstr., Curr.Cont., Excerp.Med., Film Lit.Ind. (1985-), Ind.Med., Lang.& Lang.Behav.Abstr., Mid.East: Abstr.& Ind., Psychoanal.Abstr., Psychol.Abstr., Sci.Cit.Ind., Soc.Work Res.& Abstr., Sociol.Abstr., SSCI, Yrbk.Assoc.Educ.& Rehab.Blind.
—BLDSC shelfmark: 6946.273000.
Incorporates (1952-19??): Psychoanalysis.
Description: Covers contemporary psychoanalytical theory and practice, and psychoanalytical themes in art, film and literature.
Refereed Serial

150 US ISSN 0079-7294
H9
PSYCHOANALYTIC STUDY OF SOCIETY. a. price varies. Analytic Press, Inc., 365 Broadway, Hillsdale, NJ 07642. TEL 800-926-6579. FAX 201-666-2394. Eds. Drs. L. Bryce Boyer, Simon A. Grolnick. (back issues avail.)
Description: Devoted to the application of psychoanalysis to the social sciences, literature, and the arts.

155.4 US ISSN 0079-7308
BF721 CODEN: PYACAZ
PSYCHOANALYTIC STUDY OF THE CHILD. 1945. a. price varies. Yale University Press, 92A Yale Sta., New Haven, CT 06520. TEL 203-432-0940. Ed. Dr. Albert J. Solnit. **Indexed:** Biol.Abstr., Educ.Ind., Excerp.Med., Ind.Med., Psychoanal.Abstr., Psychol.Abstr., SSCI, Yrbk.Assoc.Educ.& Rehab.Blind.

152.05 US ISSN 0889-6313
QP360 CODEN: PSYBEC
PSYCHOBIOLOGY. 1973. q. $68 (foreign $74). Psychonomic Society, Inc., 1710 Fortview Rd., Austin, TX 78704. TEL 512-462-2442. Ed. Paul E. Gold. adv.; illus.; circ. 1,300. (also avail. in microform from KTO,UMI; back issues avail.; reprint service avail. from UMI) **Indexed:** Biol.Abstr., Chem.Abstr., Curr.Adv.Ecol.Sci., Curr.Cont., Dairy Sci.Abstr., Ergon.Abstr., Excerp.Med., Nutr.Abstr., Psychol.Abstr.
—BLDSC shelfmark: 6946.276530.
Formerly: Physiological Psychology (ISSN 0090-5046)
Description: Includes articles on all of the allied fields of the neurosciences that are related directly to behavior and experience. Experimental, review and theoretical papers are published.
Refereed Serial

150 US ISSN 0363-891X
D16.16 CODEN: PSRVD2
PSYCHOHISTORY REVIEW. vol.5, 1976. 3/yr. $22 to individuals; institutions $44. Sangamon State University, c/o Larry Shiner, Ed., Springfield, IL 62794-9243. adv.; bk.rev.; circ. 600. (also avail. in microform from UMI; back issues avail.; reprint service avail. from UMI) **Indexed:** Hist.Abstr., Lang.& Lang.Behav.Abstr., Psychol.Abstr., Soc.Work Res.& Abstr.
—BLDSC shelfmark: 6946.277400.
Formerly: Group for the Use of Psychology in History. Newsletter (ISSN 0162-9999)

150 NE ISSN 0079-7324
PSYCHOLOGEN ADRESBOEK. 1960. irreg., latest 1992. fl.35. Nederlands Instituut van Psychologen - Netherlands Psychological Association, Postbus 75362, 1070 AJ Amsterdam, Netherlands. TEL 020-6791526. FAX 020-6733256. adv.; circ. 7,000.

150 JA ISSN 0033-2852
BF1 CODEN: PYLGAY
PSYCHOLOGIA/PUSHIKOROGIA; an international journal of psychology in the Orient. (Text in English) 1957. q. $40 to individuals; institutions $60. Psychologia Society - Pushikorogia-kai, Dept. of Educational Psychology, Faculty of Education, Kyoto University, Yoshida Honmachi, Sakyo-ku, Kyoto 606, Japan. FAX 81-75-753-3020. Ed. Noboru Sakano. adv.; bk.rev.; index; circ. 900. (back issues avail.) **Indexed:** Lang.& Lang.Behav.Abstr., Mid.East: Abstr.& Ind., Psychol.Abstr., Sociol.Abstr., SSCI.
—BLDSC shelfmark: 6946.278000.

370.15 150 CS
PSYCHOLOGIA A PATOPSYCHOLOGIA DIETATA. 1966. bi-m. 60 Kcs. (Ministry of Education of the Slovak Socialist Republic) Slovenske Pedagogicke Nakladatelstvo, Sasinkova 5, 815 60 Bratislava, Czechoslovakia. (Subscr. to: Slovart, Gottwaldovo nam. 6, 805-32 Bratislava, Czechoslovakia) Ed. Karol Adamovic. circ. 3,500. **Indexed:** Psychol.Abstr.

370.15 CS
PSYCHOLOGIA A SKOLA. 1972. irreg. (approx. 2/yr.). price varies. Slovenske Pedagogicke Nakladatelstvo, Sasinkova 5, 815 60 Bratislava, Czechoslovakia.

150 370 PL
PSYCHOLOGIA-PEDAGOGIKA. 1961. irreg., no.81, 1988. price varies. Adam Mickiewicz University Press, Nowowiejskiego 55, 61-734 Poznan, Poland. TEL 527-380. FAX 61-526425. TELEX 413260 UAMPL. bk.rev. **Indexed:** Psychol.Abstr.
Formerly: Uniwersytet im. Adama Mickiewicza w Poznaniu. Wydzial Historyczny. Prace. Seria Psychologia-Pedagogika (ISSN 0083-4216)
Description: Contains current research results of one author in the field of psychology, including monographs and Ph.D. works.

150 GW
PSYCHOLOGIA UNIVERSALIS FORSCHUNGSERGEBNISSE AUS DEM GESAMTGEBIET DER PSYCHOLOGIE. 1952. irreg., no.49, 1987. price varies. Verlag Anton Hain GmbH, Savignystr. 53, 6000 Frankfurt a.M. 1, Germany. Ed.Bd. **Indexed:** Psychol.Abstr.

PSYCHOLOGIA WYCHOWAWCZA/EDUCATIONAL PSYCHOLOGY. see *EDUCATION*

150 BE ISSN 0033-2879
BF30 CODEN: PBELAN
PSYCHOLOGICA BELGICA. (Supplement avail.) (Text in Dutch, English, French; summaries in English) 1954. s-a. 1000 Fr. (effective 1992). Societe Belge de Psychologie - Belgische Vereniging voor Psychologie, Tiensestraat 102, B-3000 Leuven, Belgium. FAX 016-286000. (Subscr. to: Editions Peeters s.p.r.l., Bondegnotenlaan 153, B-3000 Leuven, Belgium. TEL 016-235170) Eds. A. Marcoen, S. Bredart. adv.; bk.rev.; abstr.; cum.index; circ. 450. (back issues avail.) **Indexed:** Biol.Abstr., C.I.S. Abstr., Curr.Cont., Psychol.Abstr., SSCI.
—BLDSC shelfmark: 6946.287000.

152 US ISSN 1040-3590
PSYCHOLOGICAL ASSESSMENT: A JOURNAL OF CONSULTING AND CLINICAL PSYCHOLOGY. 1989. q. $125 to non-members (foreign $143); members $50; institutions $250 (foreign $286) (effective 1992). American Psychological Association, 750 First St., N.E., Washington, DC 20002-4242. TEL 202-336-5500. FAX 202-336-5568. Ed. Alan E. Kazdin. circ. 4,100. **Indexed:** Psychol.Abstr., Psycscan C.P.
—BLDSC shelfmark: 6946.293500.
Description: Original empirical articles concerning clinical assessment and evaluations.
Refereed Serial

150.19 SA
PSYCHOLOGICAL ASSOCIATION OF SOUTH AFRICA. NEWSLETTER. q. free. Psychological Association of South Africa, P.O. Box 2729, Pretoria, South Africa. TEL 012-326-1981.
Formerly: Psychological Institute of the Republic of South Africa. Newsletter.

150 SA
PSYCHOLOGICAL ASSOCIATION OF SOUTH AFRICA. PROCEEDINGS. (Text in Afrikaans, English) 1962. a. free. Psychological Association of South Africa, P.O. Box 2729, Pretoria, South Africa. TEL 012-326-1981.
Formerly: Psychological Institute of the Republic of South Africa. Proceedings.

PSYCHOLOGY

150　　　　　　　US　　ISSN 0033-2909
BF1　　　　　　　　　CODEN: PSBUAI
PSYCHOLOGICAL BULLETIN. 1904. bi-m. $115 to non-members (foreign $133); members $45; institutions $230 (foreign $266) (effective 1992). American Psychological Association, 750 First St., N.E., Washington, DC 20002-4242. TEL 202-336-5568. FAX 202-336-5568. Ed. John C. Masters. adv.; charts; illus.; index; circ. 7,600. (also avail. in microform from MIM,UMI; reprint service avail. from UMI,KTO) **Indexed:** Acad.Ind., Adol.Ment.Hlth.Abstr., ASSIA, Biol.Abstr., C.I.J.E., Child Devel.Abstr., Crim.Just.Abstr., Curr.Adv.Ecol.Sci., Curr.Cont., Educ.Admin.Abstr., Ergon.Abstr., Ind.Med., M.L.A., Mid.East: Abstr.& Ind., Nutr.Abstr., Pers.Lit., Psychol.Abstr., Psyscan C.P., Psyscan D.P., Psyscan, Soc.Sci.Ind., Soc.Work Res.& Abstr., Sp.Ed.Needs Abstr., SSCI, Stud.Wom.Abstr.
—BLDSC shelfmark: 6946.300000.
Description: Comprehensive and integrative reviews and interpretations of critical substantive and methodological issues and practical problems from all the areas of psychology.
Refereed Serial

370.15 150　　　　US　　ISSN 1047-840X
BF1
▼**PSYCHOLOGICAL INQUIRY;** an international journal of peer commentary and review. 1990. q. $37.50 to individuals (foreign $62.50); institutions $135 (foreign $160). Lawrence Erlbaum Associates, Inc., 365 Broadway, Hillsdale, NJ 07642. TEL 201-666-4110. FAX 201-666-2394. Ed. Lawrence A. Pervin.
—BLDSC shelfmark: 6946.380000.
Refereed Serial

616.89　　　　　　　US　　ISSN 0048-5748
　　　　　　　　　　　　CODEN: PSYIA
PSYCHOLOGICAL ISSUES. 1959. irreg., no.57, 1990. price varies. International Universities Press, Inc., 59 Boston Post Rd., Box 1524, Madison, CT 06443-1524. TEL 203-245-4000. Ed. Herbert Schlesinger. illus. **Indexed:** Biol.Abstr., Ind.Med., Mid.East: Abstr.& Ind., Psychol.Abstr., SSCI.
—BLDSC shelfmark: 6946.400000.
Formerly: Psychological Issues. Monograph (ISSN 0079-7359)
Refereed Serial

150　　　　　　　US　　ISSN 0033-2925
BF173.A2
PSYCHOLOGICAL PERSPECTIVES; a Jungian review. 1970. s-a. $18 (foreign $21). C.G. Jung Institute of Los Angeles, 10349 W. Pico Blvd., Los Angeles, CA 90064. TEL 310-556-1193. FAX 310-556-1193. Ed. Ernest L. Rossi. adv.; bk.rev.; film rev.; index; circ. 18,000. (also avail. in microform from UMI; reprint service avail. from UMI) **Indexed:** Psychol.Abstr.
—BLDSC shelfmark: 6946.510000.
Description: Journal of Jungian thought featuring articles, interviews, poetry, and fiction.

150 152　　　　　US　　ISSN 0033-2933
BF1　　　　　　　　　CODEN: PYRCAI
PSYCHOLOGICAL RECORD; a quarterly journal in theoretical and experimental psychology. 1937. q. $20 to individuals; students $10; institutions $55 (effective 1992). Kenyon College, Gambier, OH 43022-9623. TEL 614-427-5377. FAX 614-427-4950. Ed. Charles E. Rice. adv.; bk.rev.; index; circ. 1,500. (also avail. in microform from UMI; back issues avail.; reprint service avail. from UMI,ISI) **Indexed:** Adol.Ment.Hlth.Abstr., ASSIA, Biol.Abstr., Child Devel.Abstr., Crim.Just.Abstr., Curr.Adv.Ecol.Sci., Curr.Cont., Ind.Med., Lang.& Lang.Behav.Abstr., Mid.East: Abstr.& Ind., Nutr.Abstr., Psychol.Abstr., Sci.Cit.Ind., Soc.Sci.Ind., SSCI.
—BLDSC shelfmark: 6946.520000.

150　　　　　　　US　　ISSN 0033-2941
BF21　　　　　　　　CODEN: PYRTAZ
PSYCHOLOGICAL REPORTS. 1955. bi-m. (2 vols./yr.). $210. Dr. C.H. Ammons & Dr. R.B. Ammons, Eds. & Pubs., Box 9229, Missoula, MT 59807. bk.rev.; charts; illus.; stat.; index; circ. 1,800. (also avail. in microform) **Indexed:** Adol.Ment.Hlth.Abstr., Biol.Abstr., CERDIC, Chic.Per.Ind., CINAHL, Commun.Abstr., Crim.Just.Abstr., Curr.Cont., Curr.Lit.Fam.Plan., Dent.Ind., Ergon.Abstr., Excerp.Med., Ind.Med., Lang.& Lang.Behav.Abstr., Mid.East: Abstr.& Ind., PSI, Psychol.Abstr., Res.High.Educ.Abstr., Risk Abstr., Sage Fam.Stud.Abstr., Sci.Cit.Ind., Soc.Sci.Ind., SSCI, Stud.Wom.Abstr.
—BLDSC shelfmark: 6946.525000.

150　　　　　　　GW　　ISSN 0340-0727
BF3　　　　　　　　　CODEN: PSREDJ
PSYCHOLOGICAL RESEARCH; an international journal of perception, learning and communication. 1921. 4/yr. DM.388($207) Springer-Verlag, Heidelberger Platz 3, D-1000 Berlin 33, Germany. TEL 030-8207-1. (Also Heidelberg, Tokyo, Vienna, and New York) Ed. E. Scheerer. cum.index: vols.1-36. (also avail. in microform from UMI; reprint service avail. from ISI) **Indexed:** Biol.Abstr., Curr.Cont., Ind.Med., Mid.East: Abstr.& Ind., Psychol.Abstr., SSCI.
—BLDSC shelfmark: 6946.527000.
Supersedes: Psychologische Forschung.

150　　　　　　　SW　　ISSN 0555-5620
BF21.A1　　　　　　　CODEN: PRBUDE
PSYCHOLOGICAL RESEARCH BULLETIN. (Text in English) 1961. irreg. (approx. 8/yr.). SEK 120 includes irreg. Monograph Series; subscription is suspended during 1991, but subscribers already on mailing list will continue to receive forthcoming issues free of charge. Lunds Universitet, Department of Psychology, Paradisgatan 5 P, 223 50 Lund, Sweden. TEL 046-10 87 55. FAX 46-46-10-42-09. Ed.Bd. bibl.; charts; cum.index; circ. 475. **Indexed:** Psychol.Abstr.
—BLDSC shelfmark: 6946.528000.
Description: Empirical psychological studies, frequently concerned with personality.

150　　　　　　　II　　ISSN 0970-6097
BF76.5
PSYCHOLOGICAL RESEARCH JOURNAL. 1977. s-a. Rs.50($20) (effective 1991). Psychological Research Academy, Suite 9, 37 Syed Amir Ali Ave., Calcutta 700019, India. Ed.Bd. adv.; bk.rev.; index. **Indexed:** G.Indian Per.Lit., Indian Psychol.Abstr., Psychol.Abstr.

150　　　　　　　US　　ISSN 0033-295X
BF1　　　　　　　　　CODEN: PSRVAX
PSYCHOLOGICAL REVIEW. 1894. q. $65 to non-members (foreign $77); members $26; institutions $130 (foreign $154) (effective 1992). American Psychological Association, 750 First St., N.E., Washington, DC 20002-4242. TEL 202-336-5500. FAX 202-336-5568. Ed. Walter Kintsch. adv.; bibl.; charts; index; circ. 6,000. (also avail. in microform from MIM,UMI; reprint service avail. from KTO) **Indexed:** Acad.Ind., ASSIA, Biol.Abstr., C.I.J.E., Child Devel.Abstr., Cont.Pg.Manage., Curr.Adv.Ecol.Sci., Curr.Cont., Curr.Lit.Fam.Plan, Ergon.Abstr., Ind.Med., Lang.& Lang.Behav.Abstr., M.L.A., Mid.East: Abstr.& Ind., Psychol.Abstr., Psyscan D.P., Soc.Sci.Ind., Soc.Work Res.& Abstr., Sp.Ed.Needs Abstr., SSCI, Yrbk.Assoc.Educ.& Rehab.Blind.
—BLDSC shelfmark: 6946.530000.
Description: Includes articles that make theoretical contributions to all areas of scientific psychology.
Refereed Serial

150.19　　　　　　UK　　ISSN 0956-7976
BF1　　　　　　　　　CODEN: PSYSET
▼**PSYCHOLOGICAL SCIENCE.** 1990. 6/yr. $50 to individuals; institutions $100. (American Psychological Society) Cambridge University Press, Edinburgh Bldg., Shaftesbury Rd., Cambridge CB2 2UR, England. TEL 0223-312393. FAX 0223-315052. TELEX 851817256. (U.S. addr.: Cambridge University Press, 40 W. 20th St., New York, NY 10011) Ed. William Estes. **Indexed:** Psychol.Abstr.
—BLDSC shelfmark: 6946.530300.

150　　　　　　　II　　ISSN 0033-2968
BF1
PSYCHOLOGICAL STUDIES. (Text in English) 1956. 3/yr. Rs.170($30) Department of Psychology, University of Calicut, Calicut 673 635, Kerala, India. Ed. K. Kunhikrishnan. adv.; bk.rev.; charts; illus.; stat.; index; circ. 500. (reprint service avail. from ISI) **Indexed:** Psychol.Abstr., Sci.Cit.Ind., SSCI.
—BLDSC shelfmark: 6946.531100.

150　　　　　　　AT
PSYCHOLOGICAL TEST BULLETIN. 1964. 2/yr. (foreign Aus.$46). Australian Council for Educational Research, P.O. Box 210, Hawthorn, Vic. 3122, Australia. TEL 03-819-1400. FAX 03-819-5502. Ed. John Elkins. circ. 400.
Formerly: Bulletin for Psychologists.
Description: Articles dealing with the use and interpretation of tests in educational, clinical, industrial and research contexts.

PSYCHOLOGIE ET EDUCATION. see *EDUCATION*

152.8　　　　　　FR　　ISSN 0296-8770
PSYCHOLOGIE ET PSYCHOMETRIE. s-a. 80 F. Editions Scientifiques et Psychologiques, 6 bis, rue Andre Chenier, 92130 Issy-les-Moulineaux, France. TEL 46-45-38-12. FAX 40-95-73-32. TELEX 270 105 F. Eds. Pierre Favreau, Francis Van Dam.
—BLDSC shelfmark: 6946.532080.

150　　　　　　　FR　　ISSN 0033-2984
BF2　　　　　　　　　CODEN: PSFRAT
PSYCHOLOGIE FRANCAISE. 1956. 4/yr. 490 F. (Societe Francaise de Psychologie) Dunod, 15 rue Gossin, 92543 Montrouge Cedex, France. TEL 33-1-40-92-65-00. FAX 33-1-40-92-65-97. TELEX 270 004. (Subscr. to: Centrale des Revues, 11 rue Gossin, 92543 Montrouge Cedex, France. TEL 33-1-46-56-52-66) Ed. C. Bonnet. bibl.; charts; illus.; index; circ. 2,800. (reprint service avail. from SWZ) **Indexed:** Biol.Abstr., Lang.& Lang.Behav.Abstr., Psychol.Abstr., SSCI.
—BLDSC shelfmark: 6946.532200.
Description: Publishes reviews of original investigations, articles covering theoretical reflection regarding the practice of psychology.

150　　　　　　　GW　　ISSN 0340-1677
PSYCHOLOGIE HEUTE. 1974. m. DM.72. Verlag Julius Beltz, Am Hauptbahnhof 10, Postfach 100154, 6940 Weinheim, Germany. TEL 06201-60070. FAX 06201-17464. TELEX 465500-BELTZD. Ed. Heiko Ernst. adv.; bk.rev.; bibl.; charts; illus.; stat.; index; circ. 70,000. **Indexed:** Excerp.Med.
Description: Covers the behavioral sciences.

301.1 150　　　　GW　　ISSN 0170-0537
PSYCHOLOGIE UND GESELLSCHAFTSKRITIK. 1977. 4/yr. DM.40($25) Initiative Kritischer Psychologinnen und Psychologen, Buergerbuschweg 47, 2900 Oldenburg, Germany. TEL 0441-64126. Ed.Bd. adv.; bk.rev.; index; circ. 2,500. (back issues avail.)
Description: Critique of mainstream psychology in theory and practice; social foundation of psychology.

150　　　　　　　GW　　ISSN 0079-7405
PSYCHOLOGIE UND PERSON. 1961. irreg., no.26, 1990. price varies. Ernst Reinhardt, GmbH und Co., Verlag, Kemnatenstr. 46, 8000 Munich 19, Germany. TEL 089-1783005.

158　　　　　　　CS　　ISSN 0033-300X
HF5548.8　　　　　　CODEN: PSVPB2
PSYCHOLOGIE V EKONOMICKE PRAXI/APPLIED INDUSTRIAL PSYCHOLOGY; casopis pro pomoc hospodarske praxi. (Text in Czech or Slovak; summaries in English, German, Russian) 1966. q. 35 Kcs.($13.20) Universita Karlova, Filosoficka Fakulta, Nam. Krasnoarmejcu 1, 11638 Prague 1, Czechoslovakia. (Subscr. to: Artia, Ve Smeckach 30, 111 27 Prague 1, Czechoslovakia) Ed. Zbynek Bures. bk.rev.; abstr.; bibl.; charts; illus.; stat.; index; circ. 4,000. (tabloid format; also avail. in microform) **Indexed:** C.I.S. Abstr., Ergon.Abstr., Psychol.Abstr.

054.1　　　　　　　FR
PSYCHOLOGIES.* 1970. m. 9 F. per no. Loft International, 1 rue Lord Byron, 75008 Paris, France. Ed. Jacques Mousseau. adv.; bk.rev.; illus.; index; circ. 80,000. **Indexed:** Curr.Cont., Pt.de Rep. (1979-), SSCI.
Formerly (until 1983): Psychologie (ISSN 0032-1583)

PSYCHOLOGY

150   GW   ISSN 0033-3018
BF3
PSYCHOLOGISCHE BEITRAEGE; Vierteljahresschrift fuer alle Gebiete der Psychologie. (Text in German; summaries in English and French) 1953. 4/yr. DM.121. (Deutsche Gesellschaft fuer Psychologie) Verlag Anton Hain GmbH, Savignystr. 53, 6000 Frankfurt a.M. 1, Germany. Ed.Bd. adv.; bk.rev.; abstr.; bibl.; charts; index, cum.index every 10 yrs.; circ. 600. **Indexed:** Biol.Abstr., Curr.Cont., Ergon.Abstr., Ger.J.Psych., Psychol.Abstr., SSCI.
—BLDSC shelfmark: 6946.533500.

150   GW   ISSN 0033-3042
BF3
PSYCHOLOGISCHE RUNDSCHAU. (Text in German; summaries in English) 1949. q. DM.48. (Deutsche Gesellschaft fuer Psychologie) Verlag fuer Psychologie Dr. C.J. Hogrefe, Rohnsweg 25, Postfach 3751, 3400 Goettingen, Germany. TEL 0551-54044. (Co-Sponsor: Berufsverband Deutscher Psychologen) Ed. W. Prinz. adv.; bk.rev.; abstr.; charts; index; circ. 5,500. (reprint service avail. from SWZ) **Indexed:** Child Devel.Abstr., Psychol.Abstr., SSCI.

150   UK   ISSN 0952-8229
THE PSYCHOLOGIST. vol.34, 1981. m. £39. British Psychological Society, St. Andrews House, 48 Princess Rd., E., Leicester LE1 7DR, England. TEL 0533-549568. FAX 0533-470787. Eds. Mary Boyle, Ray Bull. adv.; bk.rev.; abstr.; circ. 17,000. (also avail. in microform; reprint service avail. from ISI,SWZ,UMI) **Indexed:** Br.Hum.Ind., Curr.Adv.Ecol.Sci., Curr.Cont., Ergon.Abstr., Psychol.Abstr., SSCI.
—BLDSC shelfmark: 6946.534680.
Formerly: British Psychological Society. Bulletin (ISSN 0007-1692)

150   US   ISSN 0033-3077
BF1   CODEN: PYCHBR
PSYCHOLOGY; a journal of human behavior. 1964. q. $18 (foreign $21.50). Penn State University, 201 White Oak Dr., White Oak, PA 15131. Ed. Dr. Cash Kowalski. adv.; bk.rev.; circ. 4,000. (also avail. in microform from UMI; reprint service avail. from UMI) **Indexed:** Biol.Abstr., C.I.J.E., Commun.Abstr., Curr.Cont., Lang.& Lang.Behav.Abstr., Psychol.Abstr.
—BLDSC shelfmark: 6946.535200.
Description: Devoted to the basic research, theory, and techniques in the general field of psychology.

PSYCHOLOGY AND AGING. see *GERONTOLOGY AND GERIATRICS*

150   US
PSYCHOLOGY AND DEVELOPING SOCIETIES. 1989. s-a. $26 to individuals; institutions $52. Sage Publications, Inc., 2455 Teller Rd., Newbury Park, CA 91320. TEL 805-499-0721. FAX 805-499-0871. Ed. Durganand Sinha. abstr. (back issues avail.)
Description: Provides an international forum for psychologists concerned with problems of developing societies. Publishes theoretical, empirical, and review papers which help to further our understanding of the problems of these societies.

155   US   ISSN 0887-0446
R726.7   CODEN: PSHEE4
PSYCHOLOGY & HEALTH; an international journal. 1987. 4/yr. (in 1 vol.; 4 nos./vol.). $94. Harwood Academic Publishers, 270 Eighth Ave., New York, NY 10011. TEL 212-206-8900. FAX 212-645-2459. TELEX 236735 GOPUB UR. (Subscr. to: Box 786, Cooper Sta., New York, NY 10276. TEL 800-545-8398; UK subscr. to: P.O. Box 90, Reading, Berkshire RG1 8JL, England. TEL 0734-560-080) Ed. Dr. John Weinman. (also avail. in microform) **Indexed:** Psychol.Abstr.
—BLDSC shelfmark: 6946.535325.
Description: Health psychology forum dealing with the psychological and social factors in the etiology and outcome of physical illnesses. Promotes physical well-being through health education, prevention and behavior change.
Refereed Serial

301.1 150   US   ISSN 0742-6046
PSYCHOLOGY & MARKETING. 1984. q. $195 (foreign $270). John Wiley & Sons, Inc., Journals, 605 Third Ave., New York, NY 10158. TEL 212-850-6000. FAX 212-850-6088. TELEX 12-7063. Ed. Ronald Cohen. adv.; circ. 700. **Indexed:** Psychol.Abstr.
—BLDSC shelfmark: 6946.535340.
Description: Promotes understanding of the nature and operation of psychological principles as applied to strategies in the marketing industry.

370.15 301 613.7   US   ISSN 0885-7423
GV706
PSYCHOLOGY AND SOCIOLOGY OF SPORT: CURRENT SELECTED RESEARCH. 1986. a. $57.50. A M S Press, Inc., 56 E. 13th St., New York, NY 10003. TEL 212-777-4700. FAX 212-995-5413. Eds. Lee Vander Velden, James H. Humphrey. index. (back issues avail.)
—BLDSC shelfmark: 6946.535430.
Description: Research on contemporary problems of interest to behavioral scientists in the area of sport.

370.15 150   US   ISSN 0033-3085
LB1101
PSYCHOLOGY IN THE SCHOOLS. 1964. q. $35 to individuals; libraries $100. Clinical Psychology Publishing Co., Inc., 4 Conant Sq., Brandon, VT 05733. TEL 802-247-6871. FAX 802-247-6853. Ed. Dr. Gerald B. Fuller. adv.; bk.rev.; bibl.; index; circ. 1,700. (also avail. in microform from MIM,UMI; back issues avail.) **Indexed:** Adol.Ment.Hlth.Abstr., C.I.J.E., Cont.Pg.Educ., Educ.Ind., Except.Child.Educ.Abstr., Lang.& Lang.Behav.Abstr., Psychol.Abstr., Sp.Ed.Needs Abstr., SSCI.
—BLDSC shelfmark: 6946.536400.
Refereed Serial

152.5   US   ISSN 0079-7421
BF683   CODEN: PYLMA
PSYCHOLOGY OF LEARNING AND MOTIVATION: ADVANCES IN RESEARCH AND THEORY. 1967. irreg., vol.26, 1990. Academic Press, Inc., 1250 Sixth Ave., San Diego, CA 92101. TEL 619-231-0926. FAX 619-699-6715. Ed. K.W. Spence. (reprint service avail. from ISI) **Indexed:** Educ.Ind., SSCI.
—BLDSC shelfmark: 6946.535700.

PSYCHOLOGY OF MUSIC. see *MUSIC*

155 305.4   UK   ISSN 0361-6843
HQ1206   CODEN: PWOQDY
PSYCHOLOGY OF WOMEN QUARTERLY. 1976. q. $34 to individuals; institutions $89. (American Psychological Association, Division 35) Cambridge University Press, Edinburgh Bldg., Shaftesbury Rd., Cambridge CB2 2RU, England. TEL 0223-312393. FAX 0223-315052. TELEX 851817256. (North American addr.: 40 W. 20th St., New York, NY 10011) Ed. Judith Worell. adv. (also avail. in microform from UMI) **Indexed:** Abstr.Anthropol., Adol.Ment.Hlth.Abstr., ASSIA, C.I.J.E., Child Devel.Abstr., Curr.Cont., Curr.Lit.Fam.Plan., Human Resour.Abstr., Lang.& Lang.Behav.Abstr., Psychol.Abstr., Res.High.Educ.Abstr., Sage Pub.Admin.Abstr., Sage Urb.Stud.Abstr., Soc.Sci.Ind., Soc.Work Res.& Abstr., Sociol.Abstr., Sp.Ed.Needs Abstr., SSCI, Stud.Wom.Abstr., Wom.Stud.Abstr. (1976-).
—BLDSC shelfmark: 6946.538000.

150   PK   ISSN 0033-3093
PSYCHOLOGY QUARTERLY. (Text in English) 1964. q. Rs.30($15) Government College, Psychology Department, Lahore, Pakistan. Ed. Syed Azhar Ali Rizvi. bk.rev.; charts; stat.; circ. 300. **Indexed:** CINAHL, Psychol.Abstr.
Formerly: Journal of Psychology.

150   US   ISSN 0033-3107
BF1   CODEN: PSTOAM
PSYCHOLOGY TODAY. 1967-1989 (Dec.); resumed 1991. m. $17.95 (effective 1992). Sussex Publishers Inc., 24 E. 23rd St., 5th Fl., New York, NY 10010. TEL 212-260-7210. FAX 212-260-7445. (Subscr. to: Box 55046, Boulder, CO 80322. TEL 800-234-8361) Ed. Owen Lipstein. adv.; bk.rev.; bibl.; charts; illus.; stat.; index; circ. 884,224. (also avail. in microform from MIM) **Indexed:** Acad.Ind., ASSIA, Biol.Dig., Bk.Rev.Ind. (1973-), CCR, Child.Bk.Rev.Ind. (1973-), CMI, Crim.Just.Abstr., Curr.Cont., Curr.Lit.Fam.Plan., Except.Child.Educ.Abstr., Excerp.Med., Film Lit.Ind. (1983-), Fut.Surv., G.Soc.Sci.& Rel.Per.Lit., High.Educ.Curr.Aware.Bull., Hlth.Ind., Mag.Ind., Mid.East: Abstr.& Ind., Peace Res.Abstr., Pers.Lit., PMR, R.G., Soc.Sci.Ind., Sportsearch, SSCI, TOM.
●Also available online. Vendor(s): DIALOG.
Refereed Serial

150   NE   ISSN 0033-3115
DE PSYCHOLOOG. 1966. m. fl.95 to individuals; institutions fl.175. (Nederlands Instituut van Psychologen - Netherlands Psychological Association) Van Gorcum en Co. B.V., P.O. Box 43, 9400 AA Assen, Netherlands. TEL 05920-46864. FAX 05920-72064. Ed.Bd. adv.; bk.rev.; abstr.; bibl.; index, cum.index; circ. 7,000. **Indexed:** Psychol.Abstr.
—BLDSC shelfmark: 6946.539300.

616.89   GW
PSYCHOMED. q. DM.98 (foreign DM.108). Quintessenz Verlags GmbH, Ifenpfad 2-4, 1000 Berlin 42, Germany. TEL 030-74006-0. FAX 030-7415080.

150   US   ISSN 0033-3123
BF1
PSYCHOMETRIKA; a journal devoted to the development of psychology as a quantitative rational science. 1936. q. $70. c/o Cynthia Null, Department of Psychology, College of William and Mary, Williamsburg, VA 23185. TEL 804-221-3882. FAX 804-221-3896. Ed. Lawrence Hubert. bk.rev.; abstr.; bibl.; charts; index; circ. 2,200. (also avail. in microform from MIM,UMI; reprint service avail. from UMI) **Indexed:** Biol.Abstr., C.I.J.E., Child Devel.Abstr., Commun.Abstr., Compumath, Curr.Cont., Ergon.Abstr., J.Cont.Quant.Meth., Math.R., Mid.East: Abstr.& Ind., Psychol.Abstr., Psycscan, SSCI.
—BLDSC shelfmark: 6946.540000.

PSYCHOMUSICOLOGY; a journal of research in music cognition. see *MUSIC*

150   US   ISSN 0090-5054
BF1   CODEN: BPNSBY
PSYCHONOMIC SOCIETY. BULLETIN. 1973. bi-m. $85 (foreign $93). Psychonomic Society, Inc., 1710 Fortview Rd., Austin, TX 78704. TEL 512-462-2442. adv.; circ. 1,300. (also avail. in microform from KTO,UMI; back issues avail.; reprint service avail. from UMI) **Indexed:** Biol.Abstr., Curr.Adv.Ecol.Sci., Curr.Cont., Ergon.Abstr., M.L.A., Mid.East: Abstr.& Ind., Psychol.Abstr., SSCI.
—BLDSC shelfmark: 2685.140000.
Description: Short-report journal, publishing articles by society members.

PSYCHOPHYSIOLOGY. see *MEDICAL SCIENCES*

301.1 150   SZ   ISSN 1013-5987
PSYCHOSCOPE. (Text in French and German) 1980. 10/yr. 64 SFr. (students 38 SFr.). Foederation der Schweizer Psychologen (FSP), Administration B S P, Caecilienstr. 26, CH-3000 Berne 14, Switzerland. TEL 031-460469. FAX 031-460477. Ed. Pia Somogyi. adv.; bk.rev.; circ. 3,400.
Formerly: Schweizer Psychologen. Bulletin.

PSYCHOSOCIAL EPIDEMIOLOGY SERIES. see *MEDICAL SCIENCES — Communicable Diseases*

PSYCHOSOCIAL NEWS. see *MEDICAL SCIENCES — Hematology*

150 301   US   ISSN 0147-5622
RC439.5
PSYCHOSOCIAL REHABILITATION JOURNAL. 1976. 4/yr. $39 to individuals; institutions $75; students $22. Boston University, Sargent College of Allied Health Professions, International Association of Psychosocial Rehabilitation Services and the Department of Rehabilitation Counseling, 730 Commonwealth Ave., Boston, MA 02215. TEL 617-353-3549. FAX 617-353-7700. Eds. William Anthony, George Wolkon. adv.; bk.rev.; circ. 1,300. (also avail. in microfilm; reprint service avail. from UMI) **Indexed:** Adol.Ment.Hlth.Abstr., C.I.N.L., Community Ment.Health Rev., Ind.Med., Nurs.Abstr., Psychol.Abstr., Rehabil.Lit.
—BLDSC shelfmark: 6946.553500.
  Description: Provides information relevant to the rehabilitation of persons with severe psychiatric disability.
  Refereed Serial

301.1 150   GW   ISSN 0171-3434
PSYCHOSOZIAL;* Zeitschrift fuer Analyse, Praevention und Therapie psychosozialer Konflikte und Krankheiten. 1978. q. DM.32. Verlag Julius Beltz, Am Hauptbahnhof 10, 6940 Weinheim, Germany. Ed.Bd. adv.; bk.rev.; circ. 4,500.
—BLDSC shelfmark: 6946.558030.

616.89   SZ   ISSN 0251-737X
CODEN: PSYTEW
PSYCHOTHERAPIES. (Text in French) 1981. q. 84 SFr.($60) (Medicine et Hygiene) Editions Medecine et Hygiene, Case Postale 456, CH-1211 Geneva 4, Switzerland. TEL 022-469355. FAX 022-475610. Ed.Bd. adv.; bk.rev.; circ. 900. (reprint service avail. from UMI)
—BLDSC shelfmark: 6946.558400.

616.89   US
PSYCHOTHERAPY. 1963. q. $60 to individuals (foreign $70); institutions $75 (foreign $85); students $35 (foreign $40). American Psychological Association, 750 First St., N.E., Washington, DC 20003-4242. TEL 202-336-5500. FAX 202-336-5568. adv.; bk.rev.; charts; index; circ. 6,000. (reprint service avail. from UMI,ISI) **Indexed:** Adol.Ment.Hlth.Abstr., Biol.Abstr., Psychol.Abstr., Psycscan C.P., SSCI.
  Former titles (until 1984): Psychotherapy: Theory, Research and Practice (ISSN 0033-3204); Psychotherapy (ISSN 0090-144X)

616.89   US
PSYCHOTHERAPY BULLETIN. 1968. 4/yr. $8 to non-members. American Psychological Association, 750 First St., N.E., Washington, DC 20002-4242. TEL 202-336-5500. FAX 202-336-5568. adv.; bk.rev.; circ. 5,000.

616.89   US   ISSN 0164-078X
PSYCHOTHERAPY DIGEST. 1976. bi-m. $15. Box 1167, Del Mar, CA 92014. Ed. Victor Kops. bk.rev.; circ. 1,000. (looseleaf format; back issues avail.)

616.89   US   ISSN 0163-1543
PSYCHOTHERAPY FINANCES. 1974. m. $48. Ridgewood Financial Institute, Inc., Box 509, Ridgewood, NJ 07451. TEL 201-427-3366. FAX 201-427-3644. Ed. Herbert Klein. bk.rev.; circ. 7,000.
  Formerly (until 1977): Psychotherapy Economics (ISSN 0092-184X)

616.89   US   ISSN 0731-7158
RC455.2.P73
PSYCHOTHERAPY IN PRIVATE PRACTICE; innovations in clinical methods and management, consultation and practice management. 1983. q. $32 to individuals; institutions $60; libraries $125. Haworth Press, Inc., 10 Alice St., Binghamton, NY 13904. TEL 800-342-9678. FAX 607-722-1424. TELEX 4932599. Ed. Robert D. Weitz. adv.; bk.rev.; circ. 613. (also avail. in microfiche from HAW; back issues avail.; reprint service avail. from HAW) **Indexed:** Behav.Abstr., Bull.Signal., Chicago Psychoanal.Lit.Ind., P.A.I.S., Psychol.Abstr., Soc.Work Res.& Abstr.
—BLDSC shelfmark: 6946.559400.
  Description: Covers issues and methods in the development of private practice for psychotherapists.
  Refereed Serial

301.1 150   US   ISSN 1047-9848
PSYCHOTHERAPY LETTER; resource exchange for psychotherapy professionals. m. $67 (Canada $77; elsewhere $87). Manisses Communications Group, Inc., 205 Governor St., Box 3357, Providence, RI 02906-0757. TEL 800-333-7771. FAX 401-861-6370.
  Formerly (until 1992): Psychotherapy Today.

616.89   US   ISSN 0738-6176
CODEN: PSPAEW
PSYCHOTHERAPY PATIENT; a quarterly journal of attribute-focused practice. 1984. q. $36 to individuals; institutions $60; libraries $105. Haworth Press, Inc., 10 Alice St., Binghamton, NY 13904. TEL 800-342-9678. FAX 607-722-1424. TELEX 4932599. Ed. Mark Stern. adv.; bk.rev.; circ. 475. (also avail. in microfiche from HAW; back issues avail.; reprint service avail. from HAW) **Indexed:** Psychol.Abstr., Soc.Work Res.& Abstr.
—BLDSC shelfmark: 6946.559300.
  Description: Devotes each issue to diagnostic, behavioral, and phenomenological groupings.
  Refereed Serial

616.89   US   ISSN 1050-3307
RC475
▼**PSYCHOTHERAPY RESEARCH.** 1991. q. $30 to individuals; institutions $60. (Society for Psychotherapy Research) Guilford Publications, Inc., 72 Spring St., 4th Fl., New York, NY 10012. TEL 212-431-9800. FAX 212-966-6708. Ed. Klaus Grawe. adv.
—BLDSC shelfmark: 6946.559430.
  Description: International communication on empirical findings in research on psychotherapeutic process and outcome.
  Refereed Serial

156   DK   ISSN 0107-1211
PSYKE & LOGOS. (Text in Danish; abstracts in English) 1980. 2/yr. DKK 245 (students DKK 180; foreign DKK 282). Dansk Psykologisk Forlag, Hans Knudsens Plads 1A, 2100 Copenhagen O, Denmark. TEL 31-182757. FAX 31-185758. Ed.Bd. bk.rev.; circ. 600. (back issues avail.) **Indexed:** Psychol.Abstr.
—BLDSC shelfmark: 6946.559790.

614.58 150   SW   ISSN 0033-3212
PSYKISK HAELSA/MENTAL HEALTH. 1960. q. SEK 185. Svenska Foereningen foer Psykisk Haelsovaard - Swedish Association for Mental Health, Box 45246, S-104 30 Stockholm, Sweden. TEL 08-23-19-25. FAX 08-7917563. Ed. Birgitta Nordelius. bk.rev.; circ. 6,000. **Indexed:** Psychol.Abstr.

150   DK
PSYKOLOG NYT. 1947. s-m. DKK 900. Dansk Psykologforening - Danish Psychological Association, Bjerregaards Sidevej 4, 2500 Valby, Denmark. TEL 01-163355. FAX 01-440855. Ed. Ida Schioerring. adv.; bk.rev.; tr.lit.; circ. 3,250. **Indexed:** Psychol.Abstr.
  Formerly: Dansk Psykolognyt (ISSN 0011-6432)

150   DK   ISSN 0107-3060
PSYKOLOGISK LABORATORIUM. FORSKNINGSRAPPORT. (Text in Danish; summaries in English) 1983. irreg. free. University of Copenhagen, Department of Psychology, Njalsgade 94, 2300 Copenhagen S, Denmark. Ed. Benny Karpauschof. circ. 200.

370.15 150   DK   ISSN 0906-219X
PSYKOLOGISK PAEDAGOGISK RAADGIVNING/JOURNAL OF SCHOOL PSYCHOLOGY; tidsskrift for paedagogisk psykologi og raadgivning. 1964. 6/yr. plus monographs. DKK 275 (students DKK 195; foreign DKK 225.40). Dansk Psykologisk Forlag, Hans Knudsen Plads 1A, 2100 Copenhagen OE, Denmark. TEL 31-182757. FAX 31-185758. Ed. Bjoern Glaesel. adv.; bk.rev.; abstr.; bibl.; index; circ. 1,400. (back issues avail.) **Indexed:** C.I.J.E., Psychol.Abstr., Soc.Work Res.& Abstr., SSCI.
  Formerly: Skolepsychologi (ISSN 0037-6493)

150   DK   ISSN 0906-2483
PSYKOLOGISK SET. 1982. 4/yr. DKK 140 (foreign DKK 114.75). Dansk Psykologisk Forlag, Hans Knudsens Plads 1A, 2100 Copenhagen O, Denmark. TEL 31-18-27-57. FAX 31-185758. Ed. Jan Enggaard. **Indexed:** Psychol.Abstr.
  Formerly: Psykologi.

150   HU   ISSN 0079-7456
BF636.A1
PSZICHOLOGIA A GYAKORLATBAN. 1963. irreg., vol.45, 1985. price varies. (Magyar Tudomanyos Akademia) Akademiai Kiado, Publishing House of the Hungarian Academy of Sciences, P.O. Box 24, H-1363 Budapest, Hungary.

150   HU   ISSN 0079-7464
PSZICHOLOGIAI TANULMANYOK. (Text in Hungarian; summaries in English and German) 1958. irreg., vol.15, 1979. price varies. (Magyar Tudomanyos Akademia) Akademiai Kiado, Publishing House of the Hungarian Academy of Sciences, P.O. Box 24, H-1363 Budapest, Hungary. **Indexed:** Psychol.Abstr.

150   US
PUBLICATIONS FOR THE ADVANCEMENT OF THEORY AND HISTORY IN PSYCHOLOGY. 1980. irreg. price varies. Ablex Publishing Corporation, 355 Chestnut St., Norwood, NJ 07648. TEL 201-767-8450. FAX 201-767-6717. TELEX 135-393. Ed. David Bakan.

150   NZ   ISSN 0079-7731
PUBLICATIONS IN PSYCHOLOGY. 1952. irreg., no.29, 1983. exchange basis. (Victoria University of Wellington, Department of Psychology) Victoria University Press, P.O. Box 600, Wellington, New Zealand. Eds. A.R. Forbes, M.J. White. circ. 100. **Indexed:** Psychol.Abstr.

PUDDING MAGAZINE; international journal of applied poetry. see *LITERATURE — Poetry*

PULSE OF THE PLANET. see *ENVIRONMENTAL STUDIES*

616.89   IT
QUADRANGOLO. 1974. q. L.45000. (Centro Studi Psicologici "Lo Spazio") Bulzoni Editore, Via dei Liburni 14, 00185 Rome, Italy. (Co-sponsor: Societa Italiana di Psicoterapia di Gruppo) Ed. Emiliana Mazzonis.

150   US   ISSN 0033-5010
BF173.A2
QUADRANT; the journal of contemporary Jungian thought. 1967. s-a. $25 to individuals; institutions $55. C.G. Jung Foundation for Analytical Psychology, Inc., 28 E. 39th St., New York, NY 10016. TEL 212-697-6430. FAX 201-767-6717. TELEX 135-393. (Subscr. to: Ablex Publishing, 355 Chestnut St., Norwood, NJ 07648. TEL 201-767-8455) Ed. Dr. Stephen Martin. adv.; bk.rev.; charts; illus.; circ. 2,000. (controlled). (reprint service avail.) **Indexed:** M.L.A., Psychoanal.Abstr., Psychol.Abstr.
—BLDSC shelfmark: 7168.025000.

152   UK   ISSN 0272-4987
QP351   CODEN: QJEADO
QUARTERLY JOURNAL OF EXPERIMENTAL PSYCHOLOGY. SECTION A: HUMAN EXPERIMENTAL PSYCHOLOGY. 1948. 4/yr. £50($95) to individuals; institutions £200($380). (Experimental Psychology Society) Lawrence Erlbaum Associates, Ltd., 27 Palmeira Mansions, Church Rd., Hove, E. Sussex BN3 2FA, England. TEL 0273-207411. FAX 0273-205612. Ed. Glyn W. Humphreys. adv.; bk.rev.; bibl.; charts; index; circ. 1,600. **Indexed:** ASSIA, Biol.Abstr., Br.Educ.Ind., Curr.Adv.Cell & Devel.Biol., Curr.Cont., Dent.Ind., Ind.Med., Mid.East: Abstr.& Ind., Psychol.Abstr., SSCI.
—BLDSC shelfmark: 7190.100000.
  Supersedes in part (in 1981): Quarterly Journal of Experimental Psychology (ISSN 0033-555X)
  Description: Presents original papers in all branches of human experimental psychology without limitation.
  Refereed Serial

PSYCHOLOGY

152 UK ISSN 0272-4995
QP351 CODEN: QJEBDT
QUARTERLY JOURNAL OF EXPERIMENTAL PSYCHOLOGY. SECTION B: COMPARATIVE AND PHYSIOLOGICAL PSYCHOLOGY. (Text in English; abstracts in French, Spanish) 1981. q. £27.50($53) to individuals; institutions £90($170). (Experimental Psychology Society) Lawrence Erlbaum Associates, Ltd., 27 Palmeira Mansions, Church Rd., Hove, E. Sussex BN3 2FA, England. TEL 0273-207411. FAX 0273-205612. Ed. A. Dickinson. adv.; bk.rev.; index. **Indexed:** ASSIA, Biol.Abstr., Curr.Adv.Cell & Devel.Biol., Dent.Ind., Ind.Med., Psychol.Abstr, SSCI.
—BLDSC shelfmark: 7190.200000.
Supersedes in part (in 1981): Quarterly Journal of Experimental Psychology (ISSN 0033-555X)
Description: Features articles on any topic within the field of animal psychology, not only on such traditional topics as conditioning, learning and motivation, but also on any aspect of animal behavior, comparative psychology and ethology.
Refereed Serial

QUARTERLY REVIEW OF FILM AND VIDEO. see *MOTION PICTURES*

150 GW
R K W KONTAKT. bi-m. Rationalisierungs-Kuratorium der Deutschen Wirtschaft e.V., Landesgruppe Bayern, Augustenstr. 84, Postfach 20 20 08, 8000 Munich 2, Germany. circ. 2,500.

301.1 150 IT
RASSEGNA DI PSICOLOGIA. 1984. N.S. 3/yr. L.40000 (foreign L.65000)(effective 1992). (Universita di Roma La Sapienza, Dipartimenti di Psicologia e Psicologia dei Processi di Sviluppo e Socializzazione) Franco Angeli Editore, Via Monza 106, 20127 Milan, Italy. TEL 02-2827651. Eds. C. Pontecorvo Pipermo, P. Bonaiuto.

READING AND WRITING; an interdisciplinary journal. see *LINGUISTICS*

READING PSYCHOLOGY; an international quarterly. see *EDUCATION — Teaching Methods And Curriculum*

READINGS; a journal of reviews and commentary in mental health. see *MEDICAL SCIENCES — Psychiatry And Neurology*

REALITY CHANGE; a magazine for people who want to change their lives. see *NEW AGE PUBLICATIONS*

614.58 616.8 340 GW ISSN 0724-2247
RECHT & PSYCHIATRIE. 1983. q. DM.43. Psychiatrie Verlag, Thomas-Mann-Str. 49a, 5300 Bonn 1, Germany. TEL 0228-695540. Ed. Ingeborg Rakete. circ. 900. (back issues avail.)
Description: Examines law and psychiatry.

150 371.9 US ISSN 0090-5550
RM930.A1
REHABILITATION PSYCHOLOGY. 1954. q. $32 to individuals; institutions $58. (American Psychological Association, Division of Rehabilitation Psychology) Springer Publishing Company, 536 Broadway, New York, NY 10012. TEL 212-431-4370. FAX 212-941-7842. Ed. Myron Eisenberg. adv.; bk.rev.; film rev.; charts; circ. 1,500. (back issues avail.) **Indexed:** Behav.Med.Abstr., Curr.Cont., Excerp.Med., Psychol.Abstr., Rehabil.Lit., SSCI, Yrbk.Assoc.Educ.& Rehab.Blind.
—BLDSC shelfmark: 7350.290000.

150 301 UY ISSN 0797-9754
BF5
RELACIONES. 1984. m. $24. Editorial Periodica S.R.L., Avda. Luis A. de Herrera, 1042, Ap. 708, 11300 Montevideo, Uruguay. Ed. Saul Paciuk. adv.; bk.rev.; circ. 4,000.

616.89 GW ISSN 0344-9602
REPORT PSYCHOLOGIE. 1974. 10/yr. DM.105 (foreign DM.120). Deutscher Psychologen Verlag GmbH, Heilsbachstr. 22, 5300 Bonn 1, Germany. TEL 0228-640726. FAX 0228-643118. adv.; bk.rev.; circ. 17,500.

301.1 150 US ISSN 0034-4907
HM251 CODEN: RRSPD4
REPRESENTATIVE RESEARCH IN SOCIAL PSYCHOLOGY. 1970. s-a. $10 to individuals; institutions $20. University of North Carolina at Chapel Hill, Department of Psychology, Social Psychology Graduate Students, Davie Hall, Campus Box 3270, Chapel Hill, NC 27599-3270. TEL 919-962-7636. FAX 919-962-2537. Eds. Nancy Yovetich, Jim Casebolt. adv.; bk.rev.; circ. 300. (also avail. in microform from PMC) **Indexed:** Adol.Ment.Hlth.Abstr., Curr.Cont., Psychol.Abstr., SSCI.
—BLDSC shelfmark: 7692.000000.

RESEARCH AND TEACHING IN DEVELOPMENTAL EDUCATION. see *EDUCATION*

150 616.8 362.7 US ISSN 0362-2428
BF1 CODEN: RCPBDC
RESEARCH COMMUNICATIONS IN PSYCHOLOGY, PSYCHIATRY AND BEHAVIOR. 1976. q. $85 (foreign $95). P J D Publications Ltd., Box 966, Westbury, NY 11590. TEL 516-626-0650. Ed.Bd. adv.; bk.rev.; abstr.; charts; illus.; index. (reprint service avail. from ISI) **Indexed:** Biol.Abstr., Chem.Abstr., Curr.Adv.Ecol.Sci., Curr.Cont., Curr.Lit.Fam.Plan., Excerp.Med., Psychol.Abstr.
—BLDSC shelfmark: 7736.550000.
Description: Information of value to experimental psychologists, psychiatrists, behavioral scientists, psychopharmacologists and basic and clinical scientists.
Refereed Serial

RESEARCH IN COMMUNITY AND MENTAL HEALTH; an annual compilation of research. see *PUBLIC HEALTH AND SAFETY*

301.18 US ISSN 0191-3085
HD28
RESEARCH IN ORGANIZATIONAL BEHAVIOR; an annual series of analytical essays and critical reviews. 1979. a. $63.50 to institutions. J A I Press Inc., 55 Old Post Rd., No. 2, Box 1678, Greenwich, CT 06836-1678. TEL 203-661-7602. Eds. Barry M. Staw, L.L. Cummings. **Indexed:** ASCA, Int.Lab.Doc., Psychol.Abstr., SSCI.
—BLDSC shelfmark: 7750.600000.

RESEARCH SYMPOSIUM ON THE PSYCHOLOGY AND ACOUSTICS OF MUSIC. PROCEEDINGS. see *MUSIC*

616.8 US
REVIEW OF BEHAVIOR THERAPY: THEORY & PRACTICE. 1973. biennial. price varies. Guilford Publications, Inc., 72 Spring St., 4th Fl., New York, NY 10012. TEL 212-431-9800. FAX 212-966-6708. Ed.Bd. (back issues avail.) **Indexed:** Biol.Abstr., Psychol.Abstr.
Formerly: Annual Review of Behavior Therapy: Theory and Practice (ISSN 0091-6595)
Description: Critical analyses of new developments in the theory and practice of behavior therapy.

150.19 US ISSN 0361-1531
CODEN: REXPB4
REVIEW OF EXISTENTIAL PSYCHOLOGY AND PSYCHIATRY. 1961. 3/yr. $30 to individuals; institutions $68. Box 23220, Seattle, WA 98102. TEL 206-524-3880. Ed. Keith Hoeller. adv.; bk.rev.; circ. 800. **Indexed:** Curr.Cont., Phil.Ind., Psychol.Abstr.
—BLDSC shelfmark: 7790.550000.
Formerly: Human Inquiries.
Description: Original essays and translations from the fields of literature and philosophy as well as psychology and psychiatry, presenting an existential and phenomenological approach to the understanding of human experience.
Refereed Serial

302.05 US ISSN 0270-1987
BF698
REVIEW OF PERSONALITY AND SOCIAL PSYCHOLOGY. 1980. a. $36 clothbound; $17.95 paperback. (Society for Personality and Social Psychology) Sage Publications, Inc., 2455 Teller Rd., Newbury Park, CA 91320. TEL 805-449-0721. FAX 805-499-0871. Ed. Clyde Hendrick. **Indexed:** Psychol.Abstr.
—BLDSC shelfmark: 7793.849400.

150 CI ISSN 0352-1605
BF8.S4 CODEN: RPSHDY
REVIJA ZA PSIHOLOGIJU. 1971. s-a. $15 (typically set in Mar.). Drustvo Psihologa S R Hrvatske - Croatian Psychological Association, Salajeva 3, Zagreb, Croatia. TEL 041-613-155. FAX 041-513-834. Ed. Vladimir Kolesaric. adv.; bk.rev.; circ. 1,000. **Indexed:** Psychol.Abstr.
Description: Publishes original scientific papers, theoretical contributions and critical surveys of research in all fields of psychology and related disciplines as well as relevant professional papers and news.

370.15 150 AG
REVISTA ARGENTINA DE PSICOPEDAGOGIA. 1981. fortn. $30. Fundacion Suzuki, Charlone 1689, San Miguel, 1663 Buenos Aires, Argentina. TEL 664-0771. Dir. Elizabeth J. Calvo de Suzuki. adv.; bk.rev.; abstr.; bibl.; circ. 500.
Supersedes (1975-1981): Revista de Psicopedagogia.

301.1 150 CU ISSN 0257-4322
REVISTA CUBANA DE PSICOLOGIA. (Text in Spanish; summaries in English, Spanish) 3/yr. $17 in N. America; S. America $18; Europe $22. Universidade de La Habana, Calle I No. 302, Entre 15 y 17, Havana 4, Cuba. TEL 32-5556-60. (Dist. by: Ediciones Cubanas, Obispo No. 527, Apdo. 605, Havana, Cuba)

616.89 BL
REVISTA DE PSICANALISE INTEGRAL. 1978. a. $4. (Sociedad Internacional de Trilogia Analitica - International Society of Analytical Trilogy) Proton Editora Ltda., Av. Rebouças 3115, C.E.P. 05401, Sao Paolo, SP, Brazil. Ed. Marc Andre R. Keppe. adv.; circ. 1,500.
Formerly: Analytical Trilogy.

616.89 AG ISSN 0034-8740
RC321
REVISTA DE PSICOANALISIS. (Text in Spanish; summaries in English and French) 1943. 6/yr. $80. Asociacion Psicoanalitica Argentina, Rodriguez Pena 1674, Buenos Aires, Argentina. bk.rev.; abstr.; index; circ. 2,000. (processed) **Indexed:** Excerp.Med., Psychoanal.Abstr., Psychol.Abstr.
—BLDSC shelfmark: 7870.130000.

150 PE ISSN 0254-9247
REVISTA DE PSICOLOGIA. 1983. s-a. $12.80. Pontificia Universidad del Peru, Departamento de Humanidades, Fondo Editorial, Apdo. 1761, Lima 100, Peru. Ed. Cecilia Thorne. adv.; circ. 1,000.

157 BL ISSN 0048-7740
REVISTA DE PSICOLOGIA NORMAL E PATOLOGICA. 1976-1979; N.S. 1979. irreg. Pontificia Universidade Catolica de Sao Paulo, Faculdade de Psicologia, Rua Monte Alegre 984, Sao Paulo, Brazil.

150 RM ISSN 0034-8759
BF8.R7
REVISTA DE PSIHOLOGIE. 1955. 4/yr. 100 lei($45) (Academia Romana) Editura Academiei Romane, Calea Victoriei 125, 79717 Bucharest, Rumania. (Dist. by: Rompresfilatelia, Export-Import Presa, Calea Grivitei 64-66, P.O. Box 12-201, 78104 Bucharest, Rumania) Ed. Constantin Voicu. bk.rev.; index; circ. 1,400. **Indexed:** Biol.Abstr., C.I.S. Abstr., Child Devel.Abstr., Ergon.Abstr., Lang.& Lang.Behav.Abstr., Nutr.Abstr., Psychol.Abstr.

150 CK ISSN 0120-0534
BF5 CODEN: RLPSBM
REVISTA LATINOAMERICANA DE PSICOLOGIA. 1969. 3/yr. $15 to individuals; institutions $25. Foundation for the Advancement of Psychology, Apdo. 92621, Bogota, Colombia. Ed. Ruben Ardila. adv.; bk.rev.; abstr.; bibl.; illus.; stat.; index; circ. 2,500. **Indexed:** Biol.Abstr., Curr.Cont., Psychol.Abstr., SSCI.
Description: International journal of all areas of psychology.

| 150 | MX | ISSN 0185-4534 |

REVISTA MEXICANA DE ANALISIS DE LA CONDUCTA/MEXICAN JOURNAL OF BEHAVIOR ANALYSIS. (Text in English and Spanish) 1975. 3/yr. $20 to individuals (Europe $25); institutions $35 (Europe $40). (Mexican Society of Behavior Analysis) Editorial Trillas, Apdo. Postal 21-182, 04000 Mexico, D.F., Mexico. TEL 5 547632. Ed. Florente Lopez. adv. contact: Florente Lopez. bk.rev.; bibl.; charts; illus.; stat.; index; circ. 1,000. (back issues avail.) Indexed: Adol.Ment.Hlth.Abstr., Curr.Cont., Psychol.Abstr.
  Description: Presents original research in behavior analysis and technical notes on diverse subjects of interest to behavioral scientists.

150.19   PO

REVISTA PORTUGUESA DE PSICANALISE. 1985. irreg., no.9, 1990. price varies. (Sociedade Portuguesa de Psicanalise) Edicoes Afrontamento, Lda., Rua de Costa Cabral, 859, Apdo. 2009, 4201 Porto Codex, Portugal. TEL 489271. FAX 491777. Eds. Carlos Amaral Dias, Jaime Milheiro.

150   UY

REVISTA URUGUAYA DE PSICOLOGIA. 1978. s-a. $10 (or exchange basis). (Asociacion de Psicologos Universitarios del Uruguay) Editorial Imago S.R.L., Gregorio Suarez 2719, Montevideo, Uruguay. Ed. Ricardo Landeira. bk.rev. Indexed: Psychol.Abstr.

150   SG

REVUE AFRICAINE ET MALGACHE DE PSYCHOLOGIE.* q. 5000 Fr.CFA. Association Generale des Psychologues Francophones d'Afrique et de Madagascar, c/o Secretariat Technique Permanent de la Conference des Ministeres de l'Education, Union Senegalaise de Banque, Dakar, Senegal.

| 150 370.15 | BE | ISSN 0035-0826 |
| LB1051.A2 | | CODEN: RBPPAA |

REVUE BELGE DE PSYCHOLOGIE ET DE PEDAGOGIE. 1934. q. 750 Fr. 40 rue du Disque, 1020 Brussels, Belgium. Ed. Gerard Goosens. bk.rev.; bibl.; charts. (reprint service avail. from ISI/UMI) Indexed: Lang.& Lang.Behav.Abstr., Psychol.Abstr.

301.1   CN   ISSN 0080-2492

REVUE CANADIENNE DE PSYCHO-EDUCATION. (Text in French; summaries in English and French) 1964. biennial. Can.$15 to individuals; institutions Can.$25. Universite de Montreal, Ecole de Psycho-Education, 750 bd. Gouin est., Montreal, Que. H2C 1A6, Canada. TEL 514-382-2500. FAX 514-385-9825. Ed. Serge Larivee. bk.rev.; circ. 600. Indexed: Canadiana, Psychol.Abstr., Pt.de Rep. (1983-), RADAR.
  —BLDSC shelfmark: 7896.219000.

158   FR
BF636.A1

REVUE EUROPEENE DE PSYCHOLOGIE APPLIQUEE/EUROPEAN REVIEW OF APPLIED PSYCHOLOGY. 1951. q. 350 F. Editions du Centre de Psychologie Appliquee, 48 Av. Victor Hugo, 75783 Paris Cedex 16, France. TEL 45-01-83-26. Eds. Robert Lepez, Claire Mays. adv.; bk.rev.; bibl.; charts; illus.; index; circ. 1,000. Indexed: Child Devel.Abstr., Excerp.Med., INSPEC, Psychol.Abstr., SSCI.
  Formerly (until 1991): Revue de Psychologie Appliquee (ISSN 0035-1709)

616.89   FR   ISSN 0035-2942
BF173.A2

REVUE FRANCAISE DE PSYCHANALYSE. (Includes special number: Congres de Psychanalyse des Langues Romanes. Rapports) 1927. bi-m. 570 F. (foreign 780 F.). (Societe Psychanalytique de Paris) Presses Universitaires de France, Departement des Revues, 14 av. du Bois-de-l'Epine, B.P. 90, 91003 Evry cedex, France. TEL 1-60-77-82-05. FAX 1-60-79-20-45. TELEX PUF 600 474 F. Ed.Bd. adv.; abstr.; bibl.; charts; index. (reprint service avail. from KTO) Indexed: Excerp.Med., Ind.Med., Psychoanal.Abstr., Psychol.Abstr., SSCI.
  —BLDSC shelfmark: 7904.280000.
  Description: Covers all aspects of psychoanalysis.

150.19   FR

REVUE INTERNATIONALE D'HISTOIRE DE LA PSYCHANALYSE. a. 290 F. (foreign 340 F.). Presses Universitaires de France, Departement des Revues, 14 av. du Bois-de-l'Epine, 91003 Evry Cedex, France. TEL 1-60-77-82-05. FAX 1-60-79-20-45. TELEX PUF 600 474 F. Ed.Bd.

REVUE INTERNATIONALE DE PYSCHOPATHOLOGIE. see *MEDICAL SCIENCES — Psychiatry And Neurology*

301.1 150   RM
BF1

REVUE ROUMAINE DE PSYCHOLOGIE. (Text in English, French, German, Russian or Spanish) 1964. s-a. 60 lei($45) (Academia Romana) Editura Academiei Romane, Calea Victoriei 125, 79717 Bucharest, Rumania. (Dist. by: Rompresfilatelia, Export-Import Presa, Calea Grivitei 64-66, P.O. Box 12-201, 78104 Bucharest, Rumania) bk.rev.; charts; circ. 750. Indexed: Child Devel.Abstr., Ergon.Abstr., Psychol.Abstr.
  Formerly (until 1990): Revue Romaine des Sciences Sociales. Serie de Psychologie (ISSN 0035-3892)

REVUE ZAIROISE DE PSYCHOLOGIE ET DE PEDAGOGIE. see *EDUCATION*

616.89   IT   ISSN 0391-996X

RICERCHE DI PSICOLOGIA. (Text in Italian; summaries in English and Italian) 1968. q. L.88000 (foreign L.110000)(effective 1992). (Universita degli Studi di Milano, Istituto di Psicologia) Franco Angeli Editore, Viale Monza 106, 20127 Milan, Italy. TEL 02-28-27-651. Ed. Marcello Cesa-Bianchi. adv.; bk.rev. Indexed: Anim.Behav.Abstr., Psychol.Abstr.
  Formerly (until 1972): Annali di Psicologia.

616.89   IT   ISSN 0035-6492

RIVISTA DI PSICOANALISI/JOURNAL OF THE ITALIAN PSYCHOANALYTICAL SOCIETY. (Editions in English, Italian) 1955. q. L.70000($114) to individuals; institutions and libraries L.90000. (Societa Psicoanalitica Italiana) Ghedini Editore, Via della Signora, 6, 20122 Milan, Italy. TEL 706707. FAX 02-781150. TELEX 353113 GHEDI-I. Ed. Antonio Valdina. bk.rev.; bibl.; charts; index; circ. 1,500. (reprint service avail. from ISI) Indexed: Psychol.Abstr.
  —BLDSC shelfmark: 7992.732000.
  Description: Covers research and study in the field of psychoanalysis.

150   IT   ISSN 0035-6506

RIVISTA DI PSICOLOGIA. (Text in Italian; summaries in English) 1905. q. $12. (Societa Italiana di Psicologia) Casa Editrice Giunti-Barbera, 34 via Gioberti, 50121 Florence, Italy. Ed.Bd. bk.rev.; bibl.; charts; index; circ. 1,500. Indexed: Psychol.Abstr.

150.19   IT

RIVISTA DI PSICOLOGIA ANALITICA. 1970. s-a. L.50000. Casa Editirice Astrolabio, Via Gallonio 8, 00 161 Rome, Italy. TEL 4270177. FAX 06-429590. Ed. A. Carotenuto. bk.rev.; circ. 1,500.
  Description: Covers research and study in the field of analytical psychology.

RIVISTA DI PSICOLOGIA DELL'ARTE. see *ART*

150   II

S A M I K S A. (Text in English) 1947. q. $15. Indian Psychoanalytical Society, 14 Parsibagan Lane, Calcutta 700 009, India. TEL 35-8788. (Affiliate: International Psychoanalytical Association) Ed. Dr. S. Banerji. adv.; bk.rev.; circ. 300. (back issues avail.) Indexed: Excerp.Med., Psychol.Abstr.
  Description: Presents scientific discussion of various aspects of psychoanalysis and related subjects.

155.3   CN   ISSN 0844-3718

S I E C C A N JOURNAL. 1986. q. Can.$30 to individuals; institutions Can.$40; students Can.$15. Sex Information and Education Council of Canada, 850 Coxwell Ave., East York, Ont. M4C 5R1, Canada. TEL 416-466-5304. FAX 416-778-0785. Ed. F. Michael Barrett. bk.rev.; circ. 1,000.
  Description: Includes scholarly articles, research papers, reviews, conference announcements and special theme issue.

155.3   CN   ISSN 0381-873X

S I E C C A N NEWSLETTER. 1965. irreg. (2-3/yr.). Can.$30 to individuals; institutions Can.$40; students Can.$15. Sex Information and Education Council of Canada, 850 Coxwell Ave., East York, Ont. M4C 5R1, Canada. TEL 416-446-5304. FAX 416-778-0785. Ed. F. Michael Barrett. bk.rev.; film rev.; circ. 1,000.
  Description: Features practical teaching and counselling ideas, articles, media reports and commentary.

S O L O. (Surviving Our Leukemia on Our Own) see *MEDICAL SCIENCES — Cancer*

150 301.2   US

SAGE SERIES IN CROSS CULTURAL RESEARCH AND METHODOLOGY. 1977. irreg. $39.95 clothbound; paperback $19.95. Sage Publications, Inc., 2455 Teller Rd., Newbury Park, CA 91320. TEL 805-499-0721. FAX 805-499-0871. (And: Sage Publications, Ltd., 6 Bonhill St., London EC2A 4PU, England) Eds. Walter J. Lonner, John W. Berry.
  Formerly: Cross Cultural Research and Methodology Series.

SALUD Y FAMILIA. see *MEDICAL SCIENCES*

152   CN   ISSN 0833-0247

SANS FRONTIERES - LES FORCES PSYCHOLOGIQUES. (Text in French) 1986. s-a. Can.$9.10. Institut de Formation et de Reeducation de Montreal, 55 Boulevard Gouin W., Montreal, Que. H3L 1H9, Canada. TEL 514-331-6861. FAX 514-331-7303. Ed. Julien Alain. circ. 1,000. (back issues avail.)
  Description: Psychological practices based on theoretical models, and clinical applications.

150   CN   ISSN 0383-6320
                CODEN: SMQUEK

SANTE MENTALE AU QUEBEC. (Text in French; summaries in English and French) 1976. 2/yr. Can.$18 to individuals; institutions Can.$28; students Can.$15. Revue Sante Mentale au Quebec, C.P. 548, Succ. Place d'Armes, Montreal, Que. H2Y 3H3, Canada. TEL 514-844-5536. Ed.Bd. Indexed: Pt.de Rep. (1982-), Soc.Work Res.& Abstr.
  Description: Covers experimental and clinical research, new theoretical approaches and intervention programs in the mental health field.

301.1 150   US   ISSN 0740-0853
BF204

SAYBROOK REVIEW. 1978. irreg. $10. Saybrook Institute, Graduate School and Research Center, 1550 Sutter St., San Francisco, CA 94109. TEL 415-441-5034. FAX 415-441-7556. Ed. Rudy Melone. bk.rev.; circ. 600. (back issues avail.) Indexed: Psychol.Abstr.
  Formerly: Humanistic Psychology Review.
  Description: Presents scholarly papers on a single topic in psychology or human science by invited scholars.

150   SW   ISSN 0345-1402
                CODEN: NTBEDQ

SCANDINAVIAN JOURNAL OF BEHAVIOUR THERAPY/NORDISK TIDSKRIFT FOER BETEENDETERAPI. (Text in English and Swedish; summaries in English) 1971. q. SEK 100($17) Swedish Association for Behaviour Therapy, University of Uppsala, Department of Psychiatry, Ulleraaker, S-750 17 Uppsala, Sweden. Ed. Lars-Goeran Oest. adv.; bk.rev.; charts; illus.; circ. 1,000. (back issues avail.) Indexed: Behav.Med.Abstr., Psychol.Abstr.
  —BLDSC shelfmark: 8087.490000.

150   SW   ISSN 0036-5564
BF1   CODEN: SJPYA2

SCANDINAVIAN JOURNAL OF PSYCHOLOGY. (Text in English) 1960. q. SEK 590. Almqvist & Wiksell Periodical Company, Box 638, S-101 28 Stockholm, Sweden. Ed. Kenneth Hugdahl. adv.; bibl.; charts; illus.; index. cum.index every 5 yrs.; circ. 1,400. (tabloid format) Indexed: Adol.Ment.Hlth.Abstr., ASCA, ASSIA, Biol.Abstr., Child Devel.Abstr., Curr.Cont., Dent.Ind., Ergon.Abstr., Ind.Med., Lang.& Lang.Behav.Abstr., Mid.East: Abstr.& Ind., Psychol.Abstr., Risk Abstr., SSCI.
  —BLDSC shelfmark: 8087.520000.

SCHIEDSMANNS ZEITUNG. see *LAW*

370.15 150   US

SCHOOL PRACTITIONER SERIES. irreg. (approx. 3-4/yr.). Guilford Publications, Inc., 72 Spring St., 4th Fl., New York, NY 10012. TEL 212-431-9800. FAX 212-966-6708.
  Description: Provides focused, readable, and prescriptive accounts of techniques for changing children's behavior.

SCHOOL PSYCHOLOGY INTERNATIONAL. see *EDUCATION — Teaching Methods And Curriculum*

PSYCHOLOGY

370.15   US   ISSN 1045-3830
LB1027.55   CODEN: SPSQE5
SCHOOL PSYCHOLOGY QUARTERLY. 1960. q. $30 to individuals; institutions $60. (American Psychological Association, Division of School Psychology) Guilford Publications, Inc., 72 Spring St., 4th Fl., New York, NY 10012. TEL 212-431-9800. FAX 212-966-6708. Ed. Thomas R. Kratochwill. adv.; index. **Indexed:** Psychol.Abstr.
—BLDSC shelfmark: 8092.926500.
Formerly: Professional School Psychology (ISSN 0079-5933)
Description: Focuses on the scientific understanding of school psychology; covers new concepts in enhancing life experiences of children, families and schools.
Refereed Serial

370.15   US   ISSN 0279-6015
LB1051
SCHOOL PSYCHOLOGY REVIEW. 1972. 4/yr. $40 to individuals; institutions $60. National Association of School Psychologists, 8455 Colesville Rd., Ste. 1000, Silver Spring, MD 20910. TEL 301-608-0500. FAX 301-608-2514. Ed. Edward S. Shapiro. adv.; bk.rev.; abstr.; bibl.; charts; stat.; circ. 15,600. (also avail. in microform from UMI; back issues avail.; reprint service avail. from UMI) **Indexed:** C.I.J.E., Cont.Pg.Educ., Educ.Ind., Psychol.Abstr.
—BLDSC shelfmark: 8092.926600.
Formerly (until 1979): School Psychology Digest (ISSN 0160-5569)
Description: Covers research, training, and practice in school psychology.

150   SZ
SCHWEIZERISCHE ZEITSCHRIFT FUER PSYCHOLOGIE/REVUE SUISSE DE PSYCHOLOGIE. (Text in French and German; abstracts in English, German) 1942. 4/yr. 66 Fr. (Societe Suisse de Psychologie) Verlag Hans Huber, Laengassstr. 76, CH-3000 Berne 9, Switzerland. TEL 031-24-25-33. FAX 031-24-33-80. TELEX 911886-HAHU. Eds. Dr. A. Lang, Dr. W.J. Perrig. bk.rev.; abstr.; bibl.; charts; circ. 1,000. **Indexed:** Biol.Abstr., Ger.J.Psych., Psychol.Abstr., Risk Abstr., SSCI.
Formerly: Schweizerische Zeitschrift fuer Psychologie (ISSN 0036-7869)

150   CN
SCIENCE ET COMPORTEMENT; revue internationale et multidisciplinaire. (Text in French; summaries in English) 1970. q. Can.$50($58) (foreign $64). Association Scientifique pour la Modification du Comportement, 7401 rue Hochelaga, Montreal, Que. H1N 3M5, Canada. TEL 514-253-8200. Ed. Andre Marchand. bk.rev.; circ. 600. (tabloid format) **Indexed:** Psychol.Abstr., Pt.de Rep. (1983-).
Formerly: Revue de Modification du Comportement (ISSN 0383-056X)

SELECTION AND DEVELOPMENT REVIEW. see *BUSINESS AND ECONOMICS — Management*

301.1 150   UK   ISSN 0306-0497
SELF & SOCIETY; European journal of humanistic psychology. 1973. bi-m. £10. (Association for Humanistic Psychology in Britain) Gale Centre Publications, Whitakers Way, Loughton, Essex 1G10 1SJ, England. TEL 081-508-9344. FAX 081-508-1240. Ed. David Jones. adv.; bk.rev.; circ. 1,200.
—BLDSC shelfmark: 8235.350000.
Description: Discusses human potential and research work in psychology and sociology; promotes a holistic view of life and the importance of the individual.

150 360   US
SELF HELP REPORTER NEWSLETTER. 1977. q. $10. National Self Help Clearinghouse, 25 W. 43rd St., Rm. 620, New York, NY 10036. TEL 212-642-2944. Ed. Audrey Gartner. bk.rev.; circ. 1,000.
Description: Covers trends in the burgeoning self-help movement, describes mutual support group activities, and discusses the theoretical underpinnings of self-help mutual support.

SELF-HELP SOURCEBOOK; finding and forming mutual aid self-help groups. see *SOCIAL SERVICES AND WELFARE*

155   UK   ISSN 0143-7526
SENSORY PERCEPTION AND INFORMATION PROCESSING. 1980. m. £65. Sheffield University Biomedical Information Service (SUBIS), The University, Sheffield S10 2TN, England. TEL 0742-768555. FAX 0742-739826. TELEX 547216-UGSHEF-G.
Description: Current awareness service for researchers. Studies auditory, visual, touch, olfactory and taste perceptions.

150.18   US   ISSN 0894-4520
QP431
SENSORY SYSTEMS. English translation of: Sensornye Sistemy. 1987. q. $375 (foreign $440)(effective 1992). (Russian Academy of Sciences, RU) Plenum Publishing Corp., Consultants Bureau, 233 Spring St., New York, NY 10013-1578. TEL 212-620-8468. FAX 212-463-0742. TELEX 23-421139. Ed. M.A. Ostrovskii. bibl.; illus.; index. (also avail. in microfilm from JSC; back issues avail.)
—BLDSC shelfmark: 0420.807000.
Refereed Serial

155.937   US   ISSN 0275-3510
SERIES IN DEATH EDUCATION, AGING, AND HEALTH CARE. Variant title: Death Education Series. 1979. irreg., unnumbered, latest 1984. price varies. Hemisphere Publishing Corporation (Subsidiary of: Taylor & Francis Group), 1900 Frost Rd., Ste. 101, Bristol, PA 19007-1598. TEL 215-785-5800. FAX 215-785-5515. Ed. Hannelore Wass. bibl.; charts; illus.; index. (back issues avail.; reprint service avail. from UMI)
Refereed Serial

300   US   ISSN 0740-3593
SEX OVER FORTY; a practical, authoritative newsletter directed to the sexual concerns of the mature adult. 1982. m. $36. D K T International, Inc., Box 1600, Chapel Hill, NC 27515. Eds. Drs. Douglas Whitehead, Shirley Zussman. bk.rev.; circ. 40,000.

155.3 301   US   ISSN 0360-0025
HQ768   CODEN: SROLDH
SEX ROLES; a journal of research. 1975. s-m. (in 2 vols.). $425 (foreign $495)(effective 1992). Plenum Publishing Corp., 233 Spring St., New York, NY 10013-1578. TEL 212-620-8000. FAX 212-463-0742. TELEX 23-421139. Ed. Sue Rosenberg Zalk. adv.; bk.rev.; bibl.; charts. (also avail. in microfilm from JSC; back issues avail.) **Indexed:** Adol.Ment.Hlth.Abstr., ASCA, ASSIA, C.I.J.E., Child Devel.Abstr., Commun.Abstr., Curr.Cont., Excerp.Med., Lang.& Lang.Behav.Abstr., Mid.East: Abstr.& Ind., Psychol.Abstr., Res.High.Educ.Abstr., Risk Abstr., Sage Fam.Stud.Abstr., Soc.Sci.Ind., Soc.Work Res.& Abstr., Sociol.Abstr., Sp.Ed.Needs Abstr., SSCI, Stud.Wom.Abstr., Wom.Stud.Abstr. (1975-).
—BLDSC shelfmark: 8254.457000.
Refereed Serial

155.3 610   UK   ISSN 0267-4653
SEXUAL AND MARITAL THERAPY. 1986. 3/yr. $74 to individuals; institutions $180. (Association of Sexual and Marital Therapists) Carfax Publishing Co., P.O. Box 25, Abingdon, Oxfordshire OX14 3UE, England. TEL 0235-555335. FAX 0235-553559. (U.S. subscr. addr.: Carfax Publishing Co., Box 2025, Dunnellon, FL 32630) Eds. P. d'Ardenne, A.J. Riley. adv.; bk.rev.; illus.; stat.; index, cum.index. (also avail. in microfiche; back issues avail.) **Indexed:** ASSIA, Curr.Adv.Ecol.Sci., Psychol.Abstr., Stud.Wom.Abstr.
—BLDSC shelfmark: 8254.483000.

155.937 618   US
SHARE NEWSLETTER. 1978. bi-m. $12 (donation). Share Pregnancy & Infant Loss Support National Office, St. Joseph Health Center, 300 First Capital Dr., 63301, MO 63301. TEL 314-947-5000. Ed. Mary Florea. bk.rev.; film rev.; bibl.; circ. 4,500. (looseleaf format)
Description: Provides guidance in bereavement following the death of a baby through miscarriage, stillbirth or newborn death. Includes writing from parents and information on support groups.

150   JA   ISSN 0386-1058
BF8.J3   CODEN: SHHYDJ
SHINRIGAKU HYORON/JAPANESE PSYCHOLOGICAL REVIEW. (Text in Japanese; some summaries in English or German) 1957. q. 5000 Yen to individuals; institutions 7000 Yen. Kyoto University, Faculty of Letters, Department of Psychology - Kyoto Daigaku Bungakubu Shinrigaku Kyushitsu, 54 Shogoin Kawara-cho, Sakyo-ku, Kyoto 606, Japan. Ed. Toshitsugu Hirano. illus. **Indexed:** Psychol.Abstr.
—BLDSC shelfmark: 4661.150000.

150   JA   ISSN 0021-5236
   CODEN: SHKEA5
SHINRIGAKU KENKYU/JAPANESE JOURNAL OF PSYCHOLOGY. (Text in Japanese; summaries in English) 1928. bi-m. $98. (Japanese Psychological Association) Japan Scientific Societies Press, 6-2-10 Hongo, Bunkyo-ku, Tokyo 113, Japan. TEL 3814-2001. FAX 3814-2002. TELEX 2722268 BCJSP J. (Dist. by: Business Center for Academic Societies Japan, Koshin Bldg., 6-16-3 Hongo, Bunkyo-ku, Tokyo 113, Japan; Dist. in U.S. by: International Specialized Book Services, Inc., 5602 N.E. Hassalo St., Portland, OR 97213) adv.; bk.rev.; abstr.; charts; illus.; index; circ. 4,000. **Indexed:** Biol.Abstr., Curr.Cont., Ind.Med., Psychol.Abstr., SSCI.
—BLDSC shelfmark: 4658.300000.

150.19   AU   ISSN 1015-1184
SIGMUND FREUD HOUSE BULLETIN. (Text in English) 1975. 2/yr. $30. Sigmund Freud Gesellschaft, Berggasse 19, A-1090 Vienna, Austria. TEL 311596. FAX 340279. Ed. Dr. Hans Lobner. bk.rev.; bibl.; circ. 1,000. **Indexed:** Psychol.Abstr.
Description: Contains papers on research in psychoanalysis, and the history of psychoanalysis including Freud's life and work.

616.89   IS   ISSN 0334-9330
RC321
SIHOT/DIALOGUE; Israel journal of psychotherapy. (Text in Hebrew; summaries in English and Hebrew) 1986. q. $45. P.O. Box 63, Kfar-Saba 44100, Israel. TEL 052-971637. FAX 02434434. (Co-sponsors: Israel Association of Psychotherapy; Israel Psychological Association) Eds. A. Shalev, E. Chen. adv.; bk.rev.; circ. 2,500.

SIMULATION & GAMING; an international journal of theory, design and research. see *SOCIOLOGY*

SINISTRALIAN. see *CLUBS*

616.89   NO   ISSN 0049-0563
SINNETS HELSE. 1920. 8/yr. NOK 145. Mental Barnehjelp, Arbiens Gt. 1, Oslo 2, Norway. Ed. Kirsten Weidemann Ycharff. adv.; bk.rev.; bibl.; circ. 12,000.

160 410   IT   ISSN 1120-9550
SISTEMI INTELLIGENTI; rivista quadrimestrale di scienze cognitive e intelligenza artificiale. 1989. 3/yr. L.90000. Societa Editrice Il Mulino, Strada Maggiore, 37, 40125 Bologna, Italy. TEL 051-256011. FAX 051-256034. Ed. Domenico Parisi. adv.; index; circ. 1,900. (back issues avail.)

156   US   ISSN 1046-4964
HM133   CODEN: SGREE3
SMALL GROUP RESEARCH; an international journal of theory, investigation and application. 1970. q. $45 to individuals; institutions $118. Sage Publications, Inc., 2455 Teller Rd., Newbury Park, CA 91320. TEL 805-499-0721. FAX 805-499-0871. (And: Sage Publications, Ltd., 6 Bonhill St., London EC2A 4PU, England) Eds. Charles Garvin, Richard Brian Polley. adv.; bk.rev.; charts; index; circ. 1,100. (also avail. in microform from UMI; back issues avail.; reprint service avail. from UMI) **Indexed:** Abstr.Soc.Work., Adol.Ment.Hlth.Abstr., ASCA, ASSIA, C.I.J.E., Commun.Abstr., Curr.Cont., Educ.Admin.Abstr., Lang.& Lang.Behav.Abstr., Mid.East: Abstr.& Ind., Psychol.Abstr., Sage Fam.Stud.Abstr., Sage Pub.Admin.Abstr., Sage Urb.Stud.Abstr., Soc.Work Res.& Abstr., SSCI.
—BLDSC shelfmark: 8309.995000.
Formerly: Small Group Behavior (ISSN 0090-5526); Incorporates: International Journal of Small Group Research (ISSN 8756-0275); Comparative Group Studies (ISSN 0010-4108)

PSYCHOLOGY 4047

340 US ISSN 0272-765X
K23
SOCIAL ACTION AND THE LAW. 1973. 4/yr. $20 to individuals; institutions $30. c/o Robert Buckhout, Pub., Brooklyn College, Center for Responsive Psychology, Brooklyn, NY 11210. TEL 718-780-5960. Ed. Frnak J. Sotolongo. adv.; bk.rev.; circ. 1,000. (also avail. in microfiche) **Indexed:** C.L.I., ERIC, I.R.L., Lang.& Lang.Behav.Abstr., Psychol.Abstr., Sociol.Abstr.
—BLDSC shelfmark: 8318.041070.

301.1 130 NZ ISSN 0301-2212
HM1 CODEN: SBHPAF
SOCIAL BEHAVIOR AND PERSONALITY; an international journal. 1973. q. $130. Society for Personality Research (Inc.), P.O. Box 1539, Palmerston North, New Zealand. TEL 64-6-355-5736. FAX 64-6-355-5736. Ed. Robert A.C. Stewart. adv.; circ. 1,600. (also avail. in microform from UMI; reprint service avail. from ISI) **Indexed:** ASCA, ASSIA, Biol.Abstr., C.I.J.E., Child Devel.Abstr., Curr.Cont., High.Educ.Abstr., Ind.Med., Lang.& Lang.Behav.Abstr., Psychol.Abstr., Sociol.Abstr., Sportsearch, SSCI.
—BLDSC shelfmark: 8318.054500.
Incorporates (1984-1991): Psychology and Human Development (ISSN 1011-5021); (1978-1990): Third Force Psychology.
Description: Publishes papers on all aspects of social psychology and personality.

155 US ISSN 0278-016X
BF311
SOCIAL COGNITION; a journal of social, personality and developmental psychology. 1982. q. $33 to individuals; institutions $85. Guilford Publications, Inc., 72 Spring St., 4th Fl., New York, NY 10012. TEL 212-431-9800. FAX 212-966-6708. Ed. David J. Schneider. adv.; bk.rev.; index; circ. 600. (back issues avail.) **Indexed:** Biol.Abstr., Curr.Cont., Psychol.Abstr., Sociol.Educ.Abstr., Sp.Ed.Needs Abstr.
—BLDSC shelfmark: 8318.073000.
Description: Examines the role of cognitive process in the study of personality, development and social behavior.
Refereed Serial

150 301.1 US
HM251
SOCIAL PSYCHOLOGICAL APPLICATIONS TO SOCIAL ISSUES. biennial. (Society for the Psychological Study of Social Issues) Plenum Publishing Corp., 233 Spring St., New York, NY 10013-1578. TEL 212-620-8000. FAX 212-463-0742. **Indexed:** Psychol.Abstr.
Formerly: Applied Social Psychology Annual (ISSN 0196-4151)
Refereed Serial

SOCIAL SERVICE JOBS. see OCCUPATIONS AND CAREERS

SOCIETY AND ANIMALS; social scientific studies of the human experience of other animals. see ANIMAL WELFARE

155.3 US
SOCIETY NEWSLETTER. q. $10. Society for the Scientific Study of Sex, Box 208, Mt. Vernon, IA 52314. TEL 319-895-8407. Ed. Andrew Behrendt. circ. 1,200.

SOMATOSENSORY AND MOTOR RESEARCH. see BIOLOGY — Physiology

150 SA ISSN 0081-2463
BF1 CODEN: SAJPDL
SOUTH AFRICAN JOURNAL OF PSYCHOLOGY/SUID-AFRIKAANSE TYDSKRIF VIR SIELKUNDE. (Text and summaries in Afrikaans, English) 1970. q. R.72($45) (Psychological Association of South Africa) Bureau for Scientific Publications, Box 1758, Pretoria 0001, South Africa. TEL 012-322-6422. Ed. K.F. Mauer. bk.rev.; bibl.; charts; illus.; stat.; circ. 1,200. **Indexed:** Arts & Hum.Cit.Ind., Biol.Abstr., CINAHL, Ergon.Abstr., Ind.S.A.Per., Psychol.Abstr., Sociol.Educ.Abstr., Sp.Ed.Needs Abstr., Stud.Wom.Abstr.
—BLDSC shelfmark: 8339.750000.
Incorporates (in July 1983): Psychologia Africana (ISSN 0079-7332); (in Jan. 1979): South African Psychologist; Which was formerly: Journal of Behavioural Science (ISSN 0075-4145)

370.15 150 US
SOVIET JOURNAL OF PSYCHOLOGY. English translation of: Psikhologicheskii Zhurnal. 1988. bi-m. $375 to individuals (foreign $450); institutions $600 (foreign $700). International Universities Press, Inc., Journal Department, 59 Boston Post Rd., Box 1524, Madison, CT 06443-1524. TEL 203-245-4000. FAX 203-245-0775. Ed. B.F. Lomov. bk.rev. **Indexed:** Psychol.Abstr.
Supersedes (1988-1990): Soviet Psychiatry and Psychology Today (ISSN 0892-7200)
Description: Presents Soviet studies in psychology, screened for scientific standards, innovative approach, and current interests. Features a broad range of topics.
Refereed Serial

301.1 616.8 360 GW ISSN 0171-4538
SOZIALPSYCHIATRISCHE INFORMATIONEN. 1971. q. DM.45. Psychiatrie-Verlag, Celsiusstr. 112, D-5300 Bonn 1, Germany. TEL 0228-252021. Ed. Dr. Haselbeck. adv.; circ. 2,000. (back issues avail.)
Description: A journal for people working in psychiatry: psychiatrists, doctors, social workers and nurses.

SPECIAL SERVICES IN THE SCHOOLS. see EDUCATION — Special Education And Rehabilitation

150.19 790.1 US ISSN 0888-4781
GV706.4 CODEN: SPPSEU
THE SPORT PSYCHOLOGIST. Short title: T S P. 1987. q. $36 to individuals (foreign $40); institutions $80 (foreign $84); students $24 (foreign $28). (International Society of Sport Psychology) Human Kinetics Publishers, Inc., Box 5076, Champaign, IL 61825-5076. TEL 217-351-5076. FAX 217-351-2674. Ed. Dr. Robin S. Vealey. adv.; bibl.; charts; circ. 800. (back issues avail.) **Indexed:** Phys.Ed.Ind., Psychol.Abstr., Sociol.Abstr., Sportsearch (1987-).
—BLDSC shelfmark: 8419.638000.
Description: Designed for education and clinical sport psychologists. Focuses on applied research and practical application of results in providing psychological services to coaches and athletes.
Refereed Serial

150 SZ ISSN 0253-4533
P37
SPRACHE & KOGNITION; Zeitschrift fuer Sprach- und Kognitionspsychologie und ihre Grenzgebiete. (Text in German; summaries in English and German) 1982. q. 125 Fr. Verlag Hans Huber, Laenggassstr. 76, Postfach, CH-3000 Berne 9, Switzerland. TEL 031-24-25-33. FAX 031-24-33-80. TELEX 911886-HAHU. adv.; bk.rev.; index; circ. 800. **Indexed:** Ger.J.Psych., Psychol.Abstr.
—BLDSC shelfmark: 8419.869250.

150 US ISSN 0362-0522
BF173.A2 CODEN: SAATDM
SPRING (DALLAS); a journal of archetype and culture. 1941. a. $13.50 to individuals; institutions $16. Spring Publications, Inc., Box 222069, Dallas, TX 75222. TEL 214-943-4093. FAX 214-943-4520. Eds. Charles Boer, Ross Miller. adv.; bk.rev.; circ. 1,500. (back issues avail.) **Indexed:** PMR, Psychol.Abstr.
Description: Examines new directions in understanding dreams, syndromes, and psychosomatic disorders. Includes historical and biographical research on C. G. Jung, with a critical examination of basic Jungian ideas and post-Jungian controversy.

155 US
SPRINGER SERIES IN COGNITIVE DEVELOPMENT. 1982. irreg. price varies. Springer-Verlag, 175 Fifth Ave., New York, NY 10010. TEL 212-460-1500. (Also Berlin, Heidelberg, Tokyo and Vienna)

301.1 150 US
SPRINGER SERIES IN SOCIAL PSYCHOLOGY. irreg. price varies. Springer-Verlag, 175 Fifth Ave., New York, NY 10010. TEL 212-460-1500. (Also Berlin, Heidelberg, Tokyo and Vienna) Ed. R.F. Kidd.

150 SW ISSN 0345-0139
CODEN: RPUSB7
STOCKHOLMS UNIVERSITET. PSYKOLOGISKA INSTITUTIONEN. REPORT SERIES. (Text in English) 1954. irreg. (approx. 20/yr.) $25. Stockholms Universitet, Psykologiska Institutionen, S-106 91 Stockholm, Sweden. FAX 468-159342. Ed.Bd. index; circ. 500. **Indexed:** Psychol.Abstr.

150 US ISSN 1053-2161
BF575.S75
STRESS AND EMOTION. (Subseries of: Series in Clinical and Community Psychology) 1975. irreg., vol.14, 1991. price varies. Hemisphere Publishing Corporation (Subsidiary of: Taylor & Francis Group), 1900 Frost Rd., Ste. 101, Bristol, PA 19007-1598. TEL 215-785-5800. FAX 215-785-5515. Eds. C.D. Spielberger, I.G. Sarason. bibl.; charts; illus.; index. (back issues avail.; reprint service avail. from UMI) **Indexed:** Psychol.Abstr.
—BLDSC shelfmark: 8474.128650.
Formerly (until no.14, 1991): Stress and Anxiety (ISSN 0364-1112)
Refereed Serial

STRESS MASTER. see NEW AGE PUBLICATIONS

362.2 SW ISSN 0280-2783
STRESSFORSKNINGSRAPPORTER. (Text in English, Swedish) 1967. irreg., vol.231, 1991. SEK 300 (effective 1992). Karolinska Institutet, Institut foer Stressforskning, P.O. Box 60205, S-104 01 Stockholm, Sweden. TEL 46-08-7286400. FAX 46-08-344143. index. (back issues avail.)
—BLDSC shelfmark: 8474.141000.
Description: Interdisciplinary research in stress and work, health services, and psychosocial issues.

370.15 150 IT ISSN 0393-6163
STUDI DI PSICOLOGIA DELL'EDUCAZIONE. 1982. q. L.35000. Casa Editrice Armando s.r.l., P.za S. Sonnino 13, 00153 Rome, Italy. TEL 06-5817245. FAX 06-5818564. Ed. Renzo Titone. bibl.; charts; illus.; stat. **Indexed:** Psychol.Abstr.

150 CS ISSN 0039-3320
CODEN: STPSAK
STUDIA PSYCHOLOGICA; journal for basic research in psychological sciences. (Text and summaries in English, French, German, Russian and Slovak) 1958. 5/yr. 100 Kcs.($20) (Slovenska Akademia Vied) Veda, Publishing House of the Slovak Academy of Sciences, Klemensova 19, 814 30 Bratislava, Czechoslovakia. (Dist. in Western countries by: John Benjamins B.V., Amsteldijk 44, Amsterdam, Netherlands) Ed. Dr. Damian Kovac. bk.rev.; charts; illus.; index; circ. 1,300. **Indexed:** ASCA, Biol.Abstr., Child Devel.Abstr., Curr.Cont., Psychol.Abstr., SSCI.
Description: Publishes original experimental and theoretical studies about results of investigations carried out in Czechoslovakia and abroad in the field of basic psychological research.

STUDIA PSYCHOLOGICA ET PAEDAGOGICA; series altera. see EDUCATION

150 PL ISSN 0081-685X
CODEN: SPSLBL
STUDIA PSYCHOLOGICZNE. (Text in Polish; summaries in English and Russian) 1956. s.a. $24. (Polska Akademia Nauk, Komitet Nauk Psychologicznych) Ossolineum, Publishing House of the Polish Academy of Sciences, Rynek 9, Wroclaw, Poland. TELEX 0712771 OSS PL. (Dist. by: Ars Polona-Ruch, Krakowskie Przedmiescie 7, Warsaw, Poland) Ed. Janusz Reykowski. **Indexed:** Lang.& Lang.Behav.Abstr., Psychol.Abstr.
Description: Works concerning historical and experimental psychology, theoretical and methodological problems, social perception, personal communication.

150 370 RM
▼**STUDIA UNIVERSITATIA "BABES-BOLYAI". PSICHOLOGIA - PEDAGOGIA.** 1990. s-a. exchange basis. Universitatea "Babes-Bolyai", Biblioteca Centrala Universitara, Str. Clinicilor Nr. 2, Cluj-Napoca, Rumania.

155.4 AU ISSN 0255-6715
STUDIEN ZUR KINDERPSYCHOANALYSE. JAHRBUCH. 1981. a. DM.28. (Oesterreichische Studiengesellschaft fuer Kinderpsychoanalyse) Verband der Wissenschaftlichen Gesellschaften Oesterreichs, Lindengasse 37, A-1070 Vienna, Austria. TEL 932166. circ. 450.

STUDIENHEFTE PSYCHOLOGIE IN ERZIEHUNG UND UNTERRICHT. see EDUCATION — Higher Education

370.15 GW ISSN 0173-0975
STUDIENREIHE PAEDAGOGISCHE PSYCHOLOGIE. 1978. irreg. price varies. Ernst Reinhardt GmbH und Co., Verlag, Kemnatenstr. 46, 8000 Munich 19, Germany. TEL 089-1783005. Ed. R. Dieterich.

PSYCHOLOGY

STUDIES IN EDUCATION AND PSYCHOLOGY. see *EDUCATION*

STUDIES IN EDUCATIONAL EVALUATION. see *EDUCATION*

150 410 100 NE
STUDIES IN LINGUISTICS AND PHILOSOPHY. 1978. irreg. price varies. Kluwer Academic Publishers, P.O. Box 17, 3300 AA Dordrecht, Netherlands. TEL 078-334911. FAX 078-334254. TELEX 29245. (Dist. by: Kluwer Academic Publishers Group, P.O. Box 322, 3300 AH Dordrecht, Netherlands; U.S. address: P.O. Box 358, Accord Station, Hingham, MA 02018-0358) Ed.Bd. **Indexed:** Math.R.
  Formerly: Synthese Language Library.

150.19 100 US
STUDIES IN THE PSYCHOANALYTIC WRITINGS OF ERNEST BECKER. irreg. Peter Lang Publishing, Inc., 62 W. 45th St., 4th Fl., New York, NY 10036. TEL 212-302-6740. FAX 212-302-7574. Ed. Barry R. Arnold.
  Description: Elucidates the contributions of Ernest Becker to the fields of psychoanalysis, religion, and philosophy.

STUDIES IN THE PSYCHOLOGY OF RELIGION. see *RELIGIONS AND THEOLOGY*

STUDIES IN THEORETICAL PSYCHOLINGUISTICS. see *LINGUISTICS*

SUCCESS (NEW YORK); the magazine for achievers. see *OCCUPATIONS AND CAREERS*

150.19 US
SUGGESTION QUARTERLY. 1962. q. membership only. Association to Advance Ethical Hypnosis, c/o Nell R. Orndorf, M.A., 2675 Oakwood Dr., Cuyahoga Falls, OH 44221. bk.rev.; circ. 1,200.

157.744 US ISSN 0363-0234
RC569 CODEN: SLBEDP
SUICIDE AND LIFE-THREATENING BEHAVIOR. 1970. q. $35 to individuals; institutions $110. (American Association of Suicidology) Guilford Publications, Inc., 72 Spring St., 4th Fl., New York, NY 10012. TEL 212-431-9800. FAX 212-966-6708. Ed. Ronald W. Maris. adv.; bk.rev.; abstr.; bibl.; index; circ. 1,700. (also avail. in microform from UMI; back issues avail.; reprint service avail. from ISI,UMI) **Indexed:** Abstr.Crim.& Pen., Adol.Ment.Hlth.Abstr., ASCA, Biol.Abstr., C.I.J.E., CERDIC, Community Ment.Health Rev., Curr.Cont., Excerp.Med., Human Resour.Abstr., Ind.Med., Lang.& Lang.Behav.Abstr., Psychol.Abstr., Sage Fam.Stud.Abstr., Sage Urb.Stud.Abstr., Sociol.Abstr., SSCI.
  —BLDSC shelfmark: 8514.141000.
  Former titles: Suicide (ISSN 0360-1390); Life Threatening Behavior (ISSN 0047-4592)
  Description: Biological, statistical, psychological and sociological approaches to the full range of suicide issues.
  Refereed Serial

150 US ISSN 0891-4451
SYSTEMS RESEARCH IN PSYCHOLOGY. 1982. irreg., vol.4, 1990. Gordon & Breach Science Publishers, 270 Eighth Ave., New York, NY 10011. TEL 212-206-8900. FAX 212-645-2459. TELEX 236735 GOPUB UR. (Subscr. to: Box 786, Cooper Sta., New York, NY 10276. TEL 800-545-8398; UK addr.: P.O. Box 90, Reading, Berkshire RG1 8JL, England. TEL 0734-560-080) Ed.Bd. (also avail. in microform)
  —BLDSC shelfmark: 8589.425500.
  Refereed Serial

155.3 301.4157 US ISSN 0884-9749
T V - T S TAPESTRY; the journal for persons interested in crossdressing & transsexualism. 1978. q. $40 to individuals; libraries $30. International Foundation for Gender Education, Inc., Box 367, Wayland, MA 01778. TEL 617-899-2212. FAX 617-899-5703. Ed. Merissa Sherrill Lynn. adv.; bk.rev.; circ. 10,000. (back issues avail.)

150 US
TAKING SIDES: CLASHING VIEWS ON CONTROVERSIAL ISSUES IN HUMAN SEXUALITY. irreg., 3rd ed., 1991. $11.95. Dushkin Publishing Group, Inc., Sluice Dock, Guilford, CT 06437-9989. TEL 203-453-4351. FAX 203-453-6000. Ed. Robert T. Francoeur. illus.

150 US
TAKING SIDES: CLASHING VIEWS ON CONTROVERSIAL MORAL ISSUES. irreg., 3rd ed., 1992. $11.95. Dushkin Publishing Group, Inc., Sluice Dock, Guilford, CT 06437-9989. TEL 203-453-4351. FAX 203-453-6000. Ed. Stephen Satris. illus.

150 US
TAKING SIDES: CLASHING VIEWS ON CONTROVERSIAL PSYCHOLOGICAL ISSUES. irreg., 6th ed., 1990. $11.95. Dushkin Publishing Group, Inc., Sluice Dock, Guilford, CT 06437-9989. TEL 203-453-4351. FAX 203-453-6000. Eds. Joseph Rubinstein, Brent Slife. illus.

TALK OF THE MONTH. see *NEW AGE PUBLICATIONS*

TAROT NETWORK NEWS. see *NEW AGE PUBLICATIONS*

150 371.3 US ISSN 0098-6283
BF77
TEACHING OF PSYCHOLOGY. 1974. q. $25 to individuals (foreign $40); institutions $90 (foreign $115). (American Psychological Association, Division Two) Lawrence Erlbaum Associates, Inc., 365 Broadway, Hillside, NJ 07642. TEL 201-666-4110. FAX 201-666-2394. Ed. Charles L. Brewer. adv.; bk.rev.; film rev.; bibl.; charts; index; circ. 3,200. (also avail. in microform from UMI; back issues avail; reprint service avail. from UMI) **Indexed:** ASCA, C.I.J.E., Cont.Pg.Educ., Curr.Cont., Educ.Ind., ERIC, Psychol.Abstr., Psychol.R.G., SSCI.
  —BLDSC shelfmark: 8614.330000.
  Description: Dedicated to improving the learning-teaching process at all educational levels: from secondary through college and graduate school, to continuing education.
  Refereed Serial

150 US ISSN 0887-0217
TEACHING THINKING & PROBLEM SOLVING NEWSLETTER. 1979. bi-m. $28 to individuals (foreign $48); institutions $48 (foreign $68). (American Psychological Association, Clinical Psychology) Lawrence Erlbaum Associates, Inc., 365 Broadway, Hillsdale, NJ 07642. TEL 201-666-4110. FAX 201-666-2394. (Co-publisher: Research for Better Schools) Ed. Francine S. Beyer. bk.rev.; circ. 700. (tabloid format; back issues avail.)
  Formerly (until 1985): Problem Solving.
  Description: Covers current ideas and emerging programs in the area of education.
  Refereed Serial

616.89 610 370 IT
TERAPIA FAMILIARE. 1977. q. L.50000($50) Istituto di Terapia Familiare, Via Reno 30, 00198 Rome, Italy. TEL 8554261. Ed. Maurizio Andolfi. adv.; bk.rev.; cum.index 1977-1986; circ. 3,000. (back issues avail.) **Indexed:** Psychol.Abstr.

157 US
TERRAP TIMES; a quarterly publication for people with phobias. 1970. q. $18 (foreign $20). T.S.C. Management Corporation, 648 Menlo Ave., No. 5, Menlo Park, CA 94025. TEL 800-274-6242. Ed. Kathy Anderson. adv.; bk.rev.; circ. 2,500. (back issues avail.)
  Description: For people with phobias. Features include a support column, helpful hints and a question and answer column.

375 371.3 US ISSN 0361-025X
TESTS IN PRINT. 1961. irreg., no.3, 1983. price varies. Buros Institute of Mental Measurements, 135 Bancroft, University of Nebraska-Lincoln, Lincoln, NE 68588-0348. TEL 402-472-6203. FAX 402-472-6207. (Dist. by: University of Nebraska Press, 901 N. 17th St., Lincoln, NE 68588-0520) bibl.; cum.index. (back issues avail.)

THANATOLOGY ABSTRACTS. see *PSYCHOLOGY — Abstracting, Bibliographies, Statistics*

155.937 US
THANATOLOGY LIBRARIAN; news of books on death, bereavement, loss & grief. 1979. s-a. $15. Center for Thanatology Research and Education Inc., 391 Atlantic Ave., Brooklyn, NY 11217-1701. TEL 718-858-3026. Ed. Roberta Halporn. bk.rev.; circ. 4,000. (back issues avail.)

156 GW ISSN 0934-5272
HM291
THEMENZENTRIERTE INTERAKTION. (Text and summaries in English and German) 1987. s-a. DM.20 (students DM.12). Matthias Gruenewald Verlag GmbH, Max-Hufschmidt-Str. 4a, 6500 Mainz, Germany. TEL 06131-839055. FAX 06131-834322. adv.; bk.rev. (back issues avail.)

614.58
THEORETICAL ISSUES IN COGNITIVE SCIENCE. 1986. irreg. price varies. Ablex Publishing Corporation, 355 Chestnut St., Norwood, NJ 07648. TEL 201-767-8450. FAX 201-767-6717. TELEX 135-393. Ed. Zenon Pylyshyn.

150 US ISSN 0894-2528
BF1001 CODEN: THPAEX
THEORETICAL PARAPSYCHOLOGY. 1974. 4/yr. (in 1 vol., 4 nos./vol.). $77. Gordon and Breach Science Publishers, 270 Eighth Ave., New York, NY 10011. TEL 212-206-8900. FAX 212-645-2459. TELEX 236735 GOPUB UR. (Subscr. to: Box 786, Cooper Sta., New York, NY 10276. TEL 800-545-8398; UK subscr. to: P.O. Box 90, Reading, Berkshire RG1 8JL, England. TEL 0734-560-080) adv.; bk.rev. (also avail. in microform from MIM) **Indexed:** Psychol.Abstr.
  —BLDSC shelfmark: 8814.562200.
  Former titles: Psychoenergetics (ISSN 0278-6060); Psychoenergetic Systems (ISSN 0305-7224)
  Refereed Serial

THEORIA; a Swedish journal of philosophy. see *PHILOSOPHY*

150 US
THEORIEN DER PSYCHOLOGIE. vol.6, 1983. irreg. price varies. Springer-Verlag, 175 Fifth Ave., New York, NY 10010. TEL 212-460-1500. Ed. E. Scheerer.

370.15 150 UK ISSN 0959-3543
  CODEN: THPSEJ
▼**THEORY & PSYCHOLOGY.** 1990. q. £25($41) to individuals; institutions £60($99). Sage Publications Ltd., 6 Bonhill St., London EC2A 4PU, England. TEL 071-374-0645. FAX 071-374-8741. Ed. Henderikus J. Stam. adv.: color page £150; trim 193 x 114; adv. contact: Bernie Folan. bk.rev.
  —BLDSC shelfmark: 8814.628600.
  Description: Focuses on theoretical developments within and across specific sub-areas of psychology.

155 618.92 US
THEORY AND RESEARCH IN BEHAVIORAL PEDIATRICS. 1982. irreg., vol.5, 1991. price varies. Plenum Publishing Corp., 233 Spring St., New York, NY 10013-1578. TEL 202-620-8000. FAX 212-463-0742. TELEX 23-421139. Ed.Bd. (back issues avail.)
  Refereed Serial

150 JA ISSN 0040-8743
BF1 CODEN: TPSFAD
TOHOKU PSYCHOLOGICA FOLIA. (Text in European languages) 1933. a. exchange basis. Tohoku Daigaku, Bungakubu Shinrigaku Kyoshitsu - Tohoku University, Faculty of Arts and Letters, Department of Psychology, Kawauchi, Sendai-shi, Miyagi-ken 980, Japan. Ed. Kinya Maruyama. charts; illus.; index; circ. 525. **Indexed:** Biol.Abstr., Child Devel.Abstr., Curr.Cont., Psychol.Abstr.

TOPIQUE - REVUE FREUDIENNE. see *MEDICAL SCIENCES — Psychiatry And Neurology*

150 NE ISSN 0167-7411
B1
TOPOI; an international review of philosophy. 1982. s-a. $129.50. Kluwer Academic Publishers, Postbus 17, 3300 AA Dordrecht, Netherlands. TEL 078-334911. FAX 078-334254. TELEX 29245. (Dist. by: Kluwer Academic Publishers Group, P.O. Box 322, 3300 AH Dordrecht, Netherlands; N. America dist. addr.: Box 358, Accord Station, Hingham, MA 02018-0358. TEL 617-871-6600) Ed. Ermanno Bencivenga. adv.; bk.rev.; index. (reprint service avail. from SWZ) **Indexed:** Arts & Hum.Cit.Ind., Curr.Cont., Math.R., Phil.Ind.
  —BLDSC shelfmark: 8867.499800.

TOTAL HEALTH. see *NUTRITION AND DIETETICS*

616.8 370   US   ISSN 0362-1537
RC489.T7
TRANSACTIONAL ANALYSIS JOURNAL. 1962. q. $35.
International Transactional Analysis Association,
1772 Vallejo St., San Francisco, CA 94123.
TEL 415-885-5992. FAX 415-885-5998. Ed.
Howard Douglas. adv.; bk.rev.; abstr.; charts; index;
circ. 5,000. (also avail. in microform from UMI; back
issues avail.) **Indexed:** ASCA, Curr.Cont.,
Psychol.Abstr., SSCI.
  Formerly: Transactional Analysis Bulletin (ISSN
0041-1051)

150   US
TRANSENDER.* 6/yr. free. Live and Learn, Box 6061,
Sherman Oaks, CA 91413-6061.
TEL 818-995-7121. Ed. Rich Monosson. adv.; illus.

614.58   US
TRANSITIONS IN MENTAL RETARDATION. 1984. irreg.
price varies. Ablex Publishing Corporation, 355
Chestnut St., Norwood, NJ 07648.
TEL 201-767-8450. FAX 201-767-6717. TELEX
135-393. Eds. James Mulick, Richard Antonak.

150   FR   ISSN 0041-1868
T58.A2   CODEN: TRHUAH
TRAVAIL HUMAIN. (Text in French; occasionally in
English) 1937. q. 330 F. (foreign 410 F.). Presses
Universitaires de France, Departement des Revues,
14 av. du Bois-de-l'Epine, B.P.90, 91003 Evry
Cedex, France. TEL 1-60-77-82-05.
FAX 1-60-79-20-45. TELEX PUF 600 474 F. Ed.Bd.
bk.rev.; charts; illus.; index; circ. 1,500. (reprint
service avail. from KTO) **Indexed:** ASCA, Biol.Abstr.,
C.I.S. Abstr., Chem.Abstr., Child Devel.Abstr.,
Curr.Cont., Ergon.Abstr., Excerp.Med., Int.Lab.Doc.,
P.A.I.S.For.Lang.Ind., Psychol.Abstr., SSCI.
—BLDSC shelfmark: 9027.300000.
  Description: Covers ergonomics, organization of
work, personnel recruitment, and occupational health
and safety.

137.7   FR   ISSN 0041-2864
TRIBUNE GRAPHOLOGIQUE; l'annuaire de la
graphologie. 1950. a. 8 F. Institut International de
Recherches Graphologiques, Pave du Roy, 77780
Bourron Marlotte, France. Ed. H. Ostrach. adv.;
bk.rev.; bibl.; charts; circ. 1,000. (tabloid format)

157   GW
TRIERER PSYCHOLOGISCHE BERICHTE. (Text and
summaries in English and German) 1974. irreg.
free. Universitaet Trier, Fachgebiet Psychologie,
5500 Trier, Germany. TEL 0651-201-2970.
FAX 0651-25135. Eds. Horst Graeser, Reinhold
Scheller. cum.index: 1974-1988.

150   FI   ISSN 0356-8741
TURUN YLIOPISTO. PSYKOLOGIAN TUTKIMUKSIA. 1969.
irreg. price varies. Turun Yliopisto, Psykologian
Laitos - University of Turku, Dept. of Psychology,
Arwidssonink 1, SF-20500 Turku 50, Finland. Ed.
Kirsti Lagerspetz. circ. 500.
  Supersedes in part: Turun Yliopisto. Psykologian
Laitos. Reports (ISSN 0082-7037)

370.15 150   US
▼**TUTORIAL MONOGRAPHS IN COGNITIVE SCIENCE.**
1991. irreg. price varies. Ablex Publishing
Corporation, 355 Chestnut St., Norwood, NJ
07648. TEL 201-767-8450. FAX 201-767-6717.
TELEX 135-393. Ed. Nigel Shadbolt.

150.19   US   ISSN 8756-4963
TYPE REPORTER; a monthly publication on
psychological type. 1984. 8/yr. $16. Type Reporter,
Inc., 524 N. Paxton St., Alexandria, VA 22304.
TEL 703-823-3730. Ed. Susan Scanlon. bk.rev.;
charts; illus.; circ. 3,000. (back issues avail.)

301.1 150   SA   ISSN 0256-8896
U N I S A PSYCHOLOGIA. (Text in Afrikaans, English)
1974. s-a. R.6.60($4.50) University of South Africa,
Department of Psychology, P.O. Box 392, Pretoria
0001, South Africa. FAX 012-429-3221. TELEX
350068. Ed. J. Erasmus. adv.; bk.rev.; circ. 5,000.
(back issues avail.)

U S S R REPORT: LIFE SCIENCES. see *MEDICAL
SCIENCES*

150   DK   ISSN 0105-2691
UDKAST; dansk tidsskrift for kritisk
samfundsvidenskab. 1973. 2/yr. DKK 140
(students DKK 105; foreign DKK 114.75). Dansk
Psykologisk Forlag, Hans Knudsens Plads 1A, 2100
Copenhagen O, Denmark. TEL 31-182757.
FAX 31-185758. Ed. Sven Moerch. index; circ. 500.
(back issues avail.) **Indexed:** Psychol.Abstr.
—BLDSC shelfmark: 9079.653800.

370.15 616.8   US
UNDERSTANDING PEOPLE. 1987. m. $47. Cromwell -
Sloan Publishing Company, 63 Vine Rd., Stamford,
CT 06905-2012. TEL 203-323-6839. Ed. Paul
Sloan. bk.rev.; abstr.; charts; illus.; circ. 2,700. (back
issues avail.)

370.15   SP   ISSN 0212-9728
UNIVERSIDAD DE MURCIA. ANALES DE PSICOLOGIA.
(Text in English, Spanish) 1955. s-a. 2000 ptas.
Universidad de Murcia, Secretariado de
Publicaciones e Intercambio Cientifico, Santo Cristo
1, 30001 Murcia, Spain. TEL 968-239450. Ed.
Manuel Ato Garcia.
  Supersedes in part (in 1984): Universidad de
Murcia. Filosofia y Letras. Anales (ISSN 0463-9863)

150 301   NZ   ISSN 0069-3774
**UNIVERSITY OF CANTERBURY. DEPARTMENT OF
PSYCHOLOGY AND SOCIOLOGY. RESEARCH
PROJECTS.** 1956. irreg. (2-3/yr.). price varies.
University of Canterbury, Department of Psychology,
Christchurch, New Zealand. Ed. B.G. Stacey. circ.
250. **Indexed:** Psychol.Abstr.

150   FI   ISSN 0359-0216
**UNIVERSITY OF TURKU. PSYCHOLOGICAL RESEARCH
REPORTS.** (Text in English) 1963. irreg. price varies.
Turun Yliopisto, Psykologian Laitos - University of
Turku, Department of Psychology, Arwidssonink 1,
SF-20500 Turku 50, Finland. Ed. Kirsti Lagerspetz.
circ. 500.
  Supersedes in part: Turun Yliopisto. Psykologian
Laitos. Reports (ISSN 0082-7037)

150   CS   ISSN 0083-419X
BF26   CODEN: PSYAD8
**UNIVERZITA KOMENSKEHO. FILOZOFICKA FAKULTA.
ZBORNIK: PSYCHOLOGICA.** (Text in Slovak;
summaries in English, German and Russian) 1961.
irreg. exchange basis. Univerzita Komenskeho,
Filozoficka Fakulta, c/o Ustredna Kniznica
Filozofickej Fakulty, Gondova 2, 818 01 Bratislava,
Czechoslovakia. Ed. Jukius Boros. circ. 400. **Indexed:**
Psychol.Abstr.
  Description: Covers all aspects of psychology.

370.14 150   PL   ISSN 0208-4562
**UNIWERSYTET GDANSKI. WYDZIAL HUMANISTYCZNY.
ZESZYTY NAUKOWE. PSYCHOLOGIA.** (Text in Polish;
summaries in English, Russian) 1978. irreg. price
varies. Uniwersytet Gdanski, Wydzial Humanistyczny,
c/o Biblioteka Glowna, Ul. Armii Krajowej 110,
81-824 Sopot, Poland. TEL 51-0061. TELEX 051
2247 BMOR PL. (Dist. by: Ars Polona-Ruch,
Krakowskie Przedmiescie 7, 00-680 Warsaw,
Poland) circ. 250.
  Description: Each volume covers a particular field
of interest, such as creativity, attitudes toward
religion, motivation of achievement, and family
psychology.

150 370   PL   ISSN 0083-4408
LB1051
**UNIWERSYTET JAGIELLONSKI. ZESZYTY NAUKOWE.
PRACE PSYCHOLOGICZNO-PEDAGOGICZNE.** 1957.
irreg., vol.34, 1983. price varies. Panstwowe
Wydawnictwo Naukowe, Miodowa 10, 00-251
Warsaw, Poland. (Dist. by: Ars Polona, Krakowskie
Przedmiescie 7, 00-068 Warsaw, Poland) Ed. Maria
Susulowska. illus.

158.7   PL   ISSN 0208-5569
**UNIWERSYTET SLASKI W KATOWICACH. PRACE
NAUKOWE. PSYCHOLOGICZNE PROBLEMY
FUNKCJONOWANIA CZLOWIEKA W SYTUACJI PRACY.**
(Text in Polish; summaries in English and Russian)
1980. irreg. price varies. Wydawnictwo Uniwersytetu
Slaskiego, Ul. Bankowa 14, 40-007 Katowice,
Poland. TEL 48-32-596-915. FAX 48-32-599-605.
TELEX 0315584 USKPL. (Dist. by: CHZ Ars Polona,
P.O. Box 1001, 00-950 Warsaw, Poland)
  Description: Provides social psychological studies
of human behaviour at work, especially on
interpersonal relations, trust, injustice, leadership
and attitudes to work, stress and resistance to
change, employees appraisal.

UOMINI E IDEE; rivista di letteratura, sociologia e arte.
see *LITERATURE*

VEDANTA KESARI. see *PHILOSOPHY*

616.89   GW   ISSN 0721-7234
VERHALTENSTHERAPIE UND PSYCHOSOZIALE PRAXIS.
1968. q. DM.60. Deutsche Gesellschaft fuer
Verhaltenstherapie, Postfach 1343, Belthlestr. 15,
D-7400 Tuebingen, Germany. TEL 07071-41211.
adv.; bk.rev.; circ. 7,000. (back issues avail.)

**VIERTELJAHRESSCHRIFT FUER HEILPAEDAGOGIK UND
IHRE NACHBARGEBIETE.** see *EDUCATION — Special
Education And Rehabilitation*

301.1 150 364   US   ISSN 0886-6708
HV6250
VIOLENCE AND VICTIMS. 1986. q. $28 to individuals;
institutions $54. Springer Publishing Company, 536
Broadway, New York, NY 10012.
TEL 212-431-4370. FAX 212-941-7842. Ed.
Roland Maiuro. adv.; bk.rev. (back issues avail.)
Indexed: Crim.Just.Abstr., Excerp.Med.,
Psychol.Abstr., Sage Fam.Stud.Abstr., Sage
Urb.Stud.Abstr., Sociol.Abstr., SOPODA.
—BLDSC shelfmark: 9237.751000.

150.19 069 910   US   ISSN 0892-4996
VISITOR BEHAVIOR. 1986. q. $12 to individuals;
institutions $20. Center for Social Design, Box
1111, Jacksonville, AL 36265. TEL 205-782-5640.
FAX 205-782-5640. Ed. Stephen Bitgood. adv.;
bk.rev.; circ. 500. (back issues avail.)
  Description: Deals with all areas of visitor studies,
covering research, evaluation, graphics and labels,
orientation and circulation, and architectural design.

VITA DELL'INFANZIA. see *EDUCATION*

VITA NUOVA; realta spiritica. see *SCIENCES:
COMPREHENSIVE WORKS*

616.89   US   ISSN 0042-8272
RC475
VOICES; the art and science of psychotherapy. 1965. q.
$30 to individuals; institutions $60. (American
Academy of Psychotherapists) Guilford Publications,
Inc., 72 Spring St., 4th Fl., New York, NY 10012.
TEL 212-431-9800. FAX 212-966-6708. Ed.
Edward Tick. adv.; bk.rev.; illus.; cum.index; circ.
2,000. (also avail. in microform from UMI; audio
cassette; reprint service avail. from UMI) **Indexed:**
Psychol.R.G.
—BLDSC shelfmark: 9251.465000.

150   RU   ISSN 0042-8841
BF8.R8   CODEN: VOPSAI
VOPROSY PSIKHOLOGII. (Text in Russian; summaries in
English) 1955. bi-m. 7.80 Rub. (Akademiya
Pedagogicheskikh Nauk S.S.S.R.) Izdatel'stvo
Pedagogica, Ul. Pavla Korchagina 7, Moscow,
Russia. (Subscr. to: Mezhdunarodnaya Kniga,
Moscow, G-200, Russia) Ed. A. M. Matyushkin.
index. **Indexed:** Biol.Abstr., Child Devel.Abstr.,
Curr.Cont., Int.Aerosp.Abstr., Psychol.Abstr., SSCI.
—BLDSC shelfmark: 0044.130000.

VYCHOVAVATEL. see *EDUCATION*

616.58   US   ISSN 0042-9511
W A W NEWSLETTER. 1966. 3/yr. William Alanson
White Psychoanalytic Institute, 20 W. 74th St., New
York, NY 10023. TEL 212-873-0725.
FAX 212-362-6967. Ed. Ira Moses. bk.rev.; illus.;
circ. 7,010.

150 616.8   US   ISSN 0083-8977
W P S PROFESSIONAL HANDBOOK SERIES. 1965. irreg.
price varies. Western Psychological Services, 12031
Wilshire Blvd., Los Angeles, CA 90025.
TEL 310-478-2061. FAX 310-478-7838. Ed. Janet
Hansen.

614.58 616.8   GW   ISSN 0173-3524
WERKSTATTSCHRIFTEN ZUR SOZIALPSYCHIATRIE.
1973. irreg. DM.19.80 per no. Psychiatrie-Verlag
GmbH, Thomas-Mann-Str. 49a, 5300 Bonn 1,
Germany. TEL 0228-695540. FAX 0228-695595.
Ed.Bd. adv.; bk.rev.; circ. 1,200.
  Description: Presents articles of general interest
for those in the community mental health system.

PSYCHOLOGY

370.15 150   NR   ISSN 0331-0515
WEST AFRICAN JOURNAL OF EDUCATIONAL AND VOCATIONAL MEASUREMENT. 1973. s-a. £N5. West African Examinations Council, Test Development and Research Division, P.M.B. 1076, Yaba, Lagos, Nigeria. Ed.Bd. adv.; circ. 250. **Indexed:** Psychol.Abstr.

WEST BENGAL. BUREAU OF EDUCATIONAL AND PSYCHOLOGICAL RESEARCH. see *EDUCATION*

WINGSPAN: JOURNAL OF THE MALE SPIRIT. see *MEN'S STUDIES*

158 305.4   US   ISSN 0270-3149
RC451.4.W6   CODEN: WOTHDJ
WOMEN & THERAPY; a feminist quarterly of research and opinion. 1982. q. $36 to individuals; institutions $75; libraries $150. Haworth Press, Inc., 10 Alice St., Binghamton, NY 13904. TEL 800-342-9678. FAX 607-722-1424. TELEX 4932599. Eds. Esther Rothblum, Ellen Cole. adv.; bk.rev.; circ. 351. (also avail. in microfiche from HAW; back issues avail.; reprint service avail. from HAW) **Indexed:** Alt.Press Ind., Biol.Abstr., Bull.Signal., Psychol.Abstr., Soc.Work Res.& Abstr., Stud.Wom.Abstr., Wom.Stud.Abstr. (1982-).
—BLDSC shelfmark: 9343.276000.
Formerly: Women - Counseling Therapy and Mental Health Services.
Description: Explores the multidimensional relationship between women and therapy, and feminist in orientation. Publishes descriptive, theoretical, clinical, and empirical perspectives on the topic and the therapeutic process.
Refereed Serial

WORK AND OCCUPATIONS; an international sociological journal. see *SOCIOLOGY*

158.7   UK   ISSN 0267-8373
HF5548.85
WORK AND STRESS. 1987. q. £77($132) Taylor & Francis Ltd., Rankine Rd., Basingstoke, Hants RG24 OPR, England. TEL 0256-840366. FAX 0256-479438. TELEX 858540. Ed. Dr. Tom Cox. (back issues avail.) **Indexed:** ASSIA, Psychol.Abstr.
—BLDSC shelfmark: 9348.102000.
Description: Features academic papers relating to stress, health and safety, and associated areas and scholarly articles of concern to the policy-makers, managers and trades unionists who have to deal with such issues.
Refereed Serial

WORLD COUNCIL FOR GIFTED AND TALENTED CHILDREN. YEARBOOK. see *EDUCATION — Special Education And Rehabilitation*

616.89 614.582   US
WORLD FEDERATION FOR MENTAL HEALTH. NEWSLETTER. 5/yr. membership. World Federation for Mental Health, 1021 Prince St., Alexandria, VA 22314. TEL 703-684-7722. FAX 703-684-5968. Ed. Eugene B. Brody. circ. 3,000.

150.19   GW   ISSN 0344-8274
WUNDERBLOCK; Zeitschrift fuer Psychoanalyse. 1978. irreg. DM.55. Verlag der Wunderblock, Konstanzer Strasse 11, 1000 Berlin 31, Germany. TEL 8831122. Eds. Dr. Norbert Haas, Dr. Verena Haas. adv.; bk.rev. (back issues avail.)

510   PL
WYZSZA SZKOLA PEDAGOGICZNA IM. KOMISJI EDUKACJI NARODOWEJ W KRAKOWIE. ROCZNIK NAUKOWO-DYDAKTYCZNY. PRACE PSYCHOLOGICZNE. 1963. irreg., no.2, 1988. price varies. Wydawnictwo Naukowe W S P, Ul. Karmelicka 41, 31-128 Krakow, Poland. TEL 33-78-20. (Co-sponsor: Ministerstwo Edukacji Narodowej)

150   PL   ISSN 0208-9564
WYZSZA SZKOLA PEDAGOGICZNA, OPOLE. ZESZYTY NAUKOWE. SERIA A. PSYCHOLOGIA. (Text in Polish; summaries in English) 1979. irreg., vol.6, 1990. price varies; also exchange basis. Wyzsza Szkola Pedagogiczna, Opole, Oleska 48, 45-951 Opole, Poland. TEL 48 77 383-87. (Dist. by: Ars Polona-Ruch, Krakowskie Przedmiescie 7, Warsaw, Poland)
—BLDSC shelfmark: 9512.478998.

150   CC   ISSN 1000-6648
BF8.C5
XINLI KEXUE TONGXUN/INFORMATION ON PSYCHOLOGICAL SCIENCES. (Text in Chinese) 1965. bi-m. $41. Zhongguo Xinli Xuehui, 3663 Zhongshan Beilu, Shanghai 200062, People's Republic of China. TEL 2577577. (Dist. in US by: China Books & Periodicals, Inc., 2929 24th St., San Francisco, CA 94110. TEL 415-282-2994) Ed. Zhu Manshu. **Indexed:** Psychol.Abstr.

155   CC   ISSN 0439-755X
XINLI XUEBAO/ACTA PSYCHOLOGICA SINICA. (Text in Chinese; summaries in English) 1956. q. Y6.80($9) per no. Science Press, Marketing and Sales Department, 16 Donghuangchenggen Beijie, Beijing 100707, People's Republic of China. TEL 4010642. FAX 4012180. TELEX 210247-SPBJ-CN. adv.; circ. 32,000. **Indexed:** Psychol.Abstr.
Description: Covers the basic theories of psychology, general, medical, physiological, child, and educational psychology. Also covers the history of psychology, and contains evaluations of academic studies and information on current academic activities.
Refereed Serial

YOGA INTERNATIONAL. see *NEW AGE PUBLICATIONS*

Z U M A - NACHRICHTEN. see *SOCIOLOGY*

616.89   PK
ZEHAN. (Text in Urdu) 1978. q. Rs.12($1.50) Psychope, G.P.O. Box 1964, Lahore, Pakistan. Ed. Dr. Syed Azhar Ale Rizvi. adv.; bk.rev.; circ. 500.

150 158   GW   ISSN 0932-4089
ZEITSCHRIFT FUER ARBEITS- UND ORGANISATIONSPSYCHOLOGIE.* Short title: A & O. 1956. q. DM.98. Verlag fuer Psychologie Dr. C.J. Hogrefe, Rohnsweg 25, Postfach 3751, 3400 Goettingen 1, Germany. TEL 0551-54044. Ed. Carl Graf Hoyas. adv.; bk.rev.; bibl.; charts; circ. 800. (reprint service avail. from SWZ) **Indexed:** C.I.S. Abstr., Dok.Arbeitsmed., Ger.J.Psych., Psychol.Abstr.
Former titles (until 1987): Psychologie und Praxis; Psychologie und Praxis Arbeits- und Organisationspsychologie; Psychologie und Praxis (ISSN 0033-2992)

152   SZ   ISSN 0170-1789
ZEITSCHRIFT FUER DIFFERENTIELLE UND DIAGNOSTISCHE PSYCHOLOGIE. 1980. q. 104 Fr. (foreign DM.114). (Deutschen Gesellschaft fuer Psychologie) Verlag Hans Huber, Laengsasstr. 76, CH-3000 Berne 9, Switzerland. TEL 031-24-25-33. FAX 031-24-33-80. (North American orders: Hans Huber Publishers Inc., 14, Bruce Park Ave., Toronto, Ont. M4P 2S3, Canada) adv.; circ. 800. **Indexed:** Psychol.Abstr.
—BLDSC shelfmark: 9457.686000.

370.15 150   GW   ISSN 0049-8637
L31   CODEN: ZEPPBI
ZEITSCHRIFT FUER ENTWICKLUNGSPSYCHOLOGIE UND PAEDAGOGISCHE PSYCHOLOGIE. (Text in German; summaries in English) 1969. q. DM.68. Verlag fuer Psychologie Dr. C.J. Hogrefe, Rohnsweg 25, Postfach 3751, 3400 Goettingen, Germany. TEL 0551-54044. Ed. H. Mandl. adv.; bk.rev.; abstr.; bibl.; circ. 2,400. **Indexed:** Child Devel.Abstr., Curr.Cont., Ger.J.Psych., Psychol.Abstr., SSCI.
—BLDSC shelfmark: 9458.600000.

152   GW   ISSN 0044-2712
BF3
ZEITSCHRIFT FUER EXPERIMENTELLE UND ANGEWANDTE PSYCHOLOGIE. (Summaries in English and French) 1953. 4/yr. DM.168. Verlag fuer Psychologie Dr. C.J. Hogrefe, Rohnsweg 25, Postfach 3751, 3400 Goettingen, Germany. TEL 0551-54044. Ed. G. Luer. adv.; bk.rev.; bibl.; charts; illus.; circ. 800. **Indexed:** Curr.Cont., Excerp.Med., Ger.J.Psych., Ind.Med., Lang.& Lang.Behav.Abstr., Psychol.Abstr., SSCI.

150   GW   ISSN 0342-393X
ZEITSCHRIFT FUER INDIVIDUALPSYCHOLOGIE. 1976. q. DM.68. Ernst Reinhardt, GmbH und Co., Verlag, Kemnatenstr. 46, 8000 Munich 19, Germany. TEL 089-1783005. Ed.Bd. adv.; bk.rev.; circ. 2,400. (reprint service avail. from ISI and UMI) **Indexed:** Psychoanal.Abstr., Psychol.Abstr.

157   GW   ISSN 0084-5345
ZEITSCHRIFT FUER KLINISCHE PSYCHOLOGIE - FORSCHUNG UND PRAXIS. (Text in German; summaries in English) 1972. q. DM.84. (Berufsverband Deutscher Psychologen) Verlag fuer Psychologie Dr. C.J. Hogrefe, Rohnsweg 25, Postfach 3751, 3400 Goettingen, Germany. TEL 0551-54044. Ed. U. Baumann. adv.; bk.rev.; circ. 2,000. **Indexed:** Excerp.Med., Ger.J.Psych., Psychol.Abstr., SSCI.
—BLDSC shelfmark: 9467.775000.

ZEITSCHRIFT FUER KLINISCHE PSYCHOLOGIE UND PSYCHOTHERAPIE. see *MEDICAL SCIENCES — Psychiatry And Neurology*

137.7   AU
ZEITSCHRIFT FUER MENSCHENKUNDE. ZENTRALBLATT FUER SCHRIFTPSYCHOLOGIE UND SCHRIFTVERGLEICHUNG. 1925. q. S.380. Universitaets Verlagsbuchhandlung GmbH, Servitengasse 5, A-1092 Vienna, Austria. TEL 0222-348124. FAX 0222-310-2805. adv.; bk.rev.; charts; cum.index every 2 yrs.; circ. 1,000.
Former titles: Zeitschrift fuer Menschenkunde und Zentralblatt fuer Graphologie, Ausdruckswissenschaft und Charakterkunde (ISSN 0044-3085) & Zeitschrift fuer Menschenkunde und Zentralblatt fuer Graphologie.

370.15   SZ   ISSN 1010-0652
LB1051   CODEN: ZPPSE5
ZEITSCHRIFT FUER PAEDAGOGISCHE PSYCHOLOGIE. (Text in English and German) 1987. q. 104 Fr. Verlag Hans Huber, Laenggasstr. 76, CH-3000 Berne 9, Switzerland. TEL 031-242533. FAX 031-243380. Ed.Bd. bk.rev.; circ. 500. (back issues avail.) **Indexed:** Psychol.Abstr., Sp.Ed.Needs Abstr.

150   GW   ISSN 0044-3409
QP351
ZEITSCHRIFT FUER PSYCHOLOGIE; mit Zeitschrift fuer angewandte Psychologie. 1890. 4/yr. DM.96. Johann Ambrosius Barth Verlag, Leipzig - Heidelberg, Salomonstr. 18b, 7010 Leipzig, England. TEL 70131. Ed. Dr. Klix. adv.; bk.rev.; bibl.; charts; illus.; index; circ. 1,300. (reprint service avail. from SWZ) **Indexed:** Biol.Abstr., Ger.J.Psych., Ind.Med., Psychol.Abstr., SSCI.
—BLDSC shelfmark: 9485.100000.
Incorporates: Zeitschrift fuer Angewandte Psychologie.

ZEITSCHRIFT FUER PSYCHOSOMATISCHE MEDIZIN UND PSYCHOANALYSE. BEIHEFTE. see *MEDICAL SCIENCES — Psychiatry And Neurology*

ZEITSCHRIFT FUER SEXUALFORSCHUNG. see *MEDICAL SCIENCES*

301.1   SZ   ISSN 0049-867X
ZEITSCHRIFT FUER SOZIALPSYCHOLOGIE. (Text in German; summaries in English) 1970. q. 98 Fr. Verlag Hans Huber, Laenggassstr. 76, CH-3000 Berne 9, Switzerland. TEL 031-24-25-33. FAX 031-24-33-80. TELEX 911886-HAHU. Ed.Bd. adv.; bk.rev.; abstr.; bibl.; circ. 800. **Indexed:** Can.Rev.Comp.Lit., Curr.Cont., Ger.J.Psych., Psychol.Abstr., SSCI.
—BLDSC shelfmark: 9486.380000.

616.89   GW   ISSN 0723-9505
ZEITSCHRIFT FUER SYSTEMISCHE THERAPIE. q. DM.56 (foreign DM.64). Verlag Modernes Lernen - Dortmund, Borgmann KG, Hohestr. 39, 4600 Dortmund 1, Germany. TEL 0231-128008. FAX 0231-125640. Ed. Juergen Hargens.
—BLDSC shelfmark: 9486.409000.

616.89   GW   ISSN 0176-9855
ZEITSCHRIFT FUER TRANSAKTIONSANALYSE IN THEORIE UND PRAXIS. (Text in German; summaries in English) 1984. q. DM.48. (Deutsch Gesellschaft fuer Transaktions-Analyse e.V.) Junfermann-Verlag, Imadstr. 40, Postfach 1840, 4790 Paderborn, Germany. TEL 05251-34034. FAX 05251-36371. index. (back issues avail.)

PSYCHOLOGY — ABSTRACTING, BIBLIOGRAPHIES, STATISTICS

150   CC   ISSN 1000-6729
ZHONGGUO XINLI WEISHENG ZAZHI/CHINESE MENTAL HEALTH JOURNAL. (Text in Chinese; abstracts in English) 1987. bi-m. $28 to individuals; institutions $50. Beijing Yike Daxue, Jingshen Weisheng Yanjiusuo - Beijing Medical University, Institute of Mental Health, Huayuan Beilu, Beijing 100083, People's Republic of China. TEL 2010890. (Co-sponsor: Chinese Mental Health Association) Ed. Peng Ruicong. adv.
● Also available online. Vendor(s): DIALOG.
Refereed Serial

301.1 370 300 610   GW   ISSN 0724-3766
ZWISCHENSCHRITTE; Beiträge zu einer morphologischen Psychologie. 1982. s-a. DM.20. Arbeitskreis Morphologische Psychologie e.V., Postfach 410273, 5000 Cologne 41, Germany. TEL 0221-449956. adv.; bk.rev.; bibl.; film rev.; play rev.; illus.; circ. 1,500. (back issues avail.)

PSYCHOLOGY — Abstracting, Bibliographies, Statistics

310 150   JA   ISSN 0385-7417
BF76.5
BEHAVIORMETRIKA. (Text mainly in English) 1974. a. price varies. Nihon Kodo Keiryo Gakkai - Behaviormetric Society of Japan, 6-7, Minamiazabu 4-chome, Minato-ku, Tokyo 106, Japan. (Or: 1255 Howard St., San Francisco, CA 94103) Ed. Haruo Yanai. Indexed: J.Cont.Quant.Meth., Lang.& Lang.Behav.Abstr., Psychol.Abstr.
—BLDSC shelfmark: 1878.070000.

016 150   AG   ISSN 0523-1698
BIBLIOGRAFIA ARGENTINA DE PSICOLOGIA.* irreg., nos. 5-6, 1970. Ministerio de Cultura y Educacion, Direccion de Bibliotecos, 538 Calle 7, La Plata, Argentina.

150 011   US   ISSN 0360-277X
Z7203
BIBLIOGRAPHIC GUIDE TO PSYCHOLOGY. (Text in various languages) a. $170 (foreign $195). G.K. Hall & Co., 70 Lincoln St., Boston, MA 02111. TEL 617-423-3990. FAX 617-423-3999. TELEX 94-0037.
Formerly: Psychology Book Guide.
Description: Lists all aspects of psychology catalogued during the past year by the Research Libraries of the N Y P L; includes additional entries from LC MARC tapes.

301.1 016   GW   ISSN 0303-5999
BIBLIOGRAPHIE DER DEUTSCHSPRACHIGEN PSYCHOLOGISCHEN LITERATUR. a. DM.314. Vittorio Klostermann, Frauenlobstr. 22, Postfach 900601, 6000 Frankfurt a.M. 90, Germany. TEL 069-774011. FAX 069-708038. Ed. J. Dambauer.

150   US   ISSN 0742-681X
BIBLIOGRAPHIES AND INDEXES IN PSYCHOLOGY. 1984. irreg. price varies. Greenwood Press, Inc. (Subsidiary of: Greenwood Publishing Group Inc.), 88 Post Rd. W., Box 5007, Westport, CT 06881-5007. TEL 203-226-3571. FAX 203-222-1502.
—BLDSC shelfmark: 1993.097470.

616.89 150   US
BIBLIOGRAPHIES IN THE HISTORY OF PSYCHOLOGY AND PSYCHIATRY. 1982. irreg. Kraus International Publications, (Subsidiary of: Kraus Organization Ltd.), Route 100, Millwood, NY 10546. TEL 914-762-2200. Ed. Robert H. Wozniak.

BIBLIOGRAPHY OF EDUCATION THESES IN AUSTRALIA.
see EDUCATION — Abstracting, Bibliographies, Statistics

ERGONOMICS ABSTRACTS. see ENGINEERING — Abstracting, Bibliographies, Statistics

150 016   CN   ISSN 0705-5870
BF1
GERMAN JOURNAL OF PSYCHOLOGY. (Text in English) 1977. q. Can.$74 to institutions; individuals Can.$49. (International Union of Psychological Science) Hogrefe & Huber Publishers, 14 Bruce Park Ave., Toronto, Ont. M4P 2S3, Canada. TEL 416-482-6339. FAX 416-484-4200. Ed. G. Luer. adv.; bk.rev.; abstr.; tr.lit.; circ. 2,000. Indexed: Psychol.Abstr.
Description: Summaries and abstracts of psychological work done currently in German-speaking countries.

150 016   II   ISSN 0250-9679
INDIAN PSYCHOLOGICAL ABSTRACTS. (Text in English) 1972. q. Rs.30 to individuals; institutions Rs.50($10). Indian Council of Social Science Research, 35 Ferozshah Rd., New Delhi 110 001, India. TEL 381571. TELEX 31-61083-ISSR-IN. (Co-sponsor: Indian Psychological Association) Ed. Udai Pareek. adv.; bk.rev.; abstr.; circ. 550. (back issues avail.)
—BLDSC shelfmark: 4428.180000.
Description: Short abstracts of research work in psychology from an Indian perspective.

150 370   SP   ISSN 0213-019X
Z7161.A15
INDICE ESPANOL DE CIENCIAS SOCIALES. SERIES A: PSYCHOLOGY AND EDUCATIONAL SCIENCES. 1979. a. 5000 ptas. or exchange basis. Instituto de Informacion y Documentacion en Ciencias Sociales y Humanidades, Pinar, 25, 28006 Madrid, Spain.
● Also available online.
Also available on CD-ROM.
Supersedes in part (in 1982): Indice Espanol de Ciencias Sociales (ISSN 0211-1373)

310 510   JA
NIHON KODO KEIRYO GAKKAI TAIKAI HAPPYO RONBUN SHOROKUSHU. (Text in Japanese) 1973. a. Nihon Kodo Keiryo Gakkai - Behaviormetric Society of Japan, 6-7, Minami-Azabu 4-chome, Minato-ku, Tokyo 106, Japan. abstr.
Description: Contains abstracts from the annual meeting of the society.

P A S C A L EXPLORE. E 65: PSYCHOLOGIE, PSYCHOPATHOLOGIE, PSYCHIATRIE. see MEDICAL SCIENCES — Abstracting, Bibliographies, Statistics

370.15 150   SW   ISSN 0346-5039
Z5815.S8
PEDAGOGISK DOKUMENTATION. 1971. irreg. Malmoe School of Education, Inst. foer Pedagogik och Specialmetodik, Box 23501, S-20045 Malmoe, Sweden. Ed. Aake Bjerstedt. (back issues avail.)

150 016 614   US   ISSN 0270-3114
RA421   CODEN: PHSEDF
PREVENTION IN HUMAN SERVICES; summaries, reviews & index to the world's literature in community mental health. 1976. s-a. $36 to individuals; institutions $95; libraries $160. Haworth Press, Inc., 10 Alice St., Binghamton, NY 13904. TEL 800-342-9678. FAX 607-722-1424. TELEX 4932599. Ed. Robert Hess. adv.; B&W page $300. bk.rev.; abstr.; bibl.; illus.; cum.index; circ. 233. (also avail. in microfiche from HAW; back issues avail.; reprint service avail. from HAW) Indexed: Abstr.Health Care Manage.Stud, Adol.Ment.Hlth.Abstr., Biol.Abstr., Chicago Psychoanal.Lit.Ind., Child Devel.Abstr., Excerpt.Med., Hosp.Lit.Ind., Lang.& Lang.Behav.Abstr., Past.Care & Couns.Abstr., Psychol.Abstr., Ref.Zh., Rehabil.Lit., Soc.Work Res.& Abstr., Sociol.Abstr.
Formerly (until 1981): Community Mental Health Review (ISSN 0363-1605)
Description: Devoted to the application of the philosophy of prevention in mental health and other human services.
Refereed Serial

150 016   US   ISSN 0033-2887
BF1
PSYCHOLOGICAL ABSTRACTS. 1927. m. $1245 to institutions & non-members (foreign $1290); members $622 (effective 1992). American Psychological Association, 750 First St., N.E., Washington, DC 20002-4242. TEL 202-336-5500. FAX 202-336-5568. Ed. Lois Granick. adv.; abstr.; cum.index; circ. 3,300. (also avail. in microform from MIM,UMI; reprint service avail. from UMI,KTO) Indexed: Ergon.Abstr., JAMA, Popul.Ind.
● Also available online. Vendor(s): BRS, DIMDI, Data-Star (PSYC), DIALOG (File no.11/PsycINFO), Orbit Information Technologies.
Also available on CD-ROM. Producer(s): American Psychological Association, SilverPlatter (PsycLIT).
—BLDSC shelfmark: 6946.290000.
Description: Nonevaluative summaries of the serial literature in psychology and related disciplines.

152 573   US   ISSN 0272-0582
PSYCHOLOGICAL CINEMA REGISTER; films and video in the behavioral sciences. Abbreviated title: P C R 1944. a. Pennsylvania State University, Audio-Visual Services, University Park, PA 16802. TEL 800-826-0132. FAX 814-863-2574. circ. 9,000.

616.89 011   GW   ISSN 0722-1533
PSYCHOLOGISCHER INDEX; Referatedienst ueber die psychologische Literatur aus den deutschsprachigen Laendern. 1981. q. DM.192. (Universitaet Trier, Zentralstelle fuer Psychologische Information und Dokumentation) Verlag fuer Psychologie Dr. C.J. Hogrefe, Rohnsweg 25, D-3400 Goettingen, Germany. TEL 0551-54044. (back issues avail.)

370.15 150
PSYCINFO NEWS. 1981. q. free. American Psychological Association, PsycINFO User Services, 750 First St., N.E., Washington, DC 20002-4242. TEL 800-374-2722. FAX 202-336-5633. Ed.Bd. circ. 8,000.
Description: Contains search tips and news about forthcoming and existing PsycINFO products.

152 011   US   ISSN 0891-0685
PSYCSCAN: APPLIED EXPERIMENTAL AND ENGINEERING PSYCHOLOGY. 1989. q. $30 to non-members (foreign $42); members 16; institutions $60 (foreign $84) (effective 1992). American Psychological Association, 750 First St., N.E., Washington, DC 20002-4242. TEL 202-336-5500. FAX 202-336-5568. Ed. Lois Granick. circ. 1,000.
● Also available online.
Description: Abstracts derived from the PsycINFO Database. Topics include: human factors, ergonomics, computer applications, environment, safety and accidents, transportation and flight, and working conditions.

150   US   ISSN 0271-7506
BF636.A1
PSYCSCAN: APPLIED PSYCHOLOGY. 1981. q. $30 to non-members (foreign $42); members $16; institutions $60 (foreign $84). American Psychological Association, 750 First St., N.E., Washington, DC 20002-4242. TEL 202-336-5500. FAX 202-336-5568. circ. 2,100.
—BLDSC shelfmark: 6946.559600.
Description: Abstracts from a cluster of subscriber-selected journals in general area of applied psychology.

157   US   ISSN 0197-1484
RC467
PSYCSCAN: CLINICAL PSYCHOLOGY. 1980. q. $30 to non-members (foreign $42); members $16; institutions $60 (foreign $84) (effective 1992). American Psychological Association, 750 First St., N.E., Washington, DC 20002-4242. TEL 202-336-5500. FAX 202-336-5568. Ed. Lois Granick. circ. 5,700. (back issues avail.)
—BLDSC shelfmark: 6946.559700.
Description: Abstracts from subscriber-selected journals of interest to clinical psychologists.

150   US   ISSN 0197-1492
PSYCSCAN: DEVELOPMENTAL PSYCHOLOGY. 1980. q. $30 to non-members (foreign $42); members $16; institutions $60 (foreign $84). American Psychological Association, 750 First St., N.E., Washington, DC 20002-4242. TEL 202-336-5500. FAX 202-336-5568. circ. 1,800.
—BLDSC shelfmark: 6946.559750.
Description: Abstracts from subscriber-selected journals of interest to developmental psychologists.

4052 PUBLIC ADMINISTRATION

155   US
PSYCSCAN: LEARNING AND COMMUNICATION DISORDERS AND MENTAL RETARDATION. 1982. q. $30 to non-members; members $16; institutions $60. American Psychological Association, 750 First St., N.E., Washington, DC 20002-4242. TEL 202-336-5500. FAX 202-336-5568. Ed. Lois Granick. circ. 1,500.
   Formerly: Psycscan: Learning Disabilities - Mental Retardation (ISSN 0730-1928)
   Description: Abstracts of articles on learning disorders, communication disorders, and mental retardation, drawn from PsycINFO's annual coverage of more than 1,300 journals.

150.19 011   US   ISSN 0889-5236
PSYCSCAN: PSYCHOANALYSIS. 1985. q. $30 to non-members (foreign $42); members $16; institutions $60 (foreign $84) (effective 1992). American Psychological Association, 750 First St., N.E., Washington, DC 20002-4242. TEL 202-336-5500. FAX 202-336-5568. Ed. Dr. Lois Granick. circ. 4,000.
   Formerly: Psychoanalysis Abstracts.
   Description: Produced in collaboration with APA Division 39 (Psychoanalysis). Full coverage of Psychological Abstracts is reviewed annually and journals are selected for PsycScan.

STATNI VEDECKA KNIHOVNA. VYBER NOVINEK. SERIE F: PEDAGOGIKA, PSYCHOLOGIE. see *EDUCATION — Abstracting, Bibliographies, Statistics*

155.937
THANATOLOGY ABSTRACTS. biennial. $20 per no. Foundation of Thanatology, Foundation Book & Periodical Division, Box 1191, Brooklyn, NY 11202-1202. Ed. Dr. Otto Margolis. adv. (back issues avail.)
   Formerly: Funeral Service Abstracts.
   Description: Covers articles from 120 magazines.

PUBLIC ADMINISTRATION

see also Public Administration–Computer Applications; Public Administration–Municipal Government; Housing and Urban Planning; Social Services and Welfare

A P S A NEWSLETTER. (Australasian Political Studies Association) see *POLITICAL SCIENCE*

350   IT
ABRUZZO NOTIZIE; notiziario sull'attivita legislativa del Consiglio Regionale. 1975. s-m. free. Servizio Informazione Stampa e Pubbliche Relazioni, Via Michele Jacobucci, 4, 67100 L'Aquila, Italy. circ. 9,500. (back issues avail.)

350   TS
ABU DHABI. AL-JARIDAH AL-RASMIYYAH/ABU DHABI. OFFICIAL GAZETTE. (Text in Arabic) 1968. m. Executive Council, General Secretary, P.O. Box 19, Abu Dhabi, United Arab Emirates. TEL 666444. circ. 1,200.
   Description: Covers legislative and legal matters in the Emirate of Abu Dhabi.

ACCOUNTING FOR GOVERNMENT CONTRACTS: COST ACCOUNTING STANDARDS. see *BUSINESS AND ECONOMICS — Accounting*

ACCOUNTING FOR GOVERNMENT CONTRACTS: FEDERAL ACQUISITION REGULATION. see *BUSINESS AND ECONOMICS — Accounting*

ACCOUNTING FOR PUBLIC UTILITIES. see *BUSINESS AND ECONOMICS — Accounting*

350   FR
ADJOINTS TECHNIQUES DES VILLES DE FRANCE. 1971. q. (Association des Adjoints Techniques des Villes de France) Idexpo, 21 av. de la Division-Leclerc, 94230 Cachan, France. adv.

350   SP
ADMINISTRACION PUBLICA. 3/yr. $44. (Centro de Estudios Constitucionales) Edisa, Lopez de Hoyos, 141, 28002 Madrid, Spain. TEL 415-97-12.

ADMINISTRACION Y DESARROLLO. see *POLITICAL SCIENCE*

350   IE   ISSN 0001-8325
JA26
ADMINISTRATION. 1953. q. £25. Institute of Public Administration, 57-61 Lansdowne Rd., Dublin 4, Ireland. Ed. Frank Litton. adv.; bk.rev.; charts; index. cum.index every 5 yrs.; circ. 1,800. **Indexed:** A.B.C.Pol.Sci., Curr.Cont., Rural Recreat.Tour.Abstr., Sage Pub.Admin.Abstr., World Agri.Econ.& Rural Sociol.Abstr.
—BLDSC shelfmark: 0681.950000.

ADMINISTRATION AND POLICY JOURNAL. see *POLITICAL SCIENCE*

ADMINISTRATION AND POLITICAL SCIENCES REVIEW/MAJALLAT AL-ULUM AL-IDARIYYAH WAL-SIYASIYYAH. see *POLITICAL SCIENCE*

350   US   ISSN 0095-3997
JA3
ADMINISTRATION AND SOCIETY. 1969. q. $45 to individuals; institutions $125. Sage Publications, Inc., 2455 Teller Rd., Newbury Park, CA 91320. TEL 805-499-0721. FAX 805-499-0871. TELEX 516-1000799. (And: Sage Publications, Ltd., 6 Bonhill St., London EC2A 4PU, England) Ed. Gary L. Wamsley. adv.; abstr.; bibl.; charts; tr.lit.; index; circ. 1,200. (also avail. in microfilm from UMI; back issues avail.) **Indexed:** A.B.C.Pol.Sci., Amer.Hist.& Life, BPIA, Bus.Ind., C.I.J.E., Curr.Cont., E.I., Energy Ind., Energy Info.Abstr., Hist.Abstr., Int.Polit.Sci.Abstr., Manage.Cont., Mid.East: Abstr.& Ind., P.A.I.S., Pers.Lit., Sage Pub.Admin.Abstr., Sage Urb.Stud.Abstr., SSCI, Tr.& Indus.Ind.
—BLDSC shelfmark: 0681.957000.
   Formerly: Journal of Comparative Administration (ISSN 0021-9932)
   Description: Deals with administration, bureaucracy, public organization, and public policy, and the impact these have on politics and society.

350   BG
ADMINISTRATIVE AFFAIRS IN BANGLADESH. 1979. a. $5. University of Dhaka, Center for Administrative Studies, Arts Faculty Bldg., Rm. 4036, Dhaka 2, Bangladesh.

350 301.15   US   ISSN 0001-8392
HD28   CODEN: ASCQAG
ADMINISTRATIVE SCIENCE QUARTERLY. 1956. q. $47 to individuals (foreign $47); institutions $70 (foreign $77); students $25 (foreign $32). Cornell University, Johnson Graduate School of Management, 425 Caldwell Hall, Ithaca, NY 14853-2602. TEL 607-255-5581. FAX 607-255-7524. TELEX WUI 6713054. Ed. John H. Freeman. adv.; bk.rev.; charts; illus.; index; cum.index; circ. 5,445. (also avail. in microform from UMI; back issues avail.) **Indexed:** A.B.C.Pol.Sci., ABI Inform, Account.Ind. (1974-), Amer.Hist.& Life, ASSIA, B.P.I., Bibl.Ind., BPIA, Bus.Ind., C.I.J.E., CINAHL, Commun.Abstr., Cont.Pg.Manage., Curr.Cont., Deep Sea Res.& Oceanogr.Abstr., E.I., Econ.Abstr., Educ.Admin.Abstr., Hist.Abstr., Int.Polit.Sci.Abstr., Key to Econ.Sci., Manage.Cont., Med.Care Rev., Mgmt.& Market.Abstr., Mid.East: Abstr.& Ind., Oper.Res.Manage.Sci., P.A.I.S., Pers.Lit., Pers.Manage.Abstr., Psychol.Abstr., Psycscan, Qual.Contr.Appl.Stat., Res.High.Educ.Abstr., Sage Pub.Admin.Abstr., SCIMP (1978-), Soc.Sci.Ind., Soc.Work Res.& Abstr., Sociol.Abstr., SSCI.
●Also available online. Vendor(s): BRS, DIALOG, Dow Jones/News Retrieval, Information Access Company.
—BLDSC shelfmark: 0696.517000.

350   II
ADMINISTRATOR. (Text in English) 1956. q. Rs.200($40) (effective 1992). (Lal Bahadur Shastri National Academy of Administration) M s Wiley Eastern Limited Publishers, 4835/24, Ansari Road, Darya Ganj, New Delhi - 110 002, India. bk.rev.; bibl.
   Formerly: Lal Bahadur Shastri National Academy of Administration. Journal.

ADVANCE LOCATOR FOR CAPITOL HILL. see *POLITICAL SCIENCE*

ADVOCATE'S ADVOCATE. see *POLITICAL SCIENCE*

354.6   MR   ISSN 0007-9588
JQ1871.A1
AFRICAN ADMINISTRATIVE STUDIES. French edition: Cahiers Africains d'Administration Publique. (Editions in English, French) 1966. s-a. $40. Centre Africain de Formation et de Recherche Administratives pour le Developpement - African Training and Research Centre in Administration for Development, P.O. Box 310, Tangier, Morocco. TEL 936601. FAX 9-941415. TELEX 33664M. **Indexed:** Curr.Cont.Africa, Mid.East: Abstr.& Ind., Rural Recreat.Tour.Abstr., World Agri.Econ.& Rural Sociol.Abstr.
—BLDSC shelfmark: 0732.270000.

AFRICANUS; journal for development administration. see *POLITICAL SCIENCE*

350   TG
AGENCE TOGOLAISE DE PRESSE. BULLETIN D'INFORMATION. w. Agence Togolaise de Presse, 35 rue Binger, Lome, Togo.

350 370   US   ISSN 1058-1324
▼**AID FOR EDUCATION REPORT.** 1991. s-m. $169. (Community Development Services, Inc.) C D Publications, 8204 Fenton St., Silver Spring, MD 20901. TEL 301-588-6380. FAX 301-588-6385.
   Description: Public and private funding opportunities for all levels of education, plus updates on application deadlines, eligibility criteria for upcoming programs, funding levels and budget trends.

350   TS
AL-AIN. 1986. m. Municipal Government, P.O. Box 1003, Al-Ain, United Arab Emirates. TEL 635111. Ed. Musaad Ismail. circ. 1,000.
   Formerly (until 1988): Majallat Baladiat al-Ain.
   Description: Covers the activities of the municipality and local groups.

350   US   ISSN 0892-9084
HA221
ALABAMA COUNTY DATA BOOK. 1976. a. $6. Department of Economic and Community Affairs, Box 250347, Montgomery, AL 36125-0347. TEL 205-284-8630. FAX 205-284-8670. Ed. Parker Collins. charts; stat.; circ. 5,000. **Indexed:** SRI.

ALAN GUTTMACHER INSTITUTE. WASHINGTON MEMO. see *MEDICAL SCIENCES — Obstetrics And Gynecology*

353.9   US   ISSN 0095-3865
HJ11
ALASKA. LEGISLATURE. BUDGET AND AUDIT COMMITTEE. ANNUAL REPORT.. 1965. a. free. Legislative Budget and Audit Committee, Box W, Juneau, AK 99811. circ. 200. Key Title: Annual Report - State of Alaska, Legislative Budget and Audit Committee.

353.9   US   ISSN 0092-1858
JK9530
ALASKA BLUE BOOK. 1973. biennial. $12. Department of Education, Division of Libraries, Archives & Museums, Box G, Juneau, AK 99811. TEL 907-465-2910. FAX 907-465-2665. illus.; stat.; circ. 3,000.

350   US
ALASKA LEGISLATIVE DIGEST. 1971. w. (Jan.-Jun.). $230. Information & Research Service, 3037 S. Circle, Anchorage, AK 99507. TEL 907-349-7711. FAX 907-522-1761. Ed. Tim Bradner.
   Description: Provides analytical and interpretive coverage of Alaska legislative session, interim activity and administrative action.

353.9   US
JK9549.04
ALASKA OMBUDSMAN REPORT. 1975. a. Office of Ombudsman, Box 113000, Juneau, AK 99811-3000. TEL 907-465-4970. FAX 907-465-3330. circ. 3,000.
   Formerly: Alaska. Office of Ombudsman. Report of the Ombudsman (ISSN 0363-5376)

ALLAM ES IGAZGATAS. see *LAW*

PUBLIC ADMINISTRATION 4053

350   CN
ALLIANCE (OTTAWA). (Text in English and French) 1966. bi-m. Public Service Alliance of Canada, 233 Gilmour St., Ottawa, Ont. K2P 0P1, Canada. TEL 613-560-4235. FAX 613-236-1654. Ed. Nancy Mitchell. charts; illus.; circ. 136,000.
Formerly: Argus-Journal (ISSN 0004-1211)

350 352   GW   ISSN 0722-5474
ALTERNATIVE KOMMUNALPOLITIK; Fachzeitschrift fuer gruene und alternative Politik. 1982. bi-m. DM.48. Verein zur Foerderung der Kommunalpolitischen Arbeit, Herforder Str. 92, 4800 Bielefeld 1, Germany. TEL 0521-177517. FAX 0521-177568. adv.; bk.rev.; circ. 4,000. (back issues avail.)

350   BH
AMANDALA. 1970. w. $50 (effective Jul. 1991). Amandala Press, 3304 Partridge St., Belize City, Belize. TEL 02-77276. FAX 02-75934. (Subscr. to: Box 15, Belize City, Belize) Ed. Evan X. Hyde. circ. 8,500.
Description: Community service publication.

350   US   ISSN 1049-7285
E838   CODEN: APROEY
▼**AMERICAN PROSPECT**; a journal for the liberal imagination. 1990. q. $25 to individuals; institutions $60. New Prospect, Inc., Box 7645, Princeton, NJ 08543-7645. TEL 609-497-2474. FAX 609-497-0075. Eds. Robert Kuttner, Paul Starr. adv.; bk.rev.; circ. 10,000. **Indexed:** P.A.I.S., Sage Pub.Admin., Sociol.Abstr.
—BLDSC shelfmark: 0853.330000.

350 600   US   ISSN 0360-6899
TD1
AMERICAN PUBLIC WORKS ASSOCIATION. DIRECTORY. biennial. membership. American Public Works Association, 1313 E. 60th St, Chicago, IL 60637. TEL 312-667-2200.
Former titles (1959-1968): American Public Works Association. Yearbook (ISSN 0096-025X); Public Works Engineers' Yearbook.

353   US   ISSN 0275-0740
JK1
AMERICAN REVIEW OF PUBLIC ADMINISTRATION. 1967. q. $22 to individuals in U.S. and Canada (elsewhere $25); institutions in U.S. and Canada $40 (elsewhere $50). University of Missouri, Kansas City, Henry W. Bloch School of Business and Public Administration, L.P. Cookingham Institute of Public Affairs, Kansas City, MO 64110.
FAX 816-235-2312. (Co-sponsors: University of Missouri, Columbia; University of Missouri, St. Louis) Ed. John Clayton Thomas. adv.; bk.rev.; bibl.; circ. 500. (also avail. in microform from UMI; back issues avail.) **Indexed:** A.B.C.Pol.Sci., ABI Inform, BPIA, Bus.Ind., Manage.Cont., P.A.I.S., Pers.Lit., PSI, Sage Pub.Admin.Abstr., Tr.& Indus.Ind.
●Also available online. Vendor(s): DIALOG.
Formerly (until 1981): Midwest Review of Public Administration (ISSN 0026-346X)

350   US
AMERICAN SOCIETY FOR PUBLIC ADMINISTRATION. SECTION ON INTERNATIONAL AND COMPARATIVE ADMINISTRATION. OCCASIONAL PAPERS. 1974. irreg., latest 1985. $3 per no. American Society for Public Administration, Section on International and Comparative Administration, 1120 G St., N.W., Ste. 540, Washington, DC 20005. TEL 202-393-7878. Ed. Prof. Louis A. Picard. circ. 550. (back issues avail.; reprint service avail. from KTO)

350   IT   ISSN 0044-8141
AMMINISTRARE. 1986. 3/yr. L.100000. (Istituto per la Scienza dell' Amministrazione Pubblica) Societa Editrice Il Mulino, Strada Maggiore, 37, 40125 Bologna, Italy. TEL 051-256011. FAX 051-256034. Ed. Ettore Rotelli. adv.; index; circ. 1,200. (back issues avail.)

350   IT   ISSN 0303-9722
AMMINISTRAZIONE ITALIANA. 1945. m. L.195000 (foreign L.280000). Societa Tipografica Barbieri, Noccioli & C., Casella Postale 427, 50053 Empoli, Italy. TEL 0571-920394. FAX 0571-920859. Eds. Antonio Romano, Giovanni la Torre. adv.; bk.rev.; index; circ. 3,800.
Description: Covers local and national Italian administration.

350   SZ   ISSN 0003-2115
AMTLICHER ANZEIGER. 1968. w. H. Akerets Erben AG, Postfach, 8600 Duebendorf, Switzerland. adv.; bk.rev.; circ. 12,100.

350   GW
AMTSBLATT DER REGIERUNG VON UNTERFRANKEN. 1956. s-m. DM.36. Regierung von Unterfranken, Peterplatz 9, Postfach 6349, 8700 Wuerzburg, Germany. bk.rev.; circ. 1,100.

350   GW   ISSN 0934-8964
AMTSBLATT DER STADT MOENCHENGLADBACH. 1975. 3/m. DM.30. Presse- und Informationsamt, Rathaus Abtei, 4050 Moenchengladbach 1, Germany. TEL 02161-25-2464. FAX 02161-23890. TELEX 852788-STMG-D. circ. 1,300. (back issues avail.)

350   GW
AMTSBLATT DES LANDKREISES DILLINGEN AN DER DONAU. bi-m. Landkreis Dillingen an der Donau, Grosse Allee 24, D-8880 Dillingen, Germany. TEL 09071-51-138.

350   GW
AMTSBLATT DES LANDKREISES HOF. 1972. s-m. DM.75. Landratsamt Hof, Schaumbergstr. 14, 8670 Hof, Germany. TEL 09281-57-0. FAX 09281-58340. TELEX 9281816-LRA-HOF. circ. 550.

350   GW
AMTSBLATT GROSSE KREISSTADT LEINFELDEN. 1976. w. DM.65. Nussbaum Verlag GmbH, Postfach 1340, D-7252 Weil der Stadt, Germany. TEL 07033-2001. circ. 16,000.
Description: Official information of the municipality of Leinfelden-Echterdingen.

658   II   ISSN 0003-2964
ANDHRA PRADESH PRODUCTIVITY COUNCIL. TARGET. 1961. s-a. Rs.6. Andhra Pradesh Productivity Council, P.O. Box No. 21 (10-1-200, A.C. Guards), Hyderabad 500004, Andhra Pradesh, India. Ed. S. Rajagopala Reddi. adv.; bk.rev.; circ. 1,000.
Formerly: Andhra Pradesh Productivity Council. Journal.

350   GW
DIE ANGESTELLTENVERSICHERUNG. Short title: A V. 1954. m. DM.30. Bundesversicherungsanstalt fuer Angestellte, Dezernat fuer Presse- und Oeffentlichkeitsarbeit, Postfach, 1000 Berlin 88, Germany. Ed. Joachim Kusch. bk.rev.; charts; stat.; circ. 23,000. **Indexed:** World Bibl.Soc.Sec.
Description: Covers social insurance laws and regulations, government reform, events. Includes announcements of events.

350   US   ISSN 0278-4289
ANNALS OF PUBLIC ADMINISTRATION. 1982. irreg., vol.5, 1983. $35. Marcel Dekker, Inc., 270 Madison Ave., New York, NY 10016. TEL 212-696-9000. FAX 212-685-4540. TELEX 421419. Ed. Jack Rabin.

350   BE   ISSN 0066-2461
ANNUAIRE ADMINISTRATIF ET JUDICIAIRE DE BELGIQUE/ADMINISTRATIEF EN GERECHTELIJK JAARBOEK VOOR BELGIE. 1869. a. 57100 Fr. Etablissements Emile Bruylant, 67 rue de la Regence, 1000 Brussels, Belgium. TEL 02-512-9845. circ. 3,000.

ANNUAIRE DE L'ADMINISTRATION DES D.R.I.R.. see *ENERGY*

916.7   GO
ANNUAIRE NATIONAL OFFICIEL DE LA REPUBLIQUE GABONAISE. 1973. a. 5000 Fr.CFA. Agence Havas Gabon, B.P. 213, Libreville, Gabon. adv.; illus.; stat.; circ. 5,000.

350   UK
ANNUAL CATALOGUE OF GOVERNMENT PUBLICATIONS. a. H.M.S.O., P.O. Box 276, London SW8 5DT, England. circ. 6,600.

350   US
▼**ANNUAL EDITIONS: PUBLIC ADMINISTRATION.** 1990. a. $11.95. Dushkin Publishing Group, Inc., Sluice Dock, Guilford, CT 06437-9989. TEL 203-453-4351. FAX 203-453-6000. Ed. Howard R. Balanoff. illus.
Refereed Serial

350   US
ANNUAL EDITIONS: STATE & LOCAL GOVERNMENT. 1978. a. $11.95. Dushkin Publishing Group, Inc., Sluice Dock, Guilford, CT 06437-9989. TEL 203-453-4351. FAX 203-453-6000. Ed. Bruce Stinebrickner.
Refereed Serial

350   US   ISSN 0731-339X
H50
ANNUAL GUIDE TO PUBLIC POLICY EXPERTS. a. $14.95. Heritage Foundation, 214 Massachusetts Ave., N.E., Washington, DC 20002. TEL 202-546-4400. FAX 202-546-8328. Eds. Robert Huberty, Barbara Hohbach.

350 320   US
ANNUAL REPORT ON PRIVATIZATION. a. $10. Reason Foundation, 3415 S. Sepulveda Blvd., Ste. 400, Los Angeles, CA 90034-6060. TEL 310-391-2245. FAX 310-391-4395. circ. 10,000.

350   IT   ISSN 0084-6619
ANNUARIO AMMINISTRATIVO ITALIANO/ITALIAN ADMINISTRATIVE DIRECTORY. 1968. a. L.156000. Guida Monaci S.p.A., Via Vitorchiano 107, 00189 Rome, Italy. TEL 06-3288805. FAX 06-3275693. TELEX 623324 MONACI.
Description: Directory of all Italian administrative activities.

350   AG   ISSN 0301-7818
LAW
ARGENTINA. CONGRESO DE LA NACION. BIBLIOTECA. BOLETIN LEGISLATIVO. 1976. irreg. Congreso de la Nacion, Biblioteca, Rivadavia 1850, 1033 Buenos Aires, Argentina.

333.7   AG   ISSN 0302-5705
QH113
ARGENTINA. SERVICIO NACIONAL DE PARQUES NACIONAL. ANALES. 1945. irreg. 25000p. Servicio Nacional de Parques Nacionales, Santa Fe 690, Buenos Aires, Argentina. illus.; circ. 4,000.
Supersedes: Argentina. Direccion General de Parques Nacionales. Anales de Parques Nacionales (ISSN 0518-4614)

350 340   LE   ISSN 0570-8915
L'ARGUS DE LA LEGISLATION LIBANAISE. (Text mainly in French, occasionally in English) 1954. q. $270. Bureau of Lebanese and Arab Documentation, P.O. Box 165403, Beirut, Lebanon. (Subscr. to: Bureau of Documentation, c/o Marcel Tawil, Postfach 2412, 7850 Loerrach, Germany) circ. 1,000.
Description: Translations of the main legislative texts published in the Lebanese official gazette, and translation of Lebanese legislative documents, including all modifications.

350 320   US   ISSN 0744-7477
ARIZONA CAPITOL TIMES. 1945. w. $32. Arizona News Service, 14 North 18th Ave., Phoenix, AZ 85007. TEL 602-258-7026. Ed. Ned Creighton. (newspaper)
Formerly: Arizona Legislative Review.
Description: Covers Arizona political, legislative and state agency news.

350 340 320   US   ISSN 0273-2742
ARKANSAS REPORT. 1983. m. $70. Wallace Associates, Box 1836, Little Rock, AR 72203-1826. TEL 501-376-1364. Ed. Douglas Wallace. circ. 493.
Description: Reports on political, legislative, and state government news in Arkansas.

350 340   US
ARKANSAS REPORT - WEEKLY LEGISLATIVE EDITION. 1987. w. $150. Wallace Associates, Box 1836, Little Rock, AR 72203-1836. TEL 501-376-1364. Ed. Douglas Wallace. circ. 125.

350   US
ARKANSAS STATE DIRECTORY. 1973. biennial. $7.50. Heritage Press, 4200 Heritage Dr., North Little Rock, AR 72117. TEL 501-945-0866. FAX 501-945-5000. adv.; circ. 4,000.

ARTS & CULTURAL TIMES. see *ART*

PUBLIC ADMINISTRATION

350   HK   ISSN 0259-8272
ASIAN JOURNAL OF PUBLIC ADMINISTRATION. (Text in English) 1979. 2/yr. HK.$80 (Southeast Asia $20; elsewhere $25). Hong Kong University, Department of Political Science, Pokfulam Rd., Hong Kong. TEL 852-859-2393. FAX 852-858-3550. Eds. J. Scott, T. Lui. bk.rev.; circ. 500. (back issues avail.)
Indexed: Human.Resour.Abstr., Int.Polit.Sci.Abstr., Sage Pub.Admin.Abstr., Sage Urb.Stud.Abstr.

350   UK   ISSN 0305-2044
ASSOCIATION OF COUNTY COUNCILS. YEARBOOK. a. £5. Association of County Councils, Eaton House, 66A Eaton Sq., London SW1W 9BH, England. TEL 071-235-1200. FAX 071-235-8458. adv.; circ. 5,000.

350   IT   ISSN 0004-606X
ASTE GIUDIZIARIE. 1949. m. L.3360. Istituto Vendite Giudiziarie di Roma, Via della Cava Aurelia 98, Rome, Italy. Ed. R.F. Santagati. adv.; circ. 20,000.

350   GW
AUSBILDUNG PRUEFUNG FORTBILDUNG; Zeitschrift fuer die staatliche und kommunale Verwaltung. 1975. m. DM.94. Kommunalschriften-Verlag J. Jehle Muenchen GmbH, Kirschstr. 14, Postfach 50 03 68, 8000 Munich 50, Germany. Ed.Bd. adv.; bk.rev.; circ. 2,500. (back issues avail.)

AUSTIN REPORT. see *POLITICAL SCIENCE*

350   AT
AUSTRALIA. PUBLIC SERVICE BOARD. ANNUAL REPORT. 1924. a. price varies. Australian Government Publishing Service, G.P.O. Box 84, Canberra, A.C.T. 2601, Australia. circ. 4,500.

350   AT   ISSN 0157-6178
AUSTRALIA. PUBLIC SERVICE BOARD. BULLETIN. Short title: P S B Bulletin. 1978. bi-m. free. Australian Government Publishing Service, G.P.O. Box 84, Canberra, A.C.T. 2601, Australia. circ. 18,000. (back issues avail.)

354.9   AT   ISSN 0313-6647
JA26
AUSTRALIAN JOURNAL OF PUBLIC ADMINISTRATION. 1938. q. Aus.$60 (foreign Aus.$50). Royal Institute of Public Administration Australia, G.P.O. Box 904, Sydney, N.S.W. 2001, Australia. TEL 02-228-5225. FAX 02-241-1920. Ed. Roger Wettenhall. adv.; bk.rev.; charts; stat.; cum.index 1938-1976; circ. 5,700. **Indexed:** ASSIA, Aus.P.A.I.S., Curr.Cont., Sage Pub.Admin.Abstr., SSCI.
—BLDSC shelfmark: 1811.500000.
Formerly: Public Administration (ISSN 0033-328X)

B & P A. (Business & Public Affairs) see *BUSINESS AND ECONOMICS*

350   US
BACKGROUNDER UPDATE. irreg., no.175, 1992. $1.50 per no. Heritage Foundation, 214 Massachusetts Ave., N.E., Washington, DC 20002. TEL 202-546-4400. FAX 202-546-8328. (looseleaf format; back issues avail.)
●Also available online. Vendor(s): Mead Data Central.

354.43   GW   ISSN 0340-3505
BADEN - WUERTTEMBERGISCHE VERWALTUNGSPRAXIS. 1974. m. DM.169. W. Kohlhammer GmbH, Hessbruehlstr. 69, Postfach 800430, 7000 Stuttgart 80, Germany. TEL 0711-7863-1. Eds. Max Goegler, Kurt Gerhardt. adv.; bk.rev.; circ. 2,000. **Indexed:** CERDIC.
Formed by the merger of: Baden - Wuerttembergisches Verwaltungsblat (ISSN 0005-3724) & Verwaltungspraxis.

350   BA
BAHRAIN. MINISTRY OF INFORMATION. OFFICIAL GAZETTE/BAHRAIN. WIZARAT AL-ISTI'LAMAT. AL-JARIDAH AL-RASMIYAH. (Text in Arabic) 1957. w. Ministry of Information, P.O. Box 253, Isa Town, Bahrain. TEL 681555. FAX 682777. TELEX 8399.

348   US   ISSN 0092-0959
KF015
BALDWIN'S OHIO LEGISLATIVE SERVICE. 1971. m. $290. Banks - Baldwin Law Publishing Co., University Center, Box 1974, Cleveland, OH 44106. TEL 216-721-7373. FAX 216-721-8055.
Description: Contains the text of new legislation; case notes and other annotations; bill status and Index to Bills; selected analyses prepared by the Ohio Legislative Service Commission; and research aids.

351   BG
BANGLADESH. MINISTRY OF FOREIGN AFFAIRS. LIST OF THE DIPLOMATIC CORPS AND OTHER FOREIGN REPRESENTATIVES. (Text in English) irreg. Tk.5.75. Ministry of Foreign Affairs, Dhaka, Bangladesh.

350   BG
BANGLADESH JOURNAL OF PUBLIC ADMINISTRATION. 1987. s-a. Tk.40($10) (£7). Bangladesh Public Administration Training Centre, Attn: Asst. Publication Officer, Molla Mosharraf Hossain, Savar, Dhaka 1343, Bangladesh. TEL 831711-20-251. TELEX 632228-PATC-BJ. Ed. Mustafa Abdur Rahman. bk.rev.; abstr.; bibl.; charts; circ. 750.
●Also available online.
Incorporates: Administrative Science Review (ISSN 0001-8406)
Description: Contains articles, research, and comments.

350   BB   ISSN 0377-144X
J137
BARBADOS. LEGISLATURE. HOUSE OF ASSEMBLY. MINUTES OF PROCEEDINGS. w. Legislature, House of Assembly, Bridgetown, Barbados, W.I.

350   BB   ISSN 0377-1458
J137
BARBADOS. LEGISLATURE. SENATE. MINUTES OF PROCEEDINGS. w. Legislature, Senate, Bridgetown, Barbados, W.I.

320 350   GW   ISSN 0723-7022
BAYERISCHE BUERGERMEISTER. 1917. m. DM.123.50. Kommunalschriften-Verlag J. Jehle Muenchen GmbH, Kirschstr. 14, D-8000 Munich 50, Germany. Ed.Bd. circ. 2,500. (back issues avail.)
—BLDSC shelfmark: 1871.160000.

BAYERISCHE VERWALTUNGSBLAETTER; Zeitschrift fuer oeffentliches Recht und oeffentliche Verwaltung. see *LAW*

354.43   GW   ISSN 0934-6465
BAYERISCHES STAATSMINISTERIUM DES INNERN. ALLGEMEINES MINISTERIALBLATT. 1949. bi-w. DM.110. Staatsministerium des Innern, Odeonsplatz 3, 8000 Munich 22, Germany. TEL 089-2192-01. FAX 089-21921-2271. TELEX 524540-BYIM-D. bk.rev.; circ. 8,500.
Formerly (until 1988): Bayerisches Staatsministerium des Innern. Ministerialamtsblatt der Bayerischen Innern Verwaltung (ISSN 0005-7185)

352   GW   ISSN 0005-741X
DER BEAMTE IN RHEINLAND-PFALZ; Zeitschrift fuer Angehoerige des oeffentlichen Dienstes. 1949. m. membership. Deutscher Beamtenbund, Landesbund Rheinland-Pfalz, Adam-Karrillon-Str. 62, Postfach 1706, 6500 Mainz 1, Germany. Ed. Hans Eberhard Hielscher. adv.; circ. 30,000.

363.6   AU   ISSN 0520-9048
BEGRIFFSBESTIMMUNGEN FUER DIE BUNDESSTATISTIKEN DER OESTERREICHISCHEN ELEKTRIZITAETSWIRTSCHAFT. (Issued in cooperation with Osterreichische Elektrizitaetswirtschafts-A.G.) 1955. a. S.550. Bundesministerium fuer Wirtschaftliche Angelegenheiten, Bundeslastverteiler, Dienststelle Statistik, Am Hof 6a, A-1010 Vienna, Austria. circ. 500.
Formerly: Brennstoffstatistik der Waermekraftwerke fuer die Oeffentliche Elektrizitaetsversorgung in Oesterreich.

350   NE   ISSN 0166-9222
BELEIDSANALYSE. (Text in Dutch, English) 1972. q. fl.37. Ministerie van Financien, Afdeling Beleidsevaluatie en Instrumentatie - Ministry of Finance, Korte Voorhout 7, 2511 CW The Hague, Netherlands. TEL 70-3427372. FAX 70-3427934. (Dist. by: S D Uitgeverij, Chr. Plantijnstraat 1, The Hague, Netherlands) Eds. H.O. Korte, J.C. Hellendoorn. bk.rev.; circ. 2,500. (back issues avail.)
Indexed: Key to Econ.Sci.

350 331   BE
BELGIUM. HOGE RAAD VOOR DE MIDDENSTAND. JAARVERSLAG VAN DE SECRETARIS GENERAAL. French edition: Belgium. Conseil Superieur des Classes Moyennes. Rapport Annuel du Secretaire General (ISSN 0067-5393) (Text in Dutch) 1951. a. free. Hoge Raad voor de Middenstand, Zaveltoren, J. Stevensstraat 7, B-1000 Brussels, Belgium.

BELGIUM. MINISTERE DE LA PREVOYANCE SOCIALE. RAPPORT GENERAL SUR LA SECURITE SOCIALE. see *SOCIAL SERVICES AND WELFARE*

354   NR
BENDEL STATE. MINISTRY OF INFORMATION, SOCIAL DEVELOPMENT AND SPORTS. ESTIMATE. a. £N5. Ministry of Information, Social Development and Sports, Printing and Stationery Division, P.M.B. 1099, Benin City, Nigeria. (Orders to: Bendel State Government Printer, Government Press, Benin City, Nigeria)
Formerly: Bendel State. Ministry of Home Affairs and Information. Mid-Western State Estimates.

350   BE   ISSN 0005-8777
BENELUX PUBLIKATIEBLAD/BULLETIN BENELUX. (Belgium Netherlands Luxembourg) (Supplement to: Textes de Base Benelux - Basic Benelux Texts) (Text in Dutch, French) 1958. irreg. (approx. 3/yr.) 1.60 Fr. per page. B E N E L U X Economic Union, Rue de la Regence 39, B-1000 Brussels, Belgium. (looseleaf format)
—BLDSC shelfmark: 2834.520000.

350   NE   ISSN 0165-7194
BESTUURSWETENSCHAPPEN. 1947. 7/yr. fl.130 to individuals; institutions fl.155; students fl.80. V N G Uitgeverij, P.O. Box 30435, 2500 GK The Hague, Netherlands. TEL 070-3738888. FAX 070-3651826. adv.; index; circ. 1,000.
Indexed: Excerp.Med., Key to Econ.Sci.

350 028.5   GW   ISSN 0932-5492
BETREFF. 1957. bi-m. (Deutsche Beamtenbund Jugend) Verlagsanstalt des Deutsche Beamtenbundes, Dreizehnmorgenweg 36, Postfach 205005, 5300 Bonn 2, Germany. TEL 228-811-255. FAX 0228-631720. bk.rev.; circ. 45,000.

350 330   US   ISSN 0894-9697
BILL SHIPP'S GEORGIA. 1987. w. $195. Word Merchants, Inc., 1901 Powers Ferry Road, No. 270, Marietta, GA 30067-9403. TEL 404-984-0151. FAX 404-984-0370. Ed. Bill Shipp.
Description: Covers Georgia government, politics and business.

353.002   US   ISSN 0882-1593
E185.615
BLACK ELECTED OFFICIALS; a national roster. 1970. a. $32.50. Joint Center for Political Studies, Inc., 1301 Pennsylvania Ave., N.W., Ste.400, Washington, DC 20004. stat.; index; circ. 5,000. **Indexed:** SRI.
Formerly: National Roster of Black Elected Officials (ISSN 0092-2935)

350   US
BLUE SKY NEWS. a. free. North American Securities Administrators Association, Inc., 555 New Jersey Ave., N.W., Ste. 750, Washington, DC 20001-2029. circ. 300.

350   MH
BOLETIM OFICIAL. (Text in Portuguese) 1838. w. Rua da Imprensa Nacional, CP 33, Macao. TEL 853-573822. FAX 853-596802. Ed. Antonio de Vasconcelos Mendes Liz.

PUBLIC ADMINISTRATION 4055

351   US   ISSN 0068-0125
JK2403
BOOK OF THE STATES. 1935. biennial. $79. Council of State Governments, Iron Works Pike, Box 11910, Lexington, KY 40578-9989. TEL 606-231-1939. Ed. Carlton Currens. index; circ. 11,000. (also avail. in microfiche from KTO) **Indexed:** SRI.
Description: Comprehensive reference of indexed information developed especially for: government officials, libraries, business and industry, schools, reporters and editors.

350   FR
BOTTIN ADMINISTRATIF. 1943. a. $175. Societe Bottin, 31 Cours de Juilliottes, 94706 Maisons-Alfort Cedex, France. TEL 1-49-81-56-56. FAX 1-49-77-85-28. TELEX 262 407.

353.002   US   ISSN 1041-6722
JK6
BRADDOCK'S FEDERAL-STATE-LOCAL GOVERNMENT DIRECTORY. 1975. irreg. (every 2-4 yrs.). $63.45. Braddock Communications, Inc., 909 N. Washington St., Alexandria, VA 22314-1555. TEL 703-549-6500. Eds. Paul A. Arnold, Thomas W. Jacobson.
Description: Provides list of middle and top level officials in the Bush Administration, photos and brief biographies of all members of Congress, the Supreme Court, and the executive officers of all the states.

631.6   BL   ISSN 0101-5680
BRAZIL. DEPARTAMENTO NACIONAL DE OBRAS CONTRA AS SECAS. RELATORIO. Cover title: Relatoria D N O C S. 1945. a. free. Departamento Nacional de Obras Contra as Secas, Av. Duque de Caixias 1700, Fortaleza-Ceara 60000, Brazil. bk.rev.; charts; illus.; stat. (processed) **Indexed:** Biol.Abstr.

350   CN
BRITISH COLUMBIA. LEGISLATIVE ASSEMBLY. DEBATES (HANSARD DAILY). d. (during sessions). Can.$196. Legislative Assembly, Parliament Bldgs., Victoria, B.C. V8V 1X4, Canada. (Subscr. to: Crown Publications, 546 Yates St., Victoria, B.C. V8W 1K8, Canada. TEL 604-386-4636)

350   CN
BRITISH COLUMBIA. LEGISLATIVE ASSEMBLY. DEBATES (HANSARD PAPERBOUND). irreg. Can.$46.40. Legislative Assembly, Parliament Bldgs., Victoria, B.C. V8V 1X4, Canada. (Dist. by: Crown Publications, 546 Yates St., Victoria, B.C. V8W 1K8, Canada. TEL 604-386-4636)

350   CN
BRITISH COLUMBIA. LEGISLATIVE ASSEMBLY. JOURNALS. a. price varies. Legislative Assembly, Parliament Bldgs., Victoria, B.C. V8V 1X4, Canada. (Subscr. to: Crown Publications, 546 Yates St., Victoria, B.C. V8W 1K8, Canada. TEL 604-386-4636) (back issues avail.)

350   CN
BRITISH COLUMBIA. LEGISLATIVE ASSEMBLY. THIRD READING BILLS. w. Can.$75. Legislative Assembly, Parliament Bldgs., Victoria, B.C. V8V 1X4, Canada. (Subscr. to: Crown Publications, 546 Yates St., Victoria, B.C. V8W 1K8, Canada. TEL 604-386-4636)

350   CN
BRITISH COLUMBIA. OFFICE OF THE OMBUDSMAN. PUBLIC REPORT SERIES. irreg. price varies. Office of the Ombudsman, Parliament Bldgs., Victoria, B.C. V8V 1X4, Canada. (Subscr. to: Crown Publications, 546 Yates St., Victoria, B.C. V8W 1K8, Canada. TEL 604-386-4636) (back issues avail.)

BRITISH COLUMBIA LIST; of official personnel in Federal, Provincial and Municipal Governments in the Province of British Columbia. 1978. biennial. Can.$97.50. B and C List (1982) Ltd., 301-1177 W. Broadway, Vancouver, B.C. V6H 4A5, Canada. TEL 604-732-4646. FAX 604-732-3756. Ed. Shirley Hymen. adv.; circ. 15,000.

051   US
THE BRONX REPORT; a message from Bronx Borough President. (Text in English, Spanish) q. free. Office of Borough President Fernando Ferrer, The Bronx County Bldg., 851 Grand Concourse, Bronx, NY 10451. Ed. Vlint Roswell.

350   US   ISSN 0896-3584
BUDGET AND THE REGION; a regional analysis of the President's budget request. 1976. a. price varies. Northeast - Midwest Institute, 218 D St., S.E., Washington, DC 20003. TEL 202-544-5200. FAX 202-544-0043. charts. (back issues avail.)
Description: Details the federal budget request for federal and state policy makers and staff.

354.666   LB
BUDGET OF THE GOVERNMENT OF LIBERIA.* 1960. a. Bureau of the Budget, Monrovia, Liberia.

BUILDING PERMIT ACTIVITY IN FLORIDA. see *BUILDING AND CONSTRUCTION*

363.6   FR   ISSN 0154-0033
BULLETIN OFFICIEL DU MINISTERE DE L'ENVIRONNEMENT ET DU CADRE DE VIE ET DU MINISTERE DES TRANSPORTS. irreg. 288 F. Direction des Journaux Officiels, 26 rue Desaix, 75727 Paris, France. TEL 1-45-78-61-44. (Co-sponsor: Ministere des Transports)

354.43   GW   ISSN 0007-5930
DIE BUNDESVERWALTUNG. 1951. m. DM.39. (Deutscher Beamtenbund, Verband der Beamten der Obersten Bundesbehoerden) Stollfuss Verlag Bonn, Dechenstr. 7-11, Postfach 2428, 5300 Bonn 1, Germany. TEL 0228-724-0. TELEX 8869477. adv.; circ. 9,500.

350   IT
BUROCRAZIA; rivista mensile di attualita politica e amministrativa. 1946. m. L.50000. Casella Postale No. 727, I-00100 Rome-Centro, Italy. TEL 64.80.202. Ed. Luciano Pascucci. index.

C B D WEEKLY RELEASE. see *BUSINESS AND ECONOMICS*

350.6   CN
C C P A NEWSLETTER. m. membership. Canadian Center for Policy Alternatives, 251 Laurier Ave., W., Ste. 904, Ottawa, Ont. K1P 5J6, Canada. TEL 613-563-1341.
Description: Devoted to the development of progressive alternatives to current social and economic policies.

C I S FEDERAL REGISTER INDEX. (Congressional Information Service) see *PUBLIC ADMINISTRATION — Abstracting, Bibliographies, Statistics*

C O G E L GUARDIAN. (Council on Governmental Ethics Laws) see *LAW*

C P E R. (California Public Employee Relations) see *BUSINESS AND ECONOMICS — Labor And Industrial Relations*

C S I CONGRESSIONAL RECORD REPORT. see *LAW*

C S I FEDERAL REGISTER. see *LAW*

363.3   US   ISSN 0743-8494
C S P A STATESIDE. q. free to members. National Governors Association, Council of State Planning Agencies, 400 N. Capitol St., N.W., Ste. 295, Washington, DC 20001. TEL 202-624-5386. Ed. Jan Lipkin.

350   MR
CAHIERS AFRICAINS D'ADMINISTRATION PUBLIQUE. English edition: African Administrative Studies (ISSN 0007-9588) (Editions in Arabic, English, French) 1966. s-a. $40. Centre Africain de Formation et de Recherche Administratives pour le Developpement, P.O. Box 310, Tangier, Morocco. TEL 936601. FAX 9-941415. TELEX 33664M. bk.rev.; bibl.; circ. 2,000.

350   II   ISSN 0045-3838
CALCUTTA GAZETTE. (Published in 11 parts plus supplement) (Text in English) 1784. w. Rs.206.50. (Commerce & Industries Department) West Bengal Government Press, Publication Branch, 38 Gopal Nagar Rd., Alipore, Calcutta 27, India.

CALCUTTA JOURNAL OF POLITICAL STUDIES. see *POLITICAL SCIENCE*

312   US
CALIFORNIA COUNTY. 1985. bi-m. $22. G M W Communications, Inc., 1831 V St., Sacramento, CA 95818. TEL 916-443-7133. FAX 916-443-4954. adv.; circ. 6,793.
Description: Covers public finance, social services, hospital operations, public works, state mandates, corrections and other county government and special district affairs.

300 978 350   US   ISSN 0068-5615
HC107.C2
CALIFORNIA HANDBOOK; a comprehensive guide to sources of current information and action. 1969. irreg., 6th ed., 1990. $35. California Institute of Public Affairs, Box 189040, Sacramento, CA 95818. TEL 916-442-CIPA. FAX 916-442-2478. (Affiliate: The Claremont Graduate School) Ed. Thaddeus C. Trzyna. index; circ. 2,500.
Description: Directory of organizations and a bibliography of books, periodicals, and reports which provide information about the state and its problems, organized by subject and indexed by sources of information.

350   US   ISSN 0738-694X
CALIFORNIA IN PRINT. 1981. s-m. $75. Government Research, 815 N. La Brea, Ste. 197, Inglewood, CA 90302. TEL 213-678-3851. Ed. Jerry Jeffe.
Description: Lists publications released for public distribution by the California State Legislature, in addition to executive and judicial documents received by the State Legislature.

CALIFORNIA JOURNAL; the monthly analysis of state government and politics. see *POLITICAL SCIENCE*

CALIFORNIA JOURNAL NEWSFILE. see *POLITICAL SCIENCE*

350 333.33   US   ISSN 0891-382X
CALIFORNIA PLANNING AND DEVELOPMENT REPORT. 1986. m. $179. Torf Fulton Associates, 1275 Sunny Crest Ave., Ventura, CA 93003-1212. TEL 805-642-7838. Ed. William Fulton. circ. 500.
●Also available online. Vendor(s): Information Access Company, NewsNet.
Description: Covers local government, real estate and urban planning issues.

CALIFORNIA POLITICAL WEEK; calpeek. see *POLITICAL SCIENCE*

CALIFORNIA PRIDE. see *LABOR UNIONS*

CALIFORNIA PUBLIC AGENCY PRACTICE. see *LAW*

CALIFORNIA STATE BOARD OF EQUALIZATION. REPORTS. see *BUSINESS AND ECONOMICS — Public Finance, Taxation*

CALIFORNIA TAXATION. see *BUSINESS AND ECONOMICS — Public Finance, Taxation*

328 920   US   ISSN 0068-6530
CALIFORNIANS IN CONGRESS. 1955. biennial. free. (California Congressional Recognition Program) Claremont McKenna College, Department of Government, Claremont, CA 91711. TEL 714-621-8000. Eds. Alan Heslop, Florence Adams. circ. 2,500. (back issues avail.)

CAMERA DEI DEPUTATI. BOLLETTINO DI INFORMAZIONI COSTITUZIONALI E PARLAMENTARI. see *LAW — Constitutional Law*

350   US   ISSN 0890-3956
CAMPAIGN CALIFORNIA REPORT. 1977. q. $20 includes membership. Campaign California, 926 J St., Ste. 1400, Sacramento, CA 95814. FAX 916-447-8957. Ed. Karl Ory. circ. 35,000. (back issues avail.)
Formerly: Economic Democrat (ISSN 0746-2603)

350   CN   ISSN 0382-1161
JL25
CANADA. COMMISSIONER OF OFFICIAL LANGUAGES. ANNUAL REPORT. (Text in English and French) 1971. a. free. Office of the Commissioner of Official Languages, Rm. 1421 110 O'Connor St., Ottawa, Ont. K1A 0T8, Canada. TEL 613-995-0730. Ed.Bd.

PUBLIC ADMINISTRATION

350 CN
CANADA. DEPARTMENT OF CONSUMER & CORPORATE AFFAIRS. ANNUAL REPORT. (Text in English & French) 1968. a. free. Department of Consumer & Corporate Affairs, Ottawa, Ont. K1A 0C9, Canada. TEL 819-953-5055. charts; stat.; circ. 2,000.

CANADA. LAW REFORM COMMISSION. ANNUAL REPORT. see *LAW*

537 CN ISSN 0825-0170
CANADA. NATIONAL ENERGY BOARD. INFORMATION BULLETINS. 1984. irreg. National Energy Board, 311-6th Ave. S.W., Calgary, Alta. T2P 3H2, Canada. TEL 403-292-4800. FAX 403-292-5503.
Formerly (until 1983): Canada. National Energy Board. Staff Papers.

350 CN
CANADA. NATIONAL ENERGY BOARD. REGULATORY AGENDA. (Text in English and French) 1982. q. free. National Energy Board, 311 6th Ave. S.W., Calgary, Alberta T2P 3H2, Canada. TEL 403-292-4800. FAX 403-292-5503. circ. 1,500.
Description: Provides information on recent hearing reports, forthcoming regulatory actions, and the status of ongoing proceedings.

350.722 CN
CANADA. TREASURY BOARD SECRETARIAT. ESTIMATES. PART I: GOVERNMENT EXPENDITURES PLAN/CANADA. CONSEIL DU TRESOR. BUDGET DES DEPENSES. PARTIE I: PLAN DE DEPENSES DU GOUVERNEMENT. (Text in English, French) 1977. a. free. Treasury Board, 140 O'Connor St., Ottawa, Ont. K1A 0R5, Canada. TEL 613-995-2855. charts; stat.
Formerly: Canada. Treasury Board Secretariat. Federal Expenditure Plan (ISSN 0706-6007)

354 CN
CANADA. TREASURY BOARD SECRETARIAT. ESTIMATES. PART II: ESTIMATES/CANADA. CONSEIL DU TRESOR. PARTIE II: BUDGET DES DEPENSES PRINCIPAL. a. Can.$60. Treasury Board, 140 O'Connor St., Ottawa, Ont. K1A 0R5, Canada. TEL 613-997-2560. stat.

CANADIAN FEDERAL GOVERNMENT HANDBOOK. see *BIOGRAPHY*

350 CN ISSN 0045-4893
CANADIAN GOVERNMENT PROGRAMS AND SERVICES. m. Can.$345. C C H Canadian Ltd., 6 Garamond Ct., Don Mills, Ont. M3C 1Z5, Canada. TEL 416-441-2992. FAX 416-444-9011. index.
Description: Authoritative guide to federal government organizations, programs and services, government relations. Information on all departments: their structure, key personnel with addresses and phone numbers, jurisdictions, responsibilities, budgets, etc.

350.6 CN ISSN 0229-2548
JL148
CANADIAN PARLIAMENTARY REVIEW. French edition (ISSN 0229-2556) (Editions in English, French) 1978. q. Can.$20. House of Commons, Parliamentary Relations Secretariat, Confederation Bldg., House of Parliament, PO Box 950, Ottawa, Ont. K1A 0A6, Canada. FAX 613-992-3674. (Co-sponsor: Commonwealth Parliamentary Association, Canadian Region) Ed. Gary Levy. adv.; bk.rev.; circ. 3,500. Indexed: Can.Per.Ind., CMI, P.A.I.S.

354.7 CN ISSN 0008-4840
CANADIAN PUBLIC ADMINISTRATION/ADMINISTRATION PUBLIQUE DU CANADA. (Text in English, French) 1958. q. Can.$75. Institute of Public Administration of Canada, 897 Bay St., Toronto, Ont. M5S 1Z7, Canada. TEL 416-923-7319. FAX 416-923-8994. Ed. V.S. Wilson. bk.rev.; bibl.; index; circ. 4,200. (also avail. in microfilm from MML) Indexed: A.B.C.Pol.Sci., Amer.Hist.& Life, ASSIA, BPIA, Bus.Ind., Can.Per.Ind., CMI, Curr.Cont., Educ.Admin.Abstr., Hist.Abstr., Ind.Can.L.P.L., Int.Polit.Sci.Abstr., Manage.Cont., P.A.I.S., P.A.I.S.For.Lang.Ind., PHRA, Pub.Admin.Abstr., Sage Pub.Admin.Abstr., SSCI.
—BLDSC shelfmark: 3044.150000.

CANADIAN UNION OF PUBLIC EMPLOYEES. THE PUBLIC EMPLOYEE. see *LABOR UNIONS*

359 US
CAPITOL GOVERNMENT REPORTS WEEKLY. 1980. w. $200. Capitol Government Reports, Box 602, Santa Fe, NM 87504. TEL 505-988-9835. FAX 505-982-0153. Ed. Jack Flynn.
Description: Reports on New Mexico government and politics.

350 330 US
CAPITOL UPDATE. 1981. fortn. $50. Texas State Directory Press, Inc., Box 12186, Capitol Sta., Austin, TX 78711. TEL 512-477-5698. FAX 512-473-2447. Ed. Nancy Barnes.
Description: Reports on Texas government, politics and business.

350 IT ISSN 0008-610X
U4
CARABINIERE. 1948. m. L.3800. Comando Generale dell'Arma dei Carabinieri, Viale Romania 45, 00196 Rome, Italy. Ed. Arnaldo Ferrara. adv.; bk.rev.; charts; illus.; stat.; circ. 175,000.

350 US
CAROLINA REPORT. 1986. m. $48. Broach, Mijeski and Associates, Box 12074, Rock Hill, SC 29731. TEL 803-323-2200. Ed. Glen Broach.
Description: Covers South Carolina electoral politics, legislative affairs and public policy issues.

309.1 SG
CARTE D'IDENTITE DU SENEGAL. 1971. a. free. Ministere de l'Information et de Telecommunications, Direction de l'Information, 58 Bd. de la Republique, Dakar, Senegal. illus.; stat.

350 IT
CASALECCHIO NOTIZIE. 1973. 9/yr. free. Comune di Casalecchio di Reno (BO), Via Porrettana 266, Casalecchio di Reno (BO), Italy. TEL 051-598111. FAX 051-592671. circ. 14,000. (tabloid format; back issues avail.)

350 CJ
CAYMAN ISLANDS. GOVERNMENT INFORMATION SERVICES. ANNUAL REPORT. 1972. a. C.$10($12.20) Government Information Services, Tower Bldg., 3rd Fl., Georgetown, Grand Cayman, British W.I. FAX 809-949-8487. Ed. E. Patricia Ebanks. circ. 2,000.
Description: Official report on operations of Cayman Islands Government, giving a comprehensive picture of life in the islands.

328 CJ ISSN 0300-4740
CAYMAN ISLANDS. LEGISLATIVE ASSEMBLY. MINUTES. 1966. irreg. price varies. Legislative Assembly, PO Box 890, Grand Cayman, Cayman Islands, British W.I. (processed)

350 IT
CE D R E S DOCUMENTI. 1981. q. free. Centro Documentazione e Ricerche Economico-Sociali, Via Galimberti 2-A, 15100 Alessandria, Italy. Ed. Carlo Beltrame. bk.rev.; circ. 1,500.

350 FR ISSN 0221-5918
CENTRE NATIONAL DE LA RECHERCHE SCIENTIFIQUE. ANNUAIRE EUROPEEN D'ADMINISTRATION PUBLIQUE. a. (Universite de Droit, d'Economie et des Sciences d'Aix-Marseille, Centre de Recherches Administratives) Editions du C N R S, 1 Place Aristide Briand, 92195 Meudon Cedex, France. TEL 1-45-34-75-50. FAX 1-46-26-28-49. TELEX LABOBEL 204 135 F. (Subscr. to: Presses du C N R S, 20-22, rue Saint Amand, 75015 Paris, France. TEL 1-45-33-16-00) adv.; bk.rev.; index; circ. 1,500 (controlled).

350 CN
CHAPTER 290. 1982. q. Can.$25. (Municipal Officers' Association of British Columbia) Beaudell Publishing, 200-880 Douglas St., Victoria, B.C. V8W 2B7, Canada. TEL 604-383-7032. FAX 604-384-3000. Ed. R.A. Beauchamp. adv.; bk.rev.; circ. 600.

353.9 015 US ISSN 0077-9296
Z1223.5.M57
CHECKLIST OF OFFICIAL PUBLICATIONS OF THE STATE OF NEW YORK. (Title varies: Vols. 1-15 as Official Publications of the State of New York; Supplement avail.) 1947. m. $6 (foreign $12.50); or exchange basis. New York State Library, Collection, Acquisitions and Processing, Albany, NY 12230. author index for vols. 1-23; circ. 1,500.
Description: Monthly listing of monographs and serials published within the most recent two years received and catalogued by the New York State Library.

350 CC ISSN 1001-599X
CHENGSHI GONGYONG SHIYE/PUBLIC UTILITIES. (Text in Chinese) 1987. bi-m. $18. Shanghai Gongyong Shiye Yanjiusuo - Shanghai Municipal Research Institute of Public Utilities, 706 Hengshan Road, Shanghai 200030, People's Republic of China. TEL 4314037. FAX 0086-21-3217616. Ed. Cai Junshi. adv.; B&W page $350, color page $1000. circ. 4,000.

350 US ISSN 0250-6114
F1402
CHIEFS OF STATE AND CABINET MINISTERS OF THE AMERICAN REPUBLICS. q. $4. Organization of American States, General Secretariat, Department of Publications, 1889 F St., N.W., Washington, DC 20006. TEL 703-941-1617.

CHINA DIRECTORY (YEAR)/ZHONGGUO ZUZHIBIE RENMINGBU/CHUGOKU SOSHIKIBETSU JINMEIBO. see *POLITICAL SCIENCE — International Relations*

350 US ISSN 0009-7543
CITIZEN (DENVER). 1941. m. $7.50. Colorado Association of Public Employees, 1390 Logan St., Rm. 402, Denver, CO 80203. TEL 303-832-1001. Ed. Phillip Christie. adv.; circ. 12,000. (tabloid format)
Description: Commentary, editorials, news, articles, and announcements on the financial, policy, and membership issues that affect the Colorado Association of Public Employees and Colorado state employees.

350 US
CITIZEN'S GUIDE TO LOCAL GOVERNMENT. a. $25. Washington Research Council, 906 S. Columbia, Ste. 350, Olympia, WA 98501. TEL 206-357-6643.

350 IT
CITTA DI SARONNO. 1967. bi-m. free. Comune, Via Roma, 20, Saronno (VA), Italy. circ. 15,000. (tabloid format; back issues avail.)

350 US ISSN 0885-940X
HJ275
CITY & STATE. 1985. bi-w. $70 to non-government subscribers; government subscribers $35; free to qualified personnel (effective Jul. 1992). Crain Communications, Inc. (Chicago), 740 N. Rush St., Chicago, IL 60611-2590. TEL 312-649-5260. FAX 312-649-5228. (Subscr. to: 965 E. Jefferson, Detroit, MI 48207-3185. TEL 800-678-9595) Ed. Ellen Shubart. adv.; circ. 45,777 (controlled). (tabloid format; also avail. in microfiche; back issues avail.)
Description: Covers the business side of state and local government for top, executive and financial government officials.

350 658 US
▼**CITY & STATE'S (YEAR) RESOURCE GUIDE.** 1990. a. Crain Communications, Inc. (Chicago), 740 N. Rush St., Chicago, IL 60611-2590. TEL 312-649-5215. FAX 312-649-5228. Ed. Ellen Shubart. adv.; circ. 46,000.
Description: Features a listing of goods and services provided by the companies servicing the government market. Includes financial services, public works products and services, computer hardware and software brands, and telecommunications equipment and systems.

PUBLIC ADMINISTRATION 4057

352.16   CN
CIVIC PUBLIC WORKS REFERENCE MANUAL AND BUYER'S GUIDE. (Includes 4 directories: Reference Manual & Buyers Guide for Grounds Maintenance & General Operations; Reference Manual & Buyers Guide for Solid Waste Management & Office Equipment; Reference Manual & Buyers Guide for Roads, Streets & Highways; Reference Manual & Buyers Guide for Water & Sewage) 1954. q. Can.$25. Maclean-Hunter Ltd., Business Publication Division, Maclean-Hunter Bldg., 777 Bay St., Toronto, Ont. M5W 1A7, Canada. TEL 416-596-5953. Ed. Clifford Allum.
   Former titles: Civic Municipal Reference Manual and Purchasing Guide (ISSN 0069-4258); Civic Administration's Municipal Reference Manual and Purchasing Guide.

CIVIL AIRCRAFT ACCIDENT REPORTS. see *TRANSPORTATION — Air Transport*

331.88   NR
CIVIL SERVANT.* 1971. m. £N216. Nigeria Civil Service Union, 23 Tokunboh St., P.O. Box 862, Lagos, Nigeria. illus.

350   US
CIVIL SERVICE NEWS. irreg. free. U.S. Office of Personnel Management, Office of Public Policy, 1900 E St., Rm. 5F10, Washington, DC 20415. TEL 202-632-1212. (processed)
   Formerly: Civil Service News Releases (ISSN 0009-8019)

CIVIL SERVICE NEWS. see *LABOR UNIONS*

350.6   PH   ISSN 0300-3620
JQ1412
CIVIL SERVICE REPORTER. (Text in English) 1956. q. free. Civil Service Commission, National Government Center, Constitution Hills, Diliman, Quezon City, Philippines. Ed. Marilou T. Cruz. bk.rev.; charts; illus.; stat.; circ. 1,000.

350   UK   ISSN 0302-329X
CIVIL SERVICE YEAR BOOK. a. £14. (Cabinet Office) H.M.S.O., P.O. Box 276, London SW8 5DT, England. TEL 01-873-9090. FAX 01-873-0011.
   Formerly: British Imperial Calendar and Civil Service List.

350 340   US
CODE OF MARYLAND REGULATIONS. Short title: C O M A R. 1976. a. $600. Division of State Documents, Box 802, Annapolis, MD 21404. TEL 301-974-2486. FAX 301-974-2546. Ed. Robert J. Colborn, Jr. circ. 300.
   ●Also available online.
   Description: Compilation of all Maryland agency regulations, governor's executive orders and Ethics Commission opinions.

350   CK
COLOMBIA. DEPARTAMENTO ADMINISTRATIVO NACIONAL DE ESTADISTICA. DIVISION POLITICO-ADMINISTRATIVA. 1953. irreg. Departamento Administrativo Nacional de Estadistica, Banco Nacional de Datos, Centro Administrativo Nacional, Apdo. Aereo 80043, Avenida Eldorado, Bogota, Colombia. illus.

350   US
COLORADO. DEPARTMENT OF ADMINISTRATION. DIVISION OF ACCOUNTS & CONTROL. COMPREHENSIVE ANNUAL FINANCIAL REPORT. 1876. a. free. Department of Administration, Division of Accounts & Control, 110 16th St., Ste. 1100, Denver, CO 80202. TEL 303-520-4190. FAX 303-620-4232. circ. 400.

COLORADO STATESMAN. see *POLITICAL SCIENCE*

350   RE
COMMENTAIRES DES PRINCIPALES DECISIONS DU TRIBUNAL ADMINISTRATIF DE LA REUNION. (Subseries of: Dossiers du Centre d'Etudes) 1974. a. 100 F. Centre Universitaire de la Reunion, Centre d'Etudes Administratives, 24, 26 av. de la Victoire, Saint-Denis, Reunion. circ. 250.

350   US
COMMENTS AND CORRECTIONS. 1981. m. $27. Box 65902, Salt Lake City, UT 84165. TEL 801-262-0677. Ed. Robert W. Lee.
   Description: Comments on various local, national and international issues, including those affecting the Salt Lake City area.

354.94   AT
COMMONWEALTH GOVERNMENT DIRECTORY. 1973. irreg. price varies. Australian Government Publishing Service, G.P.O. Box 84, Canberra, A.C.T. 2601, Australia.
   Formerly: Australian Government Directory.

350   AT
COMMONWEALTH OF AUSTRALIA GAZETTE: GENERAL. w. Aus.$280. Australian Government Publishing Service, G.P.O. Box 84, Canberra, A.C.T. 2601, Australia. (also avail. in microfilm from BHP)

350   AT
COMMONWEALTH OF AUSTRALIA GAZETTE: PERIODIC. irreg. Australian Government Publishing Service, G.P.O. Box 84, Canberra, A.C.T. 2601, Australia.

354.94   AT
COMMONWEALTH OF AUSTRALIA GAZETTE: PUBLIC SERVICE. w. Aus.$307. Australian Government Publishing Service, G.P.O. Box 84, Canberra, A.C.T. 2601, Australia. stat.
   Formerly: Commonwealth of Australia Gazette.

350   AT
COMMONWEALTH OF AUSTRALIA GAZETTE: SPECIAL. irreg. Australian Government Publishing Service, G.P.O. Box 84, Canberra A.C.T. 2601, Australia.

350   MW
COMMONWEALTH PARLIAMENTARY ASSOCIATION. MALAWI BRANCH. CONFERENCE. REPORT OF PROCEEDINGS. irreg., 12th, 1980. Commonwealth Parliamentary Association, Malawi Branch, c/o Parliament of Malawi, PO Box 80, Zomba, Malawi.

350   MW
COMMONWEALTH PARLIAMENTARY ASSOCIATION. MALAWI BRANCH. EXECUTIVE COMMITTEE. ANNUAL REPORT. (Text in English) a. Commonwealth Parliamentary Association, Malawi Branch, c/o Parliament of Malawi, PO Box 80, Zomba, Malawi.

350   AT   ISSN 0045-7639
COMMONWEALTH PROFESSIONAL. no.231, 1971. m. $0.20 per no. Professional Officers' Association, 132-136 Albert Rd., 4th Fl., S. Melbourne, Vic. 3205, Australia. Ed. P. Gerrand. adv.; bk.rev.; charts; illus.; circ. 7,000.

350   AT   ISSN 0313-5136
COMMONWEALTH RECORD. 1976. w. Aus.$145. Australian Government Publishing Service, G.P.O. Box 84, Canberra, A.C.T. 2601, Australia. bibl. **Indexed:** INIS Atomind.
   Supersedes: Australian Government Weekly Digest.

354   CN
COMMUNICATOR (ST. JOHN'S). 1976. 3/yr. free. Newfoundland Association of Public Employees, PO Box 1085, St. John's, Nfld. A1C 5M5, Canada. TEL 709-754-0700. FAX 709-754-0726. Ed. Brenda M. White. bk.rev.; illus.; circ. 17,000.
   Former titles: N A P E Journal (ISSN 0381-6826); N A P E News (ISSN 0318-1723)

350 352.7
COMMUNITY AFFAIRS. 1979. bi-m. free. Department of Community Affairs, 318 Forum Bldg., Harrisburg, PA 17120. TEL 717-787-2340. FAX 717-787-6074. Ed. Robert Sabbato, Jr. charts; illus.; circ. 24,000. (tabloid format)
   Former titles (until 1987): D C A Reports.
   Description: Reports on government issues and other relevant information for state and local government officials and agencies, as well as nonprofit organizations.

COMMUNITY DEVELOPMENT JOURNAL. see *SOCIAL SERVICES AND WELFARE*

350   US   ISSN 1050-3250
▼**COMMUNITY HEALTH FUNDING REPORT.** 1990. s-m. $219. (Community Development Services, Inc.) C D Publications, 8204 Fenton St., Silver Spring, MD 20910-2889. TEL 301-588-6380. FAX 301-588-6385. Ed. Mary Lehman. (back issues avail.)
   Description: Reviews of public and private health grant opportunities, including reports on eligibility requirements, funding levels and deadlines.

COMMUNITY RELATIONS REPORT. see *COMMUNICATIONS*

COMMUNITY SPIRIT MAGAZINE (CARMEL). see *ENVIRONMENTAL STUDIES*

350   IT
COMUNI D'ITALIA; rivista mensile di dottrina, giurisprudenza e tecnica amministrativa. 1964. m. (11/yr.). L.180000 (effective 1992). Maggioli Editore, Via Crimera, 1, Casella Postale 290, 47037 Rimini, Italy. TEL 0541-626777. FAX 0541-622020. Ed. Francesco Savelli.

350   MX   ISSN 0185-8114
COMUNIDAD INFORMATICA. 1988. q. free or exchange basis. Instituto Nacional de Estadistica, Geografia e Informatica, Secretaria de Programacion y Presupuesto, Prol. Heroe de Nacozri 2301 Sur, Puerta 11, planta baja, Aguascaliente, 20290 Ags., Mexico. TEL 491-822-32. FAX 491-807-39. circ. 500.

350 320   US
CONGRESS. 1978. q. free. Dirksen Congressional Center, 301 S. Fourth St., Ste. A, Pekin, IL 61554. TEL 309-347-7113. FAX 309-347-6432. Ed. Linda Sams. bk.rev.; illus.
   Formerly: Dirksen Congressional Center. Report.
   Description: Covers activities of the center relating to the study of Congress and its leaders.

CONGRESS AND THE NATION. see *POLITICAL SCIENCE*

CONGRESS AND THE PRESIDENCY. see *POLITICAL SCIENCE*

CONGRESS OF MICRONESIA. HOUSE OF REPRESENTATIVES. JOURNAL. see *LAW*

CONGRESS OF MICRONESIA. SENATE. JOURNAL. see *LAW*

352   US   ISSN 0733-0200
CONGRESSIONAL ACTIVITIES. 1935. w. $1250. Oliphant Washington Service, Box 9808, Friendship Sta., Washington, DC 20016. TEL 202-338-3616. Ed. John Oliphant. circ. 100.

CONGRESSIONAL QUARTERLY SERVICE. WEEKLY REPORT. see *POLITICAL SCIENCE*

350   US   ISSN 0069-892X
CONGRESSIONAL RECORD DIGEST AND TALLY OF ROLL CALL VOTES.* 1961. irreg. (8-9/yr.). free to contributors. Americans for Constitutional Action, 7100 Sussex Pl., Alexandria, VA 22307. circ. 5,000.

350.6   US   ISSN 0193-8029
JK1
CONGRESSIONAL RESEARCH SERVICE REVIEW. 10/yr. U.S. Library of Congress, Congressional Research Service, Washington, DC 20540. TEL 202-707-5000. (Dist. by: Supt. of Documents, GPO, Washington, DC 20402) Ed. Karen Q. Wirt. **Indexed:** Ind.U.S.Gov.Per., P.A.I.S., Pers.Lit.

CONGRESSIONAL STAFF DIRECTORY. see *POLITICAL SCIENCE*

351 328.73   US   ISSN 0191-1422
JK1083
CONGRESSIONAL YELLOW BOOK; who's who in Congress, including committees and key staff aides. 1975. q. $185. Monitor Publishing Company, 104 Fifth Avenue, 2nd Fl, New York, NY 10011. TEL 212-627-4140. FAX 212-645-0931. Ed. Jodie Scheiber. illus.; maps; circ. 13,000.
   Formerly (until 1976): Directory of Key Congressional Aides.
   Description: Lists all US Senators and Representatives, including photographs and biographical information; legislative responsibilities for key staff aides; committee and subcommittee assignments; maps with district boundaries and Congressional delegations; and top staff in Congressional support agencies.

353.9   US   ISSN 0010-6119
CONNECTICUT GOVERNMENT. vol.23, 1970. s-a. free. University of Connecticut, Institute of Public Service, Storrs, CT 06269-4014. TEL 203-486-2828. charts; circ. controlled. **Indexed:** Sage Pub.Admin.Abstr.
   Description: Reprints of articles on questions of public policy which are of interest to Connecticut state and local government officials and employees.

PUBLIC ADMINISTRATION

350.6   US
CONSOLIDATED FEDERAL FUNDS REPORT. 1981. a. price varies. U.S. Bureau of the Census, Data User Services Division, Washington, DC 20233. TEL 301-763-1584. (Subscr. to: Supt. of Documents, Washington, DC 20402) (Co-sponsor: Office of Management and Budget) circ. 7,000.

CONSUMER VIEWS. see *CONSUMER EDUCATION AND PROTECTION*

350   US
CONTEMPORARY GOVERNMENT SERIES. irreg. price varies. Houghton Mifflin Co., One Beacon St., Boston, MA 02107. TEL 617-725-5000.

CONTEMPORARY WALES; an annual review of economic and social research. see *SOCIAL SCIENCES: COMPREHENSIVE WORKS*

CONTRACT MANAGEMENT. see *BUSINESS AND ECONOMICS — Management*

COOK POLITICAL REPORT. see *POLITICAL SCIENCE*

350   CN   ISSN 0703-7384
CORPUS ADMINISTRATIVE INDEX. 1972. 4/yr. Can.$419. Corpus Information Services, Division of Southam Business Communications Inc., 1450 Don Mills Rd., Don Mills, Ont. M3B 2X7, Canada. TEL 416-445-6641. FAX 416-442-2200. Ed. Charlotte Toal.

363.6 658   US
CORRECTIONAL INDUSTRIES ASSOCIATION NEWSLETTER. 1973. q. membership. Correctional Industries Association, Inc., Council of State Governments, Box 11910, Lexington, KY 40578. FAX 606-231-1943. Ed. Gail Manning. adv.; circ. 1,500.

011   UK   ISSN 0070-1211
COUNCILS, COMMITTEES AND BOARDS; a handbook of advisory, consultative, executive and similar bodies in British public life. 1970. biennial, no.7, 1989. £67.50($150) C.B.D. Research Ltd., 15 Wickham Rd., Beckenham, Kent BR3 2JS, England. TEL 081-650-7745. (Dist. in U.S. by: Gale Research Co., Penobscot Bldg., Detroit, MI 48226) Ed. L. Sellar. index; circ. 2,000.
—BLDSC shelfmark: 3481.250000.

352   US   ISSN 0011-0353
COUNTY PROGRESS; the business magazine for county officials. 1923. m. $17.50. (County Judges and Commissioners Association of Texas) Coursey Publishing Co., Box 519, Brownwood, TX 76804. TEL 915-643-2995. Ed. Robert Tindol. adv.; illus.; circ. 1,800.

CUADERNOS HISTORICOS. see *HISTORY — History Of North And South America*

350   US
CURRENT GOVERNMENTS REPORTS. (Published in several series, avail. separately) a. U.S. Bureau of the Census, Data User Services Division, Washington, DC 20233. TEL 301-763-4100. (Subscr. to: Supt. of Documents, Washington, DC 20402)

350 331   US
CURRENT GOVERNMENTS REPORTS: COUNTY GOVERNMENT EMPLOYMENT. (Series GE-4) a. price varies. U.S. Bureau of the Census, Data User Services Division, Washington, DC 20233. TEL 301-763-4100. (Subscr. to: Supt. of Documents, Washington, DC 20402) (also avail. in microfiche)
●Also available online. Vendor(s): CompuServe Consumer Information Service, DIALOG.

CURRENT GOVERNMENTS REPORTS: FINANCES OF EMPLOYEE RETIREMENT SYSTEMS OF STATE AND LOCAL GOVERNMENTS. see *BUSINESS AND ECONOMICS — Public Finance, Taxation*

CURRENT GOVERNMENTS REPORTS: FINANCES OF SELECTED PUBLIC EMPLOYEE RETIREMENT SYSTEMS. see *BUSINESS AND ECONOMICS — Public Finance, Taxation*

956.4   CY   ISSN 0011-4456
CYPRUS BULLETIN. (Editions in Arabic, English, French, German, Greek, Spanish) 1964. fortn. free. Press and Information Office, Nicosia, Cyprus. TEL 446981. FAX 453730. TELEX 2526PIONIC. circ. 28,000.

352   GW   ISSN 0721-8206
D B B NACHRICHTEN FUER DEN OEFFENTLICHEN DIENST. 1952. q. membership. Deutscher Beamtenbund, Landesbund Bremen e.V., Dobbenweg 9, 2800 Bremen 1, Germany. Ed. Ingo A. Riemer. adv.; bk.rev.; stat.; circ. 10,000.
Formerly: Beamte im Lande Bremen (ISSN 0005-7401)

353.9   US
D E S ACTIVITIES REPORT. 1973. a. Department of Economic Security, Box 6123, Phoenix, AZ 85005. TEL 602-542-4791. illus.
Formerly: Arizona. Department of Economic Security. Annual Report (ISSN 0094-0712)

DEBATE/HIWAR. see *POLITICAL SCIENCE*

353   US   ISSN 0011-7323
HJ10
DECISIONS OF THE COMPTROLLER GENERAL OF THE UNITED STATES. m. $24. U.S. General Accounting Office, 441 G St., N.W., Washington, DC 20548. TEL 202-655-4000. (Dist. by: Supt. of Documents, Washington, DC 20402)

DEFENSE ORGANIZATION SERVICE. see *MILITARY*

350 340   SJ
DEMOCRATIC REPUBLIC OF THE SUDAN GAZETTE/JARIDAH AL-RASMIYAH LI-JUMHURIYAT AL-SUDAN AL-DIMUQRATIYAH. (Text in Arabic and English) m. Attorney General, Attorney General's Chambers, PO Box 302, Khartoum, Sudan.

350 340   SJ
DEMOCRATIC REPUBLIC OF THE SUDAN GAZETTE. LEGISLATIVE SUPPLEMENT. Variant title: Democratic Republic of the Sudan Gazette. Special Legislative Supplement. Arabic edition: Mulhaq al-Tashri lil-Jaridah al-Rasmiyah li-Jumhuriyat al-Sudan al-Dimuqratiyah. irreg. Attorney General, Attorney General's Chambers, PO Box 302, Khartoum, Sudan.

350   GW
DENKMALPFLEGE INFORMATIONEN; Bayerisches Landesamt fuer Denkmalpflege. 1974. irreg. Bayerisches Landesamt fuer Denkmalpflege, Hofgraben 4, 8000 Munich 22, Germany. TEL 089-2114-213. FAX 089-2114-300. Eds. Michael Petzet, Karlheinz Hemmeter. bk.rev.; circ. 3,000 (controlled).

350   DK   ISSN 0108-979X
JS6151
DENMARK. INDENRIGSMINISTERIET. INDENRIGSMINISTERIETS AFGOERELSER OG UDTALELSER OM KOMMUNALE FORHOLD. 1981. a. DKK 50. Indenrigsministeriet, Christiansborg Slotsplads 1, 1218 Copenhagen K, Denmark. TEL 33-923380. FAX 33-111239.

350 352.7   UK   ISSN 0951-385X
DEPARTMENT OF TOWN AND COUNTRY PLANNING. WORKING PAPER SERIES. 1987. irreg. University of Newcastle-upon-Tyne, Department of Town and Country Planning, Newcastle-upon-Tyne NE1 7RU, England. TEL 091-232-8511. FAX 091-261-1182. Ed. Tim Shaw.
—BLDSC shelfmark: 9350.967000.

350 690   US   ISSN 0099-1694
HD3840
DESARROLLO NACIONAL. (Text in Spanish) 1954. 6/yr. $75. Intercontinental Publications, Inc., 25 Sylvan Rd. S., Box 5017, Westport, CT 06880. TEL 203-226-7463. FAX 203-222-8793. Ed. Philip Anderson. adv.; illus.; circ. 22,000 (controlled).
Formerly: Servicios Publicos (ISSN 0037-2706)
Description: Infrastructure development news for government officials, construction companies and engineers in Latin America.

350   GW   ISSN 0340-8604
DEUTSCHE NOTAR-ZEITSCHRIFT. 1948. m. DM.132. (Bundesnotarkammer) C.H. Beck'sche Verlagsbuchhandlung, Wilhelmstr. 9, 8000 Munich 40, Germany. TEL 089-38189-338. FAX 089-38189-398. TELEX 5215085-BECK-D. Ed.Bd. adv.; circ. 8,000.
—BLDSC shelfmark: 3573.170000.

DEUTSCHES VERWALTUNGSBLATT. see *LAW*

350   PH   ISSN 0115-7000
DEVELOPMENT ADMINISTRATION JOURNAL. (Text in English) 1981. s-a. (Mindanao State University, College of Community Development and Public Administration) Mindanao State University, University Research Center, P.O. Box 5594, Iligan City 9200, Philippines.

350   II   ISSN 0251-317X
DEVELOPMENT POLICY AND ADMINISTRATIVE REVIEW. (Text in English) 1975. s-a. Rs.30($8) Harishchandra Mathur State Institute of Public Administration, Jaipur 302017, Rajasthan, India. Ed. M.L. Mehta. Indexed: Rural Recreat.Tour.Abstr., Sage Pub.Admin.Abstr., World Agri.Econ.& Rural Sociol.Abstr.

DIALOGUER. see *SOCIOLOGY*

350   US
DIALOGUES IN PUBLIC POLICY. Variant title: Brookings Dialogues in Public Policy. 1982. irreg. price varies. Brookings Institution, 1775 Massachusetts Ave., N.W., Washington, DC 20036-2188. TEL 202-797-6255. FAX 202-797-6004.

350   GT
DIARIO DE CENTRO AMERICA. 1880. irreg. $54. 18 Calle No. 6-72, Zona 1, Guatemala. Ed. Luis Mendizabal R. adv.; bk.rev.; circ. 10,000.
Formerly: Guatemalteco.

363.6   AT   ISSN 0725-2455
LAW
DIARY OF SOCIAL LEGISLATION AND POLICY. 1980. a. Aus.$8. Australian Institute of Family Studies, 300 Queen St., Melbourne, Vic. 3000, Australia. TEL 03-608-6888. FAX 03-600-0886. (Co-sponsors: National Institute of Economic & Industry Research; Social Policy Research Centre) index; circ. 500. (back issues avail.)
Description: Summary of legislative and administrative changes by Australian state and federal governments.

034 350   FR
DICTIONNAIRE DES COMMUNES (LAVAUZELLE ET CIE). quadrennial. 270 F. per no. Editions Charles Lavauzelle, Le Prouet, B.P. 8, 87350 Panazol, France. FAX 55-30-66-67. TELEX 580995 F.

350   GW
DIE DIENSTSTELLEN DES FREISTAATES BAYERN IN DEN KREISFREIEN STAEDTEN UND LANDKREISEN. 1980. a. DM.18. Neuhauser Str. 51, 8000 Munich 2, Germany. Ed.Bd.

350   US   ISSN 0733-0227
DIGEST OF ACTIVITIES OF CONGRESS. 1935. w. $300. Oliphant Washington Service, Box 9808, Friendship Sta., Washington, DC 20016. TEL 202-338-3616. Ed. John Oliphant. circ. 200.
●Also available online. Vendor(s): NewsNet.

323.4   CY
DIMOSIOS YPALLILOS/CIVIL SERVANT. fortn. Cyprus Civil Servants Association, 3 Dem. Severis Ave., Nicosia, Cyprus. TEL 02-442393. circ. 11,000.

362   US
DIRECTORY OF NEBRASKA SERVICES. 1983? a. free. Department of Public Institutions, Box 94728, Lincoln, NE 68509. TEL 402-471-4567. FAX 402-479-5145. Ed. Dale B. Johnson. circ. 1,500.
Formerly: D P I Yellow Pages (ISSN 0360-4357)

352   US
DIRECTORY OF NEW MEXICO MUNICIPAL OFFICIALS. a. $25. New Mexico Municipal League, 1229 Paseo de Peralta, Box 846, Santa Fe, NM 87504-0846. TEL 505-982-5573. FAX 505-984-1392. Ed. William F. Fulginiti. adv.; circ. 1,400.
Formerly: Directory of Municipal Officials of New Mexico (ISSN 0070-5888)
Description: Names, addresses of all incorporated municipalities and elected and appointed officials in New Mexico.

350   US
DIRECTORY OF OKLAHOMA. 1907. biennial. $10. Department of Libraries, 200 N.E. 18th St., Oklahoma City, OK 73105. TEL 405-521-2502. FAX 405-525-7804. Ed. Patricia Lester. circ. 7,500.
Description: State almanac.

352 US
DIRECTORY OF REGIONAL COUNCILS. 1969. a. $100 to non-members; members $30. National Association of Regional Councils, 1700 K St. N.W., Washington, DC 20006. TEL 202-457-0710. FAX 202-296-9352. Ed. Beverly Nykwest. adv.; maps; circ. 2,000.
 Former titles: National Association of Regional Councils. Directory (ISSN 0095-1455); Regional Council Directory (ISSN 0190-2334); Directory of Regional Councils (ISSN 0070-6205)
 Description: Lists names, addresses, and phone numbers of regional councils throughout the US. Includes state maps with jurisdictional boundaries.

353.9 US ISSN 0440-4947
JK9330
DIRECTORY OF STATE, COUNTY, AND FEDERAL OFFICIALS. 1964. a. price varies. Legislative Reference Bureau, State Capitol, Honolulu, HI 96813. TEL 808-587-0690.

350 340 US ISSN 1042-4172
KF8700.A19
DIRECTORY OF STATE COURT CLERKS & COUNTY COURTHOUSES (YEAR). a. $65. Want Publishing Co., 1511 K St., N.W., Washington, DC 20005. TEL 202-783-1887. FAX 202-393-5106.

350 US
DIRECTORY OF TENNESSEE MUNICIPAL OFFICIALS. a. $50. University of Tennessee, Municipal Technical Advisory Service, 600 Henley, Ste. 120, Knoxville, TN 37996-4105. TEL 615-974-0411.

350 SP ISSN 0214-4131
DISPOSICIONES GENERALES. fortn. (with s-a cumulations). 23,280 ptas. Boletin Oficial del Estado, Trafalgar, 29, 28071 Madrid, Spain. TEL 446-60-00. FAX 5933916. index.

350 US ISSN 0748-1179
JK2701
DISTRICT COUNCIL JOURNAL. 1983. 11/yr. $53. Patrick Publishing Company, 1742 Massachusetts Ave., S.E., Washington, DC 20003. TEL 202-547-3104. Ed. Tom Chorlton.
 Description: Report and analysis of District of Columbia government legislative activity.

350 SP ISSN 0012-4494
JA26
DOCUMENTACION ADMINISTRATIVA. 1958. q. 2420 ptas.($30) Instituto Nacional de Administracion Publica, Zurbano, 42, 28071 Madrid, Spain. (Alt. addr.: Gabinete Tecnico, Trafalgar, 29, 28010 Madrid, Spain) (Co-sponsor: Ministerio para las Administraciones Publicas) adv.; bk.rev.; bibl.; charts; cum.index; circ. 2,500. **Indexed:** Int.Lab.Doc.
 —BLDSC shelfmark: 3609.800000.

DOCUMENTS TO THE PEOPLE OF NEW YORK STATE. see *LIBRARY AND INFORMATION SCIENCES*

354.729 DR
DOMINICAN REPUBLIC. OFICINA NACIONAL DE PRESUPUESTO. EJECUCION PRESUPUESTARIA. INFORME.* a. Oficina Nacional de Presupuesto, Santo Domingo, Dominican Republic. charts; stat.
 Formerly: Dominican Republic. Oficina Nacional de Presupuesto. Ejecucion del Presupuesto.

354 DR
DOMINICAN REPUBLIC SECRETARIA DE ESTADO DE OBRAS PUBLICAS Y COMUNICACIONES. OPC. 1972. irreg. free. Secretaria de Estado de Obras Publicas y Comunicaciones, c/o Director General de Programacion y Proyectos, Santo Domingo, Dominican Republic. adv.; index; circ. 1,000.
 Formerly: Dominican Republic. Secretaria de Obras Publicas y Comunicaciones. Estadistica (ISSN 0070-7066)

350 TS
DUBAI. HUKUMAT DUBAI. AL-JARIDAH AL-RASMIYYAH/DUBAI. GOVERNMENT OF DUBAI. OFFICIAL GAZETTE. (Text in Arabic, English) 1965. 6/yr. Hukumat Dubai - Government of Dubai, P.O. Box 446, Dubai, United Arab Emirates. TEL 531073. Ed. Ablah al-Rusan. circ. 500.
 Description: Publishes all local laws and local government decisions.

E E I WASHINGTON LETTER. (Edison Electric Institute) see *ENGINEERING — Electrical Engineering*

ECONOMIC DEVELOPMENT QUARTERLY. see *BUSINESS AND ECONOMICS — Economic Systems And Theories, Economic History*

350 US ISSN 0278-8381
HA203
ECONOMIC INDICATORS (CHARLESTON). 1981. quinquennial. $25. West Virginia Research League, Inc., 405 Capitol St., Ste. 414, Charleston, WV 25301. TEL 304-346-9451. Ed. Sarah F. Roach. (looseleaf format) **Indexed:** Mag.Ind.
 Description: Presents quantitative data comparing important public policy functions in West Virginia and all states.

ECONOMIC OPPORTUNITY REPORT; the independent weekly source for news of all economic opportunity programs. see *SOCIAL SERVICES AND WELFARE*

320 US ISSN 0145-8124
KF4886.A45
ELECTION ADMINISTRATION REPORTS. 1971. 24/yr. $147. 5620 33rd St., N.W., Washington, DC 20015. TEL 202-244-5844. Ed. Richard Smolka. bk.rev. (back issues avail.)
 Formerly (until 1976): Electionews.
 Description: Covers all developments in election law and administration, voting machines and devices, and judicial decisions affecting elections.

ELECTRONIC PUBLIC INFORMATION NEWSLETTER. see *LIBRARY AND INFORMATION SCIENCES — Computer Applications*

350 FR ISSN 0422-9932
ELU LOCAL. 1960. m. membership. Mouvement National des Elus Locaux, 36 rue de Laborde, 75008 Paris, France. adv.; circ. 14,000.

EMERGENCY PREPAREDNESS NEWS; contingency planning, crisis management, disaster relief. see *CIVIL DEFENSE*

EMPIRE STATE REPORT; the magazine of politics and public policy in New York State. see *POLITICAL SCIENCE*

350 CK
ENCUENTRO NACIONAL DE INVESTIGADORES EN ADMINISTRACION. MEMORIAS. no.3, 1983. irreg. Universidad de Antioquia, Facultad de Ciencias Economicas, Apdo. Aereo 1226, Medellin, Colombia. (Co-sponsor: Facultad de Administracion de Empresas)

351 US ISSN 0092-8380
JK468.C7
ENCYCLOPEDIA OF GOVERNMENTAL ADVISORY ORGANIZATIONS. 1973. irreg. 8th ed., 1991. $485. Gale Research Inc., 835 Penobscot Bldg., Detroit, MI 48226. TEL 313-961-2242. FAX 313-961-6083. TELEX 810-221-7086. Ed. Donna Batten.
 —BLDSC shelfmark: 3738.592300.
 Description: Directory of contractors, consultants and other advisory businesses and organizations for the U.S. government.

ENCYCLOPEDIC DICTIONARY OF AMERICAN GOVERNMENT. see *POLITICAL SCIENCE*

350 336 UK ISSN 0263-774X
H97
ENVIRONMENT AND PLANNING C: GOVERNMENT & POLICY. 1983. 4/yr. £85($140) Pion Ltd., 207 Brondesbury Park, London NW2 5JN, England. TEL 081-459-0066. FAX 081-451-6454. TELEX 94016265-PION-G. Eds. R.J. Bennett, H. Wolman. bk.rev.; index. **Indexed:** Energy Rev., I D A, Sage Pub.Admin.Abstr., Sage Urb.Stud.Abstr., SSCI.
 —BLDSC shelfmark: 3791.105600.
 Description: Multidisciplinary, international approach to the study of theoretical economic, political, legal, fiscal and social issues related to government activities.

350 614.7 US
THE ENVIRONMENTAL CONTRACT OPPORTUNITY REPORT. Variant title: T E C O R. w. $274. United Communications Group, 11300 Rockville Pike, Ste. 1100, Rockville, MD 20852-3030. TEL 301-816-8950. FAX 301-816-8945. Ed. Nancy Becker.
 Description: Presents environmental contract opportunities and awards from federal, state and local agencies.

350 HK
ENVIRONMENTAL HONG KONG (YEAR). (Text in English) a. HK.$17. Government Publication Centre, G.P.O. Bldg., Ground Fl., Connaught Place, Hong Kong, Hong Kong. TEL 5-8428801. (Subscr. to: Director of Information Services, Information Services Dept., 1 Battery Path, G-F, Central, Hong Kong) Ed.Bd.

350 US
ERNIE MILLS' LEGISLATIVE REPORT. d. (during session); w. (during interim). $400 (30-day session); $550(60-day session). Box 5141, Santa Fe, NM 87502. TEL 505-988-3991. Ed. Ernie Mills.
 Description: Reports on New Mexico legislative activity and politics.

350 US
ESSAYS IN PUBLIC WORKS HISTORY. 1976. irreg., no.15, 1987. $20. Public Works Historical Society, 1313 E. 60th St., Chicago, IL 60637. TEL 312-667-2200. FAX 312-667-2304. Ed. Howard Rosen.
 Description: Monographs detailing the planning and financing of public works.

ESTADISTICA PANAMENA. SITUACION ECONOMICA. SECCION 342. CUENTAS NACIONALES. see *BUSINESS AND ECONOMICS — Economic Situation And Conditions*

350 EI
EUROPEAN COMMUNITIES. DIARIO OFICIAL. (Supplements avail.) 1986. d. price varies. (European Communities) Boletin Oficial del Estado, Trafalgar, 29, 28071 Madrid, Spain. TEL 5382100. (also avail. in microfiche)

350 US
EXCELSIOR. q. Department of State, Division of Information Services, 162 Washington Ave., Albany, NY 12231.
 Former titles: State and Local; Newsvane.

F C N L WASHINGTON NEWSLETTER. (Friends Committee on National Legislation) see *POLITICAL SCIENCE*

F E W'S NEWS AND VIEWS. (Federally Employed Women Inc.) see *WOMEN'S INTERESTS*

350 II ISSN 0085-1795
F M U OCCASIONAL LECTURES. no.2, 1971. irreg. price varies. Indian Institute of Public Administration, Financial Management Unit, Indraprastha Estate, Ring Rd., New Delhi 110002, India.

FEDERAL ADMINISTRATIVE LAW. see *LAW*

350 US ISSN 1050-3242
FEDERAL ASSISTANCE MONITOR. 1986. s-m. $239. (Community Development Services, Inc.) C D Publications, 8204 Fenton St., Silver Spring, MD 20910-2889. TEL 301-588-6380. FAX 301-588-6385. Ed. David Kittross. index. (back issues avail.)
 Description: Covers federal regulations, funding availability, legislative developments affecting funding of social and economic programs.

350 US ISSN 0898-0071
FEDERAL BUDGET REPORT. 1981. fortn. $245. Government Information Services, 1611 N. Kent St., Ste. 508, Arlington, VA 22209. TEL 703-528-1000. FAX 703-528-6060. Ed. Stan Collender.
 Description: Analysis of congressional and presidential budget activities.

FEDERAL CONTRACTS REPORT. see *BUSINESS AND ECONOMICS — Production Of Goods And Services*

353 US ISSN 0014-9071
HD8008.A1
FEDERAL EMPLOYEE. 1917. m. $15. National Federation of Federal Employees, 1016 16th St., N.W., Washington, DC 20036. TEL 202-862-4400. Ed. James M. Peirce, Jr. adv.; illus.; circ. 80,000. **Indexed:** Pers.Lit.
 Description: Focuses on civil service work.

351 US ISSN 0071-4127
JK671
FEDERAL EMPLOYEES' ALMANAC. 1954. a. $7.95. Federal Employees' News Digest, Inc., Box 1996, Marion, OH 43305-1996. TEL 703-533-3031. FAX 703-533-3946. Eds. Don Mace, Joseph Young. circ. 100.

PUBLIC ADMINISTRATION

351 US ISSN 0430-1692
HD8008.A1
FEDERAL EMPLOYEES' NEWS DIGEST. Variant title: Weekly Federal Employees News Digest. 1951. w. $49. Federal Employees' News Digest, Inc., 510 N. Washington St., Ste. 200, Falls Church, VA 22046. TEL 703-533-3031. FAX 703-533-3946. (Subscr. to: Box 1995,. Marion, OH 43305-1995. TEL 800-347-6969) Ed. Don Mace. s-a. index; circ. 35,000. (back issues avail.) **Indexed:** Pers.Lit.
Incorporates (in 1991): F P G Weekly News Update (ISSN 0745-841X)

350 US ISSN 0270-563X
JK6
FEDERAL EXECUTIVE DIRECTORY. bi-m. $180. Carroll Publishing Company, 1058 Thomas Jefferson St., N.W., Washington, DC 20007. TEL 202-333-8620. FAX 202-337-7020.
Description: Directory of key officials in executive and legislative branches of U.S. federal government.

350 US ISSN 1056-7275
FEDERAL EXECUTIVE DIRECTORY ANNUAL. a. $127. Carroll Publishing Company, 1058 Thomas Jefferson St., N.W., Washington, DC 20007. TEL 202-333-8620. FAX 202-337-7020.
Description: Covers both the executive and legislative branches of federal government plus their regional field offices.

363.5 US
FEDERAL FUNDS INFORMATION FOR STATES NEWSLETTER. 8/yr. $250. National Governors' Association, 444 N. Capitol St. N.W., Ste. 295, Washington, DC 20001. TEL 202-624-5849. (Co-sponsor: National Conference of State Legislatures)

350 378 US ISSN 0194-2247
FEDERAL GRANTS & CONTRACTS WEEKLY; project opportunities in research, training and services. 1977. w. $349 (foreign $399). Capitol Publications Inc., 1101 King St., Ste. 444, Alexandria, VA 22314. TEL 703-683-4100. FAX 703-739-6517. Ed. Leslie Ratzlaff. index. (looseleaf format)
●Also available online. Vendor(s): NewsNet.
Incorporates (in 1991): S C I Grants News.
Description: Provides funding news, analysis, profiles of key agencies, updates on new legislation and regulations, budget development.

350 340 AT ISSN 1036-3661
FEDERAL LEGISLATION ANNOTATIONS. 2/yr. $265. Butterworths Pty. Ltd., 271-273 Lane Cove Rd., P.O. Box 345, North Ryde, N.S.W. 2113, Australia. TEL 02-335-4444. FAX 02-335-4655.
Formerly: Annotations to the Acts and Regulations of the Australian Parliament.

350 US
FEDERAL ORGANIZATION SERVICE. base vol. (plus updates every 6 weeks). $500. Carroll Publishing Company, 1058 Thomas Jefferson St., N.W., Washington, DC 20007. TEL 202-333-8620. FAX 202-337-7020. (looseleaf format)
Formerly: Federal Organization Service - Civil.
Description: Organization charts identifying who's who in over 1,600 departments and offices of the civil branch of the federal government.

FEDERAL PROCUREMENT UPDATE. see BUSINESS AND ECONOMICS

350 US ISSN 0742-1729
JK723.E9
FEDERAL REGIONAL EXECUTIVE DIRECTORY. s-a. $130. Carroll Publishing Company, 1058 Thomas Jefferson St., N.W., Washington, DC 20007. TEL 202-333-8620. FAX 202-337-7020.
Description: Directory of key officials in regional field offices of US Cabinet departments, Congress, the courts, and federal administrative agencies.

920 US ISSN 1061-3153
▼**FEDERAL REGIONAL YELLOW BOOK;** who's who in the federal government's departments, agencies, courts, military installations and service academies outside of Washington, DC. 1992. a. $116. Monitor Publishing Company (Washington), 1301 Pennsylvania Ave., N.W., Ste. 1000, Washington, DC 20004. TEL 202-347-7757. FAX 202-628-3430. (And: 104 Fifth Ave., 2nd Fl., New York, NY 10011. TEL 212-627-4140) Ed. Debra Mayberry.

FEDERAL REGULATORY DIRECTORY. see POLITICAL SCIENCE

FEDERAL RESEARCH IN PROGRESS DATABASE. see ENGINEERING

340 US
FEDERAL RULES SERVICE. 1939. m. $826. Callaghan & Co., 155 Pfingsten Rd., Deerfield, IL 60015. TEL 800-323-8067.

350 US
FEDERAL STAFF DIRECTORY. 1982. s-a. $59. Staff Directories Ltd., Box 62, Mount Vernon, VA 22121. TEL 703-739-0900. FAX 703-739-0234. Ed. Ann L. Brownson.
●Also available on CD-ROM.
Description: Lists 28,000 federal, executive and military personnel from the White House, to Departments and independent agencies, including 2,600 biographies of key decision makers. Also includes descriptions of each agency responsibility with symbols to indicate which positions are presidential appointments.

353 US ISSN 1053-4652
FEDERAL STAFFING DIGEST. 1968. q. $6.50 (typically set in Oct.). U.S. Office of Personnel Management, 1900 E St., N.W., Washington, DC 20415-0001. TEL 202-606-0960. FAX 202-606-0390. Ed. J. Michael Carmichael. bk.rev.; illus.; circ. 30,000. (back issues avail.) **Indexed:** Ind.U.S.Gov.Per.
Incorporates (as of 1989): Recruiting Highlights; Former titles (until 1989): Spotlight on Affirmative Employment Programs & E E O Spotlight; Equal Opportunity in Federal Employment; Equal Opportunity in Federal Government (ISSN 0013-9777)
Description: Covers labor markets, employment trends, recruiting and examining, personnel literature, and Federal employment policy and procedures.

353 US ISSN 0014-9233
FEDERAL TIMES. 1965. w. $48. Army Times Publishing Co., 6883 Commercial Dr., Springfield, VA 22159. TEL 703-750-2000. Ed. Marianne Lester. adv.; bk.rev.; illus.; circ. 31,000. (tabloid format; also avail. in microform from UMI; reprint service avail. from UMI) **Indexed:** Pers.Lit.
Description: Discusses civil service work.

350.6 US ISSN 0145-6202
JK6
FEDERAL YELLOW BOOK; who's who in the federal departments and agencies. 1976. q. $185. Monitor Publishing Company, 104 Fifth Avenue, 2nd Fl..W., Ste. 1000, New York, NY 10011. TEL 212-627-4140. FAX 212-645-0931. Ed. Mary Forschler. adv.; circ. 12,000.
Description: Lists administrators and top staff aides in the Executive Office of the President, Office of Management and Budget, the Cabinet, the National Security Council, 14 Cabinet-level departments, more than 60 federal agencies, and Federal Information Centers in 72 cities.

THE FEDERALIST. see HISTORY — History Of North And South America

FEDNEWS. see LABOR UNIONS

350 SA ISSN 0015-0495
FIAT LUX. (Editions in Afrikaans and English) 1966. m. (10/yr.). free. Administration House of Delegates, Private Bag X54330, Durban 4000, South Africa. FAX 374261. Ed. Sandra Nielson. illus.; index every 2 yrs; circ. 16,000. **Indexed:** Ind.S.A.Per.
Description: Reflects the administration's perspective of the South African Indian community.

350 FJ
FIJI ROYAL GAZETTE. w. $80. Government Printing Department, P.O. Box 98, Suva, Fiji. (also avail. in microfilm from KTO)

350 FJ
FIJI TODAY. a. free. Ministry of Information, Broadcasting, Television and Telecommunications, Government Bldgs., Suva, Fiji.
Formerly: Fiji Information.

FINANZA LOCALE; rivista mensile di contabilita e tributi degli enti locale e delle regioni. see BUSINESS AND ECONOMICS — Public Finance, Taxation

FISCAL LETTER. see BUSINESS AND ECONOMICS — Public Finance, Taxation

FLORIDA ADMINISTRATIVE PRACTICE. see LAW

350 US
FLORIDA INSIGHT. 1989. fortn. $95. Florida Communications Network, Inc., Box 2099, Gainesville, FL 32602. Ed. Jon Mills.
Description: Reports on all facets of government and politics in Florida, including the state legislature.

015 US ISSN 0430-7801
FLORIDA PUBLIC DOCUMENTS. 1968. m. with annual cum. free to qualified libraries. State Library, Documents Section, Tallahassee, FL 32399. TEL 904-487-2651. bibl.; circ. controlled.
Formerly: Florida State Documents (ISSN 0071-6014)

350 DK ISSN 0107-9670
JN7261
FOLKETINGETS HAANDBOG. 1956. irreg., latest 1988. DKK 98 per no. (Folketing, Praesidium) Schultz Information A-S, Ottiliavej 18, 2500 Valby, Denmark. Ed. Kristian Hvidt. illus.; circ. 1,000.

FONCTION PUBLIQUE. see LABOR UNIONS

FOODLINES; a chronicle of hunger and poverty in America. see SOCIAL SERVICES AND WELFARE

350 US
FOREIGN GOVERNMENT OFFICES IN CALIFORNIA; a directory. 1978. irreg., 5th ed. 1991. $15. California Institute of Public Affairs, Box 189040, Sacramento, CA 95818. TEL 916-442-CIPA. FAX 916-442-2478. (Affiliate: The Claremont Graduate School) circ. 600.
Description: Lists California consulates, trade missions, and tourist offices of the 90 countries officially represented in California, and nearest source of information for all countries not represented in California.

350 FR
FRANCE. CONSEIL NATIONAL DE LA COMPTABILITE. BULLETIN TRIMESTRIEL. 1970. q. 29 F. Conseil National de la Comptabilite, c/o Imprimerie Nationale, Establissement de Douai, Route d'Auby, 59128 Flers-en-Escrebieux, France.

350 FR ISSN 0071-8513
FRANCE. CONSEIL NATIONAL DE LA COMPTABILITE. RAPPORT D'ACTIVITE. 1962. irreg., no.8, 1975. price varies. Conseil National de la Comptabilite, c/o Imprimerie Nationale, Etablissement de Douai. Route d'Auby, 59128 Flers-en-Escrebieux, France.

355 FR
FRANCE. INSTITUT INTERNATIONAL D'ADMINISTRATION PUBLIQUE. REVUE FRANCAISE D'ADMINISTRATION PUBLIQUE. q. 275 Fr. (Institut International d'Administration Publique) Documentation Francaise, 29-31 Quai Voltaire, 75340 Paris Cedex 07, France. TEL 1-4015-7000.

363.6 FR
FRANCE. MINISTERE DE L'ENVIRONNEMENT ET DU CADRE DE VIE. INSPECTION GENERALE DE L'EQUIPEMENT. a. Direction des Journaux Officiels, 26 rue Desaix, 75727 Paris Cedex 15, France. TEL 1-45-78-61-44. TELEX 201176 FDIRJO PARIS. (also avail. in microfiche)
●Also available on CD-ROM.

350 614 FR
RA440.87.F8
FRANCE. MINISTERE DES AFFAIRES SOCIALES ET DE L'INTEGRATION. BULLETIN OFFICIEL. w. Ministere des Affaires Sociales et de l'Integration, 1 place de Fontenoy, 75350 Paris Cedex 07, France. FAX 40-56-73-15. (Subscr. to: Direction des Journaux Officiels, 26 rue Desaix, 75727 Paris Cedex 15, France)
Formerly: France. Ministere des Affaires Sociales et de la Solidarite Nationale. Secretariat d'Etat Charge de la Sante. Bulletin Officiel (ISSN 0758-1998)

350 331.11 FR ISSN 0759-0083
FRANCE. MINISTERE DES AFFAIRES SOCIALES ET DE LA SOLIDARITE NATIONALE. MINISTERE CHARGE DE L'EMPLOI. CONVENTIONS COLLECTIVES. w. Ministere des Affaires Sociales et de la Solidarite Nationale, Ministere Charge de l'Emploi, 1 place de Fontenoy, 75700 Paris, France. (Subscr. to: Direction des Journaux Officiels, 26 rue Desaix, 75727 Paris Cedex 15, France). charts.

PUBLIC ADMINISTRATION

328.44   FR
FRANCE. PARLEMENT. ASSEMBLEE NATIONALE. BULLETIN. 1972. w. free. Parlement, Assemblee Nationale, Service de la Communication, Palais-Bourbon, 75355 Paris, France. FAX 40-63-69-65. circ. 6,700.

328.44   FR
FRANCE. PARLEMENT. ASSEMBLEE NATIONALE. BULLETIN DES COMMISSIONS. (Supplement avail.) irreg. 100 F. Parlement, Assemblee Nationale, Service de la Communication, Palais Bourbon, 75355 Paris, France.
  Description: Provides summaries of the works of the Commissions.

FRANCE FORUM. see *POLITICAL SCIENCE*

353.9 379.12   US
FROM THE STATE CAPITALS. CONSTRUCTION POLICIES. 1946. w. $215 (foreign $235)(effective Dec. 1990). Wakeman-Walworth, Inc., 300 N. Washington St., Alexandria, VA 22314. TEL 703-549-8606. FAX 703-549-1372. (processed)
  Formerly: Construction Policies (ISSN 0749-2766); Incorporates: From the State Capitals. Construction: Institutional (ISSN 0741-3491); From the State Capitals. Airport Construction and Financing (ISSN 0734-1636); Which was formerly: From the State Capitals. School Construction (ISSN 0734-1164)
  Description: Reports construction projects sponsored by state and local governments in the US. Includes facility planning, financial and regulatory issues, codes, right-to-know laws, affirmative action programs.

353   US   ISSN 0734-1202
FROM THE STATE CAPITALS. FEDERAL ACTION AFFECTING THE STATES. 1946. w. $215 (foreign $235)(effective Dec. 1990). Wakeman-Walworth, Inc., 300 N. Washington St., Alexandria, VA 22314. TEL 703-549-8606. FAX 703-549-1372. (processed)
  Description: Reports on key developments in Washington that impact on states, such as federal regulatory programs, court rulings and program funding.

353.9   US   ISSN 0741-3475
FROM THE STATE CAPITALS. GENERAL TRENDS. 1946. w. $215 (foreign $235)(effective Dec. 1990). Wakeman-Walworth, Inc., 300 N. Washington St., Alexandria, VA 22314. TEL 703-549-8606. FAX 703-549-1372. (processed)
  Former titles: From the State Capitals. General Fiscal Bulletin; From the State Capitals. General Bulletin (ISSN 0016-1691)
  Description: Reviews important areas of state legislation such as drug abuse, abortion, tax policies, environmental issues.

333.78   US   ISSN 0734-113X
FROM THE STATE CAPITALS. PARKS AND RECREATION TRENDS. 1946. w. $215 (foreign $235)(effective Dec. 1990). Wakeman-Walworth, Inc., 300 N. Alexandria St., Alexandria, VA 22314. TEL 703-549-8606. FAX 703-549-1732. (processed)
  Incorporates: From the State Capitals. Fish and Game Regulations (ISSN 0734-1067)
  Description: Reports on latest state and local park environmental and conservation regulation, wildlife protection, parkland development projects, taxes, licensing and fees, bicycle and hiking paths, liquor bans, city parks.

FROM THE STATE CAPITALS. PUBLIC EMPLOYEE POLICY. see *BUSINESS AND ECONOMICS — Personnel Management*

363.6 353   US   ISSN 0016-1888
FROM THE STATE CAPITALS. PUBLIC UTILITIES. 1946. w. $215 (foreign $235)(effective Dec. 1990). Wakeman-Walworth, Inc., 300 N. Washington St., Alexandria, VA 22314. TEL 703-549-8606. FAX 703-549-1372.
  ●Also available online. Vendor(s): WESTLAW.
  Description: Reports on all forms of public utilities.

FUTURE CHOICES. see *CHILDREN AND YOUTH — About*

FUTURES; the journal of forecasting, planning and policy. see *TECHNOLOGY: COMPREHENSIVE WORKS*

353   US   ISSN 0016-3414
HJ9701
G A O REVIEW. 1967. q. $11. U.S. General Accounting Office, 441 G St. N.W., Washington, DC 20548. TEL 202-655-4000. (Dist. by: Supt. of Documents, Washington, DC 20402) Ed. John D. Heller. bk.rev.; illus.; circ. 7,000. (also avail. in microform from MIM,UMI; reprint service avail. from UMI) **Indexed:** BPIA, Bus.Ind., Ind.U.S.Gov.Per., P.A.I.S., Pers.Lit., Tr.& Indus.Ind.

G M V. (Government and Military Video) see *COMMUNICATIONS — Video*

350   AT
G O: GOVERNMENT OFFICERS MAGAZINE OF ADMINISTRATION AND PURCHASING. 1983. m. Aus.$45. Peter Isaacson Publications Pty. Ltd., 45-50 Porter St., Prahran, Vic. 3181, Australia. TEL 03-520-5555. FAX 03-521-3647. Ed. Lawrence Hulse. adv.; bk.rev.; circ. 13,000. (back issues avail.)
  Description: Comprehensive coverage of key issues, relevant news, management trends and administration programs for decision makers in government.

353   US   ISSN 0016-3619
G R A REPORTER. 1949. q. $30 (effective Jan. 1991). Governmental Research Association, Inc., 315 Samford Hall, Samford University, Birmingham, AL 35229. TEL 205-870-2482. illus.; circ. 300.

350   MG
GAZETIM-PANJAKAN'NY REPOBLIKA DEMOKRATIKA MALAGASY/JOURNAL OFFICIEL DE LA REPUBLIQUE DEMOCRATIQUE DE MADAGASCAR. (Issued in 3 parts) (Text in French or Malagasy) w. Impr. National, B.P. 38, Antananarivo, Malagasy Republic. Ed. Samuel Ramaroson.

350   TZ   ISSN 0856-0323
GAZETTE OF THE UNITED REPUBLIC OF TANZANIA. (Text in English and Swahili) 1940. w. EAs.340. Government Publications Agency, P.O. Box 1801, Dar es Salaam, Tanzania. Ed. H. Hadji. circ. 6,000. (tabloid format)

350   GW
DIE GEMEINDE (STUTTGART); Zeitschrift fuer die Staedte und Gemeinden, fuer Stadtraete, Gemeinderaete und Ortschaftsraete. 1877. s-m. DM.160. Gemeindetag Baden-Wuerttemberg, Panoramastr. 33, 7000 Stuttgart 1, Germany. TEL 0711-228960. Ed. Christian Steger. adv.; bk.rev.; stat.; circ. 5,000. (tabloid format)

GENERAL ACCOUNTING OFFICE REPORTS AND TECHNOLOGY. see *BUSINESS AND ECONOMICS — Accounting*

GERMAN BRIEF. see *BUSINESS AND ECONOMICS*

001.4   GW
GERMANY (FEDERAL REPUBLIC, 1949-). BUNDESMINISTERIUM FUER FORSCHUNG UND TECHNOLOGIE. BUNDESBERICHT FORSCHUNG.* 1979. irreg. free. Verlag Dr. Heger, Goethestr. 54, 53 Bonn-Bad Godesberg, Germany. **Indexed:** Nutr.Abstr.
  Formerly: Germany (Federal Republic, 1949-). Bundesministerium fuer Bildung und Wissenschaft. Forschungsbericht der Bundesregierung.

354   GW
GERMANY (FEDERAL REPUBLIC, 1949-). PRESSE- UND INFORMATIONSAMT BULLETIN ARCHIVE SUPPLEMENT. (Text in English) 1974. irreg. Presse und Informationsamt - Press and Information Office, Welckerstr. 11, 5300 Bonn, Germany.

GILDEA REVIEW. see *ENVIRONMENTAL STUDIES*

GOETIKUSS. see *EDUCATION*

350 320   US   ISSN 0884-9072
F866.2
GOLDEN STATE REPORT.* 1985. m. $35. 3031 Fillmore St., San Francisco, CA 94123-4009. TEL 916-448-2653. Ed. Ed Mendle.
  Description: Reports on California state government and politics.

GOODS AND SERVICES BULLETIN. see *BUSINESS AND ECONOMICS — Production Of Goods And Services*

350 340   US   ISSN 0739-6937
GOTHERMAN'S OHIO MUNICIPAL SERVICE. bi-m. $135. Banks - Baldwin Law Publishing Co., University Center, Box 1974, Cleveland, OH 44106. TEL 216-721-7373. FAX 216-721-8055. Ed. John E. Gotherman.
  Description: Commentary on municipal tort liability, municipal financing, environmental and property law affecting municipalities, and public employee collective bargaining; judicial and legislative developments tracked.

920 350   FR
GOUVERNEMENT ET LES CABINETS MINISTERIELS. (Pocket Edition) 6/yr. 135.68 F. Informations Rapides de l'Administration Francaise, 27, rue Jasmin, 75016 Paris, France. Dir. M. Saulgeot.

350   US
GOVERNING GEORGIA. 1984. q. free. University of Georgia, Carl Vinson Institute of Government, Terrel Hall, Athens, GA 30602. TEL 404-542-2736. FAX 404-542-9301. Ed. Ann Allen.
  Formerly: Comment.
  Description: Reports on issues and events affecting Georgia state and local government.

350   UK   ISSN 0140-5764
GOVERNMENT AND MUNICIPAL CONTRACTORS. 1935. a. £30. Benn Business Information Services Ltd., P.O. Box 20, Sovereign Way, Tonbridge, Kent TN9 1RQ, England. TEL 0732-362666. FAX 0732-770483. TELEX 95162-BENTON-G. adv.; bk.rev.; circ. 5,000.
  —BLDSC shelfmark: 4203.880000.
  Former titles: Sell's Government and Municipal Contractors Register (ISSN 0072-5129); Government and Municipal Contractors Register.
  Description: Directory of manufacturers, services and suppliers.

350 320   US   ISSN 1054-5859
KF4945.A15
GOVERNMENT AND POLITICS ALERT. 1989. 6/yr. $87.50. Government Research Service, 701 Jackson, Topeka, KS 66603. TEL 913-232-7720. FAX 913-232-1615. Ed. Lynn Hellebust.
  Formerly (until 1990): Legislative Information Alert (ISSN 1044-9094)
  Description: Provides news and information about new publications, videos and databases dealing with Congress, state legislatures and lobbying in particular, as well as American government and politics in general.

353   US   ISSN 0072-5153
GOVERNMENT CONTRACTS MONOGRAPHS. 1961. irreg., no.13, 1980. price varies. George Washington University, Government Contracts Program, 2100 Pennsylvania Ave., N.W., Ste. 250, Washington, DC 20052. TEL 202-223-2772. FAX 202-223-1387.

GOVERNMENT CONTRACTS REPORTS. see *LAW*

GOVERNMENT EMPLOYEE RELATIONS REPORT. see *BUSINESS AND ECONOMICS — Labor And Industrial Relations*

GOVERNMENT EQUIPMENT NEWS. see *BUSINESS AND ECONOMICS — Trade And Industrial Directories*

350   US   ISSN 0017-2626
JK1   CODEN: GVEXAW
GOVERNMENT EXECUTIVE; federal government's business magazine. 1969. 12/yr. $48. National Journal, Inc. (Subsidiary of: Times Mirror Company), 1730 M St., N.W., Ste. 1100, Washington, DC 20036. TEL 202-857-1400. FAX 202-833-8069. Ed. Timothy B. Clark. adv.; bk.rev.; charts; illus.; index; circ. 60,000. (also avail. in microform from UMI; reprint service avail. from UMI) **Indexed:** Air Un.Lib.Ind., BPIA, Bus.Ind., Pers.Lit., Sage Pub.Admin.Abstr., Tr.& Indus.Ind.

350   MF
GOVERNMENT GAZETTE OF MAURITIUS. (Text in English) irreg., no.34, 1981. Government Printing Office, Elizabeth II Ave., Port Louis, Mauritius. index.

350   MF
GOVERNMENT GAZETTE OF MAURITIUS. LEGAL SUPPLEMENT. ACT. (Text in English) irreg., no.2, 1981. Government Printing Office, Elizabeth II Ave., Port Louis, Mauritius.

PUBLIC ADMINISTRATION

350   MF
GOVERNMENT GAZETTE OF MAURITIUS. LEGAL SUPPLEMENT. GOVERNMENT NOTICE. (Text in English) irreg. Government Printing Office, Elizabeth II Ave., Port Louis, Mauritius.

350   MF
GOVERNMENT GAZETTE OF MAURITIUS. LEGAL SUPPLEMENT. PROCLAMATION. (Text in English) irreg., no.3, 1981. Government Printing Office, Elizabeth II Ave., Port Louis, Mauritius.

350   MF
GOVERNMENT GAZETTE OF MAURITIUS. SPECIAL LEGAL SUPPLEMENT. A BILL. (Text in English) irreg., no.7, 1981. Government Printing Office, Elizabeth II Ave., Port Louis, Mauritius.

350 380   CN
▼**GOVERNMENT GREEN GUIDE.** 1991. a. Can.$30($30) (effective Jan. 1991). Momentum Magazines, 4040 Credit View Dr., Unit 11, Box 6900, Mississauga, Ont. L5C 348, Canada. TEL 416-569-6900. FAX 416-569-6915. Ed. Terry Hrynyshyn. adv.; circ. 17,000 (controlled).

350   US   ISSN 0072-517X
HJ389.5
GOVERNMENT IN HAWAII; a handbook of financial statistics. 1954. a. $5. Tax Foundation of Hawaii, 201 Merchant St., Ste. 901, Honolulu, HI 96813-2929. Ed. Lowell L. Kalapa. circ. 3,500.
Indexed: Vert.File Ind.

GOVERNMENT INFORMATION QUARTERLY; an international journal of resources, services, policies, and practices. see *LIBRARY AND INFORMATION SCIENCES*

353 338.9   US   ISSN 0017-2642
GOVERNMENT PRODUCT NEWS. 1962. m. $45 (free to qualified personnel). Penton Publishing (Subsidiary of: Pittway Company), 1100 Superior Ave., Cleveland, OH 44114-2543. TEL 216-696-7000. FAX 216-696-8765. (Subscr. to: Box 95759, Cleveland, OH 44101) Ed. Leslie Drahos. adv.; tr.lit.; circ. 85,000 (controlled). (tabloid format; also avail. in microform from UMI; reprint service avail. from UMI) Indexed: Tr.& Indus.Ind.
●Also available online. Vendor(s): DIALOG.
Former titles: Government Product News and Purchasing Digest; Government Purchasing Digest (ISSN 0017-2650)
Description: News, ideas, applications and literature of products and services utilized in government functions.

363.6   US   ISSN 0737-5255
JK404
GOVERNMENT PROGRAMS AND PROJECTS DIRECTORY. irreg. $145. Gale Research Inc., 835 Penobscot Bldg., Detroit, MI 48226. TEL 800-877-4253. FAX 313-961-6083. TELEX 810-221-7086. Ed. Anthony T. Kruzas, Kay Gill.
Description: Irregularly updated guide on American government programs and projects.

350   US   ISSN 0277-9390
CODEN: GPRVDI
GOVERNMENT PUBLICATIONS REVIEW; an international journal of issues and information resources. 1974. 6/yr. £160 (effective 1992). Pergamon Press, Inc., Journals Division, 660 White Plains Rd., Tarrytown, NY 10591-5153. TEL 914-524-9200. FAX 914-333-2444. (And: Headington Hill Hall, Oxford OX3 0BW, England. TEL 0865-794141) Ed. Steven Zink. adv.; bk.rev.; charts; circ. 1,500. (also avail. in microform from MIM,UMI; back issues avail.; reprint service avail. from UMI) Indexed: Amer.Hist.& Life, Bk.Rev.Ind. (1980-), Child.Bk.Rev.Ind. (1980-), Curr.Cont., Hist.Abstr., Int.Lab.Doc., Leg.Info.Manage.Ind., LHTN, Lib.Lit., Mid.East: Abstr.& Ind., P.A.I.S., SSCI.
—BLDSC shelfmark: 4206.023000.
Formerly: Government Publications Review Including Acquisitions Guide; Formed by the 1982 merger of: Government Publications Review. Part A: Research Articles (ISSN 0196-335X); Government Publications Review. Part B: Acquisitions Guide to Significant Government Publications at All Levels (ISSN 0196-3368); Supersedes in part: Government Publications Review (ISSN 0093-061X)
Description: Covers production, distribution, library handling, bibliographic control, accessibility and use of government information in all formats and at all levels.
Refereed Serial

350.712   CN   ISSN 0046-6220
GOVERNMENT PURCHASING GUIDE. (Text in English, French) 1969. m. Can.$35($50) Moorshead Publications Ltd., 1300 Don Mills Rd., North York, Ont. M3B 3M8, Canada. TEL 416-445-5600. FAX 416-445-8149. Ed. Caroline Butler. adv.; circ. 20,000 (controlled). (back issues avail.)
Description: For those who initiate, specify, review or purchase for all levels of government.

GOVERNMENT RELATIONS. see *BUSINESS AND ECONOMICS — Management*

GOVERNMENT STANDARD. see *LABOR UNIONS*

350   US
GOVERNMENTAL AFFAIRS NEWSLETTER. 1966. 11/yr. $15. University of Missouri, Governmental Affairs Program, Professional Bldg., Rm. 206, Columbia, MO 65211. TEL 314-882-6401. Ed. Richard Dohm.
Description: Covers Missouri government and politics.

350   US   ISSN 0072-520X
JK3
GOVERNMENTAL RESEARCH ASSOCIATION DIRECTORY; directory of organizations and individuals professionally engaged in governmental research and related activities. 1938. a. $30 (effective Jan. 1991). Governmental Research Association, Inc., 315 Samford Hall, Samford University, Birmingham, AL 35229. TEL 205-870-2482. index; circ. 700.

GOVERNMENTAL RISK MANAGEMENT MANUAL. see *INSURANCE*

350   US
GRADUATE PROGRAMS IN PUBLIC AFFAIRS AND PUBLIC ADMINISTRATION. Variant titles: Directory: Graduate Programs in Public Affairs and Administration. Programs in Public Affairs and Administration. 1972. biennial. $12.50. National Association of Schools of Public Affairs and Administration, 1120 G St., N.W., Ste. 520, Washington, DC 20005. TEL 202-628-8965. FAX 202-626-4978. TELEX 4972105 NASPAA DC. Ed. Alfred M. Zuck. circ. 1,500. Indexed: C.I.J.E.
Formerly: Graduate School Programs in Public Affairs and Public Administration (ISSN 0094-6648)

GRADUATE SCHOOL JOURNAL. see *EDUCATION — School Organization And Administration*

350   UK
GREAT BRITAIN. HOUSE OF COMMONS. PARLIAMENTARY DEBATES. irreg. £190. H.M.S.O., P.O. Box 276, London SW8 5DT, England. (Dist. by: UNIPUB, 4611-F Assembly Dr., Lantham, MD 20706-4391. TEL 301-459-7666) index. (also avail. in microfiche from BHP)
Description: Transcripts of the oral arguments presented in the House of Commons.

350   UK   ISSN 0072-7032
GREAT BRITAIN. PUBLIC WORKS LOAN BOARD. REPORT. 1875. a. £4.20. Public Works Loan Board, Royex House, London EC2V 7LR, England. (Avail. from: H.M.S.O., P.O. Box 276, London SW8 5DT, England) circ. 500.

352 300   UK   ISSN 0072-7350
GREATER LONDON PAPERS; problems of government of greater London. 1961. irreg., latest 1976. price varies. London School of Economics and Political Science, Houghton St., Aldwych, London WC2A 2AE, England.

350   GH   ISSN 0379-8658
JA26
GREENHILL JOURNAL OF ADMINISTRATION. 1974. q. NC.13($16) Ghana Institute of Management and Public Administration, P.O. Box 50, Achimota, Ghana. Ed. K.A. Owusu-Ansah. adv.; bk.rev.; bibl.; illus.; index; circ. 1,000. Indexed: Curr.Cont.Africa.

GUIDE TO ARKANSAS FUNDING SOURCES. see *BUSINESS AND ECONOMICS — Management*

350   US
▼**GUIDE TO GOVERNMENT CONTRACTING.** 1991. base vol. (plus m. updates). $325. Commerce Clearing House, Inc., 4025 W. Peterson Ave., Chicago, IL 60646. TEL 312-583-8500.

353.9   US   ISSN 0072-8454
JQ6121
GUIDE TO GOVERNMENT IN HAWAII. 1961. irreg., 9th ed., 1989. price varies. Legislative Reference Bureau, State Capitol, Honolulu, HI 96813. TEL 808-587-0690.

353.9   US   ISSN 0091-0716
JK6630
GUIDE TO NEBRASKA STATE AGENCIES. 1973. irreg. Nebraska Publications Clearinghouse, 1420 P St., NE, Lincoln, NE 68508. Ed. Karen Lusk. circ. 300. (also avail. in microfiche)

354   II
H C M STATE INSTITUTE OF PUBLIC ADMINISTRATION. (Text in English) 1975. s-a. $8. Harishchandra Mathur State Institute of Public Administration, Jaipur 302004, India.

HARVARD JOURNAL OF LAW AND PUBLIC POLICY. see *LAW*

350 336   US
HAWAII. LEGISLATIVE AUDITOR. SPECIAL REPORTS. 1965. irreg. (3-5/yr.). free. Office of the Auditor, State Capitol, Honolulu, HI 96813. TEL 808-548-2450. charts; stat.

350   US   ISSN 0073-1277
HAWAII. LEGISLATIVE REFERENCE BUREAU. REPORT. 1951. irreg. free. Legislative Reference Bureau, State Capitol, Honolulu, HI 96813. TEL 808-587-0690.

350 331   US   ISSN 0194-2352
HEALTH GRANTS & CONTRACTS WEEKLY; selected federal project opportunities. 1978. w. $320 (foreign $370). Capitol Publications Inc., 1101 King St., Ste. 444, Alexandria, VA 22314. TEL 703-683-4100. FAX 703-739-6517. Ed. Leslie Ratzlaff. (looseleaf format)
●Also available online. Vendor(s): NewsNet.
Description: Alerts health researchers, administrators and fundseekers to the latest funding announcements for federal health grants and contracts. Includes facts on scope of work, eligibility, amount of funds, application deadline and contact officers.

350   US   ISSN 0272-1155
HERITAGE LECTURES. 1980. irreg., latest 1989. price varies. Heritage Foundation, 214 Massachusetts Ave., N.E., Washington, DC 20002. TEL 202-546-4400. FAX 202-546-8328. index. (back issues avail.)
●Also available online. Vendor(s): Mead Data Central.

HOME OFFICE LIST OF PUBLICATIONS. see *PUBLISHING AND BOOK TRADE*

350   HO
HONDURAS. CONGRESO NACIONAL. BOLETIN. irreg., no.18, 1982. Congreso Nacional, Oficina de Boletines y Publicaciones, Tegucigalpa, Honduras.

350   HK
HONG KONG. BUILDING DEVELOPMENT DEPARTMENT. BUILDING STATISTICS. (Text in English) m. HK.$20. (Buildings Ordinance Office) Government Publication Centre, G.P.O. Bldg., Ground Fl., Connaught Place, Hong Kong, Hong Kong. TEL 5-8428801. (Subscr. to: Director of Information Services, Information Services Dept., 1 Battery Path, G-F, Central, Hong Kong) Ed.Bd.

350   HK
HONG KONG. GOVERNMENT PUBLICATION CENTRE. INQUIRY REPORTS. (Editions in Chinese, English) irreg., latest 1984. price varies. Government Publication Centre, G.P.O. Bldg., Ground Fl., Connaught Place, Hong Kong, Hong Kong. TEL 842-8801. (Subscr. to: Director of Information Services, Information Services Dept., 1 Battery Path, G-F, Central, Hong Kong) Ed.Bd.

HONG KONG. LAW REFORM COMMISSION. REPORT. see *LAW — Judicial Systems*

350   HK
HONG KONG. LEGISLATIVE COUNCIL. FINANCE COMMITTEE. REPORT. (Text in English) a. HK.$160. (Finance Committee) Government Publication Centre, G.P.O. Bldg., Ground Fl., Connaught Place, Hong Kong, Hong Kong. TEL 842-8801. (Subscr. to: Director of Information Services, Information Services Dept., 1 Battery Path, G-F, Central, Hong Kong) Ed.Bd.

350   HK
HONG KONG. LEGISLATIVE COUNCIL. PROCEEDINGS. (Editions in Chinese, English) w. price varies. Government Publication Centre, G.P.O. Bldg., Ground Fl., Connaught Place, Hong Kong, Hong Kong. TEL 842-8801. (Subscr. to: Director of Information Services, Information Services Dept., 1 Battery Path, G-F, Central, Hong Kong) Ed.Bd.

350   HK
HONG KONG. LEGISLATIVE COUNCIL. PUBLIC WORKS SUB-COMMITTEE. REPORT. (Text in English) a. HK.$200. (Public Works Sub-Committee) Government Publication Centre, G.P.O. Bldg., Ground Fl., Connaught Place, Hong Kong, Hong Kong. TEL 842-8801. (Subscr. to: Director of Information Services, Information Services Dept., 1 Battery Path, G-F, Central, Hong Kong) Ed.Bd.

350   HK
HONG KONG. PUBLIC SERVICE COMMISSION. CHAIRMAN'S REPORT. (Text in English) a. HK.$35. Government Publications Centre, G.P.O. Bldg., Ground Fl., Connaught Place, Hong Kong, Hong Kong. TEL 842-8801. FAX 845-9078. (Subscr. to: Director of Information Services, Information Services Dept., 1 Battery Path, G-F, Central, Hong Kong) Ed.Bd.

350.6   HK
HONG KONG. STANDING COMMISSION ON CIVIL SERVICE SALARIES AND CONDITIONS OF SERVICE. CIVIL SERVICE PAY. (Editions in Chinese and English) irreg., no.20, 1988. price varies. Government Publication Centre, G.P.O. Bldg., Ground Fl., Connaught Place, Hong Kong, Hong Kong. TEL 842-8801. (Subscr. to: Director of Information Services, Information Services Dept., 1 Battery Path, G-F, Central, Hong Kong) Ed.Bd.

350   HK
HONG KONG. TELEVISION ADVISORY BOARD. ANNUAL REPORT. (Editions in Chinese, English) a. HK.$45. Government Publication Centre, G.P.O. Bldg., Ground Fl., Connaught Place, Hong Kong, Hong Kong. (Subscr. to: Director of Information Services, Information Services Dept., 1 Battery Path, G-F, Central, Hong Kong) Ed.Bd.

350   HK
HONG KONG. URBAN COUNCIL. PROCEEDINGS. (Editions in Chinese, English) m. price varies. Government Publications Centre, G.P.O. Building, Ground Floor, Connaught Place, Hong Kong, Hong Kong. TEL 842-8801. FAX 845-9078. (Subscr. to: Director of Information Services, Information Services Dept., 1 Battery Path, G-F, Central Hong Kong) Ed.Bd.

350   HK
HONG KONG GOVERNMENT GAZETTE. w. HK.$1456. Government Information Services, Beaconsfield House, Queen's Rd., Central, Victoria, Hong Kong. TEL 842-8801. (Subscr. to: Director of Information Services, Information Services Department, 1 Battery Path, G-F, Central, Hong Kong) (also avail. in microfilm from BHP)
    Description: Latest Hong Kong legislation, notices, tenders and appointments.

350   US
HORIZONS (COLUMBUS); the newsletter of the Mid-Ohio Regional Planning Commission. 1969. q. free. Mid-Ohio Regional Planning Commission, 285 E. Main St., Columbus, OH 43215-5272. TEL 614-228-2663. FAX 614-621-2401. Ed. Jan Hiltner. illus.; tr.lit.; circ. 5,300. **Indexed:** Chem.Abstr.
    Former titles (until 1990): Mid-Ohio Review; Regional Review.

HOTLINE (FALLS CHURCH). see *POLITICAL SCIENCE*

350   UK
HOUSE MAGAZINE OF PARLIAMENT.* 1976. w. £75. European Parliament Review, 7 Marsham St., Westminster, London SW1P 3DW, England. Ed. Russel Dexter. adv.; bk.rev.; circ. controlled.

350   US
HUDSON OPINION. irreg. Hudson Institute, Herman Kahn Center, 5395 Emerson Way, Box 26-919, Indianapolis, IN 46226-0919. TEL 317-545-1000. FAX 317-545-9639. TELEX 855477.

350   US   ISSN 0073-3873
HUMAN RESOURCES RESEARCH ORGANIZATION. PROFESSIONAL PAPERS. 1966. irreg. free. Human Resources Research Organization, 1100 S. Washington St., Alexandria, VA 22314. TEL 703-549-3611. (also avail. in microform from NTI) **Indexed:** Psychol.Abstr.

350   HK
I C A C. COMMISSIONER'S ANNUAL REPORT. (Editions in Chinese, English) 1985. a. HK.$18. (Independent Commission Against Corruption) Government Publication Centre, G.P.O. Bldg., Ground Fl., Connaught Place, Hong Kong, Hong Kong. TEL 842-8801. (Subscr. to: Director of Information Services, Information Services Dept., 1 Battery Path, G-F, Central, Hong Kong) Ed.Bd.

350   II
I I P A NEWSLETTER. (Text in English) 1957. m. Rs.3($1) Indian Institute of Public Administration, Indraprastha Estate, Ring Rd., New Delhi 110002, India. Ed. T.N. Chaturvedi.

350   UK   ISSN 0958-5222
I P M S BULLETIN. 1925. m. £19.50 (foreign £31). Institution of Professionals, Managers and Specialists, 75-79 York Rd., London SE1 7AQ, England. TEL 071-928-9951. FAX 071-928-5996. Ed. Charles Harvey. adv.; bk.rev.; illus.; index; circ. 88,641.
    Former titles: I P C S Bulletin (ISSN 0265-0975); (until Jun. 1982): State Service (ISSN 0039-0151)

350   SU
AL-IDARAH AL-AAMAH. (Text in Arabic; summaries in English) a. SRl.20($8) Ma'had al-Idarah al-Aamah - Institute of Public Administration, P.O. Box 25, Riyadh 11141, Saudi Arabia. TEL 471160. abstr.
    Description: Publishes research on a variety of issues in public administration.

350   TS
AL-IDARAH WAL-TANMIYAH/ADMINISTRATION AND DEVELOPMENT. (Text in Arabic) 1986. Institute of Administration and Development, P.O. Box 779, Abu Dhabi, United Arab Emirates. TEL 654665. TELEX 23718. Ed. Said Khalifa al-Ghaith. circ. 2,000.
    Description: Presents research and analysis on administration and development in the U.A.E.

350   MK
AL-IDARI; dawriyyah mutakhassisah fi majal al-idarah al-aamah. q. 8 ORI. to individuals; institutions 20 ORI. Wizarat Shu'un al-Diwan al-Sultani, Ma'had al-Idarah al-Aamah - Ministry of Diwan Affairs, Institute of Public Administration, P.O. Box 4994, Ruwi, Muscat, Sultanate of Oman. TEL 602065. TELEX 2275 MBDIWAN.

350   BL
IMPRENSA OFICIAL DO ESTADO DO RIO DE JANEIRO. 1975. d. Cr.$4,800. (Secretaria Extraordinaria de Comunicacao Social) Imprensa Oficial, Rua Margues de Olinda, 15, Niteroi, Rio de Janeiro, Brazil. TEL 021-719-1122. adv.; circ. 17,900. (tabloid format; also avail. in microfilm)

IMPRESA PUBBLICA; municipalizzazione. see *PUBLIC ADMINISTRATION — Municipal Government*

350   RW
IMVAHO. (Text in Kinyarwanda) 1960. w. Office Rwandais d'Information, B.P. 83, Kigali, Rwanda. TEL 75724. TELEX 557. circ. 51,000.

INDEPENDENT GASOLINE MARKETING. see *PETROLEUM AND GAS*

INDEX TO THE CODE OF FEDERAL REGULATIONS. see *PUBLIC ADMINISTRATION — Abstracting, Bibliographies, Statistics*

350   II   ISSN 0073-6171
INDIA. CENTRAL VIGILANCE COMMISSION. REPORT. (Text in English and Hindi) 1965. a. free. Central Vigilance Commission, No.3, Dr. Rajendra Prasad Road, New Delhi, India. circ. controlled.

354   II
INDIA. DEPARTMENT OF ECONOMIC AFFAIRS. BUDGET DIVISION. KEY TO THE BUDGET DOCUMENTS. (Text in English) a. Department of Economic Affairs, Budget Division, New Delhi, India.

INDIA. DEPARTMENT OF POWER. REPORT. see *ENERGY*

354   II   ISSN 0445-6831
INDIA. PARLIAMENT. PUBLIC ACCOUNTS COMMITTEE. REPORT ON THE ACCOUNTS. (Each report covers various agencies of the government.) (Text in English) 1947. a. Parliament, Public Accounts Committee, Lok Sabha Secretariat, New Delhi, India.

351.1   II   ISSN 0073-6236
INDIA. UNION PUBLIC SERVICE COMMISSION REPORT. (Report year ends Mar. 31) (Text in English) 1951. a. Union Public Service Commission, Minto Rd., New Delhi, India.

350   II   ISSN 0019-5561
JQ201
INDIAN JOURNAL OF PUBLIC ADMINISTRATION. (Text in English) 1955. q. Rs.60($25) Indian Institute of Public Administration, Indraprastha Estate, Ring Rd., New Delhi 110002, India. Ed. T.N. Chaturvedi. adv.; bk.rev.; abstr.; bibl.; index. (back issues avail.; reprint service avail. from SWZ) **Indexed:** A.B.C.Pol.Sci., ASSIA, E.I., Int.Lab.Doc., Rural Recreat.Tour.Abstr., World Agri.Econ.& Rural Sociol.Abstr.
    —BLDSC shelfmark: 4420.350000.

350   US
INDIANA ISSUES. 1989. s-m. $80. David L. Lantz, Ed. & Pub., 7802 Cannonade Dr., Indianapolis, IN 46217. TEL 317-887-0970.
    Description: Reports on public policy issues affecting Indiana.

350   US
INDIANA LEGISLATIVE INSIGHT. 1989. 48/yr. $295. Box 383, Noblesville, IN 46060. TEL 317-773-8715. FAX 317-773-8715. Ed. Edward D. Feigenbaum.
    Description: Reports on activities in the legislative and executive branches of Indiana state government and on state politics.

353.9   US
INDIANA UNIVERSITY. SCHOOL OF PUBLIC AND ENVIRONMENTAL AFFAIRS. REVIEW. 1979. 2/yr. Indiana University, School of Public and Environmental Affairs, Bloomington, IN 47405. Ed. Carlyn Johnson. bk.rev.; circ. 2,000.
    Supersedes (1975-1979): Indiana Public Management (ISSN 0099-1023)

350   IO
INDONESIA. DEPARTEMEN PENERANGAN. SIARAN UMUM. irreg. Department of Information - Departemen Penerangan, Direktorat Publikasi, Jl. Merdeka Barat 7, Jakarta, Indonesia.

350   BE
INFORMAT; journal des Fonctionnaires. (Text in Dutch and French) 10/yr. C A S, 146 rue Jourdan, 1060 Brussels, Belgium. adv.; circ. 5,000.

INFORMATIONS RAPIDES DE L'ADMINISTRATION FRANCAISE. see *BIOGRAPHY*

INFORMATIZATION AND THE PUBLIC SECTOR; an international journal on the development, adoption, use and effects of information technologies. see *COMMUNICATIONS*

INFOS FEDERALES. see *TRANSPORTATION*

350   US
INSIDE (HELENA, MT). 1985. q. free. Department of Commerce, 1424 Ninth Ave., Helena, MT 59620. TEL 406-444-3494. FAX 406-444-2903. Ed. Alene Gorecki. circ. 2,000.
    Supersedes (in 1986): Montana Community News; Montana Planning News.

350 320   US   ISSN 0884-030X
INSIDE ALABAMA POLITICS.* 1984. 39/yr. $83. Inside Alabama Politics, Inc., 2465 Commercial Park Dr., Mobile, AL 36606-2031. Ed. Bessie Ford.

PUBLIC ADMINISTRATION

350 320   US   ISSN 1052-8857
INSIDE MICHIGAN POLITICS. 1988. bi-w. $160. 2812 Mersey Lane, Ste. J, Lansing, MI 48911. TEL 517-394-2441. FAX 517-487-3830. Ed. William S. Ballenger. circ. 1,025.
    Description: Covers Michigan government, politics and business.

350   US
INSIDE THE WHITE HOUSE. 1983. w. $495 (foreign $545). Inside Washington Publishers, Box 7167, Benjamin Franklin Sta., Washington, DC 20044. TEL 703-892-8500. FAX 703-685-2606. Ed. Peter Busowski.
    Formerly: Inside the Administration.
    Description: Reports on national administration, economic, trade and regulatory policies.

350   FR
INSTITUT INTERNATIONAL D'ADMINISTRATION PUBLIQUE. DOSSIERS ET DEBATS. 1979. a. 70 F. Institut International d'Administration Publique - International Institute of Public Administration, 2, av. de l'Observatoire, 75006 Paris, France. FAX 46-33-26-38. TELEX 204826 DOCFRAN. (Subscr. to: La Documentation Francaise, 29-31 Quai Voltaire, 75340 Paris Cedex 07, France) Ed. Jacques Ziller. circ. 1,000.
    Formerly: Institut International d'Administration Publique. Annee Administrative (ISSN 0984-8673)
    Description: Provides details on the organization and operation of public administration in France and other European countries.

INSTITUT ZA JAVNO UPRAVO. VESTNIK. see *LAW*

350   IE   ISSN 0073-9596
JN1400
INSTITUTE OF PUBLIC ADMINISTRATION, DUBLIN. ADMINISTRATION YEARBOOK AND DIARY. (Text mainly in English; some Irish) 1967. a. £25. Institute of Public Administration, 59 Lansdowne Rd., Dublin 4, Ireland. Ed. James O'Donnell. adv.; circ. 9,500.
    —BLDSC shelfmark: 4567.800900.

350   IE   ISSN 0073-9588
INSTITUTE OF PUBLIC ADMINISTRATION, DUBLIN. ANNUAL REPORT. (Text mainly in English; some Irish) 1958. a. free. Institute of Public Administration, 57-61 Lansdowne Rd., Dublin 4, Ireland. Ed. Jim O'Donnell. circ. 2,000.

354   SJ   ISSN 0073-9618
INSTITUTE OF PUBLIC ADMINISTRATION, KHARTOUM. OCCASIONAL PAPERS. 1964. irreg. Institute of Public Administration, P.O. Box 1492, Khartoum, Sudan.

354   SJ   ISSN 0073-9626
INSTITUTE OF PUBLIC ADMINISTRATION, KHARTOUM. PROCEEDINGS OF THE ANNUAL ROUND TABLE CONFERENCE. (Text in Arabic or English) 1959. irreg. Institute of Public Administration, P.O. Box 1492, Khartoum, Sudan.

350   CR   ISSN 0073-9944
INSTITUTO CENTROAMERICANO DE ADMINISTRACION PUBLICA. SERIE 100. ASPECTOS HUMANOS DE LA ADMINISTRACION. 1965. irreg., latest 1983. price varies. Instituto Centroamericano de Administracion Publica, Apdo. 10025, San Jose, Costa Rica.

350   CR   ISSN 0073-9952
INSTITUTO CENTROAMERICANO DE ADMINISTRACION PUBLICA. SERIE 200. CIENCIA DE LA ADMINISTRACION. 1960. irreg. price varies. Instituto Centroamericano de Administracion Publica, Apdo. 10025, San Jose, Costa Rica.

350   CR   ISSN 0073-9960
INSTITUTO CENTROAMERICANO DE ADMINISTRACION PUBLICA. SERIE 300: INVESTIGACION. 1968. irreg. price varies. Instituto Centroamericano de Administracion Publica, Apdo. 10025, San Jose, Costa Rica.

350   CR   ISSN 0073-9979
INSTITUTO CENTROAMERICANO DE ADMINISTRACION PUBLICA. SERIE 400: ECONOMIA Y FINANZAS. 1968. irreg. price varies. Instituto Centroamericano de Administracion Publica, Apdo. 10025, San Jose, Costa Rica.

350   CR   ISSN 0073-9995
INSTITUTO CENTROAMERICANO DE ADMINISTRACION PUBLICA. SERIE 600: INFORMES DE SEMINARIOS. 1964. irreg. price varies. Instituto Centroamericano de Administracion Publica, Apdo. 10025, San Jose, Costa Rica.

350   CR   ISSN 0074-0004
INSTITUTO CENTROAMERICANO DE ADMINISTRACION PUBLICA. SERIE 700: MATERIALES DE INFORMACION. 1966. irreg. free. Instituto Centroamericano de Administracion Publica, Apdo. 10025, San Jose, Costa Rica.

350   CR   ISSN 0074-0012
INSTITUTO CENTROAMERICANO DE ADMINISTRACION PUBLICA. SERIE 800: METODOLOGIA DE LA ADMINISTRACION. 1964. irreg. price varies. Instituto Centroamericano de Administracion Publica, Apdo. 10025, San Jose, Costa Rica.

350   CR   ISSN 0074-0020
INSTITUTO CENTROAMERICANO DE ADMINISTRACION PUBLICA. SERIE 900: MISCELANEAS. 1965. irreg. price varies. Instituto Centroamericano de Administracion Publica, Apdo. 10025, San Jose, Costa Rica.

350   UK   ISSN 0956-0998
▼**THE INTERNATIONAL DIRECTORY OF GOVERNMENT.** 1990. triennial. $275. Europa Publications Ltd., 18 Bedford Sq., London WC1B 3JN, England. TEL 071-580-8236. FAX 071-636-1664. TELEX 21540-EUROPA-G.
    Description: Provides detailed information on every government in the world.

350   BE   ISSN 0074-6479
INTERNATIONAL INSTITUTE OF ADMINISTRATIVE SCIENCES. REPORTS OF THE INTERNATIONAL CONGRESS. 1910. triennial since 1947; 21st, 1989, Marrakerk. price varies. International Institute of Administrative Sciences, 1 rue Defacqz, Bte.11, B-1050 Brussels, Belgium.

350   US   ISSN 0047-0724
HJ9701   CODEN: IJGADG
INTERNATIONAL JOURNAL OF GOVERNMENT AUDITING/REVUE INTERNATIONALE DE LA VERIFICATION DES COMPTES PUBLICS/REVISTA INTERNACIONAL DE ENTIDADES FISCALIZADORAS SUPERIORES. (Text in Arabic, English, French, German and Spanish) 1974. q. $5. International Organization of Supreme Audit Institutions, c/o U.S. General Accounting Office, 441 G St., N.W., Rm. 7848, Washington, DC 20548. TEL 202-275-4707. FAX 202-275-4021. TELEX USGAOWSH 7108229273. Ed. Donald R. Drach. adv.; bk.rev.; illus.; index; circ. 6,500. (also avail. in microform from UMI; reprint service avail. from UMI) **Indexed:** ABI Inform, Account.& Data Proc.Abstr., Account.Ind. (1974-), BPIA, Bus.Ind., Manage.Cont., Mid.East: Abstr.& Ind., Tr.& Indus.Ind.

350   US   ISSN 0190-0692
JA1.A1   CODEN: IJPADR
INTERNATIONAL JOURNAL OF PUBLIC ADMINISTRATION. 1979. 9/yr. $287.50 to individuals; institutions $575. Marcel Dekker Journals, 270 Madison Ave., New York, NY 10016. TEL 212-696-9000. FAX 212-685-4540. TELEX 421419. (Subscr. to: Box 10018, Church St. Sta., New York, NY 10249) Eds. Jack Rabin, Thomas Vocino. (also avail. in microform from RPI) **Indexed:** ABI Inform, BPIA, Manage.Cont., Pers.Lit., PSI, Sage Pub.Admin.Abstr., Sage Urb.Stud.Abstr., SSCI.
    —BLDSC shelfmark: 4542.507000.

350 658   UK   ISSN 0020-8523
INTERNATIONAL REVIEW OF ADMINISTRATIVE SCIENCES. French edition: Revue Internationale des Sciences Administratives. (Editions in English, French, Spanish) q. £38($63) to individuals; institutions £92($152). (International Institute of Administrative Sciences) Sage Publications Ltd., 6 Bonhill St., London EC2A 4PU, England. TEL 071-374-0645. FAX 071-374-8741. (Orders for French edition to: Etablissement Emile Bruylant, rue de la Regence 67, B-1000 Brussels, Belgium; Orders for Spanish edition to: I N A P, Santa Engracia 7, E-28010, Madrid, Spain.) Ed. Kenneth Kernaghan. adv.: color page £150; trim 193 x 114; adv. contact: Bernie Folan. bk.rev.; bibl.; index. cum.index every 5 yrs.; circ. 6,000 (English ed.); 5,000 (French ed.). (reprint service avail. from KTO) **Indexed:** A.B.C.Pol.Sci., ASSIA, BPIA, Cont.Pg.Manage., E.I., Int.Lab.Doc., Key to Econ.Sci., Manage.Cont., Mid.East: Abstr.& Ind., P.A.I.S., P.A.I.S.For.Lang.Ind.
    —BLDSC shelfmark: 4545.900000.
    Description: Presents comparative studies and national monographs on international administration, national civil services, controls on central government, administrative reform, public finance, regionalization and the history of administration.

INTERNATIONAL SECURITY DIRECTORY; world defense, police & fire headquarters, security companies, their products and supplies. see *CRIMINOLOGY AND LAW ENFORCEMENT — Security*

350   IT   ISSN 0074-9435
INTERNATIONAL UNION OF LATIN NOTARIES. PROCEEDINGS OF CONGRESS. 1948. biennial, Amsterdam - 19 Congress, 1989. International Union of Latin Notaries., Notaio Federico Guasti, Via Localtelli n. 5, 20124 Milan, Italy. TEL 864151. adv.; bk.rev.

350   US   ISSN 0074-106X
INTER-UNIVERSITY CASE PROGRAM. CASE STUDY. (Title varies: I C P Case Series; at head of title: Cases in Public Administration and Policy Information) 1951. irreg. price varies. Inter-University Case Program, Inc., Box 229, Syracuse, NY 13210. Ed. E.A. Bock.

350   US
IOWA LEGISLATIVE NEWS SERVICE BULLETIN. 1979. d.(during session); w.(between sessions). $250. Iowa Legislative News Service, Box 8370, Des Moines, IA 50301. TEL 515-288-4676. Ed. Jo von Stein. (delivery service avail.)
●Also available online.
    Description: Reports on bill introductions, standing committee meetings and interim committee meetings.

350   IQ
IRAQ. MINISTRY OF INFORMATION. INFORMATION SERIES. irreg., no.72, 1977. Ministry of Information, Baghdad, Iraq.

350   IQ
IRAQ GOVERNMENT GAZETTE. (Editions in Arabic and English) 1922. w. (English ed.) irreg. (Arabic ed.). Ministry of Information, Baghdad, Iraq. circ. 4,450 (4,000 Arabic ed.; 450 English ed.).

350   IE
IRIS OIFIGIUIL. (Text in English and Irish) 1922. s-w. £312. Stationery Office, Bishop St., Dublin 8, Ireland. Ed. B. Murray. circ. 600.

IRISH LAW REPORTS MONTHLY. see *LAW*

350   IS
ISRAEL. COMMISSIONER FOR COMPLAINTS FROM THE PUBLIC (OMBUDSMAN). ANNUAL REPORT. (Editions in Hebrew, occasionally in English) 1972. a. free. Commissioner for Complaints from the Public, Jerusalem, Israel. FAX 02-387768. circ. 2,000.

350   IS
ISRAEL GOVERNMENT YEAR BOOK. a. $35. I B R T Ltd., 17 Aza St., Jerusalem 92381, Israel. TEL 02-631622. FAX 02-630138.
    Description: Comprehensive coverage of issues and events of the preceding year.

354   IV
IVORY COAST. DIRECTION DU BUDGET SPECIAL D'INVESTISSEMENT ET D'EQUIPMENT. RAPPORT DE PRESENTATION DU BUDGET SPECIAL D'INVESTISSEMENT ET D'EQUIPMENT.* a. Direction du Budget Special d'Investissement et d'Equipement, Imprimerie Nationale, 7 av. Marchand, B.P. V 87, Abidjan, Ivory Coast. stat.

J C P S CONGRESSIONAL DISTRICT FACT BOOK. (Joint Center for Political Studies, Inc.) see *POLITICAL SCIENCE*

350   IS   ISSN 0021-3705
DS101
J N F ILLUSTRATED; journal of land reclamation, afforestation and environmental improvement. (Editions in English, French, German and Spanish) 1927. a. free. Jewish National Fund, P.O. Box 283, Jerusalem, Israel. TEL 02-291333. FAX 02-291311. Ed. Lenny Labensohn. charts; illus.; circ. 30,000.

350   TS
AL-JARIDAH AL-RASMIYYAH LI-DAWLAT AL-IMARAT AL-ARABIYYAH AL-MUTTAHIDAH/UNITED ARAB EMIRATES. OFFICIAL GAZETTE. (Text in Arabic) 1971. m. Wizarat al-Dawlah li-Shu'un Majlis al-Wuzara' - State Ministry of Cabinet Affairs, P.O. Box 899, Abu Dhabi, United Arab Emirates. TEL 651113. FAX 661172. Ed. Ahmad Muhammad Hamza. cum.index 1971-1985; circ. 13,000.
  Description: Publishes laws and governmental decisions from all U.A.E. Ministries.

JINGJI GAIGE/ECONOMIC REFORM. see *BUSINESS AND ECONOMICS — Economic Systems And Theories, Economic History*

JINGJI JUECE BAO/ECONOMIC POLICYMAKING. see *BUSINESS AND ECONOMICS — Economic Systems And Theories, Economic History*

350   MC
JOURNAL DE MONACO. 1858. w. 260 F. Ministry of State, Monaco. FAX 93-15-82-17. Ed. Rainier Imperti.

JOURNAL OF COLLECTIVE NEGOTIATIONS IN THE PUBLIC SECTOR. see *BUSINESS AND ECONOMICS — Labor And Industrial Relations*

350   CE   ISSN 0047-2360
JOURNAL OF DEVELOPMENT ADMINISTRATION. 1970. s-a. Rs.60($15) Sri Lanka Institute of Development Administration (SLIDA), c/o Additional Director (R.C. and P.), 28-10, Longdon Place, Colombo 07, Sri Lanka. Ed. K.P. Vimaladharma. bk.rev.; bibl.; charts; circ. 1,000. **Indexed:** Sri Lanka Sci.Ind.

350 320   US   ISSN 0276-8739
H97
JOURNAL OF POLICY ANALYSIS AND MANAGEMENT. 1981. 4/yr. $145 to institutions (foreign $195). (Association for Public Policy Analysis and Management) John Wiley & Sons, Inc., Journals, 605 Third Ave., New York, NY 10158-0012. TEL 212-850-6000. FAX 212-850-6088. Ed. David L. Weimer. adv.; bk.rev.; index; circ. 2,700. (also avail. in microform from RPI; back issues avail.; reprint service avail. from RPI) **Indexed:** A.B.C.Pol.Sci., Abstr.Health Care Manage.Stud., Amer.Bibl.Slavic & E.Eur.Stud., Amer.Hist.& Life, BPIA, Bus.Ind., Curr.Cont., Deep Sea Res.& Oceanogr.Abstr., Energy Ind., Energy Info.Abstr., Fut.Surv., Hist.Abstr., Human Resour.Abstr., INIS Atomind., J.of Econ.Lit., Med.Care Rev., Mid.East: Abstr.& Ind., P.A.I.S., Sage Pub.Admin.Abstr., Sage Urb.Stud.Abstr., Soc.Sci.Ind., Soc.Work Res.& Abstr., SSCI, Tr.& Indus.Ind.
  —BLDSC shelfmark: 5040.841400.
  Supersedes (1929-1981): Public Policy (Cambridge) (ISSN 0033-3646); (1953-1980): Policy Analysis (ISSN 0098-2067)
  Description: Encompasses issues and practices in policy analysis and public management for practitioners, researchers, economists, operations researchers, and consultants.

350   PK   ISSN 0047-2751
HC440.5.A1
JOURNAL OF RURAL DEVELOPMENT AND ADMINISTRATION (PARD). (Text in English) vol.12, 1977. q. $15. Pakistan Academy for Rural Development, Academy Town, Peshawar, Pakistan. TEL 40296. Ed. Hasan Medhi Naqvi. bk.rev.; bibl.; charts; stat.; circ. 1,000. **Indexed:** Irr.& Drain.Abstr., Poult.Abstr., Rural Devel.Abstr., Rural Ext.Educ.& Tr.Abstr., Soils & Fert., SSCI, World Agri.Econ.& Rural Sociol.Abstr.
  Formerly: Academy Quarterly.

JOURNAL OF STATE AND ADMINISTRATION. see *POLITICAL SCIENCE*

JOURNAL OF STATE GOVERNMENT; the in-depth journal of state affairs. see *POLITICAL SCIENCE*

350 320   GV   ISSN 0533-5701
JOURNAL OFFICIEL DE GUINEE. 1958. fortn. $16. Patrice Lumumba Printing Office, B.P. 156, Conakry, Guinea. adv.; illus.; stat.; circ. 700.

350   IV
JOURNAL OFFICIEL DE LA COTE D'IVOIRE. w. Service Autonome des Journaux Officiels, B.P. V70, Abidjan, Ivory Coast. TEL 22-67-76. circ. 1,000. (also avail. in microfilm from KTO)

350   FT
JOURNAL OFFICIEL DE LA REPUBLIQUE DE DJIBOUTI. (Text in French) 1977. irreg. 5720 Fr.CFA. Secretaire General du Gouvernement, Djibouti, Djibouti. (Subscr. to: Impr. Administrative, B.P. 268, Djibouti, Djibouti) adv.

350   CM
JOURNAL OFFICIEL DE LA REPUBLIQUE DU CAMEROUN. (Text in French) fortn. B.P. 1603, Yaounde, Cameroun. TEL 23-12-77. TELEX 8403. circ. 4,000. (also avail. in microfilm from BHP)

350   NG
JOURNAL OFFICIEL DE LA REPUBLIQUE DU NIGER. 1960. fortn. B.P. 116, Naimey, Niger. TEL 72-39-30. Ed. Bonkoula Aminatou Mayaki. circ. 800.

350   SG
JOURNAL OFFICIEL DE LA REPUBLIQUE DU SENEGAL. 1856. w. Rufisque, Senegal.

350   GO
JOURNAL OFFICIEL DE LA REPUBLIQUE GABONAISE. 1959. fortn. B.P. 563, Libreville, Gabon. Ed. Emmanuel Obame.

350   DM
JOURNAL OFFICIEL DE LA REPUBLIQUE POPULAIRE DU BENIN. fortn. Porto-Novo, Benin.

350   RW
JOURNAL OFFICIEL DE LA REPUBLIQUE RWANDAISE. (Text in French) vol.18, 1979. s-m. Service des Affaires Juriques de la Presidence de la Republique, Kigali, Rwanda. (Subscr. to: Imprimerie Nationale du Rwanda, B.P. 351, Kigali, Rwanda)

350   UV
JOURNAL OFFICIEL DU BURKINA. w. B.P. 568, Ouagadougou, Burkina Faso.

350   MR
JOURNAL PARLEMENTAIRE.* 1977. m. Editions La Porte, 281 av. Mohammed V, Rabat, Morocco. adv.

JUDICIAL STAFF DIRECTORY. see *LAW*

JURISPRUDENTIE VOOR GEMEENTEN. see *LAW*

350   KE   ISSN 0075-5761
K I A OCCASIONAL PAPERS. 1968. irreg., latest no. 4. price varies. Kenya Institute of Administration, P.O. Lower Kabete, Nairobi, Kenya. Ed. H.K.M. Wacirah.

352   NR
KADUNA STATE. MINISTRY OF WORKS. REPORT.* 1960. a. price varies. Ministry of Works, Kaduna, Nigeria.
  Formerly: North-Central State. Ministry of Works. Report (ISSN 0078-1762)

354.6   GH   ISSN 0022-7862
KAKYEVOLE. (Text in Nzema) 1956. m. NC.3.60. Information Services Department, P.O. Box 745, Accra, Ghana. Ed. J.M. Ngoah. adv.; circ. 10,000.

354.669   NR
KANO STATE OF NIGERIA GAZETTE. 1967. irreg. free. Government Printing Press, P.O. Box 469, Kano, Nigeria. circ. 3,500.
  Continues: Northern Nigeria Gazette.

KARNATAKA. DEPARTMENT OF TOURISM. ANNUAL REPORT. see *TRAVEL AND TOURISM*

320   US
KENTUCKY DIRECTORY OF BLACK ELECTED OFFICIALS. 1970. quadrennial. free. Commission on Human Rights, 500 Mero St., Ste. 832, Frankfort, KY 40601. TEL 502-564-3550. circ. 2,000.

350   US
KENTUCKY HORIZONS. 1988. m. $10. Legislative Research Commission, State Capitol, Rm. 300, Frankfort, KY 40601. TEL 502-564-8100. Ed. Peggy Hyland.
  Description: Covers emerging policy issues and innovative solutions to problems.

350 320   US
KENTUCKY JOURNAL. 1989. 10/yr. $20. (Kentucky Center for Public Issues) Robert F. Sexton, Ed.& Pub., 167 West Main St., Ste. 310, Lexington, KY 40507. TEL 606-255-5361. FAX 606-233-0760. adv.; bk.rev.; circ. 3,000. (newspaper)
  Description: Features ideas, research and current information on public policy in Kentucky.

338.9   KE
KENYA. MINISTRY OF FINANCE AND PLANNING. BUDGET SPEECH BY MINISTER FOR FINANCE AND PLANNING. (Text in English) a. Ministry of Finance and Planning, P.O. Box 30007, Nairobi, Kenya. (Dist. by: Government Printing and Stationery Department, P.O. Box 30128, Nairobi, Kenya)
  Former titles: Kenya. Ministry of Finance and Economic Planning. Budget Speech; Kenya. Ministry of Finance. Speech Delivered to the National Assembly, Presenting the Budget.

354   KE
KENYA. MINISTRY OF FINANCE AND PLANNING. PLAN IMPLEMENTATION REPORT. 1973. irreg. Ministry of Finance and Planning, P.O. Box 30007, Nairobi, Kenya. (Dist. by: Government Printing and Stationery Department, P.O. Box 30128, Nairobi, Kenya)

350   KE
KENYA. OFFICE OF THE DISTRICT COMMISSIONER. ANNUAL REPORT. a. Office of the District Commissioner, S. Nyanza District, P.O. Box 1, Homa Bay, Kenya.

350   KE   ISSN 0075-5931
KENYA. PUBLIC ACCOUNTS COMMITTEE. ANNUAL REPORT. a. EAs.34. Government Printing and Stationery Department, P.O. Box 30128, Nairobi, Kenya.

350   KE
KENYA GAZETTE. (Text in English) w. EAs.1385 in East Africa; EAs.1835 elsewhere. Government Printing and Stationery Department, P.O. Box 30128, Nairobi, Kenya. index. (also avail. in microfilm from KTO)

350   KE
KENYA GAZETTE SUPPLEMENT. (Issued in 3 parts: Acts, Bills and Legislative Supplement) (Text in English) irreg. Government Printing and Stationery Department, P.O. Box 30128, Nairobi, Kenya. index.

KNIGHT'S LOCAL GOVERNMENT REPORTS. see *LAW*

350   DK   ISSN 0085-2589
KONGELIG DANSK HOF- OG STATSKALENDER; STATSHAANDBOG FOR KONGERIGET DANMARK. 1734. a. price varies. Schultz Information A-S, Ottiliavej 18, DK-2500 Valby, Denmark. Eds. Herluf Nielsen, Morten Estrup. adv.; circ. 2,000.
  Description: Handbook covering all state employees down to wage rate 20 (the level of assistant leaders).

KUTLWANO/MUTUAL UNDERSTANDING. see *POLITICAL SCIENCE*

354.536   KU   ISSN 0023-575X
KUWAIT AL-YOUM. 1954. w. kD. 15. Ministry of Information, P.O. Box 193, Kuwait. FAX 2467770. TELEX 46151 MI KT. circ. 5,000.
  Description: Arabic language review of Kuwaiti official decrees, laws, decisions, and tenders.

LABOR (YEAR). see *BUSINESS AND ECONOMICS — Labor And Industrial Relations*

363.6 US
LAMPPOST. 1977. irreg. (every 2-3 mos.). Orange and Rockland Utilities, Inc., One Blue Hill Plaza, Pearl River, NY 10965. TEL 914-577-2546. Ed. Jonathan L. Yoder. circ. 4,000.
  Description: Company and utility news for employees and utility professionals.

LAND RIGHTS NEWS; a newspaper for Aboriginals people and their supporters. see *POLITICAL SCIENCE — Civil Rights*

354.4 AU ISSN 0023-7876
LANDESAMTSBLATT FUER DAS BURGENLAND. 1921. w. S.200. Amt der Burgenlaendischen Landesregierung, Landesamtsdirektion, Freiheitsplatz 1, A-7001 Eisenstadt, Austria. adv.; bk.rev.; index. (looseleaf format)

350 GW
LANDESHAUPTSTADT STUTTGART. AMTSBLATT. 1901. w. DM.26.40. Landeshauptstadt Stuttgart, Presse- und Informationsamt, Rathaus, Postfach 106034, 7000 Stuttgart 10, Germany. FAX 0711-2167705. bk.rev.; charts; circ. 62,000. (back issues avail.)
  Formerly: Stuttgart. Amtsblatt.

DER LANDKREIS. see *HOUSING AND URBAN PLANNING*

350 US
LANE STUDIES IN REGIONAL GOVERNMENT. irreg. price varies. University of California Press, 2120 Berkeley Way, Berkeley, CA 94720. TEL 415-642-4247. FAX 415-643-7127.
  Refereed Serial

350 301 CN ISSN 0709-7751
P40
LANGUAGE AND SOCIETY/LANGUE ET SOCIETE. (Text in English and French) 1979. q. free. Office of the Commissioner of Official Languages, Rm. 1421 110 O'Connor St., Ottawa, Ont. K1A 0T8, Canada. TEL 613-995-0730. **Indexed:** Amer.Bibl.Slavic & E.Eur.Stud.

LEGAL ISSUES, GOVERNMENT PROGRAMS & THE ELDERLY (FLORIDA); a handbook for the advocates. see *LAW — Legal Aid*

350 US
LEGISCON STATEHOUSE REPORT. 1975. w. $300. Box 1643, Baton Rouge, LA 70821. TEL 504-343-9828. FAX 504-338-5243. Ed. James A. Lee.
  Description: Covers Louisiana executive branch activity, interim legislative action and judicial decisions affecting state government.

350 US
LEGISLATIVE FINANCE PAPERS. 1985. irreg. (approx. 4/yr.). price varies. National Conference of State Legislatures, 1560 Broadway, Ste. 700, Denver, CO 80202-5140. TEL 303-830-2200. FAX 303-863-8003.
  Description: Comprehensive studies on state tax revenue and expenditure issues.

350 US
LEGISLATIVE GAZETTE. 1978. w.(except Jul.-Aug.). $99. Research Foundation of State University of New York, Box 7023, Albany, NY 12225. TEL 518-473-9732. Ed. Glenn C. Doty. adv.; circ. 18,000.
  Description: Covers New York legislative and related state government activity.

LEGISLATIVE STUDIES QUARTERLY. see *POLITICAL SCIENCE*

LEISURE MANAGER. see *LEISURE AND RECREATION*

350 LB
LIBERIA. INSTITUTE OF PUBLIC ADMINISTRATION. ANNUAL REPORT.* 1973. a. free. Institute of Public Administration, Monrovia, Liberia. circ. 200.

354 LB
LIBERIA. MINISTRY OF ACTION FOR DEVELOPMENT AND PROGRESS. ANNUAL REPORT.* a. Ministry of Action for Development and Progress, Monrovia, Liberia.

354 LB ISSN 0304-7326
HD4366.L5
LIBERIA. MINISTRY OF PUBLIC WORKS. ANNUAL REPORT.* (Text in English) a. Ministry of Public Works, Monrovia, Liberia.

350 LB
LIBERIA. OFFICE OF NATIONAL PLANNING. ANNUAL REPORT TO THE PRESIDENT ON THE OPERATION AND ACTIVITIES.* 1961. a. Ministry of Planning and Economic Affairs, Randall St., P.O. Box 9016, Monrovia, Liberia.
  Formerly: Liberia. Bureau of Economic Research and Statistics. Annual Report to the President on the Operation and Activities.

LIBRARY ADMINISTRATOR'S DIGEST. see *LIBRARY AND INFORMATION SCIENCES*

LOBBYING RESOURCE DIRECTORY; a practical guide to sources of information and assistance for lobbyists, legislative advocates and citizen activists. see *LAW*

350 AT
LOCAL GOVERNMENT PLANNING & ENVIRONMENT SERVICE N S W. (Volume A: Local Government Act & Index; Volume B: Legislation & Acts; Volume C: Commentary) 3 base vols. (vols. A & B updated 6/yr.; vol. C updated 4/yr.). $555. Butterworths Pty. Ltd., 271-273 Lane Cove Rd., P.O. Box 345, N. Ryde, N.S.W. 2113, Australia. TEL 02-335-4444. FAX 02-335-4655. (looseleaf format)

340 352 AT ISSN 0076-0242
LAW
LOCAL GOVERNMENT REPORTS OF AUSTRALIA. 1956. irreg. Law Book Co. Ltd., 44-50 Waterloo Rd., North Ryde, N.S.W. 2112, Australia. TEL 02-887-0177. FAX 02-888-9706. TELEX ASBOOK 27995. Ed. Kenneth Gifford.
  ●Also available online.
  Description: Reports decisions relating to environmental control, local government, valuation of land, compensation, town planning and powers and duties of statutory authorities throughout Australia. Includes decisions of the NSW Land and Environment Court from authorized reports.

LOKAAL & MONDIAL - VAKMATIG. see *POLITICAL SCIENCE — International Relations*

350 340 US
LOUISIANA ADMINISTRATIVE CODE. a. $821 includes supplement. Division of Administration, Office of the State Register, Box 94095, Baton Rouge, LA 70804-9095. TEL 504-342-5015. Ed. Suzanne McAndrew. circ. 2,000. (back issues avail.)

350 340 US
LOUISIANA REGISTER. 1975. m. $80. Division of Administration, Office of the State Register, Box 94095, Baton Rouge, LA 70804-9095. TEL 504-342-5015. Ed. Suzanne McAndrew. index; circ. 957. (back issues avail.)

350 US
M A P A ANNUAL REPORT. a. free. Omaha - Council Bluffs Metropolitan Area Planning Agency, 2222 Cuming St., Omaha, NE 68102-4328. TEL 402-444-6866. FAX 402-342-0949. circ. 1,000.

350 US
M A P A COMMUNITY ASSISTANCE REPORT. a. free. Omaha - Council Bluffs Metropolitan Area Planning Agency, 2222 Cuming St., Omaha, NE 68102-4328. TEL 402-444-6866. FAX 402-342-0949. circ. 1,000.

350 320 US
M I R S LEGISLATIVE REPORT. 1961. d. $1200. Michigan Information and Research Service, Inc., 421 West Ionia, Lansing, MI 48933. TEL 517-482-2125. FAX 517-482-1307. Ed. Todd W. Carter.
  Description: Summarizes news regarding Michigan elections, politics, legislative and state government issues. Includes bill status information, committee and meeting schedules, and other related information and services.

M S B A IN BRIEF. (Minnesota State Bar Association) see *LAW*

350 320 US ISSN 0732-0205
MCCARVILLE - HILL REPORT. 1980. 48/yr. $104. McCarville - Hill Publications, Box 30647, Midwest City, OK 73140. TEL 405-737-6021. FAX 405-737-0058. Eds. Mike McCarville, Neva Hill.
  Former titles: McCarville - Gray Report & McCarville Report.
  Description: Report on Oklahoma government and politics.

MCGRAW-HILL'S WASHINGTON REPORT ON MEDICINE AND HEALTH. see *MEDICAL SCIENCES*

MAINE ADMINISTRATIVE PROCEDURE. see *LAW*

MAINE REGISTER: STATE YEARBOOK AND LEGISLATIVE MANUAL. see *PUBLIC ADMINISTRATION — Municipal Government*

350 IO ISSN 0125-9652
MAJALAH ADMINISTRASI NEGARA; Indonesian journal of public administration. 1959. q. Rps.6000. Lembaga Administrasi Negara, Jl. Veteran 10, Jakarta, Indonesia. adv.; bibl.; illus.; circ. 1,000.

350 JO ISSN 1010-0709
AL-MAJALLAH AL-ARABIYYAH LIL-IDARAH/ARAB JOURNAL OF ADMINISTRATION. (Text in Arabic) 1977. q. $30 to individuals; institutions $50. Arab Administrative Development Organization - Al-Munathamah al-Arabiyyah lil-Tanmiah al-Idariyyah, P.O. Box 17159, Amman, Jordan. TEL 814118. FAX 816972. TELEX 21594 ARADO JO. Ed. Ahmed Sakr Ashour. adv.; bk.rev.; circ. 2,000. (back issues avail.)
  Description: Covers contemporary issues in administrative policy and practice, including case studies, responses to problems, development of administrative sciences in the Arab world, as well as a review of relevant experiences from international literature.
  Refereed Serial

350 MW
MALAWI. ECONOMIC PLANNING DIVISION. MID-YEAR ECONOMIC REVIEW. (Text in English) 1971. a. Government Printer, P.O. Box 37, Zomba, Malawi.

350 MW
MALAWI. GOVERNMENT PRINTER. CATALOGUE OF PUBLICATIONS. (Text in English) 1974. q. Government Printer, P.O. Box 37, Zomba, Malawi.

350 MW
MALAWI GAZETTE SUPPLEMENT CONTAINING ACTS. (Text in English) irreg. Government Printer, P.O. Box 37, Zomba, Malawi.

350 MW
MALAWI GAZETTE SUPPLEMENT CONTAINING BILLS. (Text in English) irreg. Government Printer, P.O. Box 37, Zomba, Malawi.

350 MW
MALAWI GAZETTE SUPPLEMENT CONTAINING REGULATIONS, RULES, ETC.. (Text in English) irreg. Government Printer, P.O. Box 37, Zomba, Malawi.

350 MW
MALAWI GOVERNMENT DIRECTORY. (Text in English) a. Government Printer, P.O. Box 37, Zomba, Malawi.

350 MW
MALAWI GOVERNMENT GAZETTE. (Text in English) vol.4, 1967. w. K.12.60. Ministry of Finance, Government Printer, P.O. Box 37, Zomba, Malawi. index.

350 658 II ISSN 0047-570X
MANAGEMENT IN GOVERNMENT. 1969. q. Rs.80($28) Department of Administrative Reforms and Public Grievances, Sardar Patel Bhawan, Parliament St., New Delhi 110 001, India. TEL 311646. Ed. S.K. Muttoo. bk.rev.; abstr.; bibl.; charts; illus.; circ. 2,000. **Indexed:** Key to Econ.Sci.

333 US
MANAGING THE NATION'S PUBLIC LANDS. 1980. a. U.S. Department of the Interior, Bureau of Land Management, Washington, DC 20240.
  Description: Describes management of U.S. public lands. Includes Bureau's accomplishments, issues, goals for the preceding fiscal year.

PUBLIC ADMINISTRATION 4067

363.6   AT
MANPOWER SERVICES GUIDE. 1980. a. free. Australian Government Publishing Service, G.P.O. Box 84, Canberra, A.C.T. 2601, Australia. circ. 100,000.

338.9 350   FR   ISSN 0542-6685
MARCHES PUBLICS; la revue de l'achat public. 1953. 8/yr. 360 F. (foreign 390 F.). Ministere de l'Economie des Finances et du Budget, Commission Centrale des Marches, Tour de Lyon, 185 rue de Bercy, 75572 Paris Cedex 12, France. TEL 48-39-56-00. FAX 43-44-90-14. (Subscr. to: Documentation Francaise, 29-31 Quai Voltaire, 75340 Paris Cedex 07, France) Ed. Bernard Gosselin. bk.rev.; bibl.; stat.; index. cum.index; circ. 6,000. (back issues avail.)
—BLDSC shelfmark: 5369.870000.

MARK SIEGEL AND ASSOCIATES WASHINGTON INSIDER. see *POLITICAL SCIENCE*

141 310   US   ISSN 0094-4491
JK3831
MARYLAND MANUAL; a guide to Maryland state government. Title varies: Manual-State of Maryland. 1896. biennial. $20. State Archives, 350 Rowe Blvd., Annapolis, MD 21401. TEL 301-974-3916. FAX 301-974-3895. Ed. Diane P. Frese. charts; illus.; stat.; index; circ. 8,000. (back issues avail.)

348   US   ISSN 0360-2834
MARYLAND REGISTER. 1974. fortn. $85. Division of State Documents, Box 802, Annapolis, MD 21404. TEL 301-974-2486. FAX 301-974-2546. Ed. Robert J. Colborn, Jr. index; circ. 3,700.
Description: Official text of all proposed, adopted and emergency regulations, court rules, governor's executive orders, agency hearing and meeting notices and state contract information.

350 340   US   ISSN 0360-2834
MARYLAND REGISTER. STATE CONTRACT SUPPLEMENT. 1985. fortn. $120. Division of State Documents, Box 802, Annapolis, MD 21404. TEL 301-974-2486. FAX 301-974-2546. Ed. Robert J. Colborn, Jr. circ. 2,200.
Description: State contract bid solicitation and award information.

350 320   US   ISSN 1042-1564
MARYLAND REPORT. 1989. bi-w. $200. Bancroft Information Group, Inc., Box 65360, Baltimore, MD 21209. TEL 301-358-0658. FAX 301-358-0658. Ed. Bruce L. Bortz. (also avail. in microfiche from BHP)
Description: News, analysis of Maryland government, politics and business.

350   MF
MAURITIUS. LEGISLATIVE ASSEMBLY. DEBATES. (Text in English) irreg., 4th session, no.9, 1980. Government Printing Office, Elizabeth II Ave., Port Louis, Mauritius.

350   MF   ISSN 0076-5503
MAURITIUS. LEGISLATIVE ASSEMBLY. SESSIONAL PAPER. irreg., latest 1972. price varies. Government Printing Office, Elizabeth II Ave., Port Louis, Mauritius.

MAURITIUS. MINISTRY OF WORKS AND INTERNAL COMMUNICATIONS. REPORT. see *TRANSPORTATION*

350   MF
MAURITIUS. OMBUDSMAN. REPORT. (Text in English) irreg., latest 1980. Government Printing Office, Elizabeth II Ave., Port Louis, Mauritius.

350   MF
MAURITIUS. PUBLIC SERVICE COMMISSION. REPORT. (Text in English) triennial, latest 1978. Government Printing Office, Elizabeth II Ave., Port Louis, Mauritius.

334   FR   ISSN 0025-9179
MEMORIAL DES PERCEPTEURS ET RECEVEURS DES COMMUNES. 1826. m. 450 F. Publications Paul Dupont, 38 rue Croix des Petits Champs, 75001 Paris, France. index.

MICHIGAN. DEPARTMENT OF SOCIAL SERVICES. ASSISTANCE PAYMENTS STATISTICS. see *SOCIAL SERVICES AND WELFARE*

MICHIGAN STATE EMPLOYEES' RETIREMENT SYSTEM FINANCIAL AND STATISTICAL REPORT. see *BUSINESS AND ECONOMICS — Labor And Industrial Relations*

350   DK   ISSN 0085-3461
MINISTERIALTIDENDE FOR KONGERIGET DANMARK. 1871. w. DKK 475. Justisministeriet, Sekretariatet for Retsinformation, Axeltorv 6, 5. sal, DK-1609 Copenhagen V, Denmark. TEL 33-32-52-22. FAX 33-91-28-01. index; circ. 2,007.
●Also available online.
Formerly (until 1977): Ministerialtidende for Kongeriget Danmark. Afdeling A (ISSN 0901-5000)
Description: Official organ for promulgating Departmental circulars and Departmental orders, etc., which may not require promulgation by law.

350 340   US
MINNESOTA ADMINISTRATIVE PROCEDURE. 1987. base vol. (plus suppl.) $75. Butterworth Legal Publishers (Salem) (Subsidiary of: Reed International PLC), 90 Stiles Rd., Salem, NH 03079. TEL 800-548-4001. FAX 603-898-9858. Ed.Bd.
Description: Explanation of state administrative procedure in Minnesota, with special attention to the contested case, the adjudicative process and how rules are made by state agencies.

350   US
MINNESOTA GOVERNMENT REPORT. 1978. s-w. $240. Box 441, Willernie, MN 55090. TEL 612-296-6561. Ed. Jean L. Dawson.
Description: Covers Minnesota state government, including appellate court activity.

340   US
MINNESOTA GUIDEBOOK TO STATE AGENCY SERVICES. 1977. quadrennial. $18. Department of Administration, Print Communications Division, 117 University Ave., St. Paul, MN 55155. TEL 612-297-3000. Ed. Robin PanLener. index; circ. 12,500.

MINNESOTA RULES. see *LAW*

MINNESOTA RULES. SUPPLEMENT. see *LAW*

MINNESOTA STATE REGISTER. see *LAW*

350   GW
MITTEILUNGEN DER FACHHOCHSCHULE DES BUNDES. 1979. q. free. Fachhochschule des Bundes fuer Oeffentliche Verwaltung, Bernhard-Feilchenfeld-Str. 9-11, 5000 Cologne 51, Germany. TEL 0221-3670-0. FAX 0221-3670-185. Ed.Bd. adv.; bk.rev.; circ. 900. (back issues avail.)
Description: Information and news of the German Federal Institute for Public Administration. Covers curriculum, activities, events.

350   US
MONTANA. DEPARTMENT OF COMMERCE. PROFESSIONAL AND OCCUPATIONAL LICENSING BUREAU. PUBLIC SAFETY DIVISION. BIENNIAL REPORT. biennial. Department of Commerce, Professional and Occupational Licensing Bureau, Public Safety Division, 111 N. Jackson, Helena, MT 59620-0407. TEL 406-444-3737.
Formerly: Montana. Department of Business Regulation. Annual Report (ISSN 0093-8246)

MONTANA. OFFICE OF THE LEGISLATIVE AUDITOR. STATE OF MONTANA BOARD OF INVESTMENTS. REPORT ON EXAMINATION OF FINANCIAL STATEMENTS. see *BUSINESS AND ECONOMICS — Investments*

350   BG
MONTHLY PRATIRODHA. 1976. s-m. Tk.36. Ministry of Home Affairs, Jatiya Gram Pratirakaha Committee, Khilgoan, Dhaka 1219, Bangladesh. Ed. Jahangir Habibullah. adv.; bk.rev.
Formerly: Pakshika Pratirodha.

350   CN
MUNICIPAL OPEN LINE. 1964. m. Can.$10. Union of Nova Scotia Municipalities, Suite 132-136 Roy Bldg., 1657 Barrington St., Halifax, N.S. B3J 2A1, Canada. TEL 902-423-8331. FAX 902-425-5592. Ed. Ken Simpson. bk.rev.; circ. 880.

350   UK   ISSN 0077-4456
N A L G O ANNUAL REPORT. 1906. a. National and Local Government Officers Association, NALGO House, 1 Mabledon Place, London WC1H 9AJ, England. TEL 01-388 2366. FAX 01-387-6692. Ed. John D. Daly. circ. 2,500.
Description: Details municipal issues: economics, service conditions, education, finance, law and welfare.

350.6 663.1   US
N C S L A MINUTES OF ANNUAL MEETING. 1937. a. $25. National Conference of State Liquor Administrators, 301 Centennial Mall, S., Lincoln, NE 68509. TEL 402-471-2571. Ed. Randy Yarbrough. circ. 100.

350.6 663.1   US
N C S L A OFFICIAL DIRECTORY. a. $5. National Conference of State Liquor Administrators, 300 Centennial Mall, S., Lincoln, NE 68509. TEL 402-471-2571. Ed. Randy Yarbrough. circ. 100.
Description: Directory of all state agencies administrating alcoholic beverage laws.

350   US   ISSN 0899-5052
N C S L CONFERENCE REPORT. q. $20 (Canada $23). National Conference of State Legislatures, 1560 Broadway, Ste. 700, Denver, CO 80202-5140. TEL 303-830-2200. FAX 303-863-8003.
Description: Communicates to legislators, staff, and those wanting to keep abreast of the many varied services and activities of the NCSL.

350   US   ISSN 0898-4298
N C S L FEDERAL UPDATE. 1975. 15/yr. $35 (Canada $38). National Conference of State Legislatures, 1560 Broadway, Ste. 700, Denver, CO 80202. TEL 303-830-2200. FAX 303-863-8003.
Former titles (until 1987): Capital to Capital; Dateline Washington.
Description: Informs legislators and legislative staff on federal issues.

350   UK
N H S ECONOMIC REVIEW (YEAR). (National Health Service) 1983. a. £10. Birmingham Research Park, Vincent Dr., Birmingham B15 2SQ, England. TEL 021-471 4444. FAX 021-414-1120. circ. 750. (back issues avail.)
Description: Sets in context the economic issues confronting the National Health Service (NHS) by taking a broad look at the activities and staffing of the health service, along with the challenges in health care for the present and coming years.

N S F BULLETIN. (U.S. National Science Foundation) see *SCIENCES: COMPREHENSIVE WORKS*

352.7   TS
NASHRAT AL-ISKAN WAL-ASHGHAL/WORKS AND HOUSING BULLETIN. (Text in Arabic) 1988. m. free. Wizarat al-Ashgal al-Aamah wal-Iskan, Al-Lajnah al-I'lamiyyah - Ministry of Pulbic Works and Housing, Information Committee, P.O. Box 878, Abu Dhabi, United Arab Emirates. TEL 651778. FAX 665598. TELEX 23833 EM. Ed. Muhammad Yusuf al-Awadi. adv.; illus.; stat.; circ. 1,000.
Formerly: United Arab Emirates. Ministry of Public Works and Housing. News Bulletin.
Description: News of ministry activities.

NATIONAL ARCHIVES OF ZAMBIA. CALENDARS OF THE DISTRICT NOTEBOOKS. see *HISTORY — History Of Africa*

350   US
NATIONAL ASSOCIATION OF REGIONAL COUNCILS. REGIONAL REPORTER. m. membership. National Association of Regional Councils, 1700 K St. N.W., Washington, DC 20006. TEL 202-296-0710. FAX 202-296-9352. Ed. Beverly Nykwest. circ. 2,000. (newspaper)
Incorporates (1986-1989): National Association of Regional Councils. News and Notes; Which supersedes: Director's News; Incorporates (1975-1989): National Association of Regional Councils. Washington Report (ISSN 0196-4003); Which supersedes: National Service to Regional Councils. Special Reports (ISSN 0028-0135); Which incorporates: Regional Review Quarterly (ISSN 0034-3382)

353.008   US
NATIONAL ASSOCIATION OF REGULATORY UTILITY COMMISSIONERS. ANNUAL REPORT ON UTILITY AND CARRIER REGULATION. a. $70. National Association of Regulatory Utility Commissioners, 1102 Interstate Commerce Commission Bldg., Box 684, Washington, DC 20044-0684. TEL 202-898-2200. FAX 202-898-2213.

PUBLIC ADMINISTRATION

363.6 352   US   ISSN 0027-8645
HD2766.A3
NATIONAL ASSOCIATION OF REGULATORY UTILITY COMMISSIONERS. BULLETIN. Short title: N A R U C Bulletin. Variant title: Blue Bulletin. 1916. w. $100. National Association of Regulatory Utility Commissioners, 1102 Interstate Commerce Commission Bldg., Box 684, Washington, DC 20044-0684. TEL 202-898-2200. FAX 202-898-2213. Ed. Paul Rodgers. index; circ. 1,600.
   Formerly: National Association of Railroad and Utilities Commissioners. Bulletin.

350   US
NATIONAL BALLOT ISSUES MONITOR. 1989. m. $300. Ballot Monitor Corporation, 1043 Cecil Pl., N.W., Washington, DC 20007. TEL 202-337-0061. Ed. Richard Glaub.
   Description: Provides latest information on important initiative and referenda measures throughout the United States.

NATIONAL CONTRACT MANAGEMENT JOURNAL (1980). see BUSINESS AND ECONOMICS — Management

350 690   US   ISSN 0360-7941
HD3840
NATIONAL DEVELOPMENT. 1954. 6/yr. $75. Intercontinental Publications, Inc., 25 Sylvan Rd. S., Box 5017, Westport, CT 06880. TEL 203-226-7463. FAX 203-222-8793. Ed. Daniel Wasserman. adv.; illus.; circ. 22,000 (controlled).
   Incorporating: Modern Engineering Technology; **Formerly:** Modern Government (ISSN 0026-7791)
   Description: Infrastructure development news for government representatives, construction companies and engineers in developing countries of Asia, Middle East and Africa.

350   AT   ISSN 1030-6641
JQ4021
NATIONAL GUIDE TO GOVERNMENT; and the bureaucracy. 1983. q. Aus.$165. Information Australia, 45 Flinders Lane, Melbourne, Vic. 3000, Australia. TEL 03 654 2800. Ed. Carol Chandler. circ. 800.

NATIONAL HOUSING REGISTER. see HOUSING AND URBAN PLANNING

NATIONAL ORDER OF WOMEN LEGISLATORS NEWS & VIEWS. see WOMEN'S INTERESTS

350   UK
NATIONAL UNION FOR CIVIL AND PUBLIC SERVANTS. JOURNAL. 1923. m. £12. National Union for Civil and Public Servants, 124-130 Southwark St., London SE1 OTU, England. TEL 01-928-9671. FAX 01-401-2693. Ed. Nick Wright. adv.; bk.rev.; illus.; circ. 130,000.
   Incorporates: Whip (ISSN 0043-485X); Former titles (until 1987): Opinion; Civil Service Opinion (ISSN 0009-8027)

336.782   US
NEBRASKA. DEPARTMENT OF ADMINISTRATIVE SERVICES. ANNUAL FISCAL REPORT. Cover title: State of Nebraska Annual Fiscal Report. 1966. a. free. Department of Administrative Services, Lincoln, NE 68509. TEL 402-471-3593. illus.; stat.; circ. 350.
   Former titles: Nebraska. Accounting Division. Annual Fiscal Report; Nebraska. Accounting Division. Annual Report of Receipts and Disbursements (ISSN 0090-628X)

NEUE MITTE; Stimme der Katholiken in Wirtschaft und Verwaltung. see RELIGIONS AND THEOLOGY — Roman Catholic

353.9   US
NEVADA. OFFICE OF LEGISLATIVE AUDITOR. BIENNIAL REPORT. (Subseries of: Nevada. Legislative Counsel Bureau. Bulletin) 1974. biennial. Office of Legislative Auditor, Carson City, NV 89710. TEL 702-885-5622. stat.
   Formerly: Nevada. Office of Fiscal Analyst. Annual Report (ISSN 0092-6841)

353.9 015   US
NEVADA OFFICIAL PUBLICATIONS. 1953. q. free. State Library, Capitol Complex, Carson City, NV 89710. Ed. Ann Brinkmeyer. bibl.; index. cum.index; circ. 525. (processed) **Indexed:** P.A.I.S.
   Formerly: Nevada State Library. Official Nevada Publications (ISSN 0028-4106)
   Description: Listing of all new Nevada state, county and city documents added to the State Library collection.

350   US
NEW DIRECTIONS IN PUBLIC ADMINISTRATION RESEARCH. 1987. s-a. $33. Florida Atlantic University, College of Urban and Public Affairs, 220 S.E. Second Ave., Fort Lauderdale, FL 33301. TEL 305-355-5219. Ed. Jay Mendell. circ. 300. (back issues avail.) **Indexed:** Int.Polit.Sci.Abstr., P.A.I.S.
   Description: Covers new methods and research fields in public administration.

340   US
NEW HAMPSHIRE CODE OF ADMINISTRATIVE RULES ANNOTATED. 1984. 6 base vols. (plus suppl. 1-2/yr.). $300. Butterworth Legal Publishers (Salem) (Subsidiary of: Reed International PLC), 90 Stiles Rd., Salem, NH 03079. TEL 800-548-4001. FAX 603-898-9858. Ed.Bd. (looseleaf format)
   Description: Codification of the administrative rules of 24 selected agencies and departments.

NEW HAMPSHIRE REGISTER: STATE YEARBOOK AND LEGISLATIVE MANUAL. see PUBLIC ADMINISTRATION — Municipal Government

350   US
NEW JERSEY COMPREHENSIVE ANNUAL FINANCIAL REPORT. a. Department of the Treasury, Division of Budget and Accounting, Office of Management and Budget, CN 221, Trenton, NJ 08625.
   Formerly: State of New Jersey Annual Financial Report.

350   US   ISSN 0300-6069
KFN2240
NEW JERSEY REGISTER. 1969. fortn. $75. Office of Administrative Law, CN 301, Trenton, NJ 08625. TEL 609-588-6601. Ed. N. Olsson. cum.index; circ. 2,900.

350 340   US
NEW MEXICO LOCAL AND FEDERAL RULES HANDBOOK. 1976. 2 base vols. (plus q. suppl.). $135. Butterworth Legal Publishers (Salem) (Subsidiary of: Reed International PLC), 90 Stiles Rd., Salem, NH 03079. TEL 800-548-4001. FAX 603-898-9858. Ed.Bd. (looseleaf format)
   Description: Complete and current compilation of rules applicable to New Mexico practice.

NEW RESOURCES. see BIBLIOGRAPHIES

NEW SOUTH WALES. DEPARTMENT OF AGRICULTURE. ANNUAL REPORT. see AGRICULTURE

350   AT   ISSN 0155-6320
NEW SOUTH WALES, AUSTRALIA, GOVERNMENT GAZETTE. 1845. w. Aus.$320. N.S.W. Government Printing Office, 390 Harris St., Ultimo, N.S.W. 2007, Australia. FAX 612-660-4940. TELEX AA73420. stat.; cum.index; circ. 1,800.

352   US
NEW YORK (STATE) DEPARTMENT OF STATE. MANUAL FOR THE USE OF THE LEGISLATURE OF THE STATE OF NEW YORK; New York State Legislative manual. 1827. biennial. $20. Department of State, Division of Information Services, 162 Washington Ave., Albany, NY 12231. Dir. Maureen L. Bigness. circ. 15,500.
   Description: Information on executive, legislative and judicial branches of state government; state and federal constitutions.

350   US
NEW YORK (STATE) LEGISLATIVE COMMISSION ON EXPENDITURE REVIEW. PROGRAM AUDITS. 1971. irreg. free. Legislative Commission on Expenditure Review, 111 Washington Ave., Albany, NY 12210. Dir. James J. Haag. circ. 1,000.

NEW YORK EMPLOYER'S ALERT. see BUSINESS AND ECONOMICS — Labor And Industrial Relations

NEW YORK EMPLOYER'S GUIDE. see BUSINESS AND ECONOMICS — Labor And Industrial Relations

350   US
NEW YORK RED BOOK. 1895. biennial. $50. New York Legal Publishing Corp., 6 Charles Park, Guilderland, NY 12084. TEL 800-541-2681. FAX 518-456-0828. Ed. George A. Mitchell. circ. 15,000.

353.9   US
NEW YORK SEA GRANT INSTITUTE. ANNUAL REPORT. 1973-1986; resumed 1992. a. New York Sea Grant Institute, Dutchess Hall, State University of New York at Stony Brook, Stony Brook, NY 11794-5001. TEL 516-632-6905. adv.; bk.rev.; illus.; circ. 1,500.
   Formerly: New York State Sea Grant Program. Annual Report (ISSN 0360-3326)

353.97   US   ISSN 0883-1548
Q224.3.U62
NEW YORK STATE MUSEUM. BIENNIAL REPORT. biennial. free. New York State Museum, 3140 Cultural Education Center, Albany, NY 12230. circ. 1,000.
   Formerly: New York State Science Service. Biennial Report.

338.9   US   ISSN 0077-9423
NEW YORK STATE URBAN DEVELOPMENT CORPORATION. ANNUAL REPORT. 1969-1975; resumed 1977. a. free. Urban Development Corporation, 1515 Broadway, New York, NY 10036. TEL 212-930-0305. FAX 212-930-0444. circ. controlled.

350   UK
NEWS FOR INDUSTRY, COMMERCE AND EDUCATION. 1985. q. Bradford and Ilkley Community College, Great Horton Rd., Bradford W., Yorkshire BD7 1AY, England. TEL 0274-753089. FAX 0274-753173. Ed. R.T. Sweeney. adv.; circ. 9,499.

NEWS ON WOMEN IN GOVERNMENT. see WOMEN'S INTERESTS

NGUOI DAI BIEU NHAN DAN/PEOPLE'S DEPUTY. see POLITICAL SCIENCE

350   BE
NIEUW KLIMAAT. (Text in Dutch) 1958. bi-m. 300 Fr. Verbond Vlaams Overheidspersoneel, Rykeklazenstraat, 45, B-1000 Brussels, Belgium. Ed. P. Stoppie. adv.; bk.rev.; circ. 6,500.

350   JA
NIPPON GYOSEI KENKYU NENPO/JAPANESE SOCIETY FOR PUBLIC ADMINISTRATION. ANNALS.* (Text in Japanese) a. Nippon Gyosei Gakkai - Japanese Society for Public Administration, c/o Faculty of Law, University of Tokyo, Tokyo Daigaku Hogakubu, Motofuji-cho, Bunkyo-ku, Tokyo 113, Japan. bibl.

354.4   DK   ISSN 0029-1285
NORDISK ADMINISTRATIVT TIDSSKRIFT. (Text in Danish, Norwegian and Swedish) 1919. q. DKK 225. Nordiske Administrative Forbund, c/o Indenrigsministeriet, Christiansborg Stotsplads 1, DK-1218 Copenhagen K, Denmark. Ed. Marius Ibsen. adv.; bk.rev.; bibl.; charts; stat.; circ. 2,400. **Indexed:** Amer.Hist.& Life, Hist.Abstr.

NORDRHEIN-WESTFAELISCHE VERWALTUNGBLAETTER; Zeitschrift fuer Oeffentliches Recht und Oeffentliche Verwaltung. see LAW

350   GW
▼**NORDRHEIN-WESTFALEN. FINANZMINISTERIUM. FINANZ REPORT.** 1991. q. Finanzministerium des Landes Nordrhein-Westfalen, Jaegerhofstr. 6, 4000 Duesseldorf 30, Germany. TEL 0211-49722325. FAX 0211-49722300. TELEX 2114101-FMNRW-D. Ed.Bd. circ. 40,000.

350   US
NORTH CAROLINA. SECRETARY OF STATE. DIRECTORY OF STATE AND COUNTY OFFICIALS. 1936. a. Secretary of State, 300 N. Salisbury St., Raleigh, NC 27603-5909. TEL 919-733-7355. Ed. John L. Cheney, Jr.

353.9   US
NORTH CAROLINA. STATE GOALS AND POLICY BOARD. ANNUAL REPORT. 1972. a. free. Department of Administration, State Goals and Policy Board, 116 W. Jones St., Raleigh, NC 27603-8003. TEL 919-733-4131. FAX 919-733-9571. Ed. Marge Tubbs. stat.; circ. 3,000.
   Formerly: North Carolina. Council on State Goals and Policy. Annual Report (ISSN 0093-9730)

350 340 US ISSN 0883-7783
KFN7457
NORTH CAROLINA LAW MONITOR.* 1985. s-m. $245. State Capital Services Inc., 3600 Glenwood Ave. K, No.100, Raleigh, NC 27612-4951. TEL 919-787-7006. Ed. Susan Kelly Nichols. circ. 1,000. (back issues avail.)

350 US
NORTH CAROLINA MANUAL. 1901. biennial. Secretary of State, 300 N. Salisbury St., Raleigh, NC 27603-5909. TEL 919-733-7355. Ed. John L. Cheney, Jr. circ. 5,000 (controlled).

NORTH KOREA DIRECTORY (YEAR). see *POLITICAL SCIENCE — International Relations*

NORTHEAST REGIONAL SCIENCE REVIEW. see *HOUSING AND URBAN PLANNING*

323 UK
NORTHERN IRELAND. COMMISSIONER FOR COMPLAINTS. ANNUAL REPORT. 1970. a. price varies. H.M.S.O. (N. Ireland), Progressive House, 33 Wellington Place, Belfast BT1 6HN, Northern Ireland. (Dist. by: H.M. Stationery Office, Chichester House, Chichester St., Belfast, Northern Ireland) circ. 170.

350 531.6 US
NORTHWEST PUBLIC POWER BULLETIN. 1946. m. $25. Northwest Public Power Association, Box 4576, Vancouver, WA 98662-0576. TEL 206-694-6553. Ed. Don Noel. adv.; charts; illus.; stat.; circ. 4,309.

350 200 US ISSN 0883-3648
K14
NOTRE DAME JOURNAL OF LAW, ETHICS & PUBLIC POLICY. 1984. s-a. $16. Thomas J. White Center on Law and Government, Notre Dame Law School, Rm. 341, Notre Dame, IN 46556. TEL 219-239-5913. FAX 219-239-6371. Ed. Ted Kommers. adv.; circ. 1,000. (also avail. in microform from WSH; reprint service avail. from WSH) Indexed: C.L.I., Leg.Per.
—BLDSC shelfmark: 6175.405000.
Description: Examines the application of religious teachings and philosophy to public policy and legal issues.

354 CN
NOVA SCOTIA. DEPARTMENT OF ECONOMIC DEVELOPMENT. ANNUAL REPORT. 1971. a. free. Department of Industry, Trade and Technology, P.O. Box 519, Halifax, N.S. B3J 2R7, Canada. TEL 902-424-8920. FAX 902-424-5739. TELEX 019-22548. Ed. Linda Laffin. circ. 300 (controlled).
Former titles: Nova Scotia. Department of Industry, Trade and Technology. Annual Report; Nova Scotia. Department of Development. Annual Report.

354.716 CN
NOVA SCOTIA. OFFICE OF THE OMBUDSMAN. ANNUAL REPORT. 1971. a. free. Office of the Ombudsman, Lord Nelson Bldg., Ste.300, 5675 Spring Garden Rd., P.O. Box 2152, Halifax, N.S. B3J 3B7, Canada. TEL 902-424-6780. Ed. Guy R. MacLean. circ. 500.

350 FR
O E C D. SOCIAL POLICY STUDIES SERIES. irreg. no.7, 1990. price varies. Organization for Economic Cooperation and Development, 2 rue Andre-Pascal, 75775 Paris Cedex 16, France. TEL 45-24-82-00. FAX 45-24-85-00. (U.S. orders to: O.E.C.D. Publications and Information Center, 2001 L St., N.W., Ste. 700, Washington, DC 20036-4910. TEL 202-785-6323) (also avail. in microfiche)

350 US
O M B WATCHER. (Office of Management and Budget) 1983. bi-m. $35 to individuals & community organizations; national & governmental organizations $100. O M B Watch, 1731 Connecticut Ave., N.W., Washington, DC 20009-1146. TEL 202-234-8494. FAX 202-234-8584. Ed. Gary D. Bass.
Description: News of OMB activities.

354 SP
OBRAS PUBLICAS. 1957. m. 750 ptas. Ministerio de Obras Publicas y Urbanismo, Servicio de Publicaciones, Avda. del Generalisimo 3, Madrid 3, Spain. illus.; index.
Formerly: Spain. Ministerio de Obras Publicas. Boletin de Informacion (ISSN 0490-334X)

349 GW ISSN 0029-859X
LAW
DIE OEFFENTLICHE VERWALTUNG; Zeitschrift fuer oeffentliches Recht und Verwaltungswissenschaft. 1948. s-m. DM.394. W. Kohlhammer GmbH, Hessbruehlstr. 69, Postfach 800430, 7000 Stuttgart 80, Germany. TEL 0711-7863-1. Ed. Heinrich Siedentopf. adv.; bk.rev.; abstr. Indexed: Dok.Str.
—BLDSC shelfmark: 6236.900000.

354.4 AU ISSN 0029-8581
DAS OEFFENTLICHE HAUSHALTSWESEN IN OESTERREICH. 1961. q. S.240($12) Gesellschaft fuer das Oeffentliche Haushaltswesen, Schenkenstr. 4, A-1010 Vienna, Austria. adv.; bk.rev.; circ. 600.

350 GY ISSN 0030-0314
OFFICIAL GAZETTE OF GUYANA. 1966. w. $533. Ministry of Information, Public Communications Agency, 18 Brickdam, P.O. Box 1023, Georgetown, Guyana. adv.; stat.; circ. 1,156. (looseleaf format)

388.324 US
OHIO GOVERNMENT DIRECTORY - OHIO TRUCKING TIMES. 1950. biennial. $5. Ohio Trucking Association, 50 W. Broad St., Ste. 1111, Columbus, OH 43215. TEL 614-221-5375. FAX 614-221-3717. Ed. David F. Bartosic. adv.; bk.rev.; illus.; circ. 8,000.
Former titles: Ohio Truck Times; (until 1974): Ohio Trucking News (ISSN 0030-1191)

350 US ISSN 0163-0008
OHIO MONTHLY RECORD. (Supplement to: Ohio Administrative Code, Approved Edition) 1977. m. $325. Banks - Baldwin Law Publishing Co., University Center, Box 1974, Cleveland, OH 44106. TEL 216-721-7373. FAX 216-721-8055. cum.index. (looseleaf format)
Description: Contains the full text of new administrative agency rules, with research aids--including notes to recent Ohio and federal court decisions and agency opinions.

350 US
OHIO STATE UNIVERSITY. SCHOOL OF PUBLIC ADMINISTRATION. WORKING PAPER SERIES. 1972. irreg. free. Ohio State University, Administrative Science Research, 1775 College Rd., Columbus, OH 42310. TEL 614-422-8696. circ. controlled.

350 020 US
OKLAHOMA GOVERNMENT PUBLICATIONS; a checklist. 1977. q. free. Department of Libraries, 200 N.E. 18th St., Oklahoma City, OK 73105. TEL 405-521-2502. FAX 405-525-7804. Ed. Vicki Sullivan. circ. 450.
Formerly: Oklahoma Government Documents.

350 US
OKLAHOMA STATE AGENCIES, BOARDS, COMMISSIONS, COURTS, INSTITUTIONS, LEGISLATURE AND OFFICERS. 1953. a. free. Department of Libraries, Legislative Reference Division, 200 N.E. 18th St., Oklahoma City, OK 73105. TEL 405-521-2521. FAX 405-525-7804. Ed. Peggy Coe. circ. 1,000.
Description: Contact directory of state government agencies, entities and personnel.

ONDERWIJS & WELZIJN - VAKMATIG. see *SOCIAL SERVICES AND WELFARE*

350 CN ISSN 0227-3268
ONTARIO. FEDERAL CABINET. ORDERS-IN-COUNCIL. w. Can.$383. Carswell Publications, Corporate Plaza, 2075 Kennedy Rd., Scarborough, Ont. M1T 3V4, Canada. TEL 416-609-8000. FAX 416-298-5094.

350 CN ISSN 0318-0743
JS1721.O58
ONTARIO. PROVINCIAL-MUNICIPAL AFFAIRS SECRETARIAT. MUNICIPAL DIRECTORY. French edition (ISSN 0832-6363) (Text in English and French) 1948. a. Can.$7.50. Ministry of Municipal Affairs and Housing, Provincial-Municipal Affairs Secretariat, 777 Bay St., 13th Fl., Toronto, Ont. M5G 2E5, Canada. TEL 416-585-4286. charts; stat.; index.

350 UK ISSN 0030-3852
OPPORTUNITIES. 1963. w. Lind House Magazines Ltd., Link House, Dingwall Rd., Croydon CR9 2TA, England. circ. 53,000. (tabloid format)

OPSTINA; casopis za teoriju i praksu razvoja opstine. see *POLITICAL SCIENCE*

ORAL HISTORY SERIES. see *HISTORY — History Of North And South America*

350 US
OREGON BLUE BOOK. 1904. biennial. $8. Secretary of State, 136 State Capitol, Salem, OR 97310. TEL 503-373-7414. FAX 503-373-7414. circ. 25,000.
Description: Record of Oregon's government, businesses, and people. Chronicles its society, providing a sense of how Oregonians live their lives.

350 GW ISSN 0323-3049
ORGANISATION; Zeitschrift fuer Leitungs- und Verwaltungsorganisation der sozialistischen Staatsorgans. 1967. bi-m. DM.30. Staatsverlag der DDR, Otto-Grotewohl Str. 17, 1086 Berlin, Germany.

354 TH ISSN 0475-2015
ORGANIZATIONAL DIRECTORY OF THE GOVERNMENT OF THAILAND.* (Text in English and Thai) irreg. (Translation & Secretarial Office) Office of the Prime Minister, Government House, Nakhon Pathom Rd., Bangkok 10300, Thailand.

354.669 NR
OYO STATE. ESTIMATES INCLUDING BUDGET SPEECH AND MEMORANDUM. Short title: Oyo State of Nigeria Estimates. a. £N40. Government Printer, Ibadan, Nigeria.
Formerly: Western State. Estimates Including Budget Speech and Memorandum.

340.05 NR
OYO STATE OF NIGERIA GAZETTE. (Supplements accompany some numbers) irreg. £N30. Government Printer, Ibadan, Nigeria. TEL 411216.
Formerly: Western State. Gazette.

350 331.1 US
P E R B NEWS. 1968. m. $15. Public Employment Relations Board, 50 Wolf Rd., Albany, NY 12205. FAX 518-457-2664. Ed. R. Rosen. circ. 200.

P S A REPORTER. (Public Service Association of New South Wales) see *LABOR UNIONS*

350.6 UK ISSN 0144-4212
HD4645
P S L G. (Public Service & Local Government) 1977. m. £8.50. Patey Doyle (Publishing) Ltd., Wilmington House, Church Hill, Wilmington, Dartford DA2 7EF, England. Ed. Alan Pickstock. illus.; circ. 20,000.
—BLDSC shelfmark: 6969.230000.

350 PK ISSN 0078-8333
PAKISTAN. NATIONAL ASSEMBLY. DEBATES. OFFICIAL REPORT. (Text in English) 1962. irreg. Rs.0.50. National Assembly, Islamabad, Pakistan. (Dist. by: Manager of Publications, Government of Pakistan, 2nd Fl., Ahmad Chamber, Tariq Rd., P.E.C.H.S., Karachi 29, Pakistan)

350 PN
PANAMA. TRIBUNAL ELECTORAL. MEMORIA. irreg. Tribunal Electoral, Panama, Panama.

350 US ISSN 0078-9151
JK8201
PAPERS IN PUBLIC ADMINISTRATION. 1962. irreg., no.33, 1977. price varies. Arizona State University, Center for Public Affairs, Tempe, AZ 85281. TEL 602-965-3926. Ed. Richard A. Eribes. index; circ. 750.
Supersedes (in 1970): Arizona State University. Governmental Finance Institute. Proceedings (ISSN 0072-5196)

354 PP
PAPUA NEW GUINEA. PUBLIC SERVICE COMMISSION. REPORT.. a. free. Public Service Commission, P.O. Ward Strip, NCD, Papua New Guinea. TEL 27-1285. FAX 259564. Ed. Karo Rupa.
Formerly: Papua New Guinea. Public Service Board. Report (ISSN 0078-9399)

PARKS AND RECREATION; journal of park and recreation management. see *CONSERVATION*

350 UK
PARLIAMENTARY BULLETIN FOR LOCAL GOVERNMENT EXECUTIVES. 1949. w. £38. Parliamentary and Common Market News Services, 19 Kingsdown Rd., Surbiton KT6 6JZ, England.

PUBLIC ADMINISTRATION

350   UK
PARLIAMENTARY YEAR BOOK.* 1979. a. £14.95($27) Blake's (Parliamentary Division) Ltd., 12-14 High Road Lane, London N2 9JP, England. TEL 44-1-450 9322. Ed. Joyce Blake. adv.; bk.rev.; circ. 5,500.

350   BX
PELITA BRUNEI. (Text in Malay) 1956. w. free. Information Department, Prime Minister's Office, Istana Nurul Iman, Bandar Seri Begawan 2041, Brunei Darussalam. circ. 45,000. (newspaper)

350   US
PENNSYLVANIA CHAMBER OF BUSINESS AND INDUSTRY. LEGISLATIVE DIRECTORY. a. $8 to non-members; members $4. Pennsylvania Chamber of Business and Industry, 222 N. Third St., Harrisburg, PA 17101. TEL 800-326-3252. FAX 717-255-3298.
  Description: Provides information and addresses of Pennsylvania elected officials at state and federal levels.

PENNSYLVANIA CHAMBER OF BUSINESS AND INDUSTRY. LEGISLATIVE REPORTER. see *LAW*

350   BL
PERFIL DA ADMINISTRACAO FEDERAL. 1974. s-a. $12 per no. Editora Visao Ltda., Rua Alvaro de Carvalho, 354, 1o andar, 01050 Sao Paulo, Brazil. TEL 256-5011. FAX 258-1919. adv.; circ. 31,000.

350 920   BL
PERFIS PARLAMENTARES. 1977. irreg. Camara dos Deputados, Brasilia, Brazil. circ. 2,000.

354.8   BL   ISSN 0006-9469
PERNAMBUCO. SECRETARIA DO SANEAMENTO, HABITACAO E OBRAS. BOLETIM TECNICO. bi-m. free. Secretaria do Saneamento, Habitacao e Obras, Av. Cruz Cabuga 1111, Recife, Pernambuco, Brazil. adv.; bk.rev.; charts; illus.; stat.

PERSPECTIVES ON POLITICAL SCIENCE. see *POLITICAL SCIENCE*

350   PH   ISSN 0031-7675
JA26
PHILIPPINE JOURNAL OF PUBLIC ADMINISTRATION. 1957. q. P.120($25) University of the Philippines, College of Public Administration, PARDEC-SAAC Building, P.O. Box 198, Don Mariano Marcos Ave., Diliman, Quezon City, Philippines. TEL 95-13-53. TELEX CPAUP. Ed. Victoria A. Bautista. bk.rev.; bibl.; charts; index; circ. 420. (also avail. in microform from UMI; reprint service avail. from UMI) **Indexed:** A.B.C.Pol.Sci., Hist.Abstr., Ind.Phil.Per., Lang.& Lang.Behav.Abstr.
  —BLDSC shelfmark: 6455.900000.
  Formerly: University of the Philippines. College of Public Administration. (Publication) (ISSN 0079-9254)

350   PH
PHILIPPINES. DEPARTMENT OF PUBLIC INFORMATION. POLICY STATEMENTS. irreg., no.13, 1977. Department of Public Information, c/o Bureau of National and Foreign Information, U P L Building, PO Box 3396, Intramuros, Manila, Philippines.

350 020.6   PH
PHILIPPINES. NATIONAL PRINTING OFFICE. ITEMIZATION OF PERSONAL SERVICES AND ORGANIZATIONAL CHARTS. a. National Printing Office, Boston St., Port Area, Manila, Philippines.

350   PH
PHILIPPINES. PUBLIC INFORMATION OFFICE. OFFICIAL GAZETTE. 1905. w. P.410($79) National Printing Office, Boston St., Port Area, Manila, Philippines. Ed. Elpidio de Peralta. circ. 1,400. (back issues avail.)

POLICY AND POLITICS. see *EDUCATION — Higher Education*

350   US
POLICY FORUM. 1988. q. free. University of Illinois at Urbana-Champaign, Institute of Government and Public Affairs, 1201 W. Nevada St., Urbana, IL 61801. TEL 217-333-3340. FAX 217-244-4817. Ed. Anna J. Merritt.
  Description: Analysis of current Illinois policy issues.

350 320   CN   ISSN 0226-5893
JL1
POLICY OPTIONS/OPTIONS POLITIQUES. (Text in English, French) 1979. 10/yr. Can.$29.95 (US Can.$34.95; elsewhere Can.$39.95). Institute for Research on Public Policy, P.O. Box 3670, Halifax South, N.S. B3J 3K6, Canada. TEL 902-494-3801. FAX 902-494-6458. Ed. Walter Stewart. bk.rev.; circ. 3,500. **Indexed:** Can.Per.Ind., CMI.
  —BLDSC shelfmark: 6543.326650.
  Description: Forum for views on Canadian public policy.

350   US   ISSN 0163-108X
H1
POLICY STUDIES REVIEW ANNUAL. 1977. a. $89.95. Transaction Publishers, Transaction Periodicals Consortium, Department 3092, Rutgers University, New Brunswick, NJ 08903. TEL 908-932-2280. FAX 908-932-3138. Ed. Ray C. Rist. bibl.
  —BLDSC shelfmark: 6543.329500.
  Description: Presents research and analysis in a wide variety of policy areas, including defense and national security, health care cost containment, work and labor information, the environment, immigration, and poverty.

350   US   ISSN 8756-9248
POLITICAL PULSE. 1985. fortn. $230. 926 J St., Rm. 1218, Sacramento, CA 95814. TEL 916-446-2048. FAX 916-446-5302. Ed. Bud Lembke. circ. 700.
  Description: News of California politics and government.

POLITICAL REPORT. see *POLITICAL SCIENCE*

353   US   ISSN 0362-4765
JA88.U6
POLITICAL SCIENCE UTILIZATION DIRECTORY. 1975. irreg. $4 to individuals; institutions $8. Policy Studies Organization, University of Illinois, 361 Lincoln Hall, Urbana, IL 61801. TEL 217-359-8541. Eds. Stuart Nagel, Marian Neef. bibl.; charts; stat.; index; circ. 2,400. (reprint service avail. from UMI)
  Description: Describes how political science has been, and can be used in federal, state, and local government agencies.

POLITICS AND THE LIFE SCIENCES. see *MEDICAL SCIENCES*

POPULATION TRENDS AND PUBLIC POLICY. see *POPULATION STUDIES*

350   IT
POTERE LOCALE. 1967. s-m. L.10000. Lega per le Autonomie ed i Poteri Locali, Via Cesare Balbo 43, 00184 Rome, Italy. Ed. Goffredo Broglio. adv.; circ. 45,000.

350   II
PRASHASNIKA. (Text in English and Hindi) 1972. q. Rs.20($5) Harishchandra Mathur State Institute of Public Administration, Jaipur, Rajasthan, India. Ed. M.L. Mehta. bk.rev.; bibl.

350 340   SZ   ISSN 0254-9441
PRAXIS DES BUNDESGERICHTS. (Text in German) 1904. 11/yr. 160 Fr. Helbing und Lichtenhahn Verlag AG, Freie Str. 82, CH-4051 Basel, Switzerland. TEL 064-268626. FAX 064-245780. TELEX 981195-SAG-CH. (Subscr. to: Sauerlaender AG, Postfach, CH-5001 Aarau, Switzerland)

PREVISIONS GLISSANTES DETAILLEES EN PERSPECTIVES SECTORIELLES (VOL.36): SERVICES PUBLICS. see *BUSINESS AND ECONOMICS — Economic Situation And Conditions*

PRINCE EDWARD ISLAND. DEPARTMENT OF COMMUNITY AND CULTURAL AFFAIRS. ANNUAL REPORT. see *ENVIRONMENTAL STUDIES*

330   CN
PRINCE EDWARD ISLAND. DEPARTMENT OF INDUSTRY. ANNUAL REPORT. 1950. a. free. Department of Industry, P.O. Box 2000, Charlottetown, P.E.I. C1A 7N8, Canada. TEL 902-368-4240. FAX 902-368-4224. TELEX 014-44154. stat.; circ. 200.
  Formerly: Prince Edward Island. Department of Industry and Commerce. Annual Commerce.

338.9 380   CN   ISSN 0079-5151
PRINCE EDWARD ISLAND. PUBLIC UTILITIES COMMISSION. ANNUAL REPORT. 1961. a. free. Public Utilities Commission, P.O. Box 577, Charlottetown, P.E.I. C1A 7L1, Canada. TEL 902-892-3501. FAX 902-566-4076. Ed. Linda Webber. circ. 325.

350   IT   ISSN 0391-2655
PROBLEMI DI AMMINISTRAZIONE PUBBLICA; trimestrale del FORMEZ. 1976. q. L.110000. (Centro di Formazione e Studi per il Mezzogiorno) Societa Editrice Il Mulino, Strada Maggiore, 37, 40125 Bologna, Italy. TEL 051-256011. FAX 051-256034. Ed. Giovanni Marongiu. adv.; circ. 1,900. (back issues avail.)

352   PL   ISSN 0079-5801
JS6132.A15
PROBLEMY RAD NARODOWYCH. STUDIA I MATERIALY. (Text in Polish; summaries in French and Russian) 1964. 4/yr. price varies. (Polska Akademia Nauk, Instytut Panstwa i Prawa) Ossolineum, Publishing House of the Polish Academy of Sciences, Rynek 9, Wroclaw, Poland. TELEX 0712771 OSS PL. (Dist. by: Ars Polona-Ruch, Krakowskie Przedmiescie 7, Warsaw, Poland) Ed. B. Zawadzka. circ. 1,600. (also avail. in microfilm)
  —BLDSC shelfmark: 6617.957300.
  Description: Theoretical papers on various aspects of activities of the People's Town Council, territorial governments and administration.

354.71   CN   ISSN 0318-0646
PROFESSIONAL INSTITUTE OF THE PUBLIC SERVICE OF CANADA. COMMUNICATIONS. (Text in English and French) 1975. bi-m. Professional Institute of the Public Service of Canada, 53 Auriga Dr., Nepean, Ont. K2E 8C3, Canada. TEL 613-228-6310. FAX 613-228-9048. circ. 24,000.

350.6   UK
PROFESSIONAL OFFICER. 1986. m. £5 to non-members. Federated Union of Managerial and Professional Officers, Terminus House, The High, Harlow, Essex CM20 1TZ, England. TEL 0274-434444. FAX 0279-451176. Ed. David Candler. adv.; bk.rev.; circ. 14,000. (back issues avail.)

350   IT
PROVINCIA NUOVA. 1971. bi-m. Amministrazione Provinciale, Corso V. Emanuele 17, 26100 Cremona, Italy. Ed.Bd. adv.; illus.

350   CN
PROVINCIAL LEGISLATIVE RECORD. m. Can.$150. C C H Canadian Ltd., 6 Garamond Court, Don Mills, Ont. M3C 1Z5, Canada. TEL 416-441-2292. FAX 416-444-9011. index.
  Formerly: Provincial Pulse Newsletter.
  Description: Complete reporting of the status of legislation for the Canadian provinces and territories, including all proclamations.

350   IT
PUBBLICA AMMINISTRAZIONE OGGI; il mensile della tecnologia e dell'innovazione. 1987. m. (10/yr.) L.118000 (effective 1992). Maggioli Editore, Via Crimea, 1, Casella Postale 290, 47037 Rimini, Italy. TEL 0541-626777. FAX 0541-622020. Ed. Dario Tiengo.

350   IT   ISSN 0393-9413
PUBBLICO ESERCIZIO. 1986. m. L.73000 (foreign L.128000). (Federazione Italiana Pubblici Esercizi) Etas s.r.l., Via Mecenate 91, 20138 Milan, Italy. TEL 02-580841. FAX 02-5064867. Ed. Toni Liguori. circ. 151,051. (back issues avail.)

350 UK ISSN 0033-3298
CODEN: PUADDD
PUBLIC ADMINISTRATION. 1923. q. £38($80) to individuals; institutions £69($140). Basil Blackwell Ltd., 108 Cowley Rd., Oxford OX4 1JF, England. TEL 0865-791100. FAX 0865-791347. TELEX 837022-OXBOOK-G. Ed. R.A.W. Rhodes. adv.; bk.rev.; index. cum.index 1953-1962; circ. 4,650. (also avail. in microform from UMI; reprint service avail. from UMI) Indexed: A.B.C.Pol.Sci., Account.& Data Proc.Abstr., Amer.Hist.& Life, ASSIA, BPIA, Br.Hum.Ind., Curr.Cont., Educ.Admin.Abstr., Geo.Abstr., Int.Polit.Sci.Abstr., Key to Econ.Sci., Manage.Cont., Mid.East: Abstr.& Ind., P.A.I.S., Pers.Lit., PSI, Rural Recreat.Tour.Abstr., Sci.Abstr., Soc.Sci.Ind., SSCI, Stud.Wom.Abstr., Tr.& Indus.Ind., World Agri.Econ.& Rural Sociol.Abstr.
—BLDSC shelfmark: 6962.400000.

350 US
PUBLIC ADMINISTRATION AND PUBLIC POLICY. 1978. irreg., vol.46, 1992. Marcel Dekker, Inc., 270 Madison Ave., New York, NY 10016. TEL 212-696-9000. FAX 212-685-4540. TELEX 1419.

350 US
▼**PUBLIC ADMINISTRATION BRIEFING.** 1990. m. Kentucky State University, School of Public Affairs, Center for Public Policy Research, Frankfort, KY 40601. TEL 502-227-6117. Ed. Manindra Mohapatra.

350 US ISSN 0734-9149
JA1
PUBLIC ADMINISTRATION QUARTERLY. 1977. q. $25 to individuals; libraries $40. Southern Public Administration Education Foundation, c/o Dr. Jack Rabin, Pennsylvania State University at Harrisburg, Division of Public Affairs, Middletown, PA 17057. TEL 717-948-6363, 717-948-6363. FAX 717-540-1383. Eds. Jack Rabin, Thomas Vocino. bk.rev.; circ. 1,300. (also avail. in microform from UMI; reprint service avail. from UMI) Indexed: ABI Inform, BPIA, Manage.Cont., Pers.Lit., Sage Pub.Admin.Abstr., Sage Urb.Stud.Abstr.
—BLDSC shelfmark: 6962.595000.
Formerly: Southern Review of Public Administration (ISSN 0147-8168)

354.3 PK ISSN 0033-3344
PUBLIC ADMINISTRATION REVIEW. (Text in English) 1963. 2/yr. Rs.100($30) National Institute of Public Administration, Regional Office, 190-Scotch Corner, Upper Mall, Lahore, Pakistan. Ed. Ahmad Iftikhar. bk.rev. (also avail. in microform from UMI; reprint service avail. from UMI) Indexed: A.B.C.Pol.Sci., Curr.Cont., Deep Sea Res.& Oceanogr.Abstr., Educ.Admin.Abstr., Fut.Surv., Hist.Abstr., L.R.I., Leg.Per., Pers.Lit., PSI, Soc.Sci.Ind., Tr.& Indus.Ind.

350 US ISSN 0033-3352
JK1
PUBLIC ADMINISTRATION REVIEW. 1940. bi-m. $80 (foreign $130). American Society for Public Administration, 1120 G St., N.W., Ste. 500, Washington, DC 20005. TEL 202-393-7878. FAX 202-638-4952. Ed. David Rosenbloom. adv.; bk.rev.; index. cum.index (published irregularly); circ. 20,000. (also avail. in microform from MIM,UMI; reprint service avail. from UMI,KTO) Indexed: A.B.C.Pol.Sci., ABI Inform, Acad.Ind., ASSIA, B.P.I., Bk.Rev.Ind. (1965-), BPIA, C.L.I., Child.Bk.Rev.Ind. (1965-), Hum.Ind., L.R.I., Manage.Cont., Mid.East: Abstr.& Ind., P.A.I.S., Sage Pub.Admin.Abstr., Sage Urb.Stud.Abstr., Soc.Sci.Ind., Soc.Work Res.& Abstr., SSCI.
—BLDSC shelfmark: 6962.600000.
Description: Presents authoritative research and articles on current issues.

350 US ISSN 0033-3360
JK4601
PUBLIC ADMINISTRATION SURVEY. 1953. q. free to libraries. University of Mississippi, Public Policy Research Center, University, MS 38677. TEL 601-232-5408. Ed. D.B. Brammer. circ. 1,800. Indexed: P.A.I.S., Sage Pub.Admin.Abstr.

350 US ISSN 0149-8797
JK1
PUBLIC ADMINISTRATION TIMES. 1978. m. $25 (foreign $35). American Society for Public Administration, 1120 G St., N.W., Ste. 500, Washington, DC 20005. TEL 202-393-7878. FAX 202-638-4952. Ed. Sheila McCormick. circ. 18,000. (reprint service avail. from UMI) Indexed: Pers.Lit.
Former titles (1951-1978): Public Administration News and Views (ISSN 0033-3328); A S P A News and Views (ISSN 0360-4233); Incorporates: Public Administration Recruiter (ISSN 0033-3336)
Description: Reports on current developments, innovative programs, and relevant issues in the field of public service.

PUBLIC AFFAIRS COMMENT. see SOCIAL SCIENCES: COMPREHENSIVE WORKS

350 UK ISSN 0952-7095
PUBLIC DOMAIN. 1986. a. £30. (Public Finance Foundation) Chapman & Hall, 3 Robert St., London WC2N 6BH, England. TEL 071-895-8823. FAX 071-895-8825. Ed. Michaela Lavender. adv.; bibl.; charts; circ. 2,000. (back issues avail.)
—BLDSC shelfmark: 6963.362000.
Description: Reviews finance and policy trends in public services.

PUBLIC EMPLOYEE NEWSLETTER. see OCCUPATIONAL HEALTH AND SAFETY

PUBLIC EMPLOYEE PRESS. see LABOR UNIONS

350.7 GW ISSN 0033-3476
PUBLIC FINANCE/FINANCES PUBLIQUES. (Text in English; summaries in English, French and German) 1946. 3/yr. DM.170. (Foundation Journal Public Finance, NE) Foundation Public Finance, c/o Prof. Dieter Biehl, Goethestr. 13, 6240 Koenigstein, Germany. Ed.Bd. adv.; bibl.; charts; index; circ. 1,700. (reprint service avail. from SWZ,UMI) Indexed: ASSIA, Curr.Cont., J.of Econ.Lit., Mid.East: Abstr.& Ind., P.A.I.S., SSCI.
—BLDSC shelfmark: 6963.400000.
Description: Devoted to the study of fiscal theory and policy and related problems.

350 UK
PUBLIC GENERAL ACTS & GENERAL SYNOD MEASURES. a. price varies. H.M.S.O., P.O. Box 276, London SW8 5DT, England.

PUBLIC INTEREST BRIEFS. see LAW — Legal Aid

350 US ISSN 1061-7639
JK1
THE PUBLIC MANAGER; the journal for practitioners. 1972. q. $26 to individuals; institutions $45. Bureaucrat, Inc., 12007 Titian Way, Potomac, MD 20854. TEL 301-279-9445. FAX 301-251-5872. Ed. Thomas W. Novotny. adv.; bk.rev.; index; circ. 4,500. (also avail. in microform from UMI; reprint service avail. from UMI) Indexed: A.B.C.Pol.Sci., ABI Inform, B.P.I, BPIA, Bus.Ind., Curr.Cont., Human Resour.Abstr., Sage Pub.Admin.Abstr., Sage Urb.Stud.Abstr., SSCI, Tr.& Indus.Ind., Urb.Aff.Abstr.
Formerly (until Spring 1992): Bureaucrat (ISSN 0045-3544)

350 UK ISSN 0954-0962
HC251
PUBLIC MONEY AND MANAGEMENT; policy journal of the public sector. 1981. q. £26.50($52.50) to individuals; institutions £99($182.50). (Public Finance Foundation) Basil Blackwell Ltd., 108 Cowley Rd., Oxford OX4 1JF, England. TEL 0865-791100. FAX 0865-791347. TELEX 837022-OXBOOK-G. (Subscr. addr.: c/o Marston Book Services, P.O. Box 87, Oxford OX2 0DT, England) illus.; circ. 2,350.
—BLDSC shelfmark: 6967.781000.
Formerly: Chartered Institute of Public Finance and Accountancy. Public Money (ISSN 0261-1252)

353.03 973 US ISSN 0079-7626
J80
PUBLIC PAPERS OF THE PRESIDENTS OF THE UNITED STATES. a. price varies. U.S. Office of the Federal Register, National Archives and Records Administration, Washington, DC 20408. TEL 202-523-5240. (Dist. by: Superintendent of Documents, Box 371954, Pittsburgh, PA 15250-7954) index. (back issues avail.)

350 658 US ISSN 1044-8039
JF1411
PUBLIC PRODUCTIVITY AND MANAGEMENT REVIEW. 1975. q. $52 to individuals; institutions $82. (American Society for Public Administration and the National Center for Public Productivity, Section on Management Science) Jossey-Bass Inc., Publishers, 350 Sansome St., 5th Fl., San Francisco, CA 94104. TEL 415-433-1767. FAX 415-433-0499. Ed. Marc Holzer. bk.rev.; circ. 1,450. (also avail. in microform from UMI; back issues avail.) Indexed: ABI Inform, Account.& Data Proc.Abstr., Anbar, B.P.I., BPIA, CINAHL, Pers.Lit., Pers.Manage.Abstr., Sage Pub.Admin.Abstr., Sage Urb.Stud.Abstr., Urb.Aff.Abstr.
—BLDSC shelfmark: 6968.392000.
Formerly: Product Productivity Review (ISSN 0361-6681)
Description: Offers public and non-profit sector professionals useful information on enhancing their organizations' productivity, case examples of successful practices and updates on public administration research and legislation.
Refereed Serial

PUBLIC ROADS; a journal of highway research and development. see ENGINEERING — Civil Engineering

354.9 NZ ISSN 0110-5191
PUBLIC SECTOR. 1978. q. NZ.$50 (foreign NZ.$55). New Zealand Institute of Public Administration, P.O. Box 5032, Lambton Quay, Wellington, New Zealand. TEL 04-389-8776. adv.; bk.rev.; charts; cum.index; circ. 1,135. (also avail. in microform from MIM) Indexed: P.A.I.S.
Formerly (until vol.40, 1978): New Zealand Journal of Public Administration (ISSN 0028-8357)

350 CN ISSN 0700-2092
PUBLIC SECTOR. 1977. w. Can.$497. Ottawa Bureau Inc., 9 Antares Dr., Nepean, Ont. K2E 7V5, Canada. TEL 613-226-6491. FAX 613-521-2520. Ed. Peter Menyasz. quarterly index.

350 338 US
PUBLIC SECTOR. 1976. q. free. Auburn University, Center for Governmental Services, 2232 Haley Center, Auburn University, Auburn, AL 36849. TEL 205-844-1913. FAX 205-844-1919. Ed. Charles Spindler. bibl.; charts; illus.; stat.; circ. 3,000. (controlled). (back issues avail.) Indexed: A.B.C.Pol.Sci.
Description: Covers current issues of interest to government officials such as: growth management, tax reform, economic development and solid waste management.

354.7 CN ISSN 0380-3988
PUBLIC SECTOR MANAGEMENT/MANAGEMENT ET SECTEUR PUBLIC. (Text in English, French) 1979. 6/yr. Can.$20. Institute of Public Administration of Canada, 897 Bay St., Toronto, Ont. M5S 1Z7, Canada. TEL 416-923-7319. FAX 416-923-8994. Eds. Joe Galimberti, Marie Fortier-Balogh. circ. 3,500.
Formerly (until 1990): Institute of Public Administration of Canada. Bulletin.

354.9 NZ
PUBLIC SECTOR RESEARCH PAPERS. 1979. irreg. NZ.$15 per paper. New Zealand Institute of Public Administration, P.O. Box 5032, Lambton Quay, Wellington, New Zealand.

350 SA ISSN 0033-376X
HD8013.S6
PUBLIC SERVANT/STAATSAMPTENAAR. (Text in Afrikaans, English) 1920. m. R.1.20 per no. Public Servants Association of South Africa - Vereniging van Staatsamptenare van Suid-Afrika, P.S.A. Bldg., 563 Belvedere St., P.O. Box 40404, Arcadia 0007, South Africa. TEL 012-323-4481. FAX 012-325-7434. Ed. J.C. Olivier. adv.; bk.rev.; circ. 78,000 (controlled). Indexed: Ind.S.A.Per.

350.6 GY
PUBLIC SERVANT. vol.4, 1977. m. Guyana Public Service Union, 160 Regent Rd. & New Garden St., Georgetown, Guyana. TEL 2-61770.

PUBLIC ADMINISTRATION

350.6 331.8 NZ ISSN 0110-6945
PUBLIC SERVICE ASSOCIATION JOURNAL. Short title: P S A Journal. 1913. 10/yr. New Zealand Public Service Association, Private Bag, Wellington, New Zealand. TEL 04-474-655. FAX 04-4711-992. Ed. Pat Martin. adv.; bk.rev.; record rev.; circ. 65,000.
   Description: Covers economic and social issues, international trade union news, personality profiles, health and safety, and PSA news.

350 AT ISSN 0033-3786
PUBLIC SERVICE REVIEW. 1888. m. Aus.$10. Public Service Association of South Australia Inc., 82 Gilbert St., Adelaide, S.A. 5000, Australia. FAX 08-231-1265. Ed. Adrian Butterworth. adv.; bk.rev.; illus.; circ. 23,000.

PUBLIC UTILITIES FORTNIGHTLY. see *ENGINEERING — Electrical Engineering*

PUBLIC UTILITIES LAW ANTHOLOGY. see *LAW*

PUBLIC UTILITIES NEWSLETTER. see *OCCUPATIONAL HEALTH AND SAFETY*

PUBLIC WORKS HISTORICAL SOCIETY NEWSLETTER. see *HISTORY — History Of North And South America*

363.6 US ISSN 0146-5473
PUBLIC WORKS NEWS. 1969. w. $350. Reynolds Publishing Co., Inc., Box 733, Glen Echo, MD 20812. Ed. William F. Reynolds.

350 SZ ISSN 0080-7249
PUBLICUS; Schweizer Jahrbuch des Oeffentlichen Lebens. (Text in French and German) 1958. a. 70 Fr. per no. Schwabe und Co. AG, Steinentorstr. 13, CH-4010 Basel, Switzerland. TEL 061-2725523. FAX 061-2725573. Ed. Josef Niederberger. adv.; index; circ. 6,500.
   Description: Summaries include science and culture, sports, economic and political organizations in Switzerland.

PUBLIUS; the journal of federalism. see *POLITICAL SCIENCE*

354.6 NR ISSN 0001-8333
QUARTERLY JOURNAL OF ADMINISTRATION. Short title: Q J A. 1966. q. £N30($40) (outside Nigeria) (typically one in Jan.) 1869. w. Can.$53 Obafemi Awolowo University, Faculty of Administration, Ile-Ife, Nigeria. TEL 036-23029. Ed. Dele Olowu. adv.; bk.rev.; bibl.; charts; illus.; stat.; index; circ. 2,000. (also avail. in microform from UMI; reprint service avail. from UMI) **Indexed:** A.B.C.Pol.Sci., Int.Lab.Doc., Int.Polit.Sci.Abstr., Mid.East: Abstr.& Ind., Rural Recreat.Tour.Abstr., World Agri.Econ.& Rural Sociol.Abstr.
   —BLDSC shelfmark: 7187.600000.
   Formerly: Administration.
   Description: Devoted to the study, research, dissemination and exchange of knowledge and information on all aspects of administration, management, and policy studies.

971 CN ISSN 0033-5983
QUEBEC OFFICIAL GAZETTE. (In Three Parts) (Text in French; Part 2 also in English) 1869. w. Can.$53 for Part 1; Can. $77 for Part 2. Ministere des Communications, Direction Generale des Publications Gouverementales, 2e etage, 1279 boul. Charest Ouest, Quebec, Que. G1N 4K7, Canada. TEL 413-643-3895. Ed. George Lapierre. cum.index; circ. 9,000 (3,000 Part 1; 5,000 Part 2 (French); 1,000 Part 2 (English)).

354 AT
QUEENSLAND. LAND ADMINISTRATION COMMISSION. ANNUAL REPORT. a. Queensland. Government Printer, Brisbane, Australia. illus.; stat.

QUESTE ISTITUZIONI; cronache del sistema politica. see *POLITICAL SCIENCE*

QUORUM REPORT. see *POLITICAL SCIENCE*

R A NEWS. (Recreation Association of the Public Service of Canada) see *CLUBS*

350 UK ISSN 0144-6525
R I P A REPORT. 1980. q. membership. Royal Institute of Public Administration, 3 Birdcage Walk, London SW1H 9JH, England. TEL 071-222-2248. FAX 071-222-2249. Ed. Ivor Shelley. circ. controlled. **Indexed:** BPIA, Nutr.Abstr.

350 NE ISSN 0033-7056
R P A BULLETIN. (Mededelingen over Rijkspersoneelsaangelegenheden) 1959. 3/m. free. Ministerie van Binnenlandse Zaken - Ministry of the Interior, Schedeldoekshaven 200, 2500 EA The Hague, Netherlands. circ. 4,000.

350 DK ISSN 0107-8747
RASP. 1981. irreg. DKK 45 per no. (Aalborg Universitetscenter) Aalborg Universitetsforlag, Aalborg, Denmark.

RATING AND VALUATION REPORTER. see *LAW*

353 320 US ISSN 0034-1185
RECENT PUBLICATIONS ON GOVERNMENTAL PROBLEMS. 1932. m. $30 (foreign $33). (Charles E. Merriam Center for Public Administration) Merriam Center Library, 1313 E. 60th St., Chicago, IL 60637. TEL 312-947-2164. Ed. Charlotte Ullman. bk.rev.; cum.index avail.; circ. 500. (back issues avail.) **Indexed:** P.A.I.S.
   —BLDSC shelfmark: 7305.082000.
   Description: Includes listings of books, monographs, government documents, guides and selected articles from relevant periodicals.

350 UK ISSN 0034-2076
RED TAPE. 1911. m. £4 (foreign £5). Civil and Public Services Association, 160 Falcon Rd., London SW11 2LN, England. TEL 071-924-2727. FAX 071-924-1847. Ed. Barry A. Reamsbotton. adv.; bk.rev.; circ. 160,000.

RED TAPE. see *LABOR UNIONS*

350 US
▼**REFERENCE GUIDES TO THE STATE CONSTITUTIONS OF THE UNITED STATES.** 1990. irreg. price varies. Praeger Publishing (Subsidiary of: Greenwood Publishing Group Inc.), 88 Post Rd. W., Box 5007, Westport, CT 06881-5007. TEL 203-226-3571. FAX 203-222-1502.

350 FR ISSN 0337-7091
JN2301
REGARDS SUR L'ACTUALITE; mensuel de la vie publique en France. 1974. 10/yr. 250 F. Documentation Francaise, 29-31 Quai Voltaire, 75340 Paris, France. TEL 1-40-15-70-00. bibl. (also avail. in microfiche)
   —BLDSC shelfmark: 7336.440000.

REGIONAL AND INDUSTRIAL RESEARCH SERIES. see *BUSINESS AND ECONOMICS*

REGIONE ABRUZZO. see *SOCIAL SERVICES AND WELFARE*

350 SW
REGISTER OVER GAELLANDE S F S-FOERFATTNINGAR. a. Allmaenna Foerlaget, 106 47 Stockholm, Sweden. TEL 08-739-9630. FAX 08-739-9548.

350 329.9 US
RENMIN ZHENGXIE BAO/JOURNAL OF THE C P P C C. (Text in Chinese) 2/w. $96.50. (Zhongguo Renmin Zhengzhi Xieshang Huiyi, CC - Chinese People's Political Consultative Conference) China Books & Periodicals, Inc., 2929 24th St., San Francisco, CA 94110. TEL 415-282-2994. FAX 415-282-0994.

350 SP
RENTA NACIONAL DE ESPANA; y su distribucion provincial (year). no.10, 1976. irreg. Banco de Bilbao, Servicio de Estudios, Apartado 21, Bilbao, Spain. charts; stat.

350 RE
REPERTOIRE DES TEXTES LEGISLATIFS ET REGLEMENTAIRES ET DES REPONSES AUX QUESTIONS ECRITES CONCERNANT LA REUNION. 1975. a. 100 F. Centre Universitaire de la Reunion, Center d'Etudes Administratives, 24, 26 av. de la Victoire, Saint-Denis, Reunion. circ. 150.

350 FR
REPERTOIRE PERMANENT DE L'ADMINISTRATION FRANCAISE. 1945. a., 48th ed., 1990. 126.48 F. Documentation Francaise, 29-31 Quai Voltaire, 75340 Paris, France. TEL 1-40-15-70-00. circ. 10,000. (also avail. in microfiche)
   Formerly: France. Delegation Generale a la Recherche Scientifique et Technique. Repertoire Permanent de l'Administration Publique (ISSN 0080-1186)

350 SE
REPUBLIC OF SEYCHELLES OFFICIAL GAZETTE. (Text in English) irreg. SRI.151.20. Government Printing Office, c/o Seychelles National Bookshop, Albert St., Victoria, Seychelles. adv.; circ. 800.
   Supersedes: Seychelles Government Gazetta.

350 SI
REPUBLIC OF SINGAPORE GOVERNMENT GAZETTE. (Text in English) w. Singapore National Printers Ltd., 303 Upper Serangoon Road, P.O. Box 485, Singapore 1334, Singapore. TEL 2820611. FAX 2854894. TELEX 24462.

RESEARCH IN PUBLIC POLICY ANALYSIS AND MANAGEMENT. see *SOCIOLOGY*

350 CR
REVISTA CENTROAMERICANA DE ADMINISTRACION PUBLICA. 1981. irreg., no. 16, 1989. $3. Instituto Centroamericano de Administracion Publica, Apdo. Postal 10025, San Jose, Costa Rica. TEL 506-22-3133. FAX 506-23-2843. TELEX 2180 ICAP CR.

350 BL ISSN 0034-7612
JA5
REVISTA DE ADMINISTRACAO PUBLICA. (Text in Portuguese; summaries in English) 1967. q. $29.40 in S. America; N. America $33.60; elsewhere $45.50. Fundacao Getulio Vargas, C.P. 9052, 22250 Rio de Janeiro, R.J., Brazil. TELEX 21-36811. Ed. Ana Maria Marquesini. bk.rev.; bibl.; circ. 3,000.
   —BLDSC shelfmark: 7835.650000.

350 PR ISSN 0034-7620
JA5
REVISTA DE ADMINISTRACION PUBLICA. 1964. s-a. $4. Universidad de Puerto Rico, Escuela Graduada de Administracion Publica, Apartado 21839, Estacion U.P.R, Rio Piedras, PR 00931. TEL 809-764-0000. Ed. Emerito Rivera Torres. bk.rev.; circ. 1,000. **Indexed:** A.B.C.Pol.Sci.
   Description: Promotes the study, research and dissemination of information in the field of public affairs and public administration.

350 SP ISSN 0034-7639
K19
REVISTA DE ADMINISTRACION PUBLICA. 1950. 3/yr. 900 ptas.($17) (Centro de Estudios Constitucionales) Libreria Europa, Plaza de la Marina Espanola 9, Apdo. de Correos 50877, 28013 Madrid, Spain. TEL 91-5325069. Ed.Bd. bk.rev.; abstr.; bibl.; index. cum.index; circ. 2,300. **Indexed:** A.B.C.Pol.Sci., P.A.I.S.For.Lang.Ind.
   —BLDSC shelfmark: 7835.700000.

350 BL ISSN 0034-9240
JL2445 **CODEN:** RSPUEC
REVISTA DO SERVICO PUBLICO. 1937. q. Cr.$35($10) Departamento Administrativo do Pessoal Civil, Esplanada dos Ministerios, Bloco 7, Brasilia, Brazil. charts.

354.4 658 FR ISSN 0035-0672
JA11
REVUE ADMINISTRATIVE. 1948. bi-m. 665 F. (foreign 790 F.)(effective 1992). Bureau 203, 2 rue de Viarmes, 75001 Paris, France. TEL 42-36-23-90. Dir. Robert Catherine. adv.; bk.rev.; bibl.; rec.rev.; tr.lit.; index. (also avail. in microform from SWZ; reprint service avail. from SCH) **Indexed:** P.A.I.S.For.Lang.Ind.
   —BLDSC shelfmark: 7882.700000.

REVUE BELGE DE SECURITE SOCIALE. see *SOCIAL SERVICES AND WELFARE*

350 FR
REVUE DE DROIT SANITAIRE ET SOCIAL. 1958. q. 490 F. (foreign 560 F.). Editions Sirey-Diffusion Dalloz, 11 rue Soufflot, 75240 Paris Cedex 05, France. TEL 40-51-54-54. FAX 45-87-37-48. TELEX 206446F. (Subscr. to: 35, rue Tournefort, 75240 Paris Cedex 05, France) Ed. M. Elie Alfandari. bk.rev.; index.
   Former titles: Revue Trimestrielle de Droit Sanitaire et Social (ISSN 0035-4325); Revue de l'Aide Sociale.

350 340 FR ISSN 0337-7393
REVUE DE JURISPRUDENCE FISCALE. 1832. m. 670 F. Editions Francis Lefebvre, 5 rue Jacques Bingen, 75017 Paris, France.

350   AE
REVUE DE LA FONCTION PUBLIQUE. 1963. q. Direction Generale de la Fonction Publique, Palais du Gouvernement, Algiers, Algeria.

350   FR
REVUE DES COMMUNES ET DES ETABLISSEMENTS PUBLICS. 1908. 11/yr. Ed. P. Maraval, 32 220 Saint-Pons, France. adv.; circ. 27,900.

350   FR   ISSN 0152-7401
JS41
REVUE FRANCAISE D'ADMINISTRATION PUBLIQUE. 1967. q. 310 F. (foreign 395 F.). Institut International d'Administration Publique - International Institute of Public Administration, 2 Avenue de l'Observatoire, 75006 Paris, France. TELEX 204826 DOCFRAN. (Subscr. to: La Documentation Francaise, 29-31 Quai Voltaire, 75340 Paris Cedex 07, France) Ed. Jacques Ziller. adv.; bk.rev.; abstr.; bibl.; circ. 2,300. (also avail. in microform) **Indexed:** A.B.C.Pol.Sci., Rural Recreat.Tour.Abstr., SCIMP (1982-), World Agri.Econ.& Rural Sociol.Abstr.
—BLDSC shelfmark: 7902.240000.
Formerly (until 1977): Institut International d'Administration Publique. Bulletin (ISSN 0020-2355)
Description: Details on all aspects of public administration: broadcasting, city management and international cooperation, defense administration, immigration and health, civil servants, telecommunications, environment, etc.

RISKWATCH. see *INSURANCE*

350   IT
RIVISTA TRIMESTRALE DI SCIENZA DELL'AMMINISTRAZIONE. (Text in English, French and Italian) 1954; N.S. q. L.95000 (foreign L.110000)(effective 1992). Franco Angeli Editore, Viale Monza 106, 20127 Milan, Italy. TEL 02-28-27-651. Ed. Giorgio Freddi. adv.; bk.rev.; bibl.; charts; illus.; index; circ. 1,500.
Formerly: Scienza e la Tecnica della Organizzazione Nella Pubblicac Amministrazione (ISSN 0036-8873)

ROLE OF STATE LEGISLATURES IN THE FREEDOM STRUGGLE. see *POLITICAL SCIENCE*

353.9   US
ROSTER - CALIFORNIA STATE, COUNTY, CITY AND TOWNSHIP OFFICIALS STATE OFFICIALS OF THE UNITED STATES. Variant title: California Roster. a. $8.72. Office of Procurement, Dept. of General Services Publications, Box 1015, N. Highlands, CA 95660. TEL 916-445-3441. Ed. Kathy Mitchell. circ. 25,000.

351   RW
RWANDA. DIRECTION GENERALE DE LA STATISTIQUE. RAPPORT ANNUEL. a. Direction Generale de la Statistique, B.P. 46, Kigali, Rwanda.
Formerly: Rwanda. Direction Generale de la Documentation et de la Statistique. Rapport Annuel (ISSN 0080-5033)

354.6   SA   ISSN 0036-0767
JA26
S A I P A; journal of public administration-tydskrif vir publieke administrasie. (Text in Afrikaans, English; summaries in English) 1965. q. R.20 (effective Apr. 1991). South African Institute of Public Administration - Suid-Afrikaanse Instituut vir Publieke Administrasie, P.O. Box 2752, Pretoria 0001, South Africa. TEL 012-202-2851. FAX 326-5362. TELEX 321710. Ed. A. Viljoen. bk.rev.; circ. 2,000. **Indexed:** A.B.C.Pol.Sci., Ind.S.A.Per.
—BLDSC shelfmark: 8070.240000.

350   US   ISSN 1049-7838
JS39
S D A C C COUNTY COMMENT. 1953. m. $10. Association of County Commissioners, 207 E. Capitol, Ste. 203, Pierre, SD 57501. TEL 605-224-4554. Ed. Susan Comer. adv.; bk.rev.; circ. 1,150.
Former titles: S D A C C County Government; (until vol.36, no.5, 1990): South Dakota Journal of County Government.

350   BE
S O D I P A. (Text in Dutch) 1953. 11/yr. free. Sociaal Dienstbetoon Voor Het Personeel der Stad Antwerpen, 22 Hopland, 2000 Antwerp, Belgium. Ed. H. Schepers. adv.; circ. 18,200.

SAIGAI NO JITTAI TO SHOBO NO GENKYO/ANNUAL REPORT OF FIRE AND DISASTER PREVENTION. see *FIRE PREVENTION*

350 320   XM
ST. VINCENT GOVERNMENT INFORMATION SERVICE NEWS BULLETIN.* vol.6, 1974. m. free. Government Information Service, Kingstown, St. Vincent and the Grenadines, West Indies.

350   US
SALARY AND FRINGE BENEFITS SURVEY OF TENNESSEE MUNICIPALITIES. a. $15. University of Tennessee, Municipal Technical Advisory Service, 600 Henley, Ste. 120, Knoxville, TN 37996-4105. TEL 615-974-0411.

350   SM   ISSN 0036-4223
SAN MARINO (REPUBBLICA) BOLLETTINO UFFICIALE. 1924. 12/yr. L.20000. Dipartimento Affari Istituzionali, San Marino. bk.rev.; index; circ. 1,100.

350 327   SM
SAN MARINO (REPUBBLICA). DIPARTIMENTO AFFARI ESTERI. NOTIZIA. 1978. q. free. Dipartimento Affari Esteri, Ufficio Stampa, San Marino. Ed. Pier Roberto De Biagi.
Formerly: San Marino (Repubblica). Segreteria di Stato per gli Affari Esteri. Notizia; **Supersedes** (1959-1978): San Marino (Repubblica). Segreteria di Stato per gli Affari Esteri. Notiziario (ISSN 0558-4477)

338 381   CN   ISSN 0080-6498
SASKATCHEWAN. DEPARTMENT OF INDUSTRY AND COMMERCE. REPORT FOR THE FISCAL YEAR.* 1957. a. free. Government Printing Co., 2005 8th St., Regina, Sask. S4P 3V7, Canada. TEL 306-566-9393.

SCHIEDSMANNS ZEITUNG. see *LAW*

350   GW
SCHRIFTEN ZUR OEFFENTLICHEN VERWALTUNG UND OEFFENTLICHEN WIRTSCHAFT. (Text in German; summaries in English, French, Russian) 1974. irreg. price varies. Nomos Verlagsgesellschaft mbH und Co. Kg., Postfach 610, 7570 Baden-Baden, Germany. Eds. P. Eichhorn, P. Friedrich.

350.6   GW   ISSN 0342-7722
SCHWARTZSCHE VAKANZEN-ZEITUNG. 1871. 3/m. DM.57.60. Verlag Otto Schwartz und Co., Annastr. 7, 3400 Goettingen, Germany. TEL 0551-31051. FAX 0551-372812.

354.4   SZ   ISSN 0036-7990
SCHWEIZERISCHES ZENTRALBLATT FUER STAATS- UND GEMEINDEVERWALTUNG. (Supplement: Zeitschrift fuer Oeffentliche Fuersorge) m. 102 SFr. (foreign 120 SFr.). Orell Fuessli Graphische Betriebe AG, Dietzingerstr. 3, CH-8036 Zurich, Switzerland. Ed.Bd. circ. 1,750.

SCIENCE AND GOVERNMENT REPORT. see *POLITICAL SCIENCE*

350   UK   ISSN 0305-6562
JS4101
SCOTLAND'S REGIONS. 1933. a. £2. William Culross & Son Ltd., Queen St., Coupar Angus, Perthshire, Scotland.
Incorporates: County and Municipal Year Book for Scotland (ISSN 0070-1300)

SENATE HISTORY. see *HISTORY — History Of North And South America*

350   SG
SENEGAL D'AUJOURD'HUI. m. Ministry of Culture and Communications, 58 blvd de la Republique, B.P. 4027, Dakar, Senegal. circ. 5,000.

350.6   FR
SERVICE ECONOMIQUE FONCTIONNAIRE. 1961. q. 132 av. Jules Cantini, 13008 Marseille, France. TEL 9179-4138. Ed. Rene Monduel.
Formerly: Fonctionnaire National.

354.611   TI   ISSN 0035-4120
SERVIR; revue Tunisienne du service public. (Text in Arabic and French) 1967-1976, resumed 1985. s-a. 2 din. for 6 nos. Ecole Nationale d'Administration, Centre de Recherches et d'Etudes Administratives, 24 Ave. du Dr. Calmette, Mutuelleville, 1060 Tunis, Tunisia. abstr.; stat.; circ. 2,000. (tabloid format; back issues avail.)

SEYCHELLES. MINISTRY OF FINANCE. BUDGET ADDRESS. see *BUSINESS AND ECONOMICS — Public Finance, Taxation*

353.9   US   ISSN 0037-3672
JK3501
SHIELD; Civil Service news. 1935. w. $21.25. (New Jersey Civil Service Association) New Jersey Shield Publishing Co., Inc., Box 505, Fairview, NJ 07022-0505. FAX 201-945-3490. Ed. Ronald Page. adv.; bk.rev.; circ. 30,000. (tabloid format) **Indexed:** DM & T.

350   TS
AL-SIJIL AL-SHAHRI LI-AHDATH DAWLAT AL-IMARAT AL-ARABIYYAH AL-MUTTAHIDAH/MONTHLY RECORD FOR THE EVENTS OF THE UNITED ARAB EMIRATES. (Text in Arabic) 1979. m. Ministry of Information and Culture, Information Department, P.O. Box 17, Abu Dhabi, United Arab Emirates. TEL 453000. circ. 1,000 (controlled).
Description: Reports activities of the rulers of the U.A.E., legislative, civil service, cabinet, and economic developments, and international concerns.

350 320   US
SIMMONS POLITICAL REPORT. 1984. w. $52. Box 783, Jefferson City, MO 65102. TEL 314-635-2225. Ed. Jame Simmons.
Description: Reports on Missouri state politics.

350   SI   ISSN 0129-3109
SINGAPORE GOVERNMENT DIRECTORY. 1960. biennial. S.$10. Ministry of Communications and Information, Psychological Defense & Publicity Division, PSA Building, 30th Fl., 460 Alexandra Rd., Singapore 0511, Singapore. circ. 8,500.

350   YU   ISSN 0037-7147
SLUZBEN VESNIK NA SOCIJALISTICKA REPUBLIKA MAKEDONIJA. (Text in Macedonian) 1945. irreg. 380 din. Socijalisticki Savez Radnog Naroda SR Makedonije, 29 Noemvri 10a, Skopje, Yugoslavia. Ed. Petar Janevski.

354 954   II   ISSN 0037-9786
SOCIETY FOR THE STUDY OF STATE GOVERNMENTS. JOURNAL. 1968. q. Society for the Study of State Governments, Kopparti Pl., Karaundi, Varanasi 221005, Uttar Pradesh, India.
Description: Covers the political and constitutional developments of India.

350   US   ISSN 0038-0121
HD82
SOCIO-ECONOMIC PLANNING SCIENCES; an international journal of public sector decision-making. 1967. 4/yr. £170($255) (effective 1992). Pergamon Press, Inc., Journals Division, 660 White Plains Rd., Tarrytown, NY 10591-5153. TEL 914-524-9200. FAX 914-333-2444. (And: Headington Hill Hall, Oxford OX3 0BW, England. TEL 0865-794141) Ed. Barnett R. Parker. adv.; bk.rev.; charts; illus.; stat.; index; circ. 1,700. (also avail. in microform from MIM,UMI; back issues avail.) **Indexed:** A.B.C.Pol.Sci., Abstr.Health Care Manage.Stud., ASCA, ASSIA, BPIA, Bus.Ind., C.I.J.E., C.R.E.J., Cont.Pg.Manage., Curr.Cont., Educ.Admin.Abstr., Excerp.Med., Geo.Abstr., J.Cont.Quant.Meth., Lang.& Lang.Behav.Abstr., Manage.Cont., Med.Care Rev., Mid.East: Abstr.& Ind., Oper.Res.Manage.Sci., P.A.I.S., Qual.Contr.Appl.Stat., Risk Abstr., Rural Devel.Abstr., Rural Recreat.Tour.Abstr., Sage Pub.Admin.Abstr., Sage Urb.Stud.Abstr., SSCI, Tr.& Indus.Ind., W.R.C.Inf., World Agri.Econ.& Rural Sociol.Abstr.
—BLDSC shelfmark: 8319.576000.
Refereed Serial

SOLID WASTE & POWER; the magazine of waste management solutions. see *ENERGY*

350   SO
SOMALI INSTITUTE OF PUBLIC ADMINISTRATION NEWSLETTER.* (Text in English) 1969. q. Somali Institute of Public Administration, Mogadishu, Somalia. bibl.

PUBLIC ADMINISTRATION

350 US
SOURCE BOOK OF AMERICAN STATE LEGISLATION. 1976. biennial. $99. American Legislative Exchange Council, 214 Massachusetts Ave., N.E., Ste. 240, Washington, DC 20002. TEL 202-547-4646. FAX 202-547-8142. Ed. Noel Card. circ. 7,500.
  Description: Compendium of model state legislation, with analysis in the areas of: tax and fiscal policy, education, health care, energy, environment, labor, housing, welfare, civil justice, criminal justice, substance abuse, agriculture, telecommunications, transportation, and insurance.

354.9 AT ISSN 0038-2906
SOUTH AUSTRALIAN GOVERNMENT GAZETTE. 1839. w. Aus.$135 (typically set in June). Government Printer, 282 Richmond Rd., Netley, S.A. 5037, Australia. TEL 08-226-4701. FAX 08-226-4729. adv.; charts; stat.; s-a index; circ. 1,850. **Indexed:** AESIS.

350 320 US
▼**SOUTH CAROLINA FORUM.** 1990. 3/yr. $18.75. University of South Carolina, Institute of Public Affairs, Gambrell Hall, Columbia, SC 29208. TEL 803-777-8156. Ed. Pinkie Whitfield.
  Description: Covers public policy issues and practical government problems in South Carolina.

350 UK
SOUTHAMPTON CITY NEWS. 1973. m. Southampton City Council, Civic Centre, Southampton SO9 4XR, England. TEL 0703-223855. FAX 0703-234537. TELEX 477915. adv.; circ. 92,000 (controlled).
  Formerly: Now in Southampton.

350 US ISSN 0362-3475
SOUTHEAST MICHIGAN COUNCIL OF GOVERNMENTS. ANNUAL REPORT. 1970. a. free. Southeast Michigan Council of Governments, 660 Plaza Dr., No. 1900, Detroit, MI 48226. TEL 313-961-4266. FAX 313-961-4869. Ed. Alma Simmons. illus.; circ. 11,000. Key Title: Annual Report - Southeast Michigan Council of Governments.

SOVETSKAYA MILITSIYA. see *MILITARY*

350 SP
SPAIN. BOLETIN OFICIAL DEL ESTADO. 1936. d. (except Sun.). 25607 ptas. (foreign 28600 ptas.)(effective 1992). Boletin Oficial del Estado, Trafalgar, 29, 28071 Madrid, Spain. TEL 5382100. FAX 5382348. index. (also avail. in microfilm from BHP,KTO; microfiche)
  ●Also available online.
  Formerly: Spain. Ministerio de Relaciones con las Cortes y de la Secretaria del Gobierno. Boletin Oficial del Estado (ISSN 0212-033X)

363.6 SP
SPAIN. MINISTERIO DE LA VIVIENDA. SERIE 3: VIVIENDA. 1974 (no. 1010). irreg. Ministerio de la Vivienda, Secretaria General Tecnica, Madrid, Spain.

350.6 CE
SRI LANKA GOVERNMENT GAZETTE. (Text in English) 1802. w. Government Press, P.O. Box 507, Colombo, Sri Lanka. TEL 1-93611. circ. 54,000.
  Description: Official government bulletin.

350 GW ISSN 0932-8955
STADT DUISBURG. VERWALTUNGSBERICHT. 1963. a. Amt fuer Statistik, Der Oberstadtdirektor, Bismarckstr. 150-158, 4100 Duisburg 1, Germany. TEL 0203-2833085. FAX 0203-2834404.

354.43 GW
STADT UND GEMEINDE. 1946. m. DM.120. (Deutscher Staedte- und Gemeindebund) Verlag Otto Schwartz und Co., Annastr. 7, 3400 Goettingen, Germany. TEL 0551-31051. FAX 0551-372812. adv.; bk.rev.; index; circ. 7,000 (controlled).
  Former titles: Staedte- und Gemeindebund (ISSN 0342-7706); Staedtebund (ISSN 0038-903X)

331.795 NO ISSN 0800-658X
STAFO-NYTT. 1925. m. (8/yr.). Statstjenestemannsforbundet, Postbox 9038, M-0134 Oslo 1, Norway. Ed. Tryque Christensen. adv.; circ. 15,000.
  Formerly: Statstjenestemannen.

352 FR
STANDING CONFERENCE OF LOCAL AND REGIONAL AUTHORITIES OF EUROPE. OFFICIAL REPORTS OF DEBATES. (Reports of 1st-3rd Sessions never published. Former name of issuing body: European Conference of Local and Regional Authorities) 1962. a. $18. Standing Conference of Local and Regional Authorities of Europe, Publications Section, Strasbourg, France. (Dist. in U.S. by: Manhattan Publishing Co., P.O. Box 650 Croton-on-Hudson, NY 10520) (Affiliate: Council of Europe) bk.rev.
  Former titles: European Conference of Local and Regional Authorities. Official Reports of Debates; European Conference of Local Authorities. Official Reports of Debates (ISSN 0071-2620)

352 FR
STANDING CONFERENCE OF LOCAL AND REGIONAL AUTHORITIES OF EUROPE. TEXTS ADOPTED. (For 1st and 2nd Sessions, Documents and Texts Adopted issued in one vol. Former name of issuing body: European Conference of Local and Regional Authorities) 1957. a. $5. Standing Conference of Local and Regional Authorities of Europe, Publications Section, Strasbourg, France. (Dist. in U.S. by: Manhattan Publishing Co., P.O.Box 650, Croton-on-Hudson, NY 10520) bk.rev.
  Former titles: European Conference of Local and Regional Authorities. Texts Adopted; European Conference of Local Authorities. Texts Adopted (ISSN 0071-2639)

350 US ISSN 0561-8630
STATE ADMINISTRATIVE OFFICIALS: CLASSIFIED BY FUNCTION. (Supplements Book of the States) 1957. biennial. $30. Council of State Governments, Iron Works Pike, Box 11910, Lexington, KY 40578-9989. TEL 606-231-1939. FAX 606-231-1858.
  Formerly: Administrative Officials Classified by Functions (ISSN 0191-9458)
  Description: Lists names, titles, addresses, and telephone numbers of thousands of administrators in more than 130 areas of state government.

350 317 US ISSN 1047-3394
HA203
▼**STATE AND LOCAL STATISTICS SOURCES.** 1990. irreg. $135. Gale Research Inc., 835 Penobscot Bldg., Detroit, MI 48226-4094. TEL 313-961-2242. FAX 313-961-6083. TELEX 810-221-7086. Eds. M. Balachandran, S. Balachandran.

STATE ARTS AGENCY DIRECTORY. see *BUSINESS AND ECONOMICS — Trade And Industrial Directories*

STATE BUDGET AND TAX NEWS. see *BUSINESS AND ECONOMICS — Public Finance, Taxation*

350 US ISSN 0585-1173
JK5330
STATE DIRECTORY OF KENTUCKY. 1965. a. $14 to individuals; libraries $12 (effective 1992). Directories, Inc., Box 187, Pewee Valley, KY 40056. Ed. Mary McKay Wright. circ. 5,000.

350 US
STATE ELECTIVE OFFICIALS AND THE LEGISLATURES. (Supplements Book of the States) biennial. $30. Council of State Governments, Iron Works Pike, Box 11910, Lexington, KY 40578-9989. TEL 606-231-1939.
  Description: Lists names, parties, addresses, and districts of state legislators, as well as elected officials with state-wide jurisdiction.

350 US
STATE-FEDERAL ISSUE BRIEFS. 1986. irreg., vol.2, no.9, 1989. $6.50. National Conference of State Legislatures, 1560 Broadway, Ste. 700, Denver, CO 80202-5140. TEL 303-830-2200. FAX 303-863-8003.
  Description: Describes congressional, White House, and federal agency issues that affect state legislatures.

350 320 US ISSN 0888-8590
JK2403
STATE GOVERNMENT (WASHINGTON); guide to current issues and activities. 1985. a. $15.95. Congressional Quarterly Inc., 1414 22nd St., N.W., Washington, DC 20037. TEL 202-887-8500. FAX 202-728-1863. Ed. Thad L. Beyle.
  Description: Collection of articles concerning state government reprinted from various publications. Topics include closed primaries, school reform, legislature, and ethics.

STATE GOVERNMENT NEWS; the monthly magazine covering all facets of state government. see *POLITICAL SCIENCE*

328 353.9 US ISSN 0190-6623
STATE GOVERNMENT RESEARCH CHECKLIST. 1947. bi-m. $20. Council of State Governments, Iron Works Pike, Box 11910, Lexington, KY 40578-9989. TEL 606-231-1939. bibl.; circ. 1,800. (reprint service avail. from ISI,UMI) **Indexed:** C.L.I., Leg.Per., Manage.Cont.
  Formerly (until 1979): Legislative Research Checklist (ISSN 0024-0486)
  Description: Lists reports by legislative research agencies, other study committees and commissions in the states, and independent organizations that have published material appropriate for review by state agencies.

STATE HOUSE WATCH. see *SOCIAL SERVICES AND WELFARE*

350 US
▼**STATE LEGAL ISSUES QUARTERLY.** 1991. q. $50. Federation of Tax Administrators, 444 N. Capitol St., N.W., Washington, DC 20001. TEL 202-624-5890. Ed. Audrey Maynard. circ. 1,000.

350 US ISSN 0195-6639
JK2495
STATE LEGISLATIVE LEADERSHIP, COMMITTEES AND STAFF. (Supplements Book of States) biennial. $30 to individuals; state officials $21. Council of State Governments, Iron Works Pike, Box 11910, Lexington, KY 40578-9989. TEL 606-231-1939.
  Formerly: Principal Legislative Staff Offices.
  Description: Supplies the names, telephone numbers, and organizational patterns of state legislative leaders, legislative committees and chairpersons, principal legislative staff officers, and staff members.

350 US
STATE LEGISLATIVE REPORT. 1980. irreg., (10-12/yr.). $30. National Conference of State Legislatures, 1560 Broadway, Ste. 700, Denver, CO 80202. TEL 303-830-2200. FAX 303-863-8003. Ed. Karen Hansen.
  Description: Reports on current and emerging state fiscal issues.

STATE LEGISLATIVE SOURCEBOOK; a resource guide to legislative information in the fifty states. see *LAW*

STATE LEGISLATURES. see *POLITICAL SCIENCE*

350 US
STATE OF LOUISIANA PUBLIC DOCUMENTS. 1948. s-a. free. State Library, Recorder of Documents, State Library, Box 131, Baton Rouge, LA 70821. TEL 504-342-4929. FAX 504-342-3547. Ed. Grace Moore. circ. 300.
  Formerly: Public Documents - State of Louisiana (ISSN 0099-2410)

STATE POLICY REPORTS. see *BUSINESS AND ECONOMICS — Public Finance, Taxation*

350 US ISSN 0899-2207
JK2403
STATE YELLOW BOOK; who's who in the executive, and legislative branches of the 50 State Governments. 1973. s-a. $185. Monitor Publishing Company, 104 Fifth Avenue, 2nd Fl., New York, NY 10011. TEL 202-347-7757. FAX 202-628-3430. Ed. Imogene Akins. circ. 3,800.
  Formerly: State Information Book.
  Description: Reflects the most recent changes in elected and appointed government personnel at the state level. Includes Executive and Legislative Branches, profiles of all 50 states and their counties.

331.7 US ISSN 0091-1402
JK6655
STATEHOUSE OBSERVER. 1972. m. free. State Personnel Department, Box 94905, Lincoln, NE 68509. TEL 402-471-4112. Ed. Marcia Donnelson. stat.; illus.; circ. 18,000. (also avail. in microfiche)

350 DK ISSN 0902-6681
HJ56
STATENS LAANTAGNING OG GAELD. 1924. a. DKK 45 (typically set in Mar.). Finansministeriet - Ministry of Finance, Christiansborg Slotsplads 1, 1109 DK-Copenhagen K, Denmark. TEL 45-33-929200. FAX 45-33-328030. TELEX 16140 BUDGET DK. (Dist. by: Statens Informationstjeneste, Bredgade 20, P.O. Box 1103, II09 Copenhagen K, Denmark) circ. 3,500.
   Formerly: Danske Statslaan (ISSN 0105-4554)
   Description: Reports on the Danish government's borrowing and debt.

STATUTORY TIME LIMITATIONS: WASHINGTON STATE. see *LAW*

STEINE SPRECHEN. see *CONSERVATION*

350 AU ISSN 0039-1050
STEIRISCHE GEMEINDE-NACHRICHTEN. 1948. m. Steiermaerkischer Gemeindebund, Burgring 18, A-8010 Graz, Austria. Ed. Dr. Hermine Jarz. adv.; bk.rev.; charts; stat.; index.

350 UK
STRATHCLYDE REGIONAL COUNCIL. ANNUAL REPORT & FINANCIAL STATEMENT. 1980. a. free. Strathclyde Regional Council, Public Relations Department, Strathclyde House, 20 India St., Glasgow G2 4PF, Scotland. Ed. Robert Calderwood. circ. 10,000.
   Formerly: Strathclyde's Budget (ISSN 0260-8065)

350 GW
STUDIENFUEHRER. 1979. s-a. Fachhochschule des Bundes fuer Oeffentliche Verwaltung, Bernhard-Feilchenfeld-Str. 9-11, 5000 Cologne 51, Germany. TEL 0221-3670-0. FAX 0221-3670185.

354.624 SJ
SUDAN. MINISTRY OF FINANCE AND NATIONAL ECONOMY. ANNUAL BUDGET SPEECH, PROPOSALS FOR THE GENERAL BUDGET AND THE DEVELOPMENT BUDGET. a. Ministry of Finance and National Economy, Box 298, Khartoum, Sudan.

354.624 SJ
SUDAN. MINISTRY OF FINANCE AND NATIONAL ECONOMY. GENERAL BUDGET: REVIEW, PRESENTATION AND ANALYSIS. irreg. Ministry of Finance and National Economy, Box 298, Khartoum, Sudan.

350 SJ
SUDAN JOURNAL OF ADMINISTRATION AND DEVELOPMENT. (Text in Arabic or English) 1965. a. Institute of Public Administration, P.O. Box 1492, Khartoum, Sudan.

353.9 US ISSN 0070-1157
KF165
SUGGESTED STATE LEGISLATION. 1941. a. $30. Council of State Governments, Iron Works Pike, Box 11910, Lexington, KY 40578-9989. TEL 606-231-1939. cum.index; circ. 5,500. (also avail. in microfiche from WSH) **Indexed:** C.L.I., Leg.Per.
   Description: Provides a source of legislative ideas and drafting assistance for state government officials.

350 US
SUMMARY OF NEW LAWS. a. $15. University of Tennessee, Municipal Technical Advisory Service, 600 Henley, Ste. 120, Knoxville, TN 37996-4105. TEL 615-974-0411.
   Formerly: Summary of Public Acts of Interest to Municipal Officials.

SURVEY OF ARTS ADMINISTRATION TRAINING. see *ART*

354 SQ
SWAZILAND. MINISTRY OF FINANCE. RECURRENT ESTIMATES OF PUBLIC EXPENDITURE. (Report year ends Mar. 31.) a. Ministry of Finance Office, Box 443, Mbabane, Swaziland.
   Formerly: Swaziland. Central Statistical Office. Recurrent Estimates of Public Expenditure.

354.4 FR ISSN 0039-8462
T P
ANNALES. 1881. m. 600 F. (Federation Nationale des Travaux Publics et des Syndicats Affilies) Centre de l'Industrie Francaise des Travaux Publics, 3 rue de Berri, 75008 Paris, France. adv.; bk.rev.; bibl.; illus.; circ. 1,600.

354.3 II ISSN 0039-9310
TAMIL NADU INFORMATION. (Text in English and Tamil) 1947. m. Rs.225. Director of Information and Public Relations, Fort St. George, Madras 9, India. adv.; bk.rev.; illus.; circ. 6,000.
   Formerly: Madras Information.

350 330 IQ
TANMIAT AL-RAFIDAIN/RAFIDAIN DEVELOPMENT. Cover title: Journal of Tanmiat al-Rafidain. (Text in Arabic, English; summaries in English) vol.12, 1990. 4/yr. ID.15 to individuals; institutions ID.25. (Mosul University, Faculty of Administration and Economics) Majallat Tanmiat al-Rafidain, P.O. Box 78, Mosul, Iraq. TEL 814433. TELEX 8011. Ed. Kubais Said Fahady. adv.; abstr.
   Description: Publishes research papers in the fields of administration, economics, accountancy and statistics.
   Refereed Serial

350 015 GW ISSN 0082-1829
TASCHENBUCH DES OEFFENTLICHEN LEBENS: Deutschland. 1950. a. DM.106.20 price varies. Festland-Verlag Gmbh, Postfach 200561, Basteistr. 88, 5300 Bonn 2, Germany. TEL 0228-362021. Ed. Heinz H. Hey. adv.; circ. 18,000.

354.9 AT ISSN 0039-9795
TASMANIAN GOVERNMENT GAZETTE. 1836. w. Aus.$250. Tasmanian Government Printer, G.P.O. Box 307-C, Hobart 7001, Australia. adv.; circ. 1,400.

TAYLOR'S ENCYCLOPEDIA OF GOVERNMENT OFFICIALS. FEDERAL AND STATE. see *ENCYCLOPEDIAS AND GENERAL ALMANACS*

350 US
TEACHING GEORGIA GOVERNMENT. 1979. q. free. University of Georgia, Carl Vinson Institute of Government, Terrell Hall, Athens, GA 30602. TEL 404-542-2736. Eds. Edwing L. Jackson, Inge Whittle.
   Description: News of current developments and issues in Georgia government. Provides a forum for teachers to share ideas about teaching citizenship and government.

TEACHING PUBLIC ADMINISTRATION. see *EDUCATION — Teaching Methods And Curriculum*

350 IT
TECNOLOGIE DEI SERVIZI PUBBLICI. 1980. bi-w. L.80000($139) (foreign L.160000). (Comitato Regionale Imprese Pubbliche Enti Locali) Stammer S.p.A, Centro Commerciale Milano San Felice, 20090 Segrate-Milan, Italy. TEL 02 7530651. FAX 02-7530587. TELEX 321083 STAMMER. Ed. Girolamo Bellina. adv.; circ. 6,000.

TENNESSEE EMPLOYMENT LAW UPDATE. see *BUSINESS AND ECONOMICS — Labor And Industrial Relations*

350 US ISSN 0194-1240
TENNESSEE JOURNAL. 1974. w. $167. M. Lee Smith Publishers & Printers, 162 Fourth Ave. N., Box 2678, Nashville, TN 37219. TEL 615-242-7395. FAX 615-256-6601. Ed. Bradford N. Forrister. circ. 1,400.
   Description: Insider's newsletter on Tennessee government and politics.

350 320 US
TEXAS AGENDA. 1989. s-m. $95. Decision - Strategies Group, Inc., Box 90422, Austin, TX 78709. TEL 512-892-6995. Ed. Hilary Hylton.
   Description: Covers Texas government, politics and business.

TEXAS GOVERNMENT NEWSLETTER. see *POLITICAL SCIENCE*

353 US ISSN 0040-4640
TEXAS PUBLIC EMPLOYEE. 1946. m. $5. Texas Public Employees Association, Drawer 12217, Capitol Sta., Austin, TX 78711. TEL 512-476-2691. Ed. Randy Roberts. adv.; illus.; circ. 20,000. (tabloid format)

PUBLIC ADMINISTRATION 4075

350.6 US ISSN 0363-7530
JK4830
TEXAS STATE DIRECTORY. 1940. a. $24.95. Texas State Directory Press, Inc., Box 12186, Austin, TX 78711. TEL 512-477-5698. FAX 512-473-2447. Ed. Julie F. Sayers. adv.; circ. 10,000.

352 US ISSN 0040-473X
JS39
TEXAS TOWN & CITY. 1914. m. $15. Texas Municipal League, 1020 Southwest Tower, Austin, TX 78701. TEL 512-478-6601. FAX 512-320-1301. Ed. Karla Vining. adv.; bk.rev.; illus.; index; circ. 11,800.
   Indexed: Sage Pub.Admin.Abstr., Sage Urb.Stud.Abstr.

350 320 US ISSN 0890-5924
TEXAS WEEKLY. 1984. 50/yr. $150. P P S, Inc., Box 5306, Austin, TX 78763. TEL 512-322-9332. FAX 512-453-0027. Ed. Sam Kinch, Jr.
   Description: Reports on Texas government and politics.

354.3 TH ISSN 0040-5353
THAI JOURNAL OF DEVELOPMENT ADMINISTRATION. (Text in English and Thai) 1960. q. $15. National Institute of Development Administration, Research Center, Klongchan, Bangkok 24, Thailand. Ed. Juree Vichit-Vadakan. adv.; bk.rev.; abstr.; charts; illus.; stat.; index; circ. 1,500.
   Formerly: Thai Journal of Public Administration.

THIRD WORLD PLANNING REVIEW. see *BUSINESS AND ECONOMICS — International Development And Assistance*

THIS WEEK IN WASHINGTON. see *SOCIAL SERVICES AND WELFARE*

331.795 NO
TJENESTEMANNSBLADET. 10/yr. Norsk Tjenestemannslag, Hammersborg Torg 1, Oslo 1, Norway. adv.; circ. 34,561.

350 NE ISSN 0018-1129
HET TORENTJE; personeelsblad van het Ministerie van Binnenlandse Zaken. 1947. m. free. Ministerie van Binnenlandse Zaken - Ministry of the Interior, Schedeldoekshaven 200, 2500 EA The Hague, Netherlands. bk.rev.; illus.; index; circ. 6,000.

350 MP
▼**TORIYN MEDEELEL/STATE INFORMATION.** (Text in Mongolian) 1991. q. State Little Hural, Ulan Bator, Mongolia.
   Description: Covers presidential and governmental decrees, state laws, and parliamentary news.

354 NZ
TOTALISATOR AGENCY BOARD. ANNUAL REPORT. 1951. a. free. Totalisator Agency Board, 106-110 Jackson St., Petore, New Zealand. TEL 644-576-6999. FAX 644-576-6942. Ed. B.D. Longhurst. illus.; circ. 1,600.

TRENDS IN COMMUNICATIONS POLICY. see *COMMUNICATIONS — Telephone And Telegraph*

TRENTINO; rivista della provincia autonoma di Trento. see *ENVIRONMENTAL STUDIES*

350 TR
TRINIDAD AND TOBAGO GAZETTE. 1962. w. T.T.$18. Government Printer, 121 Victoria Ave., Port-of-Spain, Trinidad & Tobago, W.I.

350 388.31 001.3 GW
UEBER BERG UND TAL. 1936. bi-m. Stuttgarter Strassenbahnen AG, Postfach 801006, 7000 Stuttgart 80, Germany. Ed. Peter Brodbeck. circ. 6,000.

350 690.028 IT
L'UFFICIO TECNICO; rivista mensile di tecnica edilizia e urbanistica per amministrazioni pubbliche, professionisti e costruttori. 1979. m. (11/yr.). L.85000 to individuals; institutions L.175000(effective 1992). Maggioli Editore, Via Crimera 1, Casella Postale 290, 47037 Rimini, Italy. TEL 0541-626777. FAX 0541-622020. Dir. Ermete Dalprato.

PUBLIC ADMINISTRATION

350 320   SW
UMEAA STUDIES IN POLITICS AND PUBLIC ADMINISTRATION. (Text in English or Swedish; summaries in English) 1978. irreg., no.9, 1984. price varies. Liber Forlag, S-205 10, Malmo, Sweden. Ed. Sten Berglund.

355.03   US   ISSN 0091-6919
UA23.2
U.S. DEPARTMENT OF DEFENSE. DEFENSE DEPARTMENT REPORT;* a statement by the Secretary of Defense to the Congress on the budget and defense programs. 1968. a. price varies. U.S. Department of Defense, The Pentagon, Washington, DC 20301. TEL 202-545-6700. (Orders to: Supt. of Documents, Washington, DC 20402) (also avail. in microfiche) **Indexed:** C.I.S. Ind. Key Title: Statement of Secretary of Defense Before the House Armed Services Committee on the Defense Budget and Program.

353.3   US   ISSN 0011-7331
HD181
U.S. DEPARTMENT OF THE INTERIOR. DECISIONS OF THE DEPARTMENT OF THE INTERIOR. 1955. a. $65 five-year subscr. U.S. Department of the Interior, Washington, DC 20240. TEL 703-235-3799. (Orders to: Printing Clerk, OHA, BT 3, 4015 Wilson Blvd. Arlington, VA 22203) Ed. Rachael Cubbage. (also avail. in microform) Key Title: Decisions of the Department of the Interior.

350   US   ISSN 0145-1502
KF6233.32
U.S. GENERAL ACCOUNTING OFFICE. OFFICE OF THE GENERAL COUNSEL. DIGESTS OF UNPUBLISHED DECISIONS OF THE COMPTROLLER GENERAL OF THE UNITED STATES. w.? U.S. General Accounting Office, Office of the General Counsel, 441 G. St., N.W., Rm. 4133, Washington, DC 20548. TEL 202-275-5028.

338.973   US
HC110.P63
U.S. GENERAL SERVICES ADMINISTRATION. CATALOG OF FEDERAL DOMESTIC ASSISTANCE. 1971. s-a. $38. U.S. General Services Administration, 300 Seventh St., S.W. , Reporters Bldg., Rm. 101, Washington, DC 20407. TEL 202-708-5126. FAX 202-401-8233. (Subscriptions to: Supt. of Documents, Washington, DC 20402) (also avail. in magnetic tape; avail. on floppy disc) Key Title: Catalog of Federal Domestic Assistance.
●Also available online.
Former titles: U.S. Office of Management and Budget. Catalog of Federal Domestic Assistance (ISSN 0097-7799); Continues: U.S. Office of Economic Opportunity. Catalog of Federal Domestic Assistance.

U.S. LIBRARY OF CONGRESS. CONGRESSIONAL RESEARCH SERVICE. DIGEST OF PUBLIC GENERAL BILLS AND RESOLUTIONS. see *LAW*

U.S. NATIONAL PARK SERVICE. FEDERAL ARCHEOLOGY: THE CURRENT PROGRAM. see *ARCHAEOLOGY*

328.73   US   ISSN 0095-2109
T174.5
U.S. OFFICE OF TECHNOLOGY ASSESSMENT ANNUAL REPORT TO THE CONGRESS. 1974. a. free. U.S. Office of Technology Assessment, Washington, DC 20510. TEL 202-224-8996. FAX 202-228-6098. (Dist. by: Supt. of Documents, Government Printing Office, Washington, DC 20402) circ. 5,000. Key Title: Annual Report to the Congress by the Office of Technology Assessment.

350   US   ISSN 0511-4187
J80
U.S. OFFICE OF THE FEDERAL REGISTER. WEEKLY COMPILATION OF PRESIDENTIAL DOCUMENTS. 1965. w. $55. U.S. Office of the Federal Register, National Archives and Records Administration, Washington, DC 20408. TEL 202-523-5240. (Orders to: Supt. of Documents, Box 371954, Pittsburgh, PA 15250-7954) index; circ. 7,000. **Indexed:** P.A.I.S.

353   US   ISSN 0092-1904
JK421
UNITED STATES GOVERNMENT MANUAL. 1934. a. $23. U.S. Office of the Federal Register, National Archives and Records Administration, Washington, DC 20408. TEL 202-523-5240. (Dist. by: Supt. of Documents, Box 371954, Pittsburgh, PA 15250-7950) circ. 61,000. (also avail. in microform from UMI,BHP; magnetic tape)
Former titles (until 1973): United States Government Organization Manual (ISSN 0083-1174); (until 1948): United States Government Manual.

350 658   CK   ISSN 0465-4773
UNIVERSIDAD DE MEDELLIN. FACULTAD DE CIENCIAS ADMINISTRATIVAS. REVISTA. 1973. q. Universidad de Medellin, Facultad de Ciencias Administrativas, Calle 31, No. 83b-150, Medellin, Colombia. Ed. Orlando Vasquez Castro. charts; illus.

350   PN
UNIVERSIDAD DE PANAMA. FACULTAD DE ADMINISTRACION PUBLICA Y COMERCIO. REVISTA. q. Universidad de Panama, Facultad de Administracion Publica y Comercio, Panama, Panama. illus.

UNIVERSIDAD DE SEVILLA. INSTITUTO GARCIA OVIEDO. PUBLICACIONES. see *LAW*

350   AG
UNIVERSIDAD NACIONAL DEL LITORAL. FACULTAD DE CIENCIAS DE LA ADMINISTRACION. REVISTA. 1969. a. Universidad Nacional del Litoral, Facultad de Ciencias de la Administracion, 25 de Mayo, 1783, Santa Fe, Argentina.

UNIVERSITAET HOHENHEIM. AMTLICHE MITTEILUNGEN. see *EDUCATION — Higher Education*

350   ZR
UNIVERSITE NATIONALE DU ZAIRE, KINSHASA. INSTITUT DE RECHERCHES ECONOMIQUES ET SOCIALES. DOCUMENT DU MOIS. (Text in French) 1974. q. $15. Universite Nationale du Zaire, Kinshasa, Institut de Recherches Economiques et Sociale, B.P. 257, Kinshasa 11, Zaire. Ed.Bd.

350 320 010   US   ISSN 0041-9443
UNIVERSITY OF CALIFORNIA. INSTITUTE OF GOVERNMENTAL STUDIES LIBRARY. ACCESSIONS LIST. 1963. m. free. University of California, Berkeley, Institute of Governmental Studies, 109 Moses Hall, Berkeley, CA 94720. TEL 415-642-8274. Ed. Jack Leister. circ. 250. (processed; reprint service avail. from UMI)

350   US   ISSN 0194-2670
UNIVERSITY OF NEW MEXICO. DIVISION OF GOVERNMENT RESEARCH. MONOGRAPH SERIES. 1946. irreg., vol.86, 1981. free. University of New Mexico, Division of Government Research, Albuquerque, NM 87131. TEL 505-277-3305. FAX 505-277-6540. Ed. Robert U. Anderson. bk.rev.; abstr.; circ. 600.

350
UNIVERSITY OF TEXAS, AUSTIN. LYNDON B. JOHNSON SCHOOL OF PUBLIC AFFAIRS. WORKING PAPER SERIES. vol.5, 1976. irreg. University of Texas at Austin, Lyndon B. Johnson School of Public Affairs, Austin, TX 78713-7450. TEL 512-471-4962.

350   PH
UNIVERSITY OF THE PHILIPPINES. COLLEGE OF PUBLIC ADMINISTRATION. PUBLIC ADMINISTRATION OCCASIONAL PAPERS AND SPECIAL STUDIES SERIES. (Text in English) irreg. price varies. University of the Philippines, College of Public Administration, PARDEC-SAAC Building, P.O. Box 198, Don Mariano Marcos Avenue, U.P. Diliman, Quezon City, Philippines. TEL 95-13-53. TELEX CPAUP.
Formerly: University of the Philippines. College of Public Administration. Public Administration Special Studies Series.

350 320   US   ISSN 0042-0271
UNIVERSITY OF VIRGINIA NEWS LETTER. 1925. m. $42. University of Virginia, Center for Public Service, 2015 Ivy Rd., Charlottesville, VA 22903-1795. TEL 804-924-3396. FAX 804-924-4538. Ed. Sandra H. Wiley. circ. 4,300. (looseleaf format) **Indexed:** P.A.I.S., Vert.File Ind.
Description: Focuses on specific public policy issues and their impact on state or local government in Virginia.

UNIVERSITY URBAN PROGRAMS. see *EDUCATION — Higher Education*

350   GW   ISSN 0042-0611
UNTERRICHTSBLAETTER FUER DIE BUNDESWEHRVERWALTUNG; Zeitschrift fuer Ausbildung, Fortbildung und Verwaltungspraxis mit Unterstuetzung des Bundesministers der Verteidigung. 1961. m. DM.116. (Bundesministerium der Verteidigung) R. v. Decker's Verlag, G. Schenck GmbH, Im Weiher 10, 6900 Heidelberg, Germany. Eds. H. Schellknecht, D.H. Vogt. adv.; bk.rev.; bibl.; charts; illus.; stat.; index; circ. 6,000.

URBAN AND RURAL PLANNING THOUGHT. see *ARCHITECTURE*

URBAN LAWYER; the national quarterly on urban law. see *LAW*

350   UY
URUGUAY. CONSEJO DE ESTADO. DIARIO DE SESSIONES.* 1974. irreg. Consejo de Estado, Office of the President, Edif. Libertad, Montevideo, Uruguay.

350   UY
URUGUAY. PODER LEGISLATIVO. BIBLIOTECA. ANALES PARLAMENTARIOS. 1978. q. exchange basis. Poder Legislativo, Biblioteca, Palacio Legislativo, Montevideo, Uruguay.

342.792   US   ISSN 0882-4738
KFU440.A73
UTAH. DIVISION OF ADMINISTRATIVE RULES. UTAH STATE BULLETIN. (Formerly issued by: Utah State Archives and Research Service) 1973. s-m. $135 (prices typically set in July). Division of Administrative Rules, Archives Bldg., Salt Lake City, UT 84114. TEL 801-538-3011. FAX 801-538-3844. Ed. Randy J. Fisher. circ. 500.
Former titles (until 1985): Utah. State Archives and Records Service. Utah State Bulletin; Utah. State Archives and Records Service. Administrative Rule Making Bulletin (ISSN 0093-8955)
Description: Contains the administrative rules and executive branch notices of the state government.

363.6   US   ISSN 0162-1718
UTILITIES LAW REPORTS. 3 base vols. (plus w. updates). $1845. Commerce Clearing House, Inc.,, 4025 W. Peterson Ave., Chicago, IL 60646. TEL 312-583-8500.

350   GW   ISSN 0170-7140
V O P - FACHZEITSCHRIFT FUER DIE OEFFENTLICHE VERWALTUNG. (Verwaltungsfuehrung - Organisation - Personel) 1978. bi-m. DM.95. F B O - Verlag, Postfach 316, 7570 Baden-Baden, Germany. TEL 07221-271066. FAX 07221-33228. TELEX 781280. Ed. Norbert Thom. adv.; bk.rev.; circ. 5,000. (reprint service avail. from UMI)

350   UK   ISSN 0958-0328
VACHERS PARLIAMENTARY COMPANION. 1832. q. £23. Vacher's Publications, 113 High St., Berkhamsted, Herts HP4 2DJ, England. TEL 0442-876135. FAX 0442-870148. Ed. H. Preston. (also avail. in microform from UMI)
Description: Lists personnel of the British government, and national organizations in England.

350   MG
VAOVAO. (Text in French and Malagasy) 1985. w. Ministry of Information, B.P. 271, 101 Antananarivo, Malagasy Republic. TEL 21193. Ed. Marc Rakotonoely. circ. 5,000.

350   VE
VENEZUELA. MINISTERIO DE HACIENDA. MEMORIA. a. Ministerio de Hacienda, Oficina de Relaciones Publicas, Oficina 312, Centro Simon Bolivar-Edificio Norte, Venezuela. Ed.Bd. stat.

VERMONT BAR JOURNAL AND LAW DIGEST. see *LAW*

VERSIYA. see *MILITARY*

350   GW   ISSN 0042-4498
JA44
DIE VERWALTUNG; Zeitschrift fuer Verwaltungswissenschaft. 1968. q. DM.148. Duncker und Humblot GmbH, Postfach 410329, 1000 Berlin 41, Germany. TEL 030-7900060. FAX 030-79000631. Ed.Bd. adv.; bk.rev.; index; circ. 800. **Indexed:** A.B.C.Pol.Sci, P.A.I.S.For.Lang.Ind.

PUBLIC ADMINISTRATION

350   AU
DIE VERWALTUNG DER STADT WIEN. 1863. a. S.200. Statistisches Amt der Stadt Wien, Volksgartenstr. 3, 1016 Vienna, Austria. TEL 4000-88611. FAX 4000-9997910. (Subscr. to: Jugend und Volk Verlagsgesellschaft mbH, Tiefer Graben 7-9, A-1010 Vienna, Austria) illus.; index; circ. 400. (back issues avail.)

VERWALTUNGSARCHIV; Zeitschrift fuer Verwaltungslehre, Verwaltungsrecht und Verwaltungspolitik. see *LAW*

VERZEICHNIS RHEINLAND-PFAELZISCHER RECHT- UND VERWALTUNGSVORSCHRIFTEN. see *LAW*

354.9   AT   ISSN 0042-5095
VICTORIA GOVERNMENT GAZETTE. 1851. w. Law Printer, P.O. Box 203, North Melbourne, Vic. 3051, Australia. TEL 03-320-0100. FAX 03-328-1657. adv.; bibl.; index; circ. 1,700.

VICTORIAN ADMINISTRATIVE LAW. see *LAW*

350   AT   ISSN 0158-1589
JQ5321
VICTORIAN GOVERNMENT DIRECTORY. 1971. a. Aus.$26.50 (typically set in Aug.). Information Victoria, 318 Little Bourke St., Melbourne, Vic. 3000, Australia. TEL 03-651-4100. FAX 03-651-4111.
   Formerly: Victoria, Australia. Directory of Government Departments and Authorities (ISSN 0310-8546)
   Description: Guide to state government departments, agencies, and contact officers.

352   FR   ISSN 0042-5400
VIE COMMUNALE ET DEPARTEMENTALE; revue mensuelle de l'activite locale. 1923. m. 245 F. 35 rue Marbeuf, 75008 Paris, France. Ed. V. d'Andigne. adv.; bk.rev.; bibl.; charts; illus.; stat.
   Incorporates: Revue des Finances Communales (ISSN 0035-208X)

VIE DES AFFAIRES; bulletin consacre a l'analyse des avis emis par les dirigeants d'entreprise a l'egard du droit economique et des politiques gouvernementales. see *BUSINESS AND ECONOMICS — Management*

350   VI
VIRGIN ISLANDS OF THE UNITED STATES BLUE BOOK. 1981. biennial. $5. Division of Libraries, Archives and Museums, Department of Planning and Natural Resources, 23 Dronningens Gade, St. Thomas, VI 00802. TEL 809-774-3407. FAX 809-775-1887. Ed. Jeannette Allis Bastian.
   Formerly: Virgin Island Blue Book.

340   US   ISSN 0092-1270
LAW
VIRGIN ISLANDS REGISTER. 1960. irreg., latest 1984. price varies. Equity Publishing Corporation, RR 1, Box 3, Orford, NH 03777. TEL 603-353-4351. FAX 603-353-9556. (looseleaf format)

350   IT
VOCE DI MONASTEROLO. 1968. s-a. free. Via Tridentina 5, I-24100 Bergamo, Italy. Dir. Bellini Aldo. circ. 800. (looseleaf format)

350   US
WASHINGTON (STATE). JOINT BOARD OF LEGISLATIVE ETHICS. ANNUAL REPORT. 1968. a. Joint Board of Legislative Ethics, 306 Senate Office Bldg., AS-32, Olympia, WA 98504. FAX 206-786-7520. circ. 500.

328.797   US   ISSN 0091-8253
JK9230
WASHINGTON (STATE) LEGISLATURE. PICTORIAL DIRECTORY. 1909. irreg., published each distinct legislation session. free. Legislature, Olympia, WA 98504. TEL 206-786-7550. FAX 20-786-7520. illus.; circ. 19,000. Key Title: Pictorial Directory - Washington State Legislature.

350 340   US
▼**WASHINGTON ADMINISTRATIVE LAW PRACTICE MANUAL.** 1991. base vol. (plus a. suppl.). $85. Butterworth Legal Publishers (Salem) (Subsidiary of: Reed International PLC), 90 Stiles Rd., Salem, NH 03079. TEL 800-548-4001. FAX 603-898-9858. Ed.Bd. (looseleaf format)

WASHINGTON ENVIRONMENTAL PROTECTION REPORT. see *ENVIRONMENTAL STUDIES*

350 320   US   ISSN 1045-5566
WASHINGTON JOURNAL.* 1989. fortn. $194. Media Group Northwest, Inc., Box 27739, Seattle, WA 98125-2739. TEL 206-682-3911. Ed. Dean Katz.
   Description: Issues and trends that affect Washington state business, government and politics, especially the interplay between government and business.

WASHINGTON RECREATION AND PARK ASSOCIATION. SYLLABUS. see *CONSERVATION*

350 330   US   ISSN 1042-0142
WASHINGTON REGULATORY REPORT. 1989. 10/yr. $150. Clark Boardman - Callaghan, 375 Hudson St., New York, NY 10014. TEL 212-929-7500. FAX 212-924-0460. Eds. Steve Errick, Larry Selby.
   Description: Reports on congressional and administrative agency activity affecting business.

350   US   ISSN 0192-060X
JK1118
WASHINGTON REPRESENTATIVES. 1977. a. $60. Columbia Books Inc., 1212 New York Ave., N.W., Ste. 330, Washington, DC 20005. TEL 202-898-0662. Ed.Bd.
   Formerly (until 1979): Directory of Washington Representatives of American Associations and Industry (ISSN 0147-216X)
   Description: Compilation of over 14,000 Washington lobbyists, lawyers, government relations counselors, registered foreign agents, and other advocates, organized alphabetically by person and organization.

353.9
WASHINGTON RESEARCH COUNCIL. NOTEBOOK. 1932. m. $50. Washington Research Council, 906 S. Columbia, Ste. 350, Olympia, WA 98501. TEL 206-357-6643. Ed. Richard S. Davis. stat.; index; circ. 2,500 (controlled). (looseleaf format)
   Former titles: Washington State Research Council Report; Washington State Research Council Monthly Report (ISSN 0043-0803)
   Description: Focus is on Washington state public policy issues.

350 614.8   US
WASHINGTON STATE HEALTH DATA BOOK. a. $15. Department of Health, Health Planning, Airdustrial Park, Bldg. 11, Mail Stop LL-12, Olympia, WA 98504. TEL 206-753-9659. FAX 206-753-9100.
   Description: Covers health care cost, its use and availability. Profiles hospitals and nursing homes and provides basic demographic information on the general population.

350   US   ISSN 0193-4716
WAYS & MEANS; reporting on innovative approaches to state and local government. 1976. 4/yr. $30. Center for Policy Alternatives, 1875 Connecticut Ave., N.W., Ste. 710, Washington, DC 20009. TEL 202-387-6030. FAX 202-986-2539. Ed. Sandra Martin. bk.rev.; bibl.; charts; illus.; circ. 2,000. Indexed: Urb.Aff.Abstr.
   Formerly: Conference on Alternative State and Local Public Policies. Newsletter.
   Description: Reports on policy issues such as toxic wastes, election law, small businesses, health care, corporate crime, prison construcion, worker safety, and tax reform.

350 320   US
WEEKLY REVIEW. 1970. w. $200. Louisiana News Bureau, Inc., Box 44212, Baton Rouge, LA 70804. TEL 504-343-2160. Eds. Kevin Morgan, Michael Courtney.
   Description: Review of Louisiana government and politics.

352   II   ISSN 0049-7193
WEST BENGAL. 1969. fortn. Rs.12. Department of Information and Cultural Affairs, Writers' Buildings, Calcutta 700001, India. Eds. A. Bhattachanya, S.N. Roy. adv.; illus.; circ. 6,000.

350   US
WEST VIRGINIA. LEGISLATURE. COMMISSION ON SPECIAL INVESTIGATIONS. REPORT TO THE WEST VIRGINIA LEGISLATURE. 1981. a. free. Legislature, No. 1 Players Club Dr., Ste. 501, Charleston, WV 25311-1626. TEL 304-348-2345. Ed. Gary W. Slater. circ. 300.
   Formerly: West Virginia. Legislature. Purchasing Practices and Procedures Commission. Report to the West Virginia Legislature.

350   US
WESTCHESTER PLANNING. 1973. q. free. Westchester County Department of Planning, 432 County Office Building, White Plains, NY 10601. TEL 914-682-2564. Ed. Mary R.S. Carlson. bk.rev.; illus.; circ. 2,000.
   Formerly: Westchester Planning Newsletter.
   Description: Covers planning and allied fields such as architecture, landscape architecture, law, political science, statistics and urban studies as they relate to Westchester.

354.9   AT   ISSN 0043-3489
WESTERN AUSTRALIA. GOVERNMENT GAZETTE. 1890. s-w. Aus.$410 (foreign Aus.$618)(effective 1992). Western Australia Government Printing Office, Station St., Wembley, W.A. 6014, Australia. circ. 1,350.

350   US
WHEELER REPORT. 1974. d.(during session); fortn.(during interim). $900. Wheeler News Service, 23 N. Pinckney St., Madison, WI 53703. TEL 608-257-2614. Ed. Richard Wheeler.
   Description: Reports on action taken in Wisconsin Legislature, including bill status information. Also covers attorney general opinion, agency appointments and interim committee activity.

350 320   US   ISSN 0737-9218
E839.5
WHITE HOUSE WEEKLY. 1981. 50/yr. $395. Feistritzer Publications, 4401-A Connecticut Ave., N.W., Ste. 212, Washington, DC 20008. TEL 202-362-3444. FAX 202-362-3493. Ed. David T. Chester.
   Description: Covers White House, including president and staff.

350   US
WHO IS WHO IN THE OKLAHOMA LEGISLATURE. 1963. biennial. $2. Department of Libraries, 200 N.E. 18th St., Oklahoma City, OK 73105. TEL 405-521-2502. FAX 405-525-7804. Ed. Patricia Lester. circ. 4,500.
   Description: Photographic biographical sketches of Oklahoma state legislators.

336   US   ISSN 0085-8226
WISCONSIN. DEPARTMENT OF ADMINISTRATION. ANNUAL FISCAL REPORT. 1950. a. free. Department of Administration, Bureau of Financial Operations, Box 7864, Madison, WI 53707. TEL 608-266-1694. Ed. W.J. Raftery. circ. 1,000. Indexed: SRI.

350   US
WISCONSIN. STATE ELECTIONS BOARD. BIENNIAL REPORT. 1975. biennial. $10. State Elections Board, 132 E. Wilson St., Ste. 300, Madison, WI 53702. TEL 608-266-8005. FAX 608-267-0500. circ. 100.

350   US
WISCONSIN BLUE BOOK. biennial. $8.45. Department of Administration, Document Sales, 202 S. Thornton Ave., Box 7840, Madison, WI 53707. TEL 608-266-3358.

350   US
WISCONSIN ISSUES. 1985. m. $50 (prices set in Jan.). Public Expenditure Research Foundation, 615 E. Washington Ave., Madison, WI 53703. TEL 608-255-6767. FAX 608-256-0333. Ed. Robert C. Brunner. circ. 3,000.
   Description: Policy issues related to Wisconsin state and local government.

350 336   US
WISCONSIN TAXPAYER. 1932. m. $6. Wisconsin Taxpayer Alliance, 335 West Wilson St., Madison, WI 53703-3694. TEL 608-255-4581. Ed. Beulah Poulter.
   Description: Analyzes and comments on issues dealing with Wisconsin state and local government.

350   US   ISSN 0886-9162
WORKERS' COMPENSATION JOURNAL OF OHIO. Short title: W C J O. 1986. bi-m. $125. Banks - Baldwin Law Publishing Co., University Center, 1904 Ansel Rd., Box 1974, Cleveland, OH 44106. TEL 216-721-7373. FAX 216-721-8055. Ed. Jerald D. Harris. bk.rev.
   Description: Reviews judicial, legislative, and administrative developments in Ohio workers' compensation and international tort law.

WORLD RESOURCE REVIEW. see *ENVIRONMENTAL STUDIES*

PUBLIC ADMINISTRATION — ABSTRACTING, BIBLIOGRAPHIES, STATISTICS

350.6 US ISSN 0894-1521
JF37
WORLDWIDE GOVERNMENT DIRECTORY. 1981. a. $275 softcover; hardcover $325. Cambridge Information Group Directories, Inc., 1200 Quince Orchard Blvd., Gaithersburg, MD 20878. TEL 301-590-2300. FAX 301-990-8378. TELEX 44-6194 NATSTA GAIT. (Subscr. to: 7200 Wisconsin Ave., Bethesda, MD 20878) Ed. JoAnne DuChez. adv.; circ. 2,000.
 Formerly: Lambert's Worldwide Government Directory (ISSN 0276-900X)
 Description: Covers 176 countries and over 100 international organizations. Each country listing includes Head of State and Ministers, undersecretaries, aides, legislative and judicial leaders, United Nations ambassador, and foreign diplomatic missions.

350 US ISSN 0094-3924
JK7636
WYOMING. STATE OF WYOMING ANNUAL REPORT. 1973. a. Department of Administration and Information, State Library, Supreme Court Bldg., Cheyenne, WY 82002. TEL 307-777-7504. stat.; circ. controlled.

350 US
WYOMING DATA HANDBOOK. biennial. Department of Administration and Information, Economic Analysis Division, 327 E. Emerson Bldg., Cheyenne, WY 82002. TEL 307-777-7504. charts; stat.; circ. 1,300. Indexed: SRI.

YALE JOURNAL ON REGULATION. see *LAW*

YEARBOOK OF MARYLAND LEGISLATORS. see *POLITICAL SCIENCE*

350 320 US
YELLOW SHEET REPORT. 1906. 3/wk.(between legislative sessions). $135 per month. Arizona News Service, 14 N. 18th Ave., Phoenix, AZ 85007. TEL 602-258-7026. Ed. Ned Creighton.
 Description: Covers Arizona interim legislative committee activity and other state political and governmental news.

354.3 II ISSN 0044-0515
DS401
YOJANA. (Editions in Assamese, Bengali, English, Gujarati, Hindi, Telugu, Malayalam, Marathi and Tamil) 1957. fortn. Rs.13($4) Planning Commission, Yojana Bhavan, Parliament St., Delhi 110 001, India. TEL 11-3710473. (U.S. subscr. to: M-S Inter Culture Associates, Thompson, CT 06277) Ed. D.K. Bharadwaj. adv.; bk.rev.; charts; illus.; stat.; circ. 80,000. Indexed: Acid Rain Abstr., Acid Rain Ind., Rural Recreat.Tour.Abstr., World Agri.Econ. & Rural Sociol.Abstr.

350 US
YOUR WISCONSIN GOVERNMENT. 1972. w.(during session); s-m.(during interim). $44. Wisconsin Taxpayer Alliance, 335 W. Wilson, Madison, WI 53703. TEL 608-255-4581. Ed. James R. Morgan.
 Description: Covers Wisconsin legislative issues, as well as state and local government.

YOUTH POLICY. see *CHILDREN AND YOUTH — About*

YOUTH RECORD. see *CHILDREN AND YOUTH — About*

ZAMBIA. CENTRAL STATISTICAL OFFICE. NATIONAL ACCOUNTS. see *BUSINESS AND ECONOMICS — Public Finance, Taxation*

342 ZA
ZAMBIA. COMMISSION FOR INVESTIGATIONS. ANNUAL REPORT. 1975. a. K.10. Commission for Investigations, Old Bank of Zambia Bldg., 3rd Fl., P.O. Box 50494, Ridgeway, Lusaka 10101, Zambia. (Dist. by: Government Printer, Box 136, Lusaka, Zambia) circ. 500.

ZEITSCHRIFT FUER BEAMTENRECHT. see *LAW*

350 334 GW ISSN 0344-9777
ZEITSCHRIFT FUER OEFFENTLICHE UND GEMEINWIRTSCHAFTLICHE UNTERNEHMEN. 1978. q. DM.96. Nomos Verlagsgesellschaft mbH und Co. KG, Waldseestr. 3-5, Postfach 610, 7570 Baden-Baden, Germany. Eds. Peter Eichhorn, Achim von Loesch. adv.; bk.rev.
 —BLDSC shelfmark: 9475.595000.

ZEITSCHRIFT FUER PARLAMENTSFRAGEN. see *POLITICAL SCIENCE*

350 AU
ZEITSCHRIFT FUER VERWALTUNG. 1976. bi-m. S.2690. Verlag Orac GmbH, Graben 17, A-1014 Vienna, Austria. TEL 0222-551621-0. FAX 0222-551621-79. Ed. Heinz Peter Rill. adv.: B&W page S.8800; adv. contact: Christiana Besel. circ. 5,300.

350 FR ISSN 0398-1169
ZERO - UN REFERENCES. (In 3 editions: 01 Mensuel; 01 Hebdo; 01 Digest) 1969. w. (with m. and a. supplements). 530 F. Groupe Tests, 5 place du Colonel Fabien, 75491 Paris Cedex 10, France.
Indexed: Pt.de Rep. (Feb.1989-).
 Former titles: Zero - Un Informatique; Informatique (ISSN 0073-7941)

350 CC
ZHONGGUO KEJI ZHENGCE YU GUANLI/CHINESE POLICY AND ADMINISTRATION OF SCIENCE AND TECHNOLOGY. (Text in Chinese) bi-m. Zhongguo Kexueyuan, Wenxian Qingbao Zhongxin - Chinese Academy of Sciences, Documentation Information Center, 27 Wangfujing Dajie, Beijing 100710, People's Republic of China. TEL 556180. Ed. Shi Jian.

350 CC
ZHONGGUO XINGZHENG GUANLI/CHINESE ADMINISTRATION MANAGEMENT. (Text in Chinese) m. Zhongguo Xingzheng Guanli Zazhishe, No. 22, Xi'anmen Dajie, Beijing 100017, People's Republic of China. TEL 6012886. Ed. Liu Yichang.

350 US
ZHONGHUA RENMIN GONGHEGUO. QUANGUO RENDA CHANGWEIHUI GONGBAO/CHINA, PEOPLE'S REPUBLIC. NATIONAL PEOPLE'S CONGRESS. STANDING COMMITTEE. BULLETIN. (Text in Chinese) irreg. $22.90. (Quanguo Renmin Daibiao Dahui, Changwu Weiyuanhui, CC) China Books & Periodicals, Inc., 2929 24th St., San Francisco, CA 94110. TEL 415-282-2994. FAX 415-282-0994.

350 US
ZHONGHUA RENMIN GONGHEGUO. ZUIGAO RENMIN JIANCHAYUAN GONGBAO/CHINA, PEOPLE'S REPUBLIC. SUPREME PEOPLE'S PROCURATE POST. (Text in Chinese) irreg. $10.10. (Zuigao Renmin Jianchayuan, CC) China Books & Periodicals, Inc., 2929 24th St., San Francisco, CA 94110. TEL 415-282-2994. FAX 415-282-0994.

350 US
ZHONGHUA RENMIN GONGHEGUO GUOWUYUAN GONGBAO/CHINA, PEOPLE'S REPUBLIC. STATE COUNCIL. BULLETIN. (Text in Chinese) irreg. $66.30. (Guowuyuan, CC) China Books & Periodicals, Inc., 2929 24th St., San Francisco, CA 94110. TEL 415-282-2994. FAX 415-282-0994.

350 RH
ZIMBABWE GOVERNMENT GAZETTE. w. with a. cum. $228. Department of Printing and Stationery, P.O. Box 8062, Causeway, Zimbabwe. TEL 706161.

350.6 GW ISSN 0177-1965
ZIVILDIENST; Zeitschrift fuer die Zivildienst-Leistenden. 1973. m. DM.10. (Bundesamt fuer den Zivildienst) Deutscher Gemeindeverlag GmbH, Max-Planck-Str. 12, Postfach 400263, 5000 Cologne 40, Germany. bk.rev.; circ. 54,000. (reprint service avail.)

50 STATE LEGISLATIVE REVIEW. see *POLITICAL SCIENCE*

PUBLIC ADMINISTRATION — Abstracting, Bibliographies, Statistics

A B C POL SCI; a bibliography of contents: political science and government. see *POLITICAL SCIENCE — Abstracting, Bibliographies, Statistics*

350 016 AT ISSN 0727-8926
Z7165.A8
A P A I S: AUSTRALIAN PUBLIC AFFAIRS INFORMATION SERVICE; subject index to current literature. 1945. a. (with monthly cum.). Aus.$175 (Aus.$75 for annual cum.). National Library of Australia, Publications Section, Public Programs, Parkes Place, Canberra, A.C.T. 2600, Australia. TEL 06-262-1365. FAX 06-273-4493. TELEX AA62100. index; circ. 1,500. Indexed: AESIS.
●Also available online.
 —BLDSC shelfmark: 1818.400000.
 Formerly: Australian Public Affairs Information Service (ISSN 0005-0075)
 Description: Indexes periodical literature in social sciences and humanities published in or relating to Australia.

350 SW ISSN 0065-020X
AARSBOK FOER SVERIGES KOMMUNER. (Text in Swedish; summaries in English) 1918. a. SEK 240. Statistika Centralbyraan, Distribution, S-701 89 Oerebro, Sweden. TEL 08-783-4000. circ. 3,500.

350 016 US
ABSTRACT NEWSLETTER: PROBLEM-SOLVING INFORMATION FOR STATE AND LOCAL GOVERNMENTS. w. $95 (foreign $135). U.S. National Technical Information Service, 5285 Port Royal Rd., Springfield, VA 22161. TEL 703-487-4630. FAX 703-321-8547. TELEX 64617. index. (back issues avail.)
 Former titles: Weekly Abstract Newsletter: Problem-Solving Information for State and Local Governments; Weekly Government Abstracts. Problem-Solving Information for State and Local Governments (ISSN 0364-6459); Weekly Government Abstracts. Problem Solving Technology for State and Local Governments.

350 TS
ABU DHABI. DEPARTMENT OF PLANNING. STATISTICAL YEARBOOK/ABU DHABI. DA'IRAT AL-TAKHTIT. AL-KITAB AL-IHSA'I AL-SANAWI. 1969. a. Department of Planning, Statistical Section, P.O. Box 12, Abu Dhabi, United Arab Emirates. TEL 727200. FAX 2-727749. TELEX 23194 PLANCO EM.
 Formerly: Abu Dhabi. Department of Planning. Statistical Abstract and Yearbook.
 Description: Includes statistics on climate, demographics, labor, industry, trade, transport and finance.

AFFIRMATIVE EMPLOYMENT STATISTICS. see *BUSINESS AND ECONOMICS — Abstracting, Bibliographies, Statistics*

312 US ISSN 0095-3431
HA221
ALABAMA'S VITAL EVENTS. 1971. a. $10. Department of Public Health, Center for Health Statistics, Montgomery, AL 36130. TEL 205-261-5510. FAX 205-242-3097. Ed. Dale Quinney. illus.; circ. 450. (also avail. in microfiche). Indexed: SRI.

316 AO ISSN 0066-5193
ANGOLA. DIRECCAO DOS SERVICOS DE ESTATISTICA. ANUARIO ESTATISTICO. 1933. a. Esc.100. Direccao dos Servicos de Estatistica, C.P. 1215, Luanda, Angola. circ. 1,000.

316 AO
ANGOLA. DIRECCAO DOS SERVICOS DE ESTATISTICA. INFORMACOES ESTATISTICAS. 1970. a. free. Direccao dos Servicos de Estatistica, Ministerio do Planeamento e Coordenacao Economica, C.P. 1215, Luanda, Angola. stat.; circ. 7,000.

350 IT ISSN 0390-654X
ANNUARIO DI CONTABILITA NAZIONALE TOMO 1. a. L.14000. Istituto Centrale di Statistica, Via Cesare Balbo 16, 00100 Rome, Italy.

350 IT ISSN 0390-6531
ANNUARIO DI CONTABILITA NAZIONALE TOMO 2. a. L.16000. Istituto Centrale di Statistica, Via Cesare Balbo 16, 00100 Rome, Italy.

PUBLIC ADMINISTRATION — ABSTRACTING, BIBLIOGRAPHIES, STATISTICS 4079

350 572   MX
▼ARCHIVO HISTORICO DIOCESANO DE SAN CRISTOBAL DE LAS CASAS. SERIE TECNICA. 1991. irreg., no.2, 1991. $6. Instituto de Asesoria Antropologica para la Region Maya, Archivo Historico Diocesano, Apdo. Postal 6, San Cristobal de las Casas, Chiapas C.P.29200, Mexico.
Description: Indexes official papers from civil and religious governments concerning Chiapas and colonial government in general. Covers 1596-1798.

350   AT   ISSN 1031-0533
AUSTRALIA. BUREAU OF STATISTICS. APPARENT CONSUMPTION OF FOODSTUFFS AND NUTRIENTS. 1948. a. Aus.$35 (foreign Aus.$38.60)(effective 1991). Australian Bureau of Statistics, P.O. Box 10, Belconnen, A.C.T. 2616, Australia. FAX 062-516009. TELEX 062-527911. circ. 443. (processed)
Description: Presents a general overview of the supply and utilisation of approximately 130 basic foodstuffs; level of nutrient intake and estimated supply of selected types of nutrients available for consumption.

350 319.4   AT   ISSN 0158-2496
AUSTRALIA. BUREAU OF STATISTICS. APPARENT CONSUMPTION OF SELECTED FOODSTUFFS, AUSTRALIA, PRELIMINARY. 1978. a. Aus.$10 (foreign Aus.$10.90)(effective 1991). Australian Bureau of Statistics, P.O. Box 10, Belconnen, A.C.T. 2616, Australia. circ. 285.
Description: Presents preliminary details of the apparent consumption and per capita consumption of selected food items.

350
Z7554.A77   AT   ISSN 1032-805X
AUSTRALIA. BUREAU OF STATISTICS. CATALOGUE OF PUBLICATIONS AND PRODUCTS. 1967. a. Aus.$4 (foreign Aus.$20)(effective 1991). Australian Bureau of Statistics, P.O. Box 10, Belconnen, A.C.T. 2616, Australia. circ. 2,105.
Formerly: Australia. Bureau of Statistics. Catalogue of Publications, Australia (ISSN 0727-1417)
Description: Lists publications and other standard products issued by the ABS, including a brief description of the contents of each item, as well as details of frequency, date of first issue, number of pages and price.

350   AT   ISSN 0728-6368
AUSTRALIA. BUREAU OF STATISTICS. CHILD CARE ARRANGEMENTS, AUSTRALIA. 1969. 3/yr. Aus.$15 (foreign Aus.$18.60)(effective 1991). Australian Bureau of Statistics, P.O. Box 10, Belconnen, A.C.T. 2616, Australia. TEL 062-527911. FAX 062-516009. circ. 234.
Formerly (until 1980): Australia. Bureau of Statistics. Child Care (Canberra) (ISSN 0728-6376)
Description: Focuses on the family unit with chilldren ages 0-11 years generally clasified by type and hours of childcare, multiplicity of care, day-frequency of care, number and age of children, weekly cost of care and other areas.

336.94   AT   ISSN 0725-3427
HJ90
AUSTRALIA. BUREAU OF STATISTICS. COMMONWEALTH GOVERNMENT FINANCE, AUSTRALIA. a. Aus.$10 (foreign Aus.$13.60)(effective 1991). Australian Bureau of Statistics, P.O. Box 10, Belconnen, A.C.T. 2616, Australia. TEL 062-527911. FAX 062-516009. illus.; stat.; circ. 359.
Description: Provides details of financial transactions at the federal government level.

350 319.4   AT   ISSN 0156-4722
AUSTRALIA. BUREAU OF STATISTICS. PUBLICATIONS ADVICE. 1969. s-w. Aus.$49.50 (foreign Aus.$138.60)(effective 1991). Australian Bureau of Statistics, P.O. Box 10, Belconnen, A.C.T. 2616, Australia. TEL 062-527911. FAX 062-516009. circ. 334.
Description: Lists publications released by all ABS offices on the day of issue of the Advice and those expected to be released on the following two working days. Also lists publications expected to be released by the Central Office on the three subsequent working days.

350 319.4   AT   ISSN 1031-0673
AUSTRALIA. BUREAU OF STATISTICS. PUBLICATIONS ISSUED IN (MONTH). 1961. m. Aus.$66 (foreign Aus.$81.60)(effective 1991). Australian Bureau of Statistics, P.O. Box 10, Belconnen, A.C.T. 2616, Australia. TEL 062-527911. FAX 062-516009. circ. 457.
Description: A complete list of publications issued by the ABS (Central and State Offices) during each month.

352   AT   ISSN 1031-2528
AUSTRALIA. BUREAU OF STATISTICS. QUEENSLAND OFFICE. LOCAL GOVERNMENT, QUEENSLAND. 1974. a. Aus.$16.50 (foreign Aus.$25.50). Australian Bureau of Statistics, Queensland Office, 313 Adelaide St., Brisbane, Qld. 4000, Australia. TEL 07-222-6022. FAX 07-229-6171. TELEX AA 40271.
Description: Covers all local government areas: general summary, finance, all funds, ordinary services, roads, water supply, sewerage, other services, length of roads normally open to traffic, water consumption, population served and locality supplied.

350 319.4   AT   ISSN 1035-3461
AUSTRALIA. BUREAU OF STATISTICS. SCHOOLS, AUSTRALIA. a. Aus.$20 (foreign Aus.$27.10) (effective 1991). Australian Bureau of Statistics, P.O. Box 10, Belconnen, A.C.T. 2616, Australia. TEL 062-527911. FAX 062-516009. circ. 399.
Formerly: Australia. Bureau of Statistics. National Schools Statistics Collection (ISSN 0819-5323) Formed by the merger of: National Schools Collection: Government Schools & Non-Government Schools.
Description: Covers statistics on schools, students, teaching and non-teaching staff involved in the provision or administration of primary and secondary education, in government and non-government schools.

350 319.4   AT   ISSN 1034-5671
AUSTRALIA. BUREAU OF STATISTICS. SCHOOLS, AUSTRALIA, PRELIMINARY. 1984. a. Aus.$10 (foreign Aus.$11.30)(effective 1991). Australian Bureau of Statistics, P.O. Box 10, Belconnen, A.C.T. 2616, Australia. TEL 062-527911. FAX 062-516009. circ. 277.
Formerly: National Schools Statistics Collection, Australia, Preliminary (ISSN 0816-1356)
Description: Preliminary summary statistics of primary and secondary schools, students and staff, classified by state or territory, type of school and year of education.

350 319.4   AT
AUSTRALIA. BUREAU OF STATISTICS. SOCIAL INDICATORS, AUSTRALIA. (Supplement avail.) 1976. irreg., latest 1990. Aus.$45 (foreign Aus.$55)(effective 1991). Australian Bureau of Statistics, P.O. Box 10, Belconnen, A.C.T. 2616, Australia. TEL 062-527911. FAX 062-516009. charts; circ. 845.
Description: A selection of social indicators and other statistics providing a broad background to social issues in Australia. Presents information under the following headings: Population, Families, Health, Education, Working Life, Income, Crime and Justice, Housing, and Welfare.

994 319   AT   ISSN 0312-6072
AUSTRALIA. BUREAU OF STATISTICS. WESTERN AUSTRALIAN OFFICE. LOCAL GOVERNMENT, WESTERN AUSTRALIA. 1960. a. Aus.$13.50 (foreign Aus.$17.10)(effective 1991). Australian Bureau of Statistics, Western Australian Office, 30 Terrace Rd., Perth, W.A. 6000, Australia. index; circ. 800.
Formerly: Australia. Bureau of Statistics. Western Australian Office. Abstract of Statistics of Local Government Areas. (ISSN 0067-124X)
Description: Population, by age group, at time of census. Vital statistics, dwellings, schools, hospitals and nursing homes, rural industry, manufacturing, building activity, retail census, lengths of roads, road traffic accidents, local government finance.

BADEN - WUERTTEMBERG. STATISTISCHES LANDESAMT. STATISTISCH-PROGNOSTISCHER BERICHT; Daten - Analysen - Perspektiven. see *STATISTICS*

BADEN - WUERTTEMBERG. STATISTISCHES LANDESAMT. STATISTISCHE BERICHTE. see *STATISTICS*

312   BB
BARBADOS. REGISTRATION OFFICE. REPORT ON VITAL STATISTICS & REGISTRATIONS. a., latest ed. 1981. free. Registration Office, Bridgetown, Barbados, W.I. stat.; circ. 100.

BOCHUM. AMT FUER STATISTIK, STADTFORSCHUNG UND WAHLEN. REIHE "WAHLEN IN BOCHUM". see *POLITICAL SCIENCE — Abstracting, Bibliographies, Statistics*

BOCHUM. AMT FUER STATISTIK, STADTFORSCHUNG UND WAHLEN. SONDERBERICHTE. see *HOUSING AND URBAN PLANNING — Abstracting, Bibliographies, Statistics*

BOCHUM. AMT FUER STATISTIK, STADTFORSCHUNG UND WAHLEN. STATISTICAL YEARBOOK. see *HOUSING AND URBAN PLANNING — Abstracting, Bibliographies, Statistics*

BOCHUM. AMT FUER STATISTIK, STADTFORSCHUNG UND WAHLEN. VERWALTUNGSBERICHT. see *HOUSING AND URBAN PLANNING — Abstracting, Bibliographies, Statistics*

BOCHUM. AMT FUER STATISTIK, STADTFORSCHUNG UND WAHLEN. ZUR STADTENTWICKLUNG. see *HOUSING AND URBAN PLANNING — Abstracting, Bibliographies, Statistics*

310 350   BO
BOLIVIA. INSTITUTO NACIONAL DE ESTADISTICA. ESTADISTICAS REGIONALES DEPARTAMENTALES. 1976. a. $12. Instituto Nacional de Estadistica, Casilla de Correo No. 6129, La Paz, Bolivia.

330 011   BL
BRAZIL. MINISTERIO DA FAZENDA. BOLETIM INFORMATIVO DA SECAO DE DOCUMENTACAO. 1947. bi-m. free. Ministerio da Fazenda, Delegacio no Estado do Rio de Janeiro, Secao de Documentacao, Av. Antonio Carlos 375, 14 andar, 20020 Rio de Janeiro, R.J., Brazil. circ. 1,800.
Former titles: Brazil. Ministerio da Fazenda. Nucleo Regional de Administracao. Boletim Informativo (ISSN 0006-9434); Brazil. Ministerio da Fazenda. Delegacia Estadual na Guanabara. Setor de Documentacao. Boletim Informativo.

310   BL
BRAZIL. SERVICO SOCIAL DO COMERCIO. ANUARIO ESTATISTICO. 1962. a. free. Servico Social do Comercio, Assessoria de Divulgacao e Promocao Institucional, Rua Voluntarios da Patria 169, 22270 Rio de Janeiro, Brazil. stat.

350   FR   ISSN 0293-9614
Z2169
BULLETIN SIGNALETIQUE D'INFORMATION ADMINISTRATIVE. 1982. m. 990 F. Documentation Francaise, 29-31 quai Voltaire, 75340 Paris cedex 07, France. TEL 1-4015-7000. (Subscr. to: Documentation Francaise, 124 rue Henri Barbusse, 93308 Aubervilliers) (also avail. in microfilm; back issues avail) **Indexed:** P.A.I.S.For.Lang.Ind.
●Also available online. Vendor(s): European Space Agency.

011 350   US   ISSN 0741-2878
KF70
C I S FEDERAL REGISTER INDEX. 1984. w. $595. Congressional Information Service, 4520 East-West Hwy., Bethesda, MD 20814-3389. TEL 301-654-1550. FAX 301-654-4033. TELEX 292386 CIS UR. Ed. Jim Shields. cum.index. (back issues avail.)

328 016   US   ISSN 0007-8514
C I S INDEX. 1970. m. (with q. and a. and multi-year cumulations). price varies. Congressional Information Service, 4520 East-West Hwy., Ste. 800, Bethesda, MD 20814. TEL 301-654-1550. FAX 301-654-4033. TELEX 292386 CIS UR. Ed. Aaron Lerner. abstr.; index; cum.index: 1970-74; 1975-78; 1979-82; 1983-86; 1987-1990. **Indexed:** Mid.East: Abstr.& Ind.
●Also available online. Vendor(s): DIALOG (File no.101).
Also available on CD-ROM.
Description: Abstracts and indexes to information published by congressional committees.

PUBLIC ADMINISTRATION — ABSTRACTING, BIBLIOGRAPHIES, STATISTICS

350 011 US
C S I CONGRESSIONAL RECORD ABSTRACTS: ENERGY EDITION.* d. following session of Congress. $495. (Capitol Services, Inc.) National Standards, 1200 Quince Orchard Blvd., Gaithersburg, MD 20878.

350 011 US
C S I CONGRESSIONAL RECORD ABSTRACTS: FOREIGN AFFAIRS EDITION.* d. following session of Congress. $725. (Capitol Services, Inc.) National Standards, 1200 Quince Orchard Blvd., Gaithersburg, MD 20878.

350 011 US
C S I CONGRESSIONAL RECORD ABSTRACTS: MASTER EDITION.* d. following session of Congress. $725. (Capitol Services, Inc.) National Standards, 1200 Quince Orchard Blvd., Gaithersburg, MD 20878.
●Also available online. Vendor(s): BRS, DIALOG.

350 US
C S I CONGRESSIONAL RECORD ABSTRACTS: NATIONAL DEFENSE EDITION.* d. following session of Congress. $495. (Capitol Services, Inc.) National Standards, 1200 Quince Orchard Blvd., Gaithersburg, MD 20878.

350 016 US
C S I FEDERAL INDEX;* covering the Congressional Record, Federal Register, Presidential Documents, U S Law Week. 1977. m. $595. (Capitol Services, Inc.) National Standards, 1200 Quince Orchard Blvd., Gaithersburg, MD 20878. Ed. J. Kelley Summers.
●Also available online. Vendor(s): DIALOG (File no.20).
Formerly: Federal Index Monthly (ISSN 0148-5512)

350 011 US
C S I FEDERAL REGISTER ABSTRACTS: MASTER EDITION.* d. $725. (Capitol Services, Inc.) National Standards, 1200 Quince Orchard Blvd., Gaithersburg, MD 20878. Ed. Gregory Friedman.
●Also available online. Vendor(s): BRS (FREG), BRS/Saunders Colleague, DIALOG, Orbit Information Technologies.

350 UK ISSN 0260-9762
CHARTERED INSTITUTE OF PUBLIC FINANCE AND ACCOUNTANCY. LOCAL GOVERNMENT COMPARATIVE STATISTICS. ESTIMATES. 1981. a. £55. Chartered Institute of Public Finance and Accountancy, 3 Robert St., London WC2N 6BH, England. TEL 071-895-8823. FAX 071-895-8825. (back issues avail.)
—BLDSC shelfmark: 5290.014000.

350 UK ISSN 0260-7603
CHARTERED INSTITUTE OF PUBLIC FINANCE AND ACCOUNTANCY. WASTE COLLECTION STATISTICS. ACTUALS. (Not avail. for circ. outside UK local authorities.) 1977. a. £55. Chartered Institute of Public Finance and Accountancy, 3 Robert St., London WC2N 6BH, England. TEL 071-895-8823. FAX 071-895-8825. (back issues avail.)

350 628 UK ISSN 0140-0150
CHARTERED INSTITUTE OF PUBLIC FINANCE AND ACCOUNTANCY. WASTE DISPOSAL STATISTICS. ACTUALS. (Not avail. for circ. outside UK authorities.) 1979. a. £55. Chartered Institute of Public Finance and Accountancy, 3 Robert St., London WC2N 6BH, England. TEL 071-895-8823. FAX 071-895-8825. (back issues avail.)

350 628 UK ISSN 0140-0142
CHARTERED INSTITUTE OF PUBLIC FINANCE AND ACCOUNTANCY. WASTE DISPOSAL STATISTICS. ESTIMATES. (Not avail. for circ. outside UK authorities.) 1981. a. £55. Chartered Institute of Public Finance and Accountancy, 3 Robert St., London WC2N 6BH, England. TEL 071-895-8823. FAX 071-895-8825. (back issues avail.)

011 350 US ISSN 0146-0838
Z1223.5.N55
CHECKLIST OF OFFICIAL NEW JERSEY PUBLICATIONS. 1965. bi-m. free. State Library, 185 West State St., Trenton, NJ 08625-0520. TEL 609-292-6294. Ed. Robert Lupp. circ. 600. (processed) **Indexed:** P.A.I.S.

350 CF
CONGO. CENTRE NATIONAL DE LA STATISTIQUE ET DES ETUDES ECONOMIQUES. ANNUAIRE STATISTIQUE. 1959. a. 12000 Fr.CFA. Centre National de la Statistique et des Etudes Economiques, B.P. 2031, Brazzaville, Congo. TEL 83-36-94.

350 CF
CONGO. CENTRE NATIONAL DE LA STATISTIQUE ET DES ETUDES ECONOMIQUES. BULLETIN DE STATISTIQUE. 1977. q. Centre National de la Statistique et des Etudes Economiques, B.P. 2031, Brazzaville, Congo. TEL 83-36-94. Ed. Marcel Mouelle.

350 330 CF
CONGO. CENTRE NATIONAL DE LA STATISTIQUE ET DES ETUDES ECONOMIQUES. BULLETIN TRIMESTRIEL DE LA CONJONCTURE. q. 13500 Fr.CFA. Centre National de la Statistique et des Etudes Economiques, B.P. 2031, Brazzaville, Congo. TEL 83-36-94.

350 IT ISSN 0390-6574
CONTI DEGLI ITALIANI. vol.23, 1989. a. L.15000. Istituto Centrale di Statistica, Via Cesare Balbo 16, 00100 Rome, Italy.

350 GW
DATEN UND INFORMATION. 1975. irreg. Amt fuer Statistik, Stadtforschung und Europaangelegenheiten, Der Oberstadtdirektor, Bismarckstr. 150-158, 4100 Duisburg 1, Germany. TEL 0203-283-3085. FAX 0203-2834404. TELEX 8551214. circ. 600. (back issues avail.)
Formerly: Duisburg. Amt fuer Statistik und Stadtforschung. Daten und Information (ISSN 0172-4541)

352 DK ISSN 0106-9802
HJ9056
DENMARK. DANMARKS STATISTIK. KOMMUNALE FINANSER. (Text in Danish and English) 1981. a. DKK 73.77. Danmarks Statistik, Sejroegade 11, 2100 Copenhagen OE, Denmark. TEL 31-298222. FAX 31-184801. TELEX 16236.
Formerly: Denmark. Danmarks Statistik. Kommunale Finanser for Regnskabsaaret.

350 DK ISSN 0108-8173
HC360.I5
DENMARK. DANMARKS STATISTIK. NATIONALREGNSKABSSTATISTIK. (Text in Danish and English) 1983. a. DKK 103.30. Danmarks Statistik, Sejroegade 11, 2100 Copenhagen OE, Denmark. TEL 31-298222. FAX 31-184801. TELEX 16236.

DIRECTORY OF POLITICAL PERIODICALS; a guide to newsletters, journals and newspapers. see *BUSINESS AND ECONOMICS — Trade And Industrial Directories*

350 316 FT
DJIBOUTI. DIRECTION NATIONALE DE LA STATISTIQUE. BULLETIN DE STATISTIQUE ET DE DOCUMENTATION. 1970. q. 500 F. Ministere du Commerce, des Transports et du Tourisme, Direction Nationale de la Statistique, B.P. 1846, Djibouti, Djibouti.
Former titles: Djibouti. Service de Statistique et de Documentation. Bulletin de Statistique et de Documentation; (until 1976): French Territory of the Afars and Issas. Service de Statistique et de Documentation. Bulletin de Statistique et de Documentation.

016 350 II
DOCUMENTATION IN PUBLIC ADMINISTRATION. (Text in English) 1973. q. Rs.15($5) Indian Institute of Public Administration, Indraprastha Estate, Ring Rd., New Delhi 110002, India. Ed. T.N. Chaturvedi. bibl.
Supersedes: Public Administration Abstracts and Index of Articles (ISSN 0033-331X)

EDUCATIONAL LEGISLATION INDEX. see *EDUCATION — Abstracting, Bibliographies, Statistics*

350 016 FJ ISSN 0015-0916
FIJI. GOVERNMENT PRINTING DEPARTMENT. PUBLICATIONS BULLETIN. s-a. free. Government Printing Department, Box 98, Suva, Fiji. circ. 1,000.

314 352 FI ISSN 0355-2217
FINLAND. TILASTOKESKUS. KUNNALLISVAALIT/FINLAND. STATISTIKCENTRALEN. KOMMUNALVALEN/FINLAND. CENTRAL STATISTICAL OFFICE. MUNICIPAL ELECTIONS. (Section XXIX B of Official Statistics of Finland) (Text in English, Finnish and Swedish) 1931. irreg; latest 1984. FIM 65. Tilastokeskus, Annankatu 44, SF-00100 Helsinki 10, Finland.

352 GW
GELSENKIRCHEN IM SPIEGEL DER STATISTIK. 1982. s-a. Stadt Gelsenkirchen, Amt fuer Informationsverarbeitung, Vattmannstr. 11, 4650 Gelsenkirchen, Germany. TEL 0209-1692101. circ. 350.

352 GW
GOETTINGER STATISTIK. 1950. q. Stadt Goettingen, Amt fuer Statistik und Stadtforschung, Postfach 3831, 3400 Goettingen, Germany. TEL 0551-4002353. circ. 600.

GOVERNMENT REPORTS ANNOUNCEMENTS AND INDEX ANNUAL INDEX. see *ENGINEERING — Abstracting, Bibliographies, Statistics*

016 500 US ISSN 0097-9007
Z7916
GOVERNMENT REPORTS ANNOUNCEMENTS AND INDEX JOURNAL. s-m. $495 (foreign $670). U.S. National Technical Information Service, 5285 Port Royal Rd., Springfield, VA 22161. TEL 703-487-4630. FAX 703-321-8547. TELEX 64617. index. (also avail. in microform from UMI; reprint service avail. from UMI; back issues avail.) **Indexed:** MEDOC, Sh.& Vib.Dig.
●Also available online. Vendor(s): BRS, CEDOCAR, CISTI, Data-Star, DIALOG (File no.6), European Space Agency, JICST, Orbit Information Technologies (NTIS), STN International (NTIS).
—BLDSC shelfmark: 4206.045000.
Former titles (until 1975): Government Reports Announcements (ISSN 0096-0799); Government Reports Index (ISSN 0097-9015); Incorporates: G R I (U.S. Government Reports Index) (ISSN 0041-7688)
Description: Multidisciplinary current awareness resource. Announces more than 60,000 R & D and engineering results annually.

352 336 UK ISSN 0308-1745
GREAT BRITAIN. DEPARTMENT OF THE ENVIRONMENT. LOCAL GOVERNMENT FINANCIAL STATISTICS: ENGLAND AND WALES. (Joint publication with the Welsh Office) a. price varies. H.M.S.O., P.O. Box 276, London SW8 5DT, England.

352 GW ISSN 0172-360X
HANDBUCH DER FINANZSTATISTIK. 1953. a. DM.22. Statistisches Landesamt Rheinland-Pfalz, Postfach 5427 Bad Ems, Germany. TEL 02603-71245. stat. (back issues avail.)

INDEX TO CURRENT URBAN DOCUMENTS. see *HOUSING AND URBAN PLANNING — Abstracting, Bibliographies, Statistics*

350 CN
▼**INDEX TO SELECTED CANADIAN PROVINCIAL PUBLICATIONS;** for librarians, teachers and booksellers. 1990. irreg. Can.$75. R.R. 1, Roslin, Ont. K0K 2Y0, Canada. TEL 613-477-2743. Ed. Jami van Haaften. index. (looseleaf format; also avail. on computer disk)
Description: Includes more than 2800 free or low cost Canadian provincial government publications, indexed by subject, series title adn non-book format.

011 350 US ISSN 0198-9014
KF70.A34
INDEX TO THE CODE OF FEDERAL REGULATIONS. 1977. q. $745. Congressional Information Service, 4520 East-West Hwy., Bethesda, MD 20814-3389. TEL 301-654-1550. FAX 301-654-4033. TELEX 292386 CIS UR. Ed. Lewin Chan. index.; cum.index: 1977-1979.
Description: Subject and geographic indexes to all 50 Code of Federal Regulations titles.

PUBLIC ADMINISTRATION — ABSTRACTING, BIBLIOGRAPHIES, STATISTICS 4081

350   SP
INSTITUTO NACIONAL DE ADMINISTRACION PUBLICA. SERVICIO DE BIBLIOTECA Y DOCUMENTACION. BOLETIN DE INFORMACION BIBLIOGRAFICA. 1959. m. free. Instituto Nacional de Administracion Publica, Servicio de Biblioteca y Documentacion, C. Atocha 106, 28012 Madrid, Spain. Ed. Enrique Orduna Rebollo.
Former titles: Instituto Nacional de Administracion Publica. Biblioteca. Boletin Informativo; (until 1977): Antigua Universidad de Cisneros. Instituto Nacional de Administracion Publica. Biblioteca. Boletin Informativo.

IOWA OFFICIAL REGISTER. see *POLITICAL SCIENCE — Abstracting, Bibliographies, Statistics*

350   IV
IVORY COAST. DIRECTION DE LA STATISTIQUE. BULLETIN MENSUEL DE STATISTIQUES. m. Direction de la Statistique, 01 B.P. V55, Abidjan 01, Ivory Coast. TEL 21-15-38.

350   SA
J8
JUTA - STATE LIBRARY INDEX TO THE GOVERNMENT GAZETTE. 1979. q. (annual cum.). R.256 (R.168 for annual only). Juta & Co. Ltd., P.O. Box 14373, Kenwyn 7790, South Africa. TEL 021-797-5101. FAX 021-761-5010. circ. 504. (also avail. in microfiche; back issues avail.)
Formerly: South Africa. Government Gazette Index (ISSN 0379-6078)
Description: Alphabetical index of acts, proclamations, regulations, notices and legal advertisements in the Government of South Africa Gazette.

352   GW   ISSN 0451-4874
KASSELER STATISTIK. 1970. q. Stadt Kassel, Statistisches Amt und Wahlamt, Untere Karlsstr. 8, 3500 Kassel, Germany. TEL 0561-7872299.

357   GW   ISSN 0933-632X
KOELNER STATISTISCHE NACHRICHTEN. SONDERHEFTE. 1979. irreg. Amt fuer Statistik und Einwohnerwesen, Stadthaus Chorweiler, Athener Ring 4, 5000 Cologne 71, Germany. TEL 0221-221-1887. circ. 1,000. (back issues avail.)

350   KO
KUKHOE HOEUIROK SAEGIN/INDEX TO THE NATIONAL ASSEMBLY DEBATES. Variant title: Kuk Hoe Hoe Eu Rok Saegin. (Text in Korean) 1975. irreg. free. National Assembly Library - Kukhoe Tosogwan, 1 Yoido-dong, Seoul, S. Korea. FAX 02-788-4194. circ. 1,000.

350 016   UK   ISSN 0023-6349
L O G A. (Local Government Annotations) 1966. bi-m. £5.90. (Association of London Chief Librarians) Havering Central Library. London Borough, St. Edwards Way, Romford, Essex RM1 3AR, England. Ed. Brian D. Evans. index; circ. 750. **Indexed:** P.A.I.S.
—BLDSC shelfmark: 5292.305000.
Formerly: LOGA-Local Government Abstracts.

352   GW
LANDESHAUPTSTADT KIEL. VIERTELJAHRESBERICHTE. 1955. q. DM.12. Landeshauptstadt Kiel, Fleethorn 9, Postfach 1152, D-2300 Kiel 1, Germany. TEL 0431-9011104. circ. 500.

LEGISLATIVE TRENDS; recent acquisitions received in the New York State Library. see *LAW — Abstracting, Bibliographies, Statistics*

350   SZ
LIST OF BOOKS AND ARTICLES CATALOGUED. 1964. a. free. Inter-Parliamentary Union, Place du Petit-Saconnex, B.P. 438, 1211 Geneva 19, Switzerland. TEL 022-7344150. FAX 022-733-3141. TELEX 289784 IPUCH.

600   PH
M P W BULLETIN. 1956. q. free. Ministry of Public Works, MPW Bldg., 2nd Fl., Port Area, Manila, Philippines. Ed. Nicolas R. Velas. charts; illus.; stat.; circ. 20,000.
Former titles: D P W & C Bulletin; Manila. Department of Public Works. Communications Technical Statistical Review (ISSN 0040-0998)

015   US   ISSN 0195-3443
Z1223.5.M3
MARYLAND DOCUMENTS. 1977. m. $15. Department of Legislative Reference, 90 State Circle, Annapolis, MD 21401. TEL 410-841-3810. Ed. Carol A. Carman. circ. 800.
Description: Lists all state and local publications catalogued by the state's Department of Legislative Reference; includes an index by subject, title, and other entries.

MASSACHUSETTS TAXPAYERS FOUNDATION. STATE BUDGET TRENDS. see *BUSINESS AND ECONOMICS — Abstracting, Bibliographies, Statistics*

015   US   ISSN 0091-6633
Z1223.5.M7
MISSOURI STATE GOVERNMENT PUBLICATIONS. 1972. m. $7 (free to state residents). State Library, Box 387, Jefferson City, MO 65102. TEL 314-751-3615. circ. 500.
Supersedes: Missouri State Government Documents.

353 016   US   ISSN 0362-6830
Z1223
MONTHLY CATALOG OF UNITED STATES GOVERNMENT PUBLICATIONS. m. $199 (foreign $248.75). U.S. Government Printing Office, Superintendent of Documents, Washington, DC 20402-9341. TEL 202-783-3238. FAX 202-2512-2250. index. (also avail. in microform from BLH,UMI; microfiche also avail. from Supt.Docs) **Indexed:** Fluidex.
●Also available online. Vendor(s): BRS, BRS/Saunders Colleague, DIALOG (File no.66). Also available on CD-ROM. Producer(s): SilverPlatter, H.W. Wilson.
—BLDSC shelfmark: 5936.000000.

350   GW   ISSN 0173-8895
MUELHEIMER STATISTIK. 1949. q. DM.16. Amt fuer Statistik und Stadtforschung, Von-Graefe-Str. 37, D-4300 Muelheim an der Ruhr 1, Germany. TEL 0208-4557243.

350 016   US
N T I S ALERTS: ADMINISTRATION AND MANAGEMENT. 1974. w. $125 175. U.S. National Technical Information Service, 5285 Port Royal Rd., Springfield, VA 22161. TEL 703-487-4630. FAX 703-321-8547. TELEX 64617. index. (back issues avail.)
Former titles: Abstract Newsletter: Administration and Management; Weekly Abstract Newsletter: Administration and Management; Weekly Government Abstracts. Administration and Management; Weekly Government Abstracts. Administration (ISSN 0364-7986)
Description: Contains summaries of the latest government-sponsored projects and their findings for professionals.

350   SZ
NATIONALRATSWAHLEN (YEAR)/ELECTIONS AU CONSEIL NATIONAL (YEAR). (Text in French and German) 1943. every 4 yrs. 20 Fr. Bundesamt fuer Statistik, Hallwylstr. 15, CH-3003 Bern, Switzerland. TEL 031-618836. FAX 031-617856.

371.82   US   ISSN 0097-9325
HA491
NEBRASKA STATISTICAL HANDBOOK. biennial. $15. Department of Economic Development, Division of Research, Box 94666, Lincoln, NE 68509. TEL 402-471-3111. Ed. Tom Hanson. circ. 1,000.

324   NE   ISSN 0168-5732
NETHERLANDS. CENTRAAL BUREAU VOOR DE STATISTIEK. STATISTIEK DER VERKIEZINGEN. PROVINCIALE STATEN/NETHERLANDS. CENTRAL BUREAU OF STATISTICS. ELECTION STATISTICS. PROVINCIAL COUNCILS. (Text in Dutch and English) 1946. irreg. Centraal Bureau voor de Statistiek, Prinses Beatrixlaan 428, Voorburg, Netherlands. (Dist. by: SDU - Publishers, Christoffel Plantijnstraat, The Hague)

328   NO   ISSN 0332-8023
NORWAY. STATISTISK SENTRALBYRAA. KOMMUNE OG FYLKESTINGS VALGET/NORWAY. CENTRAL BUREAU OF STATISTICS. MUNICIPAL AND COUNTY ELECTIONS. (Subseries of its Norges Offisielle Statistikk) (Text in English and Norwegian) 1902. quadrennial. NOK 75. Statistisk Sentralbyraa, Box 8131 Dep., 0033 Oslo 1, Norway. TEL 02-864500. FAX 02-864973. circ. 2,300.
Formerly: Norway. Statistisk Sentralbyraa. Kommunevalget.

350   NO   ISSN 0802-9067
NORWAY. STATISTISK SENTRALBYRAA. STORTINGSVALG/NORWAY. CENTRAL BUREAU OF STATISTICS. PARLIAMENTARY ELECTIONS. (Subseries of its Norges Offisiele Statistikk) 1894. quadrennial. price varies. Statistisk Sentralbyraa, Box 8131-Dep., 0033 Oslo 1, Norway. TEL 02-864500. FAX 02-864973. circ. 1,800.

352   GW
NUERNBERGER STATISTIK AKTUELL. 1974. m. Amt fuer Stadtforschung und Statistik, Unschlittplatz 7a, 8500 Nuremberg 1, Germany. TEL 0911-2312843. circ. 500.

350 317   CN
ONTARIO PUBLIC SECTOR; of official personnel in federal, provincial and municipal governments in the province of Ontario. 1988. biennial. Can.$117.50. 210-2175 Sheppard Ave. E., Willowdale, Ont. M2J 1W8, Canada. TEL 416-495-0700. FAX 416-495-1887. Ed. Shirley Hyman. circ. 25,000.

380   US
HD2767.07
OREGON. PUBLIC UTILITY COMMISSIONER. OREGON UTILITY STATISTICS. 1970. a. free. Public Utility Commissioner, 351 W. Summer St., N.E., Salem, OR 97310-0335. TEL 503-378-4373. FAX 503-373-7752. stat.; circ. 350.
Supersedes: Oregon Public Utility Commissioner. Statistics of Electric, Gas, Steam Heat, Telephone, Telegraph and Water Companies (ISSN 0091-0546)

PARLIAMENTARY YEAR BOOK. see *PUBLIC ADMINISTRATION*

PERSONNEL LITERATURE. see *BUSINESS AND ECONOMICS — Abstracting, Bibliographies, Statistics*

PIRMASENS ZAHLEN UND FAKTEN: STATISTISCHE JAHRBUCH STADT PIRMASENS. see *STATISTICS*

350   CN
PROFILE OF ELECTORAL DISTRICTS. irreg. Can.$50. Ministry of Finance and Corporate Relations, 1405 Douglas St., 2nd Fl., Victoria, B.C. V8V 1X4, Canada. TEL 604-387-0327. FAX 604-387-0329.
Description: Provides detailed data on the 75 new provincial electoral districts in B.C., based on the most recent Canadian Census data.

350 319   QA
QATAR YEARBOOK. (Text in English) 1976. a. free. Ministry of Information, Press and Publications Department, P.O. Box 5147, Doha, Qatar. FAX 432850. TELEX 4552 QPRESS DH - DOHA. illus.; stat.; circ. 10,000.
Description: Covers the various activities of all ministries and public institutions in Qatar, as well as many private sector industrial and commercial enterprises.

352 016   GW   ISSN 0341-2512
Z7164.R33
REFERATEBLATT ZUR RAUMENTWICKLUNG. 1975. q. DM.72. Bundesforschungsanstalt fuer Landeskunde und Raumordnung, Am Michaelshof 8, Postfach 200130, 5300 Bonn 2, Germany. TEL 0228-826-0. Ed. W. Strubelt. adv.; abstr.; bibl. (back issues avail.) **Indexed:** P.A.I.S.For.Lang.Ind.
Formerly: Referateblatt zur Raumordnung (ISSN 0034-2246)

P Q

PUBLIC ADMINISTRATION — ABSTRACTING, BIBLIOGRAPHIES, STATISTICS

350   US
RESOURCE GUIDE TO INFLUENCING STATE LEGISLATURES; an annotated bibliography. 1984. a. $20 (effective 1991). Government Research Service, 701 Jackson, Topeka, KS 66603. TEL 913-232-7720. FAX 913-232-1615. Ed. Lynn Hellebust.
Description: Focuses on the state legislative process, lobbying strategies and techniques, and related information.

016 350   US
REVIEW - S W A P.* (Sharing with a Purpose) 1972. bi-m. free. American Society for Public Administration, Section on Personnel Administration and Labor Relations, Rider College, Graduate Program for Administrators, 1120 G St., N.W., Ste. 500, Washington, DC 20005. Ed. Jack Rabin. bk.rev.; abstr.; circ. 2,200.
Formerly: S W A P.
Description: Abstracts of civil service literature relating to personnel selection research.

352   GW   ISSN 0174-2914
RHEINLAND-PFALZ. STATISTISCHES LANDESAMT RHEINLAND-PFALZ. STATISTISCHE MONATSHEFTE. 1958. m. DM.40. Statistisches Landesamt Rheinland-Pfalz, Postfach, 5427 Bad Ems, Germany. TEL 02603-71245. stat. (back issues avail.)

352   GW   ISSN 0174-2876
RHEINLAND - PFALZ HEUTE. 1977. a. DM.1. Statistisches Landesamt Rheinland-Pfalz, Postfach, 5427 Bad Ems, Germany. TEL 02603-71245. stats. (back issues avail.)

350 016   UK   ISSN 0140-4768
HN49.C6
RURAL DEVELOPMENT ABSTRACTS. 1978. q. £97($177) C.A.B. International, Wallingford, Oxon OX10 8DE, England. TEL 0491-32111. FAX 0491-33508. TELEX 847964 COMAGG G. (U.S. subscr. to: C.A.B. International, North American Office, 845 N. Park Ave., Tucson, AZ 85719. TEL 800-528-4841) circ. 500. (also avail. in microfiche; also avail. on floppy disk; back issues avail.) **Indexed:** E.I.
• Also available online. Vendor(s): BRS (ECON), CISTI, DIMDI, DIALOG, European Space Agency.
— BLDSC shelfmark: 8052.422200.
Description: Contains abstracts from world literature relating to main aspects of rural development in the Third World.

350   US   ISSN 0094-6958
JA1
SAGE PUBLIC ADMINISTRATION ABSTRACTS. 1974. q. $75 to individuals; institutions $212. Sage Publications, Inc., 2455 Teller Rd., Newbury Park, CA 91320. TEL 805-499-0721. FAX 805-499-0871. (And: Sage Publications, Ltd., 6 Bonhill St., London EC2A 4PU, England) Ed. Paul McDowell. adv.; index; circ. 500. (back issues avail.)

319   SE
SEYCHELLES. DEPARTMENT OF FINANCE. NATIONAL ACCOUNTS. a. R.5. Department of Finance, Statistics Division, P.O. Box 206, Independence House, Victoria, Republic of Seychelles.

350   SI   ISSN 0129-9786
HD9987.S57
SINGAPORE. DEPARTMENT OF STATISTICS. REPORT ON THE SURVEY OF SERVICES (YEAR). a. S.$20.40. Department of Statistics, 8 Shenton Way 10-01 Treasury Bldg., Singapore 0106, Singapore. TEL 3209702. FAX 3209689. TELEX RS 63001 STAT.

352   SA
SOUTH AFRICA. CENTRAL STATISTICAL SERVICE. LOCAL GOVERNMENT STATISTICS. (Report No. 91-05-01) irreg., latest 1987. Central Statistical Service, Private Bag X44, Pretoria 0001, South Africa. TEL 012-310-8911. FAX 012-3108500. (Dist. by: Government Printing Works, Private Bag X85, Pretoria 0001, South Africa)
Formerly: South Africa. Department of Statistics. Local Government Statistics.

352   SA
SOUTH AFRICA. CENTRAL STATISTICAL SERVICE. STATISTICS OF DEVELOPMENT BOARDS. (Report No. 13-13-10) a. Central Statistical Service, Private Bag X44, Pretoria 0001, South Africa. TEL 012-310-8911. FAX 012-310-8500. (Dist. by: Government Printing Works, Private Bag X85, Pretoria 0001, South Africa)
Former titles: South Africa. Department of Statistics. Statistics of Administration Boards; (until 1977): South Africa. Department of Statistics. Statistics of Bantu Affairs Administration Boards.

350   GW   ISSN 0172-4533
STADT DUISBURG. STATISTISCHES JAHRBUCH. 1951. a. Amt fuer Statistik, Der Oberstadtdirektor, Bismarckstr. 150-158, 4100 Duisburg 1, Germany. TEL 0203-2833085. FAX 0203-2834404.

352   GW
STADT FREIBURG IM BREISGAU. AMT FUER STATISTIK UND EINWOHNERWESEN. JAHRESHEFT. 1977. a. DM.18. Amt fuer Statistik und Einwohnerwesen, Wilhelmstr. 20A, 7800 Freiburg im Breisgau, Germany. stat.; circ. 400. (back issues avail.)
Description: Studies the development of social and economic life within municipality of Freiburg.

352   GW
STADT MANNHEIM. VIERTELJAHRESBERICHT. 1972. q. DM.8. Stadt Mannheim, Amt fuer Statistik und Stadtforschung, Postfach 103051, 6800 Mannheim 1, Germany. TEL 0621-2933810. FAX 0621-2932868. (back issues avail.)

353.9   US
STATISTICAL REVIEW OF GOVERNMENT IN UTAH. 1958. a. $11. Utah Foundation, 10 W. 100 S., No. 323, Salt Lake City, UT 84101-1544. TEL 801-364-1837. Ed. Michael Christensen. circ. 1,000. **Indexed:** SRI.
Description: Contains most-used financial and statistical information about state and local governments in Utah.

350   IT   ISSN 0075-1820
HJ9497
STATISTICHE DEI BILANCI DELLE AMMINISTRAZIONI REGIONALI, PROVINCIALI E COMUNALI. irreg. L.14000. Istituto Centrale di Statistica, Via Cesare Balbo 16, 00100 Rome, Italy.

350   IT
STATISTICHE SULLA PUBBLICA AMMINISTRAZIONE. irreg. L.21000. Istituto Centrale di Statistica, Via Cesare Balbo 16, 00100 Rome, Italy.

352 310   CN   ISSN 0702-0988
HJ9014.B7
STATISTICS RELATING TO REGIONAL AND MUNICIPAL GOVERNMENTS IN BRITISH COLUMBIA. a. Can.$15.45. Ministry of Municipal Affairs, Recreation and Culture, Victoria, B.C., Canada. (Subscr. to: Crown Publications, 546 Yates St., Victoria, B.C. V8W 1K8, Canada. TEL 604-386-4636)
Description: Provides statistics on population, area of districts, incorporation dates and financial information.

352 310   GW
STATISTISCHE MONATSHEFTE SCHLESWIG-HOLSTEIN. m. Statistisches Landesamt Schleswig-Holstein, Froebelstr. 15-17, 2300 Kiel, Germany.

352 352.7 330.9   GW
STATISTISCHE NACHRICHTEN DER STADT NUERNBERG. 1946. q. Amt fuer Stadtforschung und Statistik, Unschlittplatz 7a, 8500 Nuremberg 1, Germany. TEL 0911-2312843. Ed.Bd. circ. 600. (back issues avail.)
Description: Reports on population, housing, local economy, education and welfare.

352 310   GW
STATISTISCHER BERICHT DER STADT FRANKENTHAL. 1965. a. Stadtverwaltung Frankenthal, Postfach 2023, 6710 Frankenthal, Germany. TEL 06233-89-0. FAX 06233-89400. TELEX 465232-STFT-D. (back issues avail.)
Description: Provides statistical data about the city of Frankenthal.

357   GW
STATISTISCHER MONATSBERICHT. 1978. bi-m. DM.3. Amt fuer Statistik, Stadtforschung und Europaangelegenheiten, Der Oberstadtdirektor, Bismarckstr. 150-158, 4100 Duisburg 1, Germany. TEL 0203-283-3085. FAX 0203-2834404. TELEX 8551214. index; circ. 600. (back issues avail.)
Formerly: Duisburg. Amt fuer Statistik und Stadtforschung. Statistischer Monatsbericht (ISSN 0173-8925)

352 310   GW   ISSN 0930-3782
STATISTISCHER VIERTELJAHRESBERICHT HANNOVER. 1896. q. Landeshauptstadt Hannover, Statistisches Amt, Prinzenstr. 6, Postfach 125, 3000 Hannover 1, Germany. FAX 0511-1685129. circ. 2,400. (back issues avail.)

352 310   GW
STATISTISCHES JAHRBUCH DER STADT KOELN. 1911. a. DM.30. Stadt Koeln, Amt fuer Statistik und Einwohnerwesen, Stadthaus Chorweiler, Athener Ring 4, 5000 Cologne 71, Germany. TEL 0221-2211887. FAX 0221-2211900.

352 352.7 330.9   GW
STATISTISCHES JAHRBUCH DER STADT NUERNBERG. 1977. a. DM.30. Amt fuer Stadtforschung und Statistik, Unschlittplatz 7a, 8500 Nuremberg 1, Germany. TEL 0911-2312843. stat.; circ. 700. (back issues avail.)
Description: Contains tables on population, housing, local economy, education and welfare, plus selected data on the metropolitan area.

352 310   GW
STATISTISCHES JAHRBUCH DEUTSCHER GEMEINDEN. 1890. a. DM.105. Deutscher Staedtetag, Lindenallee 13-17, 5000 Cologne 51, Germany. TEL 0221-3771-155. FAX 0221-3771-128.

314   DK   ISSN 0107-6744
HA1489.C6
STATISTISK TIAARS-OVERSIGT FOR KOEBENHAVNS KOMMUNE. English edition: Statistical Ten-Year Review of the Municipality of Copenhagen. 1981. biennial. DKK 20. Statistisk Kontor, Vester Voldgade 87, 1552 Copenhagen V, Denmark. illus.

350   SA   ISSN 0257-5418
LAW
TRANSKEI GOVERNMENT GAZETTE INDEX. 1982. a. R.67. State Library, P.O. Box 397, Pretoria 0001, South Africa. (Co-sponsor: University of the Witwatersrand) Ed. Shelagh de Wet. circ. 48.
Formerly: Transkei Official Gazette (ISSN 0257-540X)
Description: Alphabetical index which gives subject and numeric approach to notices in the Government Gazette of the Republic of Transkei.

350   TS
UNITED ARAB EMIRATES. DA'IRAT AL-MUSHTARIAT. AL-KITAB AL-IHSA'I AL-SANAWI/UNITED ARAB EMIRATES. PURCHASING DEPARTMENT. STATISTICAL YEARBOOK. (Text in Arabic) 1986. a. Purchasing Department, Information Office, P.O. Box 838, Abu Dhabi, United Arab Emirates. TEL 212700. stat.; circ. controlled.
Description: Reports on the activities of the department, including relevant legislation and analysis of government purchases.

333   US   ISSN 0082-9110
HD183
U.S. BUREAU OF LAND MANAGEMENT. PUBLIC LAND STATISTICS. 1816. a. $3.75. U.S. Department of the Interior, Bureau of Land Management, Branch of Records and Library, Denver Service Center (D-553B), Denver Federal Center, Bldg. 50, Box 25047, Denver, CO 80225-0047. TEL 303-236-6638. (Dist. by: Supt. of Documents, Washington, DC 20402) Ed. R.E. Woerner. circ. 4,000. (also avail. in microfiche) Key Title: Public Land Statistics.

U.S. BUREAU OF THE CENSUS. CENSUS CATALOG AND GUIDE. see *POPULATION STUDIES — Abstracting, Bibliographies, Statistics*

PUBLIC ADMINISTRATION — MUNICIPAL GOVERNMENT 4083

352   US   ISSN 0082-9358
U.S. BUREAU OF THE CENSUS. CENSUS OF GOVERNMENTS. (Issued in several series) 1850. quinquennial since 1957. price varies. U.S. Bureau of the Census, Data User Services Division, Washington, DC 20233. TEL 301-763-4100. (Dist. by: Supt. of Documents, Washington, DC 20402) stat. (also avail. in microform from BHP; back issues avail.)
●Also available online. Vendor(s): CompuServe Consumer Information Service, DIALOG.
Description: Covers finance, taxes and employment.

350 016   US   ISSN 0364-8265
U.S. GENERAL ACCOUNTING OFFICE. MONTHLY LIST OF G A O REPORTS. vol.18, no.10, 1984. m. $1 per copy; free to public officials, college libraries, members of the press, faculty members, and students. U.S. General Accounting Office, 441 G. St., N.W., Washington, DC 20548. bibl.
Description: Includes legal decisions and opinions of the U.S. Comptroller General.

353 015   US   ISSN 0027-0288
Z1223.5.A1
U.S. LIBRARY OF CONGRESS. MONTHLY CHECKLIST OF STATE PUBLICATIONS. 1910. m. free to U.S. agencies which send state publications to LC Exchange and Gift Division. U.S. Library of Congress, Exchange and Gift Division, Washington, DC 20540. TEL 202-707-9468. (Dist. by: Supt. of Documents, Gov't. Printing Office, Washington, DC 20402) index; circ. 5,000.
Supersedes: Monthly List of State Publications (ISSN 0090-0087)

350 614.7 011   UK
URBAN ABSTRACTS. 1974. 12/yr. £98. London Research Centre, Parliament House, 81 Black Prince Rd., London SE1 7SZ, England. Ed. Jennifer Binnie. circ. 700. (back issues avail.)
●Also available online. Vendor(s): European Space Agency.
Also available on CD-ROM.
Formerly issued as two parts: Urban Abstracts Series 1: Policy; Urban Abstracts Series 2: Technical; Which superseded in part: Urban Abstracts (ISSN 0305-103X)
Description: Examines new books, reports, and journal articles about urban affairs.

352   US   ISSN 0300-6859
HT123
URBAN AFFAIRS ABSTRACTS. 1971. w. with s-a. and a. cumulations. $275. National League of Cities, 1301 Pennsylvania Ave., N.W., Washington, DC 20004. TEL 202-626-3130. Ed. Dennis K. Rosser. abstr.; bibl.; index; circ. 400. (processed)
Description: Summarizes articles about urban affairs from over 400 journals.

350 015   US   ISSN 0364-507X
Z1223.5.W6
WISCONSIN PUBLIC DOCUMENTS. 1916. m. (plus annual cumulation). free. State Historical Society of Wisconsin, 816 State St., Madison, WI 53706. TEL 608-262-3266. Ed. John A. Peters. index; circ. 675. (also avail. in microfiche from BHP)

350   SZ
WORLD-WIDE BIBLIOGRAPHY ON PARLIAMENTS. 1978. triennial. 40 SFr. Inter-Parliamentary Union, Place du Petit-Saconnex, B.P. 438, 1211 Geneva, Switzerland. TEL 022-7344150.
FAX 022-7333141. TELEX 414217-IPU-CH.

350 314   YU
YUGOSLAVIA. SAVEZNI ZAVOD ZA STATISTIKU. KOMUNALNI FONDOVI U GRADSKIM NASELJIMA. (Subseries of: Yugoslavia. Savezni Zavod za Statistiku. Statisticki Bilten) irreg. 4 din. Savezni Zavod za Statistiku, Kneza Milosa 20, Belgrade, Yugoslavia. TEL 681-999.

350 316   ZA
ZAMBIA. CENTRAL STATISTICAL OFFICE. FINANCIAL STATISTICS OF GOVERNMENT SECTOR (ECONOMIC AND FUNCTIONAL ANALYSIS). 1964. a. $4.50. Central Statistical Office, P.O. Box 31908, Lusaka, Zambia. TEL 211-231.
Formerly: Zambia. Central Statistical Office. Government Sector Accounts (Economic and Functional Analysis) (ISSN 0084-4527)

PUBLIC ADMINISTRATION — Computer Applications

ADMINISTRATORS' COMPUTER LETTER. see
EDUCATION — School Organization And Administration

COMPUTERS, ENVIRONMENT AND URBAN SYSTEMS. see *ENVIRONMENTAL STUDIES — Computer Applications*

350 001.6 621.381   US   ISSN 0893-052X
FEDERAL COMPUTER WEEK. 1987. w. $95. I D G Communications - F C W Publishing, 3110 Fairview Park Dr., Ste. 1040, Falls Church, VA 22042. TEL 703-876-5100. FAX 703-876-5126. Ed. Edith Holmes. adv.; circ. 60,000. (tabloid format) **Indexed:** Comput.Dtbs., Tel.Abstr., Tel.Alert.
—BLDSC shelfmark: 3901.873900.

350   US   ISSN 0738-4300
GOVERNMENT COMPUTER NEWS; the newspaper serving computer users throughout the Federal Government. 1982. bi-w. $74.95 (Canada $105.95; Mexico $98.95; elsewhere $110.95); free to qualified personnel. Cahners Publishing Company (Silver Spring) (Subsidiary of: Reed International PLC), Division of Reed Publishing (USA) Inc., 8601 Georgia Ave., Ste. 300, Silver Spring, MD 20910. FAX 301-650-2111. Ed. Thomas R. Temin. adv.; bk.rev.; circ. 80,292. (newspaper; also avail. in microform from UMI) **Indexed:** CAD CAM Abstr., Comput.Dtbs., Comput.Lit.Ind., PCR2, Pers.Lit., Tel.Abstr., Tel.Alert.
●Also available online. Vendor(s): DIALOG.
Also available on CD-ROM.
—BLDSC shelfmark: 4203.928000.
Description: For computer managers and professionals associated with computer products and services in the Federal government. Provides information on the latest technologies, computer graphics, office automation and management.

350   US   ISSN 1043-9668
JK2445.A8
GOVERNMENT TECHNOLOGY; managing state and local government in the information age. 1987. m. free to qualified personnel. G T Publications, Inc., 9719 Lincoln Village Dr., No. 500, Sacramento, CA 95827-3303. TEL 916-363-5000.
FAX 916-363-5197. Ed. Larry Madsen. adv.; circ. 56,000 (controlled). (tabloid format)
Description: For executives in state, county and local government involved in buying, managing and using information technology. Emphasis is on governmental applications of computer and telecommunications technologies.

350   NE   ISSN 0927-2011
▼**INFORMATIE EN AUTOMATISERING - VAKMATIG.** 1990. 4/yr. fl.50. V N G Uitgeverij, P.O. Box 30435, 2500 GK The Hague, Netherlands. TEL 070-3738888. FAX 070-3651826. Ed.Bd. adv.; illus; circ. 1,250. (back issues avail.)

J I C S T ONLINE INFORMATION SYSTEM. (Japanese Information Center of Science and Technology) see *SCIENCES: COMPREHENSIVE WORKS — Computer Applications*

350   FR
LETTRE INFORMATIQUE ET COLLECTIVITES LOCALES. 1985. bi-m. 1700 F. Publications du Moniteur, 17 rue d'Uzes, 75002 Paris, France. TEL 1-40-13-30-30. FAX 1-40-26-20-94. TELEX UPRESSE 680876F. circ. 800.

SOCIAL SCIENCE COMPUTER REVIEW. see *EDUCATION — Computer Applications*

PUBLIC ADMINISTRATION — Municipal Government

see also Housing and Urban Planning

352   US
A A C O G REGION. 1974. m. free. Alamo Area Council of Governments, 118 Broadway, Ste. 400, San Antonio, TX 78205. TEL 512-225-5201.
FAX 512-225-5937. Ed. Nancy A. Roth-Roffy. illus.; circ. 3,500.
Supersedes: A A C O G Newsletter; Which was formerly: A A C O G Highlights.

A P W A REPORTER. (American Public Works Association) see *ENGINEERING — Civil Engineering*

A R C ACTION. (Atlanta Regional Commission) see *HOUSING AND URBAN PLANNING*

ACROSS THE TABLE. see *BUSINESS AND ECONOMICS — Labor And Industrial Relations*

352   FR   ISSN 0001-7450
ACTION MUNICIPALE;* organe de defense et d'information des mairies. 1948. m. 85 F. Edition l'Action Municipale, 18 rue Duphot, 75001 Paris, France. Ed. Jacques Vrignaud. adv.; illus.

352   AT
ADELAIDE CITY COUNCIL MUNICIPAL REFERENCE BOOK. 1911. irreg. free. Adelaide City Council, Town Hall, King William St., Adelaide, S.A. 5000, Australia. FAX 2315838. circ. 2,000.
Formerly: Adelaide City Council Municipal Yearbook (ISSN 0084-5922)

352 173   UK   ISSN 0263-3868
ADMINISTRATOR. 1950. m. £32 to non-members (foreign £42). Institute of Chartered Secretaries and Administrators, 16 Park Cresc., London W1N 4AH, England. TEL 071-580-4741. FAX 071-323-1132. adv.; bk.rev.; charts; illus.; index; circ. 42,000.
Indexed: Intl.Mgmt.Info, World Bank.Abstr.
—BLDSC shelfmark: 0696.529000.
Formerly: Professional Administration.

352 336   US
ALABAMA. DEPARTMENT OF REVENUE. ANNUAL REPORT. 1985. a. Department of Revenue, Research and Media Affairs Division, Box 32001, Montgomery, AL 36132-0001. Ed. William E. Crawford. circ. 600.
Description: Reports on the Department of Revenue's fiscal situation.

352   US   ISSN 0002-4309
Discard
ALABAMA MUNICIPAL JOURNAL. 1943. m. $12. Alabama League of Municipalities, 535 Adams Ave., Box 1270, Montgomery, AL 36102.
TEL 205-262-2566. FAX 205-263-0200. Ed. Ann M. Roquemore. adv.; illus.; circ. 4,500.

352   US
ALASKA MUNICIPAL OFFICIALS DIRECTORY. 1958. a. $30. Alaska Municipal League, 217 2nd St., Ste. 200, Juneau, AK 99801-1267.
FAX 907-463-5480. Ed. Scott A. Burgess. circ. 1,500.
Description: Provides addresses, telephone and fax numbers, and names and titles of government officials for each of Alaska's incorporated municipalities. Other information for each municipality includes population, sales tax rate and type (if any), type and form of government, and municipality owned utilities.

352   II   ISSN 0024-5623
JS7001
ALL INDIA INSTITUTE OF LOCAL SELF GOVERNMENT. QUARTERLY JOURNAL. (Text in English) 1930. q. Rs.75($20) to non-members. All India Institute of Local Self Government, Sthanikraj Bhavan, C.D. Barfiwala Marg, Andheri (West), Bombay 400 058, India. Ed. H.D. Kopardekar. adv.; bk.rev.; charts; circ. 900. **Indexed:** P.A.I.S.

352 808.8   US
ALLIED ARTS NEWSLETTER. bi-m. Allied Arts of Seattle, 107 S. Main St., Ste. 201, Seattle, WA 98104. TEL 206-624-0432.

ALTERNATIVE KOMMUNALPOLITIK; Fachzeitschrift fuer gruene und alternative Politik. see *PUBLIC ADMINISTRATION*

AMERICAN BAR ASSOCIATION. UTILITY SECTION. NEWSLETTER. see *LAW*

PUBLIC ADMINISTRATION — MUNICIPAL GOVERNMENT

352   US   ISSN 0149-337X
HD9800.U5   CODEN: ACCOD3
AMERICAN CITY & COUNTY; administration, engineering, and operations in relation to local government. Microform edition (ISSN 0364-9814) 1909. m. $54 (foreign $124). Communication Channels, Inc., 6255 Barfield Rd., Atlanta, GA 30328-4369. TEL 404-256-9800. FAX 404-256-3116. TELEX 4611075 COMCHANI. Ed. Janet Ward. adv.; bk.rev.; charts; illus.; mkt.; tr.lit.; index; circ. 66,000. (also avail. in microform from UMI,MIM; back issues avail.; reprint service avail. from UMI) **Indexed:** A.S.& T.Ind., Avery Ind.Archit.Per., Bk.Rev.Ind. (1965-1990), Bus.Ind., Chem.Abstr., Child.Bk.Rev.Ind. (1965-1990), Eng.Ind., Excerp.Med., HRIS, Ind.Sci.Rev., Mag.Ind., Ocean.Abstr., Pollut.Abstr., R.G, Tr.& Indus.Ind., W.R.C.Inf.
●Also available online.
—BLDSC shelfmark: 0812.510000.
  Formerly: American City (ISSN 0002-7936)
  Description: Covers the issues, concepts and trends of local government and public works, including the activities and concerns of engineers and administrators of municipal, township, county and special district governments, consulting and sanitary engineers and private firms performing public services.

352   US   ISSN 1059-3659
AMERICAN CITY & COUNTY DIRECTORY OF ADMINISTRATIVE SERVICE. 1989. a. $34.95. Communication Channels, Inc., 6255 Barfield Rd., Atlanta, GA 30328-4369. TEL 404-256-9800. FAX 404-256-3116. TELEX 461105 COMCHANI. Ed. Barbara Katinsky. circ. 28,100.
  Description: Index for local government officials, providing information on a wide variety of topics from aerial photography to wastewater operation and management.

352.16   US   ISSN 0077-2151
AMERICAN CITY & COUNTY MUNICIPAL INDEX; purchasing guide for city officials and consulting engineers. 1924. a. $52.95 (foreign $82.95). Communication Channels, Inc., 6255 Barfield Rd., Atlanta, GA 30328-4369. TEL 404-256-9800. FAX 404-256-3116. TELEX 4611075 COMCHANI. Ed. Barbara Katinsky. adv.; circ. 54,000.

352   IT
AMMINISTRATORE MANAGER; mensile di politica, finanza, economia e attualita delle autonomie locali. 1985. m. (10/yr.). L.100000. Maggioli Editore, Via Crimea, 1, Casella Postale, 47037 Rimini, Italy. TEL 0541-741002. Ed.Bd.

352   DK   ISSN 0109-7822
AMSTKOMMUNERNES OEKONOMI; budget. 1978. a. DKK 75. Amstraadforeningen i Danmark, Landemarket 10, DK-1119 Copenhagen K, Denmark. FAX 01-112115. TELEX 19761. illus.; circ. 1,800.
  Formerly: Oekonomisk Oversigt for Amtskommunerne (ISSN 0105-8509)
  Description: Reports on the budget of the 14 Danish counties. Provides information about income and expenditure.

352   DK   ISSN 0109-9418
AMT- OG KOMMUNE BLADET. m. T-Press, Tordenskjoldsgade 27, 1055 Copenhagen K, Denmark. TEL 45-33-140010. FAX 45-33-123137. TELEX 21317 T-PRESS. Ed. Tommy Christiansen. circ. 22,000.

352   GW
AMTLICHER SCHULANZEIGER FUER DEN REGIERUNGSBEZIRK UNTERFRANKEN; amtliches Mitteilungsblatt fuer die Volks-, Sonder- und Berufsschulen. 1871. m. DM.28. Unterfranken, Peterplatz 9, 8700 Wuerzburg, Germany. TEL 0931-380-351. FAX 0931-179318-106. TELEX 068757-REGULRD. adv.; bk.rev.; circ. 2,500. (looseleaf format; back issues avail.)

352   GW   ISSN 0003-2131
AMTLICHES KREISBLATT FUER DEN KREIS HERZOGTUM LAUENBURG. 1883. m. DM.2.20 per no. Luebecker Nachrichten GmbH, Koenigstr. 51, 2400 Luebeck, Germany. circ. 350.

352 370 360   AU
AMTLICHES MITTEILUNGSBLATT DER MARKTGEMEINDE LEOBERSDORF. 1958. q. (Amtliche Berichterstattung der Marktgemeinde Leobersdorf) Druck- und Verlagsanstalt Gutenberg, Rathausplatz 1, 2700 Wiener Neustadt, Austria. Ed. Franz Gobec. adv.; circ. 1,600. (back issues avail.)

352   GW
AMTSBLATT DER GEMEINDE WILHELMSFELD. 1960. w. (Buergermeisteramt) Druckerei Odenwaelder Buchen Wallduern, Karl-Tranzer-Str. 2, D-6967 Buchen, Germany. TEL 06281-9211. (back issues avail.)

352   AU   ISSN 0038-8971
AMTSBLATT DER LANDESHAUPTSTADT LINZ. 1921. s-m. S.10 per no. Landeshauptstadt Linz, Pfarrgasse 9, A-4041 Linz, Austria. TEL 0732-2393-1341. FAX 0732-784424. Ed. Karin Frohner. adv.; bk.rev.; illus.; stat.; index; circ. 1,000.
  Former titles: Stadt Linz; Amtsblatt der Landeshauptstadt Linz.

352   GW
AMTSBLATT DER LANDESHAUPTSTADT MUENCHEN. 1952. 3/m. DM.37. Kommunalschriften-Verlag, Postfach 801940, 8000 Munich 80, Germany. TEL 089-416006-52. Ed. Wofgang Quadflieg.

352   AU   ISSN 0003-2239
AMTSBLATT DER STADT KAPFENBERG. 1947. q. free. Stadtgemeinde Kapfenberg, 8605 Kapfenberg, Austria. Ed. Nikolaus Prieschl.

252   GW   ISSN 0172-2522
AMTSBLATT DER STADT KOELN. 1970. w. DM.52. Oberstadtdirektor, Rathaus, 5000 Cologne 1, Germany. TEL 0221-2074. FAX 0221-6486. circ. 1,000.
  Description: Lists decisions and announcements of the town government concerning construction, planning and roads.

252   GW
AMTSBLATT DER STADT KORNTAL - MUENCHINGEN. 1978. w. Nussbaum Verlag gmbH, Merlinger Str. 20, Postfach 1340, 7252 Weil d. Stadt, Germany. TEL 07033-2001. adv.; bk.rev.; play rev, illus.; circ. 10,000.

352   GW
AMTSBLATT DES KREISES WESEL; Amtliches Verkuendungsblatt. 1975. w. Kreiseigene Druckerei, Reeser Landstr. 31, Postfach 1160, D-4230 Wesel, Germany. TEL 0281-2070. circ. 1,700.

352   GW
AMTSBLATT FUER BERLIN. 1951. w. DM.132. (Senatsverwaltung fuer Inneres) Kulturbuch Verlag GmbH, Passauerstr. 4, 1000 Berlin 30, Germany. TEL 213-60-71. FAX 213-4449. circ. 6,500. (back issues avail.)

352   AU   ISSN 0003-2271
AMTSBLATT FUER DAS LAND VORARLBERG. 1946. w. S.125. Landesregierung, Roemerstr. 15, A-6901 Bregenz, Austria. TEL 05574-511-0. FAX 05574-511-80. Ed. Klaus Rossmann. bk.rev.; circ. 1,620.

352   GW
AMTSBLATT FUER DEN LANDKREIS ROSENHEIM. 1868. s-m. DM.30. Landratsamt Rosenheim, Wittelsbacherstrasse 53, 8200 Rosenheim, Germany. circ. 400.

352   GW
AMTSBLATT FUER DEN STADT- UND LANDKREIS HEILBRONN. 1945. w. DM.23.40. Stadt Heilbronn Pressestelle, Rathaus, Postfach 3440, D-7100 Heilbronn, Germany. TEL 07131-562288. FAX 07131-562999. circ. 1,800. (looseleaf format; back issues avail.)

352   GW
AMTSBLATT FUER SCHLESWIG-HOLSTEIN. 1946. w. DM.72($40) Innenministerium, Duesternbrooker Weg 92, D-2300 Kiel 1, Germany. TEL 0431-5961. FAX 0431-596-3131. circ. 4,000. (looseleaf format)

352   GW
AMTSBLATT - STADT AUGSBURG. 1746. w. DM.30. Amt fuer Oeffentlichkeitsarbeit, Maximilianstr. 4, D-8900 Augsburg, Germany. TEL 0821-324-2170. FAX 0821-3242121. TELEX 533501. circ. 730.

352   GW   ISSN 0003-9209
JS41
ARCHIV FUER KOMMUNALWISSENSCHAFTEN. (Text in English, French, German) 1962. s-a. DM.99. (Deutsches Institut fuer Urbanistik) W. Kohlhammer GmbH, Hessbruehlstr. 69, Postfach 800430, 7000 Stuttgart 80, Germany. TEL 0711-7863-1. Ed.Bd. adv.; bk.rev.; abstr.; bibl.; charts; stat.; index; circ. 1,200. **Indexed:** A.B.C.Pol.Sci., Amer.Hist.& Life, Hist.Abstr., P.A.I.S.For.Lang.Ind.

352   IT
ARCHIVIO AMMINISTRATIVO ED URBANISTICO SUBALPINO. m. Via Fratelli di Dio 26, 28026 Omegna, Italy. Ed. Giuseppe Ravasio.

ARTS AND CULTURE FUNDING REPORT. see *ART*

352   GW
ASCHAFFENBURGER STADTZEITUNG. 1986. m. DM.32. Dalbergstr. 7, 8750 Aschaffenburg, Germany. TEL 06021-24450. Eds. Thomas Kasper, Markus Loeser. adv.; bk.rev.; circ. 25,000.

352.008   MF   ISSN 0304-6451
JS7659.M3
ASSOCIATION OF URBAN AUTHORITIES. ANNUAL BULLETIN. Added title: Local Government in Mauritius. (Text in English and French) 1962. a. Association of Urban Authorities, City Hall, Port Louis, Mauritius. circ. 200.

352   AT   ISSN 0004-9808
AUSTRALIAN MUNICIPAL JOURNAL. 1921. m. Aus.$35. Municipal Association of Victoria, G.P.O. Box 4326PP, Melbourne, Vic. 3001, Australia. TEL 03-824-8411. FAX 03-824-8404. Ed. Sarah Murray. adv.; bk.rev.; illus.; circ. 3,200. **Indexed:** Aus.P.A.I.S., Aus.Rd.Ind.
—BLDSC shelfmark: 1814.900000.

352   SP
AUTONOMIA LOCAL. bi-m. 1407 ptas. Instituto de Estudios de Administracion Local y Autonomica, Centro de Estudios Urbanos, Joaquin Garcia Morato, 7, Madrid 10, Spain.
  Formerly: Vida Local. Boletin de Informacion.

352   CN   ISSN 0709-1141
BACKGROUND. 1974. m. free. Ministry of Municipal Affairs, 777 Bay St., 13th Fl., Toronto, Ont. M5G 2E5, Canada. TEL 416-585-6255. bk.rev.; circ. controlled. (processed)

352   TS
BALADIAH RAS AL-KHAIMAH/RAS AL-KHAIMAH MUNICIPALITY. (Text in Arabic) 1977. m. Municipal Government, P.O. Box 4, Ras al-Khaimah, United Arab Emirates. TEL 32422. Ed. Saud bin Saghir al-Qusaimi. circ. 3,000.
  Description: News of municipal activities and other matters of local concern.

352   TS
AL-BALADIAT/MUNICIPALITIES. (Text in Arabic) 1980. m. General Secretariat of Municipalities, P.O. Box 3774, Abu Dhabi, United Arab Emirates. TEL 331500. FAX 214430. TELEX 23147. Ed. Muhyi al-Din A. Nafeh. circ. 2,000.

352   US   ISSN 0739-6279
JS308
BASELINE DATA REPORT. 1969. bi-m. $16.50 per no. International City - County Management Association, 777 North Capitol St., N.E. Ste. 500, Washington, DC 20002-4201. TEL 202-289-4262. Ed. Evelina Moulder. **Indexed:** P.A.I.S., Sage Pub.Admin.Abstr., SRI.
  Formerly: Urban Data Service Report (ISSN 0049-5654)
  Description: Analysis of local government data collected through surveys conducted by ICMA. Covers local government practices and activities.

352   GW
BAYERISCHES JAHRBUCH; das grosse Auskunfts- und Adressenwerk. 1887. a. DM.135. Carl Gerber Verlag, Muthmannstr. 4, 8000 Munich 45, Germany. TEL 089-32393-280. FAX 089-3231269. adv.; circ. 2,000.
  Description: Directory of Bavarian authorities.

PUBLIC ADMINISTRATION — MUNICIPAL GOVERNMENT

352 GW
BEHOERDEN SPIEGEL; Zeitung fuer Kommunen, Laender und Europabehoerden. 1988. m. DM.39. ProPress Verlag GmbH, Am Buschhof 8, 5300 Bonn 3, Germany. TEL 0228-449090. FAX 0228-444296. Ed. R. Uwe Proll. bibl.; circ. 134,000.

352 GW
BERLINER BEHOERDEN SPIEGEL; unabhaengige Zeitung fuer den oeffentlichen Dienst. 1984. m. DM.39. ProPress Verlag GmbH, Am Buschhof 8, 5300 Bonn 3, Germany. TEL 0228-449090. FAX 0228-444296. circ. 30,500.

352 GW
BLAETTER ZUR GESCHICHTE DES COBURGER LANDES. 1972. q. DM.16. Eisenacher Str. 25, 8631 Lautertal 2, Germany. TEL 09561-66922. Ed. Walter Eichhorn. circ. 1,000.

352 SA ISSN 0006-4939
BLOEMFONTEIN NUUSBRIEF/BLOEMFONTEIN NEWSLETTER. (Text in Afrikaans, English) 1965. m. free. Public Relations Officer, P.O. Box 639, Bloemfontein, South Africa. illus.; stat.; tr.lit.; index; circ. 30,500.

352 IT
BOLOGNA. 1915. m. L.1500. Comune di Bologna, Direzione dei Servizi d'Informazione, Palazzo d'Accursio, Piazza Maggiore 6, Bologna, Italy. FAX 51-228500. TELEX 51-226353 ESTERI I. Dir. Giancarlo Roversi. adv.; bk.rev.; illus.; circ. 25,000.
Indexed: Abstr.Bull.Inst.Pap.Chem.
Formerly: Comune di Bologna. Notiziario Mensile (ISSN 0010-4949)

352 GW
BONNER BEHOERDEN SPIEGEL; unabhaengige Zeitung fuer den oeffentlichen Dienst. 1984. m. DM.39. ProPress Verlag GmbH, Am Buschhof 8, 5300 Bonn 3, Germany. TEL 0228-449090. FAX 0228-444296. bibl.; circ. 27,000. (looseleaf format; back issues avail.)

352 US ISSN 0006-7946
BOSTON CITY RECORD. 1898. w. $50. One City Hall Plaza, City Hall, Rm. 808A, Boston, MA 02201. TEL 617-725-4188. FAX 617-723-6141. Ed. William D. Stanton. adv.; charts; circ. 52.
Description: Presents municipal news, public notices and advertisements of invitations for sealed bids and proposals for all purchases of materials and services estimated to exceed $2,000 in value.

352 AU ISSN 0006-8225
BOTE FUER TIROL; Amtsblatt der Behoerden Aemter und Gerichte Tirols. 1817. w. S.74. Amt der Tiroler Landesregierung, Landhaus, A 6010 Innsbruck, Tyrol, Austria. Ed. Johann Kainz. index; circ. 2,250.

352 FR
BOTTIN COMMUNES. 1978. a. $185. Societe Bottin, 31 Cours de Juilliottes, 94706 Maisons-Alfort Cedex, France. TEL 1-49-81-56-56. FAX 1-49-77-85-28. TELEX 262 407.

352 II
BRIHANMUMBAI MAHANAGARPALIKA PATRIKA. (Text in English and Marathi) 1954. m. Rs.10. Municipal Corporation of Greater Bombay, Public Relations Dept., Municipal Extension Bldg., Mahapalika Marg, Bombay 400001, India. Ed. Shri J.B. Mahajan. adv.; bk.rev.; circ. 2,000.
Formerly: Bomaby Civic Journal (ISSN 0524-0166)

352 CN
BRITISH COLUMBIA. MINISTRY OF MUNICIPAL AFFAIRS, RECREATION AND CULTURE. MUNICIPAL MANUAL. base vol. (plus irreg. suppl.). Can.$52. Ministry of Municipal Affairs, Recreation and Culture, Victoria, B.C., Canada. (Subscr. to: Crown Publications, 546 Yates St., Victoria, B.C. V8W 1K8, Canada. TEL 604-386-4636) (looseleaf format)

BRITISH COLUMBIA DECISIONS - MUNICIPAL LAW CASES. see LAW

352 GW
BUERGERBLATT DER GEMEINDE ROHRDORF. 1961. s-m. DM.10.40. O. Nussbaum Presse- und Wirtschaftsverlag, Postfach 1340, D-7252 Weil der Stadt, Germany. TEL 07033-2001. circ. 470.

352.9 US ISSN 0007-3547
BUILDING OFFICIAL AND CODE ADMINISTRATOR. 1967. bi-m. $18. Building Officials and Code Administrators International, 4051 W. Flossmoor Rd., Country Club Hills, IL 60478-5795. Ed. William J. Even. adv.; bk.rev.; charts; illus.; stat.; index, cum.index; circ. 12,000.
Formerly: Building Official.

352 US
C Q'S WASHINGTON ALERT. d. Congressional Quarterly Inc., 1414 22nd St., N.W., Washington, DC 20037. TEL 202-887-8500. FAX 202-728-1863.
●Also available online.
Description: Online database service for breaking legislation and for issues before the U.S. Congress.

C R P C INFO. (Capital Region Planning Commission) see HOUSING AND URBAN PLANNING

352 II ISSN 0008-0675
CALCUTTA MUNICIPAL GAZETTE. (Text in Bengali and English) 1924. fortn. Rs.12. Calcutta Municipal Corporation, Superintendent of Printing, 5 Surendranath Banarjee Rd., Calcutta 13, India. Ed. Shri Rabindra N. Bhatta Charyya.

352 US
CALENDAR AND BUYERS AND SERVICES GUIDE FOR LOCAL GOVERNMENTS (YEAR). a. free. Colorado Municipal League, 1660 Lincoln St., Ste. 2100, Denver, CO 80264. TEL 303-831-6411. FAX 303-860-8175.
Description: Lists firms that provide products and services to local governments. Includes the firm name, address, phone, contact person, and services performed.

CALIFORNIA CABLE LETTER; current community perspectives and directions. see COMMUNICATIONS

CALIFORNIA CONNECTIONS; a directory of private and public sector employment opportunities. see BUSINESS AND ECONOMICS — Trade And Industrial Directories

352 IT
CARPI CITTA. 1964. q. free. Comune di Carpi, Corso Alberto Pio 91, 41012 Carpi, Italy. TEL 059-649233. FAX 59-649200. (Co-sponsor: Carpi Municipal Government) adv.; circ. 22,000. (tabloid format)
Formerly (until 1988): Comune di Carpi.

CAYMAN GAZETTE. see LAW

352 US ISSN 0300-712X
CHICAGO. MUNICIPAL REFERENCE LIBRARY. CHECKLIST OF PUBLICATIONS ISSUED BY THE CITY OF CHICAGO. 1958. q. free. Municipal Reference Library, Rm. 1004, City Hall, Chicago, IL 60602. TEL 312-744-4992. circ. 1,050.

352 US ISSN 0300-7081
Z881.C53
CHICAGO. MUNICIPAL REFERENCE LIBRARY. RECENT ADDITIONS. 1958. m. free. Municipal Reference Library, Rm. 1004, City Hall, Chicago, IL 60602. TEL 312-744-4992. circ. 650.

352 UK ISSN 0264-2751
HT119
CITIES. 1983. q. £150 in UK & Europe; elsewhere £165. Butterworth - Heinemann Ltd. (Subsidiary of: Reed International PLC), Linacre House, Jordan Hill, Oxford OX2 8DP, England. TEL 0865-310366. FAX 0865-310898. TELEX 83111 BHPOXF G. (Subscr. to: Turpin Transactions Ltd., Distribution Centre, Blackhorse Rd., Letchworth, Herts SG6HN, England. TEL 0462-672555) Ed. Penny Street. adv.; bk.rev.; abstr.; illus.; index. (also avail. in microform from UMI; back issues avail.) **Indexed:** Avery Ind.Archit.Per., Environ.Abstr., I D A, P.A.I.S.
—BLDSC shelfmark: 3267.792160.
Description: Focuses on the policies and technologies affecting urban environments, and on the social, psychological and physical impact of planning policies.
Refereed Serial

330 US ISSN 0009-756X
CITIZENS' BUSINESS. 1910. irreg. $50 membership. Pennsylvania Economy League, Eastern Division, 1211 Chestnut St., Ste. 600, Philadelphia, PA 19107-4103. TEL 215-864-9562. Ed.Bd. stat.; circ. 3,000. (processed)

352 US
CITIZENS UNION FOUNDATION. OCCASIONAL PAPER SERIES. 1977. irreg. Citizens Union Foundation, Inc., 198 Broadway, New York, NY 10038. TEL 212-227-0342. FAX 212-227-0345. Dir. Jeannette Kahlenberg.
Formerly: Citizens Union Research Foundation. Occasional Paper Studies.

352 US
CITIZENS UNION REPORTS; citizens union news and comment on New York City. 1946. 4/yr. $20 to non-members. Citizens Union of the City of New York, 198 Broadway, New York, NY 10038. TEL 212-227-0342. FAX 212-227-0345. Ed. Jeannette Kahlenberg. circ. 3,000. (processed)
Formerly: Across from City Hall (ISSN 0001-5059)
Description: News articles and announcements on the legislative, political, and policy issues that affect the civic activities of this New York City people's lobby.

352 US ISSN 0193-8371
JS303.A8
CITY & TOWN (NORTH LITTLE ROCK). 1947. m. (except Feb. & Jul.). $15. Arkansas Municipal League, Box 38, North Little Rock, AR 72115. TEL 501-374-3484. Ed. Harry Hamner. adv.; bk.rev.; circ. 6,400.
Formerly: Arkansas Municipalities (ISSN 0004-1866)

352 US
CITY CLUB GADFLY. 1959. m. free. City Club of New York, 33 W. 42nd St., New York, NY 10036. TEL 212-921-9870. Ed. Louis Sepersky. bk.rev.; circ. 2,500 (controlled).
Formerly (until May 1978): City Club Comments (ISSN 0009-7721)

350 US
CITY FISCAL CONDITIONS IN (YEAR). 1983. a. $25 (members $15). National League of Cities, 1301 Pennsylvania Ave. N.W., Washington, DC 20004. TEL 202-626-3000. (back issues avail.)
Description: Survey of trends in city revenues and expenditures.

352 US ISSN 0190-0005
CITY HALL DIGEST; the municipal government newsletter. 1976. m. $54. City Hall Communications, Box 309, Seabrook, MD 20703-0309. TEL 301-557-3681. Ed. Raymond L. Bancroft. bk.rev.; charts; illus.; stat. (back issues avail.) **Indexed:** Urb.Aff.Abstr.
Description: Covers innovations and new management techniques in American city governments, including community development, public safety, environment, finances, transportation, human resources, and public relations.

352 AT
CITY OF PERTH. LORD MAYOR'S REPORT. 1970. a. City of Perth, Perth, W.A., Australia. FAX 09-2212142. illus.; stat.; circ. 2,500.
Formerly: City of Perth. Annual Report.
Description: Covers city's municipal matters. Includes financial statistics.

352 SW
CITY OF STOCKHOLM. ANNUAL FINANCIAL REPORT (YEAR). a. City of Stockholm Kammarkontor, City Hall, S-105 35 Stockholm, Sweden. TEL 46 8 785 91 83.

352 US
CITY RECORD; official journal of the City of New York. d. (M-F). $100. Department of General Services, 2223 Municipal Bldg., New York, NY 10007. TEL 212-566-4446. Ed. Virginia Bull. charts; stat.

352 SP ISSN 0210-0487
CIUDAD Y TERRITORIO. 1969. q. 3000 ptas. Instituto Nacional de Administracion Publica, Centro de Estudios para la Administracion Local, Santa Engracia, 7, 28010 Madrid, Spain. Dir. Fernando de Teran. bk.rev.; bibl.; illus.
—BLDSC shelfmark: 3268.470000.

352 II ISSN 0009-7772
CIVIC AFFAIRS. (Text in English) 1953. m. Rs.72($9) Citizen Publications, Box 188, Bhargova Estate, Kanpur 1, India. Ed. S.P. Mehra. adv.; bk.rev.; illus.; circ. 3,500.
—BLDSC shelfmark: 3268.570000.

PUBLIC ADMINISTRATION — MUNICIPAL GOVERNMENT

352 CN ISSN 0829-772X
JS1701
CIVIC PUBLIC WORKS. (Includes 4 annual directories as special issues: Grounds Maintenance and General Operations; Solid Waste Management and Office Equipment; Roads, Streets and Highways; Water and Sewage) 1949. m. Can.$31. Maclean-Hunter Ltd., Business Publication Division, Maclean-Hunter Bldg., 777 Bay St., Toronto, Ont. M5W 1A7, Canada. TEL 416-596-5953. FAX 416-593-3193. TELEX 062-19547. Ed. Clifford J. Allum. adv.; bk.rev.; bibl.; charts; illus.; mkt.; tr.lit.; index; circ. 13,500.
Formerly: Civic Administration (ISSN 0009-7764)

331.1 US
COLORADO JOB FINDER. 1979. s-m. $38. Colorado Municipal League, 1660 Lincoln St., Ste. 2100, Denver, CO 80264. TEL 303-831-6411. FAX 303-860-8175. Ed. Barbara Major. circ. 310. (back issues avail.)
Description: Lists administrative, technical and professional job openings in state and local government throughout Colorado.

352 US
COLORADO LAWS ENACTED AFFECTING MUNICIPAL GOVERNMENTS. a. $40 to non-members; members $20. Colorado Municipal League, 1660 Lincoln St., Ste. 2100, Denver, CO 80264. TEL 303-831-6411.
Description: Presents selected laws of broad municipal interest that were enacted by the Colorado General Assembly.

352 US ISSN 0010-1664
JS39
COLORADO MUNICIPALITIES. 1925. bi-m. $15 to non-members. Colorado Municipal League, 1660 Lincoln St., Ste. 2100, Denver, CO 80264. TEL 303-831-6411. FAX 303-860-8175. Ed. Kay Mariea. adv.; bk.rev.; illus.; index, cum.index; circ. 4,500. **Indexed:** P.A.I.S.
Description: Presents articles on current interests and concerns of municipal officials, activities of Colorado municipalities and individuals involved in municipal government.

352 FR ISSN 0414-1105
COMMUNES D'EUROPE. 1956. q. 80 F. Conseil des Communes et Regions d'Europe, 41 quai d'Orsay, 75007 Paris, France. Ed. F. Zaragoza. adv.; bk.rev.; circ. 10,000.

352 FR ISSN 0573-0910
COMMUNES DE FRANCE. 1959. m. 370 F. Societe de Presse des Collectivites (SOPRECO), 12 cite Malesherbes, 75009 Paris, France. TEL 45-26-30-80. FAX 42-82-94-08. Ed. Claude-Emile Guerin. adv.; bk.rev.; circ. 13,000.

352 634.9 FR
COMMUNES FORESTIERES DE FRANCE. 1931. q. 100 F. (effective Jan. 1991). Federation Nationale des Communes Forestieres de France, 13 rue du General Bertrand, 75007 Paris, France. FAX 45-67-25-99. Ed. Brigitte Deshaires. adv.; circ. 11,000.

352 US ISSN 1044-6222
COMMUNITY LEADER BRIEFINGS. (Text in English, Russian) 1989. m. free. City Leaders Institute, 3045 Thayen Pl., Boise, ID 83709. TEL 208-375-6337. FAX 208-375-6337. Ed. Wayne S. Forrey. bk.rev.; index; circ. 500. (looseleaf format; back issues avail.)
Description: Management and technical information to help mayors and council members govern cities.
Refereed Serial

352 IT
COMPENDIO DATI; patrimoniali, economici, finanziari, tecnici, produttivi e del personale. 1976. a. L.80000. Confederazione Italiana dei Servizi Pubblici degli Enti Locali, Piazza Cola di Rienzo n.80-a, I-00192 Rome, Italy.

COMPENSATION (WASHINGTON, 1982); an annual report on local government executive salaries and fringe benefits. see *BUSINESS AND ECONOMICS — Personnel Management*

352 IT ISSN 0010-4930
COMUNE DEMOCRATICO; rivista delle autonomie locali. 1945. bi-m. L.30000. Agenda della Lega per le Autonomie e i Poteri Locali, Via Cesare Balbo 43, 00184 Rome, Italy. Ed. Enzo Modica. adv.; bk.rev.; illus.; circ. 6,000.

352 IT ISSN 0010-4973
COMUNI D'EUROPA. 1952. m. L.30000 to individuals; institutions L.150000 (foreign L.40000). Associazione Italiana per il Consiglio dei Comuni d'Europa, Piazza di Trevi 86, 00187 Rome, Italy. TEL 6840461. FAX 6793275. Ed. Umberto Serafini. circ. 14,000.

352 IT
CONFEDERAZIONE ITALIANA DEI SERVIZI PUBBLICI DEGLI ENTI LOCALI. ANNUARIO. 1961? a. L.80000. Confederazione Italiana dei Servizi Pubblici degli Enti Locali, Piazza Cola di Rienzo, 80, 00192 Rome, Italy. stat.

CONGRESSIONAL LEGISLATIVE REPORTING. see *LAW*

352 AT ISSN 0728-5582
COUNCIL AND COMMUNITY. 1981. bi-m. free. Local Government Association of South Australia, G.P.O. Box 2693, Adelaide, S.A. 5001, Australia. TEL 08-223-3468. FAX 08-223-2659. TELEX 87138. Ed. Katie Thorp. adv.; bk.rev.; circ. 3,200. (back issues avail.)

350 FR
COUNCIL OF EUROPE. STUDY SERIES: LOCAL AND REGIONAL AUTHORITIES IN EUROPE. 1972. irreg. price varies. Council of Europe, Publishing and Documentation Service, 67006 Strasbourg, France. FAX 88-41-27-81. TELEX 870 943 F. (Dist. in U.S. by: Manhattan Publishing Co., 225 Lafayette St., New York, NY 10012) Ed.Bd. charts; stat.
Former titles: Council of Europe. Steering Committee on Regional and Municipal Matters. Study Series: Local and Regional Authorities in Europe; Council of Europe. Committee on Cooperation in Municipal and Regional Matters. Study Series: Local and Regional Authorities in Europe.

352 US ISSN 0742-1702
JS414
COUNTY EXECUTIVE DIRECTORY. s-a. $130. Carroll Publishing Company, 1058 Thomas Jefferson St., N.W., Washington, DC 20007. TEL 202-333-8620. FAX 202-337-7020.
Description: Directory of county officials and administrators listed by state.

352 UK
JS3260
COUNTY NEWS. 1908. s-m. £30. Association of County Councils, Eaton House, 66A Eaton Sq., London SW1 9BH, England. TEL 071-235-1200. FAX 071-235-8458. adv.; bk.rev.; abstr.; charts; illus.; stat.; index; circ. 6,167. **Indexed:** Geo.Abstr., RICS.
Formerly (until 1991): County Councils Gazette (ISSN 0011-0310)

352 US ISSN 0744-9798
COUNTY NEWS. vol.3, 1970. fortn. $75. National Association of Counties, 440 First St., N.W., Washington, DC 20001. TEL 202-393-6226. FAX 202-393-2630. Ed. Beverly Schlotterbeck. adv.; charts; illus.; stat.; circ. 27,000. (tabloid format)
Formerly: N A C O News and Views (ISSN 0027-5743)

352 BE ISSN 0011-099X
CREDIT COMMUNAL DE BELGIQUE. BULLETIN TRIMESTRIEL. (Editions in Dutch and French) 1947. q. free. Credit Communal de Belgique, 44 Bd. Pacheco, B-1000 Brussels, Belgium. Ed. L. Malvoz. bk.rev.; charts; illus.; circ. 9,000 (French ed.); 9,000 (Dutch ed.). **Indexed:** P.A.I.S.For.Lang.Ind.

352 IT
CROCEVIA; mensile di polizia municipale, stradale, amministrativa e sanitaria per i Vigili Urbani d'Italia. 1946. m. (11/yr.). L.55000 to individuals; institutions L.110000(effective 1992). Maggioli Editori, Via Crimes, 1, Casella Postale 290, 47037 Rimini, Italy. TEL 0541-626777. FAX 0541-622020. Ed. Valerio Lessi.

352 US ISSN 0011-3727
CURRENT MUNICIPAL PROBLEMS. Annual cumulation (ISSN 0161-5122) 1959. q. (plus a. cum.). $99. Callaghan & Co., 155 Pfingsten Rd., Deerfield, IL 60015. TEL 800-323-1336. Ed. Byron S. Matthews. bk.rev.; charts; cum.index; circ. 761. (also avail. in microfiche from UMI) **Indexed:** C.L.I., L.R.I., Leg.Cont., Sel.Water Res.Abstr., SSCI.

352 340 US
D.C. CODE UPDATER. 1981. m. $300. David W. Lang, Ed. & Pub., P.O. Box 3107, Crofton, MD 21114. FAX 202-457-7814. TELEX 202-497-1490. charts; cum.index; circ. 40. (back issues avail.)
Description: Listing of current changes to D.C. code and D.C. rules and regulations.

352 US
D G S DIGEST. 1989. 4/yr. free. Department of General Services, Office of Communications, Manhattan Municipal Bldg., 17th Fl. S., 1 Centre St., New York, NY 10007. TEL 212-669-7140. FAX 212-669-4664. circ. 3,500.
Formerly: D G S Reporter.
Description: Reports on agency's personnel activities, projects, achievements and awards.

352 US
D G S GREENTHUMB. 1981. 4/yr. free. Department of General Services, Office of Communications, Manhattan Municipal Bldg., 17th Fl. S., 1 Centre St., New York, NY 10007. TEL 212-669-7140. FAX 212-669-4664. Ed.Bd. circ. 3,000.
Description: Reports on Operation Greenthumb personnel, community gardens, achievements and awards.

352 US
D G S POWERLINES. 1989. s-a. free. Department of General Services, Office of Communications, Manhattan Municipal Bldg., 17th Fl. S., 1 Centre St., New York, NY 10007. TEL 212-669-7140. FAX 212-669-4664. Ed. Andrea Patterson. circ. 1,000.
Formerly: D G S Energy Manager.
Description: Reports on OEC personnel, conservation projects, achievements and awards.

352 DK ISSN 0011-6106
DANMARKS AMTSRAAD. 1970. fortn. DKK 340. Amtsraadsforeningen i Danmark, Landemarket 10, P.O. Box 1144, DK-1010 Copenhagen K, Denmark. FAX 33-146115. Ed. Ib Bjoernbak. adv.; bk.rev.; charts; circ. 3,776.

352 DK ISSN 0011-6572
DANSKE KOMMUNER. 1970. w. DKK 442. Kommunernes Landsforening - National Association of Local Authorities in Denmark, Gyldenloevesgade 11, 1600 Copenhagen V, Denmark. TEL 45-31-122788. FAX 45-31-122785. Ed. Jens Hoche. adv.; bk.rev.; illus.; stat.; index; circ. 11,500.
Supersedes: Koebstadforeningens Tidsskrift & Kommunal Tidende.

352 GW ISSN 0011-8303
DEMOKRATISCHE GEMEINDE; die Monatszeitschrift fuer Kommunalpolitik. 1949. m. DM.96. Vorwaerts-Verlag GmbH, Am Michaelshof 8-10, Postfach 20 13 64, 5300 Bonn 2, Germany. Ed. Ansgar Burghof. adv.; bk.rev.; abstr.; illus.; index; circ. 15,000. (also avail. in microform)

352 FR ISSN 0045-9984
DEPARTEMENTS ET COMMUNES. 1952. m. 371 F. (Assemblee des Presidents des Conseils Generaux) Association des Maires de France, 41 Quai d'Orsay, 75007 Paris, France. FAX 45-55-06-42. Ed. Gabriel Calamarte. adv.; bk.rev.; abstr.; index; circ. 27,500. (tabloid format)
—BLDSC shelfmark: 3553.575000.

DI C T A JOURNAL. (District Council Technical Association) see *BUILDING AND CONSTRUCTION*

352 US ISSN 0090-1989
JS451.N93
DIRECTORY: NORTH DAKOTA CITY OFFICIALS. 33rd ed. 1990. biennial. $11. North Dakota League of Cities, Box 2235, Bismarck, ND 58502. TEL 701-223-3518. Ed. Robert E. Johnson. adv.

PUBLIC ADMINISTRATION — MUNICIPAL GOVERNMENT 4087

350 US
DIRECTORY OF CITY POLICY OFFICIALS. 1984. a. $35 (members $10). National League of Cities, 1301 Pennsylvania Ave. N.W., Washington, DC 20004. TEL 202-636-3000. (back issues avail.)
Description: Lists names of mayors and council members in American cities of over 30,000 people. Includes city hall address and telephone number, population and form of government.

917.63 US ISSN 0092-0614
F379.A15
DIRECTORY OF LOUISIANA CITIES, TOWNS AND VILLAGES. irreg. $2. Department of Transportation and Development, Box 94245, Capitol Station, Baton Rouge, LA 70804. TEL 504-379-1109.

352 US ISSN 0148-7442
JS303.M5
DIRECTORY OF MICHIGAN MUNICIPAL OFFICIALS. s-a. $27 per no. Michigan Municipal League, 1675 Green Rd., Box 1487, Ann Arbor, MI 48106. TEL 313-662-3246. FAX 313-662-8083. (reprint service avail.)

352 US
DIRECTORY OF MINNESOTA CITY OFFICIALS. 1986. a. $25. League of Minnesota Cities, 183 University Ave. E., St. Paul, MN 55101-2526. TEL 612-227-5600. Ed. Jean Mehle Goad. circ. 3,500.
Formerly: Directory of Minnesota Municipal Officials.

352 US
DIRECTORY OF MUNICIPAL AND COUNTY OFFICIALS IN COLORADO (YEAR). a. $35 to non-members; members $17.50. Colorado Municipal League, 1660 Lincoln St., Ste. 2100, Denver, CO 80264. TEL 303-831-6411. FAX 303-860-8175.
Description: Lists names, titles, official addresses and telephone numbers of elected and appointed municipal and county officials. Also includes listings of selected federal and state offices and organizations, the Colorado congressional delegation, the councils of government, and the regional planning commissions.

352 US
DIRECTORY OF NORTH CAROLINA MUNICIPAL OFFICIALS. a. $30. North Carolina League of Municipalities, Box 3069, 215 N. Dawson St., Raleigh, NC 27603. TEL 919-834-1311. FAX 919-733-9519. Ed. Margot F. Christensen. circ. 1,500.

352 BL ISSN 0419-3911
DIRIGENTE MUNICIPAL. 1966. m. $70. Editora Visao Ltda., Rua Alvaro de Carvalho, 350, 2o andar, C.P. 3082, 01050 Sao Paulo, Brazil. TEL 256-5011. FAX 258-1919. TELEX 1121436. Ed. Hamilton Lucas de Oliveira. adv.; bk.rev.; circ. 15,600.

DISCIPLINE AND GRIEVANCES FOR SUPERVISORS IN LOCAL, STATE AND FEDERAL GOVERNMENT. see BUSINESS AND ECONOMICS — Labor And Industrial Relations

352 IT ISSN 0012-4737
DOCUMENTI DI VITA COMUNALE.* 1961. irreg., (approx. 3/yr.). free. Sindacato di Mogliano, Piazza Caduti 1, 31021 Magliano Veneto, Treviso, Italy. Ed. Dir. Giuseppe Marton. adv.; bk.rev.; abstr.; illus.; stat.; tr.lit.; circ. 5,500. (controlled).

352 GW
DORTMUND; Blick in die Stadt. 1950. m. DM.15.60. Krueger-Verlag, Westenhellweg 9, Postfach 102452, 4600 Dortmund 1, Germany. TEL 0231-5401-180. Ed. A. Huge.

352 GW
DORTMUNDER BEKANNTMACHUNGEN; Amtsblatt der Stadt. 1945. w. DM.24. Krueger-Verlag, Westenhellweg 9, Postfach 102452, 4600 Dortmund 1, Germany. TEL 0231-5401-180.

352 GW
▼**DRESDENER BEHOERDEN SPIEGEL;** unabhaengige Zeitung fuer den oeffentlichen Dienst. 1991. m. DM.36. ProPress Verlag GmbH, Am Buschhof 8, 5300 Bonn 3, Germany. TEL 0228-449090. FAX 0228-444296. circ. 6,000.

352 GW ISSN 0046-0796
DUESSELDORF MAGAZIN; Magazin der Landeshauptstadt. 1960. q. DM.20. Landeshauptstadt Duesseldorf, Oberstadtdirektor Presseamt, Postfach 1120, 4000 Duesseldorf 1, Germany. Ed. Hans-Joachim Neisser. adv.; bk.rev.; circ. 5,500 (controlled).

352 GW ISSN 0012-7019
DUESSELDORFER AMTSBLATT. 1946. w. DM.30. Landeshauptstadt Duesseldorf, Oberstadtdirektor Presseamt, Postfach 1120, 4000 Duesseldorf 1, Germany. TEL 0211-899-3131. FAX 0211-8994179. Ed. Hans-Joachim Neisser. adv.; bk.rev.; circ. 5,500.

352 GW ISSN 0939-4508
▼**E C PUBLIC CONTRACT LAW.** (European Community); public procurement in theory and practice. (Text in English, French, German and Italian) 1991. bi-m. DM.216. ProPress Verlag GmbH, Am Buschhof 8, 5300 Bonn 3, Germany. TEL 0228-449090. FAX 0228-444296. circ. 6,000.

352 FR
ELU D'AUJOURD'HUI. 1975. m. 180 F. 2 Place du Colonel Fabien, 75940 Paris Cedex 19, France. Ed. Robert Hue. adv.

352 310 IT ISSN 0013-6891
EMPOLI;* rassegna di vita cittadina e bollettino di statistica. 1959. s-a. L.100 per no. Casa Editrice la Toscografica, Via Pontorme 20, Empoli, Italy. Dir. Assessore G. Lombardi. adv.; charts; illus.; stat.

ENVIRONMENTAL AND URBAN ISSUES. see ENVIRONMENTAL STUDIES

352 FR
EXPERIENCES ET GESTIONS MUNICIPALES; lettre mensuelle de gestion municipale comparee. 1973. m. 370 F. (foreign 470 F.). S I D E L E R - Service d'Information et de Documentation des Elus Locaux et Regionaux, 3, villa de Longchamp, 75116 Paris, France. TEL 45-53-90-01. Ed. Jean A. Penet.

FEDERAL ELECTION CAMPAIGN FINANCING GUIDE. see BUSINESS AND ECONOMICS — Banking And Finance

352 614.8 360 US ISSN 0273-4435
HJ275
FEDERAL FUNDING GUIDE. 1976. a. (with m. supplements). $189.95. Government Information Services, 1611 N. Kent St., Ste. 508, Arlington, VA 22209. TEL 703-528-1000. FAX 703-528-6060. Eds. Charles J. Edwards, Sean K. O'Brien. (looseleaf format)
Formerly: Federal Funding Guide for Local Governments (ISSN 0362-4285)
Description: Details more than 177 federal aid programs available to state, county and municipal government, tribal governments and non-profit groups. Provides information on eligibility requirements, outlook for funding, application deadlines, allowable uses of funds and program contacts (including telephone numbers).

350 SA ISSN 0015-0347
FESTINA LENTE.* (Text in Afrikaans and English) q. free. South African Association of Municipal Employees, Municipal Employees, Pretoria Branch 1, City Hall, 0002 Pretoria, South Africa. Ed. Gerhard J. Van Niekerk. adv.; illus.

352 US
FINANCIAL CONDITION OF COLORADO MUNICIPALITIES. a. $30 to non-members; members $15. Colorado Municipal League, 1660 Lincoln St., Ste. 2100, Denver, CO 80264. TEL 303-831-6411.
Description: Reports on municipal fiscal health and what cities and towns are doing to cope with fiscal problems.

352 FI ISSN 0355-6093
FINLANDS KOMMUNALTIDSKRIFT. Finnish edition: Suomen Kunnallislehti (ISSN 0039-5544) (Text in Swedish) 1916. 10/yr. FIM 300. Suomen Kaupunkiliitto - Association of Finnish Cities, Toinen Linja 14, 00530 Helsinki 53, Finland. FAX 7712271. Ed. Hannu Taavitsainen. adv.; bk.rev.; charts; illus.; stat.; index; circ. 1,239.
Description: Covers municipal legislation, research, economy, health services and hospital administration, educational and cultural activities, social welfare, municipal engineering, local government, productivity and personnel administration and training.

FROM THE STATE CAPITALS. SCHOOL FINANCING. see EDUCATION — School Organization And Administration

352 GW
FUNDESTELLE FUER DIE KOMMUNALVERWALTUNG IN BADEN-WUERTTEMBERG. 1948. bi-w. DM.309.60. Richard Boorberg Verlag (Stuttgart), Scharrstr. 2, Postfach 800260, 7000 Stuttgart 80, Germany. Ed. Werner Frasch. (back issues avail.)

352 GW ISSN 0016-2779
DIE FUNDSTELLE; Erlaeuterungen zu allen wichtigen Vorschriften fuer die Bayerische Kommunalverwaltungen. 1947. s-m. DM.337.20. Richard Boorberg Verlag (Munich), Levelingstr. 6a, Postfach 800340, D-8000 Munich 80, Germany. Ed. Alfred Hartinger. bk.rev.; tr.lit.; index; circ. 3,500. (processed)

354 US ISSN 1051-6964
G F O A NEWSLETTER. 1949. s-m. $50 includes Government Finance Review. Government Finance Officers Association, 180 N. Michigan Ave., Ste. 800, Chicago, IL 60601. TEL 312-977-9700. FAX 312-977-4806. Ed. Bd. bk.rev.; tr.lit.; circ. 13,000. (looseleaf format)
Formerly: Municipal Finance News Letter (ISSN 0027-3481)

352 FR
GAZETTE DES COMMUNES ET DU PERSONNEL COMMUNAL.* 1934. m. 125 F. (includes subscr. to Action Municipale). Edition l' Action Municipale, 18 rue Duphot, 75001 Paris, France. adv.

352 NE ISSN 0016-6049
GEMEENTEBLAD VAN AMSTERDAM. 1858. s-w. fl.130. Stadsdrukkerij, Voormalige Stadstimmertuin 4 - 6, 1018 ET Amsterdam, Netherlands. index.

352 GW ISSN 0340-3653
GEMEINDE. 1949. m. DM.107. Deutscher Gemeindeverlag GmbH, Jaegersberg 17, 2300 Kiel 1, Germany. TEL 0431-554857. Eds. Hartmund Borchert, Wolfgang Ottens. circ. 1,700.

352 GW
GEMEINDE SCHOENAICH - RUECKSPIEGEL. 1975. a. free. Gemeinde Schoenaich, Buehlstr. 10, Postfach 1161, 7036 Schoenaich, Germany. TEL 07031-5590. FAX 07031-55999. Ed. Karl-Heinz Balzer. (looseleaf format; back issues avail.)

352 AU ISSN 0016-609X
GEMEINDEBOTE. 1963. irreg., 4-6/yr. free. Marktgemeinde Hinterbruehl. Gemeindeamt, Hauptstr. 66, A-2371 Hinterbruehl, Austria. Ed. G. Tartarotti. stat.; circ. 1,200.

352 GW ISSN 0340-3645
DER GEMEINDEHAUSHALT. m. DM.174. Verlag W. Kohlhammer, Postfach 400263, Max-Planck-Str. 12, 5000 Cologne 40, Germany. Ed. Johannes Werner Schmidt. (reprint service avail.)

352 GW ISSN 0016-612X
DIE GEMEINDEKASSE; das Blatt des Kassenverwalters fuer das Haushalts-, Kassen- und Rechnungswesen. 1950. m. DM.253.20. Richard Boorberg Verlag (Munich), Levelingstr. 6a, Postfach 800340, D-8000 Munich 80, Germany. Ed. Wilhelm Knefeli. bk.rev.; tr.lit.; index; circ. 2,500. (processed)

352 GW ISSN 0016-6170
GEMEINDEVERWALTUNG IN RHEINLAND - PFALZ. 1957. s-m. DM.237.60. Richard Boorberg Verlag (Stuttgart), Scharrstr. 2, Postfach 800260, 7000 Stuttgart 80, Germany. Eds. Walter Bogner, Hans Guenther Dehe. adv.

PUBLIC ADMINISTRATION — MUNICIPAL GOVERNMENT

352   GW   ISSN 0016-6200
GEMEINSAMES AMTSBLATT DES LANDES BADEN-WUERTTEMBERG. 1953. irreg., approx. 40/yr. DM.100. Innenministerium, Dorotheenstr. 6, Postfach 102443, 7000 Stuttgart 10, Germany. Ed. W. Schmidt. bk.rev.; index. **Indexed:** Dok.Str., INIS Atomind.

352   US
JS39
GEORGIA'S CITIES. 1951. 14/yr. $10. Georgia Municipal Association, 201 Pryor St., S.W., Atlanta, GA 30303-3606. TEL 404-688-0472. Ed. Charles C. Craig. adv.; bk.rev.; circ. 6,000.
Former titles: Urban Georgia (ISSN 0042-0875); Georgia Municipal Journal.

352   GW   ISSN 0342-3557
GESETZ UND VERORDNUNGSBLATT FUER DAS LAND HESSEN. 1945. DM.70. (Staatskanzlei) Verlag Dr. Max Gehlen GmbH und Co. KG, Daimlerstr. 12, Postfach 2463, 6380 Bad Homburg, Germany. TEL 06272-23056. FAX 06272-23055. index; circ. 8,000. **Indexed:** Dok.Str., INIS Atomind.

352   GW   ISSN 0016-9129
GESETZ- UND VERORDNUNGSBLATT FUER SCHLESWIG-HOLSTEIN. 1947. 27/yr. DM.40. Innenministerium, Duestenbrooker Weg 92, D-2300 Kiel 1, Germany. FAX 0431-596-3131. circ. 4,000. **Indexed:** Dok.Str.

352   IT
GIUSSANO. 1980. m. Comune di Giussano, Via Milano, 60, I-20034 Giussano, Italy. Ed.Bd. circ. 1,000.

352   US   ISSN 0894-3842
JK2403
GOVERNING; the states and localities. 1987. m. $48. 2300 N St., N.W., Ste. 760, Washington, DC 20037. TEL 202-862-8802. FAX 202-862-0032. (Subscr. to: Box 9092, Palm Coast, FL 32035-9092) Ed. Peter A. Harkness. index; circ. 85,000. (also avail. in microfilm)
—BLDSC shelfmark: 4203.832000.
Description: Covers emerging trends and issues in policy and politics for state and local elected and appointed officials.

352 606   US   ISSN 0883-8690
HC110.P63
GOVERNMENT ASSISTANCE ALMANAC. 1985. a. $84. Omnigraphics, Inc., 2500 Penobscot Bldg., Detroit, MI 48226. TEL 312-961-1340. FAX 313-961-1383. Ed. J. Robert Dumouchel. stat.; index.
Description: Data base of information on more than 1,200 domestic financial and non-financial assistance programs, with a cross-referenced index, application guidelines, funding summary tables, and more than 4,000 addresses and telephone numbers for federal program headquaters and field offices.

352   US   ISSN 0882-6587
GOVERNMENT MICROCOMPUTER LETTER. 1983. bi-m. $19. Innovation Groups, Inc., Box 16645, Tampa, FL 33687. TEL 813-622-8484. FAX 813-664-0051. Ed. Liz Weisherg. adv.; abstr.; bibl.; tr.lit.; circ. 2,700. (tabloid format; back issues avail.)
Description: For local governments using computer systems.

352   US
GOVERNMENTAL AFFAIRS REVIEW. m. Office of the State Comptroller, Division of Municipal Affairs, Smith State Office Bldg., Albany, NY 12236. TEL 518-474-5505. **Indexed:** Rehabil.Lit.

GREAT BRITAIN. DEPARTMENT OF THE ENVIRONMENT. LOCAL GOVERNMENT FINANCIAL STATISTICS: ENGLAND AND WALES. see *PUBLIC ADMINISTRATION — Abstracting, Bibliographies, Statistics*

352   US   ISSN 0199-1728
GREATER PORTLAND MAGAZINE. 1956. bi-m. $9.97. Greater Portland Publications Inc., Box 15490, Portland, ME 04101-7490. TEL 207-773-5000. Ed. Shirley Jacks. adv.; circ. 7,000. (back issues avail.)

352   US
GUIDE TO MANAGEMENT IMPROVEMENT PROJECTS IN LOCAL GOVERNMENT. 1977. q. $63. International City - Countu Management Association, 777 North Capitol St., N.E. Ste. 500, Washington, DC 20002-4201. TEL 800-745-8780. Ed. Catherine Swift. index; circ. 1,500.
Formerly: Guide to Productivity Improvement Projects; **Supersedes:** Jurisdictional Guide to Productivity Improvement Projects.
Description: Details projects aimed at improving services and cost savings.

352   AU
GUMPOLDSKIRCHNER NACHRICHTEN. q. Marktgemeinde Gumpoldskirchen, Gemeindeamt, A-2352 Gumpoldskirchen, Austria.

352   NE
DEN HAAG. 1946. m. free. Afdeling Voorlichting - The Hague Public Relations Department, City Hall, Burg de Monchyplein 14, 2585 BD The Hague, Netherlands. FAX 070-361-7288. adv.; charts; illus.; stat.; tr.lit.; circ. 10,000.
Formerly: S-Gravenhage (ISSN 0037-3117)

323   US   ISSN 0073-1137
JK9349.O4
HAWAII. OFFICE OF THE OMBUDSMAN. REPORT. 1971. a. free. Office of the Ombudsman, Kekuanaoa Bldg., 4th Fl., 465 S. King St., Honolulu, HI 96813. TEL 808-587-0770. Ed. Karen N. Blondin. stat.; circ. controlled.
Description: Annual report to the State Legislature; contains subject chapters, statistics, and case summaries.

352   GW
HEIDELBERGER AMTSANZEIGER. 1946. w. DM.104. Amt fuer Oeffentlichkeitsarbeit, Postfach 105520, Marktplatz 10, 6900 Heidelberg 1, Germany. TEL 06221-58491. FAX 06221-589010. TELEX 461570. Ed.Bd. circ. 63,000.

352   GW   ISSN 0932-9757
HEIMAT DORTMUND; Stadtgeschichte in Bildern und Berichten. 1986. q. DM.24. Krueger-Verlag, Westenhellweg 9, Postfach 102452, 4600 Dortmund 1, Germany. TEL 0231-5401-180. Ed. Martina Horstendahl.

352   GW
HEIMATBRIEFE DER STADT PIRMASENS. 1937. s-a. Stadtverwaltung Pirmasens, Exerzierplatz, 6780 Pirmasens, Germany. TEL 06331-842222. FAX 06331-84540. TELEX 452286. Ed. Roland Wagner. circ. 3,000.

HERNE IN ZAHLEN. JAHRESHEFT (YEAR). see *BUSINESS AND ECONOMICS — Abstracting, Bibliographies, Statistics*

HERNE IN ZAHLEN. VIERTELJAHRESBERICHTE. see *BUSINESS AND ECONOMICS — Abstracting, Bibliographies, Statistics*

352   GW
HESSEN. KOMMUNALVERWALTUNG. FUNDSTELLE. 1948. 24/yr. DM.333.60. Richard Boorberg Verlag (Stuttgart), Scharrstr. 2, 7000 Stuttgart 80, Germany. Ed. Hermann Schoenfelder.

352   GW
HESSEN - REPORT. 1988. m. Hessische Landesregierung, Bierstadter Str. 2, D-6200 Wiesbaden, Germany. TEL 06121-320. circ. 28,000.

352   US
HONOLULU EMPLOYEE JOURNAL. vol.9, 1971. bi-m. free. Office of Information & Complaint, City Hall, Honolulu, HI 96813. TEL 808-527-5782. FAX 808-523-4386. Ed. Francis A. Marzen. bk.rev.; charts; illus.; circ. 10,000.
Description: For and about city workers.

352   UK
HULL CITY COUNCIL. CIVIC NEWS. 1984. m. free. Civic News Publications, King's Building, South Church Side, Hull HU1 1RR, England. FAX 0482-214024. TELEX 592592 NEWS159. (Subscr. to: Hull City Council, Hull HU1 2AA, England) Ed. John M. Davis. adv.; bk.rev.; circ. 110,000. (tabloid format; back issues avail.)

352   US   ISSN 0047-0651
I C M A NEWSLETTER. 1919. bi-w. $115. International City - County Management Association, 777 North Capitol St., N.E. Ste. 500, Washington, DC 20002-4201. TEL 202-289-4262. Ed. Kathleen Karas. bk.rev.; charts; tr.lit.; circ. 8,000.
Description: Covers the associations's activities and local government position vacancies and appointments.

352   US
IDAHO CITIES. 1964. m. $18. Association of Idaho Cities, 3314 Grace St., Boise, ID 83703. TEL 208-344-8594. FAX 208-344-8677. Ed. William Jarocki. adv.; bk.rev.; circ. 2,250 (controlled). (processed)
Supersedes: Gem City News (ISSN 0300-8355)

352   TU
ILLER VE BELEDIYELER; aylik ilim ve meslek dergisi. 1945. m. TL.1000000. Turk Belediyecilik Dernegi, Mithat Pasa Caddesi 45-2, Ankara, Turkey. Ed. Argun Ersoz. adv.; index; circ. 3,500.

352   US   ISSN 0019-1949
ILLINOIS COUNTY AND TOWNSHIP OFFICIAL. 1940. m. $15. (Township Officials of Illinois) Stevens Publishing Co., Box 455, Astoria, IL 61501. TEL 309-329-2101. FAX 309-329-2133. (Alt. addr.: 817 LaPorte Ave., Melrose Park, IL 60164. TEL 708-562-8290) Ed. George H. Miller. adv.; illus.; circ. 12,000.

352   US   ISSN 0738-9663
ILLINOIS ISSUES; a magazine of government and politics. 1975. m. (except Aug./Sep. combined). $29.95 (foreign $44.95). Sangamon State University, Springfield, IL 62794-9243. TEL 217-786-6084. (Subscr. to: Box 251, Mt. Morris, IL 61054) (Co-sponsor: University of Illinois) Ed. Caroline Gherardini. bk.rev.; circ. 6,000. **Indexed:** P.A.I.S., Urb.Aff.Abstr.
—BLDSC shelfmark: 4365.285000.
Description: Covers political and governmental issues affecting Illinois.

352   US   ISSN 0019-2139
JS39
ILLINOIS MUNICIPAL REVIEW; * the magazine of the municipalities. 1922. m. membership. Illinois Municipal League, Box 3387, Springfield, IL 62708. TEL 217-525-1220. Ed. Steven Sargent. adv.; illus.; index; circ. 10,000.

352   IT   ISSN 0019-3003
IMPRESA PUBBLICA; municipalizzazione. (Monthly supplement avail.: Notiziario Interfederale) 1957. bi-m (with m. supplements). L.60000. Confederazione Italiana dei Servizi Pubblici degli Enti Locali, Piazza Cola di Reinzo 80, 00192 Rome, Italy. adv.; bk.rev.; charts; illus.; stat.; index; circ. 1,700. **Indexed:** P.A.I.S.For.Lang.Ind.
—BLDSC shelfmark: 4371.470000.

352   IT
L'IMPRESA PUBBLICA MUNICIPALIZZAZIONE. 1956. m. L.126000 (effective 1992). (Confederazione Italiana dei Servizi Pubblici degli Enti Locali (CISPEL)) Maggioli Editore, Via Crimea, 1, Casella Postale 290, 47037 Rimini, Italy. TEL 0541-626777. FAX 0541-622020. Ed. Renzo Santini.

352   CN
IMPROVEMENT DISTRICT MANUAL. base vol. (plus irreg. suppl.). Can.$50.75. Ministry of Municipal Affairs, Recreation and Culture, Victoria, B.C., Canada. (Subscr. to: Crown Publications, 546 Yates St., Victoria, B.C. V8W 1K8, Canada. TEL 604-386-4636)
Description: Provides a comprehensive outline on some of the common procedures that are carried out under the Municipal Act.

PUBLIC ADMINISTRATION — MUNICIPAL GOVERNMENT

352   SP
INFORMACION IBEROAMERICANA. Variant title: S I M Boletin de Informacion. 1968. q. free. Instituto Nacional de Administracion Publica, Oficina Tecnica de la O I C I, Santa Engracia 7, 28010 Madrid, Spain. (Co-sponsor: Ministerio para las Administraciones Publicas) Ed. Enrique Orduna Rebollo. adv.; bk.rev.; illus.; bibl.
    Former titles: Instituto de Estudios de Administracion Local. Oficina Tecnica de la O I C I. Boletin de Informacion & Instituto de Estudios de Administracion Local. Secretariado Iberoamericano de Municipios. Boletin de Informacion (ISSN 0210-0975)

352   IT
INFORMATICA ED ENTI LOCALI; rivista trimestrale di metodologie e tecnologie avanzate. 1984. q. L.140000 (effective 1992). Maggioli Editore, Via Crimea, 1, Casella Postale 290, 47037 Rimini, Italy. TEL 0541-626777. FAX 0541-622020. Ed. Donato Limone.

INFORMATIE EN AUTOMATISERING - VAKMATIG. see *PUBLIC ADMINISTRATION — Computer Applications*

352   GW
INFORMATION FUER ORMESHEIM. Short title: I F O. 1983. s-a. Sozialdemokratische Partei Deutschlands (SPD), Ortsverein Ormesheim, Mozartstr. 4, 6676 Mandelbachtal-Ormesheim, Germany. TEL 06893-3996. Ed. Rainer Barth. (looseleaf format)

INFORMATIONEN ZUR MODERNEN STADTGESCHICHTE (I M S). see *HOUSING AND URBAN PLANNING*

352   GW
INFORMATIONEN ZUR STADTENTWICKLUNG LUDWIGSHAFEN. 1972. irreg. Stadt Ludwigshafen, Amt fuer Stadtentwicklung, Rathausplatz 20, 6700 Ludwigshafen, Germany. TEL 0621-5042218. FAX 0621-5043453. circ. 1,000.

350   UK   ISSN 0958-4021
INLOGOV INFORMS. 1989. q. $190. (Institute of Local Government Studies) Cassell plc., Villiers House, 41-47 Strand, London,WC2N 5JE, England. (Subscr. to: Stanley House, 3 Fleets Lane, Poole, Dorset BH15 3AJ, England)
—BLDSC shelfmark: 4515.134000.
    Description: Reviews research and topics in local government.

352   US
INNOVATIVE MUNICIPAL PROGRAMS (YEAR). a. $20 to non-members; members $10. Colorado Municipal League, 1660 Lincoln St., Ste. 2100, Denver, CO 80264. TEL 303-831-6411.
    Description: Information on innovative programs submitted for judging in CML's annual Innovative Program Awards. Contains a program description and contact person for each program.

352   SP
INSTITUTO DE ESTUDIOS DE ADMINISTRACION LOCAL. CATEDRA CALVO SOTELO. CONFERENCIAS.* 1974. irreg. Instituto de Estudios de Administracion Local, Catedra Calvo Sotelo, Joaquin Garcia Morato 7, Madrid 10, Spain.

352   US   ISSN 0892-3795
IOWA COUNTY. 1972. m. $10. Iowa State Association of Counties, 701 E. Court Ave., Des Moines, IA 50309. TEL 515-244-7181. Ed. Tricia Fazzini. adv.; bk.rev.; circ. 2,000. (back issues avail.)
    Formerly: County (Des Moines) (ISSN 0199-7793)
    Description: Promotes efficient and economically sound county government for the citizens of Iowa.

336   IS
ISRAEL. KNESSET. HA-VA'ADA LE-INYANEI BIKORET HA-MEDINA. SIKUMEHA VE-HATSA'OTEHA SHEL HA-VA'ADA LE-INYANEI BIKORET HA-MEDINA LE-DIN VE-KHESHBON SHEL MEVAKER HA-MEDINA.* 1973. a. Knesset, State Control Committee, Jerusalem, Israel. Ed. Aharon Berkner. circ. controlled. (processed)

352   FR
JOURNAL D'ADMINISTRATION DES COMMUNES RURALES. 1901. m. 350 F. Publications Paul Dupont, 38 rue Croix des Petits Champs, 75001 Paris, France. Ed. Rene Dubail. adv

352   FR   ISSN 0021-8030
JOURNAL DES COMMUNES. 1828. m. 420 F. Publications Paul Dupont, 38 rue Croix des Petits Champs, 75001 Paris, France. TEL 42-36-06-87. Ed. Rene Dubail.

352   FR
JOURNAL DES MAIRES; et des conseillers municipqux. 1857. m. 315 F. 22 rue Cambaceres, 75008 Paris, France. adv.

352   FR
JOURNAL DES MAIRES ET DES CONSEILS MUNICIPAUX. 1857. m. SETAC, 22, rue Cambaceres, 75008 Paris, France. TEL 42-65-58-94. FAX 47-42-87-57. TELEX UPRESSE 680876F. circ. 12,000.

JUSTICE OF THE PEACE. see *LAW — Criminal Law*

352   DK
K C NYT. 1983. q. membership. Foreningen af Kommunale Chefer (KC), Leongangstraede 25, 4, 1468 Copenhagen K, Denmark. TEL 33-14-48-38. FAX 33-13-71-14. illus.
    Former titles: F A K E Nyt (ISSN 0109-0925); Foreningen af Kommunale Embedsmaend. Medlemsny.

352   AU   ISSN 0022-7552
KAERNTNER GEMEINDEBLATT. 1926. irreg. S.973. (Amt der Kaerntner Landesregierung) Kaertner Druck- und Verlags-Gesellschaft mbH, Viktringer Ring 28, A-9010 Klagenfurt, Austria. FAX 0463-536-32007. bk.rev.; stat.; index. (also avail. in microform)

352   AU   ISSN 0022-7579
KAERNTNER LANDES-ZEITUNG. 1949. w. S.156. Amt der Kaerntner Landesregierung, Arnulfplatz 1, A-9010 Klagenfurt, Austria. Ed. Eduard Schober.

352   US   ISSN 0022-8613
KANSAS GOVERNMENT JOURNAL. 1914. m. $18. League of Kansas Municipalities, 112 S.W. Seventh St., Topeka, KS 66603. TEL 913-354-9565. FAX 913-354-9565. Ed. E.A. Mosher. adv.; bk.rev.; illus.; stat.; index; circ. 7,700.

799   US
SK1
KENTUCKY AFIELD; the magazine. 1946. bi-m. $5. Department of Fish and Wildlife Resources, 1 Game Farm Rd., Frankfort, KY 40601. TEL 502-564-4336. Eds. Carolyn Lynn, Elaine Breeck. bk.rev.; charts; illus.; circ. 45,000.
    Formerly (until vol.47, 1991): Kentucky Happy Hunting Ground (ISSN 0023-0235)

352   US   ISSN 0453-5677
JS39
KENTUCKY CITY. 1929. m. (11/yr.). $11. Kentucky League of Cities, 2201 Regency Rd., Ste. 100, Lexington, KY 40503. TEL 606-277-2886. FAX 606-278-5766. Ed. Judy Love. adv.; illus.; circ. 4,500. (tabloid format)

352   AU   ISSN 0023-2017
KLAGENFURT; Mitteilungsblatt der Landeshauptstadt. 1951. fortn. S.120($5) Magistrat der Landeshauptstadt Klagenfurt, Rathaus, A-9010 Klagenfurt, Austria. FAX 0463-516990. Eds. Veronika Meissnitzer, Ing. Guenter Pfeistlinger. adv.; bk.rev.; bibl.; illus.; index; circ. 44,000.

352   GW
KOBLENZER BEHOERDEN SPIEGEL. 1984. m. DM.39. ProPress Verlag GmbH, Am Buschhof 8, 5300 Bonn 3, Germany. TEL 0228-449090. FAX 0228-444296. Ed. R. Uwe Proll. circ. 15,000.

352   GW
KOELNER BEHOERDEN SPIEGEL; unabhaengige Zeitung fuer den oeffentliche Dienst. 1984. m. DM.39. ProPress Verlag GmbH, Am Buschhof 8, 5300 Bonn 3, Germany. TEL 0228-449090. FAX 0228-444296. Ed. R. Uwe Proll. circ. 20,500.

352   SW   ISSN 0347-5484
KOMMUN-AKTUELT/MUNICIPAL NEWS. 1978. w. SEK 280. Svenska Kommunfoerbundet - Swedish Association of Local Authorities, Hornsgatan 15, 116 47 Stockholm, Sweden. adv.; bk.rev.; charts; illus.; circ. 46,000. (tabloid format)
    Formed by the merger of: Paa Fritid (ISSN 0346-6159) & Kommunal Tidskrift (ISSN 0023-3072) & Kommunal Skoltidning (ISSN 0023-3064) & Socialt Forum (ISSN 0049-0970) & Hygien och Miljoe. Hygien och Miljoe formerly titled (until 1974): Hygienisk Revy (ISSN 0018-8255); Kommunal Tidskrift formerly titled: Kommuneras Tidskrift; Socialt Forum formerly titled: Svenska Socialvaardsfoerbundets Tidskrift.

KOMMUNALTJAENSTEMANNEN. see *BUSINESS AND ECONOMICS — Labor And Industrial Relations*

352   DK
KOMMUNEN. 1958. fortn. Kommunen, Solvaenget 1, 2100 Copenhagen, Denmark. TEL 31 18 00 55. FAX 31-18-04-05. Ed. Erik Malling-Jensen. adv.; circ. 7,800.

KONTAK. see *BUSINESS AND ECONOMICS — Trade And Industrial Directories*

352   XV
KRANJCAN. (Text in Slovenian) 1982. m. Skupscina Obcine Kranj, Trg Revolucije 1, 64000 Kranj, Slovenia. TEL 064 25661. circ. 6,700. (back issues avail.)

352   GW
KREISAMTSBLATT DES LANDKREISES UND LANDRATSAMTES KRONACH. 1900. w. DM.8. Landratsamt Kronach, Gueterstr. 18, Postfach 1551, 8640 Kronach, Germany. TEL 09261-90-0. FAX 09261-90211. circ. 400. (looseleaf format; back issues avail.)
    Formerly: Landkreis Kronach. Amtsblatt.

352   GW
KREISPOSTILLE. 1967. q. free. Kreis Neuss, Lindenstr. 2-16, 4048 Grevenbroich 1, Germany. TEL 02181-601300. FAX 02181-601630. circ. 6,000.

352   II   ISSN 0023-5660
KURUKSHETRA; journal of community development and village democracy. (Editions in English and Hindi) 1952. fortn. Rs.5($2.40) (Ministry of Agriculture) India. Ministry of Information and Broadcasting, Publications Division, Patiala House, Tilak Marg, New Delhi 110001, India. (Subscr. in U.S. to: M-S Inter Culture Associates, Thompson, CT 06277) Ed. Ratna Juneja. adv.; bk.rev.; charts; illus.; cum.index; circ. 13,000. **Indexed:** Geo.Abstr., Rural Devel.Abstr., Rural Recreat.Tour.Abstr., Soils & Fert., World Agri.Econ. & Rural Sociol.Abstr.
    Incorporates (in June 1970): Panchayati Raj (New Delhi) (ISSN 0553-0946)

352   AU   ISSN 0023-7884
LANDESGESETZBLATT FUER DAS LAND SALZBURG. 1945. irreg. S.400. Bundesland Salzburg, Chiemseehof, A-5020 Salzburg, Austria. index; circ. 2,000. (looseleaf format)

352   SW   ISSN 0282-4485
LANDSTINGSVAERLDEN. 1914. 20/yr. SEK 315 (effective 1991). Landstingsfoerbundet - Federation of Swedish County Councils, Box 70491, S-107 26 Stockholm, Sweden. FAX 08-702-4505. Ed. Aake Ingelmo. adv.; bk.rev.; illus.; index; circ. 12,700.
    Former titles: Sveriges Landstings Tidskrift; Landstingens Tidskrift (ISSN 0023-8074)

352   GW
▼**LEIPZIGER BEHOERDEN SPIEGEL**; unabhaengige Zeitung fuer den oeffentlichen Dienst. 1990. m. DM.36. ProPress Verlag GmbH, Am Buschhof 8, 5300 Bonn 3, Germany. TEL 0228-449090. FAX 0228-444296. circ. 6,000.

352   SP
LEON. BOLETIN DE INFORMACION MUNICIPAL. 1971. q. 50 ptas. Ayuntamiento de Leon, c/o Juan Pastrana Garcia, Director, Legio VII 1, Leon, Spain.

PUBLIC ADMINISTRATION — MUNICIPAL GOVERNMENT

354　　　　　　LB　ISSN 0304-730X
HN831.L54
LIBERIA. MINISTRY OF LOCAL GOVERNMENT, RURAL DEVELOPMENT & URBAN RECONSTRUCTION. ANNUAL REPORT.* (Report year ends Sept. 30) 1972. a. Ministry of Rural Development, P.O. Box 9030, Monrovia, Liberia.
Formerly: Liberia. Department of Internal Affairs. Annual Report.

352　　　　　　　　　FR
LOCAL AND REGIONAL AUTHORITIES IN EUROPE. STUDY SERIES. (Text in English or French) 1972. irreg. (2-3/yr.). price varies. Council of Europe, Activities of the Steering Committee for Local and Regional Authorities, Publishing and Documentation Service, 67000 Strasbourg, France. (Dist. in U.S. by: Manhattan Publishing Co., 80 Brook St., Box 650, Croton, NY 10520)

352　　　　　　　　　UK
LOCAL AUTHORITY AND PUBLIC SERVICE YEARBOOK. a. £64.95($104) Kemps Publishing Group Ltd., 11 The Swan Courtyard, Charles Edward Rd., Birmingham B26 1BU, England. TEL 021-711-4144. FAX 021-711-2866. TELEX 333786-KEMPSP-G.

352 328　　　　　　　NZ
LOCAL AUTHORITY MANAGEMENT. 1975. q. NZ.$45($82) New Zealand Institute of Local Authority Management, P.O. Box 278, Wellington, New Zealand. Ed. G.W.A. Bush. adv.; bk.rev.; circ. 1,000.
Formerly: Local Authority Administration.

352　　　　　　UK　ISSN 0308-3594
JS3001
LOCAL COUNCIL REVIEW. 1950. q. £4.15. National Association of Local Councils, 108 Great Russell St., London WC1B 3LD, England. TEL 071-637-1865. adv.; bk.rev.; illus.; circ. 25,000. **Indexed:** Geo.Abstr, RICS.
—BLDSC shelfmark: 5290.011000.
Formerly: Parish Councils Review (ISSN 0031-2061)

352　　　　　　　　　PK
LOCAL GOVERNMENT. (Text in English) vol.5, 1974. m. Rs.25. Pakistan Group for the Study of Local Government, 14 Japan Mansion, Preedy St., Karachi, Pakistan. Ed. Malik M. Siddiq. adv.; bk.rev.

352　　　　　　UK　ISSN 0267-2022
LOCAL GOVERNMENT ADMINISTRATORS' OFFICIAL SOURCE BOOK. 1985. a. £25. Millbank Publications Ltd., 25 Catherine St., London WC2B 5JW, England. TEL 071-379-3036. FAX 071-240-6840. adv.; circ. 3,000.
—BLDSC shelfmark: 5290.011877.

352　　　　　　　　　UK
▼**LOCAL GOVERNMENT AND LAW.** 1991. £96 (typically set in Jan.). Monitor Press, Rectory Rd., GT Waldingfield, Sudbury, Suffolk CO10 0TL, England. TEL 0787-78607. FAX 7087-880201. Ed. Richard Clutterbuck.
Description: Reviews developments in the law as they affect those who are engaged in local government.

352　　　　　　PH　ISSN 0024-5526
JS7301.A1
LOCAL GOVERNMENT BULLETIN. 1966. bi-m. P.90($15) University of the Philippines, College of Public Administration, Local Government Center, PARDEC-SAAC Building, Don Mariano Marcos Avenue, P.O. Box 198, Diliman, Quezon City, Philippines. TEL 99-39-14. Eds. Alex Brillantes, Jr., Vicente Mariano. bk.rev.; illus.; stat.; circ. 1,000. **Indexed:** Ind.Phil.Per.

352　　　　　　UK　ISSN 0024-5534
LOCAL GOVERNMENT CHRONICLE. 1855. w. £55. Brown Knight & Truscott (Holdings) Ltd., 122 Minories, London EC3N 1NT, England. FAX 071-481-0636. Ed. Paul Keenan. adv.; bk.rev.; illus.; index; circ. 8,000. (also avail. in microform from UMI; reprint service avail.) **Indexed:** Account.& Data Proc.Abstr., ASSIA, Geo.Abstr, RICS.
—BLDSC shelfmark: 5290.013000.

352　　　　　　UK　ISSN 0305-0130
LOCAL GOVERNMENT COMPANION. 1974. a. £11. 18 Lincoln Green, Chichester, West Sussex PO19 4DN, England. Ed. E.P. Craig.
—BLDSC shelfmark: 5290.013500.

352 363.6　　　　　　SA
LOCAL GOVERNMENT IN SOUTHERN AFRICA/PLAASLIKE REGERING IN SUIDELIKE AFRIKA.* (Text in Afrikaans, English) bi-m. R.9. (South African Association of Municipal Employees) Melton Publications (Pty) Ltd., P.O. Box 3445, Randburg 2125, South Africa. Ed. J.T. Smit. adv.; bk.rev.; illus.; circ. 2,500. **Indexed:** Excerp.Med., Ind.S.A.Per., W.R.C.Inf.
Former titles: Municipal Administration and Engineering (ISSN 0027-3422); Municipal Affairs.

352　　　　　　AT　ISSN 0727-7342
LOCAL GOVERNMENT MANAGEMENT. Short title: L.G.M. 1957. bi-m. Aus.$35 (effective July 1991). Institute of Municipal Management, P.O. Box 409, S. Melbourne, Vic. 3205, Australia. TEL 03-696-5799. FAX 03-690-4217. Ed. Barrie Beattie. adv.; index; circ. 5,000 (controlled). (tabloid format; back issues avail.) **Indexed:** Aus.P.A.I.S.
Formerly (until 1984): Local Government Administration (ISSN 0024-5518)
Description: Provides articles in relation to new manament technique applicable to local government senior managers.

352　　　　　　　　　UK
LOCAL GOVERNMENT NEWS. 1979. m. £33 (foreign £44). B & M Publications (London) Ltd., Box 13, Hereford House, Bridle Path, Croydon, Surrey CR9 4NL, England. TEL 081-680-4200. FAX 081-681-5049. Ed. P. Cooper. stat.; tr.lit.; circ. 22,487. (back issues avail.)

352　　　　　　　　　UK
LOCAL GOVERNMENT POLICY MAKING. 1981. 5/yr. £755($125) (University of Birmingham, Institute of Local Government Studies) Longman Group UK Ltd., Westgate House, The High, Harlow, Essex CM20 1YR, England. TEL 0279 442601. Ed. Tim Mobbs. index. **Indexed:** Bus.Ind., Cont.Pg.Manage.
Formerly: Corporate Planning Journal (ISSN 0305-3695)

LOCAL GOVERNMENT REVIEW. see *LAW*

352　　　　　　JA　ISSN 0288-7622
JS7371.A1
LOCAL GOVERNMENT REVIEW IN JAPAN. (Text in English) 1973. a. free. General Center for Local Autonomy - Jichi Sogo Centre, Toranomon Bldg., 8th Fl., 1-7-1 Nishi-Shinbashi, Minato-ku, Tokyo 105, Japan. TEL 03-3504-0841. FAX 03-3504-0872. TELEX 02228505-JALTAS-J. Ed. Katsuomi Ohbayashi. circ. 600.
Formerly: Local Government Review (ISSN 0449-0193)
Description: Introduces problems faced by Japanese local governments. Contains articles selected and translated from publications of the bureaus of the Ministry of Home Affairs (Minister's Secretariat, Local Bureau, Local Autonomy College, and Fire Defense Agency.) Aims to promote mutual exchange between Japanese local governments and those abroad.

352　　　　　　UK　ISSN 0300-3930
LOCAL GOVERNMENT STUDIES. 1971. 6/yr. £118($185) to institutions; individuals £109. Frank Cass & Co. Ltd., Gainsborough House, 11 Gainsborough Rd., London E11 1RS, England. TEL 081-530-4226. FAX 081-530-7795. Eds. Kieron Walsh, Chris Skelcher. adv.; bk.rev.; index; circ. 1,000. **Indexed:** Account.& Data Proc.Abstr., ASSIA, Br.Hum.Ind., Curr.Cont., Sage Urb.Stud.Abstr., SSCI.
—BLDSC shelfmark: 5290.029000.
Description: Covers the study of the management of local affairs; current problems and new trends in local government.

352　　　　　　II　ISSN 0024-5615
LOCAL SELF-GOVERNMENT.* (Text in English) 1956. m. Rs.20.($4.) 1750 Sohanganj, Subzimandi, Delhi, India. Ed. H.C. Banjahi. adv.; charts; illus.

352　　　　　　US　ISSN 0164-3622
JS39
LOUISIANA MUNICIPAL REVIEW. 1938. m. $12. Louisiana Municipal Association, Box 4327, Baton Rouge, LA 70821. TEL 504-344-5001. FAX 504-344-3057. Ed. Charles J. Pasqua. adv.; bk.rev.; circ. 3,000.
Description: Devoted to municipal government issues in Louisiana, the U.S., and intergovernmental relations.

352　　　　　　　　　SZ
LUZERNER KANTONSBLATT. 1975. w. 55 Fr. (Staatskanzlei) Raeber AG, Frankenstr. 7-9, Lucerne, Switzerland. Ed.Bd. adv.; circ. 7,050.

352　　　　　　　　　US
M A P A REGIONAL DIRECTORY OF PUBLIC OFFICIALS. a. $10. Omaha - Council Bluffs Metropolitan Area Planning Agency, 2222 Cumming St., Omaha, NE 68102-4328. TEL 402-444-6866. FAX 402-342-0949. circ. 1,000.

352　　　　　　US　ISSN 0047-5262
M I S REPORTS. (Management Information Service) (Included in M I S subscription, which consists of data and inquiry services) 1946. m. price varies. International City - County Management Association, 777 North Capitol St., N.E. Ste. 500, Washington, DC 20002-4201. TEL 800-745-8780. Ed. Christine Ulrich. charts; circ. 1,600. (back issues avail.) **Indexed:** P.A.I.S., Sage Pub.Admin.Abstr., Urb.Aff.Abstr.
Description: Covers development, implementation, delivery and evaluation of local government programs and services.

MCQUILLIN MUNICIPAL LAW REPORT; a monthly review for lawyers, administrators and officials. see *LAW*

MAIL ORDER DIGEST. see *BUSINESS AND ECONOMICS — Marketing And Purchasing*

352 350　　　　　　　US
MAINE REGISTER: STATE YEARBOOK AND LEGISLATIVE MANUAL. 1822. a. $95. Tower Publishing Co., 34 Diamond St., Box 7220, Portland, ME 04112. TEL 207-774-9813. adv.; index; circ. 1,400. (avail. on diskette)
Description: Contains information on state and county officials, with complete listing of municipal, business and professional directories and organizations.

352　　　　　　US　ISSN 0025-0791
JS39
MAINE TOWNSMAN. 1939. m. $15 to non-members. Maine Municipal Association, Local Government Center, 37 Community Drive, Augusta, ME 04330. TEL 207-623-8428. FAX 207-626-5947. Ed. Michael L. Starn. adv.; bk.rev.; illus.; index; circ. 4,500.

352　　　　　　　　　GW
MANNHEIMER HEFTE. 1952. s-a. DM.5. Hauptamt, Postfach 10 30 51, D-6800 Mannheim 1, Germany. TEL 0621-2931. FAX 0621-101452. Ed. Hansjoerg Probst. circ. 2,500. (back issues avail.)

352　　　　　　US　ISSN 0361-2090
JS451.M47
MASSACHUSETTS MUNICIPAL ASSOCIATION DIRECTORY. (Supplement to: Municipal Advocate) 1964. a. $24. Massachusetts Municipal Association, 60 Temple Place, Boston, MA 02111. TEL 617-426-7272. FAX 612-695-1314. Ed. Sunny Edmunds. adv.; bk.rev.; circ. 4,200.
Description: Lists local governments and officials in the commonwealth, including city and county governments and state professional organizations.

352　　　　　　　　　II
MAYORS' NEWSLETTER. (Text in English) 1973. q. Rs.6. All India Council of Mayors, 48-B Municipal Colony, Azadpur, Delhi 110 033, India. Ed. Hira Lall Mathur. adv.; bk.rev.; circ. 2,000.

352 360　　　　　　AT
MELBOURNE. PORT COUNCIL NEWS. 1985. irreg. (3-4/yr.). free. City Council, Port Melbourne, Town Hall, Bay St., Port Melbourne, Vic. 3207, Australia. TEL 03-647-9500. FAX 03-646-4839. Ed. David Graham. circ. 4,000.
Description: Current information about council services for residents.

351　　　　　　CN　ISSN 0076-7093
JS1789
METROPOLITAN TORONTO. 1954. irreg., latest 1975. free. Municipality of Metropolitan Toronto, Clerk's Dept., 390 Bay St., 5th fl., Toronto, Ont. M5H 3Y7, Canada. TEL 416-392-8016.

PUBLIC ADMINISTRATION — MUNICIPAL GOVERNMENT

352　　　　US　　ISSN 0076-8014
MICHIGAN MUNICIPAL LEAGUE. MUNICIPAL LEGAL BRIEFS. 1961. bi-m. $25. Michigan Municipal League, 1675 Green Rd., Box 1487, Ann Arbor, MI 48106. TEL 313-662-3246. Ed. William L. Steude. circ. 700. (reprint service avail.)

352　　　　US　　ISSN 0026-2331
JS39
MICHIGAN MUNICIPAL REVIEW. 1928. 10/yr. $15. Michigan Municipal League, 1675 Green Rd., Box 1487, Ann Arbor, MI 48106. TEL 313-662-3246. Ed. Judi L. Campbell. adv.; bk.rev.; charts; illus.; mkt.; index; circ. 9,200. (also avail. in microfilm from UMI; reprint service avail. from UMI) **Indexed:** Mich.Mag.Ind., P.A.I.S.

MICROSOFTWARE NEWS. see *COMPUTERS — Microcomputers*

352　　　　US　　ISSN 0148-8546
JS39
MINNESOTA CITIES. (Supplement avail.: Loss Control Quarterly) 1916. m. $18. League of Minnesota Cities, 183 University Ave. E., St. Paul, MN 55101-2526. TEL 612-227-5600. Ed. Jean Mehle Goad. adv.; bk.rev.; charts; illus.; stat.; index; circ. 9,900. **Indexed:** P.A.I.S., Sage Pub.Admin.Abstr.
Formerly: Minnesota Municipalities (ISSN 0026-5578)
Description: Covers taxes, finances from the legislator's viewpoint, legislative programs, labor relations and court decisions.

352　　　　US　　ISSN 0026-6337
JS303.M7
MISSISSIPPI MUNICIPALITIES. 1955. m. $16. Mississippi Municipal Association, 600 E. Amite St., Jackson, MS 39202. TEL 601-353-5854. Ed. Al Sage, III. adv.; illus.; tr.lit.; circ. 3,300.

352　　　　US　　ISSN 0026-6647
JS39
MISSOURI MUNICIPAL REVIEW. 1936. 10/yr. $15. Missouri Municipal League, 1913 William St., Jefferson City, MO 65109. TEL 314-635-9134. FAX 314-635-9009. Ed. Dolores Schulte. adv.; bk.rev.; charts; illus.; index; circ. 5,550.

352　　　　AU
MITTEILUNGSBLATT DER STADT VILLACH. 1947. s-m. $115.50. Magistrat der Stadt Villach, Pressestelle, Rathaus, 9500 Villach, Austria. FAX 04242-22465. TELEX 45-516-MAGVIL-A. adv.; bk.rev.; circ. 24,500.

350　　　　US　　ISSN 0026-9980
MONTANA LEAGUE OF CITIES & TOWNS. NEWSLETTER. no.139, 1975. irreg. (3-4/yr.). free. Montana League of Cities & Towns, Box 1704, Helena, MT 59624. TEL 406-442-8768. adv.; illus.; circ. 1,200.
Formerly: Montana Municipal League. Newsletter.

352　　　　BE
MOUVEMENT COMMUNAL. (Text in French) 1919. m. 2770 Fr. Union des Villes et Communes Belges, Rue d'Arlon 53, B4, B-1040 Brussels, Belgium. Ed. M. Debauque. adv.; bk.rev.; bibl.; illus.; circ. 5,100.

352　　　　CN
MUNICIPAL ACT AND INDEX TO LOCAL GOVERNMENT LEGISLATION MANUAL. base vol. (plus irreg. suppl.). Can.$37.50. Ministry of Municipal Affairs, Recreation and Culture, Victoria, B.C., Canada. (Subscr. to: Crown Publications, 546 Yates St., Victoria, B.C. V8W 1K8, Canada. TEL 604-386-4636) (looseleaf format)
Description: A consolidation of the Municipal Act and an Index to Local Government Legislation.

352　　　　US
MUNICIPAL ADVOCATE. 1980. q. $40. Massachusetts Municipal Association, 60 Temple Pl., Boston, MA 02111. TEL 617-426-7272. FAX 617-695-1314. Ed. Adam Auster. adv.; circ. 4,525.
Description: Articles, news and information on municipal law, insurance, finance, public safety, land use and public works for mayors, town and city managers, finance committee chairmen, treasurers and other officials with purchasing authority.

352　　　　AT　　ISSN 0085-3585
MUNICIPAL ASSOCIATION OF TASMANIA. SESSION. MINUTES OF PROCEEDINGS. 1912. a. Aus.$10 to non-members. Municipal Association of Tasmania, 34 Patrick St., Hobart, Tas. 7000, Australia. TEL 002-310666. FAX 002-240086. Ed. Sue Mecklenburgh. index; circ. 200 (controlled).

352　　　　AT　　ISSN 0077-2143
MUNICIPAL ASSOCIATION OF VICTORIA. MINUTES OF PROCEEDINGS OF ANNUAL SESSION. 1879. a. free; available to member councils. Municipal Association of Victoria, G.P.O. Box 4326PP, Melbourne, Vic. 3001, Australia. TEL 03-824-8411. FAX 03-824-8404. Ed. Rob Barfus. index; circ. 4,000.

MUNICIPAL ATTORNEY. see *LAW*

352　　　　US　　ISSN 0743-6211
JS363
MUNICIPAL - COUNTY EXECUTIVE DIRECTORY ANNUAL. a. $127. Carroll Publishing Company, 1058 Thomas Jefferson St., N.W., Washington, DC 20007. TEL 202-333-8620. FAX 202-337-7020.
Description: Provides detailed listings of officials and administrators for counties with population over 25,000 and cities - over 15,000 population.

352　　　　US
MUNICIPAL ELECTION CALENDAR. a. $20 to non-members; members $10. Colorado Municipal League, 1660 Lincoln St., Ste. 2100, Denver, CO 80264. TEL 303-831-6411.
Description: Checklist of action required by the Municipal Election Code to be performed before, during and after elections.

352　　　　US　　ISSN 0742-1710
JS363
MUNICIPAL EXECUTIVE DIRECTORY. s-a. $130. Carroll Publishing Company, 1058 Thomas Jefferson St., N.W., Washington, DC 20007. TEL 202-333-8620. FAX 202-337-7020.
Description: Directory of key officials in the municipal governments of the United States.

352　363.6　　UK　　ISSN 0143-4187
TD1
MUNICIPAL JOURNAL; British public services, local government administrator, contractors' guide, public works engineer, local government journal and new technology weekly. 1893. w. £51.50. Municipal Journal Ltd., 32 Vauxhall Bridge Road, London SW2V 2SS, England. Ed. Cliff Davis Coleman. charts; film rev.; illus.; mkt.; stat.; index; circ. 10,668. **Indexed:** Br.Tech.Ind., HRIS, P.A.I.S., RICS.
—BLDSC shelfmark: 5984.400000.
Formerly: Municipal and Public Services Journal (ISSN 0027-3430); **Incorporates:** Municipal Engineering (ISSN 0027-3457); Municipal Journal (ISSN 0027-349X)

352　　　　US
MUNICIPAL LEAGUE OF KING COUNTY. ISSUE WATCH. 1911. m. membership. Municipal League of King County, 810 Third Ave., Ste. 604, Seattle, WA 98104-1651. TEL 206-622-8333. Ed. Jim Cronin. charts; stat.; index, cum.index; circ. 2,400.
Incorporates: Municipal League of Seattle and King County. Municipal News (ISSN 0027-352X)
Description: Provides balanced, non-biased coverage of government and public policy issues in the county.

340　　　　US　　ISSN 0278-1301
KF5304.A75
MUNICIPAL LITIGATION REPORTER. 1981. m. $295 (effective Oct. 1990). Strafford Publications, Inc., 1201 Peachtree St., N.E., Ste. 1150, Atlanta, GA 30361. TEL 404-881-1141. FAX 404-881-0074. cum.index: 1981-1991. (back issues avail.)
Description: Covers full spectrum of litigation involving local government entities in all 50 states and U.S. territories and possessions.

352　　　　US
MUNICIPAL MARYLAND. 1948. 10/yr. $21. Maryland Municipal League, Inc., 1212 West St., Annapolis, MD 21401. TEL 410-268-5514. Ed. Karen A. Liskey. adv.; bk.rev.; circ. 2,000.
Formerly: Maryland Municipal News (ISSN 0025-4304)
Description: Articles on the economic, legislative, law-enforcement, and social issues that affect the state's cities and towns.

352　　　　SA
MUNICIPAL REFERENCE LIBRARY BULLETIN/BULLETIN VAN DIE MUNISIPALE NASLAANBIBLIOTEEK. (Text in Afrikaans, English) 1938. m. free. Johannesburg Public Library, Market Square, Johannesburg 2001, South Africa. TEL 011-836-3787. FAX 011-836-6607. circ. 300. (back issues avail.)
Description: Current-awareness information on local government and municipal services in South Africa and elsewhere.

352　　　　UK　　ISSN 0261-5118
MUNICIPAL REVIEW AND A M A NEWS. 1930. m. £18 (foreign £36). Association of Metropolitan Authorities, 35 Great Smith St., London SW1P 3BJ, England. TEL 071-222-8100. FAX 071-222-0878. Ed. Peter Smith. adv.; bk.rev.; illus.; stat.; index; circ. 8,000. **Indexed:** RICS, Sage Pub.Admin.Abstr.
—BLDSC shelfmark: 5985.080000.
Formerly: Municipal Review (ISSN 0027-3562)

352　　　　CN　　ISSN 0027-3589
MUNICIPAL WORLD. 1891. m. Can.$36. Municipal World Inc., Box 399, St. Thomas, Ont. N5P 3V3, Canada. TEL 519-633-0031. FAX 519-633-1001. Eds. Michael J. Smither, Nasreine Canaran. adv.; bk.rev.; illus.; index; circ. 1,500. (also avail. in microfiche)

352　　　　US　　ISSN 0077-2186
JS344.C5
MUNICIPAL YEAR BOOK. 1922. a. $77.50. International City - County Management Association, 777 North Capitol, N.E. Ste. 500, Washington, DC 20002-4201. TEL 202-289-4262. Ed. Evelina Moulder. bk.rev.; circ. 16,000. **Indexed:** SRI.
—BLDSC shelfmark: 5985.412000.
Formerly: City Manager Yearbook.
Description: Provides information on local government management issues and trends, intergovernmental subjects, staffing and compensation.

352　　　　UK　　ISSN 0305-5906
MUNICIPAL YEAR BOOK. Variant title: Municipal Yearbook. 1897. a. £94. Municipal Journal Ltd., 32 Vauxhall Bridge Road, London SW1V 2SS, England. TEL 071-973-6400. FAX 071-233-5056. Ed. B. Russbridge. adv.; circ. 7,500. (also avail. in microfiche from BHP)
—BLDSC shelfmark: 5985.415000.

352　　　　US　　ISSN 1054-4062
JS141
▼**MUNICIPAL YELLOW BOOK.** 1992. s-a. $160. Monitor Publishing Co. (New York), 104 Fifth Ave., 2nd Fl., New York, NY 10011. TEL 212-627-4140. FAX 212-645-0931.
Description: Includes nearly 20,000 key elected and administrative officials in local government.

352　　　　SP
MUNICIPALIA; revista de administracion local. 1944. m. (combined Jul.-Aug.). 15000 ptas. Municipalia, S.A., Serrano, 7, 28001 Madrid, Spain. TEL 91-435-61-01. FAX 91-431-05-70. (Subscr. to: Apdo No. 103, F.D. Madrid, Spain) Dir. Hipolito Lafuente Xicola. adv.; bk.rev.; charts; illus.; stat.
Description: Essays and news on local jurisprudence in Spain.

352　　　　US　　ISSN 0027-3597
MUNICIPALITY. 1900. m. $12. League of Wisconsin Municipalities, 122 W. Washington Ave., Rm. 301, Madison, WI 53703. TEL 608-267-2380. FAX 608-267-0685. Ed. Dan Thompson. adv.; bk.rev.; charts; index; circ. 9,554. **Indexed:** P.A.I.S.

352　　　　US　　ISSN 0735-9691
N A T A T'S REPORTER. 1977. m. $36. National Association of Towns and Townships, National Center for Small Communities, 1522 K St. N.W., Ste. 600, Washington, DC 20005. TEL 202-737-5200. Ed. Ronnie J. Kweller. adv.; bk.rev.; circ. 15,000. (tabloid format; back issues avail)
Formerly: N A T A T's National Community Reporter.
Description: Covers issues concerning America's grassroots governments, including management of small towns, and federal policies affecting town governments.

PUBLIC ADMINISTRATION — MUNICIPAL GOVERNMENT

352 US
N A W REPORT. 1972. 6/yr. membership. National Association of Wholesaler - Distributors, 1725 K St., N.W., 7th Fl., Washington, DC 20006. TEL 202-872-0885. Ed. Philip Jaffa. bk.rev.; circ. 10,000.
Former titles: Channels; N A W Newsletter.

352 NE ISSN 0924-4816
JS5931
N G GEMEENTELIJK MAGAZINE. 1947. w. fl.175. V N G Uitgeverij, P.O. Box 30435, 2500 GK The Hague, Netherlands. TEL 070-3738888. FAX 070-3651826. Ed.Bd. adv.; illus.; circ. 25,000.
Indexed: Key to Econ.Sci.
Formerly (until 1990): Nederlandse Gemeente.

352 AU
NACHRICHTEN DER STADTGEMEINDE LIEZEN. 1966. q. free. Stadtgemeinde Liezen, Rathaus, A-8940 Liezen, Austria. TEL 03612-22881. FAX 03612-22881-3. Ed. Rudolf Kaltenboeck. circ. 3,500.

352 GW
NACHRICHTENBLATT FUER DAS UNTERE HAERTSFELD. 1961. w. DM.35. Gemeinde Dischingen, Marktplatz 9, 7925 Dischingen, Germany. FAX 07327-8140. adv. (looseleaf format; back issues avail.)

352 II ISSN 0027-7584
NAGARLOK; urban affairs quarterly. (Text in English) 1969. q. Rs.30($15) (Centre for Urban Studies) Indian Institute of Public Administration, Indraprastha Estate, Ring Rd., New Delhi 110002, India. Ed. P.R. Dubhashi. bk.rev.; bibl.; charts; stat. (back issues avail.)

352 US ISSN 0027-9013
JS39
NATIONAL CIVIC REVIEW. 1912. q. $30 to libraries. National Civic League, Inc., 1445 Market St., Ste. 300, Denver, CO 80202-1728. TEL 303-571-4343. Ed. David Lampe. adv.; bk.rev.; charts; circ. 4,000. (also avail. in microfiche from WSH; microfilm from WSH; reprint service avail. from UMI) **Indexed:** A.B.C.Pol.Sci., Amer.Hist.& Life, Bk.Rev.Ind. (1965-), C.L.I., Child.Bk.Rev.Ind. (1965-), Fut.Surv., Hist.Abstr., Leg.Per., P.A.I.S., Sage Pub.Admin.Abstr., So.Pac.Per.Ind.
—BLDSC shelfmark: 6021.515000.
Formerly: National Municipal Review (ISSN 0190-3799)

352 US
NATIONAL MUNICIPAL POLICY. 1951. a. $10 to non-members. National League of Cities, 1301 Pennsylvania Ave., N.W., Washington, DC 20004. TEL 202-626-3000. index.
Description: Policy statement about national urban problems and priorities for national action.

352 US ISSN 0164-5935
NATION'S CITIES WEEKLY. 1978. w. $80. National League of Cities, 1301 Pennsylvania Ave., N.W., Washington, DC 20004. TEL 202-626-3040. Ed. Alan Beals. adv.; bk.rev.; charts; illus.; index; circ. 26,500. (tabloid format; also avail. in microform from UMI; reprint service avail. from UMI) **Indexed:** Bus.Ind., Curr.Cont., Hlth.Ind., Mag.Ind., P.A.I.S., PSI, Soc.Sci.Ind., Tr.& Indus.Ind., Urb.Aff.Abstr.
Incorporates (in 1978): City Weekly (ISSN 0164-5595); **Supersedes (1963-1978):** Nation's Cities (ISSN 0028-0488)
Description: Discusses how national developments affect cities, with case studies on how local governments solve problems.

352 US ISSN 0028-1905
NEBRASKA MUNICIPAL REVIEW. 1930. m. $10. League of Nebraska Municipalities, 1335 L St., Lincoln, NE 68508. TEL 402-476-2829. Ed. Peggy Hain. adv.; illus.; stat.; circ. 3,250. **Indexed:** P.A.I.S.
Description: Contains news and feature articles on local, state and federal government issues of interest to municipal officials.

352 CN
NEW BRUNSWICK PUBLIC EMPLOYEES ASSOCIATION. NEWSLINE - BULLETIN. (Editions in English, French) 1970. irreg. free to qualified personnel. New Brunswick Public Employees Association, 238 King St., Fredericton, N.B. E3B 4Y2, Canada. TEL 506-458-8440. FAX 506-450-8481. Ed. J.A.R. Ingram. circ. 6,000. **Indexed:** Refug.Abstr.
Formerly: New Brunswick Public Employees Association. News Letter (ISSN 0381-7970)
Description: Union publication which informs, educates and promotes goals of the union and its membership.

352 330.9 US ISSN 0749-016X
NEW ENGLAND JOURNAL OF PUBLIC POLICY. 1984. s-a. $20 to individuals and libraries; institutions $100. John W. McCormack Institute of Public Affairs, University of Massachusetts at Boston, Harbor Campus, Boston, MA 02125. TEL 617-287-5550. FAX 617-287-5544. Ed. Padraig J. O'Mally. circ. 600. (back issues avail.)
—BLDSC shelfmark: 6084.008000.

350 US
NEW HAMPSHIRE MUNICIPAL PRACTICE SERIES. VOL. 2: MUNICIPAL FINANCE AND TAXATION. (Series consists of 4 vols.; Vols. 1 and 1A: Land Use Planning and Zoning; Vol. 2: Municipal Finance and Taxation; Vol. 3: Public Health, Safety and Highways) base vol. (plus a. suppl.). $70 (4-vols. set $225). Butterworth Legal Publishers (Salem) (Subsidiary of: Reed International PLC), 901 Stiles Rd., Salem, NH 03079. TEL 800-548-4001. FAX 603-898-9858. Ed. Peter J. Loughlin. (looseleaf format)
Description: Details information for municipal officials and lawyers concerning appropriations, budgets, funds, taxation, tax abatements, and exemptions.

350 US
NEW HAMPSHIRE MUNICIPAL PRACTICE SERIES. VOL. 3: PUBLIC HEALTH, SAFETY AND HIGHWAYS. (Series consists of 4 vols.; Vols. 1 and 1A: Land Use Planning and Zoning; Vol. 2: Municipal Finance and Taxation; Vol. 3: Public Health, Safety and Highways) base vol. (plus a . suppl.). $70 (4-vols. set $225). Butterworth Legal Publishers (Salem) (Subsidiary of: Reed International PLC), 90 Stiles Rd., Salem, NH 03079. TEL 800-548-4001. FAX 603-898-9858. Ed. Peter J. Loughlin. (looseleaf format)
Description: Analyzes law and regulations concerning health and sanitation, sewage disposal and water supplies, housing standards and codes, and the layout and administration of highways, roads and streets.

350 US
NEW HAMPSHIRE MUNICIPAL PRACTICE SERIES. VOLS. 1 AND 1A: LAND USE AND PLANNING. (Series consists of 4 vols.; Vols. 1 and 1A: Land Use Planning and Zoning; Vol. 2: Municipal Finance and Taxation; Vol. 3: Public Health, Safety and Highways) 2 base vols. (plus a. suppl.). $140 (4-vols. set $225). Butterworth Legal Publishers (Salem) (Subsidiary of: Reed International PLC), 90 Stiles Rd., Salem, NH 03079. TEL 800-548-4001. FAX 603-898-9858. Ed. Peter J. Loughlin. (looseleaf format)
Description: Discusses topics such as master plan, ordinance, enforcement, growth control, appeals and judicial review, variances, procedures of boards, and other state and federal controls.

352 US
▼**NEW HAMPSHIRE PRACTICE SERIES. VOLS. 13 AND 14: LOCAL GOVERNMENT LAW.** (Series consists of 14 vols.; Vols. 1 and 2: Criminal Practice and Procedure; Vol. 3: Family Law; Vols. 4, 5 and 6: Civil Practice and Procedure; Vol. 7: Wills, Trusts and Gifts; Vols. 8 and 9: Personal Injury - Tort and Insurance Practice; Vols. 10, 11 and 12: Probate Law and Procedure; Vols. 13 and 14: Local Government Law) 1990. 2 base vols. (plus a. suppl.). $120 (14-vols. set $575). Butterworth Legal Publishers (Salem) (Subsidiary of: Reed International PLC), 90 Stiles Rd., Salem, NH 03079. TEL 800-548-4001. FAX 603-898-9858. Ed. Peter J. Loughlin. (looseleaf format)
Description: Provides comprehensive coverage of the law and practice relating to cities, towns, public officials, records and meetings, municipal power and liabilities, and elections.

352 350 US
NEW HAMPSHIRE REGISTER: STATE YEARBOOK AND LEGISLATIVE MANUAL. 1768. a. $95. Tower Publishing Co., 34 Diamond St., Box 7220, Portland, ME 04112. TEL 207-774-9813. adv.; circ. 800. (avail. on diskette)
Description: Information on state and county officials and organizations. Contains complete municipal, business and professional directories.

352 US ISSN 0028-5846
JS39
NEW JERSEY MUNICIPALITIES. 1917. m. (Oct.-Jun.). $7 (members $6). New Jersey State League of Municipalities, 407 W. State St., Trenton, NJ 08618. TEL 609-695-3481. FAX 609-695-0151. Ed. Irene Gianopoulos. adv.; bk.rev.; illus.; index; circ. 8,400. **Indexed:** P.A.I.S., Sage Fam.Stud.Abstr., Sage Urb.Stud.Abstr.

352 US ISSN 0028-6257
NEW MEXICO MUNICIPAL LEAGUE. MUNICIPAL REPORTER. 1959. m. $20. New Mexico Municipal League, 1229 Paseo de Peralta, Box 846, Santa Fe, NM 87504-0846. Ed. William F. Fulginiti. adv.; bk.rev.; circ. 1,700.

352.12 US ISSN 0094-7547
HJ9013.N5e
NEW YORK (CITY). SCHEDULES SUPPORTING THE EXECUTIVE BUDGET.. 1955. a. Office of Management and Budget, 75 Park Pl., 6th Fl., New York, NY 10007. TEL 212-788-5807. circ. 500.

NEW YORK (STATE). OPINIONS OF THE COMPTROLLER. see LAW

352 US ISSN 0737-1314
JK3430
NEW YORK STATE DIRECTORY. 1983. a. $112 softcover. Cambridge Information Group Directories, Inc., 1200 Quince Orchard Blvd., Gaithersburg, MD 20878. TEL 301-590-2300. FAX 301-990-8378. TELEX 44-6194 NATSTA GAIT. (Subscr. to: 7200 Wisconsin Ave., Bethesda, MD 20878) Ed. JoAnne DuChez.
Description: Provides access to over 10,000 persons from the executive, legislative, and judicial branches of New York State Government, as well as local government officials and private sector experts concerned with New York State affairs.

352 US
NEW YORK STATE MUNICIPAL BULLETIN. 1934. bi-m. $25. Conference of Mayors and Other Municipal Officials, 119 Washington Ave., Albany, NY 12210. TEL 518-463-1185. Ed. Patricia Giannola. adv.; circ. 6,000.

353.9 US
NEW YORK STATE REGISTER. 1979. w. $40. Department of State, Division of Information Services, 162 Washington Ave., Albany, NY 12231. Dir. Maureen L. Bigness. adv.; circ. 2,500.
Supersedes (1928-1979): New York State Bulletin (ISSN 0028-7555)

352 NZ
NEW ZEALAND LOCAL GOVERNMENT. 1964. m. NZ.$51.50. Trade Publications Ltd., P.O. Box 37-549, 13 Cheshire St., Parnell, Auckland 1, New Zealand. TEL 0064-09-795500. FAX 0064-09-394825. Ed. B. Benseman. adv.; bk.rev.; illus.; circ. 2,016.

352 NZ ISSN 0028-8403
NEW ZEALAND LOCAL GOVERNMENT YEARBOOK. 1964. a. NZ.$50. Trade Publications Ltd., Box 37-549, 13 Chesire St., Parnell, Auckland 1, New Zealand. TEL 064-09-705500. FAX 064-09-394825. Ed. B. Benseman. adv.; bk.rev.; bibl.; illus.; circ. 2,344.

NEW ZEALAND TOWN PLANNING APPEALS. see LAW — Estate Planning

352 GW ISSN 0028-9779
NIEDERSAECHSISCHE GEMEINDE; Monatsschrift fuer kommunale Selbstverwaltung. 1949. m. DM.72. Niedersaechsischer Staedte-und Gemeindebund, Seelhorststr. 18, 3000 Hannover, Germany. TEL 0511-280720. FAX 0511-854107. Ed. W. Haack. adv.; bk.rev.; stat.; index; circ. 12,700 (controlled).

PUBLIC ADMINISTRATION — MUNICIPAL GOVERNMENT

352   GW   ISSN 0178-4226
NIEDERSAECHSISCHER STAEDTETAG; Nachrichten fuer kreisfreie und kreisangehoerige Staedt, Gemeinden und Samtgemeinden. 1972. m. DM.30. Verlag Otto Schwartz und Co., Annastr. 7, 3400 Goettingen, Germany. TEL 0551-31051. FAX 0551-372812. Ed. Eckehart Peil. circ. 6,450.

352   NO
NORSK KOMMUNEFORBUND. FAGBLAD.* 10/yr. Norsk Kommuneforbund, c/o Per Sletholt, Postboks 57, Tveita, Oslo 6, Norway. adv.; circ. 116,548.

352   US
NORTH DAKOTA LEAGUE OF CITIES BULLETIN. vol.41, 1973. 10/yr. $10. North Dakota League of Cities, Box 2235, Bismarck, ND 58502. TEL 701-223-3518. Ed. Robert E. Johnson. adv.; charts; illus.; circ. 2,850.

352 336   US   ISSN 0731-2385
NOTES (NEW YORK). 1914. q. $10 (free to qualified personnel). Department of Records and Information Services, 31 Chambers St., Rm. 305, New York, NY 10007. TEL 212-566-0598. FAX 212-385-4253. Ed. Jeanette Martinez. bk.rev.; circ. 5,000.

OD. see *LIBRARY AND INFORMATION SCIENCES*

352   XV
ODLOCANJE/DECISION. (Text in Slovenian) 1981. m. free. Skupscina Obcine Ravne na Koroskem, Cecovje 12-a, 62390 Ravne na Koroskem, Slovenia. TEL 062 861-821. circ. 1,200. (looseleaf format; back issues avail.)

DER OEFFENTLICHE DIENST. see *LAW*

352   AU   ISSN 0048-1424
OESTERREICHISCHE BUERGERMEISTER ZEITUNG.* vol.25, 1972. m. S.180. Zeitungsverlag Kuhn und Co., Kutschkergasse 42, A-1180 Vienna, Austria. Ed.Bd. adv.; bk.rev.; illus.; circ. 2,700.

352   AU   ISSN 0029-912X
JS4501
OESTERREICHISCHE GEMEINDE-ZEITUNG. 1934. m. S.345. (Oesterreichischer Staedtebund) Jugend und Volk Verlagsgesellschaft, Anschuetzg. 1, A-1153 Vienna, Austria. TEL 0222-8120517. FAX 0222-8120517-27. adv.; bk.rev.; stat.; circ. 6,000.

383   SA
OFFICIAL SOUTH AFRICAN MUNICIPAL YEARBOOK/AMPTELIKE SUID-AFRIKAANSE MUNISIPALE JAARBOEK; official South Africa. (Text in Afrikaans and English) 1909. a. R.145. (South African Association of Municipal Employees) Helm Publishing Co. (Pty.) Ltd., P.O. Box 41706, Craighall 2024, South Africa. TEL 011-788-0612. circ. 3,000.
   Formerly: Municipal Yearbook.

352   CN   ISSN 0833-1731
ONTARIO. MINISTRY OF MUNICIPAL AFFAIRS. ANNUAL REPORT. 1985. a. Can.$2.50. Ministry of Municipal Affairs, 777 Bay St., 17th Fl., Toronto, Ont. M5G 2E5, Canada. TEL 416-585-7020. circ. 2,500.

ONTARIO. PROVINCIAL-MUNICIPAL AFFAIRS SECRETARIAT. MUNICIPAL DIRECTORY. see *PUBLIC ADMINISTRATION*

352   US
OUTREACH. 1982. 5/yr. free. Institute for Governmental Service, University of Maryland, 2101 Woods Hall, College Park, MD 20742. TEL 301-405-6970. FAX 301-314-9646. Ed. MaryAnne S. Suehle. circ. 1,130. (back issues avail.)

P A R ANALYSIS. (Public Affairs Research Council of Louisiana, Inc.) see *POLITICAL SCIENCE*

352   US
P A R LEGISLATIVE BULLETIN. 1951. w. (during state legislative session). $100. Public Affairs Research Council of Louisiana, Inc., Box 14776, Baton Rouge, LA 70898-4776. TEL 504-926-8414. FAX 504-926-8417. Ed. Jan Carlock.
   Description: Reports on various topics being considered by the Louisiana Legislature.

352 370   US
P P F BULLETIN. 1913. irreg. (8-18/yr.). $50. Public Policy Forum, 633 W. Wisconsin Ave., Milwaukee, WI 53203-1918. TEL 414-276-8240. FAX 414-276-9962. Ed. Jean B. Tyler. charts; stat.; circ. 1,500.
   Formerly: C G R B Bulletin (Citizen's Governmental Research Bureau).
   Description: Covers the 5 county Milwaukee area.

352   US   ISSN 0162-5160
PENNSYLVANIA TOWNSHIP NEWS. 1948. m. $25 (effective 1992). Pennsylvania State Association of Township Supervisors, 3001 Gettysburg Rd., Camp Hill, PA 17011. TEL 717-763-0930. FAX 717-763-9732. Ed. Ginni Linn Gustavson. adv.; bk.rev.; circ. 12,000.

352   US   ISSN 0031-4714
JS39
PENNSYLVANIAN; the magazine of local governments. 1962. m. $17. Local Pennsylvanian, Inc., Local Government Center, 2941 N. Front St., Harrisburg, PA 17110. TEL 717-236-9526. FAX 717-236-8164. (Co-sponsors: Pennsylvania State Association of Boroughs; Pennsylvania Local Governmental Secretaries Association; Assessors' Association of Pennsylvania) Ed. Patricia F. Hazur. adv.; bk.rev.; charts; illus.; circ. 6,500. (also avail. in microfilm from UMI; reprint service avail. from UMI)
   Description: Articles, directories, indexes and announcements on governmental units at the borough and township level of the state, for governmental secretaries, administrators and clerks, county assessors, borough mayors and councilmembers.

PERSONEEL EN ORGANISATIE - VAKMATIG. see *BUSINESS AND ECONOMICS — Personnel Management*

PLANNING & ZONING NEWS. see *HOUSING AND URBAN PLANNING*

PLANNING COMMISSIONERS JOURNAL; for America's municipal & county planning boards. see *HOUSING AND URBAN PLANNING*

352 330   US   ISSN 0888-7446
PRIVATIZATION. 1986. s-m. $167. Government Information Services, 1611 N. Kent St., Ste. 508, Arlington, VA 22209. TEL 703-528-1000. FAX 703-528-6060. Ed. Laurence A. Alexander.
   Description: Covers the field of privatization and contracting-out for both the public and private sectors. Covers all services from solid waste disposal to street cleaning to general administration, with current information on comparative costs, issuing bid requests, writing contracts, and quality control in news reports, analysis and case studies.

PRIVATIZATION WATCH. see *POLITICAL SCIENCE*

352 340   US   ISSN 0893-2573
KFM4225
PUBLIC AND LOCAL ACTS OF THE LEGISLATURE OF THE STATE OF MICHIGAN. 1835. a. price varies. Legislative Council, Legislative Service Bureau, 124 W. Allegan, MNT, 4th Fl., Box 30036, Lansing, MI 48909. TEL 517-373-0170. FAX 517-373-0171. Ed. Roger W. Peters. index; circ. 2,000. (back issues avail.)

352 361.6   UK
PUBLIC AUTHORITIES DIRECTORY. 1975. a. £60. L.G.C. Communications, 122 Minories, London EC3N 1NT, England. TEL 071-623-2530. FAX 071-481-0636. Ed. Geoffrey Smith. adv.; circ. 1,200.
   Description: Reference for anyone who works in, or comes into contact with, local authorities, new towns, and health authorities.

352.1   UK   ISSN 0305-9014
HJ9701
PUBLIC FINANCE AND ACCOUNTANCY. 1896. w. £48. Chartered Institute of Public Finance and Accountancy, 3 Robert St., London WC2N 6BH, England. TEL 071-895-8823. FAX 071-895-8825. Ed. Antonia Simkins. adv.; bk.rev.; charts; illus.; stat.; index; circ. 13,000. (also avail. in microfilm from MIM; back issues avail.) **Indexed:** Account.& Data Proc.Abstr., Account.Ind. (1974-), BPIA, Bus.Ind., Cont.Pg.Manage., Hlth.Ind., RICS, Sci.Abstr, Tr.& Indus.Ind.
   —BLDSC shelfmark: 6963.420000.
   Formerly: Local Government Finance (ISSN 0024-5542)

352   US   ISSN 0033-3611
JS344
PUBLIC MANAGEMENT; devoted to the conduct of local government. 1918. m. $30. International City-County Management Association, 777 North Capitol, N.E., Ste. 500, Washington, DC 20002-4201. TEL 202-289-4262. Ed. Beth Payne. adv.; bk.rev.; bibl.; circ. 14,000. (also avail. in microform from MIM,UMI; back issues avail.; reprint service avail. from UMI) **Indexed:** Account.& Data Proc.Abstr., B.P.I., BPIA, Bus.Ind., Chic.Per.Ind., Geo.Abstr., Mag.Ind., Mid.East: Abstr.& Ind., P.A.I.S., Pers.Lit., Sage Pub.Admin.Abstr., Soc.Sci.Ind.
   —BLDSC shelfmark: 6967.700000.
   Description: Includes editorial commentary and selected departments.

352 368   US   ISSN 0891-7183
PUBLIC RISK. 1986. bi-m. $50. Public Risk Management Association, 1117 N. 19th St., Ste. 900, Arlington, VA 22209. TEL 703-528-7701. Ed. Kathleen M. Rakestraw. adv.; bk.rev.; index; circ. 2,100. (back issues avail.)
   Description: Provides news and features on public sector risk management topics. Covers association business, pooling issues and legislation.

352   US   ISSN 0033-3840
TD1   CODEN: PUWOAH
PUBLIC WORKS; city, county and state. 1896. m. $30. Public Works Journal Corporation, 200 S. Broad St., Ridgewood, NJ 07451. TEL 201-445-5800. FAX 201-445-5170. Ed. E.B. Rodie. adv.; bk.rev.; abstr.; bibl.; charts; illus.; tr.lit.; index; circ. 52,400. (also avail. in microform from UMI; reprint service avail. from UMI) **Indexed:** A.S.& T.Ind., Chem.Abstr., Energy Rev., Eng.Ind., Geotech.Abstr., HRIS, Sel.Water Res.Abstr., Tr.& Indus.Ind., W.R.C.Inf.
   —BLDSC shelfmark: 6969.780000.

628   US   ISSN 0163-9730
PUBLIC WORKS MANUAL; and catalog file. 1977. a. $20. Public Works Journal Corporation, 200 S. Broad St., Ridgewood, NJ 07451. TEL 201-445-5800. FAX 201-445-5170. Ed. E.B. Rodie. adv.; circ. 50,300. (reprint service avail. from UMI)
   Formed by the merger of: Environmental Wastes Control Manual (ISSN 0071-0946); Street and Highway Manual (ISSN 0081-5977); Water Works Manual (ISSN 0083-7717)

352   AT   ISSN 0048-6078
Q I M A. 1950. q. Institute of Municipal Administration, Queensland Division, 151 Porteus Dr., Seven Hills, Brisbane, Qld. 4170, Australia. **Indexed:** Aus.P.A.I.S.

352   US   ISSN 0892-4171
JS39
QUALITY CITIES. 1928. m. $20. Florida League of Cities, Inc., Box 1757, Tallahassee, FL 32302. TEL 904-222-9684. FAX 904-222-3806. Ed. Cecka Trueblood. adv.; bk.rev.; circ. 5,300.
   Formerly: Florida Municipal Record (ISSN 0015-4164)
   Description: Covers subjects of interest to municipal officials.

350   US   ISSN 0033-6483
QUILL (WOOD RIDGE). 1954. q. free. Municipal Clerks Association of N.J. Inc., Wood Ridge Borough, 85 Humboldt St., Wood Ridge, NJ 07075. Ed. Janet L. Lynds. circ. 1,500. (processed)

352   GW
RATHAUS; Zeitschrift fuer Kommunalpolitik. m. DM.72. Schmidt-Roemhild Verlag, Mengstr. 16, 2400 Luebeck 1, Germany. TEL 0451-1605-0. FAX 0451-1605253. TELEX 26536-MSRD.

RECYCLING TODAY (MUNICIPAL MARKET EDITION). see *ENVIRONMENTAL STUDIES — Waste Management*

352   CN
▼**REDBOOK (NORTH BURNABY).** 1949. a. Can.$50. Journal of Commerce Ltd. (Subsidiary of: Southam Business Communications Inc.), P.O. Box 82230, N. Burnaby, B.C. V5C 6E7, Canada. TEL 604-433-8184. FAX 604-433-9549. adv.; B&W page Can.$1050, color page Can.$1600; trim 8 1/2 x 11. circ. 2,008.
   Description: Directory of municipal government in British Columbia.

REGIE AUTONOME DES TRANSPORTS PARISIENS. BULLETIN DE DOCUMENTATION ET D'INFORMATION. see *TRANSPORTATION*

PUBLIC ADMINISTRATION — MUNICIPAL GOVERNMENT

352   CN
REGIONAL DISTRICT LEGISLATION; a resource manual. base vol. (plus irreg. suppl.). Can.$37.80. Ministry of Municipal Affairs, Recreation and Culture, Victoria, B.C., Canada. (Subscr. to: Crown Publications, 546 Yates St., Victoria, B.C. V8W 1K8, Canada. TEL 604-386-4636) (looseleaf format; back issues avail.)
Description: Assists regional district officials with the implementation of Bill 19.

352   US
RESEARCH IN URBAN ECONOMICS. 1981. a. $63.50 to institutions. J A I Press Inc., 55 Old Post Rd., No. 2, Box 1678, Greenwich, CT 06836-1678. TEL 203-661-7602. Ed. Bob Ebel.

352   BL   ISSN 0034-7604
REVISTA DE ADMINISTRACAO MUNICIPAL. 1954. q. $40. Instituto Brasileiro de Administracao Municipal, Largo IBAM 1, 22282 Rio de Janeiro, RJ, Brazil. TELEX 21-22638 INBM BR. Ed. Francois E. J. de Bremaeker. adv.; bk.rev.; bibl.; illus.; stat.; index, cum.index: 1965-1990; circ. 3,500.
—BLDSC shelfmark: 7835.640000.

352   SP   ISSN 0213-4675
REVISTA DE ESTUDIOS DE ADMINISTRACION LOCAL Y AUTONOMICA. q. 1000 ptas.($3.60) Instituto Nacional de Aministracion Publica, Biblioteca, C. Atocha 106, 28012 Madrid, Spain. bk.rev.; bibl.; index; circ. 3,500.
Formerly: Revista de Estudios de la Vida Local (ISSN 0034-8163)

RHEINLAND-PFALZ. STATISTISCHES LANDESAMT RHEINLAND-PFALZ. STATISTISCHE MONATSHEFTE. see PUBLIC ADMINISTRATION — Abstracting, Bibliographies, Statistics

352   IT
RIVISTA DEL PERSONALE DELL'ENTE LOCALE; bimestrale di normativa e giurisprudenza. 1987. bi-m. L.165000 (effective 1992). Maggioli Editore, Via Crimea, 1, Casella Postale 290, 47037 Rimini, Italy. TEL 0541-626777. FAX 0541-622020. Ed. Carlo Talice.

352   IT   ISSN 0035-6972
RIVISTA DELLA CITTA DI TRIESTE. 1928. m. L.2000. Comune di Trieste, Piazza Unita d'Italia, Trieste, Italy. Ed. Etrusco Carminelli. adv.; charts; illus.; stat.

352 352.7   IT
RIVISTA GIURIDICA DI URBANISTICA; trimestrale di giurisprudenza, dottrina e legislazione. 1985. q. L.100000 to individuals; institutions L.127000(effective 1992). Maggioli Editore, Via Crimea,1, Casella Postale 290, 47037 Rimini, Italy. TEL 0541-626777. FAX 0541-622020. Eds. Leopoldo Mazzarolli, Gherardo Bergonzini.

352   GW
ROSDORFER MITTEILUNGEN; fuer die Gemeinde Rosdorf mit den Ortschaften Atzenhausen, Dahlenrode, Dramfeld, Klein Wiershausen. 1965. w. (Gemeinde Rosdorf) Verlag Otto Schwartz & Co., Annastr. 7, 3400 Goettingen, Germany. TEL 0551-31051. FAX 0551-372812.

352   AU
ST. STEFANER GEMEINDENACHRICHTEN. 1977. q. Gemeinde St. Stefan ob Leoben, Gemeindeamt, A-8713 St. Stefan ob Leoben 126, Austria. FAX 03832-2250. Ed.Bd. circ. 750. (back issues avail.)

357   US
SALARIES AND FRINGE BENEFITS: BENCHMARK EMPLOYEE COMPENSATION REPORT. a. $50 to non-members; members $25. Colorado Municipal League, 1660 Lincoln St., Ste. 2100, Denver, CO 80264. TEL 303-831-6411. FAX 303-860-8175.
Description: Computerized report of employee compensation in municipalities of 3,000 population and over, as well as other jurisdictions, with comparative data of 59 key job classifications. Contains data on salaries, monetary fringe benefits and fringe benefit policies.

352   US
SALARIES AND FRINGE BENEFITS IN COLORADO CITIES AND TOWNS UNDER 3,000 POPULATION. a. $30 to non-members; members $15. Colorado Municipal League, 1660 Lincoln St., Ste. 2100, Denver, CO 80264. TEL 303-831-6411. FAX 303-860-8175.
Description: Survey of municipalities of under 3,000 population providing comparative data in tabular form on positions commonly found in cities and towns of this size. Statistical material is provided in three sections: basic municipal data, salaries, and fringe benefits.

352   US
SALARIES AND FRINGE BENEFITS: MANAGEMENT COMPENSATION REPORT FOR COLORADO CITIES. a. $30 to non-members; members $15. Colorado Municipal League, 1660 Lincoln St., Ste. 2100, Denver, CO 80264. TEL 303-831-6411. FAX 303-860-8175.
Description: Survey of Colorado cities of over 3,000 population providing comparative data in tabular form on 30 executive and administrative positions in three sections: general municipal information; salaries and fringe benefits; and job characteristics.

352   US
SALARIES AND WAGES FOR MICHIGAN MUNICIPALITIES OVER 1,000 POPULATION. 1942. a. $50. Michigan Municipal League, 1675 Green Rd., Box 1487, Ann Arbor, MI 48106. TEL 313-662-3246. (reprint service avail.)
Formed by the merger of: Salaries and Wages for Michigan Municipalities over 4,000 Population; Which was formerly: Salaries, Wages, and Fringe Benefits in Michigan Municipalities over 4,000 Population (ISSN 0080-5548) & Salaries and Wages for Michigan Municipalities under 4,000 Population. Which was formerly: Salaries and Wages for Michigan Villages and Cities 1,000-4,000 Population; Salaries, Wages and Fringe Benefits for Michigan Villages and Cities 1,000-4,000 Population (ISSN 0077-216X).

352 320   US
SAN DIEGO POLITICAL WATCH. 1987. s-m. $150. 4209 Alder Dr., San Diego, CA 92116. TEL 619-282-6582. FAX 619-282-9606. Ed. Jackie Main. circ. 150.
Formerly: Neil Good's San Diego Report.
Description: Reports on politics in city and county of San Diego.

352   CN   ISSN 0581-8435
JS1721.S3
SASKATCHEWAN MUNICIPAL DIRECTORY. 1909. a. Can.$10. Saskatchewan Community Services, 2151 Scarth St., Regina, Sask. S4P 3V7, Canada. TEL 306-787-2635. FAX 306-787-8748. Ed. Irene Rau. circ. 6,500.

SCANDINAVIAN ATLAS OF HISTORIC TOWNS. see HISTORY — History Of Europe

357   US
SEARCHLIGHT ON THE CITY COUNCIL. irreg. (6-8/yr.). membership. Citizens Union Foundation, Inc., 198 Broadway, New York, NY 10038. TEL 212-227-0342. FAX 212-227-0345. Dir. Jeannette Kahlenberg.

SEMINARS DIRECTORY; a guide to approximately 10,000 seminars and workshops held in the United States and Canada on subjects of interest to business, industry, and government. see BUSINESS AND ECONOMICS — Trade And Industrial Directories

352   IT
SERVIZI PUBBLICI LOCALI. 1972. 11/yr. L.40000. Confederazione Italiana dei Servizi Pubblici degli Enti Locali, Piazza Cola di Rienzo 80, Rome 00192, Italy. bk.rev.; bibl.
Formerly (until Jan. 1978): Notiziario Interfederale.

352   US
SISTER CITY NEWS. 1961. bi-m. $10. (Sister Cities International) Town Affiliation Association of the U.S., Inc., 120 S. Payne St., Alexandria, VA 22314. TEL 703-836-3535. FAX 703-836-4815. TELEX 4015655. Ed. Richard Oakland. adv.; bk.rev.; stat.; circ. 14,500. (tabloid format)
Formerly: T A A Newsletter (ISSN 0300-6166)

352   CI   ISSN 0037-7104
SLUZBENE NOVINE OPCINE KARLOVAC. 1964. irreg. 150 din. Skupstina Opcine Karlovac, Banjavciceva 9, Karlovac, Croatia. Ed. Vladimir Funduk.

352   CI   ISSN 0037-7120
SLUZBENI GLASNIK OPCINE ROVINJ. (Text in Croatian, Italian) 1964. irreg. 30 din. Skupstina Opcine Rovinj, Ul. Matteotti 1-1, Rovinj, Croatia. Ed. Marija Matosovic.

352   CI   ISSN 0037-7155
SLUZBENI VJESNIK OPCINE BUJE, NOVIGRAD I UMAG. (Text in Croatian, Italian) 1965. fortn. 300 din. Socijalisticki Savez Radnog Naroda Opcine Buje Novigrad i Umag, Partizanska 2, Buje, Croatia. Ed. Nada Silic.

352   CI   ISSN 0037-7163
SLUZBENI VJESNIK OPCINE KRIZEVCI. 1965. a? 200 din. Skupstina Opcine Krizevci, Ivana Zakmardija Dinakovveckog 12, Krizevci, Croatia. Ed. Branko Tinodi. circ. 200.

352.1   SA   ISSN 0038-2779
HJ9103
SOUTH AFRICAN TREASURER/SUID-AFRIKAANSE TESOURIER. (Text in Afrikaans, English) 1929. m. R.36. Institute of Municipal Treasurers and Accountants, P.O. Box 8652, Johannesburg 2000, South Africa. FAX 011-491-8346. Ed. J.R.J. Bosch. adv.; bk.rev.; charts; illus.; mkt.; pat.; tr.mk.; index; circ. 1,500. Indexed: Ind.S.A.Per.
Description: Promotes the interest of local government in the financial and allied fields.

352   US   ISSN 0300-6182
SOUTH DAKOTA MUNICIPALITIES. 1938. m. $20. South Dakota Municipal League, 214 E. Capitol, Pierre, SD 57501. TEL 605-224-8654. Ed. Aaron K. Trippler. adv.; bk.rev.; circ. 2,700. (tabloid format)

352   US
SOUTHERN CITY. a. $6. North Carolina League of Municipalities, Box 3069, 215 N. Dawson St., Raleigh, NC 27603. TEL 919-834-1311. FAX 919-733-9519. Ed. Margot F. Christensen. adv.; charts; illus.; circ. 5,550.

352   GW
SPEKTRUM (MAINZ); Veranstaltungs- und Kongressinformation der Landeshauptstadt Mainz. 1973. q. free. Kongressdirektion Mainz, Rheinstr. 66, 6500 Mainz 1, Germany. TEL 06131-242-0. FAX 06131-242105. adv.; circ. 10,000.

352   US   ISSN 0038-7711
SPOKANE, WASHINGTON. OFFICIAL GAZETTE. 1910? w. $2.35. City of Spokane, Washington, City Clerk, Municipal Bldg., 5th Fl., W. 808 Spokane Falls Blvd., Spokane, WA 99201-3333. TEL 509-456-4350. FAX 509-458-4003. Ed. Marilyn J. Montgomery. circ. 521.

352   AU   ISSN 0038-8939
STADLINGER POST. 1952. a. S.10. Gemeindeamt, A-4651 Stadl-Paura, Austria. Ed. Friedrich Urbanek. adv.; abstr.; stat.; circ. 900.

STADSBYGGNAD. see ENGINEERING — Civil Engineering

352   GW
STADT BAMBERG. MITTEILUNGSBLATT; Amtsblatt der Stadt Bamberg. 1945. s-m. DM.33.60. St. Otto Verlag GmbH, Laubanger 23, 8600 Bamberg, Germany. TEL 0951-79020. circ. 2,450.

352   GW
STADT DUISBURG. MATERIALEN ZUR STADTFORSCHUNG. 1977. irreg. Amt fuer Statistik, Der Oberstadtdirektor, Bismarckstr. 150-158, 4100 Duisburg 1, Germany. TEL 0203-2833085. FAX 0203-2834404.

352   GW   ISSN 0038-9048
JS41
DER STAEDTETAG; Zeitschrift fuer Praxis und Wissenschaft der kommunalen Verwaltung. 1948. m. DM.179.80. (Verband Kommunaler Stadtreinigungsbetriebe) W. Kohlhammer GmbH, Hessbruehlstr. 69, Postfach 800430, 7000 Stuttgart 80, Germany. TEL 0711-7863-1. adv.; bk.rev.; charts; illus.; index, cum.index; circ. 4,200. **Indexed:** Dok.Str., Excerp.Med., P.A.I.S.For.Lang.Ind.
—BLDSC shelfmark: 8426.275000.

PUBLIC ADMINISTRATION — MUNICIPAL GOVERNMENT

350 320   US   ISSN 0160-323X
JK2403
STATE AND LOCAL GOVERNMENT REVIEW; a journal of research and viewpoints on state and local government issues. 1968. 3/yr. $12 to individuals; institutions $18. University of Georgia, Carl Vinson Institute of Government, Terrell Hall, Athens, GA 30602. TEL 404-542-2736. FAX 404-542-9301. Ed. Richard W. Campbell. circ. 1,000. (back issues avail.) Indexed: A.B.C.Pol.Sci., P.A.I.S., Sage Pub.Admin.Abstr., Sage Urb.Stud.Abstr.
—BLDSC shelfmark: 8437.603000.
Supersedes: Georgia Government Review (ISSN 0016-8289)

338   US   ISSN 0276-7163
JK2482.E94
STATE EXECUTIVE DIRECTORY. 1980. 3/yr. $160. Carroll Publishing Company, 1058 Thomas Jefferson St., N.W., Washington, DC 20007. TEL 202-333-8620. FAX 202-337-7020.
Description: Directory of key officials in executive and legislative branches of state governments in the United States.

338   US   ISSN 1056-7011
STATE EXECUTIVE DIRECTORY ANNUAL. a. $127. Carroll Publishing Company, 1058 Thomas Jefferson St., N.W., Washington, DC 20007. TEL 202-333-8620. FAX 202-337-7020.
Description: Includes over 37,200 contacts with name, office address and phone number in the executive and legislative branches of state government.

352   US
STATE MUNICIPAL LEAGUE DIRECTORY. a. $25. National League of Cities, 1301 Pennsylvania Ave., N.W., Washington, DC 20004. TEL 202-626-3000. FAX 202-626-3043.
Description: Guide to the operations and functions of state municipal associations.

STATISTICS RELATING TO REGIONAL AND MUNICIPAL GOVERNMENTS IN BRITISH COLUMBIA. see *PUBLIC ADMINISTRATION — Abstracting, Bibliographies, Statistics*

STATISTISCHE MONATSHEFTE SCHLESWIG-HOLSTEIN. see *PUBLIC ADMINISTRATION — Abstracting, Bibliographies, Statistics*

STATISTISCHER BERICHT DER STADT FRANKENTHAL. see *PUBLIC ADMINISTRATION — Abstracting, Bibliographies, Statistics*

STATISTISCHER VIERTELJAHRESBERICHT HANNOVER. see *PUBLIC ADMINISTRATION — Abstracting, Bibliographies, Statistics*

STATISTISCHES JAHRBUCH DER STADT KOELN. see *PUBLIC ADMINISTRATION — Abstracting, Bibliographies, Statistics*

STATISTISCHES JAHRBUCH DEUTSCHER GEMEINDEN. see *PUBLIC ADMINISTRATION — Abstracting, Bibliographies, Statistics*

352   SW   ISSN 0039-0712
STATSANSTAELLD. 1971. w. (23/yr.). SEK 90. Statsanstaelldas Foerbund, Barnhusgatan 10, Stockholm, Sweden. TEL 08-7914100. FAX 08-211694. Ed. Ingvar Ygeman. adv.; bk.rev.; charts; illus.; tr.lit.; circ. 210,941.

352   UK
STRATHCLYDE REPORT. 1974. q. Strathclyde Regional Council, Public Relations Department, Strathclyde House, 20 India St., Glasgow G2 4PF, Scotland. Ed. Henry D.M. Dutch. adv.; circ. 953,000. (tabloid format; back issues avail.)

352.7   US
SUMMERVILLE POST. 1976. q. $10. Summerville Neighborhood Association Inc., Box 12212, Augusta, GA 30914-2212. Ed. J. Marsella Shurtleff. adv.; illus.; circ. 2,365.

352   FI   ISSN 0039-5544
SUOMEN KUNNALLISLEHTI. Swedish edition: Finlands Kommunaltidskrift (ISSN 0355-6093) (Text in Finnish) 1916. 20/yr. FIM 300. Suomen Kaupunkiliitto - Association of Finnish Cities, Toinen Linja 14, 00530 Helsinki 53, Finland. FAX 7712271. Ed. Hannu Taavitsainen. adv.; bk.rev.; charts; illus.; stat.; index; circ. 8,285.
—BLDSC shelfmark: 8543.600000.
Description: Covers municipal legislation and research in all areas of public administration in Finland.

352   IC
SVEITASTJORNARMAL. bi-m. Laugavegur 105, Reykjavik, Iceland. adv.; circ. 4,800.

352   GW
SZENE REMSCHEID. m. DM.24. R G A Buchverlag, Konrad-Adenauer-Str. 2-4, 5630 Remscheid, Germany. TEL 02191-209-0. FAX 02191-209-180. bk.rev.; circ. 10,000. (back issues avail.)

363.61   FR   ISSN 0299-7258
CODEN: TSMREA
TECHNIQUES - SCIENCES - METHODES. GENIE URBAIN RURAL. (Text in French; summaries in English) 1905. m. 470 F. (foreign 525 F.). Association Generale des Hygienistes et Techniciens Municipaux, 9 rue de Phalsbourg, 75017 Paris Cedex 17, France. TEL 44-15-15-50. FAX 43-80-65-90. Ed. J. Gillet. adv.; bk.rev.; abstr.; illus.; index; circ. 4,000. (tabloid format; back issues avail.) Indexed: Acid Pre.Dig., Acid Rain Abstr., Acid Rain Ind., Environ.Abstr., Fluidex, Ocean.Abstr., Pollut.Abstr., W.R.C.Inf.
—BLDSC shelfmark: 8745.345000.
Formerly (until 1986): Techniques et Sciences Municipales Eau (ISSN 0151-6973)

352   US
TENNESSEE GOVERNMENT OFFICIALS DIRECTORY. 1985. a. $27. M. Lee Smith Publishers & Printers, 162 Fourth Ave. N., Box 2678, Nashville, TN 37219. TEL 615-242-7395. FAX 615-256-6601. Ed. Joseph L. White.
Description: Lists all state, county and city officials including: government officials and chambers of commerce, Tennessee colleges and universities, business and professional associations, lobbyists, Capitol Hill press corps and Tennessee newspapers, magazines, radio and TV stations.

352   US
TENNESSEE PUBLIC WORKS. bi-m. Images Publications, 501 Mulberry St., Loudon, TN 37774. TEL 615-458-3560. FAX 615-458-4095. Ed. Frank Kirk. circ. 1,900.

352   US   ISSN 0040-3415
JS39
TENNESSEE TOWN AND CITY. 1950. s-m. $10. Tennessee Municipal League, 226 Capitol Blvd., Nashville, TN 37219. TEL 615-255-6416. FAX 615-255-4752. Ed. Beverly Bruninga. adv.; bk.rev.; bibl.; illus.; index; circ. 5,072. Indexed: P.A.I.S.
Description: Covers municipal and state government and plitics.

352 711   FR   ISSN 0223-5951
TERRITOIRES - CORRESPONDANCE MUNICIPALE. 1958. m. 450 F. Association pour la Democratie et l'Education Locale et Sociale, 108, rue Saint-Maur, 75011 Paris, France. Ed. Bernard Deljarrie. adv.; bk.rev.; bibl.; cum.index: 1968-1985; circ. 6,000. (also avail. in microfiche)
Formerly: Correspondance Municipale.

TIDINGS. see *SPORTS AND GAMES — Outdoor Life*

352 330.9   JA
▼**TOKYO INDUSTRY;** a graphic overview. (Text in English) 1990. a. Tokyo Metropolitan Government, Bureau of Citizens and Cultural Affairs, International Communication Division, Liaison and Protocol Section, 8-1 Nishishinjuku 2-chome, Shinjuku-ku, Tokyo 163-01, Japan. TEL 03-5388-3172. FAX 03-5388-1329. charts; stat.
Description: Provides information on characteristics and trends in the Tokyo economy, structural adjustment, manufacturing, wholesale, retail, and service industries, and agriculture, forestry, and fishing.

352   JA
DS896
TOKYO METROPOLITAN NEWS. (Editions in Chinese, English, French, Korean) 1951. q. free to public administrations. Tokyo Metropolitan Government, Bureau of Citizens and Cultural Affairs, Liaison and Protocol Section, 8-1 Nishishinjuku 2-chome, Shinjuku-ku, Tokyo 163-01, Japan. TEL 03-5388-3172. FAX 03-5388-1329. Ed.Bd. charts; illus.; stat.; circ. 5,000. Indexed: Geo.Abstr., P.A.I.S.
Formerly: Tokyo Municipal News (ISSN 0040-893X)

352 600   JA
TOKYO-TO SHIKEN KENKYU KIKAN NO KENKYU KEIKAKU. (Text in Japanese) a. Tokyo-to Somu-kyoku, Somu-bu - Tokyo Metropolitan Government, Bureau of General Affairs, General Affairs Division, 5-1 Marunouchi 3-chome, Chiyoda-ku, Tokyo 100, Japan.
Description: Publicizes the plans of research institutions under the Tokyo Metropolitan Government.

352   US   ISSN 0040-9065
TOLEDO CITY JOURNAL. 1916. w. $18. City of Toledo, One Government Center, Ste. 2140, Toledo, OH 43604. TEL 419-245-1065. Ed. Larry J. Brewer. adv.; circ. 1,000.

352   JA
TOSHI MONDAI/MUNICIPAL PROBLEMS. (Text in Japanese) 1925. m. 7800 Yen. Tokyo Institute for Municipal Research, Hibiya Koen 1-3, Chiyoda-ku, Tokyo 100, Japan. TEL 03-3591-1201. FAX 03-3591-1209. Ed. Hiroshi Toki. adv.; bk.rev.; bibl.; circ. 2,800.

352   US
TOTAL COMPENSATION REPORT. a. $20 to non-members; members $10. Colorado Municipal League, 1660 Lincoln St., Sta. 2100, Denver, CO 80264. TEL 303-831-6411.
Description: Computerized report of employee compensation plus monetary fringe benefits and the dollar value of non-monetary fringe benefits. Contains comparative data for 59 key job classifications in municipalities of 3,000 population and over and other jurisdictions.

352   US   ISSN 0748-5883
TOWN CRIER. 1984. q. National Association of Towns and Townships, National Center for Small Communities, 1522 K St., N.W., Ste. 600, Washington, DC 20005. TEL 202-737-5200. Ed. Ronnie Kweller.
Description: News about the research and educational programs for America's grassroots governments offered by the center.

352   AT   ISSN 0040-9995
LAW
TOWN PLANNING AND LOCAL GOVERNMENT GUIDE. 1956. m. Aus.$178. Law Book Co. Ltd., Head Office, 44-50 Waterloo Rd., North Ryde, N.S.W. 2113, Australia. TEL 02-887-0177. FAX 02-888-9706. TELEX ASBOOK 27995. Ed. Ken Gifford. bk.rev.
—BLDSC shelfmark: 8872.300000.

TRIBUNA DELL'IRPINIA; settimanale di attualita. see *BUSINESS AND ECONOMICS*

352   US   ISSN 1049-2119
JS39
U S MAYOR. 1934. bi-w. (24/yr.) $35. United States Conference of Mayors, 1620 Eye St., N.W., Washington, DC 20006. TEL 202-293-7330. Ed. Nicole Klimov. illus.; circ. 5,000. (back issues avail.)
Former titles: Mayor; United States Municipal News (ISSN 0041-7955)

353   FR
U T O NEWS. bi-m. United Towns Organization, 22, rue d'Alsace, 92300 Levallois, France.

352   US
UNITED STATES CONFERENCE OF MAYORS. ANNUAL MEETING; official policy resolutions. a. $10. United States Conference of Mayors, 1620 Eye St., N.W., Washington, DC 20006. TEL 202-293-7330.

PUBLIC ADMINISTRATION — PUBLIC FINANCE, TAXATION

352   US
UNITED STATES CONFERENCE OF MAYORS. PROJECTS AND SERVICES. irreg. free to qualified personnel. United States Conference of Mayors, 1620 Eye St., N.W., Washington, DC 20006. TEL 202-293-7330.
Description: Offers a variety of services, news and information covering a wide range of issues.

352   US
UNIVERSITY OF ILLINOIS. INSTITUTE OF GOVERNMENT AND PUBLIC AFFAIRS. WORKING PAPERS. 1987. irreg. University of Illinois, Urbana-Champaign Campus, Institute of Government and Public Affairs, 1201 W. Nevada St., Urbana, IL 61801. TEL 217-333-3340. Ed. Peter F. Nardulli.

352   PH
UNIVERSITY OF THE PHILIPPINES. COLLEGE OF PUBLIC ADMINISTRATION. LOCAL GOVERNMENT STUDIES. (Text in English) 1962. irreg. University of the Philippines, College of Public Administration, Local Government Center, PARDEC-SAAC Building, P.O. Box 198, Don Mariano Marcos Avenue, U.P.Diliman, Quezon City, Philippines. TEL 95-13-65. TELEX CPAUP.

352   XV   ISSN 0042-0778
URADNI VESTNIK OBCIN ORMOZ IN PTUJ. (Text in Slovenian) 1964. irreg. free. Radio-Tednik, Raiceva 6, Ptuj, Slovenia. FAX 062-771-223. Ed. Marica Fajt. circ. 11,000.

342.73   US   ISSN 0195-7686
KF5300
URBAN, STATE, AND LOCAL LAW NEWSLETTER. 1978. 4/yr. membership only. American Bar Association, Urban, State, and Local Government Law Section, 750 N. Lake Shore Dr., Chicago, IL 60611. TEL 312-988-5000. FAX 312-988-6281. Ed. James Baird. (reprint service avail.) *Indexed:* C.L.I., L.R.I.
Formerly (1978 only): State, Local, and Urban Law Newsletter (ISSN 0163-2922)
Description: Informs members on the section's activities and legal issues.

352   US   ISSN 0884-6421
KFU38
UTAH STATE DIGEST. 1985. s-m. $30. Department of Administrative Services, Division of Administrative Rules, Salt Lake City, UT 84114. Ed. Randy J. Fisher. circ. 400.
● Also available online.

352   GW
VERBANDSGEMEINDE EDENKOBEN. AMTSBLATT. 1980. w. free. Verbandsgemeinde Edenkoben, c/o Manfred Horn, Am Bachweg 3, 6732 Edenkoben, Germany. TEL 06323-80826. FAX 06323-80899. adv.; circ. 8,000. (back issues avail.)

VEREIN FUER DIE GESCHICHTE BERLINS. MITTEILUNGEN. see HISTORY — History Of Europe

352   AT   ISSN 0049-6170
VICTORIAN MUNICIPAL DIRECTORY.* 1866. s-a. Aus.$16. per no. Arnall & Jackson Pty. Ltd., 390 Barkly St., Brunswick, Vic. 3056, Australia.

352   US
VIRGINIA REVIEW. 1923. bi-m. (plus special suppl. 3-4/yr.). $14. Review Publications, Inc., Box 860, Chester, VA 23831-0860. TEL 804-748-6351. FAX 804-796-6931. Ed. A. Taylor-White. adv.; bk.rev.; illus.; circ. 3,000.
Formerly: Virginia Municipal Review (ISSN 0042-6660)

352   US   ISSN 0042-6784
JS39
VIRGINIA TOWN & CITY. 1924. m. $8. Virginia Municipal League, Box 12164, Richmond, VA 23241-0164. FAX 804-343-3758. Ed. Christine A. Everson. adv.; bk.rev.; charts; illus.; circ. 5,000.
Formerly (until 1966): Virginia Municipal Review.
Description: Features include commentary and a marketplace, product and service guide.

352   AU   ISSN 0003-2247
WELS, STADT. AMTSBLATT. 1962. m. free. Magistrat der Stadt Wels, A-4600 Wels, Austria. Ed. Wolfgang Groebner. adv.; bk.rev.; charts; illus.; stat.; circ. 23,500. (looseleaf format)

352   US   ISSN 0279-5337
TD1
WESTERN CITY. 1925. m. $15. League of California Cities, 1400 K St., Sacramento, CA 95814. TEL 916-444-5790. Ed. Victoria Clark. adv.; bk.rev.; illus.; index; circ. 9,500. *Indexed:* Cal.Per.Ind. (1978-), Hist.Abstr., P.A.I.S., Urb.Aff.Abstr.

352   CN
WESTERN MUNICIPAL PRODUCT NEWS. 1977. q. Can.$8($8) Hibernia Marketing Services, 200 Rivercrest Drive S.E., No. 240, Calgary, Alta. T2C 2X5, Canada. TEL 403-279-5151. FAX 403-236-7298. Ed. Jerry Skinner. adv.; bk.rev.; circ. 9,940. (tabloid format; back issues avail.)
Description: Covers products of interest to municipal officials in Western Canada.

352   US
WHAT'S HAPPENING FOR COMMUNITY LEADERS. (Includes irreg. supplements) 1976. m. free. Omaha - Council Bluffs Metropolitan Area Planning Agency, 2222 Cuming St., Omaha, NE 68102-4328. TEL 402-444-6866. FAX 402-342-0949. circ. 1,000.
Description: Regional data, development and public interest news for Douglas, Sarpy and Washington counties in Nebraska, Mills and Pottawattamie counties in Iowa.

352   AU
WIENER NEUSTADT. AMTSBLATT DER STATUTARSTADT. 1921. m. S.180. Magistrat, Rathaus, A-2700 Wiener Neustadt, Austria. Ed. Franz Pinczolits. adv.; circ. 19,595.
Formerly: Wiener Neustadt. Amtsblatt der Stadt (ISSN 0003-2255)
Description: Local government publication covering news and information, politics, education, commerce and industry, culture and sport. Includes reports and announcements of events and exhibitions.

352   GW
WIR BEI DER STADT. 1986. q. Stadt Nuernberg, Presse- und Informationsamt, Rathausplatz 2, 8500 Nuernberg 1, Germany. TEL 0911-2312252. FAX 0911-2313660. Ed. N. Schuergers. circ. 15,000.

352   US   ISSN 0749-6818
WISCONSIN COUNTIES. 1938. m. $19.50. Wisconsin Counties Association, 802 W. Broadway, No. 308, Madison, WI 53713-1897. Ed. Mark M. Rogacki. adv.; circ. 3,450.

WONEN EN MILIEU - VAKMATIG. see HOUSING AND URBAN PLANNING

352   US
YOUR REGION. 1967. m. free. North Central Texas Council of Governments, P.O. Drawer COG, Arlington, TX 76005-5888. TEL 817-640-3300. FAX 817-640-7806. Ed. Edwina J. Shires. bk.rev.; bibl.; circ. 5,000.
Formerly: Your Region in Action (ISSN 0049-8432)
Description: Covers activities of the Council in the 16 county Dallas-Forth Worth region.

352   GW
ZEILBERG-ECHO. 1977. w. DM.24.80. (Marktgemeinde Maroldsweisach) Linus-Wittich Verlag, Peter-Henlein-Str. 1, D-8550 Forchheim, Germany. TEL 09191-1624.

PUBLIC FINANCE, TAXATION

see Business and Economics–Public Finance, Taxation

PUBLIC HEALTH AND SAFETY

see also Birth Control; Fire Prevention; Funerals

614   US
A A W H QUARTERLY. 1953. q. $25 includes membership to individuals; libraries $250. American Association for World Health, 1129 20th St., N.W., Ste. 400, Washington, DC 20036. TEL 202-265-0286. Ed. William L. Wittenberg. bk.rev.; circ. 1,000. (back issues avail.)
Former titles: World Health News; American Association for World Health News.
Description: Focuses on current international health issues.

A C P M NEWS. (American College of Preventive Medicine) see MEDICAL SCIENCES

614   UN   ISSN 0250-8621
A F R O TECHNICAL PAPERS. French edition: Cahiers Techniques A F R O (ISSN 0250-8397) 1970. irreg. 2-4/yr. World Health Organization, Regional Office for Africa - Organisation Mondiale de la Sante. Bureau Regional de l'Afrique, B.P. No.6, Brazzaville, Congo. *Indexed:* Rural Recreat.Tour.Abstr., World Agri.Econ.& Rural Sociol.Abstr.
—BLDSC shelfmark: 0735.526500.

614   UN   ISSN 0250-8443
A F R O TECHNICAL REPORT SERIES. French edition: Serie de Rapports Techniques A F R O (ISSN 0250-8567) 1976. irreg. 3-4/yr. World Health Organization, Regional Office for Africa - Organisation Mondiale de la Sante. Bureau Regional de l'Afrique, P.O. Box 6, Brazzaville, Congo.

A H C A NOTES. (American Health Care Association) see SOCIAL SERVICES AND WELFARE

A I D S & PUBLIC POLICY JOURNAL. see MEDICAL SCIENCES — Communicable Diseases

A I D S INFORMATION EXCHANGE. see MEDICAL SCIENCES — Communicable Diseases

614.8 360   US   ISSN 0275-8407
A M S STUDIES IN MODERN SOCIETY. 1972. irreg., no.22, 1990. price varies. A M S Press, Inc., 56 E. 13th St., New York, NY 10003. TEL 212-777-4700. FAX 212-995-5413. (back issues avail.)
Description: Monographs, reference works and bibliographies on contemporary social issues.

614.8 301.16   US   ISSN 0001-2165
A P C O BULLETIN. 1935. m. $50. Associated Public-Safety Communications Officers Inc., 2040 S. Ridgewood Ave., Ste. 102, Oaytona Beach, FL 32119-2257. TEL 904-322-2500. FAX 904-322-2501. Ed. Alan Chase. adv.; bk.rev.; circ. 9,600. (back issues avail.)

A P S S NEWSLETTER. (Association of Professional Sleep Societies) see MEDICAL SCIENCES — Psychiatry And Neurology

614.8   AT   ISSN 1037-3403
ABORIGINAL AND ISLANDER HEALTH WORKER JOURNAL ; a national resource journal for aboriginal and islander community education workers. 1977. 6/yr. Aus.$26 to individuals; institutions Aus.$30. (Department of Aboriginal Affairs) Aboriginal and Islander Health Worker, P.O. Box 502, Matraville, N.S.W. 2036, Australia. TEL 02-311-3256. FAX 02-311-3393. Ed. Rose Ellis. adv.: B&W page $800; adv. contact: Rose Ellis. circ. 4,500. (back issues avail.)
Former titles: Aboriginal and Islander Health Worker & Aboriginal Health Worker (ISSN 0155-0357)

PUBLIC HEALTH AND SAFETY

614.8 US ISSN 0001-4575
HV675.A1 CODEN: AAPVB5
ACCIDENT ANALYSIS & PREVENTION. 1969. 6/yr. £265 (effective 1992). Pergamon Press, Inc., Journals Division, 660 White Plains Rd., Tarrytown, NY 10591-5153. TEL 914-524-9200. FAX 914-333-2444. (And: Headington Hill Hall, Oxford OX3 0BW, England. TEL 0865-794141) Ed. Frank A. Haight. adv.; bk.rev.; charts; illus. (also avail. in microform from MIM,UMI; back issues avail.) **Indexed:** ASCA, Biol.Abstr., C.I.S. Abstr., Curr.Cont., Ergon.Abstr., Excerp.Med., HRIS, Intl.Civil Eng.Abstr., Psychol.Abstr., Psycscan, Risk Abstr., Soft.Abstr.Eng., SSCI.
—BLDSC shelfmark: 0573.130000.
Description: Discusses industrial safety.
Refereed Serial

614.8 US ISSN 0148-6039
HA217
ACCIDENT FACTS. a. $18.95. National Safety Council, Industrial Section, 444 N. Michigan Ave., Chicago, IL 60611-3991. TEL 800-621-7619. **Indexed:** SRI.

ADMINISTRATION AND POLICY IN MENTAL HEALTH. see *MEDICAL SCIENCES*

AFRICA MEDICINE AND HEALTH. see *MEDICAL SCIENCES*

614 GW ISSN 0172-2131
AKADEMIE FUER OEFFENTLICHES GESUNDHEITSWESEN. SCHRIFTENREIHE. 1973. irrege. price varies. Akademie fuer Oeffentliches Gesundheitswesen, Auf'm Hennekamp 70, 4000 Duesseldorf 1, Germany.
Formerly: Akademie fuer Staatsmedizin, Duesseldorf. Jahrbuch (ISSN 0065-5392)

613 US ISSN 0145-6857
ALABAMA'S HEALTH. 1967. m. free. Department of Public Health, 434 Monroe St., Rm. 557, Montgomery, AL 36131-1701.
TEL 205-242-5790. FAX 205-240-3097. Ed. Arrol Sheehan. bk.rev.; circ. 2,200.
Description: Describes events and topics of interest to public health professionals.

ALBERTA. DEPARTMENT OF FAMILY AND SOCIAL SERVICES. ANNUAL REPORT. see *SOCIAL SERVICES AND WELFARE*

ALBERTA. HEALTH AND SOCIAL SERVICES DISCIPLINES COMMITTEE. ANNUAL REPORT. see *SOCIAL SERVICES AND WELFARE*

614.8 CN
ALBERTA PUBLIC SAFETY SERVICES. AGENCY INSIGHT. 1973. q. $20. Alberta Public Safety Services, 10320 146th St., Edmonton, Alta. T5N 3A2, Canada. TEL 403-427-2772. FAX 403-451-7199. Ed. Bonnie Shulman. bk.rev.; charts; illus.; tr.lit.; circ. 7,000.
Formed by the merger of: Alberta Public Safety Services News and Notes; Which was formerly: Alberta Public Safety Services. Hot Line; Alberta Disaster Services News and Notes (ISSN 0702-3138); Which was formerly: Alberta Disaster Services. Hot Line.

AMBIENTE RISORSE SALUTE; scienza, tecnica e cultura per una strategia ambientale. see *ENVIRONMENTAL STUDIES*

AMBULANCE INDUSTRY JOURNAL. see *BUSINESS AND ECONOMICS — Trade And Industrial Directories*

360 NO
AMBULANSEFORUM; tidsskrift for ambulanse og redningtjeneste. 1976. q. NOK 165. Box 51, Taasen, 0801 Oslo 8, Norway. adv.; bk.rev.; circ. 1,800.

AMERICAN COLLEGE OF TOXICOLOGY. JOURNAL. PART A. see *ENVIRONMENTAL STUDIES — Toxicology And Environmental Safety*

AMERICAN COLLEGE OF TOXICOLOGY. JOURNAL. PART B; acute toxicity data. see *PHARMACY AND PHARMACOLOGY*

AMERICAN HEALTH CARE ASSOCIATION. PROVIDER. see *SOCIAL SERVICES AND WELFARE*

AMERICAN HOSPITAL ASSOCIATION GUIDE TO THE HEALTH CARE FIELD. see *HOSPITALS — Abstracting, Bibliographies, Statistics*

613.2 US ISSN 0890-1171
CODEN: AJHPED
AMERICAN JOURNAL OF HEALTH PROMOTION. Short title: A J H P. 1986. bi-m. $49.50 in Canada & Mexico $54; Europe $67; elsewhere $78. Michael P. O'Donnell, Ed. & Pub., 1812 S Rochester Rd., Ste. 200, Rochester Hills, MI 48307-3532. TEL 313-650-9600. adv.; bk.rev.; film rev.; abstr.; charts; stat.; circ. 7,300. (back issues avail.) **Indexed:** ABI Inform., Access, Excerp.Med., Human Resour.Abstr., PSI, Psychol.Abstr., Sage Fam.Stud.Abstr.
—BLDSC shelfmark: 0824.760000.
Description: Covers the science and art of helping people change their lifestyle to move toward a state of optimal health.
Refereed Serial

AMERICAN JOURNAL OF PHARMACY (1981); and the sciences supporting public health. see *PHARMACY AND PHARMACOLOGY*

AMERICAN JOURNAL OF PREVENTIVE MEDICINE. see *MEDICAL SCIENCES*

614 US ISSN 0090-0036
RA421 CODEN: AJHEAA
AMERICAN JOURNAL OF PUBLIC HEALTH. 1911. m. $80 to individuals (foreign $120); institutions $160 (foreign $240). American Public Health Association, 1015 15th St., N.W., Washington, DC 20005. TEL 202-789-5600. Ed. Dr. Michael Ibrahim. adv.; charts; illus.; index; circ. 35,000. (also avail. in microform from UMI,MIM,PMC) **Indexed:** Abstr.Anthropol., Abstr.Health Care Manage.Stud., Abstr.Hyg., Abstr.Soc.Geront., Acad.Ind., ASSIA, Behav.Med.Abstr., Bibl.Dev.Med.& Child Neur., Biol.Abstr., Biol.Dig., C.I.J.E., C.I.N.L., C.I.S. Abstr., Chem.Abstr., CLOA, Curr.Adv.Cancer Res., Curr.Adv.Ecol.Sci., Curr.Cont., Curr.Lit.Fam.Plan., Curr.Tit.Dent., Dairy Sci.Abstr., Deep Sea Res.& Oceanogr.Abstr., Dent.Abstr., Dent.Ind., Dok.Arbeitsmed., Environ.Per.Bibl., Excerp.Med., Food Sci.& Tech.Abstr., Gen.Sci.Ind., Helminthol.Abstr., Hlth.Ind., Hosp.Lit.Ind., HRIS, Human Resour.Abstr., I.P.A., Ind.Med., Ind.Sci.Rev., Ind.Vet., INIS Atomind., Int.Nurs.Ind., Irr.& Drain.Abstr., Med.Care Rev., Medsoc, NRN, Nucl.Sci.Abstr., Nutr.Abstr., Ocean.Abstr., P.A.I.S., Phys.Ed.Ind., Popul.Ind., Protozool.Abstr., Res.High.Educ.Abstr., Risk Abstr., Rural Recreat.Tour.Abstr., Saf.Sci.Abstr., Sage Fam.Stud.Abstr., Sci.Cit.Ind., Sel.Water Res.Abstr., Small Anim.Abstr., Soc.Sci.Ind., Soc.Work.Res.& Abstr., Sp.Ed.Needs Abstr., SSCI, Stud.Wom.Abstr., Trop.Dis.Bull., Vet.Bull., W.R.C.Inf., World Agri.Econ.& Rural Sociol.Abstr.
• Also available online. Vendor(s): BRS, BRS/Saunders Colleague.
—BLDSC shelfmark: 0835.900000.
Formerly: American Journal of Public Health and the Nation's Health (ISSN 0002-9572)
Description: Contains reports of original research, demonstrations, evaluations, and other articles covering current aspects of public health.
Refereed Serial

628 US ISSN 0066-068X
AMERICAN SOCIETY OF SANITARY ENGINEERING. YEAR BOOK. 1906. a. $10 each per 2-part book. American Society of Sanitary Engineering, c/o Gael H. Dunn, Ed., Box 40362, Bay Village, OH 44140. TEL 216-835-3040. FAX 216-835-3488. adv.; cum.index: 1906-1950, 1951-1963, 1963-1970; circ. 2,700.
—BLDSC shelfmark: 9376.000000.

614.85 US
AMERISURE SAFETY NEWS. 1921. q. free to policyholders. Michigan Mutual Insurance Co., 28 W. Adams, Detroit, MI 48226. TEL 313-965-8600. FAX 313-965-7787. (Co-sponsor: Amerisure Companies) Ed. Judith Willis. circ. 5,000. (tabloid format; back issues avail.)
Former titles: Michigan Mutual Safety News; Amerisure Companies Safety News; Shopman.
Description: Provides safety tips for use in the home, on the road and at the workplace.

AMTSBLATT DES KREISES WESEL; Amtliches Verkuendungsblatt. see *PUBLIC ADMINISTRATION — Municipal Government*

614.8 AO
ANGOLA. SECRETARIA PROVINCIAL DE SAUDE, TRABALHO. PREVIDENCIA E ASSISTENCIA. SINTESE DA ACTIVIDADE DOS SERVICOS E ORGANISMOS.* 1963. irreg. (approx. a.). free. Secretaria Provincial de Saude, Trabalho, Previdencia e Assistencia, Luanda, Angola. circ. controlled. (tabloid format)

614 IT ISSN 0021-3071
ANNALI DELLA SANITA PUBBLICA. vol.23, 1970. m. L.52000. Ministero della Sanita, Piazzale dell' Industria, Rome, Italy. Ed. Dr. Fausto Federici. bk.rev.; circ. 3,000. **Indexed:** Biol.Abstr., Chem.Abstr., Helminthol.Abstr., INIS Atomind., Trop.Dis.Bull.

613.62 US ISSN 0003-4878
RC963 CODEN: AOHYA3
ANNALS OF OCCUPATIONAL HYGIENE. 1958. 6/yr. £235 (effective 1992). (British Occupational Hygiene Society, UK) Pergamon Press, Inc., Journals Division, 660 White Plains Rd., Tarrytown, NY 10591-5153. TEL 914-524-9200. FAX 914-333-2444. (And: Headington Hill Hall, Oxford OX3 0BW, England. TEL 0865-794141) Ed. John Mckellison. adv.; bk.rev.; charts; illus.; index; circ. 1,800. (also avail. in microform from MIM,UMI; back issues avail.) **Indexed:** Abstr.Hyg., Biol.Abstr., Biol.Dig., Br.Ceram.Abstr., C.I.S. Abstr., Chem.Abstr., Curr.Adv.Ecol.Sci., Curr.Cont., Ergon.Abstr., Excerp.Med., Helminthol.Abstr., Ind.Hyg.Dig., Ind.Med., Ind.Sci.Rev., Lab.Haz.Bull., Noise Pollut.Publ.Abstr., Rev.Med.& Vet.Mycol., Risk Abstr., Sci.Cit.Ind., Trop.Dis.Bull.
—BLDSC shelfmark: 1043.300000.
Description: Provides current coverage of news, issues and research in the field.
Refereed Serial

628 US
ANNUAL CONFERENCE ON ACTIVATED SLUDGE PROCESS CONTROL. PROCEEDINGS. 1981. a. Arthur Technology, Inc., Box 1236, Fond du Lac, WI 54935-6836. Ed. Robert M. Arthur.

614 US ISSN 0163-7525
RA421 CODEN: AREHDT
ANNUAL REVIEW OF PUBLIC HEALTH. 1980. a. $49 (foreign $54)(effective Jan. 1992). Annual Reviews Inc., 4139 El Camino Way, Box 10139, Palo Alto, CA 94303-0897. TEL 415-493-4400. FAX 415-855-9815. TELEX 910-290-0275. Ed. Gilbert S. Omenn. bibl.; index, cum.index. (back issues avail.; reprint service avail. from ISI) **Indexed:** Abstr.Health Care Manage.Stud., Abstr.Hyg., Adol.Ment.Hlth.Abstr., CINAHL, Curr.Cont., Deep Sea Res.& Oceanogr.Abstr., Dok.Arbeitsmed., Ind.Med., Risk Abstr., SSCI.
—BLDSC shelfmark: 1528.450000.
Description: Original reviews of critical literature and current developments in public health.
Refereed Serial

628 IT
ANNUARIO SANITARIO ITALIANO/ITALIAN SANITARY DIRECTORY. 1952. a. L.109000. Guida Monaci S.p.A., Via Vitorchiano 107, 00187 Rome, Italy. TEL 06-3288805. FAX 06-3275693. TELEX 623234 MONACI.
Formerly: Guida Monaci. Annuario Sanitario.
Description: Directory of all Italian physicians and sanitation organizations.

628 US ISSN 1047-322X
RC963.A1 CODEN: AOEHE9
APPLIED OCCUPATIONAL & ENVIRONMENTAL HYGIENE. 1986. m. $75. Applied Industrial Hygiene, Inc. (Subsidiary of: American Conference of Governmental Industrial Hygienists, Inc. (ACGIH)), 6500 Glenway Ave., Bldg. D-7, Cincinnati, OH 45211. TEL 513-661-7881. FAX 513-661-7195. Ed. Sharon Ziegler. adv.; bk.rev.; abstr.; charts; illus.; circ. 6,000. (back issues avail.) **Indexed:** Environ.Abstr., Excerp.Med.
—BLDSC shelfmark: 1576.239000.
Formerly (until vol.5, no.1, 1990): Applied Industrial Hygiene (ISSN 0882-8032)
Description: Articles of interest to the occupational and environmental safety and health professional.

PUBLIC HEALTH AND SAFETY

614   CY   ISSN 0257-3202
ARAB HEALTH. (Text in Arabic, English) 1985. 4/yr. $30. Chatila Publishing House, P.O. Box 5122, Limassol, Cyprus. TEL 357-2-476353. FAX 357-2-456252. TELEX 4990 FLY CY. (Or P.O. Box 135121, Chouran, Beirut, Lebanon) Ed. Dr. Abdul Salam Chatila. adv.; bk.rev.; circ. 15,180.
  Description: Covers articles of interest to importers and distributors of health care products and equipment, to hospital workers, and to ministries of health in the Middle East, Anglophone Africa and other countries.

614.44 613.62   GW   ISSN 0300-581X
RC963   CODEN: ASPVAS
ARBEITSMEDIZIN, SOZIALMEDIZIN, PRAEVENTIVMEDIZIN; Zeitschrift fuer Praxis, Klinik, Forschung, Begutachtung. 1966. m. DM.243.60 (foreign DM.266.40). (Deutsche Gesellschaft fuer Arbeitsmedizin) A.W. Gentner Verlag, Forststr. 131, Postfach 101742, 7000 Stuttgart 10, Germany. TEL 0711-63672-0. FAX 0711-6367211. (Co-sponsor: Oesterreichische Gesellschaft fuer Arbeitsmedizin) Ed. H. Wittgens. adv.; bk.rev.; abstr.; charts; illus.; index; circ. 3,800. **Indexed:** Abstr.Hyg., Biol.Abstr., C.I.S. Abstr., Curr.Cont., Excerp.Med., INIS Atomind., Lab.Haz.Bull., Nutr.Abstr., Trop.Dis.Bull.
 —BLDSC shelfmark: 1587.402500.
  Formerly: Arbeitsmedizin, Sozialmedizin, Arbeitshygiene (ISSN 0003-7753)

614.85   SW   ISSN 0003-7834
ARBETSMILJOE. 1970. 15/yr. SEK 135. Foereningen foer Arbetarskydd - Swedish Work Environment Association, P.O. Box 5970, S-114 89 Stockholm, Sweden. TEL 46-08-166740. FAX 46-08-8156757. Ed. Siv Soderlund. adv.; bk.rev.; charts; illus.; circ. 130,000. **Indexed:** C.I.S. Abstr.
 —BLDSC shelfmark: 1588.080000.
  Formerly: Arbetarskyddet.

ARCHIVES BELGES DE MEDECINE SOCIALE ET D'HYGIENE. see *MEDICAL SCIENCES*

ARCTIC MEDICAL RESEARCH. see *MEDICAL SCIENCES*

353.9   US   ISSN 0362-1421
RA21
ARIZONA. DEPARTMENT OF HEALTH SERVICES. ANNUAL REPORT. 1974. a. free. Department of Health Services, 1740 W. Adams St., Phoenix, AZ 85007. TEL 602-542-1000. FAX 602-542-1235. Ed. Shane Siren. illus.; circ. 500 (controlled). Key Title: Annual Report of the Arizona Department of Health Services.

ARIZONA RADIATION REGULATORY AGENCY. ANNUAL REPORT. see *ENERGY — Nuclear Energy*

ARZT IN NIEDEROESTERREICH. see *MEDICAL SCIENCES*

614.8   US   ISSN 0893-858X
ASBESTOS ABATEMENT REPORT. 1987. bi-w. $477 (foreign $499). Buraff Publications (Subsidiary of: Millin Publications, Inc.), 1350 Connecticut Ave. N.W., Ste. 1000, Washington, DC 20036. TEL 202-862-0990. FAX 202-822-8092. TELEX 285656 BNAI WSH. Ed. Rose Lally. (back issues avail.)
  ●Also available online. Vendor(s): Human Resources Information Network.
  Description: Covers developments in asbestos control.

ASIAN ENVIRONMENT; journal of environmental science and technology for balanced development. see *ENVIRONMENTAL STUDIES*

614 362.2   US
ASSOCIATION OF MENTAL HEALTH ADMINISTRATORS. NEWSLETTER. 1963. m. Association of Mental Health Administrators, 60 Revere Dr., Ste. 500, Northbrook, IL 60062. TEL 708-480-9626. Ed. James Rayball. adv.; bk.rev.; circ. 1,800 (controlled).

614   UK   ISSN 0140-4563
ASSOCIATION OF NATIONAL HEALTH SERVICE SUPPLIES OFFICERS. REFERENCE BOOK & BUYER'S GUIDE. a. £30. Sterling Publications Ltd., 86-88 Edgware Rd., London, W2 2YW, England. TEL 01-258 0066. adv.

614   AT
AUSTRALIA. DEPARTMENT OF COMMUNITY SERVICES AND HEALTH. ANNUAL REPORT (YEAR). 1954. a. Department of Community Services and Health, Box 100, Woden, A.C.T. 2606, Australia. TEL 062-898090. illus.; circ. 2,500.
  Former titles: Australia. Commonwealth Department of Health. Annual Report; Australia. Department of Health. Annual Report.

AUSTRALIAN DR WEEKLY. see *MEDICAL SCIENCES*

AUSTRALIAN FLUORIDATION NEWS. AQUA-PURA. see *WATER RESOURCES*

616.9   AT   ISSN 1035-7319
HV88   CODEN: AJPHET
AUSTRALIAN JOURNAL OF PUBLIC HEALTH. 1977. q. Aus.$70 to individuals; libraries and institutions Aus.$160. Public Health Association of Australia, G.P.O. Box 2204, Canberra, A.C.T. 2601, Australia. TEL 06-285-2373. FAX 06-282-5438. Ed. Charles Kerr. adv.; bk.rev.; circ. 2,000. (also avail. in microfilm from UMI; reprint service avail. from UMI) **Indexed:** Aus.P.A.I.S., Curr.Cont., Dent.Ind., Excerp.Med., Ind.Med., NRN, Risk Abstr., Soc.Sci.Ind., SSCI.
 —BLDSC shelfmark: 1811.650000.
  Formerly (until Dec. 1990): Community Health Studies (ISSN 0149-2047)
  Description: Publishes research reports, reviews and letters on epidemiology, health policy, health services and health promotion.
  Refereed Serial

614   AT   ISSN 0067-2165
AUSTRALIAN STUDIES IN HEALTH SERVICE ADMINISTRATION. 1968. irreg., nos. 72-74, 1992. Aus.$90 (foreign Aus.$100)(typically set Nov.-Dec.). University of New South Wales, School of Health Services Management, P.O. Box 1, Kensington, N.S.W. 2033, Australia. FAX 02-662-7698. Ed. C. Grant. circ. 300.
 —BLDSC shelfmark: 1821.800000.

614.5   US
B M F T RISIKO- UND SICHERHEITSFORSCHUNG. 1982. irreg., latest 1986. price varies. (Bundesministerium fuer Forschung und Technologie, GW) Springer-Verlag, 175 Fifth Ave., New York, NY 10010. TEL 212-460-1500. (Also Berlin, Tokyo and Vienna) **Indexed:** Chem.Abstr.

B T - L M & S. (Building Technology - Land Management & Safety) see *BUILDING AND CONSTRUCTION*

BAIERTALER. see *BUSINESS AND ECONOMICS — Small Business*

610   BB
BARBADOS. MINISTRY OF HEALTH. CHIEF MEDICAL OFFICER. ANNUAL REPORT. 1972. a. free. Ministry of Health, Bridgetown, Barbados, W.I. FAX 426-5570. Ed.Bd. charts; illus.; stat.; circ. 300.
  Former titles: Barbados. Ministry of Health and Community Services. Chief Medical Officer. Annual Report; Barbados. Ministry of Health and Welfare. Chief Medical Officer. Annual Report.

614   BE
BELGIUM. MINISTERE DE LA SANTE PUBLIQUE ET DE LA FAMILLE. BULLETIN. (Text in Dutch and French) 1936. 2/yr. 600 Fr. Ministere de la Sante Publique et de la Famille - Ministerie van Volksgezondheid en van het Gezin, Cite Administrative de l'Etat, Bibliotheque, Quartier Vesale, 1010 Brussels, Belgium. Ed.Bd. charts. **Indexed:** Trop.Dis.Bull.

BELGIUM. MINISTERE DE LA SANTE PUBLIQUE ET DE LA FAMILLE. RAPPORT ANNUEL. see *SOCIAL SERVICES AND WELFARE*

BERNIE. see *CHILDREN AND YOUTH — For*

BEZPECNOST A HYGIENA PRACE/SAFETY AND HYGIENE OF WORK. see *LABOR UNIONS*

614   SZ   ISSN 0006-4629
BLAUE KREUZ. 1896. fortn. 55 Fr. (Blue Cross of Switzerland) Blaukreuz Verlag, Lindenrain 5A, 3001 Bern, Switzerland. TEL 031-235866. FAX 031-234154. Ed.Bd. bk.rev.; illus.; circ. 4,400. (looseleaf format)

614.49   BL
BOLETIM EPIDEMIOLOGICO. 1969. s-m. free. Fundacao Servicos de Saude Publica, Centro de Investigacoes Epidemiologicas, Av. Rio Branco 251, Rio de Janeiro GB, Brazil. stat.; circ. 6,500. (processed; also avail. in record) **Indexed:** Biol.Abstr.

628   VE
BOLETIN DE SALUD PUBLICA. 1941. a. Ministerio de Sanidad y Asistencia Social, Direccion de Salud Publica, Caracas, Venezuela. (Co-sponsor: Venezuela. Oficina de los Servicios Regionales de Salud) Ed.Bd. charts; illus.
  Supersedes: Uruguay. Consejo de Salud Publica. Boletin.

614   MX
BOLETIN EPIDEMIOLOGICO. 1973. a. free. Instituto Mexicano del Seguro Social, Subdireccion General Medica, Jefatura de Servicios de Medicina Preventiva, Apdo. Postal 12976, 03001 Mexico, D.F., Mexico. stat.; circ. 2,000.
  Formerly: Boletin Epidemiologico Anual.

614   CK
BOLETIN EPIDEMIOLOGICO NACIONAL. 1975. m. Ministerio de Salud Publica, Direccion de Epidemiologia, Grupo Multidisciplinario, Calle 16 no. 7-39, Bogota, Colombia. FAX 5712112566. bk.rev.; circ. 3,000.

614   US
BORDER HEALTH/SALUD FRONTERIZA. (Text in English, Spanish) 1984. q. $12. (United States - Mexico Border Health Association) Pan American Health Organization, El Paso Field Office, 6006 N. Mesa, Ste. 600, El Paso, TX 79912. TEL 915-581-6645. FAX 915-833-4768. TELEX 749342. Ed. Dr. Herbert H. Ortega. circ. 2,500.
  Description: Covers U.S.-Mexico border public health issues.

BOSTON CYCLIST. see *SPORTS AND GAMES — Bicycles And Motorcycles*

614   BS
BOTSWANA. MINISTRY OF HEALTH. REPORT. 1973. a. Ministry of Health, Gaborone, Botswana.
  Formerly: Botswana. Department of Health. Report.

614.8   CN   ISSN 0706-4810
RA185.B7
BRITISH COLUMBIA. MINISTRY OF HEALTH. ANNUAL REPORT. 1975. a. free. Ministry of Health, Victoria, B.C., Canada. TEL 604-387-2323. circ. 4,000.
  Formerly: British Columbia. Department of Health. Annual Report (ISSN 0701-5372)

539.7   FR
BULLETIN DE LA SURETE NUCLEAIRE.. 6/yr. 225 F. (Ministere de l'Economie, du Budget et des Finances, Direction de la Prevision) Documentation Francaise, 29-31 Quai Voltaire, 75007 Paris, France. TEL 1-40-15-70-00. (Subscr. to: Documentation Francaise, 124 rue Henri Barbusse, 93308 Aubervilliers, France) (back issues avail.)
  Formerly: Surete des Installations Nucleaires. Bulletin.

614   GW   ISSN 0007-5914
BUNDESGESUNDHEITSBLATT. 1958. fortn. DM.138. (Bundesgesundheitsamt) Carl Heymanns Verlag KG, Luxemburgstr. 449, 5000 Cologne 41, Germany. TEL 0221-46010-0. FAX 0221-4601069. adv.; bk.rev.; bibl.; charts; stat.; index; circ. 2,300. **Indexed:** Biol.Abstr., C.I.S. Abstr., Dairy Sci.Abstr., Dok.Arbeitsmed., Excerp.Med., Food Sci.& Tech.Abstr., Ind.Vet., INIS Atomind., Int.Packag.Abstr., Nutr.Abstr., Packag.Sci.Tech., Vet.Bull.
 —BLDSC shelfmark: 2930.200000.

C D C - A I D S WEEKLY; a complete weekly report privately circulated. (Centers for Disease Control - Acquired Immune Deficiency Syndrome) see *MEDICAL SCIENCES — Communicable Diseases*

C F O - MAGAZINE; league issue for nurses and other people working the health and social welfare field. see *MEDICAL SCIENCES — Nurses And Nursing*

PUBLIC HEALTH AND SAFETY 4099

614.7 UK
C H E C JOURNAL. 1973. s-a. £5($9) Commonwealth Human Ecology Council, 58 Stanhope Garden, London SW7 5RF, England. TEL 071-373-6761. FAX 071-244-7470. TELEX 8951182-GECOMS-G. Ed. Zena Daysh. bk.rev.; circ. 2,000.
Former titles: C H E C News (ISSN 0307-2827); C H E C Newsletter.

614.7 UK ISSN 0142-1972
C H E C POINTS. 1978. 3/yr. membership. Commonwealth Human Ecology Council, 58 Stanhope Gardens, London SW7 5RF, England. TEL 071-373-6761. FAX 071-244-7470. TELEX 8951182-GECOMS-G.

C H R I C A NEWS. (Committee for Health Rights in Central America) see *BUSINESS AND ECONOMICS — International Development And Assistance*

614.5 US
C L E A R EXAM REVIEW. 1982. s-a. $30. Council on Licensure, Enforcement & Regulation, c/o Council of State Government, Iron Works Pike, Box 11910, Lexington, KY 40578-1910. TEL 606-231-1889. FAX 606-231-1943. Ed. Michael Rosenfeld. adv. contact: Pam Brinegar. circ. 500.
Description: Testing issues for licensure of professional and occupational trends.

362 UK
C O H S E JOURNAL. 1912. 6/yr. £15. Confederation of Health Service Employees, Glen House, High St., Banstead, Surrey, England. FAX 0737-370079. Ed. Rowena Chapman. adv.; bk.rev.; illus.; circ. 220,000. **Indexed:** ASSIA.
Formerly (until Mar. 1989): Health Services Journal (ISSN 0017-9116)

C S P DIRECTORY. (Board of Certified Safety Professionals) see *OCCUPATIONAL HEALTH AND SAFETY*

CAHIERS DE SOCIOLOGIE ET DE DEMOGRAPHIE MEDICALES. see *POPULATION STUDIES*

CALIFORNIA FIRE SERVICE. see *FIRE PREVENTION*

614.88 SA ISSN 0379-458X
CALL OF ST. JOHN/STEM VAN ST. JOHN. (Text in Afrikaans, English) 1943. biennial. Order of St. John, Priory for South Africa, Box 7137, Johannesburg 2000, South Africa. TEL 646-5520. bk.rev.; circ. 7,000.

614.8 US
CAMPUS SAFETY NEWSLETTER. 1956. 4/yr. $15. National Safety Council, Industrial Section, 444 N. Michigan Ave., Chicago, IL 60611. TEL 800-621-7619. abstr.; illus.; stat.; circ. 5,000.
Formed by the merger of: Campus Safety & College and University Newsletter; Formerly: College and University Safety Newsletter (ISSN 0010-0943)

614 360 CN ISSN 0068-7456
CANADA. DEPARTMENT OF NATIONAL HEALTH AND WELFARE. ANNUAL REPORT. (Text in English and French) 1944. a. free. Department of National Health and Welfare, Communications Branch, Brooke Claxton Bldg., Ottawa, Ont. K1A 0K9, Canada. TEL 613-952-9191. FAX 613-952-7266. circ. 10,000. **Indexed:** Med.Care Rev.

614 610 CN ISSN 0382-232X
CODEN: CDWSE9
CANADA DISEASES WEEKLY REPORT/RAPPORT HEBDOMADAIRE DES MALADIES AU CANADA. (Text in English and French) 1975. w. Department of National Health and Welfare, Laboratory Centre for Disease Control, Brooke Claxton Bldg., Ottawa, Ont. K1A 0L2, Canada. TEL 613-957-1788. Ed. Eleanor Paulson. charts; illus.; stat.; index; circ. 3,000. (back issues avail.) **Indexed:** Abstr.Hyg., Biodet.Abstr., Curr.Adv.Ecol.Sci.
—BLDSC shelfmark: 3016.432300.
Formerly: Epidemiological Bulletin (ISSN 0425-1474) - Bulletin Epidemiologique (ISSN 0382-2311).

CANADIAN HEALTH FACILITIES LAW GUIDE. see *LAW*

CANADIAN JOURNAL OF COMMUNITY MENTAL HEALTH/REVUE CANADIENNE DE SANTE MENTALE COMMUNAUTAIRE. see *PSYCHOLOGY*

614 CN ISSN 0008-4263
CODEN: CJPEA4
CANADIAN JOURNAL OF PUBLIC HEALTH. (Text in English; summaries in English and French) 1910. bi-m. Can.$48($60) (elsewhere $70). Canadian Public Health Association, 1565 Carling Ave., Ste. 400, Ottawa, Ont. K1Z 8R1, Canada. TEL 613-725-3769. FAX 613-725-9826. adv.; bk.rev.; charts; illus.; circ. 4,000. (also avail. in microform from UMI,PMC; reprint service avail. from UMI) **Indexed:** Abstr.Hyg., Bibl.Dev.Med.& Child Neur., Biol.Abstr., Biol.Dig., Chem.Abstr., CINAHL, CMI, Curr.Cont., Dairy Sci.Abstr., Dent.Ind., Dok.Arbeitsmed., Excerp.Med., Food Sci.& Tech.Abstr., Ind.Med., Ind.Vet., INIS Atomind., Med.Care Rev., NRN, Nutr.Abstr., Ocean.Abstr., Pollut.Abstr., Protozool.Abstr., Rev.Plant Path., Risk Abstr., Sel.Water Res.Abstr., Small Anim.Abstr., Sportsearch (1977-), SSCI, Trop.Dis.Bull., Vet.Bull., W.R.C.Inf.
—BLDSC shelfmark: 3035.000000.

CANADIAN MENTAL HEALTH ASSOCIATION. ANNUAL REPORT/ASSOCIATION CANADIENNE POUR LA SANTE MENTALE. RAPPORT ANNUEL. see *PSYCHOLOGY*

CANADIAN NURSE - L'INFIRMIERE CANADIENNE. see *MEDICAL SCIENCES — Nurses And Nursing*

614.88 UK ISSN 0008-7580
CASUALTY SIMULATION; to simulate realism in first aid, nursing and rescue training. 1946. 4/yr. £4. Casualties Union, 1 Grosvenor Crescent, London SW1X 7EE, England. TEL 071-235-5366. Eds. E.G. Dawson, G. Wildridge. adv.; bk.rev.; charts; illus.; index, cum.index; circ. 2,000.

614.8 UK
CAUTION MAGAZINE; industrial fire, safety and security. 1974. q. £12. Health and Safety Publishing, 32 Portland St., Cheltenham, Glos. GL52 2PB, England. FAX 0242-236336. Ed. D.G. Constantine. adv.; bk.rev.; circ. 13,433.

614 UN ISSN 0009-0131
CENTRO PAN-AMERICANO DE FEBRE AFTOSA. BOLETIN. 1963. q. free. World Health Organization, Centro Pan Americano de Febre Aftosa, Pan American Health Organization, CP 589-Z 000, 20000 Rio de Janeiro, Brazil. Ed.Bd. circ. 1,500. **Indexed:** Biol.Abstr., Vet.Bull.
—BLDSC shelfmark: 2162.050000.
Formerly: Centro Pan-Americano de Febre Aftosa. Cuadernos.
Description: Covers foot and mouth disease.

614 CS ISSN 0009-0689
CESKOSLOVENSKE ZDRAVOTNICTVI. (Text in Czech or Slovak; summaries in English and Russian) 1952. 12/yr. $45.30. (Ceskoslovenska Spolecnost pro Socialni Zdravotnictvi) Avicenum, Czechoslovak Medical Press, Malostransk nam. 28, 118 02 Prague 1, Czechoslovakia. (Dist. by: Artia, Ve Smeckach 30, 111 27 Prague 1, Czechoslovakia) (Co-sponsor: Ceskoslovenska Lekarska Spolecnost J. Ev. Purkyne) Ed. Dr. V. Bilek. adv.; bk.rev.; bibl.; charts; illus.; stat.; index. **Indexed:** Dent.Ind., Ind.Med.

CEYLON JOURNAL OF MEDICAL SCIENCE. see *MEDICAL SCIENCES*

614 FR ISSN 0069-2603
CHAMBRE SYNDICALE NATIONALE DES ENTREPRISES ET INDUSTRIES DE L'HYGIENE PUBLIQUE. ANNUAIRE. 1963. biennial. 50 F. Chambre Syndicale Nationale des Entreprises et Industries de l'Hygiene Publique, 10 rue Washington, 75008 Paris, France.

CHARTERED INSTITUTE OF PUBLIC FINANCE AND ACCOUNTANCY. ENVIRONMENTAL HEALTH STATISTICS. ACTUALS. see *PUBLIC HEALTH AND SAFETY — Abstracting, Bibliographies, Statistics*

CHEMICAL DEPENDENCY; opposing viewpoints sources. see *DRUG ABUSE AND ALCOHOLISM*

658 614.84 US
CHIEF FIRE EXECUTIVE.* bi-m. P T N Publishing Corp., 445 Broad Hollow Rd., Ste. 21, Melville, NY 11747-4722. TEL 516-845-2700. FAX 516-845-7109. Ed. Janet Kimmerly. circ. 41,000.
Description: Geared towards fire marshals, commissioners, purchasing agents, industrial safety officers and military fire officers.

CHILD SAFETY REVIEW. see *CHILDREN AND YOUTH — About*

CLEAN AIR CLARION. see *POLITICAL SCIENCE — Civil Rights*

CLEVELAND FOUNDATION. ANNUAL REPORT. see *SOCIAL SERVICES AND WELFARE*

COMBUSTION SCIENCE AND TECHNOLOGY. see *CHEMISTRY — Physical Chemistry*

613.62 EI
COMMISSION OF THE EUROPEAN COMMUNITIES. ANNUAL REPORTS ON THE PROGRESS OF RESEARCH WORK PROMOTED BY THE ECSC. French edition: Commission des Communautes Europeennes. Rapports Annuels sur l'Etat des Travaux de Recherches Encouragees par la CECA. 1967. a. Commission of the European Communities, Service de Renseignemnet et de Diffusion des Documents, 200 rue de la Loi, B-1049 Brussels, Belgium, Belgium. circ. controlled.

COMMON SENSE PEST CONTROL QUARTERLY. see *BIOLOGY — Entomology*

COMMUNITY DENTISTRY AND ORAL EPIDEMIOLOGY. see *MEDICAL SCIENCES — Dentistry*

614 BL
COMPANHIA ESTADUAL DE TECNOLOGIA DE SANEAMENTO BASICO E DE DEFESA DO MEIO AMBIENTE. DIRECTORIA RELATORIA ANUAL. 1974. a. Companhia Estadual de Tecnologia de Saneamento Basico e Defesa do Meio Ambiente, Avda. Prof. Frederico Hermann Filho 345, CEP 05459, Sao Paulo, Brazil. illus.; circ. 2,000.

614.8
COMPLIANCE PROGRAM GUIDANCE MANUALS. (Series of: Food and Cosmetics, Drugs and Biology, Veterinary Medicine, Medical and Radiological Devices) irreg. $425 for series in US, Canada, Mexico; elsewhere $850. (Department of Health and Human Services, Food and Drug Administration) U.S. National Technical Information Service, 5825 Port Royal Rd., Springfield, VA 22161. TEL 703-487-4630.
Description: Provides latest information on and helps to maintain program plans and instructions directed to FDA field operations. These plans and instructions are surveillance or compliance oriented and provide the needed direction from headquarters offices and bureaus in accomplishing FDA's regulatory obligations.

628 US ISSN 0069-8474
CONFERENCE OF STATE SANITARY ENGINEERS. REPORT OF PROCEEDINGS. 1920. a. U.S. Public Health Service, Department of Health and Human Services, Washington, DC 20201. TEL 202-245-6761.

614 US ISSN 0010-6127
CONNECTICUT HEALTH BULLETIN. 1877. q. free. Department of Health Services, 150 Washington St., Hartford, CT 06106. TEL 203-566-4800. Ed. Anita Steeves. bk.rev.; illus.; stat.; index; circ. 13,000. **Indexed:** Rehabil.Lit.

CONTINUUM OF CARE. see *HOSPITALS*

614.49 SZ ISSN 0377-3574
CODEN: CEPBDV
CONTRIBUTIONS TO EPIDEMIOLOGY AND BIOSTATISTICS. (Text in English) 1977. irreg. (approx. a.). price varies. S. Karger AG, Allschwilerstr. 10, P.O. Box, CH-4009 Basel, Switzerland. TEL 061-3061111. FAX 061-3061234. TELEX CH 962652. Ed. J. Wahrendorf. (reprint service avail. from ISI) **Indexed:** Biol.Abstr.
—BLDSC shelfmark: 3458.410000.

614 IT
CORRIERE A V I S. 1956. s-a. free. Associazione Volontari Italiani del Sangue (Turin), Via P. Baiardi, 5, 10126 Turin, Italy. TEL 011-658095. FAX 011-678831. Eds. Sandro Fisso, Piero Onida. adv.; circ. 45,000.
Description: Includes news and articles on medical subjects related to blood transfusions.

COURTS, HEALTH SCIENCE & THE LAW. see *LAW*

PUBLIC HEALTH AND SAFETY

614.8   CI   ISSN 0350-8765
COVJEK I PROMET. (Text in Serbo-Croatian; summaries in English) 1975. q. $25 to individuals; institutions $50. Istrazivacki Centar za Medicinu i Psihologiju Prometa, Sarengradska 3, 41000 Zagreb, Croatia. TEL 041 562-325. Ed. Ivo Jelcic. circ. 1,000.

614 610   CU   ISSN 0045-9178
CUADERNOS DE HISTORIA DE LA SALUD PUBLICA. 1952. s-a. $4.20. Ministerio de Salud Publica, Consejo Nacional de Sociedades Cientificas, Centro Nacional de Informacion de Ciencias Medicas, Calle 23 No. 177 e-N y O, La Rampa, Vedado, Apdo. No. 6520, Havana, Cuba. TEL 32-5556-60. (Dist. by: Ediciones Cubanas, Obispo No. 461, Apdo. 605, Havana, Cuba) circ. 3,000. **Indexed:** Biol.Abstr.

614.8   US
D E S ACTION VOICE; a focus on diethylstilbestrol exposure. 1979. q. $25. D E S Action USA, 1615 Broadway, Ste. 510, Oakland, CA 94612. TEL 415-465-4011. bk.rev.; abstr.; circ. 3,000. (back issues avail.)
  Description: Covers latest medical and legal information for D E S mothers, daughters and sons.

614.8 628.44
350.755   US   ISSN 0164-1875
D R C BOOK & MONOGRAPH SERIES. 1968. irreg., no.24, 1990. price varies. University of Delaware, Disaster Research Center, Newark, DE 19716. TEL 302-451-6618. FAX 302-451-2828. TELEX 70 99 85.
  Formerly: Ohio State University. Disaster Research Center. D R C - T R (ISSN 0078-4109)

613   US   ISSN 1043-3546
SF257   CODEN: DFESEC
DAIRY, FOOD AND ENVIRONMENTAL SANITATION; a publication for sanitarians and fieldmen. 1980. m. $100. International Association of Milk, Food and Environmental Sanitarians, Inc., 502 E. Lincoln Way, Ames, IA 50010-6666. TEL 515-232-6699. Ed. Steven K. Halstead. adv.; bk.rev.; abstr.; charts; illus.; index; circ. 3,500. (also avail. in microform from UMI; reprint service avail. from UMI) **Indexed:** Biodet.Abstr., Curr.Adv.Ecol.Sci., Dairy Sci.Abstr., Food Sci.& Tech.Abstr., Ind.Vet.
  —BLDSC shelfmark: 3514.712000.
  Former titles: Dairy and Food Sanitation (ISSN 0273-2866); Food and Fieldmen.

DENMARK. DANMARKS STATISTIK. FAERDSELSUHELD. see POPULATION STUDIES — Abstracting, Bibliographies, Statistics

614   IT   ISSN 0012-2653
DIFESA SOCIALE. (Text in Italian; summaries in English and Italian.) 1922. m. Istituto Italiano di Medicina Sociale, Via Pasquale Stanislao Mancini 28, Rome, Italy. Marafioti Renzi. bk.rev.; abstr.; index. **Indexed:** Biol.Abstr., C.I.S. Abstr., Excerp.Med., Psychol.Abstr.
  —BLDSC shelfmark: 3584.000000.
  Description: A forum that covers articles on the social issues of medicine. Includes articles on the socialization of people with handicaps, pollution issues and the elderly.

DISASTER MANAGEMENT. see CIVIL DEFENSE

614   UK
DISASTER MANAGEMENT. q. £175 (foreign £205). F M J International Publications Ltd., Queensway House, 2 Queensway, Redhill, Surrey RH1 1QS, England. TEL 0737-768611. FAX 0737-761685. TELEX 948669-TOPJNL-G.
  Description: Covers issues in contingency planning for large scale emergencies.

614.84   JA   ISSN 0006-7873
DISASTER PREVENTION/BOSAI. (Text in Japanese) 1947. bi-m. 780 Yen. Tokyo Consolidated Fire Prevention Association - Tokyo Rengo Boka Kyokai, c/o Tokyo Shobo-cho, 3-5, Otemachi Ichome, Chiyoda-ku, Tokyo 100, Japan. Ed. Bunkichi Sawaguri. adv.; circ. 12,000. **Indexed:** Abstr.J.Earthq.Eng.

628   IT
DISINFESTAZIONE. 1984. bi-m. L.60000. MO.ED.CO. s.r.l., Via Paolo da Cannobio 9, 20122 Milan, Italy. TEL 02-878577. FAX 0289010728. adv.; circ. 5,000.
  Description: Concerned with pest control.

DRINKING WATER & BACKFLOW PREVENTION. see ENGINEERING — Civil Engineering

DRUG NEWSLETTER. see PHARMACY AND PHARMACOLOGY

614.8   US
DRUGS AND BIOLOGY GUIDANCE MANUAL. (Subseries of: Compliance Program Guidance Manuals) irreg. $135 in US, Canada, Mexico; elsewhere $270. (Department of Health and Human Services, Food and Drug Administration) U.S. National Technical Information Service, 5825 Port Royal Rd., Springfield, VA 22161. TEL 703-487-4630.
  Description: Provides the latest information on and helps to maintain program plans and instructions directed to FDA field operations. These plans and instructions are surveillance or compliance oriented and provide the needed direction from headquarters offices and bureaus in accomplishing FDA's regulatory obligations.

DRUGS AND DEVICE RECALL BULLETIN. see PHARMACY AND PHARMACOLOGY

E H P. (Environmental Health Perspectives) see ENVIRONMENTAL STUDIES

ECOTOXICOLOGY AND ENVIRONMENTAL SAFETY. see ENVIRONMENTAL STUDIES — Toxicology And Environmental Safety

628   SP
EDUCACION SANITARIA. 1983. irreg., no.3, 1986. price varies. (Universidad de Navarra, Facultad de Medicina) Ediciones Universidad de Navarra, S.A., Apdo. 396, 31080 Pamplona, Spain. TEL 94 825 6850.

EDUCATION SANITAIRE ET NUTRITIONNELLE D'AFRIQUE CENTRALE. see NUTRITION AND DIETETICS

614.8   IT   ISSN 0013-2071
EDUCAZIONE ALLA SICUREZZA. 1950. q. L.600. Ente Nazionale per la Prevenzione degli Infortuni, Via Alessandria 200-E, Rome, Italy. illus.; stat.; circ. 38,000.

614   HU   ISSN 0073-4012
EGESZSEGNEVELES SZAKKONYVTARA. 1967. irreg. price varies. Medicina Kiado, Beloiannisz u. 8, 1054 Budapest, Hungary.

614   UA   ISSN 0013-2446
   CODEN: JEGPAY
EGYPTIAN PUBLIC HEALTH ASSOCIATION JOURNAL. vol.45, 1970. 6/yr. $18. Egyptian Public Health Association, Shousha Bldg., Bloc A, Apt. 116, 31 Sharia 26 July, Cairo, Egypt. Ed. Dr. S. el-Kholy. circ. 750. **Indexed:** Biol.Abstr., Chem.Abstr., Excerp.Med., Ind.Med.

EISEI KAGAKU/JAPANESE JOURNAL OF TOXICOLOGY AND ENVIRONMENTAL HEALTH. see ENVIRONMENTAL STUDIES — Toxicology And Environmental Safety

ELELMISZERVIZSGALATI KOZLEMENYEK. see FOOD AND FOOD INDUSTRIES

614.8 614.86   US
EMERGENCY RESPONSE GUIDEBOOK. a. U.S. Department of Transportation, Materials Transportation Bureau, Washington, DC 20590.
  Description: Provides information for police and fire personnel on steps to be taken in the first critical minutes after a hazardous materials transportation accident.

ENVIRONMENT ADVISOR; monthly information report on congressional and regulatory activity to control, monitor or eliminate hazards created by hazardous and toxic substances. see ENVIRONMENTAL STUDIES — Waste Management

614   UK   ISSN 0013-9270
ENVIRONMENTAL HEALTH. 1895. m. £64 (typically set in Jan.). Institution of Environmental Health Offices, Chadwick House, Rushworth St., London W1V OBN. TEL 01-261-1960. Ed. Hillary King. adv.; bk.rev.; bibl.; charts; illus.; stat.; tr.lit.; index; circ. 8,500. (also avail. in microform from UMI; reprint service avail. from UMI) **Indexed:** Abstr.Hyg., ASSIA, Biol.Abstr., Biol.Dig., C.I.S. Abstr., Curr.Adv.Ecol.Sci., Dairy Sci.Abstr., Environ.Abstr., Environ.Per.Bibl., Excerp.Med., Helminthol.Abstr., Ocean.Abstr., Pollut.Abstr., RICS, Risk Abstr., Trop.Dis.Bull., W.R.C.Inf.
  —BLDSC shelfmark: 3791.481000.
  Formerly: Public Health Inspector.
  Description: Includes articles about food hygiene, health and safety, housing, pest control, pollution, waste management, noise nuisance.

ENVIRONMENTAL HEALTH CRITERIA. see ENVIRONMENTAL STUDIES

614.7   CN   ISSN 0319-6771
ENVIRONMENTAL HEALTH REVIEW. (Text in English) 1956. q. Can.$28 (foreign $35). Canadian Institute of Public Health Inspectors, P.O. Box 1280, Sta. "A", Burlington, Ont. L7R 2H0, Canada. TEL 416-825-6211. FAX 416-825-8588. Ed. Anthony Amalfa. adv.; bk.rev.; circ. 1,500.
  —BLDSC shelfmark: 3791.501700.

628.5   US
ENVIRONMENTAL MANAGEMENT;* the journal of facilities management and industrial sanitation. 1969. 4/yr. $40. Environmental Management Association, 12835 E. Arapahoe Rd., 5th Fl., Englewood, CO 80112-3940. TEL 303-320-7855. FAX 303-393-0770. Ed. Dianna Rampy. adv.; bk.rev.; film rev.; charts; illus.; index; circ. 6,500 (controlled). **Indexed:** Energy Info.Abstr., Ocean.Abstr., Pollut.Abstr.
  Formerly: Professional Sanitation Management (ISSN 0033-0191)
  Description: Includes articles on facilities planning and design, internal building systems, maintenance and operations and building services.

ENVIRONMENTAL RADIATION SURVEILLANCE IN WASHINGTON STATE. ANNUAL REPORT. see ENVIRONMENTAL STUDIES

ENVIRONMENTAL TOXICOLOGY AND CHEMISTRY. see ENVIRONMENTAL STUDIES — Toxicology And Environmental Safety

628   US
EPI-GRAM. m. Department of Human Services, Division of Disease Control, State House, Sta. 11, Augusta, ME 04333. FAX 207-289-4172.

EPIDEMIOLOGICAL BULLETIN. see MEDICAL SCIENCES

EPIDEMIOLOGICAL SURVEILLANCE OF RABIES FOR THE AMERICAS. see VETERINARY SCIENCE

ERUUL MEND/HEALTH. see PHYSICAL FITNESS AND HYGIENE

614.7   EI
EUROPEAN ATOMIC ENERGY COMMUNITY. RESULTATS DES MESURES DE LA RADIOACTIVITE AMBIANTE DANS LES PAYS DE LA COMMUNAUTE: AIR-RETOMBEE-EAUX. (Editions in Dutch, English, French, German, Greek) 1965. irreg. price varies. Office for Official Publications of the European Communities, L-2985 Luxembourg, Luxembourg. (Dist. in U.S. by: Unipub, 4611-F Assembly Dr., Lanham, MD 20706-4391)

EUROPEAN PARLIAMENT. RESEARCH AND DOCUMENTATION PAPERS; resolutions of the European Parliament in the field of environment, public health and consumer protection. see ENVIRONMENTAL STUDIES

614.8   EI   ISSN 1010-8149
EUROPEAN SAFETY AND RELIABILITY ASSOCIATION. BULLETIN. 3/yr. Commission of the European Communities, 200 rue de la Loi, B-1049 Brussels, Belgium.
  —BLDSC shelfmark: 3811.662550.

PUBLIC HEALTH AND SAFETY

614.8 II
F R C H. NEWSLETTER. (Text in English) 1986. bi-m. $25. Foundation for Research in Community Health, 84-A, R.G. Thadani Marg, Worli, Bombay 400 018, India. TEL 22-4938601. Ed. Nagmani Rao. circ. 1,500.
Description: Carries articles related to health, including general interest features and specific informative articles.

FACTS AND ADVICE FOR AIRLINE PASSENGERS. see TRANSPORTATION — Air Transport

610 US ISSN 0160-6379
RA421
FAMILY AND COMMUNITY HEALTH; the journal of health promotion and maintenance. 1978. q. $90. Aspen Publishers, Inc., 200 Orchard Ridge Dr., Gaithersburg, MD 20878. TEL 301-417-7500. FAX 301-417-7550. (also avail. in microform from UMI; reprint service avail. from UMI) **Indexed:** Abstr.Hyg., CINAHL, FAMLI, NRN, Nurs.Abstr., Psychol.Abstr.
—BLDSC shelfmark: 3865.558000.

614.8 US ISSN 0749-310X
TX150
FAMILY SAFETY & HEALTH. 1961. q. $19 to non-members; members $15. National Safety Council, Industrial Section, 444 N. Michigan Ave., Chicago, IL 60611. TEL 800-621-7619. Ed. Laura Coyne. illus.; circ. 2,000,000. (also avail. in microform from UMI; reprint service avail. from UMI)
Formerly (until 1984): Family Safety (ISSN 0014-7397)

628 642.9 UK ISSN 0143-0645
FAR EAST HEALTH. 1980. 10/yr. £60. Reed Business Publishing Group, Carew Division (Subsidiary of: Reed International PLC), Quadrant House, The Quadrant, Sutton, Surrey SM2 5AS, England. TEL 081-661-3500. TELEX 859500. Ed. Wendy Clare. adv.; circ. 5,875. **Indexed:** ASSIA.
—BLDSC shelfmark: 3865.810000.

FEDERAL FUNDING GUIDE. see PUBLIC ADMINISTRATION — Municipal Government

610 US
FEDERAL HEALTH MONITOR. 1988. w. $78. National Health Lawyers Association, 1620 Eye St. N.W., Ste. 900, Washington, DC 20006. TEL 202-833-1100. circ. 1,000.

FEDERAL VETERINARIAN. see VETERINARY SCIENCE

FILM AUSTRALIA HEALTH & WELFARE CATALOGUE. see MOTION PICTURES

614.84 US ISSN 0145-4064
TH9111
FIREHOUSE.* 1976. m. $21. P T N Publishing Corp., 445 Broad Hollow Rd., Ste. 21, Melville, NY 11747-4722. TEL 516-845-2700. FAX 516-845-7109. Ed. Janet Kimmerly. adv.; bk.rev.; illus.; circ. 110,600. (back issues avail.)
Description: Covers historic and dramatic fires, techniques, rescues. Anything and everything about fire fighting and firefighters.

FLIGHT SAFETY FOUNDATION. ANNUAL INDEX. see TRANSPORTATION — Air Transport

FLYING SAFETY. see AERONAUTICS AND SPACE FLIGHT

614 CN ISSN 0015-5195
FOCUS: SOCIAL AND PREVENTIVE MEDICINE. 1964. 4/yr. Can.$5. (Community Health Services Association) Modern Press, 455-2nd Ave. N., Saskatoon, Sask. S7K 2C2, Canada. TEL 306-664-4289. Ed. Norine Shewchuk. bk.rev.; illus.; circ. 6,000.

FOOD & BEVERAGE NEWSLETTER. see OCCUPATIONAL HEALTH AND SAFETY

614.8 US
FOOD AND COSMETICS GUIDANCE MANUAL. (Subseries of: Compliance Program Guidance Manuals) irreg. $140 in US, Canada, Mexico; elsewhere $280. (Department of Health and Human Services, Food and Drug Administration) U.S. National Technical Information Service, 5825 Port Royal Rd., Springfield, VA 22161. TEL 703-487-4630.
Description: Provides the latest information on and helps to maintain surveillance or compliance oriented program plans and instructions directed to FDA field operations, providing needed direction from headquarter offices and bureaus in accomplishing the FDA's regulatory obligations.

613 JA ISSN 0015-6426
RA601 CODEN: SKEZAP
FOOD HYGIENIC SOCIETY OF JAPAN. JOURNAL/SHOKUHIN EISEIGAKU ZASSHI. (Text in English or Japanese) 1960. bi-m. $20. Food Hygienic Society of Japan - Nihon Shokuhin Eisei Gakkai, 2-6-1 Jingumae, Shibuya-ku, Tokyo 150, Japan. adv.; bk.rev.; abstr.; charts; illus.; index; circ. 6,000. **Indexed:** ASCA, Biol.Abstr., Chem.Abstr., Curr.Adv.Ecol.Sci., Dairy Sci.Abstr., Excerp.Med., Field Crop Abstr., Food Sci.& Tech.Abstr., Ind.Vet., Maize Abstr., Nutr.Abstr., Poult.Abstr., Triticale Abstr., Vet.Bull.
—BLDSC shelfmark: 4754.400000.

613 US ISSN 0884-0806
CODEN: FPREEP
FOOD PROTECTION REPORT. 1985. m. $135. Charles Felix Associates, Box 1581, Leesburg, VA 22075. TEL 703-777-7448. FAX 703-777-4453. Ed. Charles W. Felix. circ. 4,000.

614 610 FR ISSN 0755-4168
FRANCE. INSTITUT NATIONAL DE LA SANTE ET DE LA RECHERCHE MEDICALE. INSERM ACTUALITES. 1950. m. free. Institut National de la Sante et de la Recherche Medicale, 101 rue de Tolbiac, 75654 Paris Cedex 13, France. stat.; circ. 1,400.
Former titles: France. Institut National de la Sante et de la Recherche Medicale. Bulletin d'Information; France. Institut National de la Sante et de la Recherche Medicale. Bulletin (ISSN 0015-9603)

614 FR
FRANCE. MINISTERE DE LA SANTE ET DE LA SECURITE SOCIALE. ANNUAIRE DES STATISTIQUES SANITAIRES ET SOCIALES. 1971. a., latest 1989. 170.62 F. Documentation Francaise, 29-31 Quai Voltaire, 75340 Paris, France. TEL 1-40-15-70-00. (Co-sponsor: Ministere de la Sante)
Supersedes: France. Ministere de la Sante et de la Securite Sociale. Tableaux Statistiques "Sante et Securite Sociale; France. Ministere de la Sante. Tableaux Sante et Securite Sociale; France. Ministere de la Sante Publique et de la Securite Sociale. Annuaire Statistique de la Sante et de l'Action Sociale (ISSN 0071-8866)

614 FR
FRANCE. MINISTERE DE LA SANTE ET DE LA SECURITE SOCIALE. BULLETIN OFFICIEL. w. 110 F. Ministere de la Sante et de la Securite Sociale, 8 Av. de Segur, 75700 Paris, France.

614 FR
FRANCE. MINISTERE DE LA SANTE ET DE LA SECURITE SOCIALE. NOTES D'INFORMATION. 1969. irreg., no.145, 1980. free. Ministere de la Sante et de la Securite Sociale, Service de Press, 8 Ave. de Segur, 75700 Paris, France.
Former titles: France. Ministere de la Sante. Note d'Information (ISSN 0071-8882); (until 1969): France. Ministere des Affaires Sociales. Information Actualites.

FRANCE. MINISTERE DE LA SOLIDARITE, DE LA SANTE ET DE LA PROTECTION SOCIALE. BULLETIN OFFICIEL. see BIBLIOGRAPHIES

FRANCE. MINISTERE DES AFFAIRES SOCIALES ET DE L'INTEGRATION. BULLETIN OFFICIEL. see PUBLIC ADMINISTRATION

614 FR
FRANCE. MINISTERE DES AFFAIRES SOCIALES ET DE LA SOLIDARITE NATIONALE. BULLETIN EPIDEMIOLOGIQUE. 1983. w. free to qualified personnel. (Ministere des Affaires Sociales et de la Solidarite Nationale) Imprimerie Nationale, 25 rue de la Convention, 75732 Paris Cedex 15, France. circ. 650.
Former titles: France. Ministere de la Sante et de la Famille. Bulletin Epidemiologique & France. Ministere de la Sante et de la Securite Sociale. Bulletin Epidemiologique.

614.86 SZ
FREIE FAHRT/ROUTE LIBRE. (Text in French and German) 1923. m. 10 Fr. Schweizerischer Abstinenten-Verkehrsverband - Association Suisse des Conducteurs Abstinents, Zentralsekretariat, Langwiesstr. 22, CH-8050 Zuerich, Switzerland. Ed. Peter Ritschard-Inanen. adv.; illus.; circ. 2,000.
Former titles: Strasse und Nuechternheit (ISSN 0039-2170); Abstinenter Rad- und Motorfahrer.

FROM THE STATE CAPITALS. PUBLIC ASSISTANCE AND WELFARE TRENDS. see SOCIAL SERVICES AND WELFARE

614 US ISSN 0734-1156
FROM THE STATE CAPITALS. PUBLIC HEALTH. 1946. w. $215. Wakeman-Walworth, Inc., 300 N. Washington St., Alexandria, VA 22314. TEL 703-549-8606. FAX 703-549-1372. (processed)
Description: Covers state and local action throughout the US in health and related fields.

FROM THE STATE CAPITALS. WASTE DISPOSAL AND POLLUTION CONTROL. see ENVIRONMENTAL STUDIES — Waste Management

FROM THE STATE CAPITALS: PUBLIC SAFETY. see FIRE PREVENTION

614.8 614.7 JA ISSN 0287-1254
FUKUOKA-KEN EISEI KOGAI SENTA NENPO/FUKUOKA ENVIRONMENTAL RESEARCH CENTER. ANNUAL REPORT. 1974. a. free. Fukuoka-Ken Eisei Senta - Fukuoka Environmental Research Center, Fukuoka 818-01, Japan. Ed.Bd. circ. 500. (back issues avail.)

614.8 610 BL ISSN 0304-2138
RA463 CODEN: RFSEAK
FUNDACAO SERVICOS DE SAUDE PUBLICA. REVISTA. (Text in Portuguese; summaries in English and Portuguese) 1947. s-a. free. Fundacao Servicos de Saude Publica, Av. Rio Branco 251, 12 Andar, 20.040 Rio de Janeiro, Brazil. abstr.; index, cum.index: 1948-1979; circ. 1,000. **Indexed:** Bull.Anal.Ent.Med.Vet., Ind.Med., Trop.Dis.Bull.

610 SP ISSN 0213-9111
GASETA SANITARIA. (Text in Spanish; summaries in English) 1982. bi-m. free. (Salud Publica y Administracion Sanitaria) Ajuntament de Barcelona, Area de Salut Publica, Placa Lesseps 1, 08023 Barcelona, Spain. TEL 218 18 00. Ed. Dr. Josep Maria Anto. bk.rev.; bibl.; charts; circ. 6,000. **Indexed:** Abstr.Hyg., Ind.Med.Esp.
Formerly: Gaseta Sanitaria de Barcelona (ISSN 0212-0542)

GENETIC RESOURCE. see BIOLOGY — Genetics

GERIATRIC CARE NEWS. see GERONTOLOGY AND GERIATRICS

GERONTOLOSKO DRUSTVO S R SRBIJE. see GERONTOLOGY AND GERIATRICS

614 SZ
GESUNDHEITSPOLITISCHE INFORMATIONEN/POLITIQUE DE LA SANTE: INFORMATIONS. Short title: G P I. 1977. 4/yr. 60 Fr.($50) Schweizerische Gesellschaft fuer Gesundheitspolitik - Societe Suisse pour la Politique de la Sante (Swiss Society for Health Policy), Haldenweg 10A, CH-3074 Muri, Switzerland. FAX 031-952-6800. Ed. Gerhard Kocher. bk.rev.; abstr.; bibl.; charts; stat.; circ. 1,900. (back issues avail.)
Description: Examines health policies, medical sociology, patients' legal and human rights as well as related economic topics.

P Q

PUBLIC HEALTH AND SAFETY

613   GW   ISSN 0016-9307
GESUNDHEITSPOLITISCHE UMSCHAU. 1948. m. DM.79. Albert Amann Verlag, Richterstr. 2, Postfach 1240, 8762 Amorbach, Germany. TEL 09373-3031. FAX 09373-4134. Ed. Hans Volkhardt. adv.; bk.rev.; circ. 3,500.

GIORNALE DI IGIENE E MEDICINA PREVENTIVA. see *PHYSICAL FITNESS AND HYGIENE*

GOLDENE GESUNDHEIT. see *MEDICAL SCIENCES*

614.8   UK
GOOD HEALTH. 1986. bi-m. £7.50($10) Hawker Consumer Publishing Ltd., 13 Park House, 140 Battersea Park Rd., London SW11 4NB, England. TEL 01-720 2108. Ed. Dr. K. Hawkins. adv.; bk.rev.; circ. 25,000.

614.8   UK   ISSN 0262-5229
GREAT BRITAIN. DEPARTMENT OF EDUCATION AND SCIENCE. SAFETY IN EDUCATION. 1981. irreg. free. Department of Education and Science, Elizabeth House, York Road, London SE1 7PH, England. TEL 01-934-9000. Ed. Bernard McDonnell. bk.rev.; bibl.; charts; illus.; stat.; circ. 100,000. (back issues avail.)
—BLDSC shelfmark: 8065.748000.
Description: Accounts of local governments' good practice in educational building and management.

614 362.11   UK   ISSN 0072-6036
GREAT BRITAIN. DEPARTMENT OF HEALTH AND SOCIAL SECURITY. HOSPITAL IN-PATIENT INQUIRY. 1960. irreg. price varies. H.M.S.O., P.O. Box 276, London SW8 5DT, England. (reprint service avail. from UMI)

614   UK   ISSN 0072-6087
RA241
GREAT BRITAIN. DEPARTMENT OF HEALTH AND SOCIAL SECURITY. ON THE STATE OF THE PUBLIC HEALTH. (Annual Report of the Chief Medical Officer of the Department of Health and Social Security) 1921. a. price varies. H.M.S.O., P.O. Box 276, London SW8 5DT, England. (reprint service avail. from UMI)

614.3   UK
GREAT BRITAIN. MEDICINES COMMISSION. ANNUAL REPORT. 1971. a. price varies. Dept. of Health, Medicines Commission, Alexander Flaming House, Elephant and Castle, London SE1 6BY, England. (Orders to: Dept. of Health, Leaflets Unit, Information Div., Block 4, Canons Pk., Government Bldgs., Honeypot Ln., Stanmore HA7 1AY, England) circ. 600.
Formerly: Great Britain. Committee on Safety of Medicines. Report.
Description: Contains the reports of the Medicines Commission, the Committee on Safety of Medicines, the Veterinary Products Committee, the British Pharmacopoeia Commission, the Committee on the Review of Medicines and the Committee on Dental and Surgical Materials.

GUILDER. see *HANDICAPPED — Hearing Impaired*

614   PH
H E A P JOURNAL. 1961. q. P.2($1.25) (Health Education Association of the Philippines) Philippine Normal College, Community-School Health Education Center, Taft Ave., Manila, Philippines. Ed. Carmen F. del Rosario. bk.rev.; circ. 100.
Formerly: School Health Bulletin (ISSN 0048-9417)

H M C R I FOCUS. (Hazardous Materials Control Research Institute) see *ENVIRONMENTAL STUDIES — Waste Management*

HANDGUN CONTROL. SEMI-ANNUAL PROGRESS REPORT. see *LAW*

628   GW
HARTMANNBUND IN BADEN - WUERTTEMBERG. 1949. q. Hartmannbund - Verband der Aerzte Deutschlands e.V., Godesberger Allee 54, 5300 Bonn 2, Germany. TEL 0228-8104-0.

614   II   ISSN 0017-8241
RA312.H37
HARYANA HEALTH JOURNAL. (Text in English) 1970. q. free. State Health Education Bureau, Directorate of Health Services, 36 Madhaya Marg, Sector 7C, Chandigarh, Haryana, India. Ed. G.G. Saxena. charts; illus.; circ. controlled.
Description: Presents information about developments in medical and health services, oriented to health care professionals.

HAWAII. DEPARTMENT OF HEALTH. MENTAL HEALTH SERVICES FOR CHILDREN AND YOUTH; children's MH services branch. see *SOCIAL SERVICES AND WELFARE*

614   US   ISSN 1053-9662
HAWAII HEALTH MESSENGER. 1941. q. free. Department of Health, Communication Office, Box 3378, Honolulu, HI 96801. TEL 808-586-4442. FAX 808-586-4444. Ed. Barbara Hastings. charts; illus.; circ. 5,500 (controlled). (back issues avail.)

614   US
HAWAII HEALTH PLANNING NEWS. 1969. bi-m. free. State Health Planning and Development Agency, Box 3378, Honolulu, HI 96801. TEL 808-548-4050. Ed. Jane Pang. circ. controlled.

HAZARD MONTHLY. see *CIVIL DEFENSE*

614.8   US   ISSN 0743-8826
TA169.7
HAZARD PREVENTION. 1965. q. $45 to non-members. System Safety Society, Inc., Technology Trading Park, 5 Export Drive., Ste. A, Sterling, VA 22170-4421. TEL 703-444-6520. Ed. Sonya Kaiser. adv.; bk.rev.; circ. 1,700. (also avail. in microfiche; back issues avail.)
Description: Technical information and news of topical interest to those associated with the practice of system and product safety.

614.85   US   ISSN 0889-3454
HAZARDOUS MATERIALS NEWSLETTER. 1980. bi-m. $47 (foreign $50)(effective 1992). Hazardous Materials Publishing, Box 204, Barre, VT 05641. TEL 802-479-2307. Ed. John R. Cashman. adv.; bk.rev.; abstr.; bibl.; tr.lit.; circ. 705. (looseleaf format; back issues avail.)
Description: Addresses leak, fire, spill control for incident commanders and experienced responders, including incident causes, prevention, and remedial action.

HAZARDOUS SUBSTANCES & PUBLIC HEALTH. see *ENVIRONMENTAL STUDIES — Waste Management*

HAZARDOUS WASTE AND TOXIC TORTS LAW AND STRATEGY. see *LAW*

HAZARDOUS WASTE CONSULTANT. see *ENVIRONMENTAL STUDIES — Waste Management*

604.7   US   ISSN 0271-2601
KF3945.A15
HAZARDOUS WASTE REPORT. 1979. fortn. $475. Aspen Publishers, Inc., 200 Orchard Ridge Dr., Gaithersburg, MD 20878. TEL 301-417-7500. FAX 301-417-7550. **Indexed:** Energy Rev.

HAZARDS. see *OCCUPATIONAL HEALTH AND SAFETY*

614   JO
HEALTH/SIHHAH. (Text in Arabic) 1966. m. Ministry of Health, P.O. Box 86, Amman, Jordan. Ed. Dr. Ahmad al-Nabulsi.

614   NZ   ISSN 0017-887X
HEALTH. 1948. q. free. Department of Health, P.O. Box 5013, Wellington, New Zealand. Ed. V. Smith. charts; illus.; circ. 50,000.
Description: Covers health news and articles on a variety of health topics.

614.8 368.382   US   ISSN 0278-2715
RA410.A1
HEALTH AFFAIRS; the journal of the health policy sphere. 1981. q. $45 to individuals; institutions $75. (People-to-People Health Foundation, Inc.) Project Hope, Chevy Chase, MD 20815. TEL 301-656-7401. FAX 301-654-2845. Ed. John K. Iglehart. bk.rev.; circ. 10,000. (also avail. in microform from UMI; reprint service avail. from UMI)
Indexed: Abstr.Health Care Manage.Stud., Biostat., BPIA, Curr.Cont., Excerp.Med., Hosp.Lit.Ind., Manage.Cont., P.A.I.S., PSI.
—BLDSC shelfmark: 4274.710000.

614   UK   ISSN 0140-2986
RA421   CODEN: HEHYDD
HEALTH AND HYGIENE. 1977. q. £39. (Royal Institute of Public Health and Hygiene, Scientific & Medical Division) Macmillan Press Ltd., Houndmills, Basingstoke, Hampshire RG21 2XS, England. Ed. A.M.B. Golding. circ. 3,330. (back issues avail.)
Indexed: Abstr.Hyg., Curr.Adv.Ecol.Sci., Excerp.Med., Ind.Vet., Trop.Dis.Bull.
—BLDSC shelfmark: 4274.815000.

614   UK
HEALTH AND PERSONAL SOCIAL SERVICES STATISTICS. a. H.M.S.O., P.O. Box 276, London SW8 5DT, England. (reprint service avail. from UMI)
Formerly: Digest of Health Statistics for England and Wales (ISSN 0070-4849)

628 614.8   AT
HEALTH AND SAFETY AT WORK. 1983. bi-m. Aus.$30($30) Scriptographic Publications Pty. Ltd., P.O. Box 13, Marayong, N.S.W. 2148, Australia. TEL 02-831-5855. FAX 02-831-1248. Ed. Mitch Mitchell. circ. 5,060.
Incorporates: Safety in Australia (ISSN 0810-1167); Former titles: Health and Safety Concepts (ISSN 1030-4924) & Safety Concepts.
Description: For managers and employees in the occupational health and safety industry.

628 621.3   UK   ISSN 0142-5021
HEALTH & SAFETY NEWSLINE; for the engineering industry (UK). 1968. 8/yr. £45. Engineering Employers' Federation, Broadway House, Tothill St., London SW1H 9NQ, England. TEL 071-222-7777. FAX 071-222-2782. Ed. P.J. Reeve. bk.rev.; film rev.; index; circ. 9,000. (looseleaf format)
Formerly: (until 1984): Industrial Health and Safety.
Description: Keeps company management abreast of occupational health, safety and environmental developments in the U.K.

HEALTH AND SAFETY SCIENCE ABSTRACTS. see *PUBLIC HEALTH AND SAFETY — Abstracting, Bibliographies, Statistics*

614   UK
HEALTH AND SAFETY SPECIFIER. 1979. 3/yr. Portland Communications Ltd., 32 Portland St., Cheltenhand, Glos. GL52 2PB, England. FAX 0242-222331. Ed. D.G. Constantine. adv.; circ. 14,278.
Formerly: Health and Safety Product Information Cards.

614 360   CN
HEALTH AND SOCIAL SERVICE WORKFORCE IN ALBERTA. 1988. a. Health and Social Service Disciplines Committee, Kensington Place, 5th fl., 10011-109th St., Edmonton, Alta. T5J 3S8, Canada. TEL 403-427-2655. (back issues avail.)
Formerly: Health and Social Service Personnel Working in Alberta.
Description: Contains data and information on the health and social services of employers and self-employed professionals.

HEALTH AND SOCIAL WORK. see *SOCIAL SERVICES AND WELFARE*

HEALTH CARE COMPETITION WEEK. see *HOSPITALS*

PUBLIC HEALTH AND SAFETY 4103

614.8 US ISSN 1041-0236
CODEN: HECOER
HEALTH COMMUNICATION. 1989. q. $32.50 to individuals (foreign $57.50); institutions $115 (foreign $140). Lawrence Erlbaum Associates, Inc., 365 Broadway, Hillsdale, NJ 07642. TEL 201-666-4110. FAX 201-666-2394. Ed. Teresa L. Thompson.
—BLDSC shelfmark: 4274.953900.
Description: Features articles from scholars in communication, psychology, medicine, nursing and allied health fields.
Refereed Serial

HEALTH DEVICES. see *MEDICAL SCIENCES — Experimental Medicine, Laboratory Technique*

HEALTH EDUCATION NEWS. see *PHYSICAL FITNESS AND HYGIENE*

HEALTH FACILITIES DIRECTORY (SACRAMENTO). see *SOCIAL SERVICES AND WELFARE*

613 US
RA395.A3
HEALTH FREEDOM NEWS. 1955. m. $36 to individuals; senior citizens $24. National Health Federation, 212 W. Foothill, Monrovia, CA 91016. TEL 818-357-2181. FAX 818-303-0642. (Subscr. to: Box 688, Monrovia, CA 91016) Ed. James F. Scheer. adv.; bk.rev.; charts; illus.; stat.; circ. 25,000. (tabloid format; back issues avail.)
Former titles (until 1982): Public Scrutiny (ISSN 0743-5053); National Health Federation. Bulletin (ISSN 0027-9420)
Description: Covers educational, legislative and legal topics related to health.

HEALTH GRANTS & CONTRACTS WEEKLY; selected federal project opportunities. see *PUBLIC ADMINISTRATION*

614 US ISSN 0146-2768
RA177
HEALTH IN WISCONSIN. 1904. q. free to qualified personnel in Wisconsin. Department of Health and Social Services, Division of Health, Box 309, Madison, WI 53702. TEL 608-266-1511. Ed. Sherry L. Kasper. charts; illus.; circ. 22,000.
Former titles: Wisconsin's Health (ISSN 0043-6747); Health.

616.9 KE
HEALTH INFORMATION BULLETIN. (Text in English) 1977. q. free. Ministry of Health, Division of Communicable Diseases Control and Epidemiology, Box 20781, Nairobi, Kenya. circ. 500.

HEALTH LEGISLATION AND REGULATION. see *MEDICAL SCIENCES*

HEALTH LETTER (WASHINGTON). see *MEDICAL SCIENCES*

614 US ISSN 0735-9683
HEALTH MARKETING QUARTERLY. 1978. q. $45 to individuals; institutions $95; libraries $175. Haworth Press, Inc., 10 Alice St., Binghamton, NY 13904. TEL 800-342-9678. FAX 607-722-1424. TELEX 4932599 HAWORTH. Ed. William J. Winston. adv.; bk.rev.; abstr.; bibl.; circ. 508. (also avail. in microfiche from HAW; back issues avail.; reprint service avail. from HAW) **Indexed:** ABI Inform., Abstr.Health Care Manage.Stud., Abstr.Soc.Work, Chicago Psychoanal.Lit.Ind., Excerp.Med., Hosp.Abstr., Hosp.Lit.Ind., Med.Care Rev., Psychol.Abstr.
—BLDSC shelfmark: 4275.052850.
Former titles (until 1984): Topics in Strategic Planning for Health Care (ISSN 0731-714X); Topics in Health Care; Health and Medical Care Services Review (ISSN 0160-7618)
Description: Each issue is devoted to a select health service, and serves as a basic resource for marketing the selected service. Covers group practice marketing, mental health marketing, and long-term care marketing.
Refereed Serial

614.8 US ISSN 0899-4137
RJ102
HEALTH OF AMERICA'S CHILDREN. 1985. a. $12.95. Children's Defense Fund, 25 E St., N.W., Washington, DC 20001. TEL 202-628-8787. FAX 202-783-7324. Ed.Bd. charts; illus.
Formerly: Maternal and Child Health Data Book.
Description: Analysis of the current status of maternal and infant health, including national, state, and large city infant mortality rates, low-birthweight rates, American women's access to prenatal care, childbearing among teenagers and unmarried women, and the nation's progress on reaching the Surgeon General's objectives for maternal and infant health.

HEALTH ORGANIZATIONS OF THE U.S., CANADA AND THE WORLD; a directory of voluntary associations, professional societies and other groups concerned with health and related fields. see *MEDICAL SCIENCES*

613 US
HEALTH - P A C BULLETIN. 1968. q. $35 to individuals; institutions $45. Health Policy Advisory Center, 47 W. 14th St., 3rd fl., New York, NY 10011. TEL 212-627-1847. Ed. Ellen Bilofsky. adv.; bk.rev.; charts; illus.; stat.; tr.lit.; index; circ. 3,500. (also avail. in microform from UMI; back issues avail.)
Indexed: Alt.Press Ind., Med.Care Rev.
Supersedes (in 1987): Health and Medicine; **Formerly:** Health-Pac (ISSN 0017-9051)

614 370 NE ISSN 0168-8510
HEALTH POLICY. (Supplement avail.) (Text in English) 1979. 9/yr.(in 3 vols.; 3 nos./vol.). fl.996 (effective 1992). (European Health Policy Forum) Elsevier Science Publishers B.V., P.O. Box 211, 1000 AE Amsterdam, Netherlands. TEL 020-5803911. FAX 020-5803598. TELEX 18582 ESPA NL. (Subscr. in U.S. and Canada to: Elsevier Science Publishing Co., Inc., Box 882, Madison Sq. Sta., New York, NY 10159. TEL 212-989-5800) Ed. J.E. Blanplain. (reprint service avail. from ISI,SWZ)
Indexed: Abstr.Health Care Manage.Stud., Adol.Ment.Hlth.Abstr., ASCA, ASSIA, Cont.Pg.Educ., Curr.Cont., Excerp.Med., Hosp.Lit.Ind., P.A.I.S., Risk Abstr., Sci.Cit.Ind., SSCI.
—BLDSC shelfmark: 4275.102700.
Incorporates (in 1986): Effective Health Care (ISSN 0167-871X); **Formerly (until 1984):** Health Policy and Education (ISSN 0165-2281)
Description: Forum for discussion of health policy issues among health policy researchers, legislators, decision makers and other professionals.
Refereed Serial

614 UK ISSN 0268-1080
HEALTH POLICY AND PLANNING; a journal on health in development. 1986. q. £62($120) (London School of Hygiene and Tropical Medicine) Oxford University Press, Oxford Journals, Pinkhill House, Southfield Road, Eynsham, Oxford OX8 1JJ, England. TEL 0865-882283. FAX 0865-882890. TELEX 837330 OXPRES G. Eds. Patrick Vaughan, Gill Walt. adv.; bk.rev. **Indexed:** ASSIA, Curr.Adv.Ecol.Sci., Curr.Cont., Excerp.Med., Refug.Abstr., Rural Devel.Abstr., Sociol.Abstr., World Agri.Econ.& Rural Sociol.Abstr.
—BLDSC shelfmark: 4275.103300.
Description: Covers issues in health policy, planning, management and evaluation in the developing world.

614 US
HEALTH POLICY WEEK. 1971. w. $375. United Communications Group, 11300 Rockville Pike, Ste. 1100, Rockville, MD 20852-3030. TEL 301-816-8950. FAX 301-816-8945. Ed. Burt Schorr.
Description: Offers an inside look at federal and state government actions affecting the financing and delivery of health care services.

HEALTH PROFESSIONS REPORT; the independent bi-weekly newsletter on the education & training of medical, nursing and health professionals. see *EDUCATION*

614 CN ISSN 0833-7594
RA440.3.C2
HEALTH PROMOTION. French Edition: Promotion de la Sante (ISSN 0833-7608) (Text in English and French) 1962. q. free. Department of National Health and Welfare, Ottawa, Ont. K1A 1B4, Canada. TEL 613-954-8842. FAX 613-990-7097. Ed. K. Rawlings. bk.rev.; film rev.; circ. 14,000 (controlled) (10,000 English ed.; 4,000 French ed.). **Indexed:** Can.Per.Ind.
Formerly: Health Education (ISSN 0017-8950)

614 UK
RA427.8
HEALTH PROMOTION INTERNATIONAL. 1986. q. £62($120) (effective Jan. 1991). Oxford University Press, Pinkhill House, Southfield Road, Eynsham, Oxford OX8 1JJ, England. TEL 0865-882283. FAX 0865-882890. TELEX 837330 OXPRES G. Ed. John Catford. adv.; bk.rev.; circ. 1,500. **Indexed:** ASSIA, Excerp.Med.
Formerly (until 1989): Health Promotion (ISSN 0268-1099)
Description: Presents original articles, major reviews, and an editorial concerned with major health promotion themes.

HEALTH PSYCHOLOGY. see *PSYCHOLOGY*

614.8 UK
HEALTH, SAFETY ENVIRONMENT BULLETIN. 1976. m. £90 (foreign £100). Eclipse Publications Ltd., 18-20 Highbury Place, London N5 1QP, England. TEL 071-354-5858. FAX 071-359-4000. Ed. Rose Riddell. circ. 3,300. (reprint service avail. from UMI) **Indexed:** Br.Ceram.Abstr., Cadscan, Lab.Haz.Bull., Lead Abstr., World Surf.Coat., Zincscan.
Formerly: Health and Safety Information Bulletin (ISSN 0142-9086)

HEALTH SERVICES MANAGEMENT RESEARCH. see *MEDICAL SCIENCES*

HEALTH SERVICES RESEARCH. see *MEDICAL SCIENCES*

658 658 US ISSN 0361-0195
HEALTH SYSTEMS MANAGEMENT.* 1974. irreg., no.18, 1985. S P Medical & Scientific Books, Inc. (Subsidiary of: Spectrum Publications, Inc.), c/o Fisher, 200 Park Ave. S., New York, NY 10003-1503. Ed. Dr. Samuel Levey.

HEALTH TRENDS. see *MEDICAL SCIENCES*

614.8 US
HEALTHACTION;* for a productive life. 1985. m. (10/yr.). (Kelly Group, Ltd.) Joseph Kelly Publisher, Box 647, Charlottesville, VA 22902-0647. TEL 804-296-5676. FAX 804-296-3972. Ed. Polly Turner. circ. 550,000. (back issues avail.)
Description: Educates readers about nutrition, fitness, safety and overall wellness.

HEALTHCARE ADVERTISING REVIEW; creative forum for the people who plan and create healthcare advertising programs. see *ADVERTISING AND PUBLIC RELATIONS*

HEALTHFACTS. see *MEDICAL SCIENCES*

610 US ISSN 0736-7929
HEALTHLINE. 1981. m. $21 (foreign $33). Mosby - Year Book, Inc. (Subsidiary of: Times Mirror Company), 11830 Westline Industrial Dr., St. Louis, MO 63146. TEL 800-325-4177. FAX 314-432-1380. TELEX 44-2402. cum.index; circ. 11,000. (back issues avail.) **Indexed:** CHNI.
Description: Offers current information on health and wellness, written in nontechnical language by health care professionals and medical journalists.

HEALTHY LIFE NEWS. see *NUTRITION AND DIETETICS*

HEIM UND ANSTALT. see *FOOD AND FOOD INDUSTRIES*

614 BU ISSN 0018-8247
HIGIENA I ZDRAVEOPAZVANE. (Text in Bulgarian; summaries in English and Russian) 1958. bi-m. 24 lv.($10) (Ministerstvo na Narodnoto Zdrave) Izdatelstvo Meditsina i Fizkultura, 11, Pl. Slaveikov, Sofia, Bulgaria. (Co-sponsor: Nauchno Druzhestvo po Higiena i Organizacia na Zdraveopazvaneto) Ed. E. Efremov. adv.; bk.rev.; abstr.; charts; illus.; stat.; index; circ. 1,402. **Indexed:** Abstr.Bulg.Sci.Med.Lit., Biol.Abstr., Chem.Abstr., Excerp.Med., INIS Atomind., Nutr.Abstr.
—BLDSC shelfmark: 0391.860000.

PUBLIC HEALTH AND SAFETY

614.8 374   JA   ISSN 0912-1420
HOKEN KANRI SENTA DAYORI. (Text in Japanese) 1975. 3/yr. Nara Joshi Daigaku, Hoken Kanri Senta - Nara Women's University, Health Administration Center, Kita-Uoya-Higashi-cho, Nara-shi 630, Japan. Ed. Kimihiro Yamamoto. circ. 3,000.
 Description: Contains news of the center.

610   MX
HOMBRE Y TRABAJO; boletin de medicina, seguridad e higiene. 1976. m. Secretaria del Trabajo y Prevision Social, Direccion General de Medicina y Seguridad en el Trabajo, Calzada Azcapotzalco-La Villa No. 209, Junto Metro Ferreria, 02020 Mexico D.F, Mexico. TEL 3943344. Dir. Dr. Juan Antonio Legaspi Velasco. charts; illus.; stat.; circ. 4,000.
 Description: Covers many areas of occupational health, as well as general medicine.

HOPE HEALTH LETTER. see *PHYSICAL FITNESS AND HYGIENE*

614   US
HOPE NEWS. 1963. q. free. People-to-People Health Foundation, Inc., Project Hope Health Sciences Education Center, Millwood, VA 22646. TEL 703-837-2100. FAX 703-837-1813. Ed. Maggie Wolff Peterson. circ. 200,000.

HUANJING YU JIANKANG ZAZHI/JOURNAL OF ENVIRONMENT AND HEALTH. see *ENVIRONMENTAL STUDIES*

HUMAN ECOLOGY (PARK RIDGE). see *HOSPITALS*

HUMAN LIFE ISSUES. see *PHILOSOPHY*

HUMAN RESOURCES ADMINISTRATOR. see *HOSPITALS*

600   FR
HYGIE; international journal of health education. (Text in English, French, Spanish) 1958. q. 195 Fr. Union Internationale d'Education pour la Sante - International Union for Health Education, 15-21 rue de l'Ecole de Medecine, 75270 Paris Cedex 06, France. TEL 43-26-90-82. FAX 48-56-22-22. adv.; bk.rev.; bibl.; charts; illus.; stat.; index; circ. 4,000. (also avail. in microfilm from UMI; reprint service avail. from UMI) **Indexed:** Adol.Ment.Hlth.Abstr., Biol.Abstr., C.I.S. Abstr., Curr.Cont., Excerp.Med., FAMLI, NRN, SSCI, Trop.Dis.Bull.
 Formerly (until 1982): International Journal of Health Education (ISSN 0020-7306)
 Description: Presents theoretical research and practical papers on experiences, opinions and research leading to applications for health education internationally.

I A F C ON SCENE. (International Association of Fire Chiefs) see *FIRE PREVENTION*

I B F A N NEWS. (International Baby Food Action Network) see *CHILDREN AND YOUTH — About*

I B - 2. INFORMACJA BIEZACA; przeglad zawartosci czasopism polskich i obcojezycznych z zakresu medycyny spolecznej i organizacji ochrony zdrowia. see *MEDICAL SCIENCES*

I E E E CONFERENCE ON HUMAN FACTORS AND POWER PLANT. CONFERENCE RECORD. see *ENERGY — Nuclear Energy*

I P M PRACTITIONER; monitoring the field of pest management. (Integrated Pest Management) see *AGRICULTURE*

614   US
I S S A TODAY. 1975. m. $20. International Sanitary Supply Association, Inc., 7373 N. Lincoln Ave., Lincolnwood, IL 60646. TEL 312-982-0800. Ed. Betty A. Apelian. circ. 3,200 (controlled). (back issues avail.)

I Z A. (Illustrierte Zeitschrift fuer Arbeitssicherheit) see *OCCUPATIONAL HEALTH AND SAFETY*

IDAHO. DEPARTMENT OF HEALTH AND WELFARE. RESEARCH AND STATISTICS SECTION. QUARTERLY WELFARE STATISTICAL BULLETIN. see *SOCIAL SERVICES AND WELFARE — Abstracting, Bibliographies, Statistics*

614   IT   ISSN 0019-1639
                                CODEN: ISPRA2
IGIENE E SANITA PUBBLICA. (Text in Italian; summaries in English, French, German and Italian) 1945. bi-m. L.155000 (effective 1992). Gaetano Del Vecchio, Ed. & Pub., Via Stamira 7, 00162 Rome, Italy. TEL 06-4270948. adv.; bk.rev.; charts; illus.; index; circ. 2,000. (also avail. in microform from UMI) **Indexed:** Abstr.Hyg., Biol.Abstr., Chem.Abstr., Curr.Adv.Ecol.Sci., Excerp.Med., INIS Atomind., Trop.Dis.Bull.

IGIENE MENTALE. see *PSYCHOLOGY*

613 310   US   ISSN 0885-9914
RA448.5.I5
INDIAN HEALTH TRENDS AND SERVICES. 1969. irreg. free. U.S. Public Health Service, Resources and Services Administration, 5600 Fishers Ln., Rm. 6A-30, Rockville, MD 20857. TEL 202-545-6700. (Orders to: Supt. of Documents, Washington, DC 20402) stat.; circ. 15,000.

614   II
INDIAN JOURNAL OF ENVIRONMENTAL HEALTH. (Text in English) 1959. q. National Environmental Engineering Research Institute, Documentation and Library Services, Nehru Marg, Nagpur 440 020, India. (Affiliate: Council of Scientific and Industrial Research) Ed. S.B. Dabadghao. adv.; bk.rev.; bibl.; charts; illus.; tr.lit.; circ. 1,200. **Indexed:** Biol.Abstr., Chem.Abstr., Curr.Leather Lit., Environ.Per.Bibl., Excerp.Med., INIS Atomind., Ocean.Abstr., Pollut.Abstr., Soils & Fert., W.R.C.Inf.
 Formerly: Environmental Health (ISSN 0013-9289)

614   II   ISSN 0019-557X
RA421   CODEN: IPBHAH
INDIAN JOURNAL OF PUBLIC HEALTH. (Text in English) 1956. q. Rs.30($20) Indian Public Health Association, 110 Chittaranjan Ave., Calcutta 700 073, India. Ed. A.K. Chakraborty. adv.; bk.rev.; abstr.; charts; illus.; stat.; index; circ. 2,000. **Indexed:** Abstr.Hyg., Biol.Abstr., Chem.Abstr., Ind.Med., Ind.Vet., Small Anim.Abstr., Vet.Bull.
 —BLDSC shelfmark: 4420.400000.

THE INDIAN PRACTITIONER; a monthly journal of medicine, surgery & public health. see *MEDICAL SCIENCES*

614   US   ISSN 0019-6754
RA61
INDIANA STATE BOARD OF HEALTH BULLETIN. 1899-19??; resumed 1987. m. free. State Department of Health, Office of Public Affairs, 1330 W. Michigan St., Box 1964, Indianapolis, IN 46206. TEL 317-633-0100. FAX 317-633-0779. Ed. Mary Ann McKinney. bk.rev.; illus.; stat.; circ. 12,000. **Indexed:** Rehabil.Lit.

614   IO   ISSN 0216-3527
INDONESIAN JOURNAL OF PUBLIC HEALTH/MAJALAH KESEHATAN MASYARAKAT INDONESIA. (Text and summaries in English and Indonesian) 1969. m. Rps.3500 per no. Indonesian Public Health Association - Ikatan Ahli Kesehatan Masyarakat Indonesia, Pegangsaan Timur 16, Jakarta, Indonesia. Ed. Azrul Azwar. adv.; bk.rev.; charts; illus.; stat.; circ. 10,000.
 Former titles: Indonesian Public Health Association. Journal; Indonesian Journal of Public Health.

INDOOR AIR QUALITY UPDATE; a guide to the practical control of indoor air problems. see *ARCHITECTURE*

INDOOR POLLUTION LAW REPORTER. see *LAW*

INDUSTRIAL CRISIS QUARTERLY; international journal of industrial and organizational crises. see *BUSINESS AND ECONOMICS — Management*

614.8 340 610   US   ISSN 0890-3018
INDUSTRIAL HEALTH & HAZARDS UPDATE. 1984. m. $219 (Canada $239; elsewhere $279). Merton Allen Associates, InfoTeam Inc., Box 15640, Plantation, FL 33318-5640. TEL 305-473-9560. FAX 305-473-0544. Eds. Merton Allen, David R. Allen. (back issues avail.; reprint service avail.)
 •Also available online. Vendor(s): Data-Star, DIALOG, Human Resources Information Network, NewsNet (LA04).
 Description: Covers occupational health, safety, hazards, and related subjects. Designed for busy executives in the health, medical, environmental, legal, management, and technological fields of industry, government, commerce, and academia.

INFORMAZIONE INNOVATIVA; agenzia guindicinale di documentazione tecnica scientifica legislativa. see *ENVIRONMENTAL STUDIES*

628   IT   ISSN 0394-5871
INGEGNERIA AMBIENTALE. (Text in Italian; summaries in English, Italian) 1972. 9/yr. L.180000. (Centro di Ingegneria per la Protezione dell'Ambiente) C I P A s.r.l., Via Palladio, 26, 20135 Milan, Italy. TEL 02-58301528. FAX 02-58301550. Ed.Bd. adv.; bk.rev.; circ. 1,800. **Indexed:** Chem.Abstr., Pollut.Abstr.
 —BLDSC shelfmark: 4500.650000.
 Formerly (until 1986): Ingegneria Ambientale Inquinamento e Depurazione (ISSN 0302-7775)

628   IT
INGEGNERIA AMBIENTALE QUADERNI. (Text in Italian; summaries in English, Italian) 1984. 2/yr. L.80000. (Centro di Ingegneria per la Protezione dell'Ambiente) C I P A s.r.l., Via Palladio, 26, 20135 Milan, Italy. TEL 02-58301528. FAX 02-58301550. **Indexed:** Chem.Abstr., Pollut.Abstr.
 Formerly: Ingegneria Ambientale Inquinamento e Depurazione Quaderni.

628   IT
INGEGNERIA SANITARIA AMBIENTALE; rivista tecnica bimestrale. 1952; N.S. 1989. bi-m. L.74000 (effective 1992). (Associazione Nazionale di Ingegneria Sanitaria) Maggioli Editore, Via Crimea, 1, Casella Postale 290, 47037 Rimini, Italy. TEL 0541-626777. FAX 0541-622020. Dir. Luigi Mendia. adv.; bk.rev.; abstr.; bibl.; charts; illus.; circ. 3,800. **Indexed:** Chem.Abstr., INIS Atomind.
 Formerly: Ingegneria Sanitaria (ISSN 0020-0980)

628   AG   ISSN 0446-2424
INGENIERIA SANITARIA.* (Text in English, French, Portuguese and Spanish) 1946. q. $16. Interamerican Association of Sanitary and Environmental Engineering, Corrientes 330, 4 piso, 1378 Buenos Aires, Argentina. Ed. Osvaldo Rey. adv.; bk.rev.; circ. 8,000. **Indexed:** Pollut.Abstr.

INSTITUTE OF HEALTH EDUCATION. JOURNAL. see *MEDICAL SCIENCES*

614   JA
INSTITUTE OF PUBLIC HEALTH. ANNUAL REPORT/KOKURITSU KOSHU EISEI-IN NENPO. (Text in Japanese) 1948. a. Institute of Public Health - Kokuritsu Koshu Eisei-in, 4-6-1 Shiroganedai, Minato-ku, Tokyo 108, Japan.

614   JA   ISSN 0020-3106
                              CODEN: KEKHA7
INSTITUTE OF PUBLIC HEALTH. BULLETIN/KOKURITSU KOSHU EISEI-IN KENKYU HOKOKU. (Text in English or Japanese) 1952. q. free or exchange basis. Institute of Public Health - Kokuritsu Koshu Eisei-in, 4-6-1 Shiroganedai, Minato-ku, Tokyo 108, Japan. Ed. Dr. Takeshi Suzuki. abstr.; bibl.; charts; illus.; index; circ. 1,200. **Indexed:** Abstr.Hyg., Biol.Abstr., Chem.Abstr., Excerp.Med., Ind.Vet., INIS Atomind., Trop.Dis.Bull., Vet.Bull.
 —BLDSC shelfmark: 2584.000000.

PUBLIC HEALTH AND SAFETY 4105

614 II ISSN 0251-110X
TD1
INSTITUTION OF ENGINEERS (INDIA). ENVIRONMENTAL ENGINEERING DIVISION. JOURNAL. (Text in English) 1920. 3/yr. Rs.60($8) Institution of Engineers (India), Environmental Engineering Division, 8 Gokhale Rd., Calcutta 700 020, India. TEL 033-288334. FAX 033-288345. TELEX 0217885 IEIC IN. Ed. K.N. Majumdar. adv.; charts; illus.; index; circ. 7,000. **Indexed:** INIS Atomind., Ocean.Abstr., Pollut.Abstr.
Formerly: Institution of Engineers (India). Public Health Engineering Division. Journal (ISSN 0020-3416)

616.988 PO ISSN 0303-7762
CODEN: AIHTDH
INSTITUTO DE HIGIENE E MEDICINA TROPICAL. ANAIS. (Text and summaries in English, French and Portuguese) 1943. irreg., vol.10, 1984. price varies. Instituto de Higiene e Medicina Tropical, Centro de Documentacao e Informacao Cientifica, Rua da Junqueira, 96, Lisbon 3, Portugal. bk.rev.; circ. 1,000. **Indexed:** Abstr.Hyg., Biol.Abstr., Excerp.Med., Helminthol.Abstr., Ind.Med., Ind.Vet., Rev.Appl.Entomol., Trop.Dis.Bull., Vet.Bull.
Formerly: Lisbon. Escola Nacional de Saude de Medicina Tropical. Anais (ISSN 0075-9767)

589.9 CL ISSN 0716-1387
RA465 CODEN: BICHDZ
INSTITUTO DE SALUD PUBLICA DE CHILE. BOLETIN. (Text in Spanish; summaries in English) 1942. 2/yr. $6. Instituto de Salud Publica de Chile, Marathon 1000, Casillo 48, Santiago, Chile. Eds. J. Hernan Lobos R., Julio Garcia M. adv.; bk.rev.; bibl.; charts; illus.; circ. 628. **Indexed:** Biol.Abstr., Chem.Abstr., Ind.Med., Trop.Dis.Bull.
Formerly: Instituto Bacteriologico de Chile. Boletin (ISSN 0374-6224)

614 MX
INSTITUTO MEXICANO DEL SEGURO SOCIAL. BOLETIN ESTADISTICO. 1972. a. free. Instituto Mexicano del Seguro Social, Subdireccion General Medica, Jefatura de Servicios de Medicina Preventiva, Apdo. Postal 12976, 03001 Mexico, D.F., Mexico. circ. 2,000.

614 MX
INSTITUTO MEXICANO DEL SEGURO SOCIAL. BOLETIN SOBRE MORBILIDAD HOSPITALARIA. 1982. a. free. Instituto Mexicano del Seguro Social, Subdireccion General Medica, Jefatura de Servicios de Medicina Preventiva, Apdo. Postal 12976, 03001 Mexico, D.F., Mexico. circ. 2,000.

614 MX
INSTITUTO MEXICANO DEL SEGURO SOCIAL. BOLETIN SOBRE MORTALIDAD. 1977. a. free. Instituto Mexicano del Seguro Social, Subdireccion General Medica, Jefatura de Servicios de Medicina Preventiva, Apdo. Postal 12976, 03001 Mexico, D.F., Mexico. circ. 2,000.

614 MX
INSTITUTO MEXICANO DEL SEGURO SOCIAL. BOLETIN SOBRE MOTIVOS DE CONSULTA. 1980. a. free. Instituto Mexicano del Seguro Social, Subdireccion General Medica, Jefatura de Servicios de Medicina Preventiva, Apdo. Postal 12976, 03001 Mexico D.F., Mexico. circ. 2,000.

INSTYTUT BADAN JADROWYCH. ZAKLAD RADIOBIOLOGII I OCHRONY ZDROWIA. PRACE DOSWIADCZALNE. see *MEDICAL SCIENCES — Radiology And Nuclear Medicine*

614.86 US ISSN 0018-988X
HE5614
INSURANCE INSTITUTE FOR HIGHWAY SAFETY. STATUS REPORT. 1961. m. free. Insurance Institute for Highway Safety, 1005 North Glebe Rd., Arlington, VA 22101. TEL 703-247-1500. Ed. James H. Mooney. index; circ. 17,000. (also avail. in microform from UMI; reprint service avail. from UMI)
Formerly: I I H S Report.

INTEGRO; Gesundheits- und Sozialmagazin des V.P.O.D. see *SOCIAL SERVICES AND WELFARE*

INTERFACE (BETHESDA). see *COMPUTERS*

614 UN ISSN 0074-1892
HD7269.A6 CODEN: SSAEAW
INTERNATIONAL ATOMIC ENERGY AGENCY. SAFETY SERIES. (Text in English, French, Russian or Spanish) 1960. irreg. price varies. International Atomic Energy Agency, Wagramer Str. 5, Box 100, A-1400 Vienna, Austria. (Dist. in U.S. by: Unipub, 4611-F Assembly Dr., Lanham, MD 20706-4391) **Indexed:** Biol.Abstr., Pollut.Abstr.
—BLDSC shelfmark: 8069.140000.

614 UN ISSN 0020-6563
INTERNATIONAL DIGEST OF HEALTH LEGISLATION. (Editions in English and French) 1949. q. 150 Fr.($120) World Health Organization, Distribution and Sales, CH-1211 Geneva 27, Switzerland. TEL 022-791-2111. bibl.; charts; index; circ. 3,600 (2,600 English ed.; 1,000 French ed.). **Indexed:** Adol.Ment.Hlth.Abstr., Biol.Abstr., Cadscan, Curr.Adv.Ecol.Sci., Dairy Sci.Abstr., Food Sci.& Tech.Abstr., I.P.A., INIS Atomind., Lead Abstr., NRN, Zincscan.
—BLDSC shelfmark: 4539.600000.
Description: Allows readers to follow worldwide developments in laws and regulations designed to protect public health and the human environment.

INTERNATIONAL ENVIRONMENT AND SAFETY. see *ENVIRONMENTAL STUDIES*

INTERNATIONAL FOOD SAFETY NEWS. see *FOOD AND FOOD INDUSTRIES*

INTERNATIONAL JOURNAL OF EPIDEMIOLOGY. see *MEDICAL SCIENCES*

614 US ISSN 0020-7314
RA421 CODEN: IJUSC3
INTERNATIONAL JOURNAL OF HEALTH SERVICES. 1970. q. $36 to individuals; institutions $108. Baywood Publishing Co., Inc., 26 Austin Ave., Box 337, Amityville, NY 11701. TEL 516-691-1270. FAX 516-691-1770. Ed. Dr. Vicente Navarro. bk.rev.; abstr.; illus. (back issues avail.) **Indexed:** Abstr.Health Care Manage.Stud., Abstr.Hosp.Manage.Stud., Abstr.Hyg., ASSIA, Biol.Abstr., C.I.S. Abstr., Curr.Cont., Excerp.Med., Hosp.Lit.Ind., I D A, I.P.A., Ind.Med., INIS Atomind., Med.Care Rev., Mid.East: Abstr.& Ind., Risk Abstr., Rural Devel.Abstr., SSCI, Trop.Dis.Bull.
●Also available online.
—BLDSC shelfmark: 4542.278000.
Description: Contains current and authoritative information on the development of the health care industry worldwide.
Refereed Serial

INTERNATIONAL JOURNAL OF MASS EMERGENCIES AND DISASTERS. see *SOCIOLOGY*

INTERNATIONAL JOURNAL OF MENTAL HEALTH. see *PSYCHOLOGY*

INTERNATIONAL NARCOTICS CONTROL BOARD. REPORT FOR (YEAR). see *PHARMACY AND PHARMACOLOGY*

INTERNATIONAL PEST CONTROL; crop protection, public health, wood preservation. see *BIOLOGY — Entomology*

613 US ISSN 0272-684X
RA440.A1
INTERNATIONAL QUARTERLY OF COMMUNITY HEALTH EDUCATION. 1981. q. $36 to individuals; institutions $102. Baywood Publishing Co., Inc., 26 Austin Ave., Box 337, Amityville, NY 11701. TEL 516-691-1270. FAX 516-691-1770. Ed. Dr. George Cernada. bk.rev.; abstr.; illus. (back issues avail.) **Indexed:** Curr.Lit.Fam.Plan., NRN.
—BLDSC shelfmark: 4545.510000.
Description: Focuses on the systematic application of social science and health education theory and methodology to public health problems. Applies consumer-directed approaches to control preventive and curative health services.

INTERNATIONAL SECURITY DIRECTORY; world defense, police & fire headquarters, security companies, their products and supplies. see *CRIMINOLOGY AND LAW ENFORCEMENT — Security*

614.8 US
INTERNATIONAL SYSTEM SAFETY CONFERENCE. PROCEEDINGS. 1971. biennial. $75. System Safety Society, Inc., Technology Trading Park, 5 Export Dr., Ste. A, Sterling, VA 22170-4421.
TEL 703-444-6520. Ed.Bd. circ. 550. (back issues avail.)
Description: Technical papers on system and product safety.

614 UN
RA638
INTERNATIONAL TRAVEL AND HEALTH: VACCINATION REQUIREMENTS AND HEALTH ADVICE. French edition: Voyages Internationaux et Sante. Vaccinations Exigees et Conseils d'Hygiene. (Editions in English, French, German) a. World Health Organization, Distribution and Sales, CH-1211 Geneva 27, Switzerland. TEL 022-791-2111. circ. 15,000.
Former titles: Vaccination Certificate Requirements and Health Advice for International Travel (ISSN 0257-912X) & Vaccination Certificate Requirements for International Travel and Health Advice to Travellers (ISSN 0254-296X) & Vaccination Certificate Requirements for International Travel (ISSN 0512-3011)
Description: Serves to alert physicians, health authorities and airline and shipping companies to changes in required and recommended vaccinations that need to be communicated to travelers.

INTERNATIONAL UNION OF SCHOOL AND UNIVERSITY HEALTH AND MEDICINE. CONGRESS REPORTS. see *EDUCATION*

INVENTORY OF HEALTH & SOCIAL SERVICE PERSONNEL. see *SOCIAL SERVICES AND WELFARE*

614 IR ISSN 0304-4556
CODEN: IJPHCD
IRANIAN JOURNAL OF PUBLIC HEALTH/MAJALLE-YE BEHDASHT-E IRAN. (Text and summaries in English and Persian) 1972. q. Rs.1000($25) Iranian Public Health Association, University of Teheran, Teheran, Iran. Ed. D. Farhud. illus.; index; circ. 2,000. **Indexed:** Abstr.Hyg., Biol.Abstr., Chem.Abstr., Entomol.Abstr., Excerp.Med., Helminthol.Abstr., Nutr.Abstr., Protozool.Abstr., Rev.Appl.Entomol., Trop.Dis.Bull.
—BLDSC shelfmark: 4567.529200.

614 IS
ISRAEL. MINISTRY OF HEALTH. DIVISION OF EPIDEMIOLOGY. INFECTIOUS DISEASES SURVEILLANCE. (Text in English) s-a. Ministry of Health, Division of Epidemiology, 20 King David St., Jerusalem 91000, Israel.

614 IS
ISRAEL. MINISTRY OF HEALTH. DIVISION OF EPIDEMIOLOGY. WEEKLY EPIDEMIOLOGICAL RECORD. (Text in English) w. Ministry of Health, Division of Epidemiology, 20 King David St., Jerusalem, Israel.

610 636.089 IT ISSN 0021-2571
R61 CODEN: AISSAW
ISTITUTO SUPERIORE DI SANITA. ANNALI. (Text and summaries in English or Italian) 1960. q. L.63000 (foreign L.83000)(effective 1991). Istituto Superiore di Sanita, Viale Regina Elena 299, 00161 Rome, Italy. TEL 06-4990. FAX 06-4469938. TELEX 610071 ISTSAN I. (Subscr. to: Istituto Poligrafico e Zecca dello Stato, Direzione Commerciale - Settore Abbonamenti, Piazza Verdi 10, 00190 Rome, Italy.. TEL 06-85081) Ed. Vilma Alberani. bk.rev.; abstr.; bibl.; illus.; index, cum.index; circ. 1,000. (back issues avail.) **Indexed:** Biol.Abstr., Chem.Abstr., Dairy Sci.Abstr., Excerp.Med., Food Sci.& Tech.Abstr., Ind.Med., Ind.Vet., Nutr.Abstr., Protozool.Abstr., Rev.Appl.Entomol., Rev.Med.& Vet.Mycol., Sci.Abstr., Trop.Dis.Bull., Vet.Bull.
—BLDSC shelfmark: 1008.045000.
Formerly: Istituto Superiore di Sanita. Rendiconti.
Description: Original articles, monographs, proceedings and technical notes on health issues in many areas of public health.

614 BG
JOPSOM. (Journal of Preventive and Social Medicine) 1982. s-a. Tk.540($18) National Institute of Preventive and Social Medicine, Mohakhali, Dhaka 12, Bangladesh. Ed. Prof. M. Mobarak Ali. circ. 500. (back issues avail.)

PUBLIC HEALTH AND SAFETY

614   JM   ISSN 0021-4132
JAMAICA PUBLIC HEALTH. vol.41, 1966. q. free. Ministry of Health and Environmental Control, Bureau of Health Education, Box 478, Kingston, Jamaica, W.I. charts; illus.; circ. 40,000.

JAPANESE JOURNAL OF SANITARY ZOOLOGY/EISEI DOBUTSU. see *BIOLOGY — Zoology*

614   CC
JIANKANG WENZHAI/HEALTH DIGEST. (Text in Chinese) bi-m. Tianjin Weisheng Xuanchuan Jiaoyu-suo - Tianjin Health Education Institute, 14 Donglou Dongweili, Hexi-qu, Tianjin 300074, People's Republic of China. TEL 317495. Ed. Yang Dafeng.

614   UN   ISSN 0449-122X
TX537
JOINT F A O - W H O CODEX ALIMENTARIUS COMMISSION. REPORT OF THE SESSION. (Editions in English, French, Spanish) 1963. irreg., 18th, 1989, Geneva. $17. Food and Agriculture Organization of the United Nations, c/o UNIPUB, 4611-F Assembly Dr., Lanham, MD 20706-4391.

614   US   ISSN 0090-7421
R690
JOURNAL OF ALLIED HEALTH. 1972. q. $65 to non-members. (American Society of Allied Health Professions) University of Illinois at Chicago, College of Associated Health Professions (M-C 518), 169 CME, Box 6998, Chicago, IL 60680. TEL 312-996-6697. FAX 312-413-0086. Ed. David C. Broski. adv.; bk.rev.; circ. 2,000. (also avail. in microform from UMI,MIM; reprint service avail. from UMI) **Indexed:** Biol.Abstr., C.I.J.E., C.I.N.L., Dent.Ind., Ind.Med.
—BLDSC shelfmark: 4927.150000.
  Description: Publishes scholarly papers, reports and findings related to research and development in allied health education, practice, history and current trends.

610.28   US   ISSN 0021-9290
QP303   CODEN: JBMCBS
JOURNAL OF BIOMECHANICS. 1968. m. £490 (effective 1992). (American Society of Biomechanics) Pergamon Press, Inc., Journals Division, 660 White Plains Rd., Tarrytown, NY 10591-5153. TEL 914-524-9200. FAX 914-333-2444. (And: Headington Hill Hall, Oxford OX3 0BW, England. TEL 0865-794141) (Co-sponsor: European Society of Biomechanics) Eds. Richard A. Brand, Rik Huiskes. adv.; bk.rev.; charts; illus.; stat.; index; circ. 1,600. (also avail. in microform from MIM,UMI; back issues avail.; reprint service avail. from UMI) **Indexed:** Appl.Mech.Rev., Bioeng.Abstr., Biol.Abstr., Curr.Cont., Dent.Ind., Eng.Ind., Excerp.Med., Ind.Med., Ind.Sci.Rev., INIS Atomind., Int.Aerosp.Abstr., Sci.Abstr., Sci.Cit.Ind.
—BLDSC shelfmark: 4953.600000.
  Description: Publishes original research concerning the application of mechanics to medical and biological problems.
  Refereed Serial

JOURNAL OF COMMUNITY HEALTH; the publication for health promotion and disease prevention. see *MEDICAL SCIENCES*

JOURNAL OF ENVIRONMENTAL HEALTH. see *ENVIRONMENTAL STUDIES*

JOURNAL OF ENVIRONMENTAL PATHOLOGY, TOXICOLOGY AND ONCOLOGY. see *ENVIRONMENTAL STUDIES — Toxicology And Environmental Safety*

JOURNAL OF ENVIRONMENTAL SCIENCE AND HEALTH. PART A: ENVIRONMENTAL SCIENCE AND ENGINEERING. see *ENVIRONMENTAL STUDIES*

JOURNAL OF ENVIRONMENTAL SCIENCE AND HEALTH. PART B: PESTICIDES, FOOD CONTAMINANTS, AND AGRICULTURAL WASTES. see *ENVIRONMENTAL STUDIES*

JOURNAL OF EPIDEMIOLOGY & COMMUNITY HEALTH. see *MEDICAL SCIENCES*

613   US   ISSN 0362-028X
SF221   CODEN: JFPRDR
JOURNAL OF FOOD PROTECTION. 1937. m. $135. International Association of Milk, Food and Environmental Sanitarians, Inc., 502 E. Lincoln Way, Ames, IA 50010-6666. TEL 515-232-6699. FAX 515-232-4736. Ed. Lloyd Bullerman. adv.; bk.rev.; charts; illus.; index; circ. 3,500. (also avail. in microform from UMI; reprint service avail. from UMI) **Indexed:** Biol.Abstr., Biol.& Agr.Ind., Biotech.Abstr., Chem.Abstr., Curr.Adv.Ecol.Sci., Curr.Cont., Curr.Pack.Abstr., Dairy Sci.Abstr., Excerp.Med., Food Sci.& Tech.Abstr., Ind.Sci.Rev., Ind.Vet., Int.Packag.Abstr., Maize Abstr., Microbiol.Abstr., Nutr.Abstr., Packag.Sci.Tech., Pig News & Info., Poult.Abstr., Rev.Plant Path., Rice Abstr., Risk Abstr., Sci.Cit.Ind., Soils & Fert., Triticale Abstr., Vet.Bull., Weed Abstr.
—BLDSC shelfmark: 4984.550000.
  Formerly (until 1977): Journal of Milk and Food Technology (ISSN 0022-2747)
  Refereed Serial

JOURNAL OF HEALTH AND HUMAN RESOURCES ADMINISTRATION. see *HOSPITALS*

JOURNAL OF HEALTH & SOCIAL POLICY. see *SOCIAL SERVICES AND WELFARE*

614   NE   ISSN 0167-6296
JOURNAL OF HEALTH ECONOMICS. (Text in English) 1982. 4/yr. fl.365 (effective 1992). North-Holland (Subsidiary of: Elsevier Science Publishers B.V.), P.O. Box 211, 1000 AE Amsterdam, Netherlands. TEL 020-5803911. FAX 020-5803598. TELEX 18582 ESPA NL. (Subscr. in U.S. and Canada to: Elsevier Science Publishing Co., Inc., Box 882, Madison Sq. Sta., New York, NY 10159. TEL 212-989-5800) Ed. Joseph P. Newhouse. adv.; bk.rev. (back issues avail.; reprint service avail. from SWZ) **Indexed:** ABI Inform., Abstr.Health Care Manage.Stud., Abstr.Hyg., ASSIA, C.R.E.J., Excerp.Med., J.of Econ.Lit., Med.Care Rev., Sage Fam.Stud.Abstr., Sage Pub.Admin.Abstr., SSCI
—BLDSC shelfmark: 4996.750000.
  Description: Publishes articles related to the economics of health and medical care.
  Refereed Serial

JOURNAL OF HYGIENE, EPIDEMIOLOGY, MICROBIOLOGY AND IMMUNOLOGY. see *MEDICAL SCIENCES*

614.8 360   US   ISSN 0092-8623
JOURNAL OF MENTAL HEALTH ADMINISTRATION. 1972. s-a. $40. Association of Mental Health Administrators, 60 Revere Dr., Ste. 500, Northbrook, IL 60062. TEL 708-480-9626. Ed. James Rayball. adv.; bk.rev.; charts; illus.; stat.; index; circ. 2,000. (also avail. in microfilm from UMI) **Indexed:** Abstr.Health Care Manage.Stud., PSI, Psychol.Abstr.
—BLDSC shelfmark: 5017.685000.

628   US   ISSN 0884-0946
JOURNAL OF NATURAL HYGIENE; the science and philosophy of natural living. 1985. bi-m. $17 (foreign $30). Natural Hygiene, Inc., Box 2132, Huntington, CT 06484. TEL 203-929-1557. Ed. Jo Willard. adv.; bk.rev.; abstr.; circ. 1,850. (back issues avail.)
  Description: Covers the laws of nature and provides information on ways of maintaining or regaining health.

JOURNAL OF PESTICIDE REFORM. see *ENVIRONMENTAL STUDIES*

628   JA   ISSN 0385-1559
                        CODEN: NNGADV
JOURNAL OF PESTICIDE SCIENCE. 1976. 4/yr. 6000 Yen($40) (international ed. fl.330)(effective 1992). Pesticide Science Society of Japan, 43-11 Komagome, 1-chome, Toshima-ku, Tokyo, 170, Japan. TEL 03-3943-6021. FAX 075-753-6312. (International edition dist. outside Japan by: Elsevier Science Publishers B.V., P.O. Box 211, 1000 AE Amsterdam, Netherlands. TEL 020-5803911; Subscr. in U.S. and Canada to: Elsevier Science Publishing Co., Inc., Box 882, Madison Sq. Sta., New York, NY 10159. TEL 212-989-5800) Ed. Shozo Takahashi. adv.; bk.rev.; index; circ. 2,000. (back issues avail.) **Indexed:** Chem.Abstr., Crop Physiol.Abstr., Field Crop Abstr., Hort.Abstr., Maize Abstr., Plant Grow.Reg.Abstr., Rice Abstr., Seed Abstr., Soils & Fert., Weed Abstr.
—BLDSC shelfmark: 5030.981000.

JOURNAL OF PHARMACOEPIDEMIOLOGY. see *PHARMACY AND PHARMACOLOGY*

JOURNAL OF PUBLIC HEALTH DENTISTRY. see *MEDICAL SCIENCES — Dentistry*

JOURNAL OF PUBLIC HEALTH MEDICINE. see *SOCIAL SERVICES AND WELFARE*

614.8 178 658   US   ISSN 0197-5897
RA421   CODEN: JPPODK
JOURNAL OF PUBLIC HEALTH POLICY. 1980. q. $100 (foreign $110). Journal of Public Health Policy, Inc., 208 Meadowood Dr., South Burlington, VT 05403. TEL 802-658-0136. FAX 802-862-4011. Ed. Dr. Milton Terris. adv.; bk.rev.; circ. 1,800. (back issues avail.) **Indexed:** Abstr.Health Care Manage.Stud., Curr.Cont., Dok.Arbeitsmed., Environ.Abstr., Environ.Per.Bibl., Excerp.Med., Ind.Med., P.A.I.S., Sociol.Abstr.
—BLDSC shelfmark: 5043.570000.
  Refereed Serial

JOURNAL OF RURAL HEALTH. see *MEDICAL SCIENCES*

613   US   ISSN 0022-4391
LB3401   CODEN: JSHEA2
JOURNAL OF SCHOOL HEALTH. 1930. m. (Aug.-May). $70 to individuals; institutions $80. American School Health Association, Box 708, Kent, OH 44240. Ed. R. Morgan Pigg, Jr. adv.; bk.rev.; abstr.; bibl.; charts; stat.; index, cum.index every 10 yrs; circ. 10,000. (also avail. in microform from BLH,UMI; reprint service avail. from UMI) **Indexed:** Acad.Ind., Adol.Ment.Hlth.Abstr., Biog.Ind., Biol.Abstr., C.I.J.E., C.I.N.L., Cont.Pg.Educ., Curr.Cont., Curr.Lit.Fam.Plan., Dent.Ind., Educ.Ind., Except.Child.Educ.Abstr., Hlth.Ind., Ind.Med., Int.Nurs.Ind., Nurs.Abstr., Phys.Ed.Ind., Psychol.Abstr., Res.High.Educ.Abstr., Risk Abstr., Sp.Ed.Needs Abstr., Sportsearch (1976-), SSCI, Stud.Wom.Abstr.
—BLDSC shelfmark: 5052.650000.
  Formerly: School Physicians Bulletin.

JOURNAL OF TOXICOLOGY AND ENVIRONMENTAL HEALTH. see *ENVIRONMENTAL STUDIES — Toxicology And Environmental Safety*

JOURNAL OF TRAFFIC SAFETY EDUCATION. see *TRANSPORTATION — Automobiles*

JOURNAL OF TROPICAL MEDICINE AND HYGIENE; devoted to medical, surgical and sanitary work in warm countries. see *MEDICAL SCIENCES — Communicable Diseases*

KANSAS SPEECH - LANGUAGE - HEARING ASSOCIATION JOURNAL. see *EDUCATION — Special Education And Rehabilitation*

KEEPING THE TRUST. see *SOCIAL SERVICES AND WELFARE*

613   JA   ISSN 0022-9938
KENKO KYOIKU/PUBLIC HEALTH EDUCATION. (Text in Japanese) 1956. q. free. Kawai Pharmaceutical Co., Ltd. - Kawai Seiyaku K.K., 2-51-8 Arai, Nakano-ku, Tokyo 165, Japan. FAX 03-3385-3118. Ed. Dr. T. Shimizu. bibl.; circ. 20,000. (processed)

KOKORO TO SHAKAI/MIND AND SOCIETY. see *PSYCHOLOGY*

614.8   JA
KOKUTETSU CHUO HOKEN KANRIJOHO; health control. (Text and summaries in English, Japanese) 1955. a. free. Japanese National Railways, Central Health Institute, 2-1 Yoyogi, Shibuyaku, Tokyo 151, Japan. circ. 1,000. (back issues avail.)

614   KO   ISSN 0023-401X
RA421   CODEN: KOPOAL
KOREAN JOURNAL OF PUBLIC HEALTH/BO KUN HAK NON ZIP. (Text in English and Korean) 1964. s-a. free. Seoul National University, School of Public Health, 28 Yunkun-dong, Chongro-ku, Seoul, S. Korea. TEL 02-762-9101. Ed. Moonshik Zong. circ. 1,000. **Indexed:** Biol.Abstr. Key Title: Gonjun Bogen Jabji.

PUBLIC HEALTH AND SAFETY 4107

628   JA   ISSN 0368-5187
KOSHU EISEI/JOURNAL OF PUBLIC HEALTH PRACTICE.
(Text in Japanese) 1946. m. 21240 Yen($163) Igaku-Shoin Ltd., 5-24-3 Hongo, Bunkyo-ku, Tokyo 113-91, Japan. TEL 03-3817-5718. Ed. Shunichi Araki. circ. 3,500.
—BLDSC shelfmark: 5043.600000.

614   NE   ISSN 0075-6954
RA412.5.N4
KOSTEN EN FINANCIERING VAN DE GEZONDHEIDZORG IN NEDERLAND/COST OF HEALTH CARE IN THE NETHERLANDS. (Text in Dutch and English) 1953. irreg. Centraal Bureau voor de Statistiek, Prinses Beatrixlaan 428, Voorburg, Netherlands. (Orders to: SDU-Publishers, Christoffel Plantijnstraat, The Hague, Netherlands)

614.8   FI
KOTILAAKARI. 1889. m. FIM 231. Yhtyneet Kuvalehdet Oy, Maistraatinporti 1, 00240 Helsinki, Finland. Ed. Tarja Juntunen. circ. 55,000.

KRITISCHE MEDIZIN IM ARGUMENT. see *MEDICAL SCIENCES*

614   IS
KUPAT-HOLIM. INFORMATION SERIES: SPECIAL STUDIES AND SURVEYS ON MEDICAL MANPOWER SOCIOLOGY AND MEDICAL ECONOMICS. (Summaries in English) 1962. q. (Kupat-Holim Health Insurance Institution, Research Department) Kupat Holim Center, P.O. Box 16250, Tel Aviv, Israel. FAX 03-433-474. Ed. N. Shavitt. bk.rev.; stat.; circ. 150. (processed)
Former titles: Kupat Holim. Information Series: Special Studies on Medical Manpower and Sociology; Kupat-Holim. Information Series: Special Studies and Surveys on Medical Sociology and Health Economics; (until 1973): Kupat-Holim. Information Series. "Meida" on Medical Sociology and Health.

614   IS   ISSN 0301-4843
CODEN: SFYBAI
KUPAT-HOLIM YEARBOOK. (Editions in English and Hebrew) 1971. a. free. Kupat Holim, Health Insurance Institution of Histadrut, 101 Arlosoroff St., Tel Aviv, Israel. **Indexed:** Biol.Abstr., Chem.Abstr.

KURJOURNAL - BAD TOELZ. see *TRAVEL AND TOURISM*

614   JA   ISSN 0454-7675
TA495   CODEN: DPKBAN
KYOTO UNIVERSITY. DISASTER PREVENTION RESEARCH INSTITUTE. BULLETIN/KYOTO DAIGAKU BOSAI KENKYUJO KIYO. (Text in English) 1951. q. exchange basis. Kyoto University, Disaster Prevention Research Institute - Kyoto Daigaku Bosai Kenkyujo, Gokasho, Uji 611, Japan. Ed.Bd. circ. 650. **Indexed:** GeoRef.
—BLDSC shelfmark: 2488.000000.

614.83   US   ISSN 0277-9196
LAURISTON S. TAYLOR LECTURE SERIES. 1977. a. price varies. National Council on Radiation Protection and Measurements, 7910 Woodmont Ave., Ste. 800, Bethesda, MD 20814. TEL 301-657-2652. Ed. W. Roger Ney.

614   LB
LIBERIA. MINISTRY OF HEALTH AND SOCIAL WELFARE. ANNUAL REPORT.* a., latest 1975. Ministry of Health and Social Welfare, Monrovia, Liberia.

614.8   CN   ISSN 0714-5896
LIVING SAFETY. French edition: Famille Avertie. 1983. q. Can.$7.50. Canada Safety Council, 6-2750 Stevenage Dr., Ottawa, Ont. K1G 3N2, Canada. TEL 613-739-1535. FAX 613-739-1566. Ed. Peter Kenter. circ. 230,000 (170,000 English ed.; 60,000 French ed.).

614.86   US
LOUISIANA. DEPARTMENT OF PUBLIC SAFETY. SUMMARY OF MOTOR VEHICLE TRAFFIC ACCIDENTS. 1971. s-a. free. Department of Public Safety, Traffic Records Unit, Box 66614, Baton Rouge, LA 70896. TEL 504-925-6348. Ed. Daniel P. Ducote. charts; stat.; circ. 350. (also avail. in microfilm) **Indexed:** SRI.
Formerly: Louisiana. Department of Public Safety. Summary of Motor Vehicle Accident Reports.

362.1   ZA
LUSAKA. MEDICAL OFFICER OF HEALTH. ANNUAL REPORT. 1966. a. free. Health and Welfare Department, Medical Officer of Health, Public Health Department, Box 789, Lusaka, Zambia. stat.; circ. 300.

352.3   US
M F D REGISTER. (Milwaukee Fire Department) 1961. m. $10. Milwaukee Fire Department Athletic Association, 711 W. Wells St., Milwaukee, WI 53233. TEL 414-276-5656. Ed. Carl W. Klitzke. circ. controlled.
Description: News, articles, and announcements on issues of interest to the Milwaukee Fire Department, its retirees and affiliated organizations.

M M G. (Medizin-Mensch-Gesellschaft) see *MEDICAL SCIENCES*

M S CANADA. (Multiple Sclerosis Society of Canada) see *MEDICAL SCIENCES — Allergology And Immunology*

628   US   ISSN 1053-7899
TD788
▼**M S W MANAGEMENT;** the journal for municipal solid waste professionals. 1991. 7/yr. $60 (effective Jan. 1992). Forester Communications, Inc., 1640 Fifth St., Ste. 108, Santa Monica, CA 90401. TEL 213-576-6180. FAX 213-570-6182. Ed. Daniel Waldman. circ. 24,000 (controlled). (back issues avail.)
Description: Covers landfills, incineration, recycling and composting.

MAISONS D'ENFANTS ET D'ADOLESCENTS DE FRANCE. ALBUM-ANNUAIRE NATIONAL; publication documentaire illustree des etablissements de vacances, de repos, de soins, de cure et de prevention pour enfants et adolescents. see *CHILDREN AND YOUTH — About*

613   IR
MAJALLE-YE BEHDASHT-E JAHAN. Persian translation of: World Health (UN ISSN 0043-8502) 1974. q. $5. Iranian Public Health Association, Box 1310, Teheran, Iran. Ed. Iran Roboubi.

MASKINENTREPRENOEREN. see *BUILDING AND CONSTRUCTION*

353.9   US
MASSACHUSETTS. DEPARTMENT OF PUBLIC HEALTH. ANNUAL REPORT. 1870. a. free. Department of Public Health, 150 Tremont St., Boston, MA 02111. TEL 617-727-2700. FAX 617-727-6496. Ed. Pearl K. Russo. illus.; circ. 1,000. **Indexed:** SRI.

614.8   US
MASTER CROSS REFERENCE LIST, PART 1. Short title: M C R L - 1. q. $2110 for 1600 bpi in US, Canada, Mexico; elsewhere $4020. (Department of Defense, Defense Logistics Services) U.S. National Technical Information Service, 5825 Port Royal Rd., Springfield, VA 22161. TEL 703-487-4630. (magnetic tape)
Description: Master list of logistics reference numbers cross-referenced to their applicable national stock number(s) in the federal catalog system.

614.8   US
MASTER CROSS REFERENCE LIST, PART 2. Short title: M C R L - 2. q. $1810 for 1600 bpi in US, Canada, Mexico; elsewhere $3620. (Department of Defense, Defense Logistics Services) U.S. National Technical Information Service, 5825 Port Royal Rd., Springfield, VA 22161. TEL 703-487-4630. (magnetic tape)
Description: Master list of national stock number(s) cross-referenced to their applicable logistics reference number(s) in the federal catalog system.

614.8   US
MASTER CROSS REFERENCE LIST, PART 3. Short title: M C R L - 3. q. $1585 for 1600 bpi in US, Canada, Mexico; elsewhere $3170. (Department of Defense, Defense Logistics Services) U.S. National Technical Information Service, 5825 Port Royal Rd., Springfield, VA 22161. TEL 703-487-4630. (magnetic tape)
Description: Master list of manufacturers codes cross-referenced to their applicable logistics reference number(s) in the federal catalog system.

614   MF
MAURITIUS. MINISTRY OF HEALTH. ANNUAL REPORT. (Text in English) a. Government Printing Office, Elizabeth II Ave., Port Louis, Mauritius.

MEDICAL ADMINISTRATION EXECUTIVE. see *MEDICAL SCIENCES*

614.8   US
MEDICAL AND RADIOLOGICAL DEVICES GUIDANCE MANUAL. (Subseries of: Compliance Program Guidance Manuals) irreg. $140 in US, Canada, Mexico; elsewhere $280. (Department of Health and Human Services, Food and Drug Administration) U.S. National Technical Information Service, 5825 Port Royal Rd., Springfield, VA 22161. TEL 703-487-4630.
Description: Provides the latest information on and helps to maintain program plans and instructions directed to FDA field operations. These plans and instructions are surveillance or compliance oriented and provide the needed direction from headquarters offices and bureaus in accomplishing FDA's regulatory obligations.

MEDICAL CARE. see *MEDICAL SCIENCES*

614.8 619   US
MEDICAL DEVICE ESTABLISHMENT REGISTRATION MASTER FILE. q. $1200 in US, Canada, Mexico; elsewhere $2400. (Department of Health and Human Services, Food and Drug Administration) U.S. National Technical Information Service, 5825 Port Royal Rd., Springfield, VA 22161. TEL 703-487-4630. (magnetic tape)
Description: Contains information required to be submitted by owner-operators of medical device establishments in accordance with Section 510 of the Federal Food, Drug, and Cosmetics Act.

614.8 619   US
MEDICAL DEVICE PROBLEMS REPORT FROM THE D E N: REPORTS FROM MEDICAL DEVICE USERS. (Device Experience Network) m. $130 in US, Canada, Mexico; elsewhere $260. (Department of Health and Human Services, Food and Drug Administration) U.S. National Technical Information Service, 5825 Port Royal Rd., Springfield, VA 22161. TEL 703-487-4630.
Description: Reports are arranged by specific medical specialty such as anaesthesia, cardio-vascular or by general health areas. Each report is divided into six parts: accession number, date of report, product name, manufacturer name, serial number, and report narrative.

614.8 619   US
MEDICAL DEVICE REPORTING FROM THE D E N: REPORTS FROM MEDICAL DEVICE MANUFACTURERS. (Device Experience Network) m. $360 in US, Canada, Mexico; elsewhere $720. (Department of Health and Human Services, Food and Drug Administration) U.S. National Technical Information Service, 5825 Port Royal Rd., Springfield, VA 22161. TEL 703-487-4630.
Description: Arranged by specific medical specialty such as anaesthesia, cardio-vascular or general health areas such as general hospital. Each report is divided into six parts: accession number, date of report, product name, manufacturer name, serial number, and report narrative.

614.8   GW   ISSN 0724-8172
CODEN: MEFOET
MEDICAL FOCUS; international trade journal for medical, laboratory and hospital supplies. (Editions in Chinese and English) 1983. bi-m. DM.98. Beta Publishing, Postfach 140121, 5300 Bonn 1, Germany. TEL 0228-252061. FAX 0228-252067. TELEX 8869536-BETA-D. Ed. Gerlinde Pape. adv.: B&W page DM.6400; trim 270 x 190; adv. contact: Una Hecker. circ. 24,714 (controlled).
—BLDSC shelfmark: 5527.386000.

MEDIKAMENT & MEINUNG; Zeitschrift fuer Arzneimittel- und Gesundheitswesen. see *MEDICAL SCIENCES*

614   US
MENTAL HEALTH DIRECTORY.* 1971. a. $5. U.S. Public Health Service, Alcohol, Drug Abuse & Mental Health Administration, 5600 Fishers Lane, Rockville, MD 20857. (Orders to: Supt. of Documents, Washington, DC 20402)

MENTAL HEALTH IN AUSTRALIA. see *MEDICAL SCIENCES — Psychiatry And Neurology*

PUBLIC HEALTH AND SAFETY

MENTAL HEALTH MATTERS. see *PSYCHOLOGY*

MENTAL HEALTH STATISTICS FOR ILLINOIS. see *SOCIAL SERVICES AND WELFARE*

614   AU   ISSN 0026-010X
MERKUR MAGAZIN FUER VOLKSGESUNDHEIT. 1958. q. free. Merkur Wechselseitige Versicherungsanstalt, Neutorgasse 57, A-8010 Graz, Austria. adv.; charts; illus.; mkt.; stat.; circ. 200,000. (tabloid format)

614.8   US   ISSN 0275-6595
CODEN: MIWNE3
MICROWAVE NEWS. 1981. bi-m. $285 (foreign $315). Box 1799, Grand Central Sta., New York, NY 10163. TEL 212-517-2800. Ed. Louis Slesin. adv.; bk.rev. (back issues avail.)
—BLDSC shelfmark: 5761.220800.

614   UK   ISSN 0309-2003
MIDDLE EAST HEALTH. 1977. 10/yr. £60. Reed Business Publishing Group, Carew Division (Subsidiary of: Reed International PLC), Quadrant House, The Quadrant, Sutton, Surrey SM2 5AS, England. TEL 081-661-3500. Ed. David Powell. adv.; circ. 5,875.
—BLDSC shelfmark: 5761.375800.
Incorporates (from 1986): Middle East Dentistry; Formerly: Middle East Health Supply and Services.

MILBANK QUARTERLY. see *POLITICAL SCIENCE*

MISSOURI. DIVISION OF HIGHWAY SAFETY. HIGHWAY SAFETY PLAN. see *TRANSPORTATION — Roads And Traffic*

614.8   GW
MODERNE UNFALLVERTHUTUNG. 1956. a. DM.36. Vulcan Verlag GmbH, Hollestr. 1G, Postfach 103962, 4300 Essen 1, Germany. TEL 0201-82002-0. FAX 0201-82002-40. adv.; bk.rev.; circ. 3,500. (back issues avail.)

MONATSBERICHT DER ANGEZEITEN FLUGUNFALLUNTERSUCHUNGSSTELLE. see *TRANSPORTATION — Air Transport*

614.8   US
MONTHLY IMPORT DETENTION LIST. m. $110 in US, Canada, Mexico; elsewhere $220. (Department of Health and Human Services, Food and Drug Administration) U.S. National Technical Information Service, 5825 Port Royal Rd., Springfield, VA 22161. TEL 703-487-4630.
Description: Detentions are arranged by: product code, sample number, the product, district and port of entry, manufacturer's and shipper's names, city and country of origin, the primary and secondary reasons for detention, unit type and quantity, as well as value.

MONTHLY PRESCRIBING REFERENCE. see *MEDICAL SCIENCES*

614   UY
MORBILIDAD. irreg. Ministerio de Salud Publica, Departamento de Estadistica, Montevideo, Uruguay. stat.

614.862   US
MOTOR VEHICLE SAFETY; a report on activities under the National Traffic and Motor Vehicle Safety Act of 1966. 1966. a. U.S. National Highway Traffic Safety Administration, 400 Seventh St., N.W., Washington, DC 20590. (Prepared with: U.S. Federal Highway Administration)

628   GW   ISSN 0027-2957
MUELL UND ABFALL; Fachzeitschrift fuer Behandlung und Beseitigung von Abfaellen. 1969. m. DM.187.20. Erich Schmidt Verlag GmbH & Co. (Berlin), Genthiner Str. 30G, 1000 Berlin 30, Germany. TEL 030-2500850. FAX 030-25008521. Ed. M. Ferber. adv.; bk.rev. Indexed: Chem.Abstr.
—BLDSC shelfmark: 5982.650000.
Description: Emphasis is on sanitary engineering.

658 363.35   US   ISSN 0734-9998
MUTUAL AID; the public safety newsletter. 1981. bi-m. E M S Management Institute, Box 102, Sterling, VA 22120. TEL 703-450-6097. Ed. Joseph V. Saitta. bk.rev.; film rev.; circ. 1,000. (looseleaf format; back issues avail.)

N A C A NEWS. (National Animal Control Association) see *PETS*

614.84   UK
N A F O MAGAZINE. 1975. q. membership. National Association of Fire Officers, Hayes Court, W. Common Rd., Bromley, Kent BR2 7AU, England. circ. 5,000.

614   US
N A H S E'S RESUME.* 1972. q. $5. National Association of Health Services Executives, c/o Bernard Dickens, 1155 N. La Cienega, No. 405, Los Angeles, CA 90069-2409. adv.; bk.rev.; stat.; circ. 1,500. (back issues avail.)

N A T O ADVANCED SCIENCE INSTITUTES SERIES D: BEHAVIOURAL AND SOCIAL SCIENCES. (North Atlantic Treaty Organization) see *SOCIAL SCIENCES: COMPREHENSIVE WORKS*

N A WAY MAGAZINE. (Narcotics Anonymous) see *DRUG ABUSE AND ALCOHOLISM*

614.8   US   ISSN 0890-3417
N C A H F NEWSLETTER; quality in the health marketplace. 1977. bi-m. $15. National Council Against Health Fraud, Inc., Box 1276, Loma Linda, CA 92354. TEL 714-824-4690. FAX 714-824-4577. Ed. William T. Jarvis. bk.rev.; index; circ. 2,800. (looseleaf format; back issues avail.) Indexed: Hlth.Ind.
Description: Contains contributions from health professionals, educators, researchers and attorneys who oppose misinformation and quackery.

614.8   US
N C C E M'S OFFICIAL MONTHLY NEWSLETTER. 1983. m. $75. National Coordinating Council on Emergency Management, 7297 Lee Highway, Ste. N, Falls Church, VA 22042. FAX 703-241-5603. Ed. Shari Coffin. adv.; circ. 1,500.

614.83   US
N C R P COMMENTARY. 1982. irreg. price varies. National Council on Radiation Protection and Measurements, 7910 Woodmont Ave., Ste. 800, Bethesda, MD 20814. TEL 301-657-2652. Ed. W. Roger Ney.

614.839 621.48   US
N C R P NEWS. 1966. 3/yr. free to qualified personnel. National Council on Radiation Protection and Measurements, 7910 Woodmont Ave., Ste. 800, Bethesda, MD 20814. TEL 301-657-2652. Ed. W. Roger Ney. circ. controlled.

614.8 355.23   US   ISSN 0083-209X
CODEN: NCRDBG
N C R P REPORT. 1931. irreg., no.111, 1991. price varies. National Council on Radiation Protection and Measurements, 7910 Woodmont Ave., Ste. 800, Bethesda, MD 20814. TEL 301-657-2652. Ed. W. Roger Ney. Indexed: Biol.Abstr., Energy Info.Abstr., Environ.Abstr., GeoRef.
—BLDSC shelfmark: 6067.817100.

614.83   US
N C R P SYMPOSIUM PROCEEDINGS. 1982. irreg. $22. National Council on Radiation Protection and Measurements, 7910 Woodmont Ave., Ste. 800, Bethesda, MD 20814. TEL 301-657-2652. Ed. W. Roger Ney.

614.8   US
N E I S S DATA HIGHLIGHTS. (National Electronic Injury Surveillance System) 1973. a. free. (U.S. Consumer Product Safety Commission) U.S. National Injury Information Clearinghouse, 5401 Westbard Ave., Washington, DC 20207. TEL 202-492-6424. charts; index; circ. 3,000.
Formerly: N E I S S News (ISSN 0364-6475)

N I P H ANNALS. (National Institute for Public Health) see *MEDICAL SCIENCES — Communicable Diseases*

614   US
N R D C NEWSLINE. 1982. 5/yr. $10. Natural Resources Defense Council, Inc., 40 W. 20th St., New York, NY 10011. TEL 212-727-2700. FAX 212-727-1773. circ. 130,000.

614.8 374   JA   ISSN 0287-9549
NARA JOSHI DAIGAKU HOKEN KANRI SENTA NENPO/NARA WOMEN'S UNIVERSITY. HEALTH ADMINISTRATION CENTER. ARCHIVES OF HEALTH CARE. (Text in Japanese; table of contents in English) 1978. a. Nara Joshi Daigaku, Hoken Kanri Senta - Nara Women's University, Health Administration Center, Kita-Uoya-Higashi-cho, Nara-shi 630, Japan. Ed. Kimihiro Yamamoto. charts; circ. 500.
Formerly: Nara Joshi Daigaku Hoken Kanri Senta Kiyo.

614.8   II
NATIONAL CONFERENCE ON SAFETY. PROCEEDINGS. 1970. a. Rs.10. National Safety Council, Central Labour Institute Bldg., Sion, Bombay 22, India. Ed. A.A. Krishnan. charts; circ. 2,000.

614.83 355.23   US   ISSN 0195-7740
CODEN: PNRME9
NATIONAL COUNCIL ON RADIATION PROTECTION AND MEASUREMENTS. PROCEEDINGS OF THE ANNUAL MEETING. 15th, 1979. a. price varies. National Council on Radiation Protection and Measurements, 7910 Woodmont Ave., Ste. 800, Bethesda, MD 20814. TEL 301-657-2652.

NATIONAL DIRECTORY OF SAFETY CONSULTANTS. see *ENGINEERING*

614.8   US
NATIONAL HEALTH CARE EXPENDITURES STUDY. DATA PREVIEW. 1980. irreg. free. U.S. Department of Health and Human Services, National Center for Health Services Research, Research and Health Care Technology Assessment, 5600 Fishers Ln., 18A55, Rockville, MD 20857. Ed. Daniel C. Walden. circ. 6,500.

614   JA   ISSN 0077-5002
NATIONAL INSTITUTE OF HYGIENIC SCIENCES. BULLETIN/EISEI SHIKENJO HOKOKU. (Text in Japanese; summaries in English) 1886. a. National Institute of Hygienic Sciences - Kokuritsu Eisei Shikenjo, 1-18-1 Kamiyoga, Setagaya-ku, Tokyo 158, Japan. Ed. Hironori Takemaka. circ. 1,000. Indexed: Biol.Abstr., Chem.Abstr., Dairy Sci.Abstr., Excerp.Med., Field Crop Abstr., Food Sci.& Tech.Abstr., Hort.Abstr., Ind.Med., INIS Atomind., Rev.Plant Path., Triticale Abstr., Trop.Dis.Bull.

614   JA
NATIONAL INSTITUTE OF HYGIENIC SCIENCES. MONTHLY REPORT/KOKURITSU EISEI SHIKENJO CHOSA GEPPO. (Text in Japanese) 1968. m. free. National Institute of Hygienic Sciences - Kokuritsu Eisei Shikenjo, 1-18-1 Kamiyoga, Setagaya-ku, Tokyo 158, Japan. Ed. Y. Takenaka. bk.rev.; circ. 500.

614.8   SA   ISSN 0028-0097
NATIONAL SAFETY/NASIONALE VEILIGHEID; and occupational hygiene - en Beroepshigiene. (Text mainly in English; occasionally in Afrikaans) 1938. bi-m. R.16.50 to non-members; members R.22 (effective 1992). Safety First Association, 7 Pitcairn Rd., Blairgowrie, Johannesburg 2194, South Africa. TEL 011-782-7698. (Subscr. to: P.O. Box 56400, Pinegowrie, Transvaal 2123, South Africa) Ed. Barbara Campbell. adv.; bk.rev.; illus.; stat.; tr.lit.; circ. 2,567 (controlled). Indexed: C.I.S. Abstr.
—BLDSC shelfmark: 6032.600000.
Description: Aims to prevent accidents by promoting an awareness of accident situations as they exist in day-to-day living among members of the community.

614   US   ISSN 0028-0496
RA421
NATION'S HEALTH. 1971. 10/yr. $12 to non-members. American Public Health Association, 1015 15th St., N.W., Washington, DC 20005. TEL 202-789-5600. Ed. Kathryn Foxhall. adv.; charts; illus.; circ. 35,000. (tabloid format; also avail. in microform from UMI; reprint service avail. from UMI) Indexed: Biol.Dig., Curr.Adv.Ecol.Sci., Hlth.Ind., Med.Care Rev., Rehabil.Lit., Telegen.

614.88   NE
NEDERLANDS TIJDSCHRIFT VOOR E H B O EN REDDINGWNGWEZEN. 1912. 6/yr. fl.30.50. (Koninklijke Nationale Bond voor Reddingwezen en Eerste Hulp Bij Ongelukken "Het Oranje Kruis") S M D Educatieve Uitgevers, P.O. Box 63, 2300 AB Leiden, Netherlands. FAX 071-323340. Ed.Bd. adv.; bk.rev.; bibl.; charts; illus.; circ. 5,400.
Formerly: Reddingwezen (ISSN 0034-2114)

614.05 NE
NETHERLANDS. RIJKSINSTITUUT VOOR DE VOLKSGEZONDHEID. MEDEDELINGEN. irreg. Rijksinstituut voor Volksgezondheid en Milieuhygiene - National Institute of Public Health and Environmental Protection, Bilthoven, Netherlands. FAX 30-742971. TELEX 47215 RIVBH NL. illus.

614 CN ISSN 0838-3693
RA450.N5
NEW BRUNSWICK. DEPARTMENT OF HEALTH AND COMMUNITY SERVICES. ANNUAL REPORT. (Text in English and French) 1918. a. free. Department of Health and Community Services, Box 5100, Fredericton, N.B. E3B 5G8, Canada. TEL 506-453-2536. FAX 506-453-3983. Ed. David Gibbs. stat.; circ. 700.
  Formerly: New Brunswick. Department of Health. Annual Report.

NEW JERSEY. BUREAU OF FIRE SAFETY NEWSLETTER. see FIRE PREVENTION

NEW JERSEY STATE FIRE CODE. see FIRE PREVENTION

NEW SOUTH WALES. DEPARTMENT OF INDUSTRIAL RELATIONS AND TECHNOLOGY. SAFETY. see BUSINESS AND ECONOMICS — Labor And Industrial Relations

614 US
NEW YORK (CITY). HEALTH SYSTEMS AGENCY. QUARTERLY BULLETIN. 1969. q. free. Health Systems Agency of New York City, 275 7th Ave., 27th Fl., New York, NY 10001. TEL 212-741-8880. FAX 212-741-8305. Ed. Dudley Stone. circ. 5,000.
  Former titles (until 1985): F Y I (New York); (until 1977): Health Planning.
  Description: Provides information on New York City health care system, including medical services, primary, secondary and long term care, medical facilities planning, home health care, and substance abuse.

614 US
NEW YORK (STATE). DEPARTMENT OF HEALTH. MONOGRAPH. 1969. irreg., no.23, 1990. Department of Health, Office of Health Communications, Albany, NY 12237. charts; stat. (back issues avail.)

614
NEW YORK (STATE). HEALTH PLANNING COMMISSION, ADMINISTRATIVE PROGRAM FOR HEALTH PLANNING AND DEVELOPMENT. a. Health Planning Commission, Empire State Plaza, Tower Bldg. Rm. 1683, Albany, NY 12237.

353.9 US ISSN 0361-4018
RA981.N7
NEW YORK (STATE). MEDICAL CARE FACILITIES FINANCE AGENCY. ANNUAL REPORT. 1974. a. Medical Care Facilities Finance Agency, 3 Park Ave., New York, NY 10016. TEL 212-686-9700. charts; illus. Key Title: Annual Report - New York State Medical Care Facilities Finance Agency.

614 310 NZ
NEW ZEALAND. HEALTH STATISTICAL SERVICES. CLIENT SERVICES NEWSLETTER. bi-m? Health Statistical Services, P.O. Box 5013, Wellington, New Zealand. TEL 04-496-2049. FAX 04-496-2050.

614 NZ ISSN 0112-0212
NEW ZEALAND JOURNAL OF ENVIRONMENTAL HEALTH. 1952. q. membership. (Institute of New Zealand Health Inspectors Inc.) Percival Publishing Co. Ltd., P.O. Box 52-024, Kingsland, Auckland, New Zealand. Ed. Stephen Lawrence. adv.; bk.rev.; charts; illus.; circ. 750.
  Former titles: New Zealand Environmental Health Inspector (ISSN 0110-4969); New Zealand Sanitarian (ISSN 0048-0142)

NOVA SCOTIA. DEPARTMENT OF HEALTH. NUTRITION DIVISION. ANNUAL REPORT. see NUTRITION AND DIETETICS

NUCLEAR LEMONS. see ENERGY — Nuclear Energy

NUCLEAR PLANT JOURNAL. see ENERGY — Nuclear Energy

NUCLEAR REACTOR SAFETY. see ENERGY — Nuclear Energy

NUCLEUS (CAMBRIDGE). see POLITICAL SCIENCE

OCCUPATIONAL HEALTH IN ONTARIO. see OCCUPATIONAL HEALTH AND SAFETY

614.8 US
OCCUPATIONAL SAFETY AND HEALTH SERIES (NEW YORK). 1976. irreg., vol.23, 1991. price varies. Marcel Dekker, Inc., 270 Madison Ave., New York, NY 10016. TEL 212-696-9000. FAX 212-658-4540. TELEX 421419.
  Refereed Serial

614 GW ISSN 0029-8573
DAS OEFFENTLICHE GESUNDHEITSWESEN; Praeventivmedizin und Rehabilitation. Sozialhygiene und oeffentliche Gesundheitsdienst. 1939. m. DM.198. (Bundesverband der Aerzte des Oeffentlichen Gesundheitsdienstes e.V.) Georg Thieme Verlag, Ruedigerstr. 14, Postfach 104853, 7000 Stuttgart 10, Germany. TEL 0711-8931-0. FAX 0711-8931298. (Co-sponsors: Bundesverband der Vertrauens- und Rentenversicherungsaerzte e.V.; Zentralkomitee zur Bekaempfung der Tuberkulose; Deutsche Gesellschaft fuer Sozialhygiene und Prophylaktische Medizin) Ed.Bd. adv.; bk.rev.; abstr.; charts; illus.; index; circ. 6,400. (also avail. in microform from UMI; reprint service avail. from UMI) Indexed: Abstr.Hyg., C.I.S. Abstr., Curr.Cont., Helminthol.Abstr., Ind.Med., Ind.Vet., Nutr.Abstr., Sci.Cit.Ind., Trop.Dis.Bull., Vet.Bull.
  Formerly: Oeffentliche Gesundheitsdienst.

614 UN ISSN 0030-0632
CODEN: BOSPA8
OFICINA SANITARIA PANAMERICANA. BOLETIN. (Text in Portuguese or Spanish; summaries in English) 1922. 12/yr. (in 2 vols.). $28. Pan American Health Organization, Pan American Sanitary Bureau, Regional Office of the World Health Organization, 525 23rd St., N.W., Washington, DC 20037. TEL 202-293-8130. FAX 202-338-0869. bk.rev.; abstr.; bibl.; illus.; index; circ. 16,500. (back issues avail.) Indexed: Abstr.Hyg., Biodet.Abstr., Biol.Abstr., Chem.Abstr., Curr.Adv.Ecol.Sci., Dairy Sci.Abstr., Dent.Ind., IIS, Ind.Med., Ind.Vet., INIS Atomind., Nutr.Abstr., Protozool.Abstr., Rev.Appl.Entomol., Rural Devel.Abstr., Trop.Dis.Bull., Vet.Bull., World Bibl.Soc.Sec.
  —BLDSC shelfmark: 2186.000000.

OKLAHOMA. DEPARTMENT OF HEALTH. MONTHLY VITAL STATISTICS REPORT. see POPULATION STUDIES

614.8 BE ISSN 0771-2588
OPERATIE VEILIGHEID. French edition: Objectif Prevention (ISSN 0771-2634) 1964. m. (10/yr.). 750 Fr. Nationale Vereniging tot Voorkoming van Arbeidsongevallen (NVVA), Gachardstraat, 88, bus 4, B-1050 Brussels, Belgium. TEL 02-648-03-37. FAX 02-648-68-67. Ed. B. Schoenmaekers. adv.; bk.rev.; illus.; circ. 27,000.

613.9 US ISSN 0737-3732
OUTLOOK (SEATTLE); drug regulation and reproductive health. (Editions available in French, Spanish) 1983. q. $20 (free to developing countries). Program for Appropriate Technology in Health, 4 Nickerson St., Seattle, WA 98109. FAX 206-285-6619. TELEX 4740049 PATH UI. Ed. Jacqueline Sherris. circ. 5,000. (back issues avail.)
  —BLDSC shelfmark: 6314.495000.

OVERVIEW (OLYMPIA). see SOCIAL SERVICES AND WELFARE

P H L S LIBRARY BULLETIN. (Public Health Laboratory Service Board) see MEDICAL SCIENCES — Communicable Diseases

P H L S MICROBIOLOGY DIGEST. (Public Health Laboratory Service Board) see MEDICAL SCIENCES — Communicable Diseases

614.8 327 US
P S R MONITOR. 1984. q. membership. Physicians for Social Responsibility, 1000 16th St., N.W., Ste. 810, Washington, DC 20036. TEL 202-785-3777. Ed. Sally James. circ. 5,000.
  Description: Covers health dangers of nuclear arms testing and social and environmental costs of nuclear arms race. Recommends legislative action.

PUBLIC HEALTH AND SAFETY 4109

614.8 US ISSN 1051-2438
RA441
▼**P S R QUARTERLY.** 1991. q. $48 to individuals; institutions $85. (Physicians for Social Responsibility) Williams & Wilkins, 428 Preston St., Baltimore, MD 21202. TEL 301-528-4000. FAX 301-528-4321. Ed. Dr. Jennifer Leaning.
  —BLDSC shelfmark: 6945.943000.
  Description: Contains scientific research on the medical, public health, and bioethical problems of the post-nuclear age.
  Refereed Serial

614.8 US ISSN 0894-6264
P S R REPORTS. 1979. 3/yr. $40. Physicians for Social Responsibility, 1000 16th St., N.W., Ste. 810, Washington, DC 20036. TEL 202-785-3777. Ed. Sally James. adv.; bk.rev.; circ. 25,000.
  Formerly: P S R Newsletter.
  Description: Articles on the health and environmental impact of nuclear war, the nuclear arms race and military spending.

615 PK ISSN 0030-9834
PAKISTAN JOURNAL OF HEALTH. 1951. q. Rs.25. College of Community Medicine, 6 Birdwood Rd., Lahore, Pakistan. Ed. Dr. Shamim Raza Bokhari. adv.; bk.rev.; charts; illus.; stat. Indexed: Biol.Abstr., Chem.Abstr.

614 UN ISSN 0085-4638
RA10
PAN AMERICAN HEALTH ORGANIZATION. BULLETIN. 1967. q. $26. Pan American Health Organization, Pan American Sanitary Bureau, Regional Office of the World Health Organization, 525 23rd St., N.W., Washington, DC 20037. TEL 202-293-8129. FAX 202-338-0869. bk.rev.; abstr.; charts; stat.; index; circ. 6,000. (back issues avail.) Indexed: Abstr.Health Care Manage.Stud., Biol.Abstr., Curr.Adv.Ecol.Sci., Environ.Abstr., Excerp.Med., Helminthol.Abstr, IIS, Ind.Med., Ind.Vet., INIS Atomind., NRN, Nutr.Abstr., Protozool.Abstr., Rev.Appl.Entomol., Trop.Dis.Bull., Vet.Bull.
  —BLDSC shelfmark: 2676.205000.

614 IE ISSN 0738-3991
R727.3
PATIENT EDUCATION AND COUNSELING. 1978. 6/yr.(in 2 vols.; 3 nos./vol.). $252 (effective 1992). (International Patient Education Council) Elsevier Scientific Publishers Ireland Ltd., P.O. Box 85, Limerick, Ireland. TEL 061-61944. FAX 061-62144. TELEX 72191 ENH EI. (Subscr. in U.S. and Canada to: Elsevier Science Publishing Co., Inc., Box 882, Madison Sq. Sta., New York, NY 10159. TEL 212-989-5800) Ed. Edward E. Bartlett. Indexed: Abstr.Health Care Manage.Stud., CINAHL, Cont.Pg.Educ., Curr.Cont., Educ.Tech.Abstr., Excerp.Med., FAMLI, Hosp.Lit.Ind., I.P.A., Psychol.Abstr., Res.High.Educ.Abstr., SSCI.
  ●Also available online.
  —BLDSC shelfmark: 6412.864600.
  Incorporates (as of 1986): Patient Education Reports; Which was formerly titled: Patient Education Newsletter; (until vol.5, 1983): Patient Counselling and Health Education (ISSN 0190-2040)
  Description: For patient education researchers, managers, and others involved in patient education and counseling.
  Refereed Serial

614 US
PENNSYLVANIA CHAMBER OF BUSINESS AND INDUSTRY. CHECKLIST. m. $165 to non-members; members $115. Pennsylvania Chamber of Business and Industry, 222 N. Third St., Harrisburg, PA 17101. TEL 800-326-3252. FAX 717-255-3298.
  Description: Provides updates on legislative, regulatory and legal activities affecting environmental policy matters.

628 SP ISSN 0188-0012
PERSPECTIVAS EN SALUD PUBLICA. (Text in English, Spanish) 1987. irreg. Instituto Nacional de Salud Publica, Ave. Universidad 665, Col. Santa Maria Ahuacatitlan, C.P. 62508, Cuernavaca, Morelos, Mexico. TEL 13-17-89. FAX 13-88-90. circ. 2,000.

PERSPECTIVE (CLEVELAND). see SOCIAL SERVICES AND WELFARE

PERU. POLICIA NACIONAL. REVISTA DE LA SANIDAD. see MEDICAL SCIENCES

PEST MANAGEMENT FOR PUBLIC HEALTH. see ENGINEERING — Chemical Engineering

4110 PUBLIC HEALTH AND SAFETY

614.8 628.96   US
PESTICIDE ANALYTICAL MANUAL. irreg. $50 (base vols. $230). (Department of Health and Human Services, Food and Drug Administration) U.S. National Technical Information Service, 5825 Port Royal Rd., Springfield, VA 22161. TEL 703-487-4630.

614   UN   ISSN 0587-5943
PESTICIDE RESIDUES IN FOOD. 1966. 3/yr. price varies. Food and Agriculture Organization of the United Nations, c/o UNIPUB, 4611-F Assembly Dr., Lanham, MD 20706-4391. FAX 301-459-0056.
   Formerly: Codex Committee on Pesticide Residues. Report on the Meeting.

PHARMACY HEALTH-LINE. see *PHARMACY AND PHARMACOLOGY*

614   PH   ISSN 0048-380X
PHILIPPINE JOURNAL OF MENTAL HEALTH. (Text in English and Filipino) 1970. s-a. P.24($3.50) Philippine Mental Health Association, Box 40, 18 East Ave., Quezon City, Philippines. Ed. Loreto Paras-Sulit. adv.; bibl.; illus.; stat.; circ. 1,000.
   Indexed: Psychol.Abstr.

628 668.4   US   ISSN 1046-3046
PLASTIC WASTE STRATEGIES. 1989. m. $417. Washington Business Information, Inc., 1117 N. 19th St., Ste. 200, Arlington, VA 22209-1789. TEL 703-247-3434. FAX 703-247-3421. Ed. John Maines. (back issues avail.)
   Description: For those concerned with plastic and solid waste disposal. Covers recycling, degradability, incineration, and legal, technical, and competitive issues.

614.8   US   ISSN 0882-8768
PLAY IT SAFE. m. $7.68. Bureau of Business Practice, 24 Rope Ferry Rd., Waterford, CT 06386. TEL 203-442-4365. FAX 203-434-3341. TELEX 966420. Ed. Lori Michaelson.

POLISH JOURNAL OF OCCUPATIONAL MEDICINE AND ENVIRONMENTAL HEALTH. see *OCCUPATIONAL HEALTH AND SAFETY*

POLITECHNIKA WROCLAWSKA. INSTYTUT INZYNIERII OCHRONY SRODOWSKA. PRACE NAUKOWE. MONOGRAFIE. see *ENVIRONMENTAL STUDIES*

628.5   US   ISSN 0090-516X
                                     CODEN: PTERDY
POLLUTION TECHNOLOGY REVIEW. 1973. irreg., no.204, 1991. price varies. Noyes Data Corporation, Noyes Publications, Noyes Bldg., Mill Road at Grand Ave., Park Ridge, NJ 07656. TEL 201-391-8484. FAX 201-391-6833.
   —BLDSC shelfmark: 6544.298000.
   Formerly: Pollution Control Review (ISSN 0079-3116)

POLSKA AKADEMIA NAUK. KOMITET GOSPODARKI WODNEJ. PRACE I STUDIA. see *WATER RESOURCES*

PREHOSPITAL AND DISASTER MEDICINE; an international journal. see *MEDICAL SCIENCES*

614.44 610   UK   ISSN 0300-2659
RA421
PREVENT;* the journal for all who would prevent disease. 1973. bi-m. £5. Fitzken Publishers, 3 Alma Square, London NW8 6QD, England. Ed. Dr. J. McMurdoch. bibl.; illus.

614.8   FR   ISSN 0032-8022
PREVENTION ROUTIERE. 1957. m. 5 F.($2) Chancerel Editions, 4 rue Aumont- Thieville, 75017 Paris, France. adv.; illus.; stat.; tr.lit.; circ. 290,181.

PREVENTIVE MEDICINE; an international journal devoted to practice and theory. see *MEDICAL SCIENCES*

PREVOYANCE. see *OCCUPATIONAL HEALTH AND SAFETY*

354 614   CN
PRINCE EDWARD ISLAND. DEPARTMENT OF HEALTH AND SOCIAL SERVICES. ANNUAL REPORT. a. Department of Health and Social Services, Box 2000, Charlottetown, P.E.I. C1A 7N8, Canada. TEL 902-892-5471. FAX 902-368-5544. Ed. Carl Cooper. circ. 350.
   Formerly: Prince Edward Island. Department of Health. Annual Report (ISSN 0317-4530)

PRODUCT LIABILITY TRENDS; a monthly analysis of product liability developments. see *LAW*

643   US   ISSN 0092-7732
KF3945.A73
PRODUCT SAFETY & LIABILITY REPORTER; a weekly review of consumer safety developments. 1973. w. $785. The Bureau of National Affairs, Inc., 1231 25th St., N.W., Washington, DC 20037. TEL 202-452-4200. FAX 202-822-8092. TELEX 285656 BNAI WSH. (Subscr. to: 9435 Key West Ave., Rockville, MD 20850. TEL 800-372-1033) Ed. Stanley J. Gilbert. index. (looseleaf format; back issues avail.)
   Description: Notification and reference service providing coverage of current administrative, legislative, judicial, and industry developments relating to product safety and product liability.

600   US   ISSN 0098-7530
PRODUCT SAFETY LETTER. 1972. w. $697. Washington Business Information, Inc., c/o Karen Harrington, 1117 N. 19th St., Ste. 200, Arlington, VA 22209. TEL 703-247-3434. FAX 703-247-3421. Ed. Vincent LeClair. bk.rev.; charts; index. (looseleaf format)
   ●Also available online. Vendor(s): NewsNet.
   Description: For executives concerned with government regulation of consumer products.

614   US   ISSN 0009-1162
TN119.R6   CODEN: CHMJBP
PRODUCT SAFETY NEWS. 1973. m. $100. Institute for Product Safety, Box 1931, Durham, NC 27702. TEL 919-489-2356. FAX 919-489-2357. Ed. Verne L. Roberts. bk.rev.; abstr.; charts; illus.; stat.; cum.index: 1973-1990; circ. 350. (looseleaf format; back issues avail.)

658.56   US   ISSN 0091-8954
TS175
PRODUCT SAFETY UP TO DATE. 1973. bi-m. $19 to non-members; members $15. National Safety Council, Industrial Section, 444 N. Michigan Ave., Chicago, IL 60611. TEL 800-621-7619. Ed. Kathleen Knowles. illus.; circ. 11,000.

628   US
PROFESSIONAL SANITARIAN. irreg. (1-2/yr.). National Society of Professional Sanitarians, 1224 Hoffman Dr., Jefferson City, MO 65101.

PROFILES IN HEALTHCARE MARKETING; idea exchange for the people who plan and create healthcare marketing and PR campaigns. see *BUSINESS AND ECONOMICS — Marketing And Purchasing*

900   US
PROGRESS (COLUMBUS). 1984. 5/yr. free to qualified personnel. Department of Health, Box 118, Columbus, OH 43215. TEL 614-462-8562. charts; illus.; circ. 3,000.

618 613   CN   ISSN 0715-4356
PROLIFE NEWS. 1971. m. Can.$16.50 (typically set in Feb.). Alliance Action, B1-90 Garry St., Winnipeg, Man. R3C 4H1, Canada. TEL 204-943-5273. FAX 204-943-9283. Ed. Barbara LeBow. bk.rev.; cum.index: 1985-1990; circ. 54,000. (back issues avail.)
   Description: Covers developments in the areas of abortion, infanticide, euthanasia from a pro-life perspective.

614.49   PL   ISSN 0033-2100
PRZEGLAD EPIDEMIOLOGICZNY. (Text in Polish; summaries in English and Russian) 1947. q. $104. Panstwowy Instytut Higieny - State Institute of Hygiene, Ul. Chomiska 24, Warsaw, Poland. TEL 31-42-81. FAX 48-22-49-74-84. TELEX 81-67-12. (Dist. by: Ars Polona-Ruch, Krakowskie Przedmiescie 7, Warsaw, Poland) Ed. D. Naruszewicz - Lesiuk. adv.; bk.rev.; abstr.; charts; illus.; index, cum.index; circ. 1,080. **Indexed:** Abstr.Hyg., Biol.Abstr., Chem.Abstr., Dent.Ind., Dok.Arbeitsmed., Excerp.Med., Helminthol.Abstr., Ind.Med., Trop.Dis.Bull.
   —BLDSC shelfmark: 6940.100000.
   Description: Discusses epidemiology bacteriology, parasitology, pathology and clinical aspects of diseases.

614   JA
PUBLIC CLEANSING SERVICES IN TOKYO/SEISO JIGYO GAIYO. (Text in English) 1965. a. exchange basis. Bureau of Public Cleansing - Tokyo-to Seiso-kyoku Somu-bu, 3-8-1 Marunouchi, Chiyoda-ku, Tokyo 100, Japan. Ed.Bd. circ. 500.
   Formerly: Public Cleansing Service in Tokyo.

PUBLIC HEALTH. see *MEDICAL SCIENCES*

614   UG
PUBLIC HEALTH AND HYGIENE.* vol.4, 1972. a. Public Health Inspectors' Association, Box 46, Kampala, Uganda. Ed. Wazarwahi Bwengye. adv.; bibl.; illus.

PUBLIC HEALTH LABORATORY SERVICE BOARD. BIENNIAL REPORT. see *MEDICAL SCIENCES — Communicable Diseases*

614   US   ISSN 0079-7596
PUBLIC HEALTH MONOGRAPH.* no.3, 1951. irreg. U.S. Public Health Service, Dept. of Health Education and Welfare, Bethesda, MD 20014. TEL 301-444-6656.
   Indexed: Biol.Abstr., Ind.Med.
   Continues: Public Health Technical Monograph.

614   UN   ISSN 0555-6015
                                    CODEN: WHOPAY
PUBLIC HEALTH PAPERS. French edition: Cahiers de Sante Publique. Russian edition: Tetradi Obshchestvennogo Zdravookhranenia. Spanish edition: Cuadernos de Salud Publica. (Editions in Arabic, English, French, Russian, Spanish) 1959. irreg., no.82, 1986. World Health Organization, Distribution and Sales Service, CH-1211 Geneva 27, Switzerland. TEL 022-791-2111. circ. 12,000.
   Indexed: Abstr.Hyg., Biol.Abstr., Excerp.Med., Ind.Med., Med. Care Rev., Rural Ext.Educ.& Tr.Abstr., Rural Recreat.Tour.Abstr., So.Pac.Per.Ind., World Agri.Econ.& Rural Sociol.Abstr.

614   US   ISSN 0090-2918
RA11   CODEN: HSRPAT
PUBLIC HEALTH REPORTS; official journal of the U.S. Public Health Service. (Supplements avail.) 1878. bi-m. $12 (foreign $15). U.S. Public Health Service, Department of Health and Human Services, Parklawn Bldg., Rm. 13C-26, 5600 Fishers Ln., Rockville, MD 20857. TEL 301-443-0762. FAX 301-443-1719. (Orders to: Supt. of Documents, Washington, DC 20402-9371) Ed. Marian Priest Tebben. bibl.; charts; illus.; stat.; index; circ. 8,000. (also avail. in microform from UMI; back issues avail.; reprint service avail. from UMI) **Indexed:** Abstr.Health Care Manage.Stud., Abstr.Hyg., Acad.Ind., Amer.Stat.Ind., Bibl.Dev.Med.& Child Neur., Biotech.Abstr., C.I.N.L., Chem.Abstr., Curr.Adv.Ecol.Sci., Curr.Cont., Dent.Abstr., Dok.Arbeitsmed., Eng.Ind., Gen.Sci.Ind., Helminthol.Abstr., Hlth.Ind., Hosp.Lit.Ind., Ind.Med., Ind.U.S.Gov.Per., Mid.East: Abstr.& Ind., Nutr.Abstr., P.A.I.S., Risk Abstr., Sci.Cit.Ind., Soc.Work Res.& Abstr., SSCI, W.R.C.Inf.
   ●Also available online. Vendor(s): Mead Data Central.
   Former titles (until 1974): Health Services Reports; (until 1972): H S M H A Health Reports; (until 1970): Public Health Reports (ISSN 0033-3549)
   Description: Reports on research, activities in public health.

614   IS   ISSN 0301-0422
                                    CODEN: PBHRAM
PUBLIC HEALTH REVIEWS; an international quarterly. 1972. q. $100. Technosdar Ltd., P.O. Box 31684, Tel Aviv 61316, Israel. TEL 3-622418. FAX 3-614932. TELEX 341667 RMYM. Ed. Sigmund Geller. adv.; bk.rev.; abstr.; bibl.; index, cum.index. **Indexed:** Biol.Abstr., C.I.N.L., Curr.Adv.Ecol.Sci., Curr.Cont., Energy Ind., Energy Info.Abstr., Excerp.Med., Hosp.Lit.Ind., Ind.Med., SSCI.
   —BLDSC shelfmark: 6966.300000.
   Description: Presents reviews and critical evaluations of topics in public health, including epidemiology, environmental and occupational health. Publishes concise reports of research, surveys, long-term studies, and trends in morbidity and mortality. Also publishes proceeding and abstracts of conferences.
   Refereed Serial

PUBLIC RISK. see *PUBLIC ADMINISTRATION — Municipal Government*

628   IT
PULIZIA INDUSTRIALE E SANIFICAZIONE. 1968. m. L.60000. MO.ED.CO. s.r.l., Via Paolo da Cannobio 9, 20122 Milan, Italy. adv.; circ. 5,500.

PUBLIC HEALTH AND SAFETY 4111

614 UK
R S P A BULLETIN. 1971. m. £15. Royal Society for the Prevention of Accidents, Cannon House, The Priory Queensway, Birmingham B4 6BS, England. Ed. Elizabeth Herbert.
  Formerly: Industrial Accident Prevention Bulletin.

628 IT ISSN 0394-5391
R S RIFIUTI SOLIDI. (Text in Italian; summaries in English, Italian) 1987. 6/yr. L.150000. (Centro di Ingegneria per la Protezione dell'Ambiente) C I P A s.r.l., Via Palladio, 26, 20135 Milan, Italy. TEL 02-58301528. FAX 02-58301550.

614.8 624 US
R T E C S REGULATORY SUBFILE. REGULATIONS, RECOMMENDATIONS AND ASSESSMENTS. (Registry of Toxic Effects of Chemical Substances) q. $1500 per issue in US, Canada, Mexico; elsewhere $3000. (Department of Health and Human Services, National Institute of Occupational Safety and Health (NIOSH)) U.S. National Technical Information Service, 5825 Port Royal Rd., Springfield, VA 22161. TEL 703-487-4630. bibl. (avail. on diskette only)
  Description: Substances are listed in alphabetical order by the prime entry name. Data can be searched by RTECS accession number, CAS Registry Number, or fragment of name or synonym.

RADIATION PROTECTION DOSIMETRY. see *PHYSICS — Nuclear Physics*

614.8 US ISSN 0740-0640
CODEN: RPMAEI
RADIATION PROTECTION MANAGEMENT. (Supplement avail.: R P M Directory) 1983. bi-m. $156 to individuals; institutions $390; students $45. R S A Publications, 10 Pendleton Dr., Box 19, Hebron, CT 06248. TEL 203-228-0824. FAX 203-228-4402. Ed. Sharyn Mathews. adv.; bk.rev.; index; circ. 600. (back issues avail.) **Indexed:** Chem.Abstr.
  —BLDSC shelfmark: 7227.994000.
  Description: Covers applied health physics.

LA RADIOACTIVITE DES PRINCIPALES SOURCES D'EAU MINERALE EN BELGIQUE. ETUDE. see *WATER RESOURCES*

RAUMPLANUNG UND UMWELTSCHUTZ IM KANTON ZURICH. see *HOUSING AND URBAN PLANNING*

RECREATION CANADA. see *LEISURE AND RECREATION*

614.8 DK ISSN 0108-254X
REDNINGSHISTORISK FORENINGS INFORMATION. 1976. bi-m. membership. Redningshistorisk Forening, Postbox 101, 2770 Kastrup, Denmark. Ed. Jacob Stoppel. adv.; bk.rev.; illus.; circ. 300.
  Formerly: Redningshistorisk Forening. Information (ISSN 0108-2531)

614 CK
REGISTRO DE ORGANISMOS DE SALUD. 1976. a. Departamento Administrativo Nacional de Estadistica, Banco Nacional de Datos, Apdo. Aereo 80043, Bogota, D.E., Colombia.

614 US ISSN 0275-0902
REGULATORY WATCHDOG SERVICE. 1975. w. $893. Washington Business Information, Inc., c/o Karen Harrington, 1117 N. 19th St., Ste. 200, Arlington, VA 22209. TEL 703-247-3434. FAX 703-247-3421. Ed. Vincent LeClair. bk.rev.; index. (looseleaf format)
  Former titles: Regulatory Safety Watchdog Service; Product Safety Watchdog Service (ISSN 0146-4639)
  Description: Reports on government documents available from Congress, FDA and other federal agencies.

RENT I DANMARK. see *BUSINESS AND ECONOMICS — Management*

REPORT ON DISABILITY PROGRAMS. see *SOCIAL SERVICES AND WELFARE*

614 UN ISSN 0085-5529
RA8
REPORT ON THE WORLD HEALTH SITUATION. (Editions in Arabic, Chinese, English, French, Russian, Spanish) 1959. every 6 yrs. World Health Organization, Distribution and Sales, CH-1211 Geneva 27, Switzerland. TEL 022-791-2111. circ. 6,200.

616.89 150 US ISSN 0192-0812
RA790.A1
RESEARCH IN COMMUNITY AND MENTAL HEALTH; an annual compilation of research. 1979. a. $58.50 to institutions. J A I Press Inc., 55 Old Post Rd., No. 2, Box 1678, Greenwich, CT 06836-1678. TEL 203-661-7602. Ed. Roberta G. Simmons. **Indexed:** Chic.Per.Ind., Psychol.Abstr.
  —BLDSC shelfmark: 7736.700000.

RESEARCH IN THE SOCIOLOGY OF HEALTH CARE; a research annual. see *MEDICAL SCIENCES*

614 BE ISSN 0773-7777
RESEAU AUTOMATIQUE BELGE DE LA POLLUTION ATMOSPHERIQUE. (Text in Dutch, French) 1978. a. $7. Instituut voor Hygiene en Epidemiologie (IHE), Juliette Wytsmanstraat 14, B-1050 Brussels, Belgium. Ed.Bd. circ. 250.

REVIEWS ON ENVIRONMENTAL HEALTH. see *ENVIRONMENTAL STUDIES*

614 BL ISSN 0100-0233
RA464.B33
REVISTA BAIANA DE SAUDE PUBLICA. (Text in Portuguese; summaries in English) 1974. q. exchange basis. Secretaria da Saude do Estado da Bahia, Centro Administrativo da Bahia 4a, Av. Plataforma 06, Caixa Postal 631, 40000 Salvador, Bahia, Brazil. TEL (071)370-4273. TELEX 7136. Ed.Bd. bibl.; charts; stat.; circ. 1,000. **Indexed:** Abstr.Hyg.

614.4 CU
REVISTA CUBANA DE HIGIENE Y EPIDEMIOLOGIA. (Text in Spanish; summaries in English, French, Spanish) 1963. s-a. $10 in N. America; S. America $12; Europe $14. Ministerio de Salud Publica, Centro Nacional de Informacion de Ciencias Medicas, Calle E No. 452, e-19 y 21, Plaza de la Revolucion, Apdo. 6520, Havana, Cuba. TEL 809-32-5338. (Dist. by: Ediciones Cubanas, Obispo No. 527, Apdo. 605, Havana, Cuba) abstr.; bibl.; charts; illus.; index; circ. 1,500. **Indexed:** Abstr.Hyg., Biol.Abstr., Chem.Abstr., Dairy Sci.Abstr., Excerp.Med., Ind.Med., Trop.Dis.Bull.
  Formerly: Boletin de Higiene y Epidemiologia (ISSN 0006-629X)

614 CU ISSN 0864-3466
RA456.C7
REVISTA CUBANA DE SALUD PUBLICA. (Text in Spanish; summaries in English, French, Spanish) 1975. s-a. $10 in N. America; S. America $12; Europe $14. Ministerio de Salud Publica, Centro Nacional de Informacion de Ciencias Medicas, Calle E No. 452, e-19 y 21, Plaza de la Revolucion, Apdo. 6520, Havana, Cuba. TEL 809-32-5338. (Dist. by: Ediciones Cubanas, Obispo No. 527, Apdo. 605, Havana, Cuba) Dir. Benito Narey Ramos. bibl.; charts; illus.; index; circ. 1,500. **Indexed:** Abstr.Hyg., Curr.Adv.Ecol.Sci., Ind.Med., Popul.Ind.
  —BLDSC shelfmark: 7852.150000.
  Formerly: Revista Cubana de Administracion de Salud (ISSN 0252-1903)
  Description: Contains organ and administration news, including health surveys, automatic data processing.

REVISTA DE IGIENA, BACTERIOLOGIE, VIRUSOLOGIE, PARAZITOLOGIE, PNEUMOFTIZIOLOGIE. BACTERIOLOGIE, VIRUSOLOGIE, PARAZITOLOGIE, EPIDEMIOLOGIE. see *BIOLOGY — Microbiology*

614.8 SP ISSN 0034-8732
REVISTA DE PREVENCION. 1962. q. membership. Asociacion para la Prevencion de Accidentes, Echaide 4, 2 Piso, San Sebastian, Spain. FAX 43-42-91-32. Ed. Ramon Zamanillo Tellitu. adv.; bk.rev.; circ. 7,500. **Indexed:** C.I.S. Abstr.

614 SP ISSN 0034-8899
REVISTA DE SANIDAD E HIGIENE PUBLICA. (Text in Spanish; summaries in English) 1927. 6/yr. 2000 ptas. Ministerio de Sanidad y Consumo, Paseo del Prado 18-20, 28014 Madrid, Spain. TEL 420-00-00. FAX 4201096. TELEX 4201096. Ed. Juan Jose Artells Herrero. bk.rev.; abstr.; bibl.; charts; illus.; circ. 5,000. **Indexed:** Abstr.Hyg., Biol.Abstr., Chem.Abstr., Helminthol.Abstr., Ind.Med.Esp., Ind.Med., Protozool.Abstr., Rev.Appl.Entomol., Trop.Dis.Bull.
  —BLDSC shelfmark: 7870.600000.

614 BL ISSN 0034-8910
CODEN: RSPUB9
REVISTA DE SAUDE PUBLICA. 1967. bi-m. $40 or on exchange basis(typically set in Dec.). Universidade de Sao Paulo, Faculdade de Saude Publica, Av. Dr. Arnaldo 715, Sao Paulo, Brazil. FAX 011-852-9630. Ed. Dr. Oswaldo Paulo Forattini. bk.rev.; bibl.; charts; illus.; index; circ. 1,500. **Indexed:** Abstr.Hyg., Biol.Abstr., C.I.S. Abstr., Curr.Cont., Dent.Ind., Entomol.Abstr., Excerp.Med., Helminthol.Abstr., Ind.Med., Ind.Vet., Microbiol.Abstr., Nutr.Abstr., Protozool.Abstr., Rev.Appl.Entomol., Saf.Sci.Abstr., Soyabean Abstr., SSCI, Trop.Dis.Bull., Vet.Bull., Virol.Abstr.
  —BLDSC shelfmark: 7870.635000.
  Supersedes: Universidade de Sao Paulo. Faculdade de Higiene e Saude Publica. Archivos.
  Description: Reflects scientific advances in the public health field through original research prepared by specialists, both domestic and foreign.
  Refereed Serial

REVISTA INTERNACIONAL DEL TRABAJO. see *BUSINESS AND ECONOMICS — Labor And Industrial Relations*

614 VE ISSN 0035-0583
RA421
REVISTA VENEZOLANA DE SANIDAD Y ASISTENCIA SOCIAL. (Text in Spanish; summaries in several languages) 1936. q. free. Ministerio de Sanidad y Asistencia Social, Oficina de Publicaciones, Biblioteca y Archivo, Centro Simon Bolivar, Edificio Sur, Caracas, Venezuela. Ed. Manuel Boet. charts; illus.; stat.; index; circ. 3,000. **Indexed:** Biol.Abstr., Chem.Abstr., Ind.Med., Nutr.Abstr., Rev.Appl.Entomol.

614 FR ISSN 0398-7620
CODEN: RESPDF
REVUE D'EPIDEMIOLOGIE ET DE SANTE PUBLIQUE. (Text in French; summaries in English) 1953. bi-m. 165 ECU($195) (typically set in Jan.). Editions Masson, 120 bd. Saint-Germain, 75280 Paris Cedex 06, France. TEL 1-46-34-21-60. FAX 1-45-87-29-99. TELEX 202 671 F. Ed. Rumeau-Rouquette. bk.rev.; illus.; index; circ. 1,200. (also avail. in microform from UMI; reprint service avail. from ISI) **Indexed:** Abstr.Hyg., Bibl.Dev.Med.& Child Neur., Biol.Abstr., C.I.S. Abstr., Curr.Adv.Ecol.Sci., Curr.Cont., Excerp.Med., Helminthol.Abstr., Ind.Med., Ind.Vet., Med.Care Rev., Trop.Dis.Bull., Vet.Bull.
  —BLDSC shelfmark: 7900.109000.
  Former titles (until 1976): Revue d'Epidemiologie, Medecine Sociale et Sante Publique (ISSN 0035-2438); Revue d'Hygiene et de Medecine Sociale.

REVUE INTERNATIONALE DU TRAVAIL. see *BUSINESS AND ECONOMICS — Labor And Industrial Relations*

REVUE MEDICALE RWANDAISE. see *MEDICAL SCIENCES*

614.8 IT
RIVISTA ITALIANA DI PREVIDENZA SOCIALE. bi-m. Via Nicola Marchese, 20, Rome, Italy. Ed. U. Chiapelli.

ROHSTOFF RUNDSCHAU; Fachblatt des gesamten Handels mit Alt- und Abfallstoffen. see *TECHNOLOGY: COMPREHENSIVE WORKS*

ROTOR: BY THE INDUSTRY - FOR THE INDUSTRY. see *AERONAUTICS AND SPACE FLIGHT*

ROUTE. see *TRANSPORTATION — Automobiles*

614.8 UK
THE ROYAL LIFE SAVING SOCIETY. LIFESAVER U.K.. 1965. q. Royal Life Saving Society U.K., Mountbatten House, Studley, Warwickshire B80 7NN, England. TEL 052-785-3943. FAX 052-785-4453. Ed. Sandra Caldwell. adv.; bk.rev.; circ. 13,000. **Indexed:** Sportsearch.
  Formerly: Royal Life Saving Society - U.K. Quarterly Journal (ISSN 0048-8704)

ROYAL SOCIETY OF HEALTH JOURNAL. see *SOCIAL SERVICES AND WELFARE*

614 RW
RWANDA. MINISTERE DE LA SANTE PUBLIQUE. RAPPORT ANNUEL. a. Ministere de la Sante Publique, B.P. 84, Kigaii, Rwanda. circ. 200.

PUBLIC HEALTH AND SAFETY

614.8 — SA
S A FAMILY SAFETY/GESINSVEILIGHEID. (Text in Afrikaans, English) q. R.3. Safety First Association, 7 Pitcairn Rd., Blairgowrie, Johannesburg 2194, South Africa. TEL 011-782-7698. Ed. Barbara Campbell. adv.; tr.lit.
Description: Covers home safety topics.

S B Z - SANITAER, HEIZUNGS- UND KLIMATECHNIK. see HEATING, PLUMBING AND REFRIGERATION

614.8 — US
SAFE JOURNAL. 1967. 6/yr. $20. S A F E Association, Box 490, Yoncalla, OR 97499-0490. TEL 503-849-2977. Ed. Richard P. White, Jr. adv.; bk.rev.; circ. 1,000. Indexed: Excerp.Med.
Description: Dedicated to the preservation of human life.

614.8 — US — ISSN 0891-1797
SAFETY & HEALTH. 1919. m. $35 to non-members; members $29. National Safety Council, Industrial Section, 444 N. Michigan Ave., Chicago, IL 60611. TEL 800-621-7619. Ed. Carrie Smith. adv.; bk.rev.; abstr.; bibl.; charts; illus.; stat.; tr.lit.; index, cum.index; circ. 35,000. (also avail. in microform from UMI; reprint service avail. from UMI) Indexed: B.P.I, Bus.Ind., C.I.S. Abstr., Chem.Abstr., Hlth.Ind., Tr.& Indus.Ind.
—BLDSC shelfmark: 8065.709600.
Former titles (until 1986): National Safety and Health News (ISSN 8756-5366); (until May 1985): National Safety News (ISSN 0028-0100)
Description: For occupational safety and health professionals. Includes occupational fleet management and non-occupational traffic safety, environmental health and industrial hygiene.

614.8 — UK — ISSN 0265-4792
THE SAFETY & HEALTH PRACTITIONER. m. £40. Paramount Publishing Ltd., 17-21 Shenley Rd., Borehamwood, Herts. WD6 1RT, England. TEL 081-207-5599. FAX 081-207-2598. Ed. J. Balian. adv.; bk.rev.; circ. 12,000. Indexed: Br.Ceram.Abstr., C.I.S. Abstr., Ind.Vet., Lab.Haz.Bull., Mgmt.& Market.Abstr., World Surf.Coat.
Formerly: Safety Practitioner; Supersedes: Safety Surveyor and Protection.

614 — UK
SAFETY AND RESCUE. 1959. m. £1($7) British Safety Council, Chancellors Rd., Hammersmith, London W6 9RS, England. Ed. James Tye. adv.; bk.rev.; circ. 75,000. Indexed: C.I.S. Abstr.

614.8 350.78 — US — ISSN 0036-245X
SAFETY BRIEFS. 1938. 4/yr. free. New Jersey State Safety Council, 6 Commerce Dr., Cranford, NJ 07016-3597. TEL 201-272-7712. FAX 201-276-6622. Ed. James F. Hughes. bk.rev.; charts; stat.; circ. 19,000.

614.862 — CN — ISSN 0048-8968
SAFETY CANADA. French edition: Prevention au Canada. 1957. q. free. Canada Safety Council, 6-2750 Stevenage Dr., Ottawa, Ont., K1G 3N2, Canada. TEL 613-739-1535. FAX 613-739-1566. Ed. Heather A. Totten. bk.rev.; circ. 23,300 (20,750 English ed.; 2,550 French ed.).
Formerly: Highway Safety News.

614 — UK
SAFETY EDUCATION. 1966. 3/yr. £10 to non-members; members £4.50. Royal Society for the Prevention of Accidents, Cannon House, The Priory Queensway, Birmingham B4 6BS, England. TEL 021-200-2461. FAX 021-200-1254. Ed. Don Jones. adv.; bk.rev.; circ. 20,000.
Description: News items, informational articles, case studies, and technical advice on instruction to children and young adults in the adoption of safety practices.

614 — CN
SAFETY UPDATE.* q. free. Ontario Safety League, 21 Four Seasons Place, Etobicoke, Ont. M9B 6J8, Canada. TEL 416-593-2670.
Formerly: Ontario Safety League. News (ISSN 0700-9844)

614.88 — UK
ST. JOHN WORLD. 1927. m. $30. Order of St. John, 1 Grosvenor Crescent, London SW1X 7EF, England. TEL 01-235-5231. FAX 01-235-0796. Ed. Vic Allen. adv.; bk.rev.; film rev.; illus.; circ. 10,000.
Formerly: St. John Review (ISSN 0036-2883)

628 — JA
SAITAMA-KEN EISEI TOKEI NENPO/ANNUAL REPORT OF PUBLIC HEALTH, SAITAMA PREFECTURE. (Text in Japanese) 1950. a. free. Saitama-ken, Eisei-bu - Saitama Prefecture, Bureau of Public Health, 15-1 Takasago 3-chome, Urawa-shi, Saitama-ken 336, Japan.

614 — MX — ISSN 0036-3634
SALUD PUBLICA DE MEXICO/PUBLIC HEALTH OF MEXICO. (Includes special issue) (Text in Spanish; summaries in English and Spanish) 1959. bi-m. Mex.$50000($50) (outside Latin America $70) to individuals; students Mex.$40000($40) (outside Latin America $55). Instituto Nacional de Salud Publica, Secretaria de Salud, Av. Universidad, 665, Colonia Santa Maria Ahuacatitlad, C.P. 62508, Cuernavaca, Morelos, Mexico. TEL 73-11-01-11. FAX 73-11-01-03. bk.rev.; circ. 3,000. Indexed: Abstr.Hyg., Biol.Abstr., C.I.S. Abstr., Dairy Sci.Abstr., Excerp.Med., Helminthol.Abstr., Ind.Med., Nutr.Abstr., Trop.Dis.Bull.
—BLDSC shelfmark: 8071.800000.
Incorporates (in 1977): Investigacion en Salud Publica.

614.8 — RM
SANATATEA. 1952. m. National Council of the Red Cross, Str. Biserica Amzei 29, Bucharest, Rumania. Ed. Gheorghe M. George. circ. 140,000.

628 — BL — ISSN 0036-4312
SANEAMENTO. (Text in Portuguese; abstracts in English and French) 1947. q. exchange basis. Departamento Nacional de Obras de Saneamenento, Av. Pres. Vargas 62-11 andar, 20091 Rio de Janeiro R.J., Brazil. Ed. Dilson Ferreira Simoes. adv.; abstr.; bibl.; charts; illus.; stat.; circ. 16,000 (controlled). Indexed: Chem.Abstr.

628 — IT
SANITA PUBBLICA; rivista mensile amministrativa per gli operatori della sanita. 1981. m. (10/yr.). L.80000 to individuals; institutions L.198000(effective 1992). Maggioli Editore, Via Crimea, 1, Casella Postale 290, 47037 Rimini, Italy. TEL 0541-626777. FAX 0541-622020. Dir. Fabio Alberto Roversi-Monaco.

SANITAER UND HEIZUNGS REPORT. see HEATING, PLUMBING AND REFRIGERATION

628 — US — ISSN 0036-4436
HD9999.S383
SANITARY MAINTENANCE; the journal of the sanitary supply industry. 1943. m. $42. Trade Press Publishing Corp., 2100 W. Florist Ave., Milwaukee, WI 53209. TEL 414-228-7701. FAX 414-228-7701. Ed. Austin Weber. adv.; illus.; tr.lit.; index; circ. 17,000. (also avail. in microfilm from UMI; reprint service avail. from UMI)

614 — AE
SANTE. (Text in French) 1956. bi-m. Federation Nationale de la Sante, Maison du Peuple, Place du 1 Mai, Algiers, Algeria.

614 — RM — ISSN 0048-9107
SANTE PUBLIQUE.* (Editions also in English, German, Russian) 1958. q. 80 lei($12) Editura Medicala, c/o ILEXIM, Str. 13 Decembrie Nr. 3, P.O. Box 136-137, Bucharest, Rumania. Ed. Dr. Gh. Cadariu. bk.rev.; abstr.; bibl.; illus.; circ. 650. Indexed: Abstr.Hyg., Biol.Abstr., C.I.S. Abstr., Excerp.Med., Ind.Med., Trop.Dis.Bull.

600 — FR — ISSN 0294-0337
SCIENCES SOCIALES ET SANTE. 4/yr. 300 F. to individuals (foreign 340 F.); institutions 580 F. (foreign 720 F.); students 300 F. (foreign 390 F.). John Libbey Eurotext, 6 rue Blanche, 92129 Montrouge, France. TEL 1-47-35-85-52. FAX 1-46-57-10-09. (Dist. by: Gauthier-Villars, Centrale des Revues, 11 rue Gossin, 92543 Montrouge Cedex, France. TEL 1-46-56-52-66)
Description: Serves as an information exchange between all health care fields.

362.1 — UK
SCOTTISH HEALTH SERVICES. irreg. H.M.S.O. (Scotland), 13a Castle St., Edinburgh EH2 3AR, Scotland. (reprint service avail. from UMI)

614.8 — US
SEARCHLINES. 1979. bi-m. $25. International Association of Dive Rescue Specialists, 201 N. Link Ln., Ft. Collins, CO 80524-2712. TEL 303-482-0887. FAX 303-482-0893. Ed. Teresa D. Long. adv.; bk.rev.; circ. 2,375.
Formerly: Dive Rescue Specialist.
Description: Covers techniques, equipment and experiences pertinent to the job of public safety diver. For professional dive rescue specialists.

614.85 — IT — ISSN 0037-0657
SECURITAS; rivista di studi e documentazione sulla sicurezza nel lavoro. 1914. m. L.8000. Ente Nazionale per la Prevenzione degli Infortuni, Via Alessandria 220, Rome, Italy. Ed. Carlo Borrini. adv.; bk.rev.; abstr.; charts; illus.; stat.; tr.lit.; index; circ. 6,000. Indexed: Chem.Abstr., Trop.Dis.Bull.

SECURITY SPECIFIER. see CRIMINOLOGY AND LAW ENFORCEMENT — Security

614.8 — PO — ISSN 0049-0059
SEGURANCA. 1965. 4/yr. Esc.1200. Associacao Portuguesa de Seguradores, Av. Jose Malhoa, 1674-4 Piso, 1000 Lisbon Codex, Portugal. TEL 01-7268123. FAX 01-7262290. adv.; circ. 3,500. Indexed: C.I.S. Abstr.

SEGURIDAD SOCIAL. see SOCIAL SERVICES AND WELFARE

SEIKATSU TO KANKYO/LIFE AND ENVIRONMENT. see ENVIRONMENTAL STUDIES

614.073 — JA — ISSN 0037-1092
SEISHONEN SEKIJUJI/JAPANESE JUNIOR RED CROSS.*
1949. 6/yr. free. Japanese Red Cross Society, Junior Red Cross Section - Nihon Sekijuji Kai, 5 Shiha Koen, 3 Minato-ku, Tokyo, Japan. Ed. Keiji Shimoji. illus.; stat.; circ. 40,000.

614 — DK — ISSN 0901-9685
SEX OG SUNDHED/SEX AND HEALTH; om sexualitet, praevention og sexuelt overfoerbare sygdomme. 1986. s-a. free. Danish Family Planning Association, Aurehoejvej 2, DK-2900 Hellerup, Denmark. Ed. Marianne Soendergaard. illus.; circ. 10,000.
Former titles: Mer om Sex og Sikkerhed (ISSN 0108-7851); Mer om Koenssygdomme (ISSN 0108-7843)

613 — AA
SHENDETESIA POPULLORE.* q. $4.10. Ministere de la Sante Publique, Tirana, Albania.

613 — AA
SHENDETI.* bi-m. $6.16. Ministere de la Sante Publique, Tirana, Albania.

SHONI NO HOKEN/HEALTH FOR CHILDREN. see CHILDREN AND YOUTH — About

SICHERHEIT ZUERST. see TRANSPORTATION — Railroads

614.8 — CI — ISSN 0350-6886
SIGURNOST/SAFETY. (Text in Croatian; summaries and contents page in English) 1959. 4/yr. 1260 din.($120) Zavod za Instrazivanje i Razvoj Sigurnosti - Institute of Safety Research and Development, Proleterskih Brigada 68, 41000 Zagreb, Croatia. TEL 41-512494. FAX 41-516012. (Co-sponsor: Ministarstvo Znanosti, Tehnologije i Informatike Republike Hrvatske) Ed.Gordana Baraba. adv.; bk.rev.; charts; illus.; index, cum.index; circ. 1,500. Indexed: C.I.S. Abstr.
—BLDSC shelfmark: 8276.480000.
Formerly (until 1972): Sigurnost u Pogonu (ISSN 0037-508X)

614.8 — DK — ISSN 0108-6650
SIKKERHED. (Supplement to: Socialpaedagogernes Landsforbund. T R Information) 1981. irreg. free. Socialpaedagogernes Landsforbund, Brolaeggerstraede 9-st, 1211 Copenhagen K, Denmark. illus.

SINNETS HELSE. see PSYCHOLOGY

614 — DK — ISSN 0900-1980
SOCIAL ADMINISTRATION; lovsamling for praktikere og tilstudiebrug. 1984. a. DKK 195.20. Forlag for Social- og Sundhedssektor, Vibeholms Alle 11-15, 2605 Bronoby, Denmark.

SOCIAL WORK IN HEALTH CARE; quarterly journal of medical & psychiatric social work. see SOCIAL SERVICES AND WELFARE

613   NR   ISSN 0037-9905
SOCIETY OF HEALTH OF NIGERIA. JOURNAL.* 1966. q. $7. Nigeria Medical Council, Plot PC 13, 25 Ahmed Onidudo St., Victoria Island, P.M.B. 12611, Lagos, Nigeria. adv.

SOUTHEAST ASIAN JOURNAL OF TROPICAL MEDICINE AND PUBLIC HEALTH. see MEDICAL SCIENCES — Communicable Diseases

614   RU   ISSN 0038-5239
                          CODEN: SOZDAO
SOVETSKOE ZDRAVOOKHRANENIE/SOVIET PUBLIC HEALTH. (Text in Russian; summaries in English) 1942. m. 22.20 Rub.($16.20) (Ministerstvo Zdravookhraneniya S.S.S.R.) Izdatel'stvo Meditsina, Petroverigskii pereulok 6-8, 101838 Moscow, Russia. Ed. O.P. Shchepin. bk.rev.; abstr.; bibl.; charts; illus.; stat.; index. (microform) Indexed: Abstr.Hyg., Biol.Abstr., C.I.S. Abstr., Chem.Abstr., Curr.Dig.Sov.Press, Dent.Ind., Ind.Med., Trop.Dis.Bull., World Bibl.Soc.Sec.
  —BLDSC shelfmark: 0165.080000.
  Description: Discusses theoretical problems of social hygiene and public health organization, the main trends in the development of the socialist system of health protection, scientific bases of planning, prognosticating and management in public health service.

614 616.86   US
STATE A D M REPORTS. 10/yr. $170 to private sector; state officials $95. Intergovernmental Health Policy Project, 2021 K St., N.W., Ste. 800, Washington, DC 20006. TEL 202-872-1445.
  Formerly: State Health Reports.
  Description: Covers important research and policy developments affecting mental health, alcoholism and drug abuse programs within the fifty states.

614   US
STATE HEALTH NOTES. 1979. s-m. $195 to private sector; state officials $95. Intergovernmental Health Policy Project, 2021 K St., N.W., Ste. 800, Washington, DC 20006. TEL 202-872-1445. Ed. Linda Demkovich. charts; stat.; circ. 2,700. (tabloid format; back issues avail.)
  Description: Identifies and analyzes important health-related trends and innovations within state government.

614   SW   ISSN 0085-6738
STATUS. 1938. 8/yr. SEK 75. Riksfoerbundet foer Hjaert- och Lungsjuka - Swedish Heart and Lung Association, P.O. Box 9090, 102 72 Stockholm, Sweden. FAX 08-6682385. Ed. Tonie Andersson. adv.; bk.rev.; circ. 30,000.

614   BE
STUDIE VAN DE LUCHTKWALITEIT IN BELGIE. ZWAVEL-ROOK MEETNET. Short title: Zwavel-Rook Meetnet. (Text in Dutch, French) 1968. a. $5. Instituut voor Hygiene en Epidemiologie (IHE), Juliette Wytsmanstraat 14, B-1050 Brussels, Belgium. charts; stat.; circ. 600.
  Formerly: Instituut voor Hygiene en Epidemiologie. Zwavel-Rook Meetnet (ISSN 0378-892X)

STUDIES ON CURRENT HEALTH PROBLEMS. see MEDICAL SCIENCES

614   VN
SUC KHOE/HEALTH. fortn. Ministry of Public Health, 138 A Giang Vo St., Hanoi, Socialist Republic of Vietnam. TEL 43144. Ed. Phung Truc Phong.

614   II   ISSN 0586-1179
SWASTH HIND. (Text in English) 1957. m. Rs.6($5) Ministry of Health and Family Welfare, Central Health Education Bureau, Kotla Rd., New Delhi 110 002, India. Ed. M.L. Mehta. adv.; bk.rev.; charts; illus.; stat.; index; circ. 8,500.

614   SW   ISSN 0346-8445
SWEDEN. SJUKVAARDENS OCH SOCIALVAARDENS PLANERINGS- OCH RATIONALISERINGSINSTITUT. S P R I INFORMERAR. Short title: S P R I Informerar. 1968. 10/yr. free. Sjukvaardens och Socialvaardens Planerings- och Rationaliseringsinstitut - Swedish Planning and Rationalization Institute of the Health and Social Services, Box 70487, S-107 26 Stockholm, Sweden. TEL 08-702-4600. FAX 08-7024799.
  —BLDSC shelfmark: 8424.060000.

614   SW   ISSN 0586-1691
SWEDEN. SJUKVAARDENS OCH SOCIALVAARDENS PLANERINGS- OCH RATIONALISERINGSINSTITUT. S P R I RAPPORT. Short title: S P R I Rapport. (Text in Swedish) 1968. irreg. price varies. Sjukvaardens och Socialvaardens Planerings- och Rationaliseringsinstitut - Swedish Planning and Rationalization Institute of the Health and Social Services, Box 70487, S-107 26 Stockholm, Sweden. TEL 08-702-4600. FAX 08-702-4799.
  Indexed: Abstr.Health Care Manage.Stud.
  —BLDSC shelfmark: 8424.070000.

SWIMMING POOLS TODAY. see SPORTS AND GAMES — Outdoor Life

614.8   US
SYSTEM SAFETY SOCIETY. DIRECTORY OF CONSULTANTS. a. $50 to non-members; members $10. System Safety Society, Inc., Technology Trading Park, 5 Export Dr., Ste. A, Sterling, VA 22170-4421. TEL 703-444-6520. circ. 1,100.
  Description: Lists consultants in system and product safety.

628   ER   ISSN 0868-4103
TALLINNA TEHNIKAULIKOOL. NEUSTANOVIVSHEESYA PROTSESSY V SISTEMAKH VODOSNABZHENIYA I VODOOTVEDENIYA. (Subseries of its Toimetised) (Text in Russian; summaries in English or German) irreg. price varies. Tallinna Tehnikaulikool, Ehitajate tee 5, Tallinn, Estonia. TEL 53-72-58.
  Former titles: Polutehniline Instituut Tallinn. Neustanovivsheesya Protsessy v Sistemakh Vodosnabzheniya i Vodootvedeniya; Polutehniline Instituut Tallinn. Neustanovivsheesya Dvizheniya Zhidkosti v Trubakh (ISSN 0203-9702)

TECHNIQUES HOSPITALIERES, MEDICO-SOCIALES ET SANITAIRES. see HOSPITALS

TECHNIQUES - SCIENCES - METHODES. GENIE URBAIN RURAL. see PUBLIC ADMINISTRATION — Municipal Government

614   IT   ISSN 0040-1897
TECNICA SANITARIA. 1963. bi-m. L.60000($45) Associazione Nazionale Ufficiali Sanitari Medici Igienisti, Via Marconi 45, 40122 Bologna, Italy. Dir. Ferruccio Vivoli. adv.; bk.rev.; abstr.; bibl.; charts; illus.; stat.; index; circ. 1,000. Indexed: Food Sci.& Tech.Abstr.

TEHNOLOGIJA MESA/MEAT TECHNOLOGY; casopis industrije mesa Jugoslavije. see AGRICULTURE — Poultry And Livestock

TEMAS DE POBLACION. see POPULATION STUDIES

628 614.8   FI   ISSN 0782-3789
TERVEYS 2000. 1985. 8/yr. FIM 179. Sanoma Corporation, PL 113, SF-00381 Helsinki, Finland. Ed. Kaisa Larmela. circ. 27,178.
  Description: Results of research in health care and medical research.

614   US
TEXAS. DEPARTMENT OF HEALTH. ANNUAL REPORT. a. free. Department of Health, 1100 W. 49th St., Austin, TX 78756. TEL 512-458-7111.
  Texas. Department of Health Resources. Biennial Report (ISSN 0163-1667)

TEXAS WATER UTILITIES JOURNAL. see WATER RESOURCES

TIJDSCHRIFT VOOR SOCIALE GEZONDHEIDSZORG. see MEDICAL SCIENCES

TOKYO-TORITSU EISEI KENKYUJO KENKYU NENPO/TOKYO METROPOLITAN RESEARCH LABORATORY OF PUBLIC HEALTH. ANNUAL REPORT. see MEDICAL SCIENCES

PUBLIC HEALTH AND SAFETY   4113

614   TO   ISSN 0082-4895
TONGA. MINISTER OF HEALTH. REPORT. (Text in English and Tongan) 1951. a. $25. Government Printer, Nuku'alofa, Tongatapu, Tonga. circ. 660.

TOURING. see TRANSPORTATION — Automobiles

TOXIC CHEMICALS LITIGATION REPORTER; the national journal of record for litigation involving claims of personal injury and/or property damage from exposure to toxic chemicals. see LAW

604.7 368.5   US
TOXIC TORTS; litigation of hazardous substance cases. (Includes annual supplement) 1984. irreg. $95. Shepard's - McGraw-Hill, Inc., Box 35300, Colorado Springs, CO 80935-3530. TEL 800-525-2474.
  Description: Covers the specific hows, whys and wherefores for successfully handling chemical and hazardous waste litigation.

TOYAMA-KEN EISEI TOKEI NENPO/TOYAMA PREFECTURE. ANNUAL REPORT OF PUBLIC HEALTH. see PUBLIC HEALTH AND SAFETY — Abstracting, Bibliographies, Statistics

614.8   US   ISSN 0275-844X
    QD139.T7   CODEN: TANAD7
TRACE ANALYSIS. 1981. irreg., vol.4, 1985. Academic Press, Inc., 1250 Sixth Ave., San Diego, CA 92101. TEL 619-231-0926. FAX 619-699-6715. Ed. James F. Lawrence. (reprint service avail. from ISI)
  Refereed Serial

TRACE SUBSTANCES IN ENVIRONMENTAL HEALTH. see ENVIRONMENTAL STUDIES — Toxicology And Environmental Safety

TRANSMISSION - DISTRIBUTION HEALTH & SAFETY REPORT. see OCCUPATIONAL HEALTH AND SAFETY

614.8 380.5   US
TRANSPORTATION SAFETY RECOMMENDATIONS. m. $85 in US, Canada, Mexico; elsewhere $170. (Department of Transportation, National Transportation Safety Board) U.S. National Technical Information Service, 5825 Port Royal Rd., Springfield, VA 22161. TEL 703-487-4630.
  Description: Reports on the board's safety oversight and accident prevention activities are provided. The safety reports inform on significant transportation problems, issues, and activities.

614.8   US
TRANSPORTATION SAFETY SPECIAL REPORTS. 5/yr. $70 in US, Canada, Mexico; elsewhere $140. (Department of Transportation, National Transportation Safety Board) U.S. National Technical Information Service, 5825 Port Royal Rd., Springfield, VA 22161. TEL 703-487-4630.
  Description: Includes safety studies and reports, accident investigation reports, as well as highway and railroad accident reports.

614   US
TRENDS (WASHINGTON, 1969). 1969. m. $55. American Society of Allied Health Professions, 1101 Connecticut Ave., N.W., Ste. 700, Washington, DC 20036. TEL 202-857-1150. FAX 202-223-4579. Ed. Thomas W. Elwood. adv.; circ. 1,300.
  Formerly: Allied Health Trends.

TROPICAL PEST MANAGEMENT. see AGRICULTURE — Crop Production And Soil

TWIN CITIES GAZE; the news weekly for the gay and lesbian community. see HOMOSEXUALITY

UEBERSETZUNGEN - KERNTECHNISCHE REGELN. see ENERGY — Nuclear Energy

614.8   AU   ISSN 0049-5131
UMWELTSCHUTZ. 1963. m. S.677. Bohmann Druck und Verlag GmbH & Co. KG, Leberstr. 122, A-1110 Vienna, Austria. TEL 0222-74095. FAX 0222-74095-183. TELEX 132312. adv.; bk.rev.; illus.; circ. 14,000. Indexed: Biol.Abstr.
  —BLDSC shelfmark: 9083.500000.

PUBLIC HEALTH AND SAFETY

614   TS
UNITED ARAB EMIRATES. WIZARAT AL-SIHHAH. IDARAT AL-TIBB AL-WAQA'I. AL-TAQRIR AL-SANAWI/UNITED ARAB EMIRATES. MINISTRY OF HEALTH. PREVENTIVE MEDICINE DEPARTMENT. ANNUAL REPORT. (Text in Arabic, English) 1981. a. Wizarat al-Sihhah, Idarat al-Tibb al-Waqa'i - Ministry of Health, Preventive Medicine Department, P.O. Box 344, Abu Dhabi, United Arab Emirates. TEL 333485. stat.; circ. 1,000 (controlled).
Description: Comprehensive review of the department's activities, including communicable disease control, health education, maternal and children's health services.

U.S. CENTERS FOR DISEASE CONTROL. ABORTION SURVEILLANCE. ANNUAL SUMMARY. see *BIRTH CONTROL*

312   US   ISSN 0090-1156
RA644.B7
U.S. CENTERS FOR DISEASE CONTROL. BRUCELLOSIS SURVEILLANCE: ANNUAL SUMMARY. a. U.S. Centers for Disease Control, 1600 Clifton Rd., NE, Atlanta, GA 30333. TEL 404-329-3311. illus. Key Title: Brucellosis Surveillance; Annual Summary.

U.S. CENTERS FOR DISEASE CONTROL. DIPHTHERIA SURVEILLANCE REPORT. see *MEDICAL SCIENCES — Communicable Diseases*

615.9   US   ISSN 0098-6623
RC143
U.S. CENTERS FOR DISEASE CONTROL. FOODBORNE & WATERBORNE DISEASE OUTBREAKS. ANNUAL SUMMARY. a. U.S. Centers for Disease Control, 1600 Clifton Rd., NE, Atlanta, GA 30333. TEL 404-329-3311. Key Title: Foodborne & Waterborne Disease Outbreaks. Annual Summary.
Formerly: U.S. Centers for Disease Control. Foodborne Outbreaks. Annual Summary.

U.S. CENTERS FOR DISEASE CONTROL. LEPROSY SURVEILLANCE REPORT. see *MEDICAL SCIENCES — Communicable Diseases*

U.S. CENTERS FOR DISEASE CONTROL. LISTERIOSIS SURVEILLANCE REPORT. see *MEDICAL SCIENCES — Communicable Diseases*

U.S. CENTERS FOR DISEASE CONTROL. MALARIA SURVEILLANCE REPORT. see *MEDICAL SCIENCES — Communicable Diseases*

614.4   US   ISSN 0149-2195
RA407.3
U.S. CENTERS FOR DISEASE CONTROL. MORBIDITY AND MORTALITY WEEKLY REPORT. 1950. w. $48 (foreign $85). U.S. Department of Health and Human Services, Centers for Disease Control (MS: A28), Epidemiology Program Office, 1600 Clifton Road N.E., Atlanta, GA 30333. TEL 800-843-6356. (Subscr. to: MMS Publications, C.S.P.O. Box 9120, Waltham, MA 02254) Ed. Dr. Richard A. Goodman. circ. 84,000. (also avail. in microform from UMI) Indexed: Abstr.Hyg., Curr.Lit.Fam.Plan., Curr.Tit.Dent., Hlth.Ind., I.P.A., Ind.Med., Ind.Vet., MEDOC, Protozool.Abstr., Trop.Dis.Bull., Vet.Bull. Key Title: Morbidity and Mortality.
●Also available online. Vendor(s): BRS, NewsNet.
—BLDSC shelfmark: 6082.091000.
Formerly (until 1976): U.S. National Communicable Disease Center. Morbidity and Mortality (ISSN 0091-0031)
Description: Provides an account of communicable diseases, ranging from AIDS to malaria, on a state, regional, and national basis.

614   US
U.S. CENTERS FOR DISEASE CONTROL. SALMONELLA SURVEILLANCE. ANNUAL SUMMARY. 1962. a. free. U.S. Centers for Disease Control, Bureau of Epidemiology. Bacterial Disease Division, 1600 Clifton Rd., NE, Atlanta, GA 30333. TEL 404-329-3311. charts; stat.; circ. 3,000.

628   US
U.S. DEFENSE LOGISTICS AGENCY. D O D HAZARDOUS MATERIALS INFORMATION SYSTEM: HAZARDOUS ITEM LISTING. irreg. (base. vol. plus updates). $75. U.S. Defense Logistics Agency, Cameron Station, Alexandria, VA 22314. TEL 703-545-6700. (Orders to: Supt. of Documents, Washington, DC 20402) (microfiche)

312   US
U.S. NATIONAL CENTER FOR HEALTH STATISTICS. ADVANCE DATA FROM VITAL AND HEALTH STATISTICS. no.47, 1979. irreg. U.S. National Center for Health Statistics, 6525 Belcrest Road, Hyattsville, MD 20782. TEL 301-436-8500.
Indexed: Nutr.Abstr.

614   US   ISSN 0083-1972
U.S. NATIONAL CENTER FOR HEALTH STATISTICS. VITAL AND HEALTH STATISTICS. SERIES 10. DATA FROM THE HEALTH INTERVIEW SURVEY. 1963. irreg., no.181, 1990. price varies. U.S. National Center for Health Statistics, Scientific and Technical Information Branch, 6526 Belcrest Road, Hyattsville, MD 20782. TEL 301-436-8500. **Indexed:** Excerp.Med.

614   US
U.S. NATIONAL CENTER FOR HEALTH STATISTICS. VITAL AND HEALTH STATISTICS. SERIES 11. DATA FROM THE HEALTH AND NUTRITION EXAMINATION SURVEY. Title varies: Data from the National Health Examination Survey and the National Health and Nutrition Examination Survey. 1964. irreg., latest no.240. price varies. U.S. National Center for Health Statistics, Scientific and Technical Information Branch, 6525 Belcrest Road, Hyattsville, MD 20782. TEL 301-436-8500. **Indexed:** Excerp.Med.
Formerly: U.S. National Center for Health Statistics. Vital and Health Statistics. Series 11. Data from the Health Examination Survey (ISSN 0083-1980)

362   US
U.S. NATIONAL CENTER FOR HEALTH STATISTICS. VITAL AND HEALTH STATISTICS. SERIES 13. DATA ON HEALTH RESOURCES UTILIZATION. 1966. irreg., latest no.104. price varies. U.S. National Center for Health Statistics, Scientific and Technical Information Branch, 6525 Belcrest Road, Hyattsville, MD 20782. TEL 301-436-8500. **Indexed:** Excerp.Med.
Incorporates: U.S. National Center for Health Care Statistics. Vital and Health Statistics. Series 12. Data from the Institutional Population Surveys (ISSN 0083-1964); **Formerly:** U.S. National Center for Health Care Statistics. Vital and Health Statistics. Series 13. Data from the Hospital Discharge Survey (ISSN 0083-2006)

614   US
U.S. NATIONAL CENTER FOR HEALTH STATISTICS. VITAL AND HEALTH STATISTICS. SERIES 14. DATA ON HEALTH RESOURCES. 1968. irreg., latest no.34. price varies. U.S. National Center for Health Statistics, Scientific and Technical Information Branch, 6525 Belcrest Road, Hyattsville, MD 20782. TEL 301-436-8500. **Indexed:** Excerp.Med.
Formerly: U.S. National Center for Health Statistics. Vital and Health Statistics. Series 14. Data on Health Resources: Manpower and Facilities (ISSN 0083-1999)

614   US
UNITED STATES - MEXICO BORDER HEALTH ASSOCIATION. NEWS - NOTICIAS. 1976. m? $15. Pan American Health Organization, El Paso Field Office, 6006 N. Mesa, Ste. 600, El Paso, TX 79912. TEL 915-581-6645. TELEX 749342. Ed. Dr. Herbert H. Ortega. circ, 2,500.
Description: Reports on the activities of the Association and its membership.

628   GT
UNIVERSIDAD DE SAN CARLOS. FACULTAD DE INGENERIA. ESCUELA REGIONAL DE INGENIERIA SANITARIA. CARTA PERIODICA. 1966. irreg. Universidad de San Carlos de Guatemala, Escuela Regional de Ingenieria Sanitaria, Ciudad Universitaria, Zona 12, Guatemala. Ed. Arturo Acajabon Mendoza. bibl.; charts; illus.
Formerly: Brujula.

UNIVERSIDAD INDUSTRIAL DE SANTANDER. REVISTA - SALUD. see *MEDICAL SCIENCES*

614 350   US
UNIVERSITY OF DELAWARE. DISASTER RESEARCH CENTER. DISSERTATIONS. 1965. irreg., no.29, 1985. $25. University of Delaware, Disaster Research Center, Newark, DE 19716. TEL 302-451-6618. FAX 302-451-2838. TELEX 70 99 85.

614 350   US
UNIVERSITY OF DELAWARE. DISASTER RESEARCH CENTER. FINAL PROJECT REPORTS. no.6, 1967. irreg., no.37, 1989. price varies. University of Delaware, Disaster Research Center, Newark, DE 19716. TEL 302-451-6618. FAX 302-451-2838. TELEX 70 99 85.

614.8 628.44 350.755   US
UNIVERSITY OF DELAWARE. DISASTER RESEARCH CENTER. MISCELLANEOUS REPORTS. no.20, 1978. irreg., no.45, 1991. University of Delaware, Disaster Research Center, Newark, DE 19716. TEL 302-451-6618. FAX 302-451-2828. TELEX 70 99 85.
Formerly: Ohio State University, Columbus. Disaster Research Center. Miscellaneous Reports.

614 350   US
UNIVERSITY OF DELAWARE. DISASTER RESEARCH CENTER. PRELIMINARY PAPERS. no.5, 1973. irreg., no.157, 1990. price varies. University of Delaware, Disaster Research Center, Newark, DE 19716. TEL 302-451-6618. FAX 302-451-2838.

614.8 628.44 350.755   US
UNIVERSITY OF DELAWARE. DISASTER RESEARCH CENTER. REPORT SERIES. 1968. irreg., no.19, 1990. University of Delaware, Disaster Research Center, Newark, DE 19716. TEL 302-451-6618. FAX 302-451-2828. TELEX 70 99 85.
Formerly: Ohio State University. Disaster Research Center. Report Series (ISSN 0078-4133)
Refereed Serial

UNIVERSITY OF OCCUPATIONAL AND ENVIRONMENTAL HEALTH. JOURNAL. see *OCCUPATIONAL HEALTH AND SAFETY*

UNSCHEDULED EVENTS; research committee on disasters newsletter. see *SOCIOLOGY*

393.1   AU   ISSN 0042-0581
UNTERNEHMER. 1960. m. S.350. (Bundeskammer der Gewerblichen Wirtschaft) Oesterreichischer Wirtschaftsverlag, Nikolsdorfer Gasse 7-11, 1051 Vienna, Austria. TEL 0222-555585. TELEX 1-11669. Ed. Ernst Hofbauer. circ. 16,500.

628   US
UPDATE: WASTE DISPOSAL, RECYCLING, RESOURCE RECOVERY. m. Department of Sanitation, 51 Chambers St., New York, NY 10007.

614.8 001.6   US   ISSN 0742-938X
V D T NEWS. (Video Display Terminal); the V D T health and safety report. 1984. bi-m. $87 (foreign $97). Microwave News, Box 1799, Grand Central Station, New York, NY 10163. TEL 212-517-2802. Ed. Louis Slesin. (back issues avail.)
—BLDSC shelfmark: 9150.294270.

V F D B: ZEITSCHRIFT FUER FORSCHUNG UND TECHNIK IM BRANDSCHUTZ. (Vereinigung zur Foerderung des Deutschen Brandschutzes e.V.) see *ENGINEERING — Chemical Engineering*

614   SW
HN571
VAEL & VE. 1968. 10/yr. SEK 250. Socialstyrelsen - National Board of Health & Welfare, 106 30 Stockholm, Sweden. Ed. Anne-Marie Svedin. bk.rev.; charts; illus.; stat.; tr.lit.; circ. 10,000.
Former titles: Socialnytt (ISSN 0037-7619); Sociala Meddelanden.

VERKEHRSPSYCHOLOGISCHER INFORMATIONSDIENST. see *TRANSPORTATION — Roads And Traffic*

614.8   US
VETERINARY MEDICINE GUIDANCE MANUAL. (Subseries of: Compliance Program Guidance Manuals) irreg. $80 in US, Canada, Mexico; elsewhere $160. (Department of Health and Human Services, Food and Drug Administration) U.S. National Technical Information Service, 5825 Port Royal Rd., Springfield, VA 22161. TEL 703-487-4630.
Description: Provides the latest information on and helps to maintain surveillance or compliance oriented plans and instructions directed to FDA field operations, providing the needed direction from headquarters offices and bureaus in accomplishing FDA's regulatroy obligations.

VIGILANCIA EPIDEMIOLOGICA DE LA RABIA PARA LAS AMERICAS. see *VETERINARY SCIENCE*

614.8   US
VIRGINIA'S HEALTH. 1970. bi-m. free. Department of Health, Office of Health Education and Information, Box 2448, Ste. 245, Richmond, VA 23218. TEL 804-786-3552. FAX 804-371-6152. Ed. Dudley Olsson. circ. 6,000.

628   RU   ISSN 0042-7918
VODOSNABZHENIE I SANITARNAYA TEKHNIKA. 1913. m. 26.40 Rub. Gosstroi, Moscow, Russia. Ed. A.N. Radzivan. bk.rev.; bibl.; index; circ. 17,000. **Indexed:** C.I.S. Abstr., Chem.Abstr., Int.Build.Serv.Abstr., Pollut.Abstr.

614   US
VOLUNTEERS' VOICE FOR COMMUNITY SAFETY AND HEALTH. 1985. bi-m. $19 to non-members; members $15. National Safety Council, Industrial Section, 444 N. Michigan Ave., Chicago, IL 60611. TEL 800-621-7619. Ed. Carole Huybrecht. illus.

614.8   UN   ISSN 1010-9609
                              CODEN: WDINE8
W H O DRUG INFORMATION. (Editions in English and French) q. $40. World Health Organization, Distribution and Sales, 1211 Geneva 27, Switzerland. TEL 022-791-2111. circ. 1,500(English); 500(French).
—BLDSC shelfmark: 9311.903000.
   Description: Communicates medicinal drug information that is either developed and issued by WHO or transmitted to WHO by research and regulatory agencies throughout the world.

W H O OFFSET PUBLICATIONS. (World Health Organization) see *PUBLIC HEALTH AND SAFETY — Abstracting, Bibliographies, Statistics*

W H O TECHNICAL REPORT SERIES. (World Health Organization) see *MEDICAL SCIENCES*

W N Y F. (With New York Firefighters) see *FIRE PREVENTION*

WALK. see *TRANSPORTATION — Roads And Traffic*

614   IO
WARTA DINAS KESEHATAN. m. Dinas Kesehatan, Jl. Kesehatan 10, Jakarta, Indonesia. illus.
   Formerly: Warta Kesehatan (ISSN 0377-6549)

WARY CANARY. a news network for allergics, "sensitive birds," & environmental health advocates. see *ENVIRONMENTAL STUDIES*

WASHINGTON (STATE) DEPARTMENT OF SOCIAL AND HEALTH SERVICES. INCOME MAINTENANCE, COMMUNITY SOCIAL SERVICES AND MEDICAL ASSISTANCE.. see *SOCIAL SERVICES AND WELFARE*

WASHINGTON STATE HEALTH DATA BOOK. see *PUBLIC ADMINISTRATION*

628   UK
WASTES MANAGEMENT. 1910. m. £33 (foreign £39). Institute of Wastes Management, 14 Thetford Close, Wood Bank, Bury, Lancs. BL8 1XB, England. FAX 0604-21339. Ed. D. Taylor. adv.; bk.rev.; illus.; index; circ. 3,000. **Indexed:** Br.Tech.Ind., Excerp.Med., Pollut.Abstr., W.R.C.Inf.
   Former titles (until 1982): Solid Wastes (ISSN 0306-6509); Solid Wastes Management; Public Cleansing (ISSN 0033-3433)

628   US   ISSN 0043-1141
WATER AND WASTES DIGEST. 1961. bi-m. $10 (free to qualified personnel). Scranton Gillette Communications, Inc., 380 E. Northwest Hwy., Des Plaines, IL 60016-2282. TEL 708-298-6622. adv.; circ. 100,000. (also avail. in microform from UMI) **Indexed:** Abstr.Bull.Inst.Pap.Chem., Energy Ind., Energy Info.Abstr.
   Description: Product information and reviews in wastewater and water pollution technology, with an index of advertisers.

628   SA   ISSN 0257-8700
WATER SEWAGE AND EFFLUENT. 1980. q. R.20. Brooke Pattrick (Pty) Ltd., P.O. Box 422, Bedfordview 2008, South Africa. TEL 011-6224666. FAX 011-6167196. Ed. Helen Gow. adv.; bk.rev.; circ. 3,210. **Indexed:** Ind.S.A.Per., W.R.C.Inf.
   Description: Concerns itself with all aspects of water, the liquid life-line of mankind, agriculture and industry. Seeks to inform about issues regarding the collection, conveyance and storage of source water, and related topics.

628   UK   ISSN 0262-8104
WATERLINES; the journal of appropriate water supply and sanitation technologies. 1982. q. £14($27) to individuals; institutions £18($35). (International Development Research Centre, Canada) Intermediate Technology Publications Ltd., 103-105 Southampton Row, London WC1B 4HH, England. TEL 071-436-9761. FAX 071-436-2013. Ed. Kimberly Clarke. adv.; bk.rev. **Indexed:** Abstr.Hyg., Fluidex, I D A, Rural Devel.Abstr., Rural Ext.Educ.& Tr.Abstr., W.R.C.Inf.
—BLDSC shelfmark: 9279.428000.
   Description: Devoted entirely to low-cost water sanitation.

614   UN   ISSN 0049-8114
RA651
WEEKLY EPIDEMIOLOGICAL RECORD. (Text in English and French) 1925. w. 150 Fr.($120) World Health Organization, Distribution and Sales, CH-1211 Geneva 27, Switzerland. TEL 022-791-2111. bibl.; charts; illus.; stat.; index; circ. 7,000. (back issues avail.) **Indexed:** Abstr.Hyg., Excerp.Med., Ind.Vet., Irr.& Drain.Abstr., Protozool.Abstr., Rev.Appl.Entomol., Trop.Dis.Bull.
—BLDSC shelfmark: 9284.780000.
   Description: Essential instrument for the collation and dissemination of data, including global number of AIDS cases, useful in disease surveillance and control on a global level.

614.8 658   UK
WHO'S WHO IN THE EMERGENCY & RESCUE SERVICES (YEAR). 1988. a. £25($50) Lincoln Publications, 28 Centre Point House, St. Giles High St., London WC2 8LW, England. TEL 071-240-5562. FAX 071-497-2811. Ed. R. Feather. (back issues avail.)

WISCONSIN. DEPARTMENT OF NATURAL RESOURCES. ANNUAL WATER QUALITY REPORT TO CONGRESS. see *WATER RESOURCES*

628   GW   ISSN 0342-5967
WOHNMEDIZIN. 1962. bi-m. DM.50. Deutsche Gesellschaft fuer Wohnmedizin und Bauhygiene e.V., Postfach 368, 7513 Spoeck, Germany. bk.rev. (back issues avail.)

614.85   SW
WORKING ENVIRONMENT; arbetsmiljoe international. (Text in English) 1977. a. free. Foereningen foer Arbetarskydd - Swedish Work Environment Association, P.O. Box 5970, S-114 89 Stockholm, Sweden. TEL 46-08-156757. FAX 46-08-166740. Ed. Siv Soderlund. adv.; illus.; circ. 20,000. **Indexed:** Biol.Dig., C.I.S. Abstr., Ergon.Abstr.

WORLD FEDERATION FOR MENTAL HEALTH. NEWSLETTER. see *PSYCHOLOGY*

614   UN   ISSN 0043-8502
WORLD HEALTH/SANTE DU MONDE. (Editions in Arabic, English, French, German, Portuguese, Russian and Spanish) 1948. 6/yr. $20. World Health Organization - Organisation Mondiale de la Sante, Distribution and Sales, CH-1211 Geneva 27, Switzerland. TEL 022-791-2111. Ed. John Bland. illus.; circ. 160,000. (also avail. in microform from UMI; back issues avail.) **Indexed:** Abstr.Hyg., ASSIA, Biol.Abstr., Biol.Dig., CINAHL, Curr.Adv.Ecol.Sci., Curr.Adv.Genetics & Molec.Biol., Environ.Abstr., Environ.Per.Bibl., Gdlns, Geo.Abstr., Helminthol.Abstr., Hlth.Ind., HR Rep., Mag.Ind., Mid.East: Abstr.& Ind., Pt.de Rep. (1979-), R.G., So.Pac.Per.Ind., Telegen, Trop.Dis.Bull.
●Also available online. Vendor(s): DIALOG.
—BLDSC shelfmark: 9356.040000.
   Description: A popular magazine illustrating the human side of efforts to improve world health.

PUBLIC HEALTH AND SAFETY   4115

614   UN
WORLD HEALTH ORGANIZATION. HANDBOOK OF RESOLUTIONS AND DECISIONS OF THE WORLD HEALTH ASSEMBLY AND THE EXECUTIVE BOARD.. (Editions in Arabic, Chinese, English, French, Russian, Spanish) 1948. biennial. World Health Organization, Distribution and Sales, CH-1211 Geneva 27, Switzerland. TEL 022-791-2111. circ. 8,000.
   Formerly: World Health Organization. World Health Assembly and the Executive Board. Handbook of Resolutions and Decisions. (ISSN 0301-0740)

614   UN   ISSN 0512-3038
                              CODEN: WHOMAP
WORLD HEALTH ORGANIZATION. MONOGRAPH SERIES. 1951. irreg. World Health Organization, Distribution and Sales, CH-1211 Geneva 27, Switzerland. TEL 022-791-2111. circ. 9,000. **Indexed:** Biol.Abstr., Excerp.Med., Ind.Med., Rev.Appl.Entomol.

614   UN
WORLD HEALTH ORGANIZATION. REGIONAL OFFICE FOR AFRICA. REPORT OF THE REGIONAL COMMITTEE.. 1959. a. World Health Organization, Regional Office for Africa - Organisation Mondiale de la Sante. Bureau Regional de l'Afrique, B.P. No. 6, Brazzaville, Congo.
   Formerly: World Health Organization. Regional Office for Africa. Report of the Regional Committee. Minutes of the Plenary Session (ISSN 0512-3070)

614   UN   ISSN 0510-8837
WORLD HEALTH ORGANIZATION. REGIONAL OFFICE FOR AFRICA. REPORT OF THE REGIONAL DIRECTOR. 1951. a. World Health Organization, Regional Office for Africa - Organisation Mondiale de la Sante. Bureau Regional de l'Afrique, B.P. No. 6, Brazzaville, Congo.

614   UN
WORLD HEALTH ORGANIZATION. REGIONAL OFFICE FOR THE EASTERN MEDITERRANEAN. ANNUAL REPORT OF THE REGIONAL DIRECTOR. 1950. a. free to qualified personnel. World Health Organization, Regional Office for the Eastern Mediterranean, P.O. Box 1517, Alexandria, Egypt. FAX 4838916. TELEX 54028. circ. 3,000.
   Former titles (until 1990): World Health Organization. Regional Office for the Eastern Mediterranean. Biennial Report of Regional Director; (until 1979): World Health Organization. Regional Office for the Eastern Mediterranean. Annual Report of the Regional Director (ISSN 0512-3089)

614   UN   ISSN 0512-4921
WORLD HEALTH ORGANIZATION. REGIONAL OFFICE FOR THE WESTERN PACIFIC. ANNUAL REPORT OF THE REGIONAL DIRECTOR TO THE REGIONAL COMMITTEE FOR THE WESTERN PACIFIC. a. World Health Organization, Regional Office for the Western Pacific, P.O. Box 2932, Manila, Philippines.

614   UN   ISSN 0085-8285
WORLD HEALTH ORGANIZATION. WORK OF W H O; biennial report of the director-general to the World Health Assembly and to the United Nations. (Editions in Arabic, Chinese, English, French, Russian, Spanish) 1948. biennial. World Health Organization, Distribution and Sales, CH-1211 Geneva 27, Switzerland. TEL 791-2111. FAX 22-788-0401. TELEX 415416. circ. 8,000. **Indexed:** IIS.

614.4   US
WORLDWIDE REPORT: EPIDEMIOLOGY. irreg. (approx. 30/yr.) $7 per no. (foreign $14 per no.). U.S. Joint Publications Research Service, Box 12507, Arlington, VA 22209. TEL 703-487-4630. (Orders to: NTIS, Springfield, VA 22161)
   Former titles: World Epidemiology Review; Epidemiology Reports from the World Press.

353.9 614   US
WYOMING. DEPARTMENT OF HEALTH. ANNUAL REPORT. (Former name of issuing body: Wyoming. Department of Health and Social Services) 1975. a. Department of Health, 135 Hathaway Bldg., Cheyenne, WY 82002. TEL 307-777-7959. FAX 307-777-5402. Ed. Helen G. Levine.
   Formerly: Wyoming. Department of Health and Social Services. Annual Report (ISSN 0098-6984)

PUBLIC HEALTH AND SAFETY — ABSTRACTING, BIBLIOGRAPHIES, STATISTICS

614.7   JA   ISSN 0915-0498
YAMAGUCHI-KEN EISEI KOGAI KENKYU SENTA GYOSEKI HOKOKU. (Text in Japanese; titles and table of contents in English) 1958. a. exchange basis. Yamaguchi-ken Eisei Kogai Kenkyu Senta - Yamaguchi Prefectural Research Institute of Health, 5-67, Aoi 2-chome, Yamaguchi-shi, Yamaguchi-ken 753, Japan. TEL 0839-22-7630. FAX 0839-22-7632. charts; bibl.
   Supersedes (in 1988): Yamaguchi-ken Eisei Kenkyujo Gyoseki Hokoku (ISSN 0513-4757)
   Description: Contains original papers and research results on public health and medical issues.

628 333.91   US
YEARS AHEAD. 1982. q. $10. Pure Water of New England, 103 Union St., Watertown, MA 02172. TEL 617-924-0959. Ed. Patrick E. Mertens. circ. 10,000.

628   JA   ISSN 0912-2826
YOKOHAMA CITY INSTITUTE OF HEALTH. ANNUAL REPORT. (Text in Japanese; summaries in English) 1962. a. Yokohama City Institute of Health, 2-17, 1-chome, Takigashira, Isogo-ku, Yokohama-shi 235, Japan. circ. 300.

YOKOHAMA MEDICAL JOURNAL. see *MEDICAL SCIENCES*

614   YU   ISSN 0409-0314
ZAVOD ZA ZDRAVSTVENU ZASTITU S R SRBIJE. GLASNIK; casopis za preventivnu i socijalnu medicinu sa organizacijom zdravstvene. (Text in Serbo-Croatian; summaries in English, French and Russian) 1952. q. 120 din.($40) Zavod za Zdravstvenu Zastitu SR Srbije, Dr. Subotica 5, 11000 Belgrade, Yugoslavia. **Indexed:** Excerp.Med., Ind.Med.

614   RU   ISSN 0044-1945
                           CODEN: ZDRVA4
ZDOROV'E. 1955. m. 11.40 Rub.($8.40) Izdatel'stvo Pravda, Bumazhnyi pr., 14, 101458 GSP Moscow A-137, Russia. (Co-sponsor: Ministerstvo Zdravookhraneniya S.S.S.R.) Ed. M. Piradova. bk.rev.; bibl.; index. **Indexed:** Chem.Abstr.

614   BW   ISSN 0044-1961
                           CODEN: ZDBEA9
ZDRAVOOKHRANENIE BELORUSSII. 1924-1941; resumed 1955. m. 46.50 Rub. (Ministerstvo Zdravookhraneniya) Izdatel'stvo Polymya, Ul. Zakharova 19, Minsk, Byelarus. TEL 238-46-00. FAX 230-21-17. TELEX 411160. (Dist. by: Mezhdunarodnaya Kniga, ul. Dimitrova D.39, 113095 Moscow, Russia) Ed. N.K. Deryugo. adv.; bk.rev.; charts; illus.; index; circ. 11,000. **Indexed:** Biol.Abstr., Chem.Abstr.
   Former titles (until 1941): Meditsinsky Zhurnal B.S.S.R; (until 1938): Belorusskaya Meditsinskaya Mysl.

570   RU   ISSN 0044-197X
ZDRAVOOKHRANENIE ROSSIISKOI FEDERATSII/PUBLIC HEALTH OF THE RUSSIAN FEDERATION. 1957. m. 21.60 Rub.($10.20) (Ministerstvo Zdravookhraneniya R.S.F.S.R.) Izdatel'stvo Meditsina, Petroverigskii pereulok 6-8, 101838 Moscow, Russia. Ed. A.I. Potapov. **Indexed:** Biol.Abstr., Ind.Med., Int.Aerosp.Abstr.
   Description: Publishes scientific and practical materials on the health status of the population and on the development of public health services in autonomous republics, territories, regions and districts of the RSFSR.

614   CS   ISSN 0049-8572
ZDRAVOTNICKA PRACOVNICE. 1951. 12/yr. (plus 3 supplements) $31.20. Avicenum, Czechoslovak Medical Press, Malostranske nam. 28, 118 02 Prague 1, Czechoslovakia. (Dist. by: Artia, Ve Smeckach 30, 111 27 Prague 1, Czechoslovakia) (Co-sponsor: Ceskoslovenska Lekarska Spolecnost J. Ev. Purkyne) Ed. Dr. J. Homolka. illus. **Indexed:** Int.Nurs.Ind.

614   CS   ISSN 0044-1996
ZDRAVOTNICKE NOVINY;* tydenik pracovniku ve zdravotnictvi. vol.22, 1973. w. $52.40. Prace, Publishing House of the Trade Union Movement, Vaclavske nam. 17, 11258 Prague, Czechoslovakia. (Subscr. to: Artia, Ve Smeckach 30, 111 27 Prague 1, Czechoslovakia) Ed. Zdenek Provaznik. circ. 35,000.

614   PL   ISSN 0044-2011
RA421
ZDROWIE PUBLICZNE. 1885. m. $150. Panstwowy Zaklad Wydawnictw Lekarskich, Ul. Dluga 38-40, Warsaw, Poland. TEL 31-42-81. (Dist. by: Ars Polona-Ruch, Krakowskie Przedmiescie 7, Warsaw, Poland) bk.rev.; adv.; charts; illus.; stat.; index; circ. 2,377. **Indexed:** Biol.Abstr., Excerpt.Med., Ind.Med.
   Description: Deals with social medicine, health care organization and health policy.

ZEITSCHRIFT FUER LAERMBEKAEMPFUNG. see *PHYSICS — Sound*

ZEITSCHRIFT FUER WASSER- UND ABWASSERFORSCHUNG/JOURNAL FOR WATER AND WASTE WATER RESEARCH. see *WATER RESOURCES*

614.44 610   GW   ISSN 0934-8859
QR46   CODEN: ZHUMEO
ZENTRALBLATT FUER HYGIENE UND UMWELTMEDIZIN. irreg. (6 nos./vol.). DM.408. Gustav Fischer Verlag, Wollgrasweg 49, Postfach 720143, 7000 Stuttgart 70, Germany. TEL 0711-458030. FAX 0711-4580334. TELEX 7111488-FIBUCH. (U.S. address: Gustav Fischer New York Inc., 220 East 23rd St., Suite 909, New York, NY 10010) Ed. E. Thofern. (also avail. in microfilm from VCI) **Indexed:** Biol.Abstr., Deep Sea Res.& Oceanogr.Abstr., Dent.Ind., Excerp.Med., Helminthol.Abstr., Ind.Med., Nutr.Abstr.
   —BLDSC shelfmark: 9508.530000.
   Former titles: Zentralblatt fuer Bakteriologie, Parasitenkunde, Infektionskrankheiten und Hygiene. Series B: Krankenhaushygiene - Praeventive Medizin - Betriebshygiene (ISSN 0174-3015); Zentralblatt fuer Bakteriologie, Parasitenkunde, Infektionskrankheiten und Hygiene. Orginale Reihe B: Hygiene - Praeventive Medizin.

614   CC   ISSN 1004-1257
ZHIYE YU JIANKANG/OCCUPATION AND HEALTH. (Text in Chinese) 1985. bi-m. Y13.20. Tianjin Institute of Labor Hygiene and Occupational diseases, 221, Machangdao Street, Tianjin 300204, People's Republic of China. TEL 317375. Ed. Zhang Yinde. circ. 100,000. (controlled).
   Description: Popular science magazine for medical workers and safety-control technitians in industrial companies.

ZHONGGUO FUNU JIANKANG/CHINA WOMEN'S HEALTH. see *MEDICAL SCIENCES — Obstetrics And Gynecology*

614   CC   ISSN 1001-0580
ZHONGGUO GONGGONG WEISHENG/CHINA'S PUBLIC HEALTH. (Text in Chinese) 1985. m. $19.20. Zhonghua Yufang Yixue Hui - China Preventive Medical Society, Jixian Jie, Heping Qu, Shenyang, Liaoning 110005, People's Republic of China. TEL 363643. (Dist. overseas by: Guoji Shudian - China International Book Trading Corp., P.O. Box 399, Beijing 100044, P.R.C.. TEL 8413063) Ed. Dai Zhicheng. adv.: B&W page $300, color page $500; adv. contact: Xiying Li. circ. 10,000.

614   CC   ISSN 1001-0572
ZHONGGUO GONGGONG WEISHENG XUEBAO/CHINESE JOURNAL OF PUBLIC HEALTH. (Text in Chinese) 1982. bi-m. $12. Zhonghua Yufang Yixue Hui - China Preventive Medical Society, Jixian Jie, Heping Qu, Shenyang, Liaoning 110005, People's Republic of China. TEL 363643. (Dist. overseas by: Guoji Shudian - China International Book Trading Corp., P.O. Box 399, Beijing 100044, P.R.C.. TEL 8413063) Ed. Kan Xuegui. adv.: B&W page $300, color page $500; adv. contact: Xiying Li. circ. 3,000.
   —BLDSC shelfmark: 3180.610000.

614   CC
ZHONGGUO WEISHENG HUAKAN/CHINA HEALTH PICTORIAL. (Text in Chinese) bi-m. Liaoning Sheng Jiankang Jiaoyu-suo - Liaoning Provincial Institute of Health Education, 44-1, Jixian Jie, Heping Qu, Shenyang, Liaoning 110005, People's Republic of China. TEL 365444. Ed. Li Ren.

ZHURNAL MIKROBIOLOGII, EPIDEMIOLOGII I IMMUNOBIOLOGII/JOURNAL OF MICROBIOLOGY, EPIDEMIOLOGY AND IMMUNOBIOLOGY. see *BIOLOGY — Microbiology*

ZIVOT I ZDRAVIJE; obitelski casopis za proucavanje i promicanje prirodnih zdravstvenih nacela. see *MEDICAL SCIENCES*

614   DK   ISSN 0107-6663
ZONETERAPI OG SUNDHED.* 1981. irreg. (2-4/yr.). DKK 30 (free to libraries). Landsforeningen til Zoneterapiens Fremme, c/o Jorn Steen, Ed., Rulkehojen 40, 5260 Odense S., Denmark. illus.

614   PL
ZYCIE I ZDROWIE. 1974. fortn. $11.70. Wydawnictwo Wspolczesne R S W "Prasa-Ksiazka-Ruch", Ul. Wiejska 12, 00-420 Warsaw, Poland. TEL 48-22-285330. (Dist. by: Ars Polona-Ruch, Krakowskie Przedmiescie 7, Warsaw, Poland) illus.

PUBLIC HEALTH AND SAFETY — Abstracting, Bibliographies, Statistics

614.8 310   US
ADVANCES IN RISK ANALYSIS. 1983. irreg., vol.6, 1990. (Society for Risk Analysis) Plenum Publishing Corp., 233 Spring St., New York, NY 10013-1578. TEL 212-620-8000. FAX 212-463-0742. TELEX 23-421139. Ed.Bd. (back issues avail.)
Refereed Serial

614 600   US   ISSN 1058-675X
AMERICAN PETROLEUM INSTITUTE. HEALTH AND ENVIRONMENTAL SCIENCES DEPARTMENT. REPORTS AND OTHER PUBLICATIONS, INDEX AND ABSTRACTS. 1978. irreg. price varies. American Petroleum Institute, Central Abstracting & Information Services, 275 Seventh Ave., New York, NY 10001. **Indexed:** API Catal., API Hlth.& Environ., API Oil., API Pet.Ref., API Pet.Subst., API Transport.
   Former titles: American Petroleum Institute. Health and Environmental Sciences Department. Research Reports; American Petroleum Institute. Medicine and Biological Science Department. Medical Research Reports; American Petroleum Institute. Committee of Medicine and Environmental Health. Medical Research Reports.
Refereed Serial

312   BE   ISSN 0522-7690
RA407.5.B5
ANNUAIRE STATISTIQUE DE LA SANTE PUBLIQUE/STATISTISCH JAARBOEK VAN VOLKSGEZONDHEID. (Text in Dutch) 1950. a. free. Ministere de la Sante Publique et de la Famille, Centre de Traitement de l'Information - Ministerie van Volksgezondheid en van het Gezin, Cite Administrative de l'Etat, Quartier Vesale, 1010 Brussels, Belgium. illus.; stat.

APPLIED HEALTH PHYSICS ABSTRACTS AND NOTES. see *PHYSICS — Abstracting, Bibliographies, Statistics*

614 318   AG
ARGENTINA. MINISTERIA DE SALUD Y ACCION SOCIAL. PROGRAMA NACIONAL DE ESTADISTICAS DE SALUD. vol. 6, 1976. irreg. Ministerio de Salud y Accion Social, Alsina 301, Buenos Aires, Argentina.
   Formerly: Argentina. Secretaria de Estado de Salud Publica. Programa Nacional de Estadisticas de Salud.

AUSTRALIA. BUREAU OF STATISTICS. QUEENSLAND OFFICE. HEALTH AND WELFARE ESTABLISHMENTS, QUEENSLAND. see *SOCIAL SERVICES AND WELFARE — Abstracting, Bibliographies, Statistics*

614.86   BE   ISSN 0770-237X
HE5614.5.B4
BELGIUM. INSTITUT NATIONAL DE STATISTIQUE. STATISTIQUE DES ACCIDENTS DE LA CIRCULATION SUR LA VOIE PUBLIQUE AVEC TUES ET BLESSES. Dutch edition (ISSN 0771-0577) (Text in Dutch, French) 1954. a. 290 Fr. (foreign 390 Fr.). Institut National de Statistique, 44 rue de Louvain, B-1000 Brussels, Belgium.
   Formerly: Belgium. Institut National de Statistique. Statistique des Accidents de Roulage (ISSN 0067-5512)

PUBLIC HEALTH AND SAFETY — ABSTRACTING, BIBLIOGRAPHIES, STATISTICS

310   BE
BELGIUM. MINISTERE DE LA SANTE PUBLIQUE ET DE L'ENVIRONNEMENT. ADMINISTRATION DES ETABLISSEMENTS DE SOINS. SERVICE D'ETUDES. ANNUAIRE STATISTIQUE DES ETABLISSEMENTS DE SOINS/BELGIUM. MINISTERIE VAN VOLKSGEZONDHEID EN LEEFMILIEU. BESTUUR VOOR DE VERZORGINGSINSTELLINGEN. STUDIEDIENST. STATISTISCH JAARBOEK VAN DE VERZORGININGSINSTELLINGEN.. (In 2 parts: Liste d'Adresses - Adressenlijst; Rapport Annuel - Jaaroverzicht) (Text in Dutch, French) 1962. a. free. Ministere de la Sante Publique et de l'Environnement, Administration des Etablissements de Soins-Service d'Etudes - Ministerie van Volksgezondheid en Leefmilieu, Bestuur voor de Verzorgingsinstellingen, Cite Administrative de l'Etat, Quartier Vesale, B-1010 Brussels, Belgium. TEL 02-210-45-11. circ. 1,500.
    Former titles: Belgium. Ministere de la Sante Publique et de la Famille. Annuaire Statistique des Hopitaux; Belgium. Ministere de la Sante et de la Famille. Premiers et Principaux Resultats Statistiques de l'Enquete dans les Etablissements de Soins.

614 016   YU   ISSN 0350-0306
BILTEN DOKUMENTACIJE. ZASTITA NA RADU/BULLETIN OF DOCUMENTATION. SAFETY PRECAUTIONS. 1974. bi-m. $264. Jugoslovenski Centar za Tehnicku i Naucnu Dokumentaciju - Yugoslav Center for Technical and Scientific Documentation (YCTSD), Sl. Penezica-Krcuna 29-31, Box 724, 11000 Belgrade, Yugoslavia. Ed. Ljiljana Kojic-Bogdanovic.

614.7   US   ISSN 1047-8213
C A SELECTS. INDOOR AIR POLLUTION. 1988. s-w. $195. Chemical Abstracts Service (Subsidiary of: American Chemical Society), 2540 Olentangy River Rd., Box 3012, Columbus, OH 43210. TEL 614-447-3600. FAX 614-447-3713. TELEX 6842086.
    Formerly (until 1989): BIOSIS CAS Selects: Indoor Air Pollution.
    Description: Covers the air pollution of indoor environments. Includes pollution from chemical contaminants, particulates, and biological agents.

614   UK   ISSN 0263-2969
RA630.G73
CHARTERED INSTITUTE OF PUBLIC FINANCE AND ACCOUNTANCY. CEMETERIES & CREMATORIA STATISTICS. ACTUALS. 1982. a. £40. Chartered Institute of Public Finance and Accountancy, 3 Robert St., London WC2N 6BH, England. TEL 071-895-8823. FAX 071-895-8825. (back issues avail.)
    Incorporates (1956-1982): Chartered Institute of Public Finance and Accountancy. Crematoria Statistics. Actuals (ISSN 0534-2104); (1979-1982): Chartered Institute of Public Finance and Accountancy. Cemeteries Statistics. Actuals (ISSN 0260-9959)

614.8   UK   ISSN 0266-9552
RA566.5.G7
CHARTERED INSTITUTE OF PUBLIC FINANCE AND ACCOUNTANCY. ENVIRONMENTAL HEALTH STATISTICS. ACTUALS. 1984. a. £40. Chartered Institute of Public Finance and Accountancy, 3 Robert St., London WC2N 6BH, England. TEL 071-895-8823. FAX 071-895-8825.
—BLDSC shelfmark: 3791.507500.

CHARTERED INSTITUTE OF PUBLIC FINANCE AND ACCOUNTANCY. WASTE DISPOSAL STATISTICS. ACTUALS. see *PUBLIC ADMINISTRATION — Abstracting, Bibliographies, Statistics*

CHARTERED INSTITUTE OF PUBLIC FINANCE AND ACCOUNTANCY. WASTE DISPOSAL STATISTICS. ESTIMATES. see *PUBLIC ADMINISTRATION — Abstracting, Bibliographies, Statistics*

614   CL
CHILE. INSTITUTO NACIONAL DE ESTADISTICAS. ESTADISTICAS DE SALUD; recursos y atenciones. 1965. a. $9. Instituto Nacional de Estadisticas, Av. Bulnes 418, Casilla 498, Correo 3-Santiago, Chile.

614   NE
COMPENDIUM GEZONDHEIDSSTATISTIEK NEDERLAND/COMPENDIUM HEALTH STATISTICS OF THE NETHERLANDS. (Text in Dutch and English) 1974. irreg. Centraal Bureau voor de Statistiek, Prinses Beatrixlaan 428, Voorburg, Netherlands. (Orders to: SDU-Publishers, Christoffel Plantijnstraat, The Hague, Netherlands) (Co-sponsor: Ministry of Public Health and Environmental Hygiene) circ. 2,000.

614   CY
CYPRUS. MINISTRY OF HEALTH. DEPARTMENT OF MEDICAL & PUBLIC HEALTH SERVICES. ANNUAL REPORT. (Text in English) 1920. a. Ministry of Health, Department of Medical & Public Health Services, Nicosia, Cyprus. FAX 303498. TELEX 5734. Ed. Dr. G. Malliotis. circ. 200.

DOEDSAARSAGERNE/CAUSES OF DEATH IN DENMARK. see *POPULATION STUDIES — Abstracting, Bibliographies, Statistics*

DOKUMENTATION MEDIZIN IM UMWELTSCHUTZ. see *MEDICAL SCIENCES — Abstracting, Bibliographies, Statistics*

DOKUMENTATION SOZIALMEDIZIN, OEFFENTLICHER GESUNDHEITSDIENST, GESUNDHEITSERZIEHUNG. see *MEDICAL SCIENCES — Abstracting, Bibliographies, Statistics*

E C M T STATISTICAL REPORT ON ROAD ACCIDENTS. (European Council of Ministers of Transport) see *TRANSPORTATION — Abstracting, Bibliographies, Statistics*

610   JA
EISEI TOKEI KARA MITA AICHI-KEN NO SUGATA. 1985. a. Aichi-ken Eiseibu Somu-Ka, 1-2, 3-chome, Sannomaru, Naka-ku, Nagoya-shi, Japan. circ. 200.

ENVIRONMENTAL HEALTH REPORT. see *ENVIRONMENTAL STUDIES — Abstracting, Bibliographies, Statistics*

614 016   NE   ISSN 0924-5723
CODEN: EMPHA
EXCERPTA MEDICA. SECTION 17: PUBLIC HEALTH, SOCIAL MEDICINE & EPIDEMIOLOGY. 1955. 24/yr.(in 3 vols.; 8 nos./vol.). fl.1887 (effective 1992). Excerpta Medica (Subsidiary of: Elsevier Science Publishers), P.O. Box 548, 1000 AM Amsterdam, Netherlands. TEL 020-5803911. FAX 020-5803222. TELEX 18582 ESPA NL. (Dist. by: Elsevier Science Publishers Ireland Ltd., P.O. Box 85, Limerick, Ireland. TEL 061-61944; Subscr. in U.S. and Canada to: Elsevier Science Publishing Co., Inc., Box 882, Madison Sq. Sta., New York, NY 10159. TEL 212-989-5800) adv.; abstr.; index. cum.index. Indexed: Chem.Abstr., Popul.Ind.
    ●Also available online. Vendor(s): BRS, DIMDI, Data-Star, DIALOG, JICST.
    Also available on CD-ROM. Producer(s): SilverPlatter.
—BLDSC shelfmark: 3835.875700.
    Formerly: Excerpta Medica. Section 17: Public Health, Social Medicine and Hygiene (ISSN 0014-4215)
    Description: Covers all aspects of public health and social medicine, and includes health planning and education, epidemiology and prevention of communicable disease, public health aspects of risk populations, food and nutrition and environmental radiation, medical ethics, the influence of life style on health and the epidemiological aspects of water supply and purification.

EXCERPTA MEDICA. SECTION 35: OCCUPATIONAL HEALTH AND INDUSTRIAL MEDICINE. see *MEDICAL SCIENCES — Abstracting, Bibliographies, Statistics*

EXCERPTA MEDICA. SECTION 46: ENVIRONMENTAL HEALTH AND POLLUTION CONTROL. see *ENVIRONMENTAL STUDIES — Abstracting, Bibliographies, Statistics*

GEORGIA VITAL STATISTICS REPORT. see *POPULATION STUDIES — Abstracting, Bibliographies, Statistics*

GREECE. NATIONAL STATISTICAL SERVICE. SOCIAL WELFARE AND HEALTH STATISTICS. see *SOCIAL SERVICES AND WELFARE — Abstracting, Bibliographies, Statistics*

614.8 016   US   ISSN 0892-9351
HD7260
HEALTH AND SAFETY SCIENCE ABSTRACTS. 1973. 4/yr. $585 (foreign 615). (Institute of Safety and Systems Management) Cambridge Scientific Abstracts, 7200 Wisconsin Ave., 6th Fl., Bethesda, MD 20814. TEL 301-961-6750. FAX 301-961-6720. TELEX 910 2507547 CAMB MD. bk.rev.; abstr.; bibl.; pat.; stat.; tr.lit.; index, cum.index. (also avail. in magnetic tape; back issues avail.) Indexed: Oncol.Abstr.
    ●Also available online. Vendor(s): BRS (CSEN), Orbit Information Technologies (ORBIT).
    Also available on CD-ROM. Producer(s): Cambridge Scientific Abstracts.
    Former titles: Safety Science Abstracts Journal (ISSN 0160-1342); Safety Science Abstracts (ISSN 0092-542X)
    Description: Abstracts journal on public health, occupational safety, and industrial hygiene.

614   UN   ISSN 0085-1450
HEALTH PHYSICS RESEARCH ABSTRACTS. (Text in English) 1967. irreg. free. International Atomic Energy Agency, Wagramer Str. 5, Box 100, A-1400 Vienna, Austria. circ. 600.

HEALTH SERVICE ABSTRACTS. see *SOCIAL SERVICES AND WELFARE — Abstracting, Bibliographies, Statistics*

312 614 360   US   ISSN 0362-9279
HA331
IDAHO. DEPARTMENT OF HEALTH AND WELFARE. ANNUAL SUMMARY OF VITAL STATISTICS. Cover title: Vital Statistics, Idaho. 1946. a. $7.50. Department of Health and Welfare, Cooperative Center for Health Statistics, Statehouse, Boise, ID 83720. TEL 208-334-5976. Ed. Janet Wick. stat.illus.; circ. 800. Indexed: SRI. Key Title: Annual Summary of Vital Statistics (Boise).
    Description: Covers statistics of Idaho. Includes population census, natality, mortality, marriages and divorces, induced abortions and more.

INTERNATIONAL NARCOTICS CONTROL BOARD. STATISTICS ON PSYCHOTROPIC SUBSTANCES FOR (YEAR). see *PHARMACY AND PHARMACOLOGY — Abstracting, Bibliographies, Statistics*

614   IT
RA407.5.I8
ITALY. ISTITUTO CENTRALE DI STATISTICA. STATISTICHE SANITARIE. 1955. a. L.43000. Istituto Centrale di Statistica, Via Cesare Balbo 16, 00100 Rome, Italy. circ. 1,150.
    Formerly: Italy. Istituto Centrale di Statistica. Annuario di Statistiche Sanitarie (ISSN 0075-1758)

628 360   JA   ISSN 0911-8403
HV411
JAPAN. MINISTRY OF HEALTH AND WELFARE. STATISTICS AND INFORMATION DEPARTMENT. HANDBOOK OF HEALTH AND WELFARE STATISTICS. English edition: Health and Welfare Statistics in Japan. (Text in Japanese) 1969. a. 2100 Yen (English ed. 2000 Yen). Ministry of Health and Welfare, Statistics and Information Department - Kosei-sho Daijin Kanbo Tokei Joho-bu, 7-3 Ichigaya-Honmura cho, Shinjuku-ku, Tokyo 162, Japan. TEL 03-260-3181. (Subscr. to: Health & Welfare Statistics Association, 5-13-14 Roppongi, Minato-ku, Tokyo, Japan) Key Title: Kosei Tokei Yoran.
    Description: Includes sanitary engineering data.

614 315   JA   ISSN 0448-3952
JAPAN. MINISTRY OF HEALTH AND WELFARE. STATISTICS AND INFORMATION DEPARTMENT. STATISTICAL REPORT ON PUBLIC HEALTH ADMINISTRATION AND SERVICES/EISEI GYOSEI GYOMU HOKOKU. (Text in Japanese) 1960. a. 3600 Yen. Ministry of Health and Welfare, Statistics and Information Department - Kosei-sho Daijin Kanbo Tokei Joho-bu, 7-3 Ichigaya Honmura-cho, Shinjuku-ku, Tokyo 162, Japan. TEL 03-3260-3181. (Subscr. to: Health & Welfare Statistics and Association, 5-13-14 Roppongi, Minato-ku, Tokyo, Japan)
    Formerly: Eisei Nenpo.
    Description: Includes sanitary engineering data.

4118 PUBLIC HEALTH AND SAFETY — ABSTRACTING, BIBLIOGRAPHIES, STATISTICS

614.1   US
KENTUCKY. CABINET FOR HUMAN RESOURCES. VITAL STATISTICS REPORT. 1911. a. $10. Cabinet for Human Resources, Division of Vital Records & Health Development, 275 E. Main St., Frankfort, KY 40621. TEL 502-564-2757. FAX 502-564-2757. circ. 600. Key Title: Kentucky Annual Vital Statistics Report.
  Former titles: Kentucky. Department for Human Resources. Selected Vital Statistics and Planning Data (ISSN 0145-5990); Kentucky Vital Statistics (ISSN 0098-6739); Kentucky Vital Statistics Report.

628   UK   ISSN 0264-6714
RA412.5.G7
KEY STATISTICAL INDICATORS FOR NATIONAL HEALTH SERVICE MANAGEMENT IN WALES. 1983. a. £3. Welsh Office, Economic and Statistical Services Division, New Crown Buildings, Cathays Park, Cardiff CF1 3NQ, Wales. TEL 0222-285044. FAX 0222-825350. TELEX 498228. Ed. E. Swires-Hennessy. stat.; circ. 750. (back issues avail.)
  —BLDSC shelfmark: 5091.824700.

610   FR
MEDEXPRES. m. 450 F. (foreign 550 F.). (Ministere de la Recherche et de la Technologie (D.I.S.T.)) Editions la Simarre, Z.I. No. 2 - rue Joseph-Cugnot, 37300 Joue-les-Tours, France. TEL 47-53-53-66. FAX 47-67-45-05. (Co-sponsor: Association pour la Promotion des Publications Medicales d'Expression Francaise (A.P.P.M.F.)) bibl.
  Description: Publishes summaries of French health journals.

614 016   US   ISSN 0025-7087
RA410   CODEN: MDCRB
MEDICAL CARE REVIEW. 1944. q. $50 (foreign $60). (Foundation of the American College of Healthcare Executives) Health Administration Press, 1021 E. Huron St., Ann Arbor, MI 48104-9990. TEL 312-943-0544. FAX 708-450-1618. (Subscr. to: Order Processing Center, 1951 Cornell Ave., Melrose Park, IL 60160) Ed. Thomas Rundall. bibl.; circ. 1,300. (also avail. in microform from UMI; reprint service avail. from UMI) **Indexed**: Abstr.Health Care Manage.Stud., Hosp.Lit.Ind., I.P.A.
  —BLDSC shelfmark: 5526.910000.
  Formerly: Public Health Economics and Medical Care Abstracts.
  Description: Articles analyze, critique, and synthesize literature and research in the field of health care.
  Refereed Serial

614 310   US   ISSN 0539-7413
RA407.4.M5
MICHIGAN HEALTH STATISTICS. 1898. a. $11. Department of Public Health, Office of State Registrar and Center for Health Statistics, 3423 N. Logan St., Box 30195, Lansing, MI 48909. TEL 517-335-8705. FAX 517-335-8711. Ed. Dr. Janet Eyster. illus.; circ. 350. (also avail. in microfiche)
  Formerly: Michigan Public Health Statistics.
  Description: Longitudinal and annual natality, mortality, marriage and divorce for the state of Michigan.

312   US   ISSN 0094-5641
RA407.4.M6
MINNESOTA HEALTH STATISTICS. 1950. a. free. Department of Health, Center for Health Statistics, 717 Delaware St., S.E., Minneapolis, MN 55440. TEL 612-623-5358. FAX 612-623-5043. Ed. Linda Salkowicz. circ. 900.

MISSOURI MONTHLY VITAL STATISTICS. see *POPULATION STUDIES — Abstracting, Bibliographies, Statistics*

312   US   ISSN 0098-1974
HA471
MISSOURI VITAL STATISTICS. a. free. Department of Health, Center for Health Statistics, Box 570, Jefferson City, MO 65102. TEL 314-751-6272. Ed. Garland Land. circ. 900. (also avail. in microfiche) **Indexed**: SRI.
  Description: Contains tables and graphs.

614   US   ISSN 0077-1198
HA481
MONTANA VITAL STATISTICS. 1954. a. free. Department of Health and Environmental Sciences, Bureau of Records & Statistics, Cogswell Bldg., Helena, MT 59620. TEL 406-444-2614. FAX 406-444-2606. Ed. Sam H. Sperry. circ. 850.
  Former titles: Montana. State Department of Health. Annual Statistical Supplement (ISSN 0097-9120); Montana State Board of Health. Annual Statistical Supplement (ISSN 0097-9112)

NARCOTIC DRUGS: ESTIMATED WORLD REQUIREMENTS FOR (YEAR). see *PHYSICAL FITNESS AND HYGIENE — Abstracting, Bibliographies, Statistics*

NETHERLANDS. CENTRAAL BUREAU VOOR DE STATISTIEK. JAARSTATISTIEK VAN DE BEVOLKING/POPULATION STATISTICS. see *POPULATION STUDIES — Abstracting, Bibliographies, Statistics*

NORTH CAROLINA. DEPARTMENT OF ENVIRONMENT, HEALTH AND NATURAL RESOURCES. STATE CENTER FOR HEALTH AND ENVIRONMENTAL STATISTICS. NORTH CAROLINA VITAL STATISTICS. see *POPULATION STUDIES — Abstracting, Bibliographies, Statistics*

312.267   US   ISSN 0085-428X
RA407.4.N8
NORTH CAROLINA COMMUNICABLE DISEASE MORBIDITY STATISTICS. 1918. a. free. Department of Environment, Health and Natural Resources, Division of Epidemiology, Box 27687, Raleigh, NC 27611-7687. TEL 919-733-3419. FAX 919-733-0490. stat.; circ. 600.

373   NO   ISSN 0332-7906
NORWAY. STATISTISK SENTRALBYRAA. HELSESTATISTIKK/HEALTH STATISTICS. (Subseries of its Norges Offisielle Statistikk) (Text in Norwegian; summaries in English) a. NOK 70. Statistisk Sentralbyraa, Box 8131-Dep., 0033 Oslo 1, Norway. TEL 02-864500. FAX 02-864973. circ. 1,400.

613 616   FR   ISSN 1013-8293
NUTRICION EN SALUD PUBLICA. French edition: Nutrition de Sante Publique (ISSN 1013-8056); English edition: Public Health Nutrition (ISSN 1013-8285) (Text in Spanish) 1980. 2/yr. 240 F. for 2 yrs. Centre International de l'Enfance - International Children's Center, Chateau de Longchamp, Bois de Boulogne, 75016 Paris, France. TEL 1-45-20-79-92. FAX 1-45-25-73-67.
  Formerly (until 1989): Produccion Alimentaria - Nutricion.
  Description: Covers nutritional requirements, breast-feeding, types of diet, food, studies of dietary intake and nutritional status, indicators for nutritional surveillance, diseases and their effects, nutrition education, personnel training.

613 616   FR   ISSN 1013-8056
NUTRITION DE SANTE PUBLIQUE. English edition: Public Health Nutrition (ISSN 1013-8285); Spanish edition: Nutricion en Salud Publica (ISSN 1013-8293) 1980. 2/yr. 240 F. for 2 yrs. Centre International de l'Enfance - International Children's Center, Chateau de Longchamp, Bois de Boulogne, 75016 Paris, France. TEL 1-45-20-79-92. FAX 1-45-25-73-67.
  Formerly (until 1989): Production Alimentaire - Nutrition.
  Description: Covers nutritional requirements, breast-feeding, types of diet, food, studies of dietary intake and nutritional status, indicators for nutritional surveillance, diseases, education, personnel training and programs.

614   DK
NYHEDSINFORMATION FOR SOCIAL-, SYGEHUS- OG SUNDHEDSSEKTOR. 1982. m. DKK 320. Forlag for Social- og Sundhedssektor, Vibeholms Alle 11-15, 2605 Bronoby, Denmark. TEL 43-43-43-80. FAX 43-43-60-29. illus.
  Former titles: Informationstidsskrift for Social- og Sundhedssektor; Informationskatalog for Social- og Sundhedssektor (ISSN 0109-3487)

312   US   ISSN 0098-5651
RA407.4.O6
OKLAHOMA HEALTH STATISTICS. a. free. Department of Health, Public Health Statistics Division, Box 53551, Oklahoma City, OK 73105. TEL 405-271-5600. illus.
  Formerly (1943-1971): Public Health Statistics, State of Oklahoma (ISSN 0099-118X)

ONTARIO. MINISTRY OF LABOUR. LIBRARY. INFOLINK. see *BUSINESS AND ECONOMICS — Abstracting, Bibliographies, Statistics*

312 614   US
OREGON PUBLIC HEALTH STATISTICS REPORT. Cover title: Oregon Health Division, Vital Statistics Annual Report. Variant title: Oregon Vital Statistics. 1960. a. $10. State Health Division, c/o State Office, 1400 S.W. Fifth Ave., Portland, OR 97201. TEL 503-229-5897. stat.; circ. 600. **Indexed**: SRI.

614 314   PL   ISSN 0079-2748
POLAND. GLOWNY URZAD STATYSTYCZNY. ROCZNIK STATYSTYCZNY OCHRONY ZDROWIA/POLAND. CENTRAL STATISTICS OFFICE. YEARBOOK OF PUBLIC HEALTH STATISTICS. (Issued in its Seria Roczniki Branzowe. Branch Yearbooks) irreg., latest 1990. Glowny Urzad Statystyczny, Al. Niepodleglosci 208, 00-925 Warsaw, Poland. TEL 48 22 25-03-45.

614.8 314   PL   ISSN 0079-287X
POLAND. GLOWNY URZAD STATYSTYCZNY. WYPADKI DROGOWE. a. Glowny Urzad Statystyczny, Al. Niepodleglosci 208, 00-925 Warsaw, Poland. TEL 48 22 25-03-45.

614.8 314   PL   ISSN 0079-2888
POLAND. GLOWNY URZAD STATYSTYCZNY. WYPADKI PRZY PRACY/POLAND. CENTRAL STATISTICS OFFICE. ACCIDENTS AT WORK. a. Glowny Urzad Statystyczny, Al. Niepodleglosci 208, 00-925 Warsaw, Poland. TEL 48 22 25-03-45.

PREVENTION IN HUMAN SERVICES; summaries, reviews & index to the world's literature in community mental health. see *PSYCHOLOGY — Abstracting, Bibliographies, Statistics*

614   US   ISSN 0079-7588
PUBLIC HEALTH CONFERENCE ON RECORDS AND STATISTICS. PROCEEDINGS. no.2, 1950. irreg., no.18, 1980; no.19, 1984; latest 1989. U.S. National Center for Health Statistics, 6525 Belcrest Road, Hyattsville, MD 20782. TEL 301-436-8500.

613 616   FR   ISSN 1013-8285
PUBLIC HEALTH NUTRITION. French edition: Nutrition de Sante Publique (ISSN 1013-8056); Spanish edition: Nutricion en Salud Publica (ISSN 1013-8293) (Text in English) 1980. 2/yr. 240 F. for 2 yrs. Centre International de l'Enfance - International Childern's Center, Chateau de Longchamp, Bois de Boulogne, 75016 Paris, France. TEL 1-45-20-79-92. FAX 1-45-25-73-67.
  Formerly (until 1989): Food Production - Nutrition.
  Description: Covers nutritional requirements, breast-feeding, types of diet, food, studies of dietary intake and nutritional status, indicators for nutritional surveillance, nutritional diseases, education, personnel training, programs.

614.8 531.64   US
PUBLIC USE ENERGY STATISTICAL DATA BASE. Short title: P U E S D B. m. $200 per issue in US, Canada, Mexico; elsewhere $400. (Department of Energy, Energy Information Administration) U.S. National Technical Information Service, 5825 Port Royal Rd., Springfield, VA 22161. TEL 703-487-4630. (magnetic tape)
  Description: Provides a machine-readable "mirror image" of published energy-related information to the analyst in an efficient and concise way.

614.42 310   PR
PUERTO RICO. DEPARTMENT OF HEALTH. ANNUAL HEALTH SERVICES REPORT. (Text in Spanish) 1974. a. Department of Health, Health Facilities and Services Administration, Office of Health Statistics, PO Box 9342, Santurce, PR 00901. charts; circ. 1,500. (back issues avail.)
  Formerly: Puerto Rico. Statistics, Analysis and Control of Information. Annual Vital Statistics Report.
  Description: Information on patients, facilities, services and resources by municipality and regions.

614 360   PR
PUERTO RICO. DEPARTMENT OF HEALTH. BOLETIN ESTADISTICO. (Text in Spanish) 1979. irreg. free. Department of Health, Health Facilities and Services Administration, Office of Health Statistics, Box 9342, Santurce, PR 00908. TEL 809-721-4050. circ. 500.

REFERATIVNYI ZHURNAL. ORGANIZATSIYA I BEZOPASNOST' DOROZHNOGO DVIZHENIYA. see TRANSPORTATION — Abstracting, Bibliographies, Statistics

614.84 016   RU   ISSN 0202-9898
TH9111
REFERATIVNYI ZHURNAL. POZHARNAYA OKHRANA. 1971. m. 67 Rub. (69.40 Rub. including index). Vsesoyuznyi Institut Nauchno-Tekhnicheskoi Informatsii (VINITI), Baltiiskaya ul., 14, Moscow A-219, Russia. (Subscr. to: Mezhdunarodnaya Kniga, Dimitrova ul. 39, 113095 Moscow, Russia)

614.42   NL   ISSN 1018-0893
SOUTH PACIFIC EPIDEMIOLOGICAL AND HEALTH INFORMATION SERVICE ANNUAL REPORT. (Text in English or French) 1972. a. South Pacific Commission, B.P. D5, Noumea, Cedex, New Caledonia. TEL 26-2000. FAX 687-263818. TELEX 3138 NM SOPACOM.

368.384   IT   ISSN 0075-188X
STATISTICA DEGLI INCIDENTI STRADALI. vol.36, 1989. a. L.18000. Istituto Centrale di Statistica, Via Cesare Balbo 16, 00100 Rome, Italy.

610 015   SW   ISSN 0036-1879
SWEDEN. SJUKVAARDENS OCH SOCIALVAARDENS PLANERINGS- OCH RATIONALISERINGSINSTITUT. S P R I LITTERATURTJAENST. Short title: S P R I Litteraturtjaenst. (Text and summaries in English and Swedish) 1968. 10/yr. SEK 350. Sjukvaardens och Socialvaardens Planerings- och Rationaliseringsinstitut - Swedish Planning and Rationalization Institute of the Health and Social Services, Box 70487, S-107 26 Stockholm, Sweden. TEL 08-702-4600. FAX 08-702-4799. bibl.; index.

614.8 610   SW   ISSN 0346-8992
RA407.5.S8
SWEDEN. STATISTISKA CENTRALBYRAAN. STATISTISKA MEDDELANDEN. SUBGROUP HS (PUBLIC HEALTH AND MEDICAL CARE). (Text in Swedish; summaries in English) 1976. irreg. SEK 500 (effective 1992). Statistiska Centralbyraan, Publishing Unit, S-701 89 Oerebro, Sweden.

614   JA
TOYAMA-KEN EISEI TOKEI NENPO/TOYAMA PREFECTURE. ANNUAL REPORT OF PUBLIC HEALTH. (Text in Japanese) 1949. a. free. Toyama-ken Kosei-bu - Toyama Prefecture, Welfare Department, 1-7 Shin-Sogawa, Toyama 930, Japan. circ. 400.

UNITED ARAB EMIRATES. WIZARAT AL-SIHHAH. AL-KITAB AL-IHSA'I AL-SANAWI/UNITED ARAB EMIRATES. MINISTRY OF HEALTH. STATISTICAL YEARBOOK. see MEDICAL SCIENCES — Abstracting, Bibliographies, Statistics

317 016   US   ISSN 0278-4912
Z7553.M43
U.S. NATIONAL CENTER FOR HEALTH STATISTICS. CATALOG OF PUBLICATIONS. a. free. U.S. National Center for Health Statistics, 6525 Belcrest Road, Hyattsville, MD 20782. TEL 301-436-8500.
Formerly: U.S. National Center for Health Statistics. Current Listing and Topical Index to the Vital and Health Statistics Series (ISSN 0092-7287)

312   US   ISSN 0083-2014
RA409
U.S. NATIONAL CENTER FOR HEALTH STATISTICS. VITAL AND HEALTH STATISTICS. SERIES 1. PROGRAMS AND COLLECTION PROCEDURES. 1963. irreg. latest no.25. price varies. U.S. National Center for Health Statistics, Scientific and Technical Information Branch, 6525 Belcrest Road, Hyattsville, MD 20782. TEL 301-436-8500. **Indexed:** Chic.Per.Ind., Excerp.Med.

312   US   ISSN 0083-2057
                             CODEN: VHSBA
U.S. NATIONAL CENTER FOR HEALTH STATISTICS. VITAL AND HEALTH STATISTICS. SERIES 2. DATA EVALUATION AND METHODS RESEARCH. 1963. irreg., latest no.112. price varies. U.S. National Center for Health Statistics, Scientific and Technical Information Branch, 6525 Belcrest Road, Hyattsville, MD 20782. TEL 301-436-8500. **Indexed:** Excerp.Med., Popul.Ind.

312   US   ISSN 0083-2065
U.S. NATIONAL CENTER FOR HEALTH STATISTICS. VITAL AND HEALTH STATISTICS. SERIES 3. ANALYTICAL STUDIES. 1964. irreg., latest no.26. price varies. U.S. National Center for Health Statistics, Scientific and Technical Information Branch, 6525 Belcrest Road, Hyattsville, MD 20782. TEL 301-436-8500. **Indexed:** Excerp.Med.

312   US   ISSN 0083-2073
HA37
U.S. NATIONAL CENTER FOR HEALTH STATISTICS. VITAL AND HEALTH STATISTICS. SERIES 4. DOCUMENTS AND COMMITTEE REPORT. 1965. irreg., latest no.28. price varies. U.S. National Center for Health Statistics, Scientific and Technical Information Branch, 6525 Belcrest Road, Hyattsville, MD 20782. TEL 301-436-8500. **Indexed:** Excerp.Med.

312   US   ISSN 0083-2022
U.S. NATIONAL CENTER FOR HEALTH STATISTICS. VITAL AND HEALTH STATISTICS. SERIES 20. DATA ON MORTALITY. 1965. irreg., latest no.18. price varies. U.S. National Center for Health Statistics, Scientific and Technical Information Branch, 6525 Belcrest Road, Hyattsville, MD 20782. TEL 301-436-8500. **Indexed:** Excerp.Med.
Incorporates in part: U.S. National Center for Health Statistics. Vital and Health Statistics. Series 22. Data on Natality and Mortality Surveys (ISSN 0083-2049)

312   US   ISSN 0083-2030
U.S. NATIONAL CENTER FOR HEALTH STATISTICS. VITAL AND HEALTH STATISTICS. SERIES 21. DATA ON NATALITY, MARRIAGE, AND DIVORCE. 1964. irreg., latest no.49. price varies. U.S. National Center for Health Statistics, Scientific and Technical Information Branch, 6525 Belcrest Road, Hyattsville, MD 20782. TEL 301-436-8500. **Indexed:** Excerp.Med., Popul.Ind.
Incorporates in part: U.S. National Center for Health Statistics. Vital and Health Statistics. Series 22. Data on Natality and Mortality Surveys (ISSN 0083-2049)

614.109   US   ISSN 0083-6710
HA203
VITAL STATISTICS OF THE UNITED STATES. (In 4 vols: Vol.1 Natality; Vol.2 (2 vols.) Mortality; Vol.3 Marriage and Divorce) 1937. a. price varies. U.S. National Center for Health Statistics, 6525 Belcrest Road, Hyattsville, MD 20782. TEL 301-436-8500.

614   UN
W H O OFFSET PUBLICATIONS. (Edition in English and French) 1973. irreg. World Health Organization - Organisation Mondiale de la Sante, Distribution and Sales, 20 Ave. Appia, CH-1211 Geneva 27, Switzerland. TEL 022-791-2111. bibl.; circ. 10,000(combined). **Indexed:** Abstr.Hyg., Biol.Abstr., Dent.Ind., Ind.Med., Rural Devel.Abstr., Trop.Dis.Bull.
Description: Contains information on topics judged vital to the protection or the improvement of public health.

628 016   UN   ISSN 0083-761X
WASTE MANAGEMENT RESEARCH ABSTRACTS. (Text in English, French, Russian and Spanish) 1965. irreg. free. International Atomic Energy Agency, Wagramer Str. 5, Box 100, A-1400 Vienna, Austria. circ. 650.

614   UN   ISSN 0250-3794
RA651
WORLD HEALTH STATISTICS ANNUAL. (Text in English, French) a. $72. World Health Organization - Organisation Mondiale de la Sante, 1211 Geneva 27, Switzerland. TEL 022-791-2111. circ. 4,800. **Indexed:** IIS.
Formerly (until 1965): Annual Epidemiological and Vital Statistics.
Description: Contains life tables, changing morbidity and mortality rates for virtually every country in the world.

614   UN   ISSN 0379-8070
RA651   CODEN: WHSQDQ
WORLD HEALTH STATISTICS QUARTERLY/RAPPORT TRIMESTRIEL DE SANITARES MONDIALES. (Text in English or French) 1947. q. $72. World Health Organization, Distribution and Sales, CH-1211 Geneva 27, Switzerland. TEL 022-791-2111. circ. 5,000. **Indexed:** Abstr.Hyg., Child Devel.Abstr., Dent.Ind., Excerp.Med., I D A, IIS, Ind.Med., Popul.Ind., Trop.Dis.Bull.
Former titles: World Health Statistics Report (ISSN 0043-8510); (until 1967): Epidemiological and Vital Statistics Report.
Description: Provides fundamental health guidance based on statistical data drawn from global resources.

614.7 310   JA   ISSN 0915-048X
YAMAGUCHI-KEN EISEI KOGAI KENKYU SENTA NENPO. (Text in Japanese) 1958. a. Yamaguchi-ken Eisei Kogai Kenkyu Senta - Yamaguchi Prefectural Research Institute of Health, 5-67, Aoi 2-chome, Yamaguchi-shi, Yamaguchi-ken 753, Japan. TEL 0839-22-7630. FAX 0839-22-7632. circ. 500.
Formed by the merger of (1958-1987): Yamaguchi-ken Eisei Kenkyujo Nenpo (ISSN 0288-7436); (1974-1987): Yamaguchi-ken Kogai Senta Nenpo (ISSN 0914-031X)
Description: Annual report of the center. Reports on pollution control for air, water, noise, vibration, and offensive odors, as well as food safety and public health-related issues.

PUBLISHING AND BOOK TRADE

see also Bibliographies; Journalism; Patents, Trademarks and Copyrights; Printing

070.5   US
A B A NEWSWIRE. 1973. w. $50 to non-members; members $30. American Booksellers Association, 560 White Plains Rd., Tarrytown, NY 10591-5112. TEL 914-631-7800. Ed. Gabrielle Quaranta. adv.; circ. 8,800.

A B B W A JOURNAL; the trade publication of the Black book industry. (American Black Book Writers Association, Inc.) see BIBLIOGRAPHIES

658.896   US   ISSN 0001-0340
Z999.A1
A B BOOKMAN'S WEEKLY. (Antiquarian Bookman); for the specialist book world. (Yearbook avail.) 1948. w. $80 (Includes A B Bookman's Yearbook). Specialist Book World, Box AB, Clifton, NJ 07015. TEL 201-772-0020. FAX 201-772-9281. Ed. Jacob L. Chernofsky. adv.; bk.rev.; bibl.; illus.; tr.lit.; index, cum.index every 10 yrs; circ. 10,000. **Indexed:** Bibl.Ind., Bk.Rev.Ind. (1987-), Child.Bk.Rev.Ind. (1987-), Lib.Lit.
Formerly (until 1967): Antiquarian Bookman.

070.5   US   ISSN 0065-0005
Z990
A B BOOKMAN'S YEARBOOK. (Antiquarian Bookman); specialist book trade annual. 1949. a. $25. Specialist Book World, Box AB, Clifton, NJ 07015. TEL 201-772-0020. FAX 201-772-9281. Ed. Jacob L. Chernofsky. adv.; bk.rev.; index, cum.index; circ. 10,000.
—BLDSC shelfmark: 0537.719200.

659.1   US
A B C BLUE BOOK: U S AND CANADIAN BUSINESS PUBLICATIONS. s-a. $100 to members only. Audit Bureau of Circulations, 900 N. Meacham Rd., Schaumburg, IL 60173. TEL 708-605-0909. FAX 708-605-0909.

659.1   US
A B C BLUE BOOK: U S AND CANADIAN MAGAZINES. s-a. $180 to members only. Audit Bureau of Circulations, 900 N. Meacham Rd., Schaumburg, IL 60173. TEL 708-605-0909. FAX 708-605-0483.
Formerly: A B C Blue Book: U S and Canadian Magazines and Farm Publications.
Description: Includes publishers' circulation statements.

A B C CIRCULATION REVIEW. see JOURNALISM

PUBLISHING AND BOOK TRADE

070.5   AT
A B P A DIRECTORY OF MEMBERS. a. Aus.$12. Australian Book Publishers Association, 161 Clarence St., Sydney, N.S.W. 2000, Australia. TEL 69-2-295-422. FAX 69-2-262-1631.
   Description: Directory contains the names and addresses and types of publishing activity of the members of the Australian Book Publishers Association.

070.5   US
A S P I F NEWSLETTER. 1983. s-a. $25. Association of Small Presses in Florida, 429 Hope St., Tarpon Springs, FL 34689. Ed. John Pyros. circ. 100.

ACADEMIC LIBRARY BOOK REVIEW. see *LIBRARY AND INFORMATION SCIENCES*

070.5   CN   ISSN 1182-3968
ACTIVE VOICE. 10/yr. membership. Freelance Editors' Association of Canada, 35 Spadina Rd., Toronto, Ont. M5R 2S9, Canada. TEL 416-975-1379. FAX 416-975-1839.

AD MEDIA. see *ADVERTISING AND PUBLIC RELATIONS*

658.8   GW   ISSN 0065-2032
Z282
ADRESSBUCH FUER DEN DEUTSCHSPRACHIGEN BUCHHANDEL. 1839. a. DM.153. Buchhaendler-Vereinigung GmbH, Grosser Hirschgraben 17-21, Postfach 100442, 6000 Frankfurt a.M. 1, Germany. TEL 069-13060. TELEX 413573-BUCHV-D. adv.; circ. 4,500.

ADVANCE; editorial features directory. see *ADVERTISING AND PUBLIC RELATIONS*

070.5   CN
ADVERTISER. 1879. s-w. Can.$25($126) Kentville Publishing, P.O. Box 430, Kentville, N.S. B4N 3X4, Canada. TEL 902-678-2121. Ed. Paul Sparkes. circ. 11,073. (back issues avail.)

070.5   UK
AFRICAN BOOK WORLD AND PRESS: A DIRECTORY. (Text in English and French) 1977. irreg., latest 1989. $135. Hans Zell Publishers (Subsidiary of: Bowker-Saur Ltd. - Butterworths), P.O. Box 56, Oxford OX1 2SJ, England. TEL 0865-511428. FAX 0865-311534. TELEX 94012872-ZELL-G. (Dist. in US by: Bowker-Saur Ltd., 121 Chanlon Rd., New Providence, NJ 07974. TEL 800-521-8110) Ed. Hans M. Zell. adv.; circ. 1,500.
   Description: Comprehensive information on libraries, publishers and the retail book trade, magazines, periodicals and major newspapers, and printing industries throughout Africa.

ALKALINE PAPER ADVOCATE. see *PAPER AND PULP*

AMAZING HEROES. see *ART*

020.75   US   ISSN 0196-5654
Z990
AMERICAN BOOK COLLECTOR. 1932; N.S. 1980. m. $33 to individuals; institutions $47. Moretus Press, Inc., Box 867, Ossining, NY 10562-0867. TEL 914-941-0409. Ed. Bernard McTigue. adv.; bk.rev.; bibl.; illus.; index, cum.index; circ. 3,500. **Indexed:** Abstr.Engl.Stud., Amer.Hist.& Life, Artbibl.Mod., Bibl.Engl.Lang.& Lit., Bk.Rev.Ind. (1965-), Child.Bk.Rev.Ind. (1965-), Hist.Abstr., M.L.A.
   —BLDSC shelfmark: 0810.830000.
   Incorporates (as of 1980): Book Collector's Market (ISSN 0162-2498); Which was formerly (1974-1977): Bibliognost (ISSN 0730-3416)

070.5   US   ISSN 0065-759X
AMERICAN BOOK TRADE DIRECTORY. 1915. a. $205. R.R. Bowker, A Reed Reference Publishing Company, Division of Reed Publishing (USA) Inc., 121 Chanlon Rd., New Providence, NJ 07974. TEL 800-521-8110. FAX 908-665-6688. TELEX 138 755. (Subscr. to: Order Dept., Box 31, New Providence, NJ 07974) index. (also avail. in magnetic tape)
   ●Also available on CD-ROM. Producer(s): R.R. Bowker.
   Description: Lists bookstores, antiquarians, wholesalers, distributors, jobbers, importers, exporters, language specialists, organized by geographic location and name. Firms are classified by the major category of books they sell.

070.5   US   ISSN 0148-5903
Z477
AMERICAN BOOKSELLER. 1977. m. $49.99 to non-members; members $34.99. American Booksellers Association, 560 White Plians Rd., Tarrytown, NY 10591-5112. TEL 800-637-0037. Ed. Dan Cullen. adv.; index; circ. 10,416.

090.75 751.6   US   ISSN 0887-8978
Z700.9
AMERICAN INSTITUTE FOR CONSERVATION OF HISTORIC AND ARTISTIC WORKS. BOOK & PAPER GROUP ANNUAL. 1982. a. $15. American Institute for Conservation of Historic and Artistic Works, Book and Paper Group, 1400 16th St., N.W., Ste. 340, Washington, DC 20036. FAX 202-232-6630. Ed. Robert Espinosa. circ. 1,000.
   Description: Covers the conservation of books, documents and works of art on paper.

070.5   US   ISSN 0892-1385
AMERICAN PUBLISHING WHO'S WHO IN NEW YORK. 1987. a. American Publishing Who's Who, 781 W. Oakland Park Blvd., Ste. 103, Ft. Lauderdale, FL 33311. Ed. S. David Wilcox.

658.809   US   ISSN 0065-9959
Z1035.1
AMERICAN REFERENCE BOOKS ANNUAL. 1970. a. $85. (Literary Guild) Libraries Unlimited, Inc., Box 3988, Englewood, CO 80155-3988. TEL 800-237-6124. FAX 303-220-8843. Ed. Bodhan S. Wynar. bk.rev.; illus.; index, cum.index every 5 yrs. **Indexed:** Bk.Rev.Ind. (1977-), Chic.Per.Ind., Child.Bk.Rev.Ind. (1977-), Child.Bk.Rev.Ind., Leg.Info.Manage.Ind., Ref.Sour.
   —BLDSC shelfmark: 0853.540000.
   Formerly: Preview (ISSN 0024-4538)
   Description: Contains approximately 1,700 titles covering general reference, humanities, education, business, and technology.

070.5   US
AMERICAN RIGHT TO READ NEWSLETTER. 4/yr. free. 568 Broadway, New York, NY 10012. TEL 212-255-4009.
   Description: Features articles on issues such as book-banning attempts. Information of interest to civil libertarians and library advocates.

AMERICAN SOCIETY OF BOOKPLATE COLLECTORS AND DESIGNERS. YEAR BOOK. see *HOBBIES*

AMONG FRIENDS. see *LIBRARY AND INFORMATION SCIENCES*

001.5   CN   ISSN 0003-200X
Z990
AMPHORA. 1967. q. Can.$35. Alcuin Society, Box 3216, Vancouver, B.C. V6B 3X8, Canada. TEL 604-668-2341. Ed. Terry Dobroslavic. adv.; bk.rev.; illus.; circ. 275. (also avail. in microfiche) **Indexed:** Br.Archaeol.Abstr., Can.Per.Ind.
   —BLDSC shelfmark: 0859.453000.
   Description: Publishes articles on book art, book collecting, typography, private press publishing and related topics.

070.5   UK   ISSN 0306-7475
Z990
ANTIQUARIAN BOOK MONTHLY REVIEW. 1974. m. £22 (Europe £24; US £26). A B M R S Publications Ltd., Bullingdon House, Ste. G, 174B Cowley Rd., Oxford OX4 IUE, England. TEL 0865-794704. FAX 0865-794582. Ed. John A. Kinnane. adv.; bk.rev.; bibl.; circ. 2,500. **Indexed:** Child.Lit.Abstr.
   —BLDSC shelfmark: 1549.854000.

658.8   AU   ISSN 0003-6277
Z2105
ANZEIGER DES OESTERREICHISCHEN BUCHHANDELS. 1866. 24/yr. S.1440. Hauptverband des oesterreichischen Buchhandels, Gruenangergasse 4, A-1010 Vienna, Austria. TEL 0222-5121535. FAX 0222-5121535-21. adv.; bk.rev.; charts; illus.; index; circ. 1,700.
   Formerly: Anzeiger des Oesterreichischen Buch-, Kunst- und Musikalienhandels.

658.896   AU   ISSN 0042-3610
ANZEIGER DES VERBANDES DER ANTIQUARE OESTERREICHS. 1948. 6/yr. S.270. Hauptverband des Oesterreichischen Buchhandels, Gruenangergasse 4, A-1010 Vienna, Austria. TEL 0222-5121535. FAX 0222-512153521. adv.; bk.rev.; circ. 1,700.

028.5   US   ISSN 0003-7052
Z7401
APPRAISAL; science books for young people. 1967. q. $39. (Boston University, School of Education) Children's Science Book Review Committee, 605 Commonwealth Ave., Boston, MA 02215. TEL 617-353-4150. FAX 617-353-3924. Ed. Diane Holzheimer. bk.rev.; index, cum.index; circ. 2,600. **Indexed:** Bk.Rev.Ind. (1975-), Child.Bk.Rev.Ind. (1975-).
   Description: Reviews science books for children and young adults.

070.5   US
ARAB BOOK GUIDE INTERNATIONAL. 1986. 2/yr. $250. Inter-Crescent Publishing Co., Inc., 12021 Nieta Dr., Garden Grove, CA 92640. TEL 714-537-1000.

ARBIDO-B; offizielles Mitteilungsorgan-bulletin d'information officiel-bollettino d'informazioni officiale. see *LIBRARY AND INFORMATION SCIENCES*

ARBIDO-R; Fachorgan-revue professionnelle-rivista professionale. see *LIBRARY AND INFORMATION SCIENCES*

655   GW   ISSN 0066-6327
Z4
ARCHIV FUER GESCHICHTE DES BUCHWESENS. (Summaries in English, French and German) 1956. s-a. DM.220. (Boersenverein des Deutschen Buchhandels) Buchhaendler-Vereinigung GmbH, Grosser Hirschgraben 17-21, 6000 Frankfurt a.M. 1, Germany. TEL 069-13060. TELEX 413573-BUCHV-D. **Indexed:** M.L.A.

655.7   FR   ISSN 0758-413X
ART ET METIERS DU LIVRE; revue internationale de la Reliure, de la bibliophie et de l'estampe. 1891. bi-m. 500 F. Editions Technorama, 31 Place Saint-Ferdinand, 75017 Paris, France. TEL 1-45-74-67-43. FAX 45-72-63-21. Ed. Remy Baschet. adv.; bibl.; charts; illus.; index; circ. 4,200. (back issues avail.)
   Formerly: Reliure (ISSN 0034-4141)

ART LINE; international art news. see *ART*

686   GW   ISSN 0935-7653
ARTIKEL 5; das Wirtschaftsmagazin der Printmedien. 1987. q. DM.126. Artikel 5 Verlagsgesellschaft mbH, Eidelstedteweg 22, 2000 Hamburg 20, Germany. TEL 040-565031. FAX 040-5602920. TELEX 2162603. Ed. Guenther Baehr. adv.; bk.rev.; circ. 3,500. (back issues avail.)

ASIAN ADVERTISING AND MARKETING; the magazine for communication executives. see *ADVERTISING AND PUBLIC RELATIONS*

070.5   II   ISSN 0254-6183
ASIAN LITERARY MARKET REVIEW; the international magazine of book, magazine and audiovisual publishing. (Text in English) 1975. q. Rs.50($10) Jaffe Publishing Management Service, Kunnuparambil Bldgs., Kurichy, Kottayam 686 549, India. TEL 04826-470. Ed. K.P. Punnoose. adv.; bk.rev.; circ. 3,150. (back issues avail.)

070.5   UN
ASIAN - PACIFIC BOOK DEVELOPMENT. Short title: A B D. (Text in English) 1969. q. $13. Asian Cultural Centre for Unesco, 6, Fukuro-machi, Shinjuku-ku, Tokyo 162, Japan. TEL 269-4435. Ed. Taichi Sasaoka. bk.rev.; charts; illus.; stat.; circ. 2,000.
   Former titles: Asian Book Development (ISSN 0388-5593) & Tokyo Book Development Centre. Newsletter (ISSN 0049-4046)
   Description: Concerned with the situation and current events related to publishing and book promotion as well as with the common interests for the book-related personnel of the countries in Asia and the Pacific.

011 028   FR   ISSN 0004-5365
ASSOCIATION DES BIBLIOTHECAIRES FRANCAIS. BULLETIN D'INFORMATIONS. 1907; N.S. 1956. q. membership; institutions 350 F. Association des Bibliothecaires Francais, 4 rue de Louvois, 75002 Paris, France. bk.rev.; bibl. **Indexed:** Lib.Lit., LISA.
   —BLDSC shelfmark: 2862.220000.

070.5   US   ISSN 0276-5349
Z477
ASSOCIATION OF AMERICAN PUBLISHERS. ANNUAL REPORT. a. Association of American Publishers, 220 E. 23rd St., New York, NY 10010. TEL 212-689-8920. Key Title: Annual Report - Association of American Publishers.
Description: Summary of the Association's activities for the previous year.

071   US   ISSN 0147-0310
ASSOCIATION OF AMERICAN PUBLISHERS. EXHIBITS DIRECTORY. 1967. a. $110 to non-members; members $75. Association of American Publishers, 220 E. 23rd St., New York, NY 10010. TEL 212-689-8920. Ed. Marlene Scheuermann. circ. 700.
Continues: Directory of Exhibit Opportunities.

070.5   US   ISSN 0739-3024
Z475
ASSOCIATION OF AMERICAN UNIVERSITY PRESSES DIRECTORY. 1961. a. $14.95. Association of American University Presses, Inc., 584 Broadway, Ste. 410, New York, NY 10012. TEL 212-941-6610. Ed. Chris Terry. index; circ. controlled.

028.1   CN   ISSN 0316-5981
ATLANTIC PROVINCES BOOK REVIEW. 1974. q. Can.$9.50. St. Mary's University, Halifax, N.S. B3H 3C3, Canada. TEL 902-420-5716. Ed. Elizabeth Eve. adv.; bk.rev.; circ. 50,000. (controlled). (tabloid format; back issues avail.) Indexed: Bk.Rev.Ind. (1982-), Can.Lit.Ind., Can.Per.Ind., Child.Bk.Rev.Ind. (1982-).

659.1   US
AUDIT BUREAU OF CIRCULATIONS. BYLAWS AND RULES. (Editions in English, French) a. membership only. Audit Bureau of Circulations, 900 N. Meacham Rd., Schaumburg, IL 61073. TEL 708-605-0909. FAX 708-605-0483.

070.5   US
AUDIT REPORTS. a. Audit Bureau of Circulations, 900 N. Meacham Rd., Schaumburg, IL 60195. TEL 708-885-0910. FAX 708-605-0483.

070.5 330   US
AUSTIN BOOK OF LISTS. 1986. a. Austin Business Journal Inc., 1301 Capital of Texas Hwy., Ste. C-200, Austin, TX 78746. TEL 512-328-0180. FAX 512-328-7304.

658.8   AT
AUSTRALIAN AND NEW ZEALAND BOOKSELLERS AND PUBLISHERS. 1977. a. Aus.$55. D.W. Thorpe (Subsidiary of: Butterworths), 18 Salmon St., Port Melbourne, Vic. 3207, Australia. TEL 03-645-1511. FAX 03-645-3981. Ed. Kevin Mark. circ. 1,000.
Former titles: Australian and New Zealand Booksellers (ISSN 0810-2201) & Australian Booksellers.

070.5   AT   ISSN 0045-026X
PN101
AUSTRALIAN AUTHOR. 1969. q. Aus.$19. Australian Society of Authors Ltd., P.O. Box 1566, Strawberry Hills, N.S.W. 2012, Australia. TEL 02-318-0877. FAX 02-318-0530. Ed. Dominic O'Grady. adv.; index; circ. 2,500.

658.8   AT   ISSN 0004-8763
AUSTRALIAN BOOKSELLER AND PUBLISHER. 1921. m. Aus.$47 (includes annual edition of Australian Book Scene). D.W. Thorpe (Subsidiary of: Butterworths), 18 Salmon St., Port Melbourne, Vic. 3207, Australia. TEL 03-645-1511. FAX 03-645-3981. Ed. John Nieuwenhuizen. adv.; bk.rev.; bibl.; circ. 8,000.
—BLDSC shelfmark: 1798.050000.
Formerly: Ideas Book Trade Journal.

070.5   US
AUTHORS NEWSLETTER. bi-m. Arizona Authors' Association, 3509 E. Shea Blvd., Ste. 117, Phoenix, AZ 85028-3339. TEL 602-996-9706. FAX 602-787-8638. Ed. Cynthia Greening. adv.

AVERAGE PRICES OF BRITISH ACADEMIC BOOKS. see *LIBRARY AND INFORMATION SCIENCES*

B L M. (Bonniers Litteraera Magasin) see *LITERARY AND POLITICAL REVIEWS*

070   US   ISSN 0145-9457
B P REPORT; on the business of book publishing. 1975. w. $395. Simba Information, Inc., Box 7430, Wilton, CT 06897. TEL 203-834-0033. FAX 203-834-1771. Ed. James Milliot.
●Also available online. Vendor(s): DIALOG, NewsNet.
Incorporates (1983-1989): International Publishing Newsletter (ISSN 0740-7513) & Audio Publishing Report (ISSN 0888-4498)

028.5   SW   ISSN 0347-772X
BARNBOKEN. 1978. s-a. SEK 75. Svenska Barnboksinstitutet - Swedish Institute for Children's Books, Odengatan 61, S-113 22 Stockholm, Sweden. TEL 08-332323. FAX 08-33-24-23. Ed. Lena Kaereland. circ. 1,000.
Description: Articles and essays on children's literature by specialists; information on research in the field.

020 940 090   GW   ISSN 0067-5091
BEITRAEGE ZUR INKUNABELKUNDE. DRITTE FOLGE. 1965. irreg., vol.8, 1983. price varies. (Deutsche Staatsbibliothek Berlin) Akademie-Verlag Berlin, Leipziger Strasse 3-4, 1086 Berlin, Germany.

BELLES LETTRES; a review of books by women. see *LITERATURE*

800   US
▼**BERKELEY REVIEW OF BOOKS.** 1989. a. $20. Deserted X, 1731 10th St., Ste. A, Berkeley, CA 94710. TEL 415-528-8713. Ed. Harold David Moe. adv.; bk.rev.; circ. 1,000.

070   GW   ISSN 0005-9455
BERTELSMANN BRIEFE; Fachzeitschrift fuer Themen der Kommunikation, Medien, Kultur und Buchmarktforschung. 1960. 2/yr. free. Unternehmensverbindungen and Public Relations, Postfach 5555, 4830 Guetersloh 100, Germany. Ed. M. Harnischfeger. adv.; abstr.; bibl.; charts; stat.; index; circ. 14,000.
—BLDSC shelfmark: 1941.400000.

741.6   US
BEST IN COVERS AND POSTERS. 1975. biennial. $27.95. R C Publications, Inc., 104 Fifth Ave., 9th Fl., New York, NY 10011. TEL 212-463-0600. FAX 212-989-9891. (Subscr. to: 3200 Tower Oaks Blvd., Rockville, MD 20852. TEL 301-770-2900) illus.
Formed by the 1977 merger of: Best in Covers (ISSN 0361-2066); Best in Posters (ISSN 0360-8085)

070.5   CC
BIANJI ZHI YOU/COMPILERS' FRIEND. 1985. bi-m. Y9.6($27) (effective in Jan. 1991). (Shanxi News and Publishing Bureau) Shuhai Chubanshe - Shuhai Press, 11 Bingzhou Beilu, Taiyuan, Shanxi, People's Republic of China. TEL 440040-95. (Dist. by: China International Book Trading Corporation, P.O. Box 399, Beijing, P.R.C.; Dist. in US by: China Books & Periodicals, Inc., 2929 24th St., San Francisco, CA 94110) (Co-publisher: Shanxi Renmin Chubanshe) Eds. Zhang Ansai, Du Houqin. bk.rev.; circ. 9,300. (back issues avail.)
Formerly (until Jan. 1985): Editors' and Authors' Friend.
Description: Covers the fields of editing and publishing. Contains articles on editors' craft and techniques, researches laws in news and publishing, and comments on developments in China's publishing industry.

020.75   US   ISSN 0006-128X
Z1008.B51
BIBLIOGRAPHICAL SOCIETY OF AMERICA. PAPERS. 1904. q. $30. Bibliographical Society of America, Box 397, Grand Central Station, New York, NY 10163. TEL 212-995-9151. Ed. William S. Peterson. adv.; bk.rev.; index; circ. 1,300. (also avail. in microfilm from KTO; reprint service avail. from KTO) Indexed: Abstr.Engl.Stud., Arts & Hum.Cit.Ind., Bk.Rev.Ind. (1965-), Child.Bk.Rev.Ind. (1965-), Curr.Cont., Hist.Abstr., Hum.Ind., Ind.Bk.Rev.Hum., Lib.Lit.
—BLDSC shelfmark: 6370.550000.

BIBLIOGRAPHY NEWSLETTER. see *LIBRARY AND INFORMATION SCIENCES*

070.5 809   BE
BIBLIOLOGIA. 1983. irreg. N.V. Brepols I.G.P., Rue Baron Frans du Four 8, B-2300 Turnhout, Belgium.

PUBLISHING AND BOOK TRADE   4121

070.573   AT   ISSN 0157-3276
BIBLIONEWS AND AUSTRALIAN NOTES AND QUERIES; journal for book collectors. 1947. q. Aus.$20 (foreign Aus.$25). Book Collectors' Society of Australia, 64 Young St., Cremorne, N.S.W. 2090, Australia. TEL 953-2184. Ed. John Fletcher. adv.; bk.rev.; index, cum.index: 1947-79 (nos.1-245), 1979-83 (nos.246-260); circ. 400. (back issues avail.)
Description: For all interested in the art and craft of the book.

090 070.5 686   HU   ISSN 0067-8007
BIBLIOTHECA HUNGARICA ANTIQUA. 1960. irreg., vol.20, 1988. price varies. (Magyar Tudomanyos Akademia) Akademiai Kiado, Publishing House of the Hungarian Academy of Sciences, P.O. Box 24, H-1363 Budapest, Hungary.

090.75   US
BIG LITTLE TIMES. 1981. bi-m. $12 includes membership. (Big Little Book Club of America) Educational Research Corporation, Box 1242, Danville, CA 94526. Ed. Lawrence Lowery. adv.; bk.rev.; circ. 500.
Description: Serves as a conduit among collectors and dealers interested in children's books which preceded the comic book format.

655.7   GW   ISSN 0342-3573
BINDEREPORT; internationale Fachzeitschrift fuer Buchherstellung und Druckverarbeitung. 1886. m. DM.144. Schluetersche Verlagsanstalt GmbH und Co., Georgswall 4, Postfach 5440, 3000 Hannover 1, Germany. TEL 0511-1236-0. Ed. Eberhard Furch. adv.; bk.rev.; charts; illus.; pat.; tr.lit.; index; circ. 5,196. Indexed: Print.Abstr.
Formerly: Allgemeiner Anzeiger fuer Buchbindereien; **Incorporates:** Narichten der Fachorganisationen (ISSN 0002-5984)

655.7   SZ
BINDETECHNIK/RELIURE. (Text in French and German) 1979. m. (11/yr.). 80 Fr. Verein der Buchbindereien der Schweiz, Seestrasse 69, Postfach 337, 8712 Staefa, Switzerland. (Co-sponsors: Gewerkschaft Druck und Papier; Berufsamt fuer das Schweizerische Buchbindergewerbe) adv.; abstr.; illus.; index. Indexed: Print.Abstr.
Supersedes (1890-1979): Schweizerische Fachschrift fuer Buchbindereien (ISSN 0036-7583)
Description: Concerns bookbinding.

658.8   NE   ISSN 0167-4765
Z2435
BOEKBLAD; nieuwsblad voor het boekenvak. 1834. w. fl.334.60. Vereeniging ter Bevordering van de Belangen des Boekhandels, Frederiksplein 1, Box 15007, 1001 MA Amsterdam, Netherlands. FAX 020-220908. Ed. F. Spek. adv.; bk.rev.; bibl.; stat.; index; circ. 5,500. Indexed: Key to Econ.Sci.
Formerly: Nieuwsblad voor de Boekhandel (ISSN 0028-9965)

027.8   DK   ISSN 0006-7792
Z671
BOERN OG BOEGER. (Text in Danish; summaries in English) 1948. 8/yr. DKK 543. Danmarks Skolebiblioteksforening - Danish School Library Association, Norrebrogade 159, 2200 Copenhagen N, Denmark. FAX 35-82-17-66. Ed. Beth Juncker. adv.; bk.rev.; illus.; index; circ. 4,000.

070.5   DK   ISSN 0107-5187
BOG OG BAAND. (Supplement avail.) 1980. a. DKK 356.80 (supplement DKK 94.50). Bibliotekscentralen, Tempovej 7-11, DK-2750 Ballerup, Denmark. TEL 2-974000. FAX 2-655310.

070.5   DK   ISSN 0903-7195
BOGMARKEDET. (Includes weekly supplement: Dansk Bogfortegnelse) 1854. w. DKK 530 (typically set in Jan.). Danske Bogmarked, Landemaerket 5, 1119 Copenhagen K, Denmark. TEL 33-150844. FAX 33-156203. (Co-sponsors: Danske Forlaggerforening; Danske Boghandlerforening) Ed. Pia Rink. adv.; bk.rev.; illus.; circ. 3,700.
Formerly: Danske Bogmarked.

658.8   DK   ISSN 0006-5706
BOGORMEN. 1903. 4/yr. DKK 100. Danske Boghandler-Medhjaelperforening, Siljangade 6-8, DK-2300 Copenhagen S, Denmark. Ed. Niels Erik Knudsen. adv.; bk.rev.; illus.; index; circ. 2,300.

PUBLISHING AND BOOK TRADE

658.8   DK   ISSN 0006-5749
BOGVENNEN. 1893. a. DKK 200. (Forening for Boghaandvaerk) Christian Ejlers Forlag A-S, Brolaeggerstraede 4, 1018 Copenhagen K, Denmark. TEL 01-12 21 14. Ed.Bd. bk.rev.; illus.; index; circ. 2,000.

028   BG   ISSN 0006-5773
BOI. 1965. m. Tk.60($2) National Book Centre of Bangladesh, Grantha Bhaban 5, Bangabandhu Ave., Dhaka 1000, Bangladesh. Ed. Fazle Rabbi. adv.; bk.rev.; abstr.; charts; illus.; stat.; index; circ. 5,000.

BOOGIE WOOGIE AND BLUES COLLECTOR. see *MUSIC*

090.75   US   ISSN 0740-8439
THE BOOK; newsletter of the program in the history of the book in American culture. 1983. 3/yr. free. American Antiquarian Society, 185 Salisbury St., Worcester, MA 01609. TEL 508-755-5221. Eds. John B. Hench, David D. Hall. bk.rev.; illus.; circ. 2,300.
  Description: Contains the program, scholarly research notes, articles on research collections concerning the book in American history and culture to 1876. Also includes Society activities.

070.5   US   ISSN 0733-3005
BOOK ALERT (BRIDGEWATER). 1979. m. free. Baker and Taylor Books, 652 E. Main St., Box 6920, Bridgewater, NJ 08807-0920. TEL 908-218-0400. FAX 908-218-3980. adv.; bk.rev.; illus.; circ. 20,000. (controlled).
  Incorporates: Paperback Alert.
  Description: Prepublication announcement magazine for booksellers and librarians of adult, children's, and young adult hardcover and paperback (mass and trade) titles and spoken-word audio.

020.75   UK
BOOK AND MAGAZINE COLLECTOR. 1984. m. $70. Diamond Publishing Group Ltd., 43-45 St. Mary's Rd., Ealing, London W5 5RQ, England. TEL 081-579-1082. FAX 081-566-2024. Ed. John Dean. adv.; bibl.; cum.index. (back issues avail.)
  Indexed: Child.Lit.Abstr.

658.8   GR
▼**BOOK & MEDIA.** (Text in Greek) 1990. m. Dr.5500. Network Media Ltd., 44 Syngrou Ave., 117 42 Athens, Greece. TEL 9238672. FAX 9216847. Ed. Manto Karagianni. circ. 8,000.
  Description: Covers developments in the Greek publishing industry.

070.5   UK   ISSN 0068-0095
BOOK AUCTION RECORDS. 1902. a. £77. Dawson UK Ltd., Cannon House, Folkestone, Kent CT19 5EE, England. TEL 0303-850101. FAX 0303-850440. TELEX 96392. Ed. Wendy Y. Heath. adv.; cum.index every 5 yrs.
  Description: Priced and annotated record of books auctioned world wide.

658.809   US   ISSN 0006-7202
Z1008
BOOK CLUB OF CALIFORNIA. QUARTERLY NEWS-LETTER. 1933. q. $55 includes membership. Book Club of California, 312 Sutter St., Ste. 510, San Francisco, CA 94108. TEL 415-781-7532. Ed. Harlan Kessel. adv.; bk.rev.; cum.index; circ. 1,000. (back issues avail.)

BOOK COLLECTING WORLD. see *HOBBIES*

020.75   US
BOOK COLLECTORS' HANDBOOK OF VALUES. irreg. price varies. G. P. Putnam's Sons, 200 Madison Ave., New York, NY 10016. TEL 212-576-8900.

658.8   US
BOOK DEALERS WORLD; direct mail marketplace for book dealers and self-publishers and writers. 1980. q. $25. North American Bookdealers Exchange, Box 606, Cottage Grove, OR 97424. TEL 503-942-7455. Ed. Al Galasso. adv.; bk.rev.; circ. 20,000. (back issues avail.)

070.5 001.3   US   ISSN 0094-9426
AS30
BOOK FORUM. 1974. irreg. (approx. q.). $18 to individuals; institutions $24. Crescent Publishing Co., Inc., Box 585, Niantic, CT 06357. TEL 203-739-9497. Ed. Clarence Driskill. adv.; bk.rev.; bibl.; index; circ. 5,200. (back issues avail.)
  Indexed: Abstr.Engl.Stud., Amer.Bibl.Slavic & E.Eur.Stud., Amer.Hum.Ind., Arts & Hum.Cit.Ind., Bk.Rev.Ind. (1976-), Child.Bk.Rev.Ind. (1976-), Curr.Cont., M.L.A., Mid.East: Abstr.& Ind.
  —BLDSC shelfmark: 2248.103500.

658.8   US   ISSN 0160-970X
Z477
BOOK INDUSTRY TRENDS. Represents: Book Industry Study Group. Research Report. 1977. a. $400. Book Industry Study Group, Inc., 160 Fifth Ave., New York, NY 10010. TEL 212-929-1393. FAX 212-989-7542.
  —BLDSC shelfmark: 2248.104000.

BOOK MARK; children's literature in review with related activities for preschoolers through young adults. see *CHILDREN AND YOUTH — About*

658.8   UK   ISSN 0264-3219
BOOK MARKETING NEWS. 1981. 10/yr. £50. Book Marketing Council, 19 Bedford Sq., London WC1B 3HJ, England. TEL 01-580-6321. FAX 01-636-5375. TELEX 267160 PUBASS G. Ed. Katharine Toseland. bk.rev.; charts; illus.; stat.; tr.lit.; circ. 1,000.
  Description: Discusses trade promotions, new publications, media news, industry festivals and fairs, seminars and conferences.

070.5 658.8   US   ISSN 0891-8813
BOOK MARKETING UPDATE. 1986. bi-m. $48 (foreign $98). Open Horizons Publishing, Rt. 3, Box 205, Fairfield, IA 52556. TEL 512-472-6130. FAX 515-472-3186. Ed. John Kremer. adv.; bk.rev.; bibl.; charts; illus.; stat.; index; circ. 2,000. (back issues avail.)
  Description: Features ideas, tips, resources, case histories, and articles on book marketing, publicity, and promotions for large and small book publishers and authors.

028   US   ISSN 0006-7296
BOOK NEWS LETTER. 1944. bi-m. free. Augsburg Fortress, 426 S. Fifth St., Box 1209, Minneapolis, MN 55440. TEL 612-330-3300. Ed. Roderick D. Olson. bk.rev.; bibl.; illus.; index; circ. 30,000.

028.1   US
BOOK NEWSLETTER. irreg. (1-2/yr.). $1.50. International Publishers Co., Box 3042, New York, NY 10116. TEL 212-366-9816. FAX 212-366-9820.
  Description: Local challenges to the right to read and responses to these challenges are chronicled in this censorship newsletter.

020.75   US   ISSN 0006-730X
Z1007.B7166
BOOK-OF-THE-MONTH CLUB NEWS. 1926. 15/yr. membership. Book-Of-The-Month Club, Time & Life Bldg., 1271 Ave. of the Americas, New York, NY 10020. TEL 212-522-4200. Ed. Brigitte Weeks. bk.rev.; bibl, illus.; circ. 1,000,000.

020   US
BOOK PAGE. m. ProMotion, Inc., 107 Kenner Ave., Nashville, TN 37205-2207. TEL 615-292-8926. Ed. Ann Meador Shayne.

BOOK PARADE/BOEKPARADE. see *LIBRARY AND INFORMATION SCIENCES*

070.5   US   ISSN 1049-4456
BOOK PROMOTION HOTLINE. 1989. w. $150 (includes Book Marketing Update). Ad-Lib Publications, 51 1-2 W. Adams, Box 1102, Fairfield, IA 52556-1102. TEL 800-669-0773. FAX 515-472-3186. Ed. Marie Kiefer.
  Formerly (until 1990): Book Information Hotline.
  Description: Lists 75 to 100 key media and book marketing contacts.

659.1 070.5   US
Z475
BOOK PUBLISHING RESOURCE GUIDE. 1986. a. $25. Ad-Lib Publications, 51 1-2 W. Adams, Box 1102, Fairfield, IA 52556-1102. TEL 515-472-6617. FAX 515-472-3186. Ed.Bd. bibl.; index; circ. 2,000. (Avail. in database format for IBM-PC, Macintosh, or compatibles)
  Formerly: Book Marketing Opportunities: A Directory (ISSN 0894-1785)
  Description: Includes all major wholesalers, bookstore chains, clubs, catalogues and over 2,000 media contacts.

028.1   US
THE BOOK READER. bi-m. $20. Jay Bail, Ed. & Pub., 245 Mt. Hermon Rd., Ste. 256, Scotts Valley, CA 95066-4035. TEL 408-475-3412. (newspaper)

028.1   US   ISSN 0145-627X
BOOK TALK. 1971. irreg. (approx. 5/yr.). $10. New Mexico Book League, 8632 Horacio Pl., N.E., Albuquerque, NM 87111. TEL 505-299-8940. Ed. Carol A. Myers. adv.; bk.rev.; circ. 550. (back issues avail.)
  Description: Contains articles of interest to Southwestern booksellers and librarians. Includes reviews of 20-25 new titles having a Southwestern appeal.

070.025   CN   ISSN 0700-5296
Z485
BOOK TRADE IN CANADA/INDUSTRIE DU LIVRE AU CANADA. (Text in English, French) 1975. a. $45. Ampersand Communications Services Inc., 5606 Scobie Cr., Manotick, Ont. K4M 1B7, Canada. TEL 613-692-2080. FAX 613-692-1419. Ed. Eunice A. Thorne. circ. 2,000.
  —BLDSC shelfmark: 2248.280000.
  Formerly (until 1976): Book Publishers in Canada.
  Description: Covers the Canadian book industry: information on publishers, their programs and titles, on bookstores in Canada and on publishing related organizations.

028.1   US   ISSN 0006-7369
BOOK WORLD. Variant title: Washington Post Book World. 1972. w. $26 (foreign $31.20). Washington Post Co., 1150 15th St., N.W., Washington, DC 20071. TEL 202-334-6000. FAX 202-334-5547. TELEX 80-9522. Ed. Nina King. adv.; bk.rev.; illus.; circ. 1,165,567. (tabloid format; also avail. in microform from RPI,UMI) **Indexed:** Amer.Bibl.Slavic & E.Eur.Stud., Bk.Rev.Ind. (1967-), Child.Bk.Rev.Ind. (1967-), Mid.East: Abstr.& Ind.
  ●Also available online. Vendor(s): CompuServe Consumer Information Service, DIALOG, Dow Jones/News Retrieval, Mead Data Central, VU/TEXT Information Services, Inc..

BOOKBIRD; literature for children and young people, news from all over the world, recommendations for translation. see *CHILDREN AND YOUTH — For*

658.8   UK
BOOKDEALER; the trade weekly for books wanted and for sale. 1971. w. £40. Werner Shaw Ltd., 26 Charing Cross Rd., Ste. 34, London WC2H 0DH, England. TEL 071-240-5991. FAX 071-379-5770. Ed. Barry Shaw. adv.; bk.rev.; circ. 2,300.

BOOKENDS. see *LIBRARY AND INFORMATION SCIENCES*

020 070.5   US   ISSN 0092-7686
Z671
BOOKLEGGER. 1973-1977; resumed 1978. m. $8. Booklegger Press, 555 29th St., San Francisco, CA 94131. Eds. Celeste West, Valerie Wheat. bk.rev.; index; circ. 5,000. **Indexed:** Alt.Press Ind., CALL, Lib.Lit., Wom.Stud.Abstr. Key Title: Booklegger Magazine.

020   US
BOOKLOVER. 1983. m. $10 to individuals; institutions $20. Reading Rage Publishing Co., 151 W. 75th St., New York, NY 10023. TEL 212-362-8096. Ed. Elizabeth Timmerman. adv.; bk.rev.; circ. 50,000.

658.8   BG
BOOKMAN. (Text in Bengali or English) 1979. q. Tk.10($2) per no. Bangladesh Books International Ltd., Ittefaq Bhaban, 1 Ramkrishna Mission Rd., POB 377, Dhaka 3, Bangladesh. TEL 2-256071. bibl. (also avail. in microform from UMI; reprint service avail. from UMI)

PUBLISHING AND BOOK TRADE

070.5   US   ISSN 0068-0133
BOOKMAN'S GUIDE TO AMERICANA. 1960. irreg., 9th ed., 1986. price varies. Scarecrow Press, Inc., 52 Liberty St., Box 4167, Metuchen, NJ 08840. TEL 800-537-7107. circ. 3,000.
   Description: Alphabetically arranged compilation of quotations transcribed from recent out-of-print booksellers' catalogs. Provides the bookseller or book buyer with a record of prices asked for out-of-print titles in the comprehensive field of Americana, including factual or fictional works.

070.5   US   ISSN 0068-0141
Z1000
BOOKMAN'S PRICE INDEX; guide to the values of rare and other out-of-print books. 1964. irreg., vol.41, 1990. $199 per vol. Gale Research Inc., 835 Penobscot Bldg., Detroit, MI 48226. TEL 313-961-2242. FAX 313-961-6083. TELEX 810-221-7086. Ed. Daniel F. McGrath.
   Description: Price guide to out-of-print and rare books.

BOOKNEWS. see *LITERATURE*

070   US   ISSN 0747-847X
BOOKNOTES: RESOURCE INFORMATION FOR THE SMALL AND SELF-PUBLISHER. 1984. q. $45. INTERPUB, Box 3877, Eugene, OR 97403. TEL 503-342-6091. Ed. Cliff Martin. bk.rev.; circ. 1,400. (looseleaf format; back issues avail.)

686   UK   ISSN 0264-3693
BOOKPLATE JOURNAL. 1983. s-a. £25($45) (includes Bookplate Society Newsletter). Bookplate Society, 11 Nella Rd., London W6 9PB, England. (Subscr. to: c/o Mrs. G. Wilyman, 39 Wellington Rd., Edgbaston, Birmingham B15 2ES, England) Ed. Brian North Lee. adv.; bk.rev.; circ. 500.
   —BLDSC shelfmark: 2250.099700.
   Description: Deals with all aspects of the history, making and collecting of bookplates.

686   UK   ISSN 0309-7935
BOOKPLATE SOCIETY NEWSLETTER. 1972. q. included in subscr. to Bookplate Journal. Bookplate Society, 11 Nella Rd., London W6 9PB, England. Ed. Bryan Welch.

028.1   UK
BOOKS. 1981. m. £16. Gradegate Ltd., 43 Museum St., London WC1A 1LY, England. TEL 01 404 0304. bk.rev.
   Formerly (until 1986): Book Choice (ISSN 0261-4227)
   Description: Features new books.

028.1   JA
BOOKS AND ESSAYS/TOSHO. (Text in Japanese) 1938. m. Iwanami Shoten Publishers, 2-5-5 Hitotsubashi, Chiyoda-ku, Tokyo 101, Japan. (Overseas Distributor: Japan Publications Trading Co., Ltd., Box 5030, Tokyo International, Tokyo 100-31, Japan; or 1255 Howard St., San Francisco, CA 94103)
   Description: To stimulate an interest in reading.

658.8   UK
BOOKS AND JOURNALS WANTED LIST. 1980. m. £15.95. A A B British Book Search Services (Oxford), P.O. Box 342, Oxford, OX1 1NN, England. TEL 08-65-792610. FAX 0865-79211.

BOOKS AND LIBRARIES AT THE UNIVERSITY OF KANSAS. see *LIBRARY AND INFORMATION SCIENCES*

028.1 200   US   ISSN 0890-0841
BL1
BOOKS AND RELIGION; a quarterly review of religious books and ideas. 1971. q. $19. Trinity Church, 74 Trinity Place, New York, NY 10006. FAX 212-602-0727. Ed. Katherine Kurs. adv.; bk.rev.; bibl.; index; circ. 15,000. (tabloid format; also avail. in microform from UMI; reprint service avail. from UMI) **Indexed:** Bk.Rev.Ind. (1989-), Child.Bk.Rev.Ind. (1989-), Rel.Ind.One, Rel.Per.
   Former titles: Review of Books and Religion (ISSN 0732-5800); (1976-1980): New Review of Books and Religion (ISSN 0146-0609); Review of Books and Religion (ISSN 0048-7465)

BOOKS AT IOWA. see *LIBRARY AND INFORMATION SCIENCES*

070.5   CN
BOOKS FOR EVERYBODY. 2/yr. Key Publishers Co. Ltd., 70 The Esplanade, 4th fl., Toronto, Ont. M5E 1R2, Canada. TEL 416-360-0044. FAX 416-941-9038. Ed. Barbara Scott. adv.; circ. 400,000.

020.75   UK   ISSN 0143-909X
BOOKS FOR KEEPS. 1980. 6/yr. £11.40 (foreign £16.50). School Bookshop Association Ltd., 6 Brightfield Rd., Lee, London SE12 8QF, England. TEL 081-852-4953. Ed. Chris Powling. adv.; bk.rev.; bibl.; index; circ. 8,000. **Indexed:** Bk.Rev.Ind. (1980-), Child.Bk.Rev.Ind. (1980-), Child.Lit.Abstr.
   Incorporates (1983-1988): British Book News Children's Books (ISSN 0264-5637) & School Bookshop News.
   Description: Reviews about children's books.

028.5   UK   ISSN 0006-7482
Z1037.A1
BOOKS FOR YOUR CHILDREN. 1965. 3/yr. £2. c/o Anne Wood, Ed., P.O. Box 507, Edgbaston, Birmingham B15 3AA, England. FAX 021-452-1807. adv.; bk.rev.; illus.; index; circ. 25,000. (also avail. in microform from UMI; reprint service avail. from UMI) **Indexed:** Bk.Rev.Ind. (1986-), Child.Bk.Rev.Ind. (1986-), Child.Lit.Abstr.

028.1   CN   ISSN 0045-2564
Z1369
BOOKS IN CANADA. 1971. m. (9/yr.). Can.$19.21 to individuals (foreign Can.$27.95); institutions Can.$26.75 (foreign Can.$35). Canadian Review of Books Ltd., 33 Draper St., 2nd Fl., Toronto, Ont. M5V 2M3, Canada. TEL 416-340-9809. FAX 416-340-9813. Ed. Paul Stuewe. adv.; bk.rev.; bibl.; illus.; index; circ. 12,000. (also avail. in microfiche from MMP; back issues avail., reprint service avail. from MMP) **Indexed:** Bk.Rev.Ind. (1979-), Can.Lit.Ind., Can.Per.Ind., Child.Bk.Rev.Ind. (1979-), CMI.
   Description: A national consumer book review magazine.

028.1   UK   ISSN 0143-1285
BOOKS IN SCOTLAND. 1978. q. £8.95 (foreign £9.95). Ramsay Head Press, 15 Gloucester Place, Edinburgh EH3 6EE, Scotland. TEL 031-225 5646. Eds. Christine and Conrad Wilson. adv.; bk.rev.; circ. 3,000.
   Description: Reviews of new books by Scottish writers, books about Scots and Scotland, and books in general.

070.5   IE   ISSN 0376-6039
Z331.7
BOOKS IRELAND. (Text in English and Gaelic) 1976. 9/yr. $20. Jeremy Addis Ltd., 11 Newgrove Avenue, Dublin 4, Ireland. TEL 0353-12692185. (U.S. subscr. to: Irish Books & Media, 1433 Franklin Ave. East, Minneapolis, MN 55404-2135. TEL 612-871-3505) Ed. Jeremy Addis. adv.; bk.rev.; tr.lit.; circ. 3,180.
   —BLDSC shelfmark: 2250.201000.
   Description: Provides bibliography listings and reviews of all Irish-interest and Irish-author books, with news of Irish publishing.

070   UK
Z2005
BOOKS MAGAZINE. m. £21($40) 43 Museum St., London WC1A 1LY, England. FAX 01-242-0762. adv.; illus.; circ. 100,000. **Indexed:** Abstr.Engl.Stud., Bk.Rev.Ind. (1965-), Child.Bk.Rev.Ind. (1965-).
   Formerly: Books and Bookmen (ISSN 0006-744X)

028.1   US   ISSN 0095-3555
Z1035.A1
BOOKS - 100 REVIEWS; the West Coast review of books. Variant title: West Coast Review of Books. 1974. bi-m. $11.97. Rapport Publishing Co., Inc., 5265 Fountain Ave., Upper Terrace, Los Angeles, CA 90029. TEL 213-660-0433. FAX 213-460-2968. Ed. David Dreis. adv.; bk.rev.; circ. 70,000. **Indexed:** Bk.Rev.Ind. (1977-), Child.Bk.Rev.Ind. (1977-).
   Description: Reviews latest books and articles.

658.8   PK   ISSN 0006-7547
BOOKSELLER. 1968. m. Rps.60 (foreign $30). Bookseller (International), 26, Paisa Bazar, P.O. Box 2387, Lahore 54000, Pakistan. TEL 042-67715. FAX 042-257245. Ed. Muhammad Saeed Shaikh. adv.; bk.rev.; circ. 17,000.

658.8   UK   ISSN 0006-7539
BOOKSELLER; the organ of the book trade. 1858. w. £106. J. Whitaker & Sons Ltd., 12 Dyott St., London WC1A 1DF, England. TEL 071-836-8911. FAX 071-836-6381. Ed. Louis Baum. adv.; bibl.; illus.; circ. 16,200. (also avail. in microform from UMI) **Indexed:** Br.Ceram.Abstr., Br.Hum.Ind., Child.Lit.Abstr., Int.Lab.Doc., LISA, Print.Abstr.
   —BLDSC shelfmark: 2250.220000.

070.5 658.8   UK   ISSN 0141-917X
BOOKSELLERS ASSOCIATION OF GREAT BRITAIN AND IRELAND. CHARTER GROUP. ECONOMIC SURVEY. a. Booksellers Association of Great Britain and Ireland, 272 Vauxhall Bridge Rd, London SW1V 1BA, England. TEL 071-834-5477. FAX 071-834-8812.
   —BLDSC shelfmark: 3655.987000.

070.5   UK   ISSN 0952-1666
BOOKSELLERS ASSOCIATION OF GREAT BRITAIN AND IRELAND. DIRECTORY OF MEMBERS. a. Booksellers Association of Great Britain and Ireland, 272 Vauhall Bridge Rd., London SW1V 1BA, England. TEL 071-834-5477. FAX 071-834-8812. index.
   —BLDSC shelfmark: 3594.491000.
   Former titles: Booksellers Association of Great Britain. List of Charter Members (ISSN 0142-8934); (until 1985): Booksellers Association of Great Britain and Ireland. List of Members (ISSN 0068-0249)

070.5   UK   ISSN 0268-246X
BOOKSELLING NEWS. q. £20 to non-members. Booksellers Association of Great Britain and Ireland, 272 Vauxhall Bridge Rd., London SW1V 1BA, England. TEL 071-834-5477. FAX 071-834-8812. Ed. Lispeth Hyanis. index. 3,600. (back issues avail.)
   —BLDSC shelfmark: 2250.245000.

658.8 282   US   ISSN 0006-7563
Z479
BOOKSTORE JOURNAL. 1968. m. $43. (Christian Booksellers Association) C B A Service Corporation, 2620 Venetucci Blvd., Box 200, Colorado Springs, CO 80901. TEL 719-576-7880. FAX 719-576-0795. Ed. Todd Hafer. adv.; bk.rev.; illus.; circ. 7,500.
   Description: Trade magazine for the Christian retail industry. Provides articles on retail management, industry news, and product information.

070.5 301.412   US   ISSN 0163-1128
BOOKWOMAN. 1936. 3/yr. membership. Women's National Book Association, 5222 St. Genevieve Pl., Alexandria, VA 22310. TEL 212-675-7805. Ed. Nancy Lutz. bk.rev.; circ. 1,200.

077   YU
BORBIN INFORMATOR; list radnih ljudi NIGP Borba. m. Borba, Trg Marksa i Engelsa 7, Belgrade, Yugoslavia. Ed. Zivodar Zivkovic.

028.1 800   US   ISSN 0734-2306
BOSTON REVIEW. 1975. 6/yr. $15 to individuals; institutions $18. Boston Critic, Inc., 33 Harrison Ave., Boston, MA 02111. TEL 617-350-5353. Ed. Joshua Cohen. adv.; bk.rev.; film rev.; play rev.; illus.; index; circ. 10,000. (tabloid format; also avail. in microfilm from UMI; back issues avail.; reprint service avail. from UMI) **Indexed:** Alt.Press Ind., Bk.Rev.Ind. (1978-), Child.Bk.Rev.Ind. (1978-), M.L.A.
   Formerly (until 1982): New Boston Review (ISSN 0361-168X)
   Description: Includes literary and political essays.

THE BOWKER ANNUAL LIBRARY AND BOOK TRADE ALMANAC. see *LIBRARY AND INFORMATION SCIENCES*

BRAILLE BOOK REVIEW (LARGE PRINT EDITION). see *HANDICAPPED — Visually Impaired*

BRANDYWINE DOCUMENTS ON THE HISTORY OF BOOKS & PRINTING. see *PRINTING*

BRANDYWINE KEEPSAKE. see *PRINTING*

BRILLIANT IDEAS FOR PUBLISHERS. see *JOURNALISM*

070.5 658.8   UK
BRITAIN'S BOOK PUBLISHING INDUSTRY. 1984. a. £165. Jordan & Sons Ltd., 21 St. Thomas St., Bristol BS 1 6JS, England. TEL 0272-230600. FAX 0272-230063. TELEX 449119.
   Formerly: Book Publishers.

PUBLISHING AND BOOK TRADE

BRITISH BOOK NEWS; the British Council's monthly survey for bookbuyers throughout the world. see *BIBLIOGRAPHIES*

015   GW   ISSN 0007-2761
BUCH DER ZEIT; books and periodicals from the German Democratic Republic - Buecher und Zeitschriften aus der Deutschen Demokratischen Republik. (Text in English, German) m. Buchexport, Leninstr 16, 7010 Leipzig, Germany. TEL 7-137485. FAX 286307. TELEX 051678. adv.; bk.rev.; illus.
Description: Contains reviews of books and magazines published in eastern Germany, which can be ordered from abroad. Includes list of advertisers.

070.5   GW   ISSN 0068-3051
Z313
BUCH UND BUCHHANDEL IN ZAHLEN. 1952. a. DM.19. Boersenverein des Deutschen Buchhandels, Gr. Hirschgraben 17-21, 6000 Frankfurt a.M., Germany. FAX 069-1306-396. Ed. Juergen Bartsch. circ. 5,000.
Description: Statistical publication of the book trade. Lists book production, book prices, translations, magazine production, sales, readership. Includes list of trade societies.

658.8   GW   ISSN 0007-2796
BUCHHAENDLER HEUTE. 1947. m. DM.55. Triltsch Druck und Verlag GmbH und Co. KG, Herzogstr. 53, 4000 Duesseldorf, Germany. adv.; bk.rev.; charts; illus.; index; circ. 4,000.
Formerly: Jungbuchhandel.

070.5   GW   ISSN 0170-5105
BUCHHANDELSGESCHICHTE. ZWEITE FOLGE; Aufsaetze, Rezensionen und Berichte zur Geschichte des Buchwesens. 1979. irreg. (approx. 4/yr). DM.37.20. (Historische Kommission des Boersenvereins des Deutschen Buchhandels e.V.) Buchhaendler-Vereinigung GmbH, Grosser Hirschgraben 17-21, 6000 Frankfurt a.M. 1, Germany. TEL 069-13060. TELEX 413573-BUCHV-D. bk.rev.
—BLDSC shelfmark: 2354.966800.

686   GW   ISSN 0724-7001
BUCHWISSENSCHAFTLICHE BEITRAEGE AUS DEM DEUTSCHEN BUCHARCHIV MUENCHEN. 1950. irreg., no.35, 1991. price varies. Verlag Otto Harrassowitz, Taunusstr. 14, Postfach 2929, 6200 Wiesbaden 1, Germany. TEL 0611-530-0. FAX 0611-530570. TELEX 4186135. Eds. Ludwig Delp, Ursula Neumann.
Formerly: Buchwissenschaftliche Beitraege (ISSN 0407-5439)

655   GW   ISSN 0007-3032
BUECHERGILDE. 1924. q. free. Buechergilde Gutenberg Verlagsgesellschaft mbH, Untermainkai 66, Postfach 160165, 6000 Frankfurt a.M. 16, Germany. FAX 069-27390824. Ed. Karin Hirschfeld. bk.rev.; illus.; circ. 200,000.

028.1   SZ
BUECHERPICK; das aktuelle Buchmagazin. (Text in German) 1982. q. 14 Fr. Buecherpick Verlag AG, Postfach 146, CH-3322 Urtenen, Switzerland. TEL 031-852233. Ed. Juerg Altwegg. adv.; bk.rev.; circ. 120,000.

BUECHERSCHAU; Zeitschrift fuer Betriebs- und Gewerkschaftsbibliotheken. see *LIBRARY AND INFORMATION SCIENCES*

011   FR
BULLETIN DU BIBLIOPHILE. 1920. s-a. 395 F. Editions du Cercle de la Librairie, 35 rue Gregoire-de-Tours, 75006 Paris, France. (Co-sponsor: Association Internationale de Bibliophilie) adv.; bibl.
Formerly: Librairie Ancienne et Moderne. Bulletin (ISSN 0024-2128)

BULLETIN JUGEND UND LITERATUR. see *LIBRARY AND INFORMATION SCIENCES*

091   ET
BULLETIN OF ETHIOPIAN MANUSCRIPTS. (Text in English or Ethiopian) a. Ethiopian Manuscript Microfilm Library, Box 30274, Addis Ababa, Ethiopia.

BUREAU INTERNATIONAL DES SOCIETES GERANT LES DROITS D'ENREGISTREMENT ET DE REPRODUCTION MECANIQUE. BULLETIN. see *PRINTING*

BUSINESS BOOK REVIEW. see *BUSINESS AND ECONOMICS*

BUSINESS PUBLICATION PROFILES. see *ADVERTISING AND PUBLIC RELATIONS*

BUSINESS PUBLISHING; the magazine for desktop publishers. see *COMPUTERS — Personal Computers*

658.8   US   ISSN 0732-6599
Z475
BUY BOOKS WHERE, SELL BOOKS WHERE; a directory of out of print book dealers and their author-subject specialties. 1978. irreg., 8th ed. 1992. $29.75 (effective 1992). Ruth E. Robinson Books, Rt. 7, Box 162A, Morgantown, WV 26505. TEL 304-594-3140. Eds. Ruth E. Robinson, Daryush Farudi. adv.; circ. 3,000.

658.8   AT
C B A A NEWS. 1982. m. membership. Christian Bookselling Association of Australia Inc., P.O. Box 576, Caringbah, N.S.W. 2229, Australia. TEL 02-524-3347. FAX 02-540-3001. Ed. Tony Avent. adv.; bk.rev.; illus.tr.lit.; circ. 300. (back issues avail.)

028.5   US
C B C FEATURES; containing news of the children's book world. 1945. 2/yr. $45. Children's Book Council, Inc., 568 Broadway, New York, NY 10012-3225. TEL 212-966-1990. Ed. John Donovan. bibl.; circ. 40,000. **Indexed**: Child.Lit.Abstr.
Formerly: Calendar (ISSN 0008-0721)
Description: Lists of titles and materials, profiles of authors and publications, and feature articles pertaining to children's literature.

574 700   US
C B E VIEWS. 1978. bi-m. $38. Council of Biology Editors Inc., One Illinois Center, Ste. 200, 111 E. Wacker Dr., Chicago, IL 60601-4298. TEL 312-616-0800. adv.; bk.rev.; circ. 1,200.
Formerly (until 1977): Council of Biology Editors. Newsletter (ISSN 0164-5609)
Description: Forum for the exchange of information among authors, editors, and publishers in the life sciences.

028.5   UK   ISSN 0266-4216
C.B.F. NEWS. 1987. 3/yr. £10 membership. Children's Book Foundation, Book House, 45 East Hill, London SW18 2QZ, England. TEL 01-870-9055.
Formerly: C C B News.
Description: News about the children's book world.

028.5   UK
C B H S NEWSLETTER. s-a. Children's Books History Society, 2 Courtney Crescent, Carshalton Beeches, Surrey SM5 4LZ, England.
Description: Promotes an appreciation of children's books, and the study of their history, bibliography and literary content.

070.5 028.5   CN   ISSN 0319-0080
PN1009.A1
C C L/LITERATURE CANADIENNE POUR LA JEUNESSE. (Canadian Children's Literature) (Text in English, French) 1975. q. $24. Canadian Children's Press, University of Guelph, Dept. of English, Guelph, Ont. N1G 2W1, Canada. FAX 519-837-1315. Ed.Bd. adv.; bk.rev.; bibl.; circ. 1,000. (back issues avail.) **Indexed**: Bk.Rev.Ind. (1980-), Can.Lit.Ind., Can.Per.Ind., Child.Bk.Rev.Ind. (1980-), Child.Lit.Abstr., CMI.
—BLDSC shelfmark: 3019.405000.
Description: Presents reviews and criticism of literature for children.

070.5 020   CK   ISSN 0121-1242
Z490
C E R L A L C: EL LIBRO EN AMERICA LATINA Y EL CARIBE. 1972. q. $18 in Latin America and the Caribbean; elsewhere $22. Centro Regional para el Fomento del Libro en America Latina y el Caribe, Calle 70 No. 9-52, Apdo. Aereo 57438, Bogota, Colombia. TEL 212-60-56. FAX 255-46-14. TELEX 44637 CERLA CO. Ed. Jose Arteaga. adv.; circ. 1,000.
Incorporates (1974-1987): Boletin Bibliografico C E R L A L (ISSN 0120-1204); Former titles (until 1987): C E R L A L C: Noticias sobre el Libro y Bibliografia (ISSN 0120-0887) And (until 1978): Revista de Noticias sobre el Libro y Bibliografia (1018-239X); (until 1978): Noticias C E R L A L C (1018-2381); (until 1977): Noticias C E R L A L (0120-1158).

070.5   US
C L M P NEWSLETTER. 1967-1990; resumed 1991. q. $6. Council of Literary Magazines and Presses, 154 Christopher St., Ste. 3C, New York, NY 10014. TEL 212-714-9110. adv.; bk.rev.; circ. 1,000.
Formerly: C C L M News (ISSN 0273-3315)

070.5   CN   ISSN 0315-6621
C M P A NEWSLETTER. no.63, 1981. 8/yr. Can.$15($15) (typically set in Jun.). Canadian Magazine Publishers Association, 2 Stewart St., Toronto, Ont. M5V 1H6, Canada. TEL 416-362-2546. FAX 416-362-2547. adv.; circ. 600.

C N I D A INFORMA; boletin bimestral de informacion autoral. (Centro Nacional de Informacion - Direccion General del Derecho de Autor) see *BIBLIOGRAPHIES*

655.4   US
C O S M E P NEWSLETTER. (Committee of Small Magazine Editors & Publishers) 1969. m. $60 to non-members (effective Oct. 1991). C O S M E P, Inc., Box 420703, San Francisco, CA 94142-0703. TEL 415-922-9490. Ed. Richard Morris. bk.rev.; circ. 2,500. (back issues avail.)
Former titles (until Feb. 1981): Independent Publisher; (until Jun. 1980): C O S M E P Newsletter (ISSN 0007-8832)

028.1   US   ISSN 0590-711X
C P D A NEWS. 1956. m. Council for Periodical Distributors Associations, 60 E. 42nd St., New York, NY 10165. FAX 212-983-4699. Ed. Tilly McCardell Young. adv.; circ. 4,000 (controlled).

CABIRION: GAY BOOKS BULLETIN. see *HOMOSEXUALITY*

028.1   FR   ISSN 0338-7208
PQ1141
CAHIERS BLEUS. 1975. 3/yr. 210 F. (foreign 350 F.). Amis des Cahiers Bleus, Logis de la Folie, 2 rue Michelet, 10000 Troyes, France. TEL 25-76-11-47. FAX 25-80-80-30. circ. 1,500.
Description: Features reviews of books hot off the press.

CAHIERS D'ACTION LITTERAIRE. see *LITERATURE*

070.5 686   UK
CAMBRIDGE AUTHORS' AND PUBLISHERS' GUIDES. 1951. irreg., latest 1989. price varies. Cambridge University Press, Edinburgh Bldg., Shaftesbury Rd., Cambridge CB2 2RU, England. TEL 0223-312393. FAX 0223-315052.
Formerly: Cambridge Authors' and Printers' Guides (ISSN 0068-6603)

655.5 800   CN   ISSN 0008-2937
CANADIAN AUTHOR & BOOKMAN. 1919. q. Can.$15 to individuals; institutions Can.$25. Canadian Authors Association, 275 Slater St., 5th fl., Ottawa, Ont. K1P 5H9, Canada. TEL 613-233-2846. FAX 613-235-8237. Ed. Gordon Symons. adv.; bk.rev.; illus.; circ. 4,500. (also avail. in microfilm from CML) **Indexed**: Amer.Hum.Ind., Can.Lit.Ind., Can.Per.Ind., CMI, Ind.Bk.Rev.Hum., M.L.A.
Incorporates (in 1968): Canadian Poetry.
Description: Provides market updates on writing in Canada.

CANADIAN AUTHORS ASSOCIATION NEWSLINE. see *LITERATURE*

070.5   CN   ISSN 0576-470X
CANADIAN BOOK PRICES CURRENT. 1955. irreg. price varies. McClelland & Stewart, 481 University Ave., Ste. 900, Toronto, Ont. M5G 2E9, Canada. TEL 416-598-1114. FAX 416-598-7764.

028.1   CN   ISSN 0383-770X
F1001
CANADIAN BOOK REVIEW ANNUAL. 1975. a. Can.$98.95. Simon & Pierre Publishing Co. Ltd., P.O. Box 280, Adelaide St. Sta., Toronto, Ont. M5C 2J4, Canada. TEL 416-463-0313. FAX 416-463-4155. Ed.Bd. bk.rev.; circ. 1,100.
—BLDSC shelfmark: 3017.628000.
Description: Originial short reviews of Canadian trade titles.

PUBLISHING AND BOOK TRADE   4125

655.4 CN ISSN 0008-4859
CANADIAN PUBLISHERS DIRECTORY. (Supplement to: Quill & Quire) 1935. 2/yr. (included with subscr. to Quill and Quire). Key Publishers Co. Ltd., 70 The Esplanade, 4th fl., Toronto, Ont. M5E 1R2, Canada. TEL 416-360-0044. FAX 416-941-9038. Ed. Richard Bingham. adv.; circ. 8,000.

070.5 659.1 US ISSN 0736-9077
CODEN: CCIREV
CAPELL'S CIRCULATION REPORT; the newsletter of magazine circulation. 1982. 20/yr. $327 (foreign $377). Whitaker Newsletters Inc., 313 South Ave., Fanwood, NJ 07023. TEL 908-889-6336. FAX 908-889-6339. (Subscr. to: Box 192, Fanwood, NJ 07023-0192) Ed. Daniel Capell. (back issues avail.)
    Description: Provides current information on what's happening in circulation trends, strategies, tactics and analyses.

CARDOZO ARTS & ENTERTAINMENT LAW JOURNAL. see *LAW*

CARIBBEAN REVIEW OF BOOKS. see *LITERATURE*

070.5 UK
CASSELL AND PUBLISHERS ASSOCIATION DIRECTORY OF PUBLISHING IN THE UNITED KINGDOM, COMMONWEALTH AND OVERSEAS. 1960. a. £35. Cassell Plc., Villiers House, 41-47 Strand, London WC2N 5JE, England. (Subscr. to: Stanley House, Fleets Lane, Poole, Dorset BH15 3AJ) Ed. Jane Deam. adv.; index; circ. 5,000.
    Former titles: Cassell and Publishers Association Directory of Publishing in Great Britain, the Commonwealth, Ireland, South Africa and Pakistan; Cassell's Directory of Publishing in Great Britain, the Commonwealth, Ireland, South Africa and Pakistan (ISSN 0308-7018); Cassell's Directory of Publishing in Great Britain, The Commonwealth, Ireland and South Africa (ISSN 0069-097X)
    Description: Gives current details of all publishers in Great Britain and overseas: name, address, imprints, type of books published, key personnel, number of new titles published yearly.

070.5 UK
▼**CASSELL, PUBLISHERS ASSOCIATION AND THE FEDERATION OF EUROPEAN PUBLISHERS ASSOCIATIONS. DIRECTORY OF PUBLISHING IN CONTINENTAL EUROPE.** 1991. a. £50. Cassell Plc., Villiers House, 41-47 Strand, London WC2N 5JE, England.

CATALOG AGE. see *ADVERTISING AND PUBLIC RELATIONS*

070.5 US
Z649.F35
CATALOG OF PUBLISHER INFORMATION. 1978. s-a. Copyright Clearance Center, Inc., 27 Congress St., Salem, MA 01970. TEL 508-744-3350. FAX 508-741-2318.
    Former titles: Publishers' Photocopy Fee Catalog (ISSN 0887-2929); Permissions to Photocopy: Publishers' Fee List.
    Description: Directory of titles registered with the Copyright Clearance Center by participating publishers. Provides registered users with information needed to report photocopying activity.

070.5 IT
CATALOGO DEGLI EDITORI ITALIANI. a. L.68000. Editrice Bibliografica s.r.l., Viale Vittorio Veneto 24, 20124 Milan, Italy. TEL 02-6597950. circ. 2,315.
●Also available online.
    Description: Catalogue of Italian book publishers and distributors.

THE CATHOLIC. see *RELIGIONS AND THEOLOGY — Roman Catholic*

CENTER FOR CHILDREN'S BOOKS. BULLETIN. see *BIBLIOGRAPHIES*

070.5 BE
CERCLE BELGE DE LA LIBRAIRIE. ANNUAIRE.* 1926. a. 1060 Fr. Cercle Belge de la Librairie (CBL), 140 Blvd. Lanbermont, 1030 Brussels, Belgium.

070.5 US
CHICAGO GUIDES TO WRITING, EDITING, AND PUBLISHING. 1971. irreg., latest 1990. price varies. University of Chicago Press, 5801 S. Ellis Ave., Chicago, IL 60637. TEL 312-702-7899. (Subscr. to: 11030 Langley Ave., Chicago, IL 60628)
Refereed Serial

028.5 CN ISSN 0705-0038
CHILDRENS BOOK NEWS. 1979. 4/yr. Can.$25 (membership). Canadian Children's Book Centre, 35 Spadina Rd., Toronto, Ont. M5R 2S9, Canada. TEL 416-975-0010. FAX 416-975-1839. Ed. Debbie Rogosin. bk.rev.; illus.; circ. 35,000. **Indexed:** Bk.Rev.Ind. (1987-), Child.Bk.Rev.Ind. (1987-).
    Former titles (until 1983): Book News Times; Book Times (ISSN 0706-1064)

028.5 US ISSN 0090-7987
Z1037.A1
CHILDREN'S BOOK REVIEW SERVICE. 1972. m. (plus two supplements). $40. Children's Book Review Service Inc., 220 Berkeley Pl., No. 1-D, Brooklyn, NY 11217. Ed. Ann L. Kalkhoff. bk.rev.; circ. 300. (looseleaf format) **Indexed:** Bk.Rev.Ind. (1979-), Child.Bk.Rev.Ind. (1979-).

070.5 US ISSN 0069-3472
Z1037.A2
CHILDREN'S BOOKS: AWARDS AND PRIZES. 1969. irreg. $50. Children's Book Council, Inc., 568 Broadway, New York, NY 10012-3225. TEL 212-966-1990. Ed. John Donovan. index; circ. 6,000.
    Description: International compilation of 125 children's book awards, with sponsor's address, description of award and winners.

028.5 UK ISSN 0266-4232
CHILDREN'S BOOKS OF THE YEAR. 1971. a. Book Trust, Book House, 45 East Hill, Wandsworth, London SW18 2QZ, England. FAX 081-874-4790.
    Description: An independent selector's choice of the best children's books.

CHILDREN'S BOOKS OF THE YEAR. see *CHILDREN AND YOUTH — For*

070.5 US
CHILDREN'S BOOKS: ONE HUNDRED TITLES FOR READING AND SHARING. 1911. a. $3. New York Public Library, Office of Branch Libraries, 455 Fifth Ave., New York, NY 10016. TEL 212-340-0892. FAX 212-689-3193.
    Former titles: Children's Books and Recordings: Suggested as Holiday Gifts; Children's Books: Suggested as Holiday Gifts (ISSN 0069-3502)

070.5 808.068 700 US ISSN 0897-9790
CHILDREN'S WRITER'S AND ILLUSTRATOR'S MARKET. a. $17.95. F & W Publications, Inc., 1507 Dana Ave., Cincinnati, OH 45207. TEL 513-531-2222. FAX 513-531-4744. Ed. Lisa Carpenter.
    Description: Provides information on book publishing and magazine markets for both writers and illustrators of children's publishing. Contains advice to help market one's work.

070.5 CC
CHINA BOOKS. (Text in Chinese and English) 1981. q. Guiji Shudian, Qikan Bu, P.O. Box 339, Beijing 100044, People's Republic of China. bk.rev.

CHIPS OFF THE WRITER'S BLOCK. see *JOURNALISM*

CHRISTIAN LIBRARIAN. see *LIBRARY AND INFORMATION SCIENCES*

658.8 200 US ISSN 0749-2510
BV2369
CHRISTIAN RETAILING; the trade magazine of religious retailing. 1955. m. $24. Strang Communications Co., 600 Rinehart Rd., Lake Mary, FL 32746. TEL 407-333-0600. Ed. Brian Peterson. adv.; bk.rev.; circ. 9,800. (reprint service avail. from UMI)
    Formerly: Christian Bookseller (ISSN 0009-5273)

070.5 CC
CHUBAN FAXING YANJIU/PUBLISHING AND DISTRIBUTING RESEARCH. (Text in Chinese) bi-m. Zhongguo Chuban Kexue Yanjiusuo, No. A-7, Xirongxian Hutong, Xicheng-qu, Beijing 100031, People's Republic of China. TEL 657231. Ed. Zhao Haishen.

070.5 CC ISSN 1001-2680
CHUBAN GONGZUO/PUBLISHING AFFAIRS. (Text in Chinese) m. Xinwen Chubanshu, No. 85, Dongsi Nandajie, Beijing 100703, People's Republic of China. TEL 555415. Ed. Teng Mingdao.

070.5 CC
CHUBAN SHILIAO/HISTORICAL MATERIAL ON PUBLISHING. (Text in Chinese) 1982. q. $10. Shanghai Chuban Gongzuozhe Xiehui - Shanghai Publishers Association, 5 Shaoxing Road, Shanghai 200020, People's Republic of China. TEL 4370176. FAX 86-21-433245. Eds. Song Yuanfang, Zhao Jiabi. bk.rev.; circ. 2,500.

028.1 015 KO ISSN 0009-6245
Z464.K67
CH'ULPAN MOONWHA/KOREAN BOOK JOURNAL. (Text in Korean) 1948. m. 1,000 Won($1.50) Korean Publishers Association, 105-2 Sagan-dong, Chongno-ku, Seoul 110-190, S. Korea. TEL 02-735-2701. FAX 02-738-5414. Ed. Lee Doo-Young. adv.; bk.rev.; bibl.; circ. 1,700.

070.5 US ISSN 0888-8191
PN4784.C6 CODEN: CIRMEZ
CIRCULATION MANAGEMENT. 1986. m. $22 to individuals; free to qualified personnel (foreign $89). Ganesa Corporation, 611 Broadway, Ste. 401, New York, NY 10012-2608. TEL 212-989-2133. FAX 212-620-0396. Ed. James Fischer. adv.; bk.rev.; circ. 10,000 (controlled). (reprint service avail.)
    Description: Trade publication for circulation executives and publishers in the magazine and newsletter publishing industry. Covers subscriptions, renewals, controlled circulation, ABC, BPA, postal, fulfillment and more.

CIVIL AND MILITARY REVIEW. see *MILITARY*

CLASSIFIED ADVERTISING REPORT; the newsletter for classified publishers and advertisers. see *ADVERTISING AND PUBLIC RELATIONS*

658.8 UK
COLE'S REGISTER OF BRITISH ANTIQUARIAN & SECONDHAND BOOKDEALERS. 1986. a. £22. Clique, Ltd., 7 Pulleyn Drive, York YO2 2DY, England. TEL 0904-631752. FAX 0904-651325.

070.5 686 US ISSN 1055-9701
Z48
▼**COLOR PUBLISHING.** 1991. 6/yr. $19 (foreign $28). PennWell Publishing Co. (Westford), One Technology Park Dr., Westford, MA 01886. TEL 508-392-2157. FAX 508-692-0525. (Subscr. to: Box 2709, Tulsa, OK 74101) Ed. Frank Romano. adv.; illus.; circ. 24,000 (controlled).
    Description: Covers new developments in color publishing technology for the technical professional.

070.5 686 US
▼**COLOUR.** 1991. m. free to qualified personnel. Ulick Publishing Co., Box 8551, Bartlett, IL 60103. TEL 708-213-1300. Ed. Terry Ulick. adv.; illus.; circ. 80,000 (controlled).
    Description: Covers news of emerging color publishing technologies and new products for the technical professional.

COMIC ART COLLECTION. see *LIBRARY AND INFORMATION SCIENCES*

COMICS JOURNAL; the magazine of news & criticism. see *ART*

659.1 US
COMPARABILITY UPDATE. bi-m. Business Publications Audit of Circulations, Inc., 360 Park Ave. S., New York, NY 10010. TEL 212-532-6880. FAX 212-752-1721.

070.5 US
COMPETITIVE PUBLISHING HOTLINE. 1983. m. $150. David Foster & Associates, Inc., 360 Hayward Ave., Mt. Vernon, NY 10552. TEL 914-699-9414. adv. (back issues avail.)
    Formerly: Circulation Hotline.

COMPUTER BOOK REVIEW. see *COMPUTERS*

COMPUTERITER; microcomputer news and views for the writer-editor. see *COMPUTERS — Personal Computers*

P
Q

PUBLISHING AND BOOK TRADE

CONCEPTS IN COMMUNICATION INFORMATICS AND LIBRARIANSHIP. see *LIBRARY AND INFORMATION SCIENCES*

070.5 792   SA   ISSN 0250-2003
CONTACTS. (Text in English) 1978. a. free. Limelight Publications C.C., P.O. Box 760, Randpark Ridge 2125, South Africa. TEL 011-793-7231. FAX 011-792-2679. Ed. Jennifer van Staden. adv.; index; circ. 5,000. (back issues avail.)

CONTEMPORARY JAPANESE BOOKS. see *BIBLIOGRAPHIES*

070.5   US   ISSN 1044-2332
CODEN: RCCCEJ
COPYRIGHT CLEARANCE CENTER. REPORT. 1984. q. $10 (foreign $12). Copyright Clearance Center, Inc., 27 Congress St., Salem, MA 01970. TEL 508-744-3350. FAX 508-741-2318.
Formerly: Photocopy Authorizations Report (ISSN 0884-6146)
Description: Publicizes Copyright Clearance Center's services and activities, and reports general news of the copyright community for publishers and users of copyrighted material.

070.5   US
▼**THE CORNERSTONE (NEW PROVIDENCE).** 1992. bi-m. free to qualified personnel. R.R. Bowker, A Reed Reference Publishing Company, Division of Reed Publishing (USA) Inc., 121 Chanlon Rd., New Providence, NJ 07974. TEL 800-521-8110. FAX 908-665-6688. TELEX 138 755. (Subscr. to: Order Dept., Box 31, New Providence, NJ 07974) Ed. Valerie Berk.

070.5   CK   ISSN 0121-1390
CORREO EDITORIAL; revista informativa de la C C L. 1989. q. free. Camara Colombiana del Libro, Carrera 17A, No. 37-27, Bogota, Colombia. TEL 2886188. FAX 2873320. adv.; bk.rev.; abstr.; illus.; stat.

CRITICAL REVIEW; an interdisciplinary journal. see *LITERARY AND POLITICAL REVIEWS*

028.1   FR   ISSN 0011-1600
Z1007
CRITIQUE; revue generale des publications Francaises et etrangeres. 1946. m. 445 F. (foreign 565 F.). Editions de Minuit, 7 rue Bernard-Palissy, 75006 Paris, France. TEL 1-45-44-23-16. Ed. Jean Piel. adv.; bk.rev.; charts; play rev.; index. **Indexed:** Arts & Hum.Cit.Ind., Ind.Bk.Rev.Hum., Lang.& Lang.Behav.Abstr., M.L.A.
—BLDSC shelfmark: 3487.490000.

CUMULATIVE BOOK INDEX. see *BIBLIOGRAPHIES*

028.1   CN   ISSN 0316-9448
CURRENT CANADIAN BOOKS/LIVRES CANADIENS COURANTS. 1971. m. Can.$36. John Coutts Library Services Ltd., 6900 Kinsmen, P.O. Box 1000, Niagara Falls, Ont. L2E 7E7, Canada. TEL 416-364-9919. FAX 416-356-5064. TELEX 061-5299. Ed. John R. Grantier. circ. 100 (controlled).
Formerly: Current Canadian Imprints Catalogued.

D K NEWSLETTER; a journal of news and reviews of Indian publications in English. see *BIBLIOGRAPHIES*

070.5 658.8   GW   ISSN 0343-5598
D N V. (Der Neue Vertrieb) 1949. m. DM.144 (foreign DM.155). Presse Fachverlag, Eidelstedteweg 22, 2000 Hamburg 20, Germany. TEL 040-565031. FAX 040-5602920. adv.; bk.rev.; illus.; mkt.; tr.lit.; circ. 1,800.
Description: Trade publication for paperback book, magazine, and newspaper businesses, featuring news, reports of events, and market information.

070.5   SP   ISSN 0214-2694
DELIBROS; revista professional del libro. (English summary avail.) 1988. m (11/yr.). 6300 ptas. (foreign 11500 ptas.). Delibros, S.A., Principe de Vergara, 136, 1o, 28002 Madrid, Spain. TEL 564-13-13. FAX 564-27-40. Ed. Carmen Fernandez de Blas. adv.; bk.rev.; bibl.; illus.

DESKTOP PUBLISHING TODAY. see *PUBLISHING AND BOOK TRADE — Computer Applications*

070.5   GW
DEUTSCHES VERLAGSREGISTER; Verlage mit ihrem periodischen Schrifttum. 1970. irreg. DM.52. Stamm Verlag GmbH, Goldammerweg 16, 4300 Essen 1, Germany. Ed. Willy Stamm. adv.; bibl.; circ. 1,500.

070.5   GW
Z317
DEUTSCHSPRACHIGE VERLAGE. 1950. a. DM.110. Verlag der Schillerbuchhandlung Hans Banger, Guldenbachstr. 1, 5000 Cologne 41, Germany. TEL 0221-431641.
Formerly: Anschriften Deutscher Verlage und Auslandischer Verlage mit Deutschen Auslieferungen (ISSN 0066-4596)

090.75   US   ISSN 0012-2874
PS374.D5
DIME NOVEL ROUND-UP; devoted to the collecting, preservation and literature of the old time dime and nickel novels, libraries and popular story papers. 1931. bi-m. $10. Edward T. LeBlanc, Ed. & Pub., 87 School St., Fall River, MA 02720. TEL 508-672-2082. adv.; bk.rev.; cum.index. every 5 yrs.; circ. 400. **Indexed:** M.L.A.
Formerly: Reckless Ralph's Dime Novel Round-Up.

960 028 016   UK
DIPLOMATIC BOOKSHELF & REVIEW. 1957. m. £2. Arthur H. Thrower Ltd., 44-46 S. Ealing Rd., London W5, England. Ed. Arthur H. Thrower. adv.; bk.rev.; charts; illus.; tr.lit.; bibl. (also avail. in microform from UMI; back issues avail.; reprint service avail. from UMI)
Former titles: Diplomatic Bookshelf (ISSN 0012-3080); African Bookshelf (ISSN 0001-995X)

027.7   US   ISSN 0360-473X
Z671
DIRECTIONS (BRIDGEWATER); monthly journal for academic & research libraries. 1974. m. free. Baker & Taylor Books, 652 E. Main St., Box 6920, Bridgewater, NJ 08807-0920. TEL 908-218-0400. FAX 908-218-3980. adv.; bk.rev.; illus.; circ. 8,000 (controlled). (also avail. in microfiche)
Supersedes: Current Books for Academic Libraries (ISSN 0011-3352)
Description: Bibliographic selections from Baker and Taylor Books' academic approval program.

380 011 070.5   US   ISSN 0894-346X
Z286.D57
DIRECTORY MARKETPLACE. 1987. q. $25 (foreign $30). Todd Publications, 18 N. Greenbush Rd., W. Nyack, NY 10994. TEL 914-358-6213. Ed. Barry T. Klein. adv.; bk.rev.; circ. 25,000. (back issues avail.)
Description: Reports on new directories and reference books of interest to business and to libraries.

DIRECTORY OF AMERICAN POETS AND FICTION WRITERS. see *LITERATURE — Poetry*

070.5   US
Z475
DIRECTORY OF BOOK PRINTERS. 1984. a. $15. Ad-Lib Publications, 51 1/2 W. Adams, Box 1102, Fairfield, IA 52556-1102. TEL 515-472-6617. FAX 515-472-3186. Ed. Marie Kiefer. adv.; bibl.; charts; index; circ. 10,000. (back issues avail.)
Former titles (until 1991): Directory of Book, Catalog, and Magazine Printers (ISSN 0895-139X); Directory of Short-Run Book Printers.
Description: Includes over 900 U.S. and Canadian printers. Pinpoints specializations: quantities, sizes and bindings.

070.5   UK
DIRECTORY OF BOOK PUBLISHERS, DISTRIBUTORS AND WHOLESALERS. a. Booksellers Association of Great Britain and Ireland, 272 Vauxhall Bridge Rd., London SW1V 1BA, England. TEL 071-834-5477. FAX 071-834-8812.
Former titles: Directory of Book Publishers and Wholesalers; Directory of Book Publishers, Wholesalers and Their Terms.

070.5   CN
DIRECTORY OF CANADIAN CONSULTANTS, COPYWRITERS & CONTRACT PUBLISHERS. 1987. a. $18. 20 Tettenhall Rd., Etobicoke, Ont. M9A 2C3, Canada. TEL 416-231-7796.
Description: Listings of hard-to-find freelancers specializing in magazine and direct marketing field.

070.5   US
DIRECTORY OF EDITORS & PUBLISHERS. irreg., 20th ed., 1989-1990. Dustbooks, Box 100, Paradise, CA 95967. TEL 916-877-6110.
Description: Lists names, addresses, and phone numbers of editors and publishers, and the magazine or press with which they are associated.

659.1   US
DIRECTORY OF MARKET COMPARABILITY PROGRAMS & MEMBERSHIP. a. Business Publications Audit of Circulations, Inc., 360 Park Ave. S., New York, NY 10010. TEL 212-532-6880. FAX 212-725-1721.
Description: Serves as a guide to BPA's Market Comparability Programs and Market Classifications.

070.5   US
DIRECTORY OF MICHIGAN LITERARY PUBLISHERS. s-a. Poetry Resource Center of Michigan, 111 E. Kirby, Detroit, MI 48202. Ed. Leonard Kniffeld.
Description: Directory of literary publishers in Michigan.

070.5 011   II   ISSN 0970-9266
DIRECTORY OF PERIODICALS PUBLISHED IN INDIA. (Text in English and regional languages) 1988. biennial. Rs.500($80) Sapra & Sapra Publishers Distributors Pvt. Ltd., 51 Ring Road, Lajpat Nagar III, New Delhi 110 024, India. TEL 683-7040.
Description: Provides information on approximately 7,200 journals, bulletins, video magazines, a few widely circulated newspapers, proceedings and transactions of the learned bodies and government departments.

DIRECTORY OF POETRY PUBLISHERS. see *LITERATURE — Poetry*

020.75   US
DIRECTORY OF PUBLICATIONS RESOURCES. 1981. biennial. $12. Editorial Experts, Inc., 66 Canal Center Plaza, Ste. 200, Alexandria, VA 22314. TEL 703-683-0683. FAX 703-683-4915.
Formerly: Directory of Editorial Resources.
Description: Lists the best courses, books, periodicals, competitions, software, tools and organizations for professional publications people.

070.5   SA   ISSN 1018-7626
▼**DIRECTORY OF SOUTH AFRICAN PUBLISHERS;** with addresses and ISBN identifiers. (Text in Afrikaans, English) 1991. 2/yr. Stat Library - Staatsbiblioteek, P.O. Box 397, Pretoria 0001, South Africa. TEL 012-218931. FAX 012-325-5984. TELEX 3-22171 SA.

658.8   UK
DIRECTORY OF SPECIALIST BOOKDEALERS IN THE UK HANDLING MAINLY NEW BOOKS. 1978. triennial. £15. Peter Marcan Publications, 31 Rowliff Rd., High Wycombe, Bucks HP12 3LD, England. adv.; circ. 750.
Description: Subject classified annotated guide to specialist book outlets throughout the UK.

070.5   JA
DIRECTORY OF THE JAPANESE PUBLISHING INDUSTRY. (Text in English) 1970. biennial. free. Publishers Association for Cultural Exchange, 1-2-1 Sarugaku-cho, Chiyoda-ku, Tokyo 101, Japan. FAX 03-3233-3645. Ed. Hiroyasu Ochiai.
Formerly: Guide to Publishers and Related Industries in Japan.

070.5 296   IS
DIRECTORY OF WORLD JEWISH PRESS AND PUBLICATIONS. (Text in English) 1984. a. $23. P.O. Box 7699, Jerusalem 91 076, Israel. Ed. Yitzhak Rogow. adv.; circ. 2,000. (reprint service avail.)

658.809   US   ISSN 0012-5261
DOLPHIN BOOK CLUB NEWS. 1956. 15/yr. membership. Book-Of-The-Month Club, Time & Life Bldg., 1271 Ave. of the Americas, New York, NY 10020. TEL 212-522-4200. Dir. Laura Friedman. adv.; bk.rev.; circ. 50,000.

070.5 686.2   US
DUNN REPORT; electronic publishing & prepress systems news & views. 1983. m. $295. Dunn Technology, Inc., 1855 E. Vista Way, No. 1, Vista, CA 92084. FAX 619-758-5401. Ed. Patrice M. Dunn. (back issues avail.) **Indexed:** Print.Abstr.
Description: Focus on technological developments for the graphic arts and corporate publishing industries.

PUBLISHING AND BOOK TRADE   4127

DUNOON OBSERVER & ARGYLLSHIRE STANDARD. see *PRINTING*

070.5   US   ISSN 1042-3737
E P S I G NEWS. 4/yr. $50 or membership fee. Electronic Publishing Special Interest Group, c/o OCLC, 6565 Frantz Rd., Dublin, OH 43017-0702. —BLDSC shelfmark: 3794.398100.
Description: Covers new product announcements, user information, meeting announcements, and case studies from organizations and individuals using the Electronic Manuscript Standard for a variety of publishing ventures.

070.5   GW
E S V SORTIMENTER INFORMATIONEN RECHT - WIRTSCHAFT - TECHNIK - UMWELT - PHILOLOGIE; titel und termine. 1950. m. free. Erich Schmidt Verlag GmbH & Co. (Bielefeld), Viktoriastr. 44a, Postfach 7330, 4800 Bielefeld 1, Germany. TEL 0521-583080. adv.; circ. 2,000.
Formerly: E S V Programmbereiche Recht - Wirtschaft - Technik - Umwelt.

EDITIO; internationales Jahrbuch fuer Editionswissenschaft. see *LITERATURE*

070   BL
EDITOR (RIO DE JANEIRO). 1980. 6/yr. $30. Editora Metodos Ltda., Caixa Postal 15085, Rua Cardoso Marinho, 42, 20220 Rio de Janeiro RJ, Brazil. Ed. J.M. Lopez Barreto. circ. 3,000.

070.5   US   ISSN 0193-7383
CODEN: EDEYDQ
EDITORIAL EYE; focusing on publications standards and practices. 1978. 12/yr. $87. Editorial Experts, Inc., 66 Canal Center Plaza, Ste. 200, Alexandria, VA 22314. TEL 703-683-0683. FAX 703-683-4915. Ed. Ann R. Molpus. bk.rev.; index; circ. 2,500. (looseleaf format; back issues avail.) **Indexed:** Graph.Arts Lit.Abstr.
Description: Covers editing, proofreading, publications management and language usage. Includes reviews of publishing software.

070.5   US
EDITOR'S DIGEST. 1989. q. $15. Quadriga Publishing, 1613 Chelsea Rd., Ste. 311, San Marino, CA 91108. Ed. Bill Reinshagen. adv.; bk.rev.; circ. 400.
Description: Covers the nuts and bolts of small press publishing and editing, including literary, scholarly, professional and organization publishing.

070.5   NR   ISSN 0794-5655
EDITORS' FORUM; focusing on publications standards & practices. (Text in English) 1986. q. £N50($20) Codat Publications, P.O. Box 9400, U.I. Ibadan, Nigeria. TEL 022-314411. Ed. C.O. Adejuwon. circ. 1,000.

686 070 378   US   ISSN 0888-3173
PN4778
EDITORS' NOTES. 1982. 2/yr. $30. Council of Editors of Learned Journals, c/o Prof. John N. Serio, Department of Liberal Studies, Clarkson University, Potsdam, NY 13699-5750. (Affiliate: Modern Language Association) Ed. Edna L. Steeves. adv.; bk.rev.; circ. 450. (back issues avail.) **Indexed:** Abstr.Engl.Stud.; M.L.A.

070.5 370   US   ISSN 0013-1806
EDUCATIONAL MARKETER. 1969. 36/yr. $295. Simba Information, Inc., Box 7430, Wilton, CT 06897. TEL 203-834-0033. FAX 203-834-1771. Ed. Glenn Sanislo. adv.
●Also available online. Vendor(s): DIALOG, NewsNet.

028.1   US
ELECTRONIC BOOKSTORE FOR EXECUTIVES. m. High Tech Publishing Company, Box 1923, Brattleboro, VT 05301. TEL 802-254-3539. bk.rev.
●Also available online. Vendor(s): Data-Star, NewsNet.
Description: Covers new books of special interest to executives and managers.

ELECTRONIC PRINTING SYSTEMS: PROFESSIONAL ELECTRONIC PUBLISHING CONFERENCE PROCEEDINGS. see *PRINTING*

070.5   US   ISSN 0887-1876
ELECTRONIC PUBLISHING & PRINTING. Short title: E P & P. m. (9/yr.). $35 (Canada $45; elsewhere $60). Maclean Hunter Publishing Company, 29 N. Wacker Dr., Chicago, IL 60606. TEL 312-726-2802. FAX 312-726-2574.

ENTERTAINMENT LAW REPORTER; motion pictures, television, radio, music, theater, publishing, sports. see *LAW*

ENTERTAINMENT, PUBLISHING AND THE ARTS HANDBOOK. see *COMMUNICATIONS — Television And Cable*

090.78   US
EPHEMERA NEWS.* 1981. q. $25. Ephemera Society of America, c/o Richard Friz, Box 472, Peterborough, NH 03458. adv.; bk.rev.; bibl.; illus.; circ. 600. (tabloid format; back issues avail.)

070.483   US
EROTIC WRITER'S AND COLLECTOR'S MARKET. 1988. s-a. $14.95 per no. Michael Drax, Ed. & Pub., Box 20593, Sun Valley, NV 89433. adv.; index; circ. 1,000.
Description: Market listing of publishers and producers of erotic and sexual publications, videos, audios, software and clubs.

070   IT
ESOPO; rivista trimestrale di bibliofilia. 1979. q. L.160000. Edizioni Rovello, Via Rovello 1, 20121 Milan, Italy. FAX 02-72022884. Ed. Mario Scognamiglio. adv.; bk.rev.; circ. 4,750.

070.5   GW
DER EULENHOF BERATERBRIEF. 1982. bi-m. DM.180. Heinold Personal und Unternehmensberatung GmbH, Eulenhof, 2351 Hardebek, Germany. TEL 04324-502. FAX 04324-8146. Ed. Wolfgang Ehrhardt Heinold. adv.; bk.rev.; circ. 3,500.
Former titles: Eulenhof Basterbrief; Eulenhof Information; Eulenhof-Brief.

070.5   UK
Z1003.5.G7
THE EUROMONITOR BOOK REPORT (YEAR). 1975. biennial. £325($650) Euromonitor, 87-88 Turnmill St., London EC1M 5QU, England. TEL 071-251 8024. FAX 071-608-3149. (back issues avail.)
●Also available online.
Former titles: U K Book Report & Book Report (ISSN 0142-7628)
Description: Offers market analysis of the buying, selling and reading of books in the UK.

016 028   GW   ISSN 0014-391X
EX LIBRIS; Aktueller Buchdienst fuer Studenten und Dozenten der Rechts, Wirtschafts, und Informatik. 1963. s-a. DM.50. Ex Libris-Verlag, Schwalbenweg 21, 5020 Frechen 4, Germany. TEL 02234-63580. FAX 02234-63886. bk.rev.; bibl.; circ. 10,000.

070.5 900   US   ISSN 1042-6647
EX LIBRIS (PORTSMOUTH). 1988. bi-m. $25. New Hampshire Writers & Publishers Project, 855 Islington St., Ste. 210, Box 150, Portsmouth, NH 03802-0150. TEL 603-436-6331. Ed. Barbara Tsairis. adv.; bk.rev.; circ. 400. (back issues avail.)
Description: Articles and network by and for New Hampshire writers and publishers. Includes listings, leads and calendars.

020.75 740
790.132   FR   ISSN 0395-269X
EX LIBRIS FRANCAIS. (Text in French; summaries in English, German, Italian, Spanish) 1936. q. 145 F. Association Francaise pour la Connaissance de l'Ex Libris, Bibliotheque Municipale, 43 rue Stanislas, 54042 Nancy Cedex, France. Ed. L. Demezieres. adv.; bk.rev.; illus.; circ. 250.

097   DK   ISSN 0014-4681
EXLIBRIS-NYT. 1960. 4/yr. membership. Dansk Exlibris Selskab - Danish Bookplate Society, Postbox 1519, DK-2700 Copenhagen, Denmark. Ed. Helmer Fogedgaard. illus.; circ. 400.

070.5   II
EXPORT NEWS. (Text in English) vol.9, 1978. bi-m. Rs.30($15) People's Publishing House Private Ltd., 5E Rani Jhansi Rd., New Delhi 110055, India. bk.rev. **Indexed:** Key to Econ.Sci., So.Pac.Per.Ind.

FACHLITERATUR ZUM BUCH- UND BIBLIOTHEKSWESEN/INTERNATIONAL BIBLIOGRAPHY OF THE BOOK TRADE AND LIBRARIANSHIP. see *LIBRARY AND INFORMATION SCIENCES*

028.1   US   ISSN 0890-6823
FACTSHEET FIVE.* 1982. 6/yr. $20. Box 8615, Prairie Village, KS 66208-0615. TEL 404-876-0356. Ed. Hudson Luce. adv.; bk.rev.; music rev.; circ. 7,500. (back issues avail.)
Description: Comprehensive review of the underground and alternative press, also covering music and comic zines, poetry and small press publications, video productions, software, and electronic bulletin board services.

070.5   AG
FEDERACION ARGENTINA DE PERIODISTAS. GACETA.* 1970. a. Federacion Argentina de Periodistas, Esmeralda 356, 1035 Buenos Aires, Argentina. illus.

070.5   II
FEDERATION OF PUBLISHERS AND BOOKSELLERS ASSOCIATIONS IN INDIA. NEWSLETTER. (Text in English) 1981. q. free. Federation of Publishers and Booksellers Associations in India, 4833-24 Govind Ln., Ansari Rd., New Delhi-110002, India. Ed. Vindo Kumar. adv.; bk.rev.; index; circ. 2,000.

323.4 305.4157
070.5   US   ISSN 0741-6555
FEMINIST BOOKSTORE NEWS. 1976. bi-m. Can.$69($60) (foreign $19)(effective Jan. 1991). Box 882554, San Francisco, CA 94188. TEL 415-626-1556. FAX 415-626-8970. Ed. Carol Seajay. adv.; bk.rev.; bibl.; stat.; tr.lit.; circ. 600. (back issues avail.)
Formerly: Feminist Bookstores Newsletter.
Description: News briefs, feature articles, and reader correspondence pertaining to feminist bookselling and publishing. Reviews over 300 titles per issue.

FEMINIST COLLECTIONS; a quarterly of women's studies resources. see *WOMEN'S STUDIES*

070.5 686 011   IT
FIERA DEL LIBRO. bi-m. Edizioni Pegaso s.a.s., Galleria Mazzini, 3-13, 16121 Genoa, Italy. Ed. Marina Seveso.

FILLERS FOR PUBLICATIONS; the editorial tool that eliminates deadline pressures. see *JOURNALISM*

FINE PRINT; the review for the arts of the book. see *PRINTING*

686   US
FIRST IMPRESSIONS. 1984. 2/yr. membership. (Institute for the Book Arts) University of Alabama, Box 870252, Tuscaloosa, AL 35487-0252. TEL 205-348-4990. FAX 205-348-3746. TELEX BITNET PGOURLEY. Ed. Paula Marie Gourley. bk.rev.; circ. 2,200.
Description: Keeps the Book Arts community and collectors of fine printing and bookbinding abreast of the activities and publications of the Institute and the M.F.A. Program in the Book Arts.

090.75   US
FIRSTS: COLLECTING MODERN FIRST EDITIONS. m. Lucerne Group, 575 N. Lucerne Blvd., Los Angeles, CA 90004. TEL 213-469-9189. Ed. Robin H. Smiley.

FIVE OWLS; a publication for readers, personally and professionally involved in children's literature. see *CHILDREN AND YOUTH — About*

070.5   US
FLASH MARKET NEWS. 1940. m. $50 to non-members. National Writers Club, 1450 S. Havana, Ste. 620, Aurora, CO 80012. TEL 303-751-7844. Ed. Sandy Whelchel. circ. 1,500.

028   NE   ISSN 0015-3540
DE FLEANENDE KRIE. (Text in Frisian) 1954. 3/yr. membership. Kristlik Fryske Folks Bibleteek, Hid Heroplantsoen 1, 8701 BS Bolsward, Friesland, Netherlands. Ed.Bd. adv.; bk.rev.; bibl.; illus.

658.809   UK   ISSN 0015-5772
FOLIO. 1947. q. membership. Folio Society Ltd., 202 Great Suffolk St., London SE1 1PR, England. TEL 071-407-7411. FAX 071-378-6684. Ed. Sue Bradbury. adv.; bk.rev.; illus.; circ. 48,000. (also avail. in microfilm from UMI; reprint service avail. from UMI)

PUBLISHING AND BOOK TRADE

655.5   US   ISSN 0046-4333
PN4734
FOLIO (STAMFORD); the magazine for magazine management. 1972. m. $68 (Canada and Mexico $82). Cowles Business Media (Subsidiary of: Cowles Media Company), Six River Bend Center, 911 Hope St., Box 4949, Stamford, CT 06907-0949. TEL 203-358-9900. FAX 203-357-9014. Ed. Barbara Love. adv.; bk.rev.; index; circ. 12,000. (also avail. in microform from UMI,MIM; back issues avail.; reprint service avail. from UMI) Indexed: Tr.& Indus.Ind.
● Also available online. Vendor(s): DIALOG.
—BLDSC shelfmark: 3974.395000.

655.5   US
FOLIO: SOURCE BOOK. (Special issue of Folio magazine) a. Folio Publishing Corp. (Subsidiary of: Cowles Media Company), 911 Hope St., Six River Bend Center, Box 4949, Stamford, CT 06907-0949. Ed. Barbara Love.

070.5   US   ISSN 1043-8688
Z286.P4
FOLIO'S PUBLISHING NEWS; news magazine of magazine publishing. 1988. m. Cowles Business Media (Subsidiary of: Cowles Media Company), Six River Bend Center, 911 Hope St., Box 4949, Stamford, CT 06907-0949. TEL 203-358-9900. FAX 203-357-9014. Ed. Sean Callahan. circ. 24,000. (tabloid format; reprint service avail. from UMI)

070.5   IT
FONDAZIONE FELTRINELLI. QUADERNI. 4/yr. L.90000 (foreign L.110000)(effective 1992). Franco Angeli Editore, Viale Monza, 106, Casella Postale 17175, 20100 Milan, Italy. TEL 02-2895762.

028.1 664   UK   ISSN 0142-2545
FOOD BOOKS REVIEW; the international journal for readers of books on food technology subjects. 1978. q. £12. Food Trade Press Ltd., Station House, Hortons Way, Westerham, Kent TN16 1BZ, England. TEL 0959-563944. FAX 0959-561285. Ed. Howard Binsted. circ. 6,420.
—BLDSC shelfmark: 3977.072000.

020   US   ISSN 0098-213X
FORECAST (BRIDGEWATER); a prepublication announcement journal of hardcover and trade-paper titles (adult and children's) for public libraries. 1969. m. free. Baker & Taylor Books, 652 E. Main St., Box 6920, Bridgewater, NJ 08807-0920. TEL 908-218-0400. FAX 908-218-3980. adv.; bk.rev.; illus.; circ. 22,000 (controlled).
 Formerly: New Books Preview Bulletin.
 Description: Announcement journal of new and forthcoming adult and children's books.

070.5   DK   ISSN 0109-405X
FORLAGSVEJVISER. 1984. a. DKK 258.45. Bibliotekscentralen, Tempovej 7-11, DK-2750 Ballerup, Denmark. TEL 2-974000. FAX 2-655310.

655   FR   ISSN 0078-9666
FRANCE. IMPRIMERIE NATIONALE. ANNUAIRE.. 1962. a. Imprimerie Nationale, S.E.V.P.O., 39 rue de la Convention, 75732 Paris Cedex 15, France.

FRANCE GRAPHIQUE. see *PRINTING*

070.5 020   US
FREE MAGAZINES FOR LIBRARIES. a. McFarland & Company, Inc., Box 611, Jefferson, NC 28640. Ed. Adeline Smith.

070.5   US
▼**FREE PAPER PUBLISHER, INC..** Short title: F P P. 1990. m. $24. Free Paper Publisher, Inc., 222 S. Broad St., Box 1315, Lancaster, OH 43130. TEL 614-654-5578. FAX 614-687-9369. Ed. James L. Campbell. adv.; bk.rev.; circ. 4,000. (back issues avail.)
 Description: Trade magazine exclusively serving the free paper industry; provides sales, training, technical, and management information.

FREEDOM TO READ FOUNDATION NEWS. see *LIBRARY AND INFORMATION SCIENCES*

FREELANCE. see *LITERATURE*

FREELANCE EDITORS' ASSOCIATION OF CANADA. DIRECTORY OF MEMBERS. see *BUSINESS AND ECONOMICS — Trade And Industrial Directories*

FREELANCE WRITER'S REPORT. see *JOURNALISM*

070.5 371.42 659.1
658   US
FREELANCERS OF NORTH AMERICA. 1984. biennial. $59.95. Research Associates International, 340 E. 52nd St., New York, NY 10022. TEL 212-980-9179. Ed. Leonie Rosenstiel. adv.

FRIDAY MEMO. see *COMPUTERS*

FRIENDS OF THE NATIONAL LIBRARIES. ANNUAL REPORT. see *LIBRARY AND INFORMATION SCIENCES*

070.5 011   US
FUTUREBOOK; tomorrow's publishing scene. (Supplement to: Forthcoming Books (ISSN 0015-8119)) 3/yr. (included in Forthcoming Books). R.R. Bowker, A Reed Reference Publishing Company, Division of Reed Publishing (USA) Inc., 121 Chanlon Rd., New Providence, NJ 07974. TEL 800-521-8110. FAX 908-665-6688. TELEX 138 755. (Subscr. to: Order Dept., Box 31, New Providence, NJ 07974) Ed. Valerie Berk.

655   SY   ISSN 0072-0690
GENERAL DIRECTORY OF THE PRESS AND PERIODICALS IN JORDAN AND KUWAIT.* a. $15. Syrian Documentation Papers, P.O. Box 2712, Damascus, Syria.

655   SY   ISSN 0072-0704
GENERAL DIRECTORY OF THE PRESS AND PERIODICALS IN SYRIA.* a. $15. Syrian Documentation Papers, P.O. Box 2712, Damascus, Syria.
 Description: Consists of advertising rates and names of institutions and officials concerned with media printing and circulation.

070.5 791.4   US   ISSN 0148-7566
GET READY SHEET. 1976. bi-w. $23. Mid-York Library System, c/o Kathryn E. O'Connor, Ed., 1600 Lincoln Ave., Utica, NY 13502. TEL 315-735-8328. adv.; circ. 1,300.

GNOMON; kritische Zeitschrift fuer die gesamte klassische Altertumswissenschaft. see *CLASSICAL STUDIES*

658.8   GW   ISSN 0017-1670
GOLDMANNS MITTEILUNGEN FUER DEN BUCHHANDEL. 1955. m. Wilhelm Goldmann Verlag GmbH, Neumarkterstr. 22, 8000 Munich 80, Germany. adv.; bk.rev.; illus.; stat.; tr.lit.; circ. 12,000.

028.1   UK
THE GOOD BOOK GUIDE. 1977. 6/yr. £17 (foreign £25). Good Book Guide Ltd., 91 Great Russell St., London WC1B 3PS, England. TEL 071-580-8466. FAX 071-323-0048. Eds. Bonnie Falconer, Peter Braithwaite. bk.rev.; circ. 31,000.
 Description: An independent selection of books published in the U.K. including fiction, biography, arts, travel, and children's books accompanied by a brief review.

028 011   US
GOOD READING; a guide for serious readers. irreg., 23rd ed., 1990. $75. R.R. Bowker, A Reed Reference Publishing Company, Division of Reed Publishing (USA) Inc., 121 Chanlon Rd., New Providence, NJ 07979. TEL 800-521-8110. FAX 908-665-6688. TELEX 138 755. (Subscr. to: Order Dept., Box 31, New Providence, NJ 07974)
 Description: Recommends 3,000 enduring nonfiction and fiction titles.

028   US
GOOD READING FOR EVERYONE. 1964. m. $9. Henrichs Publications, Inc., Box 40, Sunshine Park, Litchfield, IL 62056. TEL 217-324-3425. Ed. Peggy Kuethe. circ. 5,000. (back issues avail.)
 Formerly: Good Reading (ISSN 0017-2189)
 Description: Includes articles on travel, points of interest, people, and festivals.

658.809   NE   ISSN 0017-2537
GOUDEN UREN/GOLDEN HOURS. q. membership. (Nederlandse Boekenclub - Netherlands Book Club) B.V. Uitgeversmaatschappij Succes, Prinsevinkenpark 2, Box 19999, 2500 CZ The Hague, Netherlands. Ed. C.A.M. Schinck. adv.; bk.rev.; illus.; circ. 350,000.

GOVERNMENT PUBLISHER. see *PRINTING*

DE GRAFISKE FAG. see *PRINTING*

GRAPHIC COMMUNICATIONS WORLD. see *PRINTING*

028.5   UK   ISSN 0046-6506
Z1037.A1
GROWING POINT. 1962. 6/yr. £5($12.50) Growing Point, c/o Margery Fisher, Ed., Ashton Manor, Northampton NN7 2JL, England. TEL 0604 862277. bk.rev.; illus.; index. (back issues avail.) Indexed: Bk.Rev.Ind. (1975-), Child.Bk.Rev.Ind. (1975-).

655.8   BL
GUIA DAS LIVRARIAS E PONTOS DE VENDA DE LIVROS NO BRASIL. 1976. irreg. Sindicato Nacional dos Editores de Livros, Av. Rio Branco 37, s-1503-06, 20097 Rio de Janeiro R.J., Brazil.

070.5   SP   ISSN 0072-7903
GUIA DE EDITORES Y DE LIBREROS DE ESPANA. 1983. irreg; no. 89-90. price varies. (Federacion de Gremios de Editores de Espana) CRISOL, S.A., c/o Juan Ramon Jimenez, 45-9 Iz., 28036 Madrid, Spain. FAX 91-5639276. TELEX 48457 FGEE. circ. 5,000.

070.5   BL
GUIA DOS EDITORES ASSOCIADOS. 1978. irreg. Sindicato Nacional dos Editores de Livros, Av. Rio Branco 37, s-1503-06, 20097 Rio de Janeiro R.J., Brazil. TEL 021-233-6481. FAX 021-253-8502.
 Formerly: Guia das Editoras Brasileiras.

070.5 700   US   ISSN 1055-6087
PN163
GUIDE TO LITERARY AGENTS AND ART - PHOTO REPS. a. $18.95. F & W Publications, Inc., 1507 Dana Ave., Cincinnati, OH 45207. TEL 513-531-2222. FAX 513-531-4744. Ed. Robin Gee.
 Description: Contains over 400 listings of agents and representatives across North America.

GUIDE TO MICROFORMS IN PRINT. AUTHOR - TITLE. see *BIBLIOGRAPHIES*

860   PR
GUIDE TO REVIEWS OF BOOKS FROM AND ABOUT HISPANIC AMERICA/GUIA A LAS RESENAS DE LIBROS DE Y SOBRE HISPANOAMERICA. (Text in English, Portuguese, Spanish) 1965. a. price varies. Catholic University of Puerto Rico, Encarnacion Valdes Library, Ponce, PR 00731. TEL 313-872-3160. Dir. Antonio Matos. bk.rev.; circ. 150. (back issues avail.)

070.5   US
GUILD OF BOOK WORKERS. NEWSLETTER. 1975. bi-m. $40. Guild of Book Workers, Inc., 521 Fifth Ave., 17th Fl., New York, NY 10175. TEL 212-757-6454. Ed. Margaret Johnson. adv.; bk.rev.; circ. 660. (looseleaf format; back issues avail.)

686.3   US   ISSN 0434-9245
Z1008
GUILD OF BOOK WORKERS JOURNAL. 1962. s-a. $40. Guild of Book Workers, Inc., 521 Fifth Ave., 17th Fl., New York, NY 10175. TEL 212-757-6454. Ed. Dennis Moser. bk.rev.; circ. 650. Indexed: Art & Archaeol.Tech.Abstr.
—BLDSC shelfmark: 4757.680000.

090.75   BE
GULDEN PASSER/COMPAS D'OR. (Text in Dutch, English, French, German) 1923. a. 800 Fr.($25) Vereeniging der Antwerpsche Bibliophielen - Antwerp Bibliophile Society, Museum Plantin-Moretus, Vrijdagmarkt 22-23, B-2000 Antwerp, Belgium. TEL 03-233-02-94. FAX 03-226-25-16. Eds. Francine de Nave, Marcus De Schepper. bk.rev.; circ. 1,000. (reprint service avail. from KTO)

GUTENBERG - GESELLSCHAFT. KLEINE DRUCKE. see *PRINTING*

070.5   JA
HAMBAI KAKUSHIN. (Text in Japanese) 1963. m. 12,900 Yen($200) Shyogyokai Publishing Company Ltd., 49, 2-chome Azabudai Minato-ku, Tokyo 106, Japan. TEL 03-3224-7484. FAX 03-3589-1624. Ed. Jamiyo Uchiro. circ. 85,000. (back issues avail.)

PUBLISHING AND BOOK TRADE 4129

686 US
HANDBOOK OF CIRCULATION MANAGEMENT. irreg., latest 2nd ed. $69.95. Cowles Business Media (Subsidiary of: Cowles Media Company), Six River Bend Center, 911 Hope St., Box 4949, Stamford, CT 06907-0949. TEL 203-358-9900. FAX 203-357-9014. Ed.Bd.

658.8 US
HANDBOOK OF MAGAZINE PRODUCTION. irreg., latest 2nd ed. $69.95. Cowles Business Media, Six River Bend Center, 911 Hope St., Box 4949, Stamford, CT 06907-0949. TEL 203-358-9900. Ed. Jeffery Parnau.

686 US
HANDBOOK OF MAGAZINE PUBLISHING. irreg., latest 3rd ed. $79.95. Cowles Business Media (Subsidiary of: Cowles Media Company), Six River Bend Center, 911 Hope St., Box 4949, Stamford, CT 06907-0949. TEL 203-358-9900. FAX 203-357-9014.

655 GW ISSN 0073-0165
HANDBUCH FUER DEN WERBENDEN BUCH- UND ZEITSCHRIFTENHANDEL.* 1939. a. DM.20. Bundesverband des Werbenden Buch- und Zeitschriftenhandels e.V., Pecherhaupt Str. 2C, 5307 Wachtberg, Germany.

HANDSATZLETTER; Monografien der modernen Typographie. see PRINTING

HEARTLAND CRITIQUES. see LITERARY AND POLITICAL REVIEWS

658.809 US ISSN 0018-2664
HISTORY BOOK CLUB REVIEW.* 1947. 14/yr. membership. History Book Club, Inc., 1225 S. Market St., Mechanicsburg, PA 17055-4728. TEL 800-233-1066. (Subscr. to: 45 Lexington Ave., New York, NY 10017) Dir. Nancy R.M. Whitin. adv.; bk.rev.; illus.; circ. 110,000.

070.5 US ISSN 0361-2759
Z6205
HISTORY: REVIEWS OF NEW BOOKS. 1972. q. $39 to individuals; institutions $78; foreign $84. (Helen Dwight Reid Educational Foundation) Heldref Publications, 1319 Eighteenth St., N.W., Washington, DC 20036-1802. TEL 202-296-6267. FAX 202-296-5149. Ed. Lorraine Brinca. adv.; bk.rev.; bibl.; circ. 700. (also avail. in microform; back issues avail.; reprint service avail.) Indexed: Amer.Bibl.Slavic & E.Eur.Stud., Amer.Hist.& Life, Arts & Hum.Cit.Ind., Biog.Ind., Bk.Rev.Ind. (1975-), Chic.Per.Ind., Child.Bk.Rev.Ind. (1975-), Curr.Cont., Hist.Abstr., Mid.East: Abstr.& Ind.
—BLDSC shelfmark: 4317.730000.
Description: Provides informative evaluations of books one to twelve months after their publication.
Refereed Serial

070.5 UK ISSN 0143-3237
HOME OFFICE LIST OF PUBLICATIONS. 1978. a. Home Office, 50 Queen Anne's Gate, London SW1H 9AT, England. TEL 071-273-2208. circ. 1,500.
—BLDSC shelfmark: 4326.105000.

070.5 HK
▼HONG KONG INTERNATIONAL BOOK FAIR (YEAR): FAIR CATALOGUE. (Text in English) 1991. a. HK.$10. Hong Kong Trade and Development Council, Exhibition Department, Convention Plaza Office 38F, 1 Harbour Rd., Wanchai, Hong Kong. TEL 8903067. FAX 8240249.

028.5 US ISSN 0018-5078
Z1037.A1
HORN BOOK MAGAZINE; about books for children and young adults. 1924. 6/yr. $39. Horn Book, Inc., 14 Beacon St., Boston, MA 02108-3718. TEL 617-227-1555. FAX 617-523-0299. Ed. Anita Silvey. adv.; bk.rev.; illus.; index; circ. 24,000. (also avail. in microform from UMI; reprint service avail. from UMI) Indexed: Acad.Ind., Access (1980-), Artbibl.Mod., Bk.Rev.Dig., Bk.Rev.Ind. (1965-), C.I.J.E., Child.Bk.Rev.Ind. (1965-), Child.Lit.Abstr., GdIns, Ind.Child.Mag., Lib.Lit., Mag.Ind., Media Rev.Dig., PMR, R.G.
—BLDSC shelfmark: 4328.200000.
Description: Covers juvenile literature.

070.5 US
HOT PICKS. 1988. m. free. Baker & Taylor Books, 652 E. Main St., Box 6920, Bridgewater, NJ 08807-0920. TEL 908-218-0400. FAX 908-218-3980. adv.; bk.rev.; circ. 33,000 (controlled).
Incorporates: Sound Buys.
Description: Announcement journal of mass-market and trade paperback and spoken-word audio titles for booksellers and public libraries.

070.5 338 US ISSN 0738-7415
HOW TO BE YOUR OWN PUBLISHER UPDATE. 1986. triennial. $6.95. Bibliotheca Press, c/o Prosperity & Profits Unlimited, Dist. Services, Box 570213, Houston, TX 77257. TEL 713-867-3438. Ed. A. Doyle. circ. 2,000. (looseleaf format; reprint service avail.)
Description: Covers areas of promotion, wholesale printing, and mailing approaches.

HUBEI FANGZHI. see JOURNALISM

070.5 US
HUENEFELD REPORT; for managers and planners in modest-sized book publishing houses. 1973. fortn. $88 (foreign $110). Huenefeld Company, Inc., 41 North Rd., Ste. 201, Bedford, MA 01730. TEL 617-275-1070. Ed. John Huenefeld. circ. 975. (back issues avail.)
Description: Focuses on the ups and downs of the small to modestly sized publisher.

070.5 741.5 US ISSN 1043-240X
PN6725
HUMOR AND CARTOON MARKETS. a. $16.95. F & W Publications, Inc., 1507 Dana Ave., Cincinnati, OH 45207. TEL 513-531-2222. FAX 513-531-4744. Ed. Bob Staake.
Description: Contains over 500 listings of magazine, newsletter, greeting card and comic book publishers, advertising agencies, play publishers and producers, and syndicates. Includes contests, organizations and resources.

028.1 US ISSN 0887-5499
HUNGRY MIND REVIEW; a Midwestern book review. (Supplement avail.: Hungry Mind Review Children's Book Supplement) 1986. q. $12. 1648 Grand Ave., St. Paul, MN 55105. TEL 612-699-2610. FAX 612-699-0970. Ed. Bart Schneider. adv.; bk.rev.; circ. 40,000. Indexed: Bk.Rev.Ind. (1989-), Child.Bk.Rev.Ind. (1989-).
Description: Each issue contains theme-based book reviews.

028.5 US
▼HUNGRY MIND REVIEW CHILDREN'S BOOK SUPPLEMENT. (Supplement to: Hungry Mind Review) 1991. q. $7. 1648 Grand Ave., St. Paul, MN 55105. TEL 612-699-2610. FAX 612-699-7013. Ed. Susan Marie Swanson. bk.rev.; circ. 60,000.
Description: Features reviews, articles and brief essays for parents.

I G F - JOURNAL; journal of the printing, bookbinding and paper workers in all countries. (International Graphical Federation) see PRINTING

070.5 GW
I G MEDIEN FORUM. 1862. fortn. Industriegewerkschaft Medien, Postfach 102451, 7000 Stuttgart 10, Germany. TEL 0711-2018-0. Ed. Hermann Zoller. illus. Indexed: Print.Abstr.
Former titles (until 1991): Kontrapunkt; Druck und Papier (ISSN 0012-6470); Incorporates: Forum und Technik (ISSN 0015-7708)

I P N MARKETING NEWS. (Independent Publishers Network) see BUSINESS AND ECONOMICS — Marketing And Purchasing

029 070.5 GW ISSN 0342-4634
I S B N REVIEW. (International Standard Book Number) (Text in English and German) 1977. a. price varies. (International I S B N Agency) Staatsbibliothek Preussischer Kulturbesitz, Potsdamer Str. 33, Postfach 1407, 1000 Berlin 30, Germany. TEL 030-266-2338. FAX 030-2662814. TELEX 183160-STAAB-D. adv.; bk.rev.; circ. 300. Indexed: Nutr.Abstr.
—BLDSC shelfmark: 4582.772000.

IMAGE WORLD; careers in graphic communications. see OCCUPATIONS AND CAREERS

IMPRIMERIE SYNDICALISTE. see LABOR UNIONS

IN-PLANT REPRODUCTIONS. see PRINTING

800 US
INDEPENDENT (ARLINGTON); a monthly notice of small press periodicals, books and ideas. 1978. m. $10 to individuals; institutions $12. c/o Leonard J. Andersen, 156 Pleasant St., Arlington, MA 02174. Ed.Bd. adv.; bk.rev.; circ. 800. (also avail. in microfilm from UMI; reprint service avail. from UMI)
Supersedes (1975-1976): Butt.

INDEPENDENT PUBLISHING REPORT. see JOURNALISM

028.1 US ISSN 1051-1261
INDEPENDENT SMALL PRESS REVIEW. 1989. s-a. $10 per no. Independent Small Press Review (I.S.P.R.), No. 91336 Victoria Court, Santa Barbara, CA 93190-1336. TEL 805-687-4087. FAX 805-964-3337. Ed. Janice Smythe. adv.; bk.rev.; circ. 2,000.
●Also available online.

070 US
INDEX TO MARQUIS WHO'S WHO BOOKS. a. $79.50. Marquis Who's Who, A Reed Reference Publishing Company, Division of Reed Publishing (USA) Inc., 121 Chanlon Rd., New Providence, NJ 07974. TEL 800-521-8110. FAX 908-665-6688. TELEX 138 755. (Subscr. to: R.R. Bowker, Order Dept., Box 31, New Providence, NJ 07974) (also avail. in magnetic tape)
Former titles (until 1988): Index to Who's Who Books; Index to All Books.
Description: Directs you to more than 280,000 biographies listed in the latest editions of most Marquis Who's Who publications.

655 II ISSN 0019-4433
INDIAN BOOK INDUSTRY; book production and distribution journal. (Text in English) 1969. m. Rs.100($25) (typically set in Oct). Sterling Publishers Pvt. Ltd., L-10 Green Park Extention, New Delhi 110 016, India. TEL 11-669560. FAX 11-6875545. TELEX 031-72366 SITC IN. Ed. Om Parkash Ghai. adv.; bk.rev.; bibl.; charts; illus.; tr.lit.; circ. 2,000.

028.1 II ISSN 0019-4441
INDIAN BOOK REVIEW SUPPLEMENT. 1968. q. Rs.75($20) Delhi Library Association, Box 1270, c/o Hardinge Public Library, Queen's Garden, Delhi 6, India. Ed. Shri C.P. Vashisth. bk.rev.

658.8 655 015 II ISSN 0019-6223
INDIAN PUBLISHER AND BOOKSELLER. (Text in English) 1950. m. Rs.20($4) (Federation of Publishers and Booksellers Associations in India) Popular Prakashan Pvt. Ltd., 35-C Pt. M.M. Malaviya Rd., Bombay 400 034, India. FAX 22-4940896. TELEX 011-71418 ZEB IN. Eds. Sadanand Bhatkal, Nirmala Bhatkal. adv.; bk.rev.; charts; illus.; tr.lit.
Incorporates: Booktraders Bulletin.

011 070.5 IT ISSN 0393-3903
L'INDICE. 1984. m. L.90000 (effective 1993). Indice Coop. A.r.l., Via Andrea Doria, 14, 10123 Turin, Italy. TEL 011-8121222. FAX 011-8122173. (Subscr. to: Via R. Grazioli Lante 15-A, 00195 Rome, Italy. TEL 06-316665) Ed. Filippo Maone. adv.; circ. 29,000.
Description: Reviews about 1400 books per year.

070.5 GW
INDUSTRIEGEWERKSCHAFT MEDIEN. SCHRIFTENREIHE FUER BETRIEBSRATE. 1969. irreg. exchange basis. Industriegewerkschaft Medien, Postfach 102451, 7000 Stuttgart 10, Germany. TEL 0711-2018-0. Ed.Bd. charts; illus.
Formerly: Industriegewerkschaft Druck und Papier. Schriftenreihe fuer Betriebsrate (ISSN 0170-3463)

INFO PRESSE COMMUNICATIONS; le magazine des medias et de la publicite. see ADVERTISING AND PUBLIC RELATIONS

070.5 GW ISSN 0723-4929
INFORMATION FUER DEN G M B H - GESCHAEFTSFUEHRER. (Gesellschaft mit beschraenkter Haftung); Persoenliches - Beratung - Steuern - Recht - Geld. 1982. w. DM.300. Information Verlag, Hindenburgstr. 67, 7800 Freiburg, Germany. TEL 0761-3683-150. Ed. L. Volkelt.

P
Q

PUBLISHING AND BOOK TRADE

INFORMATION INDUSTRY FACTBOOK. see *LIBRARY AND INFORMATION SCIENCES*

INFORMATION SOURCES (YEAR). see *COMPUTERS*

020 US ISSN 1041-0031
Z678.85 CODEN: ISQUEK
INFORMATION STANDARDS QUARTERLY. Abbreviated title: I S Q. 1989. q. $40 (foreign $50). National Information Standards Organization (NISO), Box 1056, Bethesda, MD 20827. TEL 301-975-2814. FAX 301-869-8071. Ed. Pat Ensor. bk.rev.; circ. 1,000. (looseleaf format; processed; back issues avail.) Indexed: LISA.
—BLDSC shelfmark: 4496.323000.
 Supersedes (in 1988): Voice of Z-39 (ISSN 0163-626X); Which was formerly (1965-1977): News About Z-39 (ISSN 0028-8942)
 Description: Reports on the activities of the organization. Includes regular status reports on standards being developed and revised, and reports news of standards activities.

INFORMATION TIMES. see *LIBRARY AND INFORMATION SCIENCES — Computer Applications*

INSIDE MEDIA; for media department of advertising. see *ADVERTISING AND PUBLIC RELATIONS*

070.5 US
INTERNAL PUBLICATIONS DIRECTORY. (Vol.5 of Working Press of the Nation) 1946. a. $150. National Research Bureau, Inc. (Chicago), 225 W. Wacker Dr., Ste. 2275, Chicago, IL 60606-1224. TEL 312-346-9097. Ed. Nancy Veatch. bk.rev.; index.
 Formerly: Gebbie House Magazine Directory (ISSN 0072-0526)

070.5 658 US ISSN 0896-6508
INTERNATIONAL ASSOCIATION OF BOOK TRADE CONSULTANTS REPORT. 1987. q. membership. International Association of Book Trade Consultants, Box 3877, Eugene, OR 97403-0877. TEL 503-342-6901. Ed. Cliff Martin. bk.rev. (back issues avail.)
 Description: Association's newsletter geared to keeping book trade consultants up-to-date and in communication.

028.1 FR ISSN 0242-035X
INTERNATIONAL ASSOCIATION OF LITERARY CRITICS. REVUE. 1969. s-a. membership. International Association of Literary Critics, 38 rue du Faubourg, St. Jacques, 75014 Paris, France. TEL 40-51-33-00. FAX 43-37-07-50. TELEX SCAM SGL 206963 F. Dir. Robert Andre. adv.; bk.rev.; abstr, bibl.; circ. 850.
 Formerly: International Association of Literary Critics. Bulletin.

INTERNATIONAL BOOK TRADE DIRECTORY; Europe, Australia, Oceania, Latin America, Africa, and Asia. see *PUBLISHING AND BOOK TRADE — Abstracting, Bibliographies, Statistics*

070.5 US ISSN 0074-6827
INTERNATIONAL LITERARY MARKET PLACE; the directory of the international book publishing industry. Variant title (1975-76, 1977-78): European Literary Market Place. 1966. a. $164. R.R. Bowker, A Reed Reference Publishing Company, Division of Reed Publishing (USA) Inc., 121 Chanlon Rd., New Providence, NJ 07974. TEL 800-521-8110. FAX 908-665-6688. TELEX 138 755. (Subscr. to: Order Dept., Box 31, New Providence, NJ 07974) index. (also avail. in magnetic tape)
 ●Also available on CD-ROM.
—BLDSC shelfmark: 4543.020000.
 Description: Arranged by function and country; lists publishers, book trade organizations, trade reference publications, agents, international events, major booksellers and libraries, and translation agencies in over 160 countries. Indexed by institution name.

070.5 SZ ISSN 0074-7556
INTERNATIONAL PUBLISHERS ASSOCIATION. PROCEEDINGS OF CONGRESS. 1896. quadrennial, 24th, 1992, New Delhi. 60 SFr.($54) International Publishers Association - Union Internationale des Editeurs (Internationale Verleger-Union), Ave. Miremont 3, CH-1206 Geneva, Switzerland. TEL 22-3463018. FAX 22-3475717. Ed. W. Gordon Graham. tr. 1,100.
 Description: Provides insights into the concerns of the international publishing community. Addresses such issues as apartheid, piracy, censorship, world trends in education, electronic publishing, and women in the publishing industry.

028.5 016 US ISSN 0146-5562
Z1037.A1
INTERRACIAL BOOKS FOR CHILDREN BULLETIN. 1967. 8/yr. $16 to individuals; institutions $24. Council on Interracial Books for Children, Inc., 1841 Broadway, New York, NY 10023-7648. TEL 212-757-5339. (Subscr. to: Box 1263, New York, NY 10023) Ed.Bd. bk.rev.; bibl.; charts; illus.; circ. 7,500. (also avail. in microfilm from UMI; back issues avail.; reprint service avail. from UMI) **Indexed:** Alt.Press Ind., Bk.Rev.Ind. (1979-1989), Chic.Per.Ind., Child.Bk.Rev.Ind. (1979-1989), Educ.Ind., Lib.Lit.
—BLDSC shelfmark: 4557.436000.
 Formerly: Interracial Books for Children (ISSN 0020-9708)

028 296 IS ISSN 0333-953X
Z449.7
ISRAEL BOOK NEWS. 1970. q. Israel Export Institute, Book and Printing Center, 29 Hamered St., P.O. Box 50084, Tel Aviv 61500, Israel. adv.; bk.rev.; circ. 2,500.
—BLDSC shelfmark: 4583.643700.
 Former titles: Jerusalem Post Literary Supplement & Israel Book World (ISSN 0021-1974)

070.5 IS ISSN 0333-6018
ISRAEL BOOK TRADE DIRECTORY; a guide to publishers, printers and ancillary book trade services in Israel. (Text in English) 1967. biennial. Israel Export Institute, Book and Printing Center, Industry House, 29 Hamered St., P.O. Box 50084, Tel Aviv, Israel. circ. 3,000.
 Former titles: Israel Book Trades Directory: A Select List; Publishers and Printers of Israel: A Select List (ISSN 0079-7820)

070.5 011 JA ISSN 0387-3927
J P G LETTER; news on English publishing in Japan and South-East Asia. (Text in English) 1973. m. 20000 Yen($150) Japan Publications Guide Service, 5-5-13 Matsushiro, Tsukubashi Ibarakiken 305, Japan. TEL 81-3-3661-8373. FAX 81-3-3667-9646. (Subscr. to: Intercontinental Marketing Corp., IPO Box 5056, Tokyo 100-31, Japan. TEL 81-3-3661-7458) Ed. Warren E. Ball. adv.; bk.rev.; illus.; circ. 600.
—BLDSC shelfmark: 5073.683300.
 Supersedes: Asia Notebook (ISSN 0004-4490)
 Description: Lists new or updated publication titles in Japan and in Southeast/East Asian countries. Also includes comments on publishers and other information sources.

JAHRBUCH DER AUKTIONSPREISE FUER BUECHER, HANDSCHRIFTEN UND AUTOGRAPHEN; Ergebnisse der Auktionen in Deutschland, den Niederlanden, Oesterreich und der Schweiz. see *MUSEUMS AND ART GALLERIES*

070.5 JA ISSN 0287-9530
HD2429.J3
JAPAN DIRECTORY OF PROFESSIONAL ASSOCIATIONS. (Text in English) 1984. irreg., 2nd ed., 1989. 30000 Yen($250) Japan Publicatins Guide Service, 5-5-13 Matsushiro, Tsukubashi Ibarakiken 305, Japan. FAX 81-3-3667-9646. (Subscr. to: Intercontinental Marketing Corp., IPO Box 5056, Tokyo 100-31, Japan. TEL 81-3-3661-7458) Ed. Warren E. Ball. adv.; stat.; tr.lit.; circ. 2,000. (also avail. on diskette)
 Description: Lists all types of associations, as well as selected institutes.

070.5 JA
JAPAN PUBLISHERS DIRECTORY. (Text in English) 1987. irreg. 6000 Yen($50) (or free with the order for Japan English Publications in Print). Japan Publications Guide Service, 5-5-13 Matsushiro, Tsukubashi Ibarakiken 305, Japan. FAX 81-3-3667-9646. (Subscri. to: Intercontinental Marketing Corp., IPO Box 5056, Tokyo 100-31, Japan. TEL 81-3-3661-7458).
 Description: Directory of Japanese publishers and others who publish material in the English language. Includes name index in romanized Japanese.

686 IS
JERFAIR NEWS; the Jerusalem International Book Fair newsletter. (Text in English) 1975. irreg. free. Jerusalem International Book Fair, Binyaney Ha'Ooma, P.O. Box 6001, Jerusalem 91060, Israel. TEL 02-528556. FAX 02-243144. TELEX 26552-JRNET-IL. Ed. Zev Birger. circ. 5,000.

070.5 FR ISSN 1156-5977
JERICHO. 1984. a. 100 F. (membership). Club des Lecteurs de Presse et Livres Meconnus, 114 rue Louis Ranvier, 42300 Roanne, France. Ed. Jacqueline Grolleau. index; circ. 250. (back issues avail.)
 Formerly: Bulletin Annuel d'Information et de Liaison entre C.L.P.L.M. (ISSN 0765-328X)

JOURNAL OF INFORMATION SCIENCE; principles and practice. see *LIBRARY AND INFORMATION SCIENCES*

686 020 US ISSN 0265-5942
PN4699
JOURNAL OF NEWSPAPER AND PERIODICAL HISTORY. 1984. 2/yr. $75 (effective Oct. 1990). Greenwood Press, Inc. (Subsidiary of: Greenwood Publishing Group Inc.), 88 Post Rd. W., Box 5007, Westport, CT 06881-9990. TEL 203-226-3571. FAX 203-222-1502. Ed. Michael Harris. adv.; bk.rev.; index; circ. 300. (also avail. in microfilm; back issues avail.)
—BLDSC shelfmark: 5022.816000.

028 296 016 US ISSN 0022-5754
Z6367
JUDAICA BOOK NEWS. 1969. s-a. $9.50. Book News, Inc. (New York), 303 W. 10th St., New York, NY 10014. TEL 212-691-3817. FAX 212-633-9731. Ed. Ernest L. Weiss. adv.; bk.rev.; bibl.; circ. 18,000. (also avail. in microform from UMI; reprint service avail. from UMI)
 Description: Devoted entirely to new and forthcoming books of Jewish interest.

028.5 UK ISSN 0022-6505
Z1037.A1
JUNIOR BOOKSHELF; a review of children's books. 1936. 6/yr. £9 (elsewhere £11). Marsh Hall, Thurstonland, Huddersfield, Yorkshire HD4 6XB, England. TEL 0484-661811. FAX 0484-510237. Ed. D.J. Morrell. adv.; bk.rev.; illus.; index; circ. 1,500. (also avail. in microform from UMI; back issues avail.; reprint service avail. from UMI) **Indexed:** Bk.Rev.Ind. (1975-), Child.Bk.Rev.Ind. (1975-), Child.Lit.Abstr., Lib.Lit., Lib.Sci.Abstr.
—BLDSC shelfmark: 5075.120000.
 Description: Offers authoritative reviews of the best new books for children.

070.5 CC ISSN 1001-5272
KEJI CHUBAN/SCIENCE AND TECHNOLOGY PUBLISHING. (Text in Chinese) bi-m. Zhongguo Chuban Gongzuozhe Xiehui - China Publishers Association, 1 Banwanzhuang Nanjie, Beijing 100037, People's Republic of China. TEL 8317766. Ed. Zhao Deming.

070.5 808 US
KEYSTROKES. 1979. q. $15. Writers Alliance, Box 2014, Setauket, NY 11733. TEL 516-751-7080. Ed. Kiel Stuart. adv.; bk.rev.; circ. 125. (back issues avail.)
 Formerly: Writers Alliance Newsletter.
 Description: Geared towards an audience of writers (fiction, poetry, journalism, research) with information on markets and computer use.

070.5　　　　　　FI　ISSN 0047-343X
Z374.7
KIRJAKAUPPALEHTI. (Text in Finnish; summaries in English) 1897. m. FIM 360 in Scandinavia; in Europe FIM 390; elsewhere FIM 440. Kirjakauppalehden Julkaisu Oy, Eerikinkatu 15-17D, 00100 Helsinki, Finland. FAX 90-6944900. Ed. Raili Tammilehto. adv.; bk.rev.; illus.; index; circ. 2,400.
   Formerly: Suomen Kirjakauppalehti - Finsk Bokhandelstidning.

028.1　　　　　　US　ISSN 0042-6598
Z477
KIRKUS REVIEWS; adult/young adult and children's book reviews. 1933. s-m. price varies. Kirkus Service, Inc., 200 Park Ave. S., New York, NY 10003. TEL 212-777-4554. Ed. Anne Larsen. bk.rev.; index; circ. 5,000. (also avail. in microform from UMI) **Indexed:** Bk.Rev.Ind. (1965-), Child.Bk.Rev.Ind. (1965-).

070.5　　　　　　US
KITCHEN SINK PIPELINE.* 1983. m. free to qualified personnel. Kitchen Sink Press, Inc., 2 Swamp Rd., Princeton, WI 54968. TEL 414-295-6922. FAX 414-295-6878. Ed. Denis Kitchen. circ. 16,000. (looseleaf format; back issues avail.)
   Description: Discusses Kitchen Sink Press publishing projects and forthcoming releases.

KLEIO. see HISTORY

028.1 011　　　　　US　ISSN 0199-2376
Z1037
KLIATT YOUNG ADULT PAPERBACK BOOK GUIDE; an annotated list of current paperback books for young adults. 1967. 3/yr. (plus 5 newsletter supplements). $33. Kliatt Paperback Book Guide, 425 Watertown St., Newton, MA 02158. TEL 617-965-4666. Eds. Doris Hiatt, Claire Rosser. adv.; bk.rev.; index; circ. 2,300. (also avail. in microform from UMI; reprint service avail. from UMI) **Indexed:** Bk.Rev.Ind. (1977-), Child.Bk.Rev.Ind. (1977-).
   Formerly: Kliatt Paperback Book Guide (ISSN 0023-2114)

070.5 947　　　　　RU
KNIGA ISSLEDOVANIYA. 1959. 2/yr. Izdatel'stvo Kniga, 50, Gorky St., 125047 Moscow, Russia. bibl.; cum.index every 2 yrs.

070.5　　　　　　CS
KNIHA. (Text in Slovak; summaries in English, German and Russian) 1976. a. price varies. Matica Slovenska, Slovenska Narodna Kniznica, Ul. L. Novomeskeho 32, 036 52 Martin, Czechoslovakia. TEL 313-71. FAX 0842-324-54. TELEX 075 331. Ed. Miroslava Domova.
   Formerly: Knizna Kultura.

028.1　　　　　　RU　ISSN 0023-2378
KNIZHNOE OBOZRENIE; review of newly published books. 1966. w. $6. (Gosudarstvennyi Komitet Soveta Ministrov po Pechati) Izdatel'stvo Kniga, 50, Gorky St., 125047 Moscow, Russia. TEL 251-19-31. Ed. A.I. Ovsyannikov. (also avail. in microform from MIM) **Indexed:** Curr.Dig.Sov.Press.

070.5　　　　　　XV
KNJIZEVNI GLASNIK MOHORJEVE DRUZBE. (Text in Slovanian) 1981. s-a. free. Mahorjeva Druzba Celje, Zidanskova 7, YU-63000 Celje, Slovenia. adv.; bk.rev.; circ. 37,000.

THE KORBIN LETTER; concerning children's books about real people, places and things. see LITERATURE

070.5 015　　　　　KO　ISSN 0075-6881
KOREAN PUBLICATIONS YEARBOOK/HANKUK CH'ULPAN YONGAM. 1963. a. 50000 Won($70) Korean Publishers Association, 105-2 Sagan-dong, Chongno-ku, Seoul 110-190, S. Korea. TEL 02-735-2701. FAX 02-738-5414. circ. 1,200. (back issues avail.)

070.5　　　　　　BE
KREATIF JAARBOOK. (Text in Flemish) a. C E D Samson (Subsidiary of: Wolters Samson Belgie n.v.), Louizalaan 485, B-1050 Brussels, Belgium. TEL 02-7231111. FAX 02-6498480. TELEX CEDSAM 64130.
   Description: Covers free-lancing in Belgium for copywriters, artists, graphic designers, photographers and illustrators.

070　　　　　　PL
KSIEGARZ. vol.19, 1975. q. $16. Stowarzyszenie Ksiegarzy Polskich, Ul. Mokotowska 4-6, 00-641 Warsaw, Poland. (Dist. by: Ars Polona-Ruch, Krakowskie Przedmiescie 7, 00-068 Warsaw, Poland) Ed. Tadeusz Hussak. adv.; bk.rev.; bibl.; illus.; index; circ. 3,500.

070.5　　　　　　AG　ISSN 0326-226X
Z519.7
L E A. (Libros de Edicion Argentina) 1982. m. $30 (foreign $100). Camara Argentina del Libro, Av. Belgrano 1580, 6 Piso, 1093 Buenos Aires, Argentina. TEL 38-8383. Ed. Jose Naveiro. adv.; illus.; circ. 4,000.

LAMBDA BOOK REPORT; a review of contemporary gay and lesbian literature. see HOMOSEXUALITY

070.5　　　　　　US　ISSN 1056-0327
LAUGHING BEAR NEWSLETTER. 1976. m. $8. Laughing Bear Press, Box 36159, Denver, CO 80236. TEL 303-989-5614. Ed. Tom Person. adv.; bk.rev.; illus.; tr.lit.; index; circ. 150. (back issues avail.)
   Description: Contains small press publishing information for publishers and writers.

028.1　　　　　　GW　ISSN 0175-8152
LAURENTIUS. 1983. 3/yr. DM.20. Laurentius Verlag, Koertingstr. 8, 3000 Hannover 1, Germany. TEL 0511-621045. (Subscr. to: Bonhoefferstr. 19, 3016 Seelze 1, Germany) Ed. Raimund Dehmlow.

070.5 020　　　　　GW　ISSN 0930-9950
LAURENTIUS SONDERHEFTE. a. Laurentius Verlag, Koertingstr. 8, 3000 Hannover 1, Germany. TEL 0511-621045. Ed. Raimund Dehmlow. adv.; bk.rev.

070.5　　　　　　UK
LEARNED PUBLISHING: A L P S P BULLETIN. 1977. q. £50 to non-members. Association of Learned and Professional Society Publishers, 48 Kelsey Lane, Beckenham, Kent BR3 3NE, England. Ed. Hazel K. Bell. adv.; bk.rev.; circ. 250.
   Formerly (until 1988): A L P S P Bulletin (ISSN 0260-9428)

018.1 860　　　　　US　ISSN 0732-8001
Z1039.M5
LECTOR. 1982. s-a. $50. Floricanto Press, 16161 Ventura Blvd., Ste. 830, Encino, CA 91436-2504. TEL 818-990-1885. Ed. Roberto Cabello-Argandona. adv.; bk.rev.; circ. 3,000. **Indexed:** Chic.Per.Ind.
   Description: Features English language reviews and information about Spanish language books published in Spain, Latin America and the US which are of interest to Hispanics in America.

070.5　　　　　　US
LEE HOWARD NEWSLETTER; for small publishers and mail order book dealers. 1979. q. $12. Selective Books, Inc., Box 1140, Clearwater, FL 34617. TEL 813-447-0100. Ed. Lee Howard. adv.; circ. 5,500. (controlled).
   Formerly: Book Business Mart.
   Description: Focuses on the self-publishing book market and mail-order book selling.

LEGAL PUBLISHING PREVIEW; reviews & listings of new & forthcoming legal products. see LAW

028.1　　　　　　GW　ISSN 0024-1083
LESESTUNDE MIT DEM GROSSEN FREIZEIT-PROGRAMM. 1924. q. free. Deutsche Buch-Gemeinschaft, Berliner Allee 6, 6100 Darmstadt, Germany. Eds. Dieter Loff, Rolf Schneider. adv.; bk.rev.; illus.; circ. 600,000. (tabloid format)

LIBRARIANS' CHRISTIAN FELLOWSHIP NEWSLETTER. see LIBRARY AND INFORMATION SCIENCES

LIBRARIAN'S WORLD. see LIBRARY AND INFORMATION SCIENCES

011 090　　　　　SZ　ISSN 0024-2152
Z990
LIBRARIUM. (Text in English, French, German and Italian) 1958. 3/yr. 120 Fr.($60) Schweizerische Bibliophilen-Gesellschaft, Im Schilf 15, CH-8044 Zurich, Switzerland. Ed. Werner G. Zimmermann. adv.; bk.rev.; illus.; index; circ. 750. **Indexed:** M.L.A.
   Description: Covers all aspects of collecting books, graphic art and autographs.

PUBLISHING AND BOOK TRADE　　4131

658.896　　　　　US　ISSN 0024-2217
THE LIBRARY BOOKSELLER; books wanted by college and university libraries. 1945. 2/m. $100 in U.S.; $75 to libraries. Scott Saifer, Pub., Box 9544, Berkeley, CA 94709-0544. TEL 415-540-6951. Ed. Gail Rusin. adv.; circ. 150.

LIBRARY JOURNAL. see LIBRARY AND INFORMATION SCIENCES

LIBRARY OF THE ECONOMISTS. see BUSINESS AND ECONOMICS

658.8　　　　　　IT　ISSN 0024-2640
Z344.A87
LIBRERIA.* 1948. bi-m. L.3000 to non-members. Associazione Librai Italiani, Piazza G.G. Belli 2, 00153 Rome, Italy. Ed. Marcello Romito. adv.; bk.rev.; illus.; circ. 4,000.

658.8　　　　　　SP　ISSN 0024-2659
LIBRERIA. no.55, 1970. 5/yr. 1500 ptas. Gremi de Libreters de Barcelona, Mallorca 274, 08037 Barcelona, Spain. TELEX 98772 CLLCE. Ed. Josep Maria Blasi i Torrado. adv.; bk.rev.; illus.; circ. 3,000.

028.1 015.45　　　　IT　ISSN 0024-2683
LIBRI E RIVISTE D'ITALIA; rassegna bibliografica mensile. English edition: Italian Books and Periodicals (ISSN 0021-2881) (Editions in French, German, Italian, Spanish) 1950. m. L.22000. Istituto Poligrafico Dello Stato, Piazza Verdi 10, Rome, Italy. bk.rev.; bibl.; index. **Indexed:** M.L.A.

070.5 806　　　　　MX　ISSN 0186-2243
Z497
LIBROS DE MEXICO. 1985. q. $40 (outside America $50). Camara Nacional de la Industria Editorial Mexicana, Holanda 13, Col. San Diego Churubusco, Coyoacan 04120, Mexico. TEL 688-7122. FAX 604-3147. Ed. Federico Krafft Vera. adv.; bibl.; circ. 6,000.
   Description: Covers trade and industry in Mexico, as well as its history.

070.5　　　　　　US
LIFTOUTS; a review of books and language work. 1983. a. $5. Preludium Publishers, 1503 Washington Ave. S., Minneapolis, NM 55454. TEL 612-333-0031. FAX 612-341-2794. Ed. Barry Casselman. adv.; bk.rev.; film rev.; play rev.; circ. 2,000. (tabloid format; back issues avail.)
   Description: Features new poetry and fiction, and recent work in translation from around the world.

070.5　　　　　　BE
LIJSTENBOEK. 1929. a. 850 BEF($8) Vereniging ter Bevordering van het Vlaamse Boekwezen - Association of Publishers of Dutch Language Books, Frankrijklei 93, B-2000 Antwerp, Belgium. index; circ. 1,500.

028.1　　　　　　GW　ISSN 0179-7417
LISTEN; Zeitschrift fuer Leserinnen und Leser. 1985. q. DM.25($16) Jordanstr. 14, 6000 Frankfurt a.M. 90, Germany. TEL 069-775592. FAX 069-702056. (U.S. addr.: M. Rosenberg Inc., 1841 Broadway, New York, NY 10023) Ed. K. Piberhofer. adv.; bk.rev.; circ. 15,000. (back issues avail.)

070.5 331.8　　　　US
LITERARY AGENT. irreg. Association of Authors' Representatives, Inc., Ten Astor Pl., 3rd fl., New York, NY 10003. TEL 212-353-3709.

LITERARY AGENTS OF NORTH AMERICA. see LITERATURE

PUBLISHING AND BOOK TRADE

070.5 US ISSN 0161-2905
PN161
LITERARY MARKET PLACE; the directory of American book publishing industry. 1940. a. $148. R.R. Bowker, A Reed Reference Publishing Company, Division of Reed Publishing (USA) Inc., 121 Chanlon Rd., New Providence, NJ 07974. TEL 800-521-8110. FAX 908-665-6688. TELEX 138 755. (Subscr. to: Order Dept., Box 31, New Providence, NJ 07974) index. (also avail. in magnetic tape)
●Also available on CD-ROM.
Formed by the 1972 merger of: Literary Market Place (ISSN 0000-1155); Names and Numbers (ISSN 0075-9899)
Description: Lists publishing and publishing-related businesses, including distributors, literary agents, small presses, events, editorial and art services, printers and binders. Includes electronic publishing and law firms that specialize in intellectual property. Also lists recent mergers and acquisitions and company reportage of publishers, i.e. divisions, subsidiaries and imprints.

LITERARY SKETCHES; a magazine of interviews, reviews and memorabilia. see *LITERATURE*

070.5 FR
LIVRAISONS. 1981. q. 120 F. 1 rue des Fosses Saint Jacques, 75005 Paris, France.

070.5 PO
LIVRARIA FIGUEIRINHAS CATALOGO. 1898. a. free. Editora Figueirinhas Lda., Rua do Almada, 47, 4000 Porto, Portugal. FAX 325907. circ. 5,000.

010 BE ISSN 0024-533X
Z990
LE LIVRE ET L'ESTAMPE. (Text in French) 1954. s-a. 1250 Fr. Societe Royale des Bibliophiles et Iconophiles de Belgique, 4 Bd. de l'Empereur, B-1000 Brussels, Belgium. Ed. A. Grisay. adv.; bk.rev.; cum.index: 1954-1985; circ. 350.

658.8 FR
LIVRES DE FRANCE. 1979. m. 424.50 F. Editions Professionnelles du Livre, 30, rue Dauphine, 75006 Paris, France. TEL 1-43-29-73-50. FAX 1-43-29-77-85. Ed. Jean-Marie Doublet. adv.; bk.rev.; bibl.; illus.; stat.; circ. 7,000.
Former titles: Bulletin du Livre; Bibliographie de la France. Livres (ISSN 0007-456X)

658.8 FR
LIVRES DU MOIS. 1979. m. Editions Professionnelles du Livre, B.P. 180, 75263 Paris Cedex 06, France. TEL 1-43-29-73-50. FAX 1-43-29-77-85.

015.46 PO ISSN 0870-5259
Z2715
LIVROS DE PORTUGAL. 1940. m. $30 (typically set in Jan.). Associacao Portuguesa de Editores e Livreiros, Av. dos Estados Unidos da America, 97 6 Esq, 1700 Lisbon, Portugal. TEL 1-8489136. FAX 1-8489377. TELEX 62735 APEL P. (Subscr. to: Dinalivro, Travessa do Convento de Jesus, 15 r/c, 1200, Lisbon, Portugal) Ed. Cristina Luisa Falcao. adv.; bk.rev.; bibl.; circ. 2,000.
Description: Covers news about the world book trade, includes interviews with publishers and book sellers, and lists a bibliography of new books and other printed materials from the previous month.

070.5 UK ISSN 0957-9656
Z284
▼**LOGOS**; the professional journal for the book world. 1990. q. $60 individuals; institutions $90. Whurr Publishers Ltd., 19b Compton Terrace, London N1 2UN, England. TEL 071-359-5979. FAX 071-226-5290. (Subscr. to: Whurr Publishers Ltd., The Distribution Centre, Blackhorse Rd., Letchworth, Herts. SG6 1HN, England; US subscr. to: Whurr Publishers Ltd., Thomas Slatner & Co., 401 Baldwin Ave., Jersey City, NJ 07306) Ed. Gordon Graham.
—BLDSC shelfmark: 5292.404000.
Description: For publishers, booksellers, librarians, and others in the international book community.

028.1 US
LOS ANGELES TIMES BOOK REVIEW. w. Los Angeles Times Inc., Times Mirror Sq., Los Angeles, CA 90053. TEL 213-237-7777. Ed. Sonja Bolle. bk.rev.; index. (also avail. in microform from UMI)
Indexed: Bk.Rev.Ind. (1982-), Child.Bk.Rev.Ind. (1982-).

070.5 NE
M N I COURANT. s-a. free. Martinus Nijhoff International, P.O. Box 269, 2501 AX The Hague, Netherlands. TEL 31-79-684400. FAX 31-79-615698. (U.S. addr.: 175 Derby St., Ste. 13, Hingham, MA 02043. TEL 800-346-3662)
Description: News of the company, with book and serial publishing updates.

M P A NEWSLETTER OF RESEARCH. (Magazine Publishers of America) see *ADVERTISING AND PUBLIC RELATIONS*

686 658.8 US
THE MAGAZINE; everything you need to know to make it in the magazine business. irreg., latest 2nd ed. $17.95. Cowles Business Media (Subsidiary of: Cowles Media Company), Six River Bend Center, 911 Hope St., Box 4949, Stamford, CT 06907-0949. TEL 203-358-9900. FAX 203-357-9014. Ed. Leonard Mogel.

028.1 US ISSN 0744-3102
Z284
MAGAZINE & BOOKSELLER; mass market retailers' and publishers' guide. 1946. m. $49 (foreign $71). North American Publishing Co. (New York), 322 Eighth Ave., 18th Fl., New York, NY 10001. TEL 212-620-7330. FAX 212-620-7335. TELEX 215-494-6735 NAPCOPHL. (Subscr. to: 401 N. Broad St., Philadelphia, PA 19108) Ed. Mark V. Hinckley. adv.; bk.rev.; stat.; circ. 22,549. (also avail. in microfiche from UMI)
Formed by the 1982 merger of: Profitways; Marketing Bestsellers (ISSN 0164-9876); Formerly: Bestsellers (ISSN 0005-9730)
Description: Directed to the marketing and distribution of magazines and paperback books through retail outlets. Explores the important "how-to's" of magazine and paperback marketing.

MAGAZINE DESIGN AND PRODUCTION. see *PRINTING*

070.5 US ISSN 0899-7039
Z286.P4
MAGAZINE ISSUES. 1982. bi-m. $20. Feredonna Communications, Box 9808, Knoxville, TN 37940. TEL 615-584-1918. Ed. Michael Scott Ward. adv.; bk.rev.; circ. 13,000. **Indexed:** ABI Inform.
Formerly (until 1988): Publishing Trade (ISSN 0730-6741)
Description: Serves publishers and key management personnel at magazine companies with circulations up to 500,000.

070.5 US
MAGAZINE PUBLISHERS ASSOCIATION. NEWSLETTER OF CIRCULATION. q. Magazine Publishers of America, 575 Lexington Ave., New York, NY 10022. TEL 212-752-0055.

070.5 US
MAGAZINE PUBLISHERS OF AMERICA. bi-m. Magazine Publishers Association, Inc., 575 Lexington Ave., New York, NY 10022. TEL 718-752-0055.

070.5 US ISSN 0895-2124
MAGAZINEWEEK; the newsweekly for the magazine industry. 1987. w. (44/yr.). $98. Lighthouse Communications Group, Inc., 233 W. Central, Natick, MA 01760. TEL 508-650-1001. FAX 508-650-4648. (Subscr. to: Box 53463 Boulder, CO 80322-3463) Ed. Donald Nicholas. adv.; circ. 12,500. (reprint service avail.)
Incorporates (in 1990): Successful Magazine Publishing (ISSN 0892-6581); Which was formerly: S M P G Newsletter.
Description: Covers all areas of the magazine industry. Provides news coverage and articles on magazine production, advertising, circulation, and management.

MAGILL'S LITERARY ANNUAL. see *LITERATURE*

020 655 HU ISSN 0025-0171
Z1007
MAGYAR KONYVSZEMLE/HUNGARIAN BOOK REVIEW; review of bookhistory, bibliography and documentation. (Summaries in English, French, German or Russian) 1876. q. $20. (Magyar Tudomanyos Akademia) Akademiai Kiado, Publishing House of the Hungarian Academy of Sciences, P.O. Box 24, H-1363 Budapest, Hungary. Eds. Gy. Kokay, Z. Havasi. adv.; bk.rev.; charts; illus.; index; circ. 1,300. **Indexed:** Amer.Hist.& Life, Hist.Abstr., Lib.Lit., Lib.Sci.Abstr. LISA, M.L.A.

MAINE ENTRY. see *LIBRARY AND INFORMATION SCIENCES*

070.5 016 US ISSN 1045-5388
Z1000
MANDEVILLE'S USED BOOK PRICE GUIDE. 1962. triennial. $89 for supplement. Price Guide Publishers, Box 82525, Kenmore, WA 98028-0525. TEL 206-783-7855. Ed. Richard L. Collins.
Formerly: Used Book Price Guide (ISSN 0083-4807)
Description: Assists in the evaluation of rare, scarce, old, and used books. Provides the background for determining the current market value of books.

MANUSCRIPTS. see *HOBBIES*

MAP REPORT. see *GEOGRAPHY*

070.5 CN ISSN 0832-512X
MASTHEAD; the magazine about magazines. 1987. 10/yr. Can.$28. North Island Sound Ltd., 1606 Sedlescomb Dr., Unit 8, Mississauga, Ont. L4X 1M6, Canada. TEL 416-625-7070. FAX 416-625-4856. Ed. Doug Bennet. adv.; stat.; circ. 4,504 (controlled). (back issues avail.)
Description: Covers news, events and issues in the Canadian periodical publishing industry.

MEDIA; Asia's media & marketing newspaper. see *ADVERTISING AND PUBLIC RELATIONS*

MEDIA ASIA. see *COMMUNICATIONS*

MEDIA-DATEN ANNUALS. see *ADVERTISING AND PUBLIC RELATIONS*

MEDIA MERGERS & ACQUISITIONS. see *COMMUNICATIONS*

MEDIENWISSENSCHAFT; Zeitschrift fuer Rezensionen ueber Veroeffentlichungen zu saemtlichen Medien. see *COMMUNICATIONS — Television And Cable*

020.75 US
MERC. 1970. m. $10. Mercantile Library Association of the City of New York, 17 E. 47th St., New York, NY 10017. TEL 212-755-6710. Ed. Nancy M. Bischoff. bk.rev.; circ. 1,600.

MICROFORM REVIEW. see *LIBRARY AND INFORMATION SCIENCES*

MIDNIGHT EXPRESS. see *LITERATURE — Science Fiction, Fantasy, Horror*

MINIATURE BOOK NEWS. see *HOBBIES*

070.5 GW
MOHR KURIER. 3/yr. Verlag J.C.B. Mohr (Paul Siebeck) Wilhelmstr. 18, Postfach 2040, 7400 Tuebingen, Germany. TEL 07071-26064. FAX 07071-51104. TELEX 7262872-MOHR-D.

MORGAN REPORT ON DIRECTORY PUBLISHING. see *BUSINESS AND ECONOMICS — Trade And Industrial Directories*

028.1 IT ISSN 0027-3384
MUNDUS.* 1965. m. L.1000. Casella Postale 2236, Rome, Italy. Ed. Karol Kleszczynski. bk.rev.

MUTUAL PIPER. see *INSURANCE*

MYOSOTIS; Zeitschrift fuer Buchwesen. see *PRINTING*

070.5 US ISSN 0893-3472
N; the newsletter for publications. 1986. 6/yr. $59. Poll Communications Group, 126 N. Third St., Minneapolis, MN 55401. TEL 612-338-7664. FAX 612-338-5423. Ed. Donn Poll. bk.rev.; charts; illus.; circ. 7,000. (back issues avail.)
Description: Provides instruction in the design, writing and editing of newsletters. Includes information on desktop publishing.

PUBLISHING AND BOOK TRADE 4133

070.5   SI   ISSN 0129-9239
N B D C S NEWS. (Text in English) 1981. q. National Book Development Council of Singapore, NBDCS Secretariat, Bukit Merah Branch Library, Bukit Merah Central, Singapore 0315, Singapore. TEL 2732730. Ed. Bee C. Gan. charts; illus.; circ. 4,000. (back issues avail.)
   Description: Contains news of relevance to Singapore's book industry as well as educational institutions and libraries.

N.S.K. NEWS BULLETIN. see *JOURNALISM*

070.5   US
N - THE NEWSLETTER FOR PUBLICATIONS. bi-m. 126 N. Third St., Ste. 200, Minneapolis, MN 55401-1678. TEL 612-338-7664. FAX 612-338-5423. Ed. Donn Poll.

N W C NEWSLETTER. see *JOURNALISM*

NANDE REKO; cuaderno de literatura popular. see *LITERATURE*

070   PL
NASZE PROBLEMY. m. 140 Zl. per no. Wydawnictwo Wspolczesne R S W "Prasa-KsiazkaRuch", Ul. Wiejska 12, 00-420 Warsaw, Poland. TEL 48-22-285330. illus.

070.5   US
NATIONAL ASSOCIATION OF SELECTIVE DISTRIBUTORS. NEWSLETTER.* m. National Association of Selective Distributors, c/o Dean Campbell, 5230 Stanton Dr., Kansas City, MO 64133. TEL 816-358-0589.

NATIONAL BRAILLE PRESS RELEASE. see *HANDICAPPED — Visually Impaired*

NATIONAL INFORMATION STANDARDS SERIES. see *LIBRARY AND INFORMATION SCIENCES*

DIE NEUE BUECHEREI; Zeitschrift fuer die oeffentlichen Buechereien in Bayern. see *LIBRARY AND INFORMATION SCIENCES*

NEUE MEDIEN; das deutsche Fach-Magazin fuer Medien und Kommunikation. see *COMMUNICATIONS — Television And Cable*

070.5   GW   ISSN 0935-7866
NEUMANN - HANDBUCH FUER DEN PRESSEVERTRIEB. 1974. a. DM.68. Presse Fachverlag, Eidelstedteweg 22, 2000 Hamburg 20, Germany. TEL 040-565031. FAX 040-5602920. Ed. Hans van Treeck. circ. 2,900.

NEW AGE RETAILER; books, music, merchandise. see *NEW AGE PUBLICATIONS*

686.3   UK   ISSN 0261-5363
NEW BOOKBINDER. 1981. a. $44 to individuals; institutions $108. (Designer Bookbinders) Carfax Publishing Co., P.O. Box 25, Abingdon, Oxfordshire OX14 3UE, England. TEL 0235-555335. FAX 0235-553559. (U.S. subscr. addr.: Carfax Publishing Co., Box 2025, Dunnellon, FL 32630) Ed.Bd. adv.; bk.rev. (back issues avail.) **Indexed:** Print.Abstr.
   —BLDSC shelfmark: 6082.280000.

NEW BOOKS QUARTERLY ON ISLAM & THE MUSLIM WORLD. see *RELIGIONS AND THEOLOGY — Islamic*

NEW LAW BOOKS REVIEWER. see *LAW*

NEW LIBRARY SCENE. see *LIBRARY AND INFORMATION SCIENCES*

070.5   US   ISSN 0271-8197
Z477
NEW PAGES; alternatives in print & media. 1979. 3/yr. $12. New Pages Press, Box 438, Grand Blanc, MI 48439. TEL 313-743-8055. FAX 313-743-2730. Ed.Bd. adv.; bk.rev.; circ. 5,000 (controlled). **Indexed:** Alt.Press Ind., Bk.Rev.Ind. (1984-), Child.Bk.Rev.Ind. (1984-).

NEW RELEASES PUBLICATIONS LIST. see *LAW*

028.1   US   ISSN 0028-7504
AP2
NEW YORK REVIEW OF BOOKS. 1963. 21/yr. $39. N Y R E V, Inc., 250 W. 57th St., New York, NY 10107. TEL 212-757-8070. FAX 212-333-5374. (Subscr. to: Box 420384, Palm Coast, FL 32142-0384) Eds. Robert Silvers, Barbara Epstein. adv.; bk.rev.; illus.; circ. 120,000. (tabloid format; also avail. in microform from UMI; reprint service avail. from UMI) **Indexed:** Acad.Ind., Alt.Press Ind., Amer.Bibl.Slavic & E.Eur.Stud., Art & Archaeol.Tech.Abstr., Arts & Hum.Cit.Ind., Bk.Rev.Dig., Bk.Rev.Ind. (1965-), Can.Lit.Ind., Child.Bk.Rev.Ind. (1965-), Curr.Cont., Film Lit.Ind. (1973-), Fut.Surv., Ind.Bk.Rev.Hum., M.L.A., Mag.Ind., Mid.East: Abstr.& Ind., R.G., RILA.
   —BLDSC shelfmark: 6089.700000.
   Description: Commentary and opinion on politics, science and culture by eminent writers.

028 655   US   ISSN 0028-7806
AP2
NEW YORK TIMES BOOK REVIEW. 1896. w. $92.40 silver halide; $78.40 vesicular. New York Times Company, 229 W. 43rd St., New York, NY 10036. TEL 212-556-1234. (Subscr. to: Box 5792, G P O, New York, NY 10087. TEL 800-631-2580) Ed. Mitchell Levitas. adv.; bk.rev.; bibl.; illus.; circ. 60,000. (also avail. in microform from UMI) **Indexed:** Amer.Bibl.Slavic & E.Eur.Stud., Bk.Rev.Ind. (1965-), Can.Lit.Ind., Child.Bk.Rev.Ind. (1965-), Curr.Cont., Gard.Lit.(1992-), Ind.Bk.Rev.Hum., Mag.Ind., R.G., TOM.
   —BLDSC shelfmark: 6089.766000.

051   US
NEW YORK TIMES BOOK REVIEW (MICROFORM EDITIONS). (Includes supplements) w. $78.40 vesicular; silver halide $92.40. (New York Times Company) University Microfilms International, Serials Data Management, 300 N. Zeeb Rd., Ann Arbor, MI 48106. TEL 800-521-0600. (microform; back issues avail.) **Indexed:** Arts & Hum.Cit.Ind.

070.5 330   US
NEW YORK UNIVERSITY BUSINESS MAGAZINE PUBLISHING SERIES. 1987. irreg. price varies. New York University Press, 70 Washington Square S., New York, NY 10012. TEL 212-998-2575. FAX 212-995-3833. TELEX 235128 NYU UR. Ed. Albert Greco.

070   NZ   ISSN 0111-834X
NEW ZEALAND PUBLISHING NEWS. 1977. 4/yr. membership. Book Publishers Association of New Zealand Inc., P.O. Box 386, Auckland 1, New Zealand. TEL 09-309-2561. FAX 09-309-7789. Ed. Gerard Reid. circ. 160.

028.1   CN   ISSN 0380-2817
NEWEST REVIEW; a journal of culture and current events in the West. 1975. bi-m. price varies. NeWest Publishers Ltd., Box 394, Sub P.O. 6, Saskatoon, Sask., S7N 0W0, Canada. TEL 306-934-1444. adv.; bk.rev.; illus.; circ. 1,000. **Indexed:** Can.Lit.Ind., Can.Per.Ind., CMI.

070.5   US
NEWS FROM HOLT.* q. free. (Library Services Department) Holt, Rinehart and Winston, Inc., c/o Harcourt Brace Jovanovich, Orlando, FL 32887. TEL 407-345-2500.

070.5 658   US
NEWS INC. 1989. m. $47.50. News Incorporated, 49 E. 21st St., New York, NY 10010-0661. TEL 212-979-4600. Ed. Gary Hoenig. adv.; bk.rev.; circ. 18,000. (back issues avail.)
   Description: Aimed at newspaper executives and managers. Covers the business side of the newspaper industry.

NEWSLETTER ON INTELLECTUAL FREEDOM. see *LIBRARY AND INFORMATION SCIENCES*

NEWSLETTER ON SERIALS PRICING ISSUES. see *LIBRARY AND INFORMATION SCIENCES*

070.5   US
Z6941
NEWSLETTERS IN PRINT; a descriptive guide to more than 8,000 subscription, membership, and free newsletters, bulletins, digests, updates, and similar serial publications issued in the United States and available in print or online. 1966. irreg., 4th ed., 1988. $175. Gale Research Inc., 835 Penobscot Bldg., Detroit, MI 48226. TEL 313-961-2242. FAX 313-961-6083. TELEX 810-221-7086. Ed. Brigitte Darnay.
   ●Also available online. Vendor(s): DIALOG, Human Resources Information Network (NIP).
   Former titles: Newsletter Directory (ISSN 0893-7656); National Directory of Newsletters and Reporting Services (ISSN 0547-6232)
   Description: Irregular updating on newsletters available in the U.S.

NEWSPAPER PUBLISHERS HANDBOOK. see *JOURNALISM*

070.5   NE   ISSN 0048-0355
NIEUWE POCKETS EN PAPERBACKS. 1961. bi-m. fl.7.50. Het Nederlandse Boek, Prinsengracht 1065, 1017 JG Amsterdam, Netherlands. Ed. Wim J. Simons. adv.; bk.rev.; bibl.; circ. 20,000.

NIGERIAN LIBRARIES. see *LIBRARY AND INFORMATION SCIENCES*

NONGYE TUSHU QINGBAO XUEKAN/AGRICULTURAL BOOKS INFORMATION JOURNAL. see *LIBRARY AND INFORMATION SCIENCES*

655   DK   ISSN 0029-1323
NORDISK EXLIBRIS TIDSSKRIFT. Short title: N E T. (Text in Danish, English or German) 1946. 4/yr. membership. Dansk Exlibris Selskab - Danish Bookplate Society, Box 1519, DK-2700 Copenhagen, Denmark. Ed. Klaus Roedel. adv.; bk.rev.; illus.; cum.index every 2 yrs. **Indexed:** Artbibl.Mod.
   Description: Facts about book plates.

020.75   SW   ISSN 0029-148X
Z993P
NORDISK TIDSKRIFT FOER BOK- OCH BIBLIOTEKSVAESEN/SCANDINAVIAN JOURNAL OF LIBRARIES. (Text in the Scandinavian languages; summaries in English) 1914. 4/yr. SEK 195($28) Almqvist & Wiksell Periodical Company, Box 638, S-101 28 Stockholm, Sweden. Ed. G. Hornwall. adv.; bk.rev.; charts; illus.; index, cum.index; circ. 750. **Indexed:** Lib.Lit., Lib.Sci.Abstr.
   Description: Covers book collecting.

NOTABLE CHILDREN'S TRADE BOOKS IN THE FIELD OF SOCIAL STUDIES. see *SOCIAL SCIENCES: COMPREHENSIVE WORKS — Abstracting, Bibliographies, Statistics*

NOTES AND QUERIES; for readers and writers, collectors and librarians. see *LITERATURE*

090   FR   ISSN 0335-752X
Z4
NOUVELLES DU LIVRE ANCIEN. 1974. q. free. Institut de Recherche et d'Histoire des Textes, Section de l'Humanisme, C.N.R.S., 40 Ave. d'Iena, 75116 Paris, France. FAX 47-23-89-39. adv.; bk.rev.; bibl.; circ. 3,100.

011   GW   ISSN 0029-4993
NOVA; Vorankuendigungen-forthcoming books-livres en preparation. (Table of contents and subtitles in English, German and Russian) 1957. s-m. free. Expolibri GmbH Leipzig, Zentrum fuer Buchwerbung & Ausstellungen, Grimmaischestr. 13-15, 7010 Leipzig, Germany. TEL 271514. FAX 293594.
   Description: Annotated list of forthcoming books from German publishers (formerly East German), which can be ordered from abroad. Subjects include: social sciences, technology, agriculture, medicine, literature, art and sport.

070.5   BL
NOVO LIVROS. vol.2, 1979. m. Cr.$18000($40) Companhia Editora Jorues Ltda., Rua dos Pinheiros 928, Sao Paulo, CEP. 05422, Brazil. Ed. Virginia Pinheiro. adv.; bk.rev.; bibl.; illus.; circ. 25,000. (tabloid format)
   Formerly: Leia Livros.

PUBLISHING AND BOOK TRADE

070.5 US ISSN 0078-2882
O.P. MARKET. (Out of Print) 1948. a. $25. (Antiquarian Bookman) A B Bookman Publications, Inc., Box AB, Clifton, NJ 07015. TEL 201-772-0020. FAX 201-772-9281. Ed. Jacob L. Chernofsky. adv.; bk.rev.; circ. 10,000.
Description: Covers the out-of-print book market.

070.5 AU ISSN 0078-3455
DAS OESTERREICHISCHE BUCH. 1947. a. Hauptverband des Oesterreichischen Buchhandels, Gruenangergasse 4, A-1010 Vienna, Austria. TEL 0222-5121535. FAX 0222-512153521.

070.5 US ISSN 0896-5730
OHIO WRITER. 1987. bi-m. $12. Ohio Writer, Box 528, Willoughby, OH 44094. Ed. Linda L. Rome. adv.; bk.rev.; circ. 650.
Description: Covers writing and writers with an Ohio connection. Includes calendar of Ohio events.

070.5760 659.1 US
OKLAHOMA PUBLISHER. m. $5. Oklahoma Press Association, 3601 N. Lincoln, Oklahoma City, OK 73105-5400. TEL 405-524-4421. Ed. Ben Blackstock. charts; circ. 1,200. (tabloid format)
Description: For Oklahoma newspaper publishers; includes news of journalism, and public relations.

020 US
ON THE ROAD (FORDS). 1989. q. $12. On the Road - Library Outreach Reporter Publications, 148 Liberty St., Fords, NJ 08863-2042. TEL 908-738-5183. Ed. Cathi Alloway. adv.; illus.
Description: Gives practical advice on how to get an author's work out to the public.

070.5 DK ISSN 0107-380X
OPLAGSBULLETIN. 1932. a. DKK 54 per no. (free to libraries). Dansk Oplagskontrol - Danish Bureau of Circulations, Frederiksberggade 5, 1459 Copenhagen K, Denmark. circ. 2,200.

686 900 FI ISSN 0358-5581
Z829.A1
OPUSCULUM; kirja- ja oppihistoriallinen aikakauskirja. Bok- och laerdomshistorisk tidskrift. (Text in Finnish and Swedish; summaries in English) 1981. q. FIM 120($23) Helsingin Yliopiston Kirjasto - Helsinki University Library, P.O. Box 312, 00171 Helsinki, Finland. Ed. Esko Haekli. bk.rev.; illus.; index; circ. 350. (back issues avail.)
Description: Contains articles on books, library history, and the history of learning.

028.1 UK
ORIGO. 1979. q. £30. Genesis Publications Ltd., Lynwood House, 51 Lynwood, Guildford, Surrey GU2 5NY, England. FAX 0483-304709. Ed. Kay Williams. bk.rev.; illus.; circ. 2,000.

070.5 UK ISSN 0048-2528
OVERSEAS BOOKS. vol.8, 1971. m. £17($55) per no. New Product Newsletter Co. Ltd., 1A Chesterfield St., London W.1., England. Ed. H.R. Vaughan. adv.; circ. 7,000.

070.5 UK ISSN 0078-7159
OVERSEAS NEWSPAPERS AND PERIODICALS. (Issued in 2 vols.: Vol. 1: Markets in Europe; Vol. 2: Markets outside Europe) 1952. biennial. £17($50) per vol. New Product Newsletter Co. Ltd., 1A Chesterfield St., London W.1., England. Ed. H.R. Vaughan. adv.; circ. 5,000. (also avail. in microfilm from UMI)

P A T E F A NEWS BULLETIN. (Printing & Allied Trades Employers Federation of Australia) see PRINTING

028.5 IT
PAGINE GIOVANI. q. Via Portuense, 112, Rome, Italy. Ed. E.F. Martinez.

028.1 IT ISSN 0030-9435
Z1007
PAIDEIA; rivista letteraria di informazione bibliografica. (Text in English, French, German and Italian) 1946. 3/yr. L.30000. Paideia Editrice, Via Corsica 132, 25125 Brescia, Italy. Ed.Bd. bk.rev.; rec.rev.; index. **Indexed:** M.L.A.

070.5 011 020 PK
PAKISTAN'S BOOKS & LIBRARIES; the only monthly magazine of its kind. (Text in English) 1989. m. Rs.200($25) M. Nayeem Siddiqui, Ed. & Pub., 305-15, F.B. Area, Karachi 75950, Pakistan. TEL 21-685858. FAX 21-200678. TELEX 23898 CROWN PK. adv.; bk.rev.; bibl.; circ. 2,000.
Description: Covers the book trade and libraries in Pakistan.

PANURGE. see LITERATURE

PAPERBACK INFERNO. see LITERATURE — Science Fiction, Fantasy, Horror

020.75 808.838 US
PAPERBACK PARADE. bi-m. $20 (foreign $26). Gryphon Publications, Box 290, Brooklyn, NY 11228-0209. adv. (back issues avail.)
Description: Covers the hobby of paperback reading and collecting.

PAPUA NEW GUINEA NATIONAL BIBLIOGRAPHY. see BIBLIOGRAPHIES

070.5 028.5 VE
PARAPARA BOLETIN INFORMATIVO. 1980. 3/yr. Bs.450($25) for all 3 Praparas. Banco del Libro, Apdo. 5893, Caracas 1010-A, Venezuela. TEL 323136. FAX 334272. circ. 300.
Supersedes in part (in 1990): Parapara.
Description: Contains information about personalities, prizes, seminars, congresses and fairs in the world of children's literature.

070.5 028.5 VE
PARAPARA REVISTA DE LITERATURA INFANTIL. 1980. w. Bs.450($25) includes all 3 Paraparas. Banco del Libro, Apdo. 5893, Caracas 1010-A, Venezuela. TEL 3230136. FAX 334272. TELEX 23635 BANLI VC. Ed. Marcela Rodriguez. circ. 1,000.
Supersedes in part (in 1990): Parapara.
Description: Contains articles on and interviews with specialists in the area of children's literature.

070.5 028.5 VE
PARAPARA SELECCION DE LIBROS PARA NINOS Y JOVENES. 1980. 3/yr. Bs.250($25) includes all 3 Paraparas. Banco del Libro, Apdo. 5893, Caracas 1010A, Venezuela. TEL 323136. FAX 334272. bk.rev.; circ. 1,000.
Supersedes in part (in 1990): Parapara.
Description: Offers a selection of books for children and young people, covering a different theme each issue.

PAROLA E IL LIBRO; the word and the book. see LIBRARY AND INFORMATION SCIENCES

PEN IN HAND. see JOURNALISM

070.5 US ISSN 0737-7843
Z6945.A2
PERIODICAL TITLE ABBREVIATIONS; covering periodical title abbreviations in science, the social sciences, the humanities, law, medicine, religion, library science, engineering, education, business, art, and many other fields. (In 3 Vols; Vol.1: By Abbreviation; Vol.2: By Title; Vol.3: New Abbreviation) 1969. irreg., 8th ed., 1991. $185 for vol.1 and vol.2; vol.3 $140. Gale Research Inc., 835 Penobscot Bldg., Detroit, MI 48226. TEL 313-961-2242. FAX 313-961-6083. TELEX 810-221-7086. Ed. Leland G. Alkire, Jr. —BLDSC shelfmark: 6426.040000.
Description: Encyclopedia of periodical title abbreviations.

PERSPECTIVES ON POLITICAL SCIENCE. see POLITICAL SCIENCE

010 760 GW ISSN 0031-7969
Z990
PHILOBIBLON. 1957. q. DM.96. (Maximilian-Gesellschaft e.V.) Dr. Ernst Hauswedell und Co. Verlag, Rosenbergstr. 113, Postfach 140155, 7000 Stuttgart 10, Germany. FAX 0711-6369010. Ed. Reimar W. Fuchs. adv.; B&W page DM.600; trim 182 x 121. bibl.; illus.; tr.lit.; index; circ. 2,000. (reprint service avail. from KTO) **Indexed:** M.L.A.

PHILOSOPHICAL BOOKS. see PHILOSOPHY

PIMS BUSINESS, INVESTOR AND GOVERNMENT RELATIONS DIRECTORY. see BUSINESS AND ECONOMICS — Banking And Finance

PIMS EUROPEAN TRADE & TECHNICAL DIRECTORY. see BUSINESS AND ECONOMICS — Trade And Industrial Directories

658.8 380.1 UK
PIMS MEDIA TOWNSLIST. 1984. q. £160. PIMS (UK) PLC., PIMS House, Mildmay Ave., London N1 4RS, England. TEL 071-226-1000. FAX 071-704-1360. (Subscr. to: 1133 Broadway, New York, NY 10010, U.S.A.)
Description: Media identified for over 1100 U.K. towns and cities.

658.8 380.1 UK
PIMS U K MEDIA DIRECTORY. 1981. m. £240. PIMS (UK) PLC., PIMS House, Mildmay Ave., London N1 4RS, England. TEL 071-226-1000. FAX 071-704-1360. (Subscr. to: 1133 Broadway, New York, NY 10010, U.S.A.)
Formerly: Pims Media Directory (ISSN 0261-5169)
Description: Lists contacts, addresses, telephone numbers for all U.K. media.

PITTSBURGH JEWISH CHRONICLE. see JOURNALISM

POLICY PUBLISHERS AND ASSOCIATIONS DIRECTORY. see POLITICAL SCIENCE

POLIGRAFIYA. see PRINTING

077 RM
PRESA NOASTRA.* 1954. m. 60 lei($12) Uniunea Ziaristilor din Republica Socialista Romania, Calea Victoriei Nr. 163, Bucharest, Rumania. (Subscr. to: ILEXIM, Str. 13 Decembrie Nr. 3, P.O. Box 136-137, Bucharest, Rumania) Ed. Petre Constaninescu.

PRESSE-PORTRAETS; das Angebot des Pressehandels. see BIBLIOGRAPHIES

658.8 GW ISSN 0341-8073
PRESSE REPORT; Magazin fuer den Presseeinzelhandel. Short title: P R. (Supplement avail.: Presse-Portraets) 1975. m. DM.58. Presse Fachverlag, Eidelstedteweg 22, 2000 Hamburg 20, Germany. TEL 040-565031. FAX 040-5602920. circ. 75,000.
Formerly (1951-1974): Zeitungs- und Zeitschriftenhandel (ISSN 0044-3832)
Description: Publication for the paperback book, magazine, and newspaper retail trade, featuring the latest news, sales strategies, businesses for sale, and new publications.

070 AU
PRESSEHANDBUCH (YEAR). 1953. a. S.957. Verband Oesterreichischer Zeitungsherausgeber und Zeitungsverleger, Schreyvogelgasse 3, A-1010 Vienna, Austria. TEL 01-5336178. FAX 01-5336178-22. Ed. Rudolf Stadler. adv.; bk.rev.; mkt.; tr.lit.; index; circ. 2,500.
Formerly: Oesterreichs Presse, Werbung, Graphik (ISSN 0030-0004)

070.5 686.2 SZ
PRINT.* (Text in French, German and Italian) vol.100, 1975. w. 45 Fr. Schweizerischer Buchdruckerverein - Societe Suisse des Maitres-Imprimeurs, Gubelstr. 28, Postfach 8391, CH-8050 Zurich, Switzerland. Ed. E. Mueller. adv.; charts; illus.; circ. 13,300.
Formerly: Schweizerische Buchdrucker-Zeitung.

PRINT AND PRODUCTION MANUAL. see PRINTING

070.5 US ISSN 0737-7436
PRINT WORLD. JOURNAL. 1978. q. $14. Journal of the Print World, 1000 Winona Rd., Meredith, NH 03253-9599. Ed. Charles Stuart Lane. adv.; bk.rev.

PRINTER'S DEVIL; graphic arts for the small press. see PRINTING

PRINTING AND BOOKBINDING TRADE REVIEW; equipment-materials-production. see PRINTING

070.5 US
PRINTING & PUBLISHING: LATIN AMERICAN INDUSTRIAL REPORT. (Avail. for each of 22 Latin American countries) 1985. a. $435 per country report. Aquino Productions, Box 15760, Stamford, CT 06901. TEL 203-325-3138. Ed. Andres C. Aquino.

PRINTING HISTORY. see PRINTING

PRIVATE LIBRARY. see LIBRARY AND INFORMATION SCIENCES

PROVIDENT BOOK FINDER. see *RELIGIONS AND THEOLOGY — Protestant*

070.5   BE
PUB MAGAZINE. (Text in Flemish) fortn. C E D Samson (Subsidiary of: Wolters Samson Belgie n.v.), Louizalaan 485, B-1050 Brussels, Belgium. TEL 02-7231111. FAX 02-6498480. TELEX CEDSAM 64130.
Description: News on advertising, marketing, and other aspects of communications and media.

070.5   BE
PUB NEWSLETTER. (Text in Flemish) 2/w. C E D Samson (Subsidiary of: Wolters Samson Belgie n.v.), Louizalaan 485, B-1050 Brussels, Belgium. TEL 02-7231111. FAX 02-6498480. TELEX CEDSAM 64130.
Description: Covers advertising, marketing, and media.

070.5   UK   ISSN 0033-3263
PUBDISCO NEWS. 1964. m. £17($50) each ed. New Product Newsletter Co. Ltd., 1A Chesterfield St., London W.1., England. Ed. H.R. Vaughan. adv.; bibl.; illus.; circ. 7,000. (also avail. in microfilm from UMI)

PUBLICATION DESIGN ANNUAL. see *ART*

PUBLICATION PROFILES. see *ADVERTISING AND PUBLIC RELATIONS*

070.5   CH
PUBLICATIONS YEARBOOK, REPUBLIC OF CHINA; including catalogs of books and records. 1977. a. NT.$700. China Publishing Company, Box 337, Taipei, Taiwan, Republic of China.

070.5   CN   ISSN 0380-8025
PUBLISHER. 1919. 10/yr. Can.$21. Canadian Community Newspapers Association, Ste. 705, 88 University Ave., Toronto, Ont. M5J 1T6, Canada. TEL 416-598-4277. FAX 416-598-4410. Ed. Maureen de Jong. adv.; bk.rev.; circ. 1,312.
Supersedes: Canadian Community Publisher (ISSN 0045-4583) & Canadian Weekly Publisher (ISSN 0008-5316)

070.5   NR
PUBLISHER. 1985. a. £N7.50($3.95) Nigerian Publishers' Association, Ile Orideth, Onireke, G.P.O. Box 2541, Ibadan, Nigeria. TEL 022-411557. Ed. Steve Falaye. circ. 2,000. (back issues avail.)

PUBLISHERS' CATALOGS ANNUAL. see *BIBLIOGRAPHIES*

070.5   US   ISSN 0742-0501
Z475
PUBLISHERS DIRECTORY. 1977. a. $245. Gale Research Inc., 835 Penobscot Bldg., Detroit, MI 48226. TEL 313-961-2242. FAX 313-961-6083. TELEX 810-221-7086. Ed. Linda Hubbard.
●Also available online. Vendor(s): DIALOG.
—BLDSC shelfmark: 7156.067900.
Former titles (until 1984): Book Publishers Directory (ISSN 0196-0903); Book Publishers of the U.S. and Canada.
Description: Book publishers of the United States and Canada.

PUBLISHERS, DISTRIBUTORS & WHOLESALERS OF THE UNITED STATES; a directory of publishers, distributors, associations, wholesalers, software producers and manufacturers listing editorial and ordering addresses, and an ISBN publisher prefix index. see *BUSINESS AND ECONOMICS — Trade And Industrial Directories*

070.5   UK
PUBLISHERS HANDBOOK. 1987. a. £25. Grosvenor Press International Ltd., Holford Mews, Cruikshank St., London WC1X 9HD, England. TEL 01-278-3000. FAX 01-278-1674. Ed. Barbara Leedham. adv.; circ. 10,000.
Description: Reference book on British publishing services.

070.5   UK   ISSN 0079-7839
PUBLISHERS IN THE UNITED KINGDOM AND THEIR ADDRESSES. 1946. a. £10.50. J. Whitaker & Sons Ltd., 12 Dyott St., London WC1A 1DF, England. TEL 071-836-8911. FAX 071-836-2909. adv.

PUBLISHERS INFORMATION BUREAU REPORT; magazine advertising expenditures. (Publishers' Information Bureau Inc.) see *ADVERTISING AND PUBLIC RELATIONS*

070.5   II
PUBLISHERS' MONTHLY. (Text in English and Hindi) 1959. m. Rs.10. S. Chand & Co. Ltd., Ravindra Mansion, Ram Nagar, New Delhi 5, India. Ed. R.C. Kumar. adv.; bk.rev.; bibl.; circ. 10,000.

070.5   US   ISSN 0884-3090
PUBLISHER'S REPORT. 1985. bi-m. $75. National Association of Independent Publishers, Box 430, Highland City, FL 33846-0430.
TEL 813-648-4420. Eds. Betty Wright, Betsey Lampe. adv.; bk.rev.; circ. 400.
Description: Furthers the visibility of independent publishing.

070.5   UK   ISSN 0953-7899
PUBLISHERS REPORTS; the independent report on international publishing. 1988. m. £185($290) P.O. Box 845, Bath BA1 3TW, England.
TEL 0225-443194. FAX 0225-443194. TELEX 94016955-PUBR-G. Ed. F. Russel-Cobb. adv.; bk.rev.
Description: Newsletter covering international publishing, especially marketing information.

658.8   US   ISSN 0000-0019
Z1219
PUBLISHERS WEEKLY; the international news magazine of book publishing. 1872. 51/yr. $119 (Canada $177, foreign $260). Cahners Publishing Company (New York), Bowker Magazine Group, Cahners Magazine Division (Subsidiary of: Reed International PLC), Division of Reed Publishing (USA) Inc., 249 W. 17th St., New York, NY 10011. TEL 212-645-0067. FAX 212-242-7216. TELEX 12-7703. (Subscr. to: Box 1979, Marion, OH 43302. TEL 800-842-1669) Ed. Nora Rawlinson. adv.; bk.rev.; bibl.; illus.; stat.; circ. 38,349. (also avail. in microform from RPI; reprint service avail. from UMI) **Indexed:** Acad.Ind., B.P.I, Bk.Rev.Ind. (1965-), Chic.Per.Ind., Child.Bk.Rev.Ind. (1965-), Child.Lit.Abstr., Curr.Lit.Fam.Plan., Gard.Lit. (1992-), Graph.Arts Lit.Abstr., Hlth.Ind., LHTN, Lib.Lit., Mag.Ind., Mid.East: Abstr.& Ind., PMR, R.G., Tr.& Indus.Ind.
—BLDSC shelfmark: 7156.080000.
Description: News and trends of interest to publishers, booksellers and librarians, including author interviews, advance book reviews, marketing and book design and manufacturing articles.

070.5 686   US   ISSN 1048-3055
Z284.
PUBLISHING & PRODUCTION EXECUTIVE. vol.2, 1988. q. $28 (foreign $35). North American Publishing Co., 401 N. Broad St., Philadelphia, PA 19108. TEL 215-238-5300. FAX 215-238-5457. Ed. Rose Blessing. circ. 33,300.
Formerly (until Nov. 1989): Publishing Technology.
Description: For printing buyers and production professionals who buy paper, prepress, printing and electronic publishing systems for book, magazine and catalogue publishers. Focuses on equipment, production techniques, computer hardware and software and related products and services.

070.5   UK   ISSN 0309-2445
Z280
PUBLISHING HISTORY. 1977. s-a. £60($100) to institutions; individuals £28($48). Chadwyck-Healey Ltd., Cambridge Place, Cambridge CB2 1NR, England. TEL 0223-311479. FAX 0223-66440. TELEX 93121 02281 CH G. (U.S. subscr. to: Chadwyck-Healey Inc., 1101 King St., Alexandria, VA 22314. TEL 800-752-0515) Ed. Michael L. Turner. adv.; bk.rev.; circ. 500. (also avail. in microform from MIM; back issues avail.) **Indexed:** Arts & Hum.Cit.Ind., Curr.Cont., Hist.Abstr.
—BLDSC shelfmark: 7156.093000.
Description: Devoted to the socio-economic and literary history of books, newspaper and magazine publishing.

070.5 658.8   US
PUBLISHING MARKETS. 1986. bi-m. $125. Cahners Publishing Company (Newton) (Subsidiary of: Reed International PLC), Division of Reed Publishing (USA) Inc., 275 Washington St., Newton, MA 02158-1630. TEL 617-964-3030. FAX 617-558-4700. (Subscr. to: 44 Cook St., Denver, CO 80206. TEL 800-662-7776) Ed. Jane Dietzel.

070.5   UK
PUBLISHING NEWS; weekly for people in the book trade. 1979. w. £60($85) (foreign £70). Gradegate Ltd., 43 Museum St., London WC1A 1LY, England. TEL 071-404-0304. Ed. Fred Newman. adv.; bk.rev.; illus.
Former titles: Book Buyer; Paperback Buyer.

PUBLISHING POYNTERS; book marketing news and ideas from Dan Poynter. see *BUSINESS AND ECONOMICS — Marketing And Purchasing*

070.5   US   ISSN 1053-8801
Z1003   CODEN: PREQEI
PUBLISHING RESEARCH QUARTERLY. 1986. q. $36 to individuals (foreign $56); institutions $72 (foreign $92). Transaction Publishers, Transaction Periodicals Consortium, Department 3092, Rutgers University, New Brunswick, NJ 08903. TEL 908-932-2280. FAX 908-932-3138. Ed. Beth Luey. bk.rev.; circ. 1,000.
—BLDSC shelfmark: 7156.094550.
Formerly: Book Research Quarterly (ISSN 0741-6148)
Description: Publishes research on or about books, the publishing and book distribution process, and the social, political, economic, and technological conditions that help shape this process.

070.5   US
PUBLISHING SYSTEMS. 1987. bi-m. $12. Technical Data Publishing Corporation, 91 N. Bertrand Rd., Box 458, Mt. Arlington, NJ 07856. TEL 201-770-2633. Ed. William M. Rowe. circ. 20,000.

070.5 658   US
PUBLISHING TRENDS AND TRENDSETTERS. 1978. 10/yr. $177. Oxbridge Communications, Inc., 150 Fifth Ave., New York, NY 10011. TEL 212-741-0231. FAX 212-633-2938. Ed. Jim Mann. bk.rev.; circ. 320. (back issues avail.)
Formerly (until 1991): Media Management Monographs (ISSN 0192-7663)
Description: Contains interviews with magazine publishing executives, analysis of publishing industry trends.

015.4 090   NE   ISSN 0014-9527
QUAERENDO; a quarterly journal from the Low Countries devoted to manuscripts and printed books. (Text mainly in English; occasionally in French and German) 1971. q. (effective 1992). E.J. Brill, P.O. Box 9000, 2300 PA Leiden, Netherlands. TEL 071-312624. FAX 071-317532. TELEX 39296 BRILL NL. (In N. America: E.J. Brill, 24 Hudson St., Kinderhook, NY 12106. TEL 800-962-4406) Ed.Bd. adv.; bk.rev.; illus.; index; circ. 750. **Indexed:** RILA.
—BLDSC shelfmark: 7168.108000.

028.1   US
QUALITY PAPERBACK BOOK CLUB REVIEW. 1974. 15/yr. membership. Quality Paperback Book Club, 485 Lexington Ave., New York, NY 10017. Ed. Susan Weinberg. circ. controlled.

686.3 747.5   AT   ISSN 0725-0711
QUEENSLAND BOOKBINDERS' GUILD. NEWSLETTER. 1980. q. Aus.$22.50 (effective Mar. 1990). Queensland Bookbinders' Guild Inc., P.O. Box 73, Annerley, Qld. 4103, Australia. TEL 07-848-3774. circ. 110. (back issues avail.)
Description: To promote, foster and practise the arts of bookbinding, graphic arts and kindred arts.

658.8   CN   ISSN 0033-6491
Z487
QUILL AND QUIRE; Canada's magazine of book news and reviews. 1935. m. Can.$48.15 (foreign Can.$55)(effective 1991). Key Publishers Co. Ltd., 70 The Esplanade, 4th fl., Toronto, Ont. M5E 1R2, Canada. TEL 416-360-0044. FAX 416-941-9038. Ed. Ted Mumford. adv.; bk.rev.; bibl.; illus.; stat.; circ. 7,000. (tabloid format; also avail. in microfiche) **Indexed:** Bk.Rev.Ind. (1980-), Can.B.P.I., Can.Lit.Ind., Can.Per.Ind., Child.Bk.Rev.Ind. (1980-), CMI.
Incorporates (in 1989): Books for Young People (ISSN 0045-2556)
Description: For booksellers, librarians and publishers.

PUBLISHING AND BOOK TRADE

070.5 808.8 011   UK   ISSN 0144-1779
RADICAL BOOKSELLER. (Includes: Radical Books of the Months) 1980. 8/yr. £15($30) Radical Bookseller Ltd., 265 Seven Sisters Rd., London N4 2DE, England. Ed. J.F. Nicol. adv.; bk.rev.; circ. 300.
—BLDSC shelfmark: 7228.090500.
Description: Trade news, literature and publications abstracts, article excerpts, and directory of small publishers of books and periodicals pertaining to avant-garde thought in economic, industrial and social politics, literature, science and education, and lifestyle, and of workshops dealing in such literature.

028   IT   ISSN 0033-8648
Z1007
RAGGUAGLIO LIBRARIO; rassegna mensile bibliografica culturale. (Former issuing body: Istituto di Propaganda Libraria) 1933. m. L.45000. Associazione Arte e Cultura, Via Terruggia 16, 20162 Milan, Italy. Dir. Giulio Madurini. adv.; bk.rev.; bibl.; illus. **Indexed:** M.L.A.

658.8   US
READING CENTER. m. Council for Periodical Distributors Association, 60 E. 42nd St., Ste. 2134, New York, NY 10165. TEL 212-818-0234. Ed. Tilly McCardell.

READINGS; a journal of reviews and commentary in mental health. see *MEDICAL SCIENCES — Psychiatry And Neurology*

RECENT PUBLICATIONS IN NATURAL HISTORY. see *SCIENCES: COMPREHENSIVE WORKS*

050   AG
REDACCION. m. Arg.$80. Editorial Replica, Distribuidora Condor, Av. Independencia, 2744, Buenos Aires, Argentina. illus.

REDACTUEL. see *JOURNALISM*

REDAKTIONS ADRESS. see *BUSINESS AND ECONOMICS — Trade And Industrial Directories*

070.5
REFERENCE REPORT.* m. $78. Educational Materials Distributors, 28 Greenbriar, Grosse Point Shores, MI 48230. Ed. E.M. Dawson.

070.5   HK
▼**REFLECTIONS;** news from Springer-Verlag Hong Kong. (Text in English) 1991. s-a. free. Springer-Verlag Hong Kong, Ltd., 701 Mirror Tower, 61 Mody Rd., Tsim Sha Tsui, Kowloon, Hong Kong. TEL 852-723-9698. FAX 852-724-2366. Ed. Maurice C. Kwong. circ. 5,000 (controlled).
Description: Features major academic activities in Asia and science-related articles.

658.8   CM
REGIONAL CENTRE FOR BOOK PROMOTION IN AFRICA. BULLETIN OF INFORMATION/CENTRE REGIONAL DE PROMOTION DU LIVRE EN AFRIQUE. BULLETIN D'INFORMATION. 1978. q. Regional Centre for Book Promotion in Africa, Box 1646, Yaounde, Cameroon.

658.8   IT   ISSN 0034-4176
REMAINDERS' BOOK ITALIANO; il servizio internazionale per l'acqisto del libro a meta del prezzo di copertina. no.3, 1967. q. Libreria Internazionale Guida, Via Port'Alba 20-21-24, Naples, Italy. adv.; illus.

655   FR
REPERTOIRE INTERNATIONAL DES EDITEURS ET DIFFUSEURS DE LANGUE FRANCAISE. a. 430 F. Editions du Cercle de la Librairie, 35 rue Gregoire de Tours, 75279 Paris Cedex 06, France. circ. 5,000.
Formerly: Livre de Langue Francaise - Repertoire des Editeurs (ISSN 0076-0110)

070.5   CN   ISSN 0712-7243
RESOURCE-MAG; a marketing report for publishing professionals. 1982. 10/yr. Can.$56. 20 Tettenhall Road, Etobicoke, Ont. M9A 2C3, Canada. TEL 416-231-7796. Ed. Lynn McFadgen. bk.rev.
Description: A marketing report focusing on advertising, circulation, news and trends for the magazine and newsletter industry.

RESOURCES IN AGING; an international newsletter featuring new developments in aging. see *GERONTOLOGY AND GERIATRICS*

RETAIL NEWSAGENT TOBACCONIST CONFECTIONER. see *TOBACCO*

028.1   BL
REVISTA DO LIVRO (SAO PAULO). 1973. bi-m. free. Circulo do Livro S.A., Caixa Postal 7413, CEP 01310 Sao Paulo, Brazil. Ed. Esnider Pizzo. adv.; bk.rev.; illus.; circ. 1,100,000.

028.1   AG
REVISTA LIBROS ELEGIDOS. 1975. m. Editorial Atlantida, S.A., Azopardo 579, Buenos Aires, Argentina. Ed. Costancio C. Vigil. adv.; bk.rev.; illus.; circ. 40,000.
Description: Contains book reviews.

028.5 028.1   FR   ISSN 0398-8384
REVUE DES LIVRES POUR ENFANTS. 1965. bi-m. 190 F. (foreign 215 F.)(effective 1992). (Centre National du Livre pour Enfants) Joie Par les Livres, 8 rue Saint-Bon, 75004 Paris, France. TEL 48-87-61-95. FAX 48-87-08-52. Ed. Ms. Claude Hubert. adv.; bk.rev.; circ. 5,000. (back issues avail.)
Formerly: Bulletin d'Analyses de Livres pour Enfants.
Description: Reviews recently published children's books and publishes articles about children's literature and libraries.

REVUE FRANCAISE D'HISTOIRE DU LIVRE. see *LIBRARY AND INFORMATION SCIENCES*

RHODE ISLAND. DEPARTMENT OF STATE LIBRARY SERVICES. NEWSLETTER. see *LIBRARY AND INFORMATION SCIENCES*

RIGHTS AND LIABILITIES OF PUBLISHERS, BROADCASTERS, AND REPORTERS. see *LAW — Civil Law*

015.498   RM   ISSN 0035-8045
ROMANIAN BOOKS. (Editions in English, French, German, Russian) 1964. q. $5. (Consiliul Culturii si Educatiei Socialiste) Centrala Editoriala, Piata Scinteii Nr. 1, 79715 Bucharest, Rumania. (Subscr. to: ICECOOP-ILEXIM, 3 Str. Decembrie, POB 1-136, 1-137, 70116 Bucharest, Rumania.) Ed. Hristu Candroveanu. adv.; bk.rev.; bibl.; illus.; circ. 6,000. (tabloid format)

ROMANTIC TRAVELING. see *TRAVEL AND TOURISM*

070.5   US
ROUND TABLE (ANDERSON). 1952. bi-m. free. Protestant Church-Owned Publishers Association, 1200 E. 5th St., Box 2499, Anderson, IN 46018. Ed. Richard Grant. circ. 500.

RUSS COCHRAN NEWSLETTER. see *ART*

070.5 685.048   US
S N A P. BULLETIN. irreg. Society of National Association Publishers, 1735 N. Lynn St, Ste. 950, Arlington, VA 22209-2022. TEL 703-524-2000.

070.5 658.048   US
S N A P. BUYERS' GUIDE. a. Society of National Association Publishers, 1735 N. Lynn St., Ste 950, Arlington, VA 22209-2022. TEL 703-524-2000.

070.5   US
S N A P SHOT. 1965. m. membership. Society of National Association Publishers, 1735 N. Lynn St., Ste. 950, Arlington, VA 22209-2022. TEL 703-524-2000. FAX 703-524-2303. Ed. Allison Parker. adv.; circ. 500.

070.5   US   ISSN 0730-2223
S P E X.* (Self-Publishers Exchange) 1981. bi-m. $20 to non-members. Marin Small-Publishers Association, 155 Cypress St,y, Ft. Bragg, CA 95437. TEL 415-924-1616. FAX 707-964-7531. Ed. John Freemont. adv.; bk.rev.; circ. 250.
Description: News, letters, notes, announcements, reviews, articles and book lists pertaining to the activities of independent authors, publishers, and printers.

S R I S NEWSLETTER. (Science Reference and Information Service) see *LIBRARY AND INFORMATION SCIENCES*

028.1   US
SAN FRANCISCO REVIEW OF BOOKS. 1975. q. $15. 555 De Haro St., No.220, San Francisco, CA 94107-2348. TEL 415-252-7708. FAX 415-252-8908. Ed. Elgy Gillespie. adv.; bk.rev.; index; circ. 10,000. (also avail. in microform from UMI; reprint service avail. from UMI) **Indexed:** Bk.Rev.Ind. (1982-), Chic.Per.Ind., Child.Bk.Rev.Ind. (1982-), New Per.Ind.

SCANDINAVIAN PUBLIC LIBRARY QUARTERLY. see *LIBRARY AND INFORMATION SCIENCES*

SCHEDARIO; periodico di letteratura giovanile. see *EDUCATION*

070.5 740   SZ   ISSN 0080-6838
SCHOENSTE SCHWEIZER BUECHER. (Text in English, French, German and Italian) 1943. a. free. Schweizerischer Buchhaendler- und Verleger-Verband, Box 9045, CH-8050 Zurich, Switzerland. (Co-sponsor: Eidgenoessisches Departement des Innern) bk.rev.

011 655   CN   ISSN 0036-634X
Z286.S37
SCHOLARLY PUBLISHING. 1969. q. Can.$25 to individuals; institutions Can.$50; students Can.$15. University of Toronto Press, Journals Department, P.O. Box 1280, 1011 Sheppard Ave. W., Downsview, Ont. M3H 5V4, Canada. TEL 705-323-3785. FAX 416-667-7832. (U.S. address: 340 Nagel Dr., Cheektowaga, NY 14225) Ed. Mark Carroll. adv.; bk.rev.; illus.; index; circ. 2,159. (also avail. in microfiche from UMI) **Indexed:** C.L.I., Curr.Cont., Hist.Abstr., Leg.Per., Lib.Lit., M.L.A., SSCI.
—BLDSC shelfmark: 8092.540500.

SCHOOL LIBRARY JOURNAL; the magazine of children, young adults & school librarians. see *LIBRARY AND INFORMATION SCIENCES*

658.8   SZ   ISSN 0036-732X
Z2775
SCHWEIZER BUCH. 1943. s-m. 300 Fr. (foreign 400 Fr.). Schweizerischer Buchhaendler- und Verleger-Verband, Postfach 9045, CH-8050 Zurich, Switzerland. (Co-sponsor: Schweizerische Landesbibliothek) adv.; bk.rev.; index; circ. 1,000.

658.8   SZ   ISSN 0036-7338
SCHWEIZER BUCHHANDEL/LIBRAIRIE SUISSE/LIBRERIA SVIZZERA. 1943. 21/yr. 120 Fr. (foreign 155 Fr.). Schweizerischer Buchhaendler- und Verleger-Verband, Baumackerstr. 42, Postfach 9045, CH-8050 Zurich, Switzerland. TEL 01-3125343. FAX 01-3113132. Ed. Franziska Schlaepfer. adv.; bk.rev.; bibl.; charts; index; circ. 3,300. **Indexed:** Key to Econ.Sci.
Description: Includes association news, reports of events, trade information, announcements of new publications, award presentations, list of events and exhibitions, letters from readers, list of advertisers, and positions available.

070.5   SZ   ISSN 0080-7230
SCHWEIZER BUCHHANDELS-ADRESSBUCH. 1966. a. 96 F. Schweizerischer Buchhaendler- und Verleger-Verband, Postfach 9045, CH-8050 Zurich, Switzerland.

SCIENCE FICTION CHRONICLE; the monthly science fiction and fantasy newsmagazine. see *LITERATURE — Science Fiction, Fantasy, Horror*

020.75   UK   ISSN 0954-8769
SCOTTISH BOOK COLLECTOR. 1987. 6/yr. £10. c/o Jennie Renton, 11a Forth St., Edinburgh EH1 3LE, Scotland. TEL 031-228-4837. adv.; bk.rev.
Description: Covers Scottish books, modern literature and trade profiles from a collector's and librarian's perspective.

091   BE   ISSN 0036-9772
Z108
SCRIPTORIUM; international review of manuscript studies. (Text in several languages) 1947. s-a. 3800 Fr. Centre d'Etudes des Manuscrits, 4 bd. de l'Empereur, B-1000 Brussels, Belgium. Ed. M. Garand. bk.rev.; bibl.; charts; illus.; index; circ. 900. **Indexed:** New Test.Abstr., RILA.
—BLDSC shelfmark: 8213.235000.

PUBLISHING AND BOOK TRADE 4137

655   JA   ISSN 0037-1009
SEIHONKAI/BOOKBINDING INDUSTRY. (Text in Japanese) 1950. m. Tokyo-to Seihon Kogyo Kumiai, 2-5 Kanda, Nishiki-cho, Chiyoda-ku, Tokyo, Japan. Ed. Tadao Toma.
Formerly: Seihon Shikokai.

028.1   II
SELECTION. bi-m. Praveen Corp., Sayajiganj, Baroda 390005, India. bk.rev.

070.5 659.1 686   US
SELLING; the publication for sales personnel. 1986. bi-m. $25. J B & Me Publishing, Box 3879, Manhattan Beach, CA 90266. TEL 310-546-1255. Ed. Marilyn Elkind. adv.; bk.rev.; charts; illus.; stat.; tr.lit.; cum.index: 1986-1989; circ. 10,000. (back issues avail.)
Former titles: Selling Space's Client Magazine; Selling Space (ISSN 0891-5857)
Description: Offers training and skills information, reports on business and demographic trends, summaries of relevant research, articles on business travel and entertainment for sales professionals.

070.5   UK   ISSN 0950-0715
Z327
SHEPPARD'S BOOK DEALERS IN BRITISH ISLES. 1951. a. £24($48) Richard Joseph Publishers Ltd., Unit 2, Monks Walk, Farnham, Surrey GU9 8HT, England. TEL 0252-734347. FAX 0252-734307. Ed. Mrs. Eshelby. adv.; circ. 2,000. (back issues avail.)
—BLDSC shelfmark: 8256.432000.
Formerly: Directory of Dealers in Secondhand and Antiquarian Books in the British Isles (ISSN 0070-5411)

070.5   UK
SHEPPARD'S BOOK DEALERS IN INDIA AND THE ORIENT. 1977. triennial. $48. Richard Joseph Publishers Ltd., Unit 2, Monks Walk, Farnham, Surrey GU9 8HT, England. TEL 0252-734347. FAX 0252-734307.
Formerly: Bookdealers in India, Pakistan and Sri Lanka (ISSN 0143-0270)

658.8   UK   ISSN 0962-2764
▼**SHEPPARD'S BOOKDEALERS IN AUSTRALIA AND NEW ZEALAND.** 1990. triennial. $48. Richard Joseph Publishers Ltd., Unit 2, Monks Walk, Farnham, Surrey GU9 8HT, England. TEL 0252-734347. FAX 0252-734307. adv.; circ. 1,000. (back issues avail.)
Description: Directory of dealers in secondhand and antiquarian books.

070.5   UK   ISSN 0963-0171
SHEPPARD'S BOOKDEALERS IN EUROPE; a directory of dealers in secondhand and antiquarian books on the continent of Europe. 1966. biennial. £48($48) Richard Joseph Publishers Ltd., Unit 2, Monks Walk, Farnham, Surrey GU9 8HT, England. TEL 0252-734347. FAX 0252-734307. adv.; circ. 1,500. (back issues avail.)
Formerly: European Bookdealers (ISSN 0071-2523)

070.5   UK   ISSN 0269-1469
Z475
SHEPPARD'S BOOKDEALERS IN NORTH AMERICA. 1954. biennial. £24($48) Richard Joseph Publishers Ltd., Unit 2, Monks Walk, Farnham, Surrey GU9 8HT, England. TEL 0252-734347. FAX 0252-734307. adv.; circ. 3,000. (back issues avail.)
—BLDSC shelfmark: 8256.432100.
Formerly: Bookdealers in North America (ISSN 0068-0109)

070.5 020   CC   ISSN 1000-0097
SHIJIE TUSHU/WORLD BOOKS. (Text in Chinese) 1956. m. $40 (effective 1992). China National Publications Import and Export Corporation, P.O. Box 88, Beijing 100704, People's Republic of China. TEL 4035458. FAX 4015664. TELEX 22313 CPC CN. Ed. Lu Bohua. adv.; bk.rev.; circ. 10,000.

665   JA   ISSN 0037-3788
SHINKAN NEWS FOR READERS/SHINKAN NYUSU. 1959. m. 2232 Yen($17) Tokyo Shuppan Hanbai Co., Ltd., 6-24 Higashigoken-cho, Shinjuku-ku, Tokyo 162, Japan. FAX 03-3267-3781. Ed. Hiromasa Kohtaki. adv.; bk.rev.; bibl.; circ. 150,000.
Description: Covers forthcoming books.

070.5   CC   ISSN 1000-4793
SHU LIN/BOOK FOREST. (Text in Chinese) 1980. m. Y16.80($41.30) Shanghai Renmin Chubanshe, Qikan Bu, 54 Shaoxing Road, Shanghai 200020, People's Republic of China. (Dist. outside China by: China International Book Trading Corp., P.O. Box 399, Beijing, P.R.C.; Dist. in US by: China Books & Periodicals, Inc., 2929 24th St., San Francisco, CA 94110) Ed. Xu Xinyuan. adv.; bk.rev.
Description: Contains book reviews and news of new books. Covers writers and their works.

070.5   US
SIGNATURE; a newsletter for the publishing industry. 1986. bi-m. free. Griffin Printing and Lithograph, Co., Inc., 544 W. Colorado St., Glendale, CA 91204-1102. TEL 818-953-9025. FAX 818-242-1172. adv.; bk.rev.; circ. 6,500 (controlled).

SINDICATO NACIONAL DOS EDITORES DE LIVROS. INFORMATIVO BIBLIOGRAFICO. see *BIBLIOGRAPHIES*

070.5   SI   ISSN 0080-9659
Z464.S55
SINGAPORE BOOK WORLD. (Text in Chinese, English and Malay) 1970. a. $10. National Book Development Council of Singapore, NBDCS Secretariat, Bukit Merah Branch Library, Bukit Merah Central, Singapore 0315. TEL 2732730. Ed. Hedwig Anuar. adv.; bk.rev.; circ. 3,000. (back issues avail.) **Indexed:** Lib.Sci.Abstr.
—BLDSC shelfmark: 8285.460000.
Description: Book reviews and articles on book trade.

020.75   MX
SISTEMA NACIONAL DE ARCHIVOS. INVENTARIOS. 1989. irreg. Archivo General de la Nacion, Tacuba No. 8, Mexico 1, D.F., Mexico.

070.5   US   ISSN 0000-0485
Z231.5.L5
SMALL PRESS; the magazine of independent book publishing. 1983. q. $29. Meckler Publishing Corporation, Colonial Hill - RFD 1, Mt. Kisco, NY 10549-5808. TEL 914-666-0069. adv.; bk.rev.; circ. 9,000. (also avail. in microform from UMI) **Indexed:** Bk.Rev.Ind. (1988-), Child.Bk.Rev.Ind. (1988-), Graph.Arts Lit.Abstr., LHTN, Lib.Lit.
—BLDSC shelfmark: 8310.105000.
Description: Dedicated to serving the independent publishing industry through articles, excerpts, and new title announcements.

028.1   US   ISSN 8756-7202
Z1215
SMALL PRESS BOOK REVIEW. 1985. bi-m. $28. Greenfield Press, Box 176, Southport, CT 06490. TEL 203-268-4878. Ed. Henry Berry. adv.; bk.rev.; circ. 3,000. (back issues avail.) **Indexed:** Bk.Rev.Ind. (1987-), Child.Bk.Rev.Ind. (1987-).
Description: Contains brief descriptive, critical reviews of all types of books published by small presses, reviews of audiocassettes and periodicals from independent presses. Includes features, a children's book section, and news notes.

070.5   US
SMALL PRESS NEWS. 1981-1985; resumed 1988. 10/yr. $10. Diane Kruchkow, Ed. & Pub., c/o Stony Hills Productions, Box 780-H, Weeks Mills, New Sharon, ME 04955. (Or Kilgour Inc., 45 Hillcrest Pl., Amherst, MA 01002) adv.; bk.rev.; bibl. (back issues avail.)

011   US   ISSN 0037-7228
SMALL PRESS REVIEW. (Supplement to International Directory of Little Magazines and Small Presses (ISSN 0092-3974)) 1967. m. $23 to individuals; institutions $29. Dustbooks, Box 100, Paradise, CA 95967. TEL 916-877-6110. Ed. Len Fulton. adv.; B&W page $150. bk.rev.; circ. 3,500. **Indexed:** ACCESS, Bk.Rev.Ind. (1980-), Child.Bk.Rev.Ind. (1980-), New Per.Ind.
Description: News, reviews and articles on small press publishing worldwide.

655 090   FR   ISSN 0081-0878
SOCIETE DES FRANCS-BIBLIOPHILES. ANNUAIRE. 1948. a. membership. 39 rue Raynouard, 75016 Paris, France.

070.5   US   ISSN 0734-8509
SOCIETY FOR SCHOLARLY PUBLISHING. PROCEEDINGS OF ANNUAL MEETINGS. 1979. a. price varies. Society for Scholarly Publishing, 10200 W. 44th Ave., Ste. 304, Wheat Ridge, CO 80033. TEL 303-422-3914. FAX 303-422-8894. circ. 1,000.
—BLDSC shelfmark: 6841.940500.
Formerly: S S P Proceedings (ISSN 0196-6146)

070.5   US
SOCIETY FOR SCHOLARLY PUBLISHING NEWSLETTER. 6/yr. Society for Scholarly Publishing, 10200 W. 44th St., Ste. 304, Wheat Ridge, CO 80033.

SOLANUS. see *LIBRARY AND INFORMATION SCIENCES*

016 260   US   ISSN 0038-7606
SPIRITUAL BOOK NEWS. 1958. 8/yr. $8. (Spiritual Book Associates) Ave Maria Press, Notre Dame, IN 46556. TEL 219-287-2838. FAX 219-239-2904. Ed. Robert Hamma. bk.rev.; circ. 9,000.
Description: Contains feature reviews of book club selections, as well as notices and reviews of other current books available in the field of spiritual reading.

658.8   NZ
SPOTLIGHT; journal for the books, gifts, greeting cards, office products, stationery and toy trades of N.Z. 1965. m. NZ.$25 (foreign NZ$106.50). Icon Press, P.O. Box 144, Opotiki, New Zealand. TEL 03-315-4886. FAX 07-315-4621. Ed. Narena Olliver. adv.; bk.rev.; circ. 3,500 (controlled). (tabloid format)
Formerly (until 1978): Spotlight: trade journal on the book, stationery, magazine, greeting cards, games and toy trade in New Zealand (ISSN 0038-8386)

STAR TRACK. see *LIBRARY AND INFORMATION SCIENCES*

686   US
STRATEGIC PLANNING FOR MAGAZINE EXECUTIVES; how to take the guesswork out of magazine publishing decisions. irreg., latest 2nd ed. $59.95. Cowles Business Media (Subsidiary of: Cowles Media Company), Six River Bend Center, 911 Hope St., Box 4949, Stamford, CT 06907-0949. TEL 203-358-9900. FAX 203-357-9014. Ed. Richard M. Koff.

STUDIA O KSIAZCE. see *LIBRARY AND INFORMATION SCIENCES*

SUECANA EXTRANEA; books on Sweden and Swedish literature in foreign languages. see *BIBLIOGRAPHIES*

658.8   SW   ISSN 0039-6451
Z407
SVENSK BOKHANDEL. 1952. fortn. (Jan.-Jul.); w. (Aug.-Dec.). SEK 650. (Svenska Bokfoerlaeggarefoereningen - Swedish Publishers' Association) Tidnings AB Svensk Bokhandel, P.O. Box 1335, S-111 83 Stockholm, Sweden. TEL 46-8-243145. FAX 46-8-149382. (Co-sponsor: Svenska Bokhandlarefoereningen - Swedish Booksellers Association) Ed. Jan-Erik Pettersson. adv.; index; circ. 4,700.

028.1   UK   ISSN 0265-8119
PT9368
SWEDISH BOOK REVIEW. 1983. s-a. $18. Swedish-English Literary Translators Association, St. David's University College, Lampeter SA48 7ED, Wales. TEL 0570-422351. FAX 0570-423782. (U.S. subscr. addr.: 260 E. St. Jose Ave., Claremont, CA 91711) Ed. Laurie Thompson. adv.; bk.rev.; illus.; circ. 1,000.
—BLDSC shelfmark: 8573.857600.
Description: Articles on Swedish writers, translations of their work, bibliographies and news of forthcoming books.

070.5   FR
SYNDICAT NATIONAL DE LA LIBRAIRIE ANCIENNE ET MODERNE. REPERTOIRE DES MEMBRES. 1930. a. 30 F. Syndicat National de la Librairie Ancienne et Moderne, 4 rue Git le Coeur, 75006 Paris, France. TEL 1-43-29-46-38.
Former titles: Guide a l'Usage des Amateurs de Livres; Guide du Livre Ancien et du Livre d'Occasion; Syndicat National de la Librairie Ancienne et Moderne. Repertoire (ISSN 0080-1100)

PUBLISHING AND BOOK TRADE

028 US
TARTAN BOOK SALES CATALOG. 1940. 12/yr. free. Brodart Co., 500 Arch St., Williamsport, PA 17705. TEL 800-233-8467. FAX 717-326-6769. Ed. Gwen Airgood. adv.; bk.rev.; bibl.; illus.; index; circ. 7,000.
  Supersedes: Tartan Book News; Book News (ISSN 0006-7288)

070.5 US ISSN 0894-9581
TELEPUBLISHING REPORT. 1987. 6/yr. $240. Telepublishing Consultants International, 284 Harvard St., Ste. 64, Cambridge, MA 02139. TEL 617-354-3919. Ed. Lawrence Kingsley. bk.rev.

686 AT ISSN 1033-6885
THOMSON'S PRINT PRODUCTION DIRECTORY. 1989. q. Aus.$315. Thomson Publications Australia, 47 Chippen St., Chippendale, N.S.W. 2008, Australia. TEL 02-699-2411. FAX 02-698-3920. Ed. Caroline Mackie. (looseleaf format)
  Description: For ad agencies, printers, graphic artists, national and retail companies.

070.5 BE
TIJDINGEN; tijdschrift voor het boekbedrijf. 1929. m. 2350 BEF. Vereniging Ter Bevordering van het Vlaamse Boekwezen - Association of Publishers of Dutch Language Books, Frankrijklei 93, Box 3, B-2000 Antwerp, Belgium. adv.; bibl.; circ. 2,000.

TIMES LITERARY SUPPLEMENT. see *LITERATURE*

070.5 US
▼**TITLES.** 1990. bi-m. $15. Larkspur Publishing, Inc., 200 Gate Five Rd., Ste. 214, Sausalito, CA 94965. TEL 415-331-1211. Ed. Christine Nordbye. circ. 60,000 (controlled). (tabloid format)
  Description: For retailers of mass market magazines, paperback books and related products. Covers merchandising and promotion techniques.

070.5 US ISSN 0193-4953
TOWERS CLUB U S A NEWSLETTER. (The Original Writers Entrepreneurial Research Service) 1974. 10/yr. $60. (Jerry Buchanan Advertising Agency) Towers Club, U.S.A., Inc., Box 2038, Vancouver, WA 98668-2038. TEL 206-574-3084. (Alt. addr.: c/o Jerry Buchanan, Ed., 9107 N.W. 11th Ave., Vancouver, WA 98665. TEL 206-574-3084) Ed. Jerry Buchanan. adv.; bk.rev.; circ. 5,700. (looseleaf format; back issues avail.)
  Description: Serving direct response marketing community information providers; insider news, tips, and sources especially for home-based entrepreneurs, plus mail order mini-clinics; success stories of self-publisher/marketers. Includes letters to the editor.

TRANSLATION REVIEW. see *LINGUISTICS*

655 BE ISSN 0041-1876
TRAVAILLEUR DU LIVRE. Dutch edition: De Boekarbeider (ISSN 0774-2797) 1945. bi-m. free to members. Centrale de l'Industrie du Livre et du Papier - Centrale der Boek- en Papiernijverheid, Galerie du Centre, Bloc 2, B-1000 Brussels, Belgium. FAX 02-2230023. Ed. Roger Sagon. charts; circ. 16,000.

070.5 UK
TRENDS IN JOURNAL SUBSCRIPTIONS. 1983. a. £10 (non-members £25). Council of Academic and Professional Publishers, 19 Bedford Square, London WC1B 3HJ, England. TEL 071-580-6321. FAX 071-636-5375. Ed. Priscilla Oakeshott. circ. 200. (back issues avail.)

070.5 US ISSN 0731-5589
TRENDS UPDATE. 1982. 4/yr. $240. Book Industry Study Group, Inc., 160 Fifth Ave., New York, NY 10010. TEL 212-929-1393. FAX 212-989-7542. Ed. Robert Winter. circ. 400.

055.1 IT
TUTTOLIBRI. 1975. w. L.1000. Editrice la Stampa S.p.A., Via Marenco 32, 10100 Turin, Italy. TEL 65681. TELEX 221121. bk.rev.; illus.

686 US ISSN 1042-105X
TYPE & PRESS. 1974. q. $4. Press of the Golden Unicorn, 24667 Heather Court, Hayward, CA 94545. Ed. Fred C. Williams. adv.; bk.rev.; circ. 1,000. (back issues avail.)

079.7 CU
U P E C. bi-m. $10 in N. America; S. America $13; Europe $15; elsewhere $21. (Union de Periodistas de Cuba) Ediciones Cubanas, Obispo No. 527, Apdo. 605, Havana, Cuba. illus.

U S B E NEWS. (Universal Serials and Book Exchange) see *LIBRARY AND INFORMATION SCIENCES*

U S REAL ESTATE REGISTER. see *REAL ESTATE*

070.5 JM
U W I P A NEWSLETTER. 1986. q. University of the West Indies Publishers' Association, P.O. Box 139, Mona, Kingston 7, Jamaica, W.I. TEL 809-927-1201. FAX 809-927-2409. (Subscr. to: P.O. Box 42, Mona, Kingston 7, Jamaica, W.I.)

028.1 GW
UEBER BUECHER. 1959. 5/yr. Georg Lingenbrink GmbH und Co., Stresemannstr. 300, 2000 Hamburg 50, Germany. TEL 040-85398-238. FAX 040-85398299. Ed. Edgar Rinize. adv.; bk.rev.; bibl.; circ. 25,000.

070.5 UN
UNESCO. STUDIES ON BOOKS AND READING. (Text in English; occasionally in Arabic, French, Spanish and Russian) irreg. free. Unesco, Division for Book Promotion, Audiovisual Archives and International Exchanges, 7 place de Fontenoy, 7500 Paris, France. TEL 33 1 568-10-00. charts; circ. 2,500.
  Indexed: IIS.

020 US ISSN 0275-9616
Z733.L735
U.S. LIBRARY OF CONGRESS. MANUSCRIPT DIVISION. ACQUISITIONS. 1979. a. free to libraries. U.S. Library of Congress, Washington, DC 20540.

028.5 US
UNITED STATES BOARD ON BOOKS FOR YOUNG PEOPLE. NEWSLETTER. 1976. s-a. $25 membership. United States Board on Books for Young People, c/o International Reading Association, 800 Barksdale Rd., Box 8139, Newark, DE 19714-8139. Ed. Alice Swinger. circ. 1,250. **Indexed:** Child Lit.Abstr.
  Formerly (until 1984): Friends of I B B Y Newsletter (International Board on Books for Young People).
  Description: Source of information on children's books from all over the world.

027.7 US ISSN 0041-9265
L11
UNIVERSITY BOOKMAN; a quarterly review. 1960. q. $7. Educational Reviewer, Inc., Box 367, Mecosta, MI 49332. Ed. Russell Kirk. bk.rev.; index; circ. 20,000. (also avail. in microform from UMI) **Indexed:** Bk.Rev.Ind. (1986-), Child.Bk.Rev.Ind. (1986-).
  Description: Multidisciplinary essays and articles on problems of American education and culture.

UNIVERSITY OF IBADAN. LIBRARY. LIBRARY RECORD. see *LIBRARY AND INFORMATION SCIENCES*

UNIVERSITY PRESS BOOK NEWS; the annotated bibliography of new university press books. see *BIBLIOGRAPHIES*

655 NE ISSN 0042-1367
UT DE SMIDTE FAN DE FRYSKE AKADEMY. (Text in Frisian) 1966. q. free to contributors. Fryske Akademy, Doelestrjitte 8, 8911 DX Ljouwert-Leeuwarden, Netherlands. TEL 058-131414. FAX 058-131409. adv.; bk.rev.; charts; illus.; circ. 3,250.

V MIRE KNIG. see *LIBRARY AND INFORMATION SCIENCES*

070.5 US
VENTURA PROFESSIONAL. m. 7502 Aaron Pl., San Jose, CA 95139. TEL 408-227-5030. FAX 408-224-9086. Ed. Gail Koffman. circ. 24,000.

VERBREITUNGSDATEN DER SCHWEIZER PRESSE. see *ADVERTISING AND PUBLIC RELATIONS*

070.5 NE
VERENIGDE NEDERLANDSE UITGEVERSBEDRIJVEN. ANNUAL REPORT. a. Verenigde Nederlandse Uitgeversbedrijven, 5-25 Ceylonpoort, 2037 AA Haarlem, Netherlands. TEL 023-304304. TELEX 41549.

658.8 NE ISSN 0042-4412
VERTEGENWOORDIGER.* 1935. 3/yr. fl.5. Vereniging van Uitgevers Vertegenwoordigers., Westerstraat 62, Wormerveer, Netherlands. Eds. P. Kluft, W. De Koning.

VIEWS & REVIEWS (NEW YORK, 1988). see *EDUCATION — Adult Education*

028.1 UK ISSN 0954-0881
VIGIL. 1988. 3/yr. £2.80. c/o John Howard Greaves, 12 Priory Mead, Bruton, Somerset BA10 0DZ, England. TEL 0749-813349. adv.; bk.rev.; illus.; circ. 250.
  Incorporates (1979-1988): Period Piece and Paperback (ISSN 0260-5333)
  Description: Focuses on the art and technique of poetry and other imaginative forms of writing. Publishes new work from contributors.

W E S AUTHORS' AND PUBLISHERS' SERVICE NEWSLETTER. (Watman Educational Services) see *EDUCATION*

WASHINGTON STATE UNIVERSITY. DAILY EVERGREEN. see *JOURNALISM*

070.5 US
WAYSTATION FOR THE S F WRITER. 1974. q. $9. Unique Graphics, 1025 55th St., Oakland, CA 94608. TEL 415-655-3024. Ed. Millea Kenin. adv.; bk.rev.; circ. 1,500. (back issues avail.)
  Formerly: Empire for the S F Writer (ISSN 0279-8085)

658.8 070.5 AT
WEEKLY BOOK NEWSLETTER. 1972. w. Aus.$180. D.W. Thorpe (Subsidiary of: Butterworths), 18 Salmon St., Port Melbourne, Vic. 3207, Australia. TEL 03-645-1511. FAX 03-645-3981. Ed. Michael Webster. circ. 2,000. (processed)
  Description: Covers publishing and bookselling industry news in Australia.

WHAT IS TO BE READ. see *LITERATURE*

WHAT'S WORKING IN DIRECT MARKETING AND FULFILLMENT. see *BUSINESS AND ECONOMICS — Marketing And Purchasing*

655 011 UK ISSN 0043-4868
Z2005
WHITAKER'S BOOKS OF THE MONTH AND BOOKS TO COME. 1970. m. £78. J. Whitaker & Sons Ltd., 12 Dyott St., London WC1A 1DF, England. TEL 071-836-8911. FAX 071-836-2909. adv.; bk.rev.; circ. 2,000. **Indexed:** Dairy Sci.Abstr.
  —BLDSC shelfmark: 9311.000500.

070.5 GW ISSN 0170-7213
WHO'S WHO AT THE FRANKFURT BOOK FAIR; an international publishers' guide. 1969. a. DM.60($45) (Frankfurt Book Fair) K.G. Saur Verlag KG, Ortlerstr. 8, Postfach 701620, 8000 Munich 70, Germany. TEL 089-76902-0. FAX 089-76902150. (N. America subscr. to: K.G. Saur, A Reed Reference Publishing Company, 121 Chanlon Rd., New Providence, NJ 07974. TEL 908-665-3576) Ed. Peter Weidhaas. adv.

070.5 658.048 US
WHO'S WHO IN S N A P. a. $80 to non-members. Society of National Association Publishers, 1735 N. Lynn St., Ste. 950, Arlington, VA 22209-2022. TEL 703-524-2000. adv.; circ. 400.

070.5 GW ISSN 0341-2253
Z119
WOLFENBUETTELER NOTIZEN ZUR BUCHGESCHICHTE. 1976. 2/yr. DM.64. (Wolfenbuetteler Arbeitskreis fuer Geschichte des Buchwesens) Verlag Otto Harrassowitz, Taunusstr. 14, Postfach 2929, 6200 Wiesbaden 1, Germany. TEL 0611-530-0. FAX 0611-530570. TELEX 4186135. Eds. Werner Arnold, Erdmann Weyrauch. circ. 750.

070.5 301.16 US
WORD WRAP. 1982. bi-m. membership. Council of Writers Organizations, Box 21797, Washington, DC 20009. TEL 301-685-2244. FAX 301-234-2868. Ed. Ruth E. Thaler-Carter. adv.; bk.rev.; circ. 35,000.
  Description: Examines various issues facing professional writers. Covers the legal questions of copyright and contracts, advice on taxes and buying computers.

PUBLISHING AND BOOK TRADE — ABSTRACTING, BIBLIOGRAPHIES, STATISTICS

070.5   UK   ISSN 0084-2664
PN12
WRITERS' AND ARTISTS' YEARBOOK; a directory for writers, artists, playwrights, writers for film, radio and television, photographers and composers. 1907. a. £8.99. A. & C. Black (Publishers) Ltd., Howard Rd., Eaton Socon, Huntingdon, Cambs PE19 3EZ, England. TEL 0480-212666. FAX 0480-405014. TELEX 32524-ACBLAC. index.
Description: Reference book for writers, artists, journalists and publishers.

070.5   AT   ISSN 0084-2680
WRITERS' AND PHOTOGRAPHERS' MARKETING GUIDE; DIRECTORY OF AUSTRALIAN AND NEW ZEALAND LITERARY AND PHOTO MARKETS. 1945. a. Aus.$12 (typically set in Jan.). Australian Writers' Professional Service, Stott House, 140 Flinders St., Melbourne, Vic. 3000, Australia. FAX 613-650-9648. Ed. J. Thornton.
Description: Directory for freelance writers and photographers.

070.5 070   US   ISSN 0749-2014
WRITERS CONNECTION. 1983. m. $18 in U.S.; Canada $24; elsewhere $32. 1601 Saratoga Sunnyvale Rd., Ste. 180, Cupertino, CA 95014. TEL 408-973-0227. FAX 408-973-1219. Ed. Jan Stiles. adv.; bk.rev.; circ. 3,000. (back issues avail.)
Description: Articles on writing nonfiction, fiction, business writing, self-publishing and publishing. Regular columns cover writers' markets, contests, events, and news for writers.

070.5   US   ISSN 0084-2710
PN137
WRITER'S HANDBOOK. 1936. a. $28.95. Writer, Inc., 120 Boylston St., Boston, MA 02116. TEL 617-423-3157. Ed. Sylvia K. Burack. (reprint service avail. from UMI, BLH)
—BLDSC shelfmark: 9364.710000.
Description: Articles of instruction on all freelance writing fields. Includes list of markets for manuscripts in all writing fields and business information for writers.

070.5 808   US
WRITERS INK. 1975. irreg. (2-4/yr.). $8 per no. (World-Wide Writers Service) Writers Ink Press, c/o Writer Unlimited Agency Inc., 186 N. Coleman Rd., Centereach, NY 11720-3072. TEL 516-744-7058. Ed. David B. Axelrod. bk.rev.; illus.; circ. 2,000.

WRITERS' JOURNAL (N. ST. PAUL). see *LITERATURE*

070.5   CN
WRITER'S LIFELINE. 1974. 3/yr. $18. Box 32, Cornwall, Ont. K6H 5R9, Canada. TEL 613-932-2135. Ed. Stephen Gill. adv.; bk.rev.; circ. 1,500.
Formerly: Lifeline (Cornwall) (ISSN 0316-0602)

070.5   US   ISSN 0084-2729
PN161
WRITER'S MARKET. 1926. a. $25.95. F & W Publications, Inc., 1507 Dana Ave., Cincinnati, OH 45207. TEL 513-531-2222. Ed. Mark Kissling. index. (reprint service avail. from UMI)
—BLDSC shelfmark: 9364.738000.
Description: Provides information on where to sell articles, books, fillers, gags, greeting cards, novels, plays, scripts and short stories.

686   US   ISSN 0895-898X
WRITER'S N W; news and reviews for the community of the printed word. 1987. q. $10. Media Weavers (Subsidiary of: Blue Heron Publishing, Inc.), 24450 N.W Hansen Rd., Hillsboro, OR 97124. TEL 503-621-3911. Eds. Linny Stovall, Dennis Stovall. adv.; bk.rev.; circ. 75,000 (controlled). (tabloid format; back issues avail.)
Formerly: Writer's Northwest Newsletter.
Description: Lists N.W. publishing and writing markets and events; includes articles on writing and publishing, new book and software reviews.

686   US   ISSN 0896-7946
PN147
WRITER'S NORTHWEST HANDBOOK; comprehensive guide to writing and publishing in Oregon, Washington, Idaho, Montana, Alaska, and British Columbia. 1986. biennial. $16.95 softcover. Media Weavers (Subsidiary of: Blue Heron Publishing, Inc.), 24450 N.W. Hansen Rd., Hillsboro, OR 97124. TEL 503-621-3911. Eds. Linny Stovall, Dennis Stovall. adv.; circ. 20,000.
Description: Lists 3,000 N.W. markets with editorial guidelines, and advertising resources, essays and interviews for writers and publishers.

070.5 800   US   ISSN 0084-2737
WRITER'S YEARBOOK. 1930. a. $3.95. F & W Publications, Inc., 1507 Dana Ave., Cincinnati, OH 45207. TEL 513-531-2222. Ed. Bruce Woods. adv.; circ. 75,000. (also avail. in microform from UMI; reprint service avail. from UMI)
Description: Articles on how and where to sell writing.

070.5 420   US
▼**WRITING RIGHT.** 1992. m. $30. Elmwood Park Publishing Co., P.O. Box 35132, Elmwood Park, IL 60635. TEL 708-453-5023. Ed. John C. Biardo.
Description: Newsletter with the sole focus on helping writers and publishers with their careers. Features writing tips, researching, promotion and publicity, book reviews, writer's conventions, book exhibit news, and sources for writers.

XEROTIC EPHEMERA. see *LITERATURE — Poetry*

020.75   US
YODELINGS. 1980. irreg. (2-3/yr.). $2. Press of Ward Schori, 2716 Noyes St., Evanston, IL 60201. Ed. Ward K. Schori. circ. 200.
Description: Concerns miniature books.

028   AU   ISSN 0044-2089
DIE ZEIT IM BUCH. 1947. q. S.140. Arbeitsgemeinschaft fuer Buch- und Schrifttum der Katholischen Aktion Oesterreichs, Stephans Platz 6-V, A-1010 Vienna, Austria. Ed. Margarete Schmid. adv.; bk.rev.; bibl.

070 384   PL   ISSN 0555-0025
ZESZYTY PRASOZNAWCZE. (Text in Polish; summaries in English, French and Russian) 1960. q. $16. (Osrodek Badan Prasoznawczych) Wydawnictwo Wspolczesne R S W "Prasa-Ksiazka-Ruch", Ul. Wiejska 12, 00-420 Warsaw, Poland. TEL 44-22-285330. (Dist. by: Ars Polona-Ruch, Krakowskie Przedmiescie 7, Warsaw, Poland) illus.

070.5   CC   ISSN 1001-8859
ZHONGGUO CHUBAN NIANJIAN/CHINA PUBLISHING YEARBOOK. (Text in Chinese) 1980. a. Y27. (China Research Institute of Publishing Science) Chinese Book Publishing House, 7A Xi Rong Xian Hu Tong, Xi Cheng District, Beijing 100031, People's Republic of China. TEL 5139134. (Co-sponsor: Publishing Association of China) Ed. Fang Houshu. adv.; circ. 5,000.
Description: Contains articles on developments in China's publishing industry. Lists publishing companies and new publications; includes addresses, telephone and telegraph numbers, and personnel.

070.5   CC
ZHONGGUO KEJI QIKAN YANJIU/CHINESE SCIENCE AND TECHNOLOGY PERIODICALS RESEARCH. (Text in Chinese) q. Zhongguo Kexueyuan, Ziran Kexue Qikan Bianji Yanjiuhui - Chinese Academy of Sciences, Natural Science Periodicals Editing Society, Zhongguancun, Beijing 100080, People's Republic of China. TEL 284303. Ed. Su Shisheng.

028.1 895.1   CC
ZHONGGUO TUSHU PINGLUN/CHINESE BOOK REVIEWS. (Text in Chinese) bi-m. $23.70. Liaoning Renmin Chubanshe, Qikan Bu, 108 Beiyi Malu, Heping-qu, Shenyang, Liaoning 110001, People's Republic of China. TEL 361304. (Dist. in US by: China Books & Periodicals, Inc., 2929 24th St., San Francisco, CA 94110. TEL 415-282-2994) Ed. Xu Lixing. bk.rev.

070.5   GW
ZWIEBEL. 1965. a. Verlag Klaus Wagenbach, Ahornstr. 4, 1000 Berlin 30, Germany. TEL 030-2115069. FAX 030-2116140.

020 070   UK
5001 HARD TO FIND PUBLISHERS. 1981. a. £30. Wm. Dawson & Sons Ltd., Cannon House, Park Farm Rd., Folkestone CT19 5EE, England. TEL 0303-850101. FAX 0303-850440. TELEX 96392.

PUBLISHING AND BOOK TRADE — Abstracting, Bibliographies, Statistics

011   US
ABRIDGED MAGAZINE INDEX. m. $975. Information Access Company, 357 Lakeside Dr., Foster City, CA 94404. TEL 800-227-8431. FAX 415-378-5499. (microform)
Description: Covers 6 years of data, indexing approximately 100 general interest periodicals.

015.6 070.5   UK   ISSN 0306-0322
Z465.7
AFRICAN BOOK PUBLISHING RECORD. (Text occasionally in French) 1975. q. £85. Hans Zell Publishers (Subsidiary of: Bowker-Saur Ltd. - Butterworths), P.O. Box 56, Oxford OX1 2SJ, England. TEL 0865-511428. FAX 0865-311534. TELEX 94012872-ZELL-G. Ed. Hans M. Zell. adv.; bk.rev.; bibl.; illus.; stat.; circ. 800 (controlled). (back issues avail.) Indexed: Curr.Cont.Africa, M.L.A.
—BLDSC shelfmark: 0732.360000.
Description: Current bibliography of African published materials. Includes features, articles, reports, news and interviews.

070 015   US   ISSN 0091-9357
Z1000
AMERICAN BOOK PRICES CURRENT. a. price varies. Bancroft-Parkman, Inc., Box 1236, Washington, CT 06793. TEL 212-737-2715. FAX 203-868-0080.
—BLDSC shelfmark: 0810.840000.

070 015   US
AMERICAN BOOK PRICES CURRENT. FOUR YEAR INDEX. quadrennial. price varies. Bancroft-Parkman, Inc., Box 1236, Washington, CT 06793. TEL 212-737-2715. FAX 203-868-0080.
Formerly: American Book Prices Current. Five Year Index.

655 011   US   ISSN 0002-7707
Z1201
AMERICAN BOOK PUBLISHING RECORD; arranged by Dewey Decimal Classification and indexed by author, title and subject. Short title: A B P R. 1960. m. with a. cumulations. $189 for m.; $189.95 for a. cum. R.R. Bowker, A Reed Reference Publishing Company, Division of Reed Publishing (USA) Inc., 121 Chanlon Rd., New Providence, NJ 07974. TEL 800-521-8110. FAX 908-665-6688. TELEX 138 755. (Subscr. to: Order Dept., Box 31, New Providence, NJ 07974) index, cum.index; circ. 7,345. Indexed: Abstr.Bull.Inst.Pap.Chem., Bibl.Engl.Lang.& Lit.
—BLDSC shelfmark: 0810.850000.
Description: Catalog records. Includes separate adult fiction and juvenile fiction sections. Included in each entry: main entry, title (italics), subtitle, author statement, publication place, publisher, publication date, collation, series statement, general note or contents note, LC Classification numbers, LC card numbers and subject tracings.

AUSTRALIAN BOOKS IN PRINT ON MICROFICHE. see *BIBLIOGRAPHIES*

AUSTRALIAN SOCIETY OF INDEXERS NEWSLETTER. see *LIBRARY AND INFORMATION SCIENCES — Abstracting, Bibliographies, Statistics*

655 011   IO   ISSN 0216-1273
BERITA BIBLIOGRAFI; Indonesian book news. 1954. m. Rps.6000($10) Yayasan Idayu - Idayu Foundation, Gedung Kebangkitan Nasional, J1 Abdulrakhman Saleh 26, P.O. Box 48-Jkt, Jakarta 10410, Indonesia. TEL 361261. TELEX 45255-SATRIA-IA. Eds. Djusna Asif. adv.; bk.rev.; bibl.; circ. 500.
Indexed: E.I.
Formerly: Berita Idayu Bibliografi; Which was formed by the merger of: Berita Bibliografi (ISSN 0005-9129) & Berita Idayu.

PUBLISHING AND BOOK TRADE — ABSTRACTING, BIBLIOGRAPHIES, STATISTICS

020 010　　　　　IT　　ISSN 0006-0941
Z1007
BIBLIOFILIA; rivista di storia del libro e di bibliografia. (Text in English, French, German and Italian) 1899. 3/yr. L.81000 (foreign L.101000). Casa Editrice Leo S. Olschki, Casella Postale 66, 50100 Florence, Italy. TEL 055-6530684. FAX 055-6530214. Ed. Luigi Balsamo. adv.; bk.rev.; illus.; circ. 1,000.
Indexed: Lib.Lit., Lib.Sci.Abstr., M.L.A.

BIBLIOGRAFIA NAZIONALE ITALIANA. see BIBLIOGRAPHIES

020.6　　　　　AU　　ISSN 0006-2022
BIBLOS; oesterreichische Zeitschrift fuer Buch- und Bibliothekswesen, Dokumentation, Bibliographie und Bibliophilie. (Text in English and German) 1952. q. S.340. Gesellschaft der Freunde der Oesterreichischen Nationalbibliothek, Josefsplatz 1, A-1015 Vienna, Austria. Ed. Dr. Magda Strebl. adv.; bk.rev.; bibl.; charts; illus.; index, cum.index every 10 yrs.; circ. 1,200. **Indexed:** Amer.Hist.& Life, Art & Archaeol.Tech.Abstr., Hist.Abstr., Lib.Lit., Lib.Sci.Abstr., P.A.I.S.For.Lang.Ind.
—BLDSC shelfmark: 2022.000000.
Description: Covers library and information science news, technical information, news from Austrian libraries, events and meetings.

658.8　　　　　NO
BOK OG SAMFUNN. (Includes supplement Norsk Bokfortegnelse - monthly edition) 1879. 24/yr. NOK 880. Norske Bokhandlerforening - Norwegian Booksellers' Association, Oevre Vollgt. 15, 0158 Oslo 1, Norway. adv.; bibl.; index.
Formerly (until 1976): Norske Bokhandlertidende (ISSN 0029-1889)

BOLETIN BIBLIOGRAFICO BOLIVIANO. see BIBLIOGRAPHIES

BOLETIN BIBLIOGRAFICO MEXICANO. see BIBLIOGRAPHIES

BOOK COLLECTOR. see HOBBIES — Abstracting, Bibliographies, Statistics

655 011　　　　　UK　　ISSN 0006-7245
BOOK EXCHANGE. 1948. m. £3($8) 9 Chandler Close, Bath BA1 4EG, England. TEL 0225-20773. Ed. F.F. Taylor. adv.; bk.rev.; circ. 1,000.
—BLDSC shelfmark: 2248.103000.

028.1 011　　　　US　　ISSN 0006-7326
Z1219
BOOK REVIEW DIGEST; an index to reviews of current books. 1905. m. (except Feb. and July) plus q. and a. cumulations. H.W. Wilson Co., 950 University Ave., Bronx, NY 10452. TEL 800-367-6770. FAX 212-538-2716. TELEX 4990003HWILSON. Ed. Martha Mooney. bk.rev.; cum.index 1905-1974; 1975-1984. (also avail. in magnetic tape)
●Also available online. Vendor(s): Wilsonline (File BRD).
Also available on CD-ROM. Producer(s): H.W. Wilson (WILSONDISC).
Description: Includes excerpts to reviews of current adult and juvenile fiction and nonfiction.

028.1　　　　　US　　ISSN 0524-0581
BOOK REVIEW INDEX; indexes all reviews in 460 periodicals. 1965. bi-m. $195. Gale Research Inc., 835 Penobscot Bldg., Detroit, MI 48226. TEL 313-961-2242. FAX 313-961-6083. TELEX 810-221-7086. Ed. Neil E. Walker. circ. 3,000. (also avail. in microfiche)
●Also available online. Vendor(s): DIALOG (File no.137).
Description: Compendium of book reviews from various periodicals.

028.1　　　　　US　　ISSN 0524-0581
Z1035.A1
BOOK REVIEW INDEX: ANNUAL CLOTHBOUND CUMULATIONS. 1965. a. $195 per vol. Gale Research Inc., 835 Penobscot Bldg., Detroit, MI 48226. TEL 313-961-2242. FAX 313-961-6083. TELEX 810-221-7086. Ed. Neil E. Walker. (back issues avail.)
Description: Annual compendium of book reviews from various periodicals.

655 020 011　　　　US　　ISSN 0006-7385
Z1035.A1
BOOKLIST. 1905. 22/yr. $60 (foreign $75). American Library Association, 50 E. Huron St., Chicago, IL 60611-2795. TEL 800-545-2433. FAX 312-440-9374. Ed. Bill Ott. adv.; bk.rev.; bibl.; index, s-a. cum.index; circ. 32,000. (also avail. in microform from UMI; back issues avail.; reprint service avail. from UMI) **Indexed:** Amer.Bibl.Slavic & E.Eur.Stud., Bk.Rev.Ind. (1965-), Chic.Per.Ind., Child.Bk.Rev.Ind. (1965-), Gard.Lit. (1992-), Leg.Info.Manage.Ind., Lib.Lit, Media Rev.Dig., Microcomp.Ind., Mid.East: Abstr.& Ind., PCR2, Ref.Sour.
—BLDSC shelfmark: 2250.068000.
Incorporates: Reference Books Bulletin; **Formerly:** Booklist and Subscription Books Bulletin.
Description: Reviews of recommended library materials for adults, young adults and children; print and non-print.

015 948　　　　　FI　　ISSN 0006-7490
Z2520
BOOKS FROM FINLAND. (Text in English) 1967. q. $35. Helsingin Yliopiston Kirjasto - Helsinki University Library, P.O. Box 312, 00171 Helsinki, Finland. Ed. Erkka Lehtola. bibl.; illus.; circ. 4,000. **Indexed:** M.L.A.
Description: Covers modern Finnish literature and writers.

BOOKS FROM KOREA. see BIBLIOGRAPHIES

943.8 057.85　　　UK　　ISSN 0006-7512
BOOKS IN POLISH OR RELATING TO POLAND. 1950. q. £13.50($27.50) Polish Library, 238-246 King St., London W6 ORF, England. TEL 01-741 0474. Ed. J. Szmidt. bibl.; index; circ. 150. (processed)
—BLDSC shelfmark: 2250.208000.

973 015　　　　　US　　ISSN 0006-7520
Z1251.S8
BOOKS OF THE SOUTHWEST; a critical checklist of current Southwestern Americana. 1957. m. $18 to individuals; institutions $30. Books West Southwest, 2452 N. Campbell, Tucson, AZ 85719. TEL 602-326-3533. Ed. W. David Laird. bk.rev.; bibl.; circ. 400.

BRANDYWINE BIBLIOGRAPHY. see PRINTING — Abstracting, Bibliographies, Statistics

015　　　　　　　UK　　ISSN 0007-1544
Z2001　　　　　　　　　CODEN: BRNBBV
BRITISH NATIONAL BIBLIOGRAPHY. 1950. w. (plus a. & interim cums.). £475 (foreign £575; a. microfiche vol. £375). British Library, National Bibliographic Service, Boston Spa, Wetherby, W. Yorkshire LS23 7BQ, England. TEL 0937-546613. FAX 0937-546586. bibl.; index; circ. 2,500.
●Also available online.
Also available on CD-ROM.
—BLDSC shelfmark: 2330.995000.
Description: Lists new books and first issues of serial titles received by the Legal Deposit Office of the British Library. All subjects are covered, including fiction and children's literature.

070.5 015　　　　AU
BUECHER (YEAR); Buecher zum lesen und schenken. 1949. a. Hauptverband des Oesterreichischen Buchhandels, Gruenangergasse 4, A-1010 Vienna, Austria. TEL 0222-5121535.
FAX 0222-512153521. adv.; bk.rev.
Former titles: Buecher fuer Sie (ISSN 0067-0634) & Aus der Schatzkammer der Buecher.

655 015　　　　　BU
BULGARSKI KNIGOPIS. SERIIA 1: KNIGI, NOTNI, GRAFICHESKI I KARTOGRAFSKI. 1897. s-m. 78 lv.($48) Narodna Biblioteka Kiril i Metodii, 11, Tolbukhin Blvd., 1504 Sofia, Bulgaria. (Dist. by: Hemus, 6, Rouski Blvd., 1000 Sofia, Bulgaria) Ed. G. Vanchurova. bibl.; index; circ. 790.
Formerly: Bulgarski Knigopis (ISSN 0007-3997)

840 028.1 011　　　FR　　ISSN 0007-4209
BULLETIN CRITIQUE DU LIVRE FRANCAIS. English edition: New French Books. 1945. m. 600 F. (foreign 800 F.). Association pour la Diffusion de la Pensee Francaise, 12 rue Pierre et Marie Curie, 75005 Paris, France. TEL 43-26-41-59. FAX 46-34-52-65. adv.; bk.rev.; index, cum.index.; circ. 5,600. (back issues avail.; also avail. on diskette)
Description: New French books, quarterly editions.

CANADA. STATISTICS CANADA. PRINTING, PUBLISHING AND ALLIED INDUSTRIES. see PRINTING — Abstracting, Bibliographies, Statistics

020.75　　　　　UK
Y CASGLWR. 3/yr. £3. Cymdeithdas Bob Owen, c/o Richard H. Lewis, 40 Maes Ceiro, Bow Street, Dyfed SY24 5BG, Wales. circ. 1,300.
Description: Covers all aspects of book collecting and bibliography.

070.5　　　　　　AG
CATALOGO COLECTIVO DE PUBLICACIONES PERIODICAS EXISTENTES EN BIBLIOTECAS CIENTIFICAS Y TECNICAS ARGENTINA. 1942; 2nd edt. 1962. irreg., suppl. 1972, 1981. $80. Consejo Nacional de Investigaciones Cientificas y Tecnicas, Moreno 433, 1091 Buenos Aires, Argentina.

011　　　　　　　SP
CATALOGO DE LIBROS ANTIGUOS Y MODERNOS. s-a. 300 ptas. Diego Gomez Florez, Ed. & Pub., Travesera de las Cortes, 305, Barcelona, 14, Spain. bibl.; illus.; circ. 3,000.

CHILDREN'S LITERATURE ABSTRACTS. see CHILDREN AND YOUTH — Abstracting, Bibliographies, Statistics

028.1 011　　　　US　　ISSN 0009-4978
Z1035　　　　　　　　　CODEN: CHOIEZ
CHOICE (MIDDLETOWN); current reviews for college libraries. 1963. m. $148. (Association of College and Research Libraries) Patricia E. Sabosik, Ed. & Pub., 100 Riverview Center, Middletown, CT 06457. TEL 203-347-6933. FAX 203-346-8586. (Affiliate: American Library Association) adv.; bk.rev.; bibl.; index; circ. 4,800. (also avail. in cards; microfilm from UMI) **Indexed:** Bibl.Ind., Bk.Rev.Dig., Bk.Rev.Ind. (1965-), Chic.Per.Ind., Child.Bk.Rev.Ind. (1965-), Leg.Info.Manage.Ind., Lib.Lit.
—BLDSC shelfmark: 3181.535000.

070.5 011　　　　　UK　　ISSN 0140-1939
CLOVER INFORMATION INDEX. 1974. 4/yr. £46 (foreign £56). Clover Publications, 32 Ickwell Road, Northill, Biggleswade, Beds. SG18 9AB, England. TEL 076272-363.
—BLDSC shelfmark: 3287.023000.
Description: A subject guide to popular periodicals.

655 011　　　　　US　　ISSN 0010-2237
Z1601
COMENTARIOS BIBLIOGRAFICOS AMERICANOS. (Text in English, Spanish) 1969. q. $62. E. Darino, Ed. & Pub., Box 1340, Madison Sq. Sta., New York, NY 10159. adv.; bk.rev.; bibl.; stat.; index; circ. 10,000. (looseleaf format; back issues avail.)
Description: Presents book reviews published in Latin America and Spain.

CORREO EDITORIAL; revista informativa de la C C L. see PUBLISHING AND BOOK TRADE

028.1 016　　　　II　　ISSN 0378-7494
CREATIVE BOOK SELECTION INDEX. (Text in English) 1972. m. Rs.144($30) K.K. Roy (Private) Ltd., 55 Gariahat Rd., P.O. Box 10210, Calcutta 700 019, India. Ed. Dr. K.K. Roy. bk.rev.; index; circ. 2,280. (looseleaf format; reprint service avail. from UMI)
Description: Reviews current fiction appearing in Indian periodicals and newspapers.

070.5 011　　　　　JA
CURRENT JAPANESE PERIODICALS FOR (YEAR). a. Japan Publications Inc., 2-1 Sarugaku-cho 1-chome, Chiyoda-ku, Tokyo 101, Japan. TEL 03-2958411. FAX 03-2958416. Ed. A. Takeuchi.
Description: Lists both English and Japanese language periodicals that are available by subscription overseas, main title alfa list with dollar prices, index by category.

028.1 011　　　　DK　　ISSN 0106-1488
DANSK ANMELDELSESINDEKS/DANISH INDEX OF REVIEWS. (Text in Danish) 1979. m. DKK 5000. Bibliotekscentralen, Tempovej 7-11, DK-2750 Ballerup, Denmark. TEL 2-974000. FAX 2-655310. circ. 130. (microfiche)
●Also available online.

PUBLISHING AND BOOK TRADE — ABSTRACTING, BIBLIOGRAPHIES, STATISTICS 4141

070.5   GW
DEUTSCHE NATIONALBIBLIOGRAPHIE. C D - R O M EDITION. 1989. 4/yr. DM.3000. (Deutsche Bibliothek) Buchhaendler-Vereinigung GmbH, Grosser Hirschgraben 17-21, 6000 Frankfurt a.M. 1, Germany. TEL 069-1306-243. TELEX 413573-BUCHV-D.
●Available only on CD-ROM.
Formerly: Deutsche Bibliographie. C D - R O M Edition.

070.5 015   GW
Z2221
DEUTSCHE NATIONALBIBLIOGRAPHIE. FUENFJAHRES-VERZEICHNIS. 1945. irreg. price varies. (Deutsche Bibliothek) Buchhaendler-Vereinigung GmbH, Grosser Hirschgraben 17-21, 6000 Frankfurt a.M. 1, Germany. TEL 069-13060. TELEX 413573-BUCHV-D. bibl.; index.
Formerly: Deutsche Bibliographie. Fuenfjahres-Verzeichnis (ISSN 0418-8233)

013 378   GW
Z5055.G29
DEUTSCHE NATIONALBIBLIOGRAPHIE. HOCHSCHULSCHRIFTEN-VERZEICHNIS. 1972. m. price varies. (Deutsche Bibliothek) Buchhaendler-Vereinigung GmbH, Grosser Hirschgraben 17-21, 6000 Frankfurt a.M. 1, Germany. TEL 069-13060. TELEX 413573-BUCHV-D. bibl.; index.
Formerly: Deutsche Bibliographie. Hochschulschriften-Verzeichnis (ISSN 0301-4665)

655 015   GW   ISSN 0323-3596
Z2221
DEUTSCHE NATIONALBIBLIOGRAPHIE. REIHE A: NEUERSCHEINUNGEN DES BUCHHANDELS.* 1931. w. DM.576. Deutsche Buecherei Leipzig, Deutscher Platz, 7010 Leipzig, Germany. adv.; index.
Description: Covers works published in Germany and German works published abroad. Includes author, title and subject index.

655 015   GW   ISSN 0323-3642
Z2221
DEUTSCHE NATIONALBIBLIOGRAPHIE. REIHE B: NEUERSCHEINUNGEN AUSSERHALB DES BUCHHANDELS.* 1931. s-m. M.408. Deutsche Buecherei Leipzig, Deutscher Platz, 7010 Leipzig, Germany. index.
Description: Covers works published in Germany and German works published abroad. Includes author, title and subject index.

070.5 015   GW
Z2221
DEUTSCHE NATIONALBIBLIOGRAPHIE. WOECHENTLICHES VERZEICHNIS. AUSGABE 1 AMTSBLATT DER DEUTSCHEN BIBLIOTHEK. 1947. w. DM.1884. (Deutsche Bibliothek) Buchhaendler-Vereinigung GmbH, Grosser Hirschgraben 17-21, 6000 Frankfurt a.M. 1, Germany. TEL 069-13060. TELEX 413573-BUCHV-D. bibl.; index.
Formerly: Deutsche Bibliographie. Woechentliches Verzeichnis. Ausgabe 1 Amtsblatt der Deutschen Bibliothek (ISSN 0170-1037)

029 070.5   GW   ISSN 0323-374X
Z2221
DEUTSCHES BUECHERVERZEICHNIS.* 1911. irreg. Deutsche Buecherei Leipzig, Deutscher Platz, 7010 Leipzig, Germany. (also avail. in microfiche from BHP)
—BLDSC shelfmark: 3576.300000.
Description: Catalog of publications of Germany and of foreign countries published in German.

DIRECTORY OF COMPANY HISTORIES OF THE BOOK INDUSTRIES/VERZEICHNIS VON JUBILAEUMSSCHRIFTEN DER GRAPHISCHEN INDUSTRIE. see *PRINTING — Abstracting, Bibliographies, Statistics*

808   US   ISSN 0095-6414
PN4820
DIRECTORY OF SMALL MAGAZINE - PRESS EDITORS AND PUBLISHERS. 1970. a. $22.95. Dustbooks, Box 100, Paradise, CA 95967. TEL 916-877-6110. Ed. Len Fulton.
Description: Lists editors and publishers of small presses and magazines.

070.5 016   US
EARTH GUILD MAIL ORDER CATALOG. 1974. s-a. $2 per no. Earth Guild Inc., Hot Springs, NC 28743. TEL 704-622-3258. adv.; bk.rev.; charts; illus.; circ. 24,000.
Formerly: Earth Guild - Grateful Union Mail Order Catalog.

THE EUROMONITOR BOOK REPORT (YEAR). see *PUBLISHING AND BOOK TRADE*

860 011   PR   ISSN 0015-0592
Z1201
FICHERO BIBLIOGRAFICO HISPANOAMERICANO. 1961. 11/yr. $70. Melcher Ediciones, c/o Margaret Melcher, Box 6000, San Juan, PR 00906. TEL 809-724-1352. FAX 809-724-2886. adv.; bk.rev.; index. (also avail. in microfilm from UMI; reprint service avail. from UMI)
Description: Lists new books in Spanish published in the Americas and Spain.

655 011   IT   ISSN 0017-0216
GIORNALE DELLA LIBRERIA. 1888. m. L.88000 to individuals; libraries L.70400(foreign L.135000). (Associazione Italiana Editori) Editrice Bibliografica s.r.l., Viale Vittorio le Veneto, 24, 20124 Milan, Italy. TEL 02-6597950. Ed. Sergio Polillo. adv.; bk.rev.; charts; stat.; index; circ. 5,000.
—BLDSC shelfmark: 4178.300000.

015   PK
ILMI A'INO. (Text in Sindhi) a. Rs.2. University of Sind, Institute of Sindhology, Jamshoro, Hyderabad 6, Pakistan.
Description: Lists books, periodicals, publishers, cultural and literary organizations in Sind.

070.5 011   SA   ISSN 0379-0584
INDEX TO SOUTH AFRICAN PERIODICALS. Short title: I S A P. (Text in Afrikaans, English) 1945. a. price varies. State Library - Staatsbiblioteek, P.O. Box 397, Pretoria 0001, South Africa. TEL 012-21-8931. FAX 012-325-5984. TELEX 3-22171 SA. circ. 350. (microfiche; back issues avail.)
●Also available online.
—BLDSC shelfmark: 4387.000000.

655 015   II   ISSN 0019-445X
Z3201
INDIAN BOOKS. (Text in English) 1968. m. Rs.95($24) Mukherjee Library, 1 Gopi Mohan Dutta Ln., Calcutta 700003, India. Ed.Bd. adv.; bk.rev.; bibl.; index; circ. 500.

070.5   GW   ISSN 0344-6190
INTERNATIONAL BOOK TRADE DIRECTORY; Europe, Australia, Oceania, Latin America, Africa, and Asia. (Text in English and German) 1978. irreg., 2nd ed., 1989. DM.498($275) K.G. Saur Verlag KG, Ortlerstr. 8, Postfach 701620, 8000 Munich 70, Germany. TEL 089-76902-0. FAX 089-76902150. (N. America subscr. to: K.G. Saur, A Reed Reference Publishing Company, 121 Chanlon Rd., New Providence, NJ 07974. TEL 908-665-3576) Ed. Michael Sachs.
Description: Lists 70,000 booksellers, bookstores, and wholesalers outside the US. Includes subject index.

070.5 016   US
INTERNATIONAL DIRECTORY OF CHILDREN'S LITERATURE. 1973. biennial. $29.95. George Kurian Reference Books, Box 519, Baldwin Place, NY 10505. Ed. Mary Beth Dunhouse. bk.rev.; circ. 3,500.
Formerly: Children's Literary Almanac (ISSN 0093-0431)

070   US   ISSN 0092-3974
Z6944.L5
INTERNATIONAL DIRECTORY OF LITTLE MAGAZINES AND SMALL PRESSES. (Supplement avail.: Small Press Review (ISSN 0037-7228)) 1965. a. $41.95 cloth; paper $25.95. Dustbooks, Box 100, Paradise, CA 95967. TEL 916-877-6110. Ed. Len Fulton. adv.; circ. 10,000.
Formerly: Directory of Little Magazines, Small Presses and Underground Newspapers (ISSN 0084-9979)
Description: Lists 5200 independent publishers, with full data on each.

090.75   UK
INTERNATIONAL RARE BOOK PRICES - EARLY PRINTED BOOKS. 1987. a. £18. Clique, Ltd., 7 Pulleyn Dr., York YO2 2DY, England. TEL 0904-631752.
Description: Bibliographic information about rare books, along with their prices and availability.

090.75   UK
INTERNATIONAL RARE BOOK PRICES - LITERATURE. 1989. a. £22. Clique, Ltd., 7 Pulleyn Dr., York YO2 2DY, England. TEL 0904-631752. (back issues avail.)
Formerly: International Rare Book Prices - 19th Century Literature.
Description: Bibliographic information about rare books, along with their prices and availability.

090.75 011   UK
INTERNATIONAL RARE BOOK PRICES - MODERN FIRST EDITION. 1987. a. £22. Clique, Ltd., 7 Pulleyn Drive, York YO2 2DY, England. TEL 0904-631752.
Description: Bibliographical information on rare books, includes prices and availability.

090.75 011   UK
INTERNATIONAL RARE BOOK PRICES - SCIENCES & MEDICINE. 1987. a. £22. Clique, Ltd., 7 Pulleyn Dr., York YO2 2DY, England. TEL 0904-631752.
Description: Bibliographic information on rare books, with prices and availability.

090.75 011   UK
INTERNATIONAL RARE BOOK PRICES - THE ARTS & ARCHITECTURE. 1987. a. £22. Clique, Ltd., 7 Pulleyn Dr., York YO2 2DY, England. TEL 0904-631752.
Description: Bibliographic information about rare books, along with prices and availability.

090.75 011   UK
INTERNATIONAL RARE BOOK PRICES - VOYAGES, TRAVEL & EXPLORATION. 1987. a. £22. Clique, Ltd., 7 Pulleyn Dr., York YO2 2DY, England. TEL 0904-631752. (back issues avail.)
Description: Bibliographic information about rare books, with prices and availability.

070.5   IT
HA40.C8
ITALY. ISTITUTO CENTRALE DI STATISTICA. STATISTICHE CULTURALI. vol.28, 1989. a. L.14000. Istituto Centrale di Statistica, Via Cesare Balbo 16, 00100 Rome, Italy. circ. 1,200.
Formerly: Italy. Istituto Centrale di Statistica. Annuario delle Statistiche Culturali (ISSN 0075-1677)

070.5 010   AE   ISSN 0066-5630
AL-KITAB AL-ARABI FI AAM/ARAB BOOK ANNUAL. (Text in Arabic; summary in English) 1961. a. ££1800($8.70) Entreprise National du Livre, 3 bd. Zirout Youcef, B.P. 49, Algiers, Algeria. TEL 2-63-97-12. TELEX 53845.

970 980 016   II   ISSN 0023-8740
LATIN AMERICAN BOOKS NEWSLETTER. (Text in English) 1970. m. R.200($58) K.K. Roy (Private) Ltd., 55 Gariahat Rd., P.O. Box 10210, Calcutta 700 019, India. Ed. John A. Gillard. bk.rev.; bibl.; index; circ. 980.

090.75 011   IT
LIBRI RARI; collezione di ristampe con nuovi apparati. 1977. irreg. latest 1987. price varies. Edizioni Il Polifilo, Via Borgonuovo 2, 20121 Milan, Italy.

655 011   FR   ISSN 0024-5348
LIVRES; bulletin bibliographique mensuel. 1949. 9/yr. 234 F. (foreign 269 F.). Centre National de Documentation Pedagogique, 29 rue d'Ulm, 75230 Paris Cedex 05, France. (Subscr. to: C.N.D.P., Abonnement, B.P. 107-05, 75224 Paris Cedex 05, France) adv.; abstr.; bibl.; index.

070.5 011   FR   ISSN 0294-0000
LIVRES HEBDO. 1979. 46/yr. 1443.80 F. Editions Professionnelles du Livre, 30 rue Dauphine, 75006 Paris, France. TEL 43-29-73-50. FAX 43-29-77-85. Ed. Jean-Marie Doublet. adv.; bk.rev.; bibl.illus.stat.circ.; 9,000.
Formerly: Bulletin du Livre et Connaissance et Formation (ISSN 0150-1402)

PUBLISHING AND BOOK TRADE — ABSTRACTING, BIBLIOGRAPHIES, STATISTICS

655 011   UK   ISSN 0024-5437
LLAIS LLYFRAU/BOOK NEWS FROM WALES. (Text in English and Welsh) 1964. q. £4 (foreign £5.50). Welsh Books Council, Castell Brychan, Aberystwyth, Dyfed SY23 2JB, Wales. TEL 0970-624151. FAX 0970-625385. Ed. John Rhys. adv.; bk.rev.; bibl.; illus.; circ. 5,000.
     Description: List of all books published in Wales during previous three months, plus reviews and articles on the Welsh literary scene.

070.5 012   US
MAGAZINE INDEX. m. price varies. Information Access Company, 362 Lakeside Dr., Foster City, CA 94404. TEL 800-227-8431. FAX 415-378-5499. (microform)
     ●Also available online. Vendor(s): BRS (MAGS), DIALOG (File no.47), Mead Data Central. Also available on CD-ROM.
     Description: Comprehensive guide to more than 350 general interest periodicals. Covers over four years of data.

655 016   US   ISSN 0026-4377
MILWAUKEE READER. 1942. s-m. $5. Milwaukee Public Library, 814 W. Wisconsin Ave., Milwaukee, WI 53233. TEL 414-278-3031. FAX 414-278-2137. Ed. Lorelei Starck. bk.rev.; circ. 4,500. (processed)

NATIONAL BIBLIOGRAPHY OF BOTSWANA. see *BIBLIOGRAPHIES*

NATIONAL UNION CATALOG. BOOKS. see *LIBRARY AND INFORMATION SCIENCES — Abstracting, Bibliographies, Statistics*

DAS NEUE BUCH; Buchprofile fuer die Katholische Buechereiarbeit. see *RELIGIONS AND THEOLOGY — Abstracting, Bibliographies, Statistics*

070.5 011   UK
NEW BUSINESS BOOKS. 1978. 12/yr. free. Alan Armstrong & Associates Ltd., 72-76 Park Rd., London NW1 4SH, England. TEL 01-258-3740.

070.5   UK
NEW EUROPEAN BOOKS. 6/yr. free. Alan Armstrong & Associates Ltd., 72-76 Park Rd., London NW1 4SH, England. TEL 01-258-3740.
     Description: Lists new books published by the office of official publications of the European Communities and those published commercially about the community.

500 655   NE
NIJHOFF INFORMATION, NEW PUBLICATIONS FROM GERMANY, AUSTRIA AND SWITZERLAND. (Text in English) 1988. m. free. Martinus Nijhoff International, P.O. Box 269, 2501 AX The Hague, Netherlands. TEL 31-79-684400. FAX 31-79-615698. TELEX 34164. (U.S. addr.: 175 Derby St., Ste. 13, Hingham, MA 02043. TEL 800-346-3662) adv.; bk.rev.; index; circ. 2,500.
     Formerly: Nijhoff Information, New Publications from West Germany, Austria and Switzerland.
     Description: Bibliographic information on all new and forthcoming scientific journals, books, monographic titles and microfiches published in Germany, Austria and Switzerland.

655 015   NE   ISSN 0029-0459
NIJHOFF INFORMATION, NEW PUBLICATIONS FROM THE NETHERLANDS. (Text in English) 1965. m. free. Martinus Nijhoff International, P.O. Box 269, 2501 AX The Hague, Netherlands. TEL 31-79-684400. FAX 31-79-615698. TELEX 34164. (U.S. addr.: 175 Derby St., Ste. 13, Hingham, MA 02043. TEL 800-346-3662) adv.; bk.rev.; index; circ. 2,500.
     Description: Bibliographic information on all new and forthcoming scientific journals, books, monographic titles and microfiches published in the Netherlands.

655 011   IT   ISSN 0029-6317
NUOVO BOLLETTINO BIBLIOGRAFICO SARDO;* archivio tradizioni popolari. 1955. bi-m. L.6000. Via S. Giovanni 402, Cagliari, Italy. Ed. Dr. Giuseppe Della Maria. bk.rev.; bibl.; index.

P E N INTERNATIONAL. see *LITERATURE — Abstracting, Bibliographies, Statistics*

070.5 070   US
PROGRESSIVE PERIODICALS DIRECTORY. 1981. irreg. $16. Progressive Education, Box 120574, Nashville, TN 37212. Ed. Craig T. Canan. index; circ. 1,500.
     Formerly: U S Progressive Periodicals Directory.
     Description: Reviews and details on 600 national social concerns periodicals.

070.5   GW
Z282
PUBLISHERS' INTERNATIONAL I S B N DIRECTORY. (International Standard Book Number) (Text in English and German) 1989. a. $315. (International ISBN Agency, Berlin) K.G. Saur Verlag KG, Ortlerstr. 8, Postfach 701620, 8000 Munich 70, Germany. TEL 089-76902-0. FAX 089-76902150. (N. America subscr. to: K.G. Saur, A Reed Reference Publishing Company, 121 Chanlon Rd., New Providence, NJ 07974. TEL 908-665-3576) adv.
     ●Also available on CD-ROM. Producer(s): K.G. Saur.
     Formed by the merger of (1962-1989): Internationales Verlagsadressbuch mit I S B N - Register (ISSN 0074-9877) & International I S B N Publishers' Directory.
     Description: Verified listings for publishers in 200 countries, indexed alphabetically, geographically, and numerically by ISBN. Includes microfilm, video and computer software publishers.

QUANGUO XIN SHUMU/NEW BOOKS CATALOG OF P R C. see *BIBLIOGRAPHIES*

028.1 016   US   ISSN 0090-7324
Z1035.1
R S R. (Reference Services Review) 1972. q. $40 to individuals; institutions $65. Pierian Press, Box 1808, Ann Arbor, MI 48106. TEL 313-434-5530. FAX 313-434-6409. Ed. Ilene Rockman. adv.; bk.rev.; bibl.; index; circ. 2,000. (back issues avail.)
     Indexed: Bk.Rev.Ind. (1973-), CALL, Child.Bk.Rev.Ind. (1973-), Hist.Abstr., Leg.Info.Manage.Ind., LHTN, Lib.Lit., Ref.Sour., Tr.& Indus.Ind.
     —BLDSC shelfmark: 7331.920000.
     Description: Devoted to the enrichment of reference knowledge and to the advancement of services in libraries.
     Refereed Serial

RADICAL BOOKSELLER. see *PUBLISHING AND BOOK TRADE*

070.5   US   ISSN 0886-0092
READERS' GUIDE ABSTRACTS. MICROFICHE EDITION. 1986. 8/yr. $675. H.W. Wilson Co., 950 University Ave., Bronx, NY 10452-9978. TEL 800-367-6770. FAX 212-538-2716. TELEX 4990003HWILSON. Ed. Robert Genovesi. film rev.; play rev.; abstr. (microfiche; also avail. in magnetic tape; back issues avail.)
     ●Also available online. Vendor(s): Wilsonline (File RGA).
     Also available on CD-ROM. Producer(s): H.W. Wilson.
     Description: Cumulative abstracting service covering general interest periodical literature.

070.5   US   ISSN 0899-1553
Z6941
READER'S GUIDE ABSTRACTS. PRINT EDITION. 1988. 10/yr. (plus s-a. cumulations). $229. H.W. Wilson Co., 950 University Ave., Bronx, NY 10452-9978. TEL 800-367-6770. FAX 212-538-2716. TELEX 4990003HWILSON. Ed. Robert Genovesi.
     Description: Cumulative abstracting service covering general interest periodical literature found in Readers' Guide.

655 011   US   ISSN 0275-682X
Z1033.R4
REPRINT BULLETIN BOOK REVIEWS. 1955. s-a. $40. Glanville Publishers, Inc., 75 Main St., Dobbs Ferry, NY 10522. TEL 914-693-5956. FAX 914-693-0402. Ed. M.C. Susan DeMaio. bk.rev.; bibl.; mkt.; cum.index; circ. 200. (processed; back issues avail.) **Indexed:** Amer.Bibl.Slavic & E.Eur.Stud., Bk.Rev.Ind. (1977-), Child.Bk.Rev.Ind. (1977-), Lib.Lit.
     Formerly (until 1966): Reprint Expediting Service Bulletin (ISSN 0034-4923)
     Description: Reviews reprints of scholarly titles of primary interest to universities and larger public libraries.

070.5   PL   ISSN 0511-1196
RUCH WYDAWNICZY W LICZBACH/POLISH PUBLISHING IN FIGURES. 1955. a. 8000 Zl.($8) (Biblioteka Narodowa, Instytut Bibliograficzny) Biblioteka Narodowa, Al. Niepodleglosci 213, 00-973 Warsaw, Poland. TEL 48-22-259271. FAX 48-22-255251. TELEX 813702 BN PL. (Dist. by: Ars Polona-Ruch, ul. Krakowskie Przedmiescie 7, 00-068 Warsaw, Poland) Ed. Krystyna Bankowska-Bober. circ. 450.
     Description: Offers official statistical data concerning books and periodicals characterized by sheets, titles, copies, subject fields and publishers.

686   GW   ISSN 0232-5616
SAECHSISCHE LANDESBIBLIOTHEK. BIBLIOGRAPHIE ILLUSTRIERTE BUECHER DER DEUTSCHEN DEMOKRATISCHEN REPUBLIK. (Text in German) 1973. a. Saechsische Landesbibliothek, Marienalle 12, 8060 Dresden, Germany. Ed. Hans-Joachim Kunz.

690 016   AG   ISSN 0037-2099
Z1007
SENALES; revista bibliografica. 1949. q. A50($18) Casilla 2484-Correo Central, 1000 Buenos Aires, Argentina. Ed. Amy Dominguez Murray. adv.; bk.rev.; bibl.; circ. 2,000.

SMALL PRESS RECORD OF BOOKS IN PRINT. see *BIBLIOGRAPHIES*

070.5 011   JA
SOUTHEAST - EAST ASIAN ENGLISH PUBLICATIONS IN PRINT. (Text in English) 1987. irreg. 25000 Yen($210) Japan Publications Guide Service, 5-5-13 Matsushiro, Tsukubashi Ibarakiken 305, Japan. FAX 81-3-3667-9646. (Subscr. to: Intercontinental Marketing Corp., IPO box 5056, Tokyo 100-31, Japan. TEL 81-3-3661-7458) adv.; circ. 1,000. (also avail. on diskette)
     Description: Excluding Japan, it covers Brunei, Burma, China, Hong Kong, Indonesia, Korea, Macao, Malaysia, Philippines, Singapore, Taiwan, Thailand and Vietnam.

015   CE
SRI LANKA NATIONAL BIBLIOGRAPHY. (Text in English, Sinhalese, Tamil) 1962. m. Rs.33. Department of National Archives, National Bibliography Branch, 7 Reid Ave., Colombo 7, Sri Lanka. circ. 200.
     Formerly (until 1973): Ceylon National Bibliography (ISSN 0009-0883)

020 296 016   US   ISSN 0039-3568
Z7070
STUDIES IN BIBLIOGRAPHY AND BOOKLORE; devoted to research in the field of Jewish bibliography. (Text in English, Hebrew and other languages) 1953. irreg. price varies. Hebrew Union College - Jewish Institute of Religion (Cincinnati), 3101 Clifton Ave., Cincinnati, OH 45220. TEL 513-221-1875. Ed.Bd. bk.rev.; bibl.; cum.index: vols. 1-16; circ. 1,100.
     Indexed: Amer.Hist. & Life, Hist.Abstr., Ind.Jew.Per., Mid.East: Abstr.& Ind.
     —BLDSC shelfmark: 8489.660000.

070.5   UK   ISSN 0265-5896
SUBJECT GUIDE: RECENT AND FORTHCOMING BRITISH BOOKS. 1983-1991. 6/yr. free. Dawson UK Ltd., Canon House, Folkestone, Kent CT19 5EE, England. TEL 0303-850101. circ. 750.
     Description: Listings of new British books, including claim information, new editions and important reprints.

SWAZILAND NATIONAL BIBLIOGRAPHY. see *BIBLIOGRAPHIES*

ULRICH'S INTERNATIONAL PERIODICALS DIRECTORY. see *BIBLIOGRAPHIES*

ULRICH'S ON MICROFICHE. see *BIBLIOGRAPHIES*

ULRICH'S PLUS; the complete International Serials database on laser disc. see *BIBLIOGRAPHIES*

ULRICH'S UPDATE. see *BIBLIOGRAPHIES*

860 011   AG
VIENTIN BIBLIOGRAPHIC SERVICE.* 1972. bi-m. Vientin S.A., Talcahuano 487, Buenos Aires, Argentina. bibl.

011　　　　　　UK　ISSN 0953-041X
Z2005
WHITAKER'S BOOK LIST. 1924. a. £57. J. Whitaker & Sons Ltd., 12 Dyott St., London WC1A 1DF, England. TEL 071-836-8911. FAX 071-836-2909.
—BLDSC shelfmark: 9311.000200.
Formerly: Whitaker's Cumulative Book List (ISSN 0140-4229)

500 016　　　　GW　ISSN 0341-8723
Z7403
WISSENSCHAFTLICHER LITERATURANZEIGER. 1961. s-a. DM.16. Verlag M. Veit M.A., Erlenweg 10, 4834 Harsewinkel 1, Germany. TEL 05247-5466. Ed. Manfred Veit. adv.; bk.rev.; circ. 4,000. (back issues avail.)

296 016　　　　IS　ISSN 0044-4774
ZIONIST LITERATURE. (Text in English and Hebrew) 1936. bi-m. free. World Zionist Organization, Central Zionist Archives, P.O. Box 92, Jerusalem 91920, Israel. Ed. Ms. S. Palmor. circ. 1,000.

PUBLISHING AND BOOK TRADE — Computer Applications

070.5　　　　　US
C D PUBLISHER NEWS. (Compact Disc) 1986. q. free. Meridian Data, Inc., 5615 Scotts Valley Dr., Scotts Valley, CA 95066. TEL 408-438-3100. FAX 408-438-6816. TELEX 998330. Ed. Monica Meyer. circ. 9,000.
Description: In-house newsletter highlights applications, industry news and upcoming events in the CD-ROM industry.

COMPUTER MEDIA DIRECTORY. see *COMPUTERS — Computer Industry Directories*

070.3　　　　　US　ISSN 0740-4085
Z286.C65
COMPUTER PUBLISHERS & PUBLICATIONS; an international directory. 1984. biennial. $199 (foreign $224). Communications Trends, Inc., 2 East Ave., Larchmont, NY 10538. TEL 914-833-0600. FAX 914-833-0558. Ed. Frederica Evan. adv.; bk.rev.
—BLDSC shelfmark: 3394.225000.
Description: Lists 250 book publishers and 1200 periodicals covering the computer field.

070.5　　　　　US　ISSN 0740-6231
COMPUTER PUBLISHING AND ADVERTISING REPORT. 1983. 24/yr. $432 (foreign $468). Communications Trends, Inc., 2 East Ave., Larchmont, NY 10538. TEL 914-833-0600. FAX 914-833-0558. Ed. Efrem Sigel. bk.rev.
Description: Provides coverage of computer publishing and distribution, international industry news, advertising campaigns for computer companies, new products and publications.

070.5　　　　　US
DATAPRO REPORTS ON ELECTRONIC PUBLISHING SYSTEMS. 1986. 2 base vols. plus m. issues. $715. Datapro Information Services Group (Subsidiary of: McGraw-Hill, Inc.), 600 Delran Pkwy., Delran, NJ 08075. TEL 800-328-2776.

DESKTOP COMMUNICATIONS. see *COMPUTERS — Microcomputers*

070.5　　　　　US
DESKTOP PUBLISHER (MAPLE GLEN). 1988. m. $18 (free to qualified personnel). Fox Pond Corp., 0841 Norristown Rd., Box 3200, Maple Glen, PA 19002. TEL 215-643-5940. FAX 215-641-9521. Ed. James S. Pennybacker. adv.; bk.rev.; circ. 15,000.
Formerly: Greater Philadelphia Desktop Publisher.
Description: Offers tips, advice and service information for Mid-Atlantic desktop publishing users.

070.5　　　　　US
DESKTOP PUBLISHING JOURNAL. 1988. m. $12.99. Linda Hanson, Ed. & Pub., 4017-C Rucker Ave., Ste. 821, Everett, WA 98201. TEL 206-568-2950. circ. 40,000. (tabloid format)

070.5　　　　　UK
DESKTOP PUBLISHING TODAY. Short title: D.P.T. Today. 1986. m. £100. Industrial Medial Ltd., Blair House, 184-190 High St., Tonbridge, Kent TN9 1BQ, England. TEL 0732-359990. FAX 0732-770049. Ed. Andrew Charlesworth. adv.; bk.rev.; circ. 10,500 (controlled).

070.5　　　　　US　ISSN 0743-2933
DESKTOP PUBLISHING USERS' REPORT. m. $90. Communications Concepts Inc., 2100 National Press Bldg., Washington, DC 20045. TEL 703-425-7751. FAX 703-425-8930. (Subscr. to: Box 1608, Springfield, VA 22151-0608) Ed. Bill Londino.
Description: Monographs on specific aspects of desktop publishing, from staffing and training to scheduling and internal SOPs.

070.5　　　　　CN　ISSN 0838-9535
ELECTRONIC COMPOSITION & IMAGING. 1987. bi-m. Can. $37($33.70) Youngblood Communications, 505 Consumers Rd., Willowdale, Ont. M2J 4V8, Canada. TEL 416-492-5777. FAX 416-492-7595. Ed. Chris Dickman. adv.; bk.rev.; tr.lit.; circ. 30,000. (back issues avail.)
Description: How-to magazine for people using desktop publishing to produce brochures, newsletters and advertising. Covers PC and Macintosh electronic prepress.

070.5　　　　　UK　ISSN 0894-3982
Z286.E43　　　　　　CODEN: EPODEU
ELECTRONIC PUBLISHING; origination, dissemination and design. 1988. q. $185 (effective 1992). John Wiley & Sons Ltd., Journals, Baffins Lane, Chichester, W. Sussex PO19 1UD, England. TEL 0243-779777. FAX 0243-775878. TELEX 86290 WIBOOK G. Eds. D. Brailsford, R. Furuta.
—BLDSC shelfmark: 3702.753200.
Description: Encompasses areas such as structured editors, authoring tools, hypermedia, document bases, production concordances and indexes, document display on workstations, electronic documents over networks, integration of text and illustrations, typface design and imaging hardware.
Refereed Serial

ELECTRONIC PUBLISHING & PRINTING. see *PUBLISHING AND BOOK TRADE*

070.5　　　　　US　ISSN 1048-3403
FAXON REPORT. q. Faxon Company, Inc., 15 Southwest Park, Westwood, MA 02090. TEL 617-329-3350. FAX 617-461-1862. TELEX 681-7238.
Formerly: Faxletter (ISSN 0882-231X)
Description: Provides news briefs and informational articles of interest to the clients of and representatives from the Faxon Company, an information-communications corporation.

G C A REVIEW. (Graphic Communications Association) see *PRINTING — Computer Applications*

GOVERNMENT PUBLISHER. see *PRINTING*

070.5　　　　　US
HUMAN RESOURCE INFORMATION NETWORK UPDATE. 1984. m. free. Executive Telecom System International (Subsidiary of: The Bureau of National Affairs, Inc.), 9585 Valparaiso Court, Indianapolis, IN 46268. TEL 800-421-8884. FAX 317-872-2059. TELEX 285656 BNAI WSH. (back issues avail.)
Description: For users of the Human Resource Information Network.

070.5　　　　　US
INFORMATION & INTERACTIVE SERVICES REPORT; the biweekly journal of record for the information industry. 1980. bi-w. $396. Telecommunications Reports (Subsidiary of: Business Research Publications, Inc.), 1333 H St., N.W., Ste. 1100-W., Washington, DC 20005. TEL 202-842-3006. FAX 202-842-30047. (Alt. addr.: 817 Broadway, 3rd Fl., New York, NY 10003. TEL 212-673-4700) Ed. Victoria Mason. adv.; index. (back issues avail.)
●Also available online. Vendor(s): NewsNet (TE41).
Formed by the merger of (Mar. 1991): Electronic Shopping News (ISSN 0893-0333); Which was formerly (until 1987): TeleServices Report (ISSN 0730-0263) & Interactivity Report (ISSN 0893-0325); Which was formerly (until 1987): International Videotex Teletext News (ISSN 0197-677X)
Description: Documents developments in the information industry.

070.5 338　　　　US　ISSN 0883-5772
INFORMATION INDUSTRY BULLETIN. 1985. w. $295. Digital Information Group, 51 Bank St., Stamford, CT 06901. TEL 203-348-2751. Ed. Chris Elwell. charts.
Description: News and analysis for executives in the business of publishing information. Includes financial and competitive statistics.

070.5 621.381　　　US
▼**MAC PUBLISHING AND PRESENTATIONS**. 1992. bi-m. $18. International Desktop Communications, Ltd., 530 Fifth Ave., 4th Fl., New York, NY 10036. TEL 212-768-7666. FAX 212-768-0288. Ed. Pauline Ores. circ. 50,000.
Description: For Macintosh desktop publishers; provides histories, product recommendations and reviews; publishes solutions and profiles on how to select and use Mac-based desktop technology.

070.5　　　　　IS
MAKINTOSH. 1988. m. $135. Israel Peled Publishing, Pinsker 64, Tel Aviv 61 332, Israel. TEL 3-295146. FAX 3-295144. circ. 5,000.

070.5 621.381　　　US　ISSN 0889-9533
MICROPUBLISHING REPORT; the industry newsletter for electronic publishing vendors. 1984. m. $295. Micro Publishing, 21150 Hawthorne Blvd., Ste. 104, Torrance, CA 90503. TEL 310-371-5787. FAX 310-542-0849. Ed. James Cavuoto. bk.rev. (back issues avail.) **Indexed:** Comput.Lit.Ind.
Incorporates: Corporate Publishing.
Description: Provides detailed analysis of market and industry trends, vendor profiles, show reports, personnel and financial briefs.

N; the newsletter for publications. see *PUBLISHING AND BOOK TRADE*

500　　　　　　US
N T I S BIBLIOGRAPHIC DATA BASE. (Supplement avail.: Subject Headings Booklet) s-m. price varies. U.S. National Technical Information Service, 5285 Port Royal Rd., Springfield, VA 22161. TEL 703-487-4630. index.
●Also available online. Vendor(s): BRS, Data-Star, DIALOG, Orbit Information Technologies, STN International.
Also available on CD-ROM. Producer(s): Dialog Information Services, O C L C, SilverPlatter.
Description: Multidisciplinary coverage of engineering as well as research and development results of scientific and technical research of the U.S. government, its contractors and foreign governments.

070.5 370　　　　US　ISSN 0888-1596
PN4784.E5
NEWS COMPUTING JOURNAL; a quarterly journal on microcomputer use in journalism and mass communication. 1984. q. $30 to individuals; libraries $100. (Duquesne University, Department of Communication) Edwards Company, Inc., 3177 Bradbury Dr., Aliquippa, PA 15001. TEL 412-375-2704. adv.; bk.rev.; cum.index: 1984-1988; circ. 620. (back issues avail.)
Description: Geared towards working journalists, and journalism educators.

NEWSLETTER DESIGN. see *JOURNALISM*

070.5　　　　　US　ISSN 0896-9841
Z286.E43　　　　　　CODEN: OPDIEW
OPTICAL PUBLISHING DIRECTORY. 3rd ed. 1988. irreg., 4th ed., 1991. $59. Learned Information, Inc., 143 Old Marlton Pike, Medford, NJ 08055-8707. TEL 609-654-6266. FAX 609-654-4309. Eds. Joseph Webb, James Sheldon.
Formerly: Optical-Electronic Publishing Directory (ISSN 0893-0317)

070.5 621.381　　　US　ISSN 0896-8209
Z286.D47
P C PUBLISHING AND PRESENTATIONS; desktop publishing. 1987. m. $36 (Canada and Mexico $48; elsewhere $96). International Desktop Communications, Ltd., 530 Fifth Ave., 4th Fl., New York, NY 10036. TEL 212-768-7666. FAX 212-768-0288. Ed. Robert Mueller. adv.; circ. 50,000.
Formerly (until 1991): P C Publishing.
Description: For IBM PC and compatible users. Feature articles cover diverse topics in desktop publishing: applications, hardware and software.

RADIO

070.5 US
P C UPGRADE; the guide to building and expanding computer systems. 6/yr. $17.95. Bedford Communications, Inc., 150 Fifth Ave., New York, NY 10011. TEL 212-807-8220. FAX 212-807-8737.
 Formerly: Desktop Publishing - Office Automation Buyer's Guide and Handbook.

070.5 US ISSN 0196-4127
PERSONAL COMPOSITION REPORT; the newsletter for users of desktop publishing, typesetting, and word & information processing. Short title: P C R. 1979. 10/yr. $60 (foreign $75). Graphic Dimensions, 134 Caversham Woods, Pittsford, NY 14534-2834. TEL 716-381-3428. Ed. Michael L. Kleper. bk.rev. (back issues avail.)
 Formerly: Digest of Information on Phototypesetting.
 Description: Covers desktop publishing, typesetting, word and information processing.

070.5 025 US ISSN 0000-1341
PLUS; plus system newsletter. 1987. q. free to all purchasers of Bowker CD-ROM products. R.R. Bowker, A Reed Reference Publishing Company, Division of Reed Publishing (USA) Inc., 121 Chanlon Rd., New Providence, NJ 07974. TEL 800-323-3288. FAX 908-665-6688. Ed. Martin Brooks.
 Description: Includes information on new CD-ROM products, conference schedules and technical reports.

PUBLISH!; the how-to magazine of desktop publishing. see COMPUTERS — Microcomputers

070.5 621.381 US
▼**QUARKXPRESS IN-DEPTH.*** 1990. m. $69. Mindcraft Publishing Corporation, Box 256, Lincoln, MA 01773-0002. TEL 508-371-1660. Ed. Matt Laurence. circ. 3,000.
 Description: Showcases hands-on application, such as newsletter, advertisement or stationery design. Includes step-by-step graphic examples to illustrate tips, tricks, special features and shortcuts.

001.6 070 651.8 US ISSN 0736-7260
Z286.E43
SEYBOLD REPORT ON PUBLISHING SYSTEMS. 1971. s-m. $336. Seybold Publications, Inc., Box 644, Media, PA 19063. TEL 215-565-2480. FAX 215-656-4659. TELEX 4991493. Ed. Stephen Edwards. bk.rev.; charts; illus.; index, cum.index. **Indexed:** Comput.Cont., Graph.Arts Lit.Abstr., P.I.R.A., Sci.Abstr.
 —BLDSC shelfmark: 8254.494000.
 Former titles: Seybold Report (ISSN 0364-5517); Editing Technology (ISSN 0046-1261)
 Description: Chronicles developments in typesetting, page make-up facilities and related electronic prepress systems.

SOFT.LETTER; trends & strategies in software publishing. see COMPUTERS — Software

WORLD PUBLISHING MONITOR. see COMPUTERS — Abstracting, Bibliographies, Statistics

621.381 070.5 US
THE YELLOWSTONE DESKTOP PUBLISHING LETTER. 1988. bi-m. $49.95 (foreign $89.95). Yellowstone Information Services, 7 View Dr., Elkview, WV 25071. TEL 304-965-5548. FAX 304-965-7785. Ed. Roger C. Thibault. index, cum.index; circ. 1,000. (back issues avail.)
 Formerly (until 1991): Desktop Publisher (Elkview).
 Description: Covers desktop publishing software and hardware, applications, and product and business news.

RADIO

see Communications–Radio

RADIOLOGY AND NUCLEAR MEDICINE

see Medical Sciences–Radiology and Nuclear Medicine

RAILROADS

see Transportation–Railroads

REAL ESTATE

see also Architecture; Building and Construction; Business and Economics–Investments; Housing and Urban Planning

333.33 US
A M O PERSPECTIVES. q. $50 to non-members; members $35. Institute of Real Estate Management, Accredited Management Organization, Box 109025, Chicago, IL 60610-9025. TEL 312-661-1953. FAX 312-661-0217.
 Description: Studies strategies for dealing with important business management situations.

333.33 US
A O M A NEWSLETTER; profile of the multi-family housing industry. 1967. m. $125 to non-members. Apartment Owners and Managers Association of America, 65 Cherry Plaza, Box 238, Watertown, CT 06795-0238. TEL 203-274-2589. Ed. Robert McGough. adv.; bk.rev.; abstr.; charts; illus.; circ. 8,618.

333.3 US
ACQUISITION COLUMBUS. m. $24 (free to qualified personnel)(effective 1992). Acquisition Columbus, 1445 Worthington Woods Blvd., Worthington, OH 43085-6707. TEL 614-841-0085. Ed. Rufus Jones. circ. controlled.
 Description: For professionals in commercial and industrial real estate.

333.3 US
ACQUISITION, NORTHEASTERN OHIO. m. Widener Publications, Inc., 9783 Ravenna Rd., Twinsburg, OH 44087-2153. TEL 216-425-4375. FAX 216-425-4306. Ed. Jeff Davis. adv.; circ. 18,000.

333.33 FR ISSN 0764-5066
ACTIVITE IMMOBILIERE. 1944. m. 350 F. Consortium d'Edition et de Publicite du Sud-Ouest, 26, avenue de Suffren, 75015 Paris, France. adv.; circ. 5,000. (looseleaf format)
 Formerly: Activite Immobiliere Commerciale et Industrielle.

L'ACTUALITE JURIDIQUE: DROIT ADMINISTRATIF. see LAW

333.33 FR
ADMINISTRER. m. 18 F. per no. 9 rue Sebastien Bottin, 75007 Paris, France. adv.; circ. 3,000.

333.33 630 CN ISSN 0701-7502
HD319.A4
AGRICULTURAL REAL ESTATE VALUES IN ALBERTA. 1971. q. Alberta Agriculture, Production Economics Branch, 3rd Fl., 7000 113th St., Edmonton, Alta. T6H 5T6, Canada. TEL 403-427-2396. FAX 403-427-5220. circ. 1,400.
 Formerly: Rural Real Estate Values in Alberta (ISSN 0383-3585)

333.33 GW
ALLGEMEINE IMMOBILIEN-ZEITUNG; Fachzeitschrift fuer Immobilienwirtschaft und Immobilienrecht. 1924. m. DM.78. (Ring Deutscher Makler e.V.) R D M-Verlags-GmbH, Moenckebergstr. 27, 2000 Hamburg 1, Germany. Ed. Gerhard Feldmann. adv.; bk.rev.; stat.; upd. 27 91365; circ. 6,700.
 Formerly: A I Z (ISSN 0001-1673)

333.3 US ISSN 0270-0484
HD251
AMERICAN REAL ESTATE AND URBAN ECONOMICS ASSOCIATION. JOURNAL. Abbreviated title: A R E U E A Journal. 1973. q. $45 to individuals; libraries $70; students $20. (American Real Estate and Urban Economics Association) Learned Hands, 77 1-2 Chestnut, Morristown, NJ 07960. TEL 812-855-7794. FAX 201-829-0757. (Subscr. to: Indiana University, School of Business, Room 428, Bloomington, IN 47401) Ed.Bd. adv.; bk.rev.; circ. 1,300. (also avail. in microfiche from UMI; back issues avail.; reprint service avail. from UMI) **Indexed:** ABI Inform, ASCA, B.P.I, J.of Econ.Lit., Risk Abstr., SSCI, Tr.& Indus.Ind.

333 332 368 US
AMERICAN SOCIETY OF APPRAISERS. NEWSLINE. m. membership. American Society of Appraisers, Box 17265, Washington, DC 20041. TEL 703-478-2228. Ed. Shirley Belz.

333.33 658 US ISSN 0892-0850
ANDREWSREPORT; for owners - developers - managers - marketers of small shopping centers. 1987. m. $147. Report Communications, 9595 Whitley Dr., Ste. 100, Indianapolis, IN 46240. TEL 317-844-9024. FAX 317-848-6953. Ed. William R. Wilburn. abstr.; circ. 900. (back issues avail.)
 Description: Current news from the shopping center industry, targeted to small center professionals.

APARTMENT AGE; the voice of the industry. see HOUSING AND URBAN PLANNING

333.33 US ISSN 0744-9143
APARTMENT MANAGEMENT NEWSLETTER; wealth building techniques for apartment owners & their managers. 1975. m. $95. Apartment Management Publishing Co., Inc., 379 W. Broadway, New York, NY 10012. TEL 212-966-8822. Ed. Harold Mann. bk.rev.; charts; tr.lit.; index; circ. 5,000. (back issues avail.)

333.33 US
APARTMENT MANAGEMENT REPORT; for managers of apartments. 1975. m. $85. Apartment Owners and Managers Association of America, 65 Cherry Plaza, Box 238, Watertown, CT 06795-0238. TEL 203-274-2589.

333.33 US ISSN 0191-8826
APARTMENT OWNER; San Fernando Valley - Ventura County - Santa Clarita - Antelope Valley. vol. 12, 1979. m. $50. Apartment Association, 14550 Archwood St., Van Nuys, CA 91405. TEL 818-787-3455. FAX 818-374-3240. Ed. MaryEllen Hughes. adv.; circ. 4,000 (controlled).

333.332 US ISSN 0003-7060
APPRAISAL DIGEST. 1950. q. $10. New York State Society of Real Estate Appraisers, 107 Washington Ave., Box 122, Albany, NY 12260. FAX 518-462-5474. (Co-sponsor: New York State Association of Realtors, Inc.) Ed. Walter F. Kresge. circ. 1,500.

333.332 CN ISSN 0003-7079
APPRAISAL INSTITUTE DIGEST. vol.4, 1970. irreg. (4-5/yr.). included in Canadian Appraiser. Appraisal Institute of Canada, 101-93 Lombard Ave., Winnipeg, Man. R3B 3B1, Canada. TEL 204-942-0751. Ed. Erin Foulkes. charts; illus.; circ. 8,200. (also avail. in microfilm from MML)

333.332 US ISSN 0003-7087
HD251 CODEN: APPJA5
APPRAISAL JOURNAL. 1932. q. $30 to non-members (foreign $35); members $25 (foreign $30). Appraisal Institute, 875 N. Michigan Ave., Ste. 2400, Chicago, IL 60611-1980. TEL 312-335-4100. FAX 312-353-4400. Ed. Jennifer Roberts. bk.rev.; abstr.; charts; illus.; stat.; index; circ. 42,000. circ. 42,000. (also avail. in microform from UMI; reprint service avail. from UMI,KTO) **Indexed:** AAR, ABI Inform, Account.Ind. (1974-), B.P.I., BPIA, Bus.Ind., Manage.Cont., Noise Pollut.Publ.Abstr., P.A.I.S., RICS, Tr.& Indus.Ind.
 —BLDSC shelfmark: 1580.130000.
 Description: Provides perspectives of professors, practitioners, and acknowledged authorities on the subject of commercial real estate appraisal.

REAL ESTATE 4145

333.33   US
APPRAISAL REPORT. q. American Society of Professional Appraisers, 100 Galleria Pkwy., Tower One, Ste. 400, Atlanta, GA 30339. TEL 404-951-1994.

333.332   US
APPRAISAL REVIEW. q. National Association of Independent Fee Appraisers, 7501 Murdoch Ave., St. Louis, MO 63119. TEL 314-781-6688. Ed. Jackie Mashburn. circ. 5,600.
Description: Subjects of interest to members of appraisal organizations.

333.33   US   ISSN 0195-4407
HD1387
APPRAISAL REVIEW AND MORTGAGE UNDERWRITING JOURNAL. 1978. q. $45. (National Association of Review Appraisers & Mortgage Underwriters) Todd Publishing, Inc., 8383 E. Evans Rd., Scottsdale, AZ 85260. TEL 602-998-7743. FAX 602-998-8022. adv.; circ. 10,000. (back issues avail.)

333.332   US
APPRAISER GRAM. vol.18, 1988. m. National Association of Independent Fee Appraisers, 7501 Murdoch Ave., St. Louis, MO 63119. TEL 314-781-6688. Ed. Jackie Mashburn. circ. 5,800. (looseleaf format)
Description: Information for members of the organization.

333.332   US   ISSN 1054-5999
HD251
APPRAISER NEWS. 1959. m. $20 (foreign $25). Appraisal Institute, 875 N. Michigan Ave., Ste. 2400, Chicago, IL 60611-1980. TEL 312-335-4100. FAX 312-335-4400. Ed. Grace M. Hayek. charts; illus.; stat.; circ. 37,800.
Formerly (until 1991): Appraiser (ISSN 0003-7095)
Description: Covers events, trends and opinions in real estate appraisal practice and related legislative, financial and economic affairs.

AREA DEVELOPMENT MAGAZINE; the executive magazine of sites and facility planning. see *BUSINESS AND ECONOMICS — Management*

ARIZONA BUSINESS & DEVELOPMENT. see *BUSINESS AND ECONOMICS — Office Equipment And Services*

ASOCIACION NACIONAL DE PROMOTORES CONSTRUCTORES DE EDIFICIOS URBANOS. ANNUAL REPORT. see *HOUSING AND URBAN PLANNING*

ASOCIACION NACIONAL DE PROMOTORES CONSTRUCTORES DE EDIFICIOS URBANOS. PROMOCION. see *HOUSING AND URBAN PLANNING*

333.332   US   ISSN 0731-0277
ASSESSMENT DIGEST. 1979. bi-m. $30. International Association of Assessing Officers, 1313 E. 60th St., Chicago, IL 60637-9990. TEL 312-947-2053. Ed. Roberta Hilleman. adv.; bk.rev.; charts; stat.; circ. 8,250.
Former titles: International Assessor; I A A O Newsletter; Assessors News Letter - A N L (ISSN 0004-508X)

526.9   CN   ISSN 0318-2126
TA527.N4
ASSOCIATION OF NEW BRUNSWICK LAND SURVEYORS. ANNUAL REPORT. 1955. a. free. Association of New Brunswick Land Surveyors, P.O. Box 22, Fredericton, N.B. E3B 4Y2, Canada. TEL 506-458-8266. FAX 506-458-8267. adv.; circ. 250 (controlled).

AUDIO ESTATE PLANNER. see *LAW — Estate Planning*

AUDIO REAL ESTATE LAWYER. see *LAW*

AUSTRALIAN TENANCY PRACTICE & PRECEDENTS. see *LAW*

B N A'S ENVIRONMENTAL DUE DILIGENCE GUIDE. see *LAW*

333.33 658   US   ISSN 0738-2170
TX980
B O M A EXPERIENCE EXCHANGE REPORT; income - expense analysis for office buildings. 1920. a. $195. Building Owners and Managers Association International, 1201 New York Ave., N.W., Ste. 300, Washington, DC 20005. TEL 202-408-2662. FAX 202-321-0181. Eds. Ellen Ku, Deidre Schexnayder. circ. 8,000. (back issues avail.)

333.33   AT
B O M A NEWS.* 1984. q. free. Building Owners & Managers Association of Australia Ltd., 98-102 Elizabeth St., Block Arcade, 3rd Fl., Melbourne, Vic. 3000, Australia. Ed. A.W. Larnach-Jones. adv.; circ. 400. (back issues avail.)

B S A ANNUAL REPORT. (Building Societies Association) see *BUILDING AND CONSTRUCTION*

BAALMAN & WELL'S LAND TITLES OFFICE PRACTICE. see *LAW*

333.33 332.1   US   ISSN 0005-5409
BANKER & TRADESMAN. 1872. w. $160. Warren Publishing Corp., 210 South St., Boston, MA 02111. TEL 617-426-4495. Ed. William A. Mallard. adv.; bk.rev.; circ. 8,006. (also avail. in microform from UMI)

333.33   GW
BAYERISCHE HAUSBESITZER-ZEITUNG. m. Zentralverband der Deutschen Haus-, Wohnungs- und Grundeigentuemer, Landesverband Bayerische Haus- und Grundbesitzer, Sonnenstr. 13, D-8000 Munich 2, Germany.

333.33   NE
BEHEER EN ONDERHOUD. 1975. m. fl.960.75. Uitgeversmaatschappij C. Misset B.V., Hanzestr. 1, 7006 RH Doetinchem, Netherlands. TEL 08340-49911. FAX 08340-43839. TELEX 45481. (Subscr. to: Postbus 4, 7000 BA Doetinchem, Netherlands) Ed. W. Pasman.
Description: Cost and management information for the management of real estate.

333.33   CC
BEIJING FANGDICHAN/BEIJING REAL ESTATE. (Text in Chinese) 1987. bi-m. Y9($6) Beijing Fangdichang Guanliju - Beijing Real Estate Administration, 1 Nanwanzi, Nanheyan, Dongcheng-qu, Beijing 100006, People's Republic of China. TEL 552102. FAX 5124104. Ed. Liang Bingliang. adv.: Color page Y4,000; adv. contact: Sunwei Wang.

333.3   GW
BERLINER HAUS- UND GRUNDBESITZ. 1963. m. DM.39.60. Verlag Adalbert Bestgen, Spessartstr. 13, Abholfach, 1000 Berlin 33, Germany. Ed. A. Bestgen. adv.; bk.rev.; circ. 4,000. (back issues avail.)

333.33   FR
BERTRAND VACANCES. 2/yr. price varies. Editions Indicateur Bertrand, 43 bd. Barbes, 75018 Paris, France. TEL 1-49-25-26-27. FAX 1-49-25-26-00. adv.: B&W page 7050 F.; trim 178 x 248; adv. contact: Philippe Juste. illus.; circ. 235,000.
Formerly: Vacances.
Description: Advertisements for the renting of vacation homes from real estate agencies and private owners.

333.33   US
▼**BIRMINGHAM COMMERCIAL REAL ESTATE REVIEW & FORECAST ANNUAL.** 1990. a. $8.95. First Publishing Inc., 2100 Riverchase Center, Ste. 110, Birmingham, AL 35244. TEL 205-733-1970. FAX 205-733-1974. Ed. Charlie Cox. adv.; circ. 18,100. (back issues avail.)
Description: Tracks and reports commercial real estate activities and trends.

333.33   US
BLACK'S BROKER - TENANT GUIDE: SOUTH FLORIDA - TREASURE COAST. 1986. s-a. $49.95. Black's Guide, Inc., 1355 Piccard Dr., Ste. 450, Rockville, MD 20850. TEL 301-948-0995. FAX 301-258-9237. Ed. David G. Hanson. adv.

333.33   US
BLACK'S BROKER - TENANT GUIDE: TAMPA BAY - SOUTHWEST FLORIDA. 1986. s-a. $49.95. Black's Guide, Inc., 1355 Piccard Dr., Ste. 450, Rockville, MD 20850. TEL 301-948-0995. FAX 301-258-9237. Ed. David G. Hanson. adv.

333.33   US
BLACK'S BROKER - TENANT GUIDE: WASHINGTON - BALTIMORE. 1978. s-a. $69.95. Black's Guide, Inc., 1355 Piccard Dr., Ste. 450, Rockville, MD 20850. TEL 301-948-0995. FAX 301-258-9237. Ed. David G. Hanson. adv.
Formerly (until 1991): Black's Guide to the Office Space Market - Washington - Baltimore.

333.33   US
BLACK'S GUIDE TO THE OFFICE SPACE MARKET: CONNECTICUT - NEW YORK SUBURBS. 1983. a. $59.95. Black's Guide, Inc., 1355 Piccard Dr., Ste. 450, Rockville, MD 20850. TEL 301-948-0995. FAX 301-258-9237. Ed. David G. Hanson. adv.

333.33   US
BLACK'S GUIDE TO THE OFFICE SPACE MARKET: DALLAS - FORT WORTH. 1984. s-a. $49.95. Black's Guide, Inc., 1355 Piccard Dr., Ste. 450, Rockville, MD 20850. TEL 301-948-0995. FAX 301-258-9237. Ed. David G. Hanson. adv.

333.33   US
BLACK'S GUIDE TO THE OFFICE SPACE MARKET: DENVER. 1982. a. $49.95. Black's Guide, Inc., 1355 Piccard Dr., Ste. 450, Rockville, MD 20850. TEL 301-948-0995. FAX 301-258-9237. Ed. David G. Hanson. adv.

333.33   US
BLACK'S GUIDE TO THE OFFICE SPACE MARKET: GREATER LOS ANGELES AREA. 1984. s-a. $59.95. Black's Guide, Inc., 1355 Piccard Dr., Ste. 450, Rockville, MD 20850. TEL 301-948-0995. FAX 301-258-9237. Ed. David G. Hanson. adv.

333.33   US
BLACK'S GUIDE TO THE OFFICE SPACE MARKET: HOUSTON. 1981. a. $49.95. Black's Guide, Inc., 1355 Piccard Dr., Ste. 450, Rockville, MD 20850. TEL 301-948-0995. FAX 301-258-9237. Ed. David G. Hanson. adv.

333.33   US
BLACK'S GUIDE TO THE OFFICE SPACE MARKET: NORTHERN NEW JERSEY. 1976. s-a. $69.95. Black's Guide, Inc., 1355 Piccard Dr., Ste. 450, Rockville, MD 20850. TEL 301-948-0995. FAX 301-258-9237. Ed. David G. Hanson. adv.

333.33   US
BLACK'S GUIDE TO THE OFFICE SPACE MARKET: PHILADELPHIA - SOUTH NEW JERSEY - DELAWARE. 1981. a. $59.95. Black's Guide, Inc., 1355 Piccard Dr., Ste. 450, Rockville, MD 20850. TEL 301-948-0995. FAX 301-258-9237. Ed. David G. Hanson. adv.
Formerly: Black's Guide to the Office Space Market: Philadelphia and Suburbs.

333.33   US
BLACK'S GUIDE TO THE OFFICE SPACE MARKET: SAN FRANCISCO BAY AREA. 1984. s-a. $49.95. Black's Guide, Inc., 1355 Piccard Dr., Ste. 450, Rockville, MD 20850. TEL 301-948-0995. FAX 301-258-9237. Ed. David G. Hanson. adv.

333.33   GW
BREMISCHE HAUSBESITZERZEITUNG. m. Zentralverband der Deutschen Haus-, Wohnungs- und Grundeigentuemer, Landesverband Bremischer Haus- und Grundbesitzervereine e.V., Am Dobben 3, D-2800 Bremen, Germany. TEL 0421-328205.

333.33   FR
BRETAGNE IMMOBILIERE. 1919. m. 5 F. per no. Federation des Associations des Proprietaires Urbains et Ruraux de la Bretagne et de l'Ouest de la France, 6. R. Saint-Louis, 35000 Rennes, France. Ed. Maitre Bellenger. adv.; circ. 11,000.

BRITISH COLUMBIA POPULATION FORECAST. see *POPULATION STUDIES*

333.33 340   CN
BRITISH COLUMBIA REAL ESTATE LAW GUIDE. m. Can.$510. C C H Canadian Ltd., 6 Garamond Ct., Don Mills, Ont. M3C 1Z5, Canada. TEL 416-441-2992. FAX 416-444-9011. Ed.Bd.
Description: Covers laws governing real estate transactions in B.C.

BROKER-DEALERS AND SECURITIES MARKETS. see *LAW*

333.33   US
BRONX REALTOR NEWS.* 1927. bi-w. membership. Bronx Board of Realtors, Inc., 1126 Pelham Pkwy. S., 1 St., Bronx, NY 10461. adv.; bk.rev.; charts; illus.; stat.; circ. 1,000.
Formerly (until 1980): Bronx Real Estate and Building News (ISSN 0007-2265)

REAL ESTATE

333.33   SI
BUILDING AND ESTATE MANAGEMENT SOCIETY. PROCEEDINGS. s-a. Building and Estate Management Society, c/o Faculty of Architecture and Building, National University of Singapore, Kent Ridge, Singapore 0511. TEL 7756666.

333.33 690   CN
BUILDING OWNER AND PROPERTY MANAGER; for the Design, Construction, Facilities & Building Management Industry. 1986. 6/yr. Can.$18. (Resident Managers Training Institute) Southam Business Communications Inc. (Subsidiary of: Southam Inc.), 1450 Don Mills Rd., Don Mills, Ont. M3B 2X7, Canada. TEL 416-442-2055. FAX 416-442-2229. Ed. Cindy Woods. circ. 30,000. (back issues avail.)
Description: News for building owners-developers, property managers and real estate developers.

333.3 332   UK   ISSN 0261-6416
BUILDING SOCIETIES ASSOCIATION. MONTHLY FIGURES PRESS RELEASE. 1978. m. £24. Building Societies Association, 3 Savile Row, London W1X 1AF, England. TEL 01-437-0655.

333.33   SZ   ISSN 0007-4675
BULLETIN IMMOBILIER. 1925. 20/yr. 38 Fr. (Federation Romande Immobiliere) I R L Lausanne SA, Case postale 2560, CH-1002 Lausanne, Switzerland. TEL 021-220041. stat.; mkt.

333.33   US   ISSN 0746-0023
HC101
BUSINESS FACILITIES. 1968. m. $30. BusFac Publishing Co., Inc., 121 Monmouth St., Box 2060, Red Bank, NJ 07701. TEL 201-842-7433. FAX 201-758-6634. Ed. Eric Peterson. adv.; charts; illus.; stat.; tr.lit.; circ. 35,000. (back issues avail.)
Formerly: A I P R (American Industrial Properties Report) (ISSN 0193-7308)

BUSINESS FIRST MAGAZINE. see *BUSINESS AND ECONOMICS — Economic Situation And Conditions*

BUSINESS OPPORTUNITIES JOURNAL. see *BUSINESS AND ECONOMICS — Investments*

333.3   US
BUSINESS PROPERTIES. q. Southeast Publishing Ventures, 528 E. Blvd., Charlotte, NC 28203-5110. TEL 704-373-0051. Ed. Tobin Roberts. circ. 15,000.

BUSINESS VENTURES. see *BUSINESS AND ECONOMICS — Investments*

BUTTERWORTHS PROPERTY LAW HANDBOOK. see *LAW*

332.1   US   ISSN 8755-3732
C A A S NEWS; newsletter on computer-assisted appraisal. 1984. 4/yr. membership. International Association of Assessing Officers, Computer-Assisted Appraisal Section, 1313 E. 60th St., Chicago, IL 60637-9990. TEL 312-947-2060. FAX 312-363-2246. Ed. Roberta Hilleman. circ. 800.
Supersedes (1981-1982): E D P.

333.33 690   UK
C A L U S RESEARCH REPORTS. (Centre for Advanced Land Use Studies) 1975. irreg., no.15, 1985. price varies. College of Estate Management, Whiteknights, Reading RG6 2AW, England.

333.3   US
C E A NEWS. m. California Escrow Association, 1717 N. Highland Ave., Ste. 604, Los Angeles, CA 90028-4485. TEL 213-461-7383. Ed. Geraldine Cassidy. adv.; circ. 4,500.

720   US   ISSN 0734-5453
CALIFORNIA HOMES AND LIFESTYLES; the magazine of architecture, the arts, and distinctive design. 1982. m. $27. Mark Marth, Ed. & Pub., 17252 Armstrong, Ste. A, Irvine, CA 92714. TEL 714-261-2680. adv.; illus.; circ. 52,000. (back issues avail.)
Formerly: California Homes; Incorporates: Southern California Home and Garden.

CALIFORNIA PLANNING AND DEVELOPMENT REPORT. see *PUBLIC ADMINISTRATION*

333.33   US
CALIFORNIA REAL ESTATE JOURNAL. bi-m. Daily Journal Corporation, 915 E. First St., Los Angeles, CA 90012-4092. TEL 213-625-2141. FAX 213-680-3682. Ed. Roger Vincent. adv.; circ. 25,000.

333.33   US   ISSN 0008-1450
CALIFORNIA REAL ESTATE MAGAZINE. 1920. m. $12. California Association of Realtors, 525 S. Virgil Ave., Los Angeles, CA 90020. TEL 213-739-8320. Ed. Patricia McLean. adv.; bk.rev.; bibl.; charts; illus.; mkt.; stat.; index; circ. 100,000. **Indexed:** Cal.Per.Ind. (1985-).

333.33 330   US
CALIFORNIA REAL ESTATE REPORTER. 1986. m. $215. Matthew Bender & Co., Inc., 11 Penn Plaza, New York, NY 10001. TEL 212-967-7707. Ed. David W. Walters.

333.33   SP
CAMARA OFICIAL DE LA PROPIEDAD URBANA DE LA PROVINCIA DE MALAGA. HOJA INFORMATIVA. 1970. m. Camara Oficial de la Propiedad Urbana de la Provincia, Carreteria, 7, Malaga, Spain.

333.33   CN   ISSN 0383-6649
CANADIAN APPRAISER/EVALUATEUR CANADIEN. 1943; N.S. 1956. q. Can.$20. Appraisal Institute of Canada, 101-93 Lombard Ave., Winnipeg, Man. R3B 3B1, Canada. TEL 204-942-0751. Ed. Erin Foulkes. adv.; bk.rev.; circ. 6,000. **Indexed:** ABI Inform, Can.B.P.I., RICS.
Formerly: A I M.

333.3   CN
CANADIAN FACILITY MANAGEMENT. 6/yr. C F M Communications, 62 Olsen Dr., Don Mills, Ont. M3A 3J3, Canada. TEL 416-447-3417. FAX 416-447-3410. Ed. Victor Clark. circ. 14,500.

333.33   CN
CANADIAN REAL ESTATE; official organ of organized real estate in Canada. (Text in English and French) 1955. m. Can.$40. Canadian Real Estate Association, Place de Ville, Tower A, 320 Queen St., 21st Fl., Ottawa, Ont. K1R 5A3, Canada. TEL 613-234-3372. FAX 613-234-2567. Ed. Debbie Lawes. adv.; bk.rev.; charts; illus.; stat.; index; circ. 89,000 (controlled). (also avail. in microfilm from UMI; reprint service avail. from UMI) **Indexed:** Can.B.P.I., RICS.
Supersedes: C R E A Reporter (ISSN 0315-3843); Canadian Realtor (ISSN 0008-4905)

333.33   CN
▼**CANADIAN REAL ESTATE ADVISER.** French edition: Conseiller Immobilier. 1992. 7/yr. Sodevco Inc., 116 Promenade du Portage, Hull, Que. J8X 2K1, Canada. TEL 819-771-5381. FAX 819-776-9973. Ed. Laurier Trahan. adv.; circ. 48,000 (21,000 Eng. ed., 27,000 Fr. ed.).

CANADIAN REAL ESTATE INCOME TAX GUIDE. see *BUSINESS AND ECONOMICS — Public Finance, Taxation*

CARLSONREPORT FOR SHOPPING CENTER MANAGEMENT. see *BUSINESS AND ECONOMICS — Management*

333.33   US
CAROLINA REAL ESTATE JOURNAL. 1981. 4/yr. $55. Shaw Publishing Inc., 128 S. Tryon St., Ste. 2200, Charlotte, NC 28202. TEL 704-375-7404. Ed. Don Sider.

333.33   US
CENTERS; upscale specialty, urban mixed-use & festival. 1989. a. $195. Jomurpa Publishing Inc., Box 1708, 7 S. Myrtle Ave., Spring Valley, NY 10977. TEL 914-426-0040. FAX 914-426-0802. (Also: 430 Mallard Dr., Santa Rosa, CA 95401) Ed. Murray Shor. adv.
Description: Information on existing and planned upscale specialty and urban mixed-use centers and festival marketplaces in the US and Canada, including portfolios of owner-developers, with names, addresses, telephone numbers. Mailing labels and custom report services also available.

333.33   US
CENTURY 21. 1976. bi-m. Home & Land, 9848-D Business Park Dr., Sacramento, CA 95827. TEL 916-366-0444. bk.rev.; circ. 500,000.

333.33   US   ISSN 1047-1413
CHARLOTTE COUNTY FLORIDA LAND OWNER.* 1989. m. $24. C.F. Cline, Ed. & Pub., Box 512241, Punta Gorda, FL 33951-2241. adv.; circ. 5,000.
Description: Records deeds from the previous month - who bought what, who sold what, and for how much. Includes information on county functions and profiles of county business people.

333.33   UK
CHARTERED SURVEYOR WEEKLY. 1868. w. £75. Builder Group plc, 1 Millharbour, London E14 9RA, England. Ed. Clive Branson. adv.; bk.rev.; charts; illus.; index; circ. 49,971. (also avail. in microfilm from UMI; reprint service avail. from UMI) **Indexed:** Bibl.Cart., Br.Tech.Ind., Build.Manage.Abstr., Eng.Ind., Forest.Abstr., Forest Prod.Abstr., Geo.Abstr., Intl.Civil Eng.Abstr., RICS, Soft.Abstr.Eng., World Agri.Econ.& Rural Sociol.Abstr.
Formerly: Chartered Surveyor (ISSN 0009-1936)

CHARTING HOUSING TRENDS. see *BUSINESS AND ECONOMICS — Banking And Finance*

CHENGXIANG JIANSHE/URBAN AND RURAL CONSTRUCTION. see *HOUSING AND URBAN PLANNING*

333.33   IT
CITTA (MILAN). m. L.18000. Altra Casa S.r.l., Via Cornelio Tacito 6, 20137 Milan, Italy. TEL 02-551871. Ed. Ivan Rizzi.

THE CLAYTON-FILLMORE REPORT; perspectives on economics and real estate. see *BUSINESS AND ECONOMICS — Economic Situation And Conditions*

CLOSING OFFICER'S GUIDE. see *LAW*

COLLIER REAL ESTATE TRANSACTIONS AND THE BANKRUPTCY CODE. see *BUSINESS AND ECONOMICS — Banking And Finance*

333.33   US   ISSN 1061-138X
COMMERCIAL INC.; the magazine for commercial real estate: East Michigan. 1987. m. $9. Commercial Inc., 138 N. Saginaw, Pontiac, MI 48342-2112. TEL 313-332-9770. FAX 313-332-3003. Ed. Bonnie M. Taube. circ. 45,000. (back issues avail.)
Description: Commercial properties for sale, lease or exchange throughout Michigan.

333.33 332.6   US   ISSN 0887-4778
HD1361
COMMERCIAL INVESTMENT REAL ESTATE JOURNAL. 1982. q. $32. Commercial Investment Real Estate Institute, 430 N. Michigan Ave., Chicago, IL 60611-4092. TEL 312-321-4460. FAX 312-329-8882. Ed. Lorene Norton Palm. adv.; index; circ. 11,000. (back issues avail.) **Indexed:** ABI Inform.
—BLDSC shelfmark: 3336.963650.
Description: Practical information for professionals on all aspects of commercial real estate.

333.33 340   US   ISSN 0736-0517
KF593.C6
COMMERCIAL LEASE LAW INSIDER; the practical, plain-English, monthly newsletter for owners, managers, attorneys and other real estate professionals. 1982. m. $206. Brownstone Publishers, Inc., 304 Park Ave. S., New York, NY 10010. TEL 212-473-8200. Ed. Seth H. Ross. index. (back issues avail.)
Description: Nationwide review of new legal developments and leasing techniques for major owners and tenants.

333.3   US
COMMERCIAL LEASING LAW AND STRATEGY. m. $155. New York Law Publishing Co., Marketing Department, 111 Eighth Ave., New York, NY 10011. TEL 212-741-8300.
Description: Provides latest developments, strategies and techniques on the business and legal aspects of commercial leasing.

333.33   US
▼**COMMERCIAL PROFILE.** 1991. q. $2.50 per no. Builder Profile Inc., 229 W. Grand Ave., Ste. 25, Bensenville, IL 60106. TEL 708-595-9142. FAX 708-595-8976. Ed. Arley Harriman. adv.; circ. 60,000.
Description: For top and middle management in Chicagoland's real estate business.

333.33 US
COMMERCIAL PROPERTY NEWS; the national newspaper for commercial property professionals. 1987. s-m. $70. Miller Freeman Inc. (New York) (Subsidiary of: United Newspapers Group), 1515 Broadway, New York, NY 10036. TEL 212-869-1300. FAX 212-302-6273. Ed. Mark Klionsky. adv.; circ. 33,740.
 Formerly: Real Estate Times.

333.33 US ISSN 0885-6133
COMMON GROUND (ALEXANDRIA). 1984. bi-m. $59 to non-members; members $39. Community Associations Institute, 1630 Duke St., Alexandria, VA 22314. TEL 703-548-8600. FAX 703-684-1581. adv.; circ. 19,099.
 Description: For volunteer board members, professional managers, accountants and attorneys who work with condominiums, townhouses and other forms of common interest ownership property.

333.33 332.6 330.9 US ISSN 0893-9136
COMMONWEALTH LETTERS; for investors in single family homes. 1978. m. $70 (foreign $82). (National Capital Corporation) CommonWealth Press, Inc., Box 21172, Tampa, FL 33622. TEL 813-287-1075. Ed. D.D. Miller. circ. 2,000. (looseleaf format; back issues avail.)
 Formerly: Jack Miller's CommonWealth Letters.
 Description: A practical guide for small investors in income-producing houses with appropriate background data in tax-economics.

333.33 US ISSN 0199-9028
COMMUNIQUE (CHICAGO). 1955. 10/yr. $25 to non-members. Women's Council of Realtors, 430 N. Michigan Ave., Chicago, IL 60611. TEL 312-329-8483. FAX 312-329-3290. Ed. Elizabeth Martinet. tr.lit.; index; circ. 18,000. (tabloid format)
 Description: Covers real estate sales techniques and management, finance and personal development. Articles are written by members and expert guest columnists.

333.33 AT ISSN 0157-5783
COMMUNITY AND REAL ESTATE NEWS.* 1978. w. Aus.$22.50. R.E.N. Nominees Pty. Ltd., P.O. Box 182, Moonee Ponds, Vic. 3039, Australia. Ed. John Dixon. adv.; circ. 82,073. (back issues avail.)

COMMUNITY ENTERPRISE. see BUSINESS AND ECONOMICS — Banking And Finance

333.33 US
HD1393.5
COMPARATIVE STATISTICS OF INDUSTRIAL OFFICE REAL ESTATE MARKETS. 1980. a. $50. Society of Industrial and Office Realtors, 777 14th St., N.W., Ste. 400, Washington, DC 20005-3271. TEL 202-737-1150. Ed. Linda Nasvaderani. circ. 7,000. (also avail. in microfiche) **Indexed**: SRI.
 Former titles: Guide to Industrial and Office Real Estate Markets & Industrial Real Estate Market Survey (ISSN 0730-0131)

COMPILATION OF NATIONALLY AVERAGED RENTAL RATES. see HOUSING AND URBAN PLANNING

333.33 US
CONDO SALES REPORT. 1982. m. $395. Yale Robbins, Inc., 31 E. 28th St., New York, NY 10016. TEL 212-683-5700. Ed. Yale Robbins. (looseleaf format; back issues avail.)
 Description: Reviews condo sales transactions with analysis of each sale.

333.33 IT
CONDOMINIO E INQUILINATO. 1973. m. L.3000 to individuals; institutions L.5000. Giuseppe Langone, Via Diaz 28, Salerno, Italy. adv.; circ. 25,300.

333.33 US
CONNECTICUT REAL ESTATE JOURNAL. 1972. m. free to qualified personnel. Brian P. Heneghan, 57 Washington St., Norwell, MA 02061. TEL 800-654-4993. FAX 617-871-1853. adv.; circ. controlled. (tabloid format; back issues avail.)
 Description: Covers commercial, industrial, and investment real estate.

333.33 340 US
CONNECTICUT REAL ESTATE LAW JOURNAL. 6/yr. $55. Butterworth Legal Publishers (Salem) (Subsidiary of: Reed International PLC), 90 Stiles Rd., Salem, NH 03079. TEL 800-548-4001. FAX 603-898-9858. cum.index. (looseleaf format; back issues avail.)
 Description: Includes case comments and Connecticut Superior Court decisions.

CONNECTICUT REAL PROPERTY STATUTES. see LAW

333.33 US
CONNECTICUT REALTOR. 1977. m. free to members. Connecticut Association of Realtors, 316 Farmington Ave., Hartford, CT 06105. TEL 203-522-7255. FAX 203-549-5934. Ed. Brad R. Durrell. adv.; circ. 14,000. (tabloid format)
 Description: Covers legislative issues affecting industry, primarily association related materials, including general issues relating to real estate.

333.33 IT ISSN 0010-7050
CONSULENTE IMMOBILIARE. 1957. s-m. L.160000($150) Pirola Editore S.p.A., Via Comelico 24, Casella Postale 10444, 20110 Milan, Italy. bk.rev.; stat.; index. cum.index; circ. 12,000.

333.33 CN
▼**CONSUMERS GUIDE.*** 1990. 6/yr. Thompson Newspapers Co. Ltd., 44 Pitt. St., Cornwall, Ont. K6J 3P3, Canada. TEL 416-286-3113. FAX 416-286-4071. adv.; circ. 727,964.

333.33 CN ISSN 0838-018X
CONTACT (MONTREAL). 1982. 4/yr. Can.$19 (effective Jan. 1990). Quebec Real Estate Association, 550 Sherbrooke W., Ste. 700, Montreal, Que. H3A 1B9, Canada. TEL 514-842-0783. FAX 514-842-1346. adv.; circ. 12,000.

340 UK ISSN 0010-8200
CONVEYANCER AND PROPERTY LAWYER. 1936. bi-m. £68. Sweet & Maxwell, South Quay Plaza, 8th Floor, 183 Marsh Wall, London E14 9FT, England. TEL 071-538-8686. FAX 071-538-9508. (Dist. in U.S. & Canada by: Carswell Co. Ltd., 233 Midland Ave., Agincourt, Ont., Canada) Ed.Bd. adv.; bk.rev.; index; circ. 2,500. (reprint service avail. from RRI) **Indexed**: C.L.I., L.R.I., Leg.Cont., Leg.Per.

333.33 US ISSN 1042-9115
CORPORATE REAL ESTATE EXECUTIVE. 1986. 9/yr. $65 (foreign $95). International Association of Corporate Real Estate Executives, 440 Columbia Dr., W. Palm Beach, FL 33409-6685. TEL 407-683-8111. FAX 407-697-4853. Ed. Kathleen B. Dempsey. adv.; bk.rev.; tr.lit.; index; circ. 3,468. (back issues avail.)
 Formerly: Corporate Real Estate Journal.
 Description: Educational and informative articles on topics of interest to heads of real estate departments in large corporations.

333.33 US ISSN 1048-7948
CORRIDOR REAL ESTATE JOURNAL. 1989. w. $84. Journal Two Publishing, Inc., 1020 N. Fairfax St., Ste. 400, Alexandria, VA 22314. TEL 703-548-0850. FAX 703-683-3687. (Affiliate: Lionmark Publications, Inc.) Ed. Robert Hickey. adv.; circ. 6,200.

333.33 UK ISSN 0011-0159
COUNTRY LANDOWNER. 1907. m. £12. Country Landowners Association, 16 Belgrave Sq., London SW1X 8PQ, England. TEL 071-824-8681. FAX 071-730-1390. Ed. John Kendall. adv.; bk.rev.; index; circ. 49,272. (tabloid format) **Indexed**: Forest.Abstr., Forest Prod.Abstr., Geo.Abstr., RICS, World Agri.Econ.& Rural Sociol.Abstr.
 —BLDSC shelfmark: 3481.880000.

333.33 BE
CRI. 10/yr. 1000 Fr. Syndicat National des Proprietaires, Rue du Lombard 76, B-1000 Brussels, Belgium. TEL 02-512-62-87.

333.33 US
CRITTENDEN REPORT. w. $387. Crittenden Research, Inc., Box 1150, Novato, CA 94948. TEL 415-382-2400.
 Description: Provides real estate developers with information on lending sources for real estate projects throughout the country.

REAL ESTATE 4147

333.33 340 US ISSN 0738-6931
D.C. REAL ESTATE REPORTER. 1979. m. $225. Land Development Institute, Ltd., 1300 N St., N.W., Washington, DC 20005. TEL 202-545-2144. FAX 202-347-4409. Ed.Bd. index; circ. 250. (back issues avail.)
 Description: Covers legislative and judicial decisions affecting land use-zoning, home ownership and rental housing in D.C.

333.33 US ISSN 0279-4195
DAILY COMMERCE. 1917. d. $143. Daily Journal Corporation (Los Angeles), 915 E. First St., Los Angeles, CA 90012. TEL 213-229-5300. FAX 213-680-3682. Ed. Nell Fields. adv.; bk.rev.; circ. 6,000. (newspaper; also avail. in microfilm)
 Former titles: Journal of Commerce Review; Journal of Commerce and Independent Review (ISSN 0021-9835)

333.33 US
DAILY TRANSCRIPT. 5/w. $75. Pioneer Printing and Publishing, 22 N. Sierra Madre, Colorado Springs, CO 80903. TEL 719-634-1593. FAX 719-632-0762.

333.33 352.7 US
DALLAS - FORT WORTH HOME BUYER'S GUIDE. 1972. bi-m. free. Home Buyer's Guide (Dallas), 5501 LBJ Frwy., Ste. 300, Dallas, TX 75240-6202. TEL 214-239-2399. Ed. Julia Jernigan. adv.; bk.rev.; charts; illus.; circ. 75,000 (controlled).
 Former titles: Living (Dallas - Fort Worth Edition) (ISSN 0741-5494) & Dallas - Fort Worth Living (ISSN 0192-8546)
 Description: New-home housing map-guide for the Dallas-Fort Worth Metroplex.

333.33 UK ISSN 0011-5894
DALTONS WEEKLY; houses, shops & businesses for sale; hotel guest house & self-catering holiday accommodation advertiser. 1870. w. £4. Daltons Weekly plc, C.I. Tower, St. George's Sq., New Malden, Surrey KT3 4JA, England. TEL 081-949-6199. FAX 081-949-2718. adv.; illus.; index; circ. 40,115.

DAYTON BUSINESS REPORTER. see BUSINESS AND ECONOMICS

333.33 US
THE DEAL MAKERS. 1979. w. $197. T D K Real Estate Advisory Group, P.O. Box 1164, Belle Mead, NJ 08502. TEL 908-281-0067. FAX 908-281-0277. adv.; bk.rev.; circ. 6,000.
 Formerly (until 1991): Retail Leasing Reporter.
 Description: For retail real estate executives. Covers retailers expansion plans, developments planned and underway, current construction and rehabilitation of existing centers.

659.1 720 FR ISSN 0291-1191
DEMEURES ET CHATEAUX. (Text and descriptions in English, French) 1978. 8/yr. 510 F. (Europe 680 F.; elswhere 900 F.). Edinot, 21, rue Cassette, 75006 Paris, France. TEL 1-42-22-03-76. FAX 55-98-55-22. (Subscr. to: B.P. 17, 19230 Pompadour, France. TEL 55-73-32-37) Ed. J.M. Reillier. adv.; bk.rev.; illus.; tr.lit.; circ. 20,000.
 Formerly: Demeures et Chateaux en France (ISSN 0180-3905)
 Description: Presents illustrated advertisements for castles, country seats and manors.

333.33 352.7 US
DENVER HOUSING GUIDE. 1974. bi-m. $12. Baker Publications, 2323 S. Troy, Ste. 103, Aurora, CO 80014. TEL 303-695-8440. FAX 303-695-8449. Ed. Patt Dodd. adv.; bk.rev.; circ. 70,000 (controlled). (back issues avail.)
 Former titles: Living - The Denver Housing Guide & Living (Denver Edition) (ISSN 0741-5508) & Denver Living (ISSN 0192-9100)

333.33 GW ISSN 0012-0995
DEUTSCHE WOHNUNGSWIRTSCHAFT. 1949. m. DM.24. (Zentralverband der Deutschen Haus, Wohnungs und Grundeigentuemer e.V.) Verlag Deutsche Wohnungswirtschaft GmbH, Cecilienallee 45, 4000 Duesseldorf 30, Germany. adv.; charts; illus.; index; circ. 7,600.

REAL ESTATE

333.33   GW   ISSN 0012-1371
DEUTSCHES VOLKSHEIMSTAETTENWERK. INFORMATIONSDIENST. 1946. s-m. DM.102. Deutsches Volksheimstaettenwerk e.V., Neefestr. 2a, 5300 Bonn, Germany. bk.rev.; stat.; index; circ. 4,800.
Incorporates: So Planen und Bauen.

333.33   AT   ISSN 0012-1525
DEVELOPER.* vol. 8, 1970. q. membership (non-members Aus.$8.40). Institute of Real Estate Development, 74 Pitt, Sidney N.S.W., Australia. Ed. E.J. Burger. adv.; stat.

DEVELOPMENT (ARLINGTON). see *BUILDING AND CONSTRUCTION*

DEVELOPMENTS; news magazine for the resort-recreational real estate and community development industries. see *HOUSING AND URBAN PLANNING*

DICTIONNAIRE PERMANENT GESTION IMMOBILIERE. see *BUSINESS AND ECONOMICS — Management*

333.33   US
▼**DIRECT SOURCE.** 1992. s-a. Metro America Office Guides, 921 S.W. Morrison St., No. 407, Portland, OR 97205. TEL 503-223-0304. FAX 503-221-6544. adv.; circ. 9,000.
Description: Contains listings of office buildings and parks in the Detroit, Michigan area. Covers real estate trends and features people, products and services.

DIRECTORY OF INTELLECTUAL PROPERTY ATTORNEYS. see *LAW*

333 658.7   US   ISSN 0732-5983
HF5430.3
DIRECTORY OF MAJOR MALLS. 1977. a. $349 (foreign $365). Jomurpa Publishing Inc., Box 1708, 7 S. Myrtle Ave., Spring Valley, NY 10977. TEL 914-426-0040. FAX 914-426-0802. (Also: 430 Mallard Dr., Santa Rosa, CA 95401; TEL 707-528-3631) Ed. Murray Shor. adv.; maps.
Description: Lists existing and planned shopping centers in the United States and Canada, over 250,000 sq.ft. of gross leasable area; includes portfolios of 48 leading owner-developers and over 250 top retailers seeking mall space. Computerized version, mailing labels, custom report services also available.

DIRECTORY OF PROPERTY INVESTORS AND DEVELOPERS. see *BUSINESS AND ECONOMICS — Investments*

333.33   US   ISSN 1048-2938
DISTRESSED PROPERTY INVESTOR'S MONTHLY. 1988. m. $70. Real Estate Publications, Inc. (Tampa), Box 20027, Tampa, FL 33622-0027. TEL 800-356-2317. Ed. Thomas J. Lucier. bk.rev.; index; circ. 1,500. (looseleaf format; back issues avail.)
Formerly: Diamonds in the Rough (ISSN 0896-0542)
Description: Provides news of investment opportunities: foreclosures, probate sales, IRS tax-seized sales, and other types of distressed property.

DISTRESSED REAL ESTATE LAW ALERT. see *LAW*

333.33   US   ISSN 0070-704X
HF5430.3
DOLLARS AND CENTS OF SHOPPING CENTERS. (Supplemental special report avail.) 1961. triennial. $225 to non-members; members $180. Urban Land Institute, 625 Indiana Ave., N.W., Ste. 400, Washington, DC 20004-2930. TEL 202-624-7000. Ed. Michael Beyard. (reprint service avail. from UMI)
—BLDSC shelfmark: 3616.580000.

DOMUS MAGAZIN. see *BUSINESS AND ECONOMICS — Investments*

333.33   US
DOUGLAS PROPERTIES INTERNATIONAL. 1989. 3/yr. $50. Jon Douglas Company, 11900 Olympic Blvd., Los Angeles, CA 90064. TEL 310-442-8002. FAX 310-271-1530. Ed. Judy Kleinberg. circ. 20,000 (controlled).
Description: Targets homeowners in the affluent areas of Santa Barbara, Ventura, Los Angeles Westside and the San Fernando Valley. Showcases the company's homes.

333.33   US   ISSN 0160-9629
HD255
E-R-C DIRECTORY. 1964. a. $35. Employee Relocation Council, 1720 N St., N.W., Washington, DC 20036. TEL 202-857-0857. Ed. Tina Lung. circ. 16,000.
Formerly: E R E A C Directory (ISSN 0071-0113)
Description: Lists real estate brokers, appraisers and relocation service companies.

333.33   NO
EIENDOMSMEGLEREN. m. Norges Eiendomsmeglerforbund, Prinsensgt. 21, 0258 Oslo 2, Norway. TEL 02-447953.

333.33   DK   ISSN 0013-2896
EJENDOMSMAEGLEREN. 1934. m. DKK 396.50. Dansk Ejendomsmaeglerforening, Stormgade 16, 1470 Copenhagen K, Denmark. Ed. Knud Pedersen. adv.; bk.rev.; abstr.; illus.; stat.; circ. 7,000. (tabloid format)

333.33   US
EMPIRE STATE REALTOR. 10/yr. New York State Association of Realtors, 130 Washington Ave., Albany, NY 12110-2298. TEL 518-463-0300. FAX 518-462-5474. Ed. Christine L. Rittner. circ. 40,000.

EQUITABLE DISTRIBUTION OF PROPERTY. see *LAW*

333.33   UK
ESTATE AGENCY NEWS. 1986. m. £12.50. Estates Press Ltd., Keenans Mill, Lords St., St. Annes on Sea, Lancs. FY8 2DF, England. TEL 0253-722142. FAX 0253-714020. Ed. David F. Perkins. adv.; bk.rev.; charts; illus.; circ. 16,000. (tabloid format; back issues avail.)

333.33   UK   ISSN 0260-1001
ESTATE AGENT; voice of the practical estate agent. 1980. 8/yr. £24. National Association of Estate Agents, 21 Jury St., Warwick CV34 4EH, England. FAX 0926-400953. Ed. Peter Cliff. adv.; bk.rev.; circ. 11,000. Indexed: Ind.S.A.Per.
Description: For realtors in the UK: dealing with residential practice and procedures.

333.33 690   IE
ESTATE & PROPERTY NEWS. 1976. m. £25. Keltic Enterprises Ltd., 45 Lower Baggot St., Dublin 2, Ireland. Ed. Leo T. Mooney. charts; illus.; stat. (back issues avail.)

333.33   UK   ISSN 0014-1240
ESTATES GAZETTE; devoted to land, commercial, industrial, residential and agricultural properties. 1858. w. £77.50. Estates Gazette Ltd., 151 Wardour St., London W1V 4BN, England. Ed. John Clayton. adv.; bk.rev.; mkt.; index; circ. 34,000. Indexed: Geo.Abstr., RICS, World Agri.Econ. & Rural Sociol.Abstr.
●Also available online. Vendor(s): Mead Data Central.
—BLDSC shelfmark: 3812.538000.
Incorporates: Property Market Review; Estates Journal; Auctioneer.

333.33   UK   ISSN 0014-1259
ESTATES TIMES. 1968. w. £35($80) Morgan-Grampian (Construction Press) Ltd., Morgan-Grampian House, 30 Calderwood St., Woolwich, London SE18 6QH, England. TEL 01-855-7777. FAX 01-854-7476. Ed. Erik Brown. adv.; circ. 29,465. (tabloid format; also avail. in microform from UMI; reprint service avail. from UMI) Indexed: RICS.
—BLDSC shelfmark: 3812.548000.
Incorporates: Commercial Property Advertiser.

333.33   UK
ESTATES TIMES DEALS DIGEST. q. Morgan-Grampian (Construction Press) Ltd., 30 Calderwood St., Woolwich, London SE18 6QH, England. TEL 01-855-7777. FAX 01-854-7476. Ed. Erik Brown. (reprint service avail.)

333.33   US
EXECUTIVE GUIDE TO SPECIALISTS IN INDUSTRIAL AND OFFICE REAL ESTATE. a. $50. Society of Industrial and Office Realtors, 777 14th St., N.W., Ste. 400, Washington, DC 20005-3271. TEL 202-737-1150. circ. 8,000.
Description: For industrial and office real estate brokers worldwide.

EXPANSION MANAGEMENT; for business-mobility decision makers. see *BUSINESS AND ECONOMICS — Economic Situation And Conditions*

333   US   ISSN 0191-2208
HD7287.67.U5
EXPENSE ANALYSIS: CONDOMINIUMS, COOPERATIVES AND PLANNED UNIT DEVELOPMENTS. a. $110. Institute of Real Estate Management, Box 109025, Chicago, IL 60610-9025. TEL 312-661-1953. Ed. Kay McGuire. Indexed: SRI.
Supersedes in part: Income-Expense Analysis. Apartments, Condominiums and Cooperatives (ISSN 0161-5262)
Description: Reports median costs for condominiums throughout the U.S.

333.33   US   ISSN 0738-2170
EXPERIENCE EXCHANGE REPORT. 1920. a. $250 to non-members; members free. Building Owners and Managers Association International, Research Department, 1201 New York Ave., N.W., Ste. 300, Washington, DC 20005. TEL 202-408-2662. FAX 202-371-0181. Ed.Bd. circ. 3,000.
Formerly (until vol.2, 1988): Trends (Washington, 1987).

333.33   US
EXTRA EQUITY FOR HOMEBUYERS.* 1984. 3/yr. Consumer Couponing Corporation, 1720 Post Rd. E., Ste. 7, Westport, CT 06880-5643. TEL 203-225-0855. circ. 250,000.
Description: Features promotional offers from national advertisers for people buying a single family home.

333.33   FR
F I A B C I PRESS. (Editions in English, French, German, Spanish) 1985. 6/yr. free. International Real Estate Federation (FIABCI), 23 ave. Bosquet, 75007 Paris, France. TEL 45-50-45-49. FAX 45-50-42-00. TELEX 201-339 F. Ed. Andrew Irvine. adv.; bk.rev.; circ. 7,500.
Description: Provides news of the Federation.

333.33   US   ISSN 0274-9882
F M O NEWS. 1964. 8/yr. $10. Federation of Mobile Home Owners of Florida, 4020 Portsmouth Rd., Largo, FL 34641. TEL 813-595-0227. FAX 813-535-9427. Ed. Charity Cicardo. adv.; circ. 126,000.
Description: Reports on the federation's lobbying and legal efforts. Contains lifestyle-oriented information.

FACILITIES PLANNING NEWS. see *ARCHITECTURE*

333.33   SW   ISSN 0348-5552
FASTIGHETSTIDNINGEN. (Text in Swedish) 1909. 20/yr. SEK 480. (Sveriges Fastighetsaegare) Fastighedstidningen, P.O. Box 1707, Regeringsgatan 67, 8 tr., S-111 87 Stockholm, Sweden. TEL 08-613-57 40. FAX 08-10-09-60. Ed. Olle Vaevare. illus.; index; circ. 23,045. (back issues avail.)

333.33 336   US
FEDERAL ESTATE AND GIFT TAX REPORTS. 1913. w. $400. Commerce Clearing House, Inc., 4025 W. Peterson Ave., Chicago, IL 60646. TEL 312-583-8500. Ed. D. Newquist.

FEDERAL HOME LOAN BANK OF ATLANTA. ANNUAL REPORT. see *BUSINESS AND ECONOMICS — Banking And Finance*

FEDERAL HOME LOAN BANK OF ATLANTA. REVIEW. see *BUSINESS AND ECONOMICS — Banking And Finance*

REAL ESTATE

333.33 US
FEDERAL INCOME TAXATION OF REAL ESTATE. supplements issued 3/yr. to update base volume. $105 for base volume and current supplement. Warren, Gorham and Lamont, One Penn Plaza, New York, NY 10119. TEL 800-950-1205. FAX 212-971-5240. (looseleaf format)
  Formerly: Robinson Federal Income Taxation of Real Estate.

333.33 340 FR
FEDERATION NATIONALE DE L'IMMOBILIERS. INFORMATIONS F N A I M: JURIDIQUES ET TECHNIQUES. m. Federation Nationale de l'Immobiliers, 129 Rue du Faubourg Saint-Honore, 75008 Paris, France. TEL 44207700.
  Formerly: Federation Nationale des Agents Immobiliers, Mandataires en Vente de Fonds de Commerce, Administrateurs de Bien, Syndics de Copropriete et Experts. Informations Juridiques.

333.33 UK
FEDERATION OF PRIVATE RESIDENTS ASSOCIATIONS. NEWSLETTER. q. Federation of Private Residents Associations, 11 Dartmouth St., London SW1, England. TEL 01-2220037.

FINANCIAL FREEDOM REPORT; the magazine for high profit investors. see *BUSINESS AND ECONOMICS — Banking And Finance*

333.3 US
FIRST TUESDAY. m. Realty Publications, Inc., 5750 Division St., Ste. 106, Riverside, CA 92506-3201. TEL 714-781-7300. Ed. Fred Crane. circ. 5,000.

333.33 US ISSN 0899-9147
HG2040.5.U5
FLEET'S GUIDE: COMMERCIAL REAL ESTATE FINANCING SOURCEBOOK. 1988. s-a (Jan., Jul.; plus s-a update newsletters Apr., Oct.). $285. Fleet Press, 3343 Duke St., Alexandria, VA 22314. TEL 703-370-3246. adv.
  Description: Provides current information regarding sources of financing for income property.

FLORIDA COMMERCIAL LANDLORD - TENANT LAW. see *LAW*

FLORIDA CONDOMINIUM LAW MANUAL. see *LAW*

333.33 352.7 US
FLORIDA GULF COAST HOMEBUYER'S GUIDE. 1979. bi-m. free. Real Estate Magazines, Inc. (Tampa), 1715 N. Westshore Blvd., Ste. 244, Tampa, FL 33607-3926. TEL 813-879-1197. FAX 813-874-3077. adv.; bk.rev.; illus.; circ. 60,000 (controlled).
  Former titles: Living (Florida Gulf Coast Edition); Florida Gulf Coast Living (ISSN 0194-8857)
  Description: Guide to all new homes, condominiums, and retirement communities.

FLORIDA MORTGAGE BROKER. see *BUSINESS AND ECONOMICS — Banking And Finance*

FLORIDA PREMISES LIABILITY. see *LAW*

333.33 US
FLORIDA REAL ESTATE. 4/yr. Shaw Publishing Inc., 128 S. Tryon St., Ste. 2200, Charlotte, NC 28202. TEL 704-375-7404. Ed. Don Sider. circ. 100,000.
  Description: Targets individuals, especially in the Northeast and Midwest, who are looking to purchase a second home in Florida.

333.33 US ISSN 0887-3208
FLORIDA REAL ESTATE AND DEVELOPMENT UPDATE; news and background information about Florida real estate, construction, development and building activities. 1986. m. $100 (foreign $135). Hank Boerner, Ed. & Pub., Box 1052, Port Washington, NY 10050. TEL 516-876-6537.

FLORIDA REAL ESTATE CLOSINGS. see *LAW*

333.33 340 US
FLORIDA REAL ESTATE CONTRACTS. 1987. base vol. (plus suppl.). $80. Butterworth Legal Publishers (Salem) (Subsidiary of: Reed International PLC), 90 Stiles Rd., Salem, NH 03079. TEL 800-548-4001. FAX 603-898-9858. (looseleaf format)

333.33 340 US
FLORIDA REAL ESTATE TRANSACTIONS. 1982. 3 base vols. (plus suppl. 2-3/yr.). $195. Butterworth Legal Publishers (Salem) (Subsidiary of: Reed International PLC), 90 Stiles Rd., Salem, NH 03079. TEL 800-548-4001. FAX 603-898-9858. (looseleaf format)

333.33 US ISSN 0199-5839
FLORIDA REALTOR.* 1925. m. $15.90. Florida Association of Realtors, Box 725025, Orlando, FL 32872-5025. TEL 407-846-2800. FAX 407-648-9249. Ed. Pam Littlefield. adv.; tr.lit.; circ. 76,243.
  Description: Provides real estate professionals with a useful combination of practical information trend analysis and insights into the industry.

FLORIDA RESIDENTIAL LANDLORD - TENANT LAW MANUAL. see *LAW*

FORECAST OF HOUSING ACTIVITY. see *BUSINESS AND ECONOMICS — Economic Situation And Conditions*

333.33 GW ISSN 0016-0784
DIE FREIE WOHNUNGSWIRTSCHAFT. 1946. 6/yr. DM.82. (Bundesverband Freier Wohnungsunternehmen e.V.) Abiszet Gesellschaft fuer Werbung und Verkaufsfoerderung mbH, Neue Weyerstr. 1-3, 5000 Cologne 1, Germany. circ. 3,000.

G D W INFORMATIONEN. see *BUILDING AND CONSTRUCTION*

333.33 340 US
GEORGIA CONDOMINIUM LAW MANUAL. 1985. base vol. (plus a. suppl.). $50. Butterworth Legal Publishers (Salem) (Subsidiary of: Reed International PLC), 90 Stiles Rd., Salem, NH 03079. TEL 800-548-4001. FAX 603-898-9858. (looseleaf format)

333.33 340 US
GEORGIA LANDLORD - TENANT LAW. 1987. base vol. (plus a. suppl.). $50. Butterworth Legal Publishers (Salem) (Subsidiary of: Reed International PLC), 90 Stiles Rd., Salem, NH 03079. TEL 800-548-4001. FAX 603-898-9858. (looseleaf format)

GEORGIA REAL ESTATE LAW LETTER. see *LAW*

333.33 796.352 US
▼**GOLF PROPERTY.** 1991. bi-m. $18. Golf Living Inc., Box 809, Hendersonville, NC 28793. TEL 800-248-6994. Ed. John Woodbury. circ. 125,000.
  Description: Covers golf course communities, resorts and properties.

333.33 US
GORDON OFFICE MARKET REPORT. q. Edward S. Gordon Co., Inc., 200 Park Ave., New York, NY 10166. TEL 212-984-8000.

333.33 US
GREATER PHILADELPHIA & SOUTHERN NEW JERSEY OFFICE BUILDINGS. a. $49. Yale Robbins, Inc., 31 E. 28th St., New York, NY 10016. TEL 212-683-5700. Ed. Yale Robbins.
  Description: Annual review of Greater Philadelphia and southern New Jersey office buildings.

333.33 US ISSN 0884-4089
GREENER PASTURES GAZETTE; the newsletter dedicated to the search for countryside Edens where the good life still exists. 1985. q. $22 (foreign $32). Greener Pastures Institute, Box 1122, Sierra Madre, CA 91025. TEL 818-355-1670. FAX 818-440-9471. Ed. William L. Seavey. adv.; bk.rev.; index; circ. 2,000. (back issues avail.)
  Description: Profiles small towns, real estate listings, information resources for individuals and families considering relocating from urban centers to far west small cities and towns.

333.33 GW
GRUNDBESITZ. m. Landesverband Hamburg, Postfach 62 04 24, D-2000 Hamburg 62, Germany. TEL 040-5239193.

DAS GRUNDEIGENTUM; Zeitschrift fuer die gesamte Grundstuecks-, Haus- und Wohnungswirtschaft. see *BUILDING AND CONSTRUCTION*

333.33 US
GUARANTOR. 1956. bi-m. Chicago Title Insurance Co., 111 W. Washington, Chicago, IL 60602. TEL 312-630-2000. Ed. Stephen Flanagan. tr.lit.; index; circ. 85,000. (back issues avail.)

HABITABEC MONTREAL; pour mieux se loger - for better living. see *HOUSING AND URBAN PLANNING*

HABITABEC QUEBEC; pour mieux se loger - for better living. see *HOUSING AND URBAN PLANNING*

333.33 US
HAMPTON STYLE. bi-m. $11.90. Parents Guide Network, Corp., 2 Park Ave., Ste. 2012, New York, NY 10016. TEL 212-213-8840. Ed. Leslie Elgort.
  Description: For homeowners in the Hamptons, New York.

333.33 GW
HAUS- UND GRUNDBESITZ. 1948. m. DM.20. (Landesverband der Hessischen Haus-, Wohnungs- und Grundeigentuemer e.V.) Verlag Haus- und Grundbesitz, Niedenau 61-63, 6000 Frankfurt a.M. 1, Germany. TEL 729458. FAX 172635.

333.33 GW
DER HAUS- UND GRUNDEIGENTUEMER. m. Zentralverband der Deutschen Haus-, Wohnungs- und Grundeigentuemer, Landesverband Westfaelischer Haus-, Wohnungs- und Grundeigentuemer e.V., Dahlenkampstr. 5, D-5800 Hagen, Germany.

333.3 US
HAWAII REALTOR JOURNAL. s-m. P M P Company, Ltd., 1034 Kilani Ave., Ste. 108, Wahiawa, HI 96786-2274. TEL 808-621-8200. FAX 808-622-3025. Ed. Peggi Murchison. circ. 11,000.

333.33 340 UK
HILL & REDMAN: LANDLORD & TENANT. (In 3 vols.) irreg. (approx. 3/yr.). $735. Butterworth & Co. (Publishers) Ltd. (Subsidiary of: Reed International PLC), 88 Kingsway, London WC2B 6AB, England. TEL 71-405-6900. FAX 71-405-1332. TELEX 95678. (US addr.: Butterworth Legal Publishers, 90 Stiles Rd., Salem, NH 03079. TEL 800-548-4001) (looseleaf format)

333.33 352.7 US
HOME & CONDO. 1980. 10/yr. $15. Gulfshore Publishing Co., Inc., Box 1000, Wettown, PA 19395. TEL 813-643-3933. FAX 813-643-5017. Ed. Linda Kelley. adv.; circ. 25,000.
  Description: For incoming home buyers and local home owners.

333.33 352.7 US
HOME FINDERS GUIDEBOOK. 1974. bi-m. free. Southeast Publishing, 12015 Park 35 Circle, Ste. 207.6, Austin, TX 78753. TEL 512-339-6281. FAX 512-832-0221. Ed. Angela Jones. adv.; bk.rev.; circ. 25,000 (controlled). (back issues avail.)
  Formerly (until 1987): Austin Living (ISSN 0741-5478)

333.33 US
HOMEBUYER'S GUIDE - DALLAS - FORT WORTH. 1972. bi-m. free. Living Partners, Ltd., Regency Center II, 5501 LBJ Frwy., Ste. 300, Dallas, TX 75240. TEL 214-239-2399. FAX 214-239-7850. adv.; circ. 70,000 (controlled).
  Description: Contains information on new house subdivisions, with information on individual builders' developments, new home products and services, moving tips, financing.

333.33 US
HOMEBUYER'S GUIDE - FLORIDA GULF COAST; complete map - guide to every new home, condominium, townhome and retirement community. 1979. bi-m. free. HomeBuyer's Guide (Tampa) (Subsidiary of: Real Estate Magazines, Inc.), 1715 N. Westshore Blvd., Ste. 244, Tampa, FL 33607-3926. TEL 813-879-1177. FAX 813-874-3077. Ed. Gigi Lynch. adv.; illus.; circ. 50,000 (controlled).
  Description: Provides information on new home communities, mortgages, interior design, new home products, and newcomer services.

REAL ESTATE

333.33   US
HOMEBUYERS GUIDE MAGAZINE. 1960. m. $20. Homebuyers Guide Real Estate Inc., 17780 Fitch, Ste. 195, Irvine, CA 92714. TEL 714-476-3055. FAX 714-476-3071. circ. 150,000.
Description: Guide to new homes in Southern California.

333.33   US
HOMEFINDERS GUIDE. 1974. m. Travel Publications, Inc., Alta Loma, CA 91701. bk.rev.; circ. 35,000 (controlled).

333.33   CN
HOMEOWNERS' GUIDE.* 1978. m. Target Market Group, 65 The East Mall, Toronto, Ont., Canada. adv.

333.33 910.09   UK   ISSN 0956-3091
HOMES ABROAD. 1974. bi-m. £9. Cresta Publishing Ltd., 387 City Rd., London EC1V 1NA, England. TEL 071-837-3909. FAX 071-833-2892. Ed. Stewart Andersen. adv.; bk.rev.; circ. 13,000.
Former titles: Homes and Travel Abroad; Homes Abroad.
Description: Guide to purchasing property overseas.

333.33   US   ISSN 1052-4703
HOMES & REAL ESTATE MAGAZINE - BILLINGS, MONTANA. 1980. m. Real Estate Publications, Inc. (Billings), Box 30516, Billings, MT 59107-0516. TEL 406-259-3534. Ed. G.L. Dangerfield. adv. (back issues avail.)
Description: Lists real estate for sale in Greater Billings area.

333.33   US   ISSN 1052-4711
HOMES & REAL ESTATE MAGAZINE - GREAT FALLS, MONTANA. 1985. m. Real Estate Publications, Inc. (Billings), Box 30516, Billings, MT 59107-0516. TEL 406-259-3534. Ed. G.L. Dangerfield. adv.
Description: Lists real estate for sale in Greater Great Falls area.

333.33   CN
HOMES MAGAZINE. 1985. 8/yr. $24. Homes Publishing Group, 178 Main St., Unionville, Ont. L3R 2G9, Canada. TEL 416-479-4663. FAX 416-479-4482. Ed. Robin Robinson. adv.; circ. 100,000.
Description: Focuses on all areas of home ownership, including buying and selling, finance, design, decor, renovation and new home buyers guide.

333.33   UK   ISSN 0018-4241
HOMES OVERSEAS. 1965. m. $52. Cresta Publishing Ltd., 387 City Rd., London EC1V 1NA, England. FAX 01-833-2892. Ed. Tim Price. adv.; bk.rev.; illus.; mkt.; circ. 12,000.
Incorporates: Time-Sharing Homes & Holidays.

333.33   UK   ISSN 0018-6473
HOUSE BUYER. 1955. m. £2 per no. Brittain Publications, 137 George Lane, S. Woodford, London E18 1AJ, England. TEL 081-530-7555. FAX 081-530-7609. Ed. Con Crowley. adv.; charts; illus.; mkt.; tr.lit.
Formerly: Houses and Estates.

HOUSING CHEAP OR ON A BUDGET NEWSLETTER. see *CONSUMER EDUCATION AND PROTECTION*

HOUSING ECONOMICS. see *BUSINESS AND ECONOMICS — Economic Situation And Conditions*

333.3 332 352.7   UK   ISSN 0955-3800
HOUSING FINANCE. 1975. q. £50. Council of Mortgage Lenders, 3 Savile Row, London W1X 1AF, England. Ed. Adrian Coles. **Indexed:** World Bank.Abstr. —BLDSC shelfmark: 4335.098829.
Formerly (until 1989): B S A Bulletin (ISSN 0261-6394)
Description: Publication on latest developments in building and housing market activity including saving and lending statistics.

333.3 332   UK
HOUSING FINANCE FACT BOOK (YEAR). 1980. a. £20. Council of Mortgage Lenders, 3 Savile Row, London W1X 1AF, England.
Former titles (until 1989): Building Society Fact Book (Year); Building Societies in (Year) (ISSN 0266-4828)
Description: Includes sections on the financial and economic environment, the savings market, the housing market, building society operations and the regulation of the mortgage market.

HOUSING POLICY DEBATE. see *HOUSING AND URBAN PLANNING*

333.33 352.7   US
HOUSTON LIVING HOUSING GUIDE. 1973. bi-m. free. Lash Publications, Inc. (Bellaire), 6700 W. Loop S., 100, Bellaire, TX 77401-4107. TEL 713-777-4636. Ed. Francine Carbajal. adv.; bk.rev.; circ. 80,000 (controlled). (back issues avail.)
Former titles: Living (Houston Edition) (ISSN 0741-5486) & Houston Living (ISSN 0192-9143)

HOW TO BUY AND SELL BUSINESS OPPORTUNITIES. see *BUSINESS AND ECONOMICS — Investments*

HYRESGAESTEN. see *HOUSING AND URBAN PLANNING*

333.33   US
I A A O UPDATE. 1978. m. membership. International Association of Assessing Officers, 1313 E. 60th St., Chicago, IL 60637-9990. TEL 312-947-2053. Ed. Eve Bjork. circ. 8,250.
Formerly (until 1987): International Association of Assessing Officers. News Bulletin (ISSN 0741-4609)

333.33   SZ
IMMOBILIA.* m. Schweizerische Verband der Immobilien-Treuhaender, Buchmattweg 4, CH-8057 Zurich, Switzerland.

333.33   GW
IMMOBILIEN-BERATER; Handbuch fuer den wirtschaftlichen Erfolg mit Haus- mit Wohnungsbesitz. 1988. bi-m. DM.160($90) Verlag Norman Rentrop, Theodor-Heuss-Str. 4, 5300 Bonn 2, Germany. TEL 0228-8205-0. FAX 0228-364411. TELEX 17228309. Ed. H.J. Oberhettinger. (looseleaf format)

333.33   GW
IMMOBILIEN VERWALTUNG HEUTE; der aktuelle Branchenbrief fuer den Haus- und Grundstuecksverwalter. 1989. m. Grabener Wirtschafts Verlag, Feldstr. 131, 2300 Kiel 1, Germany. TEL 0431-805350. Ed. Henning Grabener.

333.33   GW
IMMOBILIEN WIRTSCHAFT HEUTE; der aktuelle Branchenbrief fuer den Immobilien - Insider. 1987. bi-w. DM.180. Grabener Wirtschafts Verlag, Feldstr. 131, 2300 Kiel 1, Germany. TEL 0431-805350. Ed. Henning Grabener.

690 333   US   ISSN 0194-1941
HD7287.6.U5
INCOME - EXPENSE ANALYSIS: CONVENTIONAL APARTMENTS. 1954. a. $125. Institute of Real Estate Management, Box 109025, Chicago, IL 60610-9025. TEL 312-661-1953. Ed. Kay McGuire. **Indexed:** SRI.
Formerly: Income - Expense Analysis: Apartments; Supersedes in part: Income - Expense Analysis: Apartments, Condominiums and Cooperatives (ISSN 0161-5262); (until 1973): Apartment Building Income - Expense Analysis (ISSN 0084-6651)
Description: Detailed analysis of the financial operations of multi-family properties.

333.33 690   US
INCOME - EXPENSE ANALYSIS: FEDERALLY ASSISTED APARTMENTS. a. $110. Institute of Real Estate Management, Box 109025, Chicago, IL 60610-9025. TEL 312-661-1953. FAX 312-661-0217.
Description: Summarizes the operating experience of apartment buildings across the US that receive subsidies under one of five federal programs, drawing on a sample of over 1500 buildings.

333   US
INCOME - EXPENSE ANALYSIS: OFFICE BUILDINGS, DOWNTOWN AND SUBURBAN. 1976. a. $125. Institute of Real Estate Management, Box 109025, Chicago, IL 60610-9025. TEL 312-661-1930. Ed. Kay McGuire. **Indexed:** SRI.
Supersedes: Income - Expense Analysis: Suburban Office Buildings.
Description: Analysis of office building revenues and expenses.

333.33 690   US
INCOME - EXPENSE ANALYSIS: SHOPPING CENTERS, OPEN AND ENCLOSED. a. $125. Institute of Real Estate Management, Box 109025, Chicago, IL 60610-9025. TEL 312-661-1953. FAX 312-661-0217.
Description: For real estate professionals. Provides data for appraisals, operating comparisons and feasibility studies.

333.33   FR
INDICATEUR BERTRAND MIDI - MEDITERRANEE. m. 15 F. Editions Indicateur Bertrand, 43 bd. Barbes, 75018 Paris, France. TEL 1-49-25-26-27. FAX 1-49-25-26-00. adv.: B&W page 13050 F.; trim 270 x 210; adv. contact: Patricia Gaujoux. charts; illus.; circ. 30,000.
Formerly: Indicateur Bertrand Mediterranee.
Description: Advertisements for the sale of houses and apartments on the Mediterranean.

333.33   FR
INDICATEUR BERTRAND MONTAGNE. 8/yr. Editions Indicateur Bertrand, 43 bd. Barbes, 75018 Paris, France. TEL 1-49-25-26-27. FAX 1-49-25-26-00. adv.: B&W page 12950 F., color page 18500 F.; trim 270 x 210; adv. contact: Guy Coponat.

333.33   FR
INDICATEUR BERTRAND OUEST - SUD-OUEST. m. 15 F. per no. Editions Indicateur Bertrand, 43 bd. Barbes, 75018 Paris, France. adv.: B&W page 10120 F.; trim 270 x 210; adv. contact: Michel Joubert. charts; illus.; stat.; circ. 25,000.
Former titles: Indicateur Bertrand Ouest; Indicateur Bertrand Normandie.
Description: Advertisements for the sale of houses and apartments in the Western and South-western regions of France.

333.33   FR
INDICATEUR BERTRAND PARIS - BANLIEU. 1905. s-m. 20 F. per no. Editions Indicateur Bertrand, 43 bd. Barbes, 75018 Paris, France. adv.: B&W page 23000 F., color page 37000 F.; trim 270 x 210; adv. contact: Jacques Sarthe. circ. 30,000.
Formerly: Indicateur Bertrand (ISSN 0151-2943)
Description: Advertisements for the sale of houses and apartments in Paris and its suburbs.

333.33   FR
INDICATEUR BERTRAND RHONE-ALPES. m. 15 F. per no. Editions Indicateur Bertrand, 43 bd. Barbes, 75018 Paris, France. TEL 1-49-25-26-27. FAX 1-49-25-26-00. adv.: B&W page 22000 F.; trim 270 x 210; adv. contact: Guy Coponat. circ. 25,000.
Description: Advertisements for the sale of houses and apartments in the Rhone-Alpes region of France.

333.33   JA   ISSN 0073-7186
INDICES OF URBAN LAND PRICES AND CONSTRUCTION COST OF WOODEN HOUSES IN JAPAN. (Text in Japanese) s-a. price varies. Japan Real Estate Institute - Nihon Fudosan Kenkyusho, Kangin-Fujiya Bldg., 1-3-2 Toranomon, Minato-ku, Tokyo, Japan.

333.33   CN
INDUSTRIAL & COMMERCIAL PROPERTY - WINDSOR - ESSEX. 1959. s-a. free. Windsor-Essex County Development Commission, City Centre, Ste. 215, 333 Riverside Dr. W., Windsor, Ont. N9A 5K4, Canada. TEL 519-255-9200. FAX 519-255-9987. Ed. Lina DeMarco. circ. 600.
Former titles: Industrial Property - Windsor - Essex & Industrial Buildings - Windsor - Essex.
Description: Listing of properties available in the Windsor, Essex counties and the Town of Tilbury area.

333.33   US
INDUSTRIAL REAL ESTATE GUIDE; industrial, commercial, office. 1989. bi-m. Industrial Real Estate Guide, Inc., 7842 N. Lincoln Ave., Skokie, IL 60077. TEL 800-323-1818. FAX 312-676-0063. adv.

REAL ESTATE   4151

333.33   FR   ISSN 0046-936X
INFORMATION IMMOBILIERE. 1968. m. 165 F. Presse Immobiliere, 11 Quai Anatole-France, 75007 Paris, France. Ed. Michel Binetruy. adv.; bk.rev.; circ. 130,000.

333.33   FR
INFORMATIONS F.N.A.I.M.. 1973. m. 105 F. Federation Nationale des Agents Immobiliers et Administrateurs de Biens-Syndics d'Immeubles, 129 rue du Faubourg St. Honore, 75008 Paris, France. adv.; bk.rev.; circ. 7,000.

333.33   US
INQUILINE WORLDWIDE HOME EXCHANGES AND RENTALS;* professional executive homes. 1975. s-a. (plus q. newsletters). $30. Inquiline, Inc., Oakridge Condos, 79 Foxridge Rd., South Salem, NY 10590-9527. Ed. Benjamin T. Kernan. circ. 2,000.

333.33 647.9   US
INSIDE ISSUES. 1984. q. free. Hotel & Motel Brokers of America, 10220 N.W. Executive Hills Blvd., Ste. 610, Kansas City, MO 64153-2312. TEL 816-891-7070. FAX 816-891-7071. Ed. Robert Kralicek. circ. 28,000. (looseleaf format)
   Description: Focuses on hotel and motel real estate brokerage.

INSTITUTE ON ADVANCED TAX PLANNING FOR REAL PROPERTY TRANSACTIONS. see *BUSINESS AND ECONOMICS — Public Finance, Taxation*

INSTITUTE ON PLANNING, ZONING AND EMINENT DOMAIN. PROCEEDINGS. see *LAW*

333.33   US   ISSN 8755-6138
HD1361
INTERNATIONAL REAL ESTATE JOURNAL. 1980. 6/yr. $75. (International Real Estate Institute) Todd Publishing, Inc., 8383 E. Evans Rd., Scottsdale, AZ 85260. TEL 602-998-7743. FAX 602-998-8022. Ed.Bd. adv.; circ. 19,000. (back issues avail.)

333.33   US   ISSN 0734-5860
INVESTING IN REAL ESTATE.* 1968. m. Newsletter Bureau, Inc., Box 4096, Norwalk, CT 06855-0096. TEL 203-866-6004. Ed. Robert B. Luce. (back issues avail.)
   Formerly: Real Estate Investor (ISSN 0095-0211)

INVESTMENT ADVISER. see *BUSINESS AND ECONOMICS — Investments*

333.33   UK   ISSN 0143-6473
INVESTORS CHRONICLE HILLIER PARKER RENT INDEX. 1977. q. £1358. Hillier Parker May & Rowden, 77 Grosvenor St., London W1A 2BT, England. TEL 071-629-7666. Ed. Kiran Patel. circ. 3,000. (back issues avail.)

333.33   US   ISSN 0882-1879
ISLAND PROPERTIES REPORT. 1983. m. $39. Island Properties Report, 2257 Boston Post Rd., Guilford, CT 06437. TEL 203-458-3449. FAX 203-453-3091. Ed. Joan Kelly-Plate. bk.rev.; circ. 9,360. (back issues avail.)
   Description: Reports on Caribbean Island economy, politics, taxes and purchase regulations. Also list properties for sale.

JAPANESE INVESTMENT IN U S REAL ESTATE REVIEW. see *BUSINESS AND ECONOMICS — Investments*

JESSUP'S LAND TITLES OFFICE PRACTICE S.A.. see *LAW*

333.33   US   ISSN 0887-1922
JOHN T. REED'S REAL ESTATE INVESTOR'S MONTHLY. 1986. m. $125. Reed Publishing (Danville), 342 Bryan Dr., Danville, CA 94526. TEL 510-820-6292. (Subscr. to: Box 27311, Concord, CA 94527) Ed. John T. Reed. bk.rev.; charts; stat.; circ. 1,600. (back issues avail.)
   Description: Includes articles on real estate investment and strategy, finance, management, tax laws, and other pertinent non-tax court decisions.

JOURNAL OF FINANCIAL SERVICES RESEARCH. see *BUSINESS AND ECONOMICS — Banking And Finance*

JOURNAL OF HOUSING RESEARCH. see *HOUSING AND URBAN PLANNING*

333.33   UK   ISSN 0958-868X
                CODEN: JPFIEL
▼**JOURNAL OF PROPERTY FINANCE.** 1990. q. £90. Henry Stewart Publications, 2-3 Cornwall Terrace, Regent's Park, London NW1 4QP, England. TEL 01-935-2382. FAX 01-486-7083. adv.; bk.rev. —BLDSC shelfmark: 5042.778000.

333.33   US   ISSN 0022-3905
TX955
JOURNAL OF PROPERTY MANAGEMENT. 1934. bi-m. $35.95 (foreign $71.90). Institute of Real Estate Management, 430 N. Michigan Ave., Box 109025, Chicago, IL 60610-9025. TEL 312-329-6073. FAX 312-661-0217. Ed. Mariwyn Evans. adv.; charts; illus.; tr.lit.; index. (back issues avail.) **Indexed:** Account.Ind. (1974-), BPIA, Bus.Ind., Manage.Cont., P.A.I.S., Sage Urb.Stud.Abstr., Tr.& Indus.Ind.
   Incorporates: Operating Techniques and Products Bulletin.
   Description: Provides a forum for sharing ideas and discussing new trends that affect the asset management of investment real estate. Articles may address the management of apartments, office buildings, shopping and strip centers, mixed use properties, office-industrial properties, condominiums, and special-purpose real estate.

333.33   UK
JOURNAL OF PROPERTY VALUATION AND INVESTMENT. 1982. q. £75. Henry Stewart Publications, 2-3 Cornwall Terrace, Regent's Park, London NW1 4QP, England. TEL 01-935-2382. FAX 01-486-7083. Ed. Nick French. adv.; bk.rev.
   Formerly: Journal of Valuation (ISSN 0263-7480)

333.33 332   US   ISSN 0895-5638
HG2040   CODEN: JREEEI
JOURNAL OF REAL ESTATE FINANCE AND ECONOMICS. 1988. q. fl.180($75) to individuals; institutions fl.284 (144.50). Kluwer Academic Publishers, 101 Philip Dr., Norwell, MA 02061. TEL 617-871-6600. FAX 617-871-6528. TELEX 20090. (Subscr. to: Box 358, Accord Sta., Hingham, MA 02018-0358) Eds. James Kau, C.F. Sirmans. adv. (reprint service avail. from SWZ,UMI) **Indexed:** J.of Econ.Lit. —BLDSC shelfmark: 5047.750000.
   Description: Scholarly research in real estate finance and economics.

333.33   US   ISSN 0896-5803
JOURNAL OF REAL ESTATE RESEARCH. 1986. irreg. (1-5/yr.). 55. American Real Estate Society, c/o Theron Nelson, Dept. of Finance, University of North Dakota, Box 8233 University Station, Grand Forks, ND 58202. TEL 701-777-2396. FAX 701-777-5099. Ed. G. Donald Jud. adv.; circ. 1,500.
—BLDSC shelfmark: 5047.770000.

333.33 336.2   US   ISSN 0093-5107
HJ4181.A1
JOURNAL OF REAL ESTATE TAXATION. 1973. q. $115. Warren, Gorham and Lamont, One Penn Plaza, New York, NY 10119. TEL 800-950-1205. FAX 212-971-5240. Ed. Lester B. Snyder. bk.rev.; bibl. (also avail. in microform from UMI; reprint service avail. from RRI,UMI) **Indexed:** ABI Inform, Account.Ind. (1974-), BPIA, Bus.Ind., C.L.I., L.R.I., Leg.Cont., Leg.Per., PROMT, PSI, SSCI.
   Description: Covers all aspects of real estate tax planning. Articles are written by leading attorneys, tax accountants, and real estate authorities.

333.33   US   ISSN 0899-8930
HD268.W3
KALIS' SHOPPING CENTER LEASING DIRECTORY. 1987. s-a. $100 (foreign $105). The Atrium Bldg., Ste. 308, 4900 Leesburg Pike, Alexandria, VA 22302-1104. TEL 703-578-3051. FAX 703-578-3057.

323.4   UK   ISSN 0023-7574
HD591.A1
LAND AND LIBERTY; bi-monthly journal for land value taxation and free trade. 1894. bi-m. £7.50($13.50) Land and Liberty International Ltd., 177 Vauxhall Bridge Rd., London SW1V 1EU, England. TEL 01-834-4266. Ed. Fred Harrison. adv.; bk.rev.; charts; index; circ. 2,000. (back issues avail.) **Indexed:** P.A.I.S., RICS.

333.33 340   US   ISSN 0739-6376
KF5698.3.A15
LAND DEVELOPMENT LAW REPORTER. 1973. m. $395. Land Development Institute, Ltd., 1300 N St., N.W., Washington, DC 20005. TEL 202-545-2144. FAX 202-347-4469. Eds. Stuart Bloch, William Ingersoll. cum.index: 1973-1988; circ. 250. (looseleaf format; back issues avail.)
   Description: Covers federal agencies, state and federal court decisions, taxes and financing news relating to land development.

LAND USE FORUM; a journal of law, policy, and practice. see *LAW*

347.2   US   ISSN 0094-7598
K30
LAND USE LAW AND ZONING DIGEST. (Monthly supplement avail.: Zoning News) 1948. m. $195. American Planning Association, 1313 E. 60th St., Chicago, IL 60637. TEL 312-955-9100. FAX 312-955-8312. (And: 1776 Massachusetts Ave., N.W., Washington, DC 20036. TEL 202-872-0611) Ed. Rodney Cobb. index; circ. 1,800. (also avail. in microform from UMI; back issues avail.; reprint service avail. from UMI)
   Formerly: Zoning Digest (ISSN 0084-5566)

333.33   NE
LANDEIGENAAR; maandblad ter behartiging van de belangen van de landelijke eigendom. 1953. m. fl.88 to non-members. Uitgeverij de Landeigenaar b.v., Zwaluwenburg 6, 8084 PD 't Harde, Netherlands. FAX 05250-5601. Ed. G.R. van Woudenberg. adv.; bk.rev.; circ. 3,500.

333.33 330.9 352.7   AT   ISSN 0310-320X
LANDLINE IN AUSTRALIA. 1973. q. Real Estate Institute of Australia, P.O. Box 234, Curtin, A.C.T. 2605, Australia. TEL 06-282-4277. FAX 06-285-2444. Ed. Debra Smith. circ. 14,500. (back issues avail.) **Indexed:** AESIS.
   Description: Advocate journal on real estate industry issues.

LANDLORD REMEDIES IN FLORIDA. see *LAW*

333.33 340   US   ISSN 0883-0746
LANDLORD VS TENANT - N Y C. 1985. m. $318. Brownstone Publishers, Inc., 304 Park Ave. S., New York, NY 10010. TEL 212-473-8200. FAX 212-995-9205. Ed. Susan R. Lipp. (back issues avail.)
   Description: New cases and unreported rulings summarized for New York apartment building owners.

333.33   US
LANDOWNER. 1979. s-m. $79. (Professional Farmers of America) Oster Communications, Inc., 219 Main St., Cedar Falls, IA 50613. TEL 319-277-1278. FAX 319-277-5803. Ed. Jerry Carlson.
   Description: Provides information on the land market. Includes safe, creative ways to buy, sell or rent farm property. Also covers regional price trends and environmentally sound methods of farmland stewardship to enhance land productivity.

333.33   US
LAWYERS TITLE NEWS. 1937. q. free. Lawyers Title Insurance Corporation, Box 27567, Richmond, VA 23261. TEL 804-281-6700. FAX 804-282-5453. Ed. Eleanor Anders. circ. 80,000.

333.33   DK
VI LEJERE. 1969. q. membership. Lejernes Landsorganisation, Reventlowsgade 14,4, 1651 Copenhagen V, Denmark. FAX 31-223787. Ed. Jens Reiermann. adv.; circ. 100,000.
   Formerly (until 1985): Bolignyt (ISSN 0006-6524)

333.33 332.6   UK
LIFESTYLE AND LONDON LIVING. 1983. m. £25. Reed Publishing Services, 7-11 St. Johns Hill, London SW11, England. TEL 01-228-3344. FAX 01-924-3408. Ed. N. Keith. adv.; bk.rev.; circ. 50,000.
   Incorporates: Property and Investment; **Formerly:** London Gentleman.

REAL ESTATE

333.33   CN
LIFESTYLES MAGAZINE. 1986. m. Sun Ridge Residential Inc., 2103 Airport Dr., Ste. 110, Saskatoon, Sask. S7L 6W2, Canada. TEL 306-665-2525. FAX 306-652-6161. Ed. Keith Hanson. adv.; circ. 40,000.
    Formerly: New Homes and Renovations Magazine.
    Description: Contains photographs of log homes, floor plans, joining techniques, kit prices and contents. Articles on log home decor, energy efficiency, tools and equipment, schools and associations.

333.33   CN
LIVING GUIDE. q. 826 Erin St., Winnipeg, Man. R3G 2W4, Canada. TEL 204-775-8918.
    Description: Serves as an information source for the communities in the area, guiding future residents to their new homes and other services.

LOAN-A-HOME DIRECTORY. see *BUSINESS AND ECONOMICS — Trade And Industrial Directories*

333.33   FR   ISSN 0024-5674
LOCATIONS VACANCES. a. 30 F. Editions Indicateur Bertrand, 43 bd. Barbes, 75018 Paris, France. TEL 1-49-25-26-27. FAX 1-49-25-26-00. adv.; bk.rev.
    Description: Advertisements for the renting of vacation homes from private owners in France and elsewhere.

LOUISIANA LANDLORD & TENANT LAW. see *LAW*

LUXURY HOME IDEAS. see *INTERIOR DESIGN AND DECORATION*

M I N FAX. (Marketing Information Network) see *HOUSING AND URBAN PLANNING*

MAINE REAL ESTATE GUIDE. see *BUSINESS AND ECONOMICS — Trade And Industrial Directories*

333.33 658   US
MANAGER'S REPORT; journal for community association management. 1987. m. $18. Ivor Thomas & Associates, Inc., Box 18529, West Palm Beach, FL 33416. TEL 407-687-4700. Ed. Ivor Thomas. adv.; circ. 8,000.
    Description: News and feature articles dealing with areas of interest to individuals responsible for the management and purchasing activities of condominium, homeowner and co-operative associations.

MANAGING THE FLORIDA CONDOMINIUM. see *LAW*

333.33 747   US   ISSN 0889-9878
MANHATTAN COOPERATOR;* the co-op and condo monthly. 1981. m. $30. Manhattan Cooperator Publications, Inc., 301 E. 45th St., A, Ste. 5C, New York, NY 10017-3422. Ed. Vicki Chesler. adv.; bk.rev.; circ. 65,000. (tabloid format; back issues avail.)

333.33   US
MANHATTAN OFFICE BUILDINGS: DOWNTOWN. a. $39. Yale Robbins, Inc., 31 E. 28 St., New York, NY 10016. TEL 212-683-5700. Ed. Yale Robbins. adv.
    Description: Annual review of Manhattan's downtown office buildings.

333.33   US
MANHATTAN OFFICE BUILDINGS: MIDTOWN. a. $39. Yale Robbins, Inc., 31 E. 28 St., New York, NY 10016. TEL 212-683-5700. Ed. Yale Robbins. adv.
    Description: Annual review of Manhattan's midtown office buildings.

333.33   US
MANHATTAN OFFICE BUILDINGS: MIDTOWN SOUTH. a. 25. Yale Robbins, Inc., 31 E. 28th St., New York, NY 10016. TEL 212-683-5700.
    Description: Annual review of Manhattan's midtown south office buildings.

333.33   US
MANHATTAN REAL ESTATE EXCHANGE. 1989. m. $18. New York Construction News, Inc., 135 E. 65th St., 4th Fl., New York, NY 10021-7006. TEL 212-472-6700. FAX 212-472-6066. Ed. Charles Urstadt. circ. 50,000. (tabloid format)

333.33   US
MARKET PROFILES. 1986. a. $225 to non-members; members $185. Urban Land Institute, 625 Indiana Ave., N.W., Ste. 400, Washington, DC 20004-2930. TEL 202-624-7000. Ed. J. Thomas Black. charts; illus.; stat.

333.33 690   US   ISSN 0732-815X
TH435
MEANS SQUARE FOOT COSTS (YEAR); residential, commercial, industrial, institutional. 1980. a. $84.95. R.S. Means Company, Inc., 100 Construction Plaza, Box 800, Kingston, MA 02364-0800. TEL 800-334-3509. FAX 617-585-7466. Ed. Philip R. Waier. (also avail. in microform)
    Formerly: Appraisal Manual (ISSN 0272-0051)

333.33   FR
MEDITERRANEE IMMOBILIERE. (Text in English, French and German) m. 225 F. Publi Ric, 8 rue Richelieu, 75001 Paris, France. Ed. Gerard Lacape. circ. 25,000.

333.33   IS
MEKARKAIIN VEARCHAM/LAND AND VALUE. (Text in Hebrew) 1953. s-a. $25 per no. Israel Land Valuers Association, P.O. Box 2000, Tel Aviv 61019, Israel. TEL 03-220422. FAX 03-5235993. Ed.Bd. bk.rev.; circ. 500.

333.33   US   ISSN 0891-7698
MERCER COUNTY BOARD OF REALTORS. NEWSLINE. 1986. 11/yr. $5. Mercer County Board of Realtors, 1428 Brunswick Ave., Box 5455, Trenton, NJ 08638. TEL 609-392-3666. FAX 609-394-3939. Ed. Linda M. Mottin. adv.; circ. 3,300.
    Description: For realtors, realtor associates, and affiliate members of the Board. Covers real estate and related industries and association topics.

METRO CHICAGO OFFICE GUIDE. see *BUSINESS AND ECONOMICS — Office Equipment And Services*

333.33   US
METRO CHICAGO REAL ESTATE. 1913. bi-w. $38. Law Bulletin Publishing Co., 415 N. State St., Chicago, IL 60610-4674. TEL 312-644-7800. Ed. Jennifer Harris. adv.; bk.rev.; circ. 10,476. (also avail. in microfilm)
    Former titles: Real Estate Magazine; Chicagoland's Real Estate Advertiser (ISSN 0009-3769)

333.33   CN
METROTRENDS. 1958. a. Can.$35. Real Estate Board of Greater Vancouver, 1101 W. Broadway, Vancouver, B.C. V6H 1G2, Canada. TEL 604-736-4551. FAX 604-734-1778. Ed. Ray A. Nelson. stat.; circ. 1,000. (looseleaf format)
    Formerly (until 1984): Real Estate Trends in Metropolitan Vancouver (ISSN 0085-5405)

333.33   US   ISSN 0893-2719
MIDWEST REAL ESTATE NEWS. 1984. m. $38 (foreign $108). Communication Channels, Inc., 6255 Barfield Rd., Atlanta, GA 30324-4369. TEL 404-256-9800. FAX 404-256-3116. TELEX 4611075 COMCHANI. (And: 307 N. Michigan Ave., Chicago, IL 60601-5390. TEL 312-726-7277) Ed. Al Girardi. circ. 21,500. (tabloid format; also avail. in microform from UMI; reprint service avail. from UMI)
    ●Also available online.
    Description: Covers commercial and industrial real estate activity in 10 Midwestern states: Illinois, Indiana, Iowa, Kansas, Michigan, Minnesota, Missouri, Nebraska, Ohio, and Wisconsin.

333.33   GW
MIETER MAGAZIN. m. Berliner Mieterverein, Spichernstr. 12, Postfach 3126, D-1000 Berlin 30, Germany. TEL 030-2115099.

MINIAPPARTAMENTI. see *HOUSING AND URBAN PLANNING*

333.3   US
MINNESOTA REAL ESTATE JOURNAL. fortn. Minnesota Real Estate Journal Inc., 8900 Wentworth Ave., S. Bloomington, MN 55420. TEL 612-885-0815. FAX 612-885-0818. Ed. John Share. circ. 7,200.

333.33   US
MISSOURI REALTOR. 1937. 6/yr. $6. Missouri Association of Realtors, 2601 Bernadette Pl., Box 1327, Columbia, MO 65205. TEL 314-445-8400. FAX 314-445-7865. Ed. Pamela J. Sage. circ. 18,000. (back issues avail.)
    Description: News digest of Missouri real estate and activities of the Missouri Association of Realtors.

333.33   US
MOBILEHOME PARKS REPORT; the monthly report devoted to investment and ownership. 1980. m. $125. Parks Publishing Company, 3807 Pasadena Ave., Ste.100, Sacramento, CA 95821. TEL 916-971-0489. Ed. Thomas P. Kerr. bk.rev.; circ. 300. (back issues avail.)
    Formerly: Kerr Report (ISSN 0273-2726)
    Description: Reports on legislation, issues and trends important to owners and developers of manufactured housing communities.

333.331   US   ISSN 0195-8194
HF5549.5.R47
MOBILITY (WASHINGTON). 1980. 12/yr. $42. Employee Relocation Council, 1720 N St., N.W., Washington, DC 20036. TEL 202-857-0857. Ed. Jerry Holloman. adv.; bk.rev.; index; circ. 11,500.

333.33   US   ISSN 0895-8777
HF5430.3
MONITOR (STAMFORD). Variant title: National Mall Monitor. 1970. 10/yr. $42 (Canada $47; elsewhere $54). Monitor (Subsidiary of: Maclean Hunter Media), Four Stamford Forum, Stamford, CT 06901-3202. TEL 203-977-2900. Ed. Robert E. O'Neill. adv.; bk.rev.; circ. 33,000.
    Description: Data, studies and information on the shopping center and chain retail store market.

333.33   US   ISSN 0887-0470
HF5429.3
MONITOR'S RETAIL TENANT DIRECTORY. 1978. a. $325. Progressive Grocer Co. (Subsidiary of: Maclean Hunter Media), 4 Stamford Forum, Stamford, CT 06901. TEL 203-325-3500. Ed. Adrienne Toth. circ. 2,000. (also avail. on diskette)
    Formerly: Retail Tenant Directory.
    Description: Profiles retail tenants and their requirements.

333.33   US
MONITOR'S WEEKLY INSIDER. 1980. w. $250. Monitor (Subsidiary of: MacLean Hunter Media), Four Stamford Forum, Stamford, CT 06901-3202. TEL 203-977-2900. Ed. Vanessa Grey. circ. 500. (also avail. on floppy disk)
    Description: News on chain retail expansion plans, shopping center development, acquisition.

333.33   US   ISSN 1052-469X
MONTANA LAND MAGAZINE. 1982. q. $10 (foreign $20). Real Estate Publications, Inc. (Billings), Box 30516, Billings, MT 59107-0516. TEL 406-259-3534. Ed. G.L. Dangerfield. adv. (back issues avail.)
    Description: Lists real estate for sale throughout Montana.

333.33   CN
MONTREAL OFFICE SPACE DIRECTORY. 1988. a. En Ville Publications Ltd., 8270 Mountain Sights, Ste. 201, Montreal, Que. H4P 2B7, Canada. TEL 514-731-9517. FAX 514-731-7459. adv.; circ. 15,000.

333.33   US   ISSN 0047-813X
MORTGAGE AND REAL ESTATE EXECUTIVES REPORT. 1969. bi-w. $135. Warren, Gorham and Lamont, One Penn Plaza, New York, NY 10119. TEL 800-950-1201. FAX 212-971-5240. Ed. Alvin L. Arnold. charts; illus.; stat. (also avail. in microfilm)
    Indexed: Bank.Lit.Ind.
    Incorporates (in Sep. 1976): Condominium Report; (in Jul. 1976): Real Estate Investors Report.
    Description: Provides ideas and new updates, including analysis and forecasts of important trends and developments, investment opportunities and other money-making ideas.

MORTGAGE BANKING. see *BUSINESS AND ECONOMICS — Banking And Finance*

MORTGAGE FINANCE GAZETTE. see *BUSINESS AND ECONOMICS — Banking And Finance*

REAL ESTATE 4153

333.3 332 352.7 UK
MORTGAGE FINANCE MONTHLY. 1981. m. free. Building Societies Association, 3 Savile Row, London W1X 1AF, England.
Former titles: Savings and Loan Monthly (ISSN 0955-5870); Building Society News (ISSN 0261-5304)
Description: Reports events, trends and developments in the housing finance industry.

MORTGAGE PRODUCT SPOTLIGHT. see *BUSINESS AND ECONOMICS — Banking And Finance*

333.33 917   CN   ISSN 0713-8369
MOVING TO & AROUND ALBERTA. a. Can.$6.95. Moving Publications Ltd., 44 Upjohn Rd., Don Mills, Ont. M3B 2W1, Canada. TEL 416-441-1168. FAX 416-441-1641.

333.33 917   CN   ISSN 0228-7153
MOVING TO & AROUND MARITIMES & NEWFOUNDLAND. biennial. Can.$4.95. Moving Publications Ltd., 44 Upjohn Rd., Don Mills, Ont. M3B 2W1, Canada. TEL 416-441-1168. FAX 416-441-1641.

333.33 917.124   CN
MOVING TO & AROUND SASKATCHEWAN. 1980. 2/yr. Can.$6.95. Moving Publications Ltd., 44 Upjohn Rd., Don Mills, Ont. M3B 2W1, Canada. TEL 416-441-1168. FAX 416-441-1641. illus.
Formerly: Moving to Saskatchewan (ISSN 0225-5383)

333.33 917   CN   ISSN 0715-8114
MOVING TO & AROUND SOUTHWESTERN ONTARIO. biennial. Can.$6.95. Moving Publications Ltd., 44 Upjohn Rd., Don Mills, Ont. M3B 2W1, Canada. TEL 416-441-1168. FAX 416-441-1641.

333.33 917.13   CN   ISSN 0713-8377
MOVING TO & AROUND TORONTO & AREA. 1974. a. Can.$6.95. Moving Publications Ltd., 44 Upjohn Rd., Don Mills, Ont. M3B 2W1, Canada. TEL 416-441-1168. FAX 416-441-1641.
Former titles: Moving to Toronto and Area (ISSN 0226-7829); Moving to Toronto (ISSN 0702-9179)

333.33 917.11   CN   ISSN 0713-8407
MOVING TO & AROUND VANCOUVER & B.C. 1977. a. Can.$6.95. Moving Publications Ltd., 44 Upjohn Rd., Don Mills, Ont. M3B 2W1, Canada. TEL 416-441-1168. FAX 416-441-1641. illus.
Former titles: Moving to Vancouver and B.C; Moving to Vancouver - Victoria (ISSN 0702-9187)

333.33 917   CN   ISSN 0825-2432
MOVING TO & AROUND WINNIPEG & MANITOBA. 2/yr. Can.$6.95. Moving Publications Ltd., 44 Upjohn Rd., Don Mills, Ont. M3B 2W1, Canada. TEL 416-441-1168. FAX 416-441-1641.

333.33   CN
MOVING TO GREATER HAMILTON, C.T.T., BRANTFORD & NIAGARA. a. Can.$6.95. Moving Publications Ltd., 44 Upjohn Rd., Don Mills, Ont. M3B 2W1, Canada. TEL 416-441-1168. FAX 416-441-1641.
Formerly: Moving to Greater Hamilton and the Golden Triangle (ISSN 0843-9214)

333.33   CN   ISSN 0702-9225
MOVING TO MONTREAL/EMMENAGER A MONTREAL. 2/yr. Can.$5.95. Moving Publications Ltd., 44 Upjohn Rd., Ste. 100, Don Mills, Ont. M3B 2W1, Canada. TEL 416-441-1168. FAX 416-441-1641.

333.33 917.13   CN   ISSN 0226-7837
MOVING TO OTTAWA - HULL. (Text in English and French) 1978. a. Can.$6.95. Moving Publications Ltd., 44 Upjohn Rd., Don Mills, Ont. M3B 2W1, Canada. TEL 416-441-1168. FAX 416-441-1641. illus.

333.33   US
MR. LANDLORD; the survival newsletter for landlords and landladies. 1985. m. $59. Home Rental Publishing, Box 1366, Norfolk, VA 23501. TEL 804-495-5809. FAX 804-467-1427. Ed. Jeffrey E. Taylor. adv.; bk.rev.; circ. 15,000. (looseleaf format; back issues avail.)
Description: Aims to help landlords to attain and maintain maximum cashflow, control and gain cooperation from tenants, and to serve as a forum for rental owners to share ideas and concerns.

333.33   AT
MULTILIST REALTOR. fortn. Real Estate Institute of Queensland, P.O. Box 688, Fortitude Valley, Brisbane, Qld. 4006, Australia. TEL 07-891-5711. FAX 07-891-5742.

333.33 368   US
N A I F A CONVENTION. PROCEEDINGS. a. National Association of Independent Fee Appraisers, 7501 Murdoch St., St. Louis, MO 63119. TEL 314-781-6688.

333.33   US
N A I F A TECHNICAL MANUAL. irreg. National Association of Independent Fee Appraisers, 7501 Murdoch St., St. Louis, MO 63119. TEL 314-781-6688.

333.33   US
N A R E A APPRAISAL GUIDELINE. bi-m. National Association of Real Estate Appraisers, 8383 E. Evans Rd., Scottsdale, AZ 85260. TEL 602-948-8000. FAX 602-998-8022.

333.33   US
N A R E A REAL ESTATE APPRAISAL NEWSLETTER. q. National Association of Real Estate Appraisers, 8383 E. Evans Rd., Scottsdale, AZ 85260. TEL 602-948-8000. FAX 602-998-8022.

333.33   US
N A R E E NEWS. 1947. m. membership. National Association of Real Estate Editors, 3101 N. Central Ave., Ste. 560, Phoenix, AZ 85102. TEL 602-265-1699. FAX 602-230-8504. Ed. John Harding. bk.rev.; bibl.; charts; illus.; stat.; circ. 600.
Description: Covers journalism, real estate, housing and urban planning and consumer education and protection.

333.33   AT
N.S.W. REALTY AUCTIONEER. (New South Wales) m. Aus.$215. Ian Huntley Pty. Ltd., P.O. Box 582, Crows Nest, N.S.W. 2065, Australia. TEL 02-957-1555. Ed. Sandy Wilson. (back issues avail.)
Description: Reports on the real estate market in New South Wales, Australia.

333.33   US   ISSN 0745-0893
N Y HABITAT; for co-op, condominium and loft living. 1982. 8/yr. $30. Carol Group Ltd., 928 Broadway, New York, NY 10010. TEL 212-505-2030. FAX 212-254-6795. Ed. Carol J. Ott. adv.; charts; illus.; stat.; circ. 10,000. (back issues avail.)
Incorporates: Loft Letter.

333   US   ISSN 0161-5882
HD255
NATIONAL ASSOCIATION OF REALTORS. HOME SALES. 1976. m. $100 to non-members; members $75 (effective 1992). National Association of Realtors, Economics and Research Division, 777 14th St., N.W., Washington, DC 20005. TEL 202-383-1110. FAX 202-383-7568. Ed. Glenn E. Crellin. circ. 500,525. **Indexed:** SRI.
●Also available online.
Former titles: National Association of Realtors. Existing Home Sales; National Association of Realtors. Department of Economics and Research. Existing Home Sales Series, Annual Report.

333.33   US   ISSN 0027-9994
HD251
NATIONAL REAL ESTATE INVESTOR. 1958. m. (plus a. Directory). $70 (foreign $140). Communication Channels, Inc., 6255 Barfield Rd., Atlanta, GA 30328-4369. TEL 404-256-9800. FAX 404-256-3116. TELEX 4611075 COMCHANI. Ed. Paula S. Stephens. adv.; bk.rev.; illus.; mkt.; stat.; tr.lit.; circ. 33,000. (also avail. in microfilm from UMI; reprint service avail. from UMI) **Indexed:** ABI Inform, B.P.I, BPIA, Bus.Ind., P.A.I.S., PSI, Tr.& Indus.Ind.
●Also available online.
—BLDSC shelfmark: 6030.030000.
Description: Covers the development, investment, financing and management of commercial real estate and its allied fields.

333.33   US   ISSN 0027-9994
NATIONAL REAL ESTATE INVESTOR DIRECTORY. a. $94.95. Communication Channels, Inc., 6255 Barfield Rd., Atlanta, GA 30328. TEL 404-256-9800. FAX 404-256-3116. TELEX 4611075 COMCHANI. Ed. Barbara Katinsky. adv.; circ. 33,000. (also avail. in microform from UMI)

333.33   CN
NATIONAL REAL PROPERTY REVIEW; monthly views on real estate. 1987. m. Can.$195. Butterworths Canada Ltd., 75 Clegg Rd., Markham, Ont. L6G 1A1, Canada. TEL 800-668-6481. FAX 416-479-2826. Ed. Paul Perrell. (back issues avail.)
Formerly: National Property Review (ISSN 0836-057X)
Description: For real estate professionals. Covers practices and legislative developments in matters affecting real estate; reviews and presents recent cases.

333.33   US   ISSN 1056-9723
HD1361
NATIONAL RELOCATION AND REAL ESTATE DIRECTORY; directory of professional relocation services and professionals. 1980. a. $75. Relocation Information Service, Inc., 113 Post Rd., E., Westport, CT 06880. TEL 203-227-3800. Ed. Peter S. Featherston. adv.; bk.rev.; index; circ. 35,000. (back issues avail.)

333.3   US   ISSN 0090-1741
HD253
NATIONAL ROSTER OF REALTORS. 1962. a. $50 to realtors; all others $75. (National Association of Realtors) Stamats Communications Inc., c/o Guy H. Wendler, 427 Sixth Ave., S.E., Box 1888, Cedar Rapids, IA 52406. TEL 319-364-6032. FAX 319-365-5421. Ed. Evelyn Oldridge. adv.; illus.; circ. 9,000.

NATIONWIDE ANGLIA BUILDING SOCIETY. HOUSE PRICES. see *BUILDING AND CONSTRUCTION*

NEIGHBORING PROPERTY OWNERS. see *LAW — Estate Planning*

333.3   US   ISSN 0028-4890
NEW ENGLAND REAL ESTATE JOURNAL. 1963. w. $96. Brian P. Heneghan, 57 Washington St., Norwell, MA 02061. TEL 800-654-4993. FAX 617-871-1853. Eds. Lynn Cedrone, Ben Summers. adv.; bk.rev.; circ. 8,500. (tabloid format)
Description: Covers commercial, industrial, and investment real estate.

333.3   US
NEW ENGLAND REAL ESTATE JOURNAL - SHOPPING CENTERS. 1984. m. free to qualified personnel. Brian P. Heneghan, 57 Washington St., Norwell, MA 02061. TEL 800-654-4993. FAX 617-871-1853. adv.; bk.rev.; circ. controlled. (tabloid format; back issues avail.)

333.33   US   ISSN 1042-9689
NEW ENGLAND REAL ESTATE NEWS. 1980. bi-m. $38 (foreign $108). Communication Channels, Inc., 6255 Barfield Rd., Atlanta, GA 30328-4369. TEL 404-256-9800. FAX 404-256-3116. TELEX 4611075 COMCHANI. (And: 148 State St., Ste. 410, Boston, MA 02109-1605. TEL 617-723-2228) Ed. Don Ciandella. adv.; circ. 17,500. (tabloid format; also avail. in microform from UMI; reprint service avail. from UMI)
Formerly (until 1989): New England Real Estate Directory.
Description: Covers commercial and industrial real estate issues and activities in 6 states: Connecticut, Maine, Massachusetts, New Hampshire, Rhode Island, and Vermont, and Westchester County, NY.

333.33 659.1   US
NEW HAMPSHIRE REAL ESTATE GUIDE. 1971. m. $20. Real Estate Guide, 89 N. Main St., Box 999, Andover, MA 01810. TEL 504-475-8732. FAX 508-475-6132. Ed. Robert A. Finlayson. adv.

333.33   US
NEW HOMEOWNER. 1985. a. New Homeowner Publications, Inc., 6198 Butler Pike, Ste. 135, Blue Bell, PA 19422. FAX 215-653-0817. adv.; circ. 1,300,000.
Description: Deals with moving, remodeling and home furnishing.

333.33   US   ISSN 0192-4893
NEW HOMES MAGAZINE; for the Twin Cities and suburbs. 1973. bi-m. free. New Homes, Inc., 5500 Lincoln Dr., Ste. 195, Minneapolis, MN 55436. FAX 612-933-6310. Ed. Wendy B. Danks. adv.; circ. 60,000 (controlled).
Description: Consumer resource on Twin Cities housing with information on the effect of national trends, laws and viewpoints on the city.

REAL ESTATE

333.33 US
NEW JERSEY. DEPARTMENT OF THE TREASURY. LOCAL PROPERTY BRANCH NEWS. 1953. 6/yr. (plus annual report). free. Department of the Treasury, Division of Taxation, Local Property Branch, 50 Barrack St., Trenton, NJ 08646. TEL 609-984-3276. Ed. Gary R. Dal Corso. index; circ. 2,300.
  Formerly (until Dec. 1984): New Jersey. Department of the Treasury. Local Property and Public Utility Branch News.

333.33 US
NEW JERSEY OFFICE BUILDINGS. a. $49. Yale Robbins, Inc., 31 E. 28th St., New York, NY 10016. TEL 212-683-5700. Ed. Yale Robbins.
  Incorporates: Central New Jersey Office Buildings.
  Description: Annual review of New Jersey office buildings.

333.33 US ISSN 0028-5919
NEW JERSEY REALTOR. vol.12, 1970. m. $10. New Jersey Association of Realtors, 295 Pierson Ave., Edison, NJ 08837. TEL 201-494-5616. Ed. Donna Jean Schratwieser. adv.; illus.; circ. 17,000.

333.33 340 UK
NEW LAW FOR SURVEYORS. 1984. 2/yr. £40($70) (College of Estate Management) E. & F.N. Spon, 2-6 Boundary Row, London SE1 8HN, England. TEL 071-865-0066. FAX 071-522-9623. Ed. Vera G. McEwan.
  Formerly: New Law for General Practice Surveyors (ISSN 0264-8121)
  Description: Provides general practice surveyors with selected summaries of relevant legal developments. The first part consists of notes on recently decided cases, the second gives details of recent statutes and statutory instruments.

333.33 340 US ISSN 0898-2961
KFX2022
NEW YORK APARTMENT LAW INSIDER. 1979. m. $154. Brownstone Publishers, Inc., 304 Park Ave. S., New York, NY 10010. TEL 212-473-8200. FAX 212-995-9205. Ed. Susan R. Lipp. index. (back issues avail.)
  Description: Covers new laws, cases, and regulations for New York apartment building owners.

333.3 US
NEW YORK REAL ESTATE JOURNAL. 1989. m. $24. 57 Washington St., Norwell, MA 02061. TEL 800-654-4993. FAX 617-871-1853. adv.; bk.rev.; circ. 9,000. (tabloid format; back issues avail.)
  Description: Covers commercial, industrial, and investment real estate.

333.33 NZ ISSN 0113-4620
NEW ZEALAND PROPERTY; the magazine for property investors. 1972. m. NZ.$95 (foreign NZ$115). Profile Publishing Ltd., P.O. Box 5544, Wellesley St., Auckland, New Zealand. TEL 09-784-475. FAX 09-780-244. Ed. Tom Frewen. adv.; bk.rev.; circ. 1,500. (back issues avail.)
  Formerly (until 1987): Property (ISSN 0110-0793)
  Description: Reports on all aspects of the commercial property market, including trends, market prices, legislation and industry groups. For property investors, developers and property professionals.

333.32 NZ ISSN 0113-0315
NEW ZEALAND VALUERS' JOURNAL. 1942. q. NZ.$50 (effective Jan. 1991). New Zealand Institute of Valuers, P.O. Box 27-146, Willis St., Wellington, New Zealand. TEL 04-384-7094. FAX 04-382-9214. (Subscr. to: P.O. Box 27146, Wellington, New Zealand) Ed. T.J. Croot. adv.; bk.rev.; index, cum.index: 1942-1988; circ. 2,400.
  Formerly: New Zealand Valuer (ISSN 0027-7282)

333.33 JA
NIKKEI REAL ESTATE - TOKYO. (Text in Japanese) 1987. m. 18000 Yen. Nikkei Business Publications, Inc., 3-3-23, Misakicho, Chiyoda-ku, Tokyo 101, Japan. TEL 03-5210-8502. FAX 03-5210-8119. Ed. Keiichi Nagasawa. adv.; circ. 15,393.
  Description: Contains current news and information on the fast-changing Tokyo metropolitan real estate market.

333.33 GW
NORDDEUTSCHE HAUSBESITZER-ZEITUNG. m. Verband Schleswig-Holsteinischer Haus-, Wohnungs- und Grundeigentuemer e.V., Sophienblatt 3, Postfach 4327, D-2300 Kiel 1, Germany.

333.33 US
NORTH CAROLINA HOUSING NETWORK; the monthly magazine for North Carolina housing professionals. 1985. m. $39. Leo Douglas, Inc., 9607 Gayton Rd., Ste. 201, Richmond, VA 23233. Ed. D.J. Kingrey. adv.; stat.; illus.; circ. 23,971.
  Description: Covers the design, construction, sale, and financing of homes in the State of North Carolina.

333.33 US ISSN 1047-8833
▼**NORTHEAST REAL ESTATE NEWS.** 1990. 8/yr. $38 (foreign $108). Communication Channels, Inc., 6255 Barfield Rd., Atlanta, GA 30328-4369. TEL 404-256-9800. FAX 404-256-3116. TELEX 4611075 COMCHANI. (And: 5 Penn Plaza, New York, NY 10001-1810. TEL 212-613-9700) Ed. Dora Hatras. circ. 18,000. (tabloid format)
  Description: Covers commercial and industrial real estate activity in New York, New Jersey, Pennsylvania and Delaware.

333.33 US
NORTHERN NEW ENGLAND REAL ESTATE JOURNAL. 1973. m. free to qualified personnel. Brian P. Heneghan, 57 Washington St., Norwell, MA 02061. TEL 800-654-4993. FAX 617-871-1853. adv.; bk.rev.; circ. controlled. (tabloid format; back issues avail.)
  Description: Covers commercial, industrial, and investment real estate in Maine, New Hampshire, and Vermont.

333.33 US
NORTHWEST RELOCATION NEWS. q. $24. Greener Pastures Institute, Box 1122, Sierra Madre, CA 91024. (tabloid format)
  Description: Features interviews with residents of towns in Oregon, Idaho and Washington and detailed information on respective communities.

333.33 CN
NOVA SCOTIA REAL PROPERTY PRACTICE MANUAL. 1988. 2/yr. Can.$140. Butterworths Canada Ltd., 75 Clegg Rd., Markham, Ont. L6G 1A1, Canada. TEL 800-668-6481. FAX 416-479-2826. Ed. Chales W. MacIntosh. circ. 185. (looseleaf format; back issues avail.)
  Description: Treatment of practice and procedure of Nova Scotia real property law.

333.33 UK ISSN 0078-3048
OCCASIONAL PAPERS IN ESTATE MANAGEMENT. 1966. irreg., no.11, 1978. price varies. College of Estate Management, Whiteknights, Reading RG6 2AW, England.

333.33 AU ISSN 0029-9189
OESTERREICHISCHE HAUSBESITZ. 1926. 11/yr. S.90. Reformverband Oesterreichischer Hausbesitzer, Trattnerhof 1, A-1010 Vienna, Austria. Ed. Friedrich Ruttar. adv.; bk.rev.

333.33 AU
OESTERREICHISCHE IMMOBILIEN-ZEITUNG. bi-w. Landesinnung Wien der Immobilien- und Vermoegenstreuhaender, Salesianergasse 1, A-1030 Vienna, Austria. TEL 725611.

333.33 US ISSN 0733-1266
OFFICE GUIDE TO ORLANDO;* a guide to office space, products and services. 1982. q. $30. Zink Media Group, Ltd., 701 E. Washington St., Ste. 200, Orlando, FL 32801-2939. TEL 407-839-6100. FAX 407-839-4077. Ed. Sherry L. Valle. adv.; circ. 12,026.
  Description: Office and industrial space directory listing available square footage, costs maps, and leasing contacts. Telecommunications, interior design, office equipment, and new products and services are featured regularly, as well as articles on health and stress in the office, employee motivators, and stress and management skills and techniques.

OFFICE OF THRIFT SUPERVISION. see *BUSINESS AND ECONOMICS — Banking And Finance*

OLD-HOUSE JOURNAL. see *BUILDING AND CONSTRUCTION*

OLD-HOUSE JOURNAL CATALOG. see *BUILDING AND CONSTRUCTION*

333.33 US
ORANGE COUNTY APARTMENT NEWS. 1961. m. $36. (Apartment Association of Orange County) Orange County Multi-Housing Services Corporation, 12900 Garden Grove Blvd., No. 101, Garden Grove, CA 92643-2001. FAX 714-638-3784. Ed. Shelli L. Stewart. adv.; bk.rev.; charts; stat.; tr.lit.; circ. 6,000.
  Formerly: Orange County Apartment House News (ISSN 0030-4247)

ORANGE COUNTY REPORT. see *BUSINESS AND ECONOMICS — Domestic Commerce*

333.33 CN
OTTAWA REAL ESTATE NEWS. 1988. m. O R E N Publishing Ltd., 880 Wellington St., Ste. 616, Ottawa, Ont. K1R 6K7, Canada. TEL 613-232-2661. FAX 613-232-2922. Ed. Mark Buckshon. adv.; circ. 3,500. (tabloid format)

333.33 658 US
P M A DIRECTORY. 1968. a. $50. Property Management Association, 8811 Colesville Rd., Ste. G106, Silver Spring, MD 20910. TEL 301-587-6543. Ed. T. Cohn. circ. 2,500.
  Description: Listing of members and property management resources.

333.33 690 US
PERSPECTIVE (INDIANAPOLIS). 1985. bi-m. (free to qualified personnel). Resort Condominiums International, Inc., Box 80229, Indianapolis, IN 46280-0229. TEL 317-871-9567. FAX 317-871-9699. Ed. Jill Rush. adv.; circ. 7,000 (controlled).
  Description: Reports on events and trends in the resort-condominium development, vacation-ownership, and or exchange and travel industries on an international, federal and state-wide basis.

333.33 FR
PERSPECTIVES IMMOBILIERES. bi-m. (5/yr.). 350 F. (foreign 500 F.). Federation Nationale de l'Immobilier, 129, rue du Faubourg Saint-Honore, 75008 Paris, France. TEL 44-20-77-00. FAX 1-42-25-80-84. Ed. Catherine Vergnolle. adv.; bk.rev.
  Description: Covers the activities of the National Federation of Real Estate Agents, new innovations, interviews, etc.

333.33 690 FI
PIENTALO. 6/yr. (Finnish Small House Realty Association) Suomen Rakennuslehti Oy, Mannheimerintie 40, 00100 Helsinki, Finland. TEL 358-0-499455. FAX 358-0-407893. adv.; circ. 82,000.

PLANS DE MAISONS DU QUEBEC. see *INTERIOR DESIGN AND DECORATION*

333.33 US
PRIME REAL ESTATE. 1987. bi-m. $19.95. Prime Publishing Company, Inc., 4141 State St., No. E14, Santa Barbara, CA 93110. Ed. Michael Colin. adv.; circ. 40,000.
  Description: Features luxury residential real estate in the US. Provides localized feature articles and pertinent market information for consumers and brokers.

333 GW
PRIVATES EIGENTUM. 1960. m. membership. (Vereinigung der Haus-, Grund- und Wohnungseigentuemer Frankfurt am Main e.V.) KB-Werbung GmbH, Mainzer Landstr. 174, D-6000 Frankfurt-Main 1, Germany. TEL (0611)73 95 36. Ed. K. Rupp. adv.; bk.rev.; circ. 20,000.

PROBATE & PROPERTY. see *LAW*

333.33 340 US ISSN 0891-2599
PROFESSIONAL APARTMENT MANAGEMENT. 1988. m. $168. Brownstone Publishers, Inc., 304 Park Ave. S., New York, NY 10010. TEL 212-473-8200. FAX 212-995-9205. Ed. Glenn S. Demby. (back issues avail.)
  Description: Covers how to successfully manage an apartment community. Includes legal advice on leasing, maintenance, and employee relations.

333.33 — US
▼**PROFESSIONAL REPORT OF INDUSTRIAL AND OFFICE REAL ESTATE.** 1991. bi-m. $40 (foreign $45). Society of Industrial and Office Realtors, 777 14th St., N.W., Ste. 400, Washington, DC 20005-3271. TEL 202-737-1150. Ed. Linda Nasvaderani. circ. 2,500.
  Description: Industry news in the fields of industrial and office real estate.

333.33 — FR
PROMOTION IMMOBILIERE; hommes et logements. 1961. bi-m. (plus 2 special nos.) 50 F. Federation Nationale des Promoteurs-Constructeurs (F.N.P.C.), 106 rue de l'Universite, 75007 Paris, France. Ed. Jean Veillerot. adv.; bk.rev.; bibl.; charts; illus.; stat.; circ. 8,000.

333.33 — US — ISSN 0033-1287
PROPERTIES. 1937. m. $10. Properties Magazine Publishing Co., 4900 Euclid Ave., Cleveland, OH 44103. TEL 216-431-7666. Ed. Gene E. Bluhm. adv.; bk.rev.; charts; illus.; stat.; tr.lit.; index; circ. 2,100. (tabloid format)

333.33 — FR
PROPERTIES DE FRANCE. 6/yr. 50 F. per no. Editions Indicateur Bertrand, 43 bd. Barbes, 75018 Paris, France. TEL 1-49-25-26-27. FAX 1-49-25-26-00. adv.; circ. 50,000.
  Description: Advertises luxury houses and apartments for sale or rent in France.

333.33 — UK
PROPERTY CONFIDENTIAL. 1962. m. £127. Fleet Street Publications Ltd., 3 Fleet St., London EC4Y 1AU, England. Ed. Kerry Stephenson.

333.33 — UK
PROPERTY GUIDE. 1978. m. free. Clarendon Advertising Ltd., Burley Hill House, Burley Rd., Leeds LS4 2PX, England. FAX 0532-744740. Ed. R.J. Fletcher. adv.; circ. 40,000.
  Formerly: Property Fortnightly.
  Description: Describes property in the North of England.

333.33 — UK — ISSN 0033-1309
K16
PROPERTY JOURNAL. 1970. 6/yr. £12.80. British Property Federation, 35 Catherine Pl., London S.W.1, England. TEL 071-828-0111. FAX 071-834-3442. Ed. Helen McCarthy. adv.; bk.rev.; index; circ. 2,000. **Indexed:** RICS.
  —BLDSC shelfmark: 6927.307000.

PROPERTY LAW AND PRACTICE IN QUEENSLAND. see LAW

333.33 — UK — ISSN 0263-7472
PROPERTY MANAGEMENT. 1982. q. £75. Henry Stewart Publications, 2-3 Cornwall Terrace, Regent's Park, London NW1 4QP, England. TEL 01-935-2382. FAX 01-486-7083. Ed. Brenda Rouse. adv.; bk.rev.
  —BLDSC shelfmark: 6927.309700.

333.33 658 — US
PROPERTY MANAGEMENT ASSOCIATION. BULLETIN. 1975. m. $100. Property Management Association, 8811 Colesville Rd., Ste. G106, Silver Spring, MD 20910. TEL 301-587-6543. Ed. John P. Bachner. circ. 1,200.
  Description: Covers property management, association activities, and business management personnel.

333.33 — US — ISSN 1049-2372
HD1394
PROPERTY MANAGEMENT MONTHLY; serving decision-makers of income-producing properties. 1984. m. $18 (effective Feb. 1991). Adler Group, 8601 Georgia Ave., Ste. 400, Silver Spring, MD 20910. TEL 301-588-0681. FAX 301-588-6314. Ed. Laura O. Zaner. adv.; bk.rev.; circ. 6,000. (back issues avail.)
  Formerly: Apartment and Office Management News.
  Description: Provides information to anyone involved in the management of commercial and residential real estate.

333.33 — UK
PROPERTY REGISTER. 1978. m. £250. Tophill Press, 49 High St., Sevenoaks, Kent TN13 1L8, England. TEL 0732-743300. FAX 0732-743006. Ed. Arthur Hill. adv.; circ. controlled.
  Formerly: Commercial Property Register.

333.33 — HK
PROPERTY REVIEW; a summary of supply, vacancies, rentals and purchase prices. (Text in Chinese and English) 1975. a. HK.$100 (effective 1991). Rating and Valuation Department, 500 Hennessy Rd., Hennessy Centre, 26th Fl., Causeway Bay, Hong Kong. FAX 8459078. (Subscr. to: Director of Information Services, Information Services Department, 4 & 4A Queens's Rd. Central, Beaconsfield House, Hong Kong. TEL 8428777) circ. 1,000.

333.33 — UK — ISSN 0305-5752
PROPERTY STUDIES IN THE U.K. AND OVERSEAS. 1974. irreg., no.9, 1984. price varies. College of Estate Management, Whiteknights, Reading RG6 2AW, England. Eds. A.W. Davidson, J.E. Leonard.

333.332 — US — ISSN 0731-0285
HJ4101
PROPERTY TAX JOURNAL. 1982. q. $30 to members (foreign $35); non-members $55 (foreign $65). International Association of Assessing Officers, 1313 E. 60th St., Chicago, IL 60637-9990. TEL 312-947-2053. Ed. Annie Aubrey. circ. 1,000. (also avail. in microform from UMI; reprint service avail. from UMI) **Indexed:** ABI Inform, P.A.I.S.
  —BLDSC shelfmark: 6927.313100.
  Formerly (1966-1981): Assessors Journal (ISSN 0004-5071)

333.33 — IT — ISSN 0033-1422
PROPRIETA EDILIZIA LOMBARDA. 1901. m. L.9000. Federazione Lombarda Proprieta Edilizia, Via Meravigli 3, 20121 Milan, Italy. Dir. Giulio di Patrizio. adv.; circ. 20,000.

333.33 001.6
621.381 — US — ISSN 1052-5521
QUARTERLY BYTE. 1985. q. $30 (foreign $35). Appraisal Institute, 875 N. Michigan Ave., Ste. 2400, Chicago, IL 60611-1980. TEL 312-335-4100. FAX 312-335-4400. Ed. Mary J. Dum. circ. 2,300. **Indexed:** Comput.Lit.Ind.
  Description: Tips, programs and software reviews for the computer-using real estate appraiser.

333.33 747 — US
QUEST: MANHATTAN PROPERTIES & COUNTRY ESTATES.* 1987. m. free to qualified personnel. Quest Magazines, Inc., 1046 Madison Ave., New York, NY 10021-0137. FAX 212-288-4536. Ed. Heather Cohane. circ. 102,000 (controlled).
  Description: Contains advertisements for real estate and interior design, celebrity interviews, photos of social events, with focus on Manhattan.

333.33 — US
R E E ACTION. 7/yr. membership. Real Estate Educators Association, One Illinois Center, No. 200, 111 E. Wacker Dr., Chicago, IL 60601-4298. TEL 312-616-0800. adv.; bk.rev.; circ. 1,200. (looseleaf format)
  Description: Articles on real estate education. Includes association news.

333.33 — US
R E I S REPORT: INDUSTRIAL MARKET SERVICE. 1980. irreg. price varies. R E I S Reports, Inc., 11 E. 36th St., 7th fl., New York, NY 10016-3318. TEL 212-247-4433. FAX 212-713-0966. Ed. Lloyd Lynford.

333.33 — US
R E I S REPORT: RESIDENTIAL MARKET SERVICE. 1980. irreg. price varies. R E I S Reports, Inc., 11 E. 36th St., 7th fl., New York, NY 10016-3318. TEL 212-247-4433. FAX 212-713-0966. Ed. Lloyd Lynford. stat. (also avail. in looseleaf format; back issues avail.)

333.3 — US
R E I S REPORTS: OFFICE MARKET SERVICE. (Real Estate Information Service) 1980. irreg. price varies. R E I S Reports, Inc., 11 E. 36th St., 7th fl., New York, NY 10016-3318. TEL 212-481-8500. Ed. Lloyd Lynford. stat. (looseleaf format; back issues avail.)

REAL ESTATE 4155

333.33 — US
R E I S REPORTS: RETAIL MARKET SERVICE. (Real Estate Information Service) 1980. irreg. price varies. R E I S Reports, Inc., 11 E. 36th St., 7th fl., New York, NY 10016. TEL 212-481-8500. Ed. Lloyd Lynford. stat. (back issues avail.)

332.6 333.33 — US — ISSN 0095-1374
HG5095
R.E.I.T. FACT BOOK. 1974. irreg. $75. National Association of Real Estate Investment Trusts, Inc., 1129 20th St., N.W., Ste.705, Washington, DC 20036. TEL 202-785-8717. Ed. Victoria J. Baker. illus.; circ. 3,500.

333.33 332.6 — US
R.E.I.T. REPORT. 1981. q. membership. National Association of Real Estate Investment Trusts, Inc., 1129 20th St., N.W., Ste. 705, Washington, DC 20036. TEL 202-785-8717. Ed. Victoria J. Baker. adv.; bk.rev.; circ. 2,000.

333.33 — UK
R R V MONTHLY. 1928. m. £28($50) Institute of Revenues, Rating and Valuation, 41 Doughty St., London WC1, England. TEL 071-831-3505. FAX 071-831-2048. Ed. Colin Farrington. adv.; bk.rev.; abstr.; tr.lit.; index; circ. 6,000. **Indexed:** RICS.
  Former titles: R V A Monthly & Rating and Valuation (ISSN 0483-9889)

333.33 — US
R T C REPORT. (Resolution Trust Corporation) 1986. bi-w. $315. Land Development Institute, Ltd., 1300 N St., N.W., Washington, DC 20005. TEL 202-545-2144. FAX 202-347-4469. Eds. Stuart Bloch, William Ingersoll.
  Formerly (unitl 1989): Real Estate Opportunity Report.
  Description: Covers news relating to the RTC, federal regulation of financial institutions, and the real estate industry, including real estate and loan asset sales, contracting, and thrift resoluriona.

RAND MCNALLY PLACES RATED ALMANAC. see HOUSING AND URBAN PLANNING

REAL ESTATE ACCOUNTING AND TAXATION. see BUSINESS AND ECONOMICS — Accounting

333.33 333.9 — US
REAL ESTATE ANALYSIS AND PLANNING SERVICE. s-a. Dodge - McGraw-Hill, 24 Hartwell Ave., Lexington, MA 02173. TEL 617-863-5100. FAX 617-860-6332. TELEX 200 284.

333.33 — US
HD1387.A1
REAL ESTATE APPRAISER. 1935. 3/yr. $30 (foreign $35). Appraisal Institute, 875 N. Michigan Ave., Ste. 2400, Chicago, IL 60611-1980. TEL 312-335-4100. FAX 312-335-4400. Ed. Gerri Rothbauer. bk.rev.; index; circ. 19,000. **Indexed:** ABI Inform., B.P.I., BPIA, Bus.Ind., P.A.I.S., RICS, Tr.& Indus.Ind.
  Former titles: Real Estate Appraiser and Analyst (ISSN 0271-258X); Real Estate Appraiser (ISSN 0034-0677); Residential Appraiser.

333.33 — ISSN 0744-642X
HD1361
REAL ESTATE BUSINESS. 1982. q. $20. Realtors National Marketing Institute, Real Estate Brokerage Council, Residential Sales Council, Box 300, Wheaton, IL 60189-0300. TEL 708-752-0500. FAX 708-752-0525. Ed. Pierce Hollingsworth. adv.; bk.rev.; circ. 25,000. (back issues avail.)
  Description: News and educational articles for designated realtors.

333.33 — US — ISSN 0164-5781
REAL ESTATE CENTER JOURNAL. 1987. q. $20. Real Estate Center, Texas A&M University, College Sta., TX 77843-2115. TEL 409-845-0369. Ed. David S. Jones. illus.; circ. 70,000.
  Supersedes (1979-1986): Tierra Grande.

333.33 — US
REAL ESTATE CENTER LAW LETTER. 1986. q. $20. Texas A & M University, Real Estate Center, College Station, TX 77843-2115. TEL 409-845-0369. Ed. Shirley E. Bovey. circ. 5,600. (back issues avail.)
  Description: Covers new laws, regulations, relevant court cases and rulings with impact on Texas real estate.

R

REAL ESTATE

333.33 621.381   US
REAL ESTATE COMPUTER REVIEW. m. 1564 A Fitzgerald Dr., Ste. 404, Pinole, CA 94088. TEL 415-799-6156. Ed. Michael J. Hanrahan. circ. 1,200.

333.33   US
REAL ESTATE COORDINATOR. (In 8 vols.) bi-w. $705. Research Institute of America, Inc., 90 Fifth Ave., New York, NY 10011. TEL 212-645-4800. FAX 212-337-4279. (Subscr. to: 111 Radio Circle, Mt. Kisco, NY 10459) (looseleaf format)

333.3   US   ISSN 0098-8936
HD268.N5
REAL ESTATE DIRECTORY OF MANHATTAN. a. $625. T R W R E D I Property Data, 475 Fifth Ave., Ste. 1901, New York, NY 10017. TEL 212-532-2705.
  Formerly: Real Estate Directory of the Borough of Manhattan.

333.33   US
REAL ESTATE EDUCATORS ASSOCIATION. JOURNAL. 1988. a. membership. Real Estate Educators Association, One Illinois Center, No. 200, 111 E. Wacker Dr., Chicago, IL 60601-4298. TEL 312-616-0800. adv.; circ. 1,200.
  Description: Articles on real estate education. Includes a membership directory.

333.33   US
REAL ESTATE EDUCATORS ASSOCIATION. PROCEEDINGS. 1985. a. $18. Real Estate Educators Association, One Illinois Center, No. 200, 111 E. Wacker Dr., Chicago, IL 60601-4298. TEL 312-616-0800. (back issues avail.)
  Description: Academic research papers on a wide variety of real estate topics.

333.33   US   ISSN 0748-318X
HD1361
REAL ESTATE FINANCE. 1984. q. $88. Federal Research Press, 155 Federal St., 13th fl., Boston, MA 02110. Ed. Barbara Grzincic. bk.rev.; illus. **Indexed:** ABI Inform.
  —BLDSC shelfmark: 7303.280150.
  Incorporates (1985-1986): Real Estate Finance Law Journal.

330   US   ISSN 0898-0209
REAL ESTATE FINANCE JOURNAL. 1903. q. $110. Warren, Gorham and Lamont, One Penn Plaza, New York, NY 10119. TEL 800-950-1201. FAX 212-971-5240. Ed. William Zucker. adv. **Indexed:** ABI Inform.
  —BLDSC shelfmark: 7303.280180.
  Description: Provides analysis of current real estate financing events and issues, giving forecasts on important regulatory trends.

333.33   US   ISSN 0742-0021
REAL ESTATE FINANCE TODAY. 1984. fortn. $85. Mortgage Bankers Association of America, 1125 15th St., N.W., Washington, DC 20005. TEL 202-861-6555. Ed. Richard Helgerson. adv.; illus.; circ. 16,000.

333.33   US   ISSN 0891-9852
REAL ESTATE FINANCING UPDATE. 1985. m. $135. Warren, Gorham and Lamont, One Penn Plaza, New York, NY 10119. TEL 800-950-1201. FAX 212-971-5240.
  Description: Provides analysis of hard financial data and legislative information that affect real estate finance.

333.33   US
REAL ESTATE FOR PROFESSIONAL PRACTITIONERS: A WILEY SERIES. 1973-1989; suspended. irreg., latest 1989. price varies. John Wiley & Sons, Inc., 605 Third Ave., New York, NY 10158-0012. TEL 212-850-6000. FAX 212-850-6088. TELEX 12-7063. Ed. D. Clurman.

333.33   US   ISSN 0034-0707
REAL ESTATE FORUM. 1946. m. $65. Real Estate Forum, Inc., 12 W. 37th St., New York, NY 10018. TEL 212-563-6460. FAX 212-967-1498. Ed. Michael Desiato. adv.; charts; illus.; circ. 27,000.
  Description: Provides national coverage of real estate investment and development news.

333.33   US   ISSN 0034-0715
REAL ESTATE INSIDER; weekly newsletter. 1968. bi-w. $229. Atcom, Inc., Atcom Bldg., 2315 Broadway, New York, NY 10024-4397. TEL 212-873-5900. FAX 212-799-1728. Eds. Jean DeSapio, Michael Schau. bk.rev.; charts; tr.lit.; circ. 1,000. (reprint service avail. from UMI)
  Description: For owners, managers and brokers of real estate firms.

333.33   AT
REAL ESTATE INSTITUTE OF QUEENSLAND. ANNUAL REPORT. no.62, 1981. a. Real Estate Institute of Queensland, P.O. Box 688, Fortitude Valley, Brisbane, Qld. 4006, Australia. TEL 07-8915711. FAX 07-8915742. circ. 4,200.

333.33   US   ISSN 0145-1022
REAL ESTATE INVESTING LETTER. 1976. m. $96. Management Resources, Inc., 379 W. Broadway, New York, NY 10012. TEL 212-966-8966. bk.rev.; charts. (back issues avail.)
  Formerly: Real Estate Investor Letter.

333.33   US   ISSN 0034-0723
REAL ESTATE INVESTMENT IDEAS. s-m. $69. Macmillan Information Company Inc., 910 Sylvan Ave., Englewood Cliffs, NJ 07632. TEL 800-562-0245. FAX 201-816-3569. adv.; bk.rev.

333.33   US   ISSN 0034-0731
REAL ESTATE INVESTMENT PLANNING. 1966. base vol. (plus m. updates and Real Estate Planning Ideas). $264. Warren, Gorham & Lamont, Inc., 210 South Street, Boston, MA 02111. TEL 617-423-2020. FAX 617-423-2026. adv.; bk.rev. (looseleaf format)

333.33   US   ISSN 0034-0693
REAL ESTATE INVESTMENT PLANNING CHECKLIST AND FORMS. 1971. base vol. (plus q. updates). $264. Warren, Gorham & Lamont, Inc., 210 South Street, Boston, MA 02111. TEL 617-423-2020. FAX 617-423-2026. adv.; bk.rev. (looseleaf format)

333.33   US
REAL ESTATE INVESTMENT SITUATIONS. m. $195 (foreign $220). High Tech Publishing Company, Box 1923, Brattleboro, VT 05301. TEL 802-254-3539. ●Also available online. Vendor(s): Data-Star, NewsNet.
  Description: Analyzes emerging situations in the worldwide real estate markets having special investment potential.

333.33   US   ISSN 0146-0595
HD251
REAL ESTATE ISSUES. vol.2, 1976. s-a. $24 to individuals; university faculty and students $18. American Society of Real Estate Counselors, 430 N. Michigan Ave., Chicago, IL 60611. TEL 312-329-8427. FAX 312-329-8881. Ed. Rocky Tarantello. adv.; bk.rev.; index; circ. 1,600. (also avail. in microform from UMI) **Indexed:** ABI Inform.

333.33   JM
REAL ESTATE JAMAICA. 1985. bi-m. J.$30($2.10) per issue. Financial & Economic Resources Ltd., 12 Merrick Ave., Kingston 10, Jamaica, W.I. TEL 809-929-2993. FAX 809-968-1188. Ed. Marilyn DeLisser. adv.

333.33   AT   ISSN 0048-685X
REAL ESTATE JOURNAL (BRISBANE). 1963. m. Aus.$66. Real Estate Institute of Queensland, P.O. Box 688, Fortitude Valley, Brisbane, Qld. 4006, Australia. TEL 07-891-5711. FAX 07-891-5742. Ed. Diane Mangan. adv.; circ. 4,800.

333.33   AT   ISSN 0034-074X
REAL ESTATE JOURNAL (SYDNEY SOUTH). 1923. bi-m. Aus.$21. Real Estate Institute of New South Wales, P.O. Box A624, Sydney South, N.S.W. 2000, Australia. Ed. R. St.J. Baker. adv.; bk.rev.; illus.; tr.lit.; index; circ. 4,500. (tabloid format)
  —BLDSC shelfmark: 7303.280500.

333.33   US   ISSN 0748-3163
REAL ESTATE LEASING REPORT. 1984. m. $96. Federal Research Press, 155 Federal St., 13th fl., Boston, MA 02110.

333.33   US
REAL ESTATE NEWS. 1927. m. $30. Real Estate News Corp., 2600 W. Peterson Ave., Chicago, IL 60659. FAX 312-465-7218. Ed. Steven Polydoris. adv.; bk.rev.; circ. 9,500.
  Description: Magazine for real estate, building, financing and investment.

333.33   CN
REAL ESTATE NEWS. 1970. w. Can.$91. Toronto Real Estate Board, 1400 Don Mills Rd., Don Mills, Ont. M3B 3N1, Canada. TEL 416-443-8113. FAX 443-9185. Ed. Leslie Ironstone-Gordon. adv.; bk.rev.; charts; illus.; stat.; circ. 86,000.

333.33 352.7   CN
REAL ESTATE NEWS AND BUYERS GUIDE. 1977. w. free. Brabant Newspapers Ltd., P.O. Box 9208, 333 Arvin Ave., Stoney Creek, Ont., Canada. TEL 416-561-1090. FAX 416-664-3102. Ed. David Butler. adv.; circ. 60,660. (back issues avail.)

333.33   US
REAL ESTATE NEWSLETTER. (In 2 editions: Suburban and Manhattan and Outer Boroughs) 1969. w. $109 per ed. L L & I L Publishing, Inc., 1615 Northern Blvd., Manhasset, NY 11030. TEL 516-365-3650. Ed. Ivan Levine. adv.; tr.lit.; circ. 3,710. (reprint service avail.) **Indexed:** ABI Inform.

333.33   AT   ISSN 1033-3363
THE REAL ESTATE PRICE GUIDE. 1989. m. Aus.$275. H W W Pty. Ltd. (Horan Wall & Walker), 15-19 Prospect St., Surry Hills, N.S.W. 2010, Australia. TEL 02-331-6600. FAX 02-360-6357.

333.33   US   ISSN 0034-0774
REAL ESTATE RECORD AND BUILDER'S GUIDE. 1868. w. & q. $590. T R W R E D I Property Data, 475 Fifth Ave., Ste. 1901, New York, NY 10017. TEL 212-532-2705. Ed. Venice Kelly. circ. 1,300.

333.33   US   ISSN 0079-9890
HD251
REAL ESTATE REPORTS. 1966. irreg., no.36, 1982. price varies. University of Connecticut, Center for Real Estate & Urban Economic Studies, U-41 RE, Rm. 426, 368 Fairfield Rd., Storrs, CT 06269. TEL 203-486-3227. FAX 203-486-0349. Ed. Katherine A. Stadtmueller. circ. 500. (also avail. in microfiche; Braille)
  —BLDSC shelfmark: 7303.281000.

333   JA   ISSN 0532-7776
REAL ESTATE RESEARCH/FUDOSAN KENKYU. 1959. q. Japan Real Estate Institute - Nihon Fudosan Kenkyusho, Kangin-Fujiya Bldg., 1-3-2 Toranomon, Minato-ku, Tokyo, Japan.

333.33   US   ISSN 0034-0790
HD251
REAL ESTATE REVIEW. 1971. q. $88. Warren, Gorham and Lamont, One Penn Plaza, New York, NY 10119. TEL 800-950-1201. FAX 212-971-5240. Ed. Norman Weinberg. adv.; bk.rev. (also avail. in microform from UMI; reprint service avail. from RRI,UMI) **Indexed:** ABI Inform, B.P.I, Bank.Lit.Ind., BPIA, Bus.Ind., C.L.I., Curr.Cont., Leg.Per., Manage.Cont. P.A.I.S., RICS, Risk Abstr., SSCI, Tr.& Indus.Ind.
  —BLDSC shelfmark: 7303.281500.
  Description: Provides expert advice from the leaders of the real estate field who share the insights, opinions and techniques that have made significant changes in the industry.
  Refereed Serial

333.33   US
HD1382.5
REAL ESTATE SOURCEBOOK. 1982. a. $288. National Register Publishing Co., A Reed Reference Publishing Company, Division of Reed Publishing (USA) Inc., 121 Chanlon Rd., New Providence, NJ 07974. TEL 800-521-8110. FAX 908-665-6688. TELEX 138 755. (Subscr. to: R.R. Bowker, Order Dept., Box 31, New Providence, NJ 07974)
  Formerly: Directory of Real Estate Investors (ISSN 0277-9986)
  Description: International guide to major investors, developers, brokers, and financing opportunities.

REAL ESTATE 4157

333.33 US
REAL ESTATE SYNDICATION NEWS. w. $387. Crittenden Research, Inc., Box 1150, Novato, CA 94948. TEL 415-382-2400. Ed. John L. Ecklein.
Description: Reports on public and private real estate syndicators. Covers deal structures, contact names, broker and dealer reports, REITs, and MLPs.

333.33 US ISSN 0162-7538
REAL ESTATE TAX IDEAS. 1971. m. $98. Warren, Gorham and Lamont, One Penn Plaza, New York, NY 10119. TEL 800-950-1205. FAX 212-971-5240. Ed. Joel E. Miller. (looseleaf format; also avail. in microform from UMI) **Indexed:** Bus.Ind.
Description: Provides expert analysis of the current marketplace and regulatory agencies. Shows how to make use of the existing tax structure and achieve the most profitable tax treatment possible.

333.33 HK ISSN 1012-3253
REAL ESTATE TIMES/FANGDICHAN DAO BAO. (Text in Chinese) m. HK.$144. Economic Information & Agency, 342 Hennessy Road, 10th Fl., Hong Kong. TEL 5-738217 ext. 37. FAX 852-5-8388304. TELEX 60647 EICC HX.

333.33 US ISSN 0034-0804
HD251
REAL ESTATE TODAY. 1968. 10/yr. $25. National Association of Realtors (Chicago), 430 N. Michigan Ave., Chicago, IL 60611. TEL 312-329-8458. FAX 312-329-5978. adv.; bk.rev.; charts; illus.; index; circ. 775,855. (also avail. in microform from UMI; reprint service avail. from UMI) **Indexed:** B.P.I., Bus.Ind., Mag.Ind., Tr.& Indus.Ind.
Description: Serves as a forum of ideas, opinions, and practical applications in all areas of residential, commercial-investment, and brokerage-management real estate. Also covers association activities and interests.

333.33 US
REAL ESTATE U S A. 1988. bi-m. free to qualified personnel. Great Western Financial Corporation, 8484 Wilshire Blvd., Beverly Hills, CA 90211. Ed. Kevin Hawkins. bk.rev.; circ. 37,000.
Formerly: Great Western Real Estate Digest.
Description: Aimed at real estate professionals. Covers residential real estate issues, news, trends, statistics.

333.3 CN
REAL ESTATE VICTORIA. 1977. w. Can.$103. Circulation Department, 1609 Blanshard St., Victoria, B.C. V8V 2J5, Canada. TEL 604-382-9171. FAX 604-382-9172. Ed. Glenda Turner. adv.; circ. 20,000.

333.3 US
REAL ESTATE WEEK. s-m. Box 6119, Novato, CA 94948. TEL 415-382-2406. FAX 415-382-2416. Ed. Casey Elston. circ. 20,400.

333.33 US
REAL ESTATE WEEKLY. 1957. w. $49. Hagedorn Communications Corp., One Madison Ave., 35th Fl., New York, NY 10010. TEL 212-679-1234. Ed. Therese Fitzgerald. adv.; charts; illus.; tr.lit.; circ. 7,450.

333.33 658 US
REAL ESTATE WEST. (Including in each issue special supplement "California Real Estate") 1976. 6/yr. $36. Grier & Company, 825 E. Speer Blvd., Ste. 300, Denver, CO 80218-3719. TEL 303-744-6692. Ed.Bd. adv.; bk.rev.; circ. 14,500.

333.33 CN ISSN 0703-4687
REAL PROPERTY REPORTS. 1977. 12/yr. (in 6 vols.). Can.$108. Carswell Publications, Corporate Plaza, 2075 Kennedy Rd., Scarborough, Ont. M1T 3V4, Canada. TEL 416-609-8000. FAX 416-298-5094. Ed. Sirje Sellers. **Indexed:** C.L.I., Ind.Can.L.P.L., L.R.I.

333.33 US
REALIST FLYER. * m. National Association of Real Estate Brokers, 1629 K St. NW, Ste. 605, Washington, DC 20006. TEL 202-785-4477.

333.33 US ISSN 0279-6309
REALTOR NEWS. 1980. bi-w. $12. National Association of Realtors (Chicago), 430 N. Michigan Ave., Chicago, IL 60611. TEL 312-329-8449. Ed. Bill Adkinson. adv.; charts; stat.; circ. 116,545. (tabloid format; back issues avail.)
Description: Provides current news and information on the real estate industry.

333.33 US
REALTOR VOICE. 1920. w. $10 to non-members. Metropolitan Indianapolis Board of Realtors, 1912 N. Meridian St., Indianapolis, IN 46202. TEL 317-926-1912. FAX 317-921-3295. Eds. Stephen J. Sullivan, Becky Gianakos. adv.; circ. 4,000.
Formerly (until 1991): Metropolitan Indianapolis Realtor (ISSN 0887-1620)
Description: Community real estate magazine.

333.33 US ISSN 0888-5427
REALTORS LAND INSTITUTE. (Consists of: Journal Edition and News Edition, numbered consecutively) 1944. m. (exc. Jul.-Aug.). $30 to non-members. Realtors Land Institute, 430 N. Michigan Ave., Chicago, IL 60611. TEL 312-329-8446. FAX 312-329-8633. adv.; circ. 2,500.
Formerly: Farm and Land Realtor.
Description: Focuses on land sales, brokerage management, and land development.

333.33 US
REALTY. 1950. fortn. $15. Leader Observer, Inc., 80-34 Jamaica Ave., Woodhaven, NY 11421. TEL 718-296-2233. Ed. Lester A. Sobel. adv.; bk.rev.; illus.; circ. 8,000. (tabloid format)
Formerly: Realty and Chain Store Renting Leads (ISSN 0034-1053)

333.33 IT
REALTY; le piu belle case da ammirare e da acquistare. (Text in Italian, English, French, German, Spanish) 1989. s-a. L.50000 (foreign L.80000). F C Editore S.r.l., Via Vivaio, 24, 20122 Milan, Italy. TEL 02-76009001. FAX 02-781346. Ed. Fabrizio Capsoni. adv.; circ. 30,000.
Description: Depicts real estate, art, and antiques for sale in Europe.

333.33 US ISSN 0034-1045
HG1
REALTY AND BUILDING. 1888. w. $35. Realty and Building, Inc., 311 W. Superior St., Ste. 316, Chicago, IL 60610. TEL 312-944-1204. FAX 312-944-1824. Ed. John C. Sutler. adv.; bk.rev.; illus.; circ. 9,000.
Description: Covers real estate ownership finance, construction, sale, and management, primarily in the greater Chicago metropolitan area.

333 US ISSN 0090-399X
HD253
REALTY BLUEBOOK. (In 2 vols.: Vol.1 Real Estate; Vol.2 Financing Tables) 1966. a. $25 (prices typically set. in Jan.). Professional Publishing Corp., 122 Paul Dr., San Rafael, CA 94903. TEL 415-472-1964, 415-472-1964. FAX 415-472-2069. Ed. R.W. de Heer. circ. 100,000.
Description: Covers real estate and amortization. including sales techniques, financing, checklists, contract clauses and tax information.

RECHTSPFLEGER - STUDIENHEFTE. see LAW

333.33 US
REGISTRY REVIEW. 1978. w. $139. Real Data Corporation, 36 Bay St., Box 240, Manchester, NH 03105. TEL 603-669-3822. FAX 603-645-0072. Ed. Irvin Tolles. adv.; index. (tabloid format)
Description: Real estate and credit information for New Hampshire.

THE RELOCATION REPORT. see BUSINESS AND ECONOMICS — Personnel Management

333.33 CN
RENOVER. 1988. 4/yr. Can.$3.95 per no. Publicor Inc., 7 Chemin Bates, Outremont, Que. H2V 1A6, Canada. TEL 514-270-1100. FAX 514-270-6900. Ed. Boris Brumat. adv.; circ. 24,563.

333.33 352.7 UK ISSN 0263-7499
RENT REVIEW AND LEASE RENEWAL. 1980. q. £75. Henry Stewart Publications, 2-3 Cornwall Terrace, Regent's Park, London NW1 4QP, England. TEL 01-935-2382. FAX 01-486-7083. Ed. Brenda Rouse. adv.; bk.rev.
—BLDSC shelfmark: 7364.255200.
Formerly (until 1982): Rent Review (ISSN 0260-907X)

333.33 CN
RENTERS NEWS. w. 1575 Trinity Dr., Unit no.1, Mississauga, Ont. L5T 1K4, Canada. TEL 416-564-1646. FAX 416-564-3287.

333.33 US ISSN 0731-7999
HD251
RESEARCH IN REAL ESTATE. 1981. a. $63.50 to institutions. J A I Press Inc., 55 Old Post Rd., No. 2, Box 1678, Greenwich, CT 06836-1678. TEL 203-661-7602. Ed. C.F. Sirmans.

333.3 US
RESOLUTION TRUST REPORTER. 26/yr. Dorset Group, Inc., 212 W. 35th St., New York, NY 10001. TEL 212-563-4405. FAX 212-563-8879. Ed. Mark Fogarty.

333.3 US
RESORT DEVELOPMENT & OPERATION. 10/yr. C H B Company, Inc., Box 5627, Bellingham, WA 98227-5627. TEL 206-676-4146. Ed. Carl Burlingame. adv.; circ. 4,000.

333.33 301.435 US
▼**RETIREMENT COMMUNITY BUSINESS.** 1992. q. Great River Publishing, Inc., 2600 Poplar, Ste. 519, Memphis, TN 38112. TEL 901-324-1009. Ed. Sherry Campbell. adv.: B&W page $1640; trim 8 1/2 x 11. circ. 8,000.
Description: Provides news of management decisions, marketing tactics, legal concerns, product news and profiles of executives, construction and development.

RETIREMENT HOUSING REPORT. see GERONTOLOGY AND GERIATRICS

333.33 US
RETIREMENT REAL ESTATE REPORT. q. Health & Wealth Guardian, Ltd., 462 S. Gilbert Rd., Mesa, AZ 85204. TEL 602-829-8888. FAX 602-835-5741.

333.33 FR ISSN 0048-7953
REVUE DE L'HABITAT FRANCAIS. 1959. m. 156 F. Societe Parisienne d'Editions et de Publications Immobilieres, 274 bd. Saint-Germain, 75007 Paris, France. Ed. Jean Leveque. adv.; stat.; circ. 24,630.

REVUE DES LOYERS ET DES FERMAGES. see HOUSING AND URBAN PLANNING

RHODE ISLAND LAWYERS WEEKLY. see LAW

333.33 US
RHODES REAL ESTATE REVIEW. 1989. 8/yr. $56. 30 Broadway, Hawthorne, NY 10532. TEL 800-253-1005. Ed. Chris Maffucci. circ. 3,500.
Description: Covers zoning and planning law, environmental law, and real property law.

333.33 US ISSN 0035-5275
LAW
RIGHT OF WAY; the magazine for the right of way professional. 1954. bi-m. $16. International Right of Way Association, 13650 S. Gramercy Place, Gardena, CA 90249-2465. TEL 213-538-0233. FAX 213-538-1471. adv.; bk.rev.; charts; illus.; cum.index: 1954-1984; circ. 9,500. **Indexed:** Energy Info.Abstr., Environ.Abstr.
Description: Technical articles covering subjects of interest to right of way professionals in acquisition management of real estate for the public sector.

ROCKY MOUNTAIN MINERAL LAW INSTITUTE. PROCEEDINGS. see MINES AND MINING INDUSTRY

333.33 US
ROULAC'S STRATEGIC REAL ESTATE. m. $297. (Roulac Real Estate Consulting Group) Deloitte, Haskins & Sells, 50 Fremont St., 27th Fl., San Francisco, CA 94105. TEL 415-433-0300. Ed. Terry Humo.
Formerly: Questor Strategic Real Estate Letter.

REAL ESTATE

333.33 US
RURAL PROPERTY BULLETIN; national marketplace for rural property. 1981. m. $12. Rural Property Bulletin, Box 510, Escalante, UT 84726. TEL 801-826-4908. Ed. Bruce A. Weaver. adv.; circ. 16,000. (tabloid format)
Description: Lists all types of rural real estate and businesses for sale throughout the US.

333.33 US
S F (WOBURN). (Square Foot) 1987. m. $38. Mass High Tech, 500 W. Cummings Park, Ste.3500, Woburn, MA 01801-6514. TEL 617-935-1100. Ed. John Heymann. circ. 7,000.

333.33 352.7 US ISSN 0741-3432
SAN ANTONIO LIVING. 1978. bi-m. free. Lash Publications, Inc. (San Antonio), 12451 Starcrest, San Antonio, TX 78216-2957. TEL 512-545-4663. Ed. Gerry Brawner. adv.; bk.rev.; circ. 40,000 (controlled). (back issues avail.)

SAN JOSE POST-RECORD; daily legal, & commercial real estate & financial news. see *LAW*

333.33 SZ
SCHWEIZERISCHE HAUSEIGENTUEMER. bi-w. Schweizerischer Hauseigentuemerverband, Muehlebachstr. 70, CH-8008 Zurich, Switzerland.

333.33 SZ
SCHWEIZERISCHER BURGENVEREIN. (Text in German) vol.45, 1972. bi-m. Association Suisse Chateaux et Ruines, Balderngasse 9, CH-8039 Zurich, Switzerland. charts; illus.

333.33 US
SEA SHELTERS.* 1982. m. Coastland Times, P.O. Drawer 400, Manteo, NC 27954. TEL 919-473-2105. Ed. Darel LaPrade. adv.; circ. 20,000.

SEALES CAYMAN LETTER; an investment, economic and real estate review of the tax-free Cayman Islands. see *BUSINESS AND ECONOMICS — Investments*

333.33 US
SECOND HOME.* 1986. m. $24. Second Home Publications Inc., c/o Muhlfeld-Wolff, Inc., 111 Fifth Ave., New York, NY 10003. Dir. Martin J. Wolff. circ. 100,000.

SECONDARY MORTGAGE MARKET GUIDE. see *BUSINESS AND ECONOMICS — Banking And Finance*

SECONDARY MORTGAGE MARKETS. see *BUSINESS AND ECONOMICS — Banking And Finance*

333.33 FR
SEMAINE IMMOBILIERE. (Bi-m. supplement avail.) 1962. w. 10 F. per no. Editions Indicateur Bertrand, 43 bd. Barbes, 75018 Paris, France. TEL 1-49-25-26-27. FAX 1-49-25-26-00. adv.: B&W page 11000 F.; trim 320 x 210; adv. contact: Michel Joubert. bk.rev.; circ. 40,000. (looseleaf format)
Former titles: Locations and Ventes (ISSN 0024-5666); Locations.
Description: Advertisements for the sale and renting of houses and apartments in Paris and its suburbs.

333.33 US ISSN 0049-0393
SHOPPING CENTER WORLD. 1972. m. (plus a. Directory). $60 (foreign $130). Communication Channels, Inc., 6255 Barfield Rd., Atlanta, GA 30328-4369. TEL 404-256-9800. FAX 404-256-3116. TELEX 4611075 COMCHANI. Ed. Teresa DeFranks. adv.; charts; illus.; tr.lit.; circ. 37,000. (also avail. in microform from UMI; reprint service avail. from UMI)
Incorporates (1975-1991): Shopping Center World Product and Service Directory.
Description: Serves the fields of building, development, construction, design, financing, leasing, management and promotion of shopping centers, chain stores, and the related product and service industries.

SOUTH AFRICAN HOME OWNER. see *ARCHITECTURE*

333.33 352.7 US
HD266.F6
SOUTH FLORIDA HOME BUYER'S GUIDE. 1981. bi-m. free. Home Buyer's Guide (Deerfield Beach), (Subsidiary of: Real Estate Magazines, Inc.), 2151 W. Hillsboro Blvd., Ste. 300, Deerfield Beach, FL 33442. TEL 305-428-5602. Ed. Diana Tafel. adv.; bk.rev.; circ. 70,000 (controlled). (back issues avail.)
Formerly: South Florida Living (North Edition) (ISSN 0741-3440)

333.33 US ISSN 0192-1630
SOUTHEAST REAL ESTATE NEWS. 1972. m. $38 (foreign $108). Communication Channels, Inc., 6255 Barfield Rd., Atlanta, GA 30328-4369. TEL 404-256-9800. FAX 404-256-3116. TELEX 4611075 COMCHANI. Ed. Coles P. McKagen. adv.; illus.; circ. 19,000. (tabloid format; also avail. in microform from UMI; reprint service avail. from UMI)
●Also available online.
Description: Covers commercial and industrial real estate activity in Alabama, Florida, Georgia, Kentucky, Maryland, Mississippi, North Carolina, South Carolina, Tennessee, Virginia, West Virginia, and Washington, D.C.

333.3 US
SOUTHERN CALIFORNIA PROPERTY GUIDE. m. R & B Publishing (Santa Monica), 1337 Ocean Ave., Santa Monica, CA 90401-1027. TEL 213-458-6506. Ed. Jean Dergiman.

333.33 US
▼**SOUTHERN COMMERCIAL REAL ESTATE REVIEW AND FORECAST**. 1992. a. First Publishing Inc., 2100 Riverchase Ctr., Ste. 110, Birmingham, AL 35244. TEL 205-733-1970. FAX 205-733-1974.
Description: Tracks and reports commercial real estate activities and trends.

333.33 US ISSN 0192-9194
SOUTHWEST REAL ESTATE NEWS. 1973. bi-m. $38 (foreign $108). Communication Channels, Inc., 6255 Barfield Rd., Atlanta, GA 30328-4369. TEL 404-256-9800. FAX 404-256-3116. TELEX 4611075 COMCHANI. (And: 18601 LBJ, Ste. 240, Mesquite (Dallas), TX 75150. TEL 214-270-6651) Ed. Jim Mitchell. adv.; illus.; circ. 13,000. (tabloid format; also avail. in microform from UMI; reprint service avail. from UMI)
●Also available online.
Formerly: Texas Real Estate News.
Description: Serves the field of commercial real estate in a nine-state geographic area, including Arizona, Arkansas, Colorado, Louisiana, New Mexico, Oklahoma, California, Nevada and Texas. All aspects of commercial real estate markets are covered.

333.33 US ISSN 0039-2545
STROUT WORLD.* 1960. m. free. Strout Realty, Inc., 2951 S. Campbell Ave., Apt.A, Springfield, MO 65807-3632. Ed. Ralph Bannigan. bk.rev.; circ. 1,200 (controlled). (tabloid format)

STRUCTURING FOREIGN INVESTMENT IN U.S. REAL ESTATE. see *LAW*

333.33 690 UK
STUDIES IN CONSTRUCTION ECONOMY. 1978. irreg., no.3, 1981. price varies. College of Estate Management, Whiteknights, Reading RG6 2AW, England.

SUPERINTENDENT OF INSURANCE ANNUAL REPORT. see *INSURANCE*

333.33 UK ISSN 0952-5793
SURVEYING TECHNICIAN. (Supplement avail.) 1970. bi-m. £15. Society of Surveying Technicians, Drayton House, 30 Gordon St., London WC1H 0BH, England. TEL 071-388-8008. FAX 071-383-7554. Ed. Tony Davey. adv.; bk.rev.; circ. 4,500. **Indexed:** RICS.
—BLDSC shelfmark: 8552.600000.

333.33 AT ISSN 1035-4670
▼**SYDNEY RESIDENTIAL AUCTION MARKET REPORT**. 1990. m. Aus.$550 per issue. H W W Pty. Ltd. (Horan Wall & Walker), 15-19 Prospect St., Surry Hills, N.S.W. 2010, Australia. TEL 02-331-6600. FAX 02-360-6357.

333.33 AT
▼**SYDNEY RESIDENTIAL AUCTION MARKET STUDY**. 1990. a. Aus.$3000. H W W Pty. Ltd. (Horan Wall & Walker), 15-19 Prospect St., Surry Hills, N.S.W. 2010, Australia. TEL 02-331-6600. FAX 02-360-6357.
Formerly: Sydney Residential Auction Market Survey (ISSN 1034-7046)

T V CLOSE UP. see *COMMUNICATIONS — Television And Cable*

333.33 US
TAX MANAGEMENT REAL ESTATE. (Subseries of: Tax Management Real Estate Series) 1984. m. $683 includes Tax Management Real Estate Journal. Tax Management, Inc. (Subsidiary of: The Bureau of National Affairs, Inc.), 1231 25th St., N.W., Washington, DC 20037. TEL 202-452-4556. FAX 202-452-4096. TELEX 285656 BNAI WSH. (Subscr. to: 9435 Key West Ave., Rockville, MD 20850. TEL 800-372-1033) Ed. Glenn Davis.
●Also available online. Vendor(s): WESTLAW (File TM-RE, TM-RE-OLD, TM-REJ).
Description: Real estate tax reference service consisting of a series of portfolios written by tax practitioners, with a monthly journal covering new developments in the field.

333.33 US ISSN 8755-0628
KF6535.A15
TAX MANAGEMENT REAL ESTATE JOURNAL. (Subseries of: Tax Management Real Estate Series) 1984. m. $299. Tax Management, Inc. (Subsidiary of: The Bureau of National Affairs, Inc.), 1231 25th St., N.W., Washington, DC 20037. TEL 202-452-4200. FAX 202-822-8092. TELEX 285656 BNAI WSH. (Subscr. to: 9435 Key West Ave., Rockville, MD 20850. TEL 800372-1033) Ed. Glenn Davis. index. (back issues avail.) **Indexed:** Account.Ind. (1984-), C.L.I.
●Also available online. Vendor(s): WESTLAW (File TM-REJ).
Description: Covers judicial, legislative, and administrative developments in the real estate area.

333.33 US ISSN 0274-9491
TENNESSEE REALTOR. 1970. q. $5. Tennessee Association of Realtors, Box 121980, Nashville, TN 37212-1980. FAX 615-320-0452. Ed. Stephen Harding. adv.; circ. 14,300.

TEXAS REAL ESTATE LAW REPORTER. see *LAW*

333.33 US
TEXAS REALTOR. 1948. 11/yr. $15. Texas Association of Realtors, Box 2246, Austin, TX 78768-2246. TEL 512-480-8200. FAX 512-370-2390. Ed. Meri Houtchens-Kitchens. adv.; circ. 44,767.

333.33 CN
THUNDER BAY REAL ESTATE NEWS. 1983. w. Can.$100($60) North Superior Publishing Inc., 1145 Barton St., Thunder Bay, Ont. P7B 5N3, Canada. TEL 807-623-2348. FAX 807-623-7515. Ed. Scott A. Sumner. circ. 31,000. (tabloid format; back issues avail.)

TIMESHARING LAW REPORTER. see *LAW*

TORRENS SYSTEM IN N.S.W.. see *LAW*

TRESPASS TO TRY TITLE. see *LAW*

333.33 US
TRI-STATE REAL ESTATE JOURNAL. 1984. w. $84. Lionmark Publications, Inc., 236 W. Route 38, Box 1008, Moorestown, NJ 08057-0908. TEL 609-866-1300. FAX 609-866-1912. Ed. Richard T. Kantor. adv.; circ. 7,000 (controlled). (tabloid format)
Description: Devoted to commercial, industrial and residential real estate in New Jersey, Pennsylvania, and Delaware.

333.33 CN ISSN 0835-6386
U - CHOOSE: A GUIDE TO HOMES FOR SENIORS IN CANADA (EASTERN - ATLANTIC PROVINCE EDITION). biennial. Moving Publications Ltd., 44 Upjohn Rd., Don Mills, Ont. M3B 2W1, Canada. TEL 416-441-1168. FAX 416-441-1641.

REAL ESTATE — ABSTRACTING, BIBLIOGRAPHIES, STATISTICS

333.33   CN   ISSN 0835-6378
U - CHOOSE: A GUIDE TO HOMES FOR SENIORS IN CANADA (ONTARIO EDITION). biennial. Can.$12.95. Moving Publications Ltd., 44 Upjohn Rd., Don Mills, Ont. M3B 2W1, Canada. TEL 416-441-1168. FAX 416-441-1641.

333.33   CN   ISSN 0835-6394
U - CHOOSE: A GUIDE TO HOMES FOR SENIORS IN CANADA (WESTERN EDITION). biennial. Can.$12.95. Moving Publications Ltd., 44 Upjohn Rd., Don Mills, Ont. M3B 2W1, Canada. TEL 416-441-1168. FAX 416-441-1646.

333.33 659.1   US
U S REAL ESTATE REGISTER. 1967. a. $49. Barry Inc., Box 551, Wilmington, MA 01887. TEL 508-658-0441. FAX 508-657-8691. adv.; circ. 11,000.
    Formerly: Industrial-Commercial Real Estate Managers' Directory.

333.33   SI
UNIBEAM. a. Building and Estate Management Society, c/o Faculty of Architecture and Building, National University of Singapore, Kent Ridge, Singapore 0511, Singapore. TEL 7756666.

333.33   BE
UNION DES PROFESSIONS IMMOBILIERES DE BELGIQUE. BULLETIN MENSUEL - MAANDBLAD. m. Union des Professions Immobilieres de Belgique, Ave. Albert I 29, B-1060 Brussels, Belgium. TEL 3445768.

333.33   US
UNIQUE HOMES;* the national magazine of luxury real estate. 1973. 8/yr. $24.97. Unique Homes, Inc., 801 Second Ave., No. 11, New York, NY 10017-4706. TEL 212-599-3377. Ed. Rick Goodwin. adv.; circ. 70,746. (back issues avail.)

U.S. FEDERAL HOME LOAN BANK BOARD. REPORT. see *BUSINESS AND ECONOMICS — Banking And Finance*

U.S. FEDERAL HOME LOAN BANK BOARD. TRENDS IN THE SAVINGS AND LOAN FIELD. see *BUSINESS AND ECONOMICS — Banking And Finance*

333.33   US
UNITEDLAND. 1946. m. free. United National Real Estate, Inc., 4700 Belleview, Kansas City, MO 64112. TEL 816-753-4212. Ed. Jack R. Waln. circ. 1,500.
    Formerly: United Way.

333.33   US   ISSN 0068-5968
UNIVERSITY OF CALIFORNIA, BERKELEY. CENTER FOR REAL ESTATE AND URBAN ECONOMICS. REPRINT SERIES. 1948. irreg., latest no.68. price varies. University of California, Berkeley, Center for Real Estate and Urban Economics, 156 Barrows Hall, Berkeley, CA 94720.

333.3   US
UNIVERSITY OF CALIFORNIA, BERKELEY. CENTER FOR REAL ESTATE AND URBAN ECONOMICS. WORKING PAPER. 1950. irreg., no.169, 1988. price varies. University of California, Berkeley, Center for Real Estate and Urban Economics, 156 Barrows Hall, Berkeley, CA 94720.
    Formerly: University of California, Berkeley. Center for Real Estate and Urban Economics. Research Report (ISSN 0068-5976)

333.33   US
UNIVERSITY OF CONNECTICUT. CENTER FOR REAL ESTATE AND URBAN ECONOMIC STUDIES. ANNUAL REPORT. 1965. a. University of Connecticut, Center for Real Estate and Urban Economic Studies, U-41 RE, Rm. 426, 368 Fairfield Rd., Storrs, CT 06269. TEL 203-486-3227. FAX 203-486-0349.

333.33   US   ISSN 0069-9047
HD251
UNIVERSITY OF CONNECTICUT. CENTER FOR REAL ESTATE AND URBAN ECONOMIC STUDIES. GENERAL SERIES. 1968. irreg., no.18, 1985. price varies. University of Connecticut, Center for Real Estate and Urban Economic Studies, U-41 RE, Rm. 426, 368 Fairfield Rd., Storrs, CT 06269. TEL 203-486-3227. FAX 203-486-0349. Ed. Katherine A. Stadtmueller. circ. 300.

URBAN LAND INSTITUTE PROJECT REFERENCE FILE. see *HOUSING AND URBAN PLANNING*

333.33 368   US   ISSN 0042-238X
VALUATION MAGAZINE. 1942. s-a. $8. American Society of Appraisers, Box 17265, Washington, DC 20041. TEL 703-478-2228. Ed. Shirley Belz. bk.rev.; charts; circ. 6,500. **Indexed:** Account.Ind. (1974-), BPIA, Bus.Ind.

333.332   UK   ISSN 0042-2428
VALUER. 1927. 10/yr. £30. Incorporated Society of Valuers & Auctioneers, Three Cadogan Gate, London SW1X OAS, England. TEL 071-235-2282. FAX 071-235-4390. Ed. Margaret Powley-Baker. adv.; bk.rev.; charts; illus.; index; circ. 9,000. **Indexed:** RICS.
    Incorporates: Land and Property-Auctions.

333.332   AT
VALUER AND LAND ECONOMIST. 1930. q. Aus.$50. Australian Institute of Valuers and Land Economists, 6 Campion St., Deakin, A.C.T. 2600, Australia. TEL 06-2822411. FAX 06-28521944. Ed. Yvonne Watkinson. adv.; bk.rev.; charts; cum.index every 2 yrs.; circ. 7,000. **Indexed:** Aus.P.A.I.S., Aus.Rd.Ind., RICS.
    Formerly: Valuer (ISSN 0042-241X)

333.33 340   GW
VERBRAUCHER UND RECHT. 1986. bi-m. DM.98. Werner-Verlag GmbH, Karl-Rudolf-Str. 172, Postfach 105354, 4000 Duesseldorf 1, Germany. TEL 0211-38798-0. FAX 0211-383104.

333.33 659.1   US
VERMONT REAL ESTATE GUIDE. 1971. m. $20. Real Estate Guide, 89 N. Main St., Box 999, Andover, MA 01810. TEL 508-475-8732. FAX 508-475-6132. Ed. Robert A. Finlayson. adv.; circ. 15,000.

333.33   AT
VICTORIAN REAL ESTATE JOURNAL. 1938. q. Aus.$20. Real Estate Institute of Victoria Ltd., P.O. Box 443, Camberwell, Vic. 3124, Australia. TEL 03-882-9188. FAX 03-882-8112. Ed. Graham Stanley. adv.; bk.rev.; abstr.; stat.; index, cum.index; circ. 2,500 (controlled). **Indexed:** RICS.
    Formerly: Real Estate and Stock Journal (ISSN 0034-0669)

VIRGINIA CONDOMINIUM LAW. see *LAW*

VIRGINIA RESIDENTIAL LANDLORD AND TENANT LAW. see *LAW*

333.33   GW   ISSN 0179-7948
W I - WOHNUNGSWIRTSCHAFTLICHE INFORMATIONEN. 1949. w. DM.120. Gesamtverband der Wohnungswirtschaft e.V., Bismarkstr. 7, 5000 Cologne 1, Germany. TEL 0221-57989-0. FAX 0221-5798999. bk.rev.; circ. 4,000.

333.33   US
WASHINGTON REAL ESTATE NEWS. 1953. q. free. Department of Licensing, Real Estate Division, Box 9015, Olympia, WA 98504. TEL 206-586-4602. Ed. Lynnel P. McKnight. bibl.; illus.; circ. 60,000 (controlled).

333.33 690   SA
WEEKEND PROPERTY HOME FINDER. 1974. w. free. Devonshire Pl., P.O. Box 950, Durban 4000, South Africa. FAX 305-7568. Ed. Colin Vineall. adv.; bk.rev.; circ. 63,000.

333.33   US
WELCOME HOMEOWNER. 1987. q. $12. Welcome Homeowner, Inc., 12444 Victory Blvd., Ste. 316, N. Hollywood, CA 91606. TEL 818-508-1202. Ed. Ellen Tuck Meli. adv.; circ. 200,000.
    Description: Publication for all new homeowners in Southern California within two weeks of escrow closing.

333.33   US
WESTCHESTER - CONNECTICUT OFFICE BUILDINGS. a. $49. Yale Robbins, Inc., 31 E. 28th St., New York, NY 10016. TEL 212-683-5700. Ed. Yale Robbins. adv.
    Formed by the merger of: Westchester Office Buildings & Connecticut Office Buildings.
    Description: Annual review of Westchester County and Connecticut office buildings.

333.33   US   ISSN 0043-339X
WESTCHESTER REALTOR. 1926. m. $10. Westchester County Board of Realtors, Inc., 59 S. Broadway, White Plains, NY 10601. TEL 914-681-0833. FAX 914-681-6044. Ed. Glenn J. Kalinoski. adv.; bk.rev.; charts; illus.; circ. 4,500.

333.33   GW
WESTDEUTSCHER TUERMER. m. Haus-, Wohungs- und Grundeigentuermerverband Ruhr e.V., Huyssenallee 50, D-4300 Essen, Germany.

333.33   US   ISSN 0043-4124
WESTERN REAL ESTATE NEWS. 1964. s-m. $80. (Business Extension Bureau) B E B Publications, 500 S. Airport Blvd., S. San Francisco, CA 94080. TEL 415-737-5700. FAX 415-737-9080. Ed. Leila K. Moavero. adv.; bk.rev.; charts; illus.; circ. 12,500. (also avail. in microform from UMI; reprint service avail.)

333.33   US   ISSN 0511-8719
WHERE TO RETIRE ON A SMALL INCOME. biennial. $4.95. Harian Publications, One Vernon Ave., Floral Park, NY 11001. TEL 516-437-3440. Ed. Norman D. Ford. charts; illus.

333.33   CN
WINNIPEG INDUSTRIAL - COMMERCIAL REAL ESTATE GUIDE. s-m. Harvard Publishing Co., 315 Queenston St., 2nd Fl., Winnipeg, Man. R3N 0W9, Canada. TEL 204-488-6419. FAX 204-489-2602. Ed. Guy Rochon. circ. 15,000.

333.3   US
WISCONSIN COUNTY LANDS.* 1967. 10/yr. $25. Box 311, Lake Delton, WI 53940-0311. Ed. Sheila R. Whaley. adv.; illus.; circ. 2,000.

333.33   SZ
WOHNEIGENTUM. bi-w. Schweizerische Zentralstelle fuer Eigenheim- und Wohnbaufoerderung, Stampfenbachstr. 73, CH-8035 Zurich, Switzerland. TEL 01-3632240.

DER WOHNUNGSEIGENTUEMER. see *BUILDING AND CONSTRUCTION*

333.33   US
YANKEE HOMES.* 1985. 12/yr. $25. Yankee Publishing, Inc., Box 520, Dublin, NH 03444-0520. TEL 603-563-8111. Ed. Jim Collins. circ. 35,000. (back issues avail.)

333.33   GW   ISSN 0340-7497
ZEITSCHRIFT FUER MIET- UND RAUMRECHT. 1948. m. DM.228. Werner-Verlag GmbH, Karl-Rudolf-Str. 172, Postfach 105354, 4000 Duesseldorf 1, Germany. TEL 0211-38798-0. FAX 0211-383104. Eds. Dr. Groothold, Helga Lehmann.
—BLDSC shelfmark: 9472.500000.

333.33   CC
ZHONGGUO FANGDI XINXI/CHINA REAL ESTATE NEWS. (Text in Chinese) m. Zhongguo Fangdi Chanye Xiehui - China Real Estate Society, A-3 Congshanli, Xidan, Beijing 100031, People's Republic of China. TEL 6013301. Ed. Han Lidong.

333.33   CC
ZHONGGUO FANGDICHAN/CHINESE REAL ESTATE. (Text in Chinese) m. Tianjin-shi Fangdichan Guanli-ju - Tianjin Municipal Administration of Real Estate, 50 Munan Dao, Heping Qu, Tianjin 300050, People's Republic of China. TEL 399464. Ed. Kang Tianjin.

ZONING NEWS. see *HOUSING AND URBAN PLANNING*

REAL ESTATE — Abstracting, Bibliographies, Statistics

333.33   AT
BONDI JUNCTION CITYSCOPE. 1988. 3/yr. Aus.$665 (renewals Aus.$505). Cityscope Publications Pty. Ltd., P.O. Box 807, Manly, N.S.W. 2095, Australia. TEL 02-976-2233. FAX 02-976-2263. Ed. Neil Speirs. adv.; maps. (looseleaf format)
    Description: Contains complete property index of all buildings within the Bondi Junction - Double Bay business districts in eastern Sydney. Includes descriptions, historical information, developments, ownership, prices, sales histories, exact boundaries, and more.

REAL ESTATE — ABSTRACTING, BIBLIOGRAPHIES, STATISTICS

333.33   AT
BRISBANE CITYSCOPE. 1986. 3/yr. Aus.$825 (renewals Aus.$665). Cityscope Publications Pty. Ltd., P.O. Box 807, Manly, N.S.W. 2095, Australia. TEL 02-976-2233. FAX 02-976-2263. Ed. Neil Speirs. adv.; maps; circ. 170. (looseleaf format)
●Also available online.
Description: Contains complete property index of all buildings within the Brisbane Central Business District. Includes descriptions, historical information developments, ownership, prices, sales histories, exact boundaries, and more.

BUILDING, CONSTRUCTION AND REAL ESTATE SECTORS. SURVEY. see *BUILDING AND CONSTRUCTION — Abstracting, Bibliographies, Statistics*

333.33   AT
BURKE ROAD CITYSCOPE. 1988. 3/yr. Aus.$635 1st yr., renewals Aus.$475. Cityscope Publications Pty. Ltd., P.O. Box 807, Manly, N.S.W. 2095, Australia. TEL 02-976-2233. FAX 02-976-2263. Ed. Neil Speirs. maps.
Description: Contains complete property index of all buildings within the Camberwell Juction District Centre in eastern Melbourne. Includes descriptions, historical information, developments, ownership, tenancies, prices, sales history, exact boundaries, and more.

333.33   AT
▼**CANBERRA CITYSCOPE.** 1991. 3/yr. Aus.$795 (renewals Aus.$635). Cityscope Publications Pty. Ltd., P.O. Box 807, Manly, N.S.W. 2095, Australia. TEL 02-976-223. FAX 02-976-2263. Ed. Neil Speirs. adv.; maps. (looseleaf format)
Description: Contains a complete property index of all buildings within the Canberra City Centre, plus the outlying Town Centre districts of Woden, Belconnen and Tuggeranong. Includes descriptions, historical information, developments, ownership, prices, sales histories, exact boundaries, and more.

333.33   AT
CHATSWOOD CITYSCOPE. 1987. 3/yr. Aus.$705 (renewals Aus.$545). Cityscope Publications Pty. Ltd., P.O. Box 807, Manly, N.S.W. 2095, Australia. TEL 02-976-2233. FAX 02-976-2263. Ed. Neil Speirs. adv.; maps; circ. 147. (looseleaf format)
Description: Contains complete property index of all commercial buildings within the Chatswood Central Business District and the Willoughby municipality in northern Sydney. Includes descriptions, historical information, developments, ownership, prices, sales histories, exact boundaries and more.

333.33   AT
GOLD COAST CITYSCOPE. 1989. 3/yr. Aus.$790 (renewals Aus.$630). Cityscope Publications Pty. Ltd., P.O. Box 807, Manly, N.S.W. 2095, Australia. TEL 02-976-2233. FAX 02-976-2263. Ed. Neil Speirs. adv.; maps. (looseleaf format)
Description: Contains a complete property index of the commercial centers of the Gold Coast towns in South Queensland. Includes descriptions, historical information, developments, ownership, prices, sales histories, exact boundaries, and more.

333.33   AT   ISSN 0816-6153
HOME LOAN AFFORDABILITY IN AUSTRALIA. 1985. q. Aus.$20. Real Estate Institute of Australia, P.O. Box 234, Curtin, A.C.T. 2605, Australia. TEL 06-282-4277. FAX 06-285-2444. Ed. Phillip Malone. circ. 2,000.
Description: Examines ratio between average monthly home loan repayments and median family income.

333.33   MH
MACAO. DIRECCAO DOS SERVICOS DE ESTATISTICA E CENSOS. INDICADORES ESTATISTICOS - OPERACOES SOBRE IMOVEIS E SOCIEDADES/MACAO. CENSUS AND STATISTICS DEPARTMENT. STATISTICAL DATA - TRANSACTIONS CONCERNING REAL ESTATE AND COMPANIES. (Text in Chinese, Portuguese) 1986. q. free. Direccao dos Servicos de Estatistica e Censos, Rua Inacio Baptista, No.4D-6, P.O. Box 3022, Macao. TEL 550935. FAX 561884.

333.33 310   MH
MACAO. DIRECCAO DOS SERVICOS DE ESTATISTICA E CENSOS. RELATORIO ANUAL DA CONSTRUCAO CIVIL/MACAO. CENSUS AND STATISTICS DEPARTMENT. CIVIL CONSTRUCTION IN MACAO (ANNUAL REPORT). (Text in Chinese, Portuguese) 1984. a. free. Direccao dos Servicos de Estatistica e Censos, Rua Inacio Baptista, No.4D-6, P.O. Box 3022, Macao. TEL 550935. FAX 561884.
Description: Provides a convenient source of information for those engaged in analyzing the housing market, including information on the structure and operating characteristics of all buildings.

333.33   AT   ISSN 0818-1152
MARKET FACTS. 1973. m. Aus.$195 (includes Annual Review of Major Residential Property Markets in Australia). Real Estate Institute of Australia, P.O. Box 234, Curtin, A.C.T. 2605, Australia. TEL 06-282-4277. FAX 06-285-2444. Ed. Julian Roberston. circ. 1,000. (back issues avail.)
Incorporates: Market Facts (Brisbane) (ISSN 0811-3564); Market Facts (Adelaide) (ISSN 0811-3513); Market Facts (Melbourne) (ISSN 0811-3556); Market Facts (Perth) (ISSN 0811-353X); Markets Facts (Hobart-Launceston). Market Facts (Canberra) (ISSN 0811-3521); Market Facts (Newcastle) (0811-3270); Market Facts (Sydney) (ISSN 0811-3548).
Description: Reports the state of residential propertie markets in major Australian cities.

352.7   AT
MARKET FACTS (NORTHERN TERRITORY: DARWIN - ALICE SPRINGS). 1986. q. Aus.$60. Real Estate Institute of Australia, P.O. Box 234, Curtin, A.C.T 2605, Australia. TEL 06-282-4277. FAX 05-285-2444. circ. 250. (back issues avail.)

333.33   AT
MELBOURNE CITYSCOPE. 1976. 3/yr. Aus.$995 (renewals Aus.$835). Cityscope Publications Pty. Ltd., P.O. Box 807, Manly, N.S.W. 2095, Australia. TEL 02-976-2233. FAX 02-976-2263. Ed. Neil Speirs. adv.; charts; illus.; maps; circ. 381. (looseleaf format)
●Also available online.
Description: Contains complete property index of all buildings within the Melbourne Central Business District. Includes descriptions, historical information, developments, ownership, prices, sales histories, exact boundaries, and more.

333.33   AT
NORTH RYDE CITYSCOPE. 1989. a. Aus.$300. Cityscope Publications Pty. Ltd., P.O. Box 807, Manly, N.S.W. 2095, Australia. TEL 02-976-2233. FAX 02-976-2263. Ed. Neil Speirs. adv.; maps. (looseleaf format)
Description: Contains complete index of all industrial properties within the Ryde municipality of Sydney. Includes descriptions, improvements, occupants, ownership, prices, sales histories, exact boundaries, zoning, and more.

333.33   AT
NORTH SYDNEY CITYSCOPE. 1980. 3/yr. Aus.$800 (renewals Aus.$640). Cityscope Publications Pty. Ltd., P.O. Box 807, Manly, N.S.W. 2095, Australia. TEL 02-976-2233. FAX 02-976-2263. Ed. Neil Speirs. adv.; charts; illus.; circ. 254. (looseleaf format)
●Also available online.
Description: Contains complete property index of all commercial buildings within the North Sydney municipality. Includes descriptions, sales history, developments, ownership, historical information, prices, exact boundaries, and more.

333.33   AT
PARRAMATTA CITYSCOPE. 1982. 3/yr. Aus.$775 (renewals Aus.$615). Cityscope Publications Pty. Ltd., P.O. Box 430, Milsons Point, N.S.W. 2061, Australia. TEL 02-976-2233. FAX 02-976-2263. Ed. Neil Speirs. adv.; charts; illus.; maps; circ. 168. (looseleaf format)
Description: Contains complete property index of all buildings within the Parramatta Central Business District in western Sydney. Includes descriptions, historical information, developments, ownership, prices, sales histories, exact boundaries, and more.

333.33   AT
ST. KILDA ROAD CITYSCOPE. 1984. 3/yr. Aus.$690 (renewals Aus.$530). Cityscope Publications Pty. Ltd., P.O. Box 870, Manly, N.S.W. 2095, Australia. TEL 02-976-2233. FAX 02-976-2263. Ed. Neils Speirs. adv.; charts; illus.; maps; circ. 191. (looseleaf format)
●Also available online.

333.33   SA
SOUTH AFRICA. CENTRAL STATISTICAL SERVICE. STATISTICAL NEWS RELEASE. TRANSFERS OF RURAL IMMOVABLE PROPERTY. (No. P1141) a., latest 1989. Central Statistical Service, Private Bag X44, Pretoria 0001, South Africa. TEL 012-310-8911. FAX 012-3108500.
Former titles: South Africa. Central Statistical Service. Transfers of Rural Immovable Property; South Africa. Department of Statistics. Transfers of Rural Immovable Property.

333.33   AT
▼**SOUTHBANK CITYSCOPE.** 1991. 3/yr. Aus.$720 (renewals Aus.$560). Cityscope Publications Pty. Ltd., P.O. Box 807, Manly, N.S.W. 2095, Australia. TEL 02-976-2233. FAX 02-976-2263. Ed. Neil Speirs. adv.; maps. (looseleaf format)
Description: Contains a complete property index of all buildings within the Southbank commercial area across the Yarra River from the City of Melbourne. Includes descriptions, historical information, developments, ownership, prices, sales histories, exact boundaries, and more.

333.33   AT
▼**SPRING HILL CITYSCOPE.** 1990. 3/yr. Aus.$710 (renewals Aus.$550). Cityscope Publications Pty. Ltd., P.O. Box 807, Manly, N.S.W. 2095, Australia. TEL 02-976-2233. FAX 02-976-2263. Ed. Neil Speirs. adv.; maps. (looseleaf format)
Description: Contains a complete property index of all buildings within the commercial centers of Spring Hill, Fortitude Valley and Coronation Drive, adjoining Brisbane city. Includes descriptions, historical information, developments, ownership, prices, sales histories, exact boundaries, and more.

333.33   AT
SYDNEY CITYSCOPE. 1975. 3/yr. Aus.$990 (renewals Aus.$830). Cityscope Publications Pty. Ltd., P.O. Box 807, Manly, N.S.W. 2095, Australia. TEL 02-976-2233. TELEX 02-976-2263. Ed. Neil Speirs. adv.; charts; illus.; maps; circ. 443. (looseleaf format)
●Also available online.
Description: Contains complete property index of all commercial buildings within the Sydney Central Business District. Includes descriptions, historical information, developments, ownership, prices, sales histories, exact boundaries, and more.

333.33   AT
SYDNEY CITYSCOPE UNIT REPORT. 1989. 3/yr. Aus.$665 (renewals Aus.$495). Cityscope Publications Pty. Ltd., P.O. Box 807, Manly, N.S.W. 2095, Australia. TEL 02-976-2233. FAX 02-976-2263. Ed. Neil Speirs. adv.; maps. (looseleaf format)
Description: Contains a complete property index of all residential apartments within the Sydney Central Business District. Includes descriptions, historical information, developments, ownership, prices, sales histories, exact boundaries, and more.

TITLE NEWS. see *INSURANCE — Abstracting, Bibliographies, Statistics*

RELIGIONS AND THEOLOGY

see also Religions and Theology–Buddhist; Religions and Theology–Eastern Orthodox; Religions and Theology–Islamic; Religions and Theology–Judaic; Religions and Theology–Protestant; Religions and Theology–Roman Catholic; Religions and Theology–Other Denominations and Sects

200   KE
A A C C BULLETIN. (Text in English and French) 1983. q. EAs.36($2.10) All Africa Conference of Churches, P.O. Box 14205, Nairobi, Kenya. Ed. Maxime V. Rafransoa. adv.; bk.rev.; circ. 1,000. **Indexed:** HR Rep.
   Formed by the 1983 merger of: A A C C Quarterly Bulletin; A A C C Newsletter.

200   KE
A A C C MAGAZINE. (Text in English and French) q. All Africa Conference of Churches, Communication Unit, P.O. Box 14205, Nairobi, Kenya. **Indexed:** HR Rep.

268   US   ISSN 0277-1071
A A R ACADEMY SERIES. 1974. irreg. (American Academy of Religion) Scholars Press, Box 15399, Atlanta, GA 30333-0399. TEL 404-646-4757. FAX 404-636-8301. Ed. Susan Thistlethwaite.
   Formerly: A A R Dissertation Series.
   Description: Monographs on a wide range of subjects within the academic study of religion.

200   US   ISSN 0084-6287
A A R STUDIES IN RELIGION. 1970. irreg., no.34, 1984. (American Academy of Religion) Scholars Press, Box 15399, Atlanta, GA 30333-0399. TEL 404-636-4757. FAX 404-636-8301. Ed. Lawrence Cunningham.
   —BLDSC shelfmark: 8491.431000.
   Description: Monographs on a wide variety of topics in the academic study of religion.

200   US
A C P NEWSLOG. 1960. bi-m. membership only. Associated Church Press, Box 162, Ada, MI 49301-0162. TEL 616-676-1190. Ed. John Stapert. circ. 700.
   Description: Covers association news, awards, management features, and member publication information.

200   UK
A C T. 1970. irreg. (1-2/yr.). Ashram Community Trust, 178 Abbeyfield Rd., Sheffield S4 7AY, England. TEL 0742-436688. Ed. Rev. John Vincent.
   Description: Studies radical discipleship, community living, Bible study.

200 621.38   US   ISSN 0300-7022
A D R I S NEWSLETTER. 1971. q. $10 (foreign $15). (Association for the Development of Religious Information Services) St. Louis University, Department of Theological Studies, 3601 Lindell Boulevard, St. Louis, MO 63108. TEL 314-658-2588. Ed. Richard F. Smith. bk.rev.; abstr.; bibl.; index; circ. 425. **Indexed:** CERDIC.
   —BLDSC shelfmark: 0696.615000.
   Description: Aims to provide current and retrospective bibliographical and informational control in religion-theology and related fields. Includes calendar of events, news about recent reference materials in religion, and listings of recent articles.

200   AT
A.D. 2000. 1988. 11/yr. Aus.$25 (foreign Aus.$40). Freedom Publishing Co., 582 Queensberry St., N. Melbourne, Vic. 3051, Australia. TEL 03-326-5757. FAX 03-328-2877. Ed. B.A. Santamaria. circ. 7,000.

283 276   KE   ISSN 0001-1134
BX1675.A1
A F E R. (African Ecclesial Review) 1959. bi-m. KShs.270($24) (Amecea Pastoral Institute) Gaba Publications, P.O. Box 4002, Eldoret, Kenya. Ed. Felician Rwehikiza. bk.rev.; index; circ. 2,500. (back issues avail.) **Indexed:** Canon Law Abstr., Cath.Ind., New Test.Abstr., Rel.Ind.One.
   Description: Embraces scripture, religion and development.

266 276   US
A I M INTERNATIONAL. 1917. q. free. Africa Inland Mission International, Box 178, Pearl River, NY 10965. TEL 914-735-4014. FAX 914-735-1814. Ed. Ted Barnett. bk.rev.; illus.; circ. 39,000. (also avail. in microfilm)
   Former titles: Inland Africa (ISSN 0020-1464); Hearing and Doing (1896-1916).
   Description: Covers the mission's ministries, its personnel and the national church through which it serves.

A L L NEWS. (American Life Lobby) see *BIRTH CONTROL*

200   KE
A P S BULLETIN. (All Africa Press Service) (Text in English) 1979. w. EAs.562.60($150) Africa Church Information Service, Box 14205, Nairobi, Kenya. TEL 743644. FAX 2542-742352. TELEX 22175. bk.rev.; circ. 350.
   Description: Covers church and secular events with integrity, giving news an African perspective. Includes the continent's leading news and in-depth feature articles that probe behind the headlines in religion, socio-economics, culture, political development and even environmental issues.

200   US
A T L A MONOGRAPH SERIES. no.22, 1985. irreg., latest no.27. (American Theological Library Association) Scarecrow Press, Inc., 52 Liberty St., Box 4167, Metuchen, NJ 08840. TEL 800-537-7107. Ed. Dr. Kenneth E. Rowe.

255   NO   ISSN 0400-227X
BX8037
AARBOK FOR DEN NORSKE KIRKE. 1951. a. NOK 78. Kirkens Informationstjeneste, Underhaugsveien 15, Oslo 3, Norway. FAX 02-697280. Ed. Gunnar Westermoen. stat.; index; circ. 4,000.
   Description: Events within the Church of Norway, with a full account of the clerical districts and church organisations and institutions.

ABINGDON CLERGY INCOME TAX GUIDE. see *BUSINESS AND ECONOMICS — Public Finance, Taxation*

ACADEMIA; Zeitschrift fuer Politik und Kultur. see *LITERARY AND POLITICAL REVIEWS*

ACADEMY OF RELIGION AND PSYCHICAL RESEARCH. PROCEEDINGS. see *PARAPSYCHOLOGY AND OCCULTISM*

264   US   ISSN 0276-2358
ACCENT ON WORSHIP. 1981. irreg., 4/yr. membership. Liturgical Conference, 1017 12th St., N.W., Washington, DC 20005-4091. TEL 202-898-0885.
   Former titles (until 1981): Accent on Liturgy (ISSN 0272-7951); (until 1980): Living Worship (ISSN 0360-6224)
   Description: Provides news of the Liturgical Conference with articles on liturgical experiences.

ACCEPTANCE NEWSLETTER. see *HOMOSEXUALITY*

ACCION; revista Paraguaya de reflexion y dialogo. see *SOCIAL SCIENCES: COMPREHENSIVE WORKS*

249   US   ISSN 0001-5083
ACT. 1947. m. (bi-m. Jan.-Feb.; Jul.-Aug.). $8. Christian Family Movement, 314 Sixth St., Box 272, Ames, IA 50010. TEL 515-232-7432. Ed. Paul Leingang. bk.rev.; circ. 2,500. (looseleaf format)
   Description: For family life network; covers topics of importance to families and has a Christian and social justice orientation.

200   DK   ISSN 0106-0937
AS281
ACTA JUTLANDICA. 1929. s-a. $80. (Learned Society) Aarhus University Press, Aarhus University, DK-8000 Aarhus C, Denmark.
TEL 45-86-19-70-33. FAX 45-86-19-8433.

ACTA PHILOSOPHICA ET THEOLOGICA. see *PHILOSOPHY*

200   NE   ISSN 0065-1672
ACTA THEOLOGICA DANICA. (Text in English and German) 1958. irreg., vol.24, 1988. price varies. E. J. Brill, P.O. Box 9000, 2300 PA Leiden, Netherlands. TEL 071-312624. FAX 071-317532. TELEX 39296 BRILL NL. (In N. America: E.J. Brill, 24 Hudson St., Kinderhook, NY 12106. TEL 800-962-4406) Ed.Bd.

266 284   AT   ISSN 1033-1913
ACTION AFRICA. 1987. q. free. Africa Evangelical Fellowship, P.O. Box 292, 47 Castle St., Castle Hill, N.S.W. 2154, Australia. TEL 02-899-1617. FAX 02-899-4447. (U.K. addr.: 35 Kingfisher Court Harnbridge Rd., Newbury Berks RG14 5SJ, England) Ed. Rev. William A. Walker. circ. 4,500. (tabloid format; back issues avail.)
   Description: Christian missions in Africa, especially South of Sahara, targetted to Christian community.

200   UK   ISSN 0143-3253
ACTION NEWSLETTER. 1969. 10/yr. $10. World Association for Christian Communication, 357 Kennington Lane, London SE11 5QY, England. TEL 071-582-9139. FAX 071-735-0340. TELEX 8812669-WACC-G. Ed. Ann Shakespeare. bk.rev.; circ. 2,200.

ACTION SOCIALE. see *POLITICAL SCIENCE*

200   US
ADULT QUARTERLY. 1981. q. $3.20 (large print edition $8). Associate Reformed Presbyterian Center, Office of Christian Education, 1 Cleveland St., Greenville, SC 29601. TEL 803-232-8297. Ed. W.H.F. Kuykendall. (large print ed. in 16 pt.)
   Description: Includes lesson topics, scripture portions, and daily Bible readings.

200   AT   ISSN 0001-8619
ADVANCE AUSTRALIA.* 1965. q. Aus.$0.75 per no. Knights of the Southern Cross, P.O. Box 42, Hackett, A.C.T. 2601, Australia. Ed. H. Octigan. adv.; bk.rev.; illus.; circ. 14,000.

ADVENT. see *HOMOSEXUALITY*

200   TZ   ISSN 0856-0048
AFRICA THEOLOGICAL JOURNAL. 1968. 3/yr. $27 (foreign $25). All Africa Lutheran Churches Information and Coordination Centre, P.O. Box 314, Arusha, Tanzania. TELEX 42054 LUTHA TZ. Ed. Mutembe Gaetan. adv.; bk.rev.; circ. 1,500. **Indexed:** CERDIC, New Test.Abstr., Rel.& Theol.Abstr. (1988-), Rel.Ind.One.
   —BLDSC shelfmark: 0732.189700.

200   KE
AFRICAN CHRISTIAN. fortn. African Church Information Service, P.O. Box 14205, Nairobi, Kenya.
TEL 62974. TELEX 22175.
   Description: Covers church news and developments in Africa.

200 282   NR
AFRICAN JOURNAL OF BIBLICAL STUDIES. 1986. s-a. $20. Nigerian Association for Biblical Studies, c/o Department of Religious Studies, University of Ibadan, Oyo State, Nigeria. Ed. S.O. Oyin Abogunrin. adv.; bk.rev.; circ. 500.

200   US
AGAPE (FRANKLIN). 1985. m. $5. Starthrowers, 615 Throwbridge, Box 192, Franklin, LA 70538.

AGAPE (LOS ANGELES). see *NEW AGE PUBLICATIONS*

266   GW
AHA; Gossner Mission fuer Kinder und Jugendliche. a. Gossner Mission, Fennstr. 31, 1190 Berlin-Schoeneweiche, Germany.
TEL 00372-6351198. circ. 7,000. (back issues avail.)

267   NE   ISSN 0002-3744
AKTIE; maandblad voor jongeren. 1951. 11/yr. fl.42. Stichting Youth for Christ Nederland, Postbus 273, 3970 AG Diebergen, Netherlands.
FAX 03438-15674. Ed. Leo Blokhuis. adv.; bk.rev.; circ. 8,000.
   Formerly: Jeugd in Aktie.
   Description: Christian youth magazine.

200   GR
AKTINES/BEAM. (Text in Greek) 1938. m. Christian Union, Odos Karytsi, 105 61 Athens, Greece.
TEL 02-3235023. circ. 10,000.
   Description: Promotes Christian civilization.

RELIGIONS AND THEOLOGY

200 GW
AKTION; Zeitung junger Arbeiter. 1949. m. DM.11.40. Christliche Arbeiter-Jugend, Huettmannstr. 52, 4300 Essen 1, Germany. TEL 0201-621065. adv.; bk.rev.
Former titles: C A J Christliche Arbeiter-Jugend; Junge Christliche Arbeitnehmer. Befreiung (ISSN 0022-622X)

200 US ISSN 0272-7250
ALBANIAN CATHOLIC BULLETIN/BULETINI KATOLIK SHQIPTAR. (Text in Albanian, English) 1980. a. donations. Albanian Catholic Institute "Daniel Dajani, S.J.", University of San Francisco, Xavier Hall, San Francisco, CA 94117. FAX 415-387-1867. Ed. Gjon Sinishta. bk.rev.; circ. 1,500. (back issues avail.)
Description: To assist the rebuilding of the Catholic Church in Albania and to promote the dissemination of knowledge of Albania's national, cultural and religious heritage.

200 UK
ALCUIN. 1897. q. $27. Alcuin Club, All Saints' Vicarage, Highlands Rd., Runcorn, Cheshire WA7 4PS, England. TEL 0928-575-666. FAX 0928-581868. Ed. T.R. Barker. bk.rev.; circ. 900.

200 NE ISSN 0002-5267
ALGEMEEN MACONNIEK TIJDSCHRIFT. 1946. m. membership. Grand East of the Netherlands, Fluwelenburgwal 22, The Hague, Netherlands. Ed. Wim G. Ket. adv.; bk.rev.; illus.; circ. 6,800.

266 KE
ALL AFRICA CONFERENCE OF CHURCHES. REFUGEE DEPARTMENT. PROGRESS REPORT. irreg., latest 1974. All Africa Conference of Churches, Refugee Department, Pioneer House, Government Rd., P.O. Box 20301, Nairobi, Kenya.

266 KE
ALL AFRICA CONFERENCE OF CHURCHES. REFUGEE DEPARTMENT. PROJECT LIST. irreg., latest 1977. All Africa Conference of Churches, Refugee Department, Pioneer House, Government Rd., P.O. Box 20301, Nairobi, Kenya.

ALL-CHURCH PRESS NEWSPAPERS. see *JOURNALISM*

ALLIANCE REVIEW. see *EDUCATION*

266 MX ISSN 0002-628X
ALMAS. 1950. m. $5. (Misioneros de Guadalupe) Editora Escalante, Cordoba 17, Apdo. 24-550, Mexico 7, D. F., Mexico. FAX 5-533-6564. Ed. Jose Chavez Calderon. illus.; circ. 225,000.

200 SP
▼**ALTERNATIVA 2000.** 1990. bi-m. 2500 ptas.($25) (typically set in Jan.). Juan Antonio Monroy, Ed. & Pub., Apdo. 2029, 28080 Madrid, Spain. TEL 91-5721862. circ. 3,000.

ALTERNATIVE. see *POLITICAL SCIENCE*

L'ALTRA EUROPA. see *ART*

200 US
AMANECER; Christian reflection in the new Nicaragua. (English ed.) 1988. bi-m. $20. New York Circus Publications, Box 681, Audubon Sta., New York, NY 10032. TEL 212-928-7600. FAX 212-928-2757. Ed. Rigoberto Avila. circ. 3,000. (back issues avail.)
Description: Theology documents and testimonies of Christians in Nicaragua.

213 US ISSN 0882-2123
AMBASSADOR REPORT. 1977. q. $20. Box 60068, Pasadena, CA 91116. TEL 818-798-6112. Ed. John Trechak. bk.rev.; circ. 2,500. (back issues avail.)

200 US
AMERICAN ACADEMY OF RELIGION. ANNUAL MEETING. a. Scholars Press, Box 15399, Atlanta, GA 30333-0399. TEL 404-636-4757. FAX 404-636-8301. (Co-sponsor: Society of Biblical Literature)
Description: Meeting program of the annual meeting of the American Academy of Religion and Society of Biblical Literature.

200 US ISSN 0002-7189
BV1460
AMERICAN ACADEMY OF RELIGION. JOURNAL. 1933. q. $60. (American Academy of Religion) Scholars Press, Box 15399, Atlanta, GA 30333-0399. TEL 404-363-4757. FAX 404-636-8301. Ed. William Scott Green. adv.; bk.rev.; bibl.; index, cum.index: 1933-1979; circ. 7,200. (also avail. in microform from UMI; microfiche) **Indexed:** Amer.Hist.& Life, Arts & Hum.Cit.Ind., Bibl.Ind., Bk.Rev.Ind. (1990-), CERDIC, Child.Bk.Rev.Ind. (1990-), Curr.Cont., Hist.Abstr., Hum.Ind., Mid.East: Abstr.& Ind., New Test.Abstr., Old Test.Abstr., Rel.& Theol.Abstr. (1968-), Rel.Ind.One, Rel.Per., SSCI.
—BLDSC shelfmark: 4683.740000.
Formerly: Journal of Bible and Religion.
Description: Academic journal of religion.

200 US
AMERICAN BAPTIST WOMAN. 1956. 3/yr. $6. American Baptist Women's Ministries, Box 851, Valley Forge, PA 19482-0851. TEL 215-768-2283. FAX 215-768-2275. Ed. Carolyn Dick. adv.; bk.rev.; circ. 8,000.

220 US ISSN 0006-0801
BV2370
AMERICAN BIBLE SOCIETY RECORD. 1818. m. $3 donation. American Bible Society, 1865 Broadway, New York, NY 10023. TEL 212-408-1480. FAX 212-408-1456. Ed. Clifford P. Macdonald. illus.; index; circ. 270,000.
Formerly: Bible Society Record.
Description: Contains news and articles concerning worldwide Bible mission.

200 100 US ISSN 0194-3448
BR1
AMERICAN JOURNAL OF THEOLOGY & PHILOSOPHY. 1980. 3/yr. $25 (foreign $30). c/o Tyron Inbody, Ed., United Theological Seminary, 1810 Harrard Blvd., Daytona, OH 45406-4599. TEL 404-526-4038. (Subscr. to: Box 2009, Highlands, NC 28741) (Co-sponsors: Purdue University and University of Kansas, Hall Center for the Humanities) index; circ. 450. (back issues avail.) **Indexed:** Phil.Ind., Rel.& Theol.Abstr. (1989-), Rel.Ind.One.
—BLDSC shelfmark: 0838.700000.
Description: Provides a forum for the discussion of issues in American theology and its dialogue with philosophy.

AMERICAN LEPROSY MISSIONS ANNUAL REPORT. see *MEDICAL SCIENCES — Communicable Diseases*

291.2 US ISSN 0740-0446
AMERICAN UNIVERSITY STUDIES. SERIES 7. THEOLOGY AND RELIGION. 1984. irreg. Peter Lang Publishing, Inc., 62 W. 45th St., 4th Fl., New York, NY 10036. TEL 212-302-6740. Ed. Michael Flamini.
—BLDSC shelfmark: 0858.078100.

200 US
AMERICAN WALDENSIAN SOCIETY. NEWSLETTER. 1906. s-a. membership. American Waldensian Society, 475 Riverside Dr., Rm. 1850, New York, NY 10115. TEL 212-870-2671. Ed. Rev. Frank G. Gibson, Jr. bk.rev.; circ. 3,000.
Formerly: American Waldensian Aid Society. Newsletter (ISSN 0894-9999)
Description: Updates on Waldensian ministry in Italy, Argentina and Uruguay, and ministry exchanges between Waldensian and US churches.

200 IT ISSN 0003-1739
AMICIZIA EBRAICO-CRISTIANA DI FIRENZE. BOLLETTINO. 1951. q. free. Amicizia Ebraico-Cristiana di Firenze, Casella Postale 282, 50100 Florence, Italy. Ed. Ines Zilli Gay. bk.rev.; bibl.; circ. 500.

AMICO DELL'ARTE CRISTIANA. see *ART*

200 FR ISSN 0003-1909
AMITIES SPIRITUELLES. BULLETIN. 1919. q. 40 F. (foreign 45 F.). Association de Amities Spirituelles, B.P. 236, 75624 Paris Cedex 13, France. Ed. Jacques Sardin. bk.rev.; circ. 1,200.
Description: Objective is to shed light on issues in Christianity and spirituality.

200 UK ISSN 0003-2018
AMPLEFORTH JOURNAL. 1895. 2/yr. £10. Ampleforth Abbey, York YO6 4EN, England. TEL 04393-206. FAX 04393-770. Ed. J. Felix Stephens. adv.; bk.rev.; charts; illus.; circ. 3,400. (back issues avail.)
—BLDSC shelfmark: 0859.470000.
Description: News about Ampleforth Abbey and community, also religious articles and comment.

200 NE ISSN 0169-0272
AMSTERDAM STUDIES IN THEOLOGY. 1979. irreg. Editions Rodopi B.V., Keizersgracht 302-304, 1016 EX Amsterdam, Netherlands. TEL 020-6227507. FAX 020-6380948. (US and Canada subscr. to: 233 Peachtree St., N.E., Ste. 404, Atlanta GA 30303-1504. TEL 800-225-3998)

200 US
ANAHATA NADA/SOUNDLESS SOUND. 1974. q. $1. (Sri Chinmoy Centre) AUM Publications, 85-42 160th St., Jamaica, NY 11432. TEL 718-523-1166. (Subscr. to: Box 32433, Jamaica, NY 11431) Ed. David Burke. bk.rev.; illus.

209 BE ISSN 0003-2468
BX4655
ANALECTA BOLLANDIANA; revue critique d'hagiographie. (Text in English, French, German, Italian, Latin) 1882. s-a. 3000 Fr. Societe des Bollandistes, 24 bd. Saint-Michel, B-1040 Brussels, Belgium. bk.rev.; index, cum. index every 20 yrs. (vols. 1-100); circ. 1,000. **Indexed:** CERDIC, M.L.A.
Description: Studies about saints' lives up to 1500.

809 AU
ANALECTA CARTUSIANA; review for Carthusian history and spirituality. (Text in various languages) 1970. irreg., no.112, 1990. DM.65 per no. Universitaet Salzburg, Institut fuer Englische Sprache, Akademiestr. 24, A-5020 Salzburg, Austria. Ed. James Hogg. circ. 300. (back issues avail.) **Indexed:** M.L.A.

ANALECTA ORDINIS CARMELITARUM. see *RELIGIONS AND THEOLOGY — Roman Catholic*

207.11 US ISSN 0003-2980
ANDREWS UNIVERSITY SEMINARY STUDIES. (Text in English, French, German) 1963. 3/yr. $16 to individuals (foreign $19); institutions $22 (foreign $25); students $13 (foreign $16). Andrews University Press, Berrien Springs, MI 49104. TEL 616-471-6023. FAX 616-471-9751. (Subscr. to: Seminary Bldg., Berrien Springs, MI 49104. TEL 616-471-6395) Ed. Kenneth A. Strand. bk.rev.; charts; illus.; index; circ. 750. (tabloid format) **Indexed:** CERDIC, Mid.East: Abstr.& Ind., New Test.Abstr., Old Test.Abstr., Rel.& Theol.Abstr. (1969-), Rel.Ind.One, Rel.Per.
—BLDSC shelfmark: 0900.420000.

200 FR ISSN 0751-6460
ANGE GARDIEN. 1891. 6/yr. 120 F.($24) Association de l'Ange Gardien, 28 rue du Bon Pasteur, B.P. 4384, 69242 Lyon Cedex 04, France. TEL 78-28-48-89. Ed. Louis Chauffour. circ. 4,500.

200 209 US ISSN 0003-3286
BR1
ANGLICAN THEOLOGICAL REVIEW. 1918. q. $20 to individuals; institutions $25. Anglican Theological Review, Inc., 600 Haven St., Evanston, IL 60201. TEL 708-864-6024. FAX 708-328-9624. Ed. Richard E. Wentz. adv.; bk.rev.; abstr.; index, cum.index every 10 yrs.; circ. 1,600. (also avail. in microform from UMI; reprint service avail. from UMI) **Indexed:** Amer.Hist.& Life, Bull.Signal, CERDIC, Hist.Abstr., New Test.Abstr., Old Test.Abstr., Rel.& Theol.Abstr. (1968-), Rel.Ind.One.
—BLDSC shelfmark: 0902.770000.

200 FR ISSN 0066-2860
ANNUAIRE DES INSTITUTS DE RELIGIEUSES EN FRANCE. 1959. irreg., latest 1980. 50 F. Service National des Vocations Francais, 106 rue du Bac, 75341 Paris, France.

209 GW ISSN 0003-5157
ANNUARIUM HISTORIAE CONCILIORUM; Internationale Zeitschrift fuer Konziliengeschichtsforschung. (Text in English, French, German, Italian & Spanish) 1969. s-a. DM.140. Ferdinand Schoeningh, Juehenplatz 1-3, 4790 Paderborn, Germany. adv.; bk.rev. **Indexed:** CERDIC.
—BLDSC shelfmark: 1541.530000.

200 GW ISSN 0003-519X
DIE ANREGUNG; Seelsorglicher Dienst in der Welt von heute. 1948. m. DM.3.50 per no. Steyler Verlag, Bahnhofstr. 9, 4054 Nettetal 2, Germany. FAX 02157-120222. Ed.Bd. bk.rev.

260 GW
ANRUF. 1896. m. DM.24. (Deutscher Verband der Jugendbuende fuer Entschiedenes Christentum e.V.) Born-Verlag, Leuschnerstr. 72-74, Postfach 420220, 3500 Kassel, Germany. TEL 0561-40950. FAX 0561-4095-112. Ed. Gerhard Fitting. adv.; bk.rev.; illus.

248.83 GW
ANSAETZE;* E S G - Nachrichten. 1953. 10/yr. DM.35. Evangelische Studentengemeinde in der Bundesrepublik Deutschland, Tunisstr. 3, 5000 Cologne 1, Germany. TEL 0221-235427. FAX 0221-256674. (Co-sponsors: Bundesministerium fuer Jugend, Familie, Frauen und Gesundheit) Ed. Friedhelm Quade. adv.; bk.rev.; circ. 600. (processed)
Formerly: E S G - Nachrichten (ISSN 0012-7981)

200 US ISSN 0735-0864
ANSELM STUDIES; an occasional journal. 1983. irreg. price varies. Kraus International Publications (Subsidiary of: Kraus Organization Ltd.), Route 100, Millwood, NY 10546. TEL 914-762-2200.
—BLDSC shelfmark: 1542.003000.

207.11 GW ISSN 0003-5270
ANSTOESSE; aus der Arbeit der Evangelischen Akademie Hofgeismar. 1954. 4/yr. DM.16. Evangelische Akademie von Kurhessen-Waldeck, Schloesschen Schoenburg, 3520 Hofgeismar, Germany. bk.rev.; index; circ. 2,000.

200 GW ISSN 0003-6285
ANZEIGER DES REICHES DER GERECHTIGKEIT; Menschenfreundliche Zeitung fuer Jedermann. (Summaries in Dutch, English, French, Italian, Portuguese and Spanish) 1938. m. DM.16. (Menschenfreundliche Gesellschaft) Verlag der Engel des Herrn, Baeckerweg 12, Postfach 3608, 6000 Frankfurt 1, Germany. Ed. Miss Roulin. circ. 120,000.

266 FR
APPEL DE L'AFRIQUE. 1967. 4/yr. free. Societe des Missions Africaines, 36 rue Miguel Hidalgo, 75019 Paris, France. circ. 40,000.
Formerly: Almanach Noir.

200 GW
ARBEITEN ZUR GESCHICHTE DES PIETISMUS. 1979. irreg. Vandenhoeck und Ruprecht, Robert-Bosch-Breite 6, Postfach 3753, 3400 Goettingen, Germany. TEL 0551-6959-0. FAX 0551-695917. Ed.Bd.

200 GW
ARBEITEN ZUR KIRCHLICHEN ZEITGESCHICHTE. REIHE B; Darstellung. 1975. irreg. Vandenhoeck und Ruprecht, Robert-Bosch-Breite 6, Postfach 3753, 3400 Goettingen, Germany. TEL 0551-6959-0. FAX 0551-695917. Ed.Bd.

200 GW
ARBEITEN ZUR PASTORALTHEOLOGIE. 1962. irreg. (Verlagsbuchhandlung) Vandenhoeck und Ruprecht, Robert-Bosch-Breite 6, Postfach 3753, 3400 Goettingen, Germany. TEL 0551-6959-0. FAX 0551-695917. Ed.Bd.

200 GW ISSN 0066-5711
ARBEITEN ZUR THEOLOGIE. REIHE 1. 1960. irreg., vol.70, 1986. price varies. Calwer Verlag, Scharnhauserstr.44, 7000 Stuttgart 70, Germany. TEL 0711-452019. FAX 0711-4560660.

200 GW ISSN 0723-2446
ARBEITSGEMEINSCHAFT NEUE RELIGIOESE GRUPPEN. FORUM; Materialen und Beitraege zum religioesen Dialog. 1981. a. DM.3. Arbeitsgemeinschaft Neue Religioese Gruppen e.V., Stahlgurstr. 38, 6000 Frankfurt a.M. 1, Germany. TEL 0649-594694. (back issues avail.)

ARCHAEOLOGY AND BIBLICAL RESEARCH. see *ARCHAEOLOGY*

243 GW ISSN 0066-6386
BX1970.A1
ARCHIV FUER LITURGIEWISSENSCHAFT. 1950. a. DM.218. Abt-Herwegen-Institut fuer Liturgische und Monastische Forschung, Abtei Maria Laach, D-5471 Maria Laach, Germany. Ed. Emmanuel v. Severus. bk.rev.; circ. 800. **Indexed:** CERDIC, New Test.Abstr., Rel.Ind.One.

209 GW ISSN 0066-6432
BR857.R5
ARCHIV FUER MITTELRHEINISCHE KIRCHENGESCHICHTE. 1949. a. DM.60. Gesellschaft fuer Mittelrheinische Kirchengeschichte, Karmeliterplatz 1, 5400 Koblenz, Germany. Ed. Friedhelm Juergensmeier. circ. 1,900. **Indexed:** Bibl.Cart.

270 GW ISSN 0003-9381
BR300
ARCHIV FUER REFORMATIONSGESCHICHTE/ARCHIVE FOR REFORMATION HISTORY; Internatonale Zeitschrift zur Erforschung der Reformation und ihrer Weltwirkungen. (Text in English and German) 1904. s-a. DM.100. (Verein fuer Reformations Geschichte) Guetersloher Verlagshaus Gerd Mohn, Carl-Bertelsmann-Str. 256, Postfach 1343, 4830 Guetersloh 100, Germany. TEL 05241-862-0. FAX 05241-740548. (Co-sponsor: American Society for Reformation Research) Ed.Bd. bk.rev.; circ. 800. (also avail. in microform from PMC; reprint service avail. from KTO) **Indexed:** Amer.Hist.& Life, Arts & Hum.Cit.Ind., M.L.A., Rel.& Theol.Abstr. (1970-), Rel.Ind.One, Rel.Per.
—BLDSC shelfmark: 1640.700000.

200 150 GW ISSN 0084-6724
ARCHIV FUER RELIGIONSPSYCHOLOGIE. vol.4, 1929. irreg., vol.19, 1989. price varies. (Internationale Gesellschaft fuer Religionspsychologie) Vandenhoeck und Ruprecht, Robert-Bosch-Breite 6, Postfach 37 53, 3400 Goettingen, Germany. TEL 0551-6959-0. FAX 0551-695917. Ed.Bd.
—BLDSC shelfmark: 1623.900000.

209 GW ISSN 0066-6491
BR857.S6
ARCHIV FUER SCHLESISCHE KIRCHENGESCHICHTE. 1949. a. DM.25. (Institut fuer Ostdeutsche Kirchen- und Kulturgeschichte) Verlag August Lax, Postfach 10 08 65, 3200 Hildesheim, Germany. circ. 900. (reprint service avail. from CIP) **Indexed:** Numis.Lit.
—BLDSC shelfmark: 1623.910000.

291.64 US
ARCHIVE FOR REFORMATION HISTORY. LITERATURE REVIEW/ARCHIV FUER REFORMATIONSGESCHICHTE. LITERATURBERICHT. 1972. a. $26. American Society for Reformation Research, 6477 San Bonita, St. Louis, MO 63105.

260 IT ISSN 0066-6688
ARCHIVIO ITALIANO PER LA STORIA DELLA PIETA. (Text in language of contributor) 1951. irreg., vol.8, 1980. price varies. Edizioni di Storia e Letteraturas.r.l., Via Lancellotti 18, 00186 Rome, Italy. Ed. Romana Guarnieri.

200 HK ISSN 1011-8101
AREOPAGUS; a living encounter with today's religious world. 1987. q. $24. Tao Fang Shan Christian Centre, P.O. Box 33, Shatin, New Territories, Hong Kong. TEL 852-691-1904. FAX 852-694-0354. Ed. John G. LeMond. adv.; bk.rev.; circ. 1,000. (also avail. in microfilm from UMI) **Indexed:** Rel.Ind.One.
—BLDSC shelfmark: 1664.088000.
Incorporates (in 1987): Update (Aarhus) (ISSN 0108-7029); New Religious Movements Up-Date (ISSN 0105-9998)
Description: Provides a forum for communications between the good news of Jesus Christ and the people of faith both in major world religions and new religious movements.

200 949.5 GR
ARISTOTELION PANEPISTEMION THESSALONIKES. THEOLOGIKE SCHOLE. EPISTEMONIKE EPETERIS. 1953. a. Theologike Schole Panepistemiou Thessalonikes, Serron 39, Triandria, Saloniki, Greece. **Indexed:** Chem.Abstr.

200 DK ISSN 0107-363X
ARKEN. 1979. bi-m. DKK 10 per no. (Teologiske Fakultet) Forlaget Arken, Koebmagergade 44-46, 1150 Copenhagen K, Denmark. illus.
Formerly: Teologiske Fakultet. Bladet.

200 DK ISSN 0107-4520
ARKEN-TRYK. no.15, 1982. irreg. price varies. (Teologiske Fakultet) Forlaget Arken, Koebmagegade 44-46, 1150 Copenhagen K, Denmark.

ARMARIUM CODICUM INSIGNIUM. see *HISTORY — History Of Europe*

ARMONIA DI VOCI. see *MUSIC*

ARTE CRISTIANA; rivista internazionale di storia dell'arte e di arti liturgiche. see *ART*

200 800 DK ISSN 0905-7749
ASLAN. 1989. q. DKK 40. Aslan amba, Liljevej 8, DK-3600 Frederikssund, Denmark. TEL 45-42313213. Ed. Gunhild Lindstroem. circ. 800.
Description: Focuses on books with religious and ethical relevancy for children, youth and adults.

ASOCIACION. see *CHILDREN AND YOUTH — About*

ASSEMBLEE NOUVELLE. see *MUSIC*

200 060 FR ISSN 0066-8907
ASSOCIATION DES AMIS DE PIERRE TEILHARD DE CHARDIN. BULLETIN. 1966. a. Association des Amis de Pierre Teilhard de Chardin, 38 rue Geoffroy-Saint-Hilaire, 75005 Paris, France. bibl.

378 US
ASSOCIATION FOR PROFESSIONAL EDUCATION FOR MINISTRY. REPORT OF THE BIENNIAL MEETING. 1950. biennial. $10. Association for Professional Education for Ministry, c/o Oliver Williams, Pres., University of Notre Dame, Notre Dame, IN 46556. TEL 219-239-5000. (Subscr. to: Joseph Kelly, Treas., St. Bernard's Seminary, 2260 Lake Ave., Rochester, NY 14612) Ed. Gaylord Noyce. circ. 400.

230 IT
ASSOCIATION INTERNATIONALE D'ETUDES PATRISTIQUES. BULLETIN D'INFORMATION ET DE LIAISON. (Text in English, French) 1968. irreg. (1-2/yr.). 50 F. per no. for libraries only. Brepols Publisher, c/o A. Di Berardino, Sec. Gen., Institutum Patristicum Augustinianum, Via S. Uffizio, 25, 00193 Rome, Italy. (Subscr. to: B. Gain, 14 rue Saint Louis, 57158 Montigny Les Metz, France) Ed. A. di Berardino. bk.rev.; bibl.; circ. 800.

ASSOCIATION OF BRITISH THEOLOGICAL AND PHILOSOPHICAL LIBRARIES. BULLETIN. see *LIBRARY AND INFORMATION SCIENCES*

268 US ISSN 0362-1472
BV4019
ASSOCIATION OF THEOLOGICAL SCHOOLS IN THE UNITED STATES AND CANADA. BULLETIN. 1937. biennial. $23. Association of Theological Schools, 10 Summit Park Dr., Pittsburgh, PA 15275-1103. TEL 412-788-6505. Ed. Gail B. King. circ. 2,000.
Formerly: American Association of Theological Schools in the United States and Canada. Bulletin (ISSN 0065-7360)

268 US
ASSOCIATION OF THEOLOGICAL SCHOOLS IN THE UNITED STATES AND CANADA. DIRECTORY. 1918. a. $5. Association of Theological Schools, 10 Summit Park Dr., Pittsburgh, PA 15275-1103. TEL 412-788-6505. Ed. Gail B. King.
Formerly: American Association of Theological Schools in the United States and Canada. Directory (ISSN 0065-7379)

200 VC
ATHEISM AND FAITH. (Text in English, French, Spanish) 1966. q. $30. Pontifical Council for Dialogue with Non-Believers, 00120 Vatican City (Rome), State of the Vatican City. TEL 001139-6987273. FAX 698-7165. Ed. Paul Poupard. bk.rev.; circ. 1,000.
Formerly: Atheism and Dialogue.
Description: Contains articles on modern atheism and religious indifference, dialogue with non-believers, and science-faith relationships.

ATHEIST. see *PHILOSOPHY*

RELIGIONS AND THEOLOGY

967.5 200   BD   ISSN 0563-4245
AU COEUR DE L'AFRIQUE. 1961. bi-m. 900 Fr.CFA (300 Fr.CFA to students and teachers of religion). Association des Conference des Ordinaires du Rwanda et Burundi, B.P. 1390, Bujumbura, Burundi. Ed. Adrien Ntabona. adv.; bk.rev.; circ. 1,000.
Indexed: CERDIC.

200   UK   ISSN 0004-7481
AUDENSHAW PAPERS. 1967. 6/yr. £5.50 (foreign £9). Hinksey Centre, Westminster College, Oxford OX2 9AT, England. Ed. Deborah Padfield. bk.rev.; circ. 3,000. **Indexed:** CERDIC.
Supersedes: Christian Comment.

260   GW
AUFTRAG UND WEG. 1915. bi-m. DM.15. (Deutscher Verband der Jugenbuende fuer Entschiedenes Christentum e.V.) Born-Verlag, Leuschnerstr. 72-74, Postfach 420220, 3500 Kassel, Germany. TEL 0561-40950. FAX 0561-4095-112. Ed. Dieter Velten. bk.rev.; circ. 4,000.

200   GW
AUFWAERTS (GIESSEN); die Zeitschrift mit den guten Nachrichten. 1909. m. DM.5.40. Brunnen Verlag GmbH, Postfach 5205, 6300 Giessen 1, Germany. Ed. Ralf Tibusek. bk.rev.

200   GW
DIE AUSLESE. 1958. 4/yr. DM.6.20. Dr. Krueger Verlag, Am Schiessberg 19, 6348 Herborn, Germany. TEL 02772-2427. Ed. Hans-Joachim Krueger. adv.; bk.rev.; circ. 21,000 (controlled).

    AT   ISSN 0588-3237
AUSTRALIAN & NEW ZEALAND SOCIETY FOR THEOLOGICAL STUDIES. COLLOQUIUM. 1964. s-a. Aus.$35. Australian and New Zealand Society for Theological Studies, c/o Dr. Gregory C. Jenks, St. Francis' Theological College, 233 Milton Rd., P.O. Box 1261, Australia. TEL 07-369-4286. FAX 61-7-369-4691. Ed. James Haire. adv.; bk.rev.; circ. 500. (back issues avail.) **Indexed:** Aus.P.A.I.S., Rel.& Theol.Abstr., Rel.Ind.One.
Description: Features issues in biblical studies, theology, ethics, church history.

200   AT
AUSTRALIAN BEACON. 1968. m. Aus.$20 (foreign Aus.$30). P.O. Box 88, Para Hills, S.A. 5096, Australia. TEL 08-2637156. Ed. John S. MacKenzie. adv.; circ. 1,000.
Description: For Christians concerned with the state of the Church today.

220   AT   ISSN 0045-0308
BS410
AUSTRALIAN BIBLICAL REVIEW. 1951. a. Aus.$8 per issue. Fellowship for Biblical Studies, c/o Joint Theological Library, Ormond College, Parkville, Vic. 3052, Australia. Eds. M. O'Brien, N.M. Watson. bk.rev.; circ. 375. **Indexed:** CERDIC, New Test.Abstr., Old Test.Abstr., Rel.& Theol.Abstr. (1976-), Rel.Ind.One.
—BLDSC shelfmark: 1797.800000.

AUSTRALIAN CHURCHES OF CHRIST HISTORICAL SOCIETY. DIGEST. see HISTORY — History Of Australasia And Other Areas

200   AT   ISSN 1030-617X
AUSTRALIAN JOURNAL OF LITURGY. 1987. s-a. Aus.$15. Australian Academy of Liturgy, St. Michael's Vicarage, 32 Dalgetty Rd., Beaumaris, Vic. 3193, Australia. TEL 08-278-3417. (Subscr. to: 5, Carrick St., Woodlands 6018, Australia) Ed. R. Wesley Hartley. adv.; bk.rev.; index; circ. 250. (back issues avail.)
—BLDSC shelfmark: 1809.180000.
Description: Christian liturgy and worship with particular reference to Australia. Ecumenical in scope.

200 283   AT   ISSN 0812-0811
AUSTRALIAN LECTIONARY (YEAR). 1978. a. Aus.$4.50. Anglican Information Office, St. Andrews House, 1st Fl., Sydney Sq., N.S.W. 2000, Australia. TEL 02-265-1537. FAX 02-261-2864. Ed. Gilbert Sinden. circ. 15,000. (back issues avail.)

AUSTRALIAN RADIO TIMES. see COMMUNICATIONS — Radio

200   US   ISSN 0890-5541
AVALOKA; a journal of traditional religion and culture. 1986. s-a. $12 (foreign $15). 249 Maynard N.W., Grand Rapids, MI 49504. TEL 616-453-1653. Ed. Arthur Versluis. bk.rev.; circ. 500.
Description: Presents esoteric studies of traditional religions, includes work of Guenon, Burckhardt, and Coomaraswamy.

200   UK
AWARE. 1900. m. £20.40($66.60) Paternoster Press Ltd., Paternoster House, 3 Mount Radford Crescent, Exeter EX2 4JW, England. (Dist. in U.S. & Canada by: Paternoster Press, P.O. Box 11127, Birmingham, AL 35202) Ed. J. Ingleby. adv.; bk.rev.; illus.; circ. 2,100. (tabloid format; also avail. in microform from UMI)
Former titles: Aware Harvester; Harvester (ISSN 0017-8217); Incorporates: Witness.
Description: Publishes contemporary articles and practical input for local church life.

297.89   CN   ISSN 0708-5052
BAHA'I STUDIES. 1976. irreg. Can.$5 per no. Association for Baha'i Studies, 34 Copernicus St., Ottawa, Ont. K1N 7K4, Canada. TEL 613-233-1903. Ed.Bd. circ. 2,000.

297.89   IS   ISSN 0045-1320
BAHA'I WORLD. (Text primarily in English; occasional articles in French, German and Persian) 1925. irreg., vol.19, 1991. price varies. Baha'i World Centre, P.O. Box 155, Haifa 31001, Israel. FAX 04-358280. TELEX 46626-BAYT IL. (Dist. in U.S. by: Baha'i Publishing Trust, 415 Linden Ave., Wilmette, IL 60091) Ed. Sherna Deamer. circ. 15,000.

970 001   US   ISSN 0067-3129
BAMPTON LECTURES IN AMERICA. 1949. irreg., no.20, 1978. price varies. Columbia University Press, 562 W. 113th St., New York, NY 10025. TEL 212-678-6777.

200   UK   ISSN 0950-8368
BAND OF HOPE CHRONICLE. 1877. q. United Kingdom Band of Hope Union, 25 F Copperfield St., London SE1 0EN, England. Ed. G.T. Ruston. circ. 1,000.

200 950   II   ISSN 0253-9365
BANGALORE THEOLOGICAL FORUM. (Text in English) 1968. q. Rs.25($10) United Theological College, 17 Miller's Rd., Bangalore, S. India 560 046, India. TEL 575844. Ed. Eric J. Lott. adv.; bk.rev.; abstr.; circ. 550. (also avail. in microform from UMI; back issues avail.) **Indexed:** New Test.Abstr., Rel.& Theol.Abstr. (1989-), Rel.Ind.One.

200   UK
BANNER OF TRUTH. 1955. 11/yr. £9.50($18) (typically set in Jan.). Banner of Truth Trust Publishers, 3 Murrayfield Rd., Edinburgh EH12 6EL, Scotland. TEL 031-337-7310. FAX 031-346-7484. (U.S. addr.: Box 621, Carlisle, PA 17013. TEL 717-249-5747) bk.rev.; circ. 6,000.
Description: Exposition and application of the historic reformed Christian faith.

200   US
BAPTIST COURIER. w. $8. Baptist Courier, Inc., Box 2168, Greenville, SC 29602.
Description: Forum and news on religion.

200   US
THE BAPTIST STANDARD. 1888. w. $9.85. Baptist Standard Publishing Company, Box 660267, Dallas, TX 75266-0267. TEL 214-630-4571. FAX 214-638-8535. adv.; bk.rev.; circ. 264,411.

BASIS. see MILITARY

200   SZ   ISSN 0005-6189
BASLER PREDIGTEN; eine monatliche Predigtfolge. 1936. m. 24.80 Fr. Friedrich Reinhardt Verlag, Missionsstr. 36, CH-4012 Basel, Switzerland. Ed.Bd. circ. 3,500.

BASTA!. see POLITICAL SCIENCE — International Relations

200   GW   ISSN 0005-6618
DAS BAUGERUEST; Mitarbeiterzeitschrift fuer ausserschul. Jugendbildung. 1949. 4/yr. DM.22. Verein zur Foerderung Evangelischer Jugendarbeit e.V., Hummelsteiner Weg 100, 8500 Nuernberg, Germany. Ed. Gernard Bucke. bk.rev.; bibl.; tr.lit.; index; circ. 2,600. (avail. on records)

200   GW   ISSN 0005-707X
BAYERISCHE KRIPPENFREUND. 1917. q. DM.20.60($15) (Verband Bayerische Krippenfreunde) Anton H. Konrad Verlag, Schulstr. 5, P.O.B. 1206, D-7912 Weissenhorn, Germany. TEL 07309-2657. Ed. Erich Lidel. circ. 5,000. (back issues avail.)

200   NE   ISSN 0005-7312
DE BAZUIN. 1911. w. fl.150. Stichting De Bazuin, P.O. Box 2456, 3500 GL Utrecht, Netherlands. Ed. J. Kuhlmann. adv.; bk.rev.; illus.; circ. 5,000 (controlled). **Indexed:** CERDIC.

BEACON (NEW YORK). see PHILOSOPHY

200 919.406   AT
BECOMING. 1986. 4/yr. free. Aboriginal Apostolate Programme, 2nd Fl., 154 Elizabeth St., Sydney, N.S.W. 2000, Australia. TEL 02-264-7302. Ed. Pamela Barker. adv.; circ. 300.
Description: Encourages networking between church personnel working in Aboriginal communities.

200 333.7   US   ISSN 1050-0332
BEFRIENDING CREATION. 1985. 11/yr. $15. Friends Committee on Unity with Nature, 608 E. 11th St., Davis, CA 95616-2000. TEL 916-758-5407. Ed. Chris Laning. circ. 500.
Formerly (until 1988): Unity with Nature Newsletter.
Description: Provides news and information to members about our spiritual relations with the environment.

280   GW
DIE BEIDEN TUERME; Niederaltaicher Rundbrief. 1965. s-a. free. Benediktinerabtei Niederaltaich, 8351 Niederaltaich, Germany. Ed. P. Bonifaz Pfister. circ. 4,500.

BEITRAEGE ZUR GESCHICHTE DER PHILOSOPHIE UND THEOLOGIE DES MITTELALTERS. NEUE FOLGE. see PHILOSOPHY

266   GW   ISSN 0342-1341
BEITRAEGE ZUR GESCHICHTE DES ALTEN MOENCHTUMS UND DES BENEDIKTINERORDENS. 1912. irreg. price varies. Aschendorffsche Verlagsbuchhandlung, Soesterstr. 13, 4400 Muenster, Germany. TEL 0251-690-0. FAX 0251-690405. Ed. Emmanuel v. Severus.

200   GW
BEITRAEGE ZUR GESCHICHTE DES BISTUMS REGENSBURG. 1967. a. DM.30. Verein fuer Regensburger Bistumsgeschichte e.V., Petersweg 11-13, Postfach 11 02 28, 8400 Regensburg, Germany. TEL 0941-58813.

230   GW   ISSN 0067-5172
BEITRAEGE ZUR OEKUMENISCHEN THEOLOGIE. 1967. irreg., vol.20, 1981. price varies. Ferdinand Schoeningh, Juehenplatz 1, 4790 Paderborn, Germany. TEL 05251-29010. FAX 05251-2901-67. TELEX 936929. Ed. Heinrich Fries. circ. 500.
Description: Scholarly publication about the ecumenical movement in the Catholic Church and the beliefs of contemporary theologians. Each issue covers a distinctive topic.

200   US   ISSN 0005-8327
BELARUSKAJA CARKVA. 1956. s-a. $4. Belaruskaja Vydaveckaja Siabrynia, 3006 Logan Blvd., Chicago, IL 60647. Ed. Vaclau Panucevic. bk.rev.; charts; illus.; index; circ. 500.

260   GW
BERCKERS KATHOLISCHER TASCHENKALENDER. 1955. a. DM.12. Verlag Butzon und Bercker, Hoogeweg 71, Postfach 215, 4178 Kevelaer, Germany. circ. 20,000.
Former titles: Berckers Taschenkalender; Berckers Katholischer Taschenkalender.

220   UK
BEREAN EXPOSITOR. 1909. bi-m. £3.50($8) Berean Publishing Trust, 10 Dukes Close, Cranleigh, Surrey GU6 7JU, England. TEL 0483-272016. Ed. Stuart Allen. circ. 750.
Description: General Bible subjects for Bible students.

RELIGIONS AND THEOLOGY 4165

200 US ISSN 0005-8890
BEREAN SEARCHLIGHT. 1940. m. (except Jul.). free. Berean Bible Society, 7609 W. Belmont Ave., Chicago, IL 60635. TEL 312-456-7889. Ed. Paul M. Sadler. bk.rev.; charts; illus.; circ. 22,500. (also avail. in microfilm from UMI; reprint service avail.)

200 GW ISSN 0174-2477
BERLINER ISLAMSTUDIEN. 1981. irreg., vol.5, 1992. price varies. (Institut fuer Islamwissenschaft der Freien Universitaet Berlin) Franz Steiner Verlag Wiesbaden GmbH, Birkenwaldstr. 44, Postfach 101526, 7000 Stuttgart 1, Germany. TEL 0711-2582-0. FAX 0711-2582290. TELEX 723636-DAZD. Ed.Bd.

220 296 IS ISSN 0005-979X
BS410
BET MIKRA. (Text in Hebrew) 1956. q. $25. World Jewish Bible Center, P.O. Box 7024, Jerusalem, Israel. TEL 02-715112. Ed. Ben-Zion Luria. bk.rev.; circ. 1,400. **Indexed:** Ind.Heb.Per., Rel.& Theol.Abstr. (1977-).

200 US
BETHELITE CHALLENGER. vol.2, 1989. bi-m. (Bethelite Institutional Baptist Church) Joyce F. Roberts, Ed. & Pub., 447 Elton St., Brooklyn, NY 11208. adv.

220 418.02 AT
BEYOND WORDS. 1986. q. $8. Wycliffe Bible Translators Australia, Graham Rd., Kangaroo Ground, Vic. 3097, Australia. TEL 03-712-2777. FAX 61-3-712-2799. Ed. Bruce Grayden. bk.rev.; circ. 9,500.

220 IT ISSN 0006-0585
BS410
BIBBIA E ORIENTE; rivista per la conoscenza della Bibbia. (Supplements avail.) 1959. q. $72. (Centro Studi Arti Grafiche) Editrice Sardini, 25040 Bornato (Brescia), Italy. FAX 030-7254348. TELEX 030-725123. Ed. Fausto Sardini. adv.; bk.rev.; illus.; index. **Indexed:** New Test.Abstr., Old Test.Abstr., Rel.& Theol.Abstr.

220 GW
BIBEL IM JAHR. 1964. a. DM.13.80. Katholisches Bibelwerk e.V., Silberburgstr. 121, 7000 Stuttgart 1, Germany. TEL 0711-626001. FAX 0711-616682. Ed. F.J. Ortkemper. adv.; bk.rev.; illus.; index.

220 SW ISSN 0006-0607
BIBEL-JOURNALEN. 1952. bi-m. SEK 50. Ryska Bibelsaellskapet - Russian Bible Society, P.O. Box 1801, 70 118 Oerebro, Sweden. FAX 019-11-10-16. Ed. Ingemar Hallzon. illus.; circ. 15,000.

220 GW ISSN 0006-0615
BIBEL UND GEMEINDE. 1900. q. DM.28($12) Bibelbund e.V., Breite Str. 16, 5300 Bonn, Germany. Ed. Dr. Thomas Schirrmacher. bk.rev.; circ. 3,500 (controlled).
—BLDSC shelfmark: 1947.808000.
Description: Theological journal of German fundamentalism.

220 282 GW ISSN 0006-0623
BIBEL UND KIRCHE. 1946. q. DM.25. Katholisches Bibelwerk E.V., Silberburgstr. 121, 7000 Stuttgart 1, Germany. TEL 0711-626001. FAX 0711-616682. Ed. F.J. Ortkemper. adv.; bk.rev.; abstr.; index; circ. 25,000. **Indexed:** CERDIC, New Test.Abstr., Old Test.Abstr.
—BLDSC shelfmark: 1947.810000.

220 GW ISSN 0006-064X
BIBEL UND LITURGIE. 1926. q. DM.44. Am Wehrhahn 100, Postfach 6213, 4000 Duesseldorf 1, Germany. TEL 0521-78720. (Subscr. to: Cornelsen Verlagskontor, Kammerratsheide 66, 4800 Bielefeld 1, Germany) (Co-sponsor: Oesterreichisches Katholisches Bibelwerk) Ed. Norbert W. Hoeslinger. adv.; bk.rev.; abstr.; bibl.; tr.lit.; index; circ. 3,000. **Indexed:** CERDIC, New Test.Abstr., Old Test.Abstr.
—BLDSC shelfmark: 1947.820000.

200 GW ISSN 0933-9949
BIBELREPORT. 1968. q. DM.6. Deutsche Bibelgesellschaft, Balinger Str. 31, 7000 Stuttgart 80, Germany. TEL 0711-7181-0. FAX 0711-7181-126. TELEX 7255299-BIBL-D. Ed. Juergen Simon. bk.rev.; illus.; circ. 84,000. (back issues avail.)
Description: Magazine of the Bible societies in Germany and Austria.

266 SW ISSN 0006-0658
BIBELTROGNA VAENNERS MISSIONSTIDNING. 1912. m. SEK 120. Missionssaellskapet Bibeltrogna Vaenner, P.O. Box 6160, S-102 33 Stockholm, Sweden. Ed. Rune Karlsson. bk.rev.; index; circ. 2,700.

200 US ISSN 0746-0104
BIBLE ADVOCATE. 1863. m. free. (Church of God (Seventh Day), General Conference) Bible Advocate Press, 330 W. 152nd Ave., Broomfield, CO 80020. FAX 303-452-0657. (Subscr. to: Box 33677, Denver, CO 80233) Ed. Jerry Griffin. index; circ. 16,000. (back issues avail.)
Description: Features articles on Bible doctrine, current issues in today's world, and other material that will enrich the spiritual lives of those who seek to know about God.

220 UK
BIBLE EXPLORATION MATERIAL AND ANNUAL PROJECT. a. £2.95. National Christian Education Council, Robert Denholm House, Nutfield, Redhill, Surrey RH1 4HW, England. TEL 0737-822411. FAX 0737-822116. Ed. D. Trenaman. circ. 2,000.
Former titles: Bible Exploration Material and Annual Scripture Project; Scripture Examination Material and Annual Scripture Project.

220 US ISSN 0006-0739
BIBLE FRIEND; of biblical faith and Christ's teaching. 1903. m. $4. Osterhus Publishing House, Inc., 4500 W. Broadway, Minneapolis, MN 55422. TEL 612-537-8335. Ed. Mrs. Cyrus Osterhus. illus.; circ. 10,000.

220 US
BIBLE-IN-LIFE FRIENDS. w. David C. Cook Publishing Co., 850 N. Grove Ave., Elgin, IL 60120. TEL 312-741-2400. Ed. Ramona Warren.
Description: Aimed at children aged 6-8.

220 SW ISSN 0347-2787
BIBLE RESEARCHER. (Text in English, French, German, Polish and Swedish; summaries in English) 1975. m. SEK 120($20) European Human Rights, Marknadsvagen 289 2tr, S-183 34 Taby, Sweden. TEL 08-7681398. Ed. Ditlieb Felderer. bk.rev.; circ. 1,000. (back issues avail.)

200 US ISSN 8755-6316
BS410
BIBLE REVIEW. 1985. bi-m. $24 (foreign $28). Biblical Archaeology Society, 3000 Connecticut Ave., N.W., Ste. 300, Washington, DC 20008. TEL 202-387-8888. FAX 202-483-3423. (Subscr. to: Box 10105, Des Moines, IA 50340) Ed. Hershel Shanks. adv.; bk.rev.; cum.index: 1985-1987; circ. 40,000. (also avail. in talking book; back issues avail.) **Indexed:** Old Test.Abstr.
—BLDSC shelfmark: 1947.824660.
Description: Articles written by scholars and edited for an audience on Bible interpretation, and exegesis.

220 US
BIBLE SCIENCE NEWSLETTER. 1963. 9/yr. $25. Bible Science Association, Box 32457, Minneapolis, MN 55432-0457. TEL 612-755-8606. Ed. Paul A. Bartz. bk.rev.; illus.; circ. 15,000.

200 US ISSN 0006-081X
BIBLE STANDARD AND HERALD OF CHRIST'S KINGDOM. French edition: Etendard de la Bible et Heraut du Royaume de Christ. (Editions also in Danish and Polish) 1920. m. $1. Laymen's Home Missionary Movement, Box 679, Chester Springs, PA 19425. TEL 215-827-7665. Ed. Bernard W. Hedman. circ. 4,000. **Indexed:** CERDIC.
Description: Highlights mission work.

200 UK
BIBLE STUDY MONTHLY. 1924. bi-m. free to members. Bible Fellowship Union, 11 Lyncroft Gardens, Hounslow, Middlesex, England. bk.rev.
Description: Bible history, archaeology, prophecy, devotional from a pre-millennial outlook.

BIBLE-TIME. see *CHILDREN AND YOUTH* — For

220 US ISSN 0006-0836
BIBLE TODAY; a periodical promoting scripture for life & ministry. 1962. bi-m. $18. Liturgical Press, St. John's Abbey, Collegeville, MN 56321. TEL 612-363-2213. Ed. Sr. Diane Bergant. adv.; bk.rev.; illus.; index; circ. 9,315. (also avail. in microform from UMI; back issues avail.; reprint service avail. from UMI) **Indexed:** Cath.Ind., New Test.Abstr., Old Test.Abstr.

266 US
BIBLES FOR THE WORLD NEWS. 1966. q. free to donors. Bibles for the World, Inc., Box 805, Wheaton, IL 60189. TEL 708-668-7733. Ed.Bd. bk.rev.; circ. 30,000.
Description: Focuses on missions and missionary work.

220 IT ISSN 0006-0879
BIBLIA REVUO. (Text in Esperanto) 1964. q. $6. Internacia Asocio de Bibliistoj Kaj Orientalistoj, Piazza Duomo 4, 48100 Ravenna, Italy. Dir. Angelo Duranti. adv.; bk.rev.; charts; illus.; circ. 3,000. **Indexed:** New Test.Abstr., Old Test.Abstr.

BIBLICAL ARCHAEOLOGIST. see *ARCHAEOLOGY*

BIBLICAL ARCHAEOLOGY REVIEW. see *ARCHAEOLOGY*

220 US
BIBLICAL ERRANCY; the only national periodical focusing on biblical errors, contradictions and fallacies, while providing a hearing for apologists. 1983. m. $12 in U.S.; Canada $14 (effective May 1991). Dennis McKinsey, Ed. & Pub., 3158 Sherwood Park Dr., Springfield, OH 45505. TEL 513-323-6146. circ. 330. (back issues avail.)
Description: Exposes and critiques fallacies and contradictions in the Bible. Includes letters from readers and critics.

220 IS ISSN 0792-4739
BIBLICAL POLEMICS. (Text in English) 1988. m. $35. Jerusalem Institute of Biblical Polemics, P.O. Box 13099, Jerusalem 91130, Israel. TEL 02-250173. FAX 02-253881. Ed. Shmuel Golding. bk.rev.
Description: Attempts to educate and present information to refute Christian missionaries.

220 US ISSN 0067-6535
BS410
BIBLICAL RESEARCH. 1956. a. $5. (Chicago Society of Biblical Research) Franciscan Publishers, Franciscan Center, Pulaski, WI 54162. TEL 414-822-5833. FAX 414-822-5423. Ed. David E. Aune. index; circ. 700. (also avail. in microform from UMI; back issues avail.) **Indexed:** CERDIC, New Test.Abstr., Old Test.Abstr., Rel.& Theol.Abstr. (1967-), Rel.Ind.One.
—BLDSC shelfmark: 1947.855000.

200 US ISSN 0277-0474
BIBLICAL SCHOLARSHIP IN NORTH AMERICA. irreg. (Society of Biblical Literature) Scholars Press, Box 15399, Atlanta, GA 30333-0399. TEL 404-636-4757. FAX 404-636-8301. Ed. Kent Harold Richards.
—BLDSC shelfmark: 1947.855400.
Description: Monographs on important biblical scholars in the United States.

230 IE ISSN 0006-0917
BIBLICAL THEOLOGY. 1950. s-a. $3. Donegal Democrat, Ballyshannon, Co. Donegal, Ireland. Eds. Rev. Dr. J. Thompson, Rev. R.D. Drysdale. bk.rev.; circ. 250.

220 US ISSN 0146-1079
BS410
BIBLICAL THEOLOGY BULLETIN. 1971. 4/yr. $15 to individuals (foreign $18); institutions and libraries $25. Biblical Theology Bulletin, Inc., c/o Theology Department, St. John's University, Jamaica, NY 11439. Eds. David M. Bossman, Leland J. White. adv.; bk.rev.; abstr.; bibl.; index, cum.index; circ. 1,800. (also avail. in microform from UMI; reprint service avail. UMI) **Indexed:** Bk.Rev.Ind. (1982-), CERDIC, Child.Bk.Rev.Ind. (1982-), New Test.Abstr., Old Test.Abstr., Rel.& Theol.Abstr. (1977-), Rel.Ind.One, Rel.Per.
—BLDSC shelfmark: 1947.856000.

RELIGIONS AND THEOLOGY

230   US   ISSN 0006-0925
BIBLICAL VIEWPOINT. 1967. s-a. $4 (foreign $6). Bob Jones University, Greenville, SC 29614. TEL 803-242-5100. Ed. Stewart Custer. bk.rev.; bibl.; circ. 1,500. **Indexed**: Chr.Per.Ind., Rel.& Theol.Abstr. (1968-).
—BLDSC shelfmark: 1947.858000.
Description: Exposition on the books of the Bible.

220   SW   ISSN 0345-1453
BIBLICUM; tidskrift foer biblisk tro och forskning. 1972. q. (plus 3 supplements). SEK 100. Stiftelsen Biblicum, S. Rudbecksgatan 6, 752 36 Uppsala, Sweden. FAX 031-116230. TELEX 018-506925. Ed. Ingemar Furberg. bk.rev.; circ. 1,000.
—BLDSC shelfmark: 1947.858500.
Supersedes: Foer Biblisk Tro (ISSN 0015-5217)

200   SP   ISSN 0067-740X
BIBLIOTECA DE TEOLOGIA. 1964. irreg., no.18, 1987. price varies. (Universidad de Navarra, Facultad de Teologia) Ediciones Universidad de Navarra, S.A., Apdo. 396, 31080 Pamplona, Spain. TEL 94 825 6850.

200   SW
BIBLIOTECA THEOLOGIAE PRACTICAE. (Text in Swedish; summaries in English or German) 1957. irreg., no.44, 1989. price varies. Almqvist & Wiksell International, P.O. Box 638, S-101 28 Stockholm, Sweden. Eds. Carl-Gustaf Andren, Aake Andren.

209   PL   ISSN 0519-8658
BIBLIOTEKA PISARZY REFORMACYJNYCH. (Text in Latin and Polish) 1958. irreg., vol.16, 1988. price varies. (Polska Akademia Nauk, Instytut Filozofii i Socjologii) Panstwowe Wydawnictwo Naukowe, Ul. Miodowa 10, 00-251 Warsaw, Poland. (Dist. by: Ars Polona, Krakowskie Przedmiescie 7, 00-068 Warsaw, Poland) Ed. L. Szczucki. circ. 350.

BIBLIOTHECA DISSIDENTIUM. see *BIBLIOGRAPHIES*

200   BE
BIBLIOTHECA EPHEMERIDUM THEOLOGICARUM LOVANIENSIUM. vol.31, 1972. irreg., vol.99, 1991. Leuven University Press, Krakenstraat 3, B-3000 Leuven, Belgium. TEL 016-284175. FAX 016-284176. **Indexed**: Rel.Ind.Two.

200   NE
BIBLIOTHECA HUMANISTICA & REFORMATORICA. (Text in English, French or German) 1971. irreg., vol.52, 1992. price varies. De Graaf Publishers, P.O. Box 6, 2420 AA Nieuwkoop, Netherlands. TEL 01725-71461.

220   SZ   ISSN 0582-1673
BIBLISCHE BEITRAEGE. 1961. irreg., no.13, 1977. price varies. Universitaetsverlag, Perolles 42, CH-1700 Fribourg, Switzerland. TEL 037-246812. adv.; illus.; circ. 1,750.

220   GW   ISSN 0523-5154
BIBLISCHE UNTERSUCHUNGEN. 1967. irreg., vol.21, 1990. price varies. Verlag Friedrich Pustet, Gutenbergstr. 8, 8400 Regensburg 1, Germany. FAX 0941-948652. Eds. Jost Eckert, Josef Hainz. circ. 800.

220   GW   ISSN 0006-2014
BS410
BIBLISCHE ZEITSCHRIFT. N.S. 1957. s-a. DM.60. Ferdinand Schoeningh, Juehenplatz 1, Postfach 2540, 4790 Paderborn, Germany. TEL 05251-29010. FAX 05251-2901-35. TELEX 936929-FS-PB. Eds. J. Schreiner, R. Schnackenburg. adv.; bibl.; index. (also avail. in microform from UMI; reprint service avail. from UMI) **Indexed**: Arts & Hum.Cit.Ind., CERDIC, Curr.Cont., New Test.Abstr., Old Test.Abstr., Rel.& Theol.Abstr. (1968-), Rel.Ind.One, Rel.Per.
—BLDSC shelfmark: 2020.800000.
Description: Collection of articles concerning the Old and the New Testament. Includes reviews and criticisms.

220   GW
BIBLISCHES SEMINAR. 1967. irreg. price varies. Calwer Verlag, Scharnhauserstr. 44, 7000 Stuttgart 70, Germany. TEL 0711-452019. FAX 0711-4560660.

230 201   NE   ISSN 0006-2278
BIJDRAGEN; tijdschrift voor filosofie en theologie. (Text in Dutch, English, French and German) 1938. 4/yr. fl.95 to individuals; institutions fl.145; students fl.25. Stichting Bijdragen, Keizersgracht 105, 1015 CH Amsterdam, Netherlands. TEL 020-6272621. Ed.Bd. bk.rev.; index; circ. 500. **Indexed**: CERDIC, Int.Z.Bibelwiss, New Test.Abstr., Old.Test.Abstr., Rel.& Theol.Abstr. (1968-), Rel.Ind.One.
—BLDSC shelfmark: 2057.400000.
Description: Covers systematic theology, the history of dogma and theology, liturgical science, spirituality and applied theology, biblical studies, church history, cannon law and the social sciences.

266 338.91   NE   ISSN 0006-2308
BIJEEN; maandblad over internationale samenleving, bijzonder op het terrein van godsdienst en ontwikkeling. 1968. m. (11/yr.) fl.58.50. Stichting Gezamenlijke Missiepubliciteit, Postbus 750, 5201 AT 's-Hertogenbosch, Netherlands. FAX 073-218512. Ed.Bd. adv.; bk.rev.; film rev.; play rev.; charts; illus.; circ. 35,000. (processed; also avail. in microfiche) **Indexed**: CERDIC.

200   US   ISSN 0195-265X
BILLY JAMES HARGIS' CHRISTIAN CRUSADE; international Christian newspaper. 1969. m. free. Church of Christian Crusade, Box 977, Tulsa, OK 74102. TEL 918-665-2345. Ed. Billy James Hargis. bk.rev.; circ. 55,000. (also avail. in microfilm from UMI)
Formerly: Christian Crusade Weekly; **Supersedes**: Weekly Crusader (ISSN 0509-9498)

270 940   GW   ISSN 0341-9479
BLAETTER FUER WUERTTEMBERGISCHE KIRCHENGESCHICHTE. 1886. a. DM.70. Verein fuer Wuerttembergische Kirchengeschichte, Gaensheidestr. 4, Postfach 101342, 7000 Stuttgart 10, Germany. FAX 0711-2149236. Eds. Martin Brecht, Hermann Ehmer. bk.rev.; index; circ. 1,250. **Indexed**: Amer.Hist.& Life, Hist.Abstr.
—BLDSC shelfmark: 2110.130000.

200   GW
BLAUES KREUZ. 1897. m. DM.31.20. (Blaues Kreuz in Deutschland e.V.) Blaukreuz Verlag, Freiligrathstr. 27, 5600 Wuppertal 2, Germany. Ed. Alexander Schubert. circ. 5,000.

261   US   ISSN 0006-4696
HN39.U6
BLESSINGS OF LIBERTY. 1956. q. $3. Foundation for Religious Action in the Social and Civil Order, Box 1829, Pinehurst, NC 28374. Ed. Charles W. Lowry. bk.rev.; circ. 1,100.

BOA SEMENTE. see *CHILDREN AND YOUTH — For*

200   NE   ISSN 0006-5439
BODE VAN HET HEIL IN CHRISTUS. 1858. m. fl.42.50. Uitgeverij H. Medema, Box 113, 8170 AC Vaassen, Netherlands. TEL 31-5788-4995. FAX 31-5788-3099. Ed. H.P. Medema. bk.rev.; circ. 2,700.
Formerly: Bode des Heils.

200   YU   ISSN 0006-5714
BOGOSLOVLJE. (Text in Serbo-Croatian) 1926. s-a. $15. Pravoslavni Bogoslovski Fakultet u Beogradu, 7 Jula 2, Belgrade, Yugoslavia. TEL 011-630-268. FAX 182-780. Ed. B. Simic. bk.rev.; circ. 1,200.
Description: Presents articles by Orthodox and non-Orthodox theologians on various contemporary theological issues.

200   MH
BOLETIM ECLESIAL. (Text in Portuguese) m. Camara Eclesiastica, Macao. TEL 853-73059. Ed. Rev. Americo Casado.

200   SP
BOLETIN OFICIAL ECLESIASTICO DEL ARZOBISPADO CASTRENSE DE ESPANA. 1950. m. 2500 ptas.($10) Arrolispado Castrense de Orpana, Nuncio 13, 28005 Madrid, Spain. bk.rev.; bibl.; index; circ. controlled.
Formerly (until Jan. 1986): Boletin Oficial de la Jurisdiccion Eclesiastica Castrense.

268   IT   ISSN 0300-4589
BOLLETTINO DI COLLEGAMENTO; fra comunita cristiane in Italia. 1969. m. c/o Tony Sansone, Via delle Cascine 22, 50144 Florence, Italy. Eds. Maurizio Matteuzzi, Tony Sansone. bk.rev.; film rev.; bibl.; index; circ. 3,000.

BOLLINGEN SERIES. see *PHILOSOPHY*

BOOKS AND RELIGION; a quarterly review of religious books and ideas. see *PUBLISHING AND BOOK TRADE*

200   US
BOOKS OF ORAL TRADITION. (Text in Arabic, English, Hebrew) 1980. irreg. Quantal Publishing, Box 1598-B, Goleta, CA 93117. TEL 805-964-7293. Ed. Ken Bartlett. circ. 3,000. (back issues avail.)
Description: Basic guidance to practical psychotherapy of religions and mythologies.

BOOKSTORE JOURNAL. see *PUBLISHING AND BOOK TRADE*

200 100   US
BOSTON UNIVERSITY STUDIES IN PHILOSOPHY AND RELIGION. 1980. irreg., no.12, 1991. University of Notre Dame Press, Notre Dame, IN 46556. TEL 219-239-6346. Ed. Leroy S. Rouner. **Indexed**: Rel.Ind.Two.

200   GW   ISSN 0068-0443
BOTSCHAFT DES ALTEN TESTAMENTS; Erlauterungen Alttestamentlicher Schriften. 1958. irreg., vol.7-8, 1980. price varies. Calwer Verlag, Scharnhauserstr. 44, 7000 Stuttgart 70, Germany. TEL 0711-452019. FAX 0711-4560660.

200   GW   ISSN 0176-8573
BOTSCHAFT HEUTE. m. DM.114. Bergmoser und Hoeller Verlag GmbH, Karl-Friedrich-Str. 76, 5100 Aachen, Germany. TEL 0241-17309-21. FAX 0241-17309-34. circ. 3,600. (looseleaf format; back issues avail.)
Description: Publication of interest to preachers. Features ideas for topics, songs, psalms, prayers, Bible excerpts, and liturgical texts for sermons on all Sundays and special celebrations.

200   IT   ISSN 0391-6723
BOZZE. 1978. bi-m. L.35000 (foreign L.52500)(effective 1991). Edizioni Dedalo s.r.l., Casella Postale 362, 70100 Bari, Italy. TEL 080-371555. FAX 080-371979. Dir. Raniero La Valle. circ. 9,000.

200   GW
BRENNPUNKT SEELSORGE; Beitraege zur biblischen Lebensberatung. 1979. bi-m. DM.15. Brunnen Verlag GmbH, Postfach 5205, 6300 Giessen 1, Germany. Ed. Horst-Klaus Hofmann. bk.rev.

200   US
BRETHREN JOURNAL.* m. Rt. 3, Box 558N, Brenham, TX 77833. TEL 409-830-8762.

377 200   UK   ISSN 0141-6200
BRITISH JOURNAL OF RELIGIOUS EDUCATION. 1934. 3/yr. £17.50($32) (effective Sep. 1991). Christian Education Movement, Royal Buildings, Victoria St., Derby DE1 1GW, England. TEL 021-414-4836. FAX 021-414-4865. Ed. Dr. J.M. Hull. adv.; bk.rev.; charts; index; circ. 4,000. (also avail. in microform from UMI; back issues avail., reprint service avail. from UMI) **Indexed**: Abstr.Musl.Rel., Br.Educ.Ind., CERDIC, Cont.Pg.Educ., Rel. & Theol.Abstr.
—BLDSC shelfmark: 2324.200000.
Supersedes (in 1978): Learning for Living (ISSN 0023-9704) & Religion in Education.

207 268.8   US   ISSN 0068-2721
BROADMAN COMMENTS; INTERNATIONAL SUNDAY SCHOOL LESSONS. 1945. a. or q. $7.95. Broadman Press, 127 Ninth Ave., N., Nashville, TN 37234. TEL 615-251-2000. Ed. Donald F. Ackland. circ. 17,000.
Description: Supplementary reading on International Sunday School lessons for adults.

266   US   ISSN 0007-2494
BROWN GOLD. 1943. m. $7. New Tribes Mission Publications, 1000 E. First St., Sanford, FL 32771-1487. TEL 407-323-3430. FAX 407-330-0376. Ed. Macon G. Hare. illus.; circ. 46,000.

266   GW
▼**BRUECKENSCHLAG**; Berichte aus der Mission fuer Dankopferringe und Kollektenvereine. 1990. q. Vereinigte Evangelische Mission, Rudolfstr. 137, 5600 Wuppertal 2, Germany. TEL 0202-89004-0. FAX 0202-89004-79.

BUDDHIST - CHRISTIAN STUDIES. see *RELIGIONS AND THEOLOGY — Buddhist*

266   FR   ISSN 0007-4330
BULLETIN DE L'OEUVRE APOSTOLIQUE. 1913. q. 25 F. Oeuvre Apostolique pour les Missions de Fondation Francaise a l'Etranger, 8 Av. Daniel Lesueur, 75007 Paris, France. Ed. L. Fromy. circ. 1,000.

230   BE   ISSN 0007-442X
BULLETIN DE THEOLOGIE ANCIENNE ET MEDIEVALE. s-a. 900 Fr.($30) Abbaye du Mont-Cesar, 202 Mechelse Straat, B-3000 Louvain, Belgium. Ed. E. Manning. bk.rev.; bibl.; index.

200   GO
BULLETIN EVANGELIQUE D'INFORMATION ET DE PRESSE. m. B.P. 80, Libreville, Gabon.

220   GR
BULLETIN OF BIBLICAL STUDIES. (Text in English, French, German and Greek) 1971; N.S. 1980. s-a. $10. Artos Zoes Publications, Efranoros 12, 116 35 Athens, Greece. TEL 7015379. Ed. S. Agouridis. bk.rev.; circ. 1,000. **Indexed:** New Test.Abstr.

BUNYAN STUDIES. see *LITERATURE*

230   SP   ISSN 0521-8195
BR7
BURGENSE; collectanea scientifica. (Text in French, Latin and Spanish) 1960. s-a. 2000 ptas.($28) (Facultad de Teologie) Ediciones Aldecoa, Martinez del Compo, 10, Apartado 50, 09003 Burgos, Spain. Ed. Nicolas Lopez Martinez. bk.rev.; bibl.; circ. 600. **Indexed:** CERDIC, New Test.Abstr., Old Test.Abstr.
—BLDSC shelfmark: 2931.623000.

BURIED HISTORY. see *ARCHAEOLOGY*

200   US   ISSN 0007-6309
BURNING BUSH. 1902. bi-m. $2. Metropolitan Church Association, 323 Broad St., Lake Geneva, WI 53147. TEL 414-248-6786. Ed. E.L. Adams. circ. 600.
Description: Contains sermons, editorials, seasonal poetry, religious articles, children's stories, and news from missions abroad.

C A L C REPORT. (National Clergy and Laity Concerned) see *POLITICAL SCIENCE — International Relations*

266   US
C B M FREUNDESBRIEF. 1961. bi-m. free. Christian Blind Mission International Inc., 450 E. Park Ave., Greenville, SC 29601. TEL 803-239-0065. FAX 803-239-0069. circ. 110,000.

200   SZ
C C I A BACKGROUND INFORMATION. 1975. irreg. (approx. 2/yr.). $20. World Council of Churches, Commission of the Churches on International Affairs, 150 Route de Ferney, Box 2100, 1211 Geneva 2, Switzerland. FAX 022-7910361. TELEX 415730-OIK-CH. circ. 2,000.

200 297   GW   ISSN 0721-0035
C I B E D O - BEITRAEGE ZUM GESPRAECH ZWISCHEN CHRISTEN UND MUSLIMEN. 1978. bi-m. DM.30. C I B E D O, Guiollettstr. 35, 6000 Frankfurt a.M. 1, Germany. TEL 069-726491. FAX 069-723052. Ed. Weisse Vaeter. bk.rev.; circ. 1,000. (back issues avail.)
Formerly: Cibedo - Dokumentation und Texte.

C L S QUARTERLY. see *LAW*

C M D S. (Christian Medical & Dental Society) see *MEDICAL SCIENCES*

200   GW   ISSN 0935-0373
C-MAGAZIN. 1987. q. DM.24($16) Gemeinschaft Immanuel e.V., Rudolfstr. 16, 7980 Ravensburg, Germany. TEL 0751-17035. FAX 0751-23899. Ed. Rainer Straub. adv.; bk.rev.; film rev.; play rev.; illus.; circ. 4,000.
Description: Reports and news about worldwide events in Christian churches.

200 331.8   NE
C N V - OPINIE. 1947. bi-m. fl.25 to non-members; members fl.15. Christelijk Nationaal Vakverbond in Nederland, Postbus 2475, Utrecht, Netherlands. FAX 030-946544. TELEX 40646. Ed. E. Heres. bk.rev.; charts; stat.; circ. 20,000. **Indexed:** Key to Econ.Sci.
Formerly (until 1991): Evangelie en Maatschappij (ISSN 0014-3383)

200   IT
C O M - NUOVI TEMPI. w. $10. N T C News, Via Firenze, 38, 00184 Rome, Italy. Ed. Giorgio Girardet. circ. 11,000. **Indexed:** CERDIC.
Formed by the merger of: C O M & Nuovi Tempi.

200   GW   ISSN 0588-9804
C O N C I L I U M; internationale Zeitschrift fuer Theologie. 1964. bi-m. DM.76. (Stichting Concilium, NE) Matthias Gruenewald Verlag GmbH, Max-Hufschmidt-Str. 4a, 6500 Mainz-Weisenau, Germany. TEL 06131-839055. circ. 3,100. (back issues avail.)

200   US
C R E E D NEWS. 1980. q. free. Christian Rescue Effort for the Emancipation of Dissidents, 787 Princeton Kingston Rd., Princeton, NJ 08540. TEL 609-497-0224. Ed. Ernest Gordon. bk.rev.; circ. 4,500. (looseleaf format)
Description: To witness to and for the persecuted church.

200   UK
C.R. QUARTERLY REVIEW. 1903. 4/yr. £5. Fraternity of the Resurrection, House of the Ressurection, Mirfield, West Yorks. WF14 0BN, England. TEL 0924-494318.
Description: Provides articles on theology, sociology and politics. Includes community news.

200   US
C S S R BULLETIN. 4/yr. $18 to individuals; libraries $24; foreign $30. Council of Societies for the Study of Religion, Mercer University, R.O.T.C. Bldg., Macon, GA 31207. TEL 912-752-2376. Eds. Rick Busse, Watson Mills. circ. 6,000.
Description: Serves as a clearing house for information about specific activities in the field of religious studies; includes news from various societies, general announcements, information on grants, program announcements, calendar of events.

266   UK   ISSN 0308-5252
C W I HERALD; a quarterly record of Christian Witness to Israel. 1976. q. $3.50. Christian Witness to Israel, Seven Trees, 44 Lubbock Rd., Chislehurst, Kent BR7 5JX, England. FAX 01-467-3080. Ed. M.A. MacLeod. bk.rev.; circ. 12,000. (also avail. in microform from UMI; reprint service avail. from UMI)
Former titles: Herald; Immanuel's Witness (ISSN 0019-2759)

250   FR   ISSN 0008-0063
CAHIERS D'ETUDES CATHARES. 1948. q. 200 F. (foreign 250 F.). Societe du Souvenir et des Etudes Cathares, Chateau de Ferrieres, 81260 Ferrieres, France. TEL 63-74-03-53. bk.rev.; index; circ. 650. **Indexed:** CERDIC.

200   FR
CAHIERS DE LA FORMATION. q. 100 F. (foreign 130 F.). Armee du Salut, 76 rue de Rome, 75008 Paris, France. TEL 1-43-87-41-19.
Description: Studies the Bible, the history of the Church and the ethical positions of the Salvation Army.

200   CN
CAHIERS DE RECHERCHE ETHIQUE. (Text in French) 1977. irreg. price varies. Editions Fides, 165, rue Deslaurier, Ville St-Laurent, Que. H4N 2S4, Canada. TEL 514-745-4290. FAX 514-745-4299. **Indexed:** CERDIC.

243   FR   ISSN 0222-9714
CAHIERS EVANGILE. (Supplement avail.) 1951. q. 95 F. (foreign 140 F.); with supplement 175 F. (foreign 244 F.). (Service Biblique Evangile et Vie) Editions du Cerf, 29 bd. Latour Maubourg, 75340 Paris Cedex 07, France. TEL 43-26-38-32. (Subscr. to: 6 av. Vavin, 75006 Paris, France) Ed. Philippe Gruson. bk.rev.; abstr.; circ. 16,000. **Indexed:** Old Test.Abstr., Pt.de Rep.
Formerly: Cahiers Bibliques Trimestriels (ISSN 0007-960X)

261   FR   ISSN 0987-2213
CAHIERS POUR CROIRE AUJOURD'HUI. 1933. s-m. 260 F. (foreign 380 F.). Assas Editions, 14 rue d'Assas, 75006 Paris, France. TEL 44-39-48-48. FAX 40-49-01-92. Ed. Luc Pareyot. index; circ. 22,000. **Indexed:** CERDIC.
Formerly (until 1987): Cahiers de l'Actualite Religieuse et Sociale (ISSN 0007-9669)

266   US
CALL TO PRAYER. 1919. m. (10/yr.). $10 donation. World Gospel Mission, 3783 State Road 18 East, Box WGM, Marion, IN 46952. TEL 317-664-7331. Ed. Dr. Thomas H. Hermiz. circ. 40,000. (tabloid format)

220   GW
CALWER THEOLOGISCHE MONOGRAPHIEN. REIHE A: BIBELWISSENSCHAFT. 1972. irreg. no.14, 1984. price varies. Calwer Verlag, Scharnhauserstr. 44, 7000 Stuttgart 70, Germany. TEL 0711-452019. FAX 0711-4560660. Eds. Peter Stuhlmacher, Claus Westermann.

230   GW
CALWER THEOLOGISCHE MONOGRAPHIEN. REIHE B: SYSTEMATISCHE THEOLOGIE UND KIRCHENGESCHICHTE. 1973. irreg. no.10, 1986. price varies. Calwer Verlag, Scharnhauserstr. 44, 7000 Stuttgart 70, Germany. TEL 0711-452019. FAX 0711-4560660. Ed.Bd.

200   GW
CALWER THEOLOGISCHE MONOGRAPHIEN. REIHE C: PRAKTISCHE THEOLOGIE UND MISSIONSWISSENSCHAFT. 1973. irreg., vol.12, 1985. price varies. Calwer Verlag, Scharnhauserstr. 44, 7000 Stuttgart 70, Germany. TEL 0711-452019. FAX 0711-4560660. Eds. S.H. Buekle, M. Seitz.

CAMINHO. see *CHILDREN AND YOUTH — For*

CAMPANIA SACRA; rivista di storia sociale e religiosa del Mezzogiorno. see *HISTORY — History Of Europe*

200   CN   ISSN 0832-1590
CANADIAN BIBLE SOCIETY QUARTERLY NEWSLETTER. French edition (ISSN 1184-7204) (Editions in English and French) 1960. q. free. Canadian Bible Society - Societe Biblique Canadienne, 10 Carnforth Rd., Toronto, Ont. M4A 2S4, Canada. TEL 416-757-4171. FAX 416-757-3376. TELEX TOR-06-963696. circ. 150,000.
Description: Demonstrates how the Society translates, publishes and distributes the Word of God to those in need.

270   CN   ISSN 0008-3208
BR570
CANADIAN CHURCH HISTORICAL SOCIETY JOURNAL. 1950. s-a. Can.$20($20) Canadian Church Historical Society, c/o Archives, Anglican Church of Canada, 600 Jarvis St., Toronto, Ont. M4Y 2J6, Canada. FAX 416-968-7983. Ed. Ian Storey. bk.rev.; cum.index; circ. 450. (also avail. in microform from UMI) **Indexed:** Amer.Hist.& Life, CERDIC, Hist.Abstr., Rel.Ind.One, Rel.Per.
—BLDSC shelfmark: 4723.005000.

277.1   CN   ISSN 0701-4309
CANADIAN COUNCIL OF CHURCHES. RECORD OF PROCEEDINGS. 1944. triennial. Canadian Council of Churches - Conseil Canadien des Eglises, 40 St. Clair Ave. E., Toronto, Ont. M4T 1M9, Canada. TEL 416-921-4152. FAX 416-921-7478.

200   CN   ISSN 0227-8243
CANADIAN ECUMENICAL NEWS. 1976. 5/yr. Can.$10($10) Canadian Ecumenical Action, 240 W. 12th Ave., Vancouver, B.C. V6J 2G2, Canada. TEL 604-736-1613. Ed. M. Joan Craker. adv.; bk.rev.; illus.; circ. 4,000.
Formerly: B.C. Ecumenical News.
Description: An inter-faith publication aimed at promoting understanding between different faith groups, social action in perspective.

266   CN   ISSN 0316-2907
CANADIAN GIDEON. (Text in English and French) 1955. bi-m. Can.$8.50. Gideons International in Canada, 501 Imperial Rd. N., Guelph, Ont. N1H 7A2, Canada. TEL 519-823-1140. FAX 519-767-1913. Ed. Neil Bramble. illus.
Supersedes: Torch and Trumpet (ISSN 0316-2915)

RELIGIONS AND THEOLOGY

200   CN   ISSN 0316-8743
CANADIAN RELIGIOUS CONFERENCE. BULLETIN. French edition: Conference Religieuse Canadienne. Bulletin (ISSN 0316-8751) (Editions in English and French) 1955. 4/yr. Canadian Religious Conference, 324 Laurier Ave. E., Ottawa, Ont. K1N 6P6, Canada. TEL 613-236-0824. FAX 613-236-0825. Ed. Sr. Rita Montreuil.

220   CN   ISSN 0068-970X
CANADIAN SOCIETY OF BIBLICAL STUDIES. BULLETIN/SOCIETE CANADIENNE DES ETUDES BIBLIQUES. BULLETIN. (Not issued 1960-1963) 1935. a. membership. Canadian Society of Biblical Studies, Faculty of Theology, c/o Dr. John S. Kloppenborg, University of St. Micheal's College, 81 St. Mary St., Toronto, Ont. M5S 1J4, Canada. TEL 416-926-7140. Ed. Dr. John S. Kloppenborg. circ. 300.
—BLDSC shelfmark: 2434.192000.

CANNON. see *COLLEGE AND ALUMNI*

266   JM   ISSN 0008-6436
CARIBBEAN CHALLENGE. 1957. m. $7. Christian Literature Crusade Inc., Box 186, 55 Church St., Kingston, Jamaica, W.I. Ed.Bd. adv.; circ. 20,000. (tabloid format)
   Description: Christian magazine designed primarily to reach the "man in the street".

268   JM   ISSN 0253-066X
BR1
CARIBBEAN JOURNAL OF RELIGIOUS STUDIES; a forum for discussion of religious issues. 1975. s-a. J.$30($10) United Theological College of the West Indies, Golding Ave., P.O. Box 136, Mona, Kingston 7, Jamaica, W.I. Ed. Howard K. Gregory. bk.rev.; bibl.; circ. 400. **Indexed:** Rel.Ind.One.
   Description: Forum for discussion of religious and pastoral issues affecting the life of Caribbean people.

260   GW
CARITAS-KALENDER. 1924. a. DM.6.10. (Deutscher Caritasverband) Lambertus-Verlag GmbH, Woelflinstr. 4, Postfach 1026, 7800 Freiburg, Germany. TEL 0761-31566. FAX 0761-37064. Ed. Peter Gralla. adv.; circ. 55,000.

CARL NEWELL JACKSON LECTURES. see *FOLKLORE*

200   US   ISSN 0008-672X
CAROLINA CHRISTIAN. 1959. m. $8. Carolina Christian Publications, Inc., Box 5423, Sta. B, Greenville, SC 29606. Ed. David Pharr. adv.; bk.rev.; circ. 2,450.

200 323.4   FR
CATACOMBES; messager supraconfessionel de l'Eglise du silence. 1971. m. 90 F. Sergiu Grossu, Ed. & Pub., B.P. 98, 92405 Courbevoie, France. bk.rev.; circ. 10,000. (tabloid format) **Indexed:** HR Rep.

CATALOGUE OF CONFERENCES, SEMINARS, WORKSHOP. see *EDUCATION — Adult Education*

377.8   US   ISSN 0008-7726
CATECHIST. 1967. 7/yr. $17.95 (effective May 1991). Peter Li, Inc., 2451 E. River Rd., Dayton, OH 45439. TEL 513-294-5785. FAX 513-294-7840. Ed. Carl Fischer. bk.rev.; film rev.; illus.; circ. 47,537. **Indexed:** Cath.Ind., CERDIC.
   Description: Articles, announcements, and services pertaining to Catholic education.

240   SP   ISSN 0528-2772
CATEQUETICA. 4/yr. 2000 ptas.($22) Editorial Sal Terrae, Calle Guevara, 20, 39001 Santander, Spain. TEL 212617. FAX 942-215245.

200   US
CATHEDRAL COLLEGE OF THE LAITY NEWSLETTER. 1980. q. free. Cathedral College of the Laity, Washington Cathedral, Mount Saint Alban, Washington, DC 20016. TEL 202-537-6562. FAX 202-364-6605. Ed. Norene Dann Martin. bk.rev.; circ. 9,000.

222   US
CATHOLIC BIBLE QUARTERLY MONOGRAPH SERIES. 1971. irreg. price varies. Catholic Biblical Association of America, Catholic University of America, Washington, DC 20064. TEL 202-319-5519. Ed.Bd. circ. 1,000. **Indexed:** Cath.Ind., New Test.Abstr., Old Test.Abstr., Rel.Per.

CATHOLIC HEALTH ASSOCIATION OF THE UNITED STATES. GUIDEBOOK. see *HOSPITALS*

CATHOLIC HEALTH WORLD. see *HOSPITALS*

CATHOLIC NEAR EAST MAGAZINE. see *POLITICAL SCIENCE — Civil Rights*

CAUSA - U S A REPORT. see *LITERARY AND POLITICAL REVIEWS*

320   US
CENTRAL AMERICA REPORT. 1980. bi-m. $7 to individuals; institutions $11. Religious Task Force on Central America, 1747 Connecticut Ave., N.W., Washington, DC 20009. TEL 202-387-7652. Ed. Margaret Swedish. bk.rev.; illus. (tabloid format)

CENTRE; Bible data bank. see *HUMANITIES: COMPREHENSIVE WORKS — Computer Applications*

CENTRO CAMUNO DI STUDI PREISTORICI. BOLLETTINO. see *ARCHAEOLOGY*

CENTRO CAMUNO DI STUDI PREISTORICI. SYMPOSIA. see *ART*

200   FR   ISSN 0411-5562
BR23
CERCLE ERNEST RENAN. CAHIERS. 1954. bi-m. 70 F. membership. Cercle Ernest Renan, 3 rue Recamier, 75341 Paris Cedex 07, France. Ed. J. Coryne. bk.rev.; bibl.; circ. 1,000. **Indexed:** CERDIC, Int.Z.Bibelwiss., New Test.Abstr.
   Incorporates: Cercle Ernest Renan. Bulletin.

200   IT
CERTEZZE; rivista dei gruppi biblici universitari. 1953. m. L.20000 to individuals (foreign L.26000); students L.17000. Gruppi Biblici Universitari, Via Michelangelo Poggioli 9-17, 00161 Rome, Italy. TEL 06 495 7964. Ed. M. Fanelli. bk.rev.; charts; illus.; circ. 500. (back issues avail.)
   Description: Presents Christian messages. Includes dialogues and interviews on meaning and its power to transform our thoughts and actions.

200 100   US
CHALCEDON REPORT. 1965. m. donation basis. Chalcedon, Inc., Box 158, Vallecito, CA 95251. TEL 209-728-3510. FAX 209-736-0536. bk.rev.; circ. 11,000. (also avail. in microfiche; back issues avail.; reprint service avail.)
   Description: Scholarly, serious laymen, broad analysis of international social and cultural affairs from biblical perspectives.

200   UK   ISSN 0009-1014
CHALLENGE (SANDBACH); the magazine of St. Mary's Church, Sandbach. 1964. m. £2.40. St. Mary's Parochial Church Council, 55 Cookesmere Lane, Sandbach, Cheshire CW11 9BQ, England. TEL 0270-763033. FAX 0270-764719. Eds. John & Nora Williams. adv.; bk.rev.; charts; illus.; circ. 450.

200   MW
CHANCELLOR COLLEGE. DEPARTMENT OF RELIGIOUS STUDIES. STAFF SEMINAR PAPER. no.4, 1979. irreg. Chancellor College, Department of Religious Studies, Box 280, Zomba, Malawi.

CHANNELS OF BLESSING. see *HANDICAPPED — Visually Impaired*

200   FR   ISSN 0009-160X
LES CHANTIERS DU CARDINAL. 1963. q. 10 F. 106 rue du Bac, 75341 Paris Cedex 07, France. Ed. M. Poirson. adv.; illus.; circ. 75,000.

200   DK   ISSN 0108-4453
CHAOS; Dansk-Norsk tidsskrift for religionshistoriske studier. 1982. s-a. DKK 97 per no. Koebenhavns Universitet, Institut for Religionshistorie, Copenhagen, Denmark. (Subscr. to: Museum Tusculanums Forlag, Njalsgade 94, DK-2300 Copenhagen S, Denmark) (Co-sponsor: Religionshistorisk Forening) illus.

200   US   ISSN 0279-0424
CHARISMA; the magazine about Spirit-led living. 1975. m. $19.97. Strang Communications Co., 600 Rinehart Rd., Lake Mary, FL 32746. TEL 407-333-0600. Ed. Stephen Strang. adv.; bk.rev.; circ. 210,000. **Indexed:** Chr.Per.Ind., G.Soc.Sci.& Rel.Per.Lit.

CHART AND COMPASS INTERNATIONAL. see *SOCIAL SERVICES AND WELFARE*

200   CN   ISSN 0843-1736
CHASTITY AND HOLINESS MAGAZINE; Christ and integrity. 1988. s-a. Can.$10($12) (Christianic Poetic Ministry) C J L Poetic Empire Art Co., P.O. Box 22006, Thorncliffe Postal Outlet, Toronto, Ont. M4H 1N9, Canada. TEL 416-423-6781. Ed. Cecil Justin Lam. index; circ. 1,000. (back issues avail.)
   Description: Covers evangelism, integrity, purity and love, chastity and hope.

200   UK   ISSN 0009-2126
CHEERING WORDS. 1851. m. £5.50. D. Oldham, Ed. & Pub., 22 Victoria Rd., Stamford, Lincs. PE9 1HB, England. TEL 0780-63780. bk.rev.; illus.; index; circ. 4,500.

200   US
CHICAGO HISTORY OF AMERICAN RELIGION. 1973. irreg., latest 1981. price varies. University of Chicago Press, 5801 S. Ellis Ave., Chicago, IL 60637. TEL 312-702-7899. Ed. Martin E. Marty. adv.; bk.rev. (reprint service avail. from UMI,ISI) *Refereed Serial*

200   US
CHICAGO THEOLOGICAL SEMINARY REGISTER. 1908. 3/yr. $4. Chicago Theological Seminary, 5757 University Ave., Chicago, IL 60637. TEL 312-752-5757. Ed. Perry LeFevre. bk.rev.; circ. 4,000. **Indexed:** Rel.& Theol.Abstr. (1989-), Rel.Ind.One.

200   IT
LA CHIESA NEL TEMPO; rivista quadrimestrale di vita edicultura. 1985. 3/yr. L.20000. Diocesi di Reggio Calabria, Via T. Campanella, 63, 89100 Reggio Calabria, Italy. TEL 0965-21037. Ed. Antonio Denisi.

CHILDREN'S MINISTRY. see *CHILDREN AND YOUTH — About*

CHILDWORLD. see *CHILDREN AND YOUTH — About*

200   GW
CHINA HEUTE; Informationen ueber Religion und Christentum im Chinesischen Raum. 1982. bi-m. China Zentrum e.V., Arnold-Janssen-Str. 20, 5205 St. Augustin 1, Germany. TEL 02241-237432. FAX 02241-29142. TELEX 889559-STEYL-D. Ed. Roman Malek. bk.rev.; circ. 1,000. (back issues avail.)

291   HK   ISSN 0009-4668
CHING FENG; a journal on the encounter of religion and culture in Asia. (Editions in Chinese and English) 1957. q. $20. Christian Study Centre on Chinese Religion & Culture, 6-F Kiu Kin Mansion, 566 Nathan Rd., Kowloon, Hong Kong. TEL 7703310. FAX 7826869. Ed. Peter K.H. Lee. adv.; bk.rev.; circ. 1,200. (also avail. in microform from NBI,UMI; reprint service avail.) **Indexed:** Rel.& Theol.Abstr. (1987-), Rel.Ind.One.
   ●Also available online. Vendor(s): BRS, DIALOG.
—BLDSC shelfmark: 3181.123280.
   Formerly (until 1964): Quarterly Notes on Christianity and Chinese Religion.

266   US   ISSN 0199-6487
CHINMAYA MISSION WEST NEWS. m. $7. Chinmaya Mission West, Box 129, Piercy, CA 95467. TEL 707-247-3488. FAX 707-247-3422. Ed. Margaret Leuverink.

200   SZ   ISSN 0009-4994
CHOISIR; revue de reflexion chretienne. 1959. m. 74 Fr. Society of Jesus, 18 Rue Jacques-Dalphin, CH-1227 Carouge-Geneve, Switzerland. TEL 022-429880. FAX 022-429269. TELEX 421325-CHOICH. Ed.Bd. adv.; bk.rev.; index; circ. 4,300.

200   UK
CHRISM. 1965. 4/yr. £4 (typically set in Jan.). Guild of St. Raphael, St. Marylebone Church, Marylebone Rd., London NW1 5LT, England. TEL 071-935-6374. bk.rev.; circ. 1,800.
   Formerly: St. Raphael Quarterly.

200   US
CHRIST FOR THE NATIONS. vol.44, no.11, 1992. m. Christ for the Nations, Inc., 3404 Conway St., Dallas, TX 75224. TEL 214-376-1711. (Subscr. to: Box 769000, Dallas, TX 75376-9000) Ed. Mrs. Gordon Lindsay.

200　　　　　GW　ISSN 0009-5087
CHRIST UND BUCH; eine Hilfe fuer die Auswertung und Andwendung des gedruckten Wortes. 1960. q. membership. Evangelische Buchhilfe e.V., Alte Hauptstr. 14, Postfach 3180, 3502 Vellmar 3, Germany. Ed. Oskar Schnetter. bk.rev.; circ. 10,000.

200　　　　　NE　ISSN 0009-5141
CHRISTELIJK OOSTEN. (Text in Dutch; summaries in English, French, German) 1948. q. fl.67.50 to individuals; institutions fl.75. Instituut voor Oosters Christendom te Nijmegen, Erasmusplein 1, 6525 HT Nijmegen, Netherlands. Ed. A. Davids. adv.; bk.rev.; bibl.; illus.; index, cum.index; circ. 450. **Indexed:** CERDIC.
—BLDSC shelfmark: 3181.770000.

200　　　　　GW　ISSN 0009-5184
DIE CHRISTENGEMEINSCHAFT; Monatsschrift zur religioesen Erneuerung. 1924. m. DM.52. Verlag Urachhaus Johannes M. Mayer GmbH, Urachstr. 41, 7000 Stuttgart 1, Germany. FAX 0711-281379. adv.; bk.rev.; index; circ. 10,000. (processed) **Indexed:** CERDIC.
—BLDSC shelfmark: 3181.775000.

266　　　　　UK
CHRISTIAN ACTION JOURNAL. q. £10. Christian Action, St. Peter's House, 308 Kennington Lane, London SE11 5HY, England. TEL 071-735 2372. Ed. Rev. Canon Eric James. adv.; bk.rev.; circ. 1,000. (back issues avail.)

CHRISTIAN ADVERTISING FORUM. see *ADVERTISING AND PUBLIC RELATIONS*

200　　　　　US
CHRISTIAN ALERT. 1989. bi-m. $6 donation. Christian Activist Network, Box 406, Roseville, MI 48066. TEL 313-293-1616. Ed. Jan Opris. circ. 10,000.
Former titles: His Salt Shaker; Salt Shaker.

240　　　　　UK　ISSN 0264-598X
CHRISTIAN ARENA. 1948. q. £4. Universities and Colleges Christian Fellowship, 38 De Montfort St., Leicester LE1 7GP, England. Ed. J. Marsh. bk.rev.; circ. 4,500.
—BLDSC shelfmark: 3181.779400.
Formerly: Christian Graduate (ISSN 0045-6802)
Description: For Christian graduates containing articles, book reviews and news from the student world.

262　　　　　US　ISSN 0009-5281
BR1
CHRISTIAN CENTURY; an Ecumenical weekly. 1908. w. $30. Christian Century Foundation, 407 S. Dearborn St., Chicago, IL 60605. TEL 312-427-5380. Ed. James M. Wall. adv.; bk.rev.; s-a. index; circ. 38,000. (also avail. in microform from UMI) **Indexed:** Acad.Ind., Amer.Hist.& Life, Bk.Rev.Dig., Bk.Rev.Ind. (1965-), CCR, Child.Bk.Rev.Ind. (1965-), Film Lit.Ind. (1973-), G.Soc.Sci.& Rel.Per.Lit., Hist.Abstr., Hlth.Ind., Mag.Ind., Media Rev.Dig., Mid.East: Abstr.& Ind., PMR, R.G., Rel.& Theol.Abstr. (1968-), Rel.Ind.One, Rel.Per., TOM.

CHRISTIAN CHIROPRACTOR. see *MEDICAL SCIENCES — Chiropractic, Homeopathy, Osteopathy*

CHRISTIAN CHIROPRACTORS ASSOCIATION JOURNAL. see *MEDICAL SCIENCES — Chiropractic, Homeopathy, Osteopathy*

200　　　　　US
THE CHRISTIAN CHRONICLE; an international newspaper for members of Churches of Christ. 1943. m. $10. Oklahoma Christian University of Science and Arts, Box 11000, Oklahoma City, OK 73136-1100. TEL 405-425-5070. FAX 405-425-5076. Ed. Howard W. Norton. adv.; bk.rev.; illus.; circ. 114,000. (tabloid format)
Description: National and international news, features, and announcements pertaining to the members and activities of the Churches of Christ.

200　　　　　US　ISSN 0892-9300
CHRISTIAN CONQUEST. 1969. m. $10 institutional contribution. Christian Simpson Ministries, Box Z, Mobile, AL 36616. FAX 205-633-7080. illus.; circ. 92,000.
Formerly (until 1987): New Wine (ISSN 0194-438X)

266　　　　　US
CHRISTIAN EDUCATION JOURNAL. 1980. 3/yr. $10 (foreign $12). Scripture Press Ministries, Inc., Box 650, Glen Ellyn, IL 60138. FAX 708-668-3806. Ed. Ronald R. Ramsey. bk.rev.; circ. 2,400. (also avail. in microform from UMI) **Indexed:** CERDIC, Chr.Per.Ind., Rel.& Theol.Abstr. (1980-), Rel.Ind.One.
Formerly: Journal of Christian Education (ISSN 0277-9935)
Description: Promotes growth and advancenent in Christian education.

268　　　　　US
CHRISTIAN EDUCATORS JOURNAL. 1961. q. $7.50 to non-members (foreign $11); members $7 (foreign $9.50). Christian Educators Journal Association, c/o Peter Boogaart, Bus.Mgr., 1828 Mayfair N.E., Grand Rapids, MI 49503. Ed. Lorna Van Gilst. adv.; bk.rev.; illus.; circ. 5,000. (back issues avail.) **Indexed:** Chr.Per.Ind., G.Soc.Sci.& Rel.Per.Lit.

200　　　　　US　ISSN 0009-5338
BV1420
CHRISTIAN ENDEAVOR WORLD; the voice of Christian Endeavor. 1886. a. membership. International Society of Christian Endeavor, 1221 E. Broad St., Box 1110, Columbus, OH 43216. TEL 614-258-9545. FAX 614-258-1834. Ed. David G. Jackson. bk.rev.; illus.; circ. 4,200. (also avail. in microfilm)

200　　　　　UK　ISSN 0269-4689
CHRISTIAN FAMILY. 1979. m. £19.30. Elm House Christian Communications Ltd., 37 Elm Rd., New Malden, Surrey KT3 3HB, England. TEL 081-942-9761. FAX 081-949-2313. Ed. Clive Price. adv.; bk.rev.; illus.; film rev.; circ. 10,963. (back issues avail.)
Former titles: Family; (until Aug. 1980): Life of Faith Monthly; (until Feb. 1979): Life of Faith (ISSN 0024-3175)
Description: Popular Christian perspective on marriage, parenting and home affairs.

CHRISTIAN FAMILY CATALOG. see *GIFTWARE AND TOYS*

200　　　　　MW
CHRISTIAN FORUM. (Text in Chichewa or English) q. Christian Council of Malawi, Lilongwe, Malawi. (Dist. by: Christian Literature Association in Malawi, Box 503, Blantyre, Malawi)

200　　　　　UK　ISSN 0953-4385
CHRISTIAN HERALD. 1866. w. £44. Herald House Ltd., 96 Dominion Rd., Worthing, Sussex BN14 8JP, England. TEL 0903-821082. FAX 0903-821081. Ed. C.M. Reeves. adv.; bk.rev.; circ. 22,912. **Indexed:** Access, CCR, G.Soc.Sci.& Rel.Per.Lit., Mag.Ind.

200　　　　　US　ISSN 0009-5354
BR1
CHRISTIAN HERALD (CHAPPAQUA). 1878. bi-m. $15.97. Christian Herald Association, 40 Overlook Dr., Chappaqua, NY 10514. FAX 914-238-5393. Ed. Bob Chuvala. adv.; bk.rev.; charts; film rev.; illus.; record rev.; circ. 165,000. (also avail. in microform from UMI; reprint service avail. from UMI) **Indexed:** Access, Chr.Per.Ind., G.Soc.Sci.& Rel.Per.Lit., Mag.Ind.

200 900　　　　　US　ISSN 0891-9666
BR140
CHRISTIAN HISTORY MAGAZINE. 1982. q. $16. Christianity Today, Inc., 465 Gundersen Dr., Carol Stream, IL 60188. TEL 708-260-6200. Ed. Kevin Miller. adv.; bk.rev.; illus.; circ. 24,000. (back issues avail.)
Description: Covers major persons, events, issues in the history of the Christian Church.

377.8　　　　　US　ISSN 0009-5389
CHRISTIAN HOME & SCHOOL. 6/yr. $11.95. Christian Schools International, 3350 E. Paris Ave., S.E., Grand Rapids, MI 49512. TEL 616-957-1070. Ed. Gordon L. Bordewyk. adv.; bk.rev.; circ. 50,000.
Description: Aimed at contemporary Christian families. Focuses on family life and educational issues.

266　　　　　CN
CHRISTIAN INFO. 1982. m. Can.$15. Christian Info (Vancouver - Lower Midland) Society, 19414 96th Ave., No. 4, Surrey, B.C. V3T 4W2, Canada. FAX 604-888-9669. Ed. Lloyd Mackey. adv.; bk.rev.; film rev.; play rev.; circ. 22,000. (tabloid format; back issues avail.)

RELIGIONS AND THEOLOGY　4169

275　　　　　PH　ISSN 0045-6810
CHRISTIAN INSTITUTE FOR ETHNIC STUDIES IN ASIA. BULLETIN.* vol.4, 1970. irreg. (2-3/yr). Christian Institute for Ethnic Studies in Asia, Box 3167, Manila, Philippines. Eds. Alex J. Grant, Rufino Tima. bk.rev.; bibl.; charts.

CHRISTIAN IRELAND TODAY. see *SOCIOLOGY*

266　　　　　UK
CHRISTIAN IRISHMAN. 1880. 10/yr. 50p. Irish Mission of the Presbyterian Church in Ireland, Church House, Fisherwick Pl., Belfast BT1 6DW, N. Ireland. TEL 0232-320598. Ed. Rev. David J. Temple. adv.; bk.rev.; circ. 10,000.
Description: Devotional magazine provides articles on Christian living, mission, church growth, conferences and more.

291　　　　　UK　ISSN 0144-2902
BM535
CHRISTIAN JEWISH RELATIONS. 1968. s-a. £18($30) to individuals; institutions £25($40). Institute of Jewish Affairs, 11 Hertford St., London W1Y 7DX, England. TEL 01-491-3517. FAX 01-493-5838. (Co-sponsor: World Jewish Congress) adv.; bk.rev.; bibl.; circ. 1,500. (also avail. in microform from UMI) **Indexed:** CERDIC, Hist.Abstr., Rel.Ind.One.
—BLDSC shelfmark: 3181.828500.
Formerly: Christian Attitudes on Jews and Judaism (ISSN 0009-5249)
Description: Original research articles on Christian Jewish relations. Reports of advances from around the world.

260 051　　　　　US　ISSN 0009-5435
CHRISTIAN LIVING; a magazine about people and faith today. 1954. 10/yr. $19.95. Mennonite Publishing House, 616 Walnut Ave., Scottdale, PA 15683-1999. TEL 412-887-8500. FAX 412-887-3111. Ed. David Graybill. adv.; bk.rev.; illus.; index; circ. 6,700.

CHRISTIAN MANAGEMENT REPORT. see *BUSINESS AND ECONOMICS — Personnel Management*

CHRISTIAN MEDICAL & DENTAL SOCIETY JOURNAL. see *MEDICAL SCIENCES*

250　　　　　US　ISSN 0033-4138
BV4000
THE CHRISTIAN MINISTRY; a professional journal for clergy. vol.40, 1969. bi-m. $11. Christian Century Foundation, 407 S. Dearborn St., Chicago, IL 60605-1111. TEL 312-427-5380. FAX 312-427-1302. (Subscr. to: 5615 W. Cermak, Cicero, IL 60650-9969. TEL 312-762-2193) Ed. James M. Wall. adv.; bk.rev.; index; circ. 12,000. (also avail. in microform from UMI; back issues avail.) **Indexed:** G.Soc.Sci.& Rel.Per.Lit., Rel.Ind.One.
Formerlt: Pulpit.

200　　　　　US　ISSN 0744-4052
CHRISTIAN MISSIONS IN MANY LANDS. vol.33, 1970. m. (11/yr.) free. Christian Missions in Many Lands, Inc., Box 13, Spring Lake, NJ 07762. TEL 908-449-8880. Ed.Bd. bk.rev.; illus.; circ. 14,000.
Formerly: Fields (ISSN 0015-0762)

248　　　　　US
CHRISTIAN MOTHER (PITTSBURGH). 1942? q. $1. Archconfraternity of Christian Mothers, 220 37th St., Pittsburgh, PA 15201. TEL 412-683-2400. Ed. Rev. Bertin Roll. circ. 30,000.

CHRISTIAN MUSIC DIRECTORIES: RECORDED MUSIC. see *MUSIC*

200　　　　　US　ISSN 0899-7292
CHRISTIAN NEW AGE QUARTERLY. 1989. q. $12.50 (effective Jan.1, 1991). Bethsheva's Concern, Box 276, Clifton, NJ 07011-0276. Ed. Catherine Groves. adv.; bk.rev. (back issues avail.)
Description: Probes the common ground and distinctions of Christianity and the New Age movement - a forum for dialogue between the two ideologies.

RELIGIONS AND THEOLOGY

200   IS   ISSN 0009-5532
BR1110
CHRISTIAN NEWS FROM ISRAEL. (Editions in English, French and Spanish) 1949. s-a. $5. Ministry of Religious Affairs, Box 1167, 30 Jaffa St., Jerusalem, Israel. Ed. Shalom Ben-Zakkai. adv.; bk.rev.; bibl.; illus.; index; circ. 10,000. (also avail. in microfilm from UMI; reprint service avail. from UMI) **Indexed:** New Test.Abstr., Old Test.Abstr.
—BLDSC shelfmark: 3181.836000.

266   US   ISSN 1040-8088
CHRISTIAN PARENTING TODAY. 1988. 6/yr. $16.97 (foreign $21.37)(effective Jan. 1992). Good Family Magazine, Box 850, Sisters, OR 97759. TEL 503-549-8261. FAX 503-549-0153. adv.; bk.rev.; circ. 200,000.
Description: Provides parents with expert, biblically sound advice that covers every aspect of child development from birth through the teen years.

CHRISTIAN PATHWAY. see *CHILDREN AND YOUTH — For*

320.532   US
CHRISTIAN PRISONERS IN THE U.S.S.R.. 1981. a. (Society for the Study of Religion Under Communism) Keston College, U.S.A., Box 1310, Framingham, MA 01701. TEL 617-822-2965. (And: Keston College, Heathfield Rd., Keston, Kent BR2 6BA, England)
Formerly: Soviet Christian Prisoner List (ISSN 0278-1018)

200   US
CHRISTIAN RANCHMAN. 1976. m. Cowboys for Christ, Box 7557, Ft. Worth, TX 76111. TEL 817-834-6841. Ed. Ted K. Pressley. bk.rev.; circ. 38,000. (tabloid format; back issues avail.)
Description: Outreach ministry to livestock industry. Provides testimonies of what God has done in livestock people's lives.

266   US
CHRISTIAN READER. 1963. 6/yr. $12. Tyndale House Publishers, Periodicals Division, Box 220, Wheaton, IL 60189. TEL 312-668-8300. Eds. Dwight Hooten, Bonne Steffen. circ. 185,500.

CHRISTIAN RECORD TALKING MAGAZINE. see *HANDICAPPED — Visually Impaired*

207   US
CHRISTIAN RESEARCH JOURNAL. 1975. q. $14. Christian Research Institute, Box 500, San Juan Capistrano, CA 92693-0500. TEL 714-855-9926. Ed. Elliot Miller. adv.; bk.rev.; bibl.; circ. 20,000.
Former titles: Forward (San Juan Capistrano); Christian Research Institute. Newsletter (ISSN 0045-6845)

CHRISTIAN RETAILING; the trade magazine of religious retailing. see *PUBLISHING AND BOOK TRADE*

200   US   ISSN 0017-2251
BR1
CHRISTIAN SCHOLAR'S REVIEW; a Christian quarterly of the arts and sciences. 1970. q. $12 to individuals; libraries $15. c/o Calvin College, Grand Rapids, MI 49546. (Subscr. to: Circulation Department, Calvin College, Grand Rapids, MI 49546) Ed. William Hasker. adv.; bk.rev.; abstr.; bibl.; index, cum.index; circ. 4,200. (also avail. in microform from UMI; microfiche; back issues avail.) **Indexed:** Abstr.Engl.Stud., Amer.Hist.& Life, Bibl.Engl.Lang.& Lit., CERDIC, Chr.Per.Ind., G.Soc.Sci.& Rel.Per.Lit., Hist.Abstr., M.L.A., Mid.East: Abstr.& Ind., New Test.Abstr., Rel.& Theol.Abstr. (1971-), Rel.Ind.One.
—BLDSC shelfmark: 3181.920000.
Description: Peer articles, essays, and publication reviews pertaining to Christian thought and the interrelationship between Christian thought and all areas of scientific, theological, philosophical, cultural, and social scholarly interest.
Refereed Serial

CHRISTIAN SCHOOL BUILDER. see *EDUCATION — Teaching Methods And Curriculum*

200   MW
CHRISTIAN SERVICE COMMITTEE OF THE CHURCHES IN MALAWI. ANNUAL REPORT. (Text in English) a. free. Christian Service Committee of the Churches in Malawi, Box 51294, Limbe, Malawi.

CHRISTIAN SINGLES NEWS. see *SINGLES' INTERESTS AND LIFESTYLES*

CHRISTIAN SOCIALIST. see *POLITICAL SCIENCE*

200   US   ISSN 0009-5656
CHRISTIAN STANDARD. 1866. w. $16. Standard Publishing, 8121 Hamilton Ave., Cincinnati, OH 45231. TEL 513-931-4050. Ed. Sam E. Stone. bk.rev.; illus.; index, cum.index: 1866-1966; circ. 70,000. (also avail. in microfilm) **Indexed:** G.Soc.Sci.& Rel.Per.Lit.

261 300   US   ISSN 0009-5664
HN51
CHRISTIAN STATESMAN. 1867. bi-m. $10 to individuals; libraries & retirees $6. National Reform Association, 422 Seventh Ave., Patterson Heights, Beaver Falls, PA 15010. TEL 412-846-0159. Ed. Ronald H. Stegall. bk.rev.; circ. 2,000. (also avail. in microform; reprint service avail. from UMI)

266 808   CN   ISSN 0843-7602
CHRISTIAN VISION. 1989. q. $5. Skysong Press, R.R. 1, Washago, Ont. L0K 2B0, Canada. TEL 705-689-6226. Eds. Steve and Wendy Stanton. adv.; bk.rev.; circ. 500.
Description: Contains market listings, news, reviews, interviews and articles of interest to writers, poets, artists and patrons of Christian literature.

200   US   ISSN 0009-5702
CHRISTIAN WOMAN. 1933. 6/yr. $16.98. Gospel Advocate Company, 1006 Elm Hill Pike, Nashville, TN 37210. TEL 615-254-8781. FAX 615-254-7411. Ed. Sandra Humphrey. adv.; bk.rev.; illus.; index; circ. 30,000.
Description: Features, poetry, fiction, lessons, and information on issues pertaining to contemporary family life, self-improvement, motivation, parenting, and marriage for the practicing female Christian, married or single, with advice and opinion columns.

267   AT
CHRISTIAN WOMAN. 1954. 11/yr. Aus.$15 (effective Nov.1, 1991). Christian Women Communicating International, P.O. Box 520, Strathfield, N.S.W. 2135, Australia. FAX 02-742-6132. Ed. Sanna Wilson. adv.; bk.rev.; circ. 12,500.

200   US   ISSN 0009-5745
BR1
CHRISTIANITY AND CRISIS; a Christian journal of opinion. 1941. 19/yr. $24 to individuals; institutions $30. Christianity and Crisis Inc., 537 W. 121st St., New York, NY 10027. TEL 212-662-5907. Ed. Leon Howell. adv.; bk.rev.; film rev.; play rev.; illus.; index; circ. 13,000. (also avail. in microform from UMI; reprint service avail. from UMI) **Indexed:** Amer.Hist.& Life, CCR, CERDIC, G.Soc.Sci.& Rel.Per.Lit., Hist.Abstr., HR Rep., Hum.Ind., Mid.East: Abstr.& Ind., P.A.I.S., Rel.& Theol.Abstr. (1990-), Rel.Ind.One, Rel.Per.
Description: Independent ecumenical journal of opinion covering political, religious, economic, social and cultural issues with clear ethical analysis.

201 296   US
CHRISTIANITY AND JUDAISM IN ANTIQUITY. 1988. irreg., vol.7, 1991. price varies. University of Notre Dame Press, Notre Dame, IN 46556. TEL 219-239-6346. Ed. Charles Kannengiesser.

CHRISTIANITY AND LITERATURE. see *LITERARY AND POLITICAL REVIEWS*

200   US   ISSN 0009-5753
BR1
CHRISTIANITY TODAY. 1956. 15/yr. $24.95. Christianity Today, Inc., 465 Gunderson Dr., Carol Stream, IL 60188. TEL 708-260-6200. Ed. Harold Myra. adv.; bk.rev.; bibl.; index; circ. 144,000. (also avail. in microform from UMI) **Indexed:** Acad.Ind., Biog.Ind., Bk.Rev.Ind. (1990-), CCR, Chic.Per.Ind., Child.Bk.Rev.Ind. (1990-), Chr.Per.Ind., G.Soc.Sci.& Rel.Per.Lit., Mag.Ind., Mid.East: Abstr.& Ind., New Test.Abstr., Old Test.Abstr., Peace Res.Abstr., PMR, R.G., Rel.& Theol.Abstr. (1968-), Rel.Ind.One, Rel.Per.

200   US
CHRISTIANITY UNDER STRESS. 1988. irreg. Duke University Press, 6697 College Station, Durham, NC 27708. TEL 919-684-2173. FAX 919-684-8644. Ed. Sabrina Ramet.

200 323.4   US   ISSN 1044-5846
CHRISTIANS IN CRISIS. 1985. bi-m. free. Christian Forum Research Foundation, 1111 Fairgrounds Rd., Grand Rapids, MN 55744. TEL 218-326-2688. Ed. Sidney Reiners. bk.rev.; circ. 1,000 (controlled).
Description: Covers religious freedom and church-state issues internationally.

268   AU   ISSN 0009-5761
CHRISTLICH-PAEDAGOGISCHE BLAETTER; Zeitschrift fuer den katechetischen Dienst. 1887. bi-m. S.360. (Katechetisches Institut) Verlag Herder, Wollzeile 33, A-1010 Vienna, Austria. Ed. Edgar Josef Korherr. adv.; bk.rev.; abstr.; index; circ. 3,800. **Indexed:** Canon Law Abstr.

200   AU   ISSN 0009-5796
CHRISTLICHE INNERLICHKEIT; Schrift fuer Gebet und gelebtes Christentum. 1965. bi-m. S.70($5) Werk Christliche Innerlichkeit, Karmelweg 1, A-8630 Mariazell, Austria. (Affiliate: Order of Discalced Carmelite Fathers in Austria) Ed. P. Suitbert Siedl. bk.rev.; circ. 5,000.

200 051   US
CHRISTMAS (MINNEAPOLIS). 1931. a. $10.95 paper. Augsburg Fortress, 426 S. 5th St., Box 1209, Minneapolis, MN 55440. TEL 612-330-3437.

266   US   ISSN 0009-580X
CHRISTOFFEL-BLINDENMISSION. BERICHT. 1908. bi-m. free. Christian Blind Mission International Inc., 450 E. Park Ave., Greenville, SC 29601. TEL 803-239-0065. FAX 803-239-0069. illus.; circ. 500,000.
Description: Covers Christian missionary work and medical aid to the blind, the handicapped, and the hungry in Third World countries.

266   US   ISSN 8755-6901
CHRISTOPHER NEWS NOTES. 1945. 10/yr. donation. Christophers, Inc., 12 E. 48th St., New York, NY 10017. TEL 212-759-4050. Ed. Stephanie Raha. circ. 800,000.

266   UK
CHRYSOSTOM. 1960. 2/yr. £5. Society of St. John Chrysostom, Marian House, Holden Ave., London N12 8HY, England. Ed. H.E. Georgiadis. bk.rev.; cum.index every 3 yrs.; circ. 700. (tabloid format; also avail. in microform from UMI; reprint service avail. from UMI) **Indexed:** CERDIC

220   US   ISSN 0009-630X
CHURCH ADVOCATE. 1835. m. $10. Churches of God, General Conference, Box 926, Findlay, OH 45839. TEL 419-424-1961. FAX 419-424-3433. Ed. Linda Draper. bk.rev.; charts; illus.; circ. 7,200. **Indexed:** CERDIC.
Formerly (until 1889): Gospel Publisher.

200   SZ
CHURCH AND SOCIETY NEWSLETTER; Christian social thought in a future perspective. 1970. 2/yr. World Council of Churches, Department on Church and Society, 150 Route de Ferney, Box 2100, CH-1211 Geneva 2, Switzerland. TEL 022-7916111. FAX 022-791-0361. TELEX 415730-OIK-CH. circ. 5,000. **Indexed:** CERDIC, HR Rep.
Formerly (until 1984): Anticipation; Supersedes: Background Information for Church and Society.
Description: Examines technology, science and faith.

261 323   US   ISSN 0009-6334
BR516
CHURCH & STATE. 1948. m. (Sep.-Jul.). $18 (foreign $25). Americans United for Separation of Church and State, 8120 Fenton St., Silver Spring, MD 20910. TEL 301-589-3707. FAX 301-495-9173. Ed. Joseph L. Conn. bk.rev.; illus.; index; circ. 55,000. (also avail. in microform from UMI; reprint service avail. from UMI) **Indexed:** CERDIC, Mid.East: Abstr.& Ind., P.A.I.S.
—BLDSC shelfmark: 3189.733000.
Formerly (until 1951): Church and State Newsletter.
Description: Reviews church-state news and analysis; focuses on US with some international reports.

CHURCH AND SYNAGOGUE LIBRARIES. see *LIBRARY AND INFORMATION SCIENCES*

RELIGIONS AND THEOLOGY

200 UK
CHURCH ARMY. FRONTLINE NEWS. 1906. 4/yr. £2.50. Church Army, Independents Rd., Blackheath, London SE3 9LG, England. Ed. Gordon Kitney. bk.rev.; circ. 47,000.
 Former titles (until 1985): Church Army. Review & New Review; (until 1983): Church Army Review (ISSN 0009-6350)
 Description: Accounts of the Church Army, with articles on various religious viewpoints on social concerns.

200 690 CN
▼**CHURCH BUSINESS.** 1991. bi-m. Can.$18($30) (effective Jan. 1991). Momentum Magazines, 4040 Credit View Rd., Unit 11, Box 6900, Mississauga, Ont. L5C 348, Canada. TEL 416-569-6900. FAX 416-569-6915. Ed. Terry Hrynyshyn. adv.: B&W page Can.$1915, color page Can.$2750; trim 8 x 11. bk.rev.; circ. 9,959.
 Description: Covers the administration and facility management of churches for clergy, administration and property managers.

CHURCH COMPUTING NEWS. see *COMPUTERS — Microcomputers*

200 UK
CHURCH GROWTH DIGEST. 1979. 4/yr. £5. B C G A, 59 Warrington Rd., Harrow, Middlesex HA1 1SZ, England. TEL 01-863-4495.
 Description: Examines church growth in all its dimensions: numerical, spiritual, organizational and incarnational.

270 US ISSN 0009-6407
BR140
CHURCH HISTORY. 1932. q. $30. American Society of Church History, 328 Deland Ave., Indialantic, FL 32903. Ed.Bd. adv.; bk.rev.; bibl.; index, cum.index; circ. 3,400. (also avail. in microform) **Indexed:** Amer.Bibl.Slavic & E.Eur.Stud., Amer.Hist.& Life, Arts & Hum.Cit.Ind., Bk.Rev.Ind. (1965-), CERDIC, Child.Bk.Rev.Ind. (1965-), Chr.Per.Ind., Curr.Cont., Hist.Abstr., Hum.Ind., Lang.& Lang.Behav.Abstr., Old Test.Abstr., Rel.& Theol.Abstr. (1968-), Rel.Ind.One, Rel.Per., RILA.
 —BLDSC shelfmark: 3189.768000.

CHURCH LADS' AND CHURCH GIRLS' BRIGADE. ANNUAL REPORT. see *CHILDREN AND YOUTH — About*

CHURCH LAW & TAX REPORT. see *LAW*

200 US ISSN 8750-8613
CHURCH LIFE. 1887. m. $1. Episcopal Diocese of Ohio, 2230 Euclid Ave., Cleveland, OH 44115. TEL 216-771-4815. FAX 216-623-0735. Ed. Dana C. Speer. adv.; bk.rev.; illus.; circ. 23,000. (back issues avail.)

200 US
CHURCH MESSENGER/CERKOVNYJ VISTNIK. 1944. bi-w. $10. American Carpatho-Russian Orthodox Greek Catholic Diocese, 312 Garfield St., Johnstown, PA 15906. Ed. Rev. James S. Dutko. adv.; bk.rev.; film rev.; illus.; circ. 7,200.

THE CHURCH MUSIC REPORT. see *MUSIC*

200 UK ISSN 0009-6482
CHURCH OBSERVER. 1948. 3/yr. £0.50. (Church Union) Church Literature Association, Faith House, 7 Tufton St., London SW1P 3QN, England. TEL 071-222-6052. FAX 071-967-7180. Ed. Geoffrey Wright. adv.; bk.rev.; illus.; circ. 8,000. (also avail. in microfilm from UMI) **Indexed:** CERDIC.
 Description: Catholics in the Church of England.

CHURCH OF SCOTLAND BRAILLE MAGAZINE. see *HANDICAPPED — Visually Impaired*

268 UK
CHURCH POCKET BOOK AND DIARY. a. £5.99. Society for Promoting Christian Knowledge, c/o Ms. Rachel Boulding, Holy Trinity Church, Marylebone Rd., London NW1 4DU, England. TEL 071-387-5282. FAX 071-388-2352. circ. 7,000.
 Formerly: Churchman's Pocket Book and Diary (ISSN 0069-4029)

252 UK ISSN 0069-4002
CHURCH PULPIT YEAR BOOK;* sermon outlines. 1903. a. £1.75. Chansitor Publications, 181 Queen Victoria St., London EC4V 4DD, England. adv.; index; circ. 3,000.

370 US ISSN 0164-6451
CHURCH TEACHERS. 1969. 5/yr. $19.95. Harper Collins Publishers, Inc. (San Francisco), 1160 Battery St., San Francisco, CA 94111-1213. TEL 415-477-4400. FAX 415-477-4444. Ed. Shirley H. Strobel. adv.; bk.rev.; film rev.; circ. 7,500.

200 US ISSN 0009-6601
CHURCH WORLD. 1930. w. $25. Diocese of Portland, Maine, Box 698, Brunswick, ME 04011. TEL 207-729-8753. Ed. Henry Gosselin. adv.; bk.rev.; film rev.; play rev.; illus.; circ. 8,210. (tabloid format)

200 US
CHURCHES SPEAK. q. $99. Gale Research Inc., 835 Penobscot Bldg., Detroit, MI 48226. TEL 800-877-4253. FAX 313-961-6815. TELEX 810-221-7086.

267.4 US ISSN 0009-6598
BV4415
CHURCHWOMAN. 1934. bi-m. $8. Church Women United, 475 Riverside Dr., Rm. 812, New York, NY 10115. TEL 212-870-2347. FAX 212-870-2338. Ed. Margaret Schiffert. bk.rev.; illus.; circ. 7,000.
 Description: Addresses the concerns of today's women of faith: children, peacemaking, the discovery of gifts, health and wholeness, inclusive language, partnerships of empowerment, worship, land, homelessness, criminal justice, and poverty of women and children.

200 US ISSN 0578-3224
BX3401
CISTERCIAN STUDIES QUARTERLY. 1966. q. $20. Cistercian Studies, St. Joseph's Abbey, Spencer, MA 01562. TEL 508-885-3901. bk.rev.; circ. 1,500. (also avail. in microform; back issues avail.)
 Description: Review combining historical and critical studies of Western and Eastern spirituality in both monastic and lay commitment.

200 US ISSN 0009-7527
AS36
CITHARA; essays in Judaeo-Christian tradition. 1961. s-a. $6. St. Bonaventure University, Box BC, St. Bonaventure, NY 14778. TEL 716-375-2000. Ed. John Mulryan. bk.rev.; cum.index every 2 vols.; circ. 700. (also avail. in microfilm from UMI) **Indexed:** Abstr.Engl.Stud., Amer.Hist.& Life, Arts & Hum.Cit.Ind., Cath.Ind., Curr.Cont., Hist.Abstr., M.L.A.
 —BLDSC shelfmark: 3267.792080.

200 700 IT ISSN 0009-7632
CITTA DI VITA; bimestrale di religione arte e scienza. 1946. bi-m. L.50000. Piazza S. Croce 16, 50122 Florence, Italy. TEL 055-242783. Ed. Massimiliano G. Rosito. adv.; bk.rev.; bibl.; illus.; index; circ. 2,000. **Indexed:** M.L.A.
 —BLDSC shelfmark: 3268.260000.

200 900 BE
CLAIRLIEU: TIJDSCHRIFT GEWIJD AAN DE GESCHIEDENIS DER KRUISHEREN. (Editions in Dutch, English, French and German) 1943. a. 18.50. Geschiedkundige Kring "Clairlieu", Pelserstraat 33, B-3680 Maaseik, Belgium. Ed. C. Brasseur. bk.rev. **Indexed:** Amer.Hist.& Life, Hist.Abstr.
 Description: Covers history of the crosiers and spirituality.

250 US ISSN 0009-6431
BV652.A1
CLERGY JOURNAL. Cover title: Church Management: The Clergy Journal. 1924. 10/yr. $24. Church Management, Inc., Box 162527, Austin, TX 78716. Ed. Manfred Holck, Jr. adv.; bk.rev.; circ. 17,000. (also avail. in microform from UMI) **Indexed:** CCR.

200 US
CLOSER WALK; to develop a heart for God. 1981. m. $18. Walk Thru the Bible Ministries, Inc., 61 Perimeter Park, N.E., Box 80587, Atlanta, GA 30366. TEL 404-458-9300. Ed. Paula Kirk. circ. 125,000. (reprint service avail.)
 Formerly: Timeless Insights.

200 301.412 US ISSN 0896-0038
CO-LABORER. 1961. bi-m. $5.75. Women's National Auxiliary Convention, P.O. Box 5002, Antioch, TN 37011-5002. TEL 615-731-6812. Ed. Lorene Miley. bk.rev.; circ. 15,000.
 Description: To promote missions and deepen the spiritual life of women.

200 UK ISSN 0267-1557
CODEX: JOURNAL OF THE CENTRE FOR THE STUDY OF CHRISTIANITY IN ISLAMIC LANDS. 1985. a. Medan Books, c/o John Watson, 43 Churchill Ave., Walmer, Kent CT14 7SP, England.
 Description: Studies the ancient oriental churches: Armenian, Assyrian, Coptic, Syrian, Indian Orthodox and Ethiopian.

200 AG
COLECCION AMANECE.* no.4, 1976. irreg. Editora Patria Grande, Rivadavia 6251, 1406 Buenos Aires, Argentina.

200 SP ISSN 0069-505X
COLECCION CANONICA. 1959. irreg., no.102, 1989. price varies. (Universidad de Navarra, Facultad de Derecho Canonico) Ediciones Universidad de Navarra, S.A., Apdo. 396, 31080 Pamplona, Spain. TEL 94 825 6850.
 Description: Discusses canon law.

COLLABORATION. see *PHILOSOPHY*

261 US
COLORADO KAIROS. 1965. irreg. (3-4/yr.). $5. Colorado Council of Churches, 1370 Pennsylvania, Ste. 100, Denver, CO 80203. TEL 303-861-1884. FAX 303-861-1884. abstr.; bibl.; illus.; circ. 2,000.
 Formerly (until 1982): Colorado Councillor (ISSN 0010-1540); **Supersedes:** Rocky Mountain Churchman.
 Description: Lists events and membership news.

220 CN ISSN 0316-3040
COME AND SEE. 1974. bi-m. free. Nathanael Literature Distributors, 64 Hills Rd., Ajax, Ont. L1S 2W4, Canada. Ed. John van Dijk. circ. 8,100.

220 375 UK ISSN 0950-7191
COME LEARN BEGINNERS. q. £0.50. Go Teach Publications, 2 Radford Rd., Leamington Spa CV31 1LX, England. TEL 0926-26573.
 Description: Children's activity workbook for use with: Go Teach Beginners.

220 375 UK ISSN 0950-7213
COME LEARN JUNIORS. q. £0.50. Go Teach Publications, 2 Radford Rd., Leamington Spa CV31 1LX, England. TEL 0926-26573.
 Description: Children's activity workbook for use with: Go Teach Juniors.

220 375 UK ISSN 0950-7205
COME LEARN PRIMARIES. q. £0.50. Go Teach Publications, 2 Radford Rd., Leamington Spa CV31 1LX, England. TEL 0926-26573.
 Description: Children's activity workbook for use with: Go Teach Primaries.

COMMON BOUNDARY; between spirituality and psychotherapy. see *PSYCHOLOGY*

200 UK ISSN 0010-325X
COMMON GROUND. 1946. 4/yr. £10. Council of Christians and Jews, 1 Dennington Park Rd., London NW6 1AX, England. FAX 071-431-3500. Ed. Rev. Marcus Braybrooke. adv.; bk.rev.; illus.; circ. 5,000. (also avail. in microform from UMI) **Indexed:** CERDIC.
 Description: To encourage appreciation of the Jewish and Christian religious and interfaith understanding.

COMMUNAL COMPUTING NEWS. see *COMPUTERS — Microcomputers*

254.4 659.2 GW ISSN 0010-3497
COMMUNICATIO SOCIALIS; Zeitschrift fuer Publizistik in Kirche und Welt. (Text in German; summaries in English, French and Spanish) 1968-1988; resumed. q. DM.60. Ferdinand Schoeningh, Juehenplatz 1-3, 4790 Paderborn, Germany. TEL 05251-29010. TELEX 936929-FS-PB. Ed. Dr. Franz-Josef Eilers. adv.; bk.rev.; film rev. **Indexed:** CERDIC, Lang.& Lang.Behav.Abstr., So.Pac.Per.Ind.
 Description: Catholic publication dealing with mass media and religion, the Catholic press, and communication in theology. Includes list of book and magazine references.

R

4172 RELIGIONS AND THEOLOGY

230   SP   ISSN 0010-3705
COMMUNIO; commentarii internationales de ecclesia et theologia. 1968. 3/yr. 3000 ptas.($37) Estudio General Dominicano, Provincia Betica (Espana), Apdo. 820, 41080 Seville, Spain. Ed. Miguel de Burgos. bk.rev.; cum.index; circ. 500. **Indexed:** CERDIC, New Test.Abstr., Old Test.Abstr., Rel.& Theol.Abstr.
—BLDSC shelfmark: 3363.543400.

200   CS   ISSN 0010-3713
BR1A1
COMMUNIO VIATORUM; a theological journal. (Text in English, French and German) 1958. 3/yr. 15 Fr. Charles University, Protestant Theological Faculty, Jungmannova 9, 110 00 Prague 1, Czechoslovakia. (Subscr. to: Communio Viatorum, Jungmannova 9, 110 00 Prague 1, Czechoslovakia) Ed.Bd. bk.rev.; index; circ. 1,000. **Indexed:** New Test.Abstr., Rel.Ind.One, Rel.Per.

261   UK   ISSN 0045-7809
COMPASS.* 1961. m. 36p. Christian News Ltd., Centre One, Devonshire House, High St., Birmingham, B12 OLP, England. Ed. Rev. M.W. Blood. **Indexed:** So.Pac.Per.Ind.
Formerly: Christian News.

200   FR
CONCILIUM; revue international de theologie. 1965. 6/yr. 270 F. (foreign 345 F.). Editions Beauchesne, 72 rue des Saints Peres, 75007 Paris, France. TEL 45-48-80-28. FAX 42-22-59-79. **Indexed:** CERDIC.

200   UK   ISSN 0010-5236
CONCILIUM. 1965. bi-m. £34.95. S C M Press, 26-30 Tottenham Rd., London N1 4BZ, England. TEL 071-249-7262. FAX 071-249-3776. adv.; circ. 1,000. **Indexed:** Canon Law Abstr., CERDIC.
Description: International review of theology.

200   NE   ISSN 0167-1200
CONCILIUM. 6/yr. fl.98. Gooi en Sticht, Postbus 133, 3740 AC Baarn, Netherlands. TEL 02154-15320. FAX 02154-20658. circ. 2,250.

200   US   ISSN 0145-7233
BX8001
CONCORDIA JOURNAL. 1975. q. $10 (foreign $14). (Concordia Seminary) Ovid Bell Press, Inc., 801 Demun, Clayton, MO 63105. TEL 314-721-5934. FAX 314-721-5902. Ed. Quentin Wesselschmidt. adv.; bk.rev.; circ. 9,000. (also avail. in microform from UMI; back issues avail.) **Indexed:** CERDIC, Chr.Per.Ind., Int.Z.Bibelwiss., New Test.Abstr., Old Test.Abstr., Rel.& Theol.Abstr. (1978-), Rel.Ind.One.
—BLDSC shelfmark: 3399.477200.
Description: Official theological organ issued by the faculty of Concordia Seminary in St. Louis.

207.11   US
CONCORDIA THEOLOGICAL QUARTERLY. N.S. 1959. q. $10. Concordia Theological Seminary, 6600 N. Clinton St., Fort Wayne, IN 46825. TEL 219-481-2100. FAX 219-481-2121. Ed. Dr. David P. Scaer. adv.; bk.rev.; cum.index: 1959-1964; circ. 9,000. (also avail. in microfilm from UMI; reprint service avail. from UMI) **Indexed:** CERDIC, New Test.Abstr., Old Test.Abstr., Rel.& Theol.Abstr. (1983-), Rel.Ind.One, Rel.Per.
Formerly (until vol.40, no.2, 1976): Springfielder (ISSN 0038-8610)

200   UY
CONFEDERACION LATINOAMERICANA DE ASOCIACIONES CRISTIANAS DE JOVENES. CONFEDERACION. 1982. q. free. Confederacion Latinoamericana de Asociaciones Cristianas de Jovenes - Latin American Confederation of YMCAs, Colonia 1884, p.1, Montevideo, Uruguay. Ed. Edgardo G. Crovetto.

200   UY
CONFEDERACION LATINOAMERICANA DE ASOCIACIONES CRISTIANAS DE JOVENES. CONTACTO. 1982. m. free. Confederacion Latinoamericana de Asociaciones Cristianas de Jovenes - Latin American Confederation of YMCAs, Colonia 1884, p.1, Montevideo, Uruguay. Ed. Edgardo G. Crovetto.

369.4   UY
CONFEDERACION LATINOAMERICANA DE ASOCIACIONES CRISTIANAS DE JOVENES. CARTA. (Editions in English and Spanish) irreg. free. Confederacion Latinoamericana de Asociaciones Cristianas de Jovenes, Casilla 172, Montevideo, Uruguay.
Formerly: Federacion Sudamericana de Asociaciones Cristianas de Jovenes. Noticias (ISSN 0428-1039)

200   NP
CONFIDENT CHRISTIAN. (Text in English) 1982. s-a. $35 (foreign $45). Siveast Consultants, Inc., USA, c/o Dr. C.V. Ramasastry, Ed., P.O. Box 1755, Kathmandu, Nepal. (UK Subscr. to: Dr. Ramasastry, c/o Overseas Customer Service, Midland Bank plc., Poultry & Princes St., London EC2, England) adv.; bk.rev.; circ. 200.
Description: Covers religion and contains fictional serial stories.

200   SW   ISSN 0069-8946
CONIECTANEA BIBLICA. NEW TESTAMENT SERIES. (Text in English and French) 1966. irreg., no.22, 1989. price varies. Almqvist & Wiksell International, P.O. Box 638, S-101 28 Stockholm, Sweden. Eds. Birger Gerhardson, Lars Hartman.
Former titles: Acta Seminarii Neotestamentici Upsaliensis & Coniectanea Neotestamentica.

200   SW   ISSN 0069-8954
CONIECTANEA BIBLICA. OLD TESTAMENT SERIES. 1967. irreg., no.28, 1989. price varies. Almqvist & Wiksell International, P.O. Box 638, S-101 28 Stockholm, Sweden. Eds. Tryggve Mettinger, Helmer Ringgren.

CONNECTICUT HISTORICAL SOCIETY. BULLETIN. see HISTORY — History Of North And South America

CONOSCENZA. see PHILOSOPHY

200   IT   ISSN 0035-600X
CONSACRAZIONE E SERVIZIO; rivista delle religiose. 1952. m. L.20000. Unione Superiore Maggiori d'Italia, Via Zanardelli 32, Rome 00186, Italy. Dir. Zelia Pani. bk.rev.; index; circ. 12,000.
—BLDSC shelfmark: 3417.863000.
Formerly: Rivista delle Religiose.

CONSCIENCE ET LIBERTE. see POLITICAL SCIENCE — Civil Rights

200   US
CONSULTATION ON CHURCH UNION. DIGEST. 1962. irreg. (approx. every 18 mos.), latest 1988. price varies. Consultation on Church Union, Research Park, 151 Wall St., Princeton, NJ 08540-1514. Ed. David W.A. Taylor.
Former titles: Consultation on Church Union. Official Record (ISSN 0272-8958); Consultation on Church. Digest (ISSN 0589-4867)

200 610   SZ
CONTACT. (Text in English, French, Portuguese and Spanish) bi-m. 15 F. World Council of Churches, Christian Medical Commission, 150 Route de Ferney, Box 2100, CH-1211 Geneva 2, Switzerland. TEL 022-791-6111. FAX 022-791-0361. TELEX 415730-OIK-CH. Ed. David Hilton. circ. 26,000.

200   UK
CONTACT (ALDERSHOT). 1920. q. £3. Officers' Christian Union, Havelock House, Barrack Rd., Aldershot GU11 3NP, England. TEL 0252-311221. FAX 0252-311222. Ed. Sqn. Ldr. Mike Warwood. bk.rev.; circ. 4,500. **Indexed:** CERDIC.
Formerly: Practical Christianity (ISSN 0032-6364)
Description: Inspirational articles, profiles, and announcements of conferences and affiliations pertaining to the activities of Christian officers in the British armed forces.

200   FR   ISSN 0045-8325
CONTACTS; revue Francaise de l'Orthodoxie. 1949. q. 215 F.($37) Centre Ecumenique Enotikon, c/o John J. Balzon, 43 rue du Fer-a-Moulin, 75005 Paris, France. TEL 535-80-98. Ed. John J. Balzon. bk.rev.; bibl.; index; circ. 3,000. **Indexed:** CERDIC.
—BLDSC shelfmark: 3425.025000.

CONTEMPORARY CHRISTIAN MUSIC. see MUSIC

200   US   ISSN 0361-8854
CONTEXT; a commentary on the interaction of religion and culture. 1972. 22/yr. $24.95. Claretian Publications, 205 W. Monroe St., Chicago, IL 60606. TEL 312-236-7782. FAX 312-236-7320. Ed. Rev. Mark J. Brummel. circ. 7,311. (reprint service avail. from UMI) **Indexed:** Numis.Lit.

268   US
CONTINUING EDUCATOR. 1969. 4/yr. membership. Society for Advancement of Continuing Education for Ministry, c/o Univ. of Hartford, Auerbach 228, W. Hartford, CT 06117. Ed. Patricia Cremins. bk.rev.; circ. 450.
Former titles: Continuing Education; S A C E M Newsletter.

200   US   ISSN 0196-7053
CONTRIBUTIONS TO THE STUDY OF RELIGION. 1981. irreg. price varies. Greenwood Press, Inc. (Subsidiary of: Greenwood Publishing Group Inc.), 88 Post Rd. W., Box 5007, Westport, CT 06881-5007. TEL 203-226-3571. FAX 203-222-1502. Ed. Henry W. Bowden.
—BLDSC shelfmark: 3461.455000.

200   US
CONVENTION HERALD. 1955. bi-m. $5. (Inter-Church Holiness Convention) Old Paths Tract Society, 3589 New Garden Rd., Salem, OH 44460. Ed. H.E. Schmul. adv.; bk.rev.; circ. 12,500.

200   NE   ISSN 0167-5818
COPTIC STUDIES. 1978. irreg., vol.2, 1991. price varies. E.J. Brill, P.O. Box 9000, 2300 PA Leiden, Netherlands. TEL 071-312624. FAX 071-317532. TELEX 39296 BRILL NL. (In N. America: E.J. Brill, 24 Hudson St., Kinderhook, NY 12106. TEL 800-962-4406) Ed. M. Krause.

200   CN   ISSN 0229-1134
COPTOLOGIA; journal of coptic thought and orthodox spirituality. 1981. a. Can.$10($8.50) P.O. Box 235, Don Mills Postal Station, Don Mills, Ont. M3C 2S2, Canada. TEL 416-391-1774. Ed. Fayek M. Ishak. bk.rev.; circ. 450.
Description: Research publication which is mainly concerned with the Egyptological sources and multiple meaning of the coptic tradition.

200   US   ISSN 0360-649X
DT72.C7
COPTS; Christians of Egypt. 1974. 4/yr. American Coptic Association, Box 9119, Jersey City, NJ 07304. TEL 203-451-0972. Eds. Selim Naguib, Shawky F. Karas.
Description: Examines the problems facing the Christian Egyptians in Egypt (Copts), the history and culture of the Coptic people, and their contributions to civilization.

200   US   ISSN 0275-2743
CORNERSTONE (CHICAGO). 1972. bi-m. $15. Cornerstone Communications, Inc., 939 W. Wilson Ave., Chicago, IL 60640. TEL 312-989-2080. FAX 312-989-2076. Ed. Dawn Herrin. adv.; bk.rev.; circ. 32,000.
Description: Aims to communicate doctrinal truth based on scripture and to challenge people to take a cultural stand based on the teachings of the Bible.

200   BE
CORPUS CHRISTIANORUM. SERIES GRAECA. 1977. irreg. (2-3/yr.). (Centrum voor Hellenisme en Kristendom, Leuven) N.V. Brepols I.G.P., Rue Baron Francois du Four 8, B-2300 Turnhout, Belgium. (Co-publisher: Leuven University Press)

COUNSELOR (WHEATON). see CHILDREN AND YOUTH — For

COURAGE IN THE STRUGGLE FOR JUSTICE AND PEACE. see SOCIOLOGY

COURTENAY LIBRARY OF REFORMATION CLASSICS. see HISTORY — History Of Europe

COURTENAY REFORMATION FACSIMILES. see HISTORY — History Of Europe

COURTENAY STUDIES IN REFORMATION THEOLOGY. see HISTORY — History Of Europe

RELIGIONS AND THEOLOGY 4173

200 UK
COVENANTERS - THE LEADER. 1985. 6/yr. free to qualified personnel. 104 Bloom St., Manchester M1 6HU, England. TEL 061-236-2305.
Formerly: Leaders' Digest. Covenanter and Juco Leader.

200 500 UK
CREATION. 1971. 6/yr. £7 (overseas £6). Creation Science Movement, 50 Brecon Ave., Portsmouth PO6 2AW, England. bk.rev.; circ. 1,700.
Supersedes (1932-1971): Evolution Protest Movement.
Description: Discussion of Biblical and scientific evidence for creation and reasoned refutation of evolution theory.

200 US ISSN 0738-6001
QH359
CREATION - EVOLUTION. 1980. s-a. $18 (foreign $24) includes: N C S E Reports. National Center for Science Education, Box 9477, Berkeley, CA 94709-0477. TEL 510-843-3393. FAX 510-843-2237. Ed. John R. Cole. bk.rev.; bibl.; circ. 3,000. (back issues avail.)
—BLDSC shelfmark: 3487.234000.
Description: Deals exclusively with the creation - evolution controversy.

200 500 AT ISSN 0819-1530
CREATION EX NIHILO. 1978. q. Aus.$19.50. Creation Science Foundation Ltd., P.O. Box 302, Sunnybank, Qld. 4109, Australia. TEL 617-273-7650. FAX 617-273-7672. Ed. R.J. Doolan. adv.; bk.rev.; cum.index; circ. 16,000.
Description: Presents scientific and biblical evidence for creation and related subjects in a popular, easy to read format.

200 500 AT ISSN 1036-2916
CREATION EX NIHILO TECHNICAL JOURNAL. 1984. s-a. Aus.$25. Creation Science Foundation Ltd., P.O. Box 302, Sunnybank, Qld. 4109, Australia. Ed. A.A. Snelling. abstr.; charts; illus.; circ. 2,000. (back issues avail.)
Formerly: Ex Nihilo Technical Journal (ISSN 0814-6764)
Description: Technical study of the sciences as they relate to the study of biblical creation and Noah's flood.

200 500 US ISSN 0092-9166
BS651
CREATION RESEARCH SOCIETY QUARTERLY. 1964. q. $21 (foreign $25). Creation Research Society, Box 28473, Kansas City, MO 64118. adv.; bk.rev.; index; circ. 1,800. (also avail. in microfilm from UMI; back issues avail.; reprint service avail. from UMI) **Indexed:** Biol.Abstr., Chr.Per.Ind.
—BLDSC shelfmark: 3487.235000.
Description: Presents original research and reviews pertinent to the study of origins science, creation and evolution. Provides a creationist perspective.

CREATOR; the bimonthly magazine of balanced music ministries. see *MUSIC*

280 IT ISSN 0393-3598
BR140
CRISTIANESIMO NELLA STORIA; ricerche storiche esegetiche teologiche. (Text in English, French, German, Italian and Spanish; summaries in English) 1980. 3/yr. L.53000 (foreign L.65000). (Istituto per le Scienze Religiose) Centro Editoriale Dehoniano, Via Nosadella 6, 40123 Bologna, Italy. TEL 051-306811. FAX 051-341706. Ed. Prof. Giuseppe Alberigo. bk.rev.; bibl.; index; circ. 1,700. (back issues avail.) **Indexed:** Canon Law Abstr., CERDIC, New Test.Abstr., Old Test.Abstr., Rel.& Theol.Abstr.

200 UK
CRISTION. 1983. 6/yr. Cristion Publishing Company, c/o Lynn Jones, Bus. Manager, 30 Highfields, Llandaff, Cardiff CF5 2QB, Wales. TEL 0222-562816.
Description: Covers all aspects of religious life.

260 378 US
LB3609
CROSS CURRENTS: RELIGION AND INTELLECTUAL LIFE. 1976. q. $25. Association for Religion and Intellectual Life, College of New Rochelle, New Rochelle, NY 10805-2308. TEL 914-654-5425. FAX 914-654-5554. Ed.Bd. bk.rev.; circ. 5,000. **Indexed:** Rel.& Theol.Abstr. (1979-), Rel.Ind.One.
Incorporates (1950-1990): Cross Currents (ISSN 0011-1953); **Former titles** (until 1990): Religion and Intellectual Life (ISSN 0741-0549); (until 1983): N I C M Journal for Jews and Christians in Higher Education (ISSN 0362-0794)

200 FR
CROYANTS EN LIBERTE. q. 120 F. (foreign 150 F.). Societe de Presse et d'Edition, 49 rue du Faubourg-Poissionniere, 75009 Paris, France. TEL 1-42-46-37-50. FAX 1-48-24-33-67. TELEX 290 562. (Subscr. to: B.P. 63, F 77932 Perthes Cedex, France. TEL 1-64-38-01-55)

CRUSADER. see *CHILDREN AND YOUTH — For*

200 CN ISSN 0011-2186
CRUX; a quarterly journal of Christian thought and opinion. 1966. q. Can.$14($14) Regent College, 5800 University Blvd., Vancouver, B.C. V6T 2E4, Canada. TEL 604-224-3245. FAX 604-224-3097. Ed. Donald M. Lewis. adv.; bk.rev.; bibl.; charts; illus.; stat.; index, cum.index; circ. 1,000. (microform) **Indexed:** New Test.Abstr., Old Test.Abstr., Rel.& Theol.Abstr. (1970-), Rel.Ind.One.
—BLDSC shelfmark: 3490.132000.

282 US ISSN 0591-2296
CRUX OF THE NEWS. 1966. w. $59.50. Gabriel Publishing Co., Inc., 3 Enterprise Dr., Albany, NY 12204. TEL 518-465-4591. Ed. Richard A. Dowd. adv.; bk.rev.; circ. 3,400.

CRUZADA EUCARISTICA. see *CHILDREN AND YOUTH — For*

300 261 US ISSN 0891-2971
CRYSTAL RAINBOW. 1987. q. $11.75 (foreign $14). Mirrored Image, 340 Granada Dr., Winter Park, FL 32789. Ed. Louise M. Turmenne. adv.; circ. 160. (back issues avail.)
Description: Contains inspirational and religious poetry and prose. Strives to uphold the good in life, to uplift, comfort, encourage and inspire creativity and praise; to seek out the God of the Bible in daily life.

374 PE
CUADERNOS DE CAPACITACION. 1979. irreg. $40 includes Testimonios (en Historieta), Cuadernos de Estudio and Cuadernos Populares. Comision Evangelica Latinoamericana de Educacion Cristiana, Av. General Garzon 2267, Lima 11, Peru.

CUADERNOS PARA LA HISTORIA DE LA EVANGELIZACION EN AMERICA LATINA. see *HISTORY — History Of North And South America*

374 PE
CUADERNOS POPULARES. 1977. irreg. $40 includes Testimonios (en Historieta), Cuadernos de Capacitation and Cuadernos de Estudios). Comision Evangelica Latinoamericana de Educacion Cristiana, Av. General Garzon 2267, Lima 11, Peru.

200 BL
CULTURA E FE. 1978. q. Institutio de Desenvolvimento Cultural, Av. Alberto Bins 467, Caixa Postal 702, 90000 Porto Alegre, Brazil.

200 SZ
CURRENT DIALOGUE. (Text in English) 2/yr. World Council of Churches, Sub-unit on Dialogue with People of Living Faiths, 150 Route de Ferney, Box 2100, CH-1211 Geneva 2, Switzerland. TEL 022-791-6111. FAX 022-791-0361. TELEX 415730-OIK-CH. **Indexed:** Abstr.Musl.Rel.
Formerly: Church and the Jewish People.

200 US ISSN 0098-2113
CURRENTS IN THEOLOGY AND MISSION. 1974. bi-m. $13.50. Lutheran School of Theology at Chicago, 1100 E. 55th St., Chicago, IL 60615. TEL 312-753-0751. FAX 312-753-0782. Ed. Ralph W. Klein. adv.; bk.rev.; circ. 4,000. (also avail. in microform from UMI; reprint service avail. from UMI; back issues avail.) **Indexed:** CERDIC, Int.Z.Bibelwiss., New Test.Abstr., Old Test.Abstr., Rel.& Theol.Abstr. (1977-), Rel.Ind.One, Rel.Per.
—BLDSC shelfmark: 3505.203000.
Description: Contains articles and preaching helps for pastors and laity.

200 NE
CURRENTS OF ENCOUNTER. (Text in English) 1989. irreg. (approx. 2-3/yr.). price varies. Editions Rodopi B.V., Keizersgracht 302-304, 1016 EX Amsterdam, Netherlands. TEL 020-6227507. FAX 020-6380948. (US and Canada subscr. to: Eerdmans Publ. Co., 255 E. Jefferson, S.E., Grand Rapids, MI 49502) (Co-publisher: Wm. Eerdmans Publishing Co.) Ed.Bd.
Description: Presents comparative studies on Christianity and other religions, beliefs, and cultures.

200 AU ISSN 0011-4057
CURSILLO; fuer ein erlebtes Evangelium. 1964. m. S.150. Arbeitsgemeinschaft der Dioezesansekretariate der Cursillo-Bewegung, Bennogasse 21, A-1080 Vienna, Austria. FAX 0222-4081015. Ed. Josef G. Cascales. bk.rev.; bibl.
Formerly: Karat.

270 GW ISSN 0070-2234
CUSANUS-GESELLSCHAFT. BUCHREIHE. 1964. irreg. price varies. Aschendorffsche Verlagsbuchhandlung, Soesterstr. 13, 4400 Muenster, Germany. TEL 0251-690-0. FAX 0251-690405. Ed.Bd.

200 GW
D I A. (Daten, Informationen, Argumente) 1973. q. Presse- und Informationsstelle der Ev.-luth Landeskirche Hannovers, Haarstr. 6, 3000 Hannover 1, Germany. Eds. Peter Kollmar, Jens-Peter Kruse. bk.rev.; circ. 19,000.

DAILY WORD. see *HANDICAPPED — Visually Impaired*

200 IT
DALLO SCOGLIO DI SANTA RITA. 1940. m. Santuario di Santa Rita, Vicolo Sinibaldi 1, 00186 Rome, Italy. TEL 06-687-71-80. Dir. Luigi Di Giannicola. bk.rev.

200 DK
DANSK KIRKEHILSEN. 1927. bi-m. DKK 60. Dansk Kirke i Udlandet, Noerregaenget 43B, P.O. Box 83, 5100 Odense C, Denmark. TEL 66 13 95 31. Ed. Egon Christiansen. adv.; circ. 5,000.

266 DK ISSN 0011-6378
DANSK MISSIONSBLAD. 1834. m. DKK 123 (typically set in Dec.). Danske Missionsselskab - Danish Missionary Society, Strandagervej 24, DK-2900 Hellerup, Denmark. FAX 45-01-620206. Ed. Rev. Inge Tranholm-Mikkelsen. adv.; bk.rev.; abstr.; illus.; index; circ. 11,000. **Indexed:** CERDIC.

200 DK ISSN 0105-3191
DANSK TEOLOGISK TIDSSKRIFT. 1938. 4/yr. DKK 210. Forlaget Anis, Frederiksberg Alle 10-A, 1820 Frederiksberg C, Denmark. FAX 45-33-25-06-07. Ed. Mogens Mueller. adv.; bk.rev.; circ. 650. **Indexed:** New Test.Abstr., Old Test.Abstr., Rel.& Theol.Abstr. (1990-), Rel.Ind.One.

220 DK ISSN 0109-5846
DANSKE BIBELSELSKABS AARBOG. 1966. a. DKK 75. Danske Bibelselskab, Frederiksborggade 50, 1360 Copenhagen K, Denmark.
Formerly: Danske Bibelselskabs Aarsberetning.

DAUGHTERS OF SARAH. see *WOMEN'S INTERESTS*

266 UK
DAY ONE DIARY. 1928. a. £0.85. Lord's Day Observance Society, 6 Sherman Rd., Bromley, Kent BR1 3JH, England. Ed. J.G. Roberts. circ. 70,000.
Formerly: Happy Day Diary.
Description: Pocket diary with daily Bible verse based upon a theme.

DEATH AND DYING; opposing viewpoints sources. see *SOCIAL SCIENCES: COMPREHENSIVE WORKS*

RELIGIONS AND THEOLOGY

266   GW   ISSN 0011-7692
DEIN REICH KOMME. English edition: Light in the East News. 1920. bi-m. free. Licht im Osten, Missionsbund, Zuffenhauserstr. 37, Postfach 1340, 7015 Korntal-Muenchingen 1, Germany. FAX 0049-711-831-351. Ed. E. Damson. bk.rev.; bibl.; illus.; circ. 27,900.

230   SP
DELTA (BARCELONA). 1961. q. 1500 ptas. Instituto Catolico de Estudios Sociales de Barcelona, Enrique Granados, 2, 08007 Barcelona, Apartado de Correos 5217, Spain. Ed. Maria Martinell. bk.rev.; abstr.; circ. 2,700.
   Former titles (until 1989): Cuadernos de Orientacion Familiar (ISSN 0011-2453); (until 1969): Delta (Barcelona) (ISSN 0210-3869)

200   FR
DEMAIN D'AVANTAGE QU'HIER.* 15/yr. 200 F. Nouvelles Editions Latines, 1 rue Palatine, 75006 Paris, France. bk.rev.; bibl.

200   US   ISSN 0193-6883
DENOMINATIONS IN AMERICA. 1985. irreg. price varies. Greenwood Press, Inc. (Subsidiary of Greenwood Publishing Group Inc.), 88 Post Rd. W., Box 5007, Westport, CT 06881-5007. TEL 203-226-3571. FAX 203-222-1502. Ed. Harry Bowden.
  —BLDSC shelfmark: 3553.106600.

200   GW   ISSN 0174-786X
DEUTSCHE WALDENSER. q. DM.20. (Deutsche Waldenservereinigung) Quell Verlag, Furtbachstr. 12A, Postfach 103852, 7000 Stuttgart 10, Germany. TEL 0711-60100-0. circ. 1,500.

200   MY   ISSN 0012-1746
DHARMA; a quarterly devoted to universal religion, righteousness & culture. (Not issued in 1976) (Text in English) 1949. q. M.$6. Pure Life Society - Persatuan, Batu 6, Jalan Puchong, Jalan Kelang Lama P.O., 58200 Kuala Lumpur, Malaysia. TEL 03-7929391. Ed. Mother A. Mangalam. bk.rev.; illus.; circ. 3,000.
  —BLDSC shelfmark: 3579.502500.
  Description: Promotes the study of comparative theology and philosophy in its widest form. Works to establish spiritual and educational institutions, orphanages, and dispensaries.

200 110 070   US
DHARMA COMBAT; a magazine about spirituality, metaphysics, reality and other conspiracies. 1988. q. $10. Keith, Ed. & Pub., Box 20593, Sun Valley, NV 89433. adv.; bk.rev.; circ. 3,000.

200 410   US   ISSN 0167-9554
DIA REGNO/DIVINE KINGDOM: CHRISTIAN ESPERANTO MAGAZINE; Kristana Esperanto-Gazeto. (Text in Esperanto) 1908. m. membership. Kristana Esperantista Ligo Internacia, c/o Edwin C. Harler Jr., 47 Hardy Rd., Levittown, PA 19056. (Alt. addr.: 26 Rue de Pre Ventnet, F-86430 Nouaille-Maupertus, France) Ed. Philippe Cousson. adv.; bk.rev.; circ. 1,100. (back issues avail.)

240   GW   ISSN 0012-1967
DIAKONIA; internationale Zeitschrift fuer praktische Theologie. 1966. bi-m. DM.86.40 (students DM.70.20). Matthias Gruenewald Verlag GmbH, Max-Hufschmidt-Str. 4a, 6500 Mainz-Weisenau, Germany. TEL 06131-839055. Ed. Helmut Erharter. adv.; bk.rev.; bibl.; stat.; index; circ. 4,000. **Indexed:** Cath.Ind.
  —BLDSC shelfmark: 3579.687000.
  Description: Reflections and reports of church and parish life, practical theology and the influence of social changes on parishes and theology.

200   AU
DIAKONIE; Zeitschrift fuer Freunde und Mitarbeiter des Evangelischen Diakoniewerkes Gallneukirchen. 1875. bi-m. S.90. Evangelisches Diakoniewerk Gallneukirchen, Martin Boos-Strasse 4, A-4210 Gallneukirchen, Austria. TEL 07235-3251. FAX 07235-3251-201. Eds. Gerhard Gaebler, Andrea Kloesch. adv.; bk.rev.; circ. 4,000.
  Formerly: Gallneukirchner Bote (ISSN 0016-4143)

200   GW   ISSN 0341-826X
DIAKONIE. 1975. bi-m. DM.44. (Diakonisches Werk der Evang. Kirche in Deutschland und des Internationalen Verbandes fuer Innere Mission und Diakonie) Verlagswerk der Diakonie, Kniebisstr. 29, Postfach 101142, 7000 Stuttgart 10, Germany. TEL 0711-261388. circ. 2,500. **Indexed:** CERDIC.

261 258   GW   ISSN 0342-1643
DIAKONIE REPORT. 1975. s-m. free. Verlagswerk der Diakonie, Kniebisstr. 29, Postfach 101142, 7000 Stuttgart 10, Germany. TEL 0711-261388. Ed. Hans W. Kober. adv.; bk.rev.; bibl.; charts; illus.; stat.; circ. 65,000.
  Supersedes: Diakonische Werk (ISSN 0012-1983)

200   GW
DIAKONIESCHWESTER. 1904. m. DM.40. Ev. Diakonieverein e.V., Glockenstr. 8, 1000 Berlin 37, Germany. TEL 030-8018091. FAX 030-8022452. Ed. Rainer Sommer. bk.rev.; circ. 4,000 (controlled). (back issues avail.)

230   US   ISSN 0012-2033
BR1
DIALOG (ST. PAUL); a journal of theology. 1962. q. $19 to individuals; students and senior citizens $12. Dialog, Inc., 2481 Como Ave., St. Paul, MN 55108. FAX 612-641-3482. Ed. Carl E. Braaten. adv.; bk.rev.; circ. 2,300. (also avail. in microform from UMI; reprint service avail. from UMI) **Indexed:** CERDIC, New Test.Abstr., Old Test.Abstr., Rel.& Theol.Abstr. (1968-), Rel.Ind.One, Rel.Per.
  —BLDSC shelfmark: 3579.730000.

200   SP   ISSN 0210-2870
DIALOGO ECUMENICO; revista cuatrimestral de teologia ecumenica. 1966. 3/yr. 2500 ptas.($32) Universidad Pontificia, Departamento de Ediciones y Publicaciones, Apdo. de Correos 541, 37080 Salamanca, Spain. TEL 923-215140. FAX 923-213450. Dir. Adolfo Gonzalez-Montes. adv.; bk.rev.; circ. 400. **Indexed:** CERDIC.

200   US   ISSN 0891-5881
BL1
DIALOGUE & ALLIANCE. 1987. q. $20 to individuals; institutions $30; foreign $40. International Religious Foundation, Inc. (IRF), 4 West 43rd St., New York, NY 10036. TEL 212-869-6023. FAX 212-869-6424. TELEX 499 1393 NWERA. Ed. Peter Phan. adv.; bk.rev.; circ. 2,000. (also avail. in microform; back issues avail.) **Indexed:** Rel.& Theol.Abstr. (1988-), Rel.Ind.One, Rel.Per.
  —BLDSC shelfmark: 3579.775210.
  Description: Dialogue between religious traditions for purposes of promoting peace.

378 268   US   ISSN 0012-2289
DIALOGUE ON CAMPUS; linking the religious and the higher education systems. 1950. 4/yr. $5. Association for the Coordination of University Religious Affairs, Executive Committee, c/o Robert L. Johnson, Cornell United Religious Work, Anabel Taylor Hall, Ithaca, NY 14882. TEL 607-255-6004. FAX 607-255-9412. adv.; bk.rev.; bibl.; circ. 300. (looseleaf format; back issues avail.) **Indexed:** ERIC, High.Educ.Abstr.

221   GW
DIELHEIMER BLAETTER ZUM ALTEN TESTAMENT UND SEINER REZEPTION IN DER ALTEN KIRCHE. 1972. s-a. DM.7. Wissenschaftlich-Theologisches Seminar der Universitaet Heidelberg, Kisselgasse 1, 6900 Heidelberg, Germany. Eds. Bernd Jorg Diebner, Claudia Nauerth. bk.rev.; circ. 250.
  Formerly: Dielheimer Blaetter zum Alten Testament.

200   GW   ISSN 0012-2572
DIENENDER GLAUBE; Zeitschrift fuer Ordensfrauen. 1924. m. DM.54. Verlag Butzon und Bercker, Hoogeweg 71, Postfach 215, 4178 Kevelaer, Germany. Ed. Sister Christeta Hess. adv.; bk.rev.; circ. 3,800.
  Formerly: An Heiligen Quellen.

200   US
DIRECTORY OF DEPARTMENTS AND PROGRAMS OF RELIGIOUS STUDIES IN NORTH AMERICA. 1978. irreg. price varies. Council of Societies for the Study of Religion, Mercer University, R.O.T.C. Bldg., Macon, GA 31207. TEL 912-752-2376. Ed. Watson E. Mills.

266   UK
DIRECTORY OF ENGLISH-SPEAKING CHURCHES ABROAD. 1966. irreg. £2. Intercontinental Church Society, 175 Tower Bridge Rd., London SE1 2AQ, England. TEL 071-407-4588. FAX 071-407-6038. Ed. Lance Bidewell. circ. 3,000.

200   US
DIRECTORY OF FACULTY OF DEPARTMENTS AND PROGRAMS OF RELIGIOUS STUDIES IN NORTH AMERICA; contains biographical information on over 3,200 faculty members. (Suppl. to: Directory of Departments and Programs of Religious Studies in North America) 1988. irreg., 1992. $55. Council of Societies for the Study of Religion, Mercer University, R.O.T.C. Bldg., Macon, GA 31207. TEL 912-752-2376. Ed. Watson E. Mills.

200   GW
DIREKTORIUM FUER DAS BISTUM MUENSTER. a. DM.8.50. Verlag Regensberg, Daimlerweg 58, Postfach 6748, 4400 Muenster, Germany. TEL 0251-717061. FAX 0251-717725.

262.9   IT
DIRITTO ECCLESIASTICO E RASSEGNA DI DIRITTO MATRIMONIALE. (Text in Italian and Latin) 1889. q. L.90000 (foreign L.135000). Casa Editrice Dott. A. Giuffre, Via Busto Arsizio 40, 20151 Milan, Italy. TEL 02-38000905. FAX 02-38009582. Ed. S. Bianconi. bk.rev.; bibl.; index; circ. 800. **Indexed:** CERDIC.
  Formerly: Diritto Ecclesiastico (ISSN 0012-3455)

200   US   ISSN 0092-8372
BX7301
DISCIPLE (ST. LOUIS). 1862. m. $12.50. Christian Board of Publication, 1010 Convention Plaza, St. Louis, MO 63103. TEL 314-231-8500. FAX 314-231-8524. (Subscr. to: Box 179, St. Louis, MO 63166-0179) Ed. Robert L. Friedly. adv.; bk.rev.; charts; illus.; index; circ. 41,000. (reprint service avail. from UMI) **Indexed:** CERDIC.
  Supersedes: World Call (ISSN 0043-8308); Formerly (until 1974): Christian (ISSN 0009-5206)
  Description: Features, departments, profiles, and announcements pertaining to the evangelical, congregational, ministerial, and missionary work of the Christian Church.

DISCOVERY (NEW YORK). see *CHILDREN AND YOUTH — For*

230 100   IT   ISSN 0012-4257
DIVUS THOMAS; commentarium de philosophia et theologia. (Text in English, French, Italian, Latin, German and Spanish) 1880. q. L.35000($30) Collegio Alberoni, 29100 Piacenza, Italy. TEL 0523-63198. FAX 0523-63342. Ed. Perini Giuseppe, C.M. bk.rev.; index; circ. 600. **Indexed:** CERDIC, M.L.A., New Test.Abstr., Old Test.Abstr.
  —BLDSC shelfmark: 3605.220000.
  Description: Offers scholarly study in theology and philosophy, chiefly in the field of Thomistic research.

266   IV
DJELIBA; le journal des jeunes chretiens. 1974. 5/yr. 1000 F.($4) 01 B.P. 1287, Abidjan 01, Ivory Coast. TEL 21-69-79. Ed. Pierre Trichet. adv.; circ. 6,000. (back issues avail.)

200   SP
DOCUMENTS D'ESGLESIA. (Text in Catalan) fortn. 4300 ptas.($62) Publicacions de l' Abadia de Montserrat, Ausias March 92-98, Apdo. 244, 08013 Barcelona, Spain.

200   CN   ISSN 0318-0123
DONUM DEI. French edition (ISSN 0318-0131) (Editions in English and French) 1958. a. price varies. Canadian Religious Conference, 324 Laurier Ave. E., Ottawa, Ont. K1N 6P6, Canada. TEL 613-236-0824. FAX 613-236-0825. circ. 8,000 (both ed.).

266   US
DOOR OF HOPE. 1972. m. $10 donation. (Door of Hope International) Door of Hope Press, Box 10460, Glendale, CA 91209. TEL 818-500-3939. FAX 819-500-9933. Ed. Paul Popov. adv.; bk.rev.; film rev.; play rev.; bibl.; tr.lit.; circ. 25,000.

220 FR ISSN 0761-7267
DOSSIERS DE LA BIBLE. 1984. 5/yr. 105 F. (foreign 125 F.). Editions du Cerf, 29 bd. Latour Maubourg, 75340 Paris Cedex 07, France. TEL 45-50-34-07. FAX 45-56-04-17. (Subscr. to: Service Abonnements, 3 chemin des Prunais, 94350 Villier-sur-Marne, France) Ed. Philippe Gruson. bk.rev.; rec.rev.; charts; illus.; cum.index; circ. 15,000. (tabloid format) **Indexed**: Pt.de Rep. (1984-).
Formerly (until 1984): Bible et Son Message (ISSN 0006-0704)

DOUAI MAGAZINE. see COLLEGE AND ALUMNI

200 US
DOVETAIL. 1977. q. $10. Iowa Peace Network, 4211 Grand Ave., Des Moines, IA 50312. TEL 515-255-7114. Eds. Nancy and Gary T. Guthrie. bk.rev.; circ. 3,000. (looseleaf format; back issues avail.)
Formerly (until Sep. 1991): Dovetail - Peaces; Which was formed by the merger of: Peaces; Dovetail.

DREAMS & VISIONS; new frontiers in Christian fiction. see LITERATURE

200 AU ISSN 0012-6764
DRUZINA IN DOM. (Text in Slovene) m. S.2($8) Druzba Sv. Mohorja, Viktringer Ring 26, A-9020 Klagenfurt, Austria.

200 947 BU ISSN 0323-9578
DUKHOVNA AKADEMIYA SV. KLIMENT OKHRIDSKI. GODISHNIK. 1923. a. Sinodalno Izdatelstvo, Ul. Sveta Sofia 2, Sofia, Bulgaria. (Dist. by: Hemus Foreign Trade Co., 6 Ruski Blvd., 1000 Sofia, Bulgaria)
Formerly: Sofia. Universitet. Bogoslovski Fakultet. Godishnik.

200 AT
E.C.M. NEWS. (Also avail. on diskett.) 1965. bi-m. free. European Christian Mission (Australian Section) Inc., P.O. Box 15, Croydon, N.S.W. 2132, Australia. FAX 61-2-7475509. Ed. Rev. Jim Bosma. adv.; bk.rev.; circ. 4,000.
Formerly: Prayer Union.

200 GW ISSN 0175-7695
E M W - INFORMATIONEN. 1978. irreg. free. Evangelisches Missionswerk, Mittelweg 143, 2000 Hamburg 13, Germany. TEL 040-41174-0. circ. 2,000.

200 GW ISSN 0344-9106
E Z W - TEXTE; Arbeitstexte. 1970. 3/yr. (in 2 vols.). free. (Evangelische Kirche in Deutschland) Evangelische Zentralstelle fuer Weltanschauungsfragen, Hoelderlinplatz 2A, 7000 Stuttgart 1, Germany. TEL 0711-2262281. FAX 0711-2261331. adv.; circ. 15,000. (back issues avail.)

200 US
EARLY LATIN CHURCH. irreg. Peter Lang Publishing, Inc., 62 W. 45th St., 4th Fl., New York, NY 10036. TEL 212-302-6740. FAX 212-302-7574. Ed. Rev. Boniface Ramsey.
Description: Deals with Latin Christanity in the years from c. 200 to c. 600 A.D.

EARTHKEEPING ONTARIO. see AGRICULTURE

200 333.7 US ISSN 1050-0413
▼**EARTHLIGHT**; the magazine of spirituality and ecology. 1990. 4/yr. $15 (Canada & Mexico $21; elsewhere $25). (P Y M - C U N, Religious Society of Friends (Quakers)) Unity with Nature Committee of Pacific Yearly Meeting, 1558 Mercy St., Mountain View, CA 94041. TEL 916-758-5407. FAX 415-960-1767. Ed. Paul Burks. circ. 500.
Description: Provides insight, information, and inspiration on the spiritual basis of the concern we share for the well-being of our environment and our planet.

291 II ISSN 0012-8384
EAST AND WEST SERIES; an interpreter of the life of the spirit. (Text in English) m. Rs.3.($2) Gita Publishing House, 10 Sadhu Vaswani Rd., Mira Nagar, Poona 1, India. Ed. J.P. Vaswani. bk.rev.; bibl. (back issues avail.)

266 US
EAST ASIA'S MILLIONS. 1892. q. $4. Overseas Missionary Fellowship, 10 W. Dry Creek Cir., Littleton, CO 80120-4413. Ed. E. David Dougherty. bk.rev.; illus.; index; circ. 20,000. (also avail. in microform from UMI) **Indexed**: Helminthol.Abstr.
Former titles: East Asia Millions (ISSN 0012-8406); China's Millions.
Description: Covers mission work in Asia.

284 FR ISSN 0397-0736
ECHANGES; journal de l'eglise reformee...Provence, Cote d'Azur, Corse. 1955. m. 120 F. (typically set in Jan.). Association Echanges, 34 bvd des Platanes, 13009 Marseille, France. TEL 91-26-17-49. Ed. Eric Trocme. adv.; bk.rev.; film rev.; illus.; circ. 4,000. **Indexed**: Geo.Abstr., Pt.de Rep.
Formerly: Eglise Reformee Vous Parle.
Description: News about the protestant religion and theology. Provides chronilces of the parishes of Provence-Cote d'Azur.

200 GW
ECHO AUS AFRIKA UND ANDEREN ERDTEILEN. 1888. 10/yr. St. Petrus Claver Sodalitaet, Billerstr. 20, 8900 Augsburg, Germany. TEL 0821-414077. circ. 23,500.

266 CN ISSN 0318-9872
ECHO MISSIONAIRE/MISSION NEWS. (Text in English or French) 1975. bi-m. free. Comboni Missionaries, 79 Moore Ave., Kitchener, Ont. N2H 3S4, Canada. TEL 519-744-4680. Ed. Luigi Marcolongo. circ. 6,000.

266 276 NE
ECHO UIT AFRIKA EN ANDERE WERELDDELEN. 1933. bi-m. fl.15. Missiezusters van St. Petrus Claver - Missionary Sisters of St. Peter Claver, Bouillonstraat 4, 6211 LH Maastricht, Netherlands. TEL 043-212158. Ed.Bd. charts; illus.; circ. 16,000.
Formerly: Echo uit Afrika (ISSN 0012-9305)

266 UK
ECHOES. 1872. s-m. £9. Echoes of Service, 1 Widcombe Crescent, Bath, Avon BA2 6AQ, England. TEL 0225-310893. Eds. D.J. Restall, P.R. Grosvenor. circ. 10,000.
Description: Stimulates interest in various aspects of missionary work of the Christian Brethren, worldwide.

200 IT
L'ECO DELLE VALLI VALDESI. 1848. w. L.85000. Associazione Informazione Protestante, Via Pio V 15, 10125 Turin, Italy. TEL 011-655278. FAX 011-657542. Dir. Giorgio Gardiol. circ. 5,000.

200 FR ISSN 0070-8860
ECRITS LIBRES. 1955. irreg., no.16, 1973. Librairie Fischbacher, 33 rue de Seine, 75006 Paris, France. TEL 43-26-87-84.

200 US ISSN 0013-0761
ECUMENICAL COURIER. 1941. irreg., (2-4/yr.). $15 donations. United States Conference for the World Council of Churches, 475 Riverside Dr., No. 915, New York, NY 10115. TEL 212-870-2529. FAX 212-870-2528. bk.rev.; circ. 10,000.

200 IO
ECUMENICAL NEWS.* 1973. m. Council of Churches in Indonesia, Jalan Selemba Raya 10, Jakarta, Indonesia. (processed)

200 SZ
ECUMENICAL PRESS SERVICE. Short title: E P S. (Text in English and French) 1934. w. (approx. 45/yr.). 73.50 Fr.($49.50) World Council of Churches, Communications Department, Box 2100, CH-1211 Geneva 2, Switzerland. TEL 022-7916111. FAX 022-790-0361. TELEX 415730-OIK-CH. circ. 2,500. (back issues avail.) **Indexed**: CERDIC.

RELIGIONS AND THEOLOGY 4175

200 SZ ISSN 0013-0796
BX1
ECUMENICAL REVIEW. 1948. q. 39.50 Fr.($26.90) World Council of Churches, Publications Office, 150 Route de Ferney, CH-1211 Geneva 2, Switzerland. TEL 022-791-6111. FAX 022-790-0361. TELEX 415730-OIK-CH. Ed. Emilio E. Castro. adv.; bk.rev.; index; circ. 4,000. (also avail. in microfilm from UMI; reprint service avail. from UMI) **Indexed**: Arts & Hum.Cit.Ind., Bk.Rev.Ind. (1965-), CERDIC, Child.Bk.Rev.Ind. (1965-), Curr.Cont., Hum.Ind., Mid.East: Abstr.& Ind., New Test.Abstr., Old Test.Abstr., Rel. & Theol.Abstr. (1989-), Rel.Ind.One, Rel.Per.
—BLDSC shelfmark: 3659.700000.

200 US ISSN 0360-9073
ECUMENICAL TRENDS. 1972. 11/yr. $10. 475 Riverside Dr., Rm. 528, New York, NY 10115-0050. (Subscr. to: Graymoor Ecumenical Institute, Garrison, NY 10524) Ed. Patrick J. Cogan. bk.rev.; circ. 2,300. (also avail. in microform from UMI; reprint service avail. from UMI) **Indexed**: Cath.Ind., Rel.Ind.One.
—BLDSC shelfmark: 3659.702000.
Description: Provides news, opinion, documentation and features in the area of ecumenical and inter-religious activity. Directed towards those involved in ecumenism and church leadership.

200 CN ISSN 0383-4301
ECUMENISM. (Editions in English and French) 1966. q. Can.$14 (foreign $16). Canadian Centre for Ecumenism, 2065 Sherbrooke St. W., Montreal, Que. H3H 1G6, Canada. Ed.Bd. adv.; bk.rev.; circ. 1,600. (also avail. in microform from UMI) **Indexed**: Rel.& Theol.Abstr., Rel.Ind.One.
—BLDSC shelfmark: 3659.720000.

200 SA
ECUNEWS. (Not published 1990-1992) 1975. m. free. South African Council of Churches, Khotso House, 62 Sauer St., P.O. Box 4921, Johannesburg 2000, South Africa. FAX 011-492-1448. bk.rev.; circ. 3,500.

200 CN ISSN 0013-2322
L'EGLISE CANADIENNE; documents et informations. (Text in French) 1968. 15/yr. Can.$30. Revue L'Eglise Canadienne Inc., 1073 Blvd. St. Cyrille, W., Quebec, Que. G1S 4R5, Canada. TEL 418-688-1211. Ed. Rolande Parrot. adv.; bk.rev.; index; circ. 6,000. **Indexed**: CERDIC, Pt.de Rep. (1979-).
—BLDSC shelfmark: 3664.215300.
Description: Features studies and information on theological questions. Also covers life in the church in a general sense.

260 CN ISSN 0013-2349
EGLISE ET THEOLOGIE. (Text in English and French) 1970. 3/yr. Can.$35. Saint Paul University, Faculty of Theology, 223 Main St., Ottawa, Ont. K1S 1C4, Canada. TEL 613-236-1393. FAX 613-782-3005. Ed. Leo Laberge. bk.rev.; index. (also avail. in microform from UMI; reprint service avail. from UMI) **Indexed**: Bull.Signal., Canon Law Abstr., CERDIC, Int.Z.Bibelwiss., New Test.Abstr., Old Test.Abstr., Rel.& Theol.Abstr. (1974-), Rel.Ind.One, Rel.Per.
—BLDSC shelfmark: 3664.215500.

EGLISE QUI CHANTE. see MUSIC

200 IT
EKUMENISMO; trimonata internacia gazeto pri ekumenaj temoj kaj aferoj. (Text in Esperanto) 1985. q? L.10000($10) Piazza Duomo, 4, 48100 Ravenna, Italy. TEL 0544-918376. Ed. Angelo Duranti.

200 US ISSN 8756-1336
ELISABETH ELLIOT NEWSLETTER. 1982. 6/yr. $7. (Servant Ministeries) Servant Publications, Box 7711, Ann Arbor, MI 48107. TEL 313-761-8505. Ed. Stephanie Giba. bk.rev.; circ. 9,000.
Description: Inspirational articles for Christians.

200 NE ISSN 0013-6212
ELISABETHBODE. 1929. w. fl.27. Stichting Elisabethbode, Postbus 2, 7260 AA Ruurlo, Netherlands. circ. 200,000.

EMERGE!; a journal for Christian Scientists supporting lesbians and gay men. see HOMOSEXUALITY

RELIGIONS AND THEOLOGY

266   IT   ISSN 0013-6697
EMIGRATO ITALIANO.* 1903. m. L.1000($4) Congregazione dei Missionari di S. Carlo, Via Scalabrini 3, 36061 Bassano del Grappa (Vicenza), Italy. Ed. P.G.B. Saraggi. adv.; charts; stat.; index; circ. 5,000.

200   US   ISSN 1043-5816
EMORY STUDIES IN EARLY CHRISTIANITY. irreg. Peter Lang Publishing, Inc., 62 W. 45th St., 4th Fl., New York, NY 10036. TEL 212-302-6740. FAX 212-302-7574. Ed. Vernon K. Robbins.
  Description: Investigates early Christian literature including the New Testament, and Mediterranean literature which illuminates aspects of early Christianity.

200   US   ISSN 0194-5246
EMPHASIS ON FAITH AND LIVING. 1969. m. donations. Missionary Church, Inc., 3901 S. Wayne Ave., Ft. Wayne, IN 46807. TEL 219-456-4502. FAX 219-456-4903. Ed. Bob Ranson. adv.; bk.rev.; circ. 16,000. **Indexed:** G.Soc.Sci.& Rel.Per.Lit.
  Description: Communicates message and ministry of the Missionary Church.

200   FR   ISSN 0013-6921
EN AVANT. 1882. w. 210 F. (foreign 250 F.). Armee du Salut, 76 rue de Rome, 75008 Paris, France. TEL 1-43-87-41-19. Ed. J.P. Thoeni. bk.rev.; circ. 10,000.
  Description: Covers history related to the Salvation Army as well as current activities within the organization.

200   US   ISSN 0013-7081
BR1
ENCOUNTER (INDIANAPOLIS, 1956). 1956. q. $12. Christian Theological Seminary, 1000 W. 42nd St., Indianapolis, IN 46208. TEL 317-924-1331. Ed. Clark M. Williamson. adv.; bk.rev.; index; circ. 650. (also avail. in microfilm from UMI; reprint service avail. from UMI) **Indexed:** Amer.Hist.& Life, Arts & Hum.Cit.Ind., G.Soc.Sci.& Rel.Per.Lit., Hist.Abstr., Hum.Ind., Int.Z.Bibelwiss., New Test.Abstr., Old Test.Abstr., Rel.& Theol.Abstr., Rel.Ind.One.
  —BLDSC shelfmark: 3738.540000.
  Description: Discusses creative theological scholarship among believers in Christ and people of other faiths.

200 283   UK   ISSN 0958-2797
ENCOUNTER (LONDON, 1990). q. £4. United Society for the Propagation of the Gospel, Partnership House, 157 Waterloo Rd., London SE1 8XA, England. TEL 071-928-8681. FAX 071-928-2371. circ. 5,000.
  Incorporates (in 1990): United Society for the Propagation of the Gospel. Quarterly Intercession Paper.
  Description: Includes prayer and liturgical material.

200   US
ENCYCLOPEDIA OF AMERICAN RELIGIONS. irreg., latest 3rd ed. $165. Gale Research Inc., 835 Penobscot Bldg., Detroit, MI 48226. TEL 800-877-4253. FAX 313-961-6083. TELEX 810-221-7086. Ed. J. Gordon Melton.
  Description: Details approximately 1,600 religious groups of North America, ranging from Adventists to Zen Buddhists. Divided into two sections: essays and directory listings.

200   US
ENCYCLOPEDIA OF AMERICAN RELIGIONS: RELIGIOUS CREEDS. irreg. $125. Gale Research Inc., 835 Penobscot Bldg., Detroit, MI 48226. TEL 800-877-4253. FAX 313-961-6083. TELEX 810-221-7086. Ed. J. Gordon Melton.
  Description: Presents 464 religious creeds, statements of faith, and summaries of doctrine associated with the many branches of Christian, Jewish, Islamic, Hindu, and other religions practiced in United States.

200   SP
ENSENANZA DE LA RELIGION. 1982. irreg., no.2, 1986. price varies. (Universidad de Navarra, Facultad de Teologia) Ediciones Universidad de Navarra, S.A., Apdo. 396, 31080 Pamplona, Spain. TEL 94 825 6850.

250   CN
ENTRE - NOUS. (Editions in English, French) 1970. 4/yr. free. Canadian Council of Churches, 40 St. Clair Ave. E., Toronto, Ont. M4T 1M9, Canada. TEL 416-921-4152. FAX 416-921-7478. bk.rev.; circ. 3,000.
  Formerly (until 1990): Canadian Council of Churches. Council Communicator (ISSN 0045-4605)

200   AU   ISSN 0017-4602
ENTSCHLUSS; Zeitschrift fuer Praxis und Theologie. 1946. m. S.380. Lainzerstr. 138, A-1130 Vienna, Austria. TEL 0222-8049742. FAX 0222-8049743. adv.; bk.rev.; record rev.; bibl.; charts; index; circ. 8,000. **Indexed:** CERDIC.
  Formerly: Grosse Entschluss.

200 150   US   ISSN 0013-9408
ENVOY (PITTSBURGH). 1963. 6/yr. $9. Duquesne University, Institute of Formative Spirituality, 600 Forbes Ave., Pittsburgh, PA 15282. TEL 412-434-6029. Ed. Adrian van Kaam. circ. 3,000. (also avail. in microform from UMI; reprint service avail. from UMI) **Indexed:** Cath.Ind.

262   IT   ISSN 0013-9505
EPHEMERIDES LITURGICAE; commentarium bimestre de re liturgica. (Text in various languages) 1887. 5/yr. L.44500($38) Centro Liturgico Vincenziano, Via Pompeo Magno. 21, 00192 Rome, Italy. (Co-sponsor: Vincentian Fathers) adv.; bk.rev.; circ. 1,500. **Indexed:** Canon Law Abstr., CERDIC, New Test.Abstr.
  —BLDSC shelfmark: 3793.475000.

262   IT
EPHEMERIDES LITURGICAE. COLLECTIO SUBSIDIA. 1974. irreg., no.62, 1991. price varies. Centro Liturgico Vincenziano, Via Pompeo Magno, 21, 00192 Rome, Italy. TEL 3216114. FAX 3221078.

200   US   ISSN 0273-6969
BV4485
EPIPHANY JOURNAL; a journal of faith and insight. 1980. q. $22.50 (foreign $28.50). (Christ the Saviour Brotherhood) Epiphany Press, P.O. Box 2250, So. Portland, ME 04116-2250. Ed. Stephen Muratore. bk.rev.; circ. 1,800. (also avail. in microform from UMI; back issues avail.) **Indexed:** Rel.& Theol.Abstr. (1988-), Rel.Ind.One.
  ●Also available online. Vendor(s): BRS, DIALOG.
  Formerly: Epiphany.
  Description: An Orthodox journal proclaiming the living Gospel of Jesus Christ in the contemporary world.

200 901   US
EPOCHE; journal of the history of religions at U.C.L.A. 1972. a. $6. University of California, Los Angeles, Graduate Student Association, 301 Kerchoff Hall, 308 Westwood Plaza, Los Angeles, CA 90024. (Subscr. to: Department of History, UCLA, Los Angeles, CA 90024) Ed. Rick Talbott. cum.index: 1972-82; circ. 850. (back issues avail.)

200   US   ISSN 0276-2854
B785.E64
ERASMUS OF ROTTERDAM SOCIETY YEARBOOK. 1981. a. $35 to individuals; institutions $40. Erasmus of Rotterdam Society, 316 Syria Court, Ft. Washington, MD 20744. Ed. Richard L. DeMolen. bk.rev.; circ. 600.
  Description: Encourages research and writing on the life of Erasmus, a scholar and humanist of the Renaissance and Reformation.

200   GW   ISSN 0014-0201
ERMLANDBRIEFE. 1946. a. DM.10. Apostolischer Visitator fuer Klerus und Glaeubige des Ermlandes, Ermlandweg 22, 4400 Muenster, Germany. Ed. Johannes Schwalke. bk.rev.; illus.; circ. 33,000.

ERRANT NEWS. see *ART*

ESPIRITU. see *PHILOSOPHY*

200   FR   ISSN 0014-0775
ESPRIT ET VIE. (In 2 Parts: Doctrine; Pastorale) 1879. w. 390 F. (for both parts)(foreign 460 F.). B.P. 4, 52200 Langres, France. TEL 25-87-02-26. FAX 25-87-45-66. bk.rev.; bibl.; index; circ. 5,000. **Indexed:** CERDIC, New Test.Abstr.
  Formerly: Ami du Clerge.
  Description: Discusses readings, the Holy Scripture, theology, philosophy, liturgy, the history of literature, morals.

240   FR   ISSN 0396-969X
ESPRIT SAINT; revue de spiritualite. 1952. q. 35 F. Congregation du Saint-Esprit, Fraternites du Saint-Esprit, 30 rue Lhomond, 75005 Paris, France. Ed. Michel Picard. bk.rev.; bibl.; cum.index; circ. 6,000.
  Formerly: Devotion au Saint-Esprit (ISSN 0012-1711)

200 800 100   SP   ISSN 0210-0525
ESTUDIOS; revista trimestral publicada por los frailes de la orden de la merced. 1945. q. 2800 ptas.($36) Belisana, 2, 28043 Madrid, Spain. TEL 200 49 98. Dir. Luis Vazquez Fernandez. bk.rev.; circ. 500.

220   SP   ISSN 0014-1437
BS410
ESTUDIOS BIBLICOS. (Text in English, French, German, Italian, Spanish) 1941. q. 3000 ptas. (foreign 4000 ptas.). Centro de Estudios Teologicos "San Damasco", San Buenaventura, 9, 28005 Madrid, Spain. TEL 91-265 24 04. (Co-sponsor: Asociacion Biblica Espanola) Ed. Alfonso de la Fuente. bk.rev.; bibl.; circ. 600. **Indexed:** New Test.Abstr., Old Test.Abstr., Rel.Ind.One.

200   SP   ISSN 0210-1610
ESTUDIOS ECLESIASTICOS; revista de teologia. 1922. q. $44. (Compania de Jesus, Facultades de Teologia) Casa de Escritores, S.J., Pablo Aranda 3, E-28006 Madrid, Spain. FAX 341-5634073. Ed.Bd. bk.rev.; bibl. **Indexed:** Amer.Hist.& Life, Canon Law Abstr., CERDIC, Hist.Abstr., New Test.Abstr., Old Test.Abstr.

200   SP   ISSN 0210-0363
ESTUDIOS TRINITARIOS. 1967. 3/yr. 3500 ptas.($50) Ediciones Secretariado Trinitario, Filiberto Villalobos, 82, 37007 Salamanca, Spain. TEL 235602. Ed. P. Nereo Silanes. bk.rev. **Indexed:** CERDIC.

200   FR
ETENDARD DE LA BIBLE ET HERAUT DU ROYAUME DE CHRIST. English edition: Bible Standard and Herald of Christ's Kingdom (ISSN 0006-081X) 1957. bi-m. 15 F. Mouvement Missionnaire Interieur Laique, c/o Gilbert Hermetz, 2 rue du Dr. Capiaux, 62620 Barlin, France. TEL 21-25-94-86. Ed. Bernard Hedman. circ. 500.

ETHICS AND PUBLIC POLICY CENTER NEWSLETTER. see *POLITICAL SCIENCE*

200   SZ
ETHOS - DIE ZEITSCHRIFT FUER DIE GANZE FAMILIE. 1983. m. 90.40 Fr. Foerderung Christlicher Publizistik, Postfach 263, CH-9435 Heerbrugg, Switzerland. TEL 0711-724358. Ed. Bruno Schwengeler. circ. 30,000.
  Description: Family oriented magazine of Bible study.

ETUDES GREGORIENNES; revue de musicologie religieuse. see *MUSIC*

200 950   NE   ISSN 0531-1950
ETUDES PRELIMINAIRES AUX RELIGIONS ORIENTALES DANS L'EMPIRE ROMAIN. 1961. irreg., vol.113, 1990. price varies. E.J. Brill, P.O. Box 9000, 2300 PA Leiden, Netherlands. TEL 071-312624. FAX 071-317532. TELEX 39296 BRILL NL. (In N. America: E.J. Brill, 24 Hudson St., Kinderhook, NY 12106. TEL 800-962-4406) Eds. M.E.C. van Haaren. M.B. deBoer. **Indexed:** Rel.Ind.Two.
  Description: Focuses on the study of Oriental religions in all parts of the Roman Empire.

200 060   FR   ISSN 0082-2612
ETUDES TEILHARDIENNES/TEILHARDIAN STUDIES. 1969. irreg. price varies. Editions du Seuil, 27 rue Jacob, 75261 Paris Cedex 06, France. Ed. J.P. DeMoulin. **Indexed:** Rel.Ind.One.

200   PL   ISSN 0014-2298
EUHEMER; przeglad religioznawczy. (Text in Polish; summaries in English; table of contents in English and French) 1957. q. $25. Polskie Towarzystwo Religioznawcze, Palac Kultury i Nauki, Pietro XIII, pok. 13-27, 00-901 Warsaw, Poland. (Dist. by: Ars Polona, Krakowskie Przedmiescie 7, 00-068 Warsaw, Poland) bk.rev.; bibl.; illus.; index; circ. 860.
  —BLDSC shelfmark: 3827.400000.

EUNTES DOCETE. see *RELIGIONS AND THEOLOGY — Roman Catholic*

RELIGIONS AND THEOLOGY 4177

266 US
EUROPE REPORT. 1971. bi-m. free. Greater Europe Mission, Box 668, Wheaton, IL 60189. TEL 708-462-8050. Ed. Donna Lappert. adv.; bk.rev.; circ. 40,000. (tabloid format)
Former titles (until vol.18, no.5, 1988): G E M's Europe Report; Greater Europe Report.

EUROPEAN STUDIES JOURNAL. see *HISTORY — History Of Europe*

261 UK
EVANGEL. 3/yr. £9. Paternoster Press, 3 Mount Radford Crescent, Exeter EX2 4JW, England. Ed. Stephen Dray.

200 974 US
EVANGELICAL & REFORMED HISTORICAL SOCIETY NEWSLETTER. 1970. s-a. membership. Evangelical & Reformed Historical Society, Phillip Schaff Library, Lancaster Theological Seminary, 555 W. James St., Lancaster, PA 17603. Ed. John B. Payne. circ. 1,500. (back issues avail.)
Description: News about society meetings, papers presented and members' activities.

200 US
EVANGELICAL CATHOLIC. 1977. bi-m. $20 (foreign $30). Episcopal Synod of America, 6300 Ridglea Place, Ste. 910, Ft. Worth, TX 76116. TEL 412-741-8843. Ed. David Peter Mills. circ. 3,000. (back issues avail.)
Description: Addresses the clergy and laity. Covers theological issues in the Episcopal Church.

266 US ISSN 0014-3359
BV2350
EVANGELICAL MISSIONS QUARTERLY. 1964. q. $17.95. Evangelical Missions Information Service, Box 794, Wheaton, IL 60189. TEL 708-653-2158. FAX 708-653-0520. Ed. James W. Reapsome. adv.; bk.rev.; index; circ. 8,900. Indexed: CERDIC, Chr.Per.Ind., Rel.& Theol.Abstr. (1969-), Rel.Ind.One.
Description: Journal devoted to understanding evangelical Protestant missionary thought and practice.

200 UK ISSN 0014-3367
BR1
EVANGELICAL QUARTERLY. 1929. q. £13.80($44.40) Paternoster Press Ltd., Paternoster House, 3 Mount Radford Crescent, Exeter EX2 4JW, England. (Dist. in U.S. & Canada by: The Paternoster Press, P.O. Box 11127, Birminghan, Alabama 35202, U.S.A.) Ed. I. Howard Marshall. bk.rev.; index; circ. 1,100. (also avail. in microfilm from UMI; reprint service avail. from UMI) Indexed: CERDIC, Chr.Per.Ind., New Test.Abstr., Old Test.Abstr., Rel.& Theol.Abstr. (1969-), Rel.Ind.One, Rel.Per.
—BLDSC shelfmark: 3830.700000.
Description: Articles on a variety of biblical and theological topics.

200 US
EVANGELICAL REVIEW MAGAZINE; reviewing God's work through people today. 1979. q. $3. Hillwood Ministries, Inc., Rutland Rd., No. 6, Mt. Juliet, TN 37122. Ed. Robert C. Hill. adv.; bk.rev.; film rev.; circ. 100,000. (back issues avail.) Indexed: Crim.Just.Abstr.

200 UK ISSN 0144-8153
EVANGELICAL REVIEW OF THEOLOGY. 1977. q. £13.80($44.40) Paternoster Press Ltd., Paternoster House, 3 Mount Radford Cresc., Exeter EX2 4JW, England. (Dist. in U.S. & Canada by: The Paternoster Press, P.O. Box 11127, Birmingham, Alabama 35202, U.S.A.) Ed. Bruce Nicholls. bk.rev.; circ. 1,000. (also avail. in microfilm from UMI; reprint service avail. from UMI) Indexed: CERDIC, Rel.& Theol.Abstr. (1989-), Rel.Ind.One.
—BLDSC shelfmark: 3830.702000.
Description: Interprets the Christian faith for contemporary living.

200 US ISSN 0745-0486
EVANGELICAL VISITOR. 1887. m. $12 (effective 1992). (Brethren in Christ Church, Board for Media Ministries) Evangel Publishing House, 2000 Evangel Way, Box 166, Nappanee, IN 46550. TEL 219-773-3164. Ed. Glen A. Pierce. circ. 5,500. (back issues avail.)
Description: Promotes the doctrine, teaching and ministry of the Brethren in Christ Church.

243 US
EVANGELICAL WOMEN'S CAUCUS. UPDATE. 1980. q. $30 (students $15). Ecumenical & Evangelical Women's Caucus, Box 209, Hadley, NY 12835. TEL 518-696-2406. Ed. Debbie Jang. bk.rev.; circ. 600. (back issues avail.)

266 SP
EVANGELIO Y MISION. 1964. m. donation. Compania de Jesus, Plaza de San Marcos, 1, 24001 Leon, Spain. TEL 22 85 78. Ed. J. Pedraz. illus.; circ. 5,000.
Formerly: Boletin Intimo de Compania.

DER EVANGELISCHE ERZIEHER; Zeitschrift fuer Paedagogik und Theologie. see *EDUCATION*

EVANGELISCHE IMPULSE; Zeitschrift fuer die Arbeit mit alten Menschen. see *GERONTOLOGY AND GERIATRICS*

200 GW ISSN 0300-4236
EVANGELISCHE KOMMENTARE; Monatsschrift zum Zeitgeschehen in Kirche und Gesellschaft. 1968. m. DM.98. Kreuz-Verlag Zeitschriften GmbH, Breitwiesenstr. 30, Postfach 800669, 7000 Stuttgart 80, Germany. TEL 0711-78803. Ed.Bd. adv.; bk.rev.; circ. 9,600.
—BLDSC shelfmark: 3830.730000.

200 GW
EVANGELISCHE SAMMLUNG. m. Foerderverein Evangelische Sammlung Berlin e.V., Motzstr. 52, D-1000 Berlin 52, Germany. TEL 030-242252.

240 GW ISSN 0014-3502
BR4
EVANGELISCHE THEOLOGIE. 1934. bi-m. DM.68.50 (students DM.56.80). Christian Kaiser Verlag, Lilienstr. 70, 8000 Munich 80, Germany. TEL 089-483014. FAX 089-4484473. adv.; circ. 3,500. (also avail. in microform from UMI; reprint service avail. from UMI) Indexed: CERDIC, New Test.Abstr., Old Test.Abstr., Rel.& Theol.Abstr. (1991-), Rel.Ind.One, Rel.Per.

200 053.1 GW ISSN 0177-185X
EVANGELISCHER DIGEST. 1951. m. DM.97.20. Verlag Axel B. Trunkel, Landhausstr. 22, 7000 Stuttgart 10, Germany. Ed. Andrea Przyklenk. circ. 14,800. (back issues avail.)
Description: General interest subjects for senior citizens.

243 UK
EVANGELISM TODAY. 1972. m. £7. 320 Ashley Down Rd., Bristol BS7 9BQ, England. Ed. Bill Spencer. adv.; bk.rev.; circ. 5,500.
Description: News and topics of interest to praying and giving supporters of evangelism and outreach.

200 IT
EVANGELIZZARE; mensile per animatori di catechesi. 1974. m. L.25000 (foreign L.40000). Centro Editoriale Dehoniano, V. Nosadella 6, 40123 Bologna, Italy. TEL 051-306811. FAX 051-341706. adv.; bk.rev.

262.9 SP
EXCERPTA E DISSERTATIONIBUS IN IURE CANONICO. 1983. irreg., no.5, 1987. 3000 ptas. (Universidad de Navarra, Facultad de Derecho Canonico) Servicio de Publicaciones de la Universidad de Navarra, S.A., Apdo. 177, 31080 Pamplona, Spain. TEL 94 25 2700.

200 UK ISSN 0014-5246
BS410
EXPOSITORY TIMES. 1889. m. £12.50($24.95) T & T Clark, 59 George St., Edinburgh EH2 2LQ, Scotland. TEL 031-225-4703. FAX 031-220-4260. Ed. Rev. C.S. Rodd. adv.; bk.rev.; index; circ. 6,000. Indexed: Arts & Hum.Cit.Ind., Br.Hum.Ind., Curr.Cont., New Test.Abstr., Old Test.Abstr., Rel.& Theol.Abstr. 91968-), Rel.Ind.One.
—BLDSC shelfmark: 3843.370000.
Description: Interdenominational articles, sermons and book reviews for ministers, scholars and theological students.

200 AT
F A C T. (Faith and Atheism in Communist Territories) 1979. m. free. Voice of Peace, P.O. Box 339, Cronulla, N.S.W. 2230, Australia. circ. 1,800.

200 301.4157 051 US
F L G C NEWSLETTER. 1976. q. $8. Friends for Lesbian and Gay Concerns, Box 222, Sumneytown, PA 18084. TEL 215-234-8424. Ed. Bruce Grimes. bk.rev.; circ. 600. (looseleaf format)
Description: Carries articles of special interest to lesbian and gay Quakers, including current topics in same-sex marriage among Quakers.

200 US
FACT BOOK ON THEOLOGICAL EDUCATION. 1971. a. $20. Association of Theological Schools, 10 Summit Park Dr., Pittsburgh, PA 15275-1103. TEL 412-788-6505. Ed. Gail B. King. circ. 700. Indexed: SRI.

200 UK
FAITH. 1968. bi-m. £8($17) Faith - Keyway Publications, 2 Redford Ave., Wallington, Surrey SM6 9OP, England. TEL 081-776-8399. Ed. Rev. Timothy Finigan. adv.; bk.rev.; circ. 1,200.

200 US
FAITH. 1988. q. free. International Bible Society, c/o Karen Rayer, Ed., Box 62970, Colorado Springs, CO 80962-2970. TEL 719-488-9200. FAX 719-488-3840. TELEX 312284. circ. 125,000.
Description: Provides excerpts of Christian books as a ministry to friends of the International Bible Society along with updates on scripture projects worldwide.

200 SA
FAITH AND ACTION. (Text in English) 1983. q. free. Apostolic Faith Mission of South Africa, P.O. Box 89735, Lyndhurst 2106, South Africa. TEL 011-786-8550. FAX 011-887-1182. Ed. Edgar J. Gschwend. abstr.; circ. 10,000. (back issues avail.)
Formerly (until Jan. 1992): A F M Koinonia.

200 UK ISSN 0014-701X
FAITH AND FREEDOM; a journal of progressive religion. 1947. 2/yr. £10($20) Manchester College, Oxford OX1 3TD, England. TEL 01-393-9122. (Subscr. to: c/o Rev. Peter B. Godfrey, Ed., 41, Bradford Dr., Ewell, Epsom, Surrey KT19 0AQ, England; U.S. subscr. to: Meadville College, 5701 Woodlawn Ave., Chicago, IL 60637) adv.; bk.rev.; circ. 600. (also avail. in microform from UMI; reprint service avail. from UMI) Indexed: CERDIC, Rel.& Theol.Abstr. (1989-), Rel.Ind.One.
—BLDSC shelfmark: 3865.510600.

200 UK
FAITH AND HERITAGE. 1977. s-a. £1.25. Prayer Book Society, St. James Garlickhythe, Garlick Hill, London EC4 2AL, England. TEL 0406-25268. Ed. Rev. D.L. Scott. bk.rev.; circ. 7,000.

200 SZ ISSN 0512-2589
FAITH AND ORDER PAPERS. 1949. irreg., no.153, 1991. price varies. World Council of Churches, Publications Office, 150 Route de Ferney, Box 2100, CH-1211 Geneva 2, Switzerland. TEL 022-791-6111. FAX 022-791-0361. TELEX 415730-OIK-CH. (Dist. in U.S. by: World Council of Churches Distribution Center, Rt 111 & Sharadin Road, P.O. Box 346, Kutztown, PA 19530-0346) cum.index: 1910-70. Indexed: Rel.Ind.Two.

FAITH AND PHILOSOPHY. see *PHILOSOPHY*

230.05 US ISSN 0098-5449
BR1
FAITH & REASON (FRONT ROYAL). 1975. q. $20. (Christendom College) Christendom Press, 2101 Shenandoah Shores Rd., Front Royal, VA 22630. FAX 703-636-1655. Ed. Timothy T. O'Donnell. bk.rev.; circ. 1,000. Indexed: Cath.Ind., CERDIC.

266 US
FAITH & RENEWAL. 1976. 6/yr. $20 suggested contribution. Servant Ministries, Inc., Center for Pastoral Renewal, Box 8617, Ann Arbor, MI 48107. TEL 313-761-8505. FAX 313-761-1577. Ed. John Blattner. bk.rev.; index; circ. 9,000. (back issues avail.)
Formerly: Pastoral Renewal (ISSN 0744-8279)

RELIGIONS AND THEOLOGY

200   UK   ISSN 0309-1627
FAITH & WORSHIP. 1976. s-a. £3. Prayer Book Society, c/o A.C. Capey, Ed., 11 Nursery Lane, Wilmslow, Cheshire SK9 5JG, England. TEL 0625-527208. (Subscr. addr.: c/o Mr. John Skinner, 59A Kings End, Ruislip, Middlesex HA4 7DD, England. TEL 08956-37429) bk.rev.; circ. 7,000.

200   US
▼**FAITH WORKS.** 1990. q. $20. 122 N. Pearl, Buffalo, NY 14202. Eds. Ann Markle, Jack Shifflett.

200   IT   ISSN 0014-7095
FAMIGLIA CRISTIANA. (Supplement avail.: Familia T V) 1931. w. L.237000. Societa San Paolo Gruppo Periodici, S.r.l., Via Liberazione 4, 12051 Alba (Cuneo), Italy. TEL 0173-317356. FAX 0173-317423. Ed. Leonardo Zega. adv.; bk.rev.; film rev.; play rev.; charts; illus.; stat.; index, cum.index every 5 yrs.; circ. 1,189,352. (tabloid format)

FAMILIA CRISTA; revista da paz e do amor - revista mensal para a familia. see *SOCIOLOGY*

FAMILIA Y SOCIEDAD. see *SOCIOLOGY*

200   GW
FAMILIEN UND JUGEND - GOTTESDIENSTE. m. DM.96. Bergmoser und Hoeller Verlag GmbH, Karl-Friedrich-Str. 76, 5100 Aachen, Germany. TEL 0241-17309-21. FAX 0241-17309-34. circ. 5,200. (looseleaf format)
Formerly: Gottesdienste mit Kindern und Jugendlichen (ISSN 0176-8581)
Description: For use in preparing Sunday services for children and youth.

200   FR   ISSN 0014-7184
FAMILLE NOUVELLE.* 1969. q. 36 F. Editions du Levain, 205 rue Laurier Ouest, Montreal, Que. H2T 2N, Canada. bk.rev.; circ. 100. (processed)
Formerly: Orphee Contact.

268   US
FAMILY RADIO NEWS. 1966. q. free. Family Stations, Inc., 290 Hegenberger Rd., Oakland, CA 94621. TEL 800-543-1495. FAX 510-633-7983. Ed. Richard Homeres. charts; illus.; circ. 100,000.
Description: Contains articles about the ministry of Family Radio as well as the program guide for the stations served.

200   NO   ISSN 0014-8733
FAST GRUNN. 1948. bi-m. DKK 240. Lunde Forlag og Bokhandel A-S, Grensen 19, 0159 Oslo 1, Norway. FAX 02-42-10-49. Eds. Egil Sjaastad, Jon Kvalbein. adv.; bk.rev.; illus.; index; circ. 3,800.

200   US
FELLOWSHIP LIFE & LIFESTYLES. 1975. q. Fellowship of the Inner Light, 620 14th St., Virginia Beach, VA 23451. TEL 703-896-3673. FAX 804-428-6648. Eds. Myrrh and Stephen Haslam.

200   UK
FELLOWSHIP OF RECONCILIATION. ANNUAL REPORT; nonviolence: peace in action. a. free. Fellowship of Reconciliation, 40-46 Harleyford Rd., Vauxhall, London SE11 5AY, England. TEL 071-582-9054. FAX 071-582-9180.
Description: News of the fellowship's work.

260   FR   ISSN 0015-0371
FETES ET SAISONS. 1945. 10/yr. 175 F. (foreign 225 F.). Editions du Cerf, 29 bd. Latour Maubourg, 75340 Paris Cedex 07, France. TEL 44-18-12-12. FAX 45-56-04-27. (Subscr. to: Service Abonnements, 3 chemin des Prunais, 94350 Villiers-sur-Marne, France) Ed. Marc Sevin. illus.; circ. 40,000. Indexed: Pt.de Rep. (1979-).
Description: Studies Christian life, sacrements, the lives of saints, questions of education and morals, happenings in the Church.

FIDES ET HISTORIA. see *HISTORY*

200   IT
FILOSOFIA DELLA RELIGIONE. TESTI E STUDI. 1977. irreg., latest no.3. price varies. Paideia Editrice, Via Corsica 130, 25125 Brescia, Italy.

207.11   IT   ISSN 0015-2528
FIORI DI S. ANTONIO. 1951. s-m. free. Convento di Giaccherino, 51030 Pontelungo, Italy. Ed. P. Lorenzo Lazzeri. illus.; circ. 17,000.

200   US   ISSN 1047-5141
▼**FIRST THINGS;** a monthly journal of religion and public life. 1990. m. (10/yr.). $24 (effective Jan. 1992; typically set in Sept.). Institute on Religion & Public Life, 156 Fifth Ave., Ste. 400, New York, NY 10010. TEL 212-627-2288. FAX 212-627-2184. (Subscr. to: Department FT, Box 3000, Denville, NJ 07834-9847) Ed. Richard John Neuhaus. adv.; bk.rev.; index; circ. 15,000. (also avail. in microfilm; microfiche; back issues avail.; reprint service avail.)
●Also available online.
Description: Examines issues arising at the crossroads of religion and public life today.

FLASH. see *HANDICAPPED — Visually Impaired*

FLAT EARTH NEWS; the last iconoclast. see *HUMANITIES: COMPREHENSIVE WORKS*

200   US
FLOODTIDE; literature evangelism. 1948. bi-m. free. Christian Literature Crusade, Inc., Box 1449, Fort Washington, PA 19034. TEL 215-542-1242. Ed. Leona Hepburn. bk.rev.; circ. 6,500.

914.606 200   SP
FOC NOU; revista al servei dels Cristians. (Text in Catalan) 1974. m. 3500 ptas. (foreign 4500 ptas.). Publicaciones de el Ciervo, S.A., Calvet 56, 08021 Barcelona, Spain. Ed. Roser Bofill Portabella. adv.; bk.rev.; illus.; circ. 3,000.

200   UK
FOCUS (WARWICKSHIRE). 1975. q. £0.30. Christian Endeavour Union of Great Britain and Ireland, Wellesbourne House, Walton Rd., Wellesbourne, Warwickshire CV35 9JB, England. TEL 0789-470439. Ed. Sandra O'Nions. adv.; bk.rev.; circ. 2,000.
Formerly: Ascent.

200   UK   ISSN 0950-9720
FOCUS ON CHRISTIAN - MUSLIM RELATIONS. 1978. 12/yr. £7 to individuals; institutions £12. Islamic Foundation, Markfield Dawah Centre, Ratby Lane, Markfield, Leicester LE6 0RN, England. TEL 0530-244944. FAX 0530-244946.
Description: Examines Christian-Muslim relations in all the dimensions; provides Muslims with information from Christian sources.

200   US   ISSN 0894-3346
FOCUS ON THE FAMILY. 1980. m. free. Focus on the Family, Inc., 420 N. CascadeCenter Dr., Colorado Springs, CO 80903. TEL 719-531-3400. FAX 719-531-3499. Ed. Mike Yorkey. circ. 1,800,000.
Description: Presents articles intended to strengthen families and reinforce traditional Judeo-Christian values.

200   FR
FOI AUJOURD'HUI. 1977. m. 284 F. Bayard Presse, 5 rue Bayard, 75380 Paris Cedex 08, France. circ. 40,000.

200 054.1   FR   ISSN 0015-5357
FOI ET VIE. 1898. 6/yr. 190 F. Association des Amis de Foi et Vie, 139 bd. Montparnasse, 75006 Paris 6, France. Ed. Olivier Millet. adv.; bk.rev.; bibl.; charts; illus.; index; circ. 1,200. Indexed: CERDIC, New Test.Abstr., Rel.& Theol.Abstr. (1989-), Rel.Ind.One, Rel.Per.
—BLDSC shelfmark: 3964.385000.
Description: A religious and theological publication with protestant tendencies.

250   IT   ISSN 0015-5802
FOLIUM DIOCESANUM BAUZANENSE-BRIXINENSE. (Text in German, Italian and Latin) 1964. m. L.5000. Curia Episcopalis Bauzanensis-Brixinensis, 39100 Bolzano, Italy. index; circ. 800. (tabloid format)

200   UK
FOR CHRIST AND PEACE. 1951. irreg. $10. Loverseed Press, 141 Woolacombe Rd., Blackheath, London SE3, England. circ. 1,500.

200   GW
FORSCHUNGEN ZUR KIRCHEN- UND DOGMENGESCHICHTE. 1954. irreg. Vandenhoeck und Ruprecht, Robert-Bosch-Breite 6, Postfach 3753, 3400 Goettingen, Germany. TEL 0551-6959-0. FAX 0551-695917.

200   GW
FORSCHUNGEN ZUR RELIGION UND LITERATUR DES ALTEN UND NEUEN TESTAMENTS. 1930. irreg. Vandenhoeck und Ruprecht, Robert-Bosch-Breite 6, Postfach 3753, 3400 Goettingen, Germany. TEL 0551-6959-0. FAX 0551-695917. Eds. Wolfgang Schrage, Rudolf Smend.

200   GW
FORUM. BERICHTE AUS DER ARBEIT. 1955. q. DM.20. Evangelische Akademie Iserlohn, Haus Ortlohn, Berliner Platz 12, 5860 Iserlohn, Germany. FAX 02371-35299. Eds. G. Ebbrecht, R. Sareika. bk.rev.; illus.; circ. 850. (avail. on records)
Former titles: Forum Haus Ortlohn. Freundsbrief (ISSN 0015-8534); Freundsbrief.

200   US
FORUM NEWSLETTER. 1974. q. membership. National Catholic Educational Association, Department of Religious Education, 1077 30th St., N.W., Ste. 100, Washington, DC 20007. TEL 202-337-6232. FAX 202-333-6706. Ed. Michael Carotta. bk.rev.; circ. 5,702. (reprint service avail. from UMI)

200   GW   ISSN 0343-7744
FORUM RELIGION. 1975. q. DM.28. Kreuz-Verlag Zeitschriften GmbH, Breitwiesenstr. 30, 7000 Stuttgart 80, Germany. TEL 0711-78803. Ed.Bd. bk.rev.; circ. 2,500.

FORWARD. see *SOCIAL SERVICES AND WELFARE*

200   UK   ISSN 0144-378X
FOUNDATIONS. 1978. biennial. £1.50. British Evangelical Council, 113 Victoria St., St. Albans, Hertfordshire AL1 3TJ, England. TEL 0727-55655.
Indexed: Rel.& Theol.Abstr. (1989-).
—BLDSC shelfmark: 4025.280200.
Description: Articles and reviews on contemporary theological issues: biblical theology, church history and apologetics.

FOUNDER SOUNDER. see *MUSIC*

FOUR AND FIVE. see *CHILDREN AND YOUTH — For*

200   FR   ISSN 0015-9239
FOYERS MIXTES; informations et reflexions pour un oecumenisme vecu. 1968. q. 175 F.($30) (effective Jan. 1992). Centre Saint Irenee, 2 place Gailleton, 69002 Lyon, France. TEL 78-38-05-07. FAX 78-42-11-00. Ed. Rene Beaupere. adv.; bk.rev.; index; circ. 1,800.

FRANKFURTER KIRCHLICHES JAHRBUCH. see *HISTORY — History Of Europe*

200   GW   ISSN 0722-8120
FRAU UND MUTTER. 1918. every 4 weeks. DM.13.50. (Arbeitsgemeinschaft Frau und Mutter) Kreuz-Verlag Zeitschriften GmbH, Breitwiesenstr. 30, 7000 Stuttgart 80, Germany. TEL 0711-78803. circ. 70,000. (looseleaf format)

200   US
FREE GRACE BROADCASTER. no.129, 1989. q. free. (Mt. Zion Bible Church) Mt. Zion Publications, 2306 W. Wright St., Pensacola, FL 32505. TEL 904-438-6666. Ed. L.R. Shelton, Jr.

FREETHINKER. see *PHILOSOPHY*

200   US   ISSN 0882-8512
FREETHOUGHT TODAY. 1983. 10/yr. $20. Freedom from Religion Foundation, Box 750, Madison, WI 53701. TEL 608-256-5800. Ed. Annie Laurie Gaylor. adv.; circ. 4,500. (tabloid format)
Description: Chronicles freethought activism, critiques religion and monitors state-church separation.

FREEWAY; a power-line paper. see *CHILDREN AND YOUTH — For*

261   GW   ISSN 0016-0776
FREIE RELIGION; Monatsschrift fuer religioese Selbstbestimmung. 1962. m. DM.18. (Freireligioese Landesgemeinde Baden) Freireligioese Verlagsbuchhandlung, L 10, 4-6, 6800 Mannheim 1, Germany. TEL 0621-22805. Ed. Dr. Eckhart Pilick. bk.rev.; abstr.; illus.; circ. 5,000. (processed)
Indexed: CERDIC.

RELIGIONS AND THEOLOGY

200 UK ISSN 0016-1292
FRIENDLY COMPANION. 1857. m. £7.80($15) Gospel Standard Publications, 7 Brackendale Grove, Harpenden, Herts AL5 3EL, England. TEL 0582-760580. Ed. B.A. Ramsbottom. circ. 1,600.
Description: Focuses on scriptural teaching and every day experiences for young people and children.

200 US ISSN 0739-5418
A FRIENDLY LETTER. 1981. m. $19.95 (Canada & Mexico $20.95; elsewhere $22.95). Box 1361, Falls Church, VA 22041. TEL 703-845-0427. Ed. Charles Fager. adv.; bk.rev.; circ. 1,050. (back issues avail.)
Description: Editorials, profiles, historical vignettes and humorous anecdotes pertaining to Quakers and their tradition, culture, and beliefs.

200 GW ISSN 0340-6091
FROHE BOTSCHAFT; Predigten fuer jeden Sonntag des Kirchenjahres. bi-m. DM.29. Vandenhoeck und Ruprecht, Theaterstr. 13, Postfach 3753, 3400 Goettingen, Germany. TEL 0551-6959-22. FAX 0551-695917. Ed. H. Waehrisch.

267 AT
G B DIGEST. 1962. q. Aus.$0.75. Girls Brigade, 9 Albion Place, Sydney, N.S.W. 2000, Australia. Ed. J.A. Christie.

200 KE
GABA REPRINTS. (Text in English) 1970. 20/yr. EAs.60.50($8.80) (Amecea Pastoral Institute) Gaba Publications, P.O. Box 4002, Eldoret, Kenya. Ed. Felician N. Rwehikiza. circ. 1,200. (looseleaf format; back issues avail.)

GABRIEL; informatore filatelico. see *PHILATELY*

200 GW ISSN 0016-5735
GEBETSAPOSTOLAT UND SEELSORGE. 1949. 6/yr. DM.7.80. Verein zur Foerderung des Gebetsapostolates e.V., Beim Schlump 57, 2000 Hamburg 13, Germany. TEL 040-4105348. Ed. Karl Liesner. circ. 11,000.

200 NE
GEEST EN LEVEN; tijdschrift voor informatie, bezinning en gesprek. 1923. bi-m. fl.32.50. Missionarissen van het H. Hart, St. Goedelestraat 2, 5643 MK Eindhoven, Netherlands. Ed.Bd. bk.rev.; index; circ. 1,000. **Indexed:** CERDIC.
Formerly (until 1988): Ons Geestelijk Leven (ISSN 0030-2678)

200 149.3 200 GW ISSN 0016-5921
BV5015
GEIST UND LEBEN. 1927. bi-m. DM.58.80 (students DM.45). Echter-Verlag, Juliuspromenade 64, Postfach 5560, 8700 Wuerzburg 1, Germany. Ed. P. Paul Imhof. adv.; bk.rev.; circ. 5,000. (also avail. in microform from SWZ) **Indexed:** CERDIC, New Test.Abstr.

200 NE ISSN 0016-6065
GEMEENTELEVEN. 1956. m. fl.25. Remonstrantse Gemeente Groningen, Coehoornsingel 14, 9711 BS Groningen, Netherlands. TEL 050-130771. adv.; bk.rev.; circ. 500.

220 GW
GEMEINDEBIBELSCHULE; Mitarbeiterzeitschrift. 1977. m. DM.18.40. Oncken Verlag, Postfach 102829, 3500 Kassel 1, Germany. Ed. Bo Riedel. circ. 11,000. (back issues avail.)

200 NE ISSN 0016-6324
GENADEKLANKEN; nieuws voor nu. 1947. s-m. fl.5. Stichting Ga Uit, Postbus 61, 7090 AB Dinxperlo, Netherlands. circ. 80,000.

200 US
GENERAL CONVENTION OF THE NEW JERUSALEM. JOURNAL. 1817. a. $12. General Convention of the New Jerusalem, 48 Sargent St., Newton, MA 02158. Ed. Ethelwyn Worden. circ. 300.

266 IT ISSN 0016-6960
GENTES. 1927. m. L.15,000. Lega Missionaria Studenti, Via degli Astalli, 16, 00186 Rome, Italy. Dir. Cristoforo Sironi. bk.rev.; bibl.; illus.; stat.; index; circ. 10,000.

200 SZ ISSN 0016-9021
GESCHAEFTSMANN UND CHRIST. 1960. m. (10/yr.). 32 Fr. Internationale Vereinigung Christlicher Geschaeftsleute, Gruppe Zurich, Box 29, 8034 Zurich, Switzerland. TEL 01-2522500. FAX 01-2527242. Ed.Bd. bk.rev.; illus.; circ. 15,000.
Description: Devoted to Christianity's role in the business world, and the problem of applying Christian principles to the business community. Includes list of events.

248.83 IT ISSN 0017-0542
GIOVENTU EVANGELICA. 1947. bi-m. L.28000. Consiglio della Federazione della Gioventu Evangelica Italiana, Via L. Porro Lambertenghi 28, 20159 Milan, Italy. Ed. Francesca Spano. adv.; bk.rev.; illus.; circ. 3,000.

271 IT ISSN 0072-4548
GIOVENTU PASSIONISTA/PASSIONIST YOUTH; rivista di formazione e d'informazione passionista. (Text in various languages; summaries in English) 1955. irreg., no.3, 1960. $3. Edizioni E C O, 64048 S. Gabriele (Teramo), Italy. Ed. P. Natale Cavatassi.

200 100 US ISSN 0732-7781
GIST. 1975. m. $20. University of Healing Press, 1101 Far Valley Rd., Campo, CA 91906. TEL 619-478-5111. Ed. Herbert L. Beierle. circ. 3,000.
Description: Expresses the theme of the absolute archetypal nature of humanity in first person, present tense, positive.

200 GW
GLAUBE HOFFNUNG LIEBE. 1947. m. Horst Krueger, Ed. & Pub., Weidenweg 21, 5100 Aachen 1, Germany. TEL 0241-872552. circ. 3,100.

200 323.4 SZ ISSN 0254-4377
GLAUBE IN DER 2. WELT; Zeitschrift fuer Religionsfreiheit und Menschenrechte. 1973. m. 55 Fr. Institut Glaube in der 2. Welt, Postfach 9, Bergstr. 6, CH-8702 Zollikon-Zurich, Switzerland. TEL 01-3913747. FAX 01-3914426. Ed. Erich Bryner. (back issues avail.)

200 GW ISSN 0179-3551
GLAUBE UND LERNEN; Zeitschrift fuer theologische Urteilsbildung. s-a. DM.36. Vandenhoeck und Ruprecht, Theaterstr. 13, Postfach 3753, 3400 Goettingen, Germany. TEL 0551-6959-22. FAX 0551-695917. Ed.Bd. **Indexed:** Rel.& Theol.Abstr. (1989-).

266 US
GLENMARY CHALLENGE. 1937. q. Glenmary Home Missioners, Box 465618, Cincinnati, OH 45246-5618. TEL 513-874-8900. Ed. Rev. Robert R. Bond. charts; illus.; stat.; circ. 102,000.
Formerly: Glenmary's Challenge.
Description: Discusses mission work in the states.

200 UK ISSN 0017-1301
GLOUCESTER DIOCESAN GAZETTE.* 1880. m. The Rectory, Swindon, Cheltenham, Glos. GL51 9RD, England. Ed. Rev. M.E. Bennett. bk.rev.; circ. 42,000.

200 US
GLOW INTERNATIONAL. 1966. q. $22. Glow International, 599 Edison Dr., E. Windsor, NJ 08520-5207. TEL 609-426-4345. Ed. Naosherwan Anzar. adv.; bk.rev.; circ. 1,000. (back issues avail.)

200 GW ISSN 0017-1409
GNADE UND HERRLICHKEIT. vol.28, 1976. bi-m. DM.37. Paulus-Verlag Karl Geyer, Goethestr. 38, 7100 Heilbronn, Germany. TEL 07131-72090. Ed. Heinz Schumacher. **Indexed:** CERDIC.

220 375 UK ISSN 0950-7221
GO TEACH BEGINNERS. q. £1.95. Go Teach Publications, 2 Radford Rd., Leamington Spa CV31 1LX, England. TEL 0926-26573.
Description: Teachers' book for teaching scripture lessons to 3-5 year olds.

220 375 UK ISSN 0950-7248
GO TEACH JUNIORS. q. £1.95. Go Teach Publications, 2 Radford Rd., Leamington Spa CV31 1LX, England. TEL 0926-26573.
Description: Teachers' book for teaching scripture lessons to 8-12 year olds.

220 375 UK ISSN 0142-5935
GO TEACH PRIMARIES. q. £1.95. Go Teach Publications, 2 Radford Rd., Leamington Spa CV31 1LX, England. TEL 0926-26573. illus.
Description: Teachers' book for teaching scripture lessons to 5-8 year olds.

220 375 UK ISSN 0950-7256
GO TEACH YOUNG TEENS. q. £1.95. Go Teach Publications, 2 Radford Rd., Leamington Spa CV31 1LX, England. TEL 0926-26573.
Description: Teachers' book for teaching scripture lessons to over 12 year olds.

GOD'S SPECIAL PEOPLE; magazine & ministry to the handicapped & friends. see *HANDICAPPED*

251 GW ISSN 0340-6083
GOETTINGER PREDIGTMEDITATIONEN. 1946. q. DM.74. Vandenhoeck und Ruprecht, Theaterstr. 13, Postfach 3753, 3400 Goettingen, Germany. TEL 0551-6959-22. FAX 0551-695917. Ed. F. Merkel. adv.; index; circ. 4,900.

GOLDEN C F NEWS. (Crusselle-Freeman Church and Center of the Deaf) see *HANDICAPPED — Hearing Impaired*

266 SA ISSN 0017-2146
GOOD NEWS/GOEIE NUUS; the magazine with a message. (Editions in Afrikaans and English) 1951. q. R.10($5) Good News Missionary Society, Box 7848, Johannesburg, South Africa. TEL 011-729-9581. Ed. Sean O'Sullivan. circ. 5,000 (Eng. ed.); 2,500 (Afrikaans ed.).

266 UK ISSN 0262-2874
GOOD NEWS (BIRMINGHAM). 1837. s-a. £0.20 per no. Additional Curates Society for England and Wales, 246a Washwood Heath Rd., Birmingham B8 2XS, England. TEL 021-3280749. FAX 021-327-7951. Ed. A.J. Prescott. adv.; bk.rev.; illus.; circ. 20,000 (controlled). (also avail. in microform)
Formerly (until vol.48, 1981): Home Mission News.
Description: News and features of the Additional Curarates Society, which seeks to assist Anglican parishes, especially in deprived areas of England and Wales, by paying for assistant priests.

266 UK ISSN 0954-562X
GOOD NEWS (EXETER). 1939. m. £7.20($21.60) Paternoster Press Ltd., Paternoster House, 3 Mount Radford Crescent, Exeter EX2 4JW, England. (Dist. in U.S. & Canada by: The Paternoster Press, P.O. Box 11127, Birmingham, AL 35202) Ed. Robert Beale. circ. 30,000.
Formerly (until 1988): Emergency Post (ISSN 0305-005X)

200 CN
GOOD TIDINGS. 1944. m. Can.$10($15) (effective 1992). (Pentecostal Assemblies of Newfoundland) Good Tidings Press, P.O. Box 8895, Sta. A, St. John's, NF A1B 3T2, Canada. TEL 709-753-6314. FAX 709-753-4945. Ed. Roy D. King. adv.; bk.rev.; circ. 7,500. (back issues avail.)
Description: Covers the Bible, church news, missions, and Christian service.

200 US
GOSPEL ADVOCATE. 1855. m. $16.98 (effective Mar. 1991). Gospel Advocate Company, 1006 Elm Hill Pike, Nashville, TN 37210. TEL 615-254-8781. (Subscr. to: Box 150, Nashville, TN 37202) Ed. F. Furman Kearley. adv.; index; circ. 23,000.
Description: Devotional and educational material for church leaders and members.

200 CN ISSN 0829-4666
GOSPEL HERALD. 1936. m. Can.$11($12.50) Gospel Herald Foundation, 4904 King St., Beamsville, Ont. L0R 1B6, Canada. TEL 416-563-7503. Eds. Roy D. Merritt, Eugene C. Perry. adv.; bk.rev.; circ. 1,600. (also avail. in microfilm from UMI; reprint service avail. from UMI)
Description: Articles promoting New Testament Christianity, including teaching material for youth and women, and features history, news, and family life.

GOSPEL MESSENGER. see *HANDICAPPED — Visually Impaired*

RELIGIONS AND THEOLOGY

200 UK ISSN 0017-2367
GOSPEL STANDARD. 1835. m. £10.80($21) Gospel Standard Publications, 7 Brackendale Grove, Harpenden, Herts AL5 3EL, England. TEL 0582-760580. Ed. B.A. Ramsbottom. bk.rev.; circ. 2,600. **Indexed:** CERDIC.
  Description: Presents information relating to the Gospel Standard Societies includes texts of sermons delivered by its ministers, and articles concerning the doctrines and experience of grace.

266 GW
GOSSNER MISSION. 1852. bi-m. Gossner Mission, Fennstr. 31, 1190 Berlin-Schoeneweiche, Germany. TEL 00372-6351198. circ. 7,000. (back issues avail.)

200 GW ISSN 0017-2480
GOTTES WORT. 3/yr. DM.65. Echter-Verlag, Juliuspromenade 64, Postfach 5560, 8700 Wuerzburg 1, Germany. Ed. Rainer Rack.

200 GW ISSN 0343-8732
GOTTESDIENST; Information u. Handreichung der Liturgischen Institute Deutschlands, Oesterreichs u. der Schweiz. 1967. s-m. DM.48. Verlag Herder GmbH & Co. KG, Hermann-Herder-Str. 4, 7800 Freiburg im Breisgau, Germany. TEL 0651-94808-0. FAX 0651-94808-33. Ed. Eduard Nagel. bk.rev.; circ. 13,000. (back issues avail.)

250 PO ISSN 0017-2758
GRACAS DO SERVO DE DEUS: PADRE CRUZ. 1949. bi-m. Cr.$150. Causa Beatificaciao do Padre Cruz, Rua da Madalena 179, Apdo. 2661, 1117 Lisbon Codex, Portugal. Dir. P. Manuel Baptista. adv.; bk.rev.; circ. 26,200.

200 PO
GRACAS PADRE CRUZ, S.J. q. $750. Vice Postulacao - Causa do Padre Cruz, Rua da Madalena, 179-RC. Ap. 2661, 1117 Lisbon Codex, Portugal. TEL 872100. Ed. Antonio Reis.

286 UK ISSN 0046-6239
GRACE. 1833. m. £6. Grace Magazine Trust, Bethesda Baptist Church, Bury St., Stowmarket, Suffolk, England. (Subscr. to: 4-6 Beechwood Rd., Caterham, Surrey CR3 6NA, England) Ed. N. Lacey. adv.; bk.rev.; circ. 1,900.

200 US ISSN 0198-666X
GRACE THEOLOGICAL JOURNAL. 1980. s-a. $11.50 (foreign $12.50). Grace Theological Seminary, 200 Seminary Dr., Winona Lake, IN 46590. TEL 219-327-5123. FAX 219-372-5265. Ed. John J. Davis. bk.rev.; circ. 2,000. (also avail. in microfilm from UMI; microfiche from UMI; back issues avail.; reprint service avail. from UMI) **Indexed:** CERDIC, Chr.Per.Ind., New Test.Abstr., Old Test.Abstr., Rel.& Theol.Abstr. (1980-), Rel.Ind.One.
  —BLDSC shelfmark: 4206.356000.
  Description: Scholarly articles on contemporary evangelical topics focusing on the ministry and theological intellect.

GRACE TIDINGS. see *COLLEGE AND ALUMNI*

200 CN ISSN 0828-4083
GRAIL. 1985. q. Can.$14($14) to individuals; institutions Can.$22($22). University of St. Jerome's College Press, Waterloo, Ont. N2L 3G3, Canada. Ed. M.W. Higgins. bk.rev.; illus.; circ. 2,500.

230 BL ISSN 0046-6271
GRANDE SINAL. 1947. 6/yr. $55. Editora Vozes Ltda., Rua Frei Luis 100, Caixa Postal 90023, 25689 Petropolis, Rio de Janeiro, Brazil. Ed. Jose Ariovaldo da Silva. bk.rev.; abstr.; bibl.; illus.; stat.; index; circ. 2,900. (tabloid format)

GREAT BRITAIN. ROYAL ARMY CHAPLAINS' DEPARTMENT. JOURNAL. see *MILITARY*

200 UK ISSN 0957-8935
GREATER WORLD NEWSLETTER. 1928. q. free. Greater World Christian Spiritualist Association, Greater World Spiritual Centre, c/o Mrs. B. Scott, Sec., 3-5 Conway St., London W1P 5HA, England. TEL 071-436-7555. adv.; bk.rev.; circ. 6,000.
  Formerly (until 1989): Greater World (ISSN 0046-6352)
  Description: Spiritual teachings based on Christian spiritualism.

200 400 GW ISSN 0232-2900
GRIECHISCHEN CHRISTLICHEN SCHRIFTSTELLER DER ERSTEN JAHRHUNDERTE. (Text in Greek and Latin) 1953. irreg., latest 1989. (Akademie der Wissenschaften der D.D.R.) Akademie-Verlag Berlin, Leipziger Str. 3-4, 1086 Berlin, Germany. TELEX 114420-AVERL-DD.

GROUP (LOVELAND); the youth ministry magazine. see *CHILDREN AND YOUTH — About*

200 GW
GRUSS DER GROSSHEPPACHER SCHWESTERNSCHAFT; Kind und Schwester. s-a. Stiftung Grossheppacher Schwesternschaft, Oberlinstr. 4, Postfach 1124, 7056 Weinstadt, Germany. TEL 07151-68041. Ed. Willi Duerring. circ. 6,000.

200 US ISSN 0017-5331
BV4800
GUIDEPOSTS; a practical guide to successful living. 1945. m. $9.95 (effective Jan. 1991). Guideposts Associates, Inc., Box 858, 39 Seminary Hill Rd., Carmel, NY 10512. TEL 800-431-2344. FAX 914-228-2038. Eds. Ruth Stafford Peale, Norman Vincent Peale. circ. 3,750,000. (also avail. in Braille; audio cassette; record; large print edition in 18 pt.)

200 GW ISSN 0017-5730
GUSTAV - ADOLF - BLATT. 1955. irreg. (1-4/yr.). DM.5. (Evangelische Kirche in Deutschland) Gustav-Adolf-Werk, Olgastr. 8, 3500 Kassel 1, Germany. Ed. Dr. Fritz Heinrich Ryssel. bk.rev.; circ. 25,000.

200 GW
GUTE BESSERUNG. 1977. m. Bergmoser und Holler Verlag GmbH, Karl-Friedrich-Str. 76, 5100 Aachen, Germany. TEL 0241-17309. FAX 0241-1730934. TELEX 2414010. Ed. Paul Ostermann. circ. 50,000.
  Description: Publication concerned with giving strength and information to those who are ill, by means of religion and humor.

200 323.4 GW
H M K KURIER; aktuelle Berichte, Mitteilungen und Meinungen von und ueber Christen, die heute nicht in Freiheit leben. 1984. 4/yr. free. Hilfsaktion Maertyrerkirche e.V., Tuefingerstr. 3-5, Postfach 1160, 7772 Uhldingen, Germany. TEL 07556-6508. FAX 07556-8002. TELEX 733942-HMC. Ed. Hans Braun. circ. 22,000.
  Formerly: H M K Kirche.

268 US ISSN 0072-9787
HANDBOOK OF DENOMINATIONS IN THE U.S.. quinquennial. $13.95. Abingdon Press, 201 Eighth Ave., S., Box 801, Nashville, TN 37202. TEL 800-251-3320. FAX 615-749-6522.
  Description: Reference describing many religious bodies in the US, with information on their historical background and doctrines.

HARMONY (SAN FRANCISCO); voices for a just future. see *POLITICAL SCIENCE — Civil Rights*

HARVARD DIVINITY BULLETIN. see *COLLEGE AND ALUMNI*

HARVARD SEMITIC MONOGRAPHS. see *LINGUISTICS*

230 US ISSN 0017-8160
BR1
HARVARD THEOLOGICAL REVIEW. 1908. q. $25 to individuals; institutions $40. Harvard Divinity School, 45 Francis Ave., Cambridge, MA 02138. TEL 617-495-1778. FAX 617-495-9489. Ed. Helmut Koester. adv.; charts; circ. 1,900. (also avail. in microfiche; reprint service avail. from KTO) **Indexed:** Amer.Hist.& Life, Arts & Hum.Cit.Ind., CERDIC, Curr.Cont., Hist.Abstr., Hum.Ind., M.L.A., New Test.Abstr., Old Test.Abstr., Rel.& Theol.Abstr. (1971-), Rel.Ind.One, Rel.Per.
  —BLDSC shelfmark: 4270.690000.
  Description: Scholarly articles in the field of religious studies.

201 US ISSN 0073-0726
HARVARD THEOLOGICAL STUDIES. 1916. irreg., no.34, 1982. price varies. (Harvard Divinity School) Fortress Press, 426 S. 5th St., Box 1209, MN 55440. TEL 800-328-4648. (reprint service avail. from KTO)
  —BLDSC shelfmark: 4270.700000.

266 UK ISSN 0017-8829
HEALING HAND. 1850. 3/yr. free. Edinburgh Medical Missionary Society, Seven Washington Ln., Edinburgh EH11 2HA, Scotland. TEL 031-313-3828. FAX 031-313-4662. Ed. Fred Aitken. adv.; bk.rev.; circ. 2,000.
  Description: News of activities of the society, articles on medical missions.

200 UK ISSN 0017-9477
HEBREW CHRISTIAN. 1928. q. £3($4) in U.S.; Canada $5. International Messianic Jewish (Hebrew - Christian) Alliance, Shalom, Brockenhurst Rd., Ramsgate CT11 8ED, England. TEL 0843-592669. FAX 0843-590821. Ed. Rev. Ronald H. Lewis. bk.rev.; circ. 6,000. **Indexed:** CERDIC.
  Description: Advocates the pastoral care and material support (where necessary) of Jewish believers in Jesus as Messiah who are members of a recognized fellowship.

200 AU ISSN 0017-9620
HEILIGER DIENST. 1947. q. S.195. (Institutum Liturgicum) Verlag St. Peter, Postfach 113, A-5010 Salzburg, Austria. TEL 0662-844576-82. FAX 0662-844576-80. Ed. P. Winfried Bachler. adv.; bk.rev.; circ. 900. **Indexed:** CERDIC.
  Description: Covers liturgy and liturgical practice.

200 SW ISSN 0018-0335
HEMMETS VAEN; kristlig veckotidning. 1897. w. SEK 259($40) Evangeliipress, Box 1172, S-70117 Oerebro, Sweden. Ed. Stig Hallzon. adv.; bk.rev.; illus.; circ. 45,000. (tabloid format)

200 US
HERALD OF HIS COMING. 1941. m. free. Gospel Revivals, Inc., Box 886, Newton, KS 67114. TEL 316-283-7747. FAX 316-283-7747. Ed. Lois J. Stucky. circ. 120,000.
  Description: Articles on practical examples of living out and putting into practice Bible teaching, with prayers and scripture.

200 CU
HERALDO EPISCOPAL. 1938. q. $6. Iglesia Episcopal Cubana, Centro Diocesano, Calle 13, no.874 e-4 y 6, Vedado, Havana, Cuba. TEL 7-32-1120. Ed. Rev. Juan Quevedo. bk.rev.; circ. 2,000.
  Description: Channels communication between the Anglican and Christian Cuban communities and the world church.

200 NE
HERKENNING (THE HAGUE); tijdschrift voor Joden en Christenen. q. fl.39.80. Boekencentrum B.V., Scheveningseweg 72, Box 84176, The Hague, Netherlands.

200 GW ISSN 0440-7180
HERMENEUTISCHE UNTERSUCHUNGEN ZUR THEOLOGIE. (Text in English, German) irreg., vol.26, 1989. price varies. J.C.B. Mohr (Paul Siebeck), Wilhelmstr. 18, Postfach 2040, 7400 Tuebingen, Germany. TEL 07071-26064. FAX 07071-51104. TELEX 7262872-MOHR-D. Ed.Bd.

266 NE
HERNHUTTER SURINAME ZENDING. 1834. q. free. Zendingsgenootschap der Evangelische Broedergemeente, Box 19, 3700 AA Zeist, Netherlands. TEL 03404-17424. Ed.Bd. bk.rev.; illus.; circ. 150,000.
  Formerly: Suriname Zending (ISSN 0039-6141)

200 SA ISSN 0259-9422
HERVORMDE TEOLOGIESE STUDIES. (Text in Afrikaans, Dutch, English, German; abstracts in English) 1942. q. R.56.50 (typically set in Jan.). (University of Pretoria, Bureau for Publications) Nederduitsch Hervormde Kerk van Afrika, P.O. Box 5777, Pretoria 0001, South Africa. TEL 012-322-8885. FAX 012-322-7909. Ed. A.G. van Aarde. adv.; bk.rev.; circ. 900. **Indexed:** Rel.& Theol.Abstr. (1989-).
  —BLDSC shelfmark: 4300.390000.
  Description: Features articles on topics in all the theological disciplines including Bible study.

100 200   UK   ISSN 0018-1196
BX801
HEYTHROP JOURNAL; a review of philosophy and theology. 1960. q. $35 to individuals: institutions $48. Basil Blackwell Ltd., 108 Cowley Rd., Oxford OX4 1JF, England. TEL 0865-791100. FAX 0865-791347. TELEX 830722 OXBOOK G. Ed. Thomas J. Deidun. adv.; bk.rev.; bibl.; charts; illus.; index; circ. 950. (also avail. in microform from UMI; back issues avail.) **Indexed**: Arts & Hum.Cit.Ind., Canon Law Abstr., Cath.Ind., CERDIC, Curr.Cont., Int.Z.Bibelwiss., New Test.Abstr., Old Test.Abstr., Phil.Ind., Rel.& Theol.Abstr. (1979-).
Description: Features on contemporary philosophical and theological issues, including Bible, ecclesiastical history and the sociology of religion.

200   NE
HIER EN GINDER. m. fl.16. Missiethuisfront, Akkerstraat 12, 6617 BA Bergharen, Netherlands. Ed. J. van Gelder. bk.rev.; circ. 1,250.

200   CN
HINDU - CHRISTIAN STUDIES BULLETIN. 1988. a. Can.$12($10) (effective 1992). Calgary Institute for the Humanities, University of Calgary, 2500 University Dr. N.W., Calgary, Alta. T2N 1N4, Canada. TEL 403-220-7238. FAX 403-282-7822. (looseleaf format; back issues avail.)
Description: Provides a Hindu-Christian dialogue.

209   SP   ISSN 0018-215X
BR1020
HISPANIA SACRA; revista de historia eclesiastica. 1948. s-a. 3750 ptas. (foreign 4950 ptas.). Centro de Estudios Historicos (CSIC), Duque de Medinaceli, 6, 28006 Madrid, Spain. FAX 585-61-97. (Distr. by: Consejo Superior de Investigaciones Cientificas, Apdo. 14458, Vitruvio 8, Madrid 6, Spain) Ed. Jose Andres-Gallego. adv.; bk.rev.; illus.; circ. 550. (also avail. in microfilm; reprint service avail. from ISOC) **Indexed**: Amer.Hist.& Life, Hist.Abstr., Rel.Ind.One, Rel.Ind.Two.
—BLDSC shelfmark: 4315.765000.

200 974   US
HISTORIAN'S DIGEST. 1959. q. $20. United Methodist Church, General Commission on Archives & History, Box 127, Madison, NJ 07940. TEL 201-822-2787. FAX 201-408-3909. Ed. Charles Yrigoyen, Jr. circ. 1,000. (looseleaf format; back issues avail.)

HISTORIANS OF EARLY MODERN EUROPE. see HISTORY — History Of Europe

291 209   US   ISSN 0018-2710
BL1
HISTORY OF RELIGIONS; an international journal for comparative historical studies. 1961. q. $29 to individuals; institutions $58; students $20. University of Chicago Press, Journals Division, 5720 S. Woodlawn Ave., Chicago, IL 60637. TEL 312-753-3347. FAX 312-753-3347. TELEX 25-4603. (Subscr. to: Box 37005, Chicago, IL 60637) Ed. Joseph Kitagawa. adv.; bk.rev.; index; circ. 1,750. (also avail. in microform from MIM; reprint service avail. from UMI,ISI) **Indexed**: A.I.C.P., Amer.Hist.& Life, Arts & Hum.Cit.Ind., CERDIC, Curr.Cont., E.I., G.Soc.Sci.& Rel.Per.Lit., Hist.Abstr., Hum.Ind., Int.Z.Bibelwiss., Mid.East: Abstr.& Ind., New Test.Abstr., Old Test.Abstr., Rel.& Theol.Abstr. (1968-), Rel.Ind.One, Rel.Per.
—BLDSC shelfmark: 4318.420000.
Refereed Serial

200 933   IS
HOLY PLACES OF PALESTINE. (Text in various languages) 1970. irreg. Franciscan Printing Press, P.O. Box 14064, Jerusalem 91140, Israel. TEL 02-286594.

200   US
HOME ALTAR; meditations for families with children. q. $4.60. Augsburg Fortress, 426 S. 5th Str., Box 1209, Minneapolis, MN 55440. TEL 612-330-3300. Ed. Elaine M. Dunham. circ. 71,000.

249   UK   ISSN 0018-3946
HOME AND FAMILY. 1886. q. £3.50. Mothers' Union, Mary Sumner House, 24 Tufton St., Westminster, London SW1P 3RB, England. FAX 071-222-5533. Ed.Bd. adv.; bk.rev.; illus.; circ. 145,000.

HOME SCHOOL GAZETTE. see JOURNALISM

251   SP   ISSN 0439-4208
HOMILETICA. 6/yr. 2860 ptas.($37) Editorial Sal Terrae, Guevara, 20, 39001 Santander, Spain. TEL 212617. FAX 942-215245.

251   GW   ISSN 0018-4276
HOMILETISCHE MONATSHEFTE. 1925. m. DM.94. Vandenhoeck und Ruprecht, Theaterstr. 13, Postfach 3753, 3400 Goettingen, Germany. TEL 0551-6959-22. FAX 0551-695917. Ed. Wolf Dietrich Berner. adv.; bk.rev.; index; circ. 4,200.

HOMILY HELPS. 62/yr. $30. St. Anthony Messenger Press, 1615 Republic St., Cincinnati, OH 45210. TEL 513-241-5615. Ed. Rev. Hilarion Kistner. circ. 8,200. (looseleaf format)
Description: Aid to preaching for Catholic clergy.

264   US   ISSN 0732-1872
HOMILY SERVICE;* an ecumenical resource for sharing the word. 1968. m. $50. Liturgical Conference, 8750 Georgia Ave., No.123, Silver Spring, MD 20910-3831.
Description: Ecumenical resource for sharing scripture. Includes exegetical analysis of scriptural readings.

200   FR   ISSN 0018-4322
HOMME NOUVEAU. 1946. bi-m. 300 F.($40) 10 rue Rosenwald, 75015 Paris, France. TEL 45-32-10-80. FAX 45-32-10-84. Ed. M. Marcel Clement. bk.rev.; circ. 40,000.
Description: Analyzes the news in the light of the Gospel.

220   US   ISSN 0195-9085
BS543.A1
HORIZONS IN BIBLICAL THEOLOGY. 1979. s-a. $12 to individuals; institutions $15; students $8. Pittsburgh Theological Seminary, 616 N. Highland Ave., Pittsburgh, PA 15206. TEL 412-362-5610. FAX 412-363-3260. Ed.Bd. adv.; bk.rev.; circ. 500. (back issues avail.) **Indexed**: New Test.Abstr., Old Test.Abstr., Rel.& Theol.Abstr. (1979-), Rel.Ind.One.
—BLDSC shelfmark: 4326.794500.

200   NE   ISSN 0018-7119
HUIZER KERKBLAD. 1935. w. fl.16. J. Bout en Zoon, Ceintuurbaan 32-34, Huizen, Netherlands. adv.; bk.rev.; circ. 2,400.

150 301 200   US
HUMAN KINDNESS FOUNDATION NEWSLETTER; a little news. 1974. q. free. Human Kindness Foundation, Rt. 1, Box 201-N, Durham, NC 27705. TEL 919-942-2138. Ed. Bo Lozoff. circ. 21,000. (looseleaf format)
Formerly: Prison - Ashram Project Newsletter.

200 301   US
BX5800
HUMAN QUEST. 1804. bi-m. $10. (Churchman Associates, Inc.) Churchman Company, Inc., 1074 23rd Ave., N., St. Petersburg, FL 33704. TEL 813-894-0097. Ed. Edna Ruth Johnson. adv.; bk.rev.; bibl.; circ. 10,000. (also avail. in microform from UMI; back issues avail.) **Indexed**: Amer.Hist.& Life, CERDIC, Chr.Per.Ind., Hist.Abstr., Rel.Ind.One.
Former titles (until Dec. 1989): Churchman's Human Quest (ISSN 0897-8786); Churchman (ISSN 0009-6628)
Description: Dedicated to educating the public in humanistic religion, peace activism, disarmament, and separation of church and state.

200   JA   ISSN 0073-3938
HUMANITIES, CHRISTIANITY AND CULTURE. (Text in English, French, German, Japanese; summaries in English, Japanese) 1964. irreg. (approx. a.). 1,000 Yen per no. International Christian University, Institute for the Study of Christianity and Culture - Kokusai Kirisutokyo Daigaku Kirisutokyo to Bunka Kenkyujo, 3-10-2 Osawa, Mitaka, Tokyo 181, Japan. TEL 0422-33-3100. Ed. Masao Okano. circ. 1,400.
—BLDSC shelfmark: 4336.565000.
Formerly: International Christian University. Publications IV-B. Christianity and Culture.

HYMN; a journal of congregational song. see MUSIC

I C O - ICONOGRAPHISK POST; Nordisk tidskrift foer bildtolkning - Nordic iconographic review. see ART

RELIGIONS AND THEOLOGY   4181

200   US   ISSN 1051-2772
I C S A NEWSLETTER. 1983. a. free. (International Christian Studies Association) Institute for Interdisciplinary Research, 2828 Third St., Ste. 11, Santa Monica, CA 90405-4150. TEL 310-396-0517. Ed. Oskar Gruenwald. adv.; circ. 2,000. (tabloid format; back issues avail.)
Description: Covers Association, conferences, research and publishing news.

I C S NEWSLETTER. (International Catacomb Society) see ART

200   US
I E C NEWSLETTER. 1959. q. membership only. International Evangelism Crusades, 146-17 Victory Blvd., Ste. 4, Van Nuys, CA 91411. TEL 818-989-5942. FAX 818-989-5942. Ed. F.E. Strahges. circ. 500.
Description: News about IEC and its members, and church and seminary activities.

200   UK
I F E S REVIEW. 1976. 2/yr. £10($18) for 4 issues. International Fellowship of Evangelical Students, 55 Palmerston Rd., Wealdstone, Harrow, Middlesex HA3 7RR, England. TEL 081-863-8688. FAX 081-863-8229.
Formerly: Occasional Papers on Student Work.
Description: Training tool for people in student ministry.

266   US   ISSN 0018-9723
I F M A NEWS. vol.24, 1973. q. free. Interdenomination Foreign Mission Association of North America, Inc., P.O. Box 398, Wheaton, IL 60189. FAX 708-682-9278. Ed. John H. Orme. stat.; circ. 5,000.

I N R O ADS. (International Network for Religion and Animals) see ANIMAL WELFARE

200 600   US
I T E S T BULLETIN. 1969. q. $35. Institute for Theological Encounter with Science and Technology, 221 N. Grand Blvd., St. Louis, MO 63103. TEL 314-658-2703. Ed. Marianne Postiglione. bk.rev.; circ. 1,000. (back issues avail.)

200 600   US
I T E S T CONFERENCE PROCEEDINGS. 1970. irreg. (approx. 2/yr.). $14. Institute for Theological Encounter with Science and Technology, 221 N. Grand Blvd., St. Louis, MO 63103. TEL 314-658-2703. Ed. Robert Brungs. circ. 1,000. (back issues avail.)
Description: Contains edited versions of meetings on topics such as artificial intelligence, bio-technology, and law, the environment, Christian and Jewish perspectives on creation, sci-tech education in Church-related colleges and universities.

266   ZA
ICENGELO; Christian magazine in Bemba. (Text in Bemba) 1970. m. K.120. Mission Press, Box 71581, Ndola, Zambia. TEL 680456. FAX 680484. TELEX CAMIFF ZA 30054. Ed. Rev. Umberto Davoli. circ. 80,000.
Description: Covers religious, social and health topics.

ICONOGRAPHY OF RELIGIONS. see ART

ICONOGRAPHY OF RELIGIONS. SECTION 24, CHRISTIANITY. see ART

ICONOGRAPHY OF RELIGIONS. SUPPLEMENT. see ART

IGAKU TO FUKUIN/MEDICINE AND GOSPEL. see MEDICAL SCIENCES

200   SP
IGLESIA - MUNDO. 1971. fortn. Ediciones Iglesia Mundo, Jose Abascal 57, 3o, 28003 Madrid, Spain. TEL 91-4412965. FAX 91-4410654. Dir. Ricardo Pardo Zancada.

200   GW   ISSN 0019-2597
IM LANDE DER BIBEL; neue Folge der neuesten Nachrichten aus dem Morgenland. 1955. 3/yr. DM.12. (Jerusalemsverein) Berliner Missionswerk, Handjery Str. 19, 1000 Berlin 41, Germany. FAX 030-8593011. TELEX 186655-BLNMW-D. Ed. Rev. Paul E. Hoffman. bk.rev.; bibl.; illus.; circ. 9,000.

RELIGIONS AND THEOLOGY

200   GW   ISSN 0176-8565
IMAGE; Pfarrbriefmaterial. 1970. m. (11/yr.). DM.150. Bergmoser und Hoeller Verlag GmbH, Karl-Friedrich Str. 76, 5100 Aachen, Germany. TEL 0241-17309-21. circ. 7,000. (looseleaf format; back issues avail.)

IMBONGI. see *COLLEGE AND ALUMNI*

266   IS   ISSN 0302-8127
BM1
IMMANUEL; religious thought and research in Israel. (Text in English) 1972. a. $15 (foreign $17). Ecumenical Theological Research Fraternity in Israel, P.O. Box 249, Jerusalem 91002, Israel. TEL 02-254941. FAX 02-254961. Ed. Malcolm Lowe. adv.; bk.rev.; bibl.; circ. 1,000. **Indexed:** CERDIC, Curr.Cont., Ind.Artic.Jew.Stud., New Test.Abstr., Old Test.Abstr., Rel.& Theol.Abstr. (1990-), Rel.Ind.One.
—BLDSC shelfmark: 4369.633000.
    Description: Presents translations and summaries of recent academic, religious, and theological studies in Hebrew, for an international audience.

IMPACT; Asian magazine for human transformation. see *SOCIAL SCIENCES: COMPREHENSIVE WORKS*

266   GW
IMPULSE (GIESSEN); fuer missionarisches christsein. 1978. q. DM.10. Campus for Christus, Am Unteren Rain 2, 6300 Giessen, Germany. TEL 0641-72099. FAX 0641-72463. adv.; bk.rev.; circ. 15,000.

200   US   ISSN 0363-5058
IN COMMON. 1971. irreg. $2. Consultation on Church Union, Research Park, 151 Wall St., Princeton, NJ 08540-1514. Ed. David W.A. Taylor. circ. 10,000.

200   NE   ISSN 0019-3151
IN DE RECHTE STRAAT/EN LA CALLE RECTA. (Editions in Dutch and Spanish) 1958. m. (Dutch ed.); bi-m. (Spanish ed.). fl.22.75. Stichting In de Rechte Straat, Boulevard 11, 6881 HN Velp, Netherlands. TEL 3185 646050. Ed. Rev. H. J. Hegger. bk.rev.; illus.; circ. 14,000. **Indexed:** CERDIC.
    Description: Discusses dialogue and witness with the Catholic Church and helps ex-priests who left their church for reasons of conscience.

200   NE   ISSN 0019-316X
IN DE WAAGSCHAAL.* 1945. fortn. fl.17. Amaco, Egelantiersgracht 75-79, Amsterdam, Netherlands. Ed. Prof. Dr. K.H. Miskotte. circ. 2,000. **Indexed:** CERDIC.

266   GW
IN DIE WELT - FUER DIE WELT. bi-m. Vereinigte Evangelische Mission, Rudolfstr. 137, 5600 Wuppertal 2, Germany. TEL 0202-89004-0.

220   US
IN OTHER WORDS. 1943. every 6 wks. free to U.S. subscribers only. Wycliffe Bible Translators, Inc., Box 2727, Huntington Beach, CA 92647. TEL 714-969-4600. FAX 714-969-4661. TELEX 284682. Ed. Roger Garland. illus.; circ. 250,000.
    Supersedes: Translation (ISSN 0041-1221)

200   UK   ISSN 0019-3283
IN TOUCH (PINNER). 1969. q. £5 (typically set in Jan.). Grail, 125 Waxwell Lane, Pinner, Middlesex, England. TEL 081-866-050. Ed. Mary Grasar. bk.rev.; play rev.; illus.; circ. 1,100. (tabloid format)
    Formerly: Mosaic.

IN TOUCH (TORONTO). see *HANDICAPPED — Visually Impaired*

200   US
IN TUNE; the quarterly newsletter of 970 DJ. vol.6, 1990. q. W W D J, Box 970, Hackensack, NJ 07602.

200   US
INDEPENDENT LESSON SERMON QUARTERLY. q. $10. Plainfield Christian Science Church (Independent), 905 Prospect Ave., Box 5619, Plainfield, NJ 07060. TEL 908-756-4669.

209   II   ISSN 0019-4530
BR1150
INDIAN CHURCH HISTORY REVIEW. (Text in English) 1967. s-a. $5. Church History Association of India, Mackin-Chan Hall, Wilson College, Bombay 7, India. Ed. Dr. H. Grafe. bk.rev.; index; circ. 500. (back issues avail.) **Indexed:** Rel.& Theol.Abstr. (1989-), Rel.Ind.One, Rel.Per.

230   II   ISSN 0019-5685
BR1
INDIAN JOURNAL OF THEOLOGY. (Text in English) 1952. s-a. $7. Indian Journal of Theology, c/o Bishops's College, 224 Lower Circular Rd., Calcutta 700017, India. Ed.Bd. adv.; bk.rev.; bibl.; index; circ. 500. **Indexed:** Excerp.Med., New Test.Abstr., Old Test.Abstr., Rel.& Theol.Abstr., Rel.Ind.One, Rel.Per.

INNER PATHS. see *NEW AGE PUBLICATIONS*

200   UK   ISSN 0020-1723
INQUIRER. 1842. fortn. £12.50($30) Inquirer Publishing Co. Ltd., 1-6 Essex St., London W.C.2, England. Ed. Rev. K. Gilley. adv.; bk.rev.; illus.; circ. 2,500.

INSIDE MUSIC; excellence in Christian music. see *MUSIC*

INSIGHT (TORONTO). see *HANDICAPPED — Visually Impaired*

200   US
INSIGHTS FOR PREACHERS; a publication for parish pastors providing sermon resources on common lectionary texts. 1973. 4/yr. $22. King Publications, 5697 Applebutter Hill Rd., Coopersburg, PA 18036-9539. TEL 215-967-3901. Ed. Richard H. Stough, Sr. circ. 1,000. **Indexed:** Rel.& Theol.Abstr. (1988-).
    Former titles: Insights into Preaching; Insights (Springfield) (ISSN 0164-7709); Incorporates (1981-198?): Kerygma.

INSOUND. see *HANDICAPPED — Visually Impaired*

INSTITUT CATHOLIQUE DE PARIS. REVUE. see *GENERAL INTEREST PERIODICALS — France*

200 200   GW
INSTITUT FUER EUROPAEISCHE GESCHICHTE, MAINZ. VEROEFFENTLICHUNGEN. ABTEILUNG UNIVERSALGESCHICHTE UND ABTEILUNG FUER ABENDLAENDISCHE RELIGIONSGESCHICHTE. (Text in English, French, and German) irreg., vol.140, 1989. price varies. Franz Steiner Verlag Wiesbaden GmbH, Birkenwaldstr. 44, Postfach 101526, 7000 Stuttgart 1, Germany. TEL 0711-2582-0. FAX 0711-2582290. TELEX 723636-DAZD. Eds. K.O. von Aretin, P. Manns.
    Formerly: Institut fuer Europaeische Geschichte, Mainz. Veroeffentlichungen. Abteilung Universitaetsgeschichte und Abteilung fuer Abendlaendische Religionsphilosophie (ISSN 0537-7919)

200 200   GW
INSTITUT FUER EUROPAEISCHE GESCHICHTE, MAINZ. VORTRAEGE. ABTEILUNG UNIVERSALGESCHICHTE UND ABTEILUNG FUER ABENDLAENDISCHE RELIGIONSGESCHICHTE. (Text in English, French, and German) irreg., vol.83, 1988. price varies. Franz Steiner Verlag Wiesbaden GmbH, Birkenwaldstr. 44, Postfach 101526, 7000 Stuttgart 1, Germany. TEL 0711-2582-0. FAX 0711-2582290. TELEX 723636-DAZD. Eds. K.O. von Aretin, P. Manns.
    Formerly: Institut fuer Europaeische Geschichte, Mainz. Vortraege. Abteilung Universalgeschichte und Abteilung fuer Abendlaendische Religionsphilosophie (ISSN 0537-7927)

200   UY
INSTITUTO TEOLOGICO DEL URUGUAY MONSENOR MARIANO SOLER. LIBRO ANUAL. 1974. a. Instituto Teologico del Uruguay Monsenor Mariano Soler, San Fructuoso 1019, Montevideo, Uruguay. TEL 598-2-200289. circ. 500.
    Description: Contains articles on philosophy and theology. Covers conferences.

INSTRUMENTA LEXICOLOGIA LATINA. SERIES A & B. see *CLASSICAL STUDIES*

INTERCESSOR. see *ADVERTISING AND PUBLIC RELATIONS*

200   AT   ISSN 0047-0430
INTERCHANGE; papers on biblical and current questions. 1967. s-a. Aus.$15. Australian Fellowship of Evangelical Students, Graduate Fellowship of Australia, The Business Manager, 16 Mill Hill Rd., Bondi Junction, N.S.W. 2022, Australia. FAX 02-369-1688. Ed. Allan Friend. bk.rev.; circ. 1,000. **Indexed:** Phil.Ind.
—BLDSC shelfmark: 4532.600000.

200   US
INTERCHANGE. 1971. 8/yr. $10 to non-members. Episcopal Diocese of Southern Ohio, 412 Sycamore St., Cincinnati, OH 45202-4179. TEL 513-421-0311. FAX 513-421-0315. Ed. Michael R. Barwell. adv.; bk.rev.; illus.; stat.; circ. 13,500. (tabloid format; back issues avail.)

266   UK   ISSN 0264-0961
INTERCON. 1979. 3/yr. membership. Intercontinental Church Society, 175 Tower Bridge Rd., London SE1 2AQ, England. TEL 071-407-4588. FAX 071-407-6038. Ed. Lance Bidewell. bk.rev.; circ. 5,000 (controlled).

230.05   US   ISSN 0092-6558
BR1
INTERDENOMINATIONAL THEOLOGICAL CENTER, ATLANTA. JOURNAL. 1973. s-a. $6 to individuals; institutions $8. Interdenominational Theological Center, 671 Beckwith St., Atlanta, GA 30314. TEL 404-527-7727. Ed. John C. Diamond Jr. bk.rev.; circ. 2,500. **Indexed:** CERDIC, New Test.Abstr., Rel.& Theol.Abstr. (1990-), Rel.Ind.One, Rel.Per. Key Title: Journal of the Interdenominational Theological Center.
—BLDSC shelfmark: 4802.064000.

200   US   ISSN 0020-5575
INTERLIT. 1964. q. $2.50 (free to qualified personnel). David C. Cook Foundation, 850 N. Grove Ave., Elgin, IL 60120. TEL 708-741-2400. Ed. Gladys J. Peterson. bk.rev.; circ. 7,000. **Indexed:** CERDIC.

INTERNATIONAL ASSOCIATION FOR THE DEVELOPMENT OF CONSCIOUSNESS. INFORMATION BULLETIN. see *PHILOSOPHY*

367   US
INTERNATIONAL ASSOCIATION OF LIBERAL RELIGIOUS WOMEN. NEWSLETTER.* 1949. a. membership. International Association of Liberal Religious Women, c/o Tina Jas, Sec., 43 Coolidge Ave., Lexington, MA 02173. (Edit. addr.: Havikhorst 17hs, Amsterdam 1083 TM, Netherlands) Ed. Gusta Greve.
    Former titles: International Union of Liberal Christian Women. Newsletter; International League of Liberal Christian Women. Newsletter (ISSN 0074-6746)

201   NE   ISSN 0020-7047
BL51   CODEN: IJPREB
INTERNATIONAL JOURNAL FOR PHILOSOPHY OF RELIGION. 1970. 6/yr. $159. Kluwer Academic Publishers, Postbus 17, 3300 AA Dordrecht, Netherlands. TEL 078-334911. FAX 078-334254. TELEX 29245. (Dist. by: Kluwer Academic Publishers Group, P.O. Box 322, 3300 AH Dordrecht, Netherlands; N. America dist. addr.: Box 358, Accord Station, Hingham, MA 02018-0358. TEL 617-871-6600) Eds. Eugene T. Long, Frank R. Harrison III. bk.rev.; bibl. (back issues avail.; reprint service avail. from SWZ) **Indexed:** Arts & Hum.Cit.Ind., Curr.Cont., Hum.Ind., Mid.East: Abstr.& Ind., Phil.Ind., Rel.& Theol.Abstr. (1979-), Rel.Ind.One.
—BLDSC shelfmark: 4542.455000.

200 150   US   ISSN 1050-8619
▼**INTERNATIONAL JOURNAL FOR THE PSYCHOLOGY OF RELIGION.** 1991. q. $32.50 to individuals (foreign $57.50); institutions $80 (foreign $105). Lawrence Erlbaum Associates, Inc., 365 Broadway, Hillsdale, NJ 07642. TEL 201-666-4110. FAX 201-666-2394. Ed. L.B. Brown.
—BLDSC shelfmark: 4542.506200.
    Description: Forum for reporting specific results and encouraging discussion of the methods, theories, and applications of psychological research, in the broadest sense, to religions.
    Refereed Serial

268   US
INTERNATIONAL LESSON ANNUAL; commentary and teaching suggestions on the International Sunday School lessons. a. $9.50. Abingdon Press, 201 Eighth Ave., S., Box 801, Nashville, TN 37202. TEL 800-251-3320. FAX 615-749-6522. Ed. Horace R. Weaver.
Description: Detailed explanations of the Bible for every Sunday session.

200   US   ISSN 0743-5614
INTERNATIONAL PARTNERS IN PRAYER TRUMPETING NEWS. 1984. a. $.50. International Partners in Prayer, Box 570122, Houston, TX 77257. Ed. A.C. Doyle. circ. 1,600. (looseleaf format; also avail. in microfiche; back issues avail.)
Formerly: Trumpeting News.

266   SZ   ISSN 0020-8582
BV2351
INTERNATIONAL REVIEW OF MISSION. 1911. q. 39.50 Fr.($26.90) World Council of Churches, Commission on World Mission and Evangelism, 150 Route de Ferney, Box 2100, CH-1211 Geneva 2, Switzerland. TEL 022-791-6111. FAX 022-791-0361. TELEX 415730-OIK-CH. Ed. Christopher Duraisingh. adv.; bk.rev.; bibl.; index; circ. 4,000. (also avail. in microform from UMI; reprint service avail. from UMI,KTO) **Indexed:** A.I.C.P., Abstr.Musl.Rel., Amer.Hist.& Life, Br.Hum.Ind., CERDIC, Chr.Per.Ind., Hist.Abstr., Mid.East: Abstr.& Ind., Rel.& Theol.Abstr. (1968-), Rel.Ind.One, Rel.Per., So.Pac.Per.Ind.
—BLDSC shelfmark: 4547.380000.

200   IT
INTERNATIONAL SOCIETY FOR THE SOCIOLOGY OF RELIGION. 1948. biennial, 20th, Helsinki. International Society for the Sociology of Religion, Via Andreini 12, 35100 Padova, Italy. bk.rev.
Formerly: International Conference for the Sociology of Religion (ISSN 0074-297X)

INTERNATIONAL SOCIETY OF TORONTO FOR HUNGARIAN CHURCH HISTORY. NEWSLETTER/M E T E M. HIREK. see HISTORY — History Of Europe

220   US
INTERNATIONALE BIBELLEKTIONEN. (Text in German) 1919. q. $4. (German Church of God in U.S.A.) Christian Unity Press, 2211 Lincoln Ave., Box 527, York, NE 68467. TEL 402-362-5133. Ed. Rev. Fritz Friedrich. circ. 2,650. (processed)

200   SZ   ISSN 0020-9252
INTERNATIONALE KIRCHLICHE ZEITSCHRIFT. 1911. q. 64 Fr.($42) Staempfli und Cie AG, Postfach, CH-3001 Berne, Switzerland. FAX 031-276699. TELEX 911987. Ed. Hans Frei. bk.rev.; bibl.; index; circ. 600. (tabloid format) **Indexed:** CERDIC, New Test.Abstr., Old Test.Abstr.

INTERPRETATION (FLUSHING); a journal of political philosophy. see POLITICAL SCIENCE

220 230   US   ISSN 0020-9643
BR1
INTERPRETATION (RICHMOND); a journal of Bible and theology. 1947. q. $15.50 to individuals; institutions $22 (foreign $17). Union Theological Seminary in Virginia, 3401 Brook Rd., Richmond, VA 23227. TEL 804-355-0671. FAX 804-355-3919. Ed. Jack D. Kingsbury. adv.; bk.rev.; bibl.; index. cum.index: 1972-1981; 1982-1986; circ. 11,000. (also avail. in microform from UMI; back issues avail; reprint service avail. from UMI) **Indexed:** Bk.Rev.Ind. (1965-), Child.Bk.Rev.Ind. (1965-), Chr.Per.Ind., G.Soc.Sci.& Rel.Per.Lit., Hum.Ind., Ind.Artic.Jew.Stud., Int.Z.Bibelwiss., New Test.Abstr., Old Test.Abstr., Rel.& Theol.Abstr. (1967-), Rel.Ind.One, Rel.Per., Soc.Sci.Ind.
—BLDSC shelfmark: 4557.347000.
Description: Publishes articles and essays of biblical and theological interpretation for scholars, clergy, and laity of all denominations.

200   HK
INTER-RELIGIO; a network of Christian organizations for interreligious encounter in eastern Asia. (Text in English) 1982. s-a. Christian Study Center on Chinese Religion and Culture, 6-F Kiu Kin Mansion, 556 Nathan Rd., Kowloon, Hong Kong. TEL 770-3310. Ed. Brian Lawless. index; circ. 700. (back issues avail.)
Description: Guidebook to Christian organizations in East Asia.

267   JM   ISSN 0020-5087
INTER-SCHOOL & INTER-VARSITY CHRISTIAN FELLOWSHIP; for prayer and praise. m. free. Students Christian Fellowship and Scripture Union, 22 Hagley Park Plaza, Box 281, Kingston 10, Jamaica, W.I. Ed. Sam McCook. bk.rev.; circ. 800. (processed)
Formerly: Inter-School and Inter-Varsity Christian Fellowship of the West Indies.

255   BE   ISSN 0021-0978
BX1
IRENIKON. 1926. q. 1100 Fr.($35) Monastere de Chevetogne, 5590 Chevetogne, Belgium. TEL 083-21-17-63. FAX 083-21-60-45. Ed. Emmanuel Lanne. adv.; bk.rev.; bibl.; index; circ. 1,500. **Indexed:** CERDIC, Ind.Med., New Test.Abstr., Rel.Ind.One, Rel.Per.
—BLDSC shelfmark: 4567.805000.

200   IE   ISSN 0332-4427
IRISH BIBLICAL ASSOCIATION. PROCEEDINGS. 1976. a. £7($10.95) Columba Press, 93 The Rise, Mt. Merrion, Blackrock, Dublin, Ireland. FAX 01-2883770. Ed.Bd. adv.; circ. 250. (back issues avail.) **Indexed:** New Test.Abstr., Old Test.Abstr., Rel.& Theol.Abstr. (1989-).

220   UK   ISSN 0268-6112
BS543
IRISH BIBLICAL STUDIES. 1979. 4/yr. £22. Irish Biblical Studies, 26 College Green, Belfast BT7 1JT, N. Ireland. TEL 0232-325374. bk.rev.; circ. 400. **Indexed:** Rel.& Theol.Abstr. (1990-).
—BLDSC shelfmark: 4570.400000.
Description: Covers the Old and New Testament and related themes.

500   UK   ISSN 0264-6579
IRISH CHRISTIAN STUDY CENTRE. JOURNAL. 1983. a. £2.50 to individuals; institutions £10. Irish Christian Study Centre, Glenburn House, Glenburn Rd. S., Dunmurry, Belfast BT17 9JP, N. Ireland. TEL 602264. FAX 0232-301523. bk.rev.
—BLDSC shelfmark: 4802.770000.
Description: Provides encouragement for the development of Christian scholarship and research.

200   IE   ISSN 0021-1400
IRISH THEOLOGICAL QUARTERLY. 1906. q. £16.12. St. Patrick's College, Faculty of Theology, Maynooth, Co. Kildare, Ireland. TEL 01-285-222. Ed.Bd. bk.rev.; index; circ. 1,000. (also avail. in microform from UMI; reprint service avail. from UMI) **Indexed:** Canon Law Abstr., Cath.Ind., New Test.Abstr., Old Test.Abstr., Rel.& Theol.Abstr. (1968-).
—BLDSC shelfmark: 4574.870000.

ISSUES IN BIBLICAL ARCHAEOLOGY. see ARCHAEOLOGY

281   FR   ISSN 0021-2423
BX1781
ISTINA. 1954. q. 305 F. (typically set in Sep.). Centre d'Etudes Istina, 45 rue de la Glaciere, 75013 Paris, France. TEL 45-35-37-04. (Affiliate: Centre National de la Recherche Scientifique, Paris) Dir. B.D. Dupuy. bk.rev.; index; circ. 1,000. (also avail. in microfilm from UMI; back issues avail.; reprint service avail. from UMI) **Indexed:** Bull.Signal, CERDIC, New Test.Abstr., Rel.Ind.One, Rel.Per.
—BLDSC shelfmark: 4586.800000.

262.9   SP   ISSN 0021-325X
IUS CANONICUM. (Summaries in English and Latin) 1961. 2/yr. 6000 ptas.($60) (Universidad de Navarra, Instituto Martin de Azpilcueta) Servicio de Publicaciones de la Universidad de Navarra, S.A., Apdo. 177, 31080 Pamplona, Spain. TEL 94 25 2700. Ed. Tomas Rincon. bk.rev.; circ. 1,000. **Indexed:** Canon Law Abstr., CERDIC.
Description: Discusses canon law.

J P; paper for boys and girls. see CHILDREN AND YOUTH — For

200   GW   ISSN 0342-6505
JA; mit das taegliche Wort. 1953. m. DM.58.80. (Unity School of Christianity) Frick Verlag GmbH, Postfach 447, 7530 Pforzheim, Germany. TEL 07231-3571. FAX 07231-357744. Ed. Thea Jung. circ. 12,000.

RELIGIONS AND THEOLOGY   4183

200   GW   ISSN 0342-6513
JA, DAS WORT FUER ALLE. 1982. m. DM.13.50. (Berliner Stadtmission) Kreuz-Verlag Zeitschriften GmbH, Breitwiesenstr. 30, 7000 Stuttgart 80, Germany. TEL 0711-78803. circ. 40,000. (looseleaf format)

200   GW
JAHRBUCH DER HESSISCHEN KIRCHENGESCHICHTLICHEN VEREINIGUNG. 1949. a. DM.30. Ahastr. 5a, 6100 Darmstadt, Germany. TEL 06151-405233. FAX 06151-405440. TELEX 4197176-EKYN-D. Ed. Karl Dienst. index; circ. 700. (back issues avail.)

270   GW   ISSN 0075-2541
BR128.A2
JAHRBUCH FUER ANTIKE UND CHRISTENTUM. 1958. a. price varies. (Universitaet Bonn, Franz Joseph Doelger-Institut) Aschendorffsche Verlagsbuchhandlung, Soesterstr. 13, Postfach 1124, 4400 Muenster, Germany. TEL 0251-690-0. FAX 0251-690405. bk.rev. **Indexed:** Br.Archaeol.Abstr., New Test.Abstr., RILA.

270   GW   ISSN 0075-2568
BR857.B8
JAHRBUCH FUER BERLIN-BRANDENBURGISCHE KIRCHENGESCHICHTE. vol.55, 1985. a. DM.28. (Arbeitsgemeinschaft fuer Berlin-Brandenburgische Kirchengeschichte) Wichern-Verlag GmbH, Abt. CZV-Verlag, Bachstr. 1-2, 1000 Berlin 21, Germany. TEL 030-3915075. circ. 850.
—BLDSC shelfmark: 4630.380000.
Supersedes: Jahrbuch fuer Brandenburgische Kirchengeschichte.

JAHRBUCH FUER CHRISTLICHE SOZIALWISSENSCHAFTEN. see SOCIOLOGY

264 245   GW   ISSN 0075-2681
ML3168
JAHRBUCH FUER LITURGIK UND HYMNOLOGIE. 1955. a. price varies. (International Fellowship of Research in Hymnology - Internationale Arbeitsgemeinschaft fuer Hymnologie) Lutherisches Verlagshaus GmbH, Knochenhauerstr. 38-40, D-3000 Hannover 1, Germany. TEL 0511-1241-733. Ed.Bd. bk.rev.; circ. 1,000. **Indexed:** CERDIC, RILM.
—BLDSC shelfmark: 4631.640000.

JAHRBUCH FUER WESTFAELISCHE KIRCHENGESCHICHTE. see HISTORY — History Of Europe

260   GW   ISSN 0931-248X
JAHRBUCH MISSION. 1969. a. DM.6.80. (Verband Evangelischer Missionskonferenzen) Missionshilfe Verlag, Mittelweg 143, 2000 Hamburg 13, Germany. Ed. Joachim Wietzke. bk.rev.; circ. 10,000.
Formerly: Evangelische Mission Jahrbuch (ISSN 0531-4798)

268   FR
J'AIME LIRE. 1977. m. 345 F. Bayard Presse, 5, rue Bayard, 75380 Paris Cedex 08, France. circ. 180,000.
Description: Aimed at children aged 7-9.

200   JA   ISSN 0021-4353
JAPAN CHRISTIAN ACTIVITY NEWS. (Text in English) 1952. m. 3000 Yen($25) National Christian Council in Japan, Japan Christian Center, Rm. 24, 2-13-18 Nishi-Waseda, Shinjuku-ku, Tokyo 160, Japan. FAX 03-204-9495. TELEX J-27890-CCRAI. Ed.Bd. bk.rev.; circ. 600. (processed) **Indexed:** I.C.U.I.S.Abstr.

266   JA   ISSN 0021-4361
JAPAN CHRISTIAN QUARTERLY. (Text in English) 1925. q. $32. (Fellowship of Christian Missionaries) Japan Publications Trading Co., Ltd., Box 5030, Tokyo International, Tokyo 100-31, Japan. circ. 5,000. **Indexed:** M.L.A., Rel.& Theol.Abstr. (1989-), Rel.Ind.One, Rel.Per.
Description: Discusses mission work in the country.

266   JA   ISSN 0021-4531
JAPAN MISSIONARY BULLETIN. (Text in English) 1947. q. 4000 Yen($28) Oriens Institute for Religious Research, 28-5 Matsubara, 2-chome, Setagaya-ku, Tokyo 156, Japan. TEL 03-3322-7601. FAX 03-3325-5322. Ed. M. Christians. adv.; bk.rev.; charts; illus.; index; circ. 1,500.
Description: Discusses mission work in the country.

RELIGIONS AND THEOLOGY

200 UK ISSN 0307-3033
JAPAN NEWS. 1965. 4/yr. £3.50. Japan Evangelistic Band, 275 London Rd., North End, Portsmouth, Hants. PO2 9HE, England. TEL 0705-666151. circ. 2,000.
Formerly: Japan Evangelistic Band Magazine.

290 JA ISSN 0448-8954
BL2202
JAPANESE RELIGIONS. (Text in English) 1959. s-a. $20 for 2 yrs. National Christian Council of Japan, Center for the Study of Japanese Religions, Karasuma-Shimotachiuri, Kamikyo-ku, Kyoto-shi 602, Japan. FAX 075-432-1945. Ed. Yuki Hideo. bk.rev.; circ. 500. (back issues avail.) **Indexed:** Rel.& Theol.Abstr. (1967-), Rel.Ind.One.
—BLDSC shelfmark: 4661.600000.

JESUS MAESTRO. see *CHILDREN AND YOUTH — For*

220 IS ISSN 0792-3910
BS410
JEWISH BIBLE QUARTERLY. (Text in English) 1972. q. $20. Jewish Bible Quarterly, P.O. Box 29002, Jerusalem 93801, Israel. TEL 02-717863. Ed. Shimon Bakon. bk.rev.; circ. 1,400. **Indexed:** Old Test.Abstr., Rel.& Theol.Abstr. (1977-).
—BLDSC shelfmark: 4668.351280.
Former titles: Dor le-Dor (ISSN 0334-2166); Bible Readers' Union Bulletin (ISSN 0006-0771)

200 US ISSN 1044-5757
JOHN MACMURRAY STUDIES. irreg. Peter Lang Publishing, Inc., 62 W. 45th St., 4th Fl., New York, NY 10036. TEL 212-302-6740. FAX 212-302-7574. Ed. Frank G. Kirkpatrick.
Description: Deals with the thought and influence of the Scottish moral and religious philosopher, John Macmurray.

220 371.911 US
JOHN MILTON ADULT LESSONS QUARTERLY. 1935. 4/yr. free. John Milton Society for the Blind, 475 Riverside Dr., Rm. 455, New York, NY 10115. TEL 212-870-3335. Ed. Pam Toplisky. circ. braille ed. 1,500; record ed. 1,650. (Braille; also avail. in record)
Formerly: John Milton Sunday School Quarterly.
Description: Biblical studies based on the Uniform International Adult Lesson Series.

JOHN MILTON MAGAZINE. see *HANDICAPPED — Visually Impaired*

JOHN MILTON TALKING BOOK MAGAZINE. see *HANDICAPPED — Visually Impaired*

200 NE ISSN 0021-7395
JONGE KERK. 1917. m. fl.15. Apostolaat van het Gebed, Postbus 418, 6500 AK Nijmegen, Netherlands. TEL 080-222-495. FAX 080-222-593. Ed. Chr. Swueste. adv.; bk.rev.; index; circ. 15,000.

255 US ISSN 0021-7603
JOSEPHITE HARVEST. 1888. q. $2. Society of St. Joseph of the Sacred Heart, 1130 N. Calvert St., Baltimore, MD 21202. TEL 410-727-3386. FAX 410-385-2331. Ed. Earle A. Newman. adv.; circ. 40,000.

JOURNAL FOR CREATIVE CHANGE. see *PSYCHOLOGY*

200 US ISSN 0021-8294
BL1 CODEN: JSSRBT
JOURNAL FOR THE SCIENTIFIC STUDY OF RELIGION. 1961. q. $45 to non-members. Society for the Scientific Study of Religion, Pierce Hall, No. 193, Purdue Univ., West Lafayette, IN 47907-1305. TEL 317-494-6286. Ed. Armand Mauss. adv.; bk.rev.; charts; stat.; index,cum.index: 1961-1981; circ. 3,500. (also avail. in microform from UMI; reprint service avail. from UMI,KTO) **Indexed:** Abstr.Anthropol., Amer.Bibl.Slavic & E.Eur.Stud., Arts & Hum.Cit.Ind., CERDIC, Chic.Per.Ind., Curr.Cont., G.Soc.Sci.& Rel.Per.Lit., Hist.Abstr., Hum.Ind., Lang.& Lang.Behav.Abstr., Mid.East: Abstr.& Ind., Old Test.Abstr., PSI, Psychol.Abstr., Rel.& Theol.Abstr. (1967-), Rel.Ind.One, Rel.Per., Sociol.Abstr. (1961-), SSCI.
—BLDSC shelfmark: 5061.500000.

200.968 SA ISSN 1011-7601
JOURNAL FOR THE STUDY OF RELIGION. 1980. 2/yr. R.20 (foreign $30)(effective 1992). Association for the Study of Religion in Southern Africa, University of Natal, Department of Religious Studies, P.O. Box 375, Pietermaritzburg 3200, South Africa. TEL 0331-955571. Eds. M.H. Prozesky, P.S. Maxwell. adv.; bk.rev.; abstr.; bibl.; charts; stat.; index; circ. 240. (back issues avail.) **Indexed:** Ind.S.A.Per., Rel.Ind.One.
—BLDSC shelfmark: 5066.928000.
Formerly: Religion in Southern Africa.
Description: Forum for scholarly contributions on topics of contemporary significance in the academic study of religion.
Refereed Serial

200 UK ISSN 0142-064X
BS410
JOURNAL FOR THE STUDY OF THE NEW TESTAMENT. 1978. 3/yr. $29.50 to individuals; institutions $84. Sheffield Academic Press Ltd., 343 Fulwood Rd., Univ. of Sheffield, Sheffield S10 3BP, England. **Indexed:** New.Test.Abstr., Rel.& Theol.Abstr. (1979-), Rel.Ind.One.
—BLDSC shelfmark: 5066.917000.

200 UK ISSN 0143-5108
JOURNAL FOR THE STUDY OF THE NEW TESTAMENT. SUPPLEMENT SERIES. irreg. price varies. Sheffield Academic Press Ltd., 343 Fulwood Rd., University of Sheffield, Sheffield S10 3BP, England. **Indexed:** New Test.Abstr.
—BLDSC shelfmark: 5066.918000.

221 UK ISSN 0309-0892
BS410
JOURNAL FOR THE STUDY OF THE OLD TESTAMENT. 1976. 3/yr. $29.50 to individuals; institutions $84. Sheffield Academic Press Ltd., 343 Fulwood Rd., University of Sheffield, Sheffield S10 3BP, England. Ed.Bd. **Indexed:** Bull.Signal, Int.Z.Bibelwiss, New Test.Abstr., Old Test.Abstr., Rel.& Theol.Abstr. (1977-), Rel.Ind.One, Rel.Ind.Two, Rel.Per.
—BLDSC shelfmark: 5066.920000.

221 UK ISSN 0309-0787
JOURNAL FOR THE STUDY OF THE OLD TESTAMENT. SUPPLEMENT SERIES. irreg. price varies. Sheffield Academic Press Ltd., 343 Fulwood Rd., University of Sheffield, Sheffield S10 3BP, England. Ed.Bd. **Indexed:** Old Test.Abstr.
—BLDSC shelfmark: 5066.920100.

291 294.54 UG
JOURNAL OF AFRICAN RELIGION AND PHILOSOPHY; a journal of religion and philosophy in Africa. 1988. 2/yr. £12 per no. Sun Publishers, P.O. Box 16144, Wandegeya, Kampala, Uganda. Ed. L. Njinya-Mujinya. adv.; bk.rev.; circ. 5,000.
Formerly (until 1989): African Mind.
Description: Contents are theological, sociological, philosophical and, in terms of the plurality of religions and philosophies, comparative.

297.89 CN ISSN 0838-0430
BP300
JOURNAL OF BAHA'I STUDIES. 1988. q. Can.$20 to individuals; institutions $30. Association for Baha'i Studies, 34 Copernicus St., Ottawa, Ont. K1N 7K4, Canada. TEL 613-233-1903. FAX 613-233-3644. Ed.Bd. bk.rev.; circ. 2,300.

200 UK
JOURNAL OF BELIEFS AND VALUES. 1980. 2/yr. £6. National Association of Teachers in Further and Higher Education, Religious Studies Section, c/o Nicola Slee, Whitelands College, West Hill, London SW15 3SN, England. TEL 081-788-8268. FAX 081-789-7008. adv.; bk.rev.
Description: Aimed at teachers of religious education and religious studies in higher and continuing education.

220 US ISSN 0021-9231
BS410
JOURNAL OF BIBLICAL LITERATURE. 1881. q. $50 to non-members. (Society of Biblical Literature) Scholars Press, Box 15399, Atlanta, GA 30333-0399. TEL 404-636-4757. FAX 404-636-8301. Ed. John B. Collins. adv.; bk.rev.; index; circ. 7,000. (also avail. in microfilm from UMI; microfiche; reprint service avail. from UMI) **Indexed:** Arts & Hum.Cit.Ind., Bk.Rev.Ind. (1977-), CERDIC, Child.Bk.Rev.Ind. (1977-), Curr.Cont., G.Soc.Sci.& Rel.Per.Lit., Hum.Ind., Ind.Jew.Per., Mid.East: Abstr.& Ind., New Test.Abstr., Old Test.Abstr., Rel.& Theol.Abstr. (1968-), Rel.Ind.One, Rel.Per.
—BLDSC shelfmark: 4951.550000.
Description: Academic papers on biblical scholarship and interpretation.

377.8 AT ISSN 0021-9657
JOURNAL OF CHRISTIAN EDUCATION. 1958. 3/yr. Aus.$24 to individuals; institutions Aus.$36. Australian Teachers' Christian Fellowship, 16 Mill Hill Rd., Bondi Junction, N.S.W. 2022, Australia. TEL 02-369-1688. bk.rev.; bibl.; cum.index every 3 yrs.; circ. 1,000. (also avail. in microform from UMI; back issues avail) **Indexed:** Aus.Educ.Ind., Aus.P.A.I.S., Chr.Per.Ind., Cont.Pg.Educ., Educ.Ind., Rel.& Theol.Abstr. (1970-), Rel.Ind.One.
—BLDSC shelfmark: 4958.270000.

JOURNAL OF CHRISTIAN JURISPRUDENCE. see *LAW*

JOURNAL OF CHRISTIAN NURSING. see *MEDICAL SCIENCES — Nurses And Nursing*

230.05 US ISSN 0360-1420
BR1
JOURNAL OF CHRISTIAN RECONSTRUCTION. 1974. s-a. $15 to individuals; libraries $13. Chalcedon, Inc., Box 158, Vallecito, CA 95251. TEL 209-728-3510. FAX 209-736-0536. bk.rev.; circ. 2,000. (also avail. in microform from UMI; reprint service avail.) **Indexed:** Chr.Per.Ind.
—BLDSC shelfmark: 4958.280000.
Description: Scholarly and lay articles on the revitalization of the intellectual and cultural heritage of Christians in terms of standards set in the Old and New Testaments.

322 261 US ISSN 0021-969X
BV630.A1
JOURNAL OF CHURCH AND STATE. 1959. 4/yr. $20 to individuals (foreign $23); institutions $35 (foreign $40). Baylor University, J.M. Dawson Institute of Church-State Studies, Box 97308, Waco, TX 76798-7308. TEL 817-755-1510. Ed. James E. Wood, Jr. adv.; bk.rev.; index; circ. 1,700. (also avail. in microform from WSH; reprint service avail. from WSH) **Indexed:** Abstr.Bk.Rev.Curr.Leg.Per., Amer.Bibl.Slavic & E.Eur.Stud., Amer.Hist.& Life, Arts & Hum.Cit.Ind., Bk.Rev.Ind. (1980-), C.L.I., CERDIC, Child.Bk.Rev.Ind. (1980-), Chr.Per.Ind., Educ.Admin.Abstr., Hist.Abstr., L.R.I., Mid.East: Abstr.& Ind., P.A.I.S., Rel.& Theol.Abstr. (1968-), Rel.Ind.One, Rel.Per.
—BLDSC shelfmark: 4958.365000.

JOURNAL OF COMPARATIVE SOCIOLOGY AND ETHICS. see *SOCIOLOGY*

JOURNAL OF COPTIC STUDIES. see *HISTORY — History Of The Near East*

291 II ISSN 0253-7222
BL1
JOURNAL OF DHARMA; an international quarterly of world religions. 1975. q. Rs.80($28) (effective 1992). (Dharma Research Association) Dharmaram College, Centre for the Study of World Religions, Bangalore 560 029, India. TEL 812-643266. Ed. Thomas Manninezhath. adv.; bk.rev.; circ. 1,800. (also avail. in microform from UMI; reprint service avail. from ISI,UMI) **Indexed:** Arts & Hum.Cit.Ind., Curr.Cont., Phil.Ind., Rel.& Theol.Abstr. (19989-), Rel.Ind.One.

RELIGIONS AND THEOLOGY

209 UK ISSN 0022-0469
BR140
JOURNAL OF ECCLESIASTICAL HISTORY. 1953. q. $73 to individuals; institutions $141. Cambridge University Press, Edinburgh Bldg., Shaftesbury Rd., Cambridge CB2 2RU, England. TEL 0223-312393. FAX 0223-315052. TELEX 851817256. (North American orders to: Cambridge University Press, 40 W. 20th St., New York, NY 10011) Eds. Brendan Bradshaw, Peter Linehan. adv.; bk.rev.; bibl.; index. (also avail. in microform from UMI) **Indexed:** Amer.Hist.& Life, Arts & Hum.Cit.Ind., Br.Archaeol.Abstr., Br.Hum.Ind., CERDIC, Curr.Cont., G.Soc.Sci.& Rel.Per.Lit., Hist.Abstr., Hum.Ind., New Test.Abstr., Rel.& Theol.Abstr. (1967-), Rel.Ind.One, Rel.Per.
—BLDSC shelfmark: 4971.700000.
Description: Material on the history of the Christian Church as an institution and its relations with other religions and society.

260 US ISSN 0022-0558
BX1
JOURNAL OF ECUMENICAL STUDIES. 1964. 4/yr. $22 (foreign $25). Temple University, 022-38, Philadelphia, PA 19122. TEL 215-787-7714. FAX 215-787-4569. Ed. Leonard Swidler. adv.; bk.rev.; abstr.; index; circ. 1,900. (also avail. in microfilm from WSH; reprint service avail. from WSH) **Indexed:** Amer.Bibl.Slavic & E.Eur.Stud., Amer.Hist.& Life, Arts & Hum.Cit.Ind., C.L.I., Cath.Ind., CERDIC, Curr.Cont., G.Soc.Sci.& Rel.Per.Lit., Hist.Abstr., Hum.Ind., Int.Z.Bibelwiss, Leg.Per., Mid.East: Abstr.& Ind., New Test.Abstr., Old Test.Abstr., Rel.& Theol.Abstr. (1970-), Rel.Ind.One, Rel.Per.
—BLDSC shelfmark: 4973.096000.
Description: Scholarly and grassroots concern for interreligious and interideological dialogue worldwide, including English-language coverage of the literature and events from six continents.

JOURNAL OF EUROPEAN STUDIES. see HISTORY — History Of Europe

JOURNAL OF FEMINIST STUDIES IN RELIGION. see WOMEN'S STUDIES

JOURNAL OF HEALTH CARE CHAPLAINCY. see PHYSICAL FITNESS AND HYGIENE

JOURNAL OF LAW AND RELIGION. see LAW

200 157.63 US ISSN 1053-8755
▼**JOURNAL OF MINISTRY IN ADDICTION & RECOVERY.** 1992. s-a. $20. Haworth Press, Inc., 10 Alice St., Binghamton, NY 13904. TEL 800-342-9678. FAX 607-722-1424. TELEX 4932599. Ed. Jerry Albers. (also avail. in microform from HAW; reprint service avail. from HAW)
Description: Offers pastoral caregivers and others in the addiction field innovative approaches to treating a variety of addictive behaviors.

250 US ISSN 0022-3409
BV4000 CODEN: JPACA8
JOURNAL OF PASTORAL CARE. 1947. q. $20. Journal of Pastoral Care Publications, Inc., 1549 Clairmont Rd., Ste. 103, Decatur, GA 30030. TEL 404-320-0195. FAX 404-320-0849. Ed. Orlo Strunk. adv.; bk.rev.; index; circ. 14,000. (also avail. in microfilm from UMI; reprint service avail. from UMI) **Indexed:** ASSIA, CERDIC, Mid.East: Abstr.& Ind., Past.Care & Couns.Abstr., Psychol.Abstr., Rel.& Theol.Abstr. (1968-), Rel.Ind.One, Rel.Per., Soc.Work Res.& Abstr.
—BLDSC shelfmark: 5029.500000.
Description: Includes articles that reflect the cutting edges of clinical pastoral education and the pastoral counseling movements.

200 US ISSN 0196-9072
JOURNAL OF PASTORAL PRACTICE; a professional periodical for church leaders. 1978. irreg. $21. Christian Counseling & Educational Foundation, 1790 E. Willow Grove Ave., Laverock, PA 19118. Ed. Jay E. Adams. bk.rev.; circ. 600. (back issues avail.) **Indexed:** Chr.Per.Ind., Past.Care & Couns.Abstr.

JOURNAL OF PSYCHOLOGY AND CHRISTIANITY. see PSYCHOLOGY

JOURNAL OF PSYCHOLOGY AND THEOLOGY; an evangelical forum for the integration of psychology and theology. see PSYCHOLOGY

200 US ISSN 0022-4189
BR1
JOURNAL OF RELIGION. 1882. q. $23 to individuals; institutions $40; students $17. University of Chicago Press, Journals Division, 5720 S. Woodlawn Ave., Chicago, IL 60637. TEL 312-753-3347. FAX 312-702-0694. TELEX 25-4603. (Subscr. to: Box 37005, Chicago, IL 60637) Ed.Bd. adv.; bk.rev.; index; circ. 2,200. (also avail. in microform from MIM,UMI; reprint service avail. from UMI,ISI) **Indexed:** Acad.Ind., Amer.Hist.& Life, Arts & Hum.Cit.Ind., Bk.Rev.Dig., Bk.Rev.Ind., Child.Bk.Rev.Ind. (1965-), Curr.Cont., G.Soc.Sci.& Rel.Per.Lit., Hist.Abstr., Hum.Ind., Int.Z.Bibelwiss., Mid.East: Abstr.& Ind., New Test.Abstr., Old Test.Abstr., Rel.& Theol.Abstr. (1971-), Rel.Ind.One, Rel.Per., SSCI.
—BLDSC shelfmark: 5049.200000.
Refereed Serial

200 150 US ISSN 0022-4197
RC321 CODEN: JRHEAT
JOURNAL OF RELIGION AND HEALTH. 1961. q. $155 (foreign $180). (Institute of Religion) Human Sciences Press, Inc. (Subsidiary of: Plenum Publishing Corp.), 233 Spring St., New York, NY 10013-1578. TEL 212-620-8000. FAX 212-463-0742. (Co-sponsor: Institute of Health) Ed. Harry C. Meserve. adv.; bk.rev.; charts; index. (also avail. in microform from UMI; reprint service avail. from ISI,UMI) **Indexed:** Arts & Hum.Cit.Ind., Curr.Cont., Excerp.Med., G.Soc.Sci.& Rel.Per.Lit., Mid.East: Abstr.& Ind., Past.Care & Couns.Abstr., Psychol.Abstr., Rel.& Theol.Abstr. (1969-), Rel.Ind.One, SSCI.
—BLDSC shelfmark: 5049.350000.
Description: Explores contemporary modes of religious thought with emphasis on its relevance to current medical and psychological research.
Refereed Serial

JOURNAL OF RELIGION & PSYCHICAL RESEARCH; a scholarly quarterly dealing with religion, psychical research, and related topics. see PARAPSYCHOLOGY AND OCCULTISM

291 NE ISSN 0022-4200
BL2400
JOURNAL OF RELIGION IN AFRICA/RELIGION EN AFRIQUE. (Supplement avail.: Studies on Religion in Africa (ISSN 0169-9814)) (Text in English and French) 1967. 3/yr. fl.160($91.43) (effective 1992). E.J. Brill, P.O. Box 9000, 2300 PA Leiden, Netherlands. TEL 071-312624. FAX 071-317532. TELEX 39296 BRILL NL. (In N. America: E.J. Brill, 24 Hudson St., Kinderhook, NY 12106. TEL 800-962-4406) Ed. Adrian Hastings. bk.rev.; bibl.; charts; illus. **Indexed:** Amer.Hist.& Life, Arts & Hum.Cit.Ind., CERDIC, Curr.Cont.Africa, Curr.Cont., Hist.Abstr., Rel.& Theol.Abstr. (1989-), Rel.Ind.One, Rel.Per.
—BLDSC shelfmark: 5049.300000.
Description: Studies of the forms and history of religion on the African continent.

200 US ISSN 1045-5876
BV4012
JOURNAL OF RELIGION IN PSYCHOTHERAPY. 1952. q. $24 to individuals; institutions $32; libraries $60. (Princeton Theological Seminary) Haworth Press, Inc., 10 Alice St., Binghamton, NY 13904. TEL 607-722-1695. FAX 607-722-1424. TELEX 4932599. Ed. William M. Clements. adv.; bk.rev. (also avail. in microform from HAW,UMI; reprint service avail. from HAW,ISI,UMI) **Indexed:** CCR, CERDIC, Curr.Cont., G.Soc.Sci.& Rel.Per.Lit., Past.Care & Couns.Abstr., Psychol.Abstr., Rel.& Theol.Abstr. (1987-), Rel.Ind.One, Rel.Per., Soc.Work Res.& Abstr., SSCI.
Formerly (until 1990): Journal of Pastoral Psychotherapy (ISSN 0886-5477)
Description: For therapists and researchers who are interested in the role and dynamic of religion in the healing process of psychotherapy.
Refereed Serial

200 US ISSN 1047-7845
CODEN: JRTIE3
▼**JOURNAL OF RELIGIOUS & THEOLOGICAL INFORMATION.** 1991. s-a. $18 to individuals; institutions $48. Haworth Press, Inc., 10 Alice St., Binghamton, NY 13904-1580. TEL 800-342-9678. FAX 607-722-1424. TELEX 4932599. Ed. William C. Miller. (also avail. in microform from HAW; reprint service avail. from HAW)
Description: Presents articles pertaining to the production, dissemination, preservation, and bibliography of religious and theological information.
Refereed Serial

200 US ISSN 0384-9694
BJ1
JOURNAL OF RELIGIOUS ETHICS. 1973. s-a. $18 to individuals; institutions $25. (Religious Ethics, Inc.) Scholars Press, Box 15399, Atlanta, GA 30333-0399. TEL 414-636-4757. FAX 404-636-8301. Ed. James Johnson. circ. 1,200. (also avail. in microform from UMI; reprint service avail. from UMI) **Indexed:** Arts & Hum.Cit.Ind., CERDIC, Curr.Cont., Hum.Ind., Old Test.Abstr., Phil.Ind., Rel.& Theol.Abstr. (1978-), Rel.Ind.One, Rel.Per.
—BLDSC shelfmark: 5049.353000.

JOURNAL OF RELIGIOUS GERONTOLOGY. see GERONTOLOGY AND GERIATRICS

209 AT ISSN 0022-4227
BR140
JOURNAL OF RELIGIOUS HISTORY. 1960. s-a. Aus.$40 to individuals; institutions Aus.$77 (effective 1992). Association for the Journal of Religious History, History Department, University of Sydney, Sydney, N.S.W. 2006, Australia. Ed. A.E. Cahill. bk.rev.; bibl.; index. cum.index every 2 yrs.; circ. 700. (also avail. in microform from MIM) **Indexed:** Amer.Hist.& Life, Arts & Hum.Cit.Ind., Aus.P.A.I.S., CERDIC, Curr.Cont., Hist.Abstr., Mid.East: Abstr.& Ind., Rel.& Theol.Abstr. (1978-), Rel.Ind.One, Rel.Per.
—BLDSC shelfmark: 5049.355000.

200 II ISSN 0047-2735
BL1
THE JOURNAL OF RELIGIOUS STUDIES. (Text and summaries in English) 1969. s-a. Rs.30($13) Punjabi University, Department of Religious Studies, Patiala 147002, Punjab, India. TEL 78561. Ed. Wazir Singh. bk.rev.; circ. 800. **Indexed:** New Test.Abstr., Rel.Ind.One.

200 US ISSN 0193-3604
JOURNAL OF RELIGIOUS STUDIES. 1972. s-a. $4. Cleveland State University, Department of Religion, Cleveland, OH 44115. Ed. Frederick Holck. adv.; bk.rev.; illus.; circ. 1,200. (back issues avail.) **Indexed:** CERDIC, New Test.Abstr., Rel.Ind.One, Rel.Per.
Formerly: Ohio Journal of Religious Studies (ISSN 0094-5668)

700 US ISSN 0022-4235
BR1
JOURNAL OF RELIGIOUS THOUGHT. 1943. s-a. $12 to individuals; institutions $14. (Howard University, School of Divinity) Howard University Press, 1240 Randolph St., N.E., Washington, DC 20017. TEL 202-806-4935. FAX 202-806-4946. Ed. Cain H. Felder. adv.; bk.rev.; bibl.; cum.index; circ. 1,500. (also avail. in microform from UMI; reprint service avail. from UMI) **Indexed:** Amer.Hist.& Life, Hist.Abstr., Ind.Sel.Per., Mid.East: Abstr.& Ind., New Test.Abstr., Rel.& Theol.Abstr. (1966-), Rel.Ind.One, Rel.Per.
—BLDSC shelfmark: 5049.360000.
Description: Contains articles from persons of varied theological and ethnic backgrounds.

377.8 US ISSN 0160-7774
BV4012
JOURNAL OF SUPERVISION AND TRAINING IN MINISTRY. 1978. irreg., vol.8, 1986. $20. Box 6777, Chicago, IL 60680. TEL 312-942-5571. Ed. Roger Fallot. adv.; bk.rev.; circ. 1,000. **Indexed:** Rel.Ind.One, Rel.Per.
—BLDSC shelfmark: 5067.120000.
Description: Covers issues related to the training and supervision of ministers and chaplains.

RELIGIONS AND THEOLOGY

230   UK   ISSN 0022-5185
BR1
JOURNAL OF THEOLOGICAL STUDIES. 1899. s-a. £66($138) Oxford University Press, Oxford Journals, Pinkhill House, Southfield Road, Eynsham, Oxford OX8 1JJ, England. TEL 0865-882283. FAX 0865-882890. TELEX 837330 OXPRES G. Eds. Morna D. Hooker, Maurice Wiles. adv.; bk.rev.; abstr.; bibl.; charts; illus.; index; circ. 1,550. (also avail. in microform from UMI) **Indexed:** Arts & Hum.Cit.Ind., Br.Hum.Ind., CERDIC, Curr.Cont., M.L.A., New Test.Abstr., Old Test.Abstr., Rel.& Theol.Abstr. (1968-), Rel.Ind.One, Rel.Per.
—BLDSC shelfmark: 5069.070000.
Description: Academic study of Christian theology: Old and New Testaments, Church history, philosophy of religion and ethics.

200   SA   ISSN 0047-2867
BR1
JOURNAL OF THEOLOGY FOR SOUTHERN AFRICA. 1972. q. R.20 to individuals (foreign R.35 or $35); institutions and libraries R.25 (foreign R.50 or $50). c/o University of Cape Town, Department of Religious Studies, Rondebosch 7700, South Africa. TEL 021-650-3453. FAX 021-650-3726. Ed. J.W. de Gruchy. adv.; bk.rev.; abstr.; index; circ. 1,000. (also avail. in microfilm from UMI,WMP) **Indexed:** CERDIC, Ind.S.A.Per., New Test.Abstr., Old Test.Abstr., Rel.& Theol.Abstr. (1989-), Rel.Ind.One.
—BLDSC shelfmark: 5069.074000.

JOURNAL OF TRANSLATION AND TEXTLINGUISTICS. see LINGUISTICS

JOURNAL OF WOMEN AND RELIGION. see WOMEN'S INTERESTS

JR. HIGH MINISTRY MAGAZINE. see CHILDREN AND YOUTH — About

226 365   US
JUBILEE INTERNATIONAL. (Text in English, Spanish) 1981. bi-m. free. Prison Fellowship International, Box 17434, Washington, DC 20041. TEL 703-481-0000. FAX 703-481-0003. Ed. Martha Anderson. circ. 6,500.
Former titles (until 1991): Fellowship Communique (ISSN 0738-1530); (until 1983): Jubilee International (ISSN 0736-9662)
Description: Covers the worlwide activities of the Prison Fellowship ministries, with stories on the impact of ministry activities on prisoners' lives.

JUDAICA BOHEMIAE. see ETHNIC INTERESTS

200 100   BN   ISSN 0350-6398
JUKIC; zbornik radova. (Text in Croatian) 1971. a. 5500 din.($7) Zbor Franjevackih Bogoslova "Jukic", Aleja Branka Bujica 111, 71000 Sarajevo, Bosnia Hercegovina. TEL 071-453-266. circ. 1,000. (back issues avail.)

JUL I FAMILIEN. see CHILDREN AND YOUTH — For

268   AU   ISSN 0022-6289
JUNGE GEMEINDE. 1948. q. S.20. Evangelisches Jugendwerk in Oesterreich, Liechtensteinstr. 20, A-1090 Vienna, Austria. FAX 0222-34926716. Ed. M. Perko. adv.; bk.rev.; abstr.; circ. 2,000. (tabloid format)
Description: Contains information of interest to those involved in evangelical work with Austrian youth. Includes readers' letters, reports and announcements of events.

200   GW   ISSN 0022-6319
BX8001
JUNGE KIRCHE; eine Zeitschrift Europaeischer Christen. 1933. m. DM.56. Verlag Junge Kirche, Mathildenstr. 86, D-2800 Bremen 1, Germany. TEL 0421-71648. Ed.Bd. adv.; bk.rev.; index; circ. 6,800. **Indexed:** CERDIC.
Description: Christian socialist publication with articles about religion, politics, peace, and the Third World. Includes reader's letters.

268   GW   ISSN 0022-6467
JUNGSCHARHELFER; Mitarbeiterhilfe fuer Jungen- und Maedchenarbeit. 1954. q. DM.24. (Gemeindejugendwerk) Oncken Verlag, Langenbeckstr. 28-30, Postfach 102829, 3500 Kassel 1, Germany. Ed. Kay Moritz. bk.rev.; circ. 2,100. (tabloid format)

200   CU   ISSN 0864-0254
JUPRECU. 3/yr. Iglesia Presbiteriana, Salud No. 222, Lealtad y Companario, Havana 2, Cuba. TEL 809 61-1558. Dir. Francisco Marrero.

200   UK   ISSN 0306-7645
JUSTPEACE. 1936. 10/yr. £0.20 per no. Pax Christi, Christian Peace Education Centre, 9 Henry Rd., London N4 2LH, England. TEL 081-800-4612. adv.; bk.rev.; circ. 2,000.
Formerly: Pax Bulletin (ISSN 0031-3319)
Description: News items, letters, and calendar of events pertaining to Christian pacifism and the activities and members of this international Catholic peace movement.

KACIC. see HISTORY — History Of Europe

200   AU   ISSN 0022-7757
BL1
KAIROS; Zeitschrift fuer Religionswissenschaft und Theologie. 1959. q. S.190. Otto Mueller Verlag, Postfach 167, A-5021 Salzburg, Austria. TEL 881974. Ed.Bd. adv.; bk.rev.; bibl.; index; circ. 700. **Indexed:** CERDIC, New Test.Abstr., Rel.Ind.One, Rel.Per.

200   GW   ISSN 0022-779X
KAISERSWERTHER MITTEILUNGEN. 1836. 3/yr. free. Diakoniewerk Kaiserswerth, Alte Landstr. 129, 4000 Duesseldorf 31-Kaiserswerth, Germany. TEL 0211-4093718. FAX 0211-4092111. Eds. J. Degen, M. Klaemmt. bk.rev.; illus.; circ. 26,000.

200   II   ISSN 0022-8028
KALYAN. (Text in Hindi) 1927. m. Rs.38($7) Gita Press, Sagdesh Psesad Jalan, Gorakhpur, India. Ed.Bd.

KANDELAAR. see EDUCATION

KANON. see LAW

200   GW   ISSN 0022-9245
KASSELER SONNTAGSBLATT; christliches Familienblatt fuer Deutschland. 1879. w. DM.88.80. Verlag Thiele und Schwarz, Werner-Heisenberg-Str. 7, 3500 Kassel, Germany. FAX 0561-5890968. Ed. Rolf Schwarz. adv.; bk.rev.; illus.; mkt.; circ. 95,000. (tabloid format)

261   US   ISSN 0022-9288
BR535
KATALLAGETE. 1965. 2/yr. $15. Katallagete, Inc., Box 2307, College Sta., Berea, KY 40404. TEL 606-986-8218. Ed. James Y. Holloway. bk.rev.; illus.; circ. 4,500. (also avail. in microform from UMI) **Indexed:** CERDIC, Rel.& Theol.Abstr. (1989-), Rel.Ind.One, Rel.Per.
—BLDSC shelfmark: 5086.795000.

200 920   CN   ISSN 0315-8020
KATERI; Lily of the Mohawks. (Editions in English, French) 1949. q. Can.$3. Cause for the Canonization of Blessed Kateri Tekakwitha, Box 70, Kahnawake, Que. JOL 1B0, Canada. TEL 514-525-3611. Ed. Rev. Jacques Bruyere, S.J. circ. 16,800.
Description: News about Kateri's life and virtues, and about native peoples of America.

200   GW   ISSN 0176-5493
KATHOLISCHER ARBEITSKREIS FUER ZEITGESCHICHTLICHE FRAGEN. INFORMATIONSDIENST.. 1961. 6/yr. Katholischer Arbeitskreis fuer Zeitgeschichtliche Fragen e.V., Hochkreuzallee 246, 5300 Bonn 2, Germany. Ed. Albrecht Beckel. circ. 1,600.

KATOLIKUS MAGYAROK VASARNAPJA/CATHOLIC HUNGARIANS' SUNDAY. see RELIGIONS AND THEOLOGY — Roman Catholic

281.7 916.206   UA
AL-KERAZEH. (Text in Arabic) w. Coptic Orthodox Church, St. Mark's Cathedral, Anba Ruess, 222 Sharia Ramses, P.O. Box 9035, Abbasiya, Cairo, Egypt. TEL 02-2825983. TELEX 23281.

200 327   NE
KERK EN VREDE. 1925. m. fl.38. Kerk en Vrede, Oosterkade 13, 3582 AT Utrecht, Netherlands. Ed. Henk Eisma. adv.; bk.rev.; abstr.; circ. 3,100. **Indexed:** CERDIC.
Formerly: Militia Christi (ISSN 0026-4156)
Description: Discusses theological aspects of nonviolence through the subjects of social justice, confession, conscientious objection and peace education.

200   NE
KERKBODE VAN NEDERLANDS GEREFORMEERDE KERKEN. 1945. 17/yr. fl.42.50. Buijten en Schipperheijn, B.V., Valkenburgerstraat 106, 1011 NA Amsterdam C, Netherlands. FAX 020-6263956. Ed.Bd. adv.; bk.rev.; circ. 1,800. (tabloid format)
Formerly: Kerkbode van Gereformeerde Kerken in Noord en Zuid-Holland (ISSN 0023-0618)

270   NE   ISSN 0169-8451
KERKHISTORISCHE BIJDRAGEN. 1970. irreg., vol.15, 1988. price varies. E.J. Brill, P.O. Box 9000, 2300 PA Leiden, Netherlands. TEL 071-312624. FAX 071-317532. TELEX 39296 BRILL NL. (In N. America: E.J. Brill, 24 Hudson St., Kinderhook, NY 12106. TEL 800-962-4406)

200   NE   ISSN 0023-0685
KERUGMA. 1957. 6/yr. fl.46.50. Gooi en Sticht, Postbox 133, 3740 AC Baarn, Netherlands. TEL 01254-15320. FAX 02154-20658. Eds. B. Robben, A. Willems. **Indexed:** CERDIC.

266   CN   ISSN 0023-0693
KERYGMA. (Text in English, French) 1967. s-a. $12. Saint Paul University, Institute of Mission Studies, 223 Main St., Ottawa, Ont. K1S 1C4, Canada. TEL 613-236-1393. FAX 613-782-3005. Ed. Martin Roberge. bk.rev.; circ. 250. **Indexed:** New Test.Abstr.
—BLDSC shelfmark: 5090.350000.

200   GW   ISSN 0023-0707
BR4
KERYGMA UND DOGMA; Zeitschrift fuer theologische Forschung und kirchliche Lehre. 1955. q. DM.79. Vandenhoeck und Ruprecht, Theaterstr. 13, Postfach 3753, 3400 Goettingen, Germany. TEL 0551-6959-22. FAX 0551-695917. Ed.Bd. adv.; bk.rev.; index; circ. 1,300. **Indexed:** CERDIC, New Test.Abstr., Old Test.Abstr., Rel.& Theol.Abstr. (1970-), Rel.Ind.One, Rel.Per.
—BLDSC shelfmark: 5090.370000.

KEY TO CHRISTIAN EDUCATION. see EDUCATION

KIERKEGAARDIANA. see PHILOSOPHY

268   NE   ISSN 0023-1444
KIND EN ZONDAG. 1930. m. fl.78. Nederlandsche Zondagsschool Vereeniging, Bloemgracht 65, 1016 KG Amsterdam, Netherlands. Ed. C.M. Wigmans. adv.; bk.rev.; circ. 20,000.

200   GW   ISSN 0341-7190
KINDERGOTTESDIENST/LASS MICH HOEREN. 1890. q. DM.26.40. Guetersloher Verlagshaus Gerd Mohn, Carl-Bertelsmann-Str. 256, Postfach 1343, 4830 Guetersloh 100, Germany. TEL 05241-7405-0. FAX 05241-740548. (Subscr. to: Bechauf Verlag, Friedrichstr. 48, 4800 Bielefeld 1, Germany)

200   US   ISSN 0023-1614
KINGDOM DIGEST.* vol.29, 1968. m. $10. Box 171345, Irving, TX 75017-1345. bk.rev.; bibl. **Indexed:** CERDIC.

KINSHIP. see SOCIAL SERVICES AND WELFARE

KIRCHE IN MARBURG; Mitteilungen der evangelischen und Katholischen Gemeinden. see RELIGIONS AND THEOLOGY — Roman Catholic

200   GW
KIRCHE UND KONFESSION. 1962. irreg. (Konfessionskundliche Institut des Ev. Bundes) Vandenhoeck und Ruprecht, Robert-Bosch-Breite 6, Postfach 3753, 3400 Goettingen, Germany. TEL 0551-6959-0. FAX 0551-695917.

KIRCHE UND RECHT. see LAW

KIRCHENMUSIKALISCHE NACHRICHTEN. see MUSIC

DER KIRCHENMUSIKER. see MUSIC

KIRCHLICHE ZEITGESCHICHTE; Internationale Halbjahresschrift fuer Theologie und Geschichtswissenschaft. see HISTORY — History Of Europe

200   GW   ISSN 0023-1827
KIRCHLICHES AMTSBLATT FUER DAS BISTUM ESSEN. 1958. s-m. DM.34. Bishchoefliches Generalvikariat Essen, Zwoelfling 16, Postfach 100464, 4300 Essen 1, Germany. index; circ. 2,200. (looseleaf format)

200   GW
KIRCHLICHES AMTSBLATT FUER DAS BISTUM TRIER. 1853. s-m. DM.30. Bischoefliches Generalvikariat Trier, Hinter dem Dom 6, Postfach 1340, 5500 Trier, Germany. TEL 0651-71050. FAX 0651-7105498. index; circ. 3,000. (back issues avail.)
Description: Provides official documentation of Diocesan regulations and laws.

058.82   NO   ISSN 0023-186X
AP45
KIRKE OG KULTUR. 1894. bi-m. NOK 47 to individuals; institutions $67. Universitetsforlaget, P.O. Box 2959 Toeyen, N-0608 Oslo 6, Norway. TEL 472-677600. FAX 472-677575. (In U.S., dist. by: Publications Expediting Inc., 200 Meacham Ave., Elmont, NY 11003) Ed. Inge Loenning. adv.; bk.rev.; index; circ. 2,500. (back issues avail.) **Indexed:** M.L.A.
Formerly: For Kirke og Kultur.

280.4   DK   ISSN 0107-9824
KIRKEFONDETS AARBOG. 1929. a. DKK 50. Kirkefondet, Pile Alle 3, 2000 Frederiksberg, Denmark. TEL 31-233-355. adv.; illus.; circ. 6,000.
Formerly: Koebenhavnske Kirkefondets Aarbog.

280.4   DK   ISSN 0900-1433
KIRKENS UNDERVISNING; tidskrift for medarbejdere. 1985. 4/yr. DKK 100. Evangelisk Paedagogisk Samvirke, Religionspedagogisk Center, Frederiksberg Alle 10a, DK-1820 Frederiksberg C, Denmark. TEL 31-249250. FAX 33-250607. Ed. Henning Noerhoej. adv.; bk.rev.
Formerly: Episkopet (ISSN 0105-6867)

KIZITO; children's own magazine. see CHILDREN AND YOUTH — For

KNANAYAMITHRAM; a Christian magazine for children. see CHILDREN AND YOUTH — For

209   DK   ISSN 0105-4821
KOEBENHAVNS UNIVERSITET. INSTITUT FOR RELIGIONSHISTORIE. SKRIFTER. 1976. irreg. Koebenhavns Universitet, Institut for Religionshistorie, Copenhagen, Denmark.

KORRESPONDENZBLATT EVANGELISCHER SCHULEN UND HEIME. see EDUCATION

200   DK   ISSN 0107-7902
KOSMOS. English edition (ISSN 0107-7929); German edition (ISSN 0107-7937); Swedish edition (ISSN 0107-7910) 1978. m. (Danish and Swedish eds.); 6/yr. (English and German eds.). DKK 265($16) Martinus Institut, Mariendalsvej 94, DK-2000 Frederiksberg, Denmark. TEL 45-38-34-62-80. Ed.Bd. bk.rev.; circ. 1,770 (900 Danish ed., 100 English ed., 70 German ed., 700 Swedish ed.). **Indexed:** Chem.Abstr.
Formerly: Contact with the Martinus Institute of Spiritual Science.
Description: Includes articles on spiritual science based on the work of the Danish writer, Martinus.

200   NE   ISSN 0023-4389
KRACHT VAN OMHOOG. 1937. 11/yr. fl.25. Postbus 84, 4200 AB Gorinchem, Netherlands. Ed. P. Bronsveld. bk.rev.; illus.; tr.lit.; circ. 2,500.

200
KRAFT FUER DEN TAG; evangelisches Sonntagsblatt. 1948. w. DM.22. Brunnen Verlag GmbH, Postfach 5205, 6300 Giessen 1, Germany. Ed. Ralf Tibusek.

200   CS   ISSN 0023-4613
KRESTANSKA REVUE. 1927-1939; resumed 1946. 10/yr. 50 Kcs.($20) (Akademicka Y M C A) Evangelicke Nakladatelstvi, Jungmannova 9, 110 00 Prague 1, Czechoslovakia. TEL 287-20-59. (Subscr. to: Oikumene, Akademicak YMCA, Na Porici 12, 115 30 Prague 1, Czechoslovakia) Ed. Jan Simsa. bk.rev.; circ. 1,800. **Indexed:** CERDIC

200   NE
KRUISTOCHT. m. Nationaal Kruisleger, Nieuwe Boteringestraat 73, 9712 PK Groningen, Netherlands. TEL 050-181520. bk.rev.; circ. 10,000.

200   II
KUNDALINI; a quarterly magazine of international spiritual & scientific progress. (Text in English) 1977. q. Rs.16($8) Kundalini Research and Publication Trust, D-291 Sarvodaya Enclave, New Delhi 110017, India. Ed. Anil Vidyalankar. adv.; bk.rev.; circ. 4,000. (back issues avail.) **Indexed:** Ind.India.
Formerly (until 1979): Spiritual India.

200   GW
DER KURIER (LIESBORN); der christlichen mitte. 1988. m. DM.25. Christliche Mitte, Lippstaedterstr. 42, 4724 Liesborn, Germany. TEL 02523-8388. Ed. Adelgunde Mertensacker. bk.rev.

266   KO
KUSEGONGBO. (Text in Korean) 1909. m. $1. Salvation Army, C.P.O. Box 1192, Seoul 100, S. Korea. Eds. Captain Han, Kwang-Soo. circ. 15,000. (newspaper)

289.6   UK   ISSN 0023-5814
KVAKERA ESPERANTISTO. (Text in Esperanto) 1950. 2/yr. £4. Kvakera Esperantista Societo, c/o Martin Howard, Webbs Cottage, Woolpits Road, Great Saling, Braintree, Essex CM7 5DZ, England. TEL 0371-850423. adv.; bk.rev.; circ. 400.

284.1   SW   ISSN 0280-4603
KYRKANS TIDNING. 1982. w. SEK 360 (typically set in Oct.). Svenska Kyrkans Press AB, P.O. Box 341, S-1 130 Sollentuna, Sweden. TEL 08-623 65 55. FAX 08-35-88-43. Ed. Ingvar Laxvik. adv.; illus.; circ. 61,000.

262.9   SW   ISSN 0023-6136
KYRKOFOERFATTNINGAR. 1957. 5/yr. SEK 240. Verbum Forlag AB, Box 151 69, S-104 65 Stockholm, Sweden. FAX 08-6414585. Ed. Ulla Granarp. charts; index; circ. 2,500 (controlled).
—BLDSC shelfmark: 5134.981000.

209   SW   ISSN 0085-2619
BR140
KYRKOHISTORISK AARSSKRIFT. (Text in English, Swedish; summaries in English, French, German) 1900. a. SEK 175. Svenska Kyrkohistoriska Foereningen, Box 1604, S-751 46, Sweden. FAX 46-18-12-68-75. Ed. Harry Lenhammar. adv.; bk.rev.; circ. 1,000. **Indexed:** Amer.Hist.& Life, Hist.Abstr., NAA.
—BLDSC shelfmark: 5134.982000.

KYRKOMUSIKERNAS TIDNING. see MUSIC

200   IT
LABRYS. (Text in Italian; summaries in English) 1980. a. L.15000($18) Istituto di Studi Tradizionali, Via Roscetto 22, 06100 Perugia PG, Italy. Ed. Marco Pucciarini. adv.; bk.rev.

266   SW   ISSN 0345-7842
LAERARNAS MISSIONSFOERENING. MEDDELANDE TILL L M F. (Text in Danish, Norwegian, and Swedish) 1902. bi-m. SEK 60. Laerarnas Missionsfoerening, Vasaplatsen 4, 411 34 Goeteborg, Sweden. Ed. Margareta Burgen. bk.rev.; illus.; circ. 2,600.
Formerly: Laerarinnornas Missionsfoerening. Meddelande till L M F. (ISSN 0023-6322)

200   PH   ISSN 0116-4856
LANDAS; journal of Loyola School of Theology. (Text in English) 1987. s-a. P.150($18) (effective 1991). Loyola School of Theology, Loyola Institute for Studies on Development of Man and Society, Ateneo de Manila University, P.O. Box 4082, Manila, Philippines. TEL 632-99-15-61. FAX 632-921-7311. Ed. Antonio B. Lambino. bk.rev.; circ. 500.
Description: Features articles on scripture, theology, ethics and spirituality written from the perspective of authors, most of them Filipinos, working and teaching in the Philippines.

LANDMARK STUDIES. see ARCHAEOLOGY

RELIGIONS AND THEOLOGY   4187

200   VC
LATERANUM. 1976. 2/yr. $45. Pontificia Universita Lateranense, Piazza S. Giovanni in Laterano 4, 00120 Vatican City, State of the Vatican City. Ed. Marcello Bordoni. bk.rev. **Indexed:** CERDIC, Old Test.Abstr.

200 301   PE
LATINAMERICA PRESS. Spanish edition: Noticias Aliadas. (Text in English) 1969. w. (48 nos./yr.). $49.95. Noticias Aliadas, Apdo. 5594, Lima 100, Peru. Ed.Bd. bk.rev.; index. cum.index; circ. 2,500. **Indexed:** I.C.U.I.S.Abstr.

200 100   CN   ISSN 0023-9054
BX802
LAVAL THEOLOGIQUE ET PHILOSOPHIQUE. (Text in English and French) 1945. 3/yr. Can.$24 to individuals; institutions Can.$30. Presses de l'Universite Laval, Cite universitaire, Quebec, Que. G1K 7P4, Canada. TEL 418-656-3809. FAX 418-656-2600. Ed. Rene-Michel Roberge. bk.rev.; bibl.; index. cum.index; circ. 1,000. **Indexed:** Arts & Hum.Cit.Ind., Cath.Ind., CERDIC, Curr.Cont., New Test.Abstr., Old Test.Abstr., Phil.Ind., Pt.de Rep. (1983-), Rel.& Theol.Abstr. (1987-).
—BLDSC shelfmark: 5160.825000.

LAW & JUSTICE. see LAW

200   US   ISSN 1041-4460
LEADER (ANDERSON); a resource for Christian leadership. 1939. bi-m. $7. Church of God, Board of Christian Education, 1303 E. Fifth St., Box 2458, Anderson, IN 46018-2458. TEL 317-642-0257. Ed. Joseph L. Cookston. circ. 4,000.
Formerly: Christian Leadership.

266   UG   ISSN 0047-424X
LEADERSHIP; a magazine for Christian leaders in Africa. 1956. m. Sh.250($35) (typically set in Jan.). (Comboni Missionaries) Leadership Publications, Box 2522, Kampala, Uganda. TEL 221-001. FAX 221576. TELEX 61360. Ed. Rev. John M. Troy. bk.rev.; illus.; stat.; circ. 15,000. **Indexed:** Rel.& Theol.Abstr. (1980-).
Description: Examines social, moral and religious issues for the purposes of forming and informing Christian youth and adults.

377.8   UK
LEARNING TOGETHER WITH 5-7'S. q. £2.25. Scripture Union, 130 City Rd., London EC1V 2NJ, England. adv.; illus.; circ. 28,000.
Former titles: Teaching 5-7's; Teaching Primaries (ISSN 0040-0653)

377.8   UK
LEARNING TOGETHER WITH 7-11'S. q. £2.25. Scripture Union, 130 City Rd., London EC1V 2NJ, England. adv.; illus.; circ. 34,000.
Former titles: Teaching 7-10's; Teaching Juniors (ISSN 0040-0629)

377.8   UK   ISSN 0308-356X
LEARNING TOGETHER WITH 11-14'S. q. £2.25. Scripture Union, 130 City Rd., London EC1V 2NJ, England. Ed. Angela Flynn. adv.; illus.; circ. 19,000.
Former titles: Teaching 10-13's; Teaching Teenagers (ISSN 0040-067X)

200   SZ
LEBEN; monatszeitschrift der Fokolar-Bewegung in der Schweiz. (Text in German) 1974. m. 20 Fr. (Fokolar-Bewegung) Verlag Neue Stadt, Seestrasse 426, Postfach 435, Ch-8038 Zurich, Switzerland. FAX 01-4826017. circ. 2,600. (back issues avail.)

200   GW
LEBENDIGE SEELSORGE UND LEBENDIGE KATCHESE. 1949. bi-m. DM.51 (students DM.40). Echter Wuerzburg Verlag GmbH, Juliuspromenade 64, 8700 Wuerzburg 1, Germany. Eds. Lothar Roos, Werner Ruck. adv.; bk.rev.; circ. 8,000.

209   US   ISSN 0075-8531
LECTURES ON THE HISTORY OF RELIGIONS. NEW SERIES. no.9, 1971. irreg., no.11, 1977. Columbia University Press, 562 W. 113th St., New York, NY 10025. TEL 212-678-6777.

200   NE   ISSN 0024-0427
LEGIOEN VAN MARIA. 1945. q. fl.6. Senaat van Het Legioen van Maria in Nederland, Pb. 77, 5000 AB Tilburg, Netherlands. illus.

RELIGIONS AND THEOLOGY

200   TZ   ISSN 0039-9655
LENGO/TARGET. (Text in Swahili) 1968. fortn. Sh.960 (Europe Sh.3720; America Sh.4320). East African Venture (Tanzania), PO Box 9290, Dar es Salaam, Tanzania. TEL 25825. Ed. Nancy Mrwendamseke. adv.; bk.rev.; charts; illus.; circ. 30,000. (newspaper)

266.025   UK   ISSN 0075-8809
LEPROSY MISSION, LONDON. ANNUAL REPORT. 1874. a. free. Leprosy Mission, 80 Windmill Road, Brentford, Middlesex TW8 0QH, England. TEL 081-569-7292. FAX 081-569-7808. TELEX 9312133925 LM G. Ed. Donna Bowers. circ. 13,000.
    Formerly: Mission to Lepers, London. Annual Report.

200   LO
LESELINYANA LA LESOTHO. (Text in Sesotho; articles occasionally in English) 1863. fortn. Lesotho Evangelical Church, P.O. Box 7, Morija 190, Lesotho. Ed. Molefi Pitso. circ. 15,000.

200   US
LETTER FROM PLYMOUTH ROCK. 1980. m. $25. Plymouth Rock Foundation, 26 McKinley Circle, Box 425, Marlborough, NH 03455. TEL 603-876-4685. FAX 603-876-4128. Ed. Rus Walton. bk.rev.; charts; illus.; stat.; circ. 15,000. (looseleaf format; back issues avail.)
    Description: Looks at life from a biblical perspective.

266   FR   ISSN 0024-1490
LEVANT MORGENLAND. (Text in French and German) 1923. bi-m. 5 F. Action Chretienne en Orient, 7 rue du General-Offenstein, Strasbourg, France. Ed. Pasteur R. Brecheisen. illus.; circ. 12,500.

207.11   US   ISSN 0160-8770
LEXINGTON THEOLOGICAL QUARTERLY. 1964. q. free to qualified personnel or on exchange basis. Lexington Theological Seminary, 631 S. Limestone St., Lexington, KY 40508. TEL 312-434-0706. Ed. Anthony L. Dunnavant. bk.rev.; circ. 2,300. **Indexed:** CERDIC, New Test.Abstr., Old Test.Abstr., Rel.& Theol.Abstr. (1968-), Rel.Ind.One.
    Formerly: College of the Bible Quarterly (ISSN 0024-1628)

261   US   ISSN 0024-2055
BX6101
LIBERTY (HAGERSTOWN); a magazine of religious freedom. 1888. bi-m. $6.95. (International Religious Liberty Association) Review and Herald Publishing Association, 55 W. Oak Ridge Dr., Hagerstown, MD 21740. TEL 301-791-7000. Ed. Roland R. Hegstad. adv.; bk.rev.; illus.; index. cum.index; circ. 240,000. (also avail. in microform from UMI; reprint service avail. from UMI) **Indexed:** CCR.

LIBRARY LINES. see *LIBRARY AND INFORMATION SCIENCES*

200   US
LIBRARY OF RELIGIOUS PHILOSOPHY. 1989. irreg., vol.9, 1992. price varies. University of Notre Dame Press, Notre Dame, IN 46556. TEL 219-239-6346. FAX 219-239-8148. Ed. Thomas V. Morris.

200   SY
LE LIEN; revue du patriarcat Grec-Melkite Catholique. 1936. bi-m. £S200($25) St. Paul Press, P.O.B. 22249, Damascus, Syria. TEL 433129. TELEX 419413 SY CHAOUI. Ed. Patriarch Maximos Hakim, V. adv.; bk.rev.; illus.; circ. 2,500. (back issues avail.)
    Description: Covers news of the Patriarchate, ecumenism, liturgy, and other religious topics.

200   US
LIFEGLOW. 1983. bi-m. free to qualified personnel. Christian Record Services, 4444 South 52nd St., Lincoln, NE 68516. TEL 402-488-0981. Ed. Richard Kaiser. circ. 23,400. (also avail. in Braille; large print edition in 22 pt.)
    Description: Inspirational, devotional articles and stories for adults, especially senior citizens.

200   UK   ISSN 0047-4657
LIGHT (LONDON, 1969); on a new world. (Editions in English, French and Tolugo) 1967. bi-m. free. (Bexley Christadelphians Ecclesia) Light Bible Publications, 3 Dickens Close, Hartley, Dartford, Kent DA3 8DP, England. Ed. D.J. Evans. circ. 5,000. (also avail. in microform)

LIGHT BEARER. see *PARAPSYCHOLOGY AND OCCULTISM*

200 100   US   ISSN 1040-7448
BP605.T78
LIGHT OF CONSCIOUSNESS. 1977. 3/yr. $7. Truth Consciousness at Sacred Mountain Ashram, 10668 Gold Hill Rd., Boulder, CO 80302-9716. TEL 303-447-1637. Ed. Robert W. Conrow. circ. 800. (back issues avail.)
    Formerly (until vol.11, no.1, 1988): Truth Consciousness Journal (ISSN 0191-5207)

268   II   ISSN 0970-2571
LIGHT OF LIFE; all India magazine of Christian growth. (Text in English) 1957. m. $15. Christian Digest Society of India, 21 YMCA Rd., Bombay 400 008, India. Ed. P. Abraham. adv.; bk.rev.; illus.; circ. 5,000.

LINGUISTICA BIBLICA; Interdisziplinaere Zeitschrift fuer Theologie, Semiotik und Linguistik. see *LINGUISTICS*

200 800   US   ISSN 0732-1929
PN49
LITERATURE AND BELIEF. 1981. a. $5 (foreign $7). Brigham Young University, College of Humanities, Center for the Study of Christian Values in Literature, Jesse Knight Bldg., Provo, UT 84602. TEL 801-378-3073. FAX 801-378-4649. Ed. Jay Fox. bk.rev.; circ. 1,000. (also avail. in microfiche) **Indexed:** Abstr.Engl.Stud., LCR, M.L.A.
    —BLDSC shelfmark: 5276.712750.
    Description: Focuses on the moral-religious aspects of literature through scholarly critical articles, bibliographical articles, interviews, personal essays, and poetry.

LITERATURE AND THEOLOGY. see *LITERATURE*

200   IT
LITTERAE COMMUNIONIS. 1975. m. L.25000 (foreign L.60000). (Gruppi di Comunione e Liberazione) Cooperativa Editoriale Nuovo Mondo, Via Mose Bianchi 94, 20149 Milan, Italy. TEL 02-66987825. Ed. Pigi Colognesi. adv.; bk.rev.
    Formerly: Comunione e Liberazione.

200   US   ISSN 0460-1297
BL624
LITTLE LAMP; a journal for leading the spiritual life through the practice of meditation. 1967. bi-m. $18. (Blue Mountain Center of Meditation) Nilgiri Press, Box 256, Tomales, CA 94971. FAX 707-878-2375. Ed. Christine Easwaran. circ. 2,000. (back issues avail.)

200   GW   ISSN 0344-9092
LITURGIE KONKRET. 1978. m. DM.49.80. Verlag Friedrich Pustet, Gutenbergstr. 8, 8400 Regensburg 11, Germany. FAX 0941-948652. Ed.Bd.

200   GW   ISSN 0076-0048
LITURGIEWISSENSCHAFTLICHE QUELLEN UND FORSCHUNGEN. 1919. irreg. price varies. Aschendorffsche Verlagsbuchhandlung, Soesterstr. 13, 4400 Muenster, Germany. TEL 0251-690-0. FAX 0251-690405. Ed. W. Heckenbach.

264   GW   ISSN 0024-5100
LITURGISCHES JAHRBUCH. 1951. 4/yr. DM.63. (Deutsches Liturgisches Institut Trier) Aschendorffsche Verlagsbuchhandlung, Soesterstr. 13, 4400 Muenster, Germany. TEL 0251-690-0. FAX 0251-690405. Ed. Andreas Heinz. adv.; bk.rev.; index. **Indexed:** Rel.& Theol.Abstr. (1989-), Rel.Ind.One.

200   US   ISSN 0458-063X
BV169
LITURGY. 1955; N.S. 1980. q. $42. Liturgical Conference, 1017 12th St., N.W., Washington, DC 20005-4091. TEL 202-898-0885. adv.; bk.rev.; bibl. (back issues avail.) **Indexed:** Cath.Ind., CERDIC, Rel.& Theol.Abstr. (1980-).
    —BLDSC shelfmark: 5278.900000.
    Description: Focuses on the renewal of life and worship in the Christian churches.

264   UK   ISSN 0309-4308
LITURGY. 1976. 6/yr. £6. Bishops' Conference of England and Wales, Liturgy Office, 39 Eccleston Square, London SW1V 1PL, England. TEL 01-821-0553.
    Description: For priests and parish liturgy committees.

200   US   ISSN 0190-3845
LIVE (SPRINGFIELD); to live is Christ. 1928. w. $5.20. Gospel Publishing House, 1445 Boonville Ave., Springfield, MO 65802-1894. TEL 417-862-2781. circ. 160,000.

200   US   ISSN 0193-5968
BX809.F6
LIVING CITY. 1967. m. $15. Focolare Movement, Inc., Women's Branch, 99-28 64th Rd., Rego Park, NY 11374. TEL 212-904-1898. FAX 212-892-0419. (Subscr. to: Box 837, Bronx, NY 10465) Ed. Sharry Silvi. circ. 8,000. (back issues avail.)
    Description: News of a world striving for unity.

294.54
THE LIVING LIGHT PHILOSOPHY. 1968. q. $5. Serenity Spiritualist Association, 322 Upper Rd., San Rafael, CA 94903. TEL 415-472-3633. Ed. Ronald C. Cavender. circ. 300.
    Formerly (until vol.1 no.1): Serenity Sentinel.

200   US   ISSN 0890-5568
LIVING PRAYER. 1967. bi-m. $17 (foreign $22). Living Prayers, Inc., Beckley Hill, Barre, VT 05641. Ed. Sr. Mary Roman. bk.rev.; circ. 7,000. (also avail. in microform from UMI) **Indexed:** Cath.Ind.
    Formerly (until Sep.1986): Contemplative Review (ISSN 0193-8452)

200   UK   ISSN 0951-8347
LIVING STONES. 1987. 2/yr. £5. 7 Tufton St., Westminster, London SW1P 1QN, England. TEL 01-222-6952. bk.rev.
    Description: Includes material on catechism and theology.

LIVING STREAMS; the Christian writers journal. see *LITERATURE*

200   UK   ISSN 0024-5445
LLAN. (Text in Welsh) s-m. £11.50. Church in Wales Publications, Woodland Place, Penarth, South Glam CF6 2EX, Wales. Ed. Rev. Gwyn Ap Gwilym. adv.; bk.rev.; circ. 1,000.

LONERGAN STUDIES NEWSLETTER. see *PHILOSOPHY*

200   US   ISSN 0148-2009
BX4705.L7133
LONERGAN WORKSHOP. s-a. $18. Scholars Press, Box 15399, Atlanta, GA 30333-0399. TEL 404-636-4757. FAX 404-636-8301. Ed. Fred Lawrence.
    —BLDSC shelfmark: 5294.198000.
    Description: Academic papers on topics relating to the life and work of Lonergan.

200   US   ISSN 0024-6425
LOOKOUT (NEW YORK). 1909. 2/yr. $5. Seamen's Church Institute of New York and New Jersey, 241 Water St., New York, NY 10038. TEL 212-349-9090. FAX 212-349-8342. Ed. Carlyle Windley. bk.rev.; illus.; circ. 6,000.

200   GW
LOSUNGEN. a. DM.5.90. Quell Verlag, Furtbachstr. 12A, Postfach 103852, 7000 Stuttgart 10, Germany. TEL 0711-60100-0.

200 040   BE   ISSN 0024-6964
BX801
LOUVAIN STUDIES. 1966. q. 950 Fr.($24) Katholieke Universiteit Leuven, Faculty of Theology, St.Michielsstraat 2, B-3000 Leuven, Belgium. TEL 016-28-38-94. FAX 016-28-38-58. Ed. Raymond F. Collins. bk.rev.; index; circ. 1,500. (also avail. in microform from UMI; back issues avail) **Indexed:** Canon Law Abstr., Cath.Ind., CERDIC, New Test.Abstr., Old Test.Abstr., Rel.& Theol.Abstr. (1979-).
    —BLDSC shelfmark: 5296.360000.

200   US
LUIS PALAU LETTER. 1964. m. Luis Palau Evangelistic Association, Box 1173, Portland, OR 97207. TEL 503-643-0777. FAX 503-643-6851. Ed. Steve Hanberg.
    Description: Shares ministry vision and results with supporters.

200   FR   ISSN 0024-7332
LUMIERE. 1953. q. 100 F.($12) Agence Mondiale d'Information, 3 rue Geoffrey St. Hilaire, 75005 Paris, France. bk.rev. **Indexed:** Old Test.Abstr.

RELIGIONS AND THEOLOGY 4189

220 264 FR ISSN 0024-7359
LUMIERE ET VIE; revue de formation et de reflexion theologiques. 1951. 5/yr. 195 F. (foreign 225 F.)(effective 1992). Association Lumiere et Vie, 2 place Gailleton, 69002 Lyon, France. TEL 78-42-66-83. Ed. Antoine Lion. adv.; bk.rev.; index; circ. 5,000. **Indexed:** Cath.Ind., CERDIC, New Test.Abstr.
—BLDSC shelfmark: 5304.770000.

266 US
M A R C NEWSLETTER. q. free. (Missions Advanced Research & Communication Center) M A R C (Subsidiary of: World Vision International), 919 W. Huntington Dr., Monrovia, CA 91016. TEL 818-303-8811. FAX 813-301-7786. **Indexed:** CERDIC.
Description: News and articles on strategic planning for world evangelization by Christian mission agencies.

200 US ISSN 1049-152X
M A R GOSPEL MINISTRIES. 1989. s-a. $3. (Middle Atlantic Regional) M A R Press, 100 Bryant St., N.W., Washington, DC 20001. TEL 202-265-7609.
Description: Covers African American church history.

200 US ISSN 0362-0808
M S S.* (Master Sermon Series) 1970. m. $25. Cathedral Publishers, Box 129, Royal Oak, MI 48068-0129. Ed. Carl G. Howie. (looseleaf format)

230 CN ISSN 0849-0899
MCMASTER JOURNAL OF THEOLOGY. (Text in English, French) 1979. 2/yr. Can.$10. McMaster Divinity College, Hamilton, Ont. L8S 4K1, Canada. TEL 416-525-9140. FAX 416-577-4782. Ed. John Rook. bk.rev.; circ. 1,000. **Indexed:** CERDIC, Rel.& Theol.Abstr. (1990-).
Former titles: Theodolite (ISSN 0225-7270) & McMaster Theological Bulletin.
Description: Seeks to provide pastors, educators and interested laypersons with the fruits of theological, biblical and professional studies in a readable form.

200 IT ISSN 0024-9599
MADONNA DI CASTELMONTE. 1913. m. L.13000($20) (foreign L.22000). Frati Minori Cappuccini Veneti, 33040 Castelmonte (UD), Italy. TEL 32-731094. Ed. Aurelio Blasotti. illus.; circ. 60,000.

266 028.5 US
MAGAZINE FOR CHRISTIAN YOUTH!. m. $18 (Canada $20). United Methodist Publishing House, 201 Eighth Ave., S., Box 801, Nashville, TN 37202. TEL 615-749-6463. FAX 615-749-6079. adv.
Description: Religious magazine for teenagers.

MAGYAR EGYHAZTORTENETI VAZLATOK/ESSAYS IN CHURCH HISTORY IN HUNGARY. see HISTORY — History Of Europe

200 FR ISSN 0025-0937
MAISON - DIEU; revue specialisee de liturgique. 1945. 4/yr. 223 F. (foreign 275 F.). (Centre National de Pastorale Liturgique) Editions du Cerf, 29 bd. Latour Maubourg, 75340 Paris Cedex 07, France. TEL 45-50-34-07. FAX 45-56-04-27. (Subscr. to: Service Abonnements, 3 chemin des Prunais, 94350 Villiers-sur-Marne, France) Ed. Pierre-Marie Gy. adv.; bk.rev.; index; circ. 2,600. **Indexed:** CERDIC, New Test.Abstr.

266 CN ISSN 0225-7068
MANDATE. 1969. 6/yr. Can.$6.50. United Church of Canada, 85 St. Clair Ave. E., Toronto, Ont. M4T 1M8, Canada. TEL 416-925-5931. FAX 416-925-9692. Ed. Rebekah Chevalier. circ. 36,000.
Description: Covers mission and justice work in Canada and overseas.

266 CN ISSN 0225-7068
MANDATE "SPECIAL". 1977. a. Can.$1.95 per no. United Church of Canada, 85 St. Clair Ave. E., Toronto, Ont. M4T 1M8, Canada. TEL 416-925-5931. FAX 416-925-9692. Ed. Rebekah Chevalier. charts; illus.; circ. 39,000. (back issues avail.)
Formerly: Mission Magazine (ISSN 0706-5590)
Description: Focus is annual United Church mission study theme.

200 JM
MANNA. q. Jam.$70. University and Colleges Christian Fellowship, 22 Hagley Park Plaza, Box 281, Kingston 10, Jamaica, W.I. circ. 2,000.

200 SP
MANRESA; revista de investigacion e informacion ascetica y mistica. 1925. q. 1800 ptas.($22) (Loyola, Centro de Espiritualidad) Casa de Escritores S.J. (C E S I), Pablo Aranda 3, 28006 Madrid, Spain. adv.; bk.rev.; circ. 1,000. **Indexed:** Amer.Hist.& Life, CERDIC, Hist.Abstr., New Test.Abstr.

200 AU ISSN 0025-2999
MARIAHILFER PFARRBOTE. 1924. q. contribution. Pfarramt Mariahilf, Barnabitengasse 14, 1060 Vienna, Austria. Ed. Waldemar Posch. bk.rev.; abstr.; charts; illus.; stat.; index; circ. 3,000.

266 232 AU ISSN 0025-3022
MARIANNHILL. bi-m. S.30. Missionare von Mariannhill, Riedegg 1, A-4210 Gallneukirchen, Austria. Eds. Br. Franziskus Puehringer, P.A. Balling. bk.rev.; circ. 45,000. (tabloid format)

282 US
MARKINGS. 1971. 11/yr. $36.95. Thomas More Association, 205 W. Monroe St., 6th Fl., Chicago, IL 60606. TEL 312-609-8880.
Description: Homily service for priests.

200 US ISSN 1052-181X
MARTIN LUTHER KING, JR. MEMORIAL STUDIES IN RELIGION, CULTURE AND SOCIAL DEVELOPMENT. irreg. Peter Lang Publishing, Inc., 62 W. 45th St., 4th Fl., New York, NY 10036. TEL 212-302-6740. FAX 212-302-7574. Ed. Mozella G. Mitchell.
Description: Promotes scholarly research and writing in areas that reflect the interrelatedness of religion and social-cultural-political development both in the American society and in the world.

260 II ISSN 0376-6608
PK2030
MASIHI AVAZA. (Text in Hindi) vol.45, 1972. m. Rs.5. 277 Angrahpuri, Gaya, Bihar, India. bibl.; illus.

266 UK
MASTER AND THE MULTITUDE. 1853. q. £1. Open-Air Mission, 19 John St., London WC1N 2DL, England. Ed. Alan J. Greenbank. illus.; circ. 5,000.
Description: Mission work in the British Isles.

200 US
MASTER THOUGHTS. 1972. q. $15. (Invisible Ministry) Dominion Press, Box 4608, Salem, OR 97302-8608. TEL 503-362-9634. Ed. Friend Stuart. circ. 100. (looseleaf format; also avail. in microfilm; back issues avail.)
Description: Analysis and interpretations of words of Jesus Christ from King James Version.

200 GW ISSN 0721-2402
MATERIALDIENST. 1937. m. DM.48. (Evangelische Zentralstelle fuer Weltanschauungsfragen) Quell Verlag, Furtbachstr. 12A, 7000 Stuttgart 10, Germany. TEL 0711-60100-0. circ. 5,000.

200 GW
MATHILDE-ZIMMER-STIFTUNG. BLAETTER. 1906. bi-m. DM.11. (Mathilde-Zimmer-Stiftung e.V) Christlicher Zeitschriftenverlag, Bachstr. 1-2, 1000 Berlin 21, Germany. Ed. E. Zimmer. adv.; bk.rev.; circ. 2,000.

MEDIA & VALUES; a quarterly magazine - educational resource analyzing the social impact of mass media and new technologies on the family, youth and children. see COMMUNICATIONS

MEDIA DEVELOPMENT. see COMMUNICATIONS — Television And Cable

266 610 UK ISSN 0025-7370
MEDICAL MISSIONARY NEWS. 1946. q. £2. Medical Mission Sisters, 3 Blakesley Ave., Ealing, London WC5 2DN, England. Ed. Kathleen Brown. illus.; circ. 1,000.
Description: Mission work, mainly in the Third World.

200 901 US ISSN 1056-7917
MEDIEVAL AND EARLY MODERN MYSTICISM. irreg. price varies. Peter Lang Publishing, Inc., 62 W. 45th St., 4th Fl., New York, NY 10036. TEL 212-302-6740. Ed. Teresa Howe.
Description: Covers studies of Christian, Jewish, and Islamic mystical figures and their works from the 9th to the 17th centuries.

200 GW
MEDITATION; Anstoesse fuer den Christlichen Vollzug. 1975. q. DM.24. Verlag Christianopolis, Hechenbergstr. 13, 8120 Weilheim, Germany. Ed. Wolf von Fritsch. bk.rev.; bibl.; illus.; index. (back issues avail.)

200 US
MEGIDDO MESSAGE. 1914. m. $5. Megiddo Church, 481 Thurston Rd., Rochester, NY 14619-1697. TEL 716-436-1614. FAX 716-436-3627. Ed. Newton H. Payne. index. cum.index: 1915-1989; circ. 15,000. (also avail. in looseleaf format; reprint service avail. from UMI)

200 GW
MEHR FREUDE MAGAZIN. 1979. q. DM.8. Jugend fuer Christus Deutschland e.V., Postfach 1180, 6109 Muehtal, Germany. TEL 06151-145194. FAX 06151-144399. Ed. Bernd Schweinfurth. adv.; bk.rev.; circ. 24,500.

200 PP ISSN 0256-856X
MELANESIAN JOURNAL OF THEOLOGY. (Text in English) 1985. s-a. K.5($7.50) Melanesian Association of Theological Schools, c/o Martin Luther Seminary, P.O. Box 80, Lae, Papua New Guinea. TELEX 422699. Ed. Christopher Garland. adv.; bk.rev.; circ. 600. (back issues avail.) **Indexed:** Rel.& Theol.Abstr. (1990-).

200 212.5 MM
MELITA THEOLOGICA. (Text in English, French, Italian) 1947. 2/yr. $20. Theology Students' Association, University of Malta, Msida, Malta. TEL 333903. (Co-sponsor: University of Malta, Faculty of Theology) Ed. Rev. Anthony Abela. adv.; bk.rev.; index; circ. 600. **Indexed:** New Test.Abstr., Old Test. Abstr., Rel.& Theol.Abstr. (1968-).
Description: Contains articles in dogmatic and moral theology, fundamental theology, holy scripture, canon law, spiritual theology, liturgy, patrology, ecclesiastical history, christian archeology, philosophy and sociology.

MEMORIE DOMENICANE. see HISTORY

200 DK
MENIGHEDSRAADENES BLAD.* m. (11/yr.). Foreningen af Menighedsraadsmedlemmer, Vesterbro Torv 1-3, DK-8000 Aarhus C, Denmark. Ed. Joergen Ginnerup. adv.; circ. 22,000.

200 SP ISSN 0211-6561
MENSAJERO; del corazon de Jesus. 1866. m. 2350 ptas.($32) (effective Jan. 1992). Ediciones Mensajero S.A., Sancho de Azpeitia, 2, Apdo. 73, 48080 Bilbao, Spain. TEL 94-447-0358. FAX 94-447-2630. Ed. Angel Perez Gomez. adv.; bk.rev.; illus.; circ. 30,000. (back issues avail.)
Description: Covers religious and family subjects. Includes some political, social and cultural issues.

200 AU ISSN 0026-0126
MERLEG; folyoiratok es konyvek szemleje. (Text in Hungarian; summaries in English and German) 1965. q. S.346 (foreign S.386). Pastorale Ungarnhilfe der Oesterreichischen Bischofskonferenz, Boltzmanngasse 14, A-1090 Vienna, Austria. FAX 089-8643573. (Or: Distelfinkweg 21, D-8000 Munich 60) Ed. Janos Boor. adv.; bk.rev.; abstr.; bibl.; index; circ. 5,000. **Indexed:** Old Test.Abstr.
—BLDSC shelfmark: 5682.261500.

MERTON ANNUAL: STUDIES IN THOMAS MERTON, RELIGION, CULTURE, LITERATURE, AND SOCIAL CONCERNS. see LITERATURE

RELIGIONS AND THEOLOGY

THE MERTON SEASONAL: A QUARTERLY REVIEW. 1976. q. $8 (effective Apr.). Thomas Merton Center, Bellarmine College, Newburg Rd., Louisville, KY 40205-0671. TEL 502-452-8187. (Co-sponsor: International Thomas Merton Society) Ed. Robert E. Daggy. bk.rev.; bibl.; illus.; circ. 1,846. (looseleaf format; back issues avail.)
200 800 US ISSN 0899-4927
Formerly: Merton Seasonal.
Description: Studies in Thomas Merton, religion, culture, literature and social concerns.

MESSAGE (HAGERSTOWN). 1934. bi-m. $11.95. Review and Herald Publishing Association, 55 W. Oak Ridge Dr., Hagerstown, MD 21740. TEL 301-791-7000. Ed. Delbert W. Baker. bk.rev.; illus.; record rev.; index; circ. 68,000. **Indexed:** CCR.
200 US ISSN 0026-0231 BX6101
Formerly: Message Magazine (ISSN 0162-6019)

MESSAGE OF THE CROSS. 1950. q. free. Bethany Fellowship Inc., 6820 Auto Club Rd., Minneapolis, MN 55438. TEL 612-829-2543. FAX 612-829-2753. Ed. David P. Renich. adv.; bk.rev.
200 US ISSN 0746-0635
Description: Communication vehicle for college and church community.

MESSAGE OF THE OPEN BIBLE. 1920. m. (10/yr.). $6. Open Bible Standard Churches, Open Bible Publishers, 2020 Bell Ave., Des Moines, IA 50315-1096. TEL 515-288-6761. FAX 515-288-2510. Ed. Delores A. Winegar. circ. 4,550.
220 US ISSN 0889-4159

MESSAGGERO CAPPUCCINO. 1957. bi-m. L.12000($20) Messaggero Cappuccino, Via Villa Clelia 10, 40026 Imola, Italy. TEL 0542 40265. FAX 0542-40265. Ed. Venanzio Reali. bk.rev. (back issues avail.)
200 IT

MESSENGER (KANSAS CITY)/MESSAGGERO. (Text in English, Italian) 1921. m. $1. Messenger Publishing Co. (Kansas City), Box 30300h, Kansas City, MO 64112-3300. Ed. Dr. J.B. Bisceglia. adv.; bk.rev.; bibl.; illus.; circ. 1,000. (tabloid format; also avail. in microform)
200 US ISSN 0026-0363

▼**MESSENGER (REDDING).** a forum for truth. 1991. 6/yr. $36. Box 492333, Redding, CA 96049. TEL 916-221-0770. Ed. Pat Maldonado.
200 US
Description: Presents spiritual viewpoint for values in the 90's.

METHOD: JOURNAL OF LONERGAN STUDIES. see *PHILOSOPHY*

MICHAEL; for the triumph of the Immaculate. 1955. 6/yr. Can.$10 for 2 yrs. (Institut d'Action Politique Pelerins de Saint Michel) Louis Even Institute, 1101 Principale St., Rougemont, Que JOL 1M0, Canada. TEL 514-469-2209. Ed. Gilberte Cote-Mercier. circ. 35,000.
200 CN
Description: Promotes the application of the teachings of the Roman Catholic Church in every aspect of social life, especially in economics with the social credit philosophy of Scottish engineer, Clifford Hugh Douglas.

MIGRANTI-PRESS. see *POLITICAL SCIENCE*

MILITARY CHAPLAIN. see *MILITARY*

MILITARY CHAPLAINS' REVIEW. see *MILITARY*

MILLTOWN STUDIES. 1977. s-a. £9.50. Milltown Institute of Theology & Philosophy, Milltown Park, Dublin 6, Ireland. TEL 269-7257. Ed. Gervase Corcoran. adv.; bk.rev.; circ. 200. **Indexed:** New Test.Abstr., Old Test.Abstr.
200 100 IE ISSN 0332-1428 BR1
—BLDSC shelfmark: 5774.350000.

MINDANAO JOURNAL. (Text in English) 1974. irreg. (2-4/yr.). $6. Mindanao State University, University Research Center, P.O. Box 5594, Iligan City 9200, Philippines. Ed. Raymond Llorca. circ. 500. **Indexed:** Ind.Phil.Per.
500 PH ISSN 0115-2742 DS688.S9
Description: Covers the Muslim peoples of Mindanao and Muslim-Christian relations in the country.

MINDOLO WORLD. 1961. 2/yr. K.20($5) Mindolo Ecumenical Foundation, P.O. Box 21493, Kitwe, Zambia. Ed. Isaac Phiri. adv.; circ. 1,000.
267 270 ZA
Formerly: Mindolo News Letter (ISSN 0076-8901)

MINISTERIAL FORMATION. (Text in English) q. $10. World Council of Churches, Programme on Ecumenical Theological Education, 150 Route de Ferney, Box 2100, CH-1211 Geneva 2, Switzerland. TEL 022-791-6111. FAX 022-791-0361. TELEX 415730-OIK-CH. **Indexed:** Rel.Ind.One.
200 SZ

MINISTER'S MANUAL (YEAR); preaching and worship planning. a. $19.90. Church Management, Inc., Box 162427, Austin, TX 78716. Ed. Manfred Holck.
200 US ISSN 0894-3966

MINISTRIES TODAY; the magazine for Christian leaders. 1983. bi-m. $29.95. Strang Communications Co., 600 Rinehart Rd., Lake Mary, FL 32746. TEL 407-333-0600. Ed. Jamie Buckingham. circ. 30,000. **Indexed:** CCR.
200 US ISSN 0891-5725
Formerly: Ministries.

MISCELANEA COMILLAS; revista de teologia y ciencias humanas. 1943. s-a. $40. Universidad Pontificia Comillas de Madrid, Facultades de Filosofia y Letras y Teologia, E-28049 Madrid, Spain. FAX 341-7344570. Ed. Jose Joaquin Alemany. adv.; bk.rev.; circ. 400. **Indexed:** Amer.Hist.& Life, CERDIC, Hist.Abstr., New Test.Abstr.
200 100 370.1 150 SP ISSN 0210-9522 BX880

MISIONEROS JAVERIANOS. 1963. m. free. Monserrat. 9, Madrid-8, Spain. illus.; circ. 48,000. (tabloid format)
266 SP

MISSI; magazine d'information spirituelle et de solidarite internationale. 1935. 10/yr. 160 F.($32) (foreign 175 F.). 6 rue d'Auvergne, 69287 Lyon Cedex 2, France. TEL 78-37-86-30. Ed. Pierre Gerard. bk.rev.; index; circ. 15,000. **Indexed:** CERDIC.
200 FR ISSN 0026-5977

MISSIOLOGY; an international review. see *ANTHROPOLOGY*

MISSION; Nordisk missions tidsskrift. 1889. q. $25 (foreign $47). Dansk Missionraad - Danish Missionary Council, Skt. Lukas Vej 13, 2900 Hellerup, Denmark. TEL 31-612777. Ed. J. Aagaard. bk.rev.; charts; stat.; index; index; circ. 800.
266 DK
Formerly: Nordisk Missions Tidsskrift (ISSN 0029-1447)

MISSION MESSAGES. 1920. bi-m. 25 F. Procure des Missions du Levant, 32 rue Boissonade, 75014 Paris, France. Ed. Jean Delcroix. bk.rev.; illus.; stat.; circ. 4,500.
266 FR ISSN 0026-6124

MISSION PROBE. irreg. free. Uniting Church in Australia, Commission for Mission, 222 Pitt St., 5th Fl., Sydney, N.S.W. 2000, Australia. TEL 02-287-0900. FAX 02-287-0999. (Subscr. to: P.O. Box E266, St. James, N.S.W. 2000, Australia) Ed. Rev. J.P. Brown. circ. 125,000. (back issues avail.)
260 AT ISSN 0158-0531
Description: Covers mission issues within the life of the Uniting Church.

MISSION TO MILITARY GARRISONS QUARTERLY RECORD. see *MILITARY*

MISSIONARY MONTHLY. 1896. m. (9/yr.). $12.50 (typically set in Fall). Missionary Monthly, Inc., 4595 Broadmoor Ave., S.E., Ste. 237, Grand Rapids, MI 49512-5339. TEL 616-698-3080. Ed. Dick L. Van Halsema. adv.; bk.rev.; circ. 4,000.
266 US ISSN 0161-7133
Description: Coverage of missionary efforts worldwide, and the political and social issues facing them and their message.

MISSIONS-ETRANGERES. (Text in French) 1941. bi-m. Can.$5. Societe des Missions-Etrangeres, 160 Place Juge-Desnoyers, Pont-Viau, Ville de Laval, Que. H7G 1A4, Canada. TEL 514-384-0026. Ed. Hubert Laurin. charts; illus.; stat.; circ. 40,000.
266 CN ISSN 0026-6116

MISSIONSBANERET. 1921. w. DKK 235. Oerebromissionens Foerlag, Box 1623, S-701 16 Oerebro, Sweden. TELEX OEM 731555. Ed. Haakan Arenius. adv.; bk.rev.; illus.; circ. 10,000. (tabloid format)
266 SW ISSN 0026-6132

MISSIONSWISSENSCHAFTLICHE FORSCHUNGEN. 1962. irreg. price varies. Guetersloher Verlagshaus Gerd Mohn, Carl-Bertelsmann-Str. 256, Postfach 1343, 4830 Guetersloh 100, Germany. TEL 05241-7405-0. FAX 05241-740548.
266 GW ISSN 0076-9428

MLEZI; a journal for preaching and teaching religion. (Text in Swahili) 1970. bi-m. EAs.60($18) Europa Publications Ltd., 18 Bedford Sq., London WC1B 3JN, England. TEL 01-580-8236. TELEX 21540. adv.; bk.rev.; illus.; circ. 13,000.
268 TZ ISSN 0047-7583
Description: Research on problems facing those teaching in the church.

MODERN CHURCHMAN. 1911. q. £6 to non-members. Modern Churchpeople's Union, School House, Leysters, Leominster, Herefordshire HR6 0HB, England. Ed. A.O. Dyson. adv.; bk.rev.; index; circ. 1,200. (also avail. in microfilm from UMI) **Indexed:** CERDIC, Mid.East: Abstr.& Ind., New Test.Abstr., Rel.& Theol.Abstr. (1989-), Rel.Ind.One, Rel.Per.
200 UK ISSN 0026-7597 BX5011
—BLDSC shelfmark: 5886.030000.

MODERN LITURGY. 1973. 10/yr. $40. Resource Publications, Inc., 160 E. Virginia St., San Jose, CA 95112. TEL 408-286-8505. Ed. John Gallen, S.J. adv.; bk.rev.; circ. 15,000. (also avail. in microform from UMI; reprint service avail. from UMI) **Indexed:** Cath.Ind., CERDIC, Music Artic.Guide, Music Ind.
264 US ISSN 0363-504X BV169
—BLDSC shelfmark: 5888.200000.
Formerly: Folk Mass and Modern Liturgy (ISSN 0094-775X); Incorporates (in Sep. 1979): Worship Times.
Description: Professional growth magazine for church leaders, with an emphasis on liturgical resources devoted to planning worship with help from the arts.

MODERN THEOLOGY. 1984. q. £32.50($57.50) to individuals; institutions £65($127). Basil Blackwell Ltd., 108 Cowley Rd., Oxford OX4 1JF, England. TEL 0865-791100. FAX 0865-791347. TELEX 837022-OXBOOK-G. Ed.Bd. adv.; bk.rev.; circ. 800. (also avail. in microform; reprint service avail. from SWZ) **Indexed:** Rel.& Theol.Abstr. (1986-).
200 UK ISSN 0266-7177
—BLDSC shelfmark: 5898.210000.

MONDE DE LA BIBLE. see *ARCHAEOLOGY*

MONITOR MONTH; a global voice. see *COMMUNICATIONS — Television And Cable*

MONTHLY LETTER ON EVANGELISM. (Editions in English, French, German) 1956. irreg. 12 Fr. donation. World Council of Churches, Commission on World Mission and Evangelism, 150 Route de Ferney, Box 2100, CH-1211 Geneva 2, Switzerland. TEL 022-791-6111. FAX 022-791-0361. TELEX 415730-OIK-CH. Ed. Christopher Duraisingh. circ. 4,000 (all eds.). **Indexed:** CERDIC.
200 SZ

MOREANA; time trieth truth. see *HISTORY — History Of Europe*

RELIGIONS AND THEOLOGY 4191

200 GW
MORGENROTE. 1877. q. membership. Frei-religioese Gemeinde, Schillerplatz 1, 6050 Offenbach, Germany. TEL 069-885275. circ. 2,100.
Description: Trends in liberal theology; humanistic, ethical and counseling issues.

200 UK
MOUNT CARMEL. 1966. 4/yr. £7. Teresian Carmelites, Carmelite Priory, Boars Hill, Oxford OX1 5HB, England. TEL 0865-730183.
Description: Promotes personal growth in the Christian experience and practice of prayer.

200 US
MOUNT SAVIOUR CHRONICLE. 1951. s-a. free. Mount Saviour Monastery, Pine City, NY 14871. TEL 607-734-1688. Ed. Br. Pierre. bk.rev.; circ. 9,000. (back issues avail.)
Description: Newsletter of the activities and readings of the Mount Savior Monastery in New York State.

MOUNTAIN PATH. see *PHILOSOPHY*

MOUTHPIECE. see *EDUCATION — Teaching Methods And Curriculum*

200 MG
MPANOLOTSAINA. (Text in Malagasy) q. B.P. 623, 101 Antananarivo, Malagasy Republic. TEL 26845. Ed. Paul Solohery.

200 US
MUNDI MEDICINA. 1989. 3/yr. (Order of the Holy Cross) Holy Cross Monastery, Box 99, West Park, NY 12493. TEL 914-384-6660.
Description: Covers news of the Monastic community.

266 SP
MUNDO NEGRO; revista misional africana. 1960. m. 1400 ptas.($5) Misioneros Combonianos, Congregacion Misionera, Arturo Soria, 101, 28043 Madrid, Spain. FAX 91-5192550. Ed. Juan Gonzalez Nunez. adv.; bk.rev.; illus.; stat.; index; circ. 80,000 (controlled). (back issues avail.)
Description: Contains general information about the African continent (politics, economics, religion) and about Blacks in America.

226 PK ISSN 0254-7856
AL-MUSHIR/COUNSELOR. (Text in English or Urdu) 1959. q. Rs.60($15) Christian Study Centre, 126-B Murree Rd., Rawalpindi, Pakistan. Ed. Charles Amjad-Ali. bk.rev.; circ. 650.
—BLDSC shelfmark: 5990.145000.
Description: Discusses Christian-Muslim relations; Islamic, Christian theology and cultural, social issues in the context of Pakistan.

MUSIK UND KIRCHE. see *MUSIC*

200 UG ISSN 0541-4385
MUSIZI. (Text in Luganda) 1955. m. EAs.1200. Munno Publications, Box 4027, Kampala, Uganda. Ed. Rev. Francis Tebukozza. adv.; circ. 25,000.

MUZIEKBODE. see *MUSIC*

200 CK ISSN 0027-5638
BX1751A1
MYSTERIUM. 1946. q. Col.$50. Provincia Occidental Claretianos de Colombia, Apdo Aereo 51-841, Medellin, Colombia. bk.rev.; bibl.; index. (tabloid format) **Indexed:** Amer.Hist.& Life, Hist.Abstr.

N A O S; notes and materials for the linguistic study of the sacred. see *LINGUISTICS*

200 IT
N T C NEWS. (Text in English) 1973. s-m. $10. Via Firenze 38, 00184 Rome, Italy. Ed. Ed Grace. circ. 625.

266 610 GW ISSN 0027-7398
NACHRICHTEN AUS DER AERZTLICHEN MISSION. 1950. q. free. Deutsches Institut fuer Aerztliche Mission - German Institute for Medical Missions, Paul-Lechler-Str. 24, 7400 Tuebingen, Germany. TEL 07071-206-512. FAX 07071-27125. Ed. R. Bastian. bk.rev.; illus.; circ. 15,000.

200 US
NADA NETWORK; connecting monastery and marketplace. 1981. bi-m. $8. Spiritual Life Institute, Box 219, One Carmelite Way, Crestone, CO 81131. TEL 719-256-4778. Ed. Sr. Patricia McGowan. bk.rev.; film rev.; circ. 1,100. (tabloid format; back issues avail.)
Description: Explores spirituality in daily life for those wanting to be contemplative while living in the secular world.

281.7 299.932 NE ISSN 0169-9350
NAG HAMMADI STUDIES. 1971. irreg., vol.35, 1987. price varies. E.J. Brill, P.O. Box 9000, 2300 PA Leiden, Netherlands. TEL 071-312624. FAX 071-317532. TELEX 39296 BRILL NL. (In N. America: E.J. Brill, 24 Hudson St., Kinderhook, NY 12106. TEL 800-962-4406) Ed.Bd.
Supersedes: Coptic Gnostic Library (ISSN 0169-7749)
Description: Scholarly discussions of Gnostic and early Christian religious topics based upon the papyrus Gospels found at Nag Hammadi, Egypt.

200 952 JA ISSN 0386-720X
NANZAN INSTITUTE FOR RELIGION AND CULTURE. BULLETIN. (Text in English) 1977. a. free. Nanzan Institute for Religion and Culture, 18 Yamazato-cho, Showa-ku, 466 Nagoya, Japan. TEL 052-832-3111. Ed. James W. Hujig. circ. 1,200. (back issues avail.)
—BLDSC shelfmark: 2629.105000.

200 296 US
NARROW WAY. (Text in English, Greek, Hebrew) 1969. bi-m. free. Assemblies of Yahweh, Box C, Bethel, PA 19507. TEL 717-933-4518. Ed. Jacob O. Meyer. circ. 1,200. (back issues avail.)

200 AT
NATIONAL OUTLOOK; Australian Christian monthly. 1979. m. Aus.$30 (foreign Aus.$48). Outlook Media Ltd., G.P.O. Box 2134, Sydney, N.S.W. 2001, Australia. TEL 02-281-6617. FAX 02-281-5216. Ed. David Thomas. adv.; bk.rev.; circ. 3,000. (back issues avail.)
Description: Independent, ecumenical magazine concerned with social ethics, theological developments, economics, and politics.

200 RU ISSN 0028-1239
NAUKA I RELIGIYA. 1959. m. 10.20 Rub. Vsesoyuznoe Obshchestvo "Znanie", 14 Gorokhovskii Pereulok, Moscow K-16, Russia. Ed. A.S. Ivanov. bk.rev.; bibl.; illus.; stat.; circ. 285,000. **Indexed:** CERDIC, Curr.Dig.Sov.Press.

NAVY CHAPLAINS BULLETIN. see *MILITARY*

200 IT ISSN 0028-1700
NAZARETH.* vol.90, 1970. bi-m. contributions. Via Filitteria 10, 06049 Spoleto, Italy. circ. 2,000 (controlled). (processed)

270 NE ISSN 0028-2030
NEDERLANDS ARCHIEF VOOR KERKGESCHIEDENIS. 1900. 2/yr. fl.98. E.J. Brill, P.O. Box 9000, 2300 PA Leiden, Netherlands. TEL 071-312624. FAX 071-317532. TELEX 39296 BRILL NL. (In N. America: E.J. Brill, 24 Hudson St., Kinderhook, NY 12106. TEL 800-962-4406) Ed. J. Trapman, E.G.E. van der Wall. bk.rev.; bibl. **Indexed:** Amer.Hist.& Life, CERDIC, Hist.Abstr., Rel.Ind.One.
—BLDSC shelfmark: 6069.350000.
Description: Explores church history in the Netherlands.

230 NE ISSN 0028-212X
NEDERLANDS THEOLOGISCH TIJDSCHRIFT. vol.30, 1975. q. fl.78. Boekencentrum B.V., Box 84176, The Hague, Netherlands. Ed. A. van den Beld. adv.; bk.rev.; bibl.; index; circ. 800. **Indexed:** CERDIC, New Test.Abstr., Old Test.Abstr., Rel.& Theol.Abstr. (1967-), Rel.Ind.One, Rel.Per.
—BLDSC shelfmark: 6071.380000.

200 301 301 283 AT ISSN 0726-0458
NELEN YUBU. 1978. q. Aus.$15. Nelen Yubu Missiological Unit, P.O. Box 156, Drummoyne, N.S.W. 2047, Australia. TEL 02-819-7122. (Subscr. to: 4-17 Jersey Ave, Leura, N.S.W. 2780, Australia) Ed. M.J. Wilson. bk.rev.; cum.index: 1978-1985; circ. 250. (back issues avail.)

220 DK ISSN 0108-3023
NEMALAH/MYREN. 1982. q. DKK 30 per no. Dansk Bibel Institut, Frederiksborggade 1 B, 1, DK-1360 Copenhagen K, Denmark. TEL 45-31-13-55-00. Ed. Gunner Jensen. bk.rev.; circ. 400.
Description: Directed to students at the Danish Bible Institute. Presents theological and spiritual guidance.

225 SA ISSN 0254-8356
NEOTESTAMENTICA. (Text in English) 1967. 2/yr. $30. New Testament Society of South Africa - Nuwe Testamentiese Werkgemeenskap van Suid-Afrika, c/o Department of New Testament, University of the Orange Free State, P.O. Box 339, Bloemfontein 9300, South Africa. TEL 051-401-2667. FAX 051-489203. Ed. H.C. van Zyl. adv.; bk.rev.; circ. 430. (also avail. in microfiche; reprint service avail. from UMI) **Indexed:** Bull.Signal., Int.Z.Bibelwiss., New Test.Abstr., Rel.& Theol.Abstr. (1983-).
—BLDSC shelfmark: 6075.655000.
Description: Contains literary and theological reflections on New Testament texts.

276 UK ISSN 0028-2820
NET. 1866. s-a. $10. Zululand Swaziland Association, c/o W.A. Sanders, Nine Chimney House, Balsham, Cambridge CB1 6ES, England. Ed. Rev. M.T. Broadbent. bk.rev.; charts; illus.; circ. 1,000.

266 US
NETWORK (ATLANTA). 1983. q. United Presbyterian Church in the U.S.A., Mission to the World, Box 29765, Atlanta, GA 30359. Ed. Mary Lou Bohnsack. illus.; stat.; circ. 85,000. (processed)
Supersedes (1957-1983): W P M Newsletter (World Presbyterian Missions) (ISSN 0042-9783)
Description: Covers foreign mission work of the church.

200 GW ISSN 0344-7022
NEUE STADT. 1957. m. DM.29. Verlag Neue Stadt, Postfach 8306567, 8000 Munich 83, Germany. TEL 08093-2091. FAX 08093-2096. adv.; circ. 20,000. (back issues avail.)

266 SZ ISSN 0028-3495
NEUE ZEITSCHRIFT FUER MISSIONSWISSENSCHAFT/NOUVELLE REVUE DE SCIENCE MISSIONNAIRE. (Text in English, French, German and Italian) 1945. q. 41.60 Fr. Verein zur Foerderung der Missionswissenschaft - Association for Promoting Mission Studies, CH-6405 Immensee, Switzerland. TEL 041-815181. FAX 041-814209. Ed. F. Kollbrunner. adv.; bk.rev.; bibl.; illus.; index; circ. 800. **Indexed:** CERDIC, Curr.Cont.Africa, E.I.

201 GW ISSN 0028-3517
NEUE ZEITSCHRIFT FUER SYSTEMATISCHE THEOLOGIE UND RELIGIONSPHILOSOPHIE. 1959. 3/yr. $82.50 (students $30). Walter de Gruyter und Co., Genthiner Str. 13, 1000 Berlin 30, Germany. TEL 030-26005-0. FAX 030-26005251. TELEX 184027. (U.S. addr.: Walter de Gruyter, Inc., 200 Saw Mill Rd., Hawthorne, NY 10532) Ed. Carl Heinz Ratschow. adv.; bk.rev.; bibl.; index. **Indexed:** CERDIC, Rel.& Theol.Abstr. (1984-), Rel.Ind.One, Rel.Per.

200 GW ISSN 0720-3772
NEUERWERBUNG THEOLOGIE UND ALLGEMEINE RELIGIONSWISSENSCHAFT. 1973. m. DM.28. Universitaetsbibliothek Tuebingen, Theologische Abteilung, Wilhelmstr. 32, 7400 Tuebingen 1, Germany. circ. 650. (back issues avail.)

200 GW ISSN 0028-3665
NEUES LEBEN (MOERS); Christliches Monatsmagazin. 1956. m. DM.66.80. (Neues Leben Medien e.V) Brendow Verlag, Gutenbergstr. 1, 4130 Moers 1, Germany. FAX 02681-6842. Ed. Peter Schulte, Wilfried Schulte. adv.; bk.rev.; illus.; circ. 30,000.

NEW ATHENAEUM/NEUES ATHENAEUM. see *LITERATURE*

200 US ISSN 0028-4254
NEW AURORA. (Text in English and Italian) 1903. m. (except July & Aug.). $5. Association of Evangelicals for Italian Missions, 314 Richfield Rd., Upper Darby, PA 19082. TEL 215-352-2396. Ed. Rev. Anthony F. Vasquez. adv.; circ. 1,500.

200 PH
NEW CITY. 1966. m. P.90($4) (Focolare Movement for Men) New City Press, Box 332, Manila, Philippines. FAX 02-623956. Ed. Guido Mirti. adv.; circ. 10,000 (controlled).

RELIGIONS AND THEOLOGY

200　　　　　　UK　ISSN 0140-5845
NEW CITY. 1971. irreg. (1-2/yr.). £20. Urban Theology Unit, 210 Abbeyfield Road, Sheffield S4 7AZ, England. TEL 0742-435342.
　Description: Covers urban issues, the ministry in the city, liberation theology, and theological education.

200　　　　　　US
NEW CITY TIMES. vol.5, 1988. q. free. (Campus Crusade for Christ International) Here's Life Inner City, Box 4088, Grand Central Sta., New York, NY 10163. Eds. Doug Brendel, Donna Wright.
　Description: Serves as an information service and accountability report to the "Hope Partners" and donors.

200　　　　　　US　ISSN 0360-0181
NEW CONVERSATIONS. 1975. 3/yr. $10. United Church Board for Homeland Ministries, 700 Prospect Ave., Cleveland, OH 44115-1100. TEL 216-736-3800. bk.rev.; circ. 1,500.
　—BLDSC shelfmark: 6082.960000.

200　　　　　　US　ISSN 0028-453X
BX7350.A1
THE NEW DAY; featuring the works of Father Divine. 1936. bi-w. $9.25 (foreign $11.50). (Peace Mission Movement) The New Day Publishing Co., 1600 W. Oxford St., Philadelphia, PA 19121. TEL 215-763-9940. Ed. Eugen Ammann. adv.; charts; illus.; circ. 3,000. (tabloid format; also avail. in microfiche from KTO)
　Supersedes (1934-1936): Spoken Word.
　Description: Covers lectures, talks, interviews by Father and Mother Divine, correspondence, news of the Peace Mission Movement, with articles on health, psychology, science and world news.

200　　　　　　AT
NEW DAY INTERNATIONAL. 1980. 10/yr. Aus.$25 (foreign Aus.$38). House of Tabor, 7 Lynton Ave., Plympton, S.A. 5038, Australia. TEL 08-3710940. (Subscr. to: P.O. Box 564, Plympton, S.A. 5038, Australia) Ed. Geoffrey Strelan. adv.; bk.rev.; film rev.; circ. 3,500. (back issues avail.)
　Formerly (until 1986): Australia's New Day.
　Description: Covers teaching, inspirational - devotional material, news from a charismatic perspective with an emphasis on Christian unity.

220　　　　　　AT
NEW DOCUMENTS ILLUSTRATING EARLY CHRISTIANITY. 1981. irreg. Aus.$30 to individuals; institutions Aus.$35. Ancient History Documentary Research Centre, Macquarie University, N.S.W. 2109, Australia. TEL 02-805-7512. FAX 02-805-8892. TELEX AA 122377 MACUNI. Ed. G.H.R. Horsley. index; circ. 2,000. (back issues avail.)
　Description: Studies of Greek texts, inscriptions and papyri.

200　　　　　　II
NEW LEADER. (Text in English) 1887. w. 93 North Rd., St. Mary's Town, Bangalore 560 005, India. Ed. Rev. Herman D'Souza. circ. 10,000.

200　　　　　　UK
NEW LIFE (LONDON, 1971); prison service chaplaincy review. 1971. a. Home Office, 50 Queen Anne's Gate, London SW1H 9AT, England.
TEL 0522-533633. Ed. Rev. A.R. Duce. circ. 4,000.

200　　　　　　US　ISSN 0149-4244
BR1
NEW OXFORD REVIEW. 1940. m. (10/yr.). $19. New Oxford Review, Inc., 1069 Kains Ave., Berkeley, CA 94706. TEL 510-526-5374. Ed. Dale Vree. adv.; bk.rev.; illus.; circ. 7,000. (also avail. in microform from UMI; reprint service avail. from UMI) **Indexed:** Cath.Ind.
　—BLDSC shelfmark: 6084.872000.
　Formerly (until Feb. 1977): American Church News (ISSN 0002-791X)
　Description: Ecumenical Christian journal of ideas edited by lay Catholics interested in orthodoxy, evangelism, social justice, peace, and family life.

200　　　　　　CN
NEW RELIGIONS NEWSLETTER. 1978. m. $10. c/o Prof. Herbert Richardson, 81 St. Mary's St., Toronto, Ont. M5S 1J4, Canada.

200　　　　　　US　ISSN 1040-0974
NEW RELIGIOUS MOVEMENTS SERIES. 1988. irreg., no.3, 1988. price varies. Borgo Press, Box 2845, San Bernardino, CA 92406. TEL 714-884-5813. Ed. Peter B. Clarke. illus.; index.
　Description: Presents objective histories of the myriad of new religions which have sprung forth in the twentieth century; with each movement's origins, development, beliefs, practices, aims, and appeal, and the response to it from society.

225　　　　　　UK　ISSN 0028-6885
BS410
NEW TESTAMENT STUDIES. (Text in English, French and German) 1954. q. $56 to individuals; institutions $86. (Studiorum Novi Testamenti Societas) Cambridge University Press, Edinburgh Bldg., Shaftesbury Rd., Cambridge CB2 2RU, England. TEL 0223-312393. FAX 0223-315052. TELEX 851817256. (North American orders to: Cambridge University Press, 40 W. 20th St., New York, NY 10011) Ed. G.N. Stanton. adv.; bk.rev. (also avail. in microform from UMI; reprint service avail. from SWZ) **Indexed:** Arts & Hum.Cit.Ind., CERDIC, Curr.Cont., Hum.Ind., New Test.Abstr., Rel.& Theol.Abstr. (1968-), Rel.Ind.One, Rel.Per.
　—BLDSC shelfmark: 6088.862000.
　Description: Articles covering all aspects of the text and theology of the New Testament.

220　　　　　　NE　ISSN 0077-8842
NEW TESTAMENT TOOLS AND STUDIES. 1960. irreg., vol.15, 1991. price varies. E.J. Brill, P.O. Box 9000, 2300 PA Leiden, Netherlands. TEL 071-312624. FAX 071-317532. TELEX 39296 BRILL NL. (In N. America: E.J. Brill, 24 Hudson St., Kinderhook, NY 12106. TEL 800-962-4406) Ed. Bruce M. Metzger.
　Description: Presents studies of the New Testament.

200　　　　　　US
▼**NEW WINE;*** for Christians today. 1990. w. $12.95 (Canada $22.95; elsewhere $32.95). Chalice Press, Inc., 13 Oak Hill Cluster, Independence, MO 64050. TEL 800-762-4935. FAX 816-836-1942. adv.; bk.rev.; circ. 10,000.

266 284.1　　　US　ISSN 0043-8812
BV2550
NEW WORLD OUTLOOK; missions and ecumenical relationships. 1911; N.S. 1941. m. (combined Jul.-Aug. and Nov.-Dec.). $11. United Methodist Church, General Board of Global Ministries, 475 Riverside Dr., Rm. 1351, New York, NY 10115. TEL 212-870-3758. Eds. Arthur J. Moore, George M. Daniels. adv.; bk.rev.; illus.; index; circ. 38,000. (also avail. in microfilm) **Indexed:** CERDIC, Mid.East: Abstr.& Ind.
　Formerly: World Outlook.
　Description: Covers mission work around the globe.

200　　　　　　US
▼**NEW YORK CHRISTIAN TIMES;** the good news in bad times. 1990. bi-w. $36. Harvest Press, 9 Irving Pl., Brooklyn, NY 11238. TEL 718-638-6397. FAX 718-783-4941. circ. 28,000.

200 323.4　　　US　ISSN 1042-606X
NEWS NETWORK INTERNATIONAL. 1983. m. $75 (foreign $90). N N I, Inc., Box 28001, Santa Ana, CA 92799. TEL 714-775-4900. FAX 714-775-7315. TELEX 901-593-1332. Ed. Chris Woehr. bk.rev.; circ. 500. (looseleaf format; back issues avail.; reprint service avail.)
　Formerly: Open Doors News Service.
　Description: Religious freedom news and information.

NEWS SPECIAL; & the messenger. see *GENERAL INTEREST PERIODICALS — Great Britain*

200　　　　　　CN　ISSN 0703-5888
NIAGARA ANGLICAN. 1954. m. (10/yr.). Can.$10. 67 Victoria Ave. S., Hamilton, Ont. L8N 2S8, Canada. TEL 416-521-9598. FAX 416-527-1281. Ed. Larry Perks. adv. contact: Brian Trotter. bk.rev.; circ. 19,500.

200　　　　　　NR　ISSN 0029-005X
BR1463.N5
NIGERIAN CHRISTIAN. (Text in English) 1967-1982; N.S. 1984. m. $12. (Christian Council of Nigeria) Daystar Press, Box 1261, Ibadan, Nigeria. Ed. Rachel Alao. adv.; bk.rev.; illus.; circ. 1,500. **Indexed:** CERDIC.
　Description: Reports on matters of importance to Nigerian national life with critical references to Christianity in the region.

266　　　　　　IT　ISSN 0029-0173
BV3500
NIGRIZIA; fatti e problemi del mondo nero. 1883. m. L.22000($22) Missionari Combonian, Vicolo Pozzo 1, 37129 Verona, Italy. Ed. Aurelio Boscaini. adv.; bk.rev.; illus.; stat.; index; circ. 50,000. **Indexed:** CERDIC, Curr.Cont.Africa.

200　　　　　　NE　ISSN 0169-930X
NISABA; religious texts translation series. 1973. irreg., vol.17, 1989. price varies. E.J. Brill, P.O. Box 9000, 2300 PA Leiden, Netherlands. TEL 071-312614. FAX 071-317532. TELEX 39296 BRILL NL. (In N. America: E.J. Brill, 24 Hudson St., Kinderhook, NY 12106. TEL 800-962-4406)
　Description: Collection of texts in English translation, illuminating the religions of the world for students.

230　　　　　　NO　ISSN 0029-2176
NORSK TEOLOGISK TIDSSKRIFT/NORWEGIAN THEOLOGICAL JOURNAL. 1900. q. $62. Uniersitetsforlaget, P.O. Box 2959-Toeyen, 0608 Oslo 1, Norway. (U.S. address: Publications Expediting Inc., 200 Meacham Ave., Elmont, NY 11003) Ed. Svein Aage Christoffersen. adv.; bk.rev.; abstr.; index; circ. 550. **Indexed:** Amer.Hist.& Life (until 1991), CERDIC, Hist.Abstr. (until 1991), New Test.Abstr., Old Test.Abstr., Rel.& Theol.Abstr. (1989-), Rel.Ind.One, Rel.Per.

266　　　　　　NO　ISSN 0029-2214
NORSK TIDSSKRIFT FOR MISJON/NORWEGIAN JOURNAL OF MISSION AND MISSIONARY QUESTIONS. a. $56. (Egede Institute, Oslo) Universitetsforlaget, P.O. Box 2959-Toeyen, N-0608 Oslo 1, Norway. (U.S. addr.: Publications Expediting Inc., 200 Meacham Ave., Elmont, NY 11003) Ed. Notto R. Thelle. adv.; bk.rev.; index; circ. 800. (back issues avail.) **Indexed:** CERDIC.
　—BLDSC shelfmark: 6146.600000.

250　　　　　　II
NORTH INDIA CHURCHMAN. (Text in English) 1971. m. Rs.10($9) North India Churchman Board, 16 Pandit Pant Marg, New Delhi 110 001, India. TELEX 3166763-UPC-IN. Ed. Harold Williams. adv.; bk.rev.; circ. 1,200.

NOTES ON SCRIPTURE IN USE AND LANGUAGE PROGRAMS. see *LINGUISTICS*

200 301　　　　PE
NOTICIAS ALIADAS. English edition: Latinamerica Press. w. $49.95. Noticias Aliadas, Apdo. 5594, Lima 100, Peru. Dir. George Ann Potter. **Indexed:** HR Rep.

266　　　　　　NQ
NOTICIAS EVANGELICAS. bi-m. Comite Evangelico pro Ayudo al Desarrollo, Apdo. Postal 3091, Managua, Nicaragua.

NOTRE DAME JOURNAL OF LAW, ETHICS & PUBLIC POLICY. see *PUBLIC ADMINISTRATION*

230　　　　　　BE　ISSN 0029-4845
BX802
NOUVELLE REVUE THEOLOGIQUE. 1868. 6/yr. $65. (Centre de Documentation et de Recherche Religieuses) Casterman, S.A., 28 rue des Soeurs Noires, B-7500 Tournai, Belgium. (Dist. in N. America by: Aquinas Agency, 561 Fort Rd., St. Paul, MN 55102) bk.rev.; bibl.; index; circ. 4,000. **Indexed:** Canon Law Abstr., Cath.Ind., CERDIC, New Test.Abstr., Old Test.Abstr., Rel.& Theol.Abstr. (1970-).
　—BLDSC shelfmark: 6176.845000.

200　　　　　　FR　ISSN 0029-487X
NOUVELLES DE CHRETIENTE;* notes, documents. 1953. w. 40 F. Civitec, 1134 rue de Rivoli, 75001 Paris, France. Eds. Charles Pierre Doazan, Lucien Garrido.

225　　　　　NE　ISSN 0048-1009
BS410
NOVUM TESTAMENTUM; an international quarterly for New Testament and related studies. (Supplement avail.) (Text in English, French and German) 1956. q. fl.155 (effective 1992). E.J. Brill, P.O. Box 9000, 2300 PA Leiden, Netherlands. TEL 071-312624. FAX 071-317532. TELEX 39296 BRILL NL. (In N. America: E.J. Brill, 24 Hudson St., Kinderhook, NY 12106. TEL 800-962-4406) Ed. C.K. Barrett. (also avail. in microform from SWZ; reprint service avail. from SWZ) **Indexed**: Arts & Hum.Cit.Ind., CERDIC, Curr.Cont., New Test.Abstr., Rel.& Theol.Abstr. (1968-), Rel.Ind.One, Rel.Per.
—BLDSC shelfmark: 6180.445000.
Description: International coverage of New Testament studies.

225　　　　　NE　ISSN 0167-9732
NOVUM TESTAMENTUM. SUPPLEMENTS. (Supplement to: Novum Testametnum) 1958. irreg., vol.65, 1991. price varies. E.J. Brill, P.O. Box 9000, 2300 PA Leiden, Netherlands. TEL 071-312624. FAX 071-317532. TELEX 39296 BRILL NL. (In N. America: E.J. Brill, Kinderhook, NY 12106. TEL 800-962-4406) Ed.Bd. **Indexed**: Rel.Ind.One.
—BLDSC shelfmark: 6180.445200.

268 028.5　　　DK
NU PA VEJ; en bibelnoegle for junioner. 1985. q. DKK 20. Bibellaeser-Ringen, Korskaervej 25, 7000 Fredericia, Denmark. illus.
Formerly: Paa Vej (ISSN 0900-3355)

200　　　　　DR　ISSN 0029-5752
NUESTRO AMIGO. 1931. m. free. Iglesia Evangelica Dominicana, Apartado 727, Santo Domingo, Dominican Republic. Ed. Herman Gonzalez Roca. circ. 2,500. (tabloid format; also avail. in cards)

200　　　　　AG
NUEVO MUNDO. 1971. s-a. $10. Ediciones Castaneda, Centenario 1399, 1718 San Antonio de Padua, Buenos Aires, Argentina.

209　　　　　NE　ISSN 0029-5973
BL1
NUMEN; international review for the history of religions. (Supplements avail.) (Text in English, French, German and Italian) 1954. s-a. fl.115 (effective 1992). (International Association for the History of Religions) E.J. Brill, P.O. Box 9000, 2300 PA Leiden, Netherlands. TEL 071-312624. FAX 071-317532. TELEX 39296 BRILL NL. (In N. America: E.J. Brill, 24 Hudson St., Kinderhook, NY 12106. TEL 800-962-4406) Ed. Heerma van Voss. bk.rev.; bibl. (also avail. in microform from SWZ; back issues avail.; reprint service avail. from SWZ) **Indexed**: CERDIC, Curr.Cont., Mid.East: Abstr.& Ind., New Test.Abstr., Rel.& Theol.Abstr. (1980-), Rel.Ind.One, Rel.Per.
—BLDSC shelfmark: 6184.650000.
Description: Documents theological history.

200　　　　　NE　ISSN 0169-8834
NUMEN SUPPLEMENTS; studies in the history of religions. (Supplement to: Numen) 1954. irreg., vol.52, 1991. price varies. E.J. Brill, P.O. Box 9000, 2300 PA Leiden, Netherlands. TEL 071-312624. FAX 071-317532. TELEX 39296 BRILL NL. (In N. America: E.J. Brill, 24 Hudson St., Kinderhook, NY 12106. TEL 800-962-4406) Ed.Bd. **Indexed**: Rel.Ind.Two.
—BLDSC shelfmark: 6464.680000.
Formerly: Studies in the History of Religions (ISSN 0585-7260); Supersedes: Numen Supplements, Altera Series (ISSN 0169-8885)

NURTURE; journal for home and school. see EDUCATION — Teaching Methods And Curriculum

NY DAG. see CHILDREN AND YOUTH — For

266　　　　　DK　ISSN 0108-8297
NYE AAR; Kirkelige Forening for den Indre Mission i Danmark. 1906. a. DKK 48. (Kirkelig Forening) Lohses Forlag, Korskaervej 25, 7000 Fredericia, Denmark. TEL 75 93 44 55. FAX 0045-75926146. Ed. K. Lindhardt Jensen. adv.; illus.
Description: Contains reports of Den Kirkelige Forening for den Indre Mission i Danmark

200　　　　　DK　ISSN 0109-3169
NYHEDSBREV. 1983. s-a. free. Aarhus Universitet, Teologiske Fakultet, Universitetsparken, 8000 Aarhus C, Denmark. Ed. Povl Lind-Petersen. bk.rev.; circ. 2,000.
Formerly: T F Nyhedsbrev (ISSN 0108-8939)

220　　　　　DK　ISSN 0108-898X
NYT FRA BIBELSELSKABET. 1982. q. free. Danske Bibelselskab, Frederiksborggade 50, 1360 Copenhagen K, Denmark. TEL 33-127835. FAX 33-93-21-50. illus.
Formerly: Danske Bibelselskab. Medlemsbrev.

377　　　　　BE　ISSN 0770-1683
LC461
O I E C BULLETIN. (Editions in English, French, Spanish) 1969. 6/yr. 500 Fr.($15) in Europe; elsewhere 650 Fr.($20). Office International de l'Enseignement Catholique - Catholic International Education Office, 60 rue des Eburons, B-1040 Brussels, Belgium. Ed. Paulus Adams. adv.; bk.rev.; circ. 700. (processed) **Indexed**: HR Rep.
—BLDSC shelfmark: 6247.700000.
Former titles: Catholic International Education Office. Bulletin Nouvelle Serie; Catholic International Education Office. Bulletin Trimestriel (ISSN 0084-8638)
Description: Aim is to make widely known the major trends affecting education in schools today and shaping tomorrow's educational policies.

255　　　　　SP
OBISPADO DE TORTOSA. BOLETIN OFICIAL. 1858. m. 750 ptas. Obispado de Tortosa, Cruera, 9, Tortosa, Spain. Ed. Jesus Carda Pitarch. adv.; bk.rev.; bibl.; index; circ. 350.

266　　　　　US
OBLATES. 1943. 6/yr. membership. Missionary Association of Mary Immaculate, 15 S. 59th St., Belleville, IL 62223-4694. TEL 618-233-2238. Ed. Jacqueline Lowery Corn. circ. 600,000 (controlled). (back issues avail.)
Description: Articles and poetry espousing positive Christian direction for primarily middle-age to older Catholic adults.

282　　　　　CI　ISSN 0351-3947
OBNOVLJENI ZIVOT/LIFE RENEWED; dvomjesecnik za religioznu kulturu. (Text in Croatian; summaries in English, French, German, Latin) 1919-1945; resumed 1971. bi-m. $50. Filozofsko-Teoloski Insitut Druzbe Isusove - Institute of Philosophy and Theology, S.J., Jordanovac 110, 41001 Zagreb, Croatia. TEL 041-216-266. Ed. Ivan Koprek. bk.rev.; abstr.; bibl.; stat.; index; circ. 1,600. (back issues avail.)
—BLDSC shelfmark: 6197.230000.

200 947　　　US　ISSN 0731-5465
BR738.6
OCCASIONAL PAPERS ON RELIGION IN EASTERN EUROPE. 1981. irreg. (approx. 6-8/yr.) $36. Christian Association for Relationships with Eastern Europe, c/o Rosemont College, Rosemont, PA 19010. TEL 215-527-0200. FAX 215-525-2930. Ed. Paul Mojzes. bk.rev.; circ. 700. (looseleaf format; also avail. in microfilm; back issues avail.)
●Also available online. Vendor(s): BRS, DIALOG.
—BLDSC shelfmark: 6224.858500.

280　　　　　GW　ISSN 0029-8654
OEKUMENISCHE RUNDSCHAU. 1952. q. DM.38($9) (Deutscher Oekumenischer Studienausschuss) Verlag Otto Lembeck, Leerbachstr. 42, 6000 Frankfurt 1, Germany. Ed.Bd. adv.; bk.rev.; index; circ. 2,000. **Indexed**: CERDIC.
—BLDSC shelfmark: 6253.550000.

200　　　　　NE　ISSN 0169-9555
OEKUMENISCHE STUDIEN. irreg. price varies. E.J. Brill, P.O. Box 9000, 2300 PA Leiden, Netherlands. TEL 071-312624. FAX 071-317532. TELEX 39296 BRILL NL. (In N. America: E.J. Brill, 24 Hudson St., Kinderhook, NY 12106. TEL 800-962-4406)

200　　　　　GW　ISSN 0179-9959
OEKUMENISCHER INFORMATIONSDIENST. 1982. q. DM.15. Oekumenische Gesellschaft fuer G F S, Rendeler Str. 9-11, 6000 Frankfurt a.M. 60, Germany. TEL 05694-1417. Ed. Ulrich Schmithenner. adv.; bk.rev.; circ. 6,000. (back issues avail.)

OESTERREICHISCHES ARCHIV FUER KIRCHENRECHT. see LAW

200　　　　　US　ISSN 0892-5984
OF A LIKE MIND. 1983. q. $13. Reformed Congregation of the Goddess, Box 6021, Madison, WI 53716. Ed. Lynnie Levy. adv.; bk.rev.; circ. 25,000. (tabloid format; back issues avail.)

266　　　　　GW　ISSN 0030-011X
OFFENE TUEREN. 1907. bi-m. Missionshaus Bibelschule Wiedenest, Olper Str. 10, 5275 Bergneustadt, Germany. FAX 02261-409255. Ed. Daniel Herm. bk.rev.; illus.; circ. 11,000.
Description: Focus on the work of German missionaries.

268 260　　　US
OFFICIAL GUIDE TO CHRISTIAN CAMPS & CONFERENCE CENTERS. 1981. a. $9.95. Christian Camping International, Box 646, Wheaton, IL 60189. TEL 708-462-0300. FAX 708-462-0499. Ed. Jim Martin. adv.; circ. 100,000.
Former titles: Guide to Christian Camps; Christian Camping International Directory (ISSN 0069-3855); (until 1969): Christian Camp and Conference Association. International Directory.

221　　　　　SA
OLD TESTAMENT ESSAYS. (Text mainly in English; occasionally in Afrikaans, Dutch, German) 1983-198?; N.S. 1988. q. $50. (Old Testament Society of South Africa) Serva Publishers, P.O. Box 30043, Sunnyside 0132, Transvaal, South Africa. (Co-sponsor: University of South Africa, Department of Old Testament) Ed. J. Burden. adv.; bk.rev.; circ. 400. (back issues avail.) **Indexed**: Old Test.Abstr., Rel.& Theol.Abstr. (1989-).
Refereed Serial

377.8　　　　　UK　ISSN 0268-8786
ONE TO ONE. 1947. q. £5.20. Scripture Union, 130 City Rd., London EC1V 2NJ, England. TEL 071-782-0013. (Subscr. to: 9-11 Clothier Rd., Bristol BS4 5RL, England) Ed. T.J. Clutterham. charts; illus.; circ. 40,000.
Formerly: Key Notes.

200　　　　　SZ　ISSN 0303-125X
BR1
ONE WORLD. (Text in English) 1975. 10/yr. 37.50 Fr.($25) World Council of Churches, Publications Office, 150 Route de Ferney, Box 2100, CH-1211 Geneva 2, Switzerland. TEL 022-791-6111. FAX 022-791-0361. TELEX 415730-OIK-CH. Ed. Marlin van Elderen. illus.; circ. 10,000. (also avail. in microform from UMI; reprint service avail. from UMI) **Indexed**: CERDIC, Rel.Ind.One, So.Pac.Per.Ind.

200　　　　　NE　ISSN 0030-3267
OORSPRONKELIJK CHRISTENDOM. 1950. bi-m. free. Internationale Gemeenschap van Christenen, Drakenstein 39, 1083 XS Amsterdam, Netherlands. Ed. J.M. Burgers-Zijp. bk.rev.; illus.; circ. 1,450.

OPINION; the way I see it. see PHILOSOPHY

200　　　　　FR　ISSN 0030-4352
ORATORIANA.* 1960. s-a. 10 F. Oratoire de France, 75 rue de Vaugirard, 75006 Paris, France. bk.rev.; bibl.; illus.

200　　　　　GW　ISSN 0340-6407
ORIENS CHRISTIANUS; Hefte fuer die Kunde des christlichen Orients. 1911. a. price varies. Verlag Otto Harrassowitz, Taunusstr. 14, Postfach 2929, 6200 Wiesbaden 1, Germany. TEL 0611-530-0. FAX 0611-530570. TELEX 4186135. Eds. Julius Assfalg, Hubert Kaufhold. adv.; bk.rev.; circ. 400. (back issues avail.) **Indexed**: Rel.Ind.One.

RELIGIONS AND THEOLOGY

200   VC   ISSN 0030-5375
BX100
ORIENTALIA CHRISTIANA PERIODICA; commentarii de re orientali aetatis christianae sacra et profana. (Text in English, French, German, Italian, Latin and Spanish) 1935. a. L.70000($60) (foreign L.70000)(effective 1992). (Pontificio Istituto Orientale) Edizioni Orientalia Cristiana, Piazza S. Maria Maggiore 7, 00185 Rome, Italy. TEL 06-446-5589. FAX 06-446-5576. Ed. Vincenzo Poggi. bk.rev.; charts; index; circ. 1,000. (back issues avail.) **Indexed:** Amer.Bibl.Slavic & E.Eur.Stud, Bull.Signal., CERDIC, New Test.Abstr., Rel.& Theol.Abstr, Rel.Ind.One.
—BLDSC shelfmark: 6291.185000.
   Description: Covers articles in theology, patrology, liturgy, history, canon law, archaeology and similar aspects of the Christian East.

200   IT   ISSN 0472-0784
ORIENTAMENTI PASTORALI. 1953. m. L.15000. Centro di Orientamento Pastorale, c/o Franco Gualtieri, Collegio Internazionale, Via Casale S. Pio V, 20, 00165 Rome, Italy. Ed. G. Bonicelli. adv.; circ. 4,500. **Indexed:** CERDIC.
—BLDSC shelfmark: 6291.202000.

200   SZ   ISSN 0030-5502
ORIENTIERUNG; katholische Blaetter fuer weltanschauliche Information. 1937. s-m. 42 Fr. Institut fuer Weltanschauliche Fragen, Scheideggstr. 45, CH-8002 Zurich, Switzerland. TEL 01-2011196. FAX 01-2014983. Ed. N. Klein. adv.; bk.rev.; abstr.; bibl.; stat.; index, cum.index; circ. 15,000. (looseleaf format) **Indexed:** CERDIC, Old Test.Abstr., World Agri.Econ.& Rural Sociol.Abstr.

200   NR   ISSN 0030-5596
BL80.2
ORITA; Ibadan journal of religious studies. (Text in English) 1967. s-a. $16. University of Ibadan, Department of Religious Studies, Ibadan, Nigeria. Ed. J. Kenny. adv.; bk.rev.; illus.; cum.index; circ. 500 (controlled). (tabloid format) **Indexed:** Mid.East: Abstr.& Ind.

323.4 200   US   ISSN 0145-7675
THE OTHER SIDE (PHILADELPHIA); justice rooted in discipleship. 1965. bi-m. $29.50 (foreign $34.50). Other Side, Inc., 300 W. Apsley St., Philadelphia, PA 19144. TEL 215-849-2178. Ed. Mark Olson. adv.; bk.rev.; film rev.; illus.; circ. 13,000. (also avail. in microfiche from UMI; back issues avail.) **Indexed:** Chr.Per.Ind., Rel.Ind.One.
   Formerly: Freedom Now.

200   CN
▼**OTHER SIDE OF THE BOAT**. 1990. irreg. donation. Canadian Council of Churches, Youth Working Group - Conseil Canadien des Eglises, 40 St. Clair Ave. E., Ste. 201, Toronto, Ont. M4T 1M9, Canada. TEL 416-921-4152. FAX 416-921-7478. circ. 500.

200   NE   ISSN 0030-6746
OUDE PADEN.* 1937. s-m. fl.10. Dorpsstraat 19, Oegstgeest, Netherlands. Ed. Fr. Luitjes. circ. 1,200.

220   NE   ISSN 0169-7226
BS1192
OUDTESTAMENTISCHE STUDIEN. (Text in English and German) 1942. irreg., vol.28, 1992. price varies. E.J. Brill, P.O. Box 9000, 2300 PA Leiden, Netherlands. TEL 071-312624. FAX 071-317532. TELEX 39296 BRILL NL. (In N. America: E.J. Brill, 24 Hudson St., Kinderhook, NY 12106. TEL 800-962-4406) Ed. A.S. van der Woude. **Indexed:** Old Test.Abstr.

200   II
OUR LINK. (Text in English) 1954. m. $20. Union of Evangelical Students of India, 10 Millers Rd., Madras 600010, India. TEL 661478. Ed. Prema Fenn. adv.; bk.rev.; circ. 1,500.
   Formerly (until Jan. 1977): Evangelical Student.

OUR LITTLE FRIEND. see *CHILDREN AND YOUTH — For*

266   UK   ISSN 0048-2579
OXFORD MISSION. 1894. q. £4. Bocardo Press, 22 The Harrage, Romsey, Hampshire SO51 8AE, England. Ed. G. Wilson. circ. 1,800. (processed)

201   US   ISSN 0078-7272
OXFORD THEOLOGICAL MONOGRAPHS. irreg. Oxford University Press, 200 Madison Ave., New York, NY 10016. TEL 212-679-7300. Ed.Bd.

P C R INFORMATION; reports and background papers. (Programme to Combat Racism) see *POLITICAL SCIENCE — Civil Rights*

200   US   ISSN 0889-8936
BL2525
P R R C: EMERGING TRENDS. 1979. 10/yr. $35 (foreign $35). Princeton Religion Research Center, Inc., Box 229, Princeton, NJ 08542. TEL 609-921-8112. circ. 1,900. (looseleaf format; back issues avail.) **Indexed:** SRI.
   Description: Presents the results of recent surveys on religious beliefs and practices, with commentary, based on studies by Gallup and other polling organizations.

268   SP
P S. 1899. m. 1000 ptas.($4) Editorial Perpetuo Socorro, Covarrubias, 19, Madrid-10, Spain. Ed. Jose Maria Lorca. adv.; bk.rev.; illus.; circ. 14,000 (controlled).

266   US
PACIFIC CHRISTIAN COLLEGE BULLETIN. 1928. 4/yr. Pacific Christian College, 2500 E. Nutwood Ave., Fullerton, CA 92631. TEL 714-879-3901. FAX 714-526-0231. Ed. Becky Ahlberg. (tabloid format)
   Description: Articles and faculty information for students and constituency of Pacific Christian College.

PACIFIC THEOLOGICAL REVIEW. see *RELIGIONS AND THEOLOGY — Protestant*

200 294.54   AT   ISSN 1030-570X
PACIFICA; Australian theological studies. 1988. 3/yr. Aus.$30($26) to individuals; institutions Aus.$34($31)(set in Oct.). Pacifica Theological Studies Association, P.O. Box 271, Brunswick East, Vic. 3057, Australia. TEL 347-6366. Ed.Bd. adv.; bk.rev.; index; circ. 650. (back issues avail.) **Indexed:** Aus.P.A.I.S., New Test.Abstr., Old Test.Abstr., Rel.& Theol.Abstr. (1988-).
—BLDSC shelfmark: 6331.815000.
   Description: Scholarly journal covers all areas of theology, with emphasis on theological work in Australasia and Pacific Region.

255 248   IT   ISSN 0030-9214
PADRE SANTO; periodico dei Cappuccini liguri. 1912. m. Frati Minori Cappuccini, Provincia di Genova, Piazza Cappuccini 1, 16122 Genoa, Italy. Ed. Toso Domenico.

200   US   ISSN 0475-4816
LA PALABRA DIARIA. (Text in Spanish) 1955. m. $5. Unity School of Christianity, Unity Village, MO 64065. Ed. Colleen Zuck. circ. 100,000.

266   GW   ISSN 0031-0395
PALLOTTIS WERK. 1949. q. free. (Provinzialat der Pallottiner) Pallottiner Druck und Lahn-Verlag, Wiesbadener Str. 1, Postfach 1162, 6250 Limburg 1, Germany. TEL 06431-401221. Ed. P.W. Schuetzeichel. bk.rev.; circ. 60,000.
   Description: Catholic publication covering missionary work in Germany and abroad, especially Third World countries.

200   FR   ISSN 0299-6898
PANORAMA; revue de reflexion Chretienne. 1968. m. 299 F. Bayard Presse, 21 rue de Faubourg St. Antoine, 75550 Paris Cedex 11, France. adv.; bk.rev.; film rev.; illus.; circ. 96,000. **Indexed:** Pt.de Rep. (1979-).
   Formerly (until 1986): Panorama Aujourd'hui (ISSN 0048-2838)

PARABOLA; the magazine of myth and tradition. see *FOLKLORE*

PARMARTH; religious monthly. see *PHILOSOPHY*

200   LE
PAROLE DE L'ORIENT. (Text in English, French) 1970. s-a. £L10000($30) Universite Saint Esprit Kaslik, B.P. 446, Jounieh, Lebanon. Ed. P. Joseph Obeid. bk.rev.; circ. 1,000.
   Description: Examines the theology, exegeses, patrology, liturgy and history of churches in the near and Middle East.

250   UK   ISSN 0031-2436
PARSON AND PARISH; National Church News. 1938. s-a. £2. Parochial Clergy Association, 840 Walsall Rd., Birmingham B42 1ES, England. Ed. Rev. David Scott. adv.; bk.rev.; circ. 2,000.
   Description: Covers current church affairs, articles of general theological and pastoral interest, and correspondence.

PARTNERSHIP NEWS. see *SOCIAL SERVICES AND WELFARE*

250   GW   ISSN 0031-2681
PASSAUER BISTUMSBLATT; Kirchenzeitung der Dioezese Passau. 1936. w. DM.10.30 per quarter. Diozese Passau, 57707, Ed. Tilo Kotschenreuther, Domplatz 3, 8390 Passau, Germany. adv.; bk.rev.; film rev.; abstr.; illus.; circ. 40,000.

250   US   ISSN 0031-2762
PASTORAL LIFE; the magazine for today's ministry. 1952. m. $17. Society of St. Paul (Canfield), Canfield, OH 44406. TEL 216-533-5503. Ed. Anthony Chenevey. adv.; bk.rev.; illus.; index; circ. 4,000. (also avail. in microfilm from UMI; reprint service avail. from UMI) **Indexed:** Cath.Ind, CERDIC.

266   SP   ISSN 0210-3559
PASTORAL MISIONERA. 1965. 6/yr. 2550 ptas.($22) (foreign 3100 ptas.($27)). Editorial Popular, S.A., Bola, 3 bajo, 28013 Madrid, Spain. FAX 91-559-00-64. TELEX 49416-PUBL-E. Ed. Fernando Urbina de la Quintana. bk.rev.

PASTORAL PSYCHOLOGY. see *PSYCHOLOGY*

250   GW   ISSN 0031-2800
PASTORALBLAETTER. 1860. m. DM.50. Kreuz-Verlag Zeitschriften GmbH, Breitwiesenstr. 30, 7000 Stuttgart 80, Germany. TEL 0711-78803. Ed. Hans-Georg Lubkoll. adv.; circ. 3,500.
—BLDSC shelfmark: 6409.410000.

200   CR
PASTORALIA. 1974. s-a. $3.50 (foreign $4.50). Centro Evangelico Latinoamericano de Estudios Pastorales, Apartado 1307, 1000 San Jose, Costa Rica. Dir. Plutarco Bonilla A. bk.rev.; circ. 1,600.
   Supersedes (since vol.4, nos.1-2, 1977): C E L E P Ensayos Ocasionales.

250   GW   ISSN 0720-6259
PASTORALTHEOLOGIE - MONATSSCHRIFT FUER WISSENSCHAFT UND PRAXIS IN KIRCHE UND GESELLSCHAFT. 1904. m. DM.88. Vandenhoeck und Ruprecht, Theaterstr. 13, Postfach 3753, 3400 Goettingen, Germany. TEL 0551-695917. Eds. Guenter Brakelmann, Peter Stolt. adv.; bk.rev.; index; circ. 3,000. **Indexed:** CERDIC.
—BLDSC shelfmark: 6409.422000.
   Former titles: Wissenschaft und Praxis in Kirche und Gesellschaft (ISSN 0031-2827); Pastoraltheologie.

200 100   II
PATHWAY TO GOD. (Text in English) 1966. q. Rs.15 (foreign Rs.50). Academy of Comparative Philosophy and Religion, Belgaum, Hindwadi, Belgaum 590 011, India. TEL 22231. Ed. B.R. Modak. adv.; bk.rev.; circ. 1,000.

PATRISTIC AND BYZANTINE REVIEW. see *HISTORY — History Of Europe*

200   US   ISSN 0360-652X
PATRISTICS. 1972. s-a. $15 to individuals; institutions $10; students $6. North American Patristics Society, Emmanuel School of Religion, Johnson City, TN 37601. TEL 615-926-1186. Ed. Frederick W. Norris. bk.rev.; circ. 350.

266   CN   ISSN 0031-3335
PAX REGIS. 1942. s-a. $3. Westminster Abbey Ltd., Mission, B.C. V2V 4J2, Canada. TEL 604-826-8975. Ed. Alban Riley. illus.; circ. 1,500.
   Description: Articles and news for alumni of the Seminary of Christ the King, and for those interested in Roman Catholic seminary education.

364 200   US
PEACE AND JUSTICE SERIES. irreg. $5.95. Herald Press, 616 Walnut Ave., Scottdale, PA 15683-1999. TEL 412-887-8500. Ed. Michael King. bibl. (back issues avail.)

200   UK
PEACELINKS. 1971. bi-m. £3. Fellowship of Reconciliation, 40-46 Harleyford Rd., Vauxhall, London SE11 5AY, England. TEL 071-582-9054. FAX 071-582-9180. Ed. Ben Rees. bk.rev.; bibl.; illus.; circ. 3,000. (also avail. in microform from UMI)
    Formerly: Newspeace (ISSN 0048-0304)
    Description: News of the Fellowship of the Reconcilliation (England, Wales, Scotland and Northern Ireland) concerning their work and interest on issues such as Northern Ireland, Central America, and disarmament.

200   FR   ISSN 0399-5755
PELERIN. 1873. w. 740 F. Bayard Presse, 5 rue Bayard, 75380 Paris Cedex 08, France. Eds. Henry Caro, Guy Mauratille. adv.; bk.rev.; film rev.; play rev.; bibl.; illus.; mkt.; circ. 386,000.
    Former titles (until 1976): Pelerin du Vingtieme Siecle (ISSN 0031-4145); (until 1963): Pelerin (ISSN 0399-5747)

200   SA
PENDULUM. (Text in Afrikaans, English) 1974. q. R.10. (Bet-El Evangelistic Action) Bet-El Publishers, P.O. Box 23227, Innesdale, Pretoria 0031, South Africa. Ed. Robbie Engelbrecht. adv.; bk.rev.; circ. 30,000. (back issues avail.)
    Formerly: Evangelist.

200   AU   ISSN 0031-5141
PERCHTOLDSDORFER PFARRBOTE. 1950. m. contributions. Pfarramt Perchtoldsdorf, Marktplatz 14, A-2380 Perchtoldsdorf, Austria. Ed. Msgr. Karl Seemann. circ. 4,700.

200   US
PERE MARQUETTE THEOLOGY LECTURE SERIES. 1969. a. $7.95. Marquette University Press, 1324 W. Wisconsin Ave., Milwaukee, WI 53233. TEL 414-224-1564. (reprint service avail. from UMI)
    Description: Annual public lectures by theologians.

200   BL   ISSN 0031-5486
PERMANENCIA.* 1968. m. Cr.$50. Editora Permanencia, Rua Jardim Botanico 86, Rio de Janeiro, Brazil. Ed. Julio Fleichman.

PERSONA Y SOCIEDAD. see *SOCIAL SCIENCES: COMPREHENSIVE WORKS*

268   US
PERSPECTIVE (WHEATON). Variant title: Pioneer Clubs Perspective. 1967. 3/yr. $5. Pioneer Clubs, 27W130 St. Charles Rd., Box 788, Wheaton, IL 60189. TEL 708-293-1600. FAX 708-293-3053. Ed. Rebecca Powell Parat. circ. 25,000. (back issues avail.)
    Description: Provides resources for club leaders to develop leadership and relationship skills.

200   US   ISSN 0888-5281
PERSPECTIVES (GRAND RAPIDS); a journal of reformed thought. 1986. 10/yr. $15. Perspectives, c/o John Strapert, 502 Edgeworthe, Grand Rapids, MI 49546. bk.rev.; circ. 6,500 (AP). **Indexed:** CERDIC, Rel.& Theol.Abstr. (1989-), Rel.Ind.One.
    Incorporates (1951-1991): Reformed Journal (ISSN 0486-252X)

215   US   ISSN 0892-2675
BL240.2
PERSPECTIVES ON SCIENCE AND CHRISTIAN FAITH. 1949. q. $25 to individuals; institutions $35. American Scientific Affiliation, Box 668, Ipswich, MA 01938. TEL 508-356-5656. Ed. J.W. Haas, Jr. adv.; bk.rev.; abstr.; circ. 3,600. (also avail. in microform from UMI; reprint service avail. from UMI) **Indexed:** CERDIC, Chr.Per.Ind., G.Soc.Sci.& Rel.Per.Lit., Rel.& Theol.Abstr. (1968-), Rel.Ind.One, Soc.Work Res.& Abstr.
    —BLDSC shelfmark: 6428.163700.
    Formerly: American Scientific Affiliation. Journal: Evangelical Perspectives on Science and Christian Faith (ISSN 0003-0988)
    Description: Academic articles related to issues involving the interaction of science and Christian faith.

PESHITTA INSTITUTE, LEIDEN. MONOGRAPHS. see *RELIGIONS AND THEOLOGY — Judaic*

200   NE
PFARRAGO. q. fl.20. Vrije Universiteit, Theologische Fakulteit, De Boelelaan 1105, Amsterdam, Netherlands.

200   AU   ISSN 0031-6709
PFARRBRIEF; der evangelischen Gemeinden Purkersdorf. 1955. 6/yr. S.3 per no. Evangelische Pfarrgemeinde Purkersdorf, Wintergasse 13-15, A-3002 Purkersdorf, Austria. Ed. Vikar Hans Juergen Deml. adv.; circ. 1,200.

PHENOMENOLOGICAL THEOLOGY. see *PHILOSOPHY*

PHILIPPINE STUDIES; quarterly publication of Philippine thought and culture. see *HUMANITIES: COMPREHENSIVE WORKS*

PHILIPPINE WITNESS. see *POLITICAL SCIENCE — Civil Rights*

PHILOSOPHIC STUDIES IN THE UNITY OF RELIGIONS. see *PHILOSOPHY*

PHILOSOPHY AND RELIGION: A COMPARATIVE YEARBOOK. see *PHILOSOPHY*

PHILOSOPHY AND SOCIAL CRITICISM. see *HUMANITIES: COMPREHENSIVE WORKS*

200   GR   ISSN 0031-8396
PHONI TOU EVANGELIOU/VOICE OF THE GOSPEL. 1944. m. Dr.50($5) A.M.G. International, 28 Emm. Benaki St., Athens 142, Greece. Ed. George Z. Constantinidis. bk.rev.; abstr.; bibl.; illus.; index; circ. 6,500.

266 301.2   IT
PIEMME. 1927. s-m. L.16000. Missionari Comboniani, Vicolo Pozzo 1, 37129 Verona, Italy. Ed. Antonio Bonato. adv.; bk.rev.; circ. 120,000.
    Formerly: Piccolo Missionario (ISSN 0031-9600)

PILGRIMAGE: THE JOURNAL OF PSYCHOTHERAPY AND PERSONAL EXPLORATION. see *MEDICAL SCIENCES — Psychiatry And Neurology*

PIONEER CHRISTIAN MONTHLY. see *ETHNIC INTERESTS*

200   NE   ISSN 0032-0056
PIONIER. 1939. m. free. (Stichting Alliance Zendings, Centrum Parousia) C A M A - Zending, Amersfoortseweg 44, 3951 LC Maarn, Netherlands. TEL 03432-3392. Ed. A. Stringer. illus.; circ. 4,500.

PLANET WALK. see *LITERATURE*

200 300   US   ISSN 0740-9125
THE PLOUGH (FARMINGTON). 1938-1958; resumed 1983. irreg. donation. (Hutterian Brethren Service Committee, Inc.) Plough Publishing House, Spring Valley Bruderhof, R.D. 2, Box 446, Farmington, PA 15437. TEL 412-329-1100. FAX 412-329-0942. Ed. David Mow. bk.rev.; illus.; tr.lit.; index; circ. 14,000. (also avail. in Braille; back issues avail.)
    Description: Covers urgent issues, including personal committtment to Christ, children and education, community life, prison ministry, and racial justice.

268   FR
POINTS DE REPERE. 1955. 7/yr. 141 F. (Centre National de l'Enseignement Religieux (C.N.E.R.)) Bayard Presse, 5, rue Bayard, 75380 Paris Cedex 08, France. circ. 60,000.
    Formerly: Catechistes d'Aujourd'hui (ISSN 0008-7742)

207 268.8   US   ISSN 0079-2543
POINTS FOR EMPHASIS; INTERNATIONAL SUNDAY SCHOOL LESSONS IN POCKET SIZE. (Large type edition also avail.) 1917. a. $3.50 (large type ed. $4.50). Broadman Press, 127 Ninth Ave., N., Nashville, TN 37234. TEL 615-251-2000. Ed. William J. Fallis. circ. 46,000.
    Description: Supplementary reading on International Sunday School lessons for adults.

POLKA; Polish women's quarterly magazine. see *WOMEN'S INTERESTS*

200   VC
PONTE D'ORO. 1966. m. L.4500. Pontificia Opera della Santa Infanzia, Via di Propaganda 1, 00187 Rome, Italy. Ed. Giuliani Sandro. circ. 30,000.

200 360   IT
POPOLO. 1922. w. L.5000. Giunta Diocesana di A.C., Via Trento, 33170 Pordenone, Italy. (Subscr. to: Il Popolo, Casella Postale 103, Pordenone, Italy)

POTCHEFSTROOM UNIVERSITY FOR CHRISTIAN HIGHER EDUCATION. WETENSKAPLIKE BYDRAES. REEKS B: NATUURWETENSKAPPE. SERIES. see *EDUCATION — Adult Education*

200   US   ISSN 0032-6003
POWER FOR LIVING. 1942. q. $7.75. Scripture Press Publications, Inc., 1825 College Ave., Wheaton, IL 60187. TEL 708-668-6000. Ed. Donald W. Crawford. bk.rev.; illus.

200   US   ISSN 0032-6011
POWER FOR TODAY. 1955. q. $7.95. 20th Century Christian Foundation, 2809 Granny White Pike, Nashville, TN 37204. TEL 615-383-3842. Eds. Steven S. and Emily Y. Lemley. adv.; circ. 50,000. (processed; also avail. in microfilm from UMI; reprint service avail. from UMI)

PRACTICAL PAPERS FOR THE BIBLE TRANSLATOR. see *LINGUISTICS*

200   DK   ISSN 0106-6218
PRAESTEFORENINGENS BLAD. 1899. w. (50/yr.). DKK 504. Danske Praesteforening, Rosenvaengets Hovedvej 19, 2100 Copenhagen OE, Denmark. TEL 31-260555. FAX 35-430588. Ed. Jakob Grosboell. adv.; bk.rev.; circ. 3,800.

266   AT
PRAISE & PRAYER CALENDAR. bi-m. Far East Broadcasting Co., Cnr. Banksia Rd. & Willarong Rd., P.O. Box 183, Caringbah, N.S.W. 2229, Australia. TEL 02-525-6460. FAX 02-526-1250. Ed. Rev. D. Best. circ. 2,400. (back issues avail.)
    Description: Daily prayer guide.

PRAVSLAVNI MISIONAR/ORTHODOX MISSIONARY. see *RELIGIONS AND THEOLOGY — Other Denominations And Sects*

PRAXIS JURIDIQUE ET RELIGION. see *LAW*

200   UK
PRAYER BOOK SOCIETY NEWSLETTER. 1975. 5/yr. membership. Prayer Book Society, 36 The Drive, Northwood, Middlesex HA6 1HP, England. (Subscr. addr.: c/o Col. H.D. Rogers, Redlynch Lodge, Redlynch, Salisbury, Wiltshire SP5 2NJ, England) Ed. C.A. Anthony Kilmister. bk.rev.; circ. 10,500.
    Description: Campaigns for traditionalism in the Church of England and in particular for the 1662 Book of Common Prayer.

200   US   ISSN 0882-7036
PREACHING. 1985. bi-m. $24.95. Preaching Resources, Inc., 1529 Cesery Blvd., Jacksonville, FL 32211. TEL 904-743-5994. FAX 904-743-0925. Ed. Michael Duduit. adv.; bk.rev.; circ. 10,000. (back issues avail.)
    Description: Practical articles on preaching, sermon manuscripts and homiletic helps.

200   GW   ISSN 0079-4961
PREDIGTSTUDIEN. 1968. s-a. DM.36 per vol. Kreuz-Verlag, Breitwiesenstr. 30, 7000 Stuttgart 80, Germany. FAX 0711-7880310. Ed.Bd. circ. 7,000.

200   CN   ISSN 0079-4996
PRESBYTERIAN CHURCH IN CANADA. GENERAL ASSEMBLY. ACTS AND PROCEEDINGS. a. Can.$10. Presbyterian Church in Canada, General Assembly, 50 Wynford Dr., Don Mills, Ont. M3C IJ7, Canada. TEL 416-441-1111.

200   CN   ISSN 1188-5580
PRESENCE. 1962. 8/yr. Can.$26 (foreign Can.$36). Institut de Pastorale, 2715 Chemin de la Cote Sainte-Catherine, Montreal, Que. H3T 1B6, Canada. TEL 514-739-9797. FAX 514-739-1664. (Co-sponsors: Communaute Notre-Dame; Ordre des Dominicains) Ed. Louis Lesage. adv.: page Can.$480. bk.rev.; bibl.; circ. 5,500. **Indexed:** CERDIC, Pt.de Rep.
    ●Also available online.
    Former titles (until 1992): Nouveau Magazine Communaute Chretienne; Communaute Chretiene (ISSN 0010-3454)

RELIGIONS AND THEOLOGY

200   CK
PRESENCIA. 1950. m. $14. Editorial Presencia Ltda., Calle 23 no. 24-20, Bogota D.E., Colombia. Ed. Maria Carrizosa de Umana. adv.; abstr.; bibl.; circ. 15,000.

250   FR   ISSN 0032-7956
PRETRES DIOCESAINS. 1862. m. 320 F.($50) 179 rue de Tolbiac, 75013 Paris, France. bk.rev.; abstr.; bibl.; index. (tabloid format)
  Description: Intended for those involved in the clergy. Addresses problems in the Catholic church as well as spiritual issues. Features Biblical studies and a bibliographic section.

200   FR
PRIER. 1978. m. 163 bd. Malesherbes, 75017 Paris, France. TEL 1-48-88-46-00. FAX 1-42-27-29-03. TELEX 649 333. circ. 85,000.
  Description: A review of modern prayer and contemplation.

268   US   ISSN 0032-8278
PRIMARY DAYS; makes Bible truths live. vol.5, 1939. q. $7.75. Scripture Press Publications, Inc., 1825 College Ave., Wheaton, IL 60187. TEL 708-668-6000. Ed. Janice K. Briton. charts; illus.
  Description: Presents the teachings of the Bible for children ages 6-8.

268 028.5   SP
PRIMERA LUZ. 1972. m. 2200 ptas.($18) Juan Antonio Monroy, Ed. & Pub., Apdo. 2029, 28080 Madrid, Spain. TEL 91-572-18-62. bk.rev.; circ. 3,000.

200   AT
PRISM. 1968. 4/yr. Aus.$10. Lutheran Publishing House, 205 Halifax St., Adelaide, S.A. 5000, Australia. Ed. Mrs. P. Oster. circ. 1,750.

200   US   ISSN 0887-5049
PRISM (NEW BRIGHTON); a theological forum for the United Church of Christ. 1985. s-a. $10. (United Church of Christ) Prism Publishers, 3000 5th St. N.W., New Brighton, MN 55112. FAX 612-633-4315. Eds. Clyde Steckel, Elizabeth Nordbeck. circ. 1,500.

PRISMET; a Norwegian journal for pedagogy of religion. see *EDUCATION*

209 956   IS   ISSN 0032-9622
BR1070
PROCHE-ORIENT CHRETIEN. (Text in English and French) 1951. q. $20. Peres Blancs de Sainte-Anne de Jerusalem, B.P. 19079, Jerusalem, Israel. TEL 02-281992. Ed. Frans Bouwen. bk.rev.; index, cum.index: 1951-1970; circ. 900. (also avail. in microform from IDC) **Indexed:** Bull.Signal., CERDIC, Rel.& Theol.Abstr. (1990-), Rel.Ind.One.
  —BLDSC shelfmark: 6850.605500.

200   US
PROFESSIONAL APPROACHES FOR CHRISTIAN EDUCATORS. Short title: P A C E. 1989. 8/yr. $90. Our Sunday Visitor, Inc., Religious Education Department, 200 Noll Plaza, Huntington, IN 46750. TEL 800-348-2440. Ed.Bd. adv.; circ. 2,000.

PROFESSIONAL CHRISTIAN COUNSELOR. see *PSYCHOLOGY*

170   US
PROGRESS (MEDFORD). 1895. m. $2. International Reform Federation, 205 Tuckerston Rd., Ste.200, Medford, NJ 08109. TEL 609-985-7724. Ed. Samuel A. Jeanes. bk.rev.; circ. 2,800. (back issues avail.)

220   CN   ISSN 0048-5578
PROPHETIC EXPOSITOR. 1964. m. membership. British Israel World Federation (Canada) Inc., 313 Sherbourne St., Toronto, Ont., Canada. TEL 416-921-5996. Eds. D.C. Nesbit, M. McEwan. adv.; bk.rev.; abstr.; bibl.; charts; illus.; stat.; index; circ. 1,600. (processed)

200   RU
PROTESTANT. 1982. q. Mukomolni Proezd Dom 1 Korpus 2, 123290 Moscow, Russia. TEL 7-095-2599397. FAX 7-095-2926511.
  Formerly: Samizdat Review.

200   SP   ISSN 0478-6378
BX805
PROYECCION; teologia y mundo actual. 1954. q. 1250 ptas.($26) Facultad de Teologia, Granada, Apartado 2002, 18080 Granada, Spain. Ed. Ildefonro Camacho. adv.; bk.rev.; circ. 2,100. (tabloid format; back issues avail.) **Indexed:** Old Test.Abstr.
  —BLDSC shelfmark: 6938.323000.

220.48   NE   ISSN 0079-7197
PSEUDEPIGRAPHA VETERIS TESTAMENTI GRAECE. 1964. irreg., vol.4, 1977. price varies. (Rijksuniversiteit te Leiden) E.J. Brill, P.O. Box 9000, 2300 PA Leiden, Netherlands. TEL 071-312624. FAX 071-317532. TELEX 39296 BRILL NL. (In N. America: E.J. Brill, 24 Hudson ST., Kinderhook, NY 12106. TEL 800-962-4406) Eds. A.M. Denis, M. de Jonge.

PSYCHICAL STUDIES. see *PARAPSYCHOLOGY AND OCCULTISM*

200   GW   ISSN 0343-1401
PUBLIK-FORUM. 1972. fortn. DM.116. (Leserinitiative Publik e.V.) Publik Forum Verlagsgesellschaft mbH, Postfach 2010, 6370 Oberursel, Germany. TEL 06171-70030. FAX 06171-700340. Ed.Bd. adv.; bk.rev.; circ. 28,500.

250   US   ISSN 0160-838X
BV4200
PULPIT DIGEST (1978). N.S. 1972. bi-m. $10. Pulpit Publishing Co., Inc., Box 5199, Jackson, MS 39216. TEL 601-366-6469. Ed. Chas. L. Wallis. adv.; bk.rev.; index; circ. 12,000.
  Formerly: New Pulpit Digest (ISSN 0145-7969); Which was formed by the merger of: Pulpit Digest (ISSN 0033-4146); Pulpit Preaching (ISSN 0160-3515)

200   US   ISSN 0193-3914
PULPIT HELPS. 1975. m. $15. Advancing the Ministries of the Gospel International, 6815 Shallowford Rd., Chattanooga, TN 37422. TEL 800-251-7206. FAX 615-894-6863. Ed. Spiros Zodhiates. adv.; bk.rev.; illus.; circ. 210,000. (also avail. in microfiche; back issues avail.) **Indexed:** CCR.

200   US   ISSN 0195-1548
PULPIT RESOURCE. 1973. q. $28. Logos Productions Inc., 6160 Carmen Ave. East, Inver Grove Heights, MN 55076. TEL 612-451-9945. FAX 612-457-4617. Ed. Glendon E. Harris. circ. 7,500. (back issues avail.)
  Description: Resource and illustrative material for preparation of sermons for ministers, priests, and rabbis and lay speakers.

266   US   ISSN 0747-8631
PULSE (WHEATON). Logo title: World Pulse. 1967. s-m. $24.95. Evangelical Missions Information Service, Box 794, Wheaton, IL 60189. TEL 708-653-2158. FAX 708-653-0520. Ed. James W. Reapsome. circ. 3,500. **Indexed:** Int.Nurs.Ind.
  Formerly: Europe Pulse.
  Description: Contains news and commentary about missions, politics and religion worldwide.

200   CE
PUTHIYA ULAHAM. (Text in Tamil) 1976. 6/yr. Centre for Better Society, 115, 4th Cross St., Jaffna, Sri Lanka. TEL 21-22627. Ed. Rev. S.J. Emmanuel. circ. 1,500.

200   IT
QUADERNI DE IL GALLO. 1946. m. L.30000($18) (foreign L.40000)(effective Jan. 1992). Associazione Il Gallo, Casella Postale 1242, 16100 Genoa, Italy. TEL 010-592819. Dir. Germano Beringheli. bk.rev.; circ. 2,000. (also avail. in microform from UMI; reprint service avail. from UMI) **Indexed:** CERDIC.
  Formerly: Gallo (ISSN 0016-416X)

200 933   IS
QUADERNI DE "LA TERRA SANTA". (Text in various languages) 1963. irreg. Franciscan Printing Press, P.O. Box 14064, Jerusalem 91140, Israel. TEL 02-286594.

289.6   US   ISSN 0033-5096
QUAKER SERVICE BULLETIN. 1947. 3/yr. contribution $10. American Friends Service Committee, Inc., 1501 Cherry St., Philadelphia, PA 19102. TEL 215-241-7051. FAX 215-241-7275. Ed. Diane Shandor. illus.; circ. 85,000. (also avail. in microform from UMI; reprint service avail. from UMI) **Indexed:** HR Rep.
  Formerly (until 1960): Bulletin (Philadelphia) (ISSN 0033-510X)
  Description: Program activities of the committee.

266   US   ISSN 0033-6017
QUEEN OF ALL HEARTS; the true devotion magazine. 1950. bi-m. $15. Montfort Missionaries, 26 S. Saxon Ave., Bay Shore, NY 11706. TEL 516-665-0726. FAX 516-665-4349. Ed. J. Patrick Gaffney, S.M.M. bk.rev.; illus.; circ. 6,105. (back issues avail.)
  Description: Religious forum covering Christianity and missionaries.

260   GW   ISSN 0079-9084
QUELLEN UND FORSCHUNGEN ZUR WUERTTEMBERGISCHEN KIRCHENGESCHICHTE. 1967. irreg., vol.8, 1986. Calwer Verlag, Scharnhauserstr. 44, 7000 Stuttgart 70, Germany. TEL 0711-452019. FAX 0711-4560660. Eds. Martin Brecht, Gerhard Schaefer.
  —BLDSC shelfmark: 7216.115700.

THE QUEST (WHEATON). see *NEW AGE PUBLICATIONS*

QUESTION DE. see *PARAPSYCHOLOGY AND OCCULTISM*

200   SP
QUESTIONS DE VIDA CRISTIANA. (Text in Catalan) 5/yr. 4200 ptas.($62) Publicacions de l' Abadia de Montserrat, Ausia March 92-98, Apdo. 244, 08013 Barcelona, Spain.

R-A-D-A-R. see *CHILDREN AND YOUTH — For*

261 322   US
BR738.6
R C D A. (Religion in Communist Dominated Areas) 1962. q. $25 to individuals; institutions and foreign $28. Research Center for Religion & Human Rights in Closed Societies, Ltd., 475 Riverside Dr., Ste. 448, New York, NY 10115. TEL 212-870-2481. Ed. Olga S. Hurby. adv.; bk.rev.; illus.; index; circ. 3,000. (also avail. in microform from UMI; back issues avail.) **Indexed:** Mid.East: Abstr.& Ind., Rel.Ind.One.
  Formerly (until 1990): R C D A - Religion in Communist Dominated Areas (ISSN 0034-3978)

200   US
R I A L NEWS. 1949. q. free. Religion in American Life, 2 Queenston Pl., Rm. 200, Princeton, NJ 08540. TEL 201-921-3639. FAX 609-924-7597. Ed. Nicholas van Dyck. charts; illus.; stat.; circ. 1,000. (tabloid format)
  Description: Provides general information on strengthening congregation from an inter-faith perspective.

R N A NEWSLETTER. (Religion Newswriters Association) see *JOURNALISM*

R P R C COUNSELOR. (Religious Public Relations Council) see *ADVERTISING AND PUBLIC RELATIONS*

R P R C MEDIA KIT. (Religious Public Relations Council) see *ADVERTISING AND PUBLIC RELATIONS*

201 301   US   ISSN 0275-0147
RADIX. 1969. q. $10. Radix Magazine, Inc., Box 4307, Berkeley, CA 94704. TEL 415-548-5329. Ed. Sharon Gallagher. adv.; bk.rev.; film rev.; illus.; circ. 5,000. **Indexed:** Soils & Fert.
  Formerly (until 1976): Right On.

200   BN
RADOSNA VIJEST; monthly informative journal of pontifical mission aid societies. (Text in Serbo-Croatian) 1972. m. 1200 din.($2) Misijska Centrala, Radojke Lakic 7, Box 155, 71001 Sarajevo, Bosnia Hercegovina. TEL 071 36077. Ed. Zvonimir Baotic. bk.rev.; circ. 10,000. (back issues avail.)
  Description: News about missions in Africa, Asia and South America.

RASSEGNA DI LETTERATURA TOMISTICA. see *PHILOSOPHY*

RELIGIONS AND THEOLOGY

200   IT   ISSN 0033-9644
RASSEGNA DI TEOLOGIA; rivista bimestrale per un aggiornamento Cristiano teorico e pratico. 1960. bi-m. L.30000 to individuals; members and students L.15000. Editrice A.V.E, Via Aurelia 481, 00165 Rome, Italy. Ed. Antonio Barruffo. adv.; bk.rev.; bibl.; index; circ. 2,000. **Indexed:** CERDIC, New Test.Abstr.
—BLDSC shelfmark: 7295.020000.
    Formerly: Digest Cattolico.

THE RATIONALIST NEWS. see PHILOSOPHY

200   US   ISSN 0034-0987
REALITY; a national monthly of Christian belief and opinion. 1965. m. free. Reality Inc., 1 Canyon Dr., Alexandria, VA 22305. TEL 703-836-0565. (Subscr. to: Box 50, Washington, DC 20044) Ed. Paul Rader. adv.; bk.rev.; charts; illus.; circ. 9,831. (tabloid format; also avail. in microform from UMI; reprint service avail. from UMI)
    Formerly: Magazine of Reality.

200   FR   ISSN 0034-1258
RECHERCHES DE SCIENCE RELIGIEUSE. 1910. q. 234 F. (foreign 272 F.). Association Recherches de Science Religieuse, 15 rue Monsieur, 75007 Paris, France. TEL 40-61-64-00. Ed. Joseph Moingt. bk.rev.; index, cum.index: 1910-1960.; circ. 1,310. **Indexed:** Bull.Signal., CERDIC, M.L.A., New Test.Abstr., Old Test.Abstr., Rel.Ind.One, Rel.Per.
—BLDSC shelfmark: 7309.160000.

230   BE   ISSN 0034-1266
BX800.A1
RECHERCHES DE THEOLOGIE ANCIENNE ET MEDIEVALE; a journal of ancient and medieval Christian literature. (Text in English, French and German) 1929. s-a. 950 Fr.($32) Abbaye du Mont Cesar, 202 Mechelse Straat, B-3000 Louvain, Belgium. Ed. E. Manning. adv.; bk.rev.; bibl.; index. **Indexed:** CERDIC, M.L.A., New Test.Abstr., Rel.& Theol.Abstr. (1979-).

262.9 200   FR
RECHERCHES INSTITUTIONNELLES. (In 4 Series: Droit et Eglises (ISSN 0220-7818); Institutions et Histoire (ISSN 0243-2412); Culture et Religion (ISSN 0154-0416); Recherche Documentaire (ISSN 0244-6936)) irreg. CERDIC Publications, 2 rue Goethe, Palais Universitaire, F-67083 Strasbourg, France. Eds. J. Schlick, M. Zimmerman. circ. 2,000.

255   NE
RECONCILIATION INTERNATIONAL. (Text in English) 1919. 4/yr. DM.30($20) International Fellowship of Reconciliation, Spoorstraat 38, 1815 BK Alkmaar, Netherlands. TEL 072-123014. FAX 072-151102. Ed. Shelley J. Anderson. adv.; bk.rev.; circ. 1,000. (back issues avail.) **Indexed:** Alt.Press Ind.
    Formerly (until 1985): I F O R Report (ISSN 0167-174X)
    Description: Covers peace and justice issues, religious repsonse to social issues, and the relevance of nonviolent methods of social change and conflict resolution.

RECORD (NEW YORK, 1976). see HOMOSEXUALITY

200   US
REFLECTIONS (NEW HAVEN). 1965. s-a. free. Yale University, Divinity School, 409 Prospect St., New Haven, CT 06511. (Co-sponsors: Berkeley Divinity School; Institute of Sacred Music) circ. 7,500.

280   US   ISSN 0034-303X
REFORMATION REVIEW. (Vol. 22 not published) 1953. q. $10. (International Council of Christian Churches) Christian Beacon Press, Collingswood, NJ 08108. TEL 609-858-0700. Ed. J.C. Maris. bk.rev.; index; circ. 850. **Indexed:** CERDIC.
—BLDSC shelfmark: 7332.510000.

200   US
REFORMED SCOPE. 1971. m. free. Orthodox Reformed Publishing Society, 3836 30th St., Grandville, MI 49418-1604. Ed. Peter G. Elzinga. bk.rev.; circ. 750. (processed)

230   AT   ISSN 0034-3072
REFORMED THEOLOGICAL REVIEW. 1942. 3/yr. Aus.$12($15) P.O. Box 635, Doncaster, Vic. 3108, Australia. Eds. A.M. Harman, D.G. Peterson. bk.rev.; index; circ. 600. **Indexed:** CERDIC, Int.Z.Bibelwiss., New Test.Abstr., Rel.& Theol.Abstr. (1968-), Rel.Ind.One, Rel.Per.
—BLDSC shelfmark: 7332.530000.
    Description: Contains biblical and theological articles.

REFUGEES. see POLITICAL SCIENCE — Civil Rights

248.82   AU
REGENBOGEN; Zeitung fuer Maedchen und Buben. 1946. w. S.120. Bischoefliches Seelsorgeamt Klagenfurt, Waaggasse 18, A-9010 Klagenfurt, Austria. Ed. Martin Bliem. bk.rev.; illus.; circ. 45,000. (looseleaf format)
    Formerly (until Mar. 1977): Gotteskinder (ISSN 0017-2510)

250   GW   ISSN 0034-3250
REGENSBURGER BISTUMSBLATT. 1926. w. DM.25. (Bischoeflicher Stuhl Regensburg) Verlag Regensburger Bistumsblatt, Koenigsstr. 2, 8400 Regensburg 2, Germany. Ed. Anton Reiter.

200   IT   ISSN 0009-000X
REGNO - DOCUMENTI. 1966. m. L.28000 (foreign L.42000). Centro Editoriale Dehoniano, Via Nosadella 6, 40123 Bologna, Italy. TEL 051-306811. FAX 051-341706. adv.; circ. 14,000. (looseleaf format)
    Description: Covers religion and ecclesiastic issues.

200   GW
REGULAE BENEDICTI STUDIA. ANNUARIUM INTERNATIONALE. (Text in English, French and German) 1972. a. price varies. Eos Verlag, Erzabtei St. Ottilien, 8917 St. Ottilien, Germany. FAX 08193-6844. Eds. B. Jaspert, E. Manning. circ. 300.

200   BL   ISSN 0034-3633
REINO; de deus no mundo dos homens. 1943. m. Cr.$35. Promocao-Da-Familia Editora, Caixa Postal-1133, Belo Horizonte-MG., Brazil. Ed. Osvaldo Goncalves. illus.; circ. 12,000.
    Formerly: Reino dos Sagrados Coracoes.

REJOICE!; the gospel music magazine. see MUSIC

RELIGIEUSES DANS LES PROFESSIONS DE SANTE. see HOSPITALS

200   UK   ISSN 0048-721X
BL1
RELIGION; the established journal of the history, structure and theory of religion and religions. 1970. q. $131. Academic Press Ltd., 24-28 Oval Rd., London NW1 7DX, England. TEL 071-267-4466. FAX 071-482-2293. TELEX 25775-ACPRES-G. Eds. A. Cunningham, Ivan Strenski. **Indexed:** Arts & Hum.Cit.Ind., CERDIC, Curr.Cont, Mid.East: Abstr.& Ind., New Test.Abstr., Old Test.Abstr., Rel.Ind.One.
—BLDSC shelfmark: 7356.435000.
    Description: Provides a regular survey of current work in major and specific areas of enquiry; encompasses such related studies as psychology and archeology.

200   US   ISSN 1052-1151
▼**RELIGION AND AMERICAN CULTURE**; a journal of interpretation. 1991. s-a. $25. Indiana University Press, Journal Division, 601 Morton St., Bollmington, IN 47404. TEL 812-855-9449. Ed. Conrad Cherry.
    Description: Explores the interplay between religion and other spheres of American culture.

200   US   ISSN 0730-2363
RELIGION AND LIFE LETTERS. 1981. fortn. $25 (foreign $35). Spiritual Studies Center, Box 1104, Rockville, MD 20850. TEL 301-963-9243. Ed. George Leonard.

RELIGION AND LITERATURE. see LITERATURE

261 301   II   ISSN 0034-3951
RELIGION AND SOCIETY. vol.20, 1973. q. Rs.20($15) Christian Institute for the Study of Religion and Society, Publications Trust, Box 4600, 73 Miller's Rd., Bangalore 560046, India. FAX 0812-330335. Ed. J. Victor Koilpillai. adv.; bk.rev.; circ. 1,250. (also avail. in microfilm; reprint service avail. from UMI) **Indexed:** CERDIC, G.Indian Per.Lit, Rel.Ind.One, Rel.Ind.Two, Rel.Per.
—BLDSC shelfmark: 7356.455000.
    Description: Publishes articles on religious and social problems especially issues in social justice, and results of studies and discussions on these matters carried out by the institute.

200   US   ISSN 0742-6984
RELIGION & SOCIETY REPORT. 1984. m. $24. Rockford Institute, 934 N. Main St., Rockford, IL 61103-7061. TEL 815-964-5813. FAX 815-965-1826. (Subscr. to: Box 424, Mt. Morris, IL 61054; Alt. ed. addr.: Trinity Evangelical Divinity School, 2065 Half Day Rd., Deerfield, IL 60015) Ed. Harold O.J. Brown. circ. 4,000. (back issues avail.)
    Description: Covers religious issues and their effect on society, with special reports on timely topics.

200   FR   ISSN 0080-0864
RELIGION ET SCIENCES DE L'HOMME.* 1971. irreg. price varies. Editions du Centurion, 22 cours Albert 1e, 75008 Paris, France.

200 370.196   SZ
RELIGION FOR PEACE; newsletter on inter-religious dialogue and action for peace. 1974. 3/yr. $25. World Conference on Religion and Peace, International Division, 14 Chemin Auguste-Vilbert, CH-1218 Grand-Saconnex, Switzerland. TEL 22-7985162. FAX 22-7910034. Ed. John B. Taylor. circ. 2,500. (back issues avail.)
    Description: Includes youth page and reports from various committees of the conference.

200   GW
RELIGION HEUTE.* 4/yr. DM.59.20 (foreign DM.62.20). Friedrich Verlag, Im Brande 15, 3016 Seelze 6, Germany. Ed.Bd.

RELIGION HEUTE: SUPPLEMENT. see EDUCATION

200   US
RELIGION IN AMERICA. 1967. a. $30. Princeton Religion Research Center, Inc., Box 389, 47 Hulfish St., Princeton, NJ 08542. TEL 609-921-8112. (back issues avail.)

200   US
RELIGION INDEXES: THESAURUS. 1981. biennial. American Theological Library Association, Religion Indexes, 820 Church St., 3rd Fl., Evanston, IL 60201-3707. TEL 708-869-7788. Ed. Erica Treesh.
    ●Also available on CD-ROM.

200 335   UK   ISSN 0963-7494
BR738.6
RELIGION, STATE AND SOCIETY. 1973. 4/yr. $59 to individuals; institutions $164 (effective 1992). (Keston College) Carfax Publishing Co., P.O. Box 25, Abingdon, Oxfordshire OX14 3UE, England. TEL 0235-55535. FAX 0235-55359. (N. America dist. addr.: Carfax Publishing Co., Box 2025, Dunnellon, FL 32630) Ed. John Anderson. adv.; bk.rev.; bibl.; index; circ. 2,000. (also avail. in microform from UMI; reprint service avail. from UMI) **Indexed:** Abstr.Musl.Rel., CERDIC, HR Rep., Rel.Ind.One.
    Formerly (until 1992): Religion in Communist Lands (ISSN 0307-5974)
    Description: Articles on religious communities in communist and formerly communist countries, and social, cultural, ethical and religious issues influencing the emergence of the new Europe.

268   US   ISSN 0034-401X
RELIGION TEACHER'S JOURNAL. 1967. 7/yr. $14.95. Twenty-Third Publications, Box 180, Mystic, CT 06355. TEL 203-536-2611. FAX 203-572-0788. Ed. Gwen Costello. adv.; abstr.; illus.; index; circ. 39,500. (also avail. in microform from UMI; reprint service avail. from UMI) **Indexed:** Cath.Ind., CERDIC.
    Description: Help for lay persons working as church educators, and as a training vehicle for pastors to use with them.

RELIGIONS AND THEOLOGY

200 UK ISSN 0267-1700
RELIGION TODAY. 1984. 3/yr. £6($12) to individuals. Centre for New Religious Movements, King's College London, Strand, London WC2R 2LS, England. TEL 01-836-5454. Ed. Peter B. Clarke. adv.; bk.rev.; circ. 500. **Indexed:** ASSIA.
—BLDSC shelfmark: 7356.475200.
Description: Provides a forum for discussion and analysis of new religions and trends and developments within mainstream churches.

200 301 IT ISSN 0391-853X
RELIGIONE E SOCIETA; storia della chiesa e dei movimenti cattolici. 1977. irreg., latest vol.15. price varies. Edizioni Studium, Via Cassiodoro 14, 00193 Rome, Italy.

200 301 IT ISSN 0394-9397
RELIGIONI E SOCIETA; rivista di scienze sociali della religione. 1986. 2/yr. L.42000 (Europe L.55000; elsewhere L.75000). Rosenberg & Sellier, Via Andrea Doria, 14, 10123 Turin, Italy. TEL 011-561-39-07. FAX 011-532188. Ed. Bd. adv.; circ. 1,000. **Indexed:** Sociol.Abstr. (1986-).
Description: Religious forum covering theology, philosophy and sociology of religions.

200 GW
RELIGIONSPAEDAGOGISCHE PRAXIS. Short title: R P P. 1971. irreg. price varies. Calwer Verlag, Scharnhauserstr. 44, 7000 Stuttgart 70, Germany. TEL 0711-452019. FAX 0711-4560660. (Co-publisher: Koesel-Verlag) Eds. Horst Klaus Berg, Wolfgang Langer. (back issues avail.)

RELIGIONSUNTERRICHT AN HOEHEREN SCHULEN. see *EDUCATION*

200 DK ISSN 0108-1993
RELIGIONSVIDENSKABELIGT TIDSSKRIFT. (Text in Danish; summaries in English) 1982. s-a. DKK 120. Jysk Selskab for Religionsvidenskab, Aarhus Universitet, DK-8000 Aarhus G, Denmark. FAX 45-86-13-04-90. Ed.Bd. adv.; bk.rev.; circ. 350.

200 GW ISSN 0934-2192
RELIGIONSWISSENSCHAFTLICHE REIHE. 1988. a. Diagonal Verlag, Postfach 1248, 3550 Marburg, Germany. TEL 06421-681936. FAX 06421-681733. Ed.Bd.

RELIGIOUS AND INSPIRATIONAL BOOKS AND SERIALS IN PRINT. see *BIBLIOGRAPHIES*

RELIGIOUS BROADCASTING. see *COMMUNICATIONS — Television And Cable*

RELIGIOUS CONFERENCE MANAGER. see *TRAVEL AND TOURISM*

200 II
RELIGIOUS CONSULTANCY. 1978. 4/yr. Rs.135($27) K.K. Roy (Private) Ltd., 55 Gariahat Rd., P.O. Box 10210, Calcutta 700 019, India. Ed. K.K. Roy. adv.; abstr.; bibl.; index; circ. 980.

200 370 US ISSN 0034-4087
BV1460 CODEN: RLEDAN
RELIGIOUS EDUCATION; a platform for the free discussion of issues in the field of religion and their bearing on education. 1906. q. $45 (foreign $48). Religious Education Association, 409 Prospect St., New Haven, CT 06511. TEL 203-865-6141. Eds. Jack D. Spiro, Randolph Crump Miller. adv.; bk.rev.; index; circ. 4,000. (also avail. in microform from UMI; reprint service avail. from UMI) **Indexed:** Bk.Rev.Ind. (1990-), CERDIC, Child.Bk.Rev.Ind. (1990-), Cont.Pg.Educ., Curr.Cont., Educ.Ind., Ind.Jew.Per., Psychol.Abstr., Rel.& Theol.Abstr. (1967-), Rel.Ind.One.
—BLDSC shelfmark: 7356.500000.
Description: Platform for the free discussion of religious issues and their bearing on education, bringing together work by Jewish, Catholic, Orthodox, Protestant and other educators.

200 920 US
▼**RELIGIOUS LEADERS OF AMERICA.** 1991. quinquennial. $79.95. Gale Research Inc., 835 Penobscot Bldg., Detroit, MI 48226. TEL 800-877-4253. FAX 313-961-6083. TELEX 810-221-7086. Ed. J. Gordon Melton.
●Also available online. Vendor(s): Mead Data Central.

200 UK ISSN 0034-4125
BL1
RELIGIOUS STUDIES. 1965. q. $63 to individuals; institutions $131. Cambridge University Press, Edinburgh Bldg., Shaftesbury Rd., Cambridge CB2 2RU, England. TEL 0223-312393. FAX 0223-315052. TELEX 851817256. (U.S. addr.: Cambridge University Press, 40 W. 20th St., New York, NY 10011) Eds. P.A. Byrne, K. Ward. adv.; bk.rev.; index. (also avail. in microform from UMI; reprint service avail. from SWZ) **Indexed:** Arts & Hum.Cit.Ind., Bk.Rev.Ind. (1981-), Br.Hum.Ind., CERDIC, Child.Bk.Rev.Ind. (1981-), Curr.Cont., Hum.Ind., Mid.East: Abstr.& Ind., New Test.Abstr., Phil.Ind., Rel.& Theol.Abstr. (1968-), Rel.Ind.One, Rel.Per.
—BLDSC shelfmark: 7356.550000.
Description: Mainly concerned with the philosophy and history of religion.

200 PH ISSN 0115-6349
RELIGIOUS STUDIES JOURNAL. (Text in English) 1978. s-a. P.85($10.50) (De La Salle University, Religious Studies Department) De La Salle University Press, 2401 Taft Ave., Manila, Philippines. TEL 2-595177. Ed. Edward Baldwin. adv.; bk.rev.; circ. 300.
Description: Publishes scholarly articles reflecting significant quantitative or qualitative research. Includes speeches, research reports, and "state of the art" papers.

200 US ISSN 0319-485X
BL1
RELIGIOUS STUDIES REVIEW; a quarterly review of publications in the field of religion and related disciplines. 1975. q. $30 to individuals (foreign $38); institutions $36 (foreign $44). Council of Societies for the Study of Religion, Mercer University, R.O.T.C. Bldg., Macon, GA 31207. TEL 912-752-2376. Ed.Bd. adv.; bk.rev.; bibl.; circ. 2,672. **Indexed:** Bk.Rev.Ind. (1980-), CERDIC, Chic.Per.Ind., Child.Bk.Rev.Ind. (1980-), Mid.East: Abstr.& Ind., New Test.Abstr., Old Test.Abstr., Rel.& Theol.Abstr. (1989-), Rel.Ind.One, Rel.Per.
—BLDSC shelfmark: 7356.555000.

200 IT ISSN 0034-4486
RENOVATIO. 1966. q. L.4000. Gianni Baget Bozzo, Ed. & Pub., Via 12 Ottobre 14, Genoa, Italy. bk.rev.; index; circ. 1,200 (controlled). **Indexed:** CERDIC.

RES MEDICAE. see *MEDICAL SCIENCES*

266 US ISSN 1049-586X
RESCUE (KANSAS CITY). 1985. q. free. International Union of Gospel Missions, 1045 Swift Ave., Kansas City, MO 64116-4127. TEL 816-471-8020. FAX 816-471-3718. Ed. Michael Liimatta. adv.; bk.rev.; circ. 3,500.
Formerly: Horizons.
Description: Quarterly journal for ministries and individuals ministering to homeless and hurting men, women, youth and families.

200 301.4 US ISSN 1055-1158
RESEARCH IN RELIGION AND FAMILY: BLACK PERSPECTIVES. irreg. price varies. Peter Lang Publishing, Inc., 62 W. 45th St., 4th Fl., New York, NY 10036. TEL 212-302-6740. Ed. Noel Leo Erskine.
Description: Examines the goals of family and religion within the black tradition.

200 US
RESEARCH IN THE SOCIAL SCIENTIFIC STUDY OF RELIGION. 1989. a. (Abilene Christian University) J A I Press Inc., 55 Old Post Rd., No. 2, Box 1678, Greenwich, CT 06836-1678. TEL 203-661-7602.
Description: Contains approximately 9 international articles examining religion and religious organizations from a variety of social science perspectives.
Refereed Serial

200 CN ISSN 0708-2177
RESTORATION. 1947. 10/yr. Can.$4. Madonna House, Inc., Combermere, Ont. K0J 1L0, Canada. TEL 613-756-3713. Ed. Rev. David May. circ. 10,000. (also avail. in microform from UMI; reprint service avail. from UMI)

200 UK ISSN 0950-1568
RESTORATION. 1975. 6/yr. £9.45($17) Harvestime Publishing Ltd., 69 Main St., Markfield, Leicester LE6 0UT, England. TEL 0530-244956. FAX 0530-244955. Ed. Roger Day. adv.; bk.rev.; circ. 8,000.
Description: Provides a Bible-based perspective regarding social, moral and political issues affecting the world; each issue addresses a specific theme.

200 US ISSN 0034-5830
RESTORATION HERALD. 1925. m. (except Aug.). $8. Christian Restoration Association, 5664 Cheviot Rd., Cincinnati, OH 45247. TEL 513-385-0461. Ed. Thomas D. Thurman. adv.; bk.rev.; illus.; circ. 7,000. (also avail. in audio cassette)

222 US ISSN 0486-5642
RESTORATION QUARTERLY. 1958. q. $15 to individuals; institutions $20. Restoration Quarterly Corporation, Box 8227, Abilene, TX 79699. Ed. Everett Ferguson. adv.; bk.rev.; circ. 800. **Indexed:** CERDIC, New Test.Abstr., Old Test.Abstr., Rel.& Theol.Abstr. (1969-), Rel.Ind.One.
—BLDSC shelfmark: 7777.850000.

266 CN ISSN 0034-6284
REVEIL MISSIONNAIRE. 1966. bi-m. Can.$3. Missionnaires de la Consolata, 2505 W. bd. Gouin, Montreal, Que. H3M 1B5, Canada. TEL 514-334-1910. FAX 514-332-1940. Ed. Jean Pare. adv.; illus.; circ. 20,000.

REVIEW (NEW YORK). see *HOMOSEXUALITY*

200 UK
REVIEW OF RELIGIONS. 12/yr. £15. London Mosque, 16 Gressenhall Rd., London SW18 5QL, England. TEL 01-870-8517.
Description: Articles on the doctrines and teachings of Islam, which attempt to set forth a comparative appreciation of the teachings of other faiths.

200 US ISSN 0034-673X
BL1
REVIEW OF RELIGIOUS RESEARCH. 1959. 4/yr. $30. Religious Research Association, Marist Hall, Rm. 108; Catholic University of America, Washington, DC 20064. FAX 202-319-5447. (Editorial addr.: c/o D. Paul Johnson, Sociology Dept., Texas Tech. University, Lubbock, TX 79401) adv.; bk.rev.; abstr.; bibl.; stat.; index, cum.index: vols. 1-10; circ. 1,200. (also avail. in microform from UMI; reprint service avail. from UMI) **Indexed:** Arts & Hum.Cit.Ind., C.L.I., CERDIC, Curr.Cont., G.Soc.Sci.& Rel.Per.Lit., Lang.& Lang.Behav.Abstr., Leg.Per., Mid. East: Abstr.& Ind., Past.Care & Couns.Abstr., Rel.& Theol.Abstr. (1968-), Rel.Ind.One, Rel.Per., Sociol.Abstr. (1972-), SSCI.
—BLDSC shelfmark: 7794.195000.

220 AG ISSN 0034-7078
REVISTA BIBLICA. 1939. q. $24. (Sociedad Argentina de Profesores de Sagrada Escritura) Editorial Guadalupe, Mansilla 3865, 1425 Buenos Aires, Argentina. TEL 01-84-6066. FAX 01-805-4112. Dir. P. Armando Levoratti. adv.; bk.rev.; bibl.; index. cum.index; circ. 700. **Indexed:** Int.Z.Bibelwiss., New Test.Abstr., Rel.Ind.One.

200 SP ISSN 0034-8147
BX805
REVISTA DE ESPIRITUALIDAD. 1941. q. 2,000 ptas. Padres Carmelitas Descalzos, Triana 9, 28016 Madrid, Spain. Ed. Jesus Manuel Garcia Rojo. adv.; bk.rev.; bibl.; index; circ. 1,200. **Indexed:** New Test.Abstr.
—BLDSC shelfmark: 7854.420000.

220 CR
REVISTA DE INTERPRETACION BIBLICA LATINOAMERICANA. Short title: R I B L A. (Editions in Portuguese and Spanish) 1988. 3/yr. $18 in Latin America; elsewhere $30. (Departamento Ecumenico de Investigaciones) Editorial D E I, Apdo. 390-2070 Sabanilla, San Jose, Costa Rica. TEL 53-0229. FAX 53-1541. TELEX 3472 ADEI CR. (For Portuguese ed. subscr. to: Editora Vozes, Rua Frei Luis 100, 25689 Petropolis RJ, Brasil) Ed.Bd.

200 BL
REVISTA ECLESIASTICA BRASILEIRA. 1941. q. $70. Editora Vozes Ltda., Rua Frei Luis 100, Caixa Postal 90023, 25689 Petropolis, Rio de Janeiro, Brazil. Ed. Eloi Dionisio Piva. adv.; bk.rev.; bibl.; circ. 3,000. **Indexed:** Cath.Ind., New Test.Abstr., Old Test.Abstr.

262.9 SP ISSN 0034-9372
K19 CODEN: REDCE4
REVISTA ESPANOLA DE DERECHO CANONICO. (Text in French, Italian, Latin, Spanish; summaries in English, Latin, Spanish) 1946. 2/yr. 4500 ptas.($53) (Consejo Superior de Investigaciones Cientificas (C.S.I.C.), Instituto de Derecho Canonico "San Raimundo de Penafort") Universidad Pontificia, Departamento de Ediciones y Publicaciones, Apdo. de Correos 541, 37080 Salamance, Spain. TEL 923-21-51-40. FAX 923-21-34-50. Ed. Antonio Garcia y Garcia. bk.rev.; bibl.; index, cum.index every 20 yrs.; circ. 1,000. (tabloid format) **Indexed:** Canon Law Abstr., CERDIC.
  Incorporates (in 1984): Colectanea de Jurisprudencia Canonica (ISSN 0210-0711)

200 SP ISSN 0210-7112
REVISTA ESPANOLA DE TEOLOGIA. 1940. q. 3000 ptas. (foreign 4000 ptas.). Centro de Estudios Teologicos "San Damaso", San Buenaventura, 9, 28005 Madrid, Spain. TEL 91-265-24-04. Ed. Manuel Gesteira. bk.rev.; bibl.; circ. 600.
—BLDSC shelfmark: 7854.370000.

200 EC
REVISTA MENSAJERO. 1884. m. (10/yr.). S/2500($13) Ediciones Mensajero, Apdo. 17-01-4100, Quito, Ecuador. Ed.Bd. circ. 5,000.
  Description: Examines the concerns and issues of present-day Catholics living in Ecuador.

200 300 CR
REVISTA PASOS. bi-m. $12 in Latin America; elsewhere $18. (Departamento Ecumenico de Investigaciones) Editorial D E I, Apdo. 390-2070 Sabanilla, San Jose, Costa Rica. TEL 53-0229. FAX 53-1541. TELEX 3472 ADEI CR. Ed.Bd.

220 FR ISSN 0035-0907
REVUE BIBLIQUE. 1892. q. 920 F. (Ecole Biblique et Archeologique de Jerusalem) J. Gabalda et Cie, 18, rue P. et M. Curie, 75005 Paris, France. Ed. R.P. Tournay. bk.rev.; bibl.; charts; illus.; index. cum.index: 1892-1972. **Indexed:** Arts & Hum.Cit.Ind., CERDIC, Curr.Cont., New Test.Abstr., Old Test.Abstr., Rel.& Theol.Abstr. (1975-), Rel.Ind.One, Rel.Per.
—BLDSC shelfmark: 7892.820000.

274 FR ISSN 0300-9505
REVUE D'HISTOIRE DE L'EGLISE DE FRANCE. 1910. s-a. 330 F. Societe d'Histoire Religieuse de la France, 28 rue d'Assas, 75006 Paris, France. (Subscr. to: Editions BREPOLS, 23 rue des Grands-Augustins, 75006 Paris, France) Ed. M. Venard. bk.rev.; circ. 40. **Indexed:** CERDIC, Hist.Abstr.
—BLDSC shelfmark: 7919.452000.

200 FR ISSN 0035-2403
BR3
REVUE D'HISTOIRE ET DE PHILOSOPHIE RELIGIEUSES. 1921. q. 135 F. (foreign 175 F.). (Universite de Strasbourg II) Presses Universitaires de France, Departement des Revues, 14 av. du Bois-de-l'Epine, B.P.90, 91003 Evry Cedex, France. TEL 1-60-77-82-05. FAX 1-60-79-20-45. TELEX PUF 600 474 F. adv.; bk.rev.; charts; illus.; index, cum.index: vol.1, 1920-1945; vol.2, 1946-1974; circ. 1,800. (also avail. in microfilm from KTO; reprint service avail. from KTO) **Indexed:** Arts & Hum.Cit.Ind., CERDIC, Curr.Cont., Hist.Abstr., New Test.Abstr., Rel.& Theol.Abstr. (1975-), Rel.Ind.One, Rel.Per., So.Pac.Per.Ind.
  Description: Provides a scientific study of various biblical, historical, philosophical and dogmatic problems posed by the develoment of christian theological thought and its links with non-christian thought.

209 FR ISSN 0035-1423
BL3
REVUE DE L'HISTOIRE DES RELIGIONS. 1880. q. 315 F. (foreign 410 F.). Presses Universitaires de France, Departement des Revues, 14 av. du Bois-de-l'Epine, B.P.90, 91003 Evry Cedex, France. TEL 1-60-77-82-05. FAX 1-60-79-20-45. TELEX PUF 600 474 F. Dirs. A. Guillaumont, Charles Amiel. bk.rev.; index every 4 mos. (also avail. in microfilm from BHP; reprint service avail. from KTO) **Indexed:** Arts & Hum.Cit.Ind., Curr.Cont., Hist.Abstr., New Test.Abstr., Rel.Ind.One, Rel.Per.
  Description: Encompasses the general history of religions as well as a more in depth focus on particular aspects of a different religion each issue.

REVUE DE QUMRAN. see *ORIENTAL STUDIES*

230 100 SZ ISSN 0035-1784
REVUE DE THEOLOGIE ET DE PHILOSOPHIE. 1868. q. 59 Fr. A T A R, S.A., 11 rue de la Dole, CH-1211 Geneva 13, Switzerland. TEL 022-446400. FAX 022-446865. bk.rev.; index. (also avail. in microfilm from BHP) **Indexed:** Bull.Signal., CERDIC, New Test.Abstr., Old Test.Abstr., Phil.Ind., Rel.Ind.One.
—BLDSC shelfmark: 7956.070000.

230 100 SZ ISSN 0250-6971
REVUE DE THEOLOGIE ET DE PHILOSOPHIE. CAHIERS. 1977. irreg. (approx. a.) A T A R, S.A, 11 rue de la Dole, CH-1211 Geneva 13, Switzerland. TEL 022-446400. FAX 022-446865. (Dist. by: Librairie Droz S.A., 11, rue Massot, CH-1211 Geneva 12, Switzerland) **Indexed:** New Test.Abstr., Rel.Ind.One.
—BLDSC shelfmark: 2952.159000.

230 809 FR ISSN 0035-2012
BX2901
REVUE DES ETUDES AUGUSTINIENNES. (Text in various languages) 1955. q. 350 F.($44) Institut des Etudes Augustiniennes, 3 rue de l'Abbaye, 75006 Paris, France. Dir. Jean-Claude Fredouille. bk.rev.; bibl.; illus.; index; circ. 1,000. **Indexed:** Bull.Signal., CERDIC, M.L.A., New Test.Abstr., Phil.Ind.
  Formerly (until 1954): Annee Theologique Augustinienne.

REVUE MABILLON. see *RELIGIONS AND THEOLOGY — Roman Catholic*

200 CN ISSN 0700-6500
REVUE NOTRE DAME DU CAP. (Text in French) 1892. 8/yr. Can.$7. Corporation Revue Notre-Dame du Cap, 626 rue Notre Dame, Cap-de-la-Madelaine, Que. G8T 4G9, Canada. TEL 819-374-2441. Ed.Bd. adv.; bk.rev.; circ. 105,000.

230 FR ISSN 0035-4295
BX802
REVUE THOMISTE; revue doctrinale de theologie et de philosophie. 1893. q. 380 F. (Europe 450 F.; elsewhere 480 F.)(effective Jan. 1992). Association Culturelle de Publications, Dominicains de la Province de Toulouse, 1 av. Lacordaire, 31078 Toulouse, France. TEL 61-52-84-70. FAX 61-52-47-24. (Subscr. in US to: Kraus Reprint and Periodicals, Route 100, Milwood, NY 10546) Ed. Pere Serge-Thomas Bonino. adv.; bk.rev.; index; circ. 1,100. (also avail. in microfilm from BHP; reprint service avail. from KTO) **Indexed:** Bull.Signal., CERDIC, M.L.A., New Test.Abstr., Phil.Ind., Rel.& Theol.Abstr.

RHEINISCHER MERKUR; Christ und Welt. see *GENERAL INTEREST PERIODICALS — Germany*

200 AT
RHEMA LIFE. 1986. m. free. Rhema Family Church, 1 Thorogood St., Victoria Park, Perth, W.A. 6100, Australia. TEL 4701256. FAX 09-470-3670. Ed. Heather Moorhead. adv.; bk.rev.; circ. 1,100. (back issues avail.)

RICERCHE DI STORIA SOCIALE E RELIGIOSA. see *SOCIOLOGY*

200 282 IT
RICERCHE PER LA STORIA RELIGIOSA DI ROMA. irreg., vol.7, 1988. price varies. Edizioni di Storia e Letteratura s.r.l., Via Lancellotti, 18, 00186 Rome, Italy. TEL 65-40556.

RIGHT TO HOUSING REPORT. see *HOUSING AND URBAN PLANNING*

264 IT ISSN 0035-6395
RIVISTA DI PASTORALE LITURGICA. 1962. bi-m. L.33000 (foreign L.45000). Editrice Queriniana, Via Piamarta 6, 25187 Brescia, Italy. Ed. Daniele Piazzi.
—BLDSC shelfmark: 7992.220000.

RELIGIONS AND THEOLOGY 4199

274 900 IT ISSN 0035-6557
BR870
RIVISTA DI STORIA DELLA CHIESA IN ITALIA. (Text in English, French, German, Italian, Latin, Spanish) 1947. s-a. $90. Herder Editrice e Libreria s.r.l., Piazza Montecitorio 120, 00186 Rome, Italy. TEL 67 94 628. FAX 678-47-51. TELEX 621427 NATEL. Ed. Michele Maccarrone. bk.rev.; bibl.; charts; stat.; tr.lit.; index. (tabloid format) **Indexed:** Hist.Abstr.
—BLDSC shelfmark: 7992.880000.

209 IT ISSN 0035-6573
RIVISTA DI STORIA E LETTERATURA RELIGIOSA. (Text in English, French, German, Italian) 1965. 3/yr. L.68000 (foreign L.85000). (Universita di Torino, Biblioteca Erik Peterson) Casa Editrice Leo S. Olschki, Casella Postale 66, 50100 Florence, Italy. TEL 055-6530684. FAX 055-6530214. Ed.Bd. adv.; bk.rev.; circ. 1,000. **Indexed:** CERDIC, M.L.A., New Test.Abstr.

209 IT
▼**RIVISTA DI STORIA E LETTERATURA RELIGIOSA. BIBLIOTECA. STUDI.** 1990. irreg. price varies. Casa Editrice Leo S. Olschki, Casella Postale 66, 50100 Florence, Italy. TEL 055-6530684. FAX 055-6530214.

209 IT
RIVISTA DI STORIA E LETTERATURA RELIGIOSA. BIBLIOTECA. TESTI E DOCUMENTI. 1967. irreg., no.11, 1990. price varies. Casa Editrice Leo S. Olschki, Casella Postale 66, 50100 Florence, Italy. TEL 055-6530684. FAX 055-6530214. **Indexed:** Arts & Hum.Cit.Ind.

205 IT ISSN 0391-108X
ROCCA. 1940. fortn. L.70000. Pro Civitate Christiana, Via Ancaiani 3, 06081 Assisi, Italy. TEL 075-813641. Ed. Gesuino Bulla. adv.; bk.rev.; circ. 39,638.

200 US ISSN 1052-2204
ROCKWELL LECTURE SERIES. irreg. Peter Lang Publishing, Inc., 62 W. 45th St., 4th Fl., New York, NY 10036. TEL 212-302-6704. FAX 212-302-7574. Ed. Niels C. Nielsen.

ROEMISCHE HISTORISCHE MITTEILUNGEN. see *HISTORY — History Of Europe*

200 GW ISSN 0035-7812
ROEMISCHE QUARTALSCHRIFT FUER CHRISTLICHE ALTERTUMSKUNDE UND KIRCHENGESCHICHTE. 1905. s-a. DM.206. Verlag Herder GmbH und Co. KG, Hermann-Herder-Str. 4, 7800 Freiburg im Breisgau, Germany. FAX 0761-2717-520. adv.; bk.rev.; charts; illus. **Indexed:** Numis.Lit., RILA, RILA.

200 NE ISSN 0035-8169
ROND DE TAFEL; leerkrant liturgie. 1892; N.S. 1946. bi-m. fl.12. Grafische Bedrijven Berne B.V., Postbus 27, 5473 ZG Heeswijk-Dinther, Netherlands. TEL 04139-1394. FAX 04139-2270. bk.rev.; illus.; index; circ. 2,400. **Indexed:** CERDIC.
  Formerly: Offer.

ROTTENBURGER JAHRBUCH FUER KIRCHENGESCHICHTE. see *HISTORY — History Of Europe*

200 US
ROUNDTABLE REPORT. 1980. bi-m. $25. 3295 Popular Ave., Box 11467, Memphis, TN 38111. TEL 901-458-3795. Ed. Donna Mooshian Striegel.
  Formerly: Religious Round Table.

280 NE ISSN 0166-4069
RUIMZICHT. 1875. q. fl.40($19) Vereniging Hervormd Opleidingscentrum, J.W. Frisostraat 18, Postbox 14147, 3508 SE Utrecht, Netherlands. TEL 030-540248. Ed. Rev. G.J. Martens. bk.rev.; illus.; circ. 1,100.
  Formerly: Nieuw Ruimzicht (ISSN 0028-9841)

RUNDBRIEF EHEMALIGER SCHUELER UND FREUNDE DER SCHULBRUEDER. see *COLLEGE AND ALUMNI*

280 100 US ISSN 0883-1300
S C P JOURNAL. 1977. irreg. donation. Spiritual Counterfeits Project, Inc., Box 4308, Berkeley, CA 94704. TEL 415-540-0300. bk.rev.; circ. 5,000. (back issues avail.) **Indexed:** Chr.Per.Ind.

4200 RELIGIONS AND THEOLOGY

280   US   ISSN 0883-1319
S C P NEWSLETTER. 1975. q. donation basis. Spiritual Counterfeits Project, Inc., Box 4308, Berkeley, CA 94704. TEL 415-540-0330. bk.rev.; circ. 17,500. **Indexed:** Chr.Per.Ind.

200   BL   ISSN 0036-1267
S E D O C. (Servicio de Documentacao) 1968. 6/yr. $55. Editora Vozes Ltda., Rua Frei Luis 100, Caixa Postal 90023, 25689 Petropolis, Rio de Janeiro, Brazil. Ed. Antonio Moser. circ. 2,400.

266   UK
S G M NEWS. 1943. q. free. Scripture Gift Mission, Radstock House, 3 Eccleston St., London SW1W 9LZ, England. illus.; circ. 20,000.
Formerly: S G M News Digest (ISSN 0048-9859)

200   IT
S I D I C. (Editions in English and French) 1968. 3/yr. $23. Service International de Documentation Judeo-Chretienne, Via del Plebiscito 112, 00186 Rome, Italy. TEL 6795307. FAX 6786280. (Subscr. to: Dr. Eugene Fisher, Secretariat for Catholic-Jewish Relations, 1312 Massachusetts Ave., N.W., Washington, D.C. 20005) Ed.Bd. bk.rev.; bibl.index; circ. 1,500. (back issues avail.) **Indexed:** Cath.Ind.
Description: Focuses on common interests to Jews and Christians; promotes knowledge, understanding and respect amoung Christian and Jewish communities.

266   CN   ISSN 0711-6683
BV3500
S I M NOW. (Sudan Interior Mission) 1958. q. free in Canada and U.S. S I M International, 10 Huntingdale Blvd., Scarborough, Ont. M1W 2S5, Canada. TEL 416-497-2424. FAX 416-497-2444. (U.S. address: Box 7900, Charlotte, N.C., 28241) Ed. David W. Fuller. bk.rev.; circ. 125,000. (reprint service avail. from UMI) **Indexed:** Curr.Cont.Africa.
Formerly (until Jan. 1982): Africa Now (ISSN 0044-6513)

266   US   ISSN 0279-6716
S O W. (Save Our World) 1962. q. free. (Church of God World Missions) Pathway Press, Box 2250, Cleveland, TN 37320-2250. TEL 615-476-3361. FAX 615-478-7521. Ed. Christopher Moree. charts; illus.; stat.; circ. 87,000.
Description: Provides news and feature articles on international missions, to promote interest in missionary work among the constituency of the Church of God.

200   IT
SACERDOZIO REGALE; centro sacerdozio regale and apostolato della Preghiera. 1954. m. L.3500. Centro Sacerdozio Regale, Via Villanova, 14, Casa Betania, 33170 Pordenone, Italy. TEL 0434-570019. Ed. Domenico Corelli.

200 100   IT   ISSN 0036-2190
SACRA DOCTRINA. 1956. 5/yr. $80. Edizioni Studio Domenicano, Via dell'Osservanza, 72, 40136 Bologna, Italy. TEL 051-582034. FAX 51-331583. Ed. Ottorino Benetollo. adv.; bk.rev.; bibl.; index; circ. 1,500. (tabloid format) **Indexed:** CERDIC, New Test.Abstr.

SACRED ART JOURNAL; Orthodox liturgical arts. see ART

220   SP
SAGRADA BIBLIA. 1976. irreg., no.12, 1989. price varies. (Universidad de Navarra, Facultad de Teologia) Ediciones Universidad de Navarra, S.A., Apdo. 396, 31080 Pamplona, Spain. TEL 94 825 6850.

ST. JOSEPH'S MESSENGER AND ADVOCATE OF THE BLIND. see HANDICAPPED — Visually Impaired

207.11   US
ST. LUKE'S JOURNAL OF THEOLOGY. 1957. q. $10 to individuals; libraries $15. University of the South, School of Theology, Sewanee, TN 37375. TEL 615-598-1475. Ed. Chris Bryan. adv.; bk.rev.; index. cum.index: 1956-1967,1967-1977; circ. 2,850. (also avail. in microfilm from UMI; reprint service avail. from UMI) **Indexed:** CERDIC, Old Test.Abstr, Rel.& Theol.Abstr. (1989-), Rel.Ind.One, Rel.Per.
Formerly: St. Luke's Journal (ISSN 0036-309X)

207.11   AT   ISSN 0036-3103
ST. MARK'S REVIEW. 1955. q. Aus.$22 (foreign Aus.$28). St. Mark's National Theological Centre, Library, P.O. Box E67, Canberra, A.C.T. 2600, Australia. FAX 06-273-4067. Ed. Graeme Garrett. adv.; bk.rev.; cum.index; circ. 900. (also avail. in microform from UMI; reprint service avail. from UMI) **Indexed:** Aus.P.A.I.S., CERDIC, Rel.Ind.One.
—BLDSC shelfmark: 8070.191000.

200   US   ISSN 0038-8815
ST. PAUL'S PRINTER. 1958. q. $5. Society of St. Paul, 44-660 San Pablo Ave., Palm Desert, CA 92260. TEL 619-568-2200. Ed. Rev. Andrew Rank. bk.rev.; illus.; stat.; circ. 12,000.

250   AU   ISSN 0036-3162
ST. POELTNER DIOEZESANBLATT. 1785. irreg. (approx. 12/yr.). S.400. Bischoefliches Ordinariat St. Poelten, Domplatz 1, A-3101 St. Poelten, Austria. Ed. Heinrich Fasching. bk.rev.; bibl.; charts; circ. 800.

ST. WILLIBRORD STUDIES IN PHILOSOPHY AND RELIGION. see PHILOSOPHY

200   SP   ISSN 0211-4569
SAL TERRAE. m. (11/yr.). 3275 ptas.($35) Editorial Sal Terrae, Calle Guevara, 20, 39001 Santander, Spain. TEL 212617. FAX 942-215245. **Indexed:** Canon Law Abstr., CERDIC.
—BLDSC shelfmark: 8070.555000.

266   US   ISSN 0036-3480
SALESIAN. 1947. 4/yr. $2. Salesian Society, Inc., Box 30-148, Main St., New Rochelle, NY 10802. TEL 914-633-8344. FAX 914-633-7404. Ed. Rev. E.J. Cappelletti. illus.; circ. 1,600,000.
Description: Describes the various educational and developmental programs for youth which the Salesian Society sponsors worldwide.

282   US   ISSN 0883-2587
SALT; for Christians who seek social justice. 1981. 10/yr. $15. Claretian Publications, 205 W. Monroe St., Chicago, IL 60606. TEL 800-328-6565. FAX 312-236-7230. Ed. Rev. Mark J. Brummel. adv.; bk.rev.; illus.; circ. 10,067.
Description: Explores the integral tie between scripture and justice.

200   AT   ISSN 0816-0031
SALT. 1985. 10/yr. Aus.$10($10) Australian Fellowship of Evangelical Students, 16 Mill Hill Rd., Bondi Junction, N.S.W. 2022, Australia. TEL 02-369-1688. Ed. Kerry Nagel. bk.rev.; illus.; tr.lit.; circ. 800. (back issues avail.)

266   GW
DER SALUTIST. 1988. q. Heilsarmee Verlag GmbH, Salierring 27, 5000 Cologne 1, Germany. TEL 0221-208190. Ed. Johanna Alisch. illus.

200   IT   ISSN 0036-424X
SAN SALVATORE DA HORTA. 1927. bi-m. free. Chiesa Santa Rosalia, Cagliari 09124, Italy.

200   GW   ISSN 0342-1465
UNA SANCTA; Zeitschrift fuer oekumenische Bewegnung. 1946. q. DM.34. Kyrios Verlag, Postfach 15 45, D-8050 Freising, Germany. index; circ. 2,000. (back issues avail.)

200   BL   ISSN 0036-4614
SANTUARIO DE APARECIDA. 1900. w. $6.42 (foreign $45.55). (Congregacao do Santissimo Redentor) Editora Santuario, Rua Padre Claro Monteiro 342, 12570 Aparecida SP, Brazil. TEL 0125-362140. FAX 0125-362141. TELEX 125659 CSRE BR. Ed. Manoel Jose Paixao. adv.; bk.rev.; illus.; circ. 40,000.

SAPIENZA; rivista internazionale di filosofia e di teologia. see PHILOSOPHY

SAT SANDESH; the message of the masters. see PHILOSOPHY

200   CN   ISSN 0315-7970
LE SAUVEUR. 1926. 6/yr. Can.$7.49. Sanctuaire de la Reparation au Sacre-Coeur, 3650, bd. de la Rousseliere, Montreal, Que. H1A 2X9, Canada. TEL 514-642-5391. circ. 10,000.

266 610   UK   ISSN 0036-5106
SAVING HEALTH. 1962. q. £3. Medical Missionary Association, 244 Camden Rd., London NW1 9HE, England. TEL 01-485 2672. Ed. Dr. P.F. Green. adv.; bk.rev.; illus.; circ. 1,000. **Indexed:** CERDIC.

221   DK   ISSN 0901-8328
SCANDANAVIAN JOURNAL OF THE OLD TESTAMENT. s-a. $40. Aarhus University Press, University of Aarhus, Bldg. 170, DK-8000 C, Denmark.
—BLDSC shelfmark: 8087.517700.

266   CN   ISSN 0700-6802
SCARBORO MISSIONS. 1919. 9/yr. Can.$8. Scarboro Foreign Mission Society, 2685 Kingston Rd., Scarborough, Ont. M1M 1M4, Canada. TEL 416-261-7135. Ed. Rev. Gerald Curry. adv.; bk.rev.; circ. 35,000. (back issues avail.)

200   US
SCHLEIERMACHER STUDIES AND TRANSLATION. irreg., latest no.1. $49.95 per no. Edwin Mellen Press, 240 Portage Rd., Box 450, Lewiston, NY 14092. TEL 716-754-8566. FAX 716-754-4335.

200   UK   ISSN 0261-5703
SCHOOLS OF PRAYER. 1980. 3/yr. £15 per copy. Diocese of Northampton, Religious Education Service, St. Mary's R.E. Centre, 118 Bromham Rd., Bedford MK40 2QR, England. Ed. J. Glen, K. McGinnell. bk.rev.; illus.; circ. 200.

215   UK   ISSN 0954-4194
AS122
SCIENCE AND CHRISTIAN BELIEF. 1866. 2/yr. £12($37.20) (Victoria Institute, Philosophical Society of Great Britain) Paternoster Press Ltd., 3 Mount Radford Crescent, Exeter EX2 4JW, England. FAX 0392-413317. (Subscr. to: Paternoster Press, Box 11127, Birmingham, AL 35202, U.S.A.) Eds. Oliver R. Barclay, A. Brian Robins. bk.rev.; bibl.; index, cum.index every 5 yrs.; circ. 2,000. **Indexed:** CERDIC, Rel.& Theol.Abstr. (1989-).
—BLDSC shelfmark: 8131.830000.
Incorporates: Science and Faith (ISSN 0268-2885); Faith and Thought (ISSN 0014-7028)

SCIENCE ET ESPRIT. see PHILOSOPHY

SCIENCE OF RELIGION; abstracts and index of recent articles. see RELIGIONS AND THEOLOGY — Abstracting, Bibliographies, Statistics

200   UK
SCIENCE OF THOUGHT REVIEW. 1921. bi-m. £4($12) Science of Thought Press Ltd., Bosham House, Bosham, Chichester, W. Sussex PO18 8PJ, England. TEL 0243-572109. Ed. Brian Graham. bk.rev.; circ. 5,000. (back issues avail.)
Description: Devoted to the spiritual life.

SCORE (BROOKLYN); your gospel music connection. see MUSIC

280   UK   ISSN 0264-5572
SCOTTISH CHURCH HISTORY SOCIETY. RECORDS. 1923. a. £8($18) Scottish Church History Society, Grange Manse, 51 Portland Rd., Kilmarnock, Ayrshire KA1 2EQ, Scotland. TEL 0563-25311. Ed. James Kirk. bk.rev.; bibl.; index; circ. 280. (back issues avail.)
—BLDSC shelfmark: 7325.120000.
Description: Papers on history of church in Scotland including links abroad.

266   UK   ISSN 0048-9778
BV2100
SCOTTISH INSTITUTE OF MISSIONARY STUDIES BULLETIN. 1967. s-a. £2($5) Scottish Institute of Missionary Studies, Department of Religious Studies, University of Aberdeen, King's College, Aberdeen AB9 2UB, Scotland. Ed. A. F. Walls. bk.rev.; circ. 500. (processed; also avail. in microform from UMI; reprint service avail. from UMI) **Indexed:** CERDIC.

200   UK   ISSN 0143-8301
BL1
SCOTTISH JOURNAL OF RELIGIOUS STUDIES. 1980. 2/yr. £7 to individuals; institutions £15. c/o Univ. of Stirling, Dept. of Religious Studies, Stirling FK9 4LA, Scotland. TEL 0786-73171. FAX 0786-63000. TELEX 777759. adv.; bk.rev. **Indexed:** Rel.& Theol.Abstr. (1989-).
—BLDSC shelfmark: 8210.610000.
Description: Critical investigation of major religious traditions of the world.

RELIGIONS AND THEOLOGY 4201

200   FI   ISSN 0582-3226
SCRIPTA INSTITUTI DONNERIANI ABOENSIS. (Text in English, French, German) 1967. triennial. Fmk.200. Donner Institute for Research in Religious and Cultural History, Gezeliusgatan 2, P.O. Box 70, SF-20501 Turku, Finland. FAX 358-21-311290. (Dist. by: Almqvist & Wiksell International, P.O. Box 68, S-101 28 Stockholm, Sweden) Tore Ahlbaeck. circ. 550. **Indexed:** Arts & Hum.Cit.Ind.

200   SP   ISSN 0036-9764
BR7
SCRIPTA THEOLOGICA. 1969. 3/yr. 6000 ptas.($85) (Universidad de Navarra, Facultad de Teologia) Servicio de Publicaciones de la Universidad de Navarra, S.A., Apdo. 177, 31080 Pamplona, Spain. TEL 94 25 2700. Ed. Pedro Rodriguez. bk.rev. **Indexed:** New Test.Abstr., Old Test.Abstr., Rel.& Theol.Abstr. (1978-).

200   IT   ISSN 0036-9950
SE VUOI. 1960. bi-m. L.15000. Centro Sussidi Vocazionali, Via Mole 3, 00040 Castelgandolfo (Rome), Italy. (Co-sponsor: Istituto Regina degli Apostoli) Dir. Maria De Luca. bk.rev.; circ. 7,000.

THE SECOND STONE; the national newspaper for gay and lesbian Christians. see *HOMOSEXUALITY*

200   US
SEEK. 1970. w. $7.95 for sets of five for 3 mos. Standard Publishing, 8121 Hamilton Ave., Cincinnati, OH 45231. TEL 513-931-4050. Ed. Eileen H. Wilmoth. circ. 77,000.

201   IT   ISSN 0394-364X
SEGNI DEI TEMPI; rivista bimestrale per un cristianesimo migliore. 1921. bi-m. L.13000. Edizioni A.D.V., l'Araldo della Verita, 1 Via Chiantigiana 30, Falciani, 50023 Impruneta, Florence, Italy. TEL 055-2020291. Ed. Giuseppe Marrazzo. index; circ. 22,000.

230   SP   ISSN 0037-119X
SELECCIONES DE TEOLOGIA. 1962. q. 2250 ptas.($22.00) Instituto de Teologia Fundamental, Facultad de Teologia de Catalunya, Llaseres 30, Sant Cugat del Valles, Barcelona, Spain. TEL 93-301-23-50. (Subscr. to: Roger de Lluria 13, 08010 Barcelona, Spain) Ed. Xavier Alegre. adv.; index; circ. 5,000. **Indexed:** CERDIC.

131.3 200   US   ISSN 0037-1564
SELF-REALIZATION. 1925. q. $2.50. Self-Realization Fellowship, Inc., 3880 San Rafael Ave., Los Angeles, CA 90065. TEL 213-225-2471. Ed. Irene Bartram. bk.rev.; illus.; index; circ. 26,000. (back issues avail.)
Description: Features information on healing the body, mind and soul through the practical application of sprirtual principles.

200   UK
▼**SELLY OAK COLLEGES. OCCASIONAL PAPERS.** 1990. irreg. (6-9/yr.). £1 per issue. Selly Oak Colleges, Bristol Rd., Birmingham B29 6LQ, England. TEL 021-472-4231.

200   US   ISSN 0095-571X
BS410
SEMEIA; an experimental journal for biblical criticism. (Text in English, Greek and Hebrew) 1974. q. $25 to individuals; institutions $35. (Society of Biblical Literature) Scholars Press, Box 15399, Atlanta, GA 30333-0399. TEL 404-636-4757. FAX 404-636-8301. adv.; bk.rev.; bibl.; charts; illus.; cum.index; circ. 1,300. (also avail. in microfiche) **Indexed:** Arts & Hum.Cit.Ind., CERDIC, New Test.Abstr., Old Test.Abstr., Rel.& Theol.Abstr. (1977-), Rel.Ind.One.
—BLDSC shelfmark: 8237.840000.
Description: Academic papers on biblical criticism.

220 410   FR   ISSN 0154-6902
SEMIOTIQUE ET BIBLE. 1975. q. 100 F. Centre pour l'Analyse du Discours Religieux, 25 rue du Plat, 69002 Lyon Cedex, France. Ed. Jean Delorme. bk.rev.; circ. 800. **Indexed:** CERDIC, New Test.Abstr.
—BLDSC shelfmark: 8239.502300.

200   AU   ISSN 0037-2129
SENDBOTE DES HERZENS JESU. 1865. m. S.216. Jesuitenkolleg, Sillgasse 6, A-6021 Innsbruck, Austria. Ed. Josef Fiedler. bk.rev.; bibl.; illus.; index; circ. 7,000.

200   US
SEQUOIA (SAN FRANCISCO); news of religion & society. 1980. 6/yr. $16. Sequoia Interreligious News Magazine, 942 Market St., No. 707, San Francisco, CA 94102. TEL 415-434-0672. Ed. Mark MacNamara. adv.; bk.rev.; circ. 5,500. (also avail. in microfiche)
Description: Instructs local congregation members on how to live their faith in the world, while addressing today's major issues.

252   US   ISSN 0037-248X
SERMON BUILDER; preacher's professional periodical. 1953. m. $6. Church Extension Service, Inc., Box 988, Golden, CO 80401. TEL 303-279-1011. Ed. Glen Williamson. adv.; bk.rev.; circ. 5,000.

200   IT   ISSN 0037-2773
SERVIZIO DELLA PAROLA. 1968. m. (10/yr.). L.48000 (foreign L.68000). Editrice Queriniana, Via Piamarta 6, 25187 Brescia, Italy. Ed. Chino Biscontin.

SERVIZIO MIGRANTI. see *POLITICAL SCIENCE*

268   FR   ISSN 0985-5734
SEVE EGLISE AUJOURD'HUI. 1944. m. 180 F. (foreign 195 F.). Chretiens dans le Monde Rural, 9 rue du General Leclerc, 91230 Montgeron, France. TEL 1-69-03-09-09. FAX 1-69-83-23-24. Ed. Remy Fitterer. adv.; bk.rev. **Indexed:** CERDIC.
Formerly: Eglise Aujourd'hui (ISSN 0223-5854)
Description: For those who wish to prepare the future of the Church.

SHADOW. see *NEW AGE PUBLICATIONS*

SHALOM. see *RELIGIONS AND THEOLOGY — Judaic*

266   UK
SHARE. (Includes: Partners' News) 1867. 4/yr. donations. South American Missionary Society, Allen Gardiner House, Pembury Rd., Tunbridge Wells, Kent TN2 3QU, England. TEL 0892-538647. FAX 0892-525797. Ed. Derek Williams. bk.rev.; circ. 16,000. **Indexed:** CERDIC.
Formerly: Sent (ISSN 0037-2269)

200   US   ISSN 0193-8274
SHARING THE PRACTICE. 1978. q. $20. Academy of Parish Clergy, Inc., Box 930, Summerville, WV 26651. TEL 304-872-2371. (Subscr. to: Rev. Roger I. Perks, Bus. Mgr., 13500 Shaker Blvd., Ste. 601, Cleveland, OH 44120. TEL 201-295-2006) Ed. David W. Nash. adv.; bk.rev.; circ. 700. (tabloid format; also avail. in microform from UMI)
Formerly: Academy of Parish Clergy. News and Views.
Description: For members of the Clergy to share their interests and experiences.

200 808.81   US
SHARING THE VICTORY. 1982. m. $18. Fellowship of Christian Athletes, 8701 Leeds Rd., Kansas City, MO 64129. TEL 816-921-0909. FAX 816-921-8755. Ed. John Dodderidge. adv.; bk.rev.; circ. 50,000. (back issues avail.)
Description: Christian publication aimed at individuals involved in athletics at any level.

200   CC   ISSN 1000-4289
BL9.C4
SHIJIE ZONGJIAO YANJIU/STUDIES ON WORLD RELIGION. (Text in Chinese) 1979. q. $25.50. (Zhongguo Shehui Kexueyuan, Shijie Zongjiao Yanjiusuo - Chinese Academy of Social Sciences, Institute of World Religion) Zhongguo Shehui Kexueyuan Chubanshe, Gulou Xidajie A 158, Beijing, People's Republic of China. (Dist. in US by: China Books & Periodicals, Inc., 2929 24th St., San Francisco, CA 94110. TEL 415-282-2994)
—BLDSC shelfmark: 8492.007900.

200   CC   ISSN 1000-4505
SHIJIE ZONGJIAO ZILIAO. (Text in Chinese) 1980. q. $12.30. (Zhongguo Shehui Kexueyuan, Shijie Zongjiao Yanjiusuo - Chinese Academy of Social Sciences, Institute of World Religion) Shehui Kexue Zazhishe, A-158 Gulou Xidajie, Beijing 100720, People's Republic of China. (Dist. in US by: China Books & Periodicals, Inc., 2929 24th St., San Francisco, CA 94110. TEL 415-282-2994)
—BLDSC shelfmark: 8256.521000.

200   KO
SHINANGGYE/WORLD OF FAITH. (Text in Korean) 1967. m. 3500 Won($7) Full Gospel Central Church in Korea, 1-20 Yeouidodong, Youngdungpoku, Seoul, S. Korea. Ed. Wan-Ki Choi. adv.; bk.rev.; circ. 33,000.

200 919.306   PE
SHUPIHUI. 1976. 4/yr. $18. Centro de Estudios Teologicos de la Amazonia, Putmayo 355, Iquitos, Peru. TEL 233552. FAX 23-31-90. Ed. Joaquin Garcia Sanchez. bk.rev.; circ. 1,000.

SIAH MESHARIM; journal of Judaism, religion and state. see *RELIGIONS AND THEOLOGY — Judaic*

SINGLE ADULT MINISTRIES JOURNAL; ideas, resources and guidance for ministry with single adults. see *SINGLES' INTERESTS AND LIFESTYLES*

200   SA   ISSN 0257-8891
SKRIF EN KERK. (Text in Afrikaans) 1980. s-a. R.19.50 to individuals; students R.15.70; overseas R.27. University of Pretoria, Theological Faculty (Section B), Pretoria 0002, South Africa. TEL 012-4202322. FAX 012-437431. Ed. W.S. Prinsloo. bk.rev.; circ. 500.

266   AT
SKYWAVES. bi-m. Far East Broadcasting Co., Corner of Banksia & Willarong Rds., P.O. Box 183, Caringbah, N.S.W. 2229, Australia. TEL 02-525-6460. FAX 02-526-1250. Ed. Maire Atkinson. circ. 7,550. (back issues avail.)
Description: Covers the organization's projects and missionaries.

260   CI   ISSN 0037-7074
SLUZBA BOZJA; liturgijsko-pastoralna revija. 1961. q. $20. Franjevacka Visoka Bogoslovija, Makarska - Franciscan High School for Theology at Makarska, Zrtava Fasizma 1, 58300 Makarska, Croatia. TEL 059 612-259. Ed. Marko Babic. adv.; bk.rev.; index; circ. 1,400.
—BLDSC shelfmark: 8309.912880.

200   IT   ISSN 0037-7562
SOCCORSO PERPETUO DI MARIA. 1946. m. L.15000 (foreign L.25000). Santuario della Madonna del Perpetuo Soccorso, 37012 Bussolengo, Verona, Italy. illus.; circ. 8,000.

SOCIAL COMPASS; international review of sociology of religion. see *SOCIOLOGY*

SOCIAL STUDIES; Irish journal of sociology. see *SOCIOLOGY*

200 500   US
SOCIETY FOR COMMON INSIGHTS. JOURNAL. 1976. s-a. $5 to individuals; institutions $6. Society for Common Insights, c/o Kurt Johnson, Dept. of Biology, City University of New York, Convent Ave. and 138th St., New York, NY 10031. (Affiliate: National Council for the Church and Social Action) Eds. Kurt Johnson, Eric L. Quinter. bk.rev.; charts; illus. (back issues avail.) **Indexed:** CERDIC.

225   UK   ISSN 0081-1432
SOCIETY FOR NEW TESTAMENT STUDIES. MONOGRAPH SERIES. 1965. irreg., no.57, 1986. price varies. Cambridge University Press, Edinburgh Bldg., Shaftesbury Rd., Cambridge CB2 2RU, England. TEL 0223-312393. FAX 0223-315052. TELEX 851817256. Ed. G.N. Stanton. index.

221   UK
SOCIETY FOR OLD TESTAMENT STUDIES. MONOGRAPHS. 1972. irreg., no.6, 1980. price varies. Cambridge University Press, Edinburgh Bldg., Shaftesbury Rd., Cambridge CB2 2RU, England. TEL 0223-312393. FAX 0223-315052. TELEX 851817256.

200   US
SOCIETY FOR THE SCIENTIFIC STUDY OF RELIGION. MONOGRAPH SERIES. 1978. irreg., no.8, 1990. Society for the Scientific Study of Religion, Pierce Hall, No. 193, Purdue Univ., West Lafayette, IN 47907. TEL 317-494-6286.

RELIGIONS AND THEOLOGY

220 US ISSN 0145-2711
BS410
SOCIETY OF BIBLICAL LITERATURE. SEMINAR PAPERS (YEAR). a. $25. (Society of Biblical Literature) Scholars Press, Box 15399, Atlanta, GA 30333-0399. TEL 404-363-4757. FAX 404-636-8301. Ed. Gene Lovering. (back issues avail.) **Indexed:** Rel.Ind.One.
—BLDSC shelfmark: 8239.423670.
Description: Seminar papers to be given at the annual meeting of the Society of Biblical Literature meetings.

200 US ISSN 0732-4928
BJ1188.5
SOCIETY OF CHRISTIAN ETHICS. ANNUAL. 1975. a. $12. Georgetown University Press, Intercultural Center, Rm. 111, Georgetown University, Washington, DC 20057. TEL 202-687-5889. FAX 202-687-5712. Ed. Diane Yeager. adv.; circ. 850. (also avail. in microfilm) **Indexed:** Rel.Ind.Two.
Description: Scholarly articles targeted toward an audience that includes college professors in religion, the social sciences, and philosophy; professionals in law, medicine, politics, and human services; and the clergy and others working in Christian education and social action programs--with a section on professional resources available for teaching ethics.

266 FR
SOLIDAIRES - LUMIERE DU MONDE. 1920. q. 40 F. (Societe Presse et Publications Missionnaires) Oeuvre de la Propagation de la Foi, 5, rue Monsieur, 75007 Paris, France. TEL 47-83-67-95. abstr.; charts; illus.; stat.; circ. 100,000. (also avail. in microfiche from BHP)
Formed by the merger of: Lumiere du Monde (ISSN 0024-7340) & Solidaires (ISSN 0336-335X); Which was formerly: Annales de la Propagation de la Fois (ISSN 0003-4045)
Description: Focuses on mission work in the country.

230 SZ ISSN 0067-4907
SONDERBAENDE ZUR THEOLOGISCHEN ZEITSCHRIFT. 1966. irreg., no.10, 1981. price varies. Friedrich Reinhardt Verlag, Missionsstr. 36, CH-4012 Basel, Switzerland. (Dist. by: Albert J. Phiebig Books, Box 352, White Plains, NY 10602) Ed. B. Reicke. circ. 1,000.
Formerly: Beihefte zur Theologischen Zeitschrift.

DER SONNTAGSBRIEF. see *GERONTOLOGY AND GERIATRICS*

SONNTAGSCHULMITARBEITER; religionspaedagogisches Monatsblatt. see *EDUCATION*

201 AT ISSN 0038-1527
BL1
SOPHIA; a journal for discussion in philosophical theology. 1962. 3/yr. Aus.$10($12) Philosophical Theology Society, c/o School of Humanities, Deakin University, Vic. 3217, Australia. FAX 052-442777. TELEX DUNIN AA 35625. Ed.Bd. tr.lit.; circ. 750. (also avail. in microform from UMI) **Indexed:** Aus.P.A.I.S., CERDIC, M.L.A., Phil.Ind.
—BLDSC shelfmark: 8328.180000.

200 US
SOUND WORDS.* 1984. bi-m. $5. Glyn Taylor, Jr., Ed. & Pub., 302 Martin Ln., Lookout Mountain, GA 30750-3017.

260 301 US
SOURCE (SEATTLE). 1960. m. $12. Church Council of Greater Seattle, 4759 15 Ave., N.E., 3rd Fl., Seattle, WA 98105. TEL 206-525-1213. Ed. Margaret Lueders. adv.; bk.rev.; circ. 7,500. (tabloid format)
Supersedes (in 1976): Church Council of Greater Seattle. Occasional News (ISSN 0010-9924); Formerly: Council in Action.

200 027.7 MW
SOURCES FOR THE STUDY OF RELIGION IN MALAWI. (Text in English) 1979. irreg., no.11, 1984. $2.50 per no. University of Malawi, Chancellor College, Department of Religion, P.O. Box 280, Zomba, Malawi. Ed. J.C. Chakanza. circ. 200.

266 SA
SOUTH AFRICAN OUTLOOK; a journal dealing with ecumenical and racial affairs. 1870. m. R.30($40) (effective 1992). Outlook Publications (Pty) Ltd., Box 245, Rondebosch 7700, South Africa. Ed. Francis Wilson. adv.; bk.rev.; index; circ. 1,400. **Indexed:** CERDIC, HR Rep., Ind.S.A.Per.

SOUTH ASIA IN REVIEW; quarterly review of new books on South Asia. see *HISTORY — History Of Asia*

200 US
SOUTH FLORIDA FOCUS. 4/yr. $10. International Society of Divine Love, 234 W. Upsal St., Philadelphia, PA 19119. TEL 215-844-4009. illus.

200 UK
SOUTHWELL AND OXFORD PAPERS ON CONTEMPORARY SOCIETY. 1984. 4/yr. £7. Oxford Institute for Church and Society, Ripon College, Oxford OX9 9EX, England. TEL 08677-4595.
Formerly: Oxford Papers on Contemporary Society.
Description: Covers all aspects of the interaction of Christian faith and contemporary society.

200 286 US ISSN 0038-4828
BX6201
SOUTHWESTERN JOURNAL OF THEOLOGY. 1958. 3/yr. $13 (foreign $15). Southwestern Baptist Theological Seminary, Faculty, School of Theology, Box 22000 2E, Fort Worth, TX 76122. TEL 817-923-1921. Ed. Bill Tillman. adv.; bk.rev.; circ. 3,500. (also avail. in microform from UMI; reprint service avail. from UMI) **Indexed:** CERDIC, Chr.Per.Ind., New Test.Abstr., Old Test.Abstr., Rel.& Theol.Abstr. (1967-), Rel.Ind.One, Rel.Per., South.Bap.Per.Ind.
—BLDSC shelfmark: 8357.210000.

200 SA ISSN 0038-5980
THE SOWER. (Text in English) 1957. q. free. Bible Society of South Africa, P.O. Box 6215, Roggebaai, Cape Town 8012, South Africa.
FAX 021-419-4846. Ed. Rev. N.N. Turley. illus.; circ. 68,000 (controlled). (also avail. in microfiche)

268 UK
SOWER. 1919. q. £6. Sower Ltd., 10-12 High St., Great Wakering, Essex SS3 0EQ, England.
FAX 0702-216082. Ed.Bd. adv.; bk.rev.; circ. 2,000.
Formerly: New Sower; Which was formed by the 1978 merger of: Sower (ISSN 0049-1772); Christian Celebration.

200 360 AT ISSN 0158-1090
SOWER. 1956. q. Aus.$15. Bible Society in Australia, G.P.O. Box 507, Canberra, A.C.T. 2601, Australia. FAX 062-49618. TELEX 61642. Ed. Irene Voysey. illus.; circ. 75,000. (back issues avail.)
Description: Sows the seed of the Word of God through stories of Bible Society work in Australia and overseas; in translation; and production and distribution of the Scriptures.

266 UK
SPAN (LONDON). 1835. bi-m. contributions. London City Mission, 175 Tower Bridge Rd., London SE1 2AH, England. Ed. S. Seymour. bk.rev.; circ. 41,000. **Indexed:** Apic.Abstr, Fuel & Energy Abstr.
Formerly: London City Mission Magazine (ISSN 0047-5025)

200 KE
SPEARHEAD. (Text in English) 1969. 5/yr. EAs.121($17.60) (Amecea Pastoral Institute) Gaba Publications, P.O. Box 4002, Eldoret, Kenya. Ed. Felician N. Rwehikiza. circ. 2,000. (back issues avail.) **Indexed:** CERDIC.
Formerly (until 1977): Gaba Pastoral Papers.

268 UK ISSN 0305-7917
SPECTRUM. 1969. s-a. £9.90($30.60) (Association of Christian Teachers) Paternoster Press Ltd., 3 Mount Radford Crescent, Exeter, Devon EX2 4JW, England. TEL 0392-50631. FAX 0392-413317. Ed. John Shortt. adv.; bk.rev.; illus.; cum.index: vols. 1-6; circ. 600. (back issues avail.) **Indexed:** Abstr.Engl.Stud., Br.Educ.Ind., CERDIC, Excerp.Med.
—BLDSC shelfmark: 8411.168000.
Description: Provides a Christian viewpoint on education in both maintained and private sector schools and colleges.

200 255 NE ISSN 0038-7320
SPELING. 1948. q. fl.42. H. Gianotten B.V., Bredaseweg 61, 5038 NA Tilburg, Netherlands. Ed. Jo Tigcheler. bk.rev.; play rev.; illus.; circ. 2,500. **Indexed:** CERDIC.
—BLDSC shelfmark: 8411.650000.
Formerly: Carmel.

200 GW ISSN 0933-8985
SPIRITA; Zeitschrift fuer Religionswissenschaft. 1987. 3/yr. DM.18. Diagonal Verlag, Postfach 1248, 3550 Marburg, Germany. TEL 06421-681936. FAX 06421-681733. Ed.Bd. (back issues avail.)

200 155.4 US ISSN 0886-3156
SPIRITUAL MOTHERING JOURNAL; dedicated to the spirtual well-being of parent and child. 1980. q. $14. Spiritual Mothering, Inc., Box 82503, Albuquerque, NM 87198. TEL 505-266-5492. Ed. Pat Harvey. adv.; bk.rev.; circ. 1,000. (back issues avail.)
Formerly: Spiritual Mothering Newsletter.

200 IT
SPIRITUALITA CRISTIANA. 1981. irreg., latest no.20. price varies. Edizioni Studium, Via Cassiodoro 14, 00193 Rome, Italy.

266 FR ISSN 0038-7665
SPIRITUS; experience et recherche missionnaires. 1959. q. 140 F. Association de la Revue Spiritus, 40 rue La Fontaine, 75781 Paris Cedex 16, France. TEL 42-88-82-64. Ed. Joseph Gross. bk.rev.; abstr.; bibl.; index; circ. 3,500. **Indexed:** CERDIC
—BLDSC shelfmark: 8415.450000.
Description: Aims to advance the missionary vocation and improve communication among diverse churches.

266 IT ISSN 0038-8750
SQUILLA. 1925. bi-m. L.5000. Fratini Missionari di Recco, Collegio Serafico, Via S. Francesco 4, 16036 Recco, Genoa, Italy. Ed. Amelia Capurro. adv.; illus.; circ. 4,000 (controlled). (tabloid format)

200 IT ISSN 0038-8769
SQUILLA DI S. GERARDO.* 1923. bi-m. free. Parrocchia S. Gerardo, Piedimonte Etneo 95017, Sicily, Italy.

266 GW
STADT GOTTES; Illustrierte Familienzeitschrift. 1878. m. DM.22.20. (Steyler Missionare) Soverdia GmbH, Bahnhofstr. 9, Postfach 2460, 4054 Nettetal 2, Germany. TEL 02157-1202-0.
FAX 02157-1202-22. Ed. Udo Haltermann.

268.8 US ISSN 0081-4245
STANDARD LESSON COMMENTARY; international Sunday school lessons. 1954. a. $12.95 casebound; $9.95 kivar. Standard Publishing, 8121 Hamilton Ave., Cincinnati, OH 45231.
TEL 513-931-4050. Ed. James I. Fehl. circ. 180,000.
Description: Sunday-school lesson manual for teachers of adults.

266 GW
STEFANUS. 1949. bi-m. DM.36. Stefanuswerk e.V., Hauptstr. 1, Postfach 1152, 7960 Aulendorf, Germany. TEL 07525-1016. Ed. Gottfried Juen. illus.

200 IT
LA STELLA DEL MARE. 1908. m. L.15000($10) Passionisti Scala Santa, 00048 Nettuno (Rome), Italy. circ. 4,000.
Formerly: Santuario di N.S.D. Grazie e di S. Maria Goretti (ISSN 0036-4630)

200 052 KE
STEP. (Text in English) 1979. m. $33 to rest of Africa; USA, Australia & Far East $43; Europe & Asia $38 (typically set every 2 years). Youth for Christ, P.O. Box 58070, Nairobi, Kenya. Ed. Connie Kisuke. adv.; bk.rev.; circ. 50,000.
Description: Directed toward Christian Africans with news, insights, and regular features.

200 GW
STERNSINGER; diaspora. 1891. q. DM.2. Bonifatiuswerk der deutschen Katholiken Diaspora-Kinderhilfe, Kamp 22, Postfach 1169, 4790 Paderborn, Germany. TEL 05251-29960. FAX 05251-299688. Ed. Hans Dieter Huber. circ. 380,000. (back issues avail.)
Description: Religious developments in Germany and the Scandinavian countries.

266 GW ISSN 0722-6942
STEYLER MISSIONSCHRONIK. 1959. a. (Steyler Missionswissenschafliches Institut) Steyler Verlag, Bahnhofstr. 9, 4054 Nettetal 2, Germany. TEL 02157-1202-20. FAX 02157-1202-22. circ. 20,000.

RELIGIONS AND THEOLOGY   4203

200 GW
STIMME DER MAERTYRER; Nachrichten der Hilfsaktion Maertyrerkirche. 1969. m. DM.12. Hilfsaktion Maertyrerkirche e.V., Tuefingerstr. 3-5, Postfach 1160, 7772 Uhldingen 1, Germany. TEL 07556-6508. FAX 07556-8002. TELEX 733942-HMC. Ed. Hans Martin Braun. circ. 38,000 (controlled). (back issues avail.)
Description: Publication devoted to Christian Mission of the Communist world. Supports and aids suppressed Christians and brings evangelism to Communist countries. Focus on Bible study, radio and TV missions.

200 GW ISSN 0039-1492
STIMMEN DER ZEIT;* Monatsschrift fuer das Geistesleben der Gegenwart. 1865. m. DM.130.80. Verlag Herder GmbH und Co. KG, Hermann-Herder-Str. 4, 7800 Freiburg im Breisgau, Germany. Ed. Dr. Wolfgang Seibel, S.J. adv.; bk.rev.; circ. 6,000. Indexed: Cath.Ind., CERDIC, Hist.Abstr., M.L.A., New Test.Abstr.

200 IT
STORIA DELLE RELIGIONI. 1985. irreg., no.6, 1989. price varies. L'Erma di Bretschneider, Via Cassiodoro 19, 00193 Rome, Italy. TEL 06-687-41-27. FAX 06-687-41-29. Dirs. Ugo Bianchi, Giulia Piccaluga.

200 282 IT
STORICO DELLA BASILICATA. BOLLETTINO. vol.4, no.4, 1988. a. price varies. Edizioni di Storia e Letteratura, Via Lancellotti, 18, 00186 Rome, Italy. TEL 6540556. Ed. Vincenzo Verrastro. bk.rev.

200 GW
STORMARNSPIEGEL. 1973. irreg. (6-8/yr.). Kirchenkreis Stormarn, Kirchenkreisvorstand, Rockenhof 1, D-2000 Hamburg 67, Germany. TEL 040-603-143-28. bk.rev.; circ. 1,320. (back issues avail.)

248.83 US
STRAIGHT. 1951. w. $7.95 per set of 5 for 3 months. Standard Publishing, 8121 Hamilton Ave., Cincinnati, OH 45231. TEL 513-931-4050. Ed. Carla J. Crane. illus.; circ. 65,000.
Formed in two parts by the **1980** merger of: Glad and Now; Formerly (until 1977) Straight (ISSN 0039-2081)
Description: An uplifting take-home newspaper for young Christians with stories and feature articles.

200 GW
STREIFLICHTER. bi-m. DM.12. C V J M Landesverband Baden, Friedrich-Naumann-Str. 33, 7500 Karlsruhe 21, Germany. TEL 0721-757077. FAX 0721-753763. Ed. Hermann Traub. circ. 3,000. (back issues avail.)

STROMATA; antigua ciencia y fe. see PHILOSOPHY

220 IT ISSN 0039-2898
STUDI BIBLICI; collezione di argomento biblico. 1968. q. L.63000. Paideia Editrice, Via Corsica 130, 25125 Brescia, Italy. Ed. Giuseppe Scarpat. bk.rev.

200 940 IT ISSN 0394-0616
STUDI E RICERCHE SULL'ORIENTE CRISTIANO. (Text in Italian or Latin) 1978. 3/yr. L.25000 (foreign L.40000)(effective 1992). Giuseppe Sorge, Ed. & Pub., Via Panaro 11, 00199 Rome, Italy. TEL 06-860-2972. Ed. Giuseppe Sorge. bk.rev.; circ. 450. (back issues avail.)
Description: Features readings on research and study in Christianity.

270 IT
STUDI E TESTI PER LA STORIA RELIGIOSA DEL CINQUECENTO. 1986. irreg., no.3, 1990. price varies. Casa Editrice Leo S. Olschki, Casella Postale 66, 50100 Florence, Italy. TEL 055-6530684. FAX 055-6530214.

200 IT ISSN 0393-3687
STUDI ECUMENICI. 1983. q. L.35000 (foreign L.40000)(effective Jan. 1992). (Istituto di Studi Ecumenici) Asociazione Francescani Riunti per Attivita Territoriali e Religiose, Castello 2786, 30122 Venice, Italy. TEL 041-5235341. FAX 041-5228323. Ed.Bd. bk.rev.; index. (back issues avail.)
—BLDSC shelfmark: 8481.813000.

220 NE ISSN 0169-801X
STUDIA AD CORPUS HELLENISTICUM NOVI TESTAMENTI. (Text in English, French and German) 1970. irreg., vol.6, 1980. price varies. E.J. Brill, P.O. Box 9000, 2300 PA Leiden, Netherlands. TEL 071-312624. FAX 071-317532. TELEX 39296 BRILL NL. (In N. America: E.J. Brill, 24 Hudson St., Kinderhook, NY 12106. TEL 800-962-4406) Ed.Bd.

221 NE ISSN 0169-9954
STUDIA BIBLICA. 1983. irreg., vol.4, 1990. price varies. E.J. Brill, P.O. Box 9000, 2300 PA Leiden, Netherlands. TEL 071-312624. FAX 071-317532. TELEX 39296 BRILL NL. (In N. America: E.J. Brill, 24 Hudson St., Kinderhook, NY 12106. TEL 800-962-4406)

262.9 CN ISSN 0039-310X
K23
STUDIA CANONICA; a Canadian canon law review. (Text in English, French, Latin) 1967. s-a. Can.$35($35) (typically set in Jan.). Saint Paul University, Faculty of Canon Law, 223 Main St, Ottawa, Ont. K1S 1C4, Canada. TEL 613-236-1393. FAX 613-782-3005. Ed. Francis G. Morrisey. adv.; bk.rev.; circ. 1,400. (also avail. in microfiche) Indexed: Bull.Signal., C.L.I., Canon Law Abstr., Cath.Ind., CERDIC, Ind.Can.L.P.L., Leg.Per.
—BLDSC shelfmark: 8482.375000.

268 IT
STUDIA EPHEMERIDIS AUGUSTINIANUM. 1967. irreg. Institutum Patristicum Augustinianum, Via S. Uffizio, 25, 00193 Rome, Italy. FAX 6-686-6247. (back issues avail.)

220 NE ISSN 0169-8125
STUDIA IN VETERIS TESTAMENTI PSEUDEPIGRAPHA. 1970. irreg., vol.9, 1991. price varies. E.J. Brill, P.O. Box 9000, 2300 PA Leiden, Netherlands. TEL 071-312624. FAX 071-317532. TELEX 39296 BRILL NL. (In N. America: E.J. Brill, 24 Hudson St., Kinderhook, NY 12106. TEL 800-962-4406) Eds. A.M. Denis, M. de Jonge.

100 GW ISSN 0081-6663
STUDIA IRENICA. (Text in English, German) 1968. irreg., no.35, 1990. Verlag Peter Lang GmbH, Eschborner Landstr. 42-50, 6000 Frankfurt a.M. 90, Germany. TEL 069-7807050. FAX 069-785893.
Formerly (until 1971): Frankfurt am Main. Universitaet. Institut fuer Wissenschaftliche Irenik. Schriften.

240 US ISSN 0039-3207
STUDIA LITURGICA; an international ecumenical review for liturgical research and renewal. (Text in English) 1962. 2/yr. $22.50. Societas Liturgica, Box 597, Notre Dame, IN 46556. Ed. Paul F. Bradshaw. bk.rev.; circ. 1,000. (back issues avail.) Indexed: CERDIC, New Test.Abstr., Rel.& Theol.Abstr. (1979-), Rel.Ind.One, Rel.Per.
—BLDSC shelfmark: 8482.973000.

271 900 SP ISSN 0039-3258
BX2400
STUDIA MONASTICA; commentarium ad rem monasticam historice investigandam. (Text in Catalan, English, French, German, Italian, Latin, Portuguese, Spanish) 1959. s-a. 7000 ptas.($92) Publicacions de l' Abadia de Montserrat, Ausias March 92-98, Apdo. 244, 08013 Barcelona, Spain. Ed. Rev. Josep Massot Muntaner. adv.; bk.rev.; abstr.; bibl.; charts; illus.; index; circ. 800. Indexed: Arts & Hum.Cit.Ind., CERDIC, Hist.Abstr., M.L.A.
—BLDSC shelfmark: 8483.063000.

240 IT ISSN 0081-6736
STUDIA MORALIA. (Text in English, French, German, Italian, Spanish; summaries in English, French) 1963. s-a. L.40000($38) Editiones Academiae Alfonsianae, Via Merulana 31, C.P. 2458, 00100 Rome, Italy. Ed.Bd. bk.rev.; index; circ. 1,200. Indexed: CERDIC.

200 956 IS
STUDIA ORIENTALIA CHRISTIANA. COLLECTANEA. (Text in Arabic, Coptic, English, French, Italian) 1956. a. $25. (Franciscan Centre of Christian Oriental Studies in Cairo, UA) Franciscan Printing Press, P.O. Box 14064, Jerusalem 91140, Israel. TEL 02-286594. illus.
Description: Publishes scholarly articles on theological, historical, ethnological, and linguistic topics relating to Christianity in the Middle East.

281.5 956 IS
STUDIA ORIENTALIA CHRISTIANA. MONOGRAPHIAE. (Text in Arabic, Coptic, English, French, German, Italian, Latin) 1955. irreg., no.4, 1991. price varies. (Franciscan Centre of Christian Oriental Studies in Cairo, UA) Franciscan Printing Press, P.O. Box 14064, Jerusalem 91140, Israel. TEL 02-286594. illus.
Description: Publishes scholarly studies of theological, historical, ethnological, and linguistic topics relating to Christianity in the Middle East.

230 100 IT ISSN 0039-3304
STUDIA PATAVINA; rivista di scienze religiose. 1954. 3/yr. L.45000 (foreign L.55000). Seminario Vescovile, Facolta Teologica, Via del Seminario 29, 35122 Padova, Italy. TEL 049-657-099. Ed.Bd. adv.; bk.rev.; index; circ. 600. (back issues avail.) Indexed: CERDIC, New Test.Abstr., Old Test.Abstr.
—BLDSC shelfmark: 8483.115000.
Description: Emphasizes the promotion of the study of all religious disciplines; organizes meetings from many cultural institutions.

STUDIA PHILOSOPHIAE RELIGIONIS. see PHILOSOPHY

200 NE ISSN 0169-9717
STUDIA POST-BIBLICA. 1959. irreg., vol.39, 1991. price varies. E.J. Brill, P.O. Box 9000, 2300 PA Leiden, Netherlands. TEL 071-312624. FAX 071-317532. TELEX 39296 BRILL NL. (In N. America: E.J. Brill, 24 Hudson St., Kinderhook, NY 12106. TEL 800-962-4406) Ed. P.A.H. deBoer.

266 SP
STUDIA SILENSIA. (Text in English, French, German, Portuguese and Spanish) 1975. a. price varies. Abadia de Santo Domingo de Silos, Libreria de la Abadia, 09610 Burgos, Spain. Ed. Clemente de la Serna. illus.; stat.; tr.lit.; index. cum.index; circ. 1,500. (back issues avail.)

230 SW ISSN 0491-2853
STUDIA TEHOLOGICA LUNDENSIA. (Text in English, German, Swedish) 1952. irreg. price varies. Lund University Press, P.O. Box 141, S-221 00 Lund, Sweden. TEL 46-46-31-20-00. FAX 46-46-30-53-38. Ed. Goeran Gustafsson.

230 DK ISSN 0039-338X
BR1
STUDIA THEOLOGICA; Scandinavian journal of theology. (Text in English and German) 1946. s-a. DKK 240($33) (students DKK 154). Akademisk Forlag, Store Kanikestraede 8, P.O. Box 54, DK-1002 Copenhagen K, Denmark. Ed. Jens Glebe-Moeller. adv.; bk.rev.; bibl.; index. cum.index every 10 yrs.; circ. 550. (also avail. in microform from UMI) Indexed: Arts & Hum.Cit.Ind., CERDIC, Curr.Cont., M.L.A., New Test.Abstr., Rel.& Theol.Abstr. (1978-), Rel.Ind.One, Rel.Per.
—BLDSC shelfmark: 8483.227000.

STUDIAS HUMANITAS. see HISTORY — History Of Europe

200 GW
STUDIEN ZUR KIRCHENGESCHICHTE NIEDERSACHSENS. 1919. irreg. Vandenhoeck und Ruprecht, Robert-Bosch-Breite 6, Postfach 3753, 3400 Goettingen, Germany. TEL 0551-6959-0. FAX 0551-695917. Ed. Hans W. Krumwiede.

200 GW
STUDIEN ZUR UMWELT DES NEUEN TESTAMENTS. 1968. irreg. Vandenhoeck und Ruprecht, Robert-Bosch-Breite 6, Postfach 3753, 3400 Goettingen, Germany. TEL 0551-6959-0. FAX 0551-695917. Ed.Bd.

200 US
STUDIES IN AMERICAN RELIGION. 1980. irreg., latest no.57. $39.95 per no. Edwin Mellen Press, 240 Portage Rd., Box 450, Lewiston, NY 14092. TEL 716-754-8566. FAX 716-754-4335. Ed. Herbert Richardson. bibl.; index.

STUDIES IN ART AND RELIGIOUS INTERPRETATION. see ART

222 US
STUDIES IN BIBLE AND EARLY CHRISTIANITY. 1982. irreg., latest no.29. $39.95 per no. Edwin Mellen Press, 240 Portage Rd., Box 450, Lewiston, NY 14092. TEL 716-754-8566. FAX 754-4335.

RELIGIONS AND THEOLOGY

200   IS
STUDIES IN BIBLE AND EXEGESIS. 1980. irreg., vol.2, 1992. price varies. Bar-Ilan University Press, Ramat Gan 52900, Israel. TEL 03-5318401.
 Description: Contains a variety of essays on biblical literature, exegesis, historiography, and manuscript research: modern biblical scholarship from a Jewish perspective.

200   US   ISSN 0897-7828
STUDIES IN BIBLICAL GREEK. irreg. Peter Lang Publishing, Inc., 62 W. 45th St., 4th Fl., New York, NY 10036. TEL 212-302-6740. FAX 212-302-7574. Ed. D.A. Carson.
 Description: Covers the latest research into biblical Greek (Old and New Testaments).

STUDIES IN BLACK RELIGION IN AMERICA. see *ETHNIC INTERESTS*

STUDIES IN CHRISTIAN ETHICS. see *PHILOSOPHY*

266   NE   ISSN 0924-9389
STUDIES IN CHRISTIAN MISSION. 1990. irreg., no.7, 1992. price varies. E.J. Brill, P.O. Box 9000, 2300 PA Leiden, Netherlands. TEL 071-312624. FAX 071-317532. TELEX 39296 BRILL NL. (In N. America: E.J. Brill, 24 Hudson St., Kinderhook, NY 12106. TEL 800-962-4406)
 —BLDSC shelfmark: 8489.909000.
 Description: Scholarly monographs on the history of Christian missionary activities and related theological issues.

200 320   US
STUDIES IN CHURCH AND STATE. irreg. price varies. Princeton University Press, 3175 Princeton Pike, Lawrenceville, NJ 08648. TEL 609-896-1344. FAX 609-895-1081. Ed. John F. Wilson.

291   UK   ISSN 0039-3622
BL1
STUDIES IN COMPARATIVE RELIGION. 1941. q. £8.80($20) Perennial Books Ltd., Pates Manor, Bedfont, Middlesex, TW14, 8JP, England. Ed.Bd. adv.; bk.rev.; index; circ. controlled. (also avail. in microform from UMI; reprint service avail. from UMI) Indexed: Arts & Hum.Cit.Ind., CERDIC, Curr.Cont., Hum.Ind., Rel.Ind.One.
 —BLDSC shelfmark: 8490.270000.
 Formerly: Tomorrow.

200   US
STUDIES IN COMPARATIVE RELIGION. irreg., latest vol.7. $39.95 per no. Edwin Mellen Press, 240 Portage Rd., Box 450, Lewiston, NY 14092. TEL 716-754-8566. FAX 716-754-4335.

150   US   ISSN 0193-2748
BX2350.2
STUDIES IN FORMATIVE SPIRITUALITY. 1980. 3/yr. $18. Duquesne University, Institute of Formative Spirituality, 600 Forbes Ave., Pittsburgh, PA 15282. TEL 412-434-6029. Ed. Dr. Adrian Van Kaam. abstr.; bibl.; index; circ. 3,000. (also avail. in microform from UMI; reprint service avail. from UMI) Indexed: Arts & Hum.Cit.Ind., Cath.Ind., CERDIC, Curr.Cont., Hum.Ind., Psychol.Abstr., Rel.& Theol.Abstr. (1982-).
 —BLDSC shelfmark: 8490.570000.
 Supersedes (1965-1979): Humanitas (ISSN 0018-7496)

292   NE   ISSN 0169-9512
STUDIES IN GREEK AND ROMAN RELIGION. 1980. irreg., vol.7, 1991. price varies. E.J. Brill, P.O. Box 9000, 2300 PA Leiden, Netherlands. TEL 071-312624. FAX 071-317532. TELEX 39296 BRILL NL. (In N. America: E.J. Brill, 24 Hudson St., Kinderhook, NY 12106. TEL 800-962-4406) Eds. H.S. Versnel, F.T. van Straten.
 —BLDSC shelfmark: 8490.627500.
 Description: International studies in Hellenic and Roman theology.

200   NE   ISSN 0585-6914
STUDIES IN MEDIEVAL AND REFORMATION THOUGHT. 1966. irreg., vol.48, 1991. price varies. E.J. Brill, P.O. Box 9000, 2300 PA Leiden, Netherlands. TEL 071-312624. FAX 071-317532. TELEX 39296 BRILL NL. (In N. America: E.J. Brill, 24 Hudson St., Kinderhook, NY 12106. TEL 800-962-4406) Ed. H.A. Oberman. (back issues avail.)

STUDIES IN MORAL PHILOSOPHY. see *PHILOSOPHY*

200   US   ISSN 1048-8553
BX9354.2
STUDIES IN PURITAN AMERICAN SPIRITUALITY. a. $19.95 to individuals; institutions $29.95. Edwin Mellen Press, 240 Portage Rd., Box 450, Lewiston, NY 14092. TEL 800-753-2788. FAX 716-754-4335. Ed. Michael Schuldiner.
 Description: Addresses spiritual concerns that existed in Puritan America.

200   CN   ISSN 0008-4298
BL1
STUDIES IN RELIGION/SCIENCES RELIGIEUSES. (Text in English and French) 1971. q. Can.$39($43) (Canadian Corporation for Studies in Religion) Wilfrid Laurier University Press, 75 University Ave. W., Waterloo, Ont. N2L 3C5, Canada. TEL 519-884-1970. FAX 519-884-8853. Ed. Roland Chagnon. adv.; bk.rev.; charts; index; circ. 1,200. Indexed: Arts & Hum.Cit.Ind., CERDIC, M.L.A., Mid.East: Abstr.& Ind., New Test.Abstr., Old Test.Abstr., Rel.& Theol.Abstr. (1974-), Rel.Ind.One, Rel.Per.
 —BLDSC shelfmark: 8491.430000.
 Supersedes: Canadian Journal of Theology.
 Description: Offers articles covering the field of religious studies as well as reviews and critical notes on recent publications.

200   US
STUDIES IN RELIGION AND SOCIETY. 1981. irreg., latest no.28. $39.95 per no. Edwin Mellen Press, 240 Portage Rd., Box 450, Lewiston, NY 14092. TEL 716-754-8566. FAX 716-754-4335. Indexed: Rel.Ind.Two.

200   US
STUDIES IN RELIGIOUS EDUCATION. irreg., latest no.2. $39.95 per no. Edwin Mellen Press, 240 Portage Rd., Box 450, Lewiston, NY 14092. TEL 716-754-8566. FAX 716-754-4335.

230   NE   ISSN 0081-8607
STUDIES IN THE HISTORY OF CHRISTIAN THOUGHT. 1966. irreg., vol.47, 1991. price varies. E.J. Brill, P.O. Box 9000, 2300 PA Leiden, Netherlands. TEL 071-312624. FAX 071-317532. TELEX 39296 BRILL NL. (In N. America: E.J. Brill, 24 Hudson St., Kinderhook, NY 12106. TEL 800-962-4406) Ed. Heiko A. Oberman.
 Description: Covers topics in Christian theology.

266   US
STUDIES IN THE HISTORY OF MISSIONS. irreg., latest no.8. $39.95 per no. Edwin Mellen Press, 240 Portage Rd., Box 450, Lewiston, NY 14092. TEL 716-745-8566. FAX 716-754-4335.

STUDIES IN THE PSYCHOANALYTIC WRITINGS OF ERNEST BECKER. see *PSYCHOLOGY*

200   US
STUDIES IN THE PSYCHOLOGY OF RELIGION. irreg., latest no.6. $39.95 per no. Edwin Mellen Press, 240 Portage Rd., Box 450, Lewiston, NY 14092. TEL 716-754-8566. FAX 716-754-4335.

200 301.412   US
STUDIES IN WOMEN AND RELIGION. 1979. irreg., latest no.30. $39.95 per no. Edwin Mellen Press, 240 Portage Rd., Box 450, Lewiston, NY 14092. TEL 716-754-8566. FAX 716-754-4335.

200   NE   ISSN 0169-9814
STUDIES ON RELIGION IN AFRICA. (Supplement to: Journal of Religion in Africa (ISSN 0022-4200)) 1970. irreg., vol.7, 1991. price varies. E.J. Brill, P.O. Box 9000, 2300 PA Leiden, Netherlands. TEL 071-312624. FAX 071-317532. TELEX 39296 BRILL NL. (In N. America: E.J. Brill, 24 Hudson St., Kinderhook, NY 12106. TEL 800-962-4406) Ed. Adrian Hastings. bibl.

STUDIO; a journal of Christians writing. see *LITERATURE*

220   IS   ISSN 0081-8909
STUDIUM BIBLICUM FRANCISCANUM. ANALECTA. (Text in various languages) 1962. irreg., no.32, 1989. price varies. Franciscan Printing Press, P.O. Box 14064, 91140 Jerusalem, Israel. TEL 02-286594. circ. 1,000.

209   BE   ISSN 0777-8112
SUBSIDIA HAGIOGRAPHICA. 1886. irreg., no.75, 1991. price varies. Societe des Bollandistes, 24 bd. Saint-Michel, B-1040 Brussels, Belgium.
 Description: Critical studies about Saints' lives.

200   UK
SUDAN CHURCH REVIEW. 1949. 2/yr. £3. Sudan Church Association, 2A Chessel Ave., Bitterne, Southampton SO2 4DX, England. TEL 0703-447800. bk.rev.; circ. 1,700.
 Description: News from church leaders and other workers in the Sudan. Includes news from supporting groups and organizations in UK.

200   US   ISSN 0039-5188
SUNDAY DIGEST; selected reading for Christian adults. 1886. w. $3.50. David C. Cook Publishing Co., 850 N. Grove Ave., Elgin, IL 60120. TEL 312-741-2400. Ed. Judy Couchman. bk.rev.; illus.; circ. 125,000(approx.). (tabloid format) Indexed: A.I.P.P.

200   HK
SUNDAY EXAMINER. (Text in English) 1946. w. HK.$160 (foreign HK$240). 11-F, Catholic Diocese Centre, 16 Caine Rd., Hong Kong. TEL 5220487. FAX 5213095. Ed. Fr. Francis G. Doyle. adv.; circ. 2,000.

200   FR   ISSN 0750-1455
BJ2
LE SUPPLEMENT; revue d'ethique et de theologie morale. 1947. 4/yr. 195 F. (foreign 245 F.). Editions du Cerf, 29 bd. Latour Maubourg, 75340 Paris Cedex 07, France. TEL 45-50-34-07. FAX 45-56-04-27. (Subscr. to: Service Abonnements, 3 chemin des Prunais, 94350 Villiers-sur-Marne, France) Ed. Jean-Paul Durand. circ. 3,000. Indexed: Cath.Ind., CERDIC.
 —BLDSC shelfmark: 8547.205000.
 Description: Forum for exchange between theologians and theosophists.

220   SW
SVENSK EXEGETISK AARSBOK. (Text in English or Swedish) 1936. a. (Uppsala Exegetiska Saellskap) Liber Forlag, S-205 10, Malmo, Sweden. bk.rev.; illus. Indexed: New Test.Abstr., Old Test.Abstr., Rel.& Theol.Abstr. (1983-).

200   SW   ISSN 0039-6699
SVENSK PASTORAL TIDSKRIFT. 1959. w. SEK 350 to individuals; students SEK 250; foreign SEK 425. Stiftelsen Kyrkligt Forum, P.O. Box 2085, S-750 02 Uppsala 2, Sweden. FAX 018-550986. Ed. Carl Strandberg. adv.; bk.rev.; circ. 3,200.

230   SW   ISSN 0039-6761
BR6
SVENSK TEOLOGISK KVARTALSKRIFT. 1925. q. SEK 85. Liber Forlag, S-205 10, Malmoe, Sweden. Eds. Bengt Hagglund, P.E. Persson. adv.; bk.rev.; abstr.; index. cum.index every 10 yrs.; circ. 1,000. Indexed: CERDIC, New Test.Abstr., Old Test.Abstr., Rel.& Theol.Abstr. (1989-), Rel.Ind.One, Rel.Per.

266   SW   ISSN 0039-6826
SVENSK VECKOTIDNING. 1882. w. SEK 256. Svensk Veckotidning, P.O. Box 6302, 113 81 Stockholm, Sweden. FAX 46-8-33-55-57. TELEX S-142 75. Ed. Leif Nilsson. adv.; bk.rev.; play rev.; circ. 28,000. (tabloid format)

254   SW
SVENSKA KYRKANS.* 1946. 10/yr. SEK 20. Svenska Kyrkans Foersamlings- och Pastoratsfoerbund, PO Box 6626, S-11384 Stockholm, Sweden. Ed. Per Olof Nilsson. adv.; illus.; stat.; circ. 17,000.
 Supersedes in part: Foersamlings- och Pastoratsfoervaltning (ISSN 0015-5284)
 Description: Covers church administration.

200   US   ISSN 0039-7547
SWORD OF THE LORD; America's foremost revival magazine. 1934. bi-w. $12. Sword of the Lord Foundation, Box 1099, 224 Bridge Ave., Murfreesboro, TN 37133. TEL 615-893-6700. FAX 615-895-7447. Ed. Curtis Hutson. adv.; bk.rev.; index; circ. 125,000. (tabloid format)
 Description: Features include over 100 sermons, tips on soul winning and getting converts down the aisle, bible studies and answers to Bible questions, and reports of revivals from leading evangelists.

SYCAMORE TREE NEWSLETTER. see *EDUCATION — Teaching Methods And Curriculum*

RELIGIONS AND THEOLOGY 4205

SYNAPSE (BOSTON). see *LITERARY AND POLITICAL REVIEWS*

T B P'S OCTAVA; a news-journal of women's spirituality and thealogy. see *WOMEN'S INTERESTS*

200   NR   ISSN 0794-7046
T C N N RESEARCH BULLETIN. 1978. s-a. £N15($15) Theological College of Northern Nigeria, P.O. Box 64, Bukuru, Plateau State, Nigeria. Ed.Bd. circ. 200. (back issues avail.)

T Q. (Teen Quest) see *CHILDREN AND YOUTH — For*

200   CN   ISSN 0704-6421
T R A C E S. 1976. q. Can.$10. (Teachers of Religion and Christian Ethics) Saskatchewan Teachers' Federation, Box 1108, Saskatoon, Sask. S7K 3N3, Canada.
    Formerly (until 1977): T R A C E Newsletter (ISSN 0701-192X)

200   UK   ISSN 0039-8837
AP4
TABLET. 1840. w. £46.50. Tablet Publishing Co. Ltd., 1 King St. Cloister, Clifton Walk, London W6 0QZ, England. TEL 081-748-8484. FAX 081-748-1550. Ed. John Wilkins. adv.; bk.rev.; film rev.; index; circ. 16,421. (also avail. in microform from UMI; reprint service avail. from UMI) **Indexed**: Cath.Ind., CERDIC, Rural Recreat.Tour.Abstr., World Agri.Econ.& Rural Sociol.Abstr.
    —BLDSC shelfmark: 8597.450000.
    Description: Covers religion, politics, society, ethics and the arts.

296   US   ISSN 0039-9213
TALKS AND TALES. (Editions in French, Hebrew, Italian, Spanish and Yiddish) 1942. m. $3. Merkos L'Inyonei Chinuch, Inc., 770 Eastern Parkway, Brooklyn, NY 11213. Ed. Nissan Mindel. index.

268.8   US   ISSN 0082-1713
TARBELL'S TEACHER'S GUIDE; to the International Sunday School Lessons. 1905. a. $7.95. David C. Cook Publishing Co., 850 N. Grove Ave., Elgin, IL 60120. TEL 708-741-2400. Ed. William P. Barker. circ. 2,300.
    Description: Bible commentary using KJV and RSV for Sunday School teachers.

200   KE
TARGET. (Text in English) 1964. bi-m. P.O. Box 72839, Nairobi, Kenya. Ed. Rebeka Njau. circ. 17,000.

220   ISSN 8755-8769
TEACH; a newsletter for Christian teachers and church leaders. 1985. q. $15.95. Sweet Publishing, 3950 Fossil Creek Blvd., Ste. 201, Fort Worth, TX 76137-2403. TEL 817-232-5661. FAX 817-232-2030. Ed. Mary Hollingsworth. bk.rev.; circ. 9,000.

377.8   UK
TEACHING UNDER 5'S. q. £2.25. Scripture Union, 130 City Rd., London EC1V 2NJ, England. Ed. Christine Wright. adv.; illus.; circ. 20,000.
    Formerly: Teaching Beginners (ISSN 0040-0580)

266   US   ISSN 0163-3422
BV2350
TEAM HORIZONS. 1925. 6/yr. $2. Evangelical Alliance Mission (TEAM), Box 969, Wheaton, IL 60189-0969. TEL 708-653-5300. FAX 708-653-1826. Ed. Jack Kilgore. bk.rev.; charts; illus.; circ. 37,000.

TECHNICAL PAPERS FOR THE BIBLE TRANSLATOR. see *LINGUISTICS*

TEEN POWER (1979); a power-line paper. see *CHILDREN AND YOUTH — For*

220 375   UK   ISSN 0142-5943
TEEN-SEARCH. q. £0.50. Go Teach Publications, 2 Radford Rd., Leamington Spa CV31 1LX, England. TEL 0926-26573. illus.
    Description: Young peoples' workbooks for use with: Go Teach Teens.

200   NE   ISSN 0040-2133
TEGENWOORDIG. 1946. bi-m. fl.5.25. Karmel, Bloemgracht 90, Amsterdam C, Netherlands. (Subscr. to: Karmel, Rijksweg N. 35, Geleen, Netherlands) Ed.Bd. bk.rev.; illus.; circ. 17,000.
    Formerly: Scapulier.

200   UK
TEILHARD REVIEW AND JOURNAL OF COSMIC CONVERGENCE. 1966. 3/yr. £10($30) Teilhard Centre for the Future of Man, 23 Kensington Sq., London W8 5HN, England. TEL 01-937-5372. Ed. Michael Le Morvan. adv.; bk.rev.; bibl.; charts; illus.; cum.index: 1966-1971; 1972-1977; circ. 3,100. (tabloid format; also avail. in microform from UMI; reprint service avail. from UMI) **Indexed**: Cath.Ind., CERDIC, Mid.East: Abstr.& Ind.
    Former titles: Teilhard Review and Journal of Creative Evolution; (until 1981): Teilhard Review (ISSN 0040-2184)
    Description: Reprints of Teilhard's essays, and articles on Teilhard's work and related developments in science, philosophy and religion.

200   ZR
TELEMA. (Text in French) 1975. q. $40. B.P. 3277, Kinshasa-Gombe, Zaire. Ed. Boka di Mpasi. adv.; bk.rev.; circ. 4,000. **Indexed**: CERDIC, Curr.Cont.Africa, Old Test.Abstr.

200   FI   ISSN 0497-1817
BL1.A1
TEMENOS (TURKU). (Text in English, French, German) 1965. a. Fmk.150. Finnish Society for the Study of Comparative Religion, Gezeliusgatan 2, P.O. Box 70, SF 20501 Turku, Finland. FAX 358-21-311290. Ed. Tore Ahlbaeck. bk.rev.; circ. 250. **Indexed**: Arts & Hum.Cit.Ind., Rel.Ind.Two.
    —BLDSC shelfmark: 8789.760000.

200   IT
TEMI DI PREDICAZIONE - OMELIE. 1957. m. L.35000($75) (foreign L.65000). Editrice Domenican Italian, Via L. Palmieri 19, 80133 Naples, Italy. Ed. P. Reginaldo Agostino Iannarone. adv. **Indexed**: CERDIC.

TEMOIGNAGE CHRETIEN. see *LITERARY AND POLITICAL REVIEWS*

266   JA   ISSN 0040-3482
BL2222.T4
TENRIKYO. (Text in English) 1962-1970; resumed 1976. m. 600 Yen. Tenrikyo Church Headquarters, Tenrikyo Overseas Mission Department, Tenri, Nara, Japan. TEL 07436-3-1511. FAX 07436-2-0227. Ed. Y. Terada. illus.; tr.lit.; circ. 3,400. (tabloid format)

200   US   ISSN 0272-6939
TENTMAKER'S JOURNAL. 1980. q. $15. Tentmaker's Publishing Group, Inc., Box 246, Pickerington, OH 43147. TEL 614-866-3000. Ed. Steve Monroe. adv.; bk.rev.; circ. 12,000.

200   SP   ISSN 0495-1549
BX2350.65
TEOLOGIA ESPIRITUAL. 1958. 3/yr. 2000 ptas.($12) (foreign 3000 ptas.). Facultad de Teologia "San Vicente Ferrer", Seccion Dominicos, Mtro. Chapi 80, Torrente-Valencia, Spain. bk.rev.; index; circ. 700.

200   SP   ISSN 0212-1964
TEOLOGIA Y CATEQUESIS. 1982. q. 2000 ptas. (foreign 3800 ptas.). Centro de Estudios Teologicos "San Damaso", San Buenaventura, 9, 28005 Madrid, Spain. TEL 91-265-24-04. Ed. Antonio Canizares. bk.rev.; bibl.; circ. 1,000.

230   FI   ISSN 0040-3555
TEOLOGINEN AIKAKAUSKIRJA/TEOLOGISK TIDSKRIFT. (Text in Finnish and Swedish) 1896. 6/yr. FIM 200 (typically set in Aug.). Teologinen Julkaisuseura r.y., Fabianinkatu 7, SF-00130 Helsinki, Finland. TEL 90-1913036. FAX 90-1913033. Ed. Juha Seppo. adv.; bk.rev.; charts; illus.; index. cum.index; circ. 3,200.

200   YU
TEOLOSKI POGLEDI; versko naucni casopis. (Text in Serbian; summaries in English) 1968. q. $25. Srpska Patrijarsija, 7 Jula 5, 11000 Belgrade, Yugoslavia. Ed. Radovan Bigovic. bk.rev.; bibl.; circ. 1,200.

200   IS   ISSN 0040-3784
TERRA SANTA. English edition: Holy Land. French edition: Terre Sainte (ISSN 0040-3873); Spanish edition: Tierra Santa (ISSN 0333-6212) (Text in Italian) bi-m. price varies. Franciscan Printing Press, P.O. Box 14064, Jerusalem 91140, Israel. TEL 02-286594. Ed.Bd. **Indexed**: Numis.Lit.

200   US
TERRA UNA. 1972. s-a. $25. International Association for Religious Freedom, U S Chapter, Unitarian Universalist Association, 25 Beacon St., Boston, MA 02108. TEL 617-742-2100. Ed. Scott Phillips. bk.rev.; circ. 500.
    Formerly: Interdependence (ISSN 0362-4668)

262.9   IT
TESTIMONI NEL MONDO; pagine di vita spirituale. 1974. bi-m. L.34000. Edizioni O.R., Via Necchi 2, 20123 Milan, Italy. TEL 86453578. bk.rev.; circ. 2,500.

TESTIMONIANZE; quaderni mensili. see *LITERARY AND POLITICAL REVIEWS*

200   IT
IL TESTIMONIO. 1884. m. L.31000($24.80) (effective Oct. 1991). Unione Cristiana Evangelica Battista d'Italia, Piazza S. Lorenzo in Lucina, 35, 00186 Rome, Italy. TEL 06-6876124. FAX 06-6876185. Ed. Adriana Pagnotti. adv.; bk.rev.; index; circ. 1,000. (back issues avail.)

200 465   GW   ISSN 0082-3589
TEXTE UND UNTERSUCHUNGEN ZUR GESCHICHTE DER ALTCHRISTLICHEN LITERATUR. 1952. irreg., vol.136, 1989. price varies. (Akademie der Wissenschaften der DDR, Zentralinstitut fuer Alte Geschichte und Archaeologie) Akademie-Verlag Berlin, Leipziger Str. 3-4, 1086 Berlin, Germany. TELEX 114420-AVERL-DD.

200   US
TEXTS AND STUDIES IN RELIGION. 1977. irreg., latest no.58. $39.95 per no. Edwin Mellen Press, 240 Portage Rd., Box 450, Lewiston, NY 14092. TEL 716-754-8566. FAX 716-754-4335.

220   IS   ISSN 0082-3767
BS410
TEXTUS. (Text in English; summaries in Hebrew) 1960. irreg. (approx. a.). $6. (Hebrew University of Jerusalem, Bible Project) Magnes Press, The Hebrew University, Jerusalem, Israel. cum.index 1960-1966.
    —BLDSC shelfmark: 8813.785000.

200   GW   ISSN 0082-3775
TEXTUS PATRISTICI ET LITURGICI. 1964. irreg. price varies. (Institutum Liturgicum Ratisbonense) Verlag Friedrich Pustet, Gutenbergstr. 8, 8400 Regensburg 1, Germany. FAX 0941-948652. Ed. Klaus Gamber. circ. 1,000.

268   UK   ISSN 0307-8388
THEMELIOS. 1964. 3/yr. £4.50($10) Universities and Colleges Christian Fellowship, 38 De Montfort St., Leicester LE1 7GP, England. (Subscr. in U.S. to: I F E S Link, 6400 Schroeder Rd., Box 7895, Madison, WI 53707-7895) (Co-sponsor: International Fellowship of Evangelical Students) Ed. Chris Wright. bk.rev.; bibl.; circ. 5,500. (back issues avail.) **Indexed**: Old Test.Abstr., Rel.& Theol.Abstr. (1975-), Rel.Ind.One.
    —BLDSC shelfmark: 8814.477000.
    Description: International journal for theological students which espouses and defends the historic Christian faith.

200   GW   ISSN 0937-8766
▼**THEMENHEFTE GEMEINDEARBEIT**. 1990. q. DM.60. Bergmoser & Hoeller Verlag GmbH, Karl-Friedrich-Str. 76, 5100 Aachen, Germany. TEL 0241-173090. circ. 2,500.

200   SA   ISSN 0255-8858
THEOLOGIA EVANGELICA. (Text in Afrikaans, English) 1968. 3/yr. R.13.20($9) University of South Africa, Faculty of Theology, P.O. Box 392, Pretoria 0001, South Africa. FAX 012-429-2533. TELEX 350068. Ed. S. Maimela. adv.; bk.rev.; circ. 3,457. (also avail. in microfilm from UMI) **Indexed**: Ind.S.A.Per., New Test.Abstr., Rel.& Theol.Abstr. (1989-), Rel.Ind.One.

130   US   ISSN 0362-0085
THEOLOGIA 21. 1970. s-a. $15 to non-members. (Affiliated Christian Emortalists) Dominion Press, Box 4608, Salemarcos, OR 97302-8608. TEL 503-362-9634. Ed. A. Stuart Otto. bibl.; charts; illus.; stat.; circ. 100. (looseleaf format; also avail. in microform from UMI; back issues avail.; reprint service avail. from UMI)
    Formerly (until 1976): Immortality Newsletter (ISSN 0019-2783)
    Description: Articles on metaphysical Christianity.

RELIGIONS AND THEOLOGY

200　　　　　　　　HU　ISSN 0133-7599
BR9.H8
THEOLOGIAI SZEMLE. 1958. 6/yr. $40.50.
Magyarorszagi Egyhazak Okumenikus Tanacsa,
Szabadsag Ter 2-1, 1054 Budapest, Hungary. Ed.
Ottlyk Erno. bk.rev.; circ. 1,000. **Indexed:** Hist.Abstr.
(thru 1990).

200　　　　　　　　UK　ISSN 0954-2191
THEOLOGICAL BOOK REVIEW. 1988. 3/yr. £15($30)
(typically set in Oct.). Feed the Minds, Robertson
House, Leas Rd., Guildford, Surrey GU1 4QW,
England. TEL 0483-57787. FAX 0483-301387. Ed.
Charles Elliott. adv.; bk.rev.; circ. 600.
　Description: For theological librarians and
educators to aid them in current book selection.

207　　　　　　　　US　ISSN 0040-5620
BV4019
THEOLOGICAL EDUCATION. 1964. 2/yr. $7 (foreign
$8). Association of Theological Schools, 10 Summit
Park Dr., Pittsburgh, PA 15275-1103.
TEL 412-788-6505. Ed. Gail B. King. stat.; index;
circ. 4,500. (also avail. in microform from UMI)
Indexed: CERDIC, Curr.Cont., Rel.& Theol.Abstr.
(1989-), Rel.Ind.One, Rel.Per.
　—BLDSC shelfmark: 8814.523000.

268　377.9　　　　US　ISSN 0198-6856
BR1
THEOLOGICAL EDUCATOR. 1968. s-a. $8 (effective
1992). New Orleans Baptist Theological Seminary,
3939 Gentilly Blvd., New Orleans, LA 70126.
TEL 504-282-4455. FAX 504-944-4455. Ed. Paul
E. Robertson. adv.; bk.rev.; circ. 2,500. **Indexed:**
CERDIC, G.Soc.Sci.& Rel.Per.Lit., South.Bap.Per.Ind.
　—BLDSC shelfmark: 8814.523050.

200　　　　　　　　KO　ISSN 0260-3705
THEOLOGICAL NEWS. 1968. 4/yr. P.O. Box 94, Choong
Jong No, Seoul 120-650, Korea. TEL 2-393-9895.
FAX 2-393-8462.
　Description: News of interest to evangelical
theologians and theological educators. Contains
information about consultations, seminars and other
worldwide activities.

230　　　　　　　　US　ISSN 0040-5639
BX801
THEOLOGICAL STUDIES. 1940. q. $25 to individuals; to
U.S. institutions and foreign $30. (Theological
Faculties of the Society of Jesus in the U S)
Theological Studies, Inc., Georgetown University,
37th and "O" Sts., NW, Washington, DC 20057.
TEL 202-338-0754. FAX 202-687-7679. Ed.
Robert J. Daly. adv.; bk.rev.; index. cum.index: vols.
1-40; circ. 5,500. (also avail. in microform from
UMI) **Indexed:** Arts & Hum.Cit.Ind., Bk.Rev.Ind.
(1984-), Canon Law Abstr., Cath.Ind., CERDIC,
Child.Bk.Rev.Ind. (1984-), Curr.Cont., Hum.Ind.,
New Test.Abstr., Old Test.Abstr., Ref.Sour., Rel.&
Theol.Abstr. (1969-), Rel.Ind.One, Rel.Per.
　—BLDSC shelfmark: 8814.524000.
　Description: Scholarly articles, bulletins, and notes
in the various theological disciplines.

THEOLOGICAL TIMES. see *HANDICAPPED — Visually Impaired*

200　　　　　　　　GW　ISSN 0342-1457
THEOLOGIE DER GEGENWART. 1957. q. DM.38. Butzon
und Bercker GmbH, Hoogeweg 71, 4178 Kevelaer
1, Germany. TEL 02832-2906. FAX 02832-40321.
TELEX 812207-BBKEV. bk.rev.; circ. 1,350.

230　　　　　　　　GW
THEOLOGIE UND DIENST. 1973. irreg., latest no.30.
price varies. (Prediger- und Missionsseminar St.
Chrischona) Brunnen-Verlag GmbH,
Gottlieb-Daimler-str. 22, Postfach 5205, 6300
Giessen 1, Germany. Ed.Bd. circ. 3,000.

230　100　　　　　GW　ISSN 0040-5655
BX803
THEOLOGIE UND PHILOSOPHIE. 1926. q. DM.204.
Verlag Herder GmbH und Co. KG,
Hermann-Herder-Str. 4, 7800 Freiburg im Breisgau,
Germany. FAX 0761-2717-520. Ed. Hermann Josef
Sieben. adv.; bk.rev.; bibl.; index; circ. 700. **Indexed:**
Canon Law Abstr., CERDIC, New Test.Abstr., Phil.Ind.,
Rel.& Theol.Abstr.
　Formerly: Scholastik.

207　　　　　　　　AU　ISSN 0040-5663
THEOLOGISCH-PRAKTISCHE QUARTALSCHRIFT. 1848. q.
S.288. (Theologische Hochschule der Dioezese Linz)
Landesverlag, Landstr. 41, A-4010 Linz, Austria.
Ed.Bd. adv.; bk.rev.; circ. 2,800. **Indexed:** Canon Law
Abstr., CERDIC, New Test.Abstr.
　—BLDSC shelfmark: 8814.540000.

266　　　　　　　　GW　ISSN 0342-2372
THEOLOGISCHE BEITRAEGE. 1970. bi-m. DM.49.50.
Theologischer Verlag R. Brockhaus, Postfach 2220,
5657 Haan, Germany. TEL 02104-6911-0.
FAX 02104-691130. Ed.Bd. adv.; bk.rev.; circ.
4,000. **Indexed:** CERDIC, New Test.Abstr., Old
Test.Abstr.
　—BLDSC shelfmark: 8814.528500.
　Description: Non-denominational publication
containing essays on religion, ethics, and
evangelism.

230　　　　　　　　SZ　ISSN 0082-3902
THEOLOGISCHE DISSERTATIONEN. (Editions in English
and German; summaries in English or German)
1969. irreg., no.17, 1986. price varies.
(Universitaet Basel, Theologische Fakultaet) Friedrich
Reinhardt Verlag, Missionsstr. 36, CH-4012 Basel,
Switzerland. (Dist. by: Albert J. Phiebig Books, Box
352, White Plains, NY 10602) Ed. Bo Reicke.

200　　　　　　　　GW　ISSN 0040-5671
Z7753
THEOLOGISCHE LITERATURZEITUNG; Monatsschrift fuer
das gesamte Gebiet der Theologie und
Religionswissenschaft. 1876. m. DM.108 (foreign
DM.112). Evangelische Verlagsanstalt GmbH,
Burgstr. 1-5, 7010 Leipzig, Germany. TEL 295709.
FAX 295383. Ed. Dr. Ernst-Heinz Amberg. bk.rev.;
index. **Indexed:** CERDIC, New Test.Abstr., Old
Test.Abstr., Rel.& Theol.Abstr. (1979-), Rel.Ind.One,
Rel.Per.

230　　　　　　　　GW　ISSN 0040-5698
BR4
THEOLOGISCHE RUNDSCHAU. 1929. q. DM.115 to
individuals, students DM.65. Verlag J.C.B. Mohr
(Paul Siebeck), Wilhelmstr. 18, Postfach 2040,
7400 Tuebingen, Germany. TEL 07071-26064.
FAX 07071-51104. TELEX 7262872-MOHR-D. Eds.
J. Baur, L. Perlitt. adv.; bk.rev.; index. **Indexed:**
CERDIC, New Test.Abstr., Old Test.Abstr., Rel.&
Theol.Abstr. (1980-), Rel.Ind.One, Rel.Per.
　Description: Reports and reviews of problems and
developments in all theological fields.

230　　　　　　　　SZ　ISSN 0040-5701
BR4
THEOLOGISCHE ZEITSCHRIFT. 1945. bi-m. 107 Fr.
(Universitaet Basel, Theologische Fakultaet) Friedrich
Reinhardt Verlag, Missionsstr. 36, CH-4012 Basel,
Switzerland. Ed. K. Seybold. adv.; bk.rev.; abstr.;
bibl.; cum.index; circ. 750. **Indexed:** CERDIC, New
Test.Abstr., Old Test.Abstr., Rel.& Theol.Abstr.
(1975-), Rel.Ind.One.
　—BLDSC shelfmark: 8814.537000.

200　　　　　　　　UK　ISSN 0040-571X
BR1
THEOLOGY. 1920. bi-m. £15($30) Society for
Promoting Christian Knowledge, Holy Trinity Church,
Marylebone Rd., London NW1 4DU, England.
TEL 071-387-5282. FAX 071-388-2352. Ed.Bd.
adv.; bk.rev.; index; circ. 5,000. (also avail. in
microform) **Indexed:** Br.Hum.Ind., New Test.Abstr.,
Rel.& Theol.Abstr. (1968-), Rel.Ind.One.
　—BLDSC shelfmark: 8814.541000.

230　　　　　　　　US　ISSN 0040-5728
BX801
THEOLOGY DIGEST. 1953. q. $12 (foreign $14). (St.
Louis University, Department of Theological Studies)
Theology Digest,Inc., 3634 Lindell Blvd., St. Louis,
MO 63108-3395. TEL 314-658-2859. (Subscr. to:
Box 6036, Duluth, MN 55806) Ed. Bernhard Asen.
adv.; bk.rev.; restricted bibl.; cum.index:
1953-1973; circ. 4,000. (also avail. in microfilm
from UMI; back issues avail.) **Indexed:** Cath.Ind.,
CERDIC, Int.Z.Bibelwiss, Old Test.Abstr., Rel.&
Theol.Abstr. (1980-).
　—BLDSC shelfmark: 8814.543000.
　Description: Theology magazine with an
international readership.

230　　　　　　　　US　ISSN 0040-5736
BR1
THEOLOGY TODAY. 1944. q. $21. (Princeton
Theological Seminary) Theology Today, Box 29,
Princeton, NJ 08542. TEL 609-497-7714.
FAX 609-924-2973. Ed. Hugh T. Kerr. adv.; bk.rev.;
index. cum.index every 10 yrs.; circ. 14,000. (also
avail. in microform from MIM,UMI; back issues avail.;
reprint service avail. from UMI) **Indexed:** Arts &
Hum.Cit.Ind., Bk.Rev.Ind. (1965-), Bk.Rev.Mo., CCR,
CERDIC, Child.Bk.Rev.Ind. (1965-), Curr.Cont.,
G.Soc.Sci.& Rel.Per.Lit., Hum.Ind., Mid.East: Abstr.&
Ind., New Test.Abstr., Old Test.Abstr., Rel.&
Theol.Abstr. (1968-), Rel.Ind.One.
　—BLDSC shelfmark: 8814.545000.

THEORIE UND PRAXIS DER SOZIALPAEDAGOGIK. see
CHILDREN AND YOUTH — About

THEOSOFIA; brotherhood, problems of society, religion
and occult research. see *PHILOSOPHY*

THEOSOPHICAL JOURNAL. see *PHILOSOPHY*

200　　　　　　　　GW　ISSN 0177-8005
THEOSOPHIE HEUTE. 1954. 3/yr. DM.15($10)
Theosophische Gesellschaft in Deutschland, c/o
Hans Beetz, Argentinische Allee 159, 1000 Berlin
37, Germany. TEL 030-8131680. Ed. Herbert
Sandkuehler. circ. 1,200. (back issues avail.)

THEOSOPHIST. see *PHILOSOPHY*

200　　　　　　　　AT　ISSN 0049-3694
THEOSOPHY IN AUSTRALIA. 1895. q. (plus secial
issue). Aus.$10. Theosophical Society in Australia,
484 Kent St., Sydney, N.S.W. 2000, Australia.
TEL 02-264-7056. Ed. A. Miechel. bk.rev.; index
every 2 yrs.; circ. 1,450.
　Description: Publishes articles concerned with
comparative religion, philosophy and science, social
and environmental issues, poetic and inspirational
thought, written mainly by members.

131.35　　　　　　US　ISSN 0040-6074
THETA (NEW YORK); Greek: thought, life, the spirit. m.
membership. Church of Scientology of New York,
227 W. 46th St., New York, NY 10036.
TEL 212-921-1210. Ed. Tom Wells. adv.; charts;
illus.
　Description: Brochure of informational products
from the Church of Scientology.

283　　　　　　　　UK　ISSN 0143-8514
THINKING MISSION. 1972. q. £4. United Society for the
Propagation of the Gospel, Partnership House, 157
Waterloo Rd., London SE1 8XA, England.
TEL 071-928-8681. FAX 071-928-2371.
　Description: Theological reflections on mission.

200　　　　　　　　US
THREE MINUTES A DAY; reflections for each day of the
year. 1949. a. $5. Christophers, Inc., 12 E. 48th
St., New York, NY 10017. TEL 212-759-4050. Ed.
Stephanie Raha.

200　　　　　　　　UK　ISSN 0260-4892
THRESHING FLOOR; a paper for religious renewal.
1980. 6/yr. £12 (foreign £14). (Christian
Community in Great Britain) Floris Books, 15
Harrison Gardens, Edinburgh EH11 1SH, Scotland.
TEL 031-337-2372. FAX 031-346-7516. Ed. Jon
Madsen. adv.; bk.rev.; circ. 1,300.
　Formerly: Christian Community.

200　　　　　　　　IT　ISSN 0040-6686
TI SALUTO, FRATELLO!. 1946. m. free. Segretariato
Diocesano Malati, Via Longhin, 7, Casa Toniolo,
31100 Treviso (Veneto), Italy. TEL 0422-411069.
Ed. Sac. Giovanni Bordin. circ. 7,500. (processed)
　Description: Features letters of thanks from
devoted christians who have prayed for someone
with an illness. Includes articles on religious
community activities.

248.83　　　　　　SA
TIENERKOMPAS. 1951. q. R.5 (effective Jan. 1991).
Afrikaanse Christen-Studentevereniging van
Suid-Afrika, P.O. Box 25, Stellenbosch, South Africa.
Ed. P.J.L. Brink. adv.; bk.rev.; circ. 30,000.
　Former titles (until 1987): Tagtig; (until 1980):
Ons Bou (ISSN 0030-2643)

TIERRA NUEVA. see *SOCIOLOGY*

RELIGIONS AND THEOLOGY   4207

808.81   US
TIME OF SINGING; a magazine of Christian poetry. 1958. 3/yr. $9 (Canada $10.50; elsewhere $16). High Street Community Church, Box 248, Conneaut Lake, PA 16316. TEL 814-382-5911. (Subscr. to: Box 211, Cambridge Springs, PA 16403) Ed. Charles A. Waugaman. circ. 300.

200   US   ISSN 0740-9680
TIMES OF RESTORATION. 1943. bi-m. donation. Kingdom Press, Amherst, NH 03031-1505. TEL 603-673-3208. (Subscr. to: Kingdom Press, 105 Chestnut Hill Rd., Amherst NH 03031) Ed. Timothy F. Murray. bk.rev.; circ. 500.
   Former titles (until 1984): Restoration Tidings; (until 1983): Standard (ISSN 0038-9404)
   Description: Articles encouraging Christian belief and practice.

266   KE
TODAY IN AFRICA. (Text in English) 1967. bi-m. EAs.56($15) (Africa Inland Church) Kesho Publications, PO Box 60, Kijabe, Kenya. Ed. Sheldon Arensen. adv.; bk.rev.; circ. 14,000. **Indexed:** CERDIC.
   Formerly: Today (ISSN 0040-8387)
   Description: Christian magazine geared to high school youth.

200 305.412   US   ISSN 0163-1799
BV4527
TODAY'S CHRISTIAN WOMAN. 1978. bi-m. $14.95. Christianity Today, Inc., 465 Gunderson Dr., Carol Stream, IL 60188. TEL 708-260-6200. Ed. Julie Talerico. adv.; circ. 145,000. **Indexed:** CCR.

250   US   ISSN 0040-8549
TODAY'S PARISH. 1969. 7/yr. $20. Twenty-Third Publications, Box 180, Mystic, CT 06355. TEL 203-536-2611. FAX 203-572-0788. Ed. Dann Connors. adv.; bk.rev.; abstr.; illus.; circ. 22,000. **Indexed:** Cath.Ind., CERDIC.
   Description: Practical assistance in parish affairs for clergy, staff and lay workers in liturgy, music, education, computers, finance, administration and ministry.

TODAY'S SINGLE; serving the singles of America. see *SINGLES' INTERESTS AND LIFESTYLES*

266   UK   ISSN 0040-8824
TOILERS OF THE DEEP. 1886. 2/yr. £10 (effective Dec. 1991). Royal National Mission to Deep Sea Fishermen, 43 Nottingham Place, London W1M 4BX, England. TEL 071-487-5101. FAX 071-224-5240. Ed. David Saltiel. charts; illus.; circ. 40,000.

200   CN   ISSN 0826-9831
TORONTO JOURNAL OF THEOLOGY. 2/yr. Can.$25. Unviersity of Toronto Press, Journals Department, P.O. Box 1280, 1011 Sheppard Ave. W., Downsview, Ont. M3H 5V4, Canada. bk.rev. **Indexed:** Rel.& Theol.Abstr. (1988-).
   —BLDSC shelfmark: 8868.760000.

200   US   ISSN 8756-7385
TORONTO STUDIES IN RELIGION. 1987. irreg. Peter Lang Publishing, Inc., 62 W. 45th St., 4th Fl., New York, NY 10036. TEL 212-302-6740. Ed. Donald Wiebe.
   —BLDSC shelfmark: 8868.785000.
   Description: Contributes to the scholarly and academic understanding of religion.

200   US
TORONTO STUDIES IN THEOLOGY. 1978. irreg., latest vol.62. $39.95 per no. Edwin Mellen Press, 240 Portage Rd., Box 450, Lewiston, NY 14092. TEL 716-754-8566. FAX 716-754-4335.

200   IT   ISSN 0040-960X
TORRE DAVIDICA. 1957. s-a. free. Chiesa Universale Giuris-Davidica, Via Tevere 21-5, 00198 Rome, Italy. TEL (06) 845.38.40. Ed. Elvira Giro. illus.; circ. 2,000.

TOTALLY GOSPEL. see *MUSIC*

200   BE
TRADUCTIONS HEBRAIQUES DES EVANGILES. 1982. irreg., vol.5, 1985. N.V. Brepols I.G.P., Steenweg op Tielen 68, 2300 Turnhout, Belgium. TEL 014-41-54-63. FAX 014-42-89-19. TELEX 34 182.

200   UK   ISSN 0265-3788
TRANSFORMATION. 1984. q. £11.80($37.20) Paternoster Press Ltd., Paternoster House, 3 Mount Radford Crescent, Exeter EX2 4JW, England. TEL 0392-50631. Ed.Bd. circ. 1,800. (tabloid format; back issues avail.; reprint service avail. from KTO) **Indexed:** Rel.& Theol.Abstr. (1984-).
   —BLDSC shelfmark: 9020.593000.
   Description: Provides a forum for discussion on economics, development, violence, family life and other ethical issues, with a focus on Christian social ethics.

TRANSFORMATION TIMES; New Age journal. see *NEW AGE PUBLICATIONS*

200   UK
TREASURY. 1976. 12/yr. £9.36. Calvinistic Methodist Book Agency, St. David's Road, Caernarfon, Gwynedd LL55 1ER, Wales. TEL 0286-2018. FAX 0286-77823. adv.; bk.rev.
   Description: News from various churches.

200   GW
TRIERER FORUM. 1968. q. DM.10. Bischoefliches Generalvikariat Trier, Postfach 1340, 5500 Trier 1, Germany. TEL 0651-7105-469. FAX 0651-7105511. circ. 4,800. (back issues avail.)

230   GW   ISSN 0041-2945
BR4
TRIERER THEOLOGISCHE ZEITSCHRIFT. 1947. q. DM.64.80. (Theologische Fakultaet Trier) Paulinus-Verlag, Fleischstr. 62-65, 5500 Trier, Germany. TEL 0651-4604162. (Co-sponsor: Katholisch-Theologischer Fachbereich der Universitaet Mainz) bk.rev.; index. **Indexed:** Canon Law Abstr., New Test.Abstr., Old Test.Abstr.
   —BLDSC shelfmark: 9050.610300.

220   UK   ISSN 0049-4712
TRINITARIAN BIBLE SOCIETY. QUARTERLY RECORD. 1859. q. £5($10) Trinitarian Bible Society, 217 Kingston Rd., London SW19 3NN, England. FAX 081-543-6370. bk.rev.
   Incorporates: Trinitarian Bible Society. Annual Report.
   Description: Reports on Scripture publication and distribution; includes articles on Bible translation and textual questions.

280   US   ISSN 0360-3032
BR1
TRINITY JOURNAL. 1971-1978; N.S. 1980. s-a. $9 to individuals; students $8; foreign $10.50. Trinity Evangelical Divinity School, 2065 Half Day Rd., Deerfield, IL 60015. TEL 708-945-8800. FAX 708-945-8800. Ed. Douglas Moo. bk.rev.; circ. 1,000. **Indexed:** Bk.Rev.Ind., Bk.Rev.Mo., Bull.Signal., Chr.Per.Ind., Curr.Bk.Rev.Cit., G.Soc.Sci.& Rel.Per.Lit., Int.Z.Bibelwiss, New Test.Abstr., Old Test.Abstr., Rel.& Theol.Abstr. (1980-), Rel.Ind.One.
   —BLDSC shelfmark: 9050.662400.
   Formerly: Trinity Studies (ISSN 0360-2915)

266   SW   ISSN 0041-3178
TRONS SEGRAR. 1890. w. SEK 230. Helgelsefoerbundet, P.O. Box 67, 692 22 Kumla, Sweden. FAX 019-81450. Ed. Haaken Wistrand. adv.; bk.rev.; illus.; circ. 5,000.

200   AT   ISSN 0813-796X
TROWEL AND SWORD. 1954. m. Aus.$22($25) Reformed Churches Publishing House, 55 Maud Street, Geelong 3220, Australia. (Subscr. to: Trowel and Sword, POB 47, Geelong 3220, Australia) Ed. H. De Waard. adv.; bk.rev.; illus.; circ. 2,500.

200   GW
TUDUV-STUDIE. REIHE RELIGIONSWISSENSCHAFTEN. 1975. irreg. price varies. Tuduv Verlagsgesellschaft mbH, Gabelsbergerstr. 15, 8000 Munich 2, Germany.

207   UK   ISSN 0082-7118
TYNDALE BULLETIN. 1956. 2/yr. £5.95. Tyndale House, 36 Selwyn Gardens, Cambridge CB3 9BA, England. FAX 0223-464230. Ed. B.W. Winter. bk.rev.; circ. 1,100. (back issues avail.) **Indexed:** New Test.Abstr., Old Test.Abstr., Rel.& Theol.Abstr. (1968-), Rel.Ind.One.

UEBERBLICK; Zeitschrift fuer oekumenische Begegnung und internationale Zusammenarbeit. see *POLITICAL SCIENCE — International Relations*

200   HU
UJ EMBER. 1945. w. $97. Kossuth Lajos u. 1, 1053 Budapest, Hungary. TEL 117-3933. FAX 117-3471. Ed. Laszlo Lukacs. circ. 100,000.

ULTIMATE REALITY AND MEANING; interdisciplinary studies in the philosophy of understanding. see *PHILOSOPHY*

266   SA   ISSN 0041-6274
UMAFRIKA; the Zulu weekly. (Text in Zulu) 1911. w. R.60. Mariannhill Mission Institute, The Monastery, Mariannhill 3601, South Africa. TEL 031-7002720. FAX 031-7003707. (Editorial addr.: P.O. Box 11002, Mariannhill 3601, South Africa) Ed. Cyril Madlada. adv.; bk.rev.; charts; illus.; circ. 80,000. (also avail. in microfilm from PSL)
   Description: Aims to offer a Christian-based perspective on contemporary society. Functions as an instrument of communication leading to reconciliation mainly among the Zulu-speaking population of South Africa.

200   GW   ISSN 0041-6444
UNAUSFORSCHLICHER REICHTUM; Zweimonatsschrift fuer Gott und sein Wort. 1932. bi-m. DM.15($8) (Freunde Konkordanter Wortvekuendigung e.V. Pforzheim) Konkordanter-Verlag, Buechenbronner Str. 16, 7530 Pforzheim, Germany. TEL 07231-43720. Eds. Herman H. Rocke, Heinz Hoffmann. adv.; bk.rev.; index, cum.index: 1932-1967; circ. 2,000.

200   FR   ISSN 0396-2393
UNION DES SUPERIEURES MAJEURS DE FRANCE. ANNUAIRE. 1975. a. Union des Superieures Majeures des Instituts Religieux de France, 10 rue Jean-Bart, 75006 Paris, France.

207.11 371.8   US   ISSN 0041-7025
UNION SEMINARY QUARTERLY REVIEW. 1939. 4/yr. $21 to individuals; institutions $35. Union Theological Seminary, 3041 Broadway, New York, NY 10027. TEL 212-280-1361. FAX 212-280-1416. Ed.Bd. adv.; bk.rev.; bibl.; index; circ. 1,500. (also avail. in microfilm from UMI) **Indexed:** CERDIC, New Test.Abstr., Old Test.Abstr., Rel.& Theol.Abstr. (1969-), Rel.Ind.One, Rel.Per.
   —BLDSC shelfmark: 9090.773000.

200   AT
UNITARIAN PIONEER. 1950. bi-m. Aus.$4. Sydney Unitarian Church, 15 Francis St., E. Sydney, N.S.W. 2010, Australia. TEL 02-360-2038. Ed. Geoffrey R. Usher. circ. 270. (back issues avail.)

200   AT
UNITARIAN QUEST.* 1961. s-a. Aus.$6. Australian and New Zealand Unitarian Association, c/o Rev. Eric Heller-Wagner, Unitarian Meeting House, 99 Osmond Ter., Norwood, S.A. 5067, Australia. Ed. Geoffrey R. Usher. bk.rev.; circ. 200. (back issues avail)

200   GW   ISSN 0932-0180
UNITARISCHE BLAETTER. 1950. bi-m. DM.65 (foreign DM.67.50). (Religionsgemeinschaft Deutsche Unitarier e.V.) Verlag Deutsche Unitarier, Tettnangerstr. 385, 7980 Ravensburg 19, Germany. TEL 0751-62596. FAX 0751-67201. Ed. Gunde Hartmann. adv.; bk.rev.; illus.; index; circ. 2,000.
   Formerly: Glaube und Tat (ISSN 0017-1123)

268   FR
UNITE DES CHRETIENS; revue de formation et d'information oecumenique. 1971. q. 100 F. (foreign 115 F.). Secretariat National pour l'Unite des Chretiens, 80 rue de l'Abbe Carton, 75014 Paris, France. TEL 1-45-42-00-39. FAX 1-45-42-03-07. Ed. Damien Sicard. (back issues avail.) **Indexed:** CERDIC.

220   UK   ISSN 0041-719X
BV2370
UNITED BIBLE SOCIETIES. BULLETIN. 1950. irreg. (1-2/yr.). $3 per no. United Bible Societies (Reading), Reading Bridge House, Reading RG1 8PJ, England. circ. 4,700. (reprint service avail. from UMI)

RELIGIONS AND THEOLOGY

200 US ISSN 0270-9287
BX8201
UNITED METHODIST BOARD OF HIGHER EDUCATION AND MINISTRY. QUARTERLY REVIEW; a scholarly journal for reflection on ministry. 1932. q. $16. (United Methodist Board of Higher Education and Ministry) United Methodist Publishing House, 201 Eighth Ave. S., Box 801, Nashville, TN 37202. TEL 615-749-6731. Ed. Sharon Hels. adv.; bk.rev.; index. Indexed: CERDIC, G.Soc.Sci.& Rel.Per.Lit., Hum.Ind., Old Test.Abstr., Rel.& Theol.Abstr., Rel.Ind.One, Rel.Per.
—BLDSC shelfmark: 7203.503100.
Supersedes (in 1980): Religion in Life (ISSN 0034-3986)

266 UK
UNITED SOCIETY FOR THE PROPAGATION OF THE GOSPEL. YEARBOOK. 1704. a. United Society for the Propagation of the Gospel, Partnership House, 157 Waterloo Rd., London SE1 8XA, England. TEL 071-928-8681. FAX 071-928-2371.
Formerly: United Society for the Propagation of the Gospel. Annual Report - Review (ISSN 0144-9508)

200 GW
UNIVERSALE RELIGION. 1985. m. DM.47. (Centre of the World Religions e.V.) Sandila Import-Export Handels GmbH, Saegestr. 37, 7881 Herrischried, Germany. TEL 07764-334. adv.; bk.rev.; circ. 5,000. (back issues avail.)
Description: Comparative study of religions.

200 SP ISSN 0078-8759
UNIVERSIDAD DE NAVARRA. FACULTAD DE DERECHO CANONICO. MANUALES: DERECHO CANONICO. 1973. irreg., no.7, 1988. price varies. Ediciones Universidad de Navarra, S.A., Apdo. 396, 31080 Pamplona, Spain. TEL 94 825 6850.

200 CK
UNIVERSIDAD JAVERIANA. FACULTAD DE TEOLOGIA. COLECCION PROFESORES. irreg. price varies. Pontificia Universidad Javeriana, Facultad de Teologia, Apdo. Aereo 54-953, Bogota, D.E. 2, Colombia.

200 100 SP
UNIVERSIDAD PONTIFICIA COMILLAS DE MADRID. PUBLICACIONES. SERIE 1: ESTUDIOS. Theology section (ISSN 0211-2752); Philosophy section (ISSN 0211-2779); Canon section (ISSN 0211-2760) 1975. irreg., no.32, 1984. Universidad Pontificia Comillas de Madrid, Comision de Publicaciones, E-28049 Madrid, Spain. Ed. Antonio Vargas-Machuca.

230 AU ISSN 0579-7780
UNIVERSITAET INNSBRUCK. THEOLOGISCHE FAKULTAET. STUDIEN UND ARBEITEN. (Subseries of: Universitaet Innsbruck. Veroeffentlichungen) 1968. irreg., vol.10, 1974. price varies. Oesterreichische Kommissionsbuchhandlung, Maximilianstrasse 17, A-6020 Innsbruck, Austria. Ed. Hans Bernhard Meyer.

UNIVERSITE SAINT-JOSEPH. FACULTE DES LETTRES ET DES SCIENCES HUMAINES. RECHERCHES. SERIE B: ORIENT CHRETIEN. see ORIENTAL STUDIES

UNIVERSITY OF DAYTON REVIEW. see LITERARY AND POLITICAL REVIEWS

200 100 US
UNIVERSITY OF NOTRE DAME. STUDIES IN THE PHILOSOPHY OF RELIGION. 1979. irreg., no.6, 1989. University of Notre Dame Press, Notre Dame, IN 46556. TEL 219-239-6346. Ed. Frederick Crosson.

UNIVERSITY OF ST. THOMAS MAGAZINE. see COLLEGE AND ALUMNI

220 US ISSN 0042-0476
UNSEARCHABLE RICHES. 1909. bi-m. $1. Concordant Publishing Concern, 15570 Knochaven Rd., Santa Clarita, CA 91350. TEL 805-252-2112. Ed. Dean H. Hough. index, cum.index every 10 yrs; circ. 2,000.
Description: Directed to students of the scriptures.

200 GW ISSN 0930-1313
UNTERWEGS (MUNICH). 1983. q. Deutscher Katecheten Verein e.V., Preysingstr. 83c, 8000 Munich 80, Germany. TEL 089-48092242. FAX 089-48092237. bk.rev.; circ. 11,000.

790 US
UP WITH PEOPLE NEWS. 1971. q. free. Up with People, Inc., 3103 N. Campbell Ave., Tucson, AZ 85719. TEL 602-327-7351. Ed. Bruce L. Erley. illus.; circ. 100,000 (controlled).

200 RW
URUNANA. 1967. 3/yr. Grand Seminaire de Nyakibanda, B.P. 85, Butare, Rwanda. Ed. Emmanuel Uwimana.

UTOPIA 2; commune co-operation as a global dynamic. see NEW AGE PUBLICATIONS

266 284 NE ISSN 0042-1650
UW KONINKRIJK KOME: ZENDINGSBLAD. Cover title: Zendingsblad. 1906. 6/yr. fl.10. Christelijke Gereformeerde Kerken in Nederland - Mission of the Christian Reformed Churches in the Netherlands, Zendingshuis, Simon Stevinweg 144, 1222 SV Hilversum, Netherlands. TEL 035-859555. FAX 035-836641. Ed.Bd. adv.; bk.rev.; illus.; stat.; circ. 28,000.
Description: Publication of the Christian Reformed Church covering missionary activities in Third world countries.

V.C.F. NEWSLETTER. (Veterinary Christian Fellowship) see VETERINARY SCIENCE

V R B - INFORMATIE. (Vereniging van Religieus - Wetenschappelijke Bibliothecarissen) see LIBRARY AND INFORMATION SCIENCES

200 SW ISSN 0042-2010
VAAR FANA. 1905. s-m. SEK 90. Svenska Fraelsningsarmen, Kungsgatan 17, S-502 31 Boraas, Sweden. illus.

200 MG
VAOVAO F J K M. 10/yr.(Malagasy ed.); 5/yr.(French-English ed.). B.P. 623, 101 Antananarivo, Malagasy Republic. TEL 30253. Ed. Edmond Razafimahefa.

200 NE ISSN 0042-3262
VELUWS KERKBLAD. 1942. w. fl.48. Gereformeerde Kerken in Classis Harderwijk en Nijkerk, Redactie Raad, Hazeveld 21, 3862 XA Nijkerk, Netherlands. FAX 03420-13141. Ed. E.P. van der Veen. adv.; bk.rev.; circ. 6,500.

VENTURE INWARD. see NEW AGE PUBLICATIONS

200 930 IT ISSN 0391-8564
VERBA SENIORUM; collana di testi e studi patristici. irreg., latest no.10. price varies. Edizioni Studium, Via Cassiodoro 14, 00193 Rome, Italy.

266 DK ISSN 0109-0062
VERDEN RUNDT. 1982. bi-m. DKK 65. Laegmandsbevaegelsen for Ydre Mission, LYM-Landsformanden, Saxovej 11, 5210 Odense NV, Denmark. Ed. Simon Thorup. bk.rev.; illus.
Formerly: Maend og Mission.

266 GW ISSN 0342-2410
BR4
VERKUENDIGUNG UND FORSCHUNG. Supplement to: Evangelische Theologie. 2/yr. DM.35. Christian Kaiser Verlag, Lilienstr. 70, 8000 Munich 80, Germany. TEL 089-483014. FAX 089-4484473. (reprint service avail. from UMI) Indexed: CERDIC, New Test.Abstr.

200 CN ISSN 0042-434X
VERS DEMAIN. 1939. 7/yr. Can.$10($14) for 2 yrs. Institut d'Action Politique Pelerins de Saint Michel, Rougemont (Rouville), Que. JOL 1M0, Canada. TEL 514-469-2209. (U.S. addr: Pilgrims of Saint Michael, Box 38, Richford, VT 05476-0038) Ed. Gilberte Cote-Mercier. charts; illus.; circ. 35,000.
Description: Promotes the application of the teachings of the Roman Catholic Church in every aspect of social life, especially in economics with the social credit philosophy of Scottish engineer, Clifford Hugh Douglas.

220 SZ
VESTIGIA BIBLIAE. 1979. a. $152.80. (Deutsche Bibelarchiv) Verlag Peter Lang AG, Jupiterstr. 15, Postfach 277, CH-3000 Bern 15, Switzerland. TEL 031-9411122. FAX 031-9411131. adv.; bk.rev.

VETERA CHRISTIANORUM. see ARCHAEOLOGY

220 NE ISSN 0042-4935
BS410
VETUS TESTAMENTUM. (Text in English, French or German) 1951. 4/yr. fl.170($97.14) (effective 1992). (International Organization for the Study of the Old Testament) E.J. Brill, P.O. Box 9000, 2300 PA Leiden, Netherlands. TEL 071-312624. FAX 071-317532. TELEX 39296 BRILL NL. (In N. America: E.J. Brill, 24 Hudson St., Kinderhook, NY 12106. TEL 800-962-4406) Ed. J.A. Emerton. bk.rev.; bibl. (also avail. in microform from SWZ; reprint service avail. from SWZ) Indexed: Arts & Hum.Cit.Ind., Curr.Cont., New Test.Abstr., Old Test.Abstr., Rel.& Theol.Abstr. (1990-), Rel.Ind.One, Rel.Per.
—BLDSC shelfmark: 9231.470000.

221 NE ISSN 0083-5889
VETUS TESTAMENTUM. SUPPLEMENTS. 1953. irreg., vol.44, 1991. price varies. (International Organization for the Study of the Old Testament) E.J. Brill, P.O. Box 9000, 2300 PA Leiden, Netherlands. TEL 071-312624. FAX 071-317532. TELEX 39296 BRILL NL. (In N. America: E.J. Brill, 24 Hudson St., Kinderhook, NY 12106. TEL 800-962-4406)
—BLDSC shelfmark: 9231.475000.

200 BL ISSN 0507-7184
VIDA PASTORAL. 1960. bi-m. free. (Pia Sociedade de Sao Paulo) Edicoes Paulinas, R. Dr. Pinto Ferraz, 183, 04117 Sao Paulo, SP, Brazil. Ed. Angelo Songego. adv.; bk.rev.; bibl.; illus.; circ. 25,000.
Former titles: Pastoral Popular; Vida Pastoral (ISSN 0042-5265)

230 BE ISSN 0771-6842
VIE CONSACREE. 1925. bi-m. 490 Fr. Centre de Documentation et de Recherche Religieuses, Rue de Bruxelles 61, B-5000 Namur, Belgium. (Dist. by: Brepols Publishers, Baron du Fourstraat 8, B-2300 Turnhout, Belgium) bk.rev.; bibl.; index; circ. 6,000. Indexed: Canon Law Abstr., CERDIC.
—BLDSC shelfmark: 9234.950000.
Formerly (until 1965): Revue des Communautes Religieuses.

VIEWS ON EDUCATION - NEWS OF EPISCOPAL COLLEGES. see EDUCATION — Higher Education

209 NE ISSN 0042-6032
BR66
VIGILIAE CHRISTIANAE; a review of early Christian life and language. (Supplement avail.) (Text in various languages) 1947. 4/yr. fl.170($97.14) (effective 1992). E.J. Brill, P.O. Box 9000, 2300 PA Leiden, Netherlands. TEL 071-312624. FAX 071-317532. TELEX 39296 BRILL NL. (In N. America: E.J. Brill, 24 Hudson St., Kinderhook, NY 12106. TEL 800-962-4406) Ed. J. den Boeft. adv.; bk.rev.; index. (also avail. in microform from RPI,SWZ; reprint service avail. from SWZ) Indexed: Arts & Hum.Cit.Ind., Curr.Cont., M.L.A., New Test.Abstr., Rel.& Theol.Abstr. (1968-), Rel.Ind.One, Rel.Per.
—BLDSC shelfmark: 9236.080000.

209 NE ISSN 0920-623X
VIGILIAE CHRISTIANAE. SUPPLEMENT. (Text in English, French, German) 1987. irreg., vol.14, 1991. price varies. E.J. Brill, P.O. Box 9000, 2300 PA Leiden, Netherlands. TEL 071-312624. FAX 071-317532. TELEX 39296 BRILL NL. (In N. America: E.J. Brill, 24 Hudson St., Kinderhook, NY 12106. TEL 800-962-4406)
—BLDSC shelfmark: 9236.081000.

VIRTUE. see WOMEN'S INTERESTS

200 NE ISSN 0169-5606
BL1
VISIBLE RELIGION; annual for religious iconography. (Text in English, French and German) 1982. irreg., vol.7, 1990. price varies. (Rijksuniversiteit te Groningen, Institute for Religious Iconography) E.J. Brill, P.O. Box 9000, 2300 PA Leiden, Netherlands. TEL 071-312624. FAX 071-317532. TELEX 39296 BRILL NL. (In N. America: E.J. Brill, 24 Hudson St., Kinderhook, NY 12106. TEL 800-962-4406) Ed. H.G. Kippenberg. circ. 200.
—BLDSC shelfmark: 9240.895500.

RELIGIONS AND THEOLOGY 4209

200 US
VISION (COSTA MESA). q. free. Full Gospel Business Men's Fellowship International, 3150 Bear St., Box 5050, Costa Mesa, CA 92626.
TEL 714-557-9961. FAX 714-557-9961.
Description: Covers the work of the fellowship around the world.

240 IT ISSN 0042-7330
VITA CONSACRATA; rivista mensile di studio e informazione per Istituti Religiosi e Secolari. 1964. m. L.35000 (foreign L.70000). Editrice Ancora Milano, Via G.B. Niccolini 8, 20154 Milan, Italy. TEL 02-33608941. FAX 02-33608944. Dir. Severino Medici. adv.; bk.rev.; bibl.; index; circ. 1,200. **Indexed:** Canon Law Abstr.
—BLDSC shelfmark: 9241.583000.
Formerly: Vita Religiosa.

200 CN ISSN 0507-1690
VITA EVANGELICA. French edition (ISSN 0315-5048) (Text in English) 1965. irreg., no.12, 1984. price varies. Canadian Religious Conference, 324 Laurier Ave. E., Ottawa, Ont. K1N 6P6, Canada. TEL 613-236-0824. FAX 613-236-0825. circ. 6,000 (3,500 English ed.; 3,500 French ed.).

200 IT ISSN 0042-7284
LA VITA IN CRISTO E NELLA CHIESA; mensile per l'animazione liturgica. 1951. m. L.24000 (foreign L.28000)(effective Jan. 1992). Congregazione Suore Pie Discepole del Divin Maestro, Via Portuense 739, 00148 Rome, Italy. TEL 06-6530213. FAX 06-6531973. Dir. G. Oberto. adv.; bk.rev.; illus.; index; circ. 17,000.
—BLDSC shelfmark: 9241.584000.
Description: Religious forum devoted to Christians. Includes articles on the church, prayer and observance of religious holidays in modern day context.

200 IT
VITA PASTORALE. 1912. m. (11/yr.). L.19000. Societa San Paolo Gruppo Periodici s.r.l., Via Liberazione 4, 12051 Alba (Cuneo), Italy. Ed. Stefano Andreatta. adv.; circ. 33,000.

200 CI ISSN 0042-7659
VJESNIK NADBISKUPIJE SPLITSKO-MAKARSKE. (Text in Croatian) 1948. bi-m. Nadbiskupija Splitsko-Makarska, Zrinjsko-Frankopanska 14, 58001 Split, Croatia. Ed. Marijan Ivan Cagij. bk.rev.; circ. 400.
Supersedes: Vjesnik Biskupije Splitske i Makarske.

200 261 IT ISSN 0042-7780
VOCE; settimanale religioso sociale. w. L.10000. 06100 Perugia, Italy.

255 IT ISSN 0042-7888
VOCI FRATERNE. 1917. m. Via G. Amendola 5, 00185 Rome, Italy. Ed. Vacalebre Arcadio. adv.; bk.rev.; film rev.; bibl.; charts; illus.; cum.index.

200 US ISSN 0042-8159
VOICE OF LIBERTY. 1960. s-a. donation. Voice of Liberty Association, 692 Sunnybrook Dr., Decatur, GA 30033. TEL 404-633-3634. Ed. Martha O. Andrews. bk.rev.; charts; illus.; circ. 3,500. (processed) **Indexed:** CERDIC.

200 US
VOICE OF THE MARTYRS. (Editions in several languages) 1967. m. free. Christian Missions to the Communist World, Inc., Box 443, Bartlesville, OK 74005-0443. TEL 918-337-8015. FAX 918-337-9287. Ed. Rev. Richard D. Wurmbrand. bk.rev.; circ. 1,000,000.
Description: News on atrocities against and persecution of Christians and their families in communist countries. Includes language-specific translations of the English newsletter.

266 FR ISSN 0293-9932
VOIX D'AFRIQUE. (Text in French, German) 1923. 5/yr. 30. Peres Blancs Missionnaires d'Afrique, 49 rue de Romainville, 75019 Paris, France.
TEL 42-08-92-46. circ. 9,500.
Description: Tries to give objective information about the country and news of White Fathers missionaries doing work in Africa.

200 GW ISSN 0083-6923
VORREFORMATIONSGESCHICHTLICHE FORSCHUNGEN. 1902. irreg. price varies. Aschendorffsche Verlagsbuchhandlung, Soesterstr. 13, 4400 Muenster, Germany. TEL 0251-690-0.
FAX 0251-690405. Ed. Erwin Iserloh.

200 CN ISSN 0715-8726
VOX BENEDICTINA; a journal of feminine and monastic spirituality. 1984. s-a. Can.$20 to individuals; institutions Can.$30 (typically set in Oct.). Peregrina Publishing Co., 180 Sherwood Ave., Toronto, Ont. M4P 2A8, Canada. FAX 416-482-4488. Ed. Margot H. King. adv.; bk.rev.; circ. 450.
—BLDSC shelfmark: 9258.538500.

200 UK ISSN 0263-6786
VOX EVANGELICA. 1959. a. £5.70($17.40) (London Bible College) Paternoster Press Ltd., Paternoster House, 3 Mount Radford Crescent, Exeter, Devon EX2 4JW, England. (Dist. in U.S & Canada by: The Paternoster Press, P.O. Box 11127, Birmingham, Alabama 35202, U.S.A.) Ed. Antony Billington. circ. 600. (tabloid format; back issues avail.) **Indexed:** CERDIC, Old Test.Abstr., Rel.& Theol.Abstr. (1968-).

200 BN
VRELO ZIVOTA; spirituality journal. (Text in Serbo-Croatian) 1974. q. 1600 din.($2.5) Misijska Centrala, Radojke Lakic 7, PO Box 155, 71001 Sarajevo, Bosnia Hercegovina. TEL 071 36077. Ed. Zvonimir Baotic. bk.rev. (back issues avail.)
Description: Examines spiritual life, morality and experiences of saints.

200 NE ISSN 0042-9155
VRIEND VAN OUD EN JONG; Christelijk weekblad. 1880. fortn. fl.43. Uitgeverij J.J. Groen en Zoon, Pieterskerk Choorsteeg 18, Postbus 11031, Leiden, Netherlands. TEL 071-143443. FAX 071-120493. adv.

266 NQ
WABUL. m? Comite Evangelico por Ayuda al Desarrollo, Centro de Historio y Cultura, Apdo. 3091, Puerto Cabezas, Nicaragua. Ed.Bd. circ. 1,500.

200 US
THE WACO MESSENGER. 1927. w. $12.75. 504 Clifton St., Waco, TX 76704. TEL 817-799-6911. Ed. M.P. Harvey. adv.; circ. 3,000.

200 UK
WAKE-UP! (AYRSHIRE). 1922. bi-m. £10($20) Christian Israel Foundation, 11 Seagate, Irvine, Ayrshire KA12 8RH, Scotland. TEL 0294-75624. Ed. Mathew J. Browning. adv.; bk.rev.; charts; illus.; index; circ. 5,000.
Incorporates: National Message; **Formerly:** Message to the Anglo-Saxon and Celtic Peoples (ISSN 0261-7404); **Formed by the merger of:** British Israel World Federation. National Message (ISSN 0047-8962); Wake Up.
Description: Inter-denominational magazine with emphasis on necessity of close cooperation between the English-speaking and kindred peoples.

WALK AWAY; the newsletter for ex-fundamentalists. see **SOCIOLOGY**

200 100 US
WANDERER. 1867. w. $30. Wanderer Printing Co., 201 Ohio St., St. Paul, MN 55107.
TEL 612-224-5733. FAX 612-224-9666. Ed. A.J. Matt, Jr. adv.; bk.rev.; circ. 34,000. (also avail. in microfilm from UMI)

200 AT
WAR CRY. 1883. w. Aus.$41. Dinsdale Pender, 1-9 Drill St., Hawthorn, Melbourne, Vic. 3122, Australia. FAX 03-819-4864. Ed. William Allott. bk.rev.; illus.; circ. 63,306.

WARRIOR. see **CHILDREN AND YOUTH — For**

200 GW ISSN 0341-7158
WAS UND WIE?; Arbeitshilfen zur religoesen Erzeihen der 3 bis 7 jahrigen. 1972. q. DM.44.20. Guetersloher Verlagshaus Gerd Mohn, Carl-Bertelsmann-Str. 256, Postfach 1343, 4830 Guetersloh 100, Germany. TEL 05241-7405-0. FAX 05241-740548. Ed. Wolfgang Longart. circ. 6,500.

281.7 916.206 UA
WATANI. (Text in French) w. Coptic Orthodox Church, St. Mark's Cathedral, Anba Ruess, 222 Sharia Ramses, P.O. Box 9035, Abbasiya, Cairo, Egypt. TEL 02-2825983. TELEX 23281.

200 US ISSN 0890-6491
WEAVINGS; a journal of the Christian spiritual life. 1986. bi-m. $15. Upper Room, 1908 Grand Ave., Box 189, Nashville, TN 37202-0189.
TEL 615-340-7254. FAX 615-340-7006. Ed. John S. Mogabgab. bk.rev.; circ. 26,600.

268 US
WEEKLY BIBLE READER. 1965. w. $7.95 q. (5 nos./set each q.). Standard Publishing, 8121 Hamilton Ave., Cincinnati, OH 45231. TEL 513-931-4050. Ed. Ruth Frederick. circ. 104,000.

261 GW
WEG UND ZIEL. 1948. m. DM.52. (Johannische Kirche) Verlag Weg und Ziel, Teutonenstr. 14, 1000 Berlin 38, Germany. FAX 030-8034479. Ed.Bd. adv.; bk.rev.; circ. 1,400. (back issues avail.)
Description: Information about the Johannische Church and related regional news.

200 GW ISSN 0043-2040
WEGE ZUM MENSCHEN; Monatsschrift fuer Seelsorge und Beratung, heilendes und soziales Handeln. 1949. 8/yr. DM.96. Vandenhoeck und Ruprecht, Theaterstr. 13, Postfach 3753, 3400 Goettingen, Germany. TEL 0551-6959-22. FAX 0551-695917. adv.; index; circ. 3,100. **Indexed:** CERDIC.
—BLDSC shelfmark: 9286.650000.

200 GW
WEGGEFAEHRTE. 1963. s-a. DM.5. Bund Deutsch - Unitarischer Jugendliche, Hauptstr. 78, 5100 Aachen, Germany. Eds. Robert Roeber, Karsten Urban. circ. 100.

200 028.5 GW
WEITE WELT; illustrierte Kinderzeitschrift ab 10 Jahre. 1921. m. DM.22.20. (Steyler Missionare) Soverdia GmbH, Postfach 24 60, Bahnhofstr. 9, 4054 Nettetal 2, Germany. TEL 02157-1202-0.
FAX 02157-120222. Ed. P. Joachim Gloger.

200 UK
WELSH CHURCHMAN. 1973. m. £4. Church in Wales Publications, Woodland Place, Penarth, South Glam. CF6 2EX, Wales. Ed. Rev. Canon M.M. Davies. adv.; bk.rev.; circ. 30,000.

266 NE ISSN 0165-988X
BV3000
WERELD EN ZENDING; oecumenisch tijdschrift voor missiologie en missionaire praktijk. 1948. q. fl.40. Nederlandse Zendingsraad (Protestant), Prins Hendriklaan 37, 1075 BA Amsterdam, Netherlands. TEL 020-6717654. FAX 020-6755736.
(Co-sponsor: Nederlandse Missieraad (Catholic)) Ed. J. van Slageren. adv.; bk.rev.; index; circ. 2,000. **Indexed:** CERDIC.
—BLDSC shelfmark: 9295.535000.
Former titles (until 1972): Heerbaan (ISSN 0017-9531); Het Messiewerk.

WERELDBRIEF. see **POLITICAL SCIENCE — International Relations**

266 327 BE
WERELDWIJD; tijdschrift over evangelizatie en ontwikkeling. 1970. m. (10/yr.). 700 BEF. V.Z.W. Wereldwijd, Arthur Goemaerelei 69, B-2018 Antwerp, Belgium. Ed. Gie Goris. adv.; circ. 30,000. **Indexed:** CERDIC.

270 NR ISSN 0083-8187
BL2465
WEST AFRICAN RELIGION. 1963. s-a. N3($8) per no. University of Nigeria, Department of Religion, Nsukka, Nigeria. Ed. O.U. Kalu. adv.; bk.rev.; circ. 1,000. **Indexed:** CERDIC, Rel.Ind.One, Rel.Per.

230 GW
WESTFALIA SACRA; Quellen und Forschungen zur Kirchengeschichte Westfalens. 1948. irreg. price varies. Aschendorffsche Verlagsbuchhandlung, Soesterstr. 13, 4400 Muenster, Germany.
TEL 0251-690-0. FAX 0251-690405. Ed. Alois Schroeer.

R

RELIGIONS AND THEOLOGY

230   US   ISSN 0043-4388
BR1
WESTMINSTER THEOLOGICAL JOURNAL. 1938. 2/yr. $20 to individuals; institutions $30. Westminster Theological Seminary, Chestnut Hill, Philadelphia, PA 19118. TEL 215-887-5511. FAX 215-887-5404. Ed. Moises Silva. bk.rev.; index, cum.index; circ. 1,200. (also avail. in microform from UMI) **Indexed:** CERDIC, Chr.Per.Ind., Int.Z.Bibelwiss., New Test.Abstr., Old Test.Abstr., Rel.& Theol.Abstr. (1968-), Rel.Ind.One, Rel.Per.
—BLDSC shelfmark: 9304.800000.
Description: Scholarly articles on many theological issues, with emphasis on biblical studies and Reformed theology.

266   US   ISSN 0889-0781
WHEREVER. 1976. 3/yr. $3 (free to qualified personnel). Evangelical Alliance Mission (TEAM), Box 969, Wheaton, IL 60189. TEL 708-653-5300. FAX 708-653-1826. Ed. Jack Kilgore. bk.rev.; charts; illus.; circ. 14,000.

WHO'S WHO IN RELIGION. see *BIOGRAPHY*

222   GW   ISSN 0512-1604
WISSENSCHAFTLICHE UNTERSUCHUNGEN ZUM NEUEN TESTAMENT. (Text in English and German) 1950. irreg. price varies. Verlag J.C.B. Mohr (Paul Siebeck), Wilhelmstr. 18, Postfach 2040, 7400 Tuebingen, Germany. TEL 07071-26064. FAX 07071-51104. TELEX 7262872-MOHR-D. Eds. Martin Hengel, Otfried Hofius.

200   UK   ISSN 0962-2152
WOMAN ALIVE. 1982. m. £23 per no.(foreign £23). Herald House Ltd., 96 Dominion Rd., Worthing, Sussex BN14 8JP, England. TEL 0903-821082. FAX 0903-821081. Ed. Catherine Butcher. circ. 17,000.
Formerly: Christian Woman (ISSN 0269-0616)

200 301.4   SZ
WOMEN IN A CHANGING WORLD. (Text in English) 1974. s-a. World Council of Churches, Women in Church and Society, 150 Route de Ferney, Box 2100, CH-1211 Geneva 2, Switzerland. TEL 022-791-6111. FAX 022-791-0361. TELEX 415730-OIK-CH.

WOMEN'S CONCERNS REPORT. see *WOMEN'S INTERESTS*

200   NE
WOORD EN DIENST. fortn. fl.51.50. Boekencentrum B.V., Box 84176, The Hague, Netherlands. Ed. W.R. van der Zee. adv.; bk.rev.; illus.

WORD AND DEED. see *MEDICAL SCIENCES — Communicable Diseases*

200   UK
WORD IN ACTION. 1973. 3/yr. free. British and Foreign Bible Society, Stonehill Green, Westlea, Swindon SN5 7DG, England. TEL 0793-513713. FAX 0793-512539. TELEX 44283. Ed. Joy Aldred. charts; illus.; circ. 180,000. (tabloid format)
Formerly: Bible Society News (ISSN 0006-0755)

200   US
WORD IN SEASON. q. $4.60. Augsburg Fortress, 426 S. 5th St., Box 1209, Minneapolis, MN 55440. TEL 612-330-3300. Ed. Constance Lovaas Beck. circ. 143,000.

200   AT   ISSN 0813-7951
WORD OF SALVATION. 1955. m. Aus.$75($75) Reformed Churches Publishing House, 55 Maud St., Geelong 3220, Australia. FAX 52-221263. (Subscr. to: P.O. Box 47, Geelong 3220, Australia) Ed. W. Weirsma. circ. 100.

200   US
WORD ONE. 1973. 5/yr. free. Claretian Publications, 205 W. Monroe St., Chicago, IL 60606. TEL 312-236-7782. FAX 312-236-7230. Ed. Rev. Mark J. Brummel.

200   US
WORDS OF L I F E. 1984. irreg. membership. Living in Freedom Eternally, Inc., Box 353, New York, NY 10185. TEL 212-967-4828. circ. 1,800.
Description: Focuses on homosexuality in the context of Christianity.

200   AT
WORKING TOGETHER NATIONALLY. 1977. a. free. Uniting Church in Australia, National Assembly, 222 Pitt St., 5th Fl., Sydney N.S.W. 2000, Australia. TEL 02-287-0900. FAX 02-287-0999. (Subscr. to: P.O. Box E266, St. James, N.S.W. 2000, Australia) Ed. Rev. Gregor Henderson. circ. 5,500.
Description: Life and work of the Uniting Church in Australia, nationally.

200   US   ISSN 0743-2399
BV1430.I6
WORLD CHRISTIAN. 1980. 10/yr. $15. 21550 Oxnard St., Ste. 860, Woodland Hills, CA 91367. TEL 818-797-1907. FAX 818-797-1706. Ed. Verne Becker. adv.; bk.rev.; illus.; index; circ. 22,000. (also avail. in microfilm from UMI; reprint service avail. from UMI) **Indexed:** A.I.P.P., CERDIC, Chr.Per.Ind., G.Soc.Sci.& Rel.Per.Lit.
Incorporates (1941-1989): U: For University and College Students (ISSN 0893-0201); Which was formerly titled (until Dec. 1986): His Magazine; (until Oct. 1985): His (ISSN 0018-2095)

200   SZ   ISSN 0084-1676
WORLD COUNCIL OF CHURCHES. GENERAL ASSEMBLY. ASSEMBLY - REPORTS. (Text in English) 1948. irreg., 7th, 1991. price varies. World Council of Churches, Publications Office, 150 Route de Ferney, Box 2100, CH-1211 Geneva 2. TEL 022-791-6111. FAX 022-791-0361. TELEX 415730-OIK-CH. (Dist. in U.S. by: World Council of Churches Distribution Center, Rt. 111 & Sharadin Rd., Box 346, Kutztown, PA 19530-0346)

200   SZ   ISSN 0084-1684
WORLD COUNCIL OF CHURCHES. MINUTES AND REPORTS OF THE CENTRAL COMMITTEE MEETING. (Text in English) 1948. irreg. (approx. a.), 42nd, 1991. price varies. World Council of Churches, Publications Office, 150 Route de Ferney, Box 2100, CH-1211 Geneva 2, Switzerland. TEL 022-791-6111. FAX 022-791-0361. TELEX 415730-OIK-CH. (Dist. in U.S. by: World Council of Churches, Distribution Center, Rt. 222 & Sharadin Rd., Box 346, Kutztown, PA 19530-0346)

268   SZ
WORLD COUNCIL OF CHURCHES. OFFICE OF EDUCATION. EDUCATION NEWSLETTER. (Text in English) 1972. 3/yr. donations. World Council of Churches, Office of Education, 150 Route de Ferney, Box 2100, Switzerland. TEL 022-791-6111. FAX 022-791-0361. TELEX 415730-OIK-CH. (Dist. in US by: World Council of Churches, Distribution Center, Rt. 222 & Sharadin Rd., Box 346, Kutztown, PA 19530-0346) Ed. C. Payne. bk.rev.; film rev.; illus.; circ. 5,000.

204   US
BL1
WORLD FAITHS ENCOUNTER. 1980. 3/yr. $18. (World Congress of Faiths) World Congress of Faiths, 1047 Amsterdam Ave., New York, NY 10025. TEL 212-865-9117. FAX 212-316-7404. Eds. K.L.S. Rao, Alan Race. adv.; bk.rev.; circ. 750.
Indexed: Chr.Per.Ind.
Formerly (until 1991): World Faiths Insight (ISSN 0273-1266)

266   AT   ISSN 1033-2243
WORLD MISSION PARTNERS. 3/yr. free. Uniting Church in Australia, Uniting Church Word Mission, 222 Pitt St., 5th Fl., Sydney, N.S.W. 2000, Australia. TEL 02-287-0900. FAX 02-287-0999. (Subscr. to: P.O. Box E266, St. James, N.S.W. 2000, Australia) Ed. Rev. G. Brookes. circ. 25,000. (back issues avail.)
Description: Stories of Uniting Church mission work overseas and partner churches.

200   US
WORLD MISSIONARY PRESS NEWS. 1961. 6/yr. free. World Missionary Press, Inc., Box 120, New Paris, IN 46553. TEL 219-831-2111. FAX 219-831-2161. Ed. Gloria Byrnes. circ. 16,000.

266   US
WORLD - WIDE MISSIONARY CRUSADER. q. 2451 34th St., Lubbock, TX 79411. Ed. Mark Duncan.

200   US
WORLDORAMA. 10/yr. free. Pentecostal Holiness Church, World Mission Department, Box 12609, Oklahoma City, OK 73157. TEL 405-787-7110. FAX 405-789-3957. Ed. Harold Dalton. circ. 25,000.

WORLD'S WISDOM SERIES. see *PHILOSOPHY*

248   US   ISSN 0746-9241
WORLDWIDE CHALLENGE. 1974. bi-m. $12.95. Campus Crusade for Christ, Inc., Box 6710, San Bernardino, CA 92412-6710. TEL 714-886-5224. FAX 714-881-6522. (And: 100 Sunport Ln., Orlando, FL 32809. TEL 407-826-2390) Ed. Diane McDougall. adv.; illus.; circ. 110,000.
Formerly (until Oct. 1974): World-Wide Impact.

WORLDWIND. see *CHILDREN AND YOUTH — For*

220   US   ISSN 0043-941X
BV175
WORSHIP; concerned with the issues of liturgical renewal. 1926. bi-m. $22. Liturgical Press, St. John's Abbey, Collegeville, MN 56321. TEL 612-363-2213. Ed. Kevin Seasoltz. adv.; bk.rev.; index. cum.index every 25 yrs.; circ. 6,216. (also avail. in microform from UMI; reprint service avail. from UMI) **Indexed:** Canon Law Abstr., Cath.Ind., CERDIC, New Test.Abstr., Old Test.Abstr., Rel.& Theol.Abstr. (1979-), Rel.Ind.One, Rel.Per.
—BLDSC shelfmark: 9364.450000.

200   US   ISSN 0084-3644
YEARBOOK OF AMERICAN AND CANADIAN CHURCHES. 1916. a. $29.95. Abingdon Press, 201 Eighth Ave., S., Box 801, Nashville, TN 37202. TEL 800-251-3320. FAX 615-749-6522. **Indexed:** SRI.
Formerly: Yearbook of American Churches.
Description: Index for gauging trends in American and Canadian churches.

266   UK   ISSN 0951-726X
YES. 1960. 5/yr. £0.80 per no. Church Missionary Society, 157 Waterloo Rd., London SE1 8UU, England. TEL 071-928-8681. FAX 071-401-3215. TELEX 8950907 ANGCOM G. Ed. John Clark. bk.rev.; illus.; circ. 25,000.

200   UK   ISSN 0085-8374
YORK JOURNAL OF CONVOCATION. 1856. irreg. £5.50. Convocation of York, c/o Synodal Secretary, Church House, West Walls, Carlishe CA3 8UE, England. Ed. Canon D.T.I. Jenkins. circ. 400 (controlled).

267.2   US   ISSN 0020-2673
YOUNG MEN'S INSTITUTE. INSTITUTE JOURNAL. 1890. bi-m. $3. Young Men's Institute, 50 Oak St., San Francisco, CA 94102. TEL 415-621-4948. Ed. Eugene F. Driscoll. adv.; bk.rev.; illus.; circ. 4,500 (controlled).

266   US   ISSN 0044-1015
YOUR EDMUNDITE MISSIONS NEWS LETTER. 1943. bi-m. $2. (Society of Saint Edmund) Southern Missions, Inc., 1428 Broad St., Selma, AL 36701. Ed.Bd. illus.; circ. 54,500.

280   US   ISSN 1054-7126
YOUTH MINISTRY QUARTERLY (NEW HAMPTON). 1979. q. $23. (Growth Associates) Fred B. Estsbrook Company, Inc., Rte. 1, Box 142, New Hampton, NH 03266. TEL 800-637-9144. Ed. Veronica DiComo. abstr.; stat.; circ. 700.
Formerly: Catholic Youth Ministry.
Description: Religious articles, readings, program planning advice, discussion and lesson plans, news and historical sketches, and other suggestions pertaining to teenage life-style.

200   SZ
YOUTH NEWSLETTER. (Text mainly in English; occasionally in French) 1977. 4/yr. World Council of Churches, Youth Desk, 150 Route de Ferney, Box 2100, CH-1211 Geneva 2, Switzerland. TEL 022-791-6111. FAX 022-791-0361. TELEX 415730-OIK-CH. (Dist. in US by: World Council of Churches, Distribution Center, Rt. 222 & Sharadin Rd., Box 346, Kutztown, PA 19530-0346)

200   UK   ISSN 0143-0092
YSGRIFAU DIWINYDDOL. 1979. irreg. Evangelical Press of Wales, Bryntirion, Brigend, Mid Glamorgan CF31 4DX, Wales. TEL 0656-655886. FAX 0656-656095.
Formerly: Bwletin Diwinyddol.
Description: Volumes of theological essays in the Welsh language.

267.3 II ISSN 0044-1414
YUVAK. (Text in English) bi-m. Rs.10($2) National Council of YMCA's of India, PO Box No. 14, New Delhi 110001, India. Ed. D.S. Chinnadorai. adv.; circ. 2,500.
  Formerly: Association Men.

200 301 AT ISSN 0156-7470
ZADOK CENTRE. SERIES NO.1. 1977. q. Aus.$50. Zadok Institute for Christianity & Society, Blackall St., Barton, A.C.T. 2600, Australia. TEL 06-2731634. Ed. John Harris. circ. 1,000. (back issues avail.)
  Description: Extended evaluations of specific political, cultural or economic issues that deal with the subject area within the context of Christian values and beliefs.

200 301 AT ISSN 0156-7489
ZADOK CENTRE. SERIES NO.2. 1977. q. Aus.$50. Zadok Institute for Christianity & Society, Blackall St., Barton, A.C.T. 2600, Australia. TEL 06-2731634. Ed. John Harris. circ. 1,000. (back issues avail.)
  Description: Evaluations of biblical and theological issues as well as papers of general interest to promote application of Biblical truth to everyday life.

200 301 AT ISSN 0156-7500
ZADOK CENTRE READING GUIDES. 1977. a. Aus.$50. Zadok Institute for Christianity & Society, Blackall St., Barton, A.C.T. 2600, Australia. TEL 06-2731634. Ed. John Harris. bk.rev.; bibl.; circ. 1,000. (back issues avail.)
  Description: Introduces five or six significant books in a particular field to help people evaluate the subject and its implications to Christian faith.

200 301 AT ISSN 0810-9796
ZADOK PERSPECTIVES. 1983. q. Aus.$30. Zadok Institute for Christianity & Society, Blackall St., Barton, A.C.T. 2600, Australia. TEL 06-2731634. Ed. John Harris. bk.rev.; circ. 1,000. (back issues avail.)
  Description: Examines contemporary issues within the context of Christian belief.

221 GW ISSN 0044-2526
BS410
ZEITSCHRIFT FUER DIE ALTTESTAMENTLICHE WISSENSCHAFT. (Text in several languages) 1881. 3/yr. $104 (students $41.50). Walter de Gruyter und Co., Genthiner Str. 13, 1000 Berlin 30, Germany. TEL 030-26005-0. FAX 030-26005251. TELEX 184027. (U.S. addr.: Walter de Gruyter, Inc., 200 Saw Mill Rd., Hawthorne, NY 10532) Ed. Otto Kaiser. bk.rev.; abstr.; index. (also avail. in microform) Indexed: Arts & Hum.Cit.Ind., Curr.Cont., New Test.Abstr., Old Test.Abstr., Rel.& Theol.Abstr. (1969-), Rel.Ind.One, Rel.Per.
  —BLDSC shelfmark: 9446.950000.

225 GW ISSN 0044-2615
BS410
ZEITSCHRIFT FUER DIE NEUTESTAMENTLICHE WISSENSCHAFT UND DIE KUNDE DER AELTEREN KIRCHE. 1900. 2/yr. $73.50 (students $30). Walter de Gruyter und Co., Genthiner Str. 13, 1000 Berlin 30, Germany. TEL 030-26005-0. FAX 030-26005251. TELEX 184027. (U.S. addr.: Walter de Gruyter, Inc., 200 Saw Mill Rd., Hawthorne, NY 10532) Ed. Erich Graesser. adv.; bk.rev.; bibl.; index. cum.index: vols. 1-37, 1900-1938. (also avail. in microform) Indexed: CERDIC, New Test.Abstr., Rel.& Theol.Abstr. (1970-), Rel.Ind.One, Rel.Per.
  —BLDSC shelfmark: 9475.500000.

241 261 GW ISSN 0044-2674
ZEITSCHRIFT FUER EVANGELISCHE ETHIK. 1957. bi-m. DM.80.40. Guetersloher Verlagshaus Gerd Mohn, Carl-Bertelsmann-Str. 256, Postfach 1343, 4830 Guetersloh 100, Germany. TEL 05241-7405-0. FAX 05241-740548. Ed. Chr. Frey. bk.rev.; bibl. Indexed: Arts & Hum.Cit.Ind., CERDIC, Curr.Cont., Rel.& Theol.Abstr., Rel.Ind.One, Rel.Per.

200
ZEITSCHRIFT FUER GOTTESDIENST UND PREDIGT. 1983. bi-m. DM.78.60. Guetersloher Verlagshaus Gerd Mohn, Carl-Bertelsmann-Str. 256, 4830 Guetersloh 100, Germany. TEL 05241-7405-0. FAX 05241-740548. Ed. Horst Nitschke. adv.; bk.rev.; circ. 3,700.

209 GW ISSN 0044-2925
BR140
ZEITSCHRIFT FUER KIRCHENGESCHICHTE. 1889. 3/yr. DM.212. W. Kohlhammer GmbH, Hessbruehlstr. 69, Postfach 800430, 7000 Stuttgart 80, Germany. TEL 0711-7863-1. Ed. Joachim Mehlhausen. adv.; bk.rev.; abstr.; bibl.; index; circ. 950. (reprint service avail. from SCH) Indexed: CERDIC, Hist.Abstr., Rel.& Theol.Abstr. (1970-), Rel.Ind.One, Rel.Per.

200 261 SZ
BR4
ZEITSCHRIFT FUER KULTUR POLITIK KIRCHE. 1952. bi-m. 66 Fr. Postfach 7650, CH-3001 Bern, Switzerland. Ed. Hektor Leibundgut. adv.; bk.rev.; circ. 1,600. (reprint service avail.) Indexed: Rel.Ind.One, Rel.Per.
  Formerly: Reformatio (ISSN 0034-3021)

266 GW ISSN 0342-9423
ZEITSCHRIFT FUER MISSION. 1975. q. DM.28. Evangelischer Missionsverlag GmbH, Postfach 311141, 7000 Stuttgart 31, Germany. FAX 0711-83000-10. Ed. Hans W. Huppenbauer. adv.; bk.rev.; index; circ. 1,100. Indexed: CERDIC.
  Formerly (until 1974): Evangelische Missionszeitschrift (ISSN 0014-3472)

266 GW ISSN 0044-3123
BV2130
ZEITSCHRIFT FUER MISSIONSWISSENSCHAFT UND RELIGIONSWISSENSCHAFT. (Text in English, French, German) 1911. 4/yr. DM.56. Erzabtei St. Ottilien, 8917 St. Ottilien, Germany. TEL 08193-710. Ed. Thomas Kramm. adv.; bk.rev.; index. Indexed: Canon Law Abstr., CERDIC, Rel.& Theol.Abstr. (1978-), Rel.Ind.One, Rel.Per.
  —BLDSC shelfmark: 9473.120000.

200 NE ISSN 0044-3441
BL4
ZEITSCHRIFT FUER RELIGIONS- UND GEISTESGESCHICHTE/JOURNAL OF RELIGIOUS AND INTELLECTUAL HISTORY. 1948. q. fl.155($88.64) (effective 1992). E.J. Brill, P.O. Box 9000, 2300 PA Leiden, Netherlands. TEL 071-312624. FAX 071-317532. TELEX 39296 BRILL NL. (In N. America: E.J. Brill, 24 Hudson St., Kinderhook, NY 12106. TEL 800-962-4406) Ed.Bd. adv.; bk.rev.; bibl.; index.; circ. 650. Indexed: Arts & Hum.Cit.Ind., CERDIC, Hist.Abstr., New Test.Abstr., Phil.Ind., Rel.& Theol.Abstr. (1976-), Rel.Ind.One, Rel.Per.
  —BLDSC shelfmark: 9485.350000.

200 NE ISSN 0514-650X
BL4
ZEITSCHRIFT FUER RELIGIONS- UND GEISTESGESCHICHTE. BEIHEFTE. 1955. irreg., vol.30, 1985. price varies. E.J. Brill, P.O. Box 9000, 2300 PA Leiden, Netherlands. TEL 071-31224. FAX 071-317532. TELEX 39296 BRILL NL. (In N. America: E.J. Brill, 24 Hudson St., Kinderhook, NY 12106. TEL 800-962-4406) Ed. H.J. Klimkeit. Indexed: Rel.& Theol.Abstr., Rel.Ind.One.

209 SZ ISSN 0044-3484
ZEITSCHRIFT FUER SCHWEIZERISCHE KIRCHENGESCHICHTE/REVUE D'HISTOIRE ECCLESIASTIQUE SUISSE. (Text and title in French and German) 1907. a. 50 Fr. (Vereinigung fuer Schweizerische Kirchengeschichte) Editions Saint-Paul, Perolles 42, CH-1700 Fribourg, Switzerland. bk.rev.; bibl. Indexed: CERDIC.

284 GW ISSN 0340-8361
ZEITSCHRIFTENINHALTSDIENST THEOLOGIE; Indices theologici. 1975. m. DM.28 (foreign DM.40). Universitaetsbibliothek Tuebingen, Theologische Abteilung, Wilhelmstr. 32, 7400 Tuebingen 1, Germany. (Co-sponsor: Deutsche Forschungsgemeinschaft) index; circ. 960. (back issues avail.)

220 SA ISSN 0028-3568
ZIONS FREUND. vol.9, 1969. q. R.10. Good News Missionary Society, P.O. Box 7848, Johannesburg 2000, South Africa. TEL 011-729-9581. Ed. Sean O'Sullivan. circ. 1,500.
  Formerly: Neuer Zions Freund.

277 CI ISSN 0353-0434
ZNACI VREMENA; obitelski casopis za kriscansku renesansu. (Text in Croatian and Serbian) 1969. q. 50 din.($4) Centar za Istrazivanje Biblije Dokumentaciju i Informaciju, Klaiceva 40, 41000 Zagreb, Croatia. Eds. Tomislav Stefanovic, Zdenko Hlisc-Bladt. circ. 6,500 (Croatian ed.); 9,000 (Serbian ed.).

200 PL ISSN 0044-488X
AP54
ZNAK. (Text in Polish; summaries in English, French) 1946. m. $36. Spoleczny Instytut Wydawniczy "Znak", Ul. Kosciuszki 37, 30-106 Krakow, Poland. TEL 21-89-20. FAX 21-98-14. Ed. Stefan Wilkanowicz. bk.rev.; index; circ. 7,500. Indexed: CERDIC, M.L.A.

200 NE ISSN 0044-5002
ZONDAGSMIS. 1951. 60/yr. fl.19. Grafische Bedrijven Berne B.V., Postbus 27, 5473 ZG Heeswijk-Dinther, Netherlands. TEL 04139-1394. FAX 04139-2270. circ. 120,000.

250 US ISSN 0084-5558
ZONDERVAN PASTOR'S ANNUAL. 1966. a. $14.95. Zondervan Publishing House, Box 105, Grand Rapids, MI 49501-0105. TEL 616-698-6900. FAX 616-698-3454. circ. 14,000. (reprint service avail. from UMI)
  —BLDSC shelfmark: 9515.700000.
  Description: Contains planned and prepared sermons for every Sunday, Wednesday and special occasion of the year.

200 CC
ZONGJIAOXUE YANJIU/RELIGION RESEARCH. (Text in Chinese) q. Sichuan Daxue, Zongjiaoxue Yanjiusuo - Sichuan University, Religion Research Institute, Sichuan Daxue Nei, Jiugenqiao, Chengdu, Sichuan 610064, People's Republic of China. TEL 583875.

200 GW
ZUM THEMA; Materialien zur Orientierung. 10/yr. DM.5. Kreuz-Verlag Zeitschriften GmbH, Breitwiesenstr. 30, 7000 Stuttgart 80, Germany. TEL 0711-78803. Ed. Peter H. Blaschke.

215 US ISSN 0591-2385
BL240.2
ZYGON; journal of religion and science. 1966. q. $30 to individuals; institutions $42.50; students $22. (Institute on Religion in an Age of Science) Basil Blackwell Inc., 3 Cambridge Center, Cambridge, MA 02142. FAX 617-225-0430. Ed. Philip Hefner. adv.; bk.rev.; index, cum.index: vols.1-20; circ. 2,000. (also avail. in microfilm from MIM,UMI; back issues avail; reprint service avail. UMI) Indexed: Amer.Hist.& Life, Arts & Hum.Cit.Ind., Arts & Hum.Cit.Ind., Bk.Rev.Ind. (1977-), CERDIC, Child.Bk.Rev.Ind. (1977-), Curr.Cont., G.Soc.Sci.& Rel.Per.Lit., Hist.Abstr. (until 1990), Hum.Ind., New Test.Abstr., Old Test.Abstr., Phil.Ind., Psychol.Abstr., Rel.& Theol.Abstr. (1971-), Rel.Ind.One, Rel.Per., Sociol.Abstr., SSCI.
  Description: Covers scholarly work that explores positive ways of relating contemporary scientific knowledge to the world's philosophical and religious heritage.

200 028.5 GW
17; illustrierte Monatszeitschrift fuer junge Christen. 1973. m. DM.19.20. (Steyler Missionare) Soverdia GmbH, Postfach 24 60, Bahnhofstr. 9, 4054 Nettetal 2, Germany. TEL 02157-1202-0. FAX 02157-120222. Ed. P. Heinrich Schlake.

240 US ISSN 0162-6418
20TH CENTURY CHRISTIAN. 1938. m. $10.95. 20th Century Christian Foundation, 2809 Granny White Pike, Nashville, TN 37204. TEL 615-383-3842. Ed. Mike Cope. circ. 18,000.

RELIGIONS AND THEOLOGY —
Abstracting, Bibliographies, Statistics

200 US
A T L A BIBLIOGRAPHY SERIES. no.17, 1987. irreg., latest no.27. price varies. (American Theological Library Association) Scarecrow Press, Inc., 52 Liberty St., Box 4167, Metuchen, NJ 08840. TEL 800-537-7107. Ed. Kenneth E. Rowe.

RELIGIONS AND THEOLOGY — ABSTRACTING, BIBLIOGRAPHIES, STATISTICS

200   DK   ISSN 0901-4497
AARHUS UNIVERSITET. TEOLOGISKE FAKULTET. BIBLIOGRAFI. a. free. Aarhus Universitet, Teologiske Fakultet, Nordre Ringgade 1, DK-8000C Aarhus, Denmark.

250 016   US   ISSN 0733-2599
BV4012.2
ABSTRACTS OF RESEARCH IN PASTORAL CARE AND COUNSELING. 1972. a. $25 (foreign $30)(typically set in Feb.). Loyola College in Maryland, Pastoral Counseling Department, 7135 Minstrel Way, Ste.101, Columbia, MD 21045. TEL 804-282-8332. Ed. Joanne Greer. adv.; bk.rev.; circ. 400. (also avail. on diskette; back issues avail.)
—BLDSC shelfmark: 0569.165000.
Formerly: Pastoral Care and Counseling Abstracts.
Description: Presents abstracts of all research published in English-language academic psychology journals in which psychology is a variable, or which relates religion and psychology, counseling, or mental health.

ACTUALIDAD BIBLIOGRAFICA DE FILOSOFIA Y TEOLOGIA; selecciones de libros. see *PHILOSOPHY — Abstracting, Bibliographies, Statistics*

200 314   VC
ANNUARIUM STATISTICUM ECCLESIAE/STATISTIQUE DE L'EGLISE/STATISTICAL YEARBOOK OF THE CHURCH. (Text in English, French, Latin) 1969. a. L.80000. (Segretaria di Stato, Ufficio Centrale di Statistica della Chiesa) Libreria Editrice Vaticana, 00120 Vatican City (Rome), State of the Vatican City. TEL 0036-6-6983532. FAX 0036-6-6984716. charts; stat.
Formerly: Raccolta di Tavole Statistiche.
Description: Statistics on the presence and Apostolic work of the Church in various countries and continents.

ARCHIVES DE SCIENCES SOCIALES DES RELIGIONS. see *SOCIAL SCIENCES: COMPREHENSIVE WORKS — Abstracting, Bibliographies, Statistics*

271   VC
ARCHIVUM BIBLIOGRAPHICUM CARMELI TERESIANI. (Text in Latin and modern languages) 1956. a. L.50000 (effective 1991). Edizioni del Teresianum, Piazza S. Pancrazio 5-A, 00152 Rome, Italy. Ed. Father Antonio Fortes, O.C.D. circ. 400.
Formerly: Archivum Bibliographicum Carmelitanum (ISSN 0570-7242)

ASSOCIATED CHURCH PRESS. DIRECTORY. see *BUSINESS AND ECONOMICS — Trade And Industrial Directories*

200 011   AT   ISSN 1033-2626
AUSTRALASIAN RELIGION INDEX. Short title: A R I. 1989. s-a. Aus.$45 to ANZTLA members; individuals and libraries Aus.$60. Charles Stuart University - Riverina, Centre for Information Studies, P.O. Box 588, Wagga Wagga, N.S.W. 2650, Australia. TEL 069-222584. FAX 069-227333. (Co-sponsor: Australian and New Zealand Theological Library Association (ANZTLA))
Description: Author, subject and scriptural passage index to religious and theological serials and selected serials with religious and theological coverage published in Australia and New Zealand.

282   VC   ISSN 0394-9869
Z7838.M6
BIBLIOGRAFIA MISSIONARIA. 1935. a. $30. (Pontificia Universita Urbaniana, Pontificia Biblioteca Missionaria della S.C. per l'Evangelizzazione dei Popoli) Urbaniana University Press, Via Urbano VIII, 16, 00165 Rome, Italy. FAX 65-48-363. Ed. Willi Henkel. bk.rev.; circ. 1,000.
Formerly (until 1987): Bibliographia Missionaria.

200 016   AG   ISSN 0326-6680
BIBLIOGRAFIA TEOLOGICA COMENTADA DEL AREA IBEROAMERICANA. 1973. a. $70. Instituto Superior Evangelico de Estudios Teologicos, Camacua 282, 1406 Buenos Aires, Argentina. Ed. Eduardo Bierzychudek. bk.rev.; bibl.; circ. 1,000. (back issues avail.)

255 011 920   IT
BIBLIOGRAPHIA FRANCISCANA. (Annual supplement to: Collectanea Franciscana) (Text in Latin) 1931. a. price varies. Frati Minori Cappuccini, Istituto Storico, Casella Postale 90-91, Circonv. Occidentale 6850 (GRA km 65), 00163 Rome, Italy.
TEL 06-625-19-58. FAX 06-661-62-401. circ. 800.

296 016   US   ISSN 0067-6853
BIBLIOGRAPHICA JUDAICA. 1969. irreg., no.12, 1987. Hebrew Union College - Jewish Institute of Religion (Cincinnati), 3101 Clifton Ave., Cincinnati, OH 45220. TEL 513-221-1875. Ed. Herbert C. Zafren.
—BLDSC shelfmark: 1971.230000.

200   US   ISSN 0742-6836
BIBLIOGRAPHIES AND INDEXES IN RELIGIOUS STUDIES. 1984. irreg. price varies. Greenwood Press, Inc. (Subsidiary of: Greenwood Publishing Group Inc.), 88 Post Rd. W., Box 5007, Westport, CT 06881-5007. TEL 203-226-3571. FAX 203-222-1502. Ed. Gary E. Gorman.
—BLDSC shelfmark: 1993.097500.

BOOKS AND ARTICLES ON ORIENTAL SUBJECTS PUBLISHED IN JAPAN. see *ORIENTAL STUDIES — Abstracting, Bibliographies, Statistics*

294.3 011   US   ISSN 0360-6112
Z7860
BUDDHIST TEXT INFORMATION. 1974. q. $20. Institute for Advanced Studies of World Religions, Rd. 2, Route 301, Carmel, NY 10512.
TEL 914-225-1445. FAX 914-225-1485. Ed. Richard A. Gard. index; circ. 350. (back issues avail.)
—BLDSC shelfmark: 2357.254000.
Description: Details their indentification, published editions, translations, studies and reports on research planned, in-progress or completed.

BULLETIN SIGNALETIQUE. PART 519: PHILOSOPHIE. see *PHILOSOPHY — Abstracting, Bibliographies, Statistics*

200 016   FR   ISSN 0180-9296
Z7751
BULLETIN SIGNALETIQUE. PART 527: HISTOIRE ET SCIENCES DES RELIGIONS. 1947. q. 475 F. Centre National de la Recherche Scientifique, Institut de l'Information Scientifique et Technique, 54 bd. Raspail, 75270 Paris Cedex 06, France.
FAX 45487015. TELEX MSH 203104 F. cum.index.
●Also available online. Vendor(s): Telesystemes - Questel.
Formerly: Bulletin Signaletique. Part 527: Sciences Religieuse (ISSN 0007-5620)

262.9 016   IE   ISSN 0008-5650
CANON LAW ABSTRACTS; half-yearly review of periodical literature in Canon Law. 1959. s-a. £10. Canon Law Society of Great Britain and Ireland, Cathedral House, Ingrave Rd., Brentwood, Essex CM15 8AT, England. Ed. Rev. Ivan Payne. bk.rev.; circ. 1,000. **Indexed:** CERDIC, Old Test.Abstr.
—BLDSC shelfmark: 3049.500000.

282 011   US   ISSN 0008-8285
AI3
CATHOLIC PERIODICAL AND LITERATURE INDEX. 1930. q. with biennial cum. (service basis). Catholic Library Association, 461 W. Lancaster Ave., Haverford, PA 19041. TEL 215-649-5250. Ed. Anthony Prete. bk.rev.; abstr.; bibl.; circ. 1,500. (also avail. in microfilm from UMI)
Former titles: Catholic Periodical Index (ISSN 0363-6895); Guide to Catholic Literature (ISSN 0145-191X)

296   US   ISSN 0069-1607
CENTRAL CONFERENCE OF AMERICAN RABBIS. YEARBOOK. 1890. a. $20. (Central Conference of American Rabbis) C C A R Press, 192 Lexington Ave., 7th Fl., New York, NY 10016.
TEL 212-684-4990. FAX 212-689-1649. Ed. Elliot L. Stevens. cum.index: 1951-1970; circ. 1,500. (also avail. in microfilm from AJP) **Indexed:** Rel.Ind.Two.
Description: An indexed reference on modern Reform thought, including the annual summary of proceedings of CCAR conventions and conferences.

200 011   FR   ISSN 0181-7671
CENTRE PROTESTANT D'ETUDES ET DE DOCUMENTATION. BULLETIN. 1944. 10/yr. 200 F. Centre Protestant d'Etudes et de Documentation, 46 rue de Vaugirard, 75006 Paris, France. (Co-sponsor: Federation Protestante de France) Ed. Mrs. M.L. Fabre. adv.; bk.rev.; abstr.; bibl.; index; circ. 1,350. **Indexed:** CERDIC, New Test.Abstr.
Formerly: Federation Protestante de France. Centre d'Etudes et de Documentation. Bulletin (ISSN 0008-9842)

285   US   ISSN 0362-0832
CHRISTIAN INDEX (ATLANTA). 1822. w. $8 (effective Jan. 1991). Georgia Baptist Convention, Executive Committee, 2930 Flowers Rd., S., Atlanta, GA 30341. TEL 404-936-5312. FAX 404-936-5160. Ed. R. Albert Mohler, Jr. adv.; bk.rev.; circ. 76,000. (tabloid format; also avail. in microfilm; back issues avail.)

280 016   US   ISSN 0069-3871
CHRISTIAN PERIODICAL INDEX; an index to subjects, authors and book reviews. 1959. 3/yr. $95 (including annual). Association of Christian Librarians Inc., Box 4, Cedarville, OH 45314. TEL 513-766-2211. FAX 513-766-2337. Ed. Douglas J. Butler. circ. 450.
—BLDSC shelfmark: 3181.850000.

285   UK   ISSN 0266-7088
CONGREGATIONAL YEAR BOOK. 1973. a. £7 (typically set in Dec.). Congregational Federation, Congregational Centre, 4 Castle Gate, Nottingham NG1 7AS, England. TEL 0602-413801.
FAX 0602-480902. Ed. Jean Young. stat.; index; circ. 700.

016.2   US   ISSN 0270-2347
Z7755
CURRENT CHRISTIAN BOOKS. 1975. a. $54.95. (Christian Booksellers Association) C B A Service Corporation, 2620 Venetucci Blvd., Box 200, Colorado Springs, CO 80901. TEL 719-576-7880. FAX 719-576-0795. Ed. Tom Gruen. circ. 2,000. (also avail. in microfiche)
Incorporating: Current Christian Books. Authors and Titles (ISSN 0098-5554) & Current Christian Books. Titles, Authors, and Publishers (ISSN 0098-5562)
Description: Lists titles currently available in the Christian market by title and author indexes.

200   US   ISSN 1054-8688
CURRENT THOUGHTS & TRENDS. 1985. m. $36. Box 35004, Colorado Springs, CO 80935-3504. TEL 719-531-3585. FAX 719-598-7128. Ed. Dennis Cone. circ. 5,000.
●Also available online.
Formerly: Current Christian Abstracts (ISSN 0883-1440)
Description: Summaries of articles from Christian and secular periodicals dealing with contemporary religious, ethical, theological, social, economic, political, educational, and psychological trends in the church and in society.

220 016   VC
ELENCHUS OF BIBLICA. a. price varies. (Pontificio Istituto Biblico) Biblical Institute Press, Piazza della Pilotta 35, 00187 Rome, Italy. Ed. Robert North S.J.
Formerly: Elenchus Bibliographicus Biblicus (ISSN 0392-7423)
Description: Treats all areas of investigation which involve the scientific study of the Bible.

200 011   CE
GLEANINGS. (Text in English) 1982. q. Rs.16($4) Sioll School of Technology, 389 Battaramulla, Sri Lanka. (Subscr. to: Ecumenical Institute for Study & Dialogue, 490-5 Havelock Rd., Colombo 6, Sri Lanka) Ed. J.F. Newslan. circ. 400.

016 200   NE
GODSDIENST EN MAATSCHAPPIJ. 1981. bi-m. fl.30.50. Nederlands Bibliotheek en Lektuur Centrum, Scheltemastr. 5, 2597 CP Amersfoort, Netherlands. Eds. Magda van der Grijn, L.M.D. de Viet. bk.rev.; circ. 1,000.
Description: Information for public librarians on religous literature and its relation to society.

300 200 016   US   ISSN 0017-5307
Z7753
GUIDE TO SOCIAL SCIENCE AND RELIGION IN PERIODICAL LITERATURE. 1964. s-a. (triennall cum.). $85. National Periodical Library, Box 47, Flint, MI 48501. Ed. Albert M. Wells. index; circ. 500.

INDEX OF ARTICLES ON JEWISH STUDIES/RESHIMAT MA'AMARIM BE-MADA'E HA-YAHADUT. see *ETHNIC INTERESTS — Abstracting, Bibliographies, Statistics*

011 200 US ISSN 0887-1574
Z7753
INDEX TO BOOK REVIEWS IN RELIGION. Short title: I B R R. (Text in English, French, German) 1949. 3/yr. (plus a. cum.). $280 (foreign $295). American Theological Library Association, Religion Indexes, 820 Church St., 3rd Fl., Evanston, IL 60201-3707. TEL 708-869-7788. Ed. Edwina Schaufler. bk.rev.; circ. 475.
●Also available online. Vendor(s): BRS, DIALOG (File no.190), Wilsonline.
Also available on CD-ROM.

289.3 016 US ISSN 0073-5981
INDEX TO PERIODICALS OF THE CHURCH OF JESUS CHRIST OF LATTER-DAY SAINTS. 1961. a. $5 (cum.index: 1961-1970 $10). Church of Jesus Christ of Latter-day Saints, Corporation of the President, 50 E. North Temple, Salt Lake City, UT 84150. TEL 801-240-1000. (Subscr. to: Salt Lake Distribution Center, 1999 West 1700 South, Salt Lake City, UT 84104) index; circ. 5,000.
Description: From 1986 on, it includes the following periodicals: The Friend, Church News, Conference Reports, New Era, and the Ensign.

297 GW ISSN 0724-2263
Z7835.M6
ISLAMIC BOOK REVIEW INDEX. (Text in English) 1982. a. DM.65($44) Adiyok Verlag Wolfgang Behn, Rosenheimer Str. 5, 1000 Berlin 30, Germany. TEL 030-2117195. (U.S. subscr. to: Adiyok Publications W.H. Behn, 415 Herr Ave., Millersville, PA 17551. TEL 717-872-7941) Ed. Wolfgang Behn. bk.rev.; film rev.; video rev.; circ. 500. (back issues avail.)
Description: Lists reviews of periodicals and unpublished theses from 1980 to the present.

ISSUES IN THE ISLAMIC MOVEMENT. see RELIGIONS AND THEOLOGY — Islamic

284 ZA
LUTHERAN CHURCH OF CENTRAL AFRICA. STATISTICAL REPORT. (Text in English) a. Lutheran Church of Central Africa, P.O. Box CH 195, Lusaka, Zambia.

655 028.1 011 GW ISSN 0028-3118
DAS NEUE BUCH; Buchprofile fuer die Katholische Buechereiarbeit. 1925. bi-m. DM.38. Borromaeusverein, Wittelsbacherring 9, 5300 Bonn, Germany. (And: St. Michaelsbund, Herzog Wilhelmstr. 5, 8000 Munich 2, Germany) Eds. Herbert Stangl, Raimund Trell. bk.rev.; cum.index; circ. 10,000.

220 016 US ISSN 0028-6877
BS410
NEW TESTAMENT ABSTRACTS; a record of current literature. 1956. 3/yr. $27 (foreign $30). Weston School of Theology, 3 Phillips Place, Cambridge, MA 02138. TEL 202-319-5519. FAX 617-492-5833. (Subscr. to: Catholic Biblical Association of America, Catholic University of America, Washington, DC 20064) Ed. D.J. Harrington. adv.; bk.rev.; abstr.; index, cum.index: vols. 1-15 (1956-1970); circ. 2,250. (back issues avail) Indexed: Int.Z.Bibelwiss.
—BLDSC shelfmark: 6088.856000.

200 011 RU ISSN 0134-2932
NOVAYA SOVETSKAYA I INOSTRANNAYA LITERATURA PO OBSHCHESTVENNYM NAUKAM. PROBLEMY ATEIZMA I RELIGII; bibliograficheskii ukazatel' 1959. bi-m. 3.60 Rub. Akademiya Nauk S.S.S.R., Institut Nauchnoi Informatsii po Obshchestvennym Naukam, Ul. Krasikova 28-21, 117418 Moscow V-418, Russia. Ed. I.I. Kravchenko.

016 260 FR
OECUMENE; international bibliography indexed by computer. (Text and summaries in English, French, German, Italian, Spanish) 1977. biennial. 260 F.($20) CERDIC Publications, 2 rue Goethe, Palais Universitaire, F-67083 Strasbourg, France. TEL 88-25-97-09. FAX 88-37-96-92. bk.rev.; circ. 1,000. (back issues avail.)

220 US ISSN 0364-8591
BS410
OLD TESTAMENT ABSTRACTS. 1978. 3/yr. $14. Catholic Biblical Association of America, Catholic University of America, Washington, DC 20064. TEL 202-319-5519. Ed. Tgomas P. McCreesh. circ. 2,050.
—BLDSC shelfmark: 6253.837000.
Description: Summaries and bibliographical data on articles and books on the Old Testament.

PROVIDENT BOOK FINDER. see RELIGIONS AND THEOLOGY — Protestant

016 260 FR ISSN 0079-9300
R I C. (Repertoire Bibliographique des Institutions Chretiennes.) (Supplement avail: Thematic Bibliographies) 1966. s-a. 600 F. CERDIC Publications, 2 rue Goethe, Palais Universitaire, F-67083 Strasbourg, France. TEL 88-25-97-09. FAX 88-37-96-92. Eds. Jean Schlick, Marie Zimmermann. bk.rev.; circ. 1,500.
Description: Provides bibliographic references for Christian institutions, discussing organizational and theological characteristics, activities, and broader issues including church-state relations and ecumenical efforts.

200 016 US ISSN 0149-8428
Z7753
RELIGION INDEX ONE: PERIODICALS. Short title: R I O. (Text in English, French, German) 1949. s-a. (plus a. cum.). $380 (foreign $395). American Theological Library Association, Religion Indexes, 820 Church St., 3rd Fl., Evanston, IL 60201-3707. TEL 708-869-7788. Ed. Don Haymes. circ. 1,200.
●Also available online. Vendor(s): BRS (RELI), BRS/Saunders Colleague, DIALOG (File no.190), Wilsonline.
Also available on CD-ROM.
—BLDSC shelfmark: 7356.464000.
Formerly: Index to Religious Periodical Literature (ISSN 0019-4107)

200 US ISSN 0149-8436
Z7751
RELIGION INDEX TWO: MULTI-AUTHOR WORKS. Short title: R I T. (Text in English, French, German) 1970. a. $320. American Theological Library Association, Religion Indexes, 820 Church St., 3rd Fl., Evanston, IL 60201-3707. TEL 708-869-7788. Ed. Erica Treesh. circ. 600.
●Also available online. Vendor(s): BRS, BRS/Saunders Colleague, DIALOG (File no.190), Wilsonline.
Also available on CD-ROM.
—BLDSC shelfmark: 7356.465000.

200 016 US ISSN 0034-4044
BR1
RELIGIOUS & THEOLOGICAL ABSTRACTS. 1958. q. $37.50 to individuals; institutions $75 (effective 1992). Religious & Theological Abstracts Inc., 121 S. College St., Box 215, Myerstown, PA 17067. TEL 717-866-6734. Ed. William S. Sailer. abstr.; index; circ. 1,100. (also avail. in microfiche; back issues avail.)
●Also available on CD-ROM.
—BLDSC shelfmark: 7356.480000.
Description: Provides abstracts of articles from more than 300 scholarly periodicals in religion, including Christian, Jewish and other world religions, classified under Biblical, Theological, Historical or Practical headings.

200 016 II ISSN 0034-4060
RELIGIOUS BOOK REVIEW INDEX. 1970. bi-m. Rs.150.($63) K.K. Roy (Private) Ltd., 55 Gariahat Rd., P.O. Box 10210, Calcutta 700 019, India. Ed. John A. Gillard. adv.; bk.rev.; bibl.; circ. 1,000. (looseleaf format)
—BLDSC shelfmark: 9050.211000.

200 US
RESEARCH IN MINISTRY; an index to Doctor of Ministry project reports and theses. Short title: R I M. 1981. a. $45. American Theological Library Association, Religion Indexes, 820 Church St., 3rd Fl., Evanston, IL 60201-3707. TEL 708-869-7788. Ed. Barry Hopkins. abstr.; circ. 175. (looseleaf format; back issues avail.)
●Also available online. Vendor(s): Data-Star, DIALOG, Wilsonline.
Also available on CD-ROM.

200 US ISSN 0730-2371
S S C BOOKNEWS. 1973. m. free. Spiritual Studies Center, Box 1104, Rockville, MD 20850. TEL 301-963-9243. Ed. George H. Leonard. bk.rev.; circ. 3,000.

300 016 US ISSN 0036-6358
SCHOLARS' CHOICE; significant current theological literature from abroad. 1960. s-a. $4. Union Theological Seminary in Virginia, Library, 3401 Brook Rd., Richmond, VA 23227. TEL 804-355-0671. FAX 804-355-3919. Ed. John B. Trotti. bibl.; circ. 650.

200 NE ISSN 0165-8794
SCIENCE OF RELIGION; abstracts and index of recent articles. 1976. q. fl.50. Vrije Universiteit, Instituut voor Godsdienstwetenschap - Institute for the Study of Religion, Postbus 7161, 1007 MC Amsterdam, Netherlands. Eds. Remmelt Bakker, Michael Pye. circ. 350. **Indexed:** E.I.
—BLDSC shelfmark: 8152.362000.
Formerly: Science of Religion Bulletin.

200 UK ISSN 0081-1440
SOCIETY FOR OLD TESTAMENT STUDY. BOOK LIST. 1946. a. £15($27.50) Society for Old Testament Study, c/o W.S. Maney, P.O. Box YR7, Leeds LS9 7UU, England. TEL 0532-497481. FAX 0532-486983. Ed. L. Grabbe. adv.; bk.rev.; index; circ. 1,200.

STUDIES IN BIBLIOGRAPHY AND BOOKLORE; devoted to research in the field of Jewish bibliography. see PUBLISHING AND BOOK TRADE — Abstracting, Bibliographies, Statistics

200 016 UK
THEOLOGICAL AND RELIGIOUS BIBLIOGRAPHIES. 1972. irreg. £2. Theological Abstracting and Bibliographical Services, 33 Mayfield Grove, Harrogate, N. Yorkshire HG1 5HD, England. Ed. G.P. Cornish. bk.rev.; circ. 150. (also avail. in microfilm)
Formerly (until vol.3, 1981): Theological and Religious Index (ISSN 0306-087X)

200 US
TOPICS IN RELIGION: A BIBLIOGRAPHIC SERIES. irreg. price varies. Greenwood Press, Inc. (Subsidiary of: Greenwood Publishing Group Inc.), 88 Post Rd. W., Box 5007, Westport, CT 06881-5007. TEL 203-226-3571. FAX 203-222-1502. Ed. Gary E. Gorman.

200 UK
U K CHRISTIAN HANDBOOK (YEAR). (Missions Advanced Research & Communications Center) 1964. biennial. £21.99. M A R C Europe, Vision Building, 4 Footscray Rd., Eltham, London SE9 2TZ, England. TEL 081-294-1989. FAX 081-294-0014. Ed. P. Brierley, D. Longley. adv.; circ. 6,000. (back issues avail.)
Description: Contains addresses of 5,000 Christian organizations, plus information about church membership.

ZIONIST LITERATURE. see PUBLISHING AND BOOK TRADE — Abstracting, Bibliographies, Statistics

RELIGIONS AND THEOLOGY — Buddhist

see also Oriental Studies

294.3 US ISSN 0747-900X
AMERICAN BUDDHIST. 1980. m. $45 (effective Sept. 1991). American Buddhist Movement, 301 W. 45th St., New York, NY 10036. TEL 212-489-1075. Ed. Kevin O'Neil. adv.; bk.rev.; circ. 10,000. (back issues avail.)
Former titles: American Buddhist Newsletter; (until 1984): American Buddhist News.
Description: Covers Buddhism in the United States, Buddhism for beginners and advanced.

ARS BUDDHICA/BUKKYO GEIJUTSU. see ART

299 301.15 IO
ATMA JAYA RESEARCH CENTRE. SOCIO-RELIGIOUS RESEARCH REPORT/PUSAT PENELITIAN ATMA JAYA. LAPORAN PENELITIAN KEAGAMAAN. 1977. irreg. Atma Jaya Research Centre - Pusat Penelitian Atma Jaya, Jalan Jenderal Sudirman 57, P.O. Box 2639, Jakarta 10001, Indonesia. circ. controlled.

RELIGIONS AND THEOLOGY — BUDDHIST

294.3   KO
BEOP RYUN. (Text in Korean) 1968. m. 3000 Won($6) Beop Ryun Sa, 131-1 Pyoungchangdong, Jongro-Ku, Seoul, S. Korea. Ed. Park Wan III. adv.; bk.rev.; illus.; circ. 20,000.

294.3   US
BLIND DONKEY. 1975. irreg. $12 for 4 nos. (foreign $16). Diamond Sangha, Inc., 2119 Kaloa Way, Honolulu, HI 96822. Ed. Doug Codiga. bk.rev.; circ. 400.

299   AU
BODHI BAUM; Zeitschrift fuer Buddhismus. 1976. 4/yr. S.350. Octopus Verlag, Fleischmarkt 16, A-1010 Vienna, Austria. Ed. Claudia Rom. adv.; bk.rev.; bibl.; index; circ. 1,500.

294   CE   ISSN 0520-3325
BODHI LEAVES. (Includes: Wheel) (Text in English) q. Rs.150($25) Buddhist Publication Society, P.O. Box 61, 54, Sangharaja Mawatha, Kandy, Sri Lanka. (back issues avail.)

294.3 100   US
BUDDHA WORLD. 1973. q. $12. American Zen College Press, 16815 Germantown Rd., Germantown, MD 20874. TEL 301-428-0665. Ed. Barbara Abrams. circ. 1,000. (back issues avail.)
Description: Zen Buddhist philosophy, theory, history, stories; events of the American Zen College.

294.3   CN   ISSN 1181-8360
BUDDHISM AT THE CROSSROADS. 1981. irreg. $20 for 3 nos. Zen Lotus Society, 86 Vaughan Rd., Toronto, Ont. M6C 2M1, Canada. TEL 416-658-0137. FAX 416-658-5855. (Subscr. to: 1214 Packard Rd., Ann Arbor, MI 48104) Ed. Linda Klevnick. adv.; bk.rev.; circ. 2,000. (back issues avail.)
Formerly: Spring Wind (ISSN 0825-799X)
Description: Information about Buddhist culture and practice. Non-sectarian, each issue devoted to a single theme.

294.3 200   US   ISSN 0882-0945
BR128.B8
BUDDHIST - CHRISTIAN STUDIES. 1981. a. $13 to individuals (foreign $15); institutions $16 (foreign $18). (Society for Buddhist-Christian Studies, East-West Religions Project) University of Hawaii Press, Journals Department, 2840 Kolowalu St., Honolulu, HI 96822. TEL 808-956-8833. FAX 808-988-6052. Ed. David W. Chappell. adv.; bk.rev.; illus.; circ. 765. (back issues avail.; reprint service avail. from UMI) **Indexed:** Rel.& Theol.Abstr., Rel.Ind.One.
—BLDSC shelfmark: 2357.252440.
Description: Focuses on Buddhism and Christianity and their historical and contemporary interrelationship.
Refereed Serial

294.3   CE
BUDDHIST PUBLICATION SOCIETY NEWSLETTER. (Text in English) 1985. 3/yr. membership. Buddhist Publication Society, P.O. Box 61, 54, Sangharaja Mawatha, Kandy, Sri Lanka. Ed. Bhikkhu Bodhi. bk.rev.; circ. 4,000. (back issues avail.)
Description: Provides instruction, news, and information of relevance to members of the society.

294.3   II
BUDDHIST STUDIES. (Text in English, Hindi and Sanskrit) 1974. a. Rs.40. University of Delhi, Department of Buddhist Studies, Delhi 110007, India. TEL 2521521-218. Ed. Kewal Krishan Mittal. bk.rev.; circ. 200.

294.37   UK   ISSN 0265-2897
BUDDHIST STUDIES REVIEW. 1976. 2/yr. £7.50 to individuals; institutions £12.50. (Institut de Recherche Bouddhique Linh-Son, FR) Russell Webb, Ed. & Pub., 31 Russell Chambers, Bury Place, London WC1A 2JX, England. (Co-sponsor: Pali Buddhist Union) adv.; bk.rev.; circ. 400.
—BLDSC shelfmark: 2357.253800.
Formerly (until 1983): Pali Buddhist Review (ISSN 0308-3756)

BUDDHIST TEXT INFORMATION. see RELIGIONS AND THEOLOGY — Abstracting, Bibliographies, Statistics

294.3   AT   ISSN 0813-3573
CHORTEN. 1981. q. Aus.$7.50. Atisha Centre Ltd., RMB 1530, Eaglehawk, Vic. 3556, Australia. TEL 054-412705. FAX 054-425301. Dir. I. & J. Green. bk.rev.; circ. 150.
Description: Features teachings of Atisha Centre for Buddhist studies, and general Buddhist information.

299.51   CH
CHUNG-KUO FO CHIAO. (Text in Chinese) m. Shih Pu Temple, 140 Nanchang St. Sec. 2, Taipei, Taiwan, Republic of China. TEL 02-321-4734. Ed.Bd. charts; illus.
Description: Chinese Buddhist magazine.

299.51   CH
CONFUCIUS & MENCIUS SOCIETY OF THE REPUBLIC OF CHINA. JOURNAL. 1961. s-a. NT.$100($4) Confucius-Mencius Society of the Republic of China, 45, Nan Hai Rd., Taipei, Taiwan, Republic of China. Ed. Tung Chin-yue. bibl.; cum.index.

294.3   US   ISSN 0097-7209
BQ7662
CRYSTAL MIRROR; annual of Tibetan Buddhism. 1971. irreg., latest vol.7. (Tibetan Nyingma Meditation Center) Dharma Publishing, 2425 Hillside Ave., Berkeley, CA 94704. TEL 510-548-5407. illus.

DARSHANA INTERNATIONAL; an international quarterly of philosophy, psychology, sociology, psychical research, religion and mysticism. see PHILOSOPHY

294.3   US   ISSN 0894-2056
DENSAL; karma triyana dharmachakra's newsletter. 1979. q. $14. Karma Triyana Dharmachadra (K.T.D.), 352 Mead Mountain Rd., Woodstock, NY 12498. TEL 914-679-5906. Ed. Naomi Schmidt. adv.; bk.rev.; tr.lit.; circ. 2,000. (back issues avail.)
Description: Teaching and news of the Karma Kagyu Lineage of Tibetan Buddhism.

294.3   US
DHARMA VOICE. 1986. q. $10. College of Buddhist Studies, 933 S. New Hampshire Ave., Los Angeles, CA 90006. TEL 213-739-1270. Ed. Karuna Dharma. bk.rev.; circ. 500. (back issues avail.)
Description: Covers all areas of all Buddhist denominations. Includes children's page, sutras, advice column, philosophy, scholarly and popular Buddhism.

299.56 294.3   JA   ISSN 0387-5970
DHARMA WORLD. 6/yr. $22. Kosei Publishing Co. Ltd., Kosei Bldg., 2-7-1 Wada, Suginami-ku, Tokyo 166, Japan. TEL 03-53852319. FAX 03-53852331. Ed. Hiroshi Andoh.
Description: For living Buddhism and interfaith dialogue.

294   TH
THE DHARMACHAKSU/DHARMA-VISION. (Text in Thai) 1894. m. Foundation of Mahamakut Rajavidyalaya, Phra Sumeru Road, Bangkok 10200, Thailand. Ed. Wasin Indasara. circ. 5,000.
Description: Covers Buddhism and related subjects.

294.3   MP
DHARMADUTA. (Text in English) 1979. q. $8. Asian Buddhist Conference for Peace, Ulan Bator 51, Mongolia. TEL 53538. Ed. B. Wangchindorj. illus.; circ. 3,000.
Formerly: Buddhists For Peace.
Description: Contains organization news, articles on history, culture, and comparative religion, all concerning Buddhism.

294.3   II
DRELOMA. 1978. 2/yr. $10. Drepung Loseling Library Society, Lama Camp 2, Tibetan Col., Uttar Kannadia 581 411, India. TEL 102. Ed. Damdul Namgyal. adv.; bk.rev.; circ. 1,000.

294 100   JA   ISSN 0012-8708
EASTERN BUDDHIST. N.S. 1965. s-a. 3000 Yen($15) Eastern Buddhist Society, Otani University, Koyama, Kita-ku, Kyoto 603, Japan. (U.S. and Canada subscr. to: Scholars Press, P.O. Box 15288, Decatur, GA 30031) Ed.Bd. bk.rev.; illus.; circ. 1,200. **Indexed:** Arts & Hum.Cit.Ind., Curr.Cont., M.L.A., Rel.Ind.One, Rel.Per.

299.51   CC
FA YIN/DHARMAGOSO BIMONTHLY. (Text in Chinese) m. $49.50. Zhongguo Fojiao Xiehui - China Buddhism Society, 25 Fuchengmennei Dajie, Beijing 100034, People's Republic of China. (Dist. in US by: China Books & Periodicals, Inc., 2929 24th St., San Francisco, CA 94110. TEL 415-282-2994) Ed. Jing Hui.

294.3   UK
FRIENDLY WAY. 1966. q. £5. Buddhapadipa Temple, 14 Calonne Rd., Wimbledon, London SW19 5HJ, England. TEL 946-1357. Ed. P.K. Lom. bk.rev.; circ. 200.
Description: Information on Vipassana, or insight meditation, and Buddhism.

294.3   US   ISSN 0738-2294
GESAR; Buddhism in the West. 1973. irreg. (approx. q.). $12. (Tibetan Nyingma Meditation Center) Dharma Publishing, 2425 Hillside Ave., Berkeley, CA 94704. TEL 510-548-5407. Ed. Sylvia Gretchen. bk.rev.; film rev.; circ. 3,000. (back issues avail.)

294.3 821   US
GREAT TAO. 1986. q. $10 membership. American Taoist and Buddhist Association, 81 Bowery St., New York, NY 10002.

294   II
GURMAT SAGAR. (Text in Punjabi) 1964. m. Rs.12. Giani Balwaut Singh Saut Sipahi, Ed. & Pub., M-90 Raghuvir Nagar, Najaf Garh Rd., New Delhi 110027, India.

294.6   II
GURU NANAK COMMEMORATIVE LECTURES. (Text in English) 1970. a. Punjabi University, Publication Bureau, Patiala 1470002, India. Ed. Taran Singh. circ. 1,100.

ICONOGRAPHY OF RELIGIONS. SECTION 12, EAST AND CENTRAL ASIA. see ART

ICONOGRAPHY OF RELIGIONS. SECTION 13, INDIAN RELIGIONS. see ART

294.3   JA
INSTITUTE FOR THE COMPREHENSIVE STUDY OF LOTUS SUTRA. JOURNAL/HOKKE BUNKA KENKYU. (Text in English or Japanese) 1975. a. 3000 Yen. Rissho University, Institute for the Comprehensive Study of Lotus Sutra - Rissho Daigaku Hokekyo Bunka Kenkyujo, 4-2-16 Osaki, Shinagawa-ku, Tokyo 141, Japan. Ed. Zuiryu Nakamura. bk.rev.; illus.

294.3   US   ISSN 0193-600X
BQ2
INTERNATIONAL ASSOCIATION OF BUDDHIST STUDIES. JOURNAL. 1978. s-a. $25 to individuals; institutions $50; students $15. International Association of Buddhist Studies, c/o L. Lancaster, University of California, Department of Oriental, Berkeley, CA 94720. TEL 415-642-3480. Ed. Gregory Schopen. adv.; bk.rev.; circ. 500. (also avail. in microform from UMI; back issues avail.; reprint service avail. from UMI)
—BLDSC shelfmark: 4802.071000.

294.3   US
INTERNATIONAL BUDDHIST MEDITATION CENTER. MONTHLY GUIDE. 1970. 12/yr. donation. International Buddhist Meditation Center, 928 S. New Hampshire Ave., Los Angeles, CA 90006. TEL 213-384-0850. FAX 213-739-1270. circ. 1,000.
Formerly: International Buddhist Center. Monthly Guide.

INTERNATIONAL YOGA GUIDE. see PHILOSOPHY

294.44   II   ISSN 0021-4043
B162.5
JAIN JOURNAL. (Text in English) 1966. q. Rs.70. Jain Bhawan, P-25 Kalakar St., Calcutta 700007, India. Ed. Ganesh Lalwani. adv.; bk.rev.; bibl.; illus.; index; circ. 1,000.
—BLDSC shelfmark: 4644.450000.

RELIGIONS AND THEOLOGY — BUDDHIST

299.56 952   JA   ISSN 0304-1042
BL2202
JAPANESE JOURNAL OF RELIGIOUS STUDIES. (Text in English) 1960. q. 3500 Yen($20) to individuals; institutions 5000 Yen ($25). Nanzan Institute for Religion and Culture, 18 Yamazato-cho, Showa-ku, Nagoya 466, Japan. TEL 052-832-3111. Ed. Paul L. Swanson. adv.; bk.rev.; illus.; stat.; index, cum.index; circ. 600. (reprint service avail. from UMI) **Indexed:** Arts & Hum.Cit.Ind., Curr.Cont., Rel.& Theol.Abstr. (1989-), Rel.Ind.One.
—BLDSC shelfmark: 4658.650000.
Formerly: Contemporary Religions in Japan (ISSN 0010-7557)
Description: Presents academic studies of Japan's religions.

299.51   CN   ISSN 0737-769X
BL1802
JOURNAL OF CHINESE RELIGIONS. 1975. a. $15 to individuals; institutions $20. Society for the Study of Chinese Religions, Religious Studies, University of Saskatchewan, Saskatoon, Sask. S7N 0W0, Canada. FAX 306-966-8839. Ed. Julian F. Pas. bk.rev.; circ. 300.
Formerly (until 1982): Society for the Study of Chinese Religions. Bulletin.

291   JA   ISSN 0019-4344
JOURNAL OF INDIAN AND BUDDHIST STUDIES/INDOGAKU BUNKKYOGAKU KENKYU. (Text in Japanese; title in English) 1952. s-a. 9000 Yen($14) Japanese Association of Indian and Buddhist Studies - Nihon Indogaku-Bukkyogakukai, c/o Dept. of Indian Philosophy and Sanskrit Philology, Faculty of Letters, University of Tokyo, 7-3-1 Hongo, Bunkyo-ku, Tokyo 113, Japan. Ed.Bd. bibl.; illus.; index; circ. 3,000.
—BLDSC shelfmark: 5005.250000.

294.3   US
JOURNAL OF NICHIREN BUDDHISM. 1979. q. membership. Institute of Nichiren Buddhism, 301 W. 45th St., New York, NY 10036. Ed. Kevin R. O'Neil. adv.; bk.rev.; circ. 500.

294.3   CN
KARUNA: A JOURNAL OF BUDDHIST MEDITATION. 1984. 3/yr. $12. Karuna Meditation Society, P.O. Box 24468, Stn. "C", Vancouver, B.C. V5T 4M5, Canada. TEL 604-872-0431. Ed. Kristin Penn. adv.; bk.rev.; circ. 2,000. (back issues avail.)
Description: Provides articles related to meditation in daily life, the relationship between spiritual practice and social change and issues related to women and Buddhism.

KONGZI YANJIU/STUDIES ON CONFUCIUS. see *PHILOSOPHY*

294   KO
KOREAN BUDDHISM. (Text in English) irreg. Lotus Lantern International Buddhist Center, 148-5 Sokyok-dong, Chongno-ku, Seoul 110 200, S. Korea. TEL 735-5347. FAX 720-7849.
Description: Book series.

268   II   ISSN 0047-3693
B5134.K754
KRISHNAMURTI FOUNDATION. BULLETIN. (Text in English) 1970. 3/yr. Rs.15($10) Krishnamurti Foundation (India), c/o Dr. Sunanda Patwardhan, 64-65 Greenways Rd., Madras 600028, India. Ed. Sunanda Patwardhan. bk.rev.; circ. 1,300.

294.3   US
KWAN UM ZEN SCHOOL NEWSLETTER. 3/yr. $9 or membership. Kwan Um School of Zen, 528 Pound Rd., Cumberland, RI 02864. TEL 401-658-1476. FAX 401-658-1188.
Description: Presents the teachings and practices of Zen Buddhism as taught by Zen Master Seung Sahn, and facilitates communication among nearly 40 Kwan Um Zen centers and groups throughout the United States.

294   KO
LOTUS LANTERN INTERNATIONAL BUDDHIST CENTER. NEWSLETTER. (Text in English) 1987. bi-m. $15. Lotus Lantern International Buddhist Center, 148-5 Sokyok-dong, Chongno-ku, Seoul 110 200, S. Korea. TEL 735-5347. FAX 720-7849.

294.344   II   ISSN 0025-0406
MAHA BODHI; international Buddhist monthly. (Text in English) 1892. m. Rs.12($4) Maha Bodhi Society of India, 4A Bankim Chatterjee St., Calcutta 73, India. Ed.Bd. adv.; bk.rev.; illus.; index; circ. 2,500.

294.3   CE
MAHINDA. (Text in English) 1976. q. Rs.8($2) (Maha Mahinda International Dhammaduta Society) Buddhist English Speaking Society, 58 Sri Vipulasena Mawatha, Colombo 10, Sri Lanka.

294.3   US
METTA. 1972. m. free. Honpa Hongwanji Mission of Hawaii, 1727 Pali Highway, Honolulu, HI 96813. TEL 808-522-9200. FAX 808-522-9209. Ed. Rev. Yoshiaki Fujitani. bk.rev.; circ. 1,275.
Description: Gives information and personal insights on Buddhism, especially Jodo Shinshu. Includes information on events concerning Buddhism in Hawaii.

294.344   UK   ISSN 0026-3214
MIDDLE WAY. 1926. q. £8.50 (foreign £12.50). Buddhist Society, 58 Eccleston Square, London SW1V 1PH, England. TEL 071-254-3519. adv.; bk.rev.; illus.; index; circ. 2,500.
—BLDSC shelfmark: 5761.407000.

294.6   US
MORNINGLAND SPIRITUAL JOURNAL. 12/yr. $7. Morningland Publications, 2600 E. Seventh St., Long Beach, CA 90804. TEL 213-433-9906. Ed. Gopi Morningstar. adv.

294.3   US   ISSN 0896-8942
MOUNTAIN RECORD. 1981. q. $10. Dharma Communications, Inc., S. Plank Rd., Box 197MR, Mt. Tremper, NY 12457. TEL 914-688-2228. FAX 914-688-7911. Ed. Bonnie Myotai Treace. adv.; bk.rev.
Description: Covers both Eastern and Western religious traditions especially reflecting the impact of Zen Buddhism on social action, ecology, art, science and health.

299.51   HK
NEI MING. (Text in Chinese) m. free. Nei Ming Magazine Society, c/o Miu Fat Buddhist Monastery, 22 Mile, Castle Peak Rd., Lam Tei, Tuen Mun, N.T., Hong Kong. (Or: Buddhist Association of the United States, 3070 Albany Crescent, Bronx, NY 10463)

294.3   US   ISSN 0897-3962
BQ2
PACIFIC WORLD. 1985. a. free. Institute of Buddhist Studies, 1900 Addison St., Berkeley, CA 94704. TEL 510-849-2383. FAX 510-849-2158. Ed. Alfred Bloom. bk.rev.; circ. 7,000.
—BLDSC shelfmark: 5007.538100.

294.3   US
PATHWAYS (WATSONVILLE). 1979. 9/yr. $10. Hanuman Fellowship, Mount Madonna Center, 445 Summit Rd., Watsonville, CA 95076-0759. TEL 408-847-0406. Ed. Pratibha Queen. adv.; bk.rev.; circ. 600.
Formerly: Gateways.
Description: Includes information on current events and perspectives on the spiritual pathways, including teachings of the BHD and others.

PHENOMENOLOGY AND BUDDHIST THOUGHT. see *PHILOSOPHY*

294   II   ISSN 0554-9906
PRAKIT JAIN INSTITUTE RESEARCH PUBLICATION SERIES. (Text in English and Hindi) 1964. irreg. price varies. Bihar Research Institute of Prakit, Jainology, and Ahimsa, Vaishali, India. Ed. G.C. Choudhary.

294.3   US
PRIMARY POINT. 3/yr. $12 or membership. Kwan Um School of Zen, 528 Pound Rd., Cumberland, RI 02864. TEL 401-658-1476. FAX 401-658-1188. adv.
Description: Presents the practice of Zen Buddhism as taught by Zen Master Seung Sahn, and presents articles on contemporary issues in the Buddhist world.

REVIEW OF INDIAN SPIRITUALISM. see *PARAPSYCHOLOGY AND OCCULTISM*

294.5   II
SAI SUDDHA. (Text in English, Tamil or Telugu) m. All India Sai Samaj, Madras 4, Tamil Nadu, India. illus.

294.3   US
SEIKYO TIMES. (Text in English) 1981. m. $50. (Soka Gakkai International - U.S.A.) World Tribune Press, 525 Wilshire Blvd., Santa Monica, CA 90401. TEL 213-451-8811. FAX 213-451-3501. Ed. George M. Williams. circ. 33,000.
Description: Publishes study material of the Soka Gakkai International and the Soka Gakkai International - USA, lay organizations of the Nichiren Shoshu sect of Buddhism.

294.3   CN
BQ2
SHAMBHALA SUN. (Text in English) 1978. bi-m. $18. Vajradhatu, 1054 Tower Road, Halifax, N.S. B3H 2Y5, Canada. TEL 902-425-4275. FAX 902-423-2750. (U.S. addr.: 1345 Spruce St., Boulder, CO 80302. TEL 303-444-0190) Ed. Melvin McLeod. adv.; bk.rev.; circ. 6,300. (tabloid format; also avail. in microfilm)
Formerly (until Apr. 1992): Vajradhatu Sun (ISSN 0882-0813)
Description: Covers Buddhism and the contemplative world, presenting features on the arts, social issues, poetry, fiction, and news events.

294   UK
SIKH COURIER INTERNATIONAL. 1960. q. £7. Sikh Cultural Society of Great Britain, 88 Mollison Way, Edgware, Middlesex HA8 5QW, England. TEL 081-952-1215. Ed. A.S. Chhatwal. adv.; bk.rev.; circ. 5,000. **Indexed:** CERDIC.
Formerly: Sikh Courier (ISSN 0037-511X)

294.5   UK   ISSN 0266-9153
SIKH MESSENGER. 1984. 4/yr. Sikh Messenger Publications, 43 Dorset Rd., Merton Park, London SW19 3EZ, England. TEL 01-540-4148.

294   II   ISSN 0037-5128
BL2017
SIKH REVIEW; journal of enlightenment. (Text in English) 1953. m. Rs.100 for members; foreign $35 (typically set in Jan.). Sikh Cultural Centre, 116 Karnani Mansion, 25A Park St., Calcutta 700016, India. TEL 29-9656. Ed. Saran Singh. adv.; bk.rev.; circ. 5,000.
—BLDSC shelfmark: 8277.700000.

294.37   JA   ISSN 0385-6321
BQ8400
SOKA GAKKAI NEWS. (Text in English) 1975. m. free. Soka Gakkai International, SGI Culture Department, 32 Shinano-machi, Shinjuku-ku, Tokyo 160, Japan. TEL 03-3353-0616. FAX 03-3353-5129. TELEX J33145-SKG. Ed. Masuo Takikawa. bk.rev.; illus.; circ. 12,300.
Description: Provides a forum for peace, culture and education.

200 950   DK   ISSN 0904-2431
BQ1
STUDIES IN CENTRAL AND EAST ASIAN RELIGIONS. a. $24. Aarhus University Press, Aarhus University, Bldg. 170, DK-8000 Aarhus C, Denmark.
Description: Covers all aspects of religious life in Tibet, Central Asia, Mongolia, China, Korea and Japan from a variety of standpoints: philosophical, linguistic, sociological.

290   GW   ISSN 0340-6792
STUDIES IN ORIENTAL RELIGIONS. (Text in English and German) 1976. irreg., vol.20, 1991. price varies. Verlag Otto Harrassowitz, Taunusstr. 14, Postfach 2929, 6200 Wiesbaden 1, Germany. TEL 0611-530-0. FAX 0611-530570. TELEX 4186135. Eds. W. Heissig, H.J. Klimkeit.

294.3   GW   ISSN 0938-3506
TIBET UND BUDDHISMUS; Vierteljahresheft des Tibetischen Zentrums e.V. Hamburg. 1987. q. DM.20($25) Tibetisches Zentrum e.V. Hamburg, Hermann-Balk-Str. 106, 2000 Hamburg 73, Germany. TEL 040-6443585. FAX 040-6443515. Ed. Carola Roloff. bk.rev.; circ. 1,200. (back issues avail.)
Formerly (until 1990): Zentrumsnachrichten.

RELIGIONS AND THEOLOGY — EASTERN ORTHODOX

299.51　　　　II　　ISSN 0254-9808
TIBETAN BULLETIN. (Text in English) 1969. bi-m. free. Central Tibetan Secretariat, Information Office, Gangchen Kyishong, Dharamsala 176215, Himachal Pradesh, India. TEL 0091-01892-2457. FAX 0091-01892-2357. TELEX 31-66140-BDL-IN. Ed. Tsering Tashi. adv.; bk.rev.; illus.; circ. 2,000. **Indexed:** HR Rep.
　Description: Covers events in Chinese occupied Tibet, activities within the Tibetan administration in exile, international human rights initiatives on behalf of Tibetans, as well as cultural and religious topics of general interest.

294　　　　JA　　ISSN 0386-426X
TOHOKAI. 1973. m. 1200 Yen($6) Tohokai, Inc., 6-2-17 Nishitenma, Kita-ku, Osaka 530, Japan. Ed. Seigo Arashiba.

294.3　800　　　US　　ISSN 1055-484X
▼**TRICYCLE**; the Buddhist review. 1991. q. $20. Buddhist Ray, Inc., 163 W. 22nd St., New York, NY 10011. TEL 212-645-1143. FAX 212-645-1493. (Subscr. to: Department TRI, Box 3000, Denville, NJ 07834) Ed. Helen Tworkov. adv.; bk.rev.; illus.; circ. 25,000.
　Description: Independent cultural review illuminated by a Buddhist point of view. Publishes interviews, art, fiction, profiles, reports on international news, and discussions of the applications of Buddhism in contemporary American society.

294.39　　　　FR　　ISSN 0049-4739
TROISIEME CIVILISATION. 1971. m. 18 F. per no. Soka Gakkai France, 64 rue du Lycee, 92 Sceaux, France. FAX 46-60-12-12. Ed. Eiichi Yamazaki. adv.; bk.rev.; charts; illus.; circ. 7,000.
　Description: Covers buddhism, peace, culture and education.

294.3　　　　US
UDUMBARA; journal of Zen practice. 1974. irreg., vol.5, no.1, 1988. $5. Minnesota Zen Meditation Center, 3343 E. Calhoun Pkwy., Minneapolis, MN 55408. TEL 612-822-5313. Ed. Flora Taylor. bk.rev.; circ. 400.

299.51　　　　CH
UNIVERSAL DOOR/P'U MEN; to promote humanistic Buddhism; to establish humanly pure land; of the public; international; of living. (Text mostly in Chinese; occasionally in English) m. NT.$800. 270 Hsin 2nd Rd., Keelung, Taiwan 20118, Republic of China. TEL 02-426-4724. FAX 02-423-8572. Ed. Yung Yun. adv.

294.3　　　　US　　ISSN 0507-6986
BQ2
VAJRA BODHI SEA. (Text in Chinese, English) 1970. m. $40. (Dharma Realm Buddhist Association) Vajra Bodhi Sea Publication Society, City of 10,000 Buddhas, Box 217, Talmage, CA 95481-0217. TEL 707-462-0939. (Subscr. to: Gold Mountain Monastery, 800 Sacramento St., San Francisco, CA 94108) Ed. Chou Kuo Li. bk.rev.; illus.; index; circ. 4,000. (back issues avail.)
　Description: Specializes in translation of classical Chinese philosophical and Buddhist texts.

294　　　　AT　　ISSN 1036-4471
VESAK. a. donations. Australian Buddhist Mission Inc., 16 Woodhouse Drive, Ambarvale, N.S.W. 2560, Australia. TEL 046-267420. Ed. Yau Yue Kai.

294.44　　　　II　　ISSN 0042-8086
VOICE OF AHINSA; magazine of the non-violence Ahinsa cult. (Text in English) 1951. m. Rs.25 (foreign $5). World Jain Mission - Virendra Prasad Jain, Jain Bhawan, Aliganj, Etah, Uttar Pradesh 207247, India. Ed. V.P. Jain. adv.; bk.rev.; illus.; circ. 750.

294.344　　　　MY　　ISSN 0042-8094
VOICE OF BUDDHISM. (Text mainly in English; occasionally in Chinese) 1963. s-a. M.$5($5) (£3). Buddhist Missionary Society, Buddhist Temple, 123 Jalan Berhala, Brickfields, 50470 Kuala Lumpur, Malaysia. TEL 3-2741141. Ed. Tan Teik Beng. adv.; bk.rev.; illus.; circ. 6,500. (back issues avail.)
　Description: Promotes the study and practice of Buddhism through articles and printed lectures. Also assists in the opening of schools and endowment funds.

200　　　　US
WASHINGTON BUDDHIST. 1969. q. $6. Buddhist Vihara Society, 5017 16th St., N.W., Washington, DC 20011. TEL 202-723-0773. Ed. Rev. M. Dhamma. bk.rev.; circ. 700.

299.5　　　　UK　　ISSN 0144-9818
WESTERN BUDDHIST. 1979. s-a. £1.90. Scientific Buddhist Association, 30 Hollingbourne Gdns., Ealing, London W13 8EN, England. Ed. Paul Ingram. adv.; bk.rev.; circ. 550.

294.3　　　　CE　　ISSN 0049-7541
WHEEL; a series of Buddhist publications. (Includes: Bodhi Leaves) (Text in English) 1958. q. Rs.150($25) Buddhist Publication Society, P.O. Box 61, 54, Sangharaja Mawatha, Kandy, Sri Lanka. Eds. Ven. Nyanaponika Maha Thera, Bhikkhu Bodhi. circ. 4,000. (back issues avail.)

294.3　　　　US
WHEEL OF DHARMA. (Text in English, Japanese) 1973. m. $5. Buddhist Churches of America, 1710 Octavia St., San Francisco, CA 94109. TEL 415-776-5600. FAX 415-771-6293. Ed. Elson B. Snow. circ. 13,600. (tabloid format)
　Description: Propagation of Buddhism and Jodo-Shinshu religions; organizational and layman education.

294.392　　　　US　　ISSN 0043-5708
WIND BELL. 1962. 2/yr. $6. (Zen Center (San Francisco)) Wheelwright Press, 300 Page St., San Francisco, CA 94102. TEL 415-863-3136. Ed.Bd. bk.rev.; circ. 3,000. (processed)

294　　　　TH　　ISSN 0084-1781
WORLD FELLOWSHIP OF BUDDHISTS. BOOK SERIES. 1965. irreg., latest 1977. price varies. World Fellowship of Buddhists, 33 Sukhumvit Rd., Bangkok 10-110, Thailand.

294.344　　　　TH　　ISSN 0043-8464
WORLD FELLOWSHIP OF BUDDHISTS. REVIEW. q. B.160($8) World Fellowship of Buddhists, 33 Sukhumvit Rd., Between Soi 1-3, Bangkok 10-110, Thailand. Ed. Siri Buddhasukh. adv.; bk.rev.; charts; illus.; circ. 2,000.

294.3　　　　US　　ISSN 0049-8165
WORLD TRIBUNE. 1964. w. $44. (Soka Gakkai International - U.S.A.) World Tribune Press, 525 Wilshire Blvd., Box 1427, Santa Monica, CA 90401. TEL 213-451-8811. FAX 213-451-3501. Ed. George M. Williams. bk.rev.; illus.; circ. 44,000.
　Description: Publishes news and study material about the Soka Gakkai International and Soka Gakkai International - USA, lay organizations of the Nichiren Shoshu sect of Buddhism.

294.3　　　　CC
XIZANG FOJIAO/TIBETAN BUDDHISM. (Text in Tibetan) s-a. Zhongguo Fojiaohui, Xizang Fenhui - Chinese Society of Buddhism, Tibetan Chapter, 11, Niangre Lu, Lhasa, Xizang (Tibet) 850000, People's Republic of China. TEL 22282. Ed. Yixi Wangqiu.

294.3　　　　GW
YANA; Zeitschrift fuer Buddhismus u. Religioese Kultur auf Buddhistischer Grundlage. 1948. bi-m. DM.15. Altbuddhistische Gemeinde e.V., Zur Ludwigshoehe 30, 8919 Utting, Germany. bk.rev.; cum.index: 1948-1967, 1968-1988; circ. 550.

294.3　　　　SI
YOUNG BUDDHIST. (Text in Chinese and English) a. Singapore Buddhist Youth Organisations Joint Celebrations Committee, 83 Silat Rd., Singapore 3, Singapore. illus.

YOUNG EAST; a quarterly on Buddhism and Japanese culture. see ORIENTAL STUDIES

299.56　　　　GW
ZEN EXTRA. 1981. a. price varies. Zen-uitgeverij Theresiahoeve, Schneifelweg 15, 5540 Gondenbrett, Germany. TEL 06551-4846. Ed. Judith Bossert. adv.

ZHEXUE YANJIU/PHILOSOPHY STUDIES. see PHILOSOPHY

294　　　　CC
ZHONGGUO DAOJIAO/CHINESE TAOISM. (Text in Chinese) q. Zhongguo Daojiao Xiehui - Chinese Taoism Association, Baiyunguan Nei, Xibianmen Wai, Beijing 100045, People's Republic of China. TEL 363531. Ed. Li Yangzheng.

ZHONGGUO ZHEXUESHI YANJIU. see PHILOSOPHY

RELIGIONS AND THEOLOGY — Eastern Orthodox

281.9　　　　US　　ISSN 1059-1001
▼**AUTOCEPHALOUS ORTHODOX CHURCHES.** 1991. irreg., no.3, 1992. price varies. Borgo Press, Box 2845, San Bernardino, CA 92406. TEL 714-884-5813. Ed. Karl Prueter.
　Description: Histories, indexes, chronologies, directories, and guides to the independent Eastern churches.

281.9　　　　CI
GLAS SVETIH RAVNOAPOSTOLA CIRILA I MATODIJA. (Text in Serbo-Croatian written in Cyrillic alphabet) 1974. irreg. $2. Srpska Pravoslavna Eparhija Zagrebacka - Serbian Orthodox Diocese of Zagreb, Prilaz JNA 4, 41000 Zagreb, Croatia. FAX 041-421-660. adv.; bk.rev.; circ. 2,000. (back issues avail.)

281.9　　　　YU　　ISSN 0017-0925
GLASNIK. 1920. m. $25. Sveti Arhijerejski Sinod Srpske Pravoslavne Crkve, 7 Jula 5, 11000 Belgrade, Yugoslavia. Ed. Dragan Milin. adv.; bk.rev.; circ. 2,600.

281.9　　　　US
HOLAS CRAKVY/VOICE OF THE CHURCH. (Text in Byelorussian, English) 1955. s-a. $6. Byelorussian Autocephalous Orthodox Church, 401 Atlantic Ave., Brooklyn, NY 11217. TEL 718-746-1971. Ed.Bd. circ. 500.
　Description: Byelorussian Christian-Orthodox theology, practices and traditions.

281.9　917.106　　CN　　ISSN 0021-1761
ISKRA. (Text in English and Russian) 1943. fortn. Can.$40 (foreign $50). Soyuz Dukhovnykh Obshchin Krista - Union of Spiritual Communities of Christ, Box 760, Grand Forks, B.C. V0H 1H0, Canada. TEL 604-442-8252. FAX 604-442-3433. Ed. D.E. Popoff. adv.; bk.rev.; circ. 1,300. (processed; also avail. in microfilm from KTO)
　Description: Focuses on the history, culture, beliefs and present day activities of the Doukhobors.

281.9　　　　US　　ISSN 0890-099X
ORTHODOX AMERICA. 1979. 8/yr. $8 (foreign $12). (Russian Orthodox Church Outside of Russia) Nikodemos Orthodox Publication Society, Box 992132, Redding, CA 96099-2132. Ed. Mary Mansur. adv.; bk.rev.; circ. 2,300. (tabloid format)
　Description: Dedicated to traditional Eastern Orthodox Christianity containing articles on spiritual life, lives of saints, teachings of the Holy Fathers, contemporary issues and more.

281.9　　　　GW　　ISSN 0933-8586
ORTHODOXES FORUM. (Text in English, French, German, Greek) 1987. 2/yr. DM.42. (Universitaet Muenchen, Institut fuer Othodoxe Theologie) E O S Verlag, 8917 St. Ottilien, Germany. TEL 08193-71261. FAX 08193-6844. adv.; bk.rev.; bibl.; illus.; circ. 600. (back issues avail.)

281.9　　　　NE　　ISSN 0032-2415
POKROF; bi-monthly review about eastern Christianity. 1954. 5/yr. fl.20. Apostolaat voor de Oosterse Kerken, Dr. Nuijensstraat 4, 5014 RL Tilburg, Netherlands. TEL 013-368985. FAX 013-439510. Ed. P. Gabriel Muenninghoff. bk.rev.; illus.; index every 4 yrs.; circ. 1,500. **Indexed:** CERDIC.

281.9　　　　US　　ISSN 0032-7018
BX460
PRAVOSLAVNAYA RUS'; tzerkovno-obshchestvennyi organ. (Monthly supplement Pravoslavnaya Zhyzn) (Text in Russian) 1928. fortn. $30 (including supplement). Holy Trinity Monastery, Box 36, Jordanville, NY 13361. TEL 315-858-0940. bk.rev.; circ. 2,500. (tabloid format) **Indexed:** CERDIC.

281.9 248   US   ISSN 0032-6992
BX460
PRAVOSLAVNAYA ZHYZN/ORTHODOX LIFE. (Text in Russian) 1950. m. $10. Holy Trinity Monastery, Box 36, Jordanville, NY 13361. TEL 315-858-0940. circ. 2,625. (tabloid format) Indexed: Amer.Bibl.Slavic & E.Eur.Stud, CERDIC.

281.9   YU   ISSN 0032-700X
PRAVOSLAVNO MISAO. (Text in Serbo-Croatian) 1959. a. 100 din.($5) Udruzenje Pravoslavnog Svestenstva SFR Jugoslavije, Glavni Savez, Francuska 31-1, Belgrade, Yugoslavia. Ed. Dusan Strbac. bk.rev.; circ. 1,600.

281.9   CS   ISSN 0079-4937
PRAVOSLAVNY THEOLOGICKY SBORNIK. (Text in Czech or Slovak) 1967. irreg., no.4, 1974. 52 Kcs.($7) Pravoslavna Cirkev Ceskoslovenska, V jame 6, 110 00 Prague 1, Czechoslovakia. adv.; circ. 3,000.

281.9   RU   ISSN 0044-4553
RUSSKAYA PRAVOSLAVNAYA TSERKOV'. MOSKOVSKAYA PATRIARKHIYA. ZHURNAL/JOURNAL OF THE MOSCOW PATRIARCHATE. (Editions in English and Russian) 1931. m. 12 Rub. Moskovskaya Patriarkhiya, Novodevichii pr., 1, Moscow G-435, Russia. Ed. Archbishop Pitirim. bibl.; illus. **Indexed:** CERDIC, Curr.Dig.Sov.Press, Rel.& Theol.Abstr. (1989-), Rel.Ind.One.

281.9   AT
SLAVIC GOSPEL NEWS. 1970. bi-m. Slavic Gospel Association, P.O. Box 396, Noble Park, Vic. 3174, Australia. TEL 03-562-3434. Eds. Brian Harper, Ron Vogt. circ. 4,000.
   Description: Discusses and promotes Christianity in the U.S.S.R. and satellite countries.

281.9   YU   ISSN 0042-4552
UDRUZENJE PRAVOSLAVNOG SVESTENSTVA S.F.R. JUGOSLAVIJE. GLAVNI SAVEZ. VESNIK. 1949. m. 500 din. Udruzenje Pravoslavnog Svestenstva S.F.R. Jugoslavije, Glavni Savez, Francuska 31-1, Belgrade, Yugoslavia. Ed. Stanislav Mirovic. adv.; bk.rev.; circ. 3,000.

281.9   AT
VOICE OF ORTHODOXY. (Text in English and Greek) 1980. m. Aus.$20. Greek Orthodox Archdiocese of Australia, 242 Cleveland St., Redfern, N.S.W 2016, Australia. TEL 02 698 5066. FAX 02-6985368. Ed. Bishop Seraphime. bk.rev.; circ. 3,500.

RELIGIONS AND THEOLOGY — Hindu

see also Oriental Studies

297 100   II
ADVENT. (Text in English) 1944. q. Rs.10($7) Sri Aurobindo Ashram Trust, Pondicherry 605002, India. Ed. M.P. Pandit. adv.; bk.rev.; illus. **Indexed:** CERDIC.

294.5   II
ANDHRA PATRIKA PANCHANGAM. a. Andhra Patrika, 14-14-21 Mallikarjuna Rao St., Gandhinagar, Vijayawada 520 003, India. TEL 61247. adv.
   Description: Almanac for Hindu families.

181.41 610   II
ARUT PERUM JOTHI. (Hindu philosophy and Siddha medicine) (Text in English and Tamil) vol.11, 1970. m. Rs.6. Arumbakkam, Madras 29, India. Ed.Bd. adv.

BHARATYA VIDYA. see *ORIENTAL STUDIES*

BHAU VISHNU ASHETAR VEDIC RESEARCH SERIES. see *LINGUISTICS*

100 200   II   ISSN 0006-8721
BL1
BRAHMAVADIN. (Text in English) 1895. q. Rs.12.50($5) Vivekananda Rock Memorial Committee, 36 Singarachari St., Triplicane, Madras 600005, India. (Co-sponsor: Swami Vivekananda Centenary Celebration) Ed. Prof. A. Narasimhamurti. **Indexed:** Phil.Ind.

BRAHMAVIDYA. see *ORIENTAL STUDIES*

294   II   ISSN 0012-4206
DIVINE LIFE. (Text in English) vol.32, 1970. m. $4.50. Divine Life Society, Sivananda Nagar, Tehri-Garhwal 249192, Uttar Pradesh, India. Ed. Swami Krishnananda. bk.rev.; illus.; index.

294   II   ISSN 0012-4265
DIVYA VANI/DIVINE VOICE. (Text in English) 1961. m. $6. Avatar Meher Baba Mission, 1-8-7 Sriramanagar, Kakinada 3, Andhra Pradesh, India. Ed. Swami Satya Prakash Meheranada. bk.rev.; bibl.; circ. 1,000.

294.5   II
ECSTASY; inter-disciplinary journal of cultural renaissance. 1984. q. Rs.150. (Nityanand Institute of Culture) Brahmavidyapeeth, 23-354 Azadnagar, Jaiprakash Rd., Andheri, Bombay 400 058, India. Ed. M.R. Sinha. adv.; bk.rev.; charts; illus.; index; circ. 3,500.

294.5   MF
HINDU. (Text in English and French) 1981. w. Hindi Publications House, 26, Av. Drapers, Quatre Bornes, Mauritius. Ed. Krishnaduth Bhorra.

200   II
HINDU REGENERATION. (Text in English) 1971. q. Rs.10. Bharat Sevashram Sangha, Hyderabad Branch, Lower Tank Bund Rd., Hyderabad 500029, India. Ed. Swami Shantananda. adv.; circ. 1,000.

294.5   US   ISSN 0896-0801
HINDUISM TODAY. 1979. m. $24. Himalayan Academy, Box 157, Hanamaulu, HI 96715. TEL 808-822-3152. FAX 808-822-4351. Ed. Rev. Palaniswami. adv.; bk.rev.; film rev.; video rev.; circ. 41,000.
   Description: International newspaper affirming the dharma and recording the modern history of nearly a billion members of a global religion.

294.592   CN   ISSN 0706-6449
JOURNAL OF STUDIES IN THE BHAGAVADGITA. 1981. irreg. Can.$10 to individuals; institutions Can.$15. McGill University, Faculty of Religious, Montreal, Que. H3A 2A7, Canada. Ed.Bd. adv.; bk.rev. circ. 100. (back issues avail.) **Indexed:** Rel.& Theol.Abstr. (1990-), Rel,Ind.One, Rel.Per.
   —BLDSC shelfmark: 5066.896600.

294.1   US   ISSN 0276-0444
B130
MANANAM PUBLICATION SERIES. (Text in English and Sanskrit) 1978. q. $18. Chinmaya Mission West, Box 129, Piercy, CA 95467. TEL 707-247-3488. FAX 707-247-3422. Ed. Margaret Leuverink. adv.; bk.rev.; charts; illus.; circ. 1,300. (back issues avail.)

294   UK
NAMA HATTA NEWSLETTER; newsletter of the Vaisnava Community. 1981. 6/yr. £8. (International Society for Krishna Consciousness) Bhaktivedanta Books Ltd., P.O. Box 324, Borehamwood, Herts. WD6 1NB, England. TEL 081-905-1244. Ed. Kripamoya Das. adv.; bk.rev.; illus.; circ. 10,000.
   Former titles: F O L K Newsletter; F O L K Magazine (ISSN 0260-938X)

294.5   II   ISSN 0027-7770
NANAK PRAKASH PATRIKA. (Text in English, Hindi, or Panjabi) 1969. m. Rs.3. Punjabi University, Patiala 4, Punjab, India. Ed. Taran Singh. bk.rev.; circ. 600. (processed)

294   II
OSHO TIMES INTERNATIONAL. (Text in English, French, German, Hindi, Italian, Japanese, Polish, Portuguese, Spanish, Tamil) 1982. s-m. Rs.600($40) Tao Publishing (Pvt.) Ltd., 50 Koregaon Park, Poona 411 001, Maharashtra, India. TEL 666206. FAX 664181. TELEX 145-7474-LOV-IN. (Dist. in N. America by: Osho Times (USA), Box 318, Mill Valley, CA 94942; Dist. in UK by: Osho Purnima Publications, Spring House, Spring Place, London NW5 3BH, England) Ed. Chaitanya Keerti. adv.; bk.rev.; circ. 20,000. (tabloid format; back issues avail.)
   Formerly (until 1988): Rajneesh Times International.

295   II   ISSN 0048-3036
PARSIANA. 1965. m. Rs.50 (foreign Rs.100). J. R. Patel, Ed. & Pub., c/o H. L. Rochat, Navsari Chambers, 39 A.K. Nayak Marg, Fort, Bombay 4000001, India. TEL 2048730. adv.; bk.rev.; illus.; circ. 4,000. **Indexed:** Ind.India.

200   II   ISSN 0031-3467
PEACE. Telegu edition: Santi. (Text in English) 1928. m. Rs.15. Santi Asram - Mission of Peace, P.O. Totapalli Hills Pin 533446, Via Shankavaram, E. Godavari Dist., Andhra Pradesh, India. TEL 44 P.C.O.
   Description: Aims to illuminate Hinduism as well as other religions through prayer, poetry, meditations and devotions. Also covers religious activities. Propagates individual and universal peace.

294.5   II
SANTI. Variant spelling: Shanti. English edition: Peace (ISSN 0031-3467) (Text in Telugu) 1924. m. Rs.15. Santi Asram - Mission of Peace, P.O. Totapalli Hills Pin 533446, Via Shankavaram, E. Godavari Dist., Andhra Pradesh, India.
   Description: Aims to illuminate Hinduism as well as other religions through prayer, poetry, meditations, and devotion. Also covers religious activities. Advocates individual and universal peace.

297   II
SHREE GURUDEV ASHRAM NEWSLETTER. (Text in English) vol.7, 1978. m. Rs.10($6) (Shree Gurudev Ashram) Gurudev Siddhapeeth, P.O. Ganeshpuri District, Thana 401206, India. Ed. R. Pratap. illus.

SHREE HARI KATHA/GOSPEL OF GOD. see *PHILOSOPHY*

294.5   II
SIDDHA VANI. (Text in English or Hindi) 1972. a. Rs.6($1.50) Siddha Yoga Dham, S-174 Panch Shila Park, New Delhi 110017, India. Ed. Janak Nanda. adv.; illus.; circ. 2,000.

294.5   II   ISSN 0037-5950
SIVAM. (Text in Bengali) 1963. m. Rs.15. Swami Bholananda Seva Mandal, 1 Mahesh Choudhury Lane, Calcutta 25, India. Eds. Sachindra Kumar Bhattacharyya, Amulya Kishore Lodh. adv.; bk.rev.; circ. 2,000. **Indexed:** Rel.& Theol.Abstr.

297 100   II
SRI AUROBINDO. ARCHIVES AND RESEARCH. 1977. biennial. Rs.40($7.50) Sri Aurobindo Ashram Trust, Pondicherry 605002, India. Ed. H. Patel.

200   II
TAPOVAN PRASAD. (Text in English) 1968. m. $15. (Tara Cultural Trust) Chinmaya Mission, 17 Harrington Rd., Madras 600031, Tamil Nadu, India. (U.S. addr.: c/o Chinmaya Mission West, Box 397, Los Altos, CA 94023) Ed. Leela Nambiar. adv.; bk.rev.; circ. 7,000.

294.5   US
VIVEKANANDA VEDANTA SOCIETY OF CHICAGO. BULLETINS. 1930. m. free. Vivekananda Vedanta Society, 5423 S. Hyde Park Blvd., Chicago, IL 60615. TEL 312-363-0027. Ed. Swami Bhashyananda. circ. 750. (looseleaf format; back issues avail.)
   Description: Gives schedule of activities at the Vivekananda Vedanta Society and quotations from the society's teachings.

RELIGIONS AND THEOLOGY — Islamic

297   US
A M S S - I I I T NEWSBULLETIN. q. free. Association of Muslim Social Scientists, Box 669, Herndon, VA 22070. TEL 703-471-1133. FAX 703-471-3922. TELEX 901153 IIIT WASH. (Co-sponsor: International Institute for Islamic Thought) Ed. Syyid Muhammad Syeed.
   Formerly: A M S S Newsbulletin.

AL-ADALAH/JUSTICE. see *LAW*

297   SL   ISSN 0044-653X
AFRICAN CRESCENT. 1955. m. Le.4. Ahmadiyya Muslim Mission, P.O. Box 353, Freetown, Sierra Leone. Ed. Maulana Khalil Mobashir. adv.; bk.rev.; circ. 1,000.

268   NR   ISSN 0065-468X
AHMADU BELLO UNIVERSITY. CENTRE OF ISLAMIC LEGAL STUDIES. JOURNAL. 1966. irreg., vol.5, 1974. Ahmadu Bello University, Centre of Islamic Legal Studies, P.M.B. 1013, Zaria, Nigeria. (Foreign orders to: Wiley & Sons Ltd., Lincoln's Inn Archway, Carey St., London W.C. 2, England)

RELIGIONS AND THEOLOGY — ISLAMIC

297   DK   ISSN 0108-7290
AKTIV ISLAM. (Text in Danish) 1959. q. DKK 30 free to libraries. Nusrat Djahan Moske, Eriksminde Alle 2, 2650 Hvidovre, Denmark. TEL 45-31-75-35-05. FAX 45-75-00-07. Ed. Mansoor Ahmad Tariq. bk.rev.; circ. 750.
 Description: Presents various different religious issues, with particular reference to the mission of the Ahmadiyya Movement in Islam.

AL-MASAQ; studia arabo-islamica mediterranea. see *HISTORY — History Of The Near East*

297   IR
AL-TAWHID; a quarterly journal of Islamic thought and culture. (Text in English) 1983. q. £15. Sazman-e Tablighat-e Islami, P.O. Box 14155-4843, Tehran, Islamic Republic of Iran. (Dist. overseas by: Orient Distribution Services, P.O. Box 719, London SE26 6PS, England) Indexed: Rel.& Theol.Abstr. (1990-).
 Description: Covers Islamic history, economics, sociology, political science and comparative religion.

297   IO
AMANAH. fortn. Jalan Garuda 69, Kemayoran, Jakarta, Indonesia. TEL 021-410254. Ed. Maskun Iskandar. circ. 180,000.

AMERICAN JOURNAL OF ISLAMIC SOCIAL SCIENCES. see *SOCIAL SCIENCES: COMPREHENSIVE WORKS*

ANNALES ISLAMOLOGIQUES. see *ORIENTAL STUDIES*

297   MK
AL-AQIDAH. (Text in Arabic) w. P.O. Box 4001, Ruwi, Muscat, Sultanate of Oman. TEL 701000. TELEX 3399. Ed. Said as-Samhan al-Kathiri. illus.; circ. 5,000.

297   NE
ASFAR. 1977. irreg., vol.3, 1989. price varies. (Rijksuniversiteit te Leiden, Documentatiebureau Islam-Christendom) E.J. Brill, P.O. Box 9000, 2300 PA Leiden, Netherlands. TEL 071-312624. FAX 071-317532. TELEX 39296 BRILL NL. (In N. America: E.J. Brill, 24 Hudson St., Kinderhook, NY 12106. TEL 800-962-4406) Ed. P. van Koningsveld.

956 297   GW   ISSN 0170-3102
BIBLIOTHECA ISLAMICA. (Text in English and German) irreg., vol.33, 1990. price varies. (Deutsche Morgenlaendische Gesellschaft) Franz Steiner Verlag Wiesbaden GmbH, Birkenwaldstr. 44, Postfach 101526, 7000 Stuttgart 1, Germany. TEL 0711-2582-0. FAX 0711-2582290. TELEX 723636-DAZD. Ed.Bd.

297 956   UA   ISSN 0259-7373
BP1
BULLETIN CRITIQUE DES ANNALES ISLAMOLOGIQUES. 1986. a. Institut Francais d'Archeologie Orientale du Caire, P.O. Box 11562 Kasr el-Aini, 37 Sharia Shaikh Aly Youssef, Mounira, Cairo, Egypt. circ. 800.
 Description: Annual review of books recently published on Islamology throughout the world.

C I B E D O - BEITRAEGE ZUM GESPRAECH ZWISCHEN CHRISTEN UND MUSLIMEN. see *RELIGIONS AND THEOLOGY*

297.65   CN   ISSN 0707-2945
CANADIAN MUSLIM. (Text in Arabic and English) 1977. q. free. Ottawa Muslim Association, P.O. Box 2952, Sta. D, Ottawa, Ont. 51P 5W9, Canada. TEL 613-725-0004. Ed. Saeed Bokhari. adv.; bk.rev.; circ. 2,000 (controlled).

297   IT
COMUNITA ISLAMICA; Jihad periodico Islamico. (Text in French, German, Italian) 1980; N.S. 1990, Dec. bi-m. L.30000($10) (foreign L.50000). Edizioni Arktos, Via Gardezzana 57, 10022 Carmagnola, Italy. Ed. Giovanni Oggero. adv.; bk.rev.
 Formerly: Jihad.

297   CN   ISSN 0705-3754
DS35.3
CRESCENT INTERNATIONAL. 1972. s-m. $40 to individuals; institutions $60. Crescent Pak Inc., 300 Steelcase Rd. W., Unit 8, Markham, Ont. L3R 2W2, Canada. FAX 416-474-9293. Ed. Zafar Bangash. adv.; bk.rev.; circ. 12,000. (tabloid format; also avail. in microfilm; back issues avail.)
 Description: Covers the Islamic movements worldwide.

DAILY JANG LONDON. see *ETHNIC INTERESTS*

DANSALAN QUARTERLY. see *SOCIOLOGY*

297   LY
AL-DA'WAH AL-ISLAMIYYAH. (Text in Arabic, English, French) 1980. w. World Islamic Call Society, P.O. Box 2682, Tripoli, Libya. TEL 31021. TELEX 20407.

297   PK   ISSN 0002-399X
BP1
AL-DIRASAT AL-ISLAMIYYAH. (Text in Arabic) 1965. q. Rs.75($20) Islamic Research Institute, International Islamic University, P.O. Box 1035, Islamabad, Pakistan. TEL 051-850751. TELEX 54068 IIU PK. Ed. Muhammad Al-Ghazali. adv.; bk.rev.; index; circ. 3,000. (back issues avail.)
 Description: Covers Islamic law, history, political theory and philosphy as well as other topics.

297 355   TS
DIR'U AL-ISLAM. (Text in Arabic) 1988. q. exchange basis. General Command for the Armed Forces, Administration for Spiritual Instruction, P.O. Box 907, Abu Dhabi, United Arab Emirates. TEL 447999. Ed. Ahmed Khalil. circ. 1,000.
 Description: Covers Islamic topics, with an emphasis on fostering morale and Islamic customs and culture among members of the Armed Forces.

297   TS
AL-DIYA'. (Text in Arabic; supplements in English, Farsi, Urdu) 1978. q. Da'irat al-Awqaf wal-Shu'un al-Islamiyyah - Department of Endowments and Islamic Affairs, P.O. Box 3135, Dubai, United Arabi Emirates. TEL 695294. Ed. Isa Abdullah al-Mani' al-Hamadi. circ. 10,000.
 Description: Covers topics related to the Qur'an, Hadith, and Sunna, as well as Islamic jurisprudence, literature, medicine, and interviews.

297   IR
ECHO OF ISLAM. (Text in English) m. Foundation of Islamic Thought, P.O. Box 14155-3987, Tehran, Iran.
 Description: Contains current news of interest to the Muslim world. Covers political developments, Islamic uprisings, general news and views.

297   LE
FAWAZIR. irreg. £L1000 per no. Dar al-Risalah al-Islamiyyah, P.O. Box 155063, 13-6173 Beirut, Lebanon. TEL 868661. FAX 831253. TELEX 207339 LE. Ed. Faysal al-Sammak. adv.; circ. 10,000.
 Description: Covers Islamic issues from around the world.

297   PK   ISSN 0430-4055
FIKR-O-NAZAR. (Text in Urdu) 1964. q. Rs.35($15) Islamic Research Institute, International Islamic University, P.O. Box 1035, Islamabad, Pakistan. TEL 051-850751. TELEX 54068 IIU PK. Ed. Sahibzada Sajid-ur-Rehman. adv.; bk.rev.; index. (back issues avail.)
 Description: Covers Islamic law, history philosophy as well as other topics.

FREIBURGER ISLAMSTUDIEN. see *ORIENTAL STUDIES*

297   II
AL FURQAN. (Text in Urdu) 1933. m. Rs.25. 31 Naya Gaon West, Lucknow 226018, India.

297   SU
HAJJ. (Text in Arabic, English) 1947. m. Ministry of Pilgrimage Affairs and Awqaf, Sharia Omar bin al-Khatab, Riyadh 11183, Saudi Arabia. TEL 01-402-2200. TELEX 401603. Ed. Muhammad Said al-Amondi.

297   PK
HAMDARD FOUNDATION. REPORT. 1980. biennial. free. Hamdard Foundation, Nazimabad No. 3, Karachi 8, Pakistan. circ. 2,000.

297   PK   ISSN 0250-7196
BP1
HAMDARD ISLAMICUS. (Text in English) 1978. q. Rs.120($20) Hamdard Foundation, Nazimabad No. 3, Karachi 8, Pakistan. Ed. Hakim Mohammed Said. bk.rev.; circ. 2,000. Indexed: Abstr.Musl.Rel., Amer.Hist.& Life, Hist.Abstr., Mid.East: Abstr.& Ind., Rel.& Theol.Abstr. (1990-), Rel.Ind.One.
 —BLDSC shelfmark: 4241.441500.

AL-HAQQ - SHARI'AH WA QANUN. see *LAW — Judicial Systems*

291 297   II   ISSN 0970-4698
BP1
HENRY MARTYN INSTITUTE OF ISLAMIC STUDIES. BULLETIN. 1930-1986; resumed in Jan. 1991. q. $20 to individuals; institutions $25. Henry Martyn Institute of Islamic Studies, c/o Diane D'Souza, P.O. Box 153, Hyderabad, A.P. 500 001, India. Ed. Andreas D'Souza. bk.rev.; index; circ. 400. Indexed: Abstr.Musl.Rel., Rel.Ind.One.
 Supersedes: Al-Basheer; Formerly: Christian Institutes of Islamic Studies Bulletin (ISSN 0009-5397)
 Description: Aims to promote inter-faith understanding with a special focus on Islam.

297   BA
AL-HIDAYAH. (Text in Arabic) 1978. m. Ministry of Justice and Islamic Affairs, P.O. Box 450, Diplomatic Area, Manama, Bahrain. TEL 531333. Ed. Abd ar-Rahman bin Muhammad Rashid al-Khalifa.

297.7   UK   ISSN 0952-6145
AL-HILAL AL-DAWLI. (Text in Arabic) 1988. 24/yr. £20. 6 Engsleigh St., London WC1H ODS, England. TEL 01-388-2581.
 Description: Covers the Islamic movement: global affairs, reviews and commentaries from a Muslim perspective.

HOLY LAND; illustrated quarterly of the Franciscan custody of the holy land. see *RELIGIONS AND THEOLOGY — Roman Catholic*

297   CM
AL HOUDA; islamic cultural review. q. P.O. Box 1638, Yaounde, Cameroon. Ed. Ndam Njoya Adamou.

297.38   JO
HUDA AL-ISLAM. (Text in Arabic) 1956. m. Ministry of Awqaf and Islamic Affairs, P.O. Box 659, Amman, Jordan. TEL 666141. TELEX 21559. Ed. Ahmad Muhammad Hulayyel.

297   US
I S N A MATTERS; a movement for service to Islam and Muslims. irreg. Islamic Society of North America, P.O. Box 38, Plainfield, IN 46168. TEL 317-839-8157. FAX 317-839-1840.

ICONOGRAPHY OF RELIGIONS. SECTION 22, ISLAM. see *ART*

297   US
INDIAN MUSLIM RELIEF COMMITTEE. ANNUAL REPORT. a. Islamic Society of North America, Indian Muslim Relief Committee, Box 0622, Freemont, CA 94537-0622.

297   US
INVITATION. 1984. q. free. Islamic Information Center of America, Box 4052, Des Plaines, IL 60016. TEL 708-541-8184. FAX 708-824-8436. Ed. Musa Qutub. adv.; bk.rev.; circ. 8,000.

AL-IQTISAD AL-ISLAMI/ISLAMIC ECONOMY. see *BUSINESS AND ECONOMICS — Economic Situation And Conditions*

297   TS
ISHRAQAT JEEL. (Text in Arabic) 1984. a. Madrasat al-Qadisiyyah al-I'dadiyyah al-Thanawiyyah lil-Banat, Jama'at al-Tarbiyah al-Islamiyyah, P.O. Box 5246, Abu Dhabi, United Arab Emirates. TEL 477606. circ. 500.
 Description: Covers topics relating to Islamic education for girls.

297   NE   ISSN 0021-180X
AL-ISLAAM. 1947. bi-m. fl.38. Ahmadiyya Moslim Missie Holland - Ahmadiyya Moslim Djamaat Nederland - Ahmadiyya Muslim Mission Holland, Oostduinlaan 79, 2596 JJ The Hague, Netherlands. FAX 070-3242881. Ed.Bd. adv.; bk.rev.; circ. 300. (Also avail. on floppy disk)

297   TS
AL-ISLAH/REFORM. (Text in Arabic) 1978. m. Jam'iyat al-Islah wal-Tawjih al-Ijtima'i - Society of Social Reform and Guidance, P.O. Box 4663, Dubai. TEL 665962. FAX 662071. Ed. Muhammed bin Rahma al-Aamiri. circ. 15,000.
 Description: Presents an Islamic viewpoint on topics of interest to Muslims, icluding social, political, and cultural issues.

RELIGIONS AND THEOLOGY — ISLAMIC

DER ISLAM; Zeitschrift fuer Geschichte und Kultur des Islamischen Orients. see ORIENTAL STUDIES

297   RE   ISSN 0151-7163
BP1
AL ISLAM. (Text in French) 1975. m. 150 F. Centre Islamique de la Reunion, 31 rue M.A. Leblond, B.P. 437, 97459 Saint-Pierre, Reunion. TEL 25-19-65. Ed. A. Saeed Ingar. circ. 1,200. **Indexed:** So.Pac.Per.Ind.

297   IT
ISLAM; storia e civilta. 1981. q. L.15000. Accademia dell Cultura Islamica, Unione Islamica in Occidente, Corso Trieste, 90, 00198 Rome, Italy. Ed. Salvatore Bono.

297   PK
AL-ISLAM. (Text in Urdu) 1973. w. Rs.400. c/o Jamiat Ahl-e-Hadith, 106 Ravi Rd., Lahore, Pakistan. FAX 042-54072. TELEX 46426 KARAM PK. Ed. Bashir Ansari. adv.; bk.rev.; circ. 4,000 (controlled).

297   II   ISSN 0021-1826
ISLAM AND THE MODERN AGE. (Text in English) 1970. q. $20. Zakir Husain Institute of Islamic Studies, Jamia Nagar, New Delhi 110025, India. Ed. Z.H. Faruqi. adv.; bk.rev.; circ. 1,000. **Indexed:** Abstr.Musl.Rel., Ind.Islam.

297   BG   ISSN 0379-4032
BP1
ISLAM AND THE MODERN WORLD. (Text in English) 1977. q. Tk.40($8) Council for Islamic and Christian Studies and Research, G.P.O. Box 242, 16-A Larmini St., Wari, Dhaka 3, Bangladesh. Ed. A.B.M. Shamsuddoulah. bk.rev.; bibl.; circ. 1,250.

297 059.9435   IR
ISLAM CAGRISI. (Text in Turkish) no.69, 1990. m. Islam Dusunceler Merkezi, P.O. Box 1415-3899, Teheran, Iran.

ISLAM ET SOCIETES AU SUD DU SAHARA. see HISTORY — History Of Africa

ISLAM INTERNATIONAL. see POLITICAL SCIENCE

297   GW
ISLAM NACHRICHTEN. 1927. w. DM.260. Zentralinstitut Islam - Archiv - Deutschland, Postfach 1528, 4770 Soest, Germany. TEL 02921-60702. FAX 02921-65417. Ed. M. Salim Abdullah. circ. 100.
    Description: News of Islam and Muslims in Europe.

297   MR   ISSN 0851-1128
ISLAM TODAY/ISLAM AUJOURD'HUI. (Text in Arabic, English, French) 1983. 2/yr. $6. P.O. Box 755, Rabat, Morocco. FAX 002127. TELEX 31845M. Ed. Abdulaziz Bin Othman Altwaijri. circ. 15,000.

297 059.943   IR
▼**ISLAMI BAYRLAYK.** (Text in Azerbaijani) 1990. w. Hawzah-i Hunari Sazman-i Tablighat-i Islami, 213 Summaiyah St., P.O. Box 1677-15815, Teheran, Iran.

ISLAMIC CULTURE. see ORIENTAL STUDIES

297   US   ISSN 8756-2367
BP1
ISLAMIC HORIZONS; I S N A News and Perspectives. 1963. m. $20 to students; individuals $24. Islamic Society of North America, Box 38, Plainfield, IN 46168. TEL 317-839-8157. FAX 317-839-1840. Ed. Amr A. Halim. adv.; bk.rev.; stat.; circ. 30,000.

297 181.07   NE   ISSN 0169-8729
ISLAMIC PHILOSOPHY, THEOLOGY AND SCIENCE; texts and studies. 1986. irreg., vol.11, 1992. price varies. E.J. Brill, P.O. Box 9000, 2300 PA Leiden, Netherlands. TEL 071-312624. FAX 071-317532. TELEX 39296 BRILL NL. (In N. America: E.J. Brill, 24 Hudson St., Kinderhook, NY 12106. TEL 800-962-4406) Eds. H. Daiber, D. Pingree.
—BLDSC shelfmark: 4583.025950.

ISLAMIC QUARTERLY; a review of Islamic Culture. see ORIENTAL STUDIES

297   PK   ISSN 0578-8072
ISLAMIC STUDIES. (Text in English) 1962. q. Rs.75($20) Islamic Research Institute, International Islamic University, P.O. Box 1035, Islamabad, Pakistan. TEL 051-850751. TELEX 54068 IIU PK. Ed. Zafar Ishaq Ansari. adv.; bk.rev.; index; circ. 3,000. (back issues avail.) **Indexed:** Abstr.Musl.Rel.
    Description: Covers Islamic law, history, political theory and philosophy as well as other topics.

297   CN   ISSN 0266-6421
ISSUES IN THE ISLAMIC MOVEMENT. 1982. a. $17.95. Open Press (Holdings) Ltd., 300 Steelcase Road West, Unit 8, Markham, Ont. L3R 2W2, Canada. FAX 416-474-9293. Ed. Kalim Siddiqui. circ. 10,000.
—BLDSC shelfmark: 4584.301000.
    Description: Anthology of articles on Islamic issues.

297   UA
JAMI'AT AL-AZHAR. KULLIYYAT USUL AL-DIN WAL-DA'WAH AL-ISLAMIYYAH BI-TANTA. MAJALLAH/AL-AZHAR UNIVERSITY. FACULTY OF ISLAMIC THEOLOGY IN TANTA. JOURNAL. (Text in Arabic) 1987. irreg. Jami'at al-Azhar, Kulliyyat Usul al-Din wal-Da'wah al-Islamiyyah bi-Tanta - Al-Azhar University, Faculty of Islamic Theology in Tanta, Tanta, Egypt.

297   SU
JAMI'AT AL-IMAM MUHAMMAD IBN SA'UD AL-ISLAMIYYAH. MARKAZ AL-BUHUTH. MAJALLAH/ISLAMIC UNIVERSITY OF IMAM MUHAMMAD IBN SAUD. RESEARCH CENTER. JOURNAL. (Text in Arabic, English) no.3, 1984. q. Jami'at al-Imam Muhammad Ibn Sa'ud al-Islamiyyah, Markaz al-Buhuth - Islamic University of Imam Muhammad Ibn Saud, Research Center, P.O. Box 5701, Riyadh, Saudi Arabia. TEL 4054448. FAX 4020886. TELEX 401166.

297   IS   ISSN 0334-4118
DS36
JERUSALEM STUDIES IN ARABIC AND ISLAM. irreg. Magnes Press, Hebrew University, P.O. Box 7695, Jerusalem 91 076, Israel. Ed. S. Pines.
—BLDSC shelfmark: 4667.516900.

297 572   UK   ISSN 0955-2340
DS35.3
▼**JOURNAL OF ISLAMIC STUDIES.** 1990. s-a. $88. (Oxford Centre for Islamic Studies) Oxford University Press, Oxford Journals, Pinkhill House, Southfield Road, Eynsham, Oxford OX8 1JJ, England. TEL 0865-882283. FAX 0865-882890. TELEX 837330 OXPRES G. (US addr.: 200 Madison Ave., New York, NY 10016. TEL 212-679-7300) Ed. Farham Ahmad Nizami. adv.; bk.rev.; circ. 550.
—BLDSC shelfmark: 5008.550000.
    Description: Dedicated to the multi-disciplinary study of any aspect of Islam and the Islamic.

JOURNAL OF SEMITIC STUDIES. see RELIGIONS AND THEOLOGY — Judaic

JUSUR; the U C L A journal of Middle Eastern studies. see HISTORY — History Of The Near East

297   IR
KAYHAN ANDISHE/WORLD OF RELIGION. (Text in Farsi) 1985. 6/yr. Kayhan Publications, Ferdowsi Ave., P.O. Box 11365-9631, Teheran, Iran. TEL 021-310251. TELEX 212467.

297   SU
KING FAISAL CENTER FOR RESEARCH AND ISLAMIC STUDIES. NEWSLETTER. irreg. King Faisal Center for Research and Islamic Studies, P.O. Box 5149, Riyadh 11543, Saudi Arabia. TEL 4652255. TELEX 205470.

297   UK   ISSN 0268-8352
LINK INTERNATIONAL: EDUCATIONAL NEWSLETTER. 1986. 6/yr. £5 to individuals; institutions £7. Islamic Educational Publications, Muslim Community Studies, Post Box 139, Leicester LE2 2YH, England. TEL 0533-706714.

297   UA
AL-LIWA' AL-ISLAMI/ISLAMIC STANDARD. (Text in Arabic) 1982. w. 11 Sharia Sharif Pasha, Cairo, Egypt. Ed. Muhammad Ali Sheta. circ. 30,000.
    Description: Covers topics relating to Islamic fundamentalism.

M A A S JOURNAL OF ISLAMIC SCIENCE. (Muslim Association for the Advancement of Science) see ORIENTAL STUDIES

297   IR
MAHJUBAH. 1981. m. Rs.2000($18) Islamic Thought Foundation, P.O. Box 14155-3987, Tehran, Iran. circ. 30,000. (back issues avail.)
    Description: For Muslim women.

297   UA
AL-MAJALLAH AL-'ILMIYYAH LI-KULLIYYAT USUL AL-DIN WAL-DA'WAH LIL-ZAGAZIG. (Text in Arabic) 1987. a? Al-Azhar University, Faculty of Islamic Theology in Zagazig, Zagazig, Egypt.

297 378   UA
MAJALLAT AL-AZHAR. 1931. m. Al-Azhar University, Council of Islamic Research, Idarat al-Azhar, Sharia Al-Azhar, Cairo, Egypt. Ed. Muhammad Farid Wagdi. bk.rev.
    Description: Covers Islamic issues and concerns.

MAJALLAT AL-SHARI'AH WAL-QANUN. see LAW

297   TS
MANAAR AL-ISLAM. 1979. m. Ministry of Justice, Islamic Affairs and Endowments, P.O. Box 2922, Abu Dhabi, United Arab Emirates. TEL 212300. TELEX 22589 ISLAMI EM. Ed. Ali Muhammad al-Ajla. circ. 2,500.
    Description: Discusses Islamic guidance, Quranic studies, Sunna, Islamic history and literature, family issues, and news of the Islamic world.

297   KE
MAPENZI YA MUNGU. (Text in Swahili) 1943. m. K.25. East African Ahmadiyya Muslim Mission, PO Box 40554, Nairobi, Kenya. Ed. Jamil R. Rafiq. adv.; bk.rev.; circ. 4,000.

297.7   MF
MESSAGE DE L'AHMADIYYAT. 1965. m. $24. Ahmadiyya Muslim Association, Edward VII St., Rose Hill, Mauritius. Ed. Zafrullah Domun. bk.rev.; circ. 2,000.
    Formerly: Message.

297   PK
MINARET MONTHLY INTERNATIONAL. (Text in English) 1964. m. Rs.12 per no. (Europe, Africa, Asia $11/yr.; elsewhere $13/yr.) World Federation of Islamic Missions, Islamic Centre, Abdul Aleem Siddiqi Rd., Block B, N. Nazimabad, Karachi 74700, Pakistan. TEL 6644156. Ed. Muhammed Ja'fer. adv.; bk.rev.; circ. 1,200. **Indexed:** Abstr.Musl.Rel.
    Formerly (until Sep. 1976): Minaret (ISSN 0026-4415)
    Description: Explores mission work in the country.

297   IR
AL-MISBAH. 1984. q. Astan-i Quds Islamic Research Foundation, P.O. Box 366-91735, Meshed, Iran. TEL 63031.

297 955   IR
MISHKAT. (Text in Persian) 1984. q. Astan-i Quds Islamic Research Foundation, P.O. Box 366-91735, Meshed, Iran. TEL 63031.
    Description: Publishes papers in Islamic studies.

297   GW   ISSN 0930-7338
BP1
MOSLEMISCHE REVUE. 1924. q. DM.35. Zentralinstitut Islam-Archiv-Deutschland, Postfach 1528, 4770 Soest, Germany. TEL 02921-60702. FAX 02921-6541. Ed. M. Salim Abdullah. circ. 900.
    Description: Muslim theology, muslims and their life in Germany, dialogue between Christians and Moslem, news of the Islamic world.

297   UK   ISSN 0266-2183
MUHYIDDIN IBN ARABI SOCIETY. JOURNAL. 1982. s-a. £10.50 (effective June 1991). Muhyiddin Ibn Arabi Society, 23 Oakthorpe Road, Oxford OX2 7BD, England. TEL 0865-511963. bk.rev.
—BLDSC shelfmark: 4828.440000.
    Description: Translations and studies of works of Ibn Arabi.

297   SA   ISSN 0027-4860
MUSLIM AFRICA. 1969. m. $10. Islamic Missionary Society, P.O. Box 54125, Vrededorp 2141, Transvaal, South Africa. FAX 11-834-8341. Ed.Bd. adv.; circ. 5,000.
    Description: Highlights mission work in the country.

RELIGIONS AND THEOLOGY — ISLAMIC

297   SA   ISSN 0027-4887
MUSLIM DIGEST; international magazine of Muslim affairs. 1950. bi-m. $15. Makki Publications, 100 Brickfield Rd., Durban, South Africa. adv.; illus.

297.7   UK   ISSN 0267-615X
MUSLIM EDUCATIONAL QUARTERLY. 1983. 4/yr. £13.50 to individuals; institutions £19.50. Islamic Academy, 23 Metcalfe Rd., Cambridge CB4 2DB, England. TEL 0223-350976. FAX 0223-350976. adv.; bk.rev.; circ. 1,200.
—BLDSC shelfmark: 5991.137100.
    Description: Provides a forum for the exchange of ideas on education and related issues among Muslim as well as non-Muslim scholars and educationalists.

297   UK
MUSLIM HERALD. 12/yr. £10. London Mosque, 16 Gressenhall Rd., London SW18 5QL, England. TEL 01-870-8517.
    Description: Comparative study of religions. Examines the role of Islam in the world.

297   US
MUSLIM JOURNAL.* w. $30 (foreign $45). 910 W. Van Buren, Ste. 100, Chicago, IL 60607. TEL 312-243-7600.

297   II   ISSN 0027-4895
MUSLIM REVIEW. (Text in English) 1923. q. Rs.5($0.75) Madrasat-Ul-Waizeen, 16 Canning St., Lucknow, India. Ed. Shaheed Safipuri. bk.rev.; circ. 500.

297   US
MUSLIM STAR. 1953. m. $10. Federation of Islamic Associations in the United States and Canada, 25341 Five Mile Rd., Redford Township, MI 48239. TEL 313-535-0014. Ed. Nihad Hamed. adv.; bk.rev.; illus.; circ. 10,000.

297   US
MUSLIM SUNRISE. q. American Fazi Mosque, 2141 Leroy Pl., N.W., Washington, DC 20008. TEL 202-232-3737. Ed. B.M. Mirza.
    Description: Provides a platform for public opinion on current problems confronting humanity and their solution. Features articles written by scholars discussing as well as topics relating to other religions.

297   US   ISSN 0027-4909
MUSLIM WORLD; a journal devoted to the study of Islam and of Christian-Muslim relationships past and present. 1911. q. $20 individuals; institutions $30. (Duncan Black Macdonald Center) Hartford Seminary, 77 Sherman St., Hartford, CT 06105. TEL 203-232-4451. FAX 203-236-8570. Ed. Ernest Hamilton. adv.; bk.rev.; index, cum.index: vols.1-25 (1911-1935), vols.26-50 (1936-1960); circ. 1,200. (also avail. in microform from UMI; back issues avail.; reprint service avail. from UMI) **Indexed:** Amer.Bibl.Slavic & E.Eur.Stud, Amer.Hist.& Life, Curr.Cont., E.I., Hist.Abstr., Hum.Ind., M.L.A., Mid.East: Abstr.& Ind., Rel.& Theol.Abstr., Rel.Ind.One, Rel.Per.
—BLDSC shelfmark: 5991.150000.
    Formerly (until 1948): Moslem World (ISSN 0362-4641)

297.7   UK   ISSN 0260-3063
DS35.3
MUSLIM WORLD BOOK REVIEW. (Supplement avail.: Index of Islamic Literature) 1980. q. £17($44) to individuals; institutions £24($59). Islamic Foundation, Markfield Dawah Centre, Ratby Lane, Markfield, Leicester LE6 0RN, England. TEL 0530-244944. FAX 0530-244946. TELEX 341539-ISLAMF-G. (Co-sponsor: International Institute of Islamic Thought, US) Ed. M.M. Ahsan. adv.; bibl.; index; circ. 1,500. (back issues avail.)
—BLDSC shelfmark: 5991.160000.
    Description: Lists and reviews books on Islam, comparative religion, and the Muslim world, and publishes critical analyses on topics of interest to scholars of religion and Islamic studies.

297   SU
MUSLIM WORLD LEAGUE. JOURNAL/RABITAT AL-ALAM AL-ISLAMI. MAJALLAH. (Text in Arabic, English) 1973. m. $12 srl.30 to individuals; institutions Srl.100. Muslim World League, Press and Publications Department - Rabitat al-Alam al-Islami, P.O. Box 538, Mecca, Saudi Arabia. TEL 2-543-6530. FAX 2-543-1488. TELEX 60009. Eds. Abdullah A. al-Dhari, Hasan Mutahar. index; circ. 30,000.

297   UK
AL-MUSLIMUN. (Text in Arabic) w. Saudi Research and Marketing Co., Arab Press House, 182-184 High Holborn, London WC1V 7AP, England. TEL 071-831-8181. FAX 071-831-2310. TELEX 889272. (And: P.O. Box 4556, Jeddah 21412, Saudi Arabia. TEL 02-669-1888) adv.

297 070.5   UK
NEW BOOKS QUARTERLY ON ISLAM & THE MUSLIM WORLD. 1982. q. £4. Islamic Council of Europe, 16 Grosvenor Crescent, London S.W.1., England. bk.rev.

297   US
NEW TREND; independent forum for the oppressed Muslim masses. (Text in English, Urdu) 1977. m. $7.50. American Society for Education and Religion, Inc., Box 356, Kingsville, MD 21087. TEL 301-435-4046. Ed. K. Siddique. bk.rev.; film rev.; circ. 5,000. (tabloid format)
    Description: Islamic perspective on change and conflict in the world.

297   UA
NIDA AL-ISLAM. m. £E60 per no. Dar al-Fikr Lil-Nashr Wa-al-Ilam, 58 Shari 26 Yuliyu, Cairo, Egypt.

297   LE
NOOR AL-ISLAM; thiqafiyyah islamiyyah - islamic cultural magazine. (Text in Arabic, English) 1988. bi-m. $40. Imam Hussain Charitable - Cultural Foundation - Muassasat al-Imam al-Husain al-Khairiyya al-Thiqafiyya, P.O. Box 25156, Beirut, Lebanon. TEL 392317. TELEX 40512 KAMEC. Ed. Husain Al-Hakim. adv.; bk.rev.; illus.; circ. 10,000.
    Description: Discusses religious and cultural issues of interest to Muslims of all nations.

297   US
OUR ISLAM. 1980. q. $12 for 12 nos. (African Islamic Mission Inc.) A.I.M. Publications, 1390 Bedford Ave., Brooklyn, NY 11216. FAX 212-789-0530. Ed. Alhaji Obaba Muhammad. adv.; bk.rev.; circ. 12,000. (tabloid format; back issues avail.)

AL-QISTAS/SCALES. see *LAW*

QUELLEN ZUR GESCHICHTE DES ISLAMISCHEN AEGYPTENS. see *HISTORY — History Of Africa*

297   PK
QURANULHUDA. (Text in English and Urdu) 1976. m. Rs.5($34) S.M.S.A. Hayat, P.O. Box 8677, 28 Qasr-e-Batool, Shahrah-e-Iraq, Karachi 74400, Pakistan. Ed. Syed Zakir Aijaz. adv.; bk.rev.; circ. 31,000.
    Description: Presents texts from the Qur'an with exhaustive commentary.

291   PK   ISSN 0034-6721
REVIEW OF RELIGIONS. (Text in English) 1902. m. £12($20) Tehrik-i-Jadid, Rabwah, Pakistan. Ed. B.A. Rafiq. adv.; bk.rev.; index, cum.index; circ. 7,300. (also avail. in microform from UMI; reprint service avail. from UMI)
    Description: Teachings of Islam, the discussion of Islamic affairs and religion in general.

REVIEW OF RELIGIONS. see *RELIGIONS AND THEOLOGY*

REVUE DES ETUDES ISLAMIQUES. see *ORIENTAL STUDIES*

297   TS
AL-RISALAH. (Text in Arabic) 1987. m. exchange basis. Islamic Information Office, Publications Section, P.O. Box 1731, Sharjah, United Arab Emirates. TEL 372544. circ. 1,000.
    Description: Covers topics of interest to Muslims.

297   LE
AL-RISALAH AL ISLAMIAH. (Text in Arabic, English, French) 1977. m. $100. Nahhas Establishment, P.O. Box 155063-13-1672, Beirut, Lebanon. TEL 868661. TELEX 29155-29156 LE. Ed. Faysal Al Sammak. adv.
    Description: Islamic magazine dealing with the problems of Moslems around the world.

297   LE
AL-RISALAH AL-ISLAMIYYAH. 1977. irreg. £L1000 per no. Dar al-Risalah al-Islamiyyah, P.O. Box 155063, 13-6173 Beirut, Lebanon. TEL 868661. FAX 831253. TELEX 207339 LE. Ed. Faysal Al-Sammak. adv.; bk.rev.; circ. 10,000.
    Description: Covers Islamic issues all over the world.

297   MK
RISALAT AL-MASJID. (Text in Arabic) m. Diwan of Royal Court Affairs, Protocol Department, P.O. Box 6066, Muscat, Sultanate of Oman. TEL 704580. Ed. Jouma bin Muhammad bin Salem al-Wahaibi. illus.

297   LY
RISSALAT AL-JIHAD. (Text in Arabic, English, French) 1983. m. World Islamic Call Society, P.O. Box 2682, Tripoli, Lybia. TEL 31021. TELEX 20407.

297   SI   ISSN 0559-2674
SEDAR; journal of Islamic studies. 1968. biennial. S.$2. University of Singapore, Muslim Society, Yusof Ishak House, Clementi Rd., Kent Ridge, Singapore 5, Singapore. Ed. M. Dzulfighar Mohd. adv.; bibl.

297   MP
▼**SHARAPAT/COMPASSION.** (Text in Kazakh) 1991. every 3 weeks. Mongolian Muslim Society, Ulan Bator, Mongolia.

297.38   JO
SHARI'AH. (Text in Arabic) 1959. fortn. Shari'ah College, P.O. Box 585, Amman, Jordan. circ. 5,000.

297   UK
SHIA WORLD. 1976. q. free. World Federation of Khoja Shia Ithnaasheri Muslim Communities, P.O. Box 60, Warren House, Wood Lane, Stanmore, Middlesex, England. bk.rev.; circ. 3,000. (back issues avail.)

297.7   PK
SHIAH. (Text in Urdu) vol.56, 1977. w. Rs.12. Insaf Press, Railway Rd., Lahore, Pakistan.

SIMURGH. see *LITERARY AND POLITICAL REVIEWS*

297   II   ISSN 0039-3711
BP1
STUDIES IN ISLAM. (Text in English) 1964. q. $25. Indian Institute of Islamic Studies, Hamdard Nagar, Tughlaqabad, New Delhi 110 062, India. Ed. Hakim A. Hameed. adv.; bk.rev.; circ. 1,000. **Indexed:** Ind.Islam., Old Test.Abstr.

297   PK
TARJUMAN AL-HADITH. (Text in Urdu) 1969. m. Rs.300. Jamiat E Ahl A Hadees Pakistan, 53 Lawrence Rd., Lahore, Pakistan. FAX 042-54072. TELEX 46424-KARAM-PK. Ed. Sajid Mir. circ. 2,000. (back issues avail.)

TAWHID. see *GENERAL INTEREST PERIODICALS — Egyptian Arab Republic*

297   JO
THEOLOGY/SHARIA.* (Text in Arabic) 1959. m. League of Islamic Sciences, PO Box 1829, Amman, Jordan. Ed. Tayseer Dhabian.

297   NR   ISSN 0331-5975
THE TRUTH; the first Muslim weekly newspaper in Nigeria. (Text in English) 1951. w. £N52($5) (UK £3). Ahmadiyya Muslim Jamaat, 45, Idumagbo Ave., PO Box 418, Lagos, Nigeria. TEL 01-920105. FAX 01-668455. TELEX 26947 KESSAN NG. Ed. S.O. Lawal. adv.; bk.rev.; circ. 5,000. (newspaper; back issues avail.)

RELIGIONS AND THEOLOGY — JUDAIC

297 PK
UNIVERSAL MESSAGE. (Text in English) 1979. m. Rs.100($25) Islamic Research Academy, D-35, Block 5, Federal 'B' Area, Karachi 75950, Pakistan. TEL 681157. FAX 422827. Ed. Qadir Sharif. adv.; bk.rev.; bibl.; circ. 1,000 (controlled). (back issues avail.)
  Description: Teaches a better understanding of the religion, culture and history of Islam and challenges in the contemporary world.

297 400 LE
UNIVERSITE SAINT-JOSEPH. FACULTE DES LETTRES ET DES SCIENCES HUMAINES. RECHERCHES. SERIE A: LANGUE ARABE ET PENSEE ISLAMIQUE. (Previously published by its Institut des Lettres Orientales in 4 series) 1956; N.S. 1971. irreg. price varies. Dar el-Mashreq S.A.R.L., 2 rue Huvelin, PO Box 946, Beirut, Lebanon. (Subscr. to: Librairie Orientale, PO Box 946, Beirut, Lebanon)

297 IR
UNIVERSITY OF FERDOWSI. FACULTY OF THEOLOGY AND ISLAMIC STUDIES. PUBLICATION/DANESHGAH-E FERDOWSI. DANESHKADE-YE ELAHIYAT VA MA'AREF-E ESLAMI. NASHRIYEH. (Text in Persian) 1972. q. Rs.120. University of Ferdowsi, Faculty of Theology and Islamic Studies, Mashhad, Iran. Ed. Gholamreza Nafeli. bk.rev.

297 PK ISSN 0042-8132
VOICE OF ISLAM. vol.16, 1968. m. Rs.10. Jamiyat-ul-Falah Karachi, PO Box 7141, Karachi 3, Pakistan. Ed. A.A. Alam. adv.; bk.rev.; circ. 5,000.

297 UG
VOICE OF ISLAM. m. Ahmaddiya Muslim Association, PO Box 16085, Kampala, Uganda.

297 MF
VOIX DE L'ISLAM. (Text in English and French) 1951. m. Rs.5. Abdool Azize Peeroo, Ed. & Pub., Parisot Rd., Mesnil, Phoenix, Mauritius. (back issues avail.)

297 800 GW
WEISSES MINARETT. 1984. q. free. Verlag der Islam, Babenhauser Landstr. 70, 6000 Frankfurt a.M. 70, Germany. TEL 069-681062. FAX 069-686504. Ed. Hadayatullah Huebsch. bk.rev.; circ. 1,500. (back issues avail.)

200 PK ISSN 0084-2052
WORLD MUSLIM CONFERENCE. PROCEEDINGS. (Published in: Muslim World) (Text in English) biennial. World Muslim Congress - Motamar al-Alam al-Islami, Site 9-A, Gulsha-e-Iqbal, Karachi 75300, Pakistan. TEL 460712. FAX 466878. TELEX 24318-UMMAT-PK.

297 PK ISSN 0084-2060
WORLD MUSLIM GAZETTEER. (Text in English) 1964. quinquennial. $30. World Muslim Congress - Motamar Al-Alam al-Islami, Site 9-A, Block 7, Gulshan-e-Iqbal, Karachi 75300, Pakistan. TEL 460712. FAX 466878. Ed. Inamullah Khan.

297 PK ISSN 0044-0213
YAQEEN INTERNATIONAL. (Text in Arabic and English) 1952. fortn. Rs.100 (foreign Rs. 280). Darut Tasnif, Iqbal Mansion, Off Shahrah-e-Liaquat, Near Naveed Clinic, Saddar, Karachi 74400, Pakistan. TEL 524325. (Subscr. to: Darut Tasrif, Mujahidabad, Hub River Road, Karachi 1, Pakistan. TEL 226597) Ed. M.M. Ansari. bk.rev.; bibl.; circ. 5,000. (back issues avail.) **Indexed:** Abstr.Musl.Rel.
  Description: Presents Islam as taught by the Quran and Sunnah.

297 II
YOGASANA ALAYA VIJAYAM. (Text in English, Tamil) 1948. m. Rs.4. Yogazana Alayn, 462, T.H. Rd., Choolai Medu, Old Washermepet, Madras 600021, India. Ed. Pulavar B. Alwar. adv.; bk.rev.; circ. 800.

YOUTH MIRROR. see *CHILDREN AND YOUTH — For*

RELIGIONS AND THEOLOGY — Judaic

see also Ethnic Interests

A J L NEWSLETTER. (Association of Jewish Libraries) see *LIBRARY AND INFORMATION SCIENCES*

A J S REVIEW. (Association for Jewish Studies) see *ETHNIC INTERESTS*

A O J T NEWS; of the New York City public schools. (Association of Orthodox Jewish Teachers) see *EDUCATION*

AGADA; an illustrated Jewish literary magazine. see *ETHNIC INTERESTS*

296.68 IS
ALHAPEREK. q. (Ministry of Education and Culture) Shivtei Israel, Pedagogical Secretariat, 8 David Hamelech St., Jerusalem 91911, Israel. TEL 02-238377.

296 200 FR ISSN 0002-6050
ALLIANCE ISRAELITE UNIVERSELLE EN FRANCE. CAHIERS; paix et droit. 1947. 4/yr. free to qualified personnel. Alliance Israelite Universelle en France, 45 rue de la Bruyere, 75009 Paris, France. Eds. Jacques Levy, Colette Baer. bk.rev.; bibl.; circ. 5,000.

296.68 IS
ALON SHVUT; bulletin of graduates. 1969. q. $3. Yeshivat Har Etzion, Alon Shvut, Gush Etzion 90940, Israel. TEL 02-931456. FAX 02-931298. Ed. Amnon Bazak. circ. 1,000.

296 956 US
AMERICAN ACADEMY FOR JEWISH RESEARCH. MONOGRAPH SERIES. (Text in Arabic, English, French, German, Greek, Hebrew, Latin) irreg., vol.4, 1992. American Academy for Jewish Research, 3080 Broadway, New York, NY 10027. TEL 212-678-8864. FAX 212-678-8947.

296 956 US ISSN 0065-6798
DS101
AMERICAN ACADEMY FOR JEWISH RESEARCH. PROCEEDINGS OF THE A A J R. (Text in Arabic, English, French, German, Greek, Hebrew, Latin) 1929. a. $25. American Academy for Jewish Research, 3080 Broadway, New York, NY 10027. TEL 212-678-8864. FAX 212-678-8947. Ed. Namum M. Sarna. circ. 500.

296 956 US
AMERICAN ACADEMY FOR JEWISH RESEARCH. TEXT AND STUDIES SERIES. (Text in Arabic, English, French, German, Greek, Hebrew, Latin) irreg. American Academy for Jewish Research, 3080 Broadway, New York, NY 10027. TEL 212-678-8864. FAX 212-678-8947.

296 US ISSN 0741-465X
AMERICAN COUNCIL FOR JUDAISM. ISSUES. 1958. q. free. American Council for Judaism, Box 9009, Alexandria, VA 22304. TEL 703-836-2546. Ed. Allan C. Brownfeld. bk.rev.; circ. 8,000. **Indexed:** C.L.I.
  Formerly (until 1979): Brief (ISSN 0006-9922)

296 US ISSN 0740-8528
AMERICAN COUNCIL FOR JUDAISM. SPECIAL INTEREST REPORT; a digest of news items and articles in the area of the council's interest. 1968. m. American Council for Judaism, Box 9009, Alexandria, VA 22304. TEL 703-836-2546. Ed. Allan C. Brownfeld. circ. 8,000. (back issues avail.)

AMERICAN JEWISH ARCHIVES; devoted to the preservation and study of the American Jewish experience. see *ETHNIC INTERESTS*

AMERICAN JEWISH CONGRESS. CONGRESS MONTHLY; a journal of opinion and Jewish affairs. see *ETHNIC INTERESTS*

AMERICAN JEWISH WORLD; voice of Minnesota Jewry. see *ETHNIC INTERESTS*

296 US ISSN 0065-8987
E184.J5 CODEN: AJYBEM
AMERICAN JEWISH YEAR BOOK. 1899. a. $30. (Jewish Publication Society) American Jewish Committee, 165 E. 56th St., New York, NY 10022. TEL 212-751-4000. FAX 212-751-4017. Ed. David Singer. index; circ. 5,000. (also avail. in microform) **Indexed:** Amer.Bibl.Slavic & E.Eur.Stud., Sociol.Abstr., SRI.
  —BLDSC shelfmark: 0820.940000.
  Description: Compendium of articles and directories relating to Jews worldwide.

AMERICAN SEPHARDI. see *ETHNIC INTERESTS*

AMUDIM. see *ETHNIC INTERESTS*

296 NE ISSN 0169-734X
ARBEITEN ZUR GESCHICHTE DES ANTIKEN JUDENTUMS UND DES URCHRISTENTUMS. (Text in English, German) 1961. irreg., no.15, 1978. price varies. (Institutum Iudaicum, Tuebingen, GW) E.J. Brill, P.O. Box 9000, 2300 PA Leiden, Netherlands. TEL 071-312624. FAX 071-317532. TELEX 39296 BRILL NL. (In N. America: E.J. Brill, 24 Hudson St., Kinderhook, NY 12106. TEL 800-962-4406) Ed.Bd.

296 NE ISSN 0169-7390
ARBEITEN ZUR LITERATUR UND GESCHICHTE DES HELLENISTISCHEN JUDENTUMS. (Text in German) irreg., vol.22, 1991. price varies. E.J. Brill, P.O. Box 9000, 2300 PA Leiden, Netherlands. TEL 071-312624. FAX 071-317532. TELEX 39296 BRILL NL. (In N. America: E.J. Brill, 24 Hudson St., Kinderhook, NY 12106. TEL 800-962-4406) Ed. K.M. Rengstorf.

ARBEITSINFORMATIONEN UEBER STUDIENPROJEKTE AUF DEM GEBIET DER GESCHICHTE DES DEUTSCHEN JUDENTUMS UND DES ANTISEMITISMUS. see *HISTORY — History Of Europe*

296 FR ISSN 0518-2840
ARCHE. 1957. m. 80 F. 14 rue Georges Berger, 75017 Paris, France. adv.

296 FR ISSN 0003-9837
ARCHIVES JUIVES. 1965. q. 80 F. Commission Francaise des Archives Juives, B.P. 200, 75023 Paris cedex 01, France. Ed. Bernhard Blumenkranz. bibl.; index, cum.index (1965-1974; 1975-1979); circ. 650. **Indexed:** Bull.Signal., Numis.Lit.
  —BLDSC shelfmark: 1637.250000.

ASCHKENAS; Zeitschrift fuer Geschichte und Kultur der Juden. see *ETHNIC INTERESTS*

296 IS
ASPAKLARIA. (Text in English and Hebrew) 1982. q. $7 per no. Institute for Science and Halacha, 1 Hapisga St., Jerusalem, Israel. TEL 02-416505. Ed.Bd. adv.; bk.rev. **Indexed:** Ind.Heb.Per.

AUSTRALIAN JEWISH HISTORICAL SOCIETY. JOURNAL OF PROCEEDINGS. see *HISTORY — History Of Australasia And Other Areas*

AUSTRALIAN JEWISH HISTORICAL SOCIETY. NEWSLETTER. see *HISTORY — History Of Australasia And Other Areas*

296 US ISSN 0067-2742
B.G. RUDOLPH LECTURES IN JUDAIC STUDIES. 1963. a. free. Syracuse University, Jewish Studies Program, Syracuse, NY 13244-1170. TEL 315-443-3861. FAX 315-443-5390. Ed. Alan L. Berger. circ. 500 (controlled).

296 956 GW ISSN 0931-6418
BABYLON; Beitraege zur Juedischen Gegenwart. 1986. s-a. DM.20 per no. Verlag Neue Kritik KG, Kettenhofweg 53, 6000 Frankfurt 1, Germany. TEL 069-727576. Ed.Bd. (back issues avail.)

296 300 IS ISSN 0067-4109
BAR-ILAN: ANNUAL OF BAR-ILAN UNIVERSITY. (Text in Hebrew; summaries in English) 1963. a. $26. Bar-Ilan University Press, Ramat Gan 52900, Israel. TEL 03-718401. Ed.Bd. (back issues avail.) **Indexed:** Ind.Heb.Per.

296 IS ISSN 0334-1380
BARKAI. 1984. a. IS.30($15) Mifal Rabanim Ubnei Torah, P.O. Box 7524, Jerusalem, Israel. TEL 02-248113. Ed. Rabbi Shaul Yisraeli. circ. 2,000.

BATFUTZOT; newsletter on Jewish life in the Diaspora. see *ETHNIC INTERESTS*

296 IS ISSN 0334-2255
BEER-SHEVA. (Text in Hebrew; summaries in English) 1973. a. (Ben Gurion University of the Negev) Ben Gurion University of the Negev Press, P.O. Box 653, Beersheva, Israel. (Dist. by: Bialik Institute, P.O. Box 92, Jerusalem 91290, Israel. TEL 02-782203) Ed.Bd. illus.; circ. 1,000.
  Description: Scholarly monographs on topics pertaining to Biblical archaeology and the ancient Near East.

BET MIKRA. see *RELIGIONS AND THEOLOGY*

RELIGIONS AND THEOLOGY — JUDAIC

296 015   AG
BIBLIOGRAFIA TEMATICA SOBRE JUDAISMO ARGENTINO. (Text in English, Hebrew, Spanish, Yidish) 1984. irreg. price varies. (Centro de Documentacion e Informacion sobre Judaismo "Marc Turkow") A.M.I.A., Pasteur 633, 1028 Capital Fed., Buenos Aires, Argentina. TEL 490518. FAX 953-5474. (Co-sponsor: American Jewish Committee) index; circ. 200.
   Description: Covers Jewish education in Argentina, antisemitism in Argentina and the Jewish labor movement in Argentina; includes socio-historical investigation.

296   US
BINAH: STUDIES IN JEWISH HISTORY, CULTURE, AND THOUGHT. 1989. irreg. price varies. Praeger Publishers (Subsidiary of: Greenwood Publishing Group Inc.), 88 Post Rd. W., Box 5007, Westport, CT 06881-5007. TEL 203-226-3571. FAX 203-222-1502.

296   IS
BISHVILEI HAREFUAH. a. $3. Laniado Hospital, Netanya 42 150, Israel. TEL 053-21666. Ed. Rabbi Schwartz.

BITZARON: A QUARTERLY OF HEBREW LETTERS. see *LITERARY AND POLITICAL REVIEWS*

296.68   US
B'KITZUR/BRIEFS. vol.3, 1973. irreg. (2-3/yr.). free. (Solomon Schechter Day School Association) United Synagogue of America, Commission on Jewish Education, 155 Fifth Ave., New York, NY 10010. TEL 212-260-8450. Ed. Meir Efrati. bk.rev.; stat.; circ. 2,000.

296 900   NE   ISSN 0926-2261
BRILL'S SERIES IN JEWISH STUDIES. 1991. irreg., vol.5, 1992. price varies. E.J. Brill, P.O. Box 9000, 2300 PA Leiden, Netherlands. TEL 071-312624. FAX 071-317532. TELEX 39296 BRILL NL. (In N. America: E.J. Brill, 24 Hudson St., Kinderhook, NY 12106. TEL 800-962-4406) Ed. David S. Katz. (back issues avail.)
   Description: Scholarly monographs covering topics in Jewish history, language, society and culture up to the present era.

296   NE
BRILL'S SERIES IN JUDAIC STUDIES. 1991. irreg. price varies. E.J. Brill, P.O. Box 9000, 2300 PA Leiden, Netherlands. TEL 071-312624. FAX 071-317532. TELEX 39296 BRILL NL. (In N. America: E.J. Brill, 24 Hudson St., Kinderhook, NY 12106. TEL 800-962-4406)

296   US   ISSN 0007-2435
BROTHERHOOD. 1967. q. $1. National Federation of Temple Brotherhoods, 838 Fifth Ave., New York, NY 10021. TEL 212-570-0707. Ed. Av Bondarin. adv.; bk.rev.; charts; illus.; circ. 75,000 (controlled).

BROWARD JEWISH WORLD. see *ETHNIC INTERESTS*

296.81   BE   ISSN 1148-6716
BULLETIN DES ETUDES KARAITES. 1988. a. 1000 Fr. Editions Peeters s.p.r.l., Bondgenotenlaan 153, B-3000 Leuven, Belgium. TEL 016-235170. FAX 016-228500. Ed.Bd. bk.rev. (back issues avail.)

296   UK   ISSN 0954-1179
BULLETIN OF JUDAEO-GREEK STUDIES. 1987. 2/yr. £5.50 (typically set in Dec.). University of Cambridge, Faculty of Oriental Studies, Sidgwick Avenue, Cambridge CB3 9DA, England. bk.rev.; circ. 150. (back issues avail.)
   Description: Studies Jews in Greek-speaking lands and surrounding areas (all periods). Emphasis is on the origins of Judeo-Byzantine culture and on Greek-speaking Jews under Christian rule (4th to 15th centuries).

296   US
BM197.A1
C C A R JOURNAL; a reform Jewish quarterly. 1953. q. $18. (Central Conference of American Rabbis) C C A R Press, 192 Lexington Ave., 7th Fl., New York, NY 10016. TEL 212-684-4990. FAX 212-689-1649. Ed. Lawrence Englander. adv.; bk.rev.; cum.index (25 yrs.); circ. 2,200. (also avail. in microform from UMI; reprint service avail. from UMI) Indexed: Ind.Artic.Jew.Stud., Ind.Jew.Per., Rel.& Theol.Abstr. (1982-).
   Former titles (until Summer 1991): Journal of Reform Judaism (ISSN 0149-712X); C C A R Journal (ISSN 0007-7976)
   Description: Contains articles about contemporary topics that pertain to the leading memebrs of the rabbinical, scholarly, and lay communities.

C M J S CENTERPIECES. (Cohen Center for Modern Jewish Studies) see *ETHNIC INTERESTS*

CANADIAN JEWISH ARCHIVES (NEW SERIES). see *ETHNIC INTERESTS*

CANADIAN JEWISH NEWS. see *ETHNIC INTERESTS*

CENTRAL CALIFORNIA JEWISH HERITAGE. see *ETHNIC INTERESTS*

CENTRAL CONFERENCE OF AMERICAN RABBIS. YEARBOOK. see *RELIGIONS AND THEOLOGY — Abstracting, Bibliographies, Statistics*

296   US
CHICAGO STUDIES IN THE HISTORY OF JUDAISM. 1981. a. price varies. University of Chicago Press, 5801 S. Ellis Ave., Chicago, IL 60637. TEL 312-702-7899. (Subscr. to: 11030 Langley Ave., Chicago, IL 60628) Ed. Jacob Neusner.
Refereed Serial

CHOSEN PEOPLE. see *ETHNIC INTERESTS*

CHRISTIANITY AND JUDAISM IN ANTIQUITY. see *RELIGIONS AND THEOLOGY*

296   FR   ISSN 0763-062X
CLUB DES HEBRAISANTS. (Text in French, Hebrew) 1984. q. 60 F.($7) Association pour la Lecture de la Bible Hebraique, 39 Grande rue, 94130 Nogent sur Marne, France. Ed. Bernard Huck. bk.rev.; circ. 250. (back issues avail.)
   Description: Philological notes of the hebrew text of the old testament.

296   US
COALITION: THE TORAH ACTION JOURNAL. (Text in English, Yiddish) 1985. 5/yr. free. Agudath Israel of America, 84 William St., New York, NY 10038. TEL 212-797-9000. Ed. Y. Brandriss. circ. 50,000. (tabloid format; back issues avail)
   Description: Explores news and trends in the field of orthodox Jewish activism.

296   SP
COLECCION SENDA ABIERTA. SERIE 2 (AZUL): JUDAISMO. 1974. irreg. 150 ptas. (Centro de Estudios Judeo-Cristianos) Studium Ediciones, Bailen 19, Madrid 13, Spain.

COLLECTION DE LA REVUE DES ETUDES JUIVES. see *ETHNIC INTERESTS*

296   NE
COMPENDIA RERUM IUDAICARUM AD NOVUM TESTAMENTUM. sect.1, no.2, 1976. irreg. price varies. Van Gorcum en Co. B.V., P.O. Box 43, 9400 AA Assen, Netherlands. TEL 05920-46846. FAX 05920-72064.

CONFERENCE OF PRESIDENTS OF MAJOR AMERICAN JEWISH ORGANIZATIONS. ANNUAL REPORT. see *ETHNIC INTERESTS*

296   US   ISSN 0010-6542
BM197.5
CONSERVATIVE JUDAISM. 1945. q. $20. Rabbinical Assembly, 3080 Broadway, New York, NY 10027. TEL 212-678-8060. (Co-sponsor: Jewish Theological Seminary of America) Ed. Shamai Kanter. adv.; bk.rev.; cum.index: 1955-1963, 1963-1976; circ. 2,000. **Indexed:** Amer.Bibl.Slavic & E.Eur.Stud., Ind.Jew.Per., Mid.East: Abstr.& Ind., Rel.& Theol.Abstr. (1968-).
   —BLDSC shelfmark: 3418.500000.

CONTRIBUTIONS TO THE SOCIOLOGY OF JEWISH LANGUAGES. see *LINGUISTICS*

296   IS
CROSSROADS; Halacha and the modern world. (Text in English) 1988. a. $17.50. Zomet Institute, Alon Shvut, Gush Etzion 90940, Israel. TEL 02-931442. FAX 02-931889. Ed. Ezra Rosenfeld. circ. 3,000.
   Description: Examines Jewish law and ethics as they relate to modern society. Includes questions of modern technology, medicine, social services, Zionism, and the Israeli army.

296   IS
DAF LITARBUT YEHUDIT. 1974. m. free. Ministry of Education and Culture, Department of Torah Culture, D'vora Hanivia 2, Jerusalem 91911, Israel. Ed. Arie Strikovsky. bk.rev.; circ. 7,500.

DAVKE; revista Israelita. see *ETHNIC INTERESTS*

DETROIT JEWISH NEWS LTD. PARTNERSHIP. see *ETHNIC INTERESTS*

296   AT
EMET. 1973. q. Aus.$5. Australasian Union of Jewish Students, 1584 St. Kilda Rd, Melbourne, Vic. 3004, Australia. FAX 3529-8864. Eds. Arieh Doobov, David Gold. adv.; bk.rev.; circ. 1,500.
   Former titles: Kivum; Massada Quarterly (ISSN 0310-0138)

296   IS   ISSN 0303-7819
DS102.8
ENCYCLOPAEDIA JUDAICA YEAR BOOK. (Text in English) 1973. a. Keter Publishing House Ltd., Givat Shaul Industrial Area, PO Box 7145, Jerusalem, Israel. (Dist. in U.S. by: Keter Inc., 440 Park Ave. South, New York, NY 10016)

296   CN
ETHIOPIAN JEWRY REPORT. s-a. Canadian Association for Ethiopian Jews, 788 Marlee Ave., Toronto, Ont. M6B 3K1, Canada. TEL 416-782-2546.

296   NE   ISSN 0169-815X
ETUDES SUR LE JUDAISME MEDIEVAL. 1968. irreg., vol.13, 1989. price varies. E.J. Brill, P.O. Box 9000, 2300 PA Leiden, Netherlands. TEL 071-312624. FAX 071-317532. TELEX 39296 BRILL NL. (In N. America: E.J. Brill, 24 Hudson St., Kinderhook, NY 12106. TEL 800-962-4406) Ed. D.R. Blumenthal.

296   UK   ISSN 0014-3006
BM1
EUROPEAN JUDAISM. 1966. s-a. £40 (effective 1992). Pergamon Press plc, Headington Hill Hall, Oxford OX3 0BW, England. TEL 0865-794141. FAX 0865-743911. TELEX 83177 PERGAP. (And: 660 White Plains Rd., Tarrytown, NY 10591-5153. TEL 914-524-9200) Ed. Albert Friedlander. adv.; bk.rev.; cum.index; circ. 1,000. (also avail. in microform; back issues avail.) **Indexed:** Ind.Jew.Per., Mid.East: Abstr.& Ind.
   —BLDSC shelfmark: 3829.747500.
   Description: Covers all aspects of contemporary European Jewish thought.
Refereed Serial

L'EYLAH; a journal of judaism today. see *ETHNIC INTERESTS*

FOCUS SOVIET JEWRY. see *POLITICAL SCIENCE — Civil Rights*

296   US
FOUR WORLDS JOURNAL. 1983. q. $18 to individuals; institutions $28. (Four Worlds Journal) Four Worlds Press, Box 540, East Meadow, NY 11554. TEL 516-864-1912. FAX 516-864-1912. Ed. Edward Hoffman. bk.rev.; circ. 500.
   Description: Inter-disciplinary journal devoted to Jewish mysticism from a contemporary perspective.

FRANKFURTER JUDAISTISCHE BEITRAEGE. see *ETHNIC INTERESTS*

296   GW   ISSN 0938-6408
FRIEDE UEBER ISRAEL; Zeitschrift fuer Kirche und Judentum. 1903. q. free. Evang. Luth. Zentralverein fuer Zeugnis und Dienst unter Juden und Christen e.V., Archivstr. 3, 3000 Hannover 1, Germany. TEL 0511-1241-434. FAX 0511-1241499. bk.rev.; circ. 12,000. (back issues avail.)

RELIGIONS AND THEOLOGY — JUDAIC

296   IS
FRONTLINE. (Text in English) 1986. s-a. Chabad Mobile Centers, P.O. Box 1035, Upper Nazareth 17 110, Israel. TEL (06)571468.

DIE GEMEINDE. see POLITICAL SCIENCE

296   US   ISSN 0016-6669
GENESIS 2; an independent voice for Jewish renewal. 1970. q. $15. Rebirth Two Inc., 30 Old Whitfield Rd., Accord, NY 12404. TEL 716-576-1801. Ed. Lawrence Bush. adv.; bk.rev.; illus.; circ. 2,500. (tabloid format; also avail. in microfilm from AJP,UMI; back issues avail.; reprint service avail. from UMI) **Indexed:** Alt.Press Ind.
    Description: Examines disarmament, Mideast reconciliation, feminism and new currents in Jewish religious and cultural life.

GESHER; semi-quarterly review of Jewish affairs. see ETHNIC INTERESTS

296   US   ISSN 0016-9145
GESHER. (Text in English and Hebrew) a. $5. (Yeshiva University, Student Organization of Yeshiva) Rabbi Isaac Elchanan Theological Seminary, 500 W. 185th St., New York, NY 10033. TEL 212-960-5277. Ed.Bd.

HABINJAN; de opbouw. see ETHNIC INTERESTS

HABONE; le batisseur. see ETHNIC INTERESTS

296   IS   ISSN 0017-6508
HADASHOT MEHACHAIM HADATIYIM BEISRAEL. 1961. bi-m. $2. Hechal Shlomo, P.O. Box 7440, Jerusalem, Israel. Ed. Rabbi Aaron Pechenick. bk.rev.; circ. 3,000. (looseleaf format)

296   US   ISSN 0017-6532
HADOROM.* (Text in Hebrew; contents page in English) 1957. a. $10. Rabbinical Council of America, 275 Seventh Ave., New York, NY 10001. Ed. Rabbi Gdalia Schwartz. bk.rev.; circ. 1,300.

296   IS
HALICHOT. 1958. s-a. free. Religious Council of Tel Aviv - Yafa, P.O. Box 9, Tel Aviv, Israel. TEL 03-260271. Ed. Yitzhak Alfasi.

296   US   ISSN 0017-7040
HAMEVASER. 1962. m. $10 (effective Oct. 1991). Yeshiva University, Jewish Studies Division, 500 W. 185 St, New York, NY 10033. TEL 212-960-5277. Ed. Mitchel Benuck. adv.; bk.rev.; index; circ. 5,000. (tabloid format)
    Description: A student journal of traditional thought.

HARVARD JUDAIC MONOGRAPHS. see ETHNIC INTERESTS

296   GW   ISSN 0175-7016
DS101
HEBRAEISCHE BEITRAEGE ZUR WISSENSCHAFT DES JUDENTUMS; ein Referatenorgan. 1985. s-a. DM.86. (Lessing-Akademie) Verlag Lambert Schneider, Hausackerweg 16, 6900 Heidelberg, Germany. TEL 06221-21354.
    Description: Articles and summaries of works published in Israel, for those who can't read the Hebrew language.

HEBREW STUDIES; a journal devoted to Hebrew language and literature of all periods. see LINGUISTICS

HEBREW UNION COLLEGE ANNUAL. see ETHNIC INTERESTS

HEBREW UNION COLLEGE ANNUAL SUPPLEMENTS. see ETHNIC INTERESTS

296   US
HEBREW UNION COLLEGE - JEWISH INSTITUTE OF RELIGION. CHRONICLE. 1972. s-a. free. Hebrew Union College - Jewish Institute of Religion (New York), One W. 4th St., New York, NY 10012. TEL 212-674-5300. Ed. Jean Rosensaft. bk.rev.; bibl.; illus.; circ. 40,000.
    Formerly (until 1977): Hebrew Union College - Jewish Institute of Religion. Reporter.

296.67   US   ISSN 0732-0914
HERITAGE (WALTHAM). 1968. s-a. $50 to members. American Jewish Historical Society, 2 Thornton Rd., Waltham, MA 02154. TEL 617-891-8110. FAX 617-899-9208. Ed. Bernard Wax. circ. 3,600.
    Former titles (until 1984): American Jewish Historical Society. Report; (until 1976): American Jewish Historical Society. News (ISSN 0065-8944)

HILLEL GATE. see ETHNIC INTERESTS

HILLEL GUIDE TO JEWISH LIFE ON CAMPUS (YEAR). see COLLEGE AND ALUMNI

HOLY LAND; illustrated quarterly of the Franciscan custody of the holy land. see RELIGIONS AND THEOLOGY — Roman Catholic

296   US   ISSN 0441-4195
BM1
HUMANISTIC JUDAISM. 1967. q. $18 domestic; Canada $24; foreign $36. Society for Humanistic Judaism, 28611 W. 12 Mile Rd., Farmington Hills, MI 48334. TEL 313-478-7610. FAX 313-477-9014. Eds. M. Bonnie Cousens, Ruth Duskin Feldman. bk.rev.; circ. 2,500. **Indexed:** Ind.Jew.Per.

ICONOGRAPHY OF RELIGIONS. SECTION 23, JUDAISM. see ART

IGERET; national newsletter. see ETHNIC INTERESTS

377.9   US   ISSN 0019-3321
IN YOUR HANDS.* 1958. bi-m. free. United Synagogue of America, Commission on Jewish Education, 155 Fifth Ave., New York, NY 10010. TEL 212-533-7800. Ed. Dr. Morton Siegel. circ. 3,500.

INFORMATION JUIVE. see ETHNIC INTERESTS

INSTITUTE FOR AGRICULTURAL RESEARCH ACCORDING TO THE TORAH. MONTHLY BULLETIN. see AGRICULTURE

296   US
INTERCOM (NEW YORK, 1960?). (Text mainly in English; occasionally in Hebrew) vol.14, 1973. s-a. free to qualified personnel. Association of Orthodox Jewish Scientists, 1364 Coney Island Ave., Brooklyn, NY 11230. Ed. Rabbi Barry Freundel. bk.rev.; circ. 1,400. (also avail. in microform from MIM)

INTERMOUNTAIN JEWISH NEWS. see ETHNIC INTERESTS

ISRAEL BOOK NEWS. see PUBLISHING AND BOOK TRADE

296   US
J C C CIRCLE. 1946. 4/yr. $20. Jewish Community Centers Association of North America, 15 E. 26th St., New York, NY 10010. TEL 212-532-4949. FAX 212-481-4174. Ed. Shirley Frank. bk.rev.; circ. 22,000. (also avail. in microfilm from AJP)
    Formerly: J W B Circle (ISSN 0021-3780)

J T A COMMUNITY NEWS REPORTER. (Jewish Telegraphic Agency) see ETHNIC INTERESTS

296   IS
JERUSALEM STUDIES IN JEWISH THOUGHT. 1981. s-a. Jewish National and University Library, P.O. Box 503, Jerusalem 91004, Israel. TEL 02-585039. FAX 02-527741.
    Description: Jewish thought throughout history; medieval and modern Jewish philosophy and mysticism.

JEVREJSKI PREGLED. see ETHNIC INTERESTS

296   US   ISSN 0447-7049
BM1
JEWISH ACTION.* vol.28, 1974. 4/yr. $12 (foreign $35). Union of Orthodox Jewish Congregations of America, 333 Seventh Ave., 18th Fl., New York, NY 10001-5004. TEL 212-244-2011. FAX 212-268-4819. Ed. Heidi Tenzer. adv.; bk.rev.; illus.; circ. 70,000.

JEWISH AFFAIRS. see POLITICAL SCIENCE

JEWISH BIBLE QUARTERLY. see RELIGIONS AND THEOLOGY

296   US   ISSN 0075-3726
PN6067
JEWISH BOOK ANNUAL. (Text in English, Hebrew and Yiddish) 1942. a. $25. J W B Jewish Book Council, 15 E. 26th St., New York, NY 10010. TEL 212-532-4949. Ed. Jacob Kabakoff. bk.rev.; circ. 1,200. (reprint service avail. from KTO) **Indexed:** Amer.Bibl.Slavic & E.Eur.Stud, Ind.Heb.Per. —BLDSC shelfmark: 4668.351300.

JEWISH BRAILLE REVIEW. see HANDICAPPED — Visually Impaired

JEWISH CHRONICLE; the world's leading Jewish newspaper. see LITERARY AND POLITICAL REVIEWS

JEWISH CHRONICLE (YONKERS); serving Southern Westchester. see LITERARY AND POLITICAL REVIEWS

JEWISH CIVIC PRESS. see ETHNIC INTERESTS

JEWISH CURRENT EVENTS. see ETHNIC INTERESTS

296   US
JEWISH DENOMINATIONS IN AMERICA. 1988. irreg. price varies. Praeger Publishers (Subsidiary of: Greenwood Publishing Group Inc.), 88 Post Rd. W., Box 5007, Westport, CT 06881-5007. TEL 203-226-3571. FAX 203-222-1502.

JEWISH EDUCATION. see EDUCATION

296   US
JEWISH GUARDIAN. 1974. bi-m. $4.50. Neturei Karta of U.S.A. - Guardians of the Holy City, P.O. Box 2143, Brooklyn, New York, NY 11202. Ed. Mordecai Weberman. adv.; bk.rev.; illus.; circ. 10,000.

JEWISH HISTORICAL SOCIETY OF ENGLAND. ANNUAL REPORT AND ACCOUNTS FOR THE SESSION. see HISTORY — History Of Europe

JEWISH HISTORICAL SOCIETY OF ENGLAND. BULLETIN. see HISTORY — History Of Europe

JEWISH HISTORICAL STUDIES. TRANSACTIONS. see HISTORY — History Of Europe

JEWISH JOURNAL OF SAN ANTONIO. see ETHNIC INTERESTS

JEWISH JOURNAL OF SOCIOLOGY. see SOCIOLOGY

JEWISH JURISPRUDENCE SERIES. see LAW

JEWISH LANGUAGE REVIEW. see LINGUISTICS

JEWISH LAW ANNUAL. see LAW

JEWISH LAW IN CONTEXT. see LAW

296   US   ISSN 0021-6615
BM1
JEWISH OBSERVER. 1963. m. (Sep.-June). $22. Agudath Israel of America, 84 William St., New York, NY 10038. TEL 212-797-9000. Ed. Rabbi Nisson Wolpin. adv.; bk.rev.; index; circ. 16,000. (also avail. in microform from UMI; reprint service avail. from UMI)
    Description: Thought and opinion on Jewish affairs from an orthodox perspective.

JEWISH PRESS (BROOKLYN). see ETHNIC INTERESTS

296   US
JEWISH PROCLAIMER. 1981. irreg. $15 donation. National Center for Understanding Judaism, Box 651, Woodmoor Sta., Silver Spring, MD 20901. Ed. Ash Gerecht. circ. 6,000.

RELIGIONS AND THEOLOGY — JUDAIC

296   US   ISSN 0021-6682
DS101
JEWISH QUARTERLY REVIEW. 1909. q. $25 to individuals; institutions $35. Annenberg Research Institute, 420 Walnut St., Philadelphia, PA 19106. TEL 215-238-1290. FAX 215-238-1540. Ed.Bd. adv.; bk.rev.; bibl.; illus.; index; circ. 1,000. (also avail. in microfilm from UMI; reprint service avail. from UMI,KTO) **Indexed:** A.I.C.P., Amer.Hist.& Life, Arts & Hum.Cit.Ind., Curr.Cont., Hist.Abstr., Ind.Jew.Per., M.L.A., Mid.East: Abstr.& Ind., New Test.Abstr., Old Test.Abstr., Rel.& Theol.Abstr. (1968-), Rel.Ind.One, Rel.Per.
  —BLDSC shelfmark: 4668.370000.
  Description: Provides a forum for the study of religion, Judaica, Old and New Testaments, Semitics and Ancient Near Eastern Studies.

296   UK
JEWISH REVIEW (1983). 1946. 10/yr. £2.50($6) Mizrachi Federation of Great Britain and Ireland, 2B Golders Green Rd., London NW11 8LH, England. Ed. Arieh L. Handler. adv.; bk.rev.; film rev.; play rev.; rec.; rev.; abstr.; illus.; stat.; circ. 5,000. (tabloid format)
  Former titles (until 1983): Religious Zionist Movement Newsletter; (until 1976): Jewish Review (ISSN 0021-6690)

296   US
JEWISH SCIENCE INTERPRETER; a message of health and happiness through the Jewish Faith. 1922. 8/yr. $12. (Society of Jewish Science) Jewish Science Publishing Co., 54 Sunnyside Blvd., Plainview, NY 11803-1507. TEL 516-349-0022. Ed. David Goldstein. adv.; circ. 1,000.

JEWISH SOCIAL STUDIES. see *SOCIAL SCIENCES: COMPREHENSIVE WORKS*

296   US   ISSN 0021-6720
AP92
JEWISH SPECTATOR. 1935. q. $24. American Friends of the Center for Jewish Living and Values, 4391 Park Milano, Calabasas, CA 91302. TEL 818-591-7481. FAX 818-591-7267. Ed. Robert Bleiweiss. bk.rev.; circ. 3,000. (also avail. in microform from AJP)
  Description: Contains scholarly articles, religious and political opinion, fiction and poetry of interest to Jews.

JEWISH STANDARD. see *ETHNIC INTERESTS*

296   IS
JEWISH STUDIES. 1967. a. $3. Jerusalem Academy of Jewish Studies, P.O. Box 5454, Jerusalem, Israel. TEL 02-826875. Ed. Rabbi A. Carmell. adv.; bk.rev.; circ. 5,000.

JEWISH TELEGRAPH. see *ETHNIC INTERESTS*

296   SA
JEWISH TRADITION. (Text in English) 1954. m. R.18. Union of Orthodox Synagogues of South Africa, P.O. Box 27701, Yeoville 2143, South Africa. TEL 648-9136. Ed. R.I. Reznik. adv.; bk.rev.; charts; illus.; circ. 16,000. (tabloid format)
  Formerly: Federation of Synagogues of South Africa. Federation Chronicle (ISSN 0014-9314)
  Description: Official mouthpiece of South African Orthodox Jewry.

JEWISH TRANSCRIPT. see *ETHNIC INTERESTS*

296   US   ISSN 0021-6828
JEWISH VOICE. 1931. fortn. $15. Jewish Federation of Delaware, 101 Garden of Eden Rd., Wilmington, DE 19803. TEL 302-478-6200. FAX 302-478-5374. Ed. Paula Berenguttait. adv.; bk.rev.; circ. 4,200. (tabloid format; also avail. in microfiche; microfilm from AJP)

JEWISH WEEKLY NEWS. see *ETHNIC INTERESTS*

296   UK   ISSN 0075-3769
JEWISH YEAR BOOK. 1896. a. £14. Jewish Chronicle Publications Ltd., 25 Furnival St, London EC4A 1JT, England. FAX 071-405-9040. TELEX 940-11415. Ed. Stephen Massil. adv.; bk.rev.; circ. 5,000. (also avail. in microform)

296   US   ISSN 0740-5901
JEWS FOR JESUS NEWSLETTER. 1973. m. Jews for Jesus, 60 Haight St., San Francisco, CA 94102-5895. TEL 415-864-2600. Ed. Ceil Rosen. bk.rev.; illus.; circ. 230,00.

296   IS   ISSN 0334-0953
DS135.R92
JEWS OF THE SOVIET UNION; immigration and struggle in the 1980's. 1976. irreg. (Israel Public Council for Soviet Jewry, Scientist Committee) Magnes Press University, The Hebrew University, Jerusalem 91 904, Israel. FAX 02-584625. (Alt. addr.: Sprinzak Bldg., Rm.104, Rivat Gan, Jerusalem 91904) Ed. David Prital.
  Supersedes (in 1983): Jewish Intelligentsia in the USSR.

JOEDISK ORIENTERING. see *ETHNIC INTERESTS*

296   NE   ISSN 0047-2212
BM176
JOURNAL FOR THE STUDY OF JUDAISM IN THE PERSIAN, HELLENISTIC AND ROMAN PERIOD. 1970. 2/yr. fl.110($63) to individuals; institutions fl.152 ($87)(effective 1992). E.J. Brill, P.O. Box 9000, 2300 PA Leiden, Netherlands. TEL 071-312624. FAX 071-317532. TELEX 39296 BRILL NL. (In N. America: E.J. Brill, 24 Hudson St., Kinderhook, NY 12106. TEL 800-962-4406) Ed. A.S. van der Wonde. **Indexed:** Mid.East: Abstr.& Ind., New Test.Abstr., Old Test.Abstr., Rel.& Theol.Abstr. (1979-), Rel.Ind.One, Rel.Per.
  Formerly: Journal for the Study of Judaism.
  Description: International forum of scholarly discussions on the history, literature and religious ideas of Judaism in the Persian, Hellenistic and Roman period.

JOURNAL OF JEWISH MUSIC AND LITURGY. see *MUSIC*

296   UK   ISSN 0022-2097
BM1
JOURNAL OF JEWISH STUDIES. (Text in English; occasionally in French) 1948. s-a. £18($35) Oxford Centre for Postgraduate Hebrew Studies, 45 St. Giles, Oxford OX1 2LP, England. FAX 0865-735034. Ed. G. Vermes. adv.; bk.rev.; bibl.; index; circ. 1,000. (also avail. in microform from UMI; reprint service avail. from KTO) **Indexed:** Adol.Ment.Hlth.Abstr., Amer.Hist.& Life, Arts & Hum.Cit.Ind., Br.Hum.Ind., Curr.Cont., Hist.Abstr., Ind.Jew.Per., Mid.East: Abstr.& Ind., New Test.Abstr., Old Test.Abstr., Rel.& Theol.Abstr. (1970-), Rel.Ind.One, Rel.Per.
  —BLDSC shelfmark: 5009.600000.
  Description: Jewish history, literature and culture throughout the ages.

296   US   ISSN 1053-699X
BM1   CODEN: JJTPE2
JOURNAL OF JEWISH THOUGHT AND PHILOSOPHY. 4/yr. (in 2 vols., 2 nos./vol.). Harwood Academic Publishers, 270 Eighth Ave., New York, NY 10011. TEL 212-206-8900. FAX 212-206-2459. TELEX 236735 GOPUB UR. (Subscr. to: Box 786, Cooper Sta., New York, NY 10276. TEL 800-545-8398; UK subscr. to: Box 90, Reading, Berkshire RG1 8JL, England. TEL 0734-560-080) Ed. Elliot R. Wolfson. (also avail. in microform)
  Description: Provides an international forum for Jewish thought, philosophy and intellectual history, with an emphasis on contemporary issues. Covers biblical studies, mysticism, literary criticism, political theory, sociology and anthropology.
  Refereed Serial

JOURNAL OF PSYCHOLOGY AND JUDAISM. see *PSYCHOLOGY*

296 297 410   UK   ISSN 0022-4480
PJ3001
JOURNAL OF SEMITIC STUDIES. 1955. s-a. £51($99) (University of Manchester, Department of Near Eastern Studies) Oxford University Press, Oxford Journals, Pinkhill House, Southfield Road, Eynsham, Oxford OX8 1JJ, England. TEL 0865-882283. FAX 0865-882890. TELEX 837330 OXPRES G. Ed.Bd. adv.; bk.rev.; bibl.; index; circ. 800. (also avail. in microform from UMI; reprint service avail. from SWZ,UMI) **Indexed:** Amer.Hist.& Life, Arts & Hum.Cit.Ind., Br.Hum.Ind., Curr.Cont., Hist.Abstr., M.L.A., Mid.East: Abstr.& Ind., New Test.Abstr., Old Test.Abstr., Rel.& Theol.Abstr. (1967-), Rel.Ind.One, Rel.Per.
  —BLDSC shelfmark: 5063.500000.
  Description: Addresses modern and ancient Near East, with empahsis on research into the languages and literatures of the area.

296   SZ   ISSN 0022-572X
DS101
JUDAICA; Beitraege zum Verstaendnis des juedischen Schicksals in Vergangenheit und Gegenwart. 1945. q. 38 Fr. (Stiftung fuer Kirche und Judentum) Judaica Verlag, Etzelstr. 19, CH-8038 Zurich, Switzerland. Eds. Kurt Hruby, Martin Cunz. adv.; bk.rev.; circ. 600. (also avail. in microform from SWZ; reprint service avail. from SWZ) **Indexed:** Amer.Hist.& Life, CERDIC, Hist.Abstr., Old Test.Abstr.

JUDAICA BOOK NEWS. see *PUBLISHING AND BOOK TRADE*

296   US   ISSN 0022-5762
BM1
JUDAISM; a quarterly journal of Jewish life and thought. 1952. q. $20 to individuals; libraries $35. American Jewish Congress, 15 E. 84th St., New York, NY 10028. TEL 212-879-4500. Ed. Ruth Waxman. adv.; bk.rev.; index, cum.index (20 yr.); circ. 7,500. (also avail. in microform from UMI; reprint service avail. from UMI) **Indexed:** Acad.Ind., Amer.Bibl.Slavic & E.Eur.Stud, Arts & Hum.Cit.Ind., CERDIC, Curr.Cont., G.Soc.Sci.& Rel.Per.Lit., Mid.East: Abstr.& Ind., New Test.Abstr., Rel.& Theol.Abstr. (1970-), Rel.Ind.One, Rel.Per., SSCI.
  —BLDSC shelfmark: 5073.825000.

296 100   IS   ISSN 0334-6994
BM526
KABBALAH; newsletter of current research in Jewish mysticism. (Text in English) 1985. 3/yr. $12.75 to individuals; institutions $32.75. 41 Palyam St., Jerusalem 97 890, Israel. TEL 02-817-876. Ed. Hananya Goodman. (back issues avail.)

KADIMA. see *LITERARY AND POLITICAL REVIEWS*

296   SA
KASHRUT GUIDE. 1977. a. free. Union of Orthodox Synagogues of South Africa, P.O. Box 4110, Johannesburg 2000, South Africa. TEL 011-648-9136. FAX 011-648-4014. Ed. Saul Emanuel. adv.; circ. 13,000 (controlled).
  Description: Lists all Kosher food products and establishments under the supervision of the Johannesburg and Cape Town rabbinical authorities.

296   US   ISSN 0022-9644
KEEPING POSTED WITH N C S Y.* (Reporter and Leadership Editions) 1959. q. $6. National Conference of Synagogue Youth, 333 Seventh Ave., 19th Fl., New York, NY 10001-5004. TEL 212-244-2011. FAX 212-268-4819. (Co-sponsor: Union of Orthodox Jewish Congregations of America) Ed. Renee Straussad. adv.; bk.rev.; circ. 20,000.

296   US
KEREM SHLOMO. (Text in Hebrew) 1977. irreg. (10-12/yr.). $15. Bobover Congregation, 1577 48th St., Brooklyn, NY 11219. TEL 718-438-2018. Ed. Shmerel Zitronenbaum. bibl.; index; circ. 2,500. (back issues avail.)

296   IS
KFAR CHABAD. w. IS.60($68) Chabad Association, P.O. Box 41, Kfar Chabad 60978, Israel. TEL 03-984959.

KIRYAT SEFER; bibliographical quarterly. see *BIBLIOGRAPHIES*

KOL HA-T'NUAH/VOICE OF THE MOVEMENT. see *ETHNIC INTERESTS*

296 327 028.5   UK
KOLEINU. (Text mainly in English; occasionally in Hebrew) 1980. m. membership. Habonim-Dror Organization, 523 Finchley Rd., London NW3 7BD, England. TEL 01-435-9033. FAX 01-431-4503. (Co-sponsor: World Zionist Organisation. Youth and Hechalutz Department) Ed. Karen Ackerman. adv.; film rev.; circ. 300. (back issues avail.)

296   IS   ISSN 0333-8584
KOLOT. 1981. irreg. free. Israel Movement for Progressive Judaism, 13 King David St., Jerusalem, Israel. TEL 02-203448. FAX 02-203446. Ed. Yehoram Mazor. bk.rev.; circ. 2,500.

KOSHER DIRECTORY. see *ETHNIC INTERESTS*

RELIGIONS AND THEOLOGY — JUDAIC

296 980 US ISSN 0895-3503
LATIN AMERICAN REPORT. 1982. q. $12 to individuals: institutions $20. Anti-Defamation League of B'nai B'rith, Jarkow Institute for Latin America, 823 United Nations Plaza, New York, NY 10017. TEL 212-490-2525. FAX 212-867-0779. Ed. Morton M. Rosenthal. circ. 4,500.
Description: Covers developments in Latin America and the Caribbean that affect Jews.

296 US
LIBRARY OF JEWISH LAW AND ETHICS. irreg., vol.15, 1990. price varies. Ktav Publishing House, 900 Jefferson St., No. 6249, Hoboken, NJ 07030-7205. TEL 201-963-9524.

LONG ISLAND JEWISH WORLD. see *ETHNIC INTERESTS*

LUZ; la revista Israelita para toda Sudamerica. see *LITERARY AND POLITICAL REVIEWS*

MAAJAN - DIE QUELLE. see *GENEALOGY AND HERALDRY*

MABUEY HANCHAL. see *ETHNIC INTERESTS*

296.68 US
MACHBERET HAMENAHEL. 1975. m. $6. National Conference of Yeshiva Principals, 160 Broadway, New York, NY 10038. TEL 212-406-4190. Ed. Rabbi Chaim Feuerman. bk.rev.; circ. 900. (looseleaf format; back issues avail.)

296 IS
MACHSHEVET. 1971. bi-m. IS.12. P.O. Box 363, Bnei Brak, Israel. TEL 03-703186.

296 UK
MANNA. 1966. q. £8.50($25) (Europe £12; elsewhere £21.50). Manor House Trust, Sternberg Centre for Judaism, Manor House, 80 East End Rd., Finchley, London N3 2SY, England. TEL 081-346-2288. FAX 081-349-0694. Ed. Rab. Tony Bayfield. adv.; bk.rev.; illus.; circ. 2,000.
Formerly (until 1983): Living Judaism (ISSN 0024-5267)
Description: Covers a wide range of topics of Jewish interest.

296 IS ISSN 0334-8814
BS410
MEGADIM. 1986. 3/yr. $20. Yaacov Herzog Institute, Alon Shvut, Gush Etzion 90940, Israel. TEL 02-931-451. FAX 02-931-298. Eds. Yoseph Offer, Avraham Sham'ah. bk.rev.; circ. 1,500.

MENORAH. see *ETHNIC INTERESTS*

MENORAH REVIEW. see *ETHNIC INTERESTS*

296 UY
MENSAJE. vol.4, 1978. bi-m. Comite Central Israelita del Uruguay, Rio Negro 1308, Montevideo, Uruguay. Ed. Jorge Sztarcevsky. Indexed: Biol.Abstr.

296 IS
MESILOT; religious Zionism in action. (Editions in English and Hebrew) 1983. m. Society for the Advancement of Religious Zionism, Mesilot, P.O. Box 7524, Jerusalem, Israel. TEL 02-248113. FAX 02-257418. bk.rev.; circ. 1,800.

HA-MESIVTA. see *LAW*

MIAMI JEWISH TRIBUNE. see *ETHNIC INTERESTS*

296 282 IS ISSN 0792-0474
MISHKAN; a theological forum on Jewish evangelism. (Text in English) 1984. s-a. £9($15) United Christian Council in Israel, P.O. Box 116, Jerusalem 91000, Israel. TEL 02-286553. FAX 02-284561. Ed. Ole Chr. M. Kvarme. adv.; bk.rev.; circ. 700. **Indexed:** Rel.& Theol.Abstr. (1990-).
—BLDSC shelfmark: 5828.621500.
Description: Covers Biblical and theological debate on issues relating to Jewish evangelism, Hebrew-Christian and Messianic-Jewish identity, and Christian-Christian relations.

296 IS
MISHPACHA; the magazine for the Jewish family. (Text in Hebrew) m. P.O. Box 712, Bnei Brak, Israel. TEL 03-5792640. Ed.Bd.

LA-MISHPAHA. see *LINGUISTICS*

296 IS ISSN 0541-5632
MITZION TETZEH TORAH. M.T.T. 1968. irreg. (approx. 2/yr.). price varies. Mitzion Tetzeh Torah, Ltd., P.O. Box 29435, 9 Derech Haifa Rd., Tel-Aviv, Israel. Ed. G. Rachaman. adv.; bk.rev.; circ. 1,000.

296 US ISSN 0276-1114
BM195
MODERN JUDAISM. 1981. 3/yr. $26 to individuals (foreign $30); institutions $49 (foreign $53). Johns Hopkins University Press, Journals Publishing Division, 701 W. 40th St., Ste. 275, Baltimore, MD 21211. TEL 410-516-6987. FAX 410-516-6998. Ed. Steven T. Katz. adv.; bk.rev.; circ. 700. (back issues avail.) **Indexed:** Amer.Bibl.Slavic & E.Eur.Stud, Amer.Hist.& Life, Arts & Hum.Cit.Ind., Curr.Cont., Hist.Abstr., Ind.Jew.Per., Mid.East: Abstr.& Ind., Rel.& Theol.Abstr. (1988-), Rel.Ind.One.
—BLDSC shelfmark: 5887.341000.
Description: Presents articles and topics relative to the Jewish experience since the Haskala, including the Zionist movement and the establishment of the State of Israel, the rise of modern anti-semitism and its devastating climax in the Holocaust, and the implication of Jewish emancipation in Europe.

MOSHIACH TIMES. see *CHILDREN AND YOUTH — For*

MUSICA JUDAICA. see *MUSIC*

296 US
N A T A JOURNAL. 1981. s-a. free. National Association of Temple Administrators, 838 Fifth Ave., New York, NY 10021. TEL 312-525-4707. FAX 312-525-3502. Ed. Robert Mills. bk.rev.; circ. 2,500.

296 US ISSN 0300-6689
N A T E NEWS. 1955. 6/yr. membership. National Association of Temple Educators, 707 Summerly Dr., Nashville, TN 37209-4253. TEL 615-352-6800. FAX 615-352-7800. Ed. Richard M. Morin. adv.; bk.rev.; circ. 2,100.

N C J W JOURNAL. (National Council of Jewish Women) see *WOMEN'S INTERESTS*

956.940 232 296 US ISSN 0888-191X
DS150.L3
NA'AMAT WOMAN. 1926. 5/yr. $5. Na'Amat U S A, The Women's Labor Zionist Organization of America, Inc., 200 Madison Ave., New York, NY 10016. TEL 212-725-8010. Ed. Judith A. Sokoloff. adv.; bk.rev.; charts; illus.; circ. 30,000. (also avail. in microfilm from AJP)
Formerly: Pioneer Woman (ISSN 0032-0021)

NARROW WAY. see *RELIGIONS AND THEOLOGY*

296 US
NEW MENORAH: THE P'NAI OR JOURNAL OF JEWISH RENEWAL. 1979. q. $18. P'nai Or Religious Fellowship, 7318 Germantown Ave., Philadelphia, PA 19119. TEL 215-242-4074. FAX 215-247-9703. Eds. Arthur Waskow, Shana Margolin. adv.; bk.rev.; circ. 3,000.
Formerly: Menorah.
Description: For networking the emerging liturgical, spiritual, and social action concerns that arise out of the loose coalition of individuals and groups of the Jewish Renewal movement.

296 NE ISSN 0028-9833
NIEUW GELUID. 1952. 7/yr. fl.25($10) Bond Nederlands Israel, Postbus 88, 9285 ZW Buitenpost, Netherlands. TEL 05115-3053. FAX 05115-2344. Ed. G. van der Laan. bk.rev.; index; circ. 800.

296 IS ISSN 0048-0460
NIV HAMIDRASHIA. (Text in English, French, Hebrew) 1963. irreg. $20 per no. Friends of the Midrashia, Israel, 3, Achuzath Bayeth St., Tel Aviv, Israel. Eds. Israel Sadan, Alexander Carlebach. adv.; bk.rev.; circ. 5,000. **Indexed:** Ind.Heb.Per.

NOAH'S ARK; a newspaper for Jewish children. see *CHILDREN AND YOUTH — For*

NOTRE VOIX. see *POLITICAL SCIENCE*

296 FR ISSN 0029-4705
A I U LES NOUVEAUX CAHIERS. 1965. q. 160 F. Alliance Israelite Universelle en France, 45 rue la Bruyere, 75009 Paris, France. Ed. Colette Baer. adv.; bk.rev.; bibl.; circ. 2,500.
Description: Deals with Jewish history, philosophy, sociology and literature.

296 US
OHR HAKOLLEL. 1981. bi-m. $10. Zeirei Agudath Israel of America, 84 William St., New York, NY 10038. TEL 212-797-9000. FAX 212-269-2843. Ed. Yonah Weinrib. adv.; circ. 3,000. (back issues avail.)
Description: Articles of interest to the English-speaking Jewish population.

296 US ISSN 0030-2139
OLOMEINU/OUR WORLD. (Text in English, Hebrew) 1945. m. (8/yr.). $9 (foreign $11). National Society for Hebrew Day Schools, 5723 18th Ave., Brooklyn, NY 11204. TEL 718-259-1223. FAX 718-259-1795. Eds. Rabbi Yaakov Fruchter, Rabbi Nosson Scherman. illus.; circ. 17,500.

296 US ISSN 0362-2770
OPTIONS (WAYNE); the Jewish resources newsletter. 1974. m. $18. Options Publishing Co., Box 311, Wayne, NJ 07474-0311. TEL 201-694-2327. Ed. Betty J. Singer. bk.rev.; index. (back issues avail.)
Description: American Jewish resources: cultural, educational, religious and more.

296 IS ISSN 0333-6298
B'OR HA'TORAH; science, the arts and problems of modern life in the light of the Torah. (Editions in English and Hebrew) 1982. s-a. $16. Association of Religious Academics from the Soviet Union in Israel, Shamir, 6 David Yellin St., P.O. Box 5749, Jerusalem, Israel. TEL 02-385702. FAX 02-385118. (U.S. addr.: Mishulovin, 309 Kingston Ave., Brooklyn, NY 11213) Ed. Herman Branover. bk.rev.; circ. 3,000.

296 IS
ORACHOT. (Text in Hebrew) 1965. a. free. Haifa Religious Council, 4 Shmuel Ben Adia St., P.O. Box 2405, Haifa 31024, Israel. FAX 04-667623. adv.; circ. 3,000.

296 IS ISSN 0333-9270
ORAITA; torah publication for Jewish thought and Halacha. (Text in Hebrew) 1977. s-a. IS.180($6) Rabbinical College Tifereth Netanya "Yad Moshe", P.O. Box 245, Netanya 42102, Israel. Ed. Rabbi Amihud Levine. adv.; bk.rev.; circ. 2,000. (back issues avail.)

296 155.451 267 US
OUR WAY.* 1970. irreg. (3-4/yr.). $6. (Union of Orthodox Jewish Congregations of America) National Conference of Synagogue Youth, 333 Seventh Ave., 19th Fl., New York, NY 10001-5004. TEL 212-244-2011. FAX 212-268-4819. Ed. Rabbi E. Lederfeind. adv.; circ. 2,000.
Description: News and information about the Jewish deaf community, with emphasis on the youth.

OUTLOOK. see *ETHNIC INTERESTS*

PALM BEACH JEWISH WORLD. see *ETHNIC INTERESTS*

296 900 FR ISSN 0295-5652
PARDES.* (Text in French; summaries in English) 1985. s-a. 180 Fr. Editions Lattes, 24 bd. Saint-Michel, 75006 Paris, France. Eds. Shmuel Trigano, Annie Kriegel. adv.; bk.rev.; circ. 2,000. (back issues avail.)

PASSAGES. see *ETHNIC INTERESTS*

296 221 NE ISSN 0169-9008
PESHITTA INSTITUTE, LEIDEN. MONOGRAPHS. 1972. irreg., vol.5, 1989. E.J. Brill, P.O. Box 9000, 2300 PA Leiden, Netherlands. TEL 071-312624. FAX 071-317532. TELEX 39296 BRILL NL. (In N. America: E.J. Brill, 24 Hudson St., Kinderhook, NY 12106. TEL 800-962-4406)
Description: Monograph studies on the Syriac translations of the Old and New Testaments.

RELIGIONS AND THEOLOGY — JUDAIC

296 809   US   ISSN 0272-9601
PJ5001
PROOFTEXTS; a journal of Jewish literary history. 1981. 3/yr. $19 to individuals (foreign $24.70); institutions $45 (foreign $45.70). Johns Hopkins University Press, Journals Publishing Division, 701 W. 40th St., Ste. 275, Baltimore, MD 21211. TEL 410-516-6987. FAX 410-516-6998. Eds. Alan Mintz, David G. Roskies. adv.; circ. 712. (also avail. in microform from UMI; back issues avail.; reprint service avail. from UMI) Indexed: Amer.Bibl.Slavic & E.Eur.Stud, Arts & Hum.Cit.Ind., Curr.Cont., Ind.Jew.Per., M.L.A., Old Test.Abstr., Rel.& Theol.Abstr. (1985-), Rel.Ind.One.
—BLDSC shelfmark: 6927.075000.
    Description: Covers Jewish literary heritage.

296   UK
R S G B INFORM NEWSLETTER. 1973. q. £3.50. Reform Synagogues of Great Britain, Manor House, 80 East End Rd., Finchley, London N3 2SY, England. Ed.Bd. adv.; illus.; circ. 16,000.

296   US   ISSN 0079-936X
RABBINICAL ASSEMBLY, NEW YORK. PROCEEDINGS. (Text in English; occasionally in Hebrew, Yiddish) 1927-1970; resumed 1973. a. $7.50. Rabbinical Assembly, 3080 Broadway, New York, NY 10027. TEL 212-678-8060. Ed. Jules Harlow. cum.index: 1927-1968.; circ. 1,500.

296   IT   ISSN 0033-9792
DS101
RASSEGNA MENSILE DI ISRAEL. (Text in English, French, Italian) 1924. q. L.50000($65) Unione delle Comunita Israelitiche Italiane, Lungotevere Sanzio 9, Rome, Italy. Dir. Guido Fubini. bk.rev.; charts; illus.; index; circ. 1,000.

200   NE   ISSN 0034-1487
RECONSTRUCTION. 1947. m. fl.20.
Portugees-Israelietische Gemeente - Spanish and Portuguese Jewish Community at Amsterdam, Gerrit van der Veenstr. 141, 1077 DX Amsterdam, Netherlands. TEL 762041. Ed. Dr. J.Z. Baruch. bk.rev.; circ. 13,000.

296   US   ISSN 0034-1495
DS133
RECONSTRUCTIONIST. 1935. 4/yr. $20. Federation of Reconstructionist Congregations and Havurot, Box 1336, Roslyn Heights, NY 11577. Ed. Rabbi Joy Levitt. adv.; bk.rev.; index; circ. 10,500. (also avail. in microform from UMI; reprint service avail. from UMI) Indexed: HR Rep., Ind.Jew.Per., Mid.East: Abstr.& Ind.
—BLDSC shelfmark: 7310.685000.

296   US   ISSN 0482-0819
AP222
REFORM JUDAISM. 1955. q. $10 (teachers edition $15.25). Union of American Hebrew Congregations, 838 Fifth Ave., New York, NY 10021. TEL 212-249-0100. Ed. Aron Hirt-Manheimer. illus.; circ. 290,000. (also avail. in microfilm from AJP) Indexed: Ind.Jew.Per.
    Incorporates: Keeping Posted (ISSN 0022-9636)
    Description: Links the institutions and affiliates of Reform Judaism with every Reform Jew; covers developments within the Movement while interpreting world events and Jewish tradition from a Reform perspective; strives to convey the creativity, diversity, and dynamism of Reform Judaism.

296 282   US
REMNANT OF ISRAEL. 1976. a. Remnant of Israel Publications, New Hope, KY 40052.
TEL 502-325-3081. Ed. Arthur Klyber. circ. 70,000. (back issues avail.)

THE REPORTER (NEW YORK). see *SOCIAL SERVICES AND WELFARE*

REVISTA CULTULUI MOZAIC/REVIEW OF THE MOSAIC CREED. see *LITERATURE*

REVUE DES ETUDES JUIVES. see *ETHNIC INTERESTS*

ROCKY MOUNTAIN JEWISH HISTORICAL NOTES. see *ETHNIC INTERESTS*

S C A REPORT. (Synagogue Council of America) see *ETHNIC INTERESTS*

ST. LOUIS JEWISH LIGHT; the newspaper of the Jewish community of Greater St. Louis. see *ETHNIC INTERESTS*

SAN DIEGO JEWISH PRESS HERITAGE. see *ETHNIC INTERESTS*

296   IS
SANZ. 1978. m. Igud Chasidei Sanz, P.O. Box 5032, Netanya 42 150, Israel.
    Description: Topics of interest to the Sanz Jewish community.

SEMANARIO ISRAELITA; unabhaengiges juedisches Wochenblatt. see *ETHNIC INTERESTS*

SEMITIC STUDY SERIES. see *ORIENTAL STUDIES*

SHALOM. see *ETHNIC INTERESTS*

200   UK
SHALOM. 1962. 3/yr. £4 (typcially set in Nov.). Church's Ministry Among the Jews, 30C Clarence Rd., St. Albans, Herts AL1 4JJ, England. TEL 0727-833114. FAX 0727-48312. Ed. H. Roberts. bk.rev.; illus.; circ. 6,000.
    Former titles: C.M.J. Quarterly (ISSN 0007-8646); C.M.J. News.

296.68   IS   ISSN 0582-9836
SHAMATIV. q. IS.12. Organization of Religious Teachers, Rehov Harav Hertzog 36, Bat Yam 59 461, Israel. TEL 03-862495. circ. 800.

SHIRIM; a Jewish poetry journal. see *LITERATURE — Poetry*

370 200   US   ISSN 0300-7960
SHMUESSEN MIT KINDER UN YUGENT. (Text in Yiddish) 1942. m. $3. Merkos L'Inyonei Chinuch, Inc., 770 Eastern Parkway, Brooklyn, NY 11213. Ed. Nissan Mindel. illus.; index.

SHOMERNIK. see *EDUCATION*

SHVUT; Jewish problems in the USSR and Eastern Europe. see *ETHNIC INTERESTS*

296   IS   ISSN 0334-7559
BM390
SIAH MESHARIM; journal of Judaism, religion and state. (Text in Hebrew) 1986. m. IS.12($12) Hemdat - Council for Freedom of Science, Religion and Culture in Israel, P.O. Box 2160, Jerusalem 91201, Israel. TEL 02-632155. Ed. Z.W. Falk. bk.rev.; circ. 500.

296   IS
SICHAT HASHAVUA; the weekly sheet for every Jew. (Text in Hebrew) w. Young Chabad Center, P.O. Box 14, Kfar Chabad 72915, Israel. TEL 03-985588. Ed. Menachem Barod.

296.68   IS   ISSN 0334-6986
BM496.A1
SIDRA; a journal for the study of Rabbinic literature. (Text in Henbrew; summaries in English) 1985. a. $14. Bar-Ilan University, Talmud Department) Bar-Ilan University Press, Ramat Gan 52900, Israel. TEL 03-5318575. Ed. Zvi Arie Steinfeld. (back issues avail.)
    Description: Collection of research papers in various fields of Jewish oral law.

296   IS
SINAI. (Text in Hebrew) 1937. bi-m. $15. Rabbi Kook Foundation, P.O. Box 642, Jerusalem, Israel. Ed. Yitzchak Raphael. bk.rev.; circ. 1,500. (back issues avail.) Indexed: Ind.Heb.Per.

296   US   ISSN 0196-2183
BM40
SOLOMON GOLDMAN LECTURES; perspectives in Jewish learning. 1977. irreg. $7.95 cloth. Spertus College of Judaica Press, 618 S. Michigan Ave., Chicago, IL 60605. TEL 312-922-9012. FAX 312-922-6406. Ed. N. Stampfer. circ. 500.
—BLDSC shelfmark: 8327.590000.
    Supersedes: Perspectives in Jewish Learning (ISSN 0079-1016)
    Description: Subject matter is representative of the entire spectrum of Jewish studies.

SOURCES OF CONTEMPORARY JEWISH THOUGHT/MEKEVOT. see *LITERARY AND POLITICAL REVIEWS*

SOUTHWEST JEWISH CHRONICLE. see *ETHNIC INTERESTS*

SOVIET JEWISH AFFAIRS; a journal on Jewish problems in the USSR and Eastern Europe. see *POLITICAL SCIENCE*

296   IS
SRIDIM. 1982. a. $2.50. Standing Committee of the Conference of European Rabbis, P.O.B. 5324, Jerusalem 91 052, Israel. TEL 02-812859. Ed. Rabbi Moshe Rose. circ. 1,000.

296   IT
STORIA DELL'EBRAISMO IN ITALIA; studi e testi. 1980. irreg., vol.13, 1991. price varies. Casa Editrice Leo S. Olschki, Casella Postale 66, 50100 Florence, Italy. TEL 055-6530684. FAX 055-6530214.

296   NE   ISSN 0081-6914
STUDIA SEMITICA NEERLANDICA, 1956. irreg., no.17, 1975. price varies. Van Gorcum en Co. B.V., P.O. Box 43, 9400 AA Assen, Netherlands.
TEL 05920-46864. FAX 05920-72064.

STUDIES IN AMERICAN JEWISH HISTORY. see *ETHNIC INTERESTS*

STUDIES IN JUDAICA & THE HOLOCAUST. see *ETHNIC INTERESTS*

296   NE   ISSN 0169-961X
STUDIES IN JUDAISM IN LATE ANTIQUITY. 1973. irreg., vol.40, 1989. price varies. E.J. Brill, P.O. Box 9000, 2300 PA Leiden, Netherlands. TEL 071-312624. FAX 071-317532. TELEX 39296 BRILL NL. (In N. America: E.J. Brill, 24 Hudson St., Kinderhook, NY 12106. TEL 800-962-4406) Ed. J. Neusner.
—BLDSC shelfmark: 8490.805000.
    Description: The history of Jews from the period of the Second Temple to the rise of Islam.

296   NE   ISSN 0169-9660
STUDIES IN JUDAISM IN MODERN TIMES. 1978. irreg., vol.10, 1992. price varies. E.J. Brill, P.O. Box 9000, 2300 PA Leiden, Netherlands. TEL 071-312624. FAX 071-317532. TELEX 39296 BRILL NL. (In N. America: E.J. Brill, 24 Hudson St., Kinderhook, NY 12106. TEL 800-962-4406) Ed. J. Neusner. (back issues avail.)

296   NE   ISSN 0169-9962
STUDIES ON THE TEXTS OF THE DESERT OF JUDAH. 1957. irreg., vol.9, 1992. price varies. E.J. Brill, P.O. Box 9000, 2300 PA Leiden, Netherlands.
TEL 071-312624. FAX 071-317532. TELEX 39296 BRILL NL. (In N. America: E.J. Brill, 24 Hudson St., Kinderhook, NY 12106. TEL 800-962-4406) Ed. J. van der Ploeg.
    Description: Scholarly translation and evaluation of Biblical texts from the papyrii and manuscripts of Wadi Qumran.

296   US
SYNAGOGUE LIGHT - KOSHER LIFE. 1933. q. Synagogue Light, Inc., 47 Beekman St, New York, NY 10038. TEL 212-227-7543. Ed. Rabbi Meyer Hager.
    Description: Covers religious and other issues concerning the Jewish community and kosher life.

SYRACUSE JEWISH OBSERVER. see *ETHNIC INTERESTS*

296 947 956.94
913   IS   ISSN 0334-3650
DS101
TARBIZ; a quarterly for Jewish studies. (Text in Hebrew; summaries in English) 1929. q. $40. Hebrew University of Jerusalem, Jerusalem, Israel. Ed.Bd. bk.rev.; index; circ. 700. (back issues avail.) Indexed: M.L.A., Rel.& Theol.Abstr. (1968-).

296   CN   ISSN 0704-5905
BS709.4
TARGUMIC AND COGNATE STUDIES. NEWSLETTER. 1974. s-a. $5 (typically set in Jan.). University of Toronto, Department of Near Eastern Studies, Toronto, Ont. M5S 1A1, Canada.
TEL 416-585-4588. FAX 416-585-4584. Ed. E.G. Clark. circ. 200. (back issues avail.)

296   IS   ISSN 0333-6883
TECHUMIM. (Text in Hebrew) 1980. a. $16. Zomet, Alon Shvut, Gush Etzion 90 940, Israel.
TEL 02-741442. FAX 02-931889. Ed. Ezra Rosenfeld. circ. 3,000.
    Description: Collection of monographs concerning modern society and Jewish law.

296   IS
TELEM UTALMIA. 1985. 3/yr. Movement for Fulfiling Zionism in Israel, 23 Abarbanel St., Jerusalem 92 477, Israel. TEL 02-776210.

296   SA   ISSN 0040-2966
TEMPLE DAVID BULLETIN. 1969. s-m. free. Durban Progressive Jewish Congregation, 369 Ridge Rd., Durban, South Africa. adv.; bk.rev.; circ. 535. (tabloid format)
    Formerly: Temple David Review.

296   GW   ISSN 0721-8753
TEXTE UND STUDIEN ZUM ANTIKEN JUDENTUM. (Text in English, French and German) 1981. irreg. price varies. Verlag J.C.B. Mohr (Paul Siebeck), Wilhelmstr. 18, Postfach 2040, 7400 Tuebingen, Germany. TEL 07071-26064. FAX 07071-51104. TELEX 7262872-MOHR-D. Eds. Martin Hengel, Peter Schaefer.

296   NE   ISSN 0169-8370
THEOKRATIA: JAHRBUCH DES INSTITUTUM JUDAICUM DELITZSCHIANUM. 1967. irreg., vol.3, 1979. price varies. (Institutum Judaicum Delitzschianum) E.J. Brill, P.O. Box 9000, 2300 PA Leiden, Netherlands. TEL 071-312624. FAX 071-317532. TELEX 39296 BRILL NL. (In N. America: E.J. Brill, 24 Hudson St., Kinderhook, NY 12106. TEL 800-962-4406) Ed. K.H. Rengstorf.

296   IS
TORAH EDUCATION. (Text in English) 1971. q. World Zionist Organization, Department for Torah Education and Culture in the Diaspora, P.O. Box 92, Jerusalem 91920, Israel. TEL 02-527156. FAX 02-533542. Ed. Avner Tomaschoff. bk.rev.; charts; illus.; circ. 8,000.

296 305.3   US
TORCHLIGHT. 1941. q. $2. Federation of Jewish Men's Clubs Inc., 475 Riverside Dr., Ste. 244, New York, NY 10115. TEL 212-749-8100. FAX 212-316-4271. Ed. H. Manual Dobrusin. adv.; bk.rev.; illus.; circ. 40,000.
    Formerly (until 1977): Torch (ISSN 0049-416X)

296   US   ISSN 0041-0608
BM1   CODEN: TRADD2
TRADITION (NEW YORK); a journal of Orthodox Jewish thought. 1958. q. $23 to individuals; institutions $66. Rabbinical Council of America, 275 Seventh Ave., New York, NY 10001. TEL 212-243-6000. Ed. Rabbi Walter S. Wurzburger. bk.rev.; abstr.; circ. 4,000. (also avail. in microform from UMI) Indexed: Arts & Hum.Cit.Ind., Ind.Jew.Per., Mid.East: Abstr.& Ind., Old Test.Abstr., Rel.& Theol.Abstr. (1969-), Rel.Ind.One.
    —BLDSC shelfmark: 8881.070300.

296   GW   ISSN 0041-2716
DS101
TRIBUENE; Zeitschrift zum Verstaendnis d. Judentums. 1962. q. DM.28($7.55) Tribuene-Verlag, Habsburger Allee 72, 6000 Frankfurt, Germany. Ed. Axel Silenius. adv.; bk.rev.; stat.; circ. 5,000. Indexed: Phil.Ind.
    —BLDSC shelfmark: 9050.270000.

TZIVOS HASHEM CHILDREN'S NEWSLETTER. see CHILDREN AND YOUTH — For

296 327   US   ISSN 0888-3440
ULTIMATE ISSUES. 1985. q. $24. Dennis Prager, Ed. & Pub., 6020 Washington Blvd., Ste. 2, Culver City, CA 90232. TEL 310-558-3958. FAX 310-558-4241. bk.rev.; bibl.; tr.lit.; circ. 8,500. (looseleaf format; back issues avail.)

296.8   US   ISSN 0363-3810
BM21
UNION OF AMERICAN HEBREW CONGREGATIONS. STATE OF OUR UNION. biennial. Union of American Hebrew Congregations, 838 Fifth Ave., New York, NY 10021. TEL 212-249-0100.

296   US   ISSN 0041-8153
UNITED SYNAGOGUE REVIEW. 1943. biennial. $3. United Synagogue of America, 155 Fifth Ave., New York, NY 10010. TEL 212-533-7800. FAX 212-353-9439. Ed. Lois Goldrich. adv.; bk.rev.; illus.; circ. 255,000.
    Description: Serves as a vehicle for communication for the Conservative Movement in Judaism.

296   US
VOICE OF JUDAISM. 1960. irreg. free. National Jewish Information Service, c/o Rabbi Moshe M. Maggal, Ed., 3761 Decade St., Las Vegas, NV 89121. TEL 702-454-5872.
    Description: Pertains to conversion to Judaism and other items relating to Jewish events around the world.

296   CN
VOICE OF THE VAAD. 1961. q. Jewish Community Council of Montreal, 5491 Victoria Ave., Ste. 117, Montreal, Que. H3W 2P9, Canada. TEL 514-739-6363. Ed. Rabbi I.L. Hechtman. adv.; bk.rev. (tabloid format)

296   US   ISSN 0887-011X
WELLSPRINGS; a quarterly journal exploring the inner dimensions of Torah and Jewish life. 1984. q. $15. Lubavitch Youth Organization, Student Affairs Office, 770 Eastern Pkwy., Brooklyn, NY 11213. TEL 718-953-1000. FAX 718-771-6553. Ed. Baila Olidort. adv.; bk.rev.; tr.lit.; circ. 15,000. (back issues avail.)
    Description: Explores issues of contemporary and social concern through a Hasidic perspective. Includes essays and dialogues on the arts and sciences.

WESTERN STATES JEWISH HISTORY. see ETHNIC INTERESTS

296   US   ISSN 0043-7557
WOMEN'S LEAGUE OUTLOOK. 1930. q. $8. Women's League for Conservative Judaism, 48 E. 74 St., New York, NY 10021. TEL 212-628-1600. FAX 212-772-3507. Ed. Janis Sherman Popp. adv.; bk.rev.; circ. 140,000.

WOMEN'S ZIONIST ORGANIZATION OF SOUTH AFRICA. NEWS AND VIEWS. see POLITICAL SCIENCE

WORLD ZIONIST ORGANIZATION. GENERAL COUNCIL. ADDRESSES, DEBATES, RESOLUTIONS. see POLITICAL SCIENCE

296   IS   ISSN 0333-7596
YAD L'ACHIM WALL CALENDAR. (Text in English) 1970. bi-m. $15. Peylim-Yad l'Achim, 4 Yona St., P.O. Box 5195, Jerusalem, Israel. FAX 2371043. Ed.Bd. circ. 3,000. (back issues avail.)

296   US
YAD VASHEM STUDIES. (Text in English and Hebrew) 1957. a. £21 (effective 1992). (Yad Vashem Martyrs' and Heroes' Remembrance Authority, IS) Pergamon Press, Inc., Journals Division, 660 White Plains Rd., Tarrytown, NY 10591-5153. TEL 914-524-9200. FAX 914-333-2444. (And: Headington Hill Hall, Oxford OX3 0BW, England. TEL 0865-794141) Ed. Aharon Weiss. bk.rev.; index, cum.index: vols.1-20, 1957-1990; circ. 1,500. (also avail. in microform; back issues avail.) Indexed: Hist.Abstr.
    Formerly (until 1976): Yad Vashem Studies on the European Jewish Catastrophe and Resistance (ISSN 0084-3296)
    Refereed Serial

296   US   ISSN 0084-3369
YALE JUDAICA SERIES. 1948. irreg., no.26, 1989. price varies. Yale University Press, 92A Yale Sta., New Haven, CT 06520. TEL 203-432-0940.
    —BLDSC shelfmark: 9370.100000.

296   US
YEARBOOK OF RELIGIOUS ZIONISM. (Text in English and Hebrew) 1982. a. IS.30($15) Society for the Advancement of Religious Zionism, Mesilot, P.O. Box 7524, Jerusalem, Israel. TEL 02-248113. adv.; circ. 5,000.

YESHIVA UNIVERSITY SEPHARDIC BULLETIN. see ETHNIC INTERESTS

296   US   ISSN 0044-040X
DER YID; voice of American Orthodox Jewry. (Text in Yiddish) 1951. w. $40. (National Committee of Orthodox Jewish Communities) Der Yid Publishing, 13 Hooper St., Brooklyn, NY 11211. TEL 718-797-3900. FAX 718-797-1985. Ed. Sender Deutsch. adv.; bk.rev.; circ. 39,000. (tabloid format; also avail. in microform from AJP)

296   US   ISSN 0044-0418
BM198
YIDDISHE HEIM/JEWISH HOME. (Text in English, Yiddish) 1958. q. $8. (Agudas Neshei Ubnos Chabad) Kehot Publication Society, 770 Eastern Parkway, Brooklyn, NY 11213. TEL 718-493-9571. Eds. Rachel Altein, Tema Gurary. illus.; circ. 5,000.

296   FR
YOD; revue des etudes hebraiques et juives modernes et contemporaines. 1975. s-a. price varies. Institut National des Langues et Civilisations Orientales, 2 rue de Lille, 75343 Paris Cedex 07, France. TEL 49-26-42-74.
    Description: Studies the literature, history, and sociology of the Jewish people in Israel and the surrounding area in the 19th and 20th centuries.

296   IS
YOM HASHISHI. 1988. w. 19 B Keren Hayesod St., Jerusalem 94 188, Israel. Ed.Bd.

296   US   ISSN 0044-0809
BM1
YOUNG ISRAEL VIEWPOINT. 1937. m. (except July & Aug.). $5 to non-members. National Council of Young Israel, 3 West 16th St, New York, NY 10011. TEL 212-929-1525. FAX 212-727-9526. adv.; bk.rev.; circ. 40,000 (controlled). (tabloid format; also avail. in microfilm from AJP)

YOUR CHILD. see EDUCATION

ZION; a quarterly for research in Jewish history. see ETHNIC INTERESTS

RELIGIONS AND THEOLOGY — Protestant

A A B C NEWSLETTER. (American Association of Bible Colleges) see EDUCATION — Higher Education

A A C S NEWSLETTER. (American Association of Christian Schools) see EDUCATION — Guides To Schools And Colleges

285   CN
A C O P MESSENGER. 1957. m. Can.$8. Apostolic Church of Pentecost of Canada, Inc., 10333 Parkview Pl., Surrey, B.C. V3R 6P5, Canada. TEL 604-589-4141. Ed. Rev. Irvin Ellis. adv.; bk.rev.; circ. 2,000. (tabloid format)
    Formerly (until 1992): End Times Messenger.

287   US
A.M.E. CHRISTIAN RECORDER. bi-w. $15. African Methodist Episcopal Church, 500 Eighth Ave. S., Nashville, TN 37203. TEL 615-256-8548. FAX 615-244-7604.

287   US   ISSN 0360-3725
A.M.E. CHURCH REVIEW. 1884. q. $10. African Methodist Episcopal Church, 500 Eighth Ave. S., Nashville, TN 37203. TEL 615-256-7020. FAX 615-244-7604. Ed. Jamye C. Williams. bk.rev.; bibl.; charts; illus.; stat.; circ. 6,000. (also avail. in microform from UMI; back issues avail.)

283   US   ISSN 0731-7948
ABUNDANT LIFE MAGAZINE. vol.44, 1990. bi-m. Oral Roberts Evangelistic Association Inc., Box 2187, Tulsa, OK 74101. TEL 918-495-7307.

286   US   ISSN 0162-1955
ACCENT (BIRMINGHAM). 1970. m. (except July/Aug.). $11. Woman's Missionary Union, Highway 280 E., 100 Missionary Ridge, Birmingham, AL 35242-5235. TEL 205-991-4933. FAX 205-991-4990. (Subscr. to: Box 830010, Birmingham, AL 35283-0010) Ed. Jan Turrentine. circ. 107,000.
    Description: Publication of interest to members and leaders of Southern Baptist Acteens organizations.

ACTION AFRICA. see RELIGIONS AND THEOLOGY

284 282   US
ACTION INFORMATION; resources for people who care about congregations. 1975. bi-m. membership. Alban Institute, 4125 Nebraska Ave., N.W., Washington, DC 20016. TEL 202-244-7320. Ed. Celia Allison Hahn. bk.rev.; illus.; index, cum.index; circ. 7,500.

RELIGIONS AND THEOLOGY — PROTESTANT

283   AT   ISSN 0001-8147
ADELAIDE CHURCH GUARDIAN. 1906. m. Aus.$9.50. Anglican Church of Australia, Diocese of Adelaide, Anglican Church Office, 44 Currie St., Adelaide, S.A. 5000, Australia. FAX 08-211-8748. Ed. R. Douglass. adv.; bk.rev.; circ. 4,000.

220   US   ISSN 0149-8347
ADULT BIBLE STUDIES. 1967. q. $11 for inkprint; large print $11.15. (United Methodist Church, Board of Discipleship) United Methodist Publishing House, Graded Press, 201 Eighth Ave. S., Nashville, TN 37202. TEL 615-749-6417. FAX 615-749-6079. Ed. Victor J. Jacobs. circ. 600,000 inkprint; 150,000 large print. (large print edition in 14 pt.)

268   US   ISSN 0162-4156
ADULT BIBLE STUDY. American Indian edition (ISSN 1040-5186) (Editions in American Indian, English, Vietnamese) q. $4.75. Southern Baptist Convention, Sunday School Board, 127 Ninth Ave., North, Nashville, TN 37234. TEL 800-458-2772.

200   US   ISSN 1040-5186
ADULT BIBLE STUDY. AMERICAN INDIAN EDITION. (Editions in English, Vietnamese) q. $4.75. Southern Baptist Convention, Sunday School Board, 127 Ninth Ave., N., Nashville, TN 37234. TEL 800-458-2772.

268   US
ADULT BIBLE STUDY. VIETNAMESE EDITION. American Indian edition (ISSN 1040-5186) (Editions in American Indian, English) q. $6. Southern Baptist Convention, Sunday School Board, 127 Ninth Ave., N., Nashville, TN 37234. TEL 800-458-2772.
    Formerly: Adult Bible Study. Pupil. Vietnamese Edition.

268   US   ISSN 0162-4164
ADULT BIBLE TEACHER. q. $11. Southern Baptist Convention, Sunday School Board, 127 Ninth Ave., North, Nashville, TN 37234. TEL 800-458-2772.

268   US   ISSN 0162-4172
ADULT LEADERSHIP. m. $12.75. Southern Baptist Convention, Sunday School Board, 127 Ninth Ave., North, Nashville, TN 37234. TEL 800-458-2772.
    Indexed: Bk.Rev.Ind. (1965-1977), Child.Bk.Rev.Ind. (1965-1977), Sci.Abstr, South.Bap.Per.Ind.

284   US
ADULT STUDY GUIDE. q. $2.50 per no. for teacher ed.; student ed. $1.40. Messenger Publishing House, Box 850, Joplin, MO 64802. TEL 417-624-7050. illus.

268   US   ISSN 0400-5880
ADULT TEACHER. q. $11. Southern Baptist Convention, Sunday School Board, 127 Ninth Ave., North, Nashville, TN 37234. TEL 800-458-2772.

268   US   ISSN 0162-4148
ADVANCED BIBLE STUDY. q. $6.25. Southern Baptist Convention, Sunday School Board, 127 Ninth Ave., North, Nashville, TN 37234. TEL 800-458-2772.

286   NE   ISSN 0165-8603
ADVENT. 1899. m. (10/yr.) fl.2.95. (Zevende-Dags Adventisten - Seventh-Day Adventists) Stichting Uitgeverij "Veritas", Biltseweg 14, 3735 ME Bosch en Duin, Netherlands. FAX 030-281084. Ed. N. Kooren. illus. **Indexed:** CERDIC.
    Formerly: Adventbode (ISSN 0001-8767)

286   GW   ISSN 0179-7999
ADVENTECHO; Gemeindeblatt der Siebenten - Tags - Adventisten. 1895. m. DM.57.50. Saatkorn Verlag, Grindelberg 13-17, Postfach 132215, 2000 Hamburg 13, Germany. TEL 040-44187124. Ed. Gerhard Rempel. circ. 11,000.

286   JA
ADVENTIST LIFE. (Text in Japanese) m. 5520 Yen($42.46) Japan Union Conference of S.D.A., 846 Kamikawai-cho, Asahi-ku, Yokohama 241, Japan. FAX 045-921-2319.

286   US   ISSN 0161-1119
BX6101
ADVENTIST REVIEW. (Editions in English and Spanish) 1850. w. $44.97. Review and Herald Publishing Association (Silver Spring), 12501 Old Columbia Pike, Silver Spring, MD 20904-6600. TEL 301-680-6000. FAX 301-680-6638. Ed. William G. Johnsson. bk.rev.; index; circ. 43,000. (tabloid format; reprint service avail. from UMI)
    Former titles: Advent Review and Sabbath Herald (ISSN 0095-2397); Review and Herald (ISSN 0034-6381)

268   US   ISSN 0001-8783
ADVENTURE (NASHVILLE). m. in w. parts. $10. Southern Baptist Convention, Sunday School Board, 127 Ninth Ave., North, Nashville, TN 37234. TEL 800-458-2772.

284   US   ISSN 0044-6467
AFFIRM; our eternal Christ and his word for our changing and urgent needs. 1971. bi-m. contributions. Balance, Inc., c/o Walther Memorial Lutheran Church, 4040 West Fond du Lac Ave., Milwaukee, WI 53216. TEL 414-444-4133. (Subscr. to: Box 8390, St. Louis, MO 63132-0390) Ed. Rev. Thomas Baker. bk.rev.; circ. 104,000.
    Description: Dedicated to preserving theological heritage while looking at related developments in the Lutheran church.

286 209   US   ISSN 0002-4147
ALABAMA BAPTIST HISTORIAN. vol.5, 1969. s-a. $5. Alabama Baptist Historical Society, Sanford University Library, Birmingham, AL 35229. Ed. Lee N. Allen. bk.rev.; bibl.; circ. 250. **Indexed:** Amer.Hist.& Life, Hist.Abstr.
—BLDSC shelfmark: 0786.488000.

200   US   ISSN 0891-8767
ALIVE NOW; devotional reading. 1971. bi-m. $7. (United Methodist Church, General Board of Discipleship) Upper Room, 1908 Grand Ave., Box 189, Nashville, TN 37202. TEL 615-340-7218. Ed. Mary Ruth Coffman. bk.rev.; illus.; circ. 70,000. (back issues avail.)

220   UK
ALIVE TO GOD; bible guidelines for living by the spirit. 1984. q. £7.50. Scripture Union, 130 City Rd., London EC1V 2NJ, England. TEL 071-782-0013. FAX 071-782-0014. (Subscr. to: 9-11 Clothier Rd., Bristol BS4 5RL, England) Ed. Terry Clutterham. adv.; circ. 55,000.

283   UK   ISSN 0002-5623
ALL THE WORLD. 1884. q. £3.50. Salvation Army, International Headquarters, 101 Queen Victoria St., London EC4P 4EP, England. TEL 071-236-5222. FAX 071-329-3268. Ed. Connie Croly. circ. 18,000.
    Description: Reviews Salvation Army social services and Evangelism throughout the world.

266   NE   ISSN 0002-5666
ALLE DEN VOLCKE. 1907. m. fl.10. Gereformeerde Zendingsbond in de Nederlandse Hervormde Kerk - Board of the Reformed Mission League in the Netherlands Reformed Church, Faunalaan 89, 3972 PP Driebergen, Netherlands. FAX 03438-21392. Ed. T. Eikelboom. bk.rev.; illus.; circ. 44,000.

200   US   ISSN 1040-6794
ALLIANCE LIFE. 1882. fortn. $9.50. Christian and Missionary Alliance, Box 35000, Colorado Springs, CO 80935-3500. TEL 719-599-5999. FAX 719-593-8692. Ed. Maurice R. Irvin. adv.; bk.rev.; illus.; index; circ. 55,000. (also avail. in microform from UMI; back issues avail.; reprint service avail. from UMI) **Indexed:** Chr.Per.Ind., G.Soc.Sci.& Rel.Per.Lit.
    Formerly (until 1987): Alliance Witness (ISSN 0745-3256)

284 791.4   NE
ALPHA. 1976. q. Evangelische Omroep, Postbus 565, 1200 AN Hilversum, Netherlands. circ. 250,000.

284   UK
ALPHA (NEW MALDEN). 1991. m. £15.50. Elm House Christian Communications Ltd., 37 Elm Rd., New Malden, Surrey KT3 3HB, England. TEL 081-942-9761. FAX 081-949-2313. Ed. Dave Roberts. adv.; bk.rev.; charts; illus.; circ. 18,000. (back issues avail.)
    Formed by the merger of (1965-1991): 21st Century Christian (ISSN 0952-6269); Which was formerly: Buzz (ISSN 0045-3692); (1982-1991): Today (New Malden) (ISSN 0956-2648); Which had former titles (until Jan. 1989): Leadership Today (ISSN 0952-6277) And (until 1987): Today (London) (ISSN 0262-8023); (until 1982): Crusade (ISSN 0011-2127).
    Description: Covers Christian and social issues including church leadership, personal teaching. Informs and challenges leaders of all areas in church.

AMERICAN ASSOCIATION OF CHRISTIAN SCHOOLS. DIRECTORY. see EDUCATION — Guides To Schools And Colleges

286   US   ISSN 0002-757X
BX6201
AMERICAN BAPTIST. 1803. 10/yr. $9.95. American Baptist Churches in the U S A, Box 851, Valley Forge, PA 19482-0851. TEL 215-768-2216. FAX 215-768-2275. Ed. Philip E. Jenks. adv.; bk.rev.; charts; illus.; circ. 55,000.
    Formerly: Crusader and Mission.

286   US   ISSN 0091-9381
BX6207
AMERICAN BAPTIST CHURCHES IN THE U S A DIRECTORY. 1971. a. $5. American Baptist Churches in the U S A, Box 851, Valley Forge, PA 19482-0851. TEL 215-768-2000. Ed. Patricia Schlosser. circ. 6,000.
    Supersedes: American Baptist Convention. Directory (ISSN 0096-3380); American Baptist Convention. Yearbook.

286   US   ISSN 0092-3478
BX6207
AMERICAN BAPTIST CHURCHES IN THE U S A YEARBOOK. Continues: American Baptist Convention. Yearbook. 1907. a. $5. American Baptist Churches in the U S A, Box 851, Valley Forge, PA 19482-0851. TEL 215-768-2000. Ed. Daniel E. Weiss. illus.; circ. 3,500. Key Title: Yearbook of the American Baptist Churches in the U S A.

286 209   US
AMERICAN BAPTIST QUARTERLY; a Baptist journal of history, theology and ministry. 1958. q. $15. American Baptist Historical Society, Linfield College, McMinnville, OR 97128. (Subscr. to: Dr. William H. Brackney, Box 857, Valley Forge, PA 19482) Ed. Dr. William R. Millar. bk.rev.; circ. 1,200. (also avail. in microform from UMI; reprint service avail. from UMI) **Indexed:** Amer.Hist. & Life, Hist.Abstr., Rel.& Theol.Abstr. (1982-), Rel.Ind.One, Rel.Per.
    Former titles (until vol.25, 1982): Foundations (ISSN 0015-8992); Chronicle (Greensburg) (ISSN 0360-5779)

286   US   ISSN 0886-5159
BX8935
AMERICAN PRESBYTERIANS: JOURNAL OF PRESBYTERIAN HISTORY. 1901. q. $15. Presbyterian Church (U.S.A.), Presbyterian Historical Society, 425 Lombard St., Philadelphia, PA 19147. TEL 215-627-1852. FAX 215-627-0509. Ed. James H. Smylie. bk.rev.; abstr.; illus.; index, cum.index: 1901-1962; circ. 1,400. (also avail. in microfilm) **Indexed:** Amer.Hist.& Life, Arts & Hum.Cit.Ind., Curr.Cont., Hist.Abstr., Rel.& Theol.Abstr. (1966-), Rel.Ind.One, Rel.Per.
—BLDSC shelfmark: 0853.138000.
    Former titles (until 1984): Journal of Presbyterian History (ISSN 0022-3883); (until 1961): Presbyterian Historical Society Journal (ISSN 0147-3735)

AMERICAN PROTESTANT HEALTH ASSOCIATION. BULLETIN. see HOSPITALS

284   AT
ANCHOR. 1973. bi-m. Aus.$2. Redeemer Lutheran Church Waverley, 25 Cypress Ave., Glen Waverley, Vic. 3150, Australia. TEL 03-803-5715. circ. 200.
    Description: Parish circular with items to challenge, inform, encourage and update members.

RELIGIONS AND THEOLOGY — PROTESTANT

286 US ISSN 0066-1708
ANDREWS UNIVERSITY. MONOGRAPHS. 1963. 3/yr. price varies. Andrews University Press, Berrien Springs, MI 49104. TEL 616-471-6023. FAX 616-473-4472. Ed. Nancy Vyhmeister. adv.; bk.rev.

283 CN ISSN 0517-7731
ANGLICAN. 1958. m. Can.$5 (foreign Can.$8). Anglican Church of Canada, Diocese of Toronto, 135 Adelaide St. E., Toronto, Ont. M5C 1L8, Canada. TEL 416-363-6021. FAX 416-363-7678. Ed. Vivian Snead. adv.; bk.rev.; circ. 46,000. **Indexed:** CERDIC.

283 US
ANGLICAN ADVANCE. 1875. m. (except Aug.). $5 (free to Diocese residents). Episcopal Diocese of Chicago, 65 E. Huron St., Chicago, IL 60611. TEL 312-751-4200. FAX 312-787-4534. Ed. Charlyn M. Bridges. illus.; circ. 15,500. **Indexed:** CERDIC.
Formerly: Advance (Chicago) (ISSN 0001-8562)
Description: Contains news of the Diocese.

283 US
ANGLICAN AND EPISCOPAL HISTORY. 1932. q. $25. Historical Society of the Episcopal Church, c/o Rev. John F. Woolverton, Ed., Box 261, Center Sandwich, NH 03227. TEL 603-284-6584. adv.; bk.rev.; bibl.; index; circ. 1,500. (also avail. in microfilm from UMI; reprint service avail. from UMI) **Indexed:** Amer.Hist.& Life, CERDIC, Hist.Abstr., Rel.Ind.One, Rel.Per.
Formerly: Historical Magazine of the Protestant Episcopal Church (ISSN 0018-2486)

283 UK
ANGLICAN CATHOLIC. 2/yr. Anglican Society, c/o D. Thomson, Gen.Sec., 1 Whitfield Court, 72 Clarendon Gardens, Cranbrook, Ilford, Essex, England.
Formerly: English Catholic.
Description: Theological and liturgical studies concerned with traditional Anglicanism.

283 CN
ANGLICAN CHURCH OF CANADA. GENERAL SYNOD. JOURNAL. 1894. triennial. Anglican Church of Canada, 600 Jarvis St., Toronto, Ont. M4Y 2J6, Canada. TEL 416-924-9192. FAX 416-921-0211. TELEX 065-24128. circ. 450.
Formerly (until 1980): Anglican Church of Canada. General Synod. Journal of Proceedings (ISSN 0380-2469)

283 US ISSN 0003-3278
ANGLICAN DIGEST. 1958. bi-m. $15 donation. (Society for Promoting and Encouraging Arts and Knowledge, Inc.) S P E A K, Inc., Hillspeak, Eureka Springs, AR 72632-9705. TEL 501-253-9701. Ed. Rev. C. Frederick Barbee. adv.; bk.rev.; circ. 130,000. **Indexed:** CERDIC.

283 AT ISSN 1032-9234
ANGLICAN ENCOUNTER. 1970. m. Aus.$11 (foreign Aus.$26). Anglican Diocese of Newcastle, P.O. Box 817, Newcastle, N.S.W. 2300, Australia. TEL 049-26-3733. FAX 049-261968. Ed. Marion Willey. adv.; B&W page Aus.$600, color page Aus.$660; trim 27 x 40. bk.rev.; circ. 6,800. (tabloid format)
Description: Local and international news and teachings of interest to Anglican church members.

200 AT
ANGLICAN GAZETTE; magazine for the Anglican Church in Central Queensland. 1890. m. Aus.$9. Anglican Diocese of Rockhampton, P.O. Box 116, Rockhampton, Qld. 4700, Australia. TEL 079-273-188. FAX 079-224-562. adv.; bk.rev.; circ. 2,500.
Formerly: Church Gazette.

283 CN ISSN 0847-978X
ANGLICAN JOURNAL/JOURNAL ANGLICAN. (Supplement avail.: Crosstalk) (Text in English, French) 1874. m (10/yr.). Can.$7 (foreign Can.$14). Anglican Church of Canada, 600 Jarvis St., Toronto, Ont. M4Y 2J6, Canada. TEL 416-924-9192. FAX 416-921-4452. TELEX 065-24128. Ed. Carolyn Purden. adv.; bk.rev.; film rev.; illus.; circ. 274,980. (tabloid format; also avail. in microfilm from MIM,MML,UMI) **Indexed:** Can.Per.Ind., CMI.
Former titles (until 1989): Canadian Churchman (ISSN 0008-3216) & Anglican Journal - Journal Episcopal.
Description: The national newspaper of the Anglican Church of Canada.

283 CN ISSN 0820-506X
ANGLICAN MAGAZINE; living message. 1889. 7/yr. Can.$12. Anglican Church of Canada, 600 Jarvis St., Toronto, Ont. M4Y 2J6, Canada. TEL 416-924-9192. FAX 416-968-7893. TELEX 065-24128. Ed. John Bird. circ. 11,000. (back issues avail.)

283 AT
ANGLICAN MESSENGER. 1969. m. Aus.$12. Anglican Church in Western Australia, G.P.O. Box W2067, Perth, W.A. 6001, Australia. TEL 09-325-7455. FAX 09-325-6741. Ed. Rev. Bob Waterhouse. adv.: B&W page Aus.$645; adv. contact: Sue Murgatryd. bk.rev.; circ. 8,000. (tabloid format)

266 CN ISSN 0317-8765
ANGLICAN YEAR BOOK. 1900. a. Can.$24.95. (Anglican Church of Canada) Anglican Book Centre, 600 Jarvis St., Toronto, Ont. M4Y 2J6, Canada. TEL 416-924-9192. Ed. M. Lloyd. adv.; stat.; circ. 1,000.

266 UK
ANVIL; an Anglican Evangelical journal for theology and mission. 1984. 3/yr. £13.90($30.20) (foreign £15.90). c/o Rev. Canon Michael Sansom, Ed., 4d Harpenden Rd., St. Albans AL3 5AB, England. TEL 0727 833777. (Subscr. to: Mrs. J. Smith, 14 Lower Stanton Rd., Ilkeston, Derbyshire DE7 4LN, England) adv.; bk.rev.; circ. 850. (also avail. in microform from UMI)

287 US ISSN 0003-6552
EL APOSENTO ALTO. English edition: Upper Room (ISSN 0042-0735) (Editions in 41 languages) 1938. bi-m. $4.50 for inkprint; large print ed. $6.50; Chinese-English ed. $12; German ed. $10; Korean-English ed. $12.50; Spanish ed. $4.50; Thai ed. $10; other language eds. $8.50. (United Methodist Church, General Board of Discipleship) Upper Room, 1908 Grand Ave., Box 189, Nashville, TN 37212. TEL 615-340-7253. Ed. Horacio M. Rios. illus.; circ. 75,000. (large print edition in 18 pt.)

283 US ISSN 1041-3316
THE APOSTLE. 1892. m. $5. Episcopal Diocese of Alabama, Box 3319, Phenix City, AL 36868-3319. TEL 205-271-0750. Ed. Rev. William P. McLemore. circ. 13,500.
Formerly (until 1988): Alabama Churchman (ISSN 8750-9679)

260 US
ARKANSAS EPISCOPALIAN. vol.49, 1975. 9/yr. $3 donation. Episcopal Diocese of Arkansas, Box 164668, Little Rock, AR 72216-4668. TEL 501-372-2168. Ed. Julie Keller. bk.rev.; circ. 8,000 (controlled). (tabloid format)
Formerly: Arkansas Churchman.

287 US
ARKANSAS UNITED METHODIST. 1881. bi-m. $12.50. (United Methodist Church, Arkansas Area) Arkansas Methodist, Inc., Box 3547, Little Rock, AR 72203-3547. TEL 501-374-4831. FAX 501-370-4018. Ed. Jane D. Dennis. adv.; circ. 11,000.
Formerly (until 1983): Arkansas Methodist.
Description: Contains news, features and opinions relating to the United Methodist Church in Arkansas and its constituents. Includes national and international news and features on topics and events affecting the religious community.

207.11 US
ASBURY THEOLOGICAL JOURNAL. 1946. s-a. $5. Asbury Theological Seminary, 204 N. Lexington Ave., Wilmore, KY 40390-1199. TEL 606-858-3581. FAX 606-858-3581. Ed. Laurence Wood. bk.rev.; cum.index: 1946-66 in vol. 21; circ. 1,200. (also avail. in microform from UMI; reprint service avail. from UMI) **Indexed:** CERDIC, Chr.Per.Ind., Rel.& Theol.Abstr. (1988-), Rel.Ind.One.
Formerly: Asbury Seminarian (ISSN 0004-4253)
Description: Provides a scholarly forum for thorough discussion of issues relevant to Christian thought and faith, and to the nature and mission of the church. Addresses those concerns and ideas across the curriculum which interface with Christian thought, life and ministry.

285 US ISSN 0362-0816
ASSOCIATE REFORMED PRESBYTERIAN. 1976. m. $15. Associate Reformed Presbyterian, Inc., General Synod of the Associate Reformed Presbyterian Church, One Cleveland St., Greenville, SC 29601. TEL 803-232-8297. FAX 803-271-3729. Ed. Ben Johnston. adv.; bk.rev.; circ. 6,600. (also avail. in microform from UMI; back issues avail.)
Description: Devoted to the concerns of the Associate Reformed Presbyterian Church in relationship to its mission to the service of God.

286 CN ISSN 0004-6752
ATLANTIC BAPTIST. 1827. m. Can.$15($25) United Baptist Convention of the Atlantic Provinces, Board of Publication, Box 756, Kentville, N.S. B4N 3X9, Canada. TEL 902-681-6868. Ed. Rev. Michael A. Lipe. adv.; bk.rev.; illus.; index; circ. 9,500. (back issues avail.)
Description: Covers general religion and family life, devotional and social action.

284 GW ISSN 0004-7848
AUFBRUCH; evangelische Kirchenzeitung fuer Baden. 1965. w. DM.30. Evangelischer Presseverband fuer Baden e.V., Blumenstr. 7, 7500 Karlsruhe, Germany. adv.; bk.rev.; film rev.; illus.; circ. 69,000.

200 SZ ISSN 0004-7880
AUFTRAG. 1967. 6/yr. 18 Fr.($2) Kooperation Evangelischer Kirchen und Missionen, Missionstr. 21, 4003 Basel, Switzerland. Ed. Armin Mettler. illus; circ. 40,000.
Description: Covers missionary activities in Third World countries. Includes announcements of events.

284 282 GW
AUFTRAG; eine christliche Jugendzeitschrift. 1981. q. DM.21. Jugend mit einer Mission, Schlossgasse 1, 8931 Hurlach, Germany. FAX 030-8811932. Ed.Bd. adv.; bk.rev.; circ. 26,000. (back issues avail.)

268 US
AUGSBURG ADULT BIBLE STUDIES. LEADER GUIDE. 1968. q. $16. Augsburg Fortress, 426 S. Fifth St., Box 1209, Minneapolis, MN 55440. TEL 612-330-3300. circ. 8,000.
Formerly (until 1987): A L C - L C A Augsburg Adult Bible Studies. Teacher's Guide.

268 US
AUGSBURG ADULT BIBLE STUDIES. PARTICIPANT BOOK. 1968. q. $7.40. Augsburg Fortress, 426 S. Fifth St., Box 1209, Minneapolis, MN 55440. TEL 612-330-3300. circ. 75,000.
Former titles (until 1987): A L C - L C A Augsburg Adult Bible Studies. Adult Quarterly; A L C - L C A Augsburg Adult Bible Studies.

268 US
AUGSBURG HOME BIBLE STUDIES. 1968. q. $14.60. Augsburg Fortress, 426 S. Fifth St., Box 1209, Minneapolis, MN 55440. TEL 612-330-3300. circ. 750. (back issues avail.)
Former titles (until 1987): A L C - L C A Augsburg Adult Bible Studies. Home Bible Studies; A L C - L C A Augsburg Home Bible Studies; A L C - L C A Augsburg Adult Bible Studies. Home Bible Studies.

285 MQ
AUJOURD'HUI DIMANCHE. w. Presbytere de Bellevue, Fort-de-France, Martinique. TEL 714897. Ed. Pere Gauthier. circ. 12,000.

280 AT ISSN 0004-8852
AUSTRALIAN CHRISTIAN; national journal of Churches of Christ. 1898. fortn. Aus.$25. (Federal Conference of Churches of Christ) Australian Christian Board of Management, P.O. Box 101, Essendon North, Vic. 3041, Australia. FAX 02-379-0018. Ed. C.R. Ambrose. adv.; bk.rev.; index; circ. 4,600. **Indexed:** CERDIC.

AUSTRALIAN LECTIONARY (YEAR). see RELIGIONS AND THEOLOGY

285 AT ISSN 0005-0059
AUSTRALIAN PRESBYTERIAN LIFE. 1966. m. (except Jan.). Aus.$27. Presbyterian Church of Australia, National Journal Committee, 77 Shaftesbury Rd., Burwood, N.S.W. 2134, Australia. TEL 02-744-1902. Ed. Rev. R. Humphreys. adv.; bk.rev.; film rev.; illus.; circ. 3,500.

RELIGIONS AND THEOLOGY — PROTESTANT

286 US ISSN 0162-6833
AWARE. 1970. q. $9. Woman's Missionary Union, Highway 280 E., 100 Missionary Ridge, Birmingham, AL 35242-5235. TEL 205-991-4933. FAX 205-991-4990. (Subscr. to: Box 830010, Birmingham, AL 35283-0010) Ed. Barbara Massey. circ. 45,000.
Description: Publication of interest to leaders of Southern Baptist Girls in Action groups.

286 CN
B.C. FELLOWSHIP BAPTIST. 1927. m. Can.$5.25. Fellowship of Regular Baptist Churches of British Columbia, Box 800, Langley, B.C. V3A 8C9, Canada. TEL 604-888-3616. Ed. W. Gordon Reeve. bk.rev.; circ. 3,000.
Formerly: B.C. Regular Baptist (ISSN 0702-1003)

284 GW
B I M S. (Blaukreuz Information - Meinungen - Szene) 1986. q. DM.10. Blaues Kreuz in der Evangelischen Kirche, Dietrichsstr. 17a, 3000 Hannover 1, Germany. TEL 0511-651917. Ed. Guenter Blueder. adv.; bk.rev.; circ. 1,500.

285 US ISSN 0005-5557
BANNER (GRAND RAPIDS). 1866. 46/yr. $29.75. (Christian Reformed Church) C R C Publications, 2850 Kalamazoo Ave. S.E., Grand Rapids, MI 49560. TEL 616-246-0725. FAX 616-246-0834. Ed. Rev. Galen H. Meyer. adv.; bk.rev.; illus.; index; circ. 43,000. (also avail. in microform from UMI; reprint service avail. from UMI) Indexed: CERDIC, G.Soc.Sci.& Rel.Per.Lit.
Formerly: Banner of Truth.

268 US ISSN 0162-4180
BAPTIST ADULTS. q. $5.50. Southern Baptist Convention, Sunday School Board, 127 Ninth Ave., N., Nashville, TN 37234. TEL 800-458-2772.

286 US
BAPTIST AND REFLECTOR. 1835. w. $7.50. Tennessee Baptist Convention, c/o Executive Board, Box 728, Brentwood, TN 37027. TEL 615-373-2255. FAX 615-371-2014. adv.; circ. 67,000.

286 US ISSN 0005-5689
BAPTIST BULLETIN. 1933. m. (11/yr.). $10. General Association of Regular Baptist Churches, 1300 N. Meacham Rd., Schaumburg, IL 60173-4888. TEL 708-843-1600. FAX 708-843-3757. Ed. Norman Olson. adv.; bk.rev.; circ. 35,000. Indexed: G.Soc.Sci.& Rel.Per.Lit.

286 US ISSN 0005-5697
BAPTIST CHALLENGE; voice of independent Baptists. 1961. m. free. Central Baptist Church, Box 5567, Little Rock, AR 72215. TEL 501-664-3225. Ed. M.L. Moser, Jr. adv.; bk.rev.; illus.; circ. 7,300.

286 CN
BAPTIST DIRECTORY. a. Can.$10. Baptist Convention of Ontario and Quebec, 217 St. George St., Toronto, Ont. M5R 2M2, Canada. Ed. S. McDonald. circ. 1,000.
Formerly: Baptist Yearbook.

286 US ISSN 0005-5700
BAPTIST HERALD. 1923. m. (combined in Jan.-Feb. July-Aug.). $8 (Canada $10.50, elsewhere $16). North American Baptist Conference, 1 S. 210 Summit Ave., Oakbrook Terrace, IL 60181. TEL 708-495-2000. FAX 708-495-3301. Ed. Barbara J. Binder. adv.; illus.; circ. 8,500. (also avail. in microfilm from UMI) Indexed: CERDIC.

286 US
BAPTIST HERITAGE UPDATE. 1985. q. membership. Southern Baptist Convention, Historical Commission, 901 Commerce St., Ste. 400, Nashville, TN 37203-3630. TEL 615-244-0344. Ed. Kim Alley. circ. 7,000. (looseleaf format; back issues avail.)

286 209 US ISSN 0005-5719
BX6207
BAPTIST HISTORY AND HERITAGE. 1965. q. $13.45. Southern Baptist Convention, Historical Commission, 901 Commerce St., Ste. 400, Nashville, TN 37203-3630. TEL 615-244-0344. Ed. Lynn E. May, Jr. bk.rev.; charts; illus.; index; circ. 1,800. Indexed: Amer.Hist.& Life, CERDIC, Hist.Abstr., Rel.& Theol.Abstr. (1989-), Rel.Ind.One, South.Bap.Per.Ind.
—BLDSC shelfmark: 1863.140000.

286 910.03 US
BAPTIST INFORMER. 1878. m. $5. G B S C of North Carolina, 603 S. Wilmington St., Raleigh, NC 27601. TEL 919-821-7466. FAX 919-546-8301. Ed. A.D. Logan, Jr. adv.; bk.rev.; circ. 8,500. (tabloid format; back issues avail.)
Description: For black Baptists.

BAPTIST LEADER. see EDUCATION — Teaching Methods And Curriculum

266 US ISSN 0091-2743
BX6209.B37
BAPTIST MISSIONARY ASSOCIATION OF AMERICA. DIRECTORY AND HANDBOOK. 1961. a. free. Baptist News Service, Box 97, Jacksonville, TX 75766. TEL 903-586-2501. Ed. James C. Blaylock. circ. 5,000. Key Title: Directory and Handbook - Baptist Missionary Association of America.

266 UK ISSN 0067-4060
BAPTIST MISSIONARY SOCIETY, DIDCOT. ANNUAL REPORT. 1792. a. free. Baptist Missionary Society, P.O. Box 49, Baptist House, 129 Broadway, Didcot, Oxon OX11 8XA, England. TEL 0235-512077. FAX 0235-511265. TELEX 94070435-BMSB-G. circ. 24,000.
Description: Reports the work of the Baptist Missionary Society for the year.

266.6 UK ISSN 0067-4079
BAPTIST MISSIONARY SOCIETY, LONDON. OFFICIAL REPORT AND DIRECTORY OF MISSIONARIES. 1793. a. free. Baptist Missionary Society, P.O. Box 49, Baptist House, 129 Broadway, Didcot, Oxon OX11 3XA, England. TEL 0235-512077. FAX 0235-511265. circ. 6,000.
Description: Directory of committee members together with a financial report.

286 US ISSN 0005-5743
BAPTIST PROGRAM. 1927. m. $10. Southern Baptist Convention, Executive Committee, 901 Commerce, Ste. 750, Nashville, TN 37203-3630. TEL 615-244-2355. Ed. Ernest Mosley. adv.; bk.rev.; illus.; index; circ. 70,000. Indexed: South.Bap.Per.Ind.
Description: Keeps readers informed about programs and plans of the convention.

286 US ISSN 0005-5751
BAPTIST PROGRESS. 1912. w. $13. Baptist Missionary Association of Texas, Box 2085, Waxahachie, TX 75165. TEL 214-923-0756. FAX 214-923-2679. Ed. Danny Pope. adv.; bk.rev.; circ. 15,000 (controlled). (also avail. in microfilm)

286 US
BAPTIST PUBLIC RELATIONS ASSOCIATION NEWSLETTER. 1953. m. membership. Baptist Public Relations Association, Box 347, Brentwood, TN 37027. TEL 615-373-2255. Ed. Mary E. Speidel. bk.rev.; tr.lit.; circ. controlled. (looseleaf format)

286 209 UK ISSN 0005-576X
BX6276.A1
BAPTIST QUARTERLY. N.S. 1922. q. £5 to non-members; libraries £20. Baptist Historical Society, 148 Greenvale Rd., London SE9 1PQ, England. Ed. J.H.Y. Briggs. adv.; bk.rev.; illus.; index every 2 yrs. cum.index in 4 vols.: 1908-1921; 1922-1941; 1942-1964; 1965-1986; circ. 700. (also avail. in microfilm from UMI; reprint service avail. from UMI) Indexed: Amer.Hist.& Life, Br.Hum.Ind., CERDIC, Hist.Abstr., Hist.Abstr, Rel.& Theol.Abstr. (1968-), Rel.Ind.One, Rel.Per.
—BLDSC shelfmark: 1863.150000.

286 US ISSN 0005-5778
BAPTIST RECORD. 1877. w. $7.35. Mississippi Baptist Convention, Box 530, Jackson, MS 39205. TEL 601-968-3800. FAX 601-968-3928. Ed. Guy Henderson. adv.; bk.rev.; charts; illus.; record rev.; circ. 116,300. (newspaper; also avail. in microform) Indexed: CERDIC.

286 UK ISSN 0005-5786
BAPTIST TIMES. 1855. w. £27. Baptist Times Ltd., 129 The Broadway, Didcot, Oxon OX11 8XB, England. FAX 0235-512013. adv.; bk.rev.; illus.; music rev.; record rev.; circ. 12,500.

286 US ISSN 0025-4169
BAPTIST TRUE UNION; newsjournal for Maryland and Delaware Southern Baptists. 1849. bi-m. $7.50. Baptist Convention of Maryland - Delaware, 10255 Old Columbia Rd., Columbia, MD 21046-1716. TEL 301-321-7900. FAX 301-295-7040. Ed. Robert E. Allen. adv.; illus.; stat.; circ. 11,000. (tabloid format; also avail. in microfilm)
Formerly (until 1985): Maryland Baptist; Incorporates: True Union.

286 US ISSN 0888-9074
BAPTIST TRUMPET. 1940. w. $12.50. Baptist Missionary Association of Arkansas, Box 192208, Little Rock, AR 72219-2208. TEL 501-565-4601. Ed. David Tidwell. adv.; circ. 12,831. (tabloid format)

286.1 UK ISSN 0302-3184
BX6276.A1
BAPTIST UNION DIRECTORY. 1861. a. £5.50. Baptist Union of Great Britain, P.O. Box 44, 129 Broadway, Didcot, Oxforsh OX11 8RT, England. TEL 0235-512077. FAX 0235-811537. adv.; circ. 2,500.
Description: Details of accredited ministers and churches in membership with the Baptist Union of Great Britain.

286 CN ISSN 0067-4087
BX6252.W47
BAPTIST UNION OF WESTERN CANADA. YEARBOOK. 1907. a. Can.$14 (typically set in Sept.). Baptist Union of Western Canada, 838 11th Ave., S.W., Ste. 202, Calgary, Alta. T2R 0E5, Canada. TEL 403-234-9044. FAX 403-269-6755. Ed. W. Cram. circ. 700 (controlled).

286 US ISSN 0005-5808
BAPTIST WORLD. 1954. q. donation. Baptist World Alliance, Division of Communications, 6733 Curran St., McLean, VA 22101-6005. TEL 703-790-8980. Ed. Wendy Ryan. illus.; circ. 11,000. (also avail. in microform from UMI; reprint service avail. from UMI)

286 US ISSN 0067-4095
BAPTIST WORLD ALLIANCE. CONGRESS REPORTS. 1905. quinquennial; 15th, Los Angeles, 1985 (published in 1986); 16th, Seoul, 1990 (published in 1991). $11.50. Baptist World Alliance, Division of Communications, 6733 Curran St., McLean, VA 22101-6005. TEL 703-790-8980. circ. 15,000.

268 US ISSN 0195-136X
BAPTIST YOUNG ADULTS. q. $5.50. Southern Baptist Convention, Sunday School Board, 127 Ninth Ave. N., Nashville, TN 37234. TEL 800-458-2772.
Formerly (until Oct. 1979): Young Adults in Training (ISSN 0162-4806)

268 US ISSN 0162-4199
BAPTIST YOUTH. q. $5.50. Southern Baptist Convention, Sunday School Board, 127 Ninth Ave., N., Nashville, TN 37234. TEL 800-458-2772.

284 GW ISSN 0005-7282
BAYREUTHER GEMEINDEBLATT. 1922. m. DM.10. Evangelische-Lutherische Kirchengemeinde Bayreuth, Kirchplatz 2, 8580 Bayreuth, Germany. Ed. Helmut Beyer. adv.; bk.rev.; abstr.; circ. 5,500. (looseleaf format)

268 US ISSN 0198-6201
BEGINNING (NASHVILLE). 1980. q. $4. Southern Baptist Convention, Sunday School Board, 127 Ninth Ave., N., Nashville, TN 37234. TEL 800-458-2772.

284 GW
BERLIN - BRANDENBURGISCHES SONNTAGSBLATT; evangelische Wochenzeitung. 1946. w. DM.54. Wichern Verlag GmbH, Bachstr. 1-2, 1000 Berlin 21, Germany. TEL 030-3915075. Ed. Lutz Borgmann. circ. 16,000.
Formed by 1991 merger of: Berliner Sonntagsblatt & Potsdamer Kirche (ISSN 0232-5020); Formerly: Potsdamer.

284 GW ISSN 0724-6137
BERLINER THEOLOGISCHE ZEITSCHRIFT; Theologia Viatrum neue Folge. 1983. s-a. DM.46 (students DM.40). (Kirchliche Hochschule Berlin) Wichern-Verlag, Bachstr. 1-2, 1000 Berlin 21, Germany. circ. 500.
Description: Discusses theoretical and scientific problems of theology.

RELIGIONS AND THEOLOGY — PROTESTANT

268　　　　　US　ISSN 0162-4202
BIBLE BOOK STUDY FOR ADULT TEACHERS. q. $11.50. Southern Baptist Convention, Sunday School Board, 127 Ninth Ave., N., Nashville, TN 37234. TEL 800-458-2772.

268　　　　　US　ISSN 0162-4849
BIBLE BOOK STUDY FOR ADULTS. Chinese edition (ISSN 0897-0750); Korean edition (ISSN 0747-9514) q. $6. Southern Baptist Convention, Sunday School Board, 127 Ninth Ave., N., Nashville, TN 37234. TEL 800-458-2772.

268　　　　　US　ISSN 0897-0750
BIBLE BOOK STUDY FOR ADULTS. CHINESE EDITION. English edition (ISSN 0162-4849); Korean edition (ISSN 0747-9514) q. $6. Southern Baptist Convention, Sunday School Board, 127 Ninth Ave., N., Nashville, TN 37234. TEL 800-458-2772.

268　　　　　US　ISSN 0747-9514
BS410
BIBLE BOOK STUDY FOR ADULTS. KOREAN EDITION. English edition (ISSN 0162-4849); Chinese edition (ISSN 0897-0750) (Text in Korean) q. $5.50. Southern Baptist Convention, Sunday School Board, 127 Ninth Ave., N., Nashville, TN 37234. TEL 800-458-2772.

268　　　　　US　ISSN 0162-4849
BIBLE BOOK STUDY FOR ADULTS. LARGE PRINT EDITION. q. $6.75. Southern Baptist Convention, Sunday School Board, Customer Service Department, 127 Ninth Ave. N., Nashville, TN 37234. TEL 800-458-2772. (large print in 18 pt.)

268　　　　　US　ISSN 0162-4822
BIBLE BOOK STUDY FOR YOUTH. q. $6. Southern Baptist Convention, Sunday School Board, 127 Ninth Ave., N., Nashville, TN 37234. TEL 800-458-2772.
Description: Aimed at adolescents aged 12-17.

268　　　　　US　ISSN 0162-4830
BIBLE BOOK STUDY FOR YOUTH TEACHERS. q. $11.50. Southern Baptist Convention, Sunday School Board, 127 Ninth Ave., N., Nashville, TN 37234. TEL 800-458-2772.

268　　　　　US　ISSN 0162-4695
BIBLE DISCOVERERS. q. $4.50. Southern Baptist Convention, Sunday School Board, 127 Ninth Ave., N., Nashville, TN 37234. TEL 800-458-2772.
Description: Aimed at children aged 8-9.

268　　　　　US　ISSN 0162-4687
BIBLE DISCOVERERS TEACHER. q. $10. Southern Baptist Convention, Sunday School Board, 127 Ninth Ave., N., Nashville, TN 37234. TEL 800-458-2772.

283　　　　　UK　ISSN 0006-0763
BIBLE LANDS. 1899. s-a. donation. Jerusalem and the Middle East Church Association, The Old Gatehouse, Castle Hill, Farnham, Surrey GU9 0AE, England. TEL 0252-726994. Eds. Mrs. V. Wells, C. Willianson. adv.; bk.rev.; illus.; circ. 5,000.

268　　　　　US　ISSN 0162-4679
BIBLE LEARNERS. q. $4.50. Southern Baptist Convention, Sunday School Board, 127 Ninth Ave., N., Nashville, TN 37234. TEL 800-458-2772.
Description: Aimed at children 6-8 years old.

268　　　　　US　ISSN 0162-4660
BIBLE LEARNERS. TEACHER. q. $10. Southern Baptist Convention, Sunday School Board, 127 Ninth Ave., N., Nashville, TN 37234. TEL 800-458-2772.

268　　　　　US　ISSN 0162-4857
BIBLE LESSON DIGEST. q. in w. parts. $3.25. Southern Baptist Convention, Sunday School Board, 127 Ninth Ave., N., Nashville, TN 37234. TEL 800-458-2772.

268　　　　　US　ISSN 0006-078X
BIBLE SEARCHERS. 1970. q. $4.75. Southern Baptist Convention, Sunday School Board, 127 Ninth Ave. N., Nashville, TN 37234. TEL 800-458-2772.
Supersedes: Sunday School Junior Pupil.

268　　　　　US　ISSN 0006-0798
BIBLE SEARCHERS TEACHER. q. $10. Southern Baptist Convention, Sunday School Board, 127 Ninth Ave. N., Nashville, TN 37234. TEL 800-458-2772.
Formerly: Junior Teacher.

268　　　　　US　ISSN 0890-880X
BIBLE STORY TIME OLDER PUPIL. q. $5.25. Southern Baptist Convention, Sunday School Board, 127 Ninth Ave., N., Nashville, TN 37234. TEL 800-458-2772.
Description: Aimed at children aged 4-5.

268　　　　　US　ISSN 0890-8788
BIBLE STORY TIME TEACHER. q. $9.50. Southern Baptist Convention, Sunday School Board, 127 Ninth Ave., N., Nashville, TN 37234. TEL 800-458-2772.

268　　　　　US　ISSN 0890-8796
BIBLE STORY TIME YOUNGER PUPIL. q. $5.25. Southern Baptist Convention, Sunday School Board, 127 Ninth Ave. N., Nashville, TN 37234. TEL 800-458-2772.
Description: Aimed at children aged 1-3.

268　　　　　US　ISSN 0162-475X
BIBLE STUDY LEAFLET. q. in w. parts. $3.25. Southern Baptist Convention, Sunday School Board, 127 Ninth Ave., N., Nashville, TN 37234. TEL 800-458-2772.

268　　　　　US　ISSN 0162-4741
BIBLE STUDY POCKET COMMENTARY. q. $4.25. Southern Baptist Convention, Sunday School Board, 127 Ninth Ave., N., Nashville, TN 37234. TEL 800-458-2772.

268　　　　　US　ISSN 0748-5409
BIBLE STUDY SPECIAL MINISTRIES. q. $4.75. Southern Baptist Convention, Sunday School Board, 127 Ninth Ave., N., Nashville, TN 37234. TEL 800-458-2772.
Formerly: Simplified Bible Study (ISSN 0162-4644)

200　　　　　US　ISSN 0740-7998
BIBLICAL EVANGELIST; America's most conservative Christian voice. 1966. m. free. (Biblical Evangelism, An Independent Baptist Evangelistic Association) Biblical Evangelism Press, Drawer 940, Ingleside, TX 78362-0940. TEL 512-776-2867. Ed. Rev. Richard L. Sumner. adv.; bk.rev.; illus.; circ. 27,300. (tabloid format)

268　　　　　US　ISSN 0195-1351
BX6225
BIBLICAL ILLUSTRATOR. q. $13. Southern Baptist Convention, Sunday School Board, 127 Ninth Ave., N., Nashville, TN 37234. TEL 800-458-2772.
Indexed: South.Bap.Per.Ind.
Formerly: Sunday School Lesson Illustrator (ISSN 0162-4407)

266 285　　　US　ISSN 0006-0909
BIBLICAL MISSIONS. 1935. irreg. 3-6/yr. $6. Independent Board for Presbyterian Foreign Missions, 246 W. Walnut Lane, Philadelphia, PA 19144. TEL 215-438-0511. FAX 215-438-0560. Ed. Rev. William R. LeRoy. adv.; bk.rev.; illus.; circ. 3,000. **Indexed:** CERDIC.

286　　　　　US　ISSN 0279-8182
BIBLICAL RECORDER. 1833. w. $8. (Baptist State Convention of North Carolina) Biblical Recorder, Inc., Box 26568, Raleigh, NC 27611. TEL 919-847-2127. FAX 919-847-6939. (Subscr. to: Box 26568, Raleigh, NC 27511) Ed. R. Gene Puckett. adv.; circ. 75,000. (tabloid format; also avail. in magnetic tape)
Description: Covers news of churches, ministries, church staff, and denominational events.

284 900　　SW　ISSN 0346-5438
BIBLIOTHECA HISTORICO-ECCLESIASTICA LUNDENSIS. (Text in English and Swedish) 1972. irreg. price varies. Lund University Press, P.O. Box 141, S-221 00 Lund, Sweden. TEL 46-46-31-20-00. FAX 46-46-30-53-38. Ed. I. Brohed.

230　　　　　US　ISSN 0006-1921
BR1　　　　　　　CODEN: BSTQAA
BIBLIOTHECA SACRA; a theological quarterly. 1843. q. $18. Dallas Theological Seminary, 3909 Swiss Ave., Dallas, TX 75204. TEL 214-824-3094. FAX 214-841-3642. Ed. Roy B. Zuck. bk.rev.; abstr.; bibl.; index; circ. 9,000. (also avail. in microform from UMI; reprint service avail. from UMI) **Indexed:** CERDIC, Chr.Per.Ind., Int.Z.Bibelwiss., New Test.Abstr., Old Test.Abstr., Rel.& Theol.Abstr. (1967-), Rel.Ind.One, Rel.Per.
—BLDSC shelfmark: 2019.450000.
Description: Provides biblical and theological instruction to biblical scholars, pastors, teachers and serious lay bible students.

284　　　　　NE
BIBLIOTHECA UNITARIORUM. 1983. irreg., no. 2, 1988. price varies. De Graaf Publishers, P.O. Box 6, 2420 AA Nieuwkoop, Netherlands. TEL 01725-71461. Ed. Robert Dan.

BLACK MINISTRIES. see *ETHNIC INTERESTS*

283　　　　　GW　ISSN 0341-9452
BLAETTER FUER PFAELZISCHE KIRCHENGESCHICHTE UND RELIGIOESE VOLKSKUNDE. 1925. a. DM.40. Verein fuer Pfaelzische Kirchengeschichte, Kirchstr. 3, 6669 Grossbundenbach, Germany. bk.rev.; index. (back issues avail.)

284　　　　　GW
BLICK IN DIE KIRCHE. 1965. m. free to qualified personnel. Evangelisches Informationszentrum Kurhessen-Waldeck, Heinrich-Wimmer-Str. 4, 3500 Kassel, Germany. TEL 0561-31001-0. FAX 0561-3100155. Ed. Otmar Schulz. bk.rev.; circ. 17,000.

284　　　　　GW
BLICKPUNKT GEMEINDE; Mitarbeiterzeitschrift. 1977. q. DM.18.40. Oncken Verlag, Langenbeckstr. 28-30, Postfach 102829, 3500 Kassel 1, Germany. Ed. Hinrich Schmidt. circ. 2,000.

284　　　　　GW
BLICKPUNKTE; Marburger Gemeinschaftsblatt. 1970. bi-m. DM.10.50. (Deutscher Gemeinschafts-Diakonieverband) Verlag der Francke-Buchhandlung GmbH, Am Schwanhof 19, 3550 Marburg, Germany. FAX 06421-12975. circ. 8,000.
Formerly (until 1986): Marburger Gemeinschaftsblatt.

284.2　　　　SA　ISSN 0006-4947
BLOEMHEUWEL-NUUS.* (Text in Afrikaans) 1953. q. free. Nederduitse Gereformeerde Kerk, Bloemfontein - Dutch Reformed Church, Bloemfontein Bloemheuwel, 15 General Hertzog Str., Bloemfontein, South Africa. Ed. Rev. H. C. J. Flemming. adv.; bk.rev.; bibl.; circ. 1,000.

286　　　　　DK
BOERNEBLADET. 20/yr. DKK 99,50. Danmarks Folkekirkelige Soendagsskoler og Boernegudstjenester, Korshaersvej 25, 7000 Fredericia, Denmark. TEL 75-92-61-00. Ed. Bente Graugaard Nielsen. circ. 5,700.

368 284　　US　ISSN 0279-9111
BX8001
BOND. 1924. q. $4 to non-members. Lutheran Brotherhood, 625 Fourth Ave. S., Minneapolis, MN 55415. TEL 612-340-7000. Ed. Charles De Vries. illus.; circ. 540,000 (controlled).
Description: Covers member programs serving the community, the Lutheran Church, and families.

284　　　　　GW
BOTSCHAFT; Monatsschrift der Bruedergemeinden. 1853. m. DM.48. R. Brockhaus Verlag, Postfach 2220, 5657 Haan 2, Germany. (Subscr. to: R. Brockhaus Verlag, Zeitschriftenabteilung, Postfach 110152, 5600 Wuppertal 11, Germany) Ed. Manfred Klatt. adv.; bk.rev.; circ. 16,000. (back issues avail.)
Description: Christian evangelical publication covering religion, and missionary work in Germany and abroad.

BRAILLE EVANGELISM BULLETIN. see *HANDICAPPED — Visually Impaired*

260　　　　　GW
BREMER KIRCHENZEITUNG. 1928. bi-w. DM.8. (Bremische Evangelische Kirche) Carl Ed. Schuenemann KG, Zweite Schlachtpforte 7, Postfach 106067, 2800 Bremen 1, Germany. TEL 0421-36903-72. FAX 0421-36903-39. Ed. Olaf Droste. circ. 19,000.

284　　　　　US　ISSN 0747-4288
BRETHREN EVANGELIST. 1878. m. $13. Brethren Church, 524 College Ave., Ashland, OH 44805. TEL 419-289-1708. Ed. Richard C. Winfield. adv.; index; circ. 3,595. (back issues avail.)
Description: Inspirational articles and news of the Church and its ministries.

RELIGIONS AND THEOLOGY — PROTESTANT

250 UK
BRISTOL DIOCESAN NEWS. m. £1 for 100 copies. Diocese of Bristol, 23 Great George St., Bristol BS1 5QZ, England. Ed. Hugh Bunting. bk.rev.; circ. 15,000.
Formerly: Bristol Diocesan Gazette (ISSN 0045-2858)

200 FR
BULLETIN D'INFORMATION PROTESTANT. 1961. w. 450 F. Federation Protestante de France, Service d'Information, 47 rue de Clichy, 75009 Paris, France. TEL 874-15-08. Ed. Geoffroy de Turckheim. abstr.; circ. 800. (processed)
Formerly: Service Protestant Francais de Presse et d'Information (ISSN 0037-2625)

280 UK ISSN 0045-3536
BX4800
BULWARK. 1851. 6/yr. $6 (effective Jan. 1992). Scottish Reformation Society, 17 George Fourth Bridge, Edinburgh EH1 1EE, Scotland. TEL 031-220 1450. Ed. A. Sinclair Horne. bk.rev.; circ. 6,200.

266 282 SX
C C N INFORMATION. 1980. 11/yr. R.5. Council of Churches in Namibia, P.O. Box 41, Windhoek 9000, Namibia. Ed. D.J.K. Tjongarero. adv.; bk.rev.; circ. 2,000. (back issues avail.)

289 US
C J A NEWS. q. $20 membership. Christians for Justice Action, 233 North Country Rd., Mount Sinai, NY 11766. (Subscr. to: Fred Tilinski, 1822 Peach St., St. Charles MO 63303) Eds. John Nelson, Donna Schaper.
Description: Covers justice and peace issues of interest to members of the United Church of Christ.

266 US
C O R LETTER. 1986. 6/yr. $10. (National Council of the Churches of Christ) Ecumenical Networks, 475 Riverside Dr., Rm. 868, New York, NY 10115. TEL 212-870-2156. FAX 212-870-2158. Ed. Kathleen Hurty. bk.rev.; circ. 2,500.

C P F I NEWSLETTER. (Christian Pharmacists Fellowship International) see *PHARMACY AND PHARMACOLOGY*

283 AT ISSN 0007-9073
C S C NEWSLETTER. 1966. 3/yr. Aus.$5. Community of the Sisters of the Church, c/o Sister Audrey C.S.C., 82 Beevers St., Footscray, Vic. 3011, Australia. bk.rev.; circ. 2,000. Indexed: CERDIC.
Supersedes: Our Work.
Description: Features news of the members of the association, recent developments, upcoming conferences, etc.

267 UK
C W M REPORT. (Each issue has distinctive title) 1795. biennial. £2.50. Council for World Mission, 11 Carteret St., London SW1H 9DL, England. TEL 071-222-4214. FAX 071-233-1747. Ed. G.W. Duncan. circ. 15,000.
Formerly: Congregational Council for World Mission. Annual Report (ISSN 0069-8857)

283 CN ISSN 0383-6509
CALEDONIA DIOCESAN TIMES. 1960. m. Anglican Church of Canada, Diocese of Caledonia, Dawson Creek, B.C., Canada. TEL 604-782-2939. illus.

286 US ISSN 0008-1558
CALIFORNIA SOUTHERN BAPTIST. 1941. w. $9.50. California Southern Baptist Conventin, 678 E. Shaw Ave., Fresno, CA 93710. TEL 209-229-9533. FAX 209-224-2855. Ed. Mark Wyatt. adv.; bk.rev.; illus.; index; circ. 20,000.

207.11 US ISSN 0008-1779
CALVARY REVIEW. 1962. q. free. Calvary Bible College, 15800 Calvary Rd., Kansas City, MO 64147. TEL 816-322-0110. bk.rev.; circ. 17,000.

284.2 NE ISSN 0008-1787
CALVIJN. 1919. m. fl.5($3) Nederlandse Hervormde Vereniging Calvijn - Dutch Reformed Society, A. Paulownastraat 38, Dordrecht, Netherlands. Ed. G.J. Edelman. circ. 500.

230 US ISSN 0008-1795
BR1
CALVIN THEOLOGICAL JOURNAL. 1966. s-a. $15. Calvin Theological Seminary, 3233 Burton St. S.E., Grand Rapids, MI 49546. TEL 616-957-6044. Ed.Bd. bk.rev.; index; circ. 2,000. (also avail. in microform from UMI; reprint service avail. from UMI) **Indexed:** CERDIC, Chr.Per.Ind., Int.Z.Bibelwiss., New Test.Abstr., Old Test.Abstr., Rel.& Theol.Abstr. (1968-), Rel.Ind.One, Rel.Per.
—BLDSC shelfmark: 3015.800000.

284 366 CN ISSN 0410-3882
CALVINIST CONTACT. 1951. w. Can.$37.50. Calvinist Contact Publishing Ltd., 261 Martindale Rd., Unit 4, St. Catharines, Ont. L2W 1A1, Canada. TEL 416-682-8311. FAX 416-682-8313. Ed. Bert Witvoet. adv.; bk.rev.; film rev.; illus.; circ. 6,000.
Continues: Contact (ISSN 0382-5949)

286 CN ISSN 0008-2988
CANADIAN BAPTIST. 1854. m. Can.$14($20) Baptist Convention of Ontario and Quebec, 217 St. George St., Toronto, Ont. M5R 2M2, Canada. (Co-sponsor: Baptist Union of Western Canada) Ed. Dr. Larry Matthews. adv.; bk.rev.; index; circ. 16,798. (also avail. in microform) **Indexed:** Can.Per.Ind.

285 CN ISSN 0382-7658
CANADIAN FRIEND; Quaker news and thought. 1904. bi-m. Can.$15. Canadian Yearly of the Religious Society of Friends, 91A Fourth Ave., Ottawa, Ont. K1S 2L1, Canada. TEL 613-235-8553. Ed. Dorothy Parshall. bk.rev.; circ. 1,200. (back issues avail.)

283 UK
CANTERBURY CATHEDRAL CHRONICLE. 1928. a. £5. Friends of Canterbury Cathedral, Cathedral House, 8 The Precincts, Canterbury, Kent CT1 2EE, England. TEL 0227-471000. FAX 0227-762-897.
Description: Articles about the Cathedral and its environs, its history, stained glass and wall paintings.

250 UK ISSN 0260-9924
CANTERBURY DIOCESAN NEWS SERVICE. 1981. m. £3 for 100 copies. Diocese of Canterbury, Diocesan House, Canterbury, Kent CT1 1NQ, England. FAX 0227-450964. Ed. Alan Duke. adv.; bk.rev.; circ. 25,000.
Formerly (until Dec. 1980): Canterbury Diocesan Notes (ISSN 0008-5693)

CATHEDRAL. see *JOURNALISM*

704.948 US ISSN 0008-7874
CATHEDRAL AGE; an international magazine devoted to activities at and about Washington (National) Cathedral. 1925. q. $15 to non-members. Washington National Cathedral, Massachusetts and Wisconsin Aves., N.W., Washington, DC 20016. FAX 202-364-6600. Ed. Kelly Ferguson. adv.; bk.rev.; film rev.; illus.; circ. 24,000. (also avail. in microform from UMI; reprint service avail. from UMI)

200 US
EL CENTINELA. French edition: La Sentinelle. (Text in Spanish) 1896. m. $9.50. (Seventh-Day Adventists) Pacific Press Publishing Association, 1350 Kings Rd., Nampa, ID 83651. TEL 208-465-2500. FAX 208-465-2531. Ed. Tulio Peverini. circ. 140,000. (also avail. in microform from UMI)

284 572 100 SZ
CENTRE PROTESTANT D'ETUDES DE GENEVE. BULLETIN. (Text in French) 1948. bi-m. 38 F. Centre Protestant d'Etudes de Geneve, Case Postale 186, CH-1211 Geneva 3, Switzerland. Ed. Isabelle Graessle. adv.; circ. 1,300.
Description: Covers theological and ethical inquiries conducted in the different centers in French-speaking Switzerland, particularly in Geneva.

284 CS ISSN 0009-0778
CESKY BRATR. (Supplement avail.: Sbirka Kazani pro Ctene Sluzby Bozi) 1924. 10/yr. 198 Kcs. plus postage; supplement included. Cesko-Bratrska Cirkev Evangelicka, Synodi Rada, Jungmannova 9, 111 21 Prague 1, Czechoslovakia. Ed. Zdenek Susa. bk.rev.; circ. 6,000.
Description: Provides articles on theological, ethical and educational subjects; includes information on the work of local congregations and church workers.

200 CE
CEYLON CHURCHMAN. (Text in English) 1867. m. $10 (£8). Dioceses of Colombo & Kurunagala, Diocesan Office, Bauddhaloka Mawatha, Colombo 7, Sri Lanka. Ed.Bd. adv.; bk.rev.; circ. 1,500.

283 UK ISSN 0009-0999
CHALLENGE (LONDON, 1961). 1961. bi-m. £2. Anglican Pacifist Fellowship, Walters Farmhouse, Brenchley, Tonbridge TN12 7NU, England. FAX 44-532-755497. Ed. Rev. Robin Eastoe. adv.; bk.rev.; circ. 1,900. **Indexed:** Acad.Ind.
Formerly: Anglican Pacifist.

266 US
CHALLENGE (WHEATON). 1954. q. free. Conservative Baptist Home Mission Society, Box 828, Wheaton, IL 60189. TEL 708-653-4900. Ed. Dr. Jack Estep. circ. 92,000. (back issues avail.)

285 US
CHALLENGER (PETALUMA). 1961. m. free. Chinese Christian Mission, 951 Petaluma Blvd., S., Box 617, Petaluma, CA 94952. TEL 707-762-1314. FAX 707-762-1713. Ed. Cecilia Yau. circ. 9,500. (back issues avail.)

285 CN
CHANNELS. 1960. q. Can.$10. Renewal Fellowship within the Presbyterian Church in Canada, c/o Rev. J.H. Hans Kouwenberg, Ed., 4552 Cascade Ave., Prince George, B.C. V2M 6J5, Canada. adv.; bk.rev.; circ. 2,000.
Supersedes: Presbyterian Comment (ISSN 0383-7645)

284 US
CHAPLAIR.* 1977? q. membership. Assembly of Episcopal Hospitals and Chaplains, Box 487, Chesapeake City, MD 21816. circ. 800.

286 GW
CHARISMA. 1974. bi-m. contributions. Jesus-Haus, Grafenberger Allee 51-57, 4000 Duesseldorf 1, Germany. TEL 0211-667575. (Subscr. to: Charisma, P.O. Box 2213, 4000 Duesseldorf, Germany) Eds. Gerhard Bially, Klaus-Dieter Passon. circ. 30,000. (back issues avail.)
Description: Information about the Pentecostal-charismatic movement worldwide.

CHARITY AND CHILDREN; the voice of child care in North Carolina. see *CHILDREN AND YOUTH — About*

266 AT ISSN 0311-0737
CHECKPOINT. 1972. bi-m. for members only. Church Missionary Society of Australia, 93 Bathurst St., Sydney, N.S.W. 2000, Australia. FAX 02-267-3626. Ed. D. Butler. bk.rev.; illus.; circ. 8,400.
Incorporates: Going On (ISSN 0705-2316) & Discovery (ISSN 0726-6286); **Supersedes:** C M S News (ISSN 0007-8689)
Description: Explores mission work in North Australia and overseas.

200 UK
THE CHICHESTER LEAFLET. 1895. m. £4. Chichester Diocese, 9 Brunswick Sq., Hove, E. Sussex BN3 1EN, England. TEL 0273-29023. FAX 0273-821810. Ed. W.R. Pratt. bk.rev.; circ. 33,000.
Former titles: Chichester News (ISSN 0009-3785); Chichester Diocesan Leaflet.

283 UK
CHICHESTER MAGAZINE. 1988. q. £4. Chichester Diocese, 9 Brunswick Sq., Hove, E. Sussex BN3 1EN, England. TEL 0273-29023. FAX 0273-821810. Ed. W.R. Pratt. circ. 7,200.

268 US ISSN 0273-3161
CHILDREN'S BIBLE STUDY OLDER PUPIL. q. $5.25. Southern Baptist Convention, Sunday School Board, 127 Ninth Ave. N., Nashville, TN 37234. TEL 800-458-2772.
Description: Aimed at children aged 9-11.

268 US ISSN 0273-3153
CHILDREN'S BIBLE STUDY TEACHER. q. $9.50. Southern Baptist Convention, Sunday School Board, 127 Ninth Ave., N., Nashville, TN 37234. TEL 800-458-2772.
Description: Aimed at children aged 6-11.

RELIGIONS AND THEOLOGY — PROTESTANT

268　　　　　US　　ISSN 0273-317X
CHILDREN'S BIBLE STUDY YOUNGER PUPIL. 2. $5.25. Southern Baptist Convention, Sunday School Board, 127 Ninth Ave. N., Nashville, TN 37234. TEL 800-458-2772.
Description: Aimed at children aged 6-8.

268　　　　　US　　ISSN 0895-7428
M2193
CHILDREN'S CHOIR. q. $7.50. Southern Baptist Convention, Sunday School Board, 127 Ninth Ave., N., Nashville, TN 37234. TEL 800-458-2772.
Description: Aimed at children aged 6-11.

268　　　　　US　　ISSN 0162-461X
CHILDREN'S LEADERSHIP. q. $8.50. Southern Baptist Convention, Sunday School Board, 127 Ninth Ave., N., Nashville, TN 37234. TEL 800-458-2772.
Indexed: South.Bap.Per.Ind.

285　　　　　US
CHINA NEWS UPDATE. irreg. Presbyterian Church (U.S.A.), 100 Witherspoon St., Louisville, KY 40202-1396. TEL 502-569-5810.
Description: News on China and the church.

266　　　　　US　　ISSN 0009-4412
CHINA NOTES. 1962. q. $12. National Council of the Churches of Christ in the U.S.A., Division of Overseas Ministries, East Asia and the Pacific Committee, China Program, Rm. 616, 475 Riverside Dr., New York, NY 10115. TEL 212-870-2630. Ed. Franklin J. Woo. bk.rev.; film rev.; bibl.; index; circ. 2,000. (also avail. in microfilm)
Supersedes: China Bulletin.

285　　　　　US
CHINESE TODAY. (Text in Chinese) 1961. m. free. Chinese Christian Mission, 951 Petaluma Blvd., S., Box 617, Petaluma, CA 94952. TEL 707-762-1314. FAX 707-762-1713. Ed. Mandy Fung. circ. 30,000. (back issues avail.)
Formerly: Chinese Christians Today.

268　　　　　US.　　ISSN 0362-0409
ML1
CHORAL PRAISE. q. $7.25. Southern Baptist Convention, Sunday School Board, 127 Ninth Ave., N., Nashville, TN 37234. TEL 800-458-2772.

200　　　　　US　　ISSN 0412-2968
CHRIST IN OUR HOME; light for today. 1954. q. $4.60 for regular edition; large print, Braille and cassette $8. Augsburg Fortress, 426 S. Fifth St., Box 1209, Minneapolis, MN 55440. TEL 612-330-3300. Ed. Beth Ann Gaede. circ. 370,000. (also avail. in Braille; audio cassette; back issues avail.; large print edition in 20 pt.)

CHRISTEN HEUTE; Zeitung der Alt-Katholiken fuer Christen heute. see *RELIGIONS AND THEOLOGY — Roman Catholic*

268 282　　　　GW　　ISSN 0009-5192
CHRISTENLEHRE; Zeitschrift fuer den Katechetischen Dienst. 1948. m. DM.56.40 (foreign DM.60). Evangelische Verlagsanstalt GmbH, Burgstr. 1-5, 7010 Leipzig, Germany. TEL 295709. FAX 295383. Ed. Dieter Reiher. bk.rev.
—BLDSC shelfmark: 3181.778000.
Description: Contains discussions, curricula, teaching instructions and news.

283　　　　　UK
CHRISTIAN AID NEWS. 1969. q. free. (Council of Churches in Britain and Ireland) Christian Aid, P.O. Box 100, London SE1 7RT, England. TEL 071-620-4444. FAX 071-620-0719. Ed. Martin Cottingham. bk.rev.; circ. 175,000. (tabloid format; back issues avail.)
Description: Provides news of projects benefiting the poor in developing countries with funds from the British charity, Christian Aid. Also news of development-related world events and of fundraising initiatives by the charity's supporters.

285　　　　　US　　ISSN 0009-5265
CHRISTIAN BEACON. 1936. w. $12. Christian Beacon Press, 756 Haddon Ave., Collingswood, NJ 08108. TEL 609-858-0700. Ed. Carl McIntire. bk.rev.; illus.; circ. 20,000. (tabloid format)

283　　　　　US　　ISSN 0890-6793
BX5800
CHRISTIAN CHALLENGE. 1962. 9/yr. $20 (Canada $25; foreign $30). Foundation for Christian Theology, 1215 Independence Ave., S.E., Washington, DC 20003. TEL 202-547-5409. FAX 202-543-8704. Ed. Auburn Faber Traycik. adv.; bk.rev.; circ. 5,000. (also avail. in microfilm; back issues avail.)
Description: News, opinions and spirituality of Anglican and Episcopal Christianity from a traditional viewpoint.

371.3 284　　　US　　ISSN 0884-5506
CHRISTIAN EDUCATION TODAY; for teachers, superintendents, and other Christian educators. 1952. q. $10. Accent Publications, Inc., 12100 W. Sixth Ave., Denver, CO 80215. TEL 303-988-5300. (Subscr. to: Box 15337, Denver, CO 80215) Eds. Kenneth O. Gangel, Mary B. Nelson. adv.; bk.rev.; circ. 6,000.
Formerly: Success Magazine.

CHRISTIAN INDEX (ATLANTA). see *RELIGIONS AND THEOLOGY — Abstracting, Bibliographies, Statistics*

287　　　　　US　　ISSN 0744-4060
CHRISTIAN INDEX (MEMPHIS). 1867. bi-m. $15. Christian Methodist Episcopal Church, c/o Lawrence L. Reddick, III, Box 665, Memphis, TN 38101. TEL 901-345-1173. adv.; bk.rev.; circ. 7,000.
Description: Focuses on the predominantly Black, Christian Methodist Episcopal denomination.

CHRISTIAN LIBRARIAN. see *LIBRARY AND INFORMATION SCIENCES*

CHRISTIAN LIBRARIAN. see *LIBRARY AND INFORMATION SCIENCES*

CHRISTIAN MAGNIFIER. see *HANDICAPPED — Visually Impaired*

285　　　　　GH　　ISSN 0009-5478
CHRISTIAN MESSENGER. (Text in English, Ga, Twi) 1883. m. $7.16 per no. Presbyterian Book Depot, Box 3075, Accra, Ghana. TELEX 2525 PRESBY GHANA. Ed. G.B.K. Owusu. adv.; bk.rev.; bibl.; illus.; stat.; circ. 58,000. (tabloid format) **Indexed:** CERDIC.

285　　　　　US　　ISSN 8750-7765
CHRISTIAN MISSION; reporting what God is doing through indigenous missions. 1971. bi-m. Christian Aid Mission, 3045 Ivy Rd., Charlottesville, VA 22903. TEL 804-977-5650. Ed. John M. Lindner. circ. 23,000. (back issues avail.)
Description: Covers missions work outside North America being done by non-North Americans.

284　　　　　US　　ISSN 0009-5494
CHRISTIAN MONTHLY. 1950. m. $10. Apostolic Lutheran Church of America, Box 537, Brush Prairie, WA 98606-0537. TEL 206-687-7088. Ed. Alvar Helmes. circ. 1,500.

283　　　　　UK　　ISSN 0958-2630
CHRISTIAN MUSIC. 1988. q. £15. Herald House Ltd., 96 Dominion Rd., Worthing, Sussex BN14 8JP, England. TEL 0903-821082. FAX 0903-821081. Ed. Jane Hicks. circ. 5,000.

284　　　　　US　　ISSN 0009-5516
CHRISTIAN NEWS. 1968. w. (except Aug.). $20 (foreign $24). Lutheran News, Inc., Rt. 1, Box 309A, New Haven, MO 63068-9568. TEL 314-237-3110. FAX 314-237-3858. Ed. Herman Otten. bk.rev.; stat.; index; circ. 13,000. (tabloid format)
Formerly (1962-1967): Lutheran News.

283　　　　　UK　　ISSN 0958-3858
CHRISTIAN PUZZLER. 1987. q. £8.50. Herald House Ltd., 96 Dominion Rd., Worthing, Sussex BN14 8JP, England. TEL 0903-821082. FAX 0903-821081. Ed. Heather Thompson. circ. 8,500.

CHRISTIAN SINGLE. see *LEISURE AND RECREATION*

261 287　　　US　　ISSN 0164-5528
HV1
CHRISTIAN SOCIAL ACTION. 1973. m. $13.50. United Methodist Church, General Board of Church and Society, 100 Maryland Ave. N.E., Washington, DC 20002. TEL 202-488-5630. FAX 202-488-5619. Ed. Lee Ranck. adv.; bk.rev.; illus.; index; circ. 4,500. (also avail. in microfilm from UMI; back issues avail.; reprint service avail. from UMI) **Indexed:** CERDIC, Meth.Per.Ind., Rel.Ind.One, Rel.Per.
Former titles (until Dec. 1987): E - S A (ISSN 0897-0459); (until 1975): Engage - Social Action (ISSN 0090-3485); Which was formed by the merger of: Engage (ISSN 0013-7618); Social Action (ISSN 0037-7635)

CHRISTIAN TALKING MAGAZINE. see *HANDICAPPED — Visually Impaired*

283　　　　　UK
CHRISTIAN TODAY. 1978. 4/yr. £3.50 (foreign £6). c/o J. Robinson, St. Thomas Centre, Ardwick Green Nth., Manchester M12 6FZ, England. Ed.Bd. adv.; bk.rev.; circ. 500.
Formerly: Christian Statesman (ISSN 0144-073X)

285　　　　　CN　　ISSN 0835-412X
CHRISTIAN WEEK; a window on Christian faith and life in Canada. 1987. bi-w. Can.$23. Fellowship for Print Witness Inc., Box 725, Winnipeg, Man. R3C 2K3, Canada. TEL 204-943-1147. FAX 204-947-5632. Ed. Harold D. Jantz. adv.; bk.rev.; illus.; circ. 11,500. (back issues avail.)
Description: News about Canadian churches and religious organizations, religious response to international issues.

200　　　　　UK
CHRISTIAN WORDS. 1849. m. 72p. Wesleyan Reform Union, Wesleyan Reform Church House, 123 Queen St., Sheffield S1 2DU, England. adv.

282　　　　　GW
DIE CHRISTLICHE FAMILIE; eine Katholische Wochenschrift. 1885. w. Verlag Christliche Familie GmbH und Co., Ruhrtalstr. 52, D-4300 Essen 16, Germany. TEL 0201-49821. Ed. Albert E. Fischer. circ. 80,000. (back issues avail.)

284　　　　　AT　　ISSN 0728-0351
CHRISTOPHANY; Christ displayed. 1949. 5/yr. Aus.$10. Perth Bible College, Private Bag 3, Karrinyup, W.A. 6018, Australia. TEL 61-0-448-0055. FAX 61-9-448-0487. Ed. Alan F. Meers. adv.; bk.rev.; illus.; circ. 1,400. (back issues avail.)

284　　　　　GW
CHRISTUS IST SIEGER. 1972. bi-m. DM.7. Gertrud Papst, Ed. & Pub., Kinzigstr. 36, 7742 St. Georgen, Germany. TEL 07724-7353. FAX 07724-5397. (Co-sponsors: Internationale Evangelikale Laiengemeinschaft; Laymen's Evangelical Fellowship (India)) circ. 7,000. (back issues avail.)

284　　　　　GW
CHRISTUSSTAAT. 1985. s-m. DM.48($45) Universelles Leben GmbH, Marienstr. 1, Postfach 5643, 8700 Wurzburg, Germany. TEL 0931-17183. Eds. Hans Dienstknecht, Alfred Schulte. adv.; bk.rev

268　　　　　US　　ISSN 0412-4553
CHURCH ADMINISTRATION. m. $21. Southern Baptist Convention, Sunday School Board, 127 Ninth Ave., North, Nashville, TN 37234. TEL 800-458-2772.
Indexed: South.Bap.Per.Ind.

200　　　　　AT　　ISSN 0314-6200
CHURCH & NATION. 1977. s-m. Aus.$32. Uniting Church in Australia, Synod of Victoria, Board of Communication, 130 Little Collins St., Melbourne, Vic. 3000, Australia. Ed. Michael Ellemor. adv.; bk.rev.; illus.; circ. 4,600. (back issues avail.)
Former titles: New Spectator (ISSN 0300-3736); Spectator.
Description: Emphasis on Uniting Church in Victoria and Tasmania.

261 285　　　US　　ISSN 0037-7805
CHURCH AND SOCIETY. 1908. bi-m. $7.50. Presbyterian Church (U.S.A.), 100 Witherspoon St., Louisville, KY 40202-1396. TEL 502-569-5810. Ed. Rev. Kathy Lancaster. bk.rev.; bibl.; charts; illus.; circ. 5,000. (also avail. in microfilm from UMI; reprint service avail. from UMI) **Indexed:** CERDIC, Mid.East: Abstr.& Ind., Rel.Ind.One, Rel.Per.
Formerly: Social Progress.

RELIGIONS AND THEOLOGY — PROTESTANT

283   UK
CHURCH ARMY. FRONT LINE ANNUAL REPORT. 1981. a. Church Army, Independents Rd., Blackheath, London SE3 9LG, England. illus.
Formerly: Church Army. Front Line.
Description: Review of the year's work by the Church Army.

285   US   ISSN 0009-6393
CHURCH HERALD. 1826. 11/yr. $15. (Reformed Church in America) Church Herald, Inc., 6157 28th St., S.E., Grand Rapids, MI 49546-6999. TEL 616-957-1351. Ed. Jeff Japinga. adv.; illus.; circ. 40,000. (also avail. in microfilm; reprint service avail. from UMI) **Indexed:** G.Soc.Sci.& Rel.Per.Lit.

209   AT
CHURCH HERITAGE. 1978. s-a. Aus.$6. Church Records and Historical Society (NSW), P.O. Box 2395, North Parramatta, N.S.W. 2151, Australia. Ed. E.G. Clancy. bk.rev.; index; circ. 250. **Indexed:** So.Pac.Per.Ind.
Supersedes: Australasian Methodist Historical Society. Journal and Proceedings (ISSN 0084-6988)
Description: Articles on Church history in Australia and South Pacific.

CHURCH MEDIA LIBRARY MAGAZINE. see *LIBRARY AND INFORMATION SCIENCES*

284   AT   ISSN 1031-5837
CHURCH NEWS. 1862. m. Aus.$0.12 per no. Diocese of Tasmania, 125 MacQuarie St., Hobart, Tas. 7000, Australia. TEL 002-237668. (Subscr. to: G.P.O. Box 748H, Hobart, Tas. 7001, Australia) Ed. I.E.A. Booth. circ. 8,150.
Description: General reading and information on Anglican religious matters with particular emphasis on Tasmanian issues.

283   UK   ISSN 0307-7225
CHURCH OF ENGLAND. GENERAL SYNOD. REPORT OF PROCEEDINGS. 1970. 3/yr. £38. Church of England, General Synod, Church House, Great Smith St., London SW1P 3NZ, England. index.
—BLDSC shelfmark: 7663.900000.

283 270   AT   ISSN 0009-6490
CHURCH OF ENGLAND HISTORICAL SOCIETY (DIOCESE OF SYDNEY). JOURNAL. 1956. q. Aus.$15. Church of England Historical Society, G.P.O. Box 2902, Sydney, N.S.W. 2001, Australia. Ed. J. Bunyan. bk.rev.; circ. 250. (back issues avail.)
—BLDSC shelfmark: 3189.758000.

283   UK   ISSN 0007-8255
CHURCH OF ENGLAND NEWSPAPER. 1828. w. £29 (foreign £35). Christian Weekly Newspapers Ltd., 77-79 Farringdon Rd., 5th fl., London EC1M 3JY, England. FAX 071-430-9986. adv.; bk.rev.; film rev.; record rev.; illus.; circ. 11,000. (tabloid format)
Incorporates 1886-1991: Christian Week; Which was formerly (until 1987): British Weekly and Christian Record. Which was formed by the merger of: British Weekly and Christian World (ISSN 0007-1951) & Christian Record.

283   UK   ISSN 0069-3987
CHURCH OF ENGLAND YEARBOOK. 1882. a. £16.50. Church House Publishing, Church House, Great Smith St., London SW1P 3NZ, England. Ed. Mrs. Jo Linzey. adv.; circ. 3,000.
Description: Official yearbook of the Church of England. Lists holders of office in the English dioceses with details of associated organizations.

280   US
CHURCH OF GOD EVANGEL. 1910. m. (Jan., June, July, Aug., Dec.), fortn. $10. (Church of God) Pathway Press, Box 2250, Cleveland, TN 37320-2250. TEL 615-476-3361. FAX 615-478-7521. Ed. Homer G. Rhea. circ. 50,000. (also avail. in microform)

266 289.9   US   ISSN 0009-6504
CHURCH OF GOD MISSIONS. 1951. m. (except Jan. & Aug.). $7. Church of God, Missions Education Committee, Box 2337, Anderson, IN 46018. TEL 317-649-7597. Ed. Dondeena Caldwell. adv.; bk.rev.; illus.; circ. 9,000.

200   UK   ISSN 0009-6512
CHURCH OF IRELAND GAZETTE. 1850. w. 20p. Church of Ireland Press, 36 Bachelor's Walk, Lisburn BT28 1XN, Northern Ireland. Ed. Rev. C.W.M. Cooper. adv.; bk.rev.; circ. 6,000.

285.241   UK   ISSN 0069-3995
CHURCH OF SCOTLAND. YEARBOOK. 1885. a. £9.95. Saint Andrew Press, 121 George St., Edinburgh EH2 4YN, Scotland. TEL 031-225-5722. FAX 031-220-3113. TELEX CH-SCOT-727935. Ed. Rev. Andrew Herron. adv.; index; circ. 2,500.
Description: For both ministers and laymen.

268   US   ISSN 0162-4652
BV1620
CHURCH RECREATION MAGAZINE. q. $10. Southern Baptist Convention, Sunday School Board, 127 Ninth Ave., North, Nashville, TN 37234. TEL 800-458-2772. **Indexed:** Sportsearch.
Formerly: Church Recreation (ISSN 0529-7028)

283   AT   ISSN 0009-6563
CHURCH SCENE; Australian National Anglican newspaper. 1971. w. Aus.$49.50 (effective 1992). Church Press Ltd., P.O. Box 358, Carnegie, 3163, Australia. TEL 03-563-5311. FAX 03-5635991. Ed. Gerald Charles Davis. adv.; bk.rev.; illus.; circ. 4,000. (tabloid format)

283   UK   ISSN 0009-658X
CHURCH TIMES. 1863. w. £31. G.J. Palmer & Sons Ltd., 33 Upper St., London N1 6PN, England. TEL 071-359-4570. FAX 071-226-3051. adv.; bk.rev.; illus.; index; circ. 42,500. (tabloid format; also avail. in microfilm from UMI; reprint service avail. from UMI) **Indexed:** Chr.Per.Ind.

283   UK   ISSN 0009-661X
BX5011
CHURCHMAN; a journal of Anglican theology. 1879. 4/yr. £18. Church Society, Dean Wace House, 16 Rosslyn Rd., Watford, Herts. WD1 7EY, England. TEL 0923-35111. Ed. Rev. Gerald Bray. adv.; bk.rev.; index; circ. 1,200. (also avail. in microfilm from MIM) **Indexed:** CERDIC, New Test.Abstr., Old Test.Abstr., Rel.Ind.One, Rel.Per.
—BLDSC shelfmark: 3189.930000.

200   UK   ISSN 0009-6636
CHURCHMAN'S MAGAZINE. 1846. bi-m. £4. Protestant Truth Society Inc., 184 Fleet St., London E.C.4, England. Ed. Alfred Latimer Kensit. adv.; bk.rev.; illus.; circ. 3,200.

287   US   ISSN 0146-9924
BX8382.2.A1
CIRCUIT RIDER (NASHVILLE). 1976. m. $8 (free to United Methodist clergy). United Methodist Publishing House, 201 Eighth Ave. S., Box 801, Nashville, TN 37202. TEL 615-749-6731. Ed. Keith Pohl. circ. 40,000 (controlled).

287 940   UK   ISSN 0950-8732
CIRPLAN. 1955. 2/yr. £1.25. Society of Cirplanologists, 34 Fernhill Crescent, Stacksteads, Bacup, Lancs. OL13 8JU, England. Ed. Ken F. Bowden. bk.rev.; circ. 120. (processed; back issues avail.)
Description: Provides current and historical information on Methodist circuit regulations, appointments, and sermons.

CITE NOUVELLE. see *POLITICAL SCIENCE*

284   AT   ISSN 1036-4013
CLOSER CONTACT. 1987. m. Christian Radio Missionary Fellowship (CRMF), P.O. Box 46, Blackburn South, Vic. 3130, Australia. TEL 03-890-2338. FAX 03-899-1921. Ed. Robin G. Cole. circ. 100. (back issues avail.)
Description: News and information about CRMF.

CLUBHOUSE. see *CHILDREN AND YOUTH — For*

285   UK
Y COFIADUR. 1923. a. £2. Undeb Yr Annibynwyr Cymraeg, c/o Ty John Penry, Abertawe, Morgannwg SA1 4AL, Wales. TEL 52542.
Description: Covers the history of Welsh congregational churches and institutions.

200   US   ISSN 0883-6728
COLORADO EPISCOPALIAN. 1939. 8/yr. free. Diocese of Colorado, 1300 Washington St., Denver, CO 80203-2008. TEL 303-837-1173. FAX 303-837-1311. Ed. Barbara Benedict. circ. 19,000. (tabloid format)
Description: News about the Episcopal Church for members in Colorado.

266   US   ISSN 0010-3179
COMMISSION; Foreign Missions Journal. 1849. 9/yr. $8.25. Southern Baptist Convention, Foreign Mission Board, 3806 Monument Ave., Box 6767, Richmond, VA 23230. TEL 804-353-0151. FAX 804-358-0504. Ed. Leland F. Webb. illus.; index; circ. 89,000. **Indexed:** South.Bap.Per.Ind.

285   US
COMMUNIQUE (COLUMBUS); the newspaper of the Synod of the Covenant. 1974. m. (except Aug.). $3. Presbyterian Church (U.S.A.), Synod of the Covenant, 6172 Busch Blvd., Ste. 3000, Columbus, OH 43229. TEL 614-436-3310. FAX 614-846-5582. Ed. Doris Campbell. adv.; bk.rev.; circ. 9,000. (tabloid format; back issues avail.)

338.91 370.196   US
COMPASSION MAGAZINE (COLORADO SPRINGS). 1955. bi-m. free. Compassion International, Box 700, Colorado Springs, CO 80933. TEL 719-594-9900. FAX 719-594-6271. Ed. Doug LeBlanc. circ. 128,000 (controlled). (back issues avail.)
Formerly: Compassion Update (ISSN 1041-472X)
Description: News, country reports and photo features covering child development work for ministry's US supporters and friends.

285   US
CONCILIATION QUARTERLY. q. $10. Mennonite Central Committee, 21 S. 12th St., Box 500, Akron, PA 17501-0500. TEL 717-859-3889. FAX 717-859-2171. TELEX 90-2210 MENCENCOM AKRP. Ed. Alice Price.
Description: Newsletter of Mennonite conciliation service for anyone interested in conflict resolution.

209 900   US   ISSN 0010-5260
BX8001
CONCORDIA HISTORICAL INSTITUTE QUARTERLY. 1928. q. $20. (Lutheran Church - Missouri Synod) Concordia Historical Institute, 801 DeMun Ave., St. Louis, MO 63105. TEL 314-721-5934. Ed. Leroy E. Vogel. adv.; bk.rev.; charts; illus, tr.lit.; cum.index every 4 yrs.; circ. 1,700. **Indexed:** Amer.Hist.& Life, Geneal.Per.Ind., Hist.Abstr., Rel.& Theol.Abstr. (1988-), Rel.Ind.One, Rel.Per.
—BLDSC shelfmark: 3399.477000.

284   US   ISSN 0017-2154
CONFIDENT LIVING. 1941. 11/yr. $11.95. Good News Broadcasting Association, Inc., Back to the Bible, Box 82808, Lincoln, NE 68501. TEL 402-474-4567. FAX 402-474-4519. Ed. Jan Reeser. illus.; circ. 55,000. **Indexed:** G.Soc.Sci.& Rel.Per.Lit.
Formerly: Good News Broadcaster.
Description: Provides bible teaching for practical Christian living.

285   US   ISSN 0361-2376
CONGREGATIONAL JOURNAL. 1975. 2/yr. $10. American Congregational Center, 298 Fairfax Ave., Ventura, CA 93003-2118. TEL 805-644-3397. Ed. Henry David Gray. bk.rev.; circ. 1,500.

CONGREGATIONAL LIBRARY. BULLETIN. see *LIBRARY AND INFORMATION SCIENCES*

285   US   ISSN 0010-5856
BX7101
CONGREGATIONALIST. 1816. s-m. $8. National Association of Congregational Christian Churches, 6134 Kerry Ave., Cheyenne, WY 82009. TEL 313-393-9433. Ed. Mary K. Woolsey. adv.; bk.rev.; illus.; circ. 6,500.

284   AT   ISSN 1030-7052
CONTACT (BLACKBURN SOUTH). 1946. q. free. Christian Radio Missionary Fellowship, P.O. Box 46, Blackburn South, Vic. 3130, Australia. TEL 03-890-2338. FAX 03-899-1921. Ed. Robin G. Cole. circ. 1,500. (back issues avail.)
Description: Provides information and news items about the work and the staff of the Christian Radio Missionary Fellowship.

200   NE   ISSN 0010-731X
CONTACTBLAD; voor cursisten en oud-cursisten. 1948. q. free. (Zevende Dags Adventisten) E S D A Institute, Pr. Alexanderweg 1C, 3712 AD Huis Ter Heide, Netherlands. FAX 030-281084. Ed. A.F. Steens. adv.; circ. 4,000. (microfilm)

RELIGIONS AND THEOLOGY — PROTESTANT

286 US ISSN 0162-1971
CONTEMPO; a magazine for Baptist young women. 1970. m. $11. Woman's Missionary Union, Highway 280 E., 100 Missionary Ridge, Birmingham, AL 35242-5235. TEL 205-991-4933. FAX 205-991-4990. (Subscr. to: Box 830010, Birmingham AL 35283-0010) Ed. Cindy Dake. bk.rev.; circ. 68,000. (reprint service avail. from KTO)
   Description: Publication of interest to members of Southern Baptist Young Women groups.

CONTRAPUNKT; christliche Zweimonatszeitschrift fuer junge Leute. see CHILDREN AND YOUTH — For

287 UK
CORNISH METHODIST HISTORICAL ASSOCIATION JOURNAL. 1960. a. £2. c/o Barrie S. May, Pelmear Villa, Carharrack, Redruth, Cornwall TR16 5RB, England. TEL 0209-820381. bk.rev.; circ. 300.

266 IT ISSN 0394-0284
IL CRISTIANO. 1888. m. L.15000. Associazione Stampe Pubblicazioni Evangeliche (A.S.P.E.), Via Campo della Fiera, 16, 52031 Anghiari (AR), Italy. Ed. Paolo Moretti. circ. 4,200.

286 FR ISSN 0755-7205
CROIRE ET SERVIR. 1946. m. 105 Fr. Federation des Eglises Evangeliques Baptistes, 123 Av du Maine, 75014 Paris, France. TEL 1-43-22-51-57 820. Ed. Andre Thobois. bk.rev.; circ. 20,000.

284 282 070
CROSS AND QUILL. 1976. bi-m. $15 to non-members (Canada $18; elsewhere $21). Christian Writers Fellowship International, 590 W. Mercers Fernery Rd., DeLand, FL 32720. Ed. Mary Harwell Sayler. bk.rev.; index. (looseleaf format)
   Incorporates (in Oct. 1989): Christian Writers Newsletter.
   Description: Information, and market news for professional writers of material for the Christian market.

270 US ISSN 0011-1961
CROSS OF LANGUEDOC. 1960. s-a. membership. National Huguenot Society, c/o Mrs. Luther Swanstrom, 9027 S. Damen Ave., Chicago, IL 60620. TEL 312-238-0423. Ed. Ms. Edward Coleman. bk.rev.; circ. 4,000. (processed)
   Supersedes: National Huguenot Society Proceedings.

285 NZ ISSN 0113-2024
CROSSLINK. 1987. m. NZ.$15 free to members. Presbyterian and Methodist Churches of New Zealand, P.O. Box 9049, Wellington, New Zealand. TEL 801-6000. FAX 644-801-6001. Ed. Rev. R.L.D. Wiig. adv.; bk.rev.; illus.; circ. 60,000.
   Description: A monthly newspaper which seeks to relate the Christian gospel to contemporary life.

283.713 CN ISSN 0845-4795
CROSSTALK AND ANGLICAN JOURNAL EPISCOPAL. (Supplement to: Anglican Journal - Journal Anglican) 1978. 10/yr. Can.$5. Anglican Church of Canada, Diocese of Ottawa, 71 Bronson Ave., Ottawa, Ont. K1R 6G6, Canada. TEL 613-232-1451. FAX 613-232-7088. Ed. Jack Maybee. adv.; bk.rev.; circ. 16,500. (tabloid format; back issues avail.)
   Formerly: Crosstalk (ISSN 0706-8069)

261 UK ISSN 0011-2100
CRUCIBLE. 1962. q. £8. (Board for Social Responsibility of the General Synod) Church House Publishing, Church House, Great Smith St., London SW1P 3NZ, England. FAX 071-799-2714. Ed. Ian Kenway. adv.; bk.rev.; index; circ. 1,600. Indexed: CERDIC.
   —BLDSC shelfmark: 3489.870000.
   Description: Features industrial affairs, social problems, faith and morals.

286 US ISSN 0011-2151
CRUSADER (MEMPHIS). 1970. m. $2.55 for 3 mos. (typically set in Feb). Southern Baptist Convention, Brotherhood Commission, 1548 Poplar Ave., Memphis, TN 38104. Ed. James Warren. bk.rev.; illus.; circ. 67,000. Indexed: South.Bap.Per.Ind.
   Description: Provides missions education for boys 9-11 enrolled in Royal Ambassadors in Southern Baptist churches.

283 CN ISSN 0382-4314
CRUSADER (TORONTO). vol.1, 1929. 2/yr. free. Church Army in Canada, 397 Brunswick Ave., Toronto, Ont. M5R 2Z2, Canada. TEL 416-924-9279. Ed. W. Marshall. illus.; circ. 12,000.
   Continues: Anglican Crusader (ISSN 0382-4306)

CRUSADER MAGAZINE (GRAND RAPIDS). see CHILDREN AND YOUTH — For

283 UK
CRUX. 1972. m. £0.10 per issue. (Diocese of Manchester) Board of Finance, 90 Deansgate, Manchester M3 2GH, England. TEL 061-833-9521. Ed. Rev. Tim Baynes. adv.; bk.rev.; circ. 25,000. (back issues avail.)
   Description: Covers local church life.

285 US
CUMBERLAND FLAG. 1915. m. $6. General Assembly Second Cumberland Presbyterian Church, 226 Church St., Huntsville, AL 38501. TEL 205-536-7481.

285 US ISSN 0011-2976
CUMBERLAND PRESBYTERIAN. 1829. m. $6. Cumberland Presbyterian Church, Office of the General Assembly, 1978 Union Ave., Memphis, TN 38104. TEL 901-276-4572. Ed. Mark Brown. adv.; bk.rev.; illus.; circ. 7,225.

CURRICULUM PLANS. see EDUCATION

284 UK ISSN 0143-0076
Y CYLCHGRAWN EFENGYLAIDD. 1948. q. £5.80. Evangelical Press of Wales, Bryntirion, Bridgend, Mid Glamorgan CF31 4DX, Wales. TEL 0656-655886. FAX 0656-656095. Ed. Gwyn Davies. adv.; bk.rev.; illus.; circ. 900. (back issues avail.)
   Description: Contains articles on a wide range of subjects relating to the historic evangelical faith of the Christian Church and news of the contemporary religious scene.

284.2 SA
D R C NEWS. (Dutch Reformed Church) 1958. q. R.5. Nederduitse Gereformeerde Kerk in Suid-Afrika, Ecumenical Department - Dutch Reformed Church, Box 4445, Pretoria 0001, South Africa. FAX 012-322-3803. Ed. P. Rossouw. bk.rev.; circ. 2,000.
   Former titles: D R C Africa News; D R C Newsletter (ISSN 0011-5118)

220 US
DAILY BIBLE STUDY. q. $11. (United Methodist Church, Board of Discipleship) United Methodist Publishing House, Graded Press, 201 Eighth Ave. S., Nashville, TN 37202. TEL 615-749-6417. FAX 615-749-6079. (large print edition in 14 pt.)

283 UK
DAILY BREAD; practical help from the Bible. 1937. q. £7.50. Scripture Union, 130 City Rd., London EC1V 2NJ, England. TEL 071-782-0013. FAX 071-782-0014. (Subscr. to: S.U. Mail Order Dept., 9-11 Clothier Rd., Bristol BS4 5RL, England) Ed. Tony Hobbs. circ. 120,000. (audio cassette; also avail. in Braille)
   Description: Bible study geared to the individual.

DAILY DEVOTIONS FOR THE DEAF. see HANDICAPPED — Hearing Impaired

283 UK
DAILY NOTES; Bible studies for thought and action. 1923. q. £7.50. Scripture Union, 130 City Rd., London EC1V 2NJ, England. TEL 071-782-0013. FAX 071-782-0014. (Subscr. addr.: S.U. Mail Order Dept., 9-11 Clothier Rd., Bristol BS4 5RL, England) Ed. Tony Hobbs. circ. 45,000.

284 US
DAILY WALK; a guide for dynamic Christian living. 1978. m. $18. Walk Thru the Bible Ministries, Inc., 61 Perimeter Park, N.E., Box 80587, Atlanta, GA 30366. TEL 404-458-9300. Ed. Paula Kirk. abstr.; charts; illus.; circ. 220,000. (reprint service avail.)

268 UK
DAILY WATCHWORDS; the Moravian textbook with almanack. 1722. a. £1.60. Moravian Union Inc., Book Room, 5 Muswell Hill, London N10 3TJ, England. TEL 01-883 3409. Ed. B. McLeavy. circ. 5,000.

284 GW
DARUM; Evangelisches Missionswerk in Suedwestdeutschland. 1983. bi-m. DM.6. Evangelisches Missionswerk in Suedwestdeutschland e.V., Vogelsangstr. 62, 7000 Stuttgart 1, Germany. FAX 0711-63678-66. TELEX 723059-EMS-D. Ed. Joerg Schnellbach. bk.rev.; circ. 30,000. (back issues avail.)
   Description: Informations about mission and ecumenical matters concerning churches in Africa and Asia.

254 US ISSN 0045-9771
DEACON. 1970. q. $10.75. Southern Baptist Convention, Sunday School Board, 127 Ninth Ave., N., Nashville, TN 37234. TEL 800-458-2772. cum.index every 3 yrs. Indexed: South.Bap.Per.Ind.

284 US ISSN 0011-7307
BV3750
DECISION (MINNEAPOLIS). 1960. m., (except Aug.). $7. Billy Graham Evangelistic Association, 1300 Harmon Place, Minneapolis, MN 55403. TEL 612-338-0500. (Or: Box 779, Minneapolis, MN 55440) Ed. Roger C. Palms. illus.; index, cum.index; circ. 1,800,000. Indexed: CCR, Chr.Per.Ind.
   Description: Encourages, teaches and strengthens Christians; and reports on the crusade ministry of Billy Graham and associate evangelists.

283 UK ISSN 0011-7897
DELIVERER. 1889. bi-m. £2.50. Salvation Army, International Headquarters, 101 Queen Victoria St., London EC4P 4EP, England. TEL 071-236-5222. FAX 071-236-3491. Ed. Maxwell Ryan. circ. 17,000.

283 UK ISSN 0953-9301
DERBY DIOCESAN NEWS. m. Derby Diocesan Communications Committee, Derby Church House, Full St., Derby DE1 3DR, England. TEL 0332-382233. FAX 0332-292969. Ed. Rev. Donald C. McDonald. bk.rev.; circ. 36,000. (looseleaf format)

270 GW ISSN 0012-0294
DER DEUTSCHE HUGENOTT. 1929. q. DM.25. Deutscher Hugenotten-Verein e.V., Hafenplatz 9a, 3522 Bad Karlshafen 1, Germany. Ed. Jochen Desel. bk.rev.; abstr.; bibl.; illus.; circ. 1,500. Indexed: Amer.Hist.& Life, Hist.Abstr.

DEUTSCHER HUGENOTTEN-VEREIN E.V. GESCHICHTSBLAETTER. see HISTORY — History Of Europe

284 US
DEVOTIONS (CINCINNATI). 1957. q. $4.95 (large print $8.95). Standard Publishing, 8121 Hamilton Ave., Cincinnati, OH 45231. TEL 513-931-4050. Ed. Eileen H. Wilmoth. circ. 97,000.

284 US
DIACONALOGUE. 1984. q. $5. Lutheran Deaconess Association, Center for Diaconal Ministry, 1304 LaPorte Ave., Valparaiso, IN 46383. TEL 219-464-0909. Ed. Deaconess Diane Greve. bk.rev.; circ. 1,000. (back issues avail.)
   Description: Articles affirming the daily ministries of Christian service among the laity in their work places, volunteer commitments and family life.

284 GW
DIAKON. 1913. bi-m. membership. Deutscher Diakonenschaft e.V., Goethestr. 1, 4800 Bielefeld 1, Germany.

284.2 GW ISSN 0012-1975
DIAKONIE IM RHEINLAND.* 1963. Yr. DM.20. Diakonisches Werk der Evangelischen Kirche im Rheinland, Lenaustr. 41, D-4000 Dusseldorf 30, Germany. Ed. Heinz Rossig. adv.; illus.

284 GW
DIAKRISIS; Hilfe zur Unterscheidung von Geistesstroemungen in Kirche und Welt. 1980. q. DM.14($4) Theologischer Konvent Bekennender Gemeinschaften, Mainweg 12, 4800 Bielefeld 11, Germany. Ed. Peter P.J. Beyerhausfor. bk.rev.; cum.index: 1980-1984; circ. 2,000. (back issues avail.)

DIALOGUE. see GENERAL INTEREST PERIODICALS — Africa

RELIGIONS AND THEOLOGY — PROTESTANT

283   CN   ISSN 1184-6283
DIALOGUE (KINGSTON). 1960. m. Can.$5. Synod of the Diocese of Ontario, Board of Parish Services, 90 Johnson St., Kingston, Ont. K7L 1X7, Canada. TEL 613-544-4774. FAX 613-547-3745. Ed. Helene Hannah. adv.; bk.rev.; circ. 8,700.
    Formerly (until 1991): Ontario Churchman (ISSN 0030-2848)

287   SA   ISSN 0046-0265
DIMENSION. 1970. m. $25. Methodist Church of Southern Africa, P.O. Box 34632, Jeppestown 2043, Transvaal, South Africa. TEL 11-614-6325. FAX 11-614-0624. Ed. Ruth Coggin. adv.; bk.rev.; circ. 19,235. (tabloid format) **Indexed:** Cath.Ind.
    Description: Journal of the Methodist Church of Southern Africa, providing news of the activities of that Church.

286   US   ISSN 0162-6825
DIMENSION (BIRMINGHAM). 1970. q. $9. Woman's Missionary Union, Highway 280 E., 100 Missionary Ridge, Birmingham, AL 35242-5235. TEL 205-991-4933. FAX 205-991-4990. (Subscr. to: Box 830010, Birmingham, AL 35283-0010) Ed. Gina Howard. circ. 48,000.
    Description: Publication of interest to pastors and WMU missions organizations in Southern Baptist churches.

200   CN   ISSN 0382-9391
DIOCESAN TIMES. 1946. m. (exc. July-Aug.). Can.$5. (Anglican Diocese of Nova Scotia) Diocesan Times Publishing Co., 5732 College St., Halifax, N.S. B3H 1X3, Canada. TEL 902-423-8301. Ed. Lawrin C. Armstrong. adv.; circ. 17,500.

284   UK
DIRECTION. 1919. m. Elim Pentecostal Church, Box 38, Cheltenham, Gloucestershire GL50 3HN, England. TEL 051-632-4992. FAX 051-632-6725. Ed. D.J. Green. adv.; bk.rev.; circ. 30,000. (also avail. in microfiche)
    Formerly (until 1989): Elim Evangel (ISSN 0013-6182)

DIRECTORY OF MINISTRIES IN HIGHER EDUCATION. see EDUCATION — Higher Education

284   US   ISSN 0273-5865
BV4485
DISCIPLESHIP JOURNAL. 1981. bi-m. $18.97. Navigators, Box 35004, Colorado Springs, CO 80935. TEL 719-548-9222. FAX 719-598-7128. (Subscr. to: Box 54470, Boulder, CO 80323-4470) Ed. Susan Maycinik. adv.; index; circ. 88,000. **Indexed:** Chr.Per.Ind.
    Incorporates: Small Group Letter (ISSN 0742-1737)
    Description: Designed to help Christians understand and practice the teachings of the Bible.

268   US
DISCIPLESHIP TRAINING. m. $12.75. Southern Baptist Convention, Sunday School Board, 127 Ninth Ave., N., Nashville, TN 37234. TEL 800-458-2772. **Indexed:** South.Bap.Per.Ind.
    Formerly: Church Training.

286   US   ISSN 0732-9881
BX7301
DISCIPLIANA. 1941. q. $15. Disciples of Christ Historical Society, 1101 Nineteenth Ave., S., Nashville, TN 37212. TEL 615-327-1444. Ed. James M. Seale. bk.rev.; bibl.; circ. 5,500. (also avail. in microfilm)

286   US   ISSN 0162-198X
DISCOVERY (BIRMINGHAM). 1970. m. $9. Woman's Missionary Union, Hwy. 280, E., 100 Missionary Ridge, Birmingham, AL 35242-5235. TEL 205-991-4933. FAX 205-9914990. (Subscr. to: Box 830010, Birmingham, AL 35283-0010) Ed. Barbara Massey. circ. 210,000.
    Description: For girls, grades 1-6, who are members of Southern Baptist Girls in Action organization.

DOOPSGEZINDE BIJDRAGEN. see HISTORY — History Of Europe

284   US   ISSN 1044-7512
THE DOOR. 1971. bi-m. $24. Youth Specialties, 1224 Greenfield Dr., El Cajon, CA 92021. FAX 916-842-7729. Ed. Mike Yaconelli. bk.rev.; illus.; circ. 18,000. **Indexed:** Chr.Per.Ind.
    Formerly: Wittenburg Door (ISSN 0199-8285)

282   UK
THE DOOR; Diocese of Oxford Reporter. 1989. m. (Oxford Diocesan Board of Finance) Oxford Diocesan Publications Ltd., Diocesan Church House, North Hinksey, Oxford OX2 0NB, England. TEL 0865-244566. FAX 0865-790470.
    Formerly (until 1989): Oxford Diocesan Magazine.
    Description: Covers Berkshire, Buckinghamshire and Oxfordshire. Includes church news, theological articles.

284   CN   ISSN 0701-0214
DRAUDZES VESTIS. (Text in Latvian) 1953. bi-m. Can.$15. Peace Latvian Lutheran Church, 83 Main St., Ottawa, Ont. K1S 1B5, Canada. TEL 613-230-4085. Ed. Rev. Maris Ludviks. adv.; bk.rev.; circ. 170.

284   GW   ISSN 0012-608X
DREIKOENIGSBOTE. 1951. m. free. Evangelisch-Lutherische Dreikoenigsgemeinde, Oppenheimer Str. 5, 6000 Frankfurt 70, Germany. bibl.; circ. 800.

200   US   ISSN 0012-6152
BX8201
DREW GATEWAY; a journal of original scholarship on issues related to church and ministry. 1930. 2/yr. 21. Drew University Theological School, Madison, NJ 07940. TEL 201-408-3276. Ed. Janet F. Fishburn. bk.rev.; index; circ. 500. (also avail. in microform from UMI) **Indexed:** CERDIC, Rel.& Theol.Abstr. (1989-), Rel.Ind.One, Rel.Per.

284   GW
DURCHBLICK UND DIENST. 1969. m. DM.21.60. Liebenzeller Mission GmbH, Postfach 1240, 7263 Bad Liebenzell, Germany. TEL 07052-17114. circ. 5,200. (back issues avail.)

DUTCH CHURCH TRANSCRIPTS. see GENEALOGY AND HERALDRY

200   US
E.C. DOORS AND WINDOWS. 1923. 4/yr. free. Evangelical Congregational Church, Church Center, Box 186, Myerstown, PA 17067. Ed. Tim Christman. adv.; bk.rev.; illus.; circ. 4,800.
    Formerly (until vol.67, no.8, Sept. 1989): United Evangelical (ISSN 0041-7262)
    Description: Christian family paper.

284   GW
E M K AKTUELL. 1963. m. DM.28. (Evangelisch-methodische Kirche) Christliches Verlagshaus GmbH, Motorstr. 36, 7000 Stuttgart 31, Germany. TEL 0711-83000-14. FAX 0711-8300084. Ed. Walter Bolay. circ. 2,500.

266   GW
E M S - JAHRBUCH. 1984. a. free. Evangelisches Missionswerk in Suedwestdeutschland e.V., Vogelsangstr. 62, 7000 Stuttgart 1, Germany. TEL 0711-63678-0. FAX 0711-63678-66. TELEX 723059-EMS-D. Eds. Reinhilde Freise, Klaus Zoeller. circ. 5,000.

200   US
E P F NEWSLETTER. 1939. q. $25 membership. Episcopal Peace Fellowship, Box 28156, Washington, DC 20038-8156. TEL 202-783-3380. bk.rev.; circ. 3,000.

284   CN   ISSN 0831-4446
EASTERN SYNOD LUTHERAN. 1911. 10/yr. Can.$6.50($4) Evangelical Lutheran Church in Canada, Eastern Synod, 50 Queen St. N., Kitchener, Ont. N2H 6P4, Canada. FAX 519-743-4291. Ed. Jane Wahl. adv.; bk.rev.; circ. 23,000.
    Formerly: Canada Lutheran (ISSN 0008-2716)

284   US
ECU - LINK. 1986. 4/yr. $6. National Council of Churches, Communication Department, 475 Riverside Dr., Rm. 850, New York, NY 10115. TEL 212-870-2227. FAX 212-870-2030. Ed. Sarah Vilankulu. circ. 5,000.
    Description: An ecumenical newsletter to help create community among the Council's member communions. Includes news of NCC member denominations.

200   AT   ISSN 0726-4143
EDITOR'S CLIP SHEETS. 1980. m. Aus.$37.50. Mediacom Associates Inc., P.O. Box 610, Unley, S.A. 5061, Australia. (Subscr. addr.: P.O. Box 610, Unley, S.A. 5061, Australia) Ed. Rev. A.G. Nancarrow. adv.; circ. 2,500. (looseleaf format)

EDUCATION NEWSLINE. see EDUCATION

268   US   ISSN 0162-4547
ENCOUNTER!. q. $4.50. Southern Baptist Convention, Sunday School Board, 127 Ninth Ave., N., Nashville, TN 37234. TEL 800-458-2772. **Indexed:** Arts & Hum.Cit.Ind., Bk.Rev.Ind., CERDIC, G.Soc.Sci.& Rel.Per.Lit., Hist.Abstr., Mid.East: Abstr.& Ind., New Test.Abstr., Rel.& Theol.Abstr. (1981-), Rel.Ind.One

ENCOUNTER (LONDON, 1990). see RELIGIONS AND THEOLOGY

284   CN   ISSN 0702-844X
END-TIME NEWS.* 1970. irreg. Solbrekken Evangelistic Association, Box 2424, Edmonton, Alta., Canada. illus.
    Formerly: Edmonton Revival Centre. News (ISSN 0702-8458)

200   UK
ENGLISH CHURCHMAN & ST. JAMES'S CHRONICLE. 1843. fortn. £11.18 (foreign £15.60). English Churchman Trust Ltd., 22 Lesley Ave., Canterbury, Kent CT1 3LF, England. TEL 0227-781282. adv.; bk.rev.; circ. 87. (back issues avail.)
    Formerly: English Churchman (ISSN 0013-8223)

200   GW   ISSN 0013-9092
ENTSCHEIDUNG. 1963. bi-m. DM.20. (Billy Graham Evangelistic Association Deutschland e.V.) Friedrich Haenssler KG, Bismarkstr. 4, Postfach 1220, 7303 Neuhausen-Stuttgart, Germany. TEL 030-7411421. FAX 030-7419504. Ed. Irmhild Baerend. adv.; bk.rev.; bibl.; circ. 50,000.

284   GW   ISSN 0343-6519
ENTWURF; religionspaedagogische Mitteilungen. 1970. 3/yr. DM.20 (foreign DM.30). Fachgemeinschaft Evangelische Religionslehrer in Wuerttemberg, Grueningerstr. 25, 7000 Stuttgart 70, Germany. TEL 0711-45804-0. FAX 0711-45804-22. Ed. Eberhard Roehm. bk.rev.; cum.index; circ. 12,700. (back issues avail.)

284   US
EPISCOPAL CLERICAL DIRECTORY. biennial. Church Hymnal Corporation, 800 Second Ave., New York, NY 10017.

283   US   ISSN 0013-9610
BX5800
EPISCOPAL RECORDER. 1823. m. (exc. July-Aug.). $20. Episcopal Recorder, Inc., 4225 Chestnut St., Philadelphia, PA 19104. Ed. Walter G. Truesdell. adv.; bk.rev.; circ. 1,100. (also avail. in microform from UMI) **Indexed:** G.Soc.Sci.& Rel.Per.Lit.

250   UK
EPWORTH REVIEW. 1973. 3/yr. £5. Methodist Publishing House, 20 Ivatt Way, Peterbrough PE3 7PG, England. TEL 0733 332202. FAX 0733-331201. Ed. Rev. Dr. Richard G. Jones. circ. 3,500. **Indexed:** Rel.& Theol.Abstr. (1991-).

286 267   US   ISSN 0196-0911
EQUIPPING YOUTH. 1981. q. $8.50. Southern Baptist Convention, Sunday School Board, 127 Ninth Ave., N., Nashville, TN 37234. TEL 800-458-2772.

284   US   ISSN 0171-6204
ERNEUERUNG IN KIRCHE UND GESELLSCHAFT. 1977. q. DM.32. An der Schoenen Aussicht 52a, 4790 Paderborn, Germany. TEL 05251-62927. Ed. Richard Martin Schleyer. adv.; bk.rev.

284   GW
ERNEUERUNG UND ABWEHR. 1966. m. Vorstand der Evangelischen Notgemeinschaft in Deutschland, Schulstr. 19C, 8031 Wessling, Germany. TEL 08153-3782. circ. 6,500.

284   GW
ERWECKLICHE STIMME. 1960. m. Geistliches Ruestzentrum Krelingen, Krelingen 37, 3030 Waldsrode, Germany. TEL 05167-296. Ed. Heinrich Kemner. illus.; circ. 20,000.

RELIGIONS AND THEOLOGY — PROTESTANT

280 FR
ESQUISSE D'UNE PHILOSOPHIE DE LA RELIGION. 1956. irreg., no.24, 1973. 75 F. Librairie Fischbacher, 33 rue de Seine, 75006 Paris, France. **Indexed:** Canon Law Abstr.
  Formerly: Esprit et Liberte (ISSN 0071-1330)

286 US ISSN 0890-3115
ESTUDIOS BIBLICOS PARA NINOS: ALUMNOS. (Text in Spanish) q. $5.25. Southern Baptist Convention, Sunday School Board, 127 Ninth Ave., N., Nashville, TN 37234. TEL 800-458-2772.

286 US ISSN 0890-3123
ESTUDIOS BIBLICOS PARA NINOS: MAESTROS. (Text in Spanish) q. $9.50. Southern Baptist Convention, Sunday School Board, 127 Ninth Ave., N., Nashville, TN 37234. TEL 800-458-2772.

230 FR ISSN 0014-2239
ETUDES THEOLOGIQUES ET RELIGIEUSES. 1926. q. 150 F.($25) (effective 1991). Institut Protestant de Theologie, 13 rue Louis-Perrier, 34000 Montpellier, France. TEL 67-92-61-28. Ed. A. Gounelle. adv.; bk.rev.; bibl.; index; circ. 2,350. (also avail. in microfilm from UMI; reprint service avail. from UMI) **Indexed:** Arts & Hum.Cit.Ind., Bull.Signal., CERDIC, Curr.Cont., New Test.Abstr., Old Test.Abstr., Rel.Ind.One, Rel.Per.
  —BLDSC shelfmark: 3822.310000.

284 UK
EUROPEAN ACTION REPORT; voice of the Church of God in Europe. (Text in English) 1976. q. 14 Clark's Mead, Bushey Heath, Herts., England. TEL 44-81-9506539. FAX 44-81-9507429. Ed. Douglas LeRoy. circ. 5,000.

280 UK ISSN 0960-2720
▼**EUROPEAN JOURNAL OF THEOLOGY;** a new journal for a new Europe. 1991. s-a. £12($20) Rutherford House, 3 Mount Radford Cres., Exeter EX2 4JW, England. TEL 0392-50631. FAX 0392-413317. Nigel M. de S. Cameron. adv.; bk.rev.
  Description: Seeks to reflect the variety of European evangelical theology.

287 US ISSN 0162-1890
EVANGEL. w. $6.25. Free Methodist Church of North America, Box 535002, Indianapolis, IN 46253-5002. TEL 317-244-3660. FAX 317-244-1247. (back issues avail.)

286 CN ISSN 0014-3324
EVANGELICAL BAPTIST. 1953. m. Can.$9.95. Fellowship of Evangelical Baptist Churches in Canada, 679 South Gate Dr., Guelph, Ont. N1G 4S2, Canada. TEL 519-821-4830. FAX 519-821-9829. Ed. R.W. Lawson. adv.; bk.rev.; illus.; circ. 7,000.

286.1 CN ISSN 0317-266X
EVANGELICAL BAPTIST CHURCHES IN CANADA. FELLOWSHIP YEARBOOK. 1959. a. Fellowship of Evangelical Baptist Churches in Canada, 679 Southgate Dr., Guelph, Ont. N1G 4S2, Canada. TEL 519-821-4830. FAX 519-821-9829. illus. Key Title: Fellowship Yearbook.
  Formerly: Missions Digest and Year Book (ISSN 0544-439X)

285.73 US ISSN 0014-3332
BX7548.A1
EVANGELICAL BEACON. 1931. 12/yr. $12. Evangelical Free Church of America, 901 E 78th St., Minneapolis, MN 55420. TEL 612-854-1300. Ed. Carol Madison. adv.; bk.rev.; illus.; circ. 37,500.
  Description: Information, inspiration and evangelism for members.

284 US
EVANGELICAL LUTHERAN CHURCH IN AMERICA (YEAR). Short title: E L C A Yearbook. 1961. a. $14.95. (Evangelical Lutheran Church in America) Augsburg Fortress, 426 S. Fifth St., Box 1209, Minneapolis, MN 55440. TEL 612-330-3300. FAX 612-330-3455. adv.; circ. 15,000.
  Formed by the merger of: Lutheran Church in America. Yearbook & Yearbook of American Lutheran Church (ISSN 1050-477X)
  Description: Roster listings of congregations, ordained ministers, associates in ministry and agencies, and more.

283 940 UK ISSN 0421-8094
EVANGELICAL MAGAZINE OF WALES. 1955. bi-m. £8 (foreign £9.60). Evangelical Press of Wales, Bryntirion, Bridgend, Mid Glamorgan CF31 4DX, Wales. TEL 0656-655886. FAX 0656-656095. Ed. Rev. Andrew Davies. adv.; bk.rev.; bibl.; illus.; circ. 2,000. (back issues avail.)
  Description: Contains articles on a wide range of subjects relating to the historic evangelical faith of the Christian Church and news of the contemporary religious scene.

285 US ISSN 0360-8808
BR21
EVANGELICAL THEOLOGICAL SOCIETY. JOURNAL. 1958. q. $20 (effective Jan. 1991). Evangelical Theological Society, c/o Dr. Simon J. Kistemaker, Sec. Treas., 5422 Clinton Blvd., Jackson, MS 39209. TEL 601-922-4988. Ed. Dr. Ronald Youngblood. adv.; bk.rev.; circ. 2,800. (also avail. in microform from UMI; reprint service avail. from UMI) **Indexed:** CERDIC, Chr.Per.Ind., New Test.Abstr., Old Test.Abstr., Rel.& Theol.Abstr. (1983-), Rel.Ind.One.
  —BLDSC shelfmark: 4741.650000.
  Formerly: E T S Bulletin (ISSN 0071-3171)

284 960 980 GW ISSN 0177-8706
EVANGELIKALE MISSIOLOGIE. 1985. q. DM.15. Arbeitskreis fuer Evangelikale Missiologie, Hindenburgstr. 36, 7015 Korntal, Germany. (Co-sponsor: Freie Hochschule fuer Mission) Ed. Klaus Fiedler. bk.rev.; index; circ. 1,000. (back issues avail.)
  Description: Non-denominational publication covering information and discussions in all fields of missionary activities. Includes association news and events.

284 HU
EVANGELIKUS ELET. 1933. w. $35. Evangelical - Lutheran Church, Puskin u. 12, 1088 Budapest, Hungary. TEL 114-2074. Ed. Laszlo Lehel. circ. 12,000.

284 GW ISSN 0423-8346
EVANGELISCH-LUTHERISCHE LANDESKIRCHE SACHSENS. AMTSBLATT. 1949. s-m. DM.10.80. (Evangelisch-Lutherisches Landeskirchenamt Sachsens) Union-Verlag, Strasse der Befreiung 21, 8060 Dresden, Germany. Ed.Bd. bk.rev.; play rev.; abstr.; index; circ. 2,500.

266 GW
EVANGELISCH-LUTHERISCHES MISSIONSWERK IN NIEDERSACHSEN. JAHRBUCH (YEAR). 1954. a. DM.15. (Evangelisch-Lutherisch Missionswerk in Niedersachsen) Missionshandlung Hermannsburg, Harmsstr. 2-6, 3102 Hermannsburg, Germany. FAX 05052-69222. TELEX 925911-ELM-D. Ed. Ernst-August Luedemann. circ. 5,000. (back issues avail.)
  Formerly (until 1979): Die Hermannsburger Mission im Jahre (Year).
  Description: Articles about the work of the missionaries of the Missionswerk, and about the countries in which they work.

283 GW ISSN 0937-1729
EVANGELISCHE JUGEND IN BAYERN. NACHRICHTEN. 1958. s-a. DM.18. Amt fuer Evangelische Jugendarbeit, Hummelsteiner Weg 100, Postfach 450131, 8500 Nuernberg 40, Germany. TEL 0911-4304-0. FAX 0911-4304-201. circ. 1,500. (back issues avail.)

284 340 GW ISSN 0232-6310
EVANGELISCHE KIRCHE DER KIRCHENPROVINZ SACHSEN. AMTSBLATT. 1945. m. DM.0.60. Evangelisches Konsistorium Magdeburg, Am Dom 2, Postfach 122, 3010 Magdeburg, Germany. circ. 2,000.
  Description: Events and information on evangelistic churches in Western part of Germany.

284.2 GW ISSN 0014-343X
EVANGELISCHE KIRCHE IN DEUTSCHLAND. AMTSBLATT. 1946. m. DM.40. Kirchenamt der Evangelische Kirche in Deutschland, Herrenhaeuser Str. 12, 3000 Hannover- Herrenhausen, Germany. TEL 0511-7111463. Ed. Dr. D. Dahrmann. index; circ. 1,400. (tabloid format; back issues avail.)

284 GW
EVANGELISCHE KIRCHENZEITUNG. 1946. w. DM.69.60. Evangelischer Presseverband in Hessen und Nassau e.V., Postfach 100747, Neue Schlesingergasse 24, 6000 Frankfurt a.M. 1, Germany. FAX 069-299884-24. Ed. Klaus Fedler. adv.; bk.rev.; circ. 30,850.
  Formerly (until Jan. 1989): Weg und Wahrheit (ISSN 0170-6136)

284 GW ISSN 0014-3529
EVANGELISCHE LANDESKIRCHE IN WUERTTEMBERG. AMTSBLATT. 1855. s-m. DM.24 (free to qualified personnel). Evangelical-Lutheran Church of Wuerttemberg, Postfach 101342, 7000 Stuttgart, Germany. TEL 0711-2149-0. FAX 0711-2149236. Ed. Dr. Daur. index; circ. 4,500.
  Description: Focuses on curch matters including changes in constitution, by-laws, regulations, obligations for pastors and congregations.

284 GW
EVANGELISCHE LUTHERISCHE KIRCHE IN BAYERN. PFARRER- UND PFARRERINNENVEREIN. KORRESPONDENZBLATT. 1876. m. DM.25. Evangelische Lutherische Kirche in Bayern, Pfarrer- und Pfarrerinnenverein, Kronacher Str. 16, 8620 Lichtenfels, Germany. TEL 09571-2077. Ed. Werner Mueller. adv.; bk.rev.; index; circ. 3,100. (back issues avail.)

284 GW ISSN 0014-326X
EVANGELISCHE-LUTHERISCHE KIRCHE IN THUERINGEN. AMTSBLATT. 1948. s-m. DM.0.50. (Evangelische-Lutherische Kirche in Thueringen, Landeskirchenrat) Wartburg Verlag GmbH, Sophienstr. 18, 6900 Jena, Germany. bk.rev.

285 AU ISSN 0016-6154
EVANGELISCHE PFARRGEMEINDE A.B. WIEN-FAVORITEN-CHRISTUSKIRCHE. GEMEINDEBRIEF. 1963. q. contributions. Presbyterium der Evangelischen Gemeinde Wien-Favoriten-Christuskirche, Triester Str. 1, A-1100 Vienna, Austria. TEL 0222-6042390. Ed. Harald Hoeger. bk.rev.; abstr.; bibl.; illus.; stat.; circ. 3,000.

284 GW ISSN 0933-7857
EVANGELISCHER BUND; beitraege zur evangelische Orientierung. 1954. q. DM.6. Evangelischer Bund, Konfessionskundliches Institut, Postfach 1255, 6140 Bensheim 1, Germany. TEL 06251-38000. FAX 06251-2045. circ. 11,000. (back issues avail.)

284 AU ISSN 0036-6943
EVANGELISCHER BUND IN OESTERREICH. SCHRIFTENREIHE. 1956. q. Evangelischer Bund in Oesterreich, Ungargasse 9, A-1030 Vienna, Austria. Ed. Paul Weiland. circ. 8,000.
  Incorporates: Martin Luther.

284 GW
EVANGELISCHER INFORMATIONSDIENST FUER JUGEND- UND ERWACHSENBILDUNG AUF DEM LANDE. 1971. q. DM.10. Evangelische Landjugendakademie, Dieperzbergweg 13-17, 5230 Altenkirchen, Germany. TEL 02681-4377. FAX 02681-70206. bk.rev.; circ. Y. (back issues avail.)
  Formerly: Evangelischer Informationsdienst fuer Jugend- und Erwachsenbildung.

284 GW ISSN 0014-360X
EVANGELISCHES GEMEINDEBLATT FUER WUERTTEMBERG. 1905. w. DM.63.60. Evangelische Gemeindepresse GmbH, Furtbachstr. 12a, 7000 Stuttgart 1, Germany. TEL 0711-60100-25. FAX 0711-60100-76. adv.; bk.rev.; illus.; circ. 160,000.

284 GW ISSN 0177-462X
EVANGELIUM-GOSPEL; Zweimonatsschrift fuer lutherische Theologie und Kirche. (Text in English and German) 1963. 5/yr. DM.25($17.50) (International Lutheran Layman's League, US) Die Lutherische Stunde, Postfach 1162, 2724 Sottrum, Germany. FAX 04264-2437. Ed. Hans-Lutz Poetsch. adv.; bk.rev.; index; circ. 3,300.
  Description: Publication of the Lutheran Hour. Discusses religious education, Bible and Christianity.

RELIGIONS AND THEOLOGY — PROTESTANT

371.3 369.4 200 US ISSN 0891-3846
EVANGELIZING TODAY'S CHILD. 1942. bi-m. $13.95. Child Evangelism Fellowship, Box 348, Warrenton, MO 63383. FAX 314-456-2078. Ed. Elsie Lippy. adv.; bk.rev.; index; circ. 22,000. **Indexed:** Chr.Per.Ind.
 Description: Designed to give Sunday school teachers and other Christian workers instruction and tools to teach 5 to 12 year olds the Bible.

284 FR
EVANGILE ET LIBERTE. 1885. m. 185 F. Association Evangile et Liberte, c/o Pasteur Christian Mazel, Les Genets, Residence St. Michel, 84400 Apt en Luberon. TEL 90-74-56-37. adv.; bk.rev.; bibl.

284 YU ISSN 0014-3642
EVANJELICKY HLASNIK. 1965. m. 250 din. (effective 1992). Slovenska Evanjelicka A.V. Cirkva v SFR Juhoslavii, Karadziceva 2, 21000 Novi Sad, Yugoslavia. TEL 23 887-922. Ed. Rev. Ondrej Petkovsky. bk.rev.; circ. 4,200.

286 US ISSN 0014-374X
EVENT. 1970. m. $10. Southern Baptist Convention, Sunday School Board, 127 Ninth Ave. N., Nashville, TN 37234. TEL 800-458-2772. **Indexed:** Arts & Hum.Cit.Ind.
 Supersedes: Upward.

283 UK
EXETER DIOCESAN DIRECTORY. 1946. a. £2.75 (effective 1992). Diocese of Exeter, Diocesan House, Palace Gate, Exeter EX1 1HX, England. TEL 0392-72868. Ed. P. Greener. adv.; circ. 800. (back issues avail.)

286 US ISSN 0890-3093
EXPLORADORES. (Text in Spanish) q. $4.50. Southern Baptist Convention, Sunday School Board, 127 Ninth Ave., N., Nashville, TN 37234. TEL 800-458-2772.

268 US ISSN 0745-032X
EXPLORING 1. q. $4.50. Southern Baptist Convention, Sunday School Board, 127 Ninth Ave., N., Nashville, TN 37234. TEL 800-458-2772.
 Formerly (until 1982): Exploring A (ISSN 0162-4415)
 Description: Aimed at children aged 6-8.

268 US ISSN 0745-0346
EXPLORING 1 FOR LEADERS. q. $8.75. Southern Baptist Convention, Sunday School Board, 127 Ninth Ave., N., Nashville, TN 37234. TEL 800-458-2772.
 Formerly (until 1982): Exploring A for Leaders (ISSN 0162-4423)

268 US
EXPLORING 2. q. $4.50. Southern Baptist Convention, Sunday School Board, 127 Ninth Ave., N., Nashville, TN 37234. TEL 800-458-2772.
 Formerly (until 1982): Exploring C (ISSN 0162-4458)
 Description: For children in grades 4-6.

268 US ISSN 0745-0354
EXPLORING 2 FOR LEADERS. q. $8.75. Southern Baptist Convention, Sunday School Board, 127 Ninth Ave., N., Nashville, TN 37234. TEL 800-458-2772.
 Formerly (until 1982): Exploring C for Leaders (ISSN 0162-4466)

286 AG ISSN 0014-522X
EXPOSITOR BAUTISTA. vol.59, 1966. bi-m. Arg.$3.50($10) Convencion Evangelica Bautista Argentina, Rivadavia 3474, 1203 Buenos Aires, Argentina. Ed. Horacio V. Franco. adv.; charts; illus.

266 US
FAITH AND FELLOWSHIP. 1933. s-m. $10. (Church of the Lutheran Brethren) Faith and Fellowship Press, Box 655, Fergus Falls, MN 56537. TEL 218-736-7357. FAX 218-739-5514. Ed. Rev. David Rinden. bk.rev.; circ. 5,000.

286 US ISSN 0740-0659
FAITH AND MISSION. 1983. s-a. $9. Southeastern Baptist Theological Seminary, Inc., Wake Forest, NC 27587. TEL 919-556-3101. Ed. Fred A. Grissom. adv.; bk.rev.; circ. 1,000 (controlled). (back issues avail.) **Indexed:** Rel.& Theol.Abstr. (1983-), Rel.Ind.One.
 —BLDSC shelfmark: 3865.510900.

284 052 CN ISSN 0832-1191
FAITH TODAY; Canada's evangelical news-feature magazine. 1983. bi-m. Can.$16.50($19.50) Evangelical Fellowship of Canada, Box 8800, Station "B", Willowdale, Ont. M2K 2R6, Canada. TEL 416-479-5885. FAX 416-479-4742. Ed. Brian C. Stiller. adv.; bk.rev.; circ. 18,000.
 Formerly (until 1986): Faith Alive.
 Description: Informs Canadian Christians on issues facing church and society and on events and trends within the church community.

286 UK ISSN 0143-7917
FAMILY LIFE. 1979. 4/yr. £3.75. Stanborough Press Ltd., Alma Park, Grantham, Lincs. NG31 9SL, England. TEL 0476-591700. FAX 0476-77144. Ed. D.N. Marshall. illus.; circ. 25,000.

284 028.5 US
FAMILY WALK. 1983. m. $18. Walk Thru the Bible Ministries, Inc., 61 Perimeter Park, N.E., Box 80587, Atlanta, GA 30366. TEL 404-458-9300. Ed. Paula Kirk. circ. 100,000.

286 US ISSN 0162-4504
LA FE BAUTISTA. (Text in Spanish) q. $4.75. Southern Baptist Convention, Sunday School Board, 127 Ninth Ave., N., Nashville, TN 37234. TEL 800-458-2772.

284 IT
FEDELTA. 1976. m. free. Via Vespucci 3-19, 50047 Prato (Florence), Italy. Ed. Affuso Mario. bk.rev.; circ. 1,000. (back issues avail.)
 Formerly: Fedelta Apostolica.

284 FR
FEDERATION PROTESTANTE DE FRANCE. ANNUAIRE. 1952. a. 180 F. Federation Protestante de France, c/o A. Nicolas, 47 rue de Clichy, 75009 Paris, France.
 Formerly: France Prostestante (ISSN 0071-9064)

280 US ISSN 1045-3849
FELLOWSHIP TODAY. 1963. m. $7.80. (Fellowship of Christian Assemblies) Fellowship Press, 3 Peacock Path, Coram, NY 11727-2159. TEL 516-474-4862. Ed. James Mattson. adv.; bk.rev.; circ. 5,000.
 Formerly (until June 1989): Conviction Magazine.

284 GW ISSN 0015-0320
DER FESTE GRUND. 1850. m. DM.18. (Evangelische Gesellschaft fuer Deutschland e.V.) Licht und Leben Verlag GmbH, Kaiser Str. 78, 5600 Wuppertal 11, Germany. TEL 0202-784018. Ed. Herbert Becker. adv.; bk.rev.; circ. 10,000.
 Incorporates: Saemann.
 Description: Evangelical publication covering various topics in Christianity and missionary work.

266 UK ISSN 0015-4822
FLYING ANGEL. 1958. q. £0.80. Missions to Seamen, St. Michael Paternoster Royal, College Hill, London EC4R 2RL, England. TEL 071-248-5202. FAX 071-248-4761. Ed. Gillian Ennis. illus.; circ. 13,500.

286 UK ISSN 0143-7925
FOCUS (GRANTHAM). 1979. q. £2.50. Stanborough Press Ltd., Alma Park, Grantham, Lincs. NG31 9SL, England. TEL 0476-591700. FAX 0476-77144. Ed. D.N. Marshall. illus.; circ. 25,000.

284 US ISSN 1058-6784
FORWARD DAY BY DAY; a manual of daily Bible reading and devotions. Spanish edition: Dia a Dia. 1935. q. $6 for ink print (2 yrs.); large print $12; Braille & cassette free. Forward Movement Publications, 412 Sycamore St., Cincinnati, OH 45202. TEL 513-721-6659. FAX 513-421-0315. Ed. Charles Long. circ. 285,000. (also avail. in Braille; audio cassette; large print edition in 18 pt.)

139 FR
BX4843.A2
FRANCE PROTESTANTE ET LES EGLISES DE LANGUE FRANCAISE. 1922, 40th ed. a. 180 F. Librairie Fischbacher, 33 rue de Seine, 75006 Paris, France. TEL 43-26-84-87.
 Formerly: Annuaire Protestant: la France Protestante et les Eglises de Langue Francaise (ISSN 0066-362X)

283 UK ISSN 0532-579X
FRANCISCAN. 1959. 3/yr. £3. Society of St. Francis, The Friary, Hilfield, Dorchester, Dorset DT2 7BE, England. TEL 0300-341345. bk.rev.; circ. 3,500.
 Former titles: Floweret; Franciscan News.

FRIEDE UEBER ISRAEL; Zeitschrift fuer Kirche und Judentum. see *RELIGIONS AND THEOLOGY — Judaic*

284 GW
FRIEDE UND FREIHEIT. 1946. every 6 wks. DM.6. Evangelisch-Reformierte Kirche, Troendlinring 7, 7010 Leipzig, Germany. Ed.Bd. circ. 3,000.

284 GW
FRIEDENSBOTE. m. DM.7.20. Oncken Verlag, Langenbeckstr. 28-30, Postfach 102829, 3500 Kassel 1, Germany. Ed. Hinrich Schmidt. circ. 50,000. (back issues avail.)

269 266 GW
FRIEDENSGLOCKE. 1893. s-m. DM.6. Evangelisch-Methodistische Kirche in der DDR, Wiener Str. 56, 8020 Dresden, Germany. Ed. G. Roegner.

266 285 AT ISSN 1033-2235
FRONTIER NEWS. 1930. 4/yr. free. Uniting Church in Australia, Uniting Church Frontier Services, 222 Pitt St., 5th Fl., Sydney, N.S.W. 2000, Australia. TEL 02-287-0900. FAX 02-287-0999. (Subscr. to: P.O. Box E266, St. James, N.S.W. 2000, Australia) Ed. Rev. Brian Smith. bk.rev.; charts; illus.; stat.; circ. 20,000. (tabloid format; back issues avail.)
 Description: Stories of Uniting Church mission work in the outback, isolated areas of Australia.

284 GW ISSN 0016-2434
FUER ARBEIT UND BESINNUNG. 1947. s-m. DM.72. (Evangelischer Oberkirchenrat) Quell Verlag, Furtbachstr. 12A, Postfach 103852, 7000 Stuttgart 10, Germany. TEL 0711-60100-0. adv.; bk.rev.; index; circ. 3,800.

287 GW ISSN 0016-2442
FUER HEUTE. 1968. w. DM.16.80. (Evangelisch-methodistische Kirche) Christliches Verlagshaus GmbH, Motorstr. 36, 7000 Stuttgart 31, Germany. FAX 0711-8300084. circ. 18,000.
 Formed by the 1968 merger of: Gute Botschaft; Friedensglocke.

284 US ISSN 0896-5749
FUNDAMENTAL NEWS SERVICE. 1960. bi-m. $10. American Council of Christian Churches, Box 816, Valley Forge, PA 19482. TEL 215-566-8154. Ed. Donald McKnight. bk.rev.; circ. 15,000.

286 US ISSN 0016-2744
FUNDAMENTALIST. 1927. m. $3. World Baptist Fellowship, Box 13459, Arlington, TX 76094-0459. TEL 817-274-7161. Ed. Dr. Wendell Hiers. bk.rev.; circ. 8,500. **Indexed:** CERDIC.
 Description: Promotional news from the World Baptist Fellowship.

284 GW
DER GAERTNER. 1893. w. DM.72.50. Bundes-Verlag GmbH, Postfach 4065, D-5810 Witten, Germany. TEL 02302-399-43. Ed. Erhard Diehl. adv.; bk.rev.; circ. 10,000. (back issues avail.)

GATEWAY. see *SOCIAL SERVICES AND WELFARE*

GAYSPRING. see *HOMOSEXUALITY*

284 GW ISSN 0016-6073
DIE GEMEINDE (KASSEL). 1946. w. DM.88. (Bund Evangelisch-Freikirchlicher Gemeinden) Oncken Verlag, Langenbeckstr. 28-30, Postfach 102829, 3500 Kassel 1, Germany. Ed. Reinhard Schwarz. adv.; bk.rev.; abstr.; illus.; index; circ. 15,000. (tabloid format)

GEMEINDEBIBELSCHULE; Mitarbeiterzeitschrift. see *RELIGIONS AND THEOLOGY*

284 AU ISSN 0016-6111
GEMEINDEBRIEF; fuer die gemeindemitglieder der evangelischen Pfarrgemeinde Melk-Scheibbs. 1956. bi-m. DM.46. Evangelisches Pfarramt Melk, Kirchenstr. 15, Postfach 9, A-3390 Melk, Austria. TEL 069-78972-0. Ed. Britta Hubener. illus.; index; circ. 8,500. (back issues avail.)

200 NE
GEREFORMEERD KERKHISTORISCH TIJDSCHRIFT. 1973. q. fl.12.50. Gereformeerd Historisch Instituut - Reformed Historical Institute, Zestienhovensekade 409, Rotterdam 3008, Netherlands. Ed. J. Lussenburg. adv.; bk.rev.

284 230 NE ISSN 0016-8610
GEREFORMEERD THEOLOGISCH TIJDSCHRIFT. 1900. q. fl.36.80. J. H. Kok B. V., Box 130, 8260 AC Kampen, Netherlands. Ed. W. Bakker. bk.rev.; index.
Indexed: CERDIC, New Test.Abstr., Old Test.Abstr., Rel.& Theol.Abstr. (1968-).
—BLDSC shelfmark: 4161.630000.

284.2 SA ISSN 0378-407X
GEREFORMEERDE VROUEBLAD. (Text in Afrikaans) 1947. m. R.21.70. Reformed Churches in South Africa - Gereformeerde Kerke in Suid-Afrika, P.O. Box 20008, Noordbrug 2522, Potchefstroom, South Africa. Ed. Mrs. A. de Bruyn. circ. 6,900.

GESELLSCHAFT FUER DIE GESCHICHTE DES PROTESTANTISMUS IN OESTERREICH. JAHRBUCH. see HISTORY — History Of Europe

GESELLSCHAFT FUER NIEDERSAECHSISCHE KIRCHENGESCHICHTE. JAHRBUCH. see HISTORY — History Of Europe

053.1 GW ISSN 0016-934X
GETROSTER TAG/HOPEFUL DAY.* 1955. 3/yr. DM.9.90. Burckhardthaus-Laetare Verlag GmbH, Schumannstr. 161, 6050 Offenbach, Germany. circ. 35,000.

284 052 AT
GIPPSLAND ANGLICAN. 1930. m. Aus.$3.50 (typically set in Feb.). Anglican Diocese of Gippsland, Church News Board, 453 Raymond St., Sale, Vic. 3850, Australia. TEL 051-44-2044. FAX 051-44-7183. Ed. Rev. John White. adv.; bk.rev.; film rev.; circ. 4,500. (tabloid format; back issues avail.)
Description: Regional Anglican newpaper for Anglicans in the Diocese of Gippsland.

285 266 CN ISSN 0017-0720
GLAD TIDINGS. 1925. m. Can.$7. Women's Missionary Society (WD), Presbyterian Church in Canada, 50 Wynford Dr., Rm. 100, Don Mills, Ont. M3C 1J7, Canada. TEL 416-441-2840. FAX 416-441-2825. Ed. L. June Stevenson. bk.rev.; illus.; index; circ. 9,500.
Description: Covers mission work in the world.

GLASS (LEICESTER). see LITERATURE

284 GW ISSN 0323-8202
BX9798.U5
GLAUBE UND HEIMAT. 1946. w. DM.0.75 per no. (Landeskirchenrat der Evangelisch-Lutherischen Kirche in Thueringen) Wartburg Verlag GmbH, Sophienstr. 18, 6900 Jena, Germany. Ed.Bd. adv.; bk.rev.

GLORY SONGS. see MUSIC

283 CY ISSN 0256-4726
GO; the quarterly magazine of Interserve. 1872. q. £4.50. Interserve, PO Box 2140, Nicosia, Cyprus. TEL 02-452745. (Dist. in U.S. by: Box 418, Upper Darby, PA 19082-0418; Alt. U.K. addr.: 325 Kennington Rd., London SE11 4QH. TEL 071-735-8227) Ed. Jenny Taylor. circ. 13,000.
Description: International forum for the 400 ministerial partners in over ten countries in South Asia, the Middle East, and several other ethnic groups in Britain.

287 UK ISSN 0017-1700
GOLEUAD/LIGHT. 1871. w. 20p. per no. (Presbyterian Church of Wales) Y Llyfrfa, St. David's Rd., Caernarvon, Gwynedd LL55 1ER, Wales. Ed. Rev. M. Lloyd Davies. adv.; bk.rev.; circ. 5,000.

284 XV
GOLGOTSKA VEST. (Text in Slovenian) 1966. m. 2000 din. Kristusova Binkostna Cerkev, Milcinskega 73, 61000 Ljubljana, Slovenia. TEL 069-559-655. Ed. Mihael Kuzmic. circ. 300. (back issues avail.)

GOOD NEWS (NEW BERLIN). see RELIGIONS AND THEOLOGY — Roman Catholic

285 US ISSN 0436-1563
GOOD NEWS (WILMORE). 1967. bi-m. $14.95. Forum for Scriptural Christianity, Inc., 308 E. Main St., Box 150, Wilmore, KY 40390. TEL 606-858-4661. FAX 606-858-4972. Ed. James V. Heidinger II. adv.; bk.rev.; circ. 20,000. (back issues avail.)
Description: Covers United Methodist related current issues, testimonies and inspirational pieces.

268 US ISSN 0362-0417
ML1
GOSPEL CHOIR. q. $7.25. Southern Baptist Convention, Sunday School Board, 127 Ninth Ave., N., Nashville, TN 37234. TEL 800-458-2772.

283 UK
GOSPEL MAGAZINE. 1766. bi-m. £3($5) Gospel Magazine Trust, Mill Lane House, Margate, Kent CT9 1ND, England. TEL 0843 298819. Ed. Rev. M. Handford. adv.; bk.rev. (back issues avail.)
Incorporates: Protestant Beacon & British Protestant.

286 UK
GRACE BAPTIST MISSION HERALD. 1900. q. free. Grace Baptist Mission, 12 Abbey Close, Abingdon, Oxon. OX14 3JD, England. TEL 0235 20147. Ed. J.C. Richards. circ. 6,000.

268 US ISSN 0162-4512
GROWING (NASHVILLE). 1970. q. $4.50. Southern Baptist Convention, Sunday School Board, 127 Ninth Ave., N., Nashville, TN 37234. TEL 800-458-2772.

284 GW ISSN 0177-1817
GRUSS AUS DER WELTWEITEN BRUEDER-UNITAET - DAHEIM UND DRAUSSEN. q. Herrnhuter Missionshilfe e.V., Badwasen 6, 7325 Bad Boll, Germany. TEL 07164-8010. FAX 07164-80199. Ed. Rev. H. Heisler. circ. 40,000.
Formerly: Daheim und Draussen.

284 US
GUIDE FOR BIBLICAL STUDIES. 1885. q. $7. Church of the Brethren, General Board, 1451 Dundee Ave., Elgin, IL 60120. TEL 312-742-5100. FAX 708-742-6103. Ed. Julie L. Garber. adv.; circ. 17,000.
Description: Based on international Sunday school lessons for Christian teaching.

HANDBELLS; for directors and ringers. see MUSIC

268 US
HAPPY TIMES. 1964. m. $6.75. (Lutheran Church - Missouri Synod, Board for Parish Services) Concordia Publishing House, 3558 S. Jefferson Ave., St. Louis, MO 63118. TEL 314-664-7000. Ed. Earl H. Gaulke. circ. 49,000. (also avail. in microfilm)
Description: Stories and activities for Christian education.

283 US ISSN 0274-7154
HAWAIIAN CHURCH CHRONICLE. 1910. 9/yr. $6 donation. Episcopal Church in Hawaii, 229 Queen Emma Square, Honolulu, HI 96813-2304. TEL 808-536-7776. FAX 808-538-7194. Ed. Rev. John Paul Engelcke. circ. 7,900. (tabloid format)

287 US
HAWKEYE (DES MOINES). 1957. 10/yr. $5 (free to all Iowa local officers). United Methodist Church, Iowa Conference, 1019 Chestnut St., Des Moines, IA 50309. TEL 515-283-1991. Ed. Karen Tisinger. adv.; illus.; circ. 24,000. (tabloid format)
Former titles: Hawkeye United Methodist (ISSN 0017-8632); Hawkeye Methodist.

286 US
HEARTBEAT (NASHVILLE). 1961. 6/yr. free. Free Will Baptist Foreign Missions, Box 5002, Antioch, TN 37011-5002. TEL 615-361-1010. FAX 615-731-0049. Ed. Don Robirds. circ. 45,000 (controlled).
Description: News, profiles, and personal experiences pertaining to the foreign missionary work of Free Will Baptists.

HELFENDE HAENDE; Zeitschrift des diakonischen Werkes Westfalen. see SOCIAL SERVICES AND WELFARE

285 US
HELPING HAND IN BIBLE STUDY. 1884. q. $4.50. (Seventh Day Baptist Board of Christian Education) American Sabbath Tract & Communications Council, 3120 Kennedy Rd., Box 1678, Janesville, WI 53547-1678. TEL 608-752-5055. Ed. Linda Harris. circ. 2,200. (back issues avail.)
Description: Bible study lessons, based on international Bible lessons for Christian teaching, for Seventh Day Baptists.

285 CU ISSN 0864-0270
HERALDO CRISTIANO. bi-m. Iglesia Presbiteriana, Salud No. 222nd, Lealtad y Companario, Havana 2, Cuba. TEL 61-1558. Dir. Jacobo Guiribitey.

284 NE ISSN 0018-0920
HERVORMD ARNHEM.* 1905. w. fl.15. (Hervormde Gemeente Arnhem) Drukkerij J.C. Willemsen, Postbus 79, Amersfoort, Netherlands. (Subscr. address: Breyers Boekhandel, Looierstraat 1, Arnhem, Netherlands) Ed. P.M. Gerritse. adv.; bk.rev.; film rev. (looseleaf format)

284 NE ISSN 0018-0939
HERVORMD NEDERLAND. 1944. w. fl.132. Box 84410, The Hague, Netherlands. FAX 070-3584761. Ed. B. van Duyn. adv.; bk.rev.; illus.; circ. 26,500. **Indexed:** CERDIC.

284 NE ISSN 0018-0947
HERVORMD WAGENINGEN.* 1945. fortn. fl.6.75($2.) Hervormde Gemeente Kerkelijk Bureau, Markt 17, Wageningen, Netherlands. adv.; bk.rev.; bibl.; circ. 4,000.

284 SA ISSN 0259-949X
DIE HERVORMER. (Text in Afrikaans) 1909. s-m. R.24 (typically set in Jan.). Nederduitsch Hervormde Kerk van Afrika, P.O. Box 5777, Pretoria 0001, South Africa. Ed. D.J.C. van Wyk. adv.; bk.rev.; circ. 27,500.

284 GW
HESSISCHES PFARRBLATT. 1971. bi-m. DM.15. Evang. Pfarrerverein in Hessen und Nassau, Melsunger Str. 8a, 6000 Frankfurt a.M. 60, Germany. TEL 069-471820. Ed. Helmut Ludwig. index; circ. 2,700. (back issues avail.)
Description: Covers church problems and matters of the pastoral profession.

200 SA ISSN 0018-1684
HIGHWAY. (Text in Afrikaans, English) 1940. m. $10. Anglican Diocese of Kimberley and Kuruman, Box 45, Kimberley, South Africa. FAX 531-812730. Ed.Bd. adv.; circ. 2,100. (tabloid format)

286 US ISSN 0890-3247
HISTORIAS BIBLICAS PARA PREESCOLARES: ALUMNOS. (Text in Spanish) q. $5.25. Southern Baptist Convention, Sunday School Board, 127 Ninth Ave., N., Nashville, TN 37234. TEL 800-458-2772.

286 US ISSN 0890-3158
HISTORIAS BIBLICAS PARA PREESCOLARES: MAESTROS. (Text in Spanish) q. $9.50. Southern Baptist Convention, Sunday School Board, 127 Ninth Ave., N., Nashville, TN 37234. TEL 800-458-2772.

284 US ISSN 0360-9030
HISTORICAL FOOTNOTES (ST. LOUIS). 1955. q. $20. Concordia Historical Institute, 801 De Mun Ave., St. Louis, MO 63105. TEL 314-721-5934. Ed. A.R. Sueflow. bk.rev.; bibl.; circ. 1,700. **Indexed:** Hist.Abstr.

287 US
HISTORICAL HIGHLIGHTS. 1971. s-a. $10. South Georgia Conference Commission on Archives and History of the United Methodist Church, Box 407, Epworth-by-the-Sea, St. Simons Island, GA 31522. TEL 912-638-2379. Ed. Marynell S. Waite. bk.rev.; cum.index every 4 yrs.; circ. 275.
Description: Written by scholars and amateur historians for the purpose of collecting and preserving the Methodist heritage, history of the region and its relations to its roots and current world sphere.

RELIGIONS AND THEOLOGY — PROTESTANT

287 270   US
HISTORICAL MESSENGER. 1969. q. $3. United Methodist Church, Central Illinois Conference, Historical Society, Box 515, Bloomington, IL 61702-0515. TEL 309-828-5092. Ed. Vera Swantner. illus.; stat.; circ. 1,200. **Indexed:** Hist.Abstr.
   Formerly: Central Illinois Historical Messenger (ISSN 0008-9419)

200   UK
HISTORICAL SOCIETY OF THE CHURCH IN WALES. JOURNAL. 1946. a. £2. Historical Society of the Church in Wales, c/o Owen W. Jones, The Vicarage, Builth Wells, Brec, Wales. Ed. Canon David Walker. charts; stat. **Indexed:** Br.Archaeol.Abstr.

940 200   UK
HISTORICAL SOCIETY OF THE PRESBYTERIAN CHURCH OF WALES. JOURNAL. (Text in English and Welsh) 1916. a. 50p. Historical Society of the Presbyterian Church of Wales, The Manse, Caradog Rd., Aberystwyth, Dyfed, Wales. Ed. Rev. Gomer M. Roberts. bk.rev.; circ. 600.

286   US   ISSN 0018-3229
HOGAR CRISTIANO. (Text in Spanish) 1957. q. $6. Casa Bautista de Publicaciones, Box 4255, El Paso, TX 79914. TEL 915-566-9656. Ed. James R. West. illus.; circ. 30,000.

285   US   ISSN 1040-8584
HOLINESS DIGEST. s-a. membership. Christian Holiness Association, Box 100, Wilmore, KY 40390. TEL 606-858-4091. FAX 606-858-4096. Eds. Burnis Bushong, Patricia Walls. adv.; bk.rev.; circ. 5,600.
   Description: Examines the idea of biblical holiness in a secular age.

283   US   ISSN 0018-3725
HOLY CROSS. NEWSLETTER. vol.4, 1965. 3/yr. contributions. Order of the Holy Cross, Holy Cross Monastery, Box 99, West Park, NY 12493. TEL 914-384-6660. circ. 24,000. (newspaper)
   Formerly: Holy Cross News.

249 286   US   ISSN 0018-4071
HOME LIFE; a Christian family magazine. m. $11.75. Southern Baptist Convention, Sunday School Board, 127 Ninth Ave. N., Nashville, TN 37234. TEL 800-458-2772. **Indexed:** South.Bap.Per.Ind.

HORIZON (NEPTUNE). see *GERONTOLOGY AND GERIATRICS*

285   US
HORIZONS UNLIMITED. 1987. q. free. Redeeming Love Christian Center, 145 W. Rt. 59, Box 577, Nanuet, NY 10954-9963. Ed. Deborah D. Walker. circ. 27,500.
   Description: Biblically-based teachings by Clinton and Sarah Utterbach, fellowship's pastors and a variety of guest writers. Focus is on the result of practical application of biblical principles in the lives of individuals featured.

HUGUENOT TRAILS. see *HISTORY — History Of North And South America*

HUMAN DEVELOPMENT (HARTFORD). see *PSYCHOLOGY*

283   CN   ISSN 0018-7917
HURON CHURCH NEWS. 1950. 10/yr. Can.$5. Anglican Church of Canada, Diocese of Huron, 4-220 Dundas St., London, Ont. N6A 1H3, Canada. TEL 519-434-6893. FAX 519-673-4151. Ed. Rev. Roger W. McCombe. adv.; bk.rev.; illus.; circ. 26,000. (tabloid format)

284 783   DK   ISSN 0106-4940
ML3142
HYMNOLOGISKE MEDDELELSER; tidsskrift om salmer. (Text in Danish, Norwegian and Swedish; summaries in English and German) 1972. q. DKK 150. Salmehistorisk Selskab, Kobenhavns Universitet, Institut for Kirkehistorie, Koebmagergade 44-46, DK-1150 Copenhagen K, Denmark. Ed. Peter Balslev-Clausen. adv.; bk.rev.; illus.; circ. 700. (back issues avail.) **Indexed:** M.L.A.
   Description: Discusses hymnology and new hymns from Denmark, Norway, Sweden and Finland.

284   GW
IDEA-SPEKTRUM. English edition. 1979. w. DM.120($70) for German. ed.; English. ed. DM.25($8). Idea e.V., Postfach 18 20, D-6330 Wetzlar 1, Germany. TEL 06641-45022. FAX 06641-47706. TELEX 483729. Ed. Helmut Matthies. adv.; bk.rev.; circ. 15,000. (back issues avail.)

284   AG   ISSN 0019-1671
IGLESIA EVANGELICA DEL RIO DE LA PLATA. REVISTA PARROQUIAL. (Text in German, Spanish) 1895. m. Arg.$300($10) Convencion Evangelica Bautista Argentina, Rivadavia 3476, 1203 Buenos Aires, Argentina. Ed. Federico H. Schafer. adv.; bk.rev.; circ. 5,100.

284   TZ   ISSN 0019-171X
IJA WEBONERE. (Text in Haya, Swahili) vol.14, 1968. bi-m. Sh.300($30) Evangelical Lutheran Church in Tanzania, North Western Diocese, Box 277, Bukoba, Tanzania. TELEX 58387 ELCT TZ. Ed. Rev. Fidon Mwombeki. adv.; stat.; circ. X. (looseleaf format)

286   US   ISSN 0019-1868
ILLINOIS BAPTIST. 1905. w. $6. Illinois Baptist State Association, Box 3486, Springfield, IL 62708. TEL 217-786-2638. Ed. Robert J. Hastings. bk.rev.; charts; illus.; stat.; circ. 46,000. (tabloid format; also avail. in microform)

284.2   SA   ISSN 0378-4088
IMBONGI YENKOSI. (Text in Zulu) 1952. m. (11/yr.). R.3. Reformed Churches in South Africa - Gereformeerde Kerke in Suid-Afrika, P.O. Box 59, Hammanskraal 0400, South Africa. Ed. Rev. W.L. Kurpershoek. circ. 2,400.

284   GW
IMMER GRUEN. 1911. a. DM.6.20. Quell Verlag, Fuertbachstr. 12A, Postfach 103852, 7000 Stuttgart 10, Germany. TEL 0711-60100-0. Ed. Johannes Burdinski. circ. 25,000.

286   US   ISSN 0019-2821
IMPACT (WHEATON). 1943. 4/yr. $3. Conservative Baptist Foreign Mission Society, Box 5, Wheaton, IL 60189-0005. TEL 708-665-1200. Ed. Arthur Heerwagen. bk.rev.; film rev.; charts; illus.; stat.; tr.; lit.; circ. 40,375.
   Formerly: Conservative Baptist Impact.
   Description: Discusses mission work in the US.

284   US
IN SEASON.* 1974. w. $25. Cathedral Publishers, Box 129, Royal Oak, MI 48068-0129. Ed. H. Dean Lueking. circ. 2,000.

285   US   ISSN 0274-5569
INCREASE. bi-m. free. Bible Christian Union, Box 410, Hatfield, PA 19440-0410. TEL 215-361-0500. FAX 215-361-7994. Ed. George W. Murray. circ. 15,000. (back issues avail.)
   Description: Information regarding the missionary work of Bible Christian Union.

284   II
INDIAN LUTHERAN. (Text in English) vol.62, 1967. q. Rs.12. United Evangelical Lutheran Churches in India, No. 1 First St., Haddows Rd., Nungambakkam, Madras 600006, India. Ed. Dr. K. Rajaratnam. adv.; bk.rev.; circ. 1,000.
   Formerly (until 1980): Gospel Witness (ISSN 0017-2391)

287   II   ISSN 0019-6487
INDIAN WITNESS. 1871. s-m. Rs.10($6) to individuals; institutions Rs.15. Methodist Church in India, 25 Lodi Rd., New Delhi 110003, India. (U.S. subscr. address: c/o 1st United Methodist Church, 1589 W. Maple, Birmingham, MI 48010) Ed. Richard Renwick Smyth. adv.; bk.rev.; circ. 2,500.
   Description: Church news and views.

284   IO
INDONESIA. DIREKTORAT JENDERAL BIMBINGAN MASYARAKAT KRISTEN-PROTESTAN LAPORAN TAHUNAN/INDONESIA. DIRECTORATE GENERAL OF PROTESTANT AFFAIRS. ANNUAL REPORT.* a. Directorate General of Protestant Affairs, Ministry of Religious Affairs, Jalan M.H. Thamrin 6, Jakarta Pusat, Indonesia.

286 248.83   US   ISSN 0020-1944
INSIGHT (HAGERSTOWN); a magazine of Christian understanding for young Adventists. 1970. w. $31.97. (General Conference of Seventh-day Adventists) Review and Herald Publishing Association, 55 W. Oak Ridge Dr., Hagerstown, MD 21740. TEL 301-791-7000. Ed. Chris Blake. adv.; bk.rev.; illus.; circ. 24,000. (reprint service avail. from UMI) **Indexed:** Chr.Per.Ind.
   Supersedes: Youth's Instructor.

286   CN   ISSN 0383-6061
INTERCOM. 1968. irreg. Fellowship of Evangelical Baptist Churches in Canada, 679 Southgate Dr., Guelph, Ont. N1G 4S2, Canada. TEL 519-821-4830. FAX 519-821-9829.

INTERNATIONAL BULLETIN OF MISSIONARY RESEARCH. see *LIBRARY AND INFORMATION SCIENCES*

286   US   ISSN 0162-4342
EL INTERPRETE. (Text in Spanish) q. $4.50. Southern Baptist Convention, Sunday School Board, 127 Ninth Ave., N., Nashville, TN 37234. TEL 800-458-2772. **Indexed:** M.L.A.

286   US   ISSN 0740-0063
EL INTERPRETE: MAESTROS. (Text in Spanish) q. $11. Southern Baptist Convention, Sunday School Board, 127 Ninth Ave., N., Nashville, TN 37234. TEL 800-458-2772.

287   US   ISSN 0020-9678
INTERPRETER (NASHVILLE). 1957. 8/yr. $8. United Methodist Communications, 810 Twelfth Ave. S., Nashville, TN 37203-4744. TEL 615-742-5400. Ed. Laura J. Okumu. adv.; bk.rev.; charts; illus.; circ. 300,000. (also avail. in microfilm from UMI; back issues avail.) **Indexed:** Comput.Lit.Ind., Meth.Per.Ind.
   Formed by the 1969 merger of: Spotlight and Methodist Story; Methodist Story.
   Description: Directed to local church leaders containing program ideas and resources.

285 371.2   US
INTERVARSITY. 1982. q. donation basis. Inter-Varsity Christian Fellowship of the United States of America, 6400 Schroeder Rd., Box 7895, Madison, WI 53707-7895. TEL 608-274-9001. FAX 608-274-7882. Ed. Neal Kunde. circ. 50,000. (back issues avail.)

286   UK
IRISH BAPTIST. 1877. 12/yr. £9 (elsewhere £9.75). Baptist Union of Ireland, 117 Lisburn Road, Belfast BT9 7AF, N. Ireland. TEL 0232-663108. FAX 0232-663616. circ. 3,150.

286.0415   UK   ISSN 0075-0727
IRISH BAPTIST HISTORICAL SOCIETY. JOURNAL. 1969. a. £7($10) (effective Jan. 1992). Baptist Union of Ireland, 117 Lisburn Rd., Belfast BT9 7AF, N. Ireland. TEL 0232-669157. FAX 0232-663616. Ed. Joshua Thompson. bk.rev.; cum.index: vols.1-20 in prep.; circ. 250.

283   JM   ISSN 0047-1720
JAMAICA CHURCHMAN. 1970. m. 75p.($1.10) Anglican Diocese of Jamaica, Anglican Church Office, Kingston 5, Jamaica, W.I. Ed. Barbara Gloudon. adv.; illus.; circ. 6,000.

266   JA   ISSN 0021-440X
JAPAN HARVEST. (Text in English) 1951. q. $20. Japan Evangelical Missionary Association, 2-1 Kanda Surugadai, Chiyoda-ku, Tokyo 101, Japan. FAX 03-3295-6783. Ed. Don Wright. adv.; bk.rev.; charts; illus.; circ. 1,200.
   Description: Discusses mission work in the country.

284 028.5   GW
JESUS LIEBT KINDER. 1925. bi-m. DM.12. (Deutscher E C-Verband) Born-Verlag, Leuschnerstr. 72-74, 3500 Kassel, Germany. TEL 0561-40950. FAX 0561-4095-112. circ. 9,000.

268 US
JOURNAL OF CHRISTIAN EDUCATION OF THE AFRICAN METHODIST EPISCOPAL CHURCH. 1936. q. $3. African Methodist Episcopal Church, Christian Education Department, 500 Eighth Ave. S., Nashville, TN 37203. TEL 615-256-7020. FAX 615-244-7604. Ed. Rev. Edgar L. Mack. adv.; bk.rev.; charts; film rev.; illus.; rec.; rev.; circ. 6,000. (also avail. in microform from UMI; reprint service avail. from UMI)
Former titles (1980-1982): Journal of Religious Education of the African Methodist Episcopal Church (ISSN 0276-0770); (1936-1980): Journal of Religious Education (ISSN 0022-4219)

289.809   CN   ISSN 0824-5053
BX8101
JOURNAL OF MENNONITE STUDIES. (Text in English, German) 1983. a. Can.$10. University of Winnipeg, Chair of Mennonite Studies, Winnipeg, Man. R3B 2E9, Canada. TEL 204-786-9214. Ed. Harry Loewen. circ. 600. (back issues avail.)
—BLDSC shelfmark: 5017.640000.

200   US   ISSN 0361-1906
JOURNAL OF THEOLOGY. 1961. 4/yr. $5 (foreign $7). Immanuel Lutheran College, 501 Grover Rd., Eau Claire, WI 54701. (Subscr. to: 2750 Oxford St., N., Roseville, MN 55113) Ed. John Lau. bk.rev.; circ. 280.
—BLDSC shelfmark: 5069.071200.

200   AT   ISSN 0314-6235
JOURNEY (BRISBANE). 1977. m. Aus.$25($45) Uniting Church in Australia, Communications Services Unit, P.O. Box 674, Brisbane, Qld. 4001, Australia. TEL 07-377-9910. FAX 07-377-9716. Ed. Andrew Demack. adv.; bk.rev.; film rev.; charts; illus.; circ. 4,580. (also avail. in microfilm; back issues avail.)
Formerly: Life and Times.

JOURNEY (ST. LOUIS). see *CHILDREN AND YOUTH — For*

284   301.412   US   ISSN 0164-4882
JOYFUL WOMAN. 1978. bi-m. $15. Joyful Woman Ministries, Box 90028, Chattanooga, TN 37412. TEL 615-698-7318. Ed. Elizabeth Handford. adv.; bk.rev.; circ. 14,000.

266   US   ISSN 0893-1607
JUBILEE; the monthly newsletter of Prison Fellowship. 1977. m. free. Prison Fellowship, Box 17500, Washington, DC 20041-0500. TEL 703-478-0100. FAX 703-478-0452. Ed. Megs Singer. circ. 180,000.

280.4   028.5   AT   ISSN 1030-0287
JUNIOR CLUBHOUSE. 1975. m. Aus.$7.50 (foreign Aus.$10). Mission Publications of Australia, 19 Cascade St., P.O. Box 21, Lawson, N.S.W. 2783, Australia. TEL 047-59-1003. Ed. Rosemary Painter. circ. 2,000.
Description: Christian magazine for children ages 7-12.

266   UK
JUNKANOO. 1841. q. free. Methodist Church Overseas Division, 25 Marylebone Rd., London NW1 5JR, England. circ. 80,000.
Former titles (until 1991): Window (ISSN 0306-9028); At Home and Abroad (ISSN 0044-9830)
Description: Children's interests.

285.834   US   ISSN 0361-8668
KEEPING YOU POSTED. 1966. bi-m. $6. United Church of Christ, Office of Communication, 700 Prospect Ave., Cleveland, OH 44115-1100. TEL 216-736-2222. FAX 216-736-2223. Ed. Beverly J. Chain. bk.rev.; illus.; stat.; circ. 16,000.

284.2   SA   ISSN 0023-0596
KERKBLAD. (Text in Afrikaans) 1873. fortn. R.37. Reformed Churches in South Africa - Gereformeerde Kerke in Suid-Afrika, P.O. Box 20008, Noordbrug 2522, Potchefstroom, South Africa. Ed. G.T.C. Jordaan. adv.; bk.rev.; circ. 10,100.

284   SA
KERKBODE; amptelike blad van die Nederduitse Gereformeerde Kerk. (Text in Afrikaans) 1849. fortn. R.20($13.64) Tydskriftemaatskappy van die Nederduitse Gereformeerde Kerk in S.A., Nederduitse Gereformeerde Church Centre, Greys Pass, Box 1444, Cape Town, South Africa. Ed. G.S.J. Moller. adv.; bk.rev.; circ. 19,000. (back issues avail.)

284   GW
KIRCHE IM OSTEN. irreg. (approx. 1/yr.). DM.56. (Studien zur Osteuropaeischen Kirchengeschichte und Kirchenkunde) Vanderhoeck und Ruprecht, Theaterstr. 13, Postfach 3753, 3400 Goettingen, Germany. Ed. Peter Hauptmann. (back issues avail.)

284   GW   ISSN 0178-8906
KIRCHLICHER DIENST IN DER ARBEITSWELT; Zeitschrift fuer evangelische Arbeitnehmer und evangelische Industrie- und Sozialarbeit. 1959. m. DM.22($15) (Kirchlicher Dienst in der Arbeitswelt) Verlag Stimme der Arbeit, Postfach 1113, 7325 Boll, Germany. TEL 07164-2008. FAX 07164-5798. Ed. Ruediger Weiser. adv.; bk.rev.; circ. 3,500. (back issues avail.)

274   GW   ISSN 0075-6210
KIRCHLICHES JAHRBUCH FUER DIE EVANGELISCHE KIRCHE IN DEUTSCHLAND. a. price varies. Guetersloher Verlagshaus Gerd Mohn, Carl-Bertelsmann-Str. 256, Postfach 1343, 4830 Guetersloh 100, Germany. TEL 05241-7405-0. FAX 05241-740548.

289   GW
DER KRIEGSRUF. 1887. w. DM.40 (foreign DM.60). (Heilsarmee - Salvation Army) Heilsarmee Verlag GmbH, Salierring 27, 5000 Cologne 1, Germany. TEL 0221-208190. Ed. Evelin Binsch. bk.rev.; circ. 17,000.
Description: Official organ of the Salvation Army in Germany.

266   MW
KUUNIKA. (Text in Chichewa) 1960. m. 72 T. (Christian Literature Fund) Presbyterian Church of Central Africa, Nkhoma Synod, P.O. Nkhoma, Malawi. Ed. M.J. Nkhalambayhusi Chirwa. bk.rev.; circ. 6,000.

266   US
L I R S BULLETIN. 1964. 2/yr. free to qualified personnel. Lutheran Immigration and Refugee Service, 390 Park Ave. So., New York, NY 10016-8803. Ed. Lily R. Wu. circ. 3,500.
Formerly: L I R S Information Bulletin.
Description: Articles about immigration ranging from news of previous immigrants to why the church is involved in helping refugees. Updates on LIRS activities in resettlement and advocacy, and on developments in US immigration policy.

284   370.196   US
L P E A HEARTBEAT. 1988. 8/yr. Luis Palau Evangelistic Association, Box 1173, Portland, OR 97207. TEL 503-643-0777. FAX 503-643-6851. Ed. Mike Umlandt. circ. 10,000. (back issues avail.)
Description: Focuses primarily on Evangelistic ministry of LPEA worldwide.

284   GW   ISSN 0174-1764
BX8001
L W B DOKUMENTATION. REPORT. 1978. irreg. DM.22($10) (Lutheran World Federation - Geneva) Kreuz-Verlag Zeitschriften GmbH, Breitwiesenstr. 30, 7000 Stuttgart 80, Germany. TEL 0711-7880323. circ. 3,500.

280   US
LATIN AMERICA EVANGELIST. 1921. q. free. Latin America Mission, Box 52-7900, Miami, FL 33152. TEL 305-884-8400. FAX 305-885-8649. Ed. John D. Maust. circ. 32,000.
Description: Focuses on Latin America and the Christian Church there.

280   370   US
LEADER IN THE CHURCH SCHOOL TODAY. q. $12. (United Methodist Church, Board of Discipleship) United Methodist Publishing House, Graded Press, 201 Eighth Ave., S., Box 801, Nashville, TN 37202. TEL 615-749-6417. FAX 615-749-6079. Ed. Keith H. Kendall.
Formerly (until 1988): Children's Leader (ISSN 0276-3427)
Description: Articles providing help to leaders in their ministry.

284   US   ISSN 0199-7661
BV4000
LEADERSHIP (CAROL STREAM); a practical journal for church leaders. 1980. 4/yr. $22. Christianity Today, Inc., 465 Gunderson Dr., Carol Stream, IL 60188. TEL 708-260-6200. Ed. Marshall Shelley. bibl.; illus.; circ. 75,000. (also avail. in microfiche; back issues avail.) **Indexed:** CCR, Rel.& Theol.Abstr. (1980-).

LEAPING; magazine of Christian dance fellowship of Australia. see *DANCE*

284   UK
LEARNING ALL TOGETHER. 1984. q. £7.80. Scripture Union Publishing, 130 City Rd., London EC1V 2NJ, England. TEL 01-782-0013. Ed. Peter Grayston. circ. 8,500.
Description: Church curriculum material for Sunday school.

284   UK
LEARNING TOGETHER WITH UNDER 5'S. 1984. q. £7. Scripture Union Publishing, 130 City Road, London EC1V 2NJ, England. TEL 01-782-0013. Ed. Christine Wright. (back issues avail.)
Description: Sunday school material for children under 5.

266   AT   ISSN 0727-5854
LETTERSTICK. 1962. bi-m. free. Mission Publications of Australia, P.O. Box 21, 19 Cascade St., Lawson, N.S.W. 2783, Australia. Ed. Ian Lindsay. circ. 6,350.
Description: Easy English magazine for Australian aboriginal readers and other new readers.

269.2   CN
LIBERATION. 1972. q. Ken Campbell Evangelistic Association, Box 100, Milton, Ont. L9T 2Y3, Canada. TEL 416-878-8461. Ed. Ken Cambell. illus.; circ. 35,000. **Indexed:** Arts & Hum.Cit.Ind., G.Soc.Sci.& Rel.Per.Lit.
Formerly: Encounter (ISSN 0315-0097)

266.6   LB
LIBERIA BAPTIST MISSIONARY AND EDUCATIONAL CONVENTION. YEARBOOK.* (Text in English) a. Liberia Baptist Missionary and Educational Convention, Bentol City, Liberia. illus.

LIBRARIANS' CHRISTIAN FELLOWSHIP NEWSLETTER. see *LIBRARY AND INFORMATION SCIENCES*

284   GW   ISSN 0047-4584
LICHT UND LEBEN. 1889. m. DM.18. (Evangelische Gesellschaft fuer Deutschland e.V.) Licht und Leben Verlag GmbH, Kaiserstr. 78, 5600 Wuppertal 11, Germany. TEL 0202-784018. Ed. H. Becker. adv.; bk.rev.; circ. 10,000.
Description: Aims to disseminate knowledge about the Bible and Christianity. Discusses missionary activities.

283   GW
LICHTSTRAHLEN; taegliche Bibellese. 1897. a. DM.6.80. (Deutscher E C-Verband) Born-Verlag, Leuchnerstr. 72-74, 3500 Kassel, Germany. TEL 0561-40950. FAX 0561-4095-112. circ. 55,000.

286   US   ISSN 0890-0590
EL LIDER BAUTISTA. (Text in Spanish) q. $7.50. Southern Baptist Convention, Sunday School Board, 127 Ninth Ave., N., Nashville, TN 37234. TEL 800-458-2772.

284   GW
LIEBFRAUEN KALENDER. 1983. a. DM.3.50. Birken Verlag, 8055 Hallbergmoos-Girbeneck, Germany. FAX 0811-82119. Ed. Franz Habock.

274   UK   ISSN 0024-306X
LIFE AND WORK; the record of the Church of Scotland. 1879. m. £9. Church of Scotland, 121 George St., Edinburgh EH2 4YN, Scotland. FAX 031-220-3133. Ed. Peter B. MacDonald. adv.; bk.rev.; illus.; circ. 88,600. **Indexed:** CERDIC.

284   UK
LIFE INDEED. 1892. bi-m. £3.48. Faith Mission, 2 Drum St., Gilmerton, Edinburgh EH17 8QG, Scotland. Ed. Rev. Colin N. Peckham. adv.; cum.index; circ. 8,500. (back issues avail.)

RELIGIONS AND THEOLOGY — PROTESTANT

266   SA   ISSN 0024-3272
DIE LIGDRAER. 1940. fortn. R.20. Nederduitse Gereformeerde Sendingkerk - Dutch Reformed Mission Church, Private Bag X1, Belhar 7507, Cape Province, South Africa. Ed. Rev. D.P. Botha. adv.; bk.rev.; bibl.; illus.; stat.; index; circ. 16,000.

287   US   ISSN 0024-3299
LIGHT AND LIFE. 1896. m. $15 (effective Jan. 1991). Free Methodist Church of North America, Box 535002, Indianapolis, IN 46253-5002. TEL 317-244-3660. FAX 317-244-1247. Ed. Robert Haslam. adv.; bk.rev.; circ. 34,000. **Indexed:** G.Soc.Sci.& Rel.Per.Lit.
Description: Articles about Christians involved in service ministries.

284   UK
LIGHT AND LIFE. 1935. 3/yr. U F M Worldwide, 47a Fleet St., Swindon, Wiltshire SN1 1RE, England. TEL 0793-610515. Ed. A. Spredbury. circ. 7,500.
Description: Articles, biographical sketches, and profiles of the missionary ministry of the U F M Worldwide.

266   AT
LIGHT AND LIFE; news-line. 1989. bi-m. Aus.$5. Asia Pacific Christian Mission, 345 Bell St., Preston, Vic. 3072, Australia. TEL 03-480-4722. FAX 03-480-4186. Ed. R.W. Averill. circ. 8,400. (back issues avail.)
Description: Work of mission staff in partnership with nationals in the Asia-Pacific region. Informs supporters and those not involved in the work.

287   UK
LINCOLNSHIRE METHODIST HISTORY SOCIETY. JOURNAL. 1963. a. £2. Lincolnshire Methodist History Society, c/o J.S. English A.L.A., 1 Dorton Ave., Gainsborough, Lincs. DN21 1UB, England. bk.rev.; circ. 120.
Description: Covers all aspects of the history of Methodism in Lincolnshire and South Humberside.

LINK & VISITOR; a magazine for Baptist women. see *WOMEN'S INTERESTS*

268   US   ISSN 0162-4253
LIVING (NASHVILLE). q. $4.50. Southern Baptist Convention, Sunday School Board, 127 Ninth Ave., N., Nashville, TN 37234. TEL 800-458-2772.

283   US   ISSN 0024-5240
LIVING CHURCH; an independent weekly record of the news of the Church and the views of Episcopalians. 1878. w. $39.50. Living Church Foundation, Inc., 816 E. Juneau Ave., Milwaukee, WI 53202. TEL 414-276-5420. Ed. David A. Kavelage. adv.; bk.rev.; illus.; circ. 10,579.

268   US   ISSN 0162-4350
LIVING WITH PRESCHOOLERS. q. $10.75. Southern Baptist Convention, Sunday School Board, 127 Ninth Ave., N., Nashville, TN 37234. TEL 800-458-2772.

268   US   ISSN 0162-4261
LIVING WITH TEENAGERS. q. $10.75. Southern Baptist Convention, Sunday School Board, 127 Ninth Ave., N., Nashville, TN 37234. TEL 800-458-2772.

284   UK
LLANDAFF DIOCESAN DIRECTORY. a. £3. Llandaff Diocesan Board of Finance, Heol Fair, Llandaff, Cardiff CF5 2EE, Wales. TEL 0222-578899. Ed. M.J. Beasant. bibl.; index; circ. 1,000.

287   UK   ISSN 0024-5607
LOCAL PREACHERS MAGAZINE. 1850. q. membership. Methodist Local Preachers Mutual Aid Association, Head Office, Chorleywood Close, Rickmansworth, Herts WD3 4EG, England. TEL 0923-775856. Ed. D.L. Mitchell. bk.rev.; circ. 13,500.

268   LB
LOMA WEEKLY PAPER.* (Text in English, Loca) 1951. w. $1. Lutheran Church in Liberia, Loma Literacy Center, Box 1046, Wozi, Monrovia, Liberia.

LOOK!; the juniors' magazine of the Baptist Missionary Society. see *CHILDREN AND YOUTH — For*

268   US   ISSN 0162-4369
LOOK AND LISTEN. q. in w. parts. $4.50. Southern Baptist Convention, Sunday School Board, 127 Ninth Ave., N., Nashville, TN 37234. TEL 800-458-2772.

284   US
LOOKOUT (CINCINNATI). 1894. w. $18. Standard Publishing, 8121 Hamilton Ave., Cincinnati, OH 45231. TEL 513-931-4050. Ed. Simon J. Dahlman. circ. 140,000.

286   US   ISSN 0024-6743
LOUISIANA BAPTIST BUILDER. 1953. m. $5. Baptist Missionary Association of Louisiana, Box 1297, Denham Springs, LA 70727-1297. Ed. Leroy Mayfield. adv.; bk.rev.; illus.; circ. 2,500. (tabloid format)
Description: Provides information on mission work in the state.

284   IT
LA LUCE (TURIN); settimanale delle chiese valdesi e metodiste. w. L.85000. Associazione Informazione Protestante, Via S. Piov, no.15, 10125 Turin, Italy. TEL 011-655278. FAX 011-657542. Dir. Giorgio Gardiol. circ. 5,000.

284   GW   ISSN 0340-6210
BR323.5
LUTHER. 1919. 3/yr. DM.34. (Luther-Gesellschaft) Vandenhoeck und Ruprecht, Theaterstr. 13, Postfach 3753, 3400 Goettingen, Germany. TEL 0551-6959-22. FAX 0551-695917. Ed. Hans-Ludwig Slupina. adv.; bk.rev.; index; circ. 1,750. (reprint service avail. from SWZ) **Indexed:** CERDIC.
—BLDSC shelfmark: 5307.760000.

284.1   US   ISSN 0024-743X
BX8001
THE LUTHERAN; news magazine of the Evangelical Lutheran Church in America. 1860. 16/yr. $9.20. Publishing House of the Evangelical Lutheran Church in America, 426 S. 5th St., Box 1209, Minneapolis, MN 55440. TEL 800-638-3522. FAX 312-380-1465. TELEX 4900009324 LUT. Ed. Edgar R. Trexler. adv.; bk.rev.; illus.; circ. 1,150,000. (also avail. in microform from UMI) **Indexed:** CERDIC, G.Soc.Sci.& Rel.Per.Lit.
Incorporates (as of 1987): Lutheran Standard (ISSN 0024-7545)

284   US
LUTHERAN ANNUAL. 1910. a. $7.95 for paper; spiral $10.95. (Lutheran Church - Missouri Synod) Concordia Publishing House, 3558 Jefferson Ave., St. Louis, MO 63118. TEL 314-664-7000. Ed. John W. Gerber. adv.; circ. 40,000.

284   AT   ISSN 0726-4305
LUTHERAN CHURCH OF AUSTRALIA. YEARBOOK. 1967. a. Aus.$9. Lutheran Publishing House, 205 Halifax St., Adelaide, S.A. 5000, Australia. Ed. M. Oster.
Formed by the merger of: Australian Lutheran Almanac & Lutheran Almanac.

LUTHERAN CHURCHES IN CANADA. DIRECTORY. see *BUSINESS AND ECONOMICS — Trade And Industrial Directories*

280   US   ISSN 0458-497X
BR1
LUTHERAN DIGEST. 1953. q. Lutheran Digest, Inc., P.O. Box 23009, Minneapolis, MN 55423. TEL 612-435-5955. Ed. R. Schwanz. (also avail. in Braille; large print)

LUTHERAN DIGEST (LARGE PRINT EDITION). see *HANDICAPPED — Visually Impaired*

LUTHERAN EDUCATION. see *EDUCATION*

284.1   US   ISSN 0024-7456
BX8001
LUTHERAN FORUM; an independent journal. (Supplement: Una Sancta) 1967. q. $21 (includes subscr. to Forum Letter). American Lutheran Publicity Bureau, Box 327, Delhi, NY 13753. TEL 607-746-7511. Ed. Rev. Paul R. Hinlicky. adv.; bk.rev.; illus.; stat.; circ. 3,800. (also avail. in microform from UMI; back issues avail.; reprint service avail. from UMI) **Indexed:** CERDIC, Rel.& Theol.Abstr. (1989-), Rel.Ind.One.
Supersedes: American Lutheran Magazine.

284   US   ISSN 0046-4732
LUTHERAN FORUM. FORUM LETTER. 1972. m. $21 (includes subscr. to Lutheran Forum). American Lutheran Publicity Bureau, Box 327, Delhi, NY 13753. TEL 607-746-7511. Ed. Russell E. Saltzman. bk.rev.; circ. 3,800. (also avail. in microfilm from UMI; back issues avail.; reprint service avail. from UMI) **Indexed:** CERDIC.
Description: Provides readers with information and viewpoints from all sides of Lutheranism.

285   977   US   ISSN 0090-3817
BX8011.A1
LUTHERAN HISTORICAL CONFERENCE. ESSAYS AND REPORTS. 1966. biennial. $15. Lutheran Historical Conference, c/o Concordia Historical Institute, 801 DeMun Ave., St. Louis, MO 63105. TEL 314-721-5934. Ed. August R. Suelflow. circ. 350. **Indexed:** Rel.& Theol.Abstr. (1988-).
Description: Topics of concern and interest to professional Lutheran historians, librarians, and archivists.

284   US   ISSN 0460-0274
LUTHERAN HISTORICAL CONFERENCE NEWSLETTER. 1962. 3/yr. $15 to non-members. Lutheran Historical Conference, Trinity Lutheran Seminary, 2199 E. Main St., Columbus, OH 43209-2832. Ed. James L. Schaaf. bk.rev.; circ. 225. **Indexed:** Rel.Ind.One.
Description: News, announcements, and bibliographies on the activities of Lutheran church bodies, for archivists, librarians, and historians.

284   US
LUTHERAN HISTORICAL SOCIETY OF EASTERN PENNSYLVANIA. PERIODICAL. 1950. s-a. $5 membership. Lutheran Historical Society of Eastern Pennsylvania, Lutheran Theological Seminary, 7301 Germantown Ave., Philadelphia, PA 19119. Ed. Mahlon H. Hellerich. bk.rev.; circ. 550. (back issues avail.)
Formerly: Lutheran Historical Society of Eastern Pennsylvania.

285   US
LUTHERAN HOUR SERMONS. w. contribution. (Lutheran Braille Workers, Inc.) Concordia Publishing House, 3558 S. Jefferson Ave., St. Louis, MO 63118. TEL 314-647-4900. (Subscr. to: 2185 Hampton Ave., St. Louis, MO 63139) (large print edition in 18 pt.; Braille ed. avail. on request)
Description: Text of weekly sermons which have been broadcast.

284.1   US   ISSN 0360-6945
BX8001
LUTHERAN JOURNAL. 1937. q. $4. Outlook Publishing, Inc., 7317 Cahill Rd., Edina, MN 55435. TEL 612-941-6830. Ed. Armin U. Deye. adv.; bk.rev.; illus.; circ. 136,000. **Indexed:** A.I.P.P.
Former titles (1943-1947): Northwest Lutheran Journal; Lutheran Home Journal.

284   US   ISSN 0024-7464
LUTHERAN LAYMAN. 1929. 12/yr. $5. International Lutheran Laymen's League, 2185 Hampton, St. Louis, MO 63139. FAX 314-647-6923. TELEX 590083. Ed. Gerald Perschbacher. adv.; bk.rev.; illus.; circ. 90,000. (tabloid format)
Description: Contains religious news for Lutheran laity.

LUTHERAN LIBRARIES. see *LIBRARY AND INFORMATION SCIENCES*

LUTHERAN MESSENGER FOR THE BLIND. see *HANDICAPPED — Visually Impaired*

284   US   ISSN 0885-9922
BX8001
LUTHERAN PARTNERS. 1985. bi-m. $10. Augsburg Fortress, 426 S. 5th St., Box 1209, Minneapolis, MN 55440. TEL 612-330-3300. (Co-sponsor: Evangelical Lutheran Church in America (ELCA), Division for Ministry) Ed. Carl E. Linder. adv.; bk.rev.; circ. 21,500.

284.1   US   ISSN 0024-7510
LUTHERAN SENTINEL. 1917. m. $6. (Evangelical Lutheran Synod) Graphic Publishing Co., Inc., 204 N. Second Ave. W., Lake Mills, IA 50450. TEL 515-592-2000. FAX 515-592-2007. Ed. Paul G. Madson. bk.rev.; circ. 6,000.

RELIGIONS AND THEOLOGY — PROTESTANT

284.1 US ISSN 0024-7537
LUTHERAN SPOKESMAN. 1958. m. $6. Church of the Lutheran Confession (Minneapolis), 460 75th Ave., N.E., Minneapolis, MN 55432. TEL 414-425-6665. (Subscr. to: 2750 Oxford St., N., Roseville, MN 55113) Ed. Rev. Paul Fleischer. bk.rev.; circ. 2,500.
 Description: Testamentary commentary on issues relevant to the Church of the Lutheran Confession, with official notices and news pertaining to its activities.

284.1 AT ISSN 0024-7553
LUTHERAN THEOLOGICAL JOURNAL. 1966. 3/yr. Aus.$18.50. (Lutheran Church of Australia) Lutheran Publishing House, 205 Halifax St., Adelaide, S.A. 5000, Australia. Ed. Dr. J.G. Strelan. bk.rev.; circ. 630. **Indexed:** CERDIC, New Test.Abstr., Old Test.Abstr., Rel.Ind.One.

207.11 284 US
LUTHERAN THEOLOGICAL SEMINARY BULLETIN. 1921. q. free. Lutheran Theological Seminary, Gettysburg, PA 17325. TEL 717-334-6286. Ed. Richard D. Nelson. circ. 3,500. **Indexed:** Rel.& Theol.Abstr. (1989-).
 Formerly: Gettysburg Seminary Bulletin (ISSN 0362-0581)

284.1 US ISSN 0024-757X
BX8001
LUTHERAN WITNESS. 1882. m. $7.50. (Lutheran Church - Missouri Synod) Concordia Publishing House, 3358 S. Jefferson Ave., St. Louis, MO 63118. TEL 314-268-1000. Ed. David Mahsman. adv.; bk.rev.; illus.; circ. 400,000. (also avail. in Braille; audio cassette; large print) **Indexed:** G.Soc.Sci.& Rel.Per.Lit.

284 US
LUTHERAN WITNESS (LARGE PRINT EDITION). m. free. (Lutheran Church - Missouri Synod) Lutheran Library for the Blind, 1333 S. Kirkwood Rd., St. Louis, MO 63122. (also avail. in Braille; audio cassette; large print in 22 pt.)

284.1 US ISSN 0896-209X
LUTHERAN WOMAN TODAY. 1908. m. $8. Augsburg Fortress, 426 S. Fifth St., Box 1209, Minneapolis, MN 55440. TEL 800-328-4648. (Co-sponsor: Women of the Evangelical Lutheran Church in America (ELCA)) Ed. Nancy J. Stelling. bk.rev.; illus.; film rev.; index. (large print edition in 14 pt.) **Indexed:** A.I.P.P.
 Formed by the 1987 merger of: Lutheran Woman (ISSN 0024-7596) & Scope (ISSN 0036-8997)

284 266 US
LUTHERAN WOMAN'S QUARTERLY; knowing Christ and making Him known. 1942. q. $2.50. (Lutheran Church - Missouri Synod, Lutheran Women's Missionary League, 3558 S. Jefferson Ave., St. Louis, MO 63118-3910. TEL 314-664-7000. Ed. Patricia Beach. bk.rev.; circ. 200,000. (also avail. in Braille; audio cassette; back issues avail.)

284.1 GW ISSN 0024-7618
BX8001
LUTHERISCHE MONATSHEFTE. 1962. m. DM.66. Lutherisches Verlagshaus GmbH, Knochenhauerstr. 38-40, 3000 Hannover 1, Germany. TEL 0511-1241-733. adv.; bk.rev.; bibl.; charts; index; circ. 9,500. **Indexed:** CERDIC.
 —BLDSC shelfmark: 5308.125000.

284 GW ISSN 0170-3846
LUTHERISCHE THEOLOGIE UND KIRCHE. 1977. q. DM.60. Lutherische Theologischen Hochschule, Altkonigstr. 150, 6370 Oberursel, Germany. TEL 06171-24340. adv.; bk.rev.; circ. 800. (back issues avail.)
 —BLDSC shelfmark: 5308.125500.
 Description: Studies Lutheran theology.

284 GW
LUTHERJAHRBUCH. 1919. a. price varies. (Luther-Gesellschaft) Vandenhoeck und Ruprecht, Robert-Bosch-Breite 6, Postfach 3753, 3400 Goettingen, Germany. TEL 0551-6959-0. FAX 0551-695917. Ed. Helmar Junghans.

284.1 AU ISSN 0024-7626
DIE LUTHERKIRCHE; Pfarrblatt. 1948. q. free. Evangelische Gemeinde A.B. Wien-Waehring, Martinstr. 25, A-1180 Vienna, Austria. Ed. Werner Puelz. circ. 4,500.

268 SW ISSN 0345-7389
LUTHERSK BARNTIDNING. 1952. m. SEK 100. Missionssaellskapet Bibeltrogna Vaenner, P.O. Box 6160, 102 33 Stockholm, Sweden. Ed. Inga-Lisa Persson. circ. 4,000.

266 GW
M B K - MISSION. NACHRICHTEN. 1927. 6/yr. M B K - Mission e.V., Postfach 560, 4902 Bad Salzuflen 1, Germany. FAX 05222-180559. circ. 3,500. (looseleaf format; back issues avail.)
 Description: Reports on social and missionary work in Japan and Hong Kong.

288 US
M S U U NEWSLETTER: GLEANINGS. 1974. q. membership only. Ministerial Sisterhood Unitarian Universalist, c/o Universalist Unitarian Church, 740 E. Main St., Santa Paula, CA 93060. TEL 805-525-8859. Ed. Rev. Marjorie Newlin Leaming. adv.; bk.rev.; circ. 300 (controlled).
 Formerly: M S U U Newsletter (ISSN 0360-7046)
 Description: For Unitarian Universalist women ministers.

284 GW
MADJU. 1960. s-a. free. Evangelisches Missionswerk in Suedwestdeutschland e.V., Vogelsangstr. 62, 7000 Stuttgart 1, Germany. TEL 0711-63678-0. FAX 0711-63678-66. TELEX 723059-EMS-D. Ed. Klaus Zoeller. circ. 72,000. (looseleaf format; back issues avail.)

287 US ISSN 0745-0273
MAINE UNITED METHODIST. 1961. bi-m. free. United Methodist Church, Maine Annual Conference, E. Monmouth Rd., Box 277, Winthrop, ME 04364. TEL 207-377-2912. FAX 207-377-8412. Ed. Beverly J. Abbott. bk.rev.; circ. 5,000. (back issues avail.)
 Description: World, national, and local church news used as a tool for interpretation-communication of church.

200 US ISSN 0162-427X
MATURE LIVING. 1977. m. $14.25. Southern Baptist Convention, Sunday School Board, 127 Ninth Ave., N., Nashville, TN 37234. TEL 800-458-2772.

MATURE YEARS. see GERONTOLOGY AND GERIATRICS

289.709 CN ISSN 0380-0121
MENNONITE REPORTER. 1971. fortn. Can.$27. Mennonite Publishing Service, 3-312 Marsland Drive, Waterloo, Ont. N2J 3Z1, Canada. TEL 519-884-3810. FAX 519-884-3331. Ed. Ron Rempel. adv.; bk.rev.; index; circ. 12,000. (also avail. in microfilm from MML) **Indexed:** CMI.
 Continues: Canadian Mennonite Reporter (ISSN 0380-013X)
 Description: Independent inter-Mennonite news and comment.

289.709 GW ISSN 0342-1171
BX8101
MENNONITISCHE GESCHICHTSBLAETTER. 1936. a. DM.25($12.50) Mennonitischer Geschichtsverein, Weierhof, 6719 Bolanden, Germany. (Subscr. to: Christel Schultz, Blumenweg 28,6057 Dietzenbach) Eds. Heinold Fast, Hans-Juergen Goertz. bk.rev.; circ. 700.
 Description: Studies the history of the Mennonite Church.

287 MX ISSN 0026-0185
MESIAS; boletin semanal de la iglesia Metodista. vol.8, 1971. w. Iglesia Metodista el Mesias, Balderas 47, Mexico D. F., Mexico.

284.2 FR ISSN 0026-0274
MESSAGER EVANGELIQUE. (Text in French, German) 1945. w. 240 F. Eglise de la Confession d'Ausburg, La quai Saint Thomas, F-67081 Strasbourg, France. (Co-sponsor: Eglise Reforme d'Alsace et de Lorraine) Ed. Fritz Westphal. adv.; bk.rev.; illus.; circ. 20,000.

286 IT ISSN 0392-6346
MESSAGGERO AVVENTISTA. 1926. m. L.17500. (Unione Italiana delle Chiese Cristiane Avventiste) Edizioni A.D.V. l'Araldo della Verita, Via Chiantigiana 30, Falciani, 50023 Impruneta, Florence, Italy. TEL 055-2020291. Ed. Ivo Fasiori. circ. 1,600.

286 UK ISSN 0309-3654
MESSENGER (GRANTHAM). 1895. fortn. £11. Stanborough Press Ltd., Alma Park, Grantham, Lincs NG31 9SL, England. TEL 0476-591700. FAX 0476-77144. Ed. D.N. Marshall. adv.; bk.rev.; circ. 10,000.
 Formerly: British Advent Messenger (ISSN 0045-2874)

286 US
MESSENGER (OMAHA). 1911. 10/yr. $1. American Baptist Churches of Nebraska, 6404 Maple St., Omaha, NE 68104. TEL 402-556-4730. Ed. Kay Grabia. bk.rev.; illus.; circ. 5,455.
 Formerly: Nebraska Baptist Messenger.

283 UK
MESSIANIC WITNESS. 1876. q. free. Messianic Testimony, 93 Axe St., Barking, Essex IG11 7L2, England. Ed. Miss D. Steiner. bk.rev.; circ. 7,000.

289 UK
METHODIST CONFERENCE. MINUTES AND YEARBOOK. 1932. a. Methodist Publishing House, 20 Ivatt Way, Peterborough PE3 7PG, England. TEL 0733-332202. FAX 0733-331201. circ. 7,000.

691 UK
METHODIST DIARIES. 1850. a. Methodist Publishing House, 20 Ivatt Way, Peterborough PE3 7PG, England. FAX 0733-331201. circ. 5,000.

287 209 US ISSN 0026-1238
BX8235
METHODIST HISTORY. 1962. q. $12. United Methodist Church, Commission on Archives and History, Box 127, Madison, NJ 07940. TEL 201-822-2787. FAX 201-408-3909. Ed. Charles Yrigoyen, Jr. adv.; bk.rev.; charts; index; circ. 1,300. (also avail. in microfilm from UMI) **Indexed:** Amer.Hist.& Life, CERDIC, Hist.Abstr., Meth Per.Ind., Rel.& Theol.Abstr. (1970-), Rel.Ind.One, Rel.Per.
 —BLDSC shelfmark: 5746.350000.

287 UK ISSN 0026-1262
METHODIST RECORDER. 1861. w. £85 (effective Feb. 1992). Methodist Newspaper Co., Ltd., 122 Golden Lane, London E.C.1., England. FAX 071-608-3490. Ed. Michael Taylor. adv.; bk.rev.; play rev.; record rev.; charts; illus.; circ. 28,599. (tabloid format; also avail. in microfilm from WMP)

287 377.8 US
METHODIST THEOLOGICAL SCHOOL IN OHIO. STORY. s-a. free. Methodist Theological School in Ohio, Box 1204, Columbus Pike, Delaware, OH 43015-0931. TEL 614-363-1146. FAX 614-362-3235. Ed. Cassandra S. Clancy. (back issues avail.)
 Description: Contains news for students, staff, faculty, alumni, and friends of the school.

287 SW ISSN 0543-6206
METODISTKYRKANS I SVERIGE AARSBOK. 1896. a. SEK 100. (Metodistkyrkan i Sverige - United Methodist Church in Sweden) Foerlaget Sanctus, Box 5020, 102 41 Stockholm, Sweden. FAX 08-6639287. Ed. Rev. Bo Lindberg. stat.; circ. 400.

200 US ISSN 0026-2072
MICHIGAN CHRISTIAN ADVOCATE. 1873. 3/yr. (June, July, Aug.). $9. (United Methodist Church, West Michigan and Detroit Annual Conferences) Michigan Christian Advocate Publishing Co., 316 Springbrook Ave., Adrian, MI 49221. TEL 517-265-2075. Ed. Edward L. Duncan. adv.; bk.rev.; illus.; circ. 21,000.

264 US
MICHIGAN LUTHERAN. 1922. m. $6. Lutheran Church - Missouri Synod, Michigan District, 3773 Geddes Road, Ann Arbor, MI 48105. TEL 313-665-3791. FAX 313-665-0255. Ed. Walt Rummel. adv.; bk.rev.; film rev.; circ. 76,000 (controlled).
 Description: Presents the work of the Michigan District and its congregations to the membership of the church in the area, for information, motivation, and inspiration.

RELIGIONS AND THEOLOGY — PROTESTANT

285 US ISSN 0026-5314
BX6101
MINISTRY; international journal for clergy. 1928. m. $21. (General Conference of Seventh-Day Adventists) Review and Herald Publishing Association, 55 W. Oak Ridge Dr., Hagerstown, MD 21740. TEL 301-791-7000. Ed. David Newman. adv.; bk.rev.; charts; illus.; index; circ. 70,000. (reprint service avail. from UMI) **Indexed:** CCR, CERDIC.
 Description: Publishes theological and practical articles for ministers of all denominations.

266 UK
MISSION. 1922. 3/yr. Bible Churchmens Missionary Society (B.C.M.S.), 251 Lewisham Way, London SE4 1XF, England. Ed. Sue Knight. bk.rev.; circ. 6,000. (back issues avail.)

266 284 US
BV2050
MISSION HANDBOOK: U S A - CANADA PROTESTANT MINISTRIES OVERSEAS. 1951. irreg. (every 3-5 yrs.). $23.95. (Missions Advanced Research and Communication Center) M A R C (Subsidiary of: World Vision International), 919 W. Huntington Dr., Monrovia, CA 91016. TEL 818-303-8811. Eds. W. Dayton Roberts, John A. Siewert. index; circ. 1,500.
 Former titles: Mission Handbook: North American Protestant Ministries Overseas (ISSN 0093-8130); North American Protestant Ministries Overseas (ISSN 0078-1339)
 Description: Detailed data on Canadian and U S Christian missionary agencies, cross-indexed by ministry, state, province, countries of services, and church tradition. Includes interpretive essays.

200 US
MISSION STATEMENT; a witness to the good news of Jesus Christ. 1948. m. (9/yr.). $4. Episcopal Diocese of Northwestern Pennsylvania, 145 W. Sixth St., Erie, PA 16501. TEL 814-456-4203. Ed. Frances I. Rhodes. circ. 3,800.
 Former titles (until 1990): Forward; Forward in Erie (ISSN 0015-8623)

266 US ISSN 1051-3345
MISSION TODAY; Baptist young men 18 and up. vol.45, 1974. m. $10.56. Southern Baptist Convention, Brotherhood Commission, 1548 Poplar Ave., Memphis, TN 38104. Ed. Jim Burton. circ. 32,000. (tabloid format) **Indexed:** South.Bap.Per.Ind.
 Former titles: World Mission Journal (Baptist Men's Edition); Baptist Men's Journal.
 Description: Provides missions education for men in Southern Baptist churches.

266 UK ISSN 0264-1372
MISSIONARY HERALD. m. £6.30. Baptist Missionary Society, P.O. Box 49, Baptist House, 129 Broadway, Didcot, Oxon OX11 8XA. TEL 0235-512044. FAX 0235-511265. Ed. Rev. D.E. Pountain. circ. 19,500. (back issues avail.)

266 US
MISSIONARY REPORTER. 1946. q. membership. (Seventh Day Baptist Missionary Society) American Sabbath Tract & Communication Council, Seventh Day Baptist General Conference, Box 1678, Janesville, WI 53547. TEL 608-752-5055. FAX 608-752-7711. (Subscr. to: 119 Main St., Westerly, RI 02891) circ. 250. (looseleaf format)
 Description: Covers the minutes of the board meetings. Includes reports of workers on various missionary projects.

287 US ISSN 1043-0725
MISSIONARY TIDINGS. 1897. $10 (effective Sep. 1990). Free Methodist World Missions, 770 N. High School Rd., Indianapolis, IN 46214. TEL 317-244-3660. FAX 317-244-1247. (Subscr. to: Box 535002, Indianapolis, IN 46253-5002) Ed. Daniel V. Runyon. circ. 9,100. (also avail. in talking book)
 Description: Provides news and features about cross-cultural communication and world evangelization in the Free Methodist denomination.

266 US
MISSIONS; update. 1975. m. free. (Seventh Day Baptist Missionary Society) American Sabbath Tract & Communication Council, Seventh Day Baptist General Conference, Box 1678, Janesville, WI 53547. TEL 608-752-5055. FAX 608-752-7711. (Subscr. to: Seventh Day Baptist Missionary Society, 119 Main St., Westerly, RI 02891. TEL 401-596-4326) Ed. Leon R. Lawton. circ. 200. (looseleaf format)
 Description: National and international coverage of the society's activities.

266 UK
MISSIONS TO SEAMEN ANNUAL REPORT. 1856. a. free. Missions to Seamen, St. Michael Paternoster Royal, College Hill, London EC4R 2RL, England. TEL 071-248-5202. FAX 071-248-4761. Ed. Gillian Ennis. index.
 Formerly: Missions to Seamen Handbook (ISSN 0076-9401)

266 US ISSN 0279-5345
BV2520.A1
MISSIONS U S A. 1930. 8/yr. $6.50. Southern Baptist Convention, Home Mission Board, 1350 Spring St., N.W., Atlanta, GA 30309. TEL 404-873-4041. Ed. Walker L. Knight. adv.; bk.rev.; illus.; index; circ. 95,000. **Indexed:** South.Bap.Per.Ind.
 Formerly: Home Missions (ISSN 0018-408X)

284 GW
MISSIONSBLATT; Lutherische Kirchenmission (Bleckmarer Mission). 1899. m. DM.35. Lutherische Kirchenmission, Bleckmar 33, 3103 Bergen 1, Germany. TEL 05051-2098. FAX 05051-2845. Ed. Pastor Johannes Junker. bk.rev.; circ. 4,000. (back issues avail.)
 Description: Discusses mission and evangelistic work worldwide.

266 GW
MISSIONSGLOCKE DER LIEBENZELLER MISSION. 1909. m. DM.5. Liebenzell Mission, Postfach 1240, 7263 Bad Liebenzell, Germany. TEL 07052-17109. Ed. Rev. Ernst Vatter D.D. illus.; circ. 10,000. (back issues avail.)

287 US
MISSISSIPPI UNITED METHODIST ADVOCATE. 1947. fortn. $8. United Methodist Church, Mississippi Conference, Box 1093, Jackson, MS 39215. TEL 601-354-0515. Ed. Rev. J.R. Woodrick. adv.; bk.rev.; circ. 15,000. (tabloid format)
 Formerly: Mississippi Methodist Advocate (ISSN 0026-6329)

284 GW
MITTEILUNGEN DER NORDDEUTSCHEN MISSION. BREMEN. 1949. bi-m. free. Norddeutsche Mission, Vahrerstr. 243, 2800 Bremen 44, Germany. Eds. Rev. Dieter Lenz, Antje Pult.

284.2 SA ISSN 0378-410X
MOLAETSA-MOLAETSA. (Text in South Suthu, Swana) 1957. 8/yr. R.3. Reformed Churches in South Africa - Gereformeerde Kerke in Suid-Afrika, P.O. Box 59, Hammanskraal 0400, South Africa. Ed. H.A. Louw. circ. 2,450.
 Formerly: Rugama.

284 GW
MONATSHEFTE FUER EVANGELISCHE KIRCHENGESCHICHTE DES RHEINLANDES. 1952. a. DM.40. (Rheinland Verlag GmbH) Dr. Rudolf Habelt GmbH, Am Buchenhang 1, 5300 Bonn 1, Germany. Ed.Bd.

285 US ISSN 0360-6171
MONDAY MORNING. 1936. s-m. (21/yr.). $10. Presbyterian Church (U.S.A.), Church Vocations Unit, 100 Witherspoon St., Rm M014, Louisville, KY 40202-1396. TEL 212-870-3393. FAX 502-569-5018. Ed. Theodore Gill, Jr. adv.; circ. 22,000.
 Description: Forum for ministers to discuss relevant issues.

284 UK
MORAVIAN MESSAGE. m. £6.72. Moravian Union Inc., Book Room, 5 Muswell Hill, London N10 3TJ, England. TEL 01-883-3409. Ed. Rev. P. Gubi. bk.rev.; illus.; circ. 900.

268 US ISSN 0162-4288
MORE. m. in w. parts. $7.75. Southern Baptist Convention, Sunday School Board, 127 Ninth Ave., N., Nashville, TN 37234. TEL 800-458-2772.
 Description: Aimed at younger children, beginning readers.

MORE LIGHT UPDATE. see *HOMOSEXUALITY*

200 SA ISSN 0027-1454
MOSUPA - TSELA. (Text in Setswana) 1900. m. R.1($1) (Evangelical Lutheran Church in South Africa, Western Diocese) Lutheran Book Depot, P.O. Box 536, 0300 Rustenburg, Transvaal, South Africa. Ed. Rev. M. Dillhale. bk.rev.; illus.; circ. 12,000.

MULOT'SCHEN FAMILIENVERBAND. ZEITSCHRIFT; genealogische Mitteilungen fuer Hugenotten- und Waldensernachkommen. see *GENEALOGY AND HERALDRY*

284.2 SA ISSN 0378-4126
MURUMIWA. (Editions in Tsonga and Venda) 1950. bi-m. R.1.50. Reformed Churches in South Africa, Synod Soutspansberg - Gereformeerde Kerke in Suid-Afrika, P.O. Box 496, Sibasa, Venda, South Africa. Ed. G.D. Affourtit.

THE MUSIC LEADER. see *MUSIC*

268 US ISSN 0162-4377
ML1
MUSIC MAKERS (NASHVILLE). q. $4.50. Southern Baptist Convention, Sunday School Board, 127 Ninth Ave., N., Nashville, TN 37234. TEL 800-458-2772. **Indexed:** Perf.Arts Biog.Master Ind.

MUSIC TIME. see *MUSIC*

283 267.15 UK ISSN 0027-464X
MUSICAL SALVATIONIST. 1886. q. £5. Salvation Army, International Headquarters, 101 Queen Victoria St., London EC4P 4EP, England. TEL 071-387-3768. FAX 071-236-3491. Ed. Robert Redhead. circ. 23,000.

242 US ISSN 0027-5387
MY DEVOTIONS. 1958. m. $5.95. Concordia Publishing House, 3558 S. Jefferson Ave., St. Louis, MO 63118. TEL 314-664-7000. Ed. Don Hoeferkamp. illus.; circ. 70,000. (also avail. in microfilm; Braille; large print)
 Description: Selected daily devotions and Bible readings for Christian children, ages 8-13.

MY DEVOTIONS (LARGE PRINT EDITION). see *HANDICAPPED — Visually Impaired*

284 GW
N M - NORDELBISCHE MISSION; Breklumer Sonntagsblat fuers Haus. 1974. m. DM.10. Nordelbisches Zentrum fuer Weltmission und Kirchlichen Weltdienst, Agathe-Lasch Weg 16, 2000 Hamburg 52, Germany. TEL 040-883000-0. FAX 030-883000-11. Ed. Jens Waubke. bk.rev.; circ. 11,000.
 Description: Lutheran publication covering missionary work and development aid in all parts of the world, especially developing countries in the southern hemisphere. Includes letters from readers.

284 GW
NACHRICHTEN AUS DER BASLER MISSION. bi-m. free. Basler Mission Deutscher Zweig, Vogelsangstr. 62, 7000 Stuttgart 1, Germany. TEL 0711-63678-43. FAX 0711-63678-66. TELEX 723059-EMS-D. (Co-sponsor: Evangelische Missionswerk in Suedwestdeutschland) circ. 100,000. (back issues avail.)
 Description: Missionary and ecumenical affairs from Asia, Africa, Latin America; information for mission friends.

284 GW
NATHANAEL EVANGELISCHES GEMEINDEBLATT. 1950. bi-m. DM.9. Verlag Evangelisches Gemeindeblatt Berlin, Grazer Platz 4, 1000 Berlin 41, Germany. Ed. Joachim Ruff. adv.; bk.rev.; bibl.; illus.; circ. 500.
 Formerly (until 1990): Evangelisches Gemeindeblatt Berlin (ISSN 0014-3561)

266 UK ISSN 0077-3557
NATIONAL BIBLE SOCIETY OF SCOTLAND. ANNUAL REPORT. (Supplement to: Word at Work) 1860. a. free. National Bible Society of Scotland, 7 Hampton Terrace, Edinburgh EH12 5XU, Scotland. FAX 031-337-0641. circ. 1,000.

RELIGIONS AND THEOLOGY — PROTESTANT

260 US
NATIONAL COUNCIL OF THE CHURCHES OF CHRIST IN THE U.S.A. BIENNIAL REPORT. 1952. biennial. free. (National Council of the Churches of Christ in the U.S.A.) National Council of Churches, Department of Communication, 475 Riverside Dr., Rm. 850, New York, NY 10115. TEL 212-870-2227. FAX 212-870-2030. Ed. Sarah Vilankulu. circ. 2,000.
Formerly: National Council of the Churches of Christ in the U.S.A. Triennial Report (ISSN 0077-4111)
Description: Report of council activities.

284.2 SA ISSN 0024-8665
NEDERDUITSE GEREFORMEERDE KERK VAN NATAL GEMEENTE VRYHEID. MAANDBRIEF. 1965. m. free. Nederduitse Gereformeerde Kerk van Natal Gemeentevryheid, Smalstraat 82, Vryheid, Natal, South Africa. Ed. E. Oberholster. adv.; circ. 600 (controlled). (looseleaf format)

284.2 230 SA ISSN 0028-2006
BR9.A34
NEDERDUITSE GEREFORMEERDE TEOLOGIESE TYDSKRIF. 1959. q. R.67. (Nederduitse Gereformeerde Kerk in Suid-Afrika, Faculties of Theology - Dutch Reformed Church in South Africa) Nederduitse Gereformeerde Kerk Uitgewers, P.O. Box 4539, Cape Town, South Africa. Ed. J.M. Venter. bk.rev.; bibl.; index; circ. 1,800. **Indexed:** CERDIC, Old Test.Abstr.
—BLDSC shelfmark: 6069.150000.

284.2 NE ISSN 0031-5567
NEDERLANDSE HERVORMDE KERK. PERSBUREAU. WEEKBULLETIN. 1945. w. fl.150. Nederlandse Hervormde Kerk, Persbureau - Netherlands Reformed Church, Overgoo 11, Postbus 405, 2260 AK Leidschendam, Netherlands. TEL 020-131203. FAX 020-131202. Ed. J.A. Bijsterveld. bk.rev.; abstr.; circ. 1,000.

286 DK
NEMLI'. 10/yr. DKK 99. Danmarks Folkekirkelige Soendagsskoler og Boernegudstjenester, Korskaervej 25, 7000 Fredericia, Denmark. TEL 75-92-61-00. Ed. Inger Noergaard. circ. 1,481.

285 US ISSN 0199-3518
NEW HORIZONS (HORSHAM). 1935. 11/yr. Orthodox Presbyterian Church, Committee on Christian Education, 303 Horsham Rd., Ste. G, Horsham, PA 19044. Ed. Thomas E. Tyson. adv.; bk.rev.; illus. **Indexed:** CERDIC.
Formerly (until 1980): Presbyterian Guardian (ISSN 0032-7522)

NEW HORIZONS (NEW YORK). see EDUCATION — Higher Education

266 AT ISSN 1033-7903
NEW LIFE; Australia's weekly Christian newspaper. 1938. w. Aus.$30($33.50) New Life Australia Ltd., P.O. Box 267, Blackburn, Vic. 3130, Australia. TEL 03-877-4833. FAX 03-894-2240. Ed. Rev. Bob Thomas. adv.; bk.rev.; circ. 7,000. (tabloid format; back issues avail.)
Description: World and Australia news of Evangelical Christian activity.

287 AT
NEW TIMES. 1971. m. Aus.$35. (Uniting Church in Australia) New Times Incorporated, Epworth Building, 33 Pirie St., Adelaide, S.A. 5000, Australia. TEL 08-212-4066. FAX 08-231-6013. Ed. Nick Kerr. adv.; bk.rev.; illus.; circ. 5,200. **Indexed:** CERDIC.
Former titles: Central Times (ISSN 0038-2949); South Australian Methodist.

NEW WORLD OUTLOOK; missions and ecumenical relationships. see RELIGIONS AND THEOLOGY

286 NZ ISSN 0027-7177
NEW ZEALAND BAPTIST. 1881. m. NZ.$15 (foreign NZ$25). Baptist Union of New Zealand, P.O. Box 31156, Milford, Auckland 9, New Zealand. Ed. Rev. G.F. Duncan. adv.; bk.rev.; circ. 11,900. (tabloid format)

283 CN
NEWFOUNDLAND CHURCHMAN. 1888. m. Can.$5($7.50) Anglican Church of Newfoundland, 19 Kingsbridge Rd., St. John's, Nfld. A1C 3K4, Canada. TEL 709-576-6697. Ed. Hollis Hiscock. adv.; bk.rev.; circ. 33,000.

285 US ISSN 0362-1510
NEWS FROM THE CONGREGATIONAL CHRISTIAN HISTORICAL SOCIETY. 1969. s-a. membership. Congregational Christian Historical Society, Inc., 14 Beacon St., Boston, MA 02108. TEL 617-523-0470. Ed. Harold F. Worthley. bk.rev.; circ. 1,100.
Description: News and announcements pertaining to the members and activities of this Boston-based church historical society.

284 UK
NEWS PLUS CHURCH MAGAZINE OUTSET. 1980. Appleford Publishing Group, Appleford House, Appleford, Abingdon, Oxford OX14 4PB, England. Ed. G. Duffield. adv.; bk.rev.; illus.; circ. 22,500. (back issues avail.)
Formerly: News Today Church Magazine Outset.

283 UK
NEWSCAN. 1965. m. 30p. Scottish Episcopal Church, 21 Grosvenor Crescent, Edinburgh EH12 5EE, Scotland. adv.; bk.rev.; circ. 6,500. (tabloid format) *Former titles:* Outlook (ISSN 0306-2295); Scan (ISSN 0036-5475)

287 US
NEWSCOPE; the national weekly for United Methodist leaders. 1973. w. $24.95. United Methodist Publishing House, 201 Eighth Ave. S., Box 801, Nashville, TN 37202. TEL 615-749-6417. Ed. Tom Tozer. circ. 9,800.
Description: Summary of United Methodist news from the US and the world.

284 AT
NEWSFLASHES. q. Pocket Testament League of Australia (P T L), P.O. Box 253, Kingsgrove, N.S.W. 2208, Australia. TEL 02-502-2982.

284 GW
NIEDERSAECHSICHE EVANGELISCHE ZEITUNG. 1946. w. DM.51.60. Lutherhaus-Verlag GmbH, Knochenhauerstr. 38-40, D-3000 Hannover 1, Germany. Ed.Bd. adv.; bk.rev.; circ. 39,000.

284 GW ISSN 0938-3697
NORDELBISCHE STIMMEN; Monatszeitschrift fuer haupt- und ehrenamtliche Mitarbeiter in Hamburg und Schleswig-Holstein. 1977. m. DM.36($30) Evangelischer Presseverband Nord, Postfach 2060, 2300 Kiel 1, Germany. TEL 0431-9796-0. FAX 0431-9796-234. Ed. Peter Moeller. adv.; bk.rev.; index; circ. 3,000. (back issues avail.)

285 US
NOR'EASTER (SYRACUSE). 1985. bi-m. $10. Presbyterian Church (U.S.A.), Synod of the Northeast, 3049 E. Genesee St., Syracuse, NY 13224. TEL 315-446-5990. FAX 315-446-3708. Ed. Jane T. Mead. adv.; bk.rev.; circ. 125,000. (tabloid format; back issues avail.)
Description: Covers Presbyterians in the Northeast US.

200 US ISSN 0029-2435
NORTH CAROLINA CHRISTIAN ADVOCATE. 1855. w. $10. (United Methodist Church, North Carolina Conference and Western North Carolina Conference) Methodist Board of Publication, Inc., Box 508, Greensboro, NC 27402-0508. TEL 919-272-1196. Ed. Rev. C.A. Simonton, Jr. adv.; bk.rev.; circ. 16,637. (also avail. in microfiche)

280 US
NORTHEAST (PORTLAND). bi-m. Episcopal Diocese of Maine, 143 State St., Portland, ME 04101. TEL 207-772-1953. Ed. Nellie Blagden. circ. 10,000. (tabloid format; back issues avail.)
Description: Covers news and issues of the church.

284 US ISSN 0029-3512
NORTHWESTERN LUTHERAN. 1914. s-m. $8.50. (Wisconsin Evangelical Lutheran Synod) Northwestern Publishing House, 2929 N. Mayfair Rd., Milwaukee, WI 53222-4398. FAX 414-771-3708. Ed. Rev. James P. Schaefer. bk.rev.; index; circ. 63,000. **Indexed:** CERDIC.

284 AG ISSN 0029-425X
NOTICIERO DE LA FE. 1935. m. $1.50. Revista Luterana, Simbron 4667, Buenos Aires, Argentina. Ed. Ernesto Weigandt. adv.; bk.rev.; illus.; circ. 3,100.

287 UK
NOW (LONDON, 1970). 1970. 10/yr. £2.50. Methodist Church Overseas Division, 25 Marylebone Rd., London NW1 5JR, England. Ed. J. Pickard. bk.rev.; circ. 62,000. (also avail. in microform from UMI; reprint service avail. from UMI)
Formerly: Kingdom Overseas.
Description: Illustrated news journal of the world church of Methodists in the United Kingdom.

286 US
NUESTRA TAREA. (Text in Spanish) 1955. m. $11. Woman's Missionary Union, Highway 280 E., 100 Missionary Ridge, Birmingham, AL 35242-5235. TEL 205-991-4933. FAX 205-991-4990. (Subscr. to: Box 830010, Birmingham, AL 35283-0010) Eds. Eleanor Clay, Elina Cabarcas. circ. 4,500.
Description: Publication of interest to Hispanic members and leaders of Southern Baptist women's organizations.

200 SA ISSN 0029-6708
NUWE PROTESTANT.* (Text in Afrikaans) 1947. m. R.3. Nuwe Protestantse Kerk in Afrika, Box 18348, Hercules 0030, Pretoria, Transvaal, South Africa. Ed. Rev. L.P. van Sittert. bk.rev.; abstr.; illus.; circ. 1,200. **Indexed:** CERDIC.

284 028.5 370.196 US ISSN 0274-9459
O M S OUTREACH; official publication of O M S International. 1901. bi-m. membership. O M S International, Box A, Greenwood, IN 46142. TEL 317-881-6751. FAX 317-888-5275. Ed. Eleanor L. Burr. circ. 60,000. (back issues avail.)
Description: Provides information on mission work in 14 countries.

OKAY; Schuelerkalender und taegliche Bibellese. see CHILDREN AND YOUTH — For

286 976 US ISSN 0889-745X
OKLAHOMA BAPTIST CHRONICLE.* 1958. s-a. $2. (Baptist General Convention of Oklahoma, Historical Commission) Messenger Press (Oklahoma City), 3800 N. May Ave., Oklahoma City, OK 73103. TEL 405-236-4341. Ed. J.M. Gaskin. bk.rev.; circ. 400.

283 AT ISSN 0156-6296
ON BEING. 1974. 11/yr. Aus.$30. Richard Horne, 2 Denham St., Hawthorn, Vic. 3122, Australia. TEL 03-8194755. FAX 03-8183515. Ed. Daniel Batt. adv.; bk.rev.; film rev.; index; circ. 8,000. (back issues avail.)
Description: Aims to serve the Christian Church addressing social and spiritual issues of current concern.

284 US
ON THE EDGE (NEW YORK). 1978. q. free. Lutheran Community Services, Inc., 27 Park Pl., New York, NY 10007-2502. FAX 212-406-9130. Ed. Lloyd A. Berg. adv.; bk.rev.; circ. 16,000. **Indexed:** Bibl.& Ind.Geol.
Supersedes: Focus (Brooklyn); Which was formerly: Our70's.
Description: News and notes on Christian social mission from Lutheran Community Services.

268 US ISSN 0162-4385
ON THE WING. q. $4.25. Southern Baptist Convention, Sunday School Board, 127 Ninth Ave., N., Nashville, TN 37234. TEL 800-458-2772.

284.2 NE ISSN 0030-3356
OPBOUW; weekblad tot opbouw van het Gereformeerde leven. 1957. w. fl.40. Reformeerde Persvereniging Opbouwterdam, Anne Franklaan 14, 3417 GE Montfoort, Netherlands. Ed.Bd. adv.; bk.rev.; 2,800.

200 NE ISSN 0030-3402
OPEN DEUR. 1936. m. fl.17.65. Boekencentrum B.V., Box 84176, The Hague, Netherlands. (Co-sponsors: Dutch Reformed Church; Lutheran Church; Roman Catholic Church; Geref. Foundation) Ed. Eimert Pruim. bk.rev.; illus.; circ. controlled.

284 301.4157 US ISSN 0888-8833
OPEN HANDS; reconciling ministries with lesbian and gay men. 1985. q. $16. Reconciling Congregation Program Inc., 3801 N. Keeler, Chicago, IL 60641. Ed. Mark Bowman. adv.; bk.rev.; bibl.; circ. 1,500. (back issues avail.)
Formerly (until 1986): Manna for the Journey.

RELIGIONS AND THEOLOGY — PROTESTANT

268 US ISSN 0162-4296
BV4800
OPEN WINDOWS. q. $5.75. Southern Baptist Convention, Sunday School Board, 127 Ninth Ave. N., Nashville, TN 37234. TEL 800-458-2772.

268 US ISSN 0162-430X
OPUS ONE. q. $7.25. Southern Baptist Convention, Sunday School Board, 127 Ninth Ave., N., Nashville, TN 37234. TEL 800-458-2772.

268 US ISSN 0147-1597
ML1
OPUS TWO. q. $7.25. Southern Baptist Convention, Sunday School Board, 127 Ninth Ave., N., Nashville, TN 37234. TEL 800-458-2772.

283 US
OREGON EPISCOPAL CHURCH NEWS. 1861. 9/yr. $5. Episcopal Diocese of Oregon, Box 467, Lake Oswego, OR 97034. TEL 503-636-5613. Ed. Annette L. Ross-Davidson. adv.; bk.rev.; illus.; stat.; circ. 12,500. (tabloid format)
  Former titles: Oregon Episcopal Churchman; Oregon Churchman (ISSN 0030-4646)

285 US ISSN 0030-7238
OUTLOOK (WAKE FOREST). 1951. q. free. Southern Baptist Convention, Southeastern Baptist Theological Seminary, Inc., Wake Forest, NC 27587. TEL 919-556-3101. FAX 919-556-3101. Ed. Paul T. Brock. bk.rev.; index; circ. 10,000 (controlled).

283 UK
OXFORD DIOCESAN YEAR BOOK. 1857. a. £4. Oxford Diocesan Publishing Ltd., Diocesan Church House, North Hinksey, Oxford OX2 0NB, England. TEL 0865-244566. FAX 0865-790470. Ed. Rev. Peter Green. adv.; circ. 2,100.

285 US
P C A MESSENGER. 1977. 11/yr. $14.95. Presbyterian Church in America, Committee for Christian Education and Publications, 1852 Century Place, Ste. 100, Atlanta, GA 30345. TEL 404-320-3388. Ed. Robert G. Sweet. adv.; circ. 10,629.

200 US ISSN 0360-1897
PACIFIC THEOLOGICAL REVIEW. 1967. a. free to qualified personnel. San Francisco Theological Seminary, 2 Kensington Rd., San Anselmo, CA 94960. TEL 415-258-6579. FAX 415-454-2493. Ed. David Ng. adv.; bk.rev.; circ. 6,400. Indexed: CERDIC.
  Formerly: Action - Reaction (ISSN 0001-7485)
  Description: Discusses issues in theology and ministry from a reformed perspective.

284 US ISSN 0190-4639
PARACLETE. 1967. q. $5.50. (General Council of the Assemblies of God) Gospel Publishing House, 1445 Boonville Ave., Springfield, MO 65802-1894. TEL 417-862-2781. FAX 417-862-8558. Ed. David R. Bundrick. bk.rev.; index. cum.index every 2 yrs.; circ. 4,750. (also avail. in microform from UMI) Indexed: CERDIC, Rel.& Theol.Abstr. (1989-), Rel.Ind.One.
  Description: Covers the person and work of the Holy Spirit including Bible exposition, theology and history.

PARISH COMMUNICATION. see RELIGIONS AND THEOLOGY — Roman Catholic

284 US ISSN 0738-7962
PARISH TEACHER. 1977. m. (except Jul. & Aug.). $6.75. Augsburg Fortress, 426 S. 5th St., Box 1209, Minneapolis, MN 55440. TEL 612-330-3300. Ed. Rebecca Grothe. circ. 52,000.

282 283 SA ISSN 0031-2088
PARISHIONER. 1902. 10/yr. contribution. Cathedral of St. Mary the Virgin, P.O. Box 2029, Johannesburg 2000, South Africa. TEL 011-333-2537. Ed. Lynda Wyngaard. adv.; bk.rev.; circ. 1,500.

268 UK ISSN 0079-0117
PARTNERS IN LEARNING; worship and learning resources for all ages. 1968. a. £8.50. Methodist Church, Division of Education and Youth, 2 Chester House, Pages Lane, London N10 1PR, England. TEL 081-444-9845. FAX 081-365-2471. (And: National Christian Education Council, Robert Denholm House, Nutfield, Redhill RH1 4HW Surrey, England) Ed. Kathryn Schofield. circ. 20,000.

284 UK
PARTNERSHIP CHRISTIAN BRETHREN REVIEW. 1963. irreg. £15($30) (Christian Brethren Research Fellowship) Paternoster Press Ltd., 3 Mount Radford Crescent, Exeter EX2 4JW, England. TEL 0392-50631. FAX 0392-413317. (U.S. subscr. addr.: Box 11127, Birmingham, Alabama 35201) adv.; bk.rev.; circ. 800. (back issues avail.) Indexed: Rel.& Theol.Abstr. (1980-).
  Formerly: Christian Brethren Review (ISSN 0263-466X)
  Description: Articles on historical, ecclesiastical and theological subjects.

284 282 US
PATHWAYS (GARDEN GROVE).* 4/yr. New Order of Glastonbury, c/o Charlotte Schick, 2411 Llewellyn Dr., Las Vegas, NV 89102.

285 US
PEACE OFFICE NEWSLETTER. bi-m. suggested donation $5. Mennonite Central Committee, 21 S. 12th St., Box 500, Akron, PA 17501-0500. TEL 717-859-1151. FAX 717-859-2171. TELEX 90-2210 MENCENCOM AKRP. Ed. Gwen Groff.
  Description: Newsletter for those desiring more specialized information on peace, justice and related issues.

PEDALPOINT. see MUSIC

287 MY
PELITA METHODIST. 1977. m. M.$10($2) Methodist Church in Malaysia - Gereja Methodist Malaysia, Methodist Headquarters, 65 Jalan 5-31, Petaling Jaya, Selangor, Malaysia. Ed. Rev. Ng Ee Lin. adv.; bk.rev.; circ. 2,000.
  Former titles: Methodist Message (ISSN 0026-1254); Malaysia Methodist.

289.9 US ISSN 0031-4919
PENTECOSTAL MESSENGER. 1919. m. $11. Messenger Publishing House, Box 850, Joplin, MO 64802. TEL 417-624-7050. Ed. Don Allen. adv.; circ. 8,000. Indexed: CERDIC.

289.9 CN ISSN 0031-4927
PENTECOSTAL TESTIMONY. 1920. m. $22. Pentecostal Assemblies of Canada, 6745 Century Ave., Mississauga, Ont. L5N 6P7, Canada. TEL 416-542-7400. FAX 416-542-7313. Ed. Robert J. Skinner. adv.; bk.rev.; circ. 29,000. Indexed: CERDIC.

200 US ISSN 0093-531X
PERSPECTIVES IN RELIGIOUS STUDIES. 1974. q. $17. National Association of Baptist Professors of Religion, c/o C.S.S.R Office, Mercer University, R.O.T.C. Bldg., Macon, GA 31207. TEL 912-752-2376. adv.; bk.rev.; abstr.; bibl.; charts; illus.; stat.; cum.index: 1974-1983; circ. 650. (also avail. in microfilm from UMI; back issues avail.) Indexed: Bk.Rev.Mo., CERDIC, New Test.Abstr., Old Test.Abstr., Rel.& Theol.Abstr. (1975-), Rel.Ind.One, Rel.Per.
  —BLDSC shelfmark: 6428.163500.

284 GW
PIETISMUS UND NEUZEIT; Jahrbuch zur Geschichte des neueren Protestantismus. 1974. a. Vandenhoeck & Ruprecht, Robert-Bosch-Breite 6, Postfach 3753, 3400 Goettingen, Germany. index. (back issues avail.)

285.834 US
PILGRIM STATE NEWS. 1951. bi-m. free. (United Church of Christ, Massachusetts Conference) Beacon Communications Corporation, 20 Main St., Acton, MA 01720. TEL 617-875-5233. Ed. Rosemary K. Agnew. bk.rev.; illus.; circ. 4,500.
  Former titles: Pilgrim State Newsletter (ISSN 0362-0557); Until 1974: Pilgrim States News.

289.9 SA ISSN 0031-9902
PINKSTER PROTESTANT. (Text in Afrikaans and English; summaries in Afrikaans) 1958. 4/yr. R.30. Pentecostal Protestant Church - Pinkster Protestante Kerk, P.O. Box 180, Isando, Transvaal, South Africa. Ed. Pastor P.J.J. Synman. adv.; bk.rev.; circ. 5,000.

266 CN
PIONEER; Christian monthly. 1951. m. Can.$7.50. Council of the Reformed Church in Canada, 201 Paradise Rd. N., Hamilton, Ont. L8S 3T3, Canada. TEL 416-637-3434. Ed. Rev. Peter Yff. adv.; bk.rev.; circ. 2,500. (also avail. in microfilm)

283 AT ISSN 1035-1035
THE PIONEER. 1931. q. donation to cover postage. Church Army in Australia, P.O. Box 107, Frenchs Forest, N.S.W. 2086, Australia. TEL 02-451-8395. FAX 02-451-8877. Ed. Rev. W.M. Harris. circ. 6,000 (controlled). (back issues avail.)
  Description: Evangelism - news of Church Army work.

286 US
PIONEER (MEMPHIS). 1970. m. $2.64 for 3 mos. (typically set in Feb.). Southern Baptist Convention, Brotherhood Commission, 1548 Poplar Ave., Memphis, TN 38104. illus.; circ. 26,000. (also avail. in microform from UMI)
  Formerly: Probe (Memphis) (ISSN 0032-9215)
  Description: Provides missions education for boys 12-14 enrolled in Southern Baptist churches.

269.4 US ISSN 0272-0965
BR1644
PNEUMA. 1979. s-a. $24. Society for Pentecostal Studies, Box 2671, Gaithersburg, MD 20886. TEL 301-990-2083. Ed. Cecil M. Robeck. bk.rev.; circ. 600. (back issues avail.) Indexed: Rel.Ind.One.
  —BLDSC shelfmark: 6541.106000.

287 028.5 US ISSN 0278-565X
POCKETS. 1981. m. (except Jan.). $12.95. (United Methodist Church, General Board of Discipleship) Upper Room, 1908 Grand Ave., Box 189, Nashville, TN 37202. TEL 615-340-7333. FAX 615-340-7006. Ed. Janet McNish Bugg.
  Description: For children ages 6 to 12. Includes stories, scriptures, prayers, and games.

248 US ISSN 0032-4884
PORTALS OF PRAYER; daily devotions for adults. German edition: Taegliche Andachten (ISSN 0273-8562) 1937. q. $4.75. (Lutheran Library for the Blind) Concordia Publishing House, 3558 S. Jefferson Ave., St. Louis, MO 63118. TEL 314-664-7000. Ed. Rudolph F. Norden. circ. 900,000. (also avail. in microfilm; Braille; large print edition in 18 pt.)

287 PO ISSN 0032-5066
PORTUGAL EVANGELICO. 1920. m. Esc.500($12) (Igreja Evangelica Metodista Portuguesa) Rev. Ireneu da Silva Cunha, Ed. & Pub., Praca Coronel Pacheco 23, 4000 Porto, Portugal. TEL 02-2007410. (Co-sponsor: Presbyterian Church in Portugal) Ed. Jorge S. Barros Sousa. bk.rev.; illus.; circ. 2,000.

284 GW
POSENER STIMMEN. 1953. m. DM.28. Gemeinschaft Evangelischer Posener e.V., Bernhard-Riemann-Strasse 30, 2120 Lueneberg, Germany. TEL 04131-43607. circ. 4,200.

284 FR ISSN 0032-5228
POSITIONS LUTHERIENNES. 1953. q. 160 F. Association "Positions Lutheriennes", 16 rue Chauchat, 75009 Paris, France. TEL 47.70.80.30. Ed. J.N. Peres. bk.rev.; bibl.; circ. 550. Indexed: Bull.Signal., CERDIC.
  —BLDSC shelfmark: 6558.847000.

289 US
POSSIBILITIES; the magazine of hope. 1983. bi-m. free. (Crystal Cathedral) Publishing Directions, Inc., 5301 Wisconsin Ave., N.W., Ste. 720, Washington, DC 20015. TEL 202-364-8000. FAX 202-364-8910. (Subscr. to: Box 100, Garden Grove, CA 92642) Ed. Jeanne Dunn. adv.; circ. 300,000.

266 FR ISSN 0751-5987
POUR LA VERITE. 1935. m. 80 F. Union Eglises Evangeliques Libres de France, c/o Jean Pongy, 12, Impasse Viala-rue Montaury, 30000 Nimes, France. Ed. S. Lauzet. bk.rev.; circ. 1,500.

285 US
PRAYERLINE; a guide to intercession for indigenous missions. 1983. m. Christian Aid Mission, 3045 Ivy Rd., Charlottesville, VA 22903. TEL 804-977-5650. Ed. Cheryl Smith. circ. 16,500. (back issues avail.)
  Description: Covers mission work overseas conducted by non-North Americans.

PRAYERS FOR WORSHIP. see RELIGIONS AND THEOLOGY — Roman Catholic

RELIGIONS AND THEOLOGY — PROTESTANT

285 US
PRESBYTERIAN. 1954. m. (except Jan., May, Aug., & Nov.) Synod of the Sun, 920 Stemmons Frwy., Denton, TX 76205. Ed. Hal Bray. adv.; bk.rev.; illus.; circ. 117,000 (controlled). (tabloid format; also avail. in microfilm from UMI; reprint service avail. from UMI) **Indexed:** Chr.Per.Ind., Old Test.Abstr.
  Formerly: Texas Presbyterian (ISSN 0040-4616)

285 AT ISSN 0729-3542
PRESBYTERIAN BANNER. 1846. m. (except Jan.) Aus.$17. Presbyterian Church of Eastern Australia, 9 Craiglea Close, Taree, N.S.W. 2430, Australia. TEL 65-521317. Ed. Rev. W.P. Gadsby. adv.; bk.rev.; index; circ. 430. (back issues avail.)

285 UK ISSN 0032-7530
PRESBYTERIAN HERALD. m. £5. Presbyterian Church in Ireland, Church House, Fisherwick Place, Belfast, BT1 6DW, N. Ireland. FAX 0232-248377. Ed. Robert Cobain. adv.; bk.rev.; circ. 17,500. **Indexed:** CERDIC.

285 CM
PRESBYTERIAN NEWSLETTER. (Text in English) q. B.P. 19, Buea, Cameroon. TELEX 5613.

285 US ISSN 0032-7565
PRESBYTERIAN OUTLOOK. 1819. w. (except July, Aug.) $17.50. Outlook Publishers, Inc., Box C-32071, Richmond, VA 23261-2071. TEL 804-359-8442. Ed. Robert H. Bullock, Jr. adv.; bk.rev.; illus.; circ. 9,500. (also avail. in microfilm from UMI; reprint service avail. from UMI)

285 CN ISSN 0032-7573
BX8901
PRESBYTERIAN RECORD. 1876. m. Can.$11($17) Presbyterian Church in Canada, 50 Wynford Dr., Don Mills, Ont. M3C 1J7, Canada. TEL 416-441-1111. FAX 416-441-2825. Ed. John Congram. adv.; bk.rev.; film rev.; index; circ. 637,541. (also avail. in microfilm) **Indexed:** Can.Per.Ind.

285 266 US ISSN 0032-759X
BV2570.A1
PRESBYTERIAN SURVEY. 1867. m. $11. Presbyterian Church (U.S.A.), Education and Congregational Nurture Unit, Publications Service, 100 Witherspoon St., Louisville, KY 40202-1396. TEL 502-569-5637. FAX 502-569-5018. Ed. Kenneth Little. adv.; bk.rev.; charts; illus.; index; circ. 125,000. (also avail. in microfilm from UMI)
  Incorporates: Missionary Survey (founded in 1877); Today in World Missions; Home Missionary (founded in 1890); Missionary (founded in 1861).

285 US
PRESBYTERION. 1975. s-a. $6. Covenant Theological Seminary, 12330 Conway Rd., St. Louis, MO 63141. Ed.Bd. bk.rev.; circ. 600. (also avail. in microform) **Indexed:** CERDIC, Chr.Per.Ind., New Test.Abstr., Old Test.Abstr., Rel.& Theol.Abstr. (1978-), Rel.Ind.One.
  Description: Covers all theological disciplines in a scholarly, yet readable manner.

268 US
PRESCHOOL BIBLE TEACHER A. q. $8.50. Southern Baptist Convention, Sunday School Board, 127 Ninth Ave., N., Nashville, TN 37234. TEL 800-458-2772.
  Formerly (until 1982): Guide A for Preschool Teachers (ISSN 0162-4474)

268 US ISSN 0732-944X
PRESCHOOL BIBLE TEACHER B. q. $10. Southern Baptist Convention, Sunday School Board, 127 Ninth Ave., N., Nashville, TN 37234. TEL 800-458-2772.
  Formerly (until 1982): Guide B for Preschool Teachers (ISSN 0162-4482)

268 US ISSN 0732-9458
PRESCHOOL BIBLE TEACHER C. q. $10. Southern Baptist Convention, Sunday School Board, 127 Ninth Ave., N., Nashville, TN 37234. TEL 800-458-2772.
  Formerly (until 1982): Guide C for Preschool Teachers (ISSN 0162-4490)

268 US ISSN 0162-4393
PRESCHOOL LEADERSHIP. q. $8.50. Southern Baptist Convention, Sunday School Board, 127 Ninth Ave., N., Nashville, TN 37234. TEL 800-458-2772.
  Indexed: South.Bap.Per.Ind.

266 US ISSN 0162-4326
PROCLAIM (NASHVILLE). q. $11.75. Southern Baptist Convention, Sunday School Board, 127 Ninth Ave., N., Nashville, TN 37234. TEL 800-458-2772.
  Indexed: South.Bap.Per.Ind.

285 US
PROCLAIM (PETALUMA). (Text in Chinese) 1988. bi-m. free. Chinese Christian Mission, 951 Petaluma Blvd., S., Box 617, Petaluma, CA 94952. TEL 707-762-1314. FAX 707-762-1713. Ed. Cecilia Yau. circ. 18,000. (back issues avail.)

284 US
PROGRAMAIDS. q. Salvation Army, 799 Bloomfield Ave., Verona, NJ 07044. Ed. Mrs. Lt. Colonel Leon Ferraez.

286 US ISSN 0033-1139
PROMOTOR DE EDUCACION CRISTIANA. (Text in Spanish) 1949. q. $6. Casa Bautista de Publicaciones, Box 4255, El Paso, TX 79914. TEL 915-566-9656. Ed. Mario Martinez. bk.rev.; charts; illus.; index; circ. 5,000.
  Description: For leaders in church programs.

200 230 IT ISSN 0033-1767
BR5
PROTESTANTESIMO. 1946. q. L.30000 (foreign L.35000). Facolta Valdese di Teologia, Via Pietro Cossa 42, 00193 Rome, Italy. TEL 06-3210789. FAX 06-3201040. Ed. Bruno Corsani. bk.rev.; bibl.; cum.index: 1946-1988; circ. 1,000. **Indexed:** Bull.Signal., CERDIC, Int.Z.Bibelwiss, Rel.Ind.One.

284 917.306 US
PROVIDENT BOOK FINDER. 1970. 5/yr. free. (Provident Bookstores) Mennonite Publishing House, 616 Walnut Ave., Scottdale, PA 15683. TEL 412-887-8500. FAX 412-887-3111. Ed. Ron Meyer. bk.rev.; circ. 15,000. (back issues avail.)
  Description: Each issue contains over 100 reviews of new books concentrating on peace, social concerns, theology, ethics, children's books and family life.

284 GW ISSN 0341-9495
QUATEMBER; Vierteljahreshefte fuer Erneuerung und Einheit der Kirche. 1936. q. DM.29.60. Lutherisches Verlagshaus GmbH, Knochenhauer Str. 38-40, D-3000 Hannover 1, Germany. TEL 0511-1241-733. Ed. Juergen Boeckh. circ. 1,700.
  —BLDSC shelfmark: 7209.900000.

284.2 SA ISSN 0033-6637
QUO VADIS. (Text in Afrikaans) 1950. 10/yr. R.3.50. Reformed Churches in South Africa - Gereformeerde Kerke in Suid-Afrika, P.O. Box 20008, Noordbrug 2522, Potchefstroom, South Africa. circ. 7,950.

284 GW
R A B S. (Religionspaedagogik an Berufsbildenden Schulen) 1969. q. DM.32. Koesel-Verlag GmbH und Co., Fluggerstr. 2, 8000 Munich 19, Germany. TEL 089-1790080. illus.; circ. 2,400.

205 US
R E C MISSION BULLETIN. 1981. q. $5. Reformed Ecumenical Council, 2017 Eastern Ave., Ste. 201, Grand Rapids, MI 49507-3234. TEL 616-241-4424. Ed. Richard L. van Houten. circ. 700.
  Former titles: R E S Mission Bulletin; R E S World Diaconal Bulletin.

285 US
R E C NEWS EXCHANGE. 1964. m. $7. Reformed Ecumenical Council, 2017 Eastern Ave., Ste. 201, Grand Rapids, MI 49507-3234. TEL 616-241-4424. Ed. Richard L. van Houten. bk.rev.; circ. 1,200.
  Formerly: R E S News Exchange (ISSN 0033-6904)

200 US
R E C THEOLOGICAL FORUM. 1973. q. $7. Reformed Ecumenical Council, 2017 Eastern Ave., Ste. 201, Grand Rapids, MI 49507-3234. TEL 616-241-4424. Ed. Paul G. Schrotenboer. circ. 400.
  Formerly: R E S Theological Forum.

286 DK
RAADGIVEREN; boerne og juniorlederen. 10/yr. DKK 150. Danmarks Folkekirkelige Soendagsskoler og Boernegudstjenester, Korshaervej 25, 7000 Fredericia, Denmark. TEL 75-92-61-00. Ed. Ejgil Bodilsen. circ. 2,381.

260 UK ISSN 0300-3469
READER. 1904. q. £2.80. Church of England, Central Readers' Conference, Church House, Gt. Smith St., London SW1P 3NZ, England. Ed. C.A. Cull. adv.; bk.rev.; circ. 9,000.

READY. see MILITARY

289.9 CN ISSN 0034-0847
REAL LIVING. 1964. q. Can.$2.50. Pentecostal Assemblies of Canada, Men's Fellowship Ministries Department, 6745 Century Ave., Mississauga, Ont. L5N 6P7, Canada. TEL 416-542-7400. FAX 416-542-7313. Ed. Rev. Gordon R. Upton. circ. 15,000.

284 NZ ISSN 0034-107X
REAPER; New Zealand's Evangelical bi-monthly. 1923. bi-m. NZ.$25 (foreign NZ$28). Bible College of New Zealand, Inc., Private Bag, Henderson, Auckland 8, New Zealand. FAX 9-837-4209. Ed. S.C.H. Hillman. adv.; bk.rev.; circ. 4,000. (tabloid format)
  Description: Interdenominational, evangelical articles of topical and spiritual interest. Also news of the Bible College of New Zealand and its graduates.

200 UK ISSN 0034-1479
RECONCILIATION QUARTERLY. 1924. q. £7 europe £8.50; elsewhere £10.50. Fellowship of Reconciliation, 40-46 Harleyford Rd., Vauxhall, London SE11 5AY, England. TEL 01-582-9054. FAX 071-582-9180. Ed. Ben Rees. adv.; bk.rev.; illus.; circ. 1,750. (also avail. in microform from UMI; reprint service avail. from UMI) **Indexed:** CERDIC.
  Description: Each issue covers a topic of social concern such as peace and disarmament and discusses the subject with notes, articles and reviews.

285 UK ISSN 0306-7262
REFORM. 1972. 11/yr. £7.50. United Reformed Church in the United Kingdom, 86 Tavistock Place, London WC1H 9RT, England. Ed. Norman Hart. adv.; bk.rev.; film rev.; illus.; circ. 16,000.
  Formed by the merger of: Congregational Monthly (ISSN 0010-583X) & Outlook (ISSN 0030-7203)

286 UK ISSN 0034-3048
REFORMATION TODAY. 1970. 6/yr. $15. 75 Woodhill Road, Leeds LS16 7BZ, England. Ed. Erroll Hulse. bk.rev.; charts; circ. 3,000. **Indexed:** CERDIC.
  Supersedes: Christians Pathway.
  Description: Presents bible study material, biographies, and news of Reformed churches worldwide.

284 GW ISSN 0171-3469
REFORMATIONSGESCHICHTLICHE STUDIEN UND TEXTE. 1906. irreg., vol.130, 1991. price varies. Aschendorffsche Verlagsbuchhandlung, Soesterstr. 13, 4400 Muenster, Germany. TEL 0251-690-0. FAX 0251-690405. Ed. Erwin Iserloh. (also avail. in microform from BHP)

284 HU
REFORMATUS EGYHAZ. 1949. m. $35.50. Hungarian Reformed Church, Abonyi u. 21, 1146 Budapest, Hungary. TEL 122-7870. Ed. Ferenc Dusicza. circ. 1,600.

284 HU
REFORMATUSOK LAPJA. 1957. w. $37. Reformed Church, POB 424, 1395 Budapest, Hungary. TEL 117-6809. Ed. Attila P. Komlos. circ. 40,000.

284 FR ISSN 0223-5749
REFORME; hebdomadaire protestant d'information generale. 1945. w. 490 F. (effective 1992). 53-55 Avenue du Maine, 75014 Paris, France. FAX 1-43-21-42-86. Ed. Michel Leplay. adv.; bk.rev.; illus. (tabloid format)

280 US ISSN 0080-0481
REFORMED CHURCH OF AMERICA. HISTORICAL SERIES. no.2, 1970. irreg. Wm. B. Eerdmans Publishing Co., 255 Jefferson Ave., S.E., Grand Rapids, MI 49503. TEL 616-459-4591. FAX 616-459-6540. TELEX 234111.

RELIGIONS AND THEOLOGY — PROTESTANT

200   US   ISSN 0034-3064
REFORMED REVIEW. 1947. 3/yr. $10. Western Theological Seminary, Holland, MI 49423. TEL 616-392-8555. FAX 616-392-7717. Ed. James I. Cook. adv.; bk.rev.; bibl.; cum.index; circ. 2,900. (also avail. in microform from UMI; reprint service avail. from UMI) **Indexed:** CERDIC, Int.Z.Bibelwiss, New Test.Abstr., Rel.& Theol.Abstr. (1967-), Rel.Ind.One, Rel.Per.
—BLDSC shelfmark: 7332.520000.

284   SZ   ISSN 0034-3056
BX8901
REFORMED WORLD. 1971. q. 14 Fr.($9) World Alliance of Reformed Churches, P.O. Box 2100, 150, route de Ferney, 1211 Geneva 2, Switzerland. TEL 022-7916236. FAX 022-7916505. TELEX 415730-OIK-CH. Ed. Milan Opocensky. adv.; bk.rev.; index; circ. 11,500. (also avail. in microform from UMI; reprint service avail. from UMI) **Indexed:** CERDIC, Rel.& Theol.Abstr. (1971-), Rel.Ind.One, Rel.Per.
—BLDSC shelfmark: 7332.550000.
Formerly: Reformed and Presbyterian World.

284   US   ISSN 0890-8583
REFORMED WORSHIP; resources in liturgy and music. 1986. q. $20. C R C Publications, Education Department, 2850 Kalamazoo S.E., Grand Rapids, MI 49560. TEL 800-333-8300. FAX 616-246-0834. Ed. Emily Brink. bk.rev.; circ. 3,000. (back issues avail.)

280   UK   ISSN 0034-3080
REFORMER. 1930. bi-m. £3. Protestant Alliance, 77 Ampthill Road, Flitwick, Bedford MK45 1BD, England. TEL 0525-712348. Ed. Rev. A.G. Ashdown. bk.rev.; illus.; circ. 4,500.

RELIGIONSUNTERRICHT UND KONFIRMANDENUNTERRICHT FUER GEHOERLOSE UND SCHWERHOERIGE; ein Informationsdienst. see HANDICAPPED — Hearing Impaired

285   US   ISSN 1043-125X
RENEWAL NEWS. 1966. bi-m. free to qualified personnel. (Presbyterian and Reformed Renewal Ministries International) Presbyterian Renewal Publications, Box 428, Black Mountain, NC 28711-0428. Ed. Rev. R. Carter Blaisdell. bk.rev.; circ. 6,500. (tabloid format; back issues avail.)
Description: Promotes an experience of the Holy Spirit through news, teaching, and testimony.

286   US
REPORT FROM THE CAPITAL. 1946. 10/yr. $8. Baptist Joint Committee on Public Affairs, 200 Maryland Ave., N.E., Washington, DC 20002. TEL 202-544-4226. FAX 202-544-2094. Ed. Larry Chesser. bk.rev.; index; circ. 5,400. (back issues avail.) **Indexed:** South.Bap.Per.Ind.
Description: Provides news, views and articles about religious liberty and church-state separation.

284.1   US   ISSN 0360-7119
REPORTER (ST. LOUIS). 1954. w. $12. (Lutheran Church - Missouri Synod) Concordia Publishing House, 3558 S. Jefferson Ave., St. Louis, MO 63118. TEL 314-664-7000. Ed. David Mahsman. (also avail. in microform from UMI)
Formerly (until 1975): Advance (St. Louis) (ISSN 0001-8570)

268.8   CN   ISSN 0832-9354
RESOURCE; church ministries leadership magazine. 1986. bi-m. Can.$15($18) Pentecostal Assemblies of Canada, Church Ministries Department, 6745 Century Ave., Mississauga, Ont. L5N 6P7, Canada. TEL 416-542-7400. FAX 416-542-1624. Ed. Rick Hiebert. adv.; bk.rev.; circ. 14,000 (controlled).
Former titles (until 1986): Source (ISSN 0229-4931); (until 1981): Pentecostal Assemblies of Canada. Cell Pak (ISSN 0707-1868)
Description: Topics of relevance to lay and ordained church leaders; relationships, authority, finances and specialized ministries.

287   US   ISSN 0034-5725
RESPONSE (NEW YORK, 1969). 1969. m. (except July & Aug.). $7. United Methodist Church, General Board of Global Ministries, Mission Education and Cultivation Program Department, 475 Riverside Dr., Rm. 1344, New York, NY 10115. TEL 212-870-3755. Ed. Carol M. Herb. illus.; index; circ. 83,500. **Indexed:** Mid.East: Abstr.& Ind.
Supersedes (1940-1969): Methodist Woman.

286   US   ISSN 0034-6373
BX6201
REVIEW AND EXPOSITOR. 1904. q. $15 (foreign $16). Southern Baptist Theological Seminary, Faculty Club, 2825 Lexington Rd., Louisville, KY 40280. TEL 502-897-4407. Ed. R. Alan Culpepper. adv.; bk.rev.; index; circ. 6,000. (also avail. in microform from UMI; reprint service avail. from UMI) **Indexed:** CERDIC, New Test.Abstr., Old Test.Abstr., Rel.& Theol.Abstr. (1967-), Rel.Ind.One, Rel.Per., South.Bap.Per.Ind.
—BLDSC shelfmark: 7786.940000.
Formerly: Baptist Review and Expositor (ISSN 0190-5856)

266   GW
RHOENBRIEF. q. Christliche Gaestehaeuser, Tagungsstaette - Missionarisches Zentrum, 8743 Bischofsheim, Germany. TEL 09772-248. FAX 09772-8213. circ. 10,000.

284 282   AT
THE ROCK (EPPING). 1945. bi-m. Aus.$12. The Rock Newspaper Company, D.& C. Shelton, P.O. Box 551, Epping, N.S.W. 2121, Australia. TEL 02-868-4591. Ed. Rev. D.C. Shelton. (back issues avail.)
Description: Articles and news critical of Roman Catholicism; promotes Protestant Christianity.

284   NE
RONDUIT MAGAZINE. 1989. 6/yr. fl.10. Evangelische Omroep, Postbus 565, 1200 AN Hilversum, Netherlands. circ. 50,000.

266   US   ISSN 0035-9084
BV2520.A1
ROYAL SERVICE. 1906. m. $11. Woman's Missionary Union, Hwy. 280 E., 100 Missionary Ridge, Birmingham, AL 35242-5235. TEL 205-991-4933. FAX 205-991-4990. (Subscr. to: Box 830010, Birmingham, AL 35283-0010) Ed. Edna Ellison. bk.rev.; illus.; circ. 325,000.
Formerly: Our Mission Fields.
Description: Dedicated to members and leaders of Baptist women's missions organizations.

284   AT   ISSN 0725-6140
S.U. NEWS. q. Aus.$10 donation. Scripture Union (A.C.T.), Unit 5 Block 2, Shopping Centre, Cook, A.C.T. 2614, Australia. TEL 06-251-3677. FAX 06-251-2953. bk.rev.; circ. 1,800.

286   US   ISSN 0036-214X
SABBATH RECORDER. 1844. m. free. (American Sabbath Tract and Communication Council) Seventh Day Baptist Center, Box 1678, Janesville, WI 53547. TEL 608-752-5055. FAX 608-752-7711. Ed. Kevin Butler. bk.rev.; illus.; circ. 4,600. (also avail. in microfilm)
Description: Inspirational and informational news for and about Seventh Day Baptists.

286.73   US   ISSN 0098-9517
BX6101
SABBATH WATCHMAN. 1926. bi-m. $10. Religious Liberty Publishing Association, 9999 E. Mississippi Ave., Denver, CO 80231-1927. TEL 303-363-9853. FAX 303-850-0658. (Co-sponsor: Seventh-Day Adventist Church Reform Movement, American Union) Ed. L.D. Watts. bk.rev.; illus.; circ. 650.

200   UK   ISSN 0036-3111
ST. MARTIN'S REVIEW; the journal with the international outlook. 1893. m. £10. St. Martin-In-The-Fields Church, 5 St. Martins Place, London W.C.2, England. TEL 01-930-1862. Ed. Melanie Thorne. adv.; bk.rev.; play rev.; illus.; circ. 1,500.

384   UK   ISSN 0080-567X
SALVATION ARMY YEAR BOOK. 1906. a. £4.25 paperback; £8.95 hardback. (Salvation Army) Salvationist Publishing and Supplies, Ltd., Judd St., Kings Cross, London WC1H 9NN, England. TEL 071-387-1656. FAX 071-387-3768. Ed. Stanley Richardson. index; circ. 13,000.

360   UK
SALVATIONIST. 1907. w. £30.55. Salvation Army, International Headquarters, 101 Queen Victoria St., London EC4P 4EP, England. TEL 071-236-5222. FAX 071-236-3491. Ed. David Armistead. circ. 25,000.
Incorporates (in 1986): Musician.

283 362.7   GW
SCHNELLER-MAGAZIN. 1895. q. free. Evangelischer Verein fuer das Syrische Waisenhaus (Schneller-Schulen) e.V., Vogelsangstr. 62, 7000 Stuttgart 1, Germany. TEL 0711-63678-0. FAX 0711-63678-66. TELEX 723059-EMS-D. Eds. Reinhilde Freise, Klaus Zoeller. circ. 20,000. (back issues avail.)
Formerly (until 1991): Schneller Bote.
Description: Information on orphanages in Jordan and Lebanon and other Middle East issues.

284   GW   ISSN 0170-6128
SCHOENBERGER HEFTE. 1970. q. DM.9. (Evangelische Kirche in Hessen und Nassau, Religionspaedagogische Studienzentrum) Evangelischer Presseverband in Hessen und Nassau e.V., Postfach 100747, Neue Schlesingergasse 24, 6000 Frankfurt a.M. 1, Germany. TEL 069-299884-0. FAX 069-299884-24. Eds. Gerhard Brockmann, Hans Heller. bk.rev.; circ. 12,000.
Description: Articles on Protestant religious education, aimed at teachers in German high schools.

SCHRIFTENREIHE FUER DIE EVANGELISCHE FRAU. see WOMEN'S INTERESTS

SCOREBOARD ALERT; grassroots citizens working an agenda for the preservation of American values. see POLITICAL SCIENCE

286   UK   ISSN 0036-9136
SCOTTISH BAPTIST MAGAZINE. 1860. m. £4. Baptist Union of Scotland, c/o Rev. Robert Armstrong, Ed., Baptist Church House, 14 Aytoun Rd., Glasgow G41 5RT, Scotland. FAX 041-424-1422. adv.; bk.rev.; circ. 4,000.

284   UK   ISSN 0265-4547
SCOTTISH BULLETIN OF EVANGELICAL THEOLOGY. s-a. £9.50. Rutherford House, 17 Claremont Park, Edinburgh EH6 7PJ, Scotland. (Co-sponsor: Scottish Evangelical Theology Society) Ed. David Wright. adv.; bk.rev.; circ. 600.
Former titles (until 1983): Scottish Evangelical Theology Society Bulletin; Scottish Tynedale Bulletin (ISSN 0262-1053)

267   UK   ISSN 0260-0617
BX5225
SCOTTISH EPISCOPAL CHURCH YEARBOOK. 1879. a. £5. Scottish Episcopal Church, 21 Grosvenor Crescent, Edinburgh EH12 5EE, Scotland. TEL 031-225-6357. index; circ. 800.

284   SA   ISSN 0254-1807
SCRIPTURA; tydskrif vir Bybel en teologie in Suider-Afrika - journal of Bible and Theology in Southern Africa. (Text in Afrikaans and English) 1980. 6/yr. R.22.50($34) to individuals; libraries R.34($34)(effective 1992)(typically set in Oct.). University of Stellenbosch, Department of Biblical Studies - Universiteit van Stellenbosch, Departement Bybelkunde, 7600 Stellenbosch, South Africa. TEL 02231-772029. FAX 02231-772031. TELEX 520383 SA. Ed. B.C. Lategan. bk.rev.; illus.; circ. 700. (back issues avail.) **Indexed:** Ind.S.A.Per., New Test.Abstr., Rel.& Theol.Abstr. (1988-), Rel.Ind.One.
—BLDSC shelfmark: 8213.237300.
Description: Publishes articles on the Bible and theology. Emphasizes contextual theological and ethical issues, in particular those relating to South Africa.
Refereed Serial

284   IE   ISSN 0332-0618
SEARCH; Church of Ireland journal. 1978. s-a. I£5($10) Religious Education Resource Centre, Mount Argus Rd., Dublin 6W, Ireland. TEL 01-972821. Ed. M. Burrows. bk.rev.; circ. 600.
Description: For teachers in primary and secondary schools, people of responsibility in parishes, as well as the clergy.

268   US   ISSN 0048-9913
SEARCH (NASHVILLE). q. $14.25. Southern Baptist Convention, Sunday School Board, 127 Ninth Ave. N., Nashville, TN 37234. TEL 800-458-2772. bk.rev.; index. **Indexed:** South.Bap.Per.Ind.

RELIGIONS AND THEOLOGY — PROTESTANT

286 US ISSN 0739-2281
SEARCHING TOGETHER. 1972. q. $7. Word of Life Church, Box 548, St. Croix Falls, WI 54024. TEL 715-755-3560. FAX 612-465-5101. Ed. Jon Zens. adv.; bk.rev.; circ. 3,000. (also avail. in microform from UMI; back issues avail.) **Indexed:** CERDIC, Rel.& Theol.Abstr. (1988-), Rel.Ind.One, Rel.Per.
  Formerly (until 1981): Baptist Reformation Review (ISSN 0276-7945)
  Description: Explores church issues and biblical teachings. Includes new publications information.

286 US ISSN 0037-0606
BV4800
SECRET PLACE. 1938. q. $4 for inkprint; Braille $16; cassette $35; large print $6.50. American Baptist Churches in the U S A, Educational Ministries, Box 851, Valley Forge, PA 19482-0851. TEL 215-768-2000. (Cassette orders to: Shared Daily Devotions, Box 93734, Pasadena, CA 91109-9857) Ed. Michelle Esbenshade. circ. 120,000. (also avail. in Braille; audio cassette; large print edition in 14 pt.)

283 AT ISSN 0037-0754
SEE. 1966. m. Aus.$15. Anglican Media, Diocese of Melbourne, St. Paul's Cathedral Buildings, Flinders Lane, Melbourne, Vic. 3000, Australia. TEL 03-653-4220. FAX 03-650-5237. Ed. Angela Grutzner. adv.; bk.rev.; film rev.; play rev.; illus.; circ. 23,000. (tabloid format)

286 PO ISSN 0037-1874
SEMEADOR BAPTISTA. 1926. m. Esc.1000($8) Convencao Baptista Portuguesa - Portuguese Baptist Convention, Rua Luis Simoes, 7-1o Dto., 2745 Queluz, Portugal. FAX 01-436-1833. Ed. Jonatas Machado. bk.rev.; illus.; circ. 1,600. (tabloid format)

268 US ISSN 0162-4733
SENIOR ADULT BIBLE STUDY. q. $4.75. Southern Baptist Convention, Sunday School Board, 127 Ninth Ave., North, Nashville, TN 37234. TEL 800-458-2772.

285 CN ISSN 0848-1741
SERVANT MAGAZINE. 1989. 6/yr. Prairie Bible Institute, Three Hills, Alberta T0M 2A0, Canada. TEL 403-443-5511. FAX 403-443-5540. Ed. Phil R. Callaway. bk.rev.; circ. 18,000.
  Description: Features world news section related to the Church, moral issues, articles devoted to important figures, education and encouragement for today's Christian.

284 CM
SERVITEUR. m. B.P. 1405, Yaounde, Cameroon. Ed. Daniel Ako'o. circ. 3,000.

286 YU
SESTRINSKI LIST. (Text in Serbo-Croatian) 1955. m. $6. (Dobra Vest Union - Union of Baptist Churches) Rijeci Iskrene, Dravska 2, 42305 Puscine, Yugoslavia. TEL 021-369-882. Ed. Olga Dega. adv.; bk.rev.; circ. 1,400.

SHINING STAR MAGAZINE. see *CHILDREN AND YOUTH — For*

SIGNAL (STREAMWOOD). see *CHILDREN AND YOUTH — About*

286 US
SIGNS OF THE TIMES (NAMPA). 1874. m. $11.95. (Seventh-Day Adventists) Pacific Press Publishing Association, 1350 Kings Rd., Nampa, ID 83651. TEL 208-465-2500. FAX 208-465-2531. Ed. R. Greg Brothers. circ. 290,000. (also avail. in microform from UMI)

SILVER WINGS; poems. see *LITERATURE — Poetry*

286 US ISSN 0731-1478
SINGLE ADULT BIBLE STUDY. q. $6.50. Southern Baptist Convention, Sunday School Board, 127 Ninth Ave., N., Nashville, TN 37234. TEL 800-458-2772.

SINGLES SCENE (ALLARDT). see *SINGLES' INTERESTS AND LIFESTYLES*

266 US ISSN 0700-5202
SLAVNA NADEJE/GLORIOUS HOPE. (Text in English, Czech, Slovak) 1974. bi-m. Czechoslovak Baptist Convention of the United States and Canada, Rt. 1, Box 58D, Philippi, WV 26416. TEL 304-457-4287. FAX 304-457-1700. Ed. Martin Alac. circ. 1,300.

284.2 SA ISSN 0037-685X
SLINGERVEL; publication for the youth. (Text in Afrikaans) 1959. m. R.14.50. Reformed Churches in South Africa - Gereformeerde Kerke in Suid-Afrika, P.O. Box 20008, Noordbrug 2522, Potchefstroom, South Africa. Ed. P.W. Buys. bk.rev.; circ. 7,960.

284 XV
SNOPJE Z DOMACIH IN TUJIH NJIV KRSCANSKE MISLI. (Text in Slovenian) 1977. a. 1000 din. Kristusova Binkostna Cerkev, Milcinksega 73, 61000 Ljubljana, Slovenia. TEL 061-559-655. Ed. Mihael Kuzmic. circ. 250. (back issues avail.)

283 UK ISSN 0144-8722
BX1
SOBORNOST. 1928. s-a. £8($25) Fellowship of St. Alban & St. Sergius, 52 Ladbroke Grove, London W11 2PB, England. TEL 071-727-7713. Ed.Bd. adv.; bk.rev.; illus.; circ. 2,500. (also avail. in microform from UMI; reprint service avail. from UMI) **Indexed:** Arts & Hum.Cit.Ind., Br.Hum.Ind., Cath.Ind., CERDIC, Curr.Cont., New Test.Abstr., Rel.& Theol.Abstr. (1979-), Rel.Ind.One, Rel.Per.
—BLDSC shelfmark: 8318.020500.
  Incorporating (in 1979): Eastern Churches Review (ISSN 0012-8740)
  Description: Contains articles dealing with Orthodox theology and church history, with particular reference to parallels in Western (Anglican and Roman) milieux. Reports on ecumenical concerns within this area.

301 US ISSN 0731-0234
SOCIAL QUESTIONS BULLETIN. 1911. bi-m. $12. Methodist Federation for Social Action, 76 Clinton Ave., Staten Island, NY 10301. TEL 718-273-6372. Ed. Rev. George D. McClain. bk.rev.; circ. 1,500. (also avail. in microform from UMI; back issues avail.; reprint service avail. from UMI) **Indexed:** CERDIC.

284 FR ISSN 0035-3884
BX9401
SOCIETE CALVINISTE DE FRANCE. REVUE REFORMEE. 1950. q. 150 F. (typically set in Dec.). Faculte de Theologie Reformee, 33 av. Jules Ferry, 13100 Aix-en-Provence, France. Ed. Paul Wells. bk.rev.; index, cum.index every 10 yrs.; circ. 1,300. **Indexed:** New Test.Abstr., Old Test.Abstr.
—BLDSC shelfmark: 7945.300000.

384 FR ISSN 0037-9050
SOCIETE DE L'HISTOIRE DU PROTESTANTISME FRANCAIS. BULLETIN. 1852. q. 270 F. (typically set in Jan.). Societe de l'Histoire du Protestantisme Francais, 54 rue des Saints-Peres, 75007 Paris, France. Ed. Jacques Evesque. bk.rev.; bibl.; charts; illus.; stat.; index; cum.index; circ. 2,200. **Indexed:** Amer.Hist.& Life, CERDIC, Hist.Abstr.

269.4 US
SOCIETY FOR PENTECOSTAL STUDIES. NEWSLETTER. 1970. s-a. included in subscr. to members; non-members $6. Society for Pentecostal Studies, Box 2671, Gaithersburg, MD 20886. TEL 301-990-2083. Ed. Peter D. Hocken. bk.rev.; bibl. (back issues avail.)

286 DK ISSN 0109-2375
SOENDAGSKOLEKONTAKT. 1984. q. free. Danmarks Folkekirkelige Soendagsskoler og Boernegudstjenester, Korskaervej 25, 7000 Fredericia, Denmark. TEL 75-92-61-00 609. FAX 75-92-61-46. Ed. Hove Jacobsen. illus.; circ. 7,000.

284 GW
SONNTAGSGRUSS; Kraft fuer den Tag. 1928. w. DM.9.90. Christliche Verlagsanstalt GmbH, Zasiusstr. 8, Postfach 1186, 7750 Konstanz, Germany. TEL 07531-23054. FAX 07531-24284. Ed. Herbert Hartmann.

286 SA
SOUTH AFRICAN BAPTIST HANDBOOK. 1885. a. R.22($15) Baptist Union of Southern Africa, P.O. Box 1085, Roodepoort 1725, South Africa. TEL 011-760-3038. FAX 011-760-2685. circ. 1,200. (back issues avail.)

286 US ISSN 0146-0196
BX6248.S6
SOUTH CAROLINA BAPTIST HISTORICAL SOCIETY JOURNAL. 1975. a. $3. South Carolina Baptist Historical Society, Furman University Library, Greenville, SC 29613. TEL 803-294-2194. FAX 803-294-3004. Ed. J. Glenwood Clayton. circ. 200. (back issues avail.)
—BLDSC shelfmark: 4902.105000.

287 US
SOUTH CAROLINA UNITED METHODIST ADVOCATE. 1837. w. $14.25 (effective Jan. 1992). (United Methodist Church, South Carolina Conference) Southern Christian Advocate, 4908 Colonial Dr., Columbia, SC 29203. TEL 803-786-9483. Ed. Willie S. Teague. adv.; bk.rev.; illus.; circ. 12,000.
  Former titles: South Carolina Methodist Advocate (ISSN 0038-3147); Southern Christian Advocate.

286 016 US ISSN 0081-3001
SOUTHERN BAPTIST CONVENTION. ANNUAL. 1845. a. $7.50. Southern Baptist Convention, 901 Commerce, Ste. 400, Nashville, TN 37203. TEL 615-244-2355. Ed. Martin Bradley. cum.index 1845-1953; 1954-1965; circ. 35,000. (also avail. in microfilm)

286 016 US ISSN 0081-301X
SOUTHERN BAPTIST CONVENTION. HISTORICAL COMMISSION. MICROFILM CATALOGUE. 1954. irreg. free. Southern Baptist Convention, Historical Commission, 901 Commerce St., Ste. 400, Nashville, TN 37203-3630. TEL 615-244-0344. Ed. Lynn E. May, Jr. circ. 1,500.

266 US ISSN 0162-4334
BX6201
SOUTHERN BAPTIST CONVENTION. SUNDAY SCHOOL BOARD. QUARTERLY REVIEW. q. $11.25. Southern Baptist Convention, Sunday School Board, 127 Ninth Ave., N., Nashville, TN 37234. TEL 800-458-2772. bk.rev.; charts; stat.

377.8 US ISSN 0038-3848
SOUTHERN BAPTIST EDUCATOR. vol.12, 1947. 10/yr. $7.50. Southern Baptist Convention, Education Commission, 901 Commerce St., Ste. 600, Nashville, TN 37203-3620. Ed. Arthur L. Walker, Jr. bk.rev.; bibl.; stat.; index; circ. 10,900.

283 AT ISSN 0313-5861
SOUTHERN CROSS; Anglican news magazine. 1961. 11/yr. Aus.$18. Anglican Information Office, P.O. Box Q190, Queen Victoria Building, Sydney, N.S.W. 2000, Australia. TEL 02-265-1537. FAX 02-261-2864. Ed. George James Fisher. adv.; bk.rev.; film rev.; circ. 5,000. (back issues avail.)
  Description: Studies applied theology, information and debate on current issues.

286 US ISSN 0038-4917
SOUTHWESTERN NEWS. 1943. m. (Sep.-Jul.). free. Southwestern Baptist Theological Seminary, Box 22000 3e, Fort Worth, TX 76122. TEL 817-923-1921. Ed. John E. Seelig. circ. 38,000. (reprint service avail. from UMI) **Indexed:** South.Bap.Per.Ind.

286 US
SOUTHWESTERN UNION RECORD. 1902. m. $8 (typically set Jan.). Southwestern Union Conference of Seventh Day Adventists, Box 4000, Burleson, TX 76028. TEL 817-295-0476. FAX 817-447-2443. adv.; circ. 15,300.
  Description: Focuses on news and promotion of Seventh-day Adventists' churches and institutions in Arkansas, Louisiana, Oklahoma, Texas and New Mexico.

SPARK. see *HANDICAPPED — Visually Impaired*

286 US ISSN 0896-7784
SPECIAL EDUCATION LEADERSHIP. q. $8.75. Southern Baptist Convention, Sunday School Board, 127 Ninth Ave., N., Nashville, TN 37234. TEL 800-458-2772.

SPIRITUAL LIGHT. see *HANDICAPPED — Visually Impaired*

200 US ISSN 0038-9382
STANDARD (ARLINGTON HEIGHTS). 1911. m. (10/yr.). $15. Baptist General Conference, 2002 S. Arlington Heights Rd., Arlington Heights, IL 60005. TEL 708-228-0200. FAX 708-228-5376. Ed. Donald E. Anderson. adv.; bk.rev.; charts; illus.; circ. 17,000.

RELIGIONS AND THEOLOGY — PROTESTANT

284 GW ISSN 0323-4304
STANDPUNKT (BERLIN); evangelische Monatsschrift. 1973. m. DM.24.60. Fennstr. 16, 1190 Berlin, Germany. TEL 6350915. (Orders to: Buchexport, Postfach 160, 7010 Leipzig, Germany) Ed. Karl Hennig. circ. 3,000.

266 UK
STAR IN THE EAST; magazine of life and work in Bible lands. 1883. q. free. Bible Lands Society, The Old Kiln, Willow Chase, Off Amersham Road, Hazlemere, High Wycombe, Bucks. HP15 7QU, England. TEL 0494-521351. FAX 0494-462171. Ed. P.R. Emmerson. bk.rev.; circ. 70,000.
Description: Concerned with the care of needy children in the lands of the Bible. Combines reports of this work with articles on aspects of life and living in the area covered by the Society's operations.

287 US ISSN 0038-9870
BX8450
STAR OF ZION. 1876. w. $22. African Methodist Episcopal Zion Church, Box 31005, Charlotte, NC 28231. Ed. Rev. Morgan W. Tann. adv.; bk.rev.; illus.; circ. 8,000. (tabloid format; also avail. in microfilm from UMI; reprint service avail. from UMI)

200 811 US ISSN 0896-6095
STARLIGHT. 1987. q. $15. Star Books, Inc., 408 Pearson St., Wilson, NC 27893. TEL 919-237-1591. FAX 919-243-8482. Ed. Irene Burk Harrell. circ. 750. (back issues avail.)
Description: Poetry and prose focusing on Jesus Christ and the writer's Christian experience.

286 US ISSN 0162-6841
START (BIRMINGHAM). 1970. q. $11. Woman's Missionary Union, Highway 280 E., 100 Missionary Ridge, Birmingham, AL 35242-5235. TEL 205-991-4933. FAX 205-991-4990. (Subscr. to: Box 830010, Birmingham, AL 35283-0010) Ed. Kathryn Kizer. circ. 32,450. (also avail. in microfiche)
Description: For leaders of Mission Friends organizations.

284 GW
STIFTSKIRCHE; Protestantisches Gemeindeblatt fuer das Dekanat Landau. 1930. m. DM.15. Bezirkskircherat des Kirchenbezirks Landau, Westring 3, 6740 Landua 1, Germany. TEL 06341-4091. Ed. Gerd Uhrig.

284 US
STRENGTH FOR THE DAY. m. free. Lutheran Library for the Blind, 1333 S. Kirkwood Rd., St. Louis, MO 63122. TEL 800-433-3954. (also avail. in Braille; large print edition in 22 pt.)
Description: Includes religious articles and light fiction.

284.2 SA
STROOIDAK. (Text in Afrikaans) 1949. q. free. Nederduitse Gereformeerde Gemeente die Paarl - Dutch Reformed Church, Paarl, Hoofstraat 144, Paarl, South Africa. Eds. J.C.P.B. Nieuwoudt. circ. 1,000. (looseleaf format)
Formerly: Paarlse Padwyser (ISSN 0030-8455)

286 268 US ISSN 0039-2685
BX6205.B27
THE STUDENT (NASHVILLE). m. $11.25. Southern Baptist Convention, Sunday School Board, 127 Ninth Ave., N., Nashville, TN 37234. TEL 800-458-2772.
Formerly: Baptist Student.

STUDENT LEADERSHIP JOURNAL. see *EDUCATION*

284 AU
STUDIEN UND TEXTE ZUR KIRCHENGESCHICHTE UND GESCHICHTE. (Consists of two series) 1975. irreg., vol.4 (series 1), vol.3 (series 2), 1979. price varies. Boehlau Verlag GmbH & Co.KG., Sachsenplatz 4-6, Postfach 87, A-1201 Vienna, Austria. TEL 0222-3302427. FAX 0222-3302432. TELEX 114-506-SPRIW-A. Ed. Peter Barton. circ. 800. (back issues avail.) **Indexed:** Rel.Ind.Two.

268 US ISSN 0191-4219
STUDYING ADULT LIFE AND WORK LESSONS. q. $20.25. Southern Baptist Convention, Sunday School Board, 127 Ninth Ave., N., Nashville, TN 37234. TEL 800-458-2772.

285 CU ISSN 0864-0262
SU VOZ. a. Iglesia Presbiteriana, Salud No. 22nd, Lealtad y Campanario, Havana 2, Cuba. TEL 809 61-1558. Dir. Francisco Marrero.

268 US ISSN 0162-4911
SUNDAY SCHOOL ADULTS. q. $4.50. Southern Baptist Convention, Sunday School Board, 127 Ninth Ave., N., Nashville, TN 37234. TEL 800-458-2772.

268 US ISSN 0274-8568
SUNDAY SCHOOL LEADERSHIP. 1980. m. $12.75. Southern Baptist Convention, Sunday School Board, 127 Ninth Ave., N., Nashville, TN 37234. TEL 800-458-2772. bk.rev.; charts; illus.; index. **Indexed:** South.Bap.Per.Ind.
Formerly: Outreach (Nashville) (ISSN 0162-4318)

268 US ISSN 0748-5360
SUNDAY SCHOOL LESSONS SPECIAL MINISTRIES. q. $4.75. Southern Baptist Convention, Sunday School Board, 127 Ninth Ave., N., Nashville, TN 37234. TEL 800-458-2772.
Formerly: Sunday School Lessons Simplified (ISSN 0162-4873)

268 US ISSN 0585-9328
SUNDAY SCHOOL SENIOR ADULTS. q. $5.50. Southern Baptist Convention, Sunday School Board, 127 Ninth Ave., N., Nashville, TN 37234. TEL 800-458-2772.

268 US ISSN 0162-4903
SUNDAY SCHOOL YOUNG ADULTS. q. $4.50. Southern Baptist Convention, Sunday School Board, 127 Ninth Ave., N., Nashville, TN 37234. TEL 800-458-2772.

268 US
SUNDAY SCHOOL YOUTH. q. $5.50. Southern Baptist Convention, Sunday School Board, 127 Ninth Ave., N., Nashville, TN 37234. TEL 800-458-2772.
Formerly: Sunday School Youth A (ISSN 0162-4881)

268 US
SUNDAY SCHOOL YOUTH TEACHER. q. $9.50. Southern Baptist Convention, Sunday School Board, 127 Ninth Ave., N., Nashville, TN 37234. TEL 800-458-2772.
Formerly: Youth Teacher (ISSN 0162-4865)

284 US ISSN 0273-8562
TAEGLICHE ANDACHTEN. English edition: Portals of Prayer (ISSN 0032-4884) (Text and summaries in German) 1937. q. $5.50. (Lutheran Church - Missouri Synod) Concordia Publishing House, 3558 S. Jefferson Ave., St. Louis, MO 63118. TEL 314-664-7000. Ed. Rudolph F. Norden. circ. 16,000. (also avail. in microfilm)

286 AT
TASMANIAN BAPTIST ADVANCE. 1952. bi-m. Aus.$9 (effective Mar. 1992). Baptist Union of Tasmania, 22 Wellington St., Launceston, Tas. 7250, Australia. TEL 003-314104. FAX 003-313946. Ed. Laurence F. Rowston. adv.; bk.rev.; circ. 800. (back issues avail.)
Description: Covers church news, church history and general denominational interest.

TEACHER'S INTERACTION; a magazine church school workers grow by. see *EDUCATION*

TEEN TIME (LARGE PRINT EDITION). see *CHILDREN AND YOUTH — For*

284.2 NE ISSN 0040-5612
THEOLOGIA REFORMATA. 1958. 4/yr. fl.57.50 (students fl.46). (Gereformeerde Bond in de Hervormde Kerk) Drukkerij Oosterbaan en Le Cointre B.V., Postbus 25, 4460 AA Goes, Netherlands. TEL 08380-17091. Ed. J.M. Smit. adv.; bk.rev.; index; circ. 750 (controlled). **Indexed:** CERDIC.
—BLDSC shelfmark: 8814.510500.

THINKING MISSION. see *RELIGIONS AND THEOLOGY*

268 US
THIRD CENTURY METHODISM. 1962. irreg. (3-4/yr.). $5. United Methodist Historical Society of Baltimore Conference, Inc., 2200 St. Paul St., Baltimore, MD 21218. TEL 301-889-4458. Ed. Rev. Edwin Schell. circ. 800. (looseleaf format; back issues avail.)

284 UK ISSN 0309-3492
THIRD WAY (LONDON, 1977). 1977. 10/yr. £25 (Europe £28.50; elsewhere £30). Third Way Trust Ltd., 3 Mount Radford Crescent, Exeter, Devon EX2 4JW, England. TEL 0392-425992. FAX 0392-413317. Ed. Peter Cousins. adv.; bk.rev.; charts; illus.; circ. 3,500.
—BLDSC shelfmark: 8820.144000.

283 CC
TIAN FENG. (Text in Chinese) m. Zhongguo Jidujiao Xiehui - Chinese Association of Christianity, 169 Yuanmingyuan Lu., 3 Lou, Shanghai 200002, People's Republic of China. TEL 3210487. Ed. Shen Cheng'en.

284 NO ISSN 0040-7194
BX8001
TIDSSKRIFT FOR TEOLOGI OG KIRKE; Norwegian periodical for Church and theology. 1930. q. $56. Universitetsforlaget, P.O. Box 2959-Toeyen, N-0608 Oslo 1, Norway. (U.S. addr.: Publications Expediting Inc., 200 Meacham Ave., Elmont, NY 11003) Ed. Magne Saeboe. adv.; bk.rev.; bibl.; index; circ. 1,000. (back issues avail.) **Indexed:** New Test.Abstr., Old Test.Abstr.
—BLDSC shelfmark: 8828.180000.

286 US ISSN 0040-7232
TIE. 1929. bi-m. free. Southern Baptist Theological Seminary, 2825 Lexington Rd., Louisville, KY 40280. TEL 502-897-4011. Ed. David R. Wilkinson. circ. 49,000. **Indexed:** South.Bap.Per.Ind.

TIJDSCHRIFT VOOR THEOLOGIE. see *RELIGIONS AND THEOLOGY — Roman Catholic*

280.4 028.5 AT ISSN 1030-0295
TODAY (LAWSON); family magazine. 1966. m. free. Mission Publications of Australia, 19 Cascade St., P.O. Box 21, Lawson, N.S.W. 2783, Australia. TEL 047-59-1003. Ed. Kieth Painter. illus.; circ. 14,250.
Description: Family magazine for Australian aboriginal people. Includes stories, testimonies, Bible teaching and photos.

266 NR ISSN 0189-0557
TODAY'S CHALLENGE. (Text in English) 1951. bi-m. £N27($15) (Evangelical Churches of West Africa) E C W A Productions Ltd., P.M. Bag 2010, Jos, Nigeria. TEL 073-52230. Ed. Jacob Shaibu Tsado. adv.; bk.rev.; charts; illus.; circ. 20,000.
Formerly: African Challenge (ISSN 0001-9968)

280.4 028.5 AT ISSN 1030-0309
TODAY'S YOUNG LIFE. Short title: T Y L. 1979. m. free. Mission Publications of Australia, 19 Cascade St., P.O. Box 21, Lawson, N.S.W. 2783, Australia. TEL 047-59 1003. Ed. Grace Lindsay. circ. 8,250.
Description: For Australian aboriginal young people.

268 UK ISSN 0307-5982
TOGETHER (LONDON, 1956). 1956. 9/yr. £5. National Society, Church House, Great Smith St., London SW1P 3NZ, England. Ed. Pamela Egan. adv.; bk.rev.; illus.; circ. 3,000. **Indexed:** CCR, CERDIC, Curr.Cont.
Formerly: Church Teacher (ISSN 0009-6571)
Description: For those concerned with children's Christian education.

283 UK ISSN 0958-2800
▼**TOGETHER (LONDON, 1990)**. 1990. q. £4. United Society for the Propagation of the Gospel, Partnership House, 157 Waterloo Rd., London SE1 8XA, England. TEL 071-928-8681. FAX 071-928-2371.

284 305.3 CN ISSN 0316-2931
TORCH RUNNER. 1959. q. free. Christian Service Brigade of Canada, 1254 Plains Rd. E., Burlington, Ont. L7S 1W6, Canada. TEL 416-634-1841. FAX 416-634-7643. Ed. Mark Clayton. bk.rev.; circ. 8,000. (looseleaf format; back issues avail.)
Description: For the leaders of men's and boys' programs of the Christian Service Brigade.

TRACT MESSENGER. see *HANDICAPPED — Visually Impaired*

RELIGIONS AND THEOLOGY — PROTESTANT

280 380.5   CN   ISSN 0714-8100
TRANSACTION. 1982. bi-m. free. Christian Transportation Inc., 2222 S. Sheridan Way, Unit 5, Bldg. 2, Mississauga, Ont. L5J 2M4, Canada. TEL 416-822-2700. Ed. Louis G. Voyer. circ. 29,000.
    Supersedes: Postal Christian Witness; Christian Airman; Christian Bus Driver; Christian Railroader; Automotive Christian Witness.

280 380.5   CN   ISSN 0229-4362
TRANSPORTEUR; au service du personnel dans le transport et les industries connexes. (Text in French) 1983. bi-m. free. Christian Transportation, Inc., 2222 S. Sheridan Way, Unit 5, Bldg. 2, Mississauga, Ont. L5J 2M4, Canada. TEL 416-822-2700. Ed. Louis G. Voyer. circ. 6,300.
    Formerly: Bonne Nouvelle pour le Transporteur.

284   US
TRI-COUNTY LUTHERAN. 1941. m. $7. Lutheran Center Association of Southeastern Michigan, 579 E. 9 Mile Rd., Ferndale, MI 48220-1952. TEL 313-541-0788. Ed. Betty J. Mueller. adv.; bk.rev.; circ. 7,500.
    Former titles: Detroit and Suburban Lutheran (ISSN 0011-9660); Detroit Lutheran.

283   AT   ISSN 0811-2304
TRINITY OCCASIONAL PAPERS. 1981. s-a. Aus.$25. Trinity Theological College, P.O. Box 683, Toowong, Qld. 4066, Australia. TEL 07-377-9950. FAX 07-377-9716. Ed.Bd. adv.; bk.rev.; bibl.; circ. 500. (back issues avail.)
    Description: Information for ministers and church members; current theological issues.

TRINITY REVIEW. see *PHILOSOPHY*

284   GW   ISSN 0930-732X
TUTZINGER BLAETTER. 1975. q. free. Evangelische Akademie Tutzing, Schlossstr. 2-4, Postfach 227, 8132 Tutzing, Germany. TEL 08158-251-112. FAX 08158-251-133. Ed. Klaus Honigschnabel. circ. 8,500.

285   UK
TYST. (Text in Welsh) 1867. w. £10.40. Union of Welsh Independents, 11 St. Helen's Rd., Swansea, Wales. Ed. Rev. Gwyndaf Jones. adv.; bk.rev.; circ. 3,000.

U U M N NOTES. (Unitarian Universalist Musician's Network) see *MUSIC*

U U W F FEDERATION NEWSLETTER. (Unitarian Universalist Women's Federation) see *WOMEN'S INTERESTS*

U U W F JOURNAL. see *WOMEN'S INTERESTS*

284   NE   ISSN 0041-5944
UITZICHT. 1964. m. free. (Reformed Presbyterian Fellowship in the Great Congregation (Ps.40,10)) Evangelisatie-Boekhandel en Uitgeverij Horizont, Box 77, 7900 AB Hoogeveen (Dr.), Netherlands. Ed. Rev. G. Taverne. bk.rev.; charts; circ. 400.

284.2   SA   ISSN 0378-4134
UMTHOMBO WAMANDLA. (Text in Xhosa) 1972. bi-m. R.2. Reformed Churches in South Africa - Gereformeerde Kerke in Suid-Afrika, P.O. Box 400, Hammanskraal, South Africa. Ed. W.D. Graham. circ. 860.

288   UK   ISSN 0049-531X
UNITARIAN. 1905. m. £1.44. Manchester and District Association of Unitarian & Free Christian Churches Inc., c/o Keith M. Noble, Elbon House, 69 Downs Drive, Tinperley, Altrincham, Cheshire, England. Ed. Rev. John Rowland. adv.; bk.rev.; circ. 4,000.

267   UK
UNITARIAN AND FREE CHRISTIAN CHURCHES. HANDBOOK AND DIRECTORY OF THE GENERAL ASSEMBLY. 1890. a (directory); quinquennial (handbook). £5 each for Handbook or Directory. General Assembly of Unitarian Free Christian Churches, Essex Hall, 1-6 Essex St., Strand, London, WC2R 3HY, England. Ed. Matthew Smith. circ. 850.
    Formerly: Unitarian and Free Christian Churches. Yearbook of the General Assembly (ISSN 0082-7797)

288   UK   ISSN 0082-7800
BX9803
UNITARIAN HISTORICAL SOCIETY, LONDON. TRANSACTIONS. 1917. a. £5 to institutions. Unitarian Historical Society, c/o Hon. Treasurer, 58 Stoneygate Court, London Rd., Leicester LE2 2AJ, England. Ed. Alan Ruston. adv.; bk.rev.; cum.index every 4 yrs.; circ. 325. **Indexed:** Br.Hum.Ind., Hist.Abstr.
    —BLDSC shelfmark: 9012.540000.
    Description: Publishes articles, notes, original documents and reveiws on the history of Unitarianism and its historical constituency (English Presbyterianism and General Baptists).

285   US   ISSN 0362-0492
BX9801
UNITARIAN UNIVERSALIST CHRISTIAN. 1944. q. $30 (foreign $35). Unitarian Universalist Christian Fellowship, 110 Arlington St., Boston, MA 02116. TEL 617-482-2957. (Subscr. to: Box 66, Lancaster, MA 01523) Ed. Rev. Thomas D. Wintle. bk.rev.; cum.index; circ. 1,100. (also avail. in microfilm; microfiche; back issues avail.) **Indexed:** Rel.& Theol.Abstr. (1988-), Rel.Ind.One.
    —BLDSC shelfmark: 9090.790990.
    Description: Theological and liturgical articles for liberal Protestant clergy and laity.

266   US   ISSN 0082-7827
UNITARIAN UNIVERSALIST DIRECTORY. 1961. a. $16.95. Unitarian Universalist Association, Publications Department, 25 Beacon St., Boston, MA 02108. TEL 617-742-2100. adv.; circ. 2,500. (also avail. in microform from UMI)

288 900   US
UNITARIAN UNIVERSALIST HISTORICAL SOCIETY. PROCEEDINGS. 1925. a. or biennal; latest vol.21, 1989. $10 per part (2 parts per vol.). Unitarian Universalist Historical Society, c/o Conrad Wright, Harvard Divinity School, Andover Hall, Cambridge, MA 02138. TEL 617-495-9766. Ed. Richard Myers. bk.rev.; circ. 400.
    Formerly: Unitarian Historical Society. Proceedings (ISSN 0082-7819)
    Description: Scholarly articles on American, British, and Continental Unitarianism and Universalism.

286   CN   ISSN 0082-7843
UNITED BAPTIST CONVENTION OF THE ATLANTIC PROVINCES. YEARBOOK. 1963. a. price varies. United Baptist Convention of the Atlantic Provinces, 1655 Manawagonish Rd., Saint John, N.B. E2M 3Y2, Canada. TEL 506-635-1922. FAX 506-635-0366. Ed. Eugene M. Thompson. index; circ. 2,200.

268
UNITED BRETHREN. 1885. m. $13. United Brethren in Christ Church, Department of Church Services, 302 Lake St., Huntington, IN 46750. TEL 219-356-2312. Ed. Steve Dennie. circ. 5,000.

286   US   ISSN 0082-7214
UNITED CHURCH NEWS. 1985. m. (except Jan. & Aug.). $8. United Church of Christ, Office of Communication, 700 Prospect Ave., Cleveland, OH 44115-1100. TEL 216-736-2218. FAX 216-736-2223. Ed. Rev. W. Evan Golder. adv.; illus.; circ. 140,000. (tabloid format; back issues avail.)
    Description: News and features of the people, churches and agencies of The United Church of Christ.

287.92   CN   ISSN 0041-7238
BX9881.A1
UNITED CHURCH OBSERVER. 1925. m. Can.$17. United Church of Canada, 85 St. Clair Ave. E., Toronto, Ont. M4T 1M8, Canada. TEL 416-960-8500. FAX 416-960-8477. Ed. Muriel Duncan. adv.; bk.rev.; film rev.; circ. 215,000. (also avail. in microfilm from UMI) **Indexed:** Can.Per.Ind., CMI.

200   CN   ISSN 0082-7878
UNITED CHURCH OF CANADA. GENERAL COUNCIL. RECORD OF PROCEEDINGS. 1925. biennial. Can.$29.95. United Church of Canada, 85 St. Clair Ave. E., Toronto, Ont. M4T 1M8, Canada. TEL 416-925-5931. FAX 416-925-9692. circ. 4,000.
    —BLDSC shelfmark: 7326.069000.

200   CN
UNITED CHURCH OF CANADA. YEAR BOOK AND DIRECTORY. 1925. a. Can.$29.95. United Church of Canada, 85 St. Clair Ave. E., Toronto, Ont. M4T 1M8, Canada. TEL 416-925-5931. FAX 416-925-9692. circ. 4,000.
    Formerly: United Church of Canada. Year Book (ISSN 0082-7886)

200   US   ISSN 0041-7270
UNITED EVANGELICAL ACTION. 1942. bi-m. $15. National Association of Evangelicals, Box 28, Wheaton, IL 60189. TEL 708-665-0500. FAX 708-665-8575. Ed. Donald R. Brown. adv.; bk.rev.; illus.; circ. 11,000. (also avail. in microform) **Indexed:** Chr.Per.Ind., G.Soc.Sci.& Rel.Per.Lit.

285.241   UK   ISSN 0082-7908
BX9089
UNITED FREE CHURCH OF SCOTLAND. HANDBOOK. 1930. biennial. £3. United Free Church of Scotland, 11 Newton Place, Glasgow G3 7PR, Scotland. TEL 041-332-3435. Ed. E.S. Nicoll. bk.rev.; circ. 600.

284   US   ISSN 0041-7300
UNITED LUTHERAN. (Text mainly in English; occasionally in Slovak) 1894. bi-m. free. United Lutheran Society, Ross Mt. Park Rd., Box 947, Ligonier, PA 15658. TEL 412-238-9505. FAX 412-238-9506. Ed. Paul M. Payerchin, Jr. adv.; bk.rev.; circ. 5,000. (tabloid format; also avail. in microform)

287   US   ISSN 8750-7668
UNITED METHODIST CHRISTIAN ADVOCATE. 1881. s-w. $10. Advocate of the United Methodist North Alabama, Joint Board of Communication, 898 Arkadelphia Rd., Birmingham, AL 35204. TEL 205-251-9279. FAX 205-328-5228. (Co-sponsor: Alabama-West Florida Conferences) Ed. James H. Steele. adv.

287   US   ISSN 0503-3551
BX8382.2.A1
UNITED METHODIST CHURCH. GENERAL MINUTES OF THE ANNUAL CONFERENCES. 1968. a. $15.85 paperbound; cloth $21.60. United Methodist Church, General Council on Finance and Administration, 1200 Davis St., Evanston, IL 60201. TEL 708-869-3345. Ed. Daniel A. Nielsen. illus.; circ. 2,500. Key Title: General Minutes of the Annual Conferences of the United Methodist Church.
    Description: Directory of the Churches and personnel of the United Methodist Church.

287   US
UNITED METHODIST REPORTER. (Text in English and Spanish) 1847. w. $18 (typically set in Jan.). United Methodist Communications Council, Box 660275, Dallas, TX 75266. TEL 214-630-6495. FAX 214-630-0079. Ed. Spurgeon M. Dunnam, 3rd. adv.; bk.rev.; charts; illus.; circ. 450,000. (newspaper; also avail. in microfilm)
    Former titles: Texas Methodist - United Methodist Reporter; Texas Methodist (ISSN 0040-4489)

285   US   ISSN 0082-8548
UNITED PRESBYTERIAN CHURCH IN THE UNITED STATES OF AMERICA. MINUTES OF THE GENERAL ASSEMBLY. a. $4. Presbyterian Church (U.S.A.), 100 Witherspoon St., Louisville, KY 40202-1396. TEL 502-569-5810. circ. 16,000.

285   UK   ISSN 0049-5433
BX9890.U25
UNITED REFORMED CHURCH HISTORY SOCIETY. JOURNAL. 1973. s-a. £12. United Reformed Church History Society, Church House, 86 Tavistock Pl., London WC1H 9RT, England. Ed. Clyde Binfield. bk.rev.; index; circ. 500. (also avail. in microform from UMI; reprint service avail. from KTO) **Indexed:** Amer.Hist.& Life, Br.Hum.Ind., CERDIC, Hist.Abstr.
    —BLDSC shelfmark: 4910.640000.
    Former titles: Congregational Historical Society. Transactions; Presbyterian Historical Society. Journal.

285   UK
UNITED REFORMED CHURCH IN THE UNITED KINGDOM. UNITED REFORMED CHURCH YEAR BOOK. 1973. a. £7.50. United Reformed Church in the United Kingdom, 86 Tavistock Pl., London WC1H 9RT, England. adv.; circ. 2,000.
    Formerly: Congregational Church in England and Wales. Congregational Year book (ISSN 0069-8849)

RELIGIONS AND THEOLOGY — PROTESTANT

285　　　　　UK
UNITED REFORMED CHURCH POCKET DIARY. a. £2.75. United Reformed Church in the United Kingdom, 86 Tavistock Pl., London WC1H 9RT, England.

285　　　　　UK
UNITED REFORMED CHURCH, YORKSHIRE PROVINCE, PROVINCIAL HANDBOOK. 1973. a. £1.20. United Reformed Church (Yorkshire Province), 43 Hunslet Ln., Leeds LS10 1JW, England. Ed. Colin Mundy. adv.; circ. 450.
　Description: Names and addresses of churches' officers and committees.

283　　　　　UK　　ISSN 0958-2789
▼**UNITED SOCIETY FOR THE PROPAGATION OF THE GOSPEL. ISSUES.** 1990. q. £4. United Society for the Propagation of the Gospel, Partnership House, 157 Waterloo Rd., London SE1 8XA, England. TEL 071-928-8681. FAX 071-928-2371.
　Description: Focuses on major issues of justice, peace and mission.

283　　　　　UK　　ISSN 0958-2770
▼**UNITED SOCIETY FOR THE PROPAGATION OF THE GOSPEL. NEWSBRIEF.** 1990. q. £4. United Society for the Propagation of the Gospel, Partnership House, 157 Waterloo Rd., London SE1 8XA, England. TEL 071-928-8681. FAX 071-928-2371.

242　　　　　US　　ISSN 0042-0735
BV4800
UPPER ROOM; daily devotional guide, interdenominational, international. Spanish edition: El Aposento Alto (ISSN 0003-6552) (Editions in 41 languages) 1935. bi-m. $4.50 for inkprint; large print $6.50; cassette $35; Braille ed. free; Chinese-English ed. $12; German ed. $10; Korean-English ed. $12.50; Spanish ed. $4.50; Thai ed. $10; other language eds. $8.50. (United Methodist Church, General Board of Discipleship) Upper Room, 1908 Grand Ave., Box 189, Nashville, TN 37202. TEL 615-340-7250. FAX 615-340-7006. Ed. Mary Lou Redding. circ. 2,250,000. (also avail. in Braille; audio cassette; large print edition in 18 pt.)

266 284　　　　　NO
UT I ALL VERDEN. q. Norsk Luthersk Misjonssamband, Grensen 19, Oslo 1, Norway. adv.

UW KONINKRIJK KOME: ZENDINGSBLAD. see *RELIGIONS AND THEOLOGY*

284　　　　　GW
V E L K D - INFORMATION. 1969. q. Vereinigte Evangelisch-Lutherische Kirche Deutschlands, Lutherisches Kirchenamt, Postfach 510409, 3000 Hannover 51, Germany. TEL 0511-6261226. FAX 0511-6261211. TELEX 922673-VELKD-D. Ed. Juergen Jeziorowski. bk.rev.; circ. 4,500.

284.2　　　　　NE
VANDAAR. 1902. 10/yr. fl.9. Gereformeerde Kerken in Nederland, Centrum voor Zending en Werelddiakonaat - Mission and World Service of the Reformed Churches in the Netherlands, P.O. Box 200, 3830 AE Leusden, Netherlands. TEL 033-960-360. FAX 033-948-707. TELEX 79494 GKN NL. Ed.Bd. bk.rev.; illus.; index; circ. 175,000.
　Formerly (until 1975): Zending (ISSN 0044-3972)
　Description: Information on mission, world service and development cooperation.

284　　　　　US　　ISSN 0042-2568
BT734
VANGUARD (MILWAUKEE). 1954. 6/yr. membership. Lutheran Human Relations Association, 2703 N. Sherman Blvd., Milwaukee, WI 53210. TEL 414-871-7300. Ed. Joyce Caldwell. bk.rev.; illus.; circ. 10,000. (also avail. in microform from UMI; reprint service avail. from UMI)
　Description: Focuses on issues of justice.

268　　　　　US　　ISSN 0042-3459
VENTANA; missionary magazine for women. (Text in Spanish) 1931. q. $6. Casa Bautista de Publicaciones, Box 4255, El Paso, TX 79914. TEL 915-566-9656. Ed. Alicia Zorzoli. adv.; illus.; circ. 13,000.

286　　　　　AT　　ISSN 0726-4097
VICTORIAN BAPTIST WITNESS. 1921. m. Aus.$6. Baptist Union of Victoria, 227 Burwood Rd., Hawthorn, Vic. 3122, Australia. FAX 03-818-1041. Ed. Geoff Holland. adv.; bk.rev.; circ. 9,000.
　Formerly: Baptist Witness (ISSN 0005-5794)
　Description: Includes news and features of interest to Baptist Church members.

286　　　　　US　　ISSN 0083-6311
BX6248.V8
VIRGINIA BAPTIST REGISTER. 1962. a. $4.50 to non-members. Virginia Baptist Historical Society, Box 34, Univ. of Richmond, VA 23173. TEL 804-289-8437. Ed. John S. Moore. bk.rev.; cum.index every 5 yrs.; circ. 750. (also avail. in microfilm)
　Description: Covers early Virginia Baptist history.

200　　　　　US
VIRGINIA EPISCOPALIAN. 1922. m. (except Aug.). $5. Episcopal Diocese of Virginia, 110 W. Franklin, Richmond, VA 23220. TEL 804-643-8451. FAX 804-644-6928. Ed. Sarah Bartenstein. adv.; bk.rev.; circ. 28,000. (tabloid format)
　Formerly (until 1986): Virginia Churchman.

287　　　　　US
VIRGINIA UNITED METHODIST ADVOCATE. 1832. bi-w. $8. (United Methodist Church, Virginia Conference) Virginia United Methodist Communications, Inc., Box 11367, Richmond, VA 23230. TEL 804-359-9451. Ed. Alvin J. Horton. adv.; bk.rev.; circ. 18,000.
　Former titles: Virginia Advocate (ISSN 0042-6458); Virginia Methodist Advocate.

284 384.5　　　　　NE
VISIE. 1970. w. fl.56 (effective Jan. 1991). Evangelische Omroep, Postbus 565, 1200 AN Hilversum, Netherlands. Ed. H. Kamsteeg. adv.; bk.rev.; circ. 127,500.

284　　　　　AT
VISION. 1950. q. Aus.$10. Australian Baptist Missionary Society, 597 Burwood Rd., Hawthorn, Vic. 3122, Australia. FAX 03-819-1004. Ed. Grace Munro. bk.rev.; index; circ. 9,000. (back issues avail.)

284　　　　　GW　　ISSN 0933-6117
DIE VOELKER RUFEN. m. DM.6. Liebenzell Mission, Postfach 1240, 7263 Bad Liebenzell, Germany. TEL 07052-17109. Ed. Ernst Vatter. circ. 20,500.

282　　　　　US　　ISSN 0277-2272
VOICE (NEWARK). 1878. m. (except Jul. & Aug.). contributions. Episcopal Diocese of Newark, Cathedral House, 24 Rector St., Newark, NJ 07102. TEL 201-622-4306. Ed. Karen K. Lindley. bk.rev.; charts; illus.; stat.; cum.index; circ. 21,000. (newspaper)
　Formerly: Newark Churchman (ISSN 0028-8853)

287　　　　　UK　　ISSN 0042-8167
VOICE OF METHODISM. 1964. 3/yr. $1 to non-members. Voice of Methodism Association, 23 Manor House Court, Kirkby in Ashfield, Nottingham NG17 8LH, England. Ed. Oliver A. Beckerlegge. adv.; bk.rev.; circ. 6,000. Indexed: CERDIC.

266　　　　　US　　ISSN 0042-8175
VOICE OF MISSIONS.* 1898. m. (Sep.-Jun.). $6.50. (African Methodist Episcopal Church (New York)) National Religious Press, Box 2410, Grand Rapids, MI 49501-2410. Ed. Rev. John W.P. Collier, Jr. bk.rev.; illus.; circ. 3,900.

284　　　　　US
VOICE OF PROPHECY NEWS. 1942. q. free to qualified personnel. Voice of Prophecy, Inc., Box 2525, Newbury Park, CA 91319. TEL 805-373-7657. FAX 805-373-7701. TELEX 65-9245. Ed. Eldyn Karr. bk.rev.; circ. 42,000. (back issues avail.)

285.834　　　　　US
VOLUNTEERS; summer service opportunities in the United Church of Christ. 1970. a. free. United Church of Christ, Board for Homeland Ministries, Voluntary Service Office, 700 Prospect Ave., Cleveland, OH 44115. TEL 216-736-3266. FAX 216-736-3263. Ed. Susan M. Saunders. circ. 8,000. (controlled).

284.2　　　　　SA　　ISSN 0042-8728
DIE VOORLIGTER. (Text in Afrikaans) 1937. m. R.18.13. Tydskriftemaatskappy van die Nederduitse Gereformeerde Kerk, Box 2406, Pretoria 0001, South Africa. TEL 012-322-2881. FAX 012-322-3803. Ed. F.M. Gaum. adv.; bk.rev.; illus.; circ. 155,000. Indexed: CERDIC.

284　　　　　AT　　ISSN 0728-0912
VOX REFORMATA; Australasian journal for Christian scholarship. 1962. a. $7. Reformed Theological College, Association for Christian Tertiary Education, 55 Maud St., Geelong, Vic. 3220, Australia. TEL 052-222155. FAX 052-221263. Ed. W. Berends. adv.; bk.rev.; index; circ. 275. (also avail. in microfiche; back issues avail.) Indexed: CERDIC.
　—BLDSC shelfmark: 9258.570000.

283　　　　　UK　　ISSN 0043-0226
WAR CRY. 1879. w. £18.25. Salvation Army, International Headquarters, 101 Queen Victoria St., London EC4P 4EP, England. TEL 071-236-5222. FAX 071-236-3491. Ed. Trevor Howes. bk.rev.; illus.; circ. 110,000.

WAS UNS BETRIFFT; Zeitschrift fuer Kriegsdienstverweigerer und Zivildienstleistende. see *POLITICAL SCIENCE — Civil Rights*

283　　　　　US　　ISSN 0043-0544
WASHINGTON DIOCESE. 1933. m. (Sep.-Jun.). $5 to non-members; members $3. Episcopal Diocese of Washington, Episcopal Church House, Mount Saint Alban, N.W., Washington, DC 20016. TEL 202-537-6560. FAX 202-364-6605. Ed. Frances Antonucci. adv.; bk.rev.; charts; illus.; stat.; circ. 21,500. (tabloid format; also avail. in microfilm) Indexed: CERDIC.

285　　　　　US
WASHINGTON MEMO. bi-m. donation. Mennonite Central Committee, 21 S. 12th St., Box 500, Akron, PA 17501-0500. TEL 717-859-1151. FAX 717-859-2171. TELEX 90-2210 MENCENCOM AKRP. Ed. Delton Franz.
　Description: Deals with U.S. public policy issues. Includes issues of peacemaking and justice in domestic and international affairs.

284　　　　　UK
WATCHING AND WAITING. 1918. q. £2.75. Sovereign Grace Advent Testimony, 1 Donald Way, Chelmsford, Essex CM2 9JB, England. TEL 0245-268815. Ed. Stephen A. Toms. bk.rev.

284　　　　　UK
WAYMARK. 1967. 10/yr. £10. St. Mark's Unitarian Church, Castle Terrace, Edinburgh EH1 2DP, Scotland. TEL 031-667-4360. Ed. A.M. Hill. bk.rev.; circ. 500. (tabloid format; back issues avail.)

266　　　　　GW　　ISSN 0723-6204
DIE WELTMISSION; das Wort in der Welt. 1915. bi-m. DM.15. (Evangelisches Missionswerk) Missionshilfe Verlag, Mittelweg 143, 2000 Hamburg 13, Germany. Ed.Bd. bk.rev.; illus.; index; circ. 20,000.
　Former titles: Wort in der Welt (ISSN 0341-082X); Allgemeine Missionsnachrichten (ISSN 0002-5909)

287　　　　　UK
WESLEY HISTORICAL SOCIETY. LANCASHIRE AND CHESHIRE BRANCH. JOURNAL. 1964. 2/yr. Wesley Historical Society, Lancashire and Cheshire Branch, 26 Roe Cross Green, Mottram, Hyde, Cheshire SK14 6LP, England. TEL 63485.

287 270　　　　　UK　　ISSN 0043-2873
WESLEY HISTORICAL SOCIETY. PROCEEDINGS. 1897. 3/yr. £5($10) to members. Wesley Historical Society, 87 Marshall Ave., Bognor Regis, W. Sussex PO21 2TW, England. Ed. E.A. Rose. adv.; bk.rev.; charts; illus.; index, cum.index: vols.1-30 (1897-1958); circ. 1,100. Indexed: Br.Hum.Ind., CERDIC, Hist.Abstr.
　—BLDSC shelfmark: 6832.400000.

287.1　　　　　US　　ISSN 0043-289X
WESLEYAN ADVOCATE. 1842. m. $12.50. (Wesleyan Church) Wesley Press, Box 50434, Indianapolis, IN 46250-0434. TEL 317-576-1313. Ed. Wayne Caldwell. bk.rev.; circ. 21,000. Indexed: G.Soc.Sci.& Rel.Per.Lit.
　Formed by the merger of: Wesleyan Methodist (ISSN 0190-6100); Pilgrim Holiness Advocate.
　Description: Denominational magazine.

RELIGIONS AND THEOLOGY — PROTESTANT

200 US
WESLEYAN CHRISTIAN ADVOCATE. 1836. w. $14. (United Methodist Church, North and South Georgia Conferences) Wesleyan Christian Advocate, Inc., 159 Ralph McGill Blvd., Atlanta, GA 30365. TEL 404-659-0002. FAX 404-659-1727. Ed. G. Ross Freeman. adv.; bk.rev.; circ. 31,500.

287.1 US ISSN 0092-4245
BR1
WESLEYAN THEOLOGICAL JOURNAL.* 1966. s-a. $5. Wesleyan Theological Society, c/o William M. Arnett, Nazarene Theological Seminary, 1700 E. Meyer Blvd., Kansas City, MO 64131. Ed. Paul Bassett. adv.; bk.rev.; circ. 1,200. (also avail. in microform from UMI; reprint service avail. from UMI) Indexed: CERDIC, Chr.Per.Ind., Rel.& Theol.Abstr. (1983-), Rel.Ind.One.
—BLDSC shelfmark: 9298.673700.

286 US ISSN 0043-4132
WESTERN RECORDER. 1826. w. $9.54 to individuals; churches $7.50. (Kentucky Baptist Convention) Western Recorder, Inc., 10701 Shelbyville Rd., Box 43969, Middletown, KY 40253. TEL 502-244-6470. FAX 502-244-1688. Ed. Marv Knox. adv.; circ. 53,000. (tabloid format; also avail. in microform)

280 US ISSN 0197-8896
BX5800
WITNESS (DETROIT). 1974. m. $20 (foreign $25). 1249 Washington Blvd., Ste. 3115, Detroit, MI 48226-1868. TEL 313-962-2650. FAX 313-961-9005. Ed. Jeanie Wylie-Kellerman. bk.rev.; illus.; circ. 6,000. (also avail. in microfiche; microfilm) Indexed: CERDIC, Rel.Ind.One.
   Description: Concerned with peace and justice issues, and the social mission of the church and the Gospel message.

WONDER TIME. see *CHILDREN AND YOUTH — For*

286 US ISSN 0049-7959
WORD AND WAY. 1895. w. $7.50 to individuals; institutions $5. Missouri Baptist Convention, 400 E. High St., Jefferson City, MO 65101. TEL 314-635-7931. FAX 314-659-7436. Ed. Bobby S. Terry. adv.; bk.rev.; illus.; circ. 67,000. (tabloid format)
   Description: News of Missouri Baptist and Southern Baptist churches.

284 US
WORD & WITNESS. 1976. 6/yr. $43. Liturgical Publications Inc., 2875 South James Dr., New Berlin, WI 53151. TEL 414-785-1188. FAX 414-785-9567. Ed. Rev. Paul Wilson. bk.rev.; index. (looseleaf format)

284 US ISSN 0275-5270
BR1
WORD & WORLD; theology for Christian ministry. 1981. q. $18 to individuals; students and senior citizens $12. Luther Northwestern Seminary, 2481 Como Ave. West, St. Paul, MN 55108. TEL 612-641-3482. Ed. Frederick J. Gaiser. adv.; bk.rev.; index; circ. 4,000. (back issues avail.) Indexed: New Test.Abstr., Old Test.Abstr., Rel.& Theol.Abstr. (1981-), Rel.Ind.One.
—BLDSC shelfmark: 9347.841200.
   Description: Journal for pastors and scholars who seek to relate the work of theology to the ministry of the Christian church.

266 UK
WORD AT WORK. 2/yr. free. National Bible Society of Scotland, 7 Hampton Terrace, Edinburgh EH12 5XU, Scotland. FAX 031-337-0641. Ed. Colin S. Hay.

288 US
WORLD (BOSTON). 1970. 6/yr. $18. Unitarian Universalist Association, 25 Beacon St., Boston, MA 02108. TEL 617-742-2100. Ed. Linda Beyer. adv.; bk.rev.; charts; illus.; circ. 107,000.
   Formerly: Unitarian Universalist World (ISSN 0041-7122)

287 US
WORLD METHODIST HISTORICAL SOCIETY. HISTORICAL BULLETIN. 1961. q. $5. World Methodist Historical Society, Box 127, Madison, NJ 07940. FAX 201-408-3909. bk.rev.; illus.; circ. 200. (back issues avail.)
   Formerly: World Methodist Historical Society. News Bulletin.

286 UK
WORLD OUTLOOK. 1918. q. £2. Baptist Men's Movement, Kingsley, Pontesbury, Shrewsbury, Shrops. SY5 0QH, England. TEL 0743-790377. Ed. Michael Putnam. adv.; bk.rev.; circ. 1,200 (controlled). (back issues avail.)

287 US ISSN 0043-8839
BX8201
WORLD PARISH. 1948. bi-m. free. World Methodist Council, Box 518, Lake Junaluska, NC 28745. TEL 704-456-9432. FAX 704-456-9433. Ed. Joe Hale. bk.rev.; charts; illus.; circ. 18,300.

284 CN ISSN 0713-3391
WORLDVIEW. 1981. a. Can.$1.50. United Church of Canada, 85 St. Clair Ave. E., Toronto, Ont. M4T 1M8, Canada. TEL 416-925-5931. FAX 416-925-3394. Ed. Rebekah Chevalier. circ. 5,000. (back issues avail.)
   Description: For youth aged 11-15, focus is on mission, from the United Church perspective. Each issue focuses on a particular theme.

284 US
WORLDWIDE NEWS. 1917. 5/yr. free. Pocket Testament League, 11 Toll Gate Rd., Box 800, Lititz, PA 17543-7026. TEL 717-636-1919. FAX 717-626-5553. Ed. Martha L. Kitchen. circ. 15,000.
   Description: Information on the Pocket Testament League outreach, particularly scripture distribution and evangelism worldwide.

250 UK ISSN 0032-7107
WORSHIP AND PREACHING. 1970. bi-m. £8. Methodist Publishing House, 20 Ivatt Way, Peterborough PE3 7PG, England. TEL 0733-332202. FAX 0733-331201. Ed. Rev. John Lampard. adv.; bk.rev.; index; circ. 5,000.
   Supersedes: Preacher's Quarterly.

287 GW ISSN 0043-9444
WORT UND WEG; Sonntagsblatt der Evangelisch-Methodistischen Kirche. 1968. w. DM.75.20. (Evangelisch-methodistische Kirche) Christliches Verlagshaus GmbH, Motorstr. 36, 7000 Stuttgart 31, Germany. FAX 0711-8300084. Ed. Walter Bolay. adv.; bk.rev.; bibl.; illus.; stat.; circ. 15,000.
   Formed by the 1968 merger of: Evangelischer Botschaft & Evangelist.

284 028.5 AT
Y F C NEWSRELEASE. 1975. m. free. Geelong Youth for Christ, 58 McKillop St., Geelong, Vic. 3220, Australia. TEL 052-2144769. FAX 052-779614. Ed. Richard Brohier. circ. 800. (looseleaf format; back issues avail.)

200 US ISSN 0044-0388
YEVANHELSKYJ RANOK/EVANGELICAL MORNING. (Includes an English section: Ukrainian Christian Herald, Protestant monthly) 1905. q. $5. Ukrainian Evangelical Alliance of North America, 5610 Trowbridge Dr., Dunwoody, GA 30338. TEL 404-394-7795. Ed. Rev. W. Borowsky. adv.; bk.rev.; illus.; circ. 500. (reprint service avail. from UMI, ISI)

268 US ISSN 0162-4814
YOUNG ADULT BIBLE STUDY. 1970. q. $4.75. Southern Baptist Convention, Sunday School Board, 127 Ninth Ave, N., Nashville, TN 37234. TEL 800-458-2772.

YOUNG SOLDIER. see *CHILDREN AND YOUTH — For*

286 US ISSN 0196-0938
YOUTH ALIVE. q. $5.50. Southern Baptist Convention, Sunday School Board, 127 Ninth Ave., N., Nashville, TN 37234. TEL 800-458-2772.

286 US ISSN 0196-0946
THE YOUTH DISCIPLE. q. $5.50. Southern Baptist Convention, Sunday School Board, 127 Ninth Ave., N., Nashville, TN 37234. TEL 800-458-2772.

268 US ISSN 0162-4784
YOUTH IN ACTION. q. $5.50. Southern Baptist Convention, Sunday School Board, 127 Ninth Ave., N., Nashville, TN 37234. TEL 800-458-2772.

268 US ISSN 0162-4792
YOUTH IN ACTION TEACHER. q. $9.50. Southern Baptist Convention, Sunday School Board, 127 Ninth Ave., N., Nashville, TN 37234. TEL 800-458-2772.

268 US ISSN 0162-4776
YOUTH IN DISCOVERY. q. $5.50. Southern Baptist Convention, Sunday School Board, 127 Ninth Ave., N., Nashville, TN 37234. TEL 800-458-2772.

268 US ISSN 0162-4768
YOUTH IN DISCOVERY TEACHER. q. $9.50. Southern Baptist Convention, Sunday School Board, 127 Ninth Ave., N., Nashville, TN 37234. TEL 800-458-2772.

268 US ISSN 0162-4709
YOUTH LEADERSHIP. q. $8.50. Southern Baptist Convention, Sunday School Board, 127 Ninth Ave., N., Nashville, TN 37234. TEL 800-458-2772.
   Indexed: South.Bap.Per.Ind.

YOUTH MINISTRY QUARTERLY (ST. LOUIS). see *CHILDREN AND YOUTH — For*

284 GW
ZEICHEN. 1972. q. DM.10. Aktion Suehnezeichen, Jebensstr. 1, 1000 Berlin 12, Germany. TEL 030-310261. bk.rev.; circ. 12,000. (back issues avail.)

282 GW ISSN 0044-2038
BR4
ZEICHEN DER ZEIT; Evangelische Monatsschrift fuer Mitarbeiter der Kirche. 1947. m. DM.28 (foreign DM.32). Evangelische Verlagsanstalt GmbH, Burgstr. 1-5, 7010 Leipzig, Germany. TEL 295709. FAX 295383. Ed. Martin Uhle-Wettler. adv.; bk.rev.; index; circ. 7,000. Indexed: CERDIC.
   Description: Contains articles, essays, commentaries, sermons's Exegesis and news.

284 GW ISSN 0342-4316
ZEITSCHRIFT FUER BAYERISCHE KIRCHENGESCHICHTE. 1926. a. DM.27. Verein fuer Bayerische Kirchengeschichte, Veilhofstr. 28, 8500 Nuernburg 20, Germany. Ed. Horst Weigelt. bk.rev.; circ. 800.

262.9 284 GW ISSN 0044-2690
LAW
ZEITSCHRIFT FUER EVANGELISCHES KIRCHENRECHT. 1951. q. DM.132. Verlag J.C.B. Mohr (Paul Siebeck), Wilhelmstr. 18, Postfach 2040, 7400 Tuebingen, Germany. TEL 07071-26064. FAX 07071-51104. TELEX 7262872-MOHR-D. Ed.Bd. adv.; bk.rev.; index. Indexed: CERDIC.
—BLDSC shelfmark: 9459.250000.
   Description: Examines the problems of Protestant ecclesiastical law and the relation between church and state in Germany.

284 GW ISSN 0513-9147
BR4
ZEITSCHRIFT FUER THEOLOGIE UND KIRCHE. 1891. q. DM.74 to individuals; students DM.52. Verlag J.C.B. Mohr (Paul Siebeck), Wilhelmstr. 18, Postfach 2040, 7400 Tuebingen, Germany. TEL 07071-26064. FAX 07071-51104. TELEX 7262872-MOHR-D. Ed. Eberhard Juengel. adv.; index. Indexed: Arts & Hum.Cit.Ind., CERDIC, Curr.Cont., Old Test.Abstr., Rel.& Theol.Abstr. (1975-), Rel.Ind.One, Rel.Per.
   Description: Studies all areas of theological research and the teachings of the church.

284 GW
ZELTGRUSS. 1902. bi-m. Deutsche Zeltmission e.V., Sohlbacherstr. 171, Postfach 223180, 5900 Siegen, Germany. TEL 0271-83049. FAX 0271-83040. Ed. Michael Hoehn. bk.rev.; bibl.; illus.; circ. 23,000. (back issues avail.)

284 GW ISSN 0936-7136
ZUM WEITERGEBEN. 1947. q. DM.26. Evangelischen Frauenhilfe in Deutschland e.V., Alte Landstr. 179, Postfach 310206, 4000 Duesseldorf 31, Germany. TEL 0211-40648. FAX 0211-401268. Ed. Marielisa von Thadden. bk.rev.; circ. 6,500. (back issues avail.)

284 GW ISSN 0722-3234
ZUVERSICHT UND STAERKE. 1982. bi-m. DM.33.80. (Ludwig-Hofacker-Vereinigung) Haenssler Verlag, Bismarckstr. 4, Postfach 12 20, 7303 Neuhausen-Stuttgart, Germany. TEL 07158-177-149. FAX 07158-177119. Ed.Bd. circ. 300. (back issues avail.)

RELIGIONS AND THEOLOGY — Roman Catholic

200   FR   ISSN 0758-8240
A I M MONASTIC BULLETIN; aide inter-monasteres pour les jeunes eglises. English ed.: I M A Bulletin (Inter Monastic Aid). (Editions in English, Spanish) 1965. s-a. 80 F.($10) Aide Inter-Monasteres Secretariat, 7 rue d'Issy, 92170 Vanves, France.
TEL 46-64-60-05. (U.S. Center: Alliance for International Monasticism, c/o St. Scholastica Priory, 355 E. 9th St., Erie, PA 16503) Ed. Dom Marie-Bernard de Soos. bk.rev.; illus.; circ. 1,800.
Formerly: A I M Bulletin (ISSN 0007-4314)

282   BL   ISSN 0005-1934
A M.* (Ave Maria) 1898. s-m. Cr.$15($6) Editora Ave Maria Ltda, Rua Martins Francisco 646, Caixa Postal, 615, 01000 Sao Paulo, Brazil. adv.; bk.rev.; illus.; circ. 50,000 (controlled).

271   US   ISSN 0567-6630
ACADEMY OF AMERICAN FRANCISCAN HISTORY. BIBLIOGRAPHICAL SERIES. 1953. irreg., no.4, vol.1, 1978. price varies. Academy of American Franciscan History, 1712 Euclid Ave., Berkeley, CA 94709.
TEL 415-548-1755.

271   US   ISSN 0065-0633
ACADEMY OF AMERICAN FRANCISCAN HISTORY. DOCUMENTARY SERIES. 1951. irreg., vol.11, 1979. price varies. Academy of American Franciscan History, 1712 Euclid Ave., Berkeley, CA 94709.
TEL 415-548-1755.

271   US   ISSN 0065-0641
ACADEMY OF AMERICAN FRANCISCAN HISTORY. MONOGRAPH SERIES. 1953. irreg., vol.13, 1981. price varies. Academy of American Franciscan History, 1712 Euclid Ave., Berkeley, CA 94709.
TEL 415-548-1755.

271   US   ISSN 0065-065X
ACADEMY OF AMERICAN FRANCISCAN HISTORY. PROPAGANDA FIDE SERIES. 1966. irreg., vol.11, 1988. price varies. Academy of American Franciscan History, 1712 Euclid Ave., Berkeley, CA 94709.
TEL 415-548-1755. Eds. Mathias Kiemen, Alexander Wyse. index.

282   VC   ISSN 0001-5199
BX850
ACTA APOSTOLICAE SEDIS. COMMENTARIUM OFFICIALE. (Text in Latin and European languages) 1909. m. L.85000($105) (foreign L.130000)(effective 1992). (Secretariat of State) Libreria Editrice Vaticana, 00120 Vatican City (Rome), State of the Vatican City. index; circ. 6,000. **Indexed:** Cath.Ind., CERDIC.
Description: Contains official commentary of the Holy See with information on Papal activites.

ACTA MEDIAEVALIA. see HISTORY — History Of Europe

270   VC   ISSN 0065-1443
BX1528.A2
ACTA NUNTIATURAE GALLICAE. 1961. irreg. price varies. (Pontificia Istituto Biblico, Facolta di Storia Ecclesiastica) Gregorian University Press, Piazza della Pilotta, 35, 00187 Rome, Italy. (Co-sponsor: Ecole Francaise de Rome) Ed. Pierre Blet, S.J. circ. 1,000.
—BLDSC shelfmark: 0641.300000.

282   IT   ISSN 0001-6411
ACTA ORDINIS FRATRUM MINORUM. (Text in original languages) 1882. 3/yr. $12. Ordo Fratrum Minorum, Curia Generalis, Via S. Maria Mediatrice, 25, I-00165 Rome, Italy. TEL (06) 632241. Dir. Fr. Patrick McCloskey. index, cum.index; circ. controlled.
—BLDSC shelfmark: 0582.505000.

282   IT   ISSN 0001-642X
ACTA ORDINIS SANCTI AUGUSTINI; commentarium officiale. (Triennial supplement avail.) Commentarium Officiale - Fasciculus Specialis) (Text in Latin and various languages) 1956. a. L.25000 (supplement L.30000)(effective 1992). Order of Saint Augustine, Economato Generale, Via Paolo VI, 25, 00193 Rome, Italy. FAX 686-62-47. circ. 550. (back issues avail.)

282   VC
ACTA ROMANORUM PONTIFICUM. 1977. irreg. no.7-8, 1985. price varies. Biblioteca Apostolica Vaticana, 00120 Vatican City (Rome), State of the Vatican City.

ACTION INFORMATION; resources for people who care about congregations. see RELIGIONS AND THEOLOGY — Protestant

282   AG   ISSN 0587-4300
ACTUALIDAD PASTORAL; revista mensuel. (Includes special editions.) 1968. m. Arg.$500000($50) Abel Costa 261, C.C.140, 1708 Moron, Argentina. TEL 627-2806. FAX 541-814-2044. Ed. Vicente Oscar Vetrano. adv.; bk.rev.; charts; illus.; index; circ. 5,000. (looseleaf format)
—BLDSC shelfmark: 0677.070000.
Description: Covers Christianity around the world.

232   CN
ACTUALITE DIOCESAINE. 1970. m. Can.$7. Eglise Catholique, Diocese de Saint-Jean-Longueuil, c/o Suzie-Jacynthe Gravel, 740 bd. Ste-Foy, Longueuil, Que. J4K 4X8, Canada. TEL 514-679-1100. adv.; bk.rev.; circ. 8,000.
Formerly (until 1983): Rythme de Notre Eglise (ISSN 0383-0152)

282   FR   ISSN 0757-3529
ACTUALITE RELIGIEUSE DANS LE MONDE. 1953. m. (11/yr.). 330 F. (foreign 365 F.). Malesherbes Publications, 163 bd. Malesherbes, 75859 Paris Cedex 17, France. TEL 48-88-46-00.
FAX 47-64-04-53. TELEX 649 333 F. adv.; bk.rev.; film rev.; bibl.; illus.; index; circ. 30,000. (tabloid format) **Indexed:** Pt.de Rep. (1983-).
Former titles (until 1983): Informations Catholiques Internationales (ISSN 0020-0441); (until 1955): Actualite Religieuse dans le Monde (ISSN 0400-4620)

200   IT   ISSN 0001-8740
ADVENIAT. 1929. m. L.16000. Opera della Regalita' di N.S.G.C., Via L. Necchi 2, 20123 Milan, Italy. TEL 02-86453378. Ed.Bd. bk.rev.; circ. 15,000.

282   AT
THE ADVOCATE. 1868. w. 196-200 Lygon St., Carlton, Vic. 3053, Australia. TEL 03-662-1100.
FAX 03-662-1139. Ed. Peter Philp. circ. 18,000.

AFRICAN JOURNAL OF BIBLICAL STUDIES. see RELIGIONS AND THEOLOGY

282   IT
AGENDA. 1959. m. L.10000 (effective Oct. 1991). Azione Cattolica, Via del Monte 5, 40126 Bologna, Italy. FAX 51-239832. Ed. V. Prodi. circ. 3,000. (tabloid format)

282 255   IT   ISSN 0002-4066
AI NOSTRI AMICI. 1930. bi-m. L.1000. Gesuiti di Sicilia, Missioni Rettoria Casa Professa, 90134 Palermo, Italy. TEL 329-878. Ed. Carmelo Salv. Bentivegna, S.I. adv.; bk.rev.; bibl.; illus.; stat.; index; circ. 10,000.
Description: Features missionary articles written by Jesuits of Sicily.

282 267   GW   ISSN 0002-3000
AKADEMISCHE MONATSBLAETTER. 1887. m. DM.46. Kartellverband Katholischer Deutscher Studentenvereine, Postfach 1505, 4720 Beckum, Germany. bk.rev.; index; circ. 20,000. (tabloid format)

282   CN   ISSN 0316-473X
ALBERTA CATHOLIC DIRECTORY. 1920. a. Can.$12. Western Catholic Reporter, 8421 - 101 Ave., Edmonton, Alta. T6A 0L1, Canada. Ed. Glen Argan. adv.; circ. 1,500.
Description: Lists missions operating in the province.

282   US
ALIVE AND WELL SAINT PATRICK'S CATHEDRAL. vol.56, 1976. m. $6. (St. Patrick's Parish House) Cathedral Publications (New York), 14 E. 51st St., New York, NY 10022. TEL 212-753-2261. Ed. Michael Hoffman. adv.; bk.rev.; illus.; circ. 5,000.
Former titles: Alive and Well and Living in New York City Saint Patrick's Cathedral; St. Patrick's Cathedral Bulletin.

ALLGEMEINER CAECILIEN-VERBAND. SCHRIFTENREIHE. see MUSIC

282   US   ISSN 1051-7286
ALMA MARIANA. (Text in Spanish) bi-m. $4. (World Apostolate of Fatima) Blue Army of Our Lady of Fatima, U S A, Inc., Mountain View Rd., Box 976, Washington, NJ 07882-0976. TEL 908-689-1700. FAX 908-689-6279. Ed. Americo Lopez-Ortiz.
Description: Addresses the Spanish speaking community in the US and Latin American countries.

282   GW
ALT UND JUNG METTEN. 1926. s-a. DM.10. Abtei Verlag Metten, Postfach 1180, 8354 Metten, Germany. TEL 0991-382-141. Ed. P. Raban Schinabeck. bk.rev.; circ. 3,000.

282   NQ
AMANECER; reflexion Cristiana en la nueva Nicaragua. 1981. 10/yr. $25. Centro Ecumenico Antonio Valdivieso, Apdo. 3205, Managua, Nicaragua. Ed. Jose Arguello. bk.rev.; circ. 2,500.

200   FR
AME POPULAIRE. 1920. m. 120 F. Sillon Catholique, 4 Passage Olivier de Serres, 75015 Paris, France. Ed.Bd. adv.; bk.rev.; circ. 10,000.

282   US   ISSN 0002-7049
BX801
AMERICA. 1909. w (bi-w Jun.-Aug.). $33. America Press Inc., 106 W. 56th St., New York, NY 10019. TEL 212-581-4640. FAX 212-399-3596. Ed. George W. Hunt. adv.; bk.rev.; film rev.; play rev.; s-a index; circ. 35,000. (also avail. in microform (ISSN 0364-989X) from MIM,UMI) **Indexed:** A.I.P.P., Acad.Ind., Biog.Ind., Bk.Rev.Dig., Bk.Rev.Ind. (1965-), Cath.Ind, CERDIC, Child.Bk.Rev.Ind. (1965-), Film Lit.Ind. (1973-), G.Soc.Sci.& Rel.Per.Lit., HR Rep., Mag.Ind., Media Rev.Dig., Mid.East: Abstr.& Ind., Old Test.Abstr., PMR, R.G.
●Also available on CD-ROM.
—BLDSC shelfmark: 0809.660000.

282   PE
AMERICA LATINA. BOLETIN. no.15, Feb., 1978. irreg. Movimiento Internacional de Estudiantes Catolicos, Centro de Documentacion, Apartado 3564, Lima 100, Peru. illus.

282 207.11   US   ISSN 0002-7650
BX3001
AMERICAN BENEDICTINE REVIEW. 1950. 4/yr. $15. American Benedictine Review, Inc., Assumption Abbey, Box A, Richardton, ND 58652. Ed. Rev. Terrence Kardong. adv.; bk.rev.; index; circ. 1,200. (also avail. in microform from UMI; reprint service avail. from UMI) **Indexed:** Amer.Hist.& Life, Cath.Ind., Hist.Abstr., M.L.A., New Test.Abstr., Rel.& Theol.Abstr. (1989-), Rel.Per.
—BLDSC shelfmark: 0810.785000.

282 209   US   ISSN 0002-7790
E184.C3
AMERICAN CATHOLIC HISTORICAL SOCIETY OF PHILADELPHIA. RECORDS. 1886. q. $15 (effective Jan. 1991). American Catholic Historical Society of Philadelphia, 263 S. Fourth St., Box 84, Philadelphia, PA 19105. TEL 215-925-5752. Ed. Thomas R. Greene. adv.; bk.rev.; index, cum.index; circ. 850. (also avail. in microfiche from BHP; back issues avail.) **Indexed:** Cath.Ind., Hist.Abstr.
—BLDSC shelfmark: 7312.980000.

AMERICAN CATHOLIC PHILOSOPHICAL ASSOCIATION. PROCEEDINGS. see PHILOSOPHY

282   US
AMERICAN MONASTIC NEWSLETTER. 1947. 3/yr. $5. Sacred Heart Monastery, Box 364, Richardton, ND 58652. (Co-sponsor: American Benedictine Academy) Ed. Judith Sutera. circ. 965.
Description: Includes news, commentaries, reviews of interest to members of monastic communities and others associated with monastic studies.

282 020   US
AMICI. 1983. q. membership. American Friends of the Vatican Library, 157 Lakeshore Rd., Grosse Pointe Farms, MI 48236. TEL 313-885-8855. Ed. Yvonne Tata. bk.rev.; circ. 1,500. (back issues avail.)
Description: News on the Vatican library and VAL activities.

282   DR
AMIGO DEL HOGAR. no.442, 1983. m. $12. Apdo. Postal 1104, Santo Domingo, Dominican Republic. Ed. Juan Rodriquez. circ. 23,000.

RELIGIONS AND THEOLOGY — ROMAN CATHOLIC

282   FR   ISSN 0003-1895
AMITIES CATHOLIQUES FRANCAISES. N.S. 1915. q. 100 F. Comite Catholique des Amities Francaises dans le Monde, 9-11 rue Guyton de Morveau, 75013 Paris, France. TEL 45-65-96-66. FAX 1-45-81-30-81. TELEX 206293F COOPCAT. Ed. Pere Joseph Hardy. adv.; bk.rev.; bibl.; stat.; index; circ. 3,300. (tabloid format)

282   GW   ISSN 0003-2328
AMTSBLATT FUER DIE ERZDIOEZESE BAMBERG. (Text in German, Latin) 1878. s-m. DM.12. (Archdiocese Bamberg, Erzbischoefliches Ordinariat Bamberg) Sankt-Otto-Verlag GmbH, Laubanger 23, 8600 Bamberg, Germany. Ed. Alois Albrecht. bk.rev.; stat.; index; circ. 900.

AN SEARUD. see *LITERATURE*

255   IT   ISSN 0392-2855
ANALECTA AUGUSTINIANA. (Text in Latin & various languages) 1905. a. L.50000($45) (effective 1992). Order of Saint Augustine, Economato Generale, Via Paolo VI, 25, 00193 Rome, Italy. FAX 686-62-47. circ. 550. (back issues avail.)

282   IT   ISSN 0066-135X
ANALECTA BIBLICA. (Texts in various languages) 1952. irreg., no.121. price varies. (Pontificio Istituto Biblico) Editrice Pontificia Istituto Biblico, Piazza della Pilotta 35, I-00187 Rome, Italy. FAX 06-67015413. Ed. P. Karl Ploetz, SJ. circ. 300.

271   IT   ISSN 0003-2476
ANALECTA CISTERCIENSIA. (Text in English, French, German and Italian) 1945. s-a. L.70000($56) (Curia Generalis Ordinis Cisterciensis) Edizioni Cisterciensi, Piazza Tempio di Diana 14, 00153 Rome, Italy. Ed.Bd. bk.rev.; index; circ. 300. **Indexed:** M.L.A.
Formerly: Analecta Sacri Ordinis Cisterciensis.

270 282   VC   ISSN 0066-1376
ANALECTA GREGORIANA. (Text in various languages) 1930. irreg., latest vol.254. price varies. (Pontificio Istituto Biblico) Gregorian University Press, Piazza della Pilotta, 35, 00187 Rome, Italy. Ed. Angel Anton.

900 200   IT   ISSN 0394-7726
ANALECTA ORDINIS CARMELITARUM. 1909. s-a. L.30000($24) Institutum Carmelitanum, Via Sforza Pallavicini 10, 00193 Rome, Italy. TEL 06-654-3513. FAX 06-654-7200. Ed. Emanuele Boaga. adv.; circ. 450.
Description: Official documents of the Carmelite Order; also news and brief historical articles.

282   BE   ISSN 0066-1414
ANALECTA VATICANO-BELGICA. DEUXIEME SERIE. SECTION A: NONCIATURE DE FLANDRE. 1924. irreg. price varies. (Institut Historique Belge de Rome) N.V. Brepols I.G.P., Steenweg op Tielem 68, 2300 Turnhout, Belgium. TEL 014-41-54-63. FAX 014-42-89-19. TELEX 34 182. circ. controlled.
Description: Correspondence from and to nuncios in the Southern Low Countries during the 16th, 17th and 18th centuries.

274   BE   ISSN 0066-1422
ANALECTA VATICANO-BELGICA. DEUXIEME SERIE. SECTION B: NONCIATURE DE COLOGNE. 1956. irreg. price varies. (Institut Historique Belge de Rome) N.V. Brepols I.G.P., Steenweg op Tielem 68, 2300 Turnhout, Belgium. TEL 014-41-54-63. FAX 014-42-89-19. TELEX 34 182. circ. controlled.
Description: Correspondence from and to nuncios in the Southern Low Countries during the 16th, 17th and 18th centuries.

282   BE   ISSN 0066-1430
ANALECTA VATICANO-BELGICA. DEUXIEME SERIE. SECTION C: NONCIATURE DE BRUXELLES. 1956. irreg., vol.10, 1990. price varies. (Institut Historique Belge de Rome) N.V. Brepols I.G.P., Steenweg op Tielem 68, 2300 Turnhout, Belgium. TEL 014-41-54-63. FAX 014-42-89-19. TELEX 34 182. circ. controlled.
Description: Correspondence from and to nuncios in 19th century Belgium.

282   BE   ISSN 0066-1449
ANALECTA VATICANO-BELGICA. PREMIERE SERIE: DOCUMENTS RELATIFS AUX ANCIENS DIOCESES DE CAMBRAI, LIEGE, THEROUANNE ET TOURNAI. 1906. irreg., vol.32, 1987. price varies. (Institut Historique Belge de Rome) N.V. Brepols I.G.P., Steenweg op Tielen 68, 2300 Turnhout, Belgium. TEL 014-41-54-63. FAX 014-42-89-19. TELEX 34 182. circ. controlled.
Description: Letters from and supplications to the Popes concerning the Southern Low Countries during the 14th and 15th centuries.

282   US
ANCHOR; Fall River Diocesan newspaper for Southeast Massachusetts, Cape Cod & the Islands. 1957. w. $11. (Roman Catholic Diocese of Fall River) Anchor Publishing Co., 887 Highland Ave., Box 7, Fall River, MA 02722. TEL 508-675-7151. FAX 508-675-7048. Ed. Rev. John F. Moore. adv.; film rev.; illus.; circ. 30,945. (tabloid format; also avail. in microfilm; back issues avail.)

ANGELIC WARFARE DISPATCH. see *CHILDREN AND YOUTH — About*

ANGELICUM; periodicum trimestre pontificae studiorum. see *PHILOSOPHY*

282 255   GR
ANICHTI ORIZONTES-ANGHELIAFOROS. 1900. m. Dr.1500($10) Jesuit Fathers, 27 Smyrnis Str., Athens 10439, Greece. Ed. Father Gabriel Marangos. adv.; bk.rev.; bibl.; circ. 4,300.
Former titles (until 1977): Angheliaforos-Anichti Orizontes; Angheliaforos (ISSN 0003-3073)

248.83   AT
ANNALS MAGAZINE. 1889. m. (10/yr.) Aus.$20. (Missionaries of the Sacred Heart) Chevalier Press, Box 13, Kensington, N.S.W. 2033, Australia. TEL 02-6627894. FAX 02-662-1735. Ed. Paul Stenhouse. adv.; bk.rev.; bibl.; illus.; stat.; circ. 20,000. **Indexed:** Gdlns.
Formerly: Our Lady of the Sacred Heart (ISSN 0030-6878)

282   CN   ISSN 0318-434X
ANNALS OF GOOD ST. ANNE. French edition: Revue Sainte Anne. (Editions in English, French) 1876. m. Can.$8. Redemptorist Fathers, Ste-Anne de Beaupre Province, Basilica of Ste. Anne, Quebec, Que. G0A 3C0, Canada. FAX 418-827-4530. Ed. Bernard Mercier. adv.; bk.rev.; circ. 170,000 (50,000 English ed.); 120,000 French ed.).

282   FR   ISSN 0066-2488
ANNUAIRE CATHOLIQUE DE FRANCE. 1950. biennial. 480 F. Publicat, 17 bd. Poissonniere, 75002 Paris, France. adv.

282.675   ZR
ANNUAIRE DE L'EGLISE CATHOLIQUE AU ZAIRE. a. Edition du Secretariat-General, Kinshasa-Combe, Zaire. illus.

282   FR
ANNUAIRE DU DIOCESE DE LYON. 1826. a. 100 F. Archeveche de Lyon, 1 Place de Fourviere, 69321 Lyon Cedex 05, France.
Formerly (until 1972): Ordo et Annuaire de l'Archdiocese de Lyon.
Description: Discusses departments, parishes, communities, and various groups of the Diocese.

266   IT   ISSN 0066-4464
ANNUARIO CATTOLICO D'ITALIA. 1956. biennial. L.225000($300) Editoriale Italiana, Via Viglieno 10, 00192 Rome, Italy. FAX 3211359. index; circ. 8,000.
Description: Yearbook about the Catholic Church, Cadres and institutions in Italy.

282   US
THE ANTHONIAN. 1927. q. $10. St. Anthony's Guild, Paterson, NJ 07509-2948. TEL 212-594-6224. FAX 212-594-2769. Eds. Fr. Cassian Miles, Janet Gianopoulos. circ. 110,000.

282   VC   ISSN 0003-6064
ANTONIANUM. (Text in English, French, German, Italian, Latin, Spanish) 1926. q. L.55000($65) (effective 1991). Pontificio Ateneo Antonianum, Via Merulana 124, 00185 Rome, Italy. Ed. Marco Nobile. adv.; bk.rev.; abstr.; bibl.; index, cum.index; circ. 850.
Indexed: Amer.Hist.& Life, CERDIC, Hist.Abstr., Hist.Abstr., M.L.A., New Test.Abstr., Old Test.Abstr., Rel.& Theol.Abstr. (1968-).
—BLDSC shelfmark: 1552.950000.

282   GW   ISSN 0721-1937
ANZEIGER FUER DIE SEELSORGE; aeltestes Organ fuer die Kath. Pfarraemter und Krankenhaeuser Kloester. 1891. m. DM.28.80. Verlag Herder GmbH und Co. KG, Hermann-Herder-Str. 4, 7800 Freiburg, Germany. TEL 0761-2717408. FAX 0761-2717-520. Ed.Bd. circ. 28,700. (back issues avail.)

282   VC
APOLLINARIS. 1928. 2/yr. $64. Pontificia Universita Lateranense, Pontificio Istituto Utriusque Iuris, Piazza S. Giovanni in Laterno 4, 00120 Vatican City (Rome), State of the Vatican City. Ed. Tarcisio Bertone. **Indexed:** Canon Law Abstr., CERDIC.

282   CN   ISSN 0706-9928
APOSTOLAT. (Text in French) 1929. bi-m. Can.$5($6) Missionary Oblates of Mary Immaculate, 460 1st Street, Richelieu, Que. J3L 4B5, Canada. TEL 514-658-8761. FAX 514-658-7951. Ed. Rev. Jacques Saumure. circ. 25,000.
Description: Religious topics on the Roman Catholic home and missions abroad.

AQUINAS; rivista internazionale di filosofia. see *PHILOSOPHY*

282   CE
AQUINAS JOURNAL. (Text in English) 1984. s-a. Rs.100($8) (Archbishop of Colombo) Aquinas College of Higher Studies, Colombo - 8, Sri Lanka. Ed. Rev. Don Gerald Chrispin Leo. bk.rev.; circ. 500.

282   IT   ISSN 0003-7559
ARALDO DI S. ANTONIO; incontri con Papa Giovanni. 1949. w. free. Orfanotrofio Antoniano dei PP. Rogazionisti, Viale Motta, 36, 25015 Desenzano del Garda (BS), Italy. TEL 030-914-1743. FAX 030-9912306. bk.rev.; illus.; circ. 150,000.

282   US
ARCHDIOCESE OF CINCINNATI ALMANAC DIRECTORY AND BUYER'S GUIDE. 1959. a. $15. Catholic Telegraph, 100 E. Eighth St., Cincinnati, OH 45202. TEL 513-421-3131. Ed. James Stackpoole. adv.; stat.; circ. 3,000.

282   IT   ISSN 0003-8296
ARCHIDIOCESI DI MONREALE. BOLLETTINO ECCLESIASTICO. 1908. m. L.12000. Curia Arcivescovile di Monreale, Palermo, Italy. Ed. Msgr. Francesco Sparacio. bk.rev.

200   SP
ARCHIDIOCESIS DE MADRID-ALCALA. BOLETIN OFICIAL. 1878. s-m. 1500 ptas.($13) Arzobispado de Madrid, Bailen 8, 28013 Madrid, Spain. Ed. J. Gonzalez Prado. adv.; bibl.; index; circ. 1,500. (back issues avail.)

282 209   GW   ISSN 0003-9160
LAW
ARCHIV FUER KATHOLISCHES KIRCHENRECHT. (Text in German and Latin) 1857. s-a. DM.95 per no. Verlag Kirchheim und Co. GmbH, Kaiserstr. 41, Postfach 2524, 6500 Mainz, Germany. TEL 06131-671081. adv.; bibl.; index; circ. 550. **Indexed:** Canon Law Abstr., CERDIC.

282   IT   ISSN 0390-8240
ARCHIVIO PER LA STORIA DEL MOVIMENTO SOCIALE CATTOLICO IN ITALIA. BOLLETTINO. 1966. 3/yr. L.90000($69) (effective 1992). (Universita Cattolica del Sacro Cuore) Vita e Pensiero, Largo Gemelli 1, 20123 Milan, Italy. TEL 02-8856310. FAX 02-8856260. TELEX 321033 UCATMI 1. Ed. Alberto Cova.
—BLDSC shelfmark: 2234.390000.
Description: Covers history of the Social-Catholic movement in Italy.

RELIGIONS AND THEOLOGY — ROMAN CATHOLIC

900 282   IT   ISSN 0394-7734
ARCHIVIUM HISTORICUM CARMELITANUM. (Text in English, French, German, Italian, Latin, Spanish) 1961. irreg. price varies. (Order of Carmelites) Institutum Carmelitanum, Via Sforza Pallavicini 10, 00193 Rome, Italy. TEL 06-654-3513. FAX 06-654-7200. adv.; circ. 500.
   Description: Covers Carmelite history; an order in the Catholic religion.

ARCHIVO IBERO-AMERICANO; revista de estudios historicos. see *HISTORY — History Of Europe*

271   IT   ISSN 0004-0665
BX3601
ARCHIVUM FRANCISCANUM HISTORICUM. (Text in English, French, German, Italian, Latin and Spanish) 1908. s-a. L.60000. Collegio San Bonaventura, Commissione Storica, Via Vecchia di Marino 28-30, 00046 Grottaferrata (Rome), Italy. Ed. R.P. Victor Sanchez. bk.rev.; bibl.; charts; illus.; cum.index: 1908-1957; circ. 600. **Indexed:** Amer.Hist.& Life, CERDIC, Hist.Abstr., M.L.A.
—BLDSC shelfmark: 1659.210000.

282   VC   ISSN 0066-6785
BR1.AI
ARCHIVUM HISTORIAE PONTIFICAE. (Text in English, French, German, Italian, Latin or Spanish; summaries in Latin) 1963. a. price varies. (Pontificia Universita Gregoriana, Facolta di Storia Ecclesiastica) Gregorian University Press, Piazza della Pilotta, 35, 00187 Rome, Italy. Ed. Paulius Rabikauskas, S.J. adv.; bk.rev.; bibl.; circ. 750. (back issues avail.)

271   IT   ISSN 0037-8887
ARCHIVUM HISTORICUM SOCIETATIS IESU. (Text and summaries in English, French, German, Italian, Latin, Portuguese, and Spanish) 1932. s-a. $40. Institutum Historicum Societatis Iesu - Jesuit Historical Institute, Via dei Penitenzieri 20, 00193 Rome, Italy. Ed. Laszlo Szilas. bk.rev.; bibl.; cum.index: 1932-1951, 1952-1961; 1962-1981; circ. 900. **Indexed:** Amer.Hist.& Life, Hist.Abstr., So.Pac.Per.Ind.
   Description: Contains research articles on history of Jesuits worldwide.

ARCHIWA, BIBLIOTEKI I MUZEA KOSCIELNE. see *HISTORY — History Of Europe*

228   IT
ARCIDIOCESI DI REGGIO CALABRIA. RIVISTA PASTORALE. 1910. q. L.20000. Curia Metropolitan di Reggio Calabria, Via T. Campanella 63, 89100 Reggio Calabria, Italy. TEL 0965-21037. Ed. Sac. Antonino Denisi. adv.; illus.
   Formerly: Bollettino Ecclesiastico (ISSN 0006-6788)

282   US
ARKANSAS CATHOLIC. 1911. w. $10. 2500 N. Tyler, Box 7417, Little Rock, AR 72217-7417. TEL 501-664-0340. Ed. Karl Christ. adv.; circ. 14,500.

282   US   ISSN 0361-3712
BX801
ARLINGTON CATHOLIC HERALD. 1976. w. $14. Arlington Catholic Herald, Inc., 200 N. Glebe Rd., Ste. 614, Arlington, VA 22203. TEL 703-841-2590. Ed. Michael Flach. adv.; bk.rev.; illus.; circ. 40,000. (also avail. in microfilm)
   Description: Local, national, international news and features of Catholic interest.

282   CL
ARZOBISPADO DE SANTIAGO. VICARIA DE LA SOLIDARIDAD. ESTUDIOS. 1978. irreg. Arzobispado de Santiago, Vicaria de la Solidaridad, Plaza de Armas 444, Casilla 30D, Santiago, Chile.

250   SP
ARZOBISPADO DE SEVILLA. BOLETIN OFICIAL ECLESIASTICO. 1854. m. 3000 ptas. Arzobispado de Sevilla, Oficina Diocesana de Informacion, Apdo. Postal 6, Sevilla, Spain. Ed. Carlos Ros Carballar. adv.; bk.rev.; circ. 700.

282 209   IT   ISSN 0004-4970
ASPRENAS; rivista di scienze teologiche. 1953. q. L.45000($40) (effective Jan. 1991). (Facolta Teologica dell'Italia Meridionale, Sezione S. Tommaso D'Aquino, Napoli) Edizioni Dehoniane Roma, Viale Colli Aminei 2, 80131 Naples, Italy. FAX 081-7413041. Dir. Settimio Cipriani. adv.; bk.rev.; charts; illus.; circ. 1,000. **Indexed:** CERDIC.
—BLDSC shelfmark: 1746.333000.
   Description: Contains studies and research on all aspects of theological science; Bible, patristics, systematic and practical theology, ecumenism, with particular attention to their cultural contexts and their relationship to the humanities.

ASSOCIATION OF JESUIT COLLEGES AND UNIVERSITIES AND JESUIT SECONDARY EDUCATION ASSOCIATION DIRECTORY. see *EDUCATION — Higher Education*

AUFTRAG; eine christliche Lehrzeitschrift. see *RELIGIONS AND THEOLOGY — Protestant*

282   US   ISSN 0888-2274
BX2901
AUGUSTINIAN HERITAGE; a review of spirituality and tradition. 1939. s-a. $15. Augustinian Press, 214 Ashwood Rd., Box 476, Villanova, PA 19085. TEL 215-527-3330. FAX 215-527-0571. Ed. John E. Rotelle. circ. 300. (back issues avail.)
   Formerly: Tagastan.

282   US   ISSN 0094-5323
BR65.A9
AUGUSTINIAN STUDIES. (Text in various languages) 1970. a. $15. Villanova University, Augustinian Studies, Tolentine Hall, Villanova, PA 19085. TEL 215-645-7903. Ed. Allan D. Fitzgerald. bk.rev.; circ. 500. **Indexed:** Cath.Ind., Phil.Ind.
—BLDSC shelfmark: 1791.640000.

271   BE   ISSN 0004-8003
AUGUSTINIANA; revue pour l'etude de Saint Augustin et de l'Ordre des Augustins. (Text in English, French, German, Latin) 1951. s-a. 1300 Fr. Augustijns Historisch Instituut - Institut Historique Augustinien, Pere August Pakenstraat 109, 3030 Heverlee-Louvain, Belgium. Ed. T. van Bavel. bk.rev.; bibl.; index. **Indexed:** CERDIC, M.L.A.
—BLDSC shelfmark: 1791.650000.

271   IT   ISSN 0004-8011
AUGUSTINIANUM. 1961. s-a. L.50000 (foreign L.60000)(effective 1992). Order of Saint Augustine, Economato Generale, Via Paolo VI, 25, 00193 Rome, Italy. FAX 686-62-47. (Affiliate: Institutum Patristicum Augustinianum) Ed. V. Grossi. bk.rev.; index; circ. 850. (back issues avail.) **Indexed:** M.L.A., New Test.Abstr., Old Test.Abstr.
—BLDSC shelfmark: 1791.700000.

271   SP   ISSN 0004-802X
AUGUSTINUS. (Text in Spanish) 1956. q. 2800 ptas.($40) Padres Agustinos Recoletos, General Davila 5, Bajo D, 28003 Madrid, Spain. bk.rev.; index; circ. 700. (processed) **Indexed:** CERDIC, M.L.A., Phil.Ind.
   Description: Studies on the life, doctrine, thought, spirituality and influence of St. Augustine.

282   AT   ISSN 0004-8321
AUSTRALASIAN CATHOLIC RECORD. 1924. q. Aus.$30. St. Patrick's College, Manly, N.S.W., Australia. Ed.Bd. adv.; bk.rev.; index; circ. 2,500. **Indexed:** Aus.P.A.I.S., Canon Law Abstr., Cath.Ind., New Test.Abstr., Rel.& Theol.Abstr.
—BLDSC shelfmark: 1793.630000.

282   LE   ISSN 0005-1950
AVEDIK.* 1932. m. £L10($4) Armenian Catholic Patriarchate, Place Debbas, Beirut, Lebanon. Ed. Fr. Vartan Tekeyan. illus.

282   US
AYLESFORD CARMELITE NEWSLETTER. 1984. q. $2. Lay Carmelites, 8501 Bailey Road, Darien, IL 60561. TEL 708-969-5050. Ed. Rev. Aloysius Sieracki. circ. 16,000. (back issues avail.)
   Description: Deals with Carmelite spirituality and recent trends in the involvement of the laity in Carmel.

255   IT   ISSN 0005-3783
BADIA GRECA DI GROTTAFERRATA. BOLLETTINO. 1947. s-a. L.15000. (Monastero Esarchico di Grottaferrata) Badia Greca di Grottaferrata, 00046 Grottaferrata (Rome), Italy. bk.rev.; illus.; cum.index every 10 yrs.; circ. 350. **Indexed:** CERDIC.

282 249   GW   ISSN 0005-7177
BAYERISCHES SONNTAGSBLATT FUER DIE KATHOLISCHE FAMILIE. 1879. w. DM.82.80. Bayerisches Sonntagsblatt Verlags GmbH, Nymphenburger Str. 156, 8000 Munich 19, Germany. TEL 089-164139. FAX 089-162133. Eds. Guenter Beaugrand, Ursula Goldmann-Posch. adv.; bk.rev.; film rev.; abstr.; illus.; circ. 40,000. (looseleaf format)

282   IT   ISSN 0005-7436
BEATO ANGELO. 1924. m. L.7000($15) Frati Minori Cappuccini della Provincia Consentina, Covento del SS. Crocifisso, 87100 Cosenza, Italy. Dir. P. Elio Vittorino Vivacqua. adv.; bk.rev.; illus.; circ. 3,000.

200   NE   ISSN 0005-8734
BENEDICTIJNS TIJDSCHRIFT; voor Evangelische bezinning. 1937. q. fl.17.50. Sint-Adelbertabdij, Abdijlaan 26, 1935 BH Egmond-Binnen, Netherlands. adv.; bk.rev.; bibl.; circ. 2,800. **Indexed:** CERDIC.
—BLDSC shelfmark: 1891.330000.

BENEDICTINA. see *HISTORY — History Of Europe*

271   UK   ISSN 0522-8883
BENEDICTINE YEARBOOK. 1863. a. $5. English Congregation of the Order of Saint Benedict, Ampleforth Abbey, York YO6 4EN, England. FAX 043-93-770. Ed. Rev. J. Gordon Beattie. adv.; circ. 5,000.
   Supersedes: Benedictine Almanac.

282   US   ISSN 0005-8726
BENEDICTINES. 1946. s-a. $9. (Mount St. Scholastica Convent) Mount St. Scholastica, Inc., Atchison, KS 66002. TEL 913-367-6110. Ed. Sister Mary Alice Guilfoil. bk.rev.; illus.; cum.index: vols.1-9, 10-20, 21-30; circ. 800. (also avail. in microform from UMI; back issues avail.; reprint service avail. from UMI) **Indexed:** Bull.Signal., CERDIC.
—BLDSC shelfmark: 1891.400000.

282   IT
LA BIBBIA NELLA STORIA. 1984. irreg. Centro Editoriale Dehoniano, Via Nosadella 6, 40123 Bologna, Italy. TEL 051-306811. FAX 051-341706. Ed.Bd.

220 282   GW   ISSN 0006-0593
BIBEL HEUTE. 1965. q. DM.25($2) Katholisches Bibelwerk e.V., Silberburgstr. 121, 7000 Stuttgart 1, Germany. TEL 0711-626001. FAX 0711-616682. Ed. F.J. Ortkemper. adv.; bk.rev.; illus.; index, cum.index; circ. 24,000. **Indexed:** CERDIC.

220   II   ISSN 0970-2288
BS410
BIBLEBHASHYAM; Indian Biblical quarterly. (Text in English) 1975. q. Rs.20($8) Bible Bhashyam Trust, Post Box No. 1, Vadavathoor, Kottayam 686010, India. Ed. Matthew Vellanickal. adv.; bk.rev.; circ. 4,000. **Indexed:** New Test.Abstr., Old Test.Abstr.
—BLDSC shelfmark: 1947.821100.

282   BL
BIBLIA - GENTE. 1978. w. Cr.$100. (Pia Sociedade de Sao Paulo) Edicoes Paulinas, Via Raposo Tavares Km 18.5, C.P. 8107, 01051 Sao Paulo, Brazil. Ed. A.C. D'Elboux. illus.; circ. 120,000.

220   VC   ISSN 0006-0887
BS410
BIBLICA. (Text in English, French, German, Italian, Latin and Spanish) 1920. q. L.65000($60) (Pontificio Istituto Biblico) Biblical Institute Press, Piazza della Pilotta 35, 00187 Rome, Italy. Ed. S. Pisano S.J. bk.rev.; index, cum.index; vols.1-25, 26-50; circ. 1,900. **Indexed:** Arts & Hum.Cit.Ind., CERDIC, Curr.Cont., New Test.Abstr., Old Test.Abstr., Rel.& Theol.Abstr. (1977-), Rel.Ind.One, Rel.Per.
—BLDSC shelfmark: 1947.840000.
   Description: Explores the scientific study of scripture.

282   VC
BIBLICA ET ORIENTALIA. 1928. irreg., no.43, 1987. price varies. (Pontificio Istituto Biblico) Biblical Institute Press, Piazza della Pilotta 35, 00187 Rome, Italy.

RELIGIONS AND THEOLOGY — ROMAN CATHOLIC

282   VC
BIBLIOTECA APOSTOLICA VATICANA. CATALOGHI E NORME DI CATALOGAZIONE. (In seven subseries: A: Cataloghi ed Inventari di Manoscritti; B: Cataloghi di Mostre; C: Cataloghi di Stampati; D: Norme di Catalogazione; E: Cataloghi di Pubblicazioni; F: Storia delle Biblioteche Pontificie; G: Quaderni della Scualo di Biblioteconomia) 1902. irreg. price varies. Biblioteca Apostolica Vaticana, 00120 Vatican City (Rome), State of the Vatican City.

282   VC
BIBLIOTECA APOSTOLICA VATICANA. EDIZIONI ILLUSTRATE. (In 3 subseries: A: Illustrazioni di Codici; B: Illustrazioni di Documenti; C: Illustrazioni di Monumenti) 1902. irreg. price varies. Biblioteca Apostolica Vaticana, 00120 Vatican City (Rome), State of the Vatican City.

282   VC
BIBLIOTECA APOSTOLICA VATICANA. STUDI E TESTI. 1900. irreg., no.340, 1991. price varies. Biblioteca Apostolica Vaticana, 00120 Vatican City (Rome), State of the Vatican City.

282   IT
BIBLIOTHECA INSTITUTI HISTORICI SOCIETATIS IESU. 1941. irreg., latest no.48, 1988. Institutum Historicum Societatis Iesu - Jesuit Historical Institute, Via dei Penitenzieri 20, 00193 Rome, Italy. (back issues avail.)
Description: Contains research monographs on history of the Jesuits worldwide.

200   IT   ISSN 0067-8163
BIBLIOTHECA SERAPHICO-CAPUCCINA. SECTIO HISTORICA. (Multilingual text) 1932. irreg., no.41, 1991. price varies. Frati Minori Cappuccini, Istituto Storico, Cas. Post. 90-91, Circonv. Occidentale 6850 (GRA km 65), 00163 Rome, Italy. TEL 06-625-19-58. FAX 06-661-62-401. index; circ. 500.

200   BE   ISSN 0067-8279
BIBLIOTHEQUE DE LA REVUE D'HISTOIRE ECCLESIASTIQUE. (Text in Dutch, English, French and Italian) 1928. irreg. Universite Catholique de Louvain, Bureau de la Revue d'Histoire Ecclesiastique, Bibliotheque, College Erasme, B-1348 Louvain-la-Neuve, Belgium. circ. 500.

282   RM
BISERICA ORTODOXA ROMANA. 1822. m. Romanian Patriarchate, Intrarea Patriarhiei 9, Bucharest, Rumania. TEL 234449. Ed. Rev. Dumitru Soare. circ. 10,000.

282   IT
BISERICA ROMANEASCA. (Text in Rumanian) 1976. q. L.5000($25) Comunita Ortodossa Romana in Italia, Via Meravigli 14, 20123 Milan, Italy. (Co-sponsor: Fondazione Europea Dragan) adv.; bk.rev.; illus.; circ. 1,700.

282   XV   ISSN 0006-5722
BOGOSLOVNI VESTNIK. (Text in Slovenian) 1921-1944; resumed 1965. q. $20. Teoloska Fakulteta v Ljubljani, Poljanska 4, 61000 Ljubljana, Slovenia. FAX 061-329-793. Ed. Anton Stres. bk.rev.; circ. 900.
—BLDSC shelfmark: 2118.180100.

282   PH
BOLETIN ECLESIASTICO DE FILLIPINAS; official organ of the Catholic hierarchy of the Philippines. (Text in English) 1923. m. $25. University of Santo Tomas, Espana St., Manila, Philippines. Ed. Vicente Cajilie. adv.; bk.rev.; bibl.; index; circ. 1,800.

282   BO
BOLIVIA: GUIA ECLESIASTICA. 1977. irreg., latest 3rd ed. Conferencia Episcopal Boliviana, Secretariado General, Casilla 7857, La Paz, Bolivia. TEL 377878. illus.
Formerly: Guia de la Iglesia.

282   IT   ISSN 0404-9462
BOLLETTINO DI S. NICOLA. (Text mainly in Italian; occasionally in other languages) 1906. m. L.5000($8) Padri Domenicani della Basilica di S. Nicola di Bari, Basilica di S. Nicola, 70122 Bari, Italy. Ed. P. Gerardo Cioffari. bk.rev.; bibl.; index; circ. 2,000. (back issues avail.)

282   IT
BOLLETTINO PER LE RELIGIOSE DOMENICANE IN ITALIA. bi-m. Gerardo Cappelluti, Ed. & Pub., Piazza della Minerva 42, 00186 Rome, Italy.

282   IT
BOLLETTINO SALESIANO; rivista fondata da San Giovanni Bosco. 1877. s-a. free. Direzione Generale Opere Salesiane, Via della Pisana 1111, 00163 Rome, Italy. Ed. Giuseppe Costa. (back issues avail.)

266   IT   ISSN 0006-6907
BOLLETTINO VINCENZIANO. 1966. bi-m. L.20000. (Preti della Missione della Provincia di Roma) Centro Liturgico Vincenziano, Via Pompeo Magno 21, 00192 Rome, Italy. Ed. E. Fei. bk.rev.; charts; illus.; circ. 2,000.

BONDINGS. see HOMOSEXUALITY

254.4   GW   ISSN 0006-7113
BONIFATIUSBLATT. 1849. q. DM.4. Bonifatiuswerk der Deutschen Katholiken e.V., Kamp 22, 4790 Paderborn, Germany. TEL 05251-29960. FAX 05251-299688. Ed. H.D. Huber. illus.; stat.; circ. 400,000. (avail. in talking book ed.)
Description: Reports on Catholic minorities, so-called "Diaspora-Church", in Germany and Scandinavian countries.

282   CN   ISSN 0225-0233
BONNE NOUVELLE. (Text in French) 1911. 10/yr. Can.$8. Secular Franciscan Order, 5730 bd. Pie 9, Montreal, Que. H1X 2B9, Canada. TEL 514-727-8483. Ed.Bd. adv.; bk.rev.; bibl.; charts; illus.; stat.; circ. 4,000. (back issues avail.) **Indexed:** CERDIC.

282   NE   ISSN 0006-8349
BOUWEN AAN DE NIEUWE AARDE. 1953. bi-m. fl.17.50. Stichting Bouwen aan de Nieuwe Aarde, Laagstraat 372-374, 5654 PR Eindhoven, Netherlands. TEL 31-40515792. bk.rev.; circ. 3,500.
Description: Promotes renewal of the Christian church by the power of the Holy Spirit.

282   XV
BOZJE OKOLJE. (Text in Slovenian; summaries in English) 1977. bi-m. 2400 din.($6) (Sovenske Rimskokatoliske Skofije) Druzina, Cankarjevo Nabrezje 3-I, 61101 Ljubana, Slovenia. TEL 061 221324. Ed. France Orazem. circ. 2,500.

282   US
BRATSTVO/BROTHERHOOD.* (Text in English, Slovak) 1899. m. $3. Pennsylvania Slovak Catholic Union, 6611 Rockside Rd., 3rd Fl., Independence, OH 44131-2398. Ed. Stephen J. Kavulich. circ. 2,500. (tabloid format)
Description: Reports organization activities, and news of interest to Slovak speaking persons.

BRAUNAUER RUNDBRIEF. see HISTORY — History Of Europe

282   UK
BRIDGE (KINGSTON-UPON-THAMES). 1959. q. £2 (foreign £3). Sons of Divine Providence, 25 Lower Teddington Rd., Hampton Wick, Kingston-upon-Thames, Surrey KT1 4HB, England. TEL 081-977-5130. FAX 081-977-0105. circ. 4,500. (back issues avail.)
Description: Provides international news of work of organization and personnel, including publicity, information, communication with friends and supporters.

282   US
BRINGING RELIGION HOME; the newsletter that helps teach religion in the home. 1976. m. $12. Claretian Publications, 205 W. Monroe St., Chicago, IL 60606. TEL 312-236-7782. FAX 312-236-7230. Ed. Rev. Mark J. Brummel. circ. 61,414. (reprint service avail. from UMI)

282   CN   ISSN 0007-0483
BRITISH COLUMBIA CATHOLIC. 1931. w. Can.$25 (foreign Can.$40). Vancouver Archdiocese, Archibishop James Carney, 150 Robson St., Vancouver, B.C. V6B 2A7, Canada. TEL 604-683-0281. FAX 604-683-8117. Ed. F.V. Hawksell. adv.; bk.rev.; film rev.; play rev.; illus.; circ. 20,000. (tabloid format)

240   FR   ISSN 0007-4322
BULLETIN DE LITTERATURE ECCLESIASTIQUE. 1899. q. 273 F.($47) (effective Jan. 1992). Institut Catholique de Toulouse, 31 rue de la Fonderie, 31068 Toulouse cedex, France. TEL 61-36-81-00. Ed. Robert Cabie. bk.rev.; bibl.; index; circ. 850. (back issues avail.) **Indexed:** Bull.Signal., CERDIC, M.L.A., New Test.Abstr., Old Test.Abstr.

BUND DER DEUTSCHEN KATHOLISCHEN JUGEND. INFORMATIONSDIENST. see CHILDREN AND YOUTH — For

282   970.1   US
BUREAU OF CATHOLIC INDIAN MISSIONS. NEWSLETTER. 1977. 10/yr. free. Bureau of Catholic Indian Missions, 2021 H St., N.W., Washington, DC 20006. TEL 202-331-8542. Ed. Paul A. Lenz. bk.rev.; circ. 13,000.

C A F O D JOURNAL. (Catholic Fund for Overseas Development) see BUSINESS AND ECONOMICS — International Development And Assistance

282   US
C A R A SEMINARY DIRECTORY; U.S. Catholic institutions for the training of candidates for the priesthood. 1965. a. $30. Center for Applied Research in the Apostolate, Georgetown University, Box 1601, Washington, DC 20057. TEL 202-687-8080. Ed. C. Joseph O'Hara. circ. 500. (back issues avail.)

282   UK   ISSN 0262-6896
C A S NEWSLETTER. 1980. a. membership. Catholic Archives Society, c/o M.A. Kuhn-Regnier, Flat 7, Dawes House, High St., Burwash, Etchingham, Sussex TN19 7HD, England. circ. 260 (controlled).
Description: Notes about seminars, local meetings and the Society's annual conference.

C A V E NEWSLETTER. (Catholic Audio-Visual Educators) see EDUCATION — Teaching Methods And Curriculum

282   US
C C I C A ANNUAL. 1982. a. $10. Catholic Commission on Intellectual and Cultural Affairs, 262 Decio, Notre Dame, IN 46556. TEL 219-277-1053. Ed. Konrad Schaum. circ. 350. (back issues avail.)

C C N INFORMATION. (Council of Churches in Namibia) see RELIGIONS AND THEOLOGY — Protestant

C H A C INFO/INFO A C C S. (Catholic Health Association of Canada) see HOSPITALS

C H A C REVIEW. see HOSPITALS

C P F I NEWSLETTER. (Christian Pharmacists Fellowship International) see PHARMACY AND PHARMACOLOGY

282   360   US
C U S A N. 1948. s-a. membership. Catholics United for Spirtual Action, An Apostolate for Persons with Disabilities, 176 W. 8th St., Bayonne, NJ 07002. TEL 201-437-0412. Ed. Kathrin Taylor. bk.rev.; circ. 1,100. (also avail. in magnetic tape; Braille)
Description: An in-organ publication for members of Catholics United for Spiritual Action with articles by members with an autobiographical as well as a spiritual, practical and humorous orientation.

C W L NEWS. (Catholic Women's League) see WOMEN'S INTERESTS

282   CN   ISSN 0007-9774
BT690
CAHIERS DE JOSEPHOLOGIE. (Text in English and French) 1953. s-a. Can.$20. Oratoire Saint-Joseph du Mont-Royal, 3800 Chemin Reine-Marie, Montreal, Que. H3V 1H6, Canada. TEL 514-733-8211. FAX 514-733-9735. Ed. Roland Gauthier. bk.rev.; bibl.; illus.; index, cum.index: 1953-1972; circ. 1,000. **Indexed:** Cath.Ind., New Test.Abstr., Old Test.Abstr., Rel.& Theol.Abstr.
—BLDSC shelfmark: 2949.450000.

282   CM
CAMEROON PANORAMA. (Text in English) 1962. m. B.P. 46, Buea, Cameroon. TEL 32-22-40. Ed. Sr. Mercy Horgan. circ. 4,000.

RELIGIONS AND THEOLOGY — ROMAN CATHOLIC

282 255   NE   ISSN 0008-221X
CAMILLUSBODE. 1950. s-a. free. Provincialaat van de Camillianen, Heinsbergerweg 174, 6045 CK Roermond, Netherlands. Ed. P. Denneman. circ. 6,000. (tabloid format)
Formerly: St. Camillusbode.

282 255   IT   ISSN 0008-2260
CAMMINO; annali Francescani. 1869. m. $2. Viale Piave 2, Milan 20129, Italy. Ed.Bd. bk.rev.; film rev.; play rev.; illus.; circ. 15,000.

282   CN   ISSN 0703-1963
CANADIAN CANON LAW SOCIETY. (Text and summaries in Cajun, English, French) 1975. s-a. membership. Canadian Canon Law Society, 223 Main St., Ottawa, Ont. K1S 1C4, Canada. Ed. Rev. Alexandre Tache. circ. 450. (looseleaf format; back issues avail.)

282   CN   ISSN 0827-1704
CANADIAN CATHOLIC HISTORICAL STUDIES. (Text in English, French) 1933. a. Can.$30. Canadian Catholic Historical Association, 355 Church Street, Toronto, Ont. M5B 1Z8, Canada. FAX 416-977-6063. Eds. Terrence Murphy, Glenn Wright. bk.rev.; circ. 350.
Description: Features papers that were read at both the annual conferences.

282   CN   ISSN 0714-7724
CANADIAN CATHOLIC REVIEW. 1983. 11/yr. Can.$25($25) (typically set in Jan.). Canadian Catholic Review Corporation, 1437 College Dr., Saskatoon, Sask, S7N 0W6, Canada. TEL 306-966-8959. FAX 306-966-8904. Ed. Daniel Callam. adv.; bk.rev.; film rev.; index; circ. 1,500. (back issues avail.) **Indexed:** Cath.Ind.

200   CN
CANADIAN CONFERENCE OF CATHOLIC BISHOPS. NATIONAL BULLETIN ON LITURGY. 1965. 4/yr. Can.$10($12) (outside US and Canada US$25). Canadian Conference of Catholic Bishops, Publications Service - Conference des Eveques Catholiques du Canada, 90 Parent Ave, Ottawa, Ont. K1N 7BI, Canada. TEL 613-236-9461. FAX 613-238-1099. TELEX 053-3311. Ed. J. Frank Henderson. bk.rev.; cum.index: 1965-77, 1978-85; circ. 3,500. (also avail. in microfilm from UMI; back issues avail.; reprint service avail. from UMI)
Formerly: Canadian Catholic Conference. National Bulletin on Liturgy (ISSN 0084-8425)
Description: For parishes, schools, communities as they prepare, celebrate, and improve their life of worship and prayer. Primarily pastoral in scope.

282   CN
CANADIAN MESSENGER. 1891. m. $8. Apostleship of Prayer, 661 Greenwood Ave., Toronto, Ont. M4J 4B3, Canada. TEL 416-466-1195. Ed. Rev. F.J. Power. adv.; circ. 18,600.

282   CN   ISSN 0835-2003
CARAVAN; a resource for those engaged in animating adult faith formation. 1987. q. Can.$16($18) (outside US and Canada US$24). Canadian Conference of Catholic Bishops, Publications Service - Conference des Eveques Catholiques du Canada, 90 Parent Ave., Ottawa, Ont. K1N 7B1, Canada. TEL 613-236-9461. FAX 613-236-8117. TELEX 053-3311. Ed. Joanne Chafe. bk.rev.; charts; illus.; stat.; circ. 1,000.
Description: News about workshops, research, upcoming conferences.

285   PH
CARDINAL BEA STUDIES. Short title: C B S. 1970. irreg., no.7, 1977. Cardinal Bea Institute for Ecumenical Studies, Box 4082, Manila, Philippines. Ed. Pedro S. de Achutegui, S.J. circ. 750.

282   US
CARING COMMUNITY. 1985. m. National Catholic Reporter Publishing Company, Inc., 115 E. Armour Blvd., Box 419281, Kansas City, MO 64141. TEL 800-444-8910. FAX 816-931-5082. Eds. Carolyn Hoff, Rich Heffren. illus.; circ. 30,000.
Description: Newsletter of support and inspiration for homebound and hospitalized Catholics.

282   LI
CARITAS. 1989. m. Women's Catholic Union, Vilniaus 29, Kaunas 233000, Lithuania. TEL (0127) 209-683. Ed. Albina Pribushauskaite. circ. 30,000.

255   IE   ISSN 0008-6665
CARMEL. 1930. bi-m. £4.20. Discalced Carmelites, 55 Marlborough Rd., Donnybrook, Dublin 4, Ireland. Ed. Philip McParland, OCD. adv.; circ. 11,000.
Description: Aims to help people to pray and discover the presence of God in their daily lives.

282   IT   ISSN 0394-7742
CARMEL IN THE WORLD. (Text in English) 1961. 3/yr. L.12000($10) (Order of Carmelites) Institutum Carmelitanum, Via Sforza Pallavicini 10, 00193 Rome, Italy. TEL 06-654-3513. FAX 06-654-7200. Eds. Redemptus M. Valabek, O. Carm. adv.; circ. 800.
Description: Features readings on Carmelite spirituality, especially for laity.

282   IT   ISSN 0394-7750
CARMEL IN THE WORLD PAPERBACKS. (Text in English) 1982. irreg. price varies. (Order of Carmelites) Institutum Carmelitanum, Via Sforza Pallavicini 10, 00193 Rome, Italy. TEL 06-654-3513. FAX 06-654-7200. Eds. Redemptus M. Valabek, O. Carm. adv.; circ. 1,000.
Description: Forum includes Carmelite spirituality biography and popular treatment.

282   AT   ISSN 1035-0993
CARMELITE; magazine of prayer and reflection. 1983. 5/yr. Aus.$7.50. Carmelite Communication, Carmelite Centre, 214 Richardson Street, Middle Park, Vic. 3206, Australia. TEL 03-6908822. FAX 61-3-696-0207. Ed. Fr. B. Pitman. bk.rev.; circ. 2,500. (back issues avail.)

255   IT   ISSN 0008-6673
BX3201
CARMELUS; commentarii ab Instituto Carmelitano editi. (Text in English, French, German, Italian, Latin and Spanish) 1954. 2/yr. L.50000. (Order of Carmelites) Institutum Carmelitanum, Via Sforza Pallavicini 10, 00193 Rome, Italy. TEL 06-654-3513. FAX 06-654-7200. Eds. Joachim Smet, O. Carm. adv.; bk.rev.; annual bibl.; index; circ. 610. (back issues avail.)
—BLDSC shelfmark: 3053.600000.
Description: Contains original articles on theology, with emphasis on spirituality and mariology and history.

CATALYST (ST. DAVIDS). see SOCIAL SERVICES AND WELFARE

282   IT   ISSN 0391-5433
CATECHESI. 1932. m. L.28000. (Centro Catechistico Salesiano) Editrice Elle Di Ci, Corso Francia 214, 10096 Leumann (Turin), Italy. TEL 011 95-91-091. Ed. Pietro Damu. circ. 7,000. **Indexed:** CERDIC.

240   US
CATECHIST'S CONNECTION. 1984. 10/yr. National Catholic Reporter Publishing Company, Inc., 115 E. Armour Blvd., Box 419281, Kansas City, MO 64141. TEL 800-444-8910. FAX 816-931-5082. Ed. Jean Marie Hiesburger. adv.; bk.rev.; circ. 38,000. (tabloid format)
Description: Articles supporting professional and volunteer teachers of Catholic religion.

282   US   ISSN 1040-659X
CATECHUMENATE; a journal of Christian initiation. 1978. bi-m. $20. (Archdiocese of Chicago) Liturgy Training Publications, 1800 N. Hermitage Ave., Chicago, IL 60622-1101. TEL 312-486-8970. FAX 312-486-7094. Ed. Victoria Tufano. bk.rev.; index; circ. 6,100. (back issues avail.)
Formerly (until 1978): Chicago Catechumenate.
Description: Contains reflections and information for catechists of children and adults, parish staff, and parents.

282   UK
THE CATHOLIC. 1896. a. $20. Incorporated Catholic Truth Society, 38-40 Eccleston Square, London SW1V 1PD, England. TEL 071-834 4392. Ed. Christopher Ralls. adv.; bk.rev.; bibl.; circ. 25,000 (controlled).
Formerly (until July, 1989): Catholic Truth (ISSN 0411-275X); Incorporates: Catholic Book Notes.
Description: Reports for members of the society detailing publishing work carried out and financial position.

282   US
CATHOLIC ACTIVIST. 1978. m. $38. American Classical College, Box 4526, Albuquerque, NM 87196-4526. TEL 505-296-2320. Ed. C.M. Flumiani.
Description: Current history from Catholic viewpoint.

282   US   ISSN 0008-7904
CATHOLIC ADVANCE. 1901. w. $10 in Kansas; $12 outside Kansas. Catholic Diocese of Wichita, 424 N. Broadway, Wichita, KS 67202. TEL 316-269-3965. Ed. Christopher M. Riggs. adv.; bk.rev.; circ. 30,000. (also avail. in microform)
Formerly: Advance.

282   US   ISSN 0045-5970
CATHOLIC AGITATOR. 1971. 10/yr. $1. (Ammon Hennacy House of Hospitality) Los Angeles Catholic Worker, 632 N. Brittania St., Los Angeles, CA 90033. TEL 213-267-8789. Ed. Jeff Dietrich. adv.; bk.rev.; circ. 7,000.

CATHOLIC AID NEWS. see INSURANCE

282   US   ISSN 0069-1208
AY81.R6
CATHOLIC ALMANAC. 1904. a. $15.95. Our Sunday Visitor, Inc., 200 Noll Plaza, Huntington, IN 46750. TEL 219-356-8400. FAX 219-356-8472. Eds. Rev. Felician A. Foy, Rose M. Avato. index. **Indexed:** SRI.
Formerly: National Catholic Almanac.
Description: Names and addresses of all types of Catholic offices, organizations and facilities.

282   US
CATHOLIC ANSWER. 1987. bi-m. $25. Our Sunday Visitor, Inc., 200 Noll Plaza, Huntington, IN 46750. TEL 219-356-8400. FAX 219-356-8472. Ed. Fr. Peter M. Stravinskas. adv.; circ. 72,449.
Description: Supplies Catholics with answers on what the church teaches, how to live their faith, and what their Catholic heritage is.

282   UK   ISSN 0261-4316
CATHOLIC ARCHIVES. 1981. a. £2. Catholic Archives Society, c/o R.M. Gard, Ed., Flat 7, Dawes House, High St., Burwash, Etchingham, Sussex TN19 6HD, England. circ. 350. **Indexed:** CERDIC.
Description: Guide to the history and use of the archives of the Roman Catholic Church in the U.K. and Ireland.

220 282   US   ISSN 0008-7912
BS410
CATHOLIC BIBLICAL QUARTERLY. 1939. q. $15. Catholic Biblical Association of America, Catholic University of America, Washington, DC 20064. TEL 202-319-5519. Ed. John S. Kselman. adv.; bk.rev.; index, cum.index; circ. 4,230. (also avail. in microfilm) **Indexed:** Arts & Hum.Cit.Ind., Cath.Ind., CERDIC, Curr.Cont., Hum.Ind., Mid.East: Abstr.& Ind., New Test.Abstr., Old Test.Abstr., Rel.& Theol.Abstr. (1968-), Rel.Ind.One, Rel.Per.
—BLDSC shelfmark: 3093.010000.
Description: Articles and notices of a scholarly nature on the Scripture.

CATHOLIC CEMETERY. see FUNERALS

282   US   ISSN 8756-7482
CATHOLIC CHALLENGE. 1985. q. $15. Sanderleaf Publishing, Inc., 182 109th Ave., Elmont, NY 11003. TEL 516-488-7439. Ed. Rev. James P. Lisante.

282   US   ISSN 0008-7971
CATHOLIC CHRONICLE. 1934. bi-w. $15. (Catholic Diocese of Toledo) Catholic Chronicle, Inc., 2130 Madison Ave., Box 1866, Toledo, OH 43603. TEL 419-243-4178. FAX 419-243-4235. Ed. Daniel J. McCarthy. adv.; film rev.; circ. 38,000. (also avail. in microfilm)

282   XK
CATHOLIC CHRONICLE. 1957. m. EC$1. Archdiocese of Castries, c/o Benedictine Nuns, Box 778, Castries, St. Lucia, W.I. TEL 809-20790. Ed. Patrick A.B. Anthony. adv.; circ. 2,500.
Formerly: Castries Catholic Chronicle.

RELIGIONS AND THEOLOGY — ROMAN CATHOLIC

282 US
CATHOLIC COMMENTATOR. 1963. fortn. $10. Roman Catholic Diocese of Baton Rouge, 1800 S. Acadian Thruway, Baton Rouge, LA 70808. TEL 504-387-0983. FAX 504-336-8789. (Subscr. to: Box 14746, Baton Rouge, LA 70898) Ed. Laura Deavers. circ. 50,000. (tabloid format)
  Description: Covers local and world news, and diocesan communications.

280 FR
CATHOLIC COUNTER-REFORMATION IN THE XXTH CENTURY. (Text in English) 1970. m. $8. Contre Reforme Catholique, Maison Saint-Joseph, 10260-Saint-Parres-les-Vaudes, France. Ed. Frere Gerard Cousin. bk.rev.; circ. 4,500.

282 US
CATHOLIC COURIER. 1889. w. $19.50. (Roman Catholic Diocese of Rochester, N.Y.) Rochester Catholic Press Association, 1150 Buffalo Rd., Rochester, NY 14624. TEL 716-328-4340. Ed. Karen M. Franz. adv.; circ. 46,213. (tabloid format; also avail. in microfilm)
  Formerly: Courier-Journal.
  Description: Newspaper of the 12-county Rochester, NY diocese. Includes local, national and international church news, feature articles, columns and commentary.

282 US ISSN 0008-7998
BX801
CATHOLIC DIGEST. 1936. m. $14.97. University of St. Thomas, Box 64090, St. Paul, MN 55164. TEL 612-647-5298. FAX 612-647-4346. Ed. Henry Lexau. adv.; illus.; circ. 620,000. (also avail. in microform from UMI,PMC; reprint service avail. from UMI) Indexed: Cath.Ind., CERDIC.

282 US
CATHOLIC DIRECTORY (SAN DIEGO). 1936. a. $8. Roman Catholic Diocese of San Diego, Box 81869, San Diego, CA 92138. TEL 619-574-6393. FAX 619-293-3765. Ed. Dan E. Pitre. adv.; circ. 3,500.

CATHOLIC DIRECTORY (SAN FRANCISCO); Marin, San Francisco and San Mateo Counties. see BUSINESS AND ECONOMICS — Trade And Industrial Directories

267 UK ISSN 0306-5677
BX1497.A3
CATHOLIC DIRECTORY FOR SCOTLAND. 1828. a. £9.50. John S. Burns and Sons, 25 Finlas St., Possilpark, Glasgow, G22 5DS, Scotland.
  —BLDSC shelfmark: 3093.019000.
  Formerly: Catholic Directory for the Clergy and Laity in Scotland (ISSN 0069-1232)

282 UK
CATHOLIC DIRECTORY OF ENGLAND AND WALES. 1839. a. £17.50. Gabriel Communications, St. James's Building, First Floor, Oxford St., Manchester M1 6FP, England. Ed. Monsig. George Leonard. adv.

282 SA
CATHOLIC DIRECTORY OF SOUTHERN AFRICA. 1906. biennial. R.20. Southern African Catholic Bishops' Conference, Commission for Social Communications, P.O. Box 941, Pretoria 0001, South Africa. TEL 012-323-6458. FAX 012-211795. TELEX 32-0776-SA. adv.; stat.; index; circ. 1,500.
  Description: Guide to all Catholic organizations and institutions comprising the ecclesiastical territories of South Africa, Botswana, Namibia, and Swaziland.

282 US
CATHOLIC DIRECTORY OF THE ARCHDIOCESE OF BALTIMORE. 1921. a. $11. Cathedral Foundation, 320 Cathedral St., Box 777, Baltimore, MD 21201. TEL 301-547-5314. adv.; circ. 1,900.
  Formerly: Archdiocese of Baltimore. Directory.

282 US
CATHOLIC DIRECTORY OF THE DIOCESE OF ALBANY. 1957. a. $11. Albany Catholic Press Association, Inc., 40 N. Main Ave., Albany, NY 12203. TEL 518-453-6688. Ed. Barbara R. Oliver. adv.
  Description: Lists churches, staff, agencies, organizations, and institutions of Albany Roman Catholic Diocese, covering 14 counties in upstate NY.

282 377.8 UK
CATHOLIC EDUCATION. 1960. biennial. £6. Catholic Education Council for England and Wales, 41 Cromwell Rd., London SW7 2DJ, England. FAX 071-823-7545. Ed. R.F. Cunningham. circ. 1,350.

282 US ISSN 0008-8056
CATHOLIC FREE PRESS. 1951. w. $14. (Roman Catholic Bishop of Worcester) Catholic Free Press, 47 Elm St., Worcester, MA 01609. TEL 508-757-6387. FAX 508-753-7180. Ed. Gerard E. Goggins. adv.; bk.rev.; illus.; circ. 22,861. (newspaper; also avail. in microfilm)

282 UK ISSN 0008-8064
CATHOLIC GAZETTE. 1910. m. £12. Catholic Missionary Society, 114 W. Heath Rd., London NW3 7TX, England. Ed. Martin Hayes. adv.; bk.rev.; index; circ. 6,000. Indexed: CERDIC.

CATHOLIC HEALTH ASSOCIATION OF CANADA. DIRECTORY. see MEDICAL SCIENCES

282 UK ISSN 0008-8072
CATHOLIC HERALD. 1884. w. $40. Catholic Herald Ltd., Herald House, Lambs Passage, Bunhill Row, London E.C.1., England. TEL 01-588-3101. FAX 01-256-9728. TELEX 8813473-CATHER-G. Ed. Peter Stanford. adv.; bk.rev.; film rev.; music rev.; index; circ. 30,819. (also avail. in microform from MIM,WMP)

282 US
CATHOLIC HERALD.* 1870. w. $24. Milwaukee Catholic Press Apostolate, 3501 S. Lake Dr., Box 07913, Milwaukee, WI 53207-0913. TEL 414-769-3500. Ed. Thomas J. Smith. adv.; circ. 93,000.

282 270 US ISSN 0008-8080
BX1404
CATHOLIC HISTORICAL REVIEW. 1915. q. $30. (American Catholic Historical Association) Catholic University of America Press, 620 Michigan Ave., N.E., Washington, DC 20064. TEL 202-319-5052. Ed. Rev. Robert Trisco. adv.; bk.rev.; bibl.; index, cum.index: vols.1-20, 21-50; circ. 2,083. (also avail. in microfilm from UMI,PMC; reprint service avail. from KTO,UMI) Indexed: Amer.Bibl.Slavic & E.Eur.Stud., Amer.Hist.& Life, Arts & Hum.Cit.Ind., Bk.Rev.Ind. (1980-), Cath.Ind., Child.Bk.Rev.Ind. (1980-), Curr.Cont., Hist.Abstr., Hum.Ind., Mid.East: Abstr.& Ind., Old Test.Abstr., Rel.& Theol.Abstr. (1971-), RILA.
  —BLDSC shelfmark: 3093.070000.

282 II
CATHOLIC INDIA. (Text in English) q. Catholic Bishop's Conference of India, CBCI Centre, 1 Ashok Place, Goldakkhana, New Delhi 110 001, India. TEL 11-344470. TELEX 3161366.

CATHOLIC JOURNALIST. see JOURNALISM

282 US
CATHOLIC KEY. 1978. w. $18. Diocese of Kansas City, St. Joseph, 300 E. 36th St., Box 419037, Kansas City, MO 64141-6037. TEL 816-756-1850. FAX 816-756-0878. Ed. Albert de Zutter. adv.; bk.rev.; circ. 17,200. (tabloid format; back issues avail.)

CATHOLIC LAWYER. see LAW

CATHOLIC LIBRARY ASSOCIATION. NORTHERN ILLINOIS CHAPTER. NEWSLETTER. see LIBRARY AND INFORMATION SCIENCES

282 GW ISSN 0930-8679
CATHOLIC MEDIA COUNCIL. INFORMATION BULLETIN. 1972. q. free. Catholic Media Council, Publizistische Medienplanung fuer Entwicklungslaender, e.V., Anton-Kurze-Allee 2, 5100 Aachen, Germany. TEL 0241-73081. FAX 0241-73462. Ed. Hans-Peter Gohla. bk.rev.; charts; circ. 800.

CATHOLIC MEDICAL QUARTERLY. see MEDICAL SCIENCES

282 US ISSN 0008-8234
CATHOLIC MESSENGER. 1882. w. $19 (effective 1992). Roman Catholic Diocese of Davenport, 736 Federal St., Box 460, Davenport, IA 52805-0460. TEL 319-323-9959. Ed. Rev. Francis C. Henricksen. adv.; bk.rev.; circ. 23,000. (newspaper; also avail. in microform)

200 CN ISSN 0701-0788
CATHOLIC NEW TIMES. 1976. 23/yr. Can.$20($30) New Catholic Times Inc., 80 Sackville St., Toronto, Ont. M5A 3E5, Canada. TEL 416-361-0761. FAX 1-416-361-0796. Ed. Anne O'Brien. adv.; bk.rev.; circ. 11,000. (also avail. in microfiche) Indexed: Can.Per.Ind.

282 US ISSN 0278-1174
CATHOLIC NEW YORK. 1981. w. $20. (Roman Catholic Diocese of New York) Ecclesiastical Communications Corp., 1011 First Ave., New York, NY 10022. TEL 212-688-2399. FAX 212-688-2642. Ed. Anne M. Buckley. adv.; bk.rev.; circ. 131,406. (also avail. in microfiche)

282 US ISSN 0008-8277
CATHOLIC PEACE FELLOWSHIP BULLETIN. 1965. 2/yr. donation. Catholic Peace Fellowship, 339 Lafayette St., New York, NY 10012. TEL 212-673-8990. Ed. Bill Ofenloch. bk.rev.; illus.; circ. 4,000.
  Description: Reports on events and views in the peace and disarmament movement.

THE CATHOLIC PHARMACIST. see PHARMACY AND PHARMACOLOGY

282 UK ISSN 0008-8293
CATHOLIC PICTORIAL. 1962. w. £0.35 (effective Jan. 1991). Catholic Pictorial Ltd., Media House, Mann Island, Pier Head, Liverpool L3 1DQ, England. TEL 051-236-2191. FAX 051-236-2216. Ed. Rev. Paul F. Thomson. adv.; illus.; circ. 9,500. (tabloid format)

282 US
CATHOLIC QUOTE; instant inspiration. vol.37, 1974. m. $5. Rev. Jerome Pokorny, Ed. & Pub., Valparaiso, NE 68065. index; circ. 7,000. (back issues avail.)

282 CN ISSN 0383-1620
CATHOLIC REGISTER. 1893. w. Can.$20.95($38.95) (effective Jan. 1991). Canadian Register Ltd., 67 Bond St., Ste. 303, Toronto, Ont. M5B 1X6, Canada. TEL 416-362-6822. FAX 416-362-8652. Ed. Fr. Carl Matthews. adv.; bk.rev.; film rev.; abstr.; circ. 31,000. (tabloid format)
  Formerly: Canadian Register (ISSN 0008-4913)

282 US ISSN 0008-8315
CATHOLIC REVIEW (BALTIMORE). 1913. w. $25. Cathedral Foundation, Inc., 320 Cathedral St., Box 777, Baltimore, MD 21203. TEL 410-547-5327. FAX 410-385-0113. Ed. Daniel Medinger. adv.; bk.rev.; circ. 74,011. (also avail. in microfilm)

CATHOLIC REVIEW (NEW YORK). see HANDICAPPED — Visually Impaired

200 AT
CATHOLIC SCHOOL STUDIES. 1928. 2/yr. Aus.$15 (foreign Aus.$16) per no. Christian Brothers of the Australian and New Zealand Provinces, Treacy Centre, 156 The Avenue, Parkville, Vic. 3052, Australia. TEL 03-347-4111. FAX 03-347-3112. Ed. R. S. Stewart. adv.; bk.rev.; circ. 2,900. Indexed: Aus.Educ.Ind.
  Former titles: Christian Brothers of the Australian and New Zealand Provinces. Our Studies (ISSN 0045-6780); Christian Brothers Studies; Catholic School Studies.
  Description: Covers education for Australian and New Zealand Catholic schools.

282 US ISSN 0162-2102
CATHOLIC SENTINEL (ARCHDIOCESE OF PORTLAND, OREGON). w. Oregon Catholic Press, 5536 N.E. Hassalo St., Portland, OR 97213. TEL 503-281-1191. FAX 503-282-3486.

282 US ISSN 0162-0363
CATHOLIC SENTINEL (DIOCESE OF BAKER). 1906. Oregon Catholic Press, 5536 N.E. Hassalo St., Portland, OR 97213. TEL 503-281-1191. FAX 503-282-3486. Ed. Robert Pfohman. adv.; bk.rev.; film rev.; abstr.; illus.; circ. 23,142. (tabloid format; also avail. in microform)

282 US
CATHOLIC SPIRIT (AUSTIN). (Text in English, Spanish) 1983. m. $9. Diocese of Austin, Box 13327, Austin, TX 78711. TEL 512-476-4888. FAX 512-469-9537. Ed. Helen Osman. adv.; bk.rev.; circ. 25,000. (tabloid format)

RELIGIONS AND THEOLOGY — ROMAN CATHOLIC

200 US
CATHOLIC SPIRIT (WHEELING). 1934. w. $12. Catholic Diocese of Wheeling-Charleston, Box 951, Wheeling, WV 26003-0119. TEL 304-233-0880. FAX 304-233-0890. Ed. Richard Cain. adv.; bk.rev.; film rev.; circ. 4,600. (tabloid format; also avail. in microfiche)

282 UK ISSN 0008-8366
CATHOLIC STANDARD. 1938. w. 58p. The Catholic Herald, Herald House, Lambs Passage, Bunhill Row, London EC1Y 8T2, England. Ed. Peter Stanford. adv.; bk.rev.; illus.; circ. 5,000. **Indexed:** CERDIC, HR Rep.

282 GY
CATHOLIC STANDARD. 1905. w. 293 Oronoque St., Queenstown, POB 10720, Georgetown, Guyana. TEL 2-61540. Ed. Fr. Andrew Morrison. circ. 10,000.

282 US
CATHOLIC STUDY COUNCIL BULLETIN. 1985. m. $15. (National Center for Public Policy Research) Catholic Study Council, 300 Eye St., N.E., Ste. 2, Washington, DC 20002. TEL 202-543-1286. Ed. Michael G. Pauley. circ. 600.
Description: Discusses the role of religion in social problems.

282 US ISSN 0744-267X
CATHOLIC SUN.* 1883. w. $15. Syracuse Catholic Press, Inc., 421 S. Warren St., Syracuse, NY 13202-2603. TEL 315-422-8153. Ed. Jim Murphy. adv.; bk.rev.; circ. 42,500. (tabloid format; also avail. in microfilm; back issues avail.)

282 US
CATHOLIC TELEGRAPH. 1831. w. $22. (Archdiocese of Cincinnati) Catholic Telegraph, 100 E. 8th St., Cincinnati, OH 45202. TEL 513-421-3131. FAX 513-381-2242. Ed. Jim Stackpoole. adv.; bk.rev.; film rev.; circ. 32,000.

282 US
CATHOLIC TELEPHONE GUIDE. a. $27. Catholic News Publishing Co., Inc., 210 N. Ave., New Rochelle, NY 10801. TEL 914-632-1220.

282 US ISSN 0069-1267
CATHOLIC THEOLOGICAL SOCIETY OF AMERICA. PROCEEDINGS. 1946. a. $14 (foreign $16). Catholic Theological Society of America, c/o Dr. Michael McGinniss, Department of Religion, La Salle University, Box 119, 1900 W. Olney Ave., Philadelphia, PA 19141. TEL 215-951-1335. Ed. Paul Crowler. index, cum.index; circ. 1,600. (also avail. in microform from UMI; reprint service avail. from UMI) **Indexed:** Cath.Ind., CERDIC, New Test.Abstr.

200 100 US
CATHOLIC THOUGHT FROM LUBLIN. irreg. Peter Lang Publishing, Inc., 62 W. 45th St., 4th Fl., New York, NY 10036. TEL 212-302-6740. FAX 212-302-7574. Ed. Andrew Woznicki.

282 051 US ISSN 0745-6050
CATHOLIC TIMES. 1951. w. $17. Catholic Times, Inc., Box 636, Columbus, OH 43216. TEL 614-224-5195. Ed. Mike Collins. adv.; bk.rev.; film rev.; circ. 32,145. (tabloid format; also avail. in microfilm; magnetic tape; back issues avail.)
Description: Newspaper of the Diocese of Columbus.

CATHOLIC TRAVELER. see *TRAVEL AND TOURISM*

282 US
CATHOLIC TWIN CIRCLE. 1965. w. $49.95 (Canada $65). Twin Circle Publishing Co., 12700 Ventura Blvd., Studio City, CA 91604. TEL 800-421-3230. FAX 213-655-0344. Ed. Loretta Seyer. adv.; bk.rev.; film rev.; play rev.; illus.; circ. 30,000. (tabloid format)
Former titles: Catholic Twin Circle Weekly Magazine; Twin Circle Weekly Catholic Magazine; Twin Circle (ISSN 0041-4654)

CATHOLIC UNIVERSITY LAW REVIEW. see *LAW*

282 US
CATHOLIC UPDATE. m. $9. (Franciscan Friars of St. John the Baptist Province) St. Anthony Messenger Press, 1615 Republic St., Cincinnati, OH 45210. TEL 513-241-5615. Ed. Rev. Jack Wintz. circ. 326,000.
Description: Newsletter of Roman Catholic concerns and practices.

282 US ISSN 0008-8404
CATHOLIC VIRGINIAN. 1946. w. $10. Diocese of Richmond, c/o Most. Rev. Walter F. Sullivan, Bishop of Richmond, 800 Cathedral Pl., Box 26843, Richmond, VA 23261. TEL 804-359-5654. Ed. Charles E. Mahon. adv.; bk.rev.; film rev.; charts; illus.; circ. 38,827. (tabloid format)

266 GH ISSN 0008-8412
CATHOLIC VOICE. 1926. m. $72. (Archdiocese of Cape Coast) Catholic Mission Press, Box 60, Cape Coast, Ghana. Ed. Rev. Gabriel D. Mensah. illus.; circ. 6,000. **Indexed:** CERDIC.

282 US ISSN 0744-9585
CATHOLIC VOICE. 1903. fortn. $17.50. (Catholic Archbishop of Omaha, Nebraska) Catholic Voice Publishing Co., 6060 N.W. Radial Highway, Box 4010, Omaha, NE 68104. TEL 402-558-6611. FAX 402-558-6614. Ed. Stephen M. Kent. adv.; bk.rev.; circ. 69,023. (tabloid format; also avail. in microfiche; back issues avail.)

282 US
CATHOLIC WEEK. 1934. w. $10 inside diocese; outside diocese $15. 400 Government St., Box 349, Mobile, AL 36601. TEL 205-432-3529. Ed. Anna B. Crow. adv.; circ. 15,000. (tabloid format)

282 AT ISSN 0008-8420
CATHOLIC WEEKLY.* 1942. w. Aus.$46. Catholic Press Newspaper Co. Pty. Ltd., 2nd Fl., Mary Potter Wing, Ozaman Village, Cnr West & Thomas Sts., Lewisham, N.S.W. 2049, Australia. TEL 02-211-4499. FAX 02-381-2187. Ed. Ron F. Robinson. adv.; bk.rev.; illus.; circ. 21,000.
Description: Catholic family newspaper. Includes international, national and local news.

282 US ISSN 0008-8439
CATHOLIC WEEKLY. 1942. w. $19.50. Catholic Dioceses of Saginaw & Gaylord, 1520 Court St., Box 1405, Saginaw, MI 48605. TEL 517-793-7661. Ed. Kathleen Socha. adv.; bk.rev.; circ. 12,572. (back issues avail.)
Description: Coverage of current local, national and world news from a Catholic perspective.

282 US ISSN 0008-8447
CATHOLIC WITNESS. 1966. fortn. $9 to non-parish members. (Diocese of Harrisburg) Harrisburg Catholic Publishing Associates, Box 2555, 4800 Union Deposit Rd., Harrisburg, PA 17105. TEL 717-657-4804. FAX 717-657-7673. Ed. Rev. T.R. Haney. bk.rev.; illus.; circ. 64,000. (newspaper; also avail. in microfilm)
Description: National and international news of religious events.

282 US ISSN 0008-8471
CATHOLIC WORKMAN. vol.63, 1970. m. $1.50. Box 47, New Prague, MN 56071. TEL 612-758-2229. FAX 612-758-5041. Ed. Pauline O'Brien. stat.; circ. 8,300 (controlled). (tabloid format)
Description: Covers religious articles, lodge news, and activities.

282 AP2 US ISSN 1042-3494
THE CATHOLIC WORLD. 1865. bi-m. $12. (Missionary Society of St. Paul the Apostle in the State of New York) Paulist Press, 997 Macarthur Blvd., Mahwah, NJ 07430. TEL 201-825-7300. FAX 201-825-8345. Ed. Laurie Felknor. bk.rev.; index; circ. 8,000. (also avail. in microform from UMI,PMC; reprint service avail. from UMI) **Indexed:** Access (1980-), Amer.Hist.& Life, Bk.Rev.Ind. (1965-), Cath.Ind., CERDIC, Chic.Per.Ind., Child.Bk.Rev.Ind. (1965-), G.Soc.Sci.& Rel.Per.Lit., Hist.Abstr., Mag.Ind., Mid.East: Abstr.& Ind., R.G.
—BLDSC shelfmark: 3093.250000.
Former titles: New Catholic World; Catholic World (ISSN 0008-848X)

282 GW ISSN 0008-8501
CATHOLICA; vierteljahresschrift fuer Oekumenische Theologie. 4/yr. DM.76. (Johann Adam Moehler-Institut Paderborn) Aschendorffsche Verlagsbuchhandlung, Soesterstr. 13, 4400 Muenster, Germany. TEL 0251-690-0. FAX 0251-690405. Eds. Hans Joerg Urban, Peter Blaeser. adv.; bk.rev.; bibl.; index. **Indexed:** New Test.Abstr., Rel.& Theol.Abstr. (1989-), Rel.Ind.One, Rel.Per.

282 FR
CATHOLICISME HIER, AUJOURD'HUI, DEMAIN. 1935. irreg. (approx. 3/yr.). 150 F. per vol. Letouzey et Ane Editeurs, 87 bd. Raspail, 75006 Paris, France. TEL 45-48-80-14. Ed.Bd.

282 CN ISSN 0381-7466
CELEBRATE. French edition: Rassembler. 1940. 6/yr. Can.$21($24) Novalis, 6255 Hutchison St., Ste. 103, Montreal, Que. H2V 4C7, Canada. TEL 514-278-3025. FAX 514-278-3030. Ed. Bernadette Gasslein.
Formerly: Homiletic Service.
Description: For catechists, religion teachers, homilists and liturgy planners.

200 US ISSN 0094-2421
CELEBRATION: A CREATIVE WORSHIP SERVICE. 1970. m. $64.95. National Catholic Reporter Publishing Company, Inc., 115 E. Armour Blvd., Box 414281, Kansas City, MO 64141. TEL 800-444-8910. Ed. William Freburger. adv.; bk.rev.; circ. 10,500. (looseleaf format) Key Title: Celebration (Kansas City).
Description: Resource packet for complete liturgy planning.

282 FR ISSN 0240-4656
CELEBRER. (Supplements avail.) 10/yr. 200 F. (foreign 230 F.). (Centre National de Pastorale Liturgique) Editions du Cerf, 29 bd. Latour Maubourg, 75340 Paris Cedex 07, France. TEL 44-18-12-12. FAX 45-56-04-27. (Subscr. to: Service Abonnements, 3 chemin des Prunais, 94350 Villiers-sur-Marne, France)

CELEBRIAMO; rivista bimestrale di musica vocale per la liturgia. see *MUSIC*

282 US ISSN 0890-0426
CENTER FOR APPLIED RESEARCH IN THE APOSTOLATE SEMINARY FORUM. 1972. q. $10 (foreign $15). Center for Applied Research in the Apostolate, Georgetown University, Box 1601, Washington, DC 20057. TEL 202-687-8080. Ed. C. Joseph O'Hara. circ. 600. (back issues avail.)

282 US
CENTRAL CALIFORNIA REGISTER; Central California's Catholic newspaper. Short title: Register. (Text in English, Spanish) 1929. bi-w. $10. Roman Catholic Bishop of Fresno, 1550 N. Fresno St., Fresno, CA 93703. TEL 209-237-5125. (Subscr. to: Box 1668, Fresno, CA 93717) Ed. Terrence J. Schmal. adv.; bk.rev.; circ. 9,800.

CENTRE CATHOLIQUE DES INTELLECTUELS FRANCAIS. RECHERCHES ET DEBATS. see *HUMANITIES: COMPREHENSIVE WORKS*

CENTRUM JANA PAWLA II BIULETYN. see *BIOGRAPHY*

282 XV ISSN 0009-0387
CERKEV V SEDANJEM SVETU. 1967. bi-m. 7200 din.($8) Slovenske Rimskokatoliske Skofije, Cankarjevo Nabrezje 3, 6100 Ljubljana, Slovenia. TEL 061-329-793. TELEX 31776 DRUNA YU. Ed. Rafko Valencic. bk.rev.; bibl.; circ. 2,500.

282 US
CHAP-LETT. 3/yr. $15. American Catholic Correctional Chaplains, Box 888, Ashland, KY 41101. TEL 606-928-6414. Ed. Rev. John P. Noe. circ. 350.

282 BX801 US ISSN 0009-3718
CHICAGO STUDIES. 1962. 3/yr. $15. (Faculty St. Mary of the Lake Seminary) Civitas Dei Foundation, Box 665, Mundelein, IL 60060. TEL 708-566-1462. Ed. Rev. George J. Dyer. adv.; bk.rev.; index; circ. 10,000. (also avail. in microform from UMI; reprint service avail. from UMI) **Indexed:** Canon Law Abstr., Cath.Ind., CERDIC, New Test.Abstr., Old Test.Abstr., Rel.& Theol.Abstr. (1979-).
—BLDSC shelfmark: 3172.730000.

282　　　　　　　　GW　ISSN 0170-5148
CHRIST IN DER GEGENWART. 1948. w. DM.80.60. Verlag Herder GmbH und Co. KG, Hermann-Herder-Str. 4, 7800 Freiburg, Germany. TEL 0761-2717-276. FAX 0761-2717-520. Ed. Manfred Plate. index; circ. 35,200. (looseleaf format; back issues avail.)

282 266　　　　　IT　ISSN 0011-1465
CHRIST TO THE WORLD/CHRIST AU MONDE; international review of Apostolic experiences. (Editions in English, French) 1955. bi-m. L.35000($30) Christ to the World, Via di Propaganda 1c, 00187 Rome, Italy. TEL 06-6793226. Ed. Fr. Massimiliano M. Zangheratti. bk.rev.; charts; film rev.; index; circ. 4,220. **Indexed:** Cath.Ind., CERDIC.

282　　　　　　　　GW　ISSN 0930-5718
CHRISTEN HEUTE; Zeitung der Alt-Katholiken fuer Christen heute. 1873; N.S. 1956. m. DM.26. Katholisches Bistum der Alt-Katholiken in Deutschland, Gregor-Mendel-Str. 28, 5300 Bonn 1, Germany. TEL 0228-232285. (Subscr. to: Christen Heute, Erich-Ollenhauer-Str.151, 6200 Wiesbaden, Germany) bk.rev. (back issues avail.)
Formerly: Alt-Katholische Kirchenzeitung (ISSN 0002-6522)

282　　　　　　　　US　ISSN 0739-6422
CHRISTIAN LIFE COMMUNITIES HARVEST. 1967. q. $10. National Christian Life Community of the United States of America, 3601 Lindell Blvd., No. 418, St. Louis, MO 63108-3393. adv.; bk.rev.; index; circ. 1,000. (back issues avail.)
Formerly: Christian Life Communicator.

200　　　　　　　　PK　ISSN 0009-5699
CHRISTIAN VOICE; a weekly newspaper and review. (Text in English) 1950. w. Rs.25. Archdiocese of Karachi, St. Patrick's High School, Sangster Rd., Saddar, Karachi 0328, Pakistan. Ed. Fr. Augustine P. Varkey. adv.; bk.rev.; bibl.; illus.; circ. 1,200.

DIE CHRISTLICHE FRAU. see *WOMEN'S INTERESTS*

268 282　　　　　GW　ISSN 0009-5818
CHRISTOPHORUS. 1955. q. DM.50. Dr. Klaus Goebel, Egenhoferstr. 16, 8000 Munich 60, Germany. TEL 089-887857. adv.; bk.rev.; charts.

200　　　　　　　　FR　ISSN 0009-5834
CHRISTUS; revue de pratique evangelique. 1954. q. 170 F. (foreign 200 F.). Assas Editions, 14 rue d'Assas, 75006 Paris, France. TEL 44-39-48-48. FAX 40-49-01-92. Ed. C. Flipo. adv.; circ. 6,000. **Indexed:** CERDIC, Refug.Abstr.
—BLDSC shelfmark: 3182.200000.

282　　　　　　　　US　ISSN 0197-0348
BX1559.L5
CHRONICLE OF THE CATHOLIC CHURCH IN LITHUANIA. 1972. irreg. $12. Lithuanian Catholic Religious Aid, 351 Highland Blvd., Brooklyn, NY 11207. TEL 718-647-2434. FAX 718-827-6696. TELEX 510-1013171. Eds. Marian Skabeikis, Rev. Casimir Pugevicius. illus.; circ. 8,000. (back issues avail.)

282　　　　　　　　PL　ISSN 0578-0594
CHRZESCIJANSKIE STOWARZYSZENIE SPOLECZNE. INFORMATION BULLETIN. (Text in English, French and German) 1957. m. $12 or on exchange basis. Chrzescijanskie Stowarzyszenie Spoleczne - Christian Social Association, Marszalkowska 4, 00-590 Warsaw, Poland. (Dist. by: RSW "Prasa-Ksiazka-Ruch" Centrala Kolportazu Prasy i Wydawnictw, Towarowa 28, 00-958 Warsaw) Ed.Bd. adv.; circ. 950.

282　　　　　　　　PL
CHRZESCIJANSKIE STOWARZYSZENIE SPOLECZNE. MATERIALY PROBLEMOWE. 1965. m. $10. Chrzescijanskie Stowarzyszenie Spoleczne - Christian Social Association, Marszalkowska 4, 00-590 Warsaw, Poland. Ed. Jan Pawel Henne. adv.; circ. 5,000.

200 282　　　　　US　ISSN 0883-5667
CHURCH. 1985. q. $26. National Pastoral Life Center, 299 Elizabeth St., New York, NY 10012. TEL 212-431-7825. FAX 212-274-9786. Ed. Karen Sue Smith. adv.; bk.rev.; circ. 8,000. (back issues avail.)
Description: Concerned with aiding Roman Catholic pastoral ministers' continued spiritual reflection and growth. Gives practical examples of successful parish programs.

200　　　　　　　　SP　ISSN 0210-0398
BX805
CIENCIA TOMISTA. 1910. 3/yr. $40. Facultad Teologica de San Esteban, Convento de San Estaban., Apdo. 17, 37080 Salamanca, Spain. FAX 923-26-54-80. Ed. Luis Lago. bk.rev.; circ. 700. **Indexed:** Cath.Ind., CERDIC, M.L.A.

CISTERCIENSER CHRONIK. see *ARCHITECTURE*

271　　　　　　　　BE　ISSN 0774-4919
BX3401
CITEAUX; commentarii cistercienses. (Text in Dutch, English, French, German, Italian, Portuguese, Spanish) 1950. 3/yr. 1265 Fr.($33) Citeaux V.Z.W., Cistercian Abbey Nazareth, B-2960 Brecht, Belgium. Ed. J.F. Holthof. bk.rev.; bibl.; illus.; index, cum.index: 1950-74. (also avail. in microfilm) **Indexed:** Amer.Hist.& Life, Hist.Abstr., M.L.A.
Description: Articles deal with all aspects and periods of Cistercian history, art, archeology, law, economy, liturgy and spirituality.

282 255　　　　　SP　ISSN 0009-7756
CIUDAD DE DIOS; revista Agustiniana. 1881. 3/yr. 3600 ptas.($46) Ediciones Escurialenses, Real Monasterio del Escorial, 28200 San Lorenzo del Escorial, Madrid, Spain. TEL 91-890-50-11. FAX 91-890-54-21. bk.rev.; index; circ. 700. (also avail. in microfilm from UMI) **Indexed:** Amer.Hist.& Life, CERDIC, Hist.Abstr., M.L.A., New Test.Abstr.

282　　　　　　　　IT　ISSN 0009-8167
AP37
CIVILTA CATTOLICA. 1850. s-m. L.60000($75) Compagnia di Gesu, Via di Porta Pinciana 1, 00187 Rome, Italy. TEL 06-679-83-51. FAX 06-684-09-97. Ed. Gism Paolo Selvini. adv.; bk.rev.; film rev.; play rev.; bibl.; index, cum.index: 1940-1960, 1960-1970, 1970-1980; circ. 20,000. **Indexed:** Amer.Hist.& Life, Cath.Ind., CERDIC, Hist.Abstr., New Test.Abstr.

282　　　　　　　　IT　ISSN 0578-4182
CLARETIANUM; commentaria theologica. (Text in various European languages) 1961. a. L.35000($35) (effective 1991). Institutum Theologiae Vitae Religiosae, Largo Lorenzo Mossa 4, 00165 Rome, Italy. TEL 39-6-66-38-981. FAX 39-6-66-36-713. Ed. Bruno Proietti. bk.rev.; bibl.; circ. 300. **Indexed:** Canon Law Abstr., CERDIC.
—BLDSC shelfmark: 3274.375000.
Description: Theologica.

282　　　　　　　　US
CLARION HERALD. 1963. bi-w. $13. (Archdiocese of New Orleans) Clarion Herald Publishing Co., 1000 Howard Ave., Ste. 400, New Orleans, LA 70113. TEL 504-524-1618. FAX 504-596-3020. adv.; bk.rev.; circ. 64,496. (tabloid format; also avail. in microfilm)

CLUBHOUSE. see *CHILDREN AND YOUTH — For*

282　　　　　　　　IT
CODICE DEL VATICANO II. 1984. irreg. Centro Editoriale Dehoniano, Via Nosadella 6, 40123 Bologna, Italy. TEL 051-306811. FAX 051-341706.

282　　　　　　　　SP
COLECCION HISTORIA DE LA IGLESIA. 1971. irreg., no.24, 1990. price varies. (Universidad de Navarra, Departamento de Historia de la Iglesia) Ediciones Universidad de Navarra, S.A., Apdo. 396, 31080 Pamplona, Spain. TEL 92 825 6850.

282　　　　　　　　SP
COLECCION TEOLOGICA. 1970. irreg., no.69, 1990. price varies. (Universidad de Navarra, Facultad de Teologia) Ediciones Universidad de Navarra, S.A., Apdo. 396, 31080 Pamplona, Spain. TEL 94 825 6850.

282　　　　　　　　SP
COLEGIO MAYOR P. FELIPE SCIO. PUBLICACIONES. 1975. irreg. price varies. Ediciones Calasancias, Paseo de Canalejas 75, Apdo. 206, Salamanca, Spain.

282　　　　　　　　IT　ISSN 0069-5254
COLLANA RICCIANA. FONTI. 1963. irreg., no.12, 1975. price varies. Casa Editrice Leo S. Olschki, Casella Postale 66, 50100 Florence, Italy. TEL 055-6530684. FAX 055-6530214. Ed. P. di Agresti. circ. 1,000.

282　　　　　　　　IT　ISSN 0394-7769
COLLATIONES MARIALES INSTITUTI CARMELITANI. (Text in English, French, German, Italian, Latin and Spanish) 1960. irreg. price varies. (Order of Carmelites) Institutum Carmelitanum, Via Sforza Pallavicini 10, 00193 Rome, Italy. TEL 06-654-3513. FAX 06-654-7200. adv.; circ. 500.

COLLECTANEA BIBLIOGRAPHICA CARMELITANA. see *BIBLIOGRAPHIES*

271　　　　　　　　BE　ISSN 0378-4916
COLLECTANEA CISTERCIENSIA; revue de spiritualite monastique. (Text in French) 1934. q. 850 Fr.($25) Abbaye N.D. de Soleilmont, B-6220 Fleurus, Belgium. (U.S. subscr. to: Br. John Berchmans, St. Joseph's Abbey, Spencer, MA 01562; U.K. subscr. to: Fr. Camillus O'Donovan, Bethlehem Abbey, Portglenon, Ballymena, Co. Antrim BT44 8BL Ireland.) bk.rev.; bibl. (also avail. in microform from UMI) **Indexed:** Cath.Ind., CERDIC.
Description: Publishes studies on the various monastic traditions, both oriental and occidental, information pertaining to the dialogue between Christian and non-Christian monasticism, and reports on events in the monastic world, including congresses, meetings, and relevant publications.

271　　　　　　　　IT　ISSN 0010-0749
COLLECTANEA FRANCISCANA. (Annual supplement: Bibliographia Franciscana) (Text in English, French, German, Italian, Latin, Portuguese and Spanish) 1931. q. L.50000($60) (foreign L.65000)(effective 1990). Frati Minori Cappuccini, Istituto Storico, Casella Postale 90-91, Circonv. Occidentale 6850 (GRA km 65), Rome, Italy. TEL 06-625-19-58. FAX 06-62-62-401. Ed. Vincenzo Criscuolo. bk.rev.; bibl.; index, cum.index: 1931-1970; circ. 800. **Indexed:** CERDIC.

266　　　　　　　　US　ISSN 0095-4438
BV3410
COLUMBAN MISSION. 1918. m. (except Jun. & Aug.) $10. (St. Columban's Foreign Mission Society) Columban Fathers, St. Columbans, NE 68056. FAX 402-291-8693. Ed. Rev. Richard Steinhilber. bk.rev.; circ. 180,000 (controlled).
Formerly: Columban Fathers Mission.

282 249　　　　　US　ISSN 0010-1869
AP2
COLUMBIA (NEW HAVEN); America's largest Catholic family magazine. 1921. m. $6. Knights of Columbus, Drawer 1670, New Haven, CT 06507. TEL 203-772-2130. Ed. Rick NcMunn. adv.; bk.rev.; index; circ. 1,406,992. **Indexed:** Cath.Ind.
Description: Provides features and columns demonstrating how groups and families can cooperate to improve society.

266　　　　　　　　US　ISSN 0279-3652
COMBONI MISSIONS. 1948. q. $6. Comboni Missionaries of the Heart of Jesus, 8108 Beechmont Ave., Cincinnati, OH 45255. TEL 513-474-4997. FAX 513-474-0382. Ed. Jose Marques. illus.; circ. 25,000 (controlled).
Former titles: Verona Missions (ISSN 0164-4211); Verona Fathers Missions (ISSN 0042-4234)
Description: Informs readers about Third World situations and about the congregation's mission work.

262.9　　　　　　　IT　ISSN 0010-2598
COMMENTARIUM PRO RELIGIOSIS ET MISSIONARIIS. 1920. q. L.50000 (foreign L.55000). Institutum Iuridicum Claretianum - Claretian Juridical Institute, Via Giacomo Medici 5, 00153 Rome, Italy. Ed. Giuseppe Mettecoci. bk.rev.; bibl.; index; circ. 5,000. (back issues avail.) **Indexed:** Canon Law Abstr., CERDIC.
—BLDSC shelfmark: 3333.400000.
Description: Discusses canon law.

282　　　　　　　　US
COMMON GROUND (DES MOINES); a newsletter of faith, community and resources. 1922. 10/yr. $25 to individuals; institutions $100. National Catholic Rural Life Conference, 4625 Beaver Ave., Des Moines, IA 50310. TEL 515-270-2634. FAX 515-270-9449. Ed. Walter C. Clark. circ. 14,000.
Formerly: Earth Matters.

COMMONWEAL. see *LITERARY AND POLITICAL REVIEWS*

RELIGIONS AND THEOLOGY — ROMAN CATHOLIC

282　　　　　　　　VC
COMMUNICATIONES. s-a. L.32000($30) (foreign L.40000)(effective 1992). Libreria Editrice Vaticana, 00120 Vatican City (Rome), State of the Vatican City. **Indexed:** Canon Law Abstr., Cath.Ind., CERDIC.
　Description: Organ of the Pontifical Commission for the right interpretation of the Code of Canon Law.

282　　　　　　　US　　ISSN 0094-2065
BX801
COMMUNIO; international Catholic review. 1974. q. $21 to individuals (foreign $26); institutions $30. Communio, Inc., Box 1046, Notre Dame, IN 46556. TEL 219-239-7132. FAX 219-239-8609. Ed. David L. Schindler. adv.; index, cum.index; circ. 2,500. (also avail. in microform from UMI; back issues avail.; reprint service avail. from UMI) **Indexed:** Cath.Ind., Old Test.Abstr., Rel.& Theol.Abstr. (1979-), Rel.Ind.One.
　—BLDSC shelfmark: 3363.543600.
　Description: Journal of theological and cultural reflection from a Catholic perspective by noted theologians, philosophers, and other scholars.

282　　　　　　　CN　　ISSN 0010-3985
COMPANION OF ST. FRANCIS AND ST. ANTHONY. 1937. m. (except Jul.-Aug. combined). Can.$14. Conventual Franciscan Friars, Box 535, Station "F", Toronto, Ont. M4Y 2L8, Canada. TEL 416-924-6349. Ed. Friar Philip Kelly. adv.; bk.rev.; illus.; circ. 9,000.

282　378　　　　　US　　ISSN 0886-1293
COMPANY; a magazine of the American Jesuits. 1983. q. 3441 N. Ashland Ave., Chicago, IL 60657. TEL 312-281-1534. FAX 312-281-2667. Ed. E.J. Mattimoe. circ. 150,000 (controlled).

248.83　　　　　　AT
COMPASS MAGAZINE. 1967. q. Aus.$15. (Missionaries of the Sacred Heart) Chevalier Press, Box 13, Kensington, N.S.W. 2033, Australia. TEL 02-662-7894. FAX 02-662-1735. Ed. Fr. Peter Malone. bk.rev.; circ. 1,500.

282　　　　　　　　SP
COMUNIDAD; semanario de la Iglesia Diocesana, Salamanca. 1971. w. 10 ptas.($3) per no. Semanario de la Iglesia Diocesana, Iscar Peyra, 26 Obispado, 37002 Salamanca, Spain. Ed. Moises S. Ramos. circ. 6,000 (controlled).

282　　　　　　　　IT
COMUNITA E STORIA. 1974. bi-m. L.15000($10) Comunita e Storia, Via Mazzini 6a, 52100 Arezzo, Italy. Ed. Maria Grotti. bk.rev.; circ. 500.

282
CONFERENZA ITALIANA SUPERIORI MAGGIORI. NOTIZIARIO. 1960. bi-m. free. Conferenza Italiana Superiori Maggiori, Via degli Scipioni, 256B, I-00192 Rome, Italy.

282　　　　　　　US　　ISSN 0884-7010
CONSECRATED LIFE. 1975. s-a. $20. Institute on Religious Life, Box 41007, Chicago, IL 60641. TEL 312-267-1195. FAX 312-267-2044. Ed. Fr. James Downey, O.S.B. circ. 2,900. (back issues avail.)

282　　　　　　　UK　　ISSN 0262-107X
CONTACT (SUTTON COLDFIELD). 1945. bi-m. free. Society of Missionaries of Africa, 129 Lichfield Rd., Sutton Coldfield, W. Midlands B74 2SA, England. TEL 021-308-0226. FAX 021-323-2476. Ed. Rev. W. Turnbull. circ. 6,500.

248　　　　　　　US　　ISSN 0010-8685
CORD. 1951. m. $15. Franciscan Institute, St. Bonaventure University, St. Bonaventure, NY 14778. TEL 716-375-2105. Ed. Joseph Doino. adv.; bk.rev.; bibl.; illus.; circ. 1,700. **Indexed:** CERDIC.
　—BLDSC shelfmark: 3470.380000.

282　　　　　　　GW　　ISSN 0070-0320
BR302
CORPUS CATHOLICORUM. 1919. irreg. price varies. Aschendorffsche Verlagsbuchhandlung, Soesterstr. 13, 4400 Muenster, Germany. TEL 0251-690-0. FAX 0251-690405. Ed. Erwin Iserloh.

282　　　　　　　　BE
CORPUS CHRISTIANORUM. CONTINUATIO MEDIAEVALIS. 1966. irreg. (2-3/yr.). (Abbey of Steenbrugge) N.V. Brepols I.G.P., Rue Baron Francois du Four 8, B-2300 Turnhout, Belgium. Ed.Bd.

282　　　　　　　　BE
CORPUS CHRISTIANORUM. SERIES APOCRYPHORUM. 1983. irreg. (Association pour l'Etude de la Litterature Apocrypha Chretienne) N.V. Brepols I.G.P., Rue Baron Frans du Four 8, B-2300 Turnhout, Belgium.

282　　　　　　　　BE
CORPUS CHRISTIANORUM. SERIES LATINA. 1952. irreg. (6-7/yr.). (Abbey of Steenbrugge) N.V. Brepols I.G.P., Rue Baron Francois du Four 8, B-2300 Turnhout, Belgium. Ed.Bd.

282　　　　　　　　IT
COSCIENZA. 1946. m. L.20000. Movimento Ecclesiale di Impegno Culturale, Via della Conciliazione 1, 00193 Rome, Italy. Ed. Romolo Pietrobelli. bk.rev.; illus.; index; circ. 4,500. **Indexed:** CERDIC.

282　　　　　　　　CH
COSTANTINIAN; magazine for mature Catholics. (Index in English) 1951. bi-m. NT.$350($12) 73 Linsen N. Rd., Taipei 10420, Taiwan, Republic of China. Ed. John H. Liu. circ. 1,000.

377.8　371.4　　　　US　　ISSN 0160-7960
LC461　　　　　　　　　　CODEN: COVADQ
COUNSELING AND VALUES. 1956. 3/yr. $12. (Association for Religious and Value Issues in Counseling) American Association for Counseling and Development, 5999 Stevenson Ave., Alexandria, VA 22304. TEL 703-823-9800. FAX 703-823-0252. Ed. M. Harry Daniels. adv.; bk.rev. (also avail. in microform from UMI; reprint service avail. from UMI) **Indexed:** C.I.J.E., Cath.Ind., Psychol.Abstr., Soc.Work Res.& Abstr.
　—BLDSC shelfmark: 3481.320000.
　Formerly: National Catholic Guidance Conference Journal (ISSN 0027-8912)
　Description: Focused on the role of values and religion in counseling and psychology.

282　　　　　　　　IT
CREDEREOGGI. bi-m. L.27000 (foreign L.35000). Editrice Grafiche Messaggero Sant' Antonio, Via Orto Botanico, 11, 35123 Padua, Italy. TEL 049-664322. FAX 049-654066. TELEX 430855 MSA PD I. (Subscr. to: Basilica del Santo, 35123 Padua, Italy) Ed. Ugo Sartorio. circ. 10,000. (back issues avail.)

282　　　　　　　　US
CRISIS (NOTRE DAME); a journal of lay Catholic opinion. 1982. m. $19.95. Brownson Institute, Inc., Notre Dame, IN 46556. TEL 219-234-3759. Ed. Terry Hall. adv.; bk.rev.; circ. 5,000.
　Supersedes (in 1986): Catholicism in Crisis.

282　　　　　　　　IT
CRISTIANESIMO OGGI. 1969. m. (10/yr.). L.5000. Editrice Lanterna, Via Robino 71-A.R., 16142 Genova, Italy. adv.; circ. 5,000.

CRITIC (CHICAGO); a Catholic review of culture and the arts. see HUMANITIES: COMPREHENSIVE WORKS

282　　　　　　　IT　　ISSN 0011-1651
CROCE. 1952. w. Curia Vescovile, 40022 Comacchio (Ferrara), Italy.

282　　　　　　　　FR
CROIX; l'evenement. 1880. d. 1846 F. Bayard Presse, 5, rue Bayard, 75380 Paris Cedex 08, France. circ. 120,000. (tabloid format)

282　　　　　　　　DM
CROIX DE BENIN. 1946. fortn. B.P. 105, Cotonou, Benin. TEL 32-11-19. Ed. Barthelemy Cakpo Assogba.

282　366　　　　　　PH
CROSS; national Catholic magazine. (Text in English) 1945. bi-m. P.6($1) Knights of Columbus in the Philippines, P.O. Box 510, Manila, Philippines. Ed. Ben S. De Castro. adv.; bk.rev.; circ. 51,000.
　Former titles (until 1988): Crossline; (until 1986): Cross.

CROSS AND QUILL. see RELIGIONS AND THEOLOGY — Protestant

282　　　　　　　　PE
CUADERNOS DE ESTUDIO. 1979. irreg. $40 (includes subscr. to: Testimonios (en Historieta), Cuadernos de Capacitacion and Cuadernos Populares). Comision Evangelica Latinoamericana de Educacion Cristiana, Av. General Garzon 2267, Lima 11, Peru.

CURRENT ISSUES IN CATHOLIC HIGHER EDUCATION. see EDUCATION

D K K F - NYT. (Dansk Katolsk Kvinde-Forbund) see WOMEN'S INTERESTS

282　　　　　　　US　　ISSN 0011-6637
DARBININKAS. (Text in Lithuanian) 1915. w. $15. Franciscan Fathers, 341 Highland Blvd., Brooklyn, NY 11207. TEL 718-827-1352. Ed. Rev. Cornelius Bucmys. bk.rev.

DEUTSCHE KATHOLIK IN KANADA. see ETHNIC INTERESTS

282　　　　　　　GW　　ISSN 0933-0771
DIACONIA CHRISTI. 1966. q. DM.30. Internationales Diakonatszentrum, Postfach 420, 7800 Freiburg, Germany. FAX 200572. TELEX 772417. bk.rev.; bibl.; circ. 900. (back issues avail.)
　Formerly (until 1987): Diaconia XP (ISSN 0343-3218)

282　　　　　　　　NQ
DIAKONIA; servicio de la fe y promocion de la justicia. 1977. q. $25. Centro Ignaciano de Centro America, Apartado C-31, Managua, 13, Nicaragua. circ. 600. (back issues avail.) **Indexed:** CERDIC.
　Description: Religious publication that aids those involved in religion. Looks at problematic aspects that Christianity and other religions face in Latin America. Includes articles, research and other writings of sprituality.

282　388.3　　　　　GW
DIASPORA - M I V A; Verkehrshilfe des Bonifatiuswerkes. 1949. s-a. free. Bonifatiuswerk der Deutschen Katholiken e.V., Bonifatiushaus, Postfach 1169, 4790 Paderborn, Germany. TEL 05251-29960. FAX 05251-299688. Ed. Michael Henn. circ. 75,000. (back issues avail.)

282　　　　　　　PO　　ISSN 0253-1674
BR7
DIDASKALIA. (Text in various European languages; summaries in English and French) 1971. s-a. $30. (Universidade Catolica Portuguesa, Faculdade de Teologia) Didaskalia Editora, Palma de Cima, 1600 Lisbon, Portugal. TEL 7265550. TELEX 65094 UNICAP P. bk.rev.; circ. 1,000. **Indexed:** CERDIC, New Test.Abstr., Old Test.Abstr., Rel.& Theol.Abstr. (1990-).
　—BLDSC shelfmark: 3580.377000.

DIGNITY - U S A. see HOMOSEXUALITY

200　　　　　　　BE　　ISSN 0012-2866
DIMANCHE. (Text in French) 1935. w. 750 Fr.($20) 20 Place de Vannes, B-7000 Mons, Belgium. TEL 3265-352885. FAX 3265-346370. Ed. Fr. Charles Delhez. adv.; bk.rev.; film rev.; circ. 475,000.
　Description: Chain of parish-weeklies covering local news.

282　　　　　　　　GY
DIOCESAN MAGAZINE. q. 144 Almond and Oronoque Sts., Queenstown, Georgetown, Guyana.

282　　　　　　　　AU
DIOZESE GURK. JAHRBUCH/KRSKE SKOFIJE. ZBORNIK. (Text in German, Slovenian) 1979. a. S.60($5) Bischoefliches Gurker Ordinariat, Mariannenpg. 2, A-9020 Klagenfurt, Austria. FAX 0463-57770-87. Ed.Bd. adv.; bk.rev.; circ. 7,000. (back issues avail.)

282　　　　　　　　GW
DIOZESE HILDESHEIM IN VERGANGENHEIT UND GEGENWART. 1927. a. DM.30. (Verein fuer Geschichte und Kunst in Bistum Hildesheim e.V.) Bernward Verlag, Domhof 24, 3200 Hildesheim, Germany. TEL 05121-16920. bk.rev.; circ. 1,100. (back issues avail.)

DIRECT. see CHILDREN AND YOUTH — For

RELIGIONS AND THEOLOGY — ROMAN CATHOLIC

282 GW
DIRECTORIUM FUER DAS BISTUM TRIER. LITURGISCHER KALENDER. biennial. Paulinus Verlag GmbH, Fleischstr. 62, Postfach 3040, D-5500 Trier, Germany. TEL 0651-4604-162. circ. 450.

220 CN ISSN 0018-912X
DISCOVER THE BIBLE. French edition: Feuillet Biblique. 1964. w. (except July-Aug.). Can.$16. Guides Study Program, P.O. Box 2400, London, Ont. N6A 4G3, Canada. Ed. Rev. Walter Bedard. bk.rev.; bibl.; index; circ. 4,500.
Formerly: I Discover the Bible.

282 VC ISSN 0012-4222
BR1.A1
DIVINITAS. 1957. 3/yr. $20. Pontificia Accademia Teologica Romana, Piazza S. Giovanni in Laterano 4, 00184 Rome, Italy. adv.; bk.rev.; cum.index every 10 yrs. Indexed: New Test.Abstr., Rel.& Theol.Abstr. (1967-).
—BLDSC shelfmark: 3604.276000.

282 IE ISSN 0012-446X
DOCTRINE AND LIFE. 1951. 10/yr. I£29.80($47.46) Dominican Publications, 42 Parnell Sq., Dublin 1, Ireland. FAX 73-1760. Ed. Rev. Bernard Treacy. adv.; bk.rev.; index; circ. 5,000. (also avail. in microfilm from UMI; reprint service avail. from UMI) Indexed: Cath.Ind., CERDIC, New Test.Abstr., Old Test.Abstr.
—BLDSC shelfmark: 3608.030000.

282 FR ISSN 0012-4613
BX802
DOCUMENTATION CATHOLIQUE. 1919. s-m. 472 F. Bayard Presse, 5 rue Bayard, 75380 Paris Cedex 08, France. Ed. P. Claude Musnier. adv.; index; circ. 31,000. Indexed: Cath.Ind., CERDIC.

282 GW
DOM. 1946. a. DM.7.20. (St. Godehards Werk, Hildesheim) Bernward Verlag GmbH, Domhof 24, 3200 Hildesheim, Germany. TEL 05121-1692-0. circ. 6,000. (back issues avail.)

282 IT ISSN 0012-5288
DOMENICA. 1921. w. Viale Tunisi 43-C, 96100 Siracuse, Italy. Ed. Pino Filippelli.

282 BL
DOMINGO. (Supplements avail.) 1932. w. $100. (Pia Sociedade de Sao Paulo) Edicoes Paulinas, Via Raposo Tavares Km 18.5, C.P. 8107, 01051 Sao Paulo, Brazil. Ed. Virgilio Ciaccio. circ. 253,000.

282 US
DON BELL REPORTS. w. $40. Box 2223, Palm Beach, FL 33480.

282 255 NE ISSN 0012-5504
DOORTOCHT; schakel tussen mensen met een Franciscaanse visie. 1963. 6/yr. fl.20.70($4.50) (effective Jan 1991). Franciscaanse Lekenorde, Volendamlaan 22, 2547 CH The Hague, Netherlands. bk.rev.; illus.; circ. 5,500.

282 UK ISSN 0012-5806
BX801
DOWNSIDE REVIEW; a quarterly of Catholic thought. 1880. q. £16($25) Downside Abbey, Stratton on the Fosse, Bath BA3 4RH, England. Ed. Dom Daniel Rees. adv.; bk.rev.; index; circ. 600. (also avail. in microfiche; reprint service avail. from KTO) Indexed: Cath.Ind., CERDIC, M.L.A., New Test.Abstr., Old Test.Abstr., Rel.& Theol.Abstr. (1968-), Rel.Ind.One, Rel.Per.
—BLDSC shelfmark: 3620.100000.

282 US
DRAUGAS. 1909. 5/w. $80. Lithuanian Catholic Press Society, 4545 W. 63rd St., Chicago, IL 60629. TEL 312-585-9500. FAX 312-585-8284. Ed. Rev. F. Garsva. adv.; circ. 7,000.

282 XV
DRUZINA/FAMILY; verski tednik - Catholic weekly. 1952. w. 18000 din.($30) Slovenske Rimskokatoliske Skofije, P.P. 95, 61001 Ljubljana, Slovenia. TEL 061 329-793. TELEX 31776 DRUNA YU. Ed. Drago Klemencic. circ. 100,000. (back issues avail.)

266 PH
EAST ASIAN PASTORAL REVIEW; a quarterly with focus on Asia for all church ministers and theology in context, interested laity and theological students. 1979. q. $12 (effective 1992). East Asian Pastoral Institute, Box 221, U.P. Campus, Quezon City 1101, Philippines. FAX 02-921-7534. Ed. Rev. Geoffrey King, S.J. bk.rev.; circ. 2,000. Indexed: Cath.Ind., Ind.Phil.Per.
Formed by the merger of: Teaching All Nations (ISSN 0040-0564); Good Tidings (ISSN 0436-1571); Amen.

282 US
EASTERN CATHOLIC LIFE. 1965. bi-w. $10. Eastern Catholic Life Press Association, 445 Lackawanna Ave., West Paterson, NJ 07424. TEL 201-890-7794. FAX 201-890-7175. adv.; bk.rev.; circ. 12,017. (also avail. in microform)

282 US ISSN 0012-883X
EASTERN KANSAS REGISTER. 1939. w. $4. Catholic Archdiocese of Kansas City, 2220 Central, Kansas City, KS 66110. TEL 913-221-4377. Ed. Rev. Harold Wickey. adv.; bk.rev.; film rev.; circ. 31,622. (newspaper)

282 FR
EAUX - VIVES. 1941. m. 40 F. 21 bd. Voltaire, 75011 Paris, France. adv.; illus.

282 SP ISSN 0012-9038
ECCLESIA. 1941. w. 6540 ptas.($121) (effective Jan. 1992). Conferencia Episcopal Espanola, Alfonso 11, No. 4, 28014 Madrid, Spain. TEL 91-5315400. FAX 91-5225561. Ed. Jose Antonio Carro Celada. adv.; bk.rev.; film rev.; bibl.; charts; illus.; index; circ. 25,000. Indexed: CERDIC.
Description: Covers religious information and documentation.

282 IT
ECCLESIA MATER. 1963. 3/yr. L.20000 (foreign L.25000). Editrice "Cor Unum" Figlie della Chiesa, Viale Vaticano 62, 00165 Rome, Italy. Dir. Maria Teresa Sotgiu. bk.rev.; illus.; circ. 1,200.
Incorporates: Mater Ecclesiae (ISSN 0025-522X)

282 IT
ECCO TUA MADRE. 6/yr. L.10000 (foreign L.15000). Santuario "S. Maria Greca", Corso Garibaldi, 55, 70033 Corato, Italy.
Description: Catholic newsletter featuring articles on events in the church, prayers and interviews with missionaries.

282 GW ISSN 0252-2527
ECHO DER LIEBE. Dutch edition: Echo der Liefde (ISSN 0252-2543); English edition: Mirror (ISSN 0252-2535) (Editions in various languages) 1959. bi-m. DM.2($5) Kirche in Not - Ostpriesterhilfe e.V., Bischof-Kaller-Str. 3, Postfach 1209, 6240 Koenigstein 1, Germany. TEL 06174-291-0. FAX 06174-3423. TELEX 410654-KINI-D. circ. 600,000. (back issues avail.)
Description: News about the persecuted Church and refugees in Eastern Europe and the Third World.

282 US
ECHO Z AFRYKI I INNYCH KONTYNENTOW. (Text in Polish) 1892. m. $5. Missionary Sisters of St. Peter Claver, St. Mary's Mission House, 265 Century Ave., St. Paul, MN 55125. Ed. Sr. Maria Moryl. circ. 8,000.

282 CR
ECO CATOLICO. 1931. w. Avda. 10, Calles 5 y 7, Apdo. 1064, San Jose, Costa Rica. TEL 22-5903. Dir. Armando Alfaro. circ. 20,000.

282 IT
ECO DEL SANTUARIO DI N.S. DI LOURDES. 1926. m. L.10000. Santuario di N.S. di Lourdes, Via Tortona 27, 15100 Alessandria, Italy. TEL 0131-252769. Dir. Elisabetta Beltramo. circ. 5,500.

282 IT
L'ECO DI GIBILMANNA. 1919. bi-m. Arti Grafiche Siciliane, Frati Minori Cappuccini Santuario di Gibilmanna, Palermo, Italy. Ed. Vincenzo Di Bella. bk.rev.; circ. 3,000.

282 IT
L'ECO DI SAN GABRIELE. 1913. m. L.20000 (foreign L.30000). (Provincia Maria SS. della Pieta) Editoriale Eco s.r.l., Via Santuario, 187, 64048 S. Gabriele (TE), Italy. TEL 0861-97352. FAX 975655. Ed. Ciro Benedettini.

282 IT
L'ECO DI SAN GERMANO. 1957. m. free. Tipolitografia San. Lorenzo Tortona, Largo Paolo Savini, 1, 27057 Varzi, Italy. TEL 0383-52129. Ed. Don Giuseppe De Tommasi. adv.; circ. 1,100. (tabloid format; back issues avail.)
Description: Covers in Italian, religious articles and news about parish and diocesan life. Also presents the conditions of the churches that are situated in the territory of little villages.

282 248.8 US ISSN 0013-1016
EDMUNDITE. 1959. m. $1. Society of St. Edmund, St. Edmund's Novitiate, Enders Island, Mystic, CT 06355. TEL 203-572-9538. Ed. Rev. James F. Ryan. circ. 30,000.

266 US ISSN 0030-6819
EDUCATING IN FAITH. vol.56, 1970. bi-m. donations. Catholic Negro - American Mission Board, 2021 H St., N.W., Washington, DC 20006. Ed. Msgr. Paul A. Lenz. illus.; circ. 17,500.
Formerly: Our Colored Missions.
Description: Focuses on mission work.

282 FR
EGLISE A LYON. (Supplement avail.) fortn. 110 F. Archeveche de Lyon, 1 Place de Fourviere, 69321 Lyon Cedex 5, France.
Formerly: Eglise a Lyon et a Saint-Etienne.
Description: Review of the diocese.

282 MG
EGLISE CATHOLIQUE A MADAGASCAR. Cover title: Annuaire de l'Eglise Catholique a Madagascar. (Text in French or Malagasy) a. Imprimerie Catholique, 127, Arabe Lenine Vladimir, Antananarivo, Malagasy Republic.

200 CN ISSN 0381-0380
EGLISE DE MONTREAL. (Text in French) 1882. w. Can.$21. Eglise de Montreal, 2000 ouest, rue Sherbrooke, Montreal, Que. H3H 1G4, Canada. Ed. Rev. Yvan Desrochers. adv.; bibl.; index; circ. 2,500.

282 FR ISSN 0013-2330
EGLISE EN ALSACE. 1967. m. 155 F. Office Diocesain d'Information, 16 rue Brulee, 67081 Strasbourg Cedex, France. TEL 88-32-76-25. FAX 88-23-26-18. adv.; bk.rev. Indexed: CERDIC.

253 US ISSN 0013-6719
EMMANUEL; magazine of Eucharist spirituality. 1895. m. (except Jan.-Feb. & Jul.-Aug.). $18.95 (foreign $23.95). Congregation of Blessed Sacrament, 5384 Wilson Mill Rd., Cleveland, OH 44143. FAX 216-449-3862. Ed. Rev. Anthony Schueller. adv.; bk.rev.; bibl.; index; circ. 6,000. Indexed: New Test.Abstr.

282 CN ISSN 0317-851X
EN EGLISE. (Text in French) 1974. m. Can.$8. Eglise Catholique, Diocese de Chicoutimi, Office des Communications Sociales, 602, Racine Est., Chicoutimi, Que. G7H 6J6, Canada. TEL 418-543-0783. Ed. Jocelyn Girard. bk.rev.; illus.; circ. 1,450.
Description: Contains information about Catholic members and diocese life.

206 FR
EN EQUIPE A C G F AU SERVICE DE L'EVANGILE. 1976. q. 20 F. Action Catholique Generale Feminine, 98 rue de l'Universite, 75007 Paris, France. TEL 1-45-50-44-33. Ed. Jacqueline Brisse.
Formerly: En Equipe au Service de l'Evangile (ISSN 0395-1766)

282 UK
ENGLISH BENEDICTINE CONGREGATION. ORDO. 1885. a. £1. Ampleforth Abbey, York YO6 4EN, England. Ed. Rev. V. Wace. circ. 1,400.
Description: Directory of the Divine Office and Mass for use in the Abbeys and churches of this religious family.

ENVIRONMENT AND ART LETTER; a forum on architecture and the arts for the Parish. see ARCHITECTURE

RELIGIONS AND THEOLOGY — ROMAN CATHOLIC

262.9   IT   ISSN 0013-9491
EPHEMERIDES IURIS CANONICI. (Text in various languages) 1945. q. L.4000($100) Officium Libri Catholici - Catholic Book Agency, Via dei Lucchesi 20, 00187 Rome, Italy. Ed. Pius Fedele. bk.rev.; index. **Indexed:** Canon Law Abstr., CERDIC.

266   SP   ISSN 0425-1466
BT595
EPHEMERIDES MARIOLOGICAE; international revue of mariology. 1951. q. $30 (effective Jan. 1992). (Ephemerides Mariologicae) Claretian Fathers, Calle Buen Suceso, 22, 28008 Madrid, Spain. TEL 91-248-66-01. FAX 91-248-21-01. adv.; bk.rev.; index; circ. 550. (back issues avail.) **Indexed:** CERDIC, New Test.Abstr.
—BLDSC shelfmark: 3793.477000.

262.9 900   BE   ISSN 0013-9513
BR1.A1
EPHEMERIDES THEOLOGICAE LOVANIENSES; revue de theologie et de droit canon de Louvain/Leuvens tijdschrift voor theologie en kerkelijk recht/Louvain journal of theological and canonical studies. (Supplement avail.: Bibliotheca Ephemeridum Theologicarum Lovaniensium) (Text in English, French, German) 1924. q. 2000 Fr. (Katholieke Universiteit Leuven - Universite Catholique de Louvain) Editions Peeters s.p.r.l., Bondgenotenlaan 153, B-3000 Louvain, Belgium. TEL 016-235170. FAX 016-228500. bibl.; index. (back issues avail.) **Indexed:** CERDIC, New Test.Abstr., Old Test.Abstr., Rel.& Theol.Abstr. (1983-), Rel.Ind.One, Rel.Per.
—BLDSC shelfmark: 3793.500000.
Description: Publishes articles reflecting the full scope of theological research, with an international calendar of meetings and congresses.

EQUIPES ST VINCENT. see *SOCIAL SERVICES AND WELFARE*

282 255   GW   ISSN 0013-9963
BX3001
ERBE UND AUFTRAG; Benediktinische Monatsschrift. 1919. bi-m. DM.42. Beuroner Kunstverlag GmbH, 7792 Beuron 1, Germany. TEL 07466-17228. FAX 07466-17209. Ed. B. Schwank. adv.; bk.rev.; abstr.; bibl.; illus.; index; circ. 2,100. **Indexed:** New Test.Abstr., Old Test.Abstr.

ERNEUERUNG IN KIRCHE UND GESELLSCHAFT. see *RELIGIONS AND THEOLOGY — Protestant*

ESCOGE LA VIDA!. see *POPULATION STUDIES*

266   CN   ISSN 0318-7551
ESKIMO. French edition (ISSN 0318-756X) (Editions in English and French) 1944. s-a. Can.$5. Diocese of Churchill Hudson Bay, P.O. Box 10, Churchill, Man. ROB OEO, Canada. Ed. Rev. Guy Mary-Rousseliere. bk.rev.; circ. 5,400 (3,100 Fr. ed., 2,300 Eng. ed.). (also avail. in microfilm from UMI; back issues avail.)

282   CM
ESSOR DES JEUNES. m. B.P. 363, Nkongsamba, Cameroon. Ed. Jean-Boco Tchape. circ. 3,000.

200   SP   ISSN 0425-340X
ESTUDIO AGUSTINIANO. (Text in English, French, Italian, Spanish) 1914. 3/yr. $35 (effective Jan. 1991). Estudio Teologico Agustiniano, Po. de Filipinos, 7, 47007 Valladolid, Spain. TEL 983-306800. FAX 983-397896. Eds. Pio de Luis, Jose Vidal Gonzalez. bk.rev.; index; circ. 400. (back issues avail.) **Indexed:** Canon Law Abstr., CERDIC.

282   SP   ISSN 0210-7074
ESTUDIOS JOSEFINOS. 1947. s-a. 400 ptas.($15) Centro Josefino Espanol, c/o Fray Jose Antonio Carrasco, Pp. Carmelitas Descalzos, Valladolid, Spain. bk.rev.; circ. 600.

ETUDES. see *LITERARY AND POLITICAL REVIEWS*

268   US   ISSN 0743-524X
EUCHARISTIC MINISTER. 1984. m. National Catholic Reporter Publishing Company, Inc., 115 E. Armour Blvd., Box 419281, Kansas City, MO 64141. TEL 816-531-0538. FAX 816-931-5082. Eds. Carolyn Hoff, Rich Heffren. circ. 65,000. (tabloid format)
Description: Spiritual support and insights for the eucharistic minister.

282 200   VC   ISSN 0394-9850
EUNTES DOCETE. 1948. 3/yr. L.40000($40) (Pontificia Universita Urbaniana) Urbaniana University Press, Via Urbano VIII, 16, 00165 Rome, Italy. TEL 06-687-5992. FAX 06-7184611. Ed. Jezernik Maksimilijan. adv.; bk.rev.; circ. 1,000. (back issues avail.) **Indexed:** CERDIC, New Test.Abstr.

282   US   ISSN 0738-8489
EVANGELIST (ALBANY). 1926. w. $20. (Roman Catholic Diocese of Albany) Albany Catholic Press Association, Inc., 40 N. Main Ave., Albany, NY 12203. TEL 518-453-6688. Ed. James P. Breig. adv.; bk.rev.; film rev.; bibl.; stat.; circ. 61,000. (also avail. in microfilm)

282   SP
EXCERPTA E DISSERTATIONIBUS IN SACRA THEOLOGICA. 1975. irreg., no.13, 1987. 3000 ptas. (Universidad de Navarra, Facultad de Teologia) Servicio de Publicaciones de la Universidad de Navarra, S.A., Apdo. 177, 31080 Pamplona, Spain. TEL 94 25 2700.

266   US
EXTENSION. 1906. 10/yr. free. Catholic Church Extension Society of the United States, 35 E. Wacker Dr., Chicago, IL 60601. TEL 312-236-7240. FAX 312-236-5276. Ed. Bradley Collins. bk.rev.; circ. 140,000. **Indexed:** Cath.Ind., CERDIC.
Description: Discusses mission work in the US.

282   MX
FAMILIA CRISTIANA. 1953. m. Mex.$2500. Ediciones Paulinas, S.A., Apdo. 69-766, 04460 Coyoacan, Mexico D.F., Mexico. Ed. G. Emmanuel Hidalgo. adv.; circ. 80,000.

282   US
THE FAMILY (BOSTON); a Catholic perspective. 1958. m. $12. Daughters of St. Paul, 50 St. Paul's Ave., Boston, MA 02130. TEL 617-522-8911. FAX 617-524-8035. Ed. Sr. Donna William Giaimo. circ. 20,000.
Description: Practical advice on Christian family life.

282 360   AT
FAR EAST; mission magazine of the Columban fathers. 1920. m. Aus.$7. St. Columban's Mission Society, 69 Woodland St, North Essendon, Vic. 3041, Australia. TEL 03-379-3544. FAX 03-379-6040. Ed. J. Colgan. circ. 28,000.

282   US   ISSN 0014-8814
FATHERS OF THE CHURCH. 1947. irreg., vol.84, 1991. price varies. Catholic University of America Press, 620 Michigan Ave., N.E., Washington, DC 20064. TEL 202-319-5052.

220   CN   ISSN 0225-2112
FEUILLET BIBLIQUE. (Editions in English, French) 1958. w. (except Jul. & Aug.) Can.$17. Archeveche de Montreal, Centre Biblique, 2000 ouest, rue Sherbrooke, Montreal, Que. H3H 1G4, Canada. TEL 514-931-7311. Ed. Rev. Yves Guillemette. bk.rev.; bibl.; index; circ. 11,800.
Formerly: Parole-Dimanche.

282   IT
FIACCOLA. 1916. m. L.18000 (typically set in Jan.). Seminario Arcivescovile, Segretariato per il Seminario, P.za Duomo 16, 20122 Milan, Italy. (Subscr. to: Editrice Velar, via Torquato Tasso 10, 24020 Gorle (BG), Italy) bk.rev. (also avail. in microfilm from KTO; back issues avail.)

282   US   ISSN 1041-7710
FIDELIS ET VERUS/FAITHFUL AND TRUE. 1985. q. $10 for 10 issues. Children of Mary, Box 350333, Ft. Lauderdale, FL 33335-0333. Ed. Nicholas LaPoint. adv.; B&W page $200; adv. contact: John Walsh. bk.rev.; circ. 10,000. (tabloid format; back issues avail.)
Description: Exposes infiltration of church by Masons and Communists. Teaches traditional Catholic doctrine and practices, and warns of Soviet threat to U.S.A.

282   US   ISSN 0275-6145
E184.S64
FIRST CATHOLIC SLOVAK UNION OF AMERICA. MINUTES OF ANNUAL MEETING.* a. First Catholic Slovak Union, 6611 Rockside Rd., Cleveland, OH 44131-2398. Key Title: Minutes of the Annual Meeting of the First Catholic Slovak Union of the United States of America and Canada.

FIT DURCH TIP. see *CHILDREN AND YOUTH — For*

282   FR   ISSN 0015-5365
FOI ET VIE DE L'EGLISE AU DIOCESE DE TOULOUSE; semaine catholique de Toulouse. 1860. bi-m. 45 F. Archeveche de Toulouse, 1 Place Stes Scarbes, 31000 Toulouse, France. Ed. Chanoine Ducasse. adv.; bk.rev.; bibl.; index; circ. 1,800.

FRAENKISCHER HAUSKALENDER UND CARITASKALENDER. see *BIOGRAPHY*

282   FR
FRANCE CATHOLIQUE - ECCLESIA. 1925. w. 480 F. Soceval, 12 rue Edmond-Valentin, 75007 Paris, France. TEL 1-47-05-43-31. FAX 1-45-51-11-87. Ed. A. Chabadel. adv.; bk.rev.; circ. 20,000.
Formerly: France Catholique (ISSN 0015-9506)

271.3   US   ISSN 0080-5459
BX3601
FRANCISCAN STUDIES. 1941. a. $20. Franciscan Institute, St. Bonaventure University, Drawer F, St. Bonaventure, NY 14778. TEL 716-375-2105. Ed. Fr. Conrad L. Harkins. (also avail. in microform from UMI; reprint service avail. from UMI) **Indexed:** Cath.Ind., CERDIC, M.L.A., Phil.Ind., Rel.Ind.Two.

255   BE   ISSN 0015-9840
FRANCISCANA; bijdragen tot de geschiedenis van de Minderbroeders in de Nederlanden. 1946. s-a. 400 BEF. Instituut voor Franciskaanse Geschiedenis, Minderbroedersstraat 5, B-3800 Sint-Truiden, Belgium. Ed. A. Coenen. bk.rev.; bibl.; illus.; index, cum.index; circ. 250. **Indexed:** Amer.Hist.& Life, Hist.Abstr.
—BLDSC shelfmark: 4032.787000.

FRANCISCANUM; revista de las ciencias del espiritu. see *PHILOSOPHY*

282 255   NE   ISSN 0015-9794
FRANCISKAANS LEVEN; tijdschrift tot verdieping en vernieuwing van de Franciskaanse beweging in Nederland en Vlaanderen. 1917. bi-m. fl.25. Franciskaanse Samenwerking in Nederland, Oude Gracht 23, 3511 AB Utrecht, Netherlands. TEL 030-319321. Ed. G. Pellikaan. bk.rev.; bibl.; index, cum.index; circ. 1,000.
—BLDSC shelfmark: 4032.783600.

271   GW   ISSN 0016-0067
BX3601
FRANZISKANISCHE STUDIEN. (Text in various languages) 1918. q. DM.44. Dietrich Coelde Verlag GmbH, Walburgisstr. 41, Postfach 2060, 4760 Werl, Germany. TEL 02922-4011. Ed. P. Ildefons Vanderheyden. bk.rev.; circ. 300. **Indexed:** CERDIC, M.L.A.
—BLDSC shelfmark: 4033.020000.

282   IT
FRATI MINORI CAPPUCCINI. ISTITUTO STORICO. VARIA. 1973. irreg., no.15, 1987. price varies. Frati Minori Cappuccini, Istituto Storico, Casella Postale 90-91, Circonv. Occidentale 6850 (GRA km 65), 00163 Rome, Italy. TEL 06-625-19-58. FAX 06-661-62-401.

FREIBURGER ZEITSCHRIFT FUER PHILOSOPHIE UND THEOLOGIE. see *PHILOSOPHY*

282   NE   ISSN 0016-2175
FRONTLIJN; voor Katholieken in en buiten de kerk. 1953. m. fl.3.50. (Redemptorist Fathers) A. de Bot, Ed. & Pub., Sionsweg 2, 6525 EB Nijmegen, Netherlands. illus.; circ. 8,000. (tabloid format)

282   IE   ISSN 0016-3120
THE FURROW. 1950. m. I£20($40) Furrow Trust, Maynooth, Co. Kildare, Ireland. Ed. Ronan Drury. adv.; bk.rev.; film rev.; play rev.; index every 6 months; circ. 8,000. (also avail. in microform from UMI; reprint service avail. from UMI) **Indexed:** Canon Law Abstr., Cath.Ind., CERDIC, New Test.Abstr., Old Test.Abstr.
—BLDSC shelfmark: 4059.400000.

GAZETA NIEDZIELNA. see *GENERAL INTEREST PERIODICALS — Poland*

282   GW
GEIST UND AUFTRAG. (Text in German) 1921. q. Charitable Cooperation of the Missionary Sisters e.V., Postfach 2308, 4054 Nettetal 2, Germany. TEL 077-734600. Ed. Gudrun Bosek. bk.rev.; circ. 48,000.

RELIGIONS AND THEOLOGY — ROMAN CATHOLIC

282 US
GENERATION (CHICAGO); the spiritual enrichment newsletter for mature Catholics. 1980. m. $12. Claretian Publications, 205 W. Monroe St., Chicago, IL 60606. TEL 312-236-7782. FAX 312-236-7230. Ed. Rev. Mark J. Brummel. circ. 18,928. (reprint service avail. from UMI)

282 US
GEORGIA BULLETIN. 1962. w. $15. Catholic Archdiocese of Atlanta, 680 W. Peachtree St. N.W., Atlanta, GA 30308. Ed. Gretchen R. Keiser. adv.; bk.rev.; circ. 39,000.

GIDS OP MAATSCHAPPELIJK GEBIED; tijdschrift voor syndicale, culturele en sociale problemen. see *LABOR UNIONS*

282 IT ISSN 0017-1336
GIOVANI IN DIALOGO.* 1903. s-m. L.10000($7) Azione Cattolica Italiana of Milan, c/o Azione Cattolica Italiana, Via della Conciliazione 1, 00193 Rome, Italy. TEL 02-80-52-076. Dir. Catella Marino. circ. 24,000. (tabloid format; back issues avail.)

282 CE
GNANARTHAPRADEEPAYA. (Text in Sinhala) 1866. w. Colombo Catholic Press, 2 Gnanarthapradeepaya Mawatha, Borella, Colombo 8, Sri Lanka. TEL 1-695984. Ed. Rev. Fr. Bertram Dabrera. circ. 26,000.

282 284 US
GOOD NEWS (NEW BERLIN). 1973. m. $54. Liturgical Publications Inc., 2875 South James Dr., New Berlin, WI 53151. TEL 414-785-1188. FAX 414-785-9567. Ed. Rev. Joseph T. Nolan. bk.rev.; index. (looseleaf format) **Indexed**: Rehabil.Lit.
Incorporates (in 1983): Candle.
Description: Inter-denominational Christian publication.

282 US
THE GOOD NEWS LETTER (WASHINGTON). 1972. q. donation. National Institute for the Word of God, 487 Michigan Ave., N.E., Washington, DC 20017. Ed. Mary Ann C. McGuire. bk.rev.; circ. 5,000 (controlled).

282 323.4 SA ISSN 1012-5930
GRACE AND TRUTH. (Text in English) 1980. q. R.30($17) (foreign R.60). Federation of Dominicans of Southern Africa, P.O. Box 45096, 2108 Mayfair, South Africa. FAX 011-8376232. Ed. Bernard F. Connor. bk.rev.; index; circ. 500. (back issues avail.)
Description: Concerned with the development of the church and society in Southern Africa.

GRADUATE SCHOOL GUIDE. see *EDUCATION — Guides To Schools And Colleges*

282 US ISSN 8755-9323
GREEN BAY CATHOLIC COMPASS. 1978. w. $19.50 (typically set in July). (Catholic Diocese of Green Bay) Green Bay Register, Inc., 1825 Riverside Dr., Box 23825, Green Bay, WI 54305-3825. TEL 414-437-7531. FAX 414-437-0694. Ed. Tony Staley. adv.; circ. 14,500. (also avail. in microfiche)

282 VC ISSN 0017-4114
BX800.A1
GREGORIANUM. (Text in English, French, German, Italian and Spanish) 1920. q. L.70000($65) (Pontificio Istituto Biblico) Gregorian University Press, Piazza della Pilotta, 35, 00187 Rome, Italy. Ed. R.P. Dupuis. bk.rev.; bibl.; index. cum.index: vols.1-31, 1920-1950; circ. 1,200. **Indexed**: Bull.Signal., Canon Law Abstr., Cath.Ind., CERDIC, New Test.Abstr., Old Test.Abstr., Phil.Ind., Rel.& Theol.Abstr. (1968-), Rel.Ind.One, Rel.Per.
—BLDSC shelfmark: 4215.300000.
Description: A scientific review of theology and philosophy with occasional discussions problems in church history, canon law and social sciences.

282 GW
GUCKLOCH. 1973. q. free. Katholische Junge Gemeinde, Dioezesanverband Muenster, Rosenstr. 16, Postfach 1366, D-4400 Muenster, Germany. TEL 0251-495502. Ed. Thomas Dreger. (back issues avail.)

282 US
GUIDE TO RELIGIOUS MINISTRIES FOR CATHOLIC MEN AND WOMEN. 1979. a. $5. Catholic News Publishing Co., Inc., 210 N. Ave., New Rochelle, NY 10801. TEL 914-632-1220. Ed. Mari Castrovilla. adv.; tr.lit.; circ. 45,000.
Formerly: Guide to Religious Careers for Catholic Men and Women.

H L I CANADIAN REPORT. (Human Life International in Canada Inc.) see *POPULATION STUDIES*

H L I REPORTS. (Human Life International) see *POPULATION STUDIES*

H L I REPORTS. (Human Life International in Canada Inc.) see *POPULATION STUDIES*

260 US
HAWAII CATHOLIC HERALD. 1936. fortn. $15. Roman Catholic Bishop of Honolulu, 1184 Bishop St., Honolulu, HI 96813. TEL 808-533-1791. FAX 808-521-8428. Ed. Patrick Downes. adv.; bk.rev.; circ. 8,000.

282 US ISSN 0893-536X
HEARTS AFLAME; Catholic youth magazine. 1987. q. $2 (foreign $3). (World Apostolate of Fatima) Blue Army of Our Lady of Fatima, U S A, Inc., Mountain View Rd., Box 976, Washington, NJ 07882-0976. TEL 908-689-1700. FAX 908-689-6279. Ed. Sr. Mary Celeste. illus.; circ. 13,000. (back issues avail.)

282 PL ISSN 0017-9914
HEJNAL MARIACKI; miesiecznik o tematyce religijno-kulturalno-spolecznej. 1956. m. $6. Chrzescijanskie Stowarzyszenie Spoleczne - Christian Social Association, Marszalkowska 4, 00-590 Warsaw, Poland. (Dist. by: RSW "Prasa-Ksiazka-Ruch" Centrala Kolportazu Prasy i Wyndawnictw, Ul. Towarowa 28, 00-958 Warsaw) Ed. Eugeniusz Zdanowicz. adv.; illus.; circ. 5,000.

282 GW
HELIAND KORRESPONDENZ. 1969. q. DM.16. Kreis Katholischer Frauen im Heliandbund, Gabelsbergerstr. 19, 5000 Cologne 1, Germany. (Subscr. to: Lilienstr. 61, 6704 Mutterstadt, Germany) bk.rev.; circ. 1,500.

282 US ISSN 0746-4185
EL HERALDO CATOLICO. (Text in Spanish) 1979. fortn. $10. Roman Catholic Diocese of Sacramento, 5890 Newman Court, Box 19312, Sacramento, CA 95819. TEL 916-452-3344. FAX 916-736-0282. Ed. Deacon Jose Ramirez. adv.; bk.rev.; circ. 10,000. (tabloid format; also avail. in microfilm)

282 GW ISSN 0018-0645
BX803
HERDER - KORRESPONDENZ; Monatshefte fuer Gesellschaft und Religion. 1946. m. DM.162. Verlag Herder GmbH und Co. KG, Hermann-Herder-Str. 4, 7800 Freiburg im Breisgau, Germany. TEL 0761-2717-276. FAX 0761-2717-520. Ed. David A. Seeber. adv.; bk.rev.; index; circ. 9,600. **Indexed**: Cath.Ind.
—BLDSC shelfmark: 4298.710000.

282 SP
HOJA TRINITARIA. m. 800 ptas. Ediciones Secretariado Trinitario, Filiberto Villalobos, 82, 37007 Salamanca, Spain. TEL 235602.

282 296 297 956 IS
HOLY LAND; illustrated quarterly of the Franciscan custody of the holy land. 1975. q. $7. Franciscan Printing Press, P.O. Box 14064, Jerusalem 91140, Israel. TEL 02-286594. Ed. Raphael Bonanno. adv.; bk.rev.; cum.index: 1975-1984; circ. 5,000. (back issues avail.)

HOMELIFE; the Philippines' family magazine. see *GENERAL INTEREST PERIODICALS — Philippines*

250 US ISSN 0018-4268
BX801
HOMILETIC AND PASTORAL REVIEW. 1900. m. (bi-m. Aug.-Sep.). $24. Catholic Polls, Inc., 86 Riverside Dr., New York, NY 10024. TEL 212-799-2600. FAX 212-787-0351. Ed. Rev. Kenneth Baker. adv.; bk.rev.; index; circ. 14,500. (also avail. in microform from UMI; reprint service avail. from UMI) **Indexed**: Canon Law Abstr., Cath.Ind., CERDIC, New Test.Abstr., Old Test.Abstr., Rel.& Theol.Abstr.
—BLDSC shelfmark: 4326.179000.

282 HK ISSN 0073-3210
HONG KONG CATHOLIC CHURCH DIRECTORY/HSIANG-KANG T'IEN CHU CHIAO SHOU TS'E. (Text in Chinese, English) 1954. a. $2.50 (effective 1991; typically set in Dec.). Catholic Truth Society, Catholic Centre, 16-Fl., Grand Bldg., 15-18 Connaught Road, Central, Hong Kong. TEL 525-8021. FAX 521-8700. Ed. Louis Lee. adv.; circ. 2,700.
Description: Includes personnel of Curiae, churches, diocesan organizations, pious associations, Catholic schools, social services and religious congregations.

282 US ISSN 0360-9669
BR1
HORIZONS (VILLANOVA). (Text in English) 1974. s-a. Can.$30($30) Villanova University, Villanova, PA 19085. (Dist. by: Wilfrid Laurier University Press, Waterloo, Ont. N2L 3C5, Canada. TEL 519-884-1970) Ed. Walter E. Conn. adv.; bk.rev.; circ. 1,500. (also avail. in microfilm from UMI; reprint service avail. from UMI) **Indexed**: Cath.Ind., INIS Atomind., New Test.Abstr., Old Test.Abstr., Rel.& Theol.Abstr., Rel.Ind.One, Rel.Per., SSCI.
—BLDSC shelfmark: 4326.794400.
Description: Explores developments in Catholic theology, the total Christian tradition, human religious experience and the concerns of creative teaching in the college and university environment.

282 US ISSN 0018-6910
HRVATSKI KATOLICKI GLASNIK; mjesecnik za duhovnu izgradnju iseljenih Hrvata. 1942. m. $5. (Croatian Franciscan Fathers) Croatian Franciscan Press, 4851 Drexel Blvd., Chicago, IL 60615. TEL 312-268-2819. Ed. Fr. Harvoslav Ban, O.F.M. adv.; bk.rev.; illus.; circ. 3,000. **Indexed**: CERDIC.

HUMAN LIFE INTERNATIONAL. SPECIAL REPORT. see *POPULATION STUDIES*

HYMNOLOGISKE MEDDELELSER; tidsskrift om salmer. see *RELIGIONS AND THEOLOGY — Protestant*

282 704.948 IT
ICONOGRAPHIA FRANCISCANA. 1973. irreg., no.6, 1991. price varies. Frati Minori Cappuccini, Istituto Storico, Casella Postale 90-91, Circonv. Occidentale 6850 (GRA km 65), 00163 Rome, Italy. TEL 06-625-19-58. FAX 06-661-62-401.

IDEA INK; the national Catholic opinion quarterly. see *LITERARY AND POLITICAL REVIEWS*

282 SP
IGLESIA DE SEVILLA. s-a. 1000 ptas. Arzobispado de Sevilla, Oficina Diocesana de Informacion, Apdo. Postal 6, 41080 Sevilla, Spain. Ed. Carlos Ros Carballar. circ. 16,000.

282 GW ISSN 0938-3190
IM HEILIGEN DIENST; Zeitschrift fuer die liturgischen Dienste. 1960. q. DM.22. Verlag Haus Altenberg, Carl-Mosterts-Platz 1, 4000 Dusseldorf 30, Germany. TEL 0211-4693-173. FAX 0211-4693-120. Ed. Andreas Buesch. adv.; bk.rev.; circ. 3,000. (back issues avail.)
Description: Articles and information for people responsible for altar servants and youth choir members.

200 SP
IMAGENES DE LA FE. 1963. m. 3400 ptas.($32) (Pontifical University of Salamanca) Promocion Popular Cristiana, E. Jardiel Poncela 4, E-28016 Madrid, Spain. Ed. Manuel Useros. circ. 10,000.

282 FR
IMAGES DU MOIS. 1962. m. 163 bd. Malesherbes, 75849 Paris Cedex 17, France. Ed. Michel Houssin. circ. 600,000.

282 IT ISSN 0019-3186
IN FAMIGLIA; rassegna mensile delle attivita spirituali, culturali e artistiche dell'angelicum-chiesa di S. Angelo. 1925. m. L.4000. Angelicum-Convento di S.Angelo, Piazza S. Angelo 2, 20121 Milan, Italy. Ed.Bd. adv.; bk.rev. (tabloid format)

282 VC
INDEX ACTORUM ROMANORUM PONTIFICUM. 1975. irreg, no.5, 1990. price varies. Biblioteca Apostolica Vaticana, 00120 Vatican City (Rome), State of the Vatican City.

RELIGIONS AND THEOLOGY — ROMAN CATHOLIC

INFORMATION BULLETIN FOR CATHOLIC RURAL ORGANIZATIONS. see *AGRICULTURE*

282 374 IT
INFORMATORE DI URIO. 1973. bi-m. L.15000. Edizioni Ares, Via Stradivari 7, 20131 Milan, Italy. TEL 02-29526156. FAX 02-29514202. Ed. Giorgio Carimati. adv.; circ. 4,760 (controlled). (back issues avail.)

282 US ISSN 0020-1510
INLAND REGISTER. 1942. 17/yr. $15. Catholic Diocese of Spokane, Box 48, Spokane, WA 99210-0048. TEL 509-456-7140. Ed. Eric Meisfjord. adv.; bk.rev.; circ. 8,500.

282 US ISSN 0897-229X
INNER HORIZONS; thinking, feeling, living with the church. 1967. q. $5.50. Daughters of St. Paul, 50 St. Paul's Ave., Boston, MA 02130. TEL 617-522-8911. FAX 617-522-8035. Ed. Sister Mary Paula Kolar. circ. 3,000. (back issues avail.)
Formerly: Strain Forward.
Description: Publication of spirituality for Christian clergy, religions and laity.

282 UK ISSN 0020-157X
BX2597
INNES REVIEW. 1950. s-a. £10. (Scottish Catholic Historical Association) John S. Burns & Sons, 25 Finlas St., Possilpark, Glasgow N.2, Scotland. illus.; cum.index: 1950-1959; circ. 500. **Indexed:** Amer.Hist.& Life, Br.Archaeol.Abstr., Br.Hum.Ind., Hist.Abstr.
—BLDSC shelfmark: 4515.460000.

200 230 FR
INSTITUT CATHOLIQUE DE PARIS. ANNUAIRE. a. Institut Catholique de Paris, 21, rue d'Assas, 75270 Paris cedex 06, France. TEL 42-22-41-80. FAX 45-44-27-14.
Description: Lists departments and teachers of the institut.

282 BE ISSN 0770-4720
INTERFACE; lettre d'information trimestrielle. 1981. q. 1200 Fr.($35) Promotion Biblique et Informatique, Maredsous, B-5537 Denee, Belgium. TEL 82-699647. FAX 82-22-3269. Ed. R.F. Poswick. adv.; bk.rev.; circ. 6,000. (back issues avail.)

282 US ISSN 0273-6187
INTERMOUNTAIN CATHOLIC. (Text in English, Spanish) 1899. w. $11.50. Catholic Diocese of Salt Lake City, 27 "C" St., Salt Lake City, UT 84103. TEL 801-328-8641. (Subscr. to: Box 2489, Salt Lake City, UT 84110) Ed. Catherine Fagella. adv.; bk.rev.; film rev.; play rev.; index; circ. 12,700. (tabloid format; back issues avail.)

282 VC ISSN 0074-5782
INTERNATIONAL EUCHARIST CONGRESS. PROCEEDINGS. irreg., 45th 1993, Seville, Spain. Pontificio Comitato per i Congressi Eucaristici Internazionali, Palazzo S. Calisto, 00120 Vatican City (Rome), State of the Vatican City. Ed. H.E. Cardinal Edouard Gagnon.

282 GW ISSN 0341-8693
BX803
INTERNATIONALE KATHOLISCHE ZEITSCHRIFT. 1972. s-m. DM.14 per no. Communio Verlagsgesellschaft mbH, Friesenstr. 50, 5000 Cologne 1, Germany. TEL 0221-123553. FAX 0221-123754. Ed. Maimilian Greiner. adv.; bk.rev.; circ. 3,300. **Indexed:** CERDIC, New Test.Abstr., Old Test.Abstr., Rel.Ind.One.
—BLDSC shelfmark: 4554.311500.

282 IE
IRISH CATHOLIC. 1888. w. £35. Irish Catholic Ltd., 55 Lower Gardiner St., Dublin 1, Ireland. TEL 747538. FAX 364805. Ed. Nick Lundberg. adv.; bk.rev.; illus.; circ. 39,000.

282 UK ISSN 0075-0735
BX1503.A3
IRISH CATHOLIC DIRECTORY. 1838. a. £17.50. (Roman Catholic Church in All Ireland) Gabriel Communications, St. James's Building, First Floor, Oxford St., Manchester M1 6FP, England. adv.; index.

282 US
THE IRISH IN AMERICA. 1988. irreg. price varies. (Cushwa Center for the Study of American Catholicism) University of Notre Dame Press, Notre Dame, IN 46556. TEL 219-239-6346. FAX 219-239-8148.

282 MG
ISIKA MIANAKAVY. (Text in Malagasy) 1958. m. Ambatomena, 301 Fianarantsoa, Malagasy Republic. Ed. J. Ranaivomanana. circ. 21,000.

282 IT
ISTITUTO DI SCIENZE RELIGIOSE IN TRENTO. PUBBLICAZIONI. 1981. irreg. Centro Editoriale Dehoniano, Via Nosadella 6, 40123 Bologna, Italy. TEL 051-306811. FAX 051-341706. Ed.Bd.

ITALIA MISSIONARIA. see *CHILDREN AND YOUTH — For*

946 PO ISSN 0021-3209
ITINERARIUM; revista quadrimestral de cultura. 1955. 3/yr. Esc.1500($15) (Portuguese Franciscans) Editorial Franciscana, Largo da Luz, 11, 1699 Lisbon Codex, Portugal. TEL 01-7142700. Ed. Jose Antonio da Silva Soares. bk.rev.; bibl.; index. cum.index: 1955-1970; circ. 400. (back issues avail.) **Indexed:** Amer.Hist.& Life, CERDIC, Hist.Abstr.
—BLDSC shelfmark: 4588.660000.

IT'S OUR WORLD; mission news from the Holy Childhood Association. see *CHILDREN AND YOUTH — For*

282 340 IT
IUS ECCLESIAE; rivista internazionale di diritto canonico. 1989. s-a. L.70000 (foreign L.90000). Casa Editrice Dott. A. Giuffre, Via Busto Arsizio 40, 20151 Milan, Italy. TEL 02-38000905. FAX 02-38009582.

IUSTITIA. see *LAW*

282 US
JACOB'S WELL. 1974. q. $12. North American Conference of Separated and Divorced Catholics, 1100 S. Goodman St., Rochester, NY 14620. TEL 716-271-1320. Ed. Kathleen L. Kircher. circ. 3,000.
Description: Education resources pertinent to divorce recovery, remarriage and blended families.

282 AU
JAHRBUCH DER ERZDIOESE WIEN. 1950. a. S.65. (Erzbischoefliches Pastoralamt Wien) Wiener Dom-Verlag GmbH, Strozzigasse 8, Postfach 321, 1081 Vienna, Austria. FAX 483010. TELEX 111760. Ed. Johannes Pesl. adv.; illus.
Formerly: Jahrbuch fuer die Kirche von Wien.

282 GW ISSN 0075-2754
JAHRBUCH FUER SALESIANISCHE STUDIEN. 1963. a. price varies. (Arbeitsgemeinschaft fuer Salesianische Studien) Franz Sales Verlag, Rosental 1, Postfach 1361, 8078 Eichstaett, Germany. TEL 08421-5379. FAX 08421-80805. Ed. James Langelaan. bk.rev. (back issues avail.)

282 CN ISSN 0021-5740
JE CROIS; magazine populaire Catholique. (Text in French) 1960. m. Can.$11.95($13) (foreign $24). Messagers Catholiques de la Bible Inc., C.P. 1557, Quebec, Que. G1K 7Y4, Canada. TEL 418-628-3362. Ed. Lucile Dural. bk.rev.; bibl.; illus.; circ. 32,500.
Description: Provides a Christian outlook on current events.

JEDNOTA/UNION. see *ETHNIC INTERESTS*

282 II ISSN 0970-1117
JEEVADHARA. English edition (ISSN 0970-1125) 1971. m. (6 in English, 6 in Malayalam). Rs.36($15) per no. Jeevadhara Theological Society, Kottayam 686 017, Kerala, India. TEL 091-481-7430. Ed. Joseph Constantine Manalel. adv.; bk.rev.; index; circ. 1,500. (back issues avail.) **Indexed:** New Test.Abstr.
Description: International theological review.

271 US
JESUIT BULLETIN. 1922. q. Society of Jesus, Missouri Province Educational Institute, 4511 W. Pine Blvd., St. Louis, MO 63108. TEL 314-361-3388. (Subscr. to: 2001 S. Hanley, St. Louis, MO 63144) Ed. Rev. Michael Harter, S.J. circ. 33,000.

266 UK
JESUITS AND FRIENDS. 3/yr. free. Jesuit Missions, 11 Edge Hill, London SW19 4LR, England. TEL 081-946-0466. FAX 081-946-2292. Ed. Rev. D. Birchall. circ. 24,000. (back issues avail.)
Former titles (until 1985): Jesuit Missions; Missionary Magazine.

282 IT
JESUS CARITAS. 1961. q. L.20000($13) Communita Jesus Caritas, Abbazia di Sassovivo, 06034 Foligno - PG, Italy. TEL 0742 50620. adv.; bk.rev.; circ. 2,500.

282 GW ISSN 0342-6386
JETZT; Ordensfrauen, Ordensleben, Kirche - Information, Konfrontation. 1969. q. DM.20. J. Pfeiffer Verlag, Anzingerstr. 1, 8000 Munich 80, Germany. TEL 089-413001-0. FAX 089-413001-38. Ed. Hans Rotter. bk.rev.; circ. 1,000.
Description: Articles discussing problems and questions about convents and monastic life.

282 US ISSN 0021-759X
JOSEPHINUM NEWSLETTER. 1976. 4/yr. Pontifical College Josephinum, Columbus, OH 43235. TEL 614-885-5585. circ. 8,300.
Supersedes: Josephinum Review.

JURIST; studies in church order and ministry. see *LAW*

282 GW ISSN 0175-5161
K A B; Katholische Arbeitnehmer-Zeitung. 1891. m. (11/yr.). DM.5.50. Katholischen Arbeiternehmer-Bewegung Deutschlands, Bernhard-Letterhaus-Str. 28, 5000 Cologne 1, Germany. TEL 0221-729664. FAX 0221-732515. TELEX 8883049-KAB. (Co-sponsor: Katholische Arbeitnehmer-Bewegung Sueddeutschlands e.V.) Ed. Ralf Blumenthal. bk.rev.; circ. 260,000.
Former titles: Westdeutsche Arbeiter-Zeitung; Kettelerwacht; Katholische Arbeiter-Bewegung. Gemeinsame Zeitung.

266 282 GW
K M - DIE KATHOLISCHEN MISSIONEN. 1873. 6/yr. DM.20.40. (Internationales Katholisches Missionswerk (MISSIO)) Verlag Herder GmbH und Co. KG, Hermann-Herder-Str. 4, 7800 Freiburg im Breisgau, Germany. FAX 0761-2717-520. Ed. Jos. Alb. Otto. adv.; bk.rev.; abstr.; bibl.; charts; illus.; index; circ. 75,000.
Formerly: Katholischen Missionen (ISSN 0022-9407)

K S BULLETIN. (Foreningen af Katolske Skoler i Danmark) see *EDUCATION — School Organization And Administration*

282 PL ISSN 0860-410X
KALENDARZ SLOWA BOZEGO. 1979. a. Ksieza Werbisci, Ostrobramska 90, 04-118 Warsaw 44, Poland. Ed. Marek Grzech. circ. 200,000. (back issues avail.)

KAPPA GAMMA PI NEWS. see *EDUCATION — Higher Education*

282 LI
KATALIKU PASAULIS. 1989. fortn. (Lithuanian Catholic Church) Publishing House of the Episcopalian Conference, Pylimo 27, Vilnius 232001, Lithuania. TEL (0122) 222-422. Ed. Vaclovas Aliulis.

282 GW ISSN 0341-0013
KATECHETISCHE BLAETTER; Zeitschrift fuer Religionsunterricht, Gemeindekatechese, Kirchliche Jugendarbeit. 1875. m. DM.88.20. (Deutscher Katecheten-Verein e.V.) Koesel-Verlag GmbH und Co., Flueggenstr. 2, 8000 Munich 19, Germany. TEL 089-1790080. (Co-sponsor: Arbeitstelle fuer Jugendseelsorge der Deutschen Bischofskonferenz) adv.; bk.rev.; film rev.; play rev.; illus.; index; circ. 10,000. (back issues avail.)

282 NE
KATHOLIEK DOCUMENTATIE CENTRUM. JAARBOEK. (Summaries in English) 1971. a. price varies. Katholiek Documentatie Centrum, Erasmuslaan 36, 6525 GG Nijmegen, Netherlands. TEL 080-612412. (Co-sponsor: Archief voor de Geschiedenis van de Katholieke Kerk in Nederland) **Indexed:** CERDIC.

282   NE
KATHOLIEK DOCUMENTATIE CENTRUM. PUBLICATIES. 1971. irreg., vol.19, 1988. price varies. Katholiek Documentatie Centrum, Erasmuslaan 36, 6525 GG Nijmegen, Netherlands. TEL 180-612412. (back issues avail.)

282   GW
KATHOLISCHE BILDUNG. m. DM.80. (Verein Katholische Deutscher Lehrerinnen) Ferdinand Schoeningh, Juehenplatz 1, 4790 Paderborn, Germany. TEL 05251-29010. FAX 05251-2901-35. TELEX 936929-FS-PB.

282 267.4   AU   ISSN 0022-9377
KATHOLISCHE FRAUENBEWEGUNG OESTERREICHS. FUEHRUNGSBLATT. 1951. q. S.80. Katholisches Frauenwerk in Oesterreich, Spiegelgasse 3-II, A-1010 Vienna, Austria. Eds. Veronika Handschuh, Susanne Degenhart. bk.rev.; circ. 2,500.

KATHOLISCHE OEFFENTLICHE BUECHEREI; Vierteljahreszeitschrift fuer Mitarbeiter der Katholische Oeffentlichen Buechereien. see *LIBRARY AND INFORMATION SCIENCES*

282   GW
KATHOLISCHEN MILITAERBISCHOF FUER DIE DEUTSCHE BUNDESWEHR. VERORDNUNGSBLATT. (Text in German and Latin) 1965. 8/yr. Katholisches Militaerbischofsamt, Adenauerallee 115, Postfach 190199, 5300 Bonn 1, Germany. TEL 0228-221015. circ. 350.

KATHOLISCHER BERUFSVERBAND FUER PFLEGEBERUFE. MITTEILUNGSBLATT. see *MEDICAL SCIENCES*

282   GW   ISSN 0177-2872
KATHOLISCHER DIGEST; Europas grosse Kirchenzeitschrift. 1946. m. DM.97.20. Verlag Axel B. Trunkel, Landhausstr. 82, 7000 Stuttgart 10, Germany. TEL 0711-268630. Ed. Andrea Przyklenk. adv.; bk.rev.; film rev.; illus.; circ. 38,900.

200   GW   ISSN 0170-7302
KATHOLISCHES LEBEN UND KIRCHENREFORM IM ZEITALTER DER GLAUBENSSPALTUNG. 1927. irreg. price varies. Aschendorffsche Verlagsbuchhandlung, Soesterstr. 13, 4400 Muenster, Germany. TEL 0251-690-0. FAX 0251-690405. Ed. Erwin Iserloh.

201   PL
KATOLICKI UNIWERSYTET LUBELSKI. WYDZIAL TEOLOGICZNO-KANONICZNY. ROZPRAWY. (Text in Polish; summaries in English or French) 1947. irreg. price varies. Katolicki Uniwersytet Lubelski, Towarzystwo Naukowe, Ul. Gliniana 21, 20-616 Lublin, Poland. index; circ. 3,150.

200   PL   ISSN 0044-4405
AS262.L84
KATOLICKI UNIWERSYTET LUBELSKI. ZESZYTY NAUKOWE. (In four parts) (Text in Polish; summaries in English, French) 1958. q. price varies. Katolicki Uniwersytet Lubelski, Towarzystwo Naukowe, Ul. Gliniana 21, 20-616 Lublin, Poland. bk.rev.; illus.; index; circ. 1,125.

282   US
KATOLIKUS MAGYAROK VASARNAPJA/CATHOLIC HUNGARIANS' SUNDAY. (Text in Hungarian) 1894. w. $25. (Custody of St. Stephen King, Franciscan Friars) Catholic Publishing Company, 1739 Mahoning Ave., Box 2464, Youngstown, OH 44509. TEL 216-799-2600. FAX 216-799-3335. Ed. Fr. Angelus A. Ligeti. adv.; bk.rev.; circ. 3,100. (back issues avail.)

282   DK
KATOLSK ORIENTERING.* 20/yr. Bredgade 69A, Vesterbrogade 28, 3. t.v., DK-1620 Copenhagen V, Denmark. adv.; circ. 15,000.

282   GW   ISSN 0138-2543
KATOLSKI POSOL. (Text in Upper Sorbian) 1863. 24/yr. DM.8. (Towarstwo Cyrila a Metoda) Domowina Verlag, Tuchmacherstr. 27, 8600 Bautzen, Germany.

282   JA   ISSN 0387-3005
KATORIKKU KENKYU. (Text in Japanese; summaries in English) 1961. s-a. 2260 Yen. Sophia University, Theological Society - Jochi Daigaku, Kamishakujii 4-32-11, Nerima-ku, Tokyo 177, Japan. TEL 03-5991-0343. Ed. Peter Nemeshegyi. bk.rev.; circ. 1,000 (controlled). (back issues avail.)
   Description: Contains articles in all fields of Christian theology and philosophy, past and present, written by scholars born or living in Japan.

282 283   SA   ISSN 0022-9687
KEHILWENYANE; dikgang tsa bodumedi le morafe. (Text and summaries in English and Setswana) 1958. m. R.0.20 per no. (Roman Catholic Diocese of Kimberly) Kehilwenyane Publications, Box 309, Kimberley 8300, South Africa. Ed. Johannes Mogakwee. bk.rev.; abstr.; illus.; stat.; circ. 4,500. **Indexed:** CERDIC.

283   UK
KEYS OF PETER. 1969. bi-m. £4. Petrine Publications, 157 Vicarage Rd., London E10 5DU, England. TEL 081-539-3876. Ed. Ronald King. bk.rev.
   Description: Catholic publication covering religious and world affairs in relation to the Christian social order and Papal teaching.

282   TZ
KIONGOZI/LEADER; gazeti la wananchi. (Text in Swahili) 1950. fortn. EAs.20. Catholic Publishers Ltd., Box 9400, Dar es Salaam, Tanzania. TEL 29505. Ed. Anthony Chilumba. adv.; bk.rev.; circ. 50,000.
   Incorporates: Ecclesia (ISSN 0012-9046)

282   AU   ISSN 0023-1789
KIRCHE; Dioezesanblatt fuer die Kirchenprovinz Mitteleuropa. 1954. q. S.80. Verein zur Foerderung der Liberalkatholischen Kirche, Erdenweg 21, A-1140 Vienna, Austria. Ed. Rev. Rudolf Hammer. bk.rev.; circ. 600.

284   GW
KIRCHE IN MARBURG; Mitteilungen der evangelischen und Katholischen Gemeinden. 1936. m. DM.11. Gesamtverband der Evangelischen Kirchengemeinden in Marburg, Leipzigerstr. 20, 3550 Marburg 1, Germany. (Co-sponsor: Katholische Pfarrgemeinde in Marburg-Stadt) Ed.Bd. adv.; bk.rev.; illus.; circ. 4,000.
   Formerly: Gemeindebote (ISSN 0016-6103)

282   GW
KIRCHE UND SCHULE. 1972. q. Bischoefliches Generalvikariat, Breul 23, 4400 Muenster, Germany. TEL 0251-495-415. circ. 5,000.

KIRCHENMUSIKALISCHE MITTEILUNGEN. see *MUSIC*

282   GW
KIRCHENZEITUNG FUER DAS ERZBISTUM KOELN. 1946. w. DM.95.40. J.P. Bachem Verlag GmbH, Ursuelaplatz 1, D-5000 Cologne 1, Germany.

282   GW
KIRCHENZEITUNG FUER DIE DIOEZESE AUGSBURG. 1946. w. DM.18.60. St. Ulrich Verlag GmbH, Hafnerberg 2, 8900 Augsburg, Germany. TEL 0821-37031. Ed.Bd. circ. 40,000. (back issues avail.)

KOLPING BANNER. see *CLUBS*

282   GW
KONRADSBLATT. 1916. w. (Erbistum Freiburg) Badenia Druckerei und Verlags GmbH, Postfach 21 02 48, D-7500 Karlsruhe, Germany. TEL 0721-578041.
   Description: Discusses current religious issues.

282   AU   ISSN 0023-3676
KONTAKT DREI UND ZWANZIG.* 1954. bi-m. contribution. Roemisches Katholisches Pfarramt Atzgersdorf, Peter Kirchenplatz 1, A-1230 Vienna, Austria. Ed. Pfarrer Otto Novotny. bk.rev.; circ. 2,100.
   Formerly: Liesinger Pfarrblatt.

028.5   GW   ISSN 0344-5984
KONTRASTE IMPULS. 1960. q. DM.22. Verlag Herder GmbH und Co. KG, Hermann-Herder-Str. 4, 7800 Freiburg im Breisgau, Germany. FAX 0761-2717-520. Ed. Reinhold Lehmann. adv.; bk.rev.; illus.; circ. 35,000.

282   HK
KUNG KAO PO/CATHOLIC CHINESE WEEKLY. (Text in Chinese) 1928. w. 16 Caine Rd., 11th Fl., Hong Kong. TEL 5220487. FAX 5213095. Ed. Fr. Louis Ha.

282   MG
LAKROAN'I MADAGASIKARA. (Text in French and Malagasy) 1927. w. Maison Jean XXIII, Mahamasina Sud, 101 Antananarivo, Malagasy Republic. TEL 26141. Ed. Louis Rasolo. circ. 16,000.

282   UK
LANCASTER DIOCESAN DIRECTORY. 1925. a. £1.25. The Willows Church, Ribby Rd., Kirkham, Preston PR4 2BE, England. TEL 0772-683664. Ed. Rev. Dunstan Cooper. adv.; circ. 3,000.
   Description: Covers all churches and Catholic organizations in the Lancaster Diocese.

LAND AKTUELL. see *POLITICAL SCIENCE*

282 800   US
LATIN LITURGY ASSOCIATION NEWSLETTER. 1976. q. $10. Latin Liturgy Association, c/o Prof. Anthony Lo Bello, Chairman, Allegheny College, Box 29, Meadville, PA 16335. TEL 814-332-5340. adv.; bk.rev.; circ. 2,000. (back issues avail.)
   Description: Promotes the use of Latin in the rites of the Roman Catholic Church.

270   IT   ISSN 0023-902X
LAURENTIANUM. (Text in principal European languages) 1960. 3/yr. L.30000. (International College of the Capuchin Order) Collegio Internazionale S. Lorenzo da Brindisi, Circonvallazione Occidentale 6850, 00163 Rome, Italy. Ed. Davide Covi. bk.rev.; index; circ. 500. (back issues avail.) **Indexed:** Canon Law Abstr., CERDIC, M.L.A., New Test.Abstr., Old Test.Abstr.
   —BLDSC shelfmark: 5160.810000.

LEAPING; magazine of Christian dance fellowship of Australia. see *DANCE*

282   GW   ISSN 0171-4171
LEBENDIGE KATECHESE. 1981. s-a. DM.15. Echter Wuerzburg, Juliuspromenade 64, 8700 Wuerzburg, Germany. (back issues avail.)

282   GW   ISSN 0931-8887
LEBENDIGE ZELLE. 1957. 6/yr. DM.18. Landeskomitee der Katholiken in Bayern, Schaefflerstr. 9, 8000 Munich 2, Germany. TEL 089-2137288-212. circ. 5,800.

282   GW   ISSN 0023-9941
LEBENDIGES ZEUGNIS. 1946. q. membership. Bonifatiuswerk der Deutschen Katholiken e.V., Kamp 22, 4790 Paderborn, Germany. TEL 05251-29960. FAX 05251-299688. Ed. Bernhard Neumann. bk.rev.; circ. 6,000. **Indexed:** CERDIC.
   —BLDSC shelfmark: 5179.623200.
   Description: Examines topics in the fields of religion, philosophy and ethics.

282   GW
LESEPLAN JAHRESLOSUNG. a. DM.1.50. Katholisches Bibelwerk e.V., Silberburgstr. 121, 7000 Stuttgart 1, Germany. TEL 0711-626001. FAX 0711-616682.

LESOTHO CATHOLIC DIRECTORY. see *BUSINESS AND ECONOMICS — Trade And Industrial Directories*

200   LU
LETZEBURGER SONNDESBLAD. 1867. 610 Fr. Imprimerie Saint-Paul, 2 rue Christophe Plantin, L-2339 Luxembourg, Luxembourg. TEL 4993-281. FAX 49-10-78. Ed. Andre Heiderscheid.

282   AU
LICHTENTALER PFARRNACHRICHTEN. 1978. 4/yr. free. Pfarre Lichtental, Marktgasse 40, A-1090 Vienna, Austria. adv.; circ. 5,000.

282   IT
LIEB FRAUEN BOTE. (Text in German) 1950. bi-m. L.4000. Bertrand Vollmann, 39030 S. Lorenzo Sebato (BZ), Italy. circ. 4,000.

282   FR   ISSN 0024-2926
LIEN ENTRE MERES ET PERES DE PRETRES.* q. 3 F. (Diocese de Paris) Imprimerie Dalex a Montrouge, 5 et 7 rue Victor-Basch, Montrouge, France.

RELIGIONS AND THEOLOGY — ROMAN CATHOLIC

282 US ISSN 0024-3450
BX4020.A1
LIGUORIAN. 1913. m. $15. (Redemptorists, St. Louis Province) Liguori Publications, Liguori Dr., Liguori, MO 63057. TEL 314-464-2500. FAX 314-464-8449. Ed. Rev. Allen Weinert. bk.rev.; illus.; circ. 430,000. (also avail. in microfiche from UMI) **Indexed:** Cath.Ind., CERDIC.
Description: Articles on spirituality and Catholic teaching for readers of all ages.

282 US
LILY OF THE MOHAWKS. 1936. q. $3. Tekakwitha League, Auriesville, NY 12016. TEL 518-853-3153. Ed. John J. Paret. bk.rev.; circ. 10,000. (also avail. in microfilm; back issues avail.)

282 AT
THE LINK. 1979. q. free. Missionary Society of St. Paul, 477 Royal Parade, Parkville, Vic. 3052, Australia. TEL 03-387-7433. Ed. Noel Bianco. circ. 20,000. (looseleaf format; back issues avail.)
Formerly: Missionary Society of Saint Paul. Link (ISSN 0728-5493)
Description: Evangelical information from an internationl perspective.

282 CN
LITURGIE, FOI ET CULTURE. (Text in French) 1965. 4/yr. Can.$14($16) (outside US and Canada US$27). Canadian Conference of Catholic Bishops, Publications Service - Conference des Eveques Catholiques du Canada, 90 Ave. Parent, Ottawa, Ont. K1N 7B1, Canada. TEL 613-236-9461. FAX 613-236-8117. Ed. M. l'Abbe Paul Boily. bk.rev.; illus.; circ. 1,400.
Former titles: Conference des Eveques Catholiques du Canada. Bulletin National de Liturgie & Conference Catholique Canadienne. Bulletin National de Liturgie (ISSN 0384-5087)

282 783 US ISSN 1046-9990
LITURGY 90. 1970. 8/yr. $18. (Archdiocese of Chicago) Liturgy Training Publications, 1800 N. Hermitage Ave., Chicago, IL 60622-1101. TEL 312-486-8970. FAX 312-496-7094. Ed. Elizabeth Hoffman. index; circ. 6,120. (back issues avail.)
Formerly: Liturgy 80 (ISSN 1040-6603)
Description: For those who prepare liturgy in Catholic parishes, including artists and musicians. Contains articles, lists of events, and a question and answer column.

282 UK
LIVERPOOL CATHOLIC DIRECTORY. 1928. a. £1.15. Catholic Pictorial Ltd., Media House, Mann Island, Pier Head, Liverpool L3 1DQ, England. TEL 051-236-2191. FAX 051-236-2216. Ed. Rev. Tony Slingo. adv.; circ. 9,000.

377.8 US ISSN 0024-5275
BX923
LIVING LIGHT; an interdisciplinary review of Catholic religious education, catechesis and pastoral ministry. 1964. q. $29.95. United States Catholic Conference, Office for Publishing and Promotion Services, 3211 Fourth St., N.E., Washington, DC 20017-1194. TEL 202-541-3089. FAX 202-541-3091. Ed. Berard L. Marthaler. adv.; bk.rev.; index; circ. 1,200 (controlled). (also avail. in microform from UMI) **Indexed:** Cath.Ind., CERDIC, Old.Test.Abstr.
Description: Provides a forum for catechests and professional educators to identify problems and issues, report on research, encourage critical thinking, and to contribute to the decision-making in the field of religious educations and pastoral action.

282 CN ISSN 0703-6752
LIVING WITH CHRIST - COMPLETE EDITION. French edition: Prions en Eglise - Edition Complete. (Fr. ed. also avail. in large print, 11 pt.) 1966. 12/yr. Can.$10.23($13.85) Novalis, 6255 Hutchison St., Montreal, Que. H2V 4C7, Canada. TEL 514-278-3025. FAX 514-278-3030. Ed. Louise Pambrunn. circ. 94,963.
Description: Liturgical texts of the mass for Sundays and weekdays.

282 CN ISSN 0703-6760
LIVING WITH CHRIST - SUNDAY EDITION. French edition: Prions en Eglise - Edition Dominicale. 1936. bi-m., plus 2 special issues. Can.$5.85($7.95) Novalis, 6255 Hutchison St., Montreal, Que. H2V 4C7, Canada. TEL 514-278-3025. FAX 514-278-3030. Ed. Louise Pambrun.
Description: Liturgical texts for Sunday mass.

282 SP
LLUVIA DE ROSAS. 1923. bi-m. 450 ptas.($4) c/o P. Eugenio Alsina Valls, Apdo. 112, 25080 Lerida, Spain. Eds. Pages, Virgili. circ. 20,000. (also avail. in microfilm)

282 US ISSN 0024-6255
LONG ISLAND CATHOLIC. 1962. w. $18. (Catholic Diocese of Rockville Centre) Catholic Press Association, 115 Greenwich St., Hempstead, NY 11551. TEL 516-538-8800. (Subscr. to: Box 700, Hempstead, NY 11571) Ed. Msgr. Francis J. Maniscalco. adv.; bk.rev.; bibl.; charts; illus.; tr.lit.; circ. 130,000. (also avail. in microform)

282 GW
LOURDES - ROSEN. 1880. q. membership. Deutscher Lourdes-Verein, Schwalbengasse 10, 5000 Cologne 1, Germany. circ. 25,000 (controlled).

282 327 US
LUCHA - STRUGGLE; a journal of Christian reflection on struggles for liberation. 1976. bi-m. $10 to individuals (foreign $15); institutions $20 (foreign $25). New York Circus Publications, Box 37, Times Square Sta., New York, NY 10108. TEL 212-928-7600. Ed. Rigoberto Avila. adv.; bk.rev.; charts; illus.; stat.; circ. 3,000. (back issues avail.) **Indexed:** Alt.Press Ind., HR Rep.
Formerly (until 1979): New York Circus.

282 IT
LUISA LA SANTA TEREZIARIA DOMENICANA; periodico di spiritualita del divin volere. m. L.12000 (foreign L. 18000). Pia Associazione Luisa Piccarreta Piccoli Figli della Divina Volonta, Via N. Sauro, 25, 70033 Corato (Bari), Italy. TEL 080-898-2221. Ed. Suor. Assunta Marigliano.
Description: Religious forum covering various religious topics, also includes calendar of events.

268 BE ISSN 0770-2477
BX800.A1
LUMEN VITAE; revue internationale de la formation religieuse. French edition (ISSN 0024-7324) 1946. q. 1090 Fr. (International Centre for Religious Education) Lumen Vitae Press, 186 rue Washington, 1050 Brussels, Belgium. Ed. Pierre Mourlon Beernaert. bk.rev.; bibl.; index; circ. 1,800. (also avail. in microform from UMI) **Indexed:** Cath.Ind., CERDIC, Educ.Ind., New Test.Abstr., Rel.& Theol.Abstr. (1969-), Rural Recreat.Tour.Abstr., World Agri.Econ.& Rural Sociol.Abstr.

200 378 PE
M I E C SERVICO DE DOCUMENTACION. 12/yr. $18 (includes subscr. to: SPES and America Latina Boletin). Movimiento Internacional de Estudiantes Catolicos, Centro de Documentacion, Apdo. 3564, Lima 100, Peru. bk.rev.; bibl.; illus.

282 GW
M S C KONTAKTE. 1980. q. (Missionaries of Sacred Heart) Birkenverlag, Birkeneck, 8055 Hallbergmoos, Germany. TEL 0811-82205.

282 IT
MADONNA. 1954. bi-m. L.50000. Opera Madonna del Divino Amore, Via Ardeatina, Km 12, 00134 Rome, Italy. Dir. Don Pasquale Silla. circ. 1,500.

282 IT
LA MADONNA DEL DIVINO AMORE; bollettino mensile del santuario. 1932. m. Opera Madonna del Divino Amore, Via Ardeatina, Km 12, 00134 Rome, Italy. Ed. Carlo Sabatini. illus.; circ. 100,000.
Description: Deals with religious events for young people and community affairs sponsored by local church organizations.

282 IT
MADRE DI DIO; mensile mariano fondato da don Giacomo Alberione. 1932. m. L.16000($13) Societa S. Paolo (SSP), Via Alessandro Severo 56, 00145 Rome, Italy. TEL 06-5415501. FAX 06-5412249. Ed. Rev. Stefano Andreatta. adv.; bk.rev.; circ. 14,000. (back issues avail.)
Description: Religious publication covering religious news with special emphasis on the Virgin Mary.

266 SP
MADRE Y MAESTRA. 1871. m. (except Jul.-Aug. combined). 1000 ptas.($16) Misioneros del Sagrado Corazon de Jesus, Avenida Pio XII, 31, 28016 Madrid, Spain. TEL 259-96-00. Ed. Angel Gonzalez. adv.; bk.rev.; illus.; circ. 12,000.

282 IT ISSN 0024-9696
MAESTRO. 1944. m. L.35000 to non-members. Associazione Italiana Maestri Cattolici, Clivo di Monte del Gallo 50, 00165 Rome, Italy. TEL 634-651. FAX 06-6375903. Ed. Carlo Buzzi. adv.; bk.rev.; illus.; stat.; circ. 60,000.
Description: Presents articles from educators and others related to the field on the issues of school systems, the quality of education and the politics of schooling throughout Italy.

282 CN ISSN 0025-0007
MAGNIFICAT. English edition (ISSN 0381-0852) (Editions in English, French) 1965. m. contributions. Apostles of Infinite Love, Monastery of the Magnificat of the Mother of God, Box 308, St. Jovite, Que. JOT 2H0, Canada. FAX 819-688-5225. Ed.Bd. bk.rev.; illus.; circ. 4,000 (controlled). (processed) **Indexed:** Eng.Ind.

282 AT
MAJELLAN; champion of the family. 1949. q. Aus.$8. Redemptorist Congregation, P.O. Box 43, Brighton, Vic. 3186, Australia. TEL 03-592-2777. FAX 03-593-1337. Ed. Rev. W.H. Stinson. circ. 62,000. (back issues avail.)

232 SZ ISSN 0025-2972
MARIA; marianischer digest. 1950. 6/yr. 13.50 SFr. Postfach 6407, CH-3001 Bern, Switzerland. TEL 031-221380. FAX 031-223071. Ed. Josef Gruebel. adv.; bk.rev.; illus.; circ. 25,000.

200 IT
MARIA NOSTRA LUCE. 1918. m. L.3000. Centro Nazionale Associazione Mariana, Via Francesco Albergotti 75, 00167 Rome, Italy. bk.rev.; circ. 3,500.

282 US
MARIAN HELPERS BULLETIN. 1947. q. $2 membership. Association of Marian Helpers, Stockbridge, MA 01263. TEL 413-298-3691. FAX 413-298-3583. Ed.Bd. bk.rev.; circ. 1,000,000.

200 020 US ISSN 0076-4434
BT595
MARIAN LIBRARY STUDIES. NEW SERIES. (Text in language of author) 1951; N.S. 1969. a. price varies. University of Dayton, Marian Library, Dayton, OH 45469-1390. TEL 513-229-4214. FAX 513-229-4590. Ed. Theodore Koehler. circ. 200. **Indexed:** Cath.Ind., CERDIC.
Description: Presents scholarly, historical and interdisciplinary studies related to the Virgin Mary.

282 US ISSN 0464-9680
BT596
MARIAN STUDIES. 1950. a. $12. Mariological Society of America, Marian Library, Box 1390, University of Dayton, Dayton, OH 45469-1390. TEL 513-229-4214. FAX 513-229-4590. Ed. Thomas A. Thompson. adv.; bibl.; cum.index; circ. 600. (also avail. in microform from UMI; reprint service avail. from UMI) **Indexed:** Cath.Ind.
Description: Proceedings of society's annual convention.

232 AU ISSN 0025-3014
MARIANIST. 1956. q. S.60. Gesellschaft Mariae in Oesterreich und Deutschland - Marianist Catholic Order, Mistlberg 20, A-4284 Tragwein, Austria. FAX 07236-22523. illus.; circ. 3,000.

282 IT
MARIANUM. 1939. s-a. L.45000 (foreign L.65000). Pontificia Facolta Teologica Marianum, Viale Trenta Aprile 6, 00153 Rome, Italy. TEL 06-5890661. FAX 06-5880292. Ed. Ignazio M. Calabuig. adv.; bk.rev.; circ. 800. **Indexed:** M.L.A., New Test.Abstr.

RELIGIONS AND THEOLOGY — ROMAN CATHOLIC

282   CN
MARTYRS' SHRINE MESSAGE. 1937. s-a. Can.$5. Jesuit Fathers of Upper Canada, Martyrs' Shrine, Midland, Ont. L4R 4K5, Canada. TEL 705-526-3788. FAX 705-526-1546. Ed. James Mara. circ. 10,000. (back issues avail.)

266   US
MARYKNOLL FATHERS AND BROTHERS. m. donation. Maryknoll Magazine, Maryknoll, NY 10545. TEL 914-941-7590. FAX 914-945-0670. (Co-sponsor: Catholic Foreign Mission Society of America) Ed. Joseph Veneroso. illus.; index; circ. 700,000. (also avail. in microform from UMI) **Indexed:** Cath.Ind., CERDIC.
    Former titles: Maryknoll (ISSN 0025-4142); (until 1938): Field Afar (ISSN 0271-7204); Supersedes (in 1907): Channel (ISSN 0009-1456)
    Description: Covers mission work in underdeveloped countries.

282   GW   ISSN 0934-8522
MATERIALDIENST DES KONFESSIONSKUNDLICHEN INSTITUTS. 1950. bi-m. DM.25. Evangelischer Bund, Konfessionskundliches Institut, Postfach 1255, 6140 Bensheim 1, Germany. TEL 06251-38000. FAX 06251-2045. bk.rev.; circ. 6,200.
    Formerly: Evangelischer Bund. Materialdienst.
    Description: Ecumenical issues as they relate to the Roman Catholic Church.

282   PL   ISSN 0076-5244
MATERIALY ZRODLOWE DO DZIEJOW KOSCIOLA W POLSCE. 1965. irreg. price varies. Katolicki Uniwersytet Lubelski, Towarzystwo Naukowe, Ul. Gliniana 21, 20-616 Lublin, Poland. (Dist. by: Ars Polona-Ruch, Krakowskie Przedmiescie 7, Warsaw, Poland) (Co-sponsor: Instytut Geografii Historycznej Kosciola w Polsce przy K.U.L.) Ed. Jerzy Kloczowski. circ. 1,000.

MAVRICA/RAINBOW. see *CHILDREN AND YOUTH — For*

282   CK
MEDELLIN; teologia y pastoral para America Latina. 1975. q. Col.$5000($30) in U.S.; Europe $40. Consejo Episcopal Latinoamericano, Instituto Teologico Pastoral, Transversal 67, No.173-71, Apdo. Aereo 253353, Bogota DE, Colombia. TEL 671-40-04. FAX 612-19-29. TELEX 41388 CELA CO. Ed. Francisco Emilio Tamayo Ramirez. bk.rev.; film rev.; circ. 1,500. (back issues avail.)

282   US
MEDICAL MISSION NEWS. 1931. q. free. Catholic Medical Mission Board, Inc., 10 W. 17th St., New York, NY 10011. TEL 212-242-7757. FAX 212-807-9161. Ed. Leo T. Tarpey. circ. 30,000.
    Description: Distribution of medicines to 6,000 mission units in 60 countries.

MEDICAL MISSION SISTERS NEWS. see *HOSPITALS*

200   FR   ISSN 0025-8911
BR3
MELANGES DE SCIENCE RELIGIEUSE. 1944. q. 120 F.($20) (effective Jan. 1991). Institut Catholique de Lille, 60 bd. Vauban, B.P. 109, 59016 Lille Cedex, France. TEL 20-30-88-27. Ed. Gerard-Henry Baudry. bk.rev.; cum.index: vols. 1-27, 1944-1970; circ. 500. (back issues avail.) **Indexed:** Bull.Signal., CERDIC, Int.Z.Bibelwiss, M.L.A., New Test.Abstr., Old Test.Abstr., Rel.& Theol.Abstr. (1968-), Rel.Ind.One, Rel.Per.
  —BLDSC shelfmark: 5536.813000.
    Description: Covers theology, philosophy, the histories of religions, institutions, law, anthropology, sociology, pedagogy, literature and art.

282   CL   ISSN 0716-0062
MENSAJE. 1951. m. $28. (Compania de Jesus, Provincia Chilena) Residencia San Roberto Bellarmino, Almirante Barroso 24, Casilla 10445, Santiago, Chile. TEL 2-696-0653. Ed. Jose Arteaga. adv.; bk.rev.; film rev.; play rev.; bibl.; illus.; stat.; cum.index; circ. 8,000. **Indexed:** Biol.Abstr., HR Rep.
    Description: Church review that deals with social, cultural, economic and political issues of Chile and South America.

282   FR   ISSN 0026-0290
MESSAGES DU SECOURS CATHOLIQUE. 1945. m. 16 F. Editions S.O.S., 106 rue du Bac, 75341 Paris Cedex 07, France. Ed. Robert Prigent. adv.; bk.rev.; charts; illus.; stat.; circ. 975,000. (tabloid format)

267 325   AT
MESSAGGERO. (Text in Italian) 1961. m. Aus.$10. Scalabrinian Fathers, 378 Nicholson St., Fitzroy, Vic. 3068, Australia. Ed. Rev. Luciano Ferracin. adv.; circ. 6,000.

282 255   IT   ISSN 0026-0312
MESSAGGERO DI S. ANTONIO. (Editions in English, French, German, Italian, Portuguese and Spanish) 1898. m. L.19000 (foreign L.31000). (Provincia Padovana dei Frati Minori Conventuali) Editrice Grafiche Messaggero Sant' Antonio, Via Orto Botanico, 11, 35123 Padua, Italy. TEL 049-664322. FAX 049-654066. TELEX 430855 MSA PD I. (Subscr. to: Basilica del Santo, 35123 Padua, Italy) Ed. Giacomo Panteghini. adv.; bk.rev.; film rev.; circ. 1,600,000. (back issues avail.)

282   US   ISSN 0279-3911
THE MESSENGER (BELLEVILLE). 1907. w. (48/yr.). $17 (effective 1992). Roman Catholic Diocese of Belleville, Chancery Office, 222 S. Third St., Belleville, IL 62220. TEL 618-235-9601. FAX 618-235-7416. (Subscr. to: 2620 Lebanon Ave., Box 327, Belleville, IL 62221) Ed. Raphael H. Middeke. adv.; bk.rev.; film rev.; circ. 17,300. (tabloid format; also avail. in microfilm)

282   UK
MIDDLESBOROUGH DIOCESAN DIRECTORY. a. Universe Publishing Co., Ltd., 18 Crosby Rd. N., Waterloo, Liverpool L22 4OF, England. TEL 051 920 6171. Ed. Rev. Michael Dunn. circ. 3,000.

268   US   ISSN 0300-6158
MIESIECZNIK FRANCISZKANSKI. (Text in Polish) 1907? m. $6. (Catholic Order of the Franciscan Fathers) Franciscan Publishers, Franciscan Center, Pulaski, WI 54162. TEL 414-822-5833. FAX 414-822-5423. Ed. Sebastian M. Kus. circ. 3,688.

MILITAERSEELSORGE. see *MILITARY*

282   GW
MINI; Taschenkalender fur Ministranten und junge Christen. 1949. a. DM.7.50. Franz Sales Verlag, Rosental 1, Postfach 1361, 8078 Eichstaett, Germany. TEL 08421-5379. FAX 08421-80805. bk.rev.; circ. 50,000. (back issues avail.)

200   SZ
MIRJAM; Monatszeitschrift der weltoffenen Frau. 1934. m. 36 Fr. (Arbeitsstelle Bildungsdienst) Verlag U. Cavelti AG, CH-9202 Gossau, Switzerland. TEL 01-2521011. FAX 01-2611354. Ed. Annelies Schuepp. adv.; bk.rev.; film rev.; play rev.; illus.; index; circ. 16,000. (tabloid format)
    Formerly: Ancilla (ISSN 0003-2867)

282   GW   ISSN 0252-2535
MIRROR. (Text in English) 1959. bi-m. $5. Kirche in Not - Ostpriesterhilfe e.V., Bischof-Kaller-Str. 3, Postfach 1209, 6240 Konigstein 1, Germany. TEL 06174-291-0. Ed. Christine Decker. illus. (back issues avail.)
    Description: News about the persecuted Church and refugees in Eastern Europe and the Third World.

282   US
MIRROR (SPRINGFIELD). 1965. w. $10. Diocese of Springfield - Cape Girardeau, 601 S. Jefferson Ave., Springfield, MO 65806. TEL 417-866-0841. FAX 417-866-1140. (Subscr. to: Box 847, Springfield, MO 65801) Ed. Rev. Mark G. Boyer. adv.; circ. 16,300. (tabloid format)

200   VC   ISSN 0026-587X
MISCELLANEA FRANCESCANA; rivista trimestrale di scienze teologiche e di studi francescani. (Text in English, French, Italian, Latin) 1886. q. L.40000($45) (Pontificia Facolta Teologica S. Bonaventura) Casa Editrice Miscellanea Francescana, Via del Serafico 1, 00142 Rome, Italy. Ed. Orlando Todisco. bk.rev.; illus.; index; circ. 600. **Indexed:** Amer.Hist.& Life, Hist.Abstr., M.L.A., RILA.

MISHKAN; a theological forum on Jewish evangelism. see *RELIGIONS AND THEOLOGY — Judaic*

282   SP
MISIORAMA. (Supplement to: Comunidad) m. free. Semanario de la Iglesia Diocesana, Iscar Peyra, 26 Obispado, 37002 Salamanca, Spain.

262   GW
MISSIO AKTUELL. 1969. bi-m. DM.10. (Internationales Katholisches Missionswerk e.V.) MISSIO Aktuell Verlag GmbH, Goethestr. 43, 5100 Aachen, Germany. TEL 0241-76015. FAX 0241-7507237. TELEX 832719-MIRAD. Ed. Toni Goertz. adv.; bk.rev.; circ. 750,000.
    Former titles: Aktuell; Weltmission.

266   FR   ISSN 0026-6035
MISSION DE L'EGLISE. 1925. q. 80 F. Union Pontificale Missionnaire, 5 rue Monsieur, 75007 Paris, France. FAX 47-34-26-63. Ed. Mgr. Maurice Delorme. adv.; bk.rev.; bibl.; index; circ. 23,000. **Indexed:** CERDIC.

266 282
MISSION HANDBOOK. 1950. a. $4. United States Catholic Mission Association, 3029 Fourth St., N.E., Washington, DC 20017. TEL 202-832-3112. Ed. Sr. Mary Godfrey. circ. 1,500.
    Former titles: United States Catholic Mission Council. Handbook; United States Catholic Missionary Personnel Overseas (ISSN 0082-9560)

266   US
MISSION INTERCOM. 1971. m. (10/yr.). $8 (foreign $10). United States Catholic Mission Association, 3029 Fourth St., N.E., Washington, DC 20017. TEL 202-832-3112. Ed. Sr. Marge Zacharias. circ. 1,200.

266   UK
MISSION OUTLOOK. 1950. q. £5($12) Pontifical Mission Societies, 23 Eccleston Sq., London SW1V 1NU, England. Ed. F.J. McCarthy. circ. 2,000.
    Formerly: Outlook (ISSN 0030-7211)

282   UK
MISSION TODAY. 1937. q. free to members. Association for the Propagation of the Faith, 23 Eccleston Square, London SW1V 1NU, England. TEL 071-834-5680. Ed. John Corcoran. bk.rev.; circ. 220,000.
    Former titles: Missions, Missionaries and Young Churches & Missions and Missionaries.

055.1   IT
MISSIONARI DEL P.I.M.E.. 1914. m. (11/yr.). L.10000($16) Pontificio Istituto Missioni Estere, Via Mose Bianchi 94, 20149 Milan, Italy. TEL 02-4980741. FAX 02-4695193. Ed. P. Piero Gheddo. adv.; bk.rev.; circ. 20,000.

266   US   ISSN 0026-6086
MISSIONHURST. 1948. 6/yr. free to qualified personnel. (Congregation of the Immaculate Heart of Mary) Missionhurst, Inc., 4651 N. 25th St., Arlington, VA 22207-3500. TEL 703-528-3800. FAX 703-528-3804. Ed. James P. Fischler. illus.; circ. 90,000. (controlled)

266 282   IT   ISSN 0026-6108
MISSIONI DOMENICANE. 1926. m. (10/yr.). L.5000. Centro Missionario Domenicano, Piazza S. Domenico 1, 51100 Pistoia, Italy. Ed. P. Rossi Giuseppe. charts; illus.; circ. 5,000.

282   CN   ISSN 0700-4192
MISSIONS DES FRANCISCAINS. (Text in French) 1923. q. $10. Syndics Apostoliques des Freres Mineurs (Franciscains), 2080 Rene-Levesque Ouest, Montreal, Que. H3H 1R6, Canada. TEL 514-932-6094. FAX 514-259-7407. Ed. Raymond R. Lagace. circ. 6,000.

282   GW   ISSN 0179-0102
MISSIONSBLAETTER. 1888. q. free. Erzabtei St. Ottilien, 8917 St. Ottilien, Germany. TEL 08193-710. Eds. Basilius Doppelfeld, Arnold Walloschek. bk.rev.; circ. 23,000. (back issues avail.)

282   GW
MISSIONSKALENDER. 1888. a. DM.3. Erzabtei St. Ottilien, 8197 St. Ottilien, Germany. TEL 08193-710. FAX 08193-6844. Eds. Arno Muenz, Bernhard Sirch. circ. 102,000. (back issues avail.)

059   LO
MOELETSI OA BASOTHO/COUNSELLOR OF BASOTHO. (Text in Sesotho) 1933. w. R.40. (Missionary Oblates of Mary Immaculate) Mazenod Printing Works (Pty) Ltd., P.O. Mazenod, Lesotho. Ed. William Lesenya. adv.; circ. 13,000.

RELIGIONS AND THEOLOGY — ROMAN CATHOLIC

282   LO
MOELETSI OA BASOTHO. (Text in Sesotho) 1933. w. Mazenod Institute, P.O. Box MZ 18, Mazenod 160, Lesotho. TEL 62224. TELEX 4271. Ed. William Lesenya. circ. 12,000. (newspaper)
   Description: Roman Catholic weekly paper.

282   US
▼**MOMENTO CATOLICO.** (Text in English, Spanish) 1991. 12/yr. $12. Claretian Publications, 205 W. Monroe St., Chicago, IL 60606. TEL 312-236-7782. FAX 312-236-7230. Ed. Rev. Mark J. Brummel.
   Description: Focuses on specific topics of interest to the Hispanic community.

MOMENTUM (WASHINGTON). see EDUCATION

255   CN   ISSN 0026-9190
BX2400
MONASTIC STUDIES. 1963. a. Can.$25. Benedictine Priory of Montreal, 1475 Pine Ave., Montreal, Que. H3G 1B3, Canada. TEL 514-281-0659. FAX 514-281-0173. Ed. Laurence Freeman. bk.rev.; circ. 2,500. (also avail. in microform from UMI) **Indexed:** Cath.Ind.

282   IT
MONASTICA. 1960. q. contribution. Monastero di Santa Scolastica, I-00060 Civitella San Paolo (Rome), Italy. circ. 850. (back issues avail.)

282 266   IT   ISSN 0026-6094
MONDO E MISSIONE. 1872. m. (10/yr.). L.25000($38) Pontificio Istituto Missioni Estere, Via Mose Bianchi 94, 20149-Milan, Italy. TEL 02-4980741. FAX 02-4695193. Ed. P. Piero Gheddo. adv.; bk.rev.; illus.; index; circ. 50,000. **Indexed:** CERDIC.
   Formerly: Missioni Cattoliche.
   Description: Covers missionary work in the country.

262.9   IT   ISSN 0026-976X
MONITOR ECCLESIASTICUS; commentarius de re cannoica et pastorali post Vaticanum II. (Text in Latin and modern languages) 1876. q. L.5200($8.50) Agnesotti S.a.S., Piazza M. Fani 2, 01100 Viterbo, Italy. bk.rev.; circ. 1,000. **Indexed:** Canon Law Abstr., CERDIC.
   Description: Deals with canon law.

282   US
MONTANA CATHOLIC. 16/yr. $14. Roman Catholic Diocese of Helena, 515 N. Ewing, Box 1729, Helena, MT 59624. TEL 406-442-5820. FAX 406-442-5191. Ed. Gerald M. Korson. adv.; circ. 8,500. (tabloid format; back issues avail.)
   Description: News of the church in Western Montana.

282   UK   ISSN 0027-0172
MONTH. 1864. m. £14($35) 114 Mount St., London W1Y 6AH, England. TEL 071-491-7596. FAX 071-495-1673. Ed. John McDade, S.J. adv.; bk.rev.; film rev.; index; circ. 2,500. (also avail. in microform from UMI) **Indexed:** Br.Hum.Ind., Cath.Ind., CERDIC, Mid.East: Abstr.& Ind., New Test.Abstr.
   —BLDSC shelfmark: 5928.860000.
   Incorporates: Herder Correspondence.
   Description: Review of Christian thought and world affairs.

200   IT   ISSN 0077-1449
MONUMENTA HISTORICA ORDINIS MINORUM CAPUCCINORUM. (Text in Italian and Latin) 1937. irreg., no.20, 1991. price varies. Frati Minori Cappuccini, Istituto Storico, Cas. Post. 90-91, Circonv. Occidentale 6850 (GRA km 65), 00163 Rome, Italy. TEL 06-625-19-58. FAX 06-661-62-401. index; circ. 500.

282   IT
MONUMENTA HISTORICA SOCIETATIS IESU. irreg., vol.141, 1992. Institutum Historicum Societatis Iesu - Jesuit Historical Institute, Via dei Penitenzieri 20, 00193 Rome, Italy. (back issues avail.)
   Description: Editions of documents regarding early history of Jesuits and of Jesuit missions worldwide.

282   VC   ISSN 0077-1457
MONUMENTA IURIS CANONICI. (In 3 series: A: Corpus Glossatorum; B: Corpus Collectionum; C: Subsidia) 1965. irreg. price varies. Biblioteca Apostolica Vaticana, 00120 Vatican City (Rome), State of the Vatican City.

266   SP   ISSN 0210-0851
MORALIA; revista de ciencias morales. 1963. q. $30. Instituto Superior de Ciencias Morales, Felix Boix, 13, 28036 Madrid, Spain. Ed. Rev. Miguel Rubio. adv.; circ. 1,000. **Indexed:** CERDIC.
   Formerly (until vol.16, 1978): Pentecostes (ISSN 0479-9828)

266   US   ISSN 0027-1527
MOTHER CABRINI MESSENGER.* 1938. bi-m. contributions. Mother Cabrini League, Missionary Sisters of the Sacred Heart of Jesus, 434 W. Deming, Chicago, IL 60614. TEL 312-883-7329. Ed. Sister Immaculate. circ. 40,000.
   Description: Mission work in the United States.

282   GW   ISSN 0580-1400
BR4
MUENCHENER THEOLOGISCHE ZEITSCHRIFT. 1950. q. DM.48. Universitaet Muenchen, Katholisch-Theologische Fakultaet, Geschwister-School-Platz 1, 8000 Munich 2, Germany. bk.rev.; circ. 350. (back issues avail.)

282   GW   ISSN 0077-2011
MUENSTERSCHWARZACHER STUDIEN. 1965. irreg. price varies. (Benediktinerabtei Muensterschwarzach) Vier-Tuerme-Verlag, 8711 Muensterschwarzach, Germany. Ed. Pirmin Hugger. adv.; bk.rev.

282   SP   ISSN 0027-3252
MUNDO CRISTIANO. 1963. m. $64. E.P.A.L.S.A., Castellana, 210, 28046 Madrid, Spain. TEL 91-250-7720. (Dist. in U.S. by: Faxon Co., Inc., 15 Southwest Park, Westwood, MA 02090) Ed. D. Jesus Urteaga Loidi. adv.; film rev, bibl.; illus.; circ. 46,852. (avail. on records)

266   CN   ISSN 0316-8913
MY BROTHER AND I. 1968. q. Missionary Association of Mary Immaculate, Oblate Missionary Centre, Box 721, Winnipeg, Man. R3C 2K3, Canada. TEL 204-586-2906. illus.; circ. 600.
   Description: Highlights missionwork in the provinces.

282   US
MY DAILY VISITOR. 1955. bi-m. $8 (foreign $9.50). Our Sunday Visitor, Inc., 200 Noll Plaza, Huntington, IN 46750. TEL 219-356-8400. FAX 219-356-4872. Eds. William and Catherine Odell. circ. 30,000.
   Description: Daily scripture readings and meditations for increasing personal spirituality.

282 028.5   US
MY FRIEND; a catholic magazine for kids. 1979. m. (except Summer). $10. Daughters of St. Paul, 50 St. Paul Ave., Boston, MA 02130. TEL 617-522-8911. FAX 617-524-8035. Ed. Sister Anne Joan Flanagan. circ. 15,000. (back issues avail.)
   Description: Entertainment, information and Christian formation for children from the ages of six to twelve.

N C E A NOTES. (National Catholic Educational Association) see EDUCATION

282   XV
NASE OBCESTVO; glasilo zupnije Svete Trojice v Ljubljani. (Text in Slovenian) 1980. m. free. Zupnijski Urad Sveta Trojica, Trg Osvoboditve 17, p.p. 392, 61001 Ljubljana, Slovenia. TEL 061 224-864. circ. 1,000.

NASZA PRZESZLOSC. see HISTORY — History Of Europe

282   US   ISSN 0027-8920
NATIONAL CATHOLIC REGISTER. 1928. w. $49.95 (Canada $65). Twin Circle Publishing Co., 12700 Ventura Blvd., Studio City, CA 91604. TEL 800-421-3230. FAX 213-655-0344. Ed. Francis X. Maier. adv.; bk.rev.; film rev.; illus.; circ. 35,000. **Indexed:** Cath.Ind.
   Formerly: Denver Register.

282   US   ISSN 0027-8939
NATIONAL CATHOLIC REPORTER. 1964. w. $32.95. National Catholic Reporter Publishing Company, Inc., 115 E. Armour Blvd., Box 419281, Kansas City, MO 64141. TEL 800-444-8910. FAX 816-931-5082. Ed. Thomas Fox. adv.; bk.rev.; illus.; circ. 52,000. (tabloid format; also avail. in microform from UMI; reprint service avail. from UMI) **Indexed:** Access, Cath.Ind., CERDIC, Curr.Lit.Fam.Plan:, Hlth.Ind., Mag.Ind.
   Description: Independent progressive views on religious, social and moral issues.

NATIONAL FEDERATION OF CATHOLIC PHYSICIANS' GUILDS. NEWSLETTER. see MEDICAL SCIENCES

282   US
NETWORK CONNECTION; national Catholic social justice lobby. 1971. bi-m. $30 (low-income $15). Center for Educational Design and Communication, Attn: Nancy Sylvester, IHM, National Coordinator, 806 Rhode Island Ave., N.E., Washington, DC 20018. TEL 202-526-4070. FAX 202-832-4635. bk.rev.; charts; illus.; index; circ. 12,000. (tabloid format; back issues avail.)
   Formerly: Network (Washington, 1971) (ISSN 0199-5723)

282   GW   ISSN 0930-1143
NEUE GESPRAECHE; Handreichungen fuer Familien und Gruppen. bi-m. DM.9.90. (Arbeitsgemeinschaft fuer Katholische Familienbildung e.V.) Patmos Verlag GmbH, Am Wehrhahn 100, 4000 Dusseldorf, Germany. TEL 0211-16795-0. FAX 0211-16795-75.

282   GW
NEUE MITTE; Stimme der Katholiken in Wirtschaft und Verwaltung. bi-m. DM.2. K K V - Bundesverwaltung der Katholiken in Wirtschaft und Verwaltung e.V., Bismarckstr. 61, 4300 Essen 1, Germany. TEL 0201-771024. adv.; bk.rev.; circ. 12,000.

DIE NEUE ORDNUNG. see SOCIOLOGY

282 255   UK   ISSN 0028-4289
NEW BLACKFRIARS. 1920; N.S. 1964. m. £15($35) (English Dominicans) Blackfriars, Oxford OX1 3LY, England. TEL 0865-278414. Ed. Allan White. adv.; bk.rev.; index; circ. 2,000. (also avail. in microform from UMI; reprint service avail. from UMI) **Indexed:** Br.Hum.Ind., Cath.Ind., CERDIC, Mid.East: Abstr.& Ind., New Test.Abstr., Old Test.Abstr.
   —BLDSC shelfmark: 6082.270000.
   Incorporates: Blackfriars; Life of the Spirit.
   Description: Surveys theology, philosophy, sociology and the arts from the standpoint of Christian principles and their application to the modern world.

282   US
NEW CATHOLIC EXPLORER. 1960. w. $15 (typically set Jan.). Roman Catholic Diocese of Joliet, St. Charles Center, 402 S. Independence Blvd., Romeoville, IL 60441-2299. TEL 815-838-6475. FAX 815-838-8129. Ed. Patricia Lynn Morrison. adv.; bk.rev.; circ. 28,000.
   Formerly (until Aug. 1988): Joliet Catholic Explorer.

282   US
NEW CATHOLIC MISCELLANY. 1822. w. $15. Roman Catholic Diocese of Charleston, 119 Broad St., Box 818, Charleston, SC 29402. TEL 803-724-8375. FAX 803-724-8368. Ed. Philip M. Bowman. adv.; circ. 21,748. (tabloid format)

200   US   ISSN 0744-8589
BX2350.57
NEW COVENANT. 1971. 11/yr. $14.95. Servant Publications, Box 8617, Ann Arbor, MI 48107. TEL 313-761-8505. Ed. Jim Manney. adv.; bk.rev.; illus.; circ. 45,000. (back issues avail.) **Indexed:** Cath.Ind., CERDIC.
   Formerly: Pastoral Newsletter.
   Description: Articles on Catholic renewal.

282   US
NEW EARTH. 1938. 12/yr. $5. (Catholic Diocese of Fargo, Media Office) Catholic Bulletin, 244 Dayton Ave., St. Paul, MN 55102. TEL 701-235-6429. FAX 701-235-0296. Ed. Joan A. Smithwick. adv.; bk.rev.; circ. 31,000. (tabloid format)
   Formerly (until May 1980): Catholic Action News (ISSN 0008-7890)

RELIGIONS AND THEOLOGY — ROMAN CATHOLIC

282   CN   ISSN 0838-0341
NEW FREEMAN. 1900. w. Can.$17($27) New Freeman Ltd., One Bayard Dr., Saint John, N.B. E2L 3L5, Canada. TEL 506-632-9226. FAX 506-632-9272. Ed. Robert G. Merzetti. adv.; bk.rev.; circ. 6,950. (tabloid format; also avail. in microform)

282   UK   ISSN 0028-6079
NEW LIFE (LONDON, 1965). 1965. q. £10. New Life Publications, 120 A West Heath Rd., London NW3 7TY, England. FAX 081-458-7485. bk.rev.; film rev.; play rev.; circ. 650. (processed)

200   US
THE NEW WORLD. 1892. w. $25. (Catholic Archdiocese of Chicago) Chicago Catholic Publishing, 1144 W. Jackson Blvd., Chicago, IL 60607. TEL 312-243-1300. FAX 312-243-1526. Ed. Mary Gart. adv.; bk.rev.; circ. 60,000. (also avail. in microform) **Indexed:** CERDIC.
    Former titles: Chicago Catholic (ISSN 0149-970X); New World (ISSN 0028-7016)

282   NZ   ISSN 0028-8748
NEW ZEALAND TABLET; New Zealand's national Catholic weekly. 1873. w. NZ.$100. (Roman Catholic Church) New Zealand Tablet Co. Ltd., 64 Vogel St., Dunedin, New Zealand. FAX 03-477-8245. Ed. J.K. Molloy. adv.; bk.rev.; film rev.; play rev.; bibl.; illus.; circ. 9,000.

282   NZ
NEW ZEALANDIA. 1934. m. NZ.$39.60. Roman Catholic Bishop of Auckland, c/o Pompallier Diocesan Centre, 30 New Street, P.O. Box 845, Auckland, New Zealand. TEL 09-783-380. FAX 039-360-3065. Ed. Paul F. Freedman. adv.; bk.rev.; film rev.; play rev.; bibl.; circ. 14,000. (tabloid format)
    Supersedes (in 1989): Zealandia (ISSN 0044-202X)
    Description: Covers Catholic faith and spirituality, news, features, short story, scripture, family life, ecumenical news, church history, poems, counseling.

282   VN
NGUOI CONG GIAO VIET-NAM/VIETNAMESE CATHOLIC. 1984. fortn. Committee for Solidarity of Patriotic Vietnamese Catholics, 59 Trang Thi, Hanoi, Socialist Republic of Vietnam. TEL 56242. Ed. Pham Van Kham.

282 281.9   IT
NICOLAUS. vol.6, 1978. s-a. L.10000($14) Pontificia Universita S. Tommaso D'Aquino - Roma, Istituto di Teologia Ecumenica "S. Nicola", Via Bisanzio e Rainaldo 15, 70122 Bari, Italy. **Indexed:** CERDIC.

282   UG   ISSN 0048-041X
NILE GAZETTE. (Text in English; supplements in Alur, Logbara and Madi) 1958. m. EAs.6. Diocese of Arua, Box 3230, Kampala, Uganda. Ed. Rev. A. Dalfovo. illus.; circ. 7,000. (tabloid format)

NORTH AMERICAN ASSOCIATION OF CHRISTIANS IN SOCIAL WORK. PRACTICE MONOGRAPH SERIES. see *SOCIAL SERVICES AND WELFARE*

282   US
NORTH CAROLINA CATHOLIC. 1946. w. $16. (Roman Catholic Diocese of Raleigh) North Carolina Catholic, 300 Cardinal Gibbons Dr., Raleigh, NC 27606. TEL 919-821-9735. FAX 919-821-9705. Ed. William A. Mills. adv.; bk.rev.; circ. 30,000. (tabloid format; also avail. in microform; back issues avail.)

282   US
NORTH COUNTY CATHOLIC. 1946. w. $10. Diocese of Ogdensburg, Box 326, 308 Isabella St., Ogdensburg, NY 13669. TEL 315-393-2540. Ed. Mary Lou Kilian. adv.; circ. 10,000. (tabloid format)

282 028.5   US
NORTHWEST INDIANA CATHOLIC. 1987. w. $15 (effective Jan. 1992). Catholic Diocese of Gary, 9292 Broadway, Merrillville, IN 46410. TEL 219-769-9292. FAX 219-738-9034. Ed. Brian T. Olszewski. adv.; bk.rev.; circ. 27,200. (tabloid format)

200 028.5   IT   ISSN 0029-3903
NOTE DI PASTORALE GIOVANILE. 1967. m. L.35000. (Centro Catechistico Salesiano) Editrice Elle Di Ci, Corso Francia 214, 10096 Leumann (Turin), Italy. TEL 011 95-91-091. Ed. Riccardo Tonelli. bk.rev.; index, circ. 7,000. **Indexed:** CERDIC.

282   UK
NOTHAMPTON DIOCESAN DIRECTORY. a. Universe Publishing Co., Ltd., 18 Crosby Road North, Waterloo, Liverpool L22 4OF, England. TEL 051 920 6171. Ed. Rev. Roger Edmunds. circ. 3,000.

282   VC   ISSN 0029-4306
NOTITIAE. (Text in English, French and Latin) 1965. m. L.40000($45) (foreign L.50000)(effective 1992). Libreria Editrice Vaticana, 00120 Vatican City (Rome), State of the Vatican City. illus.; index. **Indexed:** Canon Law Abstr., Cath.Ind., CERDIC.
    —BLDSC shelfmark: 6173.200000.
    Description: Covers organ of the Congregation for Divine Worship and information on liturgical matters.

282   US
NOTRE DAME STUDIES IN AMERICAN CATHOLICISM. 1979. irreg., vol.11, 1991. (Cushwa Center for the Study of American Catholicism) University of Notre Dame Press, Notre Dame, IN 46556. TEL 219-239-6346. bibl.

266   CN   ISSN 0029-4578
LES NOTRES. 1960. q. Can.$5. Peres Montfortains, Procure des Missions, 4000 Bossuet, Montreal, Que. H1M 2M2, Canada. TEL 514-254-5376. Ed. A. Williamson. circ. 13,000.

282   US   ISSN 1047-2398
NOVA (NEW BERLIN). 1972. 6/yr. $51. Liturgical Publications Inc., 2875 South James Dr., New Berlin, WI 53151. TEL 414-785-1188. FAX 414-785-9567. Ed. Rev. Albert Nevins. bk.rev.; index. (looseleaf format) **Indexed:** Old Test.Abstr., Rel.& Theol.Abstr.
    Formerly: Nova et Vetera.

282   SZ   ISSN 0029-5027
AP24
NOVA ET VETERA. (Text in French) 1926. q. 50 Fr. Editions Universitaires de Fribourg, 42 Bd. de Perolles, CH-1700 Fribourg, Switzerland. Ed. Georges Cottier. bk.rev.; index. **Indexed:** CERDIC, New Test.Abstr.
    —BLDSC shelfmark: 6178.200000.

282   IT   ISSN 0078-253X
NOVARIEN. 1967. irreg. price varies. Associazione di Storia Ecclesiastica Novarese, Presso Archivio Storico Diocesano, Palazzo Vescovile, I-28100 Novara, Italy. Ed. Angelo L. Stoppa. bk.rev.; circ. 1,000.
    —BLDSC shelfmark: 6180.060000.

282   US
▼**NUESTRA PARROQUIA.** (Text in English, Spanish) 1991. m. $12. Claretian Publications, 205 W. Monroe St., Chicago, IL 60606. TEL 312-236-7782. FAX 312-236-7230. Ed. Rev. Mark J. Brummel. circ. 1,200.

282   AG   ISSN 0029-585X
NUEVA POMPEYA. 1924. m. Arg.$20000. (Santuario de la Virgen del Rosario) Orden de los Frailes Menores Capuchinos, Esquiu 974, C.C. 14-Suc.37, Buenos Aires, Argentina. Dir. R.P. Andres Guirao. index; circ. 18,000.

282   IT
NUOVA UMANITA. 1979. bi-m. L.25000 (foreign L.47000). Citta Nuova Editrice della PAMOM, Via degli Scipioni 265, 00192 Rome, Italy. Ed. Guglielmo Boselli.
    Description: Features articles on justice, solidarity and other topics in the humanities.

282   DK   ISSN 0109-0518
NYT FRA D U K. 1978. bi-m. free. Danmarks Unge Katolikker, Bredgade 67, 2 Th., 1260 Copenhagen K, Denmark. Ed.Bd. bk.rev.; illus.; circ. 800.

O E C T A REPORTER. (Ontario English Catholic Teachers Association) see *EDUCATION*

282   UK   ISSN 0144-9117
O R C NOTES. 1979. every 6 wks. free. Old Roman Catholic Church, Our Lady's Priory, 10 Barnmead Rd., Beckenham, Kent BR3 1JE, England. Ed. Archbishop-Primate F.G. Linale. bk.rev.; circ. 2,000.

266   US
OBLATE WORLD AND VOICE OF HOPE;* southern province edition. 1915. 5/yr. membership. Society of Oblate Fathers for Missions Among the Poor, Inc., Box 680, Tewksbury, MA 01876. (Subscr. to: Box 96, San Antonio, TX 78291) Ed. Thomas J. Reddy. illus.; circ. 154,400.
    Formerly: O M I Mission Magazine.
    Description: Discusses mission work among the needy.

282   US   ISSN 0029-7739
OBSERVER (ROCKFORD). 1935. s-m. $12. Catholic Diocese of Rockford, 921 W. State St., Rockford, IL 61102. TEL 815-963-3471. Ed. Owen Phelps, Jr. adv.; bk.rev.; film rev.; circ. 35,000. (newspaper; also avail. in microform) **Indexed:** High.Educ.Curr.Aware.Bull.

282   MW   ISSN 0300-4651
ODINI/WELCOME. (Text in Chichewa, English) 1950. fortn. K.13.80 (foreign K.19.80)(typically set in Jan.). (Diocese of Lilongwe) Likuni Press and Publishing House, Box 133, Lilongwe, Malawi. TEL 721-388. FAX 2721-141. Ed. P.I. Akomenti. adv.; bk.rev.; illus.; circ. 12,000. (tabloid format; also avail. in newspaper)
    Formerly (until 1984): African.

270 239   AU
OESTERREICHISCHE AKADEMIE DER WISSENSCHAFTEN. KOMMISSION ZUR HERAUSGABE DES CORPUS DER LATEINISCHEN KIRCHENVAETER. VEROEFFENTLICHUNGEN. irreg. Verlag der Oesterreichischen Akademie der Wissenschaften, Dr. Ignaz-Seipel-Platz 2, A-1010 Vienna, Austria. FAX 0222-5139541.

282   US   ISSN 0078-3854
OFFICIAL CATHOLIC DIRECTORY. 1817. a. (plus supplement). $173 to individuals; libraries $153; clergy $113. National Register Publishing Co., A Reed Reference Publishing Company, Division of Reed Publishing (USA) Inc., 121 Chanlon Rd., New Providence, NJ 07974. TEL 800-521-8110. FAX 908-665-6688. TELEX 138 755. (Subscr. to: R.R. Bowker, Order Dept., Box 31, New Providence, NJ 07974)
    Description: Lists 60,000 leaders - clergy and laity - in every Catholic institution in the USA, its possessions, and the governing body of Rome.

282   US
OFFICIAL WISCONSIN PASTORAL HANDBOOK. 1962. a. $24. Milwaukee Catholic Press Apostolate, 3501 S. Lake Dr., Box 07913, Milwaukee, WI 53207-7913. TEL 414-769-3472. Ed. William Hanel. adv.; circ. 2,300 (controlled).
    Description: Directory for all five Catholic dioceses in Wisconsin.

282   SR
OMHOOG. w. Gravenstraat 21, P.O. Box 1802, Paramaribo, Surinam. TEL 72521. Ed. S. Mulder.

282   UK   ISSN 0030-252X
BX1781
ONE IN CHRIST; a Roman Catholic ecumenical review. 1936. q. £22($42) Vita et Pax-Foundation for Unity, Regina Pacis, Turvey Abbey, Turvey, Beds. MK43 8DE, England. Ed. Paschal A. Hardiment. adv.; bk.rev.; bibl.; index; circ. 1,000. (also avail. in microform from UMI; reprint service avail. from UMI) **Indexed:** Br.Hum.Ind., Cath.Ind., CERDIC, New Test.Abstr., Old Test.Abstr., Rel.Ind.One.
    —BLDSC shelfmark: 6260.230000.
    Incorporates: Ecumenical Notes.
    Description: Offers documentation and comment on current ecumenical initiatives, with items on the theology, history and spirituality of ecumenism.

282   US   ISSN 1059-3144
▼**OPUS DEI AWARENESS NETWORK;** providing support and education to those impacted by Opus Dei. Short title: O D A N. 1991. m. $25. Opus Dei Awareness Network, Box 4333, Pittsfield, MA 01202. TEL 413-499-7168. Ed. Dianne Dinicola. circ. controlled.

282   IT   ISSN 0030-4174
ORA ET LABORA; quaderni di interesse monastico. 1947. q. L.23000 (effective 1991-92). Monastero S. Benedetto, Via Bellotti 10, 20129 Milan, Italy. TEL 02-799495. Ed.Bd. bk.rev.; bibl.; circ. 600. **Indexed:** CERDIC.

RELIGIONS AND THEOLOGY — ROMAN CATHOLIC

282   CN   ISSN 0030-4344
ORATOIRE. (Editions in English and French) 1912. bi-m. Can.$6. Oratoire Saint-Joseph du Mont-Royal, 3800 Chemin Reine-Marie, Montreal, Que. H3V 1H6, Canada. TEL 514-733-8211. FAX 514-733-9735. illus.; circ. 80,000.

282   CN
THE ORATORY. 1927. bi-m. Can.$6($6) St. Joseph's Oratory, 3800 Queen Mary Rd., Montreal, Que. H3V 1H6, Canada. TEL 514-733-8211. FAX 514-733-9735. Ed. Therese Baron. circ. 9,500.

266   CN   ISSN 0472-0490
ORIENT. 1953. bi-m. Can.$2. Missions des Peres de Sainte-Croix, 4901 rue Piedmont, Montreal, Que. H3V 1E3, Canada. FAX 514-731-7820. Ed. Marcel Descheneaux. illus.; circ. 13,000.

282   ES
ORIENTACION. 1953. w. 1a Calle Poniente 3412, San Salvador, El Salvador. TEL 24-5166. FAX 26-4979. Dir. Fr. Jesus Delgado. circ. 8,000.

ORIENTALIA CHRISTIANA ANALECTA. see *ORIENTAL STUDIES*

282.73   US
BX801
ORIGINS, C N S DOCUMENTARY SERVICE. 1971. 48/yr. $97. Catholic News Service, 3211 4th St., N.E., Washington, DC 20017. TEL 202-541-3290. FAX 202-541-3255. Ed. David Gibson. circ. 9,500. **Indexed:** Canon Law Abstr., Cath.Ind., CERDIC. **Key Title:** Origins (Washington).
•Also available online. Vendor(s): NewsNet.
Formerly: Origins, N C Documentary Service (ISSN 0093-609X)

282   VC
OSSERVATORE ROMANO. (Weekly editions in English, French, German, Italian, Portuguese, Spanish; monthly edition in Polish) 1861. d. Via del Pellegrino, 00120 Vatican City (Rome), State of the Vatican City. TEL 06-6983461. FAX 06-6983675. Ed. Sergio Trasatti.

249   CN   ISSN 0030-6843
OUR FAMILY; Canada's Catholic family monthly magazine. 1949. m. Can.$15.98($21.98) Oblates of St. Mary's Province of Canada, Box 249, Battleford, Sask. S0M 0E0, Canada. FAX 306-937-7644. Ed. Rev. Nestor Gregoire. adv.; illus.; circ. 12,000.

282   US   ISSN 0030-6886
BT595
OUR LADY'S DIGEST. 1946. 4/yr. $4 (foreign $6). LaSalette Publications, 10-330 336th Ave., Box 1022, Twin Lakes, WI 53181. Ed. Rev. Stanley Matuszewski. bk.rev.; circ. 50,000. (also avail. in microfilm from UMI) **Indexed:** CERDIC.

200   US   ISSN 0030-6924
OUR NORTHLAND DIOCESE. 1946. 22/yr. $8.70. Northland Diocese Association, Box 610, Crookston, MN 56716-0610. TEL 218-281-4050. Ed. Carol J. Evenson. adv.; bk.rev.; circ. 13,500.

282   US   ISSN 0030-6967
OUR SUNDAY VISITOR. 1912. w. $30 (foreign $40). Our Sunday Visitor, Inc., 200 Noll Plaza, Huntington, IN 46750. TEL 219-356-8400. FAX 219-356-8472. Ed. Greg Erlandson. adv.; bk.rev.; film rev.; play rev.; illus.; circ. 208,800. **Indexed:** Cath.Ind.
Description: Catholic newsmagazine.

282   US   ISSN 0030-7564
OVERVIEW (CHICAGO); a continuing survey of issues affecting Catholics. 1968. m. (11/yr.) $15.95. Thomas More Association, 205 W. Monroe, 6th Fl., Chicago, IL 60606. TEL 312-609-8880. Ed. Sara Miller. circ. 4,000.
Description: Issues pertaining to the Catholic faith.

282   UK   ISSN 0266-6014
P A X; newsletter of the Benedictines of Prinknash. 1904. q. £2.50. Prinknash Abbey, Cranham, Gloucester GL4 8EX, England. FAX 0452-812529. bk.rev.; circ. 300. (looseleaf format; back issues avail.)

266   US
P I M E WORLD. 1954. m. (except Jul. & Aug.). $3. Pontifical Institute for Foreign Missionaries (PIME), 35750 Moravian Dr., Fraser, MI 48026. FAX 313-791-8204. Ed. Rev. John J. Majka. circ. 25,000. (also avail. in microfilm from UMI; reprint service avail. from UMI) **Indexed:** CERDIC.
Formerly (until 1991): Catholic Life (ISSN 0008-8218)

266   US   ISSN 0030-9222
PADRES' TRAIL; the mission newsletter for the Southwest Franciscans. 1938. q. free to qualified personnel. (Franciscan Friars, Our Lady of Guadalupe Province) Franciscan Mission Center, Box 645, St. Michaels, AZ 86511. TEL 602-871-4171. FAX 602-871-5704. illus.; circ. 18,000. (also avail. in microfilm from MCA)
Description: Focuses on the orders mission work.

PAEPSTE UND PAPSTTUM. see *HISTORY — History Of Europe*

282   US   ISSN 0896-1727
LA PALABRA ENTRE NOSOTROS. (Text in Spanish) 1984. bi-m. $12 in U.S.; Puerto Rico $14; elsewhere $20. Word Among Us Press, Inc., Box 6003, Gaithersburg, MD 20884-6003. TEL 301-990-2060. FAX 301-990-2087. bk.rev.; circ. 25,000. (back issues avail.)

200   CL
PANORAMA DE LA TEOLOGIA LATINOAMERICANA. 1974. a. $8. (Universidad Catolica de Chile, Seminario Latinoamericano de Documentacon) Ediciones Sioweme, Apartado 332, 37080 Salamanca, Spain. circ. 3,000.

282 248.83   FR   ISSN 0031-1561
PARABOLES. 1949. 4/yr. 60 F. (foreign 70 F.) Communautes Chretiennes Universitaires, 5 rue de l'Abbaye, 75006 Paris, France. TEL 43-25-41-71. Ed. Jean-Robert Armogathe. bk.rev.; circ. 2,000.

280   US   ISSN 0279-7828
PARISH COMMUNICATION. 1981. q. $23. (Growth Associates) Fred B. Estabrook Company, Inc., Rte.1, Box 142, New Hampton, NH 03266-9713. TEL 603-744-6316. FAX 603-744-6318. Ed. Mary Streck. abstr.; stat.; circ. 1,100. (looseleaf format)
Description: Seasonal graphics, quotes from saints and modern leaders, weekly essays, puzzles, calendars, and sketches to be used in parish bulletins and newsletters.

PARISH COORDINATORS - DIRECTORS OF RELIGIOUS EDUCATION. see *EDUCATION*

282   US
PARISH FAMILY DIGEST. bi-m. 200 Noll Plaza, Huntington, IN 46750. TEL 219-356-8400. Ed. Corine B. Erlandson.
Description: General interest articles covering Catholic family and parish life.

266   US
PARISH VISITOR. 1924. q. $2. Parish Visitors of Mary Immaculate, Box 658, Monroe, NY 10950. TEL 914-783-2251. Ed. Sr. Mary Josita Worlock. circ. 4,300.
Description: Articles about the life and work of the parish visitors. Includes articles of a general religious nature.

220   IT   ISSN 0031-2398
PAROLE DI VITA. 1956. bi-m. L.21000. (Centro Catechistico Salesiano) Editrice Elle Di Ci, Corso Francia 214, 10096 Leumann (Turin), Italy. TEL 011 95-91-091. Eds. Carlo Ghidelli, Francesco Mosetto. bk.rev.; index; circ. 3,500.
—BLDSC shelfmark: 6406.943400.

250 282   IT   ISSN 0031-2428
PARROCCHIA. 1947. m. L.15000. Opera Madonna del Divino Amore, Via Ardeatina, Km 12, 00134 Rome, Italy. Dir. Pasquale Silla. bibl.; illus.; stat.; index. cum.index; circ. 8,000.

282   PE
PASTORAL ANDINA. 1974. bi-m. $20 (foreign $30). Instituto de Pastoral Andina, Apdo. 1018, Cusco, Peru. TEL 224137. FAX 51-84-225205. circ. 2,000.
Description: Current news on the Catholic Church and pastoral activities in the southern Andes of Peru.

282   GW
PASTORALBLATT. 1948. m. DM.59.38. J.P. Bachem Verlag GmbH, Postfach 108002, Ursulaplatz 1, 5000 Cologne 1, Germany. TEL 0221-16190.

282   CE
PATHUKAVALAN. (Text in Tamil) 1876. w. St. Joseph's Catholic Press, P.O. Box 2, Jaffna, Sri Lanka. TEL 21-22300. Ed. Rev. Fr E. J. Arumainayagam. circ. 7,000.

PATHWAYS (GARDEN GROVE). see *RELIGIONS AND THEOLOGY — Protestant*

282 299   BE
PATROLOGIA SYRIACA ET ORIENTALIS. 1983. irreg. N.V. Brepols I.G.P., Rue Baron Frans du Four 8, B-2300 Turnhout, Belgium.

282   US   ISSN 0897-9545
PAX CHRISTI U S A. 1975. 4/yr. membership. Pax Christi U S A, National Catholic Peace Movement, c/o Anne McCarthy, O.S.B., 348 E. 10th St., Erie, PA 16503. TEL 814-453-4955. bk.rev.; circ. 11,250.
Description: Covers the world of Christianity and peace.

200   PO
PAZ E ALEGRIA. 1907. m. Esc.250($3) Familia Franciscana Portuguesa, R. Serpa Pinto, 7, P 1200 Lisbon, Portugal. bk.rev.; circ. 3,000.
Supersedes: Alma (ISSN 0002-6239)

282   FR   ISSN 0031-4781
BX802
PENSEE CATHOLIQUE; cahiers de synthese. 1946. bi-m. 500 F. B.P. 39, 92370 Chaville, France. Ed. Yves Daoudal. bk.rev. **Indexed:** CERDIC.
—BLDSC shelfmark: 6422.040000.

282   IO
PERABA. (Text in Indonesian, Javanese) w. Bintaran Kidul 5, Yogyakarta, Indonesia. Ed. W. Kartosoeharsono.

262.9   VC   ISSN 0031-529X
PERIODICA DE RE MORALI CANONICA LITURGICA. (Text in Latin) 1905. q. L.70000($65) (Pontificio Istituto Biblico) Gregorian University Press, Piazza della Pilotta, 35, 00187 Rome, Italy. Ed. Francisco J. Urrutia. index; circ. 1,500. **Indexed:** Canon Law Abstr.
Description: Offers research, articles and timely essays on the most recent church legislation regarding collegiality, marriage, consecrated life, secularisation, etc.

PERLIN ET PINPIN. see *CHILDREN AND YOUTH — About*

282 266   FR
PEUPLES DU MONDE. 1967. 10/yr. 210 F. S O C E N D I, 8 rue Francois Villon, 75015 Paris, France. adv.; bk.rev.; illus. **Indexed:** CERDIC.

282   CN
PHILIPPINES. (Text in English and French) 1963. q. Can.$1. Centre cor Jesu (Philippines), 328, Rue Chapel, Ottawa, Ont. K1N 7Z3, Canada. Ed. Gerard Lefebvre. circ. 1,500.

255   IT
PICENUM SERAPHICUM. irreg. L.3500. Biblioteca Francescana, Conto Corrente Postale 15-27009, Falconara M. 60015, Italy.

282   US   ISSN 0744-933X
PILOT. 1829. w. $15. (Roman Catholic Archdiocese of Boston) Pilot Publishing Co., 49 Franklin St., Boston, MA 02110. TEL 617-482-4316. FAX 617-482-5647. Ed. Rev. Peter V. Conley. adv.; bk.rev.; film rev.; play rev.; circ. 38,000. (also avail. in microform)

282   US   ISSN 0032-0323
PITTSBURGH CATHOLIC. 1844. w. $11. (Catholic Diocese of Pittsburgh) Pittsburgh Catholic Publishing Associates, 100 Wood St., No. 500, Pittsburgh, PA 15222-1906. FAX 412-471-4228. Ed. William Fodiak. adv.; bk.rev.; film rev.; illus.; play rev.; circ. 121,500. (newspaper; also avail. in microform)

282   UK
PLYMOUTH DIOCESAN YEAR BOOK. a. Universe Publishing Co., Ltd., 18 Crosby Rd. N., Waterloo, Liverpool L22 4OF, England. TEL 051 920 6171. Ed. Rev. Christopher Smith. circ. 5,000.

RELIGIONS AND THEOLOGY — ROMAN CATHOLIC

266   FR   ISSN 0032-2504
POLE ET TROPIQUES; revue apostolique des missionnaires oblats. 1920. bi-m. 75 F. Missionnaires Oblats de Marie Immaculee, 145 Montee de Choulans, 69322 Lyon Cedex 05, France. Ed. Roger Daille. abstr.; illus.; mkt.; stat.; index; circ. 21,000.

270   VC
PONTIFICIA UNIVERSITA GREGORIANA. DOCUMENTA MISSIONALIA. (Text in various languages) 1964. irreg. price varies. (Pontificio Istituto Biblico) Gregorian University Press, Piazza della Pilotta, 35, 00187 Rome, Italy. Ed. Mariasusai Dhavamony.

270   VC   ISSN 0080-3979
PONTIFICIA UNIVERSITA GREGORIANA. MISCELLANEA HISTORIAE PONTIFICIAE. (Multi-language text) 1939. irreg., latest vol.57. price varies. (Pontificio Istituto Biblico) Gregorian University Press, Piazza della Pilotta, 35, 00187 Rome, Italy. Ed. Vincenzo Monachino.

266   VC   ISSN 0080-3987
PONTIFICIA UNIVERSITA GREGORIANA. STUDIA MISSIONALIA. (Multi-language text) 1943. a. price varies. (Pontificio Istituto Biblico) Gregorian University Press, Piazza della Pilotta, 35, 00187 Rome, Italy. TEL 06-678-1567. Ed. Mariasusai Dhavamony. index; circ. 600. (back issues avail.) **Indexed:** Cath.Ind., Rel.Ind.One.
Description: Contains subjects such as: Islam, Buddhism, Hinduism, religious ethnology, revelation, worship and ritual, prayers, meditation, mystique, moral and religion, etc., in Christianity and other religions.

282 262   US   ISSN 0032-4353
BX850
POPE SPEAKS; the Church documents bi-monthly. 1954. bi-m. $18 (foreign $21). Our Sunday Visitor, Inc., 200 Noll Plaza, Huntington, IN 46750. TEL 219-356-8400. FAX 219-356-8472. Ed. Rev. Albert J. Nevins. adv.; bk.rev.; bibl.; illus.; index; circ. 13,179. (also avail. in microform from UMI; reprint service avail. from UMI) **Indexed:** Cath.Ind., CERDIC. —BLDSC shelfmark: 6550.050000.
Description: Publishes documents relating to the Pope's activities.

282   UK   ISSN 0143-0149
POPE TEACHES; a monthly digest of the pastoral teaching of Pope John Paul II. 1978. m. £12($20) Incorporated Catholic Truth Society, 38-40 Eccleston Square, London SW1V 1PD, England. TEL 071-834 4392. Ed. Sally Purcell.

282   CN   ISSN 0032-664X
PRAIRIE MESSENGER. 1923. 26/yr. Can.$21.50($55) Order of St. Benedict, Inc., Muenster, Sask. SOK 2YO, Canada. TEL 306-682-5215. FAX 306-682-2284. Ed. Art Babych. adv.; bk.rev.; film rev.; illus.; circ. 10,000. (tabloid format)

282   GW   ISSN 0172-7478
PRAXIS IN DER GEMEINDE; materialien und erfahrungen. 1979. q. DM.24 (student DM.20). Matthias Gruenewald Verlag GmbH, Max-Hufschmidt-Str. 4a, 6500 Mainz-Weisenau, Germany. TEL 06131-839055. Ed. Jakob Laubach. adv.; bk.rev.; cum.index; circ. 2,000. (back issues avail.)

282 284   US   ISSN 0274-600X
PRAYERS FOR WORSHIP. 1978. q. $21. Liturgical Publications Inc., 2875 South James Dr., New Berlin, WI 53151. TEL 414-785-1188. FAX 414-785-9567. Ed. Rev. L. Koopman. (looseleaf format)

282   US
PRAYING. 1983. bi-m. $15. National Catholic Reporter Publishing Company, Inc., 115 E. Armour Blvd., Box 419281, Kansas City, MO 64141. TEL 800-444-8910. FAX 816-931-5082. Ed. Art Winter. adv.; bk.rev.; illus.; circ. 17,000.
Description: Spiritual insight aimed at helping people find God in their daily lives.

282   GW   ISSN 0032-7212
DER PREDIGER UND KATECHET. 1850. 6/yr. DM.54. Erich Wewel Verlag, Anzingerstr. 1, 8000 Munich 80, Germany. adv.; index; circ. 15,000.

282 250   IT   ISSN 0032-7727
PRESENZA PASTORALE. 1931. 10/yr. L.35000. (Collegio Assistenti) Azione Cattolica Italiana, Via della Conciliazione 1, 00193 Rome, Italy. FAX 06-6620207. Ed. Fiorino Tagliaferri. bk.rev.; bibl. **Indexed:** CERDIC.
Formerly: Assistente Ecclesiastico.

282   US   ISSN 0032-8200
BX803
PRIEST. 1945. m. (12/yr.). $30 (foreign $35). Our Sunday Visitor, Inc., 200 Noll Plaza, Huntington, IN 46750. TEL 219-356-8400. FAX 219-356-8472. Ed. Owen Campion. adv.; bk.rev.; tr.lit.; circ. 12,000. (also avail. in microform from UMI; reprint service avail. from UMI) **Indexed:** Cath.Ind., CERDIC.
Description: Homily helps, commentary, and parish product showcase for Roman Catholic priests and deacons.

282   GW   ISSN 0172-0929
PRIESTERJAHRHEFT. 1926. a. free. Bonifatiuswerk der Deutschen Katholiken e.V., Kamp 22, 4790 Paderborn, Germany. TEL 05251-29960. FAX 05251-299688. Ed. Georg Walf. circ. 20,000 (controlled).
Description: Sermon material for Catholic priests in Germany for the so-called "Diaspora-Sonntag".

250   UK
PRIESTS AND PEOPLE. 1930. m. £20. (Catholic Church) Tablet Publishing Co. Ltd., 1 King Cloisters, Clifton Walk, London W6 0QZ, England. TEL 081-748-8484. FAX 081-748-1550. Ed. David Sanders. adv.; bk.rev.; index; circ. 2,200. (also avail. in microform from UMI; reprint service avail. from UMI) **Indexed:** Canon Law Abstr., Cath.Ind., CERDIC, New Test.Abstr., Old Test.Abstr., Rel.& Theol.Abstr.
Formerly: Clergy Review (ISSN 0009-8736)

282   CN   ISSN 0383-8277
PRIONS EN EGLISE - EDITION DOMINICALE. English edition: Living with Christ - Sunday Edition. w., plus 2 special issues. Can.$5.74($7.25) Novalis, 6255 Hutchison St., Montreal, Que. H2V 4C7, Canada. TEL 514-278-3025. FAX 514-278-3030. Ed. Michel Maille.

282   US
PRO ECCLESIA MAGAZINE. 1965. q. $20. Pro Ecclesia Foundation, 509 Madison Ave., New York, NY 10022. Ed. Timothy A. Mitchell. illus.
Formerly: Pro Ecclesia; Incorporates: Common Good & Talks of Pope John Paul II. Which was formerly: Talks of Pope Paul VI.
Description: Examines attacks against the Catholic church and answers them with Catholic teachings.

282   US
PROBE (CHICAGO); feminist religious women. 1971. bi-m. $20. National Assembly of Religious Women (N.A.R.W.), 529 S. Wabash Ave., Ste. 404, Chicago, IL 60605-1608. TEL 312-663-1980. Ed. Judy Vaughan. bk.rev.; circ. 2,500. **Indexed:** CERDIC, South.Bap.Per.Ind.
Description: Includes includes theological reflection, social analysis and action suggestions.

282   BE
PROBLEMES D'HISTOIRE DES RELIGIONS. (Text in French) 1971-1989; N.S. 1990. a. price varies. (Universite Libre de Bruxelles, Institut d'Histoire des Religions et de la Laicite) Editions de l'Universite de Bruxelles, Avenue P. Heger, 26 - C.P. 163, B-1050 Brussels, Belgium. Ed. Jacques Marx. **Indexed:** CERDIC.
Formerly (until 1990): Problemes d'Histoire du CHristianisme.

282   CN   ISSN 0033-054X
PROGRESS/POSTUP. (Editions in English, Ukrainian) 1959. w. Can.$30($35) (Ukrainian Catholic Archdiocese of Winnipeg) Progress Printing & Publishing Co. Ltd., 418 Aberdeen Ave., Winnipeg, Man. R2W 1V7, Canada. TEL 204-582-1940. Ed. Rev. S. Izyk. adv.; bk.rev.; film rev.; play rev.; illus.; circ. 4,500.

282   US   ISSN 0032-9471
QUOTE...UNQUOTE; a public information service. 1980. m. free. (Catholic Traditionalist Movement, Inc.) C T M Publications, Inc., 210 Maple Ave., Box 781, Westbury, NY 11590. TEL 516-333-6470. Ed. Gommar A. De Pauw. (looseleaf format; back issues avail.)
Description: Comments from notable persons and publications about papal and Vatican affairs and activities within the context of traditional Catholicism.

282   AT   ISSN 1033-1050
R.C.I.A. RESOURCE. 1986. 6/yr. Aus.$20. (Melbourne Catechumenate Office) Resourceful Publishing Company, 406 Albert St., E. Melbourne, Vic. 3002, Australia. TEL 663-1403. FAX 639-1905. Ed. J. Shirvington. circ. 650.
Description: Resources for catechesis from the lectionary, commentary for local implementation of the Rite of Christian Initiation of Adults.

266 301   CN   ISSN 0035-3795
R N D. (Text in French) 1903. m. Can.$10. (Revue Notre-Dame) Les Missionnaires du Sacre-Coeur, C.P. 400, Sillery, Quebec, Que. G1T 2R7, Canada. TEL 418-681-3581. FAX 418-681-1139. Ed. Yvon Labbe. adv.; illus.; circ. 150,000. **Indexed:** Pt.de Rep. (1979-).

282   II   ISSN 0048-668X
RALLY. (Text in English) vol.50, 1973. m. $15. All India Catholic University Federation, 125 Sterling Rd., Madras 600 034, India. Ed. Michael Pinto. bk.rev.; circ. 1,500.

282   UK   ISSN 0033-9245
RANSOMER. 1893. 3/yr. $12. Guild of Our Lady of Ransom, 31 Southdown Rd., Wimbledon, London SW20 8QJ, England. TEL 081-947-2598. FAX 081-944-6208. Ed. Msgr. Anthony George Stark. adv.; bk.rev.; circ. 2,000 (controlled).

282 267   FR   ISSN 0034-0197
RAYONS; revue des jeunesses mariales. 1900. 10/yr. 30 F. Marian Association for Young Girls, 67 rue de Sevres, 75006 Paris, France. bibl.

282   IE   ISSN 0034-0960
REALITY. 1936. m. (11/yr.). £9.25($5) Redemptorist Publications, 75 Orwell Rd., Rathgar, Dublin 6, Ireland. TEL (01)961488. Ed. Kevin H. Donlon. bk.rev.; illus.; circ. 30,000. **Indexed:** CERDIC.

282   AT
THE RECORD. 1874. w. Aus.$60. P.O. Box 50, Northbridge, W.A. 6865, Australia. TEL 09-227-7080. FAX 09-227-7087. Ed. Patrick Cunningham. circ. 8,000. (tabloid format)

RECUSANT HISTORY. see *HISTORY — History Of Europe*

282   IT
IL REGNO. (In 2 sections: Attualita and Documenti) 1956. s-m. L.46000 (foreign L.73000). Centro Editoriale Dehoniano, Via Nosadella 6, 40125 Bologna, Italy. TEL 051-306811. FAX 051-341706. Ed. P. Alfio Filippi. circ. 13,500. **Indexed:** CERDIC.

282   IT   ISSN 0034-3498
REGNO - ATTUALITA. 1956. m. L.26000 (foreign L.39000). Centro Editoriale Dehoniano, Via Nosadella 6, 40123 Bologna, Italy. TEL 051 306811. FAX 051-341706. adv.; bk.rev.; bibl.; index. cum.index; circ. 12,000.
Description: Covers world events in church life. Features today's problem and discussions about recent events as well as original interviews.

282   GW   ISSN 0341-3322
REGNUM; internationale Vierteljahresschrift der Schoenstattbewegung. 1965. q. DM.22.40. Patris Verlag, Hoehrerstr. 109, 5414 Vallendar, Germany. TEL 0261-60409. bk.rev.; circ. 1,700. (back issues avail.)

266   US   ISSN 0048-7155
REIGN OF THE SACRED HEART. 1934. q. Priests of the Sacred Heart, 6889 S. Lovers Ln., Hales Corners, WI 53130. TEL 414-425-3383. Ed. Father Brian. illus.; circ. 430,000.

RELATIONS. see *SOCIAL SERVICES AND WELFARE*

RELIGIONS AND THEOLOGY — ROMAN CATHOLIC

282 370   IT
RELIGIONE E SCUOLA; mensile per l'animazione culturale e la ricerca religiosa. bi-m. L.40000 (foreign L.52000). Editrice Queriniana, Via Piamarta 6, 25187 Brescia, Italy. Ed. Roberto Laurita.

282   GW   ISSN 0173-0339
RELIGIONSPAEDAGOGISCHE BEITRAEGE. Short title: R p B. 1978. s-a. DM.27. Arbeitsgemeinschaft Katholischer Katechetikdozenten, c/o Prof. H.A. Zwergel, Wegmannstr. 1D, 3500 Kassel, Germany. TEL 0561-886207. Ed.Bd. bk.rev.; index; circ. 400. (back issues avail.)
Description: Catholic publication concerned with the teaching of religion. Contains articles on the Church, Bible, Catholic doctrine, and social issues.

282   IE
RELIGIOUS LIFE REVIEW. 1961. 6/yr. £17.58($28.48) Dominican Publications, 42 Parnell Sq., Upper Dorset, Dublin 1, Ireland. TEL 01-721611. FAX 01-731760.

REMNANT OF ISRAEL. see *RELIGIONS AND THEOLOGY — Judaic*

280   GW   ISSN 0340-8280
RENOVATIO; Zeitschrift fuer das interdisziplinaere Gespraech. 1945. 4/yr. DM.20. J.P. Bachem Verlag GmbH, Ursulaplatz 1, 5000 Cologne 1, Germany. (Co-sponsor: Katholische Aerztearbeit Deutschlands) Ed. Helmut-Josef Patt. bk.rev.; circ. 6,500. **Indexed**: CERDIC, New Test.Abstr.
—BLDSC shelfmark: 7364.204300.
Formerly: Katholische Gedanke (ISSN 0022-9385)

200   US   ISSN 0034-639X
BX2400
REVIEW FOR RELIGIOUS. 1942. bi-m. $15. Missouri Province Educational Institute, 3601 Lindell Blvd., St. Louis, MO 63108. (Subscr. to: P.O. Box 6070, Duluth, MN 55806) Ed. David L. Fleming, S.J. bk.rev.; index; circ. 13,066. (also avail. in microform from UMI; reprint service avail. from UMI) **Indexed**: Bk.Rev.Ind. (1965-), Cath.Ind., CERDIC, Child.Bk.Rev.Ind. (1965-), New Test.Abstr.
—BLDSC shelfmark: 7794.194000.
Description: Deals specifically with Roman Catholic priests, brothers, sisters and their particular way of life.

282   CL   ISSN 0716-033X
REVISTA CATOLICA. 1843. 4/yr. $20. Seminario Pontificio Mayor de Santiago, Chile, Casilla 3-D, Santiago, Chile. TEL 2153119. adv.; bk.rev.; circ. 1,200.

282 267   AG   ISSN 0034-9070
REVISTA DEL HOGAR.* s-m. Arg.$1.20. Jovenes de la Accion Catolica, Belgrand 239, Capillaudel Senor, Buenos Aires, Argentina. Ed. Reynaldo Dassat. (processed)

282   PE
REVISTA TEOLOGICA LIMENSE. 1966. 3/yr. $20. Facultad de Teologia Pontificia y Civil de Lima, Calle Carlos Bondy 700, Apdo. 21-0135, Lima 21, Peru. bk.rev.; circ. 700.

282   ZR
REVUE AFRICAINE DE THEOLOGIE. (Text in English, French; summaries in French) 1977. s-a. $70. Faculte de Theologie Catholique de Kinshasa, B.P. 1534, Kinshasa-Limetew, Zaire. (back issues avail.) **Indexed**: CERDIC, New Test.Abstr.

200   BE   ISSN 0035-0893
BX3001
REVUE BENEDICTINE; de critique, d'histoire et de litterature religieuses. (Text in English, French, German, Italian) 2/yr. 1950 Fr. Abbaye de Maredsous, B-5537 Denee, Belgium. TEL 082-69-91-55. FAX 082-69-96-25. Dir. Pierre Patrick Verbraken. bk.rev.; abstr.; index; circ. 1,000. (back issues avail.) **Indexed**: Bull.Signal., M.L.A., New Test.Abstr., Old Test.Abstr.
Description: Studies occidental ecclesiastical history, with emphasis on biblical, patristic and monastic texts.

209   BE   ISSN 0035-2381
BX940
REVUE D'HISTOIRE ECCLESIASTIQUE. 1900. q. 3300 Fr.($76) Universite Catholique de Louvain, Bureau de la Revue d'Histoire Ecclesiastique, Bibliotheque, College Erasme, B-1348 Louvain-la-Neuve, Belgium. Ed. Claude Soetens. adv.; bk.rev.; bibl.; charts; index. cum.index every 15-20 yrs.; circ. 250. **Indexed**: Arts & Hum.Cit.Ind., Hist.Abstr., M.L.A., New Test.Abstr., Rel.& Theol.Abstr. (1967-), Rel.Ind.One, Rel.Per.

209   FR   ISSN 0035-2217
BX802
REVUE DES SCIENCES RELIGIEUSES. 1921. q. 59 F. Universite de Strasbourg II, Faculte de Theologie Catholique, 22 rue Rene Descartes, 67084 Strasbourg, France. Ed. Dr. Jacques E. Minard. bk.rev.; index; circ. 700. (also avail. in microform from SWZ; reprint service avail. from SWZ) **Indexed**: CERDIC, New Test.Abstr., Old Test.Abstr., Rel.Ind.One, Rel.Per.
—BLDSC shelfmark: 7948.500000.

282   FR
REVUE DU ROSAIRE. 1927. 10/yr. 100 F. (foreign 135 F.). Editions du Cerf, 29 bd. Latour Maubourg, 75340 Paris Cedex 07, France. TEL 44-18-12-12. FAX 45-56-04-27. (Subscr. to: Service Abonnements, 3 chemin des Prunais, 94350 Villiers-sur-Marne, France)

248.894   BE   ISSN 0035-3620
BX2613
REVUE MABILLON. (Text in French, Latin) 1905. q. 1600 BEF. N.V. Brepols I.G.P., Steenweg op Tielen 68, 2300 Turnhout, Belgium. TEL 014-41-54-63. FAX 014-42-89-19. TELEX 34 182. Ed. Jean Becquet. adv.; bibl.; charts; illus.; index; circ. 200. (also avail. in microform from JAI) **Indexed**: Hist.Abstr.
—BLDSC shelfmark: 7926.770000.

200   BE   ISSN 0080-2654
REVUE THEOLOGIQUE DE LOUVAIN. 1970. 4/yr. 1350 Fr. Universite Catholique de Louvain, Faculte de Theologie et de Droit Canonique, Grand-Place 45, B-1348 Louvain-la-Neuve, Belgium. Ed. J. Ponthot. bk.rev.; circ. 1,300. **Indexed**: Arts & Hum.Cit.Ind., Cath.Ind., New Test.Abstr.
—BLDSC shelfmark: 7956.080000.

282   BE
REVUE THEOLOGIQUE DE LOUVAIN. CAHIERS. (Text in French) 1980. irreg., vol.9, 1987. (Universite Catholique de Louvain, Facultes de Theologie et de Droit Canonique) Editions Peeters s.p.r.l., Bondgenotenlaan 153, B-3000 Leuven, Belgium. TEL 016-235170. FAX 016-228500. TELEX 65981 PULB. **Indexed**: CERDIC, Old Test.Abstr.

282 100   IT   ISSN 0393-3849
RICERCHE STORICHE SALESIANE; rivista semestrale di storia religiosa e civile. 1982. s-a. L.20000 (foreign L.25000). (Istituto Storico Salesiano) Editrice Libreria Ateneo Salesiano, Via della Pisana, 1111, 00163 Rome, Italy. Ed. Pietro Braido. bk.rev.; circ. 500.
—BLDSC shelfmark: 7992.803000.
Description: Features study and research on the history of St. John Bosco and the Salesians. It also looks at religious history and civilization.

282   GW
RING DES WORTES; Seelsorgebrief fuer Hoergeschaedigte, Kranke und Senioren. 1958. bi-m. free. Erzbischoefliches Generalvikariat, Hauptabteilung Seelsorge, Marzellenstr. 31, 5000 Cologne 1, Germany. Ed. Karl-Heinz Stockhausen. circ. 10,500.
Description: Devotional material for hearing impaired and hospitalized people and seniors.

282   IT   ISSN 0042-7586
RIVISTA DEL CLERO ITALIANO. 1920. m. (11/yr.). L.52000($40) (effective 1992). (Universita Cattolica del Sacro Cuore) Vita e Pensiero, Largo Gemelli 1, 20123 Milan, Italy. TEL 02-8856310. FAX 02-8856260. TELEX 321033 UCATMI 1. Ed. Bruno Maggioni. adv.; bk.rev.; bibl.; index. **Indexed**: CERDIC.
—BLDSC shelfmark: 7983.400000.
Description: Looks at many different issues in theology and various religious cultures.

282   IT
RIVISTA DI ASCETICA E MISTICA. s-a. Via Cavour, 56, Florence, Italy. Ed. A. Spinillo.

282   IT
RIVISTA DI TEOLOGIA MORALE. 1969. L.37000 (foreign L.43000). Edizioni Dehoniano, Via Nosadella 6, 40123 Bologna, Italy. TEL 051-306811. FAX 051-341706. circ. 2,500.

282 248   IT   ISSN 0035-6638
RIVISTA DI VITA SPIRITUALE. 1947. bi-m. L.26000 (foreign L.35000). (Centro Interprovinciale O.C.D.) Edizioni O.C.D., Via Anagnina 662-B, 00040 Morena (Rome), Italy. TEL 06-7247482. FAX 06-7245387. Ed. R.P. Bruno Moriconi. bk.rev.; bibl.; index; circ. 2,000.
—BLDSC shelfmark: 7993.596000.

282   IT   ISSN 0035-6654
RIVISTA DIOCESANA DEL PATRIARCATO DI VENEZIA. 1918. m. L.40000. Curia Patriarcale di Venezia, San Marco 320A, 30124 Venice, Italy. TEL 041-5200333. FAX 041-5236945.

282   IT   ISSN 0035-6956
RIVISTA LITURGICA. 1914. bi-m. L.40000. (Centro Catechistico Salesiano) Editrice Elle Di Ci, Corso Francia 214, 10096 Leumann (Turin), Italy. TEL 011 95-91-091. Ed. Pelagio Visentin. bk.rev.; cum.index: 1914-1974; circ. 2,200. **Indexed**: CERDIC.
—BLDSC shelfmark: 7987.980000.

THE ROCK (EPPING). see *RELIGIONS AND THEOLOGY — Protestant*

262.9   PL   ISSN 0035-7723
BX806.P6
ROCZNIKI TEOLOGICZNO-KANONICZNE. (In six parts: 1. Holy Scripture; 2. Fundamental and Dogmatic Theology; 3. Moral Theology; 4. History of Church; 5. Canon Law; 6. Pastoral Theology) (Text in Polish; summaries in English, French, German, Italian and Latin) 1949. 6/yr. price varies. Katolicki Uniwersytet Lubelski, Towarzystwo Naukowe, Ul. Gliniana 21, 20-616 Lublin, Poland. Ed.Bd. bk.rev.; index; circ. 820. **Indexed**: CERDIC, New Test.Abstr., Old Test.Abstr.

282   US   ISSN 1046-5030
ROLA BOZA/GOD'S FIELD. (Text in English, Polish) 1923. bi-w. $8. (Polish National Catholic Church) Rola Boza Publishing Co., 529 E. Locust St., Scranton, PA 18505. TEL 717-343-6017. Ed. Rev. Bishop Anthony M. Rysz. circ. 7,200. (tabloid format)

282   US
ROMAN CATHOLIC STUDIES. irreg., latest no.5. $39.95 per no. Edwin Mellen Press, 240 Portage Rd., Box 450, Lewiston, NY 14092. TEL 716-754-8566. FAX 716-754-4335.

282   PO   ISSN 0035-8274
ROSARIO DE MARIA; publicacao mensal de espiritualidade rosario mariana. 1944. m. Esc.50($4) Dominican Convent Friars-Fatima, Secretariado Nacional do Rosario, Fatima, Portugal. Ed. L. Cerdeira. bk.rev.; illus.; index; circ. 7,000.

282   IT   ISSN 0035-8282
IL ROSARIO E LA NUOVA POMPEI. (Editions in English and Italian) 1884. bi-m. contribution. Pontificio Santuario di Pompei, Naples 80045, Italy. Ed. Fr. Salvatore Parrone. bk.rev.; circ. 300,000.

282   US   ISSN 0745-3299
ROZE MARYI. (Text in Polish) 1944. m. $6. Association of Marian Helpers, Stockbridge, MA 01263. TEL 413-298-3691. Ed. Andrew Maczynski. bk.rev.; circ. 9,500.

S A; a journal in the sociology of religion. (Sociological Analysis) see *SOCIOLOGY*

266   IE
S M A - THE AFRICAN MISSIONARY. (Text in English, Gaelic) 1914. 5/yr. I£3. S M A Fathers, Blackrock Rd., Cork, Ireland. TEL 021-292871. Ed. Fr. Peter McCawille. adv.; bk.rev.; circ. 40,000.
Formerly: African Missionary (ISSN 0044-6580)

RELIGIONS AND THEOLOGY — ROMAN CATHOLIC

282   IE
SACRED HEART MESSENGER. 1888. m. £4.80 (foreign £15). (Jesuit Fathers) Irish Messenger Publications, 37 Lower Leeson St., Dublin 2, Ireland. TEL 767491. FAX 611606. Ed. Rev. Father Patrick Carberry. charts; illus.; pat.; tr.mk.; circ. 200,000.
    Formerly: Irish Messenger of the Sacred Heart (ISSN 0021-1303)
    Description: Publication of the Apostleship of prayer- practical spirituality, family appeal, modern and balanced.

282   US
ST. ANSGAR'S BULLETIN. 1914. a. $5. St. Ansgar's Scandinavian Catholic League, 40 W. 13th St., New York, NY 10011. TEL 212-675-0400. Ed. John T. Dwight. illus.; stat.; circ. 1,400.

282   US   ISSN 0036-276X
ST. ANTHONY MESSENGER. 1893. m. $16. (Franciscan Friars of St. John the Baptist Province) St. Anthony Messenger Press, 1615 Republic St., Cincinnati, OH 45210. TEL 513-241-5615. Ed. Rev. Norman Perry. adv.; bk.rev.; film rev.; index; circ. 370,000. (also avail. in microform from UMI; reprint service avail. from UMI) **Indexed:** Cath.Ind., CERDIC.
    Description: News and features of interest to Catholic families.

200   US   ISSN 0080-5432
SAINT BONAVENTURE UNIVERSITY. FRANCISCAN INSTITUTE. PHILOSOPHY SERIES. 1944. irreg., no.16, 1972. price varies. Saint Bonaventure University, Franciscan Institute, St. Bonaventure, NY 14778. TEL 716-375-2105. Ed. Rev. George H. Marcil, O.F.M.

200   US   ISSN 0080-5440
SAINT BONAVENTURE UNIVERSITY. FRANCISCAN INSTITUTE. TEXT SERIES. 1951. irreg., no.16, 1972. price varies. Saint Bonaventure University, Franciscan Institute, St. Bonaventure, NY 14778. TEL 716-375-2105. Ed. Rev. George H. Marcil, O.F.M.

282   US   ISSN 0036-3022
ST. LOUIS REVIEW. 1941. w. $11. Catholic Archdiocese of St. Louis, 462 N. Taylor Ave., St. Louis, MO 63108. TEL 314-531-9700. FAX 314-531-2269. Ed. Rev. Edward J. Sudekum. adv.; bk.rev.; film rev.; illus.; circ. 100,000. (also avail. in microfilm)

SAINT PETER'S; the college magazine. see *COLLEGE AND ALUMNI*

200   AT   ISSN 0036-3219
SAINT VINCENT DE PAUL RECORD. 1935. q. Aus.$1. Saint Vincent de Paul Society, National Council of Australia, P.O. Box 740, Darlinghurst, N.S.W. 2010, Australia. TEL 02 683 2122. FAX 02-683-5358. Ed. John McFadden. bk.rev.; illus.; index; circ. 19,000.
    Description: Provides pictures and articles relating to society work of helping the needy in Australia or overseas.

200   FR   ISSN 0036-3243
SAINTE THERESE DE LISIEUX. ANNALES. 1925. m. 100 F. Direction du Pelerinage de Lisieux, 33 rue du Carmel, B.P. 95, 14102 Lisieux cedex, France. TEL 31-31-49-71. FAX 31-31-71-03. Ed. Pere Leon Baucher. bk.rev.; circ. 35,000.

284 282   IS
SALAM UAL KHEIR. (Text in Arabic) m. Franciscan Printing Press, P.O. Box 14064, Jerusalem 91140, Israel. TEL 02-286594.

282   IE   ISSN 0790-1216
SALESIAN BULLETIN. (Text in English) 1939. q. £5($10) Salesians of Don Bosco Media, Salesian House, St. Teresa's Rd., Dublin 12, Ireland. TEL 01-555605. FAX 01-558781. (Subscr. to: Salesian Missions, PO. Box 50, Pallaskenry, Co. Limerick, Ireland) Ed. Eddie Fitzgerald. bk.rev.; circ. 20,000. (back issues avail.)

200   VC   ISSN 0036-3502
BX800.A1
SALESIANUM. (Text in English, French, German, Italian, Latin, Spanish) 1939. q. L.50000 (foreign L.60000). Universita Pontificia Salesiana, Piazza Ateneo Salesiano 1, 00139 Rome, Italy. TEL 06-8812041. bk.rev.; circ. 800. **Indexed:** Canon Law Abstr., CERDIC, M.L.A., New Test.Abstr., Rel.& Theol.Abstr. (1979-).
    —BLDSC shelfmark: 8070.747000.
    Description: Features five sections that deal with theology, philosophy, canon law, commentaries, religious research and scientific events.

282 370   XV   ISSN 0353-0477
SALEZIJANSKI VESTNIK; glasilo salezijanske druzine. (Text in Slovenian) 1904. q. free. Salezijanski Inspektorat, Rakovniska ul. 6, 61108 Ljubljana, Slovenia. TEL 061 217-406. Ed. Tone Ciglar. circ. 7,500.
    Description: Information about the history of the Church, missions, mariology.

200 260   SP   ISSN 0036-3537
SALMANTICENSIS. 1954. 3/yr. 3600 ptas.($45) Universidad Pontificia, Departamento de Ediciones y Publicaciones, Apdo. de Correos 541, 37080 Salamanca, Spain. TEL 923-21-51-40. FAX 923-21-34-50. bk.rev.; bibl.; index; circ. 2,000 (controlled). (looseleaf format) **Indexed:** CERDIC, Hist.Abstr., Rel.Ind.One.
    —BLDSC shelfmark: 8070.950000.

282   US
SAN FRANCISCO CATHOLIC. 1859. m. $18. Archdiocese of San Francisco, Catholic Communications Center, 441 Church St., San Francisco, CA 94114. TEL 415-565-3630. Ed. Charlotte Pace. adv.; film rev.; circ. 35,000.
    Supersedes (in 1985): Monitor (ISSN 0026-9743)

200   IT
LA SAN VINCENZO IN ITALIA. 1856. bi-m. L.14000. Societa di San Vincenzo de Paoli, Consiglio Superiore Italiano, Via Pisacane 32, 20129 Milan, Italy. TEL 29526343. FAX 29526325. Ed. Antonio Strambi. bk.rev.; circ. 4,000.
    Formerly: Samaritano (ISSN 0036-3723)

282   IT   ISSN 0036-116X
SANTA CASA DI LORETO. MESSAGGIO. English edition: Shrine of the Holy House. Loreto. 1881 (Eng. ed. 1968). m. (Eng. ed. 3/yr.) L.3000($10) for Italian ed. Congregazione Universale della Santa Casa, 60025 Loreto (Ancora), Italy. TEL 071-970104. Ed. Fr. Joseph Santarelli. bk.rev.; illus.; circ. 36,000.

SANTO; rivista Antoniana di storia dottrina arte. see *HISTORY — History Of Europe*

282 255   IT   ISSN 0036-4606
SANTO DEI VOLI. 1946. bi-m. L.880($2) (Frati Minori Conventuali di Puglia, Provincia Religiosa) Santuario S. Giuseppe da Copertino, Via Piave 8, 73043 Copertino, Italy. TEL (0832) 947.011. Ed. Goffredo Giovanni Iasi. adv.; bk.rev.; film rev.; cum.index; circ. 4,500. (cards)

266   IT   ISSN 0036-4622
SANTUARIO DELLA MADONNA DELLE ROCCHE. 1920. bi-m. L.2000. Passionisti, 15074 Molare, Alessandria, Italy. bibl.; charts; illus.; stat.; index; circ. 1,000. (tabloid format)

SCHOOL EN GODSDIENST; catechetical periodical for elementary school teachers. see *EDUCATION — Teaching Methods And Curriculum*

282   NE
SCHRIFT; populair bijbeltijdschrift. 1953. bi-m. fl.35. (Paters Montfortanen) Janssen-Print, Heilige Land Stichting, Mgr. Suyslaan 4, 6564 BV Nijmegen, Netherlands. Ed. H. Manie. bk.rev.; circ. 3,000. **Indexed:** CERDIC.
    Formerly: Boek der Boeken (ISSN 0006-5544)
    Description: Catholic publication devoted to Biblical studies. Includes list of exhibitions and lectures.

282   GW
SCHULE UND MISSION; Hilfen fuer Religionsunterricht. q. DM.12. Kindermissionswerk, Stephanstr. 35, D-5100 Aachen, Germany. TEL 0241-21067. circ. 6,000.

SCRIBHINNI GAEILGENA NA BRATHAR MIONUR. see *LITERATURE*

220 282   UK   ISSN 0036-9780
BS410
SCRIPTURE BULLETIN. 1969. s-a. £4($12) (typically set in Jan.). Catholic Biblical Association of Great Britain, c/o Stephen Greenhalgh, LSU College of H.E., The Avenue, Southampton SO9 5HB, England. TEL 0703-228761. adv.; bk.rev.; circ. 550. **Indexed:** Cath.Ind., Int.Z.Bibelwiss., New Test.Abstr., Old Test.Abstr.
    —BLDSC shelfmark: 8213.240000.
    Description: Contains articles on Old and New Testament topics. Gives information on recent developments in area of biblical pastoral ministry.

282   IE   ISSN 0332-1150
SCRIPTURE IN CHURCH. 1970. q. I£30.32($49.12) Dominican Publications, 42 Parnell Sq., Upper Dorset St., Dublin 1, Ireland. TEL 01-721611. FAX 01-731760. circ. 6,200. (back issues avail.) **Indexed:** New Test.Abstr., Old Test.Abstr.

230   IT   ISSN 0036-9810
SCUOLA CATTOLICA. 1873. bi-m. L.40000($40) (foreign L.50000). Editrice Ancora Milano, Via G. B. Niccolini, 8, 20154 Milan, Italy. TEL 02-33608941. FAX 02-33608944. Ed. T. Citrini. bk.rev.; index; circ. 1,100. **Indexed:** CERDIC, New Test.Abstr., Rel.& Theol.Abstr.

282   CF
SEMAINE AFRICAINE. 1952. w. B.P. 2080, Brazzaville, Congo. Ed. Bernard Mackiza. circ. 8,000.

200   VC   ISSN 0582-6314
SEMINARIUM; a review for seminaries, ecclesiastical vocations, universities. (Text in language of authors) 1950. N.S 1961. q. L.37000($38) (foreign L.47000)(effective 1992). (Pontifical Society for Priestly Vocations) Libreria Editrice Vaticana, 00120 Vatican City, State of the Vatican City. bk.rev.; bibl.; index; circ. 2,500. **Indexed:** Cath.Ind., CERDIC.
    Description: Commentaries for seminaries, ecclesiastical vocations and universities, edited by the Congregation for Catholic Education.

282   PY
SENDERO. 2/wk. Alberdi 874, Asuncion, Paraguay. TEL 21-95941. Ed. Ilde Silvero. circ. 15,000.

248.8   IT   ISSN 0037-2439
SERAFICO VESSILLO;* bollettino fer il Terz'Ordine e fer le Vocazioni. 1955. m. L.1000. (Terz'ordine e le Vocazioni Cappuccine Salernitane) Fratelli Jovane, Via Lungomare 162, Salerno, Italy. Ed. Dir. Aldo Catalano. circ. 2,000.

282   US
SHRINE BULLETIN. 1978. 3/yr. $1. (World Apostolate of Fatima) Blue Army of Our Lady of Fatima, U S A, Inc., Mountain View Rd., Box 976, Washington, NJ 07882-0976. TEL 908-689-1700. FAX 908-689-6279. Ed. Toni Cormier.
    Description: Calendar of events and pilgrimage information about the National Blue Army Shrine of the Immaculate Heart of Mary.

SINGENDE KIRCHE; Zeitschrift fuer katholische Kirchenmusik. see *MUSIC*

248   US   ISSN 0037-590X
BX4200
SISTERS TODAY. 1929. bi-m. $15. Liturgical Press, Saint John's Abbey, Collegeville, MN 56321. TEL 612-363-2213. Ed. Sr. Mary Anthony Wagner. adv.; bk.rev.; index; circ. 7,707. (also avail. in microform from UMI; reprint service avail. from UMI) **Indexed:** A.I.P.P., Cath.Ind., CERDIC.
    —BLDSC shelfmark: 8286.424000.
    Formerly: Sponsa Regis.

SLOVAK CATHOLIC FALCON. see *ETHNIC INTERESTS*

282   US   ISSN 0892-5100
SLOWO I LITURGIA. (Text in Polish) 1970. q. $25. Polish American Liturgical Center, Box 240492, Orchard Lake, MI 48324. TEL 313-683-0409. Ed. Rev. Eugene Edyk, S.T.D. circ. 130. (looseleaf format)

SOCIAL JUSTICE REVIEW; pioneer American journal of Catholic social action. see *SOCIAL SCIENCES: COMPREHENSIVE WORKS*

SOCIAL WORK AND CHRISTIANITY; an international journal. see *SOCIAL SERVICES AND WELFARE*

RELIGIONS AND THEOLOGY — ROMAN CATHOLIC

282   EC
SOLIDARIDAD. 1982. m. Confederation of Catholic Office Staff and Students, Calle Oriente 725, Quito, Ecuador. TEL 2-216-541. circ. 15,000.

282   GW   ISSN 0176-862X
SONNTAGSDIENSTE. 1972. m. DM.96. (Liturgische Arbeitsgruppe) Bergmoser und Hoeller Verlag GmbH, Karl-Friedrich-Str. 76, 5100 Aachen, Germany. TEL 0241-17309-21. FAX 0241-1730934. TELEX 2414010. circ. 2,400. (looseleaf format; back issues avail.)

282   US   ISSN 0038-1756
SOUL. 1950. bi-m. $3 (foreign $5). (World Apostolate of Fatima) Blue Army of Our Lady of Fatima, U S A, Inc., Mountain View Rd., Box 976, Washington, NJ 07882-0976. TEL 908-689-1700. FAX 908-689-6279. Ed. Rev. Frederick L. Miller. charts; illus.; circ. 115,000.
Description: Roman Catholic Marian magazine promoting the message of Fatima and St. Louis de Montfort's total consecration to Jesus through Mary.

282   US   ISSN 0038-187X
BX1752
SOUNDS OF TRUTH AND TRADITION. 1965. irreg. free to qualified personnel. (Catholic Traditionalist Movement, Inc.) C T M Publications, Inc., 210 Maple Ave., Box 781, Westbury, NY 11590. TEL 516-333-6470. Ed. Father Gommar A. De Pauw. bk.rev. **Indexed:** CERDIC.

282   US
SOUTH TEXAS CATHOLIC. (Text in English, Spanish) w. 1200 Lantana, Corpus Christi, TX 78407. Ed. William G. Bilton.

282   SA   ISSN 0038-4011
SOUTHERN CROSS. 1920. w. R.80. (Southern African Catholic Bishops' Conference) Catholic Newspaper and Publishing Co. Ltd., Box 2372, Cape Town 8000, South Africa. TEL 021-45-5007. FAX 21-461-9330. Ed. Card. Owen McCann. adv.; bk.rev.; film rev.; illus.; circ. 12,500. (tabloid format) **Indexed:** CERDIC.

282   US   ISSN 0745-0257
SOUTHERN CROSS. 1912. w. $15. Roman Catholic Diocese of San Diego, Box 81869, San Diego, CA 92138. TEL 619-574-6393. FAX 619-293-3765. Ed. Dan E. Pitre. adv.; bk.rev.; film rev.; play rev.; illus.; tr.lit.; circ. 22,000. (back issues avail.)

282   US   ISSN 0038-4690
SOUTHWEST KANSAS REGISTER. 1966. fortn. $20. Catholic Diocese of Dodge City, Box 137, Dodge City, KS 67801. FAX 316-227-1570. Ed. Timothy F. Wenzl. adv.; bk.rev.; illus.; circ. 6,000. (tabloid format)

282   UK   ISSN 0269-8390
SOUTH WESTERN CATHOLIC HISTORY. 1983. a. £3. c/o Dominic Aidan Bellenger, Downside Abbey, Stratton-on-the-Fosse, Bath BA3 4RJ, England. TEL 0761-232206. FAX 0761-233575. bk.rev.; circ. 250.
—BLDSC shelfmark: 8352.195000.
Description: Covers architectural, theological and biographical studies of the English Roman Catholic community (1558-1950).

282   GW
SPEYER. DIOEZESE. DIREKTORIUM SPIRENSE - OFFIZIUM UND MESSFEIER. 1824. a. Bischoefliches Ordinariat Speyer, Pfaffengasse 16, 6720 Speyer, Germany. Ed. Christian Huber. circ. 2,500.

282 255   US   ISSN 0038-7592
SPIRIT & LIFE. 1905. 6/yr. $5. Benedictine Convent of Perpetual Adoration, 8300 Morganford Rd., St. Louis, MO 63123. TEL 314-638-6427. (Subscr. to: Benedictine Convent of Perpetual Adoration, Clyde, MO 64432) Ed. Sr. M. Romanus Penrose. bk.rev.; illus.; circ. 4,700. (also avail. in microform from UMI; reprint service avail. from UMI) **Indexed:** CERDIC.
Description: For readers who want short, pithy reading material which will inspire them and give them impetus to live out their Christ-life on a day-to-day basis. Aims to engender spirit and life in the Church from the stance of its Benedictine publishers.

282   US   ISSN 0038-7630
BX2350.A1
SPIRITUAL LIFE. 1955. q. $12. Washington Province of Discalced Carmelite Friars, Inc., 2131 Lincoln Rd., N.E., Washington, DC 20002. TEL 800-832-8489. FAX 202-832-8967. Ed. Rev. Steven Payne, O.C.D. bk.rev.; bibl.; circ. 14,500. (also avail. in microform from UMI; reprint service avail. from UMI) **Indexed:** Cath.Ind., CERDIC.
—BLDSC shelfmark: 8415.350000.
Description: Journal of contemporary spirituality.

282 255   NE   ISSN 0038-8904
STAD GODS. 1932. m. fl.12.20. Zusters Augustinessen van Sint Monica, Klooster De Stad Gods, Soestdijkerstraatweg 151, 1213 VZ Hilversum, Netherlands. bk.rev.; illus.; circ. 55,000.

282   GH   ISSN 0038-9374
STANDARD; national Catholic weekly. 1938. w. NC.7. (Ghana Catholic Hierarchy) Catholic Mission Press, Royal Lane, Box 60, Cape Coast, Ghana. Ed. Rev. Martin T. Peters. circ. 11,000. (processed)

940   AU   ISSN 0081-5594
STILLE SCHAR. 1953. a. S.55. (Emporer Charles League for Peace Among the Nations) Gebetsliga, Zisterzienserstift, A-3180 Lilienfeld, Austria. TEL 02762-2204-23. circ. 5,000.

STORICO DELLA BASILICATA. BOLLETTINO. see *RELIGIONS AND THEOLOGY*

250   IT   ISSN 0039-2901
BX804
STUDI CATTOLICI; mensile di studi ed attualita. 1957. m. L.50000($50) (Associazione Ricerche e Studi) Edizioni A.R.E.S., Via A. Stradivari 7, 20131 Milan, Italy. TEL 0039-02-2042156. FAX 0039-02-29514202. Ed. Cesare Cavalleri. adv.; bk.rev.; bibl.; charts; illus.; index. **Indexed:** CERDIC.

282   IT
STUDI E RICERCHE FRANCESCANE. 1972. q. L.35000($11) (Istituto Meridionale di Francescanesimo) T D C Telediffusione Cattolica, Piazza S. Eframo Vecchio 21, 80137 Naples, Italy. TEL 081-293691. FAX 081-444425. Ed. Ferdinando Mastroianni. adv.; bk.rev.; index; circ. 400. **Indexed:** CERDIC.

271   IT   ISSN 0039-3045
BX4055.A1
STUDI STORICI DELL'ORDINE DEI SERVI DI MARIA. (Text and summaries in English, French, German, Italian, Portuguese, Spanish) 1933. s-a. L.35000($29) (effective Sep. 1990). Ordine dei Servi di Maria, Istituto Storico, Viale Trenta Aprile, 6, 00153 Rome, Italy. FAX 06-5880292. (Co-sponsor: Centro Edizioni Marianum) Ed. Davide M. Montagna. adv.; bk.rev.; bibl.; charts; illus.; pat.; stat.; index; circ. 300.

282   IT   ISSN 0392-1719
STUDIA PICENA; rivista Marchigina di Storia e cultura. 1925. a. L.25000. Istituto Teologico Marchigiano, Rivista "Studia Picena", Presso Istituto Teologico Marchigiano, Via Roma 118, 61032 Fano (Pesaro), Italy. TEL 0721 804042. circ. 300. (back issues avail.)

282   GW   ISSN 0303-4224
STUDIEN UND MITTEILUNGEN ZUR GESCHICHTE DES BENEDIKTINER. ORDENS UND SEINER ZWEIGE. 1880. 2/yr. price varies. (Bayerische Benediktinerakademie) E O S Verlag, 8917 St. Ottilien, Germany. Ed. Ulrich Faust. bk.rev.; illus.; cum.index.

230   GW   ISSN 0081-7295
STUDIEN ZUR GESCHICHTE DER KATHOLISCHEN MORALTHEOLOGIE. vol.3, 1955. irreg., vol.29, 1989. price varies. Verlag Friedrich Pustet, Gutenbergstr. 8, 8400 Regensburg 1, Germany. FAX 0941-948652. Ed. Johannes Gruendel. circ. 500.

255   IT   ISSN 0562-4649
SUBSIDIA SCIENTIFICA FRANCISCALIA. (Text in French, German, Italian and Latin) 1962. irreg., no.7, 1989. price varies. Frati Minori Cappuccini, Istituto Storico, Casella Postale 90-91, Circonv. Occidentale 6850 (GRA km 65), 00163 Rome, Italy. TEL 06-625-19-58. FAX 06-661-62-401. index; circ. 500.

282   US
THE SUNDAY VISITOR. w. $17. Diocese of Lafayette-in-Indiana, Local Church of Northcentral Indiana, Box 1603, Lafayette, IN 47902. Ed. Thomas A. Russell.

200   AT   ISSN 0039-6184
SURSUM CORDA; lift up your hearts. 1955. bi-m. Aus.$6. Franciscan House of Formation of Australian - New Zealand Province, P.O. Box 79, Box Hill, Vic. 3128, Australia. Ed. Rev. Ralph Byrne. bk.rev.; index every 2 yrs.; circ. 5,100.

282   IT
SUSSIDI PATRISTICI. 1981. irreg. Institutum Patristicum Augustinianum, Via S. Uffizio, 25, 00193 Rome, Italy. (back issues avail.)

282   US
SV. PRANCISKAUS VARPELIS/BELL OF ST. FRANCIS. (Text in Lithuanian) 1942. 6/yr. $5. Franciscan Fathers of Maine, Franciscan Vicariate of St. Casimir, Kennebunkport, ME 04046. TEL 207-967-2011. FAX 207-967-5721. Ed. Paulius Jurkus. bk.rev.; circ. 1,400.

282   CN
SVITLO/LIGHT. English edition: Beacon (ISSN 0382-6384) (Text in Ukrainian) 1939. m. $15. Basilian Fathers Press, 286 Lisgar St., Toronto, Ont. M6J 3G9, Canada. TEL 416-535-6483. Ed. N. Svirsky. circ. 2,250.

282   BN
SVJETLO RIJECI/LIGHT OF THE WORD; vjerski list/religious newspaper. (Text in Croatian) 1983. m. 3 din.($0.40) Franjevacki Provincijalati, Svjetlo Rijeci, N. Pozderca 6, 71000 Sarajevo, Bosnia Hercegovinia. TEL 071 535-407. Ed.Bd. circ. 10,000(AP). (looseleaf format)

282   US   ISSN 0039-8845
BX801
TABLET. 1908. w. $20. (Roman Catholic Diocese of Brooklyn) Tablet Publishing Co., Inc., 653 Hicks St., Brooklyn, NY 11231. TEL 718-858-3838. FAX 718-858-2112. Ed. Edward Wilkinson. adv.; bk.rev.; illus.; circ. 98,000. (also avail. in microform; microfilm from KTO) **Indexed:** Cath.Ind.

282   GW   ISSN 0492-1283
TAG DES HERRN; katholisches Kirchenblatt. 1951. 52/yr. DM.0.90 per no. (Berliner Bischofskonferenz) St. Benno Verlag GmbH, Thuringer Str. 1-3, 7033 Leipzig, Germany. TEL 03741-474161. FAX 03741-470802. Ed. Gottfried Swoboda. bk.rev.; circ. 55,900.
Description: Covers news of the Catholic Church, including events, issues and questions.

282   XV
TEDEN BOZJE BESEDE; redna stolniska oznanila. (Text in Slovenian) 1970. w. 6000 din.($7) Stolni Zupnijski Urad, Dolnicarjeva, 61000 Ljubljana, Slovenia. TEL 061 310-684. Ed. Vinko Vegelj. (looseleaf format; back issues avail.)

282   RE
TEMOIGNAGE CHRETIEN DE LA REUNION. w. 21 bis rue de l'Est, 97465 Saint-Denis, Reunion. Ed. Rene Payet. circ. 2,000.

301.5   BL   ISSN 0103-314X
TEOCOMUNICACAO. 1971. 4/yr. Cz.$15,00($9) (Pontificia Universidade Catolica do Rio Grande do Sul, Instituto de Teologia) Editora da P U C R S, c/o Antoninho M. Naime, Caixa Postal 12001, 90620 Porto Alegre RS, Brazil. Ed. Urbano Zilles. bk.rev.; circ. 1,500.

282   HU   ISSN 0133-1779
TEOLOGIA. 1967. 4/yr. 60 Ft.($29.50) Teologia Kiadohivatale, Karoly Mihaly u. 4-8, 1053 Budapest 5, Hungary. FAX 36-1-117-3471. Ed. Szennay Andras. bk.rev.; circ. 4,000. **Indexed:** CERDIC.

240   CL   ISSN 0049-3449
TEOLOGIA Y VIDA. 1960. q. $30. Universidad Catolica de Chile, Facultad de Teologia, Jaime Guzman Enazuriz 3300, Casilla 316, Santiago, 22, Chile. Eds. Marciano Barrios, Cecilia Coz Canas. adv.; bk.rev.; abstr.; bibl.; cum.index: 1960-1979; circ. 700. **Indexed:** Bull.Signal., Canon Law Abstr., Cath.Ind., New Test.Abstr., Old Test.Abstr.
—BLDSC shelfmark: 8791.765000.

RELIGIONS AND THEOLOGY — ROMAN CATHOLIC

282   SP
TERESA DE JESUS. bi-m. 1100 ptas.($20) (foreign 1800 ptas.). Centro Teresianosanjuanista, Plaza de la Santa, 4, Apdo. 167, 05001 Avila, Spain. TEL 918-21-26-08. Dir. Francisco M. Tejedor.

282   VC   ISSN 0392-4556
TERESIANUM. (Text in several languages) 1947. s-a. L.50000 (effective 1992). (Pontificia Facolta Teresianum) Edizioni del Teresianum, Piazza S. Pancrazio 5-A, 00152 Rome, Italy. Ed. R.P. Virgilio Pasquetto. adv.; bk.rev.; **Indexed:** CERDIC, New Test.Abstr., Old Test.Abstr.
—BLDSC shelfmark: 8792.350000.
Formerly (until vol.33, 1982): Ephemerides Carmeliticae.

282   IT   ISSN 0040-3938
TESORO EUCARISTICO. 1917. bi-m. (except Jul.-Aug.). L.20000. Frati Minori Conventuali della Basilica di S. Francesco in Siena, Santuario delle Ss. Particole, 53100 Siena, Italy. TEL 0577-289081. Ed. P. Antonio Giannini. bk.rev.; circ. 2,000.

282   IT
TESTIMONI; quindicinale di informazione e aggiornamento per istituti di vita consacrata. 1978. bi-m. L.32000 (foreign L.47000). Centro Editoriale Dehoniano, Via Nosadella, 6, 40123 Bologna, Italy. TEL 051-306811. TELEX 361706 CICME. Ed.Bd. adv.; bk.rev.; circ. 11,000.
Description: Informs consecrated men and women on psychology and spiritual life.

900   IT   ISSN 0394-7793
TEXTUS ET STUDIA HISTORICA CARMELITANA. (Text in English, French, German, Italian, Latin and Spanish) 1954. irreg. price varies. (Order of Carmelites) Institutum Carmelitanum, Via Sforza Pallavicini 10, 00193 Rome, Italy. TEL 06-654-3513. FAX 06-654-7200. adv.; circ. 500.
Description: Forum covers a Carmelite history; critical editions.

200   CK   ISSN 0120-3649
THEOLOGICA XAVERIANA. 1950. q. Col.$7000($30) Pontificia Universidad Javeriana, Facultad de Teologia, Carrera 10, No. 65-48, Bogota 2 D.E., Colombia. Dir. Mario Gutierrez. adv.; bk.rev.; index; circ. controlled. (processed; back issues avail.)
Indexed: Bull.Signal, Canon Law Abstr.
Formerly (until 1975): Ecclesiastica Xaveriana (ISSN 0012-9054)

282   GW   ISSN 0049-366X
BR4
THEOLOGIE UND GLAUBE. 1908. q. DM.56. Ferdinand Schoeningh, Juehenplatz 1, 4790 Paderborn, Germany. TEL 05251-29010. FAX 05251-2901-35. TELEX 936929-FS-PB. Eds. Johannes Gamberoni, Winifred Schulz. adv.; bk.rev. **Indexed:** Canon Law Abstr., CERDIC, New Test.Abstr., Old Test.Abstr., Rel.& Theol.Abstr., Rel.Per.
—BLDSC shelfmark: 8814.526000.
Description: Covers a variety of theological issues, such as Church history, ethics, Bible, and liturgy.

282   GW   ISSN 0342-1430
BR4
THEOLOGISCHE QUARTALSCHRIFT. 1819. q. DM.60. Erich Wewel Verlag, Anzingerstr. 1, 8000 Munich 80, Germany. index. **Indexed:** Rel.& Theol.Abstr. (1990-), Rel.Ind.One.

230   GW   ISSN 0040-568X
BR4
THEOLOGISCHE REVUE. 6/yr. DM.135. (Universitaet Muenster, Katholisch-Theologische Fakultaet) Aschendorffsche Verlagsbuchhandlung, Soersterstr. 13, Postfach 1124, 4400 Muenster, Germany. TEL 0251-690-0. FAX 0251-690405. Eds. Erwin Iserloh, Vinzenz Pfnuer. adv.; bk.rev.; bibl.; index. **Indexed:** CERDIC, New Test.Abstr.
—BLDSC shelfmark: 8814.534000.

THOMAS; maandblad voor lichamelijke opvoeding. see EDUCATION — Teaching Methods And Curriculum

230 100   US   ISSN 0040-6325
BX801
THOMIST; a speculative quarterly review of theology and philosophy. 1939. q. $25 (foreign $35). (Dominican Fathers, Province of St. Joseph) Thomist Press, 487 Michigan Ave., N.E., Washington, DC 20017. TEL 202-529-5300. Ed. Rev. Joseph A. DiNoia. adv.; bk.rev.; bibl.; index; cum.index: vol.1-50, 1939-1986; circ. 1,000 (controlled). (also avail. in microfilm from UMI; reprint service avail. from KTO) **Indexed:** Arts & Hum.Cit.Ind., Cath.Ind., CERDIC, Curr.Cont., New Test.Abstr., Phil.Ind., Rel.& Theol.Abstr. (1969-).
—BLDSC shelfmark: 8820.234000.

282 100 378   US   ISSN 0040-6457
AP2
THOUGHT; a review of culture and ideas. 1926. q. $20 to individuals; institutions $30. (Fordham University) Fordham University Press, University Box L, Bronx, NY 10458-5172. TEL 212-579-2322. FAX 212-579-2321. Ed. G. Richard Dimler, S.J. adv.; circ. 1,200. (also avail. in microfilm from UMI; back issues avail.; reprint service avail. from UMI) **Indexed:** Amer.Bibl.Slavic & E.Eur.Stud., Bk.Rev.Ind. (1980-), Cath.Ind., CERDIC, Child.Bk.Rev.Ind. (1980-), Curr.Cont., Hist.Abstr., Hum.Ind., Ind.Bk.Rev.Hum., Mid.East: Abstr.& Ind., New Test.Abstr., Old Test.Abstr., P.A.I.S., Phil.Ind., Rel.& Theol.Abstr. (1979-).
—BLDSC shelfmark: 8820.290000.

282   US   ISSN 0040-6791
TIDINGS (LOS ANGELES); official Catholic weekly newspaper of Los Angeles. (Text mainly in English; occasionally in Spanish) 1895. w. $15. (Roman Catholic Archdiocese of Los Angeles) Tidings Corp., 1530 W. Ninth St., Los Angeles, CA 90015. TEL 213-251-3360. FAX 213-383-0863. Ed. Alfred Doblin. adv.; bk.rev.; film rev.; play rev.; circ. 45,000. (also avail. in microform)

282 284   NE   ISSN 0168-9959
TIJDSCHRIFT VOOR THEOLOGIE. (Text in Dutch; summaries in English) 1961. q. fl.67.50 (foreign fl.85). Studia Catholica Foundation, Postbus 35, 6500 AA Nijmegen, Netherlands. TEL 080-772077. Ed. T.M. Schoof. adv.; bk.rev.; index; circ. 2,000. (back issues avail.) **Indexed:** CERDIC, New Test.Abstr., Old Test.Abstr., Rel.& Theol.Abstr. (1968-1983,1990-).

282   US
TIMES REVIEW. 1936. w. $18. Box 4004, La Crosse, WI 54602-4004. TEL 608-788-1524. Ed. Rev. Bernard McGarty. adv.; circ. 30,000. (newspaper)

282 052   IE
TIMIRE AN CHROI NAOFA; Iris Oifigiuil Aspalacht na hUrnai. (Text in Irish) 1911. q. £3. Timire an Chroi Naofa, 16 Pairc Na Cabrai, Baile Atha Cliath 7, Ireland. TEL 01-309139. Ed. Fr. D.O Laoghaire, S.J. adv.; bk.rev.; bibl.; circ. 2,000.

282   US   ISSN 0891-1533
TODAY'S CATHOLIC (FORT WAYNE). 1926. w. $14 (effective Jan. 1991). Bishop John M. D'Arcy, Pub. & Ed., Box 11169, Fort Wayne, IN 46856. TEL 219-456-2824. FAX 219-744-1473. (And: 150 E. Doan Dr., Fort Wayne, IN 46806) adv.; bk.rev.; film rev.; charts; illus.; stat.; circ. 15,500. (tabloid format; also avail. in talking book; back issues avail.)
Description: Roman Catholic diocesan newspaper.

282   US   ISSN 0745-3612
TODAY'S CATHOLIC (SAN ANTONIO). (Text in English, Spanish) 1892. bi-w. $12. Box 28410, San Antonio, TX 78284. TEL 512-734-2620. FAX 5191034-2774. Ed. Martha Brinkmann. adv.; bk.rev.; circ. 23,400.
Description: Covers family oriented Catholic news.

TODAY'S CATHOLIC TEACHER. see EDUCATION

282   US
TOUCHSTONE (CHICAGO); the touchstone of the pilgrim Church's self-understanding is dialogue. 1985. q. $6.50 to qualified personnel. National Federation of Priests, 1337 W. Ohio, 3rd Fl., Chicago, IL 60622. TEL 312-226-3334. FAX 312-829-8915. Ed. Rev. Thomas G. Simons. bk.rev.; circ. 25,000. (back issues avail.)
Description: Information and news pertaining to priests, spirituality, and articles on various ministries.

282   FR
TRADITION ET PROGRES. q. 30 Fr. Trois-Puits, 51500 F. Rilly, France.

282 949.2   NE
BX1549.A1
TRAJECTA; tijdschrift voor de geshiedenis van het katholiek leven in de Nederlanden. 1959. 3/yr. fl.55. Uitgeverij Kerckebosch B.V., Postbus 122, 3700 AC Zeist, Netherlands. TEL 03404-21444. FAX 3404-12174. Ed. Th. Clemens. adv.; bk.rev.; abstr.; bibl.; index. cum.index 1959-1991; circ. 800. (reprint service avail.) **Indexed:** Amer.Hist.& Life, Hist.Abstr.
Formerly (until 1992): Archief voor de Geschiedenis van de Katholieke Kerk in Nederland (ISSN 0003-8326)
Description: Scholarly treatment of the history of Catholic life in the Low Countries.
Refereed Serial

282   US   ISSN 0041-7548
BX801
U S CATHOLIC. 1963. m. $15. Claretian Publications, 205 W. Monroe St., Chicago, IL 60606. TEL 312-236-7782. FAX 312-236-7320. Ed. Rev. Mark J. Brummel. adv.; bk.rev.; illus.; circ. 52,000. (also avail. in microform from UMI; reprint service avail. from UMI) **Indexed:** Cath.Ind., CERDIC, G.Soc.Sci.& Rel.Per.Lit., Mag.Ind., PMR, R.G.
Description: Provides informative articles on prayer, sacraments, marriage, work, parish, and society and interviews leading experts in theology, spirituality and parish life.

282   US
U S PARISH; the newsletter that makes good parishes better. 1983. m. $24.95. Claretian Publications, 205 W. Monroe St., Chicago, IL 60606. TEL 312-236-7782. FAX 312-236-7230. Ed. Rev. Mark J. Brummel. circ. 2,204.

282   GW   ISSN 0724-2778
UNA VOCE KORRESPONDENZ. (Text in German, Latin) 1970. bi-m. DM.15($7.95) Una Voce Korrespondenz Schriftleitung, Postfach 620275, 5000 Cologne 60, Germany. Ed. Rudolf Kaschewsky. bk.rev.; index; circ. 2,500. (back issues avail.)

UNDA - U S A NEWSLETTER. see COMMUNICATIONS — Television And Cable

UNITAS FRATRUM. see HISTORY — History Of Europe

282   UK   ISSN 0041-8226
UNIVERSE. 1860. w. 40p. Gabriel Communications, St. James's Building, First Floor, Oxford St., Manchester M1 6FP, England. Ed. Tom Murphy. adv.; bk.rev.; illus.; circ. 106,000. (tabloid format)
Incorporates: Catholic Times.

200   CL   ISSN 0069-3596
UNIVERSIDAD CATOLICA DE CHILE. FACULTAD DE TEOLOGIA. ANALES. 1940. a. Universidad Catolica de Chile, Facultad de Teologia, Jaime Guzman Enazuriz 3300, Casilla 316, Santiago, 22, Chile. Ed. Juan Noemi Callejas. cum.index: 1940-1969; circ. 500. **Indexed:** Bull.Signal, Cath.Ind.

282   BE
UNIVERSITE CATHOLIQUE DE LOUVAIN. FACULTE DE THEOLOGIE ET DE DROIT CANONIQUE. COLLECTION DES DISSERTATIONS PRESENTEES POUR L'OBTENTION DU GRADE DE MAITRE A LA FACULTE DE THEOLOGIE OU A LA FACULTE DE DROIT CANONIQUE. 1841. irreg. (series quarto, vol.6, 1987). Universite Catholique de Louvain, Faculte de Theologie et de Droit Canonique, Grand-Place 45, B-1348 Louvain-la-Neuve, Belgium.
Formerly: Universite Catholique de Louvain. Facultes de Theologie et de Droit Canonique. Dissertationes ad Gradum Magistri in Facultate Theologica Vel in Facultate Iuris Canonici Consequendum Conscriptae.

200   BE   ISSN 0076-1230
UNIVERSITE CATHOLIQUE DE LOUVAIN. FACULTE DE THEOLOGIE ET DE DROIT CANONIQUE. TRAVAUX DE DOCTORAT EN THEOLOGIE ET EN DROIT CANONIQUE. NOUVELLE SERIE. 1969. irreg., vol.14, 1990. exchange basis. Universite Catholique de Louvain, Faculte de Theologie et de Droit Canonique, Grand-Place 45, B-1348 Louvain-la-Neuve, Belgium. circ. 120.

RELIGIONS AND THEOLOGY — ROMAN CATHOLIC

268 US ISSN 0070-3052
UNIVERSITY OF DAYTON. SCHOOL OF EDUCATION. WORKSHOP PROCEEDINGS. 1970. irreg., latest 1971. $3.25. University of Dayton, School of Education, Dayton, OH 45469. TEL 513-229-3146. Ed. Louis J. Faerber.
Description: Covers Catholic elementary and secondary education.

264 US ISSN 0076-003X
UNIVERSITY OF NOTRE DAME. DEPARTMENT OF THEOLOGY. LITURGICAL STUDIES. 1955. irreg., no.11, 1977. price varies. University of Notre Dame Press, Notre Dame, IN 46556. TEL 219-239-6346. **Indexed:** Cath.Ind.

282 UK ISSN 0308-6305
USHAW MAGAZINE. 1891. a. £3. Ushaw College, Durham DH7 9RH, England. TEL 091-373-3966. Ed. M. Cecily Boulding. adv.; bk.rev.; circ. 600.
Description: Articles on theology, scripture, history, sociology, and Roman Catholic education.

282 900 IT ISSN 0394-7807
VACARE DEO. (Text in English, French, German, Italian, Latin and Spanish) 1956. irreg. price varies. (Order of Carmelites) Institutum Carmelitanum, Via Sforza Pallavicini 10, 00193 Rome, Italy.
TEL 06-654-3513. FAX 06-654-7200. adv.; circ. 500.
Description: Forum includes Carmelite spirituality; critical editions.

282 IT ISSN 0042-2304
VALLE SANTA DI RIETI;* periodico di cultura e propaganda Francescana. 1948. q. free. (Santuari Francescani Valle di Rieti) Convento S. Antonio al Monte, Rieti, Italy. Ed. Rev. Ettore Giustino Marini. adv.; bk.rev.; illus.; circ. 5,000.

282 US
VATICAN VOICES AND NOTABLE PAPAL QUOTES. 1979. w. $18. Truth, Inc., 3400 W. Michigan St., Milwaukee, WI 53208. TEL 414-258-2665. Ed. Rev. Cletus Healy, S.J. index; circ. 100. (looseleaf format)

200 IT
VENGA IL TUO REGNO. 1945. m. (10/yr.). L.10000. Pontificio Istituto Missioni Estere (Naples), Viale Colli Aminei 36, 80131 Naples, Italy.
TEL (081)741-0296. Ed. Luciano Numeroso. adv.; bk.rev.; circ. 10,000.
Description: Missionary magazine for families containing mainly correspondence from missionaries working in Asia, Africa, South America, and Oceania.

282 IT ISSN 0393-9901
VENITE ADOREMUS; mensile dello Studentato dei Padri Sacramentini. 1958. m. L.8000. Studentato dei Padri Sacramentini, Via Crispi 22, 63039 San Benedetto del Tronto (AP), Italy. index.

VERBUM; tijdschrift voor jongerkatechese. see EDUCATION — Teaching Methods And Curriculum

282 CI ISSN 0352-5708
VERITAS; revija svetog Antuna. (Text in Croatian) 1962. m. 8800 din.($9) Hrvatska Provincija S. Jeronima Franjevaca Konventualaca, Miskinina 31, 41000 Zagreb, Croatia. TEL 041 579-645. Ed. Ferdinand Cavar. circ. 16,000. (back issues avail.)

282 US ISSN 0042-4145
VERMONT CATHOLIC TRIBUNE. 1957. bi-w. $10. Vermont Catholic Press Association, 351 North Ave., Burlington, VT 05401-2999. TEL 802-658-6110. Ed. Neil Isakson. adv.; bk.rev.; film rev.; illus.; circ. 22,000. (also avail. in microfilm)

282 IT ISSN 0042-4242
VERONA FEDELE; settimanale cattolico della diocesi. 1946. w. L.50000. Editrice Verona Fedele, Via Pieta Vecchia 2, 37100 Verona, Italy. TEL 045-8000121. FAX 045-591745. Ed.Bd. adv.; bk.rev.; circ. 30,000.

255 IT ISSN 0042-4374
VERSO L'AZZURRO. 1963. m. free. Centro Nazionale Associazione Mariana, Via Francesco Albergotti 75, 00167 Rome, Italy. bk.rev.; circ. 2,300.

282 SP ISSN 0505-4605
VIDA NUEVA. 1958. w. 7200 ptas.($120) (foreign $140). Promociones Populares Cristianas, Enrique Jardiel Poncela, 4, Apdo. 19049, 28016 Madrid, Spain. TEL 457-35-39. FAX 457-72-12. TELEX 45051 PPC E. Dir. Vicente Alejandro Guillamon. adv.; bk.rev.

266 SP ISSN 0211-9749
VIDA RELIGIOSA. 1944. s-m. (except Jul.-Aug.). 4000 ptas.($48) for Europe and America; elsewhere $28(effective 1992). Misioneros Hijos del Inmaculado Corazon de Maria (Claretianos), Buen Suceso, 22, 28008 Madrid, Spain.
TEL 91-2482101. adv.; bk.rev.; bibl.; charts; stat.; tr.lit.; index; circ. 10,000 (controlled). (back issues avail.) **Indexed:** Canon Law Abstr., CERDIC.

282 II ISSN 0970-1079
VIDYAJYOTI JOURNAL OF THEOLOGICAL REFLECTION. 1938. m. Rs.40($14) Vidyajyoti Educational and Welfare Society (VIEWS), 4A Raj Nivas Marg, Delhi 110 054, India. Ed. S. Arokiasamy. adv.; bk.rev.; circ. 2,900. **Indexed:** Canon Law Abstr., New Test.Abstr., Old Test.Abstr.
—BLDSC shelfmark: 9234.501000.
Formerly: Clergy Monthly.
Description: Concerned with the life and thought of the church in India, inter-religious dialogue, theology and social concerns.

282 FR ISSN 0042-5362
VIE CATHOLIQUE DU BERRY. (Supplements avail.: Calendrier Litergique, Bourges (ISSN 0184-5713); Espoir de la Moisson (ISSN 0996-1445); Calendrier Litergique, Centre Bourges (ISSN 0181-1096)) 1865. w. 120 F. Association Diocesaine de Bourges, Archeveche de Bourges, 163 Blvd Malesherbes, 75017 Paris, France, France. TEL 1-47-66-01-86. TELEX 649 333. Ed. Jose de Broucker. adv.; bk.rev.; circ. 400,000.
Incorporates: Vocation (ISSN 1144-2549);
Formerly: Semaine Religiuese du Diocese de Bourges (ISSN 1141-1562)

282 CN ISSN 0318-9392
VIE OBLATE. (Text in English, French) 1942. 3/yr. Can.$20. 175 rue Main, Ottawa, Ont. K1S 1C3, Canada. TEL 613-237-0580. Ed. R. Boucher. bk.rev.; cum.index: 1942-1961, 1962-1990; circ. 500. (back issues avail.)

200 FR ISSN 0042-5613
VIE SPIRITUELLE. 1919. 5/yr. 222 F. (foreign 268 F.). Editions du Cerf, 29 bd. Latour-Maubourg, 75340 Paris Cedex 07, France. TEL 45-50-34-07. FAX 45-56-04-27. (Subscr. to: Service Abonnement, 3 chemin des Prunais, 94350 Villiers-sur-Marne, France) bk.rev.; bibl.; circ. 3,500. **Indexed:** Cath.Ind., CERDIC, Old Test.Abstr.
—BLDSC shelfmark: 9235.440000.

282 FR ISSN 0042-5621
VIE THERESIENNE. 1961. q. 100 F. Direction du Pelerinage de Lisieux, 33 rue du Carmel, B.P. 95, 14102 Lisieux cedex, France. TEL 31-34-49-71. FAX 31-31-71-03. Ed. Pere Leon Baucher. bk.rev.; circ. 470.

282 800 HU ISSN 0042-6024
VIGILIA. (Text in Hungarian; summaries in English, French and German) 1935. m. 480 Ft.($35) Vigilia, Kossuth Lajos u. 1, P.Box 111, 1364 Budapest 5, Hungary. TEL 117-7246. FAX 117-4895. (Subscr. to: Kultura, Box 149, H-1389 Budapest, Hungary) Ed. Laszlo Lukacs. bk.rev.; circ. 10,000. **Indexed:** CERDIC.

200 361 US
VISION (MILWAUKEE). 1968. 10/yr. $34 (includes Special Publications). National Association of Catholic Chaplains, 3501 S. Lake Dr., Box 07473, Milwaukee, WI 53207-0473. TEL 414-483-4898. Ed. Sr. Helen Hayes, O.S.F. bk.rev.; circ. 3,600. **Indexed:** CERDIC.
Formerly (until 1991): Camillian.
Description: Newsletter of the association; special publications on pastoral care available.

282 IT ISSN 0042-7233
VITA CATTOLICA. 1916. w. L.30000. Diocesi di Cremona, Piazza S.A.M. Zaccaria 3, 26100 Cremona, Italy. Ed. Erole Brocchieri. adv.; illus. (tabloid format)

282 GW
VITA FRATRUM. 1964. 3/yr. Provinzialat der Franziskaner, St.-Anna-Str. 19, 8000 Munich 22, Germany. TEL 089-226601. Ed. Winthir Rauch. circ. 450.

282 IT ISSN 0042-7276
VITA GIUSEPPINA. 1895. m. L.15000($20) Congregazione di S. Giuseppe (Giuseppini del Murialdo), Via degli Etruschi 7, 00185 Rome, Italy. FAX 06-445-67-25. Ed. Garuti Vittorio. adv.; bk.rev.; illus.; index. cum.index; circ. 32,000. (back issues avail.)

282 IT ISSN 0042-7365
VITA SOCIALE. 1944. bi-m. L.35000. Centro Riviste della Provincia Romana dei Frati Predicatori, Piazza S. Domenico 1, 51100 Pistoia, Italy. Ed. Marino Eugenio. bk.rev.; bibl.; illus.; stat.; index; circ. 1,000. (tabloid format) **Indexed:** CERDIC.
—BLDSC shelfmark: 9241.750000.

282 IT
VOCE DEI BERICI; settimanale di informazione dell Diocesi di Vicenza. 1949. w. L.45000. Via Vescovado 1, 36100 Vicenza, Italy. TEL 0444 545855. FAX 0444-543783. Ed. Lucio Mozzo.

200 IT ISSN 0042-7845
VOCE DELLA MADONNA DELLE GRAZIE.* 1954. w. L.800($1.50) Opera Madonna delle Grazie, Via Andria, Corato, Bari 70033, Italy. Ed. Favia Ferrara Don Giuseppe. illus.

282 945 370 IT
VOCE SERAFICA DELLA SARDEGNA. (Text in Italian-Sardinian; summaries in Italian) 1921. m. L.20000 (effective Jan. 1992). Frati Minori Cappuccini di Sardegna, Via S. Ignazio da Laconi 94, 09123 Cagliari, Italy. TEL 070-657370. Ed. P. Marco Tarcisio Mascia. adv.; bk.rev.; index; circ. 25,000. (also avail. in microfiche)
Description: Covers the Catholic religion and Capuchin information from Sardinia.

282 IT
VOCI AMICHE; bollettino parrocchiale. 1951. bi-m. Tipografia Pistoiese, Corso Gramsci 49, 51100 Pistoia, Italy. TEL 0573 20764. Ed. D. Giuseppe Vignozzi. circ. 1,200.

282 JO
VOICE OF THE HOLY LAND/SAWT EL-ARD EL-MUKADDASH. (Text in Arabic) 1986. m. 10000 din. Catholic Bureau of Press and Publication, P.O. Box 5634, Amman, Jordan. TEL 694095. FAX 692502. Ed. Raouf Najjar. adv.; bk.rev.; circ. 10,000.

282 US
VOICE OF THE SOUTHWEST; serving the Catholic Diocese of Gallup. m. $6. Diocese of Gallup, Box 1338, Gallup, NM 87305. TEL 505-863-4406. Ed. Tim Farrell.

282 260 UK ISSN 0043-1575
BX2350.A1
WAY; a quarterly review of Christian spirituality. (Supplements avail.) 1961. q. £12.80($26.50) (Society of Jesus) Way Publications, Heythrop College, 11 Cavendish Square, London W1M OAN, England. FAX 071-495-1673. Ed.Bd. bk.rev.; circ. 4,000. (also avail. in microform from UMI) **Indexed:** Cath.Ind., CERDIC, New Test.Abstr., Old Test.Abstr.
—BLDSC shelfmark: 9280.780000.

282 255 US
WAY OF ST. FRANCIS. 1948. 6/yr. $5. Franciscan Fathers of California, Inc., 109 Golden Gate Ave., San Francisco, CA 94102. TEL 415-621-8382. Ed. Fr. Simon Scanlon. adv.; bk.rev.; illus.; circ. 4,200. **Indexed:** CERDIC.
Formerly: Way-Catholic Viewpoints (ISSN 0043-1591)
Description: Franciscan spirituality and Christian humanist views on issues of the day.

282 US
WAY - UKRAINIAN CATHOLIC BI-WEEKLY. (Text in English and Ukrainian) 1939. bi-w. $15 (foreign $17)(effective Jan. 1991). (Ukrainian Catholic Archdiocese of Philadelphia) Apostolate, Inc., 827 N. Franklin St., Philadelphia, PA 19123-2004. TEL 215-922-5231. Eds. John M. Fields, Iwan Skoczylas. bk.rev.; illus.; circ. 8,300.
Formerly: Shlach (ISSN 0043-1583)

RELIGIONS AND THEOLOGY — OTHER DENOMINATIONS AND SECTS 4279

282 US
WEEKDAY HOMILY HELPS. 1981. m. $55. St. Anthony Messenger Press, 1615 Republic St., Cincinnati, OH 45210. TEL 513-241-5615. Ed. Carol Luebering. circ. 4,000. (looseleaf format)
  Description: Aid to Catholic clergy on preaching.

282 GW
WELT DES KINDES; Zeitschrift fuer Kleinkindpaedagogik und ausserschulische Erziehung. 1915. bi-m. DM.45. (Verband Katholischer Tageseinrichtungen fuer Kinder Bundesverband e.V.) Koesel-Verlag GmbH und Co., Flueggenstr. 2, 8000 Munich 19, Germany. TEL 089-179009-0. Ed. Wolfgang Liegle. circ. 11,500.

282 US
WEST TEXAS ANGELUS. (Text in English, Spanish) 1964. s-m. $10. Catholic Diocese of San Angelo, Box 1829, San Angelo, TX 76902-1829. TEL 915-653-2466. FAX 915-658-3438. Ed. Rev. Maurice J. Voity. adv.; bk.rev.; circ. 17,400. (tabloid format)
  Formerly: Texas Concho Register (ISSN 0040-425X)

282 US
WEST TEXAS CATHOLIC.* 1936. w. $8. Roman Catholic Diocese of Amarillo, c/o Bishop L.T. Matthiesen, Box 5644, Amarillo, TX 79117-5644. Ed. Deacon Leroy Behnke. adv.; circ. 8,750.
  Formerly: West Texas Register (ISSN 0043-3187)

282 CN ISSN 0512-5235
WESTERN CATHOLIC REPORTER. 1965. w. Can.$19.26($25) Great Western Press Ltd., 8421 - 101 Ave., Edmonton, Alta. T6A 0L1, Canada. TEL 403-465-8030. Ed. Glen Argan. adv.; circ. 36,000. (tabloid format)

282 UK ISSN 0262-1061
WHITE FATHERS - WHITE SISTERS. 1927. bi-m. free. Society of Missionaries of Africa, 129 Lichfield Rd., Sutton Coldfield, W. Midlands B74 2SA, England. TEL 021-308-0226. FAX 021-323-2476. Ed. Rev. W. Turnbull. bk.rev.; circ. 32,000. (back issues avail.)
  Description: Presents the missionary work of the Catholic Church in Africa.

282 333.7 US
WILDERNESS GAZETTE; coverage of the apparitions and messages of the Blessed Virgin Mary in modern times. 1988. bi-m. $7.50 (foreign $10). Yellowstone Information Services, 7 View Dr., Elkview, WV 25071. TEL 304-965-5548. FAX 034-965-7785. Ed. Roger C. Thibault. bk.rev.; circ. 1,000. (back issues avail.; reprint service avail.)
  Description: Covers the Church and the messages of the Mother of Jesus in her recent apparitions in various areas.

266 970.1 US
WIND RIVER RENDEZVOUS. 1971. q. $10. St. Stephens Indian Mission Foundation, Box 306, St. Stephens, WY 82524. FAX 307-856-6797. Ed. Ronald L. Mamot. illus.; circ. 33,000.

282 US ISSN 0745-0427
THE WITNESS (DUBUQUE). 1923. w. $12. (Archdiocese of Dubuque) Witness Publishing Company, 1229 Mt. Loretta Ave., Dubuque, IA 52003. TEL 319-588-0556. FAX 319-588-0557. (Subscr. to: Box 917, Dubuque, IA 52004-0917) Ed. Thomas J. Ralph. adv.; bk.rev.; circ. 17,736. (back issues avail.)
  Description: Provides national, international, and local news; includes announcements, op-ed, entertainment, television reviews and obituaries.

942 UK
WORCESTERSHIRE RECUSANT. 1963. s-a. membership. Worcestershire Catholic History Society, c/o Thomas Rock, More House, Haywood Drive, Tettenhall, Wolverhampton WV6 8RF, England. Ed. J.D. McEvilly. bibl.; circ. 150.

282 US ISSN 0742-4639
THE WORD AMONG US. Spanish edition: Palabra Entre Nosotros (ISSN 0896-1727) (Editions also avail. in Japanese, Polish, Portuguese) 1981. 11/yr. $18 for English ed.; Spanish ed. $12. Word Among Us Press, Inc., Box 6003, Gaithersburg, MD 20884-6003. TEL 301-990-2060. FAX 301-990-2087. (Alt. addr.: Box 2206, Gaithersburg MD 20884-0963) Ed. Anthony Bosnick. bk.rev.; circ. 190,000. (back issues avail.)
  Description: Catholic bible study and practical guide to Christian living.

282 US ISSN 0193-9211 BX801
WORD & SPIRIT. 1979. a. price varies. (St. Scholastica Priory) St. Bede's Publications, Box 545, Rt. 32, Petersham, MA 01366. TEL 508-724-3407. FAX 508-724-3574. Ed. Sr. Mary Joseph McManamon. circ. 300. (also avail. in microform from UMI; back issues avail.) **Indexed:** Cath.Ind., CERDIC, ERIC, Rel.& Theol.Abstr. (1979-). —BLDSC shelfmark: 9347.841000.
  Description: Focuses on scriptural, theological and spiritual themes, or commemorating the anniversary of a significant event in the history of Christianity.

282 299 AT ISSN 0155-6894
WORD IN LIFE. 1953. q. Aus.$20. Australian Catholic University, 179 Albert Rd., Strathfield, N.S.W. 2135, Australia. FAX 02-955-8932. Eds. C. Hill, L. Woods. bk.rev.; circ. 1,300. (back issues avail.) **Indexed:** CERDIC
  Formerly (until 1977): Our Apostolate.
  Description: Covers religious education.

WORKERS' CHALLENGE; from the workers to the workers. see BUSINESS AND ECONOMICS — Labor And Industrial Relations

282 NE
WORLD CHRISTIAN NEWS. 5/yr. $12 (foreign $14.50). Youth with a Mission, International Office, Prins Hendrikkade 50, 1012 AC Amsterdam, Netherlands.

282 947 US
WORLD LITHUANIAN ROMAN CATHOLIC DIRECTORY. 1975. irreg., latest 1986. $10. Lithuanian R.C. Priests' League, 600 Liberty Hwy., Putnam, CT 06260. TEL 203-928-9830. Ed. Victor Dabusis. adv.; stat.; circ. 1,000.

282 370 GW ISSN 0342-6378
WORT UND ANTWORT; Zeitschrift fuer Fragen des Glaubens. 1968. 4/yr. DM.32 (students DM.24). Matthias Gruenewald Verlag GmbH, Max-Hufschmidt-Str. 4a, 6500 Mainz-Weisenau, Germany. Ed. Paulus Engelhardt. adv.; bk.rev.; index; circ. 1,100. (back issues avail.)

266 US
XAVERIAN MISSIONS NEWSLETTER. 1951. bi-m. $5 donation. St. Francis Xavier Foreign Missionary Society, Inc., 101 Summer St., Holliston, MA 01746. Ed. Rev. Dominic Calarco. bk.rev.; circ. 30,000. (looseleaf format)
  Description: Carries reports on Xaverian foreign missions and on related subjects involving the work of the Xaverian missionaries. Includes correspondence from missionaries, appeals for vocations, and news of activities on the home front.

282 028.5 US
Y M I; youth and young adults of the Militia Immaculatae national newsletter. 1979. q. free. Spes Nostra Militia Immaculatae Center, 531 E. Merced Ave., W. Covina, CA 91790. TEL 818-917-0040. Ed.Bd. circ. 3,800. (back issues avail.)
  Former titles (until 1989): Youth Mission for the Immaculata International Newsletter; Youth Mission for the Immaculata National Newsletter.
  Description: Contains calendar of programs and testimonies. For spiritual formation of organization members, ages 9 to adult.

282 US
YOUTH UPDATE. m. $9. Franciscan Friars of St. John the Baptist Province) St. Anthony Messenger Press, 1615 Republic St., Cincinnati, OH 45210. TEL 513-241-5615. Ed. Carol Ann Morrow. circ. 25,000.
  Description: Newsletter on concerns of teenagers promoting Christian values.

266 US ISSN 0514-2482
ZEAL. 1952. q. free. (St. Elizabeth Mission Society) Franciscan Sisters of Allegany, Allegany, NY 14706. TEL 716-373-0200. Ed. Sr. Marie Dolores Gionta. circ. 10,000.

282 AU ISSN 0044-2895 BX803
ZEITSCHRIFT FUER KATHOLISCHE THEOLOGIE. 1877. q. S.728. (Universitaet Innsbruck, Theologische Fakultaet) Verlag Herder, Wollzeile 33, A-1010 Vienna, Austria. Ed. P. Hans Bernh Meyer. adv.; bk.rev.; bibl.; index, cum.index; circ. 900. **Indexed:** Canon Law Abstr., CERDIC, Old Test.Abstr.

280 GW
ZENTRALKOMITEE DER DEUTSCHEN KATHOLIKEN. MITTEILUNGEN. 1969. m. free. Zentralkomitee der deutschen Katholiken, Hochkreuzallee 246, 5300 Bonn 1, Germany. TEL 0228-316056. FAX 0228-384401. TELEX 172283-748. Ed. Friedrich Kronenberg. circ. 1,500.

282 GW ISSN 0179-6658
ZUR DEBATTE. 1970. bi-m. DM.21. Katholische Akademie in Bayern, Mandlstr. 23, Postfach 401008, 8000 Munich 40, Germany. TEL 089-381020. FAX 089-38102103.
  Description: Extracts of lectures given at the conferences at the academy.

282 GW ISSN 0342-6904
ZUR ZEIT; Zeitschrift der Redemptoristen. 1926. bi-m. DM.19.50 (foreign DM.23). Hofbauer-Verlag GmbH, Koelnstr. 417, 5300 Bonn 1, Germany. FAX 0228-672523. Ed.Bd. bk.rev.

RELIGIONS AND THEOLOGY — Other Denominations And Sects

281.62 US
A M A A NEWS. (Text in Armenian and English) 1967. bi-m. contributions. Armenian Missionary Association of America, Inc., 140 Forest Ave., Paramus, NJ 07652. TEL 201-265-2607. FAX 201-265-6015. Ed. Moses B. Janbazian. adv.; bk.rev.; illus.; cum.index; circ. 13,000.
  Formerly (until 1976): A M A A Newsletter; **Incorporates:** Armenian-American Outlook (ISSN 0004-2307)

289.9 UK
ACTION & RESOURCES FOR QUAKER PEACE AND SERVICE. 1984. 4/yr. free. Quaker Peace & Service, Friends House, Euston Rd., London NW1 2BJ, England. TEL 071-387-3601.
  Formerly: Action Resources (ISSN 0265-9344)

289 US
ACTS & FACTS. 1972. m. free. Institute for Creation Research, Box 2667, El Cajon, CA 92021. FAX 619-448-3469. Ed. Henry M. Morris. adv.; circ. 69,000. **Indexed:** CERDIC
  Description: Newsletter on the creation and evolution questions, including scientific articles.

289.9 DK ISSN 0109-1743
ADVANCE. (Text in English; available with French, German, Italian inserts) 1969. bi-m. membership. Church of Scientology, Advanced Organisation Saint Hill Europe and Africa, Jernbanegade 6, DK-1608 Copenhagen V, Denmark. TEL 45-33-11-11-69. Ed. Alan Graham, Michael Garbe. adv.; bk.rev.; illus; circ. 55,000.

289.9 250 US ISSN 0001-8589
ADVANCE (SPRINGFIELD); a magazine for Assemblies of God ministers and church leaders. 1965. m. $12. (General Council of the Assemblies of God) Gospel Publishing House, 1445 Boonville Ave., Springfield, MO 65802-9989. TEL 417-862-2781. Ed. Harris Jansen. adv.; bk.rev.; index, cum.index: 1965-1974, 1975-1979, 1980-1984; circ. 27,000.

289.9 US
ADVENT CHRISTIAN WITNESS. 1952. m. $11. Advent Christian General Conference of America, Box 23152, Charlotte, NC 28212. TEL 704-545-6161. FAX 704-573-0712. Ed. Rev. Robert J. Mayer. bk.rev.; illus.; circ. 4,000.
  Description: Promotes the gospel of Jesus Christ and the teaching of the Advent Christian Church.

RELIGIONS AND THEOLOGY — OTHER DENOMINATIONS AND SECTS

286 US ISSN 0360-389X
BX6101
ADVENTIST HERITAGE; a journal of Adventist history. 1974. q. $12 for 3 issues; Canada $18, elsewhere $22 for 4 issues. Loma Linda University, Riverside, Box 1158, 4700 Pierce St., Riverside, CA 92515. TEL 714-824-4942. FAX 714-824-4188. (Subscr. to: Loma Linda University Library, c/o Shirley Chipman, Heritage Rm., Loma Linda, CA, 92350) Ed. Dorothy Minchin-Comm. adv.; bk.rev.; illus.; circ. 2,000. (also avail. in microfilm from UMI; back issues avail.) **Indexed:** Amer.Hist.& Life, Hist.Abstr.
—BLDSC shelfmark: 0712.230950.

AFFINITY. see *HOMOSEXUALITY*

289.9 KE
AFROSCOPE. (Text in English and French) 1972. q. free. Association of Evangelicals of Africa and Madagascar, Box 49332, Nairobi, Kenya. FAX 254-2-710254. TELEX 23041-TRNKE. Ed. Gilbert Okoronkwoe. circ. 3,500 (2,500 English ed.; 1,000 French ed.).

200 II
AIM. (Text in English) 1970. m. Rs.50($20) Evangelical Fellowship of India, Publication Trust, 803 Deepali 92, Nehru Place, New Delhi 110, India. TEL 6431133. Ed. Rev. Francis Sunderaraj. adv.; bk.rev.; circ. 3,300.
Supersedes: Evangelical Fellowship Quarterly.
Description: Promotes partnership, the defense and confirmation of the Christian Gospel, as well as increasing Christian evangelicalism.

289 AU ISSN 0002-6514
ALTKATHOLISCHE KIRCHENZEITUNG. 1966. m. S.70($7) Altkatholische Kirche Oesterreichs, Schottenring 171312, A-1010 Vienna, Austria. TEL 0222-348394. Ed. Rudolf Repits. adv.; bk.rev.; illus.; circ. 2,700. (looseleaf format)
Formerly: Alt-Katholik.

289.9 US
AMERICAN BAHA'I. (Text in English, Persian, Spanish) 1969. 19/yr. National Spiritual Assembly of the Baha'is of the United States, 536 Sheridan Rd., Wilmette, IL 60091. TEL 708-869-9039. Ed. John Bowers. circ. 75,000. (tabloid format)
Description: Current events in the Baha'i community.

281.9 GR
ANALECTA VLATADON. irreg., latest no.50. price varies. Patriarchal Institute for Patristic Studies, Heptapyrgiou 64, 546 34 Thessaloniki, Greece.

281.9 UK ISSN 0265-1580
ANGLO ORTHODOXY. 1982. 3/yr. £3. Anglo-Orthodox Society, c/o Rev. P.S. Lansley, Hon.Sec., 31 King Coel Rd., Colchester, Essex CO3 5AQ, England. TEL 0206-562813. (Dist. by: Rev. Charles Lynch, 6454 Clarkston Rd., Clarkston, MI 48016) adv.; bk.rev.
Description: Covers Orthodox Christian faith, especially in its manifestation of traditional Anglicanism.

299.935 UK ISSN 0269-3259
ANTHROPOSOPHY TODAY. 1986. 3/yr. £7.50 to non-members. Anthroposophical Society in Great Britain, 35 Park Road, London NW1 6XT, England. TEL 071-723-4400. adv.; bk.rev.; circ. 2,800.
—BLDSC shelfmark: 1546.620000.
Former titles: Anthroposophical Review; Anthroposophical Quarterly.
Description: Covers Rudolf Steiner's anthroposophy and work arising from it.

281.9 CY
APOSTOLOS VARNAVAS. (Text in English and Greek) 1918. m. EC$5($15) Orthodox Church of Cyprus, Archbishopric of Cyprus, Nicosia, Cyprus. TEL 02-474411. FAX 02-474180. Ed. Andreas Mitsides. bk.rev.; circ. 1,500.

200 FR ISSN 0083-6184
ASSEMBLEES DE DIEU DE FRANCE. ANNUAIRE.* 1958. a. 8 F. Viens et Vois, 10 rue de Sentier, 75002 Paris, France.

281.9 GR
ATHENISIN ETHNIKON KAI KAPODISTRAKION PANEPISTEMION. THEOLOGIKE SCHOLE. EPISTEMONIKE EPETERIS. (Text in English, French and Greek) 1935. a. Athenisin Ethnikon kai Kapodistrakion, Theologike Schole, Odos Panepistimiou, Athens 143, Greece.

131.35 US ISSN 0004-7651
AUDITOR; the monthly scientology journal. 1964. m. membership. Church of Scientology Western United States, American Saint Hill Organization, 1413 N. Berendo St., Los Angeles, CA 90027-0972. TEL 213-660-5553. bk.rev.; bibl.; illus.; circ. 425,000.

289.9 DK
AUDITOR. (Editions for Africa, Europe, and U.S. avail.) 1969. m. membership. Church of Scientology, Advanced Organisation Saint Hill Europe and Africa, Jernbanegade 6, DK-1608 Copenhagen V, Denmark. Ed. Michael Garbe. bk.rev.; circ. 170,000.

AUM NAMO NARAYANAY. see *PHILOSOPHY*

255 PO
AVIVAMENTO. q. Esc.70. Casa Publicadoradas Assembleias de Deus, Av. Alm. Gago Coutinho 158, 1700 Lisbon, Portugal. Ed. Fernanco Martinez da Silva. circ. 4,000.

282 ISSN 0005-237X
AWAKE. (Editions in 66 languages) 1919. s-m. free. Watchtower Bible and Tract Society of New York, Inc., Writing Dept., 25 Columbia Hts., Brooklyn, NY 11201. TEL 718-625-3600. FAX 718-625-3062. Ed.Bd. circ. 13,110,000.

281.9 US ISSN 0278-551X
AXIOS; the orthodox journal. 1980. q. $10. Axios Newsletter, Inc., 800 S. Euclid St., Fullerton, CA 92632. TEL 714-526-4952. Ed. Daniel John Gorham. adv.; bk.rev.; circ. 8,759.

289.9 US
THE BANNER (ZANESVILLE); a newsletter for Christian Scientists. 1987. q. (plus special editions). free. 2040 Hazel Ave., Zanesville, OH 43701. bk.rev.
Description: Focuses on items of current interest and concern.

THE BAPTIST STANDARD. see *RELIGIONS AND THEOLOGY*

281 CN ISSN 0382-6384
BEACON; Ukrainian rite bi-monthly. Ukrainian edition: Svitlo - Light (ISSN 0039-7164) (Text in English) 1966. bi-m. Can.$12. (Order of Saint Basil-The-Great in Canada) Basilian Press, 265 Bering Ave., Etobicoke, Ont. M8Z 3A5, Canada. TEL 416-234-1212. Ed. Rev. Anthony Holowaychuk. adv.; bk.rev.; circ. 1,300.

268 US
BEADS OF TRUTH. 1972. s-a. $10. Three H O Foundation, 1620 Preuss Rd., Los Angeles, CA 90035. TEL 213-552-3416. Ed. S.S. Satsimran Kaur Khalsa. adv.; bk.rev.; illus.; circ. 3,000.

299.935 SZ
BEITRAEGE ZUR RUDOLF STEINER GESAMTAUSGABE. 1961. s-a. 24 Fr. Rudolf Steiner Verlag, Haus Duldeck, Postfach 135, CH-4143 Dornach, Switzerland. FAX 061-7012534. Ed. W. Kugler. circ. 2,000. (back issues avail.)
Description: Documents, notes, texts and other information from the Rudolf Steiner archives.

297.89 499.9 US
BELMONDA LETERO. (Text in Esperanto) 1973. q. membership only. Bahaa Esperanto-Ligo, RR 1, Box 29, Wilber, NE 68465. TEL 402-821-2027. Ed. June Knudsen Fritz. adv.; bk.rev.; circ. 500. (looseleaf format)
Description: News about the activities of Baha'i Esperantists around the world.

281.62 US ISSN 0199-8765
BEMA. 1980. m. membership. Diocese of the Armenian Church of America, 630 Second Ave., New York, NY 10016. TEL 212-686-0710. Ed. Michael Zeytoonian. bk.rev.; illus.; circ. 8,500. **Indexed:** CERDIC.
Supersedes: Armenian Church (ISSN 0004-2315) & Hayastanyaitz Yegeghetzy (ISSN 0017-8667)

398.7 US
BIBLE TEACHER AND LEADER. q. $14. Standard Publishing, 8121 Hamilton Ave., Cincinnati, OH 45231. TEL 513-931-4050. Ed. James I. Fehl.
Description: Sunday-school lesson manual for teachers of adults.

268.1 NE ISSN 0006-2243
BIJBELLESSEN VOOR DE SABBATSCHOOL. 1897. q. fl.5.50. (Zevende-Dags Adventisten - Seventh-Day Adventists) Stichting Uitgeverij "Veritas", Biltseweg 14, 3735 ME Bosch en Duin, Netherlands. FAX 030-281084. illus.

377 CN ISSN 0006-4327
BLACKBOARD BULLETIN. 1957. m. (10/yr.). $6. (Amish Church) Pathway Publishing Corporation, Route 4, Aylmer, Ont. N5H 2R3, Canada. Ed. Elizabeth Wengerd. illus.; circ. 13,000.

289 NE
BOODSCHAP. 1978. q. fl.20. Soefi-Orde Nederland, Hermelijnlaan 9, 1216 EB Hilversum, Netherlands. Ed. Akbar Helweg. adv.; bk.rev.; circ. 350.

289.7 CN ISSN 0006-8209
BOTE; ein mennonitsches Familienblatt. (Text and summaries in German) 1924. w. Can.$24. General Conference Mennonite Church, 600 Shaftesbury Blvd., Winnipeg, Man. R3P 0M4, Canada. TEL 204-888-6781. FAX 204-831-5675. (Co-sponsor: Conference of Mennonites in Canada) Ed. Erwin Strempler. adv.; bk.rev.; circ. 5,500. (tabloid format) **Indexed:** CERDIC.

BRAILLE STAR THEOSOPHIST. see *HANDICAPPED — Visually Impaired*

200 US
BREAKTHROUGH (WHEATON). 1971. bi-m. free. Slavic Gospel Association, Box 1122, Wheaton, IL 60189. TEL 312-690-8900. Ed. Wil Triggs. charts; illus.; circ. 60,000.
Incorporates (1927-1989): EuroVision Advance; **Formerly:** Slavic Gospel News (ISSN 0049-0709)

289.9 US ISSN 0006-9663
BX7801
BRETHREN LIFE AND THOUGHT; a quarterly journal published in the interest of the Church of the Brethren. 1955. q. $15. Brethren Journal Association and Bethany Theological Seminary, c/o Christina Bucher, Ed., Elizabethtown College, One Alpha Dr., Elizabethtown, PA 17022-2298. bk.rev.; cum.index: vols.1-26; circ. 800. (also avail. in microfilm from UMI; reprint service avail. from UMI) **Indexed:** Rel.& Theol.Abstr. (1968-), Rel.Ind.One.
—BLDSC shelfmark: 2279.732000.

266 US ISSN 0161-5238
BRETHREN MISSIONARY HERALD. 1940. m. $12.50. (Fellowship of Grace Brethren Churches) Brethren Missionary Herald, Inc., Box 544, Winona Lake, IN 46590. TEL 219-267-7158. FAX 219-267-4745. Ed. Charles W. Turner. adv.; bk.rev.; illus.; circ. 5,000. (controlled). (back issues avail.)

BRILLIANT STAR. see *CHILDREN AND YOUTH — For*

266 GW ISSN 0724-4533
DER BRUEDERBOTE. 1949. m. DM.36. (Europaeisch-Festlaendische Brueder-Unitaet - Moravian Church of Europe) Quell Verlag, Postfach 103852, 7000 Stuttgart 1, Germany. TEL 0711-60100-0. adv.; bk.rev.; illus.; circ. 1,500.

289 US ISSN 0745-1687
BUILDER (SCOTTDALE). 1950. m. $26.40. Mennonite Publishing House, 616 Walnut Ave., Scottdale, PA 15683. TEL 412-887-8500. FAX 412-887-3111. (Co-publisher: Faith and Life Press) Ed. David Hiebert. illus.; circ. 10,000.
Description: Directed to Christian educators and congregational leaders. Includes Sunday school teaching guide for each Sunday, following the Uniform Series outline.

C H I L D NEWSLETTER. (Children's Healthcare is a Legal Duty) see *CHILDREN AND YOUTH — About*

289.9 US
C O G NEWSLETTER. 1975. 8/yr. $20 suggested donation. Covenant of the Goddess, Box 1226, Berkeley, CA 94704. adv.; bk.rev.; circ. 200.
Description: Wiccan and Pagan news, original articles, poetry, music, humor, rituals, and announcements.

RELIGIONS AND THEOLOGY — OTHER DENOMINATIONS AND SECTS

289.1   GW
C Z B REPORT. 1986. bi-m. free. Christliches Zentrum Berlin e.V., Herwarthstr. 5, 1000 Berlin 45, Germany. TEL 030-772021. FAX 030-7736376. Eds. Petre Dippl, Peter Winkel. circ. 9,000.

299.6   ZR   ISSN 0008-0047
BL2400
CAHIERS DES RELIGIONS AFRICAINES. (Text in English, French) 1967. s-a. $35. Faculte de Theologie Catholique de Kinshasa, P.O. Box 712, Kinshasa - Limete, Zaire. TEL 78476. (Co-sponsor: Centr D'Etudes de Religions Africaines) Ed. Vincent Mulago. adv.; bk.rev.; bibl.; illus.; circ. 1,000. **Indexed:** A.I.C.P., CERDIC, Curr.Cont.Africa.

281.62   CN
CANADA ARMENIAN PRESS. NEWSLETTER. (Text in Armenian, English) 1963. q. contributions. Armenian Evangelical Church, 34 Glenforest Rd., Toronto, Ont. M4N 1Z8, Canada. TEL 416-489-3188. Ed. Rev. Yesai Sarmazian. adv.; bk.rev.; illus.; circ. 450.
Formerly: Canada Armenian Press (ISSN 0008-2562)

289   CN   ISSN 0820-554X
CANADIAN MESSENGER OF THE SACRED HEART. 1891. m. Can.$8. Apostleship of Prayer, 661 Greenwood Ave., Toronto, Ont. M4J 4B3, Canada. TEL 416-466-1195. Ed. Rev. F.J. Power, S.J. illus.; circ. 18,600. (back issues avail.)

289.6   CN   ISSN 1180-968X
CANADIAN QUAKER HISTORY JOURNAL. 1972. 2/yr. Can.$15 to individuals; libraries and institutions Can.$20 (students $8). Canadian Friends Historical Association, 60 Lowther Ave., Toronto, Ont. M5R 1C7, Canada. TEL 416-839-5935. Eds. Kathleen Hertzberg, Jane Zavitz. bk.rev.; bibl.; charts; illus.; stat.; index, cum.index; circ. 200.
Formerly: Canadian Quaker Historic Newsletter (ISSN 0319-3934)

CENTER FOR PROCESS STUDIES. NEWSLETTER. see *PHILOSOPHY*

289.9   US
CHILDREN OF THE EARTH; for Pagan families with kids. 4/yr. $5. Cassidy, Box 1896, Elkins, WV 25341-1896. bk.rev.; illus.

200   UK   ISSN 0009-5117
CHRISTADELPHIAN; dedicated wholly to the hope of Israel. 1864. m. £21($37.20) (effective 1992). Christadelphian Magazine and Publishing Association Ltd., 404 Shaftmoor Lane, Hall Green, Birmingham B28 8SZ, England. TEL 021-777-6328. FAX 021-778-5024. Ed. Michael Ashton. bk.rev.; illus.; index; circ. 6,700.
Description: Promotes bible study and a better understanding of Christadelphian beliefs.

284   US   ISSN 0893-8571
CHRISTIAN CONTENDER. 1983. a. $1. Christian Chamber of Commerce, Box 840555, Houston, TX 77284-0555. TEL 713-855-3357. Ed. John P. Hansen. circ. 10,000. (tabloid format; back issues avail.)

267   UK
CHRISTIAN ENDEAVOUR PROGRAMME BOOK. 1896. a. £2.50. Christian Endeavour Union of Great Britain and Ireland, Wellesbourne House, Walton Rd., Wellesbourne, Warwickshire CV35 9JB, England. TEL 0789-470439. Ed. Keith Bernhardt. adv.; bk.rev.; circ. 1,000.
Former titles: Christian Endeavour Topic Book; Christian Endeavour Year Book (ISSN 0069-3863)
Description: Covers missions and missionary work in the U.K.

298.7   US   ISSN 1080-8000
CHRISTIAN EXAMPLE. 1961. fortn. $7.50. Rod and Staff Publishers, Inc., State Rte. 172, Crockett, KY 41413. TEL 606-522-4348. FAX 606-522-4896. Ed. James L. Boll. circ. 4,800.

289.7   US   ISSN 0009-5419
CHRISTIAN LEADER. 1937. fortn. $12. (U S Conference of Mennonite Brethren Churches) Mennonite Brethren Publishing House, Box L, Hillsboro, KS 67063. Ed. Don Ratzlaff. adv.; bk.rev.; index; circ. 9,500.

281.9   GR
CHRISTIAN LITERATURE. irreg., latest vol.3. price varies. Patriarchal Institute for Patristic Studies, Heptapyrgiou 64, 546 34 Thessaloniki, Greece.

CHRISTIAN SCIENCE BIBLE LESSONS (BRAILLE EDITION). see *HANDICAPPED — Visually Impaired*

289.5   US   ISSN 0009-5613
BX6901
CHRISTIAN SCIENCE JOURNAL. 1883. m. $30. Christian Science Publishing Society, Box 11341, Des Moines, IA 50350-1341. TEL 800-456-4851. Ed. Allison W. Phinney. index. **Indexed:** CERDIC.

289.9   US
CHRISTIAN SCIENCE OPEN FORUM. m. free. 464 N. 43rd St., Seattle, WA 98103. TEL 206-632-2018.

289.5 252   US   ISSN 0145-7365
BX6901
CHRISTIAN SCIENCE QUARTERLY (INKPRINT EDITION); Bible lessons. Danish edition (ISSN 0145-739X); Dutch edition (ISSN 0145-742X); French edition (ISSN 0145-7438); German edition (ISSN 0145-7411); Greek edition (ISSN 0145-9503) Italian edition (US ISSN 0145-7373) Japanese edition (US ISSN 0145-7527) Norwegian edition (US ISSN 0145-7381) Polish edition (US ISSN 0145-7446) (Portuguese edition (ISSN 0145-7454); Spanish edition (ISSN 0145-7462); Swedish edition (ISSN 0145-7403)) 1890. q. $8. Christian Science Publishing Society, Box 11388, Des Moines, IA 50350-1388. TEL 800-456-4851. (also avail. in Braille)

289.5   US   ISSN 0009-563X
CHRISTIAN SCIENCE SENTINEL. 1898. w. $45. Christian Science Publishing Society, Box 11342, Des Moines, IA 50350-1342. TEL 800-456-4851. Ed. Allison W. Phinney. adv.; index. **Indexed:** CERDIC.

289.3   US
CHURCH NEWS (SALT LAKE CITY). 1931. w. $13. Church of Jesus Christ of Latter-day Saints, Corporation of the President, 50 E. North Temple, Salt Lake City, UT 84150. TEL 801-240-1000. FAX 801-240-1727. Ed. Dell Van Orden. circ. 225.
Description: Contains news of the Church.

289.9   US   ISSN 1047-4196
CIRCLE NETWORK NEWS; international nature spirituality networking newspaper - journal. 1980. 4/yr. $13 (foreign $24). Circle Sanctuary, Box 219, Mt. Horeb, WI 53572. TEL 608-924-2216. Ed. Dennis Carpenter. adv.; bk.rev.; illus. (tabloid format; back issues avail.)

289   UK   ISSN 0263-6743
CLARITY. 1968. bi-m. £3.50. Clarity Publications, 26 Valleyside, Hemel Hempstead, Herts, HP1 2LN, England. TEL 0442-252542. Ed. Jennifer Sprague. bk.rev.; index; circ. 165. (back issues avail.)
Description: Covers all aspects of Christianity.

266   US
COLUMBIA UNION VISITOR. 1895. s-m. $7.50. (Columbia Union Conference of Seventh-Day Adventists) Review and Herald Publishing Association, 55 W. Oak Ridge Dr., Hagerstown, MD 21740. TEL 301-791-7000. Ed. Kermit Netteberg. adv.; bk.rev.; circ. 35,000.

289   AT   ISSN 0004-9662
COMMUNION. 1962. q. Aus.$13. Liberal Catholic Church in Australia, P.O. Box 220, Glebe, N.S.W. 2037, Australia. TEL 02-660-6242. FAX 02-692-8373. (Subscr. to: Communion, P.O. Box 1371, Lane Cove, N.S.W. 2066, Australia) Ed. Rev. Ronald Rivett. bk.rev.; illus.; circ. 500. **Indexed:** CERDIC.
Formerly: Australian Liberal Catholic.
Description: Publishes articles on religious thought, poems, letters, church notices etc.

CONCORD. see *HOMOSEXUALITY*

COPTOLOGIA; journal of coptic thought and orthodox spirituality. see *RELIGIONS AND THEOLOGY*

281.9 950   BE   ISSN 0070-0398
CORPUS SCRIPTORUM CHRISTIANORUM: AETHIOPICA. (Text in Amharic) 1904. irreg., no.82, 1987. price varies. (Universitatis Catholicae Lovaniensis) Editions Peeters s.p.r.l., Bondgenotenlaan 153, B-3000 Leuven, Belgium. TEL 016-235170. FAX 016-228500. TELEX 65981 PULB. (Co-sponsor: Catholic University of America) bk.rev.

281.9 950   BE   ISSN 0070-0401
CORPUS SCRIPTORUM CHRISTIANORUM ORIENTALIUM: ARABICA. (Text in Arabic) 1903. irreg., no.47, 1987. price varies. (Universitatis Catholicae Lovaniensis) Editions Peeters s.p.r.l., Bondgenotenlaan 153, B-3000 Leuven, Belgium. TEL 016-235170. FAX 016-228500. TELEX 65981 PULB. (Co-sponsor: Catholic University of America) bk.rev.

281.9 950   BE   ISSN 0070-041X
CORPUS SCRIPTORUM CHRISTIANORUM ORIENTALIUM: ARMENIACA. (Text in Armenian) 1953. irreg., no.18, 1987. price varies. (Universitatis Catholicae Lovaniensis) Editions Peeters s.p.r.l., Bondgenotenlaan 153, B-3000 Leuven, Belgium. TEL 016-235170. FAX 016-228500. TELEX 65981 PULB. (Co-sponsor: Catholic University of America) bk.rev.

281.9 950   BE   ISSN 0070-0428
CORPUS SCRIPTORUM CHRISTIANORUM ORIENTALIUM: COPTICA. (Text in Coptic) 1906. irreg., no.42, 1980. price varies. (Universitatis Catholicae Lovaniensis) Editions Peeters s.p.r.l., Bondgenotenlaan 153, B-3000 Leuven, Belgium. TEL 016-235170. FAX 016-228500. TELEX 65981 PULB. (Co-sponsor: Catholic University of America) bk.rev.

281.9 950   BE   ISSN 0070-0436
CORPUS SCRIPTORUM CHRISTIANORUM ORIENTALIUM: IBERICA. (Text in Georgian) 1950. irreg., no.22, 1986. price varies. (Universitatis Catholicae Lovaniensis) Editions Peeters s.p.r.l., Bondgenotenlaan 153, B-3000 Leuven, Belgium. TEL 016-235170. FAX 016-228500. TELEX 65981 PULB. (Co-sponsor: Catholic University of America) bk.rev.

281.9 950   BE   ISSN 0070-0444
CORPUS SCRIPTORUM CHRISTIANORUM ORIENTALIUM: SUBSIDIA. (Text in English, French, German) 1950. irreg., no.79, 1987. price varies. (Universitatis Catholicae Lovaniensis) Editions Peeters s.p.r.l., Bondgenotenlaan 153, B-3000 Leuven, Belgium. TEL 016-235170. FAX 016-228500. TELEX 65981 PULB. (Co-sponsor: Catholic University of America) bk.rev.

281.9 950   BE   ISSN 0070-0452
CORPUS SCRIPTORUM CHRISTIANORUM ORIENTALIUM: SYRIACA. (Text in Syriac) 1903. irreg., no.208, 1987. price varies. (Universitatis Catholicae Lovaniensis) Editions Peeters s.p.r.l., Bondgenotenlaan 153, B-3000 Leuven, Belgium. TEL 016-235170. FAX 016-228500. TELEX 65981 PULB. (Co-sponsor: Catholic University of America) bk.rev.

289.9   US
COUNCIL OF THE MYSTIC ARTS. NEWSLETTER. 12/yr. $24. Council of the Mystic Arts, Spectrum of the Seven Keys, 538 Hammond Ave., San Antonio, TX 78210. illus.

285.734   US   ISSN 0011-0671
COVENANT COMPANION. 1926. m. $24. (Evangelical Covenant Church) Covenant Publications, 5101 N. Francisco Ave., Chicago, IL 60625. TEL 312-784-3000. FAX 312-784-4366. Ed. James R. Hawkinson. adv.; bk.rev.; index; circ. 24,000.

289   UK
COVENANT VOICE. 1945. m. £4 to non-members. Covenant Peoples Fellowship, 87 St. Barnabas Rd., Woodford Green, Essex IG8 7BT, England. Ed. Rev. Francis Thomas. charts; illus.; index; circ. 4,000.
Formerly (until June 1982): Brith (ISSN 0007-0211)

CRIME AND JUSTICE NETWORK NEWSLETTER. see *CRIMINOLOGY AND LAW ENFORCEMENT*

RELIGIONS AND THEOLOGY — OTHER DENOMINATIONS AND SECTS

281.0 YU
CRKVA/CHURCH; kalendar Srpske Pravoslavne Patrijarsije. (Text in Serbian) 1965. a. price varies. Sveti Arhijerejski Sinod, Sedmoga Jula 5, 11000 Beograd, Yugoslavia. TEL 011 635-699. circ. 25,000.

207 CI ISSN 0352-4000
CRKVA U SVIJETU. (Text in Croatian; summaries in English and French) 1966. q. $25. Nadbiskupija Splitsko-Makarska, Zrinjsko-Frankopanska 14, 58001 Split, Croatia. Ed. Drago Simundza. bk.rev.; circ. 2,000.

266 US ISSN 0045-9119
CROSSROADS (LE MARS). 1972. bi-m. £3($5) Middle East Christian Outreach Ltd., Box 502, Le Mars, IA 51031. TEL 712-546-5947. (UK addr.: 22 Culverden Park Rd., Tunbridge Wells, Kent TN4 9RA, England) Ed. Peter D.L. Thomson. adv.; circ. 5,000.
Description: Covers Christian Mission in the Middle East.

CULT AWARENESS NETWORK NEWS. see *PSYCHOLOGY*

289 US ISSN 0011-538X
DAILY BLESSING. 1959. q. $2. Oral Roberts Evangelistic Association Inc., Box 2187, Tulsa, OK 74101. TEL 918-495-6161. Eds. Oral Roberts, Betty Howard. circ. 425,000.

242.2 US ISSN 0092-7147
BV4810
DAILY BREAD; a devotional guide for every day of the year. 1969. a. $9.50. (Reorganized Church of Jesus Christ of Latter Day Saints) Herald Publishing House, 3225 S. Noland Rd., Box HH, Independence, MO 64055. TEL 816-252-5010. FAX 816-252-3976. Ed. Richard Brown. circ. 10,000.

200 US
DANICA; hrvatski tjednik. (Text in Croatian; summaries in Croatian and English) 1921. w. $30. (Croatian Center Association) Croatian Franciscan Press, 4851 Drexel Blvd., Chicago, IL 60615. TEL 312-268-2819. Ed. Fr. Castimir Majic. adv.; bk.rev.; circ. 5,000. (tabloid format)

289.3 US
DESERET NEWS. w. Church of Jesus Christ of Latter-day Saints, Corporation of the President, 50 E. North Temple, Salt Lake City, UT 84150. TEL 801-240-1000. FAX 801-240-1727.

289.3 US ISSN 0093-786X
BX8606
DESERET NEWS CHURCH ALMANAC. 1974. biennial. $6. Deseret News Publishing Co., Box 1257, Salt Lake City, UT 84110. TEL 801-237-2141. FAX 801-237-2121. Ed. Dell Van Orden. circ. 20,000.
Description: Covers church news of the Church of Jesus Christ of Latter-Day Saints.

281.9 US
DESERT VOICE. 1985. 5/yr. donations. (Monastery of St. Anthony the Great) St. Anthony the Great Orthodox Publications, Box 1432, Alamogordo, NM 88311-1432. (Subscr. to: 344 N. 27th St., Phoenix, AZ 85016) Ed. Rev. Fr. Bessarion Agioantonides. adv.; bk.rev.; tr.lit.; circ. 3,000. (tabloid format)
Formerly: Orthodox Southwest (ISSN 0897-7682)

261 CE ISSN 0012-2181
DIALOGUE. 1963. 3/yr. $10. Ecumenical Institute for Study and Dialogue, 490-5 Havelock Rd., Colombo 6, Sri Lanka. Ed. Fr. Aloysius Pieris. adv.; bk.rev.; circ. 1,000. **Indexed:** Rel.Ind.One.

289.3 US ISSN 0012-2157
BX8601
DIALOGUE: A JOURNAL OF MORMON THOUGHT. 1966. q. $25 to individuals; students and senior citizens $20. Dialogue Foundation, UMC 7805, University Sta., Logan, UT 84322-7805. TEL 801-750-1154. Eds. F. Ross Peterson, Mary Kay Peterson. bk.rev.; charts; illus.; index, cum.index: 1966-1987; circ. 4,000. (also avail. in microform from UMI; back issues avail.) **Indexed:** Amer.Hist.& Life, Hist.Abstr., Rel.Ind.One.
Description: Contains articles, essays, poetry, fiction and art.

299 II ISSN 0253-519X
DISCOURSE. (Text in English) 1972. m. Rs.10($10) Society of Servants of God, Yashwant Place, Satya Marg, Chanakyapuri, New Delhi 110021, India. Ed. Sundri P. Vaswani. bibl.; index; circ. 650.

200 US ISSN 0733-5369
DIVINE SLAVE GITA. (Between 1988 and 1989, incorporated in Tawagoto (ISSN 1047-4250)) q. $20. (Hohm Community) Hohm Press, Box 2501, Prescott, AZ 86302. TEL 602-778-9189. Eds. Jaya Hoy, Anthony Zuccarello. adv.; bk.rev.; circ 100 (controlled).
Description: An in-house publication chronicling the process of spiritual growth of the members of Hohm.

DRUID HENGE. see *PARAPSYCHOLOGY AND OCCULTISM*

264.01 UK ISSN 0012-8732
EASTERN CHURCHES NEWS LETTER. 1955. s-a. £3. Anglican & Eastern Churches Association, St. Dustan-in-the-West, 184 Fleet St., London EC4A 2EA, England. TEL 01-405 1929. Ed. Rev. Columba Graham Flegg. adv.; bk.rev.; record rev.; circ. 850.
Description: Includes news items, theological and historical articles, correspondence and announcements of events.

284.2 266 NE ISSN 0012-9119
ECHO; hervormd blad. 1952. 12/yr. fl.10. Hervormde Bond voor Inwendige Zending - Reformed Alliance for Home Mission, Johan van Oldenbarneveltlaan 10, Amersfoort, Netherlands. FAX 033-637093. Ed. M.E. Brak. illus.; circ. 20,000.

289.9 US
ECKANKAR JOURNAL. 1976. a. $4. Eckankar Publications, Box 27300, Minneapolis, MN 55427-0300. FAX 612-544-3754. Ed. Beverly Foster. circ. 20,000.
Former titles (until Oct. 1988): Eck Mata Journal; Eck News.
Description: Personal experience with the Holy Spirit, the Light and Sound of God.

281.9 HU ISSN 0133-0047
EGYHAZI KRONIKA; keleti orthodox egyhazi folyoirat. 1952. bi-m. 120 Ft.($2) Magyar Orthodox Adminisztratura, Petofi ter 2, 1052 Budapest, Hungary. TEL 1-184-813. Ed. Dr. Feriz Berki. circ. 500. (back issues avail.)
Description: Contains ecclesiastic news and religious articles for Christian Orthodox people.

289.3 US ISSN 0884-1136
BX8601
ENSIGN. 1971. m. $10. Church of Jesus Christ of Latter-day Saints, Corporation of the President, 50 E. North Temple, Salt Lake City, UT 84150. TEL 801-240-2947. FAX 801-240-1727. Ed.Bd. charts; illus.; circ. 585.
Formerly (until 1979): Ensign of the Church of Jesus Christ of Latter-day Saints (ISSN 0013-8606)
Description: Contains news of the Church, "Message of the First Presidency," and articles pertaining to all adult church members worldwide.

ENSIGN TALKING BOOK. see *HANDICAPPED — Visually Impaired*

298.7 US
ESTRELLA DE ESPERANZA. (Text in Spanish) 1967. m. $3.75. Rod and Staff Publishers, Inc., State Rte. 172, Crockett, KY 41413. TEL 606-522-4348. FAX 606-522-4896. Ed. Eugene G. Cambell. circ. 6,800. (back issues avail.)

261 US ISSN 0014-1682
BR1
ETERNITY; the magazine of Christian truth. 1950. m. $14.95. Foundation for Christian Living, 1716 Spruce St., Philadelphia, PA 19103. TEL 215-546-3696. Ed. Donald J. McCrory. adv.; bk.rev.; illus.; index; circ. 40,000. (also avail. in microform from UMI) **Indexed:** CCR, Chr.Per.Ind., G.Soc.Sci.& Rel.Per.Lit.

284 US ISSN 0014-3340
EVANGELICAL FRIEND. 1967. bi-m. $10.95. (Evangelical Friends Alliance) Barclay Press, 600 E. Third St., Newberg, OR 97132. TEL 503-538-7345. FAX 503-538-7033. Eds. Paul Anderson, Dan McCracken. adv.; bk.rev.; illus.; circ. 10,500.
Description: Provides articles addressing a broad range of Christian concerns and news.

200 CN ISSN 0014-3375
EVANGELICAL TRUTH. (Text in English, Ukrainian) 1939. bi-m. free. Rev. M. Fesenko, Ed. & Pub., 26 Robina Ave., Toronto, Ont. M6C 3Y6, Canada. TEL 416-654-4870. bk.rev.; illus.; circ. 1,000.

289.9 SW ISSN 0345-2980
EVANGELII HAEROLD. 1916. w. SEK 395 (typically set in Sep.). (Pingstroerelsen) Dagengruppen AB, Dagenhuset, 105 36 Stockholm, Sweden. FAX 08-6192416. Ed. Daniel Waern. adv.; circ. 20,000.

053 020 GW ISSN 0930-8873
DER EVANGELISCHE BUCHBERATER. 1947. q. DM.20. Deutscher Verband Evangelischer Buechereien e.V., Buergerstr. 2, 3400 Goettingen, Germany. FAX 0551-704415. Ed.Bd. bk.rev.; index; circ. 3,400. (back issues avail.)

200 US ISSN 0014-3626
EVANGELIST (PASADENA). (Editions in Arabic, Armenian, Dutch, English, German) 1960. q. £L5($2) Bible Land Mission, 814 E. Claremont St., Pasadena, CA 91104. TEL 818-798-7177. FAX 818-791-0036. Ed. Samuel Doctorian. bk.rev.; illus.; circ. 20,000.

248.4 SA ISSN 0014-7044
FAITH FOR DAILY LIVING; a guide to confident Christian living. (Text in English) 1960. bi-m. free. Faith for Daily Living Foundation, P.O. Box 3737, Durban, Natal, South Africa. Ed. Arnold J. Walker. circ. 120,000 (controlled).

289.73 CN ISSN 0014-7303
FAMILY LIFE. 1968. m. (11/yr.). $9. (Amish Church) Pathway Publishing Corporation, Route 4, Aylmer, Ont. N5H 2R3, Canada. bk.rev.; illus.; circ. 19,000. (also avail. in microform from UMI; back issues avail.; reprint service avail. from UMI)

266 US
FAR EAST REPORTER (HOUSTON). vol.22, 1976. bi-m. $5. Church of Houston Baptist International, Inc., Box 3333, Houston, TX 77253-3333. TEL 713-820-9111. Ed. Deanza Brock. illus.; circ. 200,000.

200 US ISSN 0014-8830
FATIMA FINDINGS; the smallest newspaper on earth for the greatest cause in heaven. 1946. m. $5 (foreign $5.50). Reparation Society of the Immaculate Heart of Mary, Inc., Fatima House, 100 E. 20th St., Baltimore, MD 21218-6091. TEL 410-685-7403. Ed. Rev. John Ryan, S.J. circ. 4,000 (controlled). (back issues avail.)
Description: Spreads knowledge of and devotion to Our Blessed Lady of Fatima and her message.

200 US ISSN 0014-9837
FELLOWSHIP IN PRAYER. 1949. bi-m. $16. Fellowship in Prayer, Inc., 291 Witherspoon St., Princeton, NJ 08542-3269. TEL 609-924-6863. Ed. Mary Ford-Grabowsky. bk.rev.; circ. 20,000. (back issues avail.)

289.9 US
FIERY SYNTHESIS. 1965. 12/yr. $10 donation. Aquarian Educational Group, Box 267, Sedona, AZ 86336. Ed. Torkum Saraydarian. bk.rev.; circ. 600.
Formerly: Blue Aquarius.

FISH DRUM. see *LITERATURE*

289 US ISSN 0015-9182
FOURSQUARE WORLD ADVANCE. 1923. bi-m. free. International Church of the Foursquare Gospel, 1910 Sunset Blvd., Ste. 200, Los Angeles, CA 90026-3282. TEL 213-484-2400. FAX 213-413-3824. Ed. Ron Williams. bk.rev.; illus.; circ. 95,000.
Formerly: Foursquare Magazine.

200 UK ISSN 0016-0334
FREE CHURCH OF SCOTLAND. MONTHLY RECORD. (Text in English and Gaelic) 1843. m. £8.20 (typically set in Oct.). Free Church of Scotland Publications Committee, 15 N. Bank St., Edinburgh 2LS, Scotland. TEL 031-226-5286. FAX 031-220-0597. Ed. Ronald C. Christie. bk.rev.; circ. 7,000. (tabloid format; reprint service avail. from UMI)

FREEDOM MAGAZINE. see *JOURNALISM*

RELIGIONS AND THEOLOGY — OTHER DENOMINATIONS AND SECTS

289.6   UK   ISSN 0016-1268
FRIEND; a Quaker weekly journal. 1843. w. £90. Friend Publications Ltd., Drayton House, 30 Gordon St., London WC1H 0BQ, England. TEL 071-387-7549. Ed. Sally Juniper. adv.; bk.rev.; illus.; index; circ. 6,000. (also avail. in microform from WMP)

289.6 248.82   US   ISSN 0009-4102
FRIEND. 1971. m. $8. Church of Jesus Christ of Latter-day Saints, Corporation of the President, 50 E. North Temple, Salt Lake City, UT 84150. TEL 801-240-2947. Ed. Vivian Paulsen. bk.rev.; illus.; index; circ. 210,000. (also avail. in Braille)
  Supersedes: Children's Friend.
  Description: Contains stories and activities for children, or parents with children - ages 3 to 11.

289.6 305.412   US   ISSN 0740-5618
BX7748.W64
FRIENDLY WOMAN; a journal for exchange of ideas, feelings, hopes and experiences by and among Quaker women. 1974. q. $12. Eugene Friendly Women, 84889 Harry Taylor Rd., Eugene, OR 97405. TEL 503-345-3962. Ed. Lois Barton. adv.; bk.rev.; circ. 1,100.

267   UK   ISSN 0071-9587
BX7676.A1
FRIENDS HISTORICAL SOCIETY. JOURNAL. 1903. a. £4($8) to individuals; institutions £6($15). Friends Historical Society, Friends House, Euston Rd., London NW1 2BJ, England. Ed. Gerald A.J. Hodgett. adv.; bk.rev.; circ. 500. **Indexed:** Amer.Hist.& Life, Br.Hum.Ind., Hist.Abstr.

289.6   US   ISSN 0016-1322
BX7601
FRIENDS JOURNAL. 1955. m. $18. (Religious Society of Friends) Friends Publishing Corp., 1501 Cherry St., Philadelphia, PA 19102. TEL 215-241-7277. FAX 215-568-1377. Ed. Vinton Deming. adv.; bk.rev.; film rev.; illus.; index; circ. 9,000. (also avail. in microform from UMI; reprint service avail. from UMI)
  Description: Includes articles on peace, social concerns, Quaker history, and spirituality. Contains poetry, news, humor, reports and classified advertisements on schools, publications, services and employment opportunities.

200   UK   ISSN 0016-1357
FRIENDS' QUARTERLY. N.S. 1946. q. £7.68($17.50) Headley Bros. Ltd., Ashford, Kent TN24 8HH, England. Ed. David Blamires. cum.index every 3 yrs.; circ. 1,175. **Indexed:** Br.Hum.Ind.
  —BLDSC shelfmark: 4038.300000.

FRIENDS' QUARTERLY (ENFIELD). see *MUSEUMS AND ART GALLERIES*

289.6   UK   ISSN 0016-1365
FRIENDS WORLD NEWS. 1939. 2/yr. free to contributors. Friends World Committee for Consultation, 4 Bying Pl., London WC1E 7JH, England. FAX 071-383-3722. Ed. Thomas F. Taylor. bk.rev.; illus.; circ. 9,100. **Indexed:** CERDIC.
  Description: Presents articles from Quakers worldwide.

242   US   ISSN 0016-2264
FRUIT OF THE VINE; Friends daily devotional readings. 1961. q. $8. (Friends Church, Northwest Yearly Meeting) Barclay Press, 600 E. Third St., Newberg, OR 97132. TEL 503-538-7345. FAX 503-538-7033. Ed. Harlow Ankeny. illus.; circ. 5,000.
  Description: Daily devotional writing by writers from the Friends Church.

200   US   ISSN 0042-8264
FULL GOSPEL BUSINESS MEN'S VOICE. 1953. m. $7.95. Full Gospel Business Men's Fellowship International, 3150 Bear St., Box 5050, Costa Mesa, CA 92626. TEL 714-754-1400. FAX 714-557-9916. Ed. Jerry Jensen. bk.rev.; circ. 500,000. (back issues avail.)
  Description: Designed to reach business men for Christ. Used by the organization's chapters and individuals as a witness tool.

289   SA   ISSN 0016-3988
GALAMUKANI!. (Text in Chichewa) 1957. m. R.8.50. Watch Tower Bible & Tract Society, Private Bag 2067, Krugersdorp 1740, South Africa. TEL 011-761-1000. FAX 011-764-4749. charts, illus.; index; circ. 5,900.

200   UK   ISSN 0072-0666
GENERAL CONFERENCE OF THE NEW CHURCH. YEARBOOK. 1789. a. £3 (typically set in Jan.). General Conference of the New Church, c/o G.S. Kuphal, Ed., 20 Red Barn Rd., Brightlingsea, Colchester, Essex CO7 0SH, England. TEL 0206-302932. circ. 500.

289.9 362.7   US   ISSN 0885-7776
GENERAL COUNCIL OF THE ASSEMBLIES OF GOD. MEMOS; leadership magazine for Women's Ministries Auxiliary. 1956. q. $5.50. Gospel Publishing House, 1445 Boonville Ave., Springfield, MO 65802-1894. TEL 417-862-2781. Ed. Linda Upton. bk.rev.; circ. 15,000.
  Formerly: Missionettes Memos.

289.9   US
GEORGIAN ANNUAL. 1989. a. $35. Georgian Church, 1908 Verde St., Bakersfield, CA 93304. TEL 805-323-3309. Eds. Dean & Lady Fauna. adv.; bk.rev.; illus. (back issues avail.)

289.9   US
GEORGIAN MONTHLY. 1976. 12/yr. $8. Georgian Church, 1908 Verde St., Bakersfield, CA 93304. TEL 805-323-3309. Eds. Dean & Lady Fauna. adv.; bk.rev.; illus. (back issues avail.)
  Formerly: Georgian Newsletter.

289   US   ISSN 0017-0739
GLAD TIDINGS OF GOOD THINGS. 1953. q. free to the blind; others $2.50. Sixteen & Vine Church of Christ, 1610 Vine St., Abilene, TX 79602. TEL 915-677-2892. Ed. Tim Conatser. circ. 350.

281.9   YU
GLAS ALMASKE PAROHIJE. 1975. irreg. Srpska Pravoslavna Parohija pri Hramu Sv. Tri Jerarha-Almaska, Almaska 11, 21000 Novi Sad, Yugoslavia. TEL 021 51-394. Ed. Mirko Tisma. circ. 500. (back issues avail.)
  Description: Provides news on religious education. Includes the history of the parish and parish church, as well as records of births, marriages and deaths.

266   US   ISSN 0731-1125
GLOBAL CHURCH GROWTH.* 1964. q. $12.50. Church Growth Center, Box 145, Corunna, IN 46730. TEL 219-281-2452. Ed. Kent Hunter. adv.; bk.rev.; stat.; cum.index every 5 yrs; circ. 3,500. **Indexed:** CERDIC, Chr.Per.Ind.
  —BLDSC shelfmark: 4195.359000.
  Former titles: Global Church Growth Bulletin (ISSN 0273-7183); Church Growth Bulletin (ISSN 0009-6385)
  Description: Focuses on missionaries and mission work.

289.7   US   ISSN 0017-2340
BX8101
GOSPEL HERALD. 1908. w. $26.95. Mennonite Publishing House, 616 Walnut Ave., Scottdale, PA 15683-1999. TEL 412-887-8500. FAX 412-887-3111. Ed. J. Lorne Peachey. illus.; circ. 22,300.
  Description: Covers weekly news and opinions of the Mennonite Church.

200   US   ISSN 0017-2383
GOSPEL TRUTH. 1938. m. contributions. Southwest Radio Church, Box 1144, Oklahoma City, OK 73101. TEL 405-235-5396. Ed. N.W. Hutchings. circ. 100,000. (also avail. in microform from UMI; reprint service avail. from UMI)

GREEK ORTHODOX CALENDAR. see *ETHNIC INTERESTS*

281.9 230   US   ISSN 0017-3894
BX200
GREEK ORTHODOX THEOLOGICAL REVIEW. 1954. q. $22 (foreign $25). (Holy Cross Greek Orthodox School of Theology, Hellenic College) Holy Cross Orthodox Press, 50 Goddard Ave., Brookline, MA 02146. TEL 617-731-3500. Ed. Rev. Dr. N.M. Vaporis. adv.; bk.rev.; cum.index every 5 yrs.; circ. 1,075. (also avail. in microform from UMI; reprint service avail. from UMI) **Indexed:** Amer.Bibl.Slavic & E.Eur.Stud., Amer.Hist.& Life, CERDIC, Hist.Abstr., New Test.Abstr., Old Test.Abstr., Rel.& Theol.Abstr. (1968-), Rel.Ind.One, Rel.Per.
  —BLDSC shelfmark: 4214.905000.

200   US
GREEK SUNDAY NEWS/KYRIAKATIKA NEA. (Text in English and Greek) 1953. fortn. $12. c/o William A. Harris, Ed., 231 Harrison Ave., Boston, MA 02111. TEL 617-426-1948. adv.; bk.rev.; circ. 20,000. (tabloid format)

GREGORIOS O PALAMAS. see *HISTORY — History Of Europe*

248.83   US   ISSN 0017-5226
GUIDE (HAGERSTOWN). 1953. w. $31.97. (Seventh-day Adventist Church) Review and Herald Publishing Association, 55 W. Oak Ridge Dr., Hagerstown, MD 21740. TEL 301-791-7000. Ed. Jeannette Johnson. adv.; illus.; index; circ. 45,000. (also avail. in microfilm from UMI; reprint service avail. from UMI)
  Description: Aimed at adolescents aged 10-16.

266   CN
HALLELUJAH!. 1949. bi-m. Can.$5. Bible Holiness Movement, Box 223, Sta. A, Vancouver, B.C. V6C 2M3, Canada. TEL 604-498-3895. Ed. Wesley H. Wakefield. bk.rev.; illus.; circ. 5,000. (back issues avail.)
  Formerly (until 1990): Truth on Fire (ISSN 0821-6371)
  Description: Magazine of aggressive evangelical Christianity and social activism.

281   AG   ISSN 0017-8640
HAY GUETRON.* (Text in Armenian and Spanish) 1932. m. $3. Institucion Administrativa de la Iglesia Armenia, Acevedo 1353, Buenos Aires, Argentina. adv.; abstr.; bibl.; illus.; circ. 1,200.

289.9   US
HEALING THOUGHTS. 6/yr. $18. Plainfield Christian Science Church (Independent), 905 Prospect Ave., Box 5619, Plainfield, NJ 07060. TEL 908-756-4669.

299   UK
HEATHEN. 1971. irreg. membership. Pagan Movement, Can y Lloer, Ffarmers, Llanwrda, Dyfed, Wales. adv.; circ. 300.

281.9   CN
HERALD/VISNYK. (Text in English, Ukrainian) 1924. m. $15 (foreign $16). Ecclesia Publishing Co., Ltd., Nine St. Johns Ave., Winninpeg, Man. R2W 1G8, Canada. TEL 204-582-0996. Ed. Rev. S. Jarmus.

289.5   US   ISSN 0018-0475
HERALD OF CHRISTIAN SCIENCE. Swedish edition: Kristen Vetenskaps Herold (ISSN 0145-7543). Spanish edition: Heraldo de la Ciencia Cristiana (ISSN 0439-0148); Dutch edition: Heraut van de Christelijke Wetenschap (ISSN 0145-756X); German edition: Herold der Christlichen Wissenschaft (ISSN 0145-7578); Italian edition: Araldo della Scienza Cristiana (ISSN 0145-7519); Portuguese edition: Arauto da Ciencia Crista (ISSN 0145-7489); Danish edition: Kristen Videnskabs Herold (US ISSN 0145-7551) Greek edition (US ISSN 0145-9511) Indonesian edition: Bentara Ilmuipengetahuan Kristen (US ISSN 0409-0810) Japanese edition (US ISSN 0145-8019) Norwegian edition: Kristen Vitenskaps Herold (US ISSN 0145-7535) 1903. m. (French, German, Spanish and Portuguese eds.); q. (other eds. and English-Braille). $23 for monthly eds., quarterly eds. $6; English-Braille ed. $1. Christian Science Publishing Society, Box 11390, Des Moines, IA 50350-1390. TEL 617-450-2000. Ed. Allison W. Phinney.

281.9   UK
HERALD OF THE SERBIAN ORTHODOX CHURCH IN WESTERN EUROPE. 1951. 4/yr. Religious Brotherhood of the Serbian Orthodox Church, 89 Lancaster Rd., London W11 1QQ, England. TEL 01-727-8367.

289.9 133 100   UK   ISSN 0141-6391
THE HERMETIC JOURNAL. 1978. a. £10($18) P.O. Box 375, Headington, Oxford OX3 5PW, England. TEL 0865-751369. Ed. Adam McLean. bk.rev.; circ. 600.

4284 RELIGIONS AND THEOLOGY — OTHER DENOMINATIONS AND SECTS

289.73   US   ISSN 0300-8851
HEROLD DER WAHRHEIT. (Text in English and German) 1912. m. $5. Amish Mennonite Publishing Association, c/o Roy Beachy, Sec.-Treas., Route 2, Box 339, Kalona, IA 52247. TEL 319-656-2006. Eds. Lester B. Miller, Jonas J. Beachy. index; circ. 975.

289.9   US   ISSN 0018-120X
HICALL. 1936. w. $5.20. (General Council of the Assemblies of God) Gospel Publishing House, 1445 Boonville, Springfield, MO 65802. TEL 417-862-2781. Ed. Deanna Harris. circ. 78,000.
   Description: Aimed at adolescents aged 12-17.

HIGH ADVENTURE; a Royal Rangers magazine for boys. see *CHILDREN AND YOUTH — For*

HUMANIST IN CANADA. see *PHILOSOPHY*

200   UK   ISSN 0018-8913
I C F QUARTERLY. 1963. q. £7 (foreign £15). Industrial Christian Fellowship, 16 Bark Hart Rd., Orpington, Kent BR6 0QD, England. TEL 0689-828042. Ed. D. Welbourn. bk.rev.; circ. 3,000.

289.9   US   ISSN 0748-2280
I S K C O N WORLD REVIEW; newspaper of the Hare Krishna Movement. 1980. m. $10 (foreign $20)(effective Mar. 1991). International Society for Krishna Consciousness, Box 99103, San Diego, CA 92169. TEL 619-273-6110. FAX 619-270-4183. Ed. Mukunda Maharaja. adv.; circ. 10,000. (tabloid format; back issues avail.)

ICONOGRAPHY OF RELIGIONS. SECTION 2, NEW ZEALAND. see *ART*

ICONOGRAPHY OF RELIGIONS. SECTION 5, AUSTRALIA. see *ART*

ICONOGRAPHY OF RELIGIONS. SECTION 7, AFRICA. see *ART*

ICONOGRAPHY OF RELIGIONS. SECTION 8, ARCTIC PEOPLES. see *ART*

ICONOGRAPHY OF RELIGIONS. SECTION 9, SOUTH AMERICA. see *ART*

ICONOGRAPHY OF RELIGIONS. SECTION 10, NORTH AMERICA. see *ART*

ICONOGRAPHY OF RELIGIONS. SECTION 11, ANCIENT AMERICA. see *ART*

ICONOGRAPHY OF RELIGIONS. SECTION 14, IRAN. see *ART*

ICONOGRAPHY OF RELIGIONS. SECTION 15, MESOPOTAMIA AND THE NEAR EAST. see *ART*

ICONOGRAPHY OF RELIGIONS. SECTION 16, EGYPT. see *ART*

ICONOGRAPHY OF RELIGIONS. SECTION 17, GREECE AND ROME. see *ART*

ICONOGRAPHY OF RELIGIONS. SECTION 19, ANCIENT EUROPE. see *ART*

ICONOGRAPHY OF RELIGIONS. SECTION 20, MANICHAEISM. see *ART*

ICONOGRAPHY OF RELIGIONS. SECTION 21, MANDAEISM. see *ART*

286 917.309   CN   ISSN 0383-2538
IEVANHEL'S'KYI HOLOS. (Text in Ukrainian) 1968. q. Can.$4. (Pentecostal Assemblies of Canada) Evangelical Voice, RR 1, Wilsonville, Ont. N0E 1Z0, Canada. TEL 519-443-7742. Dir. Rev. Walter Senko. illus.; circ. 1,200 (controlled). Key Title: Evangel's'kyj Golos.

220 289.9   SA   ISSN 0019-008X
IMBONISELO. (Text in Xhosa) 1955. s-m. R.17. Watch Tower Bible & Tract Society, Private Bag 2067, Krugersdorp 1740, South Africa. TEL 011-761-1000. FAX 011-764-4749. charts; illus.; index; circ. 16,500.

INDIAN LIFE. see *ETHNIC INTERESTS*

220 289.9   SA   ISSN 0019-0241
INQABAYOKULINDA. (Text in Zulu) 1950. s-m. R.17. Watch Tower Bible & Tract Society, Private Bag 2067, Krugersdorp 1740, South Africa. TEL 011-761-1000. FAX 011-764-4749. charts; illus.; index; circ. 40,000.

261   US   ISSN 0073-9456
INSTITUTE OF MENNONITE STUDIES SERIES. 1961. irreg. price varies. (Associated Mennonite Biblical Seminaries) Faith and Life Press, 718 Main St., Box 347, Newton, KS 67114. TEL 316-283-5100. Ed. Susan Janzen.

289.9   US   ISSN 0161-1380
INTEGRAL YOGA. 1969. q. $12. Integral Yoga Publications, Satchidananda Ashram-Yogaville, Rt. 1, Box 1720, Buckingham, VA 23921. TEL 804-969-3121. FAX 804-969-1303. Ed. Kumari de Sachy. adv.; bk.rev.; circ. 1,600.

289.9   US   ISSN 0031-4900
INTERNATIONAL PENTECOSTAL HOLINESS ADVOCATE. 1917. m. $4. International Pentecostal Holiness Church, Box 12609, Oklahoma City, OK 73157. TEL 404-245-7272. FAX 405-789-3957. (Subscr. to: Advocate Press, Box 98, Franklin Springs, GA 30639) Ed. Shirley Spencer. bk.rev.; bibl.; charts; illus.; circ. 40,000. (also avail. in microform; back issues avail.) **Indexed:** CERDIC.

299   US   ISSN 0886-6910
ISKCON REVIEW; academic perspectives on the Hare Krishna movement. 1985. a. $6. Institute for Vaishnaya Studies, c/o Steven J. Gelberg, 41 West Allens Lane, Philadelphia, PA 19119. TEL 215-242-6578. bk.rev.; circ. 1,200. (back issues avail.)

289.9   US   ISSN 0075-3602
JEHOVAH'S WITNESSES YEARBOOK. Variant title: Yearbook of Jehovah's Witnesses. (Text in 15 languages) 1927. a. (Jehovah's Witnesses, Governing Body) Watchtower Bible and Tract Society of New York, Inc., 25 Columbia Hts., Brooklyn, NY 11201. TEL 718-625-3600. index; circ. 2,000,000.
   Description: Reports on international preaching.

JOTTINGS. see *HANDICAPPED — Visually Impaired*

299.935   US   ISSN 0021-8235
BP595.A1
JOURNAL FOR ANTHROPOSOPHY. 1965. s-a. $12 (foreign $15). Anthroposophical Society in America, 529 Grant Pl., Chicago, IL 60614-3705. TEL 512-858-1669. FAX 512-858-4080. (Subscr. to: 3700 S. Ranch Rd., Ste. 12, Dripping Springs, TX 78620) Ed. Hilmar Moore. adv.; bk.rev.; circ. 1,800.
   Description: Contains articles by international contributors who directly or indirectly reflect the impact of the spiritual world on our physical world.

377.8   US   ISSN 0021-8480
LC586.A3
JOURNAL OF ADVENTIST EDUCATION. 1939. bi-m. (except July-Sep.). $14.95. General Conference of Seventh-Day Adventists, 12501 Old Columbia Pike, Silver Spring, MD 20904-6600. TEL 301-680-5075. FAX 301-680-6090. TELEX 440186. Ed. Beverly J. Rumble. adv.; bk.rev.; charts; illus.; index; circ. 7,500. (back issues avail.; reprint service avail. from UMI)
   Formerly: Journal of True Education.

289.3   US   ISSN 0094-7342
BX8601
JOURNAL OF MORMON HISTORY. 1974. a. $8.50 membership. Mormon History Association, Box 7010, University Sta., Provo, UT 84602. FAX 801-378-4048. Ed. Lavina Fielding Anderson. circ. 1,000. **Indexed:** Amer.Hist.& Life, CERDIC, Hist.Abstr.
●Also available online. Vendor(s): DIALOG (File nos.38,39).
—BLDSC shelfmark: 5020.980000.
   Description: Scholarly articles dealing with Mormon history.

200   UK   ISSN 0022-5703
JOY & LIGHT. 1843. 3/yr. £5. Lord's Day Observance Society, 6 Sherman Rd., Bromley, Kent BR1 3JH, England. Ed. J.G. Roberts. bk.rev.; circ. 20,000.
   Description: Describes the work and covers all matters of the society.

289.9   US   ISSN 0022-6718
JUNIOR TRAILS. 1926. w. $5.20. (General Council of the Assemblies of God) Gospel Publishing House, 1445 Boonville Ave., Springfield, MO 65802. TEL 417-862-2781. Ed. Sinda S. Zinn. circ. 65,000.
   Description: Fictional, illustrated sketches, verse, and informational articles on Christian ethics as they pertain to the school, family, and social lives of fifth and sixth graders.

291   II   ISSN 0047-3367
KERALA SABHA. (Text in Malayalam) 1970. m. Rs.12($0.75) Better Life Movement, Better Life Center, Aloor, Kallettumkara, Kerala 680 683, India. Ed. Fr. Thomas Vazhapilly. adv.; bk.rev.; film rev.; play rev.; abstr.; bibl.; charts; illus.; pat.; stat.; tr.lit.; cum.index; circ. 2,000 (controlled).

281.9   GR
KLERONOMIA. (Text in English, French, German, Greek, Italian) 1969. 2/yr. $32. Patriarchal Institute for Patristic Studies, Heptapyrgiou 64, 546 34 Thessaloniki, Greece. Ed. Panagiotis C. Christou. bk.rev.; bibl.; circ. 2,400. **Indexed:** CERDIC.

KOOKS MAGAZINE. see *NEW AGE PUBLICATIONS*

299   UK
KOSMON UNITY. 1946. s-a. £1($1.25) (Confraternity of Faithists) Kosmon Press, BM-KCKP, London WC1V 6XX, England. (Dist. in U.S. by: Kosmon Service Center, Box 664, Salt Lake City, UT 84110) Eds. Cyril Ward, Greta James. bk.rev.

289.9   US   ISSN 0882-4606
KOSMON VOICE. 1977. bi-m. $13.50. Universal Faithists of Kosmon, Box 154, Riverton, UT 84065-0154. TEL 801-254-6903. Ed. Erma J. Lee. bk.rev.; circ. 225.
   Formerly: Kosmon News.
   Description: Self and spiritual improvement, vegetarian diet, recipes, health, meditation, parenting, seeker discipline, letters, articles, meeting news and poetry.

289.6   SW   ISSN 0345-6005
KVAEKARTIDSKRIFT. (Text in Swedish) 1949. q. SEK 70. Vaennernas Samfund i Sverige - Society of Friends of Sweden (Quakers), Box 9166, S-102 72 Stockholm, Sweden. Ed. Ingmar Hollsing. bk.rev.; circ. 800. (reprint service avail. from CAS)
   Formerly: Nordisk Kvaekartidskrift (ISSN 0029-1404)

255   FR   ISSN 0750-3695
LETTER FROM TAIZE. (Editions in Dutch, English, French, German, Italian and Spanish) 1970. bi-m. 30 F. (foreign 40 F.). Communaute de Taize, 71250 Cluny, France.

289.9   NE   ISSN 0024-1547
LEVEND WOORD/LIVING WORD;* devoted to the restoration of New Testament Christianity. (Text in Dutch; summaries in English, French, German) 1960. m. fl.3.25($1.25) Churches of Christ, Meloenstraat 86, 2564 TK The Hague, Netherlands. Ed. Wil C. Goodheer. bk.rev.; circ. 2,000.

289.9   UK   ISSN 0024-1792
LIBERAL CATHOLIC. 1924. 3/yr. £6($13) (Liberal Catholic Church) St. Alban Press, Drayton House, 30 Gordon St., London WC1H 0BE, England. Ed. Rt. Rev. E.J. Burton. adv.; bk.rev.; illus.; circ. 500.

289.7   CN
LIEN DES FRERES MENNONITES. (Text in French) 1981. 11/yr. Can.$8. Conference of Mennonite Brethren Churches of Canada, Board of Faith and Life, 3-169 Riverton Ave., Winnipeg, Man. R2L 2E5, Canada. TEL 204-669-6575. FAX 204-654-1865. Ed. Annie Brosseau. adv.; bk.rev.; illus.; circ. 700.

200   UK
LIFELINE. 1976. m. £14 (typically set in Apr.). General Conference of the New Church, c/o G.S. Kuphal, 20 Red Barn Rd., Brightlingsea, Colchester, Essex CO7 0SH, England. TEL 061-834-4192. (Subscr. to: New Church House, 34 John Dalton St., Manchester M2 6LE, England. TEL 0206-302932) Ed. H. Heap. circ. 700.

RELIGIONS AND THEOLOGY — OTHER DENOMINATIONS AND SECTS

200 100   US
LOGOS (NEW YORK); the Swedenborg Foundation newsletter. 1968. 3/yr. free. Swedenborg Foundation, Inc., 139 E. 23rd St., New York, NY 10010. TEL 212-673-7310. FAX 212-254-0012. adv.; bk.rev.; circ. 5,000. **Indexed:** Met.Abstr., World Alum.Abstr.

220   SA
LOLEMI!. (Text in Cibemba) 1981. m. R.8.50. Watch Tower Bible & Tract Society, Private Bag 2067, Krugersdorp 1740, South Africa. TEL 011-761-1000. FAX 011-764-4749. circ. 11,000.

281.62   US   ISSN 0024-6476
LOOYS. (Text in Armenian and English) 1953. m. (10/yr.). contributions. St. James Armenian Apostolic Church, 465 Mt. Auburn St, Watertown, MA 02172. TEL 617-923-8860. circ. 1,275. (looseleaf format)

LOVETRANCE WORLD. see PHILOSOPHY

289.9   US
M C C CONTACT. 1977. q. donation basis. Mennonite Central Committee, 21 S. 12th St., Box 500, Akron, PA 17501-0500. TEL 717-859-1151. Ed.Bd. circ. 85,000. (back issues avail.)
    Description: Features articles on the work of Mennonite Central Committee, the relief, service and development agency of the Mennonite and Brethren in Christ Churches.

291   MY
MALAYSIA INTER-RELIGIOUS ORGANISATION. SUARA.* 1970. q. M.$3 (per issue). Malaysia Inter-Religious Organisation, 16 Road 49E, Petaling Jaya, Selangor, Malaysia. illus.

286   SA
MARANATHA. (Text in English) 1940. bi-m. donation. (South African Union Conference of Seventh-Day Adventists) Southern Publishing Association, Old Ottery Rd. and Clifford St., Ottery 7800, South Africa. FAX 021-739496. Ed. V.S. Wakaba.
    Supersedes (in 1992): South African Union Lantern (ISSN 0038-2795) & Suid-Afrikaanse Unie-Lantern (ISSN 0377-0796)

200   ISSN 0047-6064
MARTURION.* no.244, 1984. m. $1. People of the Living God, 2101 Prytania St., New Orleans, LA 70130. TEL 504-522-4821. Ed. H. Reigart Miller. bk.rev.; illus.

281.9   LE   ISSN 0025-4975
MASSIS. 1947. w. £L20($12) Armenian Catholic Patriarchate, Place Debbas, Beirut, Lebanon. Ed. Fr. Vartan Tekeyan. charts; illus. (tabloid format)

289.7   US   ISSN 0025-9330
MENNONITE. 1885. s-m. $20. Mennonite Church, General Conference, 722 Main St., Box 347, Newton, KS 67114. TEL 316-283-5100. FAX 316-283-0454. Ed. Muriel T. Stackley. adv.; bk.rev.; illus.; index; circ. 11,000. (also avail. in microfilm from UMI) **Indexed:** G.Soc.Sci.& Rel.Per.Lit., Rel.Per.
    Description: Devoted to teaching, motivating, and building the Christian fellowship within the context of Christian love.

289.7   CN   ISSN 0025-9349
MENNONITE BRETHREN HERALD. 1962. fortn. Can.$22. Conference of Mennonite Brethren Churches of Canada, Board of Faith and Life, 3-169 Riverton Ave., Winnipeg, Man. R2L 2E5, Canada. TEL 204-669-6575. FAX 204-654-1865. Ed. Ron Geddert. adv.; bk.rev.; illus.; index; circ. 13,500.

289.7 390   US   ISSN 0025-9357
BX8101
MENNONITE HISTORICAL BULLETIN. 1940. q. $20. Mennonite Church, Historical Committee, 1700 South Main St., Goshen, IN 46526. TEL 219-535-7477. Ed. Levi Miller. bk.rev.; cum.index every 10 yrs; circ. 400. (also avail. in microfilm from UMI) **Indexed:** Amer.Hist.& Life, CERDIC, Hist.Abstr.

290   US   ISSN 0076-6429
MENNONITE HISTORY SERIES. vol.2, 1966. irreg. (Mennonite Church, General Conference, Commission on Education) Faith and Life Press, 718 Main St., Newton, KS 67114. TEL 316-283-5100. Ed. Susan Janzen.

289.7 209   US   ISSN 0025-9365
BX8101
MENNONITE LIFE. 1946. q. $10. Bethel College, 300 E. 27th St., N. Newton, KS 67117. TEL 316-283-2500. bk.rev.; bibl.; charts; illus.; cum.index every 5 yrs.; circ. 700. (back issues avail.) **Indexed:** Amer.Bibl.Slavic & E.Eur.Stud., Amer.Hist.& Life, Hist.Abstr., Rel.& Theol.Abstr. (1989-), Rel.Ind.One.
    —BLDSC shelfmark: 5678.455700.
    Description: Articles related to Mennonite and Anabaptist history, faith, life and culture.

MENNONITE MIRROR. see LITERATURE

289.7   US   ISSN 0025-9373
BX8101
MENNONITE QUARTERLY REVIEW. (Text in English; occasionally in Dutch, German, and other languages.) 1927. q. $20. (Mennonite Historical Society) Goshen College, Goshen, IN 46526. TEL 219-535-7111. FAX 219-535-7660. (Co-sponsor: Associated Mennonite Biblical Seminaries) Ed. John S. Oyer. adv.; bk.rev.; bibl.; charts; illus.; index, cum.index every 10 yrs.; circ. 1,000. (also avail. in microfilm from AMS; reprint service avail. from AMS) **Indexed:** Amer.Bibl.Slavic & E.Eur.Stud., Amer.Hist.& Life, CERDIC, Hist.Abstr., Rel.& Theol.Abstr. (1969-), Rel.Ind.One, Rel.Per.
    —BLDSC shelfmark: 5678.456000.
    Description: Scholarly journal covering Mennonite, Amish, Hutterian Brethren, Anabaptist, Radical Reformation history and religious thought.

289.7   US   ISSN 0275-1178
BX8107
MENNONITE YEARBOOK AND DIRECTORY. 1905. a. $14.95. Mennonite Publishing House, 616 Walnut Ave., Scottdale, PA 15683-1999. TEL 412-887-8500. FAX 412-887-3111. Ed. James E. Horsch.

289.7   CN   ISSN 0025-9314
MENNONITISCHE RUNDSCHAU/MENNONITE REVIEW. (Text in German) 1877. fortn. Can.$18. Conference of Mennonite Brethren Churches of Canada, Board of Faith and Life, 3-169 Riverton Ave., Winnipeg, Man. R2L 2E5, Canada. TEL 204-669-6575. FAX 204-654-1865. Ed. Lorina Marsch. adv.; bk.rev.; illus.; index; circ. 3,800.

DER MERKURSTAB. see MEDICAL SCIENCES

286   SI   ISSN 0026-0371
MESSENGER. vol.18, 1968. M. S.$3.50. Southeast Asia Union Mission of Seventh-Day Adventists, 251 Upper Serangoon Rd., Singapore, Singapore. Ed. Loralyn Horning. illus.; circ. 2,000 (controlled).

289.9   US
MESSENGER (DUNN). m. $6.50. Pentecostal Free Will Baptist Church, Inc., Box 1568, Dunn, NC 28334. TEL 919-892-4161. Ed. Donna Hammond. bk.rev.; circ. 4,500.

282   US   ISSN 0026-0355
BX7801
MESSENGER (ELGIN). 1851. m. $12.50. Church of the Brethren, General Services Commission, 1451 Dundee Ave., Elgin, IL 60120. TEL 708-742-5100. FAX 708-742-6103. Ed. Kermon Thomasson. adv.; bk.rev.; film rev.; index; circ. 24,000.

200   US
MESSENGER (LA PORTE); official publication of the Swedenborgian Church. 1852. m. $12 (foreign $15). Swedenborgian Church, Department of Communications, 1592 N. 400 W. St., La Porte, IN 46350. TEL 617-969-4240. FAX 617-964-3258. Ed. Patte Wheat Le Van. adv.; bk.rev.; charts; illus.; index; circ. 2,000.
    Formerly: New Church Messenger (ISSN 0028-4424)

281.1   US   ISSN 0893-0872
MESSENGER (WORCESTER). 1921? m. free. Armenian Church of Our Saviour, 87 Salisbury St., Worcester, MA 01609. TEL 508-756-2931. Ed. Harold A. Gregory. bk.rev.; circ. 750. (back issues avail.)

286.5   US
MESSENGER OF TRUTH. (Text in Ukrainian) 1977. bi-m. $12. All-Ukrainian Evangelical Baptist Convention, 6751 Riverside Dr., Berwyn, IL 60402-2227. TEL 312-788-0999. Ed. O.R. Harbuziuk. bk.rev.; illus.; circ. 5,000.

200   FR   ISSN 0026-0401
MESSIDOR; la tribune de Dieu-revue de la vie totale. 1951. q. 120 F.($25) Alliance Universelle, La Prefete, B.P. 27, 84140 Montfavet, France.

METROLINE. see HOMOSEXUALITY

255   US   ISSN 0026-5802
MIRACULOUS MEDAL. 1928. q. Central Association of the Miraculous Medal, 475 E. Chelten Ave., Philadelphia, PA 19144. TEL 215-848-1010. Ed. Rev. John W. Gouldrick, C.M. illus.; circ. 340,000.

MIRROR (LANCASTER). see HISTORY — History Of North And South America

267 325   AT
MISLI/THOUGHTS. (Text in Slovenian) m. Aus.$4. Franciscan Fathers, Slovenian Chaplaincy, Baraga House, 19 A'Beckett St., Kew, Vic. 3101, Australia. Ed. Basil A. Valentine. adv.; bk.rev.; circ. 2,000.

289.9   US
MISSION AMERICA NEWSLETTER. 1983. 10/yr. (General Council of the Assemblies of God, Division of Home Missions) Gospel Publishing House, 1445 Boonville Ave., Springfield, MO 65802-1892. TEL 417-862-2781. Ed. Jeffrey B. Champion. circ. 25,000.
    Description: Covers home missions.

281   US
MODERN ORTHODOX SAINTS. 1971. irreg., vol.9, 1990. price varies. Institute for Byzantine and Modern Greek Studies, 115 Gilbert Rd., Belmont, MA 02178. TEL 617-484-6595. Ed. Constantine Cavarnos. bibl.; illus.; index; circ. 1,000.

200 289.9   SA   ISSN 0026-9093
MOLULA-QHOOA. (Text in Sesotho) 1954. s-m. R.17. Watch Tower Bible & Tract Society, Private Bag 2067, Krugersdorp 1740, South Africa. TEL 011-761-1000. FAX 011-764-4749. charts; illus.; index; circ. 16,000.

MOONCIRCLES. see WOMEN'S INTERESTS

284.6   US   ISSN 1041-0961
MORAVIAN (BETHLEHEM, 1856). 1856. m. (combined Jan.-Feb., July-Aug.) $7 to non-members (foreign $9). Moravian Church in America - North and South, Publications Commission, Box 1245, Bethlehem, PA 18016. TEL 215-867-0594. FAX 215-866-9223. Ed. Hermann I. Weinlick. adv.; bk.rev.; charts; illus.; maps; stat.; index; circ. 26,500.
    Former titles: North American Moravian (ISSN 0027-1012); Moravian and Wachovia Moravian.

200 289.9   SA   ISSN 0027-1179
MOROKAMI. (Text in Sepedi) 1966. s-m. R.17. Watch Tower Bible & Tract Society, Private Bag 2067, Krugersdorp 1740, South Africa. TEL 011-761-1000. FAX 011-764-4749. charts; illus.; index; circ. 9,500.

289.9   US   ISSN 0164-7253
MOUNTAIN MOVERS. 1959. m. $5 suggested contribution. Assemblies of God, Division of Foreign Missions, 1445 Boonville Ave., Springfield, MO 65802. TEL 417-862-2781. FAX 417-862-0085. Ed. Joyce Booze. circ. 200,000.
    Former titles: Good News Crusades (ISSN 0017-2162); Global Conquest.

289.9   SA
MUKAI!. (Text in Shona) 1982. q. Watch Tower Bible & Tract Society, Private Bag 2067, Krugersdorp 1740, South Africa. TEL 011-761-1000. FAX 011-764-4749. charts; illus.; circ. 6,200.

200   AT
MUSICIAN. 1947. fortn. Aus.$18. (Salvation Army) Dinsdale Pender, 1-9 Drill St., Hawthorn, Melbourne, Vic. 3122, Australia. FAX 03-819-4864. Ed. Cilla Bone. bk.rev.; circ. 3,900.

200   BG
NATIONAL COUNCIL OF CHURCHES, BANGLADESH. ANNUAL REPORT. (Text in Bengali, English) a. National Council of Churches, Bangladesh, 395, New Eskaton Rd., Dhaka 2, Bangladesh. stat.

RELIGIONS AND THEOLOGY — OTHER DENOMINATIONS AND SECTS

133 200   US
NATIONAL SPIRITUALIST. 1919. m. $12. (National Spiritualist Association of Churches) Summit Publishing by Stow, Box 217, Lily Dale, NY 14752-0217. TEL 716-595-2020. Ed. Sonora Pfortmiller. bibl.; illus.; circ. 3,500.

NEW AGE TEACHINGS. see *NEW AGE PUBLICATIONS*

200   UG
NEW CENTURY.* 1959. m. $25. Church of Uganda, Box 14123, Mengo, Uganda. Ed. Canon Tom T. Nabeta. adv.; bk.rev.; play rev.; circ. 10,000. (tabloid format)
   Formerly: New Day (ISSN 0028-4556)

289.9   US
NEW CHURCH LIFE; a monthly magazine devoted to the teachings revealed through Emanuel Swedenborg. 1891. m. $12. General Church of the New Jerusalem, Box 278, Bryn Athyn, PA 19009. TEL 215-947-4200. FAX 215-938-2616. Ed. Rev. Donald L. Rose. bk.rev.; circ. 1,900.
   Description: Contains sermons, religious articles and reviews, letters and church news.

200   UK
NEW CHURCH MAGAZINE. 1881. 2/yr. £2. General Conference of the New Church, c/o G.S. Kuphal, 20 Red Barn Rd., Brightlingsea, Colchester, Essex CO7 0SH, England. TEL 0206 302932. (Subscr. to: New Church College, 25 Radcliffe New Rd., Manchester M26 9LS, England. TEL 061-766-2521) Ed. B.M. Talbot.

289.33   US   ISSN 0164-5285
NEW ERA (SALT LAKE CITY). 1971. m. $8. Church of Jesus Christ of Latter-day Saints, Corporation of the President, 50 E. North Temple, Salt Lake City, UT 84150. TEL 801-240-2947. Ed. Richard Romney. circ. 185. (also avail. in microform from UMI; back issues avail.; reprint service avail. from UMI) Indexed: A.I.P.P.
   Description: Written for those between the ages of 13 and 19.

150   US   ISSN 0146-7832
NEW THOUGHT (MESA); a quarterly magazine dedicated to the spiritual enlightenment of the individual and of the world. 1916. q. $8. International New Thought Alliance, 5003 E. Broadway Rd., Mesa, AZ 85206. TEL 602-830-2461. Ed. Blaine C. Mays. adv.; bk.rev.; illus.; circ. 5,000.
   Formerly (until 1950): New Thought Bulletin (ISSN 0146-8170)

947   US
NEWSWIRE (WHEATON). 1984. bi-m. free. Slavic Gospel Association, Box 1122, Wheaton, IL 60189. TEL 312-690-8900. Ed. Wil Trlggs. bk.rev.; circ. 60,000. (processed)
   Supersedes (1976?-1983?): Sparks (Wheaton).

220 289.9   SA   ISSN 0028-9639
NHARIREYOMURINDI. (Text in Shona) 1949. s-m. R.17. Watch Tower Bible & Tract Society, Private Bag 2067, Krugersdrop 1740, South Africa. TEL 011-761-1000. FAX 011-764-4749. charts; illus.; index; circ. 20,000.

NICOLAUS. see *RELIGIONS AND THEOLOGY — Roman Catholic*

200   SW   ISSN 0029-5019
NOVA ECCLESIA. vol.54, 1975. bi-m. SEK 10($3.33) (General Church of the New Jerusalem) Bokfoerlaget Nova Ecclesia, Aladdinsvaegen 27, 161 38 Bromma, Sweden. Ed. Ragnar Boyesen. bk.rev.; circ. 300.

289.9   PO   ISSN 0029-5116
NOVAS DE ALEGRIA. Abbreviated title: N A. 1943. m. Esc.150($6) Casa Publicadora das Assembleias de Deus, Av. Alm. Gago Coutinho 158, 1700 Lisbon, Portugal. Ed. Fernando Martinez da Silva. adv.; bk.rev.; abstr.; illus.; circ. 20,000 (controlled).

220 289.9   SA   ISSN 0029-5442
NSANJA YA OLONDA. (Text in Chichewa) 1948. s-m. R.17. Watch Tower Bible & Tract Society, Private Bag 2067, Krugersdrop 1740, South Africa. TEL 011-761-1000. FAX 011-764-4749. illus.; circ. 24,500.

266   US
O C INTERNATIONAL. 1979. q. free. O C International, Inc., Box 36900, Colorado Springs, CO 80936-6900. TEL 719-592-9292. FAX 719-592-0693. Ed. Steve G. Aldrich. circ. 20,000.
   Former titles (until vol.6, no.3, 1987): Lost and Found; World Spotlight; Supersedes (1962-1979): Cable (ISSN 0007-9286)
   Description: Informs constituents about the ministry. Offers articles about missions.

200   US   ISSN 0029-7143
O L O G O S. 1949. bi-m. $4. Orthodox Lore Of the Gospel of Our Savior Mission, Box 5333, St. Louis, MO 63115. TEL 314-721-4342. Ed. Rev. George Mastrantonis. circ. 86,700.

289.4   SZ   ISSN 0030-0101
OFFENE TORE; Beitraege zu einem neuen christlichen Zeitalter. 1957. 6/yr. 22 Fr.($12) Swedenborg Verlag, Postfach 247, CH-8032 Zurich, Switzerland. TEL 01-3835944. Ed. Dr. Friedemann Horn. bk.rev.; circ. 1,000.
   —BLDSC shelfmark: 6236.570000.
   Description: Covers new religious perspectives while providing contributions to a new Christian era.

OMEGA NEW AGE DIRECTORY. see *BUSINESS AND ECONOMICS — Trade And Industrial Directories*

281.9   US   ISSN 0030-2503
ONE CHURCH/YEDINAYA TSERKOV. 1947. bi-m. $7.50. Patriarchal Parishes of the Russian Orthodox Church in the U.S.A., c/o Rt. Rev. Feodor Kovalchuk, Ed., 727 Miller Ave., Youngstown, OH 44502. TEL 216-788-0151. FAX 216-788-9361. bk.rev.; illus.; index; circ. 1,200. (also avail. in microform from UMI; reprint service avail. from UMI) Indexed: CERDIC.

220 289.9   SA   ISSN 0030-316X
ONTWAAK!. (Text in Afrikaans) 1939. s-m. R.17. Watch Tower Bible & Tract Society, Private Bag 2067, Krugersdrop 1740, South Africa. TEL 011-761-1000. FAX 011-764-4749. charts; illus.; index; circ. 27,000.

200   JA   ISSN 0030-3259
OOMOTO. (Text in English) 1956. bi-m. 1200 Yen($5) Oomoto International, Kameoka-shi, Kyoto-fu 621, Japan. TEL 07712-2-5561. bk.rev.; illus.; circ. 5,000.

294.3   US   ISSN 0891-1177
BQ9460
ORDER OF BUDDHIST CONTEMPLATIVES. JOURNAL. 1970. q. $20. Order of Buddhist Contemplatives, Shasta Abbey, Box 199, Mt. Shasta, CA 96067. TEL 916-926-4208. FAX 916-926-5796. Ed. Rev. Kinzan Learman. circ. 560. (back issues avail.)
   Former titles (until 1986): Shasta Abbey. Journal (ISSN 0732-8508); Zen Mission Society. Journal.
   Description: Articles on the practice of Buddhism.

280   US   ISSN 0048-2269
BX496.A1
ORTHODOX CHURCH. 1965. m. $8. Orthodox Church in America, 7900 W. 120 St, Palos Park, IL 60464. TEL 708-361-1684. FAX 708-923-1706. Ed. V. Rev. John Matusiak. bk.rev.; charts; illus.; circ. 34,000. (tabloid format) Indexed: CERDIC.
   Description: Covers Orthodox and ecumenical church news. Includes official annoucements.

200   US   ISSN 0145-7950
BX496.A5
ORTHODOX CHURCH IN AMERICA. YEARBOOK AND CHURCH DIRECTORY. a. $15. Orthodox Church in America, 7900 W 120 St., Palos Park, IL 60464. TEL 708-361-1684. FAX 708-923-1706. Ed. V. Rev. John Matusiak. charts; illus.; stat.; circ. 3,000. Key Title: Yearbook and Church Directory of the Orthodox Church in America.
   Supersedes: Russian Orthodox Greek-Catholic Church of America. Yearbook (ISSN 0095-2257); Russian Orthodox Greek Catholic Church of America. Yearbook and Church Directory (ISSN 0557-532X)
   Description: Complete listing of parishes and clergy, bishops, officers of church administration, institutions and publications in U.S. and Canada.

281.9   UK   ISSN 0267-8470
ORTHODOX NEWS. 1979. m. St. George Orthodox Information Service, 64 Prebend Gardens, London W6 OXU, England. TEL 081-741-9624. Ed. Andrew Bond. adv.; bk.rev.; circ. 2,500.
   Description: News service dealing with current affairs in the Orthododox Church.

200   US   ISSN 0731-2547
ORTHODOX OBSERVER. (Text and summaries in English and Greek) 1971. m. $5.50. (Greek Archdiocese of North and South America) Greek Archdiocese Press, 8 E. 79th St., New York, NY 10021. TEL 212-628-2590. FAX 212-570-4005. Ed. Jim Golding. adv.; bk.rev.; circ. 130,000. (tabloid format; also avail. in microfilm)

281.9   UK   ISSN 0950-8376
ORTHODOX OUTLOOK. 1986. bi-m. £12. 37 Salop Rd., Welshpool, Powys SY21 7EA, Wales. TEL 0938-554117. Ed. Stephen Maxfield. adv.; bk.rev.; circ. 1,000.
   Description: News about the Orthodox Church in Britain and worldwide.

281   US   ISSN 0030-5839
ORTHODOX WORD. 1965. bi-m. $12. St. Herman of Alaska Brotherhood, Box 70, Platina, CA 96076. FAX 916-343-2859. Ed. Fr. Herman Podmoshensky. adv.; bk.rev.; illus.; index; circ. 2,500. (also avail. in microfilm from UMI; reprint service avail. from UMI) Indexed: CERDIC, Rel.Per.
   Description: Covers traditional Christianity from Apostolic times. Features the lives of saints, especially of modern holy men and women, and offers spiritual guidance from ascetics and visionaries. Includes discussions of contemporary issues from an Orthodox perspective.

281   GW   ISSN 0030-6487
BX100
OSTKIRCHLICHE STUDIEN. (Text in English, French, German) 1952. q. DM.94. (Ostkirchliches Institut der Deutschen Augustiner) Augustinus Verlag, Grabenberg 2, 8700 Wuerzburg 11, Germany. TEL 0931-51157. Ed. H.M. Biedermann. adv.; bk.rev.; bibl.; index; circ. 500. Indexed: CERDIC, Hist.Abstr., New Test.Abstr., Rel.& Theol.Abstr. (1989-), Rel.Ind.One.
   Description: Studies the history and theology of the Eastern Orthodox Churches.

289.9   GW
OUR FAMILY; magazine of the New Apostolic Church. (Text in English) 1955. m. DM.38.40. Verlag Friedrich Bischoff GmbH, Postfach 110242, 6000 Frankfurt 1, Germany. FAX 069-252915. TELEX 416435-FBDV. Ed. Hellmut Wernher. circ. 70,000.
   Description: Nondenominational publication devoted to evangelism, to the promotion of faith and to the belief in God through the use of real life stories.

OUTREACH (NEW YORK). see *ETHNIC INTERESTS*

289.9   US
PAGANA. 1980. 6/yr. $12. American Mensa Ltd., Pagan-Occult-Witchcraft Special Interest Group, Box 9336, San Jose, CA 95157. TEL 415-856-6911. Ed. Valerie Voigt. adv.; bk.rev.; illus.; circ. 400.

200   FR   ISSN 0031-0972
PANPERE. (Text in Armenian) 1925. m. 100 F.($20) Union of the Armenian Evangelical Churches in France, 13 rue des Allies, F-69100 Villeurbanne, France. TEL 33-78-89-21-44. Ed. Ari Topouzkhanian. bk.rev.; circ. 2,500.

110   SA   ISSN 0031-2932
PATH OF TRUTH. Afrikaans edition: Huis van Geluk. 1937. m. free. School of Truth Ltd., South Africa Centre, 5th Fl., 253 Bree St., Johannesburg 2001, South Africa. TEL 011-333-8331. (Subscr. to: P.O. Box 6116, Johannesburg 2000, South Africa) Ed. Wille Martin. circ. 13,900 (3,450 Afrikaans ed.; 10,450 English ed.).
   Description: Contains daily reading, meditations, and metaphysics lectures.

281.9   GR
PATRIARCHAL INSTITUTE FOR PATRISTIC STUDIES. THEOLOGICAL STUDIES. irreg., latest no.5. price varies. Patriarchal Institute for Patristic Studies, Heptapyrgiou 64, 546 34 Thessaloniki, Greece. Ed. P.C. Christou.

RELIGIONS AND THEOLOGY — OTHER DENOMINATIONS AND SECTS

PEACEMAKER. see *POLITICAL SCIENCE*

200 US ISSN 0031-4250
PENDLE HILL PAMPHLETS. 1934. 6/yr. $12. (Pendle Hill, a Quaker Center for Study and Contemplation) Pendle Hill Publications, 338 Plush Mill Road, Wallingford, PA 19086. TEL 215-566-4507. FAX 215-566-3679. Ed. Rebecca Kratz Mays. circ. 1,500. (also avail. in microfilm from UMI) **Indexed:** Vert.File Ind.

PENNSYLVANIA MENNONITE HERITAGE. see *GENEALOGY AND HERALDRY*

289.9 US ISSN 0031-4897
BX6198.A7
PENTECOSTAL EVANGEL. 1913. w. $14.95. (General Council of the Assemblies of God) Gospel Publishing House, 1445 Boonville Ave., Springfield, MO 65802-1894. TEL 417-862-2781. FAX 417-862-8558. Ed. Richard G. Champion. bk.rev.; charts; illus.; index; circ. 280,000. (also avail. in microfilm) **Indexed:** A.I.P.P., G.Soc.Sci.& Rel.Per.Lit.

220 SA
▼**PHAFOGA!.** (Text in Sepedi) 1990. m. R.8.50. Watch Tower Bible & Tract Society, Private Bag 2067, Krugersdorp 1740, South Africa. TEL 011-761-1000. FAX 011-764-4749.

220 289.9 SA ISSN 0031-6806
PHAPHAMA!. (Text in Zulu) 1958. s-m. R.17. Watch Tower Bible & Tract Society, Private Bag 2067, Krugersdorp 1740, South Africa. TEL 011-761-1000. FAX 011-764-4749. charts; illus.; index; circ. 19,000.

289 US ISSN 0032-0420
PLAIN TRUTH; a magazine of understanding. Dutch edition: Echte Waarheid. French edition: Pure Verite (ISSN 0033-4588); German edition: Klar und Wahr. Spanish edition: Pura Verdad. Italian edition: Pura Verita. Norwegian edition: Dan Enkle Sannhet. 1934. m. free. (Worldwide Church of God) Ambassador Publishing Services, 300 W. Green St., Pasadena, CA 91129. (Subscr. to: Box 230001, Pasadena, CA 91123-0428) circ. 3,700,000. (also avail. in audio cassette)
Incorporates: Good News of Tomorrow's World (ISSN 0093-5026)

200 UK
PLOUGH. 1931. 2/yr. £2.40. General Conference of the New Church, c/o G.S. Kuphal, 20 Red Barn Rd., Brightlingsea, Colchester, Essex CO7 0SH, England. TEL 061-766-2521. (Subscr. to: 117 Gill Bent Rd., Cheadle Hulme, Cheshire SK8 6NH, England. TEL 0206-302932) (Co-sponsor: British New Church Federation) Ed. A. Bentley.

268 US
PLUS: MAGAZINE OF POSITIVE THINKING. 1945. 10/yr. $10 contribution. Peale Center for Christian Living, Box 8000, Pawling, NY 12564. TEL 914-855-5000. Ed. Eric Fellman. illus.; circ. 900,000.
Former titles: Magazine of Positive Thinking (ISSN 0747-217X); Creative Help for Daily Living.

PORTAL. see *PARAPSYCHOLOGY AND OCCULTISM*

281.9 YU
PRAVOSLAVLJE/ORTHODOXY; novine Srpske Patrijarsije. (Text in Serbian) 1967. s-m. $25. Srpska Patrijarsija, 7 Jula 5, 11000 Belgrade, Yugoslavia. TEL 011 635-699. FAX 011-630-865. (Co-sponsor: Sveti Arhijerijaki Sinod Srpske Provoslave Crkve) Ed. Slobodan Mileusnic. adv.; bk.rev.; circ. 27,000.

281.9 266 YU
PRAVSLAVNI MISIONAR/ORTHODOX MISSIONARY. (Text in Serbian) 1958. bi-m. 900 din.($10) Sveti Arhijerijski Sinod, Sedmog Jula 5, 11000 Belgrade, Yugoslavia. TEL 011 635-699. Ed. Irineus Bulovic. adv.; bk.rev.; circ. 32,000.

200 FR ISSN 0032-4922
PRESENCE ORTHODOXE. 1968. q. 70 F. Editions Friant, 96 bd. Auguste-Blanqui, 75013 Paris, France. abstr.; bibl. **Indexed:** CERDIC.
Formerly: Portique Saint-Denis.

259 US ISSN 0032-7700
PRESENT TRUTH AND HERALD OF CHRIST'S EPIPHANY. (Editions in French, Polish, Dano-Norwegian) 1918. bi-m. $2. Laymen's Home Missionary Movement, Box 679, Chester Springs, PA 19425. TEL 215-827-7665. Ed. Bernard W. Hedman. circ. 1,100.

200 IT ISSN 0033-0728
PROGRESSIO; Ignatian spirituality for laypeople. (Text in English, French and Spanish) 1924. 6/yr. (with s-a. supplements). $21. Christian Life Community, World Secretariat, Borgo Santo Spirito 8, Casella Postale 6139, 00195 Rome, Italy. Ed. Roswitha Cooper. illus.; index, cum.index every 10 yrs.; circ. 3,500.

289.9 051 370 US
PROPER DHARMA SEAL. 1983. q. free. (Dharma Realm Buddhist Association) Vajra Bodhi Sea Publication Society, City of 10,000 Buddhas, Box 217, Talmage, CA 95481-0217. TEL 707-462-0939. Ed. Heng Wu. circ. 10,000. (tabloid format; back issues avail.)
Description: Specializes in short articles on eastern and western ethics.

220 US ISSN 0033-1341
PROPHETIC NEWSLETTER; the news in the light of the Bible. 1959. m. contributions. World Prophetic Ministry, Inc., P.O. Drawer 907, Colton, CA 92324. TEL 714-825-2767. Ed. David Breese. illus.; circ. 12,000.

261 US
PURA VERDAD; noticiario de comprension. Dutch edition: Echte Waarheid. English edition: Plain Truth (ISSN 0032-0420); French edition: Pure Verite (ISSN 0033-4588); German edition: Klar und Wahr. Italian edition: Pura Verita. Norwegian edition: Dan Enkle Sannhet. (Text in Spanish) 1968. m. free. (Worldwide Church of God) Ambassador Publishing Services, 300 W. Green St., Pasadena, CA 91129. circ. 120,000.

289 US ISSN 0033-4588
PURE VERITE; revue de bonne comprehension. Dutch edition: Echte Waarheid. English edition: Plain Truth (ISSN 0032-0420); German edition: Klar und Wahr. Italian edition: Pura Verita. Spanish edition: Pura Verdad. Norwegian edition: Dan Enkle Sannhet. (Text in French) 1963. m. free. (Worldwide Church of God) Ambassador Publishing Services, 300 W. Green St., Pasadena, CA 91129. TEL 818-304-6150. (Subscr. to: Le Monde a Venir, B.P. 64, 75014 Paris, France) Ed. Dibar Apartian. illus.; circ. 180,000. (back issues avail.)

289.7 US ISSN 0163-7274
PURPOSE. 1968. w. $12.60. Mennonite Publishing House, 616 Walnut Ave., Scottdale, PA 15683-1999. TEL 412-887-8500. FAX 412-887-3111. Ed. James E. Horsch. bk.rev.; illus.; circ. 18,600.

QUAKER CONCERN. see *POLITICAL SCIENCE — Civil Rights*

289.6 100 UK
QUAKER ENCOUNTERS. irreg., vol.3, 1978. William Sessions Ltd., Ebor Press, York YO3 9HS, England. TEL 0904-659224. FAX 0904-64488. TELEX 57712.

289.6 US ISSN 0033-5053
BX7635.A1
QUAKER HISTORY. 1902. s-a. $15. Friends Historical Association, Haverford College Library, Haverford, PA 19041. TEL 215-896-1161. Ed. Charles L. Cherry. bk.rev.; bibl.; cum.index every 5 yrs, vol.1-79; circ. 800. (also avail. in microform from UMI) **Indexed:** CERDIC, Hist.Abstr., Rel.Ind.One, Rel.Per.
—BLDSC shelfmark: 7168.120000.
Formerly: Friends' Historical Association. Bulletin.

289.6 US ISSN 0033-5061
BX7601
QUAKER LIFE. 1960. 10/yr. $17. (Friends United Meeting (Quakers)) Friends United Press, 101 Quaker Hill Dr., Richmond, IN 47374. TEL 317-962-7573. FAX 317-966-1293. Ed. James R. Newby. adv.; bk.rev.; illus.; index; circ. 9,600. **Indexed:** CERDIC.
Formed by the merger of: American Friend & Quaker Action.

200 UK ISSN 0033-507X
QUAKER MONTHLY. 1922. m. £9.90 (foreign £12)(effective 1992). Quaker Home Service, Friends House, Euston Rd, London NW1 2BJ, England. TEL 071-387-3601. FAX 071-388-1977. Ed. Elizabeth Cave. bk.rev.; illus.; circ. 3,000. **Indexed:** CERDIC.
Formerly: Wayfarer.
Description: Theologic articles on the relationship between Quaker tenets and human experience.

QUAKER PEACE & SERVICE. ANNUAL REPORT. see *SOCIAL SERVICES AND WELFARE*

289.6 US ISSN 0033-5088
BX7601
QUAKER RELIGIOUS THOUGHT. 1959. irreg., (approx. 2/yr.). $10 for 4 nos. to individuals; institutions $12. Quaker Theological Discussion Group, 128 Tate St., Greensboro, NC 27403. Ed. Arthur Roberts. bk.rev.; circ. 500. (back issues avail.) **Indexed:** CERDIC.

QUAKER YEOMEN. see *GENEALOGY AND HERALDRY*

289.9 US
RAILROAD EVANGELIST. 1931. q. $6. (Railroad Evangelist Association, Inc.) Bartel Printing Co., 502 E. Winona Ave., Warsaw, IN 46580. TEL 317-844-3176. (Subscr. to: c/o Ann Grissom. 5272 Longstone Rd., Carmel, IN 46032) Ed. Esther Peterson. circ. 2,500.
Description: Interdenominational patriotic Christian magazine for the railroad and allied transportation industries.

211.6 US ISSN 0034-4095
BL2747.6
RELIGIOUS HUMANISM; a quarterly journal of religious and ethical humanism. 1967. q. $12. Fellowship of Religious Humanists, Box 278, Yellow Springs, OH 45387. TEL 513-324-8130. Eds. Paul and Lucinda Beattie. adv.; bk.rev.; index, cum.index: vols.1-10; circ. 1,500. (also avail. in microform from UMI; reprints avail. from UMI) **Indexed:** Arts & Hum.Cit.Ind., CERDIC, Curr.Cont., G.Soc.Sci.& Rel.Per.Lit., Phil.Ind., Phil.Ind., Rel.& Theol.Abstr. (1969-), Rel.Ind.One.
—BLDSC shelfmark: 7356.530000.
Description: Presents scholarly articles and creative verse pertaining to the practice and philosophy of this liberal ministry that espouses the dignity and worth of man and his capacity for self-realization without devine intervention.

289.2 US ISSN 0191-0167
RESTORATION WITNESS; evangelistic magazine of the Reorganized Church of Jesus Christ of Latter-Day Saints. 1963. bi-m. $10 to individuals; groups $9.60. (Reorganized Church of Jesus Christ of Latter Day Saints) Herald Publishing House, 3225 S. Noland Rd., Box HH, Independence, MO 64055. TEL 816-252-5010. Ed. Barbara Howard. adv.; illus.; tr.lit.; circ. 10,000.

289.9 US ISSN 1050-7930
BX8627
REVIEW OF BOOKS ON THE BOOK OF MORMON. 1989. a. $8.50 (typically set in Apr.). Foundation for Ancient Research and Mormon Studies, Box 7113, University Sta., Provo, UT 84602. TEL 801-378-3295. FAX 801-378-5254. Ed. Daniel C. Peterson. bk.rev.; circ. 1,200.
Description: Review of books published in the past year on the Book of Mormon.

281.9 RM
ROMANIAN ORTHODOX CHURCH NEWS. (Text in English, French) q. Piata Presei Libere 1, 71341 Bucharest, Rumania. circ. 2,000.

ROSICRUCIAN DIGEST. see *PHILOSOPHY*

281.9 US ISSN 0036-0317
BX496.A1
RUSSIAN ORTHODOX JOURNAL. 1927. m. (combined July-Aug. & Jan.-Feb.). $10. Federated Russian Orthodox Clubs of America, 10 Downs Dr. (Plains), Wilkes-Barre, PA 18705. TEL 717-825-3158. Ed. Mark Soroka. adv.; bk.rev.; illus.; index; circ. 3,800.
Description: Features articles about the organization's activities and members, and about the Orthodox faith.

RELIGIONS AND THEOLOGY — OTHER DENOMINATIONS AND SECTS

281.9 US ISSN 0222-1543
BX598.A1
RUSSKOE VOZROZHDENIE; nezavisimyi russkii pravoslavnyi natsional'nyi zhurnal. (Text in Russian) 1978. q. $28. St. Seraphim Foundation, 53 Duane Ln., Demarest, NJ 07627-1304. Ed. Faina Fujii. adv.; bk.rev.; circ. 800. (back issues avail.) **Indexed:** Amer.Bibl.Slavic & E.Eur.Stud.

289.9 US
SABBATH SENTINEL; serving the Seventh-day Christian community. 1945. m. $12. Bible Sabbath Association, R.R. 1, Box 222, Fairview, OK 73737. TEL 405-227-3200. Ed. Richard Wiedenheft. adv.; bk.rev.; bibl.; illus.; circ. 1,200. (back issues avail.)

200 US
SACRED NAME BROADCASTER. 1968. m. free. Assemblies of Yahweh, Box C, Bethel, PA 19507. TEL 717-933-4518. Ed. Jacob O. Meyer. illus.; circ. 14,000.

281.9 US
ST. MARY ARMENIAN CHURCH. BULLETIN. (Text in Armenian, English) 1965? m. St. Mary Armenian Church, Box 367, Yettem, CA 93670. Ed. Vartan Kasparian. circ. 325.

281.9 US ISSN 0897-7690
ST. PETER THE ALEUT ORTHODOX EDUCATIONAL SERIES. 1983. 6/yr. (Monastery of St. Anthony the Great) St. Anthony the Great Orthodox Publications, Box 1432, Alamogordo, NM 88311-1432. (Subscr. to: 3044 N. 27th St., Phoenix, AZ 85016) Ed. Rev. Fr. Bessarion Agioantonides. circ. 1,500. (back issues avail.)

230 US ISSN 0036-3227
BX460
ST. VLADIMIR'S THEOLOGICAL QUARTERLY. 1953; N.S. 1957. q. $20 (foreign $25). St. Vladimir's Orthodox Theological Seminary, 575 Scarsdale Rd., Crestwood, Tuckahoe, NY 10707. TEL 914-961-8313. Ed. Very Rev. John Breck. adv.; bk.rev.; bibl.; illus.; index; circ. 1,800. (also avail. in microform from UMI; reprint service avail. from UMI) **Indexed:** CERDIC, New Test.Abstr., Old Test.Abstr., Rel.& Theol.Abstr. (1967-), Rel.Ind.One, Rel.Per.
—BLDSC shelfmark: 8070.208000.
Formerly: St. Vladimir's Seminary Quarterly.
Description: Scholarly articles on Orthodox theology. Includes the history, liturgy, ecclesiology, scripture and pastoral theology of East and West, from an Orthodox perspective.

289.3 US ISSN 0036-3251
SAINTS' HERALD; family magazine of the Reorganized Church of Jesus Christ of Latter Day Saints. 1860. m. $19.80 to individuals; groups $16.40. (Reorganized Church of Jesus Christ of Latter Day Saints) Herald Publishing House, 3225 S. Noland Rd., Box HH, Independence, MO 64055. TEL 816-252-5010. Ed. Roger Yarrington. adv.; bk.rev.; illus.; tr.lit.; circ. 39,000. (also avail. in microfilm)

SALLY ANN; a Christian magazine for women. see WOMEN'S INTERESTS

284 GR ISSN 0036-357X
SALPISMA.* 1945. m. Dr.40($3) Free Evangelical Churches of Greece, 3 Alkiviadou, Athens, Greece. bk.rev.; cum. index every 4 yrs.; circ. 1,500. **Indexed:** CERDIC.

289 US ISSN 0586-7282
SALT LAKE CITY MESSENGER. 1964. irreg., no.79, 1991. free. Utah Lighthouse Ministry, 1350 S.W. Temple St., Box 1884, Salt Lake City, UT 84110. TEL 801-485-8894. Ed. Jerald Tanner. adv.; circ. 14,500. (looseleaf format)

289.9 US
SANCTUARY CIRCLES; events calendar newsletter. 1980. 8/yr. $10. Circle Sanctuary, Box 219, Mt. Horeb, WI 53572. TEL 608-924-2216.

362.8 KE
SAUTI YA VITA.* (Text in English and Swahili) 1928. m. EAs.2. (Salvation Army) Slavation Army, POB 40575, Nairobi, Kenya. Ed. M. Ogweno. circ. 15,100.

280 US ISSN 0036-8032
SCHWENKFELDIAN. 1903. 3/yr. $4 to non-members. (Schwenkfelder Church) Board of Publication of the Schwenkfelder General Conference, 1 Seminary St., Pennsburg, PA 18073. TEL 215-679-3103. Ed. Nancy MacQueen Byron. bk.rev.; illus.; circ. 1,700.

200 US ISSN 0036-8458
SCIENCE OF MIND MAGAZINE. 1927. m. $18 (foreign $25). United Church of Religious Science, Box 75127, Los Angeles, CA 90075. TEL 213-388-2181. FAX 213-388-1926. Ed. Kathleen Juline. adv.; bk.rev.; illus.; circ. 100,000. **Indexed:** CERDIC.

299 SA ISSN 0036-8466
SCIENCE OF THE SOUL. 1963. q. R.24($20) Radha Soami Satsang Beas, P.O. Box 41355, Craighall 2024, South Africa. FAX 011-728-2775. Ed.Bd. adv.; circ. 4,000. (back issues avail.)
Description: Concerns the practice of meditation taught by a living meditation master.

289.9 US ISSN 0276-7899
BR165
SECOND CENTURY; a journal of early Christian studies. 1981. q. $15 to individuals; libraries $20. Second Century Journal, Inc., c/o Prof. T.H. Olbricht, Pepperdine Univ., Malibu, CA 90265. TEL 213-456-4352. FAX 213-456-4314. Ed. Everett Ferguson. adv.; bk.rev.; circ. 650. **Indexed:** Rel.& Theol.Abstr. (1981-), Rel.Ind.One.
—BLDSC shelfmark: 8216.138000.

SELF-REALIZATION. see RELIGIONS AND THEOLOGY

200 US ISSN 0582-9348
SHAKER QUARTERLY. 1961. q. $15. United Society of Shakers, Sabbathday Lake, Poland Spring, ME 04274. TEL 207-926-4597. Ed. Nancy Marcote. bk.rev.; bibl.illus.; circ. 300. (back issues avail.)
Description: Scholarly research and news from the last remaining active Shaker community.

SHARE IT; a magazine to celebrate & promote awareness of our true identity. see NEW AGE PUBLICATIONS

299 UK ISSN 0260-0382
THE SHEPHERD; an Orthodox Christian pastoral magazine. 1980. m. contributions. St. Edward Brotherhood, St. Cyprian's Ave., Brookwood, Woking, Surrey, England. (Subscr. to: Xenia Nenchin, Box 62, Millville, NJ 08332) Ed. Fr. Alexis (Pobjoy). adv.; bk.rev.; circ. 330.

200 JA ISSN 0037-5055
SIGNS OF THE TIMES. (Text in Japanese) m. 5360 Yen($41.23) Japan Publishing House, 1966 Kamikawai-cho, Asahi-ku, Yokohama 241, Japan. FAX 045-921-4349. Ed. Yenezo Okafuji. circ. 50,000.

281.62 IS ISSN 0037-5810
BX120
SION.* (Text in Armenian) 1866. bi-m. $5. Armenian Patriarchate, Old City, Jerusalem, Israel. Ed. Ara Kalaydjian. bk.rev.; bibl.; illus.; index, cum.index; circ. 1,500.

281.9 YU ISSN 0353-1805
SLATKI GROZDOVI VINOGRADA GOSPODNJEG. (Text in Serbo-Croatian) 1987. w. free. Uprava Parohije Uspenske, Sumadijska 3-III, 21000 Novi Sad, Yugoslavia. TEL 021 28-055. Ed. N. Petrovic.

289.9 US
SOCIETE. 1986. 3/yr. $15. Technicians of the Sacred, 1317 N. San Fernando Blvd., Ste. 310, Burbank, CA 91504. Ed. Courtney Willis. circ. 1,000. (back issues avail.)
Description: Covers voodoo and other neo-African religious systems, their magic and culture.

240 US ISSN 0364-2097
BR115.W6
SOJOURNERS. 1971. m. (except Feb.-Mar.; Aug.-Sep. combined). $27. Box 29272, Washington, DC 20017. TEL 202-636-3637. FAX 202-636-3643. Ed. Jim Wallis. adv.; bk.rev.; illus.; circ. 40,000. (also avail. in microfiche) **Indexed:** Alt.Press Ind., CCR, CERDIC, Chr.Per.Ind., HR Rep., Media Rev.Dig., Peace Res.Abstr., Rel.Ind.One, Rel.Per.
Formerly: Post American (ISSN 0361-2422)
Description: Covers theological, social, cultural and political topics, and provides resources for spiritual discussion, study and renewal.

281.9 US ISSN 0038-1039
SOLIA; the herald. (Text in English and Romanian) 1936. m. $12 in U.S.; Canada $14; elsewhere $16. Romanian Orthodox Episcopate of America, 2522 Grey Tower Rd., Jackson, MI 49201-9120. TEL 517-522-4800. FAX 517-522-5907. Ed. Rt. Rev. Bishop Nathaniel Popp. bk.rev.; circ. 4,982. **Indexed:** CERDIC.

280 US ISSN 0194-7958
SOPHIA; the review of the Melkite Church in America. 1971. q. $10. (Melkite Diocese of Newton) Sophia Press, Sophia Editorial Office, 7 VFW Pkwy., Roslindale, MA 02131. Ed. John Azar. bk.rev.; illus.; circ. 12,000. **Indexed:** Cath.Ind.

281.9 UK ISSN 0950-2742
SOUROZH. 1980. 4/yr. £10($21) Russian Patriarchal Diocese of Sourozh, 94A Banbury Rd., Oxford OX2 6JT, England. TEL 0865-512701. (Subscr. to: 13 Carver Rd., Herne Hill, London SE24 9LS, England) bk.rev.; circ. 700.
Description: Covers Orthodox theology, current events, history, and ecumenical activities.

289.9 UK
SOUTH ENGLAND CONFERENCE COMMUNICATOR. 1987. 4/yr. free. South England Conference of Seventh Day Adventists, Communication Department, 25 St. John's Rd., Watford, Herts. WD1 1PY, England. TEL 0923-32728. FAX 0923-50582. adv.; bk.rev.; circ. 4,000.

250 II ISSN 0038-3465
SOUTH INDIA CHURCHMAN. 1947. m. Rs.15. Church of South India, c/o Christian Literature Society, Box 501, Park Town, Madras 600003, India. Ed. Rev. Dass Babu. adv.; bk.rev.; circ. 2,000.

SOUTHERN FRIEND. see HISTORY — History Of North And South America

289.6 US ISSN 0024-0591
SPARK (NEW YORK). 1970. 5/yr. membership. New York Yearly Meeting of the Religious Society of Friends, 15 Rutherford Place, New York, NY 10003. TEL 212-673-5750. Ed. Joseph A. Vlaskamp. bk.rev.; bibl.; charts; illus.; circ. 6,000. **Indexed:** Alt.Press Ind.

289.9 US
SPECTRUM (TAKOMA PARK). 1969. 5/yr. $25 (foreign $32). Association of Adventist Forums, Box 5330, Takoma Park, MD 20913. TEL 301-270-0423. FAX 301-270-2814. Ed. Roy Branson. bk.rev.; film rev.; bibl.; charts; illus.; cum.index every 5 yrs.; circ. 5,400. (back issues avail.)
Description: Journal of opinion and scholarship for Seventh-Day Adventist readers.

THE SPIRITUAL HEALER; journal of spiritual healing and philosophy. see NEW AGE PUBLICATIONS

286 US ISSN 0038-9447
STANDARD BEARER (SACRAMENTO).* vol.11, 1973. q. $3. (Seventh-Day Adventist Reform Movement) Northwestern Publishing Association, Box 245360, Sacramento, CA 95824-5360. TEL 916-428-2563. Ed. Alfon Sas Balbachas. adv.; illus.; circ. 1,300. **Indexed:** Rehabil.Lit.

289.9 UK ISSN 0308-4531
STELLA POLARIS. (Supplement avail.) 1950. bi-m. £7.25($14) White Eagle Publishing Trust, White Eagle Lodge, New Lands, Brewells Lane, Liss, Hants GU33 7HY, England. TEL 0730-893300. Ed. Ylana Hayward. bk.rev.; index; circ. 3,600. (back issues avail.)
Description: Provides articles on healing, astrology, and other topics of interest to followers of the teaching, such as the ancient spiritual centers. Includes stories and articles for children, poems and recipes.

STORY FRIENDS. see CHILDREN AND YOUTH — For

280 US ISSN 0081-7538
STUDIES IN ANABAPTIST AND MENNONITE HISTORY. 1929. irreg., no.32, 1991. price varies. (Mennonite Historical Society) Mennonite Publishing House, Herald Press, 616 Walnut Ave., Scottdale, PA 15683. TEL 412-887-8500. FAX 412-887-3111.
—BLDSC shelfmark: 8489.100000.

STUDIES IN ASIAN THOUGHT AND RELIGION. see PHILOSOPHY

289	US
STUDIES IN EVANGELICALISM. 1980. irreg., no.11, 1991. Scarecrow Press, Inc., 52 Liberty St., Box 4167, Metuchen, NJ 08840. TEL 800-537-7107. Eds. Kenneth E. Rowe, Donald W. Dayton.

200	US	ISSN 0039-5161
SUNDAY; the magazine for the Lord's day. 1913. 3/yr. $5 membership. Lord's Day Alliance of the U.S., 2930 Flowers Rd. S., Ste. 107, Atlanta, GA 30341. TEL 404-451-7315. Ed. James P. Wesberry. bk.rev.; charts; illus.; circ. 12,000. (also avail. in microform) **Indexed:** CERDIC.

268 289.1	US	ISSN 0039-5285
SUNDAY SCHOOL COUNSELOR. 1939. m. $11. Assemblies of God, Sunday School Department, 1445 Boonville, Springfield, MO 65802. TEL 417-862-2781. FAX 417-862-0085. Ed. Sylvia Lee. bk.rev.; cum.index: 1955-1988; circ. 35,000.

289.2	US	ISSN 0363-1370
AP2		
SUNSTONE. 1975. 6/yr. $32 for 12 nos. Sunstone Foundation, 331 S. Rio Grande, Ste. 30, Salt Lake City, UT 84101-1136. TEL 801-355-5926. Ed. Elbert Peck. adv.; bk.rev.; illus.; index; circ. 8,000. **Description:** Examines the total Mormon experience; includes scholarship, issues and art.

292	YU
SVETOSAVSKO ZVONCE. (Text in Serbian) 1968. bi-m. $10. Sveti Arhijerejski Sinod, Sedmog Jula 5, 11000 Belgrade, Yugoslavia. TEL 011 638-875. Ed. Rev. Sava Popovic. circ. 15,000.

200	US	ISSN 0039-7156
SVIT/LIGHT..(Text in English) 1910. bi-m. $3. Russian Orthodox Catholic Mutual Aid Society of U.S.A., 100 Hazle St., Wilkes-Barre, PA 18701. TEL 717-822-8591. adv.; circ. 1,500. (tabloid format) **Indexed:** CERDIC.

TALK OF THE MONTH. see *NEW AGE PUBLICATIONS*

200	US	ISSN 1047-4250
TAWAGOTO. (Between 1988-1989 incorporated Divine Slave Gita (ISSN 0733-5369)) 1975. q. $30. (Hohm Community) Hohm Press, Box 2501, Prescott, AZ 86302. TEL 602-778-9189. Eds. Angelon Young, Anthony Zuccarello. adv.; bk.rev.; film rev.; circ. 500. (back issues avail.) **Formerly:** At Hohm Newsletter. **Description:** Reflects the communication and teaching work of Lee Lozowick, and chronicles the process of spiritual growth of the members of Hohm.

281.62	LE	ISSN 0040-0297
TCHAHERT/TORCH. (Text in Armenian) 1966. s-a. $4. Armenian Evangelical Brotherhood Church, Box 4944, Beirut, Lebanon. Ed.Bd. bk.rev.; illus.; circ. 1,500.

289.9	US
THE TEN DIRECTIONS. 1979. s-a. donation (foreign $8). (Kuroda Institute) Zen Center of Los Angeles, 923 S. Normandie Ave., Los Angeles, CA 90006. TEL 213-387-2351. FAX 213-387-2377. Ed. Wendy Egyoku Nakao. adv.; bk.rev.; index; circ. 10,000. (back issues avail.) **Description:** Covers current issues, social and cultural issues of Zen Buddhism in America.

289.9	UK
TESTIMONY MAGAZINE. 1931. m. £9.75($19) Testimony Magazine Promoting Committee, 29 Bramfield Close, Norwich NR2 4EJ, England. TEL 0603-613968. Ed. R.A. Benson. bk.rev.; charts; illus.; index; circ. 2,275. (back issues avail.) **Description:** For the study and defense of the Holy Scripture.

230.19	GR	ISSN 0049-3635
THEOLOGIA. (Text in English, French, German, Greek or Italian) 1923. q. Dr.5100($30) Holy Synod of the Church of Greece, 14 Ioannou Gennadiou St., Athens 11521, Greece. TEL 72-18-327. Ed. Evangelos Theodorou. bk.rev.; bibl.; index; circ. 1,800. **Indexed:** CERDIC.

289	NZ	ISSN 0049-3708
THEOSOPHY IN NEW ZEALAND. 1900. q. NZ.$7. Theosophical Society in New Zealand, 18 Belvedere St., Epsom, Auckland 3, New Zealand. Ed. Gavin Laurie. bk.rev.; circ. 2,400. **Description:** Explores man's place in the universe through the study of religion, philosophy and science.

289.9 301.412	US
THESMOPHORIA; voice of the new women's religion. 1979. 8/yr. $10. Susan B. Anthony Coven No. 1, 5856 College Ave., Box 213, Oakland, CA 94618. TEL 415-444-7724. Ed. J. Roslund. adv.; bk.rev.; illus.; circ. 2,000. (back issues avail.) **Formerly:** Themis.

289.9	NE
THETA. 1972. m. membership. Scientology Kerk, N.Z. Voorburgwal 271, 1012 RS Amsterdam, Netherlands. Ed. R. Meijns. bk.rev.; circ. 5,000. **Formerly:** Nieuwe Theta.

289.2	US	ISSN 0273-6527
BX8601		
THIS PEOPLE. 1979. q. $11.95. Utah Alliance Publishing Inc., Box 2250, Salt Lake City, UT 84110. TEL 801-581-0881. Ed. William B. Smart. adv.; bk.rev.; circ. 20,000. **Description:** A family-oriented magazine reflecting the L.D.S. lifestyle.

281.9	ET
TINSAE. (Text in English) 1979. 3/yr. Eth.$6.25($3) Ethiopian Orthodox Mission, P.O. Box 3137, Addis Ababa, Ethiopia. Ed. Haddis Terrefe. charts; illus. **Description:** Covers activities of the Ethiopian Orthodox Church including latest news involving prominent figures of the church.

281.9	RU
▼**TOMSKIE PRAVOSLAVNYE VEDOMOSTI.** 1990. m. 10 Rub. Novosibirskaya Eparkhiya, Blagochinie Pravoslavnykh Khramov Tomskoi Oblasti, Ul. Altaiskaya 47, 634029 Tomsk, Russia. TEL 23-41-23. circ. 10,000. **Description:** Presents the history and life of the Eastern Orthodox church in Siberia.

220	SA
TORA HA KU LIBELELA. (Text in Silozi) 1949. m. R.8.50. Watch Tower Bible & Tract Society, Private Bag 2067, Krugersdorp 1740, South Africa. TEL 011-761-1000. FAX 011-764-4749.

220 289.9	SA	ISSN 0040-9391
TORA YA TEBELO. (Text in Tswana) 1961. s-m. R.17. Watch Tower Bible & Tract Society, Private Bag 2067, Krugersdorp 1740, South Africa. TEL 011-761-1000. FAX 011-764-4749. charts; illus.; index; circ. 10,500.

289.6	UK
TOWARDS WHOLENESS. 3/yr. £3. Friends Fellowship of Healing, 20 Burnet Avenue, Burpham, Guildford, Surrey GU1 1YD, England. TEL 0483-69257. bk.rev.; circ. 1,250. **Formerly:** Friends Fellowship of Healing. **Description:** Studies the practice of prayer and spiritual healing, alternative therapies, relaxation, Quaker thought and practice.

299	II
TRIBAL RELIGIONS. 1982. q. Rs.430($63) (International Institute of Tribal Religions) K.K. Roy (Private) Ltd., 55 Gariahat Rd., P.O. Box 10210, Calcutta 700 019, India. Ed. Dr. K.K. Roy. adv.; bk.rev.; abstr.; bibl.; index; circ. 980.

281.9	RU
▼**TSERKOV' I SPASENIE.** 1991. w. 0.30 Rub. per issue. Pokrovskaya Tserkov', Ul. Sovetskaya 187, 652500 Leninsk-Kuznetsk, Kemerovskaya Oblast', Russia. Ed. S. Plaksin. circ. 5,000. (newspaper)

200	SA	ISSN 0258-9052
TSHIINGAMO. (Text in Venda) 1983. m. R.8.50. Watch Tower Bible & Tract Society, Private Bag 2067, Krugersdorp 1740, South Africa. TEL 011-761-1000. FAX 011-764-4749. charts; illus.; index; circ. 1,900.

220	SA
▼**TSOGANG!.** (Text in Tswana) 1990. m. R.8.50. Watch Tower Bible & Tract Society, Private Bag 2067, Krugersdorp 1740, South Africa. TEL 011-761-1000. FAX 011-764-4749. circ. 3,000.

220 289.9	SA
TSOHA!. (Text in Sesotho) 1973. m. R.8.50. Watch Tower Bible & Tract Society, Private Bag 2067, Krugersdorp 1740, South Africa. TEL 011-761-1000. FAX 011-764-4749. charts; illus.; index; circ. 10,000.

289.9	US
U L C NEWS. vol.15, 1981. q. $5. Universal Life Church, 601 Third St., Modesto, CA 95351. TEL 209-527-8111. FAX 209-527-8116. Ed. Kirby J. Hensley. adv.; bk.rev.; illus.; circ. 100,000. **Formerly (until 1984):** Universal Life.

281.9	US
U R O B A MESSENGER.* (Text mainly in English; occasionally in Russian) 1925. bi-m. $5. United Russian Orthodox Brotherhood of America, 429 Forbes Ave., Ste. 1616, Pittsburgh, PA 15219-1604. TEL 412-261-4277. circ. 2,000. (tabloid format) **Formerly:** Russian Messenger - Russkij Vistnik (ISSN 0036-0287)

289.9	US
U S BAHA'I REPORT. 1984. q. free. National Spiritual Assembly of the Baha'is of the United States, 536 Sheridan Rd., Wilmette, IL 60091. TEL 708-869-9039. Ed. John Bowers. circ. 2,300. **Description:** Current events in the Baha'i community.

268	US	ISSN 0147-1015
BX738.U4		
UKRAINIAN ORTHODOX WORD. ENGLISH EDITION. vol.8, 1974. m. $9. Ukrainian Orthodox Church of the U.S.A., Box 495, So. Bound Brook, NJ 08880. TEL 908-356-0090. Ed. Bishop Antony. bk.rev.; film rev.; play rev.; bibl.; stat.; circ. 2,000. (tabloid format; back issues avail.)

200	US	ISSN 0041-6258
ULTREYA. 1959. m. $10. U S Cusillo Movement, National Secretariat, Box 210226, 4500 W. Davis, Dallas, TX 75211. Ed. Gerald P. Hughes. bk.rev.; illus.; circ. 6,000.

220	SA
ULUPUNGU LWA KWA KALINDA. (Text in Cibemba) 1949. s-m. R.17. Watch Tower Bible & Tract Society, Private Bag 2067, Krugersdorp 1740, South Africa. TEL 011-761-1000. FAX 011-764-4749. circ. 39,000.

658.32	US	ISSN 0360-9782
BX7245.5		
UNITED CHURCH OF CHRIST. PENSION BOARDS (ANNUAL REPORT). 1967. a. free. United Church of Christ, Pension Boards, 475 Riverside Dr., 10th fl., New York, NY 10115. TEL 212-870-2790. FAX 212-870-2877. Ed.Ed. Edmund Tortora. circ. 15,000. Key Title: Pension Boards.

28_.9	US	ISSN 0162-3567
UNITY (UNITY VILLAGE). 1889. m. $7 for inkprint ed.; Braille ed. free. Unity School of Christianity, Unity Village, MO 64065. TEL 816-524-3550. Ed. Philip White. circ. 150,000. (also avail. in Braille)

289.6	UK	ISSN 0267-6648
UNIVERSALIST. 1979. 3/yr. £3.50. Quaker Universalist Group, 35 The Bridle, Glen Parva, Leicester LE2 9HR, England. TEL 0533-783999. bk.rev. **Description:** Theology and religious history, religious experience and mysticism. Specializes in the universalist aspects of Quakerism.

200	GW	ISSN 0042-3696
VERBUM. (Text in English, French, German and Spanish) 1970. q. DM.34. (Missionswissenschaftliches Institut) Steyler Verlag, Bahnhofstr. 9, 4054 Nettetal 2, Germany. TEL 02157-1202-20. FAX 02157-1202-22. Ed. Rev. Karl Mueller. bk.rev.; abstr.; charts; pat.; tr.mk.; circ. 1,400.
—BLDSC shelfmark: 9155.809200.

281.9   US
VINEYARD.* (Text in English, Albanian) 1970. q. Albanian Orthodox Archdiocese in America, Box 650, Southbridge, MA 01550-0650.
TEL 617-764-6226. circ. 3,200. (tabloid format; back issues avail.)

281.9 949.7   YU   ISSN 0353-1783
VINOGRAD GOSPODNJI; list za duhovnu kulturu. (Text in Serbo-Croatian) 1978. 4/yr. free. Uprava Parohije Uspenske, Sumadijska 3-III, Novi Sad, Yugoslavia. TEL 021-28-055. Ed. Dusan Petrovic. (back issues avail.)
Description: Examines the history of the Serbian Orthodox Church and its theology.

289.9   US   ISSN 0042-7381
VITAL CHRISTIANITY. 1881. 12/yr. $19.95. (Church of God) Warner Press, Inc., Box 2499, Anderson, IN 46018. TEL 317-644-7721. Ed. Arlo F. Newell. adv.; illus.; circ. 25,000. **Indexed**: G.Soc.Sci.& Rel.Per.Lit.
Description: Provides instruction for adults on how to live life as a Christian.

289   US   ISSN 0049-6669
VOICE (GRANDVILLE). 1930. 6/yr. $7.50. Independent Fundamental Churches of America, Box 810, Grandville, MI 49468. TEL 616-457-5920. Ed. Paul J. Dollaske. adv.; bk.rev.; illus.; circ. 11,500.
Description: Discusses personal growth, clergy development, biblical exegesis (texural and topical), and current themes.

294.6   II
VOICE OF SAMANVAYA. (Text in English) 1976. s-a. Rs.15. C.P. Ramaswami Aiyar Foundation, Centre for Studies in Tradition, Thought and Culture of India, The Grove, Eldams Rd, Madras 18, India. Ed. K. Seshadri.

289.9   US   ISSN 0042-8213
VOICE OF THE NAZARENE. vol.19, 1970. m. free. God's Acres, Inc., Box 5175, Sun City, FL 33571-5175. FAX 813-634-6335. Ed. W.L. King. bk.rev.; illus.; circ. 9,000. (processed)

289.9   US
VOR TRU/OUR FAITH. 1978. q. $12 (foreign $16). World Tree Publications, Box 961, Payson, AZ 85547. Ed. Thorsteinn Thorarinsson. circ. 500.
Description: Contains news of the Asatru faith (the ancient religion of the Northern European peoples) in North America and articles, poems and letters.

200 289.9   SA
VUKANI!. (Text in Xhosa) 1973. m. R.8.50. Watch Tower Bible & Tract Society, Private Bag 2067, Krugersdorp 1740, South Africa.
TEL 011-761-1000. FAX 011-764-4749. charts; illus.; index; circ. 9,900.

220 289.9   SA
DIE WAGTORING. (Text in Afrikaans) 1943. s-m. R.17($5) Watch Tower Bible & Tract Society, Private Bag 2067, Krugersdorp 1740, South Africa.
TEL 011-761-1000. FAX 011-764-4749. charts; illus.; index; circ. 31,000.

267.15   CN   ISSN 0043-0218
WAR CRY. 1884. w. Can.$25($30) (Salvation Army, Canada Territorial Headquarters) Triumph Press, 455 North Service Road East, Oakville, Ont. L6H 1A5, Canada. TEL 416-844-2561. Ed. Major M. Ryan. bk.rev.; illus.; circ. 75,000. (tabloid format)

267.15   NR   ISSN 0049-688X
WAR CRY. 1921. bi-m. £N9 (typically set in Mar.-Apr.). Salvation Army in Nigeria, Territorial Headquarters, Box 125, Lagos, Nigeria. FAX 234-1-633556. Ed. C.B. Ezekwere. bk.rev.; circ. 4,500.

267.15   NZ   ISSN 0043-0242
WAR CRY. 1883. w. NZ.$52.60. Salvation Army, 204 Cuba Street, Wellington 2, New Zealand.
TEL 04-384-5649. FAX 04-384-6277. Ed. Alan M. Robb. bk.rev.; circ. 11,000. (also avail. in microfilm)

267.15   SA   ISSN 0043-0250
WAR CRY/STRYDKREET. (Text in Afrikaans and English) 1884. fortn. R.20. Salvation Army, P.O. Box 1018, Johannesburg 2000, South Africa.
TEL 011-403-3614. FAX 011-403-5638. Ed. Joan Dunwoodie. bk.rev.; illus.; circ. 6,500.

267.15   SI   ISSN 0049-6898
WAR CRY. 1971. m. S.$5. Salvation Army in Malaysia and Singapore, 207 Clemenceau Ave., Singapore-9, Singapore. Ed. James R. Sloan. charts; illus.

WAR CRY. see *RELIGIONS AND THEOLOGY*

067.15   US   ISSN 0043-0234
BX9701
WAR CRY. 1880. bi-w. $7.50 in the US: Canada $8; elsewhere $9. Salvation Army, 615 Sleiters Lane, Alexandria, VA 22313. TEL 703-684-5500. Ed. Lt. Col. Henry Gariepy. bk.rev.; circ. 350,000. (also avail. in microfilm; back issues avail.)

289.9   US
WARM LINE. 10/yr. 9527 Bay Court, Carmel, CA 93923. TEL 408-625-0825.
Description: Discusses ideas of interest to Christian Scientists in and out of the church.

289.9   US   ISSN 0043-1087
WATCHTOWER; announcing Jehovah's kingdom. (Editions in 111 languages; also avail. in Braille) 1879. s-m. (Jehovah's Witnesses, Governing Body) Watchtower Bible and Tract Society of New York, Inc., 25 Columbia Hts., Brooklyn, NY 11201. TEL 718-625-3600. circ. 15,570,000.

289.9   US
THE WAY FOURTH. 1979. q. membership. (Tayu Center) Tayu Press, Box 11554, Santa Rosa, CA 95406. TEL 707-829-9579. bk.rev.; circ. 200.
Formerly: Ganymede.
Description: Dedicated to the teachings of this spiritual tradition, with emphasis on meditation.

200   UK   ISSN 0043-1605
WAY OF LIFE; the church's ministry of healing. 1911. q. £5. Guild of Health, 26 Queen Anne St., London W1M 9LB, England. Ed.Bd. bk.rev.; index; circ. 1,900. **Indexed**: CERDIC.
Former titles: For Health; Healing.

294.37   US
WHEEL SERIES. 1973. irreg., no.3, 1982. Four Seasons Foundation, Box 31190, San Francisco, CA 94131. (Subscr. to: Subco, Box 168, Monroe, OR 97456) Ed. Donald Allen. circ. 3,000.

289   US   ISSN 0043-5007
WHITE WING MESSENGER. 1923. fortn. $9.50. (Church of God of Prophecy) White Wing Publishing House, Box 3000, Cleveland, TN 37311.
TEL 615-476-8536. Ed. Billy Murray. illus.; circ. 16,000.

289.9   US   ISSN 0190-4620
WOMAN'S TOUCH; an inspirational magazine for women. 1977. bi-m. $6. (General Council of the Assemblies of God) Gospel Publishing House, 1445 Boonville Ave., Springfield, MO 65802-1894. TEL 417-862-2781. FAX 417-862-8558. Ed. Sandra G. Clopine. circ. 20,000.
Description: Inspirational, general readership magazine for women with articles that are compatible with Christian teachings.

WORD IN LIFE. see *RELIGIONS AND THEOLOGY — Roman Catholic*

289   AT   ISSN 0158-6262
WORLD MISSIONS UPDATE. 1971. bi-m. Aus.$2. Assemblies of God World Missions, P.O. Box 254, Mitcham, Vic. 3132, Australia. FAX 613-872-3220. Ed. W. Robert McQuillan. bk.rev.; circ. 15,650.
Formerly: Garamut (ISSN 0311-0362)

200   US   ISSN 0043-8804
BP300
WORLD ORDER; a Baha'i magazine. 1966. q. $10. National Spiritual Assembly of the Baha'is of the United States, 536 Sheridan Rd., Wilmette, IL 60091. TEL 708-869-9039. FAX 708-251-3652. (Subscr. to: World Order Subscr. Service, 112 Linden Ave., Wilmette, IL 60091) Ed. Betty J. Fisher. bk.rev.; cum.index: vols.1-12; circ. 2,500. (also avail. in microform from UMI; reprint service avail. from UMI) **Indexed**: Ind.Amer.Per.Verse, Rel.Ind.One. —BLDSC shelfmark: 9356.955000.
Description: Articles intended to show the relationship between contemporary life and the teachings and philosophy of contemporary religions.

267.15   NE
WYZER. 1898. bi-m. fl.5. Leger des Heils - Salvation Army in the Netherlands, Damstr. 15, Amsterdam, Netherlands. Ed. Major K. Kerkhoven. bk.rev.; abstr.; circ. 3,500.
Formerly: Jonge Kampvechter (ISSN 0021-7387)
Description: For ages 6-14.

200 289.9   SA   ISSN 0258-9079
XIHONDZO XO RINDZA. (Text in Tsonga) 1974. s-m. R.17. Watch Tower Bible & Tract Society, Private Bag 2067, Krugersdorp 1740, South Africa.
TEL 011-761-1000. FAX 011-764-4749. charts; illus.; index; circ. 6,700.

YOGA; tidsskrift for universel religion. see *PHILOSOPHY*

289 341.1   CN
YOUNG COMPANION. 1966. 11/yr. $6. (Amish Church) Pathway Publishing Corporation, Route 4, Aylmer, Ont. N5H 2R3, Canada. Ed. Joseph Stoll. bk.rev.; bibl.; illus.; circ. 19,000.
Formerly: Ambassador of Peace.

200   SA   ISSN 0044-0787
YOUNG IDEAS. Afrikaans edition: Jong Dae. (Supplement to: The Path of Truth) 1937. m. free. School of Truth Ltd., South Africa Centre, 5th Fl., 253 Bree St., Johannesburg 2001, South Africa. TEL 011-333-8331. Ed. Gerita Gerryts-Elferink.

200   AT   ISSN 0300-3264
YOUNG SOLDIER. 1890. w. Aus.$31. (Salvation Army) Dinsdale Pender, 1-9 Drill St, Hawthorn, Melbourne, Vic. 3122, Australia. FAX 03-819-4864. Ed. Joy Goodacre. illus.; circ. 17,521.

200   UK
YOUR TOMORROW. 1918. m. £8.50($12) Prophetic Witness Movement International, 59 Baldwin Avenue, Eastbourne, E. Sussex NB21 1U1, England. Ed. Rev. Glyn L. Taylor. adv.; bk.rev.; illus.; circ. 4,500. **Indexed**: CERDIC.
Formerly: Prophetic Witness (ISSN 0033-135X); Incorporates: Prophetic News and Israel's Watchman (ISSN 0033-1333)

289.9   GW   ISSN 0921-5174
ZEN. 1980. q. fl.26. Zen-uitgeverij Theresiahoeve, Schneifelweg 15, 5540 Gondenbett, Germany. Ed. Judith Bossert. adv.; bk.rev.; circ. 1,200.

281.9   US
ZEN NOTES. 1954. 10/yr. $3 (foreign $5). First Zen Institute of America, 113 E. 30th St., New York, NY 10016. TEL 212-686-2520. Ed. Mary Farkas. bk.rev.; circ. 600. (back issues avail.)

RESPIRATORY DISEASES

see *Medical Sciences–Respiratory Diseases*

RHEUMATOLOGY

see *Medical Sciences–Rheumatology*

ROADS AND TRAFFIC

see *Transportation–Roads and Traffic*

ROMAN CATHOLICISM

see *Religions and Theology–Roman Catholic*

RUBBER

678.2 668.4   US
ADHESIVE AND SEALANT COUNCIL. NEWSLETTER. bi-m. Adhesive and Sealant Council, Inc., 1627 K St., N.W., Ste. 1000, Washington, DC 20006-1707. TEL 202-452-1500.

RUBBER 4291

678.2 668.4 US
ADHESIVE AND SEALANT COUNCIL. SEMINAR PAPERS. s-a. $75 to non-members; members $55. Adhesive and Sealant Council, Inc., 1627 K St., N.W., Ste. 1000, Washington, DC 20006-1707. TEL 202-452-1500.

678.2 668.4 US
ADHESIVE TRENDS. Variant title: Indicators. bi-m. free. Adhesive Manufacturers Association, 401 N. Michigan Ave., Chicago, IL 60611-4267. TEL 312-644-6610. FAX 312-321-6869. circ. 300 (controlled).

ANNUAL BOOK OF A S T M STANDARDS. VOLUME 09.01. RUBBER, NATURAL AND SYNTHETIC - GENERAL TEST METHODS; CARBON BLACK. see ENGINEERING — Engineering Mechanics And Materials

ANNUAL BOOK OF A S T M STANDARDS. VOLUME 09.02. RUBBER PRODUCTS, INDUSTRIAL - SPECIFICATIONS AND RELATED TEST METHODS; GASKETS; TIRES. see ENGINEERING — Engineering Mechanics And Materials

678 668 FR
ASSOCIATION FRANCAISE DES INGENIEURS ET CADRES DU CAOUTCHOUC ET DES PLASTIQUES. ANNUAIRE. 1956. biennial. membership. Association Francaise des Ingenieurs et Cadres du Caoutchouc et des Plastiques, 60 rue Auber, 94408 Vitry-Seine, France. FAX 45-21-03-50. TELEX 202963. adv.; bk.rev.
  Formerly: Association Francaise des Ingenieurs du Caoutchouc et des Plastiques. Annuaire (ISSN 0066-9229)

678.2 IT
ASSOGOMMA NOTIZIE. w. Associazione Nazionale fra le Industrie della Gomma, Cavi Elettrici ed Affini - Italian Rubber and Manufacturers Association, Via S. Vittore 36, 20123 Milan, Italy. TEL 4988168.

BAUEN MIT KUNSTSTOFFEN. see BUILDING AND CONSTRUCTION

678.2 US
BLUE BOOK OF MATERIALS, COMPOUNDING INGREDIENTS AND MACHINERY FOR RUBBER. 1936. a. $63. Lippincott & Peto, Inc., 1867 W. Market St., Akron, OH 44313. TEL 216-864-2122. Ed. Don R. Smith. adv.; circ. 4,500. (reprint service avail. from UMI)

BRITISH PLASTICS AND RUBBER MAGAZINE. see PLASTICS

BUSINESS TIMES. see BUSINESS AND ECONOMICS

678 668.4 FR ISSN 0035-3175
TS1870 CODEN: RCPLA5
CAOUTCHOUCS ET PLASTIQUES. (Summaries in English, French) 1924. m. 787 F. (foreign 900 F.). Societe d'Expansion Technique et Economique (SETE), 5, rue Jules Lefebvre, 75009 Paris, France. TEL 48-74-53-70. FAX 48-74-30-28. TELEX EDISETE 650896 F. Ed. Marc Bohy. adv.; bk.rev.; abstr.; bibl.; charts; illus.; stat.; index; circ. 7,000. (back issues avail.) Indexed: C.I.S. Abstr., Chem.Abstr., Excerp.Med., Hort.Abstr., PROMT, Soils & Fert., Weed Abstr., World Agri.Econ.& Rural Sociol.Abstr.
—BLDSC shelfmark: 3050.614000.
  Description: Provides information for the plastics manufacturing and processing industries, as well as for machine builders.

CHINA PLASTIC AND RUBBER JOURNAL/ZHONGGUO CUOLIAO XIANGJIAO; a plastic and rubber journal for P.R. China. see PLASTICS

COMPOSITE POLYMERS. see PLASTICS

678 668.4 US ISSN 0272-4685
TK5 CODEN: ICEPD2
CONFERENCE OF ELECTRICAL ENGINEERING PROBLEMS IN THE RUBBER AND PLASTICS INDUSTRIES. I E E E CONFERENCE RECORD. a. (I E E E, Industry Applications Society) Institute of Electrical and Electronics Engineers, Inc., 345 E. 47th St., New York, NY 10017-2394. TEL 212-705-7900. FAX 212-705-7682. (Subscr. to: IEEE Service Center, Box 1331, 445 Hoes Lane, Piscataway, NJ 08855-1331)
  Former titles: Electrical Engineering Problems in the Rubber and Plastics Industry Technical Conference. Record (ISSN 0732-295X); Rubber and Plastics Industry Technical Conference. Record (ISSN 0080-4762)

678.32 NO
DEKK AKTUELT. 7/yr. DKK 100.
  (Bilgummiverkstedenes Landsforbund) Forlagsassistanse A-S, Fredensborgveien 24-26, Oslo 1, Norway. Ed. Helge Dehlin. adv.; circ. 5,039.
  Description: Looks at the tire trade industry.

678.2 UK ISSN 0262-1584
TS1870 CODEN: DERTD4
DEVELOPMENTS IN RUBBER TECHNOLOGY. 1979. irreg., vol.4, 1987. Elsevier Science Publishers Ltd., Books Division, Crown House, Linton Rd., Barking, Essex IG11 8JU, England. TEL 081-594-7272. FAX 081-594-5942. TELEX 896950 APPSCI G. (Subscr. in U.S. and Canada to: Elsevier Science Publishing Co., Inc., Box 882, Madison Sq. Sta., New York, NY 10159. TEL 212-989-5800) (back issues avail.) Indexed: Chem.Abstr.
  Refereed Serial

678.2 MY
DUNLOP ESTATES NEWS. (Text in English) 1972. q. free. Dunlop Estates Bhd., P.O. Box 11395, 50744 Kuala Lumpur, Malaysia. Ed. J.M. Ho. charts; illus.; circ. 1,000.

678 US ISSN 0146-0706
TS1870 CODEN: ELASDA
ELASTOMERICS. 1917. m. $45 (foreign $115). Communication Channels, Inc., 6255 Barfield Rd., Atlanta, GA 30328-4369. TEL 404-256-9800. FAX 404-256-3116. TELEX 4611075 COMCHANI. Ed. Ann Barker. adv.; bk.rev.; charts; illus.; pat.; stat.; tr.lit.; index; circ. 16,000. (also avail. in microform from UMI; reprint service avail. from UMI) Indexed: A.S.& T.Ind., Chem.Abstr., Curr.Cont., Eng.Ind., Excerp.Med., Ind.Sci.Rev., PROMT, Sci.Cit.Ind., Text.Tech.Dig.
  Incorporates (1983-1984): Elastomerics Extra; Former titles: Rubber Age and Tire News (ISSN 0096-2333); Rubber Age (ISSN 0035-9440)
  Description: Serves manufacturers and users of rubber or rubberlike products. Features technical articles on scientific developments in the elastomers field.

678 US ISSN 0361-0640
TS1877
ELASTOMERICS RUBBER RED BOOK; directory of the rubber industry. 1936. a. $69.95. Communication Channels, Inc., 6255 Barfield Rd., Atlanta, GA 30328-4369. TEL 404-256-9800. FAX 404-256-3116. TELEX 4611075 COMCHANI. Ed. Barbara Katinsky. circ. 4,400.

678 UK ISSN 0260-5317
TS1870 CODEN: ERJTDW
EUROPEAN RUBBER JOURNAL. 1882. m. (except Aug.). £40($81) Crain Communications Inc., Cowcross Ct., 2nd Fl., 75-77 Cowcross St., London EC1M 6BP. TEL 071-608-1116. FAX 071-608-1173. TELEX 28544. (Subscr. to: Reader Service Dept., 120-126 Lavender Ave., Mitcham, Surrey CR 4 34P, England) Ed. D. Shaw. adv.; illus.; circ. 6,739. (also avail. in microform from UMI; back issues avail.) Indexed: Anal.Abstr., Br.Tech.Ind., Fluidex, Key to Econ.Sci., PROMT.
—BLDSC shelfmark: 3829.960000.
  Description: Covers commercial and technical developments pertinent to the processing and manufacturing industries.

FIRE & FLAMMABILITY BULLETIN; an international newsletter. see FIRE PREVENTION

GREATER BATON ROUGE MANUFACTURERS DIRECTORY. see BUSINESS AND ECONOMICS — Trade And Industrial Directories

338.476 AG ISSN 0533-4500
GUIA DE LA INDUSTRIA DEL CAUCHO. 1970. biennial. Arg.$3000($32) or exchange basis. Federacion Argentina de la Industria del Caucho, Av. Leandro N. Alem 1067, Piso 16, 1001 Buenos Aires, Argentina. Ed. Antonio C. Castro. circ. 3,000.

678 MX
GUIA DE LA INDUSTRIA: HULERA. 1968. a. Mex.$100000($50) Informatica Cosmos, S.A. de C.V., Fernando Arrieta 5-101, Col. Los Cipreses, 04830 Mexico D.F., Mexico. TEL 677-48-68. FAX 679-35-75. Ed. Cesar Macazaga O. adv.; circ. 5,000.

678 IT
GUIDA ALL'INDUSTRIA ITALIANA DELLA GOMMA/GUIDE TO THE ITALIAN RUBBER INDUSTRY. (Text in English, French, German and Spanish) 1962. a. L.80000. (Associazione Nazionale fra le Industrie della Gomma) Gesto s.r.l., Via C. Battisti, 21, 20122 Milan, Italy. TEL 55187571. FAX 5465310. Ed. Enzo Belli-Nicoletti. adv.
  Formerly: Annuario dell'Industria Italiana della Gomma (ISSN 0066-4499)
  Description: Directory of Italian rubber manufacturers and their suppliers.

678 GW
GUMMI, FASERN, KUNSTSTOFFE; internationale Fachzeitschrift. 1948. m. DM.244.80 (foreign DM.270). A.W. Gentner Verlag, Forststr. 131, Postfach 101742, 7000 Stuttgart 10, Germany. TEL 0711-63672-0. FAX 0711-6367211. Ed. Heinz Gupta. adv.; bk.rev.; bibl.; charts; illus.; pat.; stat.; index; circ. 5,760. Indexed: ASCA, Chem.Abstr., Curr.Cont., Dok.Arbeitsmed., Eng.Ind., Excerp.Med., Fluidex, INIS Atomind., Intl.Polym.Sci.& Tech., Packag.Sci.Tech., PROMT, Sh.& Vib.Dig.
  Formerly: Gummi, Asbest, Kunstoffe (ISSN 0176-1625)

678 GW ISSN 0017-5609
GUMMIBEREIFUNG; Fachzeitschrift fuer Vulkanisation, Runderneuerung, Reifenhandel und Zubehoer. 1924. m. DM.138. Bielefelder Verlagsanstalt GmbH & Co. KG, Niederwall 53, Postfach 1140, 4800 Bielefeld, Germany. TEL 0521-595-520. adv.; bk.rev.; bibl.; charts; illus.; mkt.; pat.; index; circ. 6,000. Indexed: C.I.S. Abstr., Chem.Abstr., RAPRA.
  Description: For the tire trade industry. Information on tire technology, retreading, marketing, and recycling.

678 SZ ISSN 0073-0076
HANDBUCH DER INTERNATIONALEN KAUTSCHUKINDUSTRIE/INTERNATIONAL RUBBER DIRECTORY/MANUEL INTERNATIONAL DE CAOUTCHOUC. (Text in English, French, German) 1955. every 10 yrs. 300 Fr. Verlag fuer Internationale Wirtschaftsliteratur GmbH, Box 30, CH-8047 Zurich, Switzerland. FAX 01-4010545. Ed. Walter Hirt.

668.4 MX ISSN 0018-7127
HULE MEXICANO Y PLASTICOS; revista tecnica industrial. 1944. m. Mex.$20000($60) Juan Solorzano Gomez, Ed. & Pub., Filomeno Mata 13-11, Colonia Centro, Delegacion Cuauhtemoc, 06000 Mexico, D.F., Mexico. TEL 5-21-57-51. adv.; bk.rev.; abstr.; bibl.; charts; illus.; mkt.; stat.; circ. 3,500. Indexed: Chem.Abstr., RAPRA.

678.2 MX
HULEQUIPO. 1978. m. Queretaro No. 229-402, Mexico 06700 DF, Mexico. Dir. Carlos Villagran Arevalo. adv.; circ. 5,000.

678.2 II ISSN 0970-2431
CODEN: IJNREZ
INDIAN JOURNAL OF NATURAL RUBBER RESEARCH. (Text in English) 1988. s-a. Rs.150($30) Rubber Research Institute of India, Kottayam 686 009, Kerala, India. TEL 0481-8311. FAX 91-481-8317. TELEX 888 285 RRII IN. Ed. M.R. Sethuraj. charts.
—BLDSC shelfmark: 4417.436000.
  Description: Features biological and technological aspects of natural rubber, including propagation techniques and planting methods, morphology and anatomy, growth and productivity and many other disciplines.

R

RUBBER

678 668.4   II   ISSN 0019-6312
INDIAN RUBBER & PLASTICS AGE. (Text in English) 1966. m. $24. Wadhera Publications, General Assurance Bldg., 232 Dr. D.N. Rd., Bombay 400 001, India. Ed. Roshanlal Wadhera. adv.; bk.rev.; circ. 12,000.

INDIAN RUBBER STATISTICS. see *RUBBER — Abstracting, Bibliographies, Statistics*

678   IT   ISSN 0019-7556
CODEN: INGOAF
INDUSTRIA DELLA GOMMA. 1957. m. L.110000. (Associazione Nazionale fra le Industrie della Gomma Cavi Elettrici ed Affini) Gesto s.r.l., Via Cesare Battisti 21, 20122 Milan, Italy. TEL 02-551875581. Ed. Dr. Enzo Belli-Nicoletti. adv.; bk.rev.; abstr.; charts; illus.; mkt.; pat.; stat.; tr.lit.; index. **Indexed:** Chem.Abstr., PROMT, RAPRA.
—BLDSC shelfmark: 4438.650000.
Description: Technical and economic news for the rubber industry.

678 668.4   FR   ISSN 0247-3518
INFORMATIONS DU CAOUTCHOUC ET DES PLASTIQUES. 1949. m. 1500 F. Union des Industries et de la Distribution des Plastiques et du Caoutchouc, 1 Square la Bruyere, 75009 Paris, France. Ed. M. Mercier. adv.; charts; illus.; mkt.; circ. 2,000. **Indexed:** RAPRA.
Formerly: Informations du Caoutchouc (ISSN 0020-0468)
Description: Periodical of economic research on plastics.

678   US   ISSN 0146-3977
TS1871   CODEN: APIPDP
INTERNATIONAL INSTITUTE OF SYNTHETIC RUBBER PRODUCERS. ANNUAL MEETING PROCEEDINGS. 1961. a. $135 in N. America; elsewhere $161. International Institute of Synthetic Rubber Producers, 2077 S. Gessner Rd., Ste. 133, Houston, TX 77063. TEL 713-783-7511. FAX 713-783-7253. TELEX 791062. Ed. R.J. Killian. circ. 350. **Indexed:** Chem.Abstr.
Description: Contains scientific papers on industrial hygiene, polymer development, raw material and product situations, and information on the business outlook.

678   II   ISSN 0047-1062
INTERNATIONAL PRESS CUTTING SERVICE: RUBBER AND RUBBER TECHNOLOGY. 1967. w. $65. International Press Cutting Service, Box 63, Allahabad 211001, India. Ed. N. Khanna. bk.rev.; index; circ. 1,200. (processed)

678   UK   ISSN 0020-8655
INTERNATIONAL RUBBER DIGEST. m. £54($108) International Rubber Study Group, 8th Fl., York House, Empire Way, Wembley HA9 0PA, England. TEL 081-903 7727. FAX 081-903-2848. TELEX 895 1293 RUBBER G. circ. 600. (reprint service avail. from MCE)
—BLDSC shelfmark: 4548.700000.
Description: Reports on the natural rubber market. Covers topical items drawn from many sources on all matters affecting the rubber industry.

678   UK
INTERNATIONAL RUBBER FORUM. a. price varies. International Rubber Study Group, 8th Fl., York House, Empire Way, Wembley HA9 0PA. TEL 081-903-7727. FAX 081-903-2848. TELEX 895 1293 RUBBER G. (reprint service avail. from MCE)

678   UK   ISSN 0074-7823
INTERNATIONAL RUBBER STUDY GROUP. SUMMARY OF PROCEEDINGS OF THE GROUP MEETINGS AND ASSEMBLIES. a. price varies. International Rubber Study Group, 8th Fl., York House, Empire Way, Wembley HA9 0PA. TEL 081-903 7727. FAX 081-903-2848. TELEX 895 1293 RUBBER G. (reprint service avail. from MCE)

JOURNAL OF ADHESION SCIENCE AND TECHNOLOGY. see *PLASTICS*

678   MY   ISSN 0127-7065
SB290   CODEN: JNRREQ
JOURNAL OF NATURAL RUBBER RESEARCH. Cover title: J N R R. (Text in English) 1928. q. M.$100($50) Rubber Research Institute of Malaysia, Publications, Library & Information Division, P.O. Box 10150, 50908 Kuala Lumpur, Malaysia. TEL 4567033. FAX 6-03-4573512. bibl.; charts; index, cum.index; circ. 1,500. **Indexed:** Agroforest.Abstr., Biol.Abstr., Chem.Abstr., Curr.Adv.Ecol.Sci., Curr.Cont., Excerp.Med., Hort.Abstr., Plant Breed.Abstr., RAPRA, Rev.Appl.Entomol., Rev.Plant Path., Rural Recreat.Tour.Abstr., Soils & Fert., Weed Abstr., World Agri.Econ.& Rural Sociol.Abstr.
—BLDSC shelfmark: 5021.230000.
Former titles (until 1986): Rubber Research Institute of Malaysia. Journal (ISSN 0035-953X); (until 1973): Kuala Lumpur. Rubber Research Institute of Malaya. Journal.
Description: Covers all aspects of natural rubber research.

678   RU   ISSN 0022-9466
TS1870
KAUCHUK I REZINA. 1927. m. 22.20 Rub. Izdatel'stvo Nauka, 90 Pforsoyuznaya ul., 117864 Moscow, Russia. (Dist. by: Mezhdunarodnaya Kniga, ul. Dimitrova D.39, 113095 Moscow, Russia) bk.rev.; bibl.; index. (tabloid format) **Indexed:** Biol.Abstr., Chem.Abstr., Intl.Polym.Sci.& Tech., RAPRA.
—BLDSC shelfmark: 0088.500000.

678   GW   ISSN 0022-9520
TS1870   CODEN: KGUKAC
KAUTSCHUK UND GUMMI. KUNSTSTOFFE. (Text in German; summaries in English) 1947. m. DM.400. (Verband der Deutschen Kautschukgesellschaften) Dr. Alfred Huethig Verlag GmbH, Im Weiher 10, Postfach 102869, 6900 Heidelberg 1, Germany. TEL 06221-489-281. FAX 06221-489279. TELEX 461727-HUEHDD. Eds. Ernst Prein, Sieghard Neufeldt. adv.; bk.rev.; abstr.; bibl.; charts; illus.; pat.; index; circ. 5,563. **Indexed:** Anal.Abstr., Chem.Abstr., Curr.Cont., Excerp.Med., INIS Atomind., PROMT, RAPRA, Risk Abstr.
—BLDSC shelfmark: 5088.050000.

KOVACH TIRE REPORT. see *TRANSPORTATION — Automobiles*

678.2   MY   ISSN 0126-8309
HD9161.M32
MALAYSIAN RUBBER PRODUCERS' COUNCIL. ANNUAL REPORT/MAJLIS PENGELUAR-PENGELUAR GETAH MALAYSIA. LAPURAN TAHUNAN. (Text in English, Malay) 1951. a. M.$12. Malaysian Rubber Producers' Council - Majlis Pengeluar-Pengeluar Getah Malaysia, P.O. Box 12688, 50786 Kuala Lumpur, Malaysia. TEL 2482677. stat.; circ. 600.
Formerly: Rubber Producers' Council of Malaysia. Annual Report.

633.895   MY   ISSN 0126-5865
MALAYSIAN RUBBER PRODUCERS' COUNCIL. MONTHLY STATISTICAL BULLETIN. (Text in English) 1952. m. M.$166. Malaysian Rubber Producers' Council - Majlis Pengeluar-Pengeluar Getah Malaysia, P.O. Box 12688, 50786 Kuala Lumpur, Malaysia. Ed.Bd. charts; stat.
Formerly: Rubber Producers' Council of Malaysia. Monthly Statistical Bulletin.

678.32   US   ISSN 0026-8496
MODERN TIRE DEALER; covering tire sales and car service. 1919. 14/yr. $55 (foreign $90) includes Facts Directory. Bill Communications, Inc. (Akron), 341 White Pond Dr., Box 3599, Akron, OH 44309-3599. TEL 216-867-4401. FAX 216-867-0019. Ed. Lloyd Stoyer. adv.; illus.; tr.lit.; circ. 30,000. (reprint service avail. from UMI) **Indexed:** Bus.Ind., PROMT, Tr.& Indus.Ind.
●Also available online. Vendor(s): DIALOG.
Description: Serves owners and managers of retail tire stores primarily in North America.

MODERN TIRE DEALER: TIRE, TOOLS & EQUIPMENT MERCHANDISING GUIDE. see *TRANSPORTATION*

MUANYAG ES GUMI/PLASTICS AND RUBBER. see *PLASTICS*

678.32   US   ISSN 0027-7045
N T D R A DEALER NEWS. 1942. m. $13. National Tire Dealers and Retreaders Association, Inc., 1250 I St., N.W., Ste. 400, Washington, DC 20005. TEL 202-789-2300. Ed. C.D. Hylton, III. adv.; circ. 6,331. **Indexed:** RAPRA.
Incorporates: Tire Dealers Survey (ISSN 0077-5886)

N V R - INFORMATIEF. (Nederlandse Vereniging van Rubber- en Kunststoffabrikanten) see *PLASTICS*

678   JA   ISSN 0029-022X
NIHON GOMU KYOKAISHI/SOCIETY OF RUBBER INDUSTRY. JOURNAL. (Text in Japanese; summaries in English and Japanese) 1929. m. 6000 Yen. Nihon Gomu Kyokai - Society of Rubber Industry, 1-5-26 Moto-Akasaka, Minato-ku, Tokyo 107, Japan. Ed. Tutomu Furuyama. adv.; bk.rev.; abstr.; bibl.; charts; pat.; cum.index; circ. 4,000. **Indexed:** RAPRA.
—BLDSC shelfmark: 4897.000000.

NOTICIERO DEL PLASTICO - ELASTOMEROS. see *PLASTICS*

OFFICIEL DES PLASTIQUES ET DU CAOUTCHOUC. see *PLASTICS*

OIL CHEMICAL RUBBER WORKERS TRADE UNION OF TURKEY. YEARBOOK. see *LABOR UNIONS*

PANORAMA PLASTICO; la revista mexicana del plastico. see *PLASTICS*

678 630   MY   ISSN 0032-096X
SB290   CODEN: RRMPA5
PLANTERS BULLETIN. 1952. q. M.$12($24) Rubber Research Institute of Malaysia, Publications, Library & Information Division, P.O. Box 10150, 50908 Kuala Lumpur, Malaysia. TEL 4567033. FAX 6-03-4573512. bk.rev.; charts; illus.; mkt.; pat.; tr.mk.; index, cum.index every 4 and 8 yrs.; circ. 6,000. **Indexed:** Biol.Abstr., Chem.Abstr., Curr.Adv.Ecol.Sci., RAPRA, Rev.Appl.Entomol.
—BLDSC shelfmark: 6525.010000.

PLASTE UND KAUTSCHUK; Zeitschrift fuer Wirtschaft, Wissenschaft und Technik der hochpolymeren Werkstoffe. see *PLASTICS*

PLASTFORUM SCANDINAVIA. see *PLASTICS*

PLASTICS AND RUBBER INTERNATIONAL. see *PLASTICS*

PLASTICS AND RUBBER WEEKLY. see *PLASTICS*

PLASTICS NEWS. see *PLASTICS*

PLASTICS, RUBBER AND COMPOSITES PROCESSING AND APPLICATIONS. see *PLASTICS*

PLASTICS, RUBBER AND LEATHER INDUSTRIES JOURNAL. see *PLASTICS*

PLASTIKA I GUMA. see *PLASTICS*

PLASTINDUSTRIEN. see *PLASTICS*

PLASTY A KAUCUK/PLASTICS AND RUBBER. see *PLASTICS*

678   FR
PNEUMATIQUE; publication d'education et de defense professionnelle. 1929. 5/yr. 80 F. Chambre Nationale du Commerce du Pneumatique et de l'Industrie du Rechapage, 94, rue Saint-Lazare, 75442 Paris Cedex 09, France. circ. 1,000.

POLIMERI; Jugoslavenski casopis za plastiku i gumu. see *PLASTICS*

678.2   US
POLY TOPICS. q. Polyurethane Manufacturers Association, Bldg. C, Ste. 20, 800 Roosevelt Rd., Glen Ellyn, IL 60137. TEL 708-858-2670.

678.4 668.4   JA   ISSN 0032-4779
POLYMER FRIENDS FOR RUBBER, PLASTICS AND FIBER/PORIMA NO TOMO. (Text in Japanese) 1964. m. 2400 Yen($6.66) Taiseisha Ltd., Publishing Division, 1-5 Kyobashi, Chuo-ku, Tokyo 104, Japan. Ed. Sadanori Itonori. adv.; charts; illus.; index; circ. 3,000.

POLYMERS AND RUBBER ASIA. see *PLASTICS*

678 668.4   CN
POLYSAR PROGRESS. 1965. q. free. Polysar Rubber Corp., 265 Front St. N., Sarnia, Ont. N7T 7M2, Canada. TEL 519-337-8251. FAX 519-339-7785. Ed. K.R. With. circ. 9,000. Indexed: RAPRA.
  Former titles: Rubber Progress; Polysar Progress (ISSN 0032-4027)
  Description: A marketing publication describing applications of Polysar synthetic rubbers and providing news about the company.

678.2 668.4
PRESSURE SENSITIVE TAPE COUNCIL. TECHNICAL SEMINAR. PROCEEDINGS.* s-a. Pressure Sensitive Tape Council, 5700 Old Orchard Rd., Skokie, IL 60077-1036. TEL 708-940-8800.

PREVISIONS GLISSANTES DETAILLEES EN PERSPECTIVES SECTORIELLES (VOL.20): TRANSFORMATION DU CAOUTCHOUC ET DES MATIERES PLASTIQUES. see *BUSINESS AND ECONOMICS — Economic Situation And Conditions*

678.2 668.4   UK   ISSN 0266-7320
TS1870   CODEN: PRPTEE
PROGRESS IN RUBBER AND PLASTICS TECHNOLOGY. q. £165. (Plastics and Rubber Institute) R A P R A Technology Ltd., Shawbury, Shrewsbury SY4 4NR, England. TEL 0939-250383. FAX 0939-251118. TELEX 35134. Ed. J. Buist. adv.; bk.rev.; abstr.; bibl.; charts; illus.; stat. (back issues avail.)
  —BLDSC shelfmark: 6924.526700.
  Supersedes: Progress of Rubber Technology (ISSN 0306-3542)
  Description: Contains in-depth reviews on topics important to the rubber and plastics industries.

678 668.4   UK   ISSN 0747-4954
HD9161.A1
R A P R A NEW TRADE NAMES IN THE RUBBER AND PLASTICS INDUSTRIES. 1926. a. £120 (effective 1992). (Rubber Research Association of Great Britain, R A P R A Technology Ltd.) Pergamon Press plc, Headington Hill Hall, Oxford OX3 0BW, England. TEL 0865-794141. FAX 0865-743911. TELEX 83177 PERGAP. (And: 660 White Plains Rd., Tarrytown, NY 10591-5153. TEL 914-524-9200) circ. 500.
  ●Also available online. Vendor(s): Orbit Information Technologies (RAPRA).
  —BLDSC shelfmark: 7291.744000.
  Formerly: New Trade Names in the Rubber and Plastics Industries (ISSN 0077-8869)
  Description: Lists over 5,000 new trade names introduced by the plastics and rubber industries worldwide.

R A P R A NEWS. (Rubber and Plastics Research Association of Great Britain) see *PLASTICS*

678   CE
R R I S L BULLETIN. (Text in English) irreg. Rs.25 (foreign Rs.160). Rubber Research Institute of Sri Lanka, Dartonfield, Agalawatta, Sri Lanka. Indexed: Biol.Abstr., Hort.Abstr., Plant Breed Abstr., Rev.Plant Path., Sri Lanka Sci.Ind.
  Supersedes: R R I C Bulletin.

RECENT ADVANCES IN CROSSLINKING & CURING. see *PLASTICS*

678.32   US   ISSN 1046-7157
RETREADING - REPAIR JOURNAL; a technical digest for tire retreaders. 1956. m. $50 (foreign $60). Tire Technical Services, Inc., Box 17203, Louisville, KY 40217. TEL 502-361-9219. FAX 502-367-9570. Ed. E.J. Wagner. adv.; index; circ. 3,000. (back issues avail.)
  Formerly (until vol.33, 1989): Retreader's Journal (ISSN 0482-430X)

678.2   AG   ISSN 0528-3280
TS1870   CODEN: CAUCDV
REVISTA CAUCHO. 1958. 4/yr. $4 per no. or exchange basis. Federacion Argentina de la Industria del Caucho, Av. Leandro N. Alem 1067, Piso 16, 1001 Buenos Aires, Argentina. Ed. Antonio C. Castro. adv.; bk.rev.; charts; illus.; stat.; circ. 1,000.

338.476   SP   ISSN 0212-2138
REVISTA DEL CAUCHO. 1958. bi-m. 6800 ptas. (foreign 10000 ptas.). (Consorcio Nacional de Industriales del Caucho) Reclamo Comercial, S.A., Casanovas, 212, 08036 Barcelona, Spain. TEL 4104372. FAX 3223812. Ed. Jorge Foix Cusco. adv.; circ. 1,500. Indexed: Ind.SST.

678 668   II
RUBBER AND PLASTICS DIGEST. (Text in English) vol.7, 1972. q. 640 Double Storey, New Rajinder Nagar, New Delhi 60, India. Ed. S.K. Bhanot. adv.; charts; illus.

678   US   ISSN 0300-6123
RUBBER & PLASTICS NEWS; the rubber industry's international newspaper. 1971. fortn. $52. Crain Communications Inc. (Akron), 1725 Merriman Rd., Ste. 300, Akron, OH 44313-3185. TEL 216-836-9180. FAX 216-836-1005. (Subscr. to: 965 E. Jefferson Ave., Detroit, MI 48207-3187. TEL 800-678-9595) Ed. Edward Noga. adv.; bk.rev.; charts; illus.; stat.; cum.index; circ. 15,867 (controlled). (tabloid format; also avail. in microfiche from UMI; reprint service avail. from UMI) Indexed: PROMT.
  —BLDSC shelfmark: 8040.030000.
  Description: Commentary, editorials, news items, and technical notes on legislative, technological, financial, and corporate issues that affect the rubber industry worldwide.

678   US   ISSN 0197-2219
RUBBER & PLASTICS NEWS II. (Supplement to Rubber & Plastics News) 1979. fortn. $52. Crain Communications Inc. (Akron), 1725 Merriman Rd., Ste. 300, Akron, OH 44313-3185. TEL 216-836-9180. FAX 216-836-1005. (Subscr. to: 965 E. Jefferson Ave., Detroit MI 48207-3187. TEL 800-678-9595) Ed. Edward Noga. (reprint service avail. from UMI) Indexed: PROMT.
  —BLDSC shelfmark: 8040.034000.

RUBBER AND PLASTICS NEWSLETTER. see *OCCUPATIONAL HEALTH AND SAFETY*

678.2   UK   ISSN 0955-8772
RUBBER AND POLYURETHANE DIRECTORY B.R.M.A.. (Text in English, French, German and Spanish) 1967. biennial. £25. British Rubber Manufacturers' Association Ltd., 90-91 Tottenham Court Rd., London W1P 0BR, England. TEL 01-580-2794. FAX 01-631-5471. TELEX 267059 BRMA G. circ. 1,000.
  Formerly: British Rubber Industry Directory.

678   II
RUBBER BOARD BULLETIN. (Text in English) 1951. q. Rs.10($3) Rubber Board, Box 280, Kottayam 686001, Kerala, India. Ed. P.K. Narayanan. Indexed: Agroforest.Abstr., Biol.Abstr., Chem.Abstr., Excerp.Med., Hort.Abstr., Indian Sci.Abstr., Plant Breed Abstr., RAPRA, Rev.Appl.Entomol., Soils & Fert., Trop.Abstr., Weed Abstr., World Agri.Econ.& Rural Sociol.Abstr.

678   US   ISSN 0035-9475
TS1870   CODEN: RCTEA4
RUBBER CHEMISTRY AND TECHNOLOGY. 1928. 5/yr. $95. American Chemical Society, Inc., Rubber Division, University of Akron, Akron, OH 44325-3801. TEL 216-375-7814. FAX 216-375-5269. Ed. C.M. Roland. adv.; bk.rev.; abstr.; charts; illus.; index; circ. 6,000. (also avail. in microform from UMI) Indexed: A.S.& T.Ind., Chem.Abstr., Curr.Cont., Eng.Ind., Fluidex, RAPRA, Text.Tech.Dig.
  —BLDSC shelfmark: 8041.000000.
  Description: Provides papers on fundamental research, technical development, and chemical engineering relating to rubber and its allied substances.

678   UK
RUBBER DEVELOPMENTS. 1947. q. free. Malaysian Rubber Producers' Research Association, Tun Abdul Razak Laboratory, Brickendonbury, Hertford SG13 8NL, England. TEL 0992-584966. FAX 0992-554837. Ed. G.M. Reader. bk.rev.; bibl.; charts; illus.; index; circ. 14,000. Indexed: Abstr.Bull.Inst.Pap.Chem., Br.Tech.Ind., Cadscan, Chem.Abstr., Eng.Ind., Fluidex, Hort.Abstr., Lead Abstr., RAPRA, World Surf.Coat., World Text.Abstr., Zincscan.
  Incorporates (1970-1990): N R Technology (ISSN 0307-9007)
  Description: A review of developments in natural rubber research, technology and use.

338.476   US
RUBBER DIRECTORY AND BUYERS GUIDE (YEAR); a directory of rubber product manufacturers and rubber industry suppliers in North America. Short title: Rubbicana (Year). 1978. a. $80. (Rubber and Plastic News) Crain Communications Inc. (Akron), 1725 Merriman Rd., Ste. 300, Akron, OH 44313-3185. TEL 216-836-9180. FAX 216-836-1005. TELEX 241 634. (Subscr. to: 965 E. Jefferson Ave., Detroit, MI 48207-3187. TEL 800-678-9595) adv.; circ. 16,500. (back issues avail.)

678   II   ISSN 0035-9491
TS1885.I5   CODEN: RUIDA4
RUBBER INDIA. (Text in English) 1949. m. Rs.200 (foreign Rs.500). All India Rubber Industries Association, Navjivan Society, Bldg. No. 3, 8th Fl., Lamington Rd., Bombay 400 008, India. TEL 022-395032. TELEX 011-75033. Ed. Dr. Peter Philip. adv.; bk.rev.; circ. 1,200. Indexed: Chem.Abstr.
  —BLDSC shelfmark: 8043.800000.
  Description: Devoted to the dissemination of information within the rubber industry.

338   US
RUBBER: LATIN AMERICAN INDUSTRIAL REPORT. (Avail. for each of 22 Latin American countries) 1985. a. $435 per country report. Aquino Productions, Box 15760, Stamford, CT 06901. TEL 203-325-3138. Ed. Andres C. Aquino.

678   II   ISSN 0035-9513
                    CODEN: RUBNAX
RUBBER NEWS. 1961. m. Rs.200($35) Polymer Publications, 59 Alli Chambers, Tamarind Ln., Fort, Bombay 400 023, India. TEL 27-07-85. Ed. D.S. Kulkarni. adv.; bk.rev.; charts; illus.; mkt.; index; circ. 1,000. Indexed: Chem.Abstr., RAPRA.

338.476 678.2   II   ISSN 0257-859X
RUBBER REPORTER. (Text in English) 1975. bi-m. Rs.125($20) 332, Hind Rajasthan Bldg., D.S. Phalke Road, Dadar, Bombay-400014, India. TEL 4110364. Ed. K.S. Mathew. adv.; bk.rev.; circ. 4,016. (Reprint service avail.)

633.895   MY   ISSN 0126-8279
SB290
RUBBER RESEARCH INSTITUTE OF MALAYSIA. ANNUAL REPORT. a. M.$25($30) Rubber Research Institute of Malaysia, Publications, Library & Information Division, 260 Jalan Ampang, 50450 Kuala Lumpur, Malaysia. circ. 1,700. Indexed: Biol.Abstr., Hort.Abstr., Rev.Plant Path.
  Formerly (until 1973): Kuala Lumpur. Rubber Research Institute of Malaya. Annual Report.

633.895   MY   ISSN 0127-9785
RUBBER RESEARCH INSTITUTE OF MALAYSIA. RUBBER GROWERS' CONFERENCE - PROCEEDINGS. biennial. M.$35($21) Rubber Research Institute of Malaysia, P.O. Box 10150, 50908 Kuala Lumpur, Malaysia. TEL 4567033. FAX 6-03-4573512. charts; illus.; circ. 2,000. Indexed: Chem.Abstr, Seed Abstr.
  Formerly: Rubber Research Institute of Malaysia. Planters Conference Proceedings (ISSN 0126-5849)

633.895   MY   ISSN 0126-9410
RUBBER RESEARCH INSTITUTE OF MALAYSIA. TECHNOLOGY BULLETIN. s-a. M.$3($2) Rubber Research Institute of Malaysia, Publications, Library & Information Division, P.O. Box 10150, 50908 Kuala Lumpur, Malaysia. TEL 4567033. FAX 6-03-4573512. circ. 1,500.

678   CE
RUBBER RESEARCH INSTITUTE OF SRI LANKA. ANNUAL REVIEW. (Text in English) a. Rs.50 (foreign Rs.320). Rubber Research Institute of Sri Lanka, Dartonfield, Agalawatta, Sri Lanka. Indexed: Biol.Abstr., Hort.Abstr., Rev.Plant Path, Weed Abstr.
  Supersedes: Rubber Research Institute of Ceylon. Annual Review.

RUBBER — ABSTRACTING, BIBLIOGRAPHIES, STATISTICS

678   668.4   CE   ISSN 0379-1130
TS1870   CODEN: JRRLDZ
RUBBER RESEARCH INSTITUTE OF SRI LANKA. JOURNAL. (Text in English) vol.53, 1976. irreg. Rs.50 (foreign Rs.320). Rubber Research Institute of Sri Lanka, Dartonfield, Agalawatta, Sri Lanka. Ed. Dr. L.M.K. Tillekerathe. adv.; bk.rev.; charts; illus.; circ. 2,500. **Indexed:** Abstr.Trop.Agri., Biol.Abstr., Chem.Abstr., Hort.Abstr., Plant Breed.Abstr., RAPRA, Rev.Plant Path., Rural Recreat.Tour.Abstr., Soils & Fert., Sri Lanka Sci.Ind., Trop.Abstr., World Agri.Econ.& Rural Sociol.Abstr.
Formerly (until 1976): Rubber Research Institute of Sri Lanka. Quarterly Journal (ISSN 0035-9521)

678.2   668.4   SA   ISSN 0258-9737
RUBBER SOUTHERN AFRICA. 1985. bi-m. R.92. George Warman Publications (Pty.) Ltd., P.O. Box 704, Cape Town 8000, South Africa. TEL 021-24-5320. FAX 021-26-1332. TELEX 5-21849 SA. Ed. Martin Wells. circ. 1,600.
Description: Contains information on rubber compounding, moulding, tire manufacturing, repair and marketing.

678   UK   ISSN 0035-9548
HD9161.A1
RUBBER STATISTICAL BULLETIN. 1946. m. £93($186) International Rubber Study Group, 8th Fl., York House, Empire Way, Wembley HA9 0PA, England. TEL 081-903-7727. FAX 081-903-2848. TELEX 895 1293 RUBBER G. mkt.; stat.; circ. 1,000. (reprint service avail. from MCE) **Indexed:** IIS, PROMT.
—BLDSC shelfmark: 8045.500000.
Description: Provides statistics on the production, consumption, import and export of natural and synthetic rubbers for many countries for the current and preceding year. Includes annual data for the previous five years.

678   UK   ISSN 0035-9564
HD9161.A1
RUBBER TRENDS; a quarterly review of production, markets, prices, etc. q. £335($635) (Economist Intelligence Unit) Business International Ltd., 40 Duke St., London W1A 1DW, England. TEL 071-493-6711. FAX 071-499-9767. TELEX 266353 EIUG. (US addr.: Business International Corp., 215 Park Ave. S., New York, NY 10003. TEL 212-460-0600) charts; stat.; cum.index. **Indexed:** Key to Econ.Sci., PROMT.
—BLDSC shelfmark: 8046.300000.
Description: Analyzes the consumer outlook, as well as trends in rubber-using industries and countries.

678   US   ISSN 0035-9572
TS1870   CODEN: RUBWAQ
RUBBER WORLD. 1889. m. $29. Lippincott & Peto, Inc., 1867 W. Market St., Akron, OH 44313. TEL 216-864-2122. Ed. Don R. Smith. adv.; bk.rev.; bibl.; charts; illus.; mkt.; stat.; tr.lit.; index; circ. 11,400. (also avail. in microform from UMI; reprint service avail. from UMI) **Indexed:** Anal.Abstr., Bus.Ind., Chem.Abstr., Eng.Ind., Fluidex, Key to Econ.Sci., PROMT, RAPRA, Rural Recreat.Tour.Abstr., SRI, Tr.& Indus.Ind., World Agri.Econ.& Rural Sociol.Abstr.
—BLDSC shelfmark: 8047.000000.

678   US
RUBBER WORLD BLUE BOOK. 1935. a. $75. Lippincott & Peto, Inc., 1867 W. Market St., Akron, OH 44313. TEL 216-864-2122. (reprint service avail. from UMI)

678.2   UK
RUBBICANA-EUROPE (YEAR). (Text in English, French and German) biennial. £60($100) R A P R A Technology Ltd., Shawbury, Shrewsbury, Shropshire SY4 4NR, England. TEL 0939-250383. FAX 0939-251118.
Description: Comprehensive listings of all sectors of the rubber and polyurethane industries. Includes suppliers, manufacturers and associations.

678.32   IT   ISSN 0393-7526
RUOTASPRING; tyre-rubber fortnightly journal. (Text in English, French, Italian) 1970. bi-m. L.72000. Minuti Luisa, Via Alatri 30, 00171 Rome, Italy. TEL 25 83 389. Ed. Riccardo Borasi. adv.; bk.rev.; bibl.; charts; illus.; stat.; circ. 9,780. (back issues avail.)

678.2   668.4   US
SEALANTS; the professional's guide. a. $16.45. Sealant, Waterproofing and Restoration Institute, 3101 Broadway, Ste. 585, Kansas City, MO 64111. TEL 816-561-8230. charts; illus.; stat.
Description: Covers joints, sealants, and specifications for the industry.

678   GW
SERVICE - JAHRBUCH. 1952. a. DM.29.80. Bielefelder Verlagsanstalt GmbH & Co. KG, Niederwall 53, Postfach 1140, 4800 Bielefeld, Germany. TEL 0521-595-520. adv.; circ. 2,000.
Formerly: Vulkaniseur - Jahrbuch (ISSN 0083-694X)

678.32   MY   ISSN 0126-5806
SIARAN PEKEBUN. q. M.$12($24) Rubber Research Institute of Malaysia, Publications, Library & Information Division, P.O. Box 10510, 50908 Kuala Lumpur, Malaysia. TEL 4567033. FAX 6-03-4573512.

678   US
SYNTHETIC RUBBER END-USE SURVEY. triennial, latest 1990. $305 in N. America; elsewhere $330. International Institute of Synthetic Rubber Producers, 2077 S. Gessner Rd., Ste. 133, Houston, TX 77063. TEL 713-783-7511. FAX 713-783-7253. TELEX 791062.
Description: Defines how major synthetic elastomers are used. Divided in geographical sections, by elastomer and by end-use category.

678   US
SYNTHETIC RUBBER MANUAL. triennial, 11th ed. $44 in N. America; elsewhere $55. International Institute of Synthetic Rubber Producers, 2077 S. Gessner Rd., Ste. 133, Houston, TX 77063. TEL 713-783-7511. FAX 713-783-7253. TELEX 791062.
Description: Lists over 2000 individual polymers and elastomers with technical and quality criteria.

678.32   US   ISSN 0082-4496
TIRE AND RIM ASSOCIATION. STANDARDS YEAR BOOK. 1927. a. $30. Tire and Rim Association, Inc., 175 Montrose Ave. W., Copley, OH 44321. TEL 216-666-8121. circ. 4,500.

338.476   388.3   US
TIRE BUSINESS. 1983. fortn. $42. Crain Communications Inc. (Akron), 1725 Merriman Rd., Ste. 300, Akron, OH 44313-5251. TEL 216-836-9180. FAX 216-836-1005. (Subscr. to: 965 E. Jefferson Ave., Detroit, MI 48207-3187) Ed. David Zielasko. circ. 21,000. (tabloid format; back issues avail.)
Description: For independent tire dealers and others involved in automotive service.

TIRE REVIEW; the magazine for progressive tire dealers. see TRANSPORTATION — Automobiles

331.8   TU
TURKIYE PETROL KIMYA, LASTIK ISCILEERI SENDIKASI. MAGAZINE. m. Turkiye Petrol, Kimya, Lastik Iscileeri Sendikasi - Oil Chemical Rubber Workers Trade Union of Turkey, Yildiz, Posta Cad P.O. Box 284, Evren Sitesi Gayrettepe, Istanbul 80280, Turkey. TEL 1748896. FAX 1747446.

678.2   629.286   AT
TYRE AND RIM ASSOCIATION OF AUSTRALIA STANDARDS MANUAL. 1958. a. Aus.$21 (effective 1991). Tyre and Rim Association of Australia, c/o F.A. & W.A. Coghlan, 795 Glenferrie Rd., Hawthorn, Vic. 3122, Australia. TEL 818 0759. FAX 03-818-0750. circ. 1,700.

678.32   UK   ISSN 0041-4859
TYRES AND ACCESSORIES. 1946. m. £12. Tyre Industry Publications Ltd., 136 Valley Rd., Clacton-on-Sea, Essex CO15 6LX, England. Ed. George Marshall. adv.; bk.rev.; illus.; circ. 6,100. **Indexed:** Chem.Abstr.

UNION DES INDUSTRIES ET DE LA DISTRIBUTION DES PLASTIQUES ET DU CAOUTCHOUC. GUIDE. see BUSINESS AND ECONOMICS — Trade And Industrial Directories

UNITED RUBBER WORKER. see LABOR UNIONS

678.2   UK   ISSN 0265-637X
URETHANES TECHNOLOGY. 1984. 6/yr. £37.50($80) Crain Communications Ltd., 20-22 Bedford Row, London WC1R 4EW, England. TEL 071-831-9511. FAX 071-430-2176. TELEX 28544. Ed. David R. Reed. circ. 3,523.
—BLDSC shelfmark: 9124.148700.
Description: Reports commercial and technical developments in the polyurethane industry on a world-wide basis.

678.2   US   ISSN 0083-5218
TS1890
VANDERBILT RUBBER HANDBOOK. 1926. irreg. $100. R.T. Vanderbilt Co., Inc., 30 Winfield St., Norwalk, CT 06855. TEL 203-853-1400. FAX 203-853-1452. TELEX 221125. Ed. Robert F. Ohm. index.
Description: Technical information for those directly connected with the compounding and processing of rubber and synthetic elastomers in their dry form.

678.2   CC   ISSN 1000-890X
XIANGJIAO GONGYE/CHINA RUBBER INDUSTRY. (Text in Chinese; table of contents in Chinese, English) m. Beijing Xiangjiao Gongye Yanjiu Shejiyuan - Beijing Research and Design Institute of Rubber Industry, Banbidian, Xijiao (West Surburb), Beijing 100039, People's Republic of China. TEL 815831.
—BLDSC shelfmark: 3180.234280.

RUBBER — Abstracting, Bibliographies, Statistics

678.2   CN   ISSN 0835-0027
CANADA. STATISTICS CANADA. RUBBER AND PLASTIC PRODUCTS INDUSTRIES. (Catalogue 33-250) (Text in English and French) 1919. a. Can.$35($42) (foreign $49). Statistics Canada, Publications Sales and Services, Ottawa, Ont. K1A 0T6, Canada. TEL 613-951-7277. FAX 613-951-1584.
Formerly (until 1985): Canada. Statistics Canada. Rubber Products Industries (ISSN 0300-0214)
Description: Annual census of manufactures.

678   FR
FRANCE. SERVICE D'ETUDE DES STRATEGIES ET DES STATISTIQUES INDUSTRIELLES. RESULTATS MENSUELS DES ENQUETES DE BRANCHE. INDUSTRIE DU CAOUTCHOUC. m. 260 F. (foreign 310 F.) (effective 1991). Service d'Etude des Strategies et des Statistiques Industrielles (SESSI), 85 Bd. du Montparnasse, 75270 Paris Cedex 06, France. TEL 45-56-42-34. FAX 45-56-40-71. stat.
Description: Follows developments in the rubber industry through the performance of selected indicators.

678   FR
FRANCE. SERVICE D'ETUDE DES STRATEGIES ET DES STATISTIQUES INDUSTRIELLES. RESULTATS TRIMESTRIELS DES ENQUETES DE BRANCHE. INDUSTRIE DE CAOUTCHOUC. q. 180 F. (foreign 210 F.)(effective 1991). Service d'Etude des Strategies et des Statistiques Industrielles (SESSI), 85 Bd. du Montparnasse, 75270 Paris Cedex 06, France. TEL 45-56-42-34. FAX 45-56-40-71. stat.
Description: Provides detailed industry-wide performance statistics for comparative evaluations.

678   II   ISSN 0073-6651
INDIAN RUBBER STATISTICS. (Text in English) 1958. a. price varies. Rubber Board, Box 280, Kottayam 686001, Kerala, India.

633.895   MY
MALAYSIA. DEPARTMENT OF STATISTICS. MONTHLY RUBBER STATISTICS OF MALAYSIA. (Text in English) m. M.$2 per no. Department of Statistics, Wisma Statistik, Block E, Jalan Cenderasari, 50514 Kuala Lumpur, Malaysia. TEL 03-2922133.

633.895   MY
MALAYSIA. DEPARTMENT OF STATISTICS. RUBBER STATISTICS HANDBOOK, MALAYSIA. (Text in English) 1988. irreg. Department of Statistics, Wisma Statistik, Block E, Jalan Cenderasari, 50514 Kuala Lumpur, Malaysia. TEL 03-2922133.

678   BL   ISSN 0025-9748
MERCADO DA BORRACHA NO BRASIL. BOLETIM MENSUAL. 1967. m. Superintendencia da Borracha, Ministerio de Industria e do Comercio, SAS QD 05-LT 05-BL. H, CEP 70070 Brasilia, DF, Brazil, Brazil. charts; mkt.; stat.; circ. 1,000. (processed)

SCIENCES: COMPREHENSIVE WORKS 4295

678 668.4 UK ISSN 0961-9305
▼**PLASTICS AND RUBBERS MATERIALS DISC.** 1991. 6/yr. £3250 (effective 1992). (Rubber and Plastics Research Association of Great Britain, R A P R A Technology Ltd.) Pergamon Press plc, Headington Hill Hall, Oxford OX3 0BW, England. TEL 0865-794141. FAX 0865-743911. TELEX 83177 PERGAP. (And: 660 White Plains Rd., Tarrytown, NY 10591-5153. TEL 914-524-9200)
● Available only on CD-ROM.
Description: CD-ROM version of R A P R A Abstracts.

678 668.4 016 UK ISSN 0033-6750
TS1870
R A P R A ABSTRACTS. 1923. m. £995 (effective 1992). (Rubber and Plastics Research Association of Great Britain, R A P R A Technology Ltd.) Pergamon Press plc, Headington Hill Hall, Oxford OX3 0BW, England. TEL 0865-794141. FAX 0865-743911. TELEX 83177 PERGAP. (And: 660 White Plains Rd., Tarrytown, NY 10591-5153. TEL 914-524-9200) Ed. C. Green. adv.; bk.rev.; abstr.; stat.; index; circ. 700. (back issues avail.) **Indexed:** Art & Archaeol.Tech.Abstr., World Surf.Coat., World Text.Abstr.
● Also available online. Vendor(s): Orbit Information Technologies (RAPRA).
Also available on CD-ROM.
—BLDSC shelfmark: 7289.500000.
Description: Provides a comprehensive up-to-date survey of current information from all around the globe, relevant to the rubber, plastics, composites and associated industries. Material is selected from over 450 journals, conference proceedings, books, trade and technical literature, standards and government publications.
Refereed Serial

R A P R A REVIEW REPORTS; current developments in materials technology and engineering. (Rubber and Plastics Research Association of Great Britain) see PLASTICS — *Abstracting, Bibliographies, Statistics*

338.476 310 US
RUBBER MANUFACTURERS ASSOCIATION. NATURAL AND SYNTHETIC RUBBER IMPORT AND EXPORT REPORT. m. $500. Rubber Manufacturers Association, 1400 K St., N.W., 9th Fl., Washington, DC 20005. TEL 202-682-4860. charts; stat.

338.476 310 US
RUBBER MANUFACTURERS ASSOCIATION. STATISTICAL REPORT. MONTHLY TIRE REPORT. 1974. m. $1000. Rubber Manufacturers Association, 1400 K St., N.W., 9th Fl., Washington, DC 20005. TEL 202-682-4860. charts; stat.
Description: Shows import-export activity of passenger car, light and heavy truck, and bus tires. Includes statistics on tire shipments.

338.476 310 US
RUBBER MANUFACTURERS ASSOCIATION. TIRE AND TUBE IMPORT AND EXPORT REPORT. m. $500. Rubber Manufacturers Association, 1400 K St., 9th Fl., Washington, DC 20005. TEL 202-682-4860. charts; stat.

678 UK
WORLD RUBBER STATISTICS HANDBOOK. irreg. £50($100) International Rubber Study Group, 8th Fl., York House, Empire Way, Wembley HA9 0PA. TEL 081-903 7727. FAX 081-903-2848. TELEX 895 1293 RUBBER G. (reprint service avail. from MCE)

338.476 US
WORLDWIDE RUBBER STATISTICS. a. $205 in N.A.; elsewhere $215. International Institute of Synthetic Rubber Producers, 2077 S. Gessner Rd., Ste. 133, Houston, TX 77063. TEL 713-783-7511. FAX 713-783-7253. TELEX 791062.
Description: Covers synthetic and natrual rubber industry. Lists producers, tabulates plant production, provides forecasts and gives statistical histories.

SCHOOL ORGANIZATION AND ADMINISTRATION

see Education–School Organization and Administration

SCIENCE FICTION, FANTASY, HORROR

see Literature–Science Fiction, Fantasy, Horror

SCIENCES: COMPREHENSIVE WORKS

508.1 US ISSN 0271-2229
Q181.A1 CODEN: AAAPEH
A A A S PUBLICATIONS CATALOG. a. free. American Association for the Advancement of Science, 1333 H St., N.W., Washington, DC 20005. TEL 202-326-6446. bk.rev. **Indexed:** Deep Sea Res.& Oceanogr.Abstr., GeoRef.
Formerly: A A A S Miscellaneous Publication.
Description: Lists current AAAS titles on AIDS, arms control, astronomy, biotechnology, chemistry, neuroscience, science education, and science policy.

500 US
A A A S REPORT: RESEARCH AND DEVELOPMENT. 1976. a. $16 to non-members; members $12.80. American Association for the Advancement of Science, 1333 H St., N.W., Washington, DC 20005. TEL 202-326-6600. circ. 2,500. (back issues avail.)
Description: Details information on the President's proposed federal research and development budget.

A B C MLADYCH PRIRODOVEDCU; zabavne naucny ctrnactidenik pro chapce a devcata. see CHILDREN AND YOUTH — For

A F P SCIENCES; information scientifique, technique, medicale. (Agence France-Presse) see MEDICAL SCIENCES

500 919.8 AT ISSN 0728-6414
A N A R E NEWS. (Australian National Antarctic Research Expedition) 1981. q. free. Department of Arts, Sport, The Environment, Tourism and Territories, Antarctic Division, Channel Highway, Kingston, Tas. 7050, Australia. Ed. S. Stallman. bk.rev.; abstr.; illus.; circ. 2,000. (tabloid format)

500 919.8 550 AT
A N A R E REPORT. (Australian National Antarctic Research Expeditions) 1950. irreg. free. Department of Arts, Sport, The Environment, Tourism and Territories, Antarctic Division, Channel Highway, Kingston, Tas. 7050, Australia. Ed. S.A. Potter. circ. 400. (back issues avail.) **Indexed:** AESIS, GeoRef.
Formerly: A N A R E Scientific Report.

500 AT ISSN 0729-6533
CODEN: ANRNDG
A N A R E RESEARCH NOTES. 1982. irreg. free. Australian National Antarctic Research Expeditions, Department of Arts, Sport, the Environment, Tourism and Territories, Antarctic Division, Channel Highway, Kingston, Tas. 7050, Australia. Ed. S.A. Potter. circ. 400. (back issues avail.) **Indexed:** AESIS.
—BLDSC shelfmark: 0897.730000.

A N U REPORTER. (Australian National University) see COLLEGE AND ALUMNI

500 AT ISSN 0312-8059
A N Z A A S CONGRESS PAPERS. 1970. a. price varies. (Australian and New Zealand Association for the Advancement of Science) University of New South Wales Library, P.O. Box 1, Kensington, N.S.W. 2033, Australia. FAX 02-313-7196. (microfiche) **Indexed:** Aus. P.A.I.S., Aus.Sci.Ind, Chem.Abstr.
—BLDSC shelfmark: 3415.150000.

A S T C NEWSLETTER. (Association of Science-Technology Centers) see MUSEUMS AND ART GALLERIES

A W I S MAGAZINE. (Association for Women in Science) see WOMEN'S INTERESTS

500 NE ISSN 0166-4786
Q4
AARDE EN KOSMOS - D J O/EARTH AND COSMOS - D J O. 1968. 8/yr. fl.65. Stichting Mens en Wetenschap, P.O. Box 108, 1270 AC Huizen, Netherlands. Ed Andries C. Sabelis. adv.; bk.rev.; index; circ. 25,000. **Indexed:** Excerp.Med., Geo.Abstr.
Formerly: Aarde en Kosmos.

500 BL ISSN 0001-3765
Q33 CODEN: AABCAD
ACADEMIA BRASILEIRA DE CIENCIAS. ANAIS. (Text in English, French and Portuguese) 1929. q. $50. Academia Brasileira de Ciencias, Rua Anfilofio de Carvalho 29, Caixa Postal 229, 20000 Rio de Janeiro, Brazil. bibl.; charts; illus.; index. **Indexed:** Abstr.Hyg., Biol.Abstr., Chem.Abstr., Curr.Adv.Ecol.Sci., Geo.Abstr., Helminthol.Abstr., Ind.Med, INIS Atomind., Math.R., Met.Abstr., Sci.Abstr., Sci.Cit.Ind., Trop.Dis.Bull.
—BLDSC shelfmark: 0860.000000.

500 PO ISSN 0001-3781
ACADEMIA DAS CIENCIAS DE LISBOA. BOLETIM. 1929. q. Academia das Ciencias de Lisboa, Rua D. Francisco Manuel de Melo 5, Lisbon 1, Portugal. (also avail. in microfiche from BHP) **Indexed:** GeoRef.

500 DR
ACADEMIA DE CIENCIAS DE LA REPUBLICA DOMINICANA. ANUARIO. (Text in English, French and Spanish; summaries in Spanish) 1975. a. $15. Academia de Ciencias de la Republica Dominicana, Calle las Damas 112, Esquina el Conde, Apdo. 932, Santo Domingo, Dominican Republic.

500 SP
ACADEMIA DE CIENCIAS EXACTAS, FISICO-QUIMICAS Y NATURALES. REVISTA. (Text in English, French, German and Spanish) 1916. q. 4000 ptas.($60) Academia de Ciencias Exactas, Fisico-Quimicas y Naturales, Facultad de Ciencias, Zaragoza, Spain. Ed. J. Casas. **Indexed:** Biol.Abstr., Chem.Abstr., Math.R.

500 510 VE
ACADEMIA DE CIENCIAS FISICAS MATEMATICAS Y NATURALES. BOLETIN. 1934. q. free on exchange basis to qualified personnel. Ministerio de Educacion de Venezuela, Academia de Ciencias Fisicas Matematicas y Naturales, Apdo. 1421, Palacio de las Academias, Caracas 101, Venezuela. Ed.Bd. bibl.; charts; illus.; circ. 1,500. **Indexed:** Biol.Abstr., Chem.Abstr., Math.R.

500 FI ISSN 0356-6927
ACADEMIA SCIENTIARUM FENNICA. YEARBOOK/SUOMALAINEN TIEDEAKATEMIA. VUOSIKIRJA. (Text in Finnish or English; summaries in English) 1977. a. Suomalainen Tiedeakatemia - Academia Scientiarum Fennica, Mariankatu 5, 00170 Helsinki 1, Finland. (Orders to: The Bookstore Tiedekirja, Kirkkokatu 14, SF-00170 Helsinki, Finland) Ed. Aarne Nyyssonen. index; circ. 1,300. (back issues avail.; reprint service avail. from UMI) **Indexed:** Biol.Abstr., Ref.Zh.
—BLDSC shelfmark: 9371.637000.
Supersedes (in 1977): Academia Scientiarum Fennica. Proceedings - Sitzungsberichte (ISSN 0065-0501)

500 BE
ACADEMIAE ANALECTA. MEDEDELINGEN VAN DE KONINKLIJKE ACADEMIE VOOR WETENSCHAPPEN, LETTEREN EN SCHONE KUNSTEN VAN BELGIE. SERIES 1: KLASSE DER WETENSCHAPPEN. (Text in Dutch and English; summaries in English) 1938. irreg. price varies. Koninklijke Academie voor Wetenschappen, Letteren en Schone Kunsten van Belgie, 1 Hertogsstraat, B-1000 Brussels, Belgium. TEL 014-41 54 63. (Dist. by: Brepols Publishers, Baron Frans du Foursstraat, B-2300 Turnhout, Belgium) Ed. G. Verbeke. circ. 700. (back issues avail.)

SCIENCES: COMPREHENSIVE WORKS

500 BU ISSN 0366-8681
Q69 CODEN: DBANAD
ACADEMIE BULGARE DES SCIENCES. COMPTES RENDUS.
(Text in English, French, German and Russian) 1948. m. 2.70 lv. per no. (Bulgarska Akademiia na Naukite) Publishing House of the Bulgarian Academy of Sciences, Akad. G. Bonchev St., Bldg. 6, 1113 Sofia, Bulgaria. (Dist. by: Hemus, 6, Rouski Blvd., 1000 Sofia, Bulgaria) illus.; index. **Indexed:** Abstr.Bulg.Sci.Med.Lit., Biol.Abstr., BSL Biol., BSL Geo., BSL Math., Chem.Abstr., Curr.Adv.Biochem., Curr.Adv.Genetics & Molec.Biol., Curr.Cont., Dairy Sci.Abstr., Excerp.Med., Geo.Abstr., Hort.Abstr., Ind.Med., INIS Atomind., Math.R., Met.Abstr., Plant Grow.Reg.Abstr., Sci.Abstr., Seed Abstr., Soils & Fert., Triticale Abstr., World Alum.Abstr.
—BLDSC shelfmark: 3369.050000.

500 FR ISSN 0065-0552
Q46
ACADEMIE DES SCIENCES. ANNUAIRE. 1917. a. Academie des Sciences, 23 Quai Conti, 75006 Paris, France.
Description: Informs reader of the present state of l'Academie des Sciences, list of prizes and grants available at the university, member addresses.

500 FR ISSN 0764-4450
QD1 CODEN: CRAMED
ACADEMIE DES SCIENCES. COMPTES RENDUS DES SCIENCES. SERIES 2: MECANIQUE, PHYSIQUE, CHIMIE, SCIENCES DE LA TERRE, SCIENCES DE L'UNIVERS.
(Text and summaries in English or French) 1835. 28/yr. 3850 F. (Academie des Sciences) Gauthier-Villars, 15 rue Gossin, 92543 Montrouge Cedex, France. TEL 33-1-40-92-65-00. FAX 33-1-40-92-65-97. TELEX 270 004. (Subscr. to: Centrale des Revues, 11 rue Gossin, 92543 Montrouge Cedex, France. TEL 33-1-46-56-52-66) Eds. P. Germain, F. Gros. charts; illus.; index; circ. 3,200. (also avail. in microform from MIM,PMC) **Indexed:** Appl.Mech.Rev., Astron.& Astrophys.Abstr., Biol.Abstr., Biotech.Abstr., Chem.Abstr., Curr.Chem.React, Curr.Cont., Deep Sea Res.& Oceanogr.Abstr., Ecol.Abstr., Ecol.Abstr., Eng.Ind., Excerp.Med., Geo.Abstr., Geotech.Abstr., Ind.Chem., Ind.Med., INIS Atomind., INSPEC, Int.Aerosp.Abstr., Mass Spectr.Bull., Math.R., Met.Abstr., Meteor.& Geoastrophys.Abstr., Nutr.Abstr., Phys.Ber., Sci.Abstr., World Alum.Abstr., Zent.Math.
—BLDSC shelfmark: 3370.042100.
Formerly: Academie des Sciences. Comptes Rendus Hebdomadaires des Seances. Series C: Sciences Chimiques (ISSN 0567-6541)
Description: Covers general mechanics, theoretical physics, magnetic resonance, electronics, solid state physics, celestial mechanics and more.

ACADEMIE DES SCIENCES. COMPTES RENDUS DES SEANCES. SERIES 3: SCIENCES DE LA VIE. see *BIOLOGY*

500 FR ISSN 0065-0560
ACADEMIE DES SCIENCES. INDEX BIOGRAPHIQUE DES MEMBRES ET CORRESPONDANTS. 1931. irreg. Academie des Sciences, 23 Quai Conti, 75006 Paris, France.

500 FR ISSN 0567-6576
Q46
ACADEMIE ET SOCIETE LORRAINES DE SCIENCES. BULLETIN. (Former name of issuing body: Academie et Societe Lorraines des Sciences) 1961. q. 110 F. Academie et Societe Lorraines des Sciences, Biologie Vegetales, B.P. 239, 54506 Vandoeuvre, France. TEL 83-91-22-53. Ed. J.F. Pierre. bk.rev.; circ. 600. (also avail. in microfilm) **Indexed:** Biol.Abstr., Bull.Signal, Chem.Abstr., Curr.Adv.Ecol.Sci., VITIS.

509 GW ISSN 0366-8258
ACADEMIE INTERNATIONALE D'HISTOIRE DES SCIENCES. COLLECTION DES TRAVAUX. (Text in English, French, German) irreg., vol.23, 1976. price varies. Franz Steiner Verlag Wiesbaden GmbH, Birkenwaldstr. 44, Postfach 101526, 7000 Stuttgart 1, Germany. TEL 0711-2582-0. FAX 0711-2582290. TELEX 723636-DAZD. **Indexed:** Math.R.

500 NE ISSN 0169-7897
ACADEMIE INTERNATIONALE D'HISTOIRE DES SCIENCES. COLLECTION DES TRAVAUX. irreg., no.35, 1991. price varies. E.J. Brill, P.O. Box 9000, 2300 PA Leiden, Netherlands. TEL 071-312624. FAX 071-317532. TELEX 39296 BRILL NL. (In N. America: E.J. Brill, 24 Hudson St., Kinderhook, NY 12106. TEL 800-962-4406)

500 940 BE ISSN 0001-4176
CODEN: AOBSAN
ACADEMIE ROYALE DES SCIENCES D'OUTRE-MER. BULLETIN DES SEANCES/KONINKLIJKE ACADEMIE VOOR OVERZEESE WETENSCHAPPEN. MEDEDELINGEN DER ZITTINGEN. (Text in Dutch, French) 1929. 4/yr. 2500 BEF. Academie Royale des Sciences d'Outre-Mer - Koninklijke Academie voor Overzeese Wetenschappen, B.P. 3, 1 rue Defacqz, B-1050 Brussels, Belgium. Ed. J.J. Symoens. bk.rev.; charts; illus.; index, cum.index every 10 yrs. **Indexed:** A.I.C.P., Abstr.Hyg., Amer.Hist.& Life, Chem.Abstr., Curr.Cont.Africa, GeoRef., Hist.Abstr., Trop.Dis.Bull.
—BLDSC shelfmark: 2895.015000.
Former titles: Academie Royale des Sciences Coloniales. Bulletin des Seances; Koninklijke Academie voor Koloniale Wetenschapen. Mededelingen der Zittingen.

ACADEMIE ROYALE DES SCIENCES, DES LETTRES ET DES BEAUX-ARTS DE BELGIQUE. ANNUAIRE. see *HUMANITIES: COMPREHENSIVE WORKS*

500 BE ISSN 0001-4141
AS242 CODEN: BCSAAF
ACADEMIE ROYALE DES SCIENCES, DES LETTRES ET DES BEAUX-ARTS DE BELGIQUE. CLASSE DES SCIENCES. BULLETIN. 1899. m. 1800 BEF. Academie Royale des Sciences des Lettres et des Beaux-Arts de Belgique, Classe des Sciences, Palais des Academies, 1 rue Ducale, B-1000 Brussels, Belgium. charts; illus.; stat.; index; circ. 1,500. **Indexed:** Anim.Breed.Abstr., Biol.Abstr., Chem.Abstr., Deep Sea Res.& Oceanogr.Abstr., Eng.Ind., Sci.Abstr.
—BLDSC shelfmark: 2444.900000.

500 BE
ACADEMIE ROYALE DES SCIENCES, DES LETTRES ET DES BEAUX-ARTS DE BELGIQUE. CLASSE DES SCIENCES. MEMOIRES. 1904. irreg. price varies. Academie Royale des Sciences, des Lettres et des Beaux-Arts de Belgique, Classe des Sciences, Palais des Academies, 1 rue Ducale, B-1000 Brussels, Belgium. (Dist. by: Librarie Alain Ferraton, 162 Ch. de Charleroi, B-1060 Brussels, Belgium) Ed.Bd. circ. 500. **Indexed:** Deep Sea Res.& Oceanogr.Abstr.

ACADEMIE SERBE DES SCIENCES ET DES ARTS. CLASSE DES SCIENCES MATHEMATIQUES ET NATURELLES. BULLETIN. SCIENCES MATHEMATIQUES. see *MATHEMATICS*

500 574 YU ISSN 0352-5740
CODEN: BASNA6
ACADEMIE SERBE DES SCIENCES ET DES ARTS. CLASSE DES SCIENCES MATHEMATIQUES ET NATURELLES. BULLETIN. SCIENCES NATURELLES. (Text in English, French, Russian) 1952. s-a. price varies. Srpska Akademija Nauka i Umetnosti, Odeljenje Prirodno-Matematickih Nauka - Serbian Academy of Sciences and Arts, Knez Mihailova 35, 11001 Belgrade, Serbia, Yugoslavia. TEL 011-187-144. FAX 182-825. TELEX 72593 SANU. (Dist. by: Prosveta, Terazije 16, Belgrade, Serbia, Yugoslavia) Ed. Vladimir Pantic. circ. 1,000. **Indexed:** Biol.Abstr., Chem.Abstr., Deep Sea Res.& Oceanogr.Abstr.
Supersedes in part: Academie Serbe des Sciences et des Arts. Classe des Sciences Mathematiques et Naturelles. Bulletin. Nouvelle Serie (ISSN 0001-4184)

500 US ISSN 0096-7750
ACADEMY OF NATURAL SCIENCES OF PHILADELPHIA. MONOGRAPHS. 1935. irreg., no.22, 1983. price varies. Academy of Natural Sciences of Philadelphia, 1900 Benjamin Franklin Pkwy., Philadelphia, PA 19103-1195. TEL 215-299-1050. FAX 215-299-1028. Ed. William F. Smith-Vaniz. bibl.; charts; illus.; stat. (back issues avail.) **Indexed:** Biol.Abstr., GeoRef.
—BLDSC shelfmark: 5914.200000.

500 US ISSN 0097-3157
QH1 CODEN: PANPA5
ACADEMY OF NATURAL SCIENCES OF PHILADELPHIA. PROCEEDINGS; original research in systematics, evolution & ecology. 1842. a. $30. Academy of Natural Sciences of Philadelphia, 1900 Benjamin Franklin Pkwy., Philadelphia, PA 19103-1195. TEL 215-299-1050. FAX 215-299-1028. Ed. William F. Smith-Vaniz. bibl.; charts; illus.; stat. (back issues avail.; reprint service avail. from KTO) **Indexed:** Biol.Abstr., Curr.Adv.Ecol.Sci., Curr.Cont., Deep Sea Res.& Oceanogr.Abstr., Excerp.Med., Geo.Abstr., GeoRef.
—BLDSC shelfmark: 6618.000000.

500 US ISSN 0097-3254
CODEN: AYSPAX
ACADEMY OF NATURAL SCIENCES OF PHILADELPHIA. SPECIAL PUBLICATIONS. 1922. irreg., no.15, 1985. price varies. Academy of Natural Sciences of Philadelphia, 1900 Benjamin Franklin Pkwy., Philadelphia, PA 19103-1195. TEL 215-299-1050. FAX 215-299-1028. Ed. William F. Smith-Vaniz. bibl.; charts; illus.; stat. (back issues avail.) **Indexed:** Biol.Abstr., GeoRef.
—BLDSC shelfmark: 8371.750000.

500.2 510 IT ISSN 0001-4419
CODEN: AATFAA
ACCADEMIA DELLE SCIENZE DI TORINO. ATTI. PART 1. CLASSE DI SCIENZE FISICHE, MATEMATICHE E NATURALI. 1865. 6/yr. price varies. Accademia delle Scienze di Torino, Via Maria Vittoria 3, 10123 Turin, Italy. (Subscr. to: Bottega d'Erasmo, via G. Ferrari 9, 10124 Turin, Italy) Ed. Vittorio Cirilli. charts; illus.; cum.index: vols. 50-100; circ. 500. **Indexed:** Appl.Mech.Rev., Biol.Abstr., Chem.Abstr., INIS Atomind., Math.R., Sci.Abstr.

500.2 510 IT ISSN 0373-3033
ACCADEMIA DELLE SCIENZE DI TORINO. MEMORIE. PART 1. CLASSE DI SCIENZE FISICHE, MATEMATICHE E NATURALI. 1977. irreg. (1-4/yr.). price varies. Accademia delle Scienze di Torino, Via Maria Vittoria 3, 10123 Turin, Italy. (Subscr. to: Bottega d'Erasmo, via G. Ferrari 9, 10124 Turin, Italy) Ed. Vittorio Cirilli. charts; illus.; circ. 500. **Indexed:** Biol.Abstr.

500 IT ISSN 0392-2219
CODEN: AALGA7
ACCADEMIA LIGURE DI SCIENZE E LETTERE. ATTI. (Text in English, French and Italian) 1890. a. L.7000($12) Accademia Ligure di Scienze e Lettere, Via Balbi 10, Palazzo Reale, 16126 Genoa, Italy. Ed. Pietro Scotti. circ. 500. **Indexed:** Biol.Abstr., Chem.Abstr., Deep Sea Res.& Oceanogr.Abstr., GeoRef, Math.R., Sci.Abstr.

ACCADEMIA NAZIONALE DEI LINCEI. CLASSE DI SCIENZE FISICHE MATEMATICHE E NATURALI. RENDICONTI. see *PHYSICS*

500 IT ISSN 0065-0765
ACCADEMIA PATAVINA DI SCIENZE LETTERE ED ARTI. COLLANA ACCADEMICA. 1966. irreg., no.6, 1975. price varies. Accademia Patavina di Scienze Lettere ed Arti, Via Accademia 7, 35139 Padua, Italy. TEL (049) 65.52.49.

500 IT
ACCADEMIA TOSCANA DI SCIENZA E LETTERE LA COLOMBARIA. ATTI E MEMORIE. N.S. 1947. a. price varies. Casa Editrice Leo S. Olschki, Casella Postale 66, 50100 Florence, Italy. TEL 055-6530684. FAX 055-6530214.

500 060 IT ISSN 0065-0781
ACCADEMIA TOSCANA DI SCIENZE E LETTERE LA COLOMBARIA. STUDI. 1953. irreg., vol.120, 1991. price varies. Casa Editrice Leo S. Olschki, Casella Postale 66, 50100 Florence, Italy. TEL 055-6530684. FAX 055-6530214. circ. 1,000. **Indexed:** Avery Ind.Archit.Per.

500 370 CN ISSN 0316-2893
ACCELERATOR NEWSLETTER. 1964. irreg (4-5/yr.). Can.$20 for 2 yrs. (Saskatchewan Science Teachers' Society) Saskatchewan Teachers' Federation, P.O. Box 1108, Saskatoon, Sask. S7K 3N3, Canada. TEL 306-525-0368. Ed. Jim Weseen. adv.; bk.rev.; illus.; stat.; circ. 300. (processed) **Indexed:** Can.Educ.Ind.
Formerly: Accelerator (Saskatoon) (ISSN 0001-446X)

500 US ISSN 0898-9621
Q180.55.E9 CODEN: ARQAEZ
ACCOUNTABILITY IN RESEARCH; policies and quality assurance. 4/yr. (in 1 vol., 4 nos./vol.). $76. Gordon & Breach Science Publishers, 270 Eighth Ave., New York, NY 10011. TEL 212-206-8900. FAX 212-645-2459. TELEX 236735 GOPUB UR. (Subscr. to: Box 786, Cooper Sta., New York, NY 10276. TEL 800-545-8398; UK subscr. to: P.O. Box 90, Reading, Berkshire RG1 8JL, England. TEL 0734-560-080) Ed. Adil Shamoo. (also avail. in microfilm; microfiche) **Indexed:** Soc.Work Res.& Abstr.
—BLDSC shelfmark: 0573.539500.
Refereed Serial

SCIENCES: COMPREHENSIVE WORKS

ACTA ACADEMIAE ABOENSIS, SERIES B: MATHEMATICA ET PHYSICA. see *MATHEMATICS*

500   BL   ISSN 0044-5967
CODEN: AAMZAZ
ACTA AMAZONICA. (Text in English, Portuguese) 1971. 4/yr. Cz.$10000($200) Instituto Nacional de Pesquisas da Amazonia, Estrada do Aleixo 1756, P.O. Box 478, Manaus, 69000 Amazonas, Brazil. TELEX 0922269. Ed. Eneas Salati. bk.rev.; circ. 1,500. **Indexed:** Abstr.Hyg., Agroforest.Abstr., Biol.Abstr., Chem.Abstr., Curr.Adv.Ecol.Sci., Deep Sea Res.& Oceanogr.Abstr., Forest.Abstr., Forest Prod.Abstr., GeoRef., INIS Atomind., Rev.Appl.Entomol., Rev.Med.& Vet.Mycol., Rural Devel.Abstr., Sel.Water Res.Abstr., Soils & Fert., Vet.Bull.
—BLDSC shelfmark: 0593.100000.
Description: Publication in pure and applied sciences including botany, agronomy, aquatic biology, tropical pathology, forest research, zoology and wood technology.

500 919 998   DK   ISSN 0065-1028
G601
ACTA ARCTICA. (Text in English, French and German) 1943. irreg. (every 3-5 yrs.). price varies. (Arktisk Institut) C.A. Reitzels Forlag, Norregade 20, DK-1165 Copenhagen K, Denmark. Ed. Helge Larsen. (back issues avail.) **Indexed:** Biol.Abstr.

500   II   ISSN 0379-5411
QD1   CODEN: ACIDBW
ACTA CIENCIA INDICA. (Text in English) 1974. q. Rs.40($30) (Society for the Progress of Science) Pragati Prakashan, c/o K.K. Mittal, Business Manager, Box 62, Meerut 250001, India. Ed. V.P. Kudesia. adv.; bk.rev.; bibl.; charts; circ. 1,000. **Indexed:** Chem.Abstr., Math.R., Sci.Abstr.

500   VE   ISSN 0001-5504
Q22   CODEN: ACVEAU
ACTA CIENTIFICA VENEZOLANA. (Text in Spanish; summaries in English and Spanish) 1950. 6/yr. Bs.300 to individuals ($50); institutions Bs.600 ($130). Asociacion Venezolana para el Avance de la Ciencia, Av. Neveri-Colina de Bello Monte, Apdo. 47286, Caracas, Venezuela. TEL 751.1420. Ed.Bd. adv.; bk.rev.; abstr.; bibl.; charts; illus.; stat.; index, cum.index; circ. 4,000. (reprint service avail. from ISI) **Indexed:** ASCA, Biol.Abstr., Biotech.Abstr., Chem.Abstr., Curr.Adv.Biochem., Curr.Adv.Cell & Devel.Biol., Curr.Adv.Ecol.Sci., Curr.Adv.Genetics & Molec.Biol., Curr.Cont., Curr.Tit.Ocean, Dairy Sci.Abstr., Dent.Ind., Excerp.Med., Field Crop Abstr., GeoRef., Helminthol.Abstr., Herb.Abstr., Ind.Med., Ind.Vet., Math.R., Nutr.Abstr., Sci.Cit.Ind., Soils & Fert., Vet.Bull, Zent.Math.
—BLDSC shelfmark: 0611.500000.
Description: Research papers and essays discussing general scientific problems, not exclusively based on original experimental results.
Refereed Serial

500.9 610   GW   ISSN 0001-5857
CODEN: ACHLAG
ACTA HISTORICA LEOPOLDINA. (Supplements avail.) 1963. irreg. price varies. (Deutsche Akademie der Naturforscher Leopoldina, Archiv fuer Geschichte der Naturforschung und Medizin) Johann Ambrosius Barth Verlag, Leipzig - Heidelberg, Salomonstr. 18b, 7010 Leipzig, Germany. TEL 70131. bibl.; charts; illus.; circ. 1,200. **Indexed:** Biol.Abstr., Math.R.

500 600   DK   ISSN 0065-1311
CODEN: AHSMA7
ACTA HISTORICA SCIENTIARUM NATURALIUM ET MEDICINALIUM. (Text in English, German) 1942. irreg., no.39, 1987. price varies. University Library, 49 Noerre Alle, DK-2200 Copenhagen N, Denmark. TEL 31-396523. FAX 31-398533. (back issues avail.) **Indexed:** GeoRef, Ind.Med.

500 616.99   PH   ISSN 0065-1370
ACTA MANILANA. (Text and summaries in English) 1965. a. P.80($15) University of Santo Tomas, Research Center for the Natural Sciences, Espana St., Manila 1008, Philippines. TEL 731-4031. FAX 010-63-2-732-7486. Ed. Fortunato Sevilla III. circ. 500. (back issues avail.) **Indexed:** Biol.Abstr., Curr.Adv.Ecol.Sci., Ind.Phil.Per., Nutr.Abstr.
—BLDSC shelfmark: 0629.750000.
Description: Papers dealing with all aspects of the natural sciences.

500 600   MX   ISSN 0567-7785
CODEN: AMXCB4
ACTA MEXICANA DE CIENCIA Y TECNOLOGIA. (Text in English or Spanish) 1967. irreg., vol.14, 1980. Instituto Politecnico Nacional, Comision de Operacion y Fomento de Actividades Academicas, Apdo. Postal 42-161, Mexico 17, D.F., Mexico. bibl.; charts; illus.; index; circ. 1,000. **Indexed:** Biol.Abstr., Math.R., Sci.Abstr.

ACTA REGIAE SOCIETATIS SCIENTIARUM ET LITTERARUM GOTHOBURGENSIS. INTERDISCIPLINARIA. see *HUMANITIES: COMPREHENSIVE WORKS*

500 610   SW   ISSN 0282-8928
ACTA UNIVERSITATIS UPSALIENSIS. (Text in various European languages) 1773. irreg. price varies. (Kungliga Vetenskaps-Societeten - Royal Society of Sciences of Uppsala) Almqvist & Wiksell International, Box 638, S-101 28 Stockholm, Sweden. bibl.; charts; illus.; index. **Indexed:** GeoRef., M.L.A.
—BLDSC shelfmark: 0586.648000.
Formerly (until 1968): Nova Acta Regiae Societatis Scientiarum Upsaliensis (ISSN 0029-5000)

ADVANCES IN X-RAY ANALYSIS. see *TECHNOLOGY: COMPREHENSIVE WORKS*

960 500   BE   ISSN 0001-9879
AFRICA TERVUREN. (Text in Dutch, English, and French) 1955. q. 650 BEF. Amis du Musee Royal de l'Afrique Centrale, 13 Steenweg Op Leuven, B-1980 Tervuren, Belgium. bk.rev.; charts; illus.; index; circ. 500. **Indexed:** M.L.A.
—BLDSC shelfmark: 0732.189500.
Formerly (until 1960): Congo Tervuren.

500   PH   ISSN 0115-5679
CODEN: AGHADE
AGHAM; D L S U Journal of Science. (Text in English) 1975. s-a. P.90($11) (De La Salle University, College of Science) De La Salle University Press, 2401 Taft Ave., Manila, Philippines. TEL 2-595177. Ed. Roberto de Padua. adv.; bk.rev.; circ. 300.
Description: Presents scientific research and reports. Contains articles, notes, communications, and reviews concerning all areas of biology, chemistry, physics, mathematics, and engineering.

500   II   ISSN 0002-1032
Q73   CODEN: AURSA9
AGRA UNIVERSITY JOURNAL OF RESEARCH (SCIENCE).. (Text in English) 1952. 3/yr. Rs.20. Agra University, Agra 282004, Uttar Pradesh, India. Ed. Dr. M. Ray. charts; illus. **Indexed:** Anim.Breed.Abstr., Biol.Abstr., Chem.Abstr., Field Crop Abstr., GeoRef., Herb.Abstr., Ind.Vet., Plant Breed.Abstr., Rev.Appl.Entomol., Rev.Plant Path., Vet.Bull.

500   AI   ISSN 0017-8683
AIASTANI KENSABANAKAN ANDES. (Text in Armenian and Russian) 1948. m. 19.20 Rub. Akademiya Nauk Armyanskoi S.S.R., Ul. Barekamutian, 24, Erevan, Armenia. Ed. Hrant G. Patikian. bk.rev.; abstr.; bibl.; charts; illus.; index, cum.index.

700   JA   ISSN 0388-7367
AS552.K343
AICHI KYOIKU DAIGAKU KENKYU HOKOKU. GEIJUTSU, HOKEN TAIIKU, KASEI, GIJUTSU KAGAKU. 1975. a. exchange basis. Aichi University of Education - Aichi Kyoiku Daigaku, 1, Hirosawa, Igaya-cho, Kariya-shi, Aichi-ken 448, Japan. circ. 600. **Indexed:** INIS Atomind.

510 500   JA   ISSN 0365-3722
Q4   CODEN: AKDSA5
AICHI KYOIKU DAIGAKU HOKOKU. SHIZEN KAGAKU/AICHI UNIVERSITY OF EDUCATION. NATURAL SCIENCE BULLETIN. (Text and summaries in English, Japanese) 1952. a. Aichi University of Education - Aichi Kyoiku Daigaku, 1, Hirosawa, Igaya-cho, Kariya-shi, Aichi-ken 448, Japan.
Formerly (until 1967): Aichi Gakugei Daigaku Kenkyu Hokoku. Shizen Kagaku (ISSN 0515-779X)

500   GW   ISSN 0304-2154
AS182
AKADEMIE DER WISSENSCHAFTEN DER D.D.R. JAHRBUCH. 1950. a. price varies. Akademie-Verlag Berlin, Leipziger Strasse 3-4, 1086 Berlin, Germany.
Formerly: Akademie der Wissenschaften. Berlin. Jahrbuch (ISSN 0065-5066)
Description: Current research and activities of the Academy.

500   GW   ISSN 0138-4112
AKADEMIE DER WISSENSCHAFTEN DER D.D.R. STUDIEN ZUR GESCHICHTE. 1975. irreg., vol.13, 1988. (Akademie der Wissenschaften der D.D.R.) Akademie-Verlag Berlin, Leipziger Str. 3-4, 1086 Berlin, Germany.
Description: Includes monographs on the history of specialized research disciplines and information on scholars and scientific schools.

500   GW   ISSN 0084-6082
AKADEMIE DER WISSENSCHAFTEN IN GOETTINGEN. JAHRBUCH. 1939. a. price varies. Vandenhoeck und Ruprecht, Robert-Bosch-Breite 6, Postfach 37 53, 3400 Goettingen, Germany. TEL 0551-6959-0. FAX 0551-695917. **Indexed:** GeoRef.

001.3 500   GW   ISSN 0084-6104
AS182   CODEN: AWLJAY
AKADEMIE DER WISSENSCHAFTEN UND DER LITERATUR, MAINZ. JAHRBUCH. a. price varies. Franz Steiner Verlag Wiesbaden GmbH, Birkenwaldstr. 44, Postfach 101526, 7000 Stuttgart 1, Germany. TEL 0711-2582-0. FAX 0711-2582290. TELEX 723636-DAZD. **Indexed:** GeoRef.

510 500   GW   ISSN 0002-2993
Q49   CODEN: AWLMA9
AKADEMIE DER WISSENSCHAFTEN UND DER LITERATUR, MAINZ. MATHEMATISCH-NATURWISSENSCHAFTLICHE KLASSE. ABHANDLUNGEN. (Text in English, French and German) 1950. irreg. price varies. (Mathematisch-Naturwissenschaftliche Klasse) Franz Steiner Verlag Wiesbaden GmbH, Birkenwaldstr. 44, Postfach 101526, 7000 Stuttgart 1, Germany. TEL 0711-2582-0. FAX 0711-291450. TELEX 723636-DAZD. abstr.; charts; illus.; index. **Indexed:** Biol.Abstr., Chem.Abstr., GeoRef.

500   GW   ISSN 0065-5538
AKADEMISCHE VORTRAEGE UND ABHANDLUNGEN. 1946. irreg., no.46, 1979. price varies. Bouvier Verlag Herbert Grundmann, Am Hof 32, Postfach 1268, 5300 Bonn 1, Germany.

500 060   AI
AKADEMIYA NAUK ARMYANSKOI S.S.R. DOKLADY. (Text in Armenian and Russian) 1944. 10/yr. Akademiya Nauk Armyanskoi S.S.R., Ul. Barekamutian, 24, Erevan, Armenia. **Indexed:** Anal.Abstr., Biol.Abstr., Chem.Abstr., GeoRef., INIS Atomind., Math.R.

AKADEMIYA NAUK ARMYANSKOI S.S.R. IZVESTIYA. SERIYA TEKHNICHESKIKH NAUK. see *TECHNOLOGY: COMPREHENSIVE WORKS*

500   BW   ISSN 0002-354X
Q60   CODEN: DBLRAC
AKADEMIYA NAUK BELARUSSKOI S.S.R. DOKLADY. (Text in Russian; contents page and summaries in English) 1957. m. 24.60 Rub. Akademiya Navuk Belarusskai S.S.R. - B.S.S.R. Academy of Sciences, Leninskii prospekt, 66, 220072 Minsk 72, Byelarus. TEL 39 48 15. TELEX 252277 NAUKA. Ed. V.P. Platonov. bibl.; charts; illus.; index; circ. 900. **Indexed:** Biol.Abstr., Crop Physiol.Abstr., Deep Sea Res.& Oceanogr.Abstr., Field Crop Abstr., Helminthol.Abstr., INIS Atomind., Met.Abstr., Triticale Abstr.
Description: Publishes scientific results in mathematics, natural sciences and engineering.

500   GS   ISSN 0002-3167
CODEN: SAKNAH
AKADEMIYA NAUK GRUZINSKOI S.S.R. SOOBSHCHENIYA. (Text in Georgian and Russian; summaries in English) 1940. m. 51.60 Rub. Akademiya Nauk Gruzinskoi S.S.R., Ul. Dzerzhinskogo, 8, Tbilisi, Georgia. Ed. E.K. Kharadze. bibl.; charts; circ. 1,400. **Indexed:** Biol.Abstr., Field Crop Abstr., Forest.Abstr., Helminthol.Abstr., Herb.Abstr., Hort.Abstr., Ind.Vet., Irr.& Drain.Abstr., Numis.Lit., Rev.Plant Path., Soils & Fert., Vet.Bull.

500   RU   ISSN 0002-3213
AS262   CODEN: VANKAM
AKADEMIYA NAUK KAZAKHSKOI S.S.R. VESTNIK. 1944. m. 29 Rub. Izdatel'stvo Nauka, 90 Profsoyuznaya ul., 117864 Moscow, Russia. Ed. Sh.E. Esenov. adv.; bk.rev.; abstr.; bibl.; charts; illus.; stat. **Indexed:** Biol.Abstr., Chem.Abstr, Crop Physiol.Abstr., Field Crop Abstr., Math.R., Triticale Abstr.

SCIENCES: COMPREHENSIVE WORKS

500   KG   ISSN 0002-3221
AS581   CODEN: INKSAD
AKADEMIYA NAUK KIRGIZSKOI S.S.R. IZVESTIYA. (Text in Russian) 1955. bi-m. $8.40. Akademiya Nauk Kirgizskoi S.S.R., Ul. 23 Parts'ezda, 265-a, Frunze, Kyrgyzstan. **Indexed:** Biol.Abstr., Chem.Abstr., GeoRef., INIS Atomind.

500   LV   ISSN 0132-6422
AS262   CODEN: LZAVAL
AKADEMIYA NAUK LATVIISKOI S.S.R. IZVESTIYA/LATVIJAS P.S.R. ZINATNU AKADEMIJAS. VESTIS. (Text in Latvian and Russian, summaries in English; contents page in English, German, Latvian and Russian) 1947. m. $25.20. Izdatel'stvo Zinatne, Turgeneva iela, 19, Riga, 226018, Latvia. Ed. V. Samsons. bk.rev.; abstr.; bibl.; charts; illus.; index. **Indexed:** Abstr.Bull.Inst.Pap.Chem., Amer.Hist.& Life, Biol.Abstr., Chem.Abstr., Crop Physiol.Abstr., Field Crop Abstr., Forest.Abstr., Forest Prod.Abstr., Hist.Abstr., Hort.Abstr., INIS Atomind., M.L.A., Mass Spectr.Bull., Math.R., Numis.Lit., Plant Breed.Abstr., Plant Grow.Reg.Abstr., Sci.Abstr., Soils & Fert., World Agri.Econ.& Rural Sociol.Abstr.

500   RU   ISSN 0002-3264
AS262   CODEN: DANKAS
AKADEMIYA NAUK S.S.S.R. DOKLADY; svodnyi vypusk. (Text in Russian; contents page in English) 1933. 36/yr. 191.40 Rub. Izdatel'stvo Nauka, 90 Profsoyuznaya ul., 117864 Moscow, Russia. (Dist. by: Mezhdunarodnaya Kniga, ul. Dimitrova D.39, 113095 Moscow, Russia) Ed. A.A. Baev. charts; illus.; index; circ. 5,250. (also avail. in microform from BHP; reprint service avail. from KTO) **Indexed:** Anal.Abstr., Art & Archaeol.Tech.Abstr., Biol.Abstr., Chem.Abstr., Comput.Rev., Cott.& Trop.Fibr.Abstr., Crop Physiol.Abstr., Cyb.Abstr., Deep Sea Res.& Oceanogr.Abstr., Dent.Ind., Field Crop Abstr., Geo.Abstr., GeoRef., Geotech.Abstr., Helminthol.Abstr., Hort.Abstr., INIS Atomind., Maize Abstr., Math.R., Met.Abstr., Meteor.& Geoastrophys.Abstr., Nutr.Abstr., Psychol.Abstr., Sci.Abstr., Soyabean Abstr., Triticale Abstr., Vet.Bull., World Alum.Abstr.
—BLDSC shelfmark: 0054.000000.

500   RU   ISSN 0002-3442
AS262   CODEN: VANSAC
AKADEMIYA NAUK S.S.S.R. VESTNIK. 1931. m. 42.60 Rub. Izdatel'stvo Nauka, 90 Profsoyuznaya ul., 117864 Moscow, Russia. Ed. M.D. Millionshchikov. bk.rev.; bibl.; charts; illus.; index; circ. 5,125. **Indexed:** Biol.Abstr., Chem.Abstr., GeoRef., Lang.& Lang.Behav.Abstr., Math.R., Psychol.Abstr.

500   KR   ISSN 0372-6436
AS262   CODEN: VNUKAC
AKADEMIYA NAUK UKRAINSKOI S.S.R. VISNYK. (Text in Ukrainian) 1928. m. 14.40 Rub. (Akademiya Nauk Ukrainskoi S.S.R., Prezidium) Izdatel'stvo Naukova Dumka, c/o Yu.A. Khramov, Dir, Ul. Repina, 3, Kiev 252 601, Ukraine. TEL 228-81-39. (Subscr. to: Mezhdunarodnaya Kniga, ul. Dimitrova 39, Moscow G-200, Russia) Ed. B.E. Paton.
—BLDSC shelfmark: 0039.800000.

AKITA-KENRITSU HAKUBUTSUKAN KENKYU HOKOKU/AKITA PREFECTURAL MUSEUM. ANNUAL REPORT. see *MUSEUMS AND ART GALLERIES*

500   JA   ISSN 0285-0257
AKITA SHIZENSHI KENKYU/AKITA NATURAL HISTORY ASSOCIATION. (Text in Japanese) 1973. a. Akita Natural History Association - Akita Shizenshi Gakkai, c/o Mr. Jun Takado, 6-36 Yabasedagoro, 2-chome, Akita-shi, Akita-ken 010, Japan.

500   US   ISSN 0002-4112
CODEN: JAASAJ
ALABAMA ACADEMY OF SCIENCE. JOURNAL. 1924. q. $20 to non-members. Auburn University Press (Auburn), Ralph Brown Draughon Library, Auburn University, Auburn, AL 36849. Ed. J.T. Bradley. adv.; bk.rev.; abstr.; illus.; circ. 1,000. (also avail. in microform from UMI; reprint service avail. from UMI) **Indexed:** Amer.Hist.& Life, Biol.Abstr., Chem.Abstr., Excerp.Med., GeoRef., Hist.Abstr., Sci.Cit.Ind.

500.9   US   ISSN 0361-1353
F901
ALASKA GEOGRAPHIC. 1972. q. $39. Alaska Geographic Society, Box 93370, Anchorage, AK 99509-3370. TEL 907-258-2515. FAX 907-278-6582. Ed. Penny Rennick. bk.rev.; charts; illus.; circ. 16,000. (back issues avail.) **Indexed:** Access, GeoRef.
—BLDSC shelfmark: 0786.527300.
Description: Natural resources of the lands of the Polar Rim and Pacific Rim.

ALBERTA RESEARCH COUNCIL. ANNUAL REPORT. see *TECHNOLOGY: COMPREHENSIVE WORKS*

ALBERTA RESEARCH COUNCIL. REPORTS. see *TECHNOLOGY: COMPREHENSIVE WORKS*

500 600   SP   ISSN 0214-0381
ALGO 2000; revista de divulgacion cientifica, tecnica y cultural. 1963. m. $50. Hogar y la Moda, S.A., Aribau 28, 08011 Barcelona, Spain. TEL 93-3237063. TELEX 50482. Ed. Oriol Puges Gibert. adv.; illus.; index; circ. 65,000.
Formerly (until 1987): Algo (ISSN 0002-5348)

500.9   GW
ALPENINSTITUT. SCHRIFTENREIHE. (Text in French, German and Italian) 1974. irreg. price varies. (Alpeninstitut fuer Umweltforschung und Entwicklungsplanung in der GFL) Nelles Verlag, Schleissheimer Str. 371 b, 8000 Munich 45, Germany. Ed. Walter Danz.
Description: Focuses on natural history.

500   NZ   ISSN 0111-1957
ALPHA. 1980. s-m. NZ.$0.50 per no. (Department of Scientific and Industrial Research) S I R Publishing, Box 399, Wellington, New Zealand. TEL 04-472-7421. FAX 04-473-1841. Ed. A. MacBean. circ. 2,000.

502   CK
AMERICA LATINA 2001; revista latinoamericana de ciencia, tecnologia y futurologia. (Text in English and Spanish) 1976. q. Col.$800($22) Editora Guadalupe Ltda., Apdo. Aereo 854, Bogota, Colombia. Ed. Horacio H. Godoy. adv.; bk.rev.; bibl.; illus.; circ. 5,000.

AMERICAN ACADEMY OF ARTS AND SCIENCES. BULLETIN. see *HUMANITIES: COMPREHENSIVE WORKS*

500   US   ISSN 0361-7874
Q181.A1
AMERICAN ASSOCIATION FOR THE ADVANCEMENT OF SCIENCE. HANDBOOK; OFFICERS, ORGANIZATION, ACTIVITIES. a. $7.50. American Association for the Advancement of Science, 1333 H St., N.W., Washington, DC 20005. TEL 202-326-6446.
Description: Lists AAAS section officers, council and committee members, and institutional affiliates. Includes information on association activities, policies and history.

500   US   ISSN 0361-1833
Q181.A1
AMERICAN ASSOCIATION FOR THE ADVANCEMENT OF SCIENCE. MEETING PROGRAM. 1972. a. $10. American Association for the Advancement of Science, 1333 H St., N.W., Washington, DC 20005. TEL 202-326-6462. Ed. Sue O'Connell. adv.; index; circ. 8,000. **Indexed:** GeoRef. Key Title: Annual Meeting - American Association for the Advancement of Science.
Description: Provides complete schedule of annual meeting program, including symposia, seminars, poster sessions, exhibits, workshops and films. All speakers and affiliations are also listed.

620 616   US   ISSN 0065-7964
AMERICAN COUNCIL OF INDEPENDENT LABORATORIES. DIRECTORY; a guide to the leading independent testing, research and inspection firms of America. 1937. biennial. $25. American Council of Independent Laboratories, Inc., 1629 K St., N.W., Washington, DC 20006. TEL 202-887-5872. FAX 202-887-0021. Ed. Joseph F. O'Neil. circ. 8,000.

AMERICAN HERITAGE OF INVENTION & TECHNOLOGY. see *TECHNOLOGY: COMPREHENSIVE WORKS*

AMERICAN MEN AND WOMEN OF SCIENCE; a biographical directory of today's leaders in physical, biological and related sciences. see *BIOGRAPHY*

500.9   US   ISSN 0003-0031
QH1   CODEN: AMNAAF
AMERICAN MIDLAND NATURALIST. 1909. q. $60 (foreign $65). University of Notre Dame, American Midland Naturalist, Notre Dame, IN 46556. TEL 219-239-7481. Ed. Robert P. McIntosh. bibl.; charts; illus.; index; circ. 1,400. (also avail. in microform from UMI,JSC,PMC) **Indexed:** Bio-Contr.News & Info., Biol.Abstr., Biol.& Agr.Ind., Chem.Abstr., Crop Physiol.Abstr., Curr.Adv.Ecol.Sci., Curr.Cont., Deep Sea Res.& Oceanogr.Abstr., Environ.Per.Bibl., Field Crop Abstr., Forest.Abstr., Forest Prod.Abstr., Gen.Sci.Ind., Geo.Abstr., Helminthol.Abstr., Herb.Abstr., Ind.Sci.Rev., INIS Atomind., Irr.& Drain.Abstr., Key Word Ind.Wildl.Res., Plant Breed.Abstr., Sci.Cit.Ind., Seed Abstr., Sel.Water Res.Abstr., Soils & Fert., Weed Abstr.
—BLDSC shelfmark: 0843.000000.
Description: Articles cover a broad spectrum of laboratory and field studies in biology, ecology, life histories, evolution and physiology.
Refereed Serial

AMERICAN MUSEUM NOVITATES. see *BIOLOGY — Zoology*

AMERICAN MUSEUM OF NATURAL HISTORY. ANNUAL REPORT. see *MUSEUMS AND ART GALLERIES*

AMERICAN MUSEUM OF NATURAL HISTORY. BULLETIN. see *BIOLOGY — Zoology*

900 500 100   US   ISSN 0065-9738
CODEN: MAPSAP
AMERICAN PHILOSOPHICAL SOCIETY. MEMOIRS. 1935. irreg., vol.197, 1991. price varies. American Philosophical Society, 104 S. Fifth St., Philadelphia, PA 19106. TEL 215-627-0706. Ed. Herman H. Goldstine. index. (reprint service avail. from UMI, ISI) **Indexed:** Biol.Abstr., GeoRef., Math.R.
—BLDSC shelfmark: 5577.100000.

900 500 100   US   ISSN 0065-9746
Q11   CODEN: TAPSAY
AMERICAN PHILOSOPHICAL SOCIETY. TRANSACTIONS. 1771. 1 vol./yr. (containing 1-7 parts published irregularly). $80. American Philosophical Society, 104 S. Fifth St, Philadelphia, PA 19106. TEL 215-440-3400. Ed. Herman H. Goldstine. index, cum.index: 1771-1960. (reprint service avail. from ISI,KTO,UMI) **Indexed:** Biol.Abstr., Deep Sea Res.& Oceanogr.Abstr., GeoRef, Math.R., SSCI.
—BLDSC shelfmark: 8894.000000.

500   US   ISSN 0003-0996
LJ85   CODEN: AMSCAC
AMERICAN SCIENTIST; published in the interest of scientific research. 1913. bi-m. $28 to individuals; institutions $45. Sigma Xi, Scientific Research Society, Box 13975, 99 Alexander Dr., Research Triangle Park, NC 27709. TEL 919-549-0097. FAX 919-549-0090. Ed. Brian Hayes. adv.; bk.rev.; bibl.; illus.; index, cum.index: vols.34-61 (1946-1973); circ. 110,000. (also avail. in microform from UMI,MIM,PMC; reprint service avail. from UMI,ISI) **Indexed:** A.S.& T.Ind., Abstr.Anthropol., Acad.Ind., Biog.Ind., Biol.Abstr., Biol.Dig., Bk.Rev.Ind. (1989-), Br.Archaeol.Abstr., CAD CAM Abstr., Cadscan, Chem.Abstr., Child.Bk.Rev.Ind. (1989-), Child Devel.Abstr., Comput. Rev., Curr.Adv.Ecol.Sci., Curr.Cont., Curr.Pack.Abstr., Deep Sea Res.& Oceanogr.Abstr., Energy Rev., Eng.Ind., Environ.Per.Bibl., Excerp.Med., Field Crop Abstr., Fut.Surv., Gen.Sci.Ind., Geo.Abstr., Helminthol.Abstr., Herb.Abstr., HRIS, Ind.Med., Ind.Sci.Rev., INIS Atomind., Key Word Ind.Wildl.Res., Lang.& Lang.Behav.Abstr., Lead Abstr., Math.R., Met.Abstr., Mid.East: Abstr.& Ind., NRN, Nucl.Sci.Abstr., Nutr.Abstr., Ocean.Abstr., Phys.Abstr., PMR, Psychol.Abstr., Ref.Sour., Sci.Abstr., Sci.Cit.Ind., Sel.Water Res.Abstr., So.Pac.Per.Ind., World Alum.Abstr., Zincscan.
—BLDSC shelfmark: 0857.000000.

AMERICANS FOR THE UNIVERSALITY OF UNESCO NEWSLETTER. see *POLITICAL SCIENCE — International Relations*

500   PE   ISSN 0003-2484
CODEN: ANCNA6
ANALES CIENTIFICOS. (Text in Spanish; summaries in English) 1963. q. S/800($18) Universidad Nacional Agraria, Apdo. 456, La Molina, Lima, Peru. Dir. Antonio Bacigalupo. adv.; index; circ. 1,000. **Indexed:** Biol.Abstr., Chem.Abstr., Nutr.Abstr.

ANALOG SCIENCE FICTION & FACT. see *LITERATURE — Science Fiction, Fantasy, Horror*

500   CC   ISSN 1000-2162
ANHUI DAXUE XUEBAO (ZIRAN KEXUE BAN)/ANHUI UNIVERSITY. JOURNAL (NATURAL SCIENCE EDITION). (Text in Chinese) q. Anhui Daxue, Xuebao Bianjibu, No. 3, Feixi Lu, Hefei, Anhui 230039, People's Republic of China. TEL 332632. Ed. Wu Dongru.

500   CC   ISSN 1001-2443
ANHUI SHIDA XUEBAO/ANHUI NORMAL UNIVERSITY. JOURNAL. (Text in Chinese) q. Anhui Shifan Daxue - Anhui Normal University, 1 Renmin Lu, Wuhu, Anhui 241000, People's Republic of China. TEL 35966. Ed. Ni Guangming.

509   UK   ISSN 0003-3790
Q1   CODEN: ANNSA8
ANNALS OF SCIENCE; a review of the history of science since the thirteenth century. 1936. bi-m. £223($380) Taylor & Francis Ltd., Rankine Rd., Basingstoke, Hants RG24 0PR, England. TEL 0256-840366. FAX 0256-479438. TELEX 858540. Ed. G.L.E. Turner. adv.; bk.rev.; bibl.; illus.; index. (also avail. in microform from MIM; microfiche from KTO) **Indexed:** Amer.Hist.& Life, Arts & Hum.Cit.Ind., Biol.Abstr., Br.Geol.Lit., Br.Hum.Ind., Cadscan, Chem.Abstr., Curr.Adv.Ecol.Sci., Curr.Cont., Deep Sea Res.& Oceanogr.Abstr., Helminthol.Abstr., Hist.Abstr., Ind.Sci.Rev., Lead Abstr., Math.R., Sci.Abstr., Sci.Cit.Ind., SSCI, Zincscan.
—BLDSC shelfmark: 1044.000000.
Description: Directed to all who are interested in the evolution of science and its impact on the development of related arts and industries.

500   FR
ANNUAIRE DES FOURNISSEURS DE LABORATOIRES DE RECHERCHES. 1967. a. Agence de Diffusion et de Publicite, 24 Place du General Catroux, 75017 Paris, France. Ed. Raymond Mery. adv.; circ. 3,500.

509   US   ISSN 0003-5335
G845   CODEN: AJUSAF
ANTARCTIC JOURNAL OF THE UNITED STATES. 1966. 5/yr. $16. U.S. National Science Foundation, Office of Polar Programs, 1800 G St. N.W., Washington, DC 20550. TEL 202-357-7817. (Orders to: Supt. of Documents, Washington, DC 20402) Ed. Winifred Reuning. charts; illus.; maps; circ. 4,500. (also avail. in microform from MIM,UMI) **Indexed:** Biol.Abstr., Curr.Adv.Ecol.Sci., Deep Sea Res.& Oceanogr.Abstr., Geo.Abstr., GeoRef., Ind.U.S.Gov.Per., INIS Atomind., Ocean.Abstr., Ref.Zh., Sci.Cit.Ind., Soils & Fert.

500   US   ISSN 0882-4347
APPLIED ORGONOMETRY; notes from the workshop of applied orgonometry. 1986. 3/yr. $25. R R P Publishers, Box 8, Easton, PA 18044-0008. TEL 215-252-1199. Ed. Jacob Meyerowitz. (looseleaf format)

500   NE   ISSN 0003-6994
TA349   CODEN: ASRHAU
APPLIED SCIENTIFIC RESEARCH; an international journal on mechanical and thermal phenomena in continua. 1947. q. $204.50. Kluwer Academic Publishers, Postbus 17, 3300 AA Dordrecht, Netherlands. TEL 078-334911. FAX 078-334254. TELEX 28245. (Dist. by: Kluwer Academic Publishers Group, P.O. Box 322, 3300 AH Dordrecht; N. America dist. addr.: Box 358, Accord Sta., Hingham, MA 02018-0358. TEL 617-871-6600) **Indexed:** Appl.Mech.Rev., Chem.Abstr., Chem.Eng.Abstr., Curr.Adv.Ecol.Sci., Curr.Cont., Eng.Ind., Fluidex, Ind.Sci.Rev., Math.R., Met.Abstr., Petrol.Abstr., Sci.Abstr., Sci.Cit.Ind., T.C.E.A., World Alum.Abstr.
—BLDSC shelfmark: 1576.900000.

APPRAISAL; science books for young people. see *PUBLISHING AND BOOK TRADE*

500 510   SU   ISSN 1015-4442
CODEN: AGSREJ
ARAB GULF JOURNAL OF SCIENTIFIC RESEARCH. (Text in English) 1983. 3/yr. SRI.100($25) Arab Bureau of Education for the Gulf States, P.O. Box 3908, Riyadh 11481, Saudi Arabia. Ed. Daham Alani. circ. 2,000. (back issues avail.) **Indexed:** Anim.Breed.Abstr., Biodet.Abstr., Cott.& Trop.Fibr.Abstr., Curr.Adv.Ecol.Sci., Environ.Per.Bibl., Excerp.Med., Herb.Abstr., I D A, Math.R., Poult.Abstr., Rev.Med.& Vet.Mycol., Sorghum & Millets Abstr., Vet.Bull.
—BLDSC shelfmark: 1583.226630.
Formed by the 1989 merger of: Arab Gulf Journal of Scientific Research. Section A: Mathematical and Physical Sciences (ISSN 0259-8930); Arab Gulf Journal of Scientific Research. Section B: Agricultural and Biological Sciences (ISSN 0259-8949); Which superseded: Arab Gulf Journal of Scientific Research (ISSN 0256-4548)

ARAB LEAGUE EDUCATIONAL, SCIENTIFIC, AND CULTURAL ORGANIZATION. INFORMATION NEWSLETTER. see *EDUCATION*

ARABIAN JOURNAL FOR SCIENCE AND ENGINEERING. see *ENGINEERING*

500   UK   ISSN 0957-4239
DS36.8
▼**ARABIC SCIENCES AND PHILOSOPHY;** a historical journal. 1991. s-a. $39 to individuals; institutions $75. Cambridge University Press, Edinburgh Bldg., Shaftesbury Rd., Cambridge CB2 2RU, England. TEL 0223-312393. FAX 0223-315052. TELEX 851817256. (U.S. addr.: Cambridge University Press, 40 W. 20th St., New York, NY 10011. TEL 212-924-3900) Eds. Basim Musallam, Roshdi Rashed.
—BLDSC shelfmark: 1583.329400.
Description: History of the Arabic sciences, mathematics and philosophy in the world of Islam between the eighth and eigtheenth centuries.

ARCHIMEDES; natural science magazine for the whole family. see *CHILDREN AND YOUTH — For*

509   GW   ISSN 0003-9519
Q125   CODEN: AHESAN
ARCHIVE FOR HISTORY OF EXACT SCIENCES. (Text in English; occasionally in French, German, Italian, Latin, Spanish) 1960. 8/yr. DM.856($510) (effective 1992). Springer-Verlag, Heidelberger Platz 3, D-1000 Berlin 33, Germany. TEL 030-8207-1. (Also Heidelberg, Tokyo, Vienna, and New York) Ed. C. Truesdell. adv.; bibl.; charts; index. (also avail. in microform from UMI; reprint service avail. from ISI) **Indexed:** Br.Archaeol.Abstr., Compumath, Curr.Cont., Ind.Sci.Rev., Math.R., Sci.Cit.Ind., SSCI, Zent.Math.
—BLDSC shelfmark: 1634.430000.
Description: Focuses on mathematics and natural philosophy. Includes examination of the physical sciences.

509   SZ   ISSN 0003-9705
Q2   CODEN: ASGVAH
ARCHIVES DES SCIENCES. (Text in English and French) 1948. 3/yr. 90 SFr. includes Compte-Rendu des Seances. Societe de Physique et d'Histoire Naturelle de Geneve, Museum d'Histoire Naturelle de Geneve, Cas Postale 434, CH-1211 Geneva, Switzerland. adv. (also avail. in microfilm from PMC) **Indexed:** Appl.Mech.Rev., Biol.Abstr., Chem.Abstr., Curr.Adv.Ecol.Sci., Helminthol.Abstr., Math.R., Sci.Abstr.
—BLDSC shelfmark: 1642.000000.

509   FR   ISSN 0302-2358
ARCHIVES INTERNATIONALES CLAUDE BERNARD.*
1971. q. 75 F. Archives Internationales Claude Bernard, 63-65 Faubourg-de-France, 87390 Coussac-Bonneval, France. Ed. Philippe Decourt. bk.rev.; circ. 1,000.

500.9   IT   ISSN 0003-9810
CODEN: AIHSAB
ARCHIVES INTERNATIONALES D'HISTOIRE DES SCIENCES. (Text in English, French, German, Italian, Russian, Spanish) 1919. N.S. 1972. 2/yr. L.60000($40) to individuals; institutions L.75000. Istituto della Enciclopedia Italiana, Piazza Paganica 4, 00186 Rome, Italy. Ed. R. Halleux. adv.; bk.rev.; bibl.; charts; illus.; index; circ. 1,200. (back issues avail.) **Indexed:** Amer.Hist.& Life, Chem.Abstr., Hist.Abstr., Math.R.
—BLDSC shelfmark: 1635.000000.

500 016   UK   ISSN 0260-9541
Z7403
ARCHIVES OF NATURAL HISTORY. 1936. 3/yr. £85($170) Society for the History of Natural History, c/o British Museum (Natural History), Cromwell Rd., London SW7 5BD, England. bk.rev.; bibl.; index; circ. 850. **Indexed:** Amer.Hist.& Life, Biol.Abstr., Deep Sea Res.& Oceanogr.Abstr., Geo.Abstr., GeoRef., Hist.Abstr., So.Pac.Per.Ind.
—BLDSC shelfmark: 1637.947000.
Formerly: Society for the Bibliography of Natural History. Journal (ISSN 0037-9778)

500   IT
ARCHIVIO DELLA CORRISPONDENZA DEGLI SCIENZIATI ITALIANI. 1985. irreg., no.6, 1989. price varies. Casa Editrice Leo S. Olschki, Casella Postale 66, 50100 Florence, Italy. TEL 055-6530684. FAX 055-6530214.

ARCHIWUM ENERGETYKI. see *ENGINEERING*

919 551   CN   ISSN 0004-0843
G600   CODEN: ATICAB
ARCTIC. (Text and summaries in English, French, Russian) 1947. q. Can.$37 to individuals (foreign US$37); institutions Can.$79 (foreign US$79). (Artic Institute of North America) University of Calgary Press, 2500 University Drive N.W., Calgary, Alberta T2N 1N4, Canada. TEL 403-220-7578. FAX 403-282-0085. TELEX 03-821545. Ed. Ona Stonkus. bk.rev.; abstr.; bibl.; charts; illus.; maps; index; circ. 2,600. (also avail. in microform from UMI; reprint service avail. from UMI; back issues avail.) **Indexed:** Abstr.Anthropol., Amer.Hist.& Life, Arct.Bibl., Biol.Abstr., Can.Per.Ind., Chem.Abstr., CMI, Curr.Adv.Ecol.Sci., Curr.Cont., Deep Sea Res.& Oceanogr.Abstr., Excerp.Med., Field Crop Abstr., Forest.Abstr., Forest Prod.Abstr., Geo.Abstr., GeoRef., Herb.Abstr., Hist.Abstr., Ind.Sci.Rev., Key Word Ind.Wildl.Res., Ocean.Abstr., Petrol.Abstr., Pollut.Abstr., Sci.Cit.Ind., Sel.Water Res.Abstr., Soils & Fert.
—BLDSC shelfmark: 1663.000000.
Description: Multi-disciplinary journal presents papers from circumpolar scientists.

550   US   ISSN 0004-0851
GB395   CODEN: ATLPAV
ARCTIC AND ALPINE RESEARCH. 1969. q. $45 to individuals (foreign $51); institutions $70 (foreign $76); students and retirees $35 (foreign $41). University of Colorado, Institute of Arctic and Alpine Research, Campus Box 450, Boulder, CO 80309-6450. TEL 303-492-3765. FAX 303-492-6388. Ed. Kathleen Salzberg. bk.rev.; bibl.; charts; illus.; stat.; index; circ. 990. (also avail. in microform from UMI; back issues avail.) **Indexed:** Abstr.Anthropol., Acid Rain Abstr., Acid Rain Ind., Biol.Abstr., Bull.Signal., Chem.Abstr., Curr.Adv.Ecol.Sci., Curr.Adv.Genetics & Molec.Biol., Curr.Cont., Deep Sea Res.& Oceanogr.Abstr., Ecol.Abstr., Environ.Per.Bibl., Field Crop Abstr., Forest.Abstr., Forest Prod.Abstr., Geo.Abstr., Geo.Abstr., GeoRef., Herb.Abstr., INIS Atomind., Irr.& Drain.Abstr., Key Word Ind.Wildl.Res., Meteor.& Geoastrophys.Abstr, Ref.Zh., Sci.Cit.Ind., Sel.Water Res.Abstr., Soils & Fert., Weed Abstr., World Agri.Econ.& Rural Sociol.Abstr.
—BLDSC shelfmark: 1663.060000.
Description: Presents original research pertaining to cold environments, both past and present.
Refereed Serial

509.798   US
ARCTIC SCIENCE CONFERENCE. PROCEEDINGS. 1950. a. price varies. American Association for the Advancement of Science, Arctic Division, Box 80271, Fairbanks, AK 99708. FAX 907-474-7290. circ. 600. **Indexed:** Biol.Abstr., GeoRef.
Former titles: Alaska Science Conference. Proceedings (ISSN 0084-6120); (1951-1969): Science in Alaska (ISSN 0191-2151)

SCIENCES: COMPREHENSIVE WORKS

500 US ISSN 0193-8509
Q11.A72 CODEN: JAASDM
ARIZONA-NEVADA ACADEMY OF SCIENCE. JOURNAL. 1959. 2/yr. $25. Arizona-Nevada Academy of Science, Office of Climatology, Arizona State University, Tempe, AZ 85287-1508. TEL 602-965-6265. FAX 602-965-2012. Eds. Leslie R. Landrum, Donald J. Pinkava. adv.; bk.rev.; charts; illus. **Indexed:** Biol.Abstr., Chem.Abstr., Excerp.Med., Field Crop Abstr., Geo.Abstr., GeoRef., Herb.Abstr., Sel.Water Res.Abstr., Soils & Fert., World Agri.Econ.& Rural Sociol.Abstr.
Formerly: Arizona Academy of Science Journal (ISSN 0004-1378)
Refereed Serial

ARTS & SCIENCES JOURNAL. see *HUMANITIES: COMPREHENSIVE WORKS*

500 600 US
ARTS AND SCIENCES NEWSLETTER. 1984. 2/yr. membership. Vermont Academy of Arts and Sciences, Box 723, Middletown Springs, VT 05757. TEL 802-235-2302. Ed. Frances B. Krouse. circ. 500.

ASCENT. see *TECHNOLOGY: COMPREHENSIVE WORKS*

500 BG
ASIATIC SOCIETY OF BANGLADESH. JOURNAL: SCIENCE. (Text in English) 1975. s-a. Tk.15($10) Asiatic Society of Bangladesh, 5 Old Secretariat Rd., Ramna, Dhaka, Bangladesh. TEL 2-239390.

500 AG ISSN 0325-2809
ASOCIACION DE CIENCIAS NATURALES DEL LITORAL. REVISTA. (Text in Spanish; summaries in English) 1970. s-a. $30. Asociacion de Ciencias Naturales del Litoral, J. Macia 1933, 3016 Santo Tome (S.Fe), Argentina. Ed. Federico Emiliani. adv.; bk.rev.; index. cum.index: 1970-1976; 1977-1981; 1982-1986; circ. 1,000. (back issues avail.) **Indexed:** Curr.Adv.Ecol.Sci.

500 600 SA ISSN 0373-4250
CODEN: ATSAAL
ASSOCIATED SCIENTIFIC AND TECHNICAL SOCIETIES OF SOUTH AFRICA. ANNUAL PROCEEDINGS. (Text in English) a. free. Associated Scientific and Technical Societies of South Africa, P.O. Box 93480, Yeoville 2143, South Africa. TEL 011-487-1512. FAX 011-648-1876. circ. controlled. (back issues avail.) **Indexed:** Biol.Abstr., Sci.Abstr.

500 CN ISSN 0066-8842
ASSOCIATION CANADIENNE-FRANCAISE POUR L'AVANCEMENT DES SCIENCES. ANNALES. 1935. a. Can.$12. Association Canadienne-Francaise pour l'Avancement des Sciences, C.P. 6060, Montreal, Que. H3C 3A7, Canada. TEL 514-342-1411. FAX 514-342-9552. circ. 4,000. **Indexed:** Arct.Bibl., Biol.Abstr., GeoRef.
Description: Summaries of all the communications presented at the association's congress.

500 CN
ASSOCIATION CANADIENNE-FRANCAISE POUR L'AVANCEMENT DES SCIENCES. CAHIERS SCIENTIFIQUES. irreg. price varies. Association Canadienne-Francaise Pour l'Avancement des Sciences, 2730 Cote Ste. Catherine, Montreal, Que. H3T 1B7, Canada. TEL 514-342-1411. FAX 514-342-9552.
Formerly: Cahiers de l'A C F A S.

500 CN ISSN 0826-4864
ASSOCIATION CANADIENNE-FRANCAISE POUR L'AVANCEMENT DES SCIENCES. INTERFACE. (Text in French) 1984. 5/yr. Can.$41.60 to individuals; institutions Can.$90.14; students Can.$20.80 (foreign Can.$78). Association Canadienne-Francaise pour l'Avancement des Sciences, 2730 Ct. Ste. Catherine, Montreal, Que. H3T 1B7, Canada. TEL 514-342-1411. FAX 514-342-9552. Ed. Sophie Malavoy. adv.: B&W page Can.$960, color page Can.$1200; trim 7 11/16 x 10 1/4; adv. contact: Pierette Lefrancois. circ. 8,000. (back issues avail.) **Indexed:** Pt.de Rep. (1988-).
Formerly: Association Canadienne-Francaise pour l'Avancement des Sciences. Bulletin (ISSN 0066-8850)
Description: A multi-disciplinary magazine addressed to members of the scientific community in the university, public, parapublic and private sectors.

500.9 ML
ASSOCIATION DES NATURALISTES DU MALI. BULLETIN. a. Association des Naturalistes du Mali, B.P. 1746, Bamako, Mali.

500 IT ISSN 0392-419X
CODEN: ANPMD3
ATENEO PARMENSE. ACTA NATURALIA. (Text and summaries in English, Italian) 1965. q. L.20000 (foreign L.25000). (Societa di Medicina e Scienze Naturali di Parma) Ateneo Parmense, Via Gramsci 14 (Ospedale Maggiore), 43100 Parma, Italy. Ed. Paolo Bobbio. charts; illus.; stat.; circ. 550. **Indexed:** Biol.Abstr., Chem.Abstr., Excerp.Med., Ind.Med., Nutr.Abstr.
Supersedes: Ateneo Parmense. Sezione 2: Acta Naturalia (ISSN 0004-654X)
Description: Presents research papers and articles on sciences. Includes various articles on oceanography, geology, and topology.

ATLANTE. see *GEOGRAPHY*

500 CN
ATLANTIC SCIENCE. 1975. bi-m. Atlantic Provinces Council on the Sciences, Memorial University of Newfoundland, P.O. Box 4200, St. John's, Nfld. A1C 5S7, Canada. TEL 709-737-8918. Ed. Joan Atkinson. circ. 3,000.
Formerly: A P I C S News.
Description: News about members of the council and research conducted by the Council.

500.9 DK ISSN 0067-0227
ATLANTIDE REPORT. SCIENTIFIC RESULTS OF THE DANISH EXPEDITION TO THE COASTS OF TROPICAL WEST AFRICA. (Text in English and French) 1950. irreg., vol.13, 1983. price varies. (Koebenhavns Universitet) Scandinavian Science Press Ltd., Langasen 4, Ganlose, 2760 Malov, Denmark. (Co-sponsor: British Museum) Eds. Joergen Knudsen, Torben Wolff. **Indexed:** Biol.Abstr., Deep Sea Res.& Oceanogr.Abstr.

500 600 614.7 AT
AUSTRALASIAN SCIENCE MAGAZINE. 1980. q. Aus.$25. (University College of Southern Queensland) U S Q Press, P.O. Box 58, Darling Heights, Toowoomba, Qld. 4350, Australia. TEL 076-31-2768. FAX 076-355550. TELEX 40010. Ed. John Cross. adv.; illus.; circ. 3,000. (back issues avail.)
Former titles: Australian Science Magazine (ISSN 0729-6924); Science Magazine (ISSN 0159-9062)
Description: Current scientific issues for students, teachers and laymen.

500 AT
AUSTRALIAN ACADEMY OF SCIENCE. ANNUAL GENERAL MEETING SYMPOSIUM. a. Australian Academy of Science, G.P.O. Box 783, Canberra, A.C.T. 2601, Australia.
Incorporates: Australian Academy of Science. Reports (ISSN 0067-1568)

500 AT ISSN 0067-1576
AUSTRALIAN ACADEMY OF SCIENCE. SCIENCE AND INDUSTRY FORUM REPORTS. 1968. 2/yr. Aus.$30 per no. Australian Academy of Science, G.P.O. Box 783, Canberra, A.C.T. 2601, Australia. circ. 1,500.

500 AT ISSN 0067-1584
AUSTRALIAN ACADEMY OF SCIENCE. YEAR BOOK. 1956. a. Aus.$30. Australian Academy of Science, G.P.O. Box 783, Canberra, A.C.T. 2601, Australia. index; circ. 1,500. **Indexed:** AESIS.
—BLDSC shelfmark: 9379.460000.

500.9 AT ISSN 0004-9840
QH1 CODEN: AUNHAO
AUSTRALIAN NATURAL HISTORY. 1921. q. Aus.$30 (foreign Aus.$42). Australian Museum, 6-8 College St., Sydney, N.S.W. 2000, Australia. Ed. Fiona Doig. adv.; bk.rev.; cum.index every 3 yrs.; circ. 20,000. **Indexed:** AESIS, Biol.Abstr., Environ.Per.Bibl., Gdlns, GeoRef.
—BLDSC shelfmark: 1815.500000.
Formerly: Australian Museum Magazine.
Description: Popular science magazine with feature articles on nature, culture and environmental issues.

500 600 AT ISSN 0815-4171
AUSTRALIAN SCIENCE AND TECHNOLOGY NEWSLETTER. m. Department of Foreign Affairs and Trade, Overseas Information Branch, P.O. Box 12, Canberra, A.C.T. 2601, Australia. FAX 06-2613900.
Formerly (until Sep. 1988): Australian Overseas Information Service. Science Newsletter (ISSN 0311-1334)

500 AU ISSN 0300-2772
AUSTRIA. BUNDESMINISTERIUM FUER WISSENSCHAFT UND FORSCHUNG. BERICHT DER BUNDESREGIERUNG AN DEN NATIONALRAT. 1968. a. free. Bundesministerium fuer Wissenschaft und Forschung, 1 Minoritenplatz 5, A-1014 Vienna, Austria. TEL 0222-53120-0. FAX 0222-53120-2217. TELEX 111157. stat. Key Title: Bericht der Bundesregierung an den Nationalrat.
Description: Report to the Austrian Parliament on the current situation of scientific research.

AUTOMATIC DOCUMENTATION AND MATHEMATICAL LINGUISTICS. see *LIBRARY AND INFORMATION SCIENCES*

600 II ISSN 0970-6607
AWISHKARA. (Text in Hindi) 1971. m. Rs.30. National Research Development Corporation, 20-22 Zamroodpur Community Centre, Kailash Colony Extension, New Delhi 110 048, India. TEL 11-6418615. TELEX 031-71358. Ed. D.N. Bhatnagar. adv.; bk.rev.; abstr.; charts; illus.; circ. 30,000. **Indexed:** Indian Sci.Abstr.

500 US ISSN 0141-6413
B A S R A JOURNAL. 1962. q. $25. British-American Scientific Research Association, UK , 13 Durwood Pl., Madison, NJ 07940. Ed. E.A. Rietman. adv.; bk.rev.; charts; illus.; circ. 100. (processed)
—BLDSC shelfmark: 1865.290000.
Formerly: British Amateur Scientific Research Association (ISSN 0005-2671)
Description: Publishes scientific papers from members and others. Its purpose is an exchange of scientific ideas, many of which are unorthodox.

500 CN
B.C. NATURALIST. vol.18, 1980. q. Can.$10. Federation of British Columbia Naturalists, 321-1367 West Broadway, Vancouver, B.C. V6H 4A9, Canada. TEL 604-737-3057. Ed. Jude Grass. adv.; bk.rev.; circ. 7,000.
Former titles: Federation of British Columbia Naturalists. Newsletter (ISSN 0046-3566); B.C. Nature Council.

500 CN
B.C. RESEARCH. ANNUAL REPORT & BROCHURE. 1944. a. free. British Columbia Research Corporation, 3650 Wesbrook Mall, Vancouver, B.C. V6S 2L2, Canada. TEL 604-224-4331. FAX 604-224-0540. circ. 2,000.
Former titles: B.C. Research. Annual Report; British Columbia Research Council. Annual Report (ISSN 0068-1652)

500 CN
B.C. RESEARCH NEWSLETTER. 3/yr. British Columbia Research Corporation, 3650 Wesbrook Mall, Vancouver, B.C. V6S 2L2, Canada. TEL 604-224-4331. FAX 604-224-0540.

B M F T JOURNAL. (Bundesministerium fuer Forschung und Technologie) see *TECHNOLOGY: COMPREHENSIVE WORKS*

509 UK ISSN 0144-6347
B S H S NEWSLETTER. 1980. 3/yr. £6($12) to non-members. British Society for the History of Science, 31 High St., Stanford in the Vale, Faringdon, Oxon SN7 8LH, England. TEL 0367-710223. FAX 0367-718963. Ed. F.A.J.L. James. bk.rev.; circ. 850.
Description: Developments in history of science, reports of meetings, forthcoming meetings.

SCIENCES: COMPREHENSIVE WORKS

001.3   CC
BAIKE ZHISHI/ENCYCLOPEDIC KNOWLEDGE. (Text in Chinese) m. Y11.04($43.10) Zhongguo Dabaike Quanshu Chubanshe - China Encyclopaedia Publishing House, 17 Fuchengmen Beidajie, Beijing 100037, People's Republic of China. TEL 8317319. (Dist. outside China by: China International Book Trading Corp., P.O. Box 2820, Beijing, P.R.C.; Dist. in US by: China Books & Periodicals, Inc., 2929 24th St., San Francisco, CA 94110) Ed. Mei Yi. adv.
Description: Popular science periodical.

500   BG   ISSN 0378-8121
Q80.B3   CODEN: JBACDF
BANGLADESH ACADEMY OF SCIENCES. JOURNAL. 1977. 2/yr. Tk.200($30) Bangladesh Academy of Sciences, c/o Department of Chemistry, Dhaka University, Dhaka 1000, Bangladesh. Ed. S.Z. Haider. bk.rev.; circ. 500. **Indexed:** Biol.Abstr., Chem.Abstr., Forest Prod.Abstr., Phys.Abstr., Sci.Abstr.
—BLDSC shelfmark: 4707.662000.

500   BG
BANGLADESH JOURNAL OF SCIENTIFIC AND INDUSTRIAL RESEARCH. (Text in English) 1964. q. $24. Bangladesh Council of Scientific and Industrial Research (BCSIR), Mirpur Road, Dhanmondi, Dhaka 1205, Bangladesh. FAX 880-2-863022. Ed. F.Z. Majid. **Indexed:** Biol.Abstr., Chem.Abstr., Crop Physiol.Abstr., Dairy Sci.Abstr., Field Crop Abstr., Food Sci.& Tech.Abstr., Herb.Abstr., Hort.Abstr., Nutr.Abstr., Phys.Abstr., Rice Abstr., Sci.Abstr., Seed Abstr., Soils & Fert., Triticale Abstr., Weed Abstr.
Formerly (until Jan. 1973): Scientific Researches (ISSN 0036-8830)
Description: Reports the findings of scientific and industrial research conducted in Bangladesh, India, Pakistan and Africa.

574.192   BG
BANGLADESH JOURNAL OF SCIENTIFIC RESEARCH. (Text in English) 1978. 2/yr. Tk.80($10) Bangladesh Association for the Advancement of Science, Department of Biochemistry, University of Dhaka, Ramna, Dhaka 2, Bangladesh. Ed. Abdul Mannan. adv.; bk.rev.; circ. 2,500. **Indexed:** Biol.Abstr., Chem.Abstr., Field Crop Abstr., Herb.Abstr., Plant Grow.Reg.Abstr.

BANGLADESH JOURNAL OF SOIL SCIENCE. see AGRICULTURE — Crop Production And Soil

500   BG
BANGLADESH SCIENCE CONFERENCE. PROCEEDINGS. a. (Bangladesh Association for the Advancement of Science) University of Dhaka, Ramna, Dhaka 2, Bangladesh.

500.9   IQ
BASRAH NATURAL HISTORY MUSEUM. BULLETIN. (Text in English; summaries in Arabic and English) 1974. irreg. exchange basis. Basrah Natural History Museum, University of Basrah, Basrah, Iraq. Ed. Khalaf al-Robaae. abstr.; bibl.; index. **Indexed:** Biol.Abstr.

500.9   IQ
BASRAH NATURAL HISTORY MUSEUM. PUBLICATION. 1976. irreg. exchange basis. Basrah Natural History Museum, University of Basrah, Basrah, Iraq. Ed. Khalaf al Robaae. **Indexed:** Biol.Abstr.

500   GW   ISSN 0084-6090
AS182   CODEN: BAWJAE
BAYERISCHE AKADEMIE DER WISSENSCHAFTEN. JAHRBUCH. 1912. a. price varies. C.H. Beck'sche Verlagsbuchhandlung, Wilhelmstr. 9, D-8000 Munich 40, Germany. TEL 089-38189-338. FAX 089-38189-398. TELEX 5215085-BECK-D. index. **Indexed:** Biol.Abstr., GeoRef.

500.9   GW   ISSN 0005-6995
AS182   CODEN: ABWMAJ
BAYERISCHE AKADEMIE DER WISSENSCHAFTEN. MATHEMATISCH-NATURWISSENSCHAFTLICHE KLASSE. ABHANDLUNGEN. 1929. irreg. Bayerische Akademie der Wissenschaften, Marstallplatz 8, 8000 Munich 22, Germany. **Indexed:** Appl.Mech.Rev., Biol.Abstr., Chem.Abstr., GeoRef., Math.R.

500 510   GW   ISSN 0340-7586
    CODEN: AMNSB2
BAYERISCHE AKADEMIE DER WISSENSCHAFTEN. MATHEMATISCH-NATURWISSENSCHAFTLICHE KLASSE. SITZUNGBERICHTE. 1871. a. (plus offprints). price varies. Bayerische Akademie der Wissenschaften, Marstallplatz 8, 8000 Munich 22, Germany. **Indexed:** Biol.Abstr., GeoRef., Math.R.
—BLDSC shelfmark: 8292.000000.

BAYERISCHE AKADEMIE DER WISSENSCHAFTEN. PHILOSOPHISCH-HISTORISCHE KLASSE. ABHANDLUNGEN, N.F.. see HUMANITIES: COMPREHENSIVE WORKS

BAYERISCHE AKADEMIE DER WISSENSCHAFTEN. PHILOSOPHISCH-HISTORISCHE KLASSE. SITZUNGSBERICHTE. see HUMANITIES: COMPREHENSIVE WORKS

500   CC   ISSN 0479-8023
BEIJING DAXUE XUEBAO (ZIRAN KEXUE BAN)/BEIJING UNIVERSITY. JOURNAL (NATURAL SCIENCE EDITION). (Text in Chinese) bi-m. Beijing Daxue, Honglou (Red Building), No. 205, Beijing University, Beijing 100871, People's Republic of China. TEL 282471. Ed. Gao Congshou.
—BLDSC shelfmark: 0663.190000.

500   CC
BEIJING KEJI DAXUE XUEBAO/BEIJING UNIVERSITY OF SCIENCE AND TECHNOLOGY. JOURNAL. (Text in Chinese) bi-m. Beijing Keji Daxue, Xuebao Bianjibu, Beijing 100083, People's Republic of China. TEL 2019944. Ed. Zhang Wenqi.

500   CC   ISSN 1001-0645
BEIJING LIGONG DAXUE XUEBAO/BEIJING UNIVERSITY OF SCIENCE AND ENGINEERING. JOURNAL. (Text in Chinese) q. Beijing Ligong Daxue, 7, Baishiqiao Lu, Beijing 100081, People's Republic of China. TEL 8416688. Ed. Mei Fengxiang.

500   CC   ISSN 0476-0301
BEIJING SHIFAN DAXUE XUEBAO (ZIRAN KEXUE BAN)/BEIJING NORMAL UNIVERSITY. JOURNAL (NATURAL SCIENCE EDITION). (Text in Chinese) q. Beijing Shifan Daxue, Xinwai Dajie, Beitaipingzhuang, Beijing 100875, People's Republic of China. TEL 2012288. Ed. Fang Fukang.
—BLDSC shelfmark: 4707.890900.

500   CC
BEIJING SHIFAN XUEYUAN XUEBAO (ZIRAN KEXUE BAN)/BEIJING NORMAL INSTITUTE. JOURNAL (NATURAL SCIENCE EDITION). (Text in Chinese) q. Beijing Shifan Xueyuan, Huayuancun, Fuchengmenwai, Beijing 100037, People's Republic of China. TEL 8414411. Ed. Mei Xiangming.

500   GW   ISSN 0232-1556
BEITRAEGE ZUR ALEXANDER-VON HUMBOLDT-FORSCHUNG. 1968. irreg., vol.11, 1987. (Akademie der Wissenschaften der DDR, Zentralinstitut fuer Geschichte) Akademie-Verlag Berlin, Leipziger Str. 3-4, 1086 Berlin, Germany.
Description: Studies various aspects of Humboldt's life.

500   GW   ISSN 0323-5130
    CODEN: BEFOD9
BEITRAEGE ZUR FORSCHUNGSTECHNOLOGIE; Schriftenreihe fuer Experimentalmethodik, Systemanalyse und Instrumentierung in der naturwissenschaftlichen, medizinischen und technischen Forschung. (Text in German; summaries in English, German and Russian) 1975. irreg., vol.19, 1989. (Akademie der Wissenschaften der DDR) Akademie-Verlag Berlin, Leipziger Str.3-4, 1086 Berlin, Germany.
Description: Studies in scientific, medicinal and technoloical research in the fields of methodology, systems analysis, testing and instrumentation.

500   GW   ISSN 0522-6570
BEITRAEGE ZUR GESCHICHTE DER WISSENSCHAFT UND DER TECHNIK. 1961. irreg., vol.21, 1990. price varies. (Deutsche Gesellschaft fuer Geschichte der Medizin, Naturwissenschaft und Technik e.V.) Franz Steiner Verlag Wiesbaden GmbH, Birkenwaldstr. 44, Postfach 101526, 7000 Stuttgart 1, Germany. TEL 0711-2582-0. FAX 0711-2582290. TELEX 723636-DAZD. illus.

500   BE   ISSN 0067-5407
BELGIUM. NATIONAAL FONDS VOOR WETENSCHAPPELIJK ONDERZOEK. JAARVERSLAG/BELGIUM. FONDS NATIONAL DE LA RECHERCHE SCIENTIFIQUE. RAPPORT ANNUEL. (Text in Dutch or French) 1928. a. Nationaal Fonds voor Wetenschappelijk Onderzoek - Fonds National de la Recherche Scientifique, Egmontstraat 5, B-1050 Brussels, Belgium. TEL 32-2-5129110. FAX 32-2-5125890. TELEX 25498 BEREFO B. (back isssues avail.)
Description: Report of activities of the National Fund for Scientific Research of Belgium.

507   BE
BELGIUM. NATIONAAL FONDS VOOR WETENSCHAPPELIJK ONDERZOEK. LIJST DER KREDIETGENIETERS/BELGIUM. FONDS NATIONAL DE LA RECHERCHE SCIENTIFIQUE. LISTES DES BENEFICIAIRES D'UNE SUBVENTION. (Text in Dutch or French; summaries in English) 1928. a. Nationaal Fonds voor Wetenschappelijk Onderzoek - Fonds National de la Recherche Scientifique, Egmontstraat 5, B-1050 Brussels, Belgium. TEL 32-2-5129110. FAX 32-2-5125890. TELEX 25498 BEREFO B. circ. 2,100.
Description: Scientific projects supported by the National Fund for Scientific Research of Belgium and its associated funds.

500   IS
BEN-GURION UNIVERSITY OF THE NEGEV. INSTITUTES FOR APPLIED RESEARCH. SCIENTIFIC ACTIVITIES.. (Text in English) 1973. irreg. free. Ben-Gurion University of the Negev, Institutes for Applied Research, P.O. Box 1025, Beersheva 84110, Israel. TEL 57-461926. FAX 57-71612. TELEX 5379-BGUCC-IL. Ed. Dorot Imber. circ. 1,500. **Indexed:** Field Crop Abstr., Herb.Abstr., Hort.Abstr.
Formerly: Ben-Gurion University of the Negev. Research and Development Authority. Applied Research Institute. Scientific Activities; Which superseded: Negev Institute for Arid Zone Research, Beer-Sheva, Israel. Report for Year (ISSN 0077-6467)

500.9   GW   ISSN 0067-5806
BERICHTE DES VEREINS NATUR UND HEIMAT UND DES NATURHISTORISCHEN MUSEUMS ZU LUEBECK. 1959. irreg. (every 2-3 yrs.). DM.30. Naturhistorisches Museum zu Luebeck, Muehlendamm 1, 2400 Luebeck, Germany. Eds. M. Diehl, G. Studnitz. circ. 800.

500   GW   ISSN 0170-6233
Q124.6   CODEN: BEWID8
BERICHTE ZUR WISSENSCHAFTSGESCHICHTE. (Text in German; summaries in English) 1978. 4/yr. DM.130. V C H Verlagsgesellschaft mbH, Postfach 101161, 6940 Weinheim, Germany. TEL 06201-602-0. FAX 06201-602328. TELEX 465516-VCHWH-D. (U.S. addr.: V C H Publishers Inc., 220 E. 23rd St., New York, NY 10010-4606) Ed. Fritz Krafft. adv.; bk.rev.; illus.; circ. 700.
—BLDSC shelfmark: 1938.400000.

500   IO   ISSN 0125-9156
BERITA ILMU PENGETAHUAN DEN TEKNOLOGI. (Text in English and Indonesian) 1957. q. Rps.600. Indonesian Institute of Sciences - Lembaga Ilmu Pengetahuan Indonesia, Jalan Jenderal Gatot Subroto 10, P.O. Box 250-JKT, Jakarta 10002, Indonesia. TEL 021-511542. Ed. Didin Sastrapradja. bk.rev.; bibl. (microform)
Formerly: Berita L.I.P.I. (ISSN 0005-9137)

500   GW   ISSN 0171-3302
BERLINER WISSENSCHAFTLICHER GESELLSCHAFT. JAHRBUCH. 1978. a. DM.48. (Berliner Wissenschaftlicher Gesellschaft e.V.) Duncker & Humblot GmbH, Dietrich-Schaefer-Weg 9, Postfach 410329, 1000 Berlin 41, Germany. FAX 030-79000631. Ed. B. Schlerath. circ. 400.

500.9 572   US   ISSN 0067-6160
    CODEN: OPBMAU
BERNICE PAUAHI BISHOP MUSEUM, HONOLULU. OCCASIONAL PAPERS. 1898. a. $35. Bishop Museum Press, 1525 Bernice St., Box 19000-A, Honolulu, HI 96817. TEL 808-848-4135. (reprint service avail. from UMI) **Indexed:** Biol.Abstr., Deep Sea Res.& Oceanogr.Abstr., GeoRef.
Description: Contains original contributions in anthropology, history, and the natural sciences of Hawaii and the Pacific.

SCIENCES: COMPREHENSIVE WORKS

500.9 572   US   ISSN 0067-6179
BERNICE PAUAHI BISHOP MUSEUM, HONOLULU. SPECIAL PUBLICATIONS. 1892. irregr. price varies. Bishop Museum Press, 1525 Bernice St., Box 19000-A, Honolulu, HI 96817. TEL 808-848-4135. (reprint service avail. from UMI) **Indexed:** Biol.Abstr., Deep Sea Res.& Oceanogr.Abstr.
— BLDSC shelfmark: 2094.263050.
Description: Popular and scholarly books on Hawaii and the Pacific Basin.

500 600   JA   ISSN 0285-1008
BESSATSU SAIENSU. Issued with: Saiensu (ISSN 0386-4324) 8/yr. price varies. Nikkei Science, Inc., 9-5 Ote-machi 1-chome, Chiyoda-ku, Tokyo 100, Japan. FAX 03-3293-2759. TELEX J22308-NIHONKEIZAI. Eds. K. Ohtake, S. Katayose. circ. 28,751.

BHAGALPUR UNIVERSITY JOURNAL. see *SOCIAL SCIENCES: COMPREHENSIVE WORKS*

500   IT
BIBLIOTECA DI STORIA DELLA SCIENZA. 1947. irreg., no.31, 1991. price varies. Casa Editrice Leo S. Olschki, Casella Postale 66, 50100 Florence, Italy. TEL 055-6530684. FAX 055-6530214.
Formerly (until 1987): Rivista di Storia delle Scienze Mediche e Naturali. Biblioteca.
Description: Examines the history of science.

500   CK
BIBLIOTECA JOSE JERONIMO TRIANA (SERIAL). (Text in English and Spanish) 1983. irreg. $20 or exchange basis. Universidad Nacional de Colombia, Instituto de Ciencias Naturales, Apdo. 7495, Bogota, D.E., Colombia. circ. 1,000.

BIBLIOTECAS, ARQUIVOS E MUSEUS. see *LIBRARY AND INFORMATION SCIENCES*

500.9 Q3   GW   ISSN 0006-2375
CODEN: BIWIAX
BILD DER WISSENSCHAFT; Das Magazin fuer Naturwissenschaft und Technik in unserer Zeit. 1964. m. DM.108.60 (students DM.90). Deutsche Verlags-Anstalt GmbH, Neckarstr. 121, Postfach 106012, 7000 Stuttgart 10, Germany. TEL 0711-2631-0. FAX 0711-2631-292. Ed. Reiner Korbmann. adv.; bk.rev.; bibl.; charts; illus.; index; circ. 128,000. **Indexed:** Biol.Abstr., Chem.Abstr., Excerp.Med., INIS Atomind., Numis.Lit.
— BLDSC shelfmark: 2058.950000.

501   CN   ISSN 0006-5099
CODEN: BLJYA3
BLUE JAY. 1942. 4/yr. Can.$18. Saskatchewan Natural History Society, Box 4348, Regina, Sask. S4P 3W6, Canada. TEL 306-780-9273. FAX 306-781-6021. Ed. Lynne Brown. adv.: B&W page Can.$800. bk.rev.; charts; illus.; circ. 2,000. **Indexed:** Biol.Abstr., Wild Life Rev.
— BLDSC shelfmark: 2114.150000.
Description: General interest scientific information dealing with the natural history of the prairie area.

501   CN
BLUE JAY NEWS. 1963. 3/yr. Can.$18 (free with subscr. to Blue Jay). Saskatchewan Natural History Society, Box 4348, Regina, Sask. S4P 3W6, Canada. TEL 306-780-9273. FAX 306-781-6021. Ed. John Pollock. adv.: B&W page Can.$200. circ. 2,000.
Formerly: Saskatchewan Natural History Society Newsletter (ISSN 0581-8443)
Description: Concerns society activities and current environmental issues in Saskatchewan.

500   GW   ISSN 0523-8226
BOETHIUS; Texte und Abhandlungen zur Geschichte der exakten Wissenschaften. 1962. irreg., vol.27, 1991. price varies. Franz Steiner Verlag Wiesbaden GmbH, Birkenwaldstr. 44, Postfach 101526, 7000 Stuttgart 1, Germany. TEL 0711-2582-0. FAX 0711-2582290. TELEX 723636-DAZD. Ed.Bd. illus.

500   TU
BOGAZICI UNIVERSITY JOURNAL: SCIENCES. (Text in English or Turkish) 1973. a. $10. Bogazici Universitesi, P.O. Box 2, Istanbul, Turkey. FAX 1656357. TELEX 26411 BOUN TR.

500   CU
BOLETIN DE EVENTOS CIENTIFICO-TECNICOS. w. Academia de Ciencias, Instituto de Documentacion e Informacion Cientifico-Tecnica (I D I C T), Capitolio Nacional, Padro y San Jose, Havana, 2, Cuba.

500 600   EC   ISSN 0253-5033
Q224.3.E2
BOLETIN S I N I C Y T. (Sistema Nacional de Informacion Cientifica y Tecnologia) 1982. s.a. free. Consejo Nacional de Ciencia y Tecnologia, Edificio Banco de Prestamos, Av. Patria 850 y 10 de Agosto, piso 9, Casilla C-0028, Quito, Ecuador. TEL 550160. FAX 593-2-569-983. TELEX 22027 CONACYT ED. (Co-sponsor: Programa Regional de Desarrollo Cientifico y Tecnologico de la Organizacion de los Estados Americanos) bk.rev.; charts; illus.; circ. 1,200.
Description: For professionals in the fields of technology. Covers all sciences related to modern technology in Ecuador.

500.9 QH1   II   ISSN 0006-6982
CODEN: JBOMAA
BOMBAY NATURAL HISTORY SOCIETY. JOURNAL. 1886. 3/yr. £40($80) Bombay Natural History Society, Hornbill House, Shahid Bhagat Singh Rd., Bombay 400023, India. TEL 244085. Ed.Bd. bk.rev.; charts; illus.; circ. 3,000. (also avail. in microfiche) **Indexed:** Bio-Contr.News & Info., Biol.Abstr., Curr.Adv.Ecol.Sci., Deep Sea Res.& Oceanogr.Abstr., Excerp.Med., Field Crop Abstr., Forest.Abstr., Forest Prod.Abstr., Geo.Abstr, Helminthol.Abstr., Herb.Abstr., Ind.Vet., Key Word Ind.Wildl.Res., Nutr.Abstr., Ornam.Hort., Rev.Appl.Entomol., Sel.Water Res.Abstr., Zoo.Rec.
— BLDSC shelfmark: 4709.900000.

500   II   ISSN 0006-7903
CODEN: TBICAQ
BOSE INSTITUTE. TRANSACTIONS.* (Text in English) 1918. q. Rs.32($7.50) Bose Institute, 93-1 Acharya Prafulla Chandra Rd., Calcutta 700009, India. Ed. Dr. D.M. Bose. (back issues avail.) **Indexed:** Biol.Abstr., Chem.Abstr., Field Crop Abstr., Herb.Abstr., Nucl.Sci.Abstr., Sci.Abstr.
— BLDSC shelfmark: 8905.000000.

BOSTON STUDIES IN THE PHILOSOPHY OF SCIENCE; Boston colloquium for the philosophy of science. see *PHILOSOPHY*

500   GW
BRAUNSCHWEIGISCHE WISSENSCHAFTLICHE GESELLSCHAFT. ABHANDLUNGEN. 1949. irreg. price varies. Verlag Erich Goltze GmbH und Co. KG, Stresemannstr. 28, 3400 Goettingen, Germany. Ed. K.H. Olsen. **Indexed:** Biol.Abstr., GeoRef, Math.R.

500 600   BL
BRAZIL. CONSELHO NACIONAL DE DESENVOLVIMENTO CIENTIFICO E TECNOLOGICO. BOLETIM. vol. 2, 1977. irreg. Conselho Nacional de Desenvolvimento Cientifico e Tecnologico, Edificio CNPQ, Av. W3 Norte, Q. 507-B, CP 11-1142, 70740 Brasilia D.F., Brazil. FAX 061-274-1950.

500   BL
BRAZIL. CONSELHO NACIONAL DE DESENVOLVIMENTO CIENTIFICO E TECNOLOGICO. PROGRAMA DO TROPICA SEMI-ARIDO (PUBLICACION). irreg. Conselho Nacional de Desenvolvimento Cientifico e Tecnologico, Programa do Tropico Semi-Arido, Av. W-3 Norte Q-507-B, 11-1142 Brasilia, Brazil. Ed. Domingos Carvalho da Silva. charts; stat.

500   BL
BRAZIL. CONSELHO NACIONAL DE DESENVOLVIMENTO CIENTIFICO E TECNOLOGICO. RELATORIO DE ATIVIDADES. 1975. irreg. Conselho Nacional de Desenvolvimento Cientifico e Tecnologico, Edificio CNPQ, Av. W3 Norte, Q. 507-B, CP 11-1142, 70740 Brasilia D.F., Brazil. FAX 061-274-1950.

500 QH7   CR   ISSN 0304-3711
CODEN: BRNSBE
BRENESIA. (Text in various languages; summaries in Spanish; abstracts in English, Spanish) 1972. 2/yr. $22 or exchange basis. Museo Nacional de Costa Rica, Departamento de Historia Natural, Box 749-1000, San Jose, Costa Rica. TEL 57-1433. Ed. Pablo Sanchez. illus.; circ. 1,000. (tabloid format) **Indexed:** Biol.Abstr., Curr.Adv.Ecol.Sci., GeoRef., Protozool.Abstr., Rev.Appl.Entomol., Rev.Plant Path., Zoo.Rec.
— BLDSC shelfmark: 2277.960000.
Supersedes: Revista Historia Natural de Costa Rica.

502   UK   ISSN 0068-1040
CODEN: PBNSAL
BRISTOL NATURALISTS' SOCIETY. PROCEEDINGS. 1862. a. £4.50. Bristol Naturalists' Society, City Museum, Bristol BS8 1RL, England. adv.; circ. 600. **Indexed:** Br.Hum.Ind., GeoRef.
— BLDSC shelfmark: 6665.000000.
Description: Studies the natural history and geology of the Bristol area.

509 QH84.2   UK   ISSN 0141-3325
BRITISH ANTARCTIC SURVEY. ANNUAL REPORT. 1970. a. £6. British Antarctic Survey, Madingley Rd., Cambridge CB3 OET, England. FAX 0223-62616. circ. 700.
— BLDSC shelfmark: 7383.680000.

509 Q125   UK   ISSN 0007-0874
CODEN: BJHSAT
BRITISH JOURNAL FOR THE HISTORY OF SCIENCE. 1962. q. $115 to institutions. (British Society for the History of Science) Cambridge University Press, Edinburgh Bldg., Shaftesbury Rd., Cambridge CB2 2RU, England. TEL 0223-312393. FAX 0223-31505. TELEX 851817256. (N. American addr.: Cambridge University Press, 40 W. 20th St., New York, NY 10011-4211. TEL 212-924-3900) Ed. David Knight. adv.; bk.rev.; charts; illus.; index; circ. 1,300. (also avail. in microform from UMI; reprint service avail. from UMI) **Indexed:** Amer.Hist. & Life, Arts & Hum.Cit.Ind., Br.Geol.Lit., Br.Hum.Ind., Bull.Signal., Chem.Abstr., Curr.Cont., GeoRef., Hist.Abstr., Hum.Ind., Ind.Sci.Rev., INIS Atomind., Math.R., Mid.East: Abstr.& Ind., Sci.Abstr., Sci.Cit.Ind., SSCI.
— BLDSC shelfmark: 2309.400000.
Refereed Serial

501 Q175   UK   ISSN 0007-0882
CODEN: BJPIA5
BRITISH JOURNAL FOR THE PHILOSOPHY OF SCIENCE. 1951. q. £33($70) (British Society for the Philosophy of Science) Oxford University Press, Oxford Journals, Pinkhill House, Southfield Rd., Eynsham, Oxford OX8 1JJ, England. TEL 0865-882283. FAX 0865-882890. TELEX 8373300 OXPRES G. Ed. Dr. Greg Hunt. adv.; bk.rev.; bibl.; index; circ. 1,750. (also avail. in microfiche; back issues avail.) **Indexed:** Arts & Hum.Cit.Ind., Br.Hum.Ind., Cont.Pg.Manage., Curr.Cont., Hum.Ind., Ind.Bk.Rev.Hum., Ind.Sci.Rev., Math.R., Phil.Ind., Psychol.Abstr., Sci.Abstr., Sci.Cit.Ind., SSCI.
— BLDSC shelfmark: 2316.000000.
Description: Addresses the study of the logic, the method, and the philosophy of science, including the social sciences.

800 700 500 AP2   US   ISSN 0007-2869
BUCKNELL REVIEW; a scholarly journal of letters, arts and science. 1941. s.a. $32. Bucknell University Press, c/o Associated University Presses, 440 Forsgate Dr., Cranbury, NJ 08512. TEL 609-655-4770. FAX 609-655-8366. Ed. Pauline Fletcher. illus.; index; circ. 500. (also avail. in microform from UMI; back issues avail.; reprint service avail. from UMI) **Indexed:** Amer.Hist.& Life, Hist.Abstr., LCR, M.L.A., Sociol.Abstr.
— BLDSC shelfmark: 2355.850000.

550 QH1   US   ISSN 0096-4131
CODEN: BBNSA3
BUFFALO SOCIETY OF NATURAL SCIENCES. BULLETIN. 1873. irreg., vol.33, 1988. price varies. Buffalo Society of Natural Sciences, 1020 Humboldt Pkwy., Buffalo, NY 14211. TEL 716-896-5200. FAX 716-897-6723. charts; illus.; circ. 500. (back issues avail.) **Indexed:** Biol.Abstr., GeoRef.

500   US
BUFFALO SOCIETY OF NATURAL SCIENCES. OCCASIONAL PAPERS. 1976. irreg., no.4, 1990. price varies. Buffalo Society of Natural Sciences, 1020 Humboldt Pkwy., Buffalo, NY 14211. TEL 716-896-5200. FAX 716-897-6723.

500   AA
BULETINI I SHKENCAVE TEKNIKE/BULLETIN DES SCIENCES TECHNIQUES. (Text in Albanian; summaries in French) q. $7.20. Enver Hoxha Universitet, Tirana, Albania.

SCIENCES: COMPREHENSIVE WORKS

500   BU   ISSN 0007-3989
AS343
BULGARSKA AKADEMIIA NA NAUKITE. SPISANIE. 1956. bi-m. 7.80 lv. Publishing House of the Bulgarian Academy of Sciences, Acad. G. Bonchev St., Bldg. 6, 1113 Sofia, Bulgaria. (Dist. by: Hemus, 6, Rouski Blvd., 1000 Sofia, Bulgaria) Ed. G. Brankov. illus.; circ. 800. **Indexed:** Biol.Abstr., BSL Biol., BSL Econ., BSL Math., Met.Abstr., World Alum.Abstr.
—BLDSC shelfmark: 0166.360000.

BULLETIN HISTORIQUE ET SCIENTIFIQUE DE L'AUVERGNE. see HISTORY — History Of Europe

BULLETIN OF LAW, SCIENCE & TECHNOLOGY. see LAW

500 300   US   ISSN 0270-4676
Q175.4   CODEN: BSTSDJ
BULLETIN OF SCIENCE TECHNOLOGY AND SOCIETY. 1981. bi-m. $25 to individuals; institutions $85 (effective 1992). 102 Materials Research Laboratory, Pennsylvania State University, University Park, PA 16802. TEL 814-865-1137. Eds. Rustum Roy, Kathleen Mourant. (also avail. in microform from MIM,UMI) **Indexed:** Curr.Adv.Ecol.Sci., Curr.Cont., Energy Rev., Eng.Ind., Risk Abstr., Sociol.Abstr., SSCI.
—BLDSC shelfmark: 2887.760000.
Refereed Serial

500.1 560   FR   ISSN 0373-2061
Q2   CODEN: BSBNAD
BULLETIN SCIENTIFIQUE DE BOURGOGNE. 1931. biennial. 100 F. Societe des Sciences Naturelles de Bourgogne, Faculte de Sciences, Departement de Biologie, 6 bd. Gabriel, F 21100-Dijon, France. (Subscr. to: Librairie de l'Universite, 17 rue de la Liberte, 21014 Dijon, France) (Co-sponsor: Universite de Dijon) Dir. J.P. Henry. bk.rev.; circ. 400. **Indexed:** Bull.Signal., GeoRef.

500   BL   ISSN 0034-7361
C E C REVISTA.* 1963. m. Cr.$2000($2) Centro de Estudos Cientificos, Caixa Postal 11585, Sao Paulo - SP, Brazil. Ed. Geraldo Lino de Campos. adv.; bk.rev.; charts; illus.; tr.lit.; circ. 1,000.

C I R A S NEWS. (Center for Industrial Research and Service) see TECHNOLOGY: COMPREHENSIVE WORKS

500   US   ISSN 0366-757X
Q183.9   CODEN: CODBA4
C O D A T A BULLETIN. 1967. q. $159. (International Council of Scientific Unions, Committee on Data for Science and Technology) Hemisphere Publishing Corporation (Subsidiary of: Taylor & Francis Group), 1900 Frost Rd., Ste. 101, Bristol, PA 19007-1598. TEL 215-785-5800. FAX 215-785-5515. Eds. Phyllis Glaeser, Edgar F. Westrum. circ. 700. **Indexed:** AESIS, Comput.Cont., Curr.Adv.Ecol.Sci., Curr.Cont., Deep Sea Res.& Oceanogr.Abstr., GeoRef.
—BLDSC shelfmark: 3292.765000.
Refereed Serial

500   FR   ISSN 0538-6918
Q10
C O D A T A NEWSLETTER. (Text in English) 1968. q. free. International Council of Scientific Unions, Committee on Data for Science and Technology, CODATA Secretariat, 51 bd. de Montmorency, 75016 Paris, France. FAX 42-88-14-66. TELEX 630553. Ed. Edgar F. Westrum, Jr. adv.; bk.rev.; bibl.; circ. 6,500. **Indexed:** Br.Ceram.Abstr.

500 600   II
C O S T E D NEWSLETTER. (Text in English) 1976. q. free. (Committee on Science and Technology in Developing Countries) Association for the Application of Science to Human Affairs (ASHA), c/o Indian Institute of Science, Bangalore 560012, India. Ed.Bd. bk.rev.; circ. 10,000.

500 600   BE   ISSN 0770-0725
C R I C RAPPORT DE RECHERCHE. (Text in Dutch, English, French) 1962. irreg. 500 BEF. Centre Nationl de Recherches Scientifiques et Techniques pour l'Industrie Cimentiere, 46 rue Cesar Franck, B-1050 Brussels, Belgium. FAX 2-640-0670. **Indexed:** Concr.Abstr.
Formerly: Centre National de Recherches Scientifiques et Techniques pour l'Industrie Cimentiere. Brussels. C R I C Rapport de Recherche (ISSN 0069-2026)

500 600   SA
C S I R ANNUAL REPORT - TECHNOLOGY IMPACT. (Text in Afrikaans, English) 1945. a. free. C S I R Corporate Communication, P.O. Box 395, Pretoria 0001, South Africa. TEL 012-841-4302. FAX 012-841-2055. circ. 10,000.
Formerly: C S I R Annual Report (ISSN 0370-8454)
Description: Features the year's research, development and implementation successes, division reports, executive overviews, and financial statements.

500   GH
C S I R HANDBOOK. 1970. irreg. Council for Scientific and Industrial Research, Box M32, Accra, Ghana. (back issues avail.)

068   AT   ISSN 0157-7204
C S I R O DIRECTORY. 1951. a. Aus.$10. Commonwealth Scientific and Industrial Research Organization, 314 Albert St., E. Melbourne, Vic. 3002, Australia. **Indexed:** AESIS.

500 600   FR   ISSN 0243-1335
CA M'INTERESSE. 1981. m. 204 F. Prisma Presse, 6 rue Daru, 75379 Paris Cedex 08, France. FAX 45-58-86-09. TELEX 616076. Ed. Axel Grant. circ. 370,777. **Indexed:** Pt.de Rep. (1991-).

500.9   FR   ISSN 0008-0039
                        CODEN: CNBNAN
CAHIERS DES NATURALISTES. 1946. q. 260 F. Naturalistes Parisiens, 45 rue de Buffon, 75005 Paris, France. Ed. Claude Dupuis. bk.rev.; bibl.; charts; illus.; index; circ. 500. **Indexed:** Bio-Contr.News & Info., Biol.Abstr., Bull.Signal., Chem.Abstr., Field Crop Abstr., GeoRef., Herb.Abstr., Zoo.Rec.
—BLDSC shelfmark: 2949.850000.

500   FR   ISSN 0008-0462
CAHIERS RATIONALISTES. (Supplement: Cahier Rationaliste) 1931. m. 325 F. (Union Rationaliste) Nouvelles Editions Rationalistes, 14 rue de l'Ecole Polytechnique, 75005 Paris, France. bk.rev.; index; circ. 9,000.
—BLDSC shelfmark: 2952.123000.

500   CK   ISSN 0366-5232
QH7   CODEN: CALDAK
CALDASIA. (Text in English, French, German and Spanish) 1942. s-a. $20 or exchange basis. Universidad Nacional de Colombia, Instituto de Ciencias Naturales, Apdo. 7495, Bogota, Colombia. Ed. Jose Luis Fernandez Alonso. bibl.; illus.; circ. 1,200. **Indexed:** Biol.Abstr., Bull.Signal, Deep Sea Res.& Oceanogr.Abstr., Excerp.Bot., Field Crop Abstr., Forest.Abstr., Geo.Abstr, GeoRef., Herb.Abstr., Potato Abstr., Ref.Zh, Seed Abstr., VITIS.

CALENDAR OF CONFERENCES, MEETINGS AND EXHIBITIONS TO BE HELD IN SOUTH AFRICA. see MEETINGS AND CONGRESSES

CALENDAR OF SCIENTIFIC AND TECHNOLOGICAL MEETINGS IN ISRAEL. see MEETINGS AND CONGRESSES

506   US   ISSN 0008-0829
Q1
CALIFORNIA ACADEMY OF SCIENCES. ACADEMY NEWSLETTER. 1940. m. membership. California Academy of Sciences, Golden Gate Park, San Francisco, CA 94118. TEL 415-750-7142. Ed. David Shaw. circ. 25,000. (back issues avail.)
Refereed Serial

500   US
CALIFORNIA ACADEMY OF SCIENCES. MEMOIRS. 1868. irreg., vol.15, 1991. California Academy of Sciences, Golden Gate Park, San Francisco, CA 94118. TEL 415-750-7243. Ed. Tom Daniel.
Refereed Serial

574 550   US   ISSN 0068-5461
Q11   CODEN: OPCAAX
CALIFORNIA ACADEMY OF SCIENCES. OCCASIONAL PAPERS. 1890. irreg., no.146, 1986. $35 (includes Proceedings). California Academy of Sciences, Golden Gate Park, San Francisco, CA 94118. TEL 415-750-7243. Ed. Tom Daniel. charts; illus.; circ. 1,000. (also avail. in microform from UMI; microfiche; back issues avail.) **Indexed:** Biol.Abstr., Curr.Adv.Ecol.Sci., Deep Sea Res.& Oceanogr.Abstr., GeoRef., Ocean.Abstr., Rev.Appl.Entomol., Zoo.Rec.
Refereed Serial

500 060   US   ISSN 0068-547X
Q11   CODEN: PCASAV
CALIFORNIA ACADEMY OF SCIENCES. PROCEEDINGS. 1854. irreg., vol.47, 1991. $35 includes Occasional Papers. California Academy of Sciences, Golden Gate Park, San Francisco, CA 94118. TEL 415-750-7243. Ed. Tom Daniel. index; circ. 1,000. (also avail. in microform from UMI) **Indexed:** Biol.Abstr., Curr.Adv.Ecol.Sci., Deep Sea Res.& Oceanogr.Abstr., GeoRef., Key Word Ind.Wildl.Res., Ocean.Abstr., Rev.Appl.Entomol., Zoo.Rec.
Refereed Serial

354   CN
CANADA. MINISTRY OF STATE FOR SCIENCE AND TECHNOLOGY. ANNUAL REPORT. 1971. a. Ministry of State for Science and Technology, 270 Albert St., Ottawa, Ont. K1A 1A1, Canada. TEL 613-997-0028. circ. 3,000.

500 026   CN   ISSN 0703-0320
Q224.3.C2
CANADA INSTITUTE FOR SCIENTIFIC AND TECHNICAL INFORMATION. ANNUAL REPORT/INSTITUT CANADIEN DE L'INFORMATION SCIENTIFIQUE ET TECHNIQUE. RAPPORT ANNUEL. a. free. (National Research Council of Canada) C.I.S.T.I. Publicity and Communications, Ottawa, Ont. K1A 0S2, Canada. TEL 613-993-3854. FAX 613-952-9112. circ. 4,000.
Formerly: National Science Library of Canada. Annual Report (ISSN 0077-5576)

500 600   CN   ISSN 0843-6673
CANADIAN AREA DEVELOPMENT. 1989. q. Can.$35($45) Mensa Media Inc., 111 Elizabeth St., Ste. 700, Toronto, Ont. M5G 1P7, Canada. TEL 416-979-7100. FAX 416-979-7682. Ed. Marion Woodlife. adv.; circ. 20,000. (back issues avail.)

500.9   CN   ISSN 0008-3550
                        CODEN: CAFNAK
CANADIAN FIELD-NATURALIST. 1879. q. Can.$35 to non-members. Ottawa Field-Naturalists' Club, Box 3264, Postal Station C, Ottawa, Ont. K1Y 4J5, Canada. TEL 613-722-3050. Ed. F.R. Cook. bk.rev.; bibl.; charts; illus.; maps; index; circ. 2,200. (back issues avail.) **Indexed:** Acid Rain Abstr., Acid Rain Ind., Biol.Abstr., Curr.Adv.Ecol.Sci., Curr.Cont., Deep Sea Res.& Oceanogr.Abstr., Environ.Abstr., Environ.Per.Bibl., Field Crop Abstr., Forest.Abstr., Geo.Abstr., GeoRef., Herb.Abstr., Ind.Sci.Rev., Ind.Vet., INIS Atomind., Key Word Ind.Wildl.Res., Sci.Cit.Ind., Soils & Fert., Vet.Bull.
—BLDSC shelfmark: 3023.000000.

500.9   CN
                        CODEN: SYLGBY
CANADIAN MUSEUM OF NATURE. SYLLOGEUS. (Text in English, French) 1972. irreg. price varies. Canadian Museum of Nature, Publishing Division, P.O. Box 3443, Station "D", Ottawa, Ont. K1P 6P4, Canada. TEL 613-990-6594. FAX 613-990-0318. circ. 1,000. (back issues avail.) **Indexed:** Biol.Abstr.
Formerly: National Museum of Natural Sciences. Syllogeus (ISSN 0704-576X)

500.9   CN   ISSN 0316-0343
CANADIAN PLAINS BULLETIN. 1970. 3/yr. Can.$5. Canadian Plains Research Center, University of Regina, Regina, Sask. S4S 0A2, Canada. TEL 306-585-4758. FAX 306-586-9862. Ed. Brian Mlazgar. bk.rev.; bibl.; circ. 4,000. (back issues avail.)
—BLDSC shelfmark: 3043.865000.

500   US   ISSN 0069-066X
AS32   CODEN: CIWYAO
CARNEGIE INSTITUTION OF WASHINGTON. YEAR BOOK. 1903. a. $7. Carnegie Institution of Washington, 1530 P St., N.W., Washington, DC 20005. TEL 202-387-6400. Ed. R. Bowers. bibl.; illus.; circ. 12,500. **Indexed:** Biol.Abstr., Chem.Abstr., GeoRef.
—BLDSC shelfmark: 9382.000000.
Description: Scientific research by the institution's astronomers, earth scientists, and biologists.

SCIENCES: COMPREHENSIVE WORKS

500.9 574 572 560   US   ISSN 0097-4463
AS36   CODEN: CIMUAU
CARNEGIE MUSEUM OF NATURAL HISTORY. ANNALS OF CARNEGIE MUSEUM. 1901. q. $25 to individuals; institutions and foreign $65. Carnegie Museum of Natural History, Office of Scientific Publications, 4400 Forbes Ave., Pittsburgh, PA 15213-4080. TEL 412-622-3287. FAX 412-622-8837. Eds. C.J. McCoy, Leonard Krishtalka. charts; illus.; index; circ. 800. (back issues avail.) **Indexed:** Biol.Abstr., Deep Sea Res.& Oceanogr.Abstr., GeoRef., Zoo.Rec. Key Title: Annals of Carnegie Museum.
—BLDSC shelfmark: 1022.000000.
Description: Contributions in organismal biology, earth sciences and anthropology.

500 574 572 560   US   ISSN 0145-9058
CODEN: BCMHD9
CARNEGIE MUSEUM OF NATURAL HISTORY. BULLETIN. 1976. irreg., no.28, 1989. price varies. Carnegie Museum of Natural History, Office of Scientific Publications, 4400 Forbes Ave., Pittsburgh, PA 15213-4080. TEL 412-622-3287. FAX 412-622-8837. Eds. C.J. McCoy, Leonard Krishtalka. bibl.; charts; illus.; index; circ. controlled. (back issues avail.) **Indexed:** Biol.Abstr., GeoRef.
—BLDSC shelfmark: 2434.550000.
Description: Monographs in organismal biology, earth sciences and anthropology.

500.9   US   ISSN 0145-9031
CODEN: SPCHDX
CARNEGIE MUSEUM OF NATURAL HISTORY. SPECIAL PUBLICATIONS. 1975. irreg., no.15, 1989. price varies. Carnegie Museum of Natural History, Office of Scientific Publications, 4400 Forbes Ave., Pittsburgh, PA 15213-4080. TEL 412-622-3287. FAX 412-622-8837. Eds. C.J. McCoy, Leonard Krishtalka. (back issues avail.) **Indexed:** Biol.Abstr.
—BLDSC shelfmark: 8373.850000.
Description: Variety of monographs in natural history.

500   CK   ISSN 0120-5986
CARTA DE COLCIENCIAS. 1978? m. Colciencias, Transversal 9A, No.133-28, Bogota, Colombia. TEL 2169800. FAX 2744460. TELEX 44305. Ed. Karin Zonszain.

500   UK   ISSN 0069-0945
CASS LIBRARY OF SCIENCE CLASSICS. 1967. irreg., no.23, 1971. price varies. Frank Cass & Co. Ltd., Gainsborough House, 11 Gainsborough Rd., London E11 1RS, England. TEL 081-530-4226. FAX 081-530-7795. (Dist. in U.S. by: ISBS, 5602 N.E. Hassalo St., Portland, OR 97213-3640).

CATALYST (VANCOUVER). see *EDUCATION — Teaching Methods And Curriculum*

500   UK   ISSN 0958-3629
CATALYST G C S E SCIENCE REVIEW. 1989. q. £12.50 (foreign £24.50). Philip Allan Publishers Ltd., Deddington, Oxfordshire OX15 OSE, England. TEL 0869-38652. FAX 0869-38803.

500   CN
CATALYST: RESEARCH AT THE UNIVERSITY OF CALGARY. 1986. 3/yr. free. University of Calgary, Research Services, Public Affairs, 2500 University Drive N.W., Calgary, Alta. T2N 1N4, Canada. TEL 403-220-3783. FAX 403-282-8413. Ed. Rosemary Frei. circ. 3,000. (tabloid format)

500.9   SP
CAZA FOTOGRAFICA. (Text in English and Spanish) 1973. bi-m. 1500 ptas. Instituto de la Caza Fotografica y Ciencias de la Naturaleza, Castello, 59, Madrid, Spain. illus.

509   DK   ISSN 0008-8994
CODEN: CENTA4
CENTAURUS; international magazine of the history of mathematics, science and technology. (Text in English, French, German) 1950. 4/yr. DKK 1085. Munksgaard International Publishers Ltd., 35 Noerre Soegade, P.O. Box 2148, DK-1016 Copenhagen K, Denmark. TEL 33-12-70-30. FAX 33-12-93-87. TELEX 10431 MUNKS DK. Ed. Kurt Moeller Pedersen. adv.; bk.rev.; bibl.; illus.; cum.index: vols.1-30, 1950-1984 in vol.32; circ. 500. (reprint service avail. from ISI) **Indexed:** Amer.Hist.& Life, Arts & Hum.Cit.Ind., Chem.Abstr., Curr.Cont., Hist.Abstr., Ind.Med., Math.R., Mid.East: Abstr.& Ind., SSCI.
—BLDSC shelfmark: 3104.000000.

500 600   FR
CENTRE DE RECHERCHES SCIENCE ET VIE. CAHIERS. (Text in English or French) 1971. q. Centre de Recherches Science et Vie, 2 rue de la Baume, 75008 Paris, France.

CENTRE NATIONAL DE DOCUMENTATION SCIENTIFIQUE ET TECHNIQUE. RAPPORT D'ACTIVITE. see *TECHNOLOGY: COMPREHENSIVE WORKS*

500   UN
CENTRO PANAMERICANO DE ZOONOSIS. MONOGRAFIAS CIENTIFICAS Y TECNICAS. (Text in Spanish) 1960. irreg. Centro Panamericano de Zoonosis, Casilla 3092, 1000 Buenos Aires, Argentina. TEL 792-4047. TELEX 24577. (Affiliate: World Health Organization)

500   CS
QH1   CODEN: PPUCA4
CESKOSLOVENSKA ACEDEMIE VED. USTAV V BRNE. PRIRODOVEDNE PRACE/ACTA SCIENTIARUM NATURALIUM ACADEMIAE SCIENTIARUM BOHEMOSLOVACAE BRNO. (Text in English, French or German; summaries in English and Russian) 1967. m. price varies. Academia, Publishing House of the Czechoslovak Academy of Sciences, Vodickova str. 40, 112 29 Prague, Czechoslovakia. TEL 23-63-065. (Subscr. to: Artia, Ve Smeckach 30, P.O. Box 790, 111 27 Prague 1, Czechoslovakia) adv. **Indexed:** Anim.Breed.Abstr., Biol.Abstr., Bull.Signal., Chem.Abstr., Curr.Adv.Ecol.Sci., Field Crop Abstr., Geo.Abstr., GeoRef., Herb.Abstr., Math.R., Plant Breed.Abstr., Ref.Zh.
Formerly: Ceskoslovenska Akademie Ved. Brnenska Zakladna. Prace (ISSN 0032-8758)

500   CS   ISSN 0069-228X
Q44   CODEN: RCAVAS
CESKOSLOVENSKA AKADEMIE VED. ROZPRAVY. M P V: RADA MATEMATICKYCH A PRIRODNICH VED. 1891. irreg., vol.99, 1989. price varies. (Cooper Academy of Sciences) Academia, Publishing House of the Czechoslovak Academy of Sciences, Vodickova 40, 112 29 Prague 1, Czechoslovakia. TEL 23-63-065. circ. 1,000. **Indexed:** Biol.Abstr., GeoRef., Math.R.

500   CS   ISSN 0009-0492
CESKOSLOVENSKA AKADEMIE VED. VESTNIK/CZECHOSLOVAK ACADEMY OF SCIENCES. BULLETIN. (Text in Czech or Slovak) 1891. bi-m. DM.168. (Czechoslovak Akademy of Science) Academia, Publishing House of the Czechoslovak Academy of Sciences, Vodickova 40, 112 29 Prague 1, Czechoslovakia. TEL 235-17-92. (Dist. in Western countries by: Kubon & Sagner, P.O. Box 34 01 80, 8000 Munich, Germany) bk.rev.; bibl.; illus.; index; circ. 1,800. **Indexed:** Biol.Abstr., Chem.Abstr.
Description: Reports on all activities of the Czechoslovak Academy of Sciences, and publishes articles on the situation and prospects of individual sciences.

500 600   CE
CEYLON INSTITUTE OF SCIENTIFIC & INDUSTRIAL RESEARCH. ANNUAL REPORT. 1956. a. $25. Ceylon Institute of Scientific & Industrial Research, 363 Bauddhaloka Mawatha, Box 787, Colombo 7, Sri Lanka. circ. 300.

001.9   CN   ISSN 0706-5337
CHAOS. 1978. 8/yr. Can.$16. Res Bureaux, Box 1598, Kingston, Ont. K7L 5C8, Canada. TEL 613-542-7277.

500 600   US
CHECKPOINT (WASHINGTON); newsletter from the frontiers of a future civilized world order. 1963. irreg., vol.11, no.1, 1984. donation. War Control Planners Inc., Box 19127, Washington, DC 20036. TEL 202-785-0708. Ed. Howard G. Kurtz. bk.rev.; illus.; circ. 3,000.

500   CC
CHENGDU DAXUE XUEBAO (ZIRAN KEXUE BAN)/CHENGDU UNIVERSITY. JOURNAL (NATURAL SCIENCE EDITION). (Text in Chinese) q. Y4.80. Chengdu Daxue - Chengdu University, Xiaojia Cun, Renmin Beilu, Chengdu, Sichuan 610081, People's Republic of China. TEL 337939. Ed. Yang Qiwei.
Description: Publishes scientific research results and technology news in the natural sciences, including food processing and industrial management.

500   CC   ISSN 0253-2263
CHENGDU KEJI DAXUE XUEBAO/CHENGDU UNIVERSITY OF SCIENCE AND TECHNOLOGY. JOURNAL. (Text in Chinese) bi-m. Chengdu Keji Daxue, Xuebao Bianjibu, Chengdu, Sichuan 610065, People's Republic of China. TEL 581554. Ed. Xu Xi.

500   US   ISSN 0009-3491
Q11
CHICAGO ACADEMY OF SCIENCES. BULLETIN. 1883. irreg., vol.14, no.4, 1989. price varies. Chicago Academy of Sciences, 2001 N. Clark St., Chicago, IL 60614. TEL 312-549-0606. Ed. Paul G. Heltne. charts; illus.; bibl.; circ. 1,019. (also avail. in microform from UMI; reprint service avail. from UMI) **Indexed:** Biol.Abstr.
Description: Booklets on natural history subjects.

CHICKADEE. see *CHILDREN AND YOUTH — For*

500   JA
CHIKUHO HAKUBUTSU/NATURHISTORICA CHIKUHOANA. (Text in Japanese) a. Society of Natural History of Chikuho - Chikuho Hakubutsu Kenkyukai, Iizuka-shiritsu Toshokan, 2-58 Nishi-machi, Iizuka-shi, Fukuoka-ken 820, Japan.

500 600   UK   ISSN 0894-2536
CHINA CENTER OF ADVANCED SCIENCE AND TECHNOLOGY SERIES. 1987. irreg., vol.8, 1990. Gordon & Breach Science Publishers, P.O. Box 90, Reading, Berkshire RG1 8JL, England. TEL 0734-560-080. FAX 0734-568-211. TELEX 849870 SCIPUB G. (US addr.: Box 786, Cooper Sta., New York, NY 10276. TEL 212-206-8900) Ed.Bd. (also avail. in microfilm; microfiche)
—BLDSC shelfmark: 6842.817800.
Refereed Serial

500 600   US   ISSN 0272-0086
E183.8.C5
CHINA EXCHANGE NEWS; a review of science, education, and academic relations with the PRC. 1973. q. free. National Academy of Sciences, Committee on Scholarly Communication with the People's Republic of China, 2101 Constitution Ave. N.W., Washington, DC 20418. TEL 202-334-2718. FAX 202-334-1774. Ed. Kathlin Smith. bk.rev.; abstr.; bibl.; stat.; circ. 4,000 (controlled).
—BLDSC shelfmark: 3180.144000.
Formerly: China Exchange Newsletter (ISSN 0145-6318); **Supersedes:** China Science Notes.

500 600   US
CHINA REPORT: SCIENCE AND TECHNOLOGY. irreg. (approx. 50/yr.). $7 per no. (foreign $14 per no.). U.S. Joint Publications Research Service, Box 12507, Arlington, VA 22209. TEL 703-487-4630. (Orders to: NTIS, Springfield, VA 22161)

500   CC
CHINESE ACADEMY OF SCIENCES. BULLETIN. Chinese edition: Zhongguo Kexueyuan Yuankan (ISSN 1000-3045) (Text in English) s-a. $146. Science Press, Marketing and Sales Department, 16 Donghuangchenggen Beijie, Beijing 100707, People's Republic of China. TEL 4010642. FAX 4012180. TELEX 210247 SPBJ CN.
Description: Publishes research results, science and technology development trends. Some of the articles are original, not translations.

951 500   US   ISSN 0361-9001
Q145
CHINESE SCIENCE. 1975. irreg. (1-2/yr.). $20 for 4 nos. History and Sociology of Science, University of Pennsylvania, Philadelphia, PA 19104-6310. TEL 215-898-7454. Ed. N. Sivin. adv.; bk.rev.; circ. 350.

SCIENCES: COMPREHENSIVE WORKS

500   CC   ISSN 1001-6538
CODEN: CSBUEF
CHINESE SCIENCE BULLETIN. Chinese edition: Kexue Tongbao (ISSN 0023-074X) (Text in English) 1980. fortn. $410 to individuals; institutions $684. Science Press, Marketing and Sales Department, 16 Donghuangchenggen Beijie, Beijing, People's Republic of China. TEL 4010642. FAX 4012180. TELEX 210247-SPBJ-CN. (U.S. addr.: Science Press New York Ltd., 63-117 Alderton St., Rego Park, NY 11374) adv.; index; circ. 5,000. (back issues avail.) —BLDSC shelfmark: 3181.086000.
Formerly (until 1988): Kexue Tongbao (Foreign Language Edition) (ISSN 0250-7862)
Description: Presents concise reports on important recent results in basic and applied sciences. Reflects the current level of development of science and technology in China.
Refereed Serial

500   CC   ISSN 1000-582X
CHONGQING DAXUE XUEBAO/CHONGQING UNIVERSITY. JOURNAL. (Text in Chinese) 1978. bi-m. $1.50 per no. Chongqing Daxue - Chongqing University, 74, Zhengjie, Shapingba, Chongqing, Sichuan 660044, People's Republic of China. (Dist. overseas by: China International Book Trading Corp., P.O. Box 399, Beijing, P.R.C.) **Indexed:** Art & Archaeol.Tech.Abstr., Cyb.Abstr.

500 600   CC
CHONGQING KEJI/CHONGQING SCIENCE AND TECHNOLOGY. (Text in Chinese) m. Chongqing Shi Kexue Jishu Weiyuanhui - Chongqing Science and Technology Commission, 236, Renmin Lu, Chongqing, Sichuan 630015, People's Republic of China. TEL 352263. Ed. Zhou Yongxin.

500   ZR   ISSN 0009-6040
CHRONIQUE DE L'I R S A C. (Text in English and French) 1966. 3/yr. $2. Institut pour la Recherche Scientifique en Afrique Centrale, Lwiro- Bukavu, Zaire. abstr.; illus.

500 600   JA   ISSN 0578-2228
CHUO DAIGAKU RIKOGAKUBU KIYO/CHUO UNIVERSITY. FACULTY OF SCIENCE AND ENGINEERING. BULLETIN. (Text in Japanese; summaries and some articles in English) 1957. a. free. Chuo Daigaku, Rikogakubu - Chuo University, Faculty of Science and Engineering, 1-13-27 Kasuga, Bunkyo-ku, Tokyo 112, Japan. FAX 03-814-0955. illus. **Indexed:** INIS Atomind. —BLDSC shelfmark: 2508.900000.
Description: Contains articles as well as full length studies, statistics, charts, graphs, tables and photographs from the faculty.

500   DR
CIENCIA. 1972. q. RD.$8($11) Universidad Autonoma de Santo Domingo, Direccion de Investigaciones Cientificas, Santo Domingo, Dominican Republic. Ed. Jose del Castillo. bibl.; charts; illus. **Indexed:** Biol.Abstr.

500 600   BL   ISSN 0084-8794
CIENCIA. (Text in Portuguese; summaries in English) vol.1, no.2, 1980. irreg. avail. on exchange. Centro Academico Piraja da Silva, Faculdade de Ciencias Medicas e Biologicas de Botucatu, C.P. 102, Rubiao-Junior, Botucatu, S.P., Brazil.

500 300   MX   ISSN 0185-075X
Q4   CODEN: CIENA3
CIENCIA. (Text in Spanish; summaries in English and Spanish) 1940. q. $78 to individuals; institutions $158. Academia de la Investigacion Cientifica, A.C., Av. San Jeronimo 260, Col. Jardines del Pedregal, Mexico, D.F. 04500, Mexico. TEL 550-6278. FAX 550-1143. (Subscr. to: Apartado Postal 69-692, 04460 Mexico D.F., Mexico) Ed. Julio Rubio. adv.; bk.rev.; index; circ. 3,000. (back issues avail.) **Indexed:** Biol.Abstr., Chem.Abstr., Deep Sea Res.& Oceanogr.Abstr., Helminthol.Abstr., INIS Atomind., Sci.Abstr.

500   CU
CIENCIA. s-a. $15 in N. and S. America; Europe $16. (Academia de Ciencias Instituto de Documentacion e Informacion Cientifico- Tecnica (Havana)) Ediciones Cubanas, Obispo No. 527, Apdo. 605, Havana, Cuba.

500   BL   ISSN 0009-6725
Q4   CODEN: CCUPAD
CIENCIA E CULTURA. (Text in English; summaries in English and Portuguese) 1949. m. Cr.$45000($65) Sociedade Brasileira para o Progresso da Ciencia, Rua Costa Carvalho 222, 05429 Sao Paulo, Brazil. TEL 011-211-50-08. FAX 011-212-13-76. TELEX 011-54164 SBCH. Ed.Bd. adv.; bk.rev.; bibl.; charts; illus., circ. 8,000. (tabloid format; also avail. in microform; reprint service avail.) **Indexed:** Biodet.Abstr., Biol.Abstr., Chem.Abstr., Curr.Cont., Deep Sea Res.& Oceanogr.Abstr., Excerp.Med., Field Crop Abstr., Helminthol.Abstr., INIS Atomind., Plant Breed.Abstr. —BLDSC shelfmark: 3195.900000.

500   AG   ISSN 0009-6733
Q4   CODEN: CIBAAH
CIENCIA E INVESTIGACION.* 1945. m. $15. Asociacion Argentina para el Progreso de las Ciencias, Avda. Alvear 1711, Piso 4, 1014 Buenos Aires, Argentina. Ed.Bd. adv.; bk.rev.; bibl.; charts; illus.; index; circ. 2,000. **Indexed:** Biol.Abstr., Chem.Abstr.

500   US   ISSN 0009-675X
Q4.C43   CODEN: CIIABJ
CIENCIA INTERAMERICANA. (Text in English, Spanish, Portuguese) 1960. 2/yr. $1 per no. Organization of American States, General Secretariat, 1889 F St. N.W., Washington, DC 20006. TEL 202-789-3386. Ed. Gelmi Arrieta. bk.rev.; charts; illus.; tr.lit.; index; circ. 5,000. (back issues avail.) **Indexed:** Deep Sea Res.& Oceanogr.Abstr., GeoRef.

500 600   MX
CIENCIA PARA TODOS. 1974. m. Mex.$130($14) Publicaciones Herrerias, S.A., Morelos, 16-3er Piso, Mexico 1, D.F., Mexico. Ed. Jose Pichel. adv.; bk.rev.; circ. 15,000.
Formerly: Ciencia Popular.

500 600   CK   ISSN 0120-1573
Q127.L38
CIENCIA TECNOLOGIA Y DESARROLLO. 1977. q. Col.$3.000($30) Colciencias, Transversal 9a No. 133-28, Bogota, Colombia. TEL 2169800. FAX 2744460. TELEX 44305. Ed. Miguel Infante Diaz. bk.rev.; charts.
Description: Covers research in all aspects of science and technology.

500 600   MX   ISSN 0185-0008
Q4   CODEN: CIDED8
CIENCIA Y DESARROLLO. 1975. bi-m. $33 (foreign $44). Consejo Nacional de Ciencia y Tecnologia, Circuito Cultural Universitario, Ciudad Universitaria, 04515 Mexico, D.F., Mexico. TEL 655-6366. FAX 655-3906. TELEX 017-74521. Ed. Mauricio Fortes. adv.; bk.rev.; bibl.; index; circ. 50,000. **Indexed:** Chem.Abstr.
—BLDSC shelfmark: 3196.570000.

500.1   EC   ISSN 0009-6768
CODEN: CINQAN
CIENCIA Y NATURALEZA. (Text and summaries in English or Spanish) 1957. s-a. exchange basis. Universidad Central del Ecuador, Instituto de Ciencias Naturales, Casilla 633, Quito, Ecuador. Dir. Francisco Latorre. bibl.; charts; illus.; index; circ. 2,500. **Indexed:** Biol.Abstr., Chem.Abstr., Field Crop Abstr., GeoRef., Herb.Abstr.

500   DR   ISSN 0378-7680
HC157.D6
CIENCIA Y SOCIEDAD. (Text in Spanish; summaries in English) 1975. q. RD.$60($30) Instituto Tecnologico de Santo Domingo, Apdo. Postal 342-9, Santo Domingo, Dominican Republic. Ed. Jose Marmol. adv.; bk.rev.; bibl.; charts; circ. 1,000.
—BLDSC shelfmark: 3196.900000.

500   CR   ISSN 0378-052X
CODEN: CITEDK
CIENCIA Y TECNOLOGIA. 1976. s-a. $20. Editorial de la Universidad de Costa Rica, Apartado 75-2060, Ciudad Universitaria Rodrigo Facio, 2050 San Pedro de Montes de Oca, San Jose, Costa Rica. TEL 506-25-3133. FAX 506-24-9367. TELEX UNICORI 2544. **Indexed:** Math.R.

500   SP   ISSN 0009-6776
Q65   CODEN: CINSAT
CIENCIAS. 1934. q. 1500 ptas. Asociacion Espanola para el Progreso de las Ciencias, Valverde 22, Madrid (13), Spain. adv.; circ. 1,500. **Indexed:** Biol.Abstr.

CIENCIAS TECNICAS FISICAS Y MATEMATICAS. see *TECHNOLOGY: COMPREHENSIVE WORKS*

500   SM
CIVILTA CIBERNETICA; rivista di sintesi scientifica, ricerca e cultura al futuro. (Text in Italian) 1981. q. L.20000($18) Istituto di Cibernetica, Via dei Cappuccini n.1, 47031 San Marino R.S.M., San Marino. TEL 0549-992071. FAX 0549-991538. (Co-sponsor: Dicastero Pubblica Istruzione) Ed. Aureliano Casali. adv.; bk.rev.; charts; stat.; circ. 10,000. (back issues avail.) **Indexed:** Cyb.Abstr.
Description: Forum for research in aspects of future technology.

500 100   US   ISSN 1042-4628
CLASSICS IN THE HISTORY AND PHILOSOPHY OF SCIENCE. irreg., latest vol.7. Gordon and Breach Scientific Publishers, 279 Eighth Ave., New York, NY 10011. TEL 212-206-8900. FAX 212-645-2459. TELEX 236735 GOPUB UR. (Subscr. to: Box 786, Cooper Sta., New York, NY 10276. TEL 800-545-8398; UK subscr. to: P.O. Box 90, Reading, Berkshire RG1 8JL, England. TEL 0734-560-080) Ed. Roger Hahn.
Refereed Serial

500   SP
COLECCION CIENCIAS, HUMANIDADES E INGENIERIA. irreg. (approx. 4/yr.) price varies. Colegio de Ingenieros de Caminos, Canales y Puertos, Almagro, 42, 28010 Madrid, Spain.

500   CK
COLECCION: DOCUMENTOS E HISTORIA DE LA CIENCIA EN COLOMBIA. irreg. price varies. Fondo Colombiano de Investigaciones Cientificas, Apdo. Aereo 051580, Bogota, Colombia. bk.rev.

500   NZ   ISSN 0112-2479
COLLECTED PAPERS FROM THE JOURNAL OF THE ROYAL SOCIETY OF NEW ZEALAND. 1984. irreg. price varies. Royal Society of New Zealand, P.O. Box 598, Wellington 1, New Zealand. TEL 04-727-421. FAX 64-4-731-841. Ed. Carolyn M. King.

500   US   ISSN 0160-0664
QH1
COLLECTIONS (BUFFALO). 1920. q. $5. Buffalo Society of Natural Sciences, 1020 Humboldt Pkwy., Buffalo, NY 14211. TEL 716-896-5200. FAX 716-897-6723. Ed. Barbara Park Leggett. illus.; circ. 6,000. **Indexed:** Biol.Abstr., GeoRef.
Formerly (until vol.56): Science on the March (ISSN 0036-8474)

500   CK   ISSN 0120-5595
COLOMBIA: CIENCIA Y TECNOLOGIA. 1982. q. Col.$2,500($20) Colciencias, Transversal 9a No. 133-28, P.O. Box 051580, Bogota, Colombia. TEL 2169800. FAX 2744460. TELEX 44305. Ed. Karin Zonszhain. adv.; charts; illus.; stat.; circ. 3,000.
Formerly: Ciencia y Tecnologia.
Description: Presents studies in science and technology.

500   US   ISSN 0096-2279
AS36   CODEN: JCOQAT
COLORADO-WYOMING ACADEMY OF SCIENCES. JOURNAL. 1929. a. $5. Colorado-Wyoming Academy of Science, c/o Clait E. Braun, Wildlife Research Center, 317 W. Prospect Rd., Ft. Collins, CO 80526. FAX 303-490-2621. abstr.; circ. 300. **Indexed:** Biol.Abstr., GeoRef.

500   FR
COMITE DES TRAVAUX HISTORIQUES ET SCIENTIFIQUES. SECTION DES SCIENCES. ACTES DU CONGRES NATIONAL DES SOCIETES SAVANTES. 1961. a. price varies. Comite des Travaux Historiques et Scientifiques, 1 rue d'Ulm, 75005 Paris, France. TEL 49-55-23-64.
Formerly: Comite des Travaux Historiques et Scientifiques. Section des Sciences. Comptes Rendus du Congres National des Societes Savantes.

500 600   SW   ISSN 0074-9540
CONGRES INTERNATIONAL D'HISTOIRE DES SCIENCES. ACTES. 1947. quadrennial. International Union of the History & Philosophy of Science, c/o Tore Frangsmyr, Office of History of Science, Uppsala University, Box 256, S-75105 Uppsala, Sweden.

CONNECT (BRATTLEBORO); the newsletter of practical science and math for K-8 teachers. see *EDUCATION — Teaching Methods And Curriculum*

SCIENCES: COMPREHENSIVE WORKS

001.3 500 US ISSN 0069-8970
CONNECTICUT ACADEMY OF ARTS AND SCIENCES. MEMOIRS. 1801. irreg., vol.21, 1987. Connecticut Academy of Arts and Sciences, Drawer 93A, Yale Sta., New Haven, CT 06520. TEL 203-432-3113. Ed. Catherine Skinner. illus. **Indexed:** Biol.Abstr.

CONNECTICUT ACADEMY OF ARTS AND SCIENCES. TRANSACTIONS. see *HUMANITIES: COMPREHENSIVE WORKS*

500 SP
CONOCER LA VIDA Y EL UNIVERSO. m. Ediciones Zeta, O'Donnell 12, 28009 Madrid, Spain. TEL 91-5220072. Dir. Manuel Toharia.

550 US ISSN 0459-8113
Q11 CODEN: LAMSAX
CONTRIBUTIONS IN SCIENCE. (Text in English; occasional summaries in Spanish) 1957. irreg., no.430, 1991. Natural History Museum of Los Angeles County, 900 Exposition Blvd., Los Angeles, CA 90007. TEL 213-744-3330. FAX 213-742-0730. circ. 2,000. **Indexed:** Biol.Abstr., Deep Sea Res.& Oceanogr.Abstr., GeoRef., Ocean.Abstr., Zoo.Rec.
Formerly: Natural History Museum of Los Angeles County. Contributions in Science (ISSN 0076-0900); Incorporates (in 1978): Science Bulletin (ISSN 0076-0935)
Refereed Serial

500 600 LV ISSN 0130-3252
CONTRIBUTIONS TO THE HISTORY OF NATURAL SCIENCES AND TECHNOLOGY IN THE BALTIC/IZ ISTORII ESTESTVOZNANIYA I TEKHNIKI PRIBALTIKI. (Text in Russian; contents in English) 1968. irreg., approx. a. 1.60 Rub. (Akademiya Nauk Latviiskoi S.S.R.) Izdatel'stvo Zinatne, Turgeneva iela, 19, Riga, Latvia. Ed. P. Valeskalns. bk.rev.; circ. 1,000. **Indexed:** Bull.Signal., Chem.Abstr., Ref.Zh.
Formerly: Contributions to the History of Science and Technology in Baltics. (ISSN 0069-9713)

CORRIERE DEL MEZZOGIORNO; Giornale indipendente di informazioni. see *POLITICAL SCIENCE*

500.9 UK ISSN 0011-023X
COUNTRY-SIDE; a wildlife magazine. 1905. 3/yr. £10. British Naturalists Association, c/o Mrs. J. Pearton, 48 Russell Way, Higham Ferrers, Northamptonshire NN9 8EJ, England. FAX 0933-314-672. (Subscr. to: Mrs. Y. Griffiths, 23 Oak Hill Close, Woodford Green, Essex, England) Ed. D. Applin. adv.; bk.rev.; illus.; stat.; circ. 14,000. **Indexed:** Farm & Garden Ind., Key Word Ind.Wildl.Res.
—BLDSC shelfmark: 3482.000000.

COURIER (PARIS). see *POLITICAL SCIENCE — International Relations*

COURTS, HEALTH SCIENCE & THE LAW. see *LAW*

500 US ISSN 0070-1416
Q11
CRANBROOK INSTITUTE OF SCIENCE, BLOOMFIELD HILLS, MICHIGAN. BULLETIN. (Each bulletin has a distinctive title) 1931. irreg., no.48, 1987. price varies. Cranbrook Institute of Science, Box 801, Bloomfield Hills, MI 48303-0801. TEL 313-645-3203. FAX 313-645-6545. Dir. Robert West. adv.; bk.rev. (reprint service avail. from UMI) **Indexed:** Biol.Abstr.
Description: Disseminates scientific information concerning Michigan and the Great Lakes region. Aimed at practicing scientists, serious students and informed laypeople.

CREATION. see *RELIGIONS AND THEOLOGY*

CREATION EX NIHILO. see *RELIGIONS AND THEOLOGY*

CREATION EX NIHILO TECHNICAL JOURNAL. see *RELIGIONS AND THEOLOGY*

CREATION RESEARCH SOCIETY QUARTERLY. see *RELIGIONS AND THEOLOGY*

500 CL ISSN 0716-0313
CRECES. 1979. m. $70. Bustos 2030, Providencia, Santiago, Chile. TEL 2-496692. TELEX 341011. Dir. Fernando Monckeberg. adv.; bk.rev.; circ. 12,000.

500 UK ISSN 0309-6149
CROYDON NATURAL HISTORY & SCIENTIFIC SOCIETY. BULLETIN. 1967. irreg. (approx. 3-4/yr). included in subscription for the Proceedings of the Croydon Natural History & Scientific Society. Croydon Natural History & Scientific Society Ltd., 96a Brighton Rd., South Croydon, Surrey CR2 6AD, England. Ed. J. Greig. bk.rev.; bibl.; circ. 850.

500.9 UK ISSN 0309-8656
CROYDON NATURAL HISTORY & SCIENTIFIC SOCIETY. PROCEEDINGS AND TRANSACTIONS. 1871. irreg. (approx. 3-4/yr.). £8 includes Bulletin. Croydon Natural History and Scientific Society Ltd., 96A Brighton Rd., South Croydon, Surrey CR2 6AD, England. Ed. R.D. Sowan. charts; illus.; cum.index; circ. 1,000. **Indexed:** Br.Archaeol.Abstr., Br.Geol.Lit.
—BLDSC shelfmark: 6688.000000.

CRUCIBLE. see *EDUCATION*

CRYPTOLOGIA; a quarterly journal devoted to all aspects of cryptology. see *MATHEMATICS*

CUADERNOS VALENCIANOS DE HISTORIA DE LA MEDICINA Y DE LA CIENCIA. see *MEDICAL SCIENCES*

500 CU ISSN 0138-7049
CUBA. MINISTERIO DE LA INDUSTRIA LIGERA. REVISTA CIENCIA Y TECNICA. (Text in German, Russian, Spanish) 1983. 3/yr. $18. Ministerio de la Industria Ligera, Emperado 302, esq. a Aguiar, Havana 10100, Cuba. TEL 60-3111. TELEX 051-1141. Ed. Ausberto Bianchi Diaz. adv.; circ. 1,000. **Indexed:** Ref.Zh.
Description: Examines research work on light industries production branches: textiles, ready-made garments, leather and shoes, perfumery and soaps, plastics and woodworking (furniture).

999 500 US
Z6005.P7
CURRENT ANTARCTIC LITERATURE. 1966. m. free to qualified personnel. U.S. National Science Foundation, Office of Polar Programs, 1800 G St. N.W., Washington, DC 20550. TEL 202-357-7817. Ed. Stuart Hibben. bk.rev.; circ. 700. **Indexed:** GeoRef.

500 II ISSN 0011-3891
Q1 CODEN: CUSCAM
CURRENT SCIENCE. (Text in English) 1932. 24/yr. Rs.175($175) Indian Academy of Sciences, C.V. Raman Avenue, P.B. No. 8005, Bangalore 560 080, India. TEL 342310. FAX 91-812-346094. TELEX 0845-2178-ACAD-IN. (Co-sponsor: Current Science Association) Ed. S. Ramaseshan. adv.; bk.rev.; illus.; index; circ. 3,000. (also avail. in microfilm from UMI; reprint service avail. from ISI and UMI) **Indexed:** Agroforest.Abstr., Anim.Breed.Abstr., Bio-Contr.News & Info., Biol.Abstr., Chem.Abstr., Cott.& Trop.Fibr.Abstr., Crop Physiol.Abstr., Curr.Cont., Curr.Leather Lit., Dairy Sci.Abstr., Excerp.Med., Fababean Abstr., Field Crop Abstr., Food Sci.& Tech.Abstr., Forest.Abstr., Forest Prod.Abstr., GeoRef., Helminthol.Abstr., Herb.Abstr., Hort.Abstr., Ind.Sci.Rev., Ind.Vet., INIS Atomind., Irr.& Drain.Abstr., Maize Abstr., Met.Abstr., Numis.Lit, Ocean.Abstr., Ornam.Hort., Plant Grow.Reg.Abstr., Pollut.Abstr., Potato Abstr., Poult.Abstr., Protozool.Abstr., Rev.Appl.Entomol., Rev.Plant Path., Rice Abstr., Sci.Abstr., Seed Abstr., Soils & Fert., Sorghum & Millets Abstr., Soyabean Abstr., Triticale Abstr., Trop.Oil Seeds Abstr., Vet.Bull., Weed Abstr.
—BLDSC shelfmark: 3504.000000.

CURRENT SCIENCE. see *CHILDREN AND YOUTH — For*

500 US ISSN 0275-9098
CURRENT TOPICS OF CONTEMPORARY THOUGHT. 1970. irreg., vol.14, 1979. price varies. Gordon & Breach Science Publishers, 270 Eighth Ave., New York, NY 10011. TEL 212-206-8900. FAX 212-645-2459. TELEX 236735 GOPUB UR. (Subscr. to: Box 786, Cooper Sta., New York, NY 10276. TEL 800-545-8398; UK subscr. to: P.O. Box 90, Reading, Berkshire RG1 8JL, England. TEL 0734-560-080) Eds. Rubin Gotesky, Ervin Laszlo.
Refereed Serial

D L S U GRADUATE JOURNAL. (De La Salle University) see *SOCIAL SCIENCES: COMPREHENSIVE WORKS*

DAEDALUS. see *MUSEUMS AND ART GALLERIES*

DAEDALUS (CAMBRIDGE). see *HUMANITIES: COMPREHENSIVE WORKS*

500 JA ISSN 0912-2346
DAITO BUNKA DAIGAKU KIYO. SHIZEN KAGAKU/DAITO BUNKA UNIVERSITY. BULLETIN. NATURAL SCIENCES. (Text and summaries in English and Japanese) a. Daito Bunka University - Daito Bunka Daigaku, 9-1, Takashimadaira, 1-chome, Itabashi-ku, Tokyo 175, Japan.

500 CC ISSN 1000-8608
DALIAN LIGONG DAXUE XUEBAO/DALIAN UNIVERSITY OF TECHNOLOGY. JOURNAL. (Text in Chinese) 1950. bi-m. $2.50 per no. Dalian Ligong Daxue - Dalian University of Technology, c/o Library, Dalian, Liaoning 116024, People's Republic of China. TEL 471511. FAX 0411-471009. TELEX 86231 DUT CN. Eds. Chan Lingxi, Zhu Cheng. circ. 1,500.
—BLDSC shelfmark: 4732.666000.

500 DK ISSN 0108-7606
DANDOKNOTATER. (Text in Danish, English) 1982. irreg. free. Undervisningsministeriet, Forskningsafdelingen, Statens Udvalg for Videnskabelig og Teknisk Information og Dokumentation - Ministry of Education, Danish Research Administration, State Committee for Scientific and Technical Information and Documentation, H.C. Andersens Boulevard 40, DK-1553 Copenhagen V, Denmark. TEL 45-33-11-43-00. FAX 45-33-32-35-01. TELEX 15652 FS. circ. 650.

500 600 IR ISSN 1011-3495
DANESHMAND. 1963. m. P.O. Box 15875-3649, Teheran, Iran. TEL 021-854969. Ed. Ali Mirzaei.

500 DK
DANISH POLAR CENTER. NEWSLETTER. (Text in English) 1979. s-a. free. Danish Polar Center, Hausergade 3, DK-1128 Copenhagen K, Denmark. TEL 33-158666. FAX 33-134976. bibl.; circ. 2,000. (back issues avail.)
Formerly: Commission for Scientific Research in Greenland. Newsletter (ISSN 0106-1372)
Description: Information on current and planned scientific research activities in Greenland.

DANYAG; journal of studies in the humanities, education and the sciences, basic and applied. see *HUMANITIES: COMPREHENSIVE WORKS*

500 600 CC
DAXUE KEJI/UNIVERSITY SCIENCE AND TECHNOLOGY. (Text in Chinese) q. Shanghai Keji Jiaoyu Chubanshe, 393 Guanshengyuan Road, Shanghai 200233, People's Republic of China. TEL 4367970. Ed. Hu Qiming.

500 CC ISSN 0255-7800
QH7
DAZIRAN/NATURE. (Text in Chinese) q. $1 per no. (Beijing Ziran Bowuguan - Beijing Natural History Museum) Daziran Zazhishe, 126 Tianqiao Nandajie, Beijing 100050, People's Republic of China. TEL 754431. Ed. Jin Jianming.
—BLDSC shelfmark: 6044.800000.

LES DEBROUILLARDS. see *CHILDREN AND YOUTH — For*

DEFENCE SCIENCE JOURNAL. see *MILITARY*

500 600 CS ISSN 0300-4414
CODEN: DVTDAE
DEJINY VED A TECHNIKY/HISTORY OF SCIENCES AND TECHNOLOGY. (Text in Czech; summaries in English, French or German) 1968. q. DM.124. (Czechoslovak Academy of Sciences) Academia, Publishing House of the Czechoslovak Academy of Sciences, Vodickova 40, 112 29 Prague 1, Czechoslovakia. TEL 235-94-69. (Dist. in Western countries by: Kubon & Sagner, P.O. Box 34 01 08, 8000 Munich, Germany) (Co-sponsor: Czechoslovak Society for the History of Sciences and Technology) Ed. Lubos Novy. bk.rev.; index; circ. 1,000. (also avail. in microform from AMP) **Indexed:** Math.R.
—BLDSC shelfmark: 3546.400000.
Description: History of natural sciences, medicine and technology, including the history of scientific institutions, conditions of scientific work, and social status of scientists.

SCIENCES: COMPREHENSIVE WORKS

500.9   US   ISSN 0084-9650
    CODEN: MDMHDZ
DELAWARE MUSEUM OF NATURAL HISTORY. MONOGRAPH SERIES. 1970. irreg. no.4, 1982. price varies. Delaware Museum of Natural History, Box 3937, Wilmington, DE 19807. TEL 302-658-9111. **Indexed:** Biol.Abstr.

500.9   US   ISSN 0084-9669
DELAWARE MUSEUM OF NATURAL HISTORY. REPRODUCTION SERIES. 1968. irreg., no.1, 1968. price varies. Delaware Museum of Natural History, Box 3937, Wilmington, DE 19807. TEL 302-658-9111. **Indexed:** Biol.Abstr.

DELFIN; eine deutsche Zeitschrift fuer Konstruktion, Analyse und Kritik. see *ART*

500   HU   ISSN 0011-7994
DELTA (BUDAPEST); magazine on natural sciences and technics. 1967. m. $12. (Magyar Kommunista Ifjusagi Szovetseg) Ifjusagi Lap-es Konyvkiado Vallalat, Revai u 16, 1374 Budapest 6, Hungary. (Subscr. to: Kultura, Box 149, H-1389 Budapest, Hungary) Ed. Tamas Varhelyi. adv.; bk.rev.; charts; illus.; circ. 70,000. **Indexed:** Can.Per.Ind.

DERECHO PENAL Y CIENCIAS PENALES. ANUARIO. see *LAW*

500   GW   ISSN 0070-3974
DEUTSCHE FORSCHUNGSGEMEINSCHAFT. DENKSCHRIFTEN ZUR LAGE DER DEUTSCHEN WISSENSCHAFT. 1957. irreg. price varies. V C H Verlagsgesellschaft mbH, Postfach 101161, 6940 Weinheim, Germany. TEL 06201-602-0. FAX 06201-602328. TELEX 465516-VCHWH-D. (U.S. addr.: V C H Publishers Inc., 220 E. 23rd St., New York, NY 10010-4606) bk.rev.

500   GW   ISSN 0070-3982
DEUTSCHE FORSCHUNGSGEMEINSCHAFT. FORSCHUNGSBERICHTE. 1957. irreg. price varies. V C H Verlagsgesellschaft mbH, Postfach 101163, 6940 Weinheim, Germany. TEL 06201-602-0. FAX 06201-602328. TELEX 465516-VCHWH-D. (U.S. addr.: V C H Publishers Inc., 220 E. 23rd St., New York, NY 10010-4606)

500   GW   ISSN 0070-3990
DEUTSCHE FORSCHUNGSGEMEINSCHAFT. KOMMISSIONENMITTEILUNGEN. 1964. irreg. price varies. V C H Verlagsgesellschaft mbH, Postfach 101163, 6940 Weinheim, Germany. TEL 06201-602-0. FAX 06201-602328. TELEX 465516-VCHWH-D. (U.S. addr.: V C H Publishers, Inc., 220 E. 23rd St., New York, NY 10010-4606) bk.rev. **Indexed:** Chem.Abstr. GeoRef.

500   GW   ISSN 0418-842X
DEUTSCHE FORSCHUNGSGEMEINSCHAFT. MEXIKO-PROJEKT; eine deutsch-mexikanische interdisziplinaere Regionalforschung im Becken von Puebla-Tlaxcala. (Text in German and Spanish) irreg., vol.21, 1991. price varies. Franz Steiner Verlag Wiesbaden GmbH, Birkenwaldstr. 44, Postfach 101526, 7000 Stuttgart 1, Germany. TEL 0711-2582-0. FAX 0711-2582290. TELEX 723636-DAZD. Ed. Wilhelm Lauer. **Indexed:** GeoRef.

DEUTSCHE LITERATURZEITUNG; fuer Kritik der internationalen Wissenschaft. see *LITERATURE*

DIE DEUTSCHE VOLKHOCHSCHULE. see *PHILOSOPHY*

500   GW   ISSN 0722-0847
DEUTSCHER FORSCHUNGSDIENST. APPLIED SCIENCE. (Text in English) m. DM.60. Deutscher Forschungsdienst GmbH, Ahrstr. 45, 5300 Bonn 2, Germany. TEL 0228-302210. FAX 0228-302270. —BLDSC shelfmark: 3576.270200.

500   GW   ISSN 0722-5318
DEUTSCHER FORSCHUNGSDIENST. BERICHTE AUS DER WISSENSCHAFT. 51/yr. DM.200. Deutscher Forschungsdienst GmbH, Ahrstr. 45, 5300 Bonn 2, Germany. TEL 0228-302210. FAX 0228-302270.

500   GW   ISSN 0722-0812
DEUTSCHER FORSCHUNGSDIENST. BERICHTE AUS DER WISSENSCHAFT (AUSLANDAUSGABE). m. DM.96. Deutscher Forschungsdienst GmbH, Ahrstr. 45, 5300 Bonn 2, Germany. TEL 0228-302210. FAX 0228-302270.

500   GW   ISSN 0722-5229
DEUTSCHER FORSCHUNGSDIENST. SONDERDIENST ANGEWANDTE WISSENSCHAFT. 25/yr. DM.120. Deutscher Forschungsdienst GmbH, Ahrstr. 45, 5300 Bonn 2, Germany. TEL 0228-302210. FAX 0228-302270.

500   GW   ISSN 0722-0820
DEUTSCHER FORSCHUNGSDIENST. SONDERDIENST ANGEWANDTE WISSENSCHAFT (AUSLANDAUSGABE). m. DM.60. Deutscher Forschungsdienst GmbH, Ahrstr. 45, 5300 Bonn 2, Germany. TEL 0228-302210. FAX 0228-302270.

500   GW   ISSN 0933-7814
DEUTSCHER FORSCHUNGSDIENST. SPECIAL SCIENCE REPORTS. (Text in English) m. DM.96. Deutscher Forschungsdienst GmbH, Ahrstr. 45, 5300 Bonn 2, Germany. TEL 0228-302210. FAX 0228-302270. —BLDSC shelfmark: 8401.730000.

500   GW   ISSN 0178-8965
DEUTSCHER FORSCHUNGSDIENST MAGAZIN. m. DM.72. Deutscher Forschungsdienst GmbH, Ahrstr. 45, 5300 Bonn 2, Germany. TEL 0228-302210. FAX 0228-302270.

DEVONSHIRE ASSOCIATION FOR THE ADVANCEMENT OF SCIENCE, LITERATURE AND ART. REPORT AND TRANSACTIONS. see *ART*

500   BG
AS472.D3   CODEN: DUSBAU
DHAKA UNIVERSITY STUDIES. PART B: SCIENCE. (Text in English) vol.18, 1970. irreg.? University of Dhaka, Department of Physics, Dhaka 1000, Bangladesh. bibl.; charts. **Indexed:** Biol.Abstr., Hist.Abstr.
    Formerly: Dacca University Studies. Part B: Science (ISSN 0253-5467)

DIALOGO; quaderni Europei di dialogica. see *PHILOSOPHY*

DIDATTICA DELLE SCIENZE E INFORMATICA NELLA SCUOLA. see *EDUCATION — Teaching Methods And Curriculum*

501 149   YU   ISSN 0350-1272
DIJALEKTIKA/DIALECTICS; casopis za metodolosko filozofske probleme matematickih, prirodnih i tehnickih nauka. 1966. q. 40 din. Univerzitet u Beogradu, Studentski trg 16, Belgrade, Serbia, Yugoslavia. Eds. Milorad Bertolino, Andrija Stojkovic. —BLDSC shelfmark: 3588.397800.

DIRASAT. SERIES A: HUMANITIES. see *HUMANITIES: COMPREHENSIVE WORKS*

500   JO   ISSN 0253-424X
DIRASAT. SERIES B: PURE AND APPLIED SCIENCES. (Consists of Series A: Humanities (ISSN 0255-8033), Series B: Pure and Applied Sciences) (Text in Arabic, English) 1974. 5/yr. each series. $60 (Series A&B $120). University of Jordan, Deanship of Academic Research, Amman, Jordan. FAX 962-6-832318. TELEX UNVJ JO 21629. circ. 1,000 (controlled). (back issues avail.)
    Description: Publishes original research contributions in the pure and applied sciences, each issue dedicated to topics in a single discipline.
    Refereed Serial

500   AT   ISSN 0727-6753
Q180.A8
DIRECTORY OF C S I R O RESEARCH PROGRAMS. a. Aus.$50. C.S.I.R.O., 314 Albert St., East Melbourne, Vic. 3002, Australia. TEL 61-3-418-7333. FAX 61-3-419-0459. index.

500   RH
DIRECTORY OF ORGANIZATIONS CONCERNED WITH SCIENTIFIC RESEARCH AND TECHNICAL SERVICES IN ZIMBABWE. 1959. triennial. Scientific Liaison Office, P.O. Box 8510, Causeway, Harare, Zimbabwe. TEL 700573. TELEX 22141.
    Formerly: Directory of Organizations Concerned with Scientific Research and Technical Services in Rhodesia.

500   UK
DIRECTORY OF PROFESSIONAL & LEARNED SOCIETIES. 1975. irreg., no.4, 1989. £85($180) C.B.D. Research Ltd., 15 Wickham Rd., Beckenham, Kent BR3 2JS, England. TEL 081-650-7745. (Dist. in U.S. by: Gale Research Co., Penobscot Bldg., Detroit, MI 48226) Ed. R.W. Adams. circ. 4,000.
    Formerly: Directory of European Associations. Part 2: National Learned, Scientific and Technical Societies (ISSN 0309-5339)

500 026   IS
DIRECTORY OF RESEARCH INSTITUTES IN ISRAEL. (Text in English; indexes in English and Hebrew) 1982. irreg. $40. ATIDIM Scientific Park, Devora Haneviah St., Tel Aviv 61430, Israel. TEL 03-492040. FAX 03-492033. TELEX 03-2332-IL. Ed. H. Mena. index; circ. 300.

500 600   SA
DIRECTORY OF RESEARCH ORGANISATIONS AND FACILITIES IN SOUTH AFRICA. 1950. irreg. price varies. Council for Scientific and Industrial Research, Division of Information Services, P.O. Box 395, Pretoria 0001, South Africa. Ed. Ingrid de Bont. circ. 800.
    Former titles (until 1986): Directory of Scientific Research Organisations in South Africa; Scientific Research Organisations in South Africa (ISSN 0080-7761)
    Description: Guide to governmental organizations, universities, statutory bodies and private companies, which undertake research in the natural, medical and economic sciences.

500 060   IS   ISSN 0334-2824
DIRECTORY OF SCIENTIFIC AND TECHNICAL ASSOCIATIONS IN ISRAEL. (Guides to Sources of Information Series, No. 2) (Text in English and Hebrew) 1962. irreg., 4th ed., 1992. $40. National Center of Scientific and Technological Information, ATIDIM Scientific Park, Devorah Haneviah St., Tel Aviv 61430, Israel. TEL 03-492040. FAX 03-492033. TELEX 03-2332-IL.
    Formerly: Directory of Scientific and Technical Associations and Institutes in Israel (ISSN 0070-6264)

500   NR   ISSN 0070-6280
DIRECTORY OF SCIENTIFIC RESEARCH IN NIGERIA. 1968. a. Science Association of Nigeria, Box 4039, Ibadan, Nigeria. Ed. Sunday O. Ajayi.

500 600   SA
DIRECTORY OF SOUTH AFRICAN ASSOCIATIONS/GIDS VAN SUID-AFRIKAANSE VERENIGINGS. 1950. irreg. price varies. Council for Scientific and Industrial Research, Division of Information Services, P.O. Box 395, Pretoria 0001, South Africa. Ed. Ingrid de Bont. circ. 800.
    Former titles (until 1985): Directory of Scientific and Technical Societies in South Africa; Scintific and Technical Societies in South Africa (ISSN 0080-7710)
    Description: Guide to associations of national or provincial scope in South Africa, excluding political and religious organizations and trade unions.

500   UK
DIRECTORY OF TECHNICAL AND SCIENTIFIC DIRECTORIES. irreg., 5th ed., 1987. £99. Longman Group UK Ltd., Westgate House, The High, Harlow, Essex CM20 1YR, England. TEL 0279 442601. (Dist. in N. America by: Oryx Press, 4041 N. Central at Indian School Rd., Phoenix, AZ 85012-3397. TEL 602-265-2651)
    Formerly: Directory of Scientific Directories (ISSN 0070-6272)

500 600   PK
DIRECTORY OF THE SCIENTISTS, TECHNOLOGISTS, AND ENGINEERS OF THE P C S I R. (Text in English) 1972. irreg. Pakistan Council of Scientific and Industrial Research, Scientific Information Centre, 39 Garden Rd., Karachi 74400, Pakistan. TEL 7725943. FAX 7729527. circ. controlled.

SCIENCES: COMPREHENSIVE WORKS

500 600   US   ISSN 0274-7529
Q1
DISCOVER (BURBANK). 1980. m. $27. Walt Disney Magazine Publishing Group, 500 S. Buena Vista, Burbank, CA 91521-6012. TEL 818-973-4320. (Subscr. to: Subscription Department, Box 420235, Palm Coast, FL 32142-0235. TEL 800-829-9132) Ed. Paul Hoffman. adv.; bk.rev.; film rev.; play rev.; charts; illus.; pat.; tr.lit.; circ. 1,000,000. (also avail. in Braille; talking book; record; microform from UMI,MCR; reprint service avail. from UMI; back issues avail.) **Indexed:** Acad.Ind., Access, Acid Rain Abstr., Acid Rain Ind., Biol.Dig., CAD CAM Abstr., Comput.Lit.Ind., Deep Sea Res.& Oceanogr.Abstr., Gdlns., Gen.Sci.Ind., GeoRef., Hlth.Ind., Ind.Sci.Rev., Mag.Ind., PMR, PROMT, Rehabil.Lit., Robomat, TOM.
●Also available online. Vendor(s): DIALOG, Mead Data Central, VU/TEXT Information Services, Inc..
—BLDSC shelfmark: 3595.870000.
Description: Science newsmagazine providing extensive coverage of science and technology in nontechnical language.

500.9 574 333.7   CN   ISSN 0319-8480
DISCOVERY. N.S. 1971. q. Can.$30. Vancouver Natural History Society, Box 3021, Vancouver, B.C. V6B 3X5, Canada. TEL 604-737-3000. Eds. Roland Wahlgren, Deborah Kerr. adv.; bk.rev.; circ. 1,500. **Indexed:** Can.Per.Ind., CMI.
Description: Covers natural history topics such as mammology, ornithology, marine biology and conservation issues.

500.9   US   ISSN 0012-3625
QH1   CODEN: DISCAH
DISCOVERY (NEW HAVEN). 1965. s-a. $10 (foreign $14)(effective 1992). Peabody Museum of Natural History, Yale University, 170 Whitney Ave., Box 6666, New Haven, CT 06511-8161. TEL 203-432-3786. Ed. Zelda Edelson. charts; illus.; circ. 700. (back issues avail.) **Indexed:** Biol.Abstr., Biol.Dig., GeoRef.
—BLDSC shelfmark: 3596.100000.
Description: Research and scientific activities in the area of natural history written for the general reader.
Refereed Serial

DISCOVERY CREW SCIENCE CLUB NEWS. see *CHILDREN AND YOUTH* — For

500 510 591   IS
DIVREI HA-AKADEMIA HA-LEUMIT HA-YISRAELIT LEMADAIM-HA-HATIVA LE-MADAEI HA-TEVA. (Text in Hebrew) 1966. irreg. price varies. Israel Academy of Sciences and Humanities, 43 Jabotinski St., P.O. Box 4040, Jerusalem 91040, Israel. TEL 02-636211. FAX 02-666059. Ed. S. Re'em. circ. 900. **Indexed:** Ind.Heb.Per.
Description: Reprints of scientific papers read at meetings of the Academy.

500   VE
DIVULGA. q. Universidad Nacional Experimental del Tachira, Comision de Cultura, Av. Universidad-Paramillo, Apdo. 436, San Cristoboal, Venezuela. Ed. Gilberto A. Labrador.

500   SW   ISSN 0347-5719
DOCUMENTA. 1972. irreg. (3-5/yr.). Kungliga Vetenskapsakademien - Royal Swedish Academy of Sciences, Box 50005, S-104 05 Stockholm, Sweden. FAX 46-8-155670. bibl.; illus.
—BLDSC shelfmark: 3609.255000.

500   FR   ISSN 0046-0478
DOCUMENTATION PAR L'IMAGE; revue des activites d'eveil. 1936. 9/yr. 284 F. Librairie Fernand Nathan, 9 rue Mechain, 75680 Paris Cedex 14, France. illus.

DOCUMENTS HISTORIQUES DES SCIENCES. see *HISTORY* — History Of Europe

DOGAR'S GENERAL KNOWLEDGE DIGEST. see *POLITICAL SCIENCE*

DONGBEI GONGXUEYUAN XUEBAO/NORTHEAST INSTITUTE OF TECHNOLOGY. JOURNAL. see *TECHNOLOGY: COMPREHENSIVE WORKS*

500   CC   ISSN 1000-1832
DONGBEI SHIDA XUEBAO (ZIRAN KEXUE BAN)/NORTHEAST NORMAL UNIVERSITY. JOURNAL (NATURAL SCIENCE EDITION). (Text in Chinese) q. Dongbei Shifan Daxue, Xuebao Bianjibu, 110, Stalin Street, Changchun, Jilin 130024, People's Republic of China. TEL 885085. Ed. Chen Ripeng.

500.9   IT   ISSN 0417-9927
                               CODEN: DRNAAF
DORIANA. (Supplement to its Annali) (Text and summaries in English, French, German, Italian and Spanish) 1949. irreg., no.265, 1989. exchange basis only. Museo Civico di Storia Naturale "Giacomo Doria", Via Brigata Liguria 9, 16121 Genoa, Italy. **Indexed:** Biol.Abstr., Bull.Signal., Curr.Adv.Ecol.Sci., Entomol.Abstr., Rev.Appl.Entomol., Zoo.Rec.
Description: Discusses natural history of the area.

500.9 913   UK   ISSN 0070-7112
DORSET NATURAL HISTORY AND ARCHAEOLOGICAL SOCIETY. PROCEEDINGS. 1877. a. £15 (effective 1991). Dorset County Museum, Dorchester, Dorset, England. Ed. J.C. Chaplin. circ. 2,100. **Indexed:** Br.Archaeol.Abstr., Br.Geol.Lit., Br.Hum.Ind., Numis.Lit.
Description: Covers all aspects of natural history, geology, archaeology, local history, biography in Dorset.

500   US
DREXEL FACULTY PUBLICATION. 1978. a. free. Drexel University, Office of Sponsored Projects, 32nd & Market Sts., Philadelphia, PA 19104. TEL 215-895-2499. FAX 215-895-1619. Ed. Dr. Kenneth N. Geller. circ. 200.
Supersedes (1971-1978): Drexel Research Conference. Summary Report (ISSN 0085-0071)

DYNAMICS AND STABILITY OF SYSTEMS. see *COMPUTERS*

600   MP
DZALUU DZOHION BUTEEGCH/YOUNG INVENTOR. (Text in Mongolian) 1981. q. $1. Editorial Office for Mongolian Youth, P.O. Box 1053, Ulan Bator 210613, Mongolia. TEL 29651. Ed. S. Batmonh. adv.; bk.rev.; circ. 21,000.

500   US
EARTH CORPS: THE DAILY PLANET. 1971. bi-m. $25. Earthwatch Expeditions, Inc., 680 Mount Auburn St., P.O. Box 403, Watertown, MA 02272. TEL 617-926-8200. FAX 617-926-8532. Ed. Peter Tyson.

500 300   US   ISSN 8750-0183
EARTHWATCH. 1980. 6/yr. $25 (foreign $35). Earthwatch Expeditions, Inc., 680 Mount Auburn St., Box 403N, Watertown, MA 02272. TEL 617-926-8200. FAX 617-926-8532. TELEX 5106006452. Ed. Mark Cherrington. illus.; circ. 50,000. **Indexed:** Energy Rev., Environ.Per.Bibl.
Description: Includes compendium of scientific research expeditions, feature stories on leading researchers, cultural heritage quesitons, and environmental and science-related topics.

EDUCATION IN SCIENCE. see *EDUCATION*

500.9   ER   ISSN 0131-5862
EESTI LOODUS/ESTONIAN NATURE. (Text in Estonian; summaries in English) 1958. m. $47 (effective 1992). (Estonian Academy of Sciences) Izdatel'stvo Perioodika, Parnu mnt. 8, 200090 Tallinn, Estonia. TEL 0142-441-262. FAX 0142-442-484. (Co-sponsor: Ministry of Environment) Ed. Ain Raitviirs. bk.rev.; abstr.; charts; illus.; maps; circ. 10,550. **Indexed:** Biol.Abstr.

500   CS
ELEKTRON. 1973. m. $0.50. (Socialisticky Svaz Mladeze C.S.S.R. - Socialist Union of Youth) Smena Publishing House, Prazska 11, 812 84 Bratislava, Czechoslovakia. TEL 406-06. Ed. Eduard Drobny. adv.; bk.rev.; circ. 55,000.
●Also available online.

507   SW   ISSN 0013-5933
ELEMENTA; tidskrift for matematik, fysik och kemi. (Text in Danish, Norwegian and Swedish) 1917. q. SEK 200 (typically set in Jan.). Stiftelsen Elementa, Stabby Alle 13, S-752 29 Uppsala, Sweden. TEL 018-512065. Ed. Gunnar Welin. adv.; bk.rev.; film rev.; bibl.; illus.; stat.; index; circ. 2,300. **Indexed:** Chem.Abstr.
—BLDSC shelfmark: 3727.000000.
Description: Presents history of science, study and teaching methods.

500   HU   ISSN 0013-6077
ELET ES TUDOMANY. 1946. w. $63. (Tudomanyos Ismeretterjeszto Tarsulat) Hirlapkiado Vallalat, Blaha Lujza ter 3, 1959 Budapest 8, Hungary. TEL 1-383-399. TELEX 22-5554. (Subscr. to: Kultura, Box 149, H-1389 Budapest, Hungary) Ed. Andras Wolfner. circ. 30,000. **Indexed:** Hung.Build.Bull.

500   US   ISSN 0013-6220
ELISHA MITCHELL SCIENTIFIC SOCIETY. JOURNAL. 1883. q. $45. North Carolina Academy of Science, NCSSM, Box 2418, Durham, NC 27715. TEL 919-286-3366. Ed. Robert R. Bryden. bibl.; charts; illus.; index; circ. 800. (also avail. in microform from UMI; reprint service avail. from UMI) **Indexed:** Anim.Breed.Abstr., Biol.Abstr., Chem.Abstr., Curr.Adv.Ecol.Sci., Deep Sea Res.& Oceanogr.Abstr., Field Crop Abstr., GeoRef., Helminthol.Abstr., Herb.Abstr., Math.R., Ocean.Abstr., Rev.Plant Path., Soils & Fert., VITIS.
—BLDSC shelfmark: 4739.000000.
Description: Publishes papers in all scientific disciplines as related to North Carolina and the Southeast.

500   UA
EL-ELM/SCIENCES MONTHLY MAGAZINE. 1976. m. Dar al-Tahrir, 24 Sharia Zakaria Ahmed, Cairo, Egypt. TEL 02-741611. FAX 02-749949. TELEX 92475 TAHRIR UN. adv.; illus.; circ. 25,000.

949.4   US   ISSN 0046-1865
DQ1
EMBASSY OF SWITZERLAND BULLETIN. (Text in English, French and German) vol.18, 1978. 3/yr. free to qualified personnel. Embassy of Switzerland, Science and Technology Section, 2900 Cathedral Ave., N.W., Washington, DC 20008. TEL 202-745-7900. FAX 202-387-2564. Ed.Bd. adv.; bk.rev.; bibl.; circ. 3,000 (controlled).

500 060   US   ISSN 0196-9110
Q11   CODEN: ENCYDI
ENCYCLIA. 1924. a. $12. Utah Academy of Sciences, Arts, and Letters, c/o Thomas F. Rogers, Ed., 4089A JKHB, Brigham Young University, Provo, UT 84602. TEL 801-378-3385. FAX 802-378-4649. circ. 1,000. **Indexed:** Arts & Hum.Cit.Ind., Chem.Abstr., Excerp.Bot., Field Crop Abstr., GeoRef., Herb.Abstr., Hort.Abstr., Lang.& Lang.Behav.Abstr., M.L.A., Math R., Rev.Plant Path., Sociol.Abstr.
Formerly (until vol.54, 1977): Utah Academy of Sciences, Arts, and Letters. Proceedings (ISSN 0083-4823)
Description: Resolutions, citations, titles, abstracts, and selected papers presented at the meeting of the Utah Academy.
Refereed Serial

500 530.4 621.366
030   US   ISSN 0898-9842
ENCYCLOPEDIA OF PHYSICAL SCIENCE & TECHNOLOGY YEARBOOK. a. Academic Press, Inc., 1250 Sixth Ave., San Diego, CA 92101. TEL 619-230-1840. FAX 619-699-6715.

500   FR   ISSN 0396-4957
ENCYCLOPEDIE D'UTOVIE;* revue mensuelle de science populaire. 1976. m. 30 F. Editions d' Utovie, Bats, 40320 Geaune, France. Dir. Jean-Marc Carite.

500   US   ISSN 0160-9327
Q1   CODEN: ENDEAS
ENDEAVOUR (TARRYTOWN). 1942; N.S. 1977. q. £65 (effective 1992). Pergamon Press, Inc., Journals Division, 660 White Plains Rd., Tarrytown, NY 10591-5153. TEL 914-524-9200. FAX 914-333-2444. (And: Headington Hill Hall, Oxford OX3 0BW, England. TEL 0865-794141) Ed. Trevor I. Williams. adv.; bk.rev.; charts; illus.; index; cum.index: 1942-1961 (in 2 vols.); circ. 10,000. (also avail. in microform from MIM,UMI; back issues avail.) **Indexed:** Anim.Breed.Abstr., Appl.Mech.Rev., Art & Archaeol.Tech.Abstr., Biodet.Abstr., Biol.Abstr., Br.Tech.Ind., C.I.S. Abstr., Cadscan, Chem.Abstr., Curr.Adv.Ecol.Sci., Curr.Biotech.Abstr., Deep Sea Res.& Oceanogr.Abstr., Eng.Ind., Excerp.Med., Fuel & Energy Abstr., Gen.Sci.Ind., HRIS, Ind.Med., Ind.Sci.Rev., Lead Abstr., Met.Abstr., Psychol.Abstr., RAPRA, Sci.Abstr., Sci.Cit.Ind., Zincscan.
—BLDSC shelfmark: 3740.000000.
Description: Records the progress of science and technology in the service of mankind.
Refereed Serial

SCIENCES: COMPREHENSIVE WORKS

ENGINEERING & SCIENCE. see *ENGINEERING*

500.9   JA   ISSN 0386-5037
ENSHU NO SHIZEN/NATURE OF ENSHU. (Text in Japanese) 1978. a. 1,000 Yen. Enshu Shizen Kenkyukai - Society for the Study of Nature, Enshu, c/o Mr. Hideo Toda, 895-3 Kanasashi, Inasa-cho, Shizuoka-ken 431-22, Japan.
    Description: Contains original papers, reviews, and commentary.

500 600   NE
EPISTEME; a series in the foundational methodological, philosophical, psychological, sociological and political aspects of the sciences, pure and applied. (Text in English) 1975. irreg. price varies. Kluwer Academic Publishers, Spuiboulevard 50, P.O. Box 17, 3300 AA Dordrecht, Netherlands. TEL 078-334911. TELEX 29245. (Dist. by: Kluwer Academic Publishers Group, P.O. Box 322, 3300 AH Dordrecht, Netherlands; N. America dist. addr.: Box 358, Accord Sta., Hingham, MA 02018-0358. TEL 617-871-6600) Ed. Mario Bunge. **Indexed:** Math.R.

500   PL   ISSN 0137-4990
ERGONOMIA. (Text in Polish; summaries in English, German and Russian) vol.5, 1983. s-a. price varies. (Polish Academy of Sciences, Committee of Ergonomics) Ossolineum, Publishing House of the Polish Academy of Sciences, Rynek 9, Wroclaw, Poland. TELEX 0712771 OSS PL. (Dist. by: Ars Polona-Ruch, Krakowskie Przedmiescie 7, Warsaw, Poland) Ed. Andrzej Jozefik. **Indexed:** Ergon.Abstr.
  —BLDSC shelfmark: 3808.450000.

500   GW   ISSN 0340-8833
ERNST-MACH-INSTITUT, FREIBURG. BERICHT. irreg. Ernst-Mach Institut, Eckerstr. 4, 7800 Freiburg, Germany.
    Formerly: Ernst-Mach-Institut, Freiburg. Wissenschaftlicher Bericht (ISSN 0071-1217).

040 500   US   ISSN 0361-5634
AS36
ESSAYS IN ARTS AND SCIENCES. 1971. a. $10 to individuals; libraries $5 (typically set in May). University of New Haven, Library, Serials Dept., West Haven, CT 06516. TEL 203-932-7364. FAX 203-932-1469. Eds. David E. E. Sloane, Joel Marks. adv.; bk.rev.; circ. 600 (controlled). **Indexed:** Abstr.Engl.Stud., M.L.A., Mid.East: Abstr.& Ind.
    Description: Features scholarly articles in the arts and sciences.

500   GW   ISSN 0935-3658
ESSENER UNIVERSITAETSBERICHTE. 1977. q. free. Essen University, Universitaetsstr. 2, 4300 Essen 1, Germany. TEL 0201-183-2085. TELEX 0201-1832151. adv.; circ. 10,000.
    Formerly (until 1987): Hochschuljournal Essen.
    Description: General information on scientific research at Essen University.

500   PO   ISSN 0870-001X
CODEN: EEDUDG
ESTUDOS ENSAIOS E DOCUMENTOS. 1950. irreg. Instituto de Investigacao Cientifica Tropical, Rua Jau 54, 1300 Lisbon, Portugal. TEL 364-5321. FAX 364-2008. (Subscr. to: Centro de Documentacao e Informacao, Rua Jua 47, 1300 Lisbon, Portugal) circ. 1,000.
  —BLDSC shelfmark: 3812.990000.

720 620 551   BL   ISSN 0101-5303
CODEN: ESTTEM
ESTUDOS TECNOLOGICOS. (In three series: Geologia; Engenharia; Arquitetura) (Text in Portuguese; summaries in English) 1976. 5/yr. Cr.$20000($24) for series; or exchange basis. (Universidade do Vale do Rio dos Sinos) Unisinos, Av. Unisinos, 950, 93010 Sao Leopoldo RS, Brazil. TEL 0512-926333. FAX 0512-921035. TELEX 524076. bibl.; charts; illus. **Indexed:** Old Test.Abstr.

500   AG   ISSN 0326-9442
ETICA & CIENCIA. (Text in English, Spanish) 1987. 2/yr. $4 per no.(effective Dec. 1991). Zagier & Urruty Publicaciones, P.O. Box 94, Sucursal 19, 1419 Buenos Aires, Argentina. TEL 541-572-1050. FAX 541-572-5766. (U.S. addr.: Box 526806, Miami, FL 33152-6806) Ed. Patricio Morales. circ. 1,500. (back issues avail.)
    Description: Includes articles on scientific ethics and moral questions of scientists.

ETUDES SCIENTIFIQUES. see *SOCIAL SCIENCES: COMPREHENSIVE WORKS*

500 600   US
EUROPE - LATIN AMERICA REPORT: SCIENCE AND TECHNOLOGY. irreg. (approx. 40/yr.). $7 per no. (foreign $14 per no.). U.S. Joint Publications Research Service, Box 12507, Arlington, VA 22209. TEL 703-487-4630. (Orders to: NTIS, Springfield, VA 22161)

500 600   UK
EUROPEAN RESEARCH CENTRES; a directory of organizations in science, technology, agriculture and medicine. triennial, 8th ed., 1990. £325. Longman Group UK Ltd., Westgate House, The High, Harlow, Essex CM20 1YR, England. TEL 0279-442601. (Dist. in U.S. & Canada by: Gale Research Co. Ltd., Book Tower, Detroit, MI 48226)

500   US
EUROPEAN SCIENCE NOTES. 1947. m. $27.50. U.S. Office of Naval Research, Branch Office, Box 39, FPO, NY 09510-0700. (Dist. by: Supt. of Docs., Government Printing Office, Washington, DC 20402) Ed. Connie R. Orendorf. circ. 6,000.

500 600   UK
EUROPEAN SOURCES OF SCIENTIFIC AND TECHNICAL INFORMATION. triennial, 9th ed., 1990. £140. Longman Group UK Ltd., Westgate House, The High, Harlow, Essex CM20 1YR, England. TEL 0279-442601. (Dist. in U.S. & Canada by: Gale Research Co. Ltd., Book Tower, Detroit, MI 48226)

EVENTOS EM POLITICA CIENTIFICA E TECNOLOGICA. see *TECHNOLOGY: COMPREHENSIVE WORKS*

600 500   II   ISSN 0531-495X
EVERYMAN'S SCIENCE. (Text in English) 1966. bi-m. Rs.36. Indian Science Congress Association, 14 Dr. Biresh Guha St., Calcutta 700017, India. TEL 44-4530. **Indexed:** INIS Atomind.
    Description: Contains popular science articles.

500   US
EXCITEMENT AND FASCINATION OF SCIENCE; reflections by eminent scientists. 1965. irreg. vol.3, 1990. $90 (foreign $95). Annual Reviews Inc., 4139 El Camino Way, Box 10139, Palo Alto, CA 94303-0897. TEL 415-493-4400. FAX 415-855-9815. TELEX 910-290-0275.

EXPERIENTIA; interdisciplinary journal for life sciences. see *BIOLOGY*

EXPERIENTIA. SUPPLEMENTUM. see *BIOLOGY*

EXPLORATIONS IN KNOWLEDGE; an international journal in the philosophy of science. see *PHILOSOPHY*

500 700 028.5   US   ISSN 0889-8197
EXPLORATORIUM QUARTERLY. 1977. q. $18 to individuals; institutions, libraries $24; foreign $36. Exploratorium, 3601 Lyon St., San Francisco, CA 94123. TEL 415-561-0395. FAX 415-561-0307. Ed. Pat Murphy. bk.rev.; circ. 8,000. (back issues avail.) **Indexed:** Vert.File Ind.
  —BLDSC shelfmark: 3842.207980.
    Formerly (until 1985): Exploratorium.
    Description: Magazine of science, art, and human perception reflecting the philosophy of the Exploratorium, a museum where people learn by doing.

500.9   US   ISSN 0014-5009
QH1   CODEN: EXPOAI
EXPLORER (CLEVELAND). 1938. q. membership or exchange basis. Cleveland Museum of Natural History, One Wade Oval Dr., University Circle, Cleveland, OH 44106. TEL 216-231-4600. Ed. Megan Harding. bk.rev.; charts; illus.; index; circ. 10,300. (talking book; back issues avail.) **Indexed:** Biol.Abstr., Biol.Dig., GeoRef.
    Description: Addresses natural history, environmental, conservation and general science topics for members of natural history museums, science centers, and schools.

500   US   ISSN 0092-9824
Q11
F A S PUBLIC INTEREST REPORT. 1946. bi-m. $25. Federation of American Scientists, 307 Massachusetts Ave., N.E., Washington, DC 20002. TEL 202-546-3300. FAX 202-675-1010. TELEX 9102509251 FAS DC UQ. Ed. Jeremy J. Stone. bk.rev.; circ. 4,000. **Indexed:** HR Rep.
    Formerly: F A S Newsletter.

FERTILISER TECHNOLOGY. see *TECHNOLOGY: COMPREHENSIVE WORKS*

FEUILLETS DU NATURALISTE. see *CHILDREN AND YOUTH — For*

FIBEROPTIC PRODUCT NEWS. see *COMMUNICATIONS — Telephone And Telegraph*

FILOSOFI OG VIDENSKABSTEORI PAA ROSKILDE UNIVERSITETSCENTER. see *PHILOSOPHY*

FILOSOFSKIE NAUKI (MOSCOW). see *PHILOSOPHY*

500.9   DK   ISSN 0015-3818
         CODEN: FLFAAN
FLORA OG FAUNA. (Text in Danish; summaries in English) 1894. q. DKK 125($18) Naturhistorisk Forening for Jylland, Natural History Museum, DK-8000 Aarhus C, Denmark. TEL 86-195177. FAX 86-195175. Ed. Thomas S. Jensen. bk.rev.; illus.; index; circ. 1,000. **Indexed:** Biol.Abstr., Deep Sea Res.& Oceanogr.Abstr., Zoo.Rec.
  —BLDSC shelfmark: 3954.900000.
    Description: Original papers on taxonomy, distribution, biology, ecology and conservation of Danish plants and animals.

500   US   ISSN 0098-4590
Q11   CODEN: FLSCAQ
FLORIDA SCIENTIST.* 1936. q. $20 to libraries; members $18. Florida Academy of Sciences, Inc., Box 33012, Indiatlantic, FL 32903-0012. TEL 407-323-1450. Eds. Dean F. and Barbara B. Martin. adv.; bk.rev.; charts; illus.; stat.; index; circ. 1,050. (also avail. in microform from UMI; back issues avail.; reprint service avail. from UMI) **Indexed:** Abstr.N.Amer.Geol., Biol.Abstr., Chem.Abstr., Deep Sea Res.& Oceanogr.Abstr., Excerp.Med., Geo.Abstr., GeoRef., Ocean.Abstr., Pollut.Abstr., Sel.Water Res.Abstr.
  —BLDSC shelfmark: 3956.130000.
    Formerly (until 1973): Florida Academy of Sciences. Quarterly Journal (ISSN 0015-3850)
    Description: Scientific and educational material in many categories of science for professionals, non-professionals, students and laypersons.

500   US
FLORIDA STATE UNIVERSITY RESEARCH IN REVIEW. 1969. q. free. Florida State University, Office of Graduate Studies and Research, 109 HMB R-23, Tallahassee, FL 32306. TEL 904-644-8634. Ed. Frank H. Stephenson. bk.rev.; charts; illus.; circ. 9,500. **Indexed:** Ind.Free Per.
    Formerly (until 1989): Florida State University Bulletin: Research in Review.
    Refereed Serial

910   CS
FOLIA FACULTATIS SCIENTIARUM NATURALIUM UNIVERSITATIS MASARYKIANAE BRUNENSIS: GEOGRAPHIA. irreg. (1-3/yr.). price varies. Masarykova Universita, Prirodovedecka Fakulta - Masaryk University, Faculty of Sciences, Kotlarska 2, 611 37 Brno, Czechoslovakia.
    Formerly: Folia Facultatis Scientiarum Naturalium Universitatis Purkynianae Brunensis: Geographia.

500 700 800   SP   ISSN 0015-5594
AS301
FOLIA HUMANISTICA; ciencias, artes, letras. 1963. 6/yr. 2000 ptas.($37) Fundacion Letamendi Forns, Muntaner 303, 08021 Barcelona, Spain. Ed. Prof. F. Arasa. bk.rev.; circ. 35,000. **Indexed:** Amer.Hist.& Life, Arts & Hum.Cit.Ind., Curr.Cont., Hist.Abstr., SSCI.
  —BLDSC shelfmark: 3970.500000.

SCIENCES: COMPREHENSIVE WORKS

500   GW   ISSN 0172-1518
Q180.G4
FORSCHUNG. 1983. 4/yr. DM.48. (Deutsche Forschungsgemeinschaft) V C H Verlagsgesellschaft mbH, Postfach 101161, 6940 Weinheim, Germany. TEL 06201-602-0. FAX 06201-602328. TELEX 465516-VCHWH-D. (U.S. addr.: V C H Publishers Inc., 220 E. 23rd St., New York, NY 10010-4606) Ed. E. Streier. adv.; bk.rev.; circ. 15,000. (back issues avail.) **Indexed:** Lang.& Lang.Behav.Abstr.

500   GW   ISSN 0176-263X
FORSCHUNG AKTUELL; Wissenschaft fuer die Praxis. 1984. 3/yr. free. Technische Universitaet Berlin, Presse- und Informationsreferat, Strasse des 17. Juni 135, 1000 Berlin 12, Germany. TEL 030-31422919. FAX 030-31423909. index. (back issues avail.)

500 378   GW   ISSN 0937-2873
▼**FORSCHUNG AN DER UNIVERSITAET BIELEFELD.** 1990. 2/yr. DM.10. Universitaet Bielefeld, Postfach 100131, 4800 Bielefeld 1, Germany. TEL 0521-1064146. FAX 0521-1064079. TELEX 932362-UNIBI. Ed. Veronika Reiss. adv.; circ. 4,000.

500   GW   ISSN 0175-0992
FORSCHUNG FRANKFURT. 1984. q. DM.15. Johann Wolfgang Goethe-University, Senckenberganlage 31, Postfach 111932, 6000 Frankfurt a.M. 11, Germany. TEL 069-7983266. FAX 069-7988530. adv.; circ. 5,000. (back issues avail.)

500   SW   ISSN 0015-7937
FORSKNING OCH FRAMSTEG. 1966. 8/yr. SEK 369. Stiftelsen Forskning och Framsteg, P.O. Box 1191, S-111 91 Stockholm, Sweden. Ed. Bjoern Fjaestad. charts; illus.; index; circ. 54,000. **Indexed:** NAA.
Description: A general interest popular science magazine.

052   SA   ISSN 0015-8054
AS611   CODEN: FHPADE
FORT HARE PAPERS. (Text and summaries in English) 1945. irreg. R.5 per no. Fort Hare University Press, Private Bag X1314, Alice, Republic of Ciskei, South Africa. FAX 0404-32011. TELEX 250863. Ed. M.J. Prins. charts; illus.; circ. 1,500. (tabloid format) **Indexed:** A.I.C.P., Biol.Abstr., Chem.Abstr., Curr.Cont., Field Crop Abstr., Herb.Abstr., I D A, Ind.S.A.Per., M.L.A., Maize Abstr., Weed Abstr., World Agri.Econ.& Rural Sociol.Abstr.
Description: Covers natural sciences, humanities, arts, education, and economics from a South African perspective.

FORTEAN TIMES; the journal of strange phenomena. see *PARAPSYCHOLOGY AND OCCULTISM*

500 333.78 639.9   UK   ISSN 0309-7560
FORTH NATURALIST AND HISTORIAN. 1976. a. £4($7) Forth Naturalist and Historian Editorial Board, University of Stirling, Stirling FK9 4LA, Scotland. TEL 0259-215091. FAX 0786-63000. Ed. L. Corbett. adv.; bk.rev.; cum.index (vols.1-5, 6-10); circ. 450. **Indexed:** Aqua.Sci.& Fish.Abstr., Biol.Abstr., Zoo.Rec.
—BLDSC shelfmark: 4017.700000.
Description: Promotes research in the natural history of central Scotland.

FORTHCOMING INTERNATIONAL SCIENTIFIC AND TECHNICAL CONFERENCES. see *MEETINGS AND CONGRESSES*

500   GW   ISSN 0937-8316
FORUM (ESSEN). 1976. bi-m. free. Gemeinnuetzige Verwaltungsgesellschaft fuer Wissenschaftspflege mbH, Postfach 230360, 4300 Essen 1, Germany. TEL 0201-7221-0. FAX 0201-714968. Ed. Norbert Schuergers. circ. 7,000.

500   GW   ISSN 0178-6563
FORUM WISSENSCHAFT; das kritische Wissenschaftsmagazine. 1984. q. DM.25. Bund Demokratischer Wissenschaftlerinnen und Wissenschaftler, Postfach 543, 3550 Marburg, Germany. TEL 06421-21395. bibl.; illus.; circ. 4,500.
Description: Deals with science and research policy, and the social responsibility of scientists.

500   FR
FRANCE. BUREAU NATIONAL D'INFORMATION SCIENTIFIQUE ET TECHNIQUE. BULLETIN D'INFORMATION.* 1975. q. free. Imprimerie Nationale, 39 rue de la Convention, 75015 Paris, France. Ed. J. Michel. bk.rev.; bibl.

FRANCIS BACON RESEARCH TRUST JOURNAL; studies in ancient wisdom. see *PHILOSOPHY*

500   US   ISSN 0016-0032
                         CODEN: JFINAB
FRANKLIN INSTITUTE. JOURNAL. 1826. 6/yr. £385($615) (effective 1992). Pergamon Press, Inc., Journals Division, 660 White Plains Rd., Tarrytown, NY 10591-5153. TEL 914-524-9200. FAX 914-333-2444. (And: Headington Hill Hall, Oxford OX3 0BW, England. TEL 0865-794141) Ed. Martin A. Pomerantz. adv.; bk.rev.; charts; illus.; stat.; s-a. index, cum.index every 10 yrs.; vols.1-280 (1826-1965) in 8 vols.; circ. 1,500. (also avail. in microform from MIM,UMI; back issues avail.) **Indexed:** A.S.& T.Ind., Appl.Mech.Rev., Biol.Abstr., Chem.Eng.Abstr., Comput.Abstr., Curr.Cont., Cyb.Abstr., Deep Sea Res.& Oceanogr.Abstr., Eng.Ind., GeoRef., Int.Aerosp.Abstr., Math R., Met.Abstr., Petrol.Abstr., Photo.Abstr., Plant Breed.Abstr., Psychol.Abstr., Sci.Abstr., Sh.& Vib.Dig., T.C.E.A., World Surf.Coat.
—BLDSC shelfmark: 4755.000000.
Description: Multi-disciplinary journal publishing papers on all aspects of pure and applied mathematics and physical sciences.
Refereed Serial

629.13   FA   ISSN 0085-0896
FRODSKAPARRIT; ANNALES SOCIETATIS SCIENTIARUM FAEROENSIS. (Text mainly in Faroese; summaries in English and occasionally in other languages) 1952. a. price varies. Foeroya Frodskaparfelag - Societas Scientiarum Faeroensis, FR-100 Torshavn, Faeroe Islands. TEL 298-15302. FAX 298-16844. Ed.Bd. index; circ. 1,000.
—BLDSC shelfmark: 4040.400000.

500   FA   ISSN 0429-7539
FRODSKAPARRIT; ANNALES SOCIETATIS SCIENTIARUM FAERONSIS. SUPPLEMENTA. (Text and summaries in Danish, English , Faroese) 1954. irreg. Foeroya Frodskaparfelag - Societas Scientiarum Faeroensis, FR-100 Torshavn, Faeroe Islands. TEL 298-15302. FAX 298-16844. index. **Indexed:** M.L.A.

500   CC   ISSN 0427-7104
Q4
FUDAN XUEBAO (ZIRAN KEXUE BAN)/FUDAN JOURNAL (NATURAL SCIENCE EDITION). (Text in Chinese) 1955. q. $1.20 per no. (Fudan Daxue - Fudan University) Fudan Daxue Chubanshe - Fudan University Press, 220 Handan Lu, Shanghai 200433, People's Republic of China. TEL 5484906. (Dist. by: China International Book Trading Corp., P.O. Box 399, Beijing, P.R.C.) **Indexed:** Chem.Abstr., INIS Atomind., Math.R., Sci.Abstr.
—BLDSC shelfmark: 4755.440000.

500   CC
FUJIAN SHIFAN DAXUE XUEBAO. (ZIRAN KEXUE BAN)/FUJIAN NORMAL UNIVERSITY. JOURNAL (NATURAL SCIENCE EDITION). (Text in Chinese) q. Fujian Shifan Daxue, 137 Shangsan Lu, Cangshan Qu, Fuzhou, Fujian 350007, People's Republic of China. (Dist. overseas by: Jiangsu Publications Import & Export Corp., 56 Gao Yun Ling, Nanjing, Jiangsu, P.R.C.)

500   JA   ISSN 0071-9781
FUKUI DAIGAKU KYOIKUGAKUBU KIYO. DAI 2-BU. SHIZEN KAGAKU/FUKUI UNIVERSITY. FACULTY OF EDUCATION. MEMOIRS. SERIES 2: NATURAL SCIENCE. (Text and summaries in English and Japanese) 1961. a. Fukui University, Faculty of Education - Fukui Daigaku Kyoikugakubu, 9-1 Bunkyo, 3-chome, Fukui-shi, Fukui-ken 910, Japan.
Description: Contains original papers.

510   JA   ISSN 0532-811X
Q4   CODEN: FKDRAN
FUKUOKA KYOIKU DAIGAKU KIYO. DAI-3-BUNSATSU. SUGAKU, RIKA, GIJUTSUKA HEN/FUKUOKA UNIVERSITY OF EDUCATION. BULLETIN. PART 3: MATHEMATICS, NATURAL SCIENCES AND TECHNOLOGY. (Text in English and Japanese; summaries in English) 1951. a. Fukuoka University of Education - Fukuoka Kyoiku Daigaku, Akama, Munakata-shi, Fukuoka-ken 811-41, Japan. **Indexed:** Biol.Abstr., Chem.Abstr., INIS Atomind.

500   JA   ISSN 0387-0855
Q4
FUKUSHIMA DAIGAKU KYOIKUGAKUBU RONSHU. RIKA HOKOKU/FUKUSHIMA UNIVERSITY. FACULTY OF EDUCATION. SCIENCE REPORTS. (Text in English and Japanese; summaries in English) 1951. a. Fukushima University, Faculty of Education - Fukushima Daigaku Kyoikugakubu, 2 Naomichi, Asakawa, Matsukawa-machi, Fukushima-shi, Fukushima-ken 960-12, Japan. **Indexed:** Chem.Abstr., INIS Atomind.
—BLDSC shelfmark: 8152.450000.

060   AG
FUNDACION BARILOCHE. MEMORIA ANUAL. a. Fundacion Bariloche, Casilla de Correo 138, San Carlos de Bariloche - Rio Negro, Argentina.

FUNDACION LA CAIXA. PANORAMA. see *MUSEUMS AND ART GALLERIES*

FUSION; Wissenschaft - Technik fuer das 21. Jahrhundert. see *ENERGY*

500 016   US   ISSN 8755-3317
CB158
FUTURES RESEARCH QUARTERLY. 1985. q. $75. World Future Society, 4916 St. Elmo Ave., Bethesda, MD 20814. TEL 301-656-8274. FAX 301-951-0394. bk.rev.; bibl.; circ. 1,700. (also avail. in microform from UMI; back issues avail.) **Indexed:** C.I.J.E., Fut.Surv.
Formerly (1967-1984): World Future Society Bulletin (ISSN 0049-8092)

500   US   ISSN 0016-3317
CB158   CODEN: FUTUAC
THE FUTURIST; a journal of forecasts, trends, and ideas about the future. 1967. bi-m. $36. World Future Society, 4916 St. Elmo Ave., Bethesda, MD 20814. TEL 301-656-8274. Ed. Edward S. Cornish. adv.; bk.rev.; charts; illus.; cum.index: 1967-1975, 1976-1980, 1981-1983, 1984-1988, 1987-1991; circ. 30,000. (also avail. in microform from UMI; back issues avail.; reprint service avail. from UMI) **Indexed:** A.I.Abstr., ABI Inform., Acad.Ind., Bk.Rev.Ind. (1978-), BPIA, Bus.Ind., C.I.J.E., Child.Bk.Rev.Ind. (1978-), Comput.Bus., Curr.Cont., Educ.Admin.Abstr., Energy Info.Abstr., Energy Rev., Environ.Abstr., Environ.Per.Bibl., Fut.Surv., INIS Atomind., Int.Lab.Doc., Lang.& Lang.Behav.Abstr., Mag.Ind., Manage.Cont., Mid.East: Abstr.& Ind., Oper.Res.Manage.Sci., Pers.Lit., PMR, PROMT, Qual.Contr.Appl.Stat., R.G., Sci.Abstr., Soc.Sci.Ind., SSCI, Telegen, Tr.& Indus.Ind.
●Also available online. Vendor(s): DIALOG.
—BLDSC shelfmark: 4060.700000.

500   IT   ISSN 0390-217X
IL FUTURO DELL'UOMO. 1974. 2/yr. L.20000. Istituto Niels Stensen, Viale Don Minzoni 25-a, I-50129 Florence, Italy. TEL 055-576551. Ed. Lodovico Galleni. bk.rev.; circ. 500. (back issues avail.)

FUTUROLOGY. see *TECHNOLOGY: COMPREHENSIVE WORKS*

500   CC   ISSN 1000-2243
FUZHOU DAXUE XUEBAO (ZIRAN KEXUE BAN)/FUZHOU UNIVERSITY. JOURNAL (NATURAL SCIENCE EDITION). (Text in Chinese) 1961. q. Y8. Fuzhou Daxue - Fuzhou University, Gongye Lu, Fuzhou, Fujian 350002, People's Republic of China. TEL 710845. (Dist. overseas by: Chinese Publications Import and Export Corp., book and Journal Department, Journal Section, P.O. Box 782, Beijing 100011, P.R.C.) Ed. Huang Jinling.
Description: Covers mathematics, computer science, physics, electrical engineering, civil engineering, chemistry and other fields of science.

G S F MENSCH UND UMWELT. see *ENVIRONMENTAL STUDIES*

500   JA   ISSN 0387-2440
GAKUJUTSU GEPPO/JAPANESE SCIENTIFIC MONTHLY. (Text in Japanese; summaries in English) 1948. m. 800 Yen. Japan Society for the Promotion of Science - Nihon Gakujutsu Shikokai, 3-1 Koji-machi, 5-chome, Chiyoda-ku, Tokyo 102, Japan. abstr. **Indexed:** INIS Atomind., Jap.Per.Ind.
Description: Contains reviews, commentary, and news.

500	YU
GALAKSIJA; casopis za popularizaciju nauke. 1972. m. $55. B I G Z, Bulevar vojvode Misica 17, Belgrade, Yugoslavia. Ed. Stanko Stojiljkovic. illus.

GDANSKIE TOWARZYSTWO NAUKOWE. WYDZIAL 3. NAUK MATEMATYCZNO-FIZYCZNO-CHEMICZNYCH. PRACE. see *MATHEMATICS*

500	US
GENERAL SYSTEMS BULLETIN. 1956. 2/yr. $10 per no. International Society for the Systems Sciences, Box 8793, College of Business, Idoha State University, Pocatello, ID 83209. TEL 208-233-6521. FAX 208-236-4367.

500 001.4	US	ISSN 0072-0798
H9		

GENERAL SYSTEMS YEARBOOK. 1956. a. $35 to non-members. International Society for the Systems Sciences, Box 8793, College of Business, Idaho State University, Pocatello, ID 83209. TEL 208-233-6521. FAX 208-236-4367. bk.rev.; circ. 2,000. (back issues avail.)

500	GW
GEORG-AUGUST-UNIVERSITAET GOETTINGEN. INFORMATIONEN. 1971. bi-m. Georg-August-Universitaet Goettingen, Wilhelmsplatz 1, 3400 Goettingen, Germany. TEL 0551-394341. FAX 0551-394251. Ed. Karola Neubert. adv.; bk.rev.; circ. 8,500.

500	US	ISSN 0016-8114
Q11		CODEN: BUCDA2

GEORGIA JOURNAL OF SCIENCE. 1943. q. $25. Georgia Academy of Science, c/o Andy C. Reese, Ed., Medical College of Georgia, Augusta, GA 30912. TEL 404-790-2056. FAX 404-721-6608. adv.; abstr.; bibl.; charts; illus.; stat.; cum.index: 1943-1967; circ. 1,000. (also avail. in microform from UMI) **Indexed:** Biol.Abstr., Field Crop Abstr., Herb.Abstr., Ind.Vet., INIS Atomind., Soils & Fert., Vet.Bull.
 Formerly (until vol.34, no.4, Sept. 1976): Georgia Academy of Science. Bulletin.
 Refereed Serial

500	GW	ISSN 0172-1526

GERMAN RESEARCH. (Text in English) 1983. 3/yr. DM.49. (Deutsche Forschungsgemeinschaft) V C H Verlagsgesellschaft mbH, Postfach 101161, 6940 Weinheim, Germany. TEL 06201-602-0. FAX 06201-602328. TELEX 465516-VCHWH-D. (U.S. addr.: V C H Publishers Inc., 220 E. 23rd St., New York, NY 10010-4606) adv.; circ. 8,000.

500 007	GW	ISSN 0072-1476

GERMAN RESEARCH SERVICE. (Text in English) 1962. m. $38. Deutscher Forschungsdienst GmbH, Ahrstr. 45, Postfach 205006, 5300 Bonn 2, Germany. TEL 0228-302210. FAX 0228-302270. Ed. Karl-Heinz Preuss. circ. 2,200.

GERMANY. BUNDESINSTITUT FUER SPORTWISSENSCHAFT. BIENNIAL REPORTS. see *SPORTS AND GAMES*

007	GW
GERMANY (FEDERAL REPUBLIC, 1949-). BUNDESMINISTERIUM FUER FORSCHUNG UND TECHNOLOGIE. B M F T FOERDERUNGSKATALOG. 1971. a. DM.30. Bundesministerium fuer Forschung und Technologie, Referat Hausinterne Datenverarbeitung und Dokumentation, Postfach 200240, 5300 Bonn 2, Germany. TEL 0228-593334. FAX 0228-593601. circ. 4,000.
 ●Also available online.

500.9	GW	ISSN 0037-5942

GESELLSCHAFT NATURFORSCHENDER FREUNDE ZU BERLIN. SITZUNGSBERICHTE. NEUE FOLGE. 1961. a. price varies. Duncker und Humblot GmbH, Postfach 410329, 1000 Berlin 41, Germany. TEL 030-7900060. FAX 030-79000631. Ed. Peter Goetz.

GESNERUS; die historisch-wissenschaftliche Zeitschrift der medizinischen und naturwissenschaftlichen Forschung. see *MEDICAL SCIENCES*

500	NE
GEWINA; tijdschrift voor de geschiedenis der geneeskunde, natuurwetenschappen, Wiskunde en techniek. 1978. 4/yr. fl.85. Erasmus Publishing B.V., Mathenesserlaan 332, 3021 HZ Rotterdam, Netherlands. TEL 010-4777484.
 FAX 010-4779580. Ed.Bd. circ. 1,000.
 Formerly: Tijdschrift voor de Geschiedenis der Geneeskunde, Natuurwetenschappen, Wiskunde en Techniek (ISSN 0167-2088)
 Description: Covers the history of mathematics, physics, engineering, medical and other sciences.

500	JA	ISSN 0533-9529
Q4		CODEN: GDGKAD

GIFU DAIGAKU KYOIKUGAKUBU KENKYU HOKOKU. SHIZEN KAGAKU/GIFU UNIVERSITY. FACULTY OF EDUCATION. SCIENCE REPORT. NATURAL SCIENCE. (Text in Japanese and English; summaries in English) 1953. a. Gifu University, Faculty of Education - Gifu Daigaku Kyoikugaku, 1-1 Yanagido, Gifu-shi, Gifu-ken 501-11, Japan. **Indexed:** Chem.Abstr., Jap.Per.Ind.

500	JA	ISSN 0388-550X

GIFU-KEN HAKUBUTSUKAN CHOSA KENKYU HOKOKU/GIFU PREFECTURAL MUSEUM. BULLETIN. (Text and summaries in Japanese and English) 1980. a. Gifu Prefectural Museum - Gifu-ken Hakubutsukan, Hyakunen Koen, Oyana, Seki-shi, Gifu-ken 501-32, Japan.
 Description: Contains research reports from the museum.

GLASGOW NATURALIST. see *BIOLOGY*

500 600	US	ISSN 0886-6236
QH344		CODEN: GBCYEP

GLOBAL BIOGEOCHEMICAL CYCLES. 1987. q. $135 to non-members (foreign $140); members $41 (foreign $46); students $20 (foreign $25). American Geophysical Union, 2000 Florida Ave., N.W., Washington, DC 20009. TEL 202-462-6900. FAX 202-328-0566. TELEX 710-882-9300. Ed. James J. McCarthy.
 —BLDSC shelfmark: 4195.352000.
 Description: Publishes papers in the broad areas of global change involving the geosphere and biosphere. Previews marine, hydrologic, atmospheric, extraterrestrial, geologic, biologic, and human causes of and response to environmental change on time scales of tens, thousands, and millions of years.
 Refereed Serial

500	NR	ISSN 0795-6770

GLOBAL SCIENCE JOURNAL; an international journal of science. (Text and summaries in English) 1988. m. Global Science Union, P.O. Box 10123, Ugbowo, Benin City, Nigeria. Ed. O.S.A. Aromose.

500	JA	ISSN 0385-7433

GOCHO/OKOCHI MEMORIAL FOUNDATION. JOURNAL. (Text in Japanese) irreg. 600 Yen. Okochi Kinenkai - Okochi Memorial Foundation, 17-1 Toranomon 1-chome, Minato-ku, Tokyo 105, Japan.
 Description: Contains reviews, commentary, and news of the foundation.

500	RU	ISSN 0041-8072

GOSUDARSTVENNAYA BIBLIOTEKA S.S.S.R. IM. V.I. LENINA. INFORMATSIONNYI BYULLETEN' NOVYKH INOSTRANNYKH KNIG, POSTUPIVSHIKH V BIBLIOTEKU. SERIYA 1: FIZIKO-MATEMATICHESKIE I KHIMICHESKIE NAUKI; NAUKI O ZEMLE; TEKHNIKA I TEKHNICHESKIE NAUK. (Text in Russian) 1956. 3/m. 18 Rub. Gosudarstvennaya Biblioteka S.S.S.R. im. V.I. Lenina, Pr. Kalinina, 3, 121019 Moscow, Russia. Ed. I.U. Bagrova. index; circ. 1,300.

500	SW	ISSN 0348-6788

GOTHENBURG STUDIES IN THE HISTORY OF SCIENCE AND IDEAS. (Subseries of Acta Universitatis Gothoburgensis) 1979. irreg., vol.12, 1991. price varies; also exchange basis. Acta Universitatis Gothoburgensis, Box 5096, S-402 22 Goeteborg, Sweden. Ed. Sven-Eric Liedman.

500	PH	ISSN 0116-6417

GRADUATE FORUM. (Text in English) biennial. (Mindanao State University, Graduate School) Mindanao State University, University Research Center, P.O. Box 5594, Iligan City 9200, Philippines. Ed. Aloysius Glenroy Lambert. circ. 500.

500 600	II
GRAM SHILP. (Text in Hindi) 1980. q. Rs.3. National Research Development Corporation, 20-22 Zamroodpur Community Centre, Kailash Colony Extension, New Delhi 110 048, India. TEL 11-6418615. TELEX 031-71358. Ed. D.N. Bhatnagar. adv.; bk.rev.; abstr.; charts; illus.; circ. 3,000.
 Description: Concerns technology.

GREAT BRITAIN. HARWELL LABORATORY. HARWELL INFORMATION BULLETIN. see *BIBLIOGRAPHIES*

500 100 200	GW
GRENZFRAGEN. 1972. irreg., vol.7, 1978. (Goerres-Gesellschaft) Karl Alber GmbH, Hermann Herder Str. 4, 7800 Freiburg, Germany. Ed. Norbert A. Luyten.

500	AU
GRENZGEBIETE DER WISSENSCHAFT. 1951. q. DM.65. Resch Verlag, Maximilianstr. 8, A-6010 Innsbruck, Austria. TEL 0512-574772. Ed. Andreas Resch. adv.; bk.rev.; circ. 1,000.

500	GW
GRUNDLAGEN DER EXAKTEN NATURWISSENSCHAFTEN. (Text in English, German) 1980. irreg. price varies. Bibliographisches Institut und F.A. Brockhaus AG, Dudenstr. 6, Postfach 100311, 6800 Mannheim 1, Germany. TEL 0621-3901-01.
 FAX 0621-3901-389. Ed. Peter Mittelstaedt.

GRUNDLAGENSTUDIEN AUS KYBERNETIK UND GEISTESWISSENSCHAFT; Humankybernetik. see *COMPUTERS — Cybernetics*

GUANGDONG MINZU XUEYUAN XUEBAO/GUANGDONG INSTITUTE OF NATIONALITIES. JOURNAL. see *SOCIAL SCIENCES: COMPREHENSIVE WORKS*

500	II
GUJARAT RESEARCH SOCIETY. JOURNAL. (Text in English, Gujarati) 1939. q. Rs.25. Gujarat Research Society, Samshodhan Sadan, Ramkrishna Mission Rd., Khar (West), Bombay 400 052, India. Ed. Dr. M.R. Shah. adv.; bk.rev.; charts; circ. 400. **Indexed:** Biol.Abstr.

500.9	JA	ISSN 0017-5668
Q4		CODEN: GDSHAU

GUNMA DAIGAKU KYOIKUGAKUBU KIYO. SHIZEN KAGAKU HEN/GUNMA UNIVERSITY. FACULTY OF EDUCATION. SCIENCE REPORTS. (Text in English and Japanese; summaries in English) 1950. a. exchange basis. Gunma University, Faculty of Education - Gunma Daigaku Kyoikugakubu, Library, 4-2 Aramaki-cho, Maebashi-shi, Gunma-ken 371, Japan. Ed.Bd. **Indexed:** Biol.Abstr., Chem.Abstr., Jap.Per.Ind.
 —BLDSC shelfmark: 8152.470000.

500 600	CC
GUOJI KEJI JIAOLIU/INTERNATIONAL SCIENCE AND TECHNOLOGY EXCHANGE. (Text in Chinese) m. Zhongguo Kexue Jishu Qingbao Yanjiusuo - Chinese Institute of Science and Technology Information, 15 Fuxing Lu, Beijing 100038, People's Republic of China. TEL 8015544. Ed. Hu Quanming.

500 600	CC
GUOWAI KEJI DONGTAI/FOREIGN SCIENCE AND TECHNOLOGY DEVELOPMENT. (Text in Chinese) m. Zhongguo Kexue Jishu Qingbao Yanjiusuo - Chinese Institute of Science and Technology Information, 15 Fuxing Lu, Beijing 100038, People's Republic of China. TEL 8015544. Ed. Bai Yiran.

500	GY
GUYANA SCIENCE TEACHERS' ASSOCIATION. NEWSLETTER. 3/yr. membership. Guyana Science Teachers' Association, c/o Honorary Secretary, Mr. B.N. Kumar, Unity Village, East Coast Demerara, Guyana.

500	UK	ISSN 0017-5897

Y GWYDDONYDD. (Text in Welsh) 1965. 3/yr. £6. University of Wales Press, 6 Gwennyth St., Cathays, Cardiff CF2 4YD, Wales. TEL 0222-231919. FAX 0222-230908. Ed. Prof. Glyn O. Phillips. adv.; bk.rev.; charts; illus.; circ. 500.
 Description: General science magazine.

SCIENCES: COMPREHENSIVE WORKS

500.9 UK ISSN 0028-9043
HABITAT (LONDON). 1959. 10/yr. £13.50 (foreign £17.50). Environment Council, 80 York Way, London N1 9AG, England. TEL 071-278-4736. FAX 071-837-9688. Ed. S.M. Joy. adv.; bk.rev.; circ. 2,350. Indexed: AESIS, Avery Ind.Archit.Per., Excerp.Med., Mid.East: Abstr.& Ind.
—BLDSC shelfmark: 4237.350000.
Formerly: News for Naturalists.
Description: Digest of environmental news and events.

500 600 TU ISSN 0072-9221
CODEN: HFMBDA
HACETTEPE FEN VE MUHENDISLIK BILIMLERI DERGISI. (Series A: Biology; Series B: Mathematics and Statistics; Series C: Chemistry, Physics, and Engineering) (Text in Turkish; summaries in English) 1971. a. TL.5000($8) University of Hacettepe, Faculty of Science - Hacettepe Universitesi, Fen Fakultesi, 06532 Beytepe, Ankara, Turkey. Ed. Suleyman Gunay. Indexed: INIS Atomind.
Description: Publishes short to medium length research papers.

500 JA ISSN 0289-4092
HAKUBUTSUKAN DAYORI/SAITO HO-ON KAI MUSEUM OF NATURAL HISTORY. NEWS. (Text in Japanese) 1981. q. free. Saito Ho-on Kai - Saito Gratitude Foundation, 20-2, Hon-cho 2-chome, Aoba-ku, Sendai 980, Japan. TEL 022-262-5506. FAX 22-262-5508.

500 GW ISSN 0072-9566
HD72
HAMBURGER JAHRBUCH FUER WIRTSCHAFTS- UND GESELLSCHAFTSPOLITIK. 1956. a. price varies. (HWWA-Institut fuer Wirtschaftsforschung Hamburg) Verlag J. C. B. Mohr (Paul Siebeck), Wilhelmstr. 18, Postfach 2040, 7400 Tuebingen, Germany. TEL 07071-26064. FAX 07071-51104. TELEX 7262872-MOHR-D. Ed.Bd.
Description: Studies the political, economic and social dilemmas created by new scientific developments.

HANDBUCH DER DATENBANKEN FUER NATURWISSENSCHAFT, TECHNIK, PATENTE. see COMPUTERS — Data Base Management

500 CC ISSN 0253-3618
HANGZHOU DAXUE XUEBAO (ZIRAN KEXUE BAN)/HANGZHOU UNIVERSITY. JOURNAL (NATURAL SCIENCE EDITION). (Text in Chinese) 1956. q. $1.50 per no. Hangzhou Daxue - Hangzhou University, 34 Tianmushan Lu, Hangzhou, Zhejiang 310028, People's Republic of China. (Dist. by: Guoji Shudian - China International Book Trading Corporation, P.O. Box 399, Beijing, P.R.C.) circ. 2,000. Indexed: Chem.Abstr., Curr.Adv.Ecol.Sci., Math.R.
●Also available online. Vendor(s): DIALOG.
—BLDSC shelfmark: 4757.876000.

500 CC ISSN 1000-5897
HARBIN KEXUE JISHU DAXUE XUEBAO/HARBIN UNIVERSITY OF SCIENCE AND TECHNOLOGY. JOURNAL. (Text in Chinese) q. Harbin Kexue Jishu Daxue, Xuebao Bianjibu, 22, Xuefu Lu, Nangang-qu, Harbin, Heilongjiang 150080, People's Republic of China. TEL 61081. Ed. Ren Shanzhi.

500 CC ISSN 1000-5617
HARBIN SHIFAN DAXUE ZIRAN KEXUE XUEBAO/HARBIN NORMAL UNIVERSITY. JOURNAL OF NATURAL SCIENCES. (Text in Chinese) q. Harbin Shifan Daxue, Xuebao Bianjibu, 24, Hexing Lu, Nangang-qu, Harbin, Heilongjiang 150080, People's Republic of China. TEL 62912. Ed. Han Junjie.

500 CC ISSN 1000-5854
HEBEI SHIFAN DAXUE XUEBAO (ZIRAN KEXUE BAN)/HEBEI NORMAL UNIVERSITY. JOURNAL (NATURAL SCIENCE EDITION). (Text in Chinese) q. Hebei Shifan Daxue - Hebei Normal University, Yuhua Lu, Shijiazhuang, Hebei 050016, People's Republic of China. TEL 49941. Ed. Jin Shixun.

500 US ISSN 0073-1595
CODEN: HSCLAA
HEIDELBERG SCIENCE LIBRARY. 1967. irreg.; unnumbered after vol.22. price varies. Springer-Verlag, 175 Fifth Ave., New York, NY 10010. TEL 212-460-1500. (Also Berlin, Heidelberg, Vienna) (reprint service avail. from ISI) Indexed: Biol.Abstr.

500 US ISSN 0371-0165
AS182 CODEN: SHWMAL
HEIDELBERGER AKADEMIE DER WISSENSCHAFTEN. MATHEMATISCH-NATURWISSENSCHAFTLICHE KLASSE. SITZUNGSBERICHTE. 1948. irreg. price varies. Springer-Verlag, 175 Fifth Ave, New York, NY 10010. TEL 212-460-1500. (Also Berlin, Heidelberg, Tokyo and Vienna) (reprint service avail. from ISI) Indexed: Nutr.Abstr.

500 US ISSN 0073-1633
HEIDELBERGER ARBEITSBUECHER. 1971. irreg. price varies. Springer-Verlag, 175 Fifth Ave., New York, NY 10010. TEL 212-460-1500. (Also Berlin, Heidelberg, Vienna) (reprint service avail. from ISI)

500 US ISSN 0073-1641
AS181 CODEN: HDJBAC
HEIDELBERGER JAHRBUECHER. 1957. a. price varies. (Universitaets-Gesellschaft Heidelberg, GW) Springer-Verlag, 175 Fifth Ave., New York, NY 10010. TEL 212-460-1500. (Also Berlin, Heidelberg, Tokyo and Vienna) Ed. H. Schipperges. (reprint service avail. from ISI) Indexed: Amer.Hist.& Life, Biol.Abstr., Hist.Abstr.

500 GW ISSN 0935-6576
HEIDELBERGER STUDIEN ZUR NATURKUNDE DER FRUEHEN NEUZEIT. irreg., vol.2, 1990. price varies. Franz Steiner Verlag Wiesbaden GmbH, Birkenwaldstr. 44, Postfach 101526, 7000 Stuttgart 1, Germany. TEL 0711-2582-0. FAX 0711-2582290. Eds. Wolf-Dieter Mueller-Jahncke, Joachim Telle.

500 US ISSN 0073-1684
CODEN: HDTSAB
HEIDELBERGER TASCHENBUECHER. 1964. irreg. price varies. Springer-Verlag, 175 Fifth Ave., New York, NY 10010. TEL 212-460-1500. (Also Berlin, Heidelberg, Tokyo and Vienna) (reprint service avail. from ISI) Indexed: Biol.Abstr.

500 CC ISSN 1001-7011
HEILONGJIANG DAXUE ZIRAN KEXUE XUEBAO/HEILONGJIANG UNIVERSITY. JOURNAL OF NATURAL SCIENCES. (Text in Chinese) q. Heilongjiang Daxue, Xuebao Bianjibu, Xuefu Lu, Nangang-qu, Harbin, Heilongjiang 150083, People's Republic of China. TEL 64941.

500 CC ISSN 1000-2472
HENAN DAXUE XUEBAO (ZIRAN KEXUE BAN)/HENAN UNIVERSITY. JOURNAL (NATURAL SCIENCE EDITION). (Text in Chinese) q. Henan Daxue, Xuebao Bianjibu, Kaifeng, Henan 475001, People's Republic of China. TEL 25966. Ed. Song Yingli.

500 CC ISSN 1000-2367
HENAN SHIFAN DAXUE XUEBAO (ZIRAN KEXUE BAN)/HENAN NORMAL UNIVERSITY. JOURNAL (NATURAL SCIENCE EDITION). (Text in Chinese) q. Henan Shifan Daxue, Xuebao Bianjibu, Xinxiang, Henan 453002, People's Republic of China. TEL 54921. Ed. Ding Chengjie.

500.9 GW ISSN 0018-0637
CODEN: HERCAS
HERCYNIA; Beitraege zur Erforschung und Pflege der Natuerlichen Ressourcen. N.S. 1963. 4/yr. DM.60 per no. (Martin-Luther-Universitaet Halle-Wittenberg, Mathematisch-Naturwissenschaftliche Fakultaet) Akademische Verlagsgesellschaft Geest und Portig K.G., Sternwartenstr. 8, 7010 Leipzig, Germany. Ed. R. Piechocki. bk.rev.; bibl.; charts; illus.; maps. Indexed: Agri.Eng.Abstr., Biol.Abstr., Chem.Abstr., Excerp.Med., Forest.Abstr., Herb.Abstr., Irr.& Drain.Abstr., Maize Abstr., Triticale Abstr., Weed Abstr.
—BLDSC shelfmark: 4298.310000.
Description: Covers biosciences, geography, plant life, and ecology.

500.9 JA ISSN 0389-5491
HIBA KAGAKU/HIBA SOCIETY OF NATURAL HISTORY. JOURNAL. (Text in Japanese) 1947. 3/yr. $30. Hiba Science Educational Foundation - Hiba Kagaku Kyoiku Shinkokai, 179-1 Setoyama, Shobara-shi, Hiroshima-ken 727, Japan.
Description: Contains original articles as well as reviews and commentary.

500 JA ISSN 0367-6439
Q4 CODEN: HUSRAK
HIROSAKI UNIVERSITY. FACULTY OF SCIENCE. SCIENCE REPORTS/HIROSAKI DAIGAKU RIKA HOKOKU. (Text in English, Japanese) 1954. 2/yr. free. Hirosaki Daigaku, Rigakubu - Hirosaki University, Faculty of Science, 3 Bunkyo-cho, Hirosaki-shi, Aomori-ken 036, Japan. FAX 0172-33-2524. Ed.Bd. circ. 500. Indexed: Biol.Abstr., Deep Sea Res.& Oceanogr.Abstr., Math.R.
—BLDSC shelfmark: 8153.300000.
Formerly: Hirosaki University. Faculty of Literature and Science. Science Reports (ISSN 0439-1705)
Description: Contains research reports written by members of the Faculty of Science and College of General Arts, Hirosaki University.

500 FR ISSN 0073-2362
HISTOIRE DE LA PENSEE. 1960. irreg. price varies. Editions Hermann, 293 rue Lecourbe, 75015 Paris, France. TEL 45-57-45-40.

500.9 FR ISSN 1141-4588
HISTOIRE DES SCIENCES ET DES TECHNIQUES. 1969. irreg., no.5, 1991. price varies. Editions de l' Ecole des Hautes Etudes en Sciences Sociales, 131 bd. St-Michel, 75005 Paris, France. TEL 43-54-47-15. FAX 43-54-80-73. (Dist. by: Centre Interinstitutionnel pour la Diffusion de Publications en Sciences Humaines, 131 bd St-Michel, 75005 Paris, France)

500 US ISSN 0761-1102
HISTOIRE DES SCIENCES ET DES TECHNIQUES. irreg., latest vol.2. Gordon and Breach Scientific Publishers, 270 Eighth Ave., New York, NY 10011. TEL 212-206-8900. FAX 212-645-2459. TELEX 236735 GOPUB UR. (Subscr. to: Box 786, Cooper Sta., New York, NY 10276. TEL 800-545-8398; UK subscr. to: P.O. Box 90, Reading, Berkshire RG1 8JL, England. TEL 0734-560-090) Eds. R. Hahn, M. Levy.
—BLDSC shelfmark: 0675.195600.
Refereed Serial

500.9 FR
HISTOIRE ET NATURE. (Text in French; summaries in English and French) 1968. s-a. 50 F. Association pour l'Histoire des Sciences de la Nature, 38 rue Geoffroy Saint-Hilaire, 75005 Paris, France. Ed. Y. Laissus. bibl.; illus.; circ. 350. (also avail. in microfilm; microfiche; back issues avail.) Indexed: Bull.Signal.
Formerly (1968-1969): Histoire et Biologie.

509 JA ISSN 0285-4821
Q124.6
HISTORIA SCIENTIARUM. (Text in English) 1962. a. 3,000 Yen. Nippon Kagakushi Gakkai - History of Science Society of Japan, Nihonbashi Chuo Bldg. 91, 16-3-91, Nihonbashi 2-chome, Chuo-ku, Tokyo 103, Japan. Indexed: Amer.Hist.& Life, Hist.Abstr., Math.R.
—BLDSC shelfmark: 4316.060950.
Formerly (until 1980): Japanese Studies in the History of Science (ISSN 0090-0176)

500 SP ISSN 0073-2494
HISTORIA Y FILOSOFIA DE LA CIENCIA. SERIE MAYOR. ENCUADERNADA. 1938. irreg. price varies. Espasa-Calpe, S.A., Carretera de Irun 12200, Apartado 547, Madrid 34, Spain.

500 SP ISSN 0073-2508
HISTORIA Y FILOSOFIA DE LA CIENCIA. SERIE MENOR. RUSTICA. 1938. irreg. price varies. Espasa-Calpe, S.A., Carretera de Irun 12200, Apartado 547, Madrid 34, Spain.

500 GW ISSN 0073-2532
HISTORIAE SCIENTIARUM ELEMENTA. (Text in English, German and Latin) 1962. irreg., vol.5, 1973. price varies. (Werner Fritsch Verlag) Theodor Ackermann, Ludwigstr. 7, D-8000 Munich 22, Germany. TEL 284787. Ed. Werner Fritsch.

500 AT
HISTORICAL RECORDS OF AUSTRALIAN SCIENCE. 1966. s-m. Aus.$30 per issue. Australian Academy of Science, G.P.O. Box 783, Canberra, A.C.T. 2601, Australia. index; circ. 1,000. Indexed: AESIS, Deep Sea Res.& Oceanogr.Abstr., INIS Atomind.
Formerly: Australian Academy of Science. Records (ISSN 0067-155X)

500 600 900　　　　　IE
HISTORICAL STUDIES IN IRISH SCIENCE AND TECHNOLOGY. (Text in English) 1980. irreg., approx. a. price varies. Royal Dublin Society, Science and Arts Dept., Ballsbridge, Dublin 4, Ireland. TEL 680645. FAX 604014. Ed. R. Charles Mollan. (back issues avail.)

500　　　　　US　　ISSN 0890-9997
QC7　　　　　　　　CODEN: HSPSEW
HISTORICAL STUDIES IN THE PHYSICAL AND BIOLOGICAL SCIENCES. 1970. s-a. $20 to individuals (foreign $24); institutions $36 (foreign $40). University of California Press, Journals Division, 2120 Berkeley Way, Berkeley, CA 94720. TEL 510-642-4191. FAX 510-643-7127. Ed. J.L. Heilbron. adv.; circ. 800. (back issues avail.) **Indexed:** Amer.Hist.& Life, Chem.Abstr., Hist.Abstr.
—BLDSC shelfmark: 4317.069800.
Formerly: Historical Studies in the Physical Sciences (ISSN 0073-2672)
Description: Covers history of physics, biology, and other sciences.
Refereed Serial

500　　　　　US
HISTORICAL STUDIES IN THE PHYSICAL SCIENCES. 1977. irreg. price varies. Johns Hopkins University Press, 701 W. 40th St., Ste. 275, Baltimore, MD 21211. TEL 401-516-6987. FAX 410-516-6998. (reprint service avail. from UMI)

500　　　　　BE
HISTORISCHE DOCUMENTEN VAN DE WETENSCHAPPEN. (Editions in Dutch and French) 1966. irreg. price varies. Belgisch Komitee voor de Geschiedenis der Wetenschappen, Koninklyke Bibliotheek, Keizerslaan 4, B-1000 Brussels, Belgium.

500 507　　　　　UK　　ISSN 0073-2753
Q125　　　　　　　　CODEN: HISCAR
HISTORY OF SCIENCE; review of literature and research. 1962. 4/yr. £61($122) Science History Publications Ltd, Halfpenny Furze, Mill Lane, Chalfont St. Giles, Bucks HP8 4NR, England. TEL 02407-2509. Ed. R.S. Porter. adv.; bk.rev.; illus.; index; circ. 800. (back issues avail.) **Indexed:** Amer.Hist.& Life, Hist.Abstr., Math.R.
—BLDSC shelfmark: 4318.460000.
Description: Review of literature and research on the history of science, medicine and technology in its intellectual and social context.

700 500　　　　　JA　　ISSN 0073-2788
AS551
HITOTSUBASHI JOURNAL OF ARTS AND SCIENCES. (Text in English, French or German) 1960. a. Hitotsubashi Daigaku, Hitotsubashi Gakkai - Hitotsubashi University, Hitotsubashi Academy, 2-1 Naka, Kunitachi-shi, Tokyo 186, Japan. Ed. Koji Arai. cum.index; circ. 900. **Indexed:** M.L.A., Math.R.

500.9　　　　　JA　　ISSN 0285-5615
HIWA KAGAKU HAKUBUTSUKAN KENKYU HOKOKU/HIWA MUSEUM FOR NATURAL HISTORY. MISCELLANEOUS REPORTS. (Text and summaries in Japanese and English) 1958. a. $10. Hiwa Museum for Natural History - Hiwa Kagaku Hakubutsukan, Hiwa, Hiwa-cho, Hiba-gun, Hiroshima-ken 727-03, Japan.

500　　　　　JA　　ISSN 0386-4464
HOKKAIDO KYOIKU DAIGAKU TAISETSUZAN SHIZEN KYOIKU KENKYU SHISETSU KENKYU HOKOKU/HOKKAIDO UNIVERSITY OF EDUCATION. TAISETSUZAN INSTITUTE OF SCIENCE. REPORTS. (Text in Japanese; summaries in English and Japanese) a. Hokkaido University of Education, Taisetsuzan Institute of Science - Hokkaido Kyoiku Daigaku Taisetsuzan Shizen Kyoiku Kenkyu Shisetsu, 9 Kitakado-cho, Asahikawa-shi, Hokkaido 070, Japan. **Indexed:** Jap.Per.Ind.

500 028.5　　　　　AA
HORIZONTI. 1979. m. Bashkimi i Rinise se Punes te Shqiperise - Union of Working Youth of Albania, Tirana, Albania. TEL 42-29204. Ed. Thanas Qerama. circ. 18,850.

500　　　　　CC　　ISSN 1000-5641
HUADONG SHIFAN DAXUE XUEBAO (ZIRAN KEXUE BAN)/EAST CHINA NORMAL UNIVERSITY. JOURNAL (NATURAL SCIENCE EDITION). (Text in Chinese) q. Huadong Shifan Daxue - East China Normal University, c/o Library, 3663 Zhongshan Beilu, Shanghai 200062, People's Republic of China. TEL 2577577.

500 600　　　　　CC　　ISSN 1000-565X
HUANAN LIGONG DAXUE XUEBAO (ZIRAN KEXUE BAN)/SOUTH-CHINA UNIVERSITY OF SCIENCE AND ENGINEERING. JOURNAL (NATURAL SCIENCE EDITION). (Text in Chinese) Huanan Ligong Daxue, Xuebao Bianjibu, Wushan, Guangzhou, Guangdong 510641, People's Republic of China. TEL 511311. Ed. Xu Bingzheng.

500　　　　　CC　　ISSN 1000-5463
HUANAN SHIFAN DAXUE XUEBAO (ZIRAN KEXUE BAN)/SOUTH-CHINA NORMAL UNIVERSITY. JOURNAL (NATURAL SCIENCE EDITION). (Text in Chinese) s-a. Huanan Shifan Daxue, Xuebao Bianjibu, Shipai, Guangzhou, Guangdong 510631, People's Republic of China. TEL 516911. Ed. Liu Weilin.

500　　　　　CC　　ISSN 1000-5013
HUAQIAO DAXUE XUEBAO (ZIRAN KEXUE BAN)/HUAQIAO UNIVERSITY. JOURNAL (NATURAL SCIENCE EDITION). (Text in Chinese) q. Y8. Huaqiao Daxue - Huaqiao University, c/o Huaqiao Daxue Tushuguan, Quanzhou, Fujian 362011, People's Republic of China. TEL 224921. (Dist. overseas by: Jiangsu Publications Import & Export Corp., 56 Gao Yun Ling, Nanjing, Jiangsu, P.R.C.) Ed. Shi Yushan.
Description: Carries scientific essays on theories of basic and applied sciences, new technologies, designs and products. Includes foreign news.

500 600　　　　　CC　　ISSN 1000-8616
HUAZHONG LIGONG DAXUE XUEBAO/CENTRAL-CHINA UNIVERSITY OF SCIENCE AND ENGINEERING. JOURNAL. (Text in Chinese) bi-m. Huazhong Ligong Daxue, Xuebao Bianjibu, Yujiashan, Wuchang-qu, Wuhan, Hubei 430074, People's Republic of China. TEL 701154. Ed. Kang Huaguang.
—BLDSC shelfmark: 4758.967800.

500　　　　　CC　　ISSN 1000-1190
HUAZHONG SHIFAN DAXUE XUEBAO (ZIRAN KEXUE BAN)/CENTRAL-CHINA NORMAL UNIVERSITY. JOURNAL (NATURAL SCIENCE EDITION). (Text in Chinese) q. Huazhong Shifan Daxue, Xuebao Bianjibu, Guizishan, Wuchang-qu, Wuhan, Hubei 430070, People's Republic of China. TEL 715601. Ed. Deng Zongqi.

500 300　　　　　GW
HUMBOLDT - UNIVERSITAET ZU BERLIN. WISSENSCHAFTLICHE ZEITSCHRIFT: REIHE GEISTES- UND SOZIALWISSENSCHAFT. (Text in English and German) 1951. 10/yr. DM.23 per no. Humboldt-Universitaet zu Berlin, Mittel Str. 7-8, 1086 Berlin, Germany. bk.rev.; charts; illus.; index, cum.index; circ. 1,000. **Indexed:** Anim.Breed.Abstr., Biol.Abstr., Chem.Abstr., Hist.Abstr., Ind.Vet., Math.R., Rural Recreat.Tour.Abstr., Vet.Bull., VITIS, World Agri.Econ.& Rural Sociol.Abstr.
Formerly: Humboldt - Universitaet zu Berlin. Wissenschaftliche Zeitschrift: Reihe Gesellschaftswissenschaft.

500　　　　　CC　　ISSN 1000-2537
　　　　　　　　　　　　CODEN: HSDXEL
HUNAN SHIFAN DAXUE XUEBAO (ZIRAN KEXUE BAN)/HUNAN NORMAL UNIVERSITY. JOURNAL (NATURAL SCIENCE EDITION). (Text in Chinese; summaries in English) 1956. q. Y8. Hunan Shifan Daxue, Xuebao Bianjibu, Yuelushan, Changsha, Hunan 410081, People's Republic of China. TEL 83131. TELEX 0097. (Dist. outside China by: China International Book Trading Corporation, P.O. Box 399, Beijing, People's Republic of China) Ed. Gong Weizhong. index; circ. 3,000. (back issues avail.; reprint service avail. from UMI) **Indexed:** Chem.Abstr.
—BLDSC shelfmark: 0663.188000.
Description: Academic journal of scientific research in the natural sciences.

500 374.1　　　　　JA　　ISSN 0911-6230
HYOGO KYOIKU DAIGAKU KENKYU KIYO. DAI-3-BUNSATSU. SHIZENKEI KYOIKU, SEIKATSU KENKOKEI KYOIKU/HYOGO UNIVERSITY OF TEACHER EDUCATION JOURNAL. SERIES 3: NATURAL SCIENCE, PRACTICAL LIFE STUDIES. (Text in English and Japanese; summaries in English) a. Hyogo University of Teacher Education - Hyogo Kyoiku Daigaku, 942-1 Shimokume, Yashiro-cho, Kato-gun, Hyogo-ken 673-14, Japan. abstr.

500　　　　　US　　ISSN 0075-0344
I A S BULLETIN. 1967. irreg. Iowa Academy of Science, Sci. 3538, University of Northern Iowa, Cedar Falls, IA 50614. TEL 319-273-2021.

I A T U L QUARTERLY. (International Association of Technological Universities Libraries) see *LIBRARY AND INFORMATION SCIENCES*

I C A C H; organo de divulgacion cultural. (Instituto de Ciencias y Artes de Chiapas) see *ART*

500　　　　　FR
I C S U NEWSLETTER; science international. (Text in English) 1964. q. International Council of Scientific Unions, 51 bd. de Montmorency, 75016 Paris, France. Ed. J. Marton-Lefevre. circ. 5,000.
Former titles: I C S U AB News (ISSN 0253-5572); (until 1980): I C S U Bulletin (ISSN 0536-132X)

500.1　　　　　SG　　ISSN 0018-9634
QH3　　　　　　　　CODEN: BASNB7
I F A N BULLETIN. SERIE A: SCIENCES NATURELLES. (Text in French; occasionally in English or other languages) 1954. q. 190 F. Institut Fondamental d'Afrique Noire - Cheikh Anta Diop, B.P. 206, Dakar, Senegal. Ed. Abdoulaye Bara Diop. bk.rev.; charts; illus. (reprint service avail. from SWZ) **Indexed:** Biol.Abstr., Deep Sea Res.& Oceanogr.Abstr., Field Crop Abstr., Geo.Abstr., Helminthol.Abstr., Herb.Abstr., Rev.Appl.Entomol.

500　　　　　US　　ISSN 0019-0144
I N F O JOURNAL; science and the unknown. 1966. q. $12 (foreign $16). International Fortean Organization, Box 367, Arlington, VA 22210-0367. TEL 703-522-9232. Ed. Raymond D. Manners. adv.; bk.rev.; illus.; cum.index: 1966-1985; circ. 2,000. (also avail. in microfilm from UMI; back issues avail.; reprint service avail. from UMI) **Indexed:** Abstr.Folk.Stud., Biol.Dig.
Description: Study of anomalies and unexplainable happenings in science and related areas.

500　　　　　FR　　ISSN 0992-0692
I N I S T - INFO. (Text in English, French) q. Institut de l'Information Scientifique et Technique, INIST - CNRS, 2 allee du Parc de Brabois, 54514 Vandoeuvre-les-Nancy Cedex, France. TEL 83-50-46-00. FAX 83-50-46-50. Ed. Nathalie Dusoulier.
—BLDSC shelfmark: 4513.955000.
Description: Information on activities, products, services of I N I S T and new technologies used for information processing.

500　　　　　BL　　ISSN 0019-0233
　　　　　　　　　　　　CODEN: ININDP
I N T INFORMATIVO. (Abstract in English and Portuguese) 1968. 3/yr. free. Instituto Nacional de Tecnologia, Av. Venezuela 82, 20081 Cais do Porto, Rio de Janeiro RJ, Brazil. FAX 021-263-9390. TELEX 21-30056 FINT BR. (Co-sponsor: Secretariat of Science and Technology) Ed. Gilda Massari Coelho. bk.rev.; circ. 3,000. **Indexed:** Chem.Abstr., INIS Atomind., Met.Abstr.

500　　　　　GW　　ISSN 0179-5775
I P N - BLAETTER. 1984. q. Institut fuer die Paedagogik der Naturwissenschaften, Olshausenstr. 62, 2300 Kiel 1, Germany. TEL 0431-8803123. FAX 0431-880-1521. bk.rev.; circ. 7,000. (back issues avail.)

500　　　　　UK　　ISSN 0308-0188
Q1　　　　　　　　CODEN: ISCRD8
I S R - INTERDISCIPLINARY SCIENCE REVIEWS. 1976. q. £35($72) individuals; institutions £115($225). Institute of Materials, 1 Carlton House Terrace, London SW1Y 5DB, England. TEL 071-839-4071. FAX 071-839-2078. Ed. Anthony Michaelis. adv.; bk.rev. **Indexed:** Chem.Abstr., Curr.Cont., Field Crop Abstr., Sci.Abstr.
—BLDSC shelfmark: 4533.357000.
Description: Covers global warming, molecular electronics, languages and the search for extra terrestrial intelligence, as well as the potential and limits of socially organized humankind for specialists and students of all scientific disciplines worldwide.

500　　　　　JA　　ISSN 0386-7668
IBARAKI DAIGAKU KYOIKUGAKUBU KIYO, SHIZEN KAGAKU/IBARAKI UNIVERSITY. FACULTY OF EDUCATION. BULLETIN. NATURAL SCIENCES. (Text in Japanese; summaries in English and Japanese) a. Ibaraki Daigaku, Kyoikugakubu - Ibaraki University, Faculty of Education, 1-1, Bunkyo 2-chome, Mito-shi, Ibaraki-ken 310, Japan. **Indexed:** Jap.Per.Ind.

IBYKUS; Zeitschrift fuer Poesie, Wissenschaft und Staatskunst. see *LITERATURE — Poetry*

SCIENCES: COMPREHENSIVE WORKS

IDAHO MUSEUM OF NATURAL HISTORY. OCCASIONAL PAPERS. see *MUSEUMS AND ART GALLERIES*

IKUTOKU KOGYO DAIGAKU KENKYU HOKOKU. B RIKOGAKU HEN/IKUTOKU TECHNICAL UNIVERSITY. RESEARCH REPORTS. PART B. SCIENCE AND TECHNOLOGY. see *TECHNOLOGY: COMPREHENSIVE WORKS*

ILLINOIS. NATURAL HISTORY SURVEY. REPORTS. see *CONSERVATION*

ILLINOIS. STATE MUSEUM. INVENTORY OF THE COLLECTIONS. see *MUSEUMS AND ART GALLERIES*

500 US ISSN 0360-0297
ILLINOIS. STATE MUSEUM. POPULAR SCIENCE SERIES. 1939. irreg., vol.9, 1978. price varies. Illinois State Museum, Springfield, IL 62706. TEL 217-782-7386. FAX 217-782-1254. illus. **Indexed:** GeoRef. Key Title: Popular Science Series.
Refereed Serial

500 US ISSN 0360-0270
CODEN: ISRIB
ILLINOIS. STATE MUSEUM. REPORTS OF INVESTIGATIONS. 1948. irreg., no.46, 1991. price varies. Illinois State Museum, Springfield, IL 62706. TEL 217-782-7386. FAX 217-782-1254. bibl.; charts; illus. **Indexed:** Biol.Abstr. Key Title: Reports of Investigations - Illinois State Museum.

557 970 570 US ISSN 0445-3395
ILLINOIS. STATE MUSEUM. SCIENTIFIC PAPERS SERIES. 1940. irreg., vol.23, 1991. price varies. Illinois State Museum, Springfield, IL 62706. TEL 217-782-7386. FAX 217-782-1254. illus.
Refereed Serial

500 US ISSN 0360-0289
ILLINOIS. STATE MUSEUM. STORY OF ILLINOIS SERIES. 1943. irreg., no.14, 1982. Illinois State Museum, Springfield, IL 62706. TEL 217-782-7386. FAX 217-782-1254.

500 US ISSN 0019-2252
Q11 CODEN: TISAAH
ILLINOIS STATE ACADEMY OF SCIENCE. TRANSACTIONS. 1908. q. membership. Illinois State Academy of Sciences, Illinois State Museum, Springfield, IL 62706. TEL 217-782-7386. Ed. Barry A. Fiedel. charts; illus.; circ. 1,400. (also avail. in microform from UMI) **Indexed:** Biol.Abstr., Chem.Abstr., Excerp.Med., Field Crop Abstr., Herb.Abstr., Ind.Vet., Math.R., Plant Breed.Abstr., Poult.Abstr., Protozool.Abstr., Rev.Plant Path., Soils & Fert., World Agri.Econ.& Rural Sociol.Abstr.
—BLDSC shelfmark: 8935.000000.
Refereed Serial

500 DK ISSN 0109-2456
ILLUSTRERET VIDENSKAB. (Editions in Danish, German, Finnish, French, Norwegian, Swedish) 1984. m. Bonniers Specialmagasiner A-S, Strandboulevarden 130, 2100 Copenhagen OE, Denmark. Ed. Birgitte Engen. illus.
Description: Examines the natural sciences and social sciences: psychology, biology, astronomy, geography, medicine, anthropology, geology and archaeology; also deals with new technology.

500 UN ISSN 0019-2872
Q1 CODEN: ISSOA8
IMPACT OF SCIENCE ON SOCIETY. (Editions in various languages) 1950. q. $65. Taylor & Francis Ltd., 4 John St., London WC1N 2ET, England. TEL 071-405-2237. (U.S. subscr. to: 1900 Frost Rd., Ste. 101, Bristol, PA 19007) (Co-publisher: Unesco) Ed. Howard J. Moore. illus.; circ. 4,185. (also avail. in microform from MIM,KTO; reprint service avail. from KTO,UMI) **Indexed:** Agroforest.Abstr., ASSIA, Biol.Abstr., C.I.J.E., Chem.Abstr., Curr.Adv.Ecol.Sci., Curr.Cont., Energy Rev., Environ.Per.Bibl., Fut.Surv., Geo.Abstr., High.Educ.Curr.Aware.Bull., Ind.Sci.Rev., Int.Lab.Doc., Key to Econ.Sci., Lang.& Lang.Behav.Abstr., Mar.Aff.Bibl., Mid.East: Abstr.& Ind., P.A.I.S., Pt.de Rep., Rural Recreat.Tour.Abstr., Sci.Cit.Ind, Soc.Sci.Ind., SSCI, Telegen, World Agri.Econ.& Rural Sociol.Abstr.
—BLDSC shelfmark: 4371.000000.
Description: Aims to stimulate wide public debate on timely issues concerning the interaction between science, technology and society.
Refereed Serial

500 SA
IMPULSE. (Not published 1974-76) 1971. q. free. University of Cape Town, Science Students' Council, Private Bag, Rondebosch 7700, South Africa. TEL 021 698531. Eds. C.L. Ward, G. Wheeler. adv.; bk.rev.; bibl.; charts; illus.; circ. 1,500.

200 AU
IMPULSE AUS WISSENSCHAFT UND FORSCHUNG. 1986. a. DM.27. Resch Verlag, Maximilianstr. 8, A-6010 Innsbruck, Austria. TEL 0512-574772. Ed. Andreas Resch. circ. 500.

500.9 US ISSN 1051-4546
AM101.C58
IN THE FIELD. 1930. bi-m. $6. (Field Museum of Natural History) Field Museum Press, Roosevelt Rd. at Lake Shore Dr., Chicago, IL 60605-2498. TEL 312-922-9410. FAX 312-427-7269. Ed. Ron Dorfman. illus.; index; circ. 24,000. (also avail. in microfiche from BHP; reprint service avail. from UMI) **Indexed:** So.Pac.Per.Ind.
Formerly (until Jun. 1990): Field Museum of Natural History Bulletin (ISSN 0015-0703); Chicago Natural History Museum. Bulletin.

500 600 II ISSN 0085-1779
INDIA. DEPARTMENT OF SCIENCE & TECHNOLOGY. ANNUAL REPORT. (Text in English) 1969. a. Ministry of Science and Technology, Department of Science & Technology, New Delhi 110 016, India. FAX 0091-652731. TELEX 3166096 DST IN. charts; stat.; circ. 5,000.
Formerly: India. Committee on Science and Technology. Annual Report.

500 II ISSN 0019-4964
Q1 CODEN: JIISAD
INDIAN INSTITUTE OF SCIENCE. JOURNAL. (Text in English) 1914. bi-m. Rs.120($40) Indian Institute of Science, Bangalore 560 012, India. TEL 812-344411.2256. FAX 812-341683. TELEX 0845-8349. Ed. M. Vijayan. adv.; bk.rev.; abstr.; bibl.; charts; illus.; index; circ. 500. (also avail. in microfilm from UMI; reprint service avail. from UMI) **Indexed:** Abstr.Hyg., Appl.Mech.Rev., Biol.Abstr., Biotech.Abstr., Chem.Abstr., Curr.Adv.Ecol.Sci., Curr.Cont, Deep Sea Res.& Oceanogr.Abstr., Eng.Ind., Excerp.Med., Forest.Abstr., Helminthol.Abstr., INIS Atomind., Int.Aerosp.Abstr., Math.R., Met.Abstr., Nutr.Abstr., Phys.Abstr., Sci.Abstr., Soils & Fert., Trop.Dis.Bull.

509 II ISSN 0019-5235
Q125 CODEN: IJHSA4
INDIAN JOURNAL OF HISTORY OF SCIENCE. 1966. q. Rs.200 (foreign 344.50 Fr.). Indian National Science Academy, Bahadur Shah Zafar Marg, New Delhi 110 002, India. TEL 61-6918925. FAX 61-6924262. TELEX 963475. (Dist. outside Sub-continent area by: J.C. Baltzer A.G., Wettsteinplatz 10, CH-4058 Basel, Switzerland) Ed. S.K. Mukherjee. bk.rev.; illus.; index; circ. 300. **Indexed:** Art & Archaeol.Tech.Abstr., Math.R.
—BLDSC shelfmark: 4414.700000.

INDIAN JOURNAL OF PHYSICS AND PROCEEDINGS OF THE INDIAN ASSOCIATION FOR THE CULTIVATION OF SCIENCE. see *PHYSICS*

500 II ISSN 0019-5669
T1 CODEN: IJOTA8
INDIAN JOURNAL OF TECHNOLOGY. (Text in English) 1963. m. Rs.300($150) (Council of Scientific and Industrial Research, Publications & Information Directorate) Scientific Publishers, P.O. Box 91, 5A, New Pali Rd., Jodhpur 342 001, India. TEL 0291-33323. Eds. S. Arunachalam, S. Hirannaiah. adv.; bibl.; charts; illus.; index; circ. 1,200. (also avail. in microform from UMI; back issues avail.; reprint service avail. from UMI) **Indexed:** Anal.Abstr., Appl.Mech.Rev., Biol.Abstr., CAD CAM Abstr., Cadscan, Ceram.Abstr., Chem.Abstr., Chem.Eng.Abstr., Curr.Cont., Dairy Sci.Abstr., Energy Ind., Energy Info.Abstr., Eng.Ind., Excerp.Med., Fluidex, Food Sci.& Tech.Abstr., Gas Abstr., Geotech.Abstr., INIS Atomind., Lead Abstr., Met.Abstr., Nutr.Abstr., Sci.Abstr., Soils & Fert., T.C.E.A., World Alum.Abstr., World Text.Abstr., Zincscan.
—BLDSC shelfmark: 4421.400000.

INDIAN NATIONAL SCIENCE ACADEMY. BIOGRAPHICAL MEMOIRS OF FELLOWS. see *BIOGRAPHY*

500 II ISSN 0378-6242
CODEN: BIDNAL
INDIAN NATIONAL SCIENCE ACADEMY. BULLETIN. 1952. irreg. price varies per issue. Indian National Science Academy, Bahadur Shah Zafar Marg, New Delhi 110002, India. abstr.; charts; illus.; circ. 600. **Indexed:** GeoRef., Sci.Abstr.
Formerly: National Institute of Sciences of India. Bulletin (ISSN 0027-9528)

500 II ISSN 0073-6600
QH301 CODEN: PIBSBB
INDIAN NATIONAL SCIENCE ACADEMY. PROCEEDINGS. (Text in English) 1935; in separate pts. since 1955. Parts A (Physical Sciences) and B (Biological Sciences) published in alternate months. Rs.500 (foreign 1005 Fr.). Indian National Science Academy, Bahadur Shah Zafar Marg, New Delhi 110 002, India. TEL 61-6918925. FAX 61-6924262. TELEX 963475. (Dist. outside Sub-continent area by: J.C. Baltzer A.G., Wettsteinplatz 10, CH-4058 Basel, Switzerland) circ. 1,000. **Indexed:** Biol.Abstr., Chem.Abstr., Cott.&Trop.Fibr.Abstr., Deep Sea Res.& Oceanogr.Abstr., Excerp.Med., Field Crop Abstr., GeoRef., Irr.& Drain.Abstr., Maize Abstr., Math.R., Met.Abstr., Nutr.Abstr., Rural Devel.Abstr., Sci.Abstr., Sci.Abstr., Soils & Fert.
—BLDSC shelfmark: 6711.800000.
Formerly: National Institute of Sciences of India. Proceedings.

500 II ISSN 0073-6619
Q73
INDIAN NATIONAL SCIENCE ACADEMY. YEAR BOOK. (Text in English) 1960. a. Rs.80($27) Indian National Science Academy, Bahadur Shah Zafar Marg, New Delhi 110002, India. circ. 1,000. **Indexed:** Biol.Abstr.
Former titles: National Institute of Sciences of India. Yearbook (ISSN 0547-7573); National Institute of Sciences of India, Calcutta. Year Book.

500 600 II ISSN 0085-1817
INDIAN SCIENCE CONGRESS ASSOCIATION. PROCEEDINGS. (Text in English) 1914. a. Rs.200. Indian Science Congress Association, 14 Dr. Biresh Guha St., Calcutta 700017, India. index; circ. 5,000. **Indexed:** Biol.Abstr.
—BLDSC shelfmark: 6844.220000.

500 II ISSN 0970-4256
INDIAN SCIENCE CRUISER. 1987. s-a. Rs.25($25) to non-members (effective 1992). Institute of Science, Education and Culture, 42-B Syed Amir Ali Avenue, Calcutta 700 017, India. Ed. Murali Mohan Biswas. adv.; bk.rev.; circ. 450.
—BLDSC shelfmark: 4429.510000.
Description: Disseminates knowledge of science and scientific information.

500 US ISSN 0073-6759
INDIANA ACADEMY OF SCIENCE. MONOGRAPH. 1969. Irreg. price varies. Indiana Academy of Science, 140 N. Senate Ave., Indianapolis, IN 46204. TEL 317-232-3686. **Indexed:** Biol.Abstr.

500 US ISSN 0073-6767
Q11 CODEN: PIACAP
INDIANA ACADEMY OF SCIENCE. PROCEEDINGS. 1891. q. $12 per no. Indiana Academy of Science, 140 N. Senate Ave., Indianapolis, IN 46204. TEL 317-232-3686. Ed. Gary Dolph. cum.index: 1891-1980, vols.1-90. **Indexed:** Biol.Abstr., Chem.Abstr., Crop Physiol.Abstr., Field Crop Abstr., GeoRef., Herb.Abstr., Maize Abstr., Seed Abstr., Soils & Fert., Soyabean Abstr., Triticale Abstr., Vet.Bull., Weed Abstr.

500 MX ISSN 0185-0261
Q23 CODEN: ICTEEB
INFORMACION CIENTIFICA Y TECNOLOGICA. 1979. m. $46 (foreign $57). Consejo Nacional de Ciencia y Tecnologia, Circuito Cultural Universitario, Cuidad Universitaria, Mexico 04515, D.F., Mexico. TEL 655-6366. FAX 655-3906. TELEX 017-74521. Ed. Juan Manuel Valero. adv.; illus.; circ. 39,000.

500 CU
INFORMACIONES ESPECIALES. fortn. Academia de Ciencias, Instituto de Documentacion e Informacion Cientifico-Tecnica (I D I C T), Capitolio Nacional, Prado y San Jose, Habana 2, Havana, Cuba.

INFORMATIKA ES TUDOMANYELEMZES. see *LIBRARY AND INFORMATION SCIENCES*

917 500   CN   ISSN 0315-2561
INFORMATION NORTH. 1968. 4/yr. included with subscr. to "Arctic". Arctic Institute of North America, University of Calgary, 2500 University Dr. N.W., Calgary, Alta. T2N 1N4, Canada. TEL 403-220-7515. FAX 403-282-4609. Ed. Karen M. McCullough. bk.rev.; circ. 2,800. (also avail. in microfilm from UMI; back issue avail.) Indexed: Can.Per.Ind., Curr.Adv.Ecol.Sci.
Formerly: Arctic Institute of North America. Newsletter (ISSN 0066-6963)
Description: Includes scholarly papers in the life, physical and social sciences, humanities, engineering and technology.
Refereed Serial

605   IR
INFORMATIONS ET NOUVEAUTES TECHNIQUES/ETTELA'AT VA TAZEHA-YE FANNI. (Text in French, Persian) 1961. irreg. free. Centre Francais d'Information Technique et Industrielle, 62 Forsat Ave., Shahreza Ave., Box 11-1555, Teheran, Iran. Eds. Aleksandr Gerigoriyans, Bahman Shahparast. circ. 800.

060   PL   ISSN 0537-667X
INFORMATOR NAUKI POLSKIEJ. 1958. a. 3450 Zl.($30) Centrum Informacji Naukowej, Technicznej i Ekonomicznej, Redakcja Informatora Nauki Polskiej, P.O. Box 355, 00-950 Warsaw, Poland. FAX 25-33-19. TELEX 813716 CINT PL. (Co-sponsor: Urzad Postepu Naukowo-Technicznego i Wdrozen) Ed. Mieczyslaw Stanczak. adv.; circ. 7,200.
—BLDSC shelfmark: 4496.720000.

INNOVATION. see *TECHNOLOGY: COMPREHENSIVE WORKS*

500   US
▼**INNOVATIONS.** 1992. q. free. Midwest Research Institute, 425 Volker Blvd., Kansas City, MO 64110. TEL 816-753-7600. FAX 816-753-8420. Ed. Deborah Beckett. circ. 5,000.
Description: Covers research and development in the areas of environment, health, renewable energy, engineering, and social and management sciences.

500 600   US   ISSN 1059-2091
▼**INNOVATIONS & IDEAS.** (Supplement avail.) 1991. a. $23.99. Publishing & Business Consultants, 951 S. Oxford, No. 109, Los Angeles, CA 90006. TEL 213-732-3477. (Subscr. to: Box 75392, Los Angeles, CA 90075) Ed. Atia Napoleon. adv.; circ. 100,000.
Previously announced as: American Innovation.
Description: Covers breakthroughs in scientific research and high technology fields, with emphasis on human applications.

INNOVATIONS-NACHRICHTEN. see *TECHNOLOGY: COMPREHENSIVE WORKS*

500   US   ISSN 0890-300X
INNOVATOR'S DIGEST. 1979. bi-w. $239 (Canada $279; elsewhere $349). InfoTeam Inc., Box 15640, Plantation, FL 33318-5640. TEL 305-473-9560. FAX 305-473-0544. (Co-sponsor: Merton Allen Associates)
●Also available online. Vendor(s): NewsNet (RD09).
—BLDSC shelfmark: 4515.491000.
Description: Covers worldwide innovative activities, accomplishments, and happenings in science, engineering, technology, manufacture, finance, management, marketing, and regulation.

500   II
    CODEN: TSSTA8
INSTITUT FRANCAIS DE PONDICHERY. PUBLICATIONS DU DEPARTEMENT D'ECOLOGIE. (Text and summaries in English, French) 1957. irreg. (approx. 3/yr.). price varies. Institut Francais de Pondichery - French Institute of Pondicherry, Box 33, Pondichery 605 001, India. TEL 413-24170. FAX 91-413-29534. TELEX 469224 FRAN IN. Ed. J.P. Pascal. index; circ. 500. Indexed: Biol.Abstr., Bull.Signal., Forest.Abstr., Forest Prod.Abstr.
Formed by the merger of: Institut Francais de Pondichery. Section Scientifique et Technique. Travaux. (ISSN 0073-8336) & Institut Francais de Pondichery. Section Scientifique et Technique. Travaux. Hors Serie (ISSN 0073-8344)

500   US   ISSN 0897-1013
INSTITUTE OF NOETIC SCIENCES. QUARTERLY BULLETIN. 1973. q. membership. Institute of Noetic Sciences, 475 Gate 5 Rd., Ste. 300, Sausalito, CA 94965. TEL 415-563-5650. Ed. Carol Guion. illus.; circ. 30,000. (back issues avail.) Indexed: PROMT.
Former titles: Institute of Noetic Sciences. Newsletter (ISSN 0888-3432); Institute of Noetic Sciences Investigations.
Description: Helps members to network through local study groups.

500   AO   ISSN 0020-3912
    CODEN: IANBBN
INSTITUTO DE INVESTIGACAO CIENTIFICA DE ANGOLA. BOLETIM. (Text in Portuguese; summaries in English, French and German) 1962. s-a. Instituto de Investigacao Cientifica de Angola, Departamento de Documentacao e Informacao, Caixa Postal 3244, Luanda, Angola. bibl.; charts. Indexed: Biol.Abstr.

500 600   AO   ISSN 0074-0098
INSTITUTO DE INVESTIGACAO CIENTIFICA DE ANGOLA. MEMORIAS E TRABALHOS. (Text in Portuguese; summaries in English, French, German) 1960. irreg., no.8, 1971. price varies. Instituto de Investigacao Cientifica de Angola, Departamento de Documentacao e Informacao, Box 3244, Luanda, Angola. abstr. (also avail. in microform)

500 600   AO   ISSN 0003-343X
Q180.A58   CODEN: RCIAA5
INSTITUTO DE INVESTIGACAO CIENTIFICA DE ANGOLA. RELATORIOS E COMMUNICACOES. 1962. irreg., no.25, 1973. Instituto de Investigacao Cientifica de Angola, Departamento de Documentacao e Informacao, Box 3244, Luanda, Angola.

500   PO
INSTITUTO DE INVESTIGACAO CIENTIFICA TROPICAL. ANUARIO DE ACTIVIDADES. 1986. a. Instituto de Investigacao Cientifica Tropical, Rua Jau, 54, 1300 Lisbon, Portugal. TEL 364-5321. FAX 364-2008. (Subscr. to: Centro de Documentacao e Informacao, Rua Jau 47, 1300 Lisbon, Portugal)

500   PO   ISSN 0870-0036
    CODEN: MIITEJ
INSTITUTO DE INVESTIGACAO CIENTIFICA TROPICAL. MEMORIAS. 1943, N.S. irreg. Instituto de Investigacao Cientifica Tropical, Rua Jau 54, 1300 Lisbon, Portugal. TEL 364-5321. FAX 364-2008. (Subscr. to: Centro de Documentacao e Informacao, Rua Jau 47, 1300 Lisbon) circ. 1,000.
Formerly: Junta de Investigacoes Cientifica do Ultramar. Memorias.

500   PO
INSTITUTO DE INVESTIGACAO CIENTIFICA TROPICAL. PLANO DE ACTIVIDADES. 1988. a. Instituto de Investigacao Cientifica Tropical, Rua Jau, 54, 1300 Lisbon, Portugal. TEL 364-5321. FAX 364-2008. (Subscr. to: Centro de Documentacao e Informacao, Rua Jau 47, 1300 Lisbon, Portugal)

500   PO
INSTITUTO DE INVESTIGACAO CIENTIFICA TROPICAL. RELATORIO DE ACTIVIDADES. 1987. a. Instituto de Investigacao Cientifica Tropical, Rua Jau, 54, 1300 Lisbon, Portugal. TEL 364-5321. FAX 364-2008. (Subscr. to: Centro de Documentacao e Informacao, Rua Jau 47, 1300 Lisbon, Portugal)

500   EC   ISSN 0010-7972
INSTITUTO ECUATORIANO DE CIENCIAS NATURALES. CONTRIBUCIONES. (Text in English and Spanish) 1937. s-a. exchange basis. Instituto Ecuatoriano de Ciencias Naturales, Apartado 408, Quito, Ecuador. Ed. Dr. M. Acosta-Solis. circ. 2,500. Indexed: Biol.Abstr.

500   DR   ISSN 0378-956X
T173.S2497
INSTITUTO TECNOLOGICO DE SANTO DOMINGO. DOCUMENTOS. 1976. irreg., no.6, 1981. free. Instituto Tecnologico de Santo Domingo, Apdo. Postal 249-2, Santo Domingo, Dominican Republic.

INTEGRATION. see *POLITICAL SCIENCE — International Relations*

INTER-AMERICAN COUNCIL FOR EDUCATION, SCIENCE, AND CULTURE. FINAL REPORT. see *EDUCATION*

500   VE   ISSN 0378-1844
Q4   CODEN: ITRCDB
INTERCIENCIA. (Text and summaries in English, Portuguese and Spanish) 1976. bi-m. $60 to institutions in developed countries; institutions in Latin America $45; individuals $18. Interciencia Association, Apdo. 51842, Caracas 1050 A, Venezuela. TEL 582-92-32-24. FAX 582-92-32-24. Ed. Dr. Marcel Roche. adv.; bk.rev.; circ. 3,000. (back issues avail.) Indexed: Biol.Abstr., Chic.Per.Ind., Crop Physiol.Abstr., Curr.Adv.Ecol.Sci., Curr.Cont., Deep Sea Res.& Oceanogr.Abstr., Energy Ind., Energy Info.Abstr., Environ.Abstr., Geo.Abstr., Helminthol.Abstr., Herb.Abstr., Hisp.Amer.Per.Ind., Ind.Sci.Rev., Ind.Vet., Plant Grow.Reg.Abstr., Sci.Cit.Ind, Vet.Bull., World Agri.Econ.& Rural Sociol.Abstr.
—BLDSC shelfmark: 4533.080000.
Description: Interdisciplinary approach to the study of science and technology.

INTERCOM (NEW YORK, 1960?). see *RELIGIONS AND THEOLOGY — Judaic*

500   IS   ISSN 0334-1100
INTERFACE. (Text in English) 1975. s-a. free. Weizmann Institute of Science, Public Affairs Department, Rehovot, Israel. TEL 08-342111. FAX 08-466966. TELEX 381300. circ. 25,000. (looseleaf format)

INTERNATIONAL CONGRESS SERIES. see *MEETINGS AND CONGRESSES*

500   FR   ISSN 0074-4387
Q10
INTERNATIONAL COUNCIL OF SCIENTIFIC UNIONS. YEAR BOOK. 1954. a. £45. International Council of Scientific Unions - Conseil International des Unions Scientifiques, 51 bd. de Montmorency, Paris 75016, France. TEL 45-25-03-29. FAX 42-88-94-31. TELEX ICSU 630553 F. (Dist. by: Portland Press Limited, 59 Portland Pl., London W1N 3AJ. TEL 071-580-5530) index; circ. 4,750.
Description: Provides historical information and a short description of every ICSU body, as well as the names and addresses of the 1800 individuals who serve as officers for the various groups and committees.

INTERNATIONAL JOURNAL OF ENERGY SYSTEMS. see *ENERGY*

INTERNATIONAL JOURNAL OF RADIATION BIOLOGY. see *MEDICAL SCIENCES — Cancer*

500   US
INTERNATIONAL JOURNAL OF SCIENCE AND TECHNOLOGY. 1971. s-a. $45. Foundation for International Development, Box 38, Plainfield, IN 46168. TEL 317-839-8157. FAX 317-839-1840. Ed. Syed Imtiaz Ahmad. adv.; bk.rev.; abstr.; index; circ. 1,000. Indexed: Abstr.Musl.Rel.
Formerly (until 1987): Muslim Scientist (ISSN 0743-085X)

INTERNATIONAL JOURNAL OF SCIENCE EDUCATION. see *EDUCATION*

500   US   ISSN 0896-2294
    CODEN: IJUSE5
INTERNATIONAL JOURNAL ON THE UNITY OF THE SCIENCES. 1988. q. $25. I C F, Box 1311, GPO, New York, NY 10116. FAX 212-244-6739. Ed. Marcelo Alonso. adv.; bk.rev.; circ. 500.
—BLDSC shelfmark: 4542.696700.
Description: Devoted to the study of values and their relationship to the sciences and the unity of knowledge.

INTERNATIONAL SOROPTIMIST. see *CLUBS*

500   PH
INTER-SCIENCE. q. exchange basis. National Science Development Board, International Relations Division, Box 3596, Manila, Philippines.

500   IT   ISSN 0393-2451
INTERSEZIONI; rivista di storia delle idee. 1981. 3/yr. L.90000. Societa Editrice Il Mulino, Strada Maggiore, 37, 40125 Bologna, Italy. TEL 051-256011. FAX 051-256034. Ed.Bd. adv.; index; circ. 1,300. (back issues avail.)

INVENT; an international publication for inventors, innovators, entrepreneurs, designers and engineers. see *TECHNOLOGY: COMPREHENSIVE WORKS*

SCIENCES: COMPREHENSIVE WORKS

500 608.7   II   ISSN 0970-0056
INVENTION INTELLIGENCE. (Text in English) 1965. m. Rs.40. National Research Development Corporation, 20-22 Zamroodpur Community Centre, Kailash Colony Extension, New Delhi 110 048, India. TEL 6420336. FAX 11-6449401. TELEX 031-71358. Ed. B. Khan. adv.; bk.rev.; abstr.; charts; illus.; tr.lit.; circ. 6,000. **Indexed:** Agri.Eng.Abstr., Food Sci.& Tech.Abstr., Indian Sci Abstr., PROMT.

INVENTIVA; periodico tecnico-scientifico-sociale. see *TECHNOLOGY: COMPREHENSIVE WORKS*

500   US
INVENTORS CLUBS OF AMERICA. NEWS. 1935. bi-m. membership only. Inventors Clubs of America, Box 450261, Atlanta, GA 30345. TEL 404-938-5089. Ed. Alexander T. Marinaccio. adv.; bk.rev.; circ. 6,000. (back issues avail.)
Description: Introduces new inventions, and presents articles to help inventors.

500 600   SP   ISSN 0210-136X
INVESTIGACION Y CIENCIA. Spanish translation of: Scientific American (US ISSN 0036-8733) 1976. m. 6600 ptas. (foreign 7300 ptas.). Prensa Cientifica, S.A., Viladomat, 291- 6o 1a, 08029 Barcelona, Spain. TEL 321-81-91. FAX 419-47-82. Eds. Francisco Gracia, Jose Maria Valderas. adv.; bk.rev.; bibl.; charts; illus.; index; circ. 40,000. (back issues avail.)

500   US   ISSN 0896-8381
Q11   CODEN: JIASEB
IOWA ACADEMY OF SCIENCE. JOURNAL. q. $20. Iowa Academy of Science, Sci. 3538, University of Northern Iowa, Cedar Falls, IA 50614. TEL 319-273-2021. Ed. Kenneth E. Windom. charts; illus.; circ. 2,100 (controlled). (also avail. in microform from UMI; reprint service avail. from UMI) **Indexed:** Biol.Abstr., Curr.Adv.Ecol.Sci., Excerp.Med., Field Crop Abstr., GeoRef., Herb.Abstr., Rev.Plant Path., Sci.Abstr., Seed Abstr., Soils & Fert.
—BLDSC shelfmark: 4802.529000.
Formerly: Iowa Academy of Science. Proceedings (ISSN 0085-2236)
Refereed Serial

507   US   ISSN 0021-0676
IOWA SCIENCE TEACHERS JOURNAL. 1963. 3/yr. $9 per vol. Iowa Academy of Science, Sci. 3538, University of Northern Iowa, Cedar Falls, IA 50614. TEL 319-273-2021. Ed. Carl Bollwinkel. adv.; bk.rev.; circ. 1,300.
Description: Presents teaching methods.
Refereed Serial

500.9   IQ
IRAQ NATURAL HISTORY MUSEUM. BULLETIN. (Text in English; summaries in Arabic and English) 1961. irreg. ID.2500 per no. Iraq Natural History Museum, University of Baghdad, Bab al-Muadham, Baghdad, Iraq. Ed. Munir K. Bunni. (back issues avail.) **Indexed:** Biodet.Abstr., Biol.Abstr., Zoo.Rec.
Former titles: Iraq Natural History Research Center and Museum. Bulletin; Iraq Natural History Museum. Bulletin (ISSN 0021-0897)

574   IQ
IRAQ NATURAL HISTORY MUSEUM. PUBLICATION. (Text in English; summaries in English and Arabic) 1950. irreg. ID.2000 per no. Iraq Natural History Museum, University of Baghdad, Bab al-Muadham, Baghdad, Iraq. Ed. Munir K. Bunni. **Indexed:** Biol.Abstr., Zoo.Rec.
Former titles: Iraq Natural History Research Centre and Museum. Publications; Iraq Natural History Museum. Publication (ISSN 0085-2260)

500   IQ
IRAQI JOURNAL OF SCIENCE. (Text and summaries in Arabic and English) 1956. 4/yr. available on exchange. University of Baghdad, College of Science, Adamiya Jadiriyah, Baghdad, Iraq. TEL 7760730. Ed. Muthana A. Shanshal. bk.rev.; charts; circ. 1,000. **Indexed:** Biol.Abstr., Chem.Abstr., Geo.Abstr., Math.R., Sci.Abstr.
Formerly (until vol.18, no.2, 1977): University of Baghdad. College of Science. Bulletin (ISSN 0067-2904)

500.9   UK   ISSN 0021-1311
CODEN: INAJA4
IRISH NATURALISTS' JOURNAL. 1925. q. $25. Irish Naturalists' Journal Committee, School of Biology and Biochemistry, Queen's Univ., Belfast BT7 1NN, N. Ireland. Ed. Robin Govier. adv.; bk.rev.; bibl.; illus.; cum.index every 3 yrs.; circ. 500. **Indexed:** Biol.Abstr., Br.Geol.Lit., Deep Sea Res.& Oceanogr.Abstr., Field Crop Abstr., Geo.Abstr., Herb.Abstr.
—BLDSC shelfmark: 4574.000000.

509   US   ISSN 0021-1753
Q1   CODEN: ISISA4
ISIS; international review devoted to the history of science and its cultural influences. 1912. 5/yr. $45 to individuals (foreign $56); institutions $110 (foreign $116); students $24 (foreign $35). (History of Science Society, Inc.) University of Chicago Press, Journals Division, 5720 S. Woodlawn Ave., Chicago, IL 60637. TEL 312-702-7600. FAX 312-702-0694. (Subscr. to: Box 37005, Chicago, IL 60637) Ed. Ronald Numbers. adv.; bk.rev.; bibl.; charts; illus.; index; circ. 4,400. (also avail. in microform from UMI; microfiche from JAI,KTO; reprint service avail. from ISI,SCH,UMI) **Indexed:** Acad.Ind., Alt.Press Ind., Amer.Hist.& Life, Arts & Hum.Cit.Ind., Biol.Abstr., Bk.Rev.Ind. (1989-), Bull.Signal., Chem.Abstr., Child.Bk.Rev.Ind. (1989-), Curr.Cont., Deep Sea Res.& Oceanogr.Abstr., Eng.Ind., Gen.Sci.Ind., Hist.Abstr., Hum.Ind., Ind.Med., Ind.Sci.Rev., Math.R., Ref.Sour., SSCI.
—BLDSC shelfmark: 4583.000000.
Refereed Serial

500   PK   ISSN 0304-5218
Q1   CODEN: IJSCDE
ISLAMABAD JOURNAL OF SCIENCES. (Text in English) 1974. irreg. Rs.95($15) Quaid-i-AzamUniversity, Department of Physics, c/o Bookshop, Bookbank and Publication Cell, Islamabad, Pakistan. TEL 812563. Ed. Dr. Kamaluddin Ahmed. **Indexed:** Biol.Abstr., Math.R., Sci.Abstr.
—BLDSC shelfmark: 4583.018000.
Formerly: University of Islamabad. Journal of Mathematics and Sciences.

500 610   TU   ISSN 1016-3360
ISLAMIC ACADEMY OF SCIENCES. JOURNAL. (Text in English) 1988. q. $30. (Islamic Academy of Sciences, JO) Anadolu Health and Research Foundation, Mithatpasha Caddesi 66-5, Yenishehir, Ankara, Turkey. TEL 1250319. FAX 3114777. TELEX 42237 HTK TR. (Co-sponsor: Kuwait Foundation for the Advancement of Sciences) Ed. Naci M. Bor. adv.; charts; illus.; stat.; circ. 1,000. (also avail. on diskette)
Description: Presents new research results in different scientific disciplines.
Refereed Serial

ISLE OF MAN NATURAL HISTORY AND ANTIQUARIAN SOCIETY. PROCEEDINGS. see *HISTORY*

500   IS   ISSN 0333-6190
ISRAEL ACADEMY OF SCIENCES AND HUMANITIES. SECTION OF SCIENCES. PROCEEDINGS. (Text in English) 1963. irreg. Israel Academy of Sciences and Humanities, 43 Jabotinski St., P.O. Box 4040, Jerusalem 91040, Israel. TEL 02-636211. FAX 02-666059. circ. 900. (back issues avail.) **Indexed:** Ind.Heb.Per.
—BLDSC shelfmark: 6741.700000.
Description: Reprints of scientific papers read at meetings of the academy.

500 600   US   ISSN 0748-5492
Q124.6
ISSUES IN SCIENCE AND TECHNOLOGY. 1984. q. $36 to individuals; institutions $65. National Academy of Sciences, 2101 Constitution Ave., N.W., Washington, DC 20418. TEL 202-334-3305. (Co-sponsors: Institute of Medicine; National Academy of Engineering) Ed. Kevin Finneran. adv.; bk.rev.; index; circ. 18,500. **Indexed:** Acad.Ind., Access (1985-1991), CAD CAM Abstr., Energy Ind., Energy Info.Abstr., Environ.Abstr., Ind.Sci.Rev., INIS Atomind., Med.Care Rev., Oper.Res.Manage.Sci., Qual.Contr.Appl.Stat., R.G., Risk Abstr., Tel.Abstr., Telegen.
—BLDSC shelfmark: 4584.325500.
Description: A journal of ideas and opinions, exploring the policy implications of new developments in science, technology and health.

500   IT
ISTITUTO COMELIANA DI LUGANO. COLLECTIO MONOGRAPHICA MINOR. 1976. irreg., vol.4, 1978. L.25000. Giardini Editori e Stampatori, Via Santa Bibbiana 28, 56100 Pisa, Italy. TEL 050 502531.

500   IT   ISSN 0075-1499
ISTITUTO E MUSEO DI STORIA DELLA SCIENZA. BIBLIOTECA. 1957. irreg., no.8, 1970. price varies. Casa Editrice Leo S. Olschki, Casella Postale 66, 50100 Florence, Italy. TEL 055-6530684. FAX 055-6530214. Ed. Paolo Galluzzi. circ. 1,000.

500   IT   ISSN 0021-2504
Q54   CODEN: RLMAAK
ISTITUTO LOMBARDO ACCADEMIA DI SCIENZE E LETTERE. RENDICONTI. A. vol.107, 1973. a. price varies. Istituto Lombardo Accademia di Scienze e Lettere, Via Borgonuovo 25, 20121 Milan, Italy. **Indexed:** Appl.Mech.Rev., Chem.Abstr., GeoRef., M.L.A., Math.R.

500   JA   ISSN 0287-3532
IWATANI NAOJI KINEN ZAIDAN KENKYU HOKOKUSHO/IWATANI NAOJI FOUNDATION. RESEARCH REPORT. (Text in Japanese; summaries in English and Japanese) 1977. a. Iwatani Naoji Kinen Zaidan - Iwatani Naoji Foundation, TBR Bldg., 10-2 Nagata-cho 2-chome, Chiyoda-ku, Tokyo 100, Japan.

500 300   JA   ISSN 0385-4132
CODEN: KKNDDL
IWATE MEDICAL UNIVERSITY SCHOOL OF LIBERAL ARTS & SCIENCES. ANNUAL REPORT/IWATE IKA DAIGAKU KYOYOBU NENPO. (Text in English, German, Japanese) 1966. a. free. Iwate Ika Daigaku Kyoyobu - Iwate Medical University School of Liberal Arts & Sciences, 16-1, 3-chome, Honcho-dori, Morioka-shi, Iwate-ken, Japan. circ. 350. (back issues avail.)
●Also available online. Vendor(s): JICST (JOIS-III).
Description: Reports of studies by faculty staff.

IWATE UNIVERSITY. FACULTY OF EDUCATION. ANNUAL REPORT/IWATE DAIGAKU KYOIKUGAKUBU KENKYU NENPO. see *SOCIAL SCIENCES: COMPREHENSIVE WORKS*

500   GW
J.C. POGGENDORFF: BIOGRAPHISCH-LITERARISCHES HANDWOERTERBUCH DER EXAKTEN NATURWISSENSCHAFTEN. vol.7, 1955. irreg., latest 1989. (Saechsische Akademie der Wissenschaften zu Leipzig) Akademie-Verlag Berlin, Leipziger Str. 3-4, 1086 Berlin, Germany. TELEX 114420-AVERL-DD.

500   PK   ISSN 0021-3888
JADEED SCIENCE. (Text in Urdu; summaries in English and German) 1956. bi-m. Rs.15($3.00) Scientific Society of Pakistan, University of Karachi, Dept. of Zoology, Karachi 32, Pakistan. Ed. Aftab Hassan. adv.; bk.rev.; illus.; circ. 2,000.

500 600   GW   ISSN 0938-152X
HD6331.2.G282
JAHRBUCH ARBEIT UND TECHNIK. 1985. a. DM.30. J.H.W. Dietz Nachf. GmbH, In der Raste 2, 5300 Bonn 1, Germany. TEL 0228-238083. Ed. Fricke Werner.

JAHRBUCH FUER BIOTECHNOLOGIE. see *BIOLOGY — Biophysics*

500   GW   ISSN 0173-7600
JAHRBUCH FUER REGIONALWISSENSCHAFT. 1980. a. DM.66. Vandenhoeck und Ruprecht, Theaterstr. 13, Postfach 3753, 3400 Goettingen, Germany. TEL 0551-6959-22. FAX 0551-695917. Ed.Bd. circ. 350.

500   TS
JAMA'AT AL-TA'RIKH AL-TABI'I. NASHRAT/EMIRATES NATURAL HISTORY GROUP BULLETIN. (Text in Arabic, English) 1977. q. Cultural Foundation, Natural History Group, P.O. Box 2380, Abu Dhabi, United Arab Emirates. TEL 215300. FAX 336059. TELEX 2214 CULCEN EM. Ed. Ian Hammer. circ. 500 (controlled).
Description: Covers topics in the natural history of the region.

SCIENCES: COMPREHENSIVE WORKS

500   JM   ISSN 1016-2054
Q29
JAMAICAN JOURNAL OF SCIENCE AND TECHNOLOGY.
1970. s-a. J.$50($20) Scientific Research Council, P.O. Box 350, Kingston 6, Jamaica, W.I. FAX 809-927-5347. TELEX 3631 SRCSTIN JA. Ed. Tara Dasgupta. adv.; bk.rev.; illus.; circ. 2,250.
Indexed: Chem.Abstr., GeoRef., Nutr.Abstr.
Formerly (until 1989): Scientific Research Council of Jamaica. Journal (ISSN 0036-8822); Supersedes: Scientific Research Council. Information.
Description: Publishes scientific papers based on original data on research of interest and relevance to Jamaica, research notes, happenings, profiles, perspectives, trends, research projects in progress and bibliographies.

JAMI'AT AL-IMARAT AL-ARABIYYAH AL-MUTTAHIDAH. MAJALLAH/UNITED ARAB EMIRATES UNIVERSITY. JOURNAL. see HUMANITIES: COMPREHENSIVE WORKS

500 610   NE   ISSN 0021-4264
R131.A1   CODEN: JNUSA6
JANUS; revue internationale de l'histoire des sciences, de la medecine, de la pharmacie et de la technique. (Text in several languages) 1896. 4/yr. membership. Foundation Janus, Joh. Verhulststraat 185, 1075 GZ Amsterdam, Netherlands. bk.rev.; bibl.; illus.; index; circ. controlled. (also avail. in microfilm from BHP) Indexed: Amer.Hist.& Life (until 1991), Chem.Abstr., Hist.Abstr., Math.R.

500   JA   ISSN 0386-2208
QH301   CODEN: PJABDW
JAPAN ACADEMY. PROCEEDINGS. SERIES B: PHYSICAL AND BIOLOGICAL SCIENCES/NIPPON GAKUSHIIN B. (Text in English) 1919. 10/yr. Nippon Gakushiin - Japan Academy, 7-32 Ueno Koen, Taito-ku, Tokyo 110, Japan. (Order from: Maruzen Co., Ltd., 3-10 Nihonbashi 2-chome, Chuo-ku, Tokyo 103, Japan; or Import and Export Dept., Box 5050, Tokyo International, Tokyo 100-31, Japan) Indexed: Anim.Breed.Abstr., Biol.Abstr., Chem.Abstr., Curr.Adv.Biochem., Curr.Adv.Cell & Devel.Biol., Curr.Adv.Ecol.Sci., Curr.Adv.Genetics & Molec.Biol., Curr.Cont., Deep Sea Res.& Oceanogr.Abstr., GeoRef., INIS Atomind., Math.R., Met.Abstr., Sci.Abstr., Sci.Cit.Ind.
—BLDSC shelfmark: 6742.100000.
Supersedes in part and continues numbering of (vol.53): Japan Academy. Proceedings (ISSN 0021-4280)

501   JA   ISSN 0453-0691
Q174
JAPAN ASSOCIATION FOR PHILOSOPHY OF SCIENCE. ANNALS. (Text in English) 1954. a. 2400 Yen. Japan Association for Philosophy of Science - Kagaku Kisoron Gakkai, c/o Dept. of Philosophy, Keio University, 2-15-45 Mita, Minato-ku, Tokyo 108, Japan. TEL 03-453-4511. FAX 03-798-7480. Indexed: Biol.Abstr., Math.R., Psychol.Abstr., Sci.Abstr.

JAPAN INSTITUTE OF NAVIGATION. JOURNAL/NIHON KOKAI GAKKAI RONBUNSHU. see TRANSPORTATION — Ships And Shipping

500 600   US
JAPAN REPORT: SCIENCE AND TECHNOLOGY. irreg. (approx. 40/yr.) $7 per no. (foreign $14 per no.). U.S. Joint Publications Research Service, Box 12507, Arlington, VA 22209. TEL 703-487-4630. (Subscr. to: NTIS, Springfield, VA 22161)

500   CC
JIANGXI KEXUE/JIANGXI SCIENCE. (Text in Chinese) q. Jiangxi Sheng Kexueyuan - Jiangxi Academy of Sciences, Pengjia Qiao, Beijing Donglu, Nanchang, Jiangxi 330029, People's Republic of China. TEL 332971. Ed. Gao Jiefu.

500   CC   ISSN 1000-5862
JIANGXI SHIFAN DAXUE XUEBAO (ZIRAN KEXUE BAN)/JIANGXI NORMAL UNIVERSITY. JOURNAL (NATURAL SCIENCE EDITION). (Text in Chinese) q. Jiangxi Shifan Daxue, Xuebao Bianjibu, Beijing Xilu, Nanchang, Jiangxi 330027, People's Republic of China. TEL 333993. Ed. Chen Dingru.

500   CC   ISSN 0529-0279
Q4.   CODEN: CLTTDI
JILIN DAXUE ZIRAN KEXUE XUEBAO/JILIN UNIVERSITY. JOURNAL OF NATURAL SCIENCE. (Text in Chinese) q. $4.40 per no. Jilin Daxue Chubanshe - Jilin University Press, Changchun, Jilin, People's Republic of China. TEL 23189. (Dist. overseas by: China International Book Trading Corp., P.O. Box 399, Beijing, P.R.C.) Indexed: Chem.Abstr.
—BLDSC shelfmark: 0663.180000.

500 610   CC
JINAN LIYI XUEBAO/JINAN UNIVERSITY. JOURNAL: MEDICAL & NATURAL SCIENCE AND TECHNOLOGY EDITION. (Text in Chinese; table of contents in English) 1979. q. Y8. Jinan Daxue, Xuebao Bianjibu - Jinan University, Journal Editorial Department, Rm. 217, 2nd Fl., Bldg. 75, Shipai, Guangzhou, Guangdong 510632, People's Republic of China. TEL 516511. (Dist. outside China by: Guoji Shudian - China International Book Trading Corp., P.O. Box 399, Beijing, P.R.C.) Ed. Wang Weiliang.

500 600   CC
JINRI KEJI/SCIENCE AND TECHNOLOGY TODAY. (Text in Chinese) m. Zhejiang Sheng Keji Qingbao Yanjiusuo - Zhejiang Provincial Institute of Science and Technology Information, 91 Huancheng Xilu, Hangzhou, Zhejiang 310006, People's Republic of China. TEL 754087. Ed. Chen Guangzhong.

500   CC
JINZHAN/PROGRESS. (Text in Chinese) bi-m. Zhongguo Kexue Jishu Qingbaosuo, Chongqing Fensuo - Chongqing Science and Technology Information Technology, Chongqing Branch, 132, Shengli Lu, Chongqing, Sichuan 630013, People's Republic of China. TEL 350455. Ed. Wang Zihe.

500   GW
JOACHIM-JUNGIUS-GESELLSCHAFT DER WISSENSCHAFTEN, HAMBURG. VEROEFFENTLICHUNGEN. 1957. irreg. Vandenhoeck und Ruprecht, Robert-Bosch-Breite 6, Postfach 3753, 3400 Goettingen, Germany. TEL 0551-6959-0. FAX 0551-695917.

500   JA   ISSN 0911-9639
JOETSU KYOIKU DAIGAKU KENKYU KIYO. DAI-3-BUNSATSU. SHIZENKEI KYOIKU, SEIKATSU KENKOEI KYOIKU/JOETSU UNIVERSITY OF EDUCATION. BULLETIN. 3. NATURAL SCIENCES AND HUMAN LIVING. (Text and summaries in English and Japanese) a. Joetsu University of Education - Joetsu Kyoiku Daigaku, 1 Yamayashiki-machi, Joetsu-shi, Niigata-ken 943, Japan.
—BLDSC shelfmark: 2597.295000.

500   GW   ISSN 0178-4757
JOHANNES GUTENBERG-UNIVERSITAET MAINZ. FORSCHUNGSMAGAZIN. 1985. s-a. DM.8. Johannes Gutenberg-Universitaet Mainz, Postfach 39 80, 6500 Mainz, Germany. FAX 06131-393382. TELEX 4187-476-UNI-D. Ed. Prof. J. Zoellner. adv.; circ. 7,000. (back issues avail.)
Description: Report on current research at the university.

500   AU   ISSN 0259-0689
JOHANNES-KEPLER-UNIVERSITAET LINZ. DISSERTATIONEN. 1974. irreg., no.84, 1990. price varies. (Johannes-Kepler-Universitaet Linz) Verband der Wissenschaftlichen Gesellschaften Oesterreichs, Lindengasse 37, A-1070 Vienna, Austria. TEL 932166.
Formerly: Johannes-Kepler-Hochschule Linz. Dissertationen.

JOSAI DAIGAKU KENKYU NENPO. SHIZEN KAGAKU HEN/JOSAI UNIVERSITY BULLETIN OF LIBERAL ARTS. NATURAL SCIENCE, HEALTH AND PHYSICAL EDUCATION. see HUMANITIES: COMPREHENSIVE WORKS

501   NE   ISSN 0925-4560
Q3   CODEN: JGPSE4
JOURNAL FOR GENERAL PHILOSOPHY OF SCIENCE/ZEITSCHRIFT FUER ALLGEMEINE WISSENSCHAFTSTHEORIE. (Text in English and German) 1969. s-a. $119.50. Kluwer Academic Publishers, Postbus 17, 3300 AA Dordrecht, Netherlands. TEL 078-334911. FAX 078-334254. TELEX 29245. (Dist by: Kluwer Academic Publishers Group, P.O. Box 322, 3300 AH Dordrecht, Netherlands; N. America dist. addr.: Box 358, Accord Station, Hingham, MA 02018-0358. TEL 617-871-6600) Eds. L. Geldsetzer, G. Koenig. adv.; bk.rev.; bibl.; index; circ. 700. (back issues avail.) Indexed: Ind.Bk.Rev.Hum., Math.R., Phil.Ind., Sci.Abstr.
—BLDSC shelfmark: 4988.600000.
Formerly: Zeitschrift fuer Allgemeine Wissenschaftstheorie (ISSN 0044-2216)

500   SY   ISSN 0379-2927
Q127.A5
JOURNAL FOR THE HISTORY OF ARABIC SCIENCE. (Text in Arabic, English, French, German) 1977. s-a. £S15($15) University of Aleppo, Institute for the History of Arabic Science, Aleppo, Syria. TEL 21-236 130. TELEX 331018 SY ALUNIV. Ed.Bd. adv.; bk.rev.; illus.; index, cum.index: 1977-1981 (vols.1-5); circ. 1,500. (back issues avail.) Indexed: Bull.Signal., Ind.Islam., Math.R., Mid.East: Abstr.& Ind.

JOURNAL FUER U F O - FORSCHUNG. see AERONAUTICS AND SPACE FLIGHT

JOURNAL OF BORDERLAND RESEARCH. see PARAPSYCHOLOGY AND OCCULTISM

JOURNAL OF COLLEGE SCIENCE TEACHING. see EDUCATION — Higher Education

JOURNAL OF COMPUTERS IN MATHEMATICS AND SCIENCE TEACHING. see MATHEMATICS — Computer Applications

500 610   US   ISSN 0884-1225
JOURNAL OF HYPERBARIC MEDICINE. 1986. q. $50. Undersea and Hyperbaric Medical Society, Inc., 9650 Rockville Pike, Bethesda, MD 20814. TEL 301-571-1818. FAX 301-571-1815. Ed. Enrico M. Camporesi.
—BLDSC shelfmark: 5004.509000.
Supersedes (1980-1985): Hyperbaric Oxygen Review (ISSN 0195-9263)

500   US   ISSN 1049-6335
▼**JOURNAL OF IDEAS.** 1990. q. $46 to individuals; institutions $138. Institute for Memetic Research, Box 16327, Panama City, FL 32406-1327. TEL 904-265-4378. Ed. Elan Moritz. index; circ. 200. (back issues avail.)
Description: Archival forum circulating and nurturing inquiry focusing on the evolution and dissemination of ideas, discovery and creative processes; also covers memetics, biological and electronic implementations of knowledge, and idea processing.
Refereed Serial

500   US   ISSN 1045-389X
TA418.9.S62   CODEN: JMSSER
▼**JOURNAL OF INTELLIGENT MATERIAL SYSTEMS AND STUCTURES.** 1990. q. $225. Technomic Publishing Co., Inc., 851 New Holland Ave., Box 3535, Lancaster, PA 17604. TEL 717-291-5609. FAX 717-295-4538. TELEX 230 753565 (TECHNOMIC UD). Ed. Craig A. Rogers. circ. 300.
—BLDSC shelfmark: 5007.538550.
Description: Publishes papers related to the science and engineering of diverse intelligent systems.
Refereed Serial

SCIENCES: COMPREHENSIVE WORKS

500   NE   ISSN 0022-1945
QH527   CODEN: JICRBF
JOURNAL OF INTERDISCIPLINARY CYCLE RESEARCH. (Text in English, French and German) 1970. 4/yr. $205. Swets Publishing Service (Subsidiary of: Swets en Zeitlinger B.V.), Heereweg 347, 2161 CA Lisse, Netherlands. TEL 31-2521-35111. FAX 31-2521-15888. TELEX 41325. (Dist. in N. America by: Swets & Zeitlinger, Box 517, Berwyn, PA 19312. TEL 215-644-4944) Ed. A. Sollberger, R. Hardeland. adv.; bk.rev.; charts; illus.; circ. 600. (also avail. in microform from SWZ; reprint service avail. from SWZ) **Indexed:** Biol.Abstr., Chem.Abstr., Curr.Adv.Ecol.Sci., Curr.Cont., Dairy Sci.Abstr., Deep Sea Res.& Oceanogr.Abstr., Excerpt.Med., GeoRef., Helminthol.Abstr., Ind.Sci.Rev., Ind.Vet., Sci.Cit.Ind, Small Anim.Abstr., Vet.Bull.
—BLDSC shelfmark: 5007.545000.

500   US   ISSN 0022-2038
Q167
JOURNAL OF IRREPRODUCIBLE RESULTS. 1955. 6/yr. $15 to individuals (foreign $30); institutions $31 (foreign $46). (Society for Basic Irreproducible Research) Blackwell Scientific Publications Inc., Three Cambridge Center, Ste. 208, Cambridge, MA 02142-1413. TEL 617-225-0401. FAX 617-225-0412. Ed. Marc Abrahams. adv.; bk.rev.; illus.; circ. 8,000. (back issues avail.) **Indexed:** Biol.Abstr., Curr.Cont., Mid.East: Abstr.& Ind., PROMT.
—BLDSC shelfmark: 5008.400000.
Description: Contains humorous articles.

574 530   II   ISSN 0970-3799
JOURNAL OF NATURAL & PHYSICAL SCIENCES. 1987. s-a. Rs.100($50) Gurukul Kangri University, Department of Mathematics, Hardwar 249 404, India. Ed. S.L. Singh. bk.rev.; circ. 200.
Description: Covers biology, chemistry, physics, and mathematics.

500   JA   ISSN 0075-4307
JOURNAL OF NATURAL SCIENCE. (Text in English and Japanese) vol.2, 1952. a. avail. on exchange basis. Tokushima Daigaku, Kyoikugakubu - Tokushima University, Faculty of Education, Tokushima-shi, Tokushima-ken 770, Japan.

500.1 510   PK   ISSN 0022-2941
Q1   CODEN: JNSMAC
JOURNAL OF NATURAL SCIENCES AND MATHEMATICS. (Text in English) 1961. s-a. Rs.150($15) Government College, Research Council, P.O. Box 1750, Lahore 54000, Pakistan. Ed. M. Zakria Butt. bk.rev.; index; circ. 250. **Indexed:** Chem.Abstr., INIS Atomind., Math.R., Poult.Abstr., Sci.Abstr.
—BLDSC shelfmark: 5021.300000.

JOURNAL OF OMAN STUDIES. see HISTORY — History Of The Near East

JOURNAL OF OMAN STUDIES SPECIAL REPORT. see HISTORY — History Of The Near East

500   PL
JOURNAL OF POLISH SCIENCE. (Text in English) 1956. q. price varies. (Polska Akademia Nauk) Ossolineum, Publishing House of the Polish Academy of Sciences, Rynek 9, 50-106 Wroclaw, Poland. TELEX 0712771 OSS PL. (Dist. by: Ars Polona-Ruch, Krakowskie Przedmiescie 7, Warsaw, Poland) Ed. M. Mossakowski. bibl.; charts; circ. 960. **Indexed:** Anal.Abstr., Biol.Abstr., Chem.Abstr., Deep Sea Res.& Oceanogr.Abstr., Field Crop Abstr., GeoRef., Herb.Abstr., Hist.Abstr., Math.R., Met.Abstr.
Former titles (until 1987): Acta Academiae Scientiarum Poloniae; Polish Academy of Sciences. Review (ISSN 0032-2776) French edition former title: Academie Polonaise des Sciences. Revue; Russian edition former title: Pol'skaya Akademiya Nauk. Zhurnal (ISSN 0032-3810).
Description: Devoted to problems of the development of science in Poland.

500   TU   ISSN 0022-4057
Q80.T8   CODEN: JPASBN
JOURNAL OF PURE AND APPLIED SCIENCES/TEMEL VE UYGULAMALI BILMLER DERGISI. Title varies: M E T U Journal of Pure and Applied Sciences. (Text in English and Turkish) 1968. irreg. (approx. 3/yr.). TL.60($5) (Turk Tarih Kurumu Basimevi) Middle East Technical University, Public Relations and Publications Office, Ismet Inonu Bulvari, Ankara, Turkey. Ed. Dogan Altinbilek. bk.rev.; abstr.; bibl.; charts; illus.; index; circ. 500. **Indexed:** Appl.Mech.Rev., Chem.Abstr., Curr.Cont., GeoRef., Math.R., Sci.Cit.Ind.

500 550 574 913   UK   ISSN 0267-8179
QE696
JOURNAL OF QUATERNARY SCIENCE. 1986. s-m. $235 (effective 1992). (Quarternary Research Association) John Wiley & Sons Ltd., Journals, Baffins Lane, Chichester, W. Sussex PO19 1UD. TEL 0243-779777. FAX 0243-775878. TELEX 86290-WIBOOK-G. Ed. P.L. Gibbard. (back issues avail.; reprint service avail. from SWZ)
—BLDSC shelfmark: 5043.752000.
Description: Acts as a forum for the exchange and integration of information and ideas from studies of the quaternary stratigraphic record, recent geological processes, the development and modification of natural ecosystems, the evolution and effects of man, and the nature and causes of climatic change.

507   US   ISSN 0022-4308
Q181.A1   CODEN: JRSTAR
JOURNAL OF RESEARCH IN SCIENCE TEACHING. 1963. 10/yr. $200 (foreign $325). (National Association for Research in Science Teaching) John Wiley & Sons, Inc., Journals, 605 Third Ave., New York, NY 10158-0012. TEL 212-850-6000. FAX 212-850-6088. TELEX 12-7063. Ed. Ronald Good. adv.; bibl.; charts; index; circ. 2,000. (also avail. in microform from RPI; back issues avail.; reprint service avail. from RPI) **Indexed:** C.I.J.E., Cont.Pg.Educ., Educ.Ind., Educ.Tech.Abstr., Energy Ind., Energy Info.Abstr., Mid.East: Abstr.& Ind., Psychol.Abstr., Res.High.Educ.Abstr., SSCI, Stud.Wom.Abstr.
—BLDSC shelfmark: 5052.030000.
Description: Research articles related to the philosophy, historical perspective, teaching strategies, curriculum development and other topics relevant to science education.
Refereed Serial

JOURNAL OF SCIENCE AND MATHEMATICS EDUCATION IN SOUTHEAST ASIA. see EDUCATION — Teaching Methods And Curriculum

500 600   PK
JOURNAL OF SCIENCE AND TECHNOLOGY. 1977. s-a. Rs.50($10) University of Peshawar, Department of Zoology, Peshawar, Pakistan. Ed. M. Nasim Siddiqi. circ. 500. **Indexed:** Biol.Abstr., INIS Atomind., Soils & Fert.

JOURNAL OF SCIENCE EDUCATION AND TECHNOLOGY. see EDUCATION

500   II   ISSN 0022-4456
T1   CODEN: JSIRAC
JOURNAL OF SCIENTIFIC AND INDUSTRIAL RESEARCH. (Text in English) 1942. m. Rs.250($100) (Council of Scientific and Industrial Research, Publications & Information Directorate) Scientific Publishers, P.O. Box 91, 5A, New Pali Rd., Jodhpur 342 001, India. TEL 0291-33323. Ed. S.S. Nathan. bk.rev. (also avail. in microform from UMI; back issues avail.; reprint service avail. from UMI) **Indexed:** Anal.Abstr., Appl.Mech.Rev., Biol.Abstr., CAD CAM Abstr., Cadscan, Ceram.Abstr., Chem.Abstr., Chem.Eng.Abstr., Crop Physiol.Abstr., Curr.Biotech.Abstr., Dairy Sci.Abstr., Energy Ind., Energy Info.Abstr., Environ.Abstr., Excerpt.Med., Field Crop Abstr., Food Sci.& Tech.Abstr., GeoRef., Herb.Abstr., Hort.Abstr., Ind.Sci.Rev., INIS Atomind., Irr.& Drain.Abstr., Lead Abstr., Nutr.Abstr., Plant Grow.Reg.Abstr., Protozool.Abstr., Rice Abstr., Risk Abstr., Robomat., Sci.Abstr., T.C.E.A., Text.Tech.Dig., Trop.Oil Seeds Abstr., Weed Abstr., World Text.Abstr., Zincscan.
—BLDSC shelfmark: 5057.000000.

500 133   US   ISSN 0892-3310
Q180.55.M4
JOURNAL OF SCIENTIFIC EXPLORATION. 1987. 2/yr. $40 to individuals; institutions $100 (effective 1992). Society for Scientific Exploration, c/o Rm. ERL 306, Stanford University, Stanford, CA 94305-4055. TEL 415-723-1438. Ed. Dr. Bernard M. Haisch.
—BLDSC shelfmark: 5057.500000.
Description: Publishes original research papers aimed at advancing the study of anomalous phenomena in all scientific subject disciplines.
Refereed Serial

JOURNAL OF SCIENTIFIC RESEARCH IN PLANTS & MEDICINES. see PHARMACY AND PHARMACOLOGY

JOURNAL OF THE EAST AFRICA NATURAL HISTORY SOCIETY AND NATIONAL MUSEUM. see BIOLOGY

500   GW
JUNGE WISSENSCHAFT. q. DM.35. Erhard Friedrich Verlag GmbH, Im Brande 15a, Postfach 100150, 3016 Seelze 6, Germany. TEL 0511-40004-0.

JUNIOR SCIENCE/KODOMO NO KAGAKU. see CHILDREN AND YOUTH — For

JUNIOR SCIENTIST. see EDUCATION — Teaching Methods And Curriculum

JUNKAN ASU NO KAGAKU GIJUTSU/NEWS OF SCIENCE AND TECHNOLOGY OF TOMORROW. see TECHNOLOGY: COMPREHENSIVE WORKS

500   GW   ISSN 0722-0456
K F A INTERN. (Kernforschungsanlage); Nachrichten und Berichte. 1970. q. free. Forschungszentrum Juelich GmbH, Postfach 1913, 5170 Juelich 1, Germany. Ed.Bd. bk.rev.; circ. 7,100. (back issues avail.)

500   JA   ISSN 0022-7625
Q4   CODEN: KAGTAT
KAGAKU/SCIENCE. (Text and summaries in Japanese) 1931. m. 10100 Yen. Iwanami Shoten Publishers, 5-5 Hitotsubashi 2-chome, Chiyoda-ku, Tokyo 101-02, Japan. FAX 03-239-9618. (Dist. overseas by: Japan Publications Trading Co., Ltd., Box 5030, Tokyo International, Tokyo 100-31, Japan; Or: 1255 Howard St., San Francisco, CA 94103) Ed. Shigeki Kobayashi. adv.; bk.rev.; charts; illus.; index; circ. 20,000. **Indexed:** Chem.Abstr., INIS Atomind., Jap.Per.Ind.

500   JA   ISSN 0368-4741
KAGAKU ASAHI/SCIENTIFIC ASAHI. (Text in Japanese) 1941. m. $119. Asahi Shimbunsha - Asahi Shimbun Publishing Co., 3-2, Tsukiji 5-chome, Chuo-ku, Tokyo 104-11, Japan. TEL 03-3545-0131. (Order to: Japan Publications Trading Co., Ltd., Box 5030, Tokyo International, Tokyo, Japan) Ed. Takashi Iida. **Indexed:** Biol.Abstr., Jap.Per.Ind.

500   JA   ISSN 0022-7633
KAGAKU GIJUTSU BUNKEN SABISU/SCIENCE AND TECHNOLOGY INFORMATION SERVICE. (Text in Japanese; table of contents in English) 1962. q. 3200 Yen. National Diet Library - Kokuritsu Kokkai Toshokan Senmon Shiryobu, 1-10-1 Nagata-cho, Chiyoda-ku, Tokyo 100, Japan. TEL 03-3581-2331. TELEX 2225393. bk.rev.; bibl.; charts; illus.; cum.index; circ. 1,300. (controlled). **Indexed:** INIS Atomind., Jap.Per.Ind.
—BLDSC shelfmark: 8134.257000.

KAGAKU GIJUTSU-CHO NENPO. see TECHNOLOGY: COMPREHENSIVE WORKS

KAGAKU GIJUTSU HAKUSHO/WHITE PAPER OF SCIENCE AND TECHNOLOGY IN JAPAN. see TECHNOLOGY: COMPREHENSIVE WORKS

KAGAKU GIJUTSU HAKUSHO NO ARAMASHI. see TECHNOLOGY: COMPREHENSIVE WORKS

KAGAKU GIJUTSU SHINKO CHOSEIHI NYUSU. see TECHNOLOGY: COMPREHENSIVE WORKS

KAGAKU GIJUTSU SHINKO CHOSEIHI SHIKEN KENKYU JISSHI KEIKAKU. see TECHNOLOGY: COMPREHENSIVE WORKS

SCIENCES: COMPREHENSIVE WORKS

500   JA   ISSN 0022-7668
KAGAKU KISORON KENKYU/JAPAN ASSOCIATION FOR PHILOSOPHY OF SCIENCE. JOURNAL. 1954. s-a. 800 Yen. Japan Association for Philosophy of Science - Kagaku Kisoron Gakkai, c/o Dept. of Philosophy, Kejo University, 2-15-45 Mita, Minato-ku, Tokyo 108, Japan. TEL 03-453-4511. FAX 03-798-7480. Ed. Hiroshi Kurosaki. bk.rev.; circ. 700. **Indexed:** Psychol.Abstr.
—BLDSC shelfmark: 4804.600000.

500 370   JA   ISSN 0386-4553
KAGAKU KYOIKU KENKYU/JOURNAL OF SCIENCE EDUCATION IN JAPAN. (Text in English and Japanese; summaries in English) 1977. q. Nihon Kagaku Kyoiku Gakkai - Japan Society for Science Education, 5-22 Shimomeguro 6-chome, Meguro-ku, Tokyo 153, Japan.

500   JA   ISSN 0386-183X
KAGAKU SARON. (Text in Japanese) 1977. bi-m. Tokai Daigaku Shuppankai - Tokai University Press, 27-4 Shinjuku 3-chome, Shinjuku-ku, Tokyo 160, Japan.

500   JA
KAGAKU SHINBUN/SCIENCE NEWS. (Text in Japanese) 1946. w. Kagaku Shinbunsha, 8-1 Hamamatsu-cho 1-chome, Minato-ku, Tokyo 105, Japan. (newspaper)

500   JA   ISSN 0289-3428
KAGAKU TETSUGAKU/PHILOSOPHY OF SCIENCE. (Text in Japanese) 1968. a. (Nihon Kagaku Tetsugakkai - Philosophy of Science Society, Japan) Waseda Daigaku Shuppanbu - Waseda University Press, 1-103 Totsuka-machi, Shinjuku-ku, Tokyo 169, Japan. **Indexed:** Jap.Per.Ind.

KAGAKU TO KOGYO (OSAKA)/SCIENCE AND INDUSTRY. see *TECHNOLOGY: COMPREHENSIVE WORKS*

509   JA   ISSN 0022-7692
KAGAKUSHI KENKYU/JOURNAL OF HISTORY OF SCIENCE. (Text in Japanese; summaries in European languages) 1949. q. $6.50. Nippon Kagakushi Gakkai - History of Science Society of Japan, Nihonbashi Chuo Bldg. 91, 16-3 Nihonbashi 2-chome, Chuo-ku, Tokyo 103, Japan. Ed. Masao Watanabe. **Indexed:** Chem.Abstr.
—BLDSC shelfmark: 5002.000000.

500 370   JA   ISSN 0389-3057
AS552.K24   CODEN: KDKDAM
KAGAWA DAIGAKU KYOIKUGAKUBU KENKYU HOKOKU. DAI-2-BU/KAGAWA UNIVERSITY. MEMOIRS. PART 2. (Text in English and Japanese; summaries in English) 1950. s-a. Kagawa Daigaku, Kyoikugakubu - Kagawa University, Faculty of Education, 1-1 Saiwai-cho, Takamatsu-shi, Kagawa-ken 760, Japan. **Indexed:** Jap.Per.Ind.

500   JA   ISSN 0389-6692
KAGOSHIMA DAIGAKU KYOIKUGAKUBU KENKYU KIYO. SHIZEN KAGAKU HEN/KAGOSHIMA UNIVERSITY. FACULTY OF EDUCATION. BULLETIN. NATURAL SCIENCE. (Text and summaries in English and Japanese) 1949. a. Kagoshima Daigaku, Kyoikugakubu - Kagoshima University, Faculty of Education, 20-6 Koorimoto 1-chome, Kagoshima-shi, Kagoshima-ken 890, Japan. **Indexed:** Chem.Abstr., Jap.Per.Ind.

510 530 540   JA   ISSN 0385-4027
   CODEN: KSBKB2
KAGOSHIMA DAIGAKU RIGAKUBU KIYO. SUGAKU, BUTSURIGAKU, KAGAKU/KAGOSHIMA UNIVERSITY. FACULTY OF SCIENCE. REPORTS. MATHEMATICS, PHYSICS, CHEMISTRY. (Text in English and Japanese; summaries in English) 1968. a. Kagoshima Daigaku, Rigakubu - Kagoshima University, Faculty of Science, 21-35 Koorimoto 1-chome, Kagoshima-shi, Kagoshima-ken 890, Japan. **Indexed:** Biol.Abstr., Chem.Abstr., Jap.Per.Ind.
—BLDSC shelfmark: 7467.170000.

500   JA   ISSN 0286-1208
   CODEN: KTDHDC
KAGOSHIMA-KENRITSU TANKI DAIGAKU KIYO. SHIZEN KAGAKU HEN/KAGOSHIMA PREFECTURAL JUNIOR COLLEGE. BULLETIN. NATURAL SCIENCES. (Text in Japanese and English; summaries in English) 1950. a. Kagoshima Prefectural Junior College - Kagoshima-kenritsu Tanki Daigaku, 44 Shimoishiki-cho, Kagoshima-shi, Kagoshima-ken 870, Japan. **Indexed:** Jap.Per.Ind.

500   II   ISSN 0022-7870
KALAIKATHIR. (Text in Tamil) 1948. m. Rs.30. G R D Trust, Foundation Avanashi Rd., Coimbatore 641 037, India. Ed. Dr. D. Padmanaban. adv.; bk.rev.; charts; illus.; index.

500.9 069   JA
KAMISHIHORO-CHO HIGASHI TAISETSU HAKUBUTSUKAN KENKYU HOKOKU/HIGASHI TAISETSU MUSEUM OF NATURAL HISTORY. BULLETIN. (Text in Japanese; summaries in English) 1975. irreg. Higashi Taisetsu Museum of Natural History - Kamishihoro-cho Higashi Taisetsu Hakubutsukan, Nukabira, Kamishihoro-cho, Kato-gun, Hokkaido 080-15, Japan.
Description: Contains original research papers.

500   JA   ISSN 0453-1906
QH188
KANAGAWA-KENRITSU HAKUBUTSUKAN KENKYU HOKOKU. SHIZEN KAGAKU/KANAGAWA PREFECTURAL MUSEUM. BULLETIN. NATURAL SCIENCE. (Text and summaries in English and Japanese) 1968. a. Kanagawa-kenritsu Hakubutsukan - Kanagawa Prefectural Museum, 5-60 Minami-nakadoori, Naka-ku, Yokohama-shi, Kanagawa-ken 231, Japan. **Indexed:** Biol.Abstr., Jap.Per.Ind.

500.9   JA   ISSN 0388-9009
KANAGAWA SHIZENSHI SHIRYO/NATURAL HISTORY REPORT OF KANAGAWA. (Text in Japanese; summaries in English and Japanese) 1980. a. Kanagawa-kenritsu Hakubutsukan - Kanagawa Prefectural Museum, 5-60 Minami-nakadoori, Naka-ku, Yokohama-shi, Kanagawa-ken 231, Japan.

500   JA   ISSN 0387-0995
Q4   CODEN: KADSAB
KANAZAWA DAIGAKU KYOIKUGAKUBU KIYO. SHIZEN KAGAKU HEN/KANAZAWA UNIVERSITY. FACULTY OF EDUCATION. BULLETIN. NATURAL SCIENCES. (Text in Japanese; summaries and some articles in English) 1952. a. Kanazawa Daigaku, Kyoikugakubu - Kanazawa University, Faculty of Education, 1-1 Marunouchi, Kanazawa-shi, Ishikawa-ken 920, Japan. **Indexed:** Biol.Abstr., GeoRef., Jap.Per.Ind.

500   JA   ISSN 0302-0479
Q4
KANAZAWA DAIGAKU KYOYOBU RONSHU. SHIZEN KAGAKU HEN/KANAZAWA UNIVERSITY. COLLEGE OF LIBERAL ARTS. ANNALS OF SCIENCE. (Text in English and Japanese; summaries in English) 1965. a. Kanazawa Daigaku, Kyoyobu - Kanazawa University, College of Liberal Arts, 1-1 Marunouchi, Kanazawa-shi, Ishikawa-ken 920, Japan. illus. **Indexed:** Biol.Abstr., INIS Atomind., Jap.Per.Ind., Math.R.
—BLDSC shelfmark: 1043.990000.

500   JA   ISSN 0022-8338
Q4   CODEN: SRKAAT
KANAZAWA UNIVERSITY. SCIENCE REPORTS/KANAZAWA DAIGAKU RIKA HOKOKU. (Text in English and French) 1951. s-a. exchange basis. Kanazawa Daigaku, Rigakubu - Kanazawa University, Faculty of Science, 1-1 Marunouchi, Kanazawa-shi, Ishikawa-ken 920, Japan. FAX 81-762-64-1059. Ed.Bd. bibl.; charts; illus.; index; circ. 500. **Indexed:** Biol.Abstr., Chem.Abstr., INIS Atomind., JTA, Math.R., Sci.Abstr.
—BLDSC shelfmark: 8155.000000.

500   JA   ISSN 0285-3205
KANSAI SHIZEN KAGAKU. (Text in Japanese) 1944. a. 1500 Yen (typically set in Apr.). Kansai Natural Science Research Society - Kansai Shizen Kagaku Kenkyukai, Kinki Nihon Tetsudo K.K., 1-55 Uehon-machi 6-chome, Tennoji-ku, Osaka-shi, Osaka-fu 543, Japan.
Description: Journal of the society. Contains reviews, commentary, and news.

500 150   US   ISSN 0022-8443
Q11   CODEN: TSASAH
KANSAS ACADEMY OF SCIENCE. TRANSACTIONS. 1868. s-a. $30 (Canada $32; elsewhere $35). Kansas Academy of Science, Box 30, Emporia State University, Emporia, KS 66801. TEL 316-343-5981. Ed. J. Robert Berg. circ. 850. **Indexed:** Biol.Abstr., Chem.Abstr., Dent.Ind., Ind.Med., Maize Abstr., Soils & Fert., VITIS.
—BLDSC shelfmark: 8976.000000.

500   PK   ISSN 0250-5363
Q80.P3   CODEN: KUJSDE
KARACHI JOURNAL OF SCIENCE. (Text in English) 1972. s-a. Rs.100($50) University of Karachi, Department of Physics, Karachi 75270, Pakistan. Eds. S.A. Husain, S.N. Hasnain. adv.; bk.rev.; abstr.; bibl.; charts; circ. 500. **Indexed:** Biol.Abstr., Chem.Abstr., Math.R., Phys.Abstr.
—BLDSC shelfmark: 5085.698300.

500   II   ISSN 0075-5168
Q1   CODEN: KUJSAB
KARNATAK UNIVERSITY, DHARWAD, INDIA. JOURNAL. SCIENCE. (Text in English) 1956. a. Rs.8($4) Karnatak University, Director, Prasaranga, Dharwad 580003, Karnataka, India. Ed. M.I. Savadatti. circ. 250. **Indexed:** Biol.Abstr., Chem.Abstr., Entomol.Abstr., GeoRef., Math.R.

500 600   US
KE-JI RIBAO/SCIENCE & TECHNOLOGY DAILY. (Text in Chinese) d. $329.40. China Books & Periodicals, Inc., 2929 24th St., San Francisco, CA 94110. TEL 415-282-2994. FAX 415-282-0994. (newspaper)

500 600   CC   ISSN 1002-1299
KE XUE. Chinese translation of: Scientific American (US ISSN 0036-8733) 1978. m. Y96($50) (effective 1992). I S T I C Chongqing, P.O. Box 2104, Chongqing, Sichuan, People's Republic of China. TEL 0121-53170. FAX 0811-352473. TELEX 62128 CBIST CN. Eds. Jonathan Piel, Liu Da. adv.; bk.rev.; circ. 20,000. (back issues avail.)

500   JA   ISSN 0911-7237
KEIO GIJUKU DAIGAKU HIYOSHI KIYO. SHIZEN KAGAKU/HIYOSHI REVIEW OF NATURAL SCIENCE. (Text in English and Japanese; summaries in English) 1985. a. Keio Gijuku Daigaku, Hiyoshi Kiyo Kanko linkai, 1-1, Hiyoshi 4-chome, Kohoku-ku, Yokohama-shi, Kanagawa-ken 223, Japan.
—BLDSC shelfmark: 4319.084000.

KEIO GIJUKU DAIGAKU RIKOGAKUBUHO. see *TECHNOLOGY: COMPREHENSIVE WORKS*

620   JA   ISSN 0286-4215
   CODEN: KSTREE
KEIO SCIENCE AND TECHNOLOGY REPORTS. (Text in English, French and German) 1948. irreg. exchange only. Keio Gijuku Daigaku, Rikogakubu - Keio University, Faculty of Science and Technology, Matsushita Memorial Library, 14-1, Hiyoshi 3-chome, Kohoku-ku, Yokohama-shi, Kanagawa-ken 223, Japan. Ed. Yasuji Ohtsuka. charts; illus.; stat.; circ. 1,000. **Indexed:** Chem.Abstr., Eng.Ind., JCT, JTA, Math.R., Phys.Abstr.
Former titles: Keio Engineering Reports; Keio University. Fujihara Memorial Faculty of Engineering. Proceedings. (ISSN 0016-2507)

500 600   CC   ISSN 1000-7857
KEJI DAOBAO/SCIENCE AND TECHNOLOGY HERALD. (Text in Chinese, English) bi-m. (New York Educational Foundation of Science and Technology, US) Zhongguo Keji Daobao-she, 19 Dahuisi, Haidian-qu, Beijing 100081, People's Republic of China. TEL 8313553. Ed. Meng Zhaoying.
—BLDSC shelfmark: 8134.282100.

500   CC   ISSN 1000-7695
KEJI GUANLI YANJIU. (Text in Chinese) bi-m. Zhongguo Kexueyuan, Guangzhou Fenyuan - Chinese Academy of Sciences, Guangzhou Branch, No. 100, Xianlie Zhonglu, Guangzhou, Guangdong 510070, People's Republic of China. TEL 775600.

500 600   CC   ISSN 1001-7348
KEJI JINBU YU DUICE. (Text in Chinese) bi-m. Hubei Sheng Kexue Jishu Weiyuanhui, Xiaohongshan, Wuchang-qu, Wuhan, Hubei 430071, People's Republic of China. TEL 813110. Ed. Chen Hongyu.

500 600   CC
KEJI KAIFA DONGTAI/SCIENCE AND TECHNOLOGY EXPLORATION TREND. (Text in Chinese) bi-m. Zhongguo Kexueyuan, Wenxian Qingbao Zhongxin - Chinese Academy of Sciences, Documentation Information Center, 27 Wangfujing Dajie, Beijing 100710, People's Republic of China. TEL 556180. Ed. Zhong Ying.

KEJI YINGYU XUEXI/LEARNING ENGLISH FOR SCIENCE & TECHNOLOGY. see *LINGUISTICS*

SCIENCES: COMPREHENSIVE WORKS

500 600   CC
KEJI YU FAZHAN/SCIENCE, TECHNOLOGY AND DEVELOPMENT. (Text in Chinese) q. Zhongguo Kexue Jishu Qingbao Yanjiusuo - Chinese Institute of Science and Technology Information, 15 Fuxing Lu, Beijing 100038, People's Republic of China. TEL 8015544. Ed. Su Zhongjie.

500 600   SA
KELVIN NEWS/KELVINNUUS. (Text in Afrikaans, English) 1977-19?? m. free. Associated Scientific and Technical Societies of South Africa, P.O. Box 93480, Yeoville 2143, South Africa. TEL 011-487-1512. FAX 011-648-1876. circ. controlled.

KENKYU GIJUTSU KEIKAKU/JOURNAL OF SCIENCE POLICY AND RESEARCH MANAGEMENT. see *BUSINESS AND ECONOMICS — Management*

550   JA
KENKYU JOSEIKIN JUKYUSHA KENKYU HOKOKUSHU. (Text in Japanese) 1984. a. Saneyoshi Shogakkai - Saneyoshi Scholarship Foundation, Nihon Bldg. 433, 6-2 Ote-machi 2-chome, Chiyoda-ku, Tokyo 100, Japan. abstr.
   Description: Research reports of the foundation.

500 100   NE   ISSN 0165-1773
KENNIS EN METHODE; tijdschrift voor wetenschapsfilosofie en methodologie. (Text in Dutch; summaries in English) 1977. 4/yr. fl.86 to individuals (foreign fl.133); institutions fl.152 (foreign fl.162)(effective 1992). Uitgeverij Boom, P.O. Box 1058, 7940 KB Meppel, Netherlands. TEL 05220-66111. FAX 05220-66198. Ed.Bd. adv.; circ. 675. **Indexed:** Phil.Ind.

500   US   ISSN 0023-0081
Q11   CODEN: TKASAT
KENTUCKY ACADEMY OF SCIENCE. TRANSACTIONS. 1939. s-a. $15 (foreign $30). Kentucky Academy of Science, c/o Vardley Wiedeman, University of Louisville, Louisville, KY 40292. TEL 502-588-5943. Ed. Branley A. Branson. charts; illus.; index; circ. 840. **Indexed:** Bibl.Agri., Biol.Abstr., Chem.Abstr., Excerp.Med., GeoRef., Helminthol.Abstr., Sci.Cit.Ind., Zoo.Rec.
—BLDSC shelfmark: 8977.000000.
Refereed Serial

500 600   KE
QH301   CODEN: KSTSDG
KENYA JOURNAL OF SCIENCES. SERIES A: PHYSICAL AND CHEMICAL SCIENCES. 1979. s-a. EAs.145($29) Kenya National Academy of Sciences, Box 39450, Nairobi, Kenya. Ed. J.O. Malo. (back issues avail.) **Indexed:** Chem.Abstr., Curr.Cont., Sci.Cit.Ind.
   Former titles: Kenya Journal of Science and Technology. Series A: Physical and Chemical Sciences (ISSN 0250-8257); Kenya Science and Technology Journal.

500 600   KE
KENYA NATIONAL ACADEMY FOR ADVANCEMENT OF ARTS AND SCIENCES. NEWSLETTER. Short title: K N A A S News. 1977. a. Kenya National Academy for Advancement of Arts and Sciences, Box 47288, Nairobi, Kenya. Ed. Francis Inganji.

500 700   KE
KENYA NATIONAL ACADEMY OF SCIENCES. ANNUAL REPORT. (Text in English) a. Kenya National Academy of Science, Box 47288, Nairobi, Kenya.
   Formerly: Kenya National Academy for Advancement of Arts and Sciences. Annual Report.

KENYA PAST AND PRESENT. see *HISTORY — History Of Africa*

500   CC   ISSN 0368-6396
KEXUE/SCIENCE. (Text in Chinese; abstract in English) 1915. bi-m. Y10.80 (foreign $10.80). Shanghai Scientific and Technical Publishers, Journal Department, 450 Ruijin 2 Lu, Shanghai 200020, People's Republic of China. Ed.Bd. adv.; circ. 4,000. ●Also available online.
   Description: Introduces the frontiers of science and technology in the world and achievements by Chinese scientists.

500   CC
KEXUE/SCIENCE. (Text in Chinese) m. Zhongguo Kexue Jishu Qingbaosuo, Chongqing Fensuo - Chinese Science and Technology Information Institute, Chongqing Branch, 132, Shengli Lu, Chongqing, Sichuan 630013, People's Republic of China. TEL 350455. Ed. Xiao Zhongyang.

500   CC
KEXUE DAGUANYUAN/GRAND VIEW GARDEN OF SCIENCE. JOURNAL. (Text in Chinese) bi-m. $0.40 per no. (Kexue Daguanyuan - Grand View Garden of Science) Guoji Shudian, Qikan Bu, Chegongzhuang Xilu 21, P.O. Box 399, Beijing 100044, People's Republic of China.

KEXUE DUI SHEHUI DE YINGXIANG/SCIENCE IMPACT ON SOCIETY. see *SOCIAL SCIENCES: COMPREHENSIVE WORKS*

500   CC   ISSN 0454-0905
KEXUE HUABAO/SCIENCE PICTORIAL. (Text in Chinese) 1926. m. $5 per no. Shanghai Scientific and Technical Publishers, Journal Department, 450 Ruijin 2 Lu, Shanghai 200020, People's Republic of China. TEL 4370160. Ed. Xu Fusheng.

500 600   CC
KEXUE JISHU YANJIU CHENGGUO GONGBAO/BULLETIN OF SCIENTIFIC AND TECHNOLOGICAL ACHIEVEMENTS. (Text in Chinese) m. Guojia Kewei, Chengguo Guanli Bangongshi - National Science Commission, Achievements Management Office, No. 15, Fuxing Lu, Beijing 100038, People's Republic of China. TEL 8015544. Ed. Wang Hongji.

500 600   CC   ISSN 1003-5680
KEXUE JISHU YU BIANZHENGFA/SCIENCE, TECHNOLOGY, AND DIALECTICS. (Text in Chinese) 1984. bi-m. Y4.20. Shanxi Sheng Ziran Bianzhengfa Yanjiuhui - Shanxi Institute of Dialectics of Nature, Bldg. 128, Shanxi Daxue, 36 Wucheng Lu, Taiyuan, Shanxi 030006, People's Republic of China. TEL 773441-417. Ed. Zhang Jiazhi. adv.; bk.rev.; circ. 2,500.
   Description: Covers the philosophy of science, theory of technology, science and society, and the history of scientific development.

500   CC
KEXUE SHIJIE/SCIENTIFIC WORLD. (Text in Chinese) m. Y20.40. Science Press, 16 Donghuangchenggen Beijie, Beijing 100707, People's Republic of China. TEL 4010642. FAX 4012180. TELEX 210247 SPBJ CN.
   Description: Popular science magazine.

500   CC
KEXUE SHIYAN/SCIENTIFIC EXPERIMENTS. (Text in Chinese) m. $0.40 per no. Guoji Shudian, Qikan Bu, Chegongzhuang Xilu 21, P.O. Box 399, Beijing 100044, People's Republic of China.

500   CC   ISSN 0023-074X
   CODEN: KHTPAT
KEXUE TONGBAO. English edition: Chinese Science Bulletin (ISSN 0250-7862) (Text in Chinese, summaries in English) 1950. s-m. Y8($15) per no. (Chinese Academy of Sciences) Science Press, Marketing and Sales Department, 16 Donghuangchenggen Beijie, Beijing 100707, People's Republic of China. TEL 4010642. FAX 4012180. TELEX 210247-SPBJ-CN. adv.; circ. 15,000. **Indexed:** Biol.Abstr., Chem.Abstr., Geo.Abstr., GeoRef., Helminthol.Abstr., Ind.Sci.Rev., Mass Spectr.Bull., Math.R., Sci.Abstr.
—BLDSC shelfmark: 5091.500000.
   Description: Presents concise reports on important recent results of scientific research in basic and applied sciences, reflecting the current level of development of science and technology in mainland China. Includes a letters column.
Refereed Serial

500   CC
KEXUE YU SHENGHUO/SCIENCE AND LIFE. (Text in Chinese) bi-m. Tianjin Kexue Jishu Chubanshe - Tianjin Science and Technology Press, 130 Shifeng Dao, Tianjin 300041, People's Republic of China. TEL 706821. Ed. Dou Xiurong.

500   CC   ISSN 1000-3398
KEXUE YU WENHUA/SCIENCE & CULTURE. (Text in Chinese) 1980. bi-m. $16.20. (Fujian Sheng Kexue Jishu Xiehui) Fujian Kexue Jishu Chubanshe - Fujian Science & Technology Publishers, 51 Hudong Lu, Fuzhou, Fujian 350003. TEL 550151. (Dist. in US by: China Books & Periodicals, Inc., 2929 24th St., San Francisco, CA 94110. TEL 415-282-2994) Ed. Zheng Qiguang.

500 630   CC   ISSN 1001-4284
KEXUE ZHIFU YU SHENGHUO/SCIENCE PROSPERITY AND LIFE. (Text in Chinese) 1978. m. Y1.00 per no. Kexue Chubanshe, Qikan Bu, 16 Donghuangchenggen Beijie, Beijing 100707, People's Republic of China. TEL 4010642. FAX 4012180. TELEX 210247-SPBJ-CN. (US office: Science Press New York, Ltd., 63-117 Alderton St., Rego Park, NY 11374. TEL 718-459-4638) Ed. Xu Tianxing. adv.; circ. 100,000.
   Former titles: Nongcun Kexue - Science in Countryside (ISSN 1000-307X); Nongcun Kexue Shiyan.
   Description: Comprehensive popular science publication for rural areas of China. Covers agricultural techniques, rural architecture, energy resources, environmental protection, life and hygiene.

500 658   CC   ISSN 1000-2995
Q180.55.M3
KEYAN GUANLI/SCIENCE RESEARCH MANAGEMENT. (Text in Chinese) 1980. bi-m. $7 per no. (Chinese Academy of Sciences, Institute of Science and Technology Policy Management) Science Press, Marketing and Sales Department, 16 Donghuangchenggen Beijie, Beijing 100707, People's Republic of China. TEL 4010642. FAX 4012180. TELEX 210247-SPBJ-CN. Ed. Luo Wei. adv.; circ. 21,000.
—BLDSC shelfmark: 8164.191700.
   Description: Explores the characteristics and laws of modern scientific development, theories and methods of science research management, scientific and technological policies, research systems, personnel training, and trends in newly emerging areas of research.

500 600   VN
KHOA HOC KY THUAT KINH TE THE GIOI/WORLD SCIENCE, TECHNOLOGY AND ECONOMY. 1982. w. 5 Ly Thuong Kiet, Hanoi, Socialist Republic of Vietnam. TEL 52931.

500   VN
KHOA HOC VA DOI SONG/SCIENCE AND LIFE. 1959. fortn. 70 Tran Hung Dao, Hanoi, Socialist Republic of Vietnam. TEL 53427. Ed. Duong Hong Dat. circ. 25,000.

500   SU   ISSN 1018-3647
Q80.S2
KING SAUD UNIVERSITY. JOURNAL. SCIENCES. (Other sections avail.: Administrative Sciences, Agricultural Sciences, Architecture and Planning, Arts, Educational Sciences, Engineering Sciences) (Text in Arabic, English) 1969. s-a. $10. King Saud University, University Libraries, P.O Box 22480, Riyadh 11495, Saudi Arabia. TEL 4676148. FAX 4676162. TELEX 401019 KSU SJ. Ed. M.O. Taha. charts; illus.; circ. 3,000. **Indexed:** Curr.Adv.Ecol.Sci., Herb.Abstr., Seed Abstr. Key Title: Magallat Gami'at al-Malik al-Sa'ud, al-'Ulum.
   Former titles (until 1989): King Saud University. College of Science. Journal (ISSN 0735-9799); University of Riyadh. Faculty of Sciences. Bulletin.
Refereed Serial

500 600   JA   ISSN 0386-4928
Q77   CODEN: KDRKBB
KINKI DAIGAKU RIKOGAKUBU KENKYU HOKOKU/KINKI UNIVERSITY. FACULTY OF SCIENCE AND TECHNOLOGY. JOURNAL. (Text in English and Japanese; summaries in English) 1966. a. Kinki Daigaku, Rikogakubu - Kinki University, Faculty of Science and Technology, 4-1 Kowakae 3-chome, Higashi-Osaka-shi, Osaka-fu 577, Japan. **Indexed:** Chem.Abstr., INIS Atomind., Jap.Per.Ind.
—BLDSC shelfmark: 4747.400000.

SCIENCES: COMPREHENSIVE WORKS 4321

500.9 913   US   ISSN 0075-6245
QH1   CODEN: KIRTA4
KIRTLANDIA. 1967. irreg., no.41, 1985. price varies. Cleveland Museum of Natural History, One Wade Oval Dr., University Circle, Cleveland, OH 44106. TEL 216-231-4600. Ed. David Brose. circ. 850. **Indexed:** Biol.Abstr., GeoRef., Zoo.Rec.
—BLDSC shelfmark: 5097.590000.

KISO, KANKYO KAGAKU KENKYU/HIROSHIMA UNIVERSITY. FACULTY OF INTEGRATED ARTS AND SCIENCES. SCIENCE REPORTS. see *ENVIRONMENTAL STUDIES*

500   JA   ISSN 0386-0655
KITAKAMI-SHIRITSU HAKUBUTSUKAN KENKYU/KITAKAMI CITY MUSEUM. BULLETIN. (Text in Japanese) 1975. irreg. Kitakami-shiritsu Hakubutsukan - Kitakami City Museum, 14-59 Tachibana, Kurosawajiri-cho, Kitakami-shi, Iwate-ken 024, Japan.

550.9   JA   ISSN 0387-964X
KITAKYUSHU-SHIRITSU SHIZENSHI HAKUBUTSUKAN KENKYU HOKOKU/KITAKYUSHU MUSEUM OF NATURAL HISTORY. BULLETIN. (Text in English and Japanese) 1979. a. universities and libraries on exchange basis. Kitakyushu-shiritsu Shizenshi Hakubutsukan - Kitakyushu Museum of Natural History, 3-6 Nishihon-machi, Yahatahigashi-ku, Kitakyushu-shi, Fukuoka-ken, Japan. FAX 093-661-7503. circ. 1,200.
Description: Covers original articles and short notes on natural history

KNOWLEDGE; dedicated to the dissemination of knowledge for the happiness, health, security, and survival of humankind. see *LITERARY AND POLITICAL REVIEWS*

500   JA   ISSN 0287-6515
KOBE DAIGAKU DAIGAKUIN SHIZEN KAGAKU KENKYUKA KIYO B/KOBE UNIVERSITY. GRADUATE SCHOOL OF SCIENCE AND TECHNOLOGY. MEMOIRS. SERIES B. (Text in Japanese; summaries in English and Japanese) 1983. a. Kobe Daigaku, Daigakuin Shizen Kagaku Kenkyuka - Kobe University, Graduate School of Science and Technology, 1-1, Rokkodai-cho, Nada-ku, Kobe-shi, Hyogo-ken 657, Japan. abstr.

500   JA   ISSN 0389-9578
KOBE TOKIWA TANKI DAIGAKU KIYO/KOBE TOKIWA COLLEGE. BULLETIN. (Text in English and Japanese) 1971. a. free. Kobe Tokiwa Tanki Daigaku - Kobe Tokiwa College, 2-6-2 Otani-cho, Nagata-ku, Kobe-shi 653, Japan. TEL 078-611-1821. FAX 078-643-4361. Ed. Reiko Shimomura. (back issues avail.)
Description: Covers topics in the fields of liberal arts, pedagogy, medical science and technology.

500   JA   ISSN 0450-609X
VK4   CODEN: KDKRDX
KOBE UNIVERSITY OF MERCANTILE MARINE. REVIEW. PART 2. MARITIME STUDIES, AND SCIENCE AND ENGINEERING. (Text in Japanese; abstracts in English) 1953. a. Kobe University of Mercantile Marine, 1-1, Fukae-Minami-machi 5-chome, Higashi-Nada-ku, Kobe-shi, Hyogo-ken 658, Japan. **Indexed:** INIS Atomind.
—BLDSC shelfmark: 7786.250000.
Formerly (until 1980): Kobe University of Mercantile Marine. Review. Part 2. Navigation, Marine Engineering, Nuclear Engineering and Scientific Section.

551.44   SP   ISSN 0214-6967
KOBIE REVISTA DE BELLAS ARTES Y CIENCIAS: SERIE CIENCIAS NATURALES. (Text in Basque and Spanish; summaries in English and French) 1969. a. 2000 ptas. Diputacion Foral de Bizkaia, Departamento de Cultura, P.O. Box 97, Bilbao, Spain. TEL 415-7217. FAX 416-2981. (back issues avail.)

500   JA   ISSN 0389-0244
CODEN: KDGAAR
KOCHI DAIGAKU GAKUJUTSU KENKYU HOKOKU. SHIZEN KAGAKU/KOCHI UNIVERSITY. RESEARCH REPORTS. NATURAL SCIENCE. (Text in English and Japanese; summaries in English) 1951. a. Kochi Daigaku - Kochi University, 5-1 Akebono-cho 2-chome, Kochi-shi, Kochi-ken 780, Japan. **Indexed:** Chem.Abstr., Jap.Per.Ind.

KOCHI DAIGAKU KYOIKUGAKUBU KENKYU HOKOKU. DAI-3-BU/KOCHI UNIVERSITY. FACULTY OF EDUCATION. BULLETIN. SERIES 3. see *EDUCATION*

500   JA   ISSN 0452-2486
CODEN: KJDSA6
KOCHI JOSHI DAIGAKU KIYO. SHIZEN KAGAKU HEN/KOCHI WOMEN'S UNIVERSITY. BULLETIN. SERIES OF NATURAL SCIENCES. (Text and summaries in English and Japanese) 1952. a. Kochi Joshi Daigaku - Kochi Women's University, 5-15 Eikokuji-cho, Kochi-shi, Kochi-ken 780, Japan. **Indexed:** Chem.Abstr., Jap.Per.Ind.
—BLDSC shelfmark: 2600.135000.

KOKURITSU KAGAKU HAKUBUTSUKAN NENPO. see *MUSEUMS AND ART GALLERIES*

500   JA   ISSN 0082-4755
KOKURITSU KAGAKU HAKUBUTSUKAN SENPO/NATIONAL SCIENCE MUSEUM. MEMOIRS. (Text in English and Japanese; summaries in English) 1968. a. exchange basis. Monbu-sho, Kokuritsu Kagaku Hakubutsukan - Ministry of Education, National Science Museum, 7-20 Ueno Koen, Taito-ku, Tokyo 110, Japan. Ed.Bd. circ. 1,000 (controlled). **Indexed:** Biol.Abstr., Curr.Adv.Ecol.Sci., GeoRef., Jap.Per.Ind.
—BLDSC shelfmark: 5627.700000.

069   JA   ISSN 0288-7975
KOMATSU-SHIRITSU HAKUBUTSUKAN KENKYU KIYO/KOMATSU CITY MUSEUM. MEMOIRS. (Text in Japanese) 1965. a. price varies. Komatsu-shiritsu Hakubutsukan - Komatsu City Museum, Rojo Koen, Marunouchi Koen-machi, Komatsu-shi, Ishikawa-ken 923, Japan. circ. 500.

500   JA   ISSN 0452-4160
Q1   CODEN: MKOUAS
KONAN DAIGAKU KIYO. RIGAKU HEN/KONAN UNIVERSITY. MEMOIRS. SCIENCE SERIES. (Text and summaries in English and Japanese) 1955. a. Konan Daigaku - Konan University, 9-1 Okamoto 8-chome, Higashi-nada-ku, Kobe-shi, Hyogo-ken 658, Japan. **Indexed:** Biol.Abstr., Chem.Abstr., INIS Atomind, Jap.Per.Ind.
—BLDSC shelfmark: 5623.200000.

001.3 500   NO   ISSN 0368-6302
AS283   CODEN: KNSFA2
KONGELIGE NORSKE VIDENSKABERS SELSKAB. FORHANDLINGER. 1926. a. Erling Skakkes gt. 47 b, N-7013 Trondheim, Norway. (U.S. addr.: Publications Expediting Inc., 200 Meacham Ave., Elmont, NY 11003) Ed. Nils Soevik. **Indexed:** A.I.C.P., Biol.Abstr., Math.R., Sci.Abstr.
—BLDSC shelfmark: 5107.000000.
Formerly: Kongelige Norske Videnskabers Selskab. Arsberetning.

001.3 500   NO   ISSN 0368-6310
CODEN: KNSSA7
KONGELIGE NORSKE VIDENSKABERS SELSKAB. SKRIFTER/ROYAL NORWEGIAN SOCIETY OF SCIENCES. PUBLICATIONS. (Text in English) 1791. irreg. price varies. Erling Skakkes gt. 47 b, N-7013 Trondheim, Norway. (U.S. addr.: Publications Expediting Inc., 200 Meacham Ave., Elmont, NY 11003) Ed. Nils Soevik. charts; illus.; stat. **Indexed:** Biol.Abstr., Chem.Abstr., Deep Sea Res.& Oceanogr.Abstr., Math.R., Sci.Abstr.
—BLDSC shelfmark: 5109.000000.

500   NE   ISSN 0065-552X
KONINKLIJKE NEDERLANDSE AKADEMIE VAN WETENSCHAPPEN. AFDELING NATUURKUNDE. VERHANDELINGEN. TWEEDE REEKS. (Text in English, French, German and Dutch) 1893. irreg., vol.87, 1989. price varies. Elsevier Science Publishers B.V., Books Division, P.O. Box 211, 1000 AE Amsterdam, Netherlands. TEL 020-5803911. FAX 020-5803705. TELEX 18582 ESPA NL. (Subscr. in U.S. and Canada to: Elsevier Science Publishing Co., Inc., Box 882, Madison Sq. Sta., New York, NY 10159. TEL 212-989-5800) Ed. A.M. Verheggen. adv.; bk.rev.; circ. 1,000.
Refereed Serial

500   HU   ISSN 0075-6946
KORUNK TUDOMANYA. 1964. irreg. price varies. (Magyar Tudomanyos Akademia) Akademiai Kiado, Publishing House of the Hungarian Academy of Sciences, Box 24, H-1363 Budapest, Hungary.

500   GW   ISSN 0023-4230
Q3   CODEN: KSMSAC
KOSMOS. 1904. m. DM.79.80 (foreign DM.82.80). (Kosmos Gesellschaft der Naturfreunde) Deutsche Verlags-Anstalt GmbH, Neckarstr. 121, Postfach 106012, 7000 Stuttgart 10, Germany. TEL 0711-7200591. FAX 0711-2631292. Ed. R. Koethe. adv.; bk.rev.; charts; illus.; index; circ. 60,000 (controlled). **Indexed:** GeoRef., INIS Atomind., Protozool.Abstr.
—BLDSC shelfmark: 5114.010000.
Description: Non-technical and popular magazine covering natural science subjects such as plants, animals, environmental protection, geology, astronomy, physics, technology, and medicine. Includes readers' comments, questions and answers.

KOTONOURA. see *MUSEUMS AND ART GALLERIES*

KULTURBERICHTE AUS NIEDEROESTERREICH. see *ART*

500   JA   ISSN 0454-6148
KUMAMOTO DAIGAKU KYOIKUGAKUBU KIYO. SHIZEN KAGAKU/KUMAMOTO UNIVERSITY. FACULTY OF EDUCATION. MEMOIRS. NATURAL SCIENCE. (Text and summaries in English and Japanese) 1953. a. Kumamoto Daigaku, Kyoikugakubu - Kumamoto University, Faculty of Education, 40-1, Kurokami 2-chome, Kumamoto-shi, Kumamoto-ken 860, Japan. FAX 096-343-1800. circ. 300. **Indexed:** Biol.Abstr., Chem.Abstr., INIS Atomind., Jap.Per.Ind.
—BLDSC shelfmark: 5593.310000.

500   JA   ISSN 0286-5769
Q4
KUMAMOTO DAIGAKU KYOYOBU KIYO. SHIZEN KAGAKU HEN/KUMAMOTO UNIVERSITY. FACULTY OF GENERAL EDUCATION. MEMOIRS. NATURAL SCIENCES. (Text and summaries in English and Japanese) 1966. a. Kumamoto Daigaku, Kyoyobu - Kumamoto University, Faculty of General Education, 40-1, Kurokami 2-chome, Kumamoto-shi, Kumamoto-ken 860, Japan. **Indexed:** Jap.Per.Ind.

500 060   SW   ISSN 0081-9956
KUNGLIGA VETENSKAPSAKADEMIEN. BIDRAG TILL KUNGLIGA VETENSKAPSAKADEMIENS HISTORIA. 1963. irreg., vol.22, 1989. Kungliga Vetenskapsakademien - Royal Swedish Academy of Sciences, Box 50005, S-104 05 Stockholm, Sweden. FAX 46-8-155670.

500   JA   ISSN 0286-9500
KUOKU/QUARK. (Text in Japanese) 1982. m. 740 Yen. Kodansha Ltd., International Division, 12-21 Otowa 2-chome, Bunkyo-ku, Tokyo 112, Japan. TEL 03-3945-1111. FAX 03-3943-7815. TELEX J34509 KODANSHA. Ed. Noriaki Hori. adv.; bk.rev.; circ. 120,000.

500.9   JA   ISSN 0913-1566
KURASHIKI-SHIRITSU SHIZENSHI HAKUBUTSUKAN KENKYU HOKOKU/KURASHIKI MUSEUM OF NATURAL HISTORY. BULLETIN. (Text in Japanese; summaries in English and Japanese) 1986. a. 430 Yen. Kurashiki-shiritsu Shizenshi Hakubutsukan - Kurashiki Museum of Natural History, 6-1 Chuo 2-chome, Kurashiki, Okayama 710, Japan. TEL 0864-25-6037. FAX 0864-25-6038. abstr. (back issues avail.)
Description: Contains mainly original papers.

KURASHIKI-SHIRITSU SHIZENSHI HAKUBUTSUKANPO. see *MUSEUMS AND ART GALLERIES*

500 069   JA   ISSN 0912-1897
KUSHIRO-SHIRITSU HAKUBUTSUKAN KIYO/KUSHIRO CITY MUSEUM. MEMOIRS. (Text in Japanese; summaries in English and Japanese) 1972. a. Kushiro-shiritsu Hakubutsukan - Kushiro City Museum, 1-7 Shunkodai, Kushiro-shi, Hokkaido 085, Japan.

SCIENCES: COMPREHENSIVE WORKS

500   HU   ISSN 0866-5192
Q180.A1
KUTATASSZERVEZESI TAJEKOZTATO/BULLETIN OF RESEARCH MANAGEMENT. (Text in Hungarian; summaries in English) 1961. 6/yr. $30 or exchange basis. Magyar Tudomanyos Akademia Konyvtara, Aranyjanos u.1, P.O. Box 7, 1361 Budapest 5, Hungary. Ed. J. Balazs.
—BLDSC shelfmark: 5131.575000.
    Former titles (until 1990): Kutatas - Fejlesztes (ISSN 0231-4231); (until 1982): Tudomanyszervezesi Tajekoztato (ISSN 0040-862X)
    Description: Contains information on the current problems of science policy and the organization, management and planning of scientific research.

500   KU   ISSN 0250-4065
T1   CODEN: ARKRDL
KUWAIT INSTITUTE FOR SCIENTIFIC RESEARCH. ANNUAL RESEARCH REPORT. 1977. a. free. Kuwait Institute for Scientific Research, P.O. Box 24885, Safat, Kuwait. FAX 4846891. TELEX KISR-KT-22299. Ed.Bd. circ. 2,000. (back issues avail.) **Indexed:** Chem.Abstr.
—BLDSC shelfmark: 1519.798000.
    Description: Contains articles meant to promote scientific and applied research in relation to industry, energy, environment, natural resources, food resources and economics.

500   KO
KWAHAK DONG-A. 1986. m. Dong-A Ilbo, 139 Sejongno, Chongno-gu, Seoul, S. Korea. TEL 02-721-7114. Ed. Kwon O-Kie. circ. 52,000.

500   KN
KWAHAKWON TONGBO/BULLETIN OF THE ACADEMY OF SCIENCES. (Text in Korean) bi-m. Korean Academy of Sciences, Pyongyang, N. Korea.

KWANSEI GAKUIN DAIGAKU RIGAKUBU TSUSHIN. see *COLLEGE AND ALUMNI*

607   PL   ISSN 0023-589X
Q4
KWARTALNIK HISTORII NAUKI I TECHNIKI/QUARTERLY JOURNAL OF THE HISTORY OF SCIENCE AND TECHNOLOGY. 1956. q. $38. Polska Akademia Nauk, Instytut Historii Nauki i Techniki, Ul. Nowy Swiat 72, Palac Staszica, 00-330 Warsaw, Poland. (Dist. by: Ars Polona, Krakowskie Przedmiescie 7, 00-068 Warsaw, Poland) bk.rev.; advtr.; charts; illus.; index, cum.index every 10 yrs.; circ. 740. (tabloid format) **Indexed:** Amer.Hist.& Life, Chem.Abstr., Hist.Abstr., Math.R.

500   JA   ISSN 0912-6449
KYODO TO KAGAKU/NATURE AND SCIENCE. (Text in Japanese) 1954. s-a. 1000 Yen. Hokkaido Kyoiku Daigaku, Sapporo Bunko Chigaku Kyoshitsu, 1-5, 5-jo 3-chome, Ainosato, Kita-ku, Sapporo, Hokkaido 064, Japan. FAX 011-778-8822.
    Description: Contains original papers, reviews, commentary, and news on nature and science.

509   JA   ISSN 0023-6004
KYOKUCHI/POLAR NEWS. (Text in Japanese) 1965. s-a. 5000 Yen (effective May 1991). Japan Polar Research Association - Nihon Kyokuchi Kenkyu Shinkokai, 1-8-7, Koji-machi, Chiyoda-ku, Tokyo 102, Japan. FAX 03-3239-7617. TELEX 0-232-4473. Ed. T. Torii. adv.; bk.rev.; charts; illus.; stat.; circ. 3,000. **Indexed:** Geo.Abstr.
    Description: Contains Antarctic and Arctic information and relevant news on geoscience and polar-science

500   JA
KYOTO-FURITSU DAIGAKU GAKUJUTSU HOKOKU. RIGAKU SEIKATSU KAGAKU/KYOTO PREFECTURAL UNIVERSITY. SCIENTIFIC REPORTS: NATURAL SCIENCE AND LIVING SCIENCE. (Text in Japanese; summaries in English) 1952. irreg., no.27, 1976. avail. on exchange. Kyoto Prefectural University - Kyoto-furitsu Daigaku, Shimogamo Hangi-cho, Sakyo-ku, Kyoto 606, Japan. **Indexed:** C.I.S. Abstr., Food Sci.& Tech.Abstr., INIS Atomind., Math.R.
    Formerly: Kyoto Prefectural University. Scientific Reports: Natural Science, Domestic Science and Social Welfare (ISSN 0075-739X)

505 605   JA   ISSN 0911-0305
           CODEN: MFETEC
KYOTO INSTITUTE OF TECHNOLOGY. FACULTY OF ENGINEERING AND DESIGN. MEMOIRS. (Text in English and European languages) 1952. a. exchange basis. Kyoto Institute of Technology, Faculty of Engineering and Design - Kyoto Kogei Sen'i Daigaku Kogeigakubu, Matsugasaki, Sakyo-ku, Kyoto 606, Japan. circ. 820. **Indexed:** Chem.Abstr., Math.R., Sci.Abstr.
—BLDSC shelfmark: 5593.345000.
    Formerly: Kyoto Technical University. Faculty of Industrial Arts. Memoirs: Science and Technology (ISSN 0453-0047)

KYOTO KYOIKU DAIGAKU KIYO. B. SHIZEN KAGAKU/KYOTO UNIVERSITY OF EDUCATION. BULLETIN. SERIES B: MATHEMATICS AND NATURAL SCIENCE. see *MATHEMATICS*

500   JA   ISSN 0287-7902
          CODEN: KSRODS
KYOTO SANGYO DAIGAKU RONSHU. SHIZEN KAGAKU KEIRETSU/ACTA HUMANISTICA ET SCIENTIFICA UNIVERSITATIS SANGIO KYOTIENSIS. NATURAL SCIENCE SERIES. (Text and summaries in English and Japanese) 1972. a. Kyoto Sangyo Daigaku - Kyoto Sangyo University, Motoyama, Kamigamo, Kita-ku, Kyoto-shi, Kyoto-fu 603, Japan. **Indexed:** Chem.Abstr.

500.2   JA   ISSN 0368-9689
Q77   CODEN: MFKPAQ
KYOTO UNIVERSITY. FACULTY OF SCIENCE. MEMOIRS. SERIES OF PHYSICS, ASTROPHYSICS, GEOPHYSICS AND CHEMISTRY. (Text in English) 1914. s-a. exchange basis. Kyoto University, Faculty of Science - Kyoto Daigaku Rigakubu, Kitashirakawa Oiwake-cho, Sakyo-ku, Kyoto 606, Japan. illus. **Indexed:** Chem.Abstr, Deep Sea Res.& Oceanogr.Abstr., JTA, Sci.Abstr.
—BLDSC shelfmark: 5597.900000.

546 531.64 536
539.7   JA   ISSN 0454-9244
QC770   CODEN: KURAAV
KYOTO UNIVERSITY. RESEARCH REACTOR INSTITUTE. ANNUAL REPORTS. (Text and summaries in English) 1968. a. donation or exchange basis. Kyoto University, Research Reactor Institute, Kumatori-cho, Sennan-gun, Osaka 590-04, Japan. FAX 0724-53-5810. Ed. Yutaka Iwata. circ. 1,000. (back issues avail.) **Indexed:** Chem.Abstr., INIS Atomind.
—BLDSC shelfmark: 1411.130000.

KYUSHU INSTITUTE OF TECHNOLOGY. BULLETIN: MATHEMATICS, NATURAL SCIENCE/KYUSHU KOGYO DAIGAKU KENKYU HOKOKU. SHIZEN KAGAKU. see *MATHEMATICS*

KYUSHU INSTITUTE OF TECHNOLOGY. BULLETIN: SCIENCE AND TECHNOLOGY/KYUSHU KOGYO DAIGAKU KENKYU HOKOKU. KOGAKU. see *TECHNOLOGY: COMPREHENSIVE WORKS*

500   US   ISSN 0882-1305
QC789.U62
L B L RESEARCH REVIEW. 1985. q. free to qualified personnel. University of California, Berkeley, Lawrence Berkeley Laboratory, Public Information Department, 1 Cyclotron Rd., Berkeley, CA 94720. TEL 510-486-6598. FAX 510-486-6641. Ed. Adrienne Kopa. bk.rev.; circ. 8,000. (back issues avail.) **Indexed:** Energy Rev., Environ.Per.Bibl., INIS Atomind.
—BLDSC shelfmark: 5162.213600.
    Formerly (until 1985): L B L News Magazine.
    Description: Review of important research accomplishments at the laboratory.

LAB TALK. see *EDUCATION — Teaching Methods And Curriculum*

LABORATORY PRACTICE; research techniques and equipment. see *MEDICAL SCIENCES — Experimental Medicine, Laboratory Technique*

LADA'AT; science for youth. see *CHILDREN AND YOUTH — For*

LANTERN; journal of art, knowledge and culture. see *EDUCATION*

LASER. see *TECHNOLOGY: COMPREHENSIVE WORKS*

500 539   US
QC789.U62
LAWRENCE BERKELEY LABORATORY. CATALOG OF RESEARCH PROJECTS. 1967. a. free. Lawrence Berkeley Laboratory, Technology Transfer Office, Bldg. 71F, Berkeley, CA 94720. TEL 415-486-6502. FAX 415-486-5401. circ. 12,500. (back issues avail.)
    Formerly: Lawrence Berkeley Laboratory. Research Highlights (ISSN 0091-9489)

500.2   UK   ISSN 0260-1036
LEEDS NATURALISTS' CLUB AND SCIENTIFIC ASSOCIATION. NEWSLETTER. 1976. s-a. £3 membership. Leeds Naturalists' Club and Scientific Association, c/o Mrs. P.P. Abbott, 73 Ridgeway, Leeds LS8 4DD, England. Ed. A. Hawkswell. bk.rev.; circ. 200.

500   UK
LEEDS PHILOSOPHICAL AND LITERARY SOCIETY. PROCEEDINGS. SCIENTIFIC. 1925. a. price varies. Leeds Philosophical and Literary Society, Central Museum, Calverley St., Leeds 2, England. Ed. H. Pantin. charts; index; circ. 650. **Indexed:** Biol.Abstr., Br.Hum.Ind., Curr.Adv.Ecol.Sci., GeoRef., Sci.Abstr.
    Description: Presents articles on any area of scientific investigation.

500   GW   ISSN 0323-4444
LEOPOLDINA; Mitteilungen der Deutschen Akademie der Naturforscher Leopoldina, Reihe 3. (Reihe 1: 1859-1923; Reihe 2: 1926-1930) 1955. a. DM.20. Deutsche Akademie der Naturforscher Leopoldina, August-Bebel-Str. 50a, 4010 Halle (S.), Germany. TEL 03746-24723. FAX 03746-21727. Ed. Benno Parthier. bk.rev.; circ. 1,500. **Indexed:** GeoRef.

500   NE   ISSN 0024-1520
LEVENDE NATUUR; tijdschrift voor natuurbehoud en natuurbeheer. (Text in Dutch; summaries in English) 1896. 6/yr. fl.45. Vereniging tot Behoud van Natuurmonumenten, Noordereinde 60, 1243 JJ 's-Graveland, Netherlands. TEL 080-225209. Ed. H.L. Schimmel. adv.; bk.rev.; charts; illus.; circ. 1,700. **Indexed:** Biol.Abstr.
    Description: Journal of nature conservation and management.

500   CC
LIAONING SHIFAN DAXUE XUEBAO (ZIRAN KEXUE BAN)/LIAONING NORMAL UNIVERSITY. JOURNAL (NATURAL SCIENCE EDITION). (Text in Chinese) q. Liaoning Shifan Daxue - Liaoning Normal University, 850 Huanghe Lu, Dalian, Liaoning 116022, People's Republic of China. TEL 401181. Ed. Zheng Yingshun.

500   US   ISSN 0075-9104
LIBRARY OF EXACT PHILOSOPHY. Short title: L E P. (Text in English and German) 1970. irreg. price varies. Springer-Verlag, 175 Fifth Ave., New York, NY 10010. TEL 212-460-1500. (Also Berlin, Heidelberg, Tokyo and Vienna) Ed. M. Bunge. (reprint service avail. from ISI)
—BLDSC shelfmark: 5198.700000.

500   LY   ISSN 0368-7481
Q1   CODEN: LBJSAP
LIBYAN JOURNAL OF SCIENCES; an international journal. (Text in English; summaries in Arabic) 1971. s-a. $3.50 to individuals; institutions $5.25. Al-Fateh University, Faculty of Science, P.O. Box 13040, Tripoli, Libya. Ed. M. J. Salem. adv.; circ. 400. **Indexed:** Biol.Abstr., Chem.Abstr., GeoRef., Math.R., Petrol.Abstr.

LIFE IN ACTION MAGAZINE. see *PHILOSOPHY*

SCIENCES: COMPREHENSIVE WORKS

500   US   ISSN 0024-3205
QH301   CODEN: LIFSAK
LIFE SCIENCES (1973). (Text in English, French and German) 1962. 52/yr. £1160 (effective 1992). Pergamon Press, Inc., Journals Division, 660 White Plains Rd., Tarrytown, NY 10591-5153. TEL 914-524-9200. FAX 914-333-2444. (And: Headington Hill, Oxford OX3 0BW, England. TEL 0865-794141) Eds. Rubin Bressler, Thomas F. Burks. adv.; charts; illus.; index; circ. 2,200. (also avail. in microform from MIM,UMI; back issues avail.) **Indexed:** Anim.Breed.Abstr., Biol.Abstr., Chem.Abstr., Curr.Cont, Dent.Ind., Geo.Abstr., Ind.Med., Nutr.Abstr., Protozool.Abstr., Psychol.Abstr.
—BLDSC shelfmark: 5208.930000.
    Formed by the merger of: Life Sciences. Part 1: Physiology and Pharmacology (ISSN 0300-9653); Life Sciences. Part 2: Biochemistry, General and Molecular (ISSN 0300-9637); Which superseded: Life Sciences.
    Refereed Serial

500   GW   ISSN 0024-3728
TP242   CODEN: LIBEAQ
LINDE BERICHTE AUS TECHNIK UND WISSENSCHAFT. English edition: Linde Reports on Science and Technology (ISSN 0024-3736) 1957. s-a. free. Linde AG, Abraham-Lincoln-Str. 21, 6200 Wiesbaden 1, Germany. Ed. Volker R. Leski. **Indexed:** INIS Atomind.
—BLDSC shelfmark: 5220.800000.

LIPPISCHE MITTEILUNGEN AUS GESCHICHTE UND LANDESKUNDE. see *HISTORY — History Of Europe*

500.9   US   ISSN 0024-5283
QH1   CODEN: LIMUAR
THE LIVING MUSEUM. (Braille and Inkprint Editions) 1939. q. free. Illinois State Museum, Springfield, IL 62706. TEL 217-782-7386. FAX 217-782-1254. illus.; index, cum.index: 1939-1955; circ. 18,000. **Indexed:** Biol.Abstr., Biol.Dig.
    Description: Describes Illinois' natural history, art, and anthropology.

500   US   ISSN 0096-9192
Q11   CODEN: PLAAA6
LOUISIANA ACADEMY OF SCIENCES. PROCEEDINGS. 1932. a. $20. Louisiana Academy of Sciences, c/o Dr. Brad Mc Pherson, Department of Biology, Centenary College, Shreveport, LA 71104. Ed. Robert Kolinsky. circ. 400. (back issues avail.) **Indexed:** Biol.Abstr., Chem.Abstr., Deep Sea Res.& Oceanogr.Abstr., Zoo.Rec.

LRABER ASARAKAKAN GITUTYUNNERI. see *HUMANITIES: COMPREHENSIVE WORKS*

509 016   SW   ISSN 0076-163X
LYCHNOS-BIBLIOTEK. STUDIES OCH KAELLSKRIFTER UDGIVNA AV LAERDOMSHISTORISKA SAMFUNDET. STUDIES AND SOURCES PUBLISHED BY THE SWEDISH HISTORY OF SCIENCE SOCIETY. 1936. irreg. price varies. (Laerdomshistoriska Samfundet - Swedish History of Science Society) Almqvist & Wiksell International, Box 638, S-101 28 Stockholm, Sweden. Ed. Gunnar Erikson. index. **Indexed:** Amer.Hist.& Life, Hist.Abstr.

509   SW   ISSN 0076-1648
Q64
LYCHNOS-LAERDOMSHISTORISKA SAMFUNDETS AARSBOK. ANNUAL OF THE SWEDISH HISTORY OF SCIENCE SOCIETY. 1936. a. price varies. (Laerdomshistoriska Samfundet) Almqvist & Wiksell International, Box 638, S-101 28 Stockholm, Sweden. Ed. Gunnar Erikson. bk.rev.; index.

500 600   GW   ISSN 0341-7727
Q49
M P G SPIEGEL. 1972. bi-m. Max-Planck-Gesellschaft zur Foerderung der Wissenschaften, Residenzstr. 1a, 8000 Munich 2, Germany. Ed.Bd. charts; illus.; circ. 20,000.
    Description: News for members of the Max-Planck Society.

505.8   US   ISSN 0076-2016
Q121
McGRAW-HILL YEARBOOK OF SCIENCE AND TECHNOLOGY. 1962. a. $80. McGraw-Hill, Inc., Professional & Reference Division, Engineering and Science Group, 11 W. 19th St., New York, NY 10011. TEL 212-337-5908. FAX 212-337-4092. TELEX 12-7960 MCGRAWH NYK. Ed. Sybil Parker.

MADA; Hebrew bimonthly of popular science. see *TECHNOLOGY: COMPREHENSIVE WORKS*

500   II   ISSN 0085-2945
MADRAS. GOVERNMENT MUSEUM. BULLETIN. NEW SERIES. (Text in English) 1931. irreg. price varies. Government Museum, Madras, Director of Museums, Pantheon Road, Egmore, Madras 600008, India.

500   RM
MAGAZIN. 1957. w. Piata Presei Libere 1, 71341 Bucharest, Rumania. Ed. Maria Costache. circ. 520,000.

500   HU   ISSN 0025-0325
MAGYAR TUDOMANY/HUNGARIAN SCIENCE. (Text in Hungarian, contents page in English, French, German and Russian) 1890. m. $30.50. (Magyar Tudomanyos Akademia) Akademiai Kiado, Publishing House of the Hungarian Academy of Sciences, P.O. Box 24, 1363 Budapest, Hungary. Ed. Bela Koepeczi. adv.; bk.rev.; illus.; index. **Indexed:** Amer.Hist.& Life, Forest.Abstr., Geo.Abstr., Hist.Abstr., Hung.Lib.& Info.Sci.Abstr., INIS Atomind., Rural Recreat.Tour.Abstr., World Agri.Econ.& Rural Sociol.Abstr.

500   II   ISSN 0025-0422
AS472.M23   CODEN: JMAHA2
MAHARAJA SAYAJIRAO UNIVERSITY OF BARODA. JOURNAL. (In 3 parts: Humanities, Social Science, Science.) (Text in English) 1952. 3/yr. (in 1 vol.). exchange basis. Maharaja Sayajirao University of Baroda, Baroda 390002, Gujarat, India. Ed. K.T.M. Hedge. adv.; bk.rev.; bibl.; charts; illus.; circ. 500. **Indexed:** Amer.Hist.& Life, Biol.Abstr., Chem.Abstr., Hist.Abstr., Nutr.Abstr., VITIS.

500 001.3   XN   ISSN 0580-4981
MAKEDONSKA AKADEMIJA NA NAUKITE I UMETNOSTITE. LETOPIS. 1969. a. Makedonska Akademija na Naukite i Umetnostite, Bulevar Krste Misrkov bb, P.O. Box 428, Skopje, Macedonia. TEL 235-506. Ed. Krum Tomovski.
    Description: Report of activities in symposia and congresses with information on scientific projects, exhibitions, publications, and membership listings.

510 570   XN   ISSN 0351-3246
QA1
MAKEDONSKA AKADEMIJA NA NAUKITE I UMETNOSTITE. ODDELENIE ZA MATEMATICKI I TEHNICKI NAUKI. PRILOZI/MACEDONIAN ACADEMY OF SCIENCES AND ARTS. SECTION OF MATHEMATICAL AND TECHNICAL SCIENCES. CONTRIBUTIONS. 1969. s-a. Makedonska Akademija na Naukite i Umetnostite, Oddelenie za matematicki i Tehnicki Nauki, Bulevar Krste Misirkov bb, P.O.Box 428, Skopje, Macedonia. TEL 235-506. Ed. Krum Tomovski. **Indexed:** Chem.Abstr., Math.R.
    Supersedes (in 1980): Makedonska Akademija na Naukite i Umetnostite. Oddelenie za Prirodno-Matematicki Nauki. Prilozi. (ISSN 0581-0833)
    Description: Research in mathematics, physics, chemistry and earth sciences.

507   UG
MAKERERE UNIVERSITY. SCIENCE FACULTY. HANDBOOK. irreg. Makerere University, Science Faculty, Box 7062, Kampala, Uganda. Ed. A.J. Lutalo. circ. 1,000.

500   MW
MALAWI JOURNAL OF SCIENCE. 1972. a. 25p. Association for the Advancement of Science of Malawi, Box 280, Zomba, Malawi. adv.; bk.rev.; circ. 1,000.

500.9   MY   ISSN 0025-1291
QH1   CODEN: MANJAM
MALAYAN NATURE JOURNAL. 1940. q. M.$50 to individuals; institutions M.100. Malayan Nature Society, Box 10750, Kuala Lumpur 50724, Malaysia. Ed. Ruth Kiew. adv.; bk.rev.; charts; illus.; maps; index; circ. 2,500. **Indexed:** Bio-Contr.News & Info., Biol.Abstr., Curr.Adv.Ecol.Sci., Forest.Abstr., Hort.Abstr., Soils & Fert., Weed Abstr.
    Description: Discusses natural history.

500   MY   ISSN 0301-0554
Q1   CODEN: MLJSA4
MALAYSIAN JOURNAL OF SCIENCE/JERNAL SAINS MALAYSIA. (Text in English) 1971. a. (University of Malaya, Faculty of Science) University of Malaya Co-operative Bookshop Ltd., P.O. Box 1127, Jalan Pantai Baru, Kuala Lumpur, Malaysia. TEL 565000. TELEX UNIMAL-MA-37453. Ed. Dr. Yong Hoi-Sen. adv.; bk.rev.; circ. 1,000. **Indexed:** Biol.Abstr., Chem.Abstr., Deep Sea Res.& Oceanogr.Abstr.
    Refereed Serial

MANITOBA SCIENCE TEACHER. see *EDUCATION*

MARATHWADA UNIVERSITY JOURNAL. see *EDUCATION — Higher Education*

500.9   JA
MARINE PARK RESEARCH STATIONS. BULLETIN/KAICHU KOEN KENKYUJO KENKYU HOKOKU. (Text in English or Japanese) 1975. s-a. exchange basis. Marine Parks Center of Japan, 1157 Kushimotocho Arita, Nishi-Muro-Gun, Kushimoto, Wakayama, Japan. Ed. Michitaka Uda. illus.; circ. 600.

500 913 581 551   GW
MARSCHENRAT ZUR FOERDERUNG DER FORSCHUNG IM KUESTENGEBIET DER NORDSEE. NACHRICHTEN. 1962. a. free. Marschenrat zur Foerderung der Forschung im Kuestengebiet der Nordsee, Viktoriastr. 26, 2940 Wilhelmshaven 1, Germany. Ed.Bd. circ. 1,200.

MARTIN-LUTHER-UNIVERSITAETT HALLE-WITTENBERG. WISSENSCHAFTLICHE ZEITSCHRIFT. MATHEMATISCH-NATURWISSENSCHAFTLICHE REIHE. see *MATHEMATICS*

500   US
Q180.U5
MARYLAND HIGH-TECH DIRECTORY (YEAR). 1963. irreg., latest 1990. $75. (Department of Economic and Employment Development) Corporate Technology Information Services, Inc., 12 Alfred St., Ste. 200, Woburn, MA 01801. TEL 617-932-3939. Ed. Mark Jacobson. adv.; circ. 2,500. (also avail. on diskette)
    Formerly (until 1989): Directory of Science Resources for Maryland (ISSN 0070-6256)

910   CS
MASARYK UNIVERSITY. FACULTY OF SCIENCES. SCRIPTA GEOGRAPHIA. (Text in English, French, German and Russian) 1971. irreg. (1-2/yr.). 6.50 Kcs. per no. Masarykova Universita, Prirodovedecka Fakulta - Masaryk University, Faculty of Sciences, Kotlarska 2, 611 37 Brno, Czechoslovakia. Ed. Stanislav Rosypal. charts; illus.; maps.
    Former titles: Scripta Facultatis Scientiarum Naturalium Universitatis Masarykianae Brunensis: Geographia; Scripta Gacultatis Scientiarum Naturalium Universitatis Purkynianae Brunensis: Geographia; (until 1970): Universita J. E. Purkyne. Prirodovedecka Fakulta. Spisy.

500 600   US   ISSN 1053-2110
Z7401
▼**MASTER'S THESES IN THE NATURAL AND TECHNICAL SCIENCES.** 1990. a. $45. Master's Theses Directories, Box 92, Cedar Falls, IA 50613. TEL 319-273-6412. FAX 319-273-2732. Ed. H.M. Silvey.

MASTER'S THESES IN THE PURE AND APPLIED SCIENCES; accepted by colleges and universities in the United States and Canada. see *SCIENCES: COMPREHENSIVE WORKS — Abstracting, Bibliographies, Statistics*

MATHEMATICAL METHODS IN THE APPLIED SCIENCES. see *MATHEMATICS*

500   GW   ISSN 0233-173X
QH149
MAURITIANA (ALTENBURG). 1958. annual. price varies. Naturkundliches Museum "Mauritianum", Postfach 216, 7400 Altenburg, Germany. Ed. Norbert Hoeser. circ. 900.
    Formerly (1986): Naturkindliches Museum "Mauritianum" Altenburg. Abhandlungen und Berichte (ISSN 0065-6631)

SCIENCES: COMPREHENSIVE WORKS

500　　　　　　　GW　　ISSN 0341-0218
Q3　　　　　　　　　　　　CODEN: MPJADF
MAX-PLANCK-GESELLSCHAFT. JAHRBUCH. 1951. a. price varies. Vandenhoeck & Ruprecht, Robert-Bosch-Breite 6, Postfach 3753, 3400 Goettingen, Germany. Eds. Ulrike Emrich, Robert Gerwin. bk.rev.; index; circ. 4,000. (back issues avail.) **Indexed:** Biol.Abstr.

500　　　　　　　GW　　ISSN 0076-5635
MAX-PLANCK-GESELLSCHAFT ZUR FOERDERUNG DER WISSENSCHAFTEN. JAHRBUCH. 1951. a. DM.95. Max-Planck-Gesellschaft zur Foerderung der Wissenschaften, Residenzstr. 1A, 8000 Munich 2, Germany. Ed. S. Deutschmann.
Description: Official report of the Max-Planck Society, with information on its 65 research institutes.

500　　　　　　　GW　　ISSN 0341-7778
MAX-PLANCK-GESELLSCHAFT ZUR FOERDERUNG DER WISSENSCHAFTEN BERICHTE UND MITTEILUNGEN. 1952. 5/yr. Max-Planck-Gesellschaft zur Foerderung der Wissenschaften, Residenzstr. 1a, Postfach 101062, 8000 Munich 2, Germany. TEL 089-2108275. Ed. E. S. Deutschmann. bibl.; charts; illus.; circ. 6,000.
—BLDSC shelfmark: 1937.348000.
Formerly: Max-Planck-Gesellschaft zur Foerderung der Wissenschaften Mitteilungen (ISSN 0025-6102)
Description: Information on selected Max-Plank institutes.

MECANICA POPULAR. see *TECHNOLOGY: COMPREHENSIVE WORKS*

MEIJI DAIGAKU KAGAKU GIJUTSU KENKYUJO HOKOKU. SOGO KENKYU/MEIJI UNIVERSITY. INSTITUTE OF SCIENCE AND TECHNOLOGY. REPORT. SPECIAL PROJECT. see *TECHNOLOGY: COMPREHENSIVE WORKS*

MEIJI DAIGAKU KAGAKU GIJUTSU KENKYUJO KIYO/MEIJI UNIVERSITY. INSTITUTE OF SCIENCE AND TECHNOLOGY. MEMOIRS. see *TECHNOLOGY: COMPREHENSIVE WORKS*

MEIJI DAIGAKU KAGAKU GIJUTSU KENKYUJO NENPO/MEIJI UNIVERSITY. INSTITUTE OF SCIENCE AND TECHNOLOGY. ANNUAL REPORT. see *TECHNOLOGY: COMPREHENSIVE WORKS*

500　　　　　　　NE　　ISSN 0543-6095
METHODOLOGY AND SCIENCE; interdisciplinary journal for the empirical study of the foundations of science and their methodology. 1968. q. fl.90 to individuals; institutions fl. 100. (Stichting Methodology and Science - Methodology and Science Foundation) Esser Scientific Press, Beeslaan 20, 2012 PK Haarlem, Netherlands. TEL 023-280290. Ed. Dr. P.H. Esser. adv.; bk.rev.; circ. 200. **Indexed:** Math.R., Phil.Ind.
—BLDSC shelfmark: 5746.450000.

500　　　　　　　NE
METHODS AND PHENOMENA; their applications in science and technology. 1975. irregr., vol.7, 1984. price varies. Elsevier Science Publishers B.V., Books Division, P.O. Box 211, 1000 AE Amsterdam, Netherlands. TEL 020-5803911. FAX 020-5803705. TELEX 18582 ESPA NL. (Subscr. in U.S. and Canada to: Elsevier Science Publishing Co., Inc., Box 882, Madison Sq. Sta., New York, NY 10159. TEL 212-989-5800) Eds. S.P. Wolsky, A.W. Czanderna.
Refereed Serial

500　　　　　　　US　　ISSN 0026-2005
AS30　　　　　　　　　　CODEN: MACDAH
MICHIGAN ACADEMICIAN. 1969. q. $40 (foreign $45). Michigan Academy of Science, Arts and Letters, 400 Fourth St., Ann Arbor, MI 48109-4816. TEL 313-936-2938. bk.rev.; illus.; circ. 1,000. (back issues avail.) **Indexed:** Abstr.Anthropol., Abstr.Engl.Stud., Amer.Bibl.Slavic & E.Eur.Stud., Amer.Hist.& Life, Biol.Abstr., Chem.Abstr., Film Lit.Ind. (1989-), GeoRef., Hist.Abstr., J.of Econ.Lit., Lang.& Lang.Behav.Abstr., M.L.A., Mich.Mag.Ind., Psychol.Abstr., Sociol.Abstr.
—BLDSC shelfmark: 5753.500000.
Supersedes: Michigan Academy of Science, Arts and Letters. Papers.
Description: Forum for scholars across the state and region. Presents papers of the academy derived from its meetings.
Refereed Serial

500　　　　　　　US
MIDWEST RESEARCH INSTITUTE. ANNUAL REPORT. 1945. a. free. Midwest Research Institute, 425 Volker Blvd., Kansas City, MO 64110. TEL 816-753-7600. FAX 816-753-8420. TELEX 910-771-2128. Ed. Mary G. Walker. circ. 13,000.
Description: Reports on research performed at MRI in a varied spectrum, including chemical and biological sciences, engineering, economics, social and management sciences, and solar energy.

500　　　　　　　JA　　ISSN 0389-9225
MIE DAIGAKU KYOIKUGAKUBU KENKYU KIYO. SHIZEN KAGAKU/MIE UNIVERSITY. FACULTY OF EDUCATION. BULLETIN. NATURAL SCIENCE. (Text and summaries in English and Japanese) a. Mie Daigaku, Kyoikugakubu - Mie University, Faculty of Education, 1515 Kamihama-cho, Tsu-shi, Mie-ken 514, Japan. **Indexed:** Jap.Per.Ind.

MINAMI-KYUSHU DAIGAKU ENGEIGAKUBU KENKYU HOKOKU. SHIZEN KAGAKU, JINBUN SHAKAI KAGAKU/MINAMI KYUSHU UNIVERSITY. FACULTY OF HORTICULTURE. BULLETIN. NATURAL SCIENCE, CULTURAL SCIENCE, AND SOCIAL SCIENCE. see *GARDENING AND HORTICULTURE*

959 398　　　　　　PH　　ISSN 0115-7329
MINDANAO STATE UNIVERSITY. U R C PROFESSIONAL PAPERS. 1981. irreg. Mindanao State University, University Research Center, P.O. Box 5594, Iligan City 9200, Philippines. Ed. Raymond Llorca.

MINERVA; a review of science, learning and policy. see *EDUCATION — Higher Education*

500　　　　　　　US　　ISSN 0026-539X
Q11　　　　　　　　　　　CODEN: JMNAAC
MINNESOTA ACADEMY OF SCIENCE. JOURNAL.* 1957. s-a. $8 per no. Minnesota Academy of Science, 350 Robert St. N., Ste. 583, St. Paul, MN 55101-1502. TEL 612-227-6361. Ed. Dr. Daniel P. Gilboe. bk.rev.; charts; illus.; stat.; circ. 1,600. (also avail. in microform from UMI; reprint service avail. from UMI) **Indexed:** Biol.Abstr., Chem.Abstr., Excerp.Med., GeoRef.
Refereed Serial

500　　　　　　　US　　ISSN 0026-5675
　　　　　　　　　　　　　CODEN: MINSB4
MINNESOTA SCIENCE. 1943. q. free. University of Minnesota, Agricultural Experiment Station, 405 Coffey Hall, St. Paul, MN 55108. TEL 612-625-7290. Ed. David L. Hansen. index; circ. 21,000 (controlled). (processed) **Indexed:** Biol.Abstr.
Formerly: Farm and Home Science.
Refereed Serial

MINNESOTA STUDIES IN THE PHILOSOPHY OF SCIENCE. see *PHILOSOPHY*

574　　　　　　　US　　ISSN 0076-9436
Q11　　　　　　　　　　　CODEN: JMSSAN
MISSISSIPPI ACADEMY OF SCIENCE. JOURNAL.* 1940. 4/yr. $25. Mississippi Academy of Sciences, Inc., 405 Briarwood Dr., Ste. 107E, Jackson, MS 39206-3029. TEL 601-977-0627. Ed. John D. Tiftickjian. circ. 1,000. (also avail. in microform from UMI) **Indexed:** Biol.Abstr., Chem.Abstr., GeoRef., Hort.Abstr.
—BLDSC shelfmark: 4828.200000.

509.43　　　　　　GW
MITTEILUNGSBLATT FUER WISSENSCHAFTLICHE LEHRKRAEFTE IM AUSLAND. 1977. m. membership. Deutscher Akademischer Austauschdienst (DAAD), Kennedyallee 50, 5300 Bonn - Bad Godesberg, Germany. TEL 02223-26030. Ed. Leonie Loreck. adv.; bk.rev.; circ. 2,600.
Formerly (1969-1976): Informationsblatt fuer Deutsche Wissenschaftler im Ausland.

500　　　　　　　JA　　ISSN 0285-8576
Q4　　　　　　　　　　　CODEN: MDKSAL
MIYAZAKI DAIGAKU KYOIKUGAKUBU KIYO. SHIZEN KAGAKU/MIYAZAKI UNIVERSITY. FACULTY OF EDUCATION. MEMOIRS. NATURAL SCIENCE. (Text in Japanese; summaries in English and Japanese) 1955. s-a. Miyazaki Daigaku, Kyoikugakubu - Miyazaki University, Faculty of Education, 1-1 Funatsuka, Miyazaki-shi, Miyazaki-ken 880, Japan. **Indexed:** Chem.Abstr., Jap.Per.Ind.
—BLDSC shelfmark: 5593.322000.

MOKHTAREIN VA MOBTAKERIN. see *TECHNOLOGY: COMPREHENSIVE WORKS*

500　　　　　　　SP
MOLL MONOGRAFIES CIENTIFIQUES. (Text in Catalan) irreg., latest no.4. 3850 ptas. Editorial Moll, Apdo. 142, 07080 Palma de Mallorca, Spain. TEL 971-72-41-76. FAX 971-72-62-52.

500　　　　　　　FR　　ISSN 0221-0436
JV1802
MONDES ET CULTURES; comptes-rendus trimestriels de l'Academie des Sciences d'Outre-Mer. 1941. q. 300 F. Academie des Sciences d'Outre-Mer, Paris, 15 rue La Perouse, 75116 Paris, France. TEL 47-20-87-93. Dir. Gilbert Mangin. adv.; bk.rev.; bibl.; charts; index. **Indexed:** Curr.Cont.Africa.
Formerly: Academie des Sciences d'Outre-Mer, Paris. Comptes Rendus des Seances (ISSN 0001-4044)

500 600　　　　　PL　　ISSN 0077-054X
MONOGRAFIE Z DZIEJOW NAUKI I TECHNIKI. (Text in Polish and French; summaries in English, French, German and Russian) 1957. irregr., vol.139, 1987. price varies. (Polska Akademia Nauk, Zaklad Historii Nauki i Techniki) Ossolineum, Publishing House of the Polish Academy of Sciences, Rynek 9, 50-106 Wroclaw, Poland. TELEX 0712771 OSS PL. (Dist. by: Ars Polona-Ruch, Krakowskie Przedmiescie 7, Warsaw, Poland) Ed. B. Suchodolski. **Indexed:** Math.R.

MONOGRAPHS ON SCIENCE, TECHNOLOGY, AND SOCIETY. see *TECHNOLOGY: COMPREHENSIVE WORKS*

MUNDUS; a quarterly review of German research contributions on Asia, Africa and Latin America - arts and science. see *ART*

595.7　　　　　　SP　　ISSN 0027-3414
QH7　　　　　　　　　　CODEN: MNBEA4
MUNIBE. (Text mainly in Spanish; occasionally in English & French) 1949. q. 4000 ptas. Sociedad de Ciencias Aranzadi, Plaza de l. Zuloaga (Museo), 20003 San Sebastian, Spain. TEL 943-42-29-45. FAX 943-42-13-16. Ed.Bd. bk.rev.; index, cum.index: 1949-1972, 1973-1977; circ. 2,500. **Indexed:** A.I.C.P., Amer.Hist.& Life, Biol.Abstr., Chem.Abstr., GeoRef., Hist.Abstr., Ind.SST.
—BLDSC shelfmark: 5983.915000.

500.9　　　　　　IT　　ISSN 0365-4389
　　　　　　　　　　　　CODEN: AMGDAN
MUSEO CIVICO DI STORIA NATURALE "GIACOMO DORIA", GENOA. ANNALI. (Text in English, French, German, Italian and Spanish) 1870. biennial. exchange basis only. Museo Civico di Storia Naturale "Giacomo Doria", Via Brigata Liguria 9, 16121 Genoa, Italy. **Indexed:** Biol.Abstr., Bull.Signal., Entomol.Abstr., Rev.Appl.Entomol., Zoo.Rec.
—BLDSC shelfmark: 1008.400000.

500　　　　　　　IT　　ISSN 0392-0062
QH7　　　　　　　　　　CODEN: BMCVD3
MUSEO CIVICO DI STORIA NATURALE, VERONA. BOLLETTINO. (Text in English, French, German and Italian; summaries in English, French and German) 1946. a. L.30000 per no. Museo Civico di Storia Naturale, Verona, Lungadige Porta Vittoria Nr. 9, 37129 Verona, Italy. Ed.Bd. circ. 600. (back issues avail.) **Indexed:** A.I.C.P., Biol.Abstr., Deep Sea Res.& Oceanogr.Abstr., GeoRef., Zoo.Rec.
Supersedes in part (since 1974): Museo Civico di Storia Naturale, Verona. Memorie (ISSN 0085-767X)

500.9　　　　　　IT
MUSEO CIVICO DI STORIA NATURALE, VERONA. MEMORIE. SERIE 2, PART 1: BIOLOGICA. 1977. irreg. price varies. Museo Civico di Storia Naturale di Verona, Lungadige Porta Vittoria, 9, 37129 Verona, Italy. TEL 045-8001987.

500.9　　　　　　IT
MUSEO CIVICO DI STORIA NATURALE, VERONA. MEMORIE. SERIE 2, PART 2: ABIOLOGICA. 1977. irreg. price varies. Museo Civico di Storia Naturale di Verona, Lungadige Porta Vittoria, 9, 37129 Verona, Italy. TEL 045-8001987.

500.9　　　　　　IT
MUSEO CIVICO DI STORIA NATURALE, VERONA. MEMORIE. SERIE 2, PART 3: PREISTORICA. 1980. irreg. price varies. Museo Civico di Storia Naturale di Verona, Lungadige Porta Vittoria, 9, 37129 Verona, Italy. TEL 045-8001987.

SCIENCES: COMPREHENSIVE WORKS

500.9   VE   ISSN 0027-3899
MUSEO DE CIENCIAS NATURALES. BOLETIN.* (Text in English and Spanish) 1955. q. free to qualified personnel. Museo de Ciencias Naturales, Plaza Morelos, Los Caobos, Caracas 101, Venezuela. Ed.Bd. bibl.; illus.; maps. **Indexed:** Biol.Abstr.

MUSEO MUNICIPAL DE HISTORIA NATURAL DE SAN RAFAEL. INSTITUTO DE CIENCIAS NATURALES. NOTAS. see *EARTH SCIENCES — Geology*

500.9   AG   ISSN 0375-1155
MUSEO MUNICIPAL DE HISTORIA NATURAL DE SAN RAFAEL. REVISTA. 1956. irreg. exchange basis. Museo Municipal de Historia Natural de San Rafael, Parque Mariano Moreno, 5600 San Rafael, Mendoza, Argentina. Ed. Humberto A. Lagiglia. bk.rev.; charts; illus.; index; circ. 1,500. **Indexed:** Biol.Abstr.
— **Former titles:** Museo de Historia Natural de San Rafael. Revista; Museo de Historia Natural de San Rafael. Revista Cientifica de Investigaciones (ISSN 0027-3902)

500.9   CL   ISSN 0027-3910
QH7
MUSEO NACIONAL DE HISTORIA NATURAL. BOLETIN. 1908. irreg., no.42, 1991. $12. Museo Nacional de Historia Natural, Casilla 787, Santiago, Chile. Ed. Daniel Frassinetti C. **Indexed:** Biol.Abstr.
— BLDSC shelfmark: 2182.000000.

500.9   CL   ISSN 0027-3945
MUSEO NACIONAL DE HISTORIA NATURAL. NOTICIARIO MENSUAL. 1956. m. $4. Museo Nacional de Historia Natural, Casilla 787, Santiago, Chile. Ed. Herman Nunez. circ. 800. **Indexed:** Biol.Abstr., GeoRef.

500   BL   ISSN 0080-3111
MUSEU NACIONAL, RIO DE JANEIRO. ARQUIVOS. (Text in Portuguese; summaries in English) 1876. irreg., no.56, 1981. exchange basis only. Museu Nacional, Quinta da Boa Vista, 20940 Rio de Janeiro, RJ, Brazil. charts; bibl.; illus. **Indexed:** Biol.Abstr., Rev.Appl.Entomol.

500.9   FR
MUSEUM NATIONAL D'HISTOIRE NATURELLE, PARIS. GRANDS NATURALISTES FRANCAIS. 1952. irreg. price varies. Museum National d'Histoire Naturelle, 38 rue Geoffroy Saint-Hillaire, 75005 Paris, France. illus.

MUSEUM OF SCIENCE MAGAZINE. see *MUSEUMS AND ART GALLERIES*

MUSEUMSNYTT. see *MUSEUMS AND ART GALLERIES*

500 910   CN   ISSN 0077-2542
G600   CODEN: MUOXD8
MUSK - OX; a journal on the North. (Text in English, French, summaries in Cree, French, Inuktitut) 1967. 2/yr. Can.$28 to individuals; institutions Can.$38. University of Saskatchewan, Department of Geological Sciences, Saskatoon, Sask. S7N 0W0, Canada. TEL 306-966-5720. FAX 306-966-8593. Ed. W.O. Kupsch. bk.rev.; index; circ. 1,100. (also avail. in microfilm from MML; back issues avail.) **Indexed:** Amer.Bibl.Slavic & E.Eur.Stud, Biol.Abstr., Can.Per.Ind., CMI, Geo.Abstr., GeoRef.
Description: Deals with scientific, cultural, economic and historical aspects of the North.

500   SP
MUY INTERESANTE. 1981. m. 3600 ptas. G & J Espana, S.A. (Subsidiary of: Gruner & Jahr USA Publishing), Marques de Villamagna 4, 28001 Madrid, Spain. TEL 341-435-8100. FAX 341-576-7781. TELEX 43419. Dir. Jose Pardina. adv.; circ. 290,000.
Description: Covers scientific subjects, putting all the latest discoveries and new technologies within the reader's reach.

500   US
N A S A FORMAL SERIES REPORTS. irreg. (approx. 415/yr.) $15 per issue in US only. (National Aeronautics and Space Administration) U.S. National Technical Information Service, 5825 Port Royal Rd., Springfield, VA 22161. TEL 703-487-4630.
Description: Reports available in the following selections: aeronautics, astronautics, chemistry and mechanics, engineering, geosciences, life sciences, mathematical and computer sciences, physics, social sciences, and space sciences.

500 600   AT   ISSN 0311-662X
N A T A NEWS. 1974. q. National Association of Testing Authorities, 688 Pacific Highway, Chatswood, N.S.W. 2067, Australia. TEL 02 411 4000. Ed. P.H. Davies. circ. 5,500. (back issues avail.)

N A T O ADVANCED SCIENCE INSTITUTES SERIES C: MATHEMATICAL AND PHYSICAL SCIENCES. (North Atlantic Treaty Organization) see *MATHEMATICS*

500   BE   ISSN 0255-7134
N A T O SCIENTIFIC PUBLICATIONS. NEWSLETTER. 1980. q. free. (North Atlantic Treaty Organization, Scientific Affairs Division) N A T O Publication Coordination Office, Elcerlyclaan 2, B-3090 Overijse, Belgium. TEL 2-6876636. Ed. B. Kester. adv.; bk.rev.; circ. 25,000.

500   CN   ISSN 0047-9551
N.B. NATURALIST/NATURALISTE DU N.B.. (Text in English, French) 1970. 4/yr. Can.$15 (foreign Can.$20). New Brunswick Federation of Naturalists, 277 Douglas Ave., Saint John, N.B. E2K 1E5, Canada. TEL 506-882-2100. Eds. D.S. Christie, M. Majka. adv.; bk.rev.; circ. 400. (processed)
Description: Covers natural history.

500   NO   ISSN 0800-4412
N D R E PUBLICATIONS. (Text and summaries in English) 1953. irreg., no.84, 1987. Norwegian Defence Research Establishment - Forsvarets Forskningsintitutt, Box 25, N-2007 Kjeller, Norway. FAX 06-807159. circ. controlled.
— BLDSC shelfmark: 6067.854000.
Formerly: Norway. Forsvaret Forskningsintitutt. N D R E Report (ISSN 0085-4301)

500   II   ISSN 0970-0188
N I S S A T NEWSLETTER. (Text in English) 1978. q. free. National Information System for Science and Technology, Society for Information Science, Technology Bhavan, New Mehrauli Rd., New Delhi 110 016, India. TEL 641-2916. TELEX 31-66096 DST IN. Ed. Ram D. Taneja. bk.rev.; circ. 4,000. **Indexed:** Ind.Sci.Rev.
— BLDSC shelfmark: 6113.623000.
Description: News about the development of information systems, centers, and networks in science and technology in India and abroad.

N J AUDUBON. (New Jersey Audubon Society) see *BIOLOGY — Ornithology*

N K H NAGAOKA-SHIRITSU KAGAKU HAKUBUTSUKANPO. see *MUSEUMS AND ART GALLERIES*

505   PH   ISSN 0115-1304
                     CODEN: NRBUDQ
N R C P RESEARCH BULLETIN. (National Research Council of Philippines) (Text in English) 1973. q. Philippine National Science Society, Bicutan, Taguig, Metro Manila, Philippines. Ed. Dr. Melecio S. Magno. illus.; circ. 1,000. **Indexed:** Chem.Abstr., Dairy Sci.Abstr., GeoRef., Ind.Phil.Per., Rural Recreat.Tour.Abstr., World Agri.Econ.& Rural Sociol.Abstr.

500   CH   ISSN 0255-4399
N S C REVIEW. (Text in English) 1965. a. free. National Science Council of the Republic of China, No. 106, Ho-Ping E. Rd., Sec. 2, Taipei, Taiwan 106, Republic of China.
— BLDSC shelfmark: 6180.567000.

500   CH
N S C SPECIAL PUBLICATION. 1978. irreg., no.6, 1989. National Science Council of the Republic of China, No. 106, Ho-Ping E.Rd., Sec. 2, Taipei, Taiwan 106, Republic of China.

500   CH   ISSN 0252-8177
                     CODEN: NSYSD6
N S C SYMPOSIUM SERIES. 1979. irreg., no.14, 1988. National Science Council of the Republic of China, 106 Ho-ping E. Rd. Sec. 2, Taipei, Taiwan 106, Republic of China. **Indexed:** Biol.Abstr.

500 350   US
N S F BULLETIN. 1974. m. (except Jul. & Aug.). free. U.S. National Science Foundation, Science Resource Studies, Washington, DC 20550. TEL 202-357-9494. Ed. Mary Wilson. Key Title: Bulletin - National Science Foundation.

500 375   US
N S S A NEWSLETTER. 1969. q. $20. National Science Supervisors Association, Box AL, Amagansett, NY 11930. TEL 516-267-3692. FAX 516-267-8621. Ed. Wallace Ryall. adv.; circ. 1,000. (tabloid format; back issues avail.)

N S T A REPORTS. (National Science Teachers Association) see *EDUCATION*

500.9   GW
N T M GESCHICHTE DER NATURWISSENSCHAFTEN, TECHNIK UND MEDIZIN. SCHRIFTENREIHE. 1960. irreg. (approx. 2/yr.). DM.76 per no. Akademische Verlagsgesellschaft Geest und Portig K.G., Sternwartenstr. 8, 7010 Leipzig, Germany. Ed.Bd. adv.; bk.rev.; bibl.; charts; illus.; index.
— **Former titles:** Geschichte der Naturwissenschaften, Technik und Medizin. Schriftenreihe (ISSN 0036-6978); Zeitschrift fuer Geschichte der Naturwissenschaften, der Technik und der Medizin.
Description: Contains authoritative articles, book reviews, new publications, list of events, and bibliographies.

NAGAOKA COLLEGE OF TECHNOLOGY. RESEARCH REPORTS/NAGAOKA KOGYO KOTO SENMON GAKKO KENKYU KIYO. see *ENGINEERING*

500   JA   ISSN 0285-6085
NAGAOKA-SHIRITSU KAGAKU HAKUBUTSUKAN KENKYU HOKOKU/NAGAOKA MUNICIPAL SCIENCE MUSEUM. BULLETIN. (Text in Japanese) 1973. a. Nagaoka-shiritsu Kagaku Hakubutsukan - Nagaoka Municipal Science Museum, 2-1 Yanagihara, Nagaoka-shi, Niigata-ken 940, Japan. **Indexed:** Jap.Per.Ind.
Description: Contains research reports from the museum.

500   JA   ISSN 0386-443X
                     CODEN: NADKBL
NAGASAKI DAIGAKU KYOIKUGAKUBU SHIZEN KAGAKU KENKYU HOKOKU/NAGASAKI UNIVERSITY. FACULTY OF EDUCATION. SCIENCE BULLETIN. (Text and summaries in English and Japanese) 1949. a. Nagasaki Daigaku, Kyoikugakubu - Nagasaki University, Faculty of Education, 1-14 Bunkyo-machi, Nagasaki-shi, Nagasaki-ken 852, Japan. **Indexed:** Chem.Abstr., INIS Atomind., Jap.Per.Ind.
— BLDSC shelfmark: 8137.200000.

500   JA   ISSN 0287-1319
Q4
NAGASAKI DAIGAKU KYOYOBU KIYO. SHIZEN KAGAKU HEN/NAGASAKI UNIVERSITY. FACULTY OF LIBERAL ARTS. BULLETIN. (Text in English, German, Japanese; summaries in English and German) 1960. s-a. free. Nagasaki Daigaku, Kyoyobu - Nagasaki University, Faculty of Liberal Arts, 1-14 Bunkyo-machi, Nagasaki-shi, Nagasaki-ken 852, Japan. circ. 200. **Indexed:** Jap.Per.Ind.

NAGOYA DAIGAKU FURUKAWA SOGO KENKYU SHIRYOKAN HOKOKU/NAGOYA UNIVERSITY FURUKAWA MUSEUM. BULLETIN. see *MUSEUMS AND ART GALLERIES*

500   JA   ISSN 0387-4532
                     CODEN: NDKBDI
NAGOYA DAIGAKU KYOYOBU KIYO B. SHIZEN KAGAKU, SHINRIGAKU/NAGOYA UNIVERSITY. COLLEGE OF GENERAL EDUCATION. RESEARCH BULLETIN B. NATURAL SCIENCE AND PSYCHOLOGY. (Text in English and Japanese; summaries in English) a. Nagoya Daigaku, Kyoyobu - Nagoya University, College of General Education, Furo-cho, Chikusa-ku, Nagoya-shi, Aichi-ken 464, Japan. **Indexed:** Chem.Abstr., Jap.Per.Ind.

500   JA   ISSN 0285-4538
                     CODEN: IGDKEB
NAGOYA KEIZAI DAIGAKU, ICHIMURA GAKUEN TANKI DAIGAKU SHIZEN KAGAKU KENKYUKAI KAISHI/NAGOYA ECONOMICS UNIVERSITY AND ICHIMURA GAKUEN JUNIOR COLLEGE. NATURAL SCIENTIFIC SOCIETY. JOURNAL. (Text and summaries in English and Japanese) 1966. a. Shizen Kagaku Kenkyukai - Natural Scientific Society, Furo-cho, Chikusa-ku, Nagoya-shi, Aichi-ken 464-01, Japan. (Co-sponsors: Nagoya Keizai Daigaku - Nagoya Economics University; Ichimura Gakuen Tanki Daigaku - Ichimura Gakuen Junior College)

SCIENCES: COMPREHENSIVE WORKS

500   JA   ISSN 0465-7772
CODEN: NSKKAB
NAGOYA-SHIRITSU DAIGAKU KYOYOBU KIYO. SHIZEN KAGAKU HEN/NAGOYA CITY UNIVERSITY. COLLEGE OF GENERAL EDUCATION. BULLETIN. NATURAL SCIENCE SECTION. (Text in English and Japanese; summaries in English) 1955. a. Nagoya-shiritsu Daigaku, Kyoyobu - Nagoya City University, College of General Education, 1-1 Yamanohata, Mizuho-cho, Mizuho-ku, Nagoya-shi, Aichi-ken 467, Japan. **Indexed:** Chem.Abstr., Jap.Per.Ind.

685.31   FI
NAHKA JA KENKA. bi-m. Kenkaetehtaitten Keskusliitto, Vuorik 4a, 00100 Helsinki 10, Finland. TEL 90-170211.

500   JA   ISSN 0914-1707
NAITO KINEN KAGAKU SHINKO ZAIDAN KENKYU HOKOKUSHU/NAITO FOUNDATION ANNUAL REPORT. (Text in Japanese; summaries in English) 1972. a. Naito Kinen Kagaku Shinko Zaidan - Naito Foundation, 42-6, Hongo 3, Bunkyo-ku, Tokyo 113, Japan.

500   JA   ISSN 0911-971X
NAITO ZAIDAN JIHO. (Text in Japanese) 1969. a. free. Naito Kinen Kagaku Shinko Zaidan - Naito Foundation, 42-6 Hongo 3, Bunkyo-ku, Tokyo 113, Japan.
   Description: Contains reviews, commentary, and news of the foundation.

500   SX
NAMIBIA SCIENTIFIC SOCIETY. NEWSLETTER. (Text in Afrikaans, English and German) 1959. m. membership. Namibia Scientific Society, 110 Leutwein St., P.O. Box 67, Windhoek 9000, Namibia. TEL 061-225372. Ed. A. Henrichsen.
   Formerly: South West Africa Scientific Society. Newsletter - S W A Wetenskaplike Vereniging. Nuusbrief - S W A Wissenschaftliche Gesellschaft. Mitteilungen (ISSN 0036-2069); Incorporates (in 1983): Botanische Mitteilungen.

500 600   CC   ISSN 0469-5097
NANJING DAXUE XUEBAO (ZIRAN KEXUE BAN)/NANJING UNIVERSITY. JOURNAL (NATURAL SCIENCE EDITION). (Text in Chinese) q. (Nanjing Daxue - Nanjing University) Nanjing Daxue Chubanshe, Nanjing, Jiangsu 210008, People's Republic of China. TEL 637651. Ed. Qu Qinyue.

500   JA   ISSN 0547-2407
CODEN: NKDSAC
NARA KYOIKU DAIGAKU KIYO. SHIZEN KAGAKU/NARA UNIVERSITY OF EDUCATION. BULLETIN. NATURAL SCIENCE. (Text and summaries in English and Japanese) 1951. a. Nara Kyoiku Daigaku - Nara University of Education, Takabatake-cho, Nara-shi, Nara-ken 630, Japan. **Indexed:** Biol.Abstr., Chem.Abstr., Jap.Per.Ind.

500   CS   ISSN 0036-5343
QH7   CODEN: SNMPAM
NARODNI MUZEUM V PRAZE. SBORNIK. RADA B: PRIRODNI VEDY/ACTA MUSEI NATIONALIS PRAGAE. (Text in Czech, English, French, German) 1937. q. 20 Kcs.($21.07) Narodni Muzeum, Prirodovedecke Muzeum, Vaclavske nam. 68, 115 79 Prague 1, Czechoslovakia. FAX 02-236-9489. (Subscr. to: P N S - Ustredni Expedice a Dovoz Tisku Prague, Zavod 01, Administrace Vyvozu Tisku, Kovpakova 26, 160 00 Prague 6, Czechoslovakia) Ed. Jiri Cejka. charts; illus.; index. **Indexed:** Biol.Abstr., Chem.Abstr.
   —BLDSC shelfmark: 8083.000000.
   Formerly: Narodni Muzeum v Praze. Sbornik: Prirodni Vedy.

NATIONAL ACADEMY OF SCIENCES. BIOGRAPHICAL MEMOIRS. see *BIOGRAPHY*

500 530   II   ISSN 0369-8203
Q73   CODEN: PAIAA3
NATIONAL ACADEMY OF SCIENCES, INDIA. PROCEEDINGS. SECTION A. PHYSICAL SCIENCES. (Text in English) 1931. m. Rs.100($30) National Academy of Sciences, 5 Lajpatra Rd., Allahabad 211002, Uttar Pradesh, India. Ed. U.S. Srivastava. adv.; bibl.; charts; circ. 500. **Indexed:** Biol.Abstr., Chem.Abstr., Curr.Cont., Mass Spectr.Bull., Math.R., Sci.Abstr.
   —BLDSC shelfmark: 6761.900000.

NATIONAL ACADEMY OF SCIENCES, INDIA. PROCEEDINGS. SECTION B. BIOLOGICAL SCIENCES. see *BIOLOGY*

500   II   ISSN 0250-541X
Q73   CODEN: NASLDX
NATIONAL ACADEMY OF SCIENCES, INDIA. SCIENCE LETTERS. (Text in English) 1978. m. Rs.100($30) National Academy of Sciences, 5 Lajpatra Rd., Allahabad 211002, Uttar Pradesh, India. Ed. U.S. Srivastava. **Indexed:** Bio-Contr.News & Info., Biol.Abstr., Curr.Cont., Field Crop Abstr., Forest.Abstr., Forest Prod.Abstr., Hort.Abstr., Ind.Vet., Maize Abstr., Plant Grow.Reg.Abstr., Potato Abstr., Rev.Plant Path., Sci.Abstr., Seed Abstr., Soils & Fert., Soyabean Abstr., Triticale Abstr., Trop.Oil Seeds Abstr., Weed Abstr.
   —BLDSC shelfmark: 6015.756000.

500   US
Q11
NATIONAL ASSOCIATION OF ACADEMIES OF SCIENCE. DIRECTORY, PROCEEDINGS AND HANDBOOK. 1977. a. $15. National Association of Academies of Science, Science Division, Northeast Missouri State University, Kirksville, MO 63501. TEL 816-785-4618. FAX 816-785-4045. (Affiliate: American Association for the Advancement of Science) Ed. James H. Shaddy. circ. 500. (back issues avail.) **Indexed:** ERIC.
   Former titles: National Association of Academies of Science. Directory and Proceedings (ISSN 0739-361X); Association of Academies of Science. Directory and Proceedings.

500 600   JA   ISSN 0388-4112
Q1   CODEN: MNDEDH
NATIONAL DEFENSE ACADEMY. MEMOIRS. MATHEMATICS, PHYSICS, CHEMISTRY, AND ENGINEERING/BOEI DAIGAKKO KIYO. RIKOGAKU HEN. (Text and summaries in English) 1955. q. Boei Daigakko - National Defense Academy, 10-20 Hashirimizu 1-chome, Yokosuka-shi, Kanagawa-ken 239, Japan. abstr. **Indexed:** Chem.Abstr., INIS Atomind., Sci.Abstr.
   —BLDSC shelfmark: 5626.650000.

500   JA   ISSN 0386-555X
NATIONAL INSTITUTE OF POLAR RESEARCH. MEMOIRS. SERIES F: LOGISTICS.. (Text and summaries in English) 1964. irreg., no.4, 1982. exchange basis. National Institute of Polar Research - Kokuritsu Kyokuchi Kenkyujo, Library, 9-10, Kaga 1-chome, Itabashi-ku, Tokyo 173, Japan. Ed. Takao Hoshiai. circ. 1,000.
   Supersedes: Japanese Antarctic Research Expedition, 1956-1962. Scientific Reports. Series F: Logistic (ISSN 0075-3408)

NATIONAL MUSEUM, BLOEMFONTEIN. MEMOIRS/NASIONALE MUSEUM, BLOEMFONTEIN. MEMOIRS. see *BIOLOGY — Zoology*

500   SA   ISSN 0067-9208
GN656   CODEN: NVNMAJ
NATIONAL MUSEUM, BLOEMFONTEIN. RESEARCH/NASIONALE MUSEUM, BLOEMFONTEIN. NAVORSINGE. (Text in Afrikaans, English; summaries in English) 1952. irreg., no.9, 1991. exchange basis. National Museum, Bloemfontein - Nasionale Museum, Bloemfontein, P.O. Box 266, Bloemfontein 9300, South Africa. TEL 051-479609. FAX 051-479681. Ed. S. Louw. abstr.; bibl.; charts; illus.; stat.; circ. 850. (back issues avail.) **Indexed:** Biol.Abstr., Ecol.Abstr., Entomol.Abstr., Zoo.Rec.
   Description: Research papers coming out of the National Museum of Bloemfontein covering all fields of interest.

507   US
NATIONAL PATTERNS OF R & D RESOURCES. a. U.S. National Science Foundation, 1800 G St., N.W., Washington, DC 20550. TEL 202-634-4622.
   Former titles: National Patterns of Science and Technology; National Patterns of R and D Resources: Funds and Manpower in the United States (ISSN 0093-8572)

500 620   US
NATIONAL RESEARCH COUNCIL. NEWSREPORT. 1951. bi-m. $10 (foreign $12). National Research Council, 2101 Constitution Ave., N.W., Washington, DC 20418. TEL 202-334-2138. (Co-sponsors: National Academy of Engineering; National Academy of Sciences; Institute of Medicine) Ed. Pepper Leeper. bk.rev.; bibl.; charts; illus.; index; circ. 19,000. (also avail. in microfilm from UMI; back issues avail.; reprint service avail. from UMI)
   Formerly: National Academy of Sciences. National Academy of Engineering. National Research Council. Institute of Medicine. News Report (ISSN 0027-8432)

500   CN
NATIONAL RESEARCH COUNCIL OF CANADA. N R C ANNUAL REPORT - RAPPORT ANNUEL DU C N R C. (Text in English & French) 1916. a. free. National Research Council of Canada, Corporate Services, M-58, Ottawa K1A 0R6, Ont., Canada. TEL 613-993-4752. Ed. Blair Johnston. circ. 6,000.
   Formerly: National Research Council of Canada. Report of the President - Rapport du President.

500   TH   ISSN 0028-0011
CODEN: JRCTAF
NATIONAL RESEARCH COUNCIL OF THAILAND. JOURNAL. (Text in English and Thai) 1960. s-a. B.100($10) (effective 1992). National Research Council of Thailand, 196 Phahonyothin Rd., Chatuchak, Bangkok 10900, Thailand. FAX 66-2-5613049. TELEX 82213-NARECOU-TH. Ed. Aphirat Arunin. charts; illus.; stat.; circ. 1,000. **Indexed:** Abstr.Hyg., Biol.Abstr., Chem.Abstr., Curr.Adv.Ecol.Sci., Excerp.Med., Field Crop Abstr., Food Sci.& Tech.Abstr., Herb.Abstr., Met.Abstr., Plant Breed.Abstr., Sci.Abstr., Soils & Fert., Trop.Dis.Bull.
   —BLDSC shelfmark: 4831.150000.

354.415   IE
NATIONAL SCIENCE COUNCIL (IRELAND). PROGRESS REPORT. 1972. irreg. Government Publications Sales Office, Sun Alliance House, Molesworth St., Dublin 2, Ireland. circ. 1,200.

500   IE   ISSN 0085-3836
NATIONAL SCIENCE COUNCIL (IRELAND). REGISTER OF SCIENTIFIC RESEARCH PERSONNEL. 1968. irreg. Government Publications Sales Office, Sun Alliance House, Molesworth St., Dublin 2, Ireland. Eds. Diarmuid Murphy, Donal O. Brolchain. circ. 800. (tabloid format)

500   CE   ISSN 0300-9254
Q4   CODEN: JNSCBH
NATIONAL SCIENCE COUNCIL OF SRI LANKA. JOURNAL. (Text in English) 1973. s-a. $27. Natural Resources, Energy and Science Authority, 47-5 Maitland Place, Colombo 7, Sri Lanka. Ed. Nimala Amarasuriya. (reprint service avail.) **Indexed:** Biol.Abstr., Chem.Abstr., Curr.Cont., Dairy Sci.Abstr., Field Crop Abstr., Food Sci.& Tech.Abstr., Herb.Abstr., Irr.& Drain.Abstr., Packag.Sci.Tech., Poult.Abstr., Ref.Zh., Soils & Fert., Sri Lanka Sci.Ind., Weed Abstr.
   —BLDSC shelfmark: 4831.170000.

NATIONAL TECHNICAL ASSOCIATION. JOURNAL. see *ETHNIC INTERESTS*

500.9   IC   ISSN 0028-0550
NATTURUFRAEDINGURINN. (Text in Icelandic; summaries in English) 1931. 4/yr. ISK 2300. Hith Islenska Naatturufrathifilag - Icelandic Natural History Society, Box 5320, 125 Reykjavik, Iceland. Ed. Pall Imsland. bk.rev.; charts; illus.; index; circ. 1,900. **Indexed:** Biol.Abstr., Chem.Abstr., Geo.Abstr., GeoRef., Ocean.Abstr., Pollut.Abstr.
   —BLDSC shelfmark: 6033.730000.
   Description: Research papers and reviews on the natural history of Iceland. Includes articles of more general interest.

500.9   DK   ISSN 0028-0585
NATUR OG MUSEUM. (Text in Danish) 1951. q. DKK 98($15) Naturhistorisk Museum, Universitetsparken, Building 210, DK-8000 Aarhus C, Denmark. Ed. Poul Hansen. charts; illus.; circ. 9,000.

500.9   GW   ISSN 0028-0593
QH5   CODEN: NTRHAA
NATUR UND HEIMAT. 1934. 4/yr. DM.20. Westfaelisches Museum fuer Naturkunde, Sentruperstr. 285, 4400 Muenster, Germany. bibl.; charts; illus.; maps. **Indexed:** Biol.Abstr.

SCIENCES: COMPREHENSIVE WORKS

500.9　　　　　　　AU　ISSN 0028-0607
NATUR UND LAND. vol.56, 1970. irreg. (4-6/yr.) S.150. Oesterreichischer Naturschutzbund, Arenbergstr. 10, A-5020 Salzburg, Austria. TEL 0662-642909. FAX 0662-643734. (Co-sponsor: Oesterreichische Gesellschaft fuer Natur- und Umweltschutz) Ed. Winfried Herbst. adv.; bk.rev.; charts; illus.; stat.; index; circ. 10,000. (also avail. in microform) Indexed: Biol.Abstr., Ecol.Abstr., Environ.Abstr.

500.9　　　　　　　GW　ISSN 0722-7795
NATUR- UND LANDSCHAFTKUNDE. 1965. q. DM.36. Bergmann-Verlag, Werlerstr. 269, Postfach 1211, 4700 Hamm, Germany. TEL 02381-51144. Ed.Bd. adv.; bk.rev.; circ. 2,900. Indexed: Agroforest.Abstr.
—BLDSC shelfmark: 6033.907000.
  Former titles: Natur- und Landschaftskunde in Westfalen; Naturkunde in Westfalen (ISSN 0028-0992)
  Description: Devoted to the protection of nature and environment in the Northrhein-Westphalia region. Articles on research and conservation of trees, forests and land. Includes magazine reviews.

500.9　　　　　　　GW　ISSN 0028-1301
QH5　　　　　　　　CODEN: NAMUAR
NATUR UND MUSEUM. 1867. m. DM.60. Senckenbergische Naturforschende Gesellschaft, Abt. Schriftentausch, Senckenberganlage 25, 6000 Frankfurt a.M. 1, Germany. TEL 069-7542-1. FAX 069-746238. TELEX 413129. Ed. Willi Ziegler. adv.; bk.rev.; charts; illus.; index; circ. 6,000.
Indexed: Biol.Abstr., Chem.Abstr., Deep Sea Res.& Oceanogr.Abstr., GeoRef., Ocean.Abstr., Pollut.Abstr.

500.9　　　　　　　NE　ISSN 0028-0631
NATURA. 1906. 10/yr. fl.47.50. Koninklijke Nederlandse Natuurhistorische Vereniging, Oude Gracht 237, 3511 NK Utrecht, Netherlands. Ed. G. Hooymans. adv.; bk.rev.; charts; illus.; index; circ. 9,000. Indexed: Biol.Abstr.
—BLDSC shelfmark: 6034.050000.
  Description: Covers all aspects of natural history.

500.9　　　　　　　VE　ISSN 0028-064X
　　　　　　　　　　CODEN: NTRCBU
NATURA; revista trimestral de divulgacion cientifica, tecnica y cultural. 1958. q. Bs.300($25) Sociedad de Ciencias Naturales la Salle, Edificio Fundacion la Salle, Av. Boyaca-Marirez, Apdo. 1930, Caracas 1010A, Venezuela. Ed. Jesus Hoyos. adv.; circ. 7,000. Indexed: GeoRef.
—BLDSC shelfmark: 6035.200000.

500　　　　　　　　IT　ISSN 0369-6243
QH7　　　　　　　　CODEN: NTRMAP
NATURA; rivista di scienze naturali. (Text in Italian) 1909. q. L.45000 membership (effective 1992). Societa Italiana di Scienze Naturali, Corso Venezia, 55, 20121 Milan, Italy. TEL 02-620-85405. (Co-sponsor: Museo Civico di Storia Naturale di Milano) Ed. Giovani Pinna. bk.rev.; index; circ. 2,000. (back issues avail.) Indexed: Biol.Abstr., Chem.Abstr., Deep Sea Res.& Oceanogr.Abstr., GeoRef., Mineral.Abstr., Zoo.Rec.

500.9　　　　　　　US　ISSN 0028-0712
QH1　　　　　　　　CODEN: NAHIAX
NATURAL HISTORY. 1900. m. $22. American Museum of Natural History, Central Park W. at 79th St., New York, NY 10024-5192. TEL 212-769-5500. FAX 212-769-5511. Ed. Alan Ternes. adv.; bk.rev.; bibl.; illus.; index; circ. 510,000. (also avail. in microform from UMI,MIM; reprint service avail. from UMI) Indexed: A.I.C.P., Abr.R.G., Abstr.Anthropol., Acad.Ind., Acid Pre.Dig., Amer.Bibl.Slavic & E.Eur.Stud., Biol.Abstr., Biol.Dig., Bk.Rev.Dig., Bk.Rev.Ind. (1965-), Child.Bk.Rev.Ind., Curr.Adv.Ecol.Sci., Curr.Cont., Deep Sea Res.& Oceanogr.Abstr., Energy Ind., Energy Info.Abstr., Energy Rev., Environ.Per.Bibl., Gard.Lit. (1992-), Gen.Sci.Ind., Helminthol.Abstr., Ind.Sci.Rev., Jun.High.Mag.Abstr., Mag.Ind., Mid.East: Abstr.& Ind., Peace Res.Abstr., R.G., So.Pac.Per.Ind., TOM.
● Also available online. Vendor(s): DIALOG.
—BLDSC shelfmark: 6038.000000.
  Incorporates: Nature Magazine.
  Description: Articles written by professional scientists and scholars on the biological sciences, ecology, anthropology, archeology, earth science and astronomy.
  Refereed Serial

505　　　　　　　　US　ISSN 0076-0943
NATURAL HISTORY MUSEUM OF LOS ANGELES COUNTY. SCIENCE SERIES. 1930. irreg., no.35, 1991. Natural History Museum of Los Angeles County, 900 Exposition Blvd., Los Angeles, CA 90007. TEL 213-744-3330. FAX 213-742-0730. bk.rev.; illus.; index; circ. 1,000. Indexed: Biol.Abstr., Deep Sea Res.& Oceanogr.Abstr.
Refereed Serial

500.9　　　　　　　UK　ISSN 0144-221X
QH1　　　　　　　　CODEN: TNHND5
NATURAL HISTORY SOCIETY OF NORTHUMBRIA. TRANSACTIONS. 1831. a. membership. Natural History Society of Northumbria, Hancock Museum, Newcastle Upon Tyne NE2 4PT, England. Ed. R.B. Clark. charts; illus.; cum.index; circ. 650. Indexed: Biol.Abstr., Geo.Abstr.
  Formerly: Natural History Society of Northumberland Durham and Newcastle Upon Tyne. Transactions (ISSN 0028-0720)
  Description: Covers all aspects of natural history of northern England.
Refereed Serial

NATURAL SCIENCES AND ENGINEERING RESEARCH COUNCIL OF CANADA. LIST OF SCHOLARSHIPS AND GRANTS IN AID OF RESEARCH/CONSEIL DE RECHERCHES EN SCIENCES NATURELLES ET EN GENIE DU CANADA. LISTE DES BOURSES ET SUBVENTIONS DE RECHERCHE. see *EDUCATION — Higher Education*

NATURAL SCIENCES AND ENGINEERING RESEARCH COUNCIL OF CANADA. REPORT OF THE PRESIDENT/CONSEIL DE RECHERCHES EN SCIENCES NATURELLES ET EN GENIE DU CANADA. RAPPORT DU PRESIDENT. see *EDUCATION — Higher Education*

500.9　　　　　　　TR
NATURALIST. 1975. bi-m. $35. (Field Naturalists Club of Trinidad & Tobago) S.M. Publications Publishing House, 20 Collens Rd., Maraval, Port-of-Spain, Republic of Trinidad & Tobago, W.I. TEL 809 622-6625. Ed. Stephen Mohammed. adv.; bk.rev.; illus.; stat.; index; circ. 20,000. (back issues avail.)
  Formerly: Trinidad Naturalist (ISSN 0379-4016)

500.9　　　　　　　CN　ISSN 0028-0798
QH3
NATURALISTE CANADIEN; revue d'ecologie et de systematique. (Text in English or French) 1868. 4/yr. Can.$24 to individuals (foreign Can.$30); institutions Can.$50. Presses de l'Universite Laval, Cite universitaire, Quebec, Que. G1K 7P4, Canada. TEL 418-656-3809. FAX 418-656-2600. Ed. Pierre Morrisset. bk.rev.; charts; illus.; index, cum.index: vols.1-96 (1868-1969); circ. 800. (also avail. in microform; reprint service avail. from UMI) Indexed: Acid Pre.Dig., Bio-Contr.News & Info., Biol.Abstr., Bull.Signal., Chem.Abstr., Deep Sea Res.& Oceanogr.Abstr., Field Crop Abstr., Forest.Abstr., Forest Prod.Abstr., Geo.Abstr., Helminthol.Abstr., Herb.Abstr., Hort.Abstr., Maize Abstr., Ocean.Abstr., Pollut.Abstr., Potato Abstr., Pt.de Rep. (1983-), Rev.Plant Path., Soils & Fert., Weed Abstr.
—BLDSC shelfmark: 6043.000000.

500　　　　　　　　JA
NATURALISTS. (Text in Japanese) 1987. irreg. Shizen Kagaku Kenkyukai, Shikoku Joshi Daigaku Seibutsugaku Kyoshitsu, 123-1 Ebisuno, Furukawa, Ojin-cho, Tokushima 771-11, Japan.

500.9　　　　　　　UK　ISSN 0028-0836
Q1　　　　　　　　　CODEN: NATUAS
NATURE; international weekly journal of science. 1869. w. £160($395) (effective 1992). Macmillan Magazines Ltd. (Subsidiary of: Macmillan Publishers Ltd.), 4 Little Essex St., London WC2R 3LF, England. TEL 071-836-6633. FAX 0256-842084. (Subscr. to: Brunel Rd., Basingstoke, Hants RG21 2XS, England. TEL 0256-29242; N. America subscr. to: Nature, Box 1733, Riverton, NJ 08077-7333. TEL 800-524-0384) Ed. John Maddox. adv.; bk.rev.; bibl.; charts; illus.; index; circ. 30,821. (also avail. in microform from UMI; Braille; talking book; reprint service avail. from UMI) Indexed: A.I.Abstr., A.I.Abstr., A.I.C.P., ABC, Abstr.Bull.Inst.Pap.Chem., Acad.Ind., Acid Pre.Dig., Acid Rain Abstr., Acid Rain Ind., AESIS, Anal.Abstr., Appl.Mech.Rev., Art & Archaeol.Tech.Abstr., Bibl.Dev.Med.& Child Neur., Biol.Abstr., Biol.Dig., Biostat., Biotech.Abstr., Biwk.Pap.Rad.Chem.& Photochem., Bk.Rev.Ind. (1982-), Br.Archaeol.Abstr., Br.Ceram.Abstr., Br.Educ.Ind., Br.Geol.Lit., Br.Tech.Ind., C.I.S. Abstr., Cadscan, Chem.Abstr., Child.Bk.Rev.Ind. (1982-), Curr.Adv.Biochem., Curr.Adv.Ecol.Sci., Curr.Biotech.Abstr., Curr.Cont., Curr.Tit.Dent., Dairy Sci.Abstr., Deep Sea Res.& Oceanogr.Abstr., Dent.Ind., Energy Info.Abstr., Eng.Ind., Environ.Abstr., Excerp.Med., Field Crop Abstr., Fluidex, Food Sci.& Tech.Abstr., Forest.Abstr., Forest Prod.Abstr., Fut.Surv., Gen.Sci.Ind., Geo.Abstr., GeoRef., Helminthol.Abstr., High.Educ.Curr.Aware.Bull., Hort.Abstr., I.P.A., Ind.Chem., Ind.Med., Ind.Sci.Rev., Int.Aerosp.Abstr., Int.Nurs.Ind., Lab.Haz.Bull., Lead Abstr., Mass Spectr.Bull., Math.R., Met.Abstr., Meteor.& Geoastrophys.Abstr., Mid.East: Abstr.& Ind., Nutr.Abstr., Peace Res.Abstr, Petrol.Abstr., Plant Breed.Abstr., PMR, Pollut.Abstr., Protozool.Abstr., Psychol.Abstr., RAPRA, Res.High.Educ.Abstr., Rev.Appl.Entomol., Rev.Plant Path., Rice Abstr., Risk Abstr., Sci.Abstr., So.Pac.Per.Ind., Telegen, Trop.Dis.Bull., Vet.Bull., ull., VITIS, W.R.C.Inf., World Alum.Abstr., World Text.Abstr., Zincscan.
—BLDSC shelfmark: 6045.000000.
Refereed Serial

NATURE AND RESOURCES; international news about research on environment, resources, and conservation of nature. see *CONSERVATION*

500.9　　　　　　　NO　ISSN 0028-0887
　　　　　　　　　　CODEN: NTUNA9
NATUREN; journal of popular natural science. 1877. bi-m. $39. (University of Bergen) Universitetsforlaget, P.O. Box 2959-Toeyen, N-0608 Oslo 1, Norway. (U.S. addr.: Publications Expediting Inc., 200 Meacham Ave., Elmont, NY 11003) Ed. Eyvind Alver. adv.; bk.rev.; charts; illus.; index; circ. 2,200. (back issues avail.) Indexed: Chem.Abstr, Curr.Adv.Ecol.Sci., GeoRef.
—BLDSC shelfmark: 6047.800000.

500.9　　　　　　　DK　ISSN 0028-0895
Q4
NATURENS VERDEN. 1917. m. DKK 285. Rhodos, International Science and Art Publishers, Strandgade 36 D, DK-1401 Copenhagen K, Denmark. TEL 45-31-543080. FAX 45-31-954742. TELEX 31502. Ed.Bd. adv.; bk.rev.; illus.; maps; index; circ. 10,000. Indexed: Biol.Abstr., Chem.Abstr., NAA, Zoo.Rec.
—BLDSC shelfmark: 6048.000000.

500　　　　　　　　BL　ISSN 0100-4700
NATUREZA EM REVISTA. 1976. s-a. price varies. Fundacao Zoobotanica do Rio Grande do Sul, Caixa Postal 1188, 90000 Porto Alegre, Rio Grande do sul, Brazil. Ed. Elisabete Monlleo Martins da Silva. adv.; bk.rev.; bibl.; illus.; circ. 10,000. Indexed: Biol.Abstr.

500　　　　　　　　SZ　ISSN 0077-6122
　　　　　　　　　　CODEN: VNGBAH
NATURFORSCHENDE GESELLSCHAFT IN BASEL. VERHANDLUNGEN/SOCIETY FOR NATURAL SCIENCES, BASEL. PROCEEDINGS. (Text in English, French, German and Italian) 1854. irreg. (approx. 1/yr.). 90 Fr.($65) Birkhaeuser Verlag, P.O. Box 133, CH-4010 Basel, Switzerland. TEL 061-737740. FAX 061-737950. TELEX 963475 BIRKH CH. (Dist. in N. America by: Springer-Verlag New York, Inc., Journal Fulfillment Services, Box 2485, Secaucus, NJ 07096-2491. TEL 201-348-4033) Ed. H. Schaefer. Indexed: A.I.C.P., Biol.Abstr., GeoRef.
—BLDSC shelfmark: 9165.000000.

SCIENCES: COMPREHENSIVE WORKS

500 SZ ISSN 0077-6130
Q67 CODEN: MNGBAK
NATURFORSCHENDE GESELLSCHAFT IN BERN. MITTEILUNGEN. (Text in German; summaries in English and French) 1843. a. 30 Fr. Naturforschende Gesellschaft in Bern, Stadt-und Universitaetsbibliothek, Muenstergasse 61, CH-3000 Berne 7, Switzerland. TEL 031-225519. FAX 031-212883. Ed. H. Hutzli. adv.; cum.index: 1944-1968 in no.26 (1969); circ. 1,400. **Indexed:** Biol.Abstr., GeoRef, VITIS.
—BLDSC shelfmark: 5860.950000.

500.9 SZ ISSN 0042-5672
Q67 CODEN: VNGZAL
NATURFORSCHENDE GESELLSCHAFT IN ZUERICH. VIERTELJAHRESSCHRIFT. 1855. q. 75 Fr. Orell Fussli AG, Dietzingerstr. 3, 8003 Zurich, Switzerland. Ed. H.H. Bosshard. adv.; bk.rev.; bibl.; charts; illus.; index. **Indexed:** Biol.Abstr., Chem.Abstr., GeoRef.
—BLDSC shelfmark: 9235.903000.

500 GW ISSN 0028-0917
Q49 CODEN: BEFBAZ
NATURFORSCHENDE GESELLSCHAFT ZU FREIBURG. BERICHTE. 1855. s-a. DM.30. Naturforschende Gesellschaft Freiburg, Albertstr. 23b, 7800 Freiburg, Germany. FAX 0761-2032463. bk.rev.; charts; illus.; index, cum.index: 1855-1955; circ. 1,300. **Indexed:** Biol.Abstr., GeoRef., VITIS.
—BLDSC shelfmark: 1923.040000.

500 551 560 SZ
NATURHISTORISCHES MUSEUM BASEL. VEROEFFENTLICHUNGEN. 1960. irreg. Naturhistorisches Museum Basel, Augustinergasse 2, 4001 Basel, Switzerland. FAX 061-2665546. Ed.Bd. circ. 7,500. (back issues avail.) **Indexed:** Biol.Abstr.

500.9 SZ ISSN 0253-4401
NATURHISTORISCHES MUSEUM BERN. JAHRBUCH. (Text in English, French or German.) 1960. triennial. 60 Fr. Naturhistorisches Museum, Bernastr. 15, CH-3005 Berne, Switzerland. TEL 031-431839. Ed.Bd. illus.; circ. 250. (back issues avail.)
—BLDSC shelfmark: 4625.160000.
Description: Contains activity reports and miscellaneous articles (original papers and reports on collections) in the fields of mineralogy, palaeontology, invertebrate and vertebrate zoology and anthropology.

500.9 AU ISSN 0083-6133
QH5 CODEN: ANMWAF
NATURHISTORISCHES MUSEUM IN WIEN. ANNALEN. (Text in English, French and German; summaries in English, French, German, Italian and Spanish) 1886. a. price varies. Naturhistorisches Museum in Wien, Burgring 7, P.F. 417, A-1014 Vienna, Austria. FAX 0222-935254. bk.rev.; index; circ. 1,100. (back issues avail.) **Indexed:** Bibl.& Ind.Geol., Bio-Contr.News & Info., Biol.Abstr., Curr.Adv.Ecol.Sci., Deep Sea Res.& Oceanogr.Abstr., GeoRef, Rev.Appl.Entomol., So.Pac.Per.Ind.

500.9 AU ISSN 0505-5164
NATURHISTORISCHES MUSEUM IN WIEN. VEROEFFENTLICHUNGEN. NEUE FOLGE. 1958. irreg. price varies. Naturhistorisches Museum in Wien, Burgring 7, P.F. 417, A-1014 Vienna, Austria. FAX 0222-935254. **Indexed:** Bibl.& Ind.Geol.
—BLDSC shelfmark: 9188.450000.

500 AU ISSN 0470-3901
NATURKUNDLICHES JAHRBUCH DER STADT LINZ. 1955. a. S.350. Naturkundliche Station der Stadt Linz, Roseggerstr. 22, A-4020 Linz, Austria. Ed. Gerhard Pfitzner. illus.; circ. 500.
—BLDSC shelfmark: 6048.300000.

500.9 GW ISSN 0028-1042
Q3 CODEN: NATWAY
DIE NATURWISSENSCHAFTEN. 1913. 12/yr. DM.248($139) (Max-Planck-Gesellschaft zur Foerderung der Wissenschaften) Springer-Verlag, Heidelberger Platz 3, D-1000 Berlin 33, Germany. TEL 030-8207-1. (Also Heidelberg, Tokyo, Vienna, and New York) (Co-sponsor: Gesellschaft Deutscher Naturforscher und Aertze) Eds. H.J. Autrum, F.L. Boschke. (also avail. in microform from UMI; reprint service avail. from ISI) **Indexed:** Anim.Breed.Abstr., Appl.Mech.Rev., Art & Archaeol.Tech.Abstr., Bio-Contr.News & Info., Biol.Abstr., Biotech.Abstr., Chem.Abstr., Chem.Infd., Curr.Adv.Ecol.Sci., Dairy Sci.Abstr., Deep Sea Res.& Oceanogr.Abstr., Excerp.Med., Field Crop Abstr., Forest.Abstr., Forest Prod.Abstr., Geo.Abstr., Helminthol.Abstr., Herb.Abstr., Hort.Abstr., Ind.Chem., Ind.Med., Ind.Vet., Mass Spectr.Bull., Nutr.Abstr., Plant Breed.Abstr., Rev.Appl.Entomol., Rev.Plant Path., Sci.Abstr, Soils & Fert., Vet.Bull., Weed Abstr.
—BLDSC shelfmark: 6049.000000.

500 370 GW ISSN 0342-5487
NATURWISSENSCHAFTEN IM UNTERRICHT. BIOLOGIE. 1952. 10/yr. DM.103.50. Erhard Friedrich Verlag GmbH, Im Brande 15, 3016 Seelze 6, Germany. Ed.Bd. **Indexed:** W.R.C.Inf.
Supersedes in part: Naturwissenschaften im Unterricht.

500.9 GW ISSN 0028-1050
Q3 CODEN: NARSAC
NATURWISSENSCHAFTLICHE RUNDSCHAU. 1948. m. DM.134.40 (students DM.51.60). Wissenschaftliche Verlagsgesellschaft mbH, Postfach 105339, 7000 Stuttgart 10, Germany. TEL 0711-2582-0. FAX 0711-2582-290. TELEX 723636-DAZ-D. Eds. H. Rotta, R. Schmid. adv.; bk.rev.; bibl.; charts; illus.; index; circ. 7,000. **Indexed:** Bibl.& Ind.Geol., Biol.Abstr., Biotech.Abstr., Chem.Abstr., Excerp.Med., Meteor.& Geoastrophys.Abstr., VITIS.
—BLDSC shelfmark: 6049.275000.
Description: Covers all fields of science: biology, medicine, pharmacy, chemistry, physics, astronomy and geography.

500 GW ISSN 0077-6157
NATURWISSENSCHAFTLICHE RUNDSCHAU. BUECHER DER ZEITSCHRIFT. 1966. irreg. price varies; special rate for subscribers of "Naturwissenschaftliche Rundschau". Wissenschaftliche Verlagsgesellschaft mbH, Postfach 105339, 7000 Stuttgart 10, Germany. TEL 0711-2582-0. FAX 0711-2582-290. TELEX 723636-DAZ-D.
Description: Covers all fields of science: biology, medicine, pharmacy, chemistry, physics, astronomy and geography.

500 GW ISSN 0077-6165
Q49 CODEN: SNSHAS
NATURWISSENSCHAFTLICHER VEREIN FUER SCHLESWIG-HOLSTEIN. SCHRIFTEN. 1870. irreg. price varies. Lipsius & Tischer, Holstenstr. 40, 2300 Kiel 1, Germany. TEL 0431-8802944. FAX 0431-8804658. Ed. Heinz Klug. bk.rev.; circ. 150. **Indexed:** Bibl.& Ind.Geol., Biol.Abstr., Deep Sea Res.& Oceanogr.Abstr.
—BLDSC shelfmark: 8094.810000.

500.9 AU
NATURWISSENSCHAFTLICHER VEREIN FUER STEIERMARK. MITTEILUNGEN. 1863. a. S.250. Naturwissenschaftlicher Verein fuer Steiermark, Universitaetsbibliothek, Universitaetsplatz 3, A-8010 Graz, Austria. Eds. A. Drescher, H.L. Holzer. bk.rev.; charts; illus.; index, cum.index; circ. 200. (back issues avail.) **Indexed:** Bibl.& Ind.Geol., Biol.Abstr., VITIS.
Description: Covers such subjects as mineralogy, petrology, geology, paleontology, geography, climatology, biology, botany and zoology.

500.9 NE ISSN 0028-1085
NATUUR EN MUSEUM. 1957. q. fl.7.50. Naturhistorisch Museum, van Sambeekstichting, M. H. Tromplaan 19, 7511 JJ Enschede, Netherlands. Ed. P. Venema. bk.rev.; circ. 2,800.

500.9 NE ISSN 0028-1093
Q4
NATUUR EN TECHNIEK/NATURE AND TECHNOLOGY; natuurwetenschappelijk en technisch maandblad/scientific and technical monthly. 1932. m. fl.125 (effective 1992). Centrale Uitgeverij en Adviesbureau B.V., Postbus 415, 6200 AK Maastricht, Netherlands. TEL 043-254044. FAX 043-216124. TELEX 56642 NATU NL. Eds. Th. J.M. Martens, G.M.N. Verschuuren. adv.; bk.rev.; illus.; index; circ. 49,000. **Indexed:** C.I.S. Abstr., Chem.Abstr., Excerp.Med.
—BLDSC shelfmark: 6051.000000.

500.9 NE ISSN 0028-1107
NATUURHISTORISCH MAANDBLAD. (Text mainly in Dutch; contributions in English, French and German; summaries in English) 1911. m. fl.160($80) (Natuurhistorisch Genootschap in Limburg) Publicatie bureau N H G, Groenstraat 106, 6074 EL Melick, Netherlands. TEL 043-213671. Ed. Douwe Th. de Graaf. bk.rev.; circ. 1,200. **Indexed:** Biol.Abstr., Rev.Appl.Entomol.
Description: Covers research in the biology and the geology of Limburg. Includes association news, reports, lists of events.

508 BE ISSN 0770-1748
NATUURWETENSCHAPPELIJK TIJDSCHRIFT. 1919. q. 1000 BEF. Natuur- en Geneeskundige Vennootschap, Krijgslaan 281 S.8, B-9000 Ghent, Belgium. Ed. Dr. L. Walschot. bk.rev.; charts; illus.; index; circ. 400. **Indexed:** Bibl.& Ind.Geol., Biol.Abstr., Bull.Signal., Chem.Abstr, Geo.Abstr.
—BLDSC shelfmark: 6053.000000.

500 BU ISSN 0028-1123
NAUCHEN ZHIVOT. (Contents page in Bulgarian, English, French and Russian) 1958. 5/yr. membership. (Suiuz na Nauchni Rabotnitsi v Bulgaria) Izdatelstvo Natsionalen Suvet na Otechestveniia Front, 32, Dondukov Blvd., Sofia, Bulgaria. Ed. Kiril Grigorov. illus.; circ. 4,000.

NAUCNI I STRUCNI SKUPOVI U JUGOSLAVII I U INOSTRANSTVU/SCIENTIFIC AND PROFESSIONAL MEETINGS IN YUGOSLAVIA AND FOREIGN COUNTRIES. see *MEETINGS AND CONGRESSES*

500 PL ISSN 0077-6181
NAUKA DLA WSZYSTKICH/SCIENCE FOR EVERYONE. 1966. irreg., vol.415, 1987. price varies. (Polska Akademia Nauk, Oddzial w Krakowie) Ossolineum, Publishing House of the Polish Academy of Sciences, Rynek 9, 50-106 Wroclaw, Poland. TELEX 0712771 OSS PL. (Dist. by Ars: Polona, Krakowskie Przedmiescie 7, 00-068 Warsaw, Poland) Ed. Franciszek Slawski.
Description: Popular-science publication. Presents the latest achievements of all domains of science.

NAUKA I RELIGIYA. see *RELIGIONS AND THEOLOGY*

500 RU ISSN 0028-1247
NAUKA I SUSPIL'STVO. (Text in Ukranian) 1951. m. $6.60. Stroiizdat, Shchosseva, rm. 60, Moscow, Russia. index.

500 LV ISSN 0028-1255
NAUKA I TEKHNIKA/ZINATNE UN TEHNIKA. (Editions in Latvian and Russian) 1960. m. $10.20. Gosudarstvennyi Nauchno-tekhnicheskii Komitet Soveta Ministrov, Riga, Latvia. charts; index. **Indexed:** Curr.Dig.Sov.Press.

500 RU ISSN 0028-1263
Q4
NAUKA I ZHIZN'; nauchno-populyarnyi zhurnal. 1934. m. 19.20 Rub. (Vsesoyuznoe Obshchestvo "Znanie") Izdatel'stvo Pravda, Nauka i Zhizn, Ul. Myasnitskaya 24, 101877 Moscow, Russia. TEL 095-923-2122. FAX 095-200-2259. Ed. I.K. Lagovsky. bk.rev.; adv.; charts; illus.; maps; index; circ. 1,313,000. **Indexed:** Biol.Abstr., Curr.Dig.Sov.Press, Int.Aerosp.Abstr.
—BLDSC shelfmark: 0119.300000.

SCIENCES: COMPREHENSIVE WORKS 4329

500   PL   ISSN 0028-1271
AS261
NAUKA POLSKA; czasopismo poswiecone rozwojowi nauki w Polsce. 1953. bi-m. $81. (Polska Akademia Nauk) Ossolineum, Publishing House of the Polish Academy of Sciences, Rynek 9, Wroclaw, Poland. TELEX 0712771 OSS PL. (Dist. by: Ars Polona-Ruch, Krakowskie Przedmiescie 7, Warsaw, Poland) Ed. A. Gieysztor. bk.rev.; charts; illus.; index; circ. 1,400. **Indexed:** Amer.Hist.& Life, Biol.Abstr., Hist.Abstr.
—BLDSC shelfmark: 6059.000000.
Description: Development and achievements of Polish science.

500   RU   ISSN 0203-4425
Q60   CODEN: NASRDH
NAUKA V S.S.S.R.. English edition: Science in the U.S.S.R. (ISSN 0203-4638); German edition: Wissenschaft in der U.D.S.S.R. (ISSN 0207-5709); Spanish edition: Ciencia en la U.R.S.S. (ISSN 0207-5717) (Editions in English, German, Russian and Spanish) 1981. bi-m. 6.60 Rub.($30) (Akademiya Nauk S.S.S.R.) Izdatel'stvo Nauka, 90, Profsoyuznaya ul., 117864 Moscow, Russia. TEL 234-3506. (Dist. by: Mezhdunarodnaya Kniga, Ul. Dimitrova D.39, 113095 Moscow, Russia; Dist. in the U.S. by: OMNI-Science in the U.S.S.R., 1965 Broadway, New York, NY 10133-0155) Ed. Rem V. Petrov. adv.; bk.rev.; circ. 115,000. **Indexed:** Chem.Abstr., Int.Aerosp.Abstr.
—BLDSC shelfmark: 0119.467300.
Description: Topics covered include: ecology, discoveries and inventions, human environment, museums, astronomy, agronomy, medical research, geochemistry, space technology and more.

500   US
NAUKOVE TOVARYSTVO IMENI SHEVCHENKA. PROCEEDINGS OF THE SECTION OF MATHEMATICS AND PHYSICS. (Text in English and Ukrainian) vol.6, 1964. irreg. price varies. Shevchenko Scientific Society, 63 Fourth Ave., New York, NY 10003. TEL 212-254-5130. circ. 500.
Supersedes in part: Naukove Tovarystvo Imeni Shevchenka. Proceedings of the Section of Mathematics, Natural Science and Medicine (ISSN 0470-5017)

500   US   ISSN 0077-6343
Q11   CODEN: PNBAAP
NEBRASKA ACADEMY OF SCIENCES. PROCEEDINGS. a. $1.50. Nebraska Academy of Sciences, 302 Morrill Hall, 14th & U Sts., Lincoln, NE 68588-0339. Ed. A.W. Zechmann. circ. 1,800. **Indexed:** Bibl.& Ind.Geol., Biol.Abstr., VITIS.

500   US   ISSN 0077-6351
                   CODEN: TNASBH
NEBRASKA ACADEMY OF SCIENCES. TRANSACTIONS. 1970. a. price varies. Nebraska Academy of Sciences, 302 Morrill Hall, 14th & U Sts., Lincoln, NE 68588-0339. Ed. Robert B. Kaul. circ. 1,800. **Indexed:** Bibl.& Ind.Geol., Biol.Abstr., VITIS.
Refereed Serial

500.9   NE
NEDERLANDS TIJDSCHRIFT VOOR NATUURKUNDE A EN B. (Issued in two parts) 6/yr. fl.130. Nederlandse Natuurkundige Vereniging, Fysisch Laboratorium, P.O. Box 5451, 1007 Al Amsterdam, Netherlands. Ed.Bd. adv.; bk.rev.; charts; illus.; Bibl.& Ind.Geol.; circ. 3,500. **Indexed:** Chem.Abstr., Phys.Abstr., Sci.Abstr.
Formerly: Nederlands Tijdschrift voor Natuurkunde (ISSN 0028-2189)

500   JA   ISSN 0287-3052
NEEDS. (Text in Japanese) 1975. a. Iwatani Naoji Kinen Zaidan - Iwatani Naoji Foundation, TBR Bldg., 10-2 Nagata-cho 2-chome, Chiyoda-ku, Tokyo 100, Japan.
Description: News of the foundation.

500   CC   ISSN 1000-1638
NEI MENGGU DAXUE XUEBAO (ZIRAN KEXUE BAN)/INNER MONGOLIAN UNIVERSITY. JOURNAL (NATURAL SCIENCE EDITION). (Text in Chinese) q. Nei Menggu Daxue - Inner Mongolian University, 1 Daxue Lu, Huhhot, Nei Menggu 010021, People's Republic of China. TEL 43141. Ed. Luo Liaofu.

500   CC   ISSN 1001-7623
NEI MENGGU SHIFAN DAXUE XUEBAO (ZIRAN KEXUE BAN)/INNER MONGOLIAN NORMAL UNIVERSITY. JOURNAL (NATURAL SCIENCE EDITION). (Editions in Chinese, English) q. Nei Menggu Shifan Daxue - Inner Mongolian Normal University, Huhhot, Nei Menggu 010022, People's Republic of China. TEL 41291.
—BLDSC shelfmark: 4769.775000.

500   JA   ISSN 0466-6089
NEICHA SUTADI/NATURE STUDY. (Text in Japanese) 1955. m. 2000 Yen (effective 1992). (Osaka-shiritsu Shizenshi Hakubutsukan - Osaka Museum of Natural History) Osaka-shiritsu Shizenshi Hakubutsukan Tomo no Kai, 1-23 Nagai Koen, Higashi-sumiyoshi-ku, Osaka-shi, Osaka-fu 546, Japan. bk.rev.
Description: Contains reviews, commentary, and news of the museum.

NEKOTORYE FILOSOFSKIE VOPROSY SOVREMENNOGO ESTESTVOZNANIYA. see *PHILOSOPHY*

500   US   ISSN 0085-3887
QL1   CODEN: NOPHD2
NEMOURIA: OCCASIONAL PAPERS OF THE DELAWARE MUSEUM OF NATURAL HISTORY. 1970. irreg., no.35, 1990. price varies. Delaware Museum of Natural History, Box 3937, Wilmington, DE 19807. TEL 302-658-9111. Ed. R. Bieler. **Indexed:** Biol.Abstr., M.L.A.

053.1 500   GW   ISSN 0028-3169
DAS NEUE ERLANGEN; Zeitschrift fuer Wissenschaft, Wirtschaft und kulturelles Leben. 1965. 3/yr. DM.13. Universitaetsbuchhandlung Rudolf Merkel, Untere Karlstr. 9-11, 8520 Erlangen, Germany. FAX 09131-862995. Ed. H. Lerche. adv.; charts; illus.; stat.; circ. 5,000.

500   GW
NEUE MUENCHNER BEITRAEGE ZUR GESCHICHTE DER MEDIZIN UND NATURWISSENSCHAFTEN. NATURWISSENSCHAFTSHISTORISCHE REIHE. 1969. irreg., vol.6, 1979. price varies. (Werner Fritsch Verlag) Theodor Ackermann, Ludwigstr. 7, D-8000 Munich 22, Germany. TEL 284787. Eds. Friedrich Klemm, Christa Habrich. index.

500.9   US   ISSN 0077-7900
NEVADA. STATE MUSEUM, CARSON CITY. NATURAL HISTORY PUBLICATIONS. 1962. irreg., no.4, 1980. price varies. Nevada State Museum, Capitol Complex, Carson City, NV 89710. TEL 702-687-4810. Ed. J. Scott Miller. circ. 1,000.

500   US   ISSN 0742-7514
NEW BOOK OF POPULAR SCIENCE ANNUAL; a science anthology with reviews of the year highlighting science news. 1964. a. $21.75. Grolier Incorporated, Sherman Turnpike, Danbury, CT 06816. TEL 203-797-3500. Ed. Joseph M. Castagno. charts; illus.; stat.; index.
Description: Contains special reports and summaries of the year's major events and trends in modern science.

500   US   ISSN 0028-5455
Q11   CODEN: BJASAS
NEW JERSEY ACADEMY OF SCIENCE. BULLETIN. 1955. s-a. $30. New Jersey Academy of Science, Beck Hall, Rm. 216, Kilmer Campus, Rutgers University, Piscataway, NJ 08854. TEL 201-463-0511. (Affiliate: American Association for the Advancement of Science) Ed. Robert Evans. charts; illus.; stat.; circ. 800. (also avail. in microform from UMI; reprint service avail. from UMI) **Indexed:** Bibl.& Ind.Geol., Biol.Abstr., Chem.Abstr, Excerp.Med.
—BLDSC shelfmark: 2646.800000.

500   US   ISSN 0028-5463
NEW JERSEY ACADEMY OF SCIENCE. NEWSLETTER. 1966. irreg. membership. New Jersey Academy of Science, Beck Hall, Rm. 216, Kilmer Campus, Rutgers Univ., Piscataway, NJ 08854. TEL 201-463-0511. Ed. Eugene Varney. bk.rev.; circ. 700.

500   UK   ISSN 0951-6026
NEW PARADIGMS NEWSLETTER. 1986. 4/yr. New Paradigms Publications, 29 Fairford Crescent, Downhead Park, Milton Keynes MK15 9AF, England. TEL 0908-607022. Ed. Alan Mayne. bk.rev.
Description: Covers science, philosophy, religion, parascience, human affairs, and technology.

500   US   ISSN 0028-6591
AS25
NEW RESEARCH CENTERS. (Supplement to: Research Centers Directory) 1965. s-a. $269. Gale Research Inc., 835 Penobscot Bldg., Detroit, MI 48226. TEL 313-961-2242. FAX 313-961-6083. TELEX 810-221-7086. Ed. Karen Hill. cum.index in each issue.
Description: Provides entries on newly formed and newly established research centers in the U.S. and Canada.

500   UK   ISSN 0028-6664
Q1   CODEN: NWSCAL
NEW SCIENTIST. 1956. w. £67($130) I P C Magazines Ltd., Holborn Group (Subsidiary of: Reed Business Publishing Ltd.), Kings Reach Tower, Stamford St., London SE1 9LS, England. TEL 071-261-5000. (Subscr. to: Oakfield House, 35 Perrymount Rd., Haywards Heath, West Sussex RH16 3DH, England) Ed. David Dickson. adv.; bk.rev.; charts; illus.; pat.; q. index; circ. 100,923. (back issues avail.) **Indexed:** A.I.Abstr., A.S.& T.Ind., ABC, Abstr.Bull.Inst.Pap.Chem., Acad.Ind., Acid Pre.Dig., Acid Rain Abstr., Acid Rain Ind., Anim.Breed.Abstr., Appl.Mech.Rev., Art & Archaeol.Tech.Abstr., Biodet.Abstr., Biol.Abstr., Biol.Dig., Bk.Rev.Ind. (1990-), BMT, Br.Archaeol.Abstr., Br.Ceram.Abstr., Br.Tech.Ind., Build.Manage.Abstr., C.I.S. Abstr., CAD CAM Abstr., Cadscan, Chem.Eng.Abstr., Child.Bk.Rev.Ind. (1990-), Copper Abstr., Curr.Adv.Biochem., Curr.Adv.Ecol.Sci., Curr.Biotech.Abstr., Curr.Cont., Dairy Sci.Abstr., Deep Sea Res.& Oceanogr.Abstr., Energy Info.Abstr., Energy Rev., Environ.Abstr., Fluidex, Forest.Abstr., Fuel & Energy Abstr., Fut.Surv., Gdlns., Gen.Sci.Ind., Geo.Abstr., Helminthol.Abstr., Herb.Abstr., High.Educ.Curr.Aware.Bull., Hort.Abstr, Ind.Sci.Rev., Int.Aerosp.Abstr., Int.Packag.Abstr., J.of Ferroc., Key to Econ.Sci., Lab.Haz.Bull., Lead Abstr., Met.Abstr., Mid.East: Abstr.& Ind., Ocean.Abstr., Paper & Bd.Abstr., Peace Res.Abstr., Pollut.Abstr., Print.Abstr., PROMT, Protozool.Abstr., Res.High.Educ.Abstr., Rev.Appl.Entomol., RICS, Risk Abstr., Robomat, Rural Devel.Abstr., Rural Recreat.Tour.Abstr., Sci.Abstr., Sel.Water Res.Abstr., So.Pac.Per.Ind., Stud.Wom.Abstr., Telegen, Trop.Dis.Bull., W.R.C.Inf., Weed Abstr., World Alum.Abstr., World Text.Abstr., Zincscan.
●Also available online. Vendor(s): VU/TEXT Information Services, Inc..
Description: Offers comprehensive coverage of a wide range of science-related fields and topics. Subjects of articles include botany, physics, evolution, nuclear power, mathematics and environmental studies.

500   US   ISSN 0077-8923
Q11   CODEN: ANYAA9
NEW YORK ACADEMY OF SCIENCES. ANNALS. 1823. irreg. price varies. New York Academy of Sciences, 2 E. 63rd St., New York, NY 10021. TEL 212-838-0230. Ed. Bill Boland. bibl.; charts; illus.; index, cum.index: 1960-1974; circ. 1,000. (also avail. in microfilm; back issues avail.; reprint service avail. from UMI) **Indexed:** Abstr.Health Care Manage.Stud., Anim.Breed.Abstr., Bibl.& Ind.Geol, Biodet.Abstr., Biol.Abstr., Biotech.Abstr., C.I.S. Abstr., Cadscan, Chem.Abstr., Curr.Adv.Cell & Devel.Biol., Curr.Adv.Ecol.Sci., Dairy Sci.Abstr., Deep Sea Res.& Oceanogr.Abstr., Dent.Ind., Excerp.Med., Field Crop Abstr., Helminthol.Abstr., Herb.Abstr., Hort.Abstr., Ind.Med., Ind.Vet., INIS Atomind., Int.Aerosp.Abstr., Lead Abstr., M.L.A., Math.R., Nutr.Abstr., Psychol.Abstr., Rev.Med.& Vet.Mycol., Sci.Cit.Ind., Soils & Fert., Telegen, Vert.Bull., Zincscan.
—BLDSC shelfmark: 1031.000000.
Refereed Serial

500   US   ISSN 0028-7113
Q11   CODEN: TNYAAE
NEW YORK ACADEMY OF SCIENCES. TRANSACTIONS. 1881. irreg. New York Academy of Sciences, 2 E. 63rd St., New York, NY 10021. Ed. Bill Boland. (also avail. in microform from UMI; back issues avail.; reprint service avail. from UMI) **Indexed:** Biol.Abstr., CAD CAM Abstr., Chem.Abstr., Curr.Adv.Ecol.Sci., Deep Sea Res.& Oceanogr.Abstr., Helminthol.Abstr., Ind.Vet., Math.R., Vet.Bull.
Refereed Serial

500.9   US
NEW YORK CITY NOTES ON NATURAL HISTORY. 1977. q. $5. Box 11, Inwood Sta., New York, NY 10034.

SCIENCES: COMPREHENSIVE WORKS

500 US
NEW YORK STATE MUSEUM. BULLETIN. 1887. irreg., no.477, 1990. price varies. New York State Museum, 3140 Cultural Education Center, Albany, NY 12230. TEL 518-474-3505. illus. **Indexed:** Bibl.& Ind.Geol., Biol.Abstr., Rev.Appl.Entomol.
Description: Reports of current research, popular and scholarly guides to the natural history of New York State.

500 US
NEW YORK STATE MUSEUM. CIRCULAR. 1928. irreg., no.54, 1990. price varies. New York State Museum, 3140 Cultural Education Center, Albany, NY 12230. charts; illus. **Indexed:** Bibl.& Ind.Geol., Biol.Abstr., Deep Sea Res.& Oceanogr.Abstr.
Formerly: New York State Museum and Science Service. Circular.
Description: Research updates, short scientific reports and indexes.

500 US
NEW YORK STATE MUSEUM. LEAFLET. Variant title: Educational Leaflet. 1949. irreg., no.30, 1990. price varies. New York State Museum, 3140 Cultural Education Center, Albany, NY 12230. charts; illus. **Indexed:** Biol.Abstr.
Description: Popular and educational booklets covering topics in anthropology, biology and geology.

500 US
NEW YORK STATE MUSEUM. MEMOIR. 1889. irreg., no.23, 1983. New York State Museum, 3140 Cultural Education Center, Albany, NY 12230. charts; illus. **Indexed:** Bibl.& Ind.Geol., Biol.Abstr.
Formerly: New York State Museum and Science Service. Memoir.
Description: Works on New York's natural history and prehistory.

500 NZ ISSN 0077-9601
NEW ZEALAND. DEPARTMENT OF SCIENTIFIC AND INDUSTRIAL RESEARCH. ANNUAL REPORT. 1927. a. price varies. D S I R Publishing, P.O. Box 9741, Wellington, New Zealand. **Indexed:** Anim.Breed.Abstr., Rev.Appl.Entomol.

500 NZ ISSN 0028-8667
NEW ZEALAND SCIENCE REVIEW. vol.15, 1957. bi-m. NZ.$40. New Zealand Association of Scientists, P.O. Box 1874, Wellington, New Zealand. FAX 4-712-070. Ed. F. Brian Shorland. adv.; bk.rev.; charts; illus.; stat.; cum.index; circ. 1,000. **Indexed:** Biol.Abstr., Chem.Abstr.
—BLDSC shelfmark: 6097.000000.
Description: Reviews on science and science policy.

NEWSCOPE - SCIENCE EDITION; a weekly science news summary and teaching quiz. see EDUCATION — Teaching Methods And Curriculum

500 600 JA ISSN 0286-0651
NEWTON/NYUTON. 1981. m. 9720 Yen. Kyoikusha Co. Ltd., 1-20, Nishi Shinjuku, Shinjuku-ku, Tokyo 160, Japan. TEL 03-344-4841. Ed. Hitoshi Takeuchi. adv.; circ. 400,000.

500 600 JA ISSN 0285-3922
CODEN: BSFADV
NICHI-FUTSU RIKOKA KAISHI/SOCIETE FRANCO-JAPONAISE DES SCIENCES PURES ET APPLIQUEES. BULLETIN. (Text in French and Japanese) 1960. a. Nichi-Futsu Rikokakai - Societe Franco-Japonaise des Sciences Pures et Appliquees, Nichi-Futsu Kaikan, 2-3 Kanda Surugadai, Chiyoda-ku, Tokyo 101, Japan.
—BLDSC shelfmark: 2739.850000.

500 NR ISSN 0029-0114
Q1 CODEN: NJSCAW
NIGERIAN JOURNAL OF SCIENCE. 1966. s-a. $35. Science Association of Nigeria, P.O. Box 4039, University of Ibadan, Ibadan, Nigeria. Ed. Sunday O. Ajayi. adv.; bk.rev.; abstr.; charts; illus.; index; circ. 2,000. (back issues avail) **Indexed:** Biol.Abstr., Chem.Abstr., Field Crop Abstr., Herb.Abstr., Hort.Abstr., Math.R., Nutr.Abstr., Rural Recreat.Tour.Abstr., Soils & Fert., World Agri.Econ.& Rural Sociol.Abstr.

500 JA ISSN 0369-3562
G1 CODEN: NDBSAL
NIHON DAIGAKU BUNRIGAKUBU SHIZEN KAGAKU KENKYUJO KENKYU KIYO/NIHON UNIVERSITY. INSTITUTE OF NATURAL SCIENCES. PROCEEDINGS. (Text in English and Japanese; summaries in English) 1965. a. Nihon Daigaku, Bunrigakubu Shizen Kagaku Kenkyujo - Nihon University, College of Humanities and Sciences, Institute of Natural Sciences, 25-40 Sakurajosui 3-chome, Setagaya-ku, Tokyo 156, Japan. **Indexed:** Chem.Abstr., Jap.Per.Ind.

NIHON DAIGAKU RIKOGAKU KENKYUJO SHOHO/NIHON UNIVERSITY. RESEARCH INSTITUTE OF SCIENCE AND TECHNOLOGY. JOURNAL. see TECHNOLOGY: COMPREHENSIVE WORKS

NIHON FUJIN KAGAKUSHA NO KAI NYUSU. see WOMEN'S INTERESTS

500 JA ISSN 0029-019X
NIHON GAKUJUTSU KAIGI GEPPO/SCIENCE COUNCIL OF JAPAN. MONTHLY REPORT. (Text in Japanese) 1960. m. Nihon Gakujutsu Kaigi - Science Council of Japan, 22-34 Roppongi 7-chome, Minato-ku, Tokyo 106, Japan. TEL 03-403-6291. FAX 03-403-6224. circ. 4,900. (looseleaf format)

500 JA ISSN 0029-0327
NIHON NO KAGAKU TO GIJUTSU/JAPAN SCIENCE AND TECHNOLOGY. (Text in Japanese) 1960. bi-m. 700 Yen per no. Nihon Kagaku Gijutsu Shinko Zaidan - Japan Science Foundation, 2-1 Kitanomaru Koen, Chiyoda-ku, Tokyo 102, Japan. Ed. Hiromitsu Miyamoto. bk.rev.

509.2 JA ISSN 0029-0335
NIHON NO KAGAKUSHA/JOURNAL OF JAPANESE SCIENTISTS. (Text in Japanese) 1966. m. 6000 Yen. Nihon Kagakusha Kaigi - Japan Scientists Association, 9-16 Yushima 1-chome, Bunkyo-ku, Tokyo 113, Japan. Ed. Harumi Kohara. adv.; bk.rev.; index; circ. 12,000.

500 600 JA ISSN 0549-2998
NIHON UNIVERSITY. RESEARCH INSTITUTE OF SCIENCE AND TECHNOLOGY. REPORT. (Text in English) 1952. s-a. exchange basis. Nihon Daigaku, Rikogaku Kenkyujo - Nihon University, Research Institute of Science and Technology, 1-8 Kanda Surugadai, Chiyoda-ku, Tokyo 101, Japan. **Indexed:** JCT, JTA, Sci.Abstr.

500 JA ISSN 0288-3422
NIIGATA DAIGAKU KYOIKUGAKUBU KIYO. SHIZEN KAGAKU HEN/NIIGATA UNIVERSITY. FACULTY OF EDUCATION. MEMOIRS. NATURAL SCIENCES. (Text and summaries in English and Japanese) 1960. a. Niigata Daigaku, Kyoikugakubu - Niigata University, Faculty of Education, 8050 Igarashi Nino-cho, Niigata-shi, Niigata-ken 950-11, Japan. **Indexed:** Biol.Abstr., Chem.Abstr., Jap.Per.Ind.
—BLDSC shelfmark: 5593.323000.

NIIHAMA KOGYO KOTO SENMON GAKKO KIYO. RIKOGAKU HEN/NIIHAMA NATIONAL COLLEGE OF TECHNOLOGY. MEMOIRS. SCIENCE AND ENGINEERING. see TECHNOLOGY: COMPREHENSIVE WORKS

500 CC ISSN 1001-5132
NINGBO DAXUE XUEBAO (ZIRAN KEXUE BAN)/NINGBO UNIVERSITY. JOURNAL (NATURAL SCIENCE EDITION). (Text in Chinese) s-a. Ningbo Daxue - Ningbo University, Ningbo, Zhejiang 315211, People's Republic of China. TEL 55545. Ed. Wang Lili.

500 JA ISSN 0914-1340
NISSAN KAGAKU SHINKO ZAIDAN JIGYO HOKOKUSHO/NISSAN SCIENCE FOUNDATION. ANNUAL REPORT. (Text in Japanese) 1975. a. Nissan Kagaku Shinko Zaidan - Nissan Science Foundation, 17-2 Ginza 6-chome, Chuo-ku, Tokyo 104, Japan.

500 JA ISSN 0911-4572
NISSAN KAGAKU SHINKO ZAIDAN KENKYU HOKOKUSHO/NISSAN SCIENCE FOUNDATION. RESEARCH PROJECTS IN REVIEW. (Text in Japanese; summaries in English and Japanese) 1979. a. Nissan Kagaku Shinko Zaidan - Nissan Science Foundation, 17-2 Ginza 6-chome, Chuo-ku, Tokyo 104, Japan.

500 JA ISSN 0078-0944
QR1 CODEN: RNIRAV
NODA INSTITUTE FOR SCIENTIFIC RESEARCH. REPORT/NODA SANGYO KAGAKU KENKYUJO KENKYU HOKOKU. (Text in English) 1957. a. free or exchange. Noda Sangyo Kagaku Kenkyujo - Noda Institute for Scientific Research, 399 Noda, Noda-shi, Chiba-ken 278, Japan. Ed. Shigetaka Ishii. bk.rev.; circ. 1,000. **Indexed:** Biol.Abstr., Chem.Abstr., Rev.Plant Path., VITIS.
Description: Technical journal specializing in microbiology and related fields.

500 US ISSN 0897-1005
NOETIC SCIENCES REVIEW. 1986. 4/yr. membership. Institute of Noetic Sciences, 475 Gate Five Rd., Ste. 300, Sausalito, CA 94965. TEL 415-331-5650. FAX 415-331-5673. Ed. Barbara McNeill. bk.rev.; illus.
Description: Contains articles, interviews, research updates, and review essays on the people and ideas in the forefront of consciousness research.

NORDICANA. see ANTHROPOLOGY

500 NO ISSN 0078-1231
NORGES TEKNISK-NATURVITENSKAPELIGE FORSKNINGSRAAD. AARSBERETNING/ROYAL NORWEGIAN COUNCIL FOR SCIENTIFIC AND INDUSTRIAL RESEARCH. ANNUAL REPORT. 1947. a. free. Norges Teknisk-Naturvitenskapelige Forskningsraad - Royal Norwegian Council for Scientific and Industrial Research, Sognsveien 72, Taasen, 0801 Oslo, Norway. TEL 47-2-237685. FAX 47-2-181139. circ. 5,000.

500 US
NORTH DAKOTA ACADEMY OF SCIENCE. PROCEEDINGS. 1947. a. $5 per no. North Dakota Academy of Science, Box 5567, University Sta., Fargo, ND 58105. TEL 701-237-8697. Ed. Roy Garvey. circ. 750. **Indexed:** Bibl.& Ind.Geol., Biol. Abstr., Chem.Abstr.

500 UK ISSN 0144-0586
QH1 CODEN: NNHJAQ
NORTHAMPTONSHIRE NATURAL HISTORY SOCIETY AND FIELD CLUB JOURNAL. 1880. a. £2. Northamptonshire Natural History Society and Field Club, c/o S.V.F. Leleux, Treas., 34 Broadway, Northampton NN1 4SF, England. Ed. C.A. Robinson. charts; illus.; circ. 500. (back issues avail.) **Indexed:** Bibl.& Ind.Geol., Br.Archaeol.Abstr., Geo.Abstr.

500 US ISSN 0029-344X
Q1 CODEN: NOSCAX
NORTHWEST SCIENCE. 1927. q. $14 to individuals; institutions $40. (Northwest Scientific Association) Washington State University Press, Pullman, WA 99164-5910. TEL 509-335-3518. Ed. Kenneth Kardong. charts; illus.; cum.index: vols. 21-46; circ. 1,250. (also avail. in microfilm from UMI; reprint service avail. from UMI) **Indexed:** Abstr.Anthropol., Bibl.Agri., Bibl.& Ind.Geol., Biol.Abstr., Chem.Abstr., Curr.Adv.Ecol.Sci., Excerp.Med., Forest.Abstr., Forest.Abstr., Forest Prod.Abstr., Geo.Abstr., Herb.Abstr., Ind.Sci.Rev., Irr.& Drain.Abstr., Ornam.Hort., Sci.Cit.Ind., Seed Abstr., Soils & Fert., W.R.C.Inf., Weed Abstr., Zoo.Rec.
—BLDSC shelfmark: 6152.000000.
Description: Research and review papers.
Refereed Serial

500 US ISSN 0550-1067
NOTICIAS DE GALAPAGOS. (Text in English, French, and Spanish) 1963. s-a. contribution. Charles Darwin Foundation for the Galapagos Isles, c/o Thomas H. Fritts, Ed., U.S. Fish and Wildlife Service, National Museum of Natural History, Washington, DC 20560. bk.rev.; circ. 2,350. **Indexed:** Biol.Abstr., Curr.Tit.Ocean, Deep Sea Res.& Oceanogr.Abstr.

500 CU
NOTICIERO DEL SISTEMA - INTERNACIONAL DE INFORMACION CIENTIFICO-TECNICA. 3/yr. $14 in N. America; S. America $16; Europe $20. (Academia de Ciencias, Instituto de Documentacion e Informacion Cientifico-Tecnica (I D I C T)) Ediciones Cubanas, Obispo No. 527, Apdo. 605, Havana, Cuba.

SCIENCES: COMPREHENSIVE WORKS 4331

500.9　　　　US　　ISSN 0029-4608
Q111　　　　　　　CODEN: NONAA2
NOTULAE NATURAE. 1939. irreg., no. 469, 1988. price varies. Academy of Natural Sciences of Philadelphia, 1900 Benjamin Franklin Pkwy., Philadelphia, PA 19103-1195. TEL 215-299-1050. FAX 215-299-1028. Ed. William F. Smith-Vaniz. abstr.; bibl.; charts; illus.; stat. (back issues avail.) **Indexed:** Biol.Abstr., Chem.Abstr., Deep Sea Res.& Oceanogr.Abstr. Key Title: Notulae Naturae of the Academy of Natural Sciences of Philadelphia.
　—BLDSC shelfmark: 6176.000000.

510　　　　　GW　　ISSN 0369-5034
Q49　　　　　　　　CODEN: NOALA4
NOVA ACTA LEOPOLDINA; Abhandlungen der Deutschen Akademie der Naturforscher Leopoldina. (Text in English and German) 1932. irreg. price varies. Deutsche Akademie der Naturforscher Leopoldina, August-Bebel-Str. 50a, 4010 Halle (S.), Germany. TEL 03746-24723. FAX 03746-21727. Ed. Werner Koehler. charts; illus.; stat. (back issues avail.) **Indexed:** Bibl.& Ind.Geol., Biol.Abstr., Chem.Abstr, Deep Sea Res.& Oceanogr.Abstr., Math.R.

NOVA SCOTIA RESEARCH FOUNDATION CORPORATION. ANNUAL REPORT. see *TECHNOLOGY: COMPREHENSIVE WORKS*

500　　　　　CN　　ISSN 0078-2521
Q21　　　　　　　　CODEN: PNSIAW
NOVA SCOTIAN INSTITUTE OF SCIENCE. PROCEEDINGS. 1862. irreg. Can.$15. Nova Scotian Institute of Science, Science Services, Killam Library, Dalhousie University, Halifax, N.S. B3H 4H8, Canada. TEL 902-424-2331. FAX 902-494-2319. Ed. A. Taylor. circ. 600. (also avail. in microfilm from CLA) **Indexed:** Bibl.& Ind.Geol., Biol.Abstr., Deep Sea Res.& Oceanogr.Abstr.
　—BLDSC shelfmark: 6779.000000.
　Description: Articles on proceedings pertaining to the natural sciences of the Atlantic Provinces.

500　　　　　GW　　ISSN 0722-0855
NOVEDADES CIENTIFICAS ALEMANAS. (Text in Spanish) m. DM.80. Deutscher Forschungsdienst GmbH, Ahrstr. 45, 5300 Bonn 2, Germany. TEL 0228-302210. FAX 0228-302270.

500　　　　　GW　　ISSN 0722-0863
NOVEDADES CIENTIFICAS ALEMANAS - CIENCIA APLICADA. (Text in Spanish) m. DM.60. Deutscher Forschungsdienst GmbH, Ahrstr. 45, 5300 Bonn 2, Germany. TEL 0228-302210. FAX 0228-302270.

500　　　　　IT　　ISSN 0394-7394
NUNCIUS; annali di storia della scienza. 1976. s-a. L.75000 (foreign L.96000). (Istituto e Museo di Storia della Scienza Firenze) Casa Editrice Leo S. Olschki, Casella Postale 66, 50100 Florence, Italy. TEL 055-6530684. FAX 055-6530214. Ed. Paolo Galluzzi.

500　　　　　IT
NUNCIUS. BIBLIOTECA. 1989. irreg., no.3, 1991. price varies. Casa Editrice Leo S. Olschki, Casella Postale 66, 50100 Florence, Italy. TEL 055-6530684. FAX 055-6530214.

O E C D. REVIEWS OF NATIONAL SCIENCE AND TECHNOLOGY POLICY. see *TECHNOLOGY: COMPREHENSIVE WORKS*

500　　　　　US
O R - M S TODAY. (Operations Research - Management Science) 1971. bi-m. $6 (foreign $12). Operations Research Society of America, Mount Royal and Guilford Aves., Baltimore, MD 21202. TEL 301-528-4146. (And: 290 Westminster St., Providence, RI 02903) (Co-sponsor: The Institute of Management Sciences (TIMS)) Ed. John Llewellyn. adv.; circ. 12,000. **Indexed:** Oper.Res.Manage.Sci., Qual.Contr.Appl.Stat.

500 600　　　　FR　　ISSN 0071-9013
Q180.F7
O R S T O M INSTITUT FRANCAIS DE RECHERCHE POUR LE DEVELOPEMENT EN COOPERATION. RAPPORT D'ACTIVITE. irreg. (Institut Francais de Recherche Scientifique pour le Developpement en Cooperation) Editions de l'O R S T O M, 72 Route d'Aulnay, 93143 Bondy Cedex, France. TEL 48-47-31-95. FAX 48-47-30-88.

500　　　　　GW　　ISSN 0078-2920
OBERHESSISCHE GESELLSCHAFT FUER NATUR- UND HEILKUNDE, GIESSEN. BERICHTE. a. Wilhelm Schmitz Verlag, Staufenbergerweg 22, 6304 Lollar, Germany. TEL 06406-2324. Ed. Ruediger Knapp. circ. 600. **Indexed:** Deep Sea Res.& Oceanogr.Abstr., GeoRef, VITIS.

500.1　　　　JA　　ISSN 0029-8190
　　　　　　　　　CODEN: NASOA5
OCHANOMIZU JOSHI DAIGAKU SHIZEN KAGAKU HOKOKU/OCHANOMIZU UNIVERSITY. NATURAL SCIENCE REPORT. (Text in English, French, German, Japanese) 1951. s-a. exchange basis only. Ochanomizu Joshi Daigaku - Ochanomizu University, 1-1 Otsuka 2-chome, Bunkyo-ku, Tokyo 112, Japan. Ed.Bd. charts; illus.; index; circ. 800. **Indexed:** Appl.Mech.Rev., Bibl.& Ind.Geol., Biol.Abstr., Chem.Abstr., Deep Sea Res.& Oceanogr.Abstr., Math.R.
　—BLDSC shelfmark: 6041.300000.
　Formerly: Ochanomizu Women's University. Natural Science Report.

500　　　　　RM　　ISSN 0029-8263
OCROTIREA NATURII SI A MEDIULUI INCONJURATOR. (Text in Rumanian; summaries in English, French, German, and Russian) 1955. s-a. 60 lei($34) (Academia Romana) Editura Academiei Romane, Calea Victoriei 125, 79717 Bucharest, Rumania. (Dist. by: Rompresfilatelia, Export-Import Presa, Calea Grivitei 64-66, P.O. Box 12-201, 78104 Bucharest, Rumania) Ed. N. Botnariuc. bk.rev.; charts; illus.; bibl.; index, cum.index. **Indexed:** Biol.Abstr.

500.9　　　　AU
OEKO.L. 1979. q. S.120. Naturkundliche Station der Stadt Linz, Rosegerstr. 22, A-4020 Linz, Austria. Ed. Gerhard Pfitzner. adv.; bk.rev.; charts; illus.; stat.; circ. 5,500. **Indexed:** Bk.Rev.Ind., Ind.Bk.Rev.Hum., RILA.
　Formerly: Apollo (ISSN 0003-6528)

001.3 500　　　AU　　ISSN 0378-8644
AS142　　　　　　　CODEN: OAWABT
OESTERREICHISCHE AKADEMIE DER WISSENSCHAFTEN. ALMANACH. 1851. a. price varies. Verlag der Oesterreichischen Akademie der Wissenschaften, Dr. Ignaz-Seipel-Platz 2, A-1010 Vienna, Austria. FAX 0222-5139541. **Indexed:** GeoRef.

OESTERREICHISCHE AKADEMIE DER WISSENSCHAFTEN, VIENNA. MATHEMATISCH-NATURWISSENSCHAFTLICHE KLASSE. DENKSCHRIFTEN. see *MATHEMATICS*

500　　　　　AU
OESTERREICHISCHE HOCHSCHULZEITUNG. 1949. m. $50. Verband der Wissenschaftlichen Gesellschaften Oesterreichs, Lindengasse 37, A-1070 Vienna, Austria. TEL 932166.

500　　　　　JA　　ISSN 0387-9844
OGASAWARA KENKYU NENPO/TOKYO METROPOLITAN UNIVERSITY. ANNUAL REPORT OF RESEARCH ON THE OGASAWARA (BONIN) ISLANDS. (Text in Japanese) 1977. a. free. Tokyo-toritsu Daigaku, Ogasawara Kenkyu linkai - Tokyo Metropolitan University, Ogasawara Research Committee, Minami-Ohsawa 1-1, Hachioji-shi, Tokyo 192-03, Japan. TEL 0426-77-1111. FAX 0426-77-2589. Ed. Kazuyoshi Miyashita. circ. 800. (back issues avail.)

507 373　　　US　　ISSN 0030-0764
OHIO ACADEMY OF SCIENCE NEWS. 1948. irreg. membership. (Junior Academy of the Ohio Academy of Science) Ohio Academy of Science, 1500 W. Third Ave., Ste. 223, Columbus, OH 43212. TEL 614-424-6045. adv.; bk.rev.; charts; illus.; stat.; circ. 10,000.
　Description: Aimed at high school science teachers.

500　　　　　US　　ISSN 0030-0950
　　　　　　　　　CODEN: OJSCA9
OHIO JOURNAL OF SCIENCE. 1901. 5/yr. $35 (foreign $40). Ohio Academy of Science, 1500 W. Third Ave., Ste. 223, Columbus, OH 43212. TEL 614-424-6045. Ed. Lee Meserue. bk.rev.; abstr.; charts; illus.; index; circ. 2,500. (back issues avail.) **Indexed:** Bibl.& Ind.Geol., Biol.Abstr., Chem.Abstr., Curr.Adv.Ecol.Sci., Curr.Cont., Deep Sea Res.& Oceanogr.Abstr., Environ.Abstr., Forest.Abstr., Forest Prod.Abstr., Geo.Abstr., Helminthol.Abstr., Hort.Abstr., Rev.Plant Path., Sel.Water Res.Abstr., World Agri.Econ.& Rural Sociol.Abstr.
　—BLDSC shelfmark: 6247.000000.

500 551 551.5　US
OHIO STATE UNIVERSITY. BYRD POLAR RESEARCH CENTER. CONTRIBUTION SERIES. 1961. irreg., no. 733, 1990. free or exchange basis. Ohio State University, Byrd Polar Research Center, 125 S. Oval Mall, Columbus, OH 43210-1308. TEL 614-292-6531.
　Formerly: Ohio State University. Institute of Polar Studies. Contribution Series (ISSN 0472-6979)
　Description: Scientific studies by the research staff of the center.
　Refereed Serial

500 551 551.5　US
OHIO STATE UNIVERSITY. BYRD POLAR RESEARCH CENTER. MISCELLANEOUS SERIES. 1958. irreg., no. 292, 1990. free or exchange basis. Ohio State University, Byrd Polar Research Center, 125 S. Oval Mall, Columbus, OH 43210-1308. TEL 614-292-6531.
　Formerly: Ohio State University. Institute of Polar Studies. Miscellaneous Series.
　Description: Articles not appropriate to the Contribution Series (i.e. abstracts, letters to the editor, non-technical articles), published by members.

500 551　　　US　　ISSN 0896-2472
OHIO STATE UNIVERSITY. BYRD POLAR RESEARCH CENTER. REPORT SERIES. 1962. irreg., no.87, 1984. price varies. Ohio State University, Byrd Polar Research Center, 103 Mendenhall, 125 S. Oval Mall, Columbus, OH 43210-1308. TEL 614-292-6531. circ. 500. **Indexed:** Bibl.& Ind.Geol., Geo.Abstr.
　Formerly: Ohio State University. Institute of Polar Studies. Report Series (ISSN 0078-415X)
　Description: Scientific investigations that are too lengthy for regular journal articles.

500　　　　　JA　　ISSN 0914-580X
OITA DAIGAKU KYOIKUGAKUBU KENKYU KIYO/OITA UNIVERSITY. FACULTY OF EDUCATION. RESEARCH BULLETIN. (Text in English and Japanese; summaries in English) 1952. s-a. Oita Daigaku, Kyoikugakubu - Oita University, Faculty of Education, 700 Dannohara, Oita-shi, Oita-ken 870-11, Japan. **Indexed:** Jap.Per.Ind.
　—BLDSC shelfmark: 7722.120000.

500　　　　　JA　　ISSN 0385-2776
　　　　　　　　　CODEN: KHHDD4
OKAYAMA RIKA DAIGAKU. HIRUZEN KENKYUJO KENKYU HOKOKU/OKAYAMA UNIVERSITY OF SCIENCE. HIRUZEN RESEARCH INSTITUTE. BULLETIN. (Text and summaries in English and Japanese) 1975. a. Okayama Rika Daigaku, Hiruzen Kenkyujo - Okayama University of Science, Hiruzen Research Institute, Kamifukuda, Kawakamimura, Maniwa-gun, Okayama-ken 717-06, Japan.
　Description: Contains original papers.

500　　　　　JA　　ISSN 0285-7685
　　　　　　　　　CODEN: ORDKDH
OKAYAMA RIKA DAIGAKU KIYO A. SHIZEN KAGAKU/OKAYAMA UNIVERSITY OF SCIENCE. BULLETIN A. NATURAL SCIENCE. (Text and summaries in English and Japanese) 1965. a. Okayama Rika Daigaku - Okayama University of Science, 1-1 Ridai-machi, Okayama-shi, Okayama-ken 700, Japan. **Indexed:** Chem.Abstr., Jap.Per.Ind., Sci.Abstr.

OKINAWA-KENRITSU HAKUBUTSUKAN KIYO/OKINAWA PREFECTURAL MUSEUM. BULLETIN. see *MUSEUMS AND ART GALLERIES*

500 600　　　US　　ISSN 0149-8711
AP2
OMNI. 1978. m. $24. Omni Publications International, Ltd., 1965 Broadway, New York, NY 10023-5965. TEL 212-496-6100. (Subscr. to: Box 3026, Harlan, IA 51593. TEL 800-289-6664) Ed. Keith Ferrell. adv.; bk.rev.; illus.; circ. 925,000. (also avail. in microfiche from UMI; reprint service avail. from UMI) **Indexed:** A.I.Abstr., Acad.Ind., Access, CAD CAM Abstr., Deep Sea Res.& Oceanogr.Abstr., Environ.Abstr., Gdlns., Hlth.Ind., Jun.High.Mag.Abstr., Mag.Ind., PMR, Robomat., Tel.Abstr., TOM.
　—BLDSC shelfmark: 6256.470000.
　Description: Offers a diverse selection of scientific, medical and technological articles and short fiction.
　Refereed Serial

SCIENCES: COMPREHENSIVE WORKS

500   CN   ISSN 0228-4642
ONTARIO SCIENCE CENTRE. NEWSCIENCE. 1976. 6/yr. Can.$10 to individuals; free to schools. Ontario Science Centre, 770 Don Mills Rd., Don Mills, Ont. M3C 1T3, Canada. TEL 416-429-4100. Ed. Carol Gold. bk.rev.; circ. 431,000.
     Formerly (until 1981): Ontario Science Centre. Centre News (ISSN 0701-7758)

500   NE   ISSN 0167-6377
T57.6.A1   CODEN: ORLED5
OPERATIONS RESEARCH LETTERS. (Text in English) 1981. 10/yr.(in 2 vols.; 5 nos./vol.) fl.696 (effective 1992). (Operations Research Society of America, US) North-Holland (Subsidiary of: Elsevier Science Publishers B.V.), P.O. Box 211, 1000 AE Amsterdam, Netherlands. TEL 020-5803911. FAX 020-5803598. TELEX 18582 ESPA NL. (Subscr. in U.S. and Canada to: Elsevier Science Publishing Co., Inc., Box 882, Madison Sq. Sta., New York, NY 10159. TEL 212-989-5800) Ed. G.L. Nemhauser. (back issues avail.; reprint service avail. from SWZ) **Indexed:** ASCA, Biostat., Compumath, Comput.Abstr., Cont.Pg.Manage., Eng.Ind., INSPEC, Int.Abstr.Oper.Res., J.Cont.Quant.Meth., Math.R., Oper.Res.Manage.Sci., Qual.Contr.Appl.Stat., Risk Abstr., Sci.Abstr.
     —BLDSC shelfmark: 6269.363800.
     Description: Covers all aspects of operations research and the management and decision sciences.
     Refereed Serial

500   FR   ISSN 0078-5601
ORDRE DES GEOMETRES-EXPERTS. ANNUAIRE. 1956. a. 1400 F. (Ordre des Geometres-Experts) Publi-Topex, 13 rue Leon Cogniet, 75017 Paris, France. Ed. Helene Alvares-Correa. adv.; circ. 3,000.

507 370   US   ISSN 0030-4794
OREGON SCIENCE TEACHER.* 1959. m. (Sep.-May). $8. Oregon Science Teachers Association, c/o Bill Marker, Ed., 700 Pringle Pkwy, S.E., Salem, OR 97310. TEL 503-667-5489. adv.; bk.rev.; illus.; circ. 600.

500 600   NR   ISSN 0474-6171
ORGANIZATION OF AFRICAN UNITY. SCIENTIFIC TECHNICAL AND RESEARCH COMMISSION. PUBLICATION. 1951. irreg. Organization of African Unity, Scientific Technical and Research Commission, P.M.B. 2359, Lagos, Nigeria.

500   US
ORGANIZATION OF AMERICAN STATES. DEPARTMENT OF SCIENTIFIC AFFAIRS. REPORT OF ACTIVITIES. 1963. irreg. Organization of American States, 1889 F St., N.W., Washington, DC 20006. TEL 703-941-1617.
     Formerly: Pan American Union. Department of Scientific Affairs. Report of Activities. (ISSN 0553-0334)

500 574   US
ORGANIZATION OF AMERICAN STATES. GENERAL SECRETARIAT. PROGRAM OF SCIENTIFIC MONOGRAPHS. (Text in Spanish and Portuguese) 1965. irreg. (5-7/yr.). $3.50 per no. Organization of American States, General Secretariat, Office of Sales & Promotion, 1889 F St., N.W., Washington, DC 20006. TEL 202-789-3338. Ed. Eva V. Chesneau. circ. 10,000. (back issues avail.) **Indexed:** Biol.Abstr., Chem.Abstr.

500   IT
ORGANIZZAZIONE SCIENTIFICA. 1973. m. Comitato Nazionale per l'Organizzazione Scientifica, Viale dell'Astronomia 30, 00144 Rome, Italy. Ed.Bd. bibl.

500   PL   ISSN 0078-6500
Q9
ORGANON. (Text in English, French, German and Russian) 1963. a. price varies. (Polska Akademia Nauk, Zaklad Historii Nauki, Edukacji i Techniki - Polish Academy of Sciences, Institute of History of Science, Education and Technics) Ossolineum, Publishing House of the Polish Academy of Sciences, Rynek 9, 50-106 Wroclaw, Poland. (Dist. by: Ars Polona, Krakowskie Przedmiescie 7, 00-068 Warsaw, Poland) (Co-sponsor: Division d'Histoire des Sciences de l'Union Internationale d'Histoire et de Philosophie des Sciences) Ed. Bogdan Suchodolski. bibl.; illus.; circ. 660.
     Description: Devoted to international research on the history of science, culture and human civilization.

200 550   US   ISSN 0093-7495
BS651   CODEN: ORIGD
ORIGINS (LOMA LINDA). 1974. s-a. $4. (Geoscience Research Institute) Loma Linda University, Loma Linda, CA 92350. TEL 714-824-4548. Ed. Ariel A. Roth. adv.; charts; illus.; circ. 1,900. (back issues avail.) **Indexed:** Bibl.& Ind.Geol., CERDIC.
     —BLDSC shelfmark: 6291.263850.
     Refereed Serial

OSAKA DENKI TSUSHIN DAIGAKU KENKYU RONSHU. SHIZEN KAGAKU HEN/OSAKA ELECTRO-COMMUNICATION UNIVERSITY. MEMOIRS. NATURAL SCIENCE. see *COMMUNICATIONS*

500 613.7   JA   ISSN 0289-8888
OSAKA JOSHI DAIGAKU KIYO. KISO RIGAKU HEN, TAIIKUGAKU HEN/OSAKA WOMEN'S UNIVERSITY. BULLETIN. SERIES OF NATURAL SCIENCE, PHYSICAL EDUCATION. (Text and summaries in English and Japanese) a. Osaka Joshi Daigaku, Kiso Rigakka - Osaka Women's University, 2-1 Daisen-cho, Sakai-shi, Osaka-fu 590, Japan. abstr.

OSAKA KOGYO DAIGAKU KIYO. RIKO HEN/OSAKA INSTITUTE OF TECHNOLOGY. MEMOIRS. SERIES A. SCIENCE AND TECHNOLOGY. see *TECHNOLOGY: COMPREHENSIVE WORKS*

500   JA   ISSN 0373-7411
OSAKA KYOIKU DAIGAKU KIYO. DAI-3-BUMON. SHIZEN KAGAKU/OSAKA KYOIKU UNIVERSITY. MEMOIRS. SERIES 3: NATURAL SCIENCE AND APPLIED SCIENCE. (Text and summaries in English and Japanese) 1952. s-a. Osaka Kyoiku Daigaku - Osaka Kyoiku University, 4-88 Minami-Kawahori-cho, Tennoji-ku, Osaka-shi, Osaka-fu 543, Japan. **Indexed:** Biol.Abstr., Chem.Abstr., INIS Atomind., Jap.Per.Ind.
     —BLDSC shelfmark: 5629.540000.

509.2   JA   ISSN 0911-209X
OSAKA NO KAGAKUSHA. (Text in Japanese) a. Nihon Kagakusha Kaigi, Osaka Shibu - Japan Scientists Association, Osaka Branch, Rm.7, 45 Bldg., 4-5 Ohmichi, Ten-nohji, Osaka 543, Japan.

500   JA   ISSN 0287-1394
OSAKA SANGYO DAIGAKU RONSHU. SHIZEN KAGAKU HEN/OSAKA INDUSTRIAL UNIVERSITY. JOURNAL. NATURAL SCIENCES. (Text in English, French, Japanese; summaries in English) 1956. q. free. Osaka Sangyo Daigaku Gakkai - Society of Osaka Sangyo University, 1-1 Nakagaikuchi 3-chome, Daito-shi, Osaka-fu 574, Japan. circ. 3,300. **Indexed:** Jap.Per.Ind.

500.9   JA   ISSN 0078-6675
OSAKA-SHIRITSU SHIZENSHI HAKUBUTSUKAN KENKYU HOKOKU/OSAKA MUSEUM OF NATURAL HISTORY. BULLETIN. (Text in English and Japanese; summaries of Japanese articles in English) 1954. a. 1200 Yen avail. on exchange basis. Osaka-shiritsu Shizenshi Hakubutsukan - Osaka Museum of Natural History, 1-23 Nagai Koen, Higashi-Sumiyoshi-ku, Osaka-shi, Osaka-fu 546, Japan. Ed. Yoshitaka Nasu. circ. 1,000. **Indexed:** Bibl.& Ind.Geol., Biol.Abstr., Curr.Adv.Ecol.Sci., Deep Sea Res.& Oceanogr.Abstr., Jap.Per.Ind.

505   JA   ISSN 0474-781X
Q1.A1   CODEN: SREOA7
OSAKA UNIVERSITY. COLLEGE OF GENERAL EDUCATION. SCIENCE REPORTS.* (Text in English, French, or German) 1953. s-a. Osaka Daigaku, Kyoyobu - Osaka University, College of General Education, 1-1 Machikaneyama-cho, Toyonaka-shi, Osaka-fu 560, Japan. Ed. Kozo Imahori. charts; illus.; circ. 1,000. **Indexed:** Biol.Abstr., INIS Atomind., JTA, Math.R., Sci.Abstr.
     —BLDSC shelfmark: 8156.300000.

500 900   US   ISSN 0369-7827
     CODEN: OSIRE3
OSIRIS (CHICAGO); a research journal devoted to the history of science and its cultural influences. 1936. a. $25. (History of Science Society) University of Chicago Press, Journals Division, 5720 S. Woodlawn Ave., Chicago, IL 60637. TEL 312-702-7600. FAX 312-702-0694. Ed. Arnold Thackray. adv.; circ. 1,000. (back issues avail.)
     —BLDSC shelfmark: 6301.020000.
     Refereed Serial

500   GW   ISSN 0340-4781
QH5   CODEN: ONMIDS
OSNABRUECKER NATURWISSENSCHAFTLICHE MITTEILUNGEN. (Text in German; summaries in English and German) 1873. a. DM.40. Naturwissenschaftlicher Verein Osnabrueck, Am Schoelerberg 8, 4500 Osnabrueck, Germany. TEL 0541-56003-0. (Co-sponsor: Naturwissentschaftliches Museum Osnabrueck) Ed.Bd. bk.rev.; illus.; stat.; circ. 900. **Indexed:** Bibl.& Ind.Geol., Numis.Lit.

500   UK   ISSN 0165-0262
OUTLOOK ON SCIENCE POLICY. 1978. m. (except Aug.). £25($40) to individuals; third world countries £58($101); institutions £81($139). (International Science Policy Foundation) Beech Tree Publishing, 10 Watford Close, Guildford, Surrey GU1 2EP, England. TEL 0483-67497. FAX 0483-67497. Ed. Maurice Goldsmith. adv.; bk.rev. (back issues avail.)
     Description: International news on public science and technology policy.

OWL. see *CHILDREN AND YOUTH — For*

500   GW   ISSN 0935-9400
P.M. PERSPEKTIVE. 1986. bi-m. DM.62.40 (foreign DM.71.40). Gruner und Jahr AG und Co., Am Baumwall 11, 2000 Hamburg 11, Germany. TEL 040-3703-0. FAX 040-37035631. Eds. G.P. Moosleitner, B. Roethlein. adv.; circ. 200,000. (back issues avail.)

P S L S. (Publication of the Society for Literature and Science) see *LITERATURE*

P T B BERICHTE. (Physikalisch Technische Bundesanstalt) see *TECHNOLOGY: COMPREHENSIVE WORKS*

PABLO LENNIS; science fiction, fantasy, science. see *LITERATURE — Science Fiction, Fantasy, Horror*

500.9   US   ISSN 0030-8641
Q1   CODEN: PADIAZ
PACIFIC DISCOVERY; a journal of nature and culture in the Pacific world. 1948. q. $12.95 (foreign $17). California Academy of Sciences, Golden Gate Park, San Francisco, CA 94118. TEL 415-750-7116. Ed. Keith Howell. bk.rev.; illus.; cum.index: vols.1-34 (1948-1981); circ. 30,000. (also avail. in microfilm from UMI; microfiche; back issues avail.) **Indexed:** Bibl.& Ind.Geol, Biol.Abstr., Cal.Per.Ind. (1984-), Deep Sea Res.& Oceanogr.Abstr., So.Pac.Per.Ind.
     —BLDSC shelfmark: 6329.100000.

570   US   ISSN 0030-8870
QH1   CODEN: PASCAP
PACIFIC SCIENCE; a quarterly devoted to the biological and physical sciences of the Pacific Region. 1947. q. $30 to individuals (foreign $35); institutions $45 (foreign $50). University of Hawaii Press, Journals Department, 2840 Kolowalu St., Honolulu, HI 96822. TEL 808-956-8833. FAX 808-988-6052. Ed. E. Alison Kay. adv.; bibl.; charts; illus.; index; circ. 703. (also avail. in microform from UMI; back issues avail.; reprint service avail. from UMI,ISI) **Indexed:** Bibl.& Ind.Geol., Biol.Abstr., Chem.Abstr., Curr.Adv.Ecol.Sci., Curr.Cont., Deep Sea Res.& Oceanogr.Abstr., Environ.Per.Bibl., Field Crop Abstr., Forest.Abstr., Forest Prod.Abstr., Geo.Abstr., Herb.Abstr., Hort.Abstr., Mineral.Abstr., Ocean.Abstr., Plant Breed.Abstr., Pollut.Abstr., Rev.Appl.Entomol., Rev.Plant Path., Sel.Water Res.Abstr., So.Pac.Per.Ind.
     —BLDSC shelfmark: 6331.000000.
     Description: Presents international and multidisciplinary reports on biological and physical sciences of the Pacific region.
     Refereed Serial

500   US
PACIFIC SCIENCE ASSOCIATION. CONGRESS AND INTER-CONGRESS PROCEEDINGS. (Proceedings published by host country.) 1920. biennial. Pacific Science Association, Box 17801, Honolulu, HI 96817. TEL 808-848-4139. FAX 808-841-8968. **Indexed:** Deep Sea Res.& Oceanogr.Abstr.
     Formerly: Pacific Science Association. Congress Proceedings (ISSN 0078-7647)

500   US   ISSN 0030-8889
PACIFIC SCIENCE ASSOCIATION. INFORMATION BULLETIN. (Supplement avail.: Pacific Research Titles) 1949. 4/yr. membership. Pacific Science Association, Box 17801, Honolulu, HI 96817. TEL 808-848-4139. FAX 808-841-8968. Ed. L.G. Eldredge. bk.rev.; bibl.; circ. 2,000.

PACT. see ARCHAEOLOGY

PAEDAGOGISCHE HOCHSCHULE KARL FRIEDRICH WILHELM WANDER. WISSENSCHAFTLICHE ZEITSCHRIFT. MATHEMATISCH-NATURWISSENSCHAFTLICHE REIHE; mathematisch-naturwissenschaftliche Reihe and thematische Reihe. see *MATHEMATICS*

505   PK   ISSN 0377-2969
Q1   CODEN: PKSPAW
PAKISTAN ACADEMY OF SCIENCES. PROCEEDINGS.. (Text in English) 1964. q. Rs.120($12) Pakistan Academy of Sciences, Constitution Avenue, G-5, Islamabad, Pakistan. TELEX 54349 COMST PK. Ed. M.M. Qurashi. bk.rev.; bibl.; charts; illus.; circ. 500. Indexed: Biol.Abstr., Chem.Abstr., Math.R., Phys.Abstr.

500   PK
PAKISTAN ASSOCIATION FOR THE ADVANCEMENT OF SCIENCE. ANNUAL REPORT. (Text in English) a. Rs.36($2) Pakistan Association for the Advancement of Science, 273 N Model Town, Lahore, Pakistan.

500   PK   ISSN 0030-9877
Q73   CODEN: PAJSAS
PAKISTAN JOURNAL OF SCIENCE. 1949. q. Rs.100($30) Pakistan Association for the Advancement of Science, 273 N Model Town, Lahore, Pakistan. Ed. Ghulam Rasool Chaudhry. decennial index. Indexed: Bibl.& Ind.Geol., Biol.Abstr., Chem.Abstr, Dairy Sci.Abstr., Food Sci.& Tech.Abstr., Herb.Abstr., Hort.Abstr., Ind.Vet., Packag.Sci.Tech., Plant Breed.Abstr., Sci.Abstr, Soils & Fert., Vet.Bull.

500   PK   ISSN 0030-9885
Q180.A1   CODEN: PSIRAA
PAKISTAN JOURNAL OF SCIENTIFIC AND INDUSTRIAL RESEARCH. (Text in English) 1958. m. Rs.800($108) Pakistan Council of Scientific and Industrial Research, 39 Garden Rd., Karachi 74400, Pakistan. TEL 7725943. FAX 7729527. Ed. J.N. Usman. adv.; bk.rev.; charts; illus.; index; circ. 800. (also avail. in microfilm from UMI; reprint service avail. from UMI) Indexed: Agri.Eng.Abstr., Bio-Contr.News & Info., Biol.Abstr., Chem.Abstr, Cott.&Trop.Fibr.Abstr., Crop Physiol.Abstr., Dairy Sci.Abstr., Deep Sea Res.& Oceanogr.Abstr., Excerp.Med., Field Crop Abstr., Food Sci.& Tech.Abstr., Forest.Abstr., Forest Prod.Abstr., Helminthol.Abstr., Herb.Abstr., Hort.Abstr., Ind.Chem., Irr.& Drain.Abstr., Maize Abstr., Mass Spectr.Bull., Nutr.Abstr., Poult.Abstr., Rev.Plant Path., Rice Abstr., Sci.Abstr., Sci.Cit.Ind, Seed Abstr., Soils & Fert., Sorghum & Millets Abstr., Soyabean Abstr., Triticale Abstr., Trop.Oil Seeds Abstr., Weed Abstr.

500   PK   ISSN 0552-9050
Q180.P25   CODEN: PJSRAV
PAKISTAN JOURNAL OF SCIENTIFIC RESEARCH. (Text in English) 1949. q. Rs.100($30) Pakistan Association for the Advancement of Science, 273 N Model Town, Lahore, Pakistan. Ed. Ghulam Rasool Chaudhry. cum.index every 10 yrs. Indexed: Bibl.& Ind.Geol., Biol.Abstr., Chem.Abstr, Dairy Sci.Abstr., Food Sci.& Tech.Abstr., Herb.Abstr., Ind.Vet., Mass Spectr.Bull., Plant Breed.Abstr., Plant Grow.Reg.Abstr., Sci.Abstr, Soils & Fert., Vet.Bull.

500   PK   ISSN 0078-8430
PAKISTAN SCIENCE CONFERENCE. PROCEEDINGS. (Text in English) a. Rs.100($30) Pakistan Association for the Advancement of Science, 273 N Model Town, Lahore, Pakistan. Ed. Ghulam Rasool Chaudry. index. Indexed: Bibl.& Ind.Geol., Biol.Abstr.

505   FR   ISSN 0180-3344
PALAIS DE LA DECOUVERTE. REVUE. 1972. m. 175 F. (effective 1991). Palais de la Decouverte, Av. Franklin D. Roosevelt, 75008 Paris, France. FAX 40-74-81-81. adv.; bk.rev.; illus.; circ. 4,000. (back issues avail.)
—BLDSC shelfmark: 7940.700000.

500 600   US   ISSN 0883-8305
                               CODEN: POCGEP
PALEOCEANOGRAPHY. 1986. bi-m. $180 to non-members (foreign $186); members $43 (foreign $49); students $22 (foreign $28). American Geophysical Union, 2000 Florida Ave., N.W., Washington, DC 20009. TEL 202-462-6900. FAX 202-328-0566. TELEX 710-882-9300. Ed. Ken Miller. abstr. (back issues avail.)
—BLDSC shelfmark: 6345.295000.
    Description: Deals with the history of the ocean system and its plants and animal life. Studies based on marine sedimentary sections from the ocean basin and margins and from those ancient sediments exposed on the continents.
Refereed Serial

500.9   FR   ISSN 0180-961X
QH147
PARC NATIONAL DE LA VANOISE. TRAVAUX SCIENTIFIQUES. (Text in French; summaries in English, German and Italian) 1970. a. 70 F. Ministere de l'Environnement, Direction de la Protection de la Nature, Parc National de la Vanoise, B.P. 705, 73007 Chambery, France. TEL 79-62-30-54. FAX 79-96-37-18. bk.rev.; circ. 600.
    Description: Works covering the history, geography, geology, biology, botany, zoology, ornithology, culture, people, economy of the Vanoise region of the French Alps.

500   US   ISSN 0031-3203
Q327   CODEN: PTNRA8
PATTERN RECOGNITION. 1968. 12/yr. £465 (effective 1992). (Pattern Recognition Society) Pergamon Press, Inc., Journals Division, 660 White Plains Rd., Tarrytown, NY 10591-5153. TEL 914-524-9200. FAX 914-333-2444. (And: Headington Hill Hall, Oxford OX3 0BW, England. TEL 0865-794141) Ed. Robert S. Ledley. adv.; bk.rev.; circ. 1,500. (also avail. in microform from MIM,UMI; back issues avail.) Indexed: A.I.Abstr., Appl.Mech.Rev., Biol.Abstr., CAD CAM Abstr., Compumath, Comput.Abstr., Comput.Cont., Curr.Cont., Eng.Ind., Excerp.Med., Geo.Abstr., Robomat, Sci.Abstr.
—BLDSC shelfmark: 6412.981000.
Refereed Serial

500.9   US   ISSN 0079-032X
QH1   CODEN: YUPBA8
PEABODY MUSEUM OF NATURAL HISTORY. BULLETIN. 1926. irreg., no.44, 1991. price varies. Peabody Museum of Natural History, Yale University, 170 Whitney Ave., Box 6666, New Haven, CT 06511-8161. TEL 203-432-3786. Eds. John Ostrom, Zelda Edelson. circ. 500. (back issues avail.; reprint service avail. from KTO) Indexed: Biol.Abstr., GeoRef. Key Title: Bulletin - Peabody Museum of Natural History.
    Supersedes (in 1967): Bulletin of Bingham Oceanographic Collection.
    Description: Consists of research in the fields of study encompassed by the Museum.

500.9   US   ISSN 0079-0338
PEABODY MUSEUM OF NATURAL HISTORY. SPECIAL PUBLICATION. 1961. irreg., no.4, 1982. price varies. Peabody Museum of Natural History, Yale University, 170 Whitney Ave., Box 6666, New Haven, CT 06511-8161. TEL 203-432-3786.
    Description: Guides to the exhibits of the Museum.

500   CK   ISSN 0031-4765
HN110.5.Z9
PENSAMIENTO Y ACCION. 1968. bi-m. Universidad Pedagogica y Tecnologica de Colombia, Fundo Especial de Publicaciones y Ayudas Educativas, Apdo. Nacional 34, Tunja, Boyaco, Colombia. Ed. E.S. Celis. adv.; bk.rev.; play rev.; charts; illus.

300 500   GT
PERSPECTIVA; ciencia-arte-tecnologia. 1983. 3/yr. Q.825($10.20) Universidad de San Carlos de Guatemala, Direccion General de Extension Universitaria, Edificio de Recursos Educativos, Ciudad Universitaria-Zona 12, Guatemala City, Guatemala. Ed. Eduardo Meyer Maldonado. bk.rev.; bibl.; charts; stat.

PERSPECTIVES ON SCIENCE AND CHRISTIAN FAITH. see *RELIGIONS AND THEOLOGY*

PETERSON'S GUIDE TO GRADUATE PROGRAMS IN THE PHYSICAL SCIENCES AND MATHEMATICS (YEAR) (BOOK 4). see *EDUCATION — Guides To Schools And Colleges*

500   PH   ISSN 0031-7683
Q75   CODEN: PJSCAK
PHILIPPINE JOURNAL OF SCIENCE. (Text in English) 1906. q. P.120($22) Industrial Technology Development Institute, P. Gil, Taft Ave., Manila, P.O. Box 744, Philippines. FAX 632-592275. Ed. Quintin L. Kintanar. bk.rev.; abstr.; bibl.; charts; index, cum.index: 1951-1970 (vols. 80-99), 1971-1975 (vols. 100-104); circ. 1,300. Indexed: Appl.Mech.Rev., Bibl.& Ind.Geol/, Biol.Abstr., Chem.Abstr., Curr.Adv.Ecol.Sci., Deep Sea Res.& Oceanogr.Abstr., Excerp.Med., Field Crop Abstr., Food Sci.& Tech.Abstr., Herb.Abstr., Hort.Abstr., Plant Breed.Abstr., Rev.Appl.Entomol.
—BLDSC shelfmark: 6456.000000.

500   PH   ISSN 0031-7799
PHILIPPINE SCIENTIFIC JOURNAL. 1947. q. P.5($5) Manila Central University, Caloocan Campus, Caloocan City, Philippines. Ed. Walfrido W. Sumpaido. adv.; bk.rev.; abstr.; charts; index; circ. 2,500.

500   PH   ISSN 0079-1466
Q76   CODEN: PHISB5
PHILIPPINE SCIENTIST. (Text in English) 1964. a. P.175($8.50) (University of San Carlos) San Carlos Publications, P.O. Box 182, 6000 Cebu City, Philippines. Ed. Joseph Baumgartner. circ. 180. (back issues avail.) Indexed: Biol.Abstr., Deep Sea Res.& Oceanogr.Abstr., Ind.Phil.Per.
—BLDSC shelfmark: 6456.170000.
    Description: Deals with research in various natural science fields, emphasizing marine biology and entomology.

500   PH
PHILIPPINES. DEPARTMENT OF SCIENCE AND TECHNOLOGY. ANNUAL REPORT. Short title: D O S T Annual Report. a. Department of Science and Technology, Information Division, Box 3596, Manila, Philippines. charts; illus.
    Former titles: Philippines. National Science and Technology Authority. Annual Report; Philippines. National Science Development Board. Annual Report.

501   US   ISSN 0031-8248
Q1   CODEN: PHSCA6
PHILOSOPHY OF SCIENCE. 1934. q. $55 per vol. Philosophy of Science Association, 503 S. Kedzie Hall, Dept. of Philosophy, Michigan State Univ., East Lansing, MI 48824-1032. TEL 517-353-9392. Ed. Merrilee Salmon. adv.; bk.rev.; bibl.; index; circ. 2,200. (also avail. in microform from UMI) Indexed: Arts & Hum.Cit.Ind., Biol.Abstr., Bull.Signal., Curr.Cont., Curr.Ind.Stat., Deep Sea Res.& Oceanogr.Abstr., Hum.Ind., Ind.Bk.Rev.Hum., Lang.& Lang.Behav.Abstr., Math.R., Phil.Ind., Psychol.Abstr., Sci.Abstr., Sci.Cit.Ind., Sociol.Abstr., SSCI.
—BLDSC shelfmark: 6465.000000.
Refereed Serial

PHYSIKALISCH-TECHNISCHEN BUNDESANSTALT BRAUNSCHWEIG UND BERLIN. JAHRESBERICHT. see *TECHNOLOGY: COMPREHENSIVE WORKS*

530   IT   ISSN 0031-9414
Q54   CODEN: PYSSA3
PHYSIS; rivista internazionale di storia della scienza. (Text in English, French, German, Italian and Spanish) 1959. 3/yr. L.75000 (foreign L.96000). Casa Editrice Leo S. Olschki, Casella Postale 66, 50100 Florence, Italy. TEL 055-6530684. FAX 055-6530214. Ed.Bd. adv; bk.rev.; illus.; circ. 1,000. Indexed: Biol.Abstr., Chem.Abstr., Helminthol.Abstr., Hist.Abstr., Numis.Lit., Ocean.Abstr., Pollut.Abstr.
—BLDSC shelfmark: 6489.355000.

SCIENCES: COMPREHENSIVE WORKS

500   CS   ISSN 0032-2423
Q44.J3   CODEN: PMFAA4
POKROKY MATEMATIKY, FYZIKY A ASTRONOMIE/PROGRESS IN MATHEMATICS, PHYSICS AND ASTRONOMY. 1956. bi-m. DM.152. (Ceskoslovenska Akademie Ved, Jednota Ceskoslovenskych Matematiku a Fyziku) Academia, Publishing House of the Czechoslovak Academy of Sciences, Vodickova 40, 112 29 Prague 1, Czechoslovakia. TEL 332-42-88. (Dist. in Western countries by: Kubon & Sagner, P.O. Box 34 01 08, 8000 Munich 34, Germany) Eds. Oldrich Kowalski, Miroslav Rozsival. bk.rev.; illus.; stat.; index; circ. 4,600. **Indexed:** Chem.Abstr., Math.R.
   Description: Publishes articles concerning mathematics, physics and astronomy (expository papers, history, philosophy, science and society, modern trends in education) news and activities of the association.

500 919   NO   ISSN 0800-0395
POLAR RESEARCH. (Text in English) 1982. s-a. NOK 80($27) Norwegian Polar Research Institute - Norsk Polar Institutt, P.O. Box 158, 1330 Oslo Lufthavn, Norway. Ed. Annemor Brekke. circ. 300. **Indexed:** Curr.Cont., Deep Sea Res.& Oceanogr.Abstr. —BLDSC shelfmark: 6542.300000.
   Description: Treats various subjects within the field of polar research.
   Refereed Serial

500   PL   ISSN 0137-6225
POLITECHNIKA WROCLAWSKA. BIBLIOTEKA GLOWNA I OSRODEK INFORMACJI NAUKOWO-TECHNICZNEJ. PRACE NAUKOWE. STUDIA I MATERIALY. (Text in Polish; summaries in English and Russian) 1974. irreg., no.2, 1977. price varies. Politechnika Wroclawska, Wybrzeze Wyspianskiego 27, 50-370 Wroclaw, Poland. FAX 22-36-64. TELEX 712254 PWRPL. (Dist. by: Ars Polona-Ruch, Krakowskie Przedmiescie 7, Warsaw, Poland) circ. 965.

500   PL   ISSN 0137-1215
POLITECHNIKA WROCLAWSKA. PRACE NAUKOZNAWCZE I PROGNOSTYCZNE. (Text in English, Polish or Russian; summaries in English and Russian) 1969. q. 3000 Zl.($48) Politechnika Wroclawska, Wybrzeze Wyspianskiego 27, 50-370 Wroclaw, Poland. FAX 22-36-64. TELEX 712559 PWRPL. (Dist. by: Ars Polona-Ruch, Krakowskie Przedmiescie 7, Warsaw, Poland) Ed. J. Galanc. circ. 450.

POLITECNICA; revista de informacion tecnico - cientifica. see *ENGINEERING*

500   SZ   ISSN 0085-4980
POLITIQUE DE LA SCIENCE. German edition: Wissenschaftspolitik. 1972. 4/yr plus 2 to 5 special thematic nos. 32 Fr. (free to qualified individuals). Office Federal de l'Education et de la Science - Bundesamt fuer Bildung und Wissenschaft - Ufficio Federale dell'Educazione e della Scienza - Federal Office for Science and Education, Wildhainweg 9, Case Postale 5675, CH-3001 Berne, Switzerland. TEL 31-619691. FAX 31-617854. bibl.; index; circ. French ed.850; German ed.1,150.
   Description: Publishes information on Swiss science policy and national and international higher education policy activities.

500 060   PL   ISSN 0079-354X
POLSKA AKADEMIA NAUK. ODDZIAL W KRAKOWIE. KOMISJE NAUKOWE. SPRAWOZDANIA Z POSIEDZEN. (Text in Polish; summaries in English and Polish) 1957. s-a. price varies. Ossolineum, Publishing House of the Polish Academy of Sciences, Rynek 9, Wroclaw, Poland. TELEX 0712771 OSS PL. Ed. Jozef Duzyk.
   Description: Contains summaries of papers presented and discussed at meetings of Scientific Commissions.

001.3 500   UK   ISSN 0079-371X
POLSKIE TOWARZYSTWO NAUKOWE NA OBCZYZNIE. ROCZNIK. 1951. a. £2. Polish Society of Arts and Sciences Abroad, 20 Princes Gate, London, S.W.7, England. Ed. B. Helczynski. circ. 600.

500   VC
PONTIFICIA ACADEMIA SCIENTIARUM. COMMENTARII. irreg. Pontificia Academia Scientiarum, Casina Pio IV, 00120 Vatican City (Rome), State of the Vatican City. TEL 698-3195. FAX 698-5218. TELEX 2024 DIRGENTEL VA.

500 574   VC
PONTIFICIA ACADEMIA SCIENTIARUM. DOCUMENTA. (Text in English, French) irreg. Pontificia Academia Scientiarum, Casina Pio IV, 00120 Vatican City (Rome), State of the Vatican City. TEL 698-3195. FAX 6985218. TELEX 2040 DIRGENTEL VA. **Indexed:** Biol.Abstr.

500 574   VC
PONTIFICIA ACADEMIA SCIENTIARUM. SCRIPTA VARIA. (Text in English, French) irreg. Pontificia Academia Scientiarum, Casina Pio IV, 00120 Vatican City (Rome), State of the Vatican City. TEL 698-3195. FAX 6985218. TELEX 2024 DIRGENTEL VA. **Indexed:** Biol.Abstr.

500   II   ISSN 0032-4639
POPULAR SCIENCE AND TECHNOLOGY. (Text in English) 1961-1977; resumed 1986. s-a. Rs.10 per no. (Ministry of Defence) Defence Scientific Information & Documentation Centre (DESIDOC), Metcalfe House, Delhi 110 054, India. FAX 11-2919151. TELEX 031-78031. Ed. Anuradha Ravi. adv.; charts; illus.; circ. 3,500.

500 600   KE
POST; a magazine for the promotion of science and technology. 3/yr.? Kenya National Academy for Advancement of Arts and Sciences, Box 47288, Nairobi, Kenya.

500.9   US   ISSN 0079-4295
QH1   CODEN: PSTLAD
POSTILLA. 1950. irreg., no.208, 1991. price varies. Peabody Museum of Natural History, Yale University, 170 Whitney Ave., Box 6666, New Haven, CT 06511-8161. TEL 203-432-3786. Eds. John Ostrom, Zelda Edelson. circ. 500. (back issues avail.) **Indexed:** Biol.Abstr., Deep Sea Res.& Oceanogr.Abstr.
   Description: Research in the fields of study encompassed by the museum.

500 600   FR   ISSN 0153-4092
POUR LA SCIENCE. French translation of: Scientific American. 1977. m. 310 F. Societe pour la Science, 8 rue Ferou, 75006 Paris, France. FAX 43-25-18-29. TELEX LIBELIN 202978F. Ed. P. Boulanger. adv.; bk.rev.; circ. 60,000. **Indexed:** Pt.de Rep. (1979-).

PRAIRIE FORUM. see *ENVIRONMENTAL STUDIES*

500   US   ISSN 0091-0376
QH540   CODEN: PRNTBZ
PRAIRIE NATURALIST. 1968. q. $10 to individuals (foreign $15); institutions $20 (foreign $25)(effective 1992). North Dakota Natural Science Society, Box 8238, University Sta., Grand Forks, ND 58202-8238. TEL 701-777-2199. FAX 701-777-2623. Ed. Paul B. Kannowski. bk.rev.; circ. 450. **Indexed:** Biol.Abstr., Wild Life Rev. —BLDSC shelfmark: 6598.551000.
   Description: Presents research on the North American grasslands and their biota.

500   XV   ISSN 0351-6652
PRESEK; list za mlade matematike, fizike, astronome in racunalnikarje. (Text in Slovenian) 1971. bi-m. $10. Drustvo Matematikov, Fizikov in Astronomov Slovenije, Podruznica Ljubljana, Jadranska 19, p.p. 64, 61111 Ljubljana, Slovenia. TEL 061-265-061. Ed. Marija Vencelj. adv.; bk.rev.; circ. 20,000.

PRIMI PIANI. see *MUSIC*

PRINCETON UNIVERSITY LIBRARY CHRONICLE. see *HUMANITIES: COMPREHENSIVE WORKS*

500   BU   ISSN 0032-8731
               CODEN: PRIRB4
PRIRODA. 1952. 6/yr. 6.80 lv.($10) (Bulgarska Akademiia na Naukite) Publishing House of the Bulgarian Academy of Sciences, Acad. G. Bonchev St., Bldg. 6, 1113 Sofia, Bulgaria. (Dist. by: Hemus, 6, Rouski Blvd., 1000 Sofia, Bulgaria) adv.; bk.rev.; abstr.; illus.; index; circ. 2,200. **Indexed:** Anim.Breed.Abstr., Biol.Abstr., BSL Biol., Chem.Abstr., Curr.Dig.Sov.Press. —BLDSC shelfmark: 0133.020000.

500   RU   ISSN 0032-874X
Q4   CODEN: PRIRA3
PRIRODA; populyarnyi estestvenno nauchnyi zhurnal. 1912. m. 27.60 Rub. (Akademiya Nauk S.S.S.R.) Izdatel'stvo Nauka, 90 Profsoyuznaya ul., 117864 Moscow, Russia. Ed. N.G. Basov. bk.rev.; bibl.; illus.; maps; index; circ. 62,000. **Indexed:** Anim.Breed.Abstr., Art & Archaeol.Tech.Abstr., Bibl.& Ind.Geol., Biol.Abstr., Chem.Abstr., Curr.Dig.Sov.Press, Int.Aerosp.Abstr., Sci.Abstr. —BLDSC shelfmark: 0133.000000.

500 300   CS
PRIRODA A SPOLOCNOST. 1953. fortn. $70. (Socialisticka Akademia Slovenskej Socialistickej Republiky - Socialist Academy of the Slovak Socialist Republic) Obzor, Ceskoslovenskej Armady 35, 815 85 Bratislava, Czechoslovakia. (Dist. by: Slovart, Gottwaldovo nam. 48, 805 32 Bratislava, Czechoslovakia) Ed. Pavel Berta. adv.; bk.rev.; illus.; circ. 22,000.

PRIRODNI VEDY VE SKOLE. see *EDUCATION*

500 370 600 700   GW   ISSN 0171-3604
PRISMA (KASSEL). 1973. s-a. DM.10. Gesamt Hochschule Kassel, Moenchebergstr. 19, 3500 Kassel, Germany. TEL 0561-8042216. FAX 0561-8042330. adv.; circ. 6,000. (back issues avail.)

PROBABLE LEVELS OF R & D EXPENDITURES: FORECAST AND ANALYSIS. see *TECHNOLOGY: COMPREHENSIVE WORKS*

500   CU   ISSN 0138-7170
PROBLEMAS DE ORGANIZACION DE LA CIENCIA. 1966. m. $25 in N. America; S. America $32; Europe $36; elsewhere $48. (Academia de Ciencias de Cuba, Instituto de Documentacion e Informacion Cientifica y Tecnica, Biblioteca Central de Ciencia y Tecnica) Ediciones Cubanas, Obispo No. 527, Apdo. 605, Havana, Cuba.

500   GW
PROBLEME DER KUESTENFORSCHUNG IM SUEDLICHEN NORDSEEGEBIET. 1940. irreg., vol.16, 1986. (Niedersechsisches Landesinstitut fuer Marschen und Kuestenforschung) Verlag A. Lax, Kreuzstr. 21, Postfach 10 08 05, 3200 Hildesheim, Germany.

500   PL   ISSN 0032-9487
PROBLEMY; miesiecznik popularno-naukowy. 1945. m. $6.60. (Towarzystwo Wiedzy Powszechnej) c o Redakcja, Ul. Krucza 6-14, 00-537 Warsaw, Poland. TEL 48-22-282133. (Dist. by: Ars Polona-Ruch, Krakowskie Przedmiescie 7, Warsaw, Poland) Ed. Hanna Dobrowolska. bk.rev.; bibl.; charts; illus.; index; circ. 30,000. —BLDSC shelfmark: 6617.943600.

PROGRES TECHNIQUE. see *TECHNOLOGY: COMPREHENSIVE WORKS*

500   CC   ISSN 1002-0071
▼**PROGRESS IN NATURAL SCIENCE;** communication of state key laboratories of China. Chinese edition: Ziran Kexue Jinzhan (ISSN 1002-008X) (Text in English) 1991. bi-m. Y36($150) to individuals; institutions $260. (National Natural Science Foundation of China) Science Press, Marketing and Sales Department, 16 Donghuangchenggen Beijie, Beijing 100707, People's Republic of China. TEL 4010642. FAX 4012180. TELEX 210247 SPBJ CN. (US office: Science Press New York, Ltd., 63-117 Alderton St., Rego Park, NY 11374. TEL 718-459-4638) —BLDSC shelfmark: 6870.260000.
   Description: Covers reviews of specialized subjects, thesis, research news and academic activities of State Key Laboratories in China.

500   BE   ISSN 0033-1082
PROMETHEE. 1950. q. 80 Fr.($2) Universite Libre de Bruxelles, Cercle des Sciences, 22 av. Heger, Brussels 5, Belgium. Dir. David Pierre. adv.; charts; illus.; circ. 2,000.

500   XV   ISSN 0033-1805
PROTEUS; ilustriran casopis za poljudno prirodoznanstvo. (Text in Slovenian) 1939. 10/yr. 80 din. Prirodoslovno Drustvo Slovenije, Novi trg 4, Ljubljana, Slovenia. Ed. France Adamic. —BLDSC shelfmark: 6936.200000.

SCIENCES: COMPREHENSIVE WORKS

500 300 AO
PUBLICACOES CULTURAIS DA COMPANHIA. (Alternating series: biology, geology, climatology, history, archaeology and ethnology) (Text in English, French and Portuguese) irreg. Museu do Dundo, Dundo, Luanda, Angola.

500 US ISSN 0079-7685
PUBLICATIONS IN MEDIEVAL SCIENCE. 1952. irreg. price varies. University of Wisconsin Press, 114 N. Murray St., Madison, WI 53715. TEL 608-262-4952. (reprint service avail. from UMI)

500 HU ISSN 0133-2929
PUBLICATIONS OF THE TECHNICAL UNIVERSITY FOR HEAVY INDUSTRY. SERIES D: NATURAL SCIENCES. (Text in English, German, Russian) irreg., vol.35, no.3, 1986. Nehezipari Muszaki Egyetem, Miskolc, Hungary. TEL 46-65111. FAX 46-69554. TELEX 62223-NMEMIS. bibl.; index; circ. 400.

500 KN
PUNSOK HWAHAK. (Text in Korean) q. Korean Academy of Sciences, Central Analytical Institute, Pyongyang, N. Korea.

500 600 JA ISSN 0386-2828
PUROMETEUSU. (Text in Japanese) 1977. bi-m. (Kagaku Gijutsu-cho - Science and Technology Agency) Sozo Co., Ltd., Torii Bldg., 6-12 Shinkawa 2-chome, Chuo-ku, Tokyo 104, Japan. **Indexed:** Jap.Per.Ind.

PURSUIT - S I T U. see *PARAPSYCHOLOGY AND OCCULTISM*

500 IT
QUADERNI DI SCIENZA. 1959. irreg., no.5, 1976. price varies. Giardini Editori e Stampatori, Via Santa Bibbiana 28, 56100 Pisa, Italy. TEL 050 502531.

500 510 028.5 US ISSN 1048-8820
▼**QUANTUM (WASHINGTON);** the student magazine of math and science. 1990. q. $18 to individuals; institutions $28. National Science Teachers Association, 1742 Connecticut Ave., N.W., Washington, DC 20009-1171. TEL 202-328-5800. (Co-sponsors: American Association of Physics Teachers; National Council of Teachers of Mathematics; U S S R Academy of Sciences) adv.; illus.; circ. 40,000 (controlled).
Description: Offers children articles, stories, puzzles and problems in the areas of science and mathematics from around the world.

500 US ISSN 0277-3791
QE696 CODEN: QSREDU
QUATERNARY SCIENCE REVIEWS; international review and research journal. 1982. 8/yr. £260 (effective 1992). Pergamon Press, Inc., Journals Division, 660 White Plains Rd., Tarrytown, NY 10591-5153. TEL 914-524-9200. FAX 914-333-2444. (And: Headington Hill Hall, Oxford OX3 0BW, England. TEL 0865-794141) Ed. D.Q. Bowen. (also avail. in microform) **Indexed:** AESIS, Br.Archaeol.Abstr., Chem.Abstr, Geo.Abstr.
—BLDSC shelfmark: 7210.220000.
Refereed Serial

500 CN ISSN 0021-6127
QUEBEC SCIENCE. (Text in French) 1969. m. Can.$25($35) Presses de l'Universite du Quebec, 2875 blvd Laurier, Ste-Foy, Que, G1V 2M3, Canada. TEL 418-657-3551. FAX 418-657-2096. TELEX 051-31623. Ed. Jacki Dallaire. adv.; bk.rev.; bibl.; charts; illus.; index; circ. 20,000. (also avail. in microform from UMI; reprint service avail. from UMI) **Indexed:** Acid Pre.Dig., Can.Per.Ind., Chem.Abstr., Pt.de Rep. (1979-).
—BLDSC shelfmark: 7210.700000.
Supersedes: Jeune Scientifique.
Description: News and features on science and technology.

QUEEN VICTORIA MUSEUM AND ART GALLERY. LAUNCESTON, TASMANIA. RECORDS. see *MUSEUMS AND ART GALLERIES*

500 600 MX ISSN 0185-5093
QUIPU; revista latinoamericana de historia de las ciencias y la tecnologia. (Text in English, French, Portuguese, Spanish; summaries in English) 1984. 3/yr. $15 to individuals; institutions $60. Sociedad Lationamericana de Historia de las Ciencias y la Tecnologia, Apdo. Postal 21-873, CP 04000 Mexico, DF, Mexico. TEL 534-46-51. FAX 525-534-46-51. Ed. Juan Jose Saldana. adv.; bk.rev.; bibl.; charts; illus.; index; circ. 2,500. (back issues avail.) **Indexed:** Amer.Hist.& Life, Bull.Signal., Hist.Abstr.
—BLDSC shelfmark: 7218.183000.
Description: Covers the history of science and technology in Latin America.

500 US ISSN 0033-6793
R & D CONTRACTS MONTHLY. (Research & Development); a continuously up-dated sales and R & D tool for all research organizations and manufacturers. (Annual Directory) 1962. m. $96. Government Data Publications, Inc., 1155 Connecticut Ave., N.W., Washington, DC 20036. Ed. Siegfried Lobel. **Indexed:** DM& T, PROMT.
Description: Coverage of sales as well as research and development intelligence. Lists recently awarded government contracts.

500 US
R & D MAGAZINE. m. Cahners Publishing Company (Des Plaines) (Subsidiary of: Reed International PLC), Division of Reed Publishing (USA) Inc., 1350 E. Touhy Ave., Box 5080, Des Plaines, IL 60017-5080. TEL 708-635-8800. Ed. Rob Cassidy. circ. 110,110.
Description: Aimed at scientists, chemists, engineers and administrators engaged in applied research and development.

500 SI ISSN 0217-6440
R & D SURVEY. (Text in English) 1983. a. free. National Science and Technology Board, 16 Science Park Drive, 01-03 The Pasteur, Singapore Science Park, Singapore 0511, Singapore. TEL 65-779-7066. FAX 65-777-1711.

R E C S A M NEWS. (Regional Centre for Education in Science and Mathematics) see *EDUCATION — Teaching Methods And Curriculum*

500 US ISSN 0033-8222
QC798.D3 CODEN: RACAAT
RADIOCARBON; an international journal of cosmogenic isotopic research. 1959. 3/yr. $73.50 to individuals; institutions $105; students $36.75 (typically set in Jan.). University Arizona, Department of Geosciences, 4717 E. Ft. Lowell Rd., Tucson, AZ 85721. TEL 602-621-8888. FAX 602-881-0554. Ed. Austin Long. adv.; bk.rev.; bibl.; charts; illus.; cum.index: 1950-1965; circ. 600. **Indexed:** A.I.C.P., Art & Archaeol.Tech.Abstr., Bibl.& Ind.Geol., Biol.Abstr., Br.Archaeol.Abstr., Chem.Abstr., Curr.Adv.Ecol.Sci., Deep Sea Res.& Oceanogr.Abstr.
—BLDSC shelfmark: 7234.460000.
Refereed Serial

RAKUNO GAKUEN DAIGAKU KIYO. SHIZEN KAGAKU HEN/COLLEGE OF DIARYING. JOURNAL: NATURAL SCIENCE. see *AGRICULTURE — Dairying And Dairy Products*

081 500 600 US
THE RAND CORPORATION'S RESEARCH PUBLICATIONS. irreg. $450 (foreign $550). Rand Corporation, Publications Department, 1700 Main St., Box 2138, Santa Monica, CA 90407-2138. TEL 213-393-0411. FAX 213-393-4818. TELEX 9103436878. **Indexed:** Geo.Abstr., I D A, Med.Care Rev., Popul.Ind.
Former titles: Rand Report Series; Rand Paper Series (ISSN 0092-2803); Rand Corporation. Paper.

RANGER RICK'S NATURESCOPE. see *EDUCATION — Teaching Methods And Curriculum*

500 SP ISSN 0034-0596
Q65 CODEN: RCFNAT
REAL ACADEMIA DE CIENCIAS EXACTAS, FISICAS Y NATURALES. REVISTA. (Text in English, French, German and Spanish) 1904. q. 5000 ptas. (effective 1992). Real Academia de Ciencias Exactas, Fisicas y Naturales, Valverde 22, 28004 Madrid, Spain. adv.; bk.rev.; circ. 800. **Indexed:** Biol.Abstr., Chem.Abstr, Deep Sea Res.& Oceanogr.Abstr., Math.R.

500 020.75 US ISSN 0738-0925
Z7403
RECENT PUBLICATIONS IN NATURAL HISTORY. 1983. q. $17 (foreign $20). American Museum of Natural History, Department of Library Services, Central Park W. at 79th St., New York, NY 10024-5192. TEL 212-769-5411. FAX 212-769-5233. Ed. Priscilla M. Watson. bk.rev.; circ. 300. (back issues avail.)
—BLDSC shelfmark: 7305.084200.
Description: Bibliographies and reviews of recent books in the natural sciences, astronomy and anthropology, classified into 26 subject areas.

500 FR ISSN 0029-5671
Q2 CODEN: RCCHBV
RECHERCHE. (Text in French; summaries in English) 1960. m. 325 F. Societe d'Editions Scientifiques, 57 rue de Seine, 75006 Paris, France. TEL 43-54-32-84. FAX 46-34-75-08. Ed. Stephane Khemis. adv.; bk.rev.; charts; illus.; index; circ. 92,000. (reprint service avail. from ISI) **Indexed:** Appl.Mech.Rev., Bio-Contr.News & Info., Biol.Abstr., Chem.Abstr., Curr.Adv.Ecol.Sci., Curr.Biotech.Abstr., Curr.Cont., Dairy Sci.Abstr., Deep Sea Res.& Oceanogr.Abstr., Energy Ind., Energy Info.Abstr., Excerp.Med., Geo.Abstr., Helminthol.Abstr., Int.Lab.Doc., Key to Econ.Sci., Lang.& Lang.Behav.Abstr., Met.Abstr., Pt.de Rep. (1979-), Risk Abstr., Sci.Abstr., World Alum.Abstr.
—BLDSC shelfmark: 7305.380000.
Incorporates: Atomes & Nucleus.

REDSTART. see *BIOLOGY — Ornithology*

REGENSBURGER UNIVERSITAETSZEITUNG. see *COLLEGE AND ALUMNI*

507 370 IS ISSN 0034-3609
REHOVOT. (Text in English) 1959. a. free. Weizmann Institute of Science, Public Affairs Department, Rehovot, Israel. TEL 08-342111. FAX 08-466966. TELEX 381300. illus.; circ. 19,000.

500 US ISSN 0034-4508
RENSSELAER ENGINEER; technical journal of the Students of the Rensselaer Student Union. 1947. q. $5. Rensselaer Student Union, Box 33, Troy, NY 12180-3590. TEL 518-266-6515. Ed. Bart Vashaw. adv.; bk.rev.; charts; illus.; circ. 5,000.

500 323.4 327 US ISSN 0895-5999
REPORT ON SCIENCE AND HUMAN RIGHTS. 1978. irreg. free. American Association for the Advancement of Science, Science and Human Rights Program, 1333 H St., N.W., Washington, DC 20005. TEL 202-326-6790. FAX 202-289-4950. Ed. Jane Cave. bk.rev.; circ. 2,500. **Indexed:** HR Rep.
Formerly (until 1987): Clearinghouse Report on Science and Human Rights (ISSN 0734-4171)

500 600 SA ISSN 0081-2412
Q180.A6
REPORT TO S C A R ON SOUTH AFRICAN ANTARCTIC RESEARCH ACTIVITIES. (Scientific Committee for Antarctic Research) 1963. a. free. Council for Scientific and Industrial Research, South African Scientific Committee for Antarctic Research, Box 395, Pretoria 0001, South Africa. TEL 27-12-86. circ. 300.

500 CH
REPUBLIC OF CHINA. NATIONAL SCIENCE COUNCIL. ANNUAL REPORT. (Text in Chinese) 1963. a. free. National Science Council of the Republic of China, 106 Ho-Ping E. Rd. Sec.2, Taipei, Taiwan 106, Republic of China.

500 CH ISSN 0250-1651
Q4 CODEN: KHFKDF
REPUBLIC OF CHINA. NATIONAL SCIENCE COUNCIL MONTHLY. (Text in Chinese) 1973. m. NT.$600($24) National Science Council of the Republic of China, 106 Ho-ping E. Rd. Sec. 2, Taipei, Taiwan 106, Republic of China. **Indexed:** Biol.Abstr., Crop Physiol.Abstr., Field Crop Abstr., Herb.Abstr., Plant Grow.Reg.Abstr. Key Title: Kexue Fazhan.
—BLDSC shelfmark: 6033.044000.

SCIENCES: COMPREHENSIVE WORKS

500 600   CH   ISSN 1017-7124
▼**REPUBLIC OF CHINA. NATIONAL SCIENCE COUNCIL. PROCEEDINGS. PART D: MATHEMATICS, SCIENCE, AND TECHNOLOGY EDUCATION.** (Text in English) 1991. s-a. NT.$120($8) National Science Council, 106 Ho-ping E. Rd. Sec.2, Taipei, Taiwan 106, Republic of China. TEL 2-737-7248. FAX 2-737-7594. Ed. Chi-Lin Yen.
—BLDSC shelfmark: 6769.886000.

500   US   ISSN 0080-1461
Q180.U5
RESEARCH AND DEVELOPMENT DIRECTORY. (Title varies: Unique 3-in-1 Research & Development Directory) 1959. a. $15. Government Data Publications, Inc., 1155 Connecticut Ave., N.W., Washington, DC 20036. Ed. Siegfried Lobel.

500   IE   ISSN 0085-5545
RESEARCH AND DEVELOPMENT IN IRELAND. 1967. irreg. £2.45. Government Publications Sales Office, Sun Alliance House, Molesworth St., Dublin 2, Ireland. Ed. Diarmuid Murphy.

RESEARCH AND DEVELOPMENT IN JAPAN AWARDED THE OKOCHI MEMORIAL PRIZE. see *TECHNOLOGY: COMPREHENSIVE WORKS*

500 007   US   ISSN 0080-1518
AS25
RESEARCH CENTERS DIRECTORY; a guide to approximately 13,000 university-related & other non-profit research organizations. 1962. a. (plus suppl.). $420 (effective July 1992). Gale Research Inc., 835 Penobscot Bldg., Detroit, MI 48226. TEL 313-961-2242. FAX 313-961-6083. TELEX 810-221-7086. Ed. Annette Piccirelli. index; circ. 2,500.
●Also available online. Vendor(s): DIALOG.
—BLDSC shelfmark: 7734.700000.
  Description: Lists research centers in the U.S.

500   UK   ISSN 0958-2029
▼**RESEARCH EVALUATION.** 1991. 3/yr. £52($90) Beech Tree Publishing, 10 Watford Close, Guildford, Surrey GU1 2EP, England. TEL 0483-67497. FAX 0483-67497. TELEX 859539-LYNXING-G. Eds. Tony van Raan, Carlos Kruytbosch. bk.rev.; bibl.; index.
—BLDSC shelfmark: 7739.920000.
Refereed Serial

500   II   ISSN 0253-9306
                    CODEN: UIRJAG
RESEARCH JOURNAL: SCIENCE. (Text in English) 1972. q. University of Indore, University House, Indore 452001, Madhya Pradesh, India.

REVISTA BRASILEIRA DE TECNOLOGIA. see *TECHNOLOGY: COMPREHENSIVE WORKS*

500   CL
REVISTA CONTRIBUCIONES CIENTIFICAS Y TECNOLOGICAS. (Text in Spanish; summaries in English) 1971. irreg. $5. Universidad de Santiago de Chile, Departamento de Investigaciones Cientificas y Tecnologicas, Avda. Ecuador 3469, Santiago, Chile. FAX 562-6813083. illus.; circ. 1,000. **Indexed:** Chem.Abstr.

500   CU   ISSN 0138-6107
REVISTA DE INFORMACION CIENTIFICA Y TECNICA CUBANA. 1969. 3/yr. $24 in N. America; S. America $25; Europe $26. (Academia de Ciencias de Cuba, Instituto de Documentacion e Informacion Cientifica y Tecnica) Ediciones Cubanas, Obispo No. 527, Apdo. 605, Havana, Cuba. adv. fr.
  Former titles (1973-1974): Boletin de Informacion Cientifica y Tecnica Cubana; (1969-1973): Boletin de Informacion Cientifica Cubana; **Supersedes** (1953-1969): Academia de Ciencias de Cuba. Instituto de Documentacion e Informacion Cientifica y Tecnica. Boletin (ISSN 0020-3831)

500 389.6   CU   ISSN 0138-8118
REVISTA DE NORMALIZACION. (Summaries in English) 1971. s-a. C.$2. Comite Estatal de Normalizacion, Centro de Informatica Aplicada a la Normalizacion, Reina 359 e Escobar y Lealtad, Habana Vieja 2, Havana C.P. 10200, Cuba. FAX 537-627-657. TELEX 512245 CEN CU. (Dist. by: Ediciones Cubanas, Obispo No. 461, Apdo. 605, Havana, Cuba) Ed. Josefa Gonzalez Lopez. adv.; circ. 1,000.
  Description: Deals with standization, metrology and quality control subjects in Cuba.

500   CU
REVISTA DOCUMENTOS DE CIENCIA Y TECNICA. irreg. exchange basis. Instituto Superior Ciencias Agropecuarias de la Habana (ISCAH), Direccion de Informacion Cientifico-Tecnica, Apdo. Postal 18-19, San Jose de las Lajas, Havana, Cuba.

REVISTA ESPANOLA DE DOCUMENTACION CIENTIFICA. see *LIBRARY AND INFORMATION SCIENCES*

500 600   FR   ISSN 0048-7996
Q2
REVUE D'HISTOIRE DES SCIENCES ET DE LEURS APPLICATIONS. 1947. q. 350 F. (foreign 470 F.). (Centre International de Synthese) Presses Universitaires de France, Departement des Revues, 14 av. du Bois-de-l'Epine, B.P.90, 91003 Evry Cedex, France. TEL 1-60-77-82-05. FAX 1-60-79-20-45. TELEX PUF 600 474 F. Ed. Michel Blay. bk.rev.; illus.; index, cum.index; circ. 800. (reprint service avail. from KTO) **Indexed:** Math.R.
—BLDSC shelfmark: 7919.998000.
  Description: For those interested in the evolution of scientific ideas and the history of scientific techniques.

500   BE   ISSN 0035-2160
Q2   CODEN: RQSCAN
REVUE DES QUESTIONS SCIENTIFIQUES. (Text in French; summaries in English) 1877. 4/yr. 1750 Fr. (effective 1992). Societe Scientifique de Bruxelles, Rue de Bruxelles 61, B-5000 Namur, Belgium. Ed. C. Courtoy. adv.; bk.rev.; charts; illus.; index; circ. 850. **Indexed:** Bibl.& Ind.Geol., Biol.Abstr., Bull.Signal., Chem.Abstr., Excerp.Med., Math.R.
—BLDSC shelfmark: 7945.000000.

378 500   FR   ISSN 0035-2241
REVUE DES SOCIETES SAVANTES DE HAUTE NORMANDIE. 1956. q. 25 F. J. Liger, Ed. & Pub., 190 rue Beauvoisine, Rouen, France. charts; illus.

REVUE IMPREVUE. see *SOCIOLOGY*

001.3 500 600   GW
RHEINISCH-WESTFAELISCHE AKADEMIE DER WISSENSCHAFTEN. VORTRAEGE NATUR-INGENIEUR-UND WIRTSCHAFTSWISSENSCHAFTEN. 1950. irreg. Westdeutscher Verlag GmbH (Opladen), Reuschenberger Str. 55, Postfach 300944, 5090 Leverkusen 3 - Opladen, Germany. TEL 02171-44741. FAX 02171-48048. **Indexed:** Bibl.& Ind.Geol., Biol.Abstr., Chem.Abstr.
  Former titles: Rheinisch-Westfaelische Akademie der Wissenschaften. Veroeffentlichungen (ISSN 0066-5754); (1950-1970): Arbeitsgemeinschaft fuer Forschung des Landes Nordrhein-Westfalen. Veroeffentlichungen.

RIJKSUNIVERSITEIT UTRECHT. WETENSCHAPPELIJK JAAVERSLAG. see *EDUCATION — Higher Education*

530 540 550   JA   ISSN 0287-718X
                  CODEN: RIGAD6
RIKAGAKKAISHI/JOURNAL OF PHYSICS, CHEMISTRY AND EARTH SCIENCE. (Text in Japanese) 1958. a. 500 Yen for members. Toyama-ken Rikagakkai, Toyama-ken Sogo Kyoiku Senta, Shotakata Toyama-shi, Toyama-ken 930, Japan.

500   JA   ISSN 0387-6837
Q77   CODEN: RDKSA8
RIKKYO DAIGAKU KENKYU HOKOKU. SHIZEN KAGAKU/ST. PAUL'S REVIEW OF SCIENCE. (Text and summaries in English) 1956. a. free. Rikkyo Daigaku, Ippan Kyoikubu - Rikkyo University, Faculty of General Education, 34-1 Nishi-Ikebukuro 3-chome, Toshima-ku, Tokyo 171, Japan. FAX 03-3986-8784. **Indexed:** Jap.Per.Ind.

500   IT
RIZA SCIENZA; scienza dell'uomo. m. L.75000. Edizioni Riza, Via Luigi Anelli, 1, 20122 Milan, Italy. TEL 02-58301022. FAX 55187511.

500   GW   ISSN 0323-4630
ROSTOCK UNIVERSITAET. WISSENSCHAFTLICHE ZEITSCHRIFT. GESELLSCHAFTS-WISSENSCHAFTLICHE REIHE. (Summaries in English) 1951. 6/yr. DM.24.40. Rostock Universitaet, Abt. Wissenschaftspublizistik, Vogelsang 13-14, 2500 Rostock 1, Germany. bk.rev.; abstr.; bibl.; charts; illus.; stat.; index; circ. 1,350(combined).
  Formerly: Rostock Universitaet. Wissenschaftliche Zeitschrift. Gesellschafts- und Sprachwissenschaftliche Reihe (ISSN 0043-6933)

500   GW   ISSN 0323-4681
Q3   CODEN: WZWRD5
ROSTOCK UNIVERSITAET. WISSENSCHAFTLICHE ZEITSCHRIFT. NATURWISSENSCHAFTLICHE REIHE. (Summaries in English) 1951. 6/yr. DM.24.40. Rostock Universitaet, Abt. Wissenschaftspublizistik, Vogelsang 13-14, 2500 Rostock 1, Germany. adv.; bk.rev.; abstr.; bibl.; charts; illus.; stat.; index; circ. 1,350(combined). **Indexed:** Bibl.& Ind.Geol., Biol.Abstr., Chem.Abstr., Dairy Sci.Abstr., Field Crop Abstr., Herb.Abstr., Ind.Vet., Plant Grow.Reg.Abstr.
  Formerly: Rostock Universitaet. Wissenschaftliche Zeitschrift. Mathematisch-Naturwissenschaftliche Reihe.

ROYAL BRITISH COLUMBIA MUSEUM MEMOIRS. see *MUSEUMS AND ART GALLERIES*

500   UK
ROYAL INSTITUTION OF GREAT BRITAIN. PROCEEDINGS. 1851. a. Royal Institution of Great Britain, 21 Albemarle St., London W1X 4BS, England. **Indexed:** Br.Archaeol.Abstr., Br.Ceram.Abstr., Br.Hum.Ind., Chem.Abstr., Deep Sea Res.& Oceanogr.Abstr., Hist.Abstr., Sci.Abstr.

500   UK
ROYAL INSTITUTION OF GREAT BRITAIN. RECORD. 1799. a. £6. Royal Institution of Great Britain, 21 Albemarle St., London W1X 4BS, England. circ. 3,000 (controlled).
  Formerly: Royal Institution of Great Britain. Annual Report.

500   UK
ROYAL INSTITUTION OF GREAT BRITAIN. ROYAL INSTITUTION LECTURES. 1853. 3/yr. Royal Institution of Great Britain, 21 Albemarle St., London, W1X 4BS, England. circ. 4,000 (controlled).

500   NE   ISSN 0924-8323
Q57   CODEN: PKNSEK
ROYAL NETHERLANDS ACADEMY OF SCIENCES. PROCEEDINGS. (Text in English) 1937. 4/yr. fl.296 (effective 1992). (Royal Netherlands Academy of Sciences - Koninklijke Nederlandse Akademie van Wetenschappen) North-Holland (Subsidiary of: Elsevier Science Publishers B.V.), P.O. Box 211, 1000 AE Amsterdam, Netherlands. TEL 020-5803911. FAX 020-5803598. TELEX 18582 ESPA NL. (Subscr. in U.S. and Canada to: Elsevier Science Publishing Co., Inc., Box 882, Madison Sq. Sta., New York, NY 10159. TEL 212-989-5800) charts; illus.; index; circ. 850. (back issues avail.) **Indexed:** Anal.Abstr., Anim.Breed.Abstr., Cadscan, Chem.Abstr., Crop Physiol.Abstr., Curr.Cont., E.I., Excerp.Med., Field Crop Abstr., Forest.Abstr., Forest Prod.Abstr., Helminthol.Abstr., Herb.Abstr., Ind.Vet., Lead Abstr., Math.R., Nutr.Abstr., Rev.Plant Path., Sci.Abstr., Vet.Bull., Weed Abstr., Zincscan.
  Formed by the 1990 merger of: Koninklijke Nederlandse Akademie van Wetenschappen. Series C: Biological and Medical Sciences. Proceedings (ISSN 0023-3374); Koninklijke Nederlandse Akademie van Wetenschappen. Series B: Palaeontology, Geology, Physics, and Chemistry. Proceedings (ISSN 0920-2250); Which was formerly (until 1983): Koninklijke Nederlandse Akademie van Wetenschappen. Series B: Physical Sciences. Proceedings (ISSN 0023-3366) Incorporates: Koninklijke Nederlandse Akademie van Wetenschappen. Afdeling Natuurkunde, Verhandelingen. Eerste Reeks (ISSN 0065-5503).
Refereed Serial

500 600   UK   ISSN 0260-2725
ROYAL SOCIETY NEWS. 1980. bi-m. Royal Society of London, 6 Carlton House Terrace, London SW1Y 5AG, England. TEL 071-839-5561. FAX 071-976-1837. TELEX 917876. circ. 3,500 (controlled).

500   CN   ISSN 0080-4517
AS42   CODEN: PRYCA4
ROYAL SOCIETY OF CANADA. PROCEEDINGS. (Text in English, French) 1882; N.S. vol.21, 1983. a. Can.$6.75. Royal Society of Canada, P.O. Box 9734, Ottawa, Ont. K1G 5J4, Canada. TEL 613-992-3468. FAX 613-992-5021. Ed. Claude Bishop. (also avail. in microform from UMI,BHP; reprint service avail. from UMI) **Indexed:** Bibl.& Ind.Geol., Can.Per.Ind., Math.R.
—BLDSC shelfmark: 6802.700000.
  Supersedes in part: Royal Society of Canada. Proceedings and Transactions (ISSN 0316-4616)

SCIENCES: COMPREHENSIVE WORKS

500   CN   ISSN 0035-9122
CODEN: TRSCAI
ROYAL SOCIETY OF CANADA. TRANSACTIONS. (Text in English, French) 1882; N.S. vol.21, 1983. a. Can.$20. Royal Society of Canada, P.O. Box 9734, Ottawa, Ont. K1G 5J4, Canada.
TEL 613-992-3468. Ed. Claude Bishop. bibl.; charts; illus.; cum.index: 1882-1957 (in several vols.); circ. 1,400. (also avail. in microform from MML; reprint service avail. from UMI) **Indexed:** Bibl.& Ind.Geol., Biol.Abstr., Chem.Abstr., Deep Sea Res.& Oceanogr.Abstr., Eng.Ind., Hist.Abstr., Hort.Abstr., Math.R., Met.Abstr., Petrol.Abstr., Rev.Plant Path., Sci.Abstr.
—BLDSC shelfmark: 8999.000000.
Supersedes in part: Royal Society of Canada. Proceedings and Transactions (ISSN 0316-4616)

ROYAL SOCIETY OF EDINBURGH. PROCEEDINGS. SECTION A (MATHEMATICS). see *MATHEMATICS*

ROYAL SOCIETY OF EDINBURGH. TRANSACTIONS. (EARTH SCIENCES). see *EARTH SCIENCES*

500   UK   ISSN 0080-4576
Q41   CODEN: RSEYAX
ROYAL SOCIETY OF EDINBURGH. YEAR BOOK. 1941. a. £10($25) Royal Society of Edinburgh, 22-24 George St., Edinburgh EH2 2PQ, Scotland.
TEL 031-225-6057. FAX 031-220-6889. Ed. T.G. Dart. circ. 1,500.

500   UK   ISSN 0035-9149
Q41   CODEN: NOREAY
ROYAL SOCIETY OF LONDON. NOTES AND RECORDS. 1938. s-a. £24 (foreign £25.50). Royal Society of London, 6 Carlton House Terr., London SW1Y 5AG, England. TEL 071-839-5561. FAX 071-976-1837. TELEX 917876. Ed. D.G. King-Hele. bk.rev.; bibl.; illus.; index. cum.index: vols.1-20, 1938-1965; circ. 1,300. (reprint service avail. from ISI) **Indexed:** Arts & Hum.Cit.Ind., Biol.Abstr., Br.Archaeol.Abstr., Curr.Cont., Hist.Abstr., Math.R.
—BLDSC shelfmark: 6165.075000.
Refereed Serial

ROYAL SOCIETY OF LONDON. PROCEEDINGS. SERIES A. MATHEMATICAL AND PHYSICAL SCIENCES. see *MATHEMATICS*

506   UK   ISSN 0080-4673
ROYAL SOCIETY OF LONDON. YEAR BOOK. 1898. a. £15. Royal Society of London, 6 Carlton House Terrace, London SW1Y 5AG, England.
TEL 071-839-5561. FAX 071-976-1837. TELEX 917876. circ. 1,400. (reprint service avail. from ISI)

500   AT   ISSN 0035-9173
CODEN: JPRSA5
ROYAL SOCIETY OF NEW SOUTH WALES. JOURNAL AND PROCEEDINGS. 1867. q. Aus.$42 (typically set in Dec.). Royal Society of New South Wales, 134 Herring Rd., North Ryde, N.S.W. 2113, Australia.
TEL 02-887-4448. (Subscr. to: P.O. Box 1525, Macquarie Centre, N.S.W. 2113, Australia) Ed. Mrs. M. Krysko V. Tryst. bk.rev.; charts; illus.; cum.index: 1862-1865, 1867-1916; circ. 900. **Indexed:** AESIS, Bibl.& Ind.Geol., Biol.Abstr., Chem.Abstr, Deep Sea Res.& Oceanogr.Abstr., Math.R., Rev.Plant Path., Sci.Abstr.
—BLDSC shelfmark: 4933.000000.

500 500   NZ   ISSN 0370-6559
CODEN: RNZBAY
ROYAL SOCIETY OF NEW ZEALAND. BULLETIN SERIES. 1910. irreg. Royal Society of New Zealand, P.O. Box 598, Wellington, New Zealand. circ. 300. **Indexed:** Deep Sea Res.& Oceanogr.Abstr.
—BLDSC shelfmark: 2701.000000.
Formerly: Royal Society of New Zealand. Bulletin.

500   NZ   ISSN 0303-6758
Q1   CODEN: JRNZAK
ROYAL SOCIETY OF NEW ZEALAND. JOURNAL. 1971. q. NZ.$140. Royal Society of New Zealand, P.O. Box 598, Wellington 1, New Zealand. Ed. Carolyn M. King. bibl.; charts; illus.; maps; index, cum.index: 1869-1971, 1976, 1981; circ. 800. **Indexed:** Bibl.& Ind.Geol., Biol.Abstr., Chem.Abstr, Curr.Adv.Ecol.Sci., Curr.Cont., Deep Sea Res.& Oceanogr.Abstr., Field Crop Abstr., Forest.Abstr., Forest Prod.Abstr., Geo.Abstr., Helminthol.Abstr., INIS Atomind., Nutr.Abstr., Petrol.Abstr., Rev.Appl.Entomol., Rev.Plant Path., Risk Abstr., So.Pac.Per.Ind., Soils & Fert., SSCI, Zoo.Rec.
—BLDSC shelfmark: 4864.630000.
Supersedes: Royal Society of New Zealand. Transactions (ISSN 0035-9181)

500   NZ   ISSN 0111-3895
ROYAL SOCIETY OF NEW ZEALAND. MISCELLANEOUS SERIES. irreg. Royal Society of New Zealand, P.O. Box 598, Wellington, New Zealand.
—BLDSC shelfmark: 5827.500000.

506   AT   ISSN 0080-469X
Q93   CODEN: PRSQAG
ROYAL SOCIETY OF QUEENSLAND, ST. LUCIA. PROCEEDINGS. 1884. a. Aus.$25. Royal Society of Queensland, P.O. Box 21, St. Lucia, Queensland 4067, Australia. TEL 07-870-1697. Ed. E.D. McKenzie. circ. 640. **Indexed:** AESIS, Bibl.& Ind.Geol., Curr.Adv.Ecol.Sci., Deep Sea Res.& Oceanogr.Abstr., Field Crop Abstr., Forest.Abstr., Forest Prod.Abstr., Herb.Abstr., Hort.Abstr., Nutr.Abstr., Rev.Appl.Entomol., Rev.Plant Path., Soils & Fert.
—BLDSC shelfmark: 6806.000000.

500   SA   ISSN 0035-919X
Q85   CODEN: TRSAAC
ROYAL SOCIETY OF SOUTH AFRICA. TRANSACTIONS. 1877. irreg., approx. 2/yr. R.50 per no. (effective 1992). Royal Society of South Africa, P.D. Hahn Building, P.O. Box 594, Cape Town, South Africa. TEL 021-650-2543. FAX 021-650-3726. TELEX 521439 SA. Ed. W.P.U. Jackson. bibl.; charts; illus.; cum.index: 1878-1909, 1909-1955, 1956-1985; circ. 800. (also avail. in microfilm from UMI) **Indexed:** Biol.Abstr., Chem.Abstr., Curr.Adv.Ecol.Sci., Curr.Cont., Deep Sea Res.& Oceanogr.Abstr., Excerp.Med., Geo.Abstr., Ind.S.A.Per., Math.R., S.A.Waterabstr., Sci.Abstr., Sel.Water Res.Abstr., W.R.C.Inf.

500   AT   ISSN 0085-5812
ROYAL SOCIETY OF SOUTH AUSTRALIA. TRANSACTIONS. 1878. a. Aus.$40. Royal Society of South Australia Inc., S.A. Museum, North Terrace, Adelaide, S.A. 5000, Australia. TEL 08-223-5360. Ed. M. Davies. index; circ. 800. **Indexed:** Abstr.Anthropol., AESIS, Anim.Behav.Abstr., Aqua.Sci.& Fish.Abstr., Biol.Abstr., Curr.Adv.Ecol.Sci., Deep Sea Res.& Oceanogr.Abstr., Ecol.Abstr., Entomol.Abstr., Field Crop Abstr., GeoRef, Herb.Abstr., Microbiol.Abstr., Mineral.Abstr., Rev.Plant Path., Soils & Fert., Zoo.Rec.
—BLDSC shelfmark: 9002.000000.
Description: Publishes original papers in natural sciences.

506   AT   ISSN 0080-4703
Q93   CODEN: PPRTA6
ROYAL SOCIETY OF TASMANIA, HOBART. PAPERS AND PROCEEDINGS. 1848. a. Aus.$27 (effective 1991). Royal Society of Tasmania, Box 1166M, Hobart, Tas. 7001, Australia. TEL 002-231422.
FAX 61-002-347139. Ed. M.R. Banks. circ. 700. **Indexed:** AESIS, Bibl.& Ind.Geol., Biol.Abstr., Curr.Adv.Ecol.Sci., Deep Sea Res.& Oceanogr.Abstr., Math.R., VITIS.
—BLDSC shelfmark: 6396.000000.

500   AT   ISSN 0035-9211
Q93   CODEN: PRSVAV
ROYAL SOCIETY OF VICTORIA. PROCEEDINGS. 1860. s-a. Aus.$65. Royal Society of Victoria, 9 Victoria St., Melbourne, Vic. 3000, Australia. FAX 03-663-2301. Ed. D. Holloway. charts; illus.; index; circ. 1,000. **Indexed:** AESIS, Agroforest.Abstr., Bibl.& Ind.Geol., Biol.Abstr., Chem.Abstr, Curr.Adv.Ecol.Sci., Deep Sea Res.& Oceanogr.Abstr., Field Crop Abstr., Forest.Abstr., Forest Prod.Abstr., Geo.Abstr., Herb.Abstr., Rev.Appl.Entomol., Rev.Plant Path., Sci.Abstr., Soils & Fert.
—BLDSC shelfmark: 6807.000000.

500   AT   ISSN 0035-922X
CODEN: JRSUAU
ROYAL SOCIETY OF WESTERN AUSTRALIA. JOURNAL. 1914. q. Aus.$40. Royal Society of Western Australia, Inc., c/o Western Australian Museum, Perth, W.A. 6000, Australia. Ed. W. Cowling. charts; illus.; index; circ. 700. **Indexed:** AESIS, Aus.Sci.Ind., Bibl.& Ind.Geol., Biol.Abstr., Chem.Abstr., Curr.Adv.Ecol.Sci., Deep Sea Res.& Oceanogr.Abstr., Field Crop Abstr., Herb.Abstr., Rev.Plant Path.
—BLDSC shelfmark: 4865.000000.
Description: Promotes science in Western Australia and counteracts the effects of specialization.

500   CC   ISSN 1001-8409
RUAN KEXUE. (Text in Chinese) q. Sichuan Keji Cujin Fazhan Yanjiu Zhongxin, 11, Renmin Nanlu, 7th Fl., Chengdu, Sichuan 610041, People's Republic of China. TEL 551129. Ed. Zhou Xinyuan.

500   AG   ISSN 0325-6146
S C A R BOLETIN. English edition: S C A R Bulletin (ISSN 0036-1097) 1959. 3/yr. (Scientific Committee on Antartic Research) Direccion Nacional del Antartico, Instituto Antartico Argentino, Cerrito 1248, 1010 Buenos Aires, Argentina. TEL 812-1689.
FAX 541-812-2039. (Published in English by: Scott Polar Research Institute, Lensfield Rd., Cambridge, England) (Co-sponsor: International Council of Scientific Unions) abstr.; bibl.; charts; illus.; stat.; index; circ. 750.

500 600   UK   ISSN 0262-7671
CODEN: SERBDD
S E R C BULLETIN. 1973. irreg. (3/yr.) free. Science and Engineering Research Council, Polaris House, North Star Ave., Swindon SN2 1ET, England. Ed. Juliet Russell. abstr.; illus.; index; circ. 14,000. (also avail. in microform)
—BLDSC shelfmark: 8242.503000.

S S M ARRT. (School Science & Mathematics Association, Inc.) see *EDUCATION — Teaching Methods And Curriculum*

S T A: ITS ROLES AND ACTIVITIES. (Science and Technology Agency) see *TECHNOLOGY: COMPREHENSIVE WORKS*

S U T BULLETIN. (Science University of Tokyo) see *TECHNOLOGY: COMPREHENSIVE WORKS*

991.1 570   MY   ISSN 0036-2131
DS646.33
SABAH SOCIETY. JOURNAL. 1961. irreg., latest vol.8, no.4, 1988. M.$20 per no. Sabah Society - Pertubuhan Sabah, P.O. Box 10547, 88806 Kota Kinabalu, Sabah, Malaysia. Ed. Patricia Regis. bk.rev.; circ. 500. (tabloid format) **Indexed:** E.I.

500   II   ISSN 0256-2499
CODEN: SAPSER
SADHANA; academy proceedings in engineering sciences. (Text in English) 1978. q. Rs.75($75) Indian Academy of Sciences, C.V. Raman Avenue, P.B. No. 8005, Bangalore 560 080, India.
TEL 342546. FAX 91-812-346094. TELEX 0845-2178-ACAD-IN. Ed. R. Narasimha. circ. 800. (also avail. in microform from UMI; reprint service avail. from ISI, UMI) **Indexed:** Chem.Abstr., Curr.Cont., Energy Ind., Energy Info.Abstr., Fluidex, Int.Aerosp.Abstr., Sci.Abstr.
—BLDSC shelfmark: 8062.798000.
Former titles (until 1984): Indian Academy of Sciences. Proceedings. Engineering Sciences (ISSN 0253-4096) And (until 1979): Indian Academy of Sciences. Proceedings. Section C. Engineering Sciences (ISSN 0250-5444).
Description: Wide-ranging, original papers and reviews of interest to engineering scientists.

500 069   JA
SADO HAKUBUTSUKAN KENKYU HOKOKU/PUBLICATIONS FROM THE SADO MUSEUM. (Text in English and Japanese; summaries in English) 1957. irreg. Sado Hakubutsukan - Sado Museum, Nakae, Yawata, Sawada-cho, Sado-gun, Niigata-ken 952-13, Japan.
Description: Contains research reports.

SCIENCES: COMPREHENSIVE WORKS

500   GW   ISSN 0080-5262
AS182
SAECHSISCHE AKADEMIE DER WISSENSCHAFTEN, LEIPZIG. JAHRBUCH. 1955 (covering 1949-53). irreg., latest 1988 (covering 1985-86). price varies. Akademie-Verlag Berlin, Leipziger Str. 3-4, 1086 Berlin, Germany. TELEX 114420-AVERL-DD. Ed. Gerald Wiemers. Indexed: Hist.Abstr.

500 510   GW   ISSN 0365-6470
CODEN: ASAWAO
SAECHSISCHE AKADEMIE DER WISSENSCHAFTEN, LEIPZIG. MATHEMATISCH-NATURWISSENSCHAFTLICHE KLASSE. ABHANDLUNGEN. 1896. irreg., vol.57, 1989. price varies. Akademie-Verlag Berlin, Leipziger Str. 3-4, 1086 Berlin, Germany. TELEX 114420-AVERL-DD. Indexed: Math.R.

510 500   GW   ISSN 0371-327X
AS182   CODEN: SSWMAU
SAECHSISCHE AKADEMIE DER WISSENSCHAFTEN, LEIPZIG. MATHEMATISCH-NATURWISSENSCHAFTLICHE KLASSE. SITZUNGSBERICHTE. 1896. irreg., vol.121, 1989. price varies. Akademie-Verlag Berlin, Leipziger Str. 3-4, 1086 Berlin, Germany. TELEX 114420-AVERL-DD. Indexed: Bibl.& Ind.Geol.

500 600   JA   ISSN 0386-4324
SAIENSU. Japanese translation of: Scientific American (US ISSN 0036-8733) (Includes supplement: Bessatsu Saiensu (ISSN 0258-1008)) (Text and summaries in Japanese) 1971. m. 10440 Yen. Nikkei Science, Inc., 9-5 Ote-machi 1-chome, Chiyoda-ku, Tokyo 100, Japan. FAX 03-3293-2759. TELEX J22308-NIHONKEIZAI.

500   MY   ISSN 0126-6039
Q1   CODEN: SAMADP
SAINS MALAYSIANA: JERNAL SAINS ALAM SEMULA; jadi. (Text in English, Malay) 1972. q. $60. Penerbit Universiti Kebangsaan Malaysia, 43600 UKM Bangi Selangor, Malaysia. TEL 8250001. Ed. H.D. Tjia. charts; index; circ. 5,000. Indexed: Chem.Abstr, GeoRef.
Description: Explores earth sciences, physical and applied sciences and quantitative studies.

500 600   PK
SA'INSU. Back cover title: Monthly Science Magazine. (Text in Sindhi) 1971. m. Rs.8. University of Sind, Institute of Sindhology, Jamshoro, Hyderabad 6, Pakistan.

SAINT LOUIS UNIVERSITY RESEARCH JOURNAL; an interdisciplinary journal in the sciences and the humanities. see HUMANITIES: COMPREHENSIVE WORKS

SAITAMA DAIGAKU KIYO. KYOIKUGAKUBU. SUGAKU, SHIZEN KAGAKU/SAITAMA UNIVERSITY. JOURNAL: MATHEMATICS AND NATURAL SCIENCES. see MATHEMATICS

500   JA   ISSN 0581-3662
SAITAMA DAIGAKU KIYO. SHIZEN KAGAKU HEN/SAITAMA UNIVERSITY. JOURNAL. NATURAL SCIENCE. (Text in Japanese; summaries in English) 1965. a. Saitama Daigaku, Kyoyobu - Saitama University, College of Liberal Arts, 255 Shimo-Okubo, Urawa-shi, Saitama-ken 338, Japan. Indexed: INIS Atomind., Jap.Per.Ind.
—BLDSC shelfmark: 4869.050000.

500.9 069   JA   ISSN 0288-5611
SAITAMA-KENRITSU SHIZENSHI HAKUBUTSUKAN KENKYU HOKOKU/SAITAMA MUSEUM OF NATURAL HISTORY. BULLETIN. (Text and summaries in English and Japanese) 1983. a. Saitama-kenritsu Shizenshi Hakubutsukan - Saitama Museum of Natural History, 1417-1 Nagatoro, Nagatoro-machi, Chichibu-gun, Saitama-ken 369-13, Japan.

500.9   JA   ISSN 0375-1821
CODEN: SHMRBL
SAITO HO-ON KAI MUSEUM OF NATURAL HISTORY. RESEARCH BULLETIN. (Text in English) 1934. a. free. Saito Gratitude Foundation - Saito Ho-on Kai, 20-2, Hon-cho 2-chome, Aoba-ku, Sendai 980, Japan. TEL 022-262-5506. FAX 022-262-5508.

500   IS
SAMUEL NEAMAN INSTITUTE FOR ADVANCED STUDIES IN SCIENCE AND TECHNOLOGY. ANNUAL REPORT. (Text in English) 1978. a. Technion - Israel Institute of Technology, Samuel Neaman Institute for Advanced Studies in Science and Technology, Technion City, Haifa 32000, Israel.

500   US
▼SAN DIEGO SOCIETY OF NATURAL HISTORY. PROCEEDINGS. 1990. irreg. price varies. San Diego Society of Natural History, San Diego Natural History Museum Library, Box 1390, San Diego, CA 92112. TEL 619-232-3821. FAX 619-232-0248.
Description: Presents papers in the biological and geological sciences.

SAN JOSE STUDIES; San Jose State University's journal of the arts, humanities, sciences, business and technology. see HUMANITIES: COMPREHENSIVE WORKS

500   SZ
SANKT GALLISCHE NATURWISSENSCHAFTLICHE GESELLSCHAFT. BERICHTE. 1860. irreg., vol.84, 1989. $20. Sankt Gallische Naturwissenschaftliche Gesellschaft, Myrtenstr. 9, CH-9010 St. Gallen, Switzerland. Ed. Oskar Keller. circ. 1,000.
Formerly: Sankt Gallische Naturwissenschaftliche Gesellschaft. Bericht ueber die Taetigkeit (ISSN 0080-6056)

SANTA BARBARA MUSEUM OF NATURAL HISTORY. MUSEUM BULLETIN. see MUSEUMS AND ART GALLERIES

500   IT   ISSN 0036-4681
SAPERE. 1935; N.S. 1974. m. L.50000 (foreign L.75000)(effective 1992). Edizioni Dedalo s.r.l., Casella Postale 362, 70100 Bari, Italy. TEL 080-371555. FAX 080-371979. Dir. Carlo Bernadini. adv.; bk.rev.; bibl.; charts; illus.; tr.lit.; circ. 48,000.
Description: Deals with everything the public should know: energy, armaments, nutrition, medicine, didactics, environment, etc.

SAPPORO IKA DAIGAKU JINBUN SHIZEN KAGAKU KIYO/SAPPORO MEDICAL COLLEGE. JOURNAL OF LIBERAL ARTS AND SCIENCES. see HUMANITIES: COMPREHENSIVE WORKS

500   JA   ISSN 0914-2401
SAPPORO-SHI SEISHONEN KAGAKUKAN KIYO. 1984. a. free. Sapporo-shi Seishonen Kagakukan - Sapporo Science Center, 2-20 Atsubetsu chuo 1-jo 5-chome, Atsubetsu-ku, Sapporo-shi, Hokkaido 004, Japan. FAX 011-894-5445. circ. 1,000.

500   CN   ISSN 0080-6587
T177.C2
SASKATCHEWAN RESEARCH COUNCIL. ANNUAL REPORT. 1947. a. free. Saskatchewan Research Council, 15 Innovation Blvd., Saskatoon, Sask. S7N 2X8, Canada. TEL 306-664-5400. FAX 306-933-7446. TELEX SARECO-074-2484. Ed. John R. MacIntosh. circ. 200,000. Indexed: Bibl.& Ind.Geol.

700 500 390   GW   ISSN 0036-6153
DD491.S4
SCHLESIEN; arts, science, folklore. 1956. q. DM.30. (Verein der Freunde und Foerderer der Stiftung Kulturwerk Schlesien e.V.) Verlag Nuernberger Presse, Marienplatz 1, 8500 Nuernberg 1, Germany. TEL 0931-53696. Ed. Eberhard Guenter Schulz. bk.rev.; bibl.; illus.; circ. 1,100.
—BLDSC shelfmark: 8090.620000.

507   II   ISSN 0036-679X
SCHOOL SCIENCE; quarterly journal for secondary schools. (Text in English) 1962. q. Rs.12($11.60) National Council of Educational Research and Training, Department of Education in Science and Mathematics, Publication Department, Sri Aurbindo Marg, New Delhi 110016, India. Ed. R.P. Singhami. adv.; bk.rev.; index; circ. 1,000.

SCHOOL SCIENCE AND MATHEMATICS; journal for all science and mathematical teachers. see EDUCATION

507 370   UK   ISSN 0036-6811
Q1   CODEN: SSCRAD
SCHOOL SCIENCE REVIEW. 1919. 4/yr. £46. Association for Science Education, College Lane, Hatfield, Herts AL10 9AA, England. FAX 07072-66532. Ed. A.A. Bishop. adv.; bk.rev.; charts; illus.; cum.index: vols.48-57, 1967-1977; circ. 19,000. (also avail. in microform from UMI; reprint service avail. from UMI) Indexed: C.I.J.E., Chem.Abstr, Cont.Pg.Educ., Dairy Sci.Abstr., Educ.Tech.Abstr., Environ.Abstr., Excerp.Med., High.Educ.Curr.Aware.Bull., Stud.Wom.Abstr.
—BLDSC shelfmark: 8093.000000.

500.9   SZ   ISSN 0036-7427
SCHWEIZER NATURSCHUTZ/PROTECTION DE LA NATURE. (Text in French and German) 1935. bi-m. membership. Schweizerischer Bund fuer Naturschutz, CH-4020 Basel, Switzerland. FAX 061-3127447. Eds. Juerg Kaenzig, Serge Monbaron. adv.; bk.rev.; illus.; index; circ. 110,000. Indexed: Biol.Abstr.

500   SZ
SCHWEIZERISCHE NATURFORSCHENDE GESELLSCHAFT. DENKSCHRIFTEN. (Text in English, French and German) 1829. irreg. price varies. (Schweizerische Naturforschende Gesellschaft) Birkhaeuser Verlag, P.O. Box 133, CH-4010 Basel, Switzerland. TEL 061-737740. FAX 061-737950. TELEX 963475 BIRKH CH. Ed. H. Schaefer. Indexed: Bibl.& Ind.Geol., Biol.Abstr., Deep Sea Res.& Oceanogr.Abstr.

500   SZ
SCHWEIZERISCHER WISSENSCHAFTSRAT. JAHRESBERICHT/CONSEIL SUISSE DE LA SCIENCE. RAPPORT ANNUEL. (Text in French, German) 1965. a. free. Schweizerischer Wissenschaftsrat, Wildhainweg 9, Postfach 2732, CH-3001 Berne, Switzerland.

500   US   ISSN 0036-8075
Q1   CODEN: SCIEAS
SCIENCE. 1880. w. (4 vols. per year). $87 to individuals; institutions $150. American Association for the Advancement of Science, 1333 H St., N.W., Washington, DC 20005. TEL 202-326-6500. Ed. Daniel Koshland. adv.; bk.rev.; abstr.; bibl.; illus.; circ. 150,000. (also avail. in microform from UMI,MIM; reprint service avail. from UMI) Indexed: A.I.Abstr., A.S.& T.Ind., ABC, Abstr.Anthropol., Abstr.Bull.Inst.Pap.Chem., Abstr.J.Earthq.Eng., Acad.Ind., Acid Pre.Dig., AESIS, Anal.Abstr., Anim.Breed.Abstr., API Abstr., Art & Archaeol.Tech.Abstr., Biol.Abstr., Biol.Dig., Biostat., Biotech.Abstr., Bk.Rev.Dig., Bk.Rev.Ind. (1965-), Br.Archaeol.Abstr., C.I.J.E., Ceram.Abstr., Chem.Abstr., Chem.Infd., Child.Bk.Rev.Ind. (1965-), Child Devel.Abstr., Comput.Rev., Curr.Adv.Ecol.Sci., Curr.Biotech.Abstr., Curr.Cont., Curr.Lit.Fam.Plan., Cyb.Abstr., Dairy Sci.Abstr., Dent.Ind., Energy Rev., Environ.Abstr., Excerp.Med., Field Crop Abstr., Food Sci.& Tech.Abstr., Forest.Abstr., Forest Prod.Abstr., Fut.Surv., Gen.Sci.Ind., Geo.Abstr., Geotech.Abstr., Helminthol Abstr., High.Educ.Curr.Aware.Bull., Hort.Abstr., I D A, Ind.Chem., Ind.Med., Ind.Sci.Rev., Ind.Vet., Int.Aerosp.Abstr., Lab.Haz.Bull., Lang.& Lang.Behav.Abstr., M.L.A., Mag.Ind., Mass Spectr.Bull., Math.R., Med.Care Rev., Met.Abstr., Meteor.& Geoastrophys.Abstr., Mid.East: Abstr.& Ind., Nutr.Abstr., Ocean.Abstr., Peace Res.Abstr., Plant Grow.Reg.Abstr., PMR, Pollut.Abstr., Popul.Ind., Poult.Abstr., Protozool.Abstr., Psychol.Abstr., R.G., Rev.Plant Path., Risk Abstr., Rural Recreat.Tour.Abstr., Sci.Abstr., Sci.Cit.Ind., So.Pac.Per.Ind., Sociol.Abstr., Soils & Fert., Tel.Abstr., Telegen, Trop.Dis.Bull., Vet.Bull., W.R.C.Inf., Weed Abstr., World Alum.Abstr.
●Also available online. Vendor(s): BRS (SCIE).
—BLDSC shelfmark: 8130.000000.
Description: Scientific research journal.
Refereed Serial

500 001.3   UA
SCIENCE AND ARTS - RESEARCH STUDIES/ULUM WA FUNUN - DIRASAT WA BUHUTH. 1989. q. Helwan University, 95 Sharia Ahmed Ouraby, Mohandiseen, Cairo, Egypt. TEL 02-344055.

SCIENCES: COMPREHENSIVE WORKS

507 372   US   ISSN 0036-8148
LB1585
SCIENCE AND CHILDREN. 1963. 8/yr. $50. National Science Teachers Association, 1742 Connecticut Ave. N.W., Washington, DC 20009. TEL 202-328-5800. Ed. Phyllis R. Marcuccio. adv.; bk.rev.; charts; film rev.; illus.; index; circ. 24,000. (also avail. in microfilm from UMI; reprint service avail. from UMI) **Indexed:** C.I.J.E., Cont.Pg.Educ., Educ.Ind., Except.Child Educ.Abstr., Media Rev.Dig., Wom.Stud.Abstr.
—BLDSC shelfmark: 8131.800000.

500   II   ISSN 0036-8156
QH1   CODEN: SCINAL
SCIENCE AND CULTURE; a monthly journal of natural and cultural sciences. (Text in English) 1935. m. Rs.100($30) (foreign Rs.100). Indian Science News Association, 92 Acharya Prafulla Chandra Rd., Calcutta 700 009, India. TEL 35-2224. Ed.Bd. adv.; bk.rev.; charts; illus.; circ. 2,000. **Indexed:** Bibl.& Ind.Geol., Biol.Abstr., Chem.Abstr., Excerp.Med., Field Crop Abstr., Food Sci.& Tech.Abstr., Herb.Abstr., Hort.Abstr., Ind.Vet., Plant Breed.Abstr., Rev.Plant Path., Rice Abstr., Sci.Abstr., Soils & Fert., Vet.Bull., Weed Abstr.

500 600   UK   ISSN 0261-7005
Q180.G7
SCIENCE AND ENGINEERING RESEARCH COUNCIL. REPORT. 1965. a. price varies. Science and Engineering Research Council, Polaris House, North Star Ave., Swindon SN2 1ET, England. Ed. Geoffrey Moore. illus.; circ. 4,000.
—BLDSC shelfmark: 7602.472000.
Formerly: Great Britain. Science Research Council. Report (ISSN 0072-7148)

500   US   ISSN 0892-9882
UA12.5   CODEN: SGSEE8
SCIENCE AND GLOBAL SECURITY; the technical basis for arms control and environmental policy initiatives. 4/yr. (in 1 vol.; 4 nos./vol.). $48. Gordon & Breach Science Publishers, 270 Eighth Ave., New York, NY 10011. TEL 212-206-8900. FAX 212-645-2459. TELEX 236735 GOPUB UR. (Subscr. to: Box 786, Cooper Sta., New York, NY 10276. TEL 800-545-8398; UK subscr. to: P.O. Box 90, Reading, Berkshire RG1 8JL, England. TEL 0734-560-080) (also avail. in microform)
—BLDSC shelfmark: 8134.055000.
Refereed Serial

SCIENCE AND GLOBAL SECURITY MONOGRAPH SERIES. see POLITICAL SCIENCE — International Relations

500   US
SCIENCE AND ITS CONCEPTUAL FOUNDATIONS. 1985. irreg., latest 1986. price varies. University of Chicago Press, 5801 S. Ellis Ave., Chicago, IL 60637. TEL 312-702-7899. (Subscr. to: 11030 Langley Ave., Chicago, IL 60628) Ed. David L. Hull.
Refereed Serial

500   UK   ISSN 0268-490X
Q175.4
SCIENCE AND PUBLIC AFFAIRS. 1986. q. £20. Royal Society of London, 6 Carlton House Terrace, London SW1Y 5AG, England. TEL 071-839-5561. FAX 071-976-1837. TELEX 917876. Ed. Walter Bodmer. circ. 630.
—BLDSC shelfmark: 8134.178100.

500   UK   ISSN 0302-3427
Q179.9
SCIENCE AND PUBLIC POLICY. 1973. bi-m. £87($139) to institutions; Third World £64($102); individuals £253($40). (International Science Policy Foundation) Beech Tree Publishing, 10 Watford Close, Guildford, Surrey GU1 2EP, England. TEL 0483-67497. FAX 0483-67497. Ed. Maurice Goldsmith. adv.; bk.rev.; bibl.; charts; illus.; index. (back issues avail.) **Indexed:** Bibl.& Ind.Geol., Curr.Cont., Energy Ind., Energy Info.Abstr., Energy Rev., Environ.Abstr., Excerp.Med., Fuel & Energy Abstr., High.Educ.Curr.Aware.Bull., Lang.& Lang.Behav.Abstr., World Agri.Econ.& Rural Sociol.Abstr.
—BLDSC shelfmark: 8134.179000.
Former titles: Science Policy (ISSN 0048-9700) & Science Policy News.
Description: Impact of science and technology on public policy.

500 600   KO
SCIENCE AND TECHNOLOGY.* (Text in English, Korean; summaries in English) 1955. irreg. exchange basis. Korea University, College of Science and Engineering, 1 Anam-Dong, Seoul 132, S. Korea.
Formerly: Goryo Daehakgyo Nonmunjip Science.

500 025.2   US   ISSN 0080-746X
SCIENCE AND TECHNOLOGY (PITTSBURGH); a purchase guide for branch and public libraries. 1960. a. $10. Carnegie Library of Pittsburgh, Science and Technology Department, 4400 Forbes Ave., Pittsburgh, PA 15213-4080. TEL 412-622-3141. FAX 412-621-1267. circ. 500. (also avail. in microform from EDR)
Formerly (until 1963): Basic Collection of Science and Technology Books.
Description: Annotated bibliography of new books in science and technology of general interest to the non-specialist.

500 600   UK
SCIENCE AND TECHNOLOGY IN CHINA. 1984. triennial. £75. Longman Group UK Ltd., Westgate House, The High, Harlow, Essex CM20 1YR, England. TEL 0279-442601. Ed. Alan M. Anderson.

500 600   JA   ISSN 0286-0406
Q177.J3   CODEN: STJAE8
SCIENCE AND TECHNOLOGY IN JAPAN. (Text in English) 1982. q. 4720 Yen($60) Three 'I' Publications Ltd., Kamakara-cho Parking Bldg., 5-16 Uchi-Kanda 1-chome, Chiyoda-ku, Tokyo 101, Japan. TEL 03-3291-3761. FAX 03-3291-3764. (Subscr. to: Maruzen Co. Ltd., Box 5050, Tokyo International 100-31, Japan) Ed. Miyakawa Yasuhiro. adv.; circ. 10,320. (back issues avail.) **Indexed:** CAD CAM Abstr., Energy Info.Abstr., JTA, Telegen.
—BLDSC shelfmark: 8134.260000.

500 600   UK
SCIENCE AND TECHNOLOGY IN JAPAN. 1984. triennial. £58($110) Longman Group UK Ltd., Westgate House, The High, Harlow, Essex CM20 1YR, England. TEL 0279-442601. Ed. Alan M. Anderson.

500 600   UK
SCIENCE AND TECHNOLOGY IN LATIN AMERICA. triennial. £75. Longman Group UK Ltd., Westagte House, The High, Harlow, Essex CM20 1YR, England. TEL 0279-442601.

500 600   UK
SCIENCE AND TECHNOLOGY IN THE MIDDLE EAST. 1982. triennial. £75. Longman Group UK Ltd., Westgate House, The Highl, Harlow, Essex CM20 1YR, England. TEL 0279-442601.

500   UK   ISSN 0952-9616
SCIENCE AND TECHNOLOGY POLICY. 1988. bi-m. £95 (foreign £103). Science Reference & Information Service, 25 Southampton Bldgs., London WC2A 1AW, England. FAX 071-323-79. TELEX 266959. (Dist. by: British Library, Publications Sales Unit, Boston Spa, Wetherby, W. Yorkshire LS23 7BQ, England. TEL 0937-546077) Ed. Mrs. Lesley Grayson. adv. contact: V. McBurney. bk.rev.
—BLDSC shelfmark: 8134.280820.
Description: Monitors the happenings in UK science policy.

500 320   UK   ISSN 0950-5431
SCIENCE AS CULTURE. 1974. 4/yr. £20($35) to individuals; institutions £40($65). Free Association Books, 26 Freegrove Rd., London N7, England. (And: Guilford Publications, Inc., 72 Spring St., 4th Fl., New York, NY 10012) (Co-publisher: Guilford Publications, Inc.) Ed.Bd. adv.; bk.rev.; circ. 750. **Indexed:** Alt.Press Ind., Curr.Cont., Lang.& Lang.Behav.Abstr., Left Ind. (1987-), Sociol.Abstr.
—BLDSC shelfmark: 8142.250000.
Former titles (until 1987): Radical Science Series; (until 1974): Radical Science Journal (ISSN 0305-0963)
Description: Explores all the ways in which science, technology and medicine are involved in shaping society's values and priorities.

500   CH
SCIENCE BULLETIN. m. free. National Science Council of the Republic of China, 106 Ho-ping E. Rd. Sec. 2, Taipei, Taiwan 106, Republic of China. **Indexed:** Bibl.& Ind.Geol.

500   UK   ISSN 0300-3361
SCIENCE CHELSEA. 1965. irreg., vol.8, 1979. £0.50($1.50) Chelsea College, Students Union, Manresa Rd., London SW3 6LX, England. Ed. P. Ansell. adv.; bk.rev.; bibl.; charts; illus.; index; circ. 1,000.

500   PR   ISSN 0164-7741
SCIENCE - CIENCIA; boletin cientifico del Sur. (Text in English, Spanish) 1973. q. free to qualified personnel. Fundacion Sala, Inc., P.O. Box 1786, Ponce, PR 00733. TEL 848-4191. Ed. Luis F. Sala. bk.rev.; charts; illus.; stat.; circ. 1,000.

500   US   ISSN 0161-3170
     CODEN: SJCREM
SCIENCE CITATION INDEX JOURNAL CITATION REPORT. Short title: S C I - J C R. (Not avail. in printed format. Includes Journal Ranking, Reference Data, and Source Data Packages) 1975. a. $495. Institute for Scientific Information, 3501 Market St., Philadelphia, PA 19104. TEL 215-386-0100.
FAX 215-386-2991. (And: 132 High St., Uxbridge, Middlesex, UB8 1DP, England) (microfiche)
Formerly: I S I Journal Citation Reports.
Description: Provides citation data to reveal the relationship between journals in the sciences.

500 300   PH   ISSN 0115-7809
SCIENCE DILIMAN. (Text in English and Filipino) 1980. a. P.45($10) University of the Philippines, Office of Research Coordination, Rm. 309 Malcolm Hall, Diliman, Quezon City, Philippines. Ed. Bienvenido T. Miranda. circ. 750. (back issues avail.) **Indexed:** Ind.Phil.Per.

507   US   ISSN 0036-8326
     CODEN: SEDUAV
SCIENCE EDUCATION. 1916. bi-m. $165 (foreign $240). John Wiley & Sons, Inc., Journals, 605 Third Ave., New York, NY 10158-0012. TEL 212-692-6000. Ed. Leopold E. Klopfer. adv.; charts; illus.; stat.; index; circ. 2,045. (also avail. in microform from RPI; back issues avail.; reprint service avail. from RPI) **Indexed:** C.I.J.E., Cont.Pg.Educ., Curr.Cont., Educ.Ind., Res.High.Educ.Abstr., SSCI.
—BLDSC shelfmark: 8142.800000.
Description: Examines the latest practices, issues and trends occuring both in America and abroad in science instruction, learning, and preparation of science teachers.
Refereed Serial

SCIENCE EDUCATION IN ZAMBIA. see EDUCATION

SCIENCE EDUCATION NEWS. see EDUCATION — Teaching Methods And Curriculum

500   BE   ISSN 0773-3429
SCIENCE ET CULTURE. 1954. bi-m. 300 Fr. Institut de Physique, B-5 Sart Tilman, 4000 Liege, Belgium. Ed. Roger Moreau. adv. **Indexed:** Chem.Abstr.
Formerly: T.V. (ISSN 0041-4476)

500.9   FR   ISSN 0036-8342
SCIENCE ET NATURE. bi-m. 20 F. Societe des Amis du Museum National d'Histoire Naturelle, 12 bis, Place Henri Bergson, 75008 Paris, France. Ed. Andre Manoury. adv.; charts; illus.; maps; index; circ. 10,000. **Indexed:** Biol.Abstr.
Description: Covers all areas of science and nature.

500   FR   ISSN 0036-8369
SCIENCE ET VIE; magazine of popular science. 1913. 12/yr. 242 F. (foreign 303 F.)(effective 1992). Excelsior Publications, 1 rue du Colonel Pierre Avia, 75503 Paris Cedex 15, France. TEL 46-48-48-48. FAX 46-48-48-09. TELEX 631 994 F. Ed. Philippe Cousin. adv. contact: Gilles de Keranflech. bk.rev.; illus.; circ. 364,855. (back issues avail.) **Indexed:** Biol.Abstr., Pt.de Rep. (1979-).

500 028.5   FR   ISSN 0992-5899
SCIENCE ET VIE JUNIOR. 1989. 11/yr. 223 F. (foreign 279 F.)(effective 1992). Excelsior Publications, 1 rue du Colonel Pierre Avia, 75503 Paris Cedex 15, France. TEL 46-48-48-48. FAX 46-48-48-09. TELEX 631 994 F. Ed. Sven Ortoli. adv. contact: Gilles de Keranflech. circ. 183,012. **Indexed:** Pt.de Rep. (1991-).
Description: Explores scientific and technical progress.

SCIENCES: COMPREHENSIVE WORKS

500 US ISSN 0048-9662
Q175.52.U5
SCIENCE FOR THE PEOPLE.* 1968. bi-m. $15 to individuals; institutions $24. Science Resource Center, Inc., Box 364, Somerville, MA 02143-0005. TEL 617-547-3580. Ed. Seth Shulman. adv.; bk.rev.; bibl.; illus.; circ. 5,000. (also avail. in microfilm; back issues avail.; reprint service avail. from UMI) **Indexed:** Alt.Press Ind., CAD CAM Abstr., Energy Info.Abstr., Environ.Abstr., Environ.Ind., Left Ind. (1982-1989), Telegen.
—BLDSC shelfmark: 8150.671000.
Description: Contains articles concerned with the effects of scientific innovations on humans. Features topics such as nutrition, health, nuclear technology and workplace safety.

500 US
SCIENCE FRONTIERS. 1977. bi-m. $7. Sourcebook Project, Box 107, Glen Arm, MD 21057. TEL 301-668-6047. Ed. William R. Corliss. adv.; bk.rev.; circ. 1,500. (back issues avail.)
Description: Digest of articles dealing with scientific anomalies and appearing in the current literature.

500 610 US ISSN 0897-8581
Q162
SCIENCE ILLUSTRATED. 1987. bi-m. $15. Science Illustrated, L.P., 8428 Holly Leaf Dr., McLean, VA 22102. TEL 703-356-1688. FAX 703-356-1688. Ed. Jane Alexander. adv.; bk.rev.; circ. 103,000. (back issues avail.)

500 CC ISSN 1001-6511
QA1 CODEN: SCASEY
SCIENCE IN CHINA. SERIES A: MATHEMATICS, PHYSICS, ASTRONOMY & TECHNOLOGICAL SCIENCES. Chinese edition: Zhongguo Kexue A (ISSN 1000-3126) (Text in English) 1952. m. £245 (with Series B: £390)(effective 1992). Science Press, Marketing and Sales Department, 16 Donghuangchenggen Beijie, Beijing 100707, People's Republic of China. TEL 4010642. FAX 4012180. TELEX 210247-SPBJ-CN. (US office: Science Press New York, Ltd., 63-117 Alderton St., Rego Park, NY 11374; Dist. overseas by: Pergamon Press plc, Headington Hill Hall, Oxford OX3 0BW, England. TEL 0865-794141) Ed.Bd. adv.; index; circ. 10,000. (back issues avail.) **Indexed:** Cadscan, Lead Abstr., Zincscan.
—BLDSC shelfmark: 8141.660000.
Formerly (until 1989): Scientia Sinica. Series A: Mathematics, Physics, Astronomy and Technological Sciences (ISSN 0253-5831)
Description: Covers mathematics, physics, astronomy, and technology. Contains mainly academic papers on scientific work.
Refereed Serial

500 CC ISSN 1001-652X
QA1 CODEN: SCBSE5
SCIENCE IN CHINA. SERIES B: CHEMISTRY, LIFE SCIENCES & EARTH SCIENCES. Chinese edition: Zhongguo Kexue B (ISSN 1000-3134) (Text in English) 1952. m. £245 (with Series A: £390)(effective 1992). Science Press, Marketing and Sales Department, 16 Donghuangchenggen Beijie, Beijing 100707, People's Republic of China. TEL 4010642. FAX 4012180. TELEX 210247-SPBJ-CN. (Dist. overseas by: Pergamon Press plc, Headington Hill Hall, Oxford OX3 0BW, England. TEL 0865-794141; And: 660 White Plains Rd., Tarrytown, NY 10591-5153. TEL 914-524-9200) Ed.Bd. adv.; index; circ. 10,000. (also avail. in microform; back issues avail.; reprint service avail. from KTO) **Indexed:** Cadscan, Lead Abstr., Triticale Abstr., Zincscan.
Formerly (until 1989): Scientia Sinica. Series B: Chemistry, Life Sciences and Earth Sciences (ISSN 0253-5823); Supersedes in part: Scientia Sinica.
Description: Covers chemistry, biology, earth science, medical science, and agronomy. Contains mainly academic papers on scientific work.
Refereed Serial

500 UK ISSN 0269-8897
Q175.4 CODEN: SCCOEW
SCIENCE IN CONTEXT. s-a. $42 to individuals; institutions $75. Cambridge University Press, Edinburgh Bldg., Shaftesbury Rd., Cambridge CB2 2RU, England. TEL 0223-312393. FAX 0223-315052. TELEX 851817256. (North American addr.: Cambridge University Press, 40 W. 20th St., New York, NY 10011) Ed. G. Freudenthal.
—BLDSC shelfmark: 8141.820000.
Description: Studies the history, philosophy, sociology and epistemology of science.

500 PP ISSN 0310-4303
SCIENCE IN NEW GUINEA. 1949. 3/yr. K.11.50. University of Papua New Guinea, Faculty of Science, Box 320, University P.O., Papua New Guinea. FAX 267-187. TELEX NE 22366. Ed. K. Singh. bk.rev.; circ. 400. **Indexed:** Bibl.& Ind.Geol., Biol.Abstr, Chem.Abstr., Food Sci.& Tech.Abstr., Geo.Abstr., Mineral.Abstr., Nutr.Abstr., Soils & Fert.
—BLDSC shelfmark: 8149.900000.
Supersedes (after 1972): Papua New Guinea Scientific Society. Annual Report and Proceedings (ISSN 0085-4697)
Description: Covers scientific research, the teaching of science and the social implications of science in New Guinea.

500 II ISSN 0036-8407
SCIENCE IN PARLIAMENT. (Text in English) 1965. q. Rs.5. Indian Parliamentary and Scientific Committee, 2 Telegraph Lane, New Delhi 1, India. Ed. Krishan Kant. adv.; bk.rev.

500 US
▼**SCIENCE LEADERSHIP TREND NOTES.** 1990. 6/yr. (Sep.-May). $12. National Science Supervisors Association, Box AL, Amagansett, NY 11930. TEL 516-267-3692. FAX 516-267-8621. Ed. Joseph Maurer. adv.; circ. 1,000. (tabloid format; back issues avail.)

500 US
SCIENCE MUSEUM OF MINNESOTA. MONOGRAPH. 1972. irreg. Science Museum of Minnesota, 30 E. 10th St., St. Paul, MN 55101. TEL 612-221-9488. Ed. Bruce R. Erickson. **Indexed:** Bibl.& Ind.Geol., Biol.Abstr.

500 US ISSN 0161-4452
Q11 CODEN: SCSPBA
SCIENCE MUSEUM OF MINNESOTA. SCIENTIFIC PUBLICATIONS, NEW SERIES. 1966. irreg. $0.55. Science Museum of Minnesota, 30 E. 10th St., St. Paul, MN 55101. TEL 612-221-9488. Ed. Bruce R. Erickson. **Indexed:** Bibl.& Ind.Geol., Biol.Abstr. Key Title: Scientific Publications of the Science Museum of Minnesota.
Supersedes: Science Museum of Minnesota. Scientific Bulletin; Formerly: Science Museum of Minnesota. Scientific Publications (ISSN 0080-5521)

500 SZ
SCIENCE NETWORKS HISTORICAL STUDIES. irreg. Birkhaeuser Verlag, P.O. Box 133, CH-4010 Basel, Switzerland. TEL 061-227400. FAX 061-227666. TELEX 963475-BIRKH-CH.

500 US ISSN 0036-8423
Q1 CODEN: SCNEBK
SCIENCE NEWS; the weekly news magazine of science. 1921. w. $39.50. Science Service, Inc., 1719 N St., N.W., Washington, DC 20036. TEL 202-785-2255. (Subscr. to: 231 W. Center St., Box 1925, Marion, OH 43305. TEL 800-347-6969) Ed. Patrick Young. adv.; bk.rev.; illus.; index; circ. 225,000. (also avail. in microform from UMI,MIM; reprint service avail. from UMI) **Indexed:** A.I.Abstr., Abr.R.G., Acad.Ind., Acid Rain Abstr., Acid Rain Ind., ASCA, Bibl.& Ind.Geol., Biol.Dig., BPIA, C.I.J.E., CAD CAM Abstr., Chem.Abstr., Deep Sea Res.& Oceanogr.Abstr., Energy Rev., Eng.Ind, Environ.Abstr., Environ.Ind., Gard.Lit. (1992-), Gen.Sci.Ind., Hlth.Ind., Jun.High.Mag.Abstr., Mag.Ind., Ocean.Abstr., Pollut.Abstr., PROMT, R.G., Telegen, TOM.
—BLDSC shelfmark: 8150.010000.
Former titles (until 1966): Science News Letter; Science News Bulletin.
Description: Covers research and development in all areas of science.

371.3 500 JM
SCIENCE NOTES AND NEWS. irreg. Association of Science Teachers of Jamaica, c/o Honorary Secretary, Olive Baxter, 46 Paddington Terrace, Kingston 6, Jamaica, W.I.

500 FR ISSN 0080-7540
SCIENCE NOUVELLE.* No.8, 1970. irreg. price varies. Editions R. Laffont, 6 Place Saint-Sulpice, 75006 Paris, France.
Formerly (until 1970): Jeune Science.

SCIENCE OF SCIENCE; an international journal of studies on scientific reasoning and scientific enterprise. *see PHILOSOPHY*

500 UN ISSN 0080-7591
SCIENCE POLICY STUDIES AND DOCUMENTS. (Text in English or French) 1965. irreg., latest no.71, 1991. price varies. Unesco, 7-9 Place de Fontenoy, 75700 Paris, France. TEL 577-16-10. (Dist. in U.S. by: Unipub, 4611-F Assembly Dr., Lanham, MD 20706-4391)

500 US ISSN 1049-7730
Q162
▼**SCIENCE PROBE!.** 1990. q. $11.95. Science Probe Inc., 500B Bi-County Blvd., Farmingdale, NY 11735. TEL 516-293-0467. FAX 516-293-3115. Ed. Forrest M. Mims III. circ. 150,000. (reprint service avail. from UMI) **Indexed:** Ind.How To Do It (1990-).
Description: Articles by and for amateur scientists, covering all areas of science; includes do-it-yourself projects and feature stories.

500 UK ISSN 0036-8504
Q1 CODEN: SCPRAY
SCIENCE PROGRESS; a review journal of current scientific advance. 1894. q. £62.50 (foreign £70). Blackwell Scientific Publications Ltd., Osney Mead, Oxford OX2 0EL, England. TEL 0865-240201. FAX 0865-721205. TELEX 83355-MEDBOK-G. Ed.Bd. adv.; bk.rev.; index; circ. 900. (also avail. in microform from MIM,UMI; back issues avail.; reprint service avail. from ISI,UMI) **Indexed:** Agri.Eng.Abstr., Anim.Breed.Abstr., ASCA, Bibl.& Ind.Geol., Biol.Abstr., Br.Tech.Ind., Chem.Abstr., Curr.Adv.Ecol.Sci., Curr.Cont., Field Crop Abstr., Herb.Abstr., Ind.Med., Ind.Vet., Mass Spectr.Bull., Plant Breed.Abstr., Rev.Plant Path., Sci.Abstr., Sci.Cit.Ind, Vet.Bull.
—BLDSC shelfmark: 8151.000000.

500 370 US ISSN 0887-2376
LB1585.3
SCIENCE SCOPE; a journal for middle-junior high science teachers. 1978. 8/yr. $50. National Science Teachers Association, 1742 Connecticut Ave., N.W., Washington, DC 20009. TEL 202-328-5800. Ed. Crystal Lal. adv.; bk.rev.; charts; illus.; tr.lit.; index; circ. 12,000. (also avail. in microform; back issues avail.)
—BLDSC shelfmark: 8164.237000.
Description: Covers teacher-developed activities for use in the science classroom as well as all disciplines.

500 TH ISSN 0303-8122
Q80.T5 CODEN: VKSTDB
SCIENCE SOCIETY OF THAILAND. JOURNAL. 1975. q. $30. Science Society of Thailand, Faculty of Science, Chulalongkorn University, Bangkok, Thailand. Ed. I-Ming Tang. index; circ. 1,000. (back issues avail.) **Indexed:** AIT Reports, Biol.Abstr., Chem.Abstr., Curr.Adv.Ecol.Sci., Dairy Sci.Abstr., Phys.Abstr., Rice Abstr., Sci.Abstr., Sci.Cit.Ind., Soils & Fert.

500 600 FI ISSN 0786-3012
SCIENCE STUDIES; a Scandinavian journal. (Text in English) 1988. 2/yr. FIM 120 to individuals; institutions FIM 160. Finnish Society for Science Studies, c/o Eva Heiskanen, Riihenkulma 3E25, 00700 Helsinki, Finland. (Subscr. to: Seppo Raiski, Department of Sociology, University of Tampere, PL 607, 33101 Tampere, Finland) Ed. Marja Alestalo. bk.rev.; circ. 300.
Description: Presents a forum for international, particularly Scandinavian contributors in the field of science and technology studies. The subject area ranges from history and philosophy of science to social studies of science and technology.

507 370 US ISSN 0036-8555
Q181
THE SCIENCE TEACHER. 1934. 9/yr. $50. National Science Teachers Association, 1742 Connecticut Ave N.W., Washington, DC 20009. TEL 202-328-5800. Ed. Juliana Texley. adv.; bk.rev.; charts; film rev.; illus.; index; circ. 26,000. (microfilm; also avail. in microfilm from UMI; reprint service avail. from UMI) **Indexed:** Acad.Ind., Biol.Dig., C.I.J.E., Cont.Pg.Educ., Educ.Ind., Media Rev.Dig.
—BLDSC shelfmark: 8164.750000.

500 II ISSN 0378-8717
SCIENCE TEACHER/VIGYAN SHIKSHAK. 1950. q. $25. All India Science Teachers' Association, Sardar Patel Vidyalaya, Lodi Estate, Road No. 3, New Delhi 110003, India. Ed. R.K. Mohta. adv.; bk.rev.; circ. 1,000.

SCIENCES: COMPREHENSIVE WORKS 4341

500   AT
SCIENCE TEACHERS ASSOCIATION OF QUEENSLAND. NEWSLETTER. 1961. 4/yr. Aus.$2 per no. Science Teachers Association of Queensland, Queensland Department of Education, P.O. Box 33, North Quay, Brisbane, Qld. 4000, Australia. Ed. Bob McAllister. adv.; bk.rev.; circ. 700.

170 600   US   ISSN 0162-2439
Q175.4
SCIENCE, TECHNOLOGY & HUMAN VALUES. 1972. q. $46 to individuals; institutions $100. Sage Publications, Inc., 2455 Teller Rd., Newbury Park, CA 91320. TEL 805-499-0721. FAX 805-499-0871. Ed. Susan E. Cozzens. bibl.; index; circ. 1,500. (also avail. in microform from RPI; back issues avail.; reprint service avail. from RPI) **Indexed:** ASCA, Curr.Cont., Lang.& Lang.Behav.Abstr., P.A.I.S., Phil.Ind., SSCI, Telegen.
—BLDSC shelfmark: 8164.850000.
    Former titles (until 1978): Newsletter on Science, Technology, and Human Values; Harvard University. Program of Public Conceptions of Science. Newsletter.
    Description: International and multidisciplinary approach to the study of science and technology, including their involvement in politics, society, and culture.

500   II   ISSN 0036-858X
Q1   CODEN: SCTYB8
SCIENCE TODAY; presenting the future perfect. (Text in English) 1966. m. Rs.120($25) Bennett, Coleman & Co. Ltd. (Bombay), Times Bldg., Dr. D.N. Rd., P.O. Box 213, Bombay 400 001, India. TEL 4150271. (U.S. subscr. address: M/s. Kalpana, 42-75 Main St., Flushing, NY 11355) Ed. Mukul Sharma. adv.; bk.rev.; charts; illus.; index; circ. 78,586. (also avail. in microform)

500   US   ISSN 1047-8043
                      CODEN: SCWAEM
▼**SCIENCE WATCH.** 1990. m. $295. Institute for Scientific Information, 3501 Market St., Philadelphia, PA 19104. TEL 215-386-0100. FAX 215-386-2991. (And: 132 High St., Uxbridge, Middlesex, UB8 1DP, England) Ed. David A. Pendlebury.
—BLDSC shelfmark: 8165.079000.
    Description: Tracks trends and developments in scientific research. Evaluates the research activities and performance of countries, universities, industrial firms, private and government labs, and other organizations.

500   US   ISSN 0043-0749
SCIENCE TRENDS. 1958. s-m. $560. Trends Publishing Inc., National Press Bldg., Washington, DC 20045. TEL 202-393-0031. FAX 202-392-1732. Ed. Arthur Kranish. bk.rev.; abstr.; charts; pat.; stat.; tr.lit. (looseleaf format; also avail. in microform from UMI; reprint service avail. from UMI)
    Formerly: Washington Science Trends.
    Description: Reports on developments in general science, education and research, and development.

SCIENCE WEEKLY. see *CHILDREN AND YOUTH — For*

500   US   ISSN 0036-8601
SCIENCE WORLD. 1959. 18/yr. (Sep.-May). $6.95. Scholastic Inc., 730 Broadway, New York, NY 10003. TEL 800-325-6149. Ed. Bonnie Price. adv.; bk.rev.; charts; illus.; tr.lit.; index; circ. 550,000. (also avail. in microform from UMI,MIM; reprint service avail. from UMI) **Indexed:** Ind.Child.Mag.
    Formerly: Senior Science and Science World.

SCIENCE YEAR. see *ENCYCLOPEDIAS AND GENERAL ALMANACS*

SCIENCELAND; to nurture scientific thinking. see *CHILDREN AND YOUTH — For*

500   JA
SCIENCEPEDIA/SAIENSUPEDIA. (Text in Japanese) 1982. 2/yr. Obunsha Publishing Co., Ltd., 55 Yokodera-cho, Shinjuku-ku, Tokyo 162, Japan.

500   US   ISSN 0036-861X
Q1   CODEN: SCNCAD
SCIENCES. 1961. 6/yr. $14.50. New York Academy of Sciences, 2 E. 63rd St., New York, NY 10021. Ed. Peter Brown. adv.; bk.rev.; illus.; index; circ. 75,000. (also avail. in microform from UMI,MIM; reprint service avail. from UMI) **Indexed:** Abstr.Anthropol., Access (1976-), Bibl.Agri., Biol.Abstr., Biol.Dig., Curr.Adv.Ecol.Sci., Curr.Pack.Abstr., Deep Sea Res.& Oceanogr.Abstr., Fut.Surv., Gard.Lit. (1992-), Gen.Sci.Ind., Helminthol.Abstr., Lang.& Lang.Behav.Abstr., Risk Abstr.
—BLDSC shelfmark: 8165.550000.
    Description: Contains a wide selection of articles on scientific subjects. Topics covered include space technology, environmental science, agriculture, electronics and computer sciences.
    Refereed Serial

500   FR   ISSN 0987-0717
SCIENCES & NATURE; le magazine qui s'aventure. 1983. m. 269 F. (foreign 359 F.). Winning Nature, 16 Place du Havre, 75009 Paris, France. TEL 42-85-06-58. FAX 40-16-02-60. Ed. Michel Dominik. adv.; bk.rev.; circ. 65,000.
    Formerly: Argonaute: Le Magazine de la Decouverte.
    Description: Covers intriguing scientific events and developments with a general, non-technical approach. Features interviews with important figures, and reports of current or recent natural phenomena.

500   FR   ISSN 0036-8636
Q2
SCIENCES ET AVENIR; revue de grande information scientifique. 1947. m. 375 F. 38 rue Greneta, 75002 Paris, France. FAX 1-42-33-35-23. Ed. Paul Ceuzin. adv.; bk.rev.; illus.; circ. 186,767. **Indexed:** Curr.Adv.Ecol.Sci., Excerp.Med., Geo.Abstr., Pt.de Rep. (1979-).
—BLDSC shelfmark: 8165.850000.
    Description: Articles covering all areas of science in a general sense: Environmental issues, technology, space explorations, medicine, etc. with an insight into future implications.

500   CL   ISSN 0036-8679
Q4   CODEN: SCNTAU
SCIENTIA; revista cientifica y tecnologica. (Text in Spanish; summaries in English) 1934. 2/yr. $10. Universidad Tecnica Federico Santa Maria, Casilla 110-V, Valparaiso, Chile. Ed. Carlos Gonzalez. charts; illus.; cum.index: 1934-1958; 1959-1968; circ. 2,000. **Indexed:** ASCA, Bibl.& Ind.Geol., Chem.Abstr., Math.R., Sci.Abstr.

500   US   ISSN 0036-8733
T1   CODEN: SCAMAC
SCIENTIFIC AMERICAN. Chinese translation: Ke Xue. Japanese translation: Saiensu (ISSN 0386-4324); Russian translation: V Mire Nauki (ISSN 0208-0621) 1845. m. $36. Scientific American, Inc., 415 Madison Ave., New York, NY 10017. TEL 212-754-0550. Ed. Jonathan Piel. adv.; bk.rev.; illus.; index, cum.index: 1948-1988; circ. 626,917. (also avail. in microform from UMI,MIM,KTO; back issues avail.) **Indexed:** A.I.Abstr., A.S.& T.Ind., Abstr.Anthropol., Abstr.Bull.Inst.Pap.Chem., Acad.Ind., Acid Pre.Dig., Amer.Bibl.Slavic & E.Eur.Stud., Appl.Mech.Rev., ASCA, Bibl.Dev.Med.& Child Neur., Biol.Abstr., Biol.Dig., Biostat., Bk.Rev.Dig., Bk.Rev.Ind. (1965-), BMT, Br.Archaeol.Abstr., Br.Rail.Bd., C.I.J.E., CAD CAM Abstr., Cadscan, Chem.Abstr., Child.Bk.Rev.Ind. (1965-), CINAHL, CMI, Comput.Lit.Ind., Curr.Adv.Ecol.Sci., Curr.Biotech.Abstr., Curr.Cont., Curr.Lit.Fam.Plan., Deep Sea Res.& Oceanogr.Abstr., Dent.Abstr., Energy Info.Abstr., Environ.Abstr., Environ.Ind., Excerp.Med., Field Crop Abstr., Fluidex, Fut.Surv., Gard.Lit. (1992-), Gas Abstr., Gdlns., Gen.Sci.Ind., Geo.Abstr., Graph.Arts Lit.Abstr., Helminthol.Abstr., Herb.Abstr., High.Educ.Curr.Aware.Bull., Ind.How To Do It (1963-), Ind.Med., Int.Aerosp.Abstr., Int.Packag.Abstr., Lang.& Lang.Behav.Abstr., Lead Abstr., Mag.Ind., Mass Spectr.Bull., Math.R., Med.Care Rev., Met.Abstr., Meteor.& Geoastrophys.Abstr., Mgmt.& Market.Abstr., Mid.East: Abstr.& Ind., NAA, Numis.Lit., Ocean.Abstr., Oper.Res.Manage.Sci., Peace Res.Abstr., Pers.Lit., Petrol.Abstr., Plant.Breed.Abstr., PMR, Pollut.Abstr., PROMT, Psychol.Abstr., Qual.Contr.Appl.Stat., R.G., Robomat, Rural Recreat.Tour.Abstr., Sage Urb.Stud.Abstr., Sci.Abstr., Sh.& Vib.Dig., So.Pac.Per.Ind., Telegen, Trop.Dis.Bull., Weed Abstr., World Alum.Abstr., Zincscan.
● Also available online. Vendor(s): BRS (SAMM).
—BLDSC shelfmark: 8175.000000.
    Description: Comprehensive collection of articles on a variety of scientific topics. Regular features include author biographies, historical news and a "how-to" section for amateur scientists.
    Refereed Serial

500 600   JA
SCIENTIFIC AND TECHNICAL INFORMATION IN FOREIGN COUNTRIES/KAIGAKI KAGAKU GIJUTSU JOHO SHIRYO. (Text in Japanese) irreg. Kagaku Gijutsu-cho, Keikaku-kyoku - Science and Technology Agency, Planning Bureau, 2-1 Kasumigaseki 2-chome, Chiyoda-ku, Tokyo 100, Japan.

500 600   CN   ISSN 0586-7746
AS40
SCIENTIFIC AND TECHNICAL SOCIETIES OF CANADA/SOCIETES SCIENTIFIQUES ET TECHNIQUES DU CANADA. 1968. biennial. Can.$26. (National Research Council of Canada) C.I.S.T.I. Publicity and Communications, Ottawa, Ont. K1A 0S2, Canada. TEL 613-993-3854. FAX 613-952-9112. circ. 675.

500   LY
SCIENTIFIC BULLETIN. m. Jamahiriya News Agency, Sharia al-Fateh, P.O. Box 2303, Tripoli, Libya. TEL 37106. TELEX 20841.

500   SJ
SCIENTIFIC INFORMATION BULLETIN. (Text in English) 1977. m. Industrial Research and Consultancy Institute, Department of Documentation and Technical Information, Box 268, Khartoum, Sudan.

SCIENTIFIC MEETINGS. see *MEETINGS AND CONGRESSES*

500   II
SCIENTIFIC OPINION. (Text in English) 1972. q. individuals Rs.10($10); institutions Rs.15($15). Narender K. Sehgal, Ed. & Pub., 465-R Model Town, Jullundur 144003, Punjab, India. adv.; bk.rev.; cum.index every 2 yrs.

500   UK   ISSN 0036-8857
Q1
SCIENTIFIC WORLD. (Editions in English, French and Russian) 1957. q. £10. World Federation of Scientific Workers, 27 Barnfield Ave., Shirley, Croydon, Surrey CR0 8SF, England. Ed. Chris Birch. adv.; bk.rev.; charts; illus.; index; circ. 30,000. **Indexed:** Biol.Dig.
—BLDSC shelfmark: 8204.400000.

SCIENCES: COMPREHENSIVE WORKS

500   US   ISSN 0890-3670
Q1
THE SCIENTIST; the newspaper for science professionals. 1986. 24/yr. $58 (foreign $79). The Scientist, Inc., 3501 Market St., Philadelphia, PA 19104-3302. TEL 215-386-0100. FAX 215-387-7542. (Subscr. to: The Scientist, 5615 W. Cermak Rd., Cicero, IL 60650) Ed. Eugene Garfield. adv.; bk.rev.; circ. 40,000. (newspaper; also avail. in microfilm from UMI) **Indexed:** Curr.Cont., Environ.Abstr., Tel.Abstr., Telegen.
—BLDSC shelfmark: 8205.010000.
Description: News and commentary on business, policy and politics of science.

500   NE   ISSN 0138-9130
Q1   CODEN: SCNTDX
SCIENTOMETRICS; an international journal for all quantitative aspects of the science of science, communication in science and science policy. (Text in English) 1979. 9/yr.(in 3 vols.; 3 nos./vol.). fl.879 (effective 1992). Elsevier Science Publishers B.V., P.O. Box 211, 1000 AE Amsterdam, Netherlands. TEL 020-5803911. FAX 020-5803598. TELEX 18582 ESPA NL. (Subscr. in U.S. and Canada to: Elsevier Science Publishing Co., Inc., Box 882, Madison Sq. Sta., New York, NY 10159. TEL 212-989-5800) (Co-publisher: Akademiai Kiado, HU) Ed. T. Braun. adv.; bk.rev.; bibl. (also avail. in microform from RPI; back issues avail.) **Indexed:** ASCA, Biol.Abstr., Compumath, Curr.Adv.Ecol.Sci., Curr.Cont., Lang.& Lang.Behav.Abstr., Lang.Teach.& Ling.Abstr., Sci.Abstr., Sociol.Abstr., SSCI.
—BLDSC shelfmark: 8205.080000.
Incorporates (in 1982): Journal of Research Communication Studies (ISSN 0378-5939)
Description: Publishes original studies, short communications, preliminary reports, review papers on scientometrics.
Refereed Serial

790.13   IT
SCIENZA DUEMILA. 1979. m. L.50000. Perodici Tattilo s.r.l., Via del Casale Piombino 30, 00135 Rome, Italy. Ed. Sebastiano Fusco. adv.; circ. 200,000.
Formerly: Test.

500   IT
SCIENZA E DOSSIER. 1985. m. (11/yr.). L.62000 (foreign L.83000). Giunti Gruppo Editoriale S.p.A., Via Vincenzo Gioberto, 34, 50121 Florence, Italy. TEL 055-66791. FAX 055-268312. TELEX 571438. Ed. Massimo Casini.

500   IT
SCIENZA E TECNICA. 1937-1951; N.S. 1957-1963; N.S. 1970. m. Societa Italiana per il Progresso delle Scienze, 202 Viale Reg. Margherita, 00198 Rome, Italy. TEL 8554156. Dir. Rocco Capasso.

500   IT
SCIENZE, LA MATEMATICA E IL LORO INSEGNAMENTO. 1964. bi-m. L.53000($53) (effective 1992). Editoriale e Finanziaria Le Monnier, S.p.A., Via A. Meucci 2, Casella Postale 202, 50100 Florence, Italy. bk.rev.
Former titles: Scienze ed il Loro Insegnamento (ISSN 0036-8903); Scienze e i Giovani.
Description: Covers the scientific and didactic aspects of mathematics and the techniques behind the science of instruction.

500   AT   ISSN 0004-9549
Q1   CODEN: SRCHAA
SEARCH; science and technology in Australia and New Zealand. 1970. m. Aus.$49 to individuals; libraries $165. (Australian and New Zealand Association for the Advancement of Science) Blackwell Scientific Publications (Australia) Pty. Ltd., P.O. Box 378, Carlton, Vic. 3053, Australia. TEL 03-347-0300. FAX 03-347-5001. TELEX 10716421. Ed. Dr. Stephen Garnett. adv.; bk.rev.; index; circ. 3,000. (also avail. in microform from UMI; reprint service avail. from UMI) **Indexed:** ASCA, Aus.Educ.Ind., Aus.Rd.Ind., Bibl.& Ind.Geol., Biol.Abstr., Curr.Adv.Ecol.Sci., Dairy Sci.Abstr., Deep Sea Res.& Oceanogr.Abstr., Field Crop Abstr., Forest.Abstr., Forest Prod.Abstr., Geo.Abstr., Herb.Abstr., Ind.Vet., Plant Breed.Abstr., Rural Recreat.Tour.Abstr., Sci.Cit.Ind., Soils & Fert., World Agri.Econ.& Rural Sociol.Abstr.
—BLDSC shelfmark: 8214.300000.
Formerly: Australian Journal of Science.
Description: Provides a forum for the discussion and debate of recent scientific and technological developments in the Asia Pacific region.

500   US
SELECTED RESEARCH IN MICROFICHE. Short title: S R I M. 1975. bi-m. $1.25 per no. U.S. Department of Commerce, National Technical Information Service, 5285 Port Royal Rd., Springfield, VA 22161. TEL 703-487-4929. cum.index. (back issues avail.)

500 600   II
SEMINAR REPORTEUR; journal of science and technology. (Text in English) 1961. m. Rs.50($30) De Indiana Overseas Publications, 1424 Chandni Chowk, Delhi 6, India. Ed. I.D. Gupta.

500   JA   ISSN 0386-5827
SENSHU SHIZEN KAGAKU KIYO/SENSHU UNIVERSITY. ASSOCIATION OF NATURAL SCIENCE. BULLETIN. (Text in English and Japanese; summaries in English) 1969. irreg. Senshu Daigaku, Shizen Kagaku Kenkyukai - Senshu University, Association of Natural Science, 1-1 Higashi-Mita 2-chome, Tama-ku, Kawasaki-shi, Kanagawa-ken 214, Japan.

500   JA   ISSN 0287-4466
SETSUNAN UNIVERSITY. SCIENTIFIC REVIEW. SERIES A, NATURAL SCIENCES/SETSUDAI GAKUJUTSU. SHIZEN KAGAKU HEN. (Text and summaries in English and Japanese) 1980. a. Setsunan Daigaku, 17-8 Ikedanaka-machi, Neyagawa-shi, Osaka-fu 572, Japan.

500   CC
SHANDONG DAXUE XUEBAO (ZIRAN KEXUE BAN)/SHANDONG UNIVERSITY. JOURNAL (NATURAL SCIENCE EDITION). (Text in Chinese) q. Shandong Daxue, Xuebao Bianjibu, No. 27, Shanda Nanlu, Jinan, Shandong 250100, People's Republic of China. TEL 643861. Ed. Wang Chengrui.

SHANGHAI JIAOTONG DAXUE XUEBAO/SHANGHAI JIAOTONG UNIVERSITY. BULLETIN. see *TECHNOLOGY: COMPREHENSIVE WORKS*

500   CC
SHANXI DAXUE XUEBAO (ZIRAN KEXUE BAN)/SHANXI UNIVERSITY. JOURNAL (NATURAL SCIENCE EDITION). (Text in Chinese) q. Shanxi Daxue, Xuebao Bianjibu, Wucheng Lu, Taiyuan, Shanxi 030006, People's Republic of China. TEL 773441. Ed. Liu Po.

SHAONIAN KEXUE/JUVENILE SCIENCE. see *CHILDREN AND YOUTH — For*

SHAONIAN KEXUE HUABAO/JUVENILE SCIENTIFIC PICTORIAL. see *CHILDREN AND YOUTH — For*

500 600   CC
SHENZHEN DAXUE XUEBAO (LIGONG BAN)/SHENZHEN UNIVERSITY. JOURNAL (SCIENCE, ENGINEERING EDITION). (Text in Chinese) 2/yr (2 nos. per issue). Y4. Shenzhen Daxue - Shenzhen University, Shenzhen, Guangdong 518060, People's Republic of China.
Description: Contains academic papers. Aims to reflect research results and promote academic exchange.

500.9   UK   ISSN 0080-9241
SHERBORN FUND FACSIMILES. (Text mainly in English; occasionally in other European languages) 1959. irreg., no.4, 1973. price varies. Society for the History of Natural History, c/o British Museum (Natural History), Cromwell Rd., London SW7 5BD, England.

500   JA   ISSN 0488-6291
    CODEN: SDKGAH
SHIGA DAIGAKU KYOIKUGAKUBU KIYO. SHIZEN KAGAKU/SHIGA UNIVERSITY. FACULTY OF EDUCATION. MEMOIRS. NATURAL SCIENCE. (Text and summaries in English, French, and Japanese) 1952. a. free. Shiga Daigaku, Kyoikugakubu - Shiga University, Faculty of Education, 5-1 Hiratsu 2-chome, Otsu-shi, Shiga-ken 520, Japan. **Indexed:** Biol.Abstr., Chem.Abstr., Jap.Per.Ind.
—BLDSC shelfmark: 5593.327100.

500 600   CC
SHIJIE FAMING/WORLD INVENTIONS. (Text in Chinese) m. Zhuanli Wenxian Chubanshe - Patent Documentation Publishers, Xueyuan Lukou, Beisanhuan Xilu, Beijing 100088, People's Republic of China. TEL 2021177. Ed. Wang Zhifu.

500 600   CC
SHIJIE KEXUE JISHU/WORLD SCIENCE AND TECHNOLOGY. (Text in Chinese) q. Zhongguo Kexueyuan, Keji Gongzuoze Shijieyu Xiehui - Chinese Academy of Sciences, Esperanto Association of Scientists and Technicians, 52 Sanlihe, Beijing 100864, People's Republic of China. TEL 868361. Ed. Shen Chenyu.

500   JA   ISSN 0586-9943
SHIMANE DAIGAKU KYOIKUGAKUBU KIYO. SHIZEN KAGAKU/SHIMANE UNIVERSITY. FACULTY OF EDUCATION. MEMOIRS. NATURAL SCIENCE. (Text in English and Japanese; summaries in English) 1972. a. Shimane Daigaku, Kyoikugakubu - Shimane University, Faculty of Education, 1060 Nishi-Kawatsu-cho, Matsue-shi, Shimane-ken 690, Japan. **Indexed:** Jap.Per.Ind.

500   JA   ISSN 0387-9925
Q1   CODEN: SDRKDX
SHIMANE DAIGAKU RIGAKUBU KIYO/SHIMANE UNIVERSITY. FACULTY OF SCIENCE. MEMOIRS. (Text in English and Japanese) 1966. a. free. Shimane Daigaku, Rigakubu - Shimane University. Faculty of Science, 1060 Nishi-Kawatsu-cho, Matsue-shi, Shimane-ken 690, Japan. TEL 0852-21-7100. FAX 0852-31-0812. Ed. Knaitaka Shaji. circ. 600. **Indexed:** Biol.Abstr., Chem.Abstr., INIS Atomind., Jap.Per.Ind., Math.R.
Description: Covers mathematics, physics, chemistry, biology, geology, and computer science.

SHIMANE IKA DAIGAKU KIYO/SHIMANE MEDICAL UNIVERSITY. BULLETIN. see *MEDICAL SCIENCES*

500.9   JA
SHIMANE NO SHIZEN. (Text in Japanese) 1976. irreg. Shimane-ken Shizen Koen Kyokai, Shimane-ken Kankyo Hokenbu Kankyo Hozenka, 1 Tono-machi, Matsue-shi, Shimane-ken 690, Japan.
Description: Contains news about the association, and about natural parks in Shimane Prefecture.

500   MP
SHINJLEH UHAAN AM'DRAL/SCIENCE AND LIFE. (Text in Mongolian) 1935. m. Academy of Sciences, Syhbaataryn Talbay, Ulan Bator, Mongolia. TEL 21794. (Co-sponsor: Society for Dissemination of Scientific Knowledge) Ed. L. Jambaldorj. circ. 20,000.

500   MP
SHINJLEH UHAANY AKADEMIYN MEDEE/ACADEMY OF SCIENCES NEWS. (Text in Mongolian) 1961. q. Academy of Sciences, Suhbaataryn Talbay 3, Ulan Bator, Mongolia. Ed. S. Norovsambuu.

505   JA   ISSN 0583-063X
    CODEN: JFSSB9
SHINSHU UNIVERSITY. FACULTY OF SCIENCE. JOURNAL/SHINSHU DAIGAKU RIGAKUBU KIYO. (Text in Japanese and European languages) 1966. s-a. exchange basis. Shinshu University, Faculty of Science - Shinshu Daigaku Rigakubu, 1-1 Asahi 3-chome, Matsumoto-shi, Nagano-ken 390, Japan. Ed. Kiyoshi Mochizuki. **Indexed:** Bibl.& Ind.Geol., Biol.Abstr., Chem.Abstr., Text.Tech.Dig.
—BLDSC shelfmark: 4749.800000.

500 069   JA   ISSN 0387-8716
SHIRETOKO HAKUBUTSUKAN KENKYU HOKOKU/SHIRETOKO MUSEUM. BULLETIN. (Text in Japanese; summaries in English and Japanese) 1979. a. Shari-choritsu Shiretoko Hakubutsukan - Shiretoko Museum, 4-1 Moto-machi, Shari-cho, Shari-gun, Hokkaido 099-41, Japan.

SHIRITSU NAGOYA KAGAKUKAN NYUSU. see *MUSEUMS AND ART GALLERIES*

SHIVAJI UNIVERSITY, KOLHAPUR, INDIA. JOURNAL. HUMANITIES AND SCIENCES. see *HUMANITIES: COMPREHENSIVE WORKS*

SHIYOU DAXUE XUEBAO (ZIRAN KEXUE BAN)/UNIVERSITY OF PETROLEUM, CHINA. JOURNAL (NATURAL SCIENCE EDITION). see *PETROLEUM AND GAS*

| 500 | | JA | ISSN 0914-6385 |

Q77
SHIZEN KAGAKU KENKYU (TOKUSHIMA)/UNIVERSITY OF TOKUSHIMA. FACULTY OF INTEGRATED ARTS AND SCIENCES. NATURAL SCIENCE RESEARCH. (Text in Japanese; summaries in English) 1988. a. Tokushima Daigaku, Sogo Kagakubu - University of Tokushima, Faculty of Integrated Arts and Sciences, 1-1 Minami-Josanjima-cho, Tokushima-shi, Tokushima-ken 770, Japan.

500   JA   ISSN 0441-0017
Q4   CODEN: SZKKAD
SHIZEN KAGAKU KENKYU (TOKYO)/HITOTSUBASHI UNIVERSITY RESEARCH SERIES. SCIENCES. (Text in Japanese) 1959. a. Hitotsubashi Daigaku - Hitotsubashi University, 2-1 Naka, Kunitachi-shi, Tokyo 186, Japan. Indexed: Jap.Per.Ind.
—BLDSC shelfmark: 4318.988000.

500   JA   ISSN 0285-8150
SHIZEN KAGAKU RONSO. (Text and summaries in Japanese) 1969. a. Kyoto Joshi Daigaku, Shizen Kagaku Hoken Taiiku Kenkyushitsu - Kyoto Women's University, Society of Natural Science and Physical Education, 35 Kita-Hiyoshi-machi, Imagumano, Higashiyama-ku, Kyoto-shi, Kyoto-fu 605, Japan. Indexed: Jap.Per.Ind.

SHIZEN KANSATSUKAI KAIHO. see ENVIRONMENTAL STUDIES

500   JA   ISSN 0385-759X
SHIZEN KYOIKUEN HOKOKU/MINISTRY OF EDUCATION. NATIONAL SCIENCE MUSEUM. INSTITUTE FOR NATURE STUDY. MISCELLANEOUS REPORTS. (Text and summaries in English and Japanese) 1969. a. Monbu-sho, Kokuritsu Kagaku Hakubutsukan, Fuzoku Shizen Kyoikuen - Ministry of Education, National Science Museum, Institute for Nature Study, 21-5 Shiroganedai 5-chome, Minato-ku, Tokyo 108, Japan.

500.9   JA   ISSN 0078-6683
SHIZENSHI KENKYU/OSAKA MUSEUM OF NATURAL HISTORY. OCCASIONAL PAPERS. (Text in English or Japanese; summaries in English) 1968. irreg. (1-3/yr.) price varies; also avail. on exchange basis. Osaka-shiritsu Shizenshi Hakubutsukan - Osaka Museum of Natural History, 1-23 Nagai Koen, Higashi-Sumiyoshi-ku, Osaka-shi, Osaka-fu 546, Japan. Ed. Yoshitaka Nasu. circ. 1,000. Indexed: Bibl.& Ind.Geol, Biol.Abstr., Rev.Appl.Entomol.

500   JA   ISSN 0286-7311
SHIZUOKA DAIGAKU KYOIKUGAKUBU KENKYU HOKOKU. SHIZEN KAGAKU HEN/SHIZUOKA UNIVERSITY. FACULTY OF EDUCATION. BULLETIN. NATURAL SCIENCES SERIES. (Text and summaries in English and Japanese) 1950. a. not commercially avail. Shizuoka Daigaku, Kyoikugakubu - Shizuoka University, Faculty of Education, 836 Oya, Shizuoka-shi, Shizuoka-ken 422, Japan. Indexed: Jap.Per.Ind.
—BLDSC shelfmark: 2507.630000.

500   JA   ISSN 0285-0435
SHIZUOKA DAIGAKU KYOYOBU KENKYU HOKOKU. SHIZEN KAGAKU HEN/SHIZUOKA UNIVERSITY. FACULTY OF LIBERAL ARTS. REPORTS: SCIENCES. (Text in English and Japanese; summaries in English) 1965. a. Shizuoka Daigaku, Kyoyobu - Shizuoka University, Faculty of Liberal Arts, 836 Oya, Shizuoka-shi, Shizuoka-ken 422, Japan. Indexed: Jap.Per.Ind.

505   JA   ISSN 0583-0923
Q77   CODEN: RFSSBT
SHIZUOKA UNIVERSITY. FACULTY OF SCIENCE. REPORTS/SHIZUOKA DAIGAKU RIGAKUBU KENKYU HOKOKU. (Text in English) 1976. a. exchange basis. Shizuoka Daigaku, Rigakubu - Shizuoka University, Faculty of Science, 836 Oya, Shizuoka-shi, Shizuoka-ken 422, Japan. TEL 054-237-111. FAX 054-237-9895. Ed.Bd. circ. 500. Indexed: Bibl.& Ind.Geol., Biol.Abstr., Chem.Abstr., INIS Atomind., Math.R., Sci.Abstr.
—BLDSC shelfmark: 7467.180000.
Description: Contains original papers on mathematics, physics, chemistry, radiochemistry, biology, and geoscience.

500   AA
SHKENCA DHE JETA/SCIENCE ET VIE; reviste tekniko shkencore. 1969. bi-m. $10. Union de la Jeunnesse du Travail d'Albanie, Rruga "Punetoret e Rilindjes", Tirana, Albania. TEL 39-46. Ed. Kudret Isai. bk.rev.; illus.; circ. 17,500.

500   CC   ISSN 0253-2743
SHULI KEXUE YU HUAXUE. (Text in Chinese) bi-m. Chongqing Shi Guangxue Jixie Yanjiusuo, 13, Changshicun, Shiqiaopu, Chongqing, Sichuan 630041, People's Republic of China. TEL 810140. Ed. Yang Keda.
—BLDSC shelfmark: 5156.555000.

500.9   TH
SIAM SOCIETY. NATURAL HISTORY BULLETIN. 1913. a. B.300($15) Siam Society, 131 Soi Asoke, Sukhumvit Rd., Bangkok, Thailand. Ed.Bd. bk.rev. (back issues avail.) Indexed: Amer.Hist.& Life, Biol.Abstr., Curr.Adv.Ecol.Sci., Hist.Abstr.

500   CC   ISSN 0490-6756
SICHUAN DAXUE XUEBAO (ZIRAN KEXUE BAN)/SICHUAN UNIVERSITY. JOURNAL (NATURAL SCIENCE EDITION). (Text in Chinese) q. Sichuan Daxue, Xuebao Bianjibu, Jiuyanqiao, Chengdu, Sichuan 610064, People's Republic of China. Ed. Liu Yingming.
—BLDSC shelfmark: 4876.275000.

500   CC   ISSN 1001-8220
SICHUAN SHIFAN XUEYUAN XUEBAO (ZIRAN KEXUE BAN)/SICHUAN NORMAL COLLEGE. JOURNAL (NATURAL SCIENCE EDITION). (Text in Chinese) q. Sichuan Shifan Xueyuan, Xuebao Bianjibu, 10, Renmin Xilu, Nanchong, Sichuan 637002, People's Republic of China. TEL 22244. Ed. Tang Zesheng.

500   CL   ISSN 0716-8136
▼SIGLO XXI CIENCIA AND TECNOLOGIA. 1990. w. $240. El Mercurio S.A.P., Av. Santa Maria 5542, Apdo. Postal 13 D, Las Condes, Chile. TEL 562-2287048. FAX 562-2289042. TELEX 341635. Ed. Nicolas Luco. adv.; circ. 60,000. (tabloid format)
Description: Covers science and technology for youth.

506   US   ISSN 0080-9578
SIGMA ZETAN. 1927. a. free to members. Sigma Zeta, c/o George W. Welker, Ed., Ball State University, Muncie, IN 47306. TEL 317-288-7542. circ. 1,200.

500   PH   ISSN 0037-5284
AS540
SILLIMAN JOURNAL; a quarterly of investigation and discussion in the humanities and in the sciences. 1954. q. P.50($12) Silliman University, Dumaguete City 6501, Philippines. Ed. Ruben P. Chavez. bk.rev.; charts; illus.; index. (also avail. in microform from UMI; reprint service avail. from UMI) Indexed: Biol.Abstr., Chem.Abstr, Ind.Phil.Per., M.L.A.
—BLDSC shelfmark: 8280.300000.
Description: Covers humanities and sciences with an emphasis on Negros, Cebu, and the Visayan region.

500   ET   ISSN 0379-2897
                         CODEN: SINTD7
SINET. (Text in English) 1978. s-a. Br.11 (foreign $12). Addis Ababa University, Faculty of Science, Box 31226, Addis Ababa, Ethiopia. TEL 553177. TELEX 21205. Ed. Mesfin Tadesse. Indexed: Bibl.& Ind.Geol., Biol.Abstr., Excerp.Med., Field Crop Abstr., Seed Abstr., Sorghum & Millets Abstr.
Description: Features review articles, research papers or short notes in science and technology and related disciplines.

500   ET
SINET NEWSLETTER. (Text in English) 1978. m. Addis Ababa University, Faculty of Science, Box 1176, Addis Ababa, Ethiopia. TEL 553177. TELEX 21205.

500   ET
SINET: PROCEEDINGS OF ANNUAL PROGRAMMES REVIEW CONFERENCE. (Text in English) 1978. a. Addis Ababa University, Faculty of Science, Box 1176, Addis Ababa, Ethiopia. TEL 553177. TELEX 21205.

500   SI
SINGAPORE. NATIONAL SCIENCE AND TECHNOLOGY BOARD. ANNUAL REPORTS. 1972. a. free. National Science and Technology Board, 16 Science Park Drive, 01-03 The Pasteur, Singapore Science Park, Singapore 0511, Singapore. TEL 7797066. FAX 7771711. charts; illus.; stat.
Formerly: Singapore. Science Council. Annual Reports.

SIPISCOPE. see JOURNALISM

SMITHSONIAN. see SOCIAL SCIENCES: COMPREHENSIVE WORKS

500   US   ISSN 0364-0175
Q179.9   CODEN: SIRRDL
SMITHSONIAN INSTITUTION RESEARCH REPORTS. 1972. 4/yr. free. Smithsonian Institution, Office of Public Affairs, 900 Jefferson Dr., Rm. 2410, Washington, DC 20560. TEL 202-357-1300. Ed. Jo Ann Webb. illus.; circ. 30,000. Indexed: Bibl.& Ind.Geol., Ind.U.S.Gov.Per.
Formerly: Smithsonian Research Reports.
Description: Smithsonian programs and research.

500   US   ISSN 0081-0339
SMITHSONIAN OPPORTUNITIES FOR RESEARCH AND STUDY IN HISTORY ART SCIENCE. Title varies: Smithsonian Research Opportunities. 1964. biennial. free. Smithsonian Institution Press, Office of Fellowships and Grants, 470 L'Enfant Plaza, Ste. 7100, Washington, DC 20560. TEL 202-287-3271. index.
Formerly: Smithsonian Institution Opportunities for Research and Advanced Study.

500 300   UK   ISSN 0306-3127
Q1
SOCIAL STUDIES OF SCIENCE; an international review of research in the social dimensions of science and technology. q. £35($58) to individuals; institutions £99($163). Sage Publications Ltd., 6 Bonhill St., London EC2A 4PU, England. TEL 071-374-0645. FAX 071-374-8741. Ed. David Edge. bk.rev.; index. (back issues avail.) bottom page #170; trim 177 x 101; adv. contact: Bernie Folan. bk.rev.; index. (back issues avail.) Indexed: A.B.C.Pol.Sci., Arts & Hum.Cit.Ind., ASCA, ASSIA, Curr.Cont., Deep Sea Res.& Oceanogr.Abstr., Excerp.Med., High.Educ.Curr.Aware.Bull., Hist.Abstr., Lang.& Lang.Behav.Abstr., Mid.East: Abstr.& Ind., Res.High.Educ.Abstr., Sociol.Abstr. (1971-), SSCI, Stud.Wom.Abstr.
—BLDSC shelfmark: 8318.214100.
Description: Publishes multidisciplinary research contributions on the study of the social dimensions of science, for historians, philosophers, sociologists, political scientists and economists.

500   AG   ISSN 0037-8437
Q33   CODEN: ASCAA2
SOCIEDAD CIENTIFICA ARGENTINA. ANALES. (Summaries in English) 1876. bi-m. $10. Sociedad Cientifica Argentina, Avda. Santa Fe 1145, 1059 Buenos Aires, Argentina. Ed. Pedro Cattaneo. adv.; bk.rev.; bibl.; charts; illus.; index; circ. 3,000. Indexed: Biol.Abstr., Chem.Abstr., Deep Sea Res.& Oceanogr.Abstr., Field Crop Abstr., Geo.Abstr. Herb.Abstr., Rev.Appl.Entomol., Rev.Plant Path.

500   AG
SOCIEDAD CIENTIFICA ARGENTINA. CICLO DE CONFERENCIAS. irreg. Sociedad Cientifica Argentina, Comision de Cursos y Conferencias, Av. Santa Fe 1145, Buenos Aires, Argentina. illus.

500.9   VE   ISSN 0037-8518
Q4   CODEN: SCNSAR
SOCIEDAD DE CIENCIAS NATURALES LA SALLE. MEMORIA. 1940. s-a. Bs.300($25) Sociedad de Ciencias Naturales la Salle, Av. Boyaca-Maripez, Apdo. 1930, Caracas 1010A, Venezuela. adv.; charts; illus.; index, cum.index: 1940-1972; circ. 1,300. (also avail. in microfirm from UMI; reprint service avail. from KTO,UMI) Indexed: Bibl.& Ind.Geol., Biol.Abstr., Chem.Abstr., Deep Sea Res.& Oceanogr.Abstr., Int.Abstr.Biol.Sci.
Incorporates: Novedades Cientificas Serie Zoologia.

509 600   BL   ISSN 0185-5107
SOCIEDAD LATINOAMERICANA DE HISTORIA DE LAS CIENCIAS Y LA TECNOLOGIA. BOLETIN INFORMATIVO. (Text in English, Spanish) 1983. 3/yr. $5. Rua Brasilia 46, ap 81, 04534 Sao Paulo SP, Brazil. Ed. Ana Maria Goldfarb. bk.rev.

SCIENCES: COMPREHENSIVE WORKS

500   IT   ISSN 0391-609X
SOCIETA E LA SCIENZA. 1977. irreg., no.8, 1986. price varies. Liguori Editore s.r.l., Via Mezzocannone 19, 80134 Naples, Italy. TEL 081-5227139. Ed. Felice Ippolito. **Indexed:** Math.R.

500.9   IT   ISSN 0037-8844
Q54   CODEN: ASIMAY
SOCIETA ITALIANA DI SCIENZE NATURALI E DEL MUSEO CIVICO DI STORIA NATURALE. ATTI. (Text in Italian; summaries in English, French, German) 1856. q. L.45000 (effective 1992). Societa Italiana di Scienze Naturali, Corso Venezia 55, 20121 Milan, Italy. TEL 02-620-85405. (Co-sponsor: Museo Civico di Storia Naturale) Ed. Giovanni Pinna. bk.rev.; charts; illus.; index; circ. 1,500. (back issues avail.) **Indexed:** Bibl.& Ind.Geol., Biol.Abstr., Chem.Abstr., Deep Sea Res.& Oceanogr.Abstr.

500.9   IT   ISSN 0376-2726
SOCIETA ITALIANA DI SCIENZE NATURALI E DEL MUSEO CIVICO DI STORIA NATURALE. MEMORIE. 1865. q. L.45000 (effective 1992). Societa Italiana di Scienze Naturali, Corso Venezia 55, 20121 Milan, Italy. TEL 02-62085405. (Co-sponsor: Museo Civico di Storia Naturale) Ed. Giovanni Pinna. circ. 1,500. (back issues avail.)

500   IT
SOCIETA ITALIANA PER IL PROGRESSO DELLE SCIENZE. ATTI DELLA RIUNIONE. 1907. biennial. L.30000 to non-members. Societa Italiana per il Progresso delle Scienze, 202 Viale Reg. Margherita, 00198 Rome, Italy. TEL 8554156.

500   IT
SOCIETA TOSCANA DI SCIENZA NATURALI. ATTI. SERIE A. 1987. a. L.50000 (effective 1992). Pacini Editore s.r.l., Via della Gherardesca 1, 56014 Ospedaletto (Pisa), Italy. TEL 050-982439. FAX 050-983906. TELEX 501926 PACINI I. Ed. L. Trevisan.

500   IT
SOCIETA TOSCANA DI SCIENZA NATURALI. ATTI. SERIE B. 1987. a. L.65000 (effective 1992). Pacini Editore s.r.l., Via della Gherardesca 1, 56014 Ospedaletto (Pisa), Italy. TEL 050-982439. FAX 050-983906. TELEX 501926 PACINI I. Ed. L. Trevisan.

500.9   FR   ISSN 0753-4655
SOCIETE D'HISTOIRE NATURELLE DU DOUBS. BULLETIN. (Text in French; summaries occasionally in English) 1899; N.S. 1968. a. membership. Societe d'Histoire Naturelle du Doubs, Institut des Sciences Naturelles, Place Leclerc, 25030 Besancon Cedex, France. Ed. Bernard Bonnet. adv.; bk.rev.; bibl.; charts; cum.index; circ. 500. **Indexed:** Biol.Abstr., VITIS.
—BLDSC shelfmark: 2742.950000.
Former titles (1968-78): Federation des Societes d'Histoire Naturelle de Franche-Comte. Bulletin (ISSN 0014-9357); Societe d'Histoire Naturelle du Doubs. Bulletin.

500 800   PL   ISSN 0459-6854
AS262.L6   CODEN: BSSEA3
SOCIETE DES SCIENCES ET DES LETTRES DE LODZ. BULLETIN. (Text in English, French, German, Russian) 1950. a. price varies. Lodzkie Towarzystwo Naukowe - Society of Arts and Sciences of Lodz, Piotrkowska 179, 90-447 Lodz, Poland. (Dist. by: Ars Polona-Ruch, Krakowskie Przedmiescie 7, 00-068 Warsaw, Poland) Ed. Jozef Matuszewski. bibl.; illus.; circ. 500. **Indexed:** Bibl.& Ind.Geol., Biol.Abstr., Math.R.

500   MR   ISSN 0037-9255
   CODEN: BSMAAT
SOCIETE DES SCIENCES NATURELLES ET PHYSIQUES DU MAROC. BULLETIN. (Text in French; summaries in English and French) 1920. s-a. DH.45($9) Societe des Sciences Naturelles et Physiques du Maroc, Institut Scientifique Cherifiens, Ave. Moulay Cherif, Rabat, Morocco. **Indexed:** Bibl.& Ind.Geol., Biol.Abstr., Bull.Signal.

500   BE   ISSN 0037-9565
Q56   CODEN: BSRSA6
SOCIETE ROYALE DES SCIENCES DE LIEGE. BULLETIN. (Text in English, French) 1843. 6/yr. 2500 Fr. (Societe Royale des Sciences de Liege) Editions Derouaux, 15 av. des Tilleuls, B-4000 Liege, Belgium. FAX 041-522169. Ed. J. Godeaux. charts. **Indexed:** Appl.Mech.Rev., Bibl.& Ind.Geol., Biol.Abstr., Chem.Abstr, Deep Sea Res.& Oceanogr.Abstr., Geo.Abstr, INIS Atomind., Math.R., Sci.Abstr.
—BLDSC shelfmark: 2751.000000.

500   FR   ISSN 0037-9581
Q46   CODEN: BSSBAS
SOCIETE SCIENTIFIQUE DE BRETAGNE. BULLETIN. 1924. q. price varies. Societe Scientifique de Bretagne, Faculte des Sciences, 35000 Rennes, France. Ed. Leon Grillet. bibl.; charts; illus.; cum.index: 1924-1973. **Indexed:** Bibl.& Ind.Geol., Biol.Abstr., Bull.Signal., Chem.Abstr., Deep Sea Res.& Oceanogr.Abstr., Sci.Abstr.

500.1   SZ   ISSN 0037-9603
   CODEN: BSVAA6
SOCIETE VAUDOISE DES SCIENCES NATURELLES. BULLETIN. (Text in French; summaries in English, German and Italian) 1844. s-a. 50 Fr.($32) Societe Vaudoise des Sciences Naturelles, Palais de Rumine, CH-1005 Lausanne, Switzerland. TEL 021-312-4334. Ed. Jean-Louis Moret. adv.; bk.rev.; bibl.; charts; illus.; index, cum.index: vols.1-50, 51-60. (Reprint service avail. from UMI) **Indexed:** Biol.Abstr., Chem.Abstr., Field Crop Abstr., Geo.Abstr., Herb.Abstr.

500.1   SZ   ISSN 0037-9611
Q67   CODEN: MSVNAU
SOCIETE VAUDOISE DES SCIENCES NATURELLES. MEMOIRES. (Text in French; summaries in English, German and Italian) 1922. irreg. price varies. Societe Vaudoise des Sciences Naturelles, Palais de Rumine, CH-1005 Lausanne, Switzerland. adv.; bibl.; charts; illus.; maps; index, cum.index: Vols.1-17. (Reprint service avail. from UMI.) **Indexed:** Bibl.& Ind.Geol., Biol.Abstr., Chem.Abstr.
Description: Scientific studies in geology, paleontology, botany, zoology, physiology, agronomy, chemistry, ecology, ethnology, mathematics, medicine, meteorology, and physics.

500.9   FR   ISSN 0336-8300
SOCIETE VERSAILLAISE DES SCIENCES NATURELLES. BULLETIN. serie 4, 1974. q. 140 F. Societe Versaillaise des Sciences Naturelles, E.N.S.H, 4 rue Hardy, R.P. no.914, 78009 Versailles Cedex, France. illus.; circ. 500. **Indexed:** Bibl.& Ind.Geol.
—BLDSC shelfmark: 2757.300000.
Formerly: Federation Francaise des Societes de Sciences Naturelles. Revue (ISSN 0014-9365)

SOCIETY FOR COMMON INSIGHTS. JOURNAL. see *RELIGIONS AND THEOLOGY*

500   US
SOCIETY FOR GENERAL SYSTEMS RESEARCH. PROCEEDINGS. 1956. a. $60. International Society for the Systems Sciences, Box 8793, College of Business, Idaho State University, Pocatello, ID 83209. TEL 208-233-6521. FAX 208-236-4367.

500   MW   ISSN 0037-993X
DT858   CODEN: SMJODY
SOCIETY OF MALAWI JOURNAL. vol. 23, 1970. s-a. $16. Society of Malawi, P.O. Box 125, Blantyre, Malawi. Ed. T. Hopper. bk.rev.; charts; illus.; stat.; index; circ. 500. **Indexed:** A.I.C.P., Biol.Abstr., Hist.Abstr. (until 1988).
Formerly: Nyasaland Journal.

301 500   NE
SOCIOLOGY OF THE SCIENCES. YEARBOOK. (Text in English) 1977. a. price varies. Kluwer Academic Publishers, Spuiboulevard 50, P.O. Box 17, 3300 AA Dordrecht, Netherlands. TEL 078-334911. FAX 078-334254. TELEX 29245. (Dist. by: Kluwer Academic Publishers Group, P.O. Box 322, 3300 AH Dordrecht; U.S. address: P.O. Box 358, Accord Station, Hingham, MA 02018-0358) Ed. R.D. Whitley.
Formerly: Sociology of the Sciences.

SOCIOLOGY OF THE SCIENCES MONOGRAPHS. see *SOCIOLOGY*

500 600   JA
SOGO GAKUJUTSU KENKYU SHUKAI. (Text in Japanese) 1976. irreg. Nihon Kagakusha Kaigi - Japan Scientists Association, 9-16 Yushima 1-chome, Bunkyo-ku, Tokyo 113, Japan.
Description: Contains research reports of the association.

SOGO KENKYUJO HOKOKU. see *TECHNOLOGY: COMPREHENSIVE WORKS*

500   UK   ISSN 0952-4762
SOLID MECHANICS ARCHIVES. (Text in English) 1976. q. £60($120) (foreign £72). (University of Waterloo, CN) Oxford University Press, Walton St., Oxford OX2 6DP, England. TEL 0865-56767. FAX 0865-56646. TELEX 837330 OXPRES G. Ed. John Roorda. adv.; circ. 500. (back issues avail.) **Indexed:** Appl.Mech.Rev., Int.Aerosp.Abstr., Math.R.
Formerly: S M Archives (ISSN 0376-7426)
Description: Collection and dissemination of recent advances and trends in various areas of solid mechanics research.

SOMERSET ARCHAEOLOGY AND NATURAL HISTORY. see *ARCHAEOLOGY*

500.9   US
SONORENSIS. 1972. q. membership. Arizona-Sonora Desert Museum, Inc., 2021 N. Kinney Rd., Tucson, AZ 85743. TEL 602-833-1380. bibl.; illus.
Formerly: A S D M Newsletter (ISSN 0044-8850)

SOOCHOW JOURNAL OF MATHEMATICS. see *MATHEMATICS*

500.9   UK   ISSN 0038-1551
SORBY NATURAL HISTORY SOCIETY NEWSLETTER. 1964. 10/yr. membership. Sorby Natural History Society, 9 Rosslyn Avenue, Aston, Sheffield, Yorkshire, England. TEL 0742-879622. Ed. L. Storer. bk.rev.; bibl.; circ. 500. (processed)
Description: Details of society meetings and local natural history news.

500.9   UK   ISSN 0260-2245
SORBY RECORD; a journal of natural history for the Sheffield area. 1958. irreg. membership. Sorby Natural History Society, 9 Rosslyn Avenue, Aston, Sheffield, Yorkshire, England. TEL 0742-879622. Ed. D. Whiteley. circ. 1,000.
—BLDSC shelfmark: 8328.610000.
Description: Articles on all aspects of natural history in the Sheffield area.

509   II
SOURCE MATERIALS ON THE HISTORY OF SCIENCE IN INDIA. irreg. price varies. Indian National Science Academy, Bahadur Zafar Marg, New Delhi 110002, India.

500 600   SA   ISSN 0081-2455
G845   CODEN: SAARCF
SOUTH AFRICAN JOURNAL OF ANTARCTIC RESEARCH. 1971. a. free. Council for Scientific and Industrial Research, South African Scientific Committee for Antarctic Research, Box 395, Pretoria 0001, South Africa. TEL 27-12-86. Ed. P.R. Condy. circ. 500. **Indexed:** Bibl.& Ind.Geol., Biol.Abstr., Chem.Abstr, Deep Sea Res.& Oceanogr.Abstr., Geo.Abstr., Ind.S.A.Per., Sci.Abstr.
—BLDSC shelfmark: 8338.700000.

SCIENCES: COMPREHENSIVE WORKS

500   SA   ISSN 0038-2353
Q85   CODEN: SAJSAR
SOUTH AFRICAN JOURNAL OF SCIENCE/SUID-AFRIKAANSE TYDSKRIF VIR WETENSKAP. 1903. m. R.120 to individuals; institutions R.211. Foundation for Research Development, P.O. Box 2600, Pretoria 0001, South Africa. Ed. G.S. Baker. adv.; bk.rev.; index; circ. 2,100. (also avail. in microform from UMI; reprint service avail. from ISI,UMI) **Indexed:** A.I.C.P., Agroforest.Abstr., Anim.Breed.Abstr., Bio-Contr.News & Info., Biol.Abstr., Chem.Abstr., Curr.Adv.Ecol.Sci., Curr.Cont., Dairy Sci.Abstr., Deep Sea Res.& Oceanogr.Abstr., Energy Ind., Energy Info.Abstr., Eng.Ind., Excerp.Med., Field Crop Abstr., Forest.Abstr., Forest Prod.Abstr., Geo.Abstr., Geotech.Abstr., Helminthol.Abstr., Herb.Abstr., Hort.Abstr., Ind.S.A.Per., Ind.Vet., Met.Abstr., Nutr.Abstr., Ocean.Abstr., Ornam.Hort., Plant Breed.Abstr., Plant Grow.Reg.Abstr., Pollut.Abstr., Protozool.Abstr., Res.High.Educ.Abstr., Rev.Plant Path., Rural Devel.Abstr., Rural Ext.Educ.& Tr.Abstr., Sci.Abstr., Seed Abstr., Sel.Water Res.Abstr., Soils & Fert., Trop.Oil Seeds Abstr., Vet.Bull., Weed Abstr., World Agri.Econ.& Rural Sociol.Abstr.
—BLDSC shelfmark: 8340.000000.
Incorporates (in 1984): Scientific Progress - Wetenskaplike Vordering (ISSN 0036-8814)

500.9   AT   ISSN 0038-2965
QH1
SOUTH AUSTRALIAN NATURALIST; a quarterly journal of natural history. 1919. q. Aus.$25 to non-members. Field Naturalists' Society of South Australia, Inc., G.P.O. Box 1594, Adelaide, S.A. 5001, Australia. Ed. R. Cook. bk.rev.; charts; illus.; maps; circ. 600. **Indexed:** AESIS, Aus.Sci.Ind., Biol.Abstr.
—BLDSC shelfmark: 8349.000000.

500   US   ISSN 0096-414X
Q11   CODEN: BSCAAD
SOUTH CAROLINA ACADEMY OF SCIENCE. BULLETIN. 1935. a. $25. South Carolina Academy of Science, c/o John L. Safko, Treas., Dept. of Physics & Astronomy, University of South Carolina, Columbia, SC 29208. TEL 803-777-6466. FAX 803-777-3065. Ed. G.T. Cowley. index; circ. 750. (back issues avail.) **Indexed:** Biol.Abstr.

500   US   ISSN 0096-378X
Q11   CODEN: PSDAA2
SOUTH DAKOTA ACADEMY OF SCIENCE. PROCEEDINGS. 1916. a. $11.25. South Dakota Academy of Science, University of South Dakota, HCR 531, Box 97, Pierre, SD 57501. TEL 605-224-7136. Ed. Carroll Hasnten. charts; illus.; circ. 350 (controlled). **Indexed:** Bibl.& Ind.Geol., Chem.Abstr., Field Crop Abstr., Geo.Abstr., Irr.& Drain.Abstr., Maize Abstr., Soils & Fert., Soyabean Abstr.
—BLDSC shelfmark: 6821.000000.
Description: Presents lectures and papers submitted at the proceedings.

500   US   ISSN 0038-3872
Q11   CODEN: BCASAD
SOUTHERN CALIFORNIA ACADEMY OF SCIENCES. BULLETIN. 1902. 3/yr. $20 (foreign $25). Southern California Academy of Sciences, 900 Exposition Blvd., Los Angeles, CA 90007. TEL 213-744-3384. Ed. Jon E. Keeley. bibl.; charts; illus.; index; circ. 700. **Indexed:** Bibl.& Ind.Geol., Biol.Abstr., Deep Sea Res.& Oceanogr.Abstr., Ocean.Abstr., Pollut.Abstr.
—BLDSC shelfmark: 2763.000000.

500   US
SOUTHERN RESEARCH INSTITUTE. ANNUAL REPORT. 1945. a. free. Southern Research Institute, Box 55305, Birmingham, AL 35255. TEL 205-581-2000. FAX 205-581-2726. Ed. R. Kenneth Kirby.

500.9   US   ISSN 0038-4909
QH1   CODEN: SWNAAB
SOUTHWESTERN NATURALIST. (Text in English and Spanish) 1953. 4/yr. $20 to individuals; institutions $30; students $15. Southwestern Association of Naturalists, c/o Dr. Paul J. Fonteyn, Biology Dept., Southwest Texas State Univ., San Marcos, TX 78666. TEL 512-245-2178. Ed. Michael L. Kennedy. adv.; bk.rev.; bibl.; charts; illus.; Bibl.& Ind.Geol.; circ. 1,400. (also avail. in microform from UMI; reprint service avail. from UMI) **Indexed:** ASCA, Biol.Abstr., Curr.Adv.Ecol.Sci., Curr.Cont., Field Crop Abstr., Forest.Abstr., Forest Prod.Abstr., Geo.Abstr., Helminthol.Abstr., Herb.Abstr., Ornam.Hort., Soils & Fert.
—BLDSC shelfmark: 8357.280000.
Description: Articles on scientific investigations on plants and animals (living and fossil) endemic to the southwestern United States, Mexico and Central America.

550 520   US
SPECTRA: C I W NEWSLETTER. 1971. 3/yr. free. Carnegie Institution of Washington, 1530 P St., N.W., Washington, DC 20005. TEL 202-387-6411. FAX 202-387-8092. Eds. R. Bowers, P. Craig. bk.rev.; circ. 3,300. (back issues avail.)
Formerly: C I W Newsletter.
Description: Features current activities of the Institution's astronomers, biologists, and earth scientists.

508   SA
SPECTRUM; natural science journal for teachers and lecturers. 1963. q. R.17.60 (foreign R.22.20). Foundation for Education, Science and Technology, P.O. Box 1758, Pretoria 0001, South Africa. TEL 012-322-6404. FAX 012-320-7803. bk.rev.; circ. 10,000. **Indexed:** Chem.Abstr., Ind.S.A.Per.

SPECTRUM; jornal Brasileiro ciencias. see TECHNOLOGY: COMPREHENSIVE WORKS

500   UK   ISSN 0155-7785
Q1   CODEN: SPSTDD
SPECULATIONS IN SCIENCE AND TECHNOLOGY; an international journal devoted to speculative papers in the physical, mathematical, biological and engineering sciences. (Text and summaries in English) 1977. 4/yr. $160. Science and Technology Letters, P.O. Box 81, Northwood, Middlesex HA6 3DN, England. TEL 09274-23586. FAX 09274-25066. Ed. Alan L. Mackay. charts; illus. **Indexed:** Bibl.& Ind.Geol., Biol.Abstr., Chem.Abstr., Comput.Abstr., Curr.Cont., Deep Sea Res.& Oceanogr.Abstr., Energy Ind., Energy Info.Abstr., Eng.Ind., Environ.Abstr., Excerp.Med., Field Crop Abstr., Lang.& Lang.Behav.Abstr., Met.Abstr., Sci.Abstr., Sci.Cit.Ind., Sci.Res.Abstr., So.Pac.Per.Ind., Solid St.Abstr.
—BLDSC shelfmark: 8411.176000.

500   GW   ISSN 0170-2971
SPEKTRUM DER WISSENSCHAFT. German translation of: Scientific American. 1978. m. DM.111.60. Moenchhofstr. 15, 6900 Heidelberg, Germany. TEL 06221-40360. FAX 06221-411119. TELEX 461842. Ed. Albrecht Kunkel. adv.; bk.rev.; index; circ. 128,764. (back issues avail.)
Incorporates: Spektrum (ISSN 0049-1861)

500   GW   ISSN 0176-3008
SPIEGEL DER FORSCHUNG. 1983. s-a. Justus Liebig Universitaet, Ludwigstr. 23, 6300 Giessen, Germany. TEL 0641-7022035. FAX 0641-7022039. Ed. Christel Lauterbach. adv.; circ. 10,000.

500 639.9   CN   ISSN 0381-4459
TD427.P4
SPILL TECHNOLOGY NEWSLETTER. 1976. q. Environment Canada, Technology Development and Technical Services Branch, Ottawa, Ont. K1A 0H3, Canada. Ed. Stella Wheatley. circ. 1,700. **Indexed:** Energy Info.Abstr., Environ.Abstr., Pollut.Abstr., Sci.Abstr.
—BLDSC shelfmark: 8413.840000.
Description: A forum for the exchange of information on spill counter measures and related matters.

500   CE   ISSN 0081-3745
CODEN: SPZEAY
SPOLIA ZEYLANICA/BULLETIN OF THE NATIONAL MUSEUMS OF SRI LANKA. (Text in English) 1904. a. price varies. Department of National Museums, Box 854, Sir Marcus Fernando Mawatha, Colombo 7, Sri Lanka. **Indexed:** Bibl.& Ind.Geol., Biol.Abstr., Deep Sea Res.& Oceanogr.Abstr.

500   US   ISSN 0172-7389
CODEN: SSSYDF
SPRINGER SERIES IN SYNERGETICS. vol.32, 1986. irreg. price varies. Springer-Verlag, 175 Fifth Ave., New York, NY 10010. TEL 212-460-1500. (Also Berlin and Heidelberg) Ed. H. Haken. **Indexed:** Chem.Abstr.

500   US   ISSN 0081-3877
SPRINGER TRACTS IN NATURAL PHILOSOPHY. 1964. irreg. price varies. Springer-Verlag, 175 Fifth Ave., New York, NY 10010. TEL 212-460-1500. (Also Berlin, Heidelberg, Tokyo and Vienna) Ed. B.D. Coleman. circ. 2,000. (reprint service avail. from ISI) **Indexed:** Math.R.
Continues: Ergebnisse der Angewandten Mathematik.

500   CE
SRI LANKA ASSOCIATION FOR THE ADVANCEMENT OF SCIENCE. PROCEEDINGS. (Text in English) 1945. a. Sri Lanka Association for the Advancement of Science, Vidya Mawatha, Colombo 7, Sri Lanka. Ed. C.L.M. Nethsingha. circ. 2,000. **Indexed:** Bibl.& Ind.Geol, Biol.Abstr., Sri Lanka Sci.Ind.

500   YU   ISSN 0081-4024
SRPSKA AKADEMIJA NAUKA I UMETNOSTI. ODELJENJE PRIRODNO-MATEMATICKIH NAUKA. POSEBNA IZDANJA. (Text in Serbo-Croatian; summaries in English, French, German or Russian) 1950. irreg., no.39, 1972. price varies. Srpska Akademija Nauka i Umetnosti, Knez Mihailova 35, 11001 Belgrade, Serbia, Yugoslavia. FAX 38-11-182-825. TELEX 72593 SANU YU. (Dist. by: Prosveta, Terazije 16, Belgrade, Serbia, Yugoslavia) circ. 500. **Indexed:** Bibl.& Ind.Geol., Biol.Abstr., Chem.Abstr., Ref.Zh.

060 500   YU
SRPSKA AKADEMIJA NAUKA I UMETNOSTI. POVREMENA IZDANJA. irreg. Srpska Akademija Nauka i Umetnosti, Knez Mihailova 35, 11001 Belgrade, Serbia, Yugoslavia. FAX 38-11-182-825. TELEX 72593 SANU YU.

SRPSKA AKADEMIJA NAUKA I UMETNOSTI SPOMENICA. see HUMANITIES: COMPREHENSIVE WORKS

500 700   US   ISSN 0039-0240
CODEN: PSIAAR
STATEN ISLAND INSTITUTE OF ARTS & SCIENCES. PROCEEDINGS. 1883. 2/yr. $6. Staten Island Institute of Arts and Sciences, 75 Stuyvesant Place, Staten Island, NY 10301. TEL 718-727-1135. FAX 718-273-5683. Ed. John-Paul Richiuso. bk.rev.; bibl.; charts; illus.; index; circ. 600. **Indexed:** GeoRef.
Description: Articles in the fields of natural history, archeology and local history of particular reference to Staten Island.

STEVENS INDICATOR. see COLLEGE AND ALUMNI

500 600   GW
STIFTERVERBAND FUER DIE DEUTSCHE WISSENSCHAFT. TAETIGKEITSBERICHT. 1950. a. membership. Stifterverband fuer die Deutsche Wissenschaft, Brucker Holt 56-60, 4300 Essen, Germany. circ. 10,000.
Supersedes: Stifterverband fuer die Deutsche Wissenschaft. Jahrbuch (ISSN 0081-5551)

500   RM   ISSN 0039-1417
STIINTA SI TEHNICA. 1949. m. 36 lei($20) (Comitetul Central al Uniunii Tineretului Comunist) Editura Scinteia, Piata Presei Libere 1, 79781 Bucharest, Rumania. (Subscr. to: ILEXIM, Str. 13 Decembrie Nr. 3, P.O. Box 136-137, Bucharest, Rumania) Ed. Ioan Eremia Albescu. bk.rev.; circ. 75,000.

SCIENCES: COMPREHENSIVE WORKS

500 620   NE   ISSN 0304-4149
QA274.A1   CODEN: STOPB7
STOCHASTIC PROCESSES AND THEIR APPLICATIONS.
1973. 8/yr.(in 4 vols.; 2 nos./vol.). fl.1288 (effective 1992). (Bernoulli Society for Mathematical Statistics and Probability) North-Holland (Subsidiary of: Elsevier Science Publishers B.V.), P.O. Box 211, 1000 AE Amsterdam, Netherlands. TEL 020-5803911. FAX 020-5803598. TELEX 18582 ESPA NL. (Subscr. in U.S. and Canada to: Elsevier Science Publishing Co., Inc., Box 882, Madison Sq. Sta., New York, NY 10159. TEL 212-989-5800) Ed. P. Jagers. (also avail. in microform from RPI; back issues avail.; reprint service avail. from SWZ) Indexed: ASCA, Biostat., Compumath, Cyb.Abstr., Int.Abstr.Oper.Res., J.Cont.Quant.Meth., Math.R., Oper.Res.Manage.Sci., Qual.Contr.Appl.Stat., Sci.Abstr., Zent.Math.
—BLDSC shelfmark: 8465.300000.
Description: Publishes papers on the theory and applications of stochastic processes.
Refereed Serial

500.9   BE
STUDIA ALGOLIGICA LOVANIENSIA. (Text in French) 1974. irreg. price varies. Editions Peeters s.p.r.l., Bondgenotenlaan 153, B-3000 Leuven, Belgium. TEL 016-235170. FAX 016-228500. TELEX 65981 PULB.

500   PL   ISSN 0081-6590
STUDIA I MATERIALY Z DZIEJOW NAUKI POLSKIEJ. SERIA C. HISTORIA NAUK MATEMATYCZNYCH, FIZYKO-CHEMICZNYCH I GEOLOGICZNO-GEOGRAFICZNYCH. (Text in Polish; summaries in French, Russian) 1957. irreg, vol.29, 1981. price varies. (Polska Akademia Nauk, Zaklad Historii Nauki, Oswiaty i Techniki) Panstwowe Wydawnictwo Naukowe, Ul. Miodowa 10, 00-251 Warsaw, Poland. (Dist. by: Ars Polona, Krakowskie Przedmiescie 7, 00-068 Warsaw, Poland) Ed. E. Olszewski. bibl.; illus.; circ. 210.

500   PL   ISSN 0081-6612
AS261
STUDIA I MATERIALY Z DZIEJOW NAUKI POLSKIEJ. SERIA E. ZAGADNIENIA OGOLNE. (Text in Polish; summaries in English, French, Russian) 1967. irreg., no.7, 1983. price varies. (Polska Akademia Nauk, Zaklad Historii Nauki, Oswiaty i Techniki) Panstwowe Wydawnictwo Naukowe, Ul. Miodowa 10, 00-251 Warsaw, Poland. (Dist. by: Ars Polona, Krakowskie Przedmiescie 7, 00-068 Warsaw, Poland) Ed. B. Jaczewski. index; circ. 260.

STUDIA LEIBNITIANA; Zeitschrift fuer Philosophie und der Wissenschaften. see *PHILOSOPHY*

STUDIA SPINOZANA; an international & interdisciplinary series. see *PHILOSOPHY*

500   GW   ISSN 0081-7384
STUDIENBUECHEREI. 1970. irreg. price varies. Deutscher Verlag der Wissenschaften, Postfach 1216, 1080 Berlin, Germany.

800 500 100   IE   ISSN 0039-3495
AP4
STUDIES; an Irish quarterly review of letters, philosophy and science. 1912. q. I£14($30) to individuals; institutions I£16($35). 35 Lr. Leeson St., Dublin 2, Ireland. TEL 01-766785. FAX 01-762984. Ed. Noel Barber. adv.; bk.rev.; cum.index: vols.1-50; circ. 1,300. (also avail. in microform from UMI; reprint service avail. from UMI) Indexed: Abstr.Engl.Stud., Br.Hum.Ind., Cath.Ind., CERDIC, Hist.Abstr., Mid.East: Abstr.& Ind., P.A.I.S.
—BLDSC shelfmark: 8484.250000.

509   US   ISSN 0039-3681
Q125   CODEN: SHPSB5
STUDIES IN HISTORY AND PHILOSOPHY OF SCIENCE. 1970. 4/yr. £140 (effective 1992). Pergamon Press, Inc., Journals Division, 660 White Plains Rd., Tarrytown, NY 10591-5153. TEL 914-524-9200. FAX 914-333-2444. (And: Headington Hill Hall, Oxford OX3 0BW, England. TEL 0865-794141) Ed. Nicholas Jardine. adv.; bk.rev.; charts; circ. 1,100. (also avail. in microform from MIM,UMI; back issues avail.) Indexed: Arts & Hum.Cit.Ind., ASCA, ASSIA, Biol.Abstr., Br.Hum.Ind., GeoRef, Hist.Abstr., Hum.Ind., Math.R., Phil.Ind., Sci.Abstr., SSCI.
—BLDSC shelfmark: 8490.652000.
Description: Concerned with the historical, social and intellectual contexts of the sciences and with their methodology and epistemology.
Refereed Serial

STUDIES IN SCIENCE AND THE HUMANITIES. see *HUMANITIES: COMPREHENSIVE WORKS*

501   US   ISSN 0081-8577
STUDIES IN THE FOUNDATIONS, METHODOLOGY AND PHILOSOPHY OF SCIENCE. 1967. irreg. price varies. Springer-Verlag, 175 Fifth Ave., New York, NY 10010. TEL 212-460-1500. (Also Berlin, Heidelberg, Tokyo and Vienna) Ed. M. Bunge. (reprint service avail. from ISI)

509   NE
STUDIES IN THE HISTORY OF MODERN SCIENCE. 1977. irreg. price varies. Kluwer Academic Publishers, P.O. Box 17, 3300 AA Dordrecht, Netherlands. TEL 078-334911. FAX 078-334254. TELEX 29245. (Dist. by: Kluwer Academic Publishers Group, P.O. Box 322, 3300 AH Dordrecht, Netherlands; U.S. address: Box 358, Accord Station, Hingham, MA 02018-0358) Ed.Bd. Indexed: Math.R.

354   SJ
SUDAN. NATIONAL COUNCIL FOR RESEARCH. SCIENCE POLICY AND ANNUAL REPORT. (Text in English) a. exchange basis. National Council for Research, Box 2404, Khartoum, Sudan.

SUDAN RESEARCH INFORMATION BULLETIN. see *HUMANITIES: COMPREHENSIVE WORKS*

SUDHOFFS ARCHIV; Zeitschrift fuer Wissenschaftsgeschichte. see *MEDICAL SCIENCES*

SUDHOFFS ARCHIV. BEIHEFTE. see *MEDICAL SCIENCES*

500   SA   ISSN 0039-4807
SUID-AFRIKAANSE AKADEMIE VIR WETENSKAP EN KUNS. NUUSBRIEF. 1961. q. R.9. Suid Afrikaanse Akademie vir Wetenskap en Kuns, P.O. Box 538, Pretoria 0001, South Africa. TEL 012-285082. FAX 012-285091. Ed. D.J.C. Geldenhuys. adv.; bibl.; illus.; circ. 2,000. (looseleaf format)

500   SA   ISSN 0254-3486
   CODEN: SATTDF
SUID AFRIKAANSE TYDSKRIF VIR NATUURWETENSKAP EN TEGNOLOGIE. (Text in Afrikaans; summaries in Afrikaans and English) 1982. q. R.44. Suid Afrikaanse Akademie vir Wetenskap en Kuns, Box 538, Pretoria 0001, South Africa. TEL 012-285082. FAX 012-285091. Ed. A. Strasheim. adv.; bk.rev.; charts; illus.; stat.; index; circ. 1,500. (back issues avail.)

SUMMARY OF WHITE PAPER ON SCIENCE AND TECHNOLOGY. see *TECHNOLOGY: COMPREHENSIVE WORKS*

500   JA   ISSN 0389-5025
QH188   CODEN: SJTKBF
SUZUGAMINE JOSHI TANDAI KENKYU SHUHO. SHIZEN KAGAKU/SUZUGAMINE WOMEN'S COLLEGE. BULLETIN. NATURAL SCIENCE. (Text and summaries in English and Japanese) 1954. a. Suzugamine Joshi Tanki Daigaku - Suzugamine Women's College, 6-18 Inokuchi 4-chome, Nishi-ku, Hiroshima-shi, Hiroshima-ken 733, Japan. Indexed: Biol.Abstr., Jap.Per.Ind.

500   GW
▼**SYMMETRY.** (Text in English) 1990. q. DM.370($190) V C H Verlagsgesellschaft mbH, Postfach 101161, 6940 Weinheim, Germany. TEL 06201-602-0. FAX 06201-602-328. TELEX 465516-VCHWH-D. (U.S. addr.: V C H Publishers Inc., 220 E. 23rd St., New York, NY 10010-4606) Ed. I. Hargittai.

500   SI   ISSN 0218-3188
SYNERGY. (Text in English) bi-m. free. National Science and Technology Board, 16 Science Park Dr., 01-03 The Pasteur, Singapore Science Park, Singapore 0511, Singapore. TEL 65-779-7066. FAX 65-777-1711.
Description: Covers national science and technology policies and news of research and development projects.

SYNTHESE; an international journal for epistemology, methodology and philosophy of science. see *PHILOSOPHY*

500   PL   ISSN 0860-2212
SZCZECINSKIE ROCZNIKI NAUKOWE/ANNALES SCIENTRAIRUM STETINENSES. (Text in Polish; summaries in English, Russian) 1986. a. price varies. (Szczecin Scientific Society) Ossolineum, Publishing House of the Polish Academy of Sciences, Rynek 9, 50-106 Wroclaw, Poland. TEL 386-25. (Dist. by: Ars Polona, Krakowskie Przedmiescie 7, 00-068 Warsaw, Poland) Ed. Eugeniusz Mietkiewicz.
Description: Papers on different research fields by scientists from the region of Szczecin Pomerania.

500 600   PL   ISSN 0082-1241
SZCZECINSKIE TOWARZYSTWO NAUKOWE. SPRAWOZDANIA. 1960. irreg. price varies. Szczecinskie Towarzystwo Naukowe, Rycerska 3, 70-537 Szczecin, Poland.

500   PL   ISSN 0137-5326
DK4600.L43
SZKICE LEGNICKIE. vol.12, 1984. irreg. price varies. (Legnickie Towarzystwo Przyjaciol Nauk) Ossolineum, Publishing House of the Polish Academy of Sciences, Rynek 9, Wroclaw, Poland. TELEX 0712771 OSS PL. (Dist. by: Ars Polona-Ruch, Krakowskie Przedmiescie 7, Warsaw, Poland) Ed. Tadeusz Guminski.
Description: Studies in the history, culture and social life of Legnica region.

500   US   ISSN 0161-0295
HD29   CODEN: TIMBD
T I M S - O R S A MEETING BULLETIN. Alternating issues called: O R S A - T I M S Bulletin. 1976. s-a. free to members. The Institute of Management Sciences, 290 Westminster St., Providence, RI 02903. TEL 401-274-2525. (And: 428 E. Preston St., Baltimore, MD 21202) (Co-sponsor: Operations Research Society of America) adv.; abstr.; circ. 17,500. (back issues avail.) Indexed: Appl.Mech.Rev., Sci.Abstr.
—BLDSC shelfmark: 6293.835000.
Supersedes: Operations Research Society of America. Meeting Bulletin (ISSN 0030-3666)

500   TH
T I S T R RESEARCH NEWS. m. Thailand Institute of Scientific and Technological Research, 196 Phahonyothin Rd., Chatuchak, Bangkok 10900, Thailand. TEL 579-4929. FAX 662-5798594. circ. 1,000.
Formerly: A S R C T Research News.

T N C - AKTUELLT. (Tekniska Nomenklaturcentralen) see *LINGUISTICS*

500.9   NE
T N O PROJECT; orgaan voor toegepaste wetenschappen. 1973. 11/yr. fl.54.15. (Netherlands Organisation for Applied Scientific Research) Insert B.V., P.B. 90053, 1006 BB Amsterdam, Netherlands. Ed.Bd. adv.; bk.rev.; illus.; tr.lit.; index; circ. 4,000. Indexed: C.I.S. Abstr., Excerp.Med., Food Sci.& Tech.Abstr., HRIS, Key to Econ.Sci., Met.Abstr., World Alum.Abstr.
Supersedes: T N O Nieuws (ISSN 0039-8446)

500   JA   ISSN 0386-6890
TAKAYAMA TANKI DAIGAKU KENKYU KIYO/TAKAYAMA JUNIOR COLLEGE. MEMOIRS. (Text in Japanese; summaries in English) 1978. a. Takayama Tanki Daigaku - Takayama Junior College, 1155 Shimobayashi-machi, Takayama-shi, Gifu-ken 506, Japan.

500.9   NZ   ISSN 0496-8026
QH197.5
TANE. 1948. a. NZ.$16 for institutions. Auckland University Field Club, c/o Botany Department, University of Auckland, Private Bag 92019, Auckland, New Zealand. Ed. Susan F. Courtney. illus.; circ. 300. **Indexed:** Biol.Abstr., Curr.Adv.Ecol.Sci.
—BLDSC shelfmark: 8601.900000.
Description: Covers natural history of northern New Zealand, particularly its offshore islands.

500   TZ   ISSN 0856-1761
                            CODEN: TJSCEY
TANZANIA JOURNAL OF SCIENCE. (Text in English) 1975. a. $30. University of Dar es Salaam, Faculty of Science, Box 35065, Dar es Salaam, Tanzania. TELEX 41327 UNISCIE TZ. Ed. E.C. NJau. bk.rev. **Indexed:** Chem.Abstr., Deep Sea Res.& Oceanogr.Abstr.
Formerly: University of Dar es Salaam. University Science Journal (ISSN 0250-5592)

500.9 370   UK   ISSN 0263-6107
TEACHING SCIENCE. 1903. 3/yr. £11. School Natural Science Society, 153 Fernside Avenue, Hanworth, Middlesex TW13 7BQ, England. (Subscr. to: Mr. A.R. Nicholls, 9 Killington Drive, Kendal, Cumbria LA9 7NY, England) Ed. A.R. Nicholls. adv.; bk.rev.; charts; illus.; index; circ. 1,500. (also avail. in microform from UMI)
—BLDSC shelfmark: 8614.334000.
Formerly (until 1982): Natural Science in Schools (ISSN 0028-0763)
Description: For science and technology teachers of children ages 5 to 13. Articles, reviews, lesson ideas.

500   UK   ISSN 0960-6076
▼**TECHNICAL UNIVERSITY OF KOSICE. TRANSACTIONS**. 1991. s-a. £60. (Technical University of Kosice) Riecansky Science Publishing Co., 7 Meadow Walk, Great Abington, Cambridge CB1 6AZ, England. TEL 0223-893295.
—BLDSC shelfmark: 9012.150000.

500   GR   ISSN 0040-4764
TECHNIKA CHRONIKA/ANNALES TECHNIQUES. (Text in Greek; summaries in English) 1932. q. $100 per no. Technical Chamber of Greece, 4 Rue Karageorgi Servias, 125 61 Athens, Greece. TEL 3222-466. FAX 3221772. TELEX 218374. bk.rev.; charts; illus.; index. **Indexed:** Sci.Abstr.
—BLDSC shelfmark: 8735.900000.

500   GW   ISSN 0323-6927
TECHNISCHEN HOCHSCHULE ZWICKAU. WISSENSCHAFTLICHE ZEITSCHRIFT. (Text in English and German) 1977. 5/yr. DM.50. Technischen Hochschule Zwickau, Dr.-Friedrichs-Ring 2a, 9541 Zwickau, Germany. adv.; circ. 400. (back issues avail.)

500   SA   ISSN 1017-4966
Q1
TECHNOBRIEF. (Text in Afrikaans, English) 1959. m. free. C S I R Corporate Communication, P.O. Box 395, Pretoria 0001, South Africa. TEL 012-8414304. FAX 012-8412055. Eds. Hoepel Scheepers, Johan van Eeden. circ. 16,000. (tabloid format) **Indexed:** Fuel & Energy Abstr., Ind.S.A.Per., Met.Abstr., World Alum.Abstr., World Text.Abstr.
Formerly (until 1991): Scientiae (ISSN 0036-8717)
Description: Highlights CSIR's achievements in scientific and technological research, development and implementation, focusing on technology transfer partnership with industry, and environmental impact issues.

600   US
TECHNOCRACY. INFORMATION BRIEFS. irreg. Technocracy Inc., Continental Headquarters, Savannah, OH 44874. TEL 419-962-4712.

TECHNOLOGIA; historical and social studies in science, technology and industry. see TECHNOLOGY: COMPREHENSIVE WORKS

500   US   ISSN 0040-1692
T171   CODEN: TEREAU
TECHNOLOGY REVIEW. 1899. 8/yr. $32. Massachusetts Institute of Technology, Association of Alumni and Alumnae, W59-200, Cambridge, MA 02139. TEL 617-253-8250. Ed. Steven Marcus. adv.; bk.rev.; illus.; circ. 92,000. (also avail. in microform from UMI; reprint service avail. from UMI) **Indexed:** A.I.Abstr., A.S.& T.Ind., ABI Inform, Acad.Ind., Acid Pre.Dig., Amer.Bibl.Slavic & E.Eur.Stud., ASCA, B.P.I., Biol.Abstr., Biol.Dig., Bk.Rev.Ind. (1978-), BPIA, Bus.Ind., CAD CAM Abstr., Chem.Abstr., Child.Bk.Rev.Ind. (1978-), Comput.Bus., Comput.Lit.Ind., Curr.Cont., Energy Info.Abstr., Energy Rev., Eng.Ind., Environ.Abstr., Environ.Per.Bibl., Excerp.Med., G.Soc.Sci.& Rel.Per.Lit., Geo.Abstr., High.Educ.Curr.Aware.Bull., Hlth.Ind., I D A, Key to Econ.Sci., Mag.Ind., Ocean.Abstr., P.A.I.S., Pollut.Abstr., PROMT, Risk Abstr., Robomat., Sage Urb.Stud.Abstr., Tel.Abstr., Telegen, Text.Tech.Dig., Tr.& Indus.Ind., 013045133p.Abstr.
●Also available online. Vendor(s): DIALOG.
—BLDSC shelfmark: 8761.000000.

500   US
TECHNOLOGY TODAY. 1949. 3/yr. free to qualified personnel. Southwest Research Institute, Drawer 28510, San Antonio, TX 78228-0510. TEL 512-684-5111. Ed. Elizabeth Douglas. illus.; circ. 10,740. **Indexed:** Br.Ceram.Abstr.
Formerly (until 1978): Tomorrow Through Research (ISSN 0040-9146)

500 790.13   RM
TEHNIUM. 1970. m. 50 lei po m. Piata Presei Libere 1, 79784 Bucharest, Rumania. TEL 90-183566. Ed. Ilie Mihaescu. adv.; bk.rev.; circ. 50,000.

500   KR
TEKHNICHESKAYA DIAGNOSTIKA I NERAZRUSHAYUSHCHII KONTROL; vsesoyuznyi nauchno-teoreticheskii zhurnal. (Text and summaries in Russian; contents page in English, Russian) 1989. 4/yr. 4.60 Rub. (Akademiya Nauk Ukrainskoi S.S.R., Otdelenie Fiziko-Tekhnicheskikh Problem Materialovedeniya) Izdatel'stvo Naukova Dumka, c/o Yu.A. Khramov, Dir., Ul. Repina 3, Kiev 252601, Ukraine. (Subscr. to: Mezhdunarodnaya Kniga, Moscow G-200, Russia) Ed. B.E. Paton.

TEKSTILEC; glasilo slovenskih tekstilcev. see TEXTILE INDUSTRIES AND FABRICS

500   FR   ISSN 0040-2419
AP20
TEL QUEL; litterature-philosophie-science-politique. 1960. q. 130 F. Editions du Seuil, 27 rue Jacob, 75261 Paris Cedex 06, France. Ed. Marcelin Pleynet. bk.rev. **Indexed:** Curr.Cont.

500   US   ISSN 0040-313X
Q11   CODEN: JTASAG
TENNESSEE ACADEMY OF SCIENCE. JOURNAL. 1926. q. $15 to non-members. Tennessee Academy of Science, 2001 Craven Ln., Prairie Peninsula, Hixson, TN 37343. TEL 615-251-1573. Ed. Libby Workman. adv.; bk.rev.; abstr.; charts; illus.; index; circ. 1,200. (also avail. in microform from AMS) **Indexed:** Biol.Abstr., Chem.Abstr., Excerp.Med., Geo.Abstr., GeoRef, Helminthol.Abstr., INIS Atomind.
Refereed Serial

301 100   CS   ISSN 1210-0250
TEORIE VEDY/THEORY OF SCIENCE. (Text in Czech or Slovak, English; summaries in English) vol.4, 1972. q. free. Ceskoslovenska Akademie Ved, Ustav Teorie a Historie Vedy - Czechoslovak Academy of Sciences, Institute for Theory and History of Science, Jilska 1, 110 00 Prague 1, Czechoslovakia. TEL 231-9115. (Co-sponsor: Vysoka Skola Ekonomicka) Ed. L. Tondl. bk.rev.; bibl.; charts; stat.; circ. 530. **Indexed:** Biol.Abstr., Phil.Ind., Ref.Zh.
Formerly (until 1990): Teorie Rozvoje Vedy; Supersedes (in 1977): Teorie a Metoda.
Description: Presents various aspects of the philosophy of science and science policy.

500   HU   ISSN 0040-3717
Q44   CODEN: TEVIAS
TERMESZET VILAGA. 1869. m. $28.50. (Tudomanyos Ismeretterjeszto Tarsulat) Hirlapkiado Vallalat, Biaha Lujza ter 3, 1959 Budapest 8, Hungary. TEL 1-382-399. TELEX 22-5554. (Subscr. to: Kultura, Box 149, H-1389 Budapest, Hungary) Ed. J. Horti. bk.rev.; charts; illus.; index; circ. 17,500. **Indexed:** Chem.Abstr.
Formerly: Termeszettudomanyi Kozlony.

500   US   ISSN 0040-4403
Q1   CODEN: TJSCAU
TEXAS JOURNAL OF SCIENCE. 1949. q. $45. Texas Academy of Science, c/o Texas Tech University, The Museum, Box 4499, Lubbock, TX 79409. TEL 806-742-2487. Ed. J. Knox Jones, Jr. charts; illus.; index; circ. 1,000. (also avail. in microform from UMI; reprint service avail. from ISI) **Indexed:** Abstr.Anthropol., Anal.Abstr., ASCA, Bio-Contr.News & Info., Biol.Abstr., Biol.Dig., Chem.Abstr., Curr.Adv.Ecol.Sci., Curr.Cont., Deep Sea Res.& Oceanogr.Abstr., GeoRef, Helminthol.Abstr., Math.R., Nutr.Abstr., Rev.Appl.Entomol., Sci.Abstr., Soils & Fert.
—BLDSC shelfmark: 8799.000000.
Refereed Serial

500   JA   ISSN 0286-5092
TEZUKAYAMA TANKI DAIGAKU KIYO. SHIZEN KAGAKU HEN/TEZUKAYAMA COLLEGE. JOURNAL. NATURAL SCIENCE. (Text and summaries in English and Japanese) 1963. a. Tezukayama Tanki Daigaku - Tezukayama Junior College, 3-1 Gakuen minami, Nara-shi, Nara-ken 631, Japan. FAX 0742-41-2941.

507 375.5   US
THINGS OF SCIENCE.* 1940. m. $24. Things of Science, Inc., Box 579, Sarasota, FL 34230-0579. Ed. Andrew E. Svenson, Jr. bk.rev.; circ. 3,500.
Description: Science kits (text and materials for experiments).

THOMAS SAY FOUNDATION MONOGRAPHS. see BIOLOGY — Entomology

500   CC   ISSN 0493-2137
TIANJIN DAXUE XUEBAO/TIANJIN UNIVERSITY. JOURNAL. (Text in Chinese) q. Tianjin Daxue - Tianjin University, Qilitai, Nankai Qu, Tianjin 300072, People's Republic of China. TEL 318116. Ed. Wu Yongshi.

509   RM
TIBISCUS. SERIA STIINTELE NATURII. (Text in Romanian; summaries in German) a. Muzeul Banatului, Piata Huniade Nr.1, Timisoara, Rumania.

500   FI   ISSN 0358-1039
TIEDE 2000. 1980. 8/yr. Fmk.254. Sanomaprint, PL 113, SF-00381 Helsinki, Finland. FAX 0-120-5599. TELEX 125848-SACOM. Ed. Jali Ruuskanen. adv.; bk.rev.; circ. 43,364.
Description: Contains articles and news relating to science in general.

500   MX   ISSN 0186-5730
TIEMPOS DE CIENCIA; revista de difusion cientifica. 1985. q. $20. Universidad de Guadalajara, Coordinacion de Difusion Cientifica, Av. Juarez y Enrique Diaz de Leon, 8 piso, C.P. 44170 Guadalajara, Jalisco, Mexico. Ed. Javier Garcia de Alba Garcia. adv.; bk.rev.

500 069   JA   ISSN 0910-4100
TOCHIGI-KENRITSU HAKUBUTSUKAN KENKYU HOKOKUSHO/TOCHIGI PREFECTURAL MUSEUM. MEMOIRS. (Text in Japanese; summaries in English and Japanese) 1983. a. Tochigi-kenritsu Hakubutsukan - Tochigi Prefectural Museum, 2-2 Mutsumi-cho, Utsunomiya-shi, Tochigi-ken 320, Japan.

500   AT
TODAY'S LIFE SCIENCES. 1989. m. Aus.$60. Thomson Publications Australia, 47 Chippen St., Chippendale, N.S.W. 2008, Australia. TEL 02-699-2411. FAX 02-698-3920. Ed. Jeremy Knibbs. circ. 7,299.

500   JA   ISSN 0910-7177
TOHOKU NO SHIZEN/NATURE OF TOHOKU. (Text in Japanese) 1985. m. Tohoku no Shizensha, Bunanoki Shuppan, 5-11 Tori-machi 5-chome, Yonezawa-shi, Yamagata-ken 992, Japan.

SCIENCES: COMPREHENSIVE WORKS

500　　　　　　JA　　ISSN 0563-6795
Q77　　　　　　　　　CODEN: TUFPBE
TOKAI UNIVERSITY. FACULTY OF SCIENCE. PROCEEDINGS. (Text in English and German; summaries in English) 1966. a. (Tokai Daigaku, Rigakubu - Tokai University, Faculty of Science) Tokai Daigaku Shuppankai - Tokai University Press, 27-4 Shinjuku 3-chome, Shinjuku-ku, Tokyo 160, Japan. **Indexed:** Chem.Abstr., INIS Atomind.
—BLDSC shelfmark: 6700.050000.

500　　　　　　JA　　ISSN 0563-6981
　　　　　　　　　　CODEN: TDKSBV
TOKUSHIMA DAIGAKU KYOYOBU KIYO. SHIZEN KAGAKU/UNIVERSITY OF TOKUSHIMA. COLLEGE OF GENERAL EDUCATION. JOURNAL OF SCIENCE. (Text in English and Japanese; summaries in English) 1966. a. Tokushima Daigaku, Kyoyobu - University of Tokushima, College of General Education, 1-1 Minami-Josanjima-cho, Tokushima-shi, Tokushima-ken 770, Japan. **Indexed:** Biol.Abstr., Chem.Abstr., Jap.Per.Ind.
—BLDSC shelfmark: 5054.300000.

500　　　　　　JA　　ISSN 0910-4828
TOKYO DAIGAKU SOGO KENKYU SHIRYOKAN GYOSEKISHU/UNIVERSITY OF TOKYO. UNIVERSITY MUSEUM. COLLECTED REPRINTS. (Text and summaries in English and Japanese) 1969. a. Tokyo Daigaku, Sogo Kenkyu Shiryokan - University of Tokyo, University Museum, 3-1 Hongo 7-chome, Bunkyo-ku, Tokyo 113, Japan.

500 574.192　　JA　　ISSN 0371-6813
　　　　　　　　　　CODEN: TGDSBH
TOKYO GAKUGEI DAIGAKU KIYO/TOKYO GAKUGEI UNIVERSITY. BULLETIN. (Consists of 6 sections) (Text and summaries in English and Japanese) 1949. a. free. Tokyo Gakugei Daigaku, Shuppan linkai - Tokyo Gakugei University, Publication Committee, 1-1 Nukui Kita-machi 4-chome, Koganei-shi, Tokyo 184, Japan. Ed. Jun Inamori. circ. 600. **Indexed:** Chem.Abstr., INIS Atomind., Jap.Per.Ind., Sci.Abstr.
—BLDSC shelfmark: 2780.401000.

500　　　　　　JA　　ISSN 0386-4006
　　　　　　　　　　CODEN: SRTUDZ
TOKYO JOSHI DAIGAKU KIYO. RONSHU. KAGAKU BUMON HOKOKU/TOKYO WOMAN'S CHRISTIAN UNIVERSITY. SCIENCE REPORTS. (Text and summaries in English and Japanese) 1950. a. Tokyo Joshi Daigaku Gakkai - Tokyo Woman's Christian University, Academic Society, 2 Zenpukuji, Suginami-ku, Tokyo 167, Japan.

500　　　　　　JA　　ISSN 0918-0753
TOKYO RIKA DAIGAKU KENKYU RONBUNSHU/SCIENCE UNIVERSITY OF TOKYO. COLLECTED PAPERS. (Text and summaries in English, German, and Japanese) 1958. a. exchange basis only. Tokyo Rika Daigaku - Science University of Tokyo, 1-3 Kagurazaka, Shinjuku-ku, Tokyo 162, Japan. circ. 200.

500 387.5　　　JA　　ISSN 0493-4474
TOKYO SHOSEN DAIGAKU KENKYU HOKOKU. SHIZEN KAGAKU/TOKYO UNIVERSITY OF MERCANTILE MARINE. JOURNAL. NATURAL SCIENCES. (Text and summaries in English and Japanese) 1951. a. Tokyo Shosen Daigaku - Tokyo University of Mercantile Marine, 1-6 Etchujima 2-chome, Koto-ku, Tokyo 135, Japan. **Indexed:** Jap.Per.Ind.
—BLDSC shelfmark: 4909.030000.

500　　　　　　JA　　ISSN 0288-2329
TOKYO-TO NO SHIZEN. (Text in Japanese) 1973. a. Tokyo-to Takao Shizen Kagaku Hakubutsukan - Takao Museum of Natural History, 2436 Takao-machi, Hachioji-shi, Tokyo 193, Japan.

TOKYO-TO SHIKEN KENKYU KIKAN NO KENKYU KEIKAKU. see *PUBLIC ADMINISTRATION — Municipal Government*

500　　　　　　JA　　ISSN 0286-8768
TOKYO-TO TAKAO SHIZEN KAGAKU HAKUBUTSUKAN KENKYU HOKOKU/TAKAO MUSEUM OF NATURAL HISTORY. SCIENCE REPORT. (Text in Japanese; summaries in English and Japanese) 1970. irreg. Tokyo-to Takao Shizen Kagaku Hakubutsukan - Takao Museum of Natural History, 2436 Takao-machi, Hachioji-shi, Tokyo 193, Japan.

TOKYO UNIVERSITY OF FISHERIES. REPORT/TOKYO SUISAN DAIGAKU RONSHU. see *FISH AND FISHERIES*

500　　　　　　JA
TORAY KAGAKU SHINKOKAI JIGYO HOKOKUSHO/TORAY SCIENCE FOUNDATION. ANNUAL REPORT. (Text mainly in Japanese, partly in English) 1960. a. free. Toray Science Foundation, Toray Bldg., 8-1, Mihama 1-chome, Urayasu, Chiba 279, Japan. FAX 0473-50-6082. abstr.; circ. 700.

500　　　　　　JA
TORAY KAGAKU SHINKOKAI KAGAKU KOENKAI KIROKU. (Text in Japanese) 1963. a. free. Toray Science Foundation, Toray Bldg., 8-1, Mihama 1-chome, Urayasu, Chiba 279, Japan. FAX 0473-50-6082. circ. 2,400.
Description: Contains proceedings from the lecture meetings sponsored by the foundation.

500　　　　　　JA
TORAY RIKA KYOIKUSHO JUSHO SAKUHINSHU. (Text in Japanese) 1969. a. free. Toray Science Foundation, Toray Bldg., 8-1, Mihama 1-chome, Urayasu, Chiba 279, Japan. FAX 0473-50-6082. circ. 14,000. **Indexed:** Chem.Abstr.
Description: Publishes works which have received the Toray Science Education Prize.

500　　　　　　CN　　ISSN 0835-0663
TORONTO OFFICE GUIDE. 1985. q. Can.$35($45) Mensa Media, 111 Elizabeth St., Ste 700, Toronto, Ont. M5G 1P7, Canada. FAX 416-979-7682. Ed. Sandra A. Wilson. adv.; illus.

500.9　　　　　UK　　ISSN 0082-5344
TORQUAY NATURAL HISTORY SOCIETY. TRANSACTIONS AND PROCEEDINGS. 1909. a. £3. Torquay Natural History Society, The Museum, Babbacombe Road, Torquay TQ1 1HG, England. TEL 0803-23975. Ed. J. Martin. circ. 600. **Indexed:** Br.Archaeol.Abstr.

500　　　　　　JA　　ISSN 0371-5965
TOTTORI DAIGAKU KYOIKUGAKUBU KENKYU HOKOKU. SHIZEN KAGAKU/TOTTORI UNIVERSITY. FACULTY OF EDUCATION. JOURNAL: NATURAL SCIENCE. (Text in English and Japanese; summaries in English) 1950. s-a. Tottori Daigaku, Kyoikugakubu - Tottori University, Faculty of Education, 4-101 Minami, Koyama-cho, Tottori-shi, Tottori-ken 680, Japan. **Indexed:** Biol.Abstr., INIS Atomind., Jap.Per.Ind.
—BLDSC shelfmark: 4743.700000.

500　　　　　　JA　　ISSN 0287-1688
TOTTORI-KENRITSU HAKUBUTSUKAN KENKYU HOKOKU/TOTTORI PREFECTURAL MUSEUM. BULLETIN. (Text in Japanese; summaries in English and Japanese) 1962. a. Tottori-kenritsu Hakubutsukan - Tottori Prefectural Museum, 2-124 Higashi-machi, Tottori-shi, Tottori-ken 680, Japan. FAX 0857-26-8041. circ. 1,000.

500　　　　　　US
Q179.9
TOUCHSTONE MAGAZINE. 1966. 3/yr. free. University of Wisconsin-Madison, University-Industry Research Program, 1215 WARF Bldg., 610 Walnut St., Madison, WI 53705. TEL 608-263-2840. FAX 608-263-2841. Ed. Jean M. Lang. charts; illus.; circ. 6,000 (controlled).
Formerly (until 1983): U I R Research Newsletter (ISSN 0041-512X)
Description: Aimed at the educated layman; contains articles on research in science and engineering conducted at the university.

500　　　　　　PL　　ISSN 0079-4805
TOWARZYSTWO NAUKOWE W TORUNIU. PRACE POPULARNONAUKOWE. (Text in Polish; summaries in English, German) 1961. irreg., no.53, 1990. price varies. Towarzystwo Naukowe w Toruniu, Ul. Wysoka 16, 87-100 Torun, Poland. TEL 48-56-23941. TELEX 552388 FSBH PL. Ed. Cecylia Iwaniszewska. circ. 6,500.

500　　　　　　PL　　ISSN 0371-375X
TOWARZYSTWO NAUKOWE W TORUNIU. SPRAWOZDANIA. 1949. a. price varies. Towarzystwo Naukowe w Toruniu - Torun Scientific Society, Ul. Wysoka 16, 87-100 Torun, Poland. TEL 48-56-23941. TELEX 552388 FSBH PL. Ed. Janusz Kryszak. circ. 700.

500　　　　　　JA　　ISSN 0285-9610
Q4　　　　　　　　　CODEN: TDKBDG
TOYAMA DAIGAKU KYOIKUGAKUBU KIYO, B. RIKAKEI/TOYAMA UNIVERSITY. FACULTY OF EDUCATION. MEMOIRS, B. NATURAL SCIENCE. (Text in English and Japanese; summaries in English) 1953. a. Toyama Daigaku, Kyoikugakubu - Toyama University, Faculty of Education, 3190 Gofuku, Toyama-shi, Toyama-ken 930, Japan. **Indexed:** Chem.Abstr., Jap.Per.Ind.
—BLDSC shelfmark: 5593.332000.

500　　　　　　JA　　ISSN 0385-812X
TOYAMA DAIGAKU KYOYOBU KIYO. SHIZEN KAGAKU HEN/TOYAMA UNIVERSITY. COLLEGE OF LIBERAL ARTS. JOURNAL: NATURAL SCIENCES. (Text and summaries in English and Japanese) 1969. s-a. Toyama Daigaku, Kyoyobu - Toyama University, College of Liberal Arts, 3190 Gofuku, Toyama-shi, Toyama-ken 930, Japan. **Indexed:** Chem.Abstr., Jap.Per.Ind.

500　　　　　　JA　　ISSN 0387-9089
TOYAMA-SHI KAGAKU BUNKA SENTA KENKYU HOKOKU/TOYAMA SCIENCE MUSEUM. BULLETIN. (Text and summaries in English and Japanese) 1979. a. Toyama-shi Kagaku Bunka Senta - Toyama Science Museum, 1-19 Nishi-nakano-machi 3-chome, Toyama-shi, Toyama-ken 939, Japan.
Description: Contains research papers.

TOYAMA TO SHIZEN. see *MUSEUMS AND ART GALLERIES*

500　　　　　　JA　　ISSN 0372-0330
Q4　　　　　　　　　CODEN: TODKBF
TOYO DAIGAKU KIYO. KYOYO KATEI HEN. SHIZEN KAGAKU/TOYO UNIVERSITY. JOURNAL. GENERAL EDUCATION. NATURAL SCIENCE. (Text in Japanese; summaries in English) a. Toyo Daigaku - Toyo University, 28-20, Hakusan 5-chome, Bunkyo-ku, Tokyo 112, Japan. **Indexed:** Jap.Per.Ind.

500　　　　　　NE
TRACTRIX; yearbook for the history of science, medicine, technology, and mathematics. (Text mainly in English; occasionally in French, German) 1989. a. fl.67. (Dutch Society for the History of Medicine, Mathematics, Science, and Technology) Editions Rodopi B.V., Keizersgracht 302-304, 1016 EX Amsterdam, Netherlands. TEL 020-6227507. FAX 020-6380948. (US and Canada subscr. to: 233 Peachtree St., N.E., Ste. 404, Atlanta, GA 30303-1504. TEL 800-225-3998) Ed. C.F. Cohen.
Description: Promotes international information for historians of science, medicine, and technology.

500.9　　　　　SA　　ISSN 0041-1752
QH1　　　　　　　　CODEN: ATVMA4
TRANSVAAL MUSEUM. ANNALS/TRANSVAAL MUSEUM. ANNALE. (Text in Afrikaans, English,) 1908. irreg., vol.35, 1989. price varies. Transvaal Museum, P.O. Box 413, Pretoria 0001, South Africa. TEL 012-322-7632. FAX 012-322-7939. Ed. Dippenaar. illus.; index; circ. 350. (tabloid format; back issues avail.; reprint service avail. from SWZ) **Indexed:** Biol.Abstr., GeoRef, Ind.S.A.Per., Zoo.Rec.
—BLDSC shelfmark: 1034.000000.
Description: Original research articles in the field of zoology. Includes information on systematics.

500　　　　　　CR　　ISSN 0069-2107
TROPICAL SCIENCE CENTER, COSTA RICA. OCCASIONAL PAPER. 1963. irreg., latest vol.16, 1987. price varies. Tropical Science Center, Calle 1, No. 442, Apdo. 8-3840, San Jose, Costa Rica. FAX 506-57-04-04. TELEX (506) 35 53 90. Ed. Joseph A. Tosi, Jr. circ. 250. **Indexed:** Chem.Abstr.

500　　　　　　US　　ISSN 0259-3637
TSUNAMI NEWSLETTER. 1968. s-a. free. International Tsunami Information Center, Box 50027, Honolulu, HI 96850-4993. TEL 808-541-1658. FAX 808-541-1678. Ed. George Pararas-Carayannis. circ. 700. (back issues avail.)
Description: Providing news and information for scientists, engineers, educators, community protection agencies and government throughout the world.

SCIENCES: COMPREHENSIVE WORKS

500 574 NZ ISSN 0041-3860
QH197 CODEN: TUATAY
TUATARA. 1947. irreg. (Victoria University of Wellington, Departments of Botany and Zoology) Victoria University Press, P.O. Box 600, Wellington, New Zealand. Eds. G.W. Gibbs, B. Sampson. adv.; bk.rev.; charts; illus.; maps; index. cum.index; circ. 500. (back issues avail.) **Indexed:** Biol.Abstr., Curr.Adv.Ecol.Sci., Deep Sea Res.& Oceanogr.Abstr., GeoRef.
—BLDSC shelfmark: 9068.000000.

500 600 HU ISSN 0237-322X
TUDOMANY. Hungarian translation of: Scientific American. 1985. m. 1176 Ft.($40) Lapkiado Vallalat, Lenin korut 9-11, 1073 Budapest 7, Hungary. (Subscr. to: Kultura, Box 149, H-1389 Budapest, Hungary) Eds. Jonathan Piel, Futasz Dezso. adv.; bk.rev.; bibl.; charts; illus.; circ. 25,000. (back issues avail.)

501 HU ISSN 0082-6707
TUDOMANYSZERVEZESI FUZETEK. 1965. irreg. price varies. (Magyar Tudomanyos Akademia) Akademiai Kiado, Publishing House of the Hungarian Academy of Sciences, Box 24, H-1363 Budapest, Hungary.

500 FI ISSN 0082-7002
CODEN: AUTUAP
TURUN YLIOPISTO. JULKAISUJA. SARJA A. I. ASTRONOMICA - CHEMICA - PHYSICA - MATHEMATICA. (Latin title: Annales Universitatis Turkuensis) (Text in English, Finnish, French and German) 1922. irreg. price varies. Turun Yliopisto - University of Turku, SF-20500 Turku 50, Finland. FAX 358-21-6335050. TELEX 62123 TYK SF. **Indexed:** INIS Atomind., Sci.Abstr.
—BLDSC shelfmark: 0963.345000.
Description: Studies astronomy, chemistry, physical sciences and mathematics.

505 LB
U L SCIENCE AND TECHNOLOGY MAGAZINE.* 1972. s-a. $2. University of Liberia, Division of Science and Technology, Monrovia, Liberia. Ed. Kabineh Koroma. adv.; illus. **Indexed:** Biol.Abstr.
Former titles: U L Science Magazine & Liberian Naturalist (ISSN 0459-2298)

500 US ISSN 0436-2225
U S - R & D. 1964. m. $96. Government Data Publications, Inc., 1155 Connecticut Ave., N.W., Washington, DC 20036. Ed. Siegfried Lobel. s-a. index.

500 600 US
U S S R REPORT: SCIENCE AND TECHNOLOGY POLICY. irreg. (approx. 30/yr.) $10 per no. (foreign $14 per no.). U.S. Joint Publications Research Service, Box 12507, Arlington, VA 22209. TEL 703-487-4630. (Orders to: NTIS, Springfield, VA 22161)

500.9 GW ISSN 0068-0885
UEBERSEE-MUSEUM, BREMEN. VEROEFFENTLICHUNGEN. REIHE A: NATURWISSENSCHAFTEN. 1949. irreg., vol.10, 1990. price varies. Uebersee-Museum, Bremen, Bahnhofsplatz 13, 2800 Bremen, Germany.

UMANA AVVENTURA. see *ART*

600 500 UN ISSN 0503-4434
UNESCO. REGIONAL OFFICE FOR SCIENCE AND TECHNOLOGY FOR AFRICA. BULLETIN. (Editions in English and French) 1966. 2/yr. free to qualified institutions or on exchange basis. Unesco, Regional Office for Science and Technology for Africa (R.O.S.T.A.), P.O. Box 30592, Nairobi, Kenya. FAX 25402521045. TELEX 22275 NAIROBI. Ed. P. Lissouba. bk.rev.; bibl.; circ. 1,500.

500 600 GW ISSN 0179-7182
UNI REPORT. 1985. s-a. DM.15. Universitaet Dortmund, August-Schmidt-Str., 4600 Dortmund 50, Germany. TEL 0231-7511. FAX 0231-751532. TELEX 822465-UNIDO-D. (Subscr. to: Rhein Ruhr Druck Sander, Hengsener Str. 8a, 4600 Dortmund 12, Germany) Ed. Kurt Jauslin. adv.; bibl.; illus.; circ. 5,000. (back issues avail.)
Description: News and essays concerning the scientific and technological research.

500 CR ISSN 1011-0275
UNICIENCIA. (Text in English, Spanish) 1984. s-a. Col.600($4.50) (effective Jan. 1991). Universidad de Costa Rica, Facultad de Ciencias Exactas y Naturales, Heredia, Costa Rica. TEL 506-376363. FAX 506-376427. Ed. Edgar Suarez. bk.rev.; bibl.; charts; illus.; stat.; circ. 300. (back issues avail.)
Description: Covers basic and applied research in biology, chemistry, physics and mathematics.

UNION LIST OF SCIENTIFIC AND TECHNICAL PERIODICALS IN ZAMBIA. see *BIBLIOGRAPHIES*

500 TS
UNITED ARAB EMIRATES UNIVERSITY. FACULTY OF SCIENCE. JOURNAL/JAMI'AT AL-IMARAT AL-ARABIYYAH AL-MUTTAHIDAH. KULLIYYAT AL-ULUM. MAJALLAH.* (Text in Arabic, English) 1988. a. exchange basis. United Arab Emirates University, Faculty of Science, P.O. Box 17771, Al-Ain, United Arab Emirates. TEL 677280. TELEX 33521 JAMEAH EM. Ed. Muhammad Izzat Khairi. circ. 500.
Description: Publishes papers in mathematics, computer science, physics, chemistry, geology and the life sciences.

UNITED KINGDOM ATOMIC ENERGY AUTHORITY. LIST OF PUBLICATIONS AVAILABLE TO THE PUBLIC. see *BIBLIOGRAPHIES*

338.973 US
U.S. NATIONAL SCIENCE FOUNDATION. FEDERAL FUNDS FOR RESEARCH DEVELOPMENT. (Subseries of: U.S. National Science Foundation. Surveys of Science Resource Series) a. U.S. National Science Foundation, Science Resource Studies, Washington, DC 20550. TEL 202-634-4622.
Former titles: U.S. National Science Foundation. Federal Funds for Research, Development, and other Scientific Activities (ISSN 0198-8700); U.S. National Science Foundation. Federal Funds for Science (ISSN 0083-2359)

500 507.2 US
Q180.U5
U.S. NATIONAL SCIENCE FOUNDATION. FISCAL YEAR AWARDS. 1951. a. free. U.S. National Science Foundation, Science Resource Studies, Washington, DC 20550. TEL 202-655-4000. (Dist. by: Supt. Doc., Washington, DC 20402) **Indexed:** Biol.Abstr.
Former titles: U.S. National Science Foundation. Grants and Awards (ISSN 0565-825X); U.S. National Science Foundation. Annual Report (ISSN 0083-2332)
Description: Provides information on recent NSF grants.

U.S. NATIONAL SCIENCE FOUNDATION. GUIDE TO PROGRAMS. see *EDUCATION — School Organization And Administration*

500 IS
UNITED STATES - ISRAEL BINATIONAL SCIENCE FOUNDATION. ANNUAL REPORT. (Text in English) 1974. biennial. free. United States - Israel Binational Science Foundation, P.O. Box 7677, Jerusalem 91076, Israel. FAX 02-633287. circ. 4,000.

500 FR ISSN 0083-3673
UNIVERS HISTORIQUE. 1970. irreg. price varies. Editions du Seuil, 27 rue Jacob, 75261 Paris Cedex 06, France. Eds. Jacques Julliard, Michel Winock.

502 DR
UNIVERSIDAD AUTONOMA DE SANTO DOMINGO. DIRECCION DE INVESTIGACIONES. D I C BOLETIN. Cover title: D I C Boletin. vol.2, 1974. m. (Direccion de Investigaciones) Imprenta de Universidad Autonoma de Santo Domingo, Edificio Dr. Defillo, Ciudad Universitaria, Dominican Republic.

500 SP ISSN 0075-7721
Q65
UNIVERSIDAD DE LA LAGUNA. FACULTAD DE CIENCIAS. ANALES. 1962. irreg. $15 to individuals; institutions $20. Universidad de la Laguna, Secretariado de Publicaciones, San Agustin, 30, 38201 La Laguna-Tenerife, Canary Islands, Spain. TEL 922-28-81-27. adv.; bk.rev.

500 SP ISSN 0213-5469
Q65 CODEN: ANCIET
UNIVERSIDAD DE MURCIA. ANALES DE CIENCIAS. 1930. irreg., latest vol.44, 1986. 750 ptas. Universidad de Murcia, Secretariado de Publicaciones e Intercambio Cientifico, Santo Cristo, 1, 30001 Murcia, Spain. TEL 968-239450.
Former titles (until 1984): Universidad de Murcia. Ciencias. Anales (ISSN 0463-9847); (until 1954): Universidad de Murcia. Anales (ISSN 0365-7973)

500 SP
UNIVERSIDAD DE SEVILLA. SERIE: CIENCIAS. 1967. irreg., latest no.29. Universidad de Sevilla, Servicio de Publicaciones, San Fernando, 4, 41004 Seville, Spain. TEL 954-22-80715. FAX 954-22-1315. charts; illus.
Formerly: Universidad Hispalense. Anales. Serie: Ciencias (ISSN 0374-5880)

500 PY
UNIVERSIDAD NACIONAL DE ASUNCION. INSTITUTO DE CIENCIAS. MEMORIA. irreg. Universidad Nacional de Asuncion, Asuncion, Paraguay.

500 PO ISSN 0066-8079
UNIVERSIDADE DE LISBOA. FACULDADE DE CIENCIAS. INSTITUTO BOTANICO. ARTIGO DE DIVULGACAO. 1945. irreg. price varies. Universidade de Lisboa, Faculdade de Ciencias, Instituto Botanico, 1294 Lisbon Codex, Portugal.

500 BL ISSN 0102-597X
QH117 CODEN: BOIBEM
UNIVERSIDADE FEDERAL DO RIO GRANDE DO SUL. INSTITUTO DE BIOCIENCIAS. BOLETIM. (Text in Portuguese; summaries in English) 1954. irreg., no.45, 1989. exchange basis. Universidade Federal do Rio Grande do Sul, Instituto de Biociencias, Biblioteca, Av. Paulo Gama, s-n, 90040 - Porto Alegre, RS, Brazil. Ed.Bd. charts; illus.; index; circ. 1,000. **Indexed:** Biol.Abstr., Chem.Abstr.
—BLDSC shelfmark: 2131.780000.
Former titles (until 1977): Universidade Federal do Rio Grande do Sul. Instituto Central de Biociencias. Boletim (ISSN 0101-0972); (until 1970): Universidade do Rio Grande do Sul. Instituto de Ciencias Naturais. Boletim (ISSN 0079-4058)

500 IT ISSN 0041-8951
UNIVERSITA DEGLI STUDI DI CAGLIARI. SEMINARIO DELLA FACOLTA DI SCIENZA. RENDICONTI. (Text in English and Italian) 1931. s-a. exchange basis. Universita degli Studi di Cagliari, Seminario della Faculta di Scienze, Via Canelles, 15, 09124 Cagliari, Italy. Ed.Bd. bibl.; charts; illus. **Indexed:** Chem.Abstr.

001.3 500 GW ISSN 0512-1523
UNIVERSITAET FRANKFURT. WISSENSCHAFTLICHE GESELLSCHAFT. SITZUNGSBERICHTE. 1962. irreg., vol.28, no. 4, 1992. price varies. (Wissenschaftliche Gesellschaft) Franz Steiner Verlag Wiesbaden GmbH, Birkenwaldstr. 44, Postfach 101526, 7000 Stuttgart 1, Germany. TEL 0711-2582-0. FAX 0711-2582990. TELEX 723636-DAZD.

500 AU ISSN 0259-0700
UNIVERSITAET SALZBURG. DISSERTATIONEN. 1970. irreg., no.29, 1990. price varies. (Universitaet Salzburg) Verband der Wissenschaftlichen Gesellschaften Oesterreichs, Lindengasse 37, A-1070 Vienna, Austria. TEL 932166.

500 AU ISSN 0379-1424
UNIVERSITAET WIEN. DISSERTATIONEN. 1967. irreg., no.214, 1990. price varies. Verband der Wissenschaftlichen Gesellschaften Oesterreichs, Lindengasse 37, A-1070 Vienna, Austria. TEL 932166.

UNIVERSITAS (ENGLISH EDITION); quarterly German review of the arts and sciences. see *LITERATURE*

UNIVERSITAS (GERMAN EDITION); Zeitschrift fuer interdisziplinaere Wissenschaft. see *LITERATURE*

UNIVERSITAS (SPANISH EDITION); revista trimestral alemana de letras, ciencias y arte. see *LITERATURE*

500 RM
UNIVERSITATEA BUCURESTI. ANALELE. STIINTELE NATURII. (Text in English, French, or Rumanian) a. $10. Universitatea Bucuresti, Bd. 6h. Gheorghi-Dej Nr. 64, Bucharest, Rumania. **Indexed:** Biol.Abstr.

SCIENCES: COMPREHENSIVE WORKS

500.2   AE   ISSN 0002-533X
UNIVERSITE D'ALGER. PUBLICATIONS SCIENTIFIQUES. SERIE B: SCIENCES PHYSIQUES.* 1954. irreg. 15 F. per no. Universite d'Alger, 2 rue Didouche-Mourad, Algiers, Algeria. charts.

500 510   MG
UNIVERSITE DE MADAGASCAR. ETABLISSEMENT D'ENSEIGNEMENT SUPERIEUR DES SCIENCES. ANNALES: SERIE SCIENCES DE LA NATURE ET MATHEMATIQUES. (Text in French) no.4, 1966. a. Universite de Madagascar, Etablissement d'Enseignement Superieur des Sciences, B.P. 138, Antananarivo, Malagasy Republic.

505   CM   ISSN 0566-201X
UNIVERSITE DE YAOUNDE. FACULTE DES SCIENCES. ANNALES. 1968. irreg. $50 for 3 vols. Universite de Yaounde, Faculte des Sciences, Box 337, Yaounde, Cameroon. FAX 237-23-53-88. TELEX 8384 KN. (Dist. by: Service Central des Bibliotheques, Services des Publications, B.P. 1312, Yaounde, Cameroon) illus.
Continues: Universite Federale du Cameroun. Faculte des Sciences. Annales.

550 919.8   US   ISSN 0069-6145
                            CODEN: CAAOA
UNIVERSITY OF COLORADO. INSTITUTE OF ARCTIC AND ALPINE RESEARCH. OCCASIONAL PAPERS. 1971. irreg., no.47, 1990. price varies. University of Colorado, Institute of Arctic and Alpine Research, Campus Box 450, Boulder, CO 80309-6450. TEL 303-492-3765. FAX 803-492-6388. Ed. Kathleen A. Salzberg. circ. 200. (also avail. in microfiche from NTI) **Indexed:** Biol.Abstr., Geo.Abstr. —BLDSC shelfmark: 6217.436000.
Description: Monograph series containing miscellaneous work performed by institute personnel and associates.
Refereed Serial

UNIVERSITY OF KANSAS. MUSEUM OF NATURAL HISTORY. MISCELLANEOUS PUBLICATIONS. see *BIOLOGY*

UNIVERSITY OF KANSAS. MUSEUM OF NATURAL HISTORY. MONOGRAPHS. see *BIOLOGY*

574 500.9   US   ISSN 0091-7958
QH1   CODEN: OPMNAK
UNIVERSITY OF KANSAS. MUSEUM OF NATURAL HISTORY. OCCASIONAL PAPERS. 1971. irreg., no.142, 1991. University of Kansas, Museum of Natural History, 602 Dyche Hall, Lawrence, KS 66045-2454. Ed. Joseph T. Collins. circ. 1,500. (reprint service avail.) **Indexed:** Biol.Abstr., Deep Sea Res.& Oceanogr.Abstr., GeoRef.
Refereed Serial

UNIVERSITY OF KANSAS. MUSEUM OF NATURAL HISTORY. PUBLIC EDUCATION SERIES. see *BIOLOGY*

UNIVERSITY OF KANSAS. MUSEUM OF NATURAL HISTORY. SPECIAL PUBLICATIONS. see *BIOLOGY*

500   KU   ISSN 0376-4818
Q80.K9   CODEN: JUKSD8
UNIVERSITY OF KUWAIT. JOURNAL (SCIENCE). (Text in English; summaries in Arabic) 1974. s-a. free. University of Kuwait, Faculty of Science, Box 5969, Kuwait. Ed. Riad Halwagy. circ. 1,000. **Indexed:** Abstr.Health.Eff.Environ.Pollut., Anal.Abstr., Appl.Ecol.Abstr., Aqua.Sci.& Fish.Abstr., Biol.Abstr., Chem.Abstr., Chem.Titles, Crop Physiol.Abstr., Dairy Sci.Abstr., Excerp.Med., Field Crop Abstr., Hort.Abstr., I.M.M.Abstr., Ind.Vet., INIS Atomind., Math.R., Microbiol.Abstr., Plant Breed.Abstr., Rev.Appl.Entomol., Sci.Abstr., Triticale Abstr., Vet.Bull.
—BLDSC shelfmark: 4911.550000.

500   NR   ISSN 0075-7713
UNIVERSITY OF LAGOS. SCIENTIFIC MONOGRAPH SERIES.* 1971. irreg. price varies. University of Lagos, Centre for Cultural Studies, Akoba, Yaba, Hiseha, Nigeria.

UNIVERSITY OF MICHIGAN. DIVISION OF RESEARCH DEVELOPMENT AND ADMINISTRATION. RESEARCH NEWS. see *EDUCATION — Higher Education*

500   US   ISSN 0897-6376
UNIVERSITY OF NEVADA. DESERT RESEARCH INSTITUTE. TECHNICAL REPORT. 1966. irreg. price varies. University of Nevada, Desert Research Institute, Social Sciences Center, Box 60220, Reno, NV 89506. TEL 702-673-7303. circ. 750. **Indexed:** Abstr.Anthropol.
Refereed Serial

500   AT   ISSN 0811-7640
UNIVERSITY OF NEW SOUTH WALES. FACULTY HANDBOOKS: SCIENCES. a? Aus.$5. University of New South Wales, P.O. Box 1, Kensington, N.S.W. 2033, Australia. TEL 02-697-2840. FAX 02-662-2163.

UNIVERSITY OF OSAKA PREFECTURE. BULLETIN. SERIES A: ENGINEERING AND NATURAL SCIENCES/OSAKA-FURITSU DAIGAKU KIYO, A. KOGAKU, SHIZEN KAGAKU. see *ENGINEERING*

378.1 700 800   US   ISSN 0041-9923
AS36
UNIVERSITY OF PORTLAND REVIEW; journal of arts and sciences. 1948. s-a. $1. University of Portland, 5000 N. Willamette Blvd., Portland, OR 97203. TEL 503-283-7911. FAX 503-283-7399. Ed. Thompson M. Faller. bk.rev.; cum.index; circ. 1,000. (tabloid format)

500   PK   ISSN 0080-9624
Q1.A1   CODEN: SURJAA
UNIVERSITY OF SIND. RESEARCH JOURNAL. SCIENCE SERIES. (Text in English) 1965. a. Rs.25($4) University of Sind, Faculty of Science, Jamshoro, Hyderabad 6, Pakistan. Ed. M. Rais Ahmed.

500 375   AT   ISSN 1036-0719
▼**UNIVERSITY OF TECHNOLOGY, SYDNEY. FACULTY OF SCIENCE HANDBOOK.** 1990. a. Aus.$5 (foreign Aus.$10). University of Technology, Sydney, P.O. Box 123, City Campus, Broadway, N.S.W. 2007, Australia. TEL 02-330-1990. FAX 02-330-1551. circ. 3,000.
Description: Contains detailed information on the faculty, schools, staff, courses, subject synopses, and general information on the university.

UNIVERSITY OF TECHNOLOGY, SYDNEY. RESEARCH AND CONSULTANCY REPORT. see *TECHNOLOGY: COMPREHENSIVE WORKS*

500   IR   ISSN 0042-0131
UNIVERSITY OF TEHERAN. FACULTY OF SCIENCE. QUARTERLY BULLETIN. (Text in English, French or Persian) 1968. q. Rs.350($10) (University of Teheran, Faculty of Science) University of Teheran Press Co., Enghelab Ave., Teheran, Iran. Ed.Bd. circ. 1,000. **Indexed:** Biol.Abstr., Chem.Abstr.

500   JA   ISSN 0289-7520
Q1   CODEN: SPCTDZ
UNIVERSITY OF TOKYO. COLLEGE OF ARTS AND SCIENCES. SCIENTIFIC PAPERS/TOKYO DAIGAKU KYOYOGAKUBU SHIZEN KAGAKU KIYO. (Text in European languages) 1951. s-a. exchange basis. University of Tokyo, College of Arts and Sciences - Tokyo Daigaku Kyoyogakubu, 8-1 Komaba 3-chome, Meguro-ku, Tokyo 153, Japan. FAX 81-3-3485-2904. TELEX 2426728 TODAIK J. Ed. Tadao Matsumoto. charts; illus.; index; circ. 460. **Indexed:** Appl.Mech.Rev., Biol.Abstr., Chem.Abstr., Curr.Adv.Ecol.Sci., Deep Sea Res.& Oceanogr.Abstr., GeoRef, INIS Atomind., Math.R., Plant Breed.Abstr., Sci.Abstr.
—BLDSC shelfmark: 8186.985000.
Formerly: University of Tokyo. College of General Education. Scientific Papers (ISSN 0040-8964)

500   JA
UNIVERSITY OF TOKYO. UNIVERSITY MUSEUM. BULLETIN/TOKYO DAIGAKU SOGO KENKYU SHIRYOKAN KENKYU HOKOKU. (Text in English) 1970. irreg. Tokyo Daigaku Shuppankai - University of Tokyo Press, 3-1, Hongo 7-chome, Bunkyo-ku, Tokyo 113, Japan.
Description: Contains original research papers.

UNIVERSITY OF WESTERN ONTARIO SERIES IN PHILOSOPHY OF SCIENCE. see *PHILOSOPHY*

500   YU   ISSN 0351-6962
UNIVERZITET SVETOZAR MARKOVIC U KRAGUJEVCU. PRIRODNO-MATEMATICKI FAKULTET. ZBORNIK RADOVA/FACULTY OF SCIENCE, KRAGUJEVAC. COLLECTION OF SCIENTIFIC PAPERS. (Text in English and Serbo-Croatian; summaries in English) 1980. a. $100. Univerzitet Svetozar Markovic, Prirodno-Matematicki Fakultet, Box 60, 34000 Kragujevac, Yugoslavia. TEL 69120. FAX 38-34-60252. circ. 100. (back issues avail.) **Indexed:** Math.R.
Description: Original scientific papers in the natural sciences and mathematics.

500   PL
UNIWERSYTET GDANSKI. ZESZYTY NAUKOWE. ROZPRAWY I MONOGRAFIE. 1978. irreg. price varies. Uniwersytet Gdanski, c/o Biblioteka Glowna, Ul. Armii Krajowej 110, 81-824 Sopot, Poland. TEL 51-0061. TELEX 051 2247 BMOR PL. (Dist. by: Ars Polona-Ruch, Krakowskie Przedmiescie 7, 00-680 Warsaw, Poland)
Description: Dissertations and monographs of the University of Gdansk.

500   JA   ISSN 0287-2900
UTAN. (Text in Japanese) 1982. m. 5400 Yen. Gakken Co. Ltd. - Gakushu Kenkyusha, 40-5, Kamiikedai 4-chome, Ota-ku, Tokyo 145, Japan. Ed. Nobuhiro Masuda.

500   JA   ISSN 0385-2415
AS552.U86   CODEN: UDKKBI
UTSUNOMIYA DAIGAKU KYOIKUGAKUBU KIYO. DAI-2-BU/UTSUNOMIYA UNIVERSITY. FACULTY OF EDUCATION. BULLETIN. SECTION 2. (Text and summaries in English and Japanese) 1950. a. Utsunomiya Daigaku, Kyoikugakubu - Utsunomiya University, Faculty of Education, 350, Mine-machi, Utsunomiya-shi, Tochigi-ken 321, Japan. **Indexed:** INIS Atomind., Jap.Per.Ind.
—BLDSC shelfmark: 2507.670000.

500   JA   ISSN 0286-6293
AS552.U86   CODEN: UDKKAH
UTSUNOMIYA DAIGAKU KYOYOBU KENKYU HOKOKU. DAI-2-BU/UTSUNOMIYA UNIVERSITY. FACULTY OF GENERAL EDUCATION. BULLETIN. SECTION 2. (Text and summaries in English and Japanese) 1968. a. Utsunomiya Daigaku, Kyoyobu - Utsunomiya University, Faculty of General Education, 350, Mine-machi, Utsunomiya-shi, Tochigi-ken 320, Japan. **Indexed:** Biol.Abstr., Chem.Abstr., Jap.Per.Ind.

500   II   ISSN 0083-5013
UTTAR PRADESH, INDIA. SCIENTIFIC RESEARCH COMMITTEE MONOGRAPH SERIES. (Text in English) irreg. price varies. Scientific Research Committee, Uttar Pradesh, Chhattar Manzil Palace, Lucknow, Uttar Pradesh, India.

500   RU   ISSN 0208-0621
V MIRE NAUKI. Russian translation of: Scientific American (US ISSN 0036-8733) 1983. m. 36 Rub.($99.50) (typically set in Jan.). Izdatel'stvo Mir, 2 Pervy Rizhsky Pereulok, 129820 Moscow, Russia. TEL 286-2588. FAX 288-9522. TELEX 411466 MIR SU. Eds. Sergey P. Kapitza, Lydia V. Shepeleva. adv.; bk.rev.; bibl.; charts; illus.; circ. 15,000.

V R B - INFORMATIE. (Vereniging van Religieus - Wetenschappelijke Bibliothecarissen) see *LIBRARY AND INFORMATION SCIENCES*

500   FI   ISSN 1235-0621
V T T PUBLICATIONS. (Text in English) 1981. irreg. Valtion Teknillinen Tutkimuskeskus, Information Service, P.O. Box 42, 02151 Espoo 15, Finland. FAX 358-0-4564374. (reprint service avail. from NTI) **Indexed:** Biol.Abstr., Chem.Abstr.
Formerly (until 1992): Technical Research Centre of Finland. Publications (ISSN 0358-5069)

500 600   GW   ISSN 0083-5080
VADEMECUM DEUTSCHER LEHR- UND FORSCHUNGSSTAETTEN. STAETTEN DER FORSCHUNG. 1954. irreg., vol.10, 1992. DM.490. Dr. Josef Raabe Verlag GmbH, Rotebuehlstr. 77, 7000 Stuttgart 1, Germany. TEL 0711-629000. FAX 0711-6290010. adv.; circ. 5,000.
●Also available online. Vendor(s): STN International.

SCIENCES: COMPREHENSIVE WORKS

500.1 UK ISSN 0049-5891
VASCULUM. 1915. q. £6. Northern Naturalists Union, Sunderland Museum & Art Gallery, Borough Rd., Sunderland, Tyne and Wear SR1 1PP, England. Eds. A. Coles, L. Jessop. bk.rev.; circ. 250. **Indexed:** Curr.Adv.Ecol.Sci., GeoRef.
—BLDSC shelfmark: 9149.000000.

VEDA, TECHNIKA A MY/SCIENCE, TECHNOLOGY AND WE. see *CHILDREN AND YOUTH — For*

500 US ISSN 0083-5846
VERSTAENDLICHE WISSENSCHAFT. (Issues not numbered consecutively) (Text in German) 1952. irreg. price varies. Springer-Verlag, 175 Fifth Ave., New York, NY 10010. TEL 212-460-1500. (Also Berlin, Heidelberg, Tokyo and Vienna) (reprint service avail. from ISI) **Indexed:** Biol.Abstr.

500 CS ISSN 0042-4544
CODEN: VESMAD
VESMIR/UNIVERSE. (Text in Czech and Slovak) 1871. m. DM.87. (Czechoslovak Academy of Sciences) Academia, Publishing House of the Czechoslovak Academy of Sciences, Vodickova 40, 112 29 Prague 1, Czechoslovakia. TEL 236-74-70. (Subscr. to: Artia, Ve Smeckach 30, 111 27 Prague 1, Czechoslovakia) Ed. Prokop Malek. bk.rev.; illus.; index; circ. 11,500. **Indexed:** Biol.Abstr., Chem.Abstr., GeoRef, Helminthol.Abstr.
—BLDSC shelfmark: 9218.500000.
Description: Covers general issues of scientific information and discoveries in science, medicine and technology.

500.9 AT ISSN 0042-5184
QH1 CODEN: VICNAW
VICTORIAN NATURALIST. 1884. bi-m. Aus.$50. Field Naturalists Club of Victoria, c/o National Herbarium, Birdwood Avenue, South Yarra, Vic. 3141, Australia. TEL 03-650-8661. Eds. Robyn Watson, Tim Offor. adv.; bk.rev.; charts; illus.; index; circ. 1,500. **Indexed:** Biol.Abstr., Forest.Abstr., Forest Prod.Abstr., Geo.Abstr., GeoRef, M.L.A.
—BLDSC shelfmark: 9232.650000.
Description: Publishes articles on all facts of natural history, primarily in Australia.

500 CE
VIDURAVA. (Text in English, Sinhala and Tamil) 1976. s-a. $8. Natural Resources, Energy & Science Authority, 47-5 Maitland Place, Colombo 7, Sri Lanka. Ed. Nimala Amarasuriya. (reprint service avail.) **Indexed:** Sri Lanka Sci.Ind.

500 II ISSN 0505-4753
CODEN: VIBBDS
VIDYA. vol.16, 1973. s-a. Rs.5. Gujarat University, P.O. Box 4010, Ahmedabad 380009, India. Ed.Bd. bibl.; charts; illus. **Indexed:** Chem.Abstr.

500 331.8 FR ISSN 0042-5427
VIE DE LA RECHERCHE SCIENTIFIQUE. 1960. m. & q. 250 F. (foreign 300 F.). Syndicat National des Chercheurs Scientifiques, 26, rue Boyer, 75020 Paris Cedex 20, France. Ed. Robert Descimon. adv.; charts; circ. 4,600.

500 FR ISSN 0762-0969
Q46
LA VIE DES SCIENCE; comptes rendus de l'Academie des Sciences - serie generale. 1984. 5/yr. 305 F. to individuals; institutions 510 F. Gauthier-Villars, 15 rue Gossin, 92543 Montrouge Cedex, France. TEL 33-1-40-92-65-00. FAX 33-1-40-92-65-97. TELEX 270 004. (Subscr. to: Centrale des Revues, 11 rue Gossin, 92543 Montrouge Cedex, France. TEL 33-1-46-56-52-66) Eds. Paul Germain, Francois Gros. index; circ. 3,200. **Indexed:** INIS Atomind.

500 600 II ISSN 0377-8487
Q73 CODEN: VBHAD6
VIGNANA BHARATHI.* (Text in English) 1975. s-a. Rs.10. Bangalore University, Department of Publications and Extension Lectures, Bangalore 560056, India. **Indexed:** GeoRef, Math.R., Sci.Abstr.
Description: Contains research articles on science and technology.

500 II ISSN 0042-6075
VIGYAN PRAGATI. (Text in Hindi; titles in English) 1952. m. $5.50. Council of Scientific and Industrial Research, Publications and Information Directorate Bldg., Hillside Road, New Delhi 110 012, India. Ed. G.P. Phondke. adv.; bk.rev.; circ. 60,000. (reprint service avail.) **Indexed:** Chem.Abstr.
Description: Presents the popularization of science in simple terms.

500 II ISSN 0042-6121
VIKRAM.* (Text in English, Hindi and Sanskrit) 1957. 4/yr. (nos.1 & 3 devoted to Physical and Biological Sciences, Agriculture, Medicine; nos.2 & 4 devoted to Arts & Indology). Rs.10. Vikram University, Registrar, Ujain, Madhya Pradesh, India. Eds. Dr. Har Swarup (Science Issue), Shri V. Venkatachalam (Arts Issue). charts; illus. **Indexed:** Abstr.Mil.Bibl., Biol.Abstr., Chem.Abstr., Math.R.

500 IC ISSN 0376-2599
CODEN: VIISA9
VISINDAFELAG ISLENDINGA. RIT/ICELANDIC SCIENTIFIC SOCIETY. OCCASIONAL PAPERS. (Text in English) 1923. irreg., latest no.45, 1988. price varies. Visindafelag Islendinga - Societas Scientiarum Islandica (Icelandic Scientific Society), University of Iceland, Haskolabokasafn - University Library, 101 Reykjavik, Iceland. (Subscr. to: Bokaverslun Sigfusar Eymundssonar, Austurstraeti 18, 101 Reykjavik, Iceland; or: Bokabud Mals og Menningar, Laugavegi 18, 101 Reykjavik, Iceland) circ. 1,000. **Indexed:** Biol.Abstr.

500 600 US ISSN 1051-8711
VISIONS (BEAVERTON). 1985. q. free. Oregon Graduate Institute of Science and Technology, 19600 N.W. Von Neumann Dr., Beaverton, OR 97006. TEL 503-690-1098. FAX 503-690-1110. Ed. Steve Dodge. adv.; bk.rev.; circ. 20,000.
Description: Understandable information about the world of science and technology.

500 700 CE
VISVA. (Text in Sinhalese) 1976. bi-m. Rs.2.50 per no. 301 Galle Rd., Colombo 3, Sri Lanka.

500 IT
VITA NUOVA; realta spiritica. 1977. bi-m. L.30000($40) Edizioni Vita Nuova, Via Venini 67, 20127 Milan, Italy. TEL 02-2893502. FAX 2-89010999. bk.rev.; illus; circ. 3,000. (back issues avail.)
Description: Examines research on the psychic and spiritual nature of the human being.

500 CE
VIYODAYA JOURNAL OF SCIENCE. (Text in English, Sinhalese, and Tamil) 1968. a. Rs.90($10) University of Sri Jayawardenapura, Nugegoda, Sri Lanka. TEL 55-2695. FAX 55-2604. Ed.Bd. bk.rev.; bibl.; illus.; stat; index. cum. index; circ. 1,000. **Indexed:** Sci.Cit.Ind., Sri Lanka Sci.Ind.
Supersedes in part (from Jul. 1987): Vidyodaya (ISSN 0042-532X).

500 947 RU ISSN 0205-9606
VOPROSY ISTORII ESTESTVOZNANYA I TEKHNIKI. 1956. 4/yr. 32 Rub. (Institut Istorii Estestvoznaniya i Tekhniki) Izdatel'stvo Nauka, 90 Profsoyuznaya ul., 117864 Moscow, Russia. TEL 234-05-84. (Subscr. addr.: Staropanskii Per. 1-5, 103012 Moscow, Russia) bk.rev.; illus.; bibl. **Indexed:** Hist.Abstr., Math.R.
—BLDSC shelfmark: 0042.750400.

500 JA ISSN 0511-0831
CODEN: WDKSAT
WAKAYAMA DAIGAKU KYOIKUGAKUBU KIYO. SHIZEN KAGAKU/WAKAYAMA UNIVERSITY. FACULTY OF EDUCATION. BULLETIN: NATURAL SCIENCE. (Text in English and Japanese; summaries in English) 1950. a. Wakayama Daigaku, Kyoikugakubu - Wakayama University, Faculty of Education, 930, Sakaedani, Wakayama-shi, Wakayama-ken 640, Japan. (Co-sponsor: Wakayama Daigaku Gakugei Gakkai - Wakayama University, Liberal Arts Society) **Indexed:** Biol.Abstr., Chem.Abstr., Jap.Per.Ind.

500 US
WAKE-ROBIN. 1970. a. free. John Burroughs Association, 15 W. 77th St., New York, NY 10024. TEL 212-769-5169. FAX 212-769-5233. Ed. Dr. Alfred Marks. bk.rev.; circ. 480. (back issues avail.)
Description: Focuses on nature-oriented and conservation essays, as well as news of the association.

500 620 JA ISSN 0372-7181
CODEN: WDRKA6
WASEDA DAIGAKU RIKOGAKU KENKYUJO HOKOKU/WASEDA UNIVERSITY. SCIENCE AND ENGINEERING RESEARCH LABORATORY. BULLETIN. (Text in Japanese and European languages) 1944. q. Waseda Daigaku, Rikogaku Kenkyujo - Waseda University, Science and Engineering Research Laboratory, 17 Kikui-cho, Shinjuku-ku, Tokyo 162, Japan. FAX 03-203-3231. charts; illus.; circ. 1,000. **Indexed:** Chem.Abstr., Eng.Ind., INIS Atomind., Jap.Per.Ind., Math.R.
—BLDSC shelfmark: 2702.700000.

500 620 JA ISSN 0285-4333
WASEDA UNIVERSITY. SCIENCE AND ENGINEERING RESEARCH LABORATORY. REPORT. (Text in English) 1973. irreg. Waseda Daigaku, Rikogaku Kenkyujo - Waseda University, Science and Engineering Research Laboratory, 17 Kikui-cho, Shinjuku-ku, Tokyo 162, Japan. FAX 03-203-3231.

500 US ISSN 0043-0439
Q11 CODEN: JWASA3
WASHINGTON ACADEMY OF SCIENCES. JOURNAL. 1899. q. $25 (foreign $35). Washington Academy of Sciences, 1101 N. Highland St., Arlington, VA 22201. FAX 703-524-1457. Ed. Bruce Hill. bk.rev.; bibl.; charts; illus.; circ. 1,000. (also avail. in microform from UMI) **Indexed:** Biol.Abstr., Biol.Dig., Chem.Abstr., Deep Sea Res.& Oceanogr.Abstr., Eng.Ind., GeoRef, Leg.Per., Math.R., Met.Abstr., Rev.Plant Path., Sci.Abstr. Key Title: Journal of the Washington Academy of Sciences.
—BLDSC shelfmark: 4913.000000.
Supersedes (in 1911): Washington Academy of Sciences. Proceedings (ISSN 0363-1095)

500 US ISSN 0740-0535
WASHINGTON FEDERAL SCIENCE NEWSLETTER. 1989. s-m. (m. Jan. & Aug.) $310 in N. America; elsewhere $400. Washington Federal Science Newsletter, Inc., 1057-B National Press Bldg., Washington, DC 20045. TEL 202-393-3640. (Subscr. to: Box 2075, Washington, DC 20013) Ed. Murray Felsher. bk.rev.; bibl.; stat.; tr.lit. (back issues avail.)
Description: Covers science and technology research being undertaken by all US agencies. Includes programs, budgets, and personnel.

500.9 JA ISSN 0389-6951
WATASHITACHI NO SHIZENSHI/NATURAL HISTORY. (Text in Japanese) 1979. 4/yr. 3000 Yen. Kitakyushu Shizenshi Tomo no Kai, Kitakyushu Shizenshi Hakubutsukan, Kokutetsu Yahataeki Bldg., 3-6, Nishi-Hon-machi, Yahatahigashi-ku, Kitakyushu-shi, Fukuoka-ken 805, Japan. FAX 093-661-7503. circ. 2,000.

WECHSELWIRKUNG; Technik Naturwissenschaft Gesellschaft. see *TECHNOLOGY: COMPREHENSIVE WORKS*

500 IS ISSN 0334-1151
WEIZMANN INSTITUTE OF SCIENCE. RESEARCH. (Text in English) 1977. s-a. free. Weizmann Institute of Science, Public Affairs Department, Rehovot, Israel. TEL 08-342111. FAX 08-466966. TELEX 381300. abstr.; circ. 6,000. (looseleaf format)

500 600 IS ISSN 0083-7849
Q80.I78
WEIZMANN INSTITUTE OF SCIENCE, REHOVOT, ISRAEL. SCIENTIFIC ACTIVITIES. (Text in English) 1953. a. Weizmann Institute of Science, Office of the Academic Secretary, Rehovot, Israel. TEL 08-342111. FAX 08-466966. TELEX 381300. circ. 3,000.

500 UK ISSN 0083-7989
WENNER GREN CENTER INTERNATIONAL SYMPOSIUM SERIES. 1962. irreg. price varies. Macmillan Press Ltd., Houndmills, Basingstoke, Hampshire RG2 2XS, England. (Dist. by: Stockton Press, 15 E. 26th St., New York, NY 10010) **Indexed:** Biol.Abstr., Chem.Abstr.
—BLDSC shelfmark: 9295.150000.

500 NR ISSN 0043-3020
WEST AFRICAN SCIENCE ASSOCIATION. JOURNAL. irreg. West African Science Association, P.O. Box 4039, University of Ibadan, Ibadan, Nigeria. TEL 400-550.

4352 SCIENCES: COMPREHENSIVE WORKS

500   **US**
WEST VIRGINIA ACADEMY OF SCIENCE. PROCEEDINGS. 1925. s-a. $20 to non-members; members $15. West Virginia Academy of Science, 237 Brooks Hall-Biology, Morgantown, WV 26506-6057. TEL 304-293-5201. FAX 304-293-6858. Ed. E.C. Keller, Jr. adv.; abstr.; cum.index: 1925-1975; circ. 425. (back issues avail.) **Indexed:** Bio-Contr.News & Info., Biol.Abstr., Field Crop Abstr., Geo.Abstr., Herb.Abstr., Math.R., Plant Breed.Abstr., Plant Grow.Reg.Abstr., Rev.Plant Path., Weed Abstr.

500   **AT**
WESTERN AUSTRALIAN NATURALIST. 1950. irreg. (3-4/yr.). Aus.$30. Western Australian Naturalists' Club, P.O. Box 156, Nedlands, W.A. 6009, Australia. FAX 610-272-8688. Ed. K.F. Kenneally. adv.; circ. 550. **Indexed:** Biol.Abstr.
Former titles: Western Australian Naturalist Scientific Journal (ISSN 0726-9609); Western Australian Naturalists' Club, Perth. Handbook (ISSN 0083-8748)

500.9   **GW**
WESTFAELISCHEN MUSEUM FUER NATURKUNDE. ABHANDLUNGEN. 1930. irreg. (2-4/yr.). price varies. Westfaelisches Museum fuer Naturkunde, Sentruperstr. 285, 4400 Muenster, Germany. charts; illus.; index. **Indexed:** Biol.Abstr.
Formerly: Landesmuseum fuer Naturkunde zu Muenster in Westfalen. Abhandlungen (ISSN 0023-7906)

500   **NE**   ISSN 0043-4442
Q4   CODEN: WSSLAH
WETENSCHAP & SAMENLEVING. 1947. bi-m. fl.55. (Vereniging van Wetenschappelijke Werkers) S S N, Van Berchenstr. 17-19, 6511 BA Nijmegen, Netherlands. Ed. Guus Termeer. adv.; bk.rev.; abstr.; circ. 1,200. **Indexed:** Chem.Abstr., Excerp.Med.
—BLDSC shelfmark: 9305.200000.

590 580 579   **AT**
WHIRRAKEE. 1967. m. (except Jan.). Aus.$16. Bendigo Field Naturalist Club, P.O. Box 396, Bendigo, Vic. 3550, Australia. Ed. R. Orr. circ. 170. (back issues avail.)
Supersedes in 1980: Bendigo Naturalist.

500 600   **US**
WHO KNOWS: A GUIDE TO WASHINGTON EXPERTS. 1978. irreg. (approx. every 18 mos.). $155. Washington Researchers Publishing (Subsidiary of: Washington Researchers, Ltd.), 2612 P St., N.W., Washington, DC 20007. TEL 202-333-3533. Ed.Bd.
Former titles: Who Knows: the Directory of Experts; (until 1986): Researcher's Guide to Washington.

WHO'S WHO IN INDIAN SCIENCE. see *BIOGRAPHY*

WHO'S WHO IN SCIENCE AND ENGINEERING. see *BIOGRAPHY*

500 600   **US**   ISSN 0887-5901
T39
WHO'S WHO IN TECHNOLOGY. 1979. biennial. $380 (Biography $95; Index $285). Gale Research Inc., Dept. 77748, Detroit, MI 48226. TEL 313-961-2242. FAX 313-961-6083. TELEX 810-221-7086. Ed. Amy Unterburger.
●Also available online. Vendor(s): Mead Data Central, Pergamon Infoline (WHOTECH).
Description: Profiles of the nation's leading scientists and engineers.

WILTSHIRE ARCHAEOLOGICAL AND NATURAL HISTORY MAGAZINE (1982). see *ARCHAEOLOGY*

WILTSHIRE ARCHAEOLOGICAL AND NATURAL HISTORY SOCIETY. ANNUAL REPORT (YEAR). see *ARCHAEOLOGY*

WISSENSCHAFT IN DEN MEDIEN. see *JOURNALISM*

500   **BN**   ISSN 0350-0012
WISSENSCHAFTLICHE MITTEILUNGEN DES BOSNISCH-HERZEGOWINISCHEN LANDESMUSEUMS. NATURWISSENSCHAFT. (Text in German) no.5, 1975. irreg. Zemaljski Muzej Bosne i Hercegovine, Vojvode Putnika 7, Sarajevo, Bosnia Hercegovina. Ed. Zeljka Bjelcic.

500   **GW**   ISSN 0720-9991
                    CODEN: WISSD5
WISSENSCHAFTSMAGAZIN. 1981. a. DM.9. Technische Universitaet Berlin, Presse- und Informationsreferat, Strasse des 17. Juni 135, 1000 Berlin 12, Germany. TEL 030-31422919. FAX 030-31423909. adv.; circ. 5,000. (back issues avail.)

WOMEN AI KEXUE/WE LOVE SCIENCE. see *CHILDREN AND YOUTH — For*

WOMEN AND MINORITIES IN SCIENCE AND ENGINEERING. see *ENGINEERING*

500 600   **US**   ISSN 1057-2821
▼**WONDER: OBSERVING & CONFRONTING THE ENIGMAS THAT SURROUND US.** 1991. a. $5. Zigguart Press, Box 394, Sound Beach, NY 11789. Ed. Norman Weisberg.
Description: For students of all ages; explores the interconnections and machineries of the universe.

500   **CN**   ISSN 0049-7886
WOOD DUCK. 1947. 9/yr. membership. Hamilton Naturalist's Club, Box 5182, Hamilton, Ont. L8S 4L3, Canada. Ed. Rob Dobos. bk.rev.; circ. 600.

500 600   **US**   ISSN 0897-926X
WORCESTER POLYTECHNIC INSTITUTE - STUDIES IN SCIENCE, TECHNOLOGY AND CULTURE. (Text in English and other West European languages) 1988. irreg. Peter Lang Publishing, Inc., 62 W. 45th St., 4th Fl., New York, NY 10036. TEL 212-302-6740. Eds. Lance Schachterle, Francis C. Lutz.
—BLDSC shelfmark: 9347.625000.

500   **PL**   ISSN 0084-3024
WROCLAWSKIE TOWARZYSTWO NAUKOWE. PRACE. SERIA B. NAUKI SCISLE. (Text in Polish; summaries in English, French, and German) 1947. irreg., no.210, 1987. price varies. Ossolineum, Publishing House of the Polish Academy of Sciences, Rynek 9, Wroclaw, Poland. TELEX 0712771 OSS PL. Ed. J. Kolbuszewski.
—BLDSC shelfmark: 6588.797000.

500   **PL**   ISSN 0371-4756
WROCLAWSKIE TOWARZYSTWO NAUKOWE. SPRAWOZDANIA. SERIA A. irreg., vol.39, 1986. price varies. Ossolineum, Publishing House of the Polish Academy of Sciences, Rynek 9, Wroclaw, Poland. TELEX 0712771 OSS PL. (Dist. by: Ars Polona-Ruch, Krakowskie Przedmiescie 7, Warsaw, Poland) Ed. A. Galos.
Description: Reports of activities and sessions of the Humanistic Section of the Wroclaw Scientific Society. Summaries of dissertations.

500.9   **PL**   ISSN 0043-9592
WSZECHSWIAT/UNIVERSE. (Text in Polish) 1882. m. $21. (Polskie Towarzystwo Przyrodnikow im. Kopernika) Panstwowe Wydawnictwo Naukowe, Miodowa 10, 00-251 Warsaw, Poland. (Dist. by: Ars Polona, Krakowskie Przedmiescie 7, 00-068 Warsaw, Poland) Ed. J. Vetulani. bk.rev.; charts; illus.; index; circ. 3,340. **Indexed:** Biol.Abstr.

500   **CC**   ISSN 0253-9888
                    CODEN: WTHPDI
WUHAN DAXUE XUEBAO (ZIRAN KEXUE BAN)/WUHAN UNIVERSITY. JOURNAL (NATURAL SCIENCE EDITION). (Text in Chinese) q. $1.20 per no. Wuhan Daxue, Xuebao Bianjibu, Luo Jia Shan, Wuchang-qu, Wuhan, Hubei 430072, People's Republic of China. TEL 812712. (Dist. by: China International Book Trading Corp., P.O. Box 399, Beijing, P.R.C.) Ed. Wang Renhui. **Indexed:** Chem.Abstr., Math.R.
—BLDSC shelfmark: 4917.469300.
Formerly: Wuhan Daxue Ziran Kexue Xuebao (ISSN 0509-397X)

500   **CC**   ISSN 0438-0479
Q4
XIAMEN DAXUE XUEBAO (ZIRAN KEXUE BAN)/XIAMEN UNIVERSITY. JOURNAL (NATURAL SCIENCE EDITION)/ACTA SCIENTIARUM UNIVERSITATIS AMOIENSIS. (Text in Chinese) 1952. q. $1.50 per no. Xiamen Daxue - Xiamen University, c/o Xiamen Daxue Tushuguan, Xiamen, Fujian 361005, People's Republic of China. TEL 25102. (Dist. outside China by: China International Book Trading Corp., P.O. Box 399, Beijing, P.R.C.) Ed. Zhou Shaomin.
—BLDSC shelfmark: 4917.469600.

XIANDAIHUA/MODERNIZATION. see *TECHNOLOGY: COMPREHENSIVE WORKS*

500 028.5   **CC**
XIAOXUE KEJI/ELEMENTARY SCHOOL SCIENCE AND TECHNOLOGY. (Text in Chinese) m. Shanghai Keji Jiaoyu Chubanshe, 393, Guanshengyuan Lu, Shanghai 200233, People's Republic of China. TEL 4367970. Ed. Yi Fangben.

500   **CC**   ISSN 1000-5471
XINAN SHIFAN DAXUE XUEBAO (ZIRAN KEXUE BAN)/SOUTHWEST NORMAL UNIVERSITY. JOURNAL (NATURAL SCIENCE EDITION). (Text in Chinese) q. Xinan Shifan Daxue, Xuebao Bianjibu, Beipei, Chongqing, Sichuan 630715, People's Republic of China. TEL 3901. Ed. Zhong Zhangcheng.
—BLDSC shelfmark: 4902.255000.

500   **US**   ISSN 0091-0287
YALE SCIENTIFIC. 1894. q. $8. (Yale University) Yale Scientific Publications, Inc., 244-A Yale Sta., New Haven, CT 06520. TEL 203-432-2374. Eds. Alison Begleiter, Greg Howard. adv.; bk.rev.; charts; illus.; stat.; index; circ. 7,000. (also avail. in microform from UMI; back issues avail.; reprint service avail. from UMI) **Indexed:** Biol.Abstr., Biol.Dig., Chem.Abstr., Deep Sea Res.& Oceanogr.Abstr., Educ.Ind., Eng.Ind., P.A.I.S., R.G.
—BLDSC shelfmark: 9370.490000.
Formerly: Yale Scientific Magazine (ISSN 0044-0140)
Refereed Serial

YAMA TO HAKUBUTSUKAN/MOUNTAIN AND MUSEUM. see *MUSEUMS AND ART GALLERIES*

500   **JA**
YAMADA CONFERENCE. PROCEEDINGS. (Text and summaries in English) 1979. irreg. Yamada Kagaku Shinko Zaidan - Yamada Science Foundation, Roto Seiyaku, 8-1 Tatsumi Nishi 1-chome, Ikuno-ku, Osaka-shi, Osaka-fu 544, Japan.

500   **JA**
YAMADA KAGAKU SHINKO ZAIDAN JIGYO HOKOKUSHO/YAMADA SCIENCE FOUNDATION ANNUAL REPORT. (Text in English and Japanese; summaries in English) 1977. a. Yamada Kagaku Shinko Zaidan - Yamada Science Foundation, Roto Seiyaku, 8-1, Tatsumi-Nishi 1-chome, Ikuno-ku, Osaka-shi, Osaka-fu 544, Japan.

500   **JA**   ISSN 0513-1693
YAMAGUCHI DAIGAKU KYOIKUGAKUBU KENKYU RONSO. DAI-2-BU. SHIZEN KAGAKU/YAMAGUCHI UNIVERSITY. FACULTY OF EDUCATION. BULLETIN, PART 2. (Text and summaries in English and Japanese) 1951. a. Yamaguchi Daigaku, Kyoikugakubu - Yamaguchi University, Faculty of Education, 1677-1, Yoshida, Yamaguchi-shi, Yamaguchi-ken 753, Japan. **Indexed:** Biol.Abstr., INIS Atomind., Jap.Per.Ind.
—BLDSC shelfmark: 2507.700000.

500   **JA**   ISSN 0387-4087
YAMAGUCHI DAIGAKU KYOYOBU KIYO. SHIZEN KAGAKU HEN/YAMAGUCHI UNIVERSITY. FACULTY OF LIBERAL ARTS. JOURNAL: NATURAL SCIENCE. (Text and summaries in English and Japanese) 1967. a. Yamaguchi Daigaku, Kyoyobu - Yamaguchi University, Faculty of Liberal Arts, 1677-1, Yoshida, Yamaguchi-shi, Yamaguchi-ken 753, Japan. **Indexed:** Jap.Per.Ind.

500   **JA**   ISSN 0385-2946
YAMAGUCHI JOSHI DAIGAKU KENKYU HOKOKU. DAI-2-BU. SHIZEN KAGAKU/YAMAGUCHI WOMEN'S UNIVERSITY. BULLETIN. SECTION 2, NATURAL SCIENCE. (Text and summaries in English and Japanese) 1975. 2/yr. Yamaguchi Joshi Daigaku - Yamaguchi Women's University, 2-1, Sakurabatake 3-chome, Yamaguchi-shi, Yamaguchi-ken 753, Japan. **Indexed:** Jap.Per.Ind.

500   **JA**   ISSN 0288-4240
YAMAGUCHI-KEN NO SHIZEN. (Text in Japanese) 1959. a. Yamaguchi-kenritsu Yamaguchi Hakubutsukan - Yamaguchi Prefectural Yamaguchi Museum, 8-2, Kasuga-cho, Yamaguchi-shi, Yamaguchi-ken 753, Japan.
Description: Publishes articles on the natural history of Yamaguchi Prefecture.

500   JA   ISSN 0288-4232
AM101.Y2858
YAMAGUCHI-KENRITSU YAMAGUCHI HAKUBUTSUKAN KENKYU HOKOKU/YAMAGUCHI PREFECTURAL YAMAGUCHI MUSEUM. BULLETIN. (Text in Japanese) 1970. a. Yamaguchi-kenritsu Yamaguchi Hakubutsukan - Yamaguchi Prefectural Yamaguchi Museum, 8-2, Kasuga-cho, Yamaguchi-shi, Yamaguchi-ken 753, Japan.
Description: Contains research reports from the museum.

500   JA   ISSN 0385-8766
Q4
YAMANASHI DAIGAKU KYOIKUGAKUBU KENKYU HOKOKU. DAI-2-BUNSATSU, SHIZEN KAGAKUKEI/YAMANASHI UNIVERSITY. FACULTY OF LIBERAL ARTS & EDUCATION. MEMOIRS. PART 2: MATHEMATICS & NATURAL SCIENCES. (Text and summaries in English and Japanese) 1950. a. Yamanashi Daigaku, Kyoikugakubu - Yamanashi University, Faculty of Liberal Arts & Education, 4-37, Takeda 4-chome, Kofu-shi, Yamanashi-ken 400, Japan. **Indexed:** Chem.Abstr., INIS Atomind., Jap.Per.Ind.
—BLDSC shelfmark: 5597.234000.

YANTAI DAXUE XUEBAO/YANTAI UNIVERSITY. JOURNAL. see HUMANITIES: COMPREHENSIVE WORKS

500   US   ISSN 0096-3291
Q9
YEARBOOK OF SCIENCE AND THE FUTURE. 1969. a. $33.95. Encyclopaedia Britannica, Inc., 310 S. Michigan Ave., Chicago, IL 60604. TEL 312-347-7000. FAX 312-347-7914. TELEX 190203. Ed. David Calhoun. index.
Formerly: Britannica Yearbook of Science and the Future (ISSN 0068-1199)

500   CC   ISSN 0255-8297
YINGYONG KEXUE XUEBAO/JOURNAL OF APPLIED SCIENCES. (Text mostly in Chinese; part in English; abstracts in English) 1983. q. $60. (Shanghai Kexue Jishu Daxue - Shanghai University of Science and Technology) Shanghai Scientific and Technical Publishers, Journal Department, 450 Ruijin 2 Lu, Shanghai 200020, People's Republic of China. TEL 4310310. Ed. Huang Hongjia.
—BLDSC shelfmark: 4947.075000.

YOGA AND TOTAL HEALTH. see PHILOSOPHY

500   JA   ISSN 0085-8366
Q77   CODEN: SYUMAS
YOKOHAMA NATIONAL UNIVERSITY. SCIENCE REPORTS. SECTION 1: MATHEMATICS, PHYSICS, CHEMISTRY/YOKOHAMA KOKURITSU DAIGAKU RIKA KIYO, DAI-1-RUI, SUGAKU, BUTSURIGAKU, KAGAKU. (Text in European languages and Japanese) 1952. a. exchange basis only. Yokohama Kokuritsu Daigaku, Kyoikugakubu - Yokohama National University, Faculty of Education, 156 Tokiwadai, Hodogaya-ku, Yokohama-shi, Kanagawa-ken 240, Japan. **Indexed:** Jap.Per.Ind., JCT, JTA, Math.R., Met.Abstr., Sci.Abstr.
—BLDSC shelfmark: 8162.000000.

500   JA   ISSN 0913-9664
YOKOHAMA-SHIRITSU DAIGAKU KIYO. SHIZEN KAGAKU HEN/YOKOHAMA CITY UNIVERSITY. JOURNAL. SERIES OF NATURAL SCIENCE. (Text and summaries in English and Japanese) 1986. a. Yokohama-shiritsu Daigaku - Yokohama City University, 4646, Mutsuura-machi, Kanazawa-ku, Yokohama-shi, Kanagawa-ken 236, Japan.

500   JA
YOKOHAMA-SHIRITSU DAIGAKU RONSO. SHIZEN KAGAKU KEIRETSU/YOKOHAMA CITY UNIVERSITY. BULLETIN: NATURAL SCIENCE. (Text in Japanese) 1949. s-a. Yokohama-shiritsu Daigaku, Gakujutsu Kenkyukai - Yokohama City University, Arts and Science Society, 22-2, Seto, Kanazawa-ku, Yokohama-shi, Kanagawa-ken 236, Japan. **Indexed:** Chem.Abstr., Jap.Per.Ind.

500   JA   ISSN 0513-2622
                 CODEN: SRYMAX
YOKOSUKA-SHI HAKUBUTSUKAN KENKYU HOKOKU. SHIZEN KAGAKU/YOKOSUKA CITY MUSEUM. SCIENCE REPORT. (Text and summaries in English and Japanese) 1956. irreg. $5. Yokosuka-shi Shizen Hakubutsukan - Yokosuka City Museum, 95 Fukadadai, Yokosuka-shi, Kanagawa-ken 238, Japan. Ed. N. Onba. circ. 1,000. (back issues avail.) **Indexed:** Biol.Abstr., Jap.Per.Ind.

500   JA   ISSN 0386-4286
AM101.Y58
YOKOSUKA-SHI HAKUBUTSUKAN SHIRYOSHU/YOKOSUKA CITY MUSEUM. MISCELLANEOUS REPORT. (Text in Japanese; summaries in English) 1978. a. Yokosuka-shi Shizen Hakubutsukan - Yokosuka City Museum, 95, Fukadadai, Yokosuka-shi, Kanagawa-ken 238, Japan.

YOKOSUKA-SHI HAKUBUTSUKANPO/YOKOSUKA CITY MUSEUM. ANNUAL REPORT. see MUSEUMS AND ART GALLERIES

YOSHIDA KAGAKU GIJUTSU ZAIDAN NYUSU/YOSHIDA FOUNDATION FOR SCIENCE AND TECHNOLOGY. NEWS. see TECHNOLOGY: COMPREHENSIVE WORKS

YOUR BIG BACKYARD. see CHILDREN AND YOUTH — For

ZAGADNIENIA INFORMACJI NAUKOWEJ. see LIBRARY AND INFORMATION SCIENCES

500   PL   ISSN 0044-1619
ZAGADNIENIA NAUKOZNAWSTWA. (Summaries in English and Russian) 1965. q. $42. (Polska Akademia Nauk, Komitet Naukoznawstwa) Ossolineum, Publishing House of the Polish Academy of Sciences, Rynek 9, Wroclaw, Poland. TELEX 0712771 OSS PL. (Dist. by: Ars Polona-Ruch, Krakowskie Przedmiescie 7, Warsaw, Poland) Ed. T. Pszczolowski. bk.rev.; index; circ. 1,000.
—BLDSC shelfmark: 9425.505000.
Description: Modern achievements in science.

500   JA   ISSN 0912-2354
ZAIDAN NYUSU/YAMADA SCIENCE FOUNDATION NEWS. (Text in English and Japanese) 1974. s-a. Yamada Kagaku Shinko Zaidan - Yamada Science Foundation, Roto Seiyaku, 8-1, Tatsumi-Nishi 1-chome, Ikuno-ku, Osaka-shi, Osaka-fu 544, Japan.

500   ZA   ISSN 0084-4950
ZAMBIA. NATIONAL COUNCIL FOR SCIENTIFIC RESEARCH. ANNUAL REPORT. 1968. a. National Council for Scientific Research, Box CH 158, Chelston, Lusaka, Zambia.

500 600   ZA   ISSN 0378-8857
Q91.Z33   CODEN: ZJSTDE
ZAMBIA JOURNAL OF SCIENCE AND TECHNOLOGY. (Text in English) 1976. q. $12.50 per no. National Council for Scientific Research, P.O. Box 310158, Chelston, 15302 Lusaka, Zambia. TEL 01-281081. TELEX ZA 40005. Ed.Bd. adv.; charts; stat.; circ. 2,500. **Indexed:** Biol.Abstr., Chem.Abstr., Curr.Cont., Dairy Sci.Abstr., Field Crop Abstr., Food Sci.& Tech.Abstr., GeoRef, Herb.Abstr., Ind.Vet., Protozool.Abstr., Vet.Bull.

ZEITSCHRIFT FUER GESCHICHTE DER ARABISCH-ISLAMISCHEN WISSENSCHAFTEN. see ORIENTAL STUDIES

500   BN   ISSN 0581-7528
QH7   CODEN: GZMND5
ZEMALJSKI MUZEJ BOSNE I HERCEGOVINE. GLASNIK. PRIRODNE NAUKE. Title also in French. (Summaries in English, French or German) 1969 N.S. a. Zemaljski Muzej Bosne i Hercegovine, Vojevode Putnika 7, Sarajevo, Bosnia Hercegovina. Ed. Zeljka Bjelic. illus.
Continues: Glasnik Zemaljskog Muzeja u Sarajevu.

500 600   CS
ZENIT. 1986. fortn. 86 Kcs. Smena Publishing House, Prazska 11, 812 84 Bratislava, Czechoslovakia. (Subscr. to: P N S, Gottwaldovo nam 6, 813 81 Bratislava) Ed. Ladislav Gyorffy. circ. 45,000.
Formerly: Zenit Pioniorov.

500   CC
ZHEJIANG DAXUE XUEBAO (ZIRAN KEXUE BAN)/ZHEJIANG UNIVERSITY. JOURNAL (NATURAL SCIENCE EDITION). (Text in Chinese) bi-m. $3.50 per no. Zhejiang Daxue - Zhejiang University, Yu Quan (Jade Spring), Hangzhou, Zhejiang 310027, People's Republic of China. TEL 582244. (Dist. by: China International Book Trading Corporation (Guoji Shudian), P.O. Box 399, Beijing, P.R.C.) Ed. Jiang Jingping. **Indexed:** Chem.Abstr., Math.R.

500   CC   ISSN 1001-8212
ZHENGZHOU DAXUE XUEBAO (ZIRAN KEXUE BAN)/ZHENGZHOU UNIVERSITY. JOURNAL (NATURAL SCIENCE EDITION). (Text in Chinese) s-a. Zhengzhou Daxue, Xuebao Bianjibu, No. 75, Daxue Lu, Zhengzhou, Henan 450052, People's Republic of China. TEL 446455. Ed. Zhang Peiqiang.

500   CC
ZHISHI CHUANG/WINDOW OF KNOWLEDGE. (Text in Chinese) bi-m. Jiangxi Kexue Jishu Chubanshe, No.5, Xinwei Lu, Nanchang, Jiangxi 330002, People's Republic of China. TEL 332459. Ed. Tang Yulong.

500   CC
ZHISHI JIUSHI LILIANG/KNOWLEDGE IS POWER. (Text in Chinese) m. $0.60 per no. Guoji Shudian, Qikan Bu, Chegongzhuang Xilu 21, P.O. Box 399, Beijing 100044, People's Republic of China.

500 600   CC
ZHONGGUO KE-JI SHILIAO/CHINA HISTORICAL MATERIALS OF SCIENCE AND TECHNOLOGY. (Text in Chinese; summaries and table of contents in English) q. 4 Yen per no. (Zhongguo Kexue Jishu Xiehui - China Association for Science and Technology) Zhongguo Kexue Jishu Chubanshe, 32, Baishiqiao Lu, Wei Gong Cun, Haidian Qu, Beijing, People's Republic of China. (Dist. outside China by: China International Book Trading Corp., P.O. Box 339, Beijing, P.R.C.; Editorial addr.: 137 Chaoyang Mennei Dajie, Beijing 100010, P.R.C.) bibl.; illus.

500 600   CC   ISSN 1000-0798
ZHONGGUO KEJI SHILIAO/HISTORICAL MATERIAL OF CHINESE SCIENCE AND TECHNOLOGY. (Text in Chinese) q. Zhongguo Kexue Jishu Xuehui - Chinese Association of Science and Technology, 137 Chaoyangmennei Dajie, Beijing 100010, People's Republic of China. TEL 896731. Ed. Wang Dezhao.

500   CC   ISSN 1000-3126
ZHONGGUO KEXUE A. English edition: Science in China. Series A (ISSN 1001-6511) (Text in Chinese; summaries in English) 1950. m. Y9.30($18) per no. (Zhongguo Kexueyuan - Academia Sinica) Science Press, Marketing and Sales Department, 16 Donghuangchenggen Beijie, Beijing 100707, People's Republic of China. TEL 4010642. FAX 4102180. TELEX 210247-SPBJ-CN. (Co-sponsor: Chinese Medical Association) adv.; circ. 10,000. (reprint service avail. from KTO) **Indexed:** AESIS, BMT, Chem.Abstr., Curr.Cont., Deep Sea Res.& Oceanogr.Abstr., Helminthol.Abstr., Int.Aerosp.Abstr., Math.R., Met.Abstr., Plant Breed.Abstr., Sci.Abstr., Soils & Fert., World Alum.Abstr., World Surf.Coat., World Text.Abstr.
—BLDSC shelfmark: 9512.742000.
Supersedes in part: Scientia Sinica.
Description: Covers mathematics, physics, astronomy, and technology. Contains mainly academic papers on scientific work.
Refereed Serial

500   CC   ISSN 1000-3134
ZHONGGUO KEXUE B. English edition: Science in China. Series B (ISSN 1001-652X) (Text in Chinese; summaries in English) 1950. m. $18 per no. (Chinese Academy of Sciences) Science Press, Marketing and Sales Department, 16 Donghuangchenggen Beijie, Beijing 100707, People's Republic of China. TEL 4010642. FAX 4012180. TELEX 210247-SPBJ-CN. (Co-sponsor: Chinese Medical Association) adv. (reprint service avail. from KTO) **Indexed:** AESIS, Biol.Abstr., BMT, Chem.Abstr., Curr.Adv.Biochem., Curr.Adv.Cell & Devel.Biol., Curr.Adv.Ecol.Sci., Curr.Adv.Genetics & Molec.Biol., Curr.Cont., Deep Sea Res.& Oceanogr.Abstr., Helminthol.Abstr., Ind.Med., Math.R., Met.Abstr., Seed Abstr., Soyabean Abstr., World Surf.Coat., World Text.Abstr.
—BLDSC shelfmark: 9512.742500.
Supersedes in part: Scientia Sinica.
Description: Covers chemistry, biology, earth science, medical science, and agronomy. Contains mainly academic papers on scientific work.
Refereed Serial

500   US
ZHONGGUO KEXUE BAO/CHINA'S SCIENCE. (Text in Chinese) d. $91.10. China Books & Periodicals, Inc., 2929 24th St., San Francisco, CA 94110. TEL 415-282-2994. FAX 415-282-0994. (newspaper)

SCIENCES: COMPREHENSIVE WORKS — ABSTRACTING, BIBLIOGRAPHIES, STATISTICS

500   CC   ISSN 1000-8217
ZHONGGUO KEXUE JIJIN/NATIONAL NATURAL SCIENCE FOUNDATION OF CHINA. BULLETIN. (Text in Chinese; summaries in English) 1987. q. Y16. (Zhongguo Kexue Jijinhui - National Natural Science Foundation of China) Science Press, Marketing and Sales Department, 16 Donghuangchenggen Beijie, Beijing 100707, People's Republic of China. TEL 4010642. FAX 4012180. TELEX 210247-SPBJ-CN. adv.; circ. 5,000.
—BLDSC shelfmark: 2641.172000.

500 600   CC   ISSN 0253-2778
ZHONGGUO KEXUE JISHU DAXUE XUEBAO/CHINA UNIVERSITY OF SCIENCE AND TECHNOLOGY. JOURNAL. (Text in Chinese) q. $2 per no. Zhongguo Kexue Jishu Daxue - China University of Science and Technology, 96 Jinzhai Lu, Hefei, Anhui 230026, People's Republic of China. (Dist. by: Guoji Shudian (China Publications Centre), Chegongzhuang Xilu 21, P.O. Box 399, Beijing, P.R.C.) **Indexed:** Cyb.Abstr., Math.R.
—BLDSC shelfmark: 4729.219400.

500   CC   ISSN 1000-3045
ZHONGGUO KEXUEYUAN YUANKAN. English edition: Chinese Academy of Sciences, Bulletin. (Issuing body also known as Academia Sinica.) (Text in Chinese; table of contents and summaries in English) 1985. q. Y22.40($40) Science Press, Marketing and Sales Department, 16 Donghuangchenggen Beijie, Beijing 100707, People's Republic of China. TEL 4010642. FAX 4012180. TELEX 210247-SPBJ-CN. Ed. Yu Zhihua. adv.; circ. 7,000.
—BLDSC shelfmark: 2444.496000.
Description: Publicizes mainland China's policies on science and technology, and shows trends and directions in the development of science in China. Also introduces the work and achievements of the Academia Sinica and its scientists.

500   CC   ISSN 0253-4088
ZHONGSHAN DAXUE XUEBAO (ZIRAN KEXUE BAN)/ACTA SCIENTIARUM NATURALIUM UNIVERSITATIS SUNYATSENI. (Text in Chinese) q. $1.30 per no. Zhongshan Daxue, Xuebao Bianjibu, Xingang Lu, Guangzhou, Guangdong 510275, People's Republic of China. TEL 020-446300. TELEX 44604-ZSUFO-CN. (Dist. outside China by: China International Book Trading Corp., P.O. Box 399, Beijing, P.R.C.) **Indexed:** Bio-Contr.News & Info., Chem.Abstr., Crop Physiol.Abstr., Curr.Adv.Ecol.Sci., Field Crop Abstr., Herb.Abstr., Hort.Abstr., Ind.Vet., Math.R., Ornam.Hort., Plant Grow.Reg.Abstr., Sci.Abstr., Seed Abstr., Trop.Oil Seeds Abstr., Weed Abstr.
Supersedes in part: Zhongshan Daxue Xuebao (ISSN 0529-6579)

500 600   CC
ZHONGWAI JISHU QINGBAO/CHINESE AND FOREIGN TECHNOLOGY INFORMATION. (Text in Chinese) m. Anhui Sheng Keji Qingbao Yanjiusuo - Anhui Provincial Institute of Science and Technology Information, Shengkewei, Building No.3, 145 Caohu Lu, Hefei, Anhui 230001, People's Republic of China. TEL 278453. Ed. Yang Qinghua.

ZHONGXUE KEJI/MIDDLE SCHOOL SCIENCE & TECHNOLOGY. see EDUCATION

500   RH
ZIMBABWE SCIENCE NEWS. 1967. m. Z.$15. Zimbabwe Scientific Association, Box 978, Harare, Zimbabwe. Ed. P.R. Morgan. adv.; bk.rev.; abstr.; bibl.; charts; illus.; index; circ. 2,750. **Indexed:** Biol.Abstr., Field Crop Abstr., Geo.Abstr., GeoRef., Herb.Abstr., Ind.S.A.Per., W.R.C.Inf.
Formerly: Rhodesia Science News (ISSN 0035-4732)

500   RH
ZIMBABWE SCIENTIFIC ASSOCIATION. TRANSACTION. (Text in English) 1901. irreg. Z.$10. Zimbabwe Scientific Association, P.O. Box 8351, Causeway, Harare, Zimbabwe. Ed. Brian Marshall. circ. 550. (back issues avail.) **Indexed:** A.I.C.P., Biol.Abstr., GeoRef., Ind.S.A.Per., Sci.Abstr., Soils & Fert.
Formerly: Rhodesia Scientific Association. Transaction.

500 600   CC
ZIRAN BIANZHENGFA TONGXUN/JOURNAL OF DIALECTICS OF NATURE. (Text in Chinese) bi-m. $1 per no. Guoji Shudian, Qikan Bu, Chegongzhuang Xilu 21, P.O. Box 399, Beijing 100044, People's Republic of China.

500.9   CC   ISSN 1000-0224
ZIRAN KEXUE SHI YANJIU/STUDIES IN THE HISTORY OF NATURAL SCIENCES. (Text in Chinese; summaries in English) 1982. q. Y10.80 per no. Science Press, Marketing and Sales Department, 16 Donghuangchenggen Beijie, Beijing 100707, People's Republic of China. TEL 4010642. FAX 4012180. TELEX 210247-SPBJ-CN. adv.; bk.rev.; circ. 6,000.
—BLDSC shelfmark: 8490.674900.
Description: Contains articles on theories of the history of science, biographies of scientists, and historical records of important scientific events in China and the world.

500   CC   ISSN 0253-9608
ZIRAN ZAZHI/NATURE JOURNAL. (Text in Chinese) m. $2.30 per no. Ziran Zazhishe, P.O. Box 040-056, Shanghai 200040, People's Republic of China. TEL 4336850. Ed. He Zongying. **Indexed:** Art & Archaeol.Tech.Abstr., Chem.Abstr.

500.9   NE
ZUIDHOLLANDS LANDSCHAP. 1972. q. fl.30. Stichting Het Zuidhollands Landschap, Schiedamsesingel 181, 3012 BB Rotterdam, Netherlands. FAX 010-4331570. Ed.Bd. adv.; bk.rev.; circ. 45,000.

3-2-1 CONTACT. see CHILDREN AND YOUTH — For

SCIENCES: COMPREHENSIVE WORKS — Abstracting, Bibliographies, Statistics

500 600 011   US
A A A S ANNUAL MEETING. ABSTRACTS OF PAPERS. a. $10 softcover. American Association for the Advancement of Science, 1333 H St., N.W., Washington, DC 20005. TEL 202-326-6400. Ed. Sue O'Connell. (reprint service avail. from UMI)

500 600   RM   ISSN 0001-365X
T4
ABSTRACTS OF ROMANIAN SCIENTIFIC AND TECHNICAL LITERATURE. Russian edition: Referativnyj Bjulleten Rumynskoj Nauchno-Tehnicheskoj Literatury. French edition: Bulletin Analytique de la Litterature Scientifique et Technique Roumaine. (Text in English) 1965. s-a. $121 or exchange basis. Institutul National de Informare si Documentare, Str. George Enescu 27-29, 70141 Bucharest, Rumania. TEL 134010. TELEX 11247 INIDR. (Dist. by: Rodipret, S.A., Piata Presei Libere nr.1, Sector 1, 71341 Bucharest, Rumania) abstr. **Indexed:** Anal.Abstr., Corros.Abstr., Hort.Abstr., Plant Breed.Abstr., World Surf.Coat., World Text.Abstr.
Description: Contains abstracts of articles published in Rumanian periodicals concerning different fields of pure and applied sciences.

ABSTRACTS OF SCIENTIFIC AND TECHNOLOGICAL PUBLICATIONS. see TECHNOLOGY: COMPREHENSIVE WORKS — Abstracting, Bibliographies, Statistics

500 016   SW   ISSN 0001-3676
ABSTRACTS OF UPPSALA DISSERTATIONS IN SCIENCE. 1961. 20/yr. price varies. Almqvist and Wiksell International, Box 638, S-101 28 Stockholm, Sweden. index. **Indexed:** Biol.Abstr., Chem.Abstr., Sci.Abstr.

ALTERNATIVE ALTERNATIVE. see SOCIOLOGY — Abstracting, Bibliographies, Statistics

APPLIED SCIENCE AND TECHNOLOGY INDEX; a cumulative subject index to English language periodicals in the fields of aeronautics and space science, computer technology and applications, chemistry, construction industry, energy resources and research, engineering, etc. see ENGINEERING — Abstracting, Bibliographies, Statistics

ASLIB BOOK GUIDE; a monthly list of recommended scientific and technical books. see BIBLIOGRAPHIES

500 600   BL
BAHIA, BRAZIL (STATE). CENTRO DE PESQUISAS E DESENVOLVIMENTO. SUMARIOS DE PERIODICOS EM CIENCIA E TECNOLOGIA. m. Cr.$20000. Centro de Pesquisas e Desenvolvimento, Km0 da BA 536, Caixa Postal 09, 42800 Camari BA, Brazil.

013   US   ISSN 0084-7712
BATTELLE MEMORIAL INSTITUTE. PUBLISHED PAPERS AND ARTICLES. 1970. a. free to qualified personnel. Battelle Memorial Institute, Communications Office, Attn.: Harry E. Templeton, Ed., 505 King Ave., Columbus, OH 43201. TEL 614-424-7818. circ. 1,000. (processed; back issues avail.; reprint service avail. from UMI)
Description: Lists titles of hundreds of staff-authored articles, papers, books, and patents published in a given year.

500   US   ISSN 0145-0379
BERKELEY PAPERS IN HISTORY OF SCIENCE. 1977. irreg., no.12, 1989. price varies. University of California, Berkeley, Office for History of Science and Technology, 470 Stephens Hall, Berkeley, CA 94720. TEL 415-642-4581. FAX 415-643-5321. Ed. J.L. Heilbron. circ. 1,000. **Indexed:** Math.R.
Description: Bibliographies of works by and about scientists, and of inventories of their published and unpublished correspondence.

500 016   YU   ISSN 0352-5945
Z7409
BIBLIOGRAFIJA JUGOSLAVIJE. CLANCI I PRILOZI U SERIJSKIM PUBLIKACIJAMA. SERIJA B: PRIRODNE, PRIMENJENE, MEDICINSKE I TEHNICKE NAUKE. 1950. m. $662 or exchange basis. Jugoslovenski Bibliografsko-Informacijski Institut (YUBIN) - Yugoslav Institute for Bibliography and Information, Terazije 26, Belgrade, Yugoslavia. FAX 11-687-760. Ed. Radomir Glavicki.
•Also available online.
Former titles (until 1985): Bibliografija Jugoslavije. Naucni i Strucni Radovi u Serijskim Publikacijama. Serija B: Prirodne, Primenjene, Medicinske i Tehnicke Nauke (ISSN 0352-2393); Bibliografija Jugoslavije. Serija B: Prirodne i Primenjene Nauke. Clanci i Prilozi u Casopisima, Listovima i Zbornicima (ISSN 0523-218X)

500 015   SZ   ISSN 0067-6829
BIBLIOGRAPHIA SCIENTIAE NATURALIS HELVETICA. (Text in French, German) 1927. a. price varies. Bibliotheque Nationale Suisse - Schweizerische Landesbibliothek, Hallwylstr. 15, CH-3003 Berne, Switzerland. Ed. Anton Caflisch. circ. 700 (controlled). (back issues avail.) **Indexed:** GeoRef.

500 011   US   ISSN 0888-7551
                     CODEN: BSTEEC
BIBLIOGRAPHIES AND INDEXES IN SCIENCE AND TECHNOLOGY. 1987. irreg. price varies. Greenwood Press, Inc. (Subsidiary of: Greenwood Publishing Group Inc.), 88 Post Rd. W., Box 5007, Westport, CT 06881-5007. TEL 203-226-3571. FAX 203-222-1502.
—BLDSC shelfmark: 1993.097520.

500 600   US
BIBLIOGRAPHIES ON THE HISTORY OF SCIENCE AND TECHNOLOGY. 1982. a. price varies. Garland Publishing, Inc., 1000A Sherman Ave., Hamden, CT 06514. TEL 800-627-6273. (And: 717 Fifth Ave., New York, NY 10022. TEL 212-751-7447) Eds. Robert Multhauf, Ellen Wells. circ. 375.

500 016   II
BIBLIOGRAPHY OF DOCTORAL DISSERTATIONS: NATURAL AND APPLIED SCIENCES. (Text in English) irreg., latest 1986. $70 price varies. Association of Indian Universities, A.I.U. House, 16 Kotla Marg., New Delhi 110 002, India. TEL 11-3310059. TELEX 31-66180-AIU-IN.

500 011   SP   ISSN 0211-4046
BOLETIN DE TRADUCCIONES. 1966. s-m. Instituto de Informacion y Documentacion en Ciencia y Tecnologia, Joaquin Costa 22, 28002 Madrid, Spain.
•Also available online.
Also available on CD-ROM.

SCIENCES: COMPREHENSIVE WORKS — ABSTRACTING, BIBLIOGRAPHIES, STATISTICS

500 016 600   UK   ISSN 0959-4922
Z7403
BRITISH REPORTS, TRANSLATIONS AND THESES. 1971. m. £84 (foreign £89). British Library, Document Supply Centre, Publishing Section, Boston Spa, Wetherby, W. Yorkshire LS23 7BQ, England. TEL 0937-546077. FAX 0937-546333. TELEX 557381. bibl.; circ. 900. (back issues avail.) Indexed: Agri.Eng.Abstr., Bio-Contr.News & Info., Br.Ceram.Abstr., Dairy Sci.Abstr., Field Crop Abstr., Fluidex, Forest.Abstr., Herb.Abstr., Int.Packag.Abstr., Mgmt.& Market.Abstr., Nutr.Abstr., Paper & Bd.Abstr., Print.Abstr., Rev.Appl.Entomol., World Text.Abstr.
—BLDSC shelfmark: 2342.160000.
Former titles: B L L D Announcement Bulletin (ISSN 0308-4094); N L L Announcement Bulletin (ISSN 0007-1749)

500   GW
BUECHER FUER DAS STUDIUM - NATURWISSENSCHAFTEN; Mathematik, Physik, Chemie, Biologie, Botanik, Zoologie, Geowissenschaften. a. Dr. Lothar Rossipaul Verlagsgesellschaft mbH, Menzingerstr. 37, 8000 Munich 19, Germany. TEL 089-179106-0. FAX 089-179106-22. Ed. Rainer Rossipaul. circ. 25,000.
Description: Bibliography of available books in the natural sciences for students.

500 600   RM
BULLETIN ANALYTIQUE DE LA LITTERATURE SCIENTIFIQUE ET TECHNIQUE ROUMAINE. Russian edition: Referativnyj Bjulleten Rumynskoj Nauchno-Tehnicheskoj Literatury. English edition: Abstracts of Romanian Scientific and Technical Literature. (Text in French) 1965. s-a. $121 or exchange basis. Institutul National de Informare si Documentare, Str. George Enescu 27-29, 70141 Bucharest, Rumania. TEL 134010. TELEX 11247 INIDR. (Dist. by: Rodipret, S.A., Piata presei Libere nr.1, Sector 1, 71341 Bucharest, Rumania) abstr.
Formerly: Bulletin Analytique de la Litterature Technique Roumaine.
Description: Contains abstracts of articles published in Rumanian periodicals in the fields of pure and applied science.

500   US
C S A UPDATE. q. Cambridge Scientific Abstracts, 7200 Wisconsin Ave., 6th Fl., Bethesda, MD 20814. TEL 301-961-6750. FAX 301-961-6720. TELEX 910 2507547.

500 016   AT   ISSN 0311-5836
C S I R O INDEX. 1952. 6/yr. Aus.$20. C.S.I.R.O., 314 Albert St., E. Melbourne, Vic. 3002, Australia. Ed. G.R. Levick. index; circ. 1,500. Indexed: Dairy Sci.Abstr., Field Crop Abstr., Helminthol.Abstr., Herb.Abstr., Rev.Appl.Entomol.
Formerly: C S I R O Abstracts (ISSN 0007-912X)

500 600   TR   ISSN 1011-4866
CARINDEX: SCIENCE & TECHNOLOGY. 1987. s-a. University of the West Indies, Main Library, St. Augustine, Trinidad and Tobago, W.I. TEL 809-662-2002. FAX 809-662-9238. TELEX 24-520 UWI-WG.
Description: Guide to science and technology literature (excluding medicine and agriculture) published in the English-speaking Caribbean.

016   CC   ISSN 0254-5179
QA1
CHINESE SCIENCE ABSTRACTS. PART A. Chinese edition: Zhongguo Kexue Wenzhai A. (Editions in Chinese, English) 1982. bi-m. $310. Science Press, Marketing and Sales Department, 16 Donghuangchenggen Beijie, Beijing 100707, People's Republic of China. TEL 4010642. FAX 4012180. TELEX 210247-SPBJ-CN. (Dist. outside China by: Pergamon Press plc, Headington Hill Hall, Oxford OX3 0BW, England, TEL 0865-794141; In U.S: Maxwell House, Fairview Park, Elmsford, NY 10523. TEL 914-592-7700) Ed.Bd. adv.; circ. 5,000.

016   CC   ISSN 0254-4903
QD1
CHINESE SCIENCE ABSTRACTS. PART B. Chinese edition: Zhongguo Kexue Wenzhai B. 1982. bi-m. $310. Science Press, Marketing and Sales Department, 16 Donghuangchenggen Beijie, Beijing 100707, People's Republic of China. TEL 4010642. FAX 4012180. TELEX 210247-SPBJ-CN. (US office: Science Press Press New York, Ltd., 63-117 Alderton St., Rego Park, NY 11374. TEL 718-459-4638; Dist. abroad by: Pergamon Press plc, Headington Hill Hall, Oxford OX3 0BW, England, TEL 0865-794141; In U.S.: Maxwell House, Fairview Park, Elmsford, NY 10523. TEL 914-592-7700) adv.; abstr.; circ. 5,000.

500 600 016   SP
CIENCIA Y TECNICA; boletin bibliografico nacional y extranjero. 1960. q. free. Diaz de Santos, S.A., Libreria Cientifico-Tecnica, Lagasca 95, 28006 Madrid, Spain. TEL 431-24-82. adv.; bk.rev.; circ. 25,000.

CONFERENCE PAPERS ANNUAL INDEX. see *MEETINGS AND CONGRESSES — Abstracting, Bibliographies, Statistics*

CONFERENCE PAPERS INDEX. see *MEETINGS AND CONGRESSES — Abstracting, Bibliographies, Statistics*

011   II   ISSN 0304-5358
CONTENTS LIST OF SOVIET SCIENTIFIC PERIODICALS. 1971. m. free. Indian National Scientific Documentation Centre, 14 Satsang Vihar Marg, New Delhi 110 067, India. Ed. B.K. Sen.

500 016   UK   ISSN 0309-8591
CROYDON BIBLIOGRAPHIES FOR REGIONAL SURVEY. 1968. irreg. included in subscription to the Proceedings of the Croydon Natural History & Scientific Society. Croydon Natural History & Scientific Society Ltd., 96a Brighton Rd., South Croydon, Surrey CR2 6AD, England. Ed. P.W. Sowan. bibl.; circ. 850.

CURRENT BIOTECHNOLOGY ABSTRACTS. see *BIOLOGY — Abstracting, Bibliographies, Statistics*

500 016   UK   ISSN 0379-4504
CURRENT LITERATURE ON SCIENCE OF SCIENCE. (Text in English) 1972. m. £25($40) to individuals; institutions £54($98). (National Institute of Science, Technology and Development Studies, Publications and Information Directorate, II) Beech Tree Publishing, 10 Watford Close, Guildford, Surrey GU1 2EP, England. TEL 0483-67497. TELEX 859539 LYNXIN G ATT PAGE. Ed. Ashok Jain. bk.rev.; abstr.; charts; stat.; circ. 500.
Formerly: Index to Literature on Science of Science.
Description: Details recent articles on fields of science and technology studies, with reference to dilemmas of developing countries.

500 020 015   UK   ISSN 0267-1948
Z7403
CURRENT RESEARCH IN BRITAIN. PHYSICAL SCIENCES. (Other vols. avail.: Biological Sciences, Humanities, Social Sciences) 1980. a. £90 (foreign £95). British Library, Document Supply Centre, Boston Spa, Wetherby, W. Yorkshire LS23 7BQ, England. TEL 0937-843434. FAX 0937-546333. TELEX 557381. Ed. Mike Bate.
●Also available online. Vendor(s): Pergamon Infoline (CRIB).
Formerly: Research in British Universities Polytechnics and Colleges. Vol.1: Physical Sciences (ISSN 0142-2472)

500   JA   ISSN 0288-6022
Q77
CURRENT SCIENCE AND TECHNOLOGY RESEARCH IN JAPAN. (Text in English) 1980. biennial. $325. Japan Information Center of Science and Technology - Nihon Kagaku Gijutsu Joho Senta, 5-2 Nagata-cho, 2-chome, Chiyoda-ku, Tokyo 100, Japan. TEL 03-3581-6411. FAX 03-3581-6446. TELEX 02223604 J. abstr.; index; circ. 600.
●Also available online. Vendor(s): JICST.
—BLDSC shelfmark: 3504.004000.

DIRECTORY OF PUBLISHED PROCEEDINGS. SERIES S E M T - SCIENCE, ENGINEERING, MEDICINE AND TECHNOLOGY. see *MEETINGS AND CONGRESSES — Abstracting, Bibliographies, Statistics*

016   PK
DIRECTORY OF SCIENTIFIC PERIODICALS OF PAKISTAN. irreg. Rs.5($1) Pakistan Scientific and Technological Information Centre, Quaid-i-Azam University Campus, Box 1217, Islamabad, Pakistan. Dir. Aejaz Ahmed Malik. circ. 500. (also avail. in microfilm)

500 016   II   ISSN 0376-8554
Z7401
DIRECTORY OF SCIENTIFIC RESEARCH IN INDIAN UNIVERSITIES. a. Rs.35. (University Grants Commission) Indian National Scientific Documentation Centre, Hillside Rd., New Delhi 110012, India. (Co-sponsor: Council of Scientific and Industrial Research)

DISSERTATION ABSTRACTS. see *HUMANITIES: COMPREHENSIVE WORKS — Abstracting, Bibliographies, Statistics*

500 300 016   US   ISSN 0419-4217
Z5053   CODEN: DABBBA
DISSERTATION ABSTRACTS INTERNATIONAL. SECTION B: PHYSICAL SCIENCES AND ENGINEERING. 1938. m. $475. University Microfilms International, Dissertation Publishing, c/o Dorie Mickelson, Mgr., 300 N. Zeeb Rd., Ann Arbor, MI 48106. TEL 313-761-4700. abstr.; index. (also avail. in microfiche from UMI; reprint service avail. from UMI) Indexed: Abstr.Bull.Inst.Pap.Chem., Agroforest.Abstr., Anim.Breed.Abstr., API Abstr., API Catal., API Hlth.& Environ., API Oil., API Pet.Ref., API Pet.Subst., API Transport., Art.Int.Abstr., Bio-Contr.News & Info., Biol.Abstr., Chem.Abstr., Crop Physiol.Abstr., Dairy Sci.Abstr., Eng.Ind., Fababean Abstr., Field Crop Abstr., Food Sci.& Tech.Abstr., Forest.Abstr., Forest Prod.Abstr., Geotech.Abstr., Helminthol.Abstr., Herb.Abstr., Hort.Abstr., Ind.Vet., Irr.& Drain.Abstr., Key Word Ind.Wildl.Res., Maize Abstr., Mass Spectr.Bull., Music Ind., Nutr.Abstr., Ornam.Hort., Packag.Sci.Tech., Pig News & Info., Plant Grow.Reg.Abstr., Potato Abstr., Poult.Abstr., Protozool.Abstr., Psychol.Abstr., RAPRA, Rice Abstr., Seed Abstr., Sh.& Vib.Dig., Sorghum & Millets Abstr., Soyabean Abstr., Triticale Abstr., Trop.Oil Seeds Abstr., Vet.Bull., Weed Abstr.
●Also available online. Vendor(s): BRS (DISS), BRS/Saunders Colleague, DIALOG (File no.35). Also available on CD-ROM. Producer(s): University Microfilms International.
—BLDSC shelfmark: 3599.040000.
Formerly: (until 1969): Dissertation Abstracts. Section B: the Sciences and Engineering (ISSN 0420-073X) Supersedes in part (in 1966): Dissertation Abstracts (ISSN 0099-3123).

DISSERTATION ABSTRACTS INTERNATIONAL. SECTION C: WORLDWIDE. see *BIBLIOGRAPHIES*

600 016   FR   ISSN 0012-4583
DOCUMENTATION - TECHNIQUE, SCIENTIFIQUE ET COMMERCIALE; revue d'information de l'edition francaise et etrangere. (Text and summaries in English, French, German) 1947. 8/yr. free. Librairie Lavoisier, 11 rue Lavoisier, 75008 Paris, France. FAX 47-40-67-02. TELEX TDL632020F. Ed. Pierre Fenouil. adv.; bk.rev.; circ. 20,000. (processed)

500 011   US   ISSN 0190-3241
HM24
FUTURE SURVEY; a monthly abstract of books, articles and reports concerning trends, forecasts and ideas about the future. (Supplement avail.: Future Survey Annual) 1979. m. $75 to individuals; libraries $115. World Future Society, 4916 St. Elmo Ave., Bethesda, MD 20814. TEL 301-656-8274. FAX 301-951-0394. Ed. Michael Marien. index; circ. 2,300. (back issues avail.; reprint service avail. from UMI) Indexed: Pers.Lit.
—BLDSC shelfmark: 4060.637000.
Formerly: Public Policy Book Forecast (ISSN 0197-9035)

GENERAL INDEX TO IRAQI PERIODICAL LITERATURE. PART A: SCIENCES AND ENGINEERING. see *ENGINEERING — Abstracting, Bibliographies, Statistics*

SCIENCES: COMPREHENSIVE WORKS — ABSTRACTING, BIBLIOGRAPHIES, STATISTICS

016 500   US   ISSN 0162-1963
Z7401
GENERAL SCIENCE INDEX. 1978. m. (except Jun. & Dec.), plus q. and a. cumulations. service basis. H.W. Wilson Co., 950 University Ave., Bronx, NY 10452. TEL 800-367-6770. FAX 212-538-2716. TELEX 4990003HWILSON. Ed. James Kochones. (also avail. in magnetic tape)
●Also available online. Vendor(s): Wilsonline (File GSI).
Also available on CD-ROM. Producer(s): H.W. Wilson (WILSONDISC).
—BLDSC shelfmark: 4111.196000.
Description: Cumulative subject index to English language periodicals covering the essential science periodicals.

011   GW   ISSN 0931-8593
GERMANY (FEDERAL REPUBLIC, 1949-). DEUTSCHER BUNDESTAG. WISSENSCHAFTLICHE DIENSTE. NEUE AUFSAETZE IN DER BIBLIOTHEK. 1962. 6/yr. Deutscher Bundestag, Verwaltung, Abteilung Wissenschaftlich Dienste, Bundeshaus, 5300 Bonn, Germany. index.
Formerly: Germany (Federal Republic, 1949-). Deutscher Bundestag. Wissenschaftliche Dienste. Aufsaetze aus Zeitschriften und Sammelwerken.

016 500   GH
GHANA SCIENCE ABSTRACTS. (Text in English) q. Council for Scientific and Industrial Research, Box M32, Accra, Ghana. Ed. J.A. Villars. abstr.; bibl. **Indexed:** Field Crop Abstr., Herb.Abstr., Nutr.Abstr.

GUIDE TO AMERICAN SCIENTIFIC AND TECHNICAL DIRECTORIES. see *TECHNOLOGY: COMPREHENSIVE WORKS — Abstracting, Bibliographies, Statistics*

500 600   HU   ISSN 0237-0808
HUNGARIAN R AND D ABSTRACTS. SCIENCE AND TECHNOLOGY. 1985. q. $50. Orszagos Muszaki Informacios Kozpont es Konyvtar (O.M.I.K.K.) - National Technical Information Centre and Library, Muzeum u. 17, Box 12, 1428 Budapest, Hungary. TEL 336-300. Ed. Zsuzsanna Bana. index. **Indexed:** Corros.Abstr., World Surf.Coat., World Text.Abstr.
Supersedes: Hungarian Technical Abstracts (ISSN 0018-7771)
Description: Covers all fields of science and technology, excluding humanities. Includes author and subject index.

500   HU
HUNGARY. KOZPONTI STATISZTIKAI HIVATAL. TUDOMANYOS KUTATAS ES FEJLESZTES. a. 230 Ft. Statisztikai Kiado Vallalat, Kazasdulo u. 2, Box 99, 1033 Budapest 3, Hungary. TEL 688-635. TELEX 22-6699. (Subscr. to: Kultura, Box 149, H-1389 Budapest, Hungary) circ. 1,000.

500 016   GW   ISSN 0020-918X
Z5051
I B R/INTERNATIONALE BIBLIOGRAPHIE DER REZENSIONEN WISSENSCHAFTLICHER LITERATUR. (International Bibliography of Book Reviews of Scholarly Literature) (Text in English, French, German) 1971. 6/yr. DM.2700. Felix Dietrich Verlag, Jahnstr. 15, Postfach 1949, 4500 Osnabrueck, Germany. FAX 0541-41255. Eds. Otto Zeller, Wolfram Zeller.
●Also available online.
—BLDSC shelfmark: 4554.090000.

500 011   AO   ISSN 0018-9863
I I C A. DOCUMENTACAO; boletim bibliografico. 1969. s-m. free to qualified personnel. Instituto de Investigacao Cientifica de Angola, Departamento de Documentacao e Informacao, C. P. 3244, Luanda, Angola.

500 600 016   II   ISSN 0304-534X
I N S D O C. RUSSIAN SCIENTIFIC AND TECHNICAL PUBLICATIONS. ACCESSIONS LIST. bi-m. free. Indian National Scientific Documentation Centre, 14 Satsang Vihar Marg, New Delhi 110 067, India.

INDEX DOCUMENTATION - ECONOMIE - SCIENCE - TECHNIQUE. see *BUSINESS AND ECONOMICS — Abstracting, Bibliographies, Statistics*

500 016   US   ISSN 0149-8088
Z7403
INDEX TO SCIENTIFIC & TECHNICAL PROCEEDINGS. Short title: I S T P. (Includes Author/Editor Index, Permuterm Subject Index, Sponsor Index, Meeting Location Index, Category Index, Contents of Proceedings Index, and Corporate Index) 1978. m. (annual cum.). $1325. Institute for Scientific Information, 3501 Market St., Philadelphia, PA 19104. TEL 215-386-0100. FAX 215-386-2991. (U.K. addr.: 132 High St., Uxbridge UB8 1DP, Middlesex, England. TEL 44-895-70016) (also avail. in magnetic tape)
●Also available online. Vendor(s): Orbit Information Technologies.
—BLDSC shelfmark: 4385.660000.
Description: Indexes proceedings of scientific conferences and titles of papers published.

010   US
INDEX TO SCIENTIFIC BOOK CONTENTS. Short title: I S B C. (Includes Contents of Books Index, Author - Editor Index, Corporate Index, Category Index, and Permuterm Subject Index) 1985. q. (with a cumulation). $1150. Institute for Scientific Information, 3501 Market St., Philadelphia, PA 19104. TEL 215-386-0100. FAX 215-386-2291. (And: 132 High St., Uxbridge, Middlesex, UB8 1DP, England. TEL 44-895-70016) (also avail. in magnetic tape)
●Also available online. Vendor(s): DIMDI (ISTP&B Search).
Description: Indexes published scientific books, book series, and proceedings.

011   US   ISSN 0360-0661
Z7403
INDEX TO SCIENTIFIC REVIEWS. Short title: I S R. (Permuterm Subject Index, Source Index, Corporate Index, and Research-Front Specialty Index) 1974. s-a.(annual cumulation). $830. Institute for Scientific Information, 3501 Market St., Philadelphia, PA 19104. TEL 215-386-0100. FAX 215-386-2291. (U.K. addr.: 132 High St., Uxbridge, Middlesex, UB8 1DP, England. TEL 44-895-70016) (also avail. in magnetic tape)
—BLDSC shelfmark: 4385.670000.
Description: Indexes review articles and surveys of scientific literature internationally.

500 600   II
INDIA. DEPARTMENT OF SCIENCE AND TECHNOLOGY. RESEARCH AND DEVELOPMENT STATISTICS. 1973. a. Rs.50. Department of Science and Technology, New Mehrauli Rd., New Delhi 110016, India. FAX 0091-652731. TELEX 3166096 DST IN. Ed. A.R. Rajeswari. charts; stat.; circ. 1,000.
Formerly: National Committee on Science and Technology. Research and Development Statistics.

500 016   II   ISSN 0019-6339
Q1   CODEN: IDSAAV
INDIAN SCIENCE ABSTRACTS. 1965. m. Rs.600($300) Indian National Scientific Documentation Centre, 14 Satsang Vihar Marg, New Delhi 110 067, India. Ed. A. Krishnan. abstr.; index; circ. 800. **Indexed:** Anim.Breed.Abstr., Chem.Abstr., Field Crop Abstr., Herb.Abstr., Hort.Abstr., Nutr.Abstr., Plant Breed.Abstr., World Surf.Coat.

INDIAN SCIENCE INDEX. SER.B CALCUTTA: PRE-MODERN PERIOD. see *TECHNOLOGY: COMPREHENSIVE WORKS — Abstracting, Bibliographies, Statistics*

500 011   SP   ISSN 0210-9409
Z7401
INDICE ESPANOL DE CIENCIA Y TECNOLOGIA/INDEX TO SPANISH SCIENCE AND TECHNOLOGY. 1980. q. 3710 ptas. (Consejo Superior de Investigaciones Cientificas) Instituto de Informacion y Documentacion en Ciencia y Tecnologia, Joaquin Costa 22, 28002 Madrid, Spain. TEL 91-5635482. FAX 91-5642644. TELEX 22628 CIDMD E. circ. 600.
●Also available online.
Also available on CD-ROM.

500 020   SP   ISSN 0214-1086
INDICE ESPANOL DE CIENCIAS SOCIALES. SERIES D: SCIENCE AND SCIENTIFIC INFORMATION. 1979. a. 5000 ptas. or exchange basis. Instituto de Informacion y Documentacion en Ciencias Sociales y Humanidades, Pinar, 25, 3, 28006 Madrid, Spain.
●Also available online.
Also available on CD-ROM.
Supersedes in part (in 1982): Indice Espanol de Ciencias Sociales (ISSN 0213-019X)

500 010   AO   ISSN 0074-008X
INSTITUTO DE INVESTIGACAO CIENTIFICA DE ANGOLA. BIBLIOGRAFICAS TEMATICAS. 1969. irreg., 1973, no.19. free to qualified personnel. Instituto de Investigacao Cientifica de Angola, Departamento de Documentacao e Informacao, Box 3244, Luanda, Angola. **Indexed:** Trop.Abstr.

INTERNATIONAL RARE BOOK PRICES - SCIENCES & MEDICINE. see *PUBLISHING AND BOOK TRADE — Abstracting, Bibliographies, Statistics*

500   JA   ISSN 0514-2253
JAPANESE PERIODICALS INDEX. SCIENCE AND TECHNOLOGY/ZASSHI KIJI SAKUIN. KAGAKU GIJUTSU HEN. (Text in Japanese and European languages) 1950. q. 20000 Yen. Kokuritsu Kokkai Toshokan, Chikuji Kankobutsu - National Diet Library, 10-1 Nagata-cho 1-chome, Chiyoda-ku, Tokyo 100, Japan. TEL 03-581-2331. TELEX 2225393. abstr.; circ. 840.

KAGAKU GIJUTSU BUNKEN TOYAMA/TOYAMA SCIENCE AND TECHNICAL DOCUMENTS. see *TECHNOLOGY: COMPREHENSIVE WORKS — Abstracting, Bibliographies, Statistics*

KAGAKU GIJUTSU FORAMU HOKOKUSHO. see *TECHNOLOGY: COMPREHENSIVE WORKS — Abstracting, Bibliographies, Statistics*

500   JA
KANAZAWA DAIGAKU RIGAKUBU RONBUN OYOBI CHOSHO MOKUROKU/KANAZAWA UNIVERSITY. FACULTY OF SCIENCE. LIST OF PUBLICATIONS. (Text in English, German, French, Japanese) 1961. quinquennial. Kanazawa Daigaku, Rigakubu - Kanazawa University, Faculty of Science, 1-1 Marunouchi, Kanazawa-shi, Ishikawa-ken 920, Japan. TEL 81-762-62-4281. FAX 81-762-64-1059. bibl.

500.9 016   SZ
KEY WORD INDEX OF WILDLIFE RESEARCH. (Text in English or German) 1974. a. 70. Swiss Wildlife Information Service, University of Zurich, Strickhofstr. 39, CH-8057 Zurich, Switzerland.

500 016   KO   ISSN 0023-4052
Q1
KOREAN SCIENTIFIC ABSTRACTS. 1969. bi-m. $30. Korea Institute for Economics and Technology, P.O.B. 205, 206-9 Cheongryangri-Dong, Dongdaimun-Ku, S. Korea. abstr.; index; circ. 700. (reprint service avail. from UMI) **Indexed:** AESIS, Anim.Breed.Abstr., BMT, Br.Ceram.Abstr., Forest.Abstr., Forest Prod.Abstr., Graph.Arts Lit.Abstr., Nutr.Abstr., Plant Breed.Abstr.

KUNI NO SHIKEN KENKYU GYOMU KEIKAKU. see *TECHNOLOGY: COMPREHENSIVE WORKS — Abstracting, Bibliographies, Statistics*

500   US   ISSN 0090-5232
Z7401
L C SCIENCE TRACER BULLET. 1972. irreg. free. U.S. Library of Congress, Science and Technology Division, Washington, DC 20540. TEL 202-707-5580.

500 015   TH   ISSN 0125-4537
LIST OF SCIENTIFIC AND TECHNICAL LITERATURE RELATING TO THAILAND. (Text in English) 1964. irreg. $5 per no. (Thai National Documentation Centre) Thailand Institute of Scientific and Technological Research, 196 Phahonyothin Rd., Chatuchak, Bangkok 10900, Thailand. TEL 579-4929. FAX 662-579-8594. circ. 500.
●Also available online.

500 600   MW   ISSN 0251-0154
                                 CODEN: LUSODO
LUSO; journal of science and technology. (Text in English) 1980. s-a. University of Malawi, Faculty of Science, Box 280, Zomba, Malawi. TEL 522222. Ed.Bd. adv.; bk.rev.; bibl.; charts; illus.; circ. 150. (back issues avail.) **Indexed:** Biol.Abstr., Chem.Abstr., Ecol.Abstr., Geo.Abstr., Hort.Abstr.

SCIENCES: COMPREHENSIVE WORKS — ABSTRACTING, BIBLIOGRAPHIES, STATISTICS   4357

500 015   HU
MAGYAR TUDOMANYOS AKADEMIA KONVYTARANAK KOZLEMENYEI. (Text in Hungarian; summaries in English, French, German, Russian) 1956. irreg. (4-6/yr.). price varies or exchange basis. Magyar Tudomanyos Akademia Konvytara, Aranyjanos u.1, P.O. Box 7, 1361 Budapest 5, Hungary. Eds. G. Fekete, L. Vekerdi.
   Formerly: Magyar Tudomanyos Akademia Konvytaranak Kiadvanyai (ISSN 0133-8862)
   Description: Monographs dealing with the history of the academy and the library. Colletions of data and general studies on the history of science and library science.

500 620   IR
MAQALAH-NAMAH-I 'ULUM/INDEX TO SCIENTIFIC PAPERS. no.4, 1983. s-a. Markazi Asnad va Madarak-i 'Ilmi, 1188 Khayaban-i Inqilab, P.O. Box 1387-01, Teheran, Iran.
   Description: Covers publications in pure and applied sciences, including engineering, technology, agriculture and medicine.

500 600   US
MASTER'S THESES IN THE PURE AND APPLIED SCIENCES; accepted by colleges and universities in the United States and Canada. 1955. a. price varies. Plenum Publishing Corp., 233 Spring St., New York, NY 10013-1578. TEL 212-620-8000. FAX 212-463-0742. TELEX 23-421139. Ed. W.H. Shafer. (back issues avail.)
   Refereed Serial

500 016   MX
MEXICO. CENTRO DE INFORMACION TECNICA Y DOCUMENTACION. INDICE DE REVISTAS. SECCION DE CIENCIA Y TECNOLOGIA. 1973. w. Mex.$356.25($18) Mexico. Servicio Nacional de Adiestramiento Rapido de la Mano de Obra en la Industria, Calzada Atzcapotzalco-la Villa 209, Mexico 16, D.F., Mexico. Ed. Gilberto Diaz Santana. circ. 154.

NATIONAL DIET LIBRARY. MONTHLY LIST OF FOREIGN SCIENTIFIC AND TECHNICAL PUBLICATIONS/KAIGAI KAGAKU GIJUTSU SHIRYO GEPPO. see
TECHNOLOGY: COMPREHENSIVE WORKS — Abstracting, Bibliographies, Statistics

500.9   UK   ISSN 0308-180X
NATURAL HISTORY BOOK REVIEWS; an international bibliography. 1976. 4/yr. £59($109) A B Academic Publishers, P.O. Box 42, Bicester, Oxon OX6 7NW, England. TEL 0869-320949. Ed.Bd. adv.; bk.rev.; illus.; index. (also avail. in microfiche)
   —BLDSC shelfmark: 6038.500000.

600 016   US   ISSN 0028-6869
Z5854   CODEN: NTBOAJ
NEW TECHNICAL BOOKS; a selective list with descriptive annotations. 1915. bi-m. $30 (foreign $35). New York Public Library, Science and Technology Research Center, Rm. 120, Fifth Ave. and 42nd St., New York, NY 10018. TEL 212-930-0920. Ed. Gloria Rohmann. bk.rev.; index; circ. 1,700. **Indexed:** Abstr.Bull.Inst.Pap.Chem., Bk.Rev.Ind. (1985-), Child.Bk.Rev.Ind. (1985-).

500 016   JA   ISSN 0916-1198
NIHON KAGAKU GIJUTSU KANKEI CHIKUJI KANKOBUTSU SORAN/DIRECTORY OF JAPANESE SCIENTIFIC PERIODICALS. (Text in English and Japanese) quinquennial. latest 1988. 15656 Yen. National Diet Library - Kokuritsu Kokkai Toshokan, 1-10-1 Nagata-cho, Chiyoda-ku, Tokyo 100, Japan. TEL 03-3581-2331. TELEX 2225393.
   Formerly (until 1988): Nihon Kagaku Gijutsu Kankei Chikuji Kankobutsu Mokuroku (ISSN 0911-0151)

NIJHOFF INFORMATION, NEW PUBLICATIONS FROM GERMANY, AUSTRIA AND SWITZERLAND. see
PUBLISHING AND BOOK TRADE — Abstracting, Bibliographies, Statistics

500 011   RU   ISSN 0134-2754
NOVAYA SOVETSKAYA LITERATURA PO OBSHCHESTVENNYM NAUKAM. NAUKOVEDENIE; bibliograficheskii ukazatel' 1947. m. 7.20 Rub. Akademiya Nauk S.S.S.R., Institut Nauchnoi Informatsii po Obshchestvennym Naukam, Ul. Krasikova 28-21, 117418 Moscow V-418, Russia. Ed. N.I. Makeshin.

500   RU   ISSN 0202-2141
OBSHCHESTVENNYE NAUKI ZA RUBEZHOM. NAUKOVEDENIE; referativnyi zhurnal. 1973. bi-m. 4.20 Rub. Akademiya Nauk S.S.S.R., Institut Nauchnoi Informatsii po Obshchestvennym Naukam, Ul. Krasikova 28-21, 117418 Moscow V-418, Russia. Ed. A.M. Kul'kin.

500 610   US
OUT-OF-PRINT SCIENTIFIC, MEDICAL AND TECHNICAL BOOKS. 1985. q. free. John P. Coll Books, Box 5626, Berkeley, CA 94705-0626. TEL 415-845-8475. Ed. John P. Coll. circ. 1,000.
   Description: Lists out-of-print academic and professional books in the pure and applied sciences and medicine.

OUTSTANDING SCIENCE TRADE BOOKS FOR CHILDREN. see *CHILDREN AND YOUTH — Abstracting, Bibliographies, Statistics*

500 016   PK   ISSN 0031-0085
PAKISTAN SCIENCE ABSTRACTS. (Text in English) 1961. q. Rps.35($14) Pakistan Scientific and Technological Information Centre, Quaid-i-Azam University Campus, Box 1217, Islamabad, Pakistan. Ed. Ghulam Hamid Khan. abstr.; pat.; index; circ. 500. (also avail. in microfilm)

016 500   MX   ISSN 0185-1004
Z7403
PERIODICA. INDICE DE REVISTAS LATINOAMERICANAS EN CIENCIAS. (Text in Spanish; key words in English) 1978. q. $190. Universidad Nacional Autonoma de Mexico, Centro de Informacion Cientifica y Humanistica, Apdo. Postal 70-392, C.P. 04510 Mexico, D.F., Mexico.
   ●Also available online.
   Also available on CD-ROM.
   Formerly (until 1979): Periodica. Indice de Revistas Mexicanas en Ciencias.

500 016   PH
PHILIPPINE SCIENCE AND TECHNOLOGY ABSTRACTS. 1960. q. $24. Science and Technology Information Institute, Scientific Library and Documentation Division, Box 3596, Manila, Philippines. FAX 822-05-64. abstr.; index; circ. 500. **Indexed:** Biol.Abstr.
   Formerly: Philippine Science and Technology Abstracts Bibliography (ISSN 0115-8724); Formed by the merger of: Philippine Abstracts (ISSN 0031-7438); Philippine Science Index.

500   US
PUBLISHED SEARCHES. (Supplement avail.) a. $55 in U.S., Canada, Mexico; elsewhere $70. U.S. National Technical Information Service, 5285 Port Royal Rd., Springfield, VA 22161. TEL 703-487-4630. (also avail. in microfiche)
   Description: Includes scientific information from over 23 other international sources as well as NTIS.

500 600   RM
REFERATIVNYJ BJULLETEN RUMYNSKOJ NAUCHNO-TEHNICHESKOJ LITERATURY. French edition: Bulletin Analytique de la Litterature Scientifique et Technique Roumaine. English edition: Abstracts of Romanian Scientific and Technical Literature. (Text in Russian) 1969. s-a. $121 or exchange basis. Institutul National de Informare si Documentare, Str. George Enescu 27-29, 70141 Bucharest, Rumania. TEL 134010. TELEX 11247 INIDR. (Dist. by: Rodipet, S.A., Piata Presei Libere nr.1, Sector 1, 71341 Bucharest, Rumania) abstr.; index.
   Description: Contains abstracts of articles published in Rumanian periodicals in the fields of pure and applied science.

500   IQ   ISSN 1012-3458
RESEARCH ABSTRACTS IN SCIENTIFIC RESEARCH COUNCIL. (Text in Arabic) 1984. irreg. free. Scientific Research Council, Jadiriyah P.O. Box 2441, Baghdad, Iraq. TELEX 213976 SR IK. Ed. Radhwan K. Abdul-Halim. circ. 500.

RESEARCH AND STUDIES. see *EDUCATION — Abstracting, Bibliographies, Statistics*

500   JA
RIKA NENPYO. (Text in Japanese) 1924. a. (University of Tokyo, Tokyo Astronomical Observatory - Tokyo Daigaku Tokyo Tenmondai) Maruzen Co., Ltd., 9-2 Nihonbashi 3-chome, Chuo-ku, Tokyo 103, Japan. stat.

500 016   RM   ISSN 0035-8096
RUMANIAN SCIENTIFIC ABSTRACTS.* 1973. s-a. (Academia de Stiinte Sociale si Politice, Office of Information and Documentation in Social and Political Sciences - Academy of Social and Political Sciences of the S.R.R) Editura Academiei Romane, Calea Victoriei 125, 79717 Bucharest, Rumania. (Subscr. to: ILEXIM, P.O. Box 136-137, 13 Decembrie St., no. 3, 11226 Bucharest, Rumania) Ed. Mircea Ioanid. bk.rev.; abstr.; index; circ. 1,000.
   Indexed: Appl.Mech.Rev., Bull.Signal, Field Crop Abstr., Herb.Abstr., Ref.Zh.

500 016   IO   ISSN 0216-4167
Q1
SARI KARANGAN INDONESIA. 1958. q. Rps.2400. Indonesian Institute of Sciences - Lembaga Ilmu Pengetahuan Indonesia, Jalan Jenderal Gatot Subroto 10, P.O. Box 250-JKT, Jakarta 10002, Indonesia. TEL 021-511542. Ed. Rachmat I. Wahono. abstr.; index; circ. 1,800. **Indexed:** Biol.Abstr., Chem.Abstr., E.I.
   —BLDSC shelfmark: 8076.050000.
   Formerly: Indonesian Abstracts (ISSN 0019-7319)

500 600 016   US   ISSN 0036-8059
Z673   CODEN: STNWAM
SCI-TECH NEWS. 1947. q. $11 to non-members. Columbia University, School of Library Service, Butler Library, 535 W. 114th St., New York, NY 10027. TEL 212-854-4011. Ed. Ellis Mount. adv.; bk.rev.; bibl.; circ. 4,300. **Indexed:** Lib.Lit., Sci.Abstr.
   —BLDSC shelfmark: 8205.300000.

500 016   US   ISSN 0098-342X
Z7403
SCIENCE BOOKS & FILMS. Variant title: A A A S Science Books and Films. 1965. 9/yr. $35. American Association for the Advancement of Science, 1333 H St., N.W., Washington, DC 20005. TEL 202-326-6454. Ed. Maria Sosa. adv.; bk.rev.; index; circ. 4,500. (also avail. in microform from UMI; reprint service avail. from UMI) **Indexed:** Bk.Rev.Ind. (1966-), Child.Bk.Rev.Ind. (1966-).
   Formerly: Science Books (ISSN 0036-8253)
   Description: Reviews of print, film, and software materials in all sciences for all age levels, for librarians and educators.

500 016   US   ISSN 0036-827X
Z7401
SCIENCE CITATION INDEX. Short title: S C I. (Includes Source Index, Citation Index, Permuterm Subject Index, and Corporate Index) 1961. 6/yr. (plus annual cum.). $10175. Institute for Scientific Information, 3501 Market St., Philadelphia, PA 19104. TEL 215-386-0100. FAX 215-386-2991. (U.K. addr.: 132 High St., Oxbridge, Middlesex, UB8 1DP, England) 10 yr. cum.index: 1955-1964, 1945-1954; 5 yr. cum.index: 1965-1969, 1970-1974, 1976-1979, 1980-1984, 1985-1989. (also avail. in magnetic tape)
   ●Also available online. Vendor(s): DIMDI, Data-Star, DIALOG (Files nos.34,432,433,434/SCISEARCH), Orbit Information Technologies.
   Also available on CD-ROM. Producer(s): Institute for Scientific Information (SCI CDE).
   —BLDSC shelfmark: 8141.802000.
   Description: Indexes the world's science and technology literature. Provides cited reference searching and related records.

500   US   ISSN 0092-315X
T14.5
SCIENCE INDICATORS. 1973. biennial. National Science Foundation, 1800 G St., N.W., Rm. L602, Washington, DC 20550. TEL 202-634-4634. FAX 202-634-4683. bibl.; charts; stat.; index; circ. 10,000.

SCIENCES: COMPREHENSIVE WORKS — COMPUTER APPLICATIONS

500 600 016　　　　US　　ISSN 0000-054X
Z7401
SCIENTIFIC AND TECHNICAL BOOKS AND SERIALS IN PRINT; an index to literature in science and technology. (Issued in 3 vols.) 1972. a. $267. R.R. Bowker, A Reed Reference Publishing Company, Division of Reed Publishing (USA) Inc., 121 Chanlon Rd., New Providence, NJ 07974. TEL 800-521-8110. FAX 908-665-6688. TELEX 138 755. (Subscr. to: Order Dept., Box 31, New Providence, NJ 07974) (also avail. in magnetic tape)
●Also available online. Vendor(s): Orbit Information Technologies (File name BIPS). Also available on CD-ROM.
—BLDSC shelfmark: 8176.628000.
　Formerly (until 1977): Scientific and Technical Books in Print (ISSN 0000-0248)
　　Description: Lists more than 135,000 currently published books and 22,000 international serials arranged by subject, author and title. Includes publisher information.

500 016　　　　TH　　ISSN 0125-4529
SCIENTIFIC SERIALS IN THAI LIBRARIES. (Text and summaries in English) 1968. a. B.2000($80) Thailand Institute of Scientific and Technological Research, 196 Phahonyothin Rd., Chatuchak, Bangkok 10900, Thailand. TEL 579-4929. FAX 662-579-8594. **Indexed**: Biol.Abstr.
●Also available online.
　Description: Lists journals and report series on science, technology, and socio-economic aspects of the sciences received by 150 libraries in Bangkok.

500 600　　　　　US
SCITECH REFERENCE PLUS; complete bibliographic information on SciTech books and serials, bibliographical data on science professionals, and corporate profiles of research and business facilities. a. $995. R.R. Bowker, A Reed Reference Publishing Company, Division of Reed Publishing (USA) Inc., 121 Chanlon Rd., New Providence, NJ 07974. TEL 908-665-2867. FAX 908-665-6688. TELEX 138 755. (Subscr. to: Order Dept., Box 31, New Providence, NJ 07974. TEL 800-323-3288) (avail. on MS-DOS version)
●Available only on CD-ROM.
　Description: Merges six definitive databases to provide access to the most current information.

500 600 016　　　US　　ISSN 0037-1343
AS36
SELECTED RAND ABSTRACTS; a quarterly guide to publications of the Rand Corporation. 1946. q. $15 to individuals; free to government agencies, libraries, and non-profit research organizations. Rand Corporation, Publications Department, 1700 Main St., Box 2138, Santa Monica, CA 90407-2138. TEL 213-393-0411. FAX 213-393-4818. TELEX 9103436878. abstr.; index; circ. 6,000. **Indexed**: Abstr.Mil.Bibl., Fluidex, Rehabil.Lit.
—BLDSC shelfmark: 8234.700000.
　Formerly (until 1962): Rand Corporation. Index of Selected Publications (ISSN 0485-9790)

500 600　　　　JA　　ISSN 0917-7574
SHINKU TANKU NENPO/ABSTRACTS OF THINK TANK REPORTS. (Text in Japanese) 1976. a. 5000 Yen. Sogo Kenkyu Kaihatsu Kiko - National Institute for Research Advancement, Shinjuku Mitsui Bldg., 2-1-1 Nishi-Shinjuku, Shinjuku-ku, Tokyo 103, Japan. TEL 03-3344-3371. FAX 03-3344-1449. TELEX 2325332 NIRA J. abstr.; circ. 1,400.
　Description: Introduces the results of research conducted at Japanese think tanks and research institutes.

016 500　　　　　CE
SRI LANKA SCIENCE INDEX. (Text in English) 1977. q. $7 (or exchange basis). (Sri Lanka Scientific and Technical Information Centre) Natural Resources, Energy and Science Authority, 47-5 Maitland Place, Colombo 7, Sri Lanka. (reprint service avail.)

STATNI VEDECKA KNIHOVNA. VYBER NOVINEK. SERIE A: PRIRODNI VEDY, ZEMEDELSTVI. see AGRICULTURE — Abstracting, Bibliographies, Statistics

500　　　　　　　　SJ
SUDAN SCIENCE ABSTRACTS. 1980. a. National Council for Research, National Documentation Centre, Box 2404, Khartoum, Sudan.

500 600 016　　　NE
TECHNISCHE UNIVERSITEIT TE DELFT. BIBLIOTHEEK. AANWINSTEN. 1952. m. fl.30 to individual; students fl.5. Technische Universiteit te Delft, Bibliotheek, P.O. Box 98, 2600 MG Delft, Netherlands. FAX 015-159007. TELEX 38070 BITUD NL. Ed. K.F. van Eijk. circ. 800. **Indexed**: Excerp.Med., Key to Econ.Sci.
　Formerly: Technische Hogeschool te Delft. Bibliotheek. Aanwinsten (ISSN 0006-1948)

016　　　　　　　TH　　ISSN 0125-0000
THAI ABSTRACTS, SERIES A. SCIENCE AND TECHNOLOGY. (Text in English) 1974. s-a. B.100($5) per no. Thailand Institute of Scientific and Technological Research, 196 Phahonyothin Road, Bang Khen, Bangkok 10900, Thailand. TEL 579-4929. FAX 662-579-8594. Ed.Bd. author and subject indexes; circ. 500.
●Also available online.
—BLDSC shelfmark: 8813.889000.

500 300 001.3　　PH
U P RESEARCH MONITOR. 1978. a. University of the Philippines, Office of Research Coordination, Rm. 309 Malcolm Hall, Diliman, Quezon City, Philippines. Ed. Bienvenido T. Miranda. circ. 750. (back issues avail.)

U P THESIS AND DISSERTATION ABSTRACTS. (University of the Philippines) see EDUCATION — Abstracting, Bibliographies, Statistics

UITGELEZEN. see SOCIAL SCIENCES: COMPREHENSIVE WORKS — Abstracting, Bibliographies, Statistics

310 500　　　　　UN
UNESCO. STATISTICS ON SCIENCE AND TECHNOLOGY/STATISTIQUES RELATIVES AUX SCIENCE ET A LA TECHNOLOGIE/ESTADISTICAS RELATIVAS A LA CIENCIA Y A LA TECNOLOGIA. (Text in English, French and Spanish) a. Unesco, Division of Statistics on Science and Technology, Office of Statistics, 7-9 Place de Fontenoy, 75700 Paris, France. TEL 33 1 568-10-00.

500 016　　　　　CN　　ISSN 0082-7657
Z7403
UNION LIST OF SCIENTIFIC SERIALS IN CANADIAN LIBRARIES/CATALOGUE COLLECTIF DES PUBLICATIONS SCIENTIFIQUES DANS LES BIBLIOTHEQUES CANADIENNES. 1957. biennial; 14th, 1990. Can.$220 (microfiche Can.$85). (National Research Council of Canada) C.I.S.T.I. Cataloguing Section, Ottawa, Ont. K1A 0S2, Canada. TEL 613-993-3449. circ. 1,000. (also avail. in microfiche)
●Also available online. Vendor(s): CISTI.
Also available on CD-ROM.

500 010　　　　　IS　　ISSN 0082-7665
Z6945
UNION LIST OF SERIALS IN ISRAEL LIBRARIES.* (Suppl. avail) 1955. irreg., 4th edt., 1975. $50. Jewish National and University Library, P.O.Box 503, Jerusalem 91004, Israel. TEL 02-660351. FAX 02-527741. TELEX 23567. Ed. Clara Hovne. circ. 400. (also avail. in magnetic tape)

500 011　　　　　GW　　ISSN 0344-0915
UNIVERSITAET HOHENHEIM FORSCHUNGSBERICHT. 1976. triennial. free. Universitaet Hohenheim, Postfach 700562, 7000 Stuttgart 70, Germany. TEL 0711-459-2001. FAX 0711-4593289. Ed. Klaus H. Grabowski. abstr.; circ. 1,500.

500 600　　　　　RU　　ISSN 0135-0617
Z7409
VSESOYUZNYI INSTITUT NAUCHNO-TEKHNICHESKOI INFORMATSII. DEPONIROVANNYE NAUCHNYE RABOTY. 1963. m. 35 Rub. Vsesoyuznyi Institut Nauchno-Tekhnicheskoi Informatsii (VINITI), Baltiiskaya ul. 14, Moscow A-219, Russia. (Subscr. to: Mezhdunarodnaya Kniga, Moscow 121200, Russia)
　Formerly: Vsesoyuznyi Institut Nauchno-Tekhnicheskoi Informatsii. Deponirovannye Rukopisi.

500　　　　　　　　GW　　ISSN 0177-5928
W L A SELECTA. (Wissenschaftlicher Literatur Anzeiger) 1985. s-a. Verlag M. Veit M.A., Erlenweg 10, 4834 Harsewinkel 1, Germany. TEL 05247-5466. adv.; circ. 4,000. (back issues avail.)

WASEDA DAIGAKU DAIGAKUIN RIKOGAKU KENKYU IHO/WASEDA UNIVERSITY. GRADUATE SCHOOL OF SCIENCE AND ENGINEERING. SYNOPSES OF SCIENCE AND ENGINEERING PAPERS. see ENGINEERING — Abstracting, Bibliographies, Statistics

WISSENSCHAFTLICHER LITERATURANZEIGER. see PUBLISHING AND BOOK TRADE — Abstracting, Bibliographies, Statistics

500 016　　　　　NE　　ISSN 0259-8264
Z7403
WORLD TRANSLATION INDEX. Abbreviated title: W T I. (Text in English, French, German) 1978. 10/yr. (plus annual cum.). fl.1350 to ITC member countries; elsewhere fl.1500. International Translations Centre (ITC), Schuttersveld 2, 2611 WE Delft, Netherlands. TEL 015-142242. FAX 015-158535. TELEX 38104-ITC-NL. (Co-sponsor: Centre National de la Recherche Scientifique, Institut de l'Information Scientifique et Technique (INIST-CNRS), Vandoeuvre-les-Nancy, France) adv.; cum.index 1967-1989; circ. 500. (back issues avail.) **Indexed**: GeoRef.
●Also available online. Vendor(s): DIALOG (File no.295), European Space Agency (File no.33/WTI).
—BLDSC shelfmark: 9360.154130.
　Formerly (until 1987): World Transindex (ISSN 0378-6803); Formed by the merger of: Bulletin Signaletique. Part 900. Bulletin des Traductions (ISSN 0007-571X); Transatom Bulletin (ISSN 0041-1086); World Index of Scientific Translations and List of Translations Notified to the International Translation Centre (ISSN 0376-6381); Which was formerly: World Index of Scientific Translations and List of Translations Notified to E T C. Which was formed by the merger of: World Index of Scientific Translations (ISSN 0043-8553); List of Translations Notified to the E T C (ISSN 0046-2829).
　Description: Gives bibliographic data of existing translations of scientific and technical literature from any language. Includes author and source index.

500　　　　　　　　ZA
ZAMBIA. NATIONAL COUNCIL FOR SCIENTIFIC RESEARCH. N C S R BIBLIOGRAPHY. Short title: N C S R Bibliography. 1976. irreg., latest 1979. K.1.50. National Council for Scientific Research, Box CH 158, Chelston, Lusaka, Zambia.

500 016　　　　　ZA
ZAMBIA SCIENCE ABSTRACTS. 1977. a. K.5. National Council for Scientific Research, Box CH 158, Chelston, Lusaka, Zambia. Ed. W.C. Mushipi.

500 016　　　　　RH
ZIMBABWE RESEARCH INDEX; register of current research in Zimbabwe. 1971. a. exchange basis. Scientific Liaison Office, P.O. Box 8510, Causeway, Harare, Zimbabwe. TEL 700573. TELEX 22141. (Subscr. to: Government Printer, P.O. Box 8062, Causeway, Harare, Zimbabwe) index; circ. 500 (controlled). (processed) **Indexed**: Anim.Breed.Abstr.
　Formerly: Rhodesia Research Index.

SCIENCES: COMPREHENSIVE WORKS — Computer Applications

600 621.381　　　US　　ISSN 0733-8074
QA76.5　　　　　　　　　CODEN: ACCSEG
ACCESS (RESEARCH TRIANGLE PARK). 1982. 6/yr. $21. L E D S Publishing Co. Inc., Box 12847, Research Triangle Park, NC 27709. TEL 919-477-3690. Ed. Leslie E. Sparks. adv.; bk.rev.; circ. 4,000. **Indexed**: Oper.Res.Manage.Sci., Qual.Contr.Appl.Stat.
　Description: Features technical articles on applications to engineering and science. Regular columns include statistics column, numerical analysis, scientific use of Amiga and Macintosh.

500　　　　　　　　US　　ISSN 0888-2231
APPLICATIONS OF COMPUTER SCIENCE SERIES. 1986. irreg. Computer Science Press, Inc., 41 Madison Ave., 37th Fl., New York, NY 10010-3546. TEL 212-576-9400. Ed. Arthur D. Friedman. (back issues avail.)

SCIENCES: COMPREHENSIVE WORKS — COMPUTER APPLICATIONS

500 301.1 016   US   ISSN 0005-7940
BF1   CODEN: BEHSAS
BEHAVIORAL SCIENCE. 1956. q. $37 to individuals; institutions $62. General Systems Science Foundation, Box 8369, La Jolla, CA 92038-8369. Ed. James G. Miller. adv.; bk.rev.; abstr.; charts; illus.; index; circ. 3,000. (also avail. in microform from UMI; reprint service avail. from UMI) **Indexed:** A.B.C.Pol.Sci., A.I.C.P., Adol.Ment.Hlth.Abstr., Amer.Hist.& Life, ASSIA, Biol.Abstr., Comput.Rev., Cont.Pg.Manage., Curr.Adv.Ecol.Sci., Curr.Cont., Educ.Admin.Abstr., Ergon.Abstr., Excerp.Med., Geo.Abstr., Hist.Abstr., Ind.Med., INIS Atomind., J.Cont.Quant.Meth., Lang.& Lang.Behav.Abstr., M.L.A., Math.R., Mid.East: Abstr.& Ind., Oper.Res.Manage.Sci., Pers.Lit., Psychol.Abstr., Qual.Contr.Appl.Stat., Sci.Abstr., Soc.Sci.Ind., Sociol.Abstr., SSCI.
—BLDSC shelfmark: 1877.850000.

BIOLOGICAL CYBERNETICS; communication and control in organisms and automata. see COMPUTERS — Cybernetics

C A SELECTS. COMPUTERS IN CHEMISTRY. see CHEMISTRY — Abstracting, Bibliographies, Statistics

001.6 539.7   SZ   ISSN 0304-2898
C E R N SCHOOL OF COMPUTING. PROCEEDINGS. (Former name of issuing body: Conseil Europeen pour la Recherche Nucleaire) 1970. a. C E R N - European Laboratory for Particle Physics, CH-1211 Geneva 23, Switzerland. Indexed: INIS Atomind.

500 600   CN   ISSN 0715-8661
C I S T I NEWS/ACTUALITES I C I S T. (Canada Institute for Scientific and Technical Information) 3/yr. (National Research Council of Canada - Institut Canadien de l'Information Scientifique et Technique) C I S T I Publicity and Communications, Ottawa, Ont. K1A 0S2, Canada. TEL 613-993-3854. FAX 613-952-9112. Ed. Elizabeth Katz.
—BLDSC shelfmark: 3267.693000.

001.64 500   ISSN 0364-5916
QD503   CODEN: CCCTD6
CALPHAD. (Computer Coupling of Phase Diagrams and Thermochemistry) 1977. q. £250 (effective 1992). Pergamon Press, Inc., Journals Division, 660 White Plains Rd., Tarrytown, NY 10591-5153. TEL 914-524-9200. FAX 914-333-2444. (And: Headington Hill Hall, Oxford OX3 0BW, England. TEL 0865-794141) Ed. Dr. Larry Kaufman. adv.; bk.rev.; circ. 1,025. (also avail. in microform from MIM,UMI) Indexed: Biol.Abstr., Chem.Abstr., Comput.Cont., Curr.Cont., INIS Atomind., Met.Abstr., Sci.Abstr., Sci.Cit.Ind., World Alum.Abstr.
—BLDSC shelfmark: 3015.540000.
Description: Covers all aspects of calculating and using phase diagrams in thermochemistry and studies of phase equilibrium.
Refereed Serial

621.381 500   AT   ISSN 0816-6013
COMMONWEALTH SCIENTIFIC AND INDUSTRIAL RESEARCH ORGANIZATION. DIVISION OF GEOMECHANICS. GEOMECHANICS COMPUTER PROGRAMS. 1972. irreg. Aus.$10 per no. C.S.I.R.O., Division of Geomechanics, Box 54, Mount Waverley, Vic. 3149, Australia.
Description: Documentation of computer programs for the solution of practical problems in geomechanics.

COMPUTATIONAL SEISMOLOGY. see EARTH SCIENCES — Geophysics

500   UK   ISSN 0266-7061
     CODEN: COABER
COMPUTER APPLICATIONS IN THE BIOSCIENCES. Short title: CABIOS. 1985. q. $160. I R L Press Ltd., P.O. Box 1, Eynsham, Oxford OX8 1JJ, England. TEL 0865-882283. FAX 0865-882890. TELEX 83147 IRL. (U.S. subscr. addr.: I R L Press, Box Q, McLean, VA 22101) Ed.Bd. adv.; bk.rev.; illus.; tr.lit.; index. (back issues avail.; reprint service avail. from SWZ) Indexed: A.I.Abstr., Biol.Abstr., CAD CAM Abstr., Chem.Abstr., Compumath, Comput.Rev., Curr.Adv.Ecol.Sci., Curr.Biotech.Abstr., Curr.Cont., Excerp.Med., Sci.Cit.Ind., Telegen.
—BLDSC shelfmark: 3393.635000.
Description: International applications-orientated journal publishing full papers, program reviews, new applications and developments for newcomers and computer-literate bioscientists.

530   NE   ISSN 0010-4655
QC52   CODEN: CPHCBZ
COMPUTER PHYSICS COMMUNICATIONS; an international journal and program library for computational physics and computer programs in physics. (Text in English) 1969. 18/yr.(in 6 vols.; 3 nos./vol.) fl.3156 (effective 1992). North-Holland (Subsidiary of: Elsevier Science Publishers B.V.), P.O. Box 211, 1000 AE Amsterdam, Netherlands. TEL 020-5803911. FAX 020-5803598. TELEX 18582 ESPA NL. (Subscr. in U.S. and Canada to: Elsevier Science Publishing Co., Inc., Box 882, Madison Sq. Sta., New York, NY 10159. TEL 212-989-5800) Ed. P.G. Burke. adv.; bk.rev.; software rev.; charts; index. (also avail. in microform from RPI; back issues avail.) Indexed: Chem.Abstr., Compumath, Comput.Rev., Curr.Cont., Cyb.Abstr., Ind.Sci.Rev., INIS Atomind., INSPEC, Math.R., Phys.Ber., Risk Abstr., Sci.Abstr., Sci.Cit.Ind.
—BLDSC shelfmark: 3394.150000.
Refereed Serial

651.8 540   US   ISSN 0097-8485
QD39.3.E46   CODEN: COCHDK
COMPUTERS & CHEMISTRY. 1977. q. £245 (effective 1992). Pergamon Press, Inc., Journals Division, 660 White Plains Rd., Tarrytown, NY 10591-5153. TEL 914-524-9200. FAX 914-333-2444. (And: Headington Hill Hall, Oxford OX3 0BW, England. TEL 0865-794141) Ed. David Edelson. adv.; bk.rev.; circ. 1,000. (also avail. in microform from MIM,UMI) Indexed: Abstr.Bull.Inst.Pap.Chem., Biol.Abstr., Cadscan, Chem.Abstr., Chem.Eng.Abstr., Compumath, Comput.Abstr., Comput.Cont., Comput.Rev., Curr.Cont., Ind.Sci.Rev., Lead Abstr., Mass Spectr.Bull., Sci.Abstr., Sci.Cit.Ind., Zincscan.
—BLDSC shelfmark: 3394.667000.
Description: Publishes papers on applications of computer techniques to chemistry and biochemistry.
Refereed Serial

COMPUTERS & MINING. see MINES AND MINING INDUSTRY

CZECHOSLOVAK NATIONAL WORKSHOP ON SEISMIC DATA ACQUISITION AND COMPUTER PROCESSING. PROCEEDINGS. see EARTH SCIENCES — Geophysics

DATA HANDLING IN SCIENCE AND TECHNOLOGY. see COMPUTERS — Data Base Management

DIRECTORY OF MINING PROGRAMS. see MINES AND MINING INDUSTRY

E Z SEARCH - MINING. see MINES AND MINING INDUSTRY

500   NE   ISSN 0167-739X
QA75.5
FUTURE GENERATION COMPUTER SYSTEMS. (Text in English) 1985. q. fl.516 (effective 1992). North-Holland (Subsidiary of: Elsevier Science Publishers B.V.), P.O. Box 211, 1000 AE Amsterdam, Netherlands. TEL 020-5803911. FAX 020-5803598. TELEX 18582 ESPA NL. (N. America dist. addr.: Elsevier Science Publishing Co., Inc., Box 882, Madison Sq. Sta., New York, NY 10159. TEL 212-989-5800) Eds. L.O. Hertzberger, S. Ward. adv.; bk.rev.; illus. Indexed: A.I.Abstr., Art.Int.Abstr., CAD CAM Abstr., Comput.Abstr., Comput.Lit.Ind., Cyb.Abstr., Sci.Abstr.
—BLDSC shelfmark: 4060.570000.
Formerly: Fifth Generation Computer Systems.
Description: Presents new developments in the field of computer systems. Includes models for new architectures and their analysis, as well as their hardware and software implementations.

HUANJING YAOGAN/REMOTE SENSING OF ENVIRONMENT. see GEOGRAPHY

621.3   UK   ISSN 0266-1616
INSPEC MATTERS. 1974. q. free. INSPEC, I.E.E., Michael Faraday House, Six Hills Way, Stevenage, Herts. SG1 2AY, England. TEL 0438-313311. FAX 0438-742840. TELEX 825578-IEESTV-G. (U.S. addr.: 445 Hoes Lane, Piscataway, NJ 08854. TEL 908-562-5549) Ed. Vic Royce. (tabloid format; back issues avail.) Indexed: Br.Ceram.Abstr., Graph.Arts Lit.Abstr.
—BLDSC shelfmark: 4518.380000.
Description: Keeps searchers up to date with changes, improvements and events of interest.

621.3   UK
INSPEC THESAURUS. biennial. £45($85) INSPEC, I.E.E., Michael Faraday House, Six Hills Way, Stevenage, Herts. SG1 2AY, England. TEL 0438-313311. FAX 0438-742840. TELEX 825578-IEESTV-G. (U.S. addr.: 445 Hoes Lane, Piscataway, NJ 08854. TEL 908-562-5549)

500   US   ISSN 0889-8308
QC53   CODEN: IICOEW
INTELLIGENT INSTRUMENTS & COMPUTERS. 1983. 6/yr. $120 (foreign $148)(effective 1992). Elsevier Science Publishing Co., Inc. (New York), 655 Ave. of the Americas, New York, NY 10010. TEL 212-989-5800. FAX 212-633-3965. TELEX 420643 AEP UI. Ed. Richard Graham. adv.; bk.rev.; charts; illus.; stat.; index; circ. 2,500. (back issues avail.)
—BLDSC shelfmark: 4531.831700.
Formerly: C A L: Computer Applications in the Laboratory (ISSN 0724-0031)
Description: Publishes practical, original papers and articles for scientists and engineers who use computers in their laboratories and field work for data acquisition, analysis, verification, word processing, and communications.
Refereed Serial

INTERNATIONAL JOURNAL OF MODERN PHYSICS C: PHYSICS AND COMPUTERS. see PHYSICS

500 350   US
J I C S T ONLINE INFORMATION SYSTEM. Short title: J O I S. (Text in English, Japanese) s-m. (Japanese Information Center of Science and Technology) U.S. National Technical Information Service, 5285 Port Royal Rd., Springfield, VA 22161. TEL 703-487-4630. (avail. in US only)
●Available only online. Vendor(s): JICST.
Description: Provides access to many monographs, journal articles and technical reports from Japan.

JAPAN SOCIETY FOR SIMULATION TECHNOLOGY. JOURNAL. see COMPUTERS — Computer Simulation

500 001.535   CC   ISSN 1001-4160
QA75.5   CODEN: JYYHE6
JISUANJI YU YINGYONG HUAXUE/COMPUTERS AND APPLIED CHEMISTRY. (Text in Chinese) 1984. q. Y7.60($7) per no. (Chinese Academy of Sciences, East China Institute of Metallurgy) Science Press, Marketing and Sales Department, 16 Donghuangchenggen Beijie, Beijing 100707, People's Republic of China. TEL 4010642. FAX 4012180. TELEX 210247-SPBJ-CN. (Co-sponsor: Chinese University of Science and Technology) adv.; circ. 4,000.
—BLDSC shelfmark: 3394.647000.
Description: Covers applied chemistry, chemical mathematics, computer advances in chemometrics, process simulation, control, artificial intelligence, optimization and graphics in chemistry, molecular modeling, structure-property correlation and data processing. Emphasis is on computational chemistry.
Refereed Serial

543 001.6   UK   ISSN 0142-0453
QD75.4.A8   CODEN: JAUCD6
JOURNAL OF AUTOMATIC CHEMISTRY. (Text in English; summaries in French and German) 1978. bi-m. £110($195) Taylor & Francis Ltd., Rankine Rd., Basingstoke, Hants RG24 0PR, England. TEL 0256-840366. FAX 0256-479438. TELEX 858540. Ed. P.B. Stockwell. Indexed: AESIS, Anal.Abstr., Br.Rail.Bd., Chem.Abstr., Dairy Sci.Abstr., Excerp.Med., Food Sci.& Tech.Abstr., Ind.Sci.Rev., Sci.Abstr., Sci.Cit.Ind., W.R.C.Inf.
—BLDSC shelfmark: 4949.560000.
Description: An international journal covering all aspects of automation and mechanization in analytical, clinical and industrial environments. Contains articles on instrumentation, management economics and the philosophy of automation.
Refereed Serial

SECURITY

540 US ISSN 0095-2338
QD1 CODEN: JCISD8
JOURNAL OF CHEMICAL INFORMATION AND COMPUTER SCIENCES. 1960. bi-m. $162 to non-members; members $20. American Chemical Society, 1155 16th St. N.W., Washington, DC 20036. TEL 800-333-9511. FAX 202-872-4615. TELEX 440159 ACSP Ul. Ed. George W.A. Milne. adv.; bk.rev.; charts; index; circ. 2,606. (also avail. in microfilm from RPI; microfiche; back issues avail.; reprint service avail. from RPI) **Indexed:** Abstr.Bull.Inst.Pap.Chem., Biol.Abstr., Chem.Abstr., Chem.Eng.Abstr., Compumath, Comput.Abstr., Comput.Cont., Curr.Cont., Deep Sea Res.& Oceanogr.Abstr., Eng.Ind., Excerp.Med., GeoRef, Ind.Med., Ind.Sci.Rev., Intl.Civil Eng.Abstr., PROMT, Risk Abstr., Sci.Abstr., Sci.Cit.Ind., Soft.Abstr.Eng., T.C.E.A.
●Also available online. Vendor(s): STN International (CJACS).
—BLDSC shelfmark: 4956.800000.
Formerly (until 1975): Journal of Chemical Documentation (ISSN 0021-9576)
Description: Publishes research papers in all areas of information and computer science relevant to chemistry and chemical technology.
Refereed Serial

JOURNAL OF COMPUTERS IN MATHEMATICS AND SCIENCE TEACHING. see *MATHEMATICS — Computer Applications*

500 620 NE ISSN 0925-5001
QA402.5 CODEN: JGOPEO
▼**JOURNAL OF GLOBAL OPTIMIZATION.** 1991. q. $91 to individuals; institutions $170.50. Kluwer Academic Publishers, Postbus 17, 3300 AA Dordrecht, Netherlands. TEL 078-334911. FAX 078-334254. TELEX 29245. (Dist. by: Kluwer Academic Publishers, P.O. Box 322, 3300 AH Dordrecht, Netherlands; N. America dist. addr.: Box 358, Accord Station, Hingham, MA 02018-0358. TEL 617-871-6600) Ed. R. Horst.
—BLDSC shelfmark: 4996.302000.
Description: International journal dealing with theoretical and computational aspects of seeking global optima and their applications in science, management, and engineering.
Refereed Serial

500 US ISSN 0885-7474
Q183.9 CODEN: JSCOEB
JOURNAL OF SCIENTIFIC COMPUTING. 1986. q. $175 (foreign $205)(effective 1992). Plenum Publishing Corp., 233 Spring St., New York, NY 10013-1578. TEL 212-620-8000. FAX 212-463-0742. TELEX 23-421139. Ed. Steven A. Orszag. adv. (also avail. in microfilm from JSC; back issues avail.) **Indexed:** Curr.Cont., INIS Atomind.
—BLDSC shelfmark: 5057.250000.
Refereed Serial

500 UK ISSN 0954-898X
CODEN: NEWKEB
▼**NETWORK - COMPUTATION IN NEURAL SYSTEMS.** 1990. q. £149($274) (effective 1992). (Institute of Physics) I O P Publishing, Techno House, Redcliffe Way, Bristol BS1 6NX, England. TEL 0272-297481. FAX 0272-294318. TELEX 449149-INSTP-G. (U.S. addr.: American Institute of Physics, Subscr. Services, 500 Sunnyside Blvd., Woodbury, NY 11797-2999) Ed. Daniel J. Amit. (also avail. in microfiche; microform; back issues avail.)
—BLDSC shelfmark: 6077.203020.
Description: Subject coverage includes: experimental neuroscience; physics; computer science; applied mathematics and engineering proposing, analysing, simulating and designing models with the aim of synthesizing the biological results.

OPTICAL MEMORY NEWS. see *COMPUTERS — Computer Engineering*

550 US
▼**PUBLIC DOMAIN SOFTWARE FOR EARTH SCIENTISTS.** 1991. a. $25 (foreign $35). Gibbs Associates, Box 706, Boulder, CO 80306. TEL 303-444-6032. Eds. Betty Gibbs, Stephen Krajewski.
Description: Contains information on public domain software from government agencies, universities, and individuals. Includes shareware programs and inexpensive software.

913 UK ISSN 0586-9668
CC1
SCIENCE AND ARCHAEOLOGY. 1970. a. £6. Research Centre for Computer Archaeology, Computer Centre, Blackheath Lane, Stafford ST18 OAD, England. TEL 0785-53511. FAX 0785-51058. (Subscr. to: 88 Caverswall Rd., Weston Coyney, Stoke-on-Trent, Staffordshire ST3 6PL, England) (Co-sponsor: Staffordshire Polytechnic) Ed. J.D. Wilcock. adv.; bk.rev.; bibl.; charts; illus.; circ. 250. (also avail. in microfiche) **Indexed:** Art & Archaeol.Tech.Abstr., Br.Archaeol.Abstr.
—BLDSC shelfmark: 8130.930000.

SCIENCE AND TECHNOLOGY (SAN DIEGO, 1987); opposing viewpoints sources. see *BIOLOGY*

500 US
SCIENTIFIC COMPUTING & AUTOMATION. 1984. 12/yr. $24. Gordon Publications, Inc., 301 Gibraltar Dr., Morris Plains, NJ 07950. TEL 201-292-5100. FAX 201-898-9281. Ed. Dan Breeman. adv.; tr.lit.; circ. 70,000. (tabloid format; reprint service avail.) **Indexed:** Comput.Lit.Ind.
Description: For scientists who work in industrial and analytical, clinical, life science research and electronics laboratories. Provides information on the latest technology available.

500 510 CC ISSN 1000-3266
SHUZHI JISUAN YU JISUANJI YINGYONG/JOURNAL ON NUMERICAL METHODS AND COMPUTER APPLICATIONS. (Text in Chinese) 1979. q. Y8.40($7) per no. (Chinese Academy of Sciences, Computer Centre) Science Press, Marketing and Sales Department, 16 Donghuangchenggen Beijie, Beijing 100707, People's Republic of China. TEL 4010642. FAX 4012180. TELEX 210247-SPBJ-CN. adv.; circ. 12,000.
Description: Contains articles on mathematic modules and calculation methods in the solution of problems through the use of the computer in various scientific and technical spheres.
Refereed Serial

SECURITY

see Criminology and Law Enforcement–Security

SHIPS AND SHIPPING

see Transportation–Ships and Shipping

SHOES AND BOOTS

see also Leather and Fur Industries

685.3 US ISSN 0003-1038
AMERICAN SHOEMAKING. 1896. m. $34. Shoe Trades Publishing Co., Box 198, Cambridge, MA 02140. TEL 617-648-8160. Ed. James D. Sutton. adv.; charts; illus.; mkt.; stat.; circ. 3,500.

685.31 380.1 US
AMERICAN SHOEMAKING DIRECTORY. a. $33. Shoe Trades Publishing Co., Box 198, Cambridge, MA 02140. TEL 617-648-8160. circ. 2,000. (back issues avail.)

APPAREL INTERNATIONAL. see *CLOTHING TRADE*

685.5 IT ISSN 0004-265X
ARS SUTORIA; cultural fashion review on Italian and international footwear. (Text in English, French, German, Italian, Spanish) 1947. 8/yr. $474. Editrice Ars s.r.l., Via Ippolito Nievo 33, 20145 Milan, Italy. circ. 50,000.

685.31 IT
AZETA CALZATURE. 1980. bi-m. L.10000. C.E.G., Via del Bosco 125, 56029 S. Croce s-Arno, Italy. Ed. Luca Tafi. adv.; circ. 25,000.

BOR- ES CIPOTECHNIKA. see *LEATHER AND FUR INDUSTRIES*

CANADIAN FOOTWEAR & LEATHER DIRECTORY. see *BUSINESS AND ECONOMICS — Trade And Industrial Directories*

685.31 675 CN ISSN 0705-1433
CANADIAN FOOTWEAR JOURNAL. (Annual Directory Number) 1888. 9/yr. Can.$30($42.50) (foreign $50). McLeish Communications, Inc., 1 rue Pacifique, Ste. Anne de Bellevue, Que. H9X 1C5, Canada. TEL 514-457-2423. FAX 514-457-2577. Ed. Barbara McLeish. adv.; illus.; stat.; index; circ. 9,000. (also avail. in microfiche from MML; reprint service avail. from MML)
Formerly: Shoe and Leather Journal (ISSN 0037-4032)
Description: Edited to meet the specialized needs of those engaged in all aspects of the footwear business and its allied trades. Features on fashion, business management, efficient buying and stock control, store design and new developments in technology, materials and manufacturing processes.

CHAUSSER. see *LEATHER AND FUR INDUSTRIES*

CLEO EN LA MODA. see *LEATHER AND FUR INDUSTRIES*

CLOTHING AND FOOTWEAR INSTITUTE YEAR BOOK AND MEMBERSHIP REGISTER. see *CLOTHING TRADE*

CLOTHING, TEXTILES, AND FOOTWEAR (YEAR). see *CLOTHING TRADE*

CUOIO PELLI MATERIE CONCIANTI. see *LEATHER AND FUR INDUSTRIES*

685.31 UK
FOOTWEAR BUSINESS INTERNATIONAL. 1971. m. membership. S A T R A Footwear Technology Centre, SATRA House, Rockingham Road, Kettering, Northants NN16 9JH, England. TEL 0536-410000. FAX 0536-410626. TELEX 34232. Ed. Vivienne Crow. adv.; bk.rev.; circ. 1,500 (controlled).
Former titles: Footwear Digest International; Footwear Digest; Shoemaking Progress.
Description: Reviews world's footwear industries, materials, machines, technology and fashion.

685.31 CN ISSN 0706-7534
FOOTWEAR FORUM. 1978. m. Can.$20. Mackirk Publications Ltd., 1448 Lawrence Ave. E., Ste. 302, Toronto, Ont. M4A 2V6, Canada. TEL 416-775-6191. FAX 416-955-9123. Ed. Karen Orme. adv.; circ. 10,000.

685.31 675 US
FOOTWEAR INDUSTRIES OF AMERICA. EXECUTIVE DIGEST. m. $60 to non-members. Footwear Industries of America, 1420 K St., N.W., Ste. 600, Washington, DC 20005. TEL 202-789-1420. Ed. Sarah Olson. circ. 900. (back issues avail.)
Description: Covers the technology, marketing, statistics and legislation of the footwear industry.

685.31 US
FOOTWEAR INDUSTRIES OF AMERICA. QUARTERLY REPORT. q. $120. Footwear Industries of America, 1420 K St., N.W., Ste. 600, Washington, DC 20005. **Indexed:** SRI.
Description: Provides data on production, foreign trade, marketing, labor, prices, consumer expenditures and quarterly trends in the footwear industry.

338 US ISSN 0095-1048
HD9787.U4
FOOTWEAR MANUAL. 1975. a. (plus Quarterly Report). $295 to non-members; libraries $200; members $130. Footwear Industries of America, 1420 K St., N.W., Ste. 600, Washington, DC 20005. Ed. Tracie Hoeffel. stat.; circ. 300. **Indexed:** SRI.
Supersedes: Facts and Figures on Footwear (ISSN 0362-3890)
Description: Analysis of today's industry including marketing, manufacturing, international trade, finance and raw materials.

685.31 US ISSN 0015-6833
FOOTWEAR NEWS. 1945. w. $48. Fairchild Publications, Inc., Footwear News, 7 W. 34th St., New York, NY 10001. TEL 212-630-4000. Ed. Dick Silverman. adv.; bk.rev.; illus.; mkt.; circ. 23,000. (also avail. in microfilm from FCM) **Indexed:** Bus.Ind., Key to Econ.Sci., PROMT, Tr.& Indus.Ind.
●Also available online. Vendor(s): DIALOG.

338.4 US ISSN 0429-0208
HD9787.U4
FOOTWEAR NEWS FACT BOOK. 1954. a. $15. Footwear News, 7 E. 12th St., New York, NY 10003. TEL 212-741-4000. illus.

SHOES AND BOOTS 4361

685.31 US
▼**FOOTWEAR PLUS.** 1990. s-a. Earnshaw Publications, Inc., 225 W. 34th St., Ste. 1212, New York, NY 10001. TEL 212-563-2742. Ed. Christina Gruber. circ. 18,000 (controlled).
  Description: For footwear retailers; covers the entire footwear market: dress, casual and athletic footwear, as well as hosiery and accessories.

685 IT
FOTO SHOE AMERICA. (Text in English) 1980. 6/yr. $30. Editoriale di Foto Shoe s.r.l., Via Leonardo da Vinci, 43, 20900 Trezzano S-N, Italy. adv.; circ. 23,000.

685 IT
FOTO SHOE 15; nuovo corriere della calzatura. (Italian ed.) 1963. m. $165. Editoriale di Foto Shoe s.r.l., Via Leonardo Da Vinci, 43, Trezzano S-N 20090, Italy. adv.; charts; illus.; circ. 14,000. (tabloid format)
  Former titles: Foto Shoe 15-3 Nuovo Corriere della Calzatura & Nuovo Corriere della Calzatura.
  Description: Covers technical information about footwear production materials, technologies, accessories and component parts.

685 IT
FOTO SHOE 15 (ENGLISH EDITION); international. 1963. m. L.50000($130) Editoriale di Foto Shoe s.r.l., Via Leonardo da Vinci, 43, 20900 Trezzano S-N, Italy. Ed. G. Fossati. adv.; illus.; circ. 18,200.
  Supersedes in part: Foto Shoe.
  Description: Deals with the allied footwear industries, materials, machines, technology and components and accessories. Also covers previews on fashion trends and writes about leading shoe fairs in Italy and abroad.

685 IT
FOTO SHOE 30. (Text in English, French, German, Italian, Spanish) 1969. m. L.125000($165) Editoriale di Foto Shoe s.r.l., Via Leonardo da Vinci, 43, 20900 Trezzano S-N, Italy. Ed. Adriano Pizzocaro. adv.; bk.rev.; illus.; circ. 20,000.
  Supersedes in part: Foto Shoe.
  Description: Covers the shoe fashion industry; distribution of the commercialization of footwear and trade fairs that are held worldwide.

685.31 SP
GUIA DE LA MODA DEL CALZADO. s-a. 2800 ptas. Prensa Tecnica, S.A., Caspe, 118-20, Barcelona 13, Spain.

HIDE AND LEATHER BULLETIN; for the tanning and shoe manufacturing industry. see LEATHER AND FUR INDUSTRIES

688.76 IT
JOGGING; photographic collection on Italian and international leisure shoes. 2/yr. $191. Editrice Ars s.r.l., Via Ippolito Nievo 33, 20145 Milan, Italy.

685.31 IT
JOLLY; photographic collection on Italian and international man footwear models. 2/yr. $191. Editrice Ars s.r.l., Via Ippolito Nievo 33, 20145 Milan, Italy.
  Formerly: Professional.

685.31 IT
JULIA; photographic collection on Italian and international woman footwear models. 4/yr. $342. Editrice Ars s.r.l., Via Ippolito Nievo 33, 20145 Milan, Italy.

685.31 IT
JUNIOR; photographic collection on Italian and international children footwear models. 2/yr. $191. Editrice Ars s.r.l., Via Ippolito Nievo 33, 20145 Milan, Italy.

KAWA TO HAKIMONO/LEATHER & FOOTWEARS. see LEATHER AND FUR INDUSTRIES

685.31 FI ISSN 0355-6999
KENKAALUSIKKA. 1962. 7/yr. FIM 330. Suomen Kenkaakauppiaiden Liitto r.y. - Finnish Shoe Retailers' Association, Fredrikinkatu 67 E 42, 00100 Helsinki 10, Finland. TEL 0-409-932. FAX 0-409-563. Ed. Jari Syrjaalaa. adv.; circ. 1,700.

KOZARSTVI/LEATHER INDUSTRY; odborny casopis pro prumysl kozedelny, obuvnicky a gumove obuvi. see LEATHER AND FUR INDUSTRIES

KOZHARSKA I OBUVNA PROMISHLENOST. see LEATHER AND FUR INDUSTRIES

685.31 RU ISSN 0023-4354
KOZHEVENNO-OBUVNAYA PROMYSHLENNOST. 1959. m. 21 Rub. Izdatel'stvo Kniga, 50, Gorky St., 125047 Moscow, Russia. adv.; bibl.; illus. **Indexed:** C.I.S. Abstr., Chem.Abstr.
  —BLDSC shelfmark: 0089.500000.

L S L; Fachzeitschrift fuer die Leder-, Kunstleder-, Schuh- und Lederwarenindustrie; das Schuhmacher-, Sottler- und Taeschnerhandwerk sowie den Fachhandel. (Leder, Schuhe, Lederwaren) see LEATHER AND FUR INDUSTRIES

685.31 SP
MODAPIEL. (Text in English and Spanish) 1969. s-a. 3400 ptas. Prensa Tecnica, S.A., Caspe 118-120, Barcelona 13, Spain. Ed. F. Canet Tomas. adv.; illus.; circ. 5,000.

685.31 UK
NATIONAL UNION OF THE FOOTWEAR, LEATHER AND ALLIED TRADES JOURNAL AND REPORT. vol.9, 1970. bi-m. £3 (foreign £4). National Union of the Footwear Leather and Allied Trades, The Grange, Earls Barton, Northampton NN6 OJH, England. FAX 0604-812496. adv.; bk.rev.; charts; illus.; stat.; circ. 5,000.
  Former titles: National Union of the Footwear, Leather and Allied Trades Monthly Journal and Report (ISSN 0028-0356); National Union of Boot and Shoe Operatives Monthly Report.

685.31 GW ISSN 0344-6026
ORTHOPAEDIE-SCHUHTECHNIK. 1949. m. DM.105.70. (Bundesinnungsverband des Orthopaedieschuhmacherhandwerkes) C. Maurer Druck und Verlag, Schubartstr. 21, Postfach 1361, 7340 Geislingen, Germany. TEL 07331-42011. FAX 07331-42284. TELEX 715153. Ed. Ingo Geisler. adv.; illus.; index; circ. 2,700.
  Formerly: Orthopaedieschuhmachermeister (ISSN 0030-5871)

ORTHOPEDISCHE SCHOENTECHNIEK. see MEDICAL SCIENCES — Orthopedics And Traumatology

685.31 US
ROUNDUP (CLARKSVILLE). 1967. bi-m. Acme Boot Co., Inc., 1002 Stafford St., Box 749, Clarksville, TN 37040. TEL 615-552-2000. Ed. Pam McCaslin. illus.; circ. 2,500 (controlled).

685.31 NE ISSN 0036-6269
SCHOEN - VISIE; vakblad voor schoenhandel en schoenindustrie. Short title: S V. 1959. 11/yr. Audet Tijdschriften bv, Postbus 16, 6500 AA Nijmegen, Netherlands. TEL 080-228316. FAX 080-239561. TELEX 48633. Eds. Ellis Faber, Alida Dijk. adv.; B&W page fl.2019; trim 210 x 297; adv. contact: Cor van Nek. charts; illus.; stat.; tr.lit.; circ. 2,810. **Indexed:** Key to Econ.Sci.
  Description: Trade magazine covering all aspects of shoes: manufacture, import, sales and repair.

685.31 NE ISSN 0036-6307
SCHOENWERELD. 1921. 6/yr. fl.60 to non-members. Verenigde Organisatie van Schoenmakers, Havenstraat 41A, 1736 KD Zijdewind, Netherlands. TEL 02262-3149. FAX 02262-1637. Ed. P.A. Idema. adv.; illus.; circ. 2,600. (reprint service avail.)
  Description: Covers national and international news of interest to members of the shoe manufacturing, sales and repair industries.

685.31 GW ISSN 0036-7044
HD9780.G3
SCHUH-KURIER. 1946. w. DM.313. Verlag Otto Sternefeld GmbH, Postfach 11 12 49, Oberkasseler Str. 100, 4000 Duesseldorf 11, Germany. TEL 0211-575096. FAX 0211-578852. TELEX 8582-043-STF-D. Ed. C. Foecking. adv.; bibl.; mkt.; pat.; tr.mk.; index; circ. 8,900. **Indexed:** Key to Econ.Sci.

685.31 AU
SCHUH-REVUE. (Includes: Taschen-Rapport) 1946. s-m. S.400. Johann L. Bondi und Sohn, Industriestr. 2, A-2380 Perchtoldsdorf, Austria. Ed. Franz Bondi. circ. 4,000.
  Formerly: Oesterreichische Schuhhaendler (ISSN 0029-9456)

685.31 AU ISSN 0036-7060
SCHUH-ZEITUNG. 1903. 24/yr. S.300. (Verband der Schuhindustrie und dem Schuhhandel) Verlag Michael Fischer, Neulerchenfelderstr. 8, 1160 Vienna, Austria. Ed. Michael Fischer. adv.; bk.rev.; abstr.; illus.; stat.; tr.lit.; circ. 4,500.

685.31 GW ISSN 0936-6121
DER SCHUHMACHER. 1947. m. DM.59. Ingo Geisler Verlag, Ahornweg 8, Postfach, 8491 Pemfling, Germany. TEL 09971-40506. FAX 09971-40504. Ed. Ingo Geisler. adv.; bk.rev.; illus.; mkt.; pat.; tr.mk.; tr.lit.; index; circ. 6,900.
  Formerly: Das Deutsche Schuhmacherhandwerk (ISSN 0012-0723)

685.31 GW
SCHUHMACHER FACHREPORT. 4/yr. free. Ingo Geisler Verlag, Ahornweg 8, Postfach, 8491 Pemfling, Germany. TEL 09971-40506. FAX 09971-40504. circ. 22,300.

685.31 GW ISSN 0036-7079
SCHUHMARKT. 1857. w. DM.187.20. (Bundesverband des Deutschen Schuheinzelhandels) Umschau Verlag Breidenstein GmbH, Stuttgarter Str. 18-24, 6000 Frankfurt a.M. 1, Germany. TEL 069-2600-0. FAX 069-2600-609. TELEX 411964. Ed. Manfred Willsch. adv.; bk.rev.; charts; illus.; stat.; tr.lit.; tr.mk.; index; circ. 9,300.

685.31 GW ISSN 0933-808X
SCHUHTECHNIK INTERNATIONAL; Fachzeitschrift fuer die Schuhindustrie. (Text in German; summaries in English) 1906. m. DM.189.40. (Deutsche Schuhfachschule Pirmasens) Dr. Alfred Huethig Verlag GmbH, Im Weiher 10, Postfach 102869, 6900 Heidelberg, Germany. TEL 06221-489-281. FAX 06221-489279. TELEX 461727-HUEHDD. Eds. Albert Wilhelm, Alexander Besching. adv.; bk.rev.; abstr.; charts; illus.; tr.lit.; index; circ. 7,088.
  Formerly: Schuhtechnik A B C (ISSN 0001-0405)

685.31 675 UK ISSN 0037-4040
SHOE AND LEATHER NEWS. 1916. w. £37($139) International Thomson Business Publishing, Greater London House, Ground Floor, Hampstead Rd., London NW1 7QZ, England. TEL 01-387-6611. FAX 01-387-7028. Ed. Alan Cork. adv.; bk.rev.; charts; illus.; mkt.; pat.; stat.; circ. 7,149. **Indexed:** PROMT.
  —BLDSC shelfmark: 8267.521000.

685.31 380.1 US
SHOE FACTORY BUYERS GUIDE; directory of suppliers to the shoe manufacturing industry. a. $32. Shoe Trades Publishing Co., Box 198, Cambridge, MA 02140. TEL 617-648-8160. adv.; circ. 200. (back issues avail.)

685.31 US ISSN 0886-0963
SHOE RETAILING TODAY. bi-m. $20 to non-members; members free. National Shoe Retailers Association, 9861 Broken Land Pkwy., Ste. 255, Columbia, MD 21046-1151. TEL 410-381-8282. FAX 410-381-1167. Ed. Cynthia Emmel.
  Formerly: N S R A News.
  Description: Covers trends in the shoe retailing industry.

684.3 UK ISSN 0080-9349
SHOE TRADES DIRECTORY. 1948. a. £40. International Thomson Business Publishing, Greater London House, Hampstead Rd., London NW1 7QZ. TEL 01-387-6611. FAX 01-387-7028. adv.
  Incorporates: Shoe Retailers Manual (ISSN 0140-5578)

685.31 US ISSN 0037-4083
SHOES ON PARADE. 1937. w. $162. Retail Reporting Bureau, 101 Fifth Ave., New York, NY 10003. TEL 212-255-9595. Ed.Bd. illus.
  Description: Shoe advertisements and styles from daily newspapers.

658.31 US
SHOW REPORTER. 1968. 6/yr. free. Show Reporter Publishing Co., Inc., 335 Boylston St., Newton Center, MA 02159. TEL 617-965-4577. Ed. Irving B. Roberts. adv.; bk.rev.; circ. 10,000.

S

SHOES AND BOOTS — ABSTRACTING, BIBLIOGRAPHIES, STATISTICS

685.31   NO
SKO. 1972. 8/yr. NOK 200. Skoraadet - Shoe Council, Nordstrandsveien 32, N-1163 Oslo 11, Norway. FAX 02-297951. adv.; charts; illus.; circ. 1,400.
    Formerly: Skotoey (ISSN 0049-0679); Formed by the merger of: Norsk Skotoey (ISSN 0029-2133); Skotoidetaljisten (ISSN 0037-6574)

658.8   DK   ISSN 0901-0114
SKO OG LAEDERVARER. 1952. m. (10/yr.). DKK 220. Danmarks Skohandlerforening - Association of Danish Shoe-Retailers, H.C. Andersens Blvd. 48, DK-1553 Copenhagen V, Denmark. FAX 45-01-931708. Ed. Helge Madsen. adv.; circ. 1,400.
    Formerly: Sko-Magasinet (ISSN 0037-6388)

685.31   SW   ISSN 0346-1300
SKOHANDLAREN. 1941. 14/yr. SEK 340. Sveriges Skohandlarfoerbund - Swedish Retailers Organisation, Kungsgatan 19, 111 43 Stockholm, Sweden. TEL 8-791-5300. FAX 8-213690. Ed. Mariette Baecklund. adv.; bk.rev.; circ. 2,100 (controlled).

685   SA   ISSN 0250-1333
SOUTH AFRICAN SHOEMAKER AND LEATHER REVIEW. Variant title: S.A. Shoemaker and Leather Review. (Text in English) 1973. bi-m. R.84. George Warman Publications (Pty.) Ltd., Box 3847, Cape Town 8000, South Africa. TEL 021-24-5320. FAX 021-26-1332. TELEX 5-21849 SA. Ed. Tessa Courtenay. adv.; circ. 1,700.
    Description: Covers shoe, leather, handbag, luggage and saddlery industries.

685.31   GW
SUEDWESTDEUTSCHER EINZELHANDEL (STUTTGART). m. Verband des Schuh-Einzelhandels Baden-Wuerttemberg e.V., Neue Weinsteige 44, 7000 Stuttgart 1, Germany. TEL 603025.

TANNER. see *LEATHER AND FUR INDUSTRIES*

685.31   FR   ISSN 0040-1196
TECHNIQUE CHAUSSURE. 1955. m. 400 F. (foreign 500 F.). Editions Charles Vincent, 7 ter, Cour des Petites-Ecuries, 75010 Paris, France. Ed. H. Thiron. adv.; circ. 3,000.

685.31   IT
TECNICA CALZATURIERA. (Text in English, Italian) vol.13, 1973. m. L.110000 (foreign L.235000)(effective 1992). Tecniche Nuove s.p.a., Via C. Menotti, 14, 20129 Milan, Italy. TEL 02-75701. FAX 02-7570205. TELEX 334647 TECHS I. Ed. Giuseppe Nardella. adv.; abstr.; illus.
    Description: Features articles on manufacturing in the shoe industry. Covers machinery, fashion and materials.

685.31   SP
TECNICA DEL CALZADO. 1968. bi-m. 2000 ptas. Prensa Tecnica, S.A., Caspe, 118-120, Barcelona, 13, Spain. Ed. F. Canet Tomas. adv.; abstr.; bibl.; charts; illus.; pat.; stat.; tr.lit.; circ. 3,000.

685.31   US
WORLD FOOTWEAR. 1987. bi-m. $45. Shoe Traders Publishing Co., Inc., Box 198, Cambridge, MA 02140. TEL 617-684-6810. FAX 617-492-0126. adv.; circ. 15,000.
    Description: Directed to shoe manufacturers worldwide.

SHOES AND BOOTS — Abstracting, Bibliographies, Statistics

685.31   UK
BRITISH FOOTWEAR MANUFACTURERS FEDERATION. STATISTICS. m. British Footwear Manufacturers Federation, 72 Dean St., London W1V 5HB, England. TEL 071-4375573.

310 685   UK   ISSN 0308-9398
FOOTWEAR INDUSTRY STATISTICAL REVIEW. 1972. a. £105. British Footwear Manufacturers Federation, 72 Dean St., London W1V 5HB, England. TEL 071-437-5573. circ. 400.

SINGLES' INTERESTS AND LIFESTYLES

051   US
ACTIVE SINGLES LIFE. 1973. m. $20 (typically set in Jan.). Voice Publishing, 3450 6th Ave. S., Box 81043, Seattle, WA 98108. TEL 206-223-0210. FAX 206-223-9514. Ed. Walt Briem. adv.; bk.rev.; film rev.; circ. 8,000.
    Description: Deals with the life styles of the single adult in the Northeast U.S. Includes self-help articles, personal ads, and features on local well known singles.

051 917.93   US   ISSN 1041-4002
ALASKAMEN U S A. vol.3, no.2, 1990. bi-m. $24.95 in US; Canada $34.95; elsewhere $37.95. AlaskaMen Magazine, Inc., 201 Danner St., Ste. 100, Anchorage, AK 99518. TEL 907-522-1492. FAX 907-344-1493. Ed. Susie Carter. adv.; illus.
    Formerly: AlaskaMen.
    Description: Introduces single men in Alaska for interested single women.

051   US
▼**ALBERTSEN'S SINGLES DIRECTORY.** 1992. a. $12. Albertsen's, Box 339, Nevada City, CA 95959. TEL 916-292-3655. FAX 916-477-0915. Ed. Ken Albertsen.

051   US
ARIZONA SINGLES. m. $12 free. Box 3424, Flagstaff, AZ 86003. TEL 602-779-0151. adv.

051   US
ATLANTA SINGLES MAGAZINE. 1977. bi-m. $9. 1780 Century Cir., N.E., Ste. 2, Atlanta, GA 30345-3020. TEL 404-636-2260. FAX 404-636-2366. adv.

051   US
CAROL'S SINGLES. 1983. m. $14. Box 13500, Akron, OH 44313-8899. TEL 216-945-8000. FAX 216-945-8331. Ed. Carol A. Thomas. adv.

051 910.03   US
CHOCOLATE SINGLES. m. $25. Box 333, Jamaica, NY 11413. adv.

051   US
CHRISTIAN SINGLES NEWS. 1987. m. $23. Christian Singles International, Box 100, Harrison, OH 45030. adv.; bk.rev.; circ. 50,000.
    Formerly: U S A Singles News.

051   US
CONTINENTAL SPECTATOR. q. $35. Box 278, Canal St. Sta., New York, NY 10013. TEL 718-625-6309. Ed. Linda Lee.
    Description: Worldwide listings of personal contact ads with photos; includes stories, and articles of interest to swingers.

051   US
DATE BOOK; personals, classified and daily listing of events for Westchester and Fairfield area singles. 1978. m. $21. Date Book Publications, Inc., Box 473, Pleasantville, NY 10570. TEL 914-769-1365. FAX 914-769-3660. Ed. Barbara Waugh. adv.; circ. 12,000. (back issues avail.)

052   UK
DATELINE MAGAZINE. 1977. 12/yr. £24. Singles Scene Ltd., c/o John Patterson, 23 Abingdon Rd., Kensington, London W8 6AH, England. TEL 071-938-1011. FAX 071-937-3146.
    Former titles: Singles; (1982-1984): Select; Singles.
    Description: Articles of interest to single people. Includes activities, meeting places, plus personal classified ads.

051   US
DI'S MEET PEOPLE. 1986. m. $14.95. Di Company, Box 247, Osseo, MN 55369. TEL 612-424-4266. adv.; circ. 49,000. (tabloid format)
    Description: For singles; includes personals.

051   US
FLORIDA SINGLES MAGAZINE AND DATE BOOK. 1978. bi-m. $17. Royal Sunshine Industries, Inc., Box 14730, N. Palm Beach, FL 33408-0730. Ed. Harold Alan. adv.; circ. 12,000. (back issues avail.)

051   US   ISSN 0882-8598
GET - TWO - GETHER. 1981. m. $15. Get - Two - Gether Inc., Box 1413, Ft. Collins, CO 80522. TEL 303-221-4544. FAX 303-224-3151. Ed. Gary F. Hirt. adv.; circ. 4,500.

296 051   US
INTERNATIONAL CONNECTOR FOR JEWISH SINGLES.* 1986. 4/yr. $14. Midwest Jewish Singles Network, 5961 Western Ave., Omaha, NE 68132-2027. Ed. Mary Fellman. adv.
    Formerly: Connector.

051   US
INTRO SINGLES CLUB. bi-w. $10 membership. Box 3006, Boston, MA 02130. adv.

296 051   US
JEWISH SINGLES MAGAZINE (BLOOMFIELD). irreg. Box 728, Bloomfield, CT 06002. TEL 203-243-1514. adv.

296 051   US
JEWISH SINGLES MAGAZINE (NEWTON). 1983. m. $20. Mark B. Golden, Ed. & Pub., Box 430933, Miami, FL 33243-0933. TEL 305-669-4404. adv.; bk.rev.; circ. 90,000.
    Formerly: Jewish Singles.

051   US
LAS VEGAS SINGLES LIFESTYLE.* m. $14.95. 4754 E. Falmingo Rd., Ste. 307, Las Vegas, NV 89121-4709. TEL 701-362-5800. adv.

051   US
LIFESTYLE. NORTHERN CALIFORNIA. bi-m. $7. 419 W. MacArthur Blvd., Oakland, CA 94609. TEL 415-420-1381. adv.

051   US
LIFESTYLE SOUTHERN CALIFORNIA; single adults news & events. 1967. m. $7. Gladys Smith & Associates, Box 5062, Sherman Oaks, CA 91413-5062. TEL 818-980-4786. Ed. R.H. Smith, Jr. adv.; bk.rev.; film rev.; play rev.; circ. 40,000. (back issues avail.)
    Formerly: Singles Critique.
    Description: Discusses relationships, medical issues, theater, wine and travel. Includes calendar of events, astrological forecasts and personals.

051   US
LONG ISLAND NIGHTLIFE.* m. $15. M J C Publishers, 770 Grand Blvd., K 10, Deer Park, NY 11729-5725. TEL 516-792-0250.

051 367   US
LONG ISLAND SINGLES CLUB. CALENDAR. m. $8. 1731 Prime St., W. Babylon, NY 11704. TEL 516-669-6541. adv.
    Description: For Long Island singles over 35.

051   US
LONG ISLAND SWINGERS MAGAZINE. 1981. q. $54. Bizzare Publishing Co., Box 25, Islip Terrace, NY 11752-0025. Ed. John Jay. adv.: B&W page $650. circ. 10,000.

051   US
METRO SINGLES LIFESTYLES; an upbeat publication for single women & single men of all ages. 1984. q. $15 for 12 nos. Box 28203, Kansas City, MO 64118. TEL 816-436-8424. Ed. Robert Huffstutter. adv.; bk.rev.; illus.; circ. 25,000. (tabloid format)
    Description: Includes 12 pages of personal ads in each issue, as well as interviews with singles, poetry and fiction.

051   US
METROLINA SINGLES MAGAZINE & DATEBOOK. 1982. m. $16. Creative Communications, Box 11627, Charlotte, NC 28220. TEL 704-542-4747. Ed. Thomas W. Nunnenkamp. adv.; circ. 5,000.
    Formerly: Metrolina Singles Datebook.
    Description: Serves the unmarried adults of the Carolinas. Provides information on local singles group; articles on relationships and other topics of interest to the unmarried.

051   US
NATIONAL SINGLES DIRECTORY. m. $20. 4818 Rosemar Rd., Parkersburg, WV 26101. TEL 304-428-3283. FAX 304-428-8090. adv.
    Formerly: S C A N (Singles Connection and Network).

051 US
NATIONAL SINGLES REGISTER. bi-m. $9. Box 567, Norwalk, CA 92633. TEL 714-773-5405. adv.

051 US
OHIO'S FINEST SINGLES; news, views, personals. 1972. m. $13. Box 770610, Cleveland, OH 44107-0030. TEL 216-521-1111. FAX 216-226-3283. Ed. Joyce N. Krost. adv.; circ. 50,000. (tabloid format)
  Formerly (until 1982): Cleveland's Finest Singles.

051 US
ON THE SCENE; Albuquerque's entertainment & lifestyles magazine. 1979. m. $18. Unicorn Publications, Inc., 3507 Wyoming N.E., Albuquerque, NM 87111. TEL 505-299-4401. Ed. Gail P. Skinner. adv.; bk.rev.; circ. 30,000. (tabloid format; back issues avail.)
  Formed by the 1987 merger of: Albuquerque's Senior Scene; Albuquerque's Singles Scene.
  Description: Covers local entertainment for all ages.

796 US
OUTDOOR SINGLES NETWORK. bi-m. $18. O S N - H C N, Box 2031, McCall, ID 83638.

051 US ISSN 1048-5554
PITTSBURGH SINGLES' LIFESTYLES. 1981. bi-m. $11.95. 300 Mt. Lebanon Blvd., 210-B, Pittsburgh, PA 15234. TEL 412-561-2277. FAX 412-561-3960. adv.; circ. 8,000.
  Formerly: Lifestyles Pittsburgh.
  Description: Articles geared to single adults aged 30 to 50. Contains a guide to local singles' events and quality personal ads.

301.412 305.3 US
PITTSBURGH SINGLES LIFESTYLES. 1981. bi-m. $12.95. Lifestyles Publishing, 300 Mt. Lebanoan Blvd., No. 210B, Pittsburgh, PA 15234. TEL 412-561-2277. FAX 412-561-3960. adv.; illus.; circ. 10,000.
  Formerly: Singles Magazine.
  Description: Provides articles on all aspects of single life.

SCARLET LETTER. see WOMEN'S INTERESTS

051 US
SINCERE SINGLES. 250. m. $15. Box 1719, Ann Arbor, MI 48106. TEL 313-476-6110. FAX 313-996-3544. adv.; circ. 10,000.
  Description: Provides personal ads for educated singles with 900 voice mail system.

SINGLE ADULT BIBLE STUDY. see RELIGIONS AND THEOLOGY — Protestant

051 202 US
SINGLE ADULT MINISTRIES JOURNAL;* ideas, resources and guidance for ministry with single adults. 10/yr. $24. Jerry D. Jones, Ed. & Pub., Box 60430, Colorado Springs, CO 80960-0430. TEL 800-452-1104. (Subscr. to: Box 730, Redmond OR 97756) adv.
  Description: Provides ideas and encouragement for those involved in ministry with single adults from a transdenominational perspective.

051 US ISSN 0887-1167
SINGLE ADULT MINISTRY INFORMATION. 1973. m. $15. Institute for Singles Dynamics, Box 11394, Kansas City, MO 64112. TEL 816-763-9401. Ed. Donald W. Davidson. bk.rev.
  Formerly: Single i.
  Description: Provides information for leaders of church singles ministries.

301.412 305.3 US
SINGLE AGAIN. 1976. 9/yr. $20. Box 384, Union City, CA 94587. TEL 510-793-6315. Ed. Len Harris. adv.; illus.; circ. 7,500.
  Description: Directed to people who are divorced, separated, or widowed.

051 US
SINGLE CONNECTIONS (FULLERTON). m. $24. Box 2527, Fullerton, CA 92633. TEL 714-773-5405. adv.

051 US
SINGLE FILE MAGAZINE; the lifestyle guide. 1982. 12/yr. $12. Single Association, Inc., Box 6706, Grand Rapids, MI 49516. TEL 616-774-8100. Ed. Penelope J. Barrett. adv.; circ. 15,000 (controlled).
  Description: Attempts to help singles meet others through personalized ads.

051 US
▼**SINGLE GENTLEMEN & WOMEN.** 1992. bi-m. $19.95. Mail Sort, Inc., 3880 Best Mill Rd., Winston-Salem, NC 27103. TEL 919-659-1100. Ed. Jill Hester. adv.: B&W page $1080. circ. 40,000 (controlled).
  Description: Profiles and color photographs submitted by single men and women.

051 US
SINGLE LIFE (LINCOLN). m. $12. Box 83289, Lincoln, NE 68501. TEL 402-466-8521. adv.

051 US
SINGLE LIFE (MILWAUKEE). bi-m. $9.99. 606 W. Wisconsin Ave., Ste. 703, Milwaukee, WI 53202. TEL 414-271-9700. adv.

051 US
SINGLE LIVING MAGAZINE; an Iowa perspective. 1989. m. $15. Box 573, Ames, IA 50010. TEL 515-292-5104. FAX 515-292-5011. Ed. Marilyn J. Kniss. adv.; circ. 15,000.

051 US
SINGLE MAGAZINE AND ENTERTAINMENT GUIDE. 1965. bi-m. $6. Box 5709, San Diego, CA 92165. TEL 619-296-6948. adv.

SINGLE PARENT. see SOCIAL SERVICES AND WELFARE

SINGLE PARENT NEWS. see CHILDREN AND YOUTH — About

636 367 US
SINGLE PET LOVERS. q. $19.95. Box 487, Laguardia, NY 11371.
  Description: Lists biographies of members, including their pet preferences.

051 808.81 US ISSN 0885-6648
THE SINGLE SCENE (GAHANNA). 1985. m. $20. Columbus Single Scene, Inc., Box 30856, Gahanna, OH 43230. TEL 614-476-8802. Ed. Jeanne Marlowe. adv.; bk.rev.; circ. 6,000. (back issues avail.)
  Description: Clearinghouse of information of interest to singles especially in OH, WV, and KY, emphasizing strategies for meeting and understanding members of the other sex and creating new relationships.

051 US
SINGLE SCENE (SCOTTSDALE). 1972. m. $8.50. 7432 E. Diamond, Scottsdale, AZ 85257. TEL 602-945-6746. Ed. Janet L. Jacobsen. adv.; bk.rev.; circ. 7,200. (tabloid format; back issues avail.)
  Single Scene: Arizona Solo (ISSN 0747-4350)
  Description: Presents a forum for single adults including news, self-help advice and a calendar of events.

301.412 305.3 US ISSN 0738-8578
SINGLE SOURCE NEWSLETTER. 1987. a. $5. Bibliotheca Press, c/o Prosperity & Profits Unlimited, Distribution Services, Box 570213, Houston, TX 77257. TEL 713-867-3438. Ed. A. Doyle. circ. 1,500. (looseleaf format; back issues avail.)

SINGLE TODAY. see LITERATURE

051 US ISSN 8756-0380
SINGLELIFE MAGAZINE; the interactive magazine for Wisconsin and Illinois. 1982. bi-m. $10. SingleLife Enterprises, Inc., 606 W. Wisconsin Ave., Ste. 703, Milwaukee, WI 53203. TEL 414-271-9700. Ed. Gail Rose. adv.; film rev.; illus.; circ. 17,000. (back issues avail.)

052 AT
SINGLES. m. Aus.$18. Associated Communications, 272 Rosslyn St., W. Melbourne, Vic. 3001, Australia. TEL 03 329 0277. (Subscr. to: P.O. Box 4516, World Trade Centre, Vic. 3005, Australia) Ed. Geoff Hawthorne. circ. 30,000.
  Description: Editorial stories on Australian singles, promoting being single.

051 US ISSN 1044-6184
SINGLES ALMANAC (BOSTON). 1981. m. $12. Dorothy Fishbein, Ed. & Pub., Box 299, Boston, MA 02134. TEL 617-964-8710. adv.; illus.; circ. 100,000. (back issues avail.)
  Description: Features personal ads, which are the predominant content of the magazine; the balance is devoted to features relevant to singles. Includes a calendar of events.

051 US ISSN 1045-5108
SINGLES ALMANAC OF NEW YORK; activities in NYC, the boros, NJ, Westchester & LI. 1968. w. $22. Almanac Publications, c/o Metropolitan Almanac, 725 Route 440, Jersey City, NJ 07304. TEL 800-237-4645. FAX 201-433-0847. Ed. Michael Brandon. adv.; bk.rev.; circ. 28,500.
  Former titles: Metropolitan Almanac; Singles Almanac of New York; New York Almanac; Metropolitan Almanac; Manhattan Almanac (ISSN 0025-2085)

051 US
SINGLES CHOICE.* 1988. m. $12. 113 McHenry Rd., Buffalo Grove, IL 60089-1796. TEL 708-255-9940. Ed. Ed Grossman. adv.; bk.rev.; circ. 40,000 (controlled).
  Description: Covers local Chicago singles scene.

051 US
SINGLES JOURNAL. bi-m. $10. 103 Cobblestone Ln., Cherry Hill, NJ 08003. TEL 609-424-3080. adv. (tabloid format)

301.435 US
SINGLE'S LIFE. 1967. m. $12. Voice Publishing, 3450 6th Ave. S., Box 81043, Seattle, WA 98108. TEL 206-223-0210. Ed. Walt Briem. adv.; illus.; circ. 10,000.
  Description: Directed to singles of all ages who are looking for companionship.

051 US
SINGLES LIFELINE. 1983. bi-m. $7. Singles Lifeline Co., Box 639, Randolph, MA 02368. TEL 617-341-8332. FAX 617-344-7207. Ed. Mark Snyder. adv.; bk.rev.; film rev.; circ. 60,000.

051 US
SINGLES MONTHLY (FORT WORTH).* 1982. m. $29. Box 167492, Irving, TX 56016-7492. TELEX 214-601-2092. Ed. Donald F. Pacheco. adv.; circ. 5,000.

051 US
SINGLES NEWS MAGAZINE (SACRAMENTO). 1975. m. $10. Box 61061, Sacramento, CA 95860. TEL 916-486-1414. adv.; circ. 22,000.

051 US
SINGLES OUTREACH SERVICES NEWSLETTER. (Former name of issuing body: Singles Outreach Support) 1985. m. $15. Singles Outreach Services, Box 12511, Albany, NY 12212. TEL 518-785-9438. Ed. Gregg Millett. adv.; circ. 5,500.
  Formerly: S O S Newsletter.
  Description: Covers educational and social activities for adult singles.

051 US
SINGLES' PAPER. m. $8 (free locally). Box 15114, Tucson, AZ 85708. TEL 602-749-9554. adv.
  Formerly: Tucson Connection.

051 202 US ISSN 0746-7982
SINGLES SCENE (ALLARDT). 1981. m. $25. Box 310, Allardt, TN 38504. TEL 615-879-4625. adv.
  Description: Geared to Christian singles or those with traditional Judeo-Christian values.

051 US
SINGLES' SERENDIPITY. 1985. bi-m. $11. Box 5794, Jacksonville, FL 32247. TEL 904-731-7111. Ed. Teri Bryson. adv.; circ. 55,000.
  Description: Lists activities and other single organizations. Includes articles and personal ads.

051 US
SINGLES TIMES. m. $24. Box 1015, Valley Stream, NY 11582. TEL 516-565-9100. adv.

051 US
SINGLES TODAY. 1987. bi-m. $25. Pederson & Associates, Inc., 2500 Mt. Moriah, No. 185, Memphis, TN 38115. TEL 901-365-3988. adv.; bk.rev.; circ. 5,000.
  Formerly (until 1989): Memphis Singles.

SMALL BUSINESS

051 US
SINGLES TRUMPET. s-m. $25. Box 460303, Aurora, CO 80015. TEL 303-745-0818. adv.

051 US
SINGLESLINE; a magazine for Colorado singles. 1980. m. $12. Lawrence L. Loos, Ed. & Pub., Box 16005, Colorado Springs, CO 80935. TEL 719-390-7503. adv.
   Description: Serves single adults in the Pikes Peak region, includes articles, events, business, and personal ads.

051 US
SOUTH FLORIDA SINGLE LIVING. 1982. bi-w. $25. Harry Baum, Ed. & Pub., 4801 S. University Dr., Davie, FL 33328. TEL 305-434-7200. FAX 305-434-7217. adv.; circ. 48,000. (tabloid format)

070.48346 301.412 US
SOUTHEAST SINGLES ASSOCIATION MONTHLY PUBLICATION. 1987. $83 to non-members. Southeast Singles Association, Inc., Box 267, Biloxi, MS 39533. TEL 601-872-1717. Ed. Hugh B. Jones. bk.rev.; circ. 1,500. (tabloid format; back issues avail.)
   Formerly (until 1991): Gulf Coast Singles Association Monthly Book.
   Description: Offers advice and guidance for adult singles and serves as a forum for communication; provides investment information worldwide.

051 US
T M'S SINGLES R S V P. (True Match); America's connection for the discriminating professional. m. $18. T M Publishing, Inc., 26009 S. Highland, Box 18000-5, Las Vegas, NV 89109. TEL 702-796-9966. FAX 702-796-5655. Ed. M.S. Bram.

051 US
TENNESSEE SINGLE LIFE. 1987. 11/yr. $16. Box 50711, Knoxville, TN 37950. adv.; circ. 15,000.

367 US
TODAY'S SINGLE; serving the singles of America. 1980. q. $10. National Association of Christian Singles, 1933 W. Wisconsin Ave., Milwaukee, WI 53233. TEL 414-344-7300. Ed. John M. Fisco, Jr. adv.; bk.rev.; circ. 12,000.

051 US
TRELLIS SINGLES MAGAZINE.* 1975. bi-m. $8. 5667 Snell Ave., Box 344, San Jose, CA 95123-1328. TEL 408-747-1455. Ed. Paul S. Reese. adv.; circ. 55,000.

051 US
TRI-STATE SINGLES CONNECTION.* 1983. bi-m. $15. 2436 Anderson Rd., Covington, KY 41017-1953. Ed. Vivian Shumate. adv.; bk.rev.; circ. 7,090. (tabloid format)
   Description: Articles and personal ads for singles.

296 US
WASHINGTON JEWISH SINGLES NEWSLETTER. 1988. m. $21. 444 N. Frederick Ave., Ste. L, Gaithersburg, MD 20877. TEL 301-990-0210. FAX 301-330-3671. Ed. Ben Levitan. adv.; bk.rev.; circ. 1,000.

051 US
WICHITA SINGLES NEWSLETTER - HEARTLAND FOUNDATION. 1985. m. $30. 3232 S. Clifton, Ste. 430, Wichita, KS 67216. Ed. Belyndae S. McGee. adv.; circ. 25,000.
   Formerly: Wichita Singles Newsletter.
   Description: Responses to personal ads.

SMALL BUSINESS

see Business and Economics–Small Business

SOCIAL SCIENCES: COMPREHENSIVE WORKS

A C S NEWSLETTER/A E C. BULLETIN. (Association for Canadian Studies) see HUMANITIES: COMPREHENSIVE WORKS

A F B INFO. (Arbeitsstelle Friedensforschung Bonn) see POLITICAL SCIENCE

300 GW ISSN 0934-8417
A F E T - MITGLIEDER - RUNDBRIEF. 1948. q. DM.20. Arbeitsgemeinschaft fuer Erziehungshilfe (AFET) e.V., Gandhistr. 2, 3000 Hannover 71, Germany. TEL 0511-511212. bk.rev.; circ. 1,200. (looseleaf format)

300 370 US ISSN 0044-9687
A T S S BULLETIN. vol.39, 1971. irreg. (5-6/yr.). membership. Association of Teachers of Social Studies in the City of New York, c/o Bell Sigelalis Pres., John Dewey High School, 50 Avenue X, Brooklyn, NY 11223. Ed. William McGinn. adv.; bk.rev.; bibl.; circ. 1,200.

300 FI ISSN 0358-5654
AABO AKADEMI. EKONOMISK-STATSVETENSKAPLIGA FAKULTETEN. MEDDELANDEN. (Text in English, Finnish, Swedish) 1956. irreg. free. Aabo Akademi, Ekonomisk-statsvetenskapliga Fakulteten - Aabo Akademi University, Faculty of Economics and Political Sciences, Henriksgatan 7, 20500 Aabo 50, Finland. TEL 921-654311. Ed. Jan Otto Andersson. circ. 200.
   Formerly: Aabo Akademi. Statsvetenskapliga Fakulteten. Meddelanden; Which was formed by the Jan. 1979 merger of: Aabo Akademi. Statsvetenskapliga Fakulteten. Meddelanden. Serie A (ISSN 0355-4031); Aabo Akademi. Statsvetenskapliga Fakulteten. Meddelanden. Serie B (ISSN 0355-4465)

001.3 II ISSN 0970-2385
ABHIGYAN. (Text in English) 1983. s-a. Rs.40($6) Foundation for Organisational Research and Education, Adhitam Kend ra, B-18, Qutab Institutional Area, New Delhi 110 016, India. TELEX 031-73215 FORE IN. Ed. N.K. Singh. adv.; bk.rev.; circ. 300. (back issues avail.) Indexed: Psychol.Abstr.
   Description: Original work in organizational and social research and public systems.

ACADEMIA DE CIENCIAS POLITICAS Y SOCIALES. BOLETIN.. see POLITICAL SCIENCE

300 AT
ACADEMY OF THE SOCIAL SCIENCES IN AUSTRALIA. ANNUAL REPORT. 1971. a. membership. Academy of the Social Sciences in Australia, G.P.O. Box 1956, Canberra, A.C.T. 2601, Australia. TEL 062-491788. FAX 062-486287. circ. 600.

056.1 PY ISSN 0001-4605
ACCION; revista Paraguaya de reflexion y dialogo. N.S. 1969. 10/yr. 3000 g.($20) Centro de Estudios Paraguayos "Antonio Guasch", Calle Guarani 2256, Casilla 1072, Asuncion, Paraguay. TEL 37 962. (Dist. by: D I P P, Box 2507, Asuncion, Paraguay. TEL 595-21-660991) (Co-sponsor: Society of Jesus) Ed. Alberto Leon. adv.; bk.rev.; illus.; circ. 2,000.
   Incorporates: Dimension.

300 FR ISSN 0335-5322
H3
ACTES DE LA RECHERCHE EN SCIENCES SOCIALES. (Text in French; summaries in English, German, Spanish) 1975. q. 185 F. (foreign 270 F.). (Maison des Sciences de l'Homme) Editions de Minuit, 7 rue Bernard-Palissy, 75006 Paris, France. TEL 42-22-37-94. (Subscr. to: Dunod, Centrale des Revues, 11 rue Gossin, 92543 Montrouge Cedex, France. TEL 1-46-56-52-66) Ed. Pierre Bourdieu. bibl.; illus. Indexed: Amer.Hist.& Life, Hist.Abstr., Lang.& Lang.Behav.Abstr., SSCI.
   —BLDSC shelfmark: 0675.315000.
   Description: Discusses leading research in the social sciences- sociology, ethnology, social psychology, psychology, social history, sociolinguistics, the economics of consumption and symbolic goods, etc.

300 610 US ISSN 0275-5742
ADVANCES IN MEDICAL SOCIAL SCIENCE; health and illness as view by anthropology, geography, history, psychology and sociology. irreg., vol.2, 1984. Gordon & Breach Science Publishers, 270 Eighth Ave., New York, NY 10011. TEL 212-206-8900. FAX 212-645-2459. TELEX 236735 GOPUB UR. (Subscr. to: Box 786, Cooper Sta., New York, NY 10276. TEL 800-545-8398; UK subscr. to: P.O. Box 90, Reading, Berkshire RG1 8JL, England. TEL 0734-560-080) Ed. Julio L. Ruffini.
   —BLDSC shelfmark: 0709.376000.
   Refereed Serial

300 US
AFRICAN-AMERICAN ISSUES CENTER DISCUSSION PAPERS. 1984. irreg., no.16, 1986. $4 per no. Boston University, African Studies Center, 270 Bay State Rd., Boston, MA 02215. TEL 617-353-3673. FAX 617-353-4975. TELEX 9103501947 BUASC. Indexed: I D A.

300 960 US
AFRICAN RESEARCH STUDIES. 1958. irreg., no.16, 1989. price varies. Boston University, African Studies Center, 270 Bay State Rd., Boston, MA 02215. TEL 617-353-3673. FAX 617-353-4975. TELEX 9103501947 BUASC. (back issues avail.)

300 PL ISSN 0002-029X
DT19.9.P6
AFRICANA BULLETIN. (Text in English and French) 1964. irreg., vol.35, 1988. price varies. (Uniwersytet Warszawski, Instytut Krajow Rozwijajacych Sie) Wydawnictwa Uniwersytetu Warszawskiego, Ul. Obozna 8, 00-032 Warsaw, Poland. Ed. Bogodar Winid. bk.rev.; abstr.; charts; illus.; stat.; circ. 1,000. Indexed: A.I.C.P., Abstr.Hyg., Amer.Hist.& Life, Curr.Cont.Africa, Geo.Abstr., Hist.Abstr., I D A, M.L.A., Rural Recreat.Tour.Abstr., Soils & Fert., Trop.Dis.Bull., World Agri.Econ.& Rural Sociol.Abstr.
   —BLDSC shelfmark: 0735.150000.

960 SL
AFRICANA RESEARCH BULLETIN. (Text in English) 1971. 2/yr. $20. University of Sierra Leone, Fourah Bay College, Institute of African Studies, Freetown, Sierra Leone. Ed. C. Magbaily Fyle. bk.rev.; bibl.; circ. 250. Indexed: M.L.A.

300 910.03 US ISSN 0882-5297
AFRO-AMERICAN CULTURE AND SOCIETY MONOGRAPH SERIES. Variant title: C A A S Monograph Series. 1980. irreg. price varies. University of California, Los Angeles, Center for Afro-American Studies, 160 Haines Hall, 405 Hilgard Ave., Los Angeles, CA 90024-1545. TEL 310-825-7403. FAX 310-206-3421.

300 UK ISSN 0144-686X
HQ1060
AGEING AND SOCIETY. 1981. q. $45 to individuals; institutions $98. Cambridge University Press, Edinburgh Bldg., Shaftesbury Rd., Cambridge CB2 2RU, England. TEL 0223-312393. FAX 0223-315052. TELEX 851817256. (North American addr.: Cambridge University Press, Journals Dept., 40 W. 20th St., New York, NY 10011. TEL 212-924-3900) (Co-sponsors: Centre for Policy on Ageing; British Society of Gerontology) Ed. Malcolm Johnson. adv.; bk.rev. (also avail. in microform from UMI; reprint service avail. SWZ) Indexed: Abstr.Soc.Geront., ASCA, ASSIA, CLOA, Curr.Cont., P.A.I.S., SSCI, World Bibl.Soc.Sec.
   —BLDSC shelfmark: 0736.225770.
   Description: Covers human ageing all over the world: theoretical and empirical research on issues such as lifestyles in later life, work and retirement, mental illness, sexuality, demography, health care and the history of old age.

300 IT ISSN 0002-094X
AGGIORNAMENTI SOCIALI. 1950. m. L.40000($35) Istituto Aggiornamenti Sociali, Piazza S. Fedele 4, 20121 Milan, Italy. Ed. Angelo Macchi. adv.; bk.rev.; bibl.; charts; stat.; index. cum.index: 1950-1979, 1980-1989; circ. 25,000. Indexed: Int.Lab.Doc.
   —BLDSC shelfmark: 0736.275000.

SOCIAL SCIENCES: COMPREHENSIVE WORKS

300 PL ISSN 0239-5622
AKADEMIA GORNICZO-HUTNICZA IM. STANISLAWA STASZICA. ZESZYTY NAUKOWE. ZAGADNIENIA SPOLECZNO-FILOZOFICZNE. (Text and summaries in English and Polish) irreg., no.42, 1991. price varies. Wydawnictwo A G H, Al. Mickiewicza 30, paw. B-5, 30-068 Krakow, Poland. (Dist. by: Ars Polona, Krakowskie Przedmiescie 7, 00-068 Warsaw, Poland)

300 330.1 PL ISSN 0208-7669
H8.P6
AKADEMIA ROLNICZA W SZCZECINIE. ZESZYTY NAUKOWE. NAUKI SPOLECZNE I EKONOMICZNE. 1976. irreg. price varies. Akademia Rolnicza, Janosika 8, 71-424 Szczecin, Poland. Ed. Marian Piech. bk.rev. **Indexed:** Chem.Abstr., Dairy Sci.Abstr., Field Crop Abstr., Nutr.Abstr., Potato Abstr., Rural Ext.Educ.& Tr.Abstr.

300 GW ISSN 0138-1059
CODEN: AAWTD2
AKADEMIE DER WISSENSCHAFTEN DER D.D.R. ABHANDLUNGEN. ABTEILUNG MATHEMATIK, NATURWISSENSCHAFTEN, TECHNIK. 1975. irreg. price varies. Akademie-Verlag Berlin, Leipziger Str. 3-4, 1086 Berlin, Germany. **Indexed:** Biol.Abstr., Chem.Abstr., Math.R.
—BLDSC shelfmark: 0539.585000.
Description: Reports on current research in mathematics, science and technologies at the Academy of Sciences.

300 BN ISSN 0350-0039
AKADEMIJA NAUKA I UMJETNOSTI BOSNE I HERCEGOVINE. ODJELJENJE DRUSTVENIH NAUKA. RADOVI. 1954. irreg., vol.23, 1989. price varies. Akademija Nauka i Umjetnosti Bosne i Hercegovine, Odjeljenje Drustvenih Nauka, Ul. 6 Novembra br. 7, P.O. Box 01-54, 7100 Sarajevo, Bosnia Hercegovina. circ. 600.

300 TK
AKADEMIYA NAUK TURKMENSKOI S.S.R. IZVESTIYA. SERIYA OBSHCHESTVENNYKH NAUK. bi-m. 13.50 Rub. (effective Jan. 1992). Akademiya Nauk Turkmenskoi S.S.R., Ul. Gogolya, 15, Ashkhabad, Turkmenistan. circ. 500.

300 BW ISSN 0321-1649
AKADEMIYA NAVUK BELARUSSKAI S.S.R. VESTSI. SERIYA GRAMADSKIKH NAVUK. (Text in Byelorussian; contents in Byelorussian, English) 1956. bi-m. 19.80 Rub. Akademiya Navuk Belarusskai S.S.R. - B.S.S.R. Academy of Sciences, Leninskii prospekt, 66, 220072 Minsk 72, Byelarus. TEL 39 48 15. TELEX 252277 NAUKA. Ed. N.V. Birillo. charts; illus.; index; circ. 610.
Description: Presents papers on problems of philosophy and law, sociology, economics, Byelorussian history, art, folklore, literature and linguistics.

300 CN
ALBERTA. ALBERTA CULTURE AND MULTICULTURALISM. ANNUAL REPORT. 1975. a. free. Alberta Culture and Multiculturalism, 10004-104 Ave., Edmonton, Alta. T5J 0K5, Canada. TEL 403-427-6530. FAX 403-427-1496. Ed. David May. circ. 500.
Formerly: Alberta. Alberta Culture. Annual Report (ISSN 0702-9659)

ALERO. see LITERATURE

300 GW ISSN 0176-9251
ALLENSBACHER BERICHTE. 1949. irreg. (2-3/mo.). DM.70. (Institut fuer Demoskopie Allensbach) Verlag fuer Demoskopie, Radolfzeller Str. 8, 7753 Allensbach, Germany. FAX 07533-3048. Eds. Elisabeth Noelle-Neumann, Edgar Piel. circ. 500. (back issues avail.)

980.1 PE
ALLPANCHIS. Variant title: Allpanchis Phuturinqa. 1969. s-a. $45. Instituto de Pastoral Andina, Area de Cultura Andina y Sociedad, Apdo. Aereo 1018, Cusco, Peru. TEL 224137. FAX 51-84-225205. Ed.Bd. adv.; bk.rev.; bibl.; charts; circ. 2,500. **Indexed:** A.I.C.P.

300 572 CN ISSN 0702-8865
ALTERNATE ROUTES; a journal of critical social research. 1977. a. Can.$10 to individuals; institutions $12. c/o Department of Sociology-Anthropology, Carleton University, Ottawa, Ont. K1S 5B6, Canada. TEL 613-788-7400. Ed.Bd. adv.; bk.rev.; circ. 300. **Indexed:** Lang.& Lang.Behav.Abstr., Left Ind. (1983-1988), Sociol.Abstr. (1980-).
Description: Multidisciplinary journal of the social sciences; focuses on contemporary issues within Canadian society.

ALTERNATIVES; perspectives on society technology and environment. see ENVIRONMENTAL STUDIES

AMERICAN ACADEMY OF POLITICAL AND SOCIAL SCIENCE. ANNALS. see POLITICAL SCIENCE

320 300 US ISSN 0002-7642
H1
AMERICAN BEHAVIORAL SCIENTIST. 1957. bi-m. $42 to individuals; institutions $132. Sage Publications, Inc., 2455 Teller Rd., Newbury Park, CA 91320. TEL 805-499-0721. FAX 805-499-0871. (U.K. addr.: Sage Publications, Ltd., 6 Bonhill St., London EC2A 8PU, England) Ed.Bd. adv.; index; circ. 1,500. (also avail. in microform from UMI; back issues avail.) **Indexed:** A.B.C.Pol.Sci., Acad.Ind., Adol.Ment.Hlth.Abstr., Amer.Hist.& Life, ASSIA, Bibl.Engl.Lang.& Lit., Bibl.Ind., Bk.Rev.Ind., C.I.J.E., Chic.Per.Ind., Commun.Abstr., Cont.Pg.Manage., Crim.Just.Abstr., Curr.Cont., Educ.Admin.Abstr., Fut.Surv., Geo.Abstr., I D A, Mid.East: Abstr.& Ind., P.A.I.S., Pers.Lit., Psychol.Abstr., Sage Pub.Admin.Abstr., Sage Urb.Stud.Abstr., Soc.Sci.Ind., Sociol.Abstr., SSCI, Urb.Aff.Abstr.
—BLDSC shelfmark: 0810.780000.
Description: Focuses, in theme-organized issues prepared under guest editors, on emerging cross-disciplinary interests, research, and problems in the social sciences.

AMERICAN BENEDICTINE REVIEW. see RELIGIONS AND THEOLOGY — Roman Catholic

AMERICAN ENTERPRISE. see POLITICAL SCIENCE

AMERICAN JOURNAL OF ECONOMICS AND SOCIOLOGY. see BUSINESS AND ECONOMICS

300 297 US ISSN 0742-6763
AMERICAN JOURNAL OF ISLAMIC SOCIAL SCIENCES. 1984. 3/yr. $30 to individuals (foreign $55); institutions $45 (foreign $70). Association of Muslim Social Scientists, Box 669, Herndon, VA 22070. TEL 703-471-1133. FAX 703-471-3922. TELEX 901153 IIIT WASH. (Co-sponsor: International Institute of Islamic Thought) Ed. Sayyid M. Syeed. adv.; bk.rev.; charts; illus.; stat.; index; circ. 3,000. (back issues avail.) **Indexed:** P.A.I.S., Rel.Ind.One, Sociol.Abstr.
—BLDSC shelfmark: 0826.830000.
Formerly (until 1984): American Journal of Islamic Studies.

AMERICAN JOURNAL OF SEMIOTICS. see HUMANITIES: COMPREHENSIVE WORKS

970 300 US ISSN 0026-3079
AMERICAN STUDIES. 1960. s-a. $15 to individuals; institutions $25 (effective Jan. 1992). (Mid-America American Studies Association) University of Kansas at Lawrence, American Studies Department, 2120 Wescoe Hall, Lawrence, KS 66045-2117. TEL 913-864-4878. FAX 913-864-4120. Eds. David Katzman, Norman Yetman. adv.; bk.rev.; charts; illus.; cum.index every 3 yrs.; circ. 1,500. (also avail. in microform from UMI) **Indexed:** Abstr.Engl.Stud., Amer.Hist.& Life, Amer.Hum.Ind., Hist.Abstr., Hum.Ind., LCR, M.L.A., P.A.I.S., Soc.Sci.Ind.
—BLDSC shelfmark: 0857.657600.
Former titles (until 1970): Midcontinent American Studies Association. Journal; (until 1961): Central Mississippi Valley American Studies Association. Journal.

300 PL ISSN 0137-3536
AMERICAN STUDIES. (Text in English) 1983. irreg., vol.8, 1989. price varies. (Uniwersytet Warszawski, Osrodek Studiow Amerykanskich) Wydawnictwa Uniwersytetu Warszawskiego, Ul. Obozna 8, 00-032 Warsaw, Poland. (Dist. by: Ars Polona, Krakowskie Przedmiescie 7, 00-068 Warsaw, Poland) Ed. Michal Rozbicki. circ. 500.

306 US ISSN 0740-0489
AMERICAN UNIVERSITY STUDIES. SERIES 11. ANTHROPOLOGY AND SOCIOLOGY. 1984. irreg. Peter Lang Publishing, Inc., 62 W. 45th St., 4th Fl., New York, NY 10036. TEL 212-302-6740. Ed. Michael Flamini.
—BLDSC shelfmark: 0858.078500.

ANALES CIENCIAS POLITICAS Y SOCIALES. see POLITICAL SCIENCE

300 GW ISSN 0171-5860
H1
ANALYSE & KRITIK; Zeitschrift fuer Sozialwissenschaften. (Text in English and German) 1979. s-a. DM.66 (students DM.48). Westdeutscher Verlag GmbH, Postfach 5829, 6200 Wiesbaden 1, Germany. TEL 0611-160230. FAX 0611-160229. TELEX 4186-928-VWV-D. Ed.Bd.
—BLDSC shelfmark: 0890.880000.

ANALYSEN; Zeitschrift zur Wissenschafts und Berufspraxis. see EDUCATION

300 CC ISSN 1001-5019
ANHUI DAXUE XUEBAO (SHEHUI KEXUE BAN)/ANHUI UNIVERSITY. JOURNAL (SOCIAL SCIENCE EDITION). (Text in Chinese) q. Anhui Daxue, Xuebao Bianjibu, No. 3, Feixi Lu, Hefei, Anhei 230039, People's Republic of China. TEL 332632. Ed. Zhu Zongyan.

300 100 CC ISSN 1001-2435
ANHUI SHIDA XUEBAO (SHEHUI KEXUE BAN)/ANHUI NORMAL UNIVERSITY. JOURNAL (SOCIAL SCIENCE EDITION). 1957. q. Y1.2 (foreign $2). Anhui Shifan Daxue - Anhui Normal University, 1 Renmin Lu, Wuhu, Anhui 241000, People's Republic of China. TEL 0553-35966. FAX 33730. TELEX 91125 ANU CN. Ed. Wen Bingmo. adv.; index; circ. 3,500. (back issues avail.)

300 FR ISSN 0242-7540
ANNUAIRE DE L'AFRIQUE DU NORD. 1962. a. price varies. (Centre National de la Recherche Scientifique) Editions du C N R S, 1 Place Aristide Briand, 92195 Meudon Cedex, France. TEL 1-45-34-75-50. FAX 1-46-26-28-49. TELEX LABOBEL 204 135 F. (Subscr. to: Presses du C N R S, 20-22, rue Saint Amand, 75015 Paris, France. TEL 1-45-33-16-00) adv.; bk.rev.; index; circ. 1,500 (controlled). **Indexed:** Curr.Cont.Africa.

969.005 910 FR ISSN 0247-400X
DT468
ANNUAIRE DES PAYS DE L'OCEAN INDIEN. (Text in French; summaries in English) 1974. a. 305 F. price varies. (Centre National de la Recherche Scientifique, Centre d'Etudes et de Recherches sur les Societes de l'Ocean Indien) Editions du C N R S, 1 Place Aristide Briand, 92195 Meudon Cedex, France. TEL 1-45-34-75-50. FAX 1-46-26-28-49. TELEX LABOBEL 204 135 F. (Subscr. to: Presses du C N R S, 20-22, rue Saint Amand, 75015 Paris, France. TEL 1-45-33-16-00) (Co-sponsor: Universite d'Aix-Marseille III (Universite de Droit d'Economie et des Sciences)) Eds. L. Favoreu, J. Benoit. adv.; bk.rev.; index; circ. 1,500. **Indexed:** Curr.Cont.Africa.

ANNUAL EDITIONS: HUMAN RESOURCES. see SOCIOLOGY

300 986.1 CK ISSN 0066-5045
ANUARIO COLOMBIANO DE HISTORIA SOCIAL Y DE LA CULTURA. 1963. irreg. exchange basis. Universidad Nacional de Colombia, Facultad de Ciencias Humanas, Departamento de Historia, Apartado Aereo 14490, Ciudad Universitaria, Bogota, D.E., Colombia. Dir. Bernardo Tovar Zambrano. circ. 5,000. **Indexed:** Hist.Abstr.

300 CR ISSN 0377-7316
F1421
ANUARIO DE ESTUDIOS CENTROAMERICANOS. 1974. 2/yr. $20. Editorial de la Universidad de Costa Rica, Apartado 75-2060, Ciudad Universitario Rodrigo Facio, 2050 San Pedro de Montes de Oca, San Jose, Costa Rica. TEL 506-25-3133. FAX 506-24-9367. TELEX UNICORI 2544. Dir. Oscar Fernandez. bk.rev.; circ. 1,000. **Indexed:** Amer.Hist.& Life, Curr.Adv.Ecol.Sci., Hisp.Amer.Per.Ind., Hist.Abstr., P.A.I.S.For.Lang.Ind.
—BLDSC shelfmark: 1563.908000.

SOCIAL SCIENCES: COMPREHENSIVE WORKS

300　　　　　SP　ISSN 0570-4324
ANUARIO IBEROAMERICANO; hechos y documentos. 1962. a. 600 ptas.($8.50) Instituto de Cooperacion Iberoamericana, Departamento de Documentacion Iberoamericana, Avda. de los Reyes Catolicas 4, Ciudad Universitaria, Madrid 28040, Spain. (back issues avail.)

300　　　　　JA
AOYAMA JOURNAL OF SOCIAL SCIENCES/AOYAMA SHAKAI KAGAKU KIYO. 1973. Aoyama-Gakuin University - Aoyama Gakuin Daigaku, 4-4-25 Shibuya, Shibuya-ku, Tokyo 150, Japan.

300　　　　　PE　ISSN 0252-1865
APUNTES; revista semestral de ciencias sociales. 1973. s-a. $12. Universidad del Pacifico, Centro de Investigacion, Av. Salaverry 2020, Jesus Maria Lima 11, Peru. TEL 712277. FAX 706121. TELEX 25650 PE CP SHERA. (Subscr. to: Libreria de la Universidad del Pacifico, Apdo. 4683, Lima 100, Peru) Ed. Jose Luis Sardon. adv.; bk.rev.; circ. 1,000. (back issues avail.) **Indexed**: Hisp.Amer.Per.Ind., P.A.I.S.For.Lang.Ind.

ARANZADI SOCIAL. see *LAW*

300　　　　　SP　ISSN 0210-1963
AP60
ARBOR; revista general de investigacion y cultura. 1944. m. 6000 ptas. (foreign 9500 ptas.). Consejo Superior de Investigaciones Cientificas (C.S.I.C.), Vitruvio, 8, 28006 Madrid, Spain. Dir. Miguel Angel Quintanilla. **Indexed**: Amer.Hist.& Life, Arts & Hum.Cit.Ind., CERDIC, Forest.Abstr., Forest Prod.Abstr., Hist.Abstr., M.L.A.
　Description: Expresses the view that scientific and technological industries must be sensitive and responsible to the needs of the society that supports them.

ARCHAEOLOGY IN MONTANA. see *ARCHAEOLOGY*

ARCHIV FUER WISSENSCHAFT UND PRAXIS DER SOZIALEN ARBEIT. see *SOCIAL SERVICES AND WELFARE*

ARCHIWUM HISTORII FILOZOFII I MYSLI SPOLECZNEJ. see *PHILOSOPHY*

053.1　　　GW　ISSN 0004-1157
DAS ARGUMENT; Zeitschrift fuer Philosophie und Sozialwissenschaften. 1959. bi-m. DM.72. Argument-Verlag GmbH, Rentzelstr. 1, 2000 Hamburg 13, Germany. TEL 040-456018. Ed. Wolfgang Fritz Haug. adv.; bk.rev.; index; circ. 10,000. **Indexed**: Lang.& Lang.Behav.Abstr., SSCI.
—BLDSC shelfmark: 1664.355000.

ARHIV ZA PRAVNE I DRUSTVENE NAUKE. see *LAW*

300　　　　　II
ASIAN ECONOMIC AND SOCIAL REVIEW; techno-economic quarterly of Asian co-operation. (Text in English) 1976; N.S. 1984. q. Rs.250($75) (Indian Institute of Asian Studies) Asian Studies Press, 23-354 Azadnagar, Jaiprakash Rd., Andheri, Bombay 400 058, India. TEL 22-6263974. Ed. M.R. Sinha. adv.; bk.rev.; charts; index; circ. 3,500. (reprint service avail.) **Indexed**: Rural Recreat.Tour.Abstr., World Agri.Econ.& Rural Sociol.Abstr.
　Incorporates: I F C E P Journal & Quarterly Journal of Indian Studies in Social Sciences (ISSN 0033-5584)

ASIAN PROFILE. see *ORIENTAL STUDIES*

300　001.3　US　ISSN 0361-3968
DS1
ASIAN THOUGHT AND SOCIETY: AN INTERNATIONAL REVIEW. 1976. 3/yr. $40. (State University of New York at Oneonta) East-West Publishing Co., 1 Bugbee Rd., Oneonta, NY 13820. TEL 607-431-3553. (Co-sponsors: Boston College; University of Hong Kong) Ed. Ignatius J.H. Ts'ao. adv.; bk.rev.; index. (back issues avail.) **Indexed**: A.B.C.Pol.Sci., E.I., Hist.Abstr.
—BLDSC shelfmark: 1742.752500.

300　　　　　UK　ISSN 0265-2587
ASSIGNATION. 1983. 4/yr. £24 (typically set in July). Aslib, Association for Information Management, Social Sciences Information Group, c/o Mrs. Hogan, Ed., National Institute of Social Work, 5 Tavistock Place, London WC1H 9SS, England. TEL 071-387-9681. FAX 071-387-7968. adv.; bk.rev.; circ. 200. (back issues avail.) **Indexed**: LISA.
—BLDSC shelfmark: 1746.654000.
　Description: Provides information on activities, sources and resources in the social sciences field.

ASSOCIATION FOR THE STUDY OF PLAY NEWSLETTER. see *PSYCHOLOGY*

300　　　　　VE
ATLANTIDA. 1974. irreg. free to qualified personnel. Universidad Simon Bolivar, Division de Sociales y Humanidades, Valle de Sartenejas, Caracas, Venezuela. circ. 1,000.

300　800　　DR
AULA.* 1972. q. RD.$6. Universidad Nacional "Pedro Henriquez Urena", Apdo. 1423, Santo Domingo, Dominican Republic. Ed. Carlos Esteban Deive. bk.rev.; bibl.; circ. 1,000.

509　150　　NE
AUSTRALASIAN STUDIES IN HISTORY AND PHILOSOPHY OF SCIENCE. 1982. irreg. price varies. Kluwer Academic Publishers, Spuiboulevard 50, P.O. Box 17, 3300 AA Dordrecht, Netherlands. TEL 078-334911. FAX 078-334254. TELEX 29245. (Dist. by: Kluwer Academic Publishers Group, P.O. Box 322, 3300 AH Dordrecht, Netherlands; U.S. address: P.O. Box 358, Accord Station, Hingham, MA 02018-0358) Ed. R.W. Home.
　Formerly: Australasian Studies in History and Philosophy.

AUSTRALIAN FEMINIST STUDIES. see *WOMEN'S INTERESTS*

AUSTRALIAN JOURNAL OF CHINESE AFFAIRS. see *ORIENTAL STUDIES*

300　　　　　AT　ISSN 1035-1132
AUSTRALIAN NATIONAL UNIVERSITY. AUSTRALIAN DEVELOPMENT STUDIES NETWORK. DEVELOPMENT BULLETIN. q. Aus.$15. Australian National University, National Centre for Development Studies, G.P.O. Box 4, Canberra, A.C.T. 2601, Australia. TEL 616-249-4705. FAX 616-257-2886. TELEX 61364.
　Formerly: Australian National University. National Centre for Development Studies. Newsletter (ISSN 0313-9980)
　Description: Provides information on development issues, development research, and development-related courses, summaries of national and international conferences, information on development-related organizations and recent publications and other resources.

300　　　　　AT
AUSTRALIAN NATIONAL UNIVERSITY. NATIONAL CENTRE FOR DEVELOPMENT STUDIES. DEMOGRAPHY TEACHING NOTES. irreg. Aus.$10 per no. Australian National University, National Centre for Development Studies, G.P.O. Box 4, Canberra, A.C.T. 2601, Australia. TEL 616-249-4705. FAX 616-257-2886.
　Formerly: Australian National University. Development Studies Centre. Demography Teaching Notes (ISSN 0157-6232)

300　　　　　AT　ISSN 1030-360X
AUSTRALIAN NATIONAL UNIVERSITY. NATIONAL CENTRE FOR DEVELOPMENT STUDIES. WORKING PAPERS. SERIES: CHINA WORKING PAPERS. (Text in English) 1987. irreg. Aus.$7 per no. Australian National University, National Centre for Development Studies, G.P.O. Box 4, Canberra, A.C.T. 2601, Australia. TEL 616-249-4705. FAX 616-257-2886. TELEX AA61364. circ. 300.

300　　　　　AT　ISSN 0816-5165
AUSTRALIAN NATIONAL UNIVERSITY. NATIONAL CENTRE FOR DEVELOPMENT STUDIES. WORKING PAPERS. SERIES: ISLANDS - AUSTRALIA WORKING PAPERS. irreg. Aus.$7. Australian National University, National Centre for Development Studies, G.P.O. Box 4, Canberra, A.C.T. 2601, Australia. TEL 616-249-4705. FAX 616-257-2886.
—BLDSC shelfmark: 4583.131700.
　Description: Covers economics, trade, development and policy issues.

300　　　　　AT　ISSN 0815-7596
AUSTRALIAN NATIONAL UNIVERSITY. NATIONAL CENTRE FOR DEVELOPMENT STUDIES. WORKING PAPERS. SERIES: N C D S WORKING PAPERS. irreg. Aus.$7. Australian National University, National Centre for Development Studies, G.P.O. Box 4, Canberra, A.C.T. 2601, Australia. TEL 616-249-4705. FAX 616-257-2886. TELEX 61364. **Indexed**: Geo.Abstr., I D A, Rural Devel.Abstr., Rural Recreat.Tour.Abstr., Triticale Abstr., World Agri.Econ.& Rural Sociol.Abstr.
　Description: Economics, trade, development and policy issues.

300　　　　　AU
AUSTRIA. BUNDESMINISTERIUM FUER SOZIALE VERWALTUNG. BERICHT UEBER DIE TAETIGKEIT. vol.28, 1972. m. S.640. (Bundesministerium fuer Soziale Verwaltung) Oesterreichische Staatsdruckerei, Rennweg 12a, A-1037 Vienna, Austria. TEL 0222-787631. charts; stat.

300　　　　　FR
AUTREMENT. 1975. 14/yr. Editions Autrement, 4 rue d'Enghien, 75010 Paris, France. TEL 47-70-12-50. adv.; circ. 20,000.

AZTLAN: A JOURNAL OF CHICANO STUDIES. see *ETHNIC INTERESTS*

300　　　　　CN　ISSN 0005-2949
F1086
B C STUDIES. 1969. q. Can.$25 to individuals (foreign Can.$30); institutions Can.$30 (foreign Can.$35). University of British Columbia, 2029 West Mall, Vancouver, B.C. V6T 1Z2, Canada. TEL 604-822-3727. Ed. Allan Smith. bk.rev.; bibl.; charts; illus.; circ. 1,000. (tabloid format; also avail. in microform from UMI,MML; microfilm; back issues avail.) **Indexed**: Abstr.Anthropol., Amer.Hist.& Life, Can.Per.Ind., CMI, Hist.Abstr.
—BLDSC shelfmark: 1871.371800.
　Description: Focuses on all aspects of human history in British Columbia.

BALKAN STUDIES. see *HISTORY — History Of Europe*

BASIC AND APPLIED SOCIAL PSYCHOLOGY. see *PSYCHOLOGY*

300　　　　　US　ISSN 0094-3673
H1
BEHAVIOR SCIENCE RESEARCH; journal of worldwide comparative studies. 1966. a. $30 to individuals; institutions $40. (Society for Cross-Cultural Research) Human Relations Area Files Press, Box 2054, Yale Sta., New Haven, CT 06520. TEL 203-777-2334. FAX 203-777-2337. Ed. Melvin Ember. bk.rev.; bibl.; charts; index; circ. 500. (processed; also avail. in microform from UMI; reprint service avail. from UMI) **Indexed**: A.I.C.P., Abstr.Anthropol., ASSIA, E.I., Psychol.Abstr., SSCI.
—BLDSC shelfmark: 1876.889000.
　Formerly: Behavior Science Notes (ISSN 0005-7886)

300　　　　　II
BEHAVIOROMETRIC. (Text in English) 1970. s-a. $7 to individuals; academic institutions $10. Council of Behavioral Research, Maharani Rd., Gaya 823002, Bihar, India. Ed. C.N. Daftuar. adv.; bk.rev.; charts; circ. 1,000. **Indexed**: Indian Psychol.Abstr., Psychol.Abstr.

300　　　　　CC
BEIJING SHEHUI KEXUE/BEIJING SOCIAL SCIENCES. (Text in Chinese) q. Beijing Shehui Kexueyuan - Beijing Academy of Social Sciences, No.6, Chegongzhuang Dajie, Fuchengmenwai, Beijing 100044, People's Republic of China. TEL 8311675. Ed. Zhou Yixing.

300　　　　　CC
BEIJING SHIFAN DAXUE XUEBAO (SHE KE BAN)/BEIJING NORMAL UNIVERSITY. JOURNAL (SOCIAL SCIENCE EDITION). (Text in Chinese; table of contents in English) bi-m. 9.60 Yen. Beijing Shifan Daxue Chubanshe - Beijing Normal University Press, Beijing 100088, People's Republic of China. (Dist. overseas by: China Publications Foreign Trade Corp., P.O. Box 782, Beijing, P.R.C.) Ed. Bai Shouyi.

SOCIAL SCIENCES: COMPREHENSIVE WORKS 4367

300   CC
BEIJING SHIFAN XUEYUAN XUEBAO (SHEHUI KEXUE BAN)/BEIJING NORMAL INSTITUTE. JOURNAL (SOCIAL SCIENCE EDITION). (Text in Chinese) bi-m. Beijing Shifan Xueyuan, Huayuancun, Fuchengmenwai, Beijing 100037, People's Republic of China. TEL 8414411. Ed. Zhang Shoukang.

300   GW
BEITRAEGE ZUR GESCHICHTE THUERINGENS. 1968. irreg. DM.1.80. (Museen der Stadt Erfurt) Sed-Bezirksleitung Erfurt, Erfurt, Germany. Ed. Horst H. Mueller. illus.

300   GW
BEITRAEGE ZUR GESELLSCHAFTS- UND BILDUNGSPOLITIK. 1976. 10/yr. DM.116.99. Deutscher Instituts Verlag GmbH, Gustav-Heinemann-Ufer 84, Postfach 510670, 5000 Cologne 51, Germany. TEL 0221-3708341. Ed. W. Schlaffke. bk.rev.; abstr.; bibl.; charts; illus.; stat.; index; circ. 2,000. (back issues avail.)

BEITRAEGE ZUR SOZIALGESCHICHTE BREMEN. see HISTORY — History Of Europe

300 500   II
BHAGALPUR UNIVERSITY JOURNAL.* (Text in English and Hindi) vol.4, 1971. q. Rs.12. Bhagalpur University, Bhagalpur 7, India. Ed.Bd.

300   PY
BIBLIOTECA CLASICOS COLORADOS. 1975. irreg. Instituto Colorado de Cultura, Asuncion, Paraguay.

300   AG
BIBLIOTECA DE CIENCIAS SOCIALES. irreg., no.2, 1982. Consejo Latinoamericano de Ciencias Sociales, Centro Internacional de Formacion de Ciencias Ambientales, Av. Callao 873, Buenos Aires, Argentina. Ed. Mario R. dos Santos.

300   AG
BIBLIOTECA DE ECONOMIA, POLITICA, SOCIEDAD. SERIE MAYOR.* irreg. Editorial Paidos, Defensa 599, Buenos Aires, 1065, Argentina.

300   AG
BIBLIOTECA DE ECONOMIA, POLITICA, SOCIEDAD. SERIE MENOR.* irreg., vol.6, 1976. Editorial Paidos, Defensa 599, Buenos Aires, 1065, Argentina.

500 001.3   FI   ISSN 0067-8481
BIDRAG TILL KAENNEDOM AV FINLANDS NATUR OCH FOLK. (Text in Finnish or Swedish) 1858. irreg. price varies. Societas Scientiarum Fennica - Finnish Society of Sciences and Letters, Marieg 5, SF-00170 Helsinki 17, Finland. Ed. Paul Fogelberg. circ. 700.

BLACK SCHOLAR; journal of black studies and research. see ETHNIC INTERESTS

BLUEPRINT FOR SOCIAL JUSTICE. see POLITICAL SCIENCE — Civil Rights

300   TU
BOGAZICI UNIVERSITY JOURNAL: MANAGEMENT, ECONOMIC AND SOCIAL SCIENCES/BOGAZICI UNIVERSITESI DERGISI: EY ONETICILIK, EKONOMI, VE SOSYAL BILIMLER. (Text in English or Turkish) 1973. a. $10. Bogazici Universitesi, P.O. Box 2, Istanbul, Turkey. FAX 1656357. TELEX 26411 BOUN TR. bibl.; stat.
Formerly: Bogazici University Journal: Social Sciences.

300   AG   ISSN 0497-0292
HC171
BOLETIN INFORMATIVO TECHINT. 1959. q. free. Organizacion Techint, Leandro N. Alem 1067, Buenos Aires, Argentina. TEL 311-1091. FAX 3136165. TELEX 9134. circ. 6,000.
Formerly: Organizacion Techint. Boletin Informativo.

300 960   US
BOSTON UNIVERSITY PAPERS ON AFRICA. 1964. irreg., no.8, 1987. Boston University, African Studies Center, 270 Bay State Rd., Boston, MA 02215. TEL 617-353-3673. FAX 617-353-4975. TELEX 910-3501947 BUASC.

BRAZIL. SERVICO NACIONAL DE APRENDIZAGEM COMERCIAL. BOLETIM TECNICO. see EDUCATION

300   UK
BRISTOL PAPERS. 1988. 2/yr. varies. University of Bristol, School of Applied Social Studies, 40 Berkeley Sq., Bristol BS8 1HY, England. TEL 0272-303030. circ. 500.

320.5   AT   ISSN 0007-2036
BROADSHEET. 1957. 4-6/yr. donation. Women's Electoral Lobby (Western Australia), c/o Women's Electoral Lobby (S.A.), Rm.2, 155 Pirie St., Adelaide, S.A. 5000, Australia. bk.rev.; bibl.; circ. 500.

300   US
BROOKINGS REPRINT SERIES. 1954? irreg. $20. Brookings Institution, 1775 Massachusetts Ave., N.W., Washington, DC 20036-2188. TEL 202-797-6255. FAX 202-797-6004.
Former titles: Brookings Pamphlet Series; Brookings Institution. Reprint (ISSN 0068-2810); Brookings Research Report Series (ISSN 0068-2829)

300   SJ
BUHUTH. (Publication suspended Aug.-Dec. 1973 and Aug. 1974-Oct. 1977) 1972. m. National Council for Research, Box 2404, Khartoum, Sudan.

300 920   II
BUILDERS OF INDIAN ANTHROPOLOGY. (Text in English) 1978. irreg. Rs.12. N.K. Bose Memorial Foundation, B-8-9 Bara Gambhir Singh, Gauriganj, Varanasi 221001, India. Ed. Surajit Sinha. circ. 500.

BULLETIN ANALYTIQUE DE DOCUMENTATION POLITIQUE, ECONOMIQUE ET SOCIALE CONTEMPORAINE. see POLITICAL SCIENCE

300   SA   ISSN 1017-6136
BULLETIN - NEWS FOR THE HUMAN SCIENCE RESEARCHER/NAVORSINGSNUUS VIR DIE GEESTESWETENSKAPLIKE. (Text in Afrikaans, English) 1975. 10/yr. free to universitites and institutions. Centre for Science Development, Human Sciences Research Council - Sentrum vir Wetenskapontwikkeling, Raad vir Geesteswetenskaplike Navorsing, Private Bag X270, Pretoria 0001, South Africa. TEL 012-202-9111. FAX 012-202-2741. Ed. J.M. larquharson. bk.rev.; circ. 3,000.
Formerly: Research Bulletin: Journal for the S A P R H S (ISSN 1011-1816)

980   UK   ISSN 0261-3050
F1401
BULLETIN OF LATIN AMERICAN RESEARCH. 1981. 3/yr. £75 (effective 1992). (Society for Latin American Studies) Pergamon Press plc, Headington Hill Hall, Oxford OX3 0BW, England. TEL 0865-794141. FAX 0865-743911. TELEX 83177 PERGAP. (And: 660 White Plains Rd., Tarrytown, NY 10591-5153. TEL 914-524-9200) Ed. Paul Cammac. adv.; bk.rev.; circ. 800. (also avail. in microfiche) **Indexed:** A.B.C.Pol.Sci., Amer.Hist.& Life, Curr.Cont., Hisp.Amer.Per.Ind., Hist.Abstr., I D A.
—BLDSC shelfmark: 2865.440000.
Supersedes (in Oct. 1981): Society for Latin America Studies. Bulletin.
Refereed Serial

BULLETIN OF SCIENCE TECHNOLOGY AND SOCIETY. see SCIENCES: COMPREHENSIVE WORKS

300   BR
BURMA RESEARCH SOCIETY. JOURNAL/MYANMA NAING NGAN THUTEITHANA ATHIN.* (Text in Burmese or English) 1911. s-a. Burma Research Society, University Library, University Estate, Yangon, Union of Myanmar. bk.rev.; charts; illus. (reprint service avail. from KTO) **Indexed:** Amer.Hist.& Life, Hist.Abstr.

300   US   ISSN 1051-4589
E185.5
C A A S REPORT. 1977. s-a. free. University of California, Los Angeles, Center for Afro-American Studies, 160 Haines Hall, 405 Hilgard Ave., Los Angeles, CA 90024-1545. TEL 310-825-7403. FAX 310-206-3421. Eds. N. Cherie Francis, M. Belinda Turcker. bk.rev.; circ. 5,500. (back issues avail.) **Indexed:** ERIC.
Formerly: C A A S Newsletter (ISSN 0197-5579)

300 910.03   US   ISSN 0882-5300
C A A S SPECIAL PUBLICATION SERIES. 1977. irreg. price varies. University of California, Los Angeles, Center for Afro-American Studies, 160 Haines Hall, 405 Hilgard Ave., Los Angeles, CA 90024-1545. TEL 310-825-7403. FAX 310-206-3421.

300   US   ISSN 0734-5119
C B A S S E NEWSLETTER. 1975. s-a. free. National Research Council, Commission on Behavioral and Social Sciences and Education, 2101 Constitution Ave., N.W., Washington, DC 20418. TEL 202-334-2300. Ed. Christine L. McShane. circ. 2,500.
Description: Reports the activities of the Commission on Behavioral and Social Sciences and Education of the National Research Council, including new projects, committee and panel memberships and reports.

C D R PROJECT PAPER. (Centre for Development Research) see BUSINESS AND ECONOMICS — International Development And Assistance

C D R RESEARCH REPORTS. (Centre for Development Research) see BUSINESS AND ECONOMICS — International Development And Assistance

C E D E J EGYPTE - MONDE ARABE. (Centre d'Etudes et de Documentation Economique, Juridique et Sociale) see LAW

300   FR   ISSN 0395-5621
C F D T MAGAZINE. (Includes weekly: Syndicalisme) 1976. m. (11/yr.) 162 F. (foreign 246 F.)(effective Jan. 1992). Confederation Francaise Democratique du Travail, 4 bd. de la Villette, 75955 Paris Cedex 19, France. TEL 42-03-81-40. Dir. Pierre Hureau. bk.rev.; film rev.; illus.
Formerly: Syndicalisme Magazine.

C Q RESEARCHER. see POLITICAL SCIENCE

C R: CENTENNIAL REVIEW. see HUMANITIES: COMPREHENSIVE WORKS

300   PO
CADERNOS DE CIENCIAS SOCIAIS. 1984. irreg., no.10-11, 1991. price varies. Edicoes Afrontamento, Lda., Rua de Costa Cabral, 859, Apdo. 2009, 4201 Porto Codex, Portugal. TEL 489271. FAX 491777. Ed. Jose Madureira Pinto.

360   BL
CADERNOS DE ESTUDOS SOCIAIS. (Text in Portuguese; summaries in English, French) 1985. s-a. (Fundacao Joaquim Nabuco) Editora Massangana, Rua Dois Irmaos, 15, Apipucos, 52071 Recife, Brazil. TEL 081-268-4611. FAX 081-268-9600. bibl.; circ. 1,000.

300   FR   ISSN 0068-4953
CAHIERS BRETONS/AR GWYR. 1958-61; 1970 N.S. m. 150 F. (foreign 175 F.). Grand College Celtique, Ker Sklerijenn, 35290 St. Onen-la-Chapelle, France. TEL 99-09-63-75. Ed. Jean Thos. bk.rev.; circ. 300.

CAHIERS D'ECONOMIE ET SOCIOLOGIE RURALES. see AGRICULTURE — Agricultural Economics

980 300   FR   ISSN 1141-7161
CAHIERS DES AMERIQUES LATINES. (Text in French, Portuguese, Spanish) 1968. 2/yr. 160 F. Institut des Hautes Etudes de l'Amerique Latine, 28 rue Saint-Guillaume, 75007 Paris, France. Ed.Bd. abstr.; bibl. **Indexed:** Amer.Hist.& Life, Hisp.Amer.Per.Ind., Hist.Abstr.
Formerly (until 1984): Cahiers des Ameriques Latines. Serie - Sciences de l'Homme (ISSN 0008-0020)

500   FR   ISSN 0768-9829
DT521
CAHIERS DES SCIENCES HUMAINES. (Text in French; summaries in English) 1963. q. 300 F. (Institut Francais de Recherche Scientifique pour le Developpement en Cooperation) Editions de l' O R S T O M, 72 Route d'Aulnay, 93143 Bondy Cedex, France. TEL 48-47-31-95. FAX 48-47-30-88. circ. 1,000. (back issues avail.) **Indexed:** Curr.Cont.Africa, Geo.Abstr., I D A, Int.Lab.Doc., Rice Abstr., Rural Recreat.Tour.Abstr., World Agri.Econ.& Rural Sociol.Abstr.
—BLDSC shelfmark: 2952.195680.
Formerly: Cahiers O R S T O M Serie Sciences Humaines (ISSN 0008-0403)

SOCIAL SCIENCES: COMPREHENSIVE WORKS

300　　　　　　　　SZ　ISSN 0008-0497
CAHIERS VILFREDO PARETO; revue europeenne des sciences sociales. Variant title: R E S S. (Text in English, French, German and Italian) 1963. irreg., no.90, 1991. 85 F. Librairie Droz S.A., 11, rue Massot, CH-1211 Geneva 12, Switzerland. TEL 022-466666. FAX 022-472391. Ed. Giovanni Busino. bk.rev.; circ. 2,000. **Indexed**: SSCI.
—BLDSC shelfmark: 7900.180000.
Description: European studies of social sciences.

CAHIERS ZAIROIS D'ETUDES POLITIQUES ET SOCIALES. see *POLITICAL SCIENCE*

300　　　　　　　　UA
CAIRO PAPERS IN SOCIAL SCIENCES. (Text in English) 1977. 4/yr. £E8($15) to individuals; institutions EL.10($25). American University in Cairo, Social Research Center, Box 2511, Cairo, Egypt. (Subscr. to: American University Cairo Library, c/o Unsworth & Co., 1831 Pennsylvania Ave., Linden, NJ 07036, U.S.A.) Ed.Bd.

300　　　　　　　　IT
CALENDARIO DEL POPOLO. 1945. m. L.40000. Nicola Teti e C., Via Enrico Noe 23, 20133 Milan, Italy. TEL 02-26680262. Ed. Franco Della Peruta. adv.; circ. 25,000.

971 300 900　　　　CN　ISSN 0043-8170
D839
CANADA & THE WORLD; the magazine for students of current events. 1934. 9/yr. (Sep.-May). Can.$20. P.O. Box 7004, Oakville, Ont. L6J 6L5, Canada. TEL 416-338-3394. Ed. Rupert J. Taylor. adv.; illus.; circ. 20,000. (also avail. in microform from UMI) **Indexed**: Can.Per.Ind., CMI.
Formerly: World Affairs.
Description: Current events for high school students.

CANADIAN ASSOCIATION OF SLAVISTS NEWSLETTER. see *HUMANITIES: COMPREHENSIVE WORKS*

CANADIAN CIRCUMPOLAR LIBRARY. BULLETIN. see *GEOGRAPHY — Abstracting, Bibliographies, Statistics*

CANADIAN ISSUES/THEMES CANADIENS. see *HUMANITIES: COMPREHENSIVE WORKS*

960　　　　　　　　CN　ISSN 0008-3968
DT19.9.C3
CANADIAN JOURNAL OF AFRICAN STUDIES/REVUE CANADIENNE DES ETUDES AFRICAINES. (Text in English, French) 1967. 3/yr. Can.$70 to individuals; students Can.$30. Canadian Association of African Studies, 294 Albert St., no. 308, Ottawa, Ont. K1P 6E6, Canada. TEL 613-237-6885. FAX 613-237-2105. Ed.Bd. adv.; bk.rev.; bibl.; circ. 950. **Indexed**: A.B.C.Pol.Sci., A.I.C.P., Abstr.Anthropol., Amer.Hist.& Life, CERDIC, Curr.Cont., Hist.Abstr., HR Rep., I D A, Int.Lab.Doc., Lang.& Lang.Behav.Abstr., M.L.A., Mid.East: Abstr.& Ind., Periodex, RADAR, Rural Devel.Abstr., Rural Recreat.Tour.Abstr., Sociol.Abstr., SSCI, World Agri.Econ.& Rural Sociol.Abstr.
—BLDSC shelfmark: 3027.900000.
Supersedes: Bulletin of African Studies in Canada.
Description: Covers African political economy, history, development, and literature. Includes papers on agriculture, rural economy and medicine.

300　　　　　　　　CN　ISSN 0225-5189
HC59
CANADIAN JOURNAL OF DEVELOPMENT STUDIES/REVUE CANADIENNE D'ETUDES DU DEVELOPPEMENT. (Text in English, French, Spanish) 1980. 3/yr. Can.$35($35) to individuals; institutions Can.$50($50). Institute for International Development and Cooperation - Institut de Developpement International et de Cooperation, 25 University Street, Ottawa, Ont. K1N 6N5, Canada. TEL 613-564-5459. FAX 613-564-9525. TELEX 0533338. Ed. Jose Havet. adv.; bk.rev.; circ. 1,000. (back issues avail.) **Indexed**: A.B.C.Pol.Sci., Amer.Hist.& Life, Curr.Cont., Hist.Abstr., I D A, Int.Lab.Doc., J.of Econ.Lit., P.A.I.S.For.Lang.Ind., P.A.I.S, Rural Devel.Abstr., Rural Ext.Educ.& Tr.Abstr., SSCI, World Agri.Econ.& Rural Sociol.Abstr.
—BLDSC shelfmark: 3031.135000.
Description: Provides an interdisciplinary forum for the discussion of a wide range of development issues. Open to all theoretical and development strategy orientations and publishes contributions dealing with all regions and countries of the developing world.

CANADIAN NOTES & QUERIES/QUESTIONS & REPONSES CANADIENNES. see *HUMANITIES: COMPREHENSIVE WORKS*

CANADIAN REVIEW OF STUDIES IN NATIONALISM. see *HISTORY*

CANADIAN SLAVONIC PAPERS/REVUE CANADIENNE DES SLAVISTES. see *HUMANITIES: COMPREHENSIVE WORKS*

CANADIAN SOCIAL STUDIES: HISTORY AND SOCIAL SCIENCE TEACHER. see *EDUCATION — Teaching Methods And Curriculum*

300　　　　　　　　MQ
CARBET; revue martiniquaise de sciences sociales. triennial. Editions Desormeaux, Rue Galieni, 97200 Fort de France, Martinique. Ed. Emile Desormeaux.

972.9 300　　　　　PR　ISSN 0008-6533
F2161
CARIBBEAN STUDIES. (Text in English, French or Spanish) 1961. q. $16 to individuals; institutions $25. Universidad de Puerto Rico, Institute of Caribbean Studies, Box B M, University Station, Rio Piedras, PR 00931. Ed. Sybil Farrell Lewis. bk.rev.; bibl.; charts; illus.; index; circ. 1,500. **Indexed**: Amer.Hist.& Life, ASSIA, Curr.Cont., Geo.Abstr., Hisp.Amer.Per.Ind., Hist.Abstr., Int.Polit.Sci.Abstr., PROMT, Soc.Sci.Ind., SSCI.
—BLDSC shelfmark: 3053.130000.

300　　　　　　　　US　ISSN 0149-6948
HM1
CASE ANALYSIS; in social science and social therapy. 1978. irreg. (approx. a.) $8 to individuals; institutions $12 (effective 1992). Progresiv Publishr, 401 E. 32nd St., Rm. 1002, Chicago, IL 60616. TEL 312-225-9181. Ed. Kenneth H. Ives. bk.rev.; charts; stat.; circ. 100. (back issues avail.) **Indexed**: Psychol.Abstr., Soc.Work.Res.& Abstr., Sociol.Abstr.
—BLDSC shelfmark: 3058.112000.
Description: Methods for, problems of, and examples of case studies in various fields of social science.

300　　　　　　　　US　ISSN 0008-7661
CATALYST (AMHERST). 1965. irreg. Can.$10. State University of New York at Amherst, Department of Sociology, Amherst, NY 14226. Ed. E. Porvell. adv.; bk.rev.; circ. 2,000. (also avail. in microform from UMI; reprint service avail. from UMI) **Indexed**: Amer.Hist.& Life, Hist.Abstr., Int.Bibl.Soc.Sci., Sociol.Abstr.
—BLDSC shelfmark: 3090.945000.

CEIBA. see *LITERATURE*

CENTRE D'HISTOIRE ECONOMIQUE ET SOCIALE DE LA REGION LYONNAISE. BULLETIN. see *HISTORY — History Of Europe*

300　　　　　　　　FR
CENTRE DE RECHERCHES ET D'ETUDES DES SITUATIONS INTERCULTURELLES. CAHIERS. 1988. a. 80 F. (effective 1992). (Universite de Toulouse II (le Mirail)) Presses Universitaires du Mirail, 56 rue du Taur, 31069 Toulouse Cedex, France. TEL 61-22-58-31. FAX 61-21-84-20. Ed. Claude Clanet. (back issues avail.)
Description: Publishes intercultural research on education and the humanities.

300　　　　　　　　CV
CENTRO DE ESTUDOS DE CABO VERDE. REVISTA: SERIE DE CIENCIAS HUMANAS. Short title: Serie de Ciencias Humanas. (At head of title, 1973- : Junta de Investigacoes do Ultramar) (Summaries in English) 1973. irreg. Centro de Estudos de Cabo Verde, Praia, Sao Tiago, Cape Verde Islands. bibl.; stat.

300　　　　　　　　UY
CENTRO DE INFORMACIONES Y ESTUDIOS DEL URUGUAY. CUADERNOS. 1976. irreg. price varies. Centro de Informaciones y Estudios de Uruguay, J. Paullier 1174, Casilla de Correo 10587, Montevideo, Uruguay. circ. 150.

322.4　　　　　　　AG　ISSN 0325-1306
CENTRO DE INVESTIGACION Y ACCION SOCIAL. REVISTA. 1961. m. $50. Centro de Investigacion y Accion Social (CIAS), O'Higgins 1331, 1426 Buenos Aires, Argentina. TEL 01-783-8300, 6597. Ed. Fernando Storni. adv.; bk.rev.; circ. 2,000.
Former titles: Centro de Investigacion y Accion Social. Boletin Mensual; (1965-1969): C I A S Centro de Investigacion y Accion (ISSN 0007-8387)

300　　　　　　　　US　ISSN 0252-9971
CENTRO DE INVESTIGACIONES REGIONALES DE MESOAMERICA. SERIE MONOGRAFICA. 1981. s-a. price varies. Centro de Investigaciones Regionales de Mesoamerica (CIRMA), Plumsock Mesoamerican Studies, Rt. 106, Box 38, S. Woodstock, VT 05071. TEL 802-457-1199. Eds. Christopher H. Lutz, Cherri M. Pancake. **Indexed**: A.I.C.P., Abstr.Anthropol., Int.Bibl.Soc.Sci.

300　　　　　　　　CS　ISSN 0069-2298
CESKOSLOVENSKA AKADEMIE VED. ROZPRAVY. S V: RADA SPOLECENSKYCH VED. 1891. irreg., vol.99, 1989. price varies. (Czechoslovak Academy of Sciences) Academia, Publishing House of the Czechoslovak Academy of Sciences, Vodickova 40, 112 29 Prague 1, Czechoslovakia. TEL 23-63-065. circ. 1,000. **Indexed**: Numis.Lit.
—BLDSC shelfmark: 8034.075000.

300　　　　　　　　US
CHEIRON NEWSLETTER. 1973. s-a. $10 to individuals; institutions $20. International Society for History of the Behavioral and Social Sciences, c/o Rare Books, Countway Library of Medicine, 10 Shattuck St., Boston, MA 02115. TEL 617-732-2170. (Co-sponsor: Cheiron Society) Ed. Eugene Taylor. adv.; bk.rev.; bibl.; circ. 500. (back issues avail.)
Description: Summarizes on-going research of historians in psychology and the behavioral and social sciences who are largely members of the Cheiron Society.

300 614.7　　　　　UK　ISSN 0144-9877
CHELMER WORKING PAPERS IN ENVIRONMENTAL PLANNING. 1979. irreg. Chelmer Institute of Higher Education, Faculty of Social Sciences, Department of Planning, Victoria Rd. S., Chelmsford, Essex CM1 1LL, England. Ed. David Crouch. **Indexed**: Geo.Abstr.

300　　　　　　　　CC
CHENGDU DAXUE XUEBAO (SHEHUI KEXUE BAN)/CHENGDU UNIVERSITY. JOURNAL (SOCIAL SCIENCE EDITION). (Text in Chinese) q. Y4.80. Chengdu Daxue - Chengdu University, Renmin Beilu, Chengdu, Sichuan 610081, People's Republic of China. (Dist. overseas by: China Publications Foreign Trade Corp., P.O. Box 782, Beijing, P.R.C.)
Description: Publishes research papers. Includes regular columns on Song dynasty literature, Sichuanese humanities, local literature and history, the Three Kingdoms and Zhuge Liang, political theses, economic and social development, library and information science, and Sichuan writers and their works.

300　　　　　　　　CC
CHENGSHI WENTI/URBAN ISSUES. (Text in Chinese) bi-m. Beijing Shehui Kexueyuan - Beijing Academy of Social Sciences, No.6, Chegongzhuang Dajie, Fuwai, Beijing 100044, People's Republic of China. TEL 890551.

300　　　　　　　　CC
CHENGSHI YANJIU/URBAN STUDIES. (Text in Chinese) bi-m. Taiyuan Shi Shehui Yanjiusuo, 20, Hanxiguan, Taiyuan, Shanxi 030002, People's Republic of China. TEL 345483. Ed. Yang Guangliang.

CHINA REPORT. see *POLITICAL SCIENCE — International Relations*

CHINESE SCHOLARLY WORKS IN ENGLISH. see *ORIENTAL STUDIES*

CHRISTIAN STATESMAN. see *RELIGIONS AND THEOLOGY*

CHRONIQUES D'ACTUALITE DE LA S.E.D.E.I.S. (Societe d'Etudes et de Documentation Economiques, Industrielles et Sociales) see *BUSINESS AND ECONOMICS — Economic Situation And Conditions*

CIENCIA. see *SCIENCES: COMPREHENSIVE WORKS*

SOCIAL SCIENCES: COMPREHENSIVE WORKS

300 BL ISSN 0304-2685
CIENCIA & TROPICO. (Abstracts in English and French) 1952. s-a. Cr.$1596 (effective Aug. 1991). (Fundacao Joaquim Nabuco) Editora Massangana, Rua Dois Irmaos, 15, Apipucos, 52071 Recife, Brazil. TEL 081-268-4611. FAX 081-268-9600. bk.rev.; abstr.; bibl.; charts; illus.; stat.; circ. 2,000.
Formerly (until 1971): Instituto Joaquim Nabuco de Pesquisas Sociais. Boletim.

300 CK
CIENCIAS SOCIALES. 1976. q. (Akademiya Nauk S.S.R., Social Sciences Section, UR) Centro de Estudios e Investigaciones Sociales, Calle 21 no. 17-42, Apdo. Aereo 11968, Bogota, Colombia. Ed. Alvaro Delgado Guzman.

300 BL
CIENCIAS SOCIAS HOJE (YEAR). irreg. (Associacao Nacional de Pos-Graduacao e Pesquisa en Ciencias Sociais) Cortez Editora, Rua Bartira, 387, 05009 Sao Paulo, SP, Brazil. Ed.Bd.

CIMARRON REVIEW. see *LITERATURE*

300 SX
CIMBEBASIA. SERIES B: CULTURAL HISTORY. (Text in English; summaries in French or German) 1962. irreg., vol.4, no.1, 1985. price varies. State Museum, Box 1203, Windhoek, Namibia. Ed. J. Kinahan. charts; illus.; circ. 400. (back issues avail.) **Indexed:** Ind.S.A.Per.

300 SX
CIMBEBASIA MEMOIRS. (Text mainly in English; summaries in French or German) 1967. irreg., no.6, 1985. price varies. State Museum, Box 1203, Windhoek, Namibia. Eds. H. Rust, J. Kinahan. circ. 400.

300 CE
CINTANA DHARA. (Text in Sinhalese) 1977. q. Rs.3.50. Pushparama Institute, Delkanda, Nugegoda, Sri Lanka.

CIRCOLO CULTURALE B.G. DUNS SCOTO DI ROCCARAINOLA. ATTI. see *ARCHAEOLOGY*

CIVILISATIONS ET SOCIETES. see *HISTORY — History Of Europe*

CIVILIZATION AND SOCIETY: STUDIES IN SOCIAL, ECONOMIC AND CULTURAL HISTORY. see *HISTORY*

300 NE ISSN 0587-5994
H1
COEXISTENCE; a review of East-West and development issues. (Text and summaries in English) 1963. q. $65.50 to individuals; institutions $144.50. Kluwer Academic Publishers, Postbus 17, 3300 AA Dordrecht, Netherlands. TEL 078-334911. FAX 078-334254. (Dist. by: Kluwer Academic Publishers Group, P.O. Box 322, 3300 AH Dordrecht, Netherlands; N. America dist. addr.: Box 358, Accord, Station, Hingham, MA 02018-0358. TEL 617-871-6600) Eds. S. White, R. Beerman. adv.; bk.rev.; index; circ. 700. (back issues avail.) **Indexed:** A.B.C.Pol.Sci., Amer.Hist.& Life, Curr.Cont., Hist.Abstr., Mid.East: Abstr.& Ind.
—BLDSC shelfmark: 3292.830000.

300 CL
COLECCION FE E HISTORIA. 1977. irreg. Instituto Latinoamericano de Doctrinas y Estudios Sociales, Departamento de Publicaciones, Almirante Barroso 6, Casilla 1446 Correo 21, Santiago, Chile.

COLOQUIO DE ESTUDOS LUSO BRASILEIROS. ANAIS. see *LINGUISTICS*

300 FI ISSN 0355-256X
COMMENTATIONES SCIENTIARUM SOCIALIUM. (Text in English, Finnish) 1972. irreg. price varies. Societas Scientiarum Fennicas - Finnish Society of Sciences and Letters, Marieg 5, SF-000170 Helsinki 17, Finland. Ed. Leif Nordberg. circ. 900. **Indexed:** Refug.Abstr.
—BLDSC shelfmark: 3336.010000.

300 EI
COMMISSION OF THE EUROPEAN COMMUNITIES. REPORT ON THE SOCIAL DEVELOPMENTS. (Published with its General Report on the Activities of the Communities) (Editions in Dutch, English, French, German) 1968. a. $25. Office for Official Publications of the European Communities, L-2985 Luxembourg, Luxembourg. (Dist. in U.S. by: Unipub, 4611-F Assembly Dr., Lanham, MD 20706-4391)
Former titles: Commission of the European Communities. Report on the Social Situation & Commission of the European Communities. Expose sur l'Evolution Sociale dans la Communaute (ISSN 0531-3724)

300 US
COMMUNITY COLLEGE SOCIAL SCIENCE NEWSLETTER. 1976. 5/yr. $25 to individuals; libraries $35; foreign $40. Community College Social Science Association, Grossmont College, Box 191303, San Diego, CA 92119. TEL 619-465-1700. Ed. Dr. Gerald Baydo. adv.; bk.rev.; film rev.; bibl.; charts; illus.; stat.; index; circ. 2,000. (tabloid format; also avail. in microform; reprint service avail. from UMI) **Indexed:** C.I.J.E.
Formerly (until vol.3): Community College Social Science Journal; Supersedes (in Oct. 1976): Community College Social Science Quarterly (ISSN 0045-7728)

301 410 UK ISSN 0143-7704
COMMUNITY STUDIES SERIES. 1980. irreg. price varies. University of Sheffield, Centre for English Cultural Tradition and Language, Sheffield S10 2TN, England. Ed. J.D.A. Widdowson. bk.rev.; circ. 1,000.
—BLDSC shelfmark: 3363.677500.

300 IT
COMO; cultura, turismo, commercio, industria. 1955. q. L.15000. Domenico Discacciati, Via Carloni 8, 22100 Como, Italy. Ed. Alberto Longatti. adv.; circ. 3,200.

CONCEPTOS BOLETIN. see *SOCIOLOGY*

055.1 IT ISSN 0010-5228
CONCILIATORE. 1952. q. L.7000. Corso di Porta Vittoria 32, 20122 Milan, Italy. Ed. Jose Franchini. adv.; bk.rev.; play rev.; bibl.; illus.; stat.

301
CONFERENCE GROUP FOR SOCIAL AND ADMINISTRATIVE HISTORY. TRANSACTIONS.* 1971. s-a. $5. Conference Group for Social and Administrative History, 639 Wisconsin St., Oshkosh, WI 54901. Ed. Werner Braatz. circ. 200. **Indexed:** Hist.Abstr.

CONFUCIUS & MENCIUS SOCIETY OF THE REPUBLIC OF CHINA. JOURNAL. see *RELIGIONS AND THEOLOGY — Buddhist*

300 CK
CONGRESO INTERNACIONAL DE VIVIENDA POPULAR. irreg.?, no.3, 1974. Col.$90. (Servicio Latino-Americano y Asiatico de Vivienda Popular) Centro de Investigacion y Educacion Popular, Carrera 5 No.33A-08, Apdo. Aereo 25916, Bogota, Colombia. TEL 2858977.

CONNEXIONS DIGEST; a social change sourcebook. see *POLITICAL SCIENCE*

CONSORTIUM ON REVOLUTIONARY EUROPE PROCEEDINGS. see *HISTORY — History Of Europe*

300 350 UK ISSN 0951-4937
HN398.W26
CONTEMPORARY WALES; an annual review of economic and social research. 1987. a. £7.50($14) University of Wales Press, 6 Gwennyth St., Cathay, Cardiff CF2 4YD, Wales. TEL 0222-231919. FAX 0222-230908. (Subscr. in U.S.: Books International Inc., P.O. Box 6096, McLean, VA 22106) (Co-sponsor: Board of Celtic Studies) Eds. Graham Day, Gareth Rees. adv.; stat.; circ. 500. (back issues avail.)
—BLDSC shelfmark: 3425.315000.
Description: An authoritative analysis of economic and social development in Wales.

CONTINUUM. see *HUMANITIES: COMPREHENSIVE WORKS*

300 BL
CONTRIBUICOES EM CIENCIAS SOCIAIS. irreg. Editora Campus Ltda. (Subsidiary of: Elsevier Science Publishers B.V.), Rua Barao de Itapagipe 55, Rio Comprido, 20261 Rio de Janeiro RJ, Brazil.

CONTRIBUTIONS IN LATIN AMERICAN STUDIES. see *HISTORY — History Of North And South America*

300 TZ
COUNCIL FOR THE SOCIAL SCIENCES IN EAST AFRICA. SOCIAL SCIENCE CONFERENCE. PROCEEDINGS. a. EAs.200($29) c/o University of Dar-es-Salaam, Faculty of Arts and Social Science, Box 35091, Dar-es-Salaam, Tanzania. charts; stat.

CRIME, LAW, AND DEVIANCE SERIES. see *CRIMINOLOGY AND LAW ENFORCEMENT*

300 PE
CRITICA ANDINA. 1978. irreg. $12 to individuals; institutions $18. Instituto de Estudios Sociales, Director de Publicaciones, Casilla Postal 790, Cusco, Peru. Dir. Marco Villasante. adv.; bk.rev.; circ. 2,000.

330 US
CRITICAL PERSPECTIVES IN SOCIAL THEORY. 1983. irreg. price varies. Praeger Publishers (Subsidiary of: Greenwood Publishing Group Inc.), 88 Post Rd. W., Box 5007, Westport, CT 06881-5007. TEL 203-226-3571. FAX 203-222-1502.

300 PE
CUADERNOS DE CAPACITACION CAMPESINA. 1975. irreg., latest no.5040. price varies. Centro de Estudios Regionales Andinos "Bartolome de Las Casas", Apdo. 4779, Cusco, Peru. TEL 084-236494. FAX 084-238255.
Formerly: Cuadernos de Capacitacion Popular.

300 SP
CUADERNOS DE ESTUDIOS GALLEGOS. a. 3000 ptas. (foreign 4500 ptas.). Consejo Superior de Investigaciones Cientificas (C.S.I.C.), C. Vitruvio 8, 28006 Madrid, Spain. TEL 261-28-33. FAX 262-96-34.

300 AG
CUADERNOS DE HISTORIA REGIONAL. 1984. 4/yr. price varies or exchange basis. (Universidad Nacional de Lujan, Departamento de Ciencias Sociales) Editorial Universitaria de Buenos Aires, Casilla de Correo 221, 6700 Lujan, Argentina. bk.rev.

CULTURA NACIONAL; revista bimestrale de politica y ciencias sociales. see *POLITICAL SCIENCE*

300 II ISSN 0011-2895
CULTURAL RESEARCH INSTITUTE. BULLETIN. (Text in Bengali or English) 1962. a. Rs.20. Cultural Research Institute, P1-4, C.I.T. Scheme, VIIM, V.I.P. Road, P.O. Kankurgachi, Calcutta 700054, India. (Affiliate: West Bengal. Sch. Castes & Tribal Welfare Department) Ed.Bd. bk.rev.; bibl.; charts; illus.; stat.; circ. 1,000. **Indexed:** A.I.C.P.

960 800 301 410 ZR ISSN 0302-5640
DT641
CULTURES AU ZAIRE ET EN AFRIQUE. Abbreviated title: Cultures. (Text in English, French) 1973. q. $16. Office National de la Recherche et du Developpement, Section des Sciences de l'Homme, B.P. 16706, Kinshasa 1, Zaire. bk.rev.; bibl.
Supersedes: Dombi.

CULTURES DU CANADA FRANCAIS. see *HISTORY — History Of North And South America*

CURRENT RESEARCH IN BRITISH STUDIES BY AMERICAN AND CANADIAN SCHOLARS. see *HUMANITIES: COMPREHENSIVE WORKS — Abstracting, Bibliographies, Statistics*

CYCLES (IRVINE). see *BUSINESS AND ECONOMICS — Economic Systems And Theories, Economic History*

SOCIAL SCIENCES: COMPREHENSIVE WORKS

300   CY   ISSN 1015-2881
THE CYPRUS REVIEW; a journal of social, economic and political issues. (Text in English) 1989. q. $20 to individuals; institutions $30. Intercollege, P.O. Box 4005, Nicosia, Cyprus. TEL 02-456892. FAX 02-456704. TELEX 4969 INTERCOL CY. (Co-sponsor: University of Indianapolis) adv.; bk.rev.; circ. 150. **Indexed:** Int.Bibli.Soc.Sci., Int.Polit.Sci.Abstr., P.A.I.S., Peace Res.Abstr., Polit.Sci.Abstr., Sociol.Abstr.
●Also available online. Vendor(s): BRS, Data-Star, DIALOG.
    Description: Middle Eastern scholarly journal facilitating small state research, and devoted to an examination of Cyprus social issues.

D L S U DIALOGUE. (De La Salle University) see HUMANITIES: COMPREHENSIVE WORKS

300 500   PH   ISSN 0115-6640
D L S U GRADUATE JOURNAL. (Text in English and Pilipino) 1987. s-a. P.85($10.50) (De La Salle University, Graduate School of Education, Arts and Sciences) De La Salle University Press, 2401 Taft Ave., Manila, Philippines. TEL 2-595177. Ed. Isagani Cruz. adv.; bk.rev.; circ. 500.
    Description: Publishes scholarly articles reflecting significant quantitative or qualitative research. Includes speeches, research reports, and "state of the art" papers.

300   AG
DAVID Y GOLIATH. 1970. irreg. $23. Consejo Latinoamericano de Ciencias Sociales, Callao 875, 1023 Buenos Aires, Argentina. Ed.Bd. bibl.; circ. 2,000.
    Formerly: C L A C S O Boletin (ISSN 0325-0431)

619 300 200   US   ISSN 0748-285X
R726.8
DEATH AND DYING; opposing viewpoints sources. 1984. a. $10.95 (sourcebook $39.95). Greenhaven Press, Inc., Box 289009, San Diego, CA 92198-0009. TEL 619-485-7424. FAX 619-485-9549. Ed. Bruno Leone. (back issues avail.)
    Description: Covers euthanasia, teen suicide, organ donation, living wills, right to die.

300   PE
DEBATES ANDINOS. irreg., latest no.3018. Centro de Estudios Regionales Andinos "Bartolome de Las Casas", Apdo. 477, Cusco, Peru. TEL 084-236494. FAX 084-238255.

300 900 400   II   ISSN 0045-9801
DECCAN COLLEGE. POSTGRADUATE & RESEARCH INSTITUTE. BULLETIN. (Text in English) a. $30. Deccan College, Postgraduate & Research Institute, Poona 411006, India. bk.rev.; circ. 500. (back issues avail.) **Indexed:** GeoRef.

DELFIN; eine deutsche Zeitschrift fuer Konstruktion, Analyse und Kritik. see ART

DERECHO Y CIENCIAS SOCIALES. see LAW

DESARROLLO ECONOMICO - REVISTA DE CIENCIAS SOCIALES. see BUSINESS AND ECONOMICS — International Development And Assistance

300   GW   ISSN 0341-7239
DEUTSCH-BRASILIANISCHE HEFTE. (Text and summaries in German, Portuguese) 1960. bi-m. DM.48. Lateinamerika-Zentrum e.V., Schumannstr. 2b, 5300 Bonn 1, Germany. TEL 0228-210788. Ed. Hermann M. Goergen. adv.; bk.rev.; circ. 8,000. **Indexed:** Maize Abstr., Soyabean Abstr., World Agri.Econ.& Rural Sociol.Abstr.

300 338   UK   ISSN 0012-155X
HD82
DEVELOPMENT AND CHANGE. 1969. q. £33($54) to individuals; institutions £90($149). (Institute of Social Studies, The Hague, NE) Sage Publications Ltd., 6 Bonhill St., London EC2A 4PU, England. TEL 071-374-0645. FAX 071-374-8741. Ed.Bd. adv.: color page £190; trim 177 x 101; adv. contact: Bernie Folan. bk.rev.; charts. **Indexed:** A.B.C.Pol.Sci., Amer.Hist.& Life, ASSIA, Commun.Abstr., Curr.Cont., E.I., Energy Ind., Energy Info.Abstr., Hist.Abstr., HR Rep., I D A, Int.Lab.Doc., J.of Econ.Lit., Key to Econ.Sci., Mid.East: Abstr.& Ind., Rice Abstr., Rural Devel.Abstr., Rural Ext.Educ.& Tr.Abstr., Rural Recreat.Tour.Abstr., Sage Fam.Stud.Abstr., Sage Urb.Stud.Abstr., SSCI, World Agri.Econ. & Rural Sociol.Abstr.
—BLDSC shelfmark: 3578.750000.
    Description: Contributes to the understanding of Third World problems. Publishes critical analysis and articles from all disciplines of the social sciences discussing current development issues.

DHAKA UNIVERSITY STUDIES. PART A: ARTS, HUMANITIES, AND SOCIAL SCIENCE. see HUMANITIES: COMPREHENSIVE WORKS

300   MX
DIALECTICA. 1976-1986; resumed 1987. 3/yr. Mex.$7500. Universidad Autonoma de Puebla, Escuela de Filosofia y Letras, Maxima Avila Camacho 229, C.P. 72000, Puebla, Mexico. Ed.Bd. bk.rev.; circ. 2,500. (tabloid format; back issues avail.)

300   AU
DIALOG. BEITRAEGE ZUR FRIEDENSFORSCHUNG. q. $51.50. Verband der Wissenschaftlichen Gesellschaften Oesterreichs, Lindengasse 37, A-1070 Vienna, Austria. TEL 932166.

DIALOGUE. see LITERATURE

300 325   US   ISSN 1044-2057
▼**DIASPORA: A JOURNAL OF TRANSNATIONAL STUDIES**. 1991. q. $24.50 to individuals (foreign $34.50); institutions $49 (foreign $59). Oxford University Press, Journals, 200 Madison Ave., New York, NY 10016. TEL 212-679-7300. FAX 212-725-2972. TELEX 6859654. (Subscr. to: Journals Fulfillment, 2001 Evans Rd., Cary, NC 27513. TEL 919-677-0977) Ed. Khachig Tololyan.
—BLDSC shelfmark: 3580.230000.
    Description: Publishes essays on diasporas and other transnational and infranational phenomena that challenge the homogeneity of the nation-state. Includes specific accounts of ancient and contemporary diasporal communities, their relations with real and imagined homelands, as well as their literatures, cultural productions, social structures, politics, and history.

300   UK   ISSN 0263-3221
DITCHLEY CONFERENCE REPORTS. 1981. 15/yr. Ditchley Foundation, Enstone, Chipping Norton, Oxfordshire OX7 4ER, England. TEL 0608-677346. FAX 0608-677399. (U.S. subscr. to: American Ditchley Foundation, 477 Madison Ave., 6th Fl., NY 10022) Ed. Heather Weeks.

300 340   UK   ISSN 0262-8015
DITCHLEY NEWSLETTER. 1981. 3/yr. Ditchley Foundation, Enstone, Chipping Norton, Oxfordshire OX7 4ER, England. TEL 0608-677346. FAX 0608-677399. (U.S. subscr. to: American Ditchley Foundation, 477 Madison Ave., 6th Fl., NY 10022) Ed. Heather Weeks. adv.; bibl.; index; circ. 1,000.
    Supersedes: Ditchley Journal (ISSN 0305-4322)

300   SP
DOCUMENTACION SOCIAL; revista de estudios sociales y de sociologia aplicada. no.13, 1974. 4/yr. 1400 ptas.($65) Caritas Espanola, San Bernardo, 99 bis, 7, 28015 Madrid, Spain. TEL (91) 445 53 00. **Indexed:** SCIMP (1989-), World Agri.Econ.& Rural Sociol.Abstr.

940   GW   ISSN 0340-3297
AS181
DOKUMENTATION OSTMITTELEUROPA. 1951; N.S. 1975. bi-m. DM.32.80. J.G.-Herder-Institut, Gisonenweg 5-7, 3550 Marburg-Lahn, Germany. circ. 550. **Indexed:** CERDIC, P.A.I.S.For.Lang.Ind.
    Formerly: Wissenschaftlicher Dienst fuer Ostmitteleuropa (ISSN 0043-6941)

DOKUMENTATIONSDIENST VORDERER ORIENT. REIHE A. see BIBLIOGRAPHIES

300 100   CC
DONGBEI SHIDA XUEBAO (ZHEXUE SHEHUI KEXUE BAN)/NORTHEAST NORMAL UNIVERSITY. JOURNAL (PHILOSOPHY, SOCIAL SCIENCE EDITION). (Text in Chinese) 1951. bi-m. Y9. Dongbei Shifan Daxue, Xuebao Bianjibu, 110, Stalin Street, Changchun, Jilin 130024, People's Republic of China.
    Description: Publishes research results in philosophy, political science, economics, history, education, linguistics, and literature.

300   CC   ISSN 1001-0505
DONGNAN DAXUE XUEBAO/SOUTHEAST UNIVERSITY. JOURNAL. (Text in Chinese) bi-m. Dongnan Daxue - Southeast University, Sibai Lou, Nanjing, Jiangsu 2100627, People's Republic of China. TEL 631700. Ed. Hong Wenkui.

300   CC
DONGNAN YA ZONGHENG. (Text in Chinese) q. Guangxi Shehui Kexueyuan, Dongnan Ya Yanjiusuo - Guangxi Academy of Social Sciences, Southeast Asian Studies Institute, No. 30, Xinzhu Lu, Nanning, Guangxi 530022, People's Republic of China. TEL 20584. Ed. Zhao Heman.

300   CC
DONG'OU/EASTERN EUROPE. (Text in Chinese) q. Beijing Waiyu Xueyuan - Beijing Foreign Language Institute, No.2, Xisanhuan Beilu, Beijing 100081, People's Republic of China. TEL 890351. Ed. Yang Yanjie.

300   CC
DONGYUE LUNCONG/DONGYUE TRIBUNE. (Text in Chinese) bi-m. $35.60. Shandong Sheng Shehui Kexueyuan - Shandong Academy of Social Sciences, No. 28, Yuhan Lu, Jinan, Shandong 250002, People's Republic of China. TEL 615540. (Dist. in US by: China Books & Periodicals, Inc., 2929 24th St., San Francisco, CA 94110. TEL 415-282-2994) Ed. Guo Molan.

149.3   GW   ISSN 0012-6063
DIE DREI; Zeitschrift fuer Anthroposophie. 1921. m. DM.59. (Anthroposophische Gesellschaft in Deutschland) Verlag Freies Geistesleben GmbH, Haussmannstr. 76, 7000 Stuttgart, Germany. TEL 0711-283255. FAX 0711-2624606. Ed. Dietrich Rapp. adv.; bk.rev.; abstr.; illus.; index; circ. 5,000.

DROIT SOCIAL. see LAW

300   MX
DUDA; lo increible es la verdad. w. Editorial Posada, S.A., Oculistas No. 43, Col. El Sifon, 09400 Mexico, D.F., Mexico.

500   HU   ISSN 0139-3669
E C S S I D BULLETIN. (Text in English) 1979. irreg. free. (European Coordination Centre for Research and Documentation in Social Science) Magyar Tudomanyos Akademia Konyvtara, Aranyjanos u.1, P.O. Box 7, 1361 Budapest 5, Hungary. Ed. G. Rossa.
—BLDSC shelfmark: 3659.637000.

300   UK   ISSN 0732-5819
E F L GAZETTE. 1978. m. $36. Loopformat Ltd., 10 Wrights Lane, Kensington, London W8 6TA, England. TEL 01-938-1818. FAX 01-937-7534. Ed. Melanie Butler. adv.; bk.rev.; circ. 5,000. (also avail. in microform from UMI,MIM) **Indexed:** Lang.Teach.& Ling.Abstr.

300   UK   ISSN 0736-2048
E L T DOCUMENTS.* 3/yr. MacMillan Magazines, Brunel Rd., Houndsmills, Basingstoke, Hants. RG21 2XS, England. Ed. C.J. Brumfit. (also avail. in microform from UMI,MIM) **Indexed:** Lang.& Lang.Behav.Abstr., Lang.Teach.& Ling.Abstr.
—BLDSC shelfmark: 3732.450000.

300   UK
E S R C DATA ARCHIVE BULLETIN. 1975. 3/yr. free. University of Essex, Economic and Social Research Council Data Archive, Colchester CO4 3SQ, England. TEL 0206-872003. FAX 0206-873598. TELEX 98440 UNILIB G. Ed. Bridget Winstanley. adv.; bk.rev.; circ. 4,000.
    Former titles: S S R C Data Archive Bulletin; S S R C Survey Archive Bulletin (ISSN 0307-1391)

SOCIAL SCIENCES: COMPREHENSIVE WORKS 4371

E S R C STUDENTSHIP HANDBOOK; postgraduate studentships in the social sciences. (Economic and Social Research Council) see EDUCATION — Guides To Schools And Colleges

EARTHWATCH. see SCIENCES: COMPREHENSIVE WORKS

300   TZ   ISSN 0424-0928
EAST AFRICAN STUDIES.* 1953. irreg. (Makerere University, Makerere Institute of Social Research, UG) East African Publishing House, POB 3209, Dores Salaam, Tanzania. charts.

EAST ASIAN SOCIAL SCIENCE MONOGRAPHS. see HISTORY — History Of Asia

940 947   US   ISSN 0012-8449
DR1
EAST EUROPEAN QUARTERLY. (Text in English, French, German) 1967. q. $15. University of Colorado, Box 29, Regent Hall, Boulder, CO 80309. TEL 813-753-4782. Ed. Stephen Fischer-Galati. adv.; bk.rev.; circ. 900. (also avail. in microform from UMI; reprint service avail. from UMI) **Indexed:** Amer.Bibl.Slavic & E.Eur.Stud., Amer.Hist.& Life, Curr.Cont., Hist.Abstr., Mid.East: Abstr.& Ind., P.A.I.S., RILA, Soc.Sci.Ind., SSCI.
—BLDSC shelfmark: 3646.320000.

ECONOMIC AND SOCIAL REVIEW. see BUSINESS AND ECONOMICS

300 330   FR   ISSN 0245-9132
HB3
ECONOMIE ET HUMANISME. 1942. q. 250 F. (foreign 330 F.). Economie et Humanisme, 14 rue Antoine Dumont, 69372 Lyon Cedex 08, France. TEL 78-61-32-23. FAX 78-69-86-96. Ed. Ph. Blancher. adv.; bk.rev.; bibl.; charts; illus.; index; circ. 5,000. **Indexed:** C.I.S. Abstr., Geo.Abstr., Int.Lab.Doc., Key to Econ.Sci., P.A.I.S.For.Lang.Ind., Pt.de Rep. (1979-), World Agri.Econ.& Rural Sociol.Abstr.
—BLDSC shelfmark: 3657.510000.
Description: Aims at providing information and reflexion to non-specialists about major socio-economic world issues.

320.351   UK   ISSN 0308-5147
ECONOMY AND SOCIETY. 1972. q. £34($68) Routledge, 11 New Fetter Lane, London EC4P 4EE, England. TEL 01-583 9855. Ed.Bd. adv.; bk.rev.; index. (also avail. in microform from UMI; reprint service avail. from UMI) **Indexed:** ASSIA, E.I., Lang.& Lang.Behav.Abstr., Mid.East: Abstr.& Ind., Sociol.Abstr. (1972-), SSCI, World Bank.Abstr.
—BLDSC shelfmark: 3659.520000.
Description: Presents Marxist-based scholarship and analysis in a variety of fields. Discussions span the social sciences, history, philosophy, economics, and literary criticism.

300   SP
EDICIONES PENINSULA. SERIE UNIVERSITARIA. HISTORIA, CIENCIA, SOCIEDAD. 1966. irreg. Ediciones 62, S.A., Provença 278, 08008 Barcelona, Spain. TEL 216-00-62.

EDUCATIONAL BOOK REVIEW. see HUMANITIES: COMPREHENSIVE WORKS

300   ER
EESTI TEADUSTE AKADEEMIA. TOIMETISED. UHISKONNATEADUSED/ESTONIAN ACADEMY OF SCIENCES. PROCEEDINGS. SOCIAL SCIENCES. (Text and summaries in English, Estonian, French, Russian) 1956. q. $22 (effective 1992). Kirjastus Perioodika, Parnu mnt. 8, pk.107, 200090 Tallinn, Estonia. TEL 0142-441-262. FAX 0142-442-484. (Subscr. to: Akateeminen Kirjakauppa 128 SF, 00101 Helsinki, Finland; or to: Bibliotekstajanst AB 200, S22100 Lund, Sweden) index; circ. 700.
Formerly: Akademiya Nauk Estonskoi S.S.R. Izvestiya. Obshchestvennye Nauki (ISSN 0373-6431)

300   US
THE EGG; an eco-justice quarterly. 1981. q. $10. Center for Religion, Ethics, and Social Policy, Anabel Taylor Hall, Cornell University, Ithaca, NY 14853. TEL 607-255-4225. FAX 607-255-2920. Ed. Dieter Hessel. bk.rev.; circ. 4,500.
Description: Promotes understanding and action on issues of ecology and social justice understood as inseparable.

300   CS
EKONOMIKA PRACE; casopis pre otazky riadenia a teorie prace. (Text in Czech or Slovak; summaries in English, Russian) 1968. bi-m. 48 Kcs.($24) (Federalne Ministerstvo Prace a Socialnych Veci Praha) Praca, Publishing House of the Slovak Trade Unions Council, Stefanikava19, 812 71 Bratislava, Czechoslovakia. TEL 7-333779. FAX 7-220046. (Subscr. to: PNS, Gottwaldovo nam. 6, 813 84 Bratislava, Czechoslovakia) (Co-sponsor: Vyskumny Ustav Socialneho Rozvoja a Prace Bratislava) Ed. Vladimir Zvolensky. bk.rev.; abstr.; bibl.; index; circ. 4,200. **Indexed:** Ergon.Abstr., Psychol.Abstr.
Formerly (until 1982): Synteza (ISSN 0586-3260)

ELDERS; een kroniek van zaken buiten de grenzen. see POPULATION STUDIES

300   ZR
ELIMU;* revue des sciences humaines. 1973. q. Universite Nationale du Zaire, Lubumbashi, B.P. 945, Lubumbashi, Zaire.
Supersedes: Syntheses.

ENCOUNTERS; a quincentenary review. see HISTORY — History Of North And South America

ENCYCLOPAEDIA AFRICANA. INFORMATION REPORT. see HISTORY — History Of Africa

ENTOURAGE. see MEDICAL SCIENCES — Psychiatry And Neurology

ESSAYS ON THE ECONOMY AND SOCIETY OF THE SUDAN. see BUSINESS AND ECONOMICS — Economic Situation And Conditions

300   HO
ESTIQUIRIN; arte-ciencia-literatura. bi-m. Editorial Guaymuras, Apdo. Postal 1843, Tegucigalpa, Honduras. Ed.Bd.

300   PE
▼**ESTUDIOS ANDINOS.** 1990. irreg., no. 3101, 1990. price varies. Centro de Estudios Regionales Andinos "Bartolome de las Casas", Apdo. 477, Cusco, Peru. TEL 084-236494. FAX 084-238255.

972.8 300   ES   ISSN 0014-1445
AP63   CODEN: ESCEES
ESTUDIOS CENTRO AMERICANOS. 1946. m. Col.50($40) Universidad Centroamericana "Jose Simeon Canas", Apdo. Postal (01) 575, San Salvador, El Salvador. FAX 503-24-0288. Ed. Ignacio Ellacuna. adv.; bk.rev.; charts; illus.; index; circ. 3,000. **Indexed:** Amer.Hist.& Life, Hist.Abstr.
—BLDSC shelfmark: 3812.738000.

300   SP   ISSN 0423-4847
ESTUDIOS DE DEUSTO. 1953. s-a. 2500 ptas.($30) Universidad de Deusto, Aptdo. 1, 48080 Bilbao, Spain. Ed. Ignacio Beobide. bk.rev.; adv.; index; circ. 400. (back issues avail.) **Indexed:** Amer.Hist.& Life, CERDIC, Hist.Abstr.

300   SP   ISSN 0210-1416
ESTUDIOS DE HISTORIA SOCIAL. (Former name of issuing body: Instituto de Estudios de Sanidad y Seguridad Social) 1977. q. 6000 ptas.($50) Ministerio de Trabajo y Seguridad Social, Centro de Publicaciones, Agustin de Bethencourt 11, 28003 Madrid, Spain. circ. 1,000.

378   CL   ISSN 0716-0321
HC191
ESTUDIOS SOCIALES. (Text in Spanish; abstracts in English) 1973. q. Esc.2500($48) Corporacion de Promocion Universitaria, Avda. Miguel Claro 1460, Casilla 1056, Correo 22, Santiago, Chile. FAX 2741828. (Co-sponsor: Fundacion Konrad Adenauer) Ed.Bd. adv.; bk.rev.; abstr.; charts; stat.; circ. 1,500. **Indexed:** Hisp.Amer.Per.Ind., Hist.Abstr., Rural Devel.Abstr.
Description: Scholarly articles on employment, education, politics and social sciences.

300   CR   ISSN 0303-9676
ESTUDIOS SOCIALES CENTROAMERICANOS. 1972. 3/yr. Cr.$250($8) (or exchange basis). Confederacion Universitaria Centro-Americana, Apdo. 37, Ciudad "Rodrigo Facio", San Jose, Costa Rica. TEL 252744. FAX 220478. TELEX 3011 COSUCA. Ed. Mario Lungo Uclesio S. adv.; bk.rev.; bibl.; charts; stat.; cum.index every 4 yrs.; circ. 2,000. (also avail. in microfiche) **Indexed:** Amer.Hist.& Life, Hisp.Amer.Per.Ind., Hist.Abstr., Int.Lab.Doc., SSCI.

300 869   BL   ISSN 0103-1821
ESTUDOS PORTUGUESES E AFRICANOS. 1983. s-a. $25. Universidade Estadual de Campinas, Instituto de Estudos da Linguagem, Caixa Postal 6045, 13081 Campinas SP, Brazil. FAX 55-192-391501. Ed. Antonio Alcir Bernardes Pecora.
Description: Presents studies in Portuguese culture and literature written in Portuguese in African countries.

300   GW   ISSN 0937-938X
▼**ETHIK UND SOZIALWISSENSCHAFTEN;** Streitforum fuer Erwaegungskultur. (Text in German; summaries in English) 1990. q. DM.98. Westdeutscher Verlag GmbH, Postfach 5829, 6200 Wiesbaden 1, Germany. TEL 0611-160230. FAX 0611-160229. index; circ. 500. (back issues avail.)

300   US   ISSN 0162-3095
BF1   CODEN: ETSOD8
ETHOLOGY AND SOCIOBIOLOGY. 1979. 6/yr. $271 to institutions (foreign $299)(effective 1992). Elsevier Science Publishing Co., Inc. (New York), 655 Ave. of the Americas, New York, NY 10010. TEL 212-989-5800. FAX 212-633-3965. TELEX 420643 AEP UI. Ed.Bd. (also avail. in microform from RPI; reprint service avail. from SWZ) **Indexed:** ASSIA, Curr.Adv.Ecol.Sci., Curr.Cont., Excerp.Med., Lang.& Lang.Behav.Abstr., Psychol.Abstr., Risk Abstr., S.S.C.I., Sociol.Abstr.
—BLDSC shelfmark: 3815.250000.
Description: Publishes new studies on ethological and sociobiological theories using comparative data, experimental results and literature reviews.

300   AT
ETHOS ANNUAL. (Supplement to: Ethos Papers) 1971. a. Victorian Association of Social Studies Teachers Inc., P.O. Box 91, Balaclava, Vic. 3183, Australia. adv.; circ. 1,500.
Supersedes in part: Ethos.

300   AT
ETHOS PAPERS; ideas for the classroom. (Supplement avail.: Ethos Annual) 1982. 3/yr. Aus.$50 to individuals; corporations $90. Victorian Association of Social Studies Teachers Inc., P.O. Box 91, Balaclava, Vic. 3183, Australia. adv.; bk.rev.; circ. 1,500.
Supersedes in part: Ethos.

300 500   FR
ETUDES SCIENTIFIQUES. bi-m. Peres Jesuites, c/o Mme Irene Kher, 8 av. Cesar-Caire, 75008 Paris, France.

980 300   NE   ISSN 0924-0608
F1401
EUROPEAN REVIEW OF LATIN AMERICAN AND CARIBBEAN STUDIES/REVISTA EUROPEA DE ESTUDIOS LATINOAMERICANOS Y DEL CARIBE. (Text in English and Spanish) 1965. s-a. fl.40($23) to individuals; institutions fl. 90($55). Interuniversitair Centrum voor Studie en Documentatie van Latijns Amerika - Center for Latin American Research and Documentation, Keizersgracht 397, 1016 EK Amsterdam, Netherlands. TEL 31-205253498. FAX 31-206255127. (Co-sponsor: Royal Institute of Linguistics and Anthropology) Ed. K. Willingham. adv.; bk.rev.; bibl.; charts; circ. 1,500. (also avail. in microfiche from IDC; back issues avail) **Indexed:** Amer.Hist.& Life, Hisp.Amer.Per.Ind., Hist.Abstr., Int.Lab.Doc., Key to Econ.Sci., P.A.I.S.For.Lang.Ind., P.A.I.S.
—BLDSC shelfmark: 3829.951000.
Former titles (until 1989): Boletin de Estudios Latinoamericanos y del Caribe (ISSN 0304-2634); Boletin de Estudios Latinoamericanos; Boletin Informativo sobre Estudios Latinoamericanos en Europa (ISSN 0006-6397)
Description: Addresses major debates and problems of historical interpretations in social science research of the Caribbean and Latin America.

EUROPEAN STUDIES. see HISTORY — History Of Europe

943   US   ISSN 0046-2802
D1050.82.U6
EUROPEAN STUDIES NEWSLETTER. 1972. bi-m. $30 to institutions. Council for European Studies, Columbia University, Box 44, Schermerhorn, New York, NY 10027. FAX 212-854-4172. Ed. Marion A. Kaplan. adv.; bk.rev.; bibl.; circ. 1,500.

SOCIAL SCIENCES: COMPREHENSIVE WORKS

300 US ISSN 0149-7189
H62.A1
EVALUATION AND PROGRAM PLANNING; an international journal. 1978. q. £155 (effective 1992). Pergamon Press, Inc., Journals Division, 660 White Plains Rd., Tarrytown, NY 10591-5153. TEL 914-524-9200. FAX 914-333-2444. (And: Headington Hill Hall, Oxford OX3 0BW, England. TEL 0865-794141) Ed. Jonathan A. Morell. adv.; circ. 1,400. (also avail. in microform from MIM,UMI) Indexed: Abstr.Health Care Manage.Stud., C.I.J.E., CINAHL, Curr.Cont., E.I., Excerp.Med., Med.Care Rev., Psychol.Abstr., Rural Ext.Educ.& Tr.Abstr., Sociol.Abstr.
—BLDSC shelfmark: 3830.565000.
Description: Assists evaluators and planners to better practice their professions.
Refereed Serial

300 US ISSN 0886-1633
H1
EVALUATION PRACTICE. 1980. q. $34 to non-members; institutions $75. (American Evaluation Association) J A I Press Inc., P.O. Box 1678, 55 Old Post Rd., Greenwich, CT 06836. TEL 805-499-0721. Ed. M.F. Midge Smith. adv.; bk.rev. **Indexed:** Educ.Admin.Abstr., Sage Pub.Admin.Abstr., Sociol.Abstr.
Former titles (until 1986): Evaluation News; E N. Evaluation News (ISSN 0191-8036)

300 US ISSN 0193-841X
HM1
EVALUATION REVIEW; a journal of applied social research. 1977. bi-m. $52 to individuals; institutions $144. Sage Publications, Inc., 2455 Teller Rd., Newbury Park, CA 91320. TEL 805-499-0721. FAX 805-499-0871. (U.K. addr.: Sage Publications, Ltd., 6 Bonhill St., London EC2A 4PU, England) Eds. Richard A. Berk, Howard E. Freeman. adv.; bk.rev.; abstr.; index; circ. 1,500. (also avail. in microform from UMI; back issues avail.) **Indexed:** Abstr.Health Care Manage.Stud., Adol.Ment.Hlth.Abstr., C.I.J.E., C.L.I., Crim.Just.Abstr., Curr.Cont., Curr.Lit.Fam.Plan., HRIS, L.R.I., Mid.East: Abstr.& Ind., P.A.I.S., Psychol.Abstr., Risk Abstr., Sage Fam.Stud.Abstr., Sage Pub.Admin.Abstr., Soc.Sci.Ind., Soc.Work Res.& Abstr., Sociol.Abstr., SSCI, World Agri.Econ.& Rural Sociol.Abstr.
—BLDSC shelfmark: 3830.618500.
Formerly (until vol.4, Feb. 1980): Evaluation Quarterly (ISSN 0145-4692)

300 VE
F A C E S. 1976. bi-m. Universidad Central de Venezuela, Facultad de Ciencias Economicas y Sociales, Caracas, Venezuela. Ed. Jose Eliseo Lopez.

300 914.4 CC
FAGUO YANJIU/ETUDES FRANCAISES. (Text in Chinese and French) 1983. irreg. (2-4/yr.) $12. (Wuhan Daxue, Faguo Wenti Yanjiusuo) Wuhan Daxue Chubanshe - Wuhan University Press, Luo Jia Shan, Wuchang, Hubei 430072, People's Republic of China. TEL 812723-840. (Dist. in US by: China Books & Periodicals, Inc., 2929 24th St., San Francisco, CA 94110) bk.rev.; circ. 2,000.
Description: Covers French social sciences. Contains articles, translations, and original records on French language, literature, history, philosophy, politics, and economics. Includes columns on academic activities and personal profiles.

300 IT
FAMIGLIA. 1965. bi-m. L.38000. Editrice la Scuola S.p.A., Via Cadorna 11, 25186 Brescia, Italy. Ed. Mario Cattaneo.

368.4 FI ISSN 0430-5205
FINLAND. KANSANELAKELAITOS. JULKAISUJA. SARJA A. (Text in Finnish and English; summaries in English) 1967. irreg., no.A25, 1990. Kansanelakelaitos - Social Insurance Institution of Finland, Research Institute for Social Security, P.O. Box 78, SF 00381 Helsinki 38, Finland. bibl.

610 368 FI ISSN 0355-4848
FINLAND. KANSANELAKELAITOS. JULKAISUJA. SARJA E. (Text in English and Finnish) 1967. irreg., no.E143, 1991. Kansanelakelaitos - Social Insurance Institution of Finland, Research Institute for Social Security, P.O. Box 78, SF-00381 Helsinki 38, Finland.

610 368.4 FI ISSN 0355-4821
FINLAND. KANSANELAKELAITOS. JULKAISUJA. SARJA M. (Text in Finnish, summaries in English) 1967. irreg., no.M79, 1991. Kansanelakelaitos - Social Insurance Institution of Finland, Research Institute for Social Security, P.O. Box 78, SF-00381 Helsinki 38, Finland.

FLORIDA STATE UNIVERSITY. CENTER FOR YUGOSLAV-AMERICAN STUDIES, RESEARCH, AND EXCHANGES. PROCEEDINGS AND REPORTS OF SEMINARS AND RESEARCH. see HISTORY — History Of Europe

300 CE
FOCUS. (Text in English) 1977. m. Rs.36. Collective, 26 Clifford Ave., Colombo 3, Sri Lanka.

300 338.91 FR ISSN 0339-0462
FOI ET DEVELOPPEMENT. (Includes special nos.) 1973. m. (10/yr.). 100 F. (foreign 120 F.). Centre Lebret, 43 ter, rue de la Glaciere, 75013 Paris, France. TEL 43-54-57-58. Ed. Fred Martinache. bk.rev.; bibl.; circ. 2,000. (back issues avail.) **Indexed:** CERDIC.

301 945 IT ISSN 0544-1374
HX15
FONDAZIONE GIANGIACOMO FELTRINELLI. ANNALI. 1958. a. price varies. Fondazione Giangiacomo Feltrinelli, Via Romagnosi 3, 20121 Milan, Italy. bk.rev.; circ. 3,000.

300 320 100 UK ISSN 0959-311X
FOR A CHANGE; for moral re-armament. 1952. m. £16($25) Grosvenor Productions Ltd., 12 Palace St., London SW1E 5JF, England. TEL 071-828-6591. FAX 071-821-5819. (Subscr. to: Tirley Garth, Tarporley, Cheshire CW8 0LZ, England; Dist. in US by: MRA Inc., 1156 15th St. N.W., Ste. 910, Washington, DC 20005-1704) Ed. Edward Peters. bk.rev.; illus.; play rev.; index; circ. 8,500. (tabloid format)
Former titles (until 1987): New World News; M R A Information Service (ISSN 0024-8320)
Description: Concerns the factor of faith in human and international relations.

300 060 370 US ISSN 0071-7274
AS911.F6
FORD FOUNDATION ANNUAL REPORT. a. free. Ford Foundation, Office of Communications, c/o Carolee Iltis, 320 E. 43rd St., New York, NY 10017. TEL 212-573-5000. (also avail. in microfiche from BHP)
Description: Lists grants and other financial data. Includes information on trustees, staff and grant applications.

300 378.3 658.15 US
FORD FOUNDATION REPORT. 1970. 3/yr. free. Ford Foundation, Office of Communications, c/o Carolee Iltis, 320 E. 43rd St., New York, NY 10017. TEL 212-573-5000. bibl.; illus.; index; circ. 40,000. (also avail. in microform from UMI; back issues avail.; reprint service avail. from UMI) **Indexed:** HR Rep.
Formerly: Ford Foundation Letter (ISSN 0015-699X)
Description: Includes news of grants and program actions.

300 IT
FORMAZIONE E SOCIETA. 1981. 3/yr. L.58000 (foreign L.75000)(effective 1992). Franco Angeli Editore, Viale Monza 106, 20127 Milan, Italy. TEL 02-2827651. Eds. G.P. Catelli, P. Guidicini.

FORUM (CAMBRIDGE). see EDUCATION — Teaching Methods And Curriculum

300 800 ZR
FORUM UNIVERSITAIRE.* 1973. q. K.150. Universite Nationale du Zaire, Junction des Etudiants, Bloc VIII No 1109, B.P. 945, Lubumbashi, Zaire. Ed. Eloko a Nongo Obhudiema. bibl.; illus.

300 323.4 UG
FORWARD (KAMPALA). 1979-1985; resumed 1986. q. EAs.400($10) Forward Publications Ltd., Box 5160, Kampala, Uganda. Ed.Bd. adv.; bk.rev.; play rev.; circ. 3,000.

300 FR
FRANCE. MINISTERE DE L'INDUSTRIE ET DE LA RECHERCHE. REPERTOIRE NATIONAL DES LABORATOIRES; LA RECHERCHE UNIVERSITAIRE. TOME 3: SCIENCES HUMAINES ET SOCIALES. 1966. irreg., latest 1982. Documentation Francaise, 29-31 Quai Voltaire, 75340 Paris 07, France. TEL 1-40-15-70-00.
Formerly: France. Delegation Generale a la Recherche Scientifique et Technique. Repertoire National des Laboratoires; la Recherche Universitaire; Sciences Exactes et Naturelles. Tome 3: Chimie (ISSN 0071-8556)

FREE ASSOCIATIONS; psychoanalysis, groups, politics, culture. see PSYCHOLOGY

300 II
FRENCH INSTITUTE, PONDICHERRY. PONDY PAPERS IN SOCIAL SCIENCES. (Text in English, summaries in French) 1989. irreg. (approx. 3/yr.) price varies. Institut Francais de Pondichery, Departement de Sciences Sociales, Box 33, Pondichery 605 001, India. TEL 24170. FAX 910413-29534. TELEX 569335 FRAN IN. Ed. J. Pouchepadass. circ. 250.

300 DK ISSN 0109-0372
FRUCTUS; forskningsnyt. 1983. q. free. Roskilde Universitetscenter, Informationskontoret, Postbox 260, 4000 Roskilde, Denmark. FAX 009-45-46-75-7401. Ed. Per Knudsen. illus.; circ. 2,500.

300 CC ISSN 0257-0289
FUDAN XUEBAO (SHEHUI KEXUE BAN)/FUDAN JOURNAL (SOCIAL SCIENCES EDITION). (Text in Chinese; table of contents in English) bi-m. Y1.50 per no. (Fudan Daxue - Fudan University) Fudan Daxue Chubanshe - Fudan University Press, 222 Handan Lu, Shanghai 200433, People's Republic of China. TEL 5484906. TELEX 33317-HUAFU-CN. (Dist. outside China by: China International Book Trading Corp., P.O. Box 399, Beijing, P.R.C.)

300 CC ISSN 1000-5285
FUJIAN SHIFAN DAXUE XUEBAO (SHEHUI KEXUE BAN)/FUJIAN NORMAL UNIVERSITY. JOURNAL (SOCIAL SCIENCE EDITION). (Text in Chinese) q. Y2.40. Fujian Shifan Daxue - Fujian Normal University, 137 Shangsan Lu, Cangshan Qu, Fuzhou, Fujian 350007, People's Republic of China. TEL 541616. (Dist. overseas by: Jiangsu Publications Import & Export Corp., 56 Gao Yun Ling, Nanjing, Jiangsu, P.R.C.) Ed. Chen Zheng.
—BLDSC shelfmark: 4755.512300.
Description: Covers research results in different fields of the social sciences, including philosophy, economics, linguistics, literature, history, education and the arts.

300 CC
FUJIAN XUEKAN. (Text in Chinese) bi-m. Fujian Sheng Shehui Kexue Lianhehui, Xiaoliucun, Huancheng Lu, Fuzhou, Fujian 350001, People's Republic of China. TEL 535984. Ed. Pan Boting.

300 BL
FUNDACAO JOAQUIM NABUCO. SERIE MONOGRAFIAS. 1975. irreg., no.31, 1989. $2.50 per no. (Fundacao Joaquim Nabuco) Editora Massangana, Rua Dois Irmaos, 15, Apipucos, 52071 Recife, Brazil. TEL 081-268-4611. FAX 081-268-9600.
Formerly: Instituto Joaquim Nabuco de Pesquisas Sociais. Serie Monografias.

300 EC
FUNDACION LOS ANDES DE ESTUDIOS SOCIALES. ANUARIO. a. Fundacion Los Andes de Estudios Sociales, Casilla 2, surcursal 12, Quito, Ecuador.

300 FR ISSN 0160-7847
Q172 CODEN: FUSCDO
FUNDAMENTA SCIENTIAE.* 1980. q. Association des Amis de Fundamentiae Scientiae, Universite Louis Pasteur, 4 Rue Blaise Pascal, 67070 Strasbourg Cedex, France. Eds. Dr. B.J. Jurdant, Dr. M. Paty. adv.; index; circ. 1,500. (also avail. in microform from MIM,UMI; reprint service avail. from UMI) **Indexed:** Biol.Abstr., Curr.Adv.Ecol.Sci., Geo.Abstr., Math.R.
—BLDSC shelfmark: 4056.010000.
Refereed Serial

FUTURESCAN. see BUSINESS AND ECONOMICS — Economic Situation And Conditions

SOCIAL SCIENCES: COMPREHENSIVE WORKS

FUTUROLOGY. see *TECHNOLOGY: COMPREHENSIVE WORKS*

300   CC
FUZHOU DAXUE XUEBAO (SHEHUI KEXUE BAN)/FUZHOU UNIVERSITY. JOURNAL (SOCIAL SCIENCE EDITION). (Text in Chinese) s-a. Fuzhou Daxue - Fuzhou University, Gongye Lu, Fuzhou, Fujian 350002, People's Republic of China. TEL 710845. Ed. Huang Zheng.

300 375   GW
▼**G E P**. (Geschichte Erziehung Politik) 1990. m. DM.60. Volk und Wissen Verlag GmbH, Lindenstr. 54 A, 1086 Berlin, Germany. TEL 0372-20343-0. circ. 11,400.

300   CC
GAIGE/REFORM. (Text in Chinese) bi-m. Chongqing Shehui Kexueyuan - Chongqing Academy of Social Sciences, 83 Zhongshan Silu, Congqing, Sichuan 630020, People's Republic of China. TEL 352445. Ed. Jiang Yiwei.

300   II
GANDHIAN PERSPECTIVES. (Text in English) 1978-19??; resumed 1991. s-a. Rs.120($24) to individuals; institutions Rs.150 ($30). (Gandhian Institute of Studies) Tara Book Agency, Kamacha, Varanasi 221010 (U.P.), India. Ed. Ali Ashraf.

300   CC
GAOXIAO SHEHUI KEXUE/SOCIAL SCIENCES IN HIGHER EDUCATION. (Text in Chinese) bi-m. Zhongguo Jiaoyu Zazhishe, 35, Damucang Hutong, Xidan, Beijing 100816, People's Republic of China. TEL 654921. Ed. Li Changzheng.

300 900   GW   ISSN 0340-613X
H5
GESCHICHTE UND GESELLSCHAFT; Zeitschrift fuer Historische Sozialwissenschaft. 1975. q. DM.78. Vandenhoeck und Ruprecht, Theaterstr. 13, Postfach 3753, 3400 Goettingen, Germany. TEL 0551-6959-22. FAX 0551-695917. Ed. Hans-Ulrich Wehler. adv.; index. **Indexed**: Amer.Hist.& Life, Arts & Hum.Cit.Ind., Curr.Cont., E.I., Hist.Abstr., INIS Atomind., SSCI.
—BLDSC shelfmark: 4162.521000.

300   GW
GESELLSCHAFT, RECHT, WIRTSCHAFT. 1978. irreg., vol.16, 1989. price varies. Bibliographisches Institut und F.A. Brockhaus AG, Dudenstr. 6, Postfach 100311, 6800 Mannheim 1, Germany. TEL 0621-3901-01. FAX 0621-3901-389. Ed.Bd. **Indexed**: Math.R.

GLEDISTA. see *HUMANITIES: COMPREHENSIVE WORKS*

GOOD GOVERNMENT; a journal of political, social & economic content. see *BUSINESS AND ECONOMICS — Economic Systems And Theories, Economic History*

300   UK   ISSN 0266-2043
H11
GREAT BRITAIN. ECONOMIC AND SOCIAL RESEARCH COUNCIL. ANNUAL REPORT. 1966. a. varies. Economic and Social Research Council, Polaris House, N. Star Ave., Swindon SN2 1UJ, England. TEL 0793-413000. FAX 0793-413001.
—BLDSC shelfmark: 1241.048000.
Former titles: Great Britain. Economic and Social Research Council. Report; (until Jan. 1984): Great Britain. Social Science Research Council. Report (ISSN 0081-0444)

300   UK
GREAT BRITAIN. ECONOMIC & SOCIAL RESEARCH COUNCIL BURSARY HANDBOOK. 1969. a. free. Economic and Social Research Council, Postgraduate Training Division, Polaris House, N. Star Ave., Swindon SN2 1UJ, England. TEL 0793-413000. FAX 0793-413001. circ. 2,000.
Formerly: Great Britain. Social Science Research Council. Bursary Scheme.

300   UK
GREAT BRITAIN. ECONOMIC & SOCIAL RESEARCH COUNCIL STUDENTSHIP HANDBOOK. 1966. a. free. Economic and Social Research Council, Training Division, Polaris House, N. Star Ave., Swindon SN2 1UJ, England. TEL 0793-413000. FAX 0793-413001.
Formerly: Great Britain. Social Science Research Council. Studentship Handbook.

300   GR   ISSN 0013-9696
H8
GREEK REVIEW OF SOCIAL RESEARCH/EPITHEORISIS KOINONIKON EREVNON. (Text in Greek) 1969. 4/yr. $30. National Center of Social Research, 1 Sophocleous St., Athens 10559, Greece. FAX 30-1-3216471. Ed. K. Tsoukalas. adv.; bk.rev.; bibl.; charts; stat.; circ. 2,000. **Indexed**: Lang.& Lang.Behav.Abstr.

300   GW
GRUNDRISS DER SOZIALWISSENSCHAFT. 1953. irreg. Vandenhoeck und Ruprecht, Robert-Bosch-Breite 6, Postfach 3753, 3400 Goettingen, Germany. TEL 0551-6959-0. FAX 0551-695917.

300 500   CC
GUANGDONG MINZU XUEYUAN XUEBAO/GUANGDONG INSTITUTE OF NATIONALITIES. JOURNAL. (In 2 Vols.: Parts 1-3 Social Sciences; Part 4: Natural Sciences) (Text in Chinese) 1980. q. Y6.10. Guangdong Minzu Xueyuan - Guangdong Institute of Nationalities, Shipai, Guangzhou, Guangdong 510633, People's Republic of China. (Dist. overseas by: China Publications Foreign Trade Corp., P.O. Box 782, Beijing, P.R.C.) bk.rev.; circ. 1,200.
Description: Publishes papers on the natural and social sciences, emphasizing minority issues in South China and the history and current conditions in Guangdong Province. The 4th issue covers natural sciences.

300   CC
GUANGDONG SHEHUI KEXUE/GUANGDONG SOCIAL SCIENCE. (Text in Chinese) q. Guangdong Sheng Shehui Kexueyuan - Guangdong Academy of Social Sciences, No.222, Yuexiu Beilu, Guangzhou, Guangdong 510050, People's Republic of China. TEL 334820. Ed. Zhang Lei.

GUIZHOU SHEHUI KEXUE (JINGJI BAN)/SOCIAL SCIENCES IN GUIZHOU (ECONOMICS EDITION). see *BUSINESS AND ECONOMICS — Economic Situation And Conditions*

300   CC
GUIZHOU SHEHUI KEXUE (WEN-SHI-ZHE BAN)/SOCIAL SCIENCES IN GUIZHOU (LITERATURE, HISTORY, PHILOSOPHY EDITION). (Text in Chinese) bi-m. $13.10. Guizhou Sheng Shehui Kexueyuan - Guizhou Academy of Social Sciences, Huangjia Sheng, Guiyang, Guizhou 550002, People's Republic of China. TEL 28566. (Dist. in US by: China Books & Periodicals, Inc., 2929 24th St., San Francisco, CA 94110. TEL 415-282-2994) Ed. Hu Jie.

300   CC
GUOWAI SHEHUI KEXUE/SOCIAL SCIENCE ABROAD. (Text in Chinese) m. Zhongguo Shehui Kexueyuan, Wenxian Qingbao Zhongxin - Chinese Academy of Social Sciences, Documentation Information Center, 5, Jianguomennei Dajie, Beijing 100732, People's Republic of China. TEL 5137744. Ed. Wu Andi.

300   CC   ISSN 1000-4785
GUOWAI SHEHUI KEXUE KUAIBAO/FOREIGN SOCIAL SCIENCE BULLETIN. (Text in Chinese) m. Zhongguo Shehui Kexueyuan, Wenxian Qingbao Zhongxin - Chinese Academy of Social Sciences, Documentation Information Center, 5, Jianguomennei Dajie, Beijing 100732, People's Republic of China. TEL 5137744. Ed. Qu Hanzhang.

GYPSY LORE SOCIETY. NEWSLETTER. see *ANTHROPOLOGY*

300   CC
HANGZHOU DAXUE XUEBAO (SHEHUI KEXUE BAN)/HANGZHOU UNIVERSITY. JOURNAL (SOCIAL SCIENCE EDITION). (Text in Chinese) q. Hangzhou Daxue - Hangzhou University, 34 Tianmushan Lu, Hangzhou, Zhejiang 310028, People's Republic of China. TEL 881224. Ed. Jin Jiang.

300   CC
HANGZHOU SHIFAN XUEYUAN XUEBAO (SHEHUI KEXUE BAN)/HANGZHOU NORMAL COLLEGE. JOURNAL (SOCIAL SCIENCE EDITION). (Text in Chinese) 4/yr. Y6. Hangzhou Shifan Xueyuan - Hangzhou Normal College, Hangzhou, Zhejiang 310012, People's Republic of China.

HARRY S. TRUMAN RESEARCH INSTITUTE FOR THE ADVANCEMENT OF PEACE. REPRINT SERIES. see *BIBLIOGRAPHIES*

HARYANA AGRICULTURAL UNIVERSITY. JOURNAL OF RESEARCH. see *AGRICULTURE*

300   CC   ISSN 1000-1565
HEBEI DAXUE XUEBAO/HEBEI UNIVERSITY. JOURNAL. (Text in Chinese) q. Hebei Daxue - Hebei University, Baoding, Hebei 071002, People's Republic of China. TEL 22929. Ed. Wang Peidong.

300   CC   ISSN 1000-5587
HEBEI SHIFAN DAXUE XUEBAO (SHEHUI KEXUE BAN)/HEBEI NORMAL UNIVERSITY. JOURNAL (SOCIAL SCIENCE EDITION). (Text in Chinese) q. Hebei Shifan Daxue - Hebei Normal University, Yuhua Lu, Shijiazhuang, Hebei 050016, People's Republic of China. TEL 49941. Ed. Jin Shixun.

300   CC   ISSN 1003-7071
HEBEI XUEKAN/HEBEI ACADEMIC JOURNAL. (Text in Chinese; table of contents in English) 1981. bi-m. Y9. Hebei Sheng Shehui Kexueyuan - Hebei Provincial Academy of Social Sciences, 9 Shiyi Lu, Shijianzhuang, Hebei 050051, People's Republic of China. TEL 335767. Ed. Chen Yaobin. adv. contact: Chen Yaobin. circ. 3,000. (reprint service avail.)

300   IS   ISSN 0333-6964
Q180.I78
HEBREW UNIVERSITY OF JERUSALEM. AUTHORITY FOR RESEARCH AND DEVELOPMENT. CURRENT RESEARCH. (Vol. 1: Research; Vol. 2: Publications) (Text in English) 1964. a. Hebrew University of Jerusalem, Jerusalem, Israel. TEL 02-630241. FAX 02-664740. Ed. S. Glatzer. author index; circ. controlled.
Formed by the merger of: Hebrew University of Jerusalem. Authority for Research and Development. Research Report: Humanities, Social Sciences, Law, Education, Social Work, Library (ISSN 0075-3645); Hebrew University of Jerusalem. Authority for Research and Development. Research Report. Science and Agriculture (ISSN 0075-3653); Hebrew University of Jerusalem. Authority for Research Report. Medicine, Pharmacy, Dental Medicine (ISSN 0075-3637)

300   CC   ISSN 1000-1980
HEHAI DAXUE XUEBAO/HEHAI UNIVERSITY. JOURNAL. (Text in Chinese) bi-m. Hehai Daxue - Hehai University, 1 Xikang Lu, Nanjing, Jiangsu 210024, People's Republic of China. TEL 632106. Ed. Xiang Darun.
—BLDSC shelfmark: 4758.435000.

300   PL   ISSN 0239-8818
D880
HEMISPHERES. (Text in English) 1984. a. price varies. (Polish Academy of Sciences, Institute of History, Centre for Studies on Non-European Countries) Ossolineum, Publishing House of the Polish Academy of Sciences, Rynek 9, 50-106 Wroclaw, Poland. TEL 386-25. (Dist. by: Ars Polona, Krakowskie Przedmiescie 7, 00-068 Warsaw, Poland) Ed. Andrzej Zajaczkowski. bk.rev.
Description: Reports and contributions concerning problems of the Third World - history, politics, sociology and culture.

300   CC   ISSN 1000-2359
HENAN SHIFAN DAXUE XUEBAO (SHEHUI KEXUE BAN)/HENAN NORMAL UNIVERSITY. JOURNAL (SOCIAL SCIENCE EDITION). (Text in Chinese) q. Henan Shifan Daxue, Xuebao Bianjibu, Xinxiang, Henan 453002, People's Republic of China. TEL 54921. Ed. Zhao Dejiao.

HISTORICAL METHODS. see *HISTORY*

300 301   UK   ISSN 0952-6951
H1
HISTORY OF THE HUMAN SCIENCES. 1988. q. £29($48) to individuals; institutions £80($132). Sage Publications Ltd., 6 Bonhill St., London EC2A 4PU, England. TEL 071-374-1645. FAX 071-374-8741. TELEX 263398. (Subscr. to: Routledge Journals, Subscr. Dept., N. Way, Andovet, Hants SP10 5BE, England) Eds. Arthur Still, Irving Velody. adv.; color page £150; trim 193 x 114; adv. contact: Bernie Folan. bk.rev.; illus.; index. (back issues avail.)
—BLDSC shelfmark: 4318.143000.
Description: Provides a forum for contemporary social science research that examines its own historical origins and interdisciplinary influences in an effort to review current practice.

SOCIAL SCIENCES: COMPREHENSIVE WORKS

300   JA   ISSN 0073-280X
H1
HITOTSUBASHI JOURNAL OF SOCIAL STUDIES. 1960. a. Hitotsubashi Daigaku, Hitotsubashi Gakkai - Hitotsubashi University, Hitotsubashi Academy, 2-1 Naka, Kunitachi-shi, Tokyo 186, Japan. Ed. D. Yui. circ. 900. **Indexed:** P.A.I.S., SSCI.

HITOTSUBASHI REVIEW/HITOTSUBASHI RONSO. see *BUSINESS AND ECONOMICS*

300   JA   ISSN 0386-4480
HOKKAIDO KYOIKU DAIGAKU KIYO. DAI-1-BU, B. SHAKAI KAGAKU HEN/HOKKAIDO UNIVERSITY OF EDUCATION. JOURNAL. SECTION 1 B. SOCIAL SCIENCE. vol.32, 1982. s-a. exchange basis. Hokkaido University of Education - Hokkaido Kyoiku Daigaku, Ainosoto 5-jo, 3-chome, Kita-ku, Sapporo 002, Hokkaido, Japan.

300   PR
HOMINES; revista latinoamericana de ciencias sociales. s-a. $15 (N. America $22, elsewhere $25). Universidad Interamericana, Departamento de Ciencias Sociales, Apdo. 1293, Hato Rey, PR 00919. Ed. Aline Frambes-Buxeda. bk.rev.

300   US   ISSN 0270-3602
HOYAN. 1979. q. $18 (Canada and Mexico $20; elsewhere $22). Hoya Society International, Inc., Box 54271, Atlanta, GA 30308. Ed. Christine M. Burton. adv.; bk.rev.; charts; illus.; index; circ. 500. (looseleaf format)
    Description: Presents nomenclatural and taxonomical research, republication of original descriptions with translation, cultural articles and society news.

300   100   CC   ISSN 1000-5579
HUADONG SHIFAN DAXUE XUEBAO (ZHEXUE SHEHUI KEXUE BAN)/EAST CHINA NORMAL UNIVERSITY. JOURNAL. (SOCIAL SCIENCE EDITION). (Text in Chinese; table of contents in English) bi-m. Y12.72. Huadong Shifan Daxue - East China Normal University, c/o Library, 3663 Zhongshan Beilu, Shanghai 200062, People's Republic of China. (Dist. outside China by: China International Book Trading Corp., P.O. Box 399, Beijing, P.R.C.) Ed. Guo Yushi.

300   CC   ISSN 1000-5455
HUANAN SHIFAN DAXUE XUEBAO (SHEHUI KEXUE BAN)/SOUTH-CHINA NORMAL UNIVERSITY. JOURNAL (SOCIAL SCIENCE EDITION). (Text in Chinese) q. Huanan Shifan Daxue, Shipai, Guangzhou, Guangdong 510631, People's Republic of China. TEL 516911. Ed. Liu Weilin.

300   CC
HUAQIAO DAXUE XUEBAO (SHEHUI KEXUE BAN)/HUAQIAO UNIVERSITY. JOURNAL (SOCIAL SCIENCE EDITION). (Text in Chinese) s-a. Huaqiao Daxue - Huaqiao University, c/o Huaqiao Daxue Tushuguan, Quanzhou, Fujian 362011, People's Republic of China. TEL 224921. Ed. Chen Juewan.

300   CC   ISSN 1000-2456
AS452.W84
HUAZHONG SHIFAN DAXUE XUEBAO (SHEHUI KEXUE BAN)/CENTRAL-CHINA NORMAL UNIVERSITY. JOURNAL (SOCIAL SCIENCE EDITION). (Text in Chinese) bi-m. Huazhong Shifan Daxue, Xuebao Bianjibu, Guizishan, Wuchang-qu, Wuhan, Hubei 430070, People's Republic of China. TEL 715601. Ed. Deng Zongqi.
    —BLDSC shelfmark: 4724.170200.

001.3   613.7   US
HUMAN ECOLOGY. ANNUAL REPORT. a. New York State College of Human Ecology, 1150 Comstock Hall, Cornell University, Ithaca, NY 14853. TEL 607-255-2216. FAX 607-255-3794.

614.7   301.3   US   ISSN 0018-7178
HM206
HUMAN ECOLOGY FORUM. 1970. q. $15 (foreign $25). New York State College of Human Ecology, 1150 Comstock Hall, Cornell University, Ithaca, NY 14850-0998. Ed. James Titus. bibl.; charts; illus.; index; circ. 5,000. (back issues avail.) **Indexed:** Energy Rev., Environ.Per.Bibl., P.A.I.S., Soc.Sci.Ind.
    —BLDSC shelfmark: 4336.063000.
    Description: Intended to inform alumni, legislators, and other key audiences about the activities, programs, and research of the college.

300   301.1   US   ISSN 1045-6767
GN365.9   CODEN: HNATER
▼**HUMAN NATURE;** an interdisciplinary biosocial perspective. 1990. q. $55 to individuals; institutions $110. Walter de Gruyter, Inc., 200 Saw Mill River Rd., Hawthorne, NY 10532. TEL 914-747-0110. FAX 914-747-1326. TELEX 646677. Ed. Jane B. Lancaster. circ. 250. (back issues avail.)
    —BLDSC shelfmark: 4336.223500.
    Description: Dedicated to advancing the interdisciplinary investigation of the biological, social, and environmental factors which underline human behavior.

HUMAN ORGANIZATION. see *ANTHROPOLOGY*

300   US   ISSN 0018-7267
H1   CODEN: HUREAA
HUMAN RELATIONS; towards the integration of the social sciences. 1947. m. $335 (foreign $390)(effective 1992). (Tavistock Institute of Human Relations, UK) Plenum Publishing Corp., 233 Spring St., New York, NY 10013-1578. TEL 212-260-8000. FAX 212-463-0742. TELEX 23-421139. Ed. Ray Loveridge. adv.; bk.rev.; bibl.; charts; index. (also avail. in microfilm from JSC) **Indexed:** A.I.C.P., ABI Inform., Abstr.Anthropol., ASSIA, BPIA, Br.Hum.Ind., Bus.Ind., Commun.Abstr., Cont.Pg.Manage., Curr.Cont., Educ.Admin.Abstr., Int.Lab.Doc., Lang.& Lang.Behav.Abstr., Manage.Cont., Mid.East: Abstr.& Ind., P.A.I.S., Peace Res.Abstr., Pers.Lit., Psychol.Abstr., Psycscan, SCIMP (1978-), Soc.Sci.Ind., SSCI, Stud.Wom.Abstr.
    —BLDSC shelfmark: 4336.400000.
    Refereed Serial

HUMAN SCIENCES RESEARCH COUNCIL. ANNUAL REPORT. see *HUMANITIES: COMPREHENSIVE WORKS*

300   001.3   SA   ISSN 1017-6136
HUMAN SCIENCES RESEARCH COUNCIL. BULLETIN. NEWS FOR THE HUMAN SCIENCES/RAAD VIR GEESTESWETENSKAPLIKE NAVORSING. BULLETIN. NUUS VIR DIE GEESTESWETENSKAPPE. (Text in Afrikaans, English) 1971. 10/yr. R.1 per no. Human Sciences Research Council, Private Bag X41, Pretoria 0001, South Africa. Ed. J.M. Farquharson. index; circ. 2,500.
    Formerly: Human Sciences Research Council. Research Bulletin - Raad vir Geesteswetenskaplike Navorsing. Navorsingsbulletin. Supersedes: Register of Research in the Human Sciences in South Africa - Register van Navorsing in die Geesteswetenskappe in Suid-Afrika.

HUMAN SETTLEMENT ISSUES. see *HOUSING AND URBAN PLANNING*

HUMANE STUDIES REVIEW. see *PHILOSOPHY*

300   PL   ISSN 0137-9666
B1
HUMANITAS. (Text in Polish; summaries in English) irreg., latest vol.7, 1987. price varies. (Polish Academy of Sciences, Institute of Philosophy and Sociology) Ossolineum, Publishing House of the Polish Academy of Sciences, Rynek 9, 50-106 Wroclaw, Poland. TEL 386-25. (Dist. by: Ars Polona, Krakowskie Przedmiescie 7, 00-068 Warsaw, Poland) Ed. Ryszard Palacz.
    Description: Original works dealing with problems of contemporary social life.

301   US   ISSN 0160-4341
HN65   CODEN: HJSRAB
HUMBOLDT JOURNAL OF SOCIAL RELATIONS. 1973. s-a. $16 to individuals; institutions $26; Humboldt State University, College of Behavioral & Social Science, Arcata, CA 95521. TEL 707-826-3716. adv.; bk.rev.; index; circ. 400. **Indexed:** Abstr.Soc.Work, Chic.Per.Ind., Lang.& Lang.Behav.Abstr., Mid.East: Abstr.& Ind., Psychol.Abstr., Sociol.Abstr. (1973-).

HUMBOLDT - UNIVERSITAET ZU BERLIN. WISSENSCHAFTLICHE ZEITSCHRIFT: REIHE GEISTES- UND SOZIALWISSENSCHAFT. see *SCIENCES: COMPREHENSIVE WORKS*

300   GW   ISSN 0933-1719
PN6149.P5   CODEN: HUMRES
HUMOR; international journal of humor research. 1988. q. $112. (W H I M: World Humor & Irony Movement) Mouton de Gruyter, Genthinerstr. 13, 1000 Berlin 30, Germany. TEL 030-260-05-140. FAX 030-26005-251. TELEX 184027. (U.S. subscr. to: Walter de Gruyter Inc., 200 Saw Mill River Rd., Hawthorne, NY 10532) Ed. Victor Raskin. bk.rev. (back issues avail.) **Indexed:** Lang.& Lang.Behav.Abstr., Sociol.Abstr.
    —BLDSC shelfmark: 4336.730500.
    Former titles: World Humor and Irony Movement Serials Yearbook; World Humor and Irony Membership Serial Yearbook; Western Humor and Irony Membership Serial Yearbook (ISSN 0737-0342)
    Description: Scholarly journal for the publication of research papers on humor as an important and universal human faculty.

300   CC   ISSN 1000-2529
HUNAN SHIFAN DAXUE XUEBAO (SHEHUI KEXUE BAN)/HUNAN NORMAL UNIVERSITY. JOURNAL (SOCIAL SCIENCE EDITION). bi-m. Hunan Shifan Daxue, Xuebao Bianjibu, Yuelushan, Changsha, Hunan 410081, People's Republic of China. TEL 83131.

HUNGARIAN STUDIES. see *HUMANITIES: COMPREHENSIVE WORKS*

300   IT   ISSN 0393-9367
HYRIA; cultura e societa della nuova europa. 1972. q. L.10000. Via Tanzillo, 4, 80035 Nola (Naples), Italy. Ed. Aristide LaRocca. bk.rev.; charts; illus.
    Description: Forum covering new social, cultural and educational ideas relating to the southern region of Italy.

300   150   UK
I & C. (Ideology and Consciousness) 1977. 2/yr. $9. I & C Publications Ltd., c/o G. Burchell, Westminster College, North Hinksey, Oxford OX2 9AT, England. Ed.Bd. adv.; bk.rev.; circ. 2,500. **Indexed:** Alt.Press Ind., Curr.Cont., Sociol.Abstr, SSCI.
    Formerly: Ideology and Consciousness (ISSN 0309-9156)

320   US
I C P S R BULLETIN. 4/yr. $15. (Inter-University Consortium for Political and Social Research) Institute for Social Research, University of Michigan, Box 1248, Ann Arbor, MI 48106. TEL 313-763-3485. Ed. Susan E. Wyman.

I C S A NEWSLETTER. (International Christian Studies Association) see *RELIGIONS AND THEOLOGY*

300   II   ISSN 0018-9049
H62.5.I5
I C S S R NEWSLETTER. (Text in English) 1969. q. free. Indian Council of Social Science Research, 35 Ferozshah Rd., New Delhi 110 001, India. TEL 381571. TELEX 31-61083-ISSR-IN. Ed. S. Saraswathi. abstr.; stat.; circ. 5,500. (back issues avail.) **Indexed:** A.I.C.P., Rural Devel.Abstr., World Agri.Econ.& Rural Sociol.Abstr., World Bibl.Soc.Sec.
    Description: Lists all projects, fellowships, contingency and other grants given to social scientists. Includes other news of relevance to social scientists in India, featuring political implications of research.

I F E P P INFORMATIONS. (Institut de Formation et d'Etudes Psycho-Sociologiques et Pedagogiques) see *PSYCHOLOGY*

I P S S BULLETIN. (Institute of Political and Social Studies) see *POLITICAL SCIENCE*

300   US
I S E R OCCASIONAL PAPERS. 1970. irreg., no.18, 1987. $2 per no. University of Alaska, Institute of Social and Economic Research, 3211 Providence Dr., Anchorage, AK 99508-4614. TEL 907-786-7710. Ed. Linda Leask. bibl.
    Formerly: I S E G R Occasional Papers.

I S E R RESEARCH NOTES. (Institute of Social and Economic Research) see *BUSINESS AND ECONOMICS*

SOCIAL SCIENCES: COMPREHENSIVE WORKS 4375

946 300   UK   ISSN 0307-3262
DP233
IBERIAN STUDIES. 1972. s-a. £12($20) in the U.K.; elsewhere £20($30). University of Keele, Centre for Iberian Studies, Keele, Staffs. ST5 5BG, England. TEL 0782-621111. FAX 0782-613847. TELEX 36113-UNKLIB-G. Ed. Dr. J. Naylon. bk.rev.; bibl.; illus.; stat.; circ. 300. **Indexed**: Amer.Hist.& Life, Hist.Abstr.
—BLDSC shelfmark: 4359.790000.
    Description: English language journal devoted to the study of Spanish and Portuguese society. Articles written by Iberian specialists from all over the world in the areas of history, politics, economics, geography, education, sociology and social anthropology.

300   AG   ISSN 0326-386X
H8.S7
IDEAS EN CIENCIAS SOCIALES. 1984. 3/yr. $30 (foreign $48). Universidad de Belgrano, Teodoro Gracia 2090, 1426 Buenos Aires, Argentina. TEL 774-2133. Ed. Avelino J. Porto. adv.; bk.rev.; bibl.; charts; stat.; circ. 1,000. (back issues avail.)
    Description: Covers politics, law and sociology in Latin America.

300   PH   ISSN 0300-4155
DS1
IMPACT; Asian magazine for human transformation. (Text in English) 1966. m. P.210($65) for Asia and Pacific Isles; $40 for Europe and N. America. Social Impact Foundation Inc., Noel St. 2948, United Paranaque 111, P.O. Box 2950, Metro Manila, Philippines. TEL 827-65-81. FAX 827-65-81. Ed. Cornelius G. Breed. adv.; bk.rev.; illus.; index; circ. 5,000. (also avail. in microform from UMI; reprint service avail. from UMI) **Indexed**: HR Rep., I.C.U.I.S.Abstr., Ind.Phil.Per., Lang.& Lang.Behav.Abstr., Sociol.Abstr.
    Description: Covers social development issues in Asia.

300 301   CN   ISSN 0228-2518
IN SUMMARY. 1979. 3/yr. free. University of Alberta, Department of Sociology, Population Research Laboratory, Edmonton, Alta. T6G 2H4, Canada. TEL 403-492-4659. FAX 403-432-7196. Ed. Ilze Hobin. circ. 650.
    Description: Newsletter of the Population Research Laboratory, with information on its research activities, publications, seminars and conferences.

300   II
IND-AFRICANA: COLLECTED RESEARCH PAPERS ON AFRICA. (Text in English) 1988. s-a. $8. University of Delhi, Department of African Studies, Delhi 100 007, India. TEL 2521521. Ed. K.K. Virmani. circ. 400.

INDEX TO INTERNATIONAL PUBLIC OPINION. see POLITICAL SCIENCE — International Relations

300 001.3   US   ISSN 0191-0574
Z7163
INDEX TO SOCIAL SCIENCES & HUMANITIES PROCEEDINGS. Short title: I S S H P. (Includes Author/Editor Index, Permuterm Subject Index, Sponsor Index, Meeting Location Index, Category Index, Contents of Proceedings, and Corporate Index.) 1979. q. (plus annual cum.). $885. Institute for Scientific Information, 3501 Market St., Philadelphia, PA 19104. TEL 215-386-0100. FAX 215-386-2991. (U.K. addr.: 132 High St. Uxbridge, Middlesex, UB8 1DP, England)
—BLDSC shelfmark: 4386.400000.
    Description: International multidisciplinary index of papers presented at social sciences and humanities professional meetings.

300   II   ISSN 0256-4491
INDIAN COUNCIL OF SOCIAL RESEARCH. ANNUAL REPORT. (Editions in English and Hindi) 1970. a. free. Indian Council of Social Science Research, National Social Science Documentation Centre, 35 Ferozshah Rd., New Delhi 110 001, India. TEL 385959. TELEX 31-61083-ISSR-IN. circ. 1,200 (both eds.). (back issues avail.)
    Description: Bulletin of the Indian Council of Social Science Research.

330 300   US   ISSN 0019-4646
HC431
INDIAN ECONOMIC AND SOCIAL HISTORY REVIEW. (Text in English) 1963. q. $36 to individuals; institutions $74. Sage Publications, Inc., 2455 Teller Rd., Newbury Park, CA 91320. TEL 805-499-0721. FAX 805-499-0871. (And: Sage Publications Pvt. Ltd., P.O. Box 4215, New Delhi 110-048, India) Ed. Dr. Dhamar Kumar. adv.; bk.rev.; cum.index: 1963-1969.; circ. 1,000. (also avail. in microform from UMI; reprint service avail. from UMI) **Indexed**: Amer.Hist.& Life, Hist.Abstr., J.of Econ.Lit., Numis.Lit.

INDIAN INSTITUTE OF PUBLIC OPINION. MONTHLY PUBLIC OPINION SURVEYS. see POLITICAL SCIENCE

300   II   ISSN 0046-9017
HT395.I5
INDIAN JOURNAL OF REGIONAL SCIENCE. (Text and summaries in English) 1968. s-a. Rs.100($20) (typically set in Jan.). (Regional Science Association, India) Indian Institute of Technology, Kharagpur, Dept. of Arch. & Regional Planning, Kharagpur 721302, West Bengal, India. TELEX 06401-201 IT KGIN. Eds. A.N. Bose, C.R. Pathak. adv.; bk.rev.; index; circ. 525. (tabloid format) **Indexed**: ASSIA.
—BLDSC shelfmark: 4421.030000.

300   US
INDIAN JOURNAL OF SOCIAL SCIENCE. 1989. q. $36 to individuals; institutions $62. (Indian Council of Social Science Research, II) Sage Publications, Inc., 2455 Teller Rd., Newbury Park, CA 91320. TEL 805-499-0721. FAX 805-499-0871. (And: Sage Publications Pvt. Ltd., P.O. Box 4215, New Delhi 110 048, India) Ed. Moonis Raza.
    Formerly: Indian Journal of Social Science Research.
    Description: Promotes scientific discussion on the diverse concerns of social science research.

300   II   ISSN 0376-9879
H1
INDIAN JOURNAL OF SOCIAL SCIENCES. (Text in English) 1971. 3/yr. $5. Society for the Study of Social Sciences, c/o Treasurer, Dept. of Sociology, Osmania University, Hyderabad 7, India.

INDIAN JOURNAL OF SOCIAL WORK. see SOCIAL SERVICES AND WELFARE

300   II   ISSN 0073-6694
INDIAN STATISTICAL INSTITUTE. ECONOMETRIC AND SOCIAL SCIENCES SERIES. RESEARCH MONOGRAPHS. irreg. Statistical Publishing Society, 204-1 Barrackpore Trunk Rd., Calcutta 700035, India. Ed. C.R. Rao.

300   SA
INDICATOR S A REPORT. Variant series title: Indicator S A Issue Focus. (Text in English) 1983. s-a. R.25($20) (University of Natal, Centre for Social and Development Studies) Indicator Project S A, Centre for Social and Development Studies, King George V Ave., Durban 4001, South Africa. TEL 031-816-2525. FAX 031-816-2359. Ed. Graham W. Howe. (back issues avail.)
    Description: In-depth analyses of specific topics in contemporary South African political, social and economic affairs.

300   SA   ISSN 0259-188X
INDICATOR SOUTH AFRICA; the barometer of social trends. 1983. q. R.150($200) includes s-a. Indicator S A Report. (University of Natal, Centre for Social and Development Studies) Indicator Project S A, Centre for Social and Development Studies, King George V Ave., Durban 4001, South Africa. TEL 031-816-2525. FAX 031-816-2359. Ed. Graham W. Howe. adv.; bk.rev.; stat.; index; circ. 1,000. (back issues avail.) **Indexed**: Ind.S.A.Per.
—BLDSC shelfmark: 4432.460000.
    Description: Monitors socio-political and economic trends in South Africa. Contributes to informed debate and regional scholarship, with data analyses, diagnosis of trends, and a policy prognosis service. Publishes objective and original research using primary statistics, investigative fieldwork, attitude surveys and documentary research.

INDUSTRIAL RELATIONS JOURNAL OF SOUTH AFRICA. see BUSINESS AND ECONOMICS — Labor And Industrial Relations

300   GW   ISSN 0936-546X
INFO3 EXTRA; Das Magazin der Zeitschrift Info3. 1976. m. DM.48. Info3 Verlag, Kirchgartenstr. 1, 6000 Frankfurt a.M. 50, Germany. TEL 069-584645. Ed. Ramon Bruell. bk.rev.; illus.; circ. 14,000. (back issues avail)

INIZIATIVA ISONTINA. see BUSINESS AND ECONOMICS — Economic Situation And Conditions

300 600   AU
INNOVATION. irreg., vol.3, 1990. varies. Verband der Wissenschaftlichen Gesellschaften Oesterreichs, Lindengasse 37, A-1070 Vienna, Austria. TEL 932166.

INQUIRY; an interdisciplinary journal of philosophy. see PHILOSOPHY

INSTITUCION FERNAN-GONZALEZ. BOLETIN. see HISTORY

INSTITUT DES HAUTES ETUDES DE L'AMERIQUE LATINE. COLLECTION DES TRAVAUX ET MEMOIRES. see HISTORY — History Of North And South America

300   PE   ISSN 0303-7495
F2212   CODEN: BIFEB5
INSTITUT FRANCAIS D'ETUDES ANDINES. BULLETIN/INSTITUTO FRANCES DE ESTUDIOS ANDINOS. BOLETIN. (Text in English, French or Spanish) 1972. s-a. $8 per no. Institut Francais d'Etudes Andines, Casilla 18-1217, Lima 18, Peru. Ed. Anne-Marie Brougere. adv.; illus.; circ. 850. **Indexed**: A.I.C.P., Geo.Abstr., Hisp.Amer.Per.Ind.
    Description: Covers many areas in earth and social sciences, including anthropology, agriculture, archaeology, ethnic history, and sociology.

300   II
▼**INSTITUT FRANCAIS DE PONDICHERY. DEPARTEMENT DE SCIENCES SOCIALES. PUBLICATIONS**. (Text and summaries in English, French) 1991. irreg. price varies. Institut Francais de Pondichery, Departement de Sciences Sociales, Box 33, Pondichery 605 001, India. TEL 24710. FAX 91-413-29534. TELEX 469224 FRAN IN. Ed. J. Pouchepadass. index; circ. 500.

300   JA   ISSN 0563-8186
INSTITUTE FOR COMPARATIVE STUDIES OF CULTURE. ANNALS. (Text in Japanese) 1955. a. 1500 Yen. Institute for Comparative Studies of Culture, c/o Tokyo Woman's Christian University, 2-6-1 Zempukuji, Suginami-ku, Tokyo 167, Japan. title index; circ. 600.
    Formerly: Institute for Comparative Studies of Culture. Publications.

300   US   ISSN 0020-2622
INSTITUTE FOR SOCIAL RESEARCH. NEWSLETTER. Abbreviated title: I S R Newsletter. 1969. 3/yr. free. University of Michigan, Institute for Social Research, Box 1248, Ann Arbor, MI 48106. TEL 313-764-7509. FAX 313-747-4575. Ed. Linda Stafford. bk.rev.; charts; illus.; circ. 30,000. (also avail. in microform from UMI; back issues avail.; reprint service avail. from UMI)

INSTITUTE OF SOCIAL AND ECONOMIC RESEARCH. REPORTS. see BUSINESS AND ECONOMICS

300   SI   ISSN 0217-7099
INSTITUTE OF SOUTHEAST ASIAN STUDIES. FIELD REPORTS SERIES. (Text in English) 1973. irreg., no.23, 1989. price varies. Institute of Southeast Asian Studies, Heng Mui Keng Terrace, Pasir Panjang, Singapore 0511, Singapore. TEL 7780955. FAX 7781735. TELEX RS 37068 ISEAS.
    Description: Field reports of research on southeast Asian economics, politics and social issues.

300   SI
INSTITUTE OF SOUTHEAST ASIAN STUDIES. MONOGRAPHS SERIES. (Text in English) 1973. irreg., no.124, 1991. price varies. Institute of Southeast Asian Studies, Heng Mui Keng Terrace, Pasir Panjang, Singapore 0511, Singapore. TEL 7780955. FAX 7781735. TELEX RS 37068 ISEAS.
    Description: Major works on southeast Asia, particularly current economics, political and social issues.

SOCIAL SCIENCES: COMPREHENSIVE WORKS

300   SI   ISSN 0073-9731
INSTITUTE OF SOUTHEAST ASIAN STUDIES. OCCASIONAL PAPER. (Text in English) 1970. irreg., no.87, 1990. price varies. Institute of Southeast Asian Studies, Heng Mui Keng Terrace, Pasir Panjang, Singapore 0511, Singapore. TEL 7780955. FAX 7781735. TELEX RS 37068 ISEAS. bibl. (back issues avail.) Indexed: Geo.Abstr.
—BLDSC shelfmark: 4582.832500.
Description: Studies on Southeast Asia, particularly current economic, political and social issues.

300   SI   ISSN 0129-8828
INSTITUTE OF SOUTHEAST ASIAN STUDIES. RESEARCH NOTES AND DISCUSSION SERIES. (Text in English) 1976. irreg., no.74, 1991. price varies. Institute of Southeast Asian Studies, Heng Mui Keng Terrace, Pasir Panjang, Singapore 0511, Singapore. TEL 7780955. FAX 7781735. TELEX RS 37068 ISEAS. bibl.; charts; stat. (back issues avail.)
—BLDSC shelfmark: 7749.741000.
Description: Short papers on current research on Southeast Asia, particularly economic, political and social issues.

300   CK
INSTITUTO COLOMBIANO DE CULTURA. GACETA; revista internacional de cultura. 1976. irreg. $3 per no. Instituto Colombiano de Cultura, Carrera 3-A no. 18-24, Apdo. Aereo 29665, Bogota, Colombia. Ed. Gloria Zea de Uribe.

918.503   PE   ISSN 0258-8536
INSTITUTO DE ESTUDIOS AYMARAS. BOLETIN. 1978. 3/yr. $6 to individuals; institutions $9, Instituto de Estudios Aymaras, Apdo. 295, Puno, Peru. Ed. D. Irarrazaval. (back issues avail.)

INSTITUTO DE INVESTIGACAO CIENTIFICA TROPICAL. COMUNICACOES. SERIE DE CIENCIAS HISTORICAS, ECONOMICAS E SOCIOLOGICAS. see HISTORY

300   RM
INSTITUTUL DE SUBINGINERI ORADEA. LUCRARI STIINTIFICE: SERIA STIINTE SOCIALE. (Text in Rumanian, occasionally in English or French; summaries in English, French, German or Rumanian) 1973. a. Institutul de Subingineri Oradea, Calea Armatei Roseii Nr. 5, 3700 Oradea, Rumania.
Formerly: Institutul Pedagogica Oradea. Lucrari Stiintifice: Seria Stiinte Sociale; which continues in part (in 1973): Institutul Pedagogica Oradea. Lucrari Stiintifice: Seria Istorie, Stiinte Sociale, Pedagogie; which superseded in part (in 1971): Institutul Pedagogic Oradea. Lucrari Stiintifice: Seria A and Seria B; which was formerly (until 1969): Institutul Pedagogic Oradea. Lucrari Stiintifice.

INSTRUCTIONAL SCIENCE; an international journal. see EDUCATION

300   NG   ISSN 0534-4751
INTER-AFRICAN CONFERENCE ON SOCIAL SCIENCE MEETING.* 1955. irreg. (Commission for Technical Co-Operation in Africa South of the Sahara) Maison de l'Afrique, B.P. 878, Niamey, Niger.

INTER-AMERICAN ECONOMIC AND SOCIAL COUNCIL. FINAL REPORT OF THE ANNUAL MEETING AT THE MINISTERIAL LEVEL. see HISTORY — History Of North And South America

INTERCOLLEGIATE REVIEW; a journal of scholarship and opinion. see LITERARY AND POLITICAL REVIEWS

INTERDISCIPLINARIA; revista de psicologia y ciencias afines/journal of psychology and related sciences. see PSYCHOLOGY

INTERFACES: LINGUISTICS, PSYCHOLOGY AND HEALTH THERAPEUTICS; an international journal of research, notes and commentary. see LINGUISTICS

INTERNATIONAL JOURNAL OF ENVIRONMENTAL STUDIES. SECTIONS A & B. see ENVIRONMENTAL STUDIES

INTERNATIONAL JOURNAL OF INDIAN STUDIES. see ORIENTAL STUDIES

INTERNATIONAL JOURNAL OF INFORMATION MANAGEMENT. see COMPUTERS — Information Science And Information Theory

300   UK   ISSN 0954-2892
CODEN: IJPOE2
INTERNATIONAL JOURNAL OF PUBLIC OPINION RESEARCH. 1989. 4/yr. £45($84) Oxford University Press, Oxford Journals, Pinkhill House, Southfield Road, Eynsham, Oxford OX8 1JJ, England. TEL 0865-882283. FAX 0865-882890. TELEX 837330 OXPRES G. Ed.Bd. adv.; bk.rev.; circ. 1,000.
—BLDSC shelfmark: 4542.509100.
Description: Provides a source of informed analysis and comment in the field of public opinion research. Covers matters of interest to both the professional and academic community.

300   US   ISSN 0889-0293
H1
INTERNATIONAL JOURNAL OF SOCIAL EDUCATION. 1945. 3/yr. $10 (foreign $13). (Indiana Council for the Social Studies) Ball State University, Department of History, Muncie, IN 47306. TEL 317-285-8700. Ed. John E. Weakland. adv.; circ. 1,100. (also avail. in microform from UMI; reprint service avail. from UMI) Indexed: Amer.Hist.& Life, C.I.J.E., ERIC, Hist.Abstr.
—BLDSC shelfmark: 4542.556000.
Formerly (until 1986): Indiana Social Studies Quarterly (ISSN 0019-6746)

INTERNATIONAL JOURNAL OF SOCIOLOGY AND SOCIAL POLICY. see SOCIOLOGY

INTERNATIONAL MIGRATION REVIEW; a quarterly studying sociological, demographic, economic, historical, and legislative aspects of human migration movements and ethnic group relations. see POPULATION STUDIES

300   US   ISSN 0160-0176
HT390
INTERNATIONAL REGIONAL SCIENCE REVIEW. 1975. 3/yr. $18 to individuals; institutions $35; students $8. Regional Research Institute, West Virginia Univ., Morgantown, WV 26506. TEL 304-293-2896. FAX 304-293-6699. Ed. Andrew Isserman. bibl.; charts; circ. 2,500. Indexed: A.B.C.Pol.Sci., ASSIA, Avery Ind.Archit.Per., Curr.Cont., Energy Ind., Energy Info.Abstr., Geo.Abstr., I D A, J.of Econ.Lit., Popul.Ind., Rural Recreat.Tour.Abstr., Sage Urb.Stud.Abstr., SSCI, World Agri.Econ.& Rural Sociol.Abstr.
—BLDSC shelfmark: 4545.785000.
Description: Multidisciplinary journal designed to strengthen the regional and spatial aspects of quantitative research in existing social science disciplines, particularly economics and geography.
Refereed Serial

INTERNATIONAL SEMIOTIC SPECTRUM. see HUMANITIES: COMPREHENSIVE WORKS

300   UK   ISSN 0020-8701
H1
INTERNATIONAL SOCIAL SCIENCE JOURNAL. Revue Internationale des Sciences Sociales. 1949. q. £24($48) to individuals; institutions £42.50($88). (Unesco) Basil Blackwell Ltd., 108 Cowley Road, Oxford OX4 1JF, England. TEL 0865-791100. FAX 0865-791347. TELEX 837022-OXBOOK-G. (Dist. in U.S. by: Bernan-Unipub, 4611-F Assembly Dr., Lanham, MD 20706-4391) Ed. A. Kazancigil. bibl.; charts; index; circ. 4,500. (also avail. in microform from MIM,UMI; reprint service avail. from UMI) Indexed: A.B.C.Pol.Sci., A.I.C.P., Abstr.Anthropol., Amer.Hist.& Life, ASSIA, C.I.J.E., Cont.Pg.Manage., Curr.Cont., E.I., Excerp.Med., Fut.Surv., Geo.Abstr., High.Educ.Curr.Aware.Bull., Hist.Abstr., I D A, Int.Lab.Doc., Lang.& Lang.Behav.Abstr., M.L.A., Mid.East: Abstr.& Ind., P.A.I.S., Psychol.Abstr., Rural Recreat.Tour.Abstr., Sage Fam.Stud.Abstr., Sage Pub.Admin.Abstr., Soc.Sci.Ind., Sociol.Abstr. (1952-), SSCI, World Agri.Econ.& Rural Sociol.Abstr.
—BLDSC shelfmark: 4549.450000.

300   US   ISSN 0278-2308
H1
INTERNATIONAL SOCIAL SCIENCE REVIEW. 1925. q. $10. Pi Gamma Mu, University of Toledo, Toledo, OH 43606. TEL 419-537-4395. (Subscr. to: 1717 Ames, Winfield, KS 67156) Ed. Panos D. Bardis. bk.rev.; index. cum.index: vols.21-25, 1946-1950; circ. 10,000. Indexed: Abstr.Soc.Work., Amer.Bibl.Slavic & E.Eur.Stud., Amer.Hist.& Life, ASSIA, Curr.Cont., Econ.Abstr., Geo.Abstr., Hist.Abstr., Int.Bibl.Soc.Sci., Int.Polit.Sci.Abstr., Key to Econ.Sci., Lang.& Lang.Behav.Abstr., Mid.East: Abstr.& Ind., P.A.I.S., Peace Res.Abstr., Sociol.Abstr., Sociol.Educ.Abstr., SSCI, Stud.Wom.Abstr., World Bibl.Soc.Sec.
—BLDSC shelfmark: 4549.459000.
Formerly (until Jan. 1982): Social Science (ISSN 0037-7848)
Description: Historical and modern, quantitative and qualitative studies in all social sciences, humanities, and related fields.

INTERNATIONAL STUDIES IN SOCIOLOGY AND SOCIAL ANTHROPOLOGY. see SOCIOLOGY

300   US   ISSN 0362-8736
H61.3
INTER-UNIVERSITY CONSORTIUM FOR POLITICAL AND SOCIAL RESEARCH. GUIDE TO RESOURCES AND SERVICES.. 1962. a. free. Inter-University Consortium for Political and Social Research, Box 1248, Ann Arbor, MI 48106. TEL 313-764-2570. FAX 313-764-8041.
●Also available online.
Description: Detailed descriptions of the 2300 data collections available from computerized social science data archive. Lists services offered, membership information, and computer access procedures.

300   IS   ISSN 0334-133X
ISRAEL SOCIAL SCIENCE RESEARCH; a multidisciplinary journal. (Text in English) 1983. s-a. $15 to individuals; institutions $25. Hubert H. Humphrey Institute for Social Ecology, Ben-Gurion University of the Negev, P.O. Box 653, Beersheva 84105, Israel. TEL 057-461112. FAX 057-71536. Ed. Stephen Sharot. bk.rev.; circ. 750. Indexed: Psychol.Abstr., Sociol.Abstr. (1983-).
Description: A forum for analytical and comparative studies on issues related to social behaviour in Israel.
Refereed Serial

300   IS
HA4560.Z9
ISRAEL STUDIES. 1981. s-a. $10. Jerusalem Institute for Israel Studies, 20A Radak St., Jerusalem 92186, Israel. TEL 02-630175. FAX 02-639814. Ed. Ora Ahimeir. bk.rev.; circ. 3,000.
Formerly (until 1988): Jerusalem Institute for Israel Studies. Discussion Papers - Research Series (ISSN 0333-9831)

ISTITUTO GIAPPONESE DI CULTURA, ROME. ANNUARIO.. see HISTORY — History Of Europe

300   IT
ISTITUTO UNIVERSITARIO ORIENTALE. DIPARTIMENTO DI SCIENZE SOCIALI. QUADERNI. 1988. irreg., no.4, 1991. price varies. Liguori Editore s.r.l., Via Mezzocannone, 19, 80134 Naples, Italy. TEL 081-5227139.

300   US   ISSN 0049-0903
H62
ITEMS. 1947. q. free. Social Science Research Council, 605 Third Ave., 17th Fl., New York, NY 10158. TEL 212-661-0280. FAX 212-370-7896. Ed. Gloria Kirchheimer. bk.rev.; circ. 8,000. (also avail. in microform; back issues avail.) Indexed: A.I.C.P., Hist.Abstr. (until 1990), Mid.East: Abstr.& Ind.

IWATE MEDICAL UNIVERSITY SCHOOL OF LIBERAL ARTS & SCIENCES. ANNUAL REPORT/IWATE IKA DAIGAKU KYOYOBU NENPO. see SCIENCES: COMPREHENSIVE WORKS

300 800 500 375   JA   ISSN 0367-7370
CODEN: IDKKBM
IWATE UNIVERSITY. FACULTY OF EDUCATION. ANNUAL REPORT/IWATE DAIGAKU KYOIKUGAKUBU KENKYU NENPO. 1950. a. Iwate University, Faculty of Education - Iwate Daigaku Kyoikubu, 3-18-8 Ueda, Morioka, Iwate 020, Japan. Ed. Y. Saito. index; circ. 450. (back issues avail.) **Indexed:** Biol.Abstr., INIS Atomind.
—BLDSC shelfmark: 1248.553500.

300   GW   ISSN 0931-4938
JAHRBUCH DER BUNDESREPUBLIK DEUTSCHLAND. 1984. a. DM.17.80. C.H. Beck'sche Verlagsbuchhandlung, Wilhelmstr. 9, 8000 Munich 40, Germany. TEL 089-381890. FAX 089-38189-398. TELEX 5215085-BECK-D. Eds. Emil Huebner, Horst-Hennek Rohlfs. index.

JAHRBUCH FUER SOZIOLOGIE UND SOZIALPOLITIK. see *SOCIOLOGY*

300   II   ISSN 0075-3548
JAWAHARLAL NEHRU UNIVERSITY. SCHOOL OF INTERNATIONAL STUDIES SERIES.* (Text in English) 1961. q. price varies. (Jawaharlal Nehru University, School of International Studies) Vikas Publishing House Pvt. Ltd., 576 Masjid Rd., Jangpura, New Delhi 110 014, India. TEL 11-624605. TELEX 31592252.
Vols. for 1972 issued by the school under its earlier name: Indian School of International Studies (ISSN 0073-666X)

296   US   ISSN 0021-6704
DS101
JEWISH SOCIAL STUDIES. 1939. q. $40 (foreign $43). Conference on Jewish Social Studies, Inc., 2112 Broadway, Rm. 206, New York, NY 10023. TEL 212-724-5336. Ed. Toby B. Gitelle. bk.rev.; index, cum.index every 25 yrs.; circ. 1,300. (also avail. in microform from MIM; reprint service avail. from KTO) **Indexed:** Abstr.Anthropol., Amer.Bibl.Slavic & E.Eur.Stud., Amer.Hist.& Life, Arts & Hum.Cit.Ind., ASSIA, Bk.Rev.Ind. (1965-), Child.Bk.Rev.Ind. (1965-), Curr.Cont., Hist.Abstr., Ind.Jew.Per., Lang.& Lang.Behav.Abstr., Mid.East: Abstr.& Ind., P.A.I.S., Soc.Sci.Ind., SSCI.
—BLDSC shelfmark: 4668.380000.

300   CC   ISSN 1000-856X
AS452.N35924
JIANGHAI XUEKAN/JOURNAL OF JIANGHAI ACADEMIA. (Text in Chinese; table of contents in English) 1985. bi-m. Y15($53.40) Jiangsu Sheng Shehui Kexueyuan, Jiangsu Xuekan Bianjibu - Jiangsu Academy of Social Sciences, 70-1, Beijing Xilu, Nanjing, Jiangsu 210024, People's Republic of China. (Dist. outside China by: China International Book Trade Corp., P.O. Box 2820, Beijing, P.R.C.; Dist. in US by: China Books & Periodicals, Inc., 2929 24th St., San Francisco, CA 94110. TEL 415-282-2994) (Co-sponsor: Jiangsu Sheng Zhexue Shehui Kexue Lianhehui) Ed. Cheng Zhongyuan. adv.
Formed by the 1988 merger of: Jianghai Xuekan (Wen-Shi-Zhe Ban) (ISSN 1000-601X) & Jianghai Xuekan (Jingji Shehui Ban) (ISSN 1000-6001)

300   CC
JIANGHAN LUNTAN/JIANGHAN FORUM. (Text in Chinese) m. Y14.40($54) Hubei Sheng Shehui Kexueyuan - Hubei Academy of Social Sciences, 81, Donghu Lu, Wuchang, Hubei 430077, People's Republic of China. (Dist. outside China by: China International Book Trading Corp., P.O. Box 399, Beijing, P.R.C.; Dist. in US by: China Books & Periodicals, Inc., 2929 24th St., San Francisco, CA 94110. TEL 415-282-2994) Ed. Rong Kaiming.

300   CC
JIANGHUAI LUNTAN/JIANGHUAI FORUM. (Text in Chinese) bi-m. $32.90. Anhui Sheng Shehui Kexueyuan - Anhui Provincial Academy of Social Sciences, Weigang, Hefei, Anhui 230053, People's Republic of China. TEL 331171. (Dist. in US by: China Books & Periodicals, Inc., 2929 24th St., San Francisco, CA 94110. TEL 415-282-2994)

300   CC   ISSN 1000-579X
AS452.N352
JIANGXI SHIFAN DAXUE XUEBAO (SHEHUI KEXUE BAN)/JIANGXI NORMAL UNIVERSITY. JOURNAL (SOCIAL SCIENCE EDITION). (Text in Chinese) q. Jiangxi Shifan Daxue, Xuebao Bianjibu, Beijing Xilu, Nanchang, Jiangxi 330027, People's Republic of China. TEL 333993. Ed. Chen Dinghe.

300   CC
JIATING - YU'ER. (Text in Chinese) m. Tianjin Shi Kexue Jishu Xiehui, 287, Heping Lu, Tianjin 300041, People's Republic of China. TEL 311552. Ed. Zhou Xiuping.

JINAN XUEBAO (ZHEXUE SHEHUI KEXUE BAN)/JINAN UNIVERSITY. JOURNAL (PHILOSOPHY & SOCIAL SCIENCES EDITION). see *PHILOSOPHY*

JINBUN SHIZEN KAGAKU RONSHU/JOURNAL OF HUMANITIES AND NATURAL SCIENCES. see *HUMANITIES: COMPREHENSIVE WORKS*

300   CC   ISSN 1000-2987
AS452.T379
JINYANG XUEKAN/JINYANG JOURNAL. (Text in Chinese) 1980. bi-m. Y1.50($30.60) (effective 1989). Shanxi Sheng Shehui Kexueyuan - Shanxi Academy of Social Sciences, 38 Bingzhou Lu, Taiyuan, Shanxi 030006, People's Republic of China. TEL 775843. (Dist. outside China by: China International Book Trading Corp., P.O. Box 399, Beijing, P.R.C.; Dist. in US by: China Books & Periodicals, Inc., 2929 24th St., San Francisco, CA 94110. TEL 415-282-2994) Ed. Kang Wenbin. adv.; bk.rev.; circ. 2,000. (back issues avail.)

300   AT
JOURNAL FOR STUDENTS OF V C E POLITICAL AND INTERNATIONAL STUDIES. 3/yr. Aus.$21 to non-members; members Aus.$16. Victorian Association of Social Studies Teachers Inc., P.O. Box 91, Balaclava, Vic. 3183, Australia.
Formerly: Journal for Students of Year 12 Politics.

JOURNAL FOR THE THEORY OF SOCIAL BEHAVIOUR. see *PSYCHOLOGY*

JOURNAL OF APPLIED SOCIAL PSYCHOLOGY. see *PSYCHOLOGY*

300   US   ISSN 0148-611X
H1
JOURNAL OF ASIAN-PACIFIC & WORLD PERSPECTIVES;* an international journal of the social sciences. 1977. s-a. $7. Asian-Pacific Services Institute, c/o Twork, 4526 Brookridge Dr., Kingsport, TN 37660. Ed. Dorothy Dye Lee. adv.; bk.rev.; charts; circ. 2,000. (also avail. in Braille; back issues avail.)

910.03   US   ISSN 0021-9347
E185.5
JOURNAL OF BLACK STUDIES. 1970. q. $42 to individuals; institutions $112. Sage Publications, Inc., 2455 Teller Rd., Newbury Park, CA 91320. TEL 805-499-0721. FAX 805-499-0871. (UK addr.: Sage Publications, Ltd., 6 Bonhill St., London EC2A 4PU, England) Ed. Molefi Kete Asante. adv.; bk.rev.; index; circ. 1,500. (also avail. in microform from UMI; back issues avail.; reprint service avail. from UMI) **Indexed:** Abstr.Soc.Work., Amer.Hist.& Life., ASSIA, Bk.Rev.Ind. (1984-), C.I.J.E., Child.Bk.Rev.Ind. (1984-), Curr.Cont.Africa, Curr.Cont., Hist.Abstr., Ind.Per.Negroes, Lang.& Lang.Behav.Abstr., P.A.I.S., PHRA, Sage Fam.Stud.Abstr., Sage Pub.Admin.Abstr., Soc.Sci.Ind., Soc.Work Res.& Abstr., Sociol.Abstr., SSCI.
—BLDSC shelfmark: 4954.200000.

JOURNAL OF CANADIAN STUDIES/REVUE D'ETUDES CANADIENNES. see *HUMANITIES: COMPREHENSIVE WORKS*

301.2   US   ISSN 0022-0027
CODEN: JCFRAL
JOURNAL OF CONFLICT RESOLUTION; research on war and peace between and within nations. 1957. q. $48 to individuals; institutions $138. Sage Publications, Inc., 2455 Teller Rd., Newbury Park, CA 91320. TEL 805-499-0721. FAX 805-499-0871. (U.K. addr.: Sage Publications, Ltd., 6 Bonhill St., London EC2A 4PU, England) Ed. Bruce M. Russett. adv.; bk.rev.; charts; author index; circ. 2,200. (also avail. in microform from UMI; back issues avail.; reprint service avail. from UMI) **Indexed:** A.B.C.Pol.Sci., Abstr.Mil.Bibl., Abstr.Soc.Work., Acad.Ind., Amer.Bibl.Slavic & E.Eur.Stud., Amer.Hist.& Life, Curr.Cont., E.I., Educ.Admin.Abstr., Hist.Abstr., Int.Polit.Sci.Abstr., J.of Econ.Lit., Mid.East: Abstr.& Ind., P.A.I.S., Peace Res.Abstr., PROMT, Psychol.Abstr., Psycscan, Soc.Sci.Ind., Soc.Work Res.& Abstr., Sociol.Abstr., Sociol.Educ.Abstr., SSCI.
Formerly: Conflict Resolution.

300 001.3   NE
JOURNAL OF DEVELOPING SOCIETIES. 1971. s-a. fl.115. E.J. Brill, P.O. Box 9000, 2300 PA Leiden, Netherlands. TEL 071-312624. FAX 071-317532. TELEX 39296 BRILL NL. (In N. America: E.J. Brill, 24 Hudson St., Kinderhook, NY 12106. TEL 800-962-4406) Ed. K. Ishwaran. (back issues avail) **Indexed:** ASSIA, E.I., Geo.Abstr., I D A, Rel.Ind.One, Rural Devel.Abstr., World Agri.Econ.& Rural Sociol.Abstr.
Formerly: Contributions to Asian Studies (ISSN 0169-796X)
Description: Analysis of Asian and Latin American societies and cultures, past and contemporary.

JOURNAL OF ETHIOPIAN STUDIES. see *HISTORY — History Of Africa*

300   US   ISSN 0092-2323
CB201
JOURNAL OF INDO-EUROPEAN STUDIES. 1973. q. $40 to individuals; institutions and libraries $80. Institute for the Study of Man, 6861 Elm St., Ste. 4H, McLean, VA 22101. TEL 703-442-8010. FAX 703-847-9524. Ed.Bd. adv.; bk.rev.; circ. 1,150. **Indexed:** A.I.C.P., Abstr.Anthropol., Amer.Bibl.Slavic & E.Eur.Stud., Arts & Hum.Cit.Ind., Br.Archaeol.Abstr., Curr.Cont., Lang.& Lang.Behav.Abstr., M.L.A., Mid.East: Abstr.& Ind., Soc.Sci.Ind., Sociol.Abstr.

300   US   ISSN 0895-7258
JOURNAL OF INDO-EUROPEAN STUDIES MONOGRAPH SERIES. irreg., latest no.6. Institute for the Study of Man, 6861 Elm St., Ste. 4H, McLean, VA 22101. TEL 703-442-8010. FAX 703-847-9524.
Description: Monographs of interest to Indo-Europeanists in the areas of historical linguistics, mythology, archeology, and anthropology.

300   JA   ISSN 0388-0508
CB251
JOURNAL OF INTERCULTURAL STUDIES. (Text in English) 1974. a. 2500 Yen($25) Kansai University of Foreign Studies, Intercultural Research Institute, 16-1 Kitakatahoko-cho, Hirakata-shi, Osaka 573, Japan. FAX 0720-55-5552. Ed. Michiharu Ito. adv.; bk.rev.; charts; illus.; circ. 1,000. **Indexed:** Lang.& Lang.Behav.Abstr., Mid.East: Abstr.& Ind.
Description: Explores the anthropological aspects any culture.

300   US   ISSN 0890-0132
BD255   CODEN: JISTE2
JOURNAL OF INTERDISCIPLINARY STUDIES; an international journal of interdisciplinary and interfaith dialogue. (Text in English, French, German) 1989. a. $15 to individuals (foreign $20); institutions $25 (foreign $30); students $10 (foreign $15). Institute for Interdisciplinary Research, 2828 Third St., Ste. 11, Santa Monica, CA 90405-4150. TEL 310-396-0517. (Co-sponsor: International Christian Studies Association) Ed. Oskar Gruenwald. adv.; bk.rev.; index, cum.index; circ. 2,000. (back issues avail.) **Indexed:** Rel.& Theol.Abstr. (1989-).
Description: Offers a scholarly forum for recovering the lost unity of Renaissance learning while affirming transcendental values and faith.

301 320   UK   ISSN 0954-1748
HC59.72.E44   CODEN: JINDEV
JOURNAL OF INTERNATIONAL DEVELOPMENT: POLICY, ECONOMICS, & INTERNATIONAL RELATIONS. 1981. bi-m. $185 (effective 1992). (University of Manchester, Institute for Development Policy and Management) John Wiley & Sons Ltd., Journals, Baffins Lane, Chichester, Sussex PO19 1UD, England. TEL 0243-779777. FAX 0243-775878. TELEX 86290 WIBOOK G. Ed.Bd. adv.; bk.rev.; circ. 400. (back issues avail.) **Indexed:** I D A, Int.Lab.Doc., Rural Devel.Abstr.
—BLDSC shelfmark: 5007.635000.
Formerly (until 1989): Manchester Papers on Development (ISSN 0260-8235)
Description: Presents scholarly research articles on the broad field of economic, political, and social development.

SOCIAL SCIENCES: COMPREHENSIVE WORKS

300   **US**   ISSN 0363-2873
JC571
JOURNAL OF LIBERTARIAN STUDIES. 1976. a. $24 to individuals; institutions $32. Center for Libertarian Studies, Box 4091, Burlingame, CA 94011-4091. FAX 415-342-9164. Ed. Murray N. Rothbard. adv.; circ. 1,000. (also avail. in microform from MIM,UMI; reprint service avail. from UMI) **Indexed:** Amer.Hist.& Life, Hist.Abstr., Phil.Ind.
—BLDSC shelfmark: 5010.320000.

300   **FJ**   ISSN 1011-3029
DU1
JOURNAL OF PACIFIC STUDIES. (Text in English) 1975. a. $6.50. University of the South Pacific, School of Social and Economic Development, P.O. Box 1168, Suva, Fiji. TEL 313-900. Ed. Nii K. Plange. bk.rev.; circ. 250. (back issues avail.)

300 960   **US**   ISSN 0888-6601
JOURNAL OF PAN AFRICAN STUDIES; an international medium of African culture and consciousness. 1987. q. $12 to individuals; institutions $20. California Institute of Pan African Studies, Box 13063, Fresno, CA 93794-3063. TEL 209-266-2550. Ed. Itibari M. Zulu. adv.; bk.rev.; circ. 1,000. (controlled). (back issues avail.)
Description: An interdisciplinary Afro-centric publication about African people throughout the world.

300   **UK**   ISSN 0143-814X
H96
JOURNAL OF PUBLIC POLICY. 1981. 4/yr. $53 to individuals; institutions $105. Cambridge University Press, Edinburgh Bldg., Shaftesbury Rd., Cambridge CB2 2RU, England. TEL 0223-312393. FAX 0223-315052. TELEX 851817256. (N. American addr.: Cambridge University Press, 40 W. 20th St., New York, NY 10011) Ed. Richard Rose. (also avail. in microform from UMI; reprint service avail. from SWZ) **Indexed:** A.B.C.Pol.Sci., ASSIA, Lang.& Lang.Behav.Abstr., Mid.East: Abstr.& Ind., P.A.I.S., Res.High.Educ.Abstr., Sage Pub.Admin.Abstr., Sage Urb.Stud.Abstr.
—BLDSC shelfmark: 5043.640000.
Description: Social scientists and policy-makers analyze the problems facing contemporary governments in their social, economic and political contexts.

JOURNAL OF REGIONAL AND LOCAL STUDIES. see HISTORY — History Of Europe

JOURNAL OF SOCIAL BEHAVIOR AND PERSONALITY. see PSYCHOLOGY

300   **JA**   ISSN 0454-2134
JOURNAL OF SOCIAL SCIENCE. (Text in English, Japanese) 1960. 3/yr. 1000 Yen per no. (typically set in Apr.). International Christian University, Social Science Research Institute - Kokusai Kiristokyo Daigaku, 3-10-2 Osawa, Mitaka, Tokyo 181, Japan. FAX 0422-33-9887. Eds. Koya Azumi, Shin Chiba. bk.rev.; circ. 650.
—BLDSC shelfmark: 5064.911000.

300   **II**   ISSN 0449-3168
JOURNAL OF SOCIAL SCIENCES. 1958. s-a. Agra University, Institute of Social Sciences, Agra 282004, Uttar Pradesh, India.

JOURNAL OF SOCIAL SCIENCES AND HUMANITIES/JINBUN GAKUHO. see HUMANITIES: COMPREHENSIVE WORKS

300   **BG**
JOURNAL OF SOCIAL STUDIES. Bengali edition: Samaj Nirikkhon. (Text in English) 1978. q. Tk.132($36) to individuals; institutions Tk.152 ($44). Centre for Social Studies - Samaj Nirikkhon Kendro, Dhaka University, Arts Building, Rm. 1107, Dhaka 1000, Bangladesh. Ed. B.K. Jahangir. adv.; bk.rev.; circ. 500. **Indexed:** Rice Abstr., Rural Devel.Abstr., Rural Recreat.Tour.Abstr., World Agri.Econ.& Rural Sociol.Abstr.

JOURNAL OF SOUTHEAST ASIA BUSINESS. see BUSINESS AND ECONOMICS — Economic Situation And Conditions

300   **UK**   ISSN 0305-7070
DT727
JOURNAL OF SOUTHERN AFRICAN STUDIES. 1974. 3/yr. £48($94) Oxford University Press, Oxford Journals, Pinkhill House, Southfield Road, Eynsham, Oxford OX8 1JJ, England. TEL 0865-882283. FAX 0865-882890. TELEX 837330 OXPRES G. Ed.Bd. bk.rev.; circ. 900. (also avail. in microform from UMI) **Indexed:** A.B.C.Pol.Sci., Amer.Hist.& Life, ASSIA, Br.Hum.Ind., Curr.Cont.Africa, Curr.Cont., Hist.Abstr., Int.Lab.Doc., Rural Devel.Abstr., Rural Recreat.Tour.Abstr., SSCI, Stud.Wom.Abstr., World Agri.Econ.& Rural Sociol.Abstr.
—BLDSC shelfmark: 5066.030000.
Description: Scholarly inquiry and exposition in the fields of economics, sociology, geography, demography, social anthropology, administration, law, political science, international relations, history, and natural sciences, as they relate to the human condition.

051   **US**   ISSN 0022-5231
L11
JOURNAL OF THOUGHT. 1966. q. $15. c/o Robert M. Lang, Ed., Leadership & Educational Policy Studies, Northern Illinois University, Dekalb, IL 60115. adv.; bk.rev.; index; circ. 500. (also avail. in microform from MIM,UMI; reprint service avail. from UMI) **Indexed:** C.I.J.E., Curr.Cont., Lang.& Lang.Behav.Abstr., Phil.Ind., Soc.Sci.Ind., Sociol.Abstr., SSCI.
—BLDSC shelfmark: 5069.300000.

JOURNAL OF UKRAINIAN STUDIES. see LITERATURE

JUDICATURE. see LAW — Judicial Systems

KALYANI; journal of humanities and social sciences of the University of Kelaniya. see HUMANITIES: COMPREHENSIVE WORKS

300   **II**   ISSN 0075-5176
KARNATAK UNIVERSITY, DHARWAD, INDIA. JOURNAL. SOCIAL SCIENCES. (Text in English) 1965. a. Rs.8($4) Karnatak University, Director, Prasaranga, Dharwad 580003, Karnataka, India. Ed. K. Chandrasekharaiah. circ. 500.

300   **PL**
KATOLICKI UNIWERSYTET LUBELSKI. WYDZIAL NAUK SPOLECZNYCH. ROZPRAWY. (Text in Polish; summaries in English or French) 1947. irreg. price varies. Katolicki Uniwersytet Lubelski, Towarzystwo Naukowe, Ul. Gliniana 21, 20-616 Lublin, Poland. index; circ. 1,025.

300   **CC**
KEJI FAZHAN YU GAIGE/SCIENCE AND TECHNOLOGY DEVELOPMENT AND REFORM. (Text in Chinese) m. Beijing Kexuexue Yanjiu Zhongxin, 6 Laohu Miao, Chenggongzhuang Xilu, Beijing 100044, People's Republic of China. TEL 8411527. Ed. Li Weiyi.

300   **US**   ISSN 0748-8815
JK1
KETTERING REVIEW; a journal of ideas and activities dedicated to improving the quality of public life in the American democracy. 1983. 4/yr. $9. Charles F. Kettering Foundation, 200 Commons Rd., Dayton, OH 45459-2799. TEL 513-434-7300. Ed. Robert J. Kingston. circ. 8,000.

300   **CC**   ISSN 0254-8763
KEXUE DUI SHEHUI DE YINGXIANG/SCIENCE IMPACT ON SOCIETY. (Text in Chinese) q. Zhongguo Kexueyuan, Keji Zhengce yu Guanli Kexue Yanjiusuo - Chinese Academy of Sciences, Research Institute of Science and Technology Policy and Management, P.O. Box 8712, Beijing 100080, People's Republic of China. TEL 289831. Ed. Shen Chenru.

300   **CC**   ISSN 1001-3210
KEXUE SHEHUI ZHUYI/SCIENTIFIC SOCIALISM. (Text in Chinese) bi-m. Zhongguo Gongyun Xueyuan, 2, Huayuancun, Haidian-qu, Beijing 100037, People's Republic of China. TEL 8314477. Ed. An Naizhang.

300   **US**   ISSN 0897-1986
T10.5
KNOWLEDGE AND POLICY; the international journal of knowledge transfer. 1988. q. $36 to individuals (foreign $56); institutions $72 (foreign $92). Transaction Publishers, Transaction Periodicals Consortium, Department 3092, Rutgers University, New Brunswick, NJ 08903. TEL 908-932-2280. FAX 908-932-3138. Ed. William N. Dunn. adv.; bk.rev.; circ. 400.
Formerly (until 1991): Knowledge in Society.
Description: Devoted to the development of an interdisciplinary science of knowledge transfer.

KOBE UNIVERSITY OF MERCANTILE MARINE. REVIEW. PART 1. STUDIES IN HUMANITIES AND SOCIAL SCIENCE. see HUMANITIES: COMPREHENSIVE WORKS

309.1   **KO**
KOREAN SOCIAL SCIENCE JOURNAL. (Text in English) 1973. a. $10. Korean National Commission for UNESCO, Box Central 64, Seoul, S. Korea. FAX 82-2-774-3956. TELEX MOCNDM-K23231-2 EXT.6364. (Co-sponsor: Korean Social Science Research Council) bibl.; stat. **Indexed:** Mid.East: Abstr.& Ind., Psychol.Abstr.
Formerly: Social Science Journal.

KULTUR UND GESELLSCHAFT; Neue historische Forschungen. see HISTORY

KULTURGEOGRAFISKE HAEFTER. see GEOGRAPHY

KYUSHU INSTITUTE OF TECHNOLOGY. BULLETIN: HUMANITIES, SOCIAL SCIENCES/KYUSHU KOGYO DAIGAKU KENKYU HOKOKU: JINBUN-SHAKAI-KAGAKU. see HUMANITIES: COMPREHENSIVE WORKS

980   **US**   ISSN 0890-7218
F1401
L A S A FORUM. 1969. q. $30 to non-members (effective 1992). Latin American Studies Association, William Pitt Union, 9th Fl., University of Pittsburgh, Pittsburgh, PA 15260. TEL 412-648-7929. FAX 412-624-7145. Ed. Reid Reading. adv.; circ. 3,350.
Formerly: Latin American Studies Association Newsletter (ISSN 0023-8805)
Description: Contains brief, research-based articles, letters and announcements, employment, research, and study opportunities, opinion pieces, and other information of interest to members.

331 960   **CN**   ISSN 0706-1706
LABOUR, CAPITAL AND SOCIETY/TRAVAIL, CAPITAL ET SOCIETE; a journal on the Third World. (Text in English, French) 1968. s-a. $12 to individuals; institutions $18; Third World countries $8. McGill University, Centre for Developing Area Studies, 3715 Peel St., Montreal, Que. H3A 1X1, Canada. TEL 514-398-3508. FAX 514-398-8432. Ed. Rosalind E. Boyd. adv.; bk.rev.; circ. 800. **Indexed:** Alt.Press Ind., ASSIA, E.I., Geo.Abstr., Human Resour.Abstr., I D A, Int.Lab.Doc., P.A.I.S., Rural Devel.Abstr., Rural Ext.Educ.& Tr.Abstr., Rural Recreat.Tour.Abstr., Soc.Sci.Ind., SSCI, World Agri.Econ.& Rural Sociol.Abstr.
—BLDSC shelfmark: 5142.065000.
Former titles (until vol.12, 1979): Manpower and Unemployment Research; Manpower and Unemployment Research in Africa. Newsletter.

918 980   **CC**
LADING MEIZHOU YANJIU/LATIN AMERICAN STUDIES. (Text in Chinese) bi-m. $17.60. Zhongguo Shehui Kexueyuan, Lading Meizhou Yanjiusuo - Chinese Academy of Social Sciences, Institute on Latin America, P.O. Box 1104, No.3, Zhangzizhong Lu, Beijing 100007, People's Republic of China. TEL 445031. (Dist. in US by: China Books & Periodicals, Inc., 2929 24th St., San Francisco, CA 94110. TEL 415-282-2994) Ed. Su Zhenxing.

300 001.3   **US**
LATIN AMERICAN MONOGRAPH AND DOCUMENT SERIES. irreg., no.10,1987. $4 (free to students). University of Pittsburgh, Center for Latin American Studies, 4-E-04 Forbes Quadrangle, University Center for International Studies, Pittsburgh, PA 15260.

SOCIAL SCIENCES: COMPREHENSIVE WORKS

970   US   ISSN 0075-8108
LATIN AMERICAN MONOGRAPHS. 1965. irreg., no.26, 1984. price varies. (University of Florida, Center for Latin American Studies) University Presses of Florida, 15 N. W. 15 St., Gainesville, FL 32603. TEL 904-392-1351. Ed.Bd. (reprint service avail. from KTO) **Indexed:** SSCI.
—BLDSC shelfmark: 5160.077000.

300   320.531   US   ISSN 0094-582X
F1401
LATIN AMERICAN PERSPECTIVES; a journal on Capitalism and Socialism. 1974. q. $38 to individuals; institutions $112. Sage Publications, Inc., 2455 Teller Rd., Newbury Park, CA 91320. TEL 805-499-0721. FAX 805-499-0871. (Subscr. to: Box 5084, Newbury Park, CA 91359) Ed. Ronald H. Chilcote. adv.; bk.rev.; circ. 1,300. (also avail. in microfiche; microform from UMI; back issues avail.) **Indexed:** A.B.C.Pol.Sci., Alt.Press Ind., Amer.Hist.& Life, Bibl.Ind., Chic.Per.Ind., Curr.Cont., Hisp.Amer.Per.Ind., Hist.Abstr., I D A, Int.Lab.Doc., Int.Polit.Sci.Abstr., Left Ind. (1982-), P.A.I.S., Peace Res.Abstr., Sage Fam.Stud.Abstr., Sociol.Abstr., SSCI.
—BLDSC shelfmark: 5160.085000.

980   300   US   ISSN 0023-8791
F1401
LATIN AMERICAN RESEARCH REVIEW; a journal to achieve greater and more systematic communication among individuals and institutions concerned with scholarly studies of Latin America. (Text in English and Spanish) 1965. 3/yr. $25 to individuals; institutions $40; students $18(effective Jan. 1991). Latin American Studies Association (Albuquerque), c/o University of New Mexico, 801 Yale N.E., Albuquerque, NM 87131. TEL 505-277-5985. FAX 505-277-5989. Ed. Gilbert W. Merkx. adv.; bk.rev.; bibl.; charts; index, cum.index; circ. 4,500. (also avail. in microform from JAI,MIM,UMI; back issues avail.; reprint service avail. from KTO) **Indexed:** A.B.C.Pol.Sci., Acad.Ind., Amer.Hist.& Life, Chic.Per.Ind., Curr.Cont., Film Lit.Ind. (1989-), Geo.Abstr., Hisp.Amer.Per.Ind., Hist.Abstr., I D A, Int.Lab.Doc., P.A.I.S., Soc.Sci.Ind., SSCI.
—BLDSC shelfmark: 5160.120000.
Description: Scholarly articles, research reports and notes, and review essays to promote and expound studies of Latin American culture, politics, and economics.

300   016   US
LATIN AMERICAN STUDIES WORKING PAPERS. (Text in English and Spanish) 1972. irreg. price varies. Indiana University, Center for Latin American & Caribbean Studies, 313 N. Jordan, Bloomington, IN 47405. (back issues avail.)

300   US
LATINOAMERICA. no.17, 1985. a. Universidad Nacional Autonoma de Mexico, Centro Coordinador y Difusor de Estudios Latinoamericanos, P.B. de la Torre I de Humanidades, Ciudad Universitaria C.P. 04510, Mexico, D.F., Mexico. Ed. Elsa Cecilia Frost. circ. 1,000. **Indexed:** Amer.Hist.& Life.

LAW AND SOCIAL INQUIRY. see *LAW*

LAW & SOCIETY REVIEW. see *LAW*

LER HISTORIA. see *HISTORY — History Of Europe*

300   GW   ISSN 0340-0425
H5
LEVIATHAN; Zeitschrift fuer Sozialwissenschaft. 1973. q. DM.79 (students DM.46). Westdeutscher Verlag GmbH, Postfach 5829, 6200 Wiesbaden 1, Germany. TEL 0611-160230. FAX 0611-160229. TELEX 4186-928-VWV-D. Ed. B.v Greiff. adv.; bk.rev. **Indexed:** P.A.I.S.For.Lang.Ind.
—BLDSC shelfmark: 5104.500000.

966.6   300   US   ISSN 0024-1989
DT621
LIBERIAN STUDIES JOURNAL.* 1968. s-a. $25. Liberian Studies Association, c/o Dr. Thomas C. Hendrix, 2025 E. Lincoln, Ste. 1203, Bloomington, IL 61701. TEL 708-848-2202. Ed. D. Elwood Dunn. bk.rev.; bibl. (back issues avail.) **Indexed:** Amer.Hist.& Life, Curr.Cont.Africa, Hist.Abstr., M.L.A.
—BLDSC shelfmark: 5186.740000.

966.6   300   US
LIBERIAN STUDIES MONOGRAPH SERIES. 1972. irreg., no.8, 1985. price varies. Arden Associates, Corp., Box 232, Lansdowne, PA 19050. charts; illus.

966.6   300   US
LIBERIAN STUDIES RESEARCH WORKING PAPERS. 1971. irreg., no.7, 1980. price varies. Arden Associates, Corp., Box 232, Lansdowne, PA 19050. bibl.

LIBERTARIAN ALLIANCE. SCIENTIFIC NOTES. see *POLITICAL SCIENCE*

LIBRARY OF LAW AND CONTEMPORARY PROBLEMS. see *LAW*

300   CC
LILUN YU XIANDAIHUI/THEORY AND MODERNIZATION. (Text in Chinese) m. Tianjin Shi Shehui Kexuejie Lianhehui, 4, Machang Dao, Heping-qu, Tianjin 300050, People's Republic of China. TEL 398649. Ed. Yu Zonghao.

300   MY
M C D S OCCASIONAL PAPER SERIES. (Text in English) 1974. irreg., latest no.6. exchange basis. Malaysian Centre for Development Studies, Prime Minister's Department, Government Complex, Block K 11 & K 12, Jalan Duta, Kuala Lumpur, Malaysia. Ed. Engku M. Anuar.

M I. (Mladi Istrazivaci Srbije) see *EDUCATION*

300   CN   ISSN 0076-1893
MCGILL UNIVERSITY, MONTREAL. CENTRE FOR DEVELOPING-AREA STUDIES. ANNUAL REPORT. 1967. a. $3. McGill University, Centre for Developing-Area Studies, 3715 Peel St., Montreal, Que. H3A 1X1, Canada. TEL 514-398-3507. FAX 514-398-8432.

MAGHREB, MACHREK, MONDE ARABE. see *POLITICAL SCIENCE*

MAISON FRANCO-JAPONAISE. BULLETIN. see *ORIENTAL STUDIES*

300   XN   ISSN 0350-1698
MAKEDONSKA AKADEMIJA NA NAUKITE I UMETNOSTITE. ODDELENIE ZA OPSTESTVENI NAUKI. PRILOZI/MACEDONIAN ACADEMY OF SCIENCES AND ARTS. SECTION OF SOCIAL SCIENCES. CONTRIBUTIONS. 1970. s-a. Makedonska Akademija na Naukite i Umetnostite, Oddelenie za Opstestveni Nauki, Bulevar Krste Misirkov bb, Box 428, Skopje, Macedonia. TEL 235-506. Ed. Ksente Bogoev.
Description: Research in economy, law, education, history, sociology and philosophy.

300   MW
MALAWI JOURNAL OF SOCIAL SCIENCE. 1972. a. $7. University of Malawi, Faculty of Social Science, Box 280, Zomba, Malawi. Ed.Bd. bk.rev.; circ. 500. (back issues avail.)
Formerly: Chancellor College. Journal of Social Science (ISSN 0302-3060)

MAN IN SOUTHEAST ASIA. see *ANTHROPOLOGY*

MANAB MON; a journal depicting the modern trends in psychology, biology, and sociology. see *PSYCHOLOGY*

MANCHESTER SCHOOL OF ECONOMIC AND SOCIAL STUDIES. see *BUSINESS AND ECONOMICS — Economic Systems And Theories, Economic History*

300   II
MANTHAN. (Text in English and Hindi) 1978. m. Rs.50($25) Deendayal Research Institute, 7E, Swami Ramtirth Nagar, New Delhi 110055, India. Ed. K.R. Malkani. adv.; bk.rev.; circ. 10,000. **Indexed:** G.Indian Per.Lit.

954.93   300   CE   ISSN 0047-5912
HC424.A1
MARGA. (Text in English) 1972. q. $25. Marga Institute, Sri Lanka Centre for Development Studies, Box 601, 61 Isipathana Mawatha, Colombo 5, Sri Lanka. FAX 1-589739. TELEX 21642-MARGA-CE. Ed. Godfrey Gunatilleke. adv.; bk.rev.; circ. 2,000. **Indexed:** HR Rep., Int.Lab.Doc., Rural Devel.Abstr., Rural Recreat.Tour.Abstr., Sri Lanka Sci.Ind., World Agri.Econ.& Rural Sociol.Abstr.
—BLDSC shelfmark: 5373.503000.
Description: Touches on social and economic problems.

MARXIST VEEKSHANAM; theoretical discussion forum. see *POLITICAL SCIENCE*

300   320.531   GW   ISSN 0171-3698
MARXISTISCHE STUDIEN. 1978. biennial. DM.32($11) Institut fuer Marxistische Studien und Forschungen, Liebigstr. 6, D-6000 Frankfurt, M.-1, Germany. Ed.Bd. circ. 3,000. (back issues avail.)

MASTER'S THESES IN THE ARTS AND SOCIAL SCIENCES. see *HUMANITIES: COMPREHENSIVE WORKS*

MATHEMATICAL SOCIAL SCIENCES. see *MATHEMATICS*

300   UG   ISSN 0047-6293
DT1
MAWAZO; the Makerere journal of the arts and social sciences. (Text in English) 1968. s-a. $6 per no. Makerere University, Faculty of Arts & Social Sciences, P.O. Box 7062, Kampala, Uganda. Ed. Mahmood Mamdani. adv.; bk.rev.; circ. 2,500. **Indexed:** Amer.Hist.& Life, Hist.Abstr., M.L.A.

MAX-PLANCK-GESELLSCHAFT. JAHRBUCH. see *SCIENCES: COMPREHENSIVE WORKS*

059.96   TZ   ISSN 0025-6234
MBIONI.* (Text in English) 1964. m. 10s.($4.20) Kivukoni College, P.O. Box 9193, Dar es Salaam, Tanzania. bk.rev.; index; circ. 4,000.

MEDDELELSER OM GROENLAND, MAN & SOCIETY. see *ANTHROPOLOGY*

MEDIA MONITOR (WASHINGTON). see *COMMUNICATIONS*

300   MM
MEDITERRANEAN SOCIAL SCIENCES NETWORK JOURNAL. 1988. 3/yr. £10.50($35) Foundation for International Studies, St. Paul St., Valletta, Malta. TEL 0356-234121. Ed. Carmel Tabone. circ. 1,500. (back issues avail.)
Formerly: Mediterranean Social Sciences Network Newsletter (ISSN 1015-5090)
Description: Provides a forum for academic dialogue among Mediterranean institutes working in the social sciences.

390   II
MEERUT UNIVERSITY SANSKRIT RESEARCH JOURNAL. (Text in English, Hindi or Sanskrit) 1976. s-a. Rs.60($10) c/o Dr. M.C. Bhartiya, IIA-220 Nehru Nagar, Ghaziabad 201001, India. Ed. M.C. Bhartiya. adv.; bk.rev.; circ. 200.
Formerly: Meerut University Sanskrit Research.

300   CC
MEIGUO YANJIU/AMERICAN STUDIES. (Text in Chinese) q. Zhongguo Shehui Kexueyuan, Meiguo Yanjiusuo - Chinese Academy of Social Sciences, Institute of American Studies, No.5, Jianguomennei Dajie, Beijing 100732, People's Republic of China. TEL 5137559. Ed. Li Zhen.

300   US   ISSN 0252-9963
F1421
MESOAMERICA. 1980. s-a. $18. Centro de Investigaciones Regionales de Mesoamerica (CIRMA), Plumsock Mesoamerican Studies, Box 38, S. Woodstock, VT 05071. TEL 802-457-1199. Eds. Christopher H. Lutz, Cherri M. Pancake. adv.; bk.rev.; cum.index. (back issues avail.) **Indexed:** A.I.C.P., Abstr.Anthropol., Hisp.Amer.Per.Ind., Int.Bibl.Soc.Sci., M.L.A., Popul.Ind., SSCI.

300   VI
MICROSTATE STUDIES. 1977. a. College of the Virgin Islands, Caribbean Research Institute, St. Thomas, VI 00801. Ed. Norwell Harrigan. circ. 200.

956   300   US   ISSN 0026-3184
DS41   CODEN: MESBEL
MIDDLE EAST STUDIES ASSOCIATION BULLETIN. 1967. 2/yr. $60 membership. Middle East Studies Association of North America, Inc., 1232 N. Cherry Ave., University of Arizona, Tucson, AZ 85721. TEL 602-621-5850. FAX 602-321-7752. Ed. Jon W. Anderson. adv.; bk.rev.; abstr.; index; circ. 2,200. **Indexed:** Amer.Bibl.Slavic & E.Eur.Stud., Amer.Hist.& Life, Hist.Abstr., Mid.East: Abstr.& Ind.

SOCIAL SCIENCES: COMPREHENSIVE WORKS

300　　　　　　　　US　　ISSN 0739-8069
H62.5.U5
MIDDLE STATES COUNCIL FOR THE SOCIAL STUDIES. JOURNAL. 1978. a. $10. Middle States Council for the Social Studies, Rider College, 2083 Lawrenceville Rd., Lawrenceville, NJ 08648-3099. TEL 609-896-5176. Eds. David Pierfy, Rodger C. Henderson. adv.; bk.rev.; circ. 1,100. (back issues avail.; reprint service avail. from UMI)
  Supersedes (1903-1978): Middle States Council for the Social Studies. Proceedings.

MIDWESTERN ARCHIVIST. see HISTORY

MIGRATION WORLD; a bi-monthly magazine focusing on the newest immigrant and refugee groups; policy and legislation; resources. see POPULATION STUDIES

MILBANK QUARTERLY. see POLITICAL SCIENCE

300　　　　　　　　CC
MINSU YANJIU/FOLK CUSTOM STUDY. (Text in Chinese) q. Shandong Daxue - Shandong University, Shandong Daxue Laoxiao, Jinan, Shandong 250100, People's Republic of China. TEL 643861. Ed. Li Wanpeng.

MINZU TUANJIE/UNITY OF NATIONALITIES. see ETHNIC INTERESTS

MODERN CHINA; an international quarterly of history and social science. see HISTORY — History Of Asia

300　　　　　　　　CE
MODERN SRI LANKA STUDIES; journal of the social sciences. (Text in English) 1970. s-a. Rs.120($20) University of Peradeniya, P.O. Box 35, Peradeniya, Sri Lanka. Eds. K. Tudor Silra, Mahinda Werake. bk.rev.; circ. 500.
  Formerly: Modern Ceylon Studies.

MONOGRAPHS IN ECONOMIC AND SOCIAL HISTORY. see BUSINESS AND ECONOMICS — Economic Systems And Theories, Economic History

301.15 331.1
MONOGRAPHS IN ORGANIZATIONAL BEHAVIOUR AND INDUSTRIAL RELATIONS. 1983. irreg., vol.10, 1989. $58.50 to institutions. J A I Press Inc., 55 Old Post Rd., No. 2, Box 1678, Greenwich, CT 06836-1678. TEL 203-661-7602. Ed. Samuel B. Bacharach. bibl.; index.

MONOGRAPHS ON SCIENCE, TECHNOLOGY, AND SOCIETY. see TECHNOLOGY: COMPREHENSIVE WORKS

MUSEE ROYAL DE L'AFRIQUE CENTRALE. ANNALES. SERIE IN 8. SCIENCES HUMAINES/KONINKLIJK MUSEUM VOOR MIDDEN-AFRIKA. ANNALEN. REEKS IN 8. MENSELIJKE WETENSCHAPPEN. see HUMANITIES: COMPREHENSIVE WORKS

300　　　　　　　　LE
AL-MUSTAQBAL AL-ARABI/ARAB FUTURE. 1978. m. $50 to individuals in Arab countries; elsewhere $70; institutions $90. Centre for Arab Unity Studies - Markaz Dirasat al-Wahdah al-Arabiyyah, PO Box 113-6001, Beirut, Lebanon. TEL 801582. FAX 802223. TELEX MARABI 23114LE. adv.; bk.rev.; circ. 8,000.

312 614 301　　　　　　　　NE
N A T O ADVANCED SCIENCE INSTITUTES SERIES D: BEHAVIOURAL AND SOCIAL SCIENCES. (Text in English) 1974. s-a. (North Atlantic Treaty Organization, Scientific Affairs Division) Kluwer Academic Publishers, Postbus 17, 3300 AA Dordrecht, Netherlands. TEL 078-334911. FAX 078-334254. TELEX 29245. (Dist. by: Kluwer Academic Publishers Group, P.O. Box 322, 3300 AH, Dordrecht, Netherlands; N. America dist. addr.: Box 358, Accord Station, Hingham, MA 02018-0358. TEL 617-871-6600) **Indexed:** Math.R.
  ●Also available online. Vendor(s): European Space Agency (File no.128).
  Formerly: N A T O Advanced Study Institutes Series D: Behavioural and Social Sciences.

N F E - W I D EXCHANGE - ASIA. NEWSLETTER. see EDUCATION

300 330　　　　　　　　NR
N I S E R OCCASIONAL PAPERS. irreg. price varies. Nigerian Institute of Social and Economic Research, P.M.B. 5, University of Ibadan, Ibadan, Nigeria. TEL 022-400501-5. TELEX 31119 NISER G. Ed. Remi Lawal.

300　　　　　　　　II
N.K. BOSE MEMORIAL FOUNDATION. NEWSLETTER. (Text in English) 1978. q. Rs.15. N.K. Bose Memorial Foundation, B-8-9 Bara Gambhir Singh, Gauriganj, Varanasi 221001, India. Ed. Baidyanath Saraswati. bk.rev.; circ. 300.

300　　　　　　　　US
N O R C REPORT. 1941. biennial. National Opinion Research Center, 1155 E. 60th St., Chicago, IL 60637. TEL 312-702-1200. Ed. Jeff Hackett.
  Formerly (until 1981): National Opinion Research Center. Report (ISSN 0077-5274)

300　　　　　　　　PP
N R I DISCUSSION PAPERS. 1976. irreg. price varies. National Research Institute, P.O. Box 5854, Boroko, NCD, Papua New Guinea. TEL 675-26-0300. FAX 675-26-0213. **Indexed:** I D A, Rural Devel.Abstr., Rural Recreat.Tour.Abstr., World Agri.Econ. & Rural Sociol.Abstr.
  Formerly: I A S E R Discussion Papers.

300　　　　　　　　PP
N R I MONOGRAPHS. 1976. irreg. price varies. National Research Institute, P.O. Box 5854, Boroko, NCD, Papua New Guinea. TEL 675-26-0300. FAX 674-26-0213. **Indexed:** Geo.Abstr.
  Formerly: I A S E R Monographs.

300　　　　　　　　PP
N R I SPECIAL PUBLICATIONS. 1981. irreg. price varies. National Research Institute, P.O. Box 5854, Boroko, NCD, Papua New Guinea. TEL 675-26-0300. FAX 675-26-0312. Ed. Jim Robbins. circ. 350. **Indexed:** Rural Devel.Abstr., World Agri.Econ.& Rural Sociol.Abstr.
  Formerly (until 1989): I A S E R Special Publications.

300　　　　　　　　IR
NAME-YE 'OLUM-E EJTEMA'I.* 1968. q. Rs.320. University of Teheran, Faculty of Social Sciences, Enghelab Ave., Teheran, Iran. TELEX 13944.
  Description: Includes different areas of social sciences such as sociological schools of thought, research articles, intellectuals and theories, the third world and its problems, research in the problems of Iran.

300　　　　　　　　SX
NAMIBIA SCIENTIFIC SOCIETY. JOURNAL. (Text in Afrikaans, English and German) 1925. a. membership. Namibia Scientific Society, 110 Leutwein St., P.O. Box 67, Windhoek 9000, Namibia. TEL 061-225372. Ed. A. Henrichsen. adv.; bk.rev.; illus.
  Formerly: South West Africa Scientific Society. Journal.

378 371　　　　　　　　CC　　ISSN 0257-5892
NANJING DAXUE XUEBAO (ZHEXUE SHEHUI KEXUE BAN)/NANJING UNIVERSITY. JOURNAL (SOCIAL SCIENCE EDITION). (Text in Chinese; table of contents in English) bi-m. Nanjing Daxue Chubanshe - Nanjing University Press, Nanjing, Jiangsu 210008, People's Republic of China. index.
  —BLDSC shelfmark: 4828.682500.
  Description: Each issue is devoted to a specific topic.

300　　　　　　　　CC　　ISSN 1001-8263
NANJING SHEHUI KEXUE/NANJING SOCIAL SCIENCES. (Text in Chinese) bi-m. Nanjing Zhexue Shehui Kexue Lianhehui, 257 Baixia Lu, Nanjing, Jiangsu 210001, People's Republic of China. TEL 408499. Ed. Lu Jianjie.

300　　　　　　　　CC　　ISSN 1001-4608
NANJING SHIFAN DAXUE XUEBAO (SHEHUI KEXUE BAN)/NANJING NORMAL UNIVERSTIY. JOURNAL (SOCIAL SCIENCE EDITION). (Text in Chinese) q. Nanjing Shifan Daxue - Nanjing Normal Universtiy, 122 Ninghai Lu, Nanjing, Jiangsu 210024, People's Republic of China. TEL 531535. Ed. Ju Siwei.

300 100　　　　　　　　CC　　ISSN 1001-4667
NANKAI XUEBAO. ZHEXUE SHEHUI KEXUE BAN/NANKAI UNIVERSITY. JOURNAL. PHILOSOPHY AND SOCIAL SCIENCES EDITION.. (Text in Chinese; table of contents in English) m. Y16.80. (Nankai Daxue - Nankai University) Nankai Xuebao Bianjibu, Balitai, Nankai-qu, Tianjin 300071, People's Republic of China. TEL 34412-538. (Dist. outside China by: China International Book Trading Corp., P.O. Box 2820, Beijing, P.R.C.) Ed. Zhu Guanghua. charts.
  —BLDSC shelfmark: 6015.333800.

300　　　　　　　　GW　　ISSN 0176-6023
NASSAUER GESPRAECHE DER FREIHERR-VOM-STEIN-GESELLSCHAFT. 1985. irreg., vol.4, 1991. price varies. Franz Steiner Verlag Wiesbaden GmbH, Birkenwaldstr. 44, Postfach 101526, 7000 Stuttgart 1, Germany. TEL 0711-2582-0. FAX 0711-2582290. TELEX 723626-DAZD.

300　　　　　　　　US　　ISSN 0077-4049
NATIONAL COUNCIL FOR THE SOCIAL STUDIES. BULLETINS. 1964. irreg. price varies. National Council for the Social Studies, 3501 Newark St., N.W., Washington, DC 20016. TEL 202-966-7840. adv. **Indexed:** Curr.Cont., SSCI.

300　　　　　　　　UK　　ISSN 0077-491X
H11
NATIONAL INSTITUTE OF ECONOMIC AND SOCIAL RESEARCH. ANNUAL REPORT. 1941. a. free. National Institute of Economic and Social Research, 2 Dean Trench St., Smith Sq., London SW1P 3HE, England. TEL 01-222-7665. FAX 01-222-1435. circ. 2,000. **Indexed:** A.I.C.P.

NATIONAL INSTITUTE OF ECONOMIC AND SOCIAL RESEARCH, LONDON. ECONOMIC AND SOCIAL STUDIES. see BUSINESS AND ECONOMICS

NATIONAL RESEARCH COUNCIL OF THAILAND. JOURNAL. see SCIENCES: COMPREHENSIVE WORKS

300 364　　　　　　　　UA　　ISSN 0028-0062
NATIONAL REVIEW OF SOCIAL SCIENCES. (Text in Arabic and English) 1964. 3/yr. 150. National Center for Social and Criminological Research, Zamalek P.O., Cairo, Egypt. Ed. Dr. Ahmed M. Khalifa. bk.rev.; charts; illus.

300　　　　　　　　CH　　ISSN 0077-5835
H8.C47
NATIONAL TAIWAN UNIVERSITY. COLLEGE OF LAW. JOURNAL OF SOCIAL SCIENCE. (Text in Chinese or English) 1950. irreg., no.34, 1986. NT.$180. National Taiwan University, College of Law, Taipei, Taiwan, Republic of China.

300 320　　　　　　　　US　　ISSN 0090-5992
DR24
NATIONALITIES PAPERS. 1972. s-a. $18. Association for the Study of Nationalities (U.S.S.R. and East Europe), Inc., c/o Michael Rywkin, Russian Area Studies, City College, Convent Ave. at 138th St., New York, NY 10031. TEL 217-581-2021. FAX 212-650-7385. (Subscr. to: Andris Skreija, Sec. Treas., Dept. of Sociology, Univ. of Nebraska at Omaha, Box 688, Omaha, NE 68182) Ed. Henry R. Huttenbach. adv.; bk.rev.; bibl.; circ. 1,200. (processed; also avail. in microfiche; reprint service avail. from UMI, ISI) **Indexed:** Amer.Bibl.Slavic & E.Eur.Stud., Amer.Hist.& Life, Hist.Abstr., HR Rep., Lang.& Lang.Behav.Abstr., M.L.A.
  —BLDSC shelfmark: 6033.449000.
  Description: Focuses on nationality and minority questions in Eastern Europe and the USSR.

330　　　　　　　　DK　　ISSN 0028-0453
HB9
NATIONALOEKONOMISK TIDSSKRIFT. (Text in Danish; occasionally in other Scandinavian languages or English; summaries in English) 1873. 3/yr. $50. Nationaloekonomisk Forening, Danmarks Nationalbank, Havnegade 5, DK-1093 Copenhagen K, Denmark. FAX 33-325460. Ed. Thorkild Davidsen. adv.; bk.rev.; bibl.; index, cum.index every 25 yrs.; circ. 2,200. (also avail. in microfilm from UMI; reprint service avail. from ISI,UMI) **Indexed:** Amer.Hist.& Life, Hist.Abstr., J.of Econ.Lit., SSCI.

NATURE, SOCIETY, AND THOUGHT; a journal of dialectical and historical materialism. see POLITICAL SCIENCE

300   YU   ISSN 0351-5699
NAUCNI PODMLADAK: DRUSTVENE NAUKE I FILOZOFIJA; strucni casopis studenata Univerziteta u Nisu. (Text in Serbo-Croatian; summaries in English) 1969. q. 2500 din. Univerzitet u Nisu, Strucno Udruzenje Studenata, Sumatovacka bb, 1800 Nis, Serbia, Yugoslavia. TEL 018-22-226. Ed. Miroslav Pavlovic. adv.; circ. 500.
   Supersedes in part (as of 1971): Naucni Podmladak: Tehnicke Nauki. Drustvene Nauki.

300   CC   ISSN 1000-5218
NEI MENGGU DAXUE XUEBAO (SHEHUI KEXUE BAN)/INNER MONGOLIAN UNIVERSITY. JOURNAL (SOCIAL SCIENCE EDITION). (Text in Chinese) q. Nei Menggu Daxue - Inner Mongolian University, 1 Daxue Donglu, Huhhot, Nei Menggu 010021, People's Republic of China. TEL 43141. Ed. Te Buxin.

300   CC
NEI MENGGU SHEHUI KEXUE/INNER MONGOLIAN SOCIAL SCIENCES. (Editions in Chinese and Mongolian) bi-m. $22.50 for Chinese ed.; Mongolian ed. $23.90. Nei Menggu Shehui Kexueyuan - Inner Mongolian Academy of Social Sciences, Daxue Donglu, Huhhot, Nei Menggu 010010, People's Republic of China. (Dist. outside China by: China International Book Trading Corp., P.O. Box 399, P.R.C.; Dist. in US by: China Books & Periodicals, Inc., 2929 24th St., San Francisco, CA 94119. TEL 415-282-2994)

300   GW
NEUES SCHRIFTTUM ZUR DEUTSCHEN LANDESKUNDE. 1941. a. DM.150. Zentralausschuss fuer Deutsche Landeskunde, Universitaet Trier, Postfach 3825, 5500 Trier, Germany. TEL 0651-2012237. Ed. Walter Sperling. index.

NEW AMERICAN (APPLETON). see POLITICAL SCIENCE

NEW ENGLAND JOURNAL OF HISTORY. see HISTORY — History Of North And South America

NEW ENGLAND JOURNAL OF HUMAN SERVICES. see SOCIAL SERVICES AND WELFARE

NEW HUMANIST. see PHILOSOPHY

NEW ZEALAND SLAVONIC JOURNAL. see HUMANITIES: COMPREHENSIVE WORKS

NEXUS: CHINA IN FOCUS. see GENERAL INTEREST PERIODICALS — China

300 330   NR   ISSN 0078-074X
NIGERIAN INSTITUTE OF SOCIAL AND ECONOMIC RESEARCH. ANNUAL REPORT. 1954. a. free. Nigerian Institute of Social and Economic Research, Private Mail Bag 5, University of Ibadan, Ibadan, Nigeria. TEL 01-410935.
   Formerly: West African Institute of Social and Economic Research. Annual Report.

300   NR
NIGERIAN INSTITUTE OF SOCIAL AND ECONOMIC RESEARCH. RESEARCH FOR DEVELOPMENT. 1981. s-a. Nigerian Institute of Social and Economic Research, Private Mail Bag 5, University of Ibadan, Ibadan, Nigeria.

300   CC   ISSN 1001-5124
AS452.H314
NINGBO DAXUE XUEBAO (SHEHUI KEXUE BAN)/NINGBO UNIVERSITY. JOURNAL (SOCIAL SCIENCE EDITION). (Text in Chinese) s-a. Ningbo Daxue - Ningbo University, Ningbo, Zhejiang 315211, People's Republic of China. TEL 55545. Ed. Mao Zihui.

300   CC
NINGXIA SHEHUI KEXUE/SOCIAL SCIENCE IN NINGXIA. (Text in Chinese) bi-m. $22.50. (Ningxia Shehui Kexueyuan - Ningxia Academy of Social Sciences) China Books & Periodicals, Inc., Yinchuan, Ningxia, People's Republic of China. (Dist. in US by: China Books & Periodicals, Inc., 2929 24th St., San Francisco, CA 94110. TEL 415-282-2994)

300   CC   ISSN 0546-9503
NONGCUN GONGZUO TONGXUN/RURAL AFFAIRS BULLETIN. (Text in Chinese) m. Nongcun Gongzuo Tongxun Zazhishe, No. 61, Fuxing Lu, Beijing 100036, People's Republic of China. TEL 815502. Ed. Zhou Hongfei.

300 910   FI   ISSN 0345-8326
NORD REFO. (Text in Danish, Norwegian and Swedish) 1969. q. free. Nordiska Institutet foer Regionalpolitisk Forskning, PO Box 257, 001 71 Helsinki, Finland. FAX 01-602927. Ed. Goesta Oscarsson. circ. 1,500. (back issues avail.)
   Description: Deals with regional questions and regional policies in the Nordic countries

300   GW   ISSN 0138-2802
NORDEUROPA STUDIEN. 1966. a. DM.10. Nordeuropa-Institut der Ernst-Moritz-Arndt Universitaet, Hans-Fallada-Str. 20, 2200 Greifswald, Germany. FAX 0822-63311. TELEX 318336-UNIG-D. bk.rev.; circ. 1,000. (back issues avail.) **Indexed:** Amer.Hist.& Life, Hist.Abstr.
   Formerly: Nordeuropa. Jahrbuch fuer Nordische Studien.
   Description: Contains studies of topics in international relations, history, culture, literature, philology, and others.

NORTH DAKOTA QUARTERLY. see HUMANITIES: COMPREHENSIVE WORKS

300   US   ISSN 0029-3474
HB1
NORTHWEST TECHNOCRAT. 1939. q. $12. Technocracy Inc., Continental Headquarters, Savannah, OH 44874. TEL 206-784-2111. (Alt. addr.: 7513 Greenwood Ave., N., Seattle, WA 98103) (back issues avail.)

NOTEBOOKS FOR STUDY AND RESEARCH. see POLITICAL SCIENCE

300   UV   ISSN 0550-0923
DT553.U7
NOTES ET DOCUMENTS VOLTAIQUES; bulletin trimestriel d'information scientifique. 1950. q. 3000 Fr.CFA. Centre National de la Recherche Scientifique et Technique, B.P. 7047, Ouagadougou, Burkina Faso. circ. 350. **Indexed:** A.I.C.P., M.L.A., P.A.I.S.For.Lang.Ind.
   Formerly (until 1963): Etudes Voltaiques.

NUEVA CACERES REVIEW. see ANTHROPOLOGY

300   AG
NUEVAS PROPUESTAS. 3/yr. $16. Universidad Catolica de Santiago del Estero, Avda. Alsina, Casilla de Correo 285, 4200 Santiago del Estero, Argentina. TEL 21-3820.

NURSING RESEARCH. see MEDICAL SCIENCES — Nurses And Nursing

300   RU
OBSHCHESTVENNYE NAUKI I SOVREMENNOST'. 1976. 6/yr. 1.60 Rub. per issue. Akademiya Nauk, Koordinatsionnyi Sovet po Obshchestvennym Naukam, Arbat 33-12, 121818 Moscow G-2, Russia. TEL 241-07-84. Ed. V.V. Sogrin. circ. 6,320.
   Formerly (until 1991): Akademiya Nauk S.S.S.R. Obshchestvennye Nauki (ISSN 0132-3458)

300   UZ   ISSN 0029-7763
OBSHCHESTVENNYE NAUKI V UZBEKISTANE. (Text in Russian and Uzbek) 1956. m. 21 Rub. Akademiya Nauk Uzbekskoi S.S.R., Ul. Kuibysheva, 15, Tashkent, Uzbekistan. Ed. P.M. Krumov. bk.rev.; bibl.; charts; illus.; stat.; circ. 1,420.

OFAKIM. see POLITICAL SCIENCE

OFFSHOOTS OF ORGONOMY. see HUMANITIES: COMPREHENSIVE WORKS

300   JA   ISSN 0386-8176
OGASAWARA KENKYU/OGASAWARA RESEARCH. (Text in Japanese; summaries in English) 1978. irreg. free. Tokyo-toritsu Daigaku, Ogasawara Kenkyu Iinkai - Tokyo Metropolitan University, Ogasawara Research Committee, Minami-Ohsawa 1-1, Hachioji-shi, Tokyo 192-03, Japan. TEL 0426-77-1111. FAX 0426-77-2589. Ed. Kazuyoshi Miyashita. circ. 800. (back issues avail.)
   Formerly: Ogasawara Research Committee. Publications.

300   VE
OPCION; revista de ciencias humanas y sociales. 1984. 4/yr. Bs.100($10) Universidad del Zulia, Facultad Experimental de Ciencias, Departamento de Ciencias Humanas, Apdo. 526, Maracalbo, Venezuela. Ed.Bd.

300   US   ISSN 0370-1093
Q11   CODEN: PORSAU
OREGON ACADEMY OF SCIENCE. PROCEEDINGS. 1943. a. $8. Oregon Academy of Science, c/o Donald Unger, Sci-Tech Div., Kerr Library, Oregon State University, Corvallis, OR 97331. TEL 503-754-4592. Eds. Clade Curran, John Mairs. circ. 200. (reprint service avail.) **Indexed:** Biol.Abstr., Chem.Abstr.

300   GW   ISSN 0170-8406
ORGANIZATION STUDIES. 4/yr. $58 to individuals; institutions $116. (European Group for Organizational Studies) Walter de Gruyter und Co., Genthiner Str. 13, 1000 Berlin 30, Germany. TEL 030-26005-0. FAX 030-26005251. TELEX 184027. (U.S. addr.: Walter de Gruyter, Inc., 200 Saw Mill Rd., Hawthorne, NY 10532) **Indexed:** ABI Inform., BPIA, Bus.Ind., CINAHL, Cont.Pg.Manage., Curr.Cont., E.I., Lang.& Lang.Behav.Abstr., PSI, Psychol.Abstr., SCIMP (1981-), SSCI.
   —BLDSC shelfmark: 6290.730000.

300   GW   ISSN 0724-5246
ORIENTIERUNGEN ZUR GESELLSCHAFTS- UND WIRTSCHAFTSPOLITIK. q. DM.75 (foreign DM.77). Gustav Fischer Verlag, Wollgrasweg 49, Postfach 720143, 7000 Stuttgart 70, Germany. TEL 0711-458030. FAX 0711-4580334. TELEX 7111488-FIBUCH-D.

300 987   VE
OTOMAQUIA; revista cultural. 1986. irreg. Apdo. de Correos 252, Barinas 5201-A, Barinas, Venezuela. Ed.Bd.

320 338   UK
P S I DISCUSSION PAPERS. 1980. irreg. £55 (subscription also includes Report Series; Studies in European Politics; Policy Studies). Policy Studies Institute, 100 Park Village East, London NW1 3SR, England. TEL 01-387-2171. FAX 01-388-0914.

P S I: REPORT SERIES. (Policy Studies Institute) see POLITICAL SCIENCE

300   PH   ISSN 0115-1169
P S S C SOCIAL SCIENCE INFORMATION. 1973. q. P.40($8) Philippine Social Science Council, P.O. Box 655, Greenhills, Metro Manila 3113, Philippines. Ed.Bd. bk.rev.; circ. 1,500.
   —BLDSC shelfmark: 8318.161100.

300   AT   ISSN 0155-9060
PACIFIC RESEARCH MONOGRAPH. irreg. price varies. Australian National University, National Centre for Development Studies, G.P.O. Box 4, Canberra, A.C.T. 2601, Australia. TEL 616-249-4705. FAX 616-257-2886. **Indexed:** Rural Devel.Abstr., Trop.Oil Seeds Abstr., World Agri.Econ.& Rural Sociol.Abstr.
   —BLDSC shelfmark: 6330.875000.
   Description: Economic development, Pacific history, politics and policy issues.

572   US   ISSN 0275-3596
DU1
PACIFIC STUDIES; an interdisciplinary journal devoted to the study of the Pacific--its islands and adjacent countries. 1977. 4/yr. $30. (Institute for Polynesian Studies) Brigham Young University, Hawaii Campus, Box 1829, Laie, HI 96762. TEL 808-293-3667. FAX 808-293-3645. TELEX 6502972475 MCIUW. Ed. Dr. Dale B. Robertson. adv.; bk.rev.; circ. 500. (back issues avail.) **Indexed:** Abstr.Anthropol., Amer.Hist.& Life, Bk.Rev.Ind. (1989-), Child.Bk.Rev.Ind. (1989-), Hist.Abstr., P.A.I.S., Sociol.Abstr.
   —BLDSC shelfmark: 6331.520000.

300   GW
PAEDAGOGISCHE HOCHSCHULE KARL FRIEDRICH WILHELM WANDER. WISSENSCHAFTLICHE ZEITSCHRIFT. GESELLSCHAFTSWISSENSCHAFTLICHE REIHE. (Text in German; summaries in English, German and Russian) 1967. a. DM.60. Paedagogische Hochschule Karl Friedrich Wilhelm Wander, Dresden, PSF 365, 8060 Dresden, Germany. (Dist. by: Buchexport, Leninstr. 16, 7010, Leipzig, Germany) circ. 500.
   Supersedes in part: Paedagogische Hochschule Karl Friedrich Wilhelm Wander. Wissenschaftliche Zeitschrift (ISSN 0138-1520)

PANJAB UNIVERSITY RESEARCH BULLETIN (ARTS). see HUMANITIES: COMPREHENSIVE WORKS

SOCIAL SCIENCES: COMPREHENSIVE WORKS

300   II   ISSN 0555-7631
Q180.I5   CODEN: RBJUAT
PANJAB UNIVERSITY RESEARCH BULLETIN (SCIENCES). (Text in English) 1950. s-a. Rs.250($25) Panjab University, Publication Bureau, Chandigarh 160 014, Union Territory, India. Ed. S. Khera. **Indexed:** Bio-Contr.News & Info., Soyabean Abstr., Triticale Abstr., Trop.Oil Seeds Abstr.
—BLDSC shelfmark: 7731.200000.
    Description: Multi-disciplinary studies of sciences, on both pre-doctoral and post-doctoral levels.

300 900 500   US   ISSN 1056-8190
HT390
PAPERS IN REGIONAL SCIENCE. 1955. q. $110. Regional Science Association International, 1 Observatory, 901 S. Mathews, Univ. of Illinois, Urbana, IL 61801-3682. TEL 217-333-8904. FAX 217-244-1785. Ed.Bd. circ. 3,000. **Indexed:** ASCA, C.R.E.J., Geo.Abstr., Rural Recreat.Tour.Abstr., SSCI, World Agri.Econ.& Rural Sociol.Abstr.
    Formerly (until 1991, vol.70): Regional Science Association. Papers (ISSN 0486-2902)
    Refereed Serial

300   CH
PAPERS IN SOCIAL SCIENCES. no.80, 1980. irreg. Academia Sinica, Sun Yat-Sen Institute for Social Sciences and Philosopy - Chung Yang Yen Chiu Yuan Chung Shan Ren Wen Sheh Hui Ko Sheyue Yen Chiu So, Nankang, Taipei 11529, Taiwan, Republic of China. TEL 886-2-782-1693.
FAX 886-2-785-4160. **Indexed:** Psychol.Abstr.

300   NQ
PENSAMIENTO PROPIO. 1982. m. C.$20000($27) in Latin America and North America; Europe $32. Coordinadora Regional de Investigaciones Economicas y Sociales, Apdo. C-163, Managua, Nicaragua. TEL 26228. FAX 26180. (Novib de Holanda) Ed. Sanda Garcia. adv.; bk.rev.; circ. 5,000. (back issues avail.)

PENSAMIENTO Y ACCION. see *SCIENCES: COMPREHENSIVE WORKS*

300 200   CL   ISSN 0716-730X
PERSONA Y SOCIEDAD. 1987. 3/yr. Esc.4500($30) to individuals; institutions Esc.5000 ($38). Instituto Latinoamericano de Doctrina y Estudios Sociales, Departamento de Publicaciones, Almirante Barroso 6, Casilla 14446, Correo 21, Santiago, Chile. TEL 02-717499. FAX 02-6986873. Ed. Francisco Lopez F.
    Description: Analyzes and discusses the problems of the relationship between faith and culture in Latin America.

PERSPECTIVA; ciencia-arte-tecnologia. see *SCIENCES: COMPREHENSIVE WORKS*

300   BL   ISSN 0101-3459
AS80.A1   CODEN: PRSVDY
PERSPECTIVAS; revista de ciencias sociais. (Text in Portuguese; summaries in English and Portuguese) 1976-1977; resumed 1980. a. $30 or exchange basis. Universidade Estadual Paulista, Av. Vicente Ferreira 1278, Caixa Postal 603, 17.500 Marilia SP, Brazil. TEL 0144-33-1844.
FAX 0144-22-2504. TELEX 111-9016-UJME-BR. bk.rev.; abstr.; charts; circ. 1,000. **Indexed:** Abstr.Anthropol., Bull.Signal., Sociol.Abstr.
—BLDSC shelfmark: 6428.107700.
    Description: Covers original articles and research in the social sciences.

300   FR   ISSN 0399-1253
DE1
PEUPLES MEDITERRANEENS - MEDITERRANEAN PEOPLES. (Text and summaries in English or French) 1977. q. 220 F. (foreign 380 F.) Institut d'Etudes Mediterraneennes, B.P. 18807, 75326 Paris Cedex 07, France. TEL 45-67-01-41. Ed. Paul Vieille. abstr.; circ. 2,000. **Indexed:** Amer.Hist.& Life, Curr.Cont.Africa, Geo.Abstr., Hist.Abstr., I D A, Lang.& Lang.Behav.Abstr.
—BLDSC shelfmark: 5534.742000.

300   PH   ISSN 0116-7081
PHILIPPINE-AMERICAN STUDIES JOURNAL. (Text in English) 1987. a. P.65($7) (De La Salle University, Dept. of History and Area Studies, American Studies Program) De La Salle University Press, 2401 Taft Ave., Manila, Philippines. TEL 2-595177. Ed. Socorro Reyes. adv.; bk.rev.; circ. 300.
    Description: Publishes scholarly articles reflecting significant quantitative or qualitative research. Includes speeches, research reports, and "state of the art" papers.

300   II   ISSN 0377-2772
HN681
PHILOSOPHY & SOCIAL ACTION. (Text in English and Hindi) 1975. q. Rs.150($50) Committee of Concerned Indian Philosophers for Social Action, Institute of Socio-Political Dynamics, M-120 Greater Kailash 1, New Delhi 110 048, India.
TEL 091-11-641-5365. Ed. Dhirendra Sharma. adv.; bk.rev.; circ. 1,000. **Indexed:** HR Rep., Lang.& Lang.Behav.Abstr., Phil.Ind., Sociol.Abstr.
—BLDSC shelfmark: 6464.805000.
    Description: Discusses development and science policies.

300   US   ISSN 0048-3931
H1
PHILOSOPHY OF THE SOCIAL SCIENCES. 1971. q. $40 to individuals; to institutions $90. Sage Publications, Inc., 2455 Teller Rd., Newbury Park, CA 91320. TEL 805-499-0721. FAX 805-499-0871. Eds. J.N. Hattiangadi, John O'Neill. adv.; bk.rev.; index; circ. 1,200. (also avail. in microform from UMI; reprint service avail. from UMI) **Indexed:** Arts & Hum.Cit.Ind., ASSIA, Can.Per.Ind., Curr.Cont., Ind.Bk.Rev.Hum., Lang.& Lang.Behav.Abstr., Mid.East: Abstr.& Ind., Phil.Ind., SSCI.
—BLDSC shelfmark: 6465.080000.
    Description: Provides articles, discussions, symposia, literature surveys, translations, and reviews of interest to both philosophers concerned with the social sciences and social scientists concerned with the philosophical foundations of their subject.

300 327   US
PITT LATIN AMERICAN SERIES. (Includes as of 1986 subseries: Cuban Studies (ISSN 0361-4441)) 1965. irreg. price varies. University of Pittsburgh Press, 127 N. Bellefield Ave., Pittsburgh, PA 15260. TEL 412-624-4111. FAX 412-624-7380. Ed. Cole Blasier.

300   US   ISSN 0192-5059
HN50
PLANTATION SOCIETY IN THE AMERICAS; an interdisciplinary journal of tropical and subtropical history and culture. 1979. 3/yr. $20 to individuals; libraries $40. Plantation Society, c/o Prof. Edward Lazzerini, Man. Ed., Department of History, University of New Orleans, New Orleans, LA 70148. TEL 504-286-6886. Ed. Thomas Fiehrer. adv.; bk.rev.; circ. 800. **Indexed:** Amer.Hist.& Life, Hist.Abstr., M.L.A.

THE PLOUGH (FARMINGTON). see *RELIGIONS AND THEOLOGY*

300   FR   ISSN 0336-1721
HT1501
PLURIEL. 1975. q. 60 F. Editions Pluriel, Mantilly, 61350 Passais-La-Conception, France.
TEL 33-38-77-23. Ed. Jean Foucher. bk.rev.

POLICY BITES. see *BUSINESS AND ECONOMICS*

POLICY STUDIES. see *POLITICAL SCIENCE*

320.531   PL   ISSN 0574-9077
POLITECHNIKA CZESTOCHOWSKA. ZESZYTY NAUKOWE. NAUKI SPOLECZNO-EKONOMICZNE. (Text in Polish; summaries in English and Russian) 1964. irreg., latest 1988. (Politechnika Czestochowska) Wydawnictwo Politechniki Czestochowskiej, Ul. Deglera 31, 42-200 Czestochowa, Poland. (Dist. by: Ars Polona-Ruch, Krakowskie Przedmiescie 7, Warsaw, Poland) Ed. Mieczyslaw Stanczyk.
    Description: Social and economic subjects on the borderline between the Marxist philosophy, sociology, political sciences and political economics.

300 330   PL   ISSN 0137-2599
POLITECHNIKA LODZKA. ZESZYTY NAUKOWE. ORGANIZACJA I ZARZADZANIE. (Text in Polish; summaries in English and Russian) 1975. irreg. price varies. Wydawnictwo Politechniki Lodzkiej, Ul. Wolczanska 219, 93-085 Lodz, Poland. (Krakowkie Przedmiescie 7, Warsaw, Poland) Ed. Jerzy Lewandowski. circ. 226.
    Description: Industrial arrangement of textile institutions.

300   PL   ISSN 0072-4718
POLITECHNIKA SLASKA. ZESZYTY NAUKOWE. NAUKI SPOLECZNE. (Text in Polish; summaries in English, German, Russian) 1964. irreg. price varies. Politechnika Slaska, Katowicka 7, 44-100 Gliwice, Poland. FAX 371655. TELEX 036304. (Dist by: Ars Polona, Krakowskie Przedmiescie 7, 00-068 Warsaw, Poland) Ed. Jozef Haber. circ. 205.

300   PL   ISSN 0860-3200
POLITECHNIKA WROCLAWSKA. INSTYTUT NAUK EKONOMICZNO-SPOLECZNYCH. PRACE NAUKOWE. KONFERENCJE. 1986. irreg., no.2, 1989. price varies. Politechnika Wroclawska, Wybrzeze Wyspianskiego 27, 50-370 Wroclaw, Poland. FAX 22-36-64. TELEX 712559 PWRPL.

300   PL   ISSN 0239-3204
POLITECHNIKA WROCLAWSKA. INSTYTUT NAUK EKONOMICZNO-SPOLECZNYCH. PRACE NAUKOWE. MONOGRAFIE. (Text in Polish; summaries in English and Russian) 1971. irreg., no.31, 1991. price varies. Politechnika Wroclawska, Wybrzeze Wyspianskiego 27, 50-370 Wroclaw, Poland. FAX 22-36-64. TELEX 712559 PWRPL. (Dist. by: Ars Polona-Ruch, Krakowskie Przedmiescie 7, Warsaw, Poland)
    Formerly: Politechnika Wroclawska. Instytut Nauk Spolecznych. Prace Naukowe. Monografie (ISSN 0324-9506)

300   PL   ISSN 0239-3212
POLITECHNIKA WROCLAWSKA. INSTYTUT NAUK EKONOMICZNO-SPOLECZNYCH. PRACE NAUKOWE. STUDIA I MATERIALY. (Text in Polish; summaries in English and Russian) 1969. irreg., no.11, 1989. price varies. Politechnika Wroclawska, Wybrzeze Wyspianskiego 27, 50-370 Wroclaw, Poland. FAX 22-36-64. TELEX 712559 PWRPL. (Dist. by: Ars Polona-Ruch, Krakowskie Przedmiescie 7, Warsaw, Poland)
    Formerly: Politechnika Wroclawska. Instytut Nauk Spolecznych. Prace Naukowe. Studia i Materialy (ISSN 0324-9514)

POLSKA AKADEMIA NAUK. ODDZIAL W KRAKOWIE. KOMISJE NAUKOWE. SPRAWOZDANIA Z POSIEDZEN. see *SCIENCES: COMPREHENSIVE WORKS*

300   PE
PONTIFICIA UNIVERSIDAD CATOLICA. REVISTA. N.S. 1977. irreg. $7.50. Pontificia Universidad Catolica, Ave. Bolivar s-n, Pueblo Libre, Apdo. 1761, Lima 21, Peru. Ed. Gerardo Alarco. bk.rev.

300   AG
PONTIFICIA UNIVERSIDAD CATOLICA ARGENTINA. FACULTAD DE CIENCIAS SOCIALES Y ECONOMICAS. CUADERNOS. 1976. Ediciones Macchi, Alsina 1535-37, 1088 Buenos Aires, Argentina. TEL 46-2506. FAX 46-0594.

300   PE
PONTIFICIA UNIVERSIDAD CATOLICA DEL PERU. DEPARTAMENTO DE CIENCIAS SOCIALES. SERIE: EDICIONES PREVIAS. no.5, 1975. irreg. Pontificia Universidad Catolica del Peru, Departamento de Ciencias Sociales, Fondo Editorial, Apdo. 1761, Lima 100, Peru. FAX 51-14-611785. Ed. Enrique Carrion.

300   VC   ISSN 0080-3960
PONTIFICIA UNIVERSITA GREGORIANA. ISTITUTO DI SCIENZE SOCIALI STUDIA SOCIALIA. 1955. irreg. price varies. (Pontificia Universita Gregoriana, School of Social Sciences) Gregorian University Press, Piazza della Pilotta, 35, 00187 Rome, Italy.
FAX 06-67015413. Ed. Sergio Bernal Restrepo, SJ. circ. 200.

POPULATION ET SOCIETES; bulletin mensuel d'informations demographiques, economiques, sociales. see *POPULATION STUDIES*

SOCIAL SCIENCES: COMPREHENSIVE WORKS 4383

300   PL   ISSN 0079-4716
POZNANSKIE TOWARZYSTWO PRZYJACIOL NAUK. KOMISJA NAUK SPOLECZNYCH. PRACE. (Text in Polish; summaries in English, French, German, Russian) 1922. irreg., vol.22, 1981. price varies. Panstwowe Wydawnictwo Naukowe, Ul.Miodowa 10, Warsaw, Poland. (Dist. by Ars Polona-Ruch, Krakowskie Przedmiescie 7, Warsaw, Poland) Ed. Wojciech R. Rzepka.

300   BN   ISSN 0032-7271
DB231
PREGLED (SARAJEVO, 1910); casopis za drustvena pitanja. 1910. m. 11000 din.($20) Univerzitet u Sarajevu, Vojvode Stepe obala 7-111, 71000 Sarajevo, Bosnia Hercegovina. TEL 213-296. Ed. Radovan Milanovic.
—BLDSC shelfmark: 6605.150000.
   Description: Discusses current social matters, mostly in the fields of sociology, history, economy and literature.

PRINCETON UNIVERSITY LIBRARY CHRONICLE. see *HUMANITIES: COMPREHENSIVE WORKS*

PRIRODA A SPOLOCNOST. see *SCIENCES: COMPREHENSIVE WORKS*

PRISM; quarterly of Egyptian culture. see *GENERAL INTEREST PERIODICALS — Egyptian Arab Republic*

PRISMA; the Indonesian indicator. see *GENERAL INTEREST PERIODICALS — Indonesia*

PRISMA: MAJALAH PEMIKIRAN SOSIAL EKONOMI. see *GENERAL INTEREST PERIODICALS — Indonesia*

300   IT
PROBLEMI DI CIVILTA. 1978. bi-m. L.30000. Societa Editrice Napoletana s.r.l., Corso Umberto I 34, 80138 Naples, Italy. Ed. D. Migliucci.

300   RU   ISSN 0079-5763
PROBLEMS OF THE CONTEMPORARY WORLD/PROBLEMES DU MONDE CONTEMPORAIN/PROBLEMAS DEL MUNDO CONTEMPORANEO. (Text in English, French, Spanish) 1969. irreg. available on exchange. (Akademiya Nauk S.S.S.R.) Izdatel'stvo Nauka, 90 Profsoyuznaya ul., 117864 Moscow, Russia. TEL 234-05-84. Ed. I. Grigulevich. circ. 750. **Indexed:** Math.R.

225   FR   ISSN 0033-0884
AP20
PROJET. 1946. q. 210 F. (foreign 230 F.). Assas Editions, 14 rue d'Assas, 75006 Paris, France. TEL 44-39-48-48. FAX 40-49-01-92. Ed. Christian Mellon. adv.; bk.rev.; bibl.; charts; index; circ. 5,200. **Indexed:** C.I.S. Abstr., Int.Lab.Doc., Pt.de Rep. (1979-), World Bibl.Soc.Sec.
—BLDSC shelfmark: 6924.930000.
   Formerly: Revue de l'Action Populaire.

PROSPECT. see *HOUSING AND URBAN PLANNING*

PSYCHOLOGY TODAY. see *PSYCHOLOGY*

300   FR   ISSN 0079-7448
PSYCHOTHEQUE.* 1969. irreg. 19.95 F. Editions Jean Pierre Delarge (Subsidiary of: Editions Universitaires B G), 77 rue de Vaugirard, 75006 Paris, France.

320.9   US   ISSN 0033-3395
JK4801
PUBLIC AFFAIRS COMMENT. 1955. q. free. University of Texas at Austin, Lyndon B. Johnson School of Public Affairs, Austin, TX 78713-7450. TEL 512-471-4962. Ed. David C. Warner. circ. 3,500. **Indexed:** P.A.I.S.

320   US   ISSN 0033-3557
H1   CODEN: PUBIBV
PUBLIC INTEREST. 1965. q. $21. National Affairs, Inc., 1112 16th St., N.W., Ste. 530, Washington, DC 20036. TEL 202-785-8555. FAX 202-467-0006. Eds: Irving Kristol, Nathan Glazer. bk.rev.; charts; circ. 6,000. (also avail. in microform from UMI; back issues avail., reprint service avail. from ISI,UMI) **Indexed:** A.B.C.Pol.Sci., ABI Inform., Acad.Ind., Avery Ind.Archit.Per., B.P.I., BPIA, C.I.J.E., Curr.Cont., Curr.Lit.Fam.Plan., Energy Ind., Energy Info.Abstr., Fut.Surv., Hist.Abstr., Lang.& Lang.Behav.Abstr., Med.Care Rev., Mid.East: Abstr.& Ind., P.A.I.S., Pers.Manage.Abstr., Soc.Sci.Ind., Soc.Work Res.& Abstr., SSCI.
—BLDSC shelfmark: 6967.100000.
   Description: Addresses domestic policy issues including education, welfare, housing and poverty.

PUBLIC OPINION QUARTERLY. see *POLITICAL SCIENCE*

300   US
PUBLIC POLICY STUDIES IN THE SOUTH; a selected research guide. 1975. irreg. $6. Southern Center for Studies in Public Policy, Clark Atlanta University, Atlanta, GA 30314. TEL 404-880-8085.

PUBLICACOES CULTURAIS DA COMPANHIA. see *SCIENCES: COMPREHENSIVE WORKS*

300 954 572   FR   ISSN 0339-1744
PURUSHARTHA. 1975. irreg., no.13, 1991. price varies. (Centre d'Etudes de l'Inde et de l'Asie du Sud) Editions de l' Ecole des Hautes Etudes en Sciences Sociales, 131 bd. St-Michel, 75005 Paris, France. TEL 43-54-47-15. FAX 43-54-80-73. (Dist. by: Centre Interinstitutionnel pour la Diffusion de Publications en Sciences Humaines, 131 bd. St-Michel, 75005 Paris, France) adv.; circ. 500.

300   CC
QILU XUEKAN. (Text in Chinese) bi-m. Qufu Shifan Daxue - Qufu Normal University, Xufu, Shandong 273165, People's Republic of China. TEL 411831. Ed. Xu Wendou.

QINGHAI MINZU XUEYUAN XUEBAO/QINGHAI INSTITUTE OF NATIONALITIES. JOURNAL. see *ORIENTAL STUDIES*

300   CC   ISSN 1000-5102
QINGHAI SHIFAN DAXUE XUEBAO (SHEHUI KEXUE BAN)/QINGHAI NORMAL UNIVERSITY. JOURNAL (SOCIAL SCIENCE EDITION). (Text in Chinese) 1960. q. Y5.60. Qinghai Shifan Daxue - Qinghai Normal University, 38 Wusi Dajie, Xining, Qinghai 810008, People's Republic of China. TEL 53511. (Dist. overseas by: China Publications Foreign Trade Corp., P.O. Box 782, Beijing, P.R.C.) Ed. Guo Hongji. bk.rev.; circ. 2,500.
   Description: Contains research papers on political science, economics, philosophy, literature, history, education, psychology, and art.

300   CC   ISSN 0529-3766
QIU SHI/SEEKING TRUTH. (Text in Chinese) s-m. $64.60. Qiu Shi Zazhishe, 2 Shatan Beijie, Beijing 100727, People's Republic of China. TEL 01-4011155. TELEX 1219. (Dist. in US by: China Books & Periodicals, Inc., 2929 24th St., San Francisco, CA 94110. TEL 415-282-2994) circ. 1,830,000.
   Formerly (until 1988): Hong Qi - Red Flag.
   Description: Theoretical journal of the Chinese Communist Party.

300   CC   ISSN 1000-7504
QIU SHI WENXUAN/SEEKING TRUTH - SELECT ARTICLES. Select translation of: Qiu Shi. (Editions in Kazakh, Korean, Mongolian, Tibetan, Uighur) m. $27.80. Heilongjiang Daxue - Heilongjiang University, 24, Xuefu Lu, Harbin, Heilongjiang 1500880, People's Republic of China. TEL 64941. (Dist. in US by: China Books & Periodicals, Inc., 2929 24th St., San Francisco, CA 94110. TEL 415-282-2994) Ed. Yu Shihui.

QUADERNI SARDI DI FILOSOFIA E SCIENZE UMANE. see *PHILOSOPHY*

300   US   ISSN 0149-192X
QUANTITATIVE APPLICATIONS IN THE SOCIAL SCIENCES. 1976. irreg., no.25, 1982. $7.50 per no. Sage Publications, Inc., 2455 Teller Rd., Newbury Park, CA 91320. TEL 805-499-0721. FAX 805-499-0871. (And Sage Publications, Ltd., 6 Bonhill St., London EC2A 4PU, England) Eds. John L. Sullivan, Richard G. Niemi. (back issues avail.)

300   CC
QUFU SHIFAN DAXUE XUEBAO/QUFU NORMAL UNIVERSITY. JOURNAL. (Text in Chinese) q. Qufu Shifan Daxue, Xuebao Bianjibu, Qufu, Shandong 273165, People's Republic of China. TEL 411831. Ed. Xu Benshun.

300   FR   ISSN 1150-1367
▼**RAISONS PRATIQUES**; epistemologie, sociologie, theorie sociale. 1990. a. price varies. Editions de l' Ecole des Hautes Etudes en Sciences Sociales, 131 bd. St-Michel, 75005 Paris, France. TEL 43-54-47-15. FAX 43-54-80-73. (Dist. by: Centre Interinstitutionnel pour la Diffusion de Publications en Sciences Humaines, 131 bd. St-Michel, 75005 Paris, France)

300   RE
RASSEMBLEMENT POUR LA REPUBLIQUE;* organe trimestriel d'informations politiques, economiques et sociales. q. 123, rue de Lille, 75007 Paris, France.

300   US   ISSN 1043-4631
H62.A1   CODEN: RTSOEG
RATIONALITY AND SOCIETY. 1989. q. $42 to individuals; institutions $96. Sage Publications, Inc., 2455 Teller Rd., Newbury Park, CA 91320. TEL 805-499-0721. FAX 805-499-0871. Ed. James S. Coleman. circ. 500. **Indexed:** PSI.
—BLDSC shelfmark: 7295.473000.
   Description: Designed to recognize the growing contributions of rational-action-based theory in the social sciences, as well as the questions and controversies surrounding this growth. Aims to stimulate these developments internationally and to serve as a forum within which the controversies can be aired.

300   IT
REALTA SOCIALE D'OGGI; rivista mensile di sintesi e documentazione sociale. 1946. m. Istituto Sociale Ambrosiano, Via della Signora 3, Milan, Italy. abstr.

300   II
RECENT TRENDS IN SOCIAL SCIENCES. 1975. irreg. Rs.24 (foreign $10). Anu Books, Shivaji Rd., Meerut 25001, India. Ed. Dr. Ram Nath Sharma. adv.; bk.rev.

300   MG
RECHERCHE ET CULTURE. 1985. s-a. University of Antananarivo, French Department, B.P. 907, 101 Antananarivo, Malagasy Republic. TEL 26600. Ed. Ginette Ramaroson. circ. 1,000.

300   FR   ISSN 0034-124X
RECHERCHE SOCIALE. 1965. q. 210 F. (foreign 240 F.). Fondation pour la Recherche Sociale (FORS), 28 rue Godefroy Cavaignee, 75011 Paris, France. TEL 40-09-15-12. FAX 40-09-15-32. Ed. Roger Benjamin. bk.rev.; bibl.; charts; tr.lit.; circ. 1,600. **Indexed:** A.B.C.Pol.Sci., Amer.Hist.& Life, Curr.Cont.Africa, Hist.Abstr., P.A.I.S.For.Lang.Ind.
—BLDSC shelfmark: 7307.500000.
   Formerly: Etudes et Documents.

300   FR   ISSN 0557-6989
E169.1
RECHERCHES ANGLAISES ET AMERICAINES. a. 75 F. Universite de Strasbourg II, Service des Periodiques, 22 rue Descartes, 67084 Strasbourg, France. Ed. A. Bleikasten. **Indexed:** Abstr.Engl.Stud., M.L.A.
   Description: Covers English and American culture, literature, and art.

RECHERCHES D'HISTOIRE ET DE SCIENCES SOCIALES/STUDIES IN HISTORY AND THE SOCIAL SCIENCES. see *HISTORY*

300   UY
REFLEXIONES DEL BATALLISMO. irreg. Revista Reflexiones, Casa del Partido Colorado, Andres Martinez Trueba 1271, Montevideo, Uruguay.

SOCIAL SCIENCES: COMPREHENSIVE WORKS

300   AT   ISSN 0158-7102
REGIONAL JOURNAL OF SOCIAL ISSUES. 1979. a. Aus.$10. Deakin University, Warrnambool, P.O. Box 423, Warrnambool, Vic. 3280, Australia. TEL 055-633-314. FAX 055-633-534. bk.rev.; circ. 200. (back issues avail.) Indexed: Aus.P.A.I.S.

RELIGION AND SOCIETY. see *RELIGIONS AND THEOLOGY*

300 100   SZ
RENCONTRES INTERNATIONALES DE GENEVE. 1947. biennial. 39 SFr. Editions de la Baconniere S.A., PO Box 185, CH-2017 Boudry, Switzerland. TEL 038-421004. (reprint service avail. from UMI)

RENOVACION. see *POLITICAL SCIENCE*

300   CC
RENSHENG YU BANLU/LIFE AND COMPANIONS. (Text in Chinese) m. Henan Sheng Shehui Kexue Lianhehui, No. 9, Fengchan Lu, Zhengzhou, Henan 450002, People's Republic of China. TEL 333739. Ed. Hu Shiyuan.

300   US   ISSN 0736-217X
REPORTING FROM THE RUSSELL SAGE FOUNDATION. 1982. 2/yr. free. Russell Sage Foundation, 112 E. 64th St., New York, NY 10021. FAX 212-371-4761. Ed. Lisa Nachtigall. circ. 10,000.

300   UN   ISSN 0080-1348
REPORTS AND PAPERS IN THE SOCIAL SCIENCES. (Editions in English and French) 1955. irreg., no.57, 1986. price varies. Unesco, 7-9 Place de Fontenoy, 75700 Paris, France. TEL 577-16-10. (Dist. in U.S. by: Unipub, 4611-F Assembly Dr., Lanham, MD 20706-4391)

300   CH   ISSN 1018-4473
▼**REPUBLIC OF CHINA. NATIONAL SCIENCE COUNCIL. PROCEEDINGS. PART C: HUMANITIES AND SOCIAL SCIENCES.** (Editions in Chinese, English) 1991. s-a. NT.$120($8) National Science Council, 106 Ho-ping E. Rd. Sec.2, Taipei, Taiwan 106, Republic of China. TEL 2-737-7248. FAX 2-737-7594. Ed. Kuo-Shu Yang.

RESEARCH IN THE SOCIAL SCIENTIFIC STUDY OF RELIGION. see *RELIGIONS AND THEOLOGY*

RESEARCH JOURNAL: HUMANITIES AND SOCIAL SCIENCES. see *HUMANITIES: COMPREHENSIVE WORKS*

RESEARCH JOURNAL OF PHILOSOPHY AND SOCIAL SCIENCES. see *PHILOSOPHY*

RESOURCES FOR FEMINIST RESEARCH/DOCUMENTATION SUR LA RECHERCHE FEMINISTE. see *WOMEN'S STUDIES*

REVIEW JOURNAL OF PHILOSOPHY AND SOCIAL SCIENCE. see *PHILOSOPHY*

918.503   PE
REVISTA ANDINA. 1983. s-a. $35 to individuals (foreign $40); institutions $45 (foreign $60). Centro de Estudios Regionales Andinos "Bartolome de las Casas", Apdo. 477, Cusco, Peru. TEL 084-236494. FAX 084-238255. adv.; bk.rev.; cum.index: 1983-1985; circ. 1,000. (back issues avail.)

300   BO
REVISTA BOLIVIANA DE INVESTIGACION. 4/yr. Universidad Autonoma "Gabriel Rene Moreno", Direccion Universitaria de Investigacion, Sta. Cruz, Bolivia.

REVISTA CANARIA DE FILOSOFIA Y CIENCIA SOCIAL. see *PHILOSOPHY*

300   EC
REVISTA CIENCIAS SOCIALES. 1977. q. S/250($20) Universidad Central del Ecuador, Escuela de Sociologia, Biblioteca, Ciudad Universitaria, Quito, Ecuador.

300   PO   ISSN 0254-1106
REVISTA CRITICA DE CIENCIAS SOCIAIS. 1978. 3/yr. Esc.2000($35) to individuals; institutions Esc.2500($50). Centro de Estudos Sociais, Faculdade de Economia, Apdo. 3087, 3000 Coimbra, Portugal. Ed. Boaventura de Sousa Santos. adv.; bk.rev.; circ. 2,000.
—BLDSC shelfmark: 7852.095500.

300   CU
REVISTA CUBANA DE CIENCIAS SOCIALES. 1983. 3/yr. $11 in N. & S. America; Europe $12; elsewhere $14. (Academia de Ciencias de Cuba, Instituto de Filosofia) Ediciones Cubanas, Obispo No. 527, Apdo. 605, Havana, Cuba. (Alt. addr.: Industria No. 2, Apdo. 2291, Zona 2, Havana, Cuba) Ed. Thalia Fung. circ. 6,000.

300   DR
REVISTA DE CIENCIAS ECONOMICAS Y SOCIALES.* 1972. q. Universidad Autonoma de Santo Domingo, Facultad de Ciencias Economicas y Sociales, Santo Domingo, Dominican Republic. stat.

300 100   BL   ISSN 0303-9862
H8
REVISTA DE CIENCIAS SOCIAIS. (Text in Portuguese; summaries in English and French) 1970. s-a. Cr.$400($12) or exchange basis. Universidade Federal do Ceara, Departamento de Ciencias Sociais e Filosofia, C.P. 1257, Fortaleza, Ceara, Brazil. Ed. Paulo Elpidio De Menezes Neto. adv.; bk.rev.; bibl.; charts; index, cum.index; circ. 3,000. Indexed: Hisp.Amer.Per.Ind., Lang.& Lang.Behav.Abstr., Psychol.Abstr.

300   PR   ISSN 0034-7817
REVISTA DE CIENCIAS SOCIALES. (Text in Spanish) 1957. s-a. $15 to individuals; institutions $20. Universidad de Puerto Rico, Centro de Investigaciones Sociales, Rio Piedras, PR 00391. Ed.Bd. adv.; bk.rev.; bibl.; charts; illus.; circ. 1,000. Indexed: Hisp.Amer.Per.Ind.

300   CR   ISSN 0482-5276
K19
REVISTA DE CIENCIAS SOCIALES. (Title varies each issue) 1956. 4/yr. $40. Editorial de la Universidad de Costa Rica, Apdo. 75-2060, Ciudad Universitaria Rodrigo Facio, San Jose, Costa Rica. TEL 506-25-3133. FAX 506-24-9367. TELEX UNICORI 2544. Dir. Daniel Camacho. Indexed: Hisp.Amer.Per.Ind., P.A.I.S.For.Lang.Ind.
—BLDSC shelfmark: 7851.048000.

300   VE
REVISTA DE CIENCIAS SOCIALES. N.S. 1974. irreg. exchange basis. Universidad del Zulia, Facultad de Ciencias Economicas y Sociales, Apdo. 526, Maracaibo 4001A, Venezuela. FAX 061-416025. Ed. N. Urdaneta de Barroso. circ. 1,000. Indexed: Hist.Abstr.

300   BL   ISSN 0100-7076
REVISTA DE CULTURA VOZES. 1907. 6/yr. $55. Editora Vozes Ltda, Rua Frei Luis 100, Caixa Postal 90023, 25689 Petropolis, Brazil. Ed. Leonardo Boff. adv.; bk.rev.; bibl.

REVISTA DE DERECHO (CONCEPCION). see *LAW*

300   BO
REVISTA DE HUMANIDADES, CIENCIAS SOCIALES Y RELACIONES INTERNACIONALES. 2/yr. Universidad Autonoma "Gabriel Rene Moreno", Dirrecion Universitaria de Investigacion, Sta. Cruz, Bolivia.

REVISTA DE INDIAS. see *HISTORY — History Of North And South America*

REVISTA DE LEGISLACION Y DOCUMENTACION EN DERECHO Y CIENCIAS SOCIALES. see *LAW*

306   CK
REVISTA FORO. q. Fundacion Foro Nacional por Colombia, Carrera 4A No. 27-62, A.A. 10141, Bogota, Colombia. TEL 2340967.

300   SP   ISSN 0379-0762
REVISTA INTERNACIONAL DE CIENCIAS SOCIALES. 1988. q. 5000 ptas.($45) Center Unesco de Catalunya, Mallorca, 285, 08037 Barcelona, Spain. FAX 457-58-51. TELEX 98314 CUNC. Ed. Ali Kazancigil. adv.; bk.rev.; circ. 1,300.

REVISTA LATINOAMERICANA DE ESTUDIOS EDUCATIVOS. see *EDUCATION*

REVISTA PASOS. see *RELIGIONS AND THEOLOGY*

300   PE   ISSN 1011-0410
H8.S7
REVISTA PERUANA DE CIENCIAS SOCIALES. 1987. 3/yr. $30. Asociacion Peruana para el Fomento de las Ciencias Sociales - Peruvian Association for the Advance of Social Sciences, Calle Roma 485, Apdo. 27-0261, Lima 27, Peru. Dir. Luis Soberon A. adv.; bk.rev.; circ. 1,000.

300   BL   ISSN 0102-8839
REVISTA SAO PAULO EM PERSPECTIVA. 1985. 4/yr. $76.10. Fundacao Sistema Estadual de Analise de Dados, Av. Casper Libero 464, 01033 Sao Paulo, Brazil. FAX 011-229-5259. TELEX 011-31390. circ. 2,000.
Formerly (until vol.5, no.2): Fundacao S E A D E. Revista.

300   BO
REVISTA TEMAS ECONOMICOS Y SOCIALES. a. Universidad Autonoma "Gabriel Rene Moreno", Direccion Universitaria de Investigacion, Sta. Cruz, Bolivia.

REVUE DE COREE. see *ORIENTAL STUDIES*

300   FR   ISSN 0336-1578
REVUE DES SCIENCES SOCIALES DE LA FRANCE DE L'EST. 1972. a. 110 F. Universite de Strasbourg II, 22 rue Descartes, 67084 Strasbourg, France. TEL 88-47-73-17. Ed. Freddy Raphael. bk.rev.
Description: Covers research in methodology and cultural anthropology and in demographic, economical, and social problems of the eastern region of France and of neighboring Europe.

300   UN
REVUE INTERNATIONALE DES SCIENCES SOCIALES. English edition: International Social Science Journal (ISSN 0020-8701) 1949. q. 368 F. (Unesco) Editions Eres, 19, rue Gustave-Courbet, 31400 Toulouse, France. TEL 61-53-88-55. FAX 45-67-82-06. Ed. A. Kazancigil. adv.; bibl.; charts; index; circ. 2,500. (also avail. in microfilm from UMI) Indexed: CERDIC, Int.Lab.Doc.
Description: Reflects broadly the diversity of theoretical approaches in all subject fields with contributions by leading scholars from various regions of the world.

300   MG
REVUE ITA. 1985. m. Ministry of Social Welfare, B.P. 681, 101 Antananarivo, Malagasy Republic. TEL 23630. Ed. Paulin Rakotoarivony. circ. 500.

300   TI   ISSN 0035-4333
H3
REVUE TUNISIENNE DES SCIENCES SOCIALES. (Text in Arabic and French) q. 2000 din. Universite de Tunis, Centre d'Etudes et de Recherches Economiques et Sociales, 23 rue d'Espagne, Tunis, Tunisia. bk.rev.; charts; stat.; cum.index: 1964-1968. Indexed: Curr.Cont.Africa, Int.Lab.Doc., Lang.& Lang.Behav.Abstr., M.L.A., Popul.Ind.

300   IT
RICERCA SOCIALE; quadrimestrale di sociologia urbana, rurale e cooperazione. 1972. 3/yr. L.69000 (foreign L.80000)(effective 1992). (Universita degli Studi di Bologna, Centro Studi Sui Problemi della Citta e del Territorio) Franco Angeli Editore, Viale Monza 106, 20127 Milan, Italy. TEL 02-2827651. Ed. Achille Ardigo. bibl.

300   IT   ISSN 0035-5623
RISVEGLIO DEL MOLISE E DEL MEZZOGIORNO; di attualita, cultura, economia, politica e problemi meridionali. 1961. m. L.30000($40) Editrice Rismol s.r.l., Via Luigi Arati 25, 00151 Rome, Italy. TEL 06-58-26790. Ed. Franco Romagnuolo. adv.; B&W page L.1500000. illus.; circ. 15,000. (back issues avail.)
Description: Deals with current events and problems facing southern Italy.

300   FR
RIVAROL AND POLITICAL. 1951. w. 600 Fr. Editions des Tuileries, 9 Passage des Marais, 75010 Paris, France. TEL 42-06-40-50. FAX 42-38-03-08. Ed. Camille Galic. adv.; bk.rev.; circ. 18,000. (also avail. in microfiche)
Formerly: Rivarol (ISSN 0035-5666)

SOCIAL SCIENCES: COMPREHENSIVE WORKS

300   IT   ISSN 0035-676X
RIVISTA INTERNAZIONALE DI SCIENZE SOCIALI. (Text in English, French, Italian) 1983. q. L.130000($100) (effective 1992). (Universita Cattolica del Sacro Cuore, Istituto di Economia) Vita e Pensiero, Largo Gemelli 1, 20123 Milan, Italy. TEL 02-8856310. FAX 02-8856260. TELEX 321033-UCATHI-1. Dir. Giancarlo Mazzocchi. adv.; bk.rev.; bibl.; charts; illus.; stat.; index. **Indexed:** Hist.Abstr., Lang.& Lang.Behav.Abstr.
   Description: Covers various areas in social sciences, with emphasis on economics.

300   US   ISSN 0886-9154
F1405.9
ROCKY MOUNTAIN COUNCIL ON LATIN AMERICAN STUDIES. PROCEEDINGS. (36th annual meeting: Fort Collins, CO) a. (Rocky Mountain Council on Latin American Studies) Center for Latin American Studies, New Mexico State University, Nason House, 1200 University Ave., Box 3JBR, Las Cruces, NM 88003. (Co-sponsor: Joint Border Research Institute at New Mexico State University) Ed. Patricia A. Sullivan.

300   PL
ROCZNIKI NAUK SPOLECZNYCH. (Text in Polish; summaries in English) 1949. a. price varies. Katolicki Uniwersytet Lubelski, Towarzystwo Naukowe, Ul. Gliniana 21, 20-616 Lublin, Poland. circ. 820.

300   US   ISSN 0085-5839
HC501
RURAL AFRICANA; current research in social sciences. irreg. $21 in U.S.; Africa $18; elsewhere $24. Michigan State University, African Studies Center, 100 Center for International Programs, E. Lansing, MI 48824-1035. TEL 517-353-1700. FAX 517-353-7254. TELEX 650-277-3148 MCI. abstr.; illus. **Indexed:** Hist.Abstr., Int.Lab.Doc., P.A.I.S., Rural Recreat.Tour.Abstr., World Agri.Econ.& Rural Sociol.Abstr.
   —BLDSC shelfmark: 8052.415000.

RUSSIAN SOCIAL SCIENCE REVIEW; a journal of translations. see *POLITICAL SCIENCE*

300   IS
S S D A NEWSLETTER. (Social Science Data Archives) (Text in Hebrew) 1983. s-a. free. Hebrew University, Faculty of Social Sciences, Mount Scopus, Jerusalem 91905, Israel. TEL 02-883007. FAX 02-322545. Ed. Michal Peleg. bk.rev.; circ. 500.
   ●Also available online.
   Formerly: Yedion (ISSN 0334-5971)

300   FI   ISSN 0358-7088
S S I D LIAISON BULLETIN. (Social Science Information and Documentation) (Text in English) 1981. irreg. (2-3/yr.) free. Helsinki School of Economics, Runeberginkatu 22-24, 00100 Helsinki, Finland. Ed.Bd. circ. 450.

300 301   AU
S W S - RUNDSCHAU. 1961. q. S.290 to individuals; institutions S.490; students S.150. Sozialwissenschaftliche Studiengesellschaft, Maria-Theresien-Str. 9, A-1090 Vienna, Austria. TEL 0222-343127. FAX 0222-3102238. Ed. C. Haerpfer. adv.; bk.rev.; charts; illus.; stat.; index; circ. 2,500. (back issues avail.) **Indexed:** Lang.& Lang.Behav.Abstr.
   Formerly: Journal fuer Sozialforschung.
   Description: Quantative and empirical research in political science, sociology and survey research.

301   US
SAGE LIBRARY OF SOCIAL RESEARCH. 1973. irreg. (5-12/yr.). Sage Publications, Inc., 2455 Teller Rd., Newbury Park, CA 91320. TEL 805-499-0721. FAX 805-499-0871. (And Sage Publications, Ltd., 6 Bonhill St., London EC2A 4PU, England)

300   KN
SAHOEKWAHAK/SOCIAL SCIENCES. (Text in Korean) bi-m. Academy of Social Sciences, Pyongyang, N. Korea.

SALMAGUNDI; a quarterly of the humanities & social sciences. see *HUMANITIES: COMPREHENSIVE WORKS*

300   BG
SAMAJ NIRIKKHON. English edition: Journal of Social Studies. (Text in Bengali) 1978. q. Tk.92($16) Centre for Social Studies - Samaj Nirikkhon Kendro, Rm. 1107, Arts Bldg., Dhaka University, Dhaka 1000, Bangladesh. TEL 500016. Ed. B.K. Jahangir. cum.index: vols.1-30 (1978-1988). (reprint service avail.)

SAN JOSE STUDIES; San Jose State University's journal of the arts, humanities, sciences, business and technology. see *HUMANITIES: COMPREHENSIVE WORKS*

966.9   NR   ISSN 0331-0523
HC517.N48
SAVANNA; a journal of the environmental & social sciences. (Text and summaries in English) 1972-1979 (vol.8, no.2); resumed 1988. s-a. £N15($18) to individuals; institutions £N.25($28). Ahmadu Bello University Press, Private Mail Bag 1094, Zaria, Nigeria. TELEX 75241-ZARABU-NIG. Ed. Audee T. Giwa. adv.; bk.rev.; bibl.; charts; illus.; index; circ. 1,000. **Indexed:** A.I.C.P., Biol.Abstr., Field Crop Abstr., Geo.Abstr., Herb.Abstr., Rural Recreat.Tour.Abstr., Soils & Fert., World Agri.Econ.& Rural Sociol.Abstr.
   Description: Multidisciplinary journal including bibliographies and articles focusing on the savanna.

300   SW   ISSN 0280-2791
HC59.69
SCANDINAVIAN JOURNAL OF DEVELOPMENT ALTERNATIVES. 1982. q. $40 to individuals; institutions $75. Bethany Books, PO Box 7444, S-103 91 Stockholm, Sweden. Ed. Franklin Vivekananda. adv.; bk.rev.; circ. 2,000. (back issues avail.) **Indexed:** Geo.Abstr., I D A, Int.Lab.Doc., P.A.I.S., Polit.Sci.Abstr., Rural Devel.Abstr., Sociol.Abstr.
   —BLDSC shelfmark: 8087.505650.
   Formerly: Scandinavian Journal of Developing Countries.
   Description: Devoted to the studies of genuine development related to basic human needs satisfaction such as socio-economic problems, conflict and peace, human rights, migration, environment, North-South relations and anthropological views.

SCANDINAVIAN JOURNAL OF SOCIAL MEDICINE. see *MEDICAL SCIENCES*

300   AU
SCHRIFTEN ZUR FRIEDENS- UND KONFLIKTFORSCHUNG. irreg., no.2, 1989. varies. Verband der Wissenschaftlichen Gesellschaften Oesterreichs, Lindengasse 37, A-1070 Vienna, Austria. TEL 932166.

SCIENCE DILIMAN. see *SCIENCES: COMPREHENSIVE WORKS*

300   PE   ISSN 0559-1414
H8
SCIENTIA ET PRAXIS.* 1964. Universidad Nacional Mayor de San Marcos, Av. Republica de Chile 295, Lima, Peru.

300 330   UK   ISSN 0269-5030
SCOTTISH ECONOMIC AND SOCIAL HISTORY. 1981. a. £6 (foreign £8). Economic and Social History Society of Scotland, University of Strathclyde, Dept. of History, Glasgow G1 1XQ, Scotland. adv.; bk.rev.; circ. 400.
   —BLDSC shelfmark: 8206.825000.

SCRIPTA HIEROSOLYMITANA. see *HUMANITIES: COMPREHENSIVE WORKS*

300   UN
SELECTIVE INVENTORY OF SOCIAL SCIENCE INFORMATION AND DOCUMENTATION SERVICES. (Text in English, French, Spanish) irreg., 3rd ed., 1988. Unesco, 7 Place de Fontenoy, 75700 Paris, France.

SEMIOTIC REVIEW OF BOOKS. see *HUMANITIES: COMPREHENSIVE WORKS*

300   CC
SHANDONG DAXUE XUEBAO (SHEHUI KEXUE BAN)/SHANDONG UNIVERSITY. JOURNAL (SOCIAL SCIENCE EDITION). (Text in Chinese) q. Shandong Daxue, Xuebao Bianjibu, No. 27, Shanda Nanlu, Jinan, Shandong 250100, People's Republic of China. TEL 643861. Ed. Yuan Shishuo.

300   CC   ISSN 1000-5323
SHANDONG GONGYE DAXUE XUEBAO (SHEHUI KEXUE BAN)/SHANDONG INDUSTRIAL UNIVERSITY. JOURNAL (SOCIAL SCIENCE EDITION) q. Shandong Gongye Daxue, Xuebao Bianjibu, No. 33, Jing 10 Lu, Jinan, Shandong, People's Republic of China. TEL 615081. Ed. Wei Bingquan.

300   CC
SHANDONG SHEHUI KEXUE/SHANDONG SOCIAL SCIENCES. (Text in Chinese) bi-m. Shandong Sheng Shehui Kexue Lianhehui, No. 28, Yuhan Lu, Jinan, Shandong 250002, People's Republic of China. TEL 61574. Ed. Liang Zijie.

300   CC
SHANDONG SHIDA XUEBAO (SHEHUI KEXUE BAN)/SHANDONG NORMAL UNIVERSITY. JOURNAL (SOCIAL SCIENCE EDITION). (Text in Chinese) bi-m. Y7.20. Shandong Shifan Daxue, Xuebao Bianjibu, Wenhua Donglu, Jinan, Shandong 250014, People's Republic of China. TEL 643711. (Dist. overseas by: China Publications Foreign Trade Corp., P.O. Box 782, Beijing, P.R.C.)
   Description: Contains research papers on literature, history, philosophy, economics, education, and middle school teaching.

300   CC   ISSN 1000-5595
SHANDONG YIKE DAXUE XUEBAO (SHEHUI KEXUE BAN)/SHANDONG UNIVERSITY OF MEDICAL SCIENCES. JOURNAL (SOCIAL SCIENCE EDITION). (Text in Chinese) q. Shandong Yike Daxue, Xuebao Bianjibu, No. 44, Wenhua Xilu, Jinan, Shandong 250012, People's Republic of China. TEL 21681. Ed. Wu Xianglian.

300   CC
SHANGHAI SHEHUI KEXUEYUAN XUESHU JIKAN/SHANGHAI ACADEMY OF SOCIAL SCIENCES. QUARTERLY JOURNAL. (Text in Chinese) q. $43.10. (Shanghai Shehui Kexueyuan - Shanghai Academy of Social Sciences) Shanghai Shehui Kexueyuan Chubanshe, No. 7, Alley 622, Huaihai Zhonglu, Shanghai 200020, People's Republic of China. (Dist. in US by: China Books & Periodicals, Inc., 2929 24th St., San Francisco, CA 94110. TEL 415-282-2994)

300   CC
SHANGHAI SHIFAN DAXUE XUEBAO (SHEHUI KEXUE BAN)/SHANGHAI NORMAL UNIVERSITY. JOURNAL (SOCIAL SCIENCE EDITION). (Text in Chinese) q. Shanghai Shifan Daxue, Xuebao Bianjibu, 10, Guilin Lu, Shanghai 200234, People's Republic of China. TEL 4700700. Ed. Wang Bangzuo.

300 100   CC   ISSN 1000-5935
SHANXI DAXUE XUEBAO (SHEHUI KEXUE BAN)/SHANXI UNIVERSITY. JOURNAL (SOCIAL SCIENCE EDITION). (Text in Chinese; table of contents in English) q. Y0.80 per no. Shanxi Daxue, Xuebao Bianjibu, Wucheng Lu, Taiyuan, Shanxi 030006, People's Republic of China. Eds. Meng Weizhi, Xu Jiugang.

301   US   ISSN 1054-0695
▼**SHAREDEBATE INTERNATIONAL;** a ShareWare diskette magazine. 1990. q. $60 (diskette $20). Applied Foresight, Inc., Box 20607, Bloomington, MN 55420. Ed. R.H. Martin. adv.; bk.rev. (also avail. on diskette)
   ●Also available online.
   Also available on CD-ROM.
   Description: Debate forum for PC users by PC users who are concerned about the present and the future.

300   CC
SHEHUI/SOCIETY. (Text in Chinese) m. Shanghai Daxue, Wenxueyuan - Shanghai University, College of Literature, 574 Xijiangwan Lu, Shanghai 200083, People's Republic of China. TEL 6664074. Ed. Li Qingyun.

300   CC
SHEHUI GONGZUO YANJIU/SOCIAL AFFAIRS STUDY. (Text in Chinese) q. Zhongguo Minzheng Lilun he Shehui Fuli Yanjiuhui - China Civil Administration Theory and Social Welfare Research Society, 7, Baiguang Lu, Xuanwu-qu, Beijing 100053, People's Republic of China. TEL 365331. Ed. Peng Chuanrong.

SOCIAL SCIENCES: COMPREHENSIVE WORKS

300   CC
SHEHUI KEXUE (LANZHOU)/SOCIAL SCIENCE. (Text in Chinese) bi-m. Y0.98 per no. Gansu Sheng Shehui Kexueyuan - Gansu Academy of Social Sciences, Shi Li Dian, Lanzhou, Gansu 730070, People's Republic of China. Eds. Wang Bugui, Dong Hanhe.

300   CC   ISSN 0257-5833
SHEHUI KEXUE (SHANGHAI)/SOCIAL SCIENCES. (Text in Chinese) 1980. m. $61.20. (Shanghai Shehui Kexueyuan - Shanghai Academy of Social Sciences) Shanghai Shehui Kexueyuan Chubanshe, No. 7, Alley 622, Huaihai Zhonglu, Shanghai 200020, People's Republic of China. (Dist. in US by: China Books & Periodicals, Inc., 2929 24th St., San Francisco, CA 94110. TEL 415-282-2994)

300   CC   ISSN 1001-6198
SHEHUI KEXUE JIKAN/SOCIAL SCIENCE JOURNAL. (Text in Chinese, English) 1979. bi-m. Y10.80($33.80) Liaoning Shehui Kexueyuan - Liaoning Academy of Social Sciences, 86, Taishan Lu, Huanggu Qu, Shenyang, Liaoning 110031, People's Republic of China. TEL 460511-363. FAX 0086-024-601899. (Dist. outside China by: China International Book Trading Corp., P.O. Box 2820, Beijing, P.R.C.; Dist. in US by: China Books & Periodicals, Inc., 2929 24th St., San Francisco, CA 94110) Ed. Wei Jianxun. bk.rev.; circ. 3,500.
—BLDSC shelfmark: 8318.163200.
   Description: Publishes academic papers on literature, history, philosophy, sociology and economics pertaining to Northeast China.

300   CC   ISSN 1000-4769
SHEHUI KEXUE YANJIU/SOCIAL SCIENCE RESEARCH. (Text in Chinese) 1979. bi-m. Y12. Sichuan Sheng Shehui Kexueyuan - Sichuan Academy of Social Sciences, Qingyang Gong, Chengdu, Sichuan 610072, People's Republic of China. TEL 769347-124. (Dist. outside China by: Guoji Shudian - China International Book Trading Corp., P.O. Box 399, Beijing, P.R.C.) Ed. Liu Changguo. adv.; bk.rev.; circ. 3,600.

300   CC   ISSN 0257-0246
SHEHUI KEXUE ZHANXIAN/SOCIAL SCIENCE FRONT. (Text in Chinese) 1978. q. $58.10. Jilin Sheng Shehui Kexueyuan - Jilin Academy of Social Sciences, 12, Jianshe Jie, Changchun, Jilin 130061, People's Republic of China. TEL-043-822828. (Dist. in US by: China Books & Periodicals, Inc., 2929 24th St., San Francisco, CA 94110. TEL 415-282-2994) Ed. Wang Shenrong. adv.; bk.rev.

300   CC   ISSN 1000-5226
SHENYANG SHIFAN XUEYUAN XUEBAO. SHEHUI KEXUE BAN/SHENYANG TEACHERS COLLEGE. JOURNAL. SOCIAL SCIENCE EDITION. (Text in Chinese; table of contents in English) q. Y6. Shenyang Shifan Xueyuan - Shenyang Teachers College, 95, Huanghe Nandajie, Huanggu Qu, Shenyang, Liaoning 110031, People's Republic of China. (Dist. outside China by: China Publications Foreign Trade Corp., P.O. Box 782, Beijing, P.R.C.)

300   JA
SHIMANE DAIGAKU HOBUNGAKUBU KIYO. BUNGAKUKA HEN/SHIMANE UNIVERSITY. FACULTY OF LAW AND LITERATURE. MEMOIRS. (Text in English, Japanese) 1973. a. Shimane Daigaku, Hobungakubu - Shimane University, Faculty of Law and Literature, 1060 Nishi-Kawazu-machi, Matsue-shi, Shimane-ken 690, Japan. Ed.Bd. circ. 400.

SHISO/THOUGHT. see *HUMANITIES: COMPREHENSIVE WORKS*

300   TH   ISSN 0304-226X
DS561
SIAM SOCIETY. JOURNAL. 1904. s-a. B.500($25) Siam Society, 131 Soi Asoke, Sukhumvit Rd., Bangkok, Thailand. Ed. Tej Bunnag. adv.; bk.rev.; bibl.; charts; illus.; cum.index: vols. 1-50; circ. 1,500. (reprint service avail. from KTO) Indexed: Amer.Hist.& Life, E.I., Hist.Abstr.

300   VE
SIC. 1938. 10/yr. Bs.700($20) (foreign Bs.1000)(effective Jan. 1992). Fundacion Centro Gumilla, Edificio Centro Valores, Local 2, Esq. Luneta, Apdo. 4838, Caracas 1010-A, Venezuela. TEL 582-563-5096. FAX 582-5618205. Ed. Arturo Sosa S.J. adv.; bk.rev.; film rev.; abstr.; bibl.; charts; illus.; stat.; index; circ. 6,500.

300   CC   ISSN 0490-6748
SICHUAN DAXUE XUEBAO (SHEHUI KEXUE BAN)/SICHUAN UNIVERSITY. JOURNAL (SOCIAL SCIENCES EDITION). (Text in Chinese; table of contents in English) 1955. q. Y7.20. Sichuan Daxue, Xuebao Bianjibu, Jiuyanqiao, Chengdu, Sichuan 610064, People's Republic of China. (Dist. outside China by: China International Book Trading Corp., P.O. Box 399, Beijing, P.R.C.) Ed. Tian Zuwu. bibl.

300   CC   ISSN 1000-5315
SICHUAN SHIFAN DAXUE XUEBAO (SHEHUI KEXUE BAN)/SICHUAN NORMAL UNIVERSITY. JOURNAL. (SOCIAL SCIENCE EDITION). bi-m. Sichuan Shifan Daxue, Xuebao Bianjibu, Shizishan, Chengdu Shiwai, Chengdu, Sichuan 610068. TEL 442612-234. Ed. Zhu Wenxian.

300   CC
SICHUAN SHIFAN XUEYUAN XUEBAO (ZHEXUE SHEHUI KEXUE BAN)/SICHUAN NORMAL COLLEGE. JOURNAL. (SOCIAL SCIENCE EDITION). (Text in Chinese) q. Sichuan Shifan Xueyuan, Xuebao Bianjibu, 10, Renmin Xilu, Nanchong, Sichuan 637000, People's Republic of China. TEL 2244-338. (Dist. overseas by: Jiangsu Publications Import & Export Corp., 56 Gao Yun Ling, Nanjing, Jiangsu, P.R.C.) Ed. Yan Zengye.

SIGNES DU PRESENT. see *BUSINESS AND ECONOMICS*

300 954.9   PK
SINDH QUARTERLY. (Text in English) 1973. q. $36, Sayid Ghulam Mustafa Shah, Ed. & Pub., 36-D Karachi Administration Co-operative Housing Society, Off Shahid Millat Rd., Karachi 8, Pakistan. TEL 43-19-83. bk.rev.; circ. 1,750.
   Description: Covers the socio-political and economic history of Sindh, Pakistan, and India.

SINTESE. see *PHILOSOPHY*

SIR ROBERT MADGWICK LECTURE SERIES (NO.). see *HUMANITIES: COMPREHENSIVE WORKS*

300   SP   ISSN 0210-0223
H8
SISTEMA. 1973. bi-m. 1300 ptas. Instituto de Tecnicas Sociales de la Fundacion Fondo Social Universitario, Apdo. Num. 502 F.D., Madrid, Spain. Dir. Elias Diaz. adv.; bk.rev.; index, cum.index every 20 nos.; circ. 8,000. Indexed: P.A.I.S.For.Lang.Ind.

300 370   SP
SISTEMA DE INDICADORES SOCIO-ECONOMICOS Y EDUCATIVOS DE LA O E I. 1980. a. 35000 ptas.($300) Organizacion de Estados Iberoamericanos para la Educacion, la Ciencia y la Cultura (OEI), C. Bravo Murillo 38, 28015 Madrid, Spain. TEL 594-43-82. circ. 1,000. (avail. only on diskette)
   Formerly: Educacion en Iberoamerica: Sistema de Indicadores Socio-Economicos y Educativos.

300   CC   ISSN 0561-7650
SIXIANG ZHANXIAN/IDEOLOGY FRONT. Variant title: Yunnan Daxue Xuebao (Shehui Kexue Ban) - Yunnan University. Journal (Social Sciences). (Text in Chinese; table of contents in English) bi-m. Y0.80 per no. (Yunnan Daxue - Yunnan University) Yunnan Renmin Chubanshe, Qikan Bu, 100, Shulin Jie, Kunming, Yunnan 650091, People's Republic of China. (Dist. outside China by: China International Book Trading Corp., P.O. Box 399, Beijing, P.R.C.; Editorial addr.: 52, Cuihu Beilu, Kunming, Yunnan 650091, P.R.C.) Ed. Zhou Gengxin.

300 947   US   ISSN 0037-6779
D377.A1
SLAVIC REVIEW; American quarterly of Soviet and East European studies. 1941. q. $50 to non-members. American Association for the Advancement of Slavic Studies, 128 Encina Commons, Stanford University, Stanford, CA 94305-6029. TEL 415-723-9668. (Alt. addr.: University of Pennsylvania, Center for Soviet and Eastern European Studies, 636 Williams Hall, Philadelphia, PA 19104-6305) Ed. Elliott Mossman. adv.; bk.rev.; bibl.; charts; index, cum.index: 1941-1964, 1965-1979; circ. 4,500. (also avail. in microform from MIM,UMI; reprint service avail. from UMI; back issues avail.) Indexed: A.B.C.Pol.Sci., Acad.Ind., Amer.Bibl.Slavic & E.Eur.Stud., Arts & Hum.Cit.Ind., Bk.Rev.Ind. (1990-), Child.Bk.Rev.Ind. (1990-), Hist.Abstr., Hum.Ind., M.L.A., P.A.I.S., Ref.Sour.
—BLDSC shelfmark: 8309.385000.
   Formerly: American Slavic and East European Review.

001.4   US   ISSN 0037-7333
AS30   CODEN: SMSNA5
SMITHSONIAN. 1970. m. $20. Smithsonian Institution, Arts & Industries Bldg., 900 Jefferson Dr., Washington, DC 20560. TEL 202-357-2888. FAX 202-786-2564. Ed. Don Moser. adv.; bk.rev.; illus.; index; circ. 2,100,000. (also avail. in microform from UMI; back issues avail.) Indexed: Abr.R.G., Abstr.Anthropol., Acad.Ind., Acid Rain Abstr., Acid Rain Ind., Arts & Hum.Cit.Ind., Biol.Dig., Bk.Rev.Ind. (1988-), CAD CAM Abstr., Child.Bk.Rev.Ind. (1988-), Curr.Cont., Curr.Lit.Fam.Plan., Deep Sea Res.& Oceanogr.Abstr., Environ.Abstr., Environ.Per.Bibl., Gard.Lit. (1992-), GeoRef., Hist.Abstr., Jun.High.Mag.Abstr., Mag.Ind., Ocean.Abstr., PMR, Pollut.Abstr., R.G., SSCI, Telegen.
●Also available online. Vendor(s): DIALOG.
—BLDSC shelfmark: 8311.450000.
   Description: Disseminates all aspects of sciences as well as history and the arts.

300 900   NE   ISSN 0081-0401
SOCIAAL-HISTORISCHE STUDIEN. (Text in Dutch; summaries in English or French) 1959. irreg., no.9, 1980. price varies. (International Institute for Social History) Van Gorcum en Co. B.V., P.O. Box 43, 9400 AA Assen, Netherlands. TEL 05920-46864. FAX 05920-72064.

370   II   ISSN 0037-7627
HN681   CODEN: SOACE2
SOCIAL ACTION. (Text in English) 1951. q. Rs.50($15) Indian Social Institute, Lodi Rd., New Delhi 110 003, India. Ed. Walter Fernandes. adv.; bk.rev.; index; circ. 2,000. (also avail. in microform from UMI; reprint service avail. from UMI) Indexed: Agroforest.Abstr., Bk.Rev.Ind., Forest.Abstr., Int.Lab.Doc., Rel.Ind.One, Rural Devel.Abstr., Rural Ext.Educ.& Tr.Abstr., Sociol.Educ.Abstr., Stud.Wom.Abstr., World Agri.Econ.& Rural Sociol.Abstr.
—BLDSC shelfmark: 8318.040000.

301 330   JM   ISSN 0037-7651
HN244
SOCIAL AND ECONOMIC STUDIES. 1953. 4/yr. $40. University of the West Indies, Institute of Social and Economic Research, Mona Campus, Kingston 7, Jamaica, W.I. TEL 809-927-1020. FAX 809-927-2409. TELEX 2123 JA. Eds. J. Edward Greene, Janet Liu Terry. adv.; bk.rev.; charts; stat.; index; circ. 2,000. (also avail. in microform from UMI; reprint service avail. from ISI,UMI) Indexed: A.I.C.P., ASCA, ASSIA, C.R.E.J., Curr.Cont., Geo.Abstr., Hist.Abstr., Hort.Abstr., I D A, Int.Lab.Doc., J.of Econ.Lit., Lang.& Lang.Behav.Abstr., P.A.I.S., Populi.Ind., Psychol.Abstr., Rural Devel.Abstr., Rural Recreat.Tour.Abstr., Soc.Sci.Ind., Sociol.Abstr., SSCI, Stud.Wom.Abstr., World Agri.Econ.& Rural Sociol.Abstr.
—BLDSC shelfmark: 8318.045000.
   Refereed Serial

SOCIAL CHANGE. see *SOCIOLOGY*

SOCIAL SCIENCES: COMPREHENSIVE WORKS

300　　　　　　　　SA　ISSN 0253-3952
HM1
SOCIAL DYNAMICS. 1975. s-a. R.25($25) to individuals; institutions R.50($44). University of Cape Town, Centre for African Studies, Rondebosch 7700, South Africa. TEL 021-6502310. FAX 021-650-3726. TELEX 521439. Ed.Bd. adv.; bk.rev.; circ. 300. **Indexed:** Geo.Abstr., Ind.S.A.Per., Lang.& Lang.Behav.Abstr., Rural Devel.Abstr., Sociol.Abstr. (1976-), World Agri.Econ.& Rural Sociol.Abstr.
—BLDSC shelfmark: 8318.081000.
Description: Topics in African Studies.

300　370　　　　　US　ISSN 0037-7724
H62.A1
SOCIAL EDUCATION. 1937. 7/yr. $55 to non-members. National Council for the Social Studies, 3501 Newark St., N.W., Washington, DC 20016. TEL 202-966-7840. Ed. Salvatore J. Natoli. adv.; bk.rev.; illus.; index; circ. 28,000. (also avail. in microform from UMI; reprint service avail. from UMI) **Indexed:** Acad.Ind., Adol.Ment.Hlth.Abstr., Amer.Bibl.Slavic & E.Eur.Stud., ASSIA, Bk.Rev.Ind. (1965-), C.I.J.E., Child.Bk.Rev.Ind. (1965-), Cont.Pg.Educ., Curr.Cont., Educ.Ind., Educ.Tech.Abstr., Hist.Abstr. (until 1990), HR Rep., Mid.East: Abstr.& Ind., SSCI.
—BLDSC shelfmark: 8318.087000.

SOCIAL EPISTEMOLOGY; a journal of knowledge, culture and policy. see *PHILOSOPHY*

300　　　　　　　UK　ISSN 0307-1022
HN1　　　　　　　　　　CODEN: SOHSEH
SOCIAL HISTORY. 1976. 3/yr. £26($52) to individuals; institutions £37($72). Routledge, 11 New Fetter Lane, London EC4P 4EE, England. FAX 01-583-0701. Eds. Janet Blackman, Keith Nield. adv.; bk.rev.; index; circ. 1,000. (reprint service avail. from KTO) **Indexed:** Arts & Hum.Cit.Ind., Hist.Abstr., Soc.Sci.Ind.
—BLDSC shelfmark: 8318.092900.
Description: Social historical writing, especially of a theoretical and polemical kind.

300　　　　　　　UK　ISSN 0961-2882
▼**SOCIAL INTELLIGENCE.** 1991. 3/yr. £53($103) Taylor Graham Publishing, 500 Chesham House, 150 Regent St., London W1R 5FA, England. Ed. Blaise Cronin. adv.; bk.rev. (back issues avail.)
—BLDSC shelfmark: 8318.116800.

361　　　　　　　　　ISSN 0037-7767
SOCIAL JUSTICE REVIEW; pioneer American journal of Catholic social action. 1908. bi-m. $15 (foreign $18). Catholic Central Union of America, 3835 Westminster Pl., St. Louis, MO 63108-3409. TEL 314-371-1653. Ed. Rev. John H. Miller. bk.rev.; circ. 1,250. (also avail. in microfilm) **Indexed:** ASSIA, Cath.Ind., CERDIC.
—BLDSC shelfmark: 8318.122000.

300　　　　　　　NE　ISSN 0378-8733
HM73
SOCIAL NETWORKS; an international journal of structural analysis. (Text and summaries in English) 1979. q. fl.319 (effective 1992). (International Network for Social Network Analysis) North-Holland (Subsidiary of: Elsevier Science Publishers B.V), P.O. Box 211, 1000 AE Amsterdam, Netherlands. TEL 020-5803911. FAX 020-5803598. TELEX 18582 ESPA NL. (Subscr. in U.S. and Canada to: Elsevier Science Publishing Co., Inc., Box 882, Madison Sq. Sta., New York, NY 10159. TEL 212-989-5800) Ed. Linton C. Freeman. adv.; bk.rev. (back issues avail.) **Indexed:** ASCA, ASSIA, Curr.Cont., J.Cont.Quant.Meth., Lang.& Lang.Behav.Abstr., Math.R., Mid.East: Abstr.& Ind., Psychol.Abstr., Sage Urb.Stud.Abstr., Sci.Cit.Ind., Sociol.Abstr., SSCI.
—BLDSC shelfmark: 8318.125300.
Description: Provides a common forum for representatives of anthropology, sociology, history, social psychology, political science, human geography, biology, economics, communications science.
Refereed Serial

300　　　　　　　UK
SOCIAL POLICY REVIEW. a. £16.95. Longman Group UK Ltd., Westgate House, The High, Harlow, Essex CM20 1YR, England. Ed. K. Jones. **Indexed:** Int.Lab.Doc.
Former titles: Yearbook of Social Policy in Britain; Yearbook of Social Studies.

300　　　　　　　US
SOCIAL PRACTICE. 1978. q. $6. Inter-University Consortium for Ethics and Aesthetics, Box 211, Winfield, IL 60190. Ed. D.A. Strickland.

300　320　　　　　US　ISSN 0037-783X
H1
SOCIAL RESEARCH; an international journal of political and social science. 1934. q. $20 to individuals; libraries and institutions $40. New School for Social Research, 65 Fifth Ave., New York, NY 10003. TEL 212-741-5600. FAX 212-741-5776. Ed. Arien Mack. adv.; bk.rev.; index; circ. 3,000. (also avail. in microform from JAI,MIM,UMI; reprint service avail. from KTO,UMI) **Indexed:** A.B.C.Pol.Sci., Amer.Bibl.Slavic & E.Eur.Stud., ASCA, ASSIA, Bk.Rev.Ind. (1965-1977), Child.Bk.Rev.Ind. (1965-1977), Commun.Abstr., Curr.Cont., E.I., Hist.Abstr., Lang.& Lang.Behav.Abstr., Mid.East: Abstr.& Ind., P.A.I.S., Peace Res.Abstr., Soc.Sci.Ind., Sociol.Abstr., SSCI.
—BLDSC shelfmark: 8318.150000.

300　　　　　　　IS　ISSN 0334-4762
SOCIAL RESEARCH REVIEW/RIV'ON LE-MEHKAR HEVRATI. (Text in Hebrew; summaries in English) 1972. q. free. Association for Publishing Social Research Review, 5 Nehardea St., Tel Aviv, Israel. FAX 03-5440892. Ed. Dr. Avraham Wolfensohn. adv.; bk.rev.; bibl.; circ. 1,000. **Indexed:** Ind.Heb.Per.

SOCIAL SCIENCE COMPUTER REVIEW. see *EDUCATION — Computer Applications*

300　　　　　　　CN
SOCIAL SCIENCE FEDERATION OF CANADA. ANNUAL REPORT. (Text in English, French) 1940. a. free. Social Science Federation of Canada, 151 Slater St., Ste. 415, Ottawa, Ont. K1P 5H3, Canada. TEL 613-238-6112. FAX 613-238-6114. circ. 600.
Formerly: Social Science Research Council of Canada. Report (ISSN 0081-0452)

300　　　　　　　US　ISSN 0145-5532
H1
SOCIAL SCIENCE HISTORY. 1976. q. $30 to individuals (foreign $38); institutions $50 (foreign $58); students $12 (foreign $20). (Social Science History Association) Duke University Press, 6697 College Station, Durham, NC 27708. TEL 919-684-2173. FAX 919-684-8644. Ed. Rus Menard. adv.; bk.rev.; circ. 1,000. (also avail. in microform from MIM; reprint service avail. from SCH) **Indexed:** Amer.Bibl.Slavic & E.Eur.Stud., ASCA, ASSIA, Hist.Abstr., Lang.& Lang.Behav.Abstr., Sage Pub.Admin.Abstr., Sage Urb.Stud.Abstr., SSCI, Stud.Wom.Abstr.
—BLDSC shelfmark: 8318.160500.
Refereed Serial

300　　　　　　　UK　ISSN 0539-0184
H1　　　　　　　　　　CODEN: SSCIBL
SOCIAL SCIENCE INFORMATION. 1954; N.S. 1961. q. £39($64) to individuals; institutions £99(163). Sage Publications Ltd., 6 Bonhill St., London EC2A 4PU, England. TEL 071-374-0645. FAX 071-374-8741. Eds. E. Almasy, A. Rocha-Perazzo. adv.: color page £150; trim 177 x 101; adv. contact: Bernie Folan. **Indexed:** A.B.C.Pol.Sci., Cont.Pg.Manage., Hist.Abstr. (until 1991), Lang.& Lang.Behav.Abstr., Psychol.Abstr., World Agri.Econ.& Rural Sociol.Abstr.
—BLDSC shelfmark: 8318.161000.
Formerly: Sciences Sociales Information - Information sur les Sciences Sociales (ISSN 0037-7864)
Description: Provides a forum for research in social anthropology, sociology of science and sociological theory.

300　　　　　　　US
SOCIAL SCIENCE JOURNAL. 1963. 4/yr. $45 to individuals; institutions $90. J A I Press Inc., 55 Old Post Rd., No. 2, Box 1678, Greenwich, CT 06836-1678. TEL 203-661-7602. Ed. Michael Katovitch. adv.; bk.rev.; bibl.; charts; illus.; stat.; index, cum.index: 1963-68, 1969-72; circ. 2,000. (also avail. in microform from JAI; back issues avail.) **Indexed:** Abstr.Soc.Work, Amer.Bibl.Slavic & E.Eur.Stud., Amer.Hist.& Life., ASCA, Chic.Per.Ind., Commun.Abstr., Curr.Cont., Econ.Abstr., Hist.Abstr., Int.Polit.Sci.Abstr., Lang.& Lang.Behav.Abstr., P.A.I.S., Peace Res.Abstr., Psychol.Abstr., Risk Abstr., Sage Pub.Admin.Abstr., Soc.Sci.Ind., Sociol.Abstr., Sociol.Educ.Abstr., SSCI, Stud.Wom.Abstr.
Formerly: Rocky Mountain Social Science Journal (ISSN 0035-7634)
Description: Contributions are welcome from all fields which have comments to make about the social sciences. Articles may be theoretical, speculative or heavily armored with statistical data or mathematical models.

300　　　　　　　UK　ISSN 0307-0042
SOCIAL SCIENCE MONOGRAPHS. 1975. irreg. price varies. (Board of Celtic Studies) University of Wales Press, 6 Gwennyth St., Cathays, Cardiff CF2 4YD, Wales. TEL 0222-231919. FAX 0222-230908. Ed. Harold Carter.

300　　　　　　　US　ISSN 0038-4941
H1
SOCIAL SCIENCE QUARTERLY. 1920. q. $25 to individuals; institutions $45. (Southwestern Social Science Association) University of Texas Press, Box 7819, Austin, TX 78713. TEL 512-471-4531. Ed. Dr. Charles M. Bonjean. adv.; bk.rev.; abstr.; bibl.; index; circ. 2,700. (also avail. in microform from KTO,MIM,UMI; reprint service avail. from UMI) **Indexed:** A.B.C.Pol.Sci., Amer.Bibl.Slavic & E.Eur.Stud., Amer.Hist.& Life, ASCA, ASSIA, Bk.Rev.Ind. (1975-), C.I.J.E., Chic.Per.Ind., Child.Bk.Rev.Ind. (1975-), Commun.Abstr., Crim.Just.Abstr., Curr.Cont., Educ.Admin.Abstr., Energy Info.Abstr., ERIC, Hist.Abstr., J.of Econ.Abstr., J.of Econ.Lit., Lang.& Lang.Behav.Abstr., Leg.Per., Mid.East: Abstr.& Ind., P.A.I.S., Popul.Ind., Res.High.Educ.Abstr., Sage Fam.Stud.Abstr., Sage Pub.Admin.Abstr., Sage Urb.Stud.Abstr., Soc.Sci.Ind., Sociol.Abstr., Sociol.Educ.Abstr., SSCI, Stud.Wom.Abstr., World Agri.Econ.& Rural Sociol.Abstr.
—BLDSC shelfmark: 8318.167000.
Formerly: Southwestern Social Science Quarterly.
Description: Dedicated to developing communication across traditional disciplinary boundaries.

300　　　　　　　US　ISSN 0049-089X
H1　　　　　　　　　　CODEN: SSREBG
SOCIAL SCIENCE RESEARCH; a quarterly journal of social science methodology and quantitative research. 1972. q. $132 (foreign $175). Academic Press, Inc., Journal Division, 1250 Sixth Ave., San Diego, CA 92101. TEL 619-230-1840. FAX 619-699-6800. TELEX 181726. Ed. James D. Wright. adv.; charts; stat.; index. (back issues avail.) **Indexed:** A.B.C.Pol.Sci., Adol.Ment.Hlth.Abstr., ASCA, ASSIA, Crim.Just.Abstr., Curr.Cont., Hist.Abstr., Lang.& Lang.Behav.Abstr., Mid.East: Abstr.& Ind., Psychol.Abstr., Soc.Sci.Ind., Sp.Ed.Needs Abstr., SSCI, Stud.Wom.Abstr.
—BLDSC shelfmark: 8318.170100.
Description: Illustrates the use of quantitative methods in the empirical solution of substantive problems, and emphasizes those concerned with issues or methods that cut across traditional disciplinary lines.

300　　　　　　　CE
SOCIAL SCIENCE REVIEW. (Text in English) 1979. q. $10 to individuals; institutions $15. Social Science Association of Sri Lanka, 120-10 Wijerama Mawatha, Colombo, Sri Lanka. **Indexed:** Crim.Just.Abstr., Sri Lanka Sci.Ind.

300　　　　　　　RU　ISSN 0049-0911
SOCIAL SCIENCES. (Editions in English, French, German, Portuguese, Spanish) 1970. q. $5.50. (Akademiya Nauk S.S.S.R.) Izdatel'stvo Nauka, 90 Profzoyuznaya ul., 117864 Moscow, Russia. Ed. I. Grigulevich. bk.rev.; bibl. **Indexed:** Hist.Abstr., Int.Lab.Doc.

SOCIAL SCIENCES: COMPREHENSIVE WORKS

300   CC   ISSN 0252-9203
HC426
SOCIAL SCIENCES IN CHINA; a quarterly journal in English. Chinese edition: Zhongguo Shehui Kexue. (Text in English) 1980. q. (Chinese ed. m.). $29 (Chinese ed. $53.40). (Zhongguo Shehui Kexueyuan - Chinese Academy of Social Sciences) Zhongguo Shehui Kexue Zazhishe, A-158 Gulou Xidajie, Beijing 100720, People's Republic of China. (Dist. overseas by: China International Book Trading Corp., P.O. Box 399, Beijing, P.R.C.; Dist. in US by: China Books & Periodicals, Inc., 2929 24th St., San Francisco, CA 94110. TEL 415-282-2994) **Indexed:** ASSIA, Geo.Abstr., Int.Lab.Doc., P.A.I.S.
—BLDSC shelfmark: 8318.187400.
Description: Academic journal on China's history, economics, anthropology and sociology.

300   JA
SOCIAL SCIENCES JOURNAL/SHAKAI KAGAKU KENKYU. (Text in Japanese) 1951. bi-m. (University of Tokyo, Institute of Social Science - Tokyo Daigaku Shakai Kagaku Kenkyujo) Japan Scientific Societies Press, 6-2-10 Hongo, Bunkyo-ku, Tokyo 113, Japan. bk.rev. **Indexed:** Hist.Abstr., Soc.Work Res.& Abstr.

300   II   ISSN 0251-348X
SOCIAL SCIENCES RESEARCH JOURNAL. (Text in English) 1976. 3/yr. Rs.30($6) Panjab University, Arts Block No. 3, Panjab University Campus, Chandigarh 160014, India.

330   II
SOCIAL SCIENCES RESEARCH SERIES. (Text in English) 1975. irreg., no.5, 1985. price varies. Indian Institute of Geography, 120-A Nehru Nagar East, Secunderabad 500 026, Andhra Pradesh, India. TEL 77680. Ed. B.N. Chaturuedi. circ. 1,000.
Supersedes: Wealth and Welfare of Andhra Pradesh Series (ISSN 0083-7776)

300   II   ISSN 0970-0293
HN681
SOCIAL SCIENTIST. (Text in English) 1972. m. Rs.100 to individuals; institutions Rs.150; students Rs.75 (foreign $50). Indian School of Social Sciences, C-20 Qutab Institutional Area (Behind Gutab Hotel), New Delhi 110 016, India. TEL 6862924. Ed. Prabhat Patnaik. adv.; bk.rev.; play rev.; bibl.; charts; illus.; stat.; index; circ. 2,000. (back issues avail.) **Indexed:** Geo.Abstr., Rural Recreat.Tour.Abstr., World Agri.Econ.& Rural Sociol.Abstr.
Description: Deals with a variety of current problems: economic policy, educational reform, social change, as well as problems in history, methodology, and social theory.

300   NR   ISSN 0081-0487
SOCIAL SCIENTIST.* 1965. a. University of Ife, Economics Society, Ile-Ife, Nigeria. **Indexed:** Geo.Abstr.

SOCIAL STUDIES OF SCIENCE; an international review of research in the social dimensions of science and technology. see *SCIENCES: COMPREHENSIVE WORKS*

300 375   US   ISSN 0586-6235
SOCIAL STUDIES PROFESSIONAL. 1969. 5/yr. membership. National Council for the Social Studies, 3501 Newark St., N.W., Washington, DC 20016. TEL 202-966-7840. (also avail. in microform from UMI; reprint service avail. from UMI)

300   US
SOCIAL STUDIES REVIEW. vol.12, 1974. 3/yr. $25. California Council for Social Studies, 1255 Vista Grande, Millbrae, CA 94030-2213. TEL 415-692-4830. Ed. Damon Nalty. adv.; circ. 2,600. (also avail. in microform from UMI; back issues avail.; reprint service avail. from UMI) **Indexed:** C.I.J.E., Chic.Per.Ind.

300   UK   ISSN 0267-0712
SOCIAL STUDIES REVIEW. 5/yr. £16.90. Philip Allan Publishers Ltd., Deddington, Oxfordshire OX5 4SE, England. TEL 0869-38652. FAX 0869-38803. (back issues avail.)

300 360   UK   ISSN 0144-0969
SOCIAL WORK INFORMATION BULLETIN. Short title: S W I B. 1976. bi-w. £26. Leicestershire Libraries and Information Service, Information Centre, Bishop St., Leicester LE1 6AA, England. TEL 0533-556699. FAX 0533-555435. Ed. Angela Hall. circ. 980.

300   NE   ISSN 0037-8097
SOCIALE WETENSCHAPPEN. vol.13, 1970. q. fl.2.50. Tilburg University, Faculty of Social Sciences, Postbus 90153, 5000 LE Tilburg, Netherlands. adv.; bk.rev.; charts; stat.; index; circ. 1,200. **Indexed:** E.I., Key to Econ.Sci.
—BLDSC shelfmark: 8318.242000.

SOCIALIST PERSPECTIVE; a quarterly journal of social sciences. see *POLITICAL SCIENCE*

300 368   CS
SOCIALNA POLITIKA. m. (Federal Ministry of Work and Social Affairs) Obzor, Ceskoslovenskej Armady 35, 815 85 Bratislava, Czechoslovakia.

300 913   FR   ISSN 0300-953X
DU1
SOCIETE DES OCEANISTES. JOURNAL. (Text in English and French) 1945. s-a. 220 F. (typically set in Feb. or Mar.). Societe des Oceanistes, Musee de l'Homme, 75116 Paris, France. bk.rev.; bibl.; illus.; cum.index: 1945-1960 in vol.16, 1960-1970 in vol.26; circ. 1,100. **Indexed:** A.I.C.P., E.I., So.Pac.Per.Ind.

300   FR   ISSN 0081-0894
SOCIETE DES OCEANISTES. PUBLICATIONS. 1951. irreg. (typically set in Feb. or Mar.). Societe des Oceanistes, Musee de l'Homme, 75116 Paris, France. bk.rev.; circ. 1,100.

300   US   ISSN 0147-2011
H1
SOCIETY; social science & modern society. 1963. bi-m. $36 to individuals (foreign $56); institutions $78 (foreign $98). Transaction Publishers, Transaction Periodicals Consortium, Department 3092, Rutgers University, New Brunswick, NJ 08903. TEL 908-932-2280. FAX 908-932-3138. Ed. Irving Louis Horowitz. adv.; bk.rev.; abstr.; bibl.; charts; illus.; stat.; index, cum.index: vols.1-5; circ. 10,000. (also avail. in microform from UMI,JAI,MIM; back issues avail.; reprint service avail. from UMI) **Indexed:** A.B.C.Pol.Sci., Acad.Ind., ASCA, Bk.Rev.Ind. (1976-), C.I.J.E., Child.Bk.Rev.Ind. (1976-), Curr.Cont., Educ.Admin.Abstr., Film Lit.Ind. (1973-), Fut.Surv., Hist.Abstr., Lang.& Lang.Behav.Abstr., Mag.Ind., Med.Care Rev., Mid.East: Abstr.& Ind., P.A.I.S., Peace Res.Abstr., PMR, PSI, R.G., Sage Pub.Admin.Abstr., Sage Urb.Stud.Abstr., SSCI.
Formerly: Trans-Action-Social Science and Modern Society (ISSN 0041-1035)
Description: Covers social science and public policy.

300   II
SOCIETY AND CHANGE. (Text in English) 1980. q. $16. 8B Madhu Gupta Lane, Calcutta 700 012, India. Ed. Buddhadeva Bhattacharyya.

300.2   II   ISSN 0037-9662
HN681
SOCIETY AND CULTURE. (Text in English) 1970. s-a. Rs.20($10) Institute of Social Studies, 179 Bipin Behari Ganguly St., Calcutta 12, India. Ed. K.L. Bhowmik. adv.; bk.rev.; bibl.; charts. **Indexed:** Hist.Abstr., Lang.& Lang.Behav.Abstr., Psychol.Abstr.

SOCIETY AND NATURAL RESOURCES. see *ENVIRONMENTAL STUDIES*

SOCIOLOGIA (ROME); rivista di scienze sociali. see *SOCIOLOGY*

300   IT
SOCIOLOGIA DEL LAVORO. q. L.82000 (foreign L.110000)(effective 1992). (Universita degli Studi di Bologna, Centro Internazionale di Documentazione e Studi Sui Problemi del Lavoro) Franco Angeli Editore, Viale Monza 106, 20127 Milan, Italy. TEL 02-2827651. Ed.Bd. **Indexed:** Int.Lab.Doc., Lang.& Lang.Behav.Abstr., Sociol.Abstr. (1981-).
Formerly (until 1978): Analisi e Documenti.

300 320   CH   ISSN 0259-3785
SOOCHOW JOURNAL OF POLITICAL SCIENCE & SOCIOLOGY. 1977. a. $15 per no. Soochow University, Soochow University Library, Wai Shuang Hsi, Shih Lin, Taipei, Taiwan, Republic of China. FAX 886-02-8829310. (reprint service avail.) Key Title: Dongwu Zhengzhi Shehui Xuebao.
Formerly: Soochow Journal of Social and Political Sciences.

300   RU
▼**SOTSIAL'NO-POLITICHESKIE NAUKI**; nauchno-teoreticheskii zhurnal. 1990. m. 1.50 Rub. per issue. Gosudarstvennyi Komitet S.S.S.R. po Narodnomy Obrazovaniyu, Prospekt Marksa 18, kom.156-157, 103009 Moscow K-9, Russia. TEL 203-25-43. Ed. V.F. Khalipov. circ. 8,652.

SOUNDINGS (KNOXVILLE); an interdisciplinary journal. see *HUMANITIES: COMPREHENSIVE WORKS*

SOUTH ASIAN SOCIAL SCIENTIST. see *ORIENTAL STUDIES*

SOUTH ASIAN STUDIES. see *ORIENTAL STUDIES*

300   SI   ISSN 0303-8246
SOUTHEAST ASIAN JOURNAL OF SOCIAL SCIENCES. 1968. s-a. S.$48($30) (National University of Singapore, Department of Sociology) Chopmen Publishers, Katong Shopping Centre, Mountbatten Rd., No. 05-28, Singapore 1543, Singapore. TEL 3441495. FAX 3440180. Ed. Peter S.J. Chen. adv.; bk.rev.; illus.; circ. 500. **Indexed:** ASSIA.
Incorporates: Southeast Asia Ethnicity and Development Newsletter; **Formerly:** South-East Asian Journal of Sociology.

300   US
SOUTHERN SOCIAL STUDIES JOURNAL. 1975. s-a. $10. Kentucky Council for the Social Studies, Morehead State University, 114 Rader Hall, Morehead, KY 40351. TEL 606-783-2347. FAX 606-783-2678. Eds. Charles Holt, Kent Freeland. adv.; bk.rev.; circ. 500. (back issues avail.) **Indexed:** C.I.J.E.
●Also available online. Vendor(s): BRS, DIALOG.
Formerly (until 1990): Southern Social Studies Quarterly (ISSN 0741-143X)
Description: Articles of interest to social studies educators of all levels.

300 976.3   US   ISSN 0735-8342
F366
SOUTHERN STUDIES: AN INTERDISCIPLINARY JOURNAL OF THE SOUTH. 1961; N.S. 1990. q. $10 (foreign $25). Northwestern State University of Louisiana, Southern Studies Institute, Natchitoches, LA 71497. TEL 318-357-6195. FAX 318-357-6125. Ed. Maxine Taylor. adv.; bk.rev.; bibl.; charts; illus.; index, cum.index: 1962-1966; circ. 400. (also avail. in microform from UMI; reprint service avail. from UMI) **Indexed:** Abstr.Engl.Stud., Amer.Hist.& Life, M.L.A.
Former titles: Louisiana Studies: an Interdisciplinary Journal of the South; Louisiana Studies (ISSN 0024-693X)
Description: Publishes original research in various fields contributing to greater knowledge and understanding of the south.
Refereed Serial

300   GW   ISSN 0171-8738
SOZIAL REPORT. (Editions in English, French, German and Spanish) m. Inter Nationes e.V., Kennedyallee 91-103, 5300 Bonn 2, Germany. TEL 0228-8800. FAX 0228-880457. TELEX 17228308-IND-D.

SOZIAL- UND WIRTSCHAFTSHISTORISCHE STUDIEN. see *BUSINESS AND ECONOMICS — Economic Systems And Theories, Economic History*

360   GW   ISSN 0038-609X
HN441
SOZIALER FORTSCHRITT. (Unabhaengige Zeitschrift fuer Sozialpolitik) 1952. m. DM.120. (Gesellschaft fuer Sozialen Fortschritt E.V., Bonn) Duncker und Humblot GmbH, Postfach 410329, 1000 Berlin 41, Germany. TEL 030-7900060.
FAX 030-79000631. Ed. Eve-Elisabeth Schewe. adv.; bk.rev.; index. **Indexed:** Int.Lab.Doc., P.A.I.S.For.Lang.Ind., World Bibl.Soc.Sec.
—BLDSC shelfmark: 8361.080000.

300   GW   ISSN 0490-1657
SOZIALGERICHTSBARKEIT. 1953. m. DM.644. Verlag Chmielorz GmbH und Co., Wilhelmstr. 42, 6200 Wiesbaden, Germany. TEL 06121-39671. circ. 966. (back issues avail.)

SOZIALPOLITISCHE INFORMATIONEN. see *POLITICAL SCIENCE*

300   GW   ISSN 0175-6559
SOZIALWISSENSCHAFTLICHE LITERATUR RUNDSCHAU; Sozialarbeit-Sozialpaedagogik-Sozialpolitik-soziale Probleme. 1978. s-a. DM.45. Karin Boellert K T-Verlag, Postfach 1406, 4800 Bielefeld, Germany. TEL 0521-885890. Ed.Bd. adv.; bk.rev.; circ. 900.

300　　　　　　　SZ
SOZIOOEKONOMISCHE FORSCHUNGEN. 1974. irreg., no.25, 1991. price varies. Paul Haupt AG, Falkenplatz 14, CH-3001 Berne, Switzerland. TEL 031-232425.

300 320　　　　GW　ISSN 0171-3159
SPAK-FORUM. 1970. 4/yr. DM.20($10) AG Spak, Adlzreiterstr. 23, 8000 Munich 2, Germany. TEL 089-774077. bk.rev.

300　　　　　　　PL
SPOLECZENSTWO OTWARTE. 1969. 10/yr. $22. Ul. Ujazdowskie 28, pok. 204, Warsaw, Poland. TEL 22-217343. (Dist. by: Ars Polona-Ruch, Krakowskie Przedmiescie 7, Warsaw, Poland)
Supersedes: Wychowanie Obywatelskie (ISSN 0512-4263)

SRI LANKA JOURNAL OF HISTORICAL AND SOCIAL STUDIES. see *HISTORY*

300　　　　　　　YU　ISSN 0081-394X
SRPSKA AKADEMIJA NAUKA I UMETNOSTI. ODELJENJE DRUSTVENIH NAUKA. GLAS. (Text in Serbo-Croatian; summaries in English, French, German or Russian) 1951. irreg. price varies. Srpska Akademija Nauka i Umetnosti, Knez Mihailova 35, 11001 Belgrade, Serbia, Yugoslavia. FAX 38-11-182-825. TELEX 72593 SANU YU. (Dist. by: Prosveta, Terzije 16, Belgrade, Serbia, Yugoslavia) circ. 1,000. **Indexed:** Amer.Hist.& Life, Art & Archaeol.Tech.Abstr., Hist.Abstr., Int.Aerosp.Abstr.

300　　　　　　　YU　ISSN 0081-3982
SRPSKA AKADEMIJA NAUKA I UMETNOSTI. ODELJENJE DRUSTVENIH NAUKA. POSEBNA IZDANJA. (Text in Serbo-Croatian; summaries in English, French, German or Russian) N.S. 1949. irreg. price varies. Srpska Akademija Nauka i Umetnosti, Knez Mihailova 35, 11001 Belgrade, Serbia, Yugoslavia. FAX 38-11-182-825. TELEX 72593 SANU YU. (Dist. by: Prosveta, Terzije 16, Belgrade, Serbia, Yugoslavia) circ. 1,000. **Indexed:** Hist.Abstr.

300 913 720　　YU　ISSN 0081-4059
SRPSKA AKADEMIJA NAUKA I UMETNOSTI. ODELJENJE DRUSTVENIH NAUKA. SPOMENIK. (Text in Serbo-Croatian; summaries in English, French, German or Russian) N.S. 1950. irreg. price varies. Srpska Akademija Nauka i Umetnosti, Knez Mihailova 35, 11001 Belgrade, Serbia, Yugoslavia. FAX 38-11-182-825. TELEX 72593 SANU YU. (Dist. by: Prosveta, Terazije 16, Belgrade, Serbia, Yugoslavia) circ. 1,000.

SRPSKA AKADEMIJA NAUKA I UMETNOSTI SPOMENICA. see *HUMANITIES: COMPREHENSIVE WORKS*

SSU YU YEN/THOUGHT AND WORDS; journal of the humanities and social sciences. see *HUMANITIES: COMPREHENSIVE WORKS*

STATNI VEDECKA KNIHOVNA. VYBER NOVINEK. SERIE C: CLOVEK A SPOLECNOST. see *BIBLIOGRAPHIES*

300　　　　　　　IT
STUDI GORIZIANI. 1923. s-a. L.12000 per no. Biblioteca Statale Isontina di Gorizia, Via Mameli 12, 34170 Gorizia, Italy. TEL 0481-531802. FAX 0481-531802. Ed.Bd. bk.rev.; bibl.; illus.; circ. 600.

300 943.8　　　PL　ISSN 0081-6574
H8
STUDIA I MATERIALY Z DZIEJOW NAUKI POLSKIEJ. SERIA A. HISTORIA NAUK SPOLECZNYCH. (Text in Polish; summaries in English, French, Russian) 1957. irreg., vol.16, 1984. price varies. (Polska Akademia Nauk, Zaklad Historii Nauki, Oswiaty i Techniki) Panstwowe Wydawnictwo Naukowe, Ul. Miodowa 10, 00-251 Warsaw, Poland. (Dist. by: Ars Polona, Krakowskie Przedmiescie 7, 00-068 Warsaw, Poland) Ed. E. Olszewski. illus.; circ. 320.

300　　　　　　　US　ISSN 0039-3606
H31
STUDIES IN COMPARATIVE INTERNATIONAL DEVELOPMENT. 1964. q. $36 to individuals (foreign $56); institutions $76 (foreign $96). Transaction Publishers, Transaction Periodicals Consortium, Department 3092, Rutgers University, New Brunswick, NJ 08903. TEL 908-932-2280. FAX 908-932-3138. Ed. John D. Martz. circ. 1,000. (also avail. in microform from MIM,UMI; reprint service avail. from UMI) **Indexed:** A.B.C.Pol.Sci., ASCA, ASSIA, Curr.Cont., Hisp.Amer.Per.Ind., Hist.Abstr., I D A, Int.Lab.Doc., Lang.& Lang.Behav.Abstr., Mid.East: Abstr.& Ind., Rural Devel.Abstr., SSCI, World Agri.Econ.& Rural Sociol.Abstr.
—BLDSC shelfmark: 8490.250000.
Description: Interdisciplinary exploration of current issues in development theory and practice.

STUDIES IN SOCIAL EXPERIMENTATION. see *SOCIOLOGY*

300　　　　　　　NE
STUDIES IN SOCIAL HISTORY. (Text in English) 1976. irreg. price varies. (International Institute for Social History) Kluwer Academic Publishers, Postbus 17, 3300 AA Dordrecht, Netherlands. TEL 078-334911. FAX 078-334254.

300　　　　　　　PL　ISSN 0860-3359
D880
STUDIES IN THE DEVELOPING COUNTRIES. (Text in English) q. $24. (Polish Academy of Sciences, Committee for Studies on Asia, Africa and Latin America) Ossolineum, Publishing House of the Polish Academy of Sciences, Rynek 9, 50-106 Wroclaw, Poland. TEL 386-25. (Dist. by: Ars Polona, Krakowskie Przedmiescie 7, 00-068 Warsaw, Poland) Ed. Jerzy Prokopczuk. bk.rev.
Description: Scientific studies on various aspects of developing countries, information, scientific reports on Asia, Africa and Latin America.

300　　　　　　　US
STUDIES IN THE HISTORY OF SCIENCE. vol.5, 1979. irreg. Burt Franklin & Co., Inc., Box 856, New York, NY 10014. TEL 212-627-0027. Ed. L. Pearce Williams.

300　　　　　　　SJ
SUDAN. ECONOMIC AND SOCIAL RESEARCH COUNCIL. OCCASIONAL PAPER. irreg., no.7, 1976. Economic and Social Research Council, P.O. Box 1166, Khartoum, Sudan. bibl.

300　　　　　　　SJ
SUDAN. NATIONAL COUNCIL FOR RESEARCH. ECONOMIC AND SOCIAL RESEARCH COUNCIL. BULLETIN. (Text in Arabic, English) 1974. irreg., no.152, 1990. National Council for Research, Economic and Social Research Council, P.O. Box 1166, Khartoum, Sudan. TEL 78805. TELEX 22342 ILIMI. **Indexed:** Rural Devel.Abstr.
Description: Presents papers on specific topics relating to agricultural, industrial, social and theoretical economics issues in the Sudan.

300 338.91　　SJ
SUDAN. NATIONAL COUNCIL FOR RESEARCH. ECONOMIC AND SOCIAL RESEARCH COUNCIL. RESEARCH METHODS. (Text in Arabic, English) 1983. irreg., no.3, 1989. National Council for Research, Economic and Social Research Council, P.O. Box 1166, Khartoum, Sudan. TEL 78805. TELEX 22342 ILIMI.

300　　　　　　　SJ
SUDAN. NATIONAL COUNCIL FOR RESEARCH. ECONOMIC AND SOCIAL RESEARCH COUNCIL. RESEARCH REPORT. (Text in Arabic, English) 1976. irreg., no.42, 1989. National Council for Research, Economic and Social Research Council, P.O. Box 1166, Khartoum, Sudan. TEL 78805. TELEX 22342 ILIMI.
Description: Presents reports on social and economic issues in the Sudan, with emphasis on the impact of modernization programs.

330.9　　　　　　SJ
SUDAN JOURNAL OF ECONOMIC AND SOCIAL STUDIES. (Text in English) 1974. s-a. $5. (University of Khartoum, Faculty of Economic and Social Studies) Khartoum University Press, PO Box 321, Khartoum, Sudan. Ed. Ahmed A. Ahmed. **Indexed:** Rural Recreat.Tour.Abstr., Soils & Fert., World Agri.Econ.& Rural Sociol.Abstr.

SUDAN RESEARCH INFORMATION BULLETIN. see *HUMANITIES: COMPREHENSIVE WORKS*

300　　　　　　　CH　ISSN 0300-3302
SUN YAT-SEN CULTURAL FOUNDATION BULLETIN/CHUNG SHAN HSUEH SHU WEN HUA CH'I K'AN. (Text in Chinese and English) 1968. s-a. NT.$250($16) per no. Sun Yat-sen Cultural Foundation, No. 23, Lane 13, Yung Kang St., Taipei, Taiwan, Republic of China. charts.

300 100　　　　CC
SUZHOU DAXUE XUEBAO (ZHEXUE SHEHUI KEXUE BAN)/SUZHOU UNIVERSITY. JOURNAL (SOCIAL SCIENCE EDITION). (Text in Chinese) 1906. q. Y8($40) Suzhou Daxue - Suzhou University, 1 Shizi Jie, Suzhou, Jiangsu 215006, People's Republic of China. TEL 0512-778805. FAX 0512-771918. TELEX 5868. (Dist. overseas by: China Publications Foreign Trade Corp., P.O. Box 782, Beijing, P.R.C.) adv.; bk.rev.
Formerly: Dongwu Daxue. Xuebao.
Description: Covers the studies of the Chinese language, Chinese and foreign literature, history, law, economics, philosophy, and psychology with special columns featuring the studies of poetry and prose of the Ming and Qing dynasties, Wu culture, and local history of Suzhou.

300　　　　　　　US
SYMBOLIC INTERACTION. 1977. s-a. $45 to individuals; institutions $90. (Society for the Study of Symbolic Interaction) J A I Press Inc., 55 Old Post Rd., No. 2, Box 1678, Greenwich, CT 06836-1678. TEL 203-661-7602. Ed. David Maines. **Indexed:** ASCA, Lang.& Lang.Behav.Abstr., Mid.East: Abstr.& Ind., Psychol.Abstr., Sociol.Abstr. (1977-).

SYNTHESE LIBRARY; monographs on epistemology, logic, methodology, philosophy of science and of knowledge, and the mathematical methods of social and behavioral sciences. see *PHILOSOPHY*

960　　　　　　　US
SYRACUSE UNIVERSITY. FOREIGN AND COMPARATIVE STUDIES. AFRICAN SERIES. (Former name of issuing body: Maxwell School of Citizenship and Public Affairs) 1971. irreg., vol.43, 1990. price varies. Syracuse University, Foreign and Comparative Studies, c/o Joanna C. Giansanti, Man. Ed., 321 Sims Hall, Syracuse, NY 13244-1230. TEL 315-443-4667. FAX 315-443-4597. **Indexed:** Geo.Abstr., Rural Devel.Abstr.
Formerly (until vol.25, 1976): Syracuse University. Program of East African Studies. Eastern African Series.

SYSTEM DYNAMICS REVIEW. see *BUSINESS AND ECONOMICS — Management*

300　　　　　　　SZ　ISSN 0080-7427
T.M.. (Tatsachen und Meinungen) 1968. irreg., no.56, 1987. price varies. (Schweizerisches Ost-Institut - Swiss Eastern Institute) Verlag SOI, Jubilaeumsstr. 41, CH-3000 Berne 6, Switzerland. TEL 031-431212. FAX 031-433891. TELEX 812713. Ed. Peter Sager.

TAGEBLATT. see *POLITICAL SCIENCE*

300　　　　　　　US
TAIWAN YANJIU/TAIWAN STUDY. (Text in Chinese) q. $16.50. China Books & Periodicals, Inc., 2929 24th St., San Francisco, CA 94110. TEL 415-282-2994. FAX 415-282-0994.
Description: Contains mainland Chinese studies of Taiwan's society.

300 972　　　　PN　ISSN 0494-7061
F1561
TAREAS. 1960. q. $15. Centro de Estudios Latinoamericanos "Justo Arosemena", Apdo. 6-3093, El Dorado, Panama, Panama. TEL 230028. FAX 692032. Ed. Ricaurte Soler. bk.rev.; circ. 1,500. (back issues avail.)
—BLDSC shelfmark: 8605.700000.

300　　　　　　　HU　ISSN 0133-0381
TARSADALOMTUDOMANYI KOZLEMENYEK. 1974. q. 100 Ft.($29) (Magyar Szocialista Munkaspart (MSZMP), Tarsadalomtudomanyi Intezet) Kossuth Konyvkiado, Steindl Imre u. 6, 1366 Budapest 5, Hungary. bk.rev. **Indexed:** World Agri.Econ.& Rural Sociol.Abstr.

SOCIAL SCIENCES: COMPREHENSIVE WORKS

329   US   ISSN 0040-1587
TECHNOCRACY DIGEST. 1934. q. $12. Technocracy Inc., Continental Headquarters, Savannah, OH 44874. TEL 419-962-4712. (Alt. addr.: 3642 Kingsway, Vancouver V5S 5M2, B.C., Canada) Ed. Elizabeth Hiebert.

300   SZ
LE TEMPS STRATEGIQUE. (Text in French) 1982. bi-m. 125 Fr. Sonor S.A., Bovy-Lysberg 2, Case Postale 418, CH-1211 Geneva 11, Switzerland. TEL 022-282448. FAX 022-219862. (Subscr. to: 15 rue des Savoises, CH-1211 Geneva 11, Switzerland) Ed. Claude Monnier. adv.; bk.rev.; bibl.; charts; illus.; circ. 6,000. (back issues avail.)

300   IT   ISSN 0040-392X
D848
TERZO MONDO/THIRD WORLD; rivista trimestrale di studi, ricerche e documentazione sui paesi afro-asiatici e latino-americani. (Text mainly in English, Italian; occasionally in French, Portuguese, Spanish) 1968. q. L.50000($40) to individuals; institutions L.60000($50). Centro Studi Terzo Mondo, Via G. B. Morgagni 39, 20129 Milan, Italy. TEL 39-2-29409041. Ed. Dr. Umberto Melotti. adv.; bk.rev.; abstr.; bibl.; index; circ. 3,500. **Indexed:** Curr.Cont.Africa.
—BLDSC shelfmark: 8796.198000.
Description: Journal on the problems of the Third World, with contributions from various social disciplines.

THEORIA; a journal of studies in the arts, humanities and social sciences. see *HUMANITIES: COMPREHENSIVE WORKS*

300 100   NE   ISSN 0040-5833
H61   CODEN: THDCBA
THEORY AND DECISION; an international journal for methods and models in the social and decision sciences. 1970. 6/yr. $273. Kluwer Academic Publishers, Postbus 17, 3300 AA Dordrecht, Netherlands. TEL 078-334911. FAX 078-334254. TELEX 29245. (Dist. by: Kluwer Academic Publishers Group, P.O. Box 322, 3300 AH Dordrecht, Netherlands; N. America distr. addr.: Box 358, Accord Station, Hingham, MA 02018-0358. TEL 617-871-6600) Ed. B. Munier. adv.; bk.rev (reprint service avail. from SWZ) **Indexed:** ASCA, Commun.Abstr., Curr.Cont., J.Cont.Quant.Meth., Lang.& Lang.Behav.Abstr., Math.R., Phil.Ind., Psychol.Abstr., Risk Abstr., Sociol.Abstr., SSCI.
—BLDSC shelfmark: 8814.627000.

300   NE
THEORY AND DECISION LIBRARY; an international series in the philosophy and methodology of the social and behavioral sciences. (Text in English) 1973. irreg. price varies. Kluwer Academic Publishers, Spuiboulevard 50, P.O. Box 17, 3300 AA Dordrecht, Netherlands. TEL 078-334911. FAX 078-334254. TELEX 29245. (Dist. by: Kluwer Academic Publishers Group, P.O. Box 322, 3300 AH Dordrecht, Netherlands; U.S. address: P.O. Box 358, Accord Station, Hingham, MA 02018-0358) Eds. Gerald Eberlein, Werner Leinfellner. **Indexed:** Psychol.Abstr.

371.3   US   ISSN 0093-3104
H1
THEORY AND RESEARCH IN SOCIAL EDUCATION. Variant title: Theory and Research. 1972. q. $35. National Council for the Social Studies, 3501 Newark St., N.W., Washington, DC 20016-3167. TEL 202-966-7840. FAX 202-966-2061. Ed. Jack R. Fraenkel. adv.; bk.rev.; circ. 900. (also avail. in microform from UMI) **Indexed:** C.I.J.E., Cont.Pg.Educ., Educ.Tech.Abstr., Psychol.Abstr., Sociol.Abstr.
Description: Covers all aspects of social studies research, including teacher training, instructional strategies, curriculum development, student involvement and social action.

300   CC
TIANFU XINLUN. (Text in Chinese) bi-m. Sichuan Sheng Zhexue Shehui Kexue Lianhehui, 30, Shiye Jie, Building No. 1, Chengdu, Sichuan 610031, People's Republic of China. TEL 661619. Ed. Fu Jiangzhong.

300   NO   ISSN 0040-716X
TIDSSKRIFT FOR SAMFUNNSFORSKNING; Norwegian journal of social research. (Text in Scandinavian languages; summaries in English) 1960. bi-m. $56 to individuals; institutions $79. Universitetsforlaget, P.O. Box 2959-Toeyen, N-0608 Oslo 1, Norway. (U.S. addr.: Publications Expediting Inc., 200 Meacham Ave., Elmont, NY 11003) Ed. Tor Bjoerklund. adv.; bk.rev.; bibl.; charts; stat.; index; circ. 1,700. (back issues avail.; reprint service avail. from ISI) **Indexed:** ASCA, Hist.Abstr. (until 1991), Lang.& Lang.Behav.Abstr., SSCI, Stud.Wom.Abstr.

TIJDSCHRIFT VOOR ECONOMISCHE EN SOCIALE GEOGRAFIE/NETHERLANDS JOURNAL OF ECONOMIC AND SOCIAL GEOGRAPHY. see *GEOGRAPHY*

TIJDSCHRIFT VOOR SOCIAAL WETENSCHAPPELIJK ONDERZOEK VAN DE LANDBOUW. see *AGRICULTURE — Agricultural Economics*

TOKAI DAIGAKU KIYO. BUNGAKUBU/TOKAI UNIVERSITY. FACULTY OF LETTERS. BULLETIN. see *LITERATURE*

300   CC
TONGYI LUNTAN/UNITED TRIBUNE. (Text in Chinese) bi-m. $29.10. Tongyi Luntan Zazhishe, 111, Nanheyan Dajie, Beijing 100006, People's Republic of China. TEL 5120085. (Dist. in US by: China Books & Periodicals, Inc. 2929 24th St., San Francisco, CA 94110. TEL 415-282-2994) Ed. Miu Qun.

TOPIC (WASHINGTON); a journal of the liberal arts. see *HUMANITIES: COMPREHENSIVE WORKS*

300   GY   ISSN 1012-8263
TRANSITION. 1978. a. G.$20($10) University of Guyana, Faculty of Social Sciences and the Institute of Development Studies, Georgetown, Guyana. TEL 2-54841. adv.; circ. 750. **Indexed:** I D A.
Description: Progressive multidisciplinary journal of Third World scholarship.

300   SZ   ISSN 0082-6022
TRAVAUX DE DROIT, D'ECONOMIQUE DE SOCIOLOGIE ET DE SCIENCES POLITIQUES. (Text in English and French) 1963. irreg., no.164, 1990. price varies. Librairie Droz S.A., 11, rue Massot, CH-1211 Geneva 12, Switzerland. TEL 022-466666. FAX 022-472391. Ed. G. Busino. circ. 800.
Description: Covers research on law, economics, political science and sociology.

300   GW
TUDUV-STUDIEN. REIHE SOZIALWISSENSCHAFTEN: 1976. irreg. price varies. Tuduv Verlagsgesellschaft mbH, Gabelsbergerstr. 15, 8000 Munich 2, Germany. adv.

300   UN   ISSN 1014-8361
HN978
U N R I S D NEWS. (Editions in English, French, Spanish) 1963. biennial. free. United Nations Research Institute for Social Development, Reference Centre, Palais des Nations, CH-1211 Geneva 10, Switzerland. FAX 29-96-96. circ. 5,500 (3,000 English ed.; 1,000 French ed.; 1,500 Spanish ed.). **Indexed:** Geo.Abstr., I D A, Rural Devel.Abstr.
Former titles (until 1989): United Nations Research Institute for Social Development. Research Notes (ISSN 0258-9834); United Nations Research Institute for Social Development. Report.

300   HU
UJ TUKOR.* 1976. w. Erzsebet krt 9-11, 1073 Budapest, Hungary. TEL 122-3058. Eds. Laszlo Gyurko, Sandor Korospataki Kiss. illus.; circ. 101,000.

UNDUGU BULLETIN. see *EDUCATION*

UNITED NATIONS. ECONOMIC AND SOCIAL COUNCIL. ANNEXES. see *BUSINESS AND ECONOMICS*

UNITED NATIONS ECONOMIC AND SOCIAL COUNCIL. OFFICIAL RECORDS. SUPPLEMENTS AND SPECIAL SUPPLEMENTS. see *BUSINESS AND ECONOMICS*

UNITED NATIONS ECONOMIC AND SOCIAL COUNCIL. RESOLUTIONS AND DECISIONS. see *BUSINESS AND ECONOMICS*

UNITED NATIONS ECONOMIC AND SOCIAL COUNCIL. SUMMARY RECORDS OF PLENARY MEETINGS. see *BUSINESS AND ECONOMICS*

UNIVERSIDAD DE SAN CARLOS. REVISTA; artes - literatura - ciencias humanas. see *ART*

300   PR
UNIVERSIDAD INTERAMERICANA DE PUERTO RICO. DEPARTAMENTO DE CIENCIAS SOCIALES. REVISTA ANALES.* 1980. a. $6. (Universidad Interamericana, Departamento de Ciencias Sociales) Antillian College Press, P.O. Box 118, Mayaguez, PR 00708. TEL 809-832-3490. Ed. Hector Feliciano. bk.rev.; circ. 2,000. **Indexed:** Sociol.Abstr.

300 900   PR
UNIVERSIDAD INTERAMERICANA DE PUERTO RICO. RECINTO DE SAN GERMAN. REVISTA DE CIENCIAS SOCIALES E HISTORIA. ANALES. 1984. a. $6. (Universidad Interamericana de Puerto Rico, Recinto de San German, Revista de Ciencias Sociales e Historia) Antillian College Press, P.O. Box 118, Mayaguez, PR 00708. TEL 809-832-3490. Ed. Gilberto Arroyo.

300   HO
UNIVERSIDAD NACIONAL AUTONOMA DE HONDURAS. INSTITUTO DE INVESTIGACIONES ECONOMICAS Y SOCIALES. BOLETIN. 1971. m. Universidad Nacional Autonoma de Honduras, Instituto de Investigaciones Economicas y Sociales, Tegucigalpa, Honduras. Ed. Victor Meza. bibl.

300   CK   ISSN 0502-949X
AS82
UNIVERSIDAD NACIONAL DE COLOMBIA. DIRECCION DE DIVULGACION CULTURAL. REVISTA. 1968. irreg. exchange basis. Universidad Nacional de Colombia, Direccion de Divulgacion Cultural, Apartado Aereo 14490, Bogota, D.E., Colombia. circ. 5,000.

300   CL
UNIVERSIDAD TECNICA DEL ESTADO. REVISTA. 1970. irreg. $4. Universidad Tecnica del Estado, Avda. Ecuador 3469, Correo 2, Santiago, Chile. illus.

500   BL
UNIVERSIDADE DO AMAZONAS. CENTRO DE PESQUISAS SOCIO-ECONOMICAS. BOLETIM TECNICO INFORMATIVO.* irreg. Universidade do Amazonas, Centro de Pesquisas Socio-Economicas, Rua Jose Paranagua 200, C.P. 348, 69000 Manaus, AM, Brazil.

300 100   BL   ISSN 0041-8870
UNIVERSIDADE FEDERAL DO CEARA. DEPARTAMENTO DE CIENCIAS SOCIAIS E FILOSOFIA. DOCUMENTOS. (Text in English, Portuguese; summaries in English) 1967. irreg., vol.8, no.2, 1977. Cr.$5($6) (Universidade Federal do Ceara, Departamento de Ciencias Sociais e Filosofia) Imprensa Universitaria do Ceara, 2762 Avda. da Universidade, C.P. 1257, Fortaleza BR Ceara, Brazil. Ed. Paulo Elpidio De Menezes Neto. adv.; bk.rev.; circ. 2,000.

300   BE   ISSN 0076-1214
UNIVERSITE CATHOLIQUE DE LOUVAIN. ECOLE DES SCIENCES POLITIQUES ET SOCIALES. COLLECTION.* (Text in Flemish, French) 1894. irreg. price varies. 1348 Louvain-la-Neuve, Belgium.

301.3   FR   ISSN 0065-4949
UNIVERSITE D'AIX-MARSEILLE I. CENTRE D'ETUDES DES SOCIETES MEDITERRANEENNES. CAHIERS. 1966. a. Universite d'Aix-Marseille I (Universite de Provence), Centre d'Etudes des Societes Mediterraneennes, Service des Publications, 13621 Aix en Provence, France.

UNIVERSITE DE DAKAR. FACULTE DES LETTRES ET SCIENCES HUMAINES. ANNALES. see *LITERATURE*

UNIVERSITE DE DROIT, ECONOMIE ET DE SCIENCES SOCIALES DE PARIS. TRAVAUX DU SEMINAIRE DE RECHERCHES SUR LES FAITS ELECTORAUX DE MONSIEUR LE PROFESSEUR ROBERT VILLERS. see *LAW*

300   FR   ISSN 0563-9727
UNIVERSITE DES SCIENCES SOCIALES DE TOULOUSE. ANNALES. 1953. a. 130 F. Universite de Toulouse I (Sciences Sociales), Place Anatole France, 31042 Toulouse, France.
—BLDSC shelfmark: 0964.500000.

SOCIAL SCIENCES: COMPREHENSIVE WORKS

300   II   ISSN 0304-2286
UNIVERSITY OF BOMBAY. JOURNAL. (Arts section in Oct.; Science section in Nov.) vol.41, 1972. s-a. Rs.12. University of Bombay, Registrar, Bombay 400032, India. Ed. V. G. Moghe. adv.; bk.rev.; abstr.; circ. 400. (back issues avail.) Indexed: Amer.Hist.& Life, Hist.Abstr., Math.R.

300   SA   ISSN 0377-8533
UNIVERSITY OF DURBAN-WESTVILLE. INSTITUTE FOR SOCIAL AND ECONOMIC RESEARCH. ANNUAL REPORT. 1973. a. free. University of Durban-Westville, Institute for Social and Economic Research, Private Bag X54001, Durban 4000, South Africa. FAX 03-820-2834. Ed. D.C. Hindson. circ. 250.
—BLDSC shelfmark: 1480.350000.

300 900   US   ISSN 0071-6197
UNIVERSITY OF FLORIDA MONOGRAPHS. SOCIAL SCIENCES. 1959. irreg., no.76, 1989. price varies. University Presses of Florida, 15 N.W. 15 St, Gainesville, FL 32603. TEL 904-392-1351. Ed.Bd.
—BLDSC shelfmark: 9110.050000.

300   GH
UNIVERSITY OF GHANA. INSTITUTE OF STATISTICAL, SOCIAL AND ECONOMIC RESEARCH. DISCUSSION PAPERS. (Text in English) 1977. irreg., no.14, 1984. University of Ghana, Institute of Statistical, Social and Economic Research, PO Box 74, Legon, Ghana.
Description: Examines farming systems research and its applications in West Africa.

UNIVERSITY OF HONG KONG. CENTRE OF ASIAN STUDIES. OCCASIONAL PAPERS AND MONOGRAPHS. see ORIENTAL STUDIES

UNIVERSITY OF KHARTOUM. DEVELOPMENT STUDIES AND RESEARCH CENTRE. DISCUSSION PAPERS. see BUSINESS AND ECONOMICS — International Development And Assistance

UNIVERSITY OF LONDON. CONTEMPORARY CHINA INSTITUTE. RESEARCH NOTES AND STUDIES. see ORIENTAL STUDIES

325.3   UK   ISSN 0076-0781
UNIVERSITY OF LONDON. INSTITUTE OF COMMONWEALTH STUDIES. ANNUAL REPORT. 1949. a. free. University of London, Institute of Commonwealth Studies, 28 Russell Sq., London WC1B 5DS, England. TEL 071-580-5876. FAX 071-255-2160.

300   UK   ISSN 0076-0773
UNIVERSITY OF LONDON. INSTITUTE OF COMMONWEALTH STUDIES. COLLECTED SEMINAR PAPERS. 1967. irreg., no.41, 1990. price varies. University of London, Institute of Commonwealth Studies, 28 Russell Sq., London WC1B 5DS, England. TEL 071-580-5876. FAX 071-255-2160. circ. 400.
Description: Papers presented to research seminars.

300.7   KE
UNIVERSITY OF NAIROBI. INSTITUTE FOR DEVELOPMENT STUDIES. RESEARCH AND PUBLICATIONS. 1969. a. free. University of Nairobi, Institute for Development Studies, P.O. Box 30197, Nairobi, Kenya. circ. 2,000.
Description: Includes current research projects, completed research seminars and workshops, theses presented by institute staff and associates, and listing of institute publications.

300   SA
UNIVERSITY OF NATAL. CENTRE FOR SOCIAL AND DEVELOPMENT STUDIES. ANNUAL REPORT. 1959. a. free. University of Natal, Centre for Social and Development Studies, Durban, South Africa. FAX 031-8162359. TELEX 6-21231 SA. Ed. S. Bekker. circ. 150.
Former titles: University of Natal. Centre for Applied Social Research. Annual Report; University of Natal. Institute for Social Research. Annual Report (ISSN 0070-7759).

300   US
UNIVERSITY OF NEW MEXICO. LATIN AMERICAN INSTITUTE. RESEARCH PAPER SERIES. 1979. irreg., no.19, 1987. University of New Mexico, Latin American Institute, 801 Yale NE, Albuquerque, NM 87131. TEL 505-277-6839. FAX 505-277-5989. bibl.; charts; stat.; cum.index; circ. 800.

300   US
UNIVERSITY OF NORTH CAROLINA, CHAPEL HILL. INSTITUTE FOR RESEARCH IN SOCIAL SCIENCE. TECHNICAL PAPERS. 1977. irreg., no.7, 1983. I R S S Publications, Manning Hall 026A, Chapel Hill, NC 27514. TEL 919-962-2211. Ed. Angell Beza.

300   US
UNIVERSITY OF NORTH CAROLINA, CHAPEL HILL. INSTITUTE FOR RESEARCH IN SOCIAL SCIENCE. WORKING PAPERS IN METHODOLOGY. 1967. irreg., no.10, 1978. I R S S Publications, Manning Hall 026A, Chapel Hill, NC 27514. Ed. Angell Beza.

300 001.3   PH   ISSN 0047-5742
AS539.5
UNIVERSITY OF SANTO TOMAS. GRADUATE SCHOOL. JOURNAL OF GRADUATE RESEARCH. Variant title: University of Santo Tomas Journal of Graduate Research. (Text in English) 1971. s-a. $10 to individuals; free to students. University of Santo Tomas, Graduate School, Espana St., Manila, Philippines. Ed. Elena P. Polo. bk.rev.; bibl.; illus.; charts; circ. 1,500.

300 375   AT   ISSN 1036-0727
▼**UNIVERSITY OF TECHNOLOGY, SYDNEY. FACULTY OF SOCIAL SCIENCES HANDBOOK.** 1990. a. Aus.$5 (foreign Aus.$10). University of Technology, Sydney, P.O. Box 123, City Campus, Broadway, N.S.W. 2007, Australia. TEL 02-330-1990. FAX 02-330-1551. circ. 3,000.
Description: Contains detailed information on the faculty, schools staff, courses, the media center, centers for information studies, publications, and information management.

300   TR
UNIVERSITY OF THE WEST INDIES, TRINIDAD. INSTITUTE OF SOCIAL & ECONOMIC RESEARCH. OCCASIONAL PAPERS: GENERAL SERIES. 1977. irreg. price varies. University of the West Indies, Institute of Social & Economic Research, St. Augustine, Republic of Trinidad & Tobago, W.I. Ed. Jack Harewood. charts; stat.; circ. 220. (back issues avail.)

300   JA   ISSN 0563-8054
UNIVERSITY OF TOKYO. INSTITUTE OF SOCIAL SCIENCE. ANNALS.* (Text in English) 1953. a. free to research and educational institutions. University of Tokyo, Institute of Social Science - Tokyo Daigaku Shakai Kagaku Kenkyujo, 7-3-1 Hongo, Bunkyo-ku, Tokyo 113, Japan. circ. 200.
—BLDSC shelfmark: 1027.900000.
Formerly: Social Science Abstracts.

301.4   US
UNIVERSITY OF WISCONSIN, MADISON. INSTITUTE FOR RESEARCH ON POVERTY. DISCUSSION PAPER SERIES. 1967. irreg. $40. University of Wisconsin-Madison, Institute for Research on Poverty, 3412 Social Science Bldg., 1180 Observatory Dr., Madison, WI 53706. TEL 608-262-6358.

301.4   US
UNIVERSITY OF WISCONSIN, MADISON. INSTITUTE FOR RESEARCH ON POVERTY. MONOGRAPH SERIES. 1970. irreg., no.32, 1986. (University of Wisconsin-Madison, Institute for Research on Poverty) Academic Press, Inc., 1250 Sixth Ave., San Diego, CA 92101. TEL 619-231-0973. FAX 619-699-6715. (reprint service avail. from ISI)

301.45   US   ISSN 0084-0769
UNIVERSITY OF WISCONSIN, MADISON. INSTITUTE FOR RESEARCH ON POVERTY. REPRINT SERIES. 1966. irreg. $25. University of Wisconsin-Madison, Institute for Research on Poverty, 3412 Social Sciences Bldg., 1180 Observatory Drive, Madison, WI 53706. TEL 608-262-6358. (reprint service avail.)

301.4   US
UNIVERSITY OF WISCONSIN, MADISON. INSTITUTE FOR RESEARCH ON POVERTY. SPECIAL REPORT SERIES. 1966. irreg. price varies. University of Wisconsin-Madison, Institute for Research on Poverty, 3412 Social Science Bldg., 1180 Observatory Dr., Madison, WI 53706. TEL 608-262-6358.
Description: Summarizes Institute projects, prepared for government agencies, committees or commissions.

300   CS
UNIVERZITA KOMENSKEHO. USTAV MARXIZMU-LENINIZMU. ZBORNIK: VEDECKY KOMUNIZMUS. (Text in Slovak; summaries in German, Russian) 1978. a. exchange basis. Univerzita Komenskeho, Ustav Marxizmu-Leninizmu, c/o Study and Information Center, Safarikovo nam. 6, 818 06 Bratislava, Czechoslovakia. Ed. Peter Kulasik. circ. 450.

URBAN AFFAIRS ASSOCIATION COMMUNICATION. see HOUSING AND URBAN PLANNING

URBAN AFFAIRS QUARTERLY. see HOUSING AND URBAN PLANNING

URBAN HISTORY YEARBOOK. see HISTORY — History Of Europe

URBAN INSTITUTE. ANNUAL REPORT. see BUSINESS AND ECONOMICS

URBAN INSTITUTE. POLICY AND RESEARCH REPORT. see BUSINESS AND ECONOMICS

300   US   ISSN 0732-7277
URBAN RESEARCH REVIEW. 1974. s-a. free. Howard University, Institute for Urban Affairs and Research, 2900 Van Ness St., N.W., Washington, DC 20008. TEL 202-806-8770. Ed. Lula A. Beatty. bk.rev.; circ. 3,000. (back issues avail.) Indexed: Urb.Aff.Abstr., Vert.File Ind.
Description: Social science newsletter for the dissemination of research findings.

UTAFITI; journal of the faculty of arts and social science. see LITERATURE

300   NP   ISSN 0887-2023
VEDIC GLOBE. (Text in English) 1982. q. $20. Siveast Consultants, Inc., U.S.A., PO. Box 1755, Kathmandu, Nepal. Ed. C.V. Ramasastry. circ. 500. (looseleaf format)
Description: Features socio-economic aspects including folklore stories of the Southeastern countries.

VERHALTENSTHERAPIE UND PSYCHOSOZIALE PRAXIS. see PSYCHOLOGY

VICTORIAN STUDIES; a journal of the humanities, arts and sciences. see HUMANITIES: COMPREHENSIVE WORKS

VIDYA BHARATHI. see HUMANITIES: COMPREHENSIVE WORKS

300   CE
VIDYODAYA JOURNAL OF SOCIAL SCIENCE. (Text in English, Sinhalese and Tamil) 1968. s-a. Rs.100($10) University of Sri Jayewardenepura, Nugegoda, Sri Lanka. TEL 55-2695. FAX 55-2604. Ed.Bd. bk.rev.; bibl.; charts; illus.; stat.; index, cum.index; circ. 1,000. Indexed: Sci.Cit.Ind., Sri Lanka Sci.Ind.
Supersedes in part (from 1987): Vidyodaya (ISSN 0042-532X)

330 300   GW   ISSN 0340-8728
VIERTELJAHRSCHRIFT FUER SOZIAL- UND WIRTSCHAFTSGESCHICHTE. (Text in English and German) 1903. 4/yr. DM.108 (supplements priced individually). Franz Steiner Verlag Wiesbaden GmbH, Birkenwaldstr. 44, Postfach 101526, 7000 Stuttgart 1, Germany. TEL 0711-2582-0. FAX 0711-2582290. TELEX 723636-DAZD. Ed.Bd. adv.; bk.rev.; cum.index: vols.21-50 (1928-1963); circ. 1,100. (back issues avail.) Indexed: Hist.Abstr., P.A.I.S.For.Lang.Ind.

330 300   GW   ISSN 0341-0846
VIERTELJAHRSCHRIFT FUER SOZIAL- UND WIRTSCHAFTSGESCHICHTE. BEIHEFTE. irreg., vol.102, 1992. price varies. Franz Steiner Verlag Wiesbaden GmbH, Birkenwaldstr. 44, Postfach 101526, 7000 Stuttgart 1, Germany. TEL 0711-2582-0. FAX 0711-2582290. TELEX 723636-DAZD. Ed.Bd.

300   VN
VIETNAM SOCIAL SCIENCE. (Text in English, French, Russian) 1984. q. Viet-Nam Institute of Social Science, 27 Tran Xuan Soan, Hanoi, Socialist Republic of Vietnam. TEL 52031. Ed. Nguyen Huu Thanh.

SOCIAL SCIENCES: COMPREHENSIVE WORKS

VIETNAMESE STUDIES. see HISTORY — History Of Asia

300　　　　　　　　US　ISSN 0507-1305
H1
VIRGINIA SOCIAL SCIENCE JOURNAL. 1966. a. $15 to individuals; institution price varies. Virginia Social Science Association, c/o Dr. Thomas Bertsch, Marketing Dept., James Madison University, Harrisonburg, VA 22807. FAX 703-568-3299. circ. 300. (back issues avail.)
Description: Provides original research articles on social science issues.

300 060　　　　　　　FR　ISSN 0083-6672
VISTI IZ SARSELIU. (Text in Ukrainian) 1963. irreg., no.31-32, 1988. $5. Societe Scientifique Sevcenko, 29, rue des Bauves, 95200 Sarcelles, France. Ed. Athanas Figol. bk.rev.; circ. 1,000.

VITA SOCIALE. see RELIGIONS AND THEOLOGY — Roman Catholic

VITAL ISSUES; the journal of African American Speeches. see POLITICAL SCIENCE

VIVANT UNIVERS; revue de la promotion humaine et chretienne en Afrique et dans le monde. see POLITICAL SCIENCE — International Relations

300　　　　　　　　GW　ISSN 0173-1955
VON DEUTSCHLAND NACH AMERIKA. irreg., vol.6, 1991. price varies. Franz Steiner Verlag Wiesbaden GmbH, Birkenwaldstr. 44, Postfach 101526, 7000 Stuttgart 1, Germany. TEL 0711-2582-0. FAX 0711-2582290. TELEX 723636-DAZD. Ed. Guenter Moltmann.

330 331.8 300　　　　GW　ISSN 0342-300X
HC281
W S I MITTEILUNGEN. 1948. m. DM.108. (Deutscher Gewerkschaftsbund, Wirtschafts- und Sozialwissenschaftliches Institut) Bund-Verlag GmbH, Hansestr. 63a, Postfach 900840, 5000 Cologne 90, Germany. Ed. Manfred H. Bobke. adv.; bk.rev.; charts; stat.; index; circ. 6,500. **Indexed:** P.A.I.S.For.Lang.Ind., World Bibl.Soc.Sec.
—BLDSC shelfmark: 9364.930000.
Formerly: W W I Mitteilungen (ISSN 0042-9872)

300　　　　　　　　GW　ISSN 0174-3120
W Z B - MITTEILUNGEN. 1978. q. free. Wissenschaftszentrum Berlin fuer Sozialforschung, Reichpietschufer 50, 1000 Berlin 30, Germany. TEL 030-25491509. FAX 030-25491684. TELEX 308897-WZB-D. Ed. Burckhard Wiebe. circ. 9,000. (back issues avail.)

300　　　　　　　　CC
WAIGUO WENTI YANJIU. (Text in Chinese) q. Dongbei Shifan Daxue, Riben Yanjiusuo - Northeast Normal University, Institute of Japanese Studies, 110, Stalin St., Changchun, Jilin 130024, People's Republic of China. TEL 885085. Ed. Song Shaoying.

300 895.1　　　　　CC
WENSHI ZHISHI/KNOWLEDGE OF LITERATURE AND HISTORY. (Text in Chinese) 1981. m. Y19.20($63) Zhonghua Shuju - Zhonghua Book Company, 36 Wangfujing Jie, Beijing 100710, People's Republic of China. TEL 554595. (Dist. in US by: China Books & Periodicals, Inc., 2929 24th St., San Francisco, CA 94110. TEL 415-282-2994) Eds. Li Kan, Chai Jianhong. abstr.; bibl.; charts; illus.; index; circ. 70,000.
Description: Concerns Chinese literature and history.

300　　　　　　　　US　ISSN 0081-8682
WEST GEORGIA COLLEGE STUDIES IN THE SOCIAL SCIENCES. 1962. a. $5. West Georgia College, School of Arts and Sciences, Carrollton, GA 30118-0001. TEL 404-836-6505. FAX 404-836-6717. Ed. Francis Conner. adv.; bk.rev.; bibl.; circ. 500. **Indexed:** Hist.Abstr.
—BLDSC shelfmark: 8491.152000.

WETENSCHAP & SAMENLEVING. see SCIENCES: COMPREHENSIVE WORKS

300　　　　　　　　GW　ISSN 0342-8990
WOCHENSCHAU FUER POLITISCHE ERZIEHUNG, SOZIAL- UND GEMEINSCHAFTSKUNDE. AUSGABE FUER SEKUNDARSTUFE I. 1949. 7/yr. DM.68.50. Wochenschau Verlag, Adolf-Damaschke-Str. 103-105, 6231 Schwalbach, Germany. Ed. Ursula Buch. bk.rev.; index.

300　　　　　　　　GW　ISSN 0342-8974
WOCHENSCHAU FUER POLITISCHE ERZIEHUNG, SOZIAL- UND GEMEINSCHAFTSKUNDE. AUSGABE FUER SEKUNDARSTUFE II. 1949. 7/yr. DM.68.50. Wochenschau Verlag, Adolf-Damaschke-Str. 103-105, 6231 Schwalbach, Germany. TEL 06196-84010. Ed. Ursula Buch. adv.; bk.rev.; charts; illus.; stat.; index. (back issues avail.)

300 960　　　　　　US
WORKING PAPERS IN AFRICAN STUDIES. 1976. irreg., no.144, 1989. $4 per no. Boston University, African Studies Center, 270 Bay State Rd., Boston, MA 02215. TEL 617-353-3673. FAX 617-353-4975. TELEX 9103501947 BUASC.

300 371.3 900　　　US　ISSN 0193-7871
WORLD EAGLE; the monthly social studies resource. 1977. 10/yr. $38.95 (effective Sep. 1991). World Eagle, Inc., 64 Washburn Ave., Wellesley, MA 02181. TEL 617-235-1415. FAX 617-237-2842. Ed. Duncan L. Gibson. index.
Description: Presents comparative data, graphs, and maps for use as a resource and reference tool for social studies teachers.

WORLD MEETINGS: SOCIAL & BEHAVIORAL SCIENCES, HUMAN SERVICES AND MANAGEMENT. see MEETINGS AND CONGRESSES

300　　　　　　　　CC　ISSN 1000-5374
WUHAN DAXUE XUEBAO (SHEHUI KEXUE BAN)/WUHAN UNIVERSITY. JOURNAL (SOCIAL SCIENCE EDITION). (Text in Chinese; table of contents in English) bi-m. Y7.20. Wuhan Daxue, Xuebao Bianjibu, Luo Jia Shan, Wuchang, Hubei 430072, People's Republic of China. TEL 812712. (Dist. outside China by: China International Book Trading Corp., P.O. Box 399, Beijing, P.R.C.) Eds. Tao Delin, Yang Xiaoyan. bk.rev.
—BLDSC shelfmark: 9365.160040.

300　　　　　　　　PL　ISSN 0239-670X
WYZSZA SZKOLA PEDAGOGICZNA, OPOLE. ZESZYTY NAUKOWE. SERIA A. NAUKI SPOLECZNO-POLITYCZNE. (Text in Polish; summaries in English) 1985. irreg., vol.4, 1990. price varies. avail. on exchange basis. Wyzsza Szkola Pedagogiczna, Opole, Oleska 48, 45-951 Opole, Poland. TEL 48-77-383-87. (Dist. by: Ars Polona-Ruch, Krakowskie Przedmiescie 7, Warsaw, Poland)
—BLDSC shelfmark: 9512.478984.

300　　　　　　　　CC　ISSN 0438-0460
XIAMEN DAXUE XUEBAO (ZHEXUE SHEHUI KEXUE BAN)/XIAMEN UNIVERSITY. JOURNAL (PHILOSOPHY AND SOCIAL SCIENCES EDITION). (Text in Chinese; table of contents in English) q. Y1.20 per no. Xiamen Daxue - Xiamen University, c/o Xiamen Daxue Tushuguan, Xiamen, Fujian 361005, People's Republic of China. TEL 25102. (Dist. outside China by: China International Book Trading Corp., P.O. Box 399, Beijing, P.R.C.) Ed. Luo Yucong.
—BLDSC shelfmark: 9367.035000.

300　　　　　　　　CC　ISSN 1000-2731
XIBEI DAXUE XUEBAO. SHEHUI KEXUE BAN/NORTHWEST UNIVERSITY. JOURNAL. SOCIAL SCIENCES EDITION. (Text in Chinese; table of contents in English) 1957. q. Y0.60 per no. Xibei Daxue - Northwest University, Xiao Nan Menwai, Xi'an, Shaanxi 710069, People's Republic of China. (Dist. outside China by: China International Book Trading Corp., P.O. Box 2820, Beijing, P.R.C.) Eds. Xu Huaidong, Zhang Tianjie.
—BLDSC shelfmark: 4834.411000.

300　　　　　　　　CC
XINAN MINZU XUEYUAN XUEBAO (ZHEXUE SHEHUI KEXUE BAN)/SOUTHWEST INSTITUTE OF NATIONALITIES. JOURNAL (PHILOSOPHY, SOCIAL SCIENCE EDITION). (Text in Chinese) bi-m. Y6. Xinan Minzu Xueyuan, Xuebao Bianjibu, Nanjiao (Southern Suburb), Chengdu, Sichuan 610041, People's Republic of China. (Dist. overseas by: China Publications Foreign Trade Corp., P.O. Box 782, Beijing, P.R.C.) Ed. Meng Zhuqun.
Description: Contains academic papers mainly focusing on minority nationalities of southwestern China. Covers politics, philosophy, economics, education, linguistics, and literature.

300　　　　　　　　CC
XINAN MINZU XUEYUAN XUEBAO (ZHEXUE SHEHUI KEXUE BAN)/SOUTHWEST CHINA NATIONALITIES COLLEGE. JOURNAL. (SOCIAL SCIENCE EDITION). (Text in Chinese) q. Xinan Minzu Xueyuan - Southwest China Nationalities College, Chengdu Shi Nanjiao, Sichuan 610041, People's Republic of China. TEL 553811-150. (Dist. overseas by: Jiangsu Publications Import & Export Corp., 56 Gao Yun Ling, Nanjing, Jiangsu, P.R.C.)

300　　　　　　　　CC　ISSN 1000-2677
XINAN SHIFAN DAXUE XUEBAO (SHEHUI KEXUE BAN)/SOUTHWEST NORMAL UNIVERSITY. JOURNAL (SOCIAL SCIENCE EDITION). (Text in Chinese) q. Xinan Shifan Daxue, Xuebao Bianjibu, Beipei Qu, Chongqing, Sichuan 630715, People's Republic of China. TEL 3901. Ed. Ji Ping.

300　　　　　　　　CC　ISSN 1000-4262
AP95.C4
XINJIANG SHEHUI KEXUE/SOCIAL SCIENCE IN XINJIANG. (Text in Chinese) 1981. q. $20.40. Xinjiang Weiwuer Zizhiqu Shehui Kexueyuan - Xinjiang Uighur Autonomous Region Academy of Social Sciences, Beijing Lu, Wulumuqi (Urumqi), Xijiang 830011, People's Republic of China. TEL 37942. (Dist. in US by: China Books & Periodicals, Inc., 2929 24th St., San Francisco, CA 94110. TEL 415-282-2994) bibl.

940 339　　　　　　CC　ISSN 1000-3576
XI'OU YANJIU/WESTERN EUROPEAN STUDIES. Variant English title: Studies in Western Europe. (Text in Chinese) 1984. bi-m. $14.40. Zhongguo Shehui Kexueyuan, Xi'ou Yanjiusuo - Chinese Academy of Social Sciences, Institute on Western Europe, No.5, Jianguomennei Dajie, Beijing 100732, People's Republic of China. (Dist. in US by: China Books & Periodicals, Inc., 2929 24th St., San Francisco, CA 94110. TEL 415-282-2994)

300　　　　　　　　CC
XIWANG/HOPE. (Text in Chinese) bi-m. Xin Shiji Chubanshe, No. 10, 4 Malu, Dashatou, Guangzhou, Guangdong 510102, People's Republic of China. TEL 335210. Ed. Chen Sang.

300　　　　　　　　CC
XIYA FEIZHOU/WEST ASIA AND AFRICA. (Text in Chinese) bi-m. Zhongguo Shehui Kexueyuan, Xiya Feizhou Yanjiusuo - Chinese Academy of Social Sciences, Institute on West Asia and Africa, No.3, Zhangzizhong Lu, Dongcheng-qu, Beijing 100007, People's Republic of China. TEL 447718. Ed. Ge Ji.

300　　　　　　　　CC
XUE HAI. (Text in Chinese) bi-m. Jiangsu Sheng Shehui Kexueyuan - Jiangsu Academy of Social Sciences, 12 Huju Beilu, Nanjing, Jiangsu 210013, People's Republic of China. TEL 637995. Ed. Chen Ling.

300　　　　　　　　CC　ISSN 0438-1033
XUESHU LUNTAN. (Text in Chinese) bi-m. Guangxi Shehui Kexueyuan - Guangxi Academy of Social Sciences, No. 30, Xinzhu Lu, Nanning, Guangxi 530022, People's Republic of China. TEL 20201. Ed. Chen Xian'an.

300　　　　　　　　CC　ISSN 1000-7326
XUESHU YANJIU/ACADEMIC RESEARCH. (Text in Chinese) 1962. bi-m. $30.60. (Guangdong Sheng Shehui Kexue Xuehui Lianhehui) Guangdong Renmin Chubanshe, Qikan Bu, Dashatou Si Ma Lu 10, Guangzhou, Guangdong, People's Republic of China. (Dist. in US by: China Books & Periodicals, Inc., 2929 24th St., San Francisco, CA 94110. TEL 415-282-2994)

XUESHU YUEKAN/ACADEMIC MONTHLY. see PETROLEUM AND GAS

300　　　　　　　　US
XUEXI/STUDY. (Text in Chinese) m. $61.20. China Books & Periodicals, Inc., 2929 24th St., San Francisco, CA 94110. TEL 415-282-2994. FAX 415-282-0994.

SOCIAL SCIENCES: COMPREHENSIVE WORKS

300   CC
XUEXI YU TANSUO/STUDY & EXPLORATION. (Text and summaries in Chinese; table of contents in English) bi-m. Y11.40($35.10) (Heilongjiang Sheng Shehui Kexueyuan - Heilongjiang Provincial Academy of Social Sciences) Xuexi yu Tansuo Zazhishe, 124 Huayuan Jie, Nangang Qu, Harbin, Heilongjiang 150006, People's Republic of China. (Dist. outside China by: China International Book Trading Corp., P.O. Box 339, Beijing, P.R.C.; Dist. in US by: China Books & Periodicals, Inc., 2929 24th St., San Francisco, CA 94110. TEL 415-282-2994) Eds. Sun Qinglin, Ji Kefei.

300 001.3   PP
YAGL-AMBU; Papua New Guinea journal of the social sciences and humanities. vol.6, 1979. q. K.10. University of Papua New Guinea, PO Box 320, University P.O., Papua New Guinea. Ed.Bd. **Indexed:** So.Pac.Per.Ind.

300   US   ISSN 0084-3326
YALE FASTBACKS. 1970. irreg. price varies. Yale University Press, 92A Yale Sta., New Haven, CT 06520. TEL 203-432-0940.

YALE SOUTHEAST ASIA STUDIES. MONOGRAPH SERIES. see ORIENTAL STUDIES

300   CC
YAN DU/CAPITAL OF YAN. (Text in Chinese) bi-m. Yanshan Chubanshe, No. 36, Fuxue Hutong, Dongcheng-qu, Beijing 100007, People's Republic of China. TEL 4014694. Ed. Song Tishui.

300   CC
YANTAI DAXUE XUEBAO (SHEHUI KEXUE BAN)/YANTAI UNIVERSITY. JOURNAL (SOCIAL SCIENCE EDITION). (Text in Chinese) q. Yantai Daxue, Xuebao Bianjibu, Yantai, Shandong 264005, People's Republic of China. TEL 248995. Ed. Yang Chunxian.

300 296   US
DS101
YIVO ANNUAL. 1946-1983; resumed 1990. a., vol.19, 1990. $36.95. (Y I V O Institute for Jewish Research) Northwestern University Press, 625 Colfax Ave., Evanston, IL 60201. TEL 708-491-5313. Ed.Bd. index; circ. 2,000. (back issues avail.) **Indexed:** Amer.Hist.& Life, Hist.Abstr., Lang.& Lang.Behav.Abstr., SSCI.
Formerly: Yivo Annual of Jewish Social Science (ISSN 0084-4209)

300   US   ISSN 0084-4217
PJ5120
YIVO BLETER/YIVO PAGES. (Text in Yiddish; summaries in English) 1931. irreg., vol.46, 1980. $15. Y I V O Institute for Jewish Research, 1048 Fifth Ave., New York, NY 10028. TEL 212-535-6700. Ed.Bd. bk.rev.; circ. 1,500. **Indexed:** Amer.Hist.& Life, Hist.Abstr.

YIVO NEWS/YEDIES FUN YIVO. see HUMANITIES: COMPREHENSIVE WORKS

100 300   JA   ISSN 0513-5621
YOKOHAMA KOKURITSU DAIGAKU JINBUN KIYO DAI-1-RUI, TETSUGAKU, SHAKAI KAGAKU/YOKOHAMA NATIONAL UNIVERSITY. HUMANITIES, SECTION 1: PHILOSOPHY AND SOCIAL SCIENCES.* (Text in Japanese; summaries in English) 1953. a. Yokohama Kokuritsu Daigaku, Shakaigaku Kyoshitsu - Yokohama National University, Department of Sociology, 156 Tokiwadai, Hodogaya-ku, Yokohama-shi, Kanagawa-ken 240, Japan.

300   CC   ISSN 1000-8691
YUNNAN SHEHUI KEXUE/SOCIAL SCIENCE IN YUNNAN. (Text in Chinese; table of contents in English) bi-m. Y3.60($27) Yunnan Shehui Kexueyuan - Yunnan Academy of Social Sciences, 45, Qixiang Lu, Kunming, Yunnan 650032, People's Republic of China. (Dist. outside China by: China International Book Trading Corp., P.O. Box 339, Beijing, P.R.C.; Dist. in US by: China Books & Periodicals, Inc., 2929 24th St., San Francisco, CA 94110) Eds. He Yaohua, Fan Zuqi.

300   RH   ISSN 0379-0622
H1
ZAMBEZIA: THE JOURNAL OF THE UNIVERSITY OF ZIMBABWE. (Supplements avail.) 1969. s-a. $12 per no. University of Zimbabwe, Publications Office, P.O. Box MP 45, Mt. Pleasant, Harare, Zimbabwe. FAX 4-732828. TELEX 26580 ZW. Ed. E.A. Ngara. adv.; bk.rev.; illus.; circ. 400. **Indexed:** Amer.Hist.& Life, Ind.S.A.Per., M.L.A.
—BLDSC shelfmark: 9426.150000.
Formerly: Zambezia: A Journal of Social Studies in Southern and Central Africa (ISSN 0514-5236); Which incorporated: University of Rhodesia. Series in Education. Occasional Paper; University of Rhodesia. Series in Humanities. Occasional Paper; University of Rhodesia. Series in Science. Occasional Paper; University of Rhodesia. Series in Social Studies. Occasional Paper.

300   YU   ISSN 0044-1937
AS346
ZBORNIK ZA DRUSTVENE NAUKE. (Text in Serbo-Croatian, written in Cyrillic alphabet) 1915. a. Matica Srpska, Matice Srpske 1, Novi Sad, Vojvodina, Yugoslavia. Ed. Miladen Stojanov. **Indexed:** A.I.C.P., Hist.Abstr., I D A.

300   GW   ISSN 0044-2429
HD2951
ZEITSCHRIFT FUER DAS GESAMTE GENOSSENSCHAFTSWESEN. 1950. 4/yr. DM.108. Vandenhoeck und Ruprecht, Theaterstr. 13, Postfach 3753, 3400 Goettingen, Germany. TEL 0551-6959-22. FAX 0551-695917. Ed. Oswald Hahn. adv.; bk.rev.; bibl.; charts; index; circ. 840. **Indexed:** Key to Econ.Sci., P.A.I.S.For.Lang.Ind.
—BLDSC shelfmark: 9462.805000.

300   GW   ISSN 0175-0488
ZEITSCHRIFT FUER ENTWICKLUNGSPAEDAGOGIK. 1978. q. DM.46. Verlag Schoeppe und Schwarzenbart, Nonnengasse 1, 7400 Tuebingen, Germany. TEL 07071-22801. Ed. Alfred K. Treml. adv.; bk.rev.; illus. (back issues avail.)

300   GW   ISSN 0930-9381
ZEITSCHRIFT FUER INTERNATIONALE ERZIEHUNGS- UND SOZIALWISSENSCHAFTLICHE FORSCHUNG. 2/yr. DM.24. Boehlau Verlag GmbH, Theodor-Heuss-Str. 76, 5000 Cologne 90, Germany.

ZEITSCHRIFT FUER OSTFORSCHUNG; Laender und Voelker im oestlichen Mitteleuropa. see HISTORY — History Of Europe

ZEITSCHRIFT FUER UMWELTPOLITIK. see ENVIRONMENTAL STUDIES

300   CC   ISSN 1001-5035
ZHEJIANG SHIFAN DAXUE XUEBAO (SHEHUI KEXUE BAN)/ZHEJIANG NORMAL UNIVERSITY. JOURNAL (SOCIAL SCIENCE EDITION). (Text in Chinese) q. Zhejiang Shifan Daxue - Zhejiang Normal University, Jinhua Shi Beijiao (Northern Suburb), Zhejiang 321004, People's Republic of China. Ed. Luo Xiangfa.

300   CC
ZHENGMING. (Text in Chinese) bi-m. Jiangxi Sheng Shehui Kexue Xuehui Lianhehui, 19 Fuzhou Lu, Nanchang, Jiangxi 330006, People's Republic of China. TEL 69402. Ed. Zheng Keqiang.

300   CC
ZHENGZHOU DAXUE XUEBAO (SHEHUI KEXUE BAN)/ZHENGZHOU UNIVERSITY. JOURNAL (SOCIAL SCIENCE EDITION). (Text in Chinese) bi-m. Zhengzhou Daxue, Xuebao Bianjibu, No. 75, Daxue Lu, Zhengzhou, Henan 450052, People's Republic of China. TEL 446455. Ed. Zhang Peiqiang.

ZHONGGUO QINGNIAN YANJIU/CHINESE YOUTH STUDY. see CHILDREN AND YOUTH — About

300   CC   ISSN 1000-5420
ZHONGGUO RENMIN DAXUE XUEBAO/CHINA PEOPLE'S UNIVERSITY. JOURNAL. (Text in Chinese) bi-m. Zhongguo Renmin Daxue, Xuebao Bianjibu, Haidian Qu, Beijing 100872, People's Republic of China. TEL 2563399. Ed. Wei Xinghua.

ZHONGGUO SHAOSHU MINZU. see ORIENTAL STUDIES

ZHONGGUO SHEHUI JINGJISHI YANJIU/JOURNAL OF CHINESE SOCIAL AND ECONOMIC HISTORY. see HISTORY — History Of Asia

300   CC   ISSN 1000-2952
ZHONGGUO SHEHUI KEXUEYUAN YANJIUSHENGYUAN XUEBAO/CHINESE ACADEMY OF SOCIAL SCIENCES. GRADUATE SCHOOL. JOURNAL. (Text in Chinese) 1985. bi-m. $30.60. Zhongguo Shehui Kexueyuan, Yanjiushengyuan, No. 131, Xibajianfang, Dongzhimenwai, Beijing 100015, People's Republic of China. TEL 472019. (Dist. in US by: China Books & Periodicals, Inc. 2929 24th St., San Francisco, CA 94110. TEL 415-282-2994) Ed. Wang Haibo.

ZHONGGUO XIZANG. see GENERAL INTEREST PERIODICALS — China

300 951   CC   ISSN 1000-5439
DS730
ZHONGNAN MINZU XUEYUAN XUEBAO (SHEHUI KEXUE BAN)/SOUTH-CENTRAL COLLEGE FOR NATIONALITIES. JOURNAL (SOCIAL SCIENCE EDITION). (Text in Chinese; table of contents in English) 1981. bi-m. Y0.50 per no. Zhongnan Minzu Xueyuan, Xuebao Bianjibu - South-Central College for Nationalities, Journal Editorial Department, No. 5, Minyuan Lu, Wuchang-qu, Wuhan, Hubei 430074, People's Republic of China. (Dist. outside China by: China International Book Trading Corp., P.O. Box 399, Beijing, P.R.C.) Eds. Yan Xuejun, Wei Ruifeng.
Description: Contains theses on all areas of social science and philosophy. Emphasizes papers on issues in Chinese history, development of minority areas in China, and aid to the poor.

300   CC   ISSN 1000-9639
AS451
ZHONGSHAN DAXUE XUEBAO (ZHEXUE SHEHUI KEXUE BAN)/SUN YAT-SEN UNIVERSITY. JOURNAL (SOCIAL SCIENCE EDITION). (Text in Chinese; table of contents in English) 1955. 4/yr. Y1.50 per no. Zhongshan Daxue, Xuebao Bianjibu, Xingang Lu, Guangzhou, Guangdong 510275, People's Republic of China. TEL 020-446300. TELEX 44604-ZSUFO-CN. (Dist. outside China by: China International Book Trading Corp., P.O. Box 399, Beijing, P.R.C.) Eds. Liao Wenhui, He Zhiping. bk.rev.; bibl.; index.
—BLDSC shelfmark: 4904.470000.
Formerly: Zhongshan Daxue Shehui Kexue Xuebao (ISSN 0412-443X); Supersedes in part: Zhongshan Daxue Xuebao (ISSN 0529-6579)

300   CC
ZHONGZHOU XUEKAN. (Text in Chinese) bi-m. $24.80. Henan Sheng Shehui Kexueyuan - Henan Academy of Social Science, 50, Wenhua Lu, Zhengzhou, Henan 450002, People's Republic of China. TEL 336507. (Dist. in US by: China Books & Periodicals, Inc., 2929 24th St., San Francisco, CA 94110. TEL 415-282-2994) Ed. Hu Siyong.

300   CC   ISSN 1001-2370
ZOUXIANG SHIJIE. (Text in Chinese) bi-m. Shandong Shengwei Xuanchuanbu, No. 484, Wei 1 Lu, Jinan, Shandong 250001, People's Republic of China. TEL 615823. Ed. Jiang Jinde.

300   SZ
ZUKUNFTSFORSCHUNG. (Text in English and German) 1972. 4/yr. 60 Fr.($50) Schweizerische Vereinigung fuer Zukunftsforschung - Swiss Association for Futures Research, Haldenweg 10A, CH-3074 Muri, Switzerland. FAX 031-952-6800. Ed. Gerhard Kocher. bk.rev.; abstr.; bibl.; charts; stat.; circ. 1,020. (back issues avail.)
Formerly: S Z F-Bulletin.
Description: Focuses on long-range planning, forecasts, strategic management and futures research.

ZWISCHENSCHRITTE; Beitraege zu einer morphologischen Psychologie. see PSYCHOLOGY

SOCIAL SCIENCES: COMPREHENSIVE WORKS — Abstracting, Bibliographies, Statistics

300   UK   ISSN 0950-2238
Z7163
A S S I A. (Applied Social Sciences Index & Abstracts) 1987. bi-m. (plus a. cum.). £425($790) (foreign £490). (Library Association Publishing Ltd.) Bowker-Saur Ltd., 59-60 Grosvenor St., London W1X 9DA, England. TEL 071-493-5841. FAX 071-499-1590. (Subscr. to: Bailey Management Services, 127 Sandgate Rd., Folkestone, Kent CT20 2BL, England. TEL 0303-850501) Ed. Peter F. Broxis. (back issues avail.)
●Also available online. Vendor(s): Data-Star (ASSI). Also available on CD-ROM. Producer(s): R.R. Bowker.
—BLDSC shelfmark: 1746.648800.
Description: Studies of social sciences, with emphasis on the needs of people and social work.

200 300 016   FR   ISSN 0335-5985
BL60
ARCHIVES DE SCIENCES SOCIALES DES RELIGIONS. (Text in English and French; occasionally in German) 1956. s-a. (Groupe de Sociologie des Religions) Editions du C N R S, 1 Place Aristide Briand, 92195 Meudon Cedex, France. TEL 1-45-34-75-50. FAX 1-46-26-28-49. TELEX LABOBEL 204 135 F. (Subscr. to: Presses du C N R S, 20-22, rue Saint Amand, 75015 Paris, France. TEL 1-45-34-16-00) Ed. J. Seguy. bk.rev.; abstr.; bibl.; charts; illus.; stat.; circ. 1,200. Indexed: A.I.C.P., Amer.Hist.& Life, Arts & Hum.Cit.Ind., Bull.Signal., Curr.Cont., Hist.Abstr., Lang.& Lang.Behav.Abstr., Rel.& Theol.Abstr. (1989-), Rel.Ind.One, Rel.Per., Sociol.Abstr. (1956-), SSCI.
—BLDSC shelfmark: 1643.110000.
Formerly: Archives de Sociologie des Religions (ISSN 0003-9659)
Description: Articles can be grouped under various headings- methodology, epistemology, status of scientific approaches to religions, classics of the sociology of religions, new religious movements.

300 314   BE   ISSN 0067-5563
BELGIUM. INSTITUT NATIONAL DE STATISTIQUE. STATISTIQUES SOCIALES. (Text in Dutch, French) 1970. irreg. (1-4/yr.). 290 Fr. (foreign 590 Fr.). Institut National de Statistique, 44 rue de Louvain, B-1000 Brussels, Belgium. **Indexed:** P.A.I.S.For.Lang.Ind.

300   NE   ISSN 0168-5988
BIBLIOGRAFIE VAN REGIONALE ONDERZOEKINGEN OP SOCIAAL-WETENSCHAPPELIJK TERREIN/BIBLIOGRAPHY OF REGIONAL STUDIES IN THE SOCIAL SCIENCES. (Text in Dutch and English) 1945. a. Centraal Bureau voor de Statistiek, Prinses Beatrixlaan 428, Voorburg, Netherlands. (Orders to: SDN - Publishers, Christoffel Plantijnstraat, The Hague)

300 015   YU   ISSN 0352-5899
BIBLIOGRAFIJA JUGOSLAVIJE. CLANCI I PRILOZI U SERIJSKIM PUBLIKACIJAMA. SERIJA A: DRUSTVENE NAUKE. 1950. m. $662 or exchange basis. Jugoslovenski Bibliografsko-Informacijski Institut (YUBIN) - Yogoslav Institute for Bibliography and Information, Terazije 26, Belgrade, Yugoslavia. FAX 11-687-760. Ed. Radomir Glavicki.
●Also available online.
Formerly (until 1985): Bibliografija Jugoslavije. Serija A: Drustvene Nauke. Clanci i Prilozi u Casopisima, Listovima i Zbornicima (ISSN 0373-6369)

BIBLIOGRAPHIC GUIDE TO EAST ASIAN STUDIES. see ORIENTAL STUDIES — Abstracting, Bibliographies, Statistics

BIBLIOGRAPHIC GUIDE TO LATIN AMERICAN STUDIES. see BIBLIOGRAPHIES

300   BE
BIBLIOGRAPHIE ETHNOGRAPHIQUE DE L'AFRIQUE SUD-SAHARIENNE; sciences humaines et sociales. 1932. a., latest 1984 (covers 1980). 1200 BEF. Musee Royal de l'Afrique Centrale, 13 Steenweg op Leuven, B-1980 Tervuren, Belgium. **Indexed:** A.I.C.P.
Formerly (until 1962): Bibliographie Ethnographique du Congo Belge et des Regions Avoisinantes.

BIBLIOGRAPHIES AND INDEXES IN LATIN AMERICAN AND CARIBBEAN STUDIES. see HISTORY — Abstracting, Bibliographies, Statistics

BIBLIOGRAPHIES COMMENTEES. see BUSINESS AND ECONOMICS — Abstracting, Bibliographies, Statistics

300 016   II
BIBLIOGRAPHY OF DOCTORAL DISSERTATIONS: SOCIAL SCIENCES AND HUMANITIES. (Text in English) 1974. irreg., latest 1988. $72. Association of Indian Universities, A.I.U. House, 16 Kotla Marg, New Delhi 110 002, India. TEL 11-3310059. TELEX 31-66180-AIU-IN. circ. 500.

BIBLIOGRAPHY OF EDUCATION THESES IN AUSTRALIA. see EDUCATION — Abstracting, Bibliographies, Statistics

300   II
BOOK REVIEW INDEX: AFRICA. (Text in English and French) 1971. a. $30. University of Delhi, Department of African Studies, Delhi 110 007, India. TEL 2521521. Ed. R.P. Sood. index; circ. 300.

300 001.3   TR   ISSN 0250-7617
CARINDEX: SOCIAL SCIENCES AND HUMANITIES. 1977. s-a. $45. University of the West Indies, Main Library, St. Augustine, Trinidad and Tobago, W.I. TEL 809-662-2002. FAX 809-662-9238. TELEX 24-520-UWI-WG. Ed. Annette Knight. bk.rev.; circ. 100. (back issues avail.)
Formerly (until 1982): Carindex: Social Sciences.
Description: Guide to the social sciences and humanities literature published in the English-speaking Caribbean. Covers periodical articles as well as conference proceedings, reports, and theses presented to the university.

CURRENT DIGEST OF THE POST-SOVIET PRESS. see POLITICAL SCIENCE — Abstracting, Bibliographies, Statistics

300 020 015   UK   ISSN 0267-1964
H62.5.G7
CURRENT RESEARCH IN BRITAIN. SOCIAL SCIENCES. (Other vols. avail.: Biological Sciences, Humanities, Physical Sciences) 1980. a. £70 (foreign £75). British Library, Document Supply Centre, Boston Spa, Wetherby, W. Yorkshire LS23 7BQ, England. TEL 0937-843434. FAX 0937-546333. TELEX 557381. Ed. Mike Bate.
Formerly: Research in British Universities Polytechnics and Colleges. Vol.3: Social Sciences (ISSN 0143-0742)

312   CY   ISSN 0253-875X
CYPRUS. DEPARTMENT OF STATISTICS AND RESEARCH. STATISTICAL ABSTRACT. (Text in English) 1955. a. £C6. Department of Statistics and Research, Ministry of Finance, Nicosia, Cyprus. TEL 02-303286. FAX 456712. bk.rev.; circ. 420.
Description: Summarized statistics concerning the economic and social conditions in Cyprus on a time series basis.

DIRECTORY OF PUBLISHED PROCEEDINGS. SERIES S S H - SOCIAL SCIENCES - HUMANITIES. see MEETINGS AND CONGRESSES — Abstracting, Bibliographies, Statistics

DISSERTATION ABSTRACTS INTERNATIONAL. SECTION A: HUMANITIES AND SOCIAL SCIENCES. see HUMANITIES: COMPREHENSIVE WORKS — Abstracting, Bibliographies, Statistics

960 300   NE   ISSN 0166-2694
DOCUMENTATIEBLAD: THE ABSTRACTS JOURNAL OF THE AFRICAN STUDIES CENTRE LEIDEN. (Text in Dutch, English, French, German) 1968. q. fl.30. Afrika-Studiecentrum - African Studies Centre, Postbus 9555, 2300 RB Leiden, Netherlands. TEL 071-273372. FAX 071-273344. Ed.Bd. abstr.; circ. 500. (processed) **Indexed:** World Agri.Econ.& Rural Sociol.Abstr.
Supersedes (in 1980): Afrika Studiecentrum. Documentatieblad (ISSN 0002-0419)

300   GW   ISSN 0936-9171
DOKUMENTATIONSDIENST ASIEN UND SUEDPAZIFIK. AUSGEWAEHLTE NEUER LITERATUR. (Text in English and German) 1975. 4/yr. DM.55. Deutsche Uebersee Institut, Uebersee Dokumentation, Neuer Jungfernstieg 21, 2000 Hamburg 36, Germany. TEL 040-3562598. Eds. Hans-Juergen Cwik, Angelika Pathak. circ. 150.

300   GW   ISSN 0938-3638
DOKUMENTATIONSDIENST ASIEN UND SUEDPAZIFIK. KURZBIBLIOGRAPHIE. (Text in English and German) 1978. irreg. Deutsche Uebersee Institut, Uebersee Dokumentation, Neuer Jungfernstieg 21, 2000 Hamburg 36, Germany. TEL 040-3562598.

300   GW   ISSN 0937-5929
DOKUMENTATIONSDIENST ASIEN UND SUEDPAZIFIK. REIHE A. (Text in English and German) 1974. irreg. Deutsche Uebersee Institut, Uebersee Dokumentation, Neuer Jungfernstieg 21, 2000 Hamburg 36, Germany. TEL 040-3562598.

300   GW   ISSN 0937-5937
DOKUMENTATIONSDIENST VORDERER ORIENT. AUSGEWAEHLTE NEUERE LITERATUR. (Text in English, French and German) 1970. 4/yr. DM.55. Deutsche Uebersee Institut, Uebersee Dokumentation, Neuer Jungfernstieg 21, 2000 Hamburg 36, Germany. TEL 040-3562598. Eds. Gerda Hansen, Marianne Schmidt-Dumont. circ. 205.

300   GW   ISSN 0938-2666
DOKUMENTATIONSDIENST VORDERER ORIENT. KURZBIBLIOGRAPHIE. (Text in English, French and German) 1978. irreg. Deutsche Uebersee Institut, Uebersee Dokumentation, Neuer Jungfernstieg 21, 2000 Hamburg 36, Germany. TEL 040-3562598.

300 016   BO
EXTENSION BIBLIOGRAFICA. 1974. irreg., no.10, 1984. price varies. Centro de Investigaciones Sociales, Casilla 6931 - C.C., La Paz, Bolivia.

FICHIER AFRIQUE. see BUSINESS AND ECONOMICS — Abstracting, Bibliographies, Statistics

314   FI
FINLAND. TILASTOKESKUS. TILASTOLLISIA TIEDONANTOJA. KULTTUURITILASTO/FINLAND. STATISTIKCENTRALEN. STATISTISKA MEDDELANDEN KULTURSTATISTIK/FINLAND. CENTRAL STATISTICAL OFFICE. STATISTICAL SURVEYS. CULTURAL STATISTICS. (Text in English, Finnish and Swedish) 1978. irreg., latest 1981. FIM 150. Tilastokeskus, Annankatu 44, SF-00100 Helsinki 10, Finland.

300   IQ   ISSN 1012-3415
GENERAL INDEX TO IRAQI PERIODICAL LITERATURE. PART B: HUMANITIES AND SOCIAL SCIENCES. (Text in Arabic, English) 1986. irreg. free. Scientific Research Council, Jadiriyah P.O. Box 2441, Baghdad, Iraq. TELEX 213976 SR IK. Ed. Radhwan K. ABdul-Halim. circ. 500.

300 016   US
GUIDE TO ALTERNATIVE PERIODICALS. 1980. a. price varies. New Pages Press, Box 438, Grand Blanc, MI 48439. TEL 313-743-8055. FAX 313-743-2730. Ed. Casey Hill. adv.; illus.

GUIDE TO SOCIAL SCIENCE AND RELIGION IN PERIODICAL LITERATURE. see RELIGIONS AND THEOLOGY — Abstracting, Bibliographies, Statistics

300   CC
GUOWAI SHEHUI KEXUE LUNWEN SUOYIN/FOREIGN SOCIAL SCIENCE DISSERTATION INDEX. (Text in Chinese) bi-m. Zhongguo Shehui Kexueyuan, Wenxian Qingbao Zhongxin - Chinese Academy of Social Sciences, Documentation Information Center, 5, Jianguomennei Dajie, Beijing 100732, People's Republic of China. TEL 5137744. Ed. Zhu Tiesheng.

I A S S I S T QUARTERLY. (International Association for Social Science Information Services and Technology) see LIBRARY AND INFORMATION SCIENCES

300 016   II   ISSN 0376-4206
I C S S R RESEARCH ABSTRACTS QUARTERLY. (Text in English) 1971. q. Rs.30 to individuals; institutions Rs.50($10). Indian Council of Social Science Research, 35 Ferozshah Rd., New Delhi 110 001, India. TEL 381571. TELEX 31-61083-ISSR-IN. Ed. S. Saraswathi. adv.; bk.rev.; abstr.; bibl.; charts; circ. 550. (back issues avail.)
—BLDSC shelfmark: 4362.094000.
Description: Abstracts reports of research projects funded by the ICSSR. Covers objectives, methodology, and major findings.

SOCIAL SCIENCES: COMPREHENSIVE WORKS — ABSTRACTING, BIBLIOGRAPHIES, STATISTICS

011 II
I C S S R UNION CATALOGUE OF SOCIAL SCIENCE PERIODICALS. (Text in English) 1973. irreg. Rs.1530($460) Indian Council of Social Science Research, National Social Science Documentation Centre, 35 Ferozshah Rd., New Delhi 110 001, India. TEL 385959. TELEX 31-61083-ISSR-IN. Ed. K.G. Tyagi. bibl.; index; circ. 1,000.
Formerly: I C S S R Union Catalogue of Social Science Periodicals - Serials.

300 IT
I D O C INTERNAZIONALE. (Text in English) 1970. 4/yr. L.25000($30) International Documentation and Communication Center, Via S. Maria dell'Anima 30, 00186 Rome, Italy. FAX 0039-6-6832766. TELEX 0402-6105943 DOCLU. Ed. Albert van Oortmerssen. adv.; bk.rev.; bibl.; circ. 1,500. (back issues avail.)

300 011 TH ISSN 0125-5827
INDEX TO THAI PERIODICAL LITERATURE. (Text in Thai) 1964. a. $16. National Institute of Development Administration, Library and Information Center, Publication and Dissemination of Information Division, Klongjan, Bangkapi, Bangkok 10240, Thailand. index; circ. 200.

016.3091 II
INDIA. MINISTRY OF EDUCATION AND SOCIAL WELFARE. DEPARTMENT OF SOCIAL WELFARE. DOCUMENTATION SERVICE BULLETIN. 1968. a. free. Ministry of Education and Social Welfare, Department of Social Welfare, Shastri Bhavan, New Delhi 110001, India. circ. controlled.

300 016 II ISSN 0250-9709
INDIAN DISSERTATION ABSTRACTS. (Text in English) 1973. q. Rs.30 to individuals; institutions Rs.50($10). Indian Council of Social Science Research, 35, Ferozshah Rd., New Delhi 110 001, India. TEL 381571. TELEX 31-61083-ISSR-IN. (Co-sponsor: Association of Indian Universities) Ed. Dinesh C. Sharma. adv.; abstr.; index; circ. 550. (back issues avail.)
Description: Abstracts of research theses in social sciences on which Ph.D. degrees were awarded by Indian universities. Features topic, methodology, and results of each project.

INTER-AMERICAN REVIEW OF BIBLIOGRAPHY/REVISTA INTERAMERICANA DE BIBLIOGRAFIA. see HUMANITIES: COMPREHENSIVE WORKS — Abstracting, Bibliographies, Statistics

JAPAN. MINISTRY OF HEALTH AND WELFARE. STATISTICS AND INFORMATION DEPARTMENT. REPORT ON SURVEY OF SOCIO-ECONOMIC ASPECTS ON VITAL EVENTS. see BUSINESS AND ECONOMICS — Abstracting, Bibliographies, Statistics

300 310 NR
NIGERIA. FEDERAL OFFICE OF STATISTICS. SOCIAL STATISTICS IN NIGERIA. a. $10. Federal Office of Statistics, P.M.B. 12528, Lagos, Nigeria.

300 NR ISSN 0078-0766
NIGERIAN INSTITUTE OF SOCIAL AND ECONOMIC RESEARCH. LIBRARY. LIST OF ACCESSIONS. 1963. q. exchange basis. Nigerian Institute of Social and Economic Research, Private Mail Bag 5, University of Ibadan, Ibadan, Nigeria.

300 011 NR
NIGERIAN JOURNAL OF SOCIAL SCIENCE RESEARCH ABSTRACTS. 1982. s-a. Nigerian Institute of Social and Economic Research, Private Mail Bag 5, University of Ibadan, Ibadan, Nigeria.

NORDIC JOURNAL ON LATIN AMERICAN STUDIES. see HISTORY — Abstracting, Bibliographies, Statistics

800 011 300 US
NOTABLE CHILDREN'S TRADE BOOKS IN THE FIELD OF SOCIAL STUDIES. 1971. a. (National Council for the Social Studies, Joint Committee Project) Children's Book Council, Inc., 568 Broadway, New York, NY 10012-3225. TEL 212-966-1990. Ed. David Riederman.
Description: Annotated bibliography of books for kindergarten to eighth grade in American and world history and culture. Includes biographies, folktales, myths and legends.

300 011 RU
NOVAYA SOVETSKAYA I INOSTRANNAYA LITERATURA PO OBSHCHESTVENNYM NAUKAM. BOLGARIYA; bibliograficheskii ukazatel' 1949. m. 4.80 Rub. Akademiya Nauk S.S.S.R., Institut Nauchnoi Informatsii po Obshchestvennym Naukam, Ul. Krasikova 28-21, 117418 Moscow V-418, Russia. Ed. L.A. Rozhnova.
Formerly: Novaya Sovetskaya i Inostrannaya Literatura po Obshchestvennym Naukam. Narodnaya Respublika Bolgariya (ISSN 0134-2991)

300 011 RU ISSN 0134-2916
Z3013
NOVAYA SOVETSKAYA I INOSTRANNAYA LITERATURA PO OBSHCHESTVENNYM NAUKAM. BLIZHNII I SREDNII VOSTOK - AFRIKA; bibliograficheskii ukazatel' 1947. m. 9.60 Rub. Akademiya Nauk S.S.S.R., Institut Nauchnoi Informatsii po Obshchestvennym Naukam, Ul. Krasikova 28-21, 117418 Moscow V-418, Russia. Ed. A.Ya. Porkhomovskii.

300 011 RU
NOVAYA SOVETSKAYA I INOSTRANNAYA LITERATURA PO OBSHCHESTVENNYM NAUKAM. CHEKHOSLOVAKIYA; bibliograficheskii ukazatel' 1949. m. 4.80 Rub. Akademiya Nauk S.S.S.R., Institut Nauchnoi Informatsii po Obshchestvennym Naukam, Ul. Krasikova 28-21, Moscow 117418, Russia. Ed. T.V. Vladislavleva.
Formerly: Novaya Sovetskaya i Inostrannaya Literatura po Obshchestvennym Naukam. Chekhoslovatskaya Sotsialisticheskaya Respublika (ISSN 0134-2967)

300 RU ISSN 0134-2975
NOVAYA SOVETSKAYA I INOSTRANNAYA LITERATURA PO OBSHCHESTVENNYM NAUKAM. GERMANSKAYA DEMOKRATICHESKAYA RESPUBLIKA. 1962. m. 10.40 Rub. Akademiya Nauk S.S.S.R., Institut Nauchnoi Informatsii po Obshchestvennym Naukam, Ul. Krasikova 28-21, Moscow 117418, Russia. Ed. I.A. Kaloeva.

300 011 RU
Z2523
NOVAYA SOVETSKAYA I INOSTRANNAYA LITERATURA PO OBSHCHESTVENNYM NAUKAM. POL'SHA; bibliograficheskii ukazatel' 1949. m. 7.20 Rub. Akademiya Nauk S.S.S.R., Institut Nauchnoi Informatsii po Obshchestvennym Naukam, Ul. Krasikova 28-21, 117418 Moscow V-418, Russia. Ed. E.Yu. Matveeva.
Formerly: Novaya Sovetskaya i Inostrannaya Literatura po Obshchestvennym Naukam. Pol'skaya Narodnaya Respublika (ISSN 0134-2924)

300 011 RU ISSN 0134-3041
NOVAYA SOVETSKAYA I INOSTRANNAYA LITERATURA PO OBSHCHESTVENNYM NAUKAM. PROBLEMY SLAVYANOVEDENIYA I BALKANISTIKI; bibliograficheskii ukazatel' 1966. bi-m. 1.20 Rub. Akademiya Nauk S.S.S.R., Institut Nauchnoi Informatsii po Obshchestvennym Naukam, Ul. Krasikova 28-21, 117418 Moscow V-418, Russia. Ed. I.A. Kaloeva.
—BLDSC shelfmark: 0133.668000.

300 011 RU
NOVAYA SOVETSKAYA I INOSTRANNAYA LITERATURA PO OBSHCHESTVENNYM NAUKAM. RUMYNIYA; bibliograficheskii ukazatel' 1949. m. 4.80 Rub. Akademiya Nauk S.S.S.R., Institut Nauchnoi Informatsii po Obshchestvennym Naukam, Ul. Krasikova 28-21, 117418 Moscow V-418, Russia. Ed. I.A. Kaloeva.
Formerly: Novaya Sovetsakaya i Inostrannaya Literatura po Obshchestvennym Naukam. Sotsialisticheskaya Respublika Rumyniya (ISSN 0202-2540)

300 011 RU ISSN 0134-3033
NOVAYA SOVETSKAYA I INOSTRANNAYA LITERATURA PO OBSHCHESTVENNYM NAUKAM. STRANY AZII I AFRIKI. OBSHCHIE PROBLEMY; bibliograficheskii ukazatel' 1947. m. 3.60 Rub. Akademiya Nauk S.S.S.R., Institut Nauchnoi Informatsii po Obshchestvennym Naukam, Ul. Krasikova 28-21, 117418 Moscow V-418, Russia. Ed. Z.A. Suprunenko.

300 011 RU
NOVAYA SOVETSKAYA I INOSTRANNAYA LITERATURA PO OBSHCHESTVENNYM NAUKAM. STRANY VOSTOCHNOI EVROPY. OBSHCHIE PROBLEMY; bibliograficheskii ukazatel' 1964. m. 4.80 Rub. Akademiya Nauk S.S.S.R., Institut Nauchnoi Informatsii po Obshchestvennym Naukam, Ul. Krasikova 28-21, 117418 Moscow V-418, Russia. Ed. I.A. Kaloeva.
Formerly: Novaya Sovetskaya i Inostrannaya Literatura po Obshchestvennym Naukam. Evropeiskie Sotsialisticheskie Strany. Obshchie Problemy (ISSN 0134-2983)

300 011 RU
NOVAYA SOVETSKAYA I INOSTRANNAYA LITERATURA PO OBSHCHESTVENNYM NAUKAM. VENGRIYA; bibliograficheskii ukazatel' 1956. m. 4.80 Rub. Akademiya Nauk S.S.S.R., Institut Nauchnoi Informatsii po Obshchestvennym Naukam, Ul. Krasikova 28-21, 117418 Moscow V-418, Russia. Ed. I.A. Kaloeva.
Formerly: Novaya Sovetskaya i Inostrannaya Literatura po Obshchestvennym Naukam. Vengerskaya Narodnaya Respublika (ISSN 0134-3017)

300 011 RU
NOVAYA SOVETSKAYA I INOSTRANNAYA LITERATURA PO OBSHCHESTVENNYM NAUKAM. YUGOSLAVIYA; bibliograficheskii ukazatel' 1956. m. 4.80 Rub. Akademiya Nauk S.S.S.R., Institut Nauchnoi Informatsii po Obshchestvennym Naukam, Ul. Krasikova 28-21, 117418 Moscow V-418, Russia. Ed. A.I. Sliva.
Formerly: Novaya Sovetskaya i Inostrannaya Literatura po Obshchestvennym Naukam. Sotsialisticheskaya Federativnaya Respublika Yugoslaviya (ISSN 0134-3009)

300 011 RU ISSN 0134-2959
Z3001
NOVAYA SOVETSKAYA I INOSTRANNAYA LITERATURA PO OBSHCHESTVENNYM NAUKAM. YUZHNAYA I YUGO-VOSTOCHNAYA AZIYA - DAL'NII VOSTOK; bibliograficheskii ukazatel' 1947. m. 9.60 Rub. Akademiya Nauk S.S.S.R., Institut Nauchnoi Informatsii po Obshchestvennym Naukam, Ul. Krasikova 28-21, 117418 Moscow V-418, Russia. Ed. A.A. Stolyarov.

300 016 TA
OBSHCHESTVENNYE NAUKI V TADZHIKISTANE; ukazatel' literatury. q. Akademiya Nauk Tadzhikskoi S.S.R., Tsentral'naya Nauchnaya Biblioteka, Ul. Aym, 121, Dushanbe, Tadzhikistan.

951 RU ISSN 0235-6821
OBSHCHESTVENNYE NAUKI ZA RUBEZHOM. KITAVEDENIE; referativnyi zhurnal. 1973. bi-m. 6 Rub. Akademiya Nauk S.S.S.R., Institut Nauchnoi Informatsii po Obshchestvennym Naukam, Ul. Krasikova 28-21, 117418 Moscow V-418, Russia. Ed. S.L. Tikhvinskii.

P A I S INTERNATIONAL IN PRINT. (Public Affairs Information Service, Inc.) see BUSINESS AND ECONOMICS — Abstracting, Bibliographies, Statistics

300 US ISSN 0730-3335
REFERENCE SOURCES FOR THE SOCIAL SCIENCES AND HUMANITIES. 1982. irreg. price varies. Greenwood Press, Inc. (Subsidiary of: Greenwood Publishing Group Inc.), 88 Post Rd. W., Box 5007, Westport, CT 06881-5007. TEL 203-226-3571. FAX 203-222-1502. Ed. Raymond G. McInnis.

015 FR ISSN 0038-7282
S P E L D INFORMATION; droit, politique, economie, sciences sociales, erudition. (Text in English, French, German) 1963. q. 90 F. Societe de Promotion a l'Etranger du Livre de Droit (S.P.E.L.D.), 6 rue Victor-Cousin, 75005 Paris, France. Ed. Denis Pedone. bk.rev.; circ. 7,000. Indexed: P.A.I.S.For.Lang.Ind.
—BLDSC shelfmark: 8411.430000.

SCITECH BOOK NEWS; an annotated bibliography of new books in science, technology, & medicine. see BIBLIOGRAPHIES

SOCIAL SERVICES AND WELFARE

016 300 US ISSN 0091-3707
Z7161
SOCIAL SCIENCES CITATION INDEX. Short title: S S C I. (Includes Source Index, Citation Index, Permuterm Subject Index, and Corporate Index) 1969. 3/yr. (includes annual cumulations). $4300. Institute for Scientific Information, 3501 Market St., Philadelphia, PA 19104. TEL 215-386-0100.
FAX 215-386-2991. (And: 132 High St., Uxbridge, Middlesex., UB8 1DP, England) cum.index: 1956-1965, 1966-1970, 1971-1975, 1976-1980, 1981-1985, 1986-1990. (also avail. in magnetic tape)
●Also available online. Vendor(s): BRS (SSCI), DIMDI, Data-Star, DIALOG (File no.7/SOCIAL SCISEARCH). Also available on CD-ROM. Producer(s): Institute for Scientific Information (SSCI).
—BLDSC shelfmark: 8318.188200.
Description: Multidisciplinary indexing of research in all fields of social sciences.

300 US ISSN 0161-3162
Z7161
SOCIAL SCIENCES CITATION INDEX JOURNAL CITATION REPORTS. Short title: S S C I - J C R. (Not avail. in printed format. Includes Journal Ranking, Reference Data, and Source Data Packages) 1977. a. $245. Institute for Scientific Information, 3501 Market St., Philadelphia, PA 19104. TEL 215-386-0100.
FAX 215-386-2991. (And 132 High St., Uxbridge, Middlesex., UB8 1DP, England) (microfiche)
Formerly: I S I Journal Citation Reports.
Description: Provides citation data of journals in the social sciences.

300 016 US ISSN 0094-4920
AI3
SOCIAL SCIENCES INDEX. 1974. q. (plus a. cum.). service basis. H.W. Wilson Co., 950 University Ave., Bronx, NY 10452. TEL 800-367-6770.
FAX 212-538-2716. TELEX 4990003HWILSON. Ed. Cheryl Ehrens. (also avail. in magnetic tape)
●Also available online. Vendor(s): Wilsonline (File SSI).
Also available on CD-ROM. Producer(s): H.W. Wilson.
—BLDSC shelfmark: 8318.191000.
Supersedes in part: Social Sciences and Humanities Index (ISSN 0037-7899)
Description: Author and subject index to periodicals in the fields of anthropology, community health and medicine, economics, geography, international relations, law, criminology and police science, political science, psychology and psychiatry, public administration, sociology, social work, and related subjects.

SUDAN. NATIONAL COUNCIL FOR RESEARCH. ECONOMIC AND SOCIAL RESEARCH COUNCIL. BIBLIOGRAPHIES. see BUSINESS AND ECONOMICS — Abstracting, Bibliographies, Statistics

972 US
SYRACUSE UNIVERSITY. FOREIGN AND COMPARATIVE STUDIES. LATIN AMERICAN SERIES. (Former name of issuing body: Maxwell School of Citizenship and Public Affairs) 1980. irreg., no.10, 1990. price varies. Syracuse University, Foreign and Comparative Studies, c/o Joanna C. Giansanti, Man. Ed., 321 Sims Hall, Syracuse, NY 13244-1230.
TEL 315-443-4667. FAX 315-443-4597. Ed. Rolena Adorno.

950 US
SYRACUSE UNIVERSITY. FOREIGN AND COMPARATIVE STUDIES. SOUTH ASIAN SERIES. (Former name of issuing body: Maxwell School of Citzenship and Public Affairs) 1976. irreg., no.14, 1990. price varies. Syracuse University, Foreign and Comparative Studies, c/o Joanna C. Giansanti, Man. Ed., 321 Sims Hall, Syracuse, NY 13244-1230.
TEL 315-443-4667. FAX 315-443-4597. Ed. Susan S. Wadley.

U P RESEARCH MONITOR. (University of the Philippines) see SCIENCES: COMPREHENSIVE WORKS — Abstracting, Bibliographies, Statistics

500 016 NE ISSN 0041-591X
UITGELEZEN. (Text in Dutch, English, French, German) 1968. m. fl.60. Ministerie van Sociale Zaken, Library and Documentation Service - Ministry of Social Affairs, P.O. Box 90801, 2509 LV The Hague, Netherlands. Ed. W. Mazure. abstr.; index; circ. 1,500 (controlled).
●Also available online.
Description: Abstracts from books, reports and articles with material of interest to policy makers in the Dutch ministry.

300 015 JM
UNIVERSITY OF THE WEST INDIES. INSTITUTE OF SOCIAL AND ECONOMIC RESEARCH. OCCASIONAL BIBLIOGRAPHY SERIES. 1974. irreg., no.9, 1987? University of the West Indies, Institute of Social and Economic Research, Mona Campus, Kingston 7, Jamaica, W.I. TEL 809-927-1020.
FAX 809-927-2409. TELEX 2123 JA.

011 II
VIKRAM RESEARCH GUIDE.* (Text in English) 1971. q. Rs.21. Vikram University, Maharaja Jiwajirao Library, P.O. 12, Ujjain, Madhya Pradesh, India. Ed. N.K. Trivedi. abstr.

300 GW ISSN 0932-3481
W Z B FORSCHUNG; Hinweise auf neue Arbeiten. 1978. 3/yr. Wissenschafts Zentrum Berlin fuer Sozialforschung, Reichpietschufer 50, 1000 Berlin 30, Germany. TEL 030-25491-0.
FAX 030-25491684. TELEX 308897-WZB-D. Ed. Heidi Hilzinger. abstr.; circ. 4,400.

300 US ISSN 0734-9033
HM206
WHOLE AGAIN RESOURCE GUIDE; periodical and resource directory. 1982. irreg., 2nd ed. 1987. $26.95. SourceNet, Box 6767, Santa Barbara, CA 93160. TEL 805-494-7123. Ed. Tim Ryan. bk.rev.; bibl.; illus.; index; circ. 5,000. (back issues avail.)
—BLDSC shelfmark: 9311.953640.
Incorporates: International Guide to Psi-Periodicals (ISSN 0277-9870)

300 016 UN
WORLD DIRECTORY OF SOCIAL SCIENCE INSTITUTIONS. (Text in English and French) 1970. irreg., 5th ed., 1990. Unesco, 7-9 Place de Fontenoy, 75700 Paris, France. TEL 577-16-10. (Dist. in U.S. by: Unipub, 4611-F Assembly Dr., Lanham, MD 20706-4391) **Indexed:** A.I.C.P.
Formerly: World Index of Social Science Institutions.

300 UN ISSN 0084-1870
WORLD LIST OF SOCIAL SCIENCE PERIODICALS. (Text in English and French) irreg., 7th ed., 1987. $30. Unesco, 7-9 Place de Fontenoy, 75700 Paris, France.

ZASSHI KIJI SAKUIN. JINBUN SHAKAI HEN/JAPANESE PERIODICALS INDEX. HUMANITIES AND SOCIAL SCIENCE SECTION. see HUMANITIES: COMPREHENSIVE WORKS — Abstracting, Bibliographies, Statistics

300 011 CC
ZHONGGUO SHEHUI KEXUE WENXIAN TILU/CHINESE SOCIAL SCIENCE DOCUMENTATIONS INDEX. (Text in Chinese) bi-m. Zhongguo Shehui Kexueyuan, Wenxian Qingbao Zhongxin - Chinese Academy of Social Sciences, Documentation Information Center, No.5, Jianguomennei Dajie, Beijing 100732, People's Republic of China. TEL 5137744. Ed. Mo Zuoqin.

SOCIAL SERVICES AND WELFARE

see also Drug Abuse and Alcoholism; Public Health and Safety

A A - B A NEWSLETTER. (American Anorexia - Bulimia Association, Inc.) see PSYCHOLOGY

A B P - ASSOCIATION BELGE DES PARALYSES. BULLETIN/B V V - BELGISCHE VERENIGING VOOR VERLAMDEN. BULLETIN. see MEDICAL SCIENCES — Psychiatry And Neurology

A C A NEWS; the provincial newsletter for seniors. (Alberta Council on Aging) see GERONTOLOGY AND GERIATRICS

360 LY
A C A R T S O D NEWSLETTER. (Text in Arabic, English, French) 1980. q. free. African Centre for Applied Research and Training in Social Development, P.O. Box 80606, Tripoli, Libya. TEL 218-21-833640.
TELEX 20803. Ed. Oscar Gasana. circ. 1,500. (back issues avail.)

360 362.41 AT ISSN 0729-8463
A C R O D NEWSLETTER. 1981. m. Aus.$60 (foreign Aus.$70). Australian Council for Rehabilitation of Disabled (ACROD), P.O. Box 60, Curtin, A.C.T. 2605, Australia. TEL 062-824333.
FAX 062-813488. Ed. Patricia Clarke. adv.; bk.rev.; circ. 1,500. (back issues avail.)

614 US
A H C A NOTES. 1972. bi-w. $150 to non-members; members $15. American Health Care Association, 1201 L St., N.W., Washington, DC 20005. TEL 202-842-4444. FAX 202-842-3860. Ed. Marla Gold. illus.; circ. 10,000.
Formerly: A H C A Weekly Notes (ISSN 0146-6321)

A H R C CHRONICLE. (Association for the Help of Retarded Children) see MEDICAL SCIENCES — Psychiatry And Neurology

A I D S UPDATE (NEW YORK). see MEDICAL SCIENCES — Communicable Diseases

360 US
A L M A SEARCHLIGHT. 1974. q. membership. Adoptees' Liberty Movement Association, Box 154, Washington Bridge Sta., New York, NY 10033. TEL 212-581-1568. Ed. Florence Fisher. circ. 50,000.

A M S STUDIES IN MODERN SOCIETY. see PUBLIC HEALTH AND SAFETY

A P I ACCOUNT. (Accountants for the Public Interest) see BUSINESS AND ECONOMICS — Accounting

360 US
A P W A NEWS. 1986. q. membership only. American Public Welfare Association, c/o Pat Reynolds, 810 First St., N.E., Ste. 500, Washington, DC 20002-4205. TEL 202-682-0100.
FAX 202-289-6555. illus.; circ. 8,000. (tabloid format)
Description: Contains articles on APWA events and projects; includes calendar, conference reports, and interviews.

360 PK ISSN 0001-2262
A P W A NEWSLETTER. 1967. 3/yr. free. All Pakistan Women's Association, Information and Research Bureau, 67-B Garden Rd., Karachi 3, Pakistan. Ed. Ishrat Aftab. charts; illus.

362.3 US ISSN 0199-9435
A R C. 1952. bi-m. $15. Association for Retarded Citizens, National Headquarters, 500 E. Border St., te. 300, Arlington, TX 76010. TEL 817-261-6003. FAX 817-277-3491. Ed. Dick Collier. adv.; bk.rev.; illus.; circ. 140,000. (tabloid format; also avail. in microform from UMI; reprint service avail. from UMI)
Former titles: Mental Retardation News (ISSN 0009-4072); Children Limited.

360 US ISSN 0001-2335
A R S HAI SIRD. 1939. a. $10. Armenian Relief Society, Inc., 80 Bigelow Ave., Watertown, MA 02172-2021. TEL 617-926-5892. FAX 617-926-4855. Ed. Arpie Balian. adv.; bk.rev.; circ. 1,000.

649 178 IT ISSN 0394-6479
A S P E. (Agenzia di Stampa sui Problemi dell'Emarginazione) 1983. fortn. L.50000 (foreign L.60000). Edizioni Gruppo Abele, Via Giolitti 21, 10123 Turin, Italy. TEL 011-839-5444.
FAX 011-8395577. adv.; cum.index: 1983-1986; circ. 7,500. (back issues avail.)
Description: Features news, surveys and documents concerning social issues, peace and environment. Reports on national and international meetings on conventions, seminars and training courses.

SOCIAL SERVICES AND WELFARE 4397

360   ET
A S W E A JOURNAL FOR SOCIAL WORK EDUCATION IN AFRICA. (Editions in English and French) 1974. s-a. Association for Social Work Education in Africa, c/o College of Social Sciences, Addis Ababa University, PO Box 1176, Addis Ababa, Ethiopia.
   Supersedes: Association for Social Work Education in Africa. Bulletin.

361.3 929   US
A T M REUNION REGISTRY. 1985. q. $50. Adoption Triangle Ministries, 1105 Cape Coral Pkwy. E., Ste. G, Cape Coral, FL 33904-9175. TEL 813-542-1342. FAX 813-549-9393. (Subscr. to: Musser Foundation, Box 1860, Cape Coral, FL 33910) Ed. Sandy Musser.
   Description: Adopted persons seeking birth parents and other family members.

360   GW
A W O MITTEILUNGEN; Kreisverband Karlsruhe. 1969. q. DM.1.60. Arbeiterwohlfahrt, Kreisverband Karlsruhe - Stadt, Kronenstr. 15, 7500 Karlsruhe 1, Germany. TEL 0721-69070. bk.rev.; bibl.; stat.; circ. 4,500. (back issues avail.)
   Formerly: A W Mitteilungen.

ABILITIES. see *HANDICAPPED — Hearing Impaired*

361   PE
ACCION CRITICA. 1976. s-a. $6. Asociacion Latinoamericana de Escuelas de Servicio Social, Centro Latinoamericano de Trabajo Social, Jr. Jorge Vanderghen No. 351, Apdo. 348, Lima, Peru. Dir. Maria Cecilia Tobon. bk.rev.

362.8   FR   ISSN 0223-5420
ACCUEILLIR. 1972. bi-m. 140 F. Service Social d'Aide aux Emigrants, 72 rue Regnault, 75640 Paris Cedex 13, France. TEL 40-77-94-47. FAX 45-84-43-05. Ed. Monique Moreira. adv.; bk.rev.; circ. 2,000.

323.4   US
ACTING OUT. 1979? q. $4. Mental Patients Liberation Front, Box 514, Cambridge, MA 02138.

360   AT   ISSN 0300-4678
ACTION (FITZROY). 1969. q. free. Brotherhood of St. Laurence, 67 Brunswick St., Fitzroy, Vic. 3065, Australia. FAX 61-03-4172691. bk.rev.; circ. 42,000.
   Description: For donors and supporters of the brotherhood on its services and advocacy for the disadvantaged.

360   US
ACTION ALERT (WASHINGTON, 19??). irreg. (4-8/yr.). $30 membership. Interfaith Impact for Justice and Peace, 110 Maryland Ave., N.E., Washington, DC 20002. TEL 202-543-2800.
   Description: Each issue covers a different topic in areas such as civil rights, world peace, poverty, environment and economics.

360   AT   ISSN 1030-7451
ACTIVNEWS. 1953. m. Activ Foundation Inc., P.O. Box 446, Jolimont, W.A. 6014, Australia. TEL 09-387-0555. FAX 09-387-0599. Ed. Lindy Markes. adv.; bk.rev.; circ. 2,700. (back issues avail.)
   Formerly: Our Children (ISSN 0048-2382)
   Description: Promotes the wide range of services for adults and children with developmental disabilities.

360   FR   ISSN 0400-471X
ACTUALITES SOCIALES HEBDOMADAIRES. 1955. w. 310 F. (foreign 630 F.)(typically set in Sep.). Actualites Sociales Hebdomadaires, s.a.r.l., 14 bd. Montmartre, 75009 Paris, France. TEL 47-70-84-59. FAX 48-00-06-74. adv.; B&W page 6250 F., color page 7140 F. bk.rev.; circ. 12,300. (looseleaf format)

361   BG   ISSN 0042-1057
ADHUNA. (Text in Bengali) 1974. m. $10. Association of Development Agencies in Bangladesh, 1-3 Block F, Lalmatia, Dhaka 1207, Bangladesh. Ed. Minar Monsur. adv.; bk.rev.; circ. 7,000.
   Former titles (until 1991): A D A B Sangbad; Adab Sangbad; Urdu Adab.
   Description: For grassroots organization of Bangladesh's NGO workers.

360   US   ISSN 0364-3107
                         CODEN: ASWODB
ADMINISTRATION IN SOCIAL WORK; the quarterly journal of human services management. 1977. q. $40 to individuals; institutions $85; libraries $175. Haworth Press, Inc., 10 Alice St., Binghamton, NY 13904. TEL 800-342-9678. FAX 607-722-1424. Ed. Simon Slavin. adv.; bk.rev.; circ. 950. (also avail. in microfiche from HAW; back issues avail.; reprint service avail. from HAW) Indexed: ABI Inform., Abstr.Health Care Manage.Stud., ASSIA, BPIA, Bull.Signal., Curr.Cont., Hosp.Lit.Ind., Human Resour.Abstr., Manage.Abstr., Manage.Cont., Mid.East: Abstr.& Ind., PSI, Psychol.Abstr., Ref.Zh., Sage Fam.Stud.Abstr., Soc.Work Res.& Abstr., Sociol.Abstr., SSCI.
   —BLDSC shelfmark: 0696.270000.
   Description: Provides current information to administrators, supervisors, managers and sub-executives in social work and related human services fields.
   Refereed Serial

362.7   US   ISSN 0273-6497
ADOPTALK. 1976. q. $30 (effective 1992). North American Council on Adoptable Children (NACAC), 1821 University Ave., Ste. N-498, St. Paul, MN 55104. FAX 612-645-0963. Ed. Roberta Frank. adv.; bk.rev.; circ. 8,000. (processed)
   Supersedes (1965-1976): National Adoptalk (ISSN 0027-8459)
   Description: Information and articles about special needs adoption, foster care, adoptive family support, resources, and federal legislation.

ADOPTED CHILD. see *CHILDREN AND YOUTH — About*

362.7   US
ADOPTION. 1989. bi-m. $30. Ulick Publishing Co., Box 8551, Bartlett, IL 60103. TEL 800-833-3460. Ed. Geoffrey Golson.
   Description: For people exploring the various options of adopting children.

362.7   UK   ISSN 0308-5759
HV875
ADOPTION AND FOSTERING. 1976. q. £18 (foreign £22)(typically set in Apr.). British Agencies for Adoption & Fostering, 11 Southwark St., London SE1 1RQ, England. TEL 071-407-8800. Ed. Barbara Fletcher. adv.; bk.rev.; stat.; cum.index; circ. 5,000. (back issues avail.) Indexed: ASSIA, Psychol.Abstr., Soc.Work Res.& Abstr.
   —BLDSC shelfmark: 0696.592000.
   Formerly: Child Adoption.
   Description: Multi-disciplinary professional look at children in danger of separation from their families or needing foster care or adoption.

362.7   US
ADOPTION FACTBOOK; United States data, issues, regulations and resources. 1985. irreg., 2nd ed., 1989. $39.95. National Council for Adoption, Inc., 1930 17th St., N.W., Washington, DC 20009-6207. TEL 202-328-1200.
   Description: Information sources for adoption and related services, especially services to young, single or troubled parents. Includes a hotline.

361 929   US
ADOPTION REFORM ORGANIZATIONS. 1985. s-a. $35. Adoption Triangle Ministries, 1105 Cape Coral Pkwy. E., Ste. G, Cape Coral, FL 33904-9175. TEL 813-542-1342. FAX 813-549-9393. (Subscr. to: Musser Foundation, Box 1860, Cape Coral, FL 33910) Ed. Sandy Musser. circ. 350. (looseleaf format)
   Description: A mailing list of active networking organizations working for adoption reform.

362   US
ADULT AND FAMILY SERVICES IN OREGON. m. Department of Human Resources, Public Welfare Division, 304 Public Service Bldg., Salem, OR 97310. TEL 503-378-2720. illus.
   Formerly: Public Welfare in Oregon (ISSN 0474-4039)

361 309.2   GH   ISSN 0515-4510
ADVANCE. 1954. q. Ministry of Social Welfare and Community Development, P.O. Box 778, Accra, Ghana. (processed)

360   US
ADVANCES IN CLINICAL REHABILITATION. 1980-1986 (vol:5); N.S. 1987. irreg. (approx. every 18 mos.). price varies. Springer Publishing Company, 536 Broadway, New York, NY 10012. TEL 212-431-4370. FAX 212-941-7842. Eds. M.C. Eisenberg, R. Grzesiak. circ. 417. Indexed: Dok.Arbeitsmed., Ind.Med., Psychol.Abstr.
   Supersedes: Annual Review of Rehabilitation (ISSN 0197-2251)

360 352.7   UK   ISSN 0950-5458
ADVISER. 1979. bi-m. £20. Shelter National Housing Aid Trust, 63 Waterloo Rd., Wolverhampton, West Midlands WV1 4QU, England. TEL 0902-310568. FAX 0902-710068. (Co-sponsor: National Association of Citizens Advice Bureau) Eds. Roman Leszczyszyn, Carolan Davidge. adv.; bk.rev.; index; circ. 3,500.
   —BLDSC shelfmark: 0712.289400.
   Former titles: Housing Aid; S N H A T News Bulletin (ISSN 0262-4885)
   Description: Guide to social security, housing, employment. Includes consumer and money advice.

THE ADVOCATE (INDIANAPOLIS). see *POLITICAL SCIENCE — Civil Rights*

360 305.4   US   ISSN 0886-1099
HV1442
AFFILIA; journal of women and social work. 1986. q. $34 to individuals; institutions $84 (effective 1991). Sage Publications, Inc., 2455 Teller Rd., Newbury Park, CA 91320. TEL 805-499-7021. FAX 805-499-0871. Eds. Bea Saunders, Betty Sancier. adv.; bk.rev.; circ. 1,000. (back issues avail.) Indexed: PSI, Sage Fam.Stud.Abstr., Soc.Work Res.& Abstr., Sociol.Abstr., Wom.Stud.Abstr. (1986-).
   —BLDSC shelfmark: 0731.720700.
   Description: Brings insight and knowledge to the field of social work from a feminist perspective and provides research and tools necessary to make significant changes and improvements in the delivery of social services.

AFN SHVEL. see *ETHNIC INTERESTS*

AGE D'OR - VIE NOUVELLE. see *GERONTOLOGY AND GERIATRICS*

360   RU   ISSN 0235-8611
QH540   CODEN: VDOSE8
▼**AKADEMIYA NAUK S.S.S.R. DAL'NEVOSTOCHNOE OTDELENIE. VESTNIK/U.S.S.R ACADEMY OF SCIENCES. FAR EASTERN BRANCH. BULLETIN.** (Text in Russian; table of contents in English) 1990. 6/yr. 9 Rub. (effective 1992). Akademiya Nauk S.S.S.R., Dal'nevostochnoe Otdelenie - U.S.S.R. Academy of Sciences, Far Eastern Branch, Ul. Leninskaya 50, Vladivostok 690600, Russia. TEL 22-25-88. Ed. Alexey V. Zhirmunsky. adv.; bk.rev.; circ. 1,000.
   —BLDSC shelfmark: 0027.740000.
   Description: Contains research papers and reviews of recent developments in all areas of science.

613   NE
AKTIVITEITENSEKTOR. MAANDBLAD; informatieblad voor bezigheidstherapie/aktiviteitenbegeleiding. 1956. m. (11/yr.). fl.79 (students fl.55). Vuga Uitgeverij BV, P.O. Box 16400, 2500 BK The Hague, Netherlands. Ed.Bd. adv.; bk.rev.; circ. 5,500.
   Formerly (until 1983): Ligament (ISSN 0024-3264)
   Description: Covers recreational therapy.

360   GW
AKTUELL JOSEFS - GESELLSCHAFT. 1986. q. Josefs - Gesellschaft e.V., Alarichstr. 40, 5000 Cologne 21, Germany. TEL 0221-88998-0. FAX 0221-8899860. circ. 50,000.
   Formerly (until 1990): Dankbrief.

360 614   CN
ALBERTA. DEPARTMENT OF FAMILY AND SOCIAL SERVICES. ANNUAL REPORT. 1945. a. free. Family and Social Services, Seventh Street Plaza, 10030 107 St., 10th fl., Edmonton, Alta. T5J 3E4, Canada. TEL 403-427-4801. FAX 422-9044. circ. 1,200.
   Former titles: Alberta. Department of Social Services. Annual Report; Alberta. Department of Social Services and Community Health. Annual Report (ISSN 0381-4327); Alberta. Department of Health and Social Development. Annual Report (ISSN 0084-6163)

SOCIAL SERVICES AND WELFARE

360 614   CN   ISSN 0707-1434
RA410.9.C2
ALBERTA. HEALTH AND SOCIAL SERVICES DISCIPLINES COMMITTEE. ANNUAL REPORT. 1977. a. free. Health and Social Services Disciplines Committee, Kensington Place, 5th Floor, 10011-109th St., Edmonton, Alta. T5J 3S8, Canada. TEL 403-427-2655. Ed. F. Rawson. circ. 800.
   Description: Gives an account of the work of the Alberta health and social services disciplines committee.

360   AT   ISSN 0706-1870
ALERT (ADELAIDE). 1980. bi-m. Aus.$19. Diabetes Association of South Australia, 114-159 Burbridge Rd., Hilton, S.A. 5033, Australia. TEL 08-2341977. Ed. P.G. Stretton. circ. 4,500.

360 616.9   US
ALERT (LOS ANGELES). m. $10 (free to qualified personnel). Universal Fellowship of Metropolitan Community Churches, c/o Rev. Steve Pieters, 5300 Santa Monica Blvd., Ste. 304, Los Angeles, CA 90029. FAX 213-464-2123. bk.rev.; circ. 1,600.
   Description: Covers AIDS related legislation, education, research and treatment.

ALL THE WORLD. see RELIGIONS AND THEOLOGY — Protestant

362.6   UK
ALMSHOUSES GAZETTE. 1950. q. 40p. National Association of Almshouses, Billingbear Lodge, Wokingham, Berkshire RG11 5RU, England. TEL 0344 52922.

ALTENHILFE; Beispiele, Informationen, Meinungen. see GERONTOLOGY AND GERIATRICS

AMBULANSEFORUM; tidsskrift for ambulanse og redningtjeneste. see PUBLIC HEALTH AND SAFETY

362.3   BE   ISSN 0002-7022
AMENTIA; la voix des parents. (Text in Dutch, French) 1963. q. 500 Fr. Association Nationale d'Aide aux Handicapes Mentaux, 13 rue Forestiere, B-1050 Brussels, Belgium. TEL 02-640-42-99. FAX 02-641-90-99. Ed. Th. Kempeneers-Foulon. adv.; bk.rev.; bibl.; illus.; circ. 8,000.

AMERICAN COUNSELOR. see EDUCATION

AMERICAN FOUNDATION FOR THE BLIND. ANNUAL REPORT. see HANDICAPPED — Visually Impaired

361.7   US   ISSN 0071-9617
AMERICAN FRIENDS SERVICE COMMITTEE. ANNUAL REPORT. 1917. a. free to contributors. American Friends Service Committee, Inc., 1501 Cherry St., Philadelphia, PA 19102. TEL 215-834-4263. FAX 215-864-0104. TELEX 247559 AFSC UR.

362.1 614   US
RA973.5
AMERICAN HEALTH CARE ASSOCIATION. PROVIDER. 1975. m. $48. American Health Care Association, 1201 L St., N.W., Washington, DC 20005. TEL 202-842-4444. FAX 202-842-3860. Ed. Marla Gold. adv.; illus.; circ. 30,000. Indexed: Abstr.Soc.Geront., CLOA, I.P.A., Med.Care Rev.
● Also available online.
   Formerly: American Health Care Association. Journal (ISSN 0360-4969)

360 610.736   US   ISSN 0749-1565
R726.8
AMERICAN JOURNAL OF HOSPICE CARE. 1983. bi-m. $42 to individuals; libraries $52. Prime National Publishing Corp., 470 Boston Post Rd., Weston, MA 02193. TEL 617-899-2702. Ed. David Lescohier. adv.; bk.rev.; charts; illus.; circ. 2,000. (back issues avail.) Indexed: Soc.Work Res.& Abstr.
   Description: Journal covering current techniques in care of terminally ill persons.
   Refereed Serial

AMERICAN JOURNAL OF ORTHOPSYCHIATRY. see PSYCHOLOGY

361.6   US   ISSN 0163-8300
AMERICAN PUBLIC WELFARE ASSOCIATION. W - MEMO. 1961. irreg. (20-25/yr.). $65 to non-members; members $65; foreign $85. American Public Welfare Association, c/o Pat Reynolds, 810 First St., N.E., Ste. 500, Washington, DC 20002-4205. TEL 202-682-0100. FAX 202-289-6555. (looseleaf format)
   Description: Covers national human service issues and policies aimed principally at state administrators.

361   US
AMERICAN RED CROSS. ANNUAL REPORT. 1901. a. free. American National Red Cross, External Communications, 17th and D Sts., N.W., Washington, DC 20006. circ. 30,000. (also avail. in microfilm from BHP)
   Formerly: American National Red Cross. Annual Report (ISSN 0080-0384)

362 610   US   ISSN 0362-4048
HD7255.A2
AMERICAN REHABILITATION. 1975. q. $5. (U.S. Rehabilitation Services Administration) U.S. Department of Education, Mary E. Switzer Bldg., Rm. 3127, 330 C St. S.W., Washington, DC 20202. TEL 202-732-1296. (Subscr. to: U.S. Supt. of Documents, Washington, DC 20402) Ed. Frank Romano. bk.rev.; circ. 8,000. (also avail. in microform from MCA,MIM) Indexed: Hlth.Ind., Ind.U.S.Gov.Per., Med.Care Rev., MEDOC, Rehabil.Lit.

360   US   ISSN 0886-1196
AMERICA'S SPIRIT. 1941. q. free to qualified personnel. United Service Organizations, Inc., U S O World Headquarters, 601 Indiana Ave., N.W., Washington, DC 20004. TEL 202-783-8121. FAX 202-638-4716. Ed. Amy E. Adler. illus.; circ. 50,000. (tabloid format; also avail. in microform from UMI)
   Formerly: Wherever They Go.

AMTLICHES MITTEILUNGSBLATT DER MARKTGEMEINDE LEOBERSDORF. see PUBLIC ADMINISTRATION — Municipal Government

362.8   UK   ISSN 0003-2840
ANCHOR.* 1947. q. $60. Apostleship of the Sea, National Board for England and Wales, Anchor House, Anlaby Rd., Hull, Yorks., England. Ed. Rev. M.F. Hardy. adv.; bk.rev.; abstr.; illus.; index; circ. 6,000.

360   IT   ISSN 0003-4568
ANNALI DELLA CARITA. 1930. m. L.20000. (Vincentian Fathers) Centro Liturgico Vincenziano, Via Pompeo Magno 21, 00192 Rome, Italy. circ. 3,000.

ANNUAIRE H L M. (Habitations a Loyer Modere) see HOUSING AND URBAN PLANNING

ANNUAL EDITIONS: HUMAN RESOURCES. see SOCIOLOGY

309.1   US   ISSN 0272-4464
HN51
ANNUAL EDITIONS: SOCIAL PROBLEMS. 1973. a. $10.95. Dushkin Publishing Group, Inc., Sluice Dock, Guilford, CT 06437-9989. TEL 203-453-4351. FAX 203-453-6000. Ed. LeRoy W. Barnes. illus. Indexed: Lang.& Lang.Behav.Abstr., Soc.Sci.Ind.
   Formerly: Annual Editions: Readings in Social Problems (ISSN 0094-9183)
   Refereed Serial

ANNUAL REPORT ON PRIVATIZATION. see PUBLIC ADMINISTRATION

ANTI-CENSORSHIP NEWSLETTER. see SOCIOLOGY

APPAREL GUILD. JOURNAL. see CLOTHING TRADE

366   FR
ARC-BOUTANT;* organe d'information des questions scolaires et familiales. 1954. m. 15 F. U.R.O,G, 28 rue de l'Ande, 31500 Toulouse, France. charts; stat.

360 300   GW   ISSN 0340-3564
ARCHIV FUER WISSENSCHAFT UND PRAXIS DER SOZIALEN ARBEIT. 1970. q. DM.60. Deutscher Verein fuer Offentliche und Private Fuersorge, Am Stockborn 1-3, 6000 Frankfurt a.M. 50, Germany. FAX 5803381. Ed. Teresa Bock. bk.rev.; circ. 800.

300   US   ISSN 0363-2903
PN6099.6
ARETE. 1970. s-w. $15. University of South Carolina, College of Social Work, Columbia, SC 29208. TEL 803-777-5291. Ed. Miriam L. Freeman. circ. 900. Indexed: Abstr.Soc.Work, Lang.& Lang.Behav.Abstr., Mid.East: Abstr.& Ind., Phys.Ed.Ind., Soc.Work Res.& Abstr., Sociol.Abstr.
   Description: Focuses on problems, issues and new developments in social work practice, social work education and social welfare.

ARKANSAS. DIVISION OF REHABILITATION SERVICES. ANNUAL REPORT. see EDUCATION — Special Education And Rehabilitation

360   US   ISSN 0004-2382
ARMENIAN WELFARE ASSOCIATION OF NEW YORK NEWS. vol.19, 1970. q. free. Armenian Welfare Association of New York, Inc., 137-41 45th Ave., Flushing, NY 11355. TEL 718-461-1504. Ed. Susan Kelekian. charts; illus.

ASSIGNMENT CHILDREN; monographs concerned with children, women and youth in development. see CHILDREN AND YOUTH — About

ASSOCIATION FRANCAISE DES AMIS D'ALBERT SCHWEITZER. CAHIERS. see PHILOSOPHY

ASSOCIATION OF GAY AND LESBIAN PSYCHIATRISTS. NEWSLETTER. see HOMOSEXUALITY

ASSOCIATION OF MENTAL HEALTH ADMINISTRATORS. NEWSLETTER. see PUBLIC HEALTH AND SAFETY

362 355.115   IT
ASSOCIAZIONE FRA MUTILATI E INVALIDI DI GUERRA. BOLLETTINO. 1918. m. Associazione fra Mutilati e Invalidi di Guerra, Piazza Adriana 3, 00193 Rome, Italy. Ed. Gerardo Agostini.

ASSOCIAZIONE NAZIONALE MUTILATI E INVALIDI DI GUERRA. SEZIONE DI ROMA. NOTIZIARIO. see MILITARY

360 362   FR
ATELIERS PROTEGES. 1960. q. 30 F. 7 bd. Chastenet-de-Gery, 96270 le Kremlin-Bicetre, France.

AUF - EINE FRAUENZEITSCHRIFT. see WOMEN'S INTERESTS

361   US
AUGUSTUS. 1978. m. $22 to individuals; institutions $45; students $17. National Center on Institutions and Alternatives, 635 Slaters Ln., Ste. G100, Alexandria, VA 22314. TEL 703-684-0373. Ed. Jerome G. Miller. bk.rev.; illus.; index; circ. 3,000. (back issues avail.)
   Formerly: Institutions, Etc. (ISSN 0276-8836)

AUSTRALIA NEW ZEALAND FOUNDATION. ANNUAL REPORT (YEAR); promoting friendship across the Tasman. see POLITICAL SCIENCE — International Relations

AUSTRALIAN AND NEW ZEALAND JOURNAL OF FAMILY THERAPY. see SOCIOLOGY

360   AT
AUSTRALIAN DEPARTMENT OF SOCIAL SECURITY. SOCIAL SECURITY JOURNAL. 1973. q. free. (Department of Social Security) Australian Government Publishing Service, G.P.O. Box 84, Canberra, A.C.T. 2601, Australia. Ed. Rosemary Lynch. bk.rev.; circ. 10,000.
   Formerly: Australian Department of Social Security. Social Security Quarterly (ISSN 0310-544X)

SOCIAL SERVICES AND WELFARE

360   AT   ISSN 0004-9557
HN841
AUSTRALIAN JOURNAL OF SOCIAL ISSUES. 1961. q. $45 to individuals; institutions $70. Australian Council of Social Service, P.O. Box 45, Railway Sq., Sydney, N.S.W. 2000, Australia. FAX 02-281-1597. Ed. Dr. Sue Kippax. adv.; bk.rev.; abstr.; bibl.; index, cum.index; circ. 1,500. (also avail. in microfilm from UMI) **Indexed:** Abstr.Soc.Work, ASSIA, Aus.P.A.I.S., Curr.Cont., Gdlns., Geo.Abstr., Int.Lab.Doc., Lang.& Lang.Behav.Abstr., Soc.Work Res.& Abstr., SSCI, World Bibl.Soc.Sec.
   Supersedes in part: A C O S S Quarterly (ISSN 0045-0391)
   Description: Articles discuss particular social issues, review conceptual problems, present empirical reports and debate policy alternatives.

360   AT
AUSTRALIAN SOCIAL SECURITY GUIDE. (In 2 vols.) 1984. 8/yr. C C H Australia Ltd., P.O. Box 230, North Ryde, N.S.W. 2113, Australia. TEL 02-888-2555. FAX 02-888-7324.

360   AT   ISSN 0312-407X
AUSTRALIAN SOCIAL WORK. 1947. q. Aus.$80. Australian Association of Social Workers, P.O. Box 84, Hawker, Canberra, A.C.T. 2614, Australia. TEL 06-255-1626. FAX 06-255-2225. Ed. Elizabeth Rabbitts. adv.; bk.rev.; charts; index; circ. 3,500. (tabloid format) **Indexed:** ASSIA, Aus.P.A.I.S., Soc.Work Res.& Abstr., Sp.Ed.Needs Abstr., Stud.Wom.Abstr.
   —BLDSC shelfmark: 1820.600000.
   Formerly: Australian Journal of Social Work (ISSN 0004-9565)

368.4   AT
AUSTRALIAN SUPERANNUATION LAW AND PRACTICE. (In 2 vols.) 1972. 10/yr. C C H Australia Ltd., P.O. Box 230, North Ryde, N.S.W. 2113, Australia. TEL 888-2555. FAX 02-888-7324.
   Former titles (until 1991): Australian Superannuation and Employment Benefits Guide; (until 1980): Australian Superannuation and Employment Benefits Planning in Action (ISSN 0310-1347)

362.6   AT
▼**AUSTRALIAN SUPERANNUATION SOURCE MATERIALS.** 1991. irreg. C C H Australia Ltd., P.O. Box 230, North Ryde, N.S.W. 2113, Australia. TEL 02-888-2555. FAX 02-888-7324.

362.7   AU
AUSTRIA. STATISTISCHES ZENTRALAMT. JUGENDWOHLFAHRTSPFLEGE. (Subseries of its: Beitraege zur Oesterreichischen Statistik) 1965. a. S.110. Oesterreichisches Statistisches Zentralamt, Hintere Zollamtsstr. 2b, 1033 Vienna, Austria.
   Description: Activity of tribunals and administrative authorities, with information on education assistance and child welfare work.

360   IT   ISSN 0392-2278
AUTONOMIE LOCALI E SERVIZI SOCIALI; vademecum a schede. 1978. 3/yr. L.100000. Societa Editrice Il Mulino, Strada Maggiore, 37, 40125 Bologna, Italy. TEL 051-256011. FAX 051-256034. Ed.Bd. adv.; index; circ. 4,000. (back issues avail.)

AUTUMN SCHOOL OF STUDIES ON ALCOHOL & DRUGS. PROCEEDINGS OF SEMINARS. see *DRUG ABUSE AND ALCOHOLISM*

360   IS   ISSN 0334-4525
AVAREYANUT VESTIYA CHEURATI/CRIME AND SOCIAL DEVIANCE. (Text in Hebrew; summaries in English) 1972. a. $14. (Bar-Ilan University, Department of Criminology) Bar-Ilan University Press, Ramat Gan 52900, Israel. Ed. Israel Nachshon. adv.; bk.rev.; abstr.; bibl.; charts; illus.; stat.; index; circ. 500. (back issues avail.) **Indexed:** Ind.Heb.Per., Sociol.Abstr.

360   IT   ISSN 0005-2566
AZIONE COOPERATIVA. 1911. fortn. free. Comitato Regionale Lombardo delle Cooperative, Via Palmanova 22, 20132 Milan, Italy. Ed. Lidia Lommi. adv.; bk.rev.; circ. controlled.

361   UK   ISSN 0260-082X
B A A F DISCUSSION SERIES. irreg. British Agencies for Adoption & Fostering, 11 Southwark St., London SE1 1RQ, England. TEL 071-407-8800.
   —BLDSC shelfmark: 3597.994500.
   Description: Presents current issues of interest to workers in the area of social service and welfare.

362.7   UK   ISSN 0260-3888
B A A F NEWS. 1981. m. British Agencies for Adoption & Fostering, 11 Southwark St., London SE1 1RQ, England. TEL 071-407-8800.
   Formerly: A B A F A News.
   Description: Includes news and information on publications, practice, policy, legislation, training events and seminars.

361   UK   ISSN 0260-0803
B A A F PRACTICE SERIES. irreg. British Agencies for Adoption & Fostering, 11 Southwark St., London SE1 1RQ, England. TEL 071-407-8800.
   —BLDSC shelfmark: 6597.420000.
   Description: Covers the major practice needs of workers in adoption, fostering and child care.

361   UK   ISSN 0260-0811
B A A F RESEARCH SERIES. irreg. British Agencies for Adoption & Fostering, 11 Southwark St., London SE1 1RQ, England. TEL 071-407-8800.
   —BLDSC shelfmark: 7769.810000.
   Description: Recent research on adoption, fostering and child care.

B A S H MAGAZINE. (Bulimia Anorexia Self-Help) see *MEDICAL SCIENCES — Psychiatry And Neurology*

352.4 362.6   UK
B L E S M A G. 1947. 3/yr. £1. (British Limbless Ex-Servicemen's Association) M & B (Felstead) Ltd., 185-187 High Rd., Chadwell Heath, Essex RM6 6NA, England. TEL 01-590-1124. Ed. R.R. Holland. adv.; bk.rev.; circ. 10,000 (controlled). (back issues avail.)
   Description: Promotes the welfare of those of either sex who have lost a limb or limbs, or one or both eyes as a result of service in any branch of Her Majesty's Forces.

360   619   US   ISSN 1042-7015
B N A SPECIAL REPORT SERIES ON WORK & FAMILY. 1988. m. $475. The Bureau of National Affairs, Inc., 1231 25th St., N.W., Washington, DC 20037. TEL 202-452-4200. FAX 202-822-8092. TELEX 285656 BNAI WSH. (Subscr. to: 9435 Key West Ave., Rockville, MD 20850. TEL 800-372-1033) Ed. Andrew B. Douglas. (back issues avail.)
   ●Also available online. Vendor(s): Human Resources Information Network.
   Description: Focuses on such work and family issues as elder care, child care, adoption assistance plans, the union's role in work and family, and psychiatric care for families.

361.77   GW
BAFF. 1970. q. Bayerisches Jugendrotkreuz, Holbeinstr. 11, 8000 Munich 86, Germany. TEL 089-9241341. FAX 089-989526. bk.rev.; circ. 10,500.
   Description: Information about Red Cross youth and youth activities for readers between the ages of 8 and 25.

DAS BAND. see *EDUCATION — Special Education And Rehabilitation*

360   AU   ISSN 0005-5999
BARMHERZIGKEIT; Blaetter fuer die Freunde des Hauses der Barmherzigkeit. 1959. q. free. Institut "Haus der Barmherzigkeit", Vinzenzg. 2-6, A-1180 Vienna, Austria. Ed. Karl Pilnacek. abstr.; circ. 800,000.

360   UK
BARNARDO NEWS. bi-m. free. Barnardo's, Tanners Lane, Barkingside, Ilford, Essex IG6 7QG, England. TEL 081-550-8822. FAX 081-551-6870. Ed. Lix Bestic. circ. 670,000.
   Description: News about child care and appeals work.

360   GW   ISSN 0171-9319
BEGEGNEN UND HELFEN. 1912. q. DM.14. Verband der Caritas-Konferenzen Deutschlands, Lorenz-Werthmann-Haus, Postfach 420, 7800 Freiburg, Germany. TEL 0761-2001. (Co-sponsor: Gemeinschaft der Vinzenzkonferenzen Deutschlands) Ed.Bd. bk.rev.; index; circ. 11,000.

362.6 363.6   BE   ISSN 0067-558X
BELGIUM. MINISTERE DE LA PREVOYANCE SOCIALE. RAPPORT GENERAL SUR LA SECURITE SOCIALE. (Text in Flemish or French) 1962. a. 325 BEF. Ministere de la Prevoyance Sociale, Rue de la Vierge Noire 3C, B-1000 Brussels, Belgium. Ed.Bd.

360   614   BE
BELGIUM. MINISTERE DE LA SANTE PUBLIQUE ET DE LA FAMILLE. RAPPORT ANNUEL. (Text in Dutch and French) 1954. a. Ministere de la Sante Publique et de la Famille, Cite Administrative de l'Etat, Bibliotheque, Quartier Vesale, 1010 Brussels, Belgium. charts; stat.

BERNIE. see *CHILDREN AND YOUTH — For*

362.7   370   GW
BERUFSAUSBILDUNG JUGENDARBEITSLOSIGKEIT. 1976. m. DM.350. U. Kurz Verlag, Korallenweg 10, Postfach 750365, 7000 Stuttgart 75, Germany. TEL 0711-442076. FAX 0711-445644. Ed. Heinz Kurz. circ. 450.

BETHPHAGE MESSENGER. see *EDUCATION — Special Education And Rehabilitation*

360   NE
DE BIJSTAANDER; personeelsblad. 1952. m. free. Gemeentelijke Sociale Dienst, Vlaardingenlaan 15, 1062 HM Amsterdam, Netherlands. TEL 020-5160828. FAX 020-174841. Ed.Bd. adv.; bk.rev.; illus.; circ. 3,400.
   Formerly: Socioscoop (ISSN 0038-0458)

BLACK CHILD ADVOCATE. see *CHILDREN AND YOUTH — About*

360   GW
BLAETTER DER WOHLFAHRTSPFLEGE; Fachzeitschrift fuer Sozialarbeit und Sozialpaedagogik in der Bundesrepublik Deutschland. 1848. m. DM.68.80. Wohlfahrtswerk fuer Baden-Wuerttemberg, Falkertstr. 29, 7000 Stuttgart 1, Germany. Ed. Gerhard Pfannendoerfer. adv.; bk.rev.; bibl.; index; circ. 5,500.

360   GW   ISSN 0067-9178
BLICK HINTER DIE FASSADE; Aspekte moderner Sozialarbeit. 1961. a. DM.90. Kodex-Verlag GmbH, Eugenstr. 16, 7000 Stuttgart 1, Germany.

362.7   DK
BOERNS TRIVSEL I TIDEN. 1905. s-m. (22/yr.). DKK 380. Boernesagens Faellsraad, Lauravej 14, St., 2500 Valby, Denmark. Ed. Claus Hegelund. adv.; circ. 4,000.
   Former titles: Boern i Tiden; Boern i Tiden - Boernesagens Tidende.
   Description: Offers articles covering the issues of the welfare of children.

362.7   US   ISSN 0889-6828
BOYS TOWN QUARTERLY. 1976. q. $10 donation. Father Flanagan's Boys Home, Boys Town, NE 68010. TEL 402-498-1301. FAX 402-498-1225. Ed. John Melingagio. illus.; circ. 600,000. (also avail. in microform from UMI)
   Supersedes: Boys Town Times.
   Description: Provides news of the programs and of the people from around the world who visit the world-famous Boys Town campus.

BRAILLE SPORTING RECORD. see *HANDICAPPED — Visually Impaired*

361.6   BL
BRASILIA. FUNDACAO DO SERVICO SOCIAL DO DISTRITO FEDERAL. RELATORIO ANUAL DAS ATIVIDADES. a. Fundacao do Servico Social do Distrito Federal, Brasilia, Brazil.

360   BL
BRAZIL. SERVICO SOCIAL DO COMERCIO. ADMINISTRACAO REGIONAL DO ESTADO DE SAO PAULO. RELATORIA ANNUAL. 1958. a. free. Servico Social do Comercio, Administracao Regional do Estado de Sao Paulo, Rua Dr. Vila Nova, 228, Sao Paulo, Brazil. illus.; circ. 2,000.

S

SOCIAL SERVICES AND WELFARE

362.8 US ISSN 1045-1005
BREAD FOR THE WORLD NEWSLETTER. 1974. 10/yr. $25. Bread for the World, 802 Rhode Island Ave., N.E., Washington, DC 20018. TEL 202-269-0200. FAX 202-529-8546. Ed. Carole Zimmerman. circ. 40,000. (back issues avail.)
 Incorporates (1980-1989): Leaven (Washington); (1986-1989): Action Alert (Washington, 1986); (1974-1989): Bread; Which was formerly (until 1986): Bread for the World (ISSN 0198-6511)
 Description: News of the movement and background articles on issues relevant to worship and world hunger.

BRIDGE. see CRIMINOLOGY AND LAW ENFORCEMENT

BRIEF AUS WAHLWIES; Mitteilungen aus dem Pestalozzi Kinder- und Jugenddorf. see CHILDREN AND YOUTH — About

361 UK
BRITISH ASSOCIATION OF SOCIAL WORKERS. ANNUAL REPORT. 1970. a. £2. British Association of Social Workers, 16 Kent St., Birmingham B5 6RD, England. adv.; bk.rev.; bibl.; tr.lit.; circ. 14,000.

361 CN
BRITISH COLUMBIA. MINISTRY OF SOCIAL SERVICES AND HOUSING. SERVICES FOR PEOPLE. ANNUAL REPORT (YEAR). 1945. a. free. Ministry of Social Services and Housing, Communications Division, Parliament Buildings, Victoria, B.C. V8V 1X4, Canada. TEL 604-387-6485. circ. 5,000.
 Former titles: British Columbia. Ministry of Human Resources. Services for People (ISSN 0317-4670); British Columbia. Department of Human Resources. Annual Report (ISSN 0068-1466)

361 UK ISSN 0045-3102
HV1 CODEN: BJSWAS
BRITISH JOURNAL OF SOCIAL WORK. 1971. 6/yr. £70($140) Oxford University Press, Oxford Journals, Pinkhill House, Southfield Road, Eynsham, Oxford OX8 1JJ, England. TEL 0865-882283. FAX 0865-882890. TELEX 837330 OXPRES G. Ed. Barbara L. Hudson. adv.; bk.rev.; abstr.; circ. 3,000. (also avail. in microform from UMI) **Indexed:** Abstr.Health Care Manage.Stud., Adol.Ment.Hlth.Abstr., ASSIA, Br.Hum.Ind., Curr.Cont., Mid.East: Abstr.& Ind., Psychol.Abstr., Sage Fam.Stud.Abstr., Sage Urb.Stud.Abstr., Soc.Work Res.& Abstr., SSCI, Stud.Wom.Abstr.
 —BLDSC shelfmark: 2324.790000.
 Description: Papers on the research and practice of every aspect of social work. Examines its principles and theories.

BRITISH POLIO FELLOWSHIP. BULLETIN. see MEDICAL SCIENCES — Psychiatry And Neurology

BROWN UNIVERSITY CHILD AND ADOLESCENT BEHAVIOR LETTER; monthly reports on the problems of children and adolescents growing up. see PSYCHOLOGY

BUND DER DEUTSCHEN KATHOLISCHEN JUGEND. INFORMATIONSDIENST. see CHILDREN AND YOUTH — For

360 FR
C A F REVUE. 1948. 8/yr. 120 F. Caisse Nationale des Allocations Familiales, 23 rue Daviel, 75634 Paris Cedex 13, France. Ed. Daniel Bequignon. bk.rev.; bibl.; charts; illus.; circ. 7,500.
 Formerly: C A F Bulletin Mensuel (ISSN 0409-6568)

C B M I FAMILY MAGAZINE. (Christian Blind Mission International Inc.) see HANDICAPPED — Visually Impaired

C E N S I S NOTE E COMMENTI. (Centro Studi Investimenti Sociali) see SOCIOLOGY

360 NQ
C E P A D. INFORME ANUAL. a. Comite Evangelico Pro-Ayuda al Desarrollo, Departamento de Documentacion y Comunicacion Popular, Managua, Nicaragua.

360 US
C J F ANNUAL REPORT. a. Council of Jewish Federations, Inc., 730 Broadway, 2nd Fl., New York, NY 10003. TEL 212-474-5000.
 Formerly: C J F Annual Review.

360 296 US
C J F ENDOWMENT REVIEW. 1983. q. $8. Council of Jewish Federations, Inc., Endowment Development Department, 730 Broadway, New York, NY 10003. TEL 212-475-5000. Ed. Donald Kent. bk.rev.; circ. 27,000.
 Description: Focuses on charitable giving.

360 320 UK ISSN 0261-0183
C S P: CRITICAL SOCIAL POLICY; a journal of socialist theory and practice in social welfare. 1981. 3/yr. £52($91) (Critical Social Policy) Longman Group UK Ltd., Westgate House, The High, Harlow, Essex CM20 1YR, England. TEL 0279-442601. Ed.Bd. adv.; bk.rev.; illus.; circ. 800. **Indexed:** ASSIA, Lang.& Lang.Behav.Abstr.
 —BLDSC shelfmark: 3487.485500.

C U S A N. (Catholics United for Spirtual Action) see RELIGIONS AND THEOLOGY — Roman Catholic

CALIFORNIA FAMILY LAW MONTHLY. see LAW — Family And Matrimonial Law

360 US
CALIFORNIA STATE PLAN FOR REHABILITATION FACILITIES. a. Health and Welfare Agency, Department of Rehabilitation, 830 K St. Mall, Sacramento, CA 95814.

362.4 CN ISSN 0045-4001
CALIPER. 1945. q. Can.$10 to individuals; institutions Can.$13. Canadian Paraplegic Association, National Office, 1500 Don Mills Rd., Suite 201, Don Mills, Ont. M3B 3K4, Canada. TEL 416-391-0203. FAX 416-391-2144. Ed. Greg Pyc. adv.; bk.rev.; film rev.; circ. 5,000.

CANADA. DEPARTMENT OF NATIONAL HEALTH AND WELFARE. ANNUAL REPORT. see PUBLIC HEALTH AND SAFETY

300 CN ISSN 0068-8584
CANADIAN COUNCIL ON SOCIAL DEVELOPMENT. ANNUAL REPORT - RAPPORT ANNUEL. (Text in English and French) 1920. a. Can.$50 membership. Canadian Council on Social Development, 55 Parkdale Ave., Box 3505, Station C, Ottawa, Ont. K1Y 4G1, Canada. TEL 613-728-1865. FAX 613-728-9387. circ. 5,000.

360 CN
CANADIAN FACT BOOK ON POVERTY/DONNEES DE BASE SUR LA PAUVRETE AU CANADA. 1975. irreg. price varies. Canadian Council on Social Development, 55 Parkdale Ave., PO Box 3505, Station C, Ottawa, Ont. K1Y 4G1, Canada. TEL 613-728-1865. FAX 613-728-9387.

CANADIAN NATIONAL INSTITUTE FOR THE BLIND. NATIONAL ANNUAL REPORT. see HANDICAPPED — Visually Impaired

362.4 CN ISSN 0068-9424
CANADIAN PARAPLEGIC ASSOCIATION. ANNUAL REPORT. 1946. a. free. Canadian Paraplegic Association, National Office, 1500 Don Mills Rd., Suite 201, Don Mills, Ont. M3B 3K4, Canada. TEL 416-391-0203. FAX 416-391-2144. circ. 5,000.

361.5 CN ISSN 0068-9572
CANADIAN RED CROSS SOCIETY. ANNUAL REPORT. (Text in English and French) 1914. a. free. Canadian Red Cross Society, National Headquarters, 5700 Cancross Court, Mississauga, Ont. L5R 3E9, Canada. TEL 416-890-1000. circ. 60,000.

361.77 CN ISSN 0700-9828
CANADIAN RED CROSS SOCIETY. MANITOBA DIVISION. NEWS AND VIEWS. 1971. q. free. Canadian Red Cross Society, Manitoba Division, 200 - 360 Broadway, Winnipeg, Man. R3C 0T6, Canada. TEL 204-982-7300. FAX 204-942-8367. Ed.Bd. circ. 4,500. (back issues avail.)
 Description: Includes information of Red Cross activities in Manitoba and around the world.

360 CN ISSN 0820-909X
CANADIAN SOCIAL WORK REVIEW/REVUE CANADIENNE DE SERVICE SOCIAL. (Text in English and French) 1974. s-a. Can.$20 to individuals (foreign Can.$24); institutions Can.$30 (foreign Can.$36). Canadian Association of Schools of Social Work, 55 Parkdale Ave., Ottawa, Ont. K1Y 6C5, Canada. TEL 613-722-2974. (Subscr. to: Wilfrid Laurier University Press, Waterloo, Ont. N2L 3C5, Canada) Eds. Roland Lecomte, Marilyn Callahan. adv.; bk.rev.; circ. 450. **Indexed:** Can.Wom.Per.Ind., Soc.Work Res.& Abstr.
 —BLDSC shelfmark: 3044.741000.
 Supersedes (in 1983): Canadian Journal of Social Work Education (ISSN 0316-8565)
 Description: Aims to enhance social work knowledge, practice and education.

360 UK ISSN 0952-8636
CARE WEEKLY; for residential & day care professionals. 1987. w. £45. Inside Communications, Nine White Lion St., Islington, London N1 9XJ, England. TEL 071-837-8727. FAX 071-278-1889. adv.; bk.rev.; circ. 25,537.

361.5 US
CARE WORLD REPORT. 1972. q. free. Care, Inc., 660 First Ave., New York, NY 10016. TEL 212-686-3110. FAX 212-686-3675. Ed. Matt De Galan. circ. 400,000.

CAREER PLANNING & ADULT DEVELOPMENT JOURNAL. see EDUCATION — Adult Education

CAREER PLANNING AND ADULT DEVELOPMENT NETWORK NEWSLETTER; a newsletter for career counselors, educators, and human resource specialists. see EDUCATION — Adult Education

CAREGIVING. see GERONTOLOGY AND GERIATRICS

CARING (WASHINGTON). see MEDICAL SCIENCES — Nurses And Nursing

360 GW ISSN 0008-6614
CARITAS; Zeitschrift fuer Caritasarbeit und Caritaswissenschaft. 1896. m. DM.70. (Deutscher Caritasverband) Lambertus-Verlag GmbH, Woelflinstr. 4, Postfach 1026, 7800 Freiburg, Germany. TEL 0761-31566. FAX 0761-37064. Ed. Thomas Becker. adv.; bk.rev.; bibl.; charts; index; circ. 2,500. **Indexed:** CERDIC, SSCi.
 —BLDSC shelfmark: 3053.290000.

361 GW ISSN 0069-0570
CARITAS; JAHRBUCH DES DEUTSCHEN CARITASVERBANDES. 1968. a. DM.21($10) Deutscher Caritasverband, Karlstr. 40, 7800 Freiburg, Germany. FAX 0761-200572.
 —BLDSC shelfmark: 3053.291000.

361 GW ISSN 0008-6622
CARITAS-KORRESPONDENZ; Informationsblaetter fuer die Caritaspraxis. 1929. m. DM.68. (Deutscher Caritasverband) Lambertus-Verlag GmbH, Woelflinstr. 4, Postfach 1026, 7800 Freiburg, Germany. TEL 0761-31566. FAX 0761-37064. Ed. Hans Harro Buehler. adv.; circ. 4,800. (processed)

360 AU
CARITAS-ZEITSCHRIFT. 1947. 6/yr. Caritas, Trauttmansdorffg. 15, A-1130 Vienna, Austria. FAX 587-157713. Ed. Wolfgang Bergmann. adv.; bk.rev.; abstr.; bibl.; circ. 12,000.
 Former titles: Caritas & Oesterreichische Caritas Zeitschrift (ISSN 0029-8980)

301.4 IT ISSN 0008-7122
CASA; rivista della famiglia - studi, esperienza, documentazioni e pagine varie per la famiglia e la casa. (Supplements avail.) 1943. m. L.35000. Istituto "la Casa", Via Lattuada 14, 20135 Milan, Italy. Ed. Paolo Liggeri. adv.; bk.rev.; illus.

360 US ISSN 0008-7246
CASE & COUNSEL; North Dakota human service report. 1966. m. free. Department of Human Services, State Capitol, 600 East Blvd., Bismarck, ND 58505. FAX 701-224-2359. Ed. Mary Jane Low. illus.; circ. 2,000. **Indexed:** Law Ofc.Info.Svc.
 Formerly: Case and Comment (Bismarck).

SOCIAL SERVICES AND WELFARE

362.8   IT   ISSN 0008-7416
CASSA DI SOCCORSO E MALATTIA PER I DIPENDENTI DELL'AZIENDA TRASPORTI MUNICIPALI DI MILANO. BOLLETTINO D'INFORMAZIONE.* 1954. bi-m. free. Cassa di Soccorso e Malattia per i Dipendenti dell' Azienda Trasporti Municipali di Milano, Via. P. Lomazzo 27, 20154 Milan, Italy.

360 282   US
CATALYST (ST. DAVIDS). bi-m. membership. North American Association of Christians in Social Work, Box 7090, St. Davids, PA 19087-7090. TEL 215-687-5777.

361   US
CATHOLIC RELIEF SERVICES. ANNUAL REPORT. a. Catholic Relief Services, 209 W. Fayette St., Baltimore, MD 21201-3403. TEL 301-625-2220. FAX 301-685-1635.
   Description: Covers various types of information including financial statements, country updates, and headquarters information.

360   US   ISSN 0886-1811
CATHOLIC WAR VETERAN. 6/yr. Catholic War Veterans, U.S.A., 419 N. Lee St., Alexandria, VA 22314. TEL 216-333-2951. Ed. William J. Gill.

360 374   UK
CENTRAL COUNCIL FOR EDUCATION AND TRAINING IN SOCIAL WORK. REPORT OF COUNCIL MEETING. 1978. irreg. free. Central Council for Education and Training in Social Work, Derbyshire House, St. Chad's St., London WC1H 8AD, England. FAX 071-278-2934. Ed. George Smith. illus.; circ. controlled.
   Supersedes (in 1988): C C E T S W Reporting; Which supersedes (with no.3, 1979): C C E T S W News (ISSN 0142-2693); Which was formerly (until 1978): C C E T S W Bulletin.

360   BG
CHAKRA. (Text in Bengali) w. 242A Nakhalpara, P.O. Box 2682, Dhaka 1215, Bangladesh. TEL 2-604568. Ed. Husneara Aziz.

362.7   AT
CHALLENGE ADVOCATE. 1956; N.S. q. free. Challenge Foundation of New South Wales, 8 Junction St., P.O. Box 229, Ryde, N.S.W. 2112, Australia. TEL 02-807-2822. FAX 02-809-5327. adv.; circ. 4,500.
   Formerly (until 1984): Sub-Normal Children's Welfare Association. Welfare News (ISSN 0049-2418)

360   FR   ISSN 0339-686X
CHAMP SOCIAL. q. 70 F. Editions Solin, 1 rue des Fosses St. Jacques, 75005 Paris, France.

360   UK   ISSN 0263-8371
CHANGES; an international journal of psychology and psychotherapy. 1983. q. £18($36) to individuals; institutions £35($70). (Psychology and Psychotherapy Association) Lawrence Erlbaum Associates Ltd., 27 Palmeira Mansions, Church Rd., Hove, E. Sussex BN3 2FA, England. TEL 0273-207411. FAX 0273-205612. Ed. Craig Newnes. adv.; bk.rev.; circ. 2,000. **Indexed:** ASSIA.
—BLDSC shelfmark: 3129.656500.
   Description: Provides a forum for the exchange of ideas, experiences and views of people working in psychology, nursing, education, medicine, and social work.
Refereed Serial

CHANNELS (EXETER); communications and management ideas for non-profit organizations. see *ADVERTISING AND PUBLIC RELATIONS*

361.73   US
▼**CHARITABLE ORGANIZATIONS OF THE U S.** 1990. biennial. $139.50. Gale Research Inc., 835 Penobscot Bldg., Detroit, MI 48226. TEL 800-877-4253. FAX 313-961-6083. TELEX 810-221-7086. Ed. Doris Morris Maxfield.

360   UK   ISSN 0590-9783
CHARITIES DIGEST (YEAR). 1882. a. £10.95. Family Welfare Association, 501-505 Kingsland Rd., London E8 4AU, England. TEL 071-254-6251. FAX 071-249-5443. Ed.Bd. adv.; circ. 6,500.
   Description: Major listing of UK charities with contact addresses.

361.7   US   ISSN 0364-0760
HV530
CHARITIES U S A. 1974. q. $25 (foreign $33). Catholic Charities U S A, 1731 King St., Ste. 200, Alexandria, VA 22314. TEL 703-549-1390. FAX 703-549-1656. Ed. Alexandra Peeler. illus.; circ. 3,000.
   Description: Focuses on social justice and social service issues of interest to US Catholic Charities members, such as poverty, family counseling, aging issues, low-income housing, emergency service, teen pregnancy, and adoption.

361.73   UK   ISSN 0265-5209
CHARITY. 1983. m. £30. Charities Aid Foundation, 48 Pembury Rd., Tonbridge, Kent TN9 2JD, England. TEL 0732-771-333. Ed. Stewart Lawrie. bk.rev.; circ. 2,500. (back issues avail.)
—BLDSC shelfmark: 3129.918670.
   Description: For people giving, receiving and managing charitable money.

361   UK
CHART AND COMPASS INTERNATIONAL. 1818. s-a. free. British Sailors' Society, 3a Orchard Place, Southampton, Hampshire SO9 7SS, England. TEL 0703-337333. FAX 0703-338333. TELEX 477986 SAILOR G. Ed. Rev. James MacDonald. bk.rev.; illus.; circ. 60,000.
   Formerly: Chart and Compass.

362.7 970.1   US
CHEROKEE VOICE. 1981. q. Cherokee Children's Home, Box 507, Cherokee, NC 28719. Ed. Stan Bienick. circ. 3,000.
   Description: Contains items of interest to the American Indian community.

362.7 155.4   UK   ISSN 0952-9136
CODEN: CABEEB
▼**CHILD ABUSE REVIEW.** 1992. 3/yr. $90. John Wiley & Sons Ltd., Journals, Baffins Lane, Chichester, Sussex PO19 1UD, England. TEL 0243-779777. FAX 0243-775878. TELEX 86290-WIBOOK-G. Eds. Kevin Browne, Margaret Lynch.
—BLDSC shelfmark: 3172.912700.
   Description: Reflects current child welfare issues and concerns.

362.7   US   ISSN 0145-935X
HV701   CODEN: CYSEDP
CHILD & YOUTH SERVICES. 1977. s-a. $40 to individuals; institutions $85; libraries $160. Haworth Press, Inc., 10 Alice St., Binghamton, NY 13904. TEL 800-342-9678. FAX 607-722-1424. Ed. Jerome Beker. adv.; bk.rev.; abstr.; bibl.; circ. 221. (also avail. in microfiche from HAW; back issues avail.; reprint service avail. from HAW) **Indexed:** Adol.Ment.Hlth.Abstr., Behav.Abstr., Biol.Abstr., Bull.Signal., C.I.J.E., Chicago Psychoanal.Lit.Ind., Child Devel.Abstr., CJPI, Crim.Just.Abstr., Educ.Ind., Except.Child Educ.Abstr., Human Resour.Abstr., Lang.& Lang.Behav.Abstr., Past.Care & Couns.Abstr., PSI, Psychol.Abstr., Ref.Zh., Rehabil.Lit., Sage Fam.Stud.Abstr., Soc.Work. Res.& Abstr., Sociol.Abstr., Sociol.Educ.Abstr., Sp.Ed.Needs Abstr., Stud.Wom.Abstr.
—BLDSC shelfmark: 3172.916000.
   Description: Each issue covers one particular topic regarding conditions of young people in our society.
Refereed Serial

CHILD CARE FOCUS. see *CHILDREN AND YOUTH — About*

CHILD HEALTH TALK. see *CHILDREN AND YOUTH — About*

362.7   US   ISSN 0009-4021
CODEN: CHWFA
CHILD WELFARE; journal of policy, practice and program. 1920. bi-m. $50 to individuals (foreign $70); institutions $60 (foreign $80). (Child Welfare League of America, Inc.) Transaction Publishers, Transaction Periodicals Consortium, Department 3092, Rutgers University, New Brunswick, NJ 08903. TEL 908-932-2280. FAX 908-932-3138. Ed. Carl Schoenberg. adv.; bk.rev.; charts; index; circ. 12,000. (also avail. in microform from MIM,UMI; reprint service avail. from KTO,UMI) **Indexed:** Acad.Ind., Adol.Ment.Hlth.Abstr., ASSIA, C.I.J.E., Child Devel.Abstr., CINAHL, Crim.Just.Abstr., Curr.Cont., Curr.Lit.Fam.Plan., Educ.Ind., Except.Child Educ.Abstr., Hlth.Ind., Ind.Med., Lang.& Lang.Behav.Abstr., P.A.I.S., PHRA, PSI, Psychol.Abstr., Sage Fam.Stud.Abstr., Soc.Sci.Ind., Soc.Work Res.& Abstr., Sp.Ed.Needs Abstr., SSCI.
—BLDSC shelfmark: 3172.950000.
   Formerly: Child Welfare League of America. Bulletin.
   Description: Presents special problems facing millions of children who are homeless, abused, new to this country, or severely disabled.

362.7   US
CHILD WELFARE LEAGUE OF AMERICA. DIRECTORY OF MEMBER AND ASSOCIATE AGENCIES. a. $14. Child Welfare League of America, Inc., 440 First St., Ste. 310, Washington, DC 20001-2085. TEL 202-638-2952. FAX 202-638-4004.
   Former titles: Child Welfare League of America. Directory of Member And Associate Agencies Listing; Child Welfare League of America. Directory of Member Agencies and Associates (ISSN 0529-1674)

362.7   JA
CHILD WELFARE QUARTERLY. q. Intercontinental Marketing Corp., P.O. Box 5056, Tokyo 100-31, Japan. TEL 86-3-3661-8373. FAX 81-3-3667-9646.

301.412   US   ISSN 1055-9221
CHILD, YOUTH, AND FAMILY FUTURES CLEARINGHOUSE. 1985. bi-m. $23.95. Children's Defense Fund, 25 E St., N.W., Washington, DC 20001. TEL 202-628-8787. FAX 202-783-7324. charts; stat. (back issues avail.)
   Formerly (until 1990): Adolescent Pregnancy Prevention Clearinghouse (ISSN 0899-5591)
   Description: Each issue examines a specific aspect of America's teen pregnancy crisis; includes strategies for pregnancy prevention, based on the theory of improving young people's ability to make the transition from childhood to adulthood.

CHILDREN AND YOUTH SERVICES REVIEW; an international multidisciplinary review of the welfare of young people. see *CHILDREN AND YOUTH — About*

562.7   FI   ISSN 0783-6244
CHILDREN IN FINLAND. irreg. FIM 10. Lastensuojelun Keskusliitto - Central Union for Child Welfare in Finland, Armfeltintie 1, 00150 Helsinki 15, Finland. FAX 0-627990. Ed. S. Utriainen.

362.8   US
CHILDREN IN HOSPITALS (NEWSLETTER). 1972. q. $10. Children in Hospitals, Inc., 31 Wilshire Pk., Needham, MA 02192. TEL 617-482-2915. Eds. Margaret King Saphier, Barbara Popper. bk.rev.; circ. 300.

CHILDREN TODAY; an interdisciplinary journal for the professions serving children. see *CHILDREN AND YOUTH — About*

362.7   US
CHILDREN'S AID SOCIETY NEWS. 1971. s-a. free. Children's Aid Society, 105 East 22 St., New York, NY 10010. TEL 212-949-4800. Ed. Rita C. Arsht. charts; illus.; circ. 35,000.
   Former titles: Children's Aid Society Newsletter; Children's Aid Society News (ISSN 0045-6667)

SOCIAL SERVICES AND WELFARE

362.7 US ISSN 0273-9615
RJ242
CHILDREN'S HEALTH CARE JOURNAL. 1973. q. $23. (Association for the Care of Children's Health) Waverly Press, Inc. (Subsidiary of: Williams & Wilkins), 428 E. Preston St., Box 64025, Baltimore, MD 21202. TEL 301-528-4000. Ed. Dr. William Rae. adv.; bk.rev.; circ. 4,000 (controlled). (also avail. in microform from UMI; reprint service avail. from UMI) **Indexed:** CINAHL, Psychol.Abstr.
—BLDSC shelfmark: 3172.990200.
Former titles: Association for the Care of Children's Health. Journal (ISSN 0274-8916); Association for the Care of Children in Hospitals. Journal (ISSN 0145-3351)

362.7 US ISSN 1057-736X
HV741
CHILDREN'S VOICE. 1985. q. $35 to individuals; institutions $50. Child Welfare League of America, Inc., 440 First St., N.W., Ste. 310, Washington, DC 20001-2085. TEL 202-638-2952. FAX 202-638-4004.
Formed by the merger of (1976-1984): Child Welfare Planning Notes; (1971-1984): Child Welfare League Newsletter (ISSN 0045-6659); (1979-1984): C W L A - Crittenton Reporter on School-Age Parenting.
Description: Reports current program and policy developments in child welfare services.

CHILDREN'S WELFARE ASSOCIATION OF VICTORIA. NEWSLETTER. see *CHILDREN AND YOUTH — About*

362.7 UK ISSN 0009-4218
CHILD'S GUARDIAN. 1887. 4/yr. free. National Society for the Prevention of Cruelty to Children, 67 Saffron Hill, London EC1N 8RS, England. TEL 071-242-1626. FAX 071-831-9562. bk.rev.; illus.; circ. 20,000.

361.73 US ISSN 1040-676X
CHRONICLE OF PHILANTHROPY. 1988. bi-w. $57.50. Chronicle of Higher Education, Inc., 1255 23rd St., N.W., Ste. 700, Washington, DC 20037. TEL 202-466-1200. FAX 202-296-2691. TELEX 892505. (Subscr. to: Box 1989, Marion, OH 43306) Ed. Philip Semas. (reprint service avail. from UMI) **Indexed:** PSI.
Description: Provides news and information for fund raisers, professional employees of foundations, corporate grant makers, and people who work for non-profit, tax-exempt organizations in health, education, religion, the arts, and social services.

362.4 AT
CITIZEN ADVOCACY NEWS. 1983. bi-m. Aus.$5. Suite 3, 266 Hay St., Subiaco, W.A. 6008, Australia. TEL 09-342-4833. Ed. Margaret Maher. circ. 180.

361.8 US
CITIZEN NEWS. 6/yr. $5. Long Beach Area Citizens Involved, 56 Park Ave., Long Beach, CA 90803. TEL 213-433-1974. Ed. Chris Conrad. adv. (tabloid format)

CIVIL AND MILITARY REVIEW. see *MILITARY*

CIVIL LIBERTARIAN; journal of civil, social and sexual liberty. see *POLITICAL SCIENCE — Civil Rights*

CIVIL SERVICE PENSIONER. see *GERONTOLOGY AND GERIATRICS*

361.73 362.5 NE ISSN 0166-3488
CLAMAVI. bi-m. contribution. Stichting Mensen in Nood - Caritas Neerlandica, Hekellaan 6, 5211 LX 's-Hertogenbosch, Netherlands. TEL 073-144544. FAX 073-132115. TELEX 50090 CARIT NL. Ed. I de Haas. bk.rev.; circ. 250,000 (controlled).
Description: Covers Dutch aid to Third World countries and Dutch hospitality to refugees. Includes lists of projects and their expenditures in different countries.

360 614.8 US
CLEVELAND FOUNDATION. ANNUAL REPORT. a. Cleveland Foundation, 1422 Euclid Ave., Ste. 1400, Cleveland, OH 44115. TEL 216-861-3810.

CLINICAL GERONTOLOGIST; the journal of aging and mental health. see *GERONTOLOGY AND GERIATRICS*

361.3 US ISSN 0091-1674
HV1 CODEN: CSWJBG
CLINICAL SOCIAL WORK JOURNAL. 1973. q. $155 (foreign $180). (National Federation of Societies for Clinical Social Work) Human Sciences Press, Inc. (Subsidiary of: Plenum Publishing Corp.), 233 Spring St., New York, NY 10013-1578. TEL 212-620-8000. FAX 212-463-0742. Ed. Jean L. Sanville. adv.; bk.rev.; index. (also avail. in microform from UMI; reprint service avail. from ISI,UMI) **Indexed:** Abstr.Soc.Work., Adol.Ment.Hlth.Abstr., ASCA, ASSIA, Child.Devel.Abstr., Curr.Cont., Mid.East: Abstr.& Ind., Psychol.Abstr., Sage Fam.Stud.Abstr., Sage Pub.Admin.Abstr., Soc.Work Res.& Abstr., Sociol.Abstr., Sp.Ed.Needs Abstr., SSCI.
—BLDSC shelfmark: 3286.381000.
Description: Devoted to clinical social work theory and practice, and provides a cross-fertilization of ideas and concepts.
Refereed Serial

361 US ISSN 0732-5223
RC336 CODEN: CLSUEH
CLINICAL SUPERVISOR; the journal of supervision in psychotherapy and mental health. 1982. q. $40 to individuals; institutions $70; libraries $150. Haworth Press, Inc., 10 Alice St., Binghamton, NY 13904. TEL 800-342-9678. FAX 607-722-1424. Ed. Carlton E. Munson. adv.; bk.rev.; circ. 584. (also avail. in microfiche from HAW; reprint service avail. from HAW) **Indexed:** Bull.Signal., Chicago Psychoanal.Lit.Ind., CINAHL, Past.Care & Couns.Abstr., Psychol.Abstr., Rehabil.Lit., Soc.Work Res.& Abstr.
—BLDSC shelfmark: 3286.387000.
Formerly (until 1983): Journal of Social Work Supervision.
Description: Reflects the concerns, needs, and interests of supervisors in a variety of professional settings. Highlights current supervisory techniques and methods.
Refereed Serial

360 SP
COLECCION CUADERNOS DE TRABAJO SOCIAL. 1973. irreg., no.4, 1974. price varies. (Universidad de Navarra, Escuela de Asistentes Sociales) Ediciones Universidad de Navarra, S.A., Apdo. 396, 31080 Pamplona, Spain. TEL 94 825 6850.

COLLEGES AND UNIVERSITIES WITH ACCREDITED SOCIAL WORK DEGREE PROGRAMS. see *EDUCATION — Guides To Schools And Colleges*

COMENIUS; wetenschappelijk tijdschrift voor demokratisering van opvoeding, onderwijs, vorming en hulpverlening. see *EDUCATION*

COMMUNICATION (LONDON, 1967). see *EDUCATION — Special Education And Rehabilitation*

362.7 CN ISSN 0319-7468
COMMUNIQUE (OTTAWA). 1965. q. free. Children's Aid Society of Ottawa-Carleton, 1370 Bank St., Ottawa, Ont. K1H 7Y3, Canada. TEL 613-733-1619. FAX 613-737-6305. bk.rev.
Formerly: C.A.S. Record (ISSN 0045-6675)

361.8 UK
COMMUNITY. 1980. q. £2.50. National Federation of Community Organizations, 8-9 Upper St., London N1 0PQ, England. TEL 01-226-0189. Ed. Bevan Jones. circ. 3,000.
Description: For volunteers involved in community groups.

360 US
COMMUNITY (ALEXANDRIA). 1977. q. $10. United Way of America, 701 N. Fairfax St., Alexandria, VA 22314. TEL 703-836-7100. Ed. Roberta A. Lewis. charts; illus.; circ. 9,000.
Former titles (until 1982): Community Focus; Community (ISSN 0045-771X)
Description: Covers issues that affect the U.S. social service system. Includes welfare reform, computer networking, marketing research data on giving, and community problem solving.

COMMUNITY (CHICAGO). see *SOCIOLOGY*

361.8 CN ISSN 0833-0816
COMMUNITY ACTION. 1985. 22/yr. Can.$28.95($35.95) (foreign $42.95). Community Action Publishers, Box 448, Don Mills, Ont. M3C 2T2, Canada. TEL 416-449-6766. FAX 416-444-5850. Ed. Leon Kumove. adv.; circ. 12,000. (tabloid format)

361 UK ISSN 0307-5508
COMMUNITY CARE; the independent voice of social work. 1974. w. £60 (foreign £75). Reed Business Publishing Group, Quadrant House, The Quadrant, Sutton, Surrey SM2 5AS, England. TEL 081-661-3500. (Subscr. to: Oakfield House, Perrymount Rd., Haywards Heath, West Sussex RH16 3DH, England) Ed. Terry Philpot. adv.; bk.rev.; s-a. index; circ. 28,303. **Indexed:** ASSIA.
—BLDSC shelfmark: 3363.598000.
Incorporates: Insight (Wallington); **Formerly:** Community Care - Social Work in Action.
Description: For social workers in the United Kingdom.

360 350 UK ISSN 0010-3802
HN1
COMMUNITY DEVELOPMENT JOURNAL. 1966. q. £34($70) Oxford University Press, Oxford Journals, Pinkhill House, Southfield Road, Eynsham, Oxford OX8 1JJ, England. TEL 0865-882283. FAX 0865-882890. TELEX 83733OO OXPRES G. Ed. Gary Craig. adv.; bk.rev.; index, cum.index; circ. 1,400. (also avail. in microform from UMI) **Indexed:** Agri.Eng.Abstr., ASSIA, Br.Hum.Ind., C.I.J.E., Curr.Cont.Africa, Curr.Cont., E.I., Geo.Abstr., I D A, Int.Lab.Doc., Lang.& Lang.Behav.Abstr., Mid.East: Abstr.& Ind., P.A.I.S., PSI, Rural Ext.Educ.& Tr.Abstr., Rural Recreat.Tour.Abstr., Sage Pub.Admin.Abstr., Soc.Sci.Ind., Soc.Work Res.& Abstr., Sociol.Abstr., SSCI, Stud.Wom.Abstr., World Agri.Econ.& Rural Sociol.Abstr.
—BLDSC shelfmark: 3363.621000.
Formerly: Community Development Bulletin.
Description: Community work and development in "developed" and "developing" countries.

301.1 362 US ISSN 0010-3853
RA790.A1 CODEN: CMHJAY
COMMUNITY MENTAL HEALTH JOURNAL. 1965. bi-m. $195 (foreign $230). (National Council of Community Mental Health Centers, Inc.) Human Sciences Press, Inc. (Subsidiary of: Plenum Publishing Corp.), 233 Spring St., New York, NY 10013-1578. TEL 212-620-8000. FAX 212-463-0742. Ed. David Cutler. adv.; bk.rev.; film rev.; abstr.; bibl.; charts; illus.; index. (also avail. in microform from UMI; back issues avail.; reprint service avail. from ISI,UMI) **Indexed:** Abstr.Health Care Manage.Stud., Abstr.Soc.Work., Adol.Ment.Hlth.Abstr., ASSIA, Biol.Abstr., CERDIC, Coll.Stud.Pers.Abstr., Crime Delinq.Abstr., Curr.Adv.Ecol.Sci., Curr.Cont., Excerp.Med., Hosp.Lit.Ind., Human Resour.Abstr., Ind.Med., Media Rev.Dig., Ment.Retard.Abstr., Mid.East: Abstr.& Ind., P.H.R.A., Psychol.Abstr., Saf.Sci.Abstr., Sci.Cit.Ind., Soc.Sci.Ind., Soc.Work Res.& Abstr., Sociol.Abstr., Sp.Ed.Needs Abstr., SSCI.
—BLDSC shelfmark: 3363.643000.
Description: Cordinates emergent approaches to mental health and social well-being, covering crisis intervention, suicide prevention, family therapy, social welfare, etc.
Refereed Serial

COMMUNITY TRANSPORT MAGAZINE; the journal for minibus & non-profit transport operators. see *TRANSPORTATION*

CONCERN. see *CHILDREN AND YOUTH — About*

361 610 US
CONCERN NEWS. 1961. 4/yr. free. Project Concern International, Box 85323, San Diego, CA 92186. TEL 619-279-9690. FAX 619-694-0294. Ed. Catherine Panos. illus.; circ. 8,000. (tabloid format)
Former titles: Project Concern News (ISSN 0033-0906); Project Concern Newsletter.

CONFLICT RESOLUTION NOTES. see *LAW*

CONNECTIONS (DAYTON). see *POLITICAL SCIENCE*

360 US
CONNECTOR. 1973. q. contribution. Minnesota State Council on Disability, 121 E. Seventh Pl., Ste. 145, St. Paul, MN 55101. TEL 612-296-6785. FAX 612-296-5935. Ed. Tom Brick. circ. 8,000.

SOCIAL SERVICES AND WELFARE

362.6   IT
CONQUISTE DEI PENSIONATI. 1953. m. L.10000. Federazione Nazionale Pensionati, Via Alessandria, 26, 00198 Rome, Italy. TEL 06-84-15-670. FAX 06-84-17-565. Ed. Carlo Candida. circ. 1,300,000.

CONSUMERS AFFAIRS COUNCIL OF TASMANIA. ANNUAL REPORT. see *CONSUMER EDUCATION AND PROTECTION*

CONTACT; voice of the Irish deaf. see *HANDICAPPED — Hearing Impaired*

CONTINUING CARE; supporting the transition into post hospital care. see *HOSPITALS*

360   US   ISSN 1055-0623
HV97.A3
CORPORATE GIVING DIRECTORY. (Section of: Taft Corporate Information System) 1981. a. $327. Taft Group, 12300 Twinbrook Pkwy., Ste. 450, Rockville, MD 20852. TEL 301-816-0210.
   Former titles: Taft Corporate Giving Directory (ISSN 0882-7176); (until 1984): Taft Corporate Directory (ISSN 0732-8958)

360   US   ISSN 0747-8003
HV97.A3
CORPORATE GIVING WATCH; news and ideas for nonprofit organizations seeking corporate funds. 1981. m. $135 includes Corporate Updates. Taft Group, 12300 Twinbrook Pkwy., Ste. 450, Rockville, MD 20852. TEL 301-816-0210.
   ●Also available online. Vendor(s): NewsNet.

361.7 380   US   ISSN 0197-937X
HV97.A3
CORPORATE 500: THE DIRECTORY OF CORPORATE PHILANTHROPY. 1980. a. $355. Public Management Institute, 358 Brannan St., San Francisco, CA 94107. TEL 415-896-1900. Ed. Kenneth Gilman. circ. 2,000.
   Description: Directory of corporate philanthropic programs, with profiles and indices.

CORRECTIONAL INDUSTRIES ASSOCIATION NEWSLETTER. see *PUBLIC ADMINISTRATION*

362 616.21   IT
CORRIERE DEI LARINGECTOMIZZATI. 1957. q. Associazione Italiana Laringectomizzati, Via Friuli 28, Milan, Italy. TEL 02-86-45-29-92. Ed. C.D. Faroldi. adv.; illus. (tabloid format)
   Description: Organizational news for laryngectomees and users of artificial speaking devices.

360   UN   ISSN 0538-8295
COST OF SOCIAL SECURITY. irreg. price varies. (International Labour Office) I L O Publications, CH-1211 Geneva 22, Switzerland. TEL 022-7996111. FAX 022-798-6358. TELEX 415647-ILO-CH. (U.S. distributor: I L O Publications Center, 49 Sheridan Ave., Albany, NY 12210)

361.74
COUNCIL COLUMNS. 1980. s-m. $60. Council on Foundations, Inc., 1828 L St., N.W., Ste. 300, Washington, DC 20036. TEL 202-466-6512. FAX 202-785-3926. Ed. Robin Hettleman. circ. 6,400. (back issues avail.)

360 327   FR
COUNCIL OF EUROPE. COMMITTEE OF INDEPENDENT EXPERTS ON THE EUROPEAN SOCIAL CHARTER. CONCLUSIONS.. (Text in English; French edition also available) 1970. biennial. price varies. Council of Europe, Publishing and Documentation Service, 67006 Strasbourg, France. (Dist. in U.S. by: Manhattan Publishing Co., Box 650, Croton-on-Hudson, N.Y. 10520)

360   US
COUNCIL ON FOUNDATIONS. ANNUAL REPORT. a. Council on Foundations, Inc., 1828 L St., N.W., Ste. 300, Washington, DC 20036. TEL 202-466-6512.

COUNSELING AND VALUES. see *RELIGIONS AND THEOLOGY — Roman Catholic*

COURIER (NEW YORK, 1954). see *PHILOSOPHY*

CRIME, LAW AND SOCIAL POLICY; an international journal. see *CRIMINOLOGY AND LAW ENFORCEMENT*

360   BL
CRITICA SOCIAL. 1974. irreg. Universidade Catolica de Minas Gerais, Escola de Servico Social, Av. Dom Jose Gaspar 500, Belo Horizonte 30000, Minas Gerais, Brazil.

360   UK
CRONER'S CARE HOME MANAGEMENT. 1986. q. £54.30($100) Croner Publications Ltd., Croner House, London Rd., Kingston-upon-Thames, Surrey KT2 6SR, England. TEL 081-547-3333. FAX 081-547-2637. (looseleaf format)
   Description: For residential care home or nursing home owners and managers.

CULTURAL RESEARCH INSTITUTE. BULLETIN. see *SOCIAL SCIENCES: COMPREHENSIVE WORKS*

300 360   US
D S S NEWSLETTER. 1960. m. free. Department of Social Services, Public Information Office, 1510 Guilford Ave., Baltimore, MD 21202. TEL 301-361-2002. FAX 301-361-3150. Ed. Sue Fitzsimmons. circ. 4,000 (controlled).

362.4   US
D V R NEWS. 1979. 2/yr. free. Department of Health and Social Services, Division of Vocational Rehabilitation, 1 W. Wilson St., Rm. 830, Box 7852, Madison, WI 53707. TEL 608-266-3956. Ed. Karen Eckland. bk.rev.; stat.; circ. 3,200. (tabloid format)
   Former titles: D V R Newsletter & Our News.

362.7   US   ISSN 0092-4199
HV854
DAY CARE AND EARLY EDUCATION. 1973. q. $90 (foreign $105). Human Sciences Press, Inc. (Subsidiary of: Plenum Publishing Corp.), 233 Spring St., New York, NY 10013-1578. TEL 212-620-8000. FAX 212-463-0742. Ed. Randa Roen Nachbar. adv.; bk.rev.; illus. (also avail. in microform from UMI; back issues avail.; reprint service avail. from ISI,UMI) **Indexed:** C.I.J.E., Cont.Pg.Educ., Educ.Ind., Except.Child Educ.Abstr., Soc.Work Res.& Abstr., Sp.Ed.Needs Abstr.
   —BLDSC shelfmark: 3535.866100.
   Description: Provides a practical and lively forum for early childhood teachers, program administrators, day care workers, and other professionals concerned with the education of young children.
   Refereed Serial

362.7   US
DAY CARE U S A. (Supplement avail.: Day Care Information Service Special Reports) fortn. $229. United Communications Group, 11300 Rockville Pike, Ste. 1100, Rockville, MD 20852-3030. TEL 301-816-8950. Ed. Charles Pekow.
   Description: Covers new programs, funding and challenges facing day care.

DEAF COMMUNITY SERVICES MAGAZINE OF SAN DIEGO. see *HANDICAPPED — Hearing Impaired*

360   BL
DEBATES SOCIAIS. 1965. s-a. membership or exchange basis. Centro Brasileiro de Cooperacao e Intercambio de Servicos Sociais, Rua Santa Luzia 685, 2 andar, 20030 Rio de Janeiro R.J., Brazil. Ed. Moacyr Velloso Cardoso de Oliveira. bk.rev.; circ. 5,000.
   Description: Examines community development.

DELIVERER. see *RELIGIONS AND THEOLOGY — Protestant*

360   DK   ISSN 0904-9398
DENMARK. SOCIALFORSKNINGSINSTITUTTET. ARBEJDSNOTATER. 1987. irreg. free. Socialforskningsinstituttet - Danish National Institute of Social Research, 28 Borgergade, DK-1300 Copenhagen, Denmark. TEL 33-139811. FAX 33-138992.

361   DK   ISSN 0107-4377
H62.5.D4
DENMARK. SOCIALFORSKNINGSINSTITUTTET. BERETNING OM SOCIALFORSKNINGSINSTITUTTETS VIRKSOMHED. Cover title: Denmark. Socialforskningsinstituttet. Socialforskningsinstituttets Virksomhed. 1960. a. price varies. Socialforskningsinstituttet - Danish National Institute of Social Research, Borgergade 28, DK-1300 Copenhagen K, Denmark. TEL 33-139811. FAX 33-138992.

301   DK   ISSN 0905-0957
DENMARK. SOCIALFORSKNINGSINSTITUTTET. PJECER. 1973. irreg., no.28, 1989. price varies. Socialforskningsinstituttet - Danish National Institute of Social Research, 28 Borgergade, DK-1300 Copenhagen K, Denmark.

360   DK   ISSN 0903-6814
DENMARK. SOCIALFORSKNINGSINSTITUTTET. RAPPORTER. 1960. irreg. price varies. Socialforskningsinstituttet - Danish National Institute of Social Research, 28 Borgergade, DK-1300 Copenhagen K, Denmark. TEL 33-139811. FAX 33-138992.

360   GW   ISSN 0012-1185
DEUTSCHER VEREIN FUER OEFFENTLICHE UND PRIVATE FUERSORGE. NACHRICHTENDIENST. vol.50, 1970. m. DM.30. Deutscher Verein fuer Oeffentliche und Private Fuersorge, Am Stockborn 1-3, 6000 Frankfurt a.M. 50, Germany. FAX 069-5803381. Ed. Prof. Dr. Teresa Bock. adv.; bk.rev.; index. (tabloid format)
   —BLDSC shelfmark: 6010.700000.

361.77   GW
DEUTSCHES ROTES KREUZ DER DEUTSCHEN DEMOKRATISCHEN REPUBLIK. 1953. m. DM.35 per no. Deutsches Rotes Kreuz, Praesidium, Kaitzer Str. 2, 8010 Dresden, Germany. adv.; bk.rev.; index; circ. 75,000.

360   US
DEVELOPMENT RESEARCH DIGEST. 1986. q. free. State Developmental Research Institutes, Department of Developmental Services, 2501 Harbour Blvd., Costa Mesa, CA 92626. Ed.Bd. bk.rev.; circ. 650.

360   CN
DEVELOPPEMENT SOCIAL EN PERSPECTIVES. (English edition Social Development Overview ceased in 1991)(Text in French) 1972. irreg. membership. Conseil Canadien du Developpement Social, 55 Ave. Parkdale, C.P. 3505, Station C, Ottawa, Ont. K1Y 4G1, Canada. TEL 613-728-1865. FAX 613-728-9387. Ed. Carolyn Brown. adv.; bk.rev.; circ. 4,000.
   Formerly (until 1985): Developpement Social.
   Description: Newsletter on activities and positions of the council.

DIAKONIE REPORT. see *RELIGIONS AND THEOLOGY*

362.3   CN   ISSN 0383-8528
DIALECT. 1977. 6/yr. free. Saskatchewan Association for Community Living, 3031 Louise St., Saskatoon, Sask. S7J 3L1, Canada. TEL 306-955-3344. FAX 306-373-3070. Ed. Karin Melberg Schwier. bk.rev.; film rev.; circ. 5,600. (back issues avail.)

DIARY OF SOCIAL LEGISLATION AND POLICY. see *PUBLIC ADMINISTRATION*

362.4   UK
DIG AROUND. 1981. q. £3 membership. Disablement Income Group, Millmead Business Centre, Millmead Rd., London N17 9QU, England. TEL 01-801 8013. Ed. Pauline Thompson. circ. 5,000.

362   GW   ISSN 0722-0014
DIGEST FUER JUGEND UND BILDUNGEINRICHTUNGEN. 8/yr. DM.36. Deutscher Forschungsdienst GmbH, Ahrstr. 45, 5300 Bonn 2, Germany. TEL 0228-302210. FAX 0228-302270.

360   UK   ISSN 0309-4413
DIRECTORY FOR DISABLED PEOPLE. 1977. irreg. $33. (Royal Association for Disability and Rehabilitation (RADAR)) Woodhead-Faulkner (Publishers) Ltd., Fitzwilliam House, 32 Trumpington St., Cambridge CB2, England. TEL 0223-66733. FAX 0223-461428. Eds. Ann Darnbrough, Derek Kinrade. (back issues avail.)
   —BLDSC shelfmark: 3593.412000.
   Description: A handbook of information and opportunities for disabled and handicapped people.

360   UK
DIRECTORY OF AIDS FOR DISABLED AND ELDERLY PEOPLE. 1986. irreg. $32. Woodhead-Faulkner (Publishers) Ltd., Fitzwilliam House, 32 Trumpington St., Cambridge CB2 1QY, England. TEL 0223-66733. FAX 0223-461428.
   Description: A wide-ranging directory of useful equipment helpful to disabled people and others with difficulties in daily living.

SOCIAL SERVICES AND WELFARE

361.7 US
DIRECTORY OF CATHOLIC CHARITIES, DIOCESAN AGENCIES AND ORGANIZATIONS. UNITED STATES, PUERTO RICO AND CANADA (YEAR). biennial. $35 non-members; members $20. Catholic Charities U S A, 1731 King St., Ste. 200, Alexandria, VA 22314. TEL 703-549-1390. FAX 703-549-1656.
Former titles: Directory. Diocesan Agencies of Catholic Charities and Catholic Charities U S A Member Institutions. United States, Puerto Rico and Canada; Directory. Diocesan Agencies of Catholic Charities and N C C C Member Institutions. United States, Puerto Rico and Canada; Directory. Diocesan Agencies of Catholic Charities. United States, Puerto Rico and Canada (ISSN 0091-1003)

360 US
DIRECTORY OF COMMUNITY RESOURCES AND SERVICES. 1943. a. $35. United Way of the Texas Gulf Coast, 2200 N. Loop West, Houston, TX 77018. TEL 713-685-2300. FAX 713-956-2868. index; circ. 1,800.
Description: Lists human services in the greater Houston area and surrounding counties.

361.6 CN ISSN 0315-0631
DIRECTORY OF COMMUNITY SERVICES IN METROPOLITAN TORONTO. 1938. a. Can.$55. Community Information Centre of Metropolitan Toronto, 590 Jarvis St., 5th Fl., Toronto, Ont. M4Y 2J4, Canada. TEL 416-392-4575. FAX 416-392-4404. circ. 5,500.

361.6 CN ISSN 0319-258X
HV110.M6
DIRECTORY OF COMMUNITY SERVICES OF GREATER MONTREAL/REPERTOIRE DES SERVICES COMMUNAUTAIRES DU GRAND MONTREAL; welfare-health-recreation. (Text in English and French) 1956. biennial. Can.$42. Information and Referral Centre of Greater Montreal Foundation - Fondation du Centre de Reference du Grand Montreal, 881 de Maisonneuve E., Montreal, Que. H2L 1Y8, Canada. TEL 514-527-1375. FAX 514-527-9712. Ed.Bd. circ. 3,500.
Formerly: Directory of Health, Welfare and Recreation Services of Greater Montreal (ISSN 0070-5640)

360 US
DIRECTORY OF FEDERAL AID FOR HEALTH AND ALLIED FIELDS. irreg. Ready Reference Press, Box 5879, Santa Monica, CA 90405.

362.6
DIRECTORY OF FEDERAL AID FOR THE AGING. irreg. Ready Reference Press, Box 5879, Santa Monica, CA 90405.

362.4 371 US
DIRECTORY OF FEDERAL AID FOR THE HANDICAPPED. irreg. Ready Reference Press, Box 5879, Santa Monica, CA 90405.

360 UK ISSN 0070-5624
DIRECTORY OF GRANT-MAKING TRUSTS. 1968. biennial. £49. Charities Aid Foundation, 48 Pembury Rd., Tonbridge, Kent TN9 2JD, England. Ed. Anne Villemur. circ. 6,000.
Description: Lists 2,500 grant-making bodies to whom charitable organizations may apply for funds.

640.73 US
DIRECTORY OF INFORMATION AND REFERRAL AGENCIES IN THE UNITED STATES AND CANADA. biennial. $26.50 to non-members; members $20. Alliance of Information and Referral Systems, Box 3546, Joliet, IL 60434-3546. TEL 815-744-6922.

DIRECTORY OF INTERNATIONAL CORPORATE GIVING IN AMERICA. see *BUSINESS AND ECONOMICS — Trade And Industrial Directories*

361.7 US ISSN 0161-2638
HV3191
DIRECTORY OF JEWISH FEDERATIONS, WELFARE FUNDS AND COMMUNITY COUNCILS. 1936. a. $10. Council of Jewish Federations, Inc., 730 Broadway, 2nd Fl., New York, NY 10003. index; circ. 1,000.
Formerly: Jewish Federations, Welfare Funds and Community Councils Directory (ISSN 0075-3734)
Description: Lists all member agencies geographically; includes names of executive directors and presidents.

DIRECTORY OF NEBRASKA SERVICES. see *PUBLIC ADMINISTRATION*

360 US ISSN 0888-7624
DIRECTORY OF NURSING HOME FACILITIES. 1982. irreg., 5th ed., 1992. $225. Health Care Investment Analysts, Inc., 300 E. Lombard St., 7th Fl., Baltimore, MD 21202. TEL 410-576-9600. FAX 410-783-0575. Ed. Sam Mongeau.
Description: Covers nearly 16,300 state licensed long-term care facilities, with complete profiles of each facility.

362.1 AT ISSN 0812-4663
DISABILITY AIDS DIRECTORY. 1984. biennial. Mount Eagle Publications, P.O. Box 84, Heidelberg, Victoria 3084, Australia. Ed. Kennith Lloyd Jones. adv.; bibl.; index; circ. 10,000.
Description: Aids and services available nationally for the disabled.

DISABILITY ISSUES. see *HANDICAPPED — Visually Impaired*

360 267 796.31 US ISSN 8755-965X
DISCOVERY Y M C A. (Young Men's Christian Association) 1982. q. $8 (free to qualified personnel). Y M C A of the U S A, 101 N. Wacker Dr., Chicago, IL 60606. TEL 312-977-0031. FAX 312-977-9063. Ed. Anthony Ripley. adv.; circ. 88,000.
Description: Concentrates on challenges and accomplishments of the 2060 YMCAs in the U.S.A. and on issues facing the movement as a whole.

362.7 GW
DISKURS. s-a. DM.48. (Deutsches Jugendinstitut) Juventa Verlag GmbH, Ehretstr. 3, 6940 Weinheim, Germany. TEL 06201-61035. FAX 06201-13135.

360 US
DOMESTIC HUMAN NEEDS NETWORKER. 10/yr. $25 contribution. Interfaith Action for Economic Justice, 110 Maryland Ave., N.E., Washington, DC 20002. TEL 202-543-2800.

360 FR ISSN 0758-6531
HN421
DONNEES SOCIALES. a. Institut National de la Statistique et des Etudes Economique, 18 bd. Adolphe Pinard, 75675 Paris cedex 14, France.
—BLDSC shelfmark: 3619.237000.
Description: Information on French society: population, employee salaries, working conditions, lifestyles, health conditions, education, welfare and social justice.

361.73 US
DONOR BRIEFING; a biweekly digest for the nonprofit fundraising community. 1986. bi-w. $163.50. Business Publishers, Inc., 951 Pershing Dr., Silver Spring, MD 20910-4464. TEL 301-587-6300. FAX 301-587-1081. Eds. Albert Copland, Amy Jo Mendelson.
Description: Provides both donors and candidates with a timely forum for news of donor activity.

362.6 DK ISSN 0107-8275
E G V INFORMATION. no.16, 1981. irreg. price varies. Ensomme Gamles Vaern Fonden, Vesterbrogade 97, 1620 Copenhagen V, Denmark. FAX 01-234623. Ed. G.W. Leeson. circ. 300.

360 FR ISSN 0760-8675
ECHANGE-SANTE; bulletin de liaison et de documentation. 1984. q. 42 ECU($50) (typically set in Jan.). (Ministere des Affaires Sociales et de la Solidarite Nationale) Masson, 120 Bd. St. Germain, 75280 Paris Cedex 06, France. TEL 1-46-34-21-60. FAX 1-45-87-29-99. TELEX 202 671 F. (also avail. in microfiche)
—BLDSC shelfmark: 3647.363900.

ECHO DE L'UNION. see *GERONTOLOGY AND GERIATRICS*

971 CN ISSN 0012-9321
ECHOES. 1902. 3/yr. Can.$3. I O D E, 40 Orchard View Blvd., Toronto, Ont. M4R 1B9, Canada. TEL 416-487-4416. Ed. Winifred Anderson. adv.; bk.rev.; illus.; tr.lit.; index; circ. 11,000.

330 US ISSN 0013-0206
ECONOMIC OPPORTUNITY REPORT; the independent weekly source for news of all economic opportunity programs. 1966. w. $307. Business Publishers, Inc., 951 Pershing Dr., Silver Spring, MD 20910-4464. TEL 301-587-6300. FAX 301-585-9075. Ed. Jay Fletcher. (looseleaf format; back issues avail.)
●Also available online. Vendor(s): NewsNet.
Description: Provides inside news from Washington on money, trends, innovations, and research results for antipoverty administrators.

360 VE ISSN 0013-0680
ECOS. 1945. bi-m. free. (Asociacion Benefico - Social Hogar Virgen de los Dolores) Editorial Sucre, Monzon a Barcenas No. 135, Caracas, Venezuela. Ed. Hermann Gonzalez-Oropeza. bk.rev.; circ. 18,000 (controlled). (looseleaf format; also avail. in record)

EDUCATION PERMANENTE. see *EDUCATION*

EMOTIONAL FIRST AID; a journal of crisis intervention. see *PSYCHOLOGY*

361 US ISSN 0071-0237
HV35
ENCYCLOPEDIA OF SOCIAL WORK. 1929. irreg. (approx. every 10 yrs.), no.18, 1987. $85. (National Association of Social Workers) N.A.S.W. Press, Publications Department, 7981 Eastern Ave., Silver Spring, MD 20910. TEL 301-565-0333. FAX 301-589-9340. Ed. Anne Minahan. circ. 25,000. **Indexed:** Abstr.Soc.Work.
Formerly: Social Work Year Book.
Description: Accesses data on the entire range of activities in social work and social welfare.

362.7 UN ISSN 0013-757X
ENFANTS DU MONDE. 1965. 5/yr. 10 F. Fonds des Nations Unies pour l'Enfance (UNICEF), Comite Francais, 35 rue Felicien David, 75016 Paris, France. TEL 45-24-60-00. FAX 40-50-09-97. TELEX 645638. Ed. Josette Marthelot Tagher. bk.rev.; charts; illus.; circ. 400,000.
Description: Aim is to promote assistance to deprived children worldwide, by exposing their unsatisfactory living conditions.

360 GW ISSN 0343-656X
ENTSCHEIDUNGEN DER SPRUCHSTELLEN FUER FUERSORGESTREITIGKEITEN. 1947. m. DM.124. Deutscher Gemeindeverlag GmbH, Max-Planck-Str. 12, Postfach 400263, 5000 Cologne 40, Germany. TEL 02234-1060. circ. 970.

EPANOUIR. see *EDUCATION — Special Education And Rehabilitation*

360 616.8 AT ISSN 0729-7823
EPILETTER. 1978? q. Aus.$10. Epilepsy Foundation of Victoria, 818 Burke Rd., Camberwell, Vic. 3124, Australia. TEL 03-813-2866. FAX 03-813-7159. Ed. Kath Walters. bk.rev.; circ. 7,500. (back issues avail.)
Description: Covers all aspects of epilepsy, including research, human interest, medicine, fundraising and welfare.

267 FR ISSN 0763-5184
EQUIPES ST VINCENT. 3/yr. 55 F. Federation Francaise des Equipes Saint-Vincent, 67 rue de Sevres, 75006 Paris, France. Ed. Mauricette Borloo. bk.rev.; circ. 4,000.
Formerly: Echos des Charites de St. Vincent de Paul (ISSN 0070-8305)

368 658.3 GW ISSN 0014-0279
DIE ERSATZKASSE. 1916. m. DM.3.70. Verband der Angestellten-Krankenkassen e.V., Frankfurter Str. 84, 5200 Siegburg, Germany. Ed. Malte Retiet. adv.; bk.rev.; illus.; stat.; circ. 5,400. **Indexed:** Excerp.Med., World Bibl.Soc.Sec.
—BLDSC shelfmark: 3810.772600.

360 FR
ESCLAVAGE; document social. 1974. q. 5 F. Equipes d'Action Contre la Traite des Femmes et des Enfants, 21 rue Sainte Croix de la Bretonnerie, 75004 Paris, France.

ESCOGE LA VIDA!. see *POPULATION STUDIES*

SOCIAL SERVICES AND WELFARE 4405

360   IT   ISSN 0014-0678
ESPERIENZA; mensile di elevazione sociale. 1951. m. membership. (Associazione Nazionale Lavoratori Anziani di Azienda) Editoriale Esperienza s.r.l., Largo Teatro Valle, 6, 00186 Rome, Italy.
FAX 06-6877012. Ed. Renzo Radice. adv.; bk.rev.; circ. 275,000.

360 917.306   US   ISSN 0737-1411
ETHNIC AMERICAN VOLUNTARY ORGANIZATIONS. 1983. irreg. price varies. Greenwood Press, Inc. (Subsidiary of: Greenwood Publishing Group Inc.), 88 Post Rd. W., Box 5007, Westport, CT 06881-5007. TEL 203-226-3571. FAX 203-222-1502.

296   FR
EUROPEAN COUNCIL OF JEWISH COMMUNITY SERVICES. EXCHANGE. (Text in English and French) 1971. q. free. European Council of Jewish Community Services, 4 bis rue de Lota, 75116 Paris, France. Ed. Nicole Goldman. circ. 4,000.
  Formerly: European Council of Jewish Community Services. Exchange Information Service (ISSN 0531-5174)

360   AU   ISSN 0253-7427
EUROSOCIAL NEWSLETTER/EUROSOCIAL BULLETIN D'INFORMATION/EUROSOCIAL NACHRICHTEN. (Text in English, French and German) 1974. 3/yr. free. European Centre for Social Welfare Policy and Research, Berggasse 17, 1090 Vienna, Austria. TEL 0222-314505-0. FAX 0222-31450519. Ed. Bernd Marin. bk.rev.; circ. 4,000. (back issues avail.)
  —BLDSC shelfmark: 3830.429300.
  Description: Examines social services and policies in Europe.

330.9   SP
EVOLUCION SOCIOECONOMICA DE ESPAÑA. Organizacion Sindical Espanola, Secretariado Central de Asuntos Economicos, Casa Sindical, Paseo del Prado 18, Madrid, Spain. illus.; stat.

361.73   US
EXCHANGE (NEW YORK). 1985. 3/yr. Funding Exchange, 666 Broadway, Ste. 500, New York, NY 10012. TEL 212-529-5300. Ed. Nan Robin. circ. 4,000. (back issues avail.)
  Formerly: Donor Update.
  Description: Covers organizational activities, social exchange issues, philanthropy, and donors.

361.73 371.42   US
EXECUTIVE SEARCH SERVICE NEWS. 1963. m. $25 to non-members. National Society of Fund Raising Executives, 1101 King St., Ste. 3000, Alexandria, VA 22314. TEL 703-684-0410. FAX 703-684-0540. Eds. Cathlene Williams, Alisa Nesmith. adv.; circ. 12,000 (controlled).
  Formerly: E S S Employment Newsletter.
  Description: Information on career opportunities in fund-raising.

361   US
EYE ON L S S I. 1988. 3/yr. free. Lutheran Social Services of Illinois, 1001 E. Touhy Ave., Des Plaines, IL 60018. TEL 708-635-4600. (Affiliate: Evangelical Lutheran Church in America) Ed. Julie B. Bokser. illus.; circ. 82,000. (tabloid format)
  Description: Introduces programs and achievements of the organization.

F C L ACTION ALERTS. (Friends Committee on Legislation of California) see *POLITICAL SCIENCE*

360   US   ISSN 0014-6137
F R I MONTHLY PORTFOLIO. 1962. m. $59. Fund Raising Institute, Div. of the Taft Group, 12300 Twinbrook Pkwy., Ste. 450, Rockville, MD 20852. TEL 301-816-0210. FAX 301-816-0811. bk.rev.; index; circ. 3,500.
  Description: Newsletter articles on sources for and examples of philanthropic fund-raising ideas and techniques. For individuals and nonprofit organizations.

362.8   US
F S C MONTHLY BULLETIN. m. free. Federation of Southern Cooperatives, Box 95, Epes, AL 35460. TEL 202-652-9676.

355   GW   ISSN 0014-6447
DIE FACKEL. 1946. m. DM.18. Verband der Kriegs- und Wehrdienstopfer, Behinderten und Sozialrentner Deutschlands e.V. (VdK), Wurzerstr. 2-4, 5300 Bonn 2, Germany. TEL 0228-820930.
FAX 0228-8209343. Ed. Joachim Faustmann. circ. 770,000.
  Description: Covers social politics, social law, laws covering pensions, health and accident insurance and other aspects of international social welfare laws.

360   NE
FACT SHEET ON THE NETHERLANDS. (Text in Dutch, English, French, German and Spanish) irreg. Ministerie van Welzijn Volksgezondheid en Cultuur, Postbus 5406, 2280 HK Rijswijk, Netherlands. TEL 070-3406015.

338.1 360   FR   ISSN 0014-6889
FAIMS ET SOIFS DES HOMMES. 1969. q. 100 F. (effective 1992). Mouvement Emmaus, 1 Passage Saint-Sebastien, 75011 Paris, France.
TEL 1-43-57-24-29. FAX 43-57-96-35. Ed. Abbe Pierre. adv.; bk.rev.; film rev.; play rev.; illus.
  Supersedes: Faim et Soif.

FAIRE FACE. see *MEDICAL SCIENCES*

FAMILIA Y SOCIEDAD. see *SOCIOLOGY*

361.3   US   ISSN 1044-3894
HV1   CODEN: FASOEN
FAMILIES IN SOCIETY; the journal of contemporary human services. 1920. m. (10/yr.) $37 to individuals; institutions $64. Family Service America, 11700 W. Lake Park Dr., Milwaukee, WI 53224. TEL 414-359-1040. FAX 414-359-1074. (Subscr. to: Subscription Department, Box 6649, Syracuse, NY 13217) Ed. Ralph J. Burant. adv.; bk.rev.; index; circ. 7,000. (also avail. in microform from JAI,MIM,UMI; back issues avail.; reprint service avail. from KTO,UMI) *Indexed:* Abstr.Health Care Manage.Stud., Abstr.Soc.Geront., Acad.Ind., ASSIA, Behav.Abstr., Bk.Rev.Ind. (1965-), Chicago Psychoanal.Lit.Ind., Child.Bk.Rev.Ind. (1965-), CLOA, Crim.Just.Abstr., Curr.Cont., Except.Child.Educ.Abstr., Hosp.Lit.Ind., Lang.& Lang.Behav.Abstr., Mid.East: Abstr.& Ind., PSI, Psychol.Abstr., Soc.Sci.Ind., Soc.Work Res.& Abstr., Sociol.Abstr., SSCI, Stud.Wom.Abstr.
  —BLDSC shelfmark: 3865.553973.
  Formerly (until Jan. 1990): Social Casework (ISSN 0037-7678)
  Description: Directed to human service professionals. Deals with the theory, practice, and management of family, individual and group counseling and therapy.

FAMILY MATTERS. see *SOCIOLOGY*

FAMILY THERAPY. see *MEDICAL SCIENCES — Psychiatry And Neurology*

FAMILY THERAPY NETWORKER. see *PSYCHOLOGY*

FAMILY THERAPY NEWS. see *PSYCHOLOGY*

FAR EAST; mission magazine of the Columban fathers. see *RELIGIONS AND THEOLOGY — Roman Catholic*

FEDERAL FUNDING GUIDE. see *PUBLIC ADMINISTRATION — Municipal Government*

360   FR   ISSN 0248-3165
FEUILLE DE ROUTE. m. 50 F. (A.T.D. Fourthworld) Editions Quart Monde, 122 av. du General Leclerc, 95480 Pierrelaye, France.

FILM AUSTRALIA HEALTH & WELFARE CATALOGUE. see *MOTION PICTURES*

360   FI
FINLAND. MINISTRY OF SOCIAL AFFAIRS AND HEALTH. PLANNING DEPARTMENT. PUBLICATIONS. (Text in Finnish) 1987. irreg. (6-8/yr). price varies. Ministry of Social Affairs and Health, Planning Department, P.O. Box 303, SF 00171 Helsinki 17, Finland. TEL 90-1601. FAX 359-0-1605403. TELEX 125073. (Subscr. to: Government Printing Centre, P.O. Box 516, SF 00101 Helsinki 10, Finland)

360   FI
FINLAND. MINISTRY OF SOCIAL AFFAIRS AND HEALTH. PLANNING DEPARTMENT. REPORTS. (Text in Finnish) 1987. irreg. (3-4/yr.). price varies. Ministry of Social Affairs and Health, Planning Department, P.O. Box 303, SF 00171 Helsinki 17, Finland. TEL 90-1601. FAX 358-0-1605403. TELEX 125073. (Subscr. to: Government Printing Centre, P.O. Box 516, SF 00101 Helsinki 10, Finland)

360   FI   ISSN 0355-4759
HA1448
FINLAND. SOSIAALIHALLITUS. HUOLTOAPU/FINLAND. NATIONAL BOARD OF SOCIAL WELFARE. HOMEHELP/FINLAND. SOCIALSTYRELSEN. SOCIALHJAELP. (Text in English, Finnish and Swedish) 1969. biennial. FIM 25. Sosiaalihallitus, Siltaarenkatu 18 C, SF-00530 Helsinki, Finland. (Dist. by: Government Printing Center, Box 516, SF-00101 Helsinki, Finland) Ed. Kyllikki Korpi. circ. 1,000.

360   FI   ISSN 0355-4767
FINLAND. SOSIAALIHALLITUS. KODINHOITOAPU/FINLAND. NATIONAL BOARD OF SOCIAL WELFARE. SOCIAL ASSISTANCE/FINLAND. SOCIALSTYRELSEN. HEMVAARDSHJAELP. (Text in English, Finnish and Swedish) 1971. biennial. FIM 21. Sosiaalihallitus, Siltasaarenkatu 18 C, SF-00530 Helsinki, Finland. (Dist. by: Government Printing Center, Box 516, SF-00101 Helsinki, Finland) Ed. Kyllikki Korpi. circ. 1,200.

360   FI   ISSN 0071-5328
FINLAND. SOSIAALIHALLITUS. SOSIAALIHUOLTOTILASTON VUOSIKIRJA/FINLAND. NATIONAL BOARD OF SOCIAL WELFARE. YEARBOOK OF SOCIAL WELFARE STATISTICS/FINLAND. SOCIALSTYRELSEN. SOCIALVAARDSSTATISTISK AARSBOK. (Section XXV B of Official Statistics of Finland) (Text in English, Finnish and Swedish) 1959. a. Sosiaalihallitus, Siltasaarenkatu 18 C, Helsinki, Finland. Ed. Kyllikki Korpi. circ. 1,100.

FITZHUGH DIRECTORY OF INDEPENDENT HOSPITALS AND PROVIDENT ASSOCIATIONS. see *MEDICAL SCIENCES*

353.9   US
FLORIDA. DEPARTMENT OF CORRECTIONS. ANNUAL REPORT. 1973. a. free. Department of Corrections, 2601 Blairstone Rd., Tallahassee, FL 32399-2500. TEL 904-488-1776. FAX 904-488-4602. Ed.Bd. stat.; circ. 3,500. *Indexed:* SRI.
  Formerly: Florida. Division of Corrections. Financial Report (ISSN 0094-6435)

362.8   DK   ISSN 0900-2537
FLYGTNINGE NYT. 1982. 8/yr. free. Dansk Flygtningehjaelp, Postbox 53, 1002 Copenhagen K, Denmark. FAX 45-33-32-84-48. Ed. Finn Slumstrup. illus.; circ. 22,000.
  Formerly: Nyt om Flygtninge (ISSN 0108-1845)

362.5   US   ISSN 0195-5705
HC79.P6
FOCUS (MADISON). 1976. 4/yr. free. University of Wisconsin-Madison, Institute for Research on Poverty, 3412 Social Science Bldg., University of Wisconsin, 1180 Observatory Dr., Madison, WI 53706. TEL 608-262-6358. cum.index: 1976-1988; circ. 5,000. (back issues avail.)
  —BLDSC shelfmark: 3964.194940.
  Formerly: Focus on Poverty Research (ISSN 0191-2186)
  Description: Provides coverage of poverty related research, events, and issues in essay form and acquaints others with the institute's work.

362.4   US
FOCUS (WASHINGTON, 1978). 1978. q. free. National Council on Disability, 800 Independence Ave. S.W., Ste. 814, Washington, DC 20591. TEL 202-267-3846. FAX 202-453-4240. (also avail. in audio cassette; large print edition in 14 pt.)
  Description: Focuses on council news and upcoming events.

FOKUS PAA FAMILIEN; Norwegian journal on family therapy. see *MEDICAL SCIENCES — Psychiatry And Neurology*

SOCIAL SERVICES AND WELFARE

616.99 362.1   FR
FONDAMENTAL. 1978. q. 40 F. Association pour la Recherche sur le Cancer (ARC), B.P. 3, 7, rue Guy Moquet, 94801 Villejuif Cedex, France. TEL 45-59-59-59. FAX 47-26-04-75. Ed. J. Crozemarie. adv.; bk.rev.
Description: French cancer information on research and prevention for the public.

360   US
FOOD & POVERTY NOTES. 1976. bi-m. $10. Maryland Food Committee, 204 E. 25th St., Baltimore, MD 21218. TEL 301-366-0600. FAX 301-366-3963. Ed. Julie Ayers. circ. 27,000.
Description: Covers various issues dealing with food assistance, advocacy and the hunger problem nationwide.

362.8   US   ISSN 0736-0010
FOODLINES; a chronicle of hunger and poverty in America. 1982. bi-m. $20. Food Research & Action Center, 1875 Connecticut Ave., N.W., Ste. 540, Washington, DC 20009. TEL 202-986-2200. FAX 202-986-2525. Ed. Ann Kittlaus. circ. 2,000.

360   GW   ISSN 0071-7835
FORTBILDUNG UND PRAXIS. (Supplement to: Wege zur Sozialversicherung) 1949. irreg. price varies. Asgard-Verlag Dr. Werner Hippe KG, Einsteinstr. 10, Postfach 1465, 5205 St. Augustin, Germany. TEL 02241-3164-0.

FORTUNE NEWS. see *CRIMINOLOGY AND LAW ENFORCEMENT*

362.7 364   GW
FORUM JUGENDHILFE. 1950. 4/yr. DM.10. Arbeitsgemeinschaft fuer Jugendhilfe, Haager Weg 44, 5300 Bonn 1, Germany. FAX 0228-285503. Eds. P. Marguard, Dieter Roettgers. adv.; bk.rev.; circ. 1,500.
Former titles: Arbeitsgemeinschaft fuer Jugendhilfe. Mitteilungen & Arbeitsgemeinschaft fuer Jugendpflege und Jugendfuersorge. Mitteilungen (ISSN 0003-7710)

360   UK
FORWARD. 1889. s-a. Sandes Soldiers & Airmen's Centers, 30-A Belmont Rd., Belfast BT4 2AN, N. Ireland. TEL 0232-652592. Ed. Hazel M. Knox. circ. 2,500.

FOSTER CARE. see *CHILDREN AND YOUTH — About*

361.73   US
▼**FOUNDATION DIRECTORY PART 2: A GUIDE TO GRANT PROGRAMS TWENTY FIVE THOUSAND DOLLARS TO ONE HUNDRED THOUSAND DOLLARS.** 1990. a. $150. Foundation Center, 79 Fifth Ave., New York, NY 10003. TEL 212-620-4230. FAX 212-691-1828.
Description: Provides current information on 4,283 foundations that maintain mid-sized grant programs.

360   US   ISSN 0741-7004
FOUNDATION GIVING WATCH; the monthly report to non-profit organizations seeking foundation support. 1981. m. $135 includes Foundation Update. Taft Group, 12300 Twinbrook Pkwy., Ste. 450, Rockville, MD 20852. TEL 301-816-0210. Ed. Louis LaBreque. index; circ. 3,100. (back issues avail.)

FOURTH WORLD JOURNAL. see *POLITICAL SCIENCE — Civil Rights*

FRAENKISCHER HAUSKALENDER UND CARITASKALENDER. see *BIOGRAPHY*

360   FR   ISSN 0184-6469
FRANCE. CAISSE NATIONALE DES ALLOCATIONS FAMILIALES. STATISTIQUES PRESTATIONS DE LOGEMENT. a. Caisse Nationale des Allocations Familiales, 23 rue Daviel, 75634 Paris Cedex 13, France.

362.4 371.9 610   CN   ISSN 0824-7226
FREEWHEELER. 1978. q. Can.$10. Canadian Paraplegic Association Ontario, 520 Sutherland Dr., Toronto, Ont. M4G 3V9, Canada. TEL 416-422-5644. FAX 416-422-5943. Ed. Kathey Smith. adv.; circ. 4,000. (back issues avail.)

362.9   NO   ISSN 0046-5143
FRIVAKT.* 1948. m. (except Aug.). NOK 15. (Velferdstjenesten for Handelsflaaten) Soelberg Trykk A-S, c/o Arne Christiansen, P.O. Box 27, 1335 Smaraya, Norway. Ed. Gunnar Sand. adv.; bk.rev.; film rev.; illus.; circ. 14,700 (controlled).

361 614   US   ISSN 0734-1601
FROM THE STATE CAPITALS. PUBLIC ASSISTANCE AND WELFARE TRENDS. 1946. w. $215 (foreign $235)(effective Dec. 1990). Wakeman-Walworth, Inc., 300 N. Washington St., Alexandria, VA 22314. TEL 703-549-8606. FAX 703-549-1372. (processed)
Description: Summary of developments in state welfare.

360   GW
FUERSORGERECHTLICHE ENTSCHEIDUNGEN. 1951. m. DM.105. Verlag Fritz Eberlein GmbH, Kestnerstrasse 44, 3000 Hannover 1, Germany. TEL 0511-810592. FAX 0511-810575. Ed. U. Harmening. circ. 1,850.

362.7   PO   ISSN 0016-3910
GAIATO; obra de rapazes, para rapazes, pelos rapazes. 1944. s-m. free. Casa do Gaiato, Paco de Sousa, 4560 Penafiel, Portugal. circ. 70,000. (tabloid format; also avail. in microform)

362.7   UK
GATEWAY. 1881. 3/yr. free. Children's Society, Edward Rudolf House, Margery St., London WC1X 0JL, England. TEL 071-837-4299. FAX 071-837-0211. Ed. Angus Stickler. adv.; bk.rev.; circ. 400,000.
Description: Discusses child welfare issues.

362.8   GW   ISSN 0016-5794
GEFAEHRDETENHILFE; Aktuelles aus Theorie und Praxis. 1959. q. DM.16. Bundesarbeitsgemeinschaft fuer Nichtsesshaftenhilfe e.V., Postfach 13 01 48, 4800 Bielefeld 13, Germany. Ed. H. Becker. adv.; bk.rev.; index; circ. 2,000.

GEISTIGE BEHINDERUNG; Fachzeitschrift der Lebenshilfe fuer geistig Behinderte. see *EDUCATION — Special Education And Rehabilitation*

GERIATRIC DIRECTORY OF GERIATRIC PUBLICATIONS. see *BUSINESS AND ECONOMICS — Trade And Industrial Directories*

GERONTOLOSKO DRUSTVO S R SRBIJE. see *GERONTOLOGY AND GERIATRICS*

360   GW   ISSN 0016-9153
GESICHERTES LEBEN. 1954. bi-m. DM.6.60. Wirtschaftsdienst Gesellschaft fuer Medien & Kommunikation mbH & Co. OHG, Lange Str. 13, 6000 Frankfurt, Germany. Ed. W. Bergemann. adv.; circ. 1,848,500.

360   UK   ISSN 0956-3229
GINGER. 1973. 6/yr. £3.50 to members; libraries £12. Gingerbread, Association for One Parent Families, 35 Wellington St., London WC2 7BN, England. TEL 071-240-0953. Ed.Bd. adv.; bk.rev.; illus.; circ. 10,000.
Description: Self-help information for one parent families in England and Wales.

361.73   US   ISSN 0436-0257
HV89
GIVING U S A; the annual compilation of total philanthropic giving estimates. 1956. a. $45. (American Association of Fund-Raising Counsel) A A F R C Trust for Philanthropy, 25 W. 43rd St., New York, NY 10036. TEL 212-354-5799. Ed. Nathan Weber. circ. 5,000. **Indexed:** SRI.
Formerly: Giving U S A Annual Report.

361.73   US   ISSN 0899-3793
HV41
GIVING U S A UPDATE. 1955. q. $35. (American Association of Fund-Raising Counsel) A A F R C Trust for Philanthropy, 25 W. 43rd St., New York, NY 10036. TEL 212-354-5799. FAX 212-768-1795. Ed. Nathan Weber. bk.rev.; circ. 5,000.
Former titles: Fund-Raising Review (ISSN 0735-8873); Giving U S A Bulletin (ISSN 0436-0257); American Association of Fund-Raising Counsel. Bulletin (ISSN 0002-743X)

361   UK   ISSN 0143-7429
GLASGOW DIRECTORY OF VOLUNTARY ORGANIZATIONS. 1980. biennial. £3.50. Glasgow Council for Voluntary Service, 11 Queens Cres., Glasgow G4 9AS, Scotland. TEL 041-332 2444. FAX 041-332-0175. adv.; illus.; circ. 2,000.

610.734   US
GOOD NEIGHBOR. 1952. bi-m. free. American Red Cross, 17th and D Sts. N.W., Washington, DC 20006. Ed. Sally Ann Stewart. circ. 80,000.
Formerly: Red Cross Newsletter (ISSN 0034-1983)
Description: Discusses services provided by the Red Cross.

361   UK
GOOD NEIGHBOURS NEWS. 1954. 13/yr. (every 4 wks.). $13. Community Publishing, 60 West St., Old Market, Bristol, England. TEL 0272-555550. FAX 0272-351481. Ed. Tony Ferrand. adv.; circ. 134,994.
Description: Contains information for and about charity work in the United Kingdom.

360 370 338   US   ISSN 1055-825X
▼**GOVERNMENT PROGRAMS.** (Supplement avail.) 1991. a. $23.99. Publishing & Business Consultants, 951 S. Oxford, No. 109, Los Angeles, CA 90006. TEL 213-732-3477. (Subscr. to: Box 75392, Los Angeles, CA 90075) Ed. Atia Napoleon. adv.; circ. 100,000.
Previously announced as: Subsidized Government Programs.
Description: Lists government programs covering education, employment, housing, families, and business.

360   JM
GRACE, KENNEDY FOUNDATION. ANNUAL REPORT. 1984. a. free. Grace, Kennedy Foundation, 64 Harbour St., P.O. Box 86, Kingston, Jamaica, W.I. TEL 809-922-3440-9. FAX 809-922-7567. TELEX 2290. (Subscr. to: One St. Lucia Cres., Kingston 5, Jamaica, W.I.) Ed. Marjorie Humphreys. circ. 500. (back issues avail.)

361   BG
GRASSROOTS. (Text in English) 1974. q. Tk.50($25) Association of Development Agencies in Bangladesh, 1-3 Block F, Lalmatia, Dhaka 1207, Bangladesh. TEL 2-327424. TELEX 642940. Ed. K.S. Huda. bk.rev.; circ. 10,000. **Indexed:** Irr.& Drain.Abstr., Rural Devel.Abstr., World Agri.Econ.& Rural Sociol.Abstr.
Former titles (until 1991): A D A B News; Association of Department Agencies of Bangladesh. Newsletter.
Description: Articles on contemporary developmental issues and problems affecting Bangladesh.

361.8   US   ISSN 0740-4832
GRASSROOTS FUNDRAISING JOURNAL. 1981. bi-m. $25. Box 11607, Berkeley, CA 94701. Eds. Kim Klein, Lisa Honig. adv.; bk.rev.; circ. 1,500. (back issues avail.) **Indexed:** Alt.Press Ind.
Description: Teaches small nonprofit organizations how to raise money in their communities.

GREAT BRITAIN. DEPARTMENT OF HEALTH AND SOCIAL SECURITY. HEALTH BUILDING NOTES. see *HOSPITALS*

GREAT BRITAIN. DEPARTMENT OF HEALTH AND SOCIAL SECURITY. HEALTH EQUIPMENT NOTES. see *HOSPITALS*

GREAT BRITAIN. DEPARTMENT OF HEALTH AND SOCIAL SECURITY. HOSPITAL IN-PATIENT INQUIRY. see *PUBLIC HEALTH AND SAFETY*

368.4   UK
GREAT BRITAIN. DEPARTMENT OF HEALTH AND SOCIAL SECURITY. SOCIAL SECURITY STATISTICS. 1973. a. price varies. H.M.S.O., P.O. Box 276, London SW8 5DT, England. illus.; stat. (reprint service avail. from UMI)

360   AT
GREEK ACTION BULLETIN. (Text in English and Greek) 1972. q. Aus.$6. Australian Greek Welfare Society, 8 Corsair St., Richmond, Vic. 3121, Australia. TEL 429-1147. circ. 210.

SOCIAL SERVICES AND WELFARE

360   UK   ISSN 0951-824X
GROUPWORK. (Text in English; summaries in French, German, Spanish) 1988. 3/yr. £27.50($60) Whiting & Birch Ltd., P.O. Box 872, Forest Hill, London SE23 3HL, England. TEL 081-699-0914. FAX 081-699-3685. Ed. Allan Brown. index; circ. 750. (back issues avail.) **Indexed:** ASSIA, Soc.Work Res.& Abstr., Sociol.Abstr.
—BLDSC shelfmark: 4220.460000.
   Description: Social work with groups of all types.

GUIDE TO ARKANSAS FUNDING SOURCES. see *BUSINESS AND ECONOMICS — Management*

362   UK   ISSN 0072-8756
GUIDE TO THE SOCIAL SERVICES. 1882. a. £10.95. Family Welfare Association, 501-505 Kingsland Rd., London E8 4AU, England. TEL 071-254-6251. FAX 071-249-5443. Ed.Bd. circ. 6,500.
   Description: Reference book on the structure and organization of the welfare state in England and Wales.

361.77   GW   ISSN 0017-5803
DIE GUTE TAT. 1954. q. (Deutsches Rotes Kreuz - German Red Cross) Sueddeutscher Verlag GmbH, Magazine Dept., Thomas-Dehler-Str. 27, D-8000 Munich 83, Germany. TEL 089-678040. FAX 089-67804-108. TELEX 5216148-EFV-D. Ed.Bd. adv.; illus.; circ. 1,378,300.

362.4   GW
DER GUTE WILLE; zur Sicherung der eingliederung Schwerbehinderter. 1967. bi-m. free. Arbeitsgemeinschaft der Deutschen Hauptfuersorgestellen, Mindenerstr. 2, Postfach 210720, 5000 Cologne 21, Germany. bk.rev.; circ. 217,600. (looseleaf format)

H E R S NEWSLETTER. (Hysterectomy Educational Resources & Services) see *WOMEN'S INTERESTS*

325   US
H I A S REPORTER. 1983. q. free. H I A S Inc., 333 Seventh Ave., New York, NY 10001-5004. Ed. Roberta Elliott. bk.rev.; illus.; circ. 11,000.
   Former titles: H I A S Bulletin (ISSN 0097-0263); U H S Bulletin (ISSN 0041-509X)

H L I CANADIAN REPORT. (Human Life International in Canada Inc.) see *POPULATION STUDIES*

H L I REPORTS. (Human Life International) see *POPULATION STUDIES*

H L I REPORTS. (Human Life International in Canada Inc.) see *POPULATION STUDIES*

360   DK
HAANDBOG FOR SOCIAL OG SUNDHEDSSEKTOR. 1982. a. (in 2 vols.). DKK 750 per vol. Forlag for Social- og Sundhedssektor, Vibeholms Alle 11-15, 2605 Bronoby, Denmark. TEL 43-43-43-80. FAX 43-43-60-29.
   Formerly: Plejehjemshaandbogen (ISSN 0108-0857); Incorporates: Bistandshaandbogen (ISSN 0108-8351)

362.7   DK
HAANDBOGEN DAGINSTITUTIONER. 1984. triennial. DKK 174. Kroghs Forlag A-S, Chr. Hansensvej 3, 7100 Vejle, Denmark. TEL 75 82 3900. adv.; circ. 3,000.
   Former titles: Haandbog for Boerne- og Ungdominstitutioner. Daginstitutioner & Haandbog for Boerne- og Ungdominstitutioner.

HABITAT WORLD. see *HOUSING AND URBAN PLANNING*

361.8   US
HAIGHT ASHBURY NEWSPAPER. 1977. 11/yr. free. Newspaper Collective, 409 Clayton St., San Francisco, CA 94117. TEL 415-863-5498. Ed.Bd. adv.; bk.rev.; circ. 6,500.

HANDICAP NEWS. see *HANDICAPPED*

362.4   DK   ISSN 0904-8081
HANDICAP - NYT. 1925. 8/yr. DKK 128. Dansk Handicap Forbund - National Association of Disabled in Denmark, Hans Knudsens Plads 1A, 2100 Copenhagen OE, Denmark. TEL 31-293555. FAX 31-293948. Ed. Keld Sogaard. adv.; circ. 18,000.
   Formerly: Vanfoerebladet (ISSN 0042-2541)
   Description: Cultural, political and social activities and aims of the handicapped.

HANDICAPPED FUNDING DIRECTORY; a guide to sources of funding in the United States for handicapped programs & services. see *HANDICAPPED*

HARICOT; newsletter for the renal patients of Australia. see *MEDICAL SCIENCES — Urology And Nephrology*

HARTMANNBUND IN BADEN - WUERTTEMBERG. see *PUBLIC HEALTH AND SAFETY*

362.7   US   ISSN 0362-6296
RJ501.H3
HAWAII. DEPARTMENT OF HEALTH. MENTAL HEALTH SERVICES FOR CHILDREN AND YOUTH; children's MH services branch. 1970. a. Department of Health, Mental Health Division, Children's Mental Health Services Branch, 3627 Kilauea Ave., Rm. 101, Honolulu, HI 96816. TEL 808-548-6335. stat.; circ. 300. Key Title: Mental Health Services for Children and Youth.

HAWAII. DEPARTMENT OF HEALTH. WAIMANO TRAINING SCHOOL AND HOSPITAL DIVISION (REPORT). see *HOSPITALS*

HAWAII'S NATIONAL GAY COMMUNITY NEWS; Hawaii and Western States. see *HOMOSEXUALITY*

HEALTH & SOCIAL SERVICE JOURNAL. see *HOSPITALS*

HEALTH AND SOCIAL SERVICE WORKFORCE IN ALBERTA. see *PUBLIC HEALTH AND SAFETY*

360   US   ISSN 0360-7283
HV687.5.U5   CODEN: HSWODK
HEALTH AND SOCIAL WORK. 1976. q. $50 to non-members; institutions and libraries $63. National Association of Social Workers, Publications Department, 7981 Eastern Ave., Silver Spring, MD 20910. TEL 301-565-0333. FAX 301-587-1321. Ed. Judith Ross. adv.; bk.rev.; index; circ. 6,500. (also avail. in microfiche from UMI; back issues avail.; reprint service avail. from UMI) **Indexed:** Abstr.Health Care Manage.Stud., Adol.Ment.Hlth.Abstr., ASSIA, Biol.Abstr., CINAHL, Dent.Ind., DSH Abstr., Except.Child Educ.Abstr., Excerp.Med., Ind.Med., Psychol.Abstr., Rehabil.Lit., Soc.Work Res.& Abstr., Soc.Work Res.& Abstr., Sociol.Abstr., Sp.Ed.Needs Abstr., World Bibl.Soc.Sec.
—BLDSC shelfmark: 4274.884000.
   Description: Examines health-related social problems and issues dealing with the client and the community.

HEALTH CARE FACILITY MANAGEMENT. see *HOSPITALS*

HEALTH CARE FINANCING REVIEW. see *MEDICAL SCIENCES*

361 610   UK   ISSN 0268-1153
    CODEN: HRTPE2
HEALTH EDUCATION RESEARCH; theory and practice. 1986. q. £80($140) I R L Press Ltd. (Subsidiary of: Oxford University Press), Pinkhill House, Southfield Road, Eynsham, Oxford OX8 1JJ, England. TEL 0865-882283. FAX 0865-882890. TELEX 837330-OXPRES-G. (U.S. subscr. addr.: I R L Press, Box Q, McLean, VA 22101) Ed. Keith Tones. adv.; bk.rev.; index. (back issues avail.; reprint service avail. from SWZ) **Indexed:** ASSIA, Biol.Abstr., Cont.Pg.Educ., Curr.Cont., Curr.Tit.Dent., Excerp.Med., Ind.Med., Psychol.Abstr., Sci.Cit.Ind., Stud.Wom.Abstr.
—BLDSC shelfmark: 4275.011440.
   Description: Promotes understanding of the processes, rationale and philosophy underlying the work of practicing health educators in an international forum.
   Refereed Serial

362.1   US   ISSN 0361-2929
RA981.C3
HEALTH FACILITIES DIRECTORY (SACRAMENTO). Spine title: Directory of Health Facilities. 1975. q. free. Department of Health Services, Licensing and Certification Division, 714-744 P St., Box 942732, Sacramento, CA 94234-7320. TEL 916-322-2810.

360   US   ISSN 0361-4468
RA407.3
HEALTH, UNITED STATES. a. price varies. U.S. National Center for Health Statistics, Scientific and Technical Information Branch, 6525 Belcrest Road, Hyattsville, MD 20782. TEL 301-436-8500.

360   GW   ISSN 0017-9868
DIE HEIMSTATT; * Werkheft Jugendsozialarbeit und Jugendpflege in Heim und Gruppe. 1953. s-a. DM.24. (Katholische Landesarbeitsgemeinschaft fuer Jugendsozialarbeit) Die Heimstatt Domus Verlag, Servatinstr. 8, Postfach 150137, 5300 Bonn 1, Germany. Ed. Dr. Karl Hugo Breuer.

360
HELFENDE HAENDE; Zeitschrift des diakonischen Werkes Westfalen. 1950. q. free. Diakonisches Werk der Evangelischen Kirche von Westfalen, Friesenring 32, 4400 Muenster, Germany. TEL 0251-2709-410. FAX 0251-2709-573. Ed. Achim Kuhlmann. bk.rev.; bibl.; charts; illus.; stat.; circ. 10,000. (back issues avail.)

HEMLOCK QUARTERLY. see *MEDICAL SCIENCES*

360 649   JA   ISSN 0018-327X
HOIKU NO TOMO. 1952. m. 5160 Yen. National Council of Social Welfare - Zenkoku Shakai Fukushi Kyogikai, 3-3-2 Kasumigaseki, Chiyoda-ku, Tokyo, Japan. Ed. Kishio Kimura. adv.; bk.rev.; circ. 35,000.

362   UK   ISSN 0260-5295
HOME CARE SERVICES, DAY CARE ESTABLISHMENTS, DAY SERVICES - SCOTLAND. 1976. a. Social Work Services Group, 43 Jeffrey St., Rm. 424, Edinburgh EH1 1DN, Scotland.
   Supersedes in part (1971-1975): Scottish Social Work Statistics (ISSN 0307-9597)

361.6   HO
HONDURAS. SECRETARIA DE TRABAJO Y PREVISION SOCIAL. BOLETIN DE ESTADISTICAS LABORALES. 1973. a. Ministerio de Trabajo y Prevision Social, Planificacion Sectorial y Estadistica Laboreal, Tegucigalpa, Honduras.

360   US   ISSN 0275-3065
HOOSHARAR - MIOUTUNE. (Text in Armenian) 1914. m. (except Jul. & Aug.). $10 to non-members. Armenian General Benevolent Union, 585 Saddle River Rd., Saddle Brook, NJ 07662. TEL 201-797-7600. Ed. Antranig Poladian. circ. 2,000.

362   US
▼**HOSPICE.** 1990. 4/yr. $45 membership. National Hospice Organization, 1901 N. Moore St., Ste. 901, Arlington, VA 22209. TEL 800-658-8898. FAX 703-525-5762. Ed. Nina Barth.
   Description: For professionals involved in hospice care for the terminally ill.

362   US
HOSPICE TODAY. 1981. q. free. Hospice of the Florida Suncoast, 300 E. Bay Dr., Largo, FL 34640. TEL 813-586-4432. Ed. Kimberly Walter. bk.rev.; circ. 36,000. (controlled).
   Formerly (until 1987): Hospice Care Newsletter.
   Description: Informs friends, volunteers, and financial supporters about the activities and programs of the agency, its services to the community, and its role as a resource and an advocate on issues related to death, grief and terminal illness.

HOUSING THE ELDERLY REPORT. see *HOUSING AND URBAN PLANNING*

360   UK
HOW TO LIVE IN BRITAIN. 1952. a. price varies. British Council, 10 Spring Gardens, London, England. TEL 071-930-8466. FAX 071-493-5035.

HUMAN RIGHTS RESOURCES. see *POLITICAL SCIENCE — Civil Rights*

S

SOCIAL SERVICES AND WELFARE

361.6 323.4   US
HUMAN SERVE CAMPAIGN NEWSLETTER. irreg. (3-4/yr.). free. Human Serve Campaign, c/o Columbia University, 622 W. 113th St., Rm. 410, New York, NY 10025. TEL 212-854-4053.

360   US
HUMAN SERVICES DIRECTORY; health and social agencies in Greater Cleveland. 1946. biennial. $15. Federation for Community Planning, 614 Superior Ave. N.W., Ste. 300, Cleveland, OH 44113-1306. TEL 216-781-2944. FAX 216-781-2988. circ. 5,000.
Formerly: Health and Welfare Directory.

360   US   ISSN 0193-9009
HV85
HUMAN SERVICES IN THE RURAL ENVIRONMENT. 1974. q. $25 to individuals (foreign $35); institutions and libraries $35 (foreign $45). Eastern Washington University, Inland Empire School of Social Work and Human Services, Cheney, WA 99004. TEL 509-359-6474. Ed. Lynne Clemmons Morris. adv.; bk.rev.; circ. 1,000. (also avail. in microform) **Indexed:** Abstr.Soc.Geront., C.I.J.E., Soc.Work Res.& Abstr.
Description: Dedicated to the concerns of people living in rural areas. Serves as an information exchange and communication forum among those interested in rural service settings, by focusing on policy and legislative developments, program models, research and evaluation projects, and innovative efforts to document aspects of rural life.

301.4   US   ISSN 0164-6079
HUMAN SERVICES REPORTER. 1978. 6/yr. free. Department of Human Services, CN 700, Trenton, NJ 08625. TEL 609-292-3703. FAX 609-393-4846. Eds. Ed Rogan, Margaret Bergmann. circ. 33,500. (tabloid format)
Incorporates (in 1978): Family.

360   PR   ISSN 0441-4144
HUMANIDAD. 1967. a. Universidad de Puerto Rico, Escuela Graduada de Trabajo Social, Rio Piedras, PR 00931. Ed. Josef R. de Caraballo. bibl.; cum.index: vols.1-8, 1967-1974; circ. 2,000.

I B I S REVIEW. (International Benefits Information Service) see INSURANCE

362.7   II   ISSN 0018-8867
I C C W NEWS BULLETIN. (Text in English) 1954. q. Rs.35. Indian Council for Child Welfare, 4 Deen Dayal Upadhayaya Marg, New Delhi 110 002, India. TEL 11-331-9539. Ed. Smt. Kusum Kapur. adv.; bibl.; charts; illus.; circ. 1,000.
Description: Covers nutrition, education, labor, health and allied disciplines relevant to the welfare of children.

360   US   ISSN 0047-1305
I F C O NEWS. 1970. q. $15 to individuals; $20 libraries and institutions. Interreligious Foundation for Community Organization, 402 W. 145th St., New York, NY 10031. TEL 212-926-5757. FAX 212-926-5842. Ed.Bd. adv.; bk.rev.; bibl.; illus.; circ. 113,000.
Description: Focuses on local, national and international community organizing efforts.

I L C O PRAXIS. see MEDICAL SCIENCES — Cancer

I P C POVERTY RESEARCH SERIES. (Institute of Philippine Culture) see SOCIOLOGY

362.4   FI   ISSN 0356-7249
I T - INVALIDITYOE. 1941. m. FIM 100. Invalidiliitto r.y., Kumpulantie 1, 00520 Helsinki, Finland. FAX 0-739-500. Ed. Voitto Korhonen. adv.; bk.rev.; illus.; circ. 39,500.
Formerly: Suomen Invalidi (ISSN 0049-2566)

ICARUS FILE. see MEDICAL SCIENCES

360   AT   ISSN 0706-5914
IMPACT (NORTH FITZROY). 1979. q. $5. Melbourne Citymission, 472 Nicholson St., North Fitzroy, Vic. 3068, Australia. TEL 03-489-9666. Ed. Peter Philp. circ. 7,000. (back issues avail.)
Description: Report on Citymission's services for families, children, homeless, young people and adults, aged persons, the terminally ill and the intellectually disabled.

360   AT
IMPACT (SYDNEY). 1971. 11/yr. $30. Australian Council of Social Service, Inc. (ACOSS), P.O. Box 45, Railway Sq., Sydney, N.S.W. 2000, Australia. TEL 02-212-3277. FAX 02-281-1597. Ed. Anna Cater. adv.; bk.rev.; circ. 1,000. **Indexed:** ASSIA, Aus.P.A.I.S., World Bibl.Soc.Sec.
Former titles: Australian Social Welfare: Impact (ISSN 0157-6321); Australian Social Welfare; Supersedes in part: A C O S S Quarterly (ISSN 0045-0391)

362.7   US
IMPACT (WESTPORT). 1982. q. free. Save the Children, Public Affairs and Communication, 54 Wilton Rd., Box 950, Westport, CT 06881. TEL 203-221-4000. FAX 203-222-1067. Ed. Lee Mullane. illus.; circ. 150,000.
Formerly (until vol.6, no.4): Lifeline (Westport).

IN TOUCH (AUSTIN). see HANDICAPPED — Visually Impaired

360   AT   ISSN 0728-6503
IN UNITY. 1949. q. Australian Council of Churches, P.O. Box C199, Clarence St., Sydney, N.S.W. 2000, Australia. FAX 02-262-4514. bk.rev.; circ. 6,500.
Incorporates (in Jan. 1978): Christian Action News.

360   IT   ISSN 0046-8819
INCHIESTA; ricerca e pratica sociale. 1971. q. L.30000 (foreign L.45000)(effective 1992). Edizioni Dedalo s.r.l., Casella Postale 362, 70100 Bari, Italy. TEL 080-371555. FAX 080-371979. Dir. Vittorio Capecchi. bk.rev.; charts; circ. 12,000.
—BLDSC shelfmark: 4374.960000.
Description: Includes research on social issues in Italy. For students, researchers, social and political workers.

362.4 616.836   US
INDEPENDENT LIVING. 1983. q. $8. Equal Opportunity Publications, Inc., 44 Broadway, Greenlawn, NY 11740. TEL 516-261-8899. FAX 516-261-8935. Ed. Anne Kelly. bk.rev.; circ. 35,000. **Indexed:** Hlth.Ind.
Former titles: Independent Living and Health Care Today; Independent Living; S H R (Social Health Review).

362.4   AT   ISSN 0815-2276
INDEPENDENT LIVING. 1984. q. Aus.$22 (foreign Aus.$34)(effective Sep. 1991). (Independent Living Centre NSW Inc.) Rala Publications, 203-205 Darling St., Bamain, N.S.W. 2041, Australia. TEL 02-555-1944. FAX 02-555-1496. (Subscr. addr.: P.O. Box 706, Ryde, N.S.W. 2112, Australia) Ed. Charlotte Smedley. adv.; bk.rev.; cum.index: 1984-1990; circ. 1,500.
Description: Information on equipment, audio-visual resources and organizations for people with disabilities, caregivers, health professionals, builders and architects.

360   US
INDEPENDENT SECTOR. ANNUAL REPORT. 1980. a. free. Independent Sector, 1828 L St., N.W., Ste. 1200, Washington, DC 20036. TEL 202-223-8100. Ed. Sharon Fitzgerald. circ. 5,000. (back issues avail.)
Description: Overview of the sector's activities: communications, research, government relations.

INDEPENDENT SECTOR. UPDATE. see EDUCATION

362.7   II
INDIAN COUNCIL FOR CHILD WELFARE. ANNUAL REPORT. (Text in English) a. Indian Council for Child Welfare, 4 Deen Dayal Upadhyaya Marg, New Delhi 110 002, India. TEL 11-331-9539.

360   II   ISSN 0019-5634
HV1   CODEN: IJSWA3
INDIAN JOURNAL OF SOCIAL WORK. (Text in English) 1940. q. Rs.120($20) (effective 1991). Tata Institute of Social Sciences, Sion-Trombay Rd., Deonar, Bombay 400 088, India. TEL 551-0400. Ed. Armaity S. Desai. adv.; bk.rev.; index; circ. 1,200. (also avail. in microfilm from UMI; back issues avail.; reprint service avail. from UMI) **Indexed:** Adol.Ment.Hlth.Abstr., ASSIA, Curr.Cont., Lang.& Lang.Behav.Abstr., Psychol.Abstr., Rehabil.Lit., Rural Ext.Educ.& Tr.Abstr., Rural Recreat.Tour.Abstr., Soc.Work Res.& Abstr., Sociol.Abstr., SSCI, Stud.Wom.Abstr., World Agri.Econ.& Rural Sociol.Abstr.
Description: Interdisciplinary study of social work and social sciences, devoted to the scientific interpretation of social problems.

INDIAN YOUTH OF AMERICA NEWSLETTER. see CHILDREN AND YOUTH — About

362.7   PO   ISSN 0870-6565
INFANCIA E JUVENTUDE. 1955. q. Esc.1500. Direccao Geral dos Servicos Tutelares de Menores, Av. Almirante Reis, No. 101, 5 Andar, 1197 Lisbon Codex, Portugal. TEL 352-47-09. FAX 52-69-85. bk.rev.; charts; illus.; stat.; circ. 900.

INFOCUS NEWSLETTER. see ETHNIC INTERESTS

361   US   ISSN 0278-2383
HV85   CODEN: IREFD9
INFORMATION AND REFERRAL. Variant title: Alliance of Information and Referral Systems. Journal. 1979. s-a. $20 to individuals; institutions $30; members $10. Alliance of Information and Referral Systems, Box 3546, Joliet, IL 60434. TEL 815-744-6922. Ed. William E. Buffum. adv.; bk.rev.; circ. 400. **Indexed:** Lang.& Lang.Behav.Abstr., LISA, Sci.Abstr.
—BLDSC shelfmark: 4481.853000.

INFORMATION JUIVE. see ETHNIC INTERESTS

362.7   GW
INFORMATIONEN UEBER JUGENDARBEIT UND JUGENDPOLITIK IM LANDKREIS MUENCHEN. 1972. m. Kreisjugendring Muenchen-Land, Burg Schwaneck, 8023 Pullach im Isartal, Germany. TEL 44140-0. bk.rev.; circ. 2,000.

360   GW   ISSN 0179-8863
INFORMATIONEN ZUM ARBEITSLOSENRECHT UND SOZIALHILFERECHT. q. DM.48. Nomos Verlagsgesellschaft mbH und Co. KG, Waldseestr. 3-5, 7570 Baden-Baden, Germany. TEL 07221-21041. FAX 07221-210427. TELEX 051-933524.
—BLDSC shelfmark: 4496.461600.

360   FR   ISSN 0046-9459
HN421
INFORMATIONS SOCIALES. 8/yr. 170 F. Caisse Nationale des Allocations Familiales, 23 rue Daviel, 75634 Paris Cedex 13, France. TEL 45-65-54-32. Ed. Daniel Bequignon. adv.; bk.rev.; circ. 12,000. **Indexed:** World Bibl.Soc.Sec.
—BLDSC shelfmark: 4496.569000.

301   IT   ISSN 0020-0816
INFORMAZIONI SOCIALI. 1946. bi-m. free. Patronato A C L I, Via G. Marcora 18-20, 00153 Rome, Italy. Dir. Domenico Rosati. adv.; illus.

360   CN   ISSN 0827-4789
INITIATIVE. (Text in English, French) 1985. 4/yr. free. Canadian Council on Social Development, 55 Parkdale Ave., Box 3505, Sta. C, Ottawa, Ont. K1Y 4G1, Canada. TEL 613-728-1865. FAX 613-728-9387. circ. 10,000.
Description: Newsletter on self-help issues.

INNOVATING. see EDUCATION — Teaching Methods And Curriculum

360   US
INSIGHTS (WASHINGTON, 1977). 1977. q. free. American Association of Retired Persons, 601 E St., N.W., Washington, DC 20049. TEL 202-434-2260. (Co-sponsors: Widowed Persons Service; Social Outreach and Support)

INSTITUT DE READAPTATION DE MONTREAL. BULLETIN. see MEDICAL SCIENCES

SOCIAL SERVICES AND WELFARE 4409

360 051   US
INSTITUTE FOR CONTEMPORARY STUDIES. LETTER. 1975. biennial. free. Institute for Contemporary Studies, 243 Kearny St., San Francisco, CA 94108. TEL 415-981-5353, 800-326-0263. FAX 415-986-4878. Ed. Robert Kendrick. bk.rev.; circ. 6,000. (back issues avail.)
Description: Summarizes the finding of the institute's latest public policy research.

362.7 371.9   UY
INSTITUTO INTERAMERICANO DEL NINO. EDUCACION ESPECIAL. INFORMES TECNICOS. irreg. Instituto Interamericano del Nino, Avda. 8 de Octubre No. 2904, Montevideo, Uruguay.

362.7 310   UY
INSTITUTO INTERAMERICANO DEL NINO. ESTADISTICA E INFORMATICA. INFORMES TECNICOS. irreg. Instituto Interamericano del Nino, Avda. 8 de Octubre No. 2904, Montevideo, Uruguay.

362.7   UY
INSTITUTO INTERAMERICANO DEL NINO. REGISTRO CIVIL. INFORMES TECNICOS. irreg. Instituto Interamericano del Nino, Avda. 8 de Octubre No. 2904, Montevideo, Urugay.

362.7   UY
INSTITUTO INTERAMERICANO DEL NINO. SERVICIO SOCIAL. INFORMES TECNICOS. irreg. Instituto Interamericano del Nino, Avda. 8 de Octubre no. 2904, Montevideo, Uruguay. circ. 600.
Formerly: Instituto Interamericano del Nino. Publicaciones sobre Servicio Social.

360   SZ
INTEGRO; Gesundheits- und Sozialmagazin des V.P.O.D. 1983. m. (10/yr.). 35 Fr. Postfach, CH-8030 Zurich, Switzerland. TEL 01-2519935.

362.3   AT   ISSN 0818-6286
INTERACTION (CANBERRA); the Australian magazine on intellectual disability. 1962. 5/yr. Aus.$20 (typically set in July). National Council on Intellectual Disability, G.P.O. Box 647, Canberra, A.C.T. 2601, Australia. FAX 06-24-70729. Ed. M. Burgess. adv.; bk.rev.; index; circ. 3,700. Indexed: ERIC, Except.Child.Educ.Abstr.
Former titles: A A M R Journal (ISSN 0814-2610) & Australian Citizen Limited (ISSN 0313-6620); (until 1975): Australian Children Limited (ISSN 0004-8844)

362.7   UY
INTERAMERICAN CHILDREN'S INSTITUTE. REPORT OF THE GENERAL DIRECTOR. a. Instituto Interamericano del Nino, Avda. 8 de Octubre no. 2904, Montevideo, Uruguay. illus.

360   BL
INTERCAMBIO; revista quadrimestral de informacao e cultura. 1965-1976; N.S. 1980; N.S. 1988. 3/yr. free. Servico Social do Comercio, Assessoria de Divulgacao e Promocao Institucional, Rua Voluntarios da Patria 169, 11o andar, 22270 Rio de Janeiro, Brazil. bibl.; circ. 2,500.
Formerly (until 1987): Brazil. Servico Social do Comercio. Boletim de Intercambio.

361   UK   ISSN 0144-3488
INTERCHANGE. 1980. irreg. (10-12/yr.). £10. Glasgow Council for Voluntary Service, 11 Queen's Cres., Glasgow G4 9AS, Scotland. TEL 041-332-2444. FAX 041-332-0175. adv.; bk.rev.; circ. 1,500.

300 320   AU   ISSN 0020-5362
INTERESSE; soziale Information. 1963. q. contribution. Pastoralamt der Dioezese Linz, Sozialreferat, Kapuzinerstr. 84, A-4020 Linz, Austria. TEL 0732-27444162. Ed. Alfred Koller. bk.rev.; circ. 4,800.

360   US
INTERFACE (TRENTON). 1975. q. free. Developmental Disabilities Council, 108-110 N. Broad St., CN 700, Trenton, NJ 08625. TEL 609-292-3745. FAX 609-292-7114. Ed. Gregory Mizanin. circ. 3,000. (also avail. in microform from UMI; reprint service avail. from UMI) Indexed: PROMT, RILM.

360
INTERFAITH IMPACT. 1984. q. $30 membership. Interfaith Impact for Justice and Peace, 110 Maryland Ave., N.E., Washington, DC 20002. TEL 202-543-2800. Ed. Christie L. Goodman. bk.rev.; circ. 10,000. (back issues avail.)
Formed by the 1990 merger of: Interfaith Action (ISSN 8755-9404) & National Impact. Update.

361.77   SZ
INTERNATIONAL COMMITTEE OF THE RED CROSS. ANNUAL REPORT - RAPPORT D'ACTIVITE - INFORME DE ACTIVIDAD - TAETIGKEITSBERICHT. (Text in Arabic, English, French, German and Spanish) a. 12 Fr. International Committee of the Red Cross, 19 Avenue de la Paix, 1202 Geneva, Switzerland.

361   US   ISSN 0074-2961
INTERNATIONAL CONFERENCE OF SOCIAL WORK. CONFERENCE PROCEEDINGS. biennial. (International Council on Social Welfare) Columbia University Press, 562 W. 113th St., New York, NY 10025. TEL 212-678-6777.

INTERNATIONAL DIRECTORY OF PRISONERS AID AGENCIES. see CRIMINOLOGY AND LAW ENFORCEMENT

361   MY   ISSN 0020-6784
INTERNATIONAL FORUM.* (Summaries in French) 1960. q. Aus.$0.08($1.20) World Council of Young Men's Service Clubs, KTM Godown No. 2A, Jalan Tun Sambanthan, 50470 Kuala Lumpur, Malaysia. Ed. John Bremner. adv.; illus.; circ. 25,000.

362.7   US
INTERNATIONAL FRIENDSHIP AND GOOD WILL BULLETIN. 1978. q. $10 to non-members; free to members. International Society of Friendship and Good Will, 211 W. Fourth Ave., Box 2637, Gastonia, NC 28053-2637. TEL 704-864-7906. Ed. S.J. Drake. adv.; bk.rev.; circ. 1,000. (back issues avail.)

360   UK   ISSN 0749-6753
CODEN: IJHMEO
INTERNATIONAL JOURNAL OF HEALTH PLANNING AND MANAGEMENT. 1986. q. $295 (effective 1992). John Wiley & Sons Ltd., Journals, Baffins Lane, Chichester, Sussex PO19 1UD, England. TEL 0243-779777. FAX 0243-775878. TELEX 86290 WIBOOK G. Ed. K. Lee. adv. (reprint service avail. from SWZ) Indexed: Abstr.Health Care Manage.Stud., Curr.Cont., Excerp.Med., Sociol.Abstr.
—BLDSC shelfmark: 4542.277600.
Description: Discusses major issues in health planning, management systems, and practices; maintains a balance between practice and theory from a variety of schools of thought.

362.2   US   ISSN 0272-4308
CODEN: IPHOD3
INTERNATIONAL JOURNAL OF PARTIAL HOSPITALIZATION. 1982. s-a. $95 (foreign $110)(effective 1992). Plenum Publishing Corp., 233 Spring St., New York, NY 10013-1578. TEL 212-620-8000. FAX 212-463-0742. TELEX 23-421139. Ed. Raymond F. Luber. adv.; bk.rev. (also avail. in microfilm from JSC; back issues avail.) Indexed: Abstr.Health Care Manage.Stud., CINAHL, Curr.Cont., Excerp.Med., Ind.Med., Psychol.Abstr.
—BLDSC shelfmark: 4542.449500.
Refereed Serial

360 364   US   ISSN 0020-8396
INTERNATIONAL PRISONERS AID ASSOCIATION. NEWSLETTER.* 1950. 3/yr. $5. International Prisoners Aid Association, c/o Badr-El-Din Ali, Exec. Dir., Visiting Scholar, CMES, Harvard University, 1737 Cambridge St., Cambridge, MA 02138. TEL 502-588-5555. bk.rev.; circ. 500. (processed)

361   US   ISSN 0538-9461
INTERNATIONAL RESCUE COMMITTEE ANNUAL REPORT. a. free. International Rescue Committee, 386 Park Ave. S., New York, NY 10016. TEL 212-679-0010.

INTERNATIONAL REVIEW OF THE RED CROSS. see LAW — International Law

INTERNATIONAL REVIEW OF VICTIMOLOGY. see CRIMINOLOGY AND LAW ENFORCEMENT

360   UK   ISSN 0020-8728
HV1
INTERNATIONAL SOCIAL WORK. (Text in English) 1958. q. £31($51) to individuals; institutions £77($127). (International Council on Social Welfare) Sage Publications Ltd., 6 Bonhill St., London EC2A 4PU, England. TEL 071-374-0645. FAX 071-374-8741. (Co-sponsors: International Association of Schools of Social Work; International Federation of Social Workers) Ed. Francis J. Turner. adv.: color page £150; trim 177 x 101; adv. contact: Bernie Folan. bk.rev.; index, cum.index: 1958-1977. (also avail. in microform from UMI; reprint service avail. from UMI) Indexed: Abstr.Soc.Work., ASSIA, I D A, Mid.East: Abstr.& Ind., PSI, Psychol.Abstr., Soc.Work Res.& Abstr., Sociol.Abstr., World Bibl.Soc.Sec.
—BLDSC shelfmark: 4549.500000.
Description: Designed to promote communication and extend knowledge in the fields of social development, social welfare and human services.

360   UK
INTERNATIONAL WHO'S WHO IN COMMUNITY SERVICE. 1974. irreg. Melrose Press Ltd., 3 Regal Lane, Soham, Ely, Cambridgeshire CB7 5BA, England. TEL 0353-721091. FAX 0353-721839.

INTERNATIONAL WORKCAMP LISTING (YEAR). see BUSINESS AND ECONOMICS — International Development And Assistance

361   CN   ISSN 0047-1321
INTERVENTION. (Text in English and French) 1969. 3/yr. Can.$42.80($40) to institutions; individuals Can.$37.45. Corporation Professionnelle des Travailleurs Sociaux du Quebec - Professional Corporation of Social Workers of Quebec, 5757 Decelles Ave., Ste. 335, Montreal, Que. H3S 2C3, Canada. TEL 514-731-2749. FAX 514-731-6785. Ed. Rene Page. adv.; bk.rev.; bibl.; circ. 2,000. (also avail. in audio cassette) Indexed: Pt.de Rep. (1983-), RADAR.
—BLDSC shelfmark: 4557.471800.
Description: Provides opportunities for members of the Corporation to publish and share the results of their research and professional experience, stimulates new ideas and serves as a source of information and continuing education.

362.7   UK
INVALID CHILDREN'S AID NATIONWIDE YEAR BOOK. a. free. 198 City Rd., London EC1V 2PH, England. FAX 01-250-1612. Ed. Linda MacDonald. adv.; circ. 3,000.
Formerly: Invalid Children's Aid Association Year Book.

360 614   CN
RA410.9.C2
INVENTORY OF HEALTH & SOCIAL SERVICE PERSONNEL. 1978. a. free. Health and Social Services Disciplines Committee, Kensington Place, 5th Floor, 10011-109th St., Edmonton, Alta. T5J 3S8, Canada. TEL 403-427-2655. FAX 403-422-9734. Ed. F. Rawson. circ. 800. (back issues avail.)
Former titles: Health and Social Services Workforce in Alberta & Health and Social Service Manpower in Alberta (ISSN 0714-1904)
Description: Contains the results of the annual survey of health and social service employers in Alberta concerning the number of personnel employed, their status, vacancy and turnover rates and recruitment difficulties.

360   IE
IRELAND. DEPARTMENT OF SOCIAL WELFARE. STATISTICAL INFORMATION ON SOCIAL WELFARE. a. Department of Social Welfare, c/o Secretary, Dublin 2, Ireland.

362   IS   ISSN 0075-1014
HA1931
ISRAEL. CENTRAL BUREAU OF STATISTICS. DIAGNOSTIC STATISTICS OF HOSPITALIZED PATIENTS. (Subseries of its Special Series) (Text in English and Hebrew) 1950. irreg. price varies. Central Bureau of Statistics, Box 13015, Jerusalem 91 130, Israel. TEL 02-21 12 11.

SOCIAL SERVICES AND WELFARE

361   IS
ISRAEL. MINISTRY OF LABOUR AND SOCIAL AFFAIRS. DEPARTMENT OF INTERNATIONAL RELATIONS. THE PRESS ON WELFARE; a selection of articles on welfare from the Israeli press. (Text in English) 1970. s-a. free. Ministry of Labour and Social Affairs, Department of International Relations, 10 Yad Harutzim St., Talpiot, P.O. Box 1260, Jerusalem, Israel.
   Formerly: Israel. Ministry of Social Welfare. Department of International Relations. The Press on Welfare.

360 314   IT
ITALY. ISTITUTO CENTRALE DI STATISTICA. STATISTICHE DELL' ASSISTENZA E DELLA PREVIDENZA SOCIALE. 1953. a. L.18000. Istituto Centrale di Statistica, Via Cesare Balbo 16, 00100 Rome, Italy. circ. 1,200.
   Formerly: Italy. Istituto Centrale di Statistica. Annuario Statistico dell' Assistenza e della Previdenza Sociale (ISSN 0075-1790)

ITINERARY (BAYONNE); the magazine for travelers with physical disabilities. see *TRAVEL AND TOURISM*

J A C S VOLUNTEER. (Joint Action in Community Services, Inc.) see *OCCUPATIONS AND CAREERS*

J C C CIRCLE. (Jewish Community Centers Association of North America) see *RELIGIONS AND THEOLOGY — Judaic*

360   GW
JAHRBUCH DES SOZIALRECHTS DER GEGENWART. a. price varies. Erich Schmidt Verlag GmbH & Co. (Bielefeld), Viktoriastr. 44a, Postfach 7330, 4800 Bielefeld, Germany. TEL 0521-5830855. Eds. G. Wannagat, W. Gitter. (back issues avail.)

361   JA
JAPANESE REPORT TO THE INTERNATIONAL COUNCIL ON SOCIAL WELFARE. 1954. a. free. International Council on Social Welfare, Japanese National Committee, 3-3-4 Kasumigaseki, Chiyoda-ku, Tokyo, Japan.
   Formerly: International Conference of Social Work. Japanese National Committee. Progress Report (ISSN 0538-6039)

JEEVAN JAUBAN. see *PHYSICAL FITNESS AND HYGIENE*

JEWISH POPULATION SERIES. see *POPULATION STUDIES*

360 296   US   ISSN 0021-6712
HV3190
JEWISH SOCIAL WORK FORUM. 1964. a. $9 (typically set in Jan.). Yeshiva University, Wurzweiler School of Social Work, Alumni Association, 2495 Amsterdam Ave., New York, NY 10033. TEL 212-960-0841. FAX 212-960-0822. Ed. Norman Linzer. adv.; bk.rev.; charts; circ. 950. *Indexed:* Abstr.Soc.Geront., Lang.& Lang.Behav.Abstr., Mid.East: Abstr.& Ind., Soc.Work Res.& Abstr., Sociol.Abstr.

362.4   UK
JOHN GROOMS NEWSLETTER. 1979. s-a. free. John Grooms Association for Disabled People, 10 Gloucester Drive, Finsbury Park N4 2LP, England. TEL 081-802-7272. adv.; circ. 40,000.

JONQUIL. see *CLUBS*

361   FR
JOURNAL DES ORPHELINS DE GUERRE. 1930. m. 14 F. Federation Nationale "les Fils des Tues", 25, rue Lavoisier, 75008 Paris, France.

JOURNAL OF ADDICTIONS & OFFENDER COUNSELING. see *CRIMINOLOGY AND LAW ENFORCEMENT*

360   US   ISSN 1052-9950
▼**JOURNAL OF ANALYTIC SOCIAL WORK.** 1992. q. $18 to individuals; institutions $24; libraries $36. Haworth Press, Inc., 10 Alice St., Binghamton, NY 13904-1580. TEL 800-342-9678. FAX 607-722-1424. Ed. Jerrold R. Brandell. (also avail. in microform from HAW; reprint service avail. from HAW)
   Description: Designed to provide social work clinicians and clinical educators with articles relevant to the practice of psychoanalytic social work with the individual client.
   Refereed Serial

362.4   US   ISSN 0047-2220
                CODEN: JRCOD3
JOURNAL OF APPLIED REHABILITATION COUNSELING. 1970. q. $15 to individuals; institutions $30. National Rehabilitation Counseling Association, 1910 Association Dr., Ste. 206, Reston, VA 22091. Ed. Arnold Wolf. adv.; bk.rev.; circ. 6,500. (also avail. in microfilm from UMI; reprint service avail. from UMI) *Indexed:* Except.Child.Educ.Abstr., Psychol.Abstr., Rehabil.Lit.
   —BLDSC shelfmark: 4947.030000.

362.7   US   ISSN 1053-8712
                CODEN: JCABEK
▼**JOURNAL OF CHILD SEXUAL ABUSE**; research, treatment & program innovations for victims, survivors & offenders. 1992. q. $24 to individuals; institutions $32; libraries $48. Haworth Press, Inc., 10 Alice St., Binghamton, NY 13904-1580. TEL 800-342-9678. FAX 607-722-1424. Ed. Robert A. Geffner. adv.; page $300. bk.rev. (also avail. in microfiche from HAW; reprint service avail. from HAW) *Indexed:* Behav.Med.Abstr., Crim.Just.Abstr., DNP, Educ.Admin.Abstr., G.Soc.Sci.& Rel.Per.Lit., Ind.Per.Art.Relat.Law, Ref.Zh., Sage Fam.Stud.Abstr., Sage Urb.Stud.Abstr., Soc.Work Res.Abstr., Sociol.Abstr., SOPODA, Stud.Wom.Abstr.
   Description: Covers research issues, clinical issues, case studies and brief reports on young victims, adult survivors and the offenders.
   Refereed Serial

JOURNAL OF GAY & LESBIAN PSYCHOTHERAPY. see *HOMOSEXUALITY*

362.8 301.415   US   ISSN 1053-8720
▼**JOURNAL OF GAY & LESBIAN SOCIAL SERVICES.** 1992. q. $15 to individuals; institutions $18; libraries $30. Haworth Press, Inc., 10 Alice St., Binghamton, NY 13904-1580. TEL 800-342-9678. FAX 607-722-1424. Ed. James Kelley. (also avail. in microform from HAW; reprint service avail. from HAW)
   Description: Focuses on policy, program and practice issues aiming to promote the well-being of homosexuals and bisexuals in contemporary society.
   Refereed Serial

360 614.8   US   ISSN 0897-7186
RA418   CODEN: JHSPEH
JOURNAL OF HEALTH & SOCIAL POLICY. 1989. q. $28 to individuals; institutions $32; libraries $60. Haworth Press, Inc., 10 Alice St., Binghamton, NY 13904. TEL 800-342-9678. FAX 607-722-1424. Ed. Marvin D. Feit. adv.; bk.rev. (also avail. in microfiche from HAW; reprint service avail. from HAW)
   —BLDSC shelfmark: 4996.731000.
   Description: Addresses health and social policy issues, concerns, and questions.
   Refereed Serial

360   US   ISSN 0883-7562
JOURNAL OF INDEPENDENT SOCIAL WORK; innovations in professional service and private practice. 1987. q. $30 to individuals; institutions $45; libraries $95. Haworth Press, Inc., 10 Alice St., Binghamton, NY 13904. TEL 800-342-9678. FAX 607-722-1424. Ed. Robert L. Barker. adv.; bk.rev.; circ. 119. (also avail. in microfiche; back issues avail.) *Indexed:* Human Resour.Abstr., Psychol.Abstr., Sage Fam.Stud.Abstr., Soc.Work Res.& Abstr., Sociol.Abstr.
   —BLDSC shelfmark: 5005.170000.
   Description: For the professional, self-employed social worker, both part-time and full-time, who is providing services outside of traditional bureaucratic agency auspice. Provides practical analyses of the economic, social, and professional trends which can affect independent social workers and their clients.
   Refereed Serial

JOURNAL OF INTELLECTUAL DISABILITY RESEARCH. see *MEDICAL SCIENCES — Psychiatry And Neurology*

JOURNAL OF MARITAL AND FAMILY THERAPY. see *PSYCHOLOGY*

JOURNAL OF MENTAL HEALTH ADMINISTRATION. see *PUBLIC HEALTH AND SAFETY*

JOURNAL OF MINORITY AGING. see *GERONTOLOGY AND GERIATRICS*

JOURNAL OF OFFENDER REHABILITATION; a multidisciplinary journal of innovation in research, services, and programs in corrections and criminal justice. see *CRIMINOLOGY AND LAW ENFORCEMENT*

360 320.531   US   ISSN 1042-8232
HV85   CODEN: JPHSER
JOURNAL OF PROGRESSIVE HUMAN SERVICES. 1978. s-a. $12 to individuals; institutions $20; libraries $25. (Institute for Social Services Alternatives, Inc.) Haworth Press, Inc., 10 Alice St., Binghamton, New York, NY 13904. TEL 800-342-9678. FAX 607-722-1424. TELEX 4932599. Ed. Mimi Abramovitz. adv.; bk.rev.; film rev.; circ. 1,000. (also avail. in microfiche from HAW; back issues avail.; reprint service avail. from HAW) *Indexed:* Alt.Press Ind., Left Ind. (1982-), Soc.Work Res.& Abstr., Sociol.Abstr.
   —BLDSC shelfmark: 5042.745000.
   Formerly (until 1990): Catalyst (New York, 1978) (ISSN 0191-040X)
   Description: Deals with social problems and human services from the progressive perspective.
   Refereed Serial

JOURNAL OF PSYCHOSOCIAL NURSING AND MENTAL HEALTH SERVICES. see *MEDICAL SCIENCES — Nurses And Nursing*

360 614   UK   ISSN 0957-4832
                CODEN: JPHME9
JOURNAL OF PUBLIC HEALTH MEDICINE. 1979. q. £55($115) Oxford University Press, Pinkhill House, Southfield Road, Eynsham, Oxford OX8 1JJ. TEL 0865-882283. FAX 0865-882890. TELEX 8373300 OXPRES G. Ed. Dr. L.J. Donaldson. adv.; bk.rev.; index; circ. 2,450. *Indexed:* Abstr.Hyg., ASSIA, Bibl.Dev.Med.& Child Neur., Curr.Adv.Ecol.Sci., Excerp.Med., Med.Care Rev., Protozool.Abstr., Rev.Plant Path., Risk Abstr., Trop.Dis.Bull.
   —BLDSC shelfmark: 5043.560000.
   Formerly: Community Medicine (ISSN 0142-2456)
   Description: Addresses the practice of community medicine.

362 615   US   ISSN 0022-4154
HD7255.A2   CODEN: JOREA
JOURNAL OF REHABILITATION.* 1935. q. $35. National Rehabilitation Association, 1910 Association Dr., Ste. 205, Reston, VA 22091-1502. TEL 703-836-0850. FAX 703-836-2209. Ed. Paul Leung. adv.; bk.rev.; illus.; pat.; index; circ. 24,000. (also avail. in microform from MIM; microfilm from KTO; reprint service avail. from KTO) *Indexed:* Adol.Ment.Hlth.Abstr., ASSIA, C.I.J.E., C.I.S. Abstr., CINAHL, Curr.Cont., Except.Child.Educ.Abstr., Excerp.Med., Hlth.Ind., Hosp.Lit.Ind., Ind.Med., Psychol.Abstr., Rehabil.Lit., Soc.Sci.Ind., SSCI.
   —BLDSC shelfmark: 5048.850000.

360   BG
JOURNAL OF SOCIAL DEVELOPMENT. (June issue is in English; Dec. issue is in Bengali.) 1966-1969; resumed in 1984. s-a. Tk.25($3) per no. University of Dhaka, Institute of Social Welfare and Research, Dhaka 1205, Bangladesh. bk.rev.; circ. 200.
   Formerly (until 1984): Social Horizon (ISSN 0037-7759)

360   RH   ISSN 1012-1080
JOURNAL OF SOCIAL DEVELOPMENT IN AFRICA. 1986. 2/yr. $30. School of Social Work, Private Bag 66022, Kopje, Harare, Zimbabwe. TEL 707414. Ed. Brigid Willmore. index; circ. 350. (back issues avail.) *Indexed:* Geo.Abstr., Soc.Work Res.& Abstr.
   —BLDSC shelfmark: 5064.752700.
   Description: Specializes in social development. Publishes critical analyses of issues affecting development and poverty, popular participation, equality and productivity. Aimed at practitioners, academics and policy makers.
   Refereed Serial

SOCIAL SERVICES AND WELFARE 4411

360 US ISSN 1053-0789
HN1 CODEN: JSDHET
▼JOURNAL OF SOCIAL DISTRESS AND THE HOMELESS. 1992. q. $80 (foreign $95). Human Sciences Press, Inc. (Subsidiary of: Plenum Publishing Corp.), 233 Spring St., New York, NY 10013. TEL 212-620-8000. FAX 212-463-0742. TELEX 23-421139. Ed. R. W. Rieber. adv.
  Description: Explores the link between social distress and issues such as homelessness, violence, and racial tension and its institutionalization in modern society.
  Refereed Serial

360 US ISSN 0148-8376
HV1 CODEN: JSSRDV
JOURNAL OF SOCIAL SERVICE RESEARCH. 1977. q. $36 to individuals; institutions $95; libraries $175. Haworth Press, Inc., 10 Alice St., Binghamton, NY 13904. TEL 800-342-9678. FAX 607-722-1424. TELEX 4932599. Ed. Shanti K. Khinduka. adv.; bk.rev.; circ. 327. (also avail. in microfiche from HAW; back issues avail.; reprint service avail. from HAW) Indexed: Adol.Ment.Hlth.Abstr., ASSIA, Behav.Abstr., Bull.Signal., Chicago Psychoanal.Lit.Ind., CJPI, Crim.Just.Abstr., Curr.Cont., Human Resour.Abstr., Lang.& Lang.Behav.Abstr., Left Ind., Past.Care & Couns.Abstr., Psychol.Abstr., Sage Pub.Admin.Abstr., Soc.Work Res.& Abstr., Sociol.Abstr., SSCI.
  —BLDSC shelfmark: 5064.913000.
  Description: Devoted to empirical research and its application to the design, delivery, and management of social services.
  Refereed Serial

JOURNAL OF SOCIAL WELFARE AND FAMILY LAW. see LAW — Family And Matrimonial Law

361.3 US ISSN 0276-3850
HV1 CODEN: JSWSDK
JOURNAL OF SOCIAL WORK AND HUMAN SEXUALITY. (In 1993 the title will change to: Journal of Family Social Work (ISSN 1052-2158)) 1981. q. $30 to individuals; institutions $75; libraries $95. Haworth Press, Inc., 10 Alice St., Binghamton, NY 13904. TEL 800-342-9678. FAX 607-722-1424. Ed. Tom Smith. adv.; bk.rev.; circ. 207. (also avail. in microfiche; back issues avail.) Indexed: Behav.Abstr., Biol.Abstr., Bull.Signal., Chicago Psychoanal.Lit.Ind., Child Devel.Abstr., Crim.Just.Abstr., Ind.Per.Art.Relat.Law, Past.Care & Couns.Abstr., Psychol.Abstr., Sage Fam.Stud.Abstr., Soc.Work Res.& Abstr., Stud.Wom.Abstr.
  —BLDSC shelfmark: 5064.918900.
  Description: Devoted to social work practice, research theory, and education, as they relate to issues in human sexuality.
  Refereed Serial

360 IS ISSN 0334-9977
JOURNAL OF SOCIAL WORK AND POLICY IN ISRAEL. (Text in English; summaries in Hebrew) a. $12 per no. Bar-Ilan University Press, Ramat Gan 52900, Israel. TEL 03-5318401. Eds. F.M. Loewenberg, M.H. Spero. (back issues avail.)
  —BLDSC shelfmark: 5064.918930.

361 US
JOURNAL OF SOCIAL WORK EDUCATION. 1965. 3/yr. membership. Council on Social Work Education, 1600 Duke St., Alexandria, VA 22314-3421. TEL 703-683-8080. Ed. F.G. Reamer. bk.rev.; charts; cum.index; circ. 3,800. (also avail. in microform from UMI; back issues avail.; reprint service avail. from UMI) Indexed: Abstr.Soc.Work., C.I.J.E., Cont.Pg.Educ., Curr.Cont., Educ.Ind., Lang.& Lang.Behav.Abstr., Mid.East: Abstr.& Ind., Res.High.Educ.Abstr., Soc.Sci.Ind., Soc.Work.Res.& Abstr., Sociol.Abstr., SSCI, Stud.Wom.Abstr.
  Formerly: Journal of Education for Social Work (ISSN 0022-0612)
  Description: Peer research articles on education in the fields of social work knowledge and social welfare, focusing on developments, innovations, and problems pertaining to social work education at the undergraduate, master's, and postgraduate levels.

360 369.4 UK ISSN 0265-0533
CODEN: JSWPEC
JOURNAL OF SOCIAL WORK PRACTICE. 1983. s-a. $44 to individuals; institutions $110. Carfax Publishing Co., P.O. Box 25, Abingdon, Oxfordshire OX14 3UE, England. TEL 0235-555335. FAX 0235-553559. (U.S. subscr. addr.: Carfax Publishing Co., Box 2025, Dunnellon, FL 32630) Ed. John Simmonds. adv.; bk.rev.; index. (also avail. in microfiche; back issues avail.) Indexed: ASSIA, Psychol.Abstr.
  —BLDSC shelfmark: 5064.919000.

JOURNAL OF SOCIOLOGY AND SOCIAL WELFARE. see SOCIOLOGY

JOURNAL OF TEACHING IN SOCIAL WORK. see EDUCATION — Teaching Methods And Curriculum

360 US ISSN 0733-6535
HV91
JOURNAL OF VOLUNTEER ADMINISTRATION. 1982. q. $29. (Association for Volunteer Administration) Johnson Publishing Co., Box 4584, Boulder, CO 80306. TEL 303-541-0238. Ed. Barbara Gilfillen. abstr.; illus.; charts; cum.index; circ. 2,000. (back issues avail.) Indexed: BPIA, Sage Pub.Admin.Abstr.
  —BLDSC shelfmark: 5072.517500.
  Supersedes (1968-1982): Volunteer Administration.
  Description: Contains articles on program management, model projects and tested techniques for successful volunteer involvement.

JUGEND BERUF GESELLSCHAFT; Journal for professionals in youth social service. see CHILDREN AND YOUTH — About

362.7 GW ISSN 0022-5940
JUGENDHILFE. 1963. 8/yr. DM.39. Luchterhand Verlag, Heddesdorferstr. 31, Postfach 2352, 5450 Neuwied 1, Germany. TEL 02631-801-00. FAX 02631-801210. adv.; charts; illus.; stat.; index.
  —BLDSC shelfmark: 5073.832000.

362.7 GW ISSN 0022-5975
JUGENDWOHL; Zeitschrift fuer Kinder- und Jugendhilfe. 1912. m. DM.62. (Deutscher Caritasverband) Lambertus-Verlag GmbH, Woelflinstr. 4, Postfach 1026, 7800 Freiburg, Germany. TEL 0761-31566. FAX 0761-37064. Ed. Hubertus Junge. adv.; bk.rev.; charts; index; circ. 2,200. (processed)
  —BLDSC shelfmark: 5073.835000.

362.4 DK
JULEHAEFTET, VANFOERES JUL. 1958. a. DKK 20. Dansk Handicap Forbund, Hans Knudsen Plads 1A, 2100 Copenhagen OE, Denmark. FAX 31-29-39-48. adv.; bk.rev.; illus.
  Formerly: Vanfoeres Jul (ISSN 0900-2863)

360 US
JUNIOR LEAGUE NEWSLINE. 1981. 3/yr. $10 (includes Junior League Review). Association of Junior Leagues International, Inc., 660 First Ave., New York, NY 10016. TEL 212-683-1515. FAX 212-481-7196. Ed. Betsey B. Steeger. adv.; circ. 184,000.
  Former titles: A J L I Newsline; A J L Newsline.
  Description: Newsletter about volunteering. Reports on activities of the association, individual leagues and league members, and other community organizations.

360 US
JUNIOR LEAGUE REVIEW. 1911. s-a. $10 (includes Junior League Newsline). Association of Junior Leagues International, Inc., 660 First Ave., New York, NY 10016. TEL 212-683-1515. FAX 212-481-7196. Ed. Betsey B. Steeger. adv.; bk.rev.; film rev.; illus.; index; circ. 184,000.
  Formerly: Junior League (ISSN 0022-6637)
  Description: Contains articles of general interest to women and trends affecting the voluntary sector. Reports on activities of the association, individual leagues and other community organizations.

JUSTICE REPORT/ACTUALITES JUSTICE. see CRIMINOLOGY AND LAW ENFORCEMENT

KALEIDOSCOPE (AKRON); international magazine of literature, fine arts and disability. see LITERATURE

360 IR
▼**KAR VA TAWSI'AH/LABOUR AND DEVELOPMENT.** (Text in English, Farsi) 1990. m. Rs.350 per no. Mu'assasah-i Kar va Ta'min-i Ijtima'i, 80 Khalid Islamboli Ave., Teheran, Iran.

360 614.8 US
KEEPING THE TRUST. 1987. q. free. Cleveland Foundation, 1422 Euclid Ave., Ste. 1400, Cleveland, OH 44115. TEL 216-861-3810. Ed. David V. Patterson. illus.; circ. 5,000.

362.7
KENTUCKY. DEPARTMENT OF HUMAN RESOURCES. ANNUAL REPORT. a. Department for Human Resources, Frankfort, KY 40601. TEL 502-564-2336.
  Incorporates: Kentucky. Department of Child Welfare. Annual Report.

360 KE ISSN 0075-594X
KENYA. PUBLIC SERVICE COMMISSION. ANNUAL REPORT. a. EAs.3. Government Printing and Stationery Department, Box 30128, Nairobi, Kenya.

360 KE
KENYA NATIONAL COUNCIL OF SOCIAL SERVICES. ANNUAL REPORT. (Text in English) a. Kenya National Council of Social Services, Box 47628, Nairobi, Kenya.

360 301 GW ISSN 0930-0775
KINDERSCHUTZ AKTUELL. 1974. q. DM.16. Deutscher Kinderschutzbund e.V., Droste Str. 14-16, 3000 Hannover 1, Germany. TEL 0511-662056. adv.; bk.rev.; circ. 40,000. (back issues avail.)

360 266 US ISSN 0023-1703
KINSHIP. 1961. q. $5. Glenmary Home Mission Sisters of America, 405 W. Parrish Ave., Box 2264, Owensboro, KY 42302-2264. TEL 513-741-8846. Ed. Sr. Christine Beckett. illus.; circ. 11,000.

362.7 GW
KLINGE. 1954. q. DM.15($3) Kinder- und Jugenddorf Klinge e.V., Klingerstr. 30, 6966 Seckach, Germany. FAX 06292-78200. Ed. Norbert Georg Mueller. bk.rev.; bibl.; illus.; circ. 9,000.
  Formerly: Jugenddorf-Zeitung (ISSN 0022-5924)
  Description: Focuses on child welfare.

362.4 IS
KOL NECEI MILCHAMA. s-a. 8 Haarbaa St., Tel Aviv, Israel.

301.4 GW ISSN 0023-2947
KOLPINGSBLATT. 1900. m. DM.15. Deutsche Kolpingsfamilie e.V., Kolpingplatz 5-11, 5000 Cologne 1, Germany. Ed. Martin Gruenewald. adv.; bk.rev.; film rev.; abstr.; illus.; stat.; circ. 204,000.

361.8 GW
KOMBA RUNDSCHAU. bi-m. Komba Gewerkschaft Schleswig-Holstein, Lerchenstr. 17, 2300 Kiel 1, Germany. TEL 0431-673318. Ed. Horst Benedixen.

KOSTEN EN FINANCIERING VAN DE GEZONDHEIDZORG IN NEDERLAND/COST OF HEALTH CARE IN THE NETHERLANDS. see PUBLIC HEALTH AND SAFETY

KRANKENDIENST; Zeitschrift fuer kath. Krankenhaeuser, Sozialstationen und Pflegeberufe. see HOSPITALS

KRITISCHE MEDIZIN IM ARGUMENT. see MEDICAL SCIENCES

KUULOVIESTI/HEARING NEWS. see HANDICAPPED — Hearing Impaired

362.8
L A CO-OPS AND THE SHARED HOUSING NETWORKER. 6/yr. $10. Cooperative Resources & Services Project, Box 27731, Los Angeles, CA 90027. TEL 213-738-1254. Ed. Lois Arkin. adv.; illus.
  Formerly: C R S Networking Newsletter.

361 NE
L V M W NIEUWS. (Text in Dutch) 1989. q. fl.35 for non-members. Landelijke Vereniging van Maatschappelijk Werkers - Netherlands Association of Social Workers, Leidseweg 80, 3581 BE Utrecht, Netherlands. TEL 030-948603. (Subscr. to: Postbus 2734, 3500 GS Utrecht, Netherlands) Ed.Bd. adv.; bk.rev.; circ. 2,500.

360 GW
L W V INFO; Bericht Nachricht. 1989. q. free. Landeswohlfahrtsverband Hessen, Standeplatz 6-10, 3500 Kassel, Germany. TEL 0561-1004-0. circ. 8,800.
  Formerly: L W V-Nachrichten.

SOCIAL SERVICES AND WELFARE

LAND AND LIFE. see *ETHNIC INTERESTS*

260 GW ISSN 0340-3270
LANDESVERSICHERUNGSANSTALT WUERTTEMBERG. MITTEILUNGEN. 1908. m. DM.105. W. Kohlhammer GmbH, Hessbruehlstr. 69, Postfach 800430, 7000 Stuttgart 80, Germany. TEL 0711-8363-1. Ed. L. Fichtner. stat.; index; circ. controlled.

362.7 GW ISSN 0937-7123
LANDSCHAFTSVERBAND WESTFALEN-LIPPE. MITTEILUNGEN DES LANDESJUGENDAMTES; Beitraege, Entscheidungen und Information zur Jugendhilfe. 1969. q. Landschaftsverband Westfalen-Lippe, Landesjugendamt, Landeshaus, Postfach 6125, 4400 Muenster, Germany. TEL 0251-591-3641. FAX 0251-591-275. TELEX 892835-LAWEL-D. Ed. Hans Joachim Stahl. bk.rev.; circ. 1,200. (back issues avail.)

362.7 FI ISSN 0786-0188
LAPSEN MAILMA/CHILD'S WORLD. 1938. m. Fmk.150($35) Lastensuojelun Keskusliitto - Central Union for Child Welfare in Finland, Armfeltintie 1, 00150 Helsinki 15, Finland. TEL 90-625901. FAX 90-627990. Ed. Soila Niklander. adv.; bk.rev.; bibl.; illus.; index; circ. 6,000.
Former titles: Lapset Ja Yhteiskunta (ISSN 0355-3736); Lapsi Ja Nuoriso (ISSN 0047-407X)

360 US
LATHAM LETTER. 1980. q. $10. Latham Foundation, Latham Plaza Bldg., Clement & Schiller Sts., Alameda, CA 94501. TEL 415-521-0920. FAX 510-521-9861. Ed. Madeleine C. Pitts. bk.rev. (back issues avail.)
Description: Promotes respect for all life through humane education.

IL LAVORATORE ELETTRICO. see *ENERGY*

LAW OF ASSOCIATIONS: AN OPERATING LEGAL MANUAL FOR EXECUTIVES AND COUNSEL. see *LAW*

360 GW ISSN 0724-3820
LEBEN UND WEG; Magazin fuer Koerperbehinderte. 1960. bi-m. DM.20. Verlag Bauland-Hohenlohe, Altkrautheimerstr. 17, 7109 Krautheim 1, Germany. TEL 06294-68109. FAX 06294-95383. Ed. G. Heiden. circ. 15,000.

360 GW
LEBENSABEND. m. Zentralverband der Sozialversicherten- der Rentner- und deren Hinterbliebenen Deutschland e.V., Bruckenweg 30, 5632 Wermelskirchen 1, Germany. TEL 02196-2760. adv.; bk.rev.; circ. 10,000. (looseleaf format)
Description: Information on social insurances for insured people and pensioners.

LEGISLATIVE ALERT. see *LAW*

LESBIAN AND GAY COUNSELLING NEWS. see *HOMOSEXUALITY*

362.5 FR
LETTER TO FRIENDS AROUND THE WORLD. (Editions in English, French, Spanish) 1981. 3/yr. $4. Fourth World Movement, Hameau de Vaux, 95540 Mery sur Oise, France. TEL 01-34646963. Ed. Ms. Alwine de Vos van Steenwijk. index; circ. 5,000. (back issues avail.)

LIAISONS SOCIALES. see *BUSINESS AND ECONOMICS — Labor And Industrial Relations*

354 LB
LIBERIA. GENERAL SERVICES AGENCY. ANNUAL REPORT.* a. General Services Agency, Box 9027, Monrovia, Liberia. stat.

354 LB
LIBERIA. MINISTRY OF LABOUR, YOUTH & SPORTS. ANNUAL REPORT.* (Text in English) a. Ministry of Labour, Youth & Sports, Camp Johnson Rd., Monrovia, Liberia. stat.

LIGHT (WHEATON). see *HANDICAPPED — Visually Impaired*

362.4 AT ISSN 1034-8883
LINK DISABILITY JOURNAL. 1980. bi-m. Aus.$25 (foreign Aus.$30). Disabled Peoples' International, South Australian Branch, G.P.O. Box 909, Adelaide. S.A. 5001, Australia. TEL 61-8-234-0708. FAX 08-234-0236. Ed. Cecilia Lim. adv.; bk.rev.; circ. 2,500. (also avail. in talking book; back issues avail.)
Description: Examines all issues relevant to disability, from the perspective of the disabled and their families.

362.41 AT ISSN 0158-5460
LINK-UP. 1980. bi-m. free. National Library of Australia, Disability Services Section, Canberra, A.C.T. 2600, Australia. TEL 06-2621251. FAX 06-273-1180. TELEX 062-62100. Ed. Susanne Bruhn. bk.rev.; circ. 1,000. (also avail. in audio cassette) Indexed: Aus.Educ.Ind., Aus.P.A.I.S. —BLDSC shelfmark: 5221.473500.
Description: National Library newsletter concerned with the provision of library services for people with disabilities in Australia and overseas.

360 UK ISSN 0266-8750
LIVERPOOL LINK; Liverpool's voluntary sector news magazine. 1966. m. (10/yr.). £5. (Liverpool Council of Social Service) Liverpool Council for Voluntary Service, 14 Castle St., Liverpool L2 ONJ, England. Ed. Deirdre Morley. adv.; bk.rev.; circ. 1,200. —BLDSC shelfmark: 5281.143200.
Supersedes (in Jul. 1984): Castle Street Circular (ISSN 0045-592X)

360 US ISSN 0896-2154
LIVING WORLD. 1985. q. $10. International Life Services, Inc., 2606 1-2 W. 8th St., Los Angeles, CA 90057. TEL 213-382-2156. Ed. Sister Paula Vandegaer. adv.; bk.rev.; circ. 30,000.
Description: Contains information on sexuality, counseling techniques, euthanasia, teenage life styles and other issues concerning family life.

360 UK
LOCAL ECONOMIC DEVELOPMENT INFORMATION SERVICE. m. £110 to non-members; members £80. Planning Exchange, 186 Bath Street, Glasgow G2 4HG, Scotland. TEL 041-332-8541. FAX 041-332-8277.

LOCAL - STATE FUNDING REPORT. see *BUSINESS AND ECONOMICS — Public Finance, Taxation*

HALOCHAME. see *MILITARY*

360 GW ISSN 0724-1429
LOCKE; fuer Auszubildende im Friseurhandwerk. 1982. q. Berufsgenossenschaft fuer Gesundheitsdienst und Wohlfahrtspflege, Pappelallee 35, 2000 Hamburg 35, Germany. TEL 040-202070. FAX 040-20207525. Ed. Eckart Wiedemann. film rev.; circ. 70,000. (back issues avail.)

LONDAM. see *MEDICAL SCIENCES*

362.4 UK
LONDON DISABILITY NEWS. m. £7. Greater London Association of Disabled People, 336 Brixton Road, London SW9 7AA, England. TEL 01-274-0107. Ed. Nick Lewis. adv.; circ. 3,000. (tabloid format)
Formerly (until 1989): G L A D Newsletter.
Description: For disabled people and those who work with them.

360 610 CN
M A P NEWS. Info A M P. (Editions in English, French) q. Medical Aid for Palestine - Aide Medicale pour la Palestine, 300 Carre St-Louis, Ste. 310, Montreal, Que. H2X 1A5, Canada. TEL 514-843-7875. FAX 514-843-3061. illus.; circ. 2,000.
Description: Reports on the events and medical conditions in the Occupied Territories.

350 AT ISSN 1035-5707
M I M S SERVICES DIRECTORY. a? Aus.$30. M I M S Australia, 48 Albany St., Crows Nest, N.S.W. 2065, Australia.
Description: Comprehensive listing of health, welfare, patient advisory and self help services nationwide.

360 US
M M I BULLETIN. q. membership. Medicaid Management Institute, c/o American Public Welfare Association, 810 First St., N.E., Ste. 500, Washington, DC 20002-4205. TEL 202-682-0100. FAX 202-289-6555.
Formerly: M I A P Bulletin.

360 PH
M S D D DIGEST. 1978. q. Department of Social Welfare and Development, Public Information Division, 389 San Rafael St., Manila, Philippines. Ed. Susan Argel.

360 US
MAIN STREET MEMORANDUM. vol.8, 1989. q. Rockford Institute, 934 N. Main St., Rockford, IL 61103. TEL 815-964-5813. FAX 815-965-1826. Ed. Michael Warder.
Description: Interprets the principles of a free society for modern America.

MALAY; dyornal ng humanidades at agham panlipunan - journal of humanities and social sciences. see *HUMANITIES: COMPREHENSIVE WORKS*

360 CN
MANITOBA SOCIAL WORKER. 1971. 8/yr. Can.$20 (effective Apr. 1991). Manitoba Association of Social Workers, 103-2015 Portage Ave., Winnipeg, Man. R3J OK3, Canada. TEL 204-888-9477. FAX 204-889-0021. Ed.Bd. adv.; bk.rev.; circ. 350. (looseleaf format; back issues avail.)

361.73 361.8 SP ISSN 0214-5979
MANOS UNIDAS. (Includes special nos.) no.44, Jul. 1978. q. 1000 ptas. (foreign $15). Campana Contra el Hambre en el Mundo, Barquillo 38-2, 28004 Madrid, Spain. TEL 91-4107500. FAX 91-3084208. Ed. Ana de Felipe. bk.rev.; charts; illus.; bibl.; circ. 60,000.

360 362.5 IT
MARGINALITA E SOCIETA. q. L.45000 (foreign L.65000)(effective 1992). Franco Angeli Editore, Viale Monza, 106, Casella Postale 17175, 20100 Milan, Italy. TEL 02-2895762. Ed. G. Pietropolli Charmet.
Formerly: Devianza ed Emarginazione.

MARRIAGE MAGAZINE. see *MATRIMONY*

360 GW ISSN 0723-2047
MATERIALIEN ZUR HEIMERZIEHUNG. 1972. q. DM.16. Internationale Gesellschaft fuer Heimerziehung, Heinrich-Hoffmannstr. 3, 6000 Frankfurt a.M. 71, Germany. TEL 069-6706250. Ed. Wolfgang Trede. index; circ. 2,000. (back issues avail.)

368.4 MF
MAURITIUS. MINISTRY OF SOCIAL SECURITY. NATIONAL SOLIDARITY AND REFORM INSTITUTIONS. 1962. a. Rs.25. Ministry of Social Security, National Solidarity and Reform Institution, Astor Court, Lislet Geoffroy St., Port Louis, Mauritius. (Orders to: Government Printing Office, Elizabeth II Ave., Port Louis, Mauritius) Ed.Bd. circ. 300.
Former titles: Mauritius. Ministry for Employment and of Social Security and National Solidarite; (until 1982): Mauritius. Ministry of Social Security. Annual Report (ISSN 0076-5538)
Description: Information on various branches of the ministry.

360 US
MEDICAID DIRECTORS' NETWORK. membership. m. State Medicaid Directors' Association, c/o American Public Welfare Association, 810 First St., N.E., Ste. 500, Washington, DC 20002-4205. TEL 202-682-0100. FAX 202-289-6555.

360 610 US ISSN 0098-3616
HD7106.U5
MEDICAID RECIPIENT CHARACTERISTICS AND UNITS OF SELECTED MEDICAL SERVICES. (NCSS Report B-4 Supplement) a. U.S. National Center for Social Statistics, U.S. Dept. of Health and Human Services, 330 Independence Ave., S.W., Washington, DC 20201. TEL 301-436-7900.

361.73 US
MEDICAL RESEARCH FUNDING BULLETIN. 1972. 3/m. $68. Science Support Center, Box 7507, New York, NY 10150. Ed. Carroll Jordon. bk.rev.; tr.lit.; circ. 2,000 (controlled). (looseleaf format)

SOCIAL SERVICES AND WELFARE 4413

MELBOURNE. PORT COUNCIL NEWS. see *PUBLIC ADMINISTRATION — Municipal Government*

360   AT   ISSN 0728-1897
MELBOURNE CITYMISSION. ANNUAL REPORT. 1855. a. Melbourne Citymission, 472 Nicholson St., North Fitzroy, Vic. 3068, Australia. TEL 03 489 9666. Ed. Peter Philp. circ. 5,000. (back issues avail.)

MENCAP NEWS. (Mentally Handicapped) see *HANDICAPPED*

MENTAL HEALTH IN CHILDREN. see *PSYCHOLOGY*

362.2   US   ISSN 0191-6750
MENTAL HEALTH REPORT. 1977. fortn. $280.54. Business Publishers, Inc., 951 Pershing Dr., Silver Spring, MD 20910-4464. TEL 301-587-6300. FAX 301-585-9075. Ed. Lisa Rabasca. (looseleaf format; back issues avail.)
●Also available online. Vendor(s): NewsNet.
Description: Provides funding and operational tips for managers of mental health programs in public and private sectors.

362   US   ISSN 0076-6453
MENTAL HEALTH STATISTICS FOR ILLINOIS. 1930. a. free. Department of Mental Health and Developmental Disabilities, 100 N. Ninth St., Rm. 207, Springfield, IL 62765. TEL 217-785-9844. Ed. John Brunk. circ. 1,000.
Formerly: Illinois. Department of Mental Health. Administrator's Data Manual.

362 368   CN   ISSN 0026-1556
METROPOLITAN PENSIONER.* 1966. m. $3. Metropolitan Pensioners Welfare Association, Box 2929, Vancouver 3, B.C., Canada. Ed. George S. Hobson. adv.; bk.rev.; abstr.; illus.; stat.; circ. 4,800.

MEXICO INDIGENA. see *HOUSING AND URBAN PLANNING*

360   US
MICHIGAN. DEPARTMENT OF SOCIAL SERVICES. ASSISTANCE PAYMENTS STATISTICS. m. Department of Social Services, Box 30037, 300 S. Capitol Ave., Lansing, MI 48909. TEL 517-373-2005. **Indexed:** SRI.

MIETERZEITUNG. see *HOUSING AND URBAN PLANNING*

MIEUX-VIVRE CHEZ LES AVEUGLES ET LES GRANDS INFIRMES. see *HANDICAPPED*

MIGRATION ACTION. see *SOCIOLOGY*

353.9   US
MISSOURI. DIVISION OF YOUTH SERVICES. ANNUAL REPORT. 1949. a. Department of Social Services, Division of Youth Services, Broadway State Office Bldg., Box 447, Jefferson City, MO 65101. TEL 314-751-3324. Ed. Mark Steward. illus.; stat.; circ. 500.
Formerly: Missouri. State Board of Training Schools. Annual Report (ISSN 0098-0110)

MITEINANDER. see *MEDICAL SCIENCES*

361 338.91   US
MONDAY DEVELOPMENTS. bi-w. $55 to non-members. (American Council for Voluntary International Action) InterAction, 1717 Massachusettes Ave., N.W., 8th Fl., Washington, DC 20036.
Description: Focuses on council member news and events, public policy updates and other news and events of interest to the PVO community.

MOSAIKK. see *ETHNIC INTERESTS*

MOTHER AND CHILD. see *WOMEN'S INTERESTS*

N A A C P ANNUAL REPORT. (National Association for the Advancement of Colored People) see *SOCIOLOGY*

368.4   US
N A D E ADVOCATE. 1978. bi-m. $40. National Association of Disability Examiners, Box 4188, Frankfort, KY 40603. TEL 502-875-8388. Ed. Lavonne Hoglund. adv.; stat.; tr.lit.; circ. 2,500. (back issues avail.)

361.7   US
N A E I R ADVANTAGE. 1982. bi-m. free. National Association for the Exchange of Industrial Resources, 560 McClure St., Box 8076, Galesburg, IL 61402. TEL 309-343-0704. FAX 309-343-0862. Ed. Jack Zavada. circ. 40,000 (controlled). (tabloid format)
Formerly: N A E I R News.
Description: Discusses corporate donations of excess inventory for use by schools and charities, and the subsequent tax benefits for the donors.

360   US
N A P C W A NETWORK. q. membership. National Association of Public Child Welfare Administrators, c/o American Public Welfare Association, 810 First St., N.E., Ste. 500, Washington, DC 20002-4205. TEL 202-682-0100. FAX 202-289-6555.

360   CN   ISSN 0820-7364
N A P O NEWS/ECHO DE L'O N A P. (Text in English and French) 1983. q. membership. National Anti-Poverty Organization, 316 - 256 King Edward Ave., Ottawa, Ont. K1N 7M1, Canada. TEL 613-789-0096. FAX 613-789-0141. bk.rev.; circ. 1,000. (back issues avail.)
Description: News on poverty, anti-poverty organizations and issues of importance to low-income Canadians.

360   US
N A R C E A CONFERENCE PROCEEDINGS. irreg. price varies. National Aging Resource Center on Elder Abuse, c/o American Public Welfare Association, 810 First St., N.E., Ste. 500, Washington, DC 20002-4205. TEL 202-682-0100. FAX 202-289-6555.

360   US
N A R C E A PROJECT REPORTS. 1986. irreg. price varies. National Aging Resource Center on Elder Abuse, c/o American Public Welfare Association, 810 First Ave., N.E., Ste. 500, Washington, DC 20002-4205. TEL 202-682-0100. FAX 202-289-6555.

360   US
N A R C E A SELECTED PUBLICATIONS. irreg. price varies. National Aging Resource Center on Elder Abuse, c/o American Public Welfare Association, 810 First St., N.E., Ste. 500, Washington, DC 20002-4205. TEL 202-682-0100. FAX 202-289-6555.

N C I V NEWSLETTER. (National Council for International Visitors) see *TRAVEL AND TOURISM*

360   UK   ISSN 0955-2170
N C V O NEWS. 1979. 10/yr. £50. National Council for Voluntary Organisations, 26 Bedford Sq., London WC1B 3HU, England. TEL 071-636-4066. FAX 071-436-3188. (back issues avail.)
Formerly (until 1989): Voluntary Action (ISSN 0143-5744)

362   US
N H O HOSPICE NEWS. 1984. 11/yr. membership only. National Hospice Organization, 1901 N. Moore St., Ste. 901, Arlington, VA 22209. TEL 800-658-8898. FAX 703-525-5762. Ed. Nina Barth. adv.; circ. 1,100.
Formerly: N H O President's Letter.
Description: Covers legal, ethical, regulatory and educational topics relevant to providers of hospice care for terminally ill patients.

360   II   ISSN 0253-6757
N I H F W TECHNICAL REPORTS. 1978. irreg. free. National Institute of Health and Family Welfare, New Mehrauli Rd., Munirka, New Delhi 110 067, India. circ. 3,000.

361.8
N R A G PAPERS. 1976. irreg., vol.7, 1987. price varies. Northern Rockies Action Group, Inc., 9 Placer St., Helena, MT 59601. Ed. Mike Schechtman. illus.; circ. 400 (controlled).

361.73   US   ISSN 0196-3295
HG177
N S F R E JOURNAL. q. $40 to non-members. National Society of Fund Raising Executives, 1101 King St., Ste. 3000, Alexandria, VA 22314. TEL 703-684-0410. FAX 703-684-0540. Ed. Cathlene Williams. adv.; bk.rev.; circ. 12,000. (back issues avail.)
Description: Provides a forum for research and the presentation of practical new ideas in the fund-raising profession.

361.73   US   ISSN 0890-2828
N S F R E NEWS. 1963. 8/yr. $25 to non-members. National Society of Fund Raising Executives, 1101 King St., Ste. 3000, Alexandria, VA 22314. TEL 703-684-0410. FAX 703-684-0540. Ed. Cathlene Williams. adv.; bk.rev.; circ. 11,000. (back issues avail.)
Description: Current events in the nonprofit fund-raising field.

360   GW   ISSN 0937-7425
NACHRICHTEN - PARITAET. 1950. m. DM.18. Deutscher Paritaetischer Wohlfahrtsverband e.V., Heinrich-Hoffmann-Str. 3, 6000 Frankfurt a.M., Germany. Ed. Inge Niemeyer. bk.rev.; index; circ. 11,200. (tabloid format)
Formerly (until 1990): D P W V - Nachrichten (ISSN 0011-510X)

362.7   US
NATIONAL ADOPTION REPORTS. bi-m. membership. National Council for Adoption, Inc., 1930 17th St. N.W., Washington, DC 20009-6207. TEL 202-328-1200.
Description: Newsletter and bulletin service on adoption matters.

362.7   US
NATIONAL ADVOCATE. 1981. bi-m. membership only. National Foster Parent Association, Inc., 4874 Bloom Ave., White Bear Lake, MN 55110. TEL 612-429-7855. Ed. Dorothy Bodlovick. bk.rev.; circ. 3,500. (back issues avail.)
Description: Contains information for foster parents and other child advocates.

360   UK
NATIONAL ASSOCIATION OF ALMSHOUSES. YEARBOOK AND STATEMENT OF ACCOUNTS. a. 50p. National Association of Almshouses, Wokingham, Berkshire RG11 5RU, England. TEL 0344 52922. Ed.Bd. stat.

361.6   US
NATIONAL CONFERENCE OF STATE SOCIAL SECURITY ADMINISTRATORS. PROCEEDINGS. 1952. a. membership only. National Conference of State Social Security Administrators, c/o Jim Larche, Deputy Dir., Employee Retirement System of Georgia, Two Northside 75, Ste. 300, Atlanta, GA 30318. TEL 404-352-6400. circ. controlled.

362.7   US
NATIONAL COUNCIL FOR ADOPTION. LEGAL NOTES. bi-w. membership. National Council for Adoption, Inc., 1930 17th St., N.W., Washington, DC 20009-6207. TEL 202-328-1200.
Formerly: National Committee for Adoption. Legal Notes.

362.7   US
NATIONAL COUNCIL FOR ADOPTION. MEMO. bi-w. National Council for Adoption, Inc., 1930 17th St., N.W., Washington, DC 20009-6207. TEL 202-328-1200.
Formerly: National Committee for Adoption. Memo.

360   UK
NATIONAL COUNCIL FOR VOLUNTARY ORGANIZATIONS. ANNUAL REPORT. a. free. National Council for Voluntary Organisations, 26 Bedford Sq., London WC1B 3HU, England. TEL 071-636-4066. FAX 071-436-3188. circ. 6,000.
Formerly: National Council of Social Service. Annual Report (ISSN 0077-409X)

NATIONAL COUNCIL NEWS. see *MEDICAL SCIENCES — Psychiatry And Neurology*

NATIONAL COUNCIL OF LA RAZA. A I D S NEWSLETTER. see *MEDICAL SCIENCES — Communicable Diseases*

SOCIAL SERVICES AND WELFARE

362.5   US
NATIONAL COUNCIL OF LA RAZA. POVERTY PROJECT NEWSLETTER. q. free. National Council of La Raza, 810 First St., N.E., Ste. 300, Washington, DC 20002-4272. TEL 202-289-1380. FAX 202-289-8173. Ed. Julie Quiroz.
   Description: Covers legislative and social welfare issues affecting the Hispanic community.

360   US
NATIONAL DIRECTORY OF PRIVATE SOCIAL AGENCIES. 1964. base vol. (plus m. supplements). $79.90. (Social Service Publications) Croner Publications, Inc., 34 Jericho Turnpike, Jericho, NY 11753. TEL 800-441-4033. FAX 516-388-4986. Ed. Carol Sixt. adv.; circ. 1,000. (looseleaf format)
   Description: Lists by field of service and geographical location. Includes addresses, telephone numbers and description of services.

360   US
NATIONAL EASTER SEAL COMMUNICATOR. vol.32, 1972. 3/yr. free. National Easter Seal Society, 70 E. Lake St., Chicago, IL 60601. TEL 312-726-6200. FAX 312-726-1494. Ed. Barbara J. Palombo. bk.rev.; circ. 10,000.
   Former titles: Easter Seal Communicator; Easter Seal Bulletin (ISSN 0012-8651)
   Description: Highlights news of the society.

361.73 658   US   ISSN 0272-0825
NATIONAL FUND RAISER. 1974. m. $79. Barnes Associates, Inc., 603 Douglas Blvd., Roseville, CA 95678. TEL 916-786-7471. Ed. W. David Barnes. bk.rev.; circ. 2,200. (back issues avail.)
   Description: For the nonprofit fund raising professional. Contains specific, "how-to" fund raising information in an easy to read format.

361   US
NATIONAL LEAGUE OF FAMILIES OF AMERICAN PRISONERS AND MISSING IN ACTION IN SOUTHEAST ASIA NEWSLETTER. 1974. bi-m. membership. National League of Families of American Prisoners and Missing in Action in Southeast Asia, 1001 Connecticut Ave. N.W., Ste. 219, Washington, DC 20036-5504. TEL 202-223-6846. Ed. Ann Mills Griffiths. circ. 15,000.
   Description: Purpose is the return of all prisoners, the fullest possible accounting for the missing and the repatriation of remains of those who died while serving in Southeast Asia.

NATIONAL LIBRARY FOR THE HANDICAPPED CHILD. NEWSLETTER. see *EDUCATION — Special Education And Rehabilitation*

360   US
NATIONAL PRO-LIFE JOURNAL. 1976. irreg. Pro-Life Publications, Box 172, Fairfax, VA 22030. Ed. Audree Ryberg.

360   US   ISSN 0164-7415
HQ767.15
NATIONAL RIGHT TO LIFE NEWS. 1973. s-m. $16. National Right to Life Committee, Inc., 419 7th St., N.W., Ste.500, Washington, DC 20004. TEL 202-626-8800. FAX 202-737-9189. Ed. Dave Andrusko. adv.; bk.rev.; film rev.; play rev.; charts; illus.; pat.; stat.; index; circ. 195,000. (tabloid format; back issues avail.)
   Description: Covers issues of abortion, infanticide, and euthanasia from medical, ethical, social and public policy perspectives.

362.7   US
NATIONAL SERVICE NEWSLETTER. 1966. s-a. $10 (contribution). National Service Secretariat, Inc., 5140 Sherrier Pl., N.W., Washington, DC 20016. TEL 202-244-5828. Ed. Donald J. Eberly. bk.rev.; circ. 1,700. (processed)
   Description: Contains current news about national service.

362.7   UK   ISSN 0077-5754
NATIONAL SOCIETY FOR PREVENTION OF CRUELTY TO CHILDREN. ANNUAL REPORT. 1885. a. National Society for the Prevention of Cruelty to Children, 67 Saffron Hill, London EC1N 8RS, England. TEL 071-242-1626. FAX 071-831-9562. circ. 90,000.

363 904.5   US   ISSN 0082-5166
NATURAL HAZARD RESEARCH WORKING PAPERS. 1968. irreg., latest no.70. $4.50. (Natural Hazards Research and Applications Information Center) University of Colorado, Institute of Behavioral Science, Campus Box 482, Boulder, CO 80309. TEL 303-492-6818. Eds. Sylvia Dane, David Butler. circ. 130. **Indexed:** Geo.Abstr.

363 904.5   US   ISSN 0193-8355
CODEN: NSOBD7
NATURAL HAZARDS OBSERVER. 1976. bi-m. free in N. America; elsewhere $15. University of Colorado, Institute of Behavioral Science, Natural Hazards Research and Applications Information Center, Campus Box 482, Boulder, CO 80309. TEL 303-492-6818. Eds. David L. Butler, Sylvia C. Dane. bk.rev.; circ. 10,200. **Indexed:** GeoRef.
   Description: Reports on new research and findings from completed projects, pertinent legislation, applications of research at federal, state, and local levels and by private agencies. Includes announcements of recent publications and future conferences.

NEBELHORN; Regionalmagazin fuer Politik und Kultur. see *BUSINESS AND ECONOMICS — Labor And Industrial Relations*

360   US
NEBRASKA. DEPARTMENT OF SOCIAL SERVICES. ANNUAL REPORT. no.38, 1974. a. Department of Social Services, Research and Finance Division, Box 95026, 301 Centennial Mall So., Lincoln, NE 68509. FAX 402-471-9455. Ed. Marvin E. Kanne. charts; stat.; circ. 500 (controlled). **Indexed:** SRI.
   Formerly: Nebraska. Department of Public Welfare. Annual Report.

NEPAL FAMILY PLANNING AND MATERNAL CHILD HEALTH BOARD. ANNUAL REPORT. see *BIRTH CONTROL*

362.5   US
NETWORKER: DOMESTIC POVERTY AND HUMAN NEEDS. 2/yr. price varies. Interfaith Impact for Justice and Peace, 110 Maryland Ave., NE, Washington, DC 20002. TEL 202-543-2800.

360   GW   ISSN 0342-9857
HV275
NEUE PRAXIS; kritische Zeitschrift fuer Sozialarbeit und Sozialpaedagogik. 1970. q. DM.96. Luchterhand Verlag, Heddesdorfer Str. 31, Postfach 1780, 5450 Neuwied 1, Germany. TEL 02631-801-0. TELEX 867853-HLVN-D. **Indexed:** Excerp.Med.

NEW CHOICES; for the best years. see *GERONTOLOGY AND GERIATRICS*

381   US
NEW DETROIT, INC. ANNUAL REPORT. 1968. a. New Detroit, Inc., One Kennedy Sq., Ste.1000, Detroit, MI 48226-3379. TEL 313-496-2000. Ed. John R. Huls. circ. 10,000.
   Former titles: New Detroit Annual Report; New Detroit Progress Report; New Detroit Incorporated.
   Description: Covers projects of nation's oldest urban coalition.

301   US
NEW DETROIT NOW. 1970. q. free. New Detroit, Inc., One Kennedy Sq., Ste. 1000, Detroit, MI 48226-3379. TEL 313-496-2000. Ed. John R. Huls. circ. 10,000.
   Description: Covers New Detroit, Inc. projects in education, crime prevention, race relations, minority business development and other local social issues and initiatives.

NEW DIRECTIONS FOR PROGRAM EVALUATION. see *EDUCATION*

360   US   ISSN 0277-996X
HV1
NEW ENGLAND JOURNAL OF HUMAN SERVICES. 1980. q. $24 to individuals; institutions $42. Osiris Press, 445 Fifth Ave., Ste. 270, New York, NY 10016-0109. TEL 212-226-5643. Ed. W. Robert Curtis. adv.; bk.rev.; charts; illus.; stat.; circ. 2,000. (also avail. in microfiche; reprint service avail from UMI) **Indexed:** Crim.Just.Abstr., Hosp.Lit.Ind., Lang.& Lang.Behav.Abstr., Med.Care Rev., P.A.I.S., Rehabil.Lit., Sage Pub.Admin.Abstr., Soc.Work Res.& Abstr., Sociol.Abstr.
—BLDSC shelfmark: 6083.990000.
   Description: Addresses issues important in management, law and public policy, specifically in the areas of health and mental health care, social services, welfare and special services to the elderly and children.

353.9   US   ISSN 0090-077X
RJ506.M4
NEW JERSEY. DEVELOPMENTAL DISABILITIES COUNCIL. ANNUAL REPORT. 1971. a. free. Developmental Disabilities Council, 108-110 N. Broad St., CN 700, Trenton, NJ 08625. TEL 609-292-3745. FAX 609-292-7114. Ed. Gregory Mizanin. circ. 3,000.
   Supersedes: New Jersey Mental Retardation Planning Board. Annual Report.

NEW MEXICO. VETERANS' SERVICE COMMISSION. REPORT. see *MILITARY*

NEW REVIEW. see *SOCIOLOGY*

NEW TECHNOLOGY IN THE HUMAN SERVICES. see *SOCIOLOGY — Computer Applications*

361   US
NEW YORK (STATE). ASSEMBLY. STANDING COMMITTEE ON CHILDREN AND FAMILIES. ANNUAL REPORT. a. State Assembly, Standing Committee on Children and Families, Room 422, State Capitol, Albany, NY 12248. TEL 518-455-5474.

NEW YORK (STATE). ASSEMBLY. STANDING COMMITTEE ON VETERANS' AFFAIRS. ANNUAL REPORT. see *MILITARY*

NEW YORK (STATE). COMMISSION ON QUALITY OF CARE FOR THE MENTALLY DISABLED. ANNUAL REPORT. see *HOSPITALS*

361   US   ISSN 0363-9835
HV98.N7
NEW YORK (STATE). DEPARTMENT OF SOCIAL SERVICES. ANNUAL REPORT. 1974. a. Department of Social Services, 40 N. Pearl St., Albany, NY 12243. **Indexed:** SRI.
   Formerly: New York (State). Board of Social Welfare. Annual Report (ISSN 0363-9843)

362.974   US   ISSN 0090-4716
HV86
NEW YORK (STATE) DEPARTMENT OF SOCIAL SERVICES. BUREAU OF DATA MANAGEMENT AND ANALYSIS. PROGRAM ANALYSIS REPORT. 1954. irreg., no.65, 1980. free. Department of Social Services, 40 N. Pearl St., Albany, NY 12243.
   Formerly: New York (State) Department of Social Services. Bureau of Research. Program Analysis Report.

362.974   US   ISSN 0162-6302
NEW YORK (STATE) DEPARTMENT OF SOCIAL SERVICES. BUREAU OF DATA MANAGEMENT AND ANALYSIS. PROGRAM BRIEF. 1961. irreg. free. Department of Social Services, 40 N. Pearl St., Albany, NY 12243. Ed. Herbert Altrasso. illus.
   Formerly: New York (State) Department of Social Services. Bureau of Research. Program Brief. (ISSN 0361-6436)

362.4   US
NEW YORK (STATE). OFFICE OF ADVOCATE FOR THE DISABLED. ANNUAL REPORT. 1980. a. free. Office of Advocate for the Disabled, One Empire State Plaza, Albany, NY 12223. FAX 518-473-6005. Ed. Alan J. Sangiacomo. circ. 6,000.

051   US
NEW YORK HABITAT TIMES. irreg. (approx. 4/yr.). free. Habitat New York City, 742 E. 6th St., New York, NY 10009-9920. TEL 212-505-2230. (Co-sponsor: Habitat for Humanity, Inc.) circ. 7,000.
   Description: Covers the work of the organizations.

SOCIAL SERVICES AND WELFARE

051 US
▼**NEW YORK MIX.** 1992. bi-w. $26. Opportunity Foundation, Inc., 120 Broadway, Ste. 948, New York, NY 10271. TEL 212-243-8000. Ed. Jonathan Rowe. adv.: B&W page $767. circ. 32,000. (tabloid format)
Description: Offers innovative solutions to urban problems - from the crisis in public education, to crime, to the decaying infrastructure, as well as promoting civic participation.

361.8 US
NEW YORK URBAN LEAGUE. ANNUAL REPORT.* a. New York Urban League, Inc., 204 W 136th St., New York, NY 10030-2696. TEL 212-730-5200.
Formerly: Urban League of Greater New York. Annual Report.

362.7 355.133 NZ
NEW ZEALAND R S A REVIEW. 1921. bi-m. NZ.$7. 181-183 Willis St., P.O. Box 27-248, Wellington, New Zealand. TEL 04-384-7994. FAX 04-384-7994. Ed. J.E. Cummings. adv. contact: J.E. Mandehl. circ. 86,005 (paid); 86,005 (controlled).

361 NZ ISSN 0080-0392
NEW ZEALAND RED CROSS SOCIETY. REPORT. 1931. a. free. New Zealand Red Cross Society Inc., P.O. Box 12-140, Wellington N., New Zealand. FAX 04-730-315.

361 CN ISSN 0078-0294
NEWFOUNDLAND. DEPARTMENT OF SOCIAL SERVICES. ANNUAL REPORT. 1950. a. free. Department of Social Services, P.O. Box 8700, Confederation Bldg., W. Block, St. John's, Nfld. A1B 4J6, Canada. TEL 709-576-3607. FAX 709-576-6996. TELEX 016-4197. circ. 500.

NEWORLD; the multicultural magazine of the arts. see *ART*

060 UN
NEWS FROM C C I V S; comprehensive newsheet on current initiatives and actions about voluntary service and relevant youth events. (Text in English and French) 1959. 4/yr. $20. Unesco, Coordinating Committee for International Voluntary Service, 1 rue Miollis, 75015 Paris, France. TEL 1-45-682731. TELEX 204461-F-UNESCO. Ed. Alexei Kruglov. illus.; circ. 3,000.
Former titles: C C I V S News; Volunteer Service Bulletin (ISSN 0007-4942); Volunteer World (ISSN 0042-8698)
Description: Publicizes the activities and ideas of CCIVS and its member organizations, as well as UNESCO and other United Nations agencies, and announcements concering voluntary service or youth.

360 AT
NEWSBEAT. 1988. q. free. Sydney City Mission, 28 Regent St., Chippendale, N.S.W. 2008, Australia. TEL 02-212-6277. FAX 02-281-3854. Ed. Kenneth B. Harrison. circ. 20,000. (back issues avail.)
Formerly: Missionbeat.
Description: Examines poverty and programs to deal with it: welfare, youth work programs and employment training.

NO. see *WOMEN'S INTERESTS*

361.73 US ISSN 0899-7640
HV1 CODEN: NVSQEQ
▼**NONPROFIT AND VOLUNTARY SECTOR QUARTERLY.** 1971. q. $56 to individuals; institutions $86. (Association of Voluntary Action Scholars) Jossey-Bass Inc., Publishers, 350 Sansome St., 5th Fl., San Francisco, CA 94104. TEL 415-433-1767. FAX 415-433-0499. Ed. Jon Van Til. bk.rev.; circ. 800. (back issues avail.; reprint service avail. from UMI)
—BLDSC shelfmark: 6117.340100.
Description: Explores the unique dynamics, needs, and concerns of today's nonprofit and voluntary organizations.
Refereed Serial

361.73 US
NONPROFIT WORLD. 1983. bi-m. $59. Society for Nonprofit Organizations, 6314 Odana Rd., Ste. One, Madison, WI 53719. TEL 608-274-9777. FAX 608-274-9978. Ed. Jill Muehrcke. adv.; bk.rev.; circ. 5,000. (back issues avail.) **Indexed:** ABI Inform., PSI.
Formerly: Nonprofit World Report (ISSN 8755-7614)
Description: Focuses on all aspects of running an effective non-profit organization, including fundraising, income generation, and legal advice.

NORCAL COMMUNITY FORUM. see *HANDICAPPED — Hearing Impaired*

360 NO ISSN 0333-1342
HV333
NORDISK SOSIALT ARBEID; professional journal for Scandinavian social workers. (Text in Danish, Norwegian, Swedish; summaries in English, Finnish) 1981. q. $33 to individuals; institutions $66. Universitetsforlaget, P.O.Box 2959-Toeyen, N-0608 Oslo 1, Norway. (U.S. addr.: Publications Expediting inc., 200 Meacham Ave., Elmont, NY 11003) Ed. Grete Stang. circ. 2,000.

360 282 US ISSN 8756-5013
NORTH AMERICAN ASSOCIATION OF CHRISTIANS IN SOCIAL WORK. PRACTICE MONOGRAPH SERIES. irreg. $6 per no. North American Association of Christians in Social Work, Box 7090, St. Davids, PA 19087-7090. TEL 215-687-5777. Ed. Alan Keith-Lucas.

362 US
HV86
NORTH DAKOTA HUMAN SERVICES; biennial report. 1973. biennial. Department of Human Services, State Capitol, 600 East Blvd., Bismarck, ND 58505. FAX 701-224-2359. circ. controlled.
Formerly: Social Sciences in North Dakota (ISSN 0094-1220)

360 301 CN
NOUVELLES PRATIQUES SOCIALES. 1989. s-a. Can.$20 (effective 1991). Presses de l'Universite du Quebec, C.P. 250, Sillery, Que. G1T 2R1, Canada. TEL 418-657-3551. FAX 418-657-2096. (back issues avail.) **Indexed:** Pt.de Rep. (1991-).

361.6 CN
NOVA SCOTIA DEPARTMENT OF COMMUNITY SERVICES (YEAR). 1964. a. Can.$12. Department of Community Services, P.O. Box 696, Halifax, N.S. B3J 2T7, Canada. TEL 902-424-4455. FAX 902-424-0502. Ed. Allan Clark. illus.; stat.; circ. 1,000.
Former titles: Social Services for Nova Scotians & Social Services in Nova Scotia (ISSN 0317-4336); Supersedes: Welfare Services in Nova Scotia.

300 FR ISSN 0154-8530
OBJECTIF ET ACTION MUTUALISTES. 1972. m. 38.50 F. Cooperative d'Information et d'Edition Mutualiste (C.I.E.M.), 255, Rue de Vaugirard, 75719 Paris Cedex 15, France. TEL 40-43-30-10. FAX 40-43-30-06. Ed. Philippe Marchal. adv.; film rev.; illus.

OCCUPATIONAL PENSIONS. see *INSURANCE*

OCCUPATIONAL THERAPY IN MENTAL HEALTH; a journal of psychosocial practice and research. see *MEDICAL SCIENCES — Psychiatry And Neurology*

614 AU ISSN 0029-9901
OESTERREICHISCHES JUGENDROTKREUZ. ARBEITSBLAETTER. 1947. bi-m. free. Oesterreichisches Jugendrotkreuz, Wiedner Hauptstr. 32, A-1041 Vienna 4, Austria. FAX 0222-58900179. Ed. Helmut Jahn. adv.; bk.rev.; illus.; index; circ. 10,000 (controlled).
Description: News and information of the Austrian Junior Red Cross.

790.1 FR ISSN 0010-2458
OFFICIEL DES COMITES D'ENTREPRISE ET SERVICES SOCIAUX. (Supplements avail.: Loisirs Magazine C.E., Lettre des C.E.) 1957. m. 410 F. (Societe Garon) Editions Garon, 60 rue du Landy, 93210 la Plaine St. Denis, France. TEL 48-20-05-55. FAX 48-20-78-08. adv.; bk.rev.; abstr.; index; circ. 11,000.

362.6 612.67 IT
OGGI DOMANI ANZIANI. 1988. q. L.30000 (foreign L.50000)(effective 1992). (Federazione Nazionale Pensionati Cisl) Franco Angeli Editore, Viale Monza, 106, Casella Postale 17175, 20100 Milan, Italy. TEL 02-2895762.

326.6 IT
OGGIDOMANI ANZIANI. q. Federazione Nazionale Pensionati, Via Alessandria, 26, 00198 Rome, Italy. TEL 06-84-15-670. FAX 06-84-17-565. circ. 1,500,000.

360 US ISSN 0277-8289
HV86
OKLAHOMA. DEPARTMENT OF HUMAN SERVICES. ANNUAL REPORT. 1936. a. free (includes Statistical Report). Commission for Human Services, Department of Human Services, Box 25352, Oklahoma City, OK 73125. TEL 405-521-3551. FAX 405-521-3551. charts; stat. **Indexed:** SRI.
Formerly (until 1979): Oklahoma. Department of Institutions, Social and Rehabilitative Services. Annual Report (ISSN 0078-4362)

OLD AGE: A REGISTER OF SOCIAL RESEARCH. see *GERONTOLOGY AND GERIATRICS*

301.435 362.6 US ISSN 0146-3640
OLDER AMERICANS REPORT. 1976. w. $294.50 (effective Sep. 1992). Business Publishers, Inc., 951 Pershing Dr., Silver Spring, MD 20910-4464. TEL 301-587-6300. FAX 301-585-9075. Ed. Nancy Aldrich. (looseleaf format; back issues avail.)
●Also available online. Vendor(s): NewsNet.
Incorporates: Aging Service News (ISSN 0197-4025)
Description: News for directors of senior citizens programs; includes funding, nutrition and social security news.

360 370 NE ISSN 0925-4862
ONDERWIJS & WELZIJN - VAKMATIG. 1980. 10/yr. fl.95. V N G Uitgeverij, P.O. Box 30435, 2500 GK The Hague, Netherlands. TEL 070-3738888. FAX 070-3651826. adv.; circ. 2,000.
Formerly (until 1990): Welzijnsinfo.

362 CN
ONTARIO. MINISTRY OF COMMUNITY AND SOCIAL SERVICES. SOCIAL ASSISTANCE REVIEW BOARD. ANNUAL REPORT OF THE BOARD. (Report Year Ends Mar. 31) a. Ministry of Community and Social Services, Social Assistance Review Board, Toronto, Ont. M7A 1E9, Canada. TEL 416-326-5104. FAX 416-326-5135. (Subscr. to: Social Assistance Review Board, 1075 Bay St., 7th Fl., Toronto, Ont. M5S 2B1, Canada)
Formerly: Ontario. Ministry of Community and Social Services. Social Assistance Review Board. Annual Report of the Chairman.

362.7 CN ISSN 0030-283X
ONTARIO ASSOCIATION OF CHILDREN'S AID SOCIETIES. JOURNAL.* 1952. m. (except Jul. & Aug.) Can.$25. Ontario Association of Children's Aid Societies, 75 Front Street E., Suite 203, Toronto, Ont. M5E 1V9, Canada. TEL 416-366-8115. FAX 416-491-5173. Ed. Diane Cresswell. bk.rev.; circ. 10,000. (back issues avail.)
Description: Tackles child welfare issues.

OPEN HOUSE. see *CHILDREN AND YOUTH — About*

OPEN MIND; the mental health magazine. see *MEDICAL SCIENCES — Nurses And Nursing*

OPTIONS (WASHINGTON). see *POPULATION STUDIES*

362.734 US
ORPHAN VOYAGE. ADOPTION SERIES. 1983. irreg. membership. Clarity Network, c/o Diana Edwards, Ed., Box 1117, St. Augustine, FL 32085. bibl.; circ. 500. (back issues avail.)
Formerly: Orphan Voyage. Log.

362.7 FR
ORPHELINAT. m. 5 F. Orphelinat Mutualiste de la Police Nationale, 19 rue du Renard, 75004 Paris, France. Ed. Paul Bareaud. adv.; circ. 66,235.

360 IS
OSIM INYAN. 1989. bi-m. (General Labor Federation of Israel) Union of Social Workers - Israel, P.O. Box 303, Tel Aviv, Israel. TEL 03-431644. Ed. Neomi Sagee.

SOCIAL SERVICES AND WELFARE

OUR REVIEW/MABAT SHELANV. see HANDICAPPED — Hearing Impaired

360 614   US
OVERVIEW (OLYMPIA). 1973. m. free. Department of Social and Health Services, MS. OB-44Q, Olympia, WA 98504. TEL 206-753-7039. Ed. Mary Vaughn. illus.

P C C SOUND CONSUMER. (Puget Consumers Co-Op) see CONSUMER EDUCATION AND PROTECTION

360   UK
P S S R U BULLETIN. irreg. free. Personal Social Services Research Unit, Cornwallis Building, The University, Canterbury, Kent CT2 7NF, England. TEL 0227-764000. FAX 0227-764327.

PAA FLUKT/NEW FUTURE. see POLITICAL SCIENCE — International Relations

362.7   US   ISSN 0737-5131
PAEDOVITA; an international journal of child-life. (Text in English, French, German, and Spanish) 1984. q. Eterna International, Inc., 27 W. 560 Warrenville Rd., Warrenville, IL 60555. TEL 708-393-2930. Ed. Stephen B. Parrish. adv.; bk.rev.; abstr.; illus.; pat.; index. **Indexed:** Int.Nurs.Ind., Psychol.Abstr.

PAKENHAM GAZETTE BERWICK GAZETTE. see AGRICULTURE

362.8 325   UN   ISSN 0031-0336
HV640.5.A6
PALESTINE REFUGEES TODAY. (Editions in Arabic, English, French, German, Spanish) 1960. q. free. United Nations Relief and Works Agency, Vienna International Centre, P.O. Box 700, A-1400 Vienna, Austria. FAX 43-1-237283. TELEX 135310 UNRA A. Ed. Lynn Failing. bk.rev.; charts; illus.; stat.; circ. 12,500. (tabloid format)

362.7   II   ISSN 0031-2096
PARIYAL KALYAN. (Text in Assamese) 1965. m. free. Assam State Social Welfare Advisory Board, Uzanbazar, Gauhati 1, Assam, India. Ed. Sri R. K. Gautam. circ. 500.
Formerly: Bala-Sevika.
Description: Covers child welfare.

200   US
PARTNERSHIP NEWS. 1983. irreg. (approx. 6/yr.). free. Partnership for the Homeless, Inc., 110 W. 32nd St., 8th Fl., New York, NY 10001-3274. TEL 212-947-3444. FAX 212-477-4663. Ed. John S. Turcott. circ. 27,609.
Description: Provides a source of information for shelter administrators, volunteers and others concerned with helping the homeless.

PATEN; Mitteilung der Vereinigung der Pflege- und Adoptiveltern im Lande Nordrhein-Westfalen. see SOCIOLOGY

PATIENTENPOST. see CHILDREN AND YOUTH — For

362.7   US   ISSN 0195-5926
PEDIATRIC SOCIAL WORK; an international journal. 1980. q. Eterna International, Inc., 27 W. 560 Warrenville Rd., Warrenville, IL 60555. TEL 708-393-2930. Ed. Allen F. Johnson. adv.; circ. 5,000. **Indexed:** Psychol.Abstr.

362.6   US
PENNSYLVANIA. ADMINISTRATION ON AGING. STATE PLAN ON AGING. 1979. a. Department of Aging, 231 State St., Harrisburg, PA 17101. TEL 717-783-8975. FAX 717-783-6842.

361.6   US
PENNSYLVANIA. DEVELOPMENTAL DISABILITIES PLANNING COUNCIL. PENNSYLVANIA STATE PLAN. 1977. a. Developmental Disabilities Planning Council, Health & Welfare Bldg., Harrisburg, PA 17120. Ed. Janeen DuChane. circ. 2,000.

PENSION FUNDS & THEIR ADVISERS. see INSURANCE

PENSION WORLD. see BUSINESS AND ECONOMICS — Banking And Finance

368.43   UK   ISSN 0048-3281
PENSIONERS VOICE. 1938. m. £6. National Federation of Retirement Pensions Associations, Melling House, 14 St. Peter St., Blackburn, Lancashire, England. Ed. Robert Stansfield. adv.; circ. 8,000.

360 640.73   AT   ISSN 1035-3615
PENSIONERS VOICE. 1956. 11/yr. Aus.$9($34) Combined Pensioners and Superannuants Association of N.S.W. Inc., Level 5, 405 Sussex St., Haumarket, N.S.W. 2000, Australia. TEL 02-281-1811. FAX 02-281-5958. Ed. Eric Cameran. adv.; bk.rev.; film rev.; play rev.; stat.; circ. 20,000. (tabloid format)
Description: Covers social services and welfare, consumer education and protection and taxation information, social security entitlements.

PENSIONS WORLD. see INSURANCE

PEOPLE AND PROGRAMS. see LAW

PEOPLENET. see EDUCATION — Special Education And Rehabilitation

PEOPLE'S MEDICAL SOCIETY NEWSLETTER. see CONSUMER EDUCATION AND PROTECTION

360   CN   ISSN 0704-5263
HV1
PERCEPTION. 1977. 4/yr. Can.$20($23) Canadian Council on Social Development, 55 Parkdale Ave., P.O. Box 3505, Sta. C, Ottawa, Ont. K1Y 4G1, Canada. TEL 613-728-1865. FAX 613-728-9387. Ed. Carolyn Brown. adv.; bk.rev.; illus.; circ. 4,500. (also avail. in microform from MIM,UMI; reprint service avail. from UMI) **Indexed:** Abstr.Soc.Work., Can.Per.Ind., CMI, P.A.I.S, Sp.Ed.Needs Abstr., SSCI, World Bibl.Soc.Sec.
Formerly: Canadian Welfare (ISSN 0008-5332)
Description: Journal of social comment.

361   US
PERSPECTIVE (CLEVELAND). 1975. irreg. free. Cleveland Foundation, 1422 Euclid Ave., Ste. 1400, Cleveland, OH 44115. TEL 216-861-3810. Ed. David V. Patterson. charts; illus.; circ. 5,000.
Former titles: Cleveland Foundation Perspective; Cleveland Foundation Quarterly.

360   US   ISSN 0480-2853
PHILANTHROPIC DIGEST. 1955. m. $79.50. Philanthropic Digest, Inc., Box 7059, Wilton, CT 06897. TEL 203-762-5746. Ed. Aline F. Anderson. circ. 500. (also avail. on diskette)

361   US
PHILANTHROPIC TRENDS DIGEST. 1983. bi-m. $48. Douglas M. Lawson Associates, Inc., 545 Madison Ave., New York, NY 10022. TEL 212-759-5660. FAX 212-759-1893. Ed. Joyce Rosen. bk.rev.; circ. 2,000.

PHILIPPINE STUDIES; quarterly publication of Philippine thought and culture. see HUMANITIES: COMPREHENSIVE WORKS

361.73 362.5
338.91   NE   ISSN 0167-6172
PLAN AND ACTION. (Text in English, French and Spanish) s-a. free. Stichting Mensen in Nood - Caritas Neerlandica, Postbus 1041, 5200 BA 's-Hertogenbosch, Netherlands. TEL 073-144544. FAX 073-132115. TELEX 50090 CARIT NL. Ed. H.A.G. Hofste. circ. 2,000 (controlled).
Description: News about the possibilities of co-sponsoring development projects in third world countries by Stichting Mensen in Nood - Caritas Neerlandica.

361.8   US
PLANNING AND ACTION NEWSLETTER. 1948. 6/yr. free. Federation for Community Planning, 614 Superior Ave. N.W., Ste. 300, Cleveland, OH 44113-1306. TEL 216-781-2944. FAX 216-781-2988. Ed. Frederic E. Markowitz. illus.; circ. 3,800.
Former titles: Federation Forum (ISSN 0300-6999); Welfare Talks.
Description: Covers the organization's current activities.

PLAY AND PARENTING CONNECTIONS. see CHILDREN AND YOUTH — About

360   US
POLICY STUDIES IN EMPLOYMENT AND WELFARE. 1969. irreg., no.39, 1983. price varies. Johns Hopkins University Press, 701 W. 40th St., Ste. 275, Baltimore, MD 21211. TEL 410-516-6900. FAX 410-516-6998. (reprint service avail. from UMI)

POPOLO. see RELIGIONS AND THEOLOGY

362.7   UK   ISSN 0032-5856
HC260.P63
POVERTY. 1966. 3/yr. £12 membership. C P A G Ltd. (Child Poverty Action Group), 1-5 Bath St., London EC1V 9PY, England. Ed. Julia Lewis. adv.; bk.rev.; circ. 7,000. **Indexed:** ASSIA, World Bibl.Soc.Sec.
—BLDSC shelfmark: 6571.450000.

301.44   US
POVERTY IN SOUTH DAKOTA. a. Economic Opportunity Office, Community Service Block Grant Program, State Government Operations, Office of the Governor, 500 E. Capitol Ave., Pierre, SD 57501. TEL 605-224-8280. Ed. George J. Mauer. illus.; stat.
Formerly (until 1975): Annual Causes and Conditions of Poverty in South Dakota (ISSN 0091-0724)

362.7   UK
POVERTY PUBLICATIONS SERIES. 3/yr. £18. C P A G Ltd. (Child Poverty Action Group), 1-5 Bath St., London EC1V 9PY, England.
Formerly: Poverty Pamphlets.

360   AT   ISSN 0810-5537
POVERTY WATCH. 1980. bi-m. Aus.$11. Victorian Council of Christian Education, 2A Chapel St., St. Kilda, Vic. 3182, Australia. TEL 03-5294377. FAX 03-5294998. Ed. Newton Daddow. adv.; bk.rev.; circ. 1,000.
Description: Social justice issues for church readership.

362.4 362.6   UK
PRACTICAL CARING. 1982. 6/yr. £7.90 (foreign £9.30)(effective Jan. 1992). A.E. Morgan Publications Ltd., Stanley House, 9 West St., Epsom, Surrey KT18 7RL, England. TEL 0372-741411. FAX 0372-744493. Ed. Charles Lloyd. circ. 3,300.
Former titles: Caring; Handicapped Living.
Description: Provides information and encouragement for caretakers of the disabled and elderly.

360   UK   ISSN 0950-3153
PRACTICE. 1987. q. £27.50($60) (British Association of Social Workers) Whiting & Birch Ltd, P.O. Box 872, Forest Hill, London SE23 3HL, England. TEL 081-699-0914. FAX 081-669-3685. Ed. Wendy Stafford. adv.; bk.rev.; index; circ. 2,000. (back issues avail.) **Indexed:** ASSIA, Soc.Work Res.& Abstr., Sociol.Abstr.
—BLDSC shelfmark: 6597.117000.
Description: Issues in social work practice.

360   GW
DIE PRAXIS; sozialpolitische Vierteljahresschrift. 1948. q. DM.10. Reichsbund der Kriegs- und Wehrdienstopfer, Behinderten, Sozialrentner und Hinterbliebenen e.V. - German Association of Victims of War and Military Service, Handicapped, Social Insurance, Pensioners and Dependants, Beethovenallee 56-58, D-5300 Bonn 2, Germany. TEL 0228-363071. FAX 0228-361550. TELEX 885557. Ed. Wolfgang Falk. circ. 8,000.

361.77   FR   ISSN 0301-0260
PRESENCE CROIX-ROUGE. 1865. 6/yr. 30 F.($5) Croix-Rouge Francaise, 17 rue Quentin Bauchart, 75384 Paris Cedex 08, France. Ed. J. Boulet. adv.; bk.rev.; charts; illus.; stat.; index; circ. 30,000. (also avail. in microform; micropaque)
Formerly: Vie et Bonte (ISSN 0042-5486)

PRIME OF LIFE. see SOCIOLOGY

362.6   US
PRIME TIMES. 1978. m. U S Old American Volunteers Programs, ACTION, 806 Connecticut Ave., N.W., Washington, DC 20525. TEL 301-443-1575. Ed. Pat Yuknavage. illus.

360   SW   ISSN 0345-9225
PRO - PENSIONAEREN. (Text in Finnish, Swedish) 1942. 10/yr. SEK 100. P.O. Box 3274, 10365 Stockholm, Sweden. TEL 08-244960. FAX 08-203358. Ed. Monica Swaerd. adv.; bk.rev.; circ. 290,667.
Formerly: Pensionaeren.

SOCIAL SERVICES AND WELFARE   4417

362.7 364   US   ISSN 0893-4231
PROTECTING CHILDREN. 1984. q. $25. American Humane Association, American Association for Protecting Children, 63 Inverness Dr. E., Englewood, CO 80112-5117. TEL 303-792-9900. FAX 303-792-5333. Ed. Robyn Alsop. adv.; bk.rev.; circ. 1,500. Indexed: Adol.Ment.Hlth.Abstr.
—BLDSC shelfmark: 6935.762300.
Formerly (until 1984): National Child Protective Services Newsletter.
Description: Includes information on topics of current concern, programs, research, state activities, legislation and conferences in the field of child welfare, specifically abuse and neglect.

PSYCHOSOZIALE UMSCHAU. see *MEDICAL SCIENCES — Psychiatry And Neurology*

360   US
PUBLIC ASSISTANCE REPORT. 1988. s-m. $209. (Community Development Services, Inc.) C D Publications, 8204 Fenton St., Silver Spring, MD 20910-2889. TEL 301-588-6380. FAX 301-588-6385. Ed. Mark Kuhn.
Formerly (until 1991): Public Assistance Success (ISSN 1050-3447); Incorporates (1988-1991): Helping the Homeless (ISSN 1050-3439)
Description: Updates on welfare legislation; plus case studies of successful job training, housing, and employment programs.

PUBLIC AUTHORITIES DIRECTORY. see *PUBLIC ADMINISTRATION — Municipal Government*

360   US   ISSN 0033-3816
HV1
PUBLIC WELFARE. 1943. q. $25 (foreign $35). American Public Welfare Association, c/o Pat Reynolds, 810 First St., N.E., Ste. 500, Washington, DC 20002-4205. TEL 202-682-0100. FAX 202-289-6555. Ed. Bill Detweiler. adv.; bk.rev.; abstr.; charts; illus.; index; circ. 8,700. (also avail. in microform from UMI; reprint service avail. from ISI, UMI) Indexed: Adol.Ment.Hlth.Abstr., Curr.Cont., Curr.Lit.Fam.Plan., Lang.& Lang.Behav.Abstr., Med. Care Rev., P.A.I.S., Soc.Sci.Ind., Soc.Work.Res.& Abstr., SSCI.
—BLDSC shelfmark: 6969.750000.
Description: Contains articles ranging from commentary by national leaders to practical features by administrators and direct service practitioners.

360   US   ISSN 0163-8297
HV89
PUBLIC WELFARE DIRECTORY. 1940. a. $70 to non-members; members $65; foreign $80. American Public Welfare Association, 810 First St., N.E., Ste. 500, Washington, DC 20002-4205. TEL 202-682-0100. FAX 202-289-6555. Ed. Amy Weinstein. circ. 5,000.
Description: Describes welfare programs and agencies in the US and Canada. Tells where to write and lists personnel contacts and phone numbers for records and administrative information, what programs are offered in each state and locality, and how federal and state programs are administered.

PUERTO RICO. DEPARTMENT OF HEALTH. BOLETIN ESTADISTICO. see *PUBLIC HEALTH AND SAFETY — Abstracting, Bibliographies, Statistics*

PUERTO RICO. DEPARTMENT OF HEALTH. INFORME ANUAL DE FACILIDADES DE SALUD. see *HOSPITALS*

PUERTO RICO. DEPARTMENT OF HEALTH. INFORME DEL REGISTRO DE PROFESIONALES DE LA SALUD. see *MEDICAL SCIENCES*

360   MY   ISSN 0552-6426
PURE LIFE SOCIETY. ANNUAL REPORT. (Text in English) 1953. a. free to membership. Pure Life Society, Batu 6, Jalan Puchong, Jalan Kelang Lama P.O., 58200 Kuala Lumpur, Malaysia. TEL 03-7929391. Ed.Bd. circ. 2,000.

360   US
Q C REVIEW. q. membership. National Association of Human Service Quality Control Directors, c/o American Public Welfare Association, 810 First St. N.E., Ste. 500, Washington, DC 20002-4205. TEL 202-682-0100. FAX 202-289-6555.

362   UK   ISSN 0260-9584
QUAKER PEACE & SERVICE. ANNUAL REPORT. 1927. a. free. Quaker Peace and Service, Friends House, Euston Rd., London NW1 2BJ, England. TEL 071-397-3601. FAX 071-388-1977. Ed. Mary Hogan. illus.
Formerly: Friends Service Council. Annual Report (ISSN 0071-9609)

RAAKPUNT. see *MEDICAL SCIENCES*

RALPH H. BLANCHARD MEMORIAL ENDOWMENT SERIES. see *INSURANCE*

362.7   UK
RAPPORT. 1970. m. £15. Community and Youth Workers' Union, Unit 202A, The Argent Center, 60 Frederick St., Hockley, Birmingham B1 3HS, England. FAX 021-236-7842. Ed. Doug Nicholls. adv.; bk.rev.; circ. 3,000.

360   IT   ISSN 0033-9601
RASSEGNA DI SERVIZIO SOCIALE. 1962. q. L.40000 (foreign L.45000). Ente Italiano di Servizio Sociale, Via Ferdinando Baldelli 41, 00146 Rome, Italy. Ed. Giuseppe Rizzo. adv.; bk.rev.; abstr.; charts; stat.; index; circ. 1,500.
—BLDSC shelfmark: 7294.740000.

360   GW
RAUTE; Magazin fuer Hilfesuchende und Helfer. 1973. q. DM.10. Bundesverband der Allgemeinen Rettungsverbaende Deutschlands e.V., Postfach 1166, D-8480 Weiden, Germany. Ed.Bd. circ. 3,000.

360   FR   ISSN 0220-9926
REALITES FAMILIALES. 1946. 4/yr. 110 F. Union Nationale des Associations Familiales, 28 place St. Georges, 75009 Paris, France. adv.; bk.rev.; film rev.; illus.; index; circ. 10,000.
Formerly: U N A F. Bulletin de Liaison (ISSN 0041-5219)

360   US   ISSN 0360-4608
HV86
RECORD (NASHVILLE). 1938. s-a. free. Department of Human Services, 400 Deaderick St., Citizens Plaza, Nashville, TN 37219. Ed. Patricia Harris. illus.; circ. 9,800.
Formerly (until 1975): Tennessee Public Welfare Record (ISSN 0040-3377)

361.77   NZ
RED CROSS NEWS. 1979. 6/yr. New Zealand Red Cross Society Inc., Box 12-140, Wellington North, New Zealand. FAX 04-730-315. adv.; illus.; circ. 7,000.

361.77   UK
RED CROSS NEWS. 1975. q. membership. British Red Cross Society, 9 Grosvenor Crescent, London SW1X 7EJ, England. TEL 071-235-5454. FAX 071-245-6315. Ed. Emily Rae. circ. 50,000. (tabloid format)

361.77   NP   ISSN 0048-7023
RED CROSS QUARTERLY/REDA KRASA TRAIMASIKA.⁎ (Text in English and Nepali) 1969. q. Nepal Red Cross Society, P.O. 217, Kathmandu, Nepal. adv.; illus.

360 350   IT
REGIONE ABRUZZO. 1972. m. free. Servizio Informazione Stampa e Pubbliche Relazioni, Via Michele Jacobucci, 4, I-67100 L'Aquila, Italy. circ. 9,500. (back issues avail.)

362.5   CN   ISSN 0034-3781
BX802
RELATIONS. 1941. m. Can.$22 (foreign $26)(effective Jan. 1992). (Peres de la Compagnie de Jesus) Revue Relations, 25 Jarry Oeust, Montreal, Que. H2P 1S6, Canada. TEL 514-387-2541. Ed. Gisele Turcot. adv.; bk.rev.; bibl.; index; circ. 8,108. (also avail. in microform from UMI; reprint service avail. from UMI) Indexed: Can.Per.Ind., Cath.Ind., CERDIC, Pt.de Rep. (1979-).
Description: Concerned with social welfare and economic justice for the poor.

RELEASE. see *ETHNIC INTERESTS*

360   US   ISSN 1043-1209
HV1553
REPORT ON DISABILITY PROGRAMS. 1978. fortn. $248.04. Business Publishers, Inc., 951 Pershing Dr., Silver Spring, MD 20910-4464. TEL 301-587-6300. FAX 301-585-9075. Ed. Lisa Rabasca. (looseleaf format; back issues avail.) Indexed: Rehabil.Lit.
●Also available online. Vendor(s): NewsNet.
Former titles: Handicapped Americans Report (ISSN 0276-2889); (until 1985): Handicapped Rights and Regulations (ISSN 0191-6734)
Description: Covers funding advice, new programs for managers of disabled programs; especially for occupational development of disabled.

REPORT ON EDUCATION OF THE DISADVANTAGED; the biweekly newsletter on Title I and other federal programs for disadvantaged children. see *EDUCATION — Special Education And Rehabilitation*

360 371.4   US
THE REPORTER (NEW YORK). 1966. q. $1 to members; non-members $5. Women's America O R T, Inc., 315 Park Ave. S., New York, NY 10010. TEL 212-505-7700. FAX 212-674-3057. Ed. Eve M. Jacobson. adv.; bk.rev.; film rev.; play rev.; illus.; circ. 150,000. (also avail. in microform from AJP)
Formerly: Women's American O R T Reporter (ISSN 0043-7514)
Description: National paper for the American Jewish woman.

RESEARCH COMMUNICATIONS IN PSYCHOLOGY, PSYCHIATRY AND BEHAVIOR. see *PSYCHOLOGY*

RESEARCH ON SOCIAL WORK PRACTICE. see *SOCIOLOGY*

360   UK   ISSN 0264-519X
RESEARCH, POLICY AND PLANNING. 1977. s-a. £20 to non-members. Social Services Research Group, c/o Roger Lightup, Ed., Manchester SSD, P.O. Box 536, Manchester M60 2AF, England. (Subscr. addr.: c/o Brian McClay, Bradford SSD, Olicana House, Chapel St., Bradford BD1 5RE, England) adv.; bk.rev.; circ. 1,000.
—BLDSC shelfmark: 7755.076200.
Supersedes (in 1983): Social Services Research Group. Journal (ISSN 0144-0640)

360   UK
RESIDENTIAL ACCOMMODATION - SCOTLAND. 1983. a. Social Work Services Group, 43 Jeffrey St., Rm. 24, Edinburgh EH1 1DN, Scotland.

361.73   US
RESPONSIVE PHILANTHROPY. 1979. q. $25. National Committee for Responsive Philanthropy, 2001 S St., N.W., Ste. 620, Washington, DC 20009. TEL 202-387-9177. FAX 202-332-5084. Ed. Beth Baker. bk.rev.; circ. 4,000. (back issues avail.)
Description: Covers changes and trends in philanthropy and fund raising, with emphasis on "social justice" and non-traditional non-profit organizations.

360   US
▼**REUNIONS - THE MAGAZINE.** 1990. q. $24. Adoption Triangle Ministries, 1105 Cape Coral Pkwy. E., Ste. G, Cape Coral, FL 33904-9175. TEL 813-542-1342. FAX 813-549-9393. (Subscr to: Musser Foundation, Box 1860, Cape Coral, FL 33910) Ed. Mary Thiele Fobian.
Description: Covers all types of reunion stories, as well as a classified section for locating missing persons.

360   SP   ISSN 0211-4364
HQ799.S7
REVISTA DE ESTUDIOS DE JUVENTUD. 1980. q. 1700 ptas. (foreign 2800 Ptas.). Instituto de la Juventud, Jose Ortega y Gaset, 71, 28006 Madrid, Spain. TEL 347-76-90. FAX 402-21-94. Ed. Magdy Martinez Soliman. bk.rev.; cum.index: 1980-1986; circ. 3,000. (back issues avail.) Indexed: Psychol.Abstr.
Formerly: De Juventud: Revista de Estudios e Investigaciones.

360   SP   ISSN 0210-4792
REVISTA DE SEGURIDAD SOCIAL. 1979. q. 6000 ptas.($50) Ministerio de Trabajo y Seguridad Social, Agustin de Bethencourt, 28003 Madrid, Spain. circ. 1,000.

SOCIAL SERVICES AND WELFARE

360   PR   ISSN 0034-8937
REVISTA DE SERVICIO SOCIAL. 1940. irreg. Facultad de la Escuela de Trabajo Social, Apdo. 6679, Santurce, PR 00914. adv.; bk.rev.; bibl.; charts; illus.; index; circ. 1,000.

360   CL   ISSN 0716-2642
REVISTA TRABAJO SOCIAL. 1970. 3/yr. $20. Pontificia Universidad Catolica de Chile, Escuela de Trabajo Social, Vicuna Mackena 4860, Casilla 114-D, Santiago, Chile. Ed. Maria Ignacia Jimenez Suarez. bk.rev.; circ. 700.
    Formerly: Trabajo Social.

REVISTA VENEZOLANA DE SANIDAD Y ASISTENCIA SOCIAL. see PUBLIC HEALTH AND SAFETY

362.6 363.6   BE   ISSN 0035-0834
REVUE BELGE DE SECURITE SOCIALE. (Text in Flemish or French) 1959. 10/yr. 900 BEF. Ministere de la Prevoyance Sociale, Rue de la Vierge Noire 3C, 1000 Brussels, Belgium. **Indexed:** Int.Lab.Doc., P.A.I.S.For.Lang.Ind., World Bibl.Soc.Sec.
    —BLDSC shelfmark: 7892.500000.

REVUE DU TRAVAIL. see BUSINESS AND ECONOMICS — Labor And Industrial Relations

360   FR   ISSN 0121-4977
REVUE FRANCAISE DE SERVICE SOCIAL. 1945. q. 200 F. (foreign 225 F.). Association Nationale des Assistants de Service Social, 15 rue de Bruxelles, 75009 Paris, France. TEL 45-26-33-79. Ed. M.T. Paillusson. adv.; bk.rev.; illus.; circ. 2,700 (controlled).
    Formerly: Feuillets de l'A N A S (ISSN 0004-5586).

REVUE INTERNATIONALE D'ACTION COMMUNAUTAIRE; international review of community development. see SOCIOLOGY

360   FR
REVUE QUART MONDE. q. 150 F. (A.T.D. Fourthworld) Editions Quart Monde, 122 av. du General-Leclerc, 95480 Pierrelaye, France. Ed. L. Join-Lambert. illus.
    Formerly: Igloos (ISSN 0019-168X)

360   US
RIGHT-TO-KNOW PLANNING GUIDE (SERIES). 1987. m. $475. The Bureau of National Affairs, Inc., 1231 25th St., N.W., Washington, DC 20037. TEL 202-452-4200. FAX 202-822-8092. TELEX 285656 BNAI WSH. (Subscr. to: 9435 Key West Ave., Rockville, MD 20850. TEL 800-372-1033) Ed. Eileen Z. Joseph. (looseleaf format; back issues avail.)
    Description: Reference service providing information on new community right-to-know and community emergency response program.

360   US
RIGHT-TO-KNOW PLANNING REPORT. (Subseries of: Right-to-Know Planning Guide) 1987. bi-w. $285 includes Right-to-Know Planning Guide. The Bureau of National Affairs, Inc., 1231 25th St., N.W., Washington, DC 20037. TEL 202-452-4200. FAX 202-822-8092. TELEX 285656 BNAI WSH. (Subscr. to: 9435 Key West Ave., Rockville, MD 20850. TEL 800-372-1033) Ed. Eileen Z. Joseph. (back issues avail.)
    Description: Provides information on new community right-to-know and community emergency response programs.

362.4   JA   ISSN 0035-5305
RIHABIRITESHON/REHABILITATION (TOKYO, 1953). (Text in Japanese) 1953. 10/yr. 260 Yen per no. Handicapped Persons Association of Japan Railways - Tetsudo Shinshosha Kyokai, 5-1 Koji-machi, Chiyoda-ku, Tokyo 102, Japan. Ed. Takeo Oshida. adv.; bk.rev.; charts; illus.; circ. 8,000.

360   IT   ISSN 0035-6522
RIVISTA DI SERVIZIO SOCIALE. (Text in Italian; abstracts in English) 1961. q. L.40000. Istituto per gli Studi Sui Servizi Sociali, Via di Villa Pamphili 84, 00152 Rome, Italy. TEL 06-5897179. Ed. Aurelia Florea. adv.; bk.rev.; bibl.; tr.lit.; index; circ. 2,000. **Indexed:** P.A.I.S.For.Lang.Ind., Sociol.Abstr.
    —BLDSC shelfmark: 7992.810000.

361.77   SW   ISSN 1101-413X
ROEDA KORSETS TIDING. 1909. 6/yr. SEK 90. Svenska Roeda Korset - Swedish Red Cross, PO Box 27316, S-102 54 Stockholm, Sweden. Ed. Marianne Roennberg. adv.; bk.rev.; abstr.; illus.; circ. 420,000. (tabloid format)
    Formerly titles: Apropaa; Apropaa Roeda Korset (ISSN 0042-2819)

361.77   NO   ISSN 0333-2985
ROEDE KORS. 1921. 8/yr. NOK 125. Norges Roede Kors - Norwegian Red Cross, P.O. Box 6875, St. Olavs Plass, 0130 Oslo 1, Norway. TEL 47-02-94-30-30. FAX 47-02-20-68-40. TELEX 76011-NORCR-N. Ed. Kirsten Skarlund. adv.; bk.rev.; illus.; circ. 53,000.
    Former titles (until 1981): Over Alle Graenser (ISSN 0030-7335); (until 1955): Norges Roede Kors (ISSN 0332-5326)

ROSTER OF AFRICA SOCIAL SCIENTISTS. see BUSINESS AND ECONOMICS — International Development And Assistance

360   AU
DAS ROTE KREUZ. 1929. q. S.10. Oesterreichisches Rotes Kreuz, Gusshausstr. 3, A-1041 Vienna, Austria. Ed. Walter Vilt. adv.; bk.rev.; illus.; circ. 40,000.

362.7   US
THE ROUNDTABLE (SOUTHFIELD). 1986. q. free. Spaulding for Children, National Resource Center for Special Needs Adoption, 16250 Northland Dr., Ste. 120, Southfield, MI 48075-4325. TEL 313-443-7080. FAX 313-443-7099. Ed. Nancy Burkhalter. bk.rev.; illus.; circ. 12,000.
    Description: Informs adoption practitioners, administrators and advocates of the center's activities and of new developments in the field of special needs adoption. Shares ideas, problems and successes.

179.3   UK
ROYAL HUMANE SOCIETY. ANNUAL REPORT. 1774. a. free. (Royal Humane Society) Blackfords Truro Cornwall, Brettenham House, Lancaster Place, London WC2E 7EP, England. TEL 01-836-8155. Ed. Maj. A.J. Dickinson. circ. 800.

360 613   UK   ISSN 0264-0325
ROYAL SOCIETY OF HEALTH JOURNAL. 1876. bi-m. £38($93) Royal Society of Health, R S H House, 38A St., George's Dr., London SW1V 8BH, England. TEL 071-630-0121. FAX 071-976-6847. Ed. Cath Hawkings. adv.; bk.rev.; bibl.; charts; illus.; index; circ. 13,000. (also avail. in microform from UMI) **Indexed:** Abstr.Hyg., ASSIA, Biol.Abstr., Br.Tech.Ind., Chem.Abstr., Curr.Adv.Ecol.Sci., Curr.Cont., Dairy Sci.Abstr., Dent.Ind., Excerp.Med., Food Sci.& Tech.Abstr., Geo.Abstr., Helminthol.Abstr., HRIS, I.P.A, Ind.Med., Ind.Vet., Nutr.Abstr., Risk Abstr., Soc.Work Res.& Abstr., SSCI, Trop.Dis.Bull., Vet.Bull., W.R.C.Inf.
    —BLDSC shelfmark: 4864.500000.
    Description: Devoted to all aspects of health care, nutrition, and social services.

S A BAROMETER; fortnightly journal of current affairs statistics. see POLITICAL SCIENCE — Civil Rights

S A S C H NEWSLETTER. (Saskatchewan Association of Special Care Homes) see MEDICAL SCIENCES

S C O L A G. (Scottish Legal Action Group) see LAW

S E T FREE. (Society for the Eradication of Television) see COMMUNICATIONS — Television And Cable

361 647.9   SZ
S K A V - FACHBLATT; Zeitschrift fuer stationaere Betreuung. (Text in French, German and Italian) 1939. bi-m. 60 Fr.($45) Schweizerischer Verband Christlicher Institutionen, Zaehringerstr. 19, 6000 Lucerne 7, Switzerland. Ed. Xaver Schorno. adv.; bk.rev.; play rev.; illus.; cum.index; circ. 1,500 (controlled). (tabloid format) **Indexed:** Excerp.Med.
    Formerly: Heim und Anstalt (ISSN 0017-9671)

360   FR   ISSN 0003-1887
S O S AMITIE FRANCE. BULLETIN NATIONAL. 1961. q. 120 F. (foreign 150 F.). S.O.S. Amitie France, 12 rue du Havre, 75009 Paris, France. TEL 42-80-25-20. Dir. Jean Nicolas Mory. adv.; bk.rev.; circ. 2,000.

362.7   AU
S O S KINDERDORF INTERNATIONAL. (Text in English and German) 1962. q. S O S Kinderdorf, International Office, Stafflerstr. 10a, A-6021 Innsbruck, Austria. TEL 5918-307. illus.
    Formerly: S O S Messenger (ISSN 0036-178X)

362.7   AU   ISSN 0023-1509
S O S KINDERDORFBOTE. 1950. q. S O S Kinderdorf, Stafflerstr. 10a, A-6021 Innsbruck, Austria. TEL 5918-307. Ed. Herbert Genser. illus.; circ. 1,000,000.

360 301   AT
S P R C NEWSLETTER. 1980. q. free. Social Policy Research Centre, c/o University of New South Wales, P.O. Box 1, Kensington, N.S.W. 2033, Australia. Ed. Jennifer Young. bk.rev.; stat.; tr.lit.; circ. 2,500. (back issues avail.)
    Formerly: S W R C Newsletter (ISSN 0159-9615)

360 301   AT
S P R C REPORTS AND PROCEEDINGS. 1980. irreg. Aus.$120 for 15 issues. Social Policy Research Centre, c/o University of New South Wales, P.O. Box 1, Kensington, N.S.W. 2033, Australia. Ed. Jennifer Young. stat. (back issues avail.)
    Formerly: S W R C Reports and Proceedings (ISSN 0159-9607)

360   SW   ISSN 0283-1910
S S R - TIDNINGEN. 1958. 41/yr; w. (Oct.-Apr.); fortn. (May-Sep.). SEK 265 to individuals; institutions Kr.385. Sveriges Socionomers Riksfoerbund - Swedish Union of Social Workers and Public Administrators, Mariedalsvaegen 4, S-112 51 Stockholm, Sweden. FAX 08-6174465. Ed. Anders Ljungberg. adv.; bk.rev.; illus.; circ. 29,000.
    Former titles: S S R - Tidningen Socionomen (ISSN 0282-1001); Socionomen (ISSN 0038-044X)

SAGE CRIMINAL JUSTICE SYSTEMS ANNUAL. see CRIMINOLOGY AND LAW ENFORCEMENT

361.8   US
ST. PAUL URBAN LEAGUE. ANNUAL REPORT. 1924. a. free. St. Paul Urban League, 401 Selby Ave., St. Paul, MN 55102. TEL 612-224-5771. Ed. Willie Mac Wilson. circ. 3,000. (tabloid format)

360   IT   ISSN 0392-4505
SALUTE E TERRITORIO. bi-m. L.45000. Regione Toscana, Via di Novoli, 26, 50127 Florence, Italy. Ed. Mariella Crocella.

360   CU
SALVACION. s-m. Ejercito de Salvacion, 96 No. 5513rd, 55 y 57 Marianao 14, Havana, Cuba.

SALVATIONIST. see RELIGIONS AND THEOLOGY — Protestant

360   II   ISSN 0036-3693
SAMAJ KALYAN. (Text in Assamese) 1956. m. Rs.3($0.90) Assam State Social Welfare Advisory Board, Uzanbazar, Gauhati 1, Assam, India. Ed. Sri R.K. Gautam. adv.; abstr.; bibl.; illus.; stat.; circ. 1,100. (tabloid format)

SANTA CRUZ ACTION NETWORK. NEWSLETTER. see HOUSING AND URBAN PLANNING

059.91   II   ISSN 0036-4835
SARVODAYA. (Text in English) 1951. m. Rs.24($8) Tamilnadu Sarvodaya Sangh, Gandhinagar, Tirupur 638603, India. Ed. Sri S. Sivan Pillay. adv.; illus.; index; circ. 1,500.
    Description: Presents Gandhi's ideal of social service.

360   CN
SASKATCHEWAN. DEPARTMENT OF SOCIAL SERVICES. ANNUAL REPORT. 1915. a. free. Department of Social Services, 1920 Broad St., Regina, Sask. S4P 3V6, Canada. TEL 306-787-3494. illus.
    Formerly: Saskatchewan. Department of Social Welfare. Annual Report (ISSN 0708-3882)

362.7   US
SAVE THE CHILDREN. ANNUAL REPORT. a. Save the Children, Public Affairs and Communication, 54 Wilton Rd., Box 950, Westport, CT 06881. TEL 203-221-4000. FAX 203-222-1067.

SCAN. see EDUCATION — Adult Education

SOCIAL SERVICES AND WELFARE

SCARLET LETTER. see *WOMEN'S INTERESTS*

SCHOOL LEAVER. see *EDUCATION*

SCHOOL SOCIAL WORK JOURNAL. see *EDUCATION — Special Education And Rehabilitation*

SCHOOL VOLUNTEERING; linking school volunteers nationwide. see *EDUCATION*

301.3   GW   ISSN 0080-7133
SCHRIFTENREIHE FUER LAENDLICHE SOZIALFRAGEN. 1951. irreg., no.113, 1991. price varies. Agrarsoziale Gesellschaft e.V., Kurze Geismarstr. 33, 3400 Goettingen, Germany. index.
—BLDSC shelfmark: 8104.346000.

360   UK   ISSN 0144-0462
SCOPE (BELFAST); a review of social policy & voluntary action in Northern Ireland. 1975. m. 50p. Northern Ireland Council for Voluntary Action, 127-131 Ormeau Rd., Belfast BT7 1SH, N. Ireland. TEL 321224. FAX 438350. Ed. Liz Law. adv.; bk.rev.; illus.; index; circ. 2,000.
—BLDSC shelfmark: 8205.700000.
Formerly: Voluntary Organisations News.

SCUGNIZZO. see *CHILDREN AND YOUTH — About*

362   UK   ISSN 0958-3467
SEARCH (YORK). 1989. q. free. Joseph Rowntree Foundation, The Homestead, 40 Water End, York YO3 6LP, England. TEL 0904-629241. FAX 0904-620072. Ed. Roland Hurst. bk.rev.; circ. 6,000 (controlled). (back issues avail.)
—BLDSC shelfmark: 8214.370000.
Description: Research and development work supported by the foundation in housing, social policy, social care, disability, local and central government relations.

338.1 360   US   ISSN 0194-4495
SEEDS; hope for the healing and hunger of poverty. 1977-1991; resumed 1992. q. $20 subscr. includes Sprouts Newsletter; libraries $40 (foreign $34). Box 6170, Waco, TX 76706-0170. TEL 817-755-7745. FAX 817-755-3740. Ed. Susan L. Hansen. adv.; bk.rev.; circ. 5,000.
Description: Offers analysis and information to understand US and world hunger and poverty issues; provides practical information for direct involvement.

360 614.8   MX   ISSN 0582-4001
SEGURIDAD SOCIAL. 1958. q. $50. Conferencia Interamericana de Seguridad Social, Calle San Ramon, Unidad Azcapotzalco, Apt. 99089, 10100 Mexico, D.F., Mexico. FAX 6838524. (Co-sponsor: Instituto Mexicano del Seguro Social) Ed.Bd. film rev.; charts; illus.; stat.; circ. 500. **Indexed:** World Bibl.Soc.Sec.

360   GW   ISSN 0724-5572
SELBSTHILFE; Zeitschrift der Bundesarbeitsgemeinschaft Hilfe fuer Behinderte. 1926. 9/yr. DM.36 (students DM.30). Verlag fuer Medizin Dr. Ewald Fischer GmbH, Fritz-Frey-Str. 21, Postfach 105767, 6900 Heidelberg 1, Germany. TEL 06221-4062-0. Ed. Dr. Rolf Bieker. bk.rev.; illus.

360   GW
SELBSTHILFE SPEKTRUM RHEIN - MAIN. 1984. a. Koordination und Entwicklung von Selbsthilfe e.V. (KES), Theodor-Stern-Kai 7, 6000 Frankfurt a.M. 70, Germany. TEL 069-63017603. FAX 069-63016301. circ. 2,000. (back issues avail.)

SELF HELP REPORTER NEWSLETTER. see *PSYCHOLOGY*

361.8 614.58   US   ISSN 8756-1425
HV547
SELF-HELP SOURCEBOOK; finding and forming mutual aid self-help groups. 1986. a. $10. Self-Help Clearinghouse, St. Clares-Riverside Medical Center, Pocono Rd., Denville, NJ 07834. TEL 201-625-7101. Eds. E. Madara, A. Meese. circ. 3,000.
Former titles (until 1986): Self-Help Group Directory (ISSN 0740-7548); Self-Help Group Sourcebook.
Description: Lists national groups, toll-free helplines and clearinghouses around the world for professionals working in the health, mental health, and social service fields. Also contains a how-to section for starting up groups.

362.6
SENIOR CITIZEN SENTINEL. 1942. q. $5. California League of Senior Citizens, 611 S. Catalina St., Ste. 400B, Los Angeles, CA 90005. TEL 213-386-7771. Ed. Kay Corbutt. adv.; bk.rev.; circ. 1,000. (tabloid format; back issues avail.)

US   ISSN 0199-7947

SENIOR NEWS/SENIOR NUUS. see *GERONTOLOGY AND GERIATRICS*

360   AF
SERAMIASHT. (Text in English, Persian or Pushto) 1977. q. Afghan Red Crescent Society, Pul-i Hartan, P.O. Box 3066, Kabul, Afghanistan. TEL 30969. TELEX 318 ARC AF.

361.5   CN   ISSN 0227-034X
SERVICE. (Text in English and French) 1940. q. free. Canadian Red Cross Society, National Headquarters, 5700 Cancross Court, Mississauga, Ont. L5R 3E9, Canada. TEL 416-890-1000. Ed.Bd. circ. 60,000.
Formerly (until 1977): Despatch (ISSN 0046-0087)

360   CN   ISSN 0037-2633
HV2
SERVICE SOCIAL. (Text in French) 1951. 3/yr. Can.$23.54 to individuals; institutions Can.$34.24; students Can.$19.26. Universite Laval, Cite Universitaire, Quebec, Que. G1K 7P4, Canada. TEL 418-656-3288. FAX 418-656-3567. Ed. Jean Louis Gendron. adv.; bk.rev.; bibl.; charts; cum.index; circ. 800. (also avail. in microform from UMI; back issues avail.; reprint service avail. from UMI) **Indexed:** P.A.I.S.For.Lang.Ind., Pt.de Rep. (1979-).
—BLDSC shelfmark: 8252.150000.

360   BE   ISSN 0037-2641
SERVICE SOCIAL DANS LE MONDE. (Text in French; summaries in English, Spanish) 1935. q. 770 Fr. (foreign 950 F.). Service Social dans le Monde, Rue de la Madeleine 57, B 1000 Brussels, Belgium. TEL 322-512-0511. FAX 322-356-9318. (Subscr. to: rue du Gouvernement 50, B 7000 Mons, Belgium. TEL 32-65-33-56-86) Ed. Marie-Anne Beauduin. adv.; bk.rev.; abstr.; cum.index (5/yr.); circ. 1,250. **Indexed:** Cath.Ind.
—BLDSC shelfmark: 8252.160000.

SETTIMANA DEL SORDO; organo di informazione dei minorati dell'udito e della parola. see *HANDICAPPED — Hearing Impaired*

360   UK   ISSN 0037-3168
SHAFTESBURY REVIEW. 1848. s-a. membership. Shaftesbury Society, 18-20 Kingston Rd., South Wimbledon, London SW19 1JZ, England. Ed. N. Slater. illus.; circ. 10,000. (also avail. in microfilm from UMI; reprint service avail. from UMI)
Formerly: Shaftesbury Newsletter.

360   JA
SHAKAI FUKUSHI NO DOKO. 1957. a. 1900 Yen. National Council of Social Welfare - Zenkoku Shakai Fukushi Kyogikai, 3-3-2 Kasumigaseki, Chiyoda-ku, Tokyo, Japan. Ed. Kishio Kimura. circ. 7,000.

362.8   US
SHARED HOUSING QUARTERLY. * 1982. q. $20. Shared Housing Resource Center, 1221 Fairmoint Ave., Philadelphia, PA 19123-2412. TEL 215-848-1220. Ed. Milton Marks. bk.rev.; circ. 500. (back issues avail.)
Description: Features articles on programs, legislation, research, financing, marketing and fund raising. Includes listings of conference and workshop dates.

301.4   US   ISSN 0037-5748
HQ1
SINGLE PARENT. 1958. bi-m. $15 to non-members. Parents Without Partners Inc., 8807 Colesville Rd., Silver Spring, MD 20910-4346. TEL 301-588-9354. FAX 301-588-9216. Ed. Ms. Rene McDonald. adv.; bk.rev.; charts; illus.; tr.lit.; circ. 110,000 (controlled). **Indexed:** PMR.
—BLDSC shelfmark: 8285.568000.
Description: Covers all aspects of single parenting. Includes stories for children of single parents.

SMALL TOWN. see *HOUSING AND URBAN PLANNING*

360   US   ISSN 0037-7317
HV1   CODEN: SMSWAW
SMITH COLLEGE STUDIES IN SOCIAL WORK. 1930. 3/yr. $16. Smith College, School for Social Work, Northampton, MA 01063. TEL 413-585-7950. FAX 413-585-2075. Ed. Joan Laird. bk.rev.; abstr.; index; circ. 2,000. **Indexed:** ASCA, ASSIA, Lang.& Lang.Behav.Abstr., Mid.East Abstr.& Ind., P.A.I.S., Psychol.Abstr., Sage Fam.Stud.Abstr., Soc.Work Res.& Abstr., SSCI.
—BLDSC shelfmark: 8311.200000.

360   UK   ISSN 0955-0801
SOCIAL CARE EDUCATION. 4/yr. membership. Social Care Association, 23a Victoria Rd., Surbiton, Surrey KT6 4JZ, England. TEL 01-390-6831. Ed. Phil Carradice.
—BLDSC shelfmark: 8318.058000.

360   GW   ISSN 0176-1714
SOCIAL CHOICE AND WELFARE. 1984. 4/yr. DM.240($144) Springer-Verlag, Heidelberger Platz 3, D-1000 Berlin 33, Germany. TEL 030-8207-1. Ed. W. Gaertner. **Indexed:** J.of Econ.Lit.
—BLDSC shelfmark: 8318.072000.

360   UK   ISSN 0961-205X
▼**SOCIAL DEVELOPMENT.** 1992. 4/yr. Basil Blackwell Ltd., 108 Cowley Rd., Oxford OX4 1JF, England. TEL 0865-791100. FAX 0865-791347. TELEX 837002-OXBOOK-G.

360   US
SOCIAL DEVELOPMENT ISSUES; alternative approaches to global human needs. 1977. 3/yr. $20 to individuals; institutions $30 (foreign $35); students $15 (foreign $18). University of Iowa, School of Social Work, Iowa City, IA 52242. TEL 319-335-4645. FAX 319-335-1711. (Subscr. to: Social Development Issues, The University of Iowa Publications Services, Grahpic Services Building, Iowa City, IA 52242) Eds. Martin Tracy, Roland Meinert. bk.rev.; bibl.; circ. 500. **Indexed:** Lang.& Lang.Behav.Abstr., Soc.Work Res.& Abstr., Sociol.Abstr.
Supersedes: Iowa Journal of Social Work (ISSN 0021-0536)
Description: Serves as a forum for achieving linkages between multiple disciplines, nations, and cultures. Attempts to advance social, cultural, political, and economic theory, policy, and practice (and their inter-relationship) in a global framework.

360 370   EI   ISSN 0255-0776
HD5764.5.A6
SOCIAL EUROPE. French edition (ISSN 0255-0792); German edition (ISSN 0255-0784) (Editions in English, French and German) 1983. 3/yr., (plus 10-12 supplements/yr.). $105. (Commission of the European Communities, Directorate-General for Employment, Social Affairs and Education) Office for Official Publications of the European Communities, L-2985 Luxembourg, Luxembourg. (Dist. in the U.S. by: Unipub, 4611-F Assembly Dr., Lanham, MD 20706-4391) circ. 7,000. (back issues avail.) **Indexed:** IIS, Int.Lab.Doc., World Bibl.Soc.Sec.
—BLDSC shelfmark: 8318.088000.
Description: Presents an overview of developments and current events in the fields of employment, education, vocational training, industrial relations and social measures; covers international conferences, research, studies and other activities stimulating debate on these issues; reports on the latest developments in national employment policies, and on the introduction of new technologies.

362   UK
SOCIAL RESPONSIBILITY; a directory of resources in the Church of England. 1950. biennial. £4.50. Board for Social Responsibility, General Synod of the Church of England, Church House, Great Smith St., London, SW1P 3NZ, England. TEL 01-222 9011. Ed. Alison Webster. circ. 1,000.
Former titles: Directory of Church of England Social Services (ISSN 0070-5268); Directory of Church of England Moral and Social Welfare Work.

SOCIAL SECURITY BULLETIN. see *INSURANCE*

SOCIAL SECURITY PRACTICE GUIDE. see *INSURANCE*

SOCIAL SECURITY REPORTER. see *INSURANCE*

SOCIAL SECURITY RULINGS, ACQUIESCENCE RULINGS ON FEDERAL OLD-AGE, SURVIVORS, DISABILITY, SUPPLEMENTAL SECURITY INCOME AND BLACK LUNG BENEFITS. see *INSURANCE*

SOCIAL SERVICES AND WELFARE

SOCIAL SERVICE JOBS. see *OCCUPATIONS AND CAREERS*

360   US   ISSN 0737-3627
HV89
SOCIAL SERVICE ORGANIZATIONS AND AGENCIES DIRECTORY. 1982. irreg. $140. Gale Research Inc., 835 Penobscot Bldg., Detroit, MI 48226. TEL 313-961-2242. FAX 3130961-6083. TELEX 810-221-7086. Ed. Anthony T. Kruzas.
Description: Guide to social service organizations and agencies.

360   US   ISSN 0037-7961
HV1   CODEN: SSRVA
SOCIAL SERVICE REVIEW; devoted to the scientific and professional interests of social work. 1927. q. $30 to individuals; institutions $51; students $21. University of Chicago Press, Journals Division, 5720 S. Woodlawn Ave., Chicago, IL 60637. TEL 312-753-3347. FAX 312-702-0694. TELEX 25-4603. (Subscr. to: Box 37005, Chicago, IL 60637) Ed. John R. Schuerman. adv.; bk.rev.; bibl.; index; circ. 3,000. (also avail. in microform from MIM,UMI; reprint service avail. from UMI,ISI) **Indexed:** Adol.Ment.Hlth.Abstr., Amer.Hist.& Life, ASCA, ASSIA, Bk.Rev.Ind. (1984-), Child.Bk.Rev.Ind. (1984-), CLOA, Curr.Cont., Excerp.Med., Hist.Abstr., Lang.& Lang.Behav.Abstr., Med.Care Rev., Mid.East: Abstr.& Ind., P.A.I.S., PSI, Sage Fam.Stud.Abstr., Sage Urb.Stud.Abstr., Soc.Sci.Ind., Soc.Work Res.& Abstr., Sociol.Abstr., Sp.Ed.Needs Abstr., SSCI.
—BLDSC shelfmark: 8318.203000.
Refereed Serial

360 362.7   UK   ISSN 0265-6957
SOCIAL SERVICES RESEARCH. 1972. q. £49 (foreign £55). University of Birmingham, Department of Social Policy and Social Work, Edgbaston, Birmingham B15 2TT, England. TEL 021 472 1301. FAX 021-4144989. Ed. Neil Thomas. bk.rev.; circ. 249. (back issues avail.) **Indexed:** ASSIA.
—BLDSC shelfmark: 8318.204830.
Formerly: Clearing House for Local Authority Social Services Research.
Description: Applied research concerned with all aspects of personal social services: articles, notes and summaries of reports.

360   UK   ISSN 0307-093X
SOCIAL SERVICES YEARBOOK. 1972. a. £43. Longman Group UK Ltd., Longman House, Burnt Mill, Harlow, Essex CM20 2JE, England. Ed. Meta Brett. adv.

300   AT   ISSN 0037-8011
SOCIAL SURVEY. 1951. m. Aus.$8($1.92) Institute of Social Order, Belloc House, 12 Sackville St., Kew, Vic. 3101, Australia. Ed. Rev. W.G. Smith. adv.; bk.rev.; abstr.; charts; illus.; stat.; index; circ. 4,000. (tabloid format) **Indexed:** Aus.P.A.I.S., Gdlns.

361   US   ISSN 0099-183X
HN30
SOCIAL THOUGHT. 1974. q. $26 (foreign $32). (Catholic University of America) Catholic Charities U S A, 1731 King St., Ste. 200, Alexandria, VA 22314. TEL 703-549-1390. FAX 703-549-1656. Ed. Eleanor Hannon Judah. adv.; bk.rev.; charts; illus.; index; circ. 1,000. (also avail. in microform from UMI; back issues avail.; reprint service avail. from UMI) **Indexed:** Adol.Ment.Hlth.Abstr., ASSIA, Cath.Ind., CERDIC, G.Soc.Sci.& Rel.Per.Lit., Lang.& Lang.Behav.Abstr., Soc.Work Res.& Abstr.
—BLDSC shelfmark: 8318.218300.

360   II   ISSN 0037-8038
SOCIAL WELFARE. (Text in English) 1954. m. $8. Central Social Welfare Board, Jeevan Deep, Parliament St., New Delhi 110 001, India. Ed. Ravindra Nair. adv.; bk.rev.; charts; illus.; circ. 5,000. **Indexed:** World Bibl.Soc.Sec.
—BLDSC shelfmark: 8318.219800.

SOCIAL WELFARE LAW. see *LAW*

360   JA
SOCIAL WELFARE SERVICES IN JAPAN. 1960. a. 2000 Yen. International Council on Social Welfare, Japanese National Committee, 3-3-4 Kasumigaseki, Chiyoda-ku, Tokyo, Japan.

360   SA   ISSN 0037-8054
SOCIAL WORK/MAATSKAPLIKE WERK. (Text in Afrikaans and English; summaries in English) 1965. q. R.40($40) (effective Jan. 1992). University of Stellenbosch, Department of Social Work, B.J. Vorster Building, Stellenbosch 7600, South Africa. TEL 02231-772078. FAX 02231-774336. (Subscr. to: P.O. Box 223, Stellenbosch, South Africa) Ed. Johan Cronje. adv.; bk.rev.; abstr.; bibl.; index; circ. 2,000. (back issues avail.) **Indexed:** Chic.Per.Ind., Ind.S.A.Per.
—BLDSC shelfmark: 8318.223100.
Description: A professional journal for social workers.

360   US   ISSN 0037-8046
HV1   CODEN: SOWOA
SOCIAL WORK. 1956. 6/yr. $51 to non-members; institutions $64. National Association of Social Workers, Publications Department, 7981 Eastern Ave., Silver Spring, MD 20910. TEL 301-565-0333. FAX 301-587-1321. Ed. Ann Hartman. adv.; bk.rev.; index; circ. 135,000. (also avail. in microform from UMI; back issues avail.; reprint service avail. from UMI) **Indexed:** Abstr.Health Care Manage.Stud., Acad.Ind., ASCA, Bk.Rev.Ind. (1980-), C.I.J.E., Child.Bk.Rev.Ind. (1980-), Crim.Just.Abstr., Curr.Cont., Except.Child.Educ.Abstr., Excerp.Med., Hosp.Lit.Ind., Lang.& Lang.Behav.Abstr., Mid.East: Abstr.& Ind., P.A.I.S., PSI, Psychol.Abstr., Rehabil.Lit., Sage Pub.Admin.Abstr., Soc.Sci.Ind., Soc.Work Res.& Abstr., Soc.Work Res.& Abstr., Sp.Ed.Needs Abstr., SSCI, Stud.Wom.Abstr., World Bibl.Soc.Sec.
—BLDSC shelfmark: 8318.221100.
Description: Includes scholarly research, critical analyses of the profession and current information on social issues.

360 282   US   ISSN 0737-5778
HV530
SOCIAL WORK AND CHRISTIANITY; an international journal. 1974. s-a. $10. North American Association of Christians in Social Work, Box 7090, St. Davids, PA 19087-7090. TEL 215-687-5777. Ed. David A. Sherwood. adv.; bk.rev.; circ. 1,200. (back issues avail.) **Indexed:** Chr.Per.Ind., Soc.Work Res.& Abstr.

360   US   ISSN 0081-055X
SOCIAL WORK AND SOCIAL ISSUES. 1969. irreg., no.5, 1977. Columbia University Press, 562 W. 113th St., New York, NY 10025. TEL 212-678-6777.

360   UK   ISSN 0261-5479
SOCIAL WORK EDUCATION. 1980. 3/yr. £19($45) Whiting & Birch Ltd., P.O. Box 872, Forest Hill, London SE23 3HL, England. TEL 081-699-0914. FAX 081-699-3685. Ed. John Warwick. index; circ. 500. (back issues avail.) **Indexed:** ASSIA, Sociol.Abstr.
—BLDSC shelfmark: 8318.223700.
Description: Covers social work education and training.

SOCIAL WORK EDUCATION REPORTER. see *EDUCATION*

361   II   ISSN 0583-7065
HV1
SOCIAL WORK FORUM. 1963. q. Indian Association of Trained Social Workers, 3 University Rd., Delhi 110007, India.

360   US   ISSN 0162-7961
LB3013.4   CODEN: SOWEEG
SOCIAL WORK IN EDUCATION; a journal for school social workers. 1978. q. $44 to non-members; institutions $53. National Association of Social Workers, Publications Department, 7981 Eastern Ave., Silver Spring, MD 20910. TEL 301-565-0333. FAX 301-587-1321. Ed. Paula Allen-Meares. adv.; bk.rev.; circ. 2,600. (also avail. in microform from UMI; reprint service avail. from UMI) **Indexed:** Adol.Ment.Hlth.Abstr., Cont.Pg.Educ., PSI, Psychol.Abstr., Soc.Work Res.& Abstr., Sociol.Abstr., Sp.Ed.Needs.Abstr.
—BLDSC shelfmark: 8318.223720.
Description: Articles for school social workers and their colleagues on problems they encounter in daily work.

360 362   US   ISSN 0098-1389
HV687.A2   CODEN: SWHCDO
SOCIAL WORK IN HEALTH CARE; quarterly journal of medical & psychiatric social work. 1975. q. $36 to individuals; institutions $85; libraries $145. Haworth Press, Inc., 10 Alice St., Binghamton, NY 13904. TEL 800-342-9678. FAX 607-722-1424. TELEX 4932599 HAWORTH. Ed. Sylvia Clarke. adv.; bk.rev.; abstr.; charts; circ. 2,000. (also avail. in microfiche from HAW; back issues avail.; reprint service avail. from HAW) **Indexed:** Abstr.Health Care Manage.Stud., Abstr.Hosp.Manage.Stud., Abstr.Soc.Geront., Adol.Ment.Hlth.Abstr., ASCA, ASSIA, Behav.Abstr., Biol.Abstr., Bull.Signal., Chicago Psychoanal.Lit.Ind., CINAHL, CLOA, Curr.Cont., Excerp.Med., Hosp.Abstr., Hosp.Lit.Ind., Ind.Med., Int.Nurs.Ind., Med.Care Rev., PSI, Psychol.Abstr., Rehabil.Lit., Sage Fam.Stud.Abstr., Sage Pub.Admin.Abstr., Soc.Work Res.& Abstr., Sociol.Abstr., Sp.Ed.Needs Abstr., SSCI.
—BLDSC shelfmark: 8318.225600.
Description: Devoted to social work, theory, practice, and administration in a wide variety of health care settings.
Refereed Serial

SOCIAL WORK INFORMATION BULLETIN. see *SOCIAL SCIENCES: COMPREHENSIVE WORKS*

360   SA
SOCIAL WORK PRACTICE/MAATSKAPLIKEWERK-PRAKTYK. (Text and summaries in Afrikaans, English) 1983. 3/yr. free. Department of Planning and Provincial Affairs, 240 Walker St., Sunnyside, Private Bag X644, Pretoria 0001, South Africa. TEL 012-421-1311. FAX 012-341-7328. TELEX 012-320397. Ed. E. Viviers. bk.rev.; cum.index; circ. 3,300.
Description: Devoted to enhancing the professionalism of social workers.

360   UK   ISSN 0037-8070
HV1
SOCIAL WORK TODAY. 1970. w. £65. British Association of Social Workers, 16 Kent St., Birmingham, B5 6RD, England. Ed. Angela Anderson. adv.; bk.rev.; index. **Indexed:** ASSIA, High.Educ.Curr.Aware.Bull., Soc.Work Res.& Abstr.
—BLDSC shelfmark: 8318.233000.
Incorporates: Residential Social Work.

362.8   US   ISSN 0160-9513
HV45   CODEN: SWGRDU
SOCIAL WORK WITH GROUPS; a journal of community and clinical practice. 1978. q. $36 to individuals; institutions $85; libraries $165. Haworth Press, Inc., 10 Alice St., Binghamton, NY 13904. TEL 800-342-9678. FAX 607-722-1424. TELEX 4932599. Ed. Roselle Kurland. adv.; bk.rev.; bibl.; circ. 768. (also avail. in microfiche from HAW; reprint service avail. from HAW,ISI; back issues avail.) **Indexed:** Adol.Ment.Hlth.Abstr., ASCA, ASSIA, Chic.Per.Ind., Curr.Cont., Lang.& Lang.Behav.Abstr., Psychol.Abstr., Soc.Work Res.& Abstr., Sociol.Abstr., Sp.Ed.Needs Abstr., SSCI.
—BLDSC shelfmark: 8318.225000.
Description: Covers the areas of groupwork in psychiatric, rehabilitative, and multipurpose social work and social services agencies.
Refereed Serial

360   CN   ISSN 0037-8089
SOCIAL WORKER/TRAVAILLEUR SOCIAL. (Text in English and French) 1932. q. Can.$32($36) (Canadian Association of Social Workers) Myropen Publications Ltd., 55 Parkdale Ave., Ottawa, Ont. K1Y 1E5, Canada. TEL 613-729-6668. FAX 613-725-3720. Ed. Nada Skerl. adv.; bk.rev.; index; circ. 13,000. (also avail. in microform from MML) **Indexed:** Soc.Work Res.& Abstr.
—BLDSC shelfmark: 8318.235000.
Description: Information about social work groups in Canada and current social welfare policy. Examines regional, national and international social issues.

360   SW   ISSN 0037-8100
SOCIALFOERFATTNINGAR. 1957. 20/yr. SEK 1240. Foerlagshuset Gothia AB, P.O. Box 15169, S-104 65 Stockholm, Sweden. FAX 08-641-4585. Ed. Bengt-Olof Bengtson. adv.; charts; index; circ. 2,000 (controlled).

SOCIALNI POLITIKA. see *POLITICAL SCIENCE*

SOCIAL SERVICES AND WELFARE

360 DK ISSN 0105-5399
SOCIALPAEDAGOGEN. vol.24, 1967. 23/yr. DKK 274.50. Socialpaedagogernes Landsforbund, Brolaeggerstraede 9-1, 1211 Copenhagen K, Denmark. adv.; circ. 12,000.
 Formerly: Boernesagspaedagogen.

361 DK ISSN 0108-6103
SOCIALRAADGIVEREN. 1938. s-m. DKK 460. Dansk Socialraadgiverforening - Danish Association of Social Workers, Toldbodgade 19 A, 1253 Copenhagen K, Denmark. FAX 33-913019. Eds. Rie Graesberg, Wittus Nielsen. adv.; bk.rev.; circ. 8,400.

360 AG ISSN 0037-8569
SOCIEDAD ESPANOLA DE SOCORROS MUTUOS Y BENEFICENCIA. BOLETIN.* 1968. irreg. (4-5/yr.) free. Sociedad Espanola de Socorros Mutuos y Beneficencia, Rodriquez No. 545, Tandil, Buenos Aires, Argentina. Ed. Ernesto Enrique Reclusa. circ. 2,000. (looseleaf format)

SOCIEDADE E ESTADO. see SOCIOLOGY

360 IS ISSN 0334-4029
SOCIETY AND WELFARE/HEVRA U-REVAHA; quarterly for social work. (Text in Hebrew and English) 1978. irreg. IS.20($15) Ministry of Labour and Social Affairs, P.O. Box 1260, Jerusalem, Israel. TEL 02-719081. Ed. Dr. Shimon Spiro. bk.rev.

301 CI ISSN 0038-0105
SOCIJALNI RAD/SOCIAL WORK; teorija i praksa. (Text in Serbo-Croatian; abstracts in English) 1961. s-a. 80000 din. Republic Institute for Social Work, c/o Visnja Gracin, Ul. 8 Maja 1945, br. 42, 41000 Zagreb, Croatia. TEL 431-555. Ed. Bozo Zaja. bk.rev.

301 GW ISSN 0038-0164
HM1.A1
SOCIOLOGIA INTERNATIONALIS; internationale Zeitschrift fuer Soziologie, Kommunikations- und Kulturforschung. (Text in English, French, German and Spanish; summaries in English) 1963. s-a. DM.112. Duncker und Humblot GmbH, Postfach 410329, 1000 Berlin 41, Germany. TEL 030-7900060. FAX 030-79000631. Ed.Bd. adv.; bk.rev. Indexed: Lang.& Lang.Behav.Abstr., Sociol.Abstr. (1963-).
 —BLDSC shelfmark: 8319.605000.

301.4 FR ISSN 0338-1757
SOLIDAIRES (PARIS). 1956. q. 70 F. (foreign 80 F.) Association Edition Solidaires, 28 place St. Georges, 75009 Paris, France. TEL 45-26-05-42. Ed. L. Marchand. adv.; bk.rev.; illus.; circ. 90,000. (back issues avail.)
 Formerly: Survivre.

360 AT ISSN 0813-4650
SOLO; Victorian newsletter for parents without partners. 1967. m. Aus.$10. (Parents Without Partners (Vic) Inc.) New Lithographics Ltd., Sunbury Cres., Surrey Hills, Vic. 3126, Australia. (Subscr. to: Parents Without Partners (Vic) Inc., 220 Canterbury Rd., Canterbury, Vic. 3156, Australia) Ed. Jan Mason. adv.; bk.rev.; circ. 8,500. (back issues avail.)

360 US ISSN 0097-9562
HD6050
SOROPTIMIST; of the Americas. 1927. 6/yr. $8. Soroptimist International of the Americas, Inc., 1616 Walnut St., Philadelphia, PA 19103. TEL 215-732-0512. FAX 215-732-7508. Ed. Darlene Friedman. adv.; bk.rev.; illus.; circ. 39,000.

360 FI ISSN 0038-1594
SOSIAALINEN AIKAKAUSKIRJA/SOCIAL REVIEW. (Text in Finnish; summaries in English) 1907. 6/yr. Fmk.120. Sosiaali- ja Terveysministerio - Ministry of Social Affairs and Health, Snellmaninkatu 4-6, Box 267, SF-00170 Helsinki 17, Finland. TEL 90-1601. FAX 90-1604328. TELEX 125073. Ed. Heikki S. von Hertzen. circ. 3,000.
 Description: Problems of public health, social welfare, social security and occupational health.

360 368 NO ISSN 0038-1608
SOSIAL TRYGD. 1937. m. (11/yr.). NOK 270. Trygdekontorenes Landsforening, Stortingsgt. 6, 0161 Oslo, Norway. TEL 02-41-59-90. FAX 04-72-42-40-75. Ed. Halina Thee. adv.; bk.rev.; bibl.; charts; illus.; circ. 7,000.

361 NO
SOSIONOMEN. 1956. 22/yr. NOK 390. Norsk Sosionomforbund, Postboks 696, 0106 Oslo 1, Norway. Ed. Barbro Sveen. adv.; bk.rev.; circ. 13,718.

362.4 FI ISSN 0049-1349
SOTAINVALIDI.* (Text in Finnish and Swedish) 1940. m. Fmk.5($2) (Disabled War Veterans Association of Finland) Veljesliitto, Kasarmikatu 34, 00130 Helsinki 13, Finland. Ed. Paivio Halminen. circ. 49,000.

SOUNDBARRIER. see HANDICAPPED — Hearing Impaired

361 US ISSN 0740-4549
HV99.N59
SOURCE BOOK: SOCIAL AND HEALTH SERVICES IN THE GREATER NEW YORK AREA. 1984. irreg., latest 1991. $39.50. (Department of Social Serivces, Human Resources Administration) Oryx Press, 4041 N. Central at Indian School Rd., Phoenix, AZ 85012-3397. TEL 602-265-2651. FAX 602-265-6250. (Co-sponsor: United Way of New York City)
 Description: Information on more than 2,000 non-profit, voluntary, public and private agencies and their 5,000 individual program sites in greater New York, with community or district location, names of directors and chairpersons.

SOUTH AFRICAN MEDICAL AND DENTAL COUNCIL. REGISTER OF SUPPLEMENTARY HEALTH SERVICES PROFESSIONS. see MEDICAL SCIENCES

360 AT ISSN 0816-9594
SOUTH AUSTRALIAN VOLUNTEERING. 1984. q. Aus.$30. Volunteer Centre of South Australia Inc., 155 Pirie St., Adelaide, S.A. 5000, Australia. TEL 08-232-0199. Ed. Marjon Martin. bk.rev.; circ. 1,000.
 Description: For organizations involving volunteers.

361.77 RU ISSN 0132-1226
SOVETSKII KRASNYI KREST/SOVIET RED CROSS. 1923. m. 13.20 Rub.($10.20) (Obshchestvo Krasnyi Krest) Izdatel'stvo Meditsina, Petroverigskii pereulok 6-8, 101838 Moscow, Russia. (Subscr. to: Mezhdunarodnaya Kniga, Moscow, G-200, Russia) Ed. I.A. Martynov. index.
 Description: Provides information on health and disease prevention, recommendations on childhood health topics, and guidance on home care for the sick.

SOWER. see RELIGIONS AND THEOLOGY

360 AU
SOZIALARBEIT IN OESTERREICH. 1965. 4/yr. S.200. Oesterreichischer Berufsverband Diplomierter Sozialarbeiterinnen, Mariahilferstr. 81, A-1060 Vienna, Austria. TEL 0222-5874656. Eds. Peter Sitte, Ursula Nader. adv.; bk.rev.; index; circ. 3,000.

360 GW ISSN 0490-1606
HV3
SOZIALE ARBEIT; deutsche Zeitschrift fuer soziale und sozialverwandte Gebiete. 1951. m. DM.82. Deutsches Zentralinstitut fuer Soziale Fragen, Miquelstr. 83, 1000 Berlin 33, Germany. TEL 030-8324041. FAX 030-8314750. adv.; bk.rev.; abstr.; bibl.; circ. 1,200. Indexed: Excerp.Med., P.A.I.S.For.Lang.Ind.
 —BLDSC shelfmark: 8361.030000.

360 GW ISSN 0340-8469
SOZIALMAGAZIN; die Zeitschrift fuer soziale Arbeit. 1976. m. DM.69 (students DM.59). Juventa Verlag GmbH, Ehretstr. 3, 6940 Weinheim, Germany. TEL 06201-61035. FAX 06201-13135. adv.; bk.rev.; index; circ. 10,000.

SOZIALPSYCHIATRISCHE INFORMATIONEN. see PSYCHOLOGY

362 GW
SOZIALRECHT & PRAXIS; Fachzeitschrift des VdK fuer Vertrauensleute der Behinderten und fuer Sozialpolitiker. 1950. m. DM.30. Verband der Kriegs- und Wehrdienstopfer, Behinderten und Sozialrentner Deutschlands e.V. (VdK), Wurzerstr. 2-4, 5300 Bonn 2, Germany. TEL 0228-820930. FAX 0228-8209343. Ed. Guenter Neuberger. circ. 15,000.
 Former titles: V D K - Mitteilungen Sozialpolitische Fachzeitschrift; V D K - Mitteilungen (ISSN 0042-1774)
 Description: Covers social politics, social law, laws covering pensions, health & accident insurance and other aspects of international social welfare laws.

SOZIALWISSENSCHAFTEN UND BERUFSPRAXIS. see SOCIOLOGY

SOZIALWISSENSCHAFTLICHE LITERATUR RUNDSCHAU; Sozialarbeit-Sozialpaedagogik-Sozialpolitik-soziale Probleme. see SOCIAL SCIENCES: COMPREHENSIVE WORKS

361.77 CN ISSN 0847-3390
SPIRIT. 1970. q. Canadian Red Cross Society, Alberta - Northwest Territories Division, 9931-106th St., Edmonton, Alta. T5K 1E2, Canada. TEL 403-423-2680. FAX 403-428-7092. Ed. Kathy Krug. illus.; circ. 2,000.
 Former titles: Action (ISSN 0382-4527); Supersedes in part: Volunteer (ISSN 0382-4551); Swim Signals (ISSN 0382-4535); Red Cross Youth (ISSN 0382-4543)

360 US
SPRINGER SERIES ON SOCIAL WORK. irreg., vol.9, 1986. price varies. Springer Publishing Company, 536 Broadway, New York, NY 10012. FAX 212-941-7842. Ed. Albert Roberts, D.S.W.

361.8 UK
STAFF OF SCOTTISH WORK DEPARTMENTS. 1979. a. Social Work Services Group, 43 Jeffrey St., Rm. 424, Edinburgh EH1 1DN, Scotland.

STAR AND GARTER MAGAZINE. see HOSPITALS

360 350 US
STATE HOUSE WATCH. 1982. 20/yr. $60 to individuals; institutions $120. Massachusetts Human Service Coalition, Inc., 37 Temple Pl., 3rd Fl., Boston, MA 02111. TEL 617-482-6119. FAX 617-695-1295. Ed. Donna Southwell. circ. 700.
 Description: Covers Massachusetts human service legislation and budgets, including housing, health care, children and families, senior citizens, disabilities and mental helath.

361 US ISSN 1055-9213
HV741
STATE OF AMERICA'S CHILDREN (YEAR); an analysis of our nation's investment in children. 1981. a. $14.95. Children's Defense Fund, 25 E St., N.W., Washington, DC 20001. TEL 202-628-8787. FAX 202-783-7324. charts; stat.; circ. 18,000.
 Former titles (until 1991): Vision for America's Future; (until 1989): Children's Defense Budget (ISSN 0736-6701)
 Description: Presents an analysis of federal programs affecting children and families. Includes recommendations for positive investments in children.

STATISTICS ON SOCIAL WORK EDUCATION IN THE UNITED STATES. see EDUCATION — Abstracting, Bibliographies, Statistics

361 IT
LA STILLA; organo di stampa dell'A.V.I.S. provinciale di Montova. 1965. m. Associazione Volontari Italiani Sangue (A.V.I.S.), c/o Ospedale "C. Poma", Via Albertoni 1, 46100 Mantova, Italy.

360 SW ISSN 0281-2851
STOCKHOLM STUDIES IN SOCIAL WORK. (Text in English) 1983. irreg. price varies. Almquist & Wiksell International, P.O. Box 638, S-101 28 Stockholm, Sweden. TELEX 12430 S. Ed. Hans Berglind. circ. 500.
 —BLDSC shelfmark: 8465.741000.

STRAFVOLLZUG IN DER SCHWEIZ. see CRIMINOLOGY AND LAW ENFORCEMENT

SOCIAL SERVICES AND WELFARE

STREETWIZE COMICS; youth rights comics. see CHILDREN AND YOUTH — For

362.8   UK
STUDENT WELFARE MANUAL. 1970. a. £15. National Union of Students, 461 Holloway Rd., London N7 6LJ, England. circ. 3,000.

STUDIENSTIFTUNG. JAHRESBERICHT. see EDUCATION — Special Education And Rehabilitation

STUDIES IN HEALTH AND HUMAN SERVICES. see PHYSICAL FITNESS AND HYGIENE

360
STUDIES IN SOCIAL POLICY AND WELFARE. no.6, 1978. irreg. £8. Heinemann Educational Books Ltd., 22 Bedford Square, London WC1B 3HH, England. Ed. Robert Pinker. bibl.

360   US   ISSN 8755-5360
STUDIES IN SOCIAL WELFARE POLICIES AND PROGRAMS. 1985. irreg. price varies. Greenwood Press, Inc. (Subsidiary of: Greenwood Publishing Group Inc.), 88 Post Rd. W., Box 5007, Westport, CT 06881-5007. TEL 203-226-3571. FAX 203-222-1502.
—BLDSC shelfmark: 8491.626000.

SUIZIDPROPHYLAXE. see MEDICAL SCIENCES — Psychiatry And Neurology

SUMMARY INFORMATION ON MASTER OF SOCIAL WORK PROGRAMS. see EDUCATION — Higher Education

SURVEY; a quarterly journal. see BUSINESS AND ECONOMICS — Management

360   SW   ISSN 0346-6019
SWEDEN. SOCIALSTYRELSEN. FOERFATTNINGSSAMLING: SOCIAL. 1976. irreg. (approx. 3/yr.). Kr.125. Socialstyrelsen - National Board of Health and Welfare, 106 30 Stockholm, Sweden. index; circ. 6,000. (looseleaf format)
Supersedes in part (1883-1976): Sweden. Medicinalvaesendet. Foerfattningssamling (ISSN 0346-5837)

360   SW   ISSN 1100-2808
SWEDEN. SOCIALSTYRELSEN. S O S - RAPPORT. irreg. (10-15/yr.). price varies. Allmaenna Foerlaget, 106 47 Stockholm, Sweden. TEL 08-739-9630. FAX 08-739-9548. charts; circ. 2,000.
Formerly: Sweden. Socialstyrelsen. Redovisar (ISSN 0346-5799)

360   US   ISSN 0730-6237
HV97.A3
TAFT FOUNDATION REPORTER. 1971. a. $327. Taft Group, 12300 Twinbrook Pkwy., Ste. 450, Rockville, MD 20852. TEL 301-816-0210.

362.4   UK
TALKING SENSE. 1956. 4/yr. £10. Sense - National Deaf-Blind and Rubella Association, 311 Grays Inn Rd., London WC1X 8PT, England. TEL 071-278-1005. FAX 071-837-3267. Ed. Helen Matson. adv.; bk.rev.; bibl.; circ. 4,000. (processed)
Former titles: National Association for Deaf - Blind and Rubella Handicapped. Newsletter; National Association for Deaf - Blind and Rubella Children. Newsletter.

362.7   AT   ISSN 0728-988X
TANDARRA. 1980. s-a. free. Berry Street - Child and Family Care, 1 Berry Street, East Melbourne, Vic. 3002, Australia. TEL 03-429-9266. FAX 03-429-5160. Ed. Jenny Reece. circ. 6,000. (back issues avail.)
Description: Information about family support and child care; news about the agency.

TEL AVIV UNIVERSITY. FACULTY OF THE HUMANITIES AND SOCIAL SCIENCES. YIDION. see HUMANITIES: COMPREHENSIVE WORKS

TELEPHONE PIONEER. see CLUBS

361.6   CR   ISSN 0492-6471
TEMAS SOCIALES. 1954. q. Ministerio de Trabajo y Prevision Social, Apartado 2041, San Jose, Costa Rica.

362   US
TEXAS. DEPARTMENT ON AGING. ANNUAL REPORT. 1982. a. free. Department on Aging, Box 12786, Capitol Sta., Austin, TX 78711. TEL 512-444-2727.
Former titles: Texas Department on Aging. Biennial Report; Texas. Department on Aging. Annual Report; Texas. Governor's Committee on Aging. Biennial Report (ISSN 0082-3058)

360   GW
THEORIE UND PRAXIS DER SOZIALEN ARBEIT. 1947. m. DM.55. Arbeiterwohlfahrt Bundesverband e.V., Oppelner Str. 130, 5300 Bonn 1, Germany. Ed. Heinz Niedrig. adv.; bk.rev.; circ. 4,000.
Formerly: Neues Beginnen (ISSN 0028-3592)
Description: News about social work and social politics.

THERAPY WEEKLY; the newspaper for the remedial professions. see HOSPITALS

360   UK
THIRD SECTOR FORTNIGHT AND INFORM. 1985. fortn. £25. Scottish Council for Voluntary Organisations, 18-19 Claremont Crescent, Edinburgh EH7 4QD, Scotland. TEL 031-556-3882. FAX 031-556-0279. adv.; circ. 1,000.
Formerly: Third Sector (ISSN 0267-3053)
Description: News and information for voluntary and community organizations in Scotland.

360   UK   ISSN 0268-4047
THIS CARING BUSINESS. 1985. 10/yr. £25($30) Careworld Publishing House Ltd., 1 St. Thomas's Rd., Hastings, East Sussex TN34 3LG, England. TEL 0424-718406. FAX 0424-718460. Ed. Michael J. Monk. adv.; bk.rev.; charts; stat.; tr.lit.; circ. 16,768. (back issues avail.)
Description: Covers commercially-oriented matters relating to long-stay health and residential care.

360   US   ISSN 0743-2437
THIS WEEK IN WASHINGTON. 1980. w. (50/yr.). $95 to non-members; members $85; foreign $105. American Public Welfare Association, 810 First St., N.E., Ste. 500, Washington, DC 20002-4205. TEL 202-682-0100. Ed. Kathy Patterson. circ. 800.
Description: Updates on legislative action, federal legislation, and personnel changes.

TINNITUS TODAY. (American Tinnitus Association) see MEDICAL SCIENCES — Otorhinolaryngology

361.7   US
TOLSTOY FOUNDATION NEWS. (Text in English and Russian) 1978. s-a. free. Tolstoy Foundation, Inc., 200 Park Ave. S., Rm. 1612, New York, NY 10003-1522. TEL 212-677-7770. FAX 212-674-0519. TELEX 66366. circ. 4,000 (paid); (controlled).

360   US
TRANSITION (YEAR); the California social services directory. a. (plus s-a. updates). $95. Crossover Communications, Inc., 255 S. Laurel St., Ventura, CA 93001-3069. TEL 805-648-3744. (also avail. on diskette)
Description: Contains descriptions, addresses and phone numbers of over 11,000 agencies in all 58 California counties.

360   US
TRANSITION NEWS. q. Crossover Communications, Inc., 255 S. Laurel St., Ventura, CA 93001-3069. TEL 805-648-3744. Ed. Betty Abramson. adv.

TRANSIZIONE. see POLITICAL SCIENCE

362   NE
TREFPUNT. 1965. 52/yr. fl.45. Ministerie van Welzijn, Volksgezondheid en Cultuur, Postbus 5406, 2280 HK Rijswijk, Netherlands. Ed. G. Zandbergen. bk.rev.; abstr.; film rev.; play rev.; index; circ. 8,000.
Indexed: Key to Econ.Sci.

TRUDOV INVALID. see INSURANCE

360   GW   ISSN 0579-5621
U.I.A.M.S. BULLETIN TRIMESTRIEL. q. $6. International Union for Moral and Social Action, Jaegerallee 5, D-4700 Hamm 1, Germany. bk.rev.; circ. 2,500.

361 362.7   UN   ISSN 1013-3194
U N I C E F POLICY REVIEW SERIES. (Text in English; occasionally Arabic, French, Spanish) 1988. irreg. price varies. United Nations Childrens Fund, 3 United Nations Plaza, Rm.H-12G, New York, NY 10017. TEL 212-326-7157. FAX 212-326-7096. TELEX 175989TRT. Ed. Dr. Pierre-Emeric Mandl. circ. 12,000. (also avail. in microform from EDR)

360   ISSN 0082-8556
U S O ANNUAL REPORT. a. free. United Service Organizations, Inc., U S O World Headquarters, 601 Indiana Ave., N.W., Washington, DC 20004. TEL 202-783-8121. Ed. Amy Adler. circ. 5,000.

UNDERVISNING OG VELFERD/EDUCATION AND WELFARE. see MILITARY

360   FR   ISSN 0041-7041
UNION SOCIALE. 1947. m. 75 F. Union Nationale Interfederale des Oeuvres Privees Sanitaires et Sociales, 103 Faubourg St.-Honore, 75008 Paris, France. Ed. M. Lepagnez. adv.; illus.; index; circ. 8,000.

UNIONIST. see LABOR UNIONS

361.8   US
UNITED COMMUNITY PLANNING CORPORATION. REPORT.* irreg., no.161, 1979. United Community Planning Corporation, c/o Boston Foundation, 1 Boston Pl., no.2400, Boston, MA 02103-4402.

361   US
UNITED FOR SERVICE. 1977. q. free. United Way International, 901 N. Pitt St., Alexandria, VA 22314. TEL 703-836-7100. FAX 703-519-1485. Ed. Cathy Seigerman. circ. 300. (looseleaf format)
Description: Covers international philanthropic activities of United Way.

361 362.7   UN   ISSN 1013-3186
UNITED NATIONS CHILDREN'S FUND. PROGRAMME DIVISION. CONFERENCE REPORTS SERIES. (Text in English) 1988. irreg. price varies. United Nations Children's Fund, Programme Division, 3 United Nations Plaza, Rm.H-12G, New York, NY 10017. TEL 212-326-7157. FAX 212-326-7096. TELEX 175989TRT. Ed. Dr. Pierre-Emeric Mandl. circ. 4,000. (also avail. in microform from EDR)

361 362.7   UN   ISSN 1013-3178
UNITED NATIONS CHILDRENS FUND. PROGRAMME DIVISION. STAFF WORKING PAPERS SERIES. 1988. irreg. (2-4/yr.). price varies. United Nations Childrens Fund, Programme Division, 3 United Nations Plaza, Rm.H-12G, New York, NY 10017. TEL 212-326-7157. FAX 212-326-7096. TELEX 175989TRT. Ed. Dr. Pierre-Emeric Mandl. circ. 4,000. (also avail. in microform from EDR)

360   UN   ISSN 0252-452X
UNITED NATIONS ECONOMIC AND SOCIAL COMMISSION FOR ASIA AND THE PACIFIC. SOCIAL DEVELOPMENT DIVISION. SOCIAL WORK EDUCATION AND DEVELOPMENT. 1966. irreg. United Nations Economic and Social Commission for Asia and the Pacific (ESCAP), Social Development Division, United Nations Bldg., Rajadamnern Ave., Bangkok 10200, Thailand.
Formerly: United Nations Economic and Social Commission for Asia and the Pacific. Social Development Division. Social Work Training and Teaching Materials Newsletter (ISSN 0085-7513)

360   US
UNITED NEIGHBORHOOD CENTERS OF AMERICA. NEWS & ROUND TABLE.* vol.36, 1972. q. $25. United Neighborhood Centers of America, Inc., 4801 Massachusetts Ave.,N.W., Ste. 400, Washington, DC 20016. TEL 202-393-3929. Ed. J.C. Stevenson. bk.rev.; play rev.; circ. 3,000. (tabloid format)
Formerly (until 1979): National Federation of Settlements and Neighborhood Centers, News and Round Table.

361.6   US   ISSN 0190-373X
HC110.P63
U.S. COMMUNITY SERVICES ADMINISTRATION. ANNUAL REPORT. 1976. a. U.S. Community Services Administration, Washington, DC 20506. TEL 202-655-4000. Key Title: Annual Report of Community Services Administration.
Formerly: U.S. Office of Economic Opportunity. Annual Report.

SOCIAL SERVICES AND WELFARE 4423

353.007 US ISSN 0091-6242
JK1672
U.S. GENERAL SERVICES ADMINISTRATION. MANAGEMENT REPORT. a. U.S. General Services Administration, Office of Public Affairs, Washington, DC 20405. TEL 202-523-1250. stat. Key Title: Management Report - General Services Administration.

362 US
U.S. NATIONAL CENTER FOR SOCIAL STATISTICS. FAIR HEARINGS IN PUBLIC ASSISTANCE. (NCSS E-8) 1970. s-a. free. U.S. National Center for Social Statistics, U.S. Department of Health, Education and Welfare, 330 Independence Ave., S.W., Washington, DC 20201. TEL 301-436-7900. stat.

362 CN
UNITED WAY OF CANADA. DIRECTORY OF MEMBERS. (Text in English and French) 1963. a. United Way of Canada, 150 Kent St., Ste. 600, Ottawa, Ont. K1P 5P4, Canada. TEL 613-236-7041. index. cum.index. (processed)
Formerly: Directory of Canadian Community Funds and Councils (ISSN 0084-9863)

362.7 340 US
UNMARRIED PARENTS TODAY. 1981. bi-m. membership. National Council for Adoption, Inc., 1930 17th St., N.W., Washington, DC 20009-2607. TEL 202-328-1200. Ed. Mary Beth Seader. (looseleaf format; back issues avail.)
Description: For social workers providing services to pregnant and parenting teens.

360 UK
UPFRONT. 1989. q. £0.60. War on Want, Fenner Brockway House, 37-39 Great Guildford St., London SE1 0ES, England. FAX 01-261-9291. TELEX 24784 WOW G. Ed. Nicky Parker. adv.; bk.rev.; circ. 5,000.

360 II ISSN 0377-6352
HN681
UPLIFT. (Text in English and Hindi) 1973. q. Rs.20($10) Low Income Family Emancipation (Life) Society, 69, Sector XII, R.K. Puram, New Delhi 110 022, India. TEL 11-600-410. Ed. T.J. Abraham. adv.; illus.; circ. 2,500.

360 352.7 US ISSN 0042-0832
HT101
URBAN AND SOCIAL CHANGE REVIEW. 1967. s-a. $8. Boston College, Graduate School of Social Work, McGuinn Hall, Rm. 109, Chestnut Hill, MA 02167. TEL 617-552-4038. Ed. Robert M. Moroney. adv.; bk.rev.; film rev.; circ. 2,500. (also avail. in microform from UMI; reprint service avail. from UMI)
Indexed: A.B.C.Pol.Sci., Abstr.Soc.Work, Adol.Ment.Hlth.Abstr., Curr.Cont., Econ.Abstr., Geo.Abstr., Hist.Abstr., Human Resour.Abstr., Lang.& Lang.Behav.Abstr., Med.Care Rev., Pers.Manage.Abstr., Sage Fam.Stud.Abstr., Sage Pub.Admin.Abstr., Sage Urb.Stud.Abstr., Sociol.Abstr., SSCI, Trans.Res.Abstr.
Formerly: Institute of Human Sciences. Review.

360 SW ISSN 0042-1553
UTE OCH HEMMA; tidning for Svenskt sjoefolk och turister. 1927. m. SEK 50. Naemnden foer Svenska Kyrkan i Utlandet, Box 205, 751 04 Uppsala, Sweden. FAX 18-176372. Ed. Lena Sjoestroem. adv.; bk.rev.; illus.; indes; circ. 12,500.
Description: Church of Sweden abroad, Seamen's and tourist's mission.

VAEL & VE. see *PUBLIC HEALTH AND SAFETY*

VANISHED CHILDREN'S ALLIANCE NEWSLETTER. see *CHILDREN AND YOUTH — About*

361.6 VE
VENEZUELA. MINISTERIO DE SANIDAD Y ASISTENCIA SOCIAL. MEMORIA Y CUENTA. 1936. a. Ministerio de Sanidad y Asistencia Social, Oficina de Publicaciones, Biblioteca y Archivo, Centro Simon Bolivar, Edificio Sur, Caracas, Venezuela. Ed. Manuel Boet. circ. 3,000.

368 AU
VERBAND DER VERSICHERUNGSUNTERNEHMUNGEN OESTERREICHS. GESCHAEFTSBERICHT. 1956. a. free. Verband der Versicherungsunternehmen Oesterreichs, Schwarzenbergplatz 7, A-1030 Vienna, Austria. Ed. Gregor Kozak. circ. 750.
Formerly: Verband der Versicherungsunternehmungen Oesterreichs. Bericht ueber das Geschaeftsjahr (ISSN 0083-5501)

360 GW
DIE VERSORGUNGSVERWALTUNG. 1949. bi-m. DM.76. (Gewerkschaft der Versorgungsverwaltung) W. Kohlhammer GmbH, Hessbruehlstr. 69, Postfach 800430, 7000 Stuttgart 80, Germany. TEL 0711-7863-1. Ed. G. Geist.
Formerly: Versorgungsbeamte (ISSN 0340-3289)

360 UK ISSN 0083-601X
VICTORIA LEAGUE FOR COMMONWEALTH FRIENDSHIP. ANNUAL REPORT. 1901. a. membership. Victoria League, 18 Northumberland Ave., London WC2N 5BJ, England.

362.6 FR ISSN 0042-5370
VIE COLLECTIVE. 1935. m. 270 F. Editions Max Brezol, 9 rue Labie, 75838 Paris Cedex 17, France. TEL 1-45-74-21-62. Ed. Max Brezol.

VISION (MILWAUKEE). see *RELIGIONS AND THEOLOGY — Roman Catholic*

VOCE DELL'EMIGRANTE. see *ETHNIC INTERESTS*

VOICE OF SILENCE NEWSLETTER. see *HANDICAPPED — Hearing Impaired*

VOICE OF THE DIABETIC; a support and information network. see *HANDICAPPED — Visually Impaired*

360 FR
VOIX DE FRANCE. 1927. m. 150 F. Union des Francais de l'Etranger, 146 bd. Haussmann, 75008 Paris, France. FAX 42-56-34-56. Ed. Bruno de Leusse. adv.; illus.

360 AU
VOLKSHILFE AKTUELL.* 1981. q. free. (Oesterreichischer Wohlfahrtsverband Volkshilfe) Erwin Schwaiger Verlag GmbH, Pichlergasse 2-10, A-1010 Vienna, Austria. Ed. Erich Weisbier. circ. 124,300. (back issues avail.)

360 US
VOLNET ELECTRONIC NEWSMAGAZINE.* 1983. bi-w. $50. National Volunteer Center, 736 Jackson Pl., N.W., Washington, DC 20503-0001. TEL 703-276-0542. Ed. Kay Drake. circ. 200.

360 US ISSN 0149-6492
HV91
VOLUNTARY ACTION LEADERSHIP.* 1975. q. $20. National Volunteer Center, 736 Jackson Pl., N.W., Washington, DC 20503-0001. TEL 703-276-0542. Ed. Brenda Hanlon. adv.; bk.rev.; circ. 2,000.
—BLDSC shelfmark: 9254.572000.
Incorporates (in 1976): Voluntary Action News (ISSN 0300-6638)

360 UK
VOLUNTARY AGENCIES DIRECTORY. 1928. a. £10.95. National Council for Voluntary Organisations, 26 Bedford Sq., London WC1B 3HU, England. TEL 071-636-4066. FAX 071-436-3188. adv.
Former titles: Voluntary Organisations; Voluntary Social Services (ISSN 0083-6907)
Description: Nearly 2,000 entries describing nationwide British voluntary and charitable agencies.

360 US
HV89
VOLUNTEER! (NEWTON, 1944); the comprehensive guide to voluntary service in the U.S. and abroad. 1944. s-a. $6.95. Commission on Voluntary Service & Action, 722 Main St., Box 347, Newton, KS 67114. (And: c/o Jan Schrock, 1451 Dundee Ave., Elgin, IL 60120) (Co-sponsor: Council on the International Educational Exchange) circ. 10,000.
Formerly (until 1985): Invest Yourself (ISSN 0148-6802)
Description: Directory of voluntary service and work camp opportunities for all ages.

362 371.9 US
VOLUNTEER (WHITE PLAINS). 1980. q. March of Dimes Birth Defects Foundation, 1275 Mamaroneck Ave., White Plains, NY 10605. TEL 914-428-7100. Ed. Judith S. Gooding. circ. 25,000.
Description: Newsletter focusing on birth defect research, education, and care.

VOLUNTEER LEADER. see *HOSPITALS*

360 US ISSN 0275-3030
HV1
VOLUNTEERING.* 1978. bi-m. membership. National Volunteer Center, 736 Jackson Pl., N.W., Washington, DC 20503-0001. TEL 703-276-0542. Ed. Brenda Hanlon. circ. 2,500.

361.8 US ISSN 0000-1325
HN90.V64
VOLUNTEERISM; the directory of organizations, training, programs and publications. 1984. irreg., 3rd., 1991. $120. R.R. Bowker, A Reed Reference Publishing Company, Division of Reed Publishing (USA) Inc., 121 Chanlon Rd., New Providence, NJ 07974. TEL 800-521-8110. FAX 908-665-6688. TELEX 138 755. (Subscr. to: Order Dept., Box 31, New Providence, NJ 07974) Ed. Harriet Clyde Kipps.
Formerly (until 1990): Community Resources Directory.
Description: Covers volunteer organizations, services and training programs that provide human services in many areas.

VOLUNTEERS; summer service opportunities in the United Church of Christ. see *RELIGIONS AND THEOLOGY — Protestant*

VOTE AND SURVEY; magazine of political, social and economic issues. see *POLITICAL SCIENCE*

362.7 UK
WAKE UP (LONDON). 2/yr. membership. National Society for the Prevention of Cruelty to Children, 67 Saffron Hill, London EC1N 8RS, England. TEL 071-242-1626. FAX 071-831-9562. illus.; circ. 10,000.
Former titles: Wings; Young N S P C C News; League of Pity Paper (ISSN 0047-4258)

361.7 US
WASHINGTON (STATE). ATTORNEY GENERAL'S OFFICE. CHARITABLE TRUST DIRECTORY. 1967. a. price varies. Attorney General's Office, c/o Sandy Stenberg, Highways-Licenses Bldg., Box 61, Olympia, WA 98504. TEL 206-753-0863. FAX 206-586-8772. Ed. Jeanette Dieckman. circ. 700.
Formerly: Washington (State). Attorney General's Office. Directory of Charitable Organizations and Trusts Registered with the Office of Attorney General (ISSN 0093-6693)

360 610 US
WASHINGTON (STATE) DEPARTMENT OF SOCIAL AND HEALTH SERVICES. INCOME MAINTENANCE, COMMUNITY SOCIAL SERVICES AND MEDICAL ASSISTANCE. vol.27, 1974. m. free. Department of Social and Health Services, Office of Program Analysis, MS. OB-34F, Olympia, WA 98504. TEL 206-753-7039. charts; stat.

WASHINGTON DIOCESE. see *RELIGIONS AND THEOLOGY — Protestant*

328 353.84 US ISSN 0149-2578
WASHINGTON SOCIAL LEGISLATION BULLETIN. 1944. s-m. $65. Child Welfare League of America, Inc., Social Legislation Information Service, 440 First St., N.W., Ste. 310, Washington, DC 20001-2085. TEL 202-638-2952. FAX 202-638-4004. Ed. Marjorie Kopp. index every 2 yrs; circ. 2,300. (also avail. in microfiche from UMI; reprint service avail. from UMI)
Formerly: Washington Bulletin (ISSN 0037-7775)
Description: Reports on federal social legislation and the activities of federal agencies in health, education, welfare, housing, employment, and other social welfare affecting children, the elderly, the handicapped, and juvenile delinquents.

S

SOCIAL SERVICES AND WELFARE

360   GW   ISSN 0043-2059
WEGE ZUR SOZIALVERSICHERUNG. 1947. m. DM.66. Asgard-Verlag Dr. Werner Hippe KG, Einsteinstr. 10, Postfach 1465, 5205 St. Augustin, Germany. TEL 02241-3164-0. Eds. W. Hippe, A. Guenther. adv.; bk.rev.; abstr.; bibl.; circ. 4,500. (tabloid format) **Indexed:** World Bibl.Soc.Sec.

360   AT   ISSN 0310-6969
WELCARE. 1973. q. Aus.$1 per no. Jewish Welfare Society Inc., 466 Punt Rd., South Yarra, Vic. 3141, Australia. Ed. Laurence A. Joseph. adv.; circ. 17,000.

360   UK
WELFARE JOURNAL. 1980. q. £15. Institute of Welfare Officers, 254 The Corn Exchange, Hanging Ditch, Manchester M4 3ES, England. TEL 061-832-1374. Ed. Lisa Davies. adv.; bk.rev.; illus.; circ. 1,500.
    Former titles: Welfare and Social Services Journal (ISSN 0261-4049); Welfare Officer.

360   UK   ISSN 0263-2098
WELFARE RIGHTS BULLETIN. 1974. 6/yr. £12($20) C P A G Ltd. (Child Poverty Action Group), 1-5 Bath St., London EC1V 9PY, England. TEL 071-253-3406.
    Description: Includes information about the rights information, practice, law, news, and reviews for the UK welfare adviser. Complements and updates the CPAG Benefit Guides to provide the fullest coverage of the workings of the UK social security system.

WELFARER. see *ETHNIC INTERESTS*

360   UK   ISSN 0043-2407
WELLDOER. 1956. q. 50p. League of Welldoers, 119-133 Limekiln Lane, Liverpool 5, England. Ed. W.J. Horn. bk.rev.; circ. 5,000.

360   GW   ISSN 0043-2644
WELTWEITE HILFE. 1951. 4/yr. free. Diakonisches Werk in Hessen und Nassau, Ederstr. 12, 6000 Frankfurt a.M. 90, Germany. FAX 069-7947-310. Ed. Juergen Albert. bk.rev.; illus.; circ. 7,000.

354   AT
WESTERN AUSTRALIA. DEPARTMENT FOR COMMUNITY SERVICES. ANNUAL REPORT. 1973. a. free. Department for Community Services, 189 Royal St., E. Perth, W.A. 6004, Australia. FAX 09-2222861. (Subscr. to: State Printer, 22 Station St., Wembley, W.A. 6014, Australia) stat.; circ. 600 (controlled).
    Formerly: Western Australia. Department for Community Welfare. Annual Report.

362.4   UK
WHEELS. 1986. q. £4. Wheels Club, Queen Elizabeth Military Hospital, Stadium Rd., Woolwich, London SE 18, England. TEL 0322-347651. (Subscr. to: 45 Castleton Ave., Bexleyheath, Kent DA7 6QT, England) Ed. Major B.H. Tinton. adv.; bk.rev.; circ. 10,000. (reprint service avail. from KTO)

362.5   US
HD9000.1
WHY; challenging hunger and poverty. 1976. q. $18. World Hunger Year, Inc., 261 W. 35th St., New York, NY 10001-1906. TEL 212-629-8850. FAX 212-868-5571. Ed. Peter Mann. adv.; bk.rev.; circ. 3,000. **Indexed:** Alt.Press Ind., HR Rep., P.A.I.S.
    Former titles (until no.46, 1989): Food Monitor (ISSN 0162-0045); (until 1985): Mini-Monitor.
    Description: Provides information to the general public, the media and policymakers on the extent and causes of hunger and poverty in the United States and abroad.

360   GW
WIDERSPRUECHE. 1981. q. DM.54. Verlag 2000 GmbH, Bleichstr. 5-7, Postfach 102062, 6050 Offenbach 1, Germany. TEL 069-821116. circ. 4,500.

361.7   UK
WILL TO CHARITY GROUP: CHARITIES BY COUNTIES AND REGIONS. 1978. a. free. Will to Charity Ltd., Equus House, Rear of 48 High St., Walton-on-Thames, Surrey KT12 1BY, England. TEL 0932-227711. FAX 0932-253988.

361.7   UK
WILL TO CHARITY GROUP: CHARITIES' STORY BOOK. no.4, 1974. a. free. Will to Charity Ltd., Equus House, Rear of 48 High St., Walton-on-Thames, Surrey KT12 1BY, England. TEL 0932-227711. FAX 0932-253988. Ed. Anne Frazer Simpson. adv.; illus.; circ. 20,000.
    Formerly: Will to Charity: Charities' Story Book.

361.7   UK
WILL TO CHARITY GROUP: HANDBOOK OF CHARITIES. 1984. a. free. Will to Charity ltd., Equus House, Rear of 48 High St., Walton-on-Thames, Surrey KT12 1BY, England. TEL 0932-227711. FAX 0932-253988.

WOMEN AGAINST RAPE NEWSLETTER. see *WOMEN'S INTERESTS*

360   AT   ISSN 0310-9062
WOMEN'S ELECTORAL LOBBY (SOUTH AUSTRALIAN) NEWSLETTER. 1972. b-m. Aus.$25. Women's Electoral Lobby (S.A.), 155 Pirie St., Rm. 2, Adelaide, S.A. 5000, Australia. TEL 0232-2245. (Subscr. to.: G.P.O. Box 2026, Adelaide, S.A. 5001, Australia) Ed. P. Brabham. bk.rev. (looseleaf format; back issues avail.)

361   US
WOODEN BELL. 4/yr. Catholic Relief Services, 209 W. Fayette St., Baltimore, MD 21201-3403. TEL 301-625-2220. FAX 301-685-1635. Ed. Geoffrey Goodnow.
    Formerly: Spectrum (New York).
    Description: Informs donors of what's happening in the world of CRS. Highlights various development programs and disaster relief efforts in different countries.

360   US
WORKPLACE IN THE COMMUNITY. 1985. q. membership. National Volunteer Center, 736 Jackson Pl., N.W., Washington, DC 20503-0001. TEL 703-276-0542. Ed. Brenda Hanlon. circ. 1,000.
    Description: Provides information on corporate volunteerism and corporate social responsibility.

369.4   NZ
WORLD COUNCIL OF SERVICE CLUBS. MINUTES OF THE GENERAL MEETING. 1962. a. free. World Council of Service Clubs, P.O. Box 240, Blenheim 7301, New Zealand. FAX 57-88968. circ. 500. (processed)
    Formerly: World Council of Young Men's Service Clubs. Minutes of the General Meeting (ISSN 0052-2678)

360   US   ISSN 0818-4984
WORLD GOODWILL NEWSLETTER. 1955. q. donation. Lucis Publishing Co., 113 University Place, 11th fl., Box 722, Cooper Sta., New York, NY 10276. TEL 212-982-8770. (In Europe: Case Postale 31, 1 Rue de Varembe (3e), 1211 Geneva 20, Switzerland; In U.K.: 3 Whitehall Court, Ste. 54, London SW1A 2EF, England) Ed. Jan Nation. bk.rev.; circ. 30,000.
    Description: Provides current information on constructive current action in world affairs as well as details on the work and program of World Goodwill.

362   FR   ISSN 0084-2044
WORLD MOVEMENT OF MOTHERS. REPORTS OF MEETINGS. 1949. a. 50 F. World Movement of Mothers - Mouvement Mondial des Meres, c/o M. de Vaublanc, Secretaire Generale, 56 rue de Passy, 75016 Paris, France. circ. 500.

362.8   US   ISSN 0197-5439
HV640
WORLD REFUGEE SURVEY. 1958. a. $8. United States Committee for Refugees, 1025 Vermont Ave., N.W., Washington, DC 20005. TEL 202-347-3507. Ed. Virginia Hamilton. bk.rev.; charts; illus.; stat.; circ. 20,000. **Indexed:** HR Rep., Refug.Abstr., SRI.
    Formerly: World Refugee Survey Report (ISSN 0162-9832)

WORLD UNION FOR THE SAFEGUARD OF YOUTH. BULLETIN. see *CHILDREN AND YOUTH — About*

301.4   FR
WORLD UNION FOR THE SAFEGUARD OF YOUTH. CONFERENCE PROCEEDINGS. (Editions in English and French) 1960. triennial, 5th, 1972, Paris. World Union for the Safeguard of Youth, 28 Place Saint-Georges, 75442 Paris Cedex 9, France.
    Formerly: World Union of Organizations for the Safeguard of Youth (ISSN 0084-2400)

362.7   US   ISSN 0043-9215
WORLD VISION. 1957. bi-m. free. 919 W. Huntington Dr., Monrovia, CA 91016. TEL 818-357-7979. FAX 818-357-0915. TELEX 6753411 WORVIS MROV. Ed. Terry Madison. bk.rev.; charts; illus.; stat.; circ. 100,651. **Indexed:** Chr.Per.Ind.
    Description: Looks at relief, development, child sponsorship, human rights and injustice in the Third World from an Evangelical Christian perspective.

WORLD'S WOMAN'S CHRISTIAN TEMPERANCE UNION. TRIENNIAL REPORT. see *DRUG ABUSE AND ALCOHOLISM*

360   US
WYOMING. DIVISION OF PUBLIC ASSISTANCE AND SOCIAL SERVICES. QUARTERLY STATISTICAL REPORT. q. $1. Division of Public Assistance and Social Services, Hathaway Bldg., 3rd Fl., 2300 Capitol Ave., Cheyenne, WY 82002. TEL 307-777-7561. FAX 307-777-7747. Ed. Paul Blatt. charts; stat.; circ. 100.

267.3   US   ISSN 0084-4292
Y M C A YEARBOOK AND OFFICIAL ROSTER. (Young Men's Christian Association) 1877. a. Y M C A of the U S A, 101 N. Wacker Dr., Chicago, IL 60606-1718. TEL 312-977-0031. FAX 312-977-9063. circ. 2,000.

361.73 360   US
YEARBOOK OF NEW YORK STATE CHARITABLE ORGANIZATIONS. irreg., latest 1990. $79.95. Independent Sector, 1828 L St., N.W. Ste. 1200, Washington, DC 20036. TEL 202-223-8100. (also avail. in microfiche)

362.7   UK   ISSN 0956-2842
YOUNG PEOPLE NOW. 1973. m. £18.60. National Youth Agency, 17-23 Albion St., Leicester LE1 6GD, England. TEL 0533-471200. FAX 0533-471043. Ed. Jackie Scott. adv.; bk.rev.; circ. 15,000. **Indexed:** ASSIA, High.Educ.Curr.Aware.Bull.
    —BLDSC shelfmark: 9421.451554.
    Formerly (until 1989): Youth in Society (ISSN 0307-1790); Incorporates: Youth Social Work Bulletin (ISSN 0307-3513)
    Description: Focuses on issues that affect young people and those who work with them.

360   US
YOUR (YEAR) GUIDE TO SOCIAL SECURITY BENEFITS. 1982. a. $19.95 hardbound; paperbound $10.95. Facts on File, Inc., 460 Park Ave. S., New York, NY 10016. TEL 212-683-2244. Ed. Leona G. Rubin.

YOUTH AND POLICY. see *CHILDREN AND YOUTH — About*

YOUTH LAW NEWS. see *LAW*

YOUTH SERVICE SURVEY. see *CHILDREN AND YOUTH — About*

362.7   US   ISSN 0196-9668
YOUTH - SERVING ORGANIZATIONS DIRECTORY. 1978. irreg., 2nd ed., 1980. $85. Gale Research Inc., 835 Penobscot Bldg., Detroit, MI 48226. TEL 313-961-2242. FAX 313-961-6083. TELEX 810-221-7086.
    Description: Guide to youth service organizations.

360 309.1   ZA
ZAMBIA. DEPARTMENT OF SOCIAL DEVELOPMENT. REPORT. 1964. irreg. (approx. a.). 30 n. Government Printer, P.O. Box 136, Lusaka, Zambia.
    Formed by the merger of: Zambia. Department of Social Welfare. Report (ISSN 0084-4667) & Zambia. Department of Community Development. Report (ISSN 0084-4608)

SOCIAL SERVICES AND WELFARE — ABSTRACTING, BIBLIOGRAPHIES, STATISTICS

360 ZA
ZAMBIA. DEPARTMENT OF SOCIAL DEVELOPMENT. SOCIAL WELFARE RESEARCH MONOGRAPHS. a. price varies. Department of Social Development, Director General, P.O. Box 71630, Ndola, Zambia.
   Formerly: Zambia. Department of Social Welfare. Social Welfare Research Monographs (ISSN 0081-0533)

360 ZA ISSN 0084-5035
ZAMBIA. PUBLIC SERVICE COMMISSION. REPORT. 1964. a. 40 n. Government Printer, P.O. Box 136, Lusaka, Zambia.

360 GW
ZEITSCHRIFT FUER DAS FUERSORGEWESEN. m. DM.111.80. (Sozialamt) Verlag Fritz Eberlein GmbH, Kestnerstr. 44, D-3000 Hannover 1, Germany. TEL 0511-810592. FAX 0511-810575. circ. 2,400.

360 SZ ISSN 0044-3204
ZEITSCHRIFT FUER OEFFENTLICHE FUERSORGE; Monatsschrift fuer oeffentliche Fuersorge und Jugendhilfe. bi-m. 49 SFr. (foreign 65 SFr.). (Schweizerische Konferenz fuer Oeffentliche Fuersorge) Orell Fuessli Graphische Betriebe AG, Dietzingerstr. 3, CH-8036 Zurich, Switzerland.
   Formerly: Armenpfleger.

ZEITSCHRIFT FUER SOZIALREFORM. see *POLITICAL SCIENCE*

ZENTRALBLATT FUER JUGENDRECHT; Jugend und Familie - Jugendhilfe - Jugendgerichtshilfe. see *CHILDREN AND YOUTH — About*

360 GW ISSN 0177-3836
ZENTRALER BEWERBERANZEIGER MARKT UND CHANCE. 1955. w. Zentralstelle fuer Arbeitsvermittlung, Feuerbachstr. 42-46, 6000 Frankfurt a.M. 1, Germany. TEL 069-71110. FAX 069-7222-555. (looseleaf format)

ZERO TO THREE. see *CHILDREN AND YOUTH — About*

ZHONGNAN MINZU XUEYUAN XUEBAO (SHEHUI KEXUE BAN)/SOUTH-CENTRAL COLLEGE FOR NATIONALITIES. JOURNAL (SOCIAL SCIENCE EDITION). see *SOCIAL SCIENCES: COMPREHENSIVE WORKS*

361.73 US ISSN 0897-5736
501(C)(3) MONTHLY LETTER. 1980. m. $42. Great Oaks Communication Services, 1508 E. Seventh St., Box 192, Atlantic, IA 50322. TEL 712-243-5257. FAX 712-243-2808. (Subscr. to: Box 17040, Des Moines, IA, 50317) Ed. Marilyn Miller. adv.; bk.rev.; charts; stat; circ. 5,000.
   Description: For non-profit organizations. Emphasizes fundraising, communication and management.

SOCIAL SERVICES AND WELFARE —
Abstracting, Bibliographies, Statistics

362.7 AT ISSN 1034-5132
AUSTRALIA. BUREAU OF STATISTICS. QUEENSLAND OFFICE. CHILD CARE ARRANGEMENTS, QUEENSLAND. 1984. irreg., latest 1987. Aus.$7.50. Australian Bureau of Statistics, Queensland Office, 313 Adelaide St., Brisbane, Qld. 4000, Australia. TEL 07-222-6022. FAX 07-229-6171. TELEX AA 40271.
   Description: Demographic and economic characteristics of family units responsible for child care services; availability of facilities; demographic characteristics of children using formal and informal child care services.

360 AT ISSN 0728-294X
AUSTRALIA. BUREAU OF STATISTICS. QUEENSLAND OFFICE. HEALTH AND WELFARE ESTABLISHMENTS, QUEENSLAND. 1970. a. Aus.$12 (foreign Aus.$17). Australian Bureau of Statistics, Queensland Office, 313 Adelaide St., Brisbane, Qld. 4000, Australia. TEL 07-222-6022. FAX 07-229-6171. TELEX AA 40271.
   Description: Lists by number, size, activities, income, operating expenditure, staff, staff-patient ratios, nature of treatment by condition of category of patients, activities in statistical divisions.

360 AT ISSN 0817-8526
AUSTRALIA. BUREAU OF STATISTICS. QUEENSLAND OFFICE. SUMMARY OF SOCIAL STATISTICS, QUEENSLAND. 1985. a. Aus.$10 (foreign Aus.$15). Australian Bureau of Statistics, Queensland Office, 313 Adelaide St., Brisbane, Qld. 4000, Australia. TEL 07-222-6022. FAX 07-229-6171. TELEX AA 40271.
   Description: Selection of social and other related statistics providing a broad background to social issues in the state.

361 314 AU
AUSTRIA. STATISTISCHES ZENTRALAMT. SOZIALHILFE. vol.360, 1974. a. S.50. Oesterreichisches Statistisches Zentralamt, Hintere Zollamtsstr. 2b, 1033 Vienna, Austria. circ. 300.
   Formerly: Austria. Statistisches Zentralamt. Oeffentliche Fuersorge.
   Description: Data on the extent and output of social assistance in Austria.

362.7 GW
BERLIN (WEST). SENATSVERWALTUNG FUER FRAUEN, JUGEND UND FAMILIE. STATISTISCHER DIENST. 1980. s-a. free. Senatsverwaltung fuer Frauen, Jugend und Familie, Am Karlsbad 8, 1000 Berlin 30, Germany. TEL 030-26041. FAX 030-2628864. circ. 400. (back issues avail.)
   Description: Annotated statistics on children's and youth services and welfare, and the situation of women in West Berlin.

300 NE
Z7164.S68
BIBLIOGRAFIE NEDERLANDSE SOCIALE WETENSCHAPPEN; vakbibliografie politieke en sociaal-culturele wetenschappen. 1972. a. fl.95. Rijksuniversiteit te Utrecht, Bureau Bibliografie Nederlandse Sociale Wetenschappen, Plompetorengracht 11, 3512 CA Utrecht, Netherlands. TEL 030-393272. Ed.Bd. bk.rev.; circ. 200.
   Formerly (until 1990): Bibliografie Nederlandse Sociologie (ISSN 0167-8272)

360 016 BL
BRAZIL. SERVICO SOCIAL DO COMERCIO. BOLETIM BIBLIOGRAFICO. 1969. s-a. free. Servico Social do Comercio, Rua Voluntarios da Patria 169, 22270 Rio de Janeiro, Brazil. charts; stat.
   Description: Social services bibliography.

360 UK
CHARITY TRENDS. 1978. a. £28.95. Charities Aid Foundation, 48 Pembury Rd., Tonbridge, Kent TN9 2JD, England. Ed. J. McQuillan. circ. 2,000.
   Formerly: Charity Statistics.

310 360 UK ISSN 0309-653X
CHARTERED INSTITUTE OF PUBLIC FINANCE AND ACCOUNTANCY. PERSONAL SOCIAL SERVICES STATISTICS. ACTUALS. 1949. a. £55. Chartered Institute of Public Finance and Accountancy, 3 Robert St., London WC2N 6BH, England. TEL 071-895-8823. FAX 071-895-8825. stat. (back issues avail.)
   Formerly: Chartered Institute of Public Finance and Accountancy. Local Health and Social Services Statistics (ISSN 0307-0506)

360 UK ISSN 0144-610X
CHARTERED INSTITUTE OF PUBLIC FINANCE AND ACCOUNTANCY. PERSONAL SOCIAL SERVICES STATISTICS. ESTIMATES. 1974. a. £55. Chartered Institute of Public Finance and Accountancy, 3 Robert St., London WC2N 6BH, England. (back issues avail.)

360 UK ISSN 0264-6544
HV9346.A5
CHARTERED INSTITUTE OF PUBLIC FINANCE AND ACCOUNTANCY. PROBATION. ESTIMATES. 1983. a. £30. Chartered Institute of Public Finance and Accountancy, 3 Robert St., London WC2N 6BH, England. TEL 071-895-8823. FAX 071-895-8825. (back issues avail.)
   —BLDSC shelfmark: 6617.256470.

360 UK ISSN 0140-8291
HV9346.A5
CHARTERED INSTITUTE OF PUBLIC FINANCE AND ACCOUNTANCY. PROBATION STATISTICS. ACTUALS. 1984. a. £35. Chartered Institute of Public Finance and Accountancy, 3 Robert St., London WC2N 6BH, England. TEL 071-895-8823. FAX 071-895-8825. (back issues avail.)

360 011 UK ISSN 0264-4088
COMMUNITY CURRENTS; the community development information digest. 1982. bi-m. £17.60. Community Development Foundation, 60 Highbury Grove, London N5 2AG, England. TEL 071-226 5375. FAX 071-704-0313. Ed. Kevin Harris. bk.rev.; abstr.; circ. 450.
   —BLDSC shelfmark: 3363.608700.

360 UK ISSN 0144-5081
HV249.S5
COMMUNITY SERVICE STATISTICS: SCOTLAND. 1980. a. Social Work Services Group, 43 Jeffrey St., Edinburgh EH1 1DN, Scotland.
   —BLDSC shelfmark: 8447.679140.

361.73 US
CORPORATE FOUNDATION PROFILES. biennial. $125. Foundation Center, 79 Fifth Ave., New York, NY 10003. TEL 212-620-4230.
   Description: Lists current information on over 250 of America's top corporate foundations. Examines corporate grantmakers with assets of $1 million or annual giving of $100,000 or more.

361.6 318 DR
DOMINICAN REPUBLIC. SECRETARIA DE SANIDAD Y ASISTENCIA PUBLICA. CUADROS ESTADISTICOS. irreg. Secretaria de Sanidad y Asistencia Publica, Ciudad Trujillo, Dominican Republic.

360 GR ISSN 0256-3630
ENQUETE ANNUELLE SUR L'ACTIVITE DES ORGANISMES DE SECURITE SOCIALE. (Text in Greek; summaries in French) 1962. a. $4. National Statistical Service of Greece, Statistical Information and Publications Division, 14-16 Lycourgou St., 10166 Athens, Greece. TEL 3244-748. FAX 3222205. TELEX 216734 ESYE GR.

318 PN
ESTADISTICA PANAMENA. SITUACION SOCIAL. SECCION 431. SERVICIOS DE SALUD. 1957. a. Bl.0.75. Direccion de Estadistica y Censo, Contraloria General, Apdo. 5213, Panama 5, Panama. FAX 63-9322. circ. 1,100.
   Formerly: Estadistica Panamena. Situacion Social. Seccion 431. Asistencia Social (ISSN 0378-262X)

362 US
FLORIDA. DEPARTMENT OF HEALTH AND REHABILITATIVE SERVICES. ANNUAL STATISTICAL REPORT. a. Department of Health and Rehabilitative Services, 1317 Winewood Blvd., Tallahassee, FL 32302. TEL 904-488-1234. **Indexed:** SRI.
   Formerly: Florida. Division of Family Services. Annual Statistical Report (ISSN 0093-6715)

010 060 US ISSN 0190-3357
Z733
FOUNDATION CENTER. ANNUAL REPORT. 1956. a. free. Foundation Center, 79 Fifth Ave., New York, NY 10003. TEL 212-620-4230.
   Formerly: Foundation Center. Report (ISSN 0548-7269)
   Description: Describes how network of cooperating libraries works to provide free, convenient access to accurate information on private funding sources to nonprofit groups and other interested individuals and organizations throughout the country.

010 060 US
FOUNDATION CENTER SOURCE BOOK PROFILES. Key title: Source Book Profiles. 1977. s-a. $350 for 500 profiles. Foundation Center, 79 Fifth Ave., New York, NY 10003. TEL 212-620-4230.
   Formerly: Foundation Center Source Book (ISSN 0362-1170)
   Description: Lists the nation's 1,000 largest foundations which hold over $89 billion in assets and award nearly $5 billion in grants annually.

010 060 US ISSN 0071-8092
AS911.A2
FOUNDATION DIRECTORY. (Supplement avail.) 1960. a. $165 hardcover; softcover $140. Foundation Center, 79 Fifth Ave., New York, NY 10003. TEL 212-620-4230. Ed. Stan Olson. charts; stat.; index; circ. 8,000. **Indexed:** ERIC.
   ●Also available online. Vendor(s): DIALOG.
   —BLDSC shelfmark: 4024.923000.
   Supersedes: American Foundation and Their Fields.
   Description: Contains current information on the nation's largest grantmakers.

SOCIAL SERVICES AND WELFARE — ABSTRACTING, BIBLIOGRAPHIES, STATISTICS

361.73 US
FOUNDATION GIVING (YEAR). a. $19.45. Foundation Center, 79 Fifth Ave., New York, NY 10003. TEL 212-620-4230.
Formerly: Foundations Today: Current Facts and Figures on Private Foundations.
Description: Provides a summary of current facts and figures on private foundations drawn from the Center's exclusive databases of foundation information.

010 060 US
FOUNDATION GRANTS INDEX. 1970. q. $125. Foundation Center, 79 Fifth Ave., New York, NY 10003. TEL 212-620-4230.
●Also available online. Vendor(s): DIALOG.
Description: Offers comprehensive coverage of over 55,000 grants of $10,000 or more.

361.73 US
FOUNDATION GRANTS TO INDIVIDUALS. 1977. biennial. $40. Foundation Center, 79 Fifth Ave., New York, NY 10003. TEL 212-620-4230.
Description: Contains information on over 2,000 independent and corporate foundations which award grants to individuals.

362.8 FR ISSN 0181-0804
FRANCE. CAISSE NATIONALE DES ALLOCATIONS FAMILIALES. STATISTIQUES ACTION SOCIALE. a. Caisse Nationale des Allocations Familiales, 23 rue Daviel, 75634 Paris Cedex 13, France. charts; stat.
Formerly: France. Caisse Nationale des Allocations Familiales. Action Sociale.

362.5 FR ISSN 0182-1598
FRANCE. CAISSE NATIONALE DES ALLOCATIONS FAMILIALES. STATISTIQUES PRESTATIONS FAMILIALES. RESULTATS GENERAUX: RECETTES, DEPENSES, BENEFICIAIRES. a. Caisse Nationale des Allocations Familiales, 23 rue Daviel, 75634 Paris Cedex 13, France. charts; stat.
Formerly: France. Caisse Nationale des Allocations Familiales. Prestations Familiales. Resultats Generaux: Recettes, Depenses, Beneficiaires.

010 060 US
GRANT GUIDES. 1972. a. $55. Foundation Center, 79 Fifth Ave., New York, NY 10003. TEL 212-620-4230. (also avail. in microfiche)
Formed by the merger of (1972-1991): Comsearch: Broad Topics; (1980-1991): Comsearch: Geographics; (1982-1991): Comsearch: Subjects. Which was formerly: Comsearch Printouts: Subjects; Supersedes in part: Comsearch Printouts; Supersedes (in 1977): Foundation Grants Index: Subjects on Microfiche (ISSN 0090-1601); Broad Topics incorporated International Philanthropy.
Description: Lists actual foundation grants categorized into 30 key areas of grantmaking.

360 GR ISSN 0253-9454
RA407.5.G73
GREECE. NATIONAL STATISTICAL SERVICE. SOCIAL WELFARE AND HEALTH STATISTICS. (Text in English and Greek) 1967. a. $7. National Statistical Service of Greece, Statistical Information and Publications Division, 14-16 Lycourgou St., 10166 Athens, Greece. TEL 3244-748. FAX 3222205. TELEX 216734 ESYE GR.

360 614 UK
HEALTH SERVICE ABSTRACTS. 1974. m. £36. Departments of Health and Social Security, Library, Rm. 96, Hannibal House, Elephant and Castle, London SE1 6TE, England. (Subscr. addr.: P.O. Box 21, Stanmore, Middlesex HA7 1AY, England) Eds. Harry Barrett, Helen Wickham.
Incorporates (in May 1985): Hospital Abstracts (ISSN 0018-5507); Current Literature on Health Services (ISSN 0141-0571); Current Literature on General Medical Practice.

IDAHO. DEPARTMENT OF HEALTH AND WELFARE. ANNUAL SUMMARY OF VITAL STATISTICS. see PUBLIC HEALTH AND SAFETY — Abstracting, Bibliographies, Statistics

361.6 US
IDAHO. DEPARTMENT OF HEALTH AND WELFARE. RESEARCH AND STATISTICS SECTION. QUARTERLY WELFARE STATISTICAL BULLETIN. q. Department of Health and Welfare, Research and Statistics Section, Statehouse, Boise, ID 83720. TEL 208-338-7000. Ed. R.V. Atwood. circ. 180.
Former titles: Idaho. Department of Health and Welfare. Bureau of Research and Statistics. Quarterly Welfare Statistical Bulletin; Idaho. Department of Health and Welfare. Bureau of Research and Statistics. Research Report (ISSN 0098-8561)

350.7 US ISSN 0019-6576
INDIANA. DEPARTMENT OF PUBLIC WELFARE. SEMI-ANNUAL STATISTICAL SERIES. 1936. s-a. $5 (free to qualified personnel). Department of Public Welfare, Research and Statistics Division, 402 W. Washington St., Rm. W386, Indianapolis, IN 46204. TEL 317-232-4360. Dir. David Webster. circ. 250.

JAPAN. MINISTRY OF HEALTH AND WELFARE. STATISTICS AND INFORMATION DEPARTMENT. HANDBOOK OF HEALTH AND WELFARE STATISTICS. see PUBLIC HEALTH AND SAFETY — Abstracting, Bibliographies, Statistics

362 315 JA ISSN 0448-4002
JAPAN. MINISTRY OF HEALTH AND WELFARE. STATISTICS AND INFORMATION DEPARTMENT. REPORT ON SURVEY OF PUBLIC ASSISTANCE. (Text in Japanese) 1960. a. 2700 Yen. Ministry of Health and Welfare, Statistics and Information Department - Kosei-sho Daijin Kanbo Tokei Joho-bu, 7-3 Ichigaya-Honmura cho, Shinjuku-ku, Tokyo 162, Japan. TEL 03-3260-3181. (Subscr. to: Health & Welfare Statistics Association, 5-13-14 Roppongi, Minato-ku, Tokyo, Japan) Key Title: Seikatsu Hogo Dotai Chosa Hokoku.

362 315 JA ISSN 0448-4029
JAPAN. MINISTRY OF HEALTH AND WELFARE. STATISTICS AND INFORMATION DEPARTMENT. REPORT ON SURVEY OF SOCIAL WELFARE INSTITUTIONS. (Issued in 2 volumes) 1960. a. 4500 Yen for vol.1; 4100 Yen for vol.2. Ministry of Health and Welfare, Statistics and Information Department - Kosei-sho Daijin Kanbo Tokei Joho-bu, 7-3 Ichigaya-Honmura cho, Shinjuku-ku, Tokyo 162, Japan. TEL 03-3260-3181. (Subscr. to: Health & Welfare Statistics Association, 5-13-14 Roppongi, Minato-ku, Tokyo, Japan) Key Title: Shakai Fukushi Shisetsu Chosa Hokoku.

362 315 JA ISSN 0448-4010
JAPAN. MINISTRY OF HEALTH AND WELFARE. STATISTICS AND INFORMATION DEPARTMENT. STATISTICAL REPORT ON SOCIAL WELFARE ADMINISTRATION AND SERVICES. 1960. a. 3100 Yen. Ministry of Health and Welfare, Statistics and Information Department - Kosei-sho Daijin Kanbo Tokei Joho-bu, 7-3 Ichigaya Honmura-cho, Shinjuku-ku, Tokyo 162, Japan. TEL 03-3260-3181. (Subscr. to: Health & Welfare Statistics Association, 5-13-14 Roppongi, Minato-ku, Tokyo, Japan) Key Title: Shakai Fukushi Gyosei Gyomu Hokoku.

361 US ISSN 0093-7835
HV86
MICHIGAN. DEPARTMENT OF SOCIAL SERVICES. PROGRAM STATISTICS. (Report year ends Sept. 30) a. Department of Social Services, Box 30037, 300 S. Capitol Ave., Lansing, MI 48909. TEL 517-373-2005. Key Title: Program Statistics - Michigan Department of Social Services.
Supersedes: Michigan. Department of Social Services. Public Assistance Statistics (ISSN 0093-6774)

360 317 US ISSN 0091-1143
HV86
MONTANA. DEPARTMENT OF SOCIAL AND REHABILITATION SERVICES. STATISTICAL REPORT. vol.36, 1974. m. free. Department of Social and Rehabilitation Services, 111 Sanders St., Helena, MT 59601. TEL 406-449-3860. charts; stat.; circ. 400.
Indexed: SRI.

010 060 US ISSN 0730-1677
AS911.A2
NATIONAL DATA BOOK OF FOUNDATIONS; a comprehensive guide to grantmaking foundations. 1975. a. $125. Foundation Center, 79 Fifth Ave., New York, NY 10003. TEL 212-620-4230. circ. 26,000.
●Also available online. Vendor(s): DIALOG.
Formerly: Foundation Center National Data Book.
Description: Provides information on over 32,000 active grantmaking foundations.

360 314.9 NE ISSN 0168-549X
HC321
NETHERLANDS. CENTRAAL BUREAU VOOR DE STATISTIEK. SOCIAAL-ECONOMISCHE MAANDSTATISTIEK. 1953. m. Centraal Bureau voor de Statistiek, Prinses Beatrixlaan 428, Voorburg, Netherlands. (Dist. by: SDU - Publishers, Christoffel Plantijnstraat, The Hague, Netherlands) circ. 1,250.
Formerly: Netherlands. Centraal Bureau voor de Statistiek. Sociale Maandstatistiek (ISSN 0470-6978)

360 336 NE ISSN 0168-4086
NETHERLANDS. CENTRAAL BUREAU VOOR DE STATISTIEK. STATISTIEK VAN DE ALGEMENE BIJSTAND/STATISTICS OF PUBLIC ASSISTANCE. (Text in Dutch and English) 1965. a. Centraal Bureau voor de Statistiek, Prinses Beatrixlaan 428, Voorburg, Netherlands. (Distb by: SDU - Publishers, Christoffel Plantijnstraat, The Hague, Netherlands)

362 NE
NETHERLANDS. CENTRAAL BUREAU VOOR DE STATISTIEK. STATISTIEK VAN DE BEJAARDENOORDEN/HOMES FOR THE AGED. (Text in Dutch and English) 1950. a. Centraal Bureau voor de Statistiek, Prinses Beatrixlaan 428, Voorburg, Netherlands. (Dist. by: SDU - Publishers, Christoffel Plantijnstraat, The Hague, Netherlands)

362.7 US
OHIO. DEPARTMENT OF HUMAN SERVICES. CHILD WELFARE STATISTICS. q. free. Department of Human Services, 30 E. Broad St., 30th Fl., Columbus, OH 43215. TEL 614-466-3366. FAX 614-466-3863. Ed. Florence C. Odita. circ. 500. (looseleaf format; back issues avail.)

360 011 US
▼**PHILANTHROPIC STUDIES INDEX.** 1991. 3/yr. £37.50($75) (Indiana University Center on Philanthropy) Indiana University Press, Journals Division, 601 N. Morton St., Bloomington, IN 47404. TEL 812-855-9449. FAX 812-855-7931. Ed. Dwight F. Burlingame.
Description: Indexes relevant books, periodical articles, dissertations and other information sources that cover philanthropy, including nonprofit management, voluntarism and fund raising.

REFUGEE ABSTRACTS. see POPULATION STUDIES — Abstracting, Bibliographies, Statistics

360 315 CH
SOCIAL AFFAIRS STATISTICS OF TAIWAN/CHUNG HUA MIN KUO T'AI-WAN SHENG SHE HUI SHIH YEH T'UNG CHI. (Text in Chinese and English) a. Department of Social Affairs, Nantou Hsien, Taiwan, Republic of China. stat.

360 315 JA
SOCIAL INDICATORS BY PREFECTURE (YEAR). 1989. a. 7100 Yen. Nihon Tokei Kyokai - Japan Statistical Association, Crest 21, 6-21, Yocho-machi, Shinjuku-ku, Tokyo 162, Japan. TEL 03-5269-3051. FAX 03-5269-3058.

360 016 US ISSN 0195-7988
HV1 CODEN: SOPODA
SOCIAL PLANNING - POLICY & DEVELOPMENT ABSTRACTS. Short title: SOPODA. 1979. 2/yr. $165. Sociological Abstracts, Inc., Box 22206, San Diego, CA 92192. TEL 619-695-8803. FAX 619-695-0416. Ed. Miriam Chall.
●Also available online. Vendor(s): BRS (SOCA), DIMDI (SA63), Data-Star (SOCA), DIALOG (File No.37). Also available on CD-ROM. Producer(s): SilverPlatter, Sociological Abstracts, Inc. (SocioFile).
Formerly: Social Welfare, Social Planning, Policy and Social Development.

360 UK ISSN 0309-4693
HV1
SOCIAL SERVICE ABSTRACTS. 1977. m. £38. Departments of Health and Social Security, Hannibal House, Elephant and Castle, London SE1 6TE, England. (Subscr. to: H.M.S.O., P.O. Box 276, London SW8 5DT, England) Ed. Janet Cockayne. (reprint service avail. from UMI) **Indexed:** CERDIC.
—BLDSC shelfmark: 8318.198100.

362 016 US ISSN 0148-0847
HV1
SOCIAL WORK RESEARCH AND ABSTRACTS. 1965. q. $60 to non-members; institutions $82. National Association of Social Workers, Publications Department, 7981 Eastern Ave., Silver Spring, MD 20910. TEL 301-565-0333. FAX 301-587-1321. Ed. Shirley M. Buttrick. adv.; abstr.; index; circ. 4,500. (also avail. in microform from UMI; back issues avail.; reprint service avail. from UMI) **Indexed:** Abstr.Health Care Manage.Stud., Adol.Ment.Hlth.Abstr., ASCA, ASSIA, CLOA, Crim.Just.Abstr., Hosp.Lit.Ind., Lang.& Lang.Behav.Abstr., Med.Care Rev., Psychol.Abstr., Rehabil.Lit., Sage Pub.Admin.Abstr., Soc.Work Res.& Abstr., Soc.Work.Res.& Abstr., Sociol.Abstr., SSCI.
● Also available online. Vendor(s): BRS (SWAB).
Formerly: Abstracts for Social Workers (ISSN 0001-3412)
Description: Resource for social work professionals for information on all subjects in social welfare.

360 FR ISSN 0764-4493
SOLIDARITE SANTE ETUDES STATISTIQUES. q. 42 ECU($50) (typically set in Jan.). (Ministere des Affaires Sociales et de l'Integration) Masson, 120 bd. Saint-Germain, 75280 Paris Cedex 06, France. TEL 1-46-34-21-60. FAX 1-45-87-29-99. TELEX 202 671 F. Ed. D. Lequet. (also avail. in microfiche)
—BLDSC shelfmark: 8327.553700.

360 310 US
SOUTH DAKOTA. STATE DEPARTMENT OF SOCIAL SERVICES. ANNUAL STATISTICAL REPORT. 1971. a. State Department of Social Services, Office of Management Information, Statistical Analysis and Reports, Richard F. Kneip Bldg., 700 Governors Dr., Pierre, SD 57501. TEL 605-773-3226. FAX 605-773-4855. stat.; circ. 300.
Formerly: South Dakota. State Department of Public Welfare. Research and Statistical Annual Report (ISSN 0099-2305)

SWEDEN. SJUKVAARDENS OCH SOCIALVAARDENS PLANERINGS- OCH RATIONALISERINGSINSTITUT. S P R I LITTERATURTJAENST. (Sjukvaardens och Socialvaardens Planerings- och Rationaliseringsinstitut) see *PUBLIC HEALTH AND SAFETY — Abstracting, Bibliographies, Statistics*

360 314 SW ISSN 0082-0326
SWEDEN. STATISTISKA CENTRALBYRAAN. STATISTISKA MEDDELANDEN. SUBGROUP S (SOCIAL WELFARE STATISTICS). (Text in Swedish; table heads and summaries in English) 1963 N.S. irreg. SEK 1000. Statistiska Centralbyraan, Publishing Unit, S-701 89 Oerebro, Sweden. circ. 1,300.

361 016 US
UNITED WAY OF AMERICA. INFORMATION CENTER. DIGEST OF SELECTED REPORTS. 1947. 2/yr. $10. United Way of America, 701 N. Fairfax St., Alexandria, VA 22314. TEL 703-836-7100. abstr.; circ. controlled.
Supersedes: United Way of America. Information Center. Bibliography of Reports and Manuals; Which was formerly: United Way of America. Information Center. Digest of Current Reports (ISSN 0090-3191)

ZEITSCHRIFTENBIBLIOGRAPHIE GERONTOLOGIE. see *GERONTOLOGY AND GERIATRICS — Abstracting, Bibliographies, Statistics*

SOCIOLOGY

see also Folklore; Social Sciences; Comprehensive Works; Social Services and Welfare

A I L A MONTHLY MAILING. (American Immigration Lawyers Association) see *LAW*

A R T I NEWS LETTER. (Agrarian Research and Training Institute) see *AGRICULTURE*

301 US ISSN 0749-6931
HM1
A S A FOOTNOTES. 9/yr. $22 (foreign $28); effective 1992. American Sociological Association, 1722 N St., N.W., Washington, DC 20036. TEL 202-833-3410. FAX 202-785-0146. (reprint service avail from UMI)
—BLDSC shelfmark: 3985.016500.
Description: Contains departmental news, activities of the ASA and the Executive Office; developments on the Washington scene; and the ASA official reports and proceedings.

ACADEMIA; Zeitschrift fuer Politik und Kultur. see *LITERARY AND POLITICAL REVIEWS*

ACADEMIE DE STIINTE A R.S.S. MOLDOVA. BULETINUL. ECONOMIE SE SOCIOLOGIE/AKADEMIYA NAUK MOLDAVSKOI S.S.R. IZVESTIYA. EKONOMIKA I SOTSIOLOGIYA. see *BUSINESS AND ECONOMICS — Economic Situation And Conditions*

614 BU ISSN 0515-2925
ACTA MEDICA ET SOCIOLOGICA. 1962. irreg., 6th, 1972, Varna; latest 9th, 1983, Barcelona, Spain. International Medical Association for the Study of Living Conditions and Health, c/o T. Tashev, Bd. D. Nestorov 15, BG-1431 Sofia, Bulgaria.

301 IT ISSN 0065-1656
ACTA SCIENTIARUM SOCIALIUM. (Text in English, French, German, Italian, Rumanian, Spanish) 1959. irreg. price varies. Societa Accademica Romena, Foro Traiano 1a, 00187 Rome, Italy.

301 NO ISSN 0001-6993
HM1.A1
ACTA SOCIOLOGICA; an international sociological journal. (Text in English) 1955. q. $73. (Scandinavian Sociological Association) Universitetsforlaget, P.O. Box 2959 Toeyen, N-0608 Oslo 1, Norway. (U.S. addr.: Publications Expediting Inc., 200 Meacham Ave., Elmont, NY 11003) Ed. Peter Heastroem. adv.; bk.rev.; charts; index; circ. 2,900. (also avail. in microform from SWZ,UMI; back issues avail.; reprint service avail. from ISI,SWZ) **Indexed:** A.B.C.Pol.Sci., Amer.Hist.& Life, ASCA, ASSIA, Bibl.Ind., Curr.Cont., E.I., Hist.Abstr., Lang.& Lang.Behav.Abstr., Mid.East: Abstr.& Ind., P.A.I.S., Soc.Sci.Ind., Sociol.Abstr. (1955-), Sp.Ed.Needs Abstr., SSCI, SSCI, Stud.Wom.Abstr.
—BLDSC shelfmark: 0663.350000.

301 MX
ACTA SOCIOLOGICA. SERIE PROMOCION SOCIAL. 1969. a. Universidad Nacional Autonoma de Mexico, Facultad de Ciencias Politicas y Sociales, Centro de Estudios del Desarrollo, Ciudad Universitaria, Villa Obregon, Mexico 20, D.F., Mexico. Ed. Ricardo Pozas Arciniega. bibl.; illus.

301 370 PL ISSN 0208-600X
HM7
ACTA UNIVERSITATIS LODZIENSIS: FOLIA SOCIOLOGICA. (Text in Polish; summaries in various languages) 1975. irreg. Wydawnictwo Uniwersytetu Lodzkiego, Ul. Jaracza 34, Lodz, Poland. (Dist. by: Ars Polona-Ruch, Krakowskie Przedmiescie 7, Warsaw, Poland)
—BLDSC shelfmark: 0585.208750.
Supersedes in part (in 1980): Uniwersytet Lodzki. Zeszyty Naukowe. Seria 3: Nauki Ekonomiczne i Socjologiczne (ISSN 0076-0374)
Description: Covers studies on culture, sociology of art, industry and occupations, basic theory of interactions and methodology.

AD MARGINEM; Randbemerkungen zur musikalischen Volkskunde. see *MUSIC*

ADMINISTRATION AND SOCIETY. see *PUBLIC ADMINISTRATION*

ADMINISTRATIVE SCIENCE QUARTERLY. see *PUBLIC ADMINISTRATION*

301 US
ADOPTOLOGIST. 1979. q. $15. Kansas City Adult Adoptees Organization, Box 11828, Kansas City, MO 64138. TEL 816-229-4075. FAX 816-356-5213. Ed. Patti Myer. circ. 250.
Description: Education regarding adoption and its life-long effects.

ADVANCES IN APPLIED SOCIAL PSYCHOLOGY. see *PSYCHOLOGY*

301.15 US ISSN 0065-2601
HM251 CODEN: AXSPAQ
ADVANCES IN EXPERIMENTAL SOCIAL PSYCHOLOGY. 1964. irreg., vol.23, 1990. Academic Press, Inc., 1250 Sixth Ave., San Diego, CA 92101. TEL 619-231-0926. FAX 619-699-6715. Ed. Leonard Berkowitz. index. (reprint service avail. from ISI) **Indexed:** Biol.Abstr., SSCI.
—BLDSC shelfmark: 0706.100000.

ADVANCES IN FAMILY INTERVENTION, ASSESSMENT AND THEORY; a research annual. see *PSYCHOLOGY*

301 US
ADVANCES IN GROUP PROCESSES. 1984. a. $63.50 to institutions. J A I Press Inc., 55 Old Post Rd., No. 2, Box 1678, Greenwich, CT 06836-1678. TEL 203-661-7602. Ed. Edward J. Lawler.

ADVANCES IN SUICIDOLOGY. see *MEDICAL SCIENCES — Psychiatry And Neurology*

ADVANCES IN THE STUDY OF COMMUNICATION AND AFFECT.. see *PSYCHOLOGY*

301 327 IT
AFFARI SOCIALI INTERNAZIONALI. 1973. q. L.82000 (foreign L.120000)(effective 1992). Franco Angeli Editore, Viale Monza 106, 20127 Milan, Italy. TEL 02-28-27-651. Ed. Pier Marcello Masotti. bk.rev.; bibl.; circ. 5,000. **Indexed:** Int.Lab.Doc.

AFRICA. see *HISTORY — History Of Africa*

301 KE
AFRICAN JOURNAL OF SOCIOLOGY. 1981. s-a. University of Nairobi, Department of Sociology, P.O. Box 30022, Nairobi, Kenya. **Indexed:** Lang.& Lang.Behav.Abstr., Sociol.Abstr. (1981-).

AFRICAN LANGUAGES AND CULTURES. see *LINGUISTICS*

301 960 ZA ISSN 0002-0168
HN771 CODEN: ASREDO
AFRICAN SOCIAL RESEARCH. 1944. s-a. University of Zambia, P.O. Box 32379, Lusaka, Zambia. Ed.Bd. adv.; bk.rev.; charts; cum.index; circ. 1,000. **Indexed:** A.I.C.P., Amer.Hist.& Life, ASSIA, Curr.Cont.Africa, Curr.Cont., Geo.Abstr., Hist.Abstr., Lang.& Lang.Behav.Abstr., Mid.East: Abstr.& Ind., Psychol.Abstr., Rural Recreat.Tour.Abstr., SSCI, World Agri.Econ.& Rural Sociol.Abstr.
Supersedes: Rhodes-Livingstone Journal.
Description: Articles in social research, with emphasis on sociology, economics, history and related disciplines.

AFRIKA SPECTRUM; deutsche Zeitschrift fuer moderne Afrikaforschung. see *POLITICAL SCIENCE*

AFRIQUE MON PAYS. see *POLITICAL SCIENCE*

AFTERWORDS; suicide: the busy professionals newsletter. see *PSYCHOLOGY*

AGORA (RAVENNA). see *PHILOSOPHY*

301.4 338.1 GW ISSN 0065-437X
AGRARSOZIALE GESELLSCHAFT. GESCHAEFTS- UND ARBEITSBERICHT. 1950. a. free. Agrarsoziale Gesellschaft e.V., Kurze Geismarstr. 33, 3400 Goettingen, Germany.
Formerly (until 1968): Agrarsoziale Gesellschaft. Arbeitsbericht.

301.4 GW ISSN 0170-7671
AGRARSOZIALE GESELLSCHAFT. KLEINE REIHE. 1970. irreg., no.45, 1991. price varies. Agrarsoziale Gesellschaft e.V., Kurze Geismarstr. 33, 3400 Goettingen, Germany. **Indexed:** Rural Recreat.Tour.Abstr., World Agri.Econ.& Rural Sociol.Abstr.

338.1 301.4 GW ISSN 0179-7603
AGRARSOZIALE GESELLSCHAFT. LAENDLICHER RAUM RUNDBRIEFE. 1950. m. DM.60. Agrarsoziale Gesellschaft e.V., Kurze Geismarstr. 33, 3400 Goettingen, Germany. index.
Formerly: Agrarsoziale Gesellschaft. Rundbriefe (ISSN 0065-4388)

301.4 GW ISSN 0344-5712
AGRARSOZIALE GESELLSCHAFT. MATERIALSAMMLUNG. 1953. irreg., no.185, 1991. price varies. Agrarsoziale Gesellschaft e.V., Kurze Geismarstr. 33, 3400 Goettingen, Germany. **Indexed:** Geo.Abstr.

SOCIOLOGY

AGRICULTURAL ECONOMICS AND RURAL SOCIOLOGY. BULLETINS. see *AGRICULTURE — Agricultural Economics*

AGRICULTURAL ECONOMICS AND RURAL SOCIOLOGY. REPORT SERIES. see *AGRICULTURE — Agricultural Economics*

AGRICULTURAL ECONOMICS AND RURAL SOCIOLOGY. SOUTHERN COOPERATIVE SERIES BULLETIN. see *AGRICULTURE — Agricultural Economics*

AGRICULTURAL ECONOMICS AND RURAL SOCIOLOGY. SPECIAL REPORTS. see *AGRICULTURE — Agricultural Economics*

AGRO SUR. see *AGRICULTURE*

AGROEKONOMIKA. see *AGRICULTURE — Agricultural Economics*

ALBERTA - EDMONTON SERIES REPORT. see *POPULATION STUDIES*

301.15   GW   ISSN 0175-9191
ALLENSBACHER JAHRBUCH DER DEMOSKOPIE. 1947. irreg. price varies. (Institut fuer Demoskopie, Allensbach) K.G. Saur Verlag KG, Ortlerstr. 8, Postfach 701620, 8000 Munich 70, Germany. TEL 089-76902-0. FAX 089-76902150. adv.; bk.rev.; circ. 3,000.
Formerly: Jahrbuch der Oeffentlichen Meinung (ISSN 0075-2347)

ALTERNATIVE RESEARCH NEWSLETTER. see *LITERARY AND POLITICAL REVIEWS*

L'ALTRA EUROPA. see *ART*

ALZHEIMER'S ASSOCIATION NEWSLETTER. see *GERONTOLOGY AND GERIATRICS*

301.4 973   US   ISSN 0044-7471
E184.O6   CODEN: AMEJEZ
AMERASIA JOURNAL. 1971. 3/yr. $15 to individuals; institutions $21. University of California, Los Angeles, Asian American Studies Center, 3230 Campbell Hall, Los Angeles, CA 90024-1546. TEL 310-825-2968. FAX 310-206-9844. Ed. Russell C. Leong. adv.; bk.rev.; charts; circ. 1,500. (also avail. in microform from UMI) **Indexed:** Amer.Hist.& Life., Arts & Hum.Cit.Ind., C.I.J.E., Curr.Cont., ERIC, Hist.Abstr.
—BLDSC shelfmark: 0809.655000.
Description: Contains information about Asian-American history and life. Includes bibliography of Asian-American studies.

301   PE   ISSN 0065-6763
AMERICA - PROBLEMA. 1968. irreg., no.15, 1991. price varies. (Instituto de Estudios Peruanos) I E P Ediciones, Horacio Urteaga 694 (Campo de Marte), Lima 11, Peru. TEL 323070. FAX 324981.

AMERICAN CROSSDRESSER. see *PSYCHOLOGY*

301.4   US
AMERICAN CULTURAL HERITAGE SERIES. irreg. $18.39. Burt Franklin & Co., Inc., Box 856, New York, NY 10014. TEL 212-627-0027. Ed. Jack Salzman.

301.4   US   ISSN 0161-1178
AMERICAN FAMILY (WASHINGTON); national newsletter on family policy and programs. 1977. 9/yr. $67 (foreign $97). Youth Policy Institute, 1221 Massachusetts Ave., Ste. B, Washington, DC 20005. TEL 202-638-2144. Ed. Martha Herr. adv.; bk.rev.; charts; index. cum.index: 1977-1983; circ. 900. **Indexed:** Soc.Work Res.& Abstr.
Description: Covers family policy and programs with special focus on issues having impact on young families with children to age 11.

AMERICAN FAMILY THERAPY ASSOCIATION NEWSLETTER. see *PSYCHOLOGY*

301.1   US   ISSN 0091-0562
RA790.A1   CODEN: AJCPCK
AMERICAN JOURNAL OF COMMUNITY PSYCHOLOGY. 1973. 6/yr. $295 (foreign $345)(effective 1992). Plenum Publishing Corp., 233 Spring St., New York, NY 10013-1578. TEL 212-620-8000. FAX 212-463-0742. TELEX 23-421139. Ed. Julian Rappaport. adv. (also avail. in microfilm from JSC; back issues avail.) **Indexed:** Adol.Ment.Hlth.Abstr., ASSIA, CINAHL, Curr.Cont., Except.Child.Educ.Abstr., Excerp.Med., Ind.Med., INIS Atomind., Mid.East: Abstr.& Ind., PSI, Psychol.Abstr., Sage Fam.Stud.Abstr., Sage Pub.Admin.Abstr., Sp.Ed.Needs Abstr., SSCI.
—BLDSC shelfmark: 0824.070000.
Refereed Serial

AMERICAN JOURNAL OF FAMILY THERAPY. see *PSYCHOLOGY*

301   US   ISSN 0002-9602
HM1
AMERICAN JOURNAL OF SOCIOLOGY. 1895. bi-m. $37 to individuals; institutions $76; students $26. University of Chicago Press, Journals Division, 5720 S. Woodlawn Ave., Chicago, IL 60637. TEL 312-753-3347. FAX 312-702-0694. TELEX 25-4603. (Subscr. to: Box 37005, Chicago IL 60637) Ed. Marta Tienda. adv.; bk.rev.; abstr.; bibl.; charts; index,cum.index: vols.1-70, 1895-1965, vols.71-75, 1965-1970, vols.76-80, 1971-1980; circ. 7,300. (also avail. in microform from MIM,UMI; reprint service avail. from UMI,ISI,SCH) **Indexed:** A.B.C.Pol.Sci., A.I.C.P., Abstr.Anthropol., Abstr.Crim.& Pen., Acad.Ind., Amer.Bibl.Slavic & E.Eur.Stud., Amer.Hist.& Life, ASSIA, Bk.Rev.Ind. (1965-), C.I.J.E., Chic.Per.Ind., Child.Bk.Rev.Ind. (1965-), CLOA, Cont.Pg.Manage., Crim.Just.Abstr., Curr.Cont., G.Soc.Sci.& Rel.Per.Lit., Geo.Abstr., Hist.Abstr., I D A, Int.Lab.Doc., Lang.& Lang.Behav.Abstr., P.A.I.S., Popul.Ind., Psychol.Abstr., Res.High.Educ.Abstr., Rural Ext.Educ.& Tr.Abstr., Rural Recreat.Tour.Abstr., Sage Fam.Stud.Abstr., Sage Urb.Stud.Abstr., Soc.Sci.Ind., Soc.Work Res.& Abstr., Sociol.Abstr. (1952-59), Sociol.Educ.Abstr., Sp.Ed.Needs Abstr., SSCI, Stud.Wom.Abstr., Trop.Dis.Bull., World Agri.Econ.& Rural Sociol.Abstr.
—BLDSC shelfmark: 0838.300000.
Description: Articles and review essays presented are of interest to scholars and students throughout the social sciences.
Refereed Serial

301   US
AMERICAN SOCIOLOGICAL ASSOCIATION. PROCEEDINGS OF ANNUAL MEETING. a. $6 (foreign $12); effective 1992. American Sociological Association, 1722 N St., N.W., Washington, DC 20036. TEL 202-833-3410. FAX 202-785-0146. (reprint service avail. from UMI)

301   US   ISSN 0003-1224
HM1   CODEN: ASRRB
AMERICAN SOCIOLOGICAL REVIEW. 1936. bi-m. $44 to individuals (foreign $50); institutions $93 (foreign $99) (effective 1992). American Sociological Association, 1722 N St., N.W., Washington, DC 20036. TEL 202-833-3410. FAX 202-785-0146. Ed. Gerald Marwell. adv.; bk.rev.; charts; circ. 15,000. (also avail. in microform from MIM,UMI; reprint service avail. from UMI,SCH) **Indexed:** A.B.C.Pol.Sci., Abstr.Anthropol., Acad.Ind., Adol.Ment.Hlth.Abstr., Amer.Bibl.Slavic & E.Eur.Stud., ASSIA, Bk.Rev.Ind. (1965-1973), C.I.J.E., Child.Bk.Rev.Ind. (1965-), Commun.Abstr., Cont.Pg.Manage., Crim.Just.Abstr., Curr.Cont., Deep Sea Res.& Oceanogr.Abstr., E.I., Educ.Admin.Abstr., G.Soc.Sci.& Rel.Per.Lit., Geo.Abstr., Hist.Abstr., Int.Lab.Doc., Lang.& Lang.Behav.Abstr., Mid.East: Abstr.& Ind., P.A.I.S., Popul.Ind., Psychol.Abstr., Rural Recreat.Tour.Abstr., Sage Fam.Stud.Abstr., Sage Urb.Stud.Abstr., SCIMP, Soc.Sci.Ind., Soc.Work Res.& Abstr., Sociol.Abstr. (1952-), SSCI, Stud.Wom.Abstr., World Agri.Econ.& Rural Sociol.Abstr.
—BLDSC shelfmark: 0857.500000.
Description: Publishes work of interest to the discipline in general: new theoretical developments, results of research advancing understanding of fundamental social processes, as well as methodological innovations.

301   US   ISSN 0003-1232
HM9
AMERICAN SOCIOLOGIST. 1965. q. $36 to individuals (foreign $56); institutions $72 (foreign $92). (American Sociological Association) Transaction Publishers, Transaction Periodicals Consortium, Department 3092, Rutgers University, New Brunswick, NJ 08903. TEL 908-932-2280. FAX 908-932-3138. Ed. Richard H. Hall. adv.; circ. 600. (also avail. in microform from MIM,UMI; reprint service avail. from SWZ,UMI) **Indexed:** Curr.Cont., E.I., Lang.& Lang.Behav.Abstr., Mid.East: Abstr.& Ind., Res.High.Educ.Abstr., Soc.Sci.Ind., Sociol.Abstr. (1966-), SSCI, Stud.Wom.Abstr.
—BLDSC shelfmark: 0857.503000.
Description: Examines the history, current status, and future prospects of sociology as a profession and discipline. Emphasizes new trends in the profession and focuses on how sociologists have shaped or influenced social policy and the intellectual issues of the age.
Refereed Serial

AMERICAN UNIVERSITY STUDIES. SERIES 16. ECONOMICS. see *POPULATION STUDIES*

301   SP   ISSN 0066-1473
ANALES DE MORAL SOCIAL Y ECONOMICA. 1962. irreg. 125 ptas. Centro de Estudios Sociales de la Santa Cruz del Valle de los Caidos, Madrid, Spain. (Dist. by: Aguilar, S.A. de Publicaciones, Juan Bravo 38, Madrid 6, Spain)

300   PO   ISSN 0003-2573
HM7
ANALISE SOCIAL. (Summaries in English and French) 1963. 5/yr. Esc.1300($45) Universidade de Lisboa, Instituto de Ciencias Sociais, Av. das Forcas Armadas, Edif. I.S.C.T.E., Ala Sul, 1 Andar, 1600 Lisbon, Portugal. Ed.Bd. bk.rev.; charts; circ. 3,000. (back issues avail.) **Indexed:** Lang.& Lang.Behav.Abstr., Sociol.Abstr.

301   PL
ANALIZY I PROBY TECHNIK BADAWCZYCH W SOCJOLOGII. (Text in Polish; summaries in English and Russian) irreg., vol.6, 1986. price varies. (Polska Akademia Nauk, Instytut Filozofii i Socjologii) Ossolineum, Publishing House of the Polish Academy of Sciences, Rynek 9, Wroclaw, Poland. TELEX 0712771 OSS PL. (Dist. by: Ars Polona-Ruch, Krakowskie Przedmiescie 7, Warsaw, Poland) Eds. Z. Gostkowski, J. Lutynski.

ANCIENT CONTROVERSY; a newsletter for society's leaders. see *POLITICAL SCIENCE*

ANCIENT GREEK CITIES REPORT. see *HOUSING AND URBAN PLANNING*

301   AU   ISSN 0587-5234
ANGEWANDTE SOZIALFORSCHUNG. 1972. q. S.370. Institut fuer Angewandte Soziologie, Lerchenfelderstr. 36, A-1080 Vienna, Austria. Ed. Henrik Kreutz. adv.; bk.rev.

301   IT   ISSN 0392-5870
ANIMAZIONE SOCIALE; mensile per gli operatori sociali. 1970. m. L.50000 (effective 1991). Edizioni Gruppo Abele, Via Giolitti 21, 10123 Turin, Italy. TEL 011-8395444. FAX 011-8395577. Ed. G.A. Ellena.
Description: Deals with social issues, as they relate to political and cultural institutions.

ANNALES DE L'EST. see *HISTORY — History Of Europe*

301   FR   ISSN 0003-441X
ANNALES - ECONOMIES, SOCIETES, CIVILISATIONS. 1929. bi-m. 70 ECU($87) (typically set in Jan.). Armand Colin (Subsidiary of: Masson), 103 bd. Saint Michel, 75005 Paris, France. Ed. Bernard Lepetit. adv.; circ. 5,000. (also avail. in microform from UMI; reprint service avail. from KTO) **Indexed:** Amer.Hist.& Life, Arts & Hum.Cit.Ind., Br.Archaeol.Abstr., C.I.S. Abstr., Curr.Cont., Geo.Abstr., I D A, Lang.& Lang.Behav.Abstr., Popul.Ind., SSCI.

ANNALES UNIVERSITATIS MARIAE CURIE-SKLODOWSKA. SECTIO I. PHILOSOPHIA-SOCIOLOGIA. see *PHILOSOPHY*

301   FR   ISSN 0066-2399
ANNEE SOCIOLOGIQUE. 1896. a. 310 F. (foreign 370 F.). Presses Universitaires de France, Departement des revues, 14 av. du Bois-de-l'Epine, B.P.90, 91003 Evry Cedex, France. TEL 1-60-77-82-05. FAX 1-60-79-20-45. TELEX PUF 600 474 F. (reprint service avail. from KTO) Indexed: A.I.C.P., CERDIC, Lang.& Lang.Behav.Abstr., P.A.I.S.For.Lang.Ind., Sociol.Abstr. (1960-).
  Description: Covers general, political, and theoretical sociology, methodologie, social and cultural anthropology, religious, demographic and family sociology, criminology.

301 309 157.63   US
ANNUAL EDITIONS: DRUGS, SOCIETY & BEHAVIOR. 1986. a. $10.95. Dushkin Publishing Group, Inc., Sluice Dock, Guilford, CT 06437-9989. TEL 203-453-4351. FAX 203-453-6000. Ed. Erich Goode. illus.

300 360   US
ANNUAL EDITIONS: HUMAN RESOURCES. 1989. a. $10.95. Dushkin Publishing Group, Inc., Sluice Dock, Guilford, CT 06437-9989. TEL 203-453-4351. FAX 203-453-6000. Ed. Fred H. Maidment. illus.
  Refereed Serial

ANNUAL EDITIONS: HUMAN SEXUALITY. see BIOLOGY

ANNUAL EDITIONS: MARRIAGE AND FAMILY. see MATRIMONY

305.8   US
▼**ANNUAL EDITIONS: RACE & ETHNIC RELATIONS.** 1991. a. $10.95. Dushkin Publishing Group, Inc., Sluice Dock, Guilford, CT 06437-9989. TEL 203-453-4351. FAX 203-453-6000. Ed. John A. Kromkowski. illus.
  Refereed Serial

301   US   ISSN 0277-9315
HM1
ANNUAL EDITIONS: SOCIOLOGY. 1972. a. $10.95. Dushkin Publishing Group, Inc., Sluice Dock, Guilford, CT 06437-9989. TEL 203-453-4351. FAX 203-453-6000. Ed. Kurt Finsterbusch. illus.; index. (back issues avail.) Indexed: Soc.Sci.Ind.
  Formerly: Annual Editions: Readings in Sociology (ISSN 0090-4236)
  Refereed Serial

301.364   US   ISSN 0160-9815
HT101
ANNUAL EDITIONS: URBAN SOCIETY. 1978. biennial. $11.95. Dushkin Publishing Group, Inc., Sluice Dock, Guilford, CT 06437-9989. TEL 203-453-4351. FAX 203-453-6000. Ed. Jeffrey M. Elliot. illus.; index. (back issues avail.)
  Formerly: Focus: Urban Society.
  Refereed Serial

301   US   ISSN 0360-0572
HM1   CODEN: ARVSDB
ANNUAL REVIEW OF SOCIOLOGY. 1975. a. $49 (foreign $54)(effective 1992). Annual Reviews Inc., 4139 El Camino Way, Box 10139, Palo Alto, CA 94303-0897. TEL 415-493-4400. FAX 415-855-9815. TELEX 910-290-0275. Ed. Judith Blake. bibl.; cum.index. (back issues avail.; reprint service avail. from ISI) Indexed: Amer.Bibl.Slavic & E.Eur.Stud., Biol.Abstr., Curr.Cont., Lang.& Lang.Behav.Abstr., PSI, Psychol.Abstr., Soc.Sci.Ind., Sociol.Abstr. (1974-), SSCI.
  —BLDSC shelfmark: 1529.100000.
  Description: Original reviews of critical literature and current developments in sociology.

301.4 360 362.7   US
ANTI-CENSORSHIP NEWSLETTER.* m. $15 (foreign $40). The Parent S I G, 1640 Via Pacifica, Ste.F-105, Corona, CA 91720. Ed. Lawrence A. Stanley. bk.rev.
  ●Also available online.
  Formerly (until 1980): Parent S I G NewsFliers.
  Description: Covers anti-censorship and pro-censorship in reference to child pornography, includes sex education, childhood sexuality and sex exploitation of children.

ANVESAK. see BUSINESS AND ECONOMICS

309.1   US   ISSN 0503-5422
HC107.A133
APPALACHIAN REGIONAL COMMISSION. ANNUAL REPORT. 1965. a. free. U.S. Appalachian Regional Commission, 1666 Connecticut Ave. N.W., Washington, DC 20235. TEL 202-673-7968. Ed. Jack Russell. circ. 3,000. (back issues avail.)
  Indexed: P.A.I.S.

301   PY   ISSN 0044-8524
AQUI. 1971. w. $50. Editorial Emegebe S.A., Alberdi 1393, Asuncion, Paraguay. TEL 448-688-443-536. FAX 448-271-495-901.
  Description: Treats themes in the political and judicial atmospheres and covers social and economic issues.

ARBEITEN ZUR SOZIALWISSENSCHAFTLICHEN PSYCHOLOGIE. see PSYCHOLOGY

ARMED FORCES AND SOCIETY; an interdisciplinary journal on military institutions, civil-military relations, arms control and peacekeeping, and conflict management. see MILITARY

301   SI
ASIAN CULTURE. 2/yr. $10. Singapore Society of Asian Studies, No. 10-319, Blk 72 Telok Blangah Height, Singapore 0410, Singapore. TEL 271-3652.

301   US
ASSOCIATION FOR THE SOCIOLOGY OF RELIGION. NEWS AND ANNOUNCEMENTS. 1965. q. $25. Association for the Sociology of Religion (Annville), Lebanon College, Annville, PA 17003. TEL 717-867-6336. FAX 717-867-6124. (Subscr. to: Marist Hall, Rm. 108, Catholic University, Washington, DC 20064) Ed. Barbara J. Denison. bk.rev.; circ. 600.
  Description: Social commentary on religion.

ASSOCIATION INTERNATIONALE D'ETUDES DU SUD-EST EUROPEEN. BULLETIN. see HISTORY — History Of Europe

360   FR   ISSN 0587-3746
ASSURE SOCIAL. 1964. bi-m. 100 F. (Union Nationale pour l'Avenir de la Medecine) B.C. Savy, 18 av. de la Marne, 92600 Asnieres, France. adv.; bk.rev.; circ. 15,000.

ATMA JAYA RESEARCH CENTRE. SOCIO-MEDICAL RESEARCH REPORT/PUSAT PENELITIAN ATMA JAYA. PENELITIAN TENTANG KEBUTUHAN KESEHATAN MASYARAKAT DAN SISTEM PELEYANAN KESEHATAN DI KECAMATAN PENJARINGAN. see MEDICAL SCIENCES

ATMA JAYA RESEARCH CENTRE. SOCIO-RELIGIOUS RESEARCH REPORT/PUSAT PENELITIAN ATMA JAYA. LAPORAN PENELITIAN KEAGAMAAN. see RELIGIONS AND THEOLOGY — Buddhist

AUFRISS. see HISTORY — History Of Europe

301.4 360 150   AT   ISSN 0814-723X
CODEN: ANZTE7
AUSTRALIAN AND NEW ZEALAND JOURNAL OF FAMILY THERAPY. 1979. q. Aus.$65($57) to individuals; institutions Aus.$82 ($86)(typically set in Aug.-Sep.). Australian and New Zealand Journal of Family Therapy Inc., P.O. Box 633, Lane Cove, N.S.W. 2066, Australia. TEL 02 879 6144. FAX 02-879-6440. Ed. Max Cornwell. adv.; bk.rev.; circ. 1,500. (back issues avail.) Indexed: Psychol.Abstr., Sage Fam.Stud.Abstr., Soc.Work Res.& Abstr.
  —BLDSC shelfmark: 1796.886500.
  Formerly: Australian Journal of Family Therapy.

301   AT   ISSN 0004-8690
HM1
AUSTRALIAN & NEW ZEALAND JOURNAL OF SOCIOLOGY. 1965. 3/yr. Aus.$42 to individuals; institutions Aus.$ 60. (Sociological Association of Australia and New Zealand) La Trobe University Press, Bundoora, Vic. 3085, Australia. Ed. Ken Demprey. adv.; bk.rev.; abstr.; index; cum.index every 2 yrs.; circ. 1,500. (also avail. in microfilm from UMI) Indexed: Amer.Hist.& Life, ASSIA, Aus.Educ.Ind., Aus.P.A.I.S., Curr.Cont., Geo.Abstr., Hist.Abstr., Lang.& Lang.Behav.Abstr., Mid.East: Abstr.& Ind., Psychol.Abstr., Res.High.Educ.Abstr., So.Pac.Per.Ind., Sociol.Abstr. (1965-), SSCI, Stud.Wom.Abstr.
  —BLDSC shelfmark: 1796.897000.

AUSTRALIAN CRICKET JOURNAL. see SPORTS AND GAMES — Ball Games

AUSTRALIAN FOLKLORE. see FOLKLORE

AZAD MAZDUR; Hindi weekly. see POLITICAL SCIENCE

301 338.91   BG
B I D S. MONOGRAPH. 1949. irreg., latest no.9. price varies. Bangladesh Unnayan Gobeshona Protishthan - Bangladesh Institute of Development Studies, G.P.O. Box 3854, E - 17 Agargoan, Sher-e-Banglanagar, Dhaka 1207, Bangladesh. TEL 325041. Ed.Bd.

B I D S. NEWSLETTER. see BUSINESS AND ECONOMICS — International Development And Assistance

301 338.91   BG
B I D S. RESEARCH REPORTS. (Text in English) irreg., latest no.72. Bangladesh Unnayan Gobeshona Protishthan - Bangladesh Institute of Development Studies, G.P.O. Box 3854, E - 17 Agargoan, Sher-e-Banglanagar, Dhaka, Bangladesh. TEL 325041. Ed.Bd.

301 338.91   BG
B I D S. WORKING PAPER. irreg., no.4, 1987. price varies. Bangladesh Unnayan Gobeshona Protishthan - Bangladesh Institute of Development Studies, G.P.O. Box 3854, E - 17 Agargoan, Sher-e-Banglanagar, Dhaka 1207, Bangladesh. TEL 325041. Ed.Bd.

301.16   US
BAD SEED. 1983. q. $15. Kicks, Box 646, Cooper Sta., NY 10003. TEL 718-789-4438. FAX 718-398-9215. Ed. Miriam Linna. bk.rev.; film rev.; circ. 1,000. (back issues avail.)
  Description: Contains studies, discussions, and research on juvenile delinquency in popular culture; film, literature, media.

300   IS   ISSN 0005-4542
BAMA'ARAKHA. 1961. m. Council of the Sephardi and Oriental Communities, P.O. Box 10, 12A Haavatzelet St., Jerusalem 91000, Israel. Ed. Yehezkel Soffer. adv.; bk.rev.; bibl.; circ. 4,000. Indexed: Ind.Heb.Per.

301   GW
BAUSTEINE FUER EINE SOZIALE ZUKUNFT.* 1977. DM.46.80. Institut fuer soziale Gegenwartsfrage, Prinz-Eugen-Str., 7800 Freiburg, Germany. circ. 300.

BEHAVIOR TODAY; the weekly newsletter for mental health & family relations professionals. see PSYCHOLOGY

BEITRAEGE ZUR NATIONALSOZIALISTISCHEN GESUNDHEITS- UND SOZIALPOLITIK. see MEDICAL SCIENCES

BEITRAEGE ZUR PSYCHOLOGIE UND SOZIOLOGIE DES KRANKEN MENSCHEN. see PSYCHOLOGY

BELARUSKAJA CARKVA. see RELIGIONS AND THEOLOGY

BELGIUM. MINISTERE DE L'EDUCATION NATIONALE. REVUE. see EDUCATION

301   US   ISSN 0067-5830
HM1
BERKELEY JOURNAL OF SOCIOLOGY; critical review. 1955. a. $8 to individuals; institutions $15 (foreign $20.50); students $6. University of California, Berkeley, Sociology Department, 410 Barrows Hall, Berkeley, CA 94720. TEL 510-642-2772. FAX 510-642-0659. (Subscr. to: 458 A Barrows Hall, Berkeley, CA 94720) Ed.Bd. adv.; bk.rev.; index; circ. 1,500. (back issues avail.) Indexed: Alt.Press Ind., Amer.Bibl.Slavic & E.Eur.Stud., Lang.& Lang.Behav.Abstr., Mid.East: Abstr.& Ind., Sociol.Abstr. (1955-), Stud.Wom.Abstr.
  —BLDSC shelfmark: 1940.350000.
  Formerly (until vol. 4, 1958): Berkeley Publications in Society and Institutions.

SOCIOLOGY

301.2   PL   ISSN 0067-7655
BIBLIOTEKA ETNOGRAFII POLSKIEJ. (Text in English or Polish; summaries in English, French or German) 1958. a. price varies. (Polska Akademia Nauk, Instytut Historii Kultury Materialnej) Ossolineum, Publishing House of the Polish Academy of Sciences, Rynek 9, 50-106 Wroclaw, Poland. TELEX 0712771 OSS PL. (Dist. by: Ars Polona-Ruch, Krakowskie Przedmiescie 7, Warsaw, Poland) Ed. Maria Frankowska.

BLACKCOUNTRYMAN. see *HISTORY — History Of Europe*

300   GW
BLAUE FEDER; alle "Thema Null"-Beitraege. 1965. m. DM.160. OHO-Verlag, Schlagweg 5, Postfach 30, 3501 Zierenberg 1, Germany. Ed. Horst Brede. adv.; bk.rev.; film rev.; play rev.; illus.; pat.; tr.lit.; circ. 200-2,000.
   Former titles: Thema Null (ISSN 0023-9968); Arbeitsmethodik Briefe.

BLAUWE WEGWIJZER. see *DRUG ABUSE AND ALCOHOLISM*

301   UY   ISSN 0006-6508
BOLETIN URUGUAYO DE SOCIOLOGIA. (Text in Spanish; summaries in English, French, Portuguese and Spanish) 1961. q. $6. Mario Bon Espasandin, Ed. & Pub., Calle Juncal 1395, Piso 2, Escritorio 5, Montevideo, Uruguay. adv.; bk.rev.; abstr.; bibl.; charts; stat.; index; circ. 1,500. **Indexed:** Lang.& Lang.Behav.Abstr.

BOULITE. see *FOLKLORE*

301   BE
BRIEVEN AAN GEZINNEN. 1979. bi-m. 65 Fr. (Katholiek Vormingswerk voor Landelijke Vrouwen) Publicarto N.V., Langestraat 170, B-1150 Brussels 15, Belgium. TEL 02-782-00-00. FAX 02-782-16-16. B.G.J.G. (De Bond van Grote en Jonge Gezinnen). bk.rev.; illus.; circ. 25,000.
   Formerly: Brieven aan Jonge Gezinnen.

301   UK
BRITISH ASSOCIATION FOR CANADIAN STUDIES. NEWSLETTER. 3/yr. £10 to individuals; institutions £15. British Association for Canadian Studies, c/o Quebec House, 59 Pall Mall, London SW1Y 5JH, England. TEL 071-976-1941. FAX 071-930-7938. (North American addr.: International Council for Canadian Studies, 2 Daly Ave., Ottawa K1N 6E2, Canada) Ed. Christopher Rolfe.

301   UK   ISSN 0269-9222
F1021
BRITISH JOURNAL OF CANADIAN STUDIES. 1977. s-a. £15 (foreign Can.$35). British Association for Canadian Studies, c/o Quebec House, 59 Pall Mall, London SW1Y 5JH, England. TEL 071-976-1941. FAX 071-930-7938. (North American addr.: International Council for Canadian Studies, 2 Daly Ave., Ottawa, Ont. K1N 6E2, Canada) Ed. Colin Nicholson. bk.rev.; index.
   —BLDSC shelfmark: 2306.900000.
   Formerly (until 1986): Bulletin of Canadian Studies.

301   UK   ISSN 0007-1315
HM1
BRITISH JOURNAL OF SOCIOLOGY. 1950. q. £30($60) to individuals; institutions £37($74). (London School of Economics) Routledge, 11 New Fetter Lane, London EC4P 4EE, England. TEL 01-583 9855. Eds. Paul Rock, Ian Roxborough. adv.; bk.rev.; index. cum.index every 10 yrs. (also avail. in microfilm) **Indexed:** A.I.C.P., Adol.Ment.Hlth.Abstr., Amer.Hist.& Life, ASSIA, Br.Hum.Ind., C.I.J.E., Commun.Abstr., Cont.Pg.Manage., Curr.Cont., E.I., Geo.Abstr., High.Educ.Curr.Aware.Bull., Hist.Abstr., Ind.Med., Int.Lab.Doc., Lang.& Lang.Behav.Abstr., Mid.East: Abstr.& Ind., P.A.I.S., Psychol.Abstr., Res.High.Educ.Abstr., SCIMP (1979-), Soc.Sci.Ind., Sociol.Abstr. (1952-), Sp.Ed.Needs Abstr., SSCI, Trop.Dis.Bull.
   —BLDSC shelfmark: 2324.800000.
   Description: Research projects and discussion notes as well as articles and papers in sociology and other related fields.

BRITISH JOURNAL OF SOCIOLOGY OF EDUCATION. see *EDUCATION*

BULLETIN OF TIBETOLOGY. see *HISTORY — History Of Asia*

C A P SULE (LEVITTOWN). (Children of Aging Parents) see *GERONTOLOGY AND GERIATRICS*

301.45   NZ
C A R E. 1972. 4/yr. NZ.$5. Citizens Association for Racial Equality, P.O. Box 10-5035, Auckland, New Zealand. Ed. Carol Symington. adv.; bk.rev.; illus.; circ. 600.
   Description: Deals with race relations.

301 360   IT
C E N S I S NOTE E COMMENTI. 1965. 12/yr. L.65000 (effective Jan. 1992). Centro Studi Investimenti Sociali, Piazza di Novella, 2-00, 00199 Rome, Italy. TEL 39-6-860911. FAX 39-6-8315200. Dir. Nadio Delai. stat.; index; circ. 4,500. (processed)
   Formerly: C E N S I S Quindicinale di Note e Commenti (ISSN 0007-8271)
   Description: Investigates and interprets the most significant events in the Italian socio-economic and cultural phenomenology and in the sectors of social policy.

C I R E S CAHIERS. (Centre Ivoirien de Recherches Economiques et Sociales) see *BUSINESS AND ECONOMICS*

C M J S CENTERPIECES. (Cohen Center for Modern Jewish Studies) see *ETHNIC INTERESTS*

C S S S DIGEST. (Center for the Study of Sport in Society) see *SPORTS AND GAMES*

301   US
C U B COMMUNICATOR. 1976. m. $50. Concerned United Birthparents, Inc., 2000 Walker St., Des Moines, IA 50317-5255. FAX 800-822-2777. Ed. Carole Anderson. adv.; bk.rev.; circ. 2,500.

301 320   BL
CADERNOS DO C.E.A.S. no.28, 1973. bi-m. $20. Centro de Estudos e Acao Social, Rua Aristides Novis 101, Salvador, Bahia, Brazil. Ed. Claudio Perani. adv.; bk.rev.; bibl.; charts; stat.; circ. 2,000. **Indexed:** HR Rep., Int.Lab.Doc., Rural Devel.Abstr.

301   BL
CADERNOS RIOARTE. 1985. 2/yr. Instituto Municipal de Arte e Cultura, Rua Rumania 20, Laranjeiras, CEP 22240 Rio de Janeiro, Brazil.

CAHIERS CRITIQUES DE THERAPIE FAMILIALE ET DE PRATIQUES DE RESEAUX. see *PSYCHOLOGY*

CAHIERS DE PRAXEMATIQUE. see *LINGUISTICS*

CAHIERS DES RELIGIONS AFRICAINES. see *RELIGIONS AND THEOLOGY — Other Denominations And Sects*

301   FR   ISSN 0008-0276
HM3
CAHIERS INTERNATIONAUX DE SOCIOLOGIE. 1946. s-a. 185 F. (foreign 255 F.). (Ecole des Hautes Etudes en Sciences Sociales) Presses Universitaires de France, Departement des Revues, 14 av. du Bois-de-l'Epine, B.P.90, 91003 Evry Cedex, France. TEL 1-60-77-82-05. FAX 1-60-79-20-45. TELEX PUF 600 474 F. Dir. G. Balandier. bk.rev.; bibl.; index; circ. 3,500. (reprint service avail. from KTO,SCH) **Indexed:** E.I., Lang.& Lang.Behav.Abstr., Pt.de Rep. (1979-), Sociol.Abstr. (1952-), SSCI.
   Description: Covers the new work on sociological theory and practice.

CAHIERS POUR CROIRE AUJOURD'HUI. see *RELIGIONS AND THEOLOGY*

CALIFORNIA FAMILY LAW: PRACTICE AND PROCEDURE. see *LAW — Family And Matrimonial Law*

301.05   US   ISSN 0162-8712
HM1
CALIFORNIA SOCIOLOGIST; a journal of sociology and social work. 1978. s-a. $8 to individuals; institutions $12. California State University, Los Angeles, Department of Sociology, 5151 State University Dr., Los Angeles, CA 90032. TEL 213-343-2200. FAX 213-343-5155. Ed. Terry R. Kandal. adv.; circ. 200. **Indexed:** Adol.Ment.Hlth.Abstr., Lang.& Lang.Behav.Abstr., Soc.Work Res.& Abstr., Sociol.Abstr.
   —BLDSC shelfmark: 3015.332000.
   Description: Publishes theoretical and empirical articles and articles on practice and social policy issues.

301   UK   ISSN 0068-6727
CAMBRIDGE PAPERS IN SOCIOLOGY. 1970. irreg., no.5, 1975. $32.50 for latest vol. Cambridge University Press, Edinburgh Bldg., Shaftesbury Rd., Cambridge CB2 2RU, England. TEL 0223-312393. FAX 0223-315052. TELEX 851817256. Eds. R.M. Blackburn, J.H. Goldthorpe. index.

301   UK   ISSN 0068-6808
CAMBRIDGE STUDIES IN SOCIOLOGY. 1968. irreg., no.10, 1978. price varies. Cambridge University Press, Edinburgh Bldg., Shaftesbury Rd., Cambridge CB2 2RU, England. TEL 0223-312393. FAX 0223-315052. TELEX 851817256. Eds. R.M. Blackburn, J.H. Goldthorpe.

CANADIAN JOURNAL OF BEHAVIOURAL SCIENCE/REVUE CANADIENNE DES SCIENCES DU COMPORTEMENT. see *PSYCHOLOGY*

CANADIAN JOURNAL OF LAW AND SOCIETY/REVUE CANADIENNE DE DROIT ET SOCIETE. see *LAW*

CANADIAN JOURNAL OF POLITICAL & SOCIAL THEORY/REVUE CANADIENNE DE THEORIE POLITIQUE ET SOCIALE. see *POLITICAL SCIENCE*

301   CN   ISSN 0318-6431
HM1
CANADIAN JOURNAL OF SOCIOLOGY/CAHIERS CANADIENS DE SOCIOLOGIE. (Text in English or French) q. $38.15 to individuals; institutions $65.40. University of Alberta, Department of Sociology, Edmonton, Alta. T6G 2E7, Canada. Ed.Bd. bk.rev. **Indexed:** Can.Wom.Per.Ind., Sociol.Abstr. (1975-).
   —BLDSC shelfmark: 3035.630000.
   Description: Covers all aspects of sociology, with particular emphasis on politics and history.

301 572   CN   ISSN 0008-4948
CANADIAN REVIEW OF SOCIOLOGY AND ANTHROPOLOGY/REVUE CANADIENNE DE SOCIOLOGIE ET D'ANTHROPOLOGIE. (Text in English, French) 1964. q. Can.$69.55 (foreign Can.$70). Canadian Sociology and Anthropology Association, Concordia University, 1455 Bd. de Maisonneuve W., Montreal, Que. H3G 1M8, Canada. TEL 514-848-8780. FAX 514-848-3494. Ed. James E. Curtis. adv.; bk.rev.; charts; index; cum.index 1964-1984; circ. 1,800. (also avail. in microform from MIM,KTO,UMI) **Indexed:** A.I.C.P., Abstr.Anthropol., Amer.Bibl.Slavic & E.Eur.Stud., Amer.Hist.& Life, ASSIA, Can.Per.Ind., CMI, Commun.Abstr., Curr.Cont., Educ.Admin.Abstr., Hist.Abstr., Lang.& Lang.Behav.Abstr., Mid.East: Abstr.& Ind., Psychol.Abstr., Rural Recreat.Tour.Abstr., Soc.Sci.Ind., Sociol.Abstr. (1964-) SSCI, Stud.Wom.Abstr., World Agri.Econ.& Rural Sociol.Abstr.
   —BLDSC shelfmark: 3044.650000.
   Description: Carries articles, commentaries and book reviews on key research findings and the current theoretical debates in the social sciences.

CASE ANALYSIS; in social science and social therapy. see *SOCIAL SCIENCES: COMPREHENSIVE WORKS*

CATALYST (TORONTO). see *POLITICAL SCIENCE — Civil Rights*

301.15   US
CENTER FOCUS. 1971. bi-m. $15. Center of Concern, 3700 13th St., N.E., Washington, DC 20017. TEL 202-635-2757. FAX 202-832-9494. Ed. John Prendergast. adv.; bk.rev.; circ. 21,000. **Indexed:** CERDIC, HR Rep.

301   US
CENTER FOR SOCIAL POLICY AND PRACTICE IN THE WORKPLACE NEWSLETTER. s-a. $6. Center for Social Policy and Practice in the Workplace, School of Social Work, Columbia University, 622 W. 113th St., New York, NY 10025. TEL 212-280-5173. FAX 212-932-7817. circ. 1,000.
   Description: Devoted to improving social policy, mental health, and rehabilitative services for working people.

CENTRE D'ETUDES ETHNOLOGIQUES. PUBLICATIONS. SERIE 2: MEMOIRES ET MONOGRAPHIES. see *ANTHROPOLOGY*

CENTRE D'ETUDES ETHNOLOGIQUES BANDUNDU. PUBLICATIONS. see *ANTHROPOLOGY*

SOCIOLOGY

301.45 **SA**
CENTRE FOR INTERGROUP STUDIES. ANNUAL REPORT. Variant title: Abe Bailey Institute of Inter-Racial Studies. Annual Report. (Text in English) 1968. a. free. Centre for Intergroup Studies, 37 Grotto Rd., Rondebosch, South Africa. TEL 021-6502503. FAX 021-6852142. TELEX 5-21439. Ed. H.W. van der Merwe. bibl.; circ. 2,200 (controlled).

CENTRE FOR URBAN AND COMMUNITY STUDIES. BIBLIOGRAPHIC SERIES. see *HOUSING AND URBAN PLANNING*

CENTRE FOR URBAN AND COMMUNITY STUDIES. MAJOR REPORT SERIES. see *HOUSING AND URBAN PLANNING*

CENTRE FOR URBAN AND COMMUNITY STUDIES. RESEARCH PAPERS. see *HOUSING AND URBAN PLANNING*

301 330.9 **BO**
CENTRO DE ESTUDIOS DE LA REALIDAD ECONOMICA Y SOCIAL. SERIE COCHABAMBA. irreg., no.6, 1985. Centro de Estudios de la Realidad Economica y Social, Casilla 10018, La Paz, Bolivia. TEL (tel.) 321643.

CENTRO DE ESTUDIOS DE LA REALIDAD ECONOMICA Y SOCIAL. SERIE ESTUDIOS REGIONALES. see *BUSINESS AND ECONOMICS — Economic Situation And Conditions*

301.35 330.9 **BO**
CENTRO DE ESTUDIOS DE LA REALIDAD ECONOMICA Y SOCIAL. SERIE ESTUDIOS URBANOS. irreg., no.9, 1982. Centro de Estudios de la Realidad Economica y Social, Casilla 10018, La Paz, Bolivia.

301 330.9 **BO**
CENTRO DE ESTUDIOS DE LA REALIDAD ECONOMICA Y SOCIAL. SERIE MOVIMIENTOS SOCIALES. irreg., no.3, 1985. Centro de Estudios de la Realidad Economica y Social, Casilla 10018, La Paz, Bolivia. TEL (tel.) 321643.

301.364 **AG** **ISSN 0326-8470**
CENTRO DE ESTUDIOS URBANOS Y REGIONALES. BOLETIN. 1986. 2/yr. $4. Ediciones C E U R, Av. Corrientes 2835, Cuerpo A, Piso 7-A, 1193 Buenos Aires, Argentina. TEL 961-8593. circ. 500.
Description: Articles and research news on urban and regional development.

301.364 **AG** **ISSN 0326-1417**
HT395.A7
CENTRO DE ESTUDIOS URBANOS Y REGIONALES. CUADERNOS. 1982. irreg. Ediciones C E U R, Av. Corrientes 2835, Piso 7 A, 1193 Buenos Aires, Argentina. TEL 961-8593. circ. 500.
Description: Monographs and short research reports on urban and regional social problems.

301.364 **AG**
CENTRO DE ESTUDIOS URBANOS Y REGIONALES. INFORMES DE INVESTIGACION. 1985. irreg. Ediciones C E U R, Av. Corrientes 2835, Piso 7 A, 1193 Buenos Aires, Argentina. TEL 961-8593. circ. 500.
Description: Research reports on Argentine and Latin American development process on urban and regional problems.

980 301 **UY**
HC121
CENTRO LATINOAMERICANO DE ECONOMIA HUMANA. PUBLICACIONES. 1958; N.S. 1976. 3/yr. Urg.$15,500($18) Centro Latinoamericano de Economia Humana, Zelmar Michelini 1220, Casilla de Correo 5021, 11100 Montevideo, Uruguay. adv.; bk.rev.; charts; tr.lit.; index, cum.index; circ. 2,000.
Formerly: Cuadernos Latinoamericanos de Economia Humana (ISSN 0011-2526)

301.4 **US**
CHANGING ISSUES IN THE FAMILY. 1981. irreg. price varies. Praeger Publishers (Subsidiary of: Greenwood Publishing Group Inc.), 88 Post Rd. W., Box 5007, Westport, CT 06881-5007. TEL 203-226-3571. FAX 203-222-1502.

301 **US** **ISSN 0300-6921**
F548.9.N3
CHICAGO REPORTER; a monthly information service on racial issues in metropolitan Chicago. 1972. m. $38. Community Renewal Society, 332 S. Michigan, Chicago, IL 60604-4301. TEL 312-427-4830. FAX 312-427-6130. Ed. Roy Larson. bk.rev.; illus.; index; circ. 3,500.
Description: Reports and comments on the social, economic and political issues of metropolitan Chicago, with a special focus on race and poverty.

CHILD ABUSE & NEGLECT; the international journal. see *CHILDREN AND YOUTH — About*

150 301 **US** **ISSN 0738-0151**
HV701 **CODEN: CASWDD**
CHILD AND ADOLESCENT SOCIAL WORK JOURNAL. 1983. bi-m. $185 (foreign $215). Human Sciences Press, Inc. (Subsidiary of: Plenum Publishing Corp.), 233 Spring St., New York, NY 10013-1578. TEL 212-620-8000. FAX 212-463-0742. Ed. Florence Lieberman. adv.; bibl. (reprint service avail. UMI) Indexed: Adol.Ment.Hlth.Abstr., ASSIA, Child Devel.Abstr., Lang.& Lang.Behav.Abstr., Psychol.Abstr., Soc.Work Res.& Abstr.
—BLDSC shelfmark: 3172.914000.
Supersedes (1972?-1981): Family and Child Mental Health Journal (ISSN 0190-230X); Which was formerly: Issues in Child Mental Health (ISSN 0362-403X); (until vol.5, 1977): Psychosocial Process (ISSN 0556-431X)
Description: Focuses on clinical social work practice with children, adolescents, and their families.
Refereed Serial

CHINA REPORT: POLITICAL, SOCIOLOGICAL, AND MILITARY AFFAIRS. see *POLITICAL SCIENCE*

301 **US** **ISSN 0895-4690**
CHINESE AMERICAN FORUM; a cultural bridge and nationwide communication. 1984. q. $12 to individuals; institutions $16. Chinese American Forum, Inc., 606 Brantford Ave., Silver Spring, MD 20904. TEL 301-622-3053. (Subscr. to: Box 4487, Silver Spring, MD 20904) Ed. S. Yen Lee. adv.; bk.rev.; circ. 500. (back issues avail.)
—BLDSC shelfmark: 3180.270350.

301 572 **US** **ISSN 0009-4625**
HM1
CHINESE SOCIOLOGY AND ANTHROPOLOGY; a journal of translations. 1968. q. $260 to institutions. M. E. Sharpe, Inc., 80 Business Park Dr., Armonk, NY 10504. TEL 914-273-1800. FAX 914-273-2106. adv.; index. (back issues avail.) Indexed: Curr.Cont., Lang.& Lang.Behav.Abstr., SSCI, Stud.Wom.Abstr.
—BLDSC shelfmark: 3181.100000.
Refereed Serial

174.24 **US**
CHOICE IN DYING. (Former names of issuing body: Concern for Dying; Concern for Dying - Society for the Right to Die) 1975. 4/yr. $15. Choice in Dying, Inc., 200 Varick St., New York, NY 10014. TEL 212-246-6973. Ed. Julia Curry. bk.rev.; illus.; circ. 160,000.
Former titles: Concern for Dying - Society for the Right to Die Newsletter; Concern for Dying Newsletter; Euthanasia News.

200 917.306 **US** **ISSN 1040-8622**
CHRISTIAN IRELAND TODAY. 1987. m. free. Christian Ireland Ministries Inc., Box 11057, Albany, NY 12211. TEL 518-329-3003. Ed. Rev. Francis G. McCloskey. circ. 763. (back issues avail.)
Description: Deals with issues of reconciliation, violence and non-violence, and cross-cultural cooperation.

CHRISTIAN JEWISH RELATIONS. see *RELIGIONS AND THEOLOGY*

CHRISTIAN SOCIAL ACTION. see *RELIGIONS AND THEOLOGY — Protestant*

CHRISTLICHE DEMOKRATIE; Vierteljahresschrift fuer Zeitgeschichte, Sozial-, Kultur- und Wirtschaftsgeschichte. see *HISTORY — History Of Europe*

CHURCH AND SOCIETY. see *RELIGIONS AND THEOLOGY — Protestant*

301 340 **II**
CITIZEN ACTION. 1981. q. Rs.480($77) K.K. Roy (Private) Ltd., 55 Geriahat Rd., P.O. Box 10210, Calcutta 700 019, India. Ed. Dr. K.K. Roy. **Indexed:** HR Rep.

CIVILIAN CONGRESS; includes a directory of persons holding executive branch-military office in Congress contrary to constitutional prohibition (Art.1, Sec.6, Cl.2) of concurrent office-holding. see *LAW*

301 **BE** **ISSN 0009-8140**
AP1
CIVILISATIONS; revue international de sciences humaines et des civilisation differerentes. (Text in English, French) 1951. s-a. 1280 Fr. (foreign 1340Fr.)(effective 1992). Universite Libre de Bruxelles, Institut de Sociologie, 44 Av. Jeanne, 1050 Brussels, Belgium. TEL 2-650-3521. FAX 2-650-3359. TELEX 23069 UNILIB B. Ed.Bd. bk.rev.; bibl.; index; circ. 1,000. (reprint service avail. from SWZ) Indexed: A.B.C.Pol.Sci., A.I.C.P., Amer.Hist.& Life, Bull.Signal., E.I., Hist.Abstr., Mid.East: Abstr.& Ind., Rural Recreat.Tour.Abstr., Sociol.Abstr., World Agri.Econ. & Rural Sociol.Abstr.

301 **FR**
CIVILISATIONS DE L'EUROPE CENTRALE ET DU SUD-EST. irreg., latest no.8. price varies. Institut National des Langues et Civilisations Orientales, 2 rue de Lille, 75343 Paris Cedex 07, France. TEL 49-26-42-74. Ed. Catherine Durandin.

301 **US** **ISSN 0730-840X**
HM1
CLINICAL SOCIOLOGY REVIEW. 1982. a. $18. (Sociological Practice Association) Michigan State University Press, 25 Manly Miles Bldg., 1405 S. Harrison Rd., East Lansing, MI 48823-5202. TEL 517-355-9543. Ed. Susan Eve. bk.rev.; circ. 750. **Indexed:** Psychol.Abstr., Soc.Work Res.& Abstr., Sociol.Abstr. (1965-).
Description: Essays concerning the practice of sociology.

301 **SP**
COLECCION FUNDACION F O E S S A. SERIE ESTUDIOS. 1969. irreg. (Fundacion Fomento de Estudios Sociales y Sociologia Aplicada) Euramerica, S.A., Mateo Inurria, 15, Madrid-16, Spain. bibl.; charts.

COLLECTIVE VOICE; a multi-issue magazine of politics and culture. see *POLITICAL SCIENCE*

COLORADO HOMES & LIFESTYLES. see *INTERIOR DESIGN AND DECORATION*

COLORADO KAIROS. see *RELIGIONS AND THEOLOGY*

COLUMBIA JOURNAL OF LAW AND SOCIAL PROBLEMS. see *LAW*

COLUMBIANA; bioregional journal for the Intermountain Northwest. see *CONSERVATION*

COMMON GROUND. see *RELIGIONS AND THEOLOGY*

301.45 **US** **ISSN 0010-3772**
COMMUNITY (CHICAGO). 1941. q. $4. Friendship House, 1746 W. Division Ave., Chicago, IL 60622. TEL 312-227-5065. FAX 312-227-5065. Ed. Albert Schorsch, III. adv.; bk.rev.; illus.; circ. 2,500. (also avail. in microform from UMI)
Description: External house organ for Friendship House, serving the homeless and needy. Focuses on race relations.

360 301.34 **AT** **ISSN 0814-401X**
COMMUNITY QUARTERLY; leading journal of community development case studies. 1984. q. Aus.$24 to individuals; institutions Aus.$26; students Aus.$18; foreign Aus.$38. P.O. Box 1042, Windsor, Vic. 3181, Australia. TEL 03-524-3384. (Co-sponsor: Employ-Working Effectively Inc.) Eds. Rod Williams, Chris Morris. adv.; bk.rev.; circ. 1,000.
Description: Publishes practical articles about community development.

SOCIOLOGY

300   US   ISSN 0277-6189
COMMUNITY SERVICE NEWSLETTER. 1943. bi-m. $25. Community Service, Inc., Box 243, Yellow Springs, OH 45387. TEL 513-767-2161. Ed. Jane Morgan. bk.rev.; circ. 350. (back issues avail.) **Indexed:** New Per.Ind.
    Formerly: Community Comments (ISSN 0010-3780)
    Description: Essays, commentary, book reviews, and announcements pertaining to the growth of small communities as a basic social institution that encompasses units of economic, social, and spiritual development.

301 572   US   ISSN 0733-4540
CB3
COMPARATIVE CIVILIZATIONS REVIEW. 1973. biennial. $20. International Society for the Comparative Study of Civilizations, Department of Sociology, Dickinson College, Carlisle, PA 17013. (Subscr. to: Stephanie Waldbauer, Program in Comparative Literature, The University of Illinois, Urbana, IL 61801) Eds. Wayne Bledsoe, Vytautas Kavolis. adv.; bk.rev.; circ. 500. **Indexed:** Abstr.Engl.Stud., Arts & Hum.Cit.Ind., Curr.Cont., M.L.A., Sociol.Abstr.
    —BLDSC shelfmark: 3363.752700.

301   US   ISSN 0195-6310
HM1
COMPARATIVE SOCIAL RESEARCH. 1978. a. $63.50 to institutions. J A I Press Inc., 55 Old Post Rd., No. 2, Box 1678, Greenwich, CT 06836-1678. TEL 203-661-7602. Ed. Richard A. Tomasson. **Indexed:** Lang.& Lang.Behav.Abstr.
    —BLDSC shelfmark: 3363.820000.
    Formerly (until vol.2): Comparative Studies in Sociology (ISSN 0164-1247)

300 900   UK   ISSN 0010-4175
H1
COMPARATIVE STUDIES IN SOCIETY AND HISTORY; an international quarterly. 1959. 4/yr. $32 to individuals; institutions $70. Cambridge University Press, Edinburgh Bldg., Shaftesbury Rd., Cambridge CB2 2RU, England. TEL 0223-312393. FAX 0223-315052. TELEX 851817256. (North American orders to: Cambridge University Press, 40 W. 20th St., New York, NY 10011. TEL 212-924-2900) Ed. Raymond Grew. adv.; bk.rev.; bibl.; charts; illus.; index. (also avail. in microform from UMI; reprint service avail. from SWZ) **Indexed:** A.B.C.Pol.Sci., A.I.C.P., Acad.Ind., Amer.Hist.& Life, Arts & Hum.Cit.Ind., ASSIA, Curr.Cont., E.I., Geo.Abstr., Hist.Abstr., Hum.Ind., Lang.& Lang.Behav.Abstr., Mid.East: Abstr.& Ind., Rural Recreat.Tour.Abstr., Sociol.Abstr., Sociol.Abstr., SSCI, World Agri.Econ.& Rural Sociol.Abstr.
    —BLDSC shelfmark: 3363.850000.
    Description: Compares change and stability in societies all over the world and in all eras: topics such as slavery, colonialism, revolution, religious movements, women's roles.

301   US   ISSN 0892-5569
HT110
COMPARATIVE URBAN AND COMMUNITY RESEARCH. a. $19.95. Transaction Publishers, Transaction Periodicals Consortium, Department 3092, Rutgers University, New Brunswick, NJ 08903. TEL 908-932-2280. FAX 908-932-3138. Ed. Michael Smith.
    —BLDSC shelfmark: 3363.878000.
    Description: Interdisciplinary review of theoretical, empirical, and applied research on the process of urbanization and community change throughout the world.

301   AG
CONCEPTOS BOLETIN. 1912. bi-m. Museo Social Argentino, Corrientes 1723, 1042 Buenos Aires, Argentina. Ed.Bd. bk.rev.; abstr.; bibl.
    Formerly: Museo Social Argentino. Boletin (ISSN 0045-3331)

301   US   ISSN 0899-9910
CONFLICT AND CONSCIOUSNESS: STUDIES IN WAR, PEACE AND SOCIAL THOUGHT. irreg. Peter Lang Publishing, Inc., 62 W. 45th St., 4th Fl., New York, NY 10036. TEL 212-302-6740. FAX 212-302-7574. Ed. Charles P. Webel.
    Description: Discusses topics on individual consciousness, personal and collective belief systems, and social practices involving coercion and violence.

CONFRONTATION - CHANGE REVIEW. see *BUSINESS AND ECONOMICS*

CONSERVATIVE REVIEW. see *POLITICAL SCIENCE*

CONTEMPORARY FAMILY THERAPY; an international journal. see *PSYCHOLOGY*

CONTEMPORARY GERMAN STUDIES: OCCASIONAL PAPERS. see *LITERATURE*

301   UK   ISSN 0069-942X
CONTEMPORARY ISSUES SERIES. 1969. a. Peter Owen Ltd., 73 Kenway Rd., London SW5 0RE, England. (Dist. in U.S. by: Humanities Press Inc., 450 Park Ave. So., New York, NY 10010)

301.15   US
CONTEMPORARY STUDIES IN APPLIED BEHAVIORAL SCIENCE. 1983. irreg., vol.4, 1986. $58.50 to institutions. J A I Press Inc., 55 Old Post Rd., No. 2, Box 1678, Greenwich, CT 06836-1678. TEL 203-661-7602. Ed. Louis A. Zurcher. bibl.; index.

301   US
CONTEMPORARY STUDIES IN SOCIOLOGY. irreg., vol.6, 1986. $58.50 to institutions. J A I Press Inc., 55 Old Post Rd., No. 2, Box 1678, Greenwich, CT 06836-1678. TEL 203-661-7602. Ed. John Clark.

301   US   ISSN 1056-1072
H1   CODEN: CDSSEN
▼**CONTENTION;** a journal of debates in society, culture, and science. 1991. 3/yr. $45. Indiana University Press, Journals Division, 601 N. Morton St., Bloomington, IN 47404. TEL 812-855-9449. FAX 812-855-7931. Ed. Nikki Keddie.
    Description: Provides a forum for debates on issues and trends in the social sciences, humanities, and natural sciences. The emphasis is on controversies to increase understanding of key issues.

CONTINUITY AND CHANGE; a journal of social structure, law and demography in past societies. see *POPULATION STUDIES*

301.4   US   ISSN 0147-1023
CONTRIBUTIONS IN FAMILY STUDIES. 1977. irreg., no.22, 1992. price varies. Greenwood Press, Inc. (Subsidiary of: Greenwood Publishing Group Inc.), 88 Post Rd. W., Box 5007, Westport, CT 06881-5007. TEL 203-226-3571. FAX 203-222-1502. Ed. Carol V.R. George.

301.4   US   ISSN 0147-1031
CONTRIBUTIONS IN INTERCULTURAL AND COMPARATIVE STUDIES. 1976. irreg. price varies. Greenwood Press, Inc. (Subsidiary of: Greenwood Publishing Group Inc.), 88 Post Rd. W., Box 5007, Westport, CT 06881-5007. TEL 203-226-3571. FAX 203-222-1502. Ed. Ann M. Pescatello.
    —BLDSC shelfmark: 3458.750000.

301   US   ISSN 0084-9278
CONTRIBUTIONS IN SOCIOLOGY. 1970. irreg., no.97, 1992. price varies. Greenwood Press, Inc. (Subsidiary of: Greenwood Publishing Group Inc.), 88 Post Rd. W., Box 5007, Westport, CT 06881-5007. TEL 203-226-3571. FAX 203-222-1502. Ed. Don Martindale.
    —BLDSC shelfmark: 3461.440000.

301   US   ISSN 0069-9667
CONTRIBUTIONS TO INDIAN SOCIOLOGY. (Text in English) N.S. 1957. s-a. $28 to individuals; institutions $62. (Institute of Economic Growth, Delhi, Asian Research Center, II) Sage Publications, Inc., 2455 Teller Rd., Newbury Park, CA 91320. TEL 805-499-0721. FAX 805-499-0871. (And: Sage Publications Pvt. Ltd., P.O. Box 4215, New Delhi 110-048, India) Ed. T.N. Madan. adv.; bk.rev.; circ. 800. **Indexed:** A.I.C.P., Rural Devel.Abstr, Sociol.Abstr. (1985-).

CONTRIBUTIONS TO THE STUDY OF POPULAR CULTURE. see *ANTHROPOLOGY*

362 301.4   US
CO-OP NETWORKER. bi-m. free. St. John's Mercy Medical Center, 615 S. New Ballas Rd., St. Louis, MO 63141. TEL 314-569-6010. Ed. Richard P. Johnson.

334   JA
COOPERATIVE LIFE/GEKKAN KYODOTAI. (Text in Japanese) 1963. m. 1000 Yen($5) Japanese Commune Movement, 2083 Sakae-cho, Imaichi-shi, Tochigi-ken 321-12, Japan. Ed. Hisao Okumura. adv.; bk.rev.; abstr.; charts; stat.; index; circ. 1,000.
    Formerly: Gekkan Kibbutz (ISSN 0016-5956)

301   US
CORPORATE COMMUNITY RELATIONS NEWSLETTER; the newsletter for the community relations professionals. 1986. m. (except combined May-Jun., Jul.-Aug.). $115. Boston College, Center for Corporate Community Relations, 36 College Rd., Chestnut Hill, MA 02167-3835. TEL 617-552-4545. FAX 617-552-8499. Ed. Susan Thomas. bk.rev.; cum.index: 1989-1991; circ. 1,200. (back issues avail.)
    Description: Trends and issues affecting corporations and how they react on society.

301   IT
CORSO DI SOCIOLOGIA. 1974; N.S. 1992. m. L.60000($60) to individuals; institutions L.60000($50). Centro Studi Terzo Mondo, Via G.B. Morgagni 39, 20129 Milan, Italy. TEL 39-2-29409041. Ed. Umberto Melotti. adv.; circ. 4,000.
    Description: Monographs on sociological, anthropological and sociobiological issues at the center of today's debate.

301   US
COUNTRY LADY'S DAYBOOK - COUNTRY CLASSIFIED.* 1975. m. $5. c/o Schultz, 12270 Volver Ave., Felton, CA 95018-8947. bibl.; illus.
    Formerly: Country Lady's Daybook; Incorporates: Country Classified.

361 300   US
COURAGE IN THE STRUGGLE FOR JUSTICE AND PEACE. 1986. 10/yr. free. United Church of Christ, Office for Church Society, 110 Maryland Ave., N.E., Washington, DC 20002. TEL 202-543-1517. bk.rev.; circ. 16,000. (back issues avail.)
    Description: Covers social justice issues.

301 370.15 150   US
CREATIVE INTELLIGENCE ENHANCEMENT. (Text in English, Japanese) q. price varies. Innovation Institute Inc., 4405 East-West Hwy., Bethesda, MD 20814. TEL 301-654-1100. adv.; bk.rev. (back issues avail.)
    Description: Covers methods for which to increase creative intelligence, and how culture affects creative insight.

CRIMINAL JUSTICE (SAN DIEGO); opposing viewpoints sources. see *CRIMINOLOGY AND LAW ENFORCEMENT*

301   IT   ISSN 0011-1546
HM7
CRITICA SOCIOLOGICA. (Text in Italian; summaries in English) 1967. q. L.50000($45) (foreign L.100000($90))(effective 1992). S I A R E S, Corso Vittorio Emanuele 24, 00186 Rome, Italy. TEL 06-6786760. Ed. Franco Ferrarotti. adv.; bk.rev.; bibl.; illus.; circ. 3,500. (also avail. in microform from UMI; reprint service avail. from UMI) **Indexed:** Lang.& Lang.Behav.Abstr., Sociol.Abstr. (1967-).
    —BLDSC shelfmark: 3487.410000.

CRITICAL SOCIOLOGY. see *LITERARY AND POLITICAL REVIEWS*

CRITIQUE OF ANTHROPOLOGY; a journal for the critical reconstruction of anthropology. see *ANTHROPOLOGY*

309 330.9   BE   ISSN 0770-0075
CRITIQUE REGIONALE; cahiers de sociologie et d'economie regionales. 1979. irreg. 1300 Fr. (Universite Libre de Bruxelles, Institut de Sociologie) Centre de Sociologie et d'Economie Regionales, 12 rue des Canoniers, B-1400 Nivelles, Belgium. FAX 02-642-3521. (Co-sponsor: Comite pour l'Etude des Problemes de l'Emploi et du Chomage)
    —BLDSC shelfmark: 3487.490400.

| 800 320 | CN | ISSN 0704-6588 |

CROSSCURRENTS. 1973. m. Can.$10. Greenwich, 516 Ave. K. South, Saskatoon, Sask., Canada. TEL 306-244-0679. Ed. Robert Fink. bk.rev.; circ. 500.
 Description: A newsletter on politics, peace, the environment, music and art.

CUADERNOS C I P C A (SERIE POPULAR). see *EDUCATION — Adult Education*

| 301 | SP | ISSN 0302-7724 |
| HN1 | | |

CUADERNOS DE REALIDADES SOCIALES. Short title: R S. 1973. irreg. 1500 ptas.($20) Instituto de Sociologia Aplicada de Madrid, Claudio Coello 141, Madrid-6, Spain. TEL 2620239. Ed. Jesus Maria Vazquez. bk.rev.; bibl.; circ. 1,000. (also avail. in microform; back issues avail.) Indexed: Sociol.Abstr. (1973-).
 Description: Covers social issues in Spain and around the world.

| 301 | NQ | ISSN 1010-528X |
| HN161 | | |

CUADERNOS DE SOCIOLOGIA. 1986. 3/yr. $20 (foreign $30). Universidad Centroamericana, Escuela de Sociologia, Apdo. 69, Managua, Nicaragua. TEL 703523 ext.292. (Co-sponsor: Asociacion Nicaraguense de Cientificos Sociales) Ed.Bd. adv.; circ. 3,000.

| 301 | | US |

CULT OBSERVER; toward an awareness of cultism in society. 1979. 10/yr. $30. American Family Foundation, Box 2265, Bonita Springs, FL 33959. TEL 212-249-7693. Ed. Robert E. Schecter. bk.rev.; circ. 1,000. (back issues avail.)
 Formerly: Advisor (Weston).

| 301 | | US | ISSN 0748-6499 |

CULTIC STUDIES JOURNAL; a journal on cults and manipulative techniques of social influence. 1984. s-a. $15 to individuals; institutions $22 (foreign $25). American Family Foundation, Box 2265, Bonita Springs, FL 33959. TEL 212-249-7693. Ed. Michael D. Langune. circ. 350. **Indexed:** Psychol.Abstr.
—BLDSC shelfmark: 3491.616700.

| 301.2 | UK | ISSN 0950-2386 |
| | | CODEN: CUSTE9 |

CULTURAL STUDIES.* 1987. 3/yr. £20($38) to individuals; institutions £37($60). Methuen Educational, Micheline Houseane, 81 Fulham Rd, London SW3 6RB, England. TEL 583 9855. Ed. John Fiske.
—BLDSC shelfmark: 3491.668420.
 Description: Provides a forum where academics, researchers, students and practitioners can consider and review patterns of power and meaning in contemporary culture, and focus for work in the interlocking areas of media, communication and cultural studies.

CULTURAL SURVIVAL. OCCASIONAL PAPERS. see *ANTHROPOLOGY*

CULTURAL SURVIVAL QUARTERLY. see *ANTHROPOLOGY*

CULTURAL SURVIVAL REPORT. see *ANTHROPOLOGY*

| 301 947 | FR | ISSN 0765-0213 |

CULTURES ET SOCIETE DE L'EST. 1985. irreg. price varies. Institut d'Etudes Slaves, 9 rue Michelet, F-75006 Paris, France. TEL 43-26-50-89. (Co-sponsor: Institut du Monde Sovietique et de l'Europe Centrale et Orientale)

| 301 | | US | ISSN 0278-1204 |
| HM1 | | | |

CURRENT PERSPECTIVES IN SOCIAL THEORY; a research annual. 1980. a. $63.50 to institutions. J A I Press Inc., 55 Old Post Rd., No. 2, Box 1678, Greenwich, CT 06836-1678. TEL 203-661-7602. Ed. John Wilson. **Indexed:** Lang.& Lang.Behav.Abstr., Sociol.Abstr. (1980-), SSCI.

| 301 | UK | ISSN 0011-3921 |
| Z7161 | | |

CURRENT SOCIOLOGY/SOCIOLOGIE CONTEMPORAINE. (Text in English and French) 1952. 3/yr. £29($48) to individuals; institutions £74($122). (International Sociological Association) Sage Publications Ltd., 6 Bonhill St., London EC2A 4PU, England. TEL 071-374-0645. FAX 071-374-8741. Ed. William Outhwaite. adv.: color page #190; trim 177 x 101; adv. contact: Bernie Folan. (reprint service avail. from KTO) Indexed: ASSIA, Curr.Cont., E.I., Int.Lab.Doc., Key to Econ.Sci., Lang.& Lang.Behav.Abstr., Mid.East: Abstr.& Ind., P.A.I.S., Psychol.Abstr., Soc.Sci.Ind., Sociol.Abstr. (1958-), Sportsearch, SSCI.
—BLDSC shelfmark: 3504.033000.
 Description: Focuses on the theory, research and methodology of contemporary international sociology. Each issue is devoted to a substantial Trend Report on a particular sociological topic.

CZLOWIEK I SPOLECZENSTWO. see *PSYCHOLOGY*

| 361 | US | ISSN 0164-1867 |

D R C HISTORICAL AND COMPARATIVE DISASTERS SERIES. 1977. irreg., no.7, 1987. University of Delaware, Disaster Research Center, Newark, DE 19716. TEL 302-451-6618. FAX 302-451-2828. TELEX 70 99 85.

D W D NEWSLETTER. (Death with Dignity) see *LAW*

| 301 649 | | US |

DADS ONLY. 1978. bi-m. (plus s-a. audio cassette tape: Dad Talk). $18.50. Family Development Foundation, Box 340, Julian, CA 92036. Ed. Paul Lewis. bk.rev.; circ. 20,000. (also avail. in audio cassette; talking book)
 Description: News, fathering, child development, marriage, and family living tips for busy dads.

| 301.2 | | RU |

DAGESTANSKII ETNOGRAFICHESKII SBORNIK. 1974. irreg. 1.49 Rub. Akademiya Nauk S.S.S.R., Dagestanskii Filial, Institut Istorii, Yazyka i Literatury, Prospekt Kalinina 77-b, kv.19, 367012 Makhachkala, Dagestan A.S., Russia. illus.

| 301 297 | | PH |

DANSALAN QUARTERLY. 1979. q. P.100($10) Dansalan College Foundation, Inc., Gowing Memorial Research Center, Marawi City 9700, Philippines.
 Description: Covers the Muslim regions of Mindanao and Sulu and the Maranao peoples.

| 301 | DK | ISSN 0905-5908 |

▼**DANSK SOCIOLOGI.** (Text in Danish; summaries in English) 1990. q. DKK 300 to individuals; institutions DKK 440. Danish Sociological Association, Copenhagen Business School, Nansensgade 19, Third Floor, DK-1366 Copenhagen K, Denmark. TEL 33-144-41-08. FAX 33-14-11-28. Ed. Heine Andersen. bk.rev.; circ. 1,000.

| 301 301.412 615.7 | | BO |

DE TEXTOS. irreg., no.10, 1985. price varies. Centro de Investigaciones Sociales, Casilla 6931 - Correo Central, La Paz, Bolivia.

DEATH STUDIES; education-counseling-care-law-ethics. see *PSYCHOLOGY*

| 301 | | PE |

DEBATES EN SOCIOLOGIA. 1977. a. $6.40. Pontificia Universidad Catolica del Peru, Departamento de Ciencias Sociales, Fondo Editorial, Apdo. 1761, Lima 100, Peru. FAX 51-14-611785. Ed. Ana Ponce. charts; illus.

| 170 | | US |

DECENCY REPORTER. 1961. 3/yr. free. Children's Legal Foundation, 2845 E. Camelback Rd., Ste. 740, Phoenix, AZ 85016. TEL 602-381-1322. FAX 602-381-1613. Ed. Beth Sonlan. bk.rev.; circ. 30,000.
 Former titles: C D L Reporter; (until Jan. 1986): National Decency Reporter (ISSN 0027-9102)

DENMARK. SOCIALFORSKNINGSINSTITUTTET. PJECER. see *SOCIAL SERVICES AND WELFARE*

DESARROLLO DE BASE. see *BUSINESS AND ECONOMICS — International Development And Assistance*

DEUTSCHE JUGEND; Zeitschrift fuer die Jugendarbeit. see *CHILDREN AND YOUTH — About*

| 301.1 | SZ | ISSN 0378-7931 |
| HM291 | | |

DEVIANCE ET SOCIETE. (Text in French; abstracts in English and German) 1977. q. 65 SFr.($47) Editions Medecine et Hygiene, 78 Av. de la Roseraie, Case Postale 456, CH-1211 Geneva 4, Switzerland. TEL 022-469355. FAX 022-475610. Ed. Philippe Robert. Indexed: Crim.Just.Abstr.
—BLDSC shelfmark: 3579.099700.

| 301 | US | ISSN 0163-9625 |
| HM1 | | CODEN: DEBEDF |

DEVIANT BEHAVIOR; an interdisciplinary journal. 1979. q. $107. Hemisphere Publishing Corporation (Subsidiary of: Taylor & Francis Group), 1900 Frost Rd., Ste. 101, Bristol, PA 19007-1598. TEL 215-785-5800. FAX 215-785-5515. Ed. Clifton D. Bryant. adv.; bk.rev.; bibl.; charts; illus.; index; circ. 300. (also avail. in microfiche from UMI; back issues avail.; reprint service avail. from UMI) Indexed: Biol.Abstr., Crim.Just.Abstr., Curr.Cont., Lang.& Lang.Behav.Abstr., Psychol.Abstr., Sociol.Abstr., SSCI.
—BLDSC shelfmark: 3579.099900.
 Description: Scientific findings on cultural norm violations from a wide variety of perspectives. *Refereed Serial*

DIALOGO; quaderni Europei di dialogica. see *PHILOSOPHY*

| 301.4 | | CR |

DIALOGO.* q. free. Universidad de Costa Rica, Centro de Estudios Sociales y Poblacion, Ciudad Universitaria Rodrigo Facio, Apdo. 75, 2050 San Pedro Montes de Oca, San Jose, Costa Rica. Eds. Mario Julio Segura Vargas, Luis Montoya Salas. illus. Indexed: HR Rep.

| 301 320 | PN | ISSN 0046-0206 |
| HN1 | | |

DIALOGO SOCIAL. 1967. m. (except Jan.) Bl.8($35) Centro de Capacitacion Social, Apdo. 9a-192, Panama, Panama. TEL 26-6971. Ed.Bd. adv.; bk.rev.; film rev.; bibl.; illus.; stat.; index, cum.index: 1967-1977; circ. 7,800.

| 301 | FR | ISSN 0012-2297 |

DIALOGUER. no.10, 1969. bi-m. 120 F. Union Feminine Civique et Sociale, 6 rue Beranger, 75003 Paris, France. FAX 40-27-08-78. Ed. Ag. Planchais. adv.; bk.rev.; bibl.; charts; illus.; circ. 30,000.

| 301 | | II |

DIBRUGARH UNIVERSITY. CENTRE FOR SOCIOLOGICAL STUDY OF THE FRONTIER REGION. NORTH EASTERN RESEARCH BULLETIN. 1970. a. Rs.5. Dibrugarh University, Centre for Sociological Study of Frontier Region, Dept. of Sociology, Rajabheta, Dibrugarh, Assam, India. Ed. S.M. Dubey. bk.rev.; bibl.; circ. 500.

| 349 | FR | ISSN 0012-2513 |

DICTIONNAIRE PERMANENT SOCIAL. 1950. fortn. 1260.66 F. Editions Legislatives et Administratives, 80, ave. de la Marne, 92546 Montrouge Cedex, France. TEL 1-40-92-68-68. FAX 1-46-56-00-15. TELEX 632 855 F. bibl.; index, cum.index; circ. 14,000. (looseleaf format)
 Description: Provides information on labor laws and social security.

DIFFERENCES; a journal of feminist cultural studies. see *WOMEN'S STUDIES*

| 301 | UN | ISSN 0392-1921 |
| AS4 | | |

DIOGENES (ENGLISH EDITION). Chinese edition (ISSN 1000-6575); French edition: Diogene (ISSN 0419-1633); Spanish edition (ISSN 0012-3048) (Editions also avail. in: Arabic, Hindi, Japanese, Portuguese) 1953. q. $40 to individuals; institutions $80. (Unesco, International Council for Philosophy and Humanistic Studies) Berg Publishers, 150 Cowley Rd., Oxford OX4 1JJ, England. TEL 0865-245104. FAX 0865-791165. Ed. Jean d'Ormesson. adv.; bk.rev.; circ. 600. (also avail. in microfiche) Indexed: Arts & Hum.Cit.Ind., Curr.Cont., Hist.Abstr., Hum.Ind., M.L.A.

DIRECTORY OF UNPUBLISHED EXPERIMENTAL MENTAL MEASURES. see *PSYCHOLOGY*

SOCIOLOGY

301   UK   ISSN 0267-4645
HV1551   CODEN: DHSOEG
DISABILITY, HANDICAP & SOCIETY. 1986. 3/yr. $55 to individuals; institutions $164. Carfax Publishing Co., P.O. Box 25, Abingdon, Oxfordshire OX14 3UE, England. TEL 0235-555335. FAX 0235-553559. (U.S. subscr. addr.: Carfax Publishing Co., Box 2025, Dunnellon, FL 32630) Ed. Len Barton. adv.; bk.rev.; illus.; stat.; index, cum.index. (also avail. in microfiche) **Indexed:** ASSIA, Curr.Adv.Ecol.Sci., Psychol.Abstr., Sp.Ed.Needs Abstr., Stud.Wom.Abstr.
—BLDSC shelfmark: 3595.421000.

DISCOURSE & SOCIETY. see *PSYCHOLOGY*

301.428   US   ISSN 0012-4230
DIVORCE CHATS. 1961. irreg. membership. United States Divorce Reform, Inc., Box 243, Kenwood, CA 95452. TEL 707-833-2550. Ed. George Partis. bk.rev.; circ. 1,500. (processed)

301.4   BO
DOCUMENTOS INSTITUCIONALES OFICIALES. 1972. irreg., no.25, 1985. price varies. Centro de Investigaciones Sociales, Casilla 6931 - C.C., La Paz, Bolivia.

DOUBLE TALK (AMELIA); newsletter for parents of multiples. see *CHILDREN AND YOUTH — About*

DROIT ET SOCIETE; revue international de theorie du droit et de societie juridique. see *LAW*

301.2   US
DUBLIN SEMINAR FOR NEW ENGLAND FOLKLIFE. ANNUAL PROCEEDINGS. 1976. a. $10. (Dublin Seminar for New England Folklife) Boston University, Scholarly Publications, 985 Commonwealth Ave., Boston, MA 02215. TEL 617-353-4106. Ed. Peter Benes. adv.; bibl.; charts; illus.; index; circ. 1,500. (back issues avail.) **Indexed:** Avery Ind.Archit.Per.

DUISBURGER STUDIEN; Geistes- und Gesellschaftswissenschaften. see *PHILOSOPHY*

379
DURAN-DURAN. 1966. q. Aus.$4. Aboriginal Education Council, 132 St. John's Road, Glebe, N.S.W. 2037, Australia. Ed. F. Paterson. bk.rev.; circ. 700.

301   AT   ISSN 0310-222X
EARTH GARDEN. 1972. q. Aus.$16. RmB 427, Trntham, Vic. 3458, Australia. FAX 054-241743. Ed. A.G. Thomas. adv.; bk.rev.; circ. 18,000. (also avail. in microfiche) **Indexed:** Gdlns, Pinpointer.

EAST EUROPE REPORT. see *POLITICAL SCIENCE*

ECONOMIA E SOCIOLOGIA. see *BUSINESS AND ECONOMICS — Economic Situation And Conditions*

301.4 330   IT
ECONOMIA, SOCIETA E ISTITUZIONI. 1989. 3/yr. L.50000. (Libera Universita Internazionale degli Studi Sociali) Maggioli Editore, Via Crimea, 1, Casella Postale 290, 47037 Rimini, Italy. TEL 0541-741002. Eds. Giovanni Palmerio, Carlo Scognamiglio.

ECONOMIC DEVELOPMENT AND CULTURAL CHANGE. see *BUSINESS AND ECONOMICS — International Development And Assistance*

ECORISSA. see *BUSINESS AND ECONOMICS*

301   UK
EDINBURGH STUDIES IN CULTURE AND SOCIETY. irreg. (approx. 2 vols./yr.). price varies. Macmillan Press Ltd., Houndmills, Basingstoke, Hampshire RG21 2XS, England. TEL 0256-29242. FAX 0256-479476. Ed.Bd.
—Formerly: Edinburgh Studies in Sociology.

EDUCATION AND SOCIETY JOURNAL. see *EDUCATION*

EDUCATION AND URBAN SOCIETY. see *EDUCATION*

ELLIS ISLAND SERIES: IMMIGRATION AND THE PLURALIST SOCIETY. see *HISTORY — History Of North And South America*

EMIGRE; non-stop design - the magazine that ignores boundaries. see *ART*

301   NE
EMMAUS; honger en dorst. 1958. 3/yr. fl.10. Stichting Emmaus Nederland, P.O. Box 175, 3720 AD Bilthoven, Netherlands. circ. 2,000.
—Formerly: Honger en Dorst.
Description: Articles about the Emmaus movement in the Netherlands and worldwide.

ENCYCLOPEDIA OF WORLD PROBLEMS AND HUMAN POTENTIAL. see *POLITICAL SCIENCE — International Relations*

301   US
ENCYCLOPEDIC DICTIONARY OF SOCIOLOGY. irreg., 3rd ed., 1985. $12.95. Dushkin Publishing Group, Inc., Sluice Dock, Guilford, CT 06437-9989. TEL 203-453-4351. FAX 203-453-6000. Ed. Richard Lachmann. illus.

ENQUIRY. see *POLITICAL SCIENCE*

301   GW   ISSN 0721-2178
ENTWICKLUNG UND ZUSAMMENARBEIT. (Editions in English, French, German and Spanish) 1965. m. DM.33. (Deutsche Stiftung fuer Internationale Entwickung) Nomos Verlagsgesellschaft mbH und Co. KG, Hans-Boeckler-Str. 5, 5300 Bonn 3, Germany. (Co-sponsor: Carl Duisberg Gesellschaft) Ed. Inga Krugmann-Randolf. adv.; bk.rev.; circ. 16,500.

301.3   US   ISSN 0013-9165
HM206   CODEN: EVBHAF
ENVIRONMENT AND BEHAVIOR. 1969. bi-m. $55 to individuals; institutions $148. (Environmental Design Research Association) Sage Publications, Inc., 2455 Teller Rd., Newbury Park, CA 91320. TEL 805-499-0721. FAX 805-499-0871. (And Sage Publications, Ltd., 6 Bonhill St., London EC2A 4PU, England) Ed. Robert B. Bechtel. adv.; abstr.; charts; illus.; index; circ. 1,500. (also avail. in microfilm from UMI; reprint service avail. from UMI; back issues avail.) **Indexed:** ASSIA, Avery Ind.Archit.Per., C.I.J.E., Curr.Adv.Ecol.Sci., Curr.Cont. E.I., Energy Rev., Environ.Per.Bibl., Excerp.Med., INIS Atomind., Lang.& Lang.Behav.Abstr., Mag.Ind., Mar.Aff.Bibl., PHRA, Psychol.Abstr., Psycscan, Res.High.Educ.Abstr., Risk Abstr., Sage Fam.Stud.Abstr., Sage Urb.Stud.Abstr., Soc.Sci.Ind., Sociol.Abstr., SSCI.
—BLDSC shelfmark: 3791.097000.
Description: Discusses the interaction of the physical environment and human behavioral systems, and covers the study, design and control of the physical environment.

ENVIRONMENT AND PLANNING D: SOCIETY & SPACE. see *HOUSING AND URBAN PLANNING*

ERA SOCIALISTA. see *POLITICAL SCIENCE*

301   NE
ERASMUS UNIVERSITEIT, ROTTERDAM. CENTRUM VOOR MAATSCHAPPIJGESCHIEDENIS. MEDEDELINGEN/INFORMATION BULLETIN. 1978. irreg., no.7, 1979. Erasmus Universiteit, Rotterdam, Centrum voor Maatschappijgeschiedenis, Postbus 1738, Rotterdam, Netherlands.

301   HU   ISSN 0014-0120
ERGONOMIA; munkaelettan, munkalelektan, munkaszociologia. 1967. q. $34.50. (Koho- es Gepipari Miniszterium - Ministry of Industry) Struktura Szervezesi Vallalat, Budapest, Hungary. (Subscr. to: Kultura, Box 149, H-1389 Budapest, Hungary) Ed. Gyorgy Garamvolgyi. adv.; bk.rev.; circ. 2,500 (approx.). **Indexed:** C.I.S. Abstr., Ergon.Abstr.

ESPERANTO-DOKUMENTOJ. NOVA SERIO. see *LINGUISTICS*

309   BO
ESTUDIOS DE POBLACION Y DESARROLLO. 1974. irreg., no.29, 1985. price varies. Centro de Investigaciones Sociales, Casilla 6931 - C.C., La Paz, Bolivia.

301   BO
ESTUDIOS DE RECURSOS HUMANOS. 1978. irreg., no.10, 1985. Centro de Investigaciones Sociales, Casilla 6931 - C.C., La Paz, Bolivia.

301.4   BO
ESTUDIOS DE SOCIOLOGIA FAMILIAR. 1975. irreg., no.7, 1985. Centro de Investigaciones Sociales, Casilla 6931 - C.C., La Paz, Bolivia.

301   VE   ISSN 1013-4069
▼**ESTUDIOS DEL DESARROLLO/DEVELOPMENT STUDIES JOURNAL.** (Text in English, Spanish) 1990. a. Bs.500($20) (foreign $25) to individuals; institutions Bs. 1000 ($40)(foreign $50). Universidad Central de Venezuela, Centro de Estudios del Desarrollo, Apdo. Postal 6622, Caracas 1010-A, Venezuela. TEL 7523266. (U.S. subscr. addr: Poba International, No. 151, Box 02-5255, Miami, FL 33102-5255, U.S.A.) Ed. Nelson Prato Barbosa. adv.; bk.rev.; circ. 1,000.
Description: Promotes discussion and thought on the present and future problems of development from an interdisciplinary perspective.

ESTUDIOS MICHOACANOS. see *HISTORY — History Of North And South America*

309   DR
ESTUDIOS SOCIALES. vol.11, 1978. q. $5. Centro de Investigacion y Accion Social, Apdo. 841, Santo Domingo R.D., Dominican Republic. Ed.Bd. bk.rev.; charts; stat.; circ. 1,000. **Indexed:** A.B.C.Pol.Sci, Amer.Hist.& Life, Hisp.Amer.Per.Ind, Hist.Abstr., Lang.& Lang.Behav.Abstr., Rural Devel.Abstr.

301   MX   ISSN 0185-4186
ESTUDIOS SOCIOLOGICOS. 1983. 3/yr. Mex.$2000($38) to individuals (foreign $46); institutions $55 (foreign $64). Colegio de Mexico, A.C., Departamento de Publicaciones, Camino al Ajusco 20, Codigo Postal 01000, Mexico, D.F., Mexico. TEL 568 6033. FAX 6526233. TELEX 1777585 COLME. Ed. Claudio Stern. adv.; circ. 2,500. (back issues avail.; reprint service avail. from Swets & Zeitlinger)

301.364   BO
ESTUDIOS URBANOS. 1973. irreg., no.6, 1979. price varies. Centro de Investigaciones Sociales, Casilla 6931 - C.C., La Paz, Bolivia.

ESTUDOS POLITICOS E SOCIAIS. see *POLITICAL SCIENCE*

ETHNIC GROUPS. see *ETHNIC INTERESTS*

ETHOS (WASHINGTON). see *ANTHROPOLOGY*

ETUDES DAHOMEENNES. see *HISTORY — History Of Africa*

301 630 230   FR   ISSN 0014-2182
HN1
ETUDES RURALES; revue trimestrielle d'histoire, geographie, sociologie et economie des campagnes. 1961. q. 230 Fr. to individuals; institutions 385 F. Editions de l' Ecole des Hautes Etudes en Sciences Sociales, 131 bd. St. Michel, 75005 Paris, France. (Dist. by: Gauthier-Villars, Centrale des Revues, 11 rue Gossin, 92543 Montrouge Cedex, France. TEL 1-46-56-52-66) Ed. I. Chiva. adv.; bk.rev.; abstr.; bibl.; charts; illus.; index; circ. 800. **Indexed:** Amer.Hist.& Life, Geo.Abstr., Hist.Abstr., Int.Lab.Doc., Rural Recreat.Tour.Abstr., SSCI, World Agri.Econ.& Rural Sociol.Abstr.

301 960   SG
ETUDES SENEGALAISES.* 1949. irreg. Institut Fondamental d'Afrique Noire, Chiek Anta Diop, Universite de Dakar, B.P. 206, Dakar, Senegal. illus. (reprint service avail. from SWZ)

300   FR   ISSN 0014-2204
ETUDES SOCIALES. 1935. 2/yr. 200 F. to non-members. Societe d'Economie et de Science Sociales, 80 Rue Vaneau, 75007 Paris, France. Ed. Edouard Secretan. bk.rev.; charts; cum.index: 1961-1967; circ. 400. (also avail. in microfilm from BHP,KTO)
—BLDSC shelfmark: 3822.040000.

300   FR   ISSN 0014-2212
ETUDES SOCIALES ET SYNDICALES. 1955. bi-m. 350 F. Association d'Etudes Economiques, Sociales et Syndicales, 15 Av. Raymond-Poincare, 75116 Paris, France. Ed. Morvan Duhamel. bk.rev.; index; circ. 3,500.
—BLDSC shelfmark: 3822.080000.

SOCIOLOGY

301   FR   ISSN 0014-2247
DX101
ETUDES TSIGANES. 1955. q. 180 F. (foreign 200 F.) to individuals; institutions 250 F. (foreign 270 F.); students 135 (foreign 150 F.). Association des Etudes Tsiganes, 2 rue d'Hautpoul, 75019 Paris, France. TEL 40-40-09-05. adv.; bk.rev.; bibl.; illus.; cum.index: 1955-1980; circ. 1,800.

301   FR   ISSN 0531-2663
EUROPEAN ASPECTS, SOCIAL STUDIES SERIES; a collection of studies relating to European integration. 1959. irreg. Council of Europe, Publishing and Documentation Service, 67000 Strasbourg, France. (Dist. in U.S. by: Manhattan Publishing Co., Box 650, Croton-on-Hudson, N.Y. 10520)

309   EI
EUROPEAN FOUNDATION FOR THE IMPROVEMENT OF LIVING AND WORKING CONDITIONS. ANNUAL REPORT. a. European Foundation for the Improvement of Living and Working Conditions, Office des Publications Officielles des Communautes Europeennes, 2 rue Mercier, Luxembourg L-2985, Luxembourg.

301   UK   ISSN 0952-391X
▼**EUROPEAN JOURNAL OF INTERCULTURAL STUDIES.** 1990. 3/yr. £35 to individuals; institutions £55; foreign £60. Trentham Books Ltd., Westview House, 734 London Rd., Oakhill, Stoke-on-Trent, Staffs. ST4 5NP, England. TEL 0782-745567. FAX 0782-745553. index; circ. 1,500.
—BLDSC shelfmark: 3829.730600.
Description: Studies majority and minority communities throughout Europe.

EUROPEAN JOURNAL OF SOCIAL PSYCHOLOGY. see *PSYCHOLOGY*

301   UK   ISSN 0003-9756
HM1.A1
EUROPEAN JOURNAL OF SOCIOLOGY/ARCHIVES EUROPEENNES DE SOCIOLOGIE/EUROPAISCHE ARCHIV FUR SOZIOLOGIE. (Text in English, French and German) 1960. s-a. $52 to individuals; $99 to institutions. Cambridge University Press, Edinburgh Bldg., Shaftesbury Rd., Cambridge CB2 2RU, England. TEL 0223-312393. FAX 0223-315052. TELEX 851817256. (N. American addr.: Cambridge University Press, 40 W. 20th St., New York, NY 10011-4211, USA. TEL 212-924-3900) Ed.Bd. adv.; bibl.; charts; illus.; stat.; index, cum.index. (also avail. in microform from UMI; reprint service avail. from SWZ) **Indexed:** Amer.Hist.& Life, ASSIA, Hist.Abstr., Lang.& Lang.Behav.Abstr., Soc.Sci.Ind., Sociol.Abstr. (1960-), SSCI.
—BLDSC shelfmark: 1634.278000.
Description: Encourages comparative studies of societies worldwide.

301   UK   ISSN 0266-7215
HM1
EUROPEAN SOCIOLOGICAL REVIEW. 1985. 3/yr. £47($90) Oxford University Press, Oxford Journals, Pinkhill House, Southfield Road, Eynsham, Oxford OX8 1JJ, England. TEL 0865-882283. FAX 0865-882890. TELEX 837330 OXPRES G. Ed. Hans Peter Blossfeld. adv.; bk.rev.; circ. 300. (back issues avail.) **Indexed:** ASSIA, Sociol.Abstr. (1985-).
—BLDSC shelfmark: 3830.108000.
Description: Aims to present papers in which research expertise is combined with substantive and theoretical significance.

EVALUATION COMMENT; the journal of educational evaluation. see *EDUCATION*

301   GW
EXILFORSCHUNG; ein internationales Jahrbuch. 1983. a. price varies. (Gesellschaft fuer Exilforschung) Edition Text und Kritik GmbH, Levelingstr. 6a, 8000 Munich 80, Germany. TEL 089-432929. FAX 089-433997.

F A O ECONOMIC AND SOCIAL DEVELOPMENT PAPER. see *BUSINESS AND ECONOMICS*

FACT SHEETS ON INSTITUTIONAL RACISM; minority outlook on current issues. see *POLITICAL SCIENCE — Civil Rights*

300   YU   ISSN 0014-7052
FACTS AND TENDENCIES/FAITS ET TENDANCES; review for social questions. (Text in English and French) 1966. a. $3.35. Konferencija za Drustvenu Aktivnost Zena Jugoslavije - Conference for Social Activities of Yugoslav Women, Bulevar Lenjina 6, 11000 Belgrade, Yugoslavia. TEL 011 62-76-42. TELEX YU 1277. Ed. Dasa Sasic. bk.rev.; bibl.; circ. 2,400.
Description: Devoted to an international seminar on the status of women. Covers general issues, women in economy, agriculture and technical and technological development.

301.42 249   BL   ISSN 0014-7125
FAMILIA CRISTA; revista da paz e do amor - revista mensal para a familia. 1934. m. Cr.$160. Pia Sociedade Filhas de Sao Paulo, Rua Domingos de Morais 678, Sao Paulo 04010, Brazil. Ed. Joana Terezinha Puntel. adv.; bk.rev.; charts; illus.; circ. 160,000.
Description: General interest magazine for family living.

301.4 200 360   CK   ISSN 0120-3215
FAMILIA Y SOCIEDAD. 1976. bi-m. $11 to U.S.; elsewhere $12. Centro de Pastoral Familiar para America Latina, Avda. 28 No. 37-21, Apdo. Aereo No. 54569, Bogota, Colombia. TEL 269 6311.

FAMILIENDYNAMIK; interdisziplinaere Zeitschrift fuer systemorientierte Praxis und Forschung. see *PSYCHOLOGY*

301.4   US   ISSN 0892-2691
FAMILY IN AMERICA. 1978. m. $21. Rockford Institute, 934 N. Main St., Rockford, IL 61103. TEL 815-964-5813. FAX 815-965-1826. Ed. Bryce Christensen. illus.; circ. 4,800. (back issues avail.)
Formerly: Persuasion at Work (ISSN 0163-5387)
Description: Reports on social problems facing the traditional family.

301 360   AT   ISSN 1030-2646
HQ706   CODEN: FAMMEL
FAMILY MATTERS. 1980. 3/yr. Aus.$30 (foreign Aus.$45)(effective 1992). Australian Institute of Family Studies, 300 Queen St., Melbourne, Vic. 3000, Australia. TEL 03-608-6888. FAX 03-600-0886. bk.rev.; circ. 2,000. **Indexed:** Aus.P.A.I.S., Soc.Work Res.& Abstr.
Former titles: Australian Institute of Family Studies. Newsletter (ISSN 0818-0229); Institute of Family Studies (ISSN 0159-9143)
Description: Research from the institute and by other Australian and international researchers on social, psychological, and legal issues involving families of all types.

301 640 150   US   ISSN 0014-7311
HQ1
FAMILY PERSPECTIVE. 1966. q. $25 to individuals (foreign $35); institutions $50 (foreign $60). Brigham Young University, Center for Studies of the Family, 922 Kimball Tower, Provo, UT 84602. TEL 801-378-2948. Ed. Stephen J. Bahr. illus.; circ. 1,000. (also avail. in microform from MIM; back issues avail.)
Description: Multidisciplinary journal publishing articles on any aspect of family life.

FAMILY PROCESS. see *PSYCHOLOGY*

301.42   US   ISSN 0197-6664
HQ1   CODEN: FCOOBE
FAMILY RELATIONS; journal of applied family & child studies. 1952. q. $45 to individuals; institutions and libraries $75. National Council on Family Relations, 3989 Central Ave., N.E., Ste. 550, Minneapolis, MN 55421-3921. TEL 612-781-9331. FAX 612-781-9348. Ed. Mark Fine. adv.; bk.rev.; charts; index; circ. 5,200. (also avail. in microform from UMI,MIM; reprint service avail. from UMI) **Indexed:** Abstr.Soc.Geront., Adol.Ment.Hlth.Abstr., Bk.Rev.Ind. (1989-), C.I.J.E., CERDIC, Child.Bk.Rev.Ind. (1989-), Child Devel.Abstr., Curr.Cont., Curr.Lit.Fam.Plan., Lang.& Lang.Behav.Abstr., Media Rev.Dig., Mid.East: Abstr.& Ind., Psychol.Abstr., Res.High.Educ.Abstr., Sage Fam.Stud.Abstr., Soc.Sci.Ind., Soc.Work Res.& Abstr., Sociol.Abstr, SSCI, Stud.Wom.Abstr.
●Also available online. Vendor(s): BRS, DIALOG.
Former titles: Family Coordinator (ISSN 0014-7214); Family Life Coordinator
Description: Covers applied scholarly articles with emphasis on family relationships across the life cycle with implications for intervention, education and public policy.

301.4 155   US
FAMILY SERVICE PERSPECTIVES; useful information for the workplace and home. 1988. q. $1. Family Service of the Cincinnati Area, 205 W. Fourth St., Cincinnati, OH 45202. TEL 513-381-6300. FAX 513-345-8551. Ed. Sheila Libecap. circ. 5,000.
Description: Provides practical information for individuals and families about the workplace and home, for better management of job and family and for nurturing healthy relationships.

FAMILY THERAPY NEWS. see *PSYCHOLOGY*

FANLIGHT NEWS. see *MEDICAL SCIENCES*

301.412 301   UK
FEMINIST PRAXIS. 1984. bi-m. £4 per no. University of Manchester, Department of Sociology, Manchester M13 9PL, England. TEL 061-275-2496. Ed. Liz Stanley. adv.; circ. 500. (back issues avail.) **Indexed:** Sociol.Abstr. (1984-), Stud.Wom.Abstr.
Formerly: Studies in Sexual Politics.
Description: Feminist research within social sciences, focusing on epistemological issues and main relationship to praxis.

FILOZOFSKI FAKULTET - ZADAR. RAZDIO FILOZOFIJE, PSIHOLOGIJE, SOCIOLOGIJE I PEDAGOGIJE. RADOVI. see *PHILOSOPHY*

301   SW
FINNISH SOCIETY FOR DEVELOPMENT STUDIES. MONOGRAPH SERIES. (Text in English) 1987. irreg. price varies. Nordiska Afrikainstitutet - Scandinavian Institue of African Studies, P.O. Box 1703, S-751 47 Uppsala, Sweden. TEL 018-155480. FAX 018-695629. circ. 1,500.

FIVE FINGERS REVIEW. see *LITERATURE*

FLORIDA PSYCHOLOGIST. see *PSYCHOLOGY*

FORUM. BERICHTE AUS DER ARBEIT. see *RELIGIONS AND THEOLOGY*

FORUM (LONDON, 1967); the journal of human relations and psycho-sexual studies. see *PSYCHOLOGY*

FORUM (LORENTON). see *LITERARY AND POLITICAL REVIEWS*

FRAME-WORK; a journal of images and culture. see *PHOTOGRAPHY*

301   US   ISSN 0736-9182
HM1
FREE INQUIRY IN CREATIVE SOCIOLOGY. 1972. s-a. $12 to individuals; institutions $20 (effective 1992). University of Central Oklahoma, Department of Sociology and Criminal Justice, 100 N. University Dr., Edmond, OK 73034. TEL 405-341-2980. FAX 405-341-4964. Ed. Joan Luxenburg. adv.; circ. 400. (also avail. in microform from UMI; reprint service avail. from UMI) **Indexed:** Lang.& Lang.Behav.Abstr., Sociol.Abstr. (1972-).
—BLDSC shelfmark: 4033.322000.
Formerly (until Jan. 1979): Free Inquiry (Norman).
Description: Publishes articles of interest to a non-specialist audience.

SOCIOLOGY

FREE LIFE. see *POLITICAL SCIENCE*

FREIE UNIVERSITAET BERLIN. OSTEUROPA-INSTITUT. PHILOSOPHISCHE UND SOZIOLOGISCHE VEROEFFENTLICHUNGEN. see *PHILOSOPHY*

FRIENDS JOURNAL. see *RELIGIONS AND THEOLOGY — Other Denominations And Sects*

FRIENDS OF YOUTH NEWSLETTER. see *CHILDREN AND YOUTH — About*

FROM THE STATE CAPITALS. CIVIL RIGHTS. see *POLITICAL SCIENCE — Civil Rights*

301 330   BL
FUNDACAO CENTRO DE PESQUISAS ECONOMICAS E SOCIAIS DO PIAUI. RELATÓRIO DE ATIVIDADES. Cover title: Fundacao Centro de Pesquisas Economicas e Sociais do Piaui. Atividades C E P R O. irreg. Fundacao Centro de Pesquisas Economicas e Sociais do Piaui, Av. Miguel Rosa 3190-S, Caixa Postal 429, 6400 Teresina-Piaui, Brazil.

301   BL
FUNDACAO JOAQUIM NABUCO. SERIE CURSOS E CONFERENCIAS. 1974. irreg., no.43, 1991. (Fundacao Joaquim Nabuco) Editora Massangana, Rua Dois Irmaos, 15, Apipucos, 52071 Recife, Brazil.
    Formerly: Instituto Joaquim Nabuco de Pesquisas Sociais. Serie Cursos e Conferencias.

301   BL
FUNDACAO JOAQUIM NABUCO. SERIE DOCUMENTOS. 1975. irreg., no.37, 1991. (Fundacao Joaquim Nabuco) Editora Massangana, Rua Dois Irmaos, 15, Apipucos, 52071 Recife, Brazil. TEL 081-268-4611. FAX 081-268-9600.
    Formerly: Instituto Joaquim Nabuco de Pesquisas Sociais. Serie Documentos.

301   BL
FUNDACAO JOAQUIM NABUCO. SERIE ESTUDOS E PESQUISAS. 1974. irreg., no.79, 1990. (Fundacao Joaquim Nabuco) Editora Massangana, Rua Dois Irmaos, 15, Apipucos, 25071 Recife, Brazil. **Indexed:** Rural Recreat.Tour.Abstr., World Agri.Econ.& Rural Sociol.Abstr.
    Formerly: Instituto Joaquim Nabuco de Pesquisas Sociais. Serie Estudos e Pesquisas.

301.4   IT
FUORIMARGINE. 1989. irreg., no.4, 1991. price varies. Liguori Editore s.r.l., Via Mezzocannone, 19, 80134 Naples, Italy. TEL 081-5227139. Ed Alberto Abruzzese.

FUTURES; the journal of forecasting, planning and policy. see *TECHNOLOGY: COMPREHENSIVE WORKS*

301   FR   ISSN 0337-307X
H3
FUTURIBLES; analyse-prevision-prospective. (Text in French; summaries in English, French) 1975. m. 580 F. (foreign 650 F.). Futuribles, sarl, 55 rue de Varenne, 75341 Paris Cedex 07, France. TEL 42-22-63-10. FAX 42-22-65-54. Ed. Hughes de Jouvenel. adv.; bk.rev.; charts; index; circ. 4,000. (also avail. in microform from UMI) **Indexed:** A.B.C.Pol.Sci., Curr.Cont., Int.Lab.Doc., Key to Econ.Sci., P.A.I.S.For.Lang.Ind., Rural Recreat.Tour.Abstr., Sociol.Abstr., World Agri.Econ.& Rural Sociol.Abstr.
    Formed by the merger of: Analyse et Prevision (ISSN 0003-262X); Prospectives (ISSN 0033-1503)
    Description: Analysis, forcasting and prospective on main contemporary problems with a pluridisciplinary approach and in a middle and long-term perspective.

301 600   US   ISSN 0164-1220
CB161
FUTURICS; a quarterly journal of futures research. 1977. q. $40 in U.S. and Canada; elsewhere $57. Minnesota Futurists, 365 Summit Ave., St. Paul, MN 55102. TEL 612-222-4548. (Subscr. to: Minnesota Futurists, ASI, Ste. 700, 245 E. 6th St., St. Paul, MN 55101) Ed. Earl C. Joseph. adv.; bk.rev.; circ. 500. (also avail. in microfilm from UMI; back issues avail.; reprint service avail. from UMI) **Indexed:** Fut.Surv.
    —BLDSC shelfmark: 4060.690000.
    Description: Contains articles dealing with alternative futures from a professional viewpoint. Devoted to advancing our understanding of possible futures.

300   II   ISSN 0016-4496
GANMITRAM. (Text in Hindi and Sanskrit) 1966. w. Rs.3. Basudeo Misra, Ed. & Pub., At 4 Post Khetasarai District, Janpur, Uttar Pradesh, India. circ. 1,800.

309   US   ISSN 0891-2432
HQ1075
GENDER AND SOCIETY. 1987. q. $38 to individuals; institutions $99. (Sociologists for Women in Society) Sage Publications, Inc., 2455 Teller Rd., Newbury Park, CA 91320. TEL 805-499-0721. FAX 805-499-0871. Ed. Margaret Andersen. adv.; bk.rev.; circ. 2,100. **Indexed:** Psychol.Abstr., Sociol.Abstr. (1987-), Sp.Ed.Needs Abstr., Wom.Stud.Abstr. (1987-).
    —BLDSC shelfmark: 4096.401500.
    Description: Focuses on the social and structural study of gender as a basic principle of the social order and as a primary social category, with emphasis on theory and research from micro- and macrostructural perspectives.

320 300   US   ISSN 0161-3340
HN29
GENERAL SOCIAL SURVEYS. 1972. a. National Opinion Research Center, 1155 E. 60th St., Chicago, IL 60637. TEL 312-753-7500. FAX 312-753-7886. Ed. Tom W. Smith. (also avail. in microfiche)
    Description: Presents survey of representative sample of U.S. population, attitudes and behavior.

GENEVA - AFRICA/GENEVE - AFRIQUE. see *POLITICAL SCIENCE — International Relations*

GEOGRAFIA URBANA. see *GEOGRAPHY*

GESELLSCHAFT UND POLITIK; Zeitschrift fuer soziales und wirtschafliches Engagement. see *POLITICAL SCIENCE*

301   GH   ISSN 0435-9380
GHANA JOURNAL OF SOCIOLOGY. 1965. s-a. $5. Ghana Sociological Association, c/o Department of Sociology, University of Ghana, Legon, Ghana. **Indexed:** Lang.& Lang.Behav.Abstr.

301   PL   ISSN 0072-5013
GORNOSLASKIE STUDIA SOCJOLOGICZNE. 1963. irreg. Slaski Instytut Naukowy, Ul. Graniczna 32, 40-956 Katowice, Poland. (Dist. by: Ars Polona-Ruch, Krakowskie Przedmiescie 7, Warsaw, Poland)

GRADUATE SCHOOL JOURNAL. see *EDUCATION — School Organization And Administration*

309 334.683   AT   ISSN 0310-2890
GRASS ROOTS; craft and self-sufficiency for down to earth people. 1973. 6/yr. Aus.$23.50. Night Owl Publishers Pty. Ltd., P.O. Box 242, Euroa, Vic. 3666, Australia. TEL 6157-94-7274. FAX 6157-947285. Ed. Megg Miller. adv.; bk.rev.; circ. 32,000. (back issues avail.) **Indexed:** Alt.Press Ind., Gdlns., Pinpointer.

GRASSROOTS DEVELOPMENT. see *BUSINESS AND ECONOMICS — International Development And Assistance*

GRAZER LINGUISTISCHE STUDIEN. see *LINGUISTICS*

301   UK   ISSN 0072-5765
GREAT BRITAIN. CENTRAL STATISTICAL OFFICE. SOCIAL TRENDS. 1970. a. (Central Statistical Office) H.M.S.O., Publications Centre, 51 Nine Elms Lane, London SW8 5DR, England. TEL 01-873-9090. FAX 01-873-8463. TELEX 297138. charts; stat.

GREAT BRITAIN. DEPARTMENT OF THE ENVIRONMENT. REPORT ON RESEARCH AND DEVELOPMENT. see *ENVIRONMENTAL STUDIES*

GREAT ISSUES OF THE DAY. see *POLITICAL SCIENCE*

051   US   ISSN 0017-3983
GREEN REVOLUTION; a voice for decentralization and balanced living. 1943. q. $50. School of Living, RR 1, Box 185A, Cochranville, PA 19330. TEL 215-593-6988. Ed. Virginia Green. bk.rev.; charts; illus.; circ. 500. (also avail. in microform from UMI; reprint service avail. from UMI) **Indexed:** Alt.Press Ind., Energy Ind., Energy Info.Abstr., New Per.Ind.
    Incorporates (1969-1979): Aquarian Research Foundation Newsletter.
    Description: For self-governing communities on the land.

301.4   FR
GROUPE FAMILIAL. 1958. q. 250 F. (foreign 280 F.). Federation Nationale des Ecole des Parents et des Educateurs, 5 impasse Bon-Secours, 75543 Paris Cedex 11, France. TEL 43-48-00-16. FAX 1-43-48-81-53. Ed. Odile Naudin. adv.; bk.rev.; bibl.; circ. 5,000. **Indexed:** Bull.Signal.
    Description: For specialists in education. Covers issues on a general theme connected with family, psychology, social work.

GRUPPENDYNAMIK; Zeitschrift fuer angewandte Sozialpsychologie. see *PSYCHOLOGY*

301.4   FR
GUIDE DES FUTURS EPOUX. 1957. q. 11 bis rue du Docteur Baudin, 28004 Chartres Cedex 92, France. Ed. Pierre Delaval. circ. 400,000 (controlled).

301   US   ISSN 0091-7052
HM47.U6
GUIDE TO GRADUATE DEPARTMENTS OF SOCIOLOGY. a. $11 to individuals (foreign $17); students $6 (foreign $12); effective 1992. American Sociological Association, 1722 N St., N.W., Washington, DC 20036. TEL 202-833-3410. FAX 202-785-0146. (reprint service avail. from UMI)

HANDLING CHILD CUSTODY CASES. see *LAW — Family And Matrimonial Law*

301   KO
HANGUK SAHOEHAK/KOREAN JOURNAL OF SOCIOLOGY. 1964. s-a. 20,000 Won($32) Korean Sociological Association, 304-28, Sachik-dong, Chongro-ku, Seoul 110-054, S. Korea. FAX 02-739-3427. Ed. Hung-Tak Lee. adv.; bk.rev.; circ. 1,000.

HARROWSMITH. see *AGRICULTURE*

301 900   US   ISSN 0146-5414
HN1
HARVEST BOOK SERIES. 1966. irreg. $16. Harvest Publishers, 1521 Shattuck Ave., Box 9503, N. Berkeley Sta., Berkeley, CA 94709. Ed. Ann Baxandall. adv.; bk.rev.; circ. 1,500. (back issues avail.) **Indexed:** Alt.Press Ind.
    Description: Dynamics of social change in the Western world and Pacific Basin.

360   US
HARVEST NEWS. 1947. 3/yr. free. (CROP, the Community Hunger Appeal of Church World Service) Church World Service, Box 968, Elkhart, IN 46515. TEL 219-264-3102. FAX 219-294-2964. Ed. Frances Jones. bk.rev.; charts; circ. 290,000.
    Formerly (until 1983): Service News (Elkhart) (ISSN 0037-2617)

301   US   ISSN 0891-7795
HEALTH, SOCIETY AND CULTURE. 1987. irreg., latest vol.1. Gordon & Breach Science Publishers, 270 Eighth Ave., New York, NY 10011. TEL 212-206-8900. FAX 212-645-2459. TELEX 236735 GOPUB UR. (Subscr. to: Box 786, Cooper Sta., New York, NY 10276. TEL 800-545-8398; UK subscr. to: P.O. Box 90, Reading, Berkshire RG1 8JL, England. TEL 0734-560-080) Ed. H.A. Baer.
    Refereed Serial

HEARD HERITAGE; Heard County, Georgia - a history of its people. see *GENEALOGY AND HERALDRY*

301   GW   ISSN 0073-1676
HEIDELBERGER SOCIOLOGICA. 1962. irreg., vol.20 1984. price varies. (Universitaet Heidelberg, Institut fuer Soziologie und Ethnologie) Verlag J.C.B. Mohr (Paul Siebeck), Wilhelmstr. 18, Postfach 2040, 7400 Tuebingen, Germany. TEL 07071-26064. FAX 07071-51104. TELEX 7262872-MOHR-D. Ed. W.E. Muehlmann.
    Description: Covers a variety of sociological issues and theories.

360   NO
HELSE OG SOSIAL FORUM. 1926. 10/yr. NOK 50. Norsk Forening for Sosialt Arbeid - Norwegian Association for Social Work, Osterhausgt. 11, 0183 Oslo 1, Norway. Ed. Barbro Sveen. adv.; bk.rev.; abstr.; illus.; circ. 6,000.
    Former titles: Sosial Forum - Sosial Arbeid; Sosialt Arbeid (ISSN 0038-1632)

HESSISCHE STIFTUNG FRIEDENS- UND KONFLIKTFORSCHUNG. MITTEILUNGEN; Bericht ueber Organisation und laufende Forschung. see *POLITICAL SCIENCE — International Relations*

SOCIOLOGY

301.4 155 US
HISPANIC AMERICAN FAMILY MAGAZINE. (Text in English, Spanish) 1987. q. $10. Hispanic American Family of the Year Foundation, 10654 Woodbrige St., N. Hollywood, CA 91602-2717. TEL 818-500-1309. Ed. Bernard Kemp. adv.; circ. 11,000.
 Description: Features articles on interests and concerns parents have and with the problems and pleasures of raising a family in today's society from the Hispanic American perspective.

HISTOIRE SOCIALE/SOCIAL HISTORY. see *HISTORY*

HISTORICAL METHODS. see *HISTORY*

HISTORICAL SOCIAL RESEARCH/HISTORISCHE SOZIALFORSCHUNG. see *HISTORY — History Of Europe*

301 US ISSN 0190-2067
HM1
HISTORY OF SOCIOLOGY: AN INTERNATIONAL REVIEW. 1978. s-a. $25. Department of Sociology, University of Kansas, Lawrence, KS 66045. TEL 913-864-4111. Eds. Alan Sica, Gerd Schroeter. adv.; bk.rev.; circ. 300. (reprint service avail. from SCH) **Indexed:** Amer.Hist.& Life, Hist.Abstr., Lang.& Lang.Behav.Abstr., Sociol.Abstr.
 Formerly: Journal of the History of Sociology.

301 309 EC
HOMBRE Y AMBIENTE; el punto de vista indigena. 1987. a.? S/1000($15) or exchange basis. Ediciones Abya - Yala, Casilla 8513, Quito, Ecuador. TEL 562633. (Dist. by: Libreria Libri Mundi, Juan Leon Mera, 851, Quito, Ecuador.) Ed. Jose E. Juncosa.

325 312 FR ISSN 0223-3290
HOMMES ET MIGRATIONS. 1950. m. 425 F. Amis de Hommes & Migrations, 40 rue de la Duee, 75020 Paris, France. TEL 47-97-26-05. FAX 47-97-99-77. Ed. Francois Gremont. bk.rev.; charts; illus.; stat.; index, cum.index; circ. 2,000. (tabloid format; reprint service avail. from SWZ) **Indexed:** Abstr.Musl.Rel., Refug.Abstr.
 —BLDSC shelfmark: 4326.270000.
 Formerly: Cahiers Nord Africains (ISSN 0018-4365)

301 FR ISSN 0563-9743
HM3
HOMO; psychologie, education, culture, societe. (Text in French; summaries in English) 1953. a. 65 F. (effective 1992). (Universite de Toulouse II (le Mirail)) Presses Universitaires du Mirail, 56 rue du Taur, 31069 Toulouse Cedex, France. TEL 61-22-58-31. Ed. J.P. Martineau. (back issues avail.) **Indexed:** Biol.Abstr., SSCI.
 —BLDSC shelfmark: 4326.330000.
 Description: Presents fundamental or applied research, methodolgical confrontation, clinical studies and essays in the fields of psychology, education, culture and society.

301 SP
HOMO SOCIOLOGICUS. 1974. irreg. Ediciones 62, S.A., Provenca 278, 08008 Barcelona, Spain. TEL 216-00-62.

HONG KONG SOCIAL AND ECONOMIC TRENDS. see *BUSINESS AND ECONOMICS — Economic Situation And Conditions*

HOT WIRE; the journal of women's music and culture. see *WOMEN'S INTERESTS*

HOUSTON REVIEW: HISTORY AND CULTURE OF THE GULF COAST. see *HISTORY — History Of North And South America*

HUMAN KINDNESS FOUNDATION NEWSLETTER; a little news. see *RELIGIONS AND THEOLOGY*

HUMAN LIFE ISSUES. see *PHILOSOPHY*

301 US ISSN 0097-9783
HQ767
HUMAN LIFE REVIEW. 1975. q. $20. Human Life Foundation, Inc., 150 E. 35th St., New York, NY 10016. TEL 212-685-5210. FAX 212-696-0309. Ed. J.P. McFadden. circ. 14,000. (also avail. in microfiche from BLH,UMI; reprint service avail. from UMI) **Indexed:** C.L.I., Curr.Lit.Fam.Plan., Leg.Per.
 Description: Covers abortion and related issues.

HUMAN NATURE; an interdisciplinary biosocial perspective. see *SOCIAL SCIENCES: COMPREHENSIVE WORKS*

HUMAN POTENTIAL. see *PSYCHOLOGY*

HUMAN QUEST. see *RELIGIONS AND THEOLOGY*

301.45 US ISSN 0018-7283
HUMAN RELATIONS NEWS OF CHICAGO.* 1959. m. free. Chicago Commission on Human Relations, 500 N. Peshigto Court, Chicago, IL 60611. TEL 312-744-4100. Ed. Rachel R. Ridley. charts; illus.; stat.; circ. 9,500. (tabloid format)

HUMAN RESOURCES ABSTRACTS; an international information service. see *SOCIOLOGY — Abstracting, Bibliographies, Statistics*

301 US ISSN 0275-0392
JC571
HUMAN RIGHTS QUARTERLY; a comparative and international journal of the social sciences, humanities and law. 1979. q. $23 to individuals (foreign $29.50); institutions $63 (foreign $69). (Urban Morgan Institute for Human Rights) Johns Hopkins University Press, Journals Publishing Division, 701 W. 40th St., Ste. 275, Baltimore, MD 21211. TEL 410-516-6987. FAX 410-516-6998. Ed. Bert B. Lockwood, Jr. adv.; bk.rev.; circ. 11,560. (also avail. in microform from UMI; back issues avail.; reprint service avail. from UMI) **Indexed:** A.B.C.Pol.Sci., Abstr.Bk.Rev.Curr.Leg.Per., Amer.Bibl.Slavic & E.Eur.Stud, Amer.Hist.& Life, BPIA, C.L.I., Curr.Cont., Foreign Leg.Per., Hist.Abstr., HR Rep., Int.Lab.Doc., Int.Polit.Sci.Abstr., L.R.I., L.R.I., Lang.& Lang.Behav.Abstr., Leg.Cont., Leg.Per., P.A.I.S., Phil.Ind., Polit.Sci.Abstr., Refug.Abstr., Rel.Ind.One, Sociol.Abstr., SSCI.
 —BLDSC shelfmark: 4336.441500.
 Formerly (until 1981): Universal Human Rights (ISSN 0163-2647)
 Description: Presents current work in rights research and policy analysis, and philosophical essays probing the fundamental nature of human rights as defined by the Universal Declaration of Human Rights.

HUMAN STRESS: CURRENT SELECTED RESEARCH. see *PSYCHOLOGY*

HUMAN STUDIES; a journal for philosophy and the social sciences. see *PHILOSOPHY*

301 US
THE HUMANIST SOCIOLOGIST. q. membership. Association for Humanist Sociology, Department of Sociology, University of North Carolina, Charlotte, NC 28223. (Subscr. to: c/o Charles McKelvey, Department of Sociology, Presbyterian College, Clinton, SC 29325)

301 US ISSN 0160-5976
HM1
HUMANITY & SOCIETY. 1977. q. $40 (foreign $45). Association for Humanist Sociology, Department of Sociology, University of North Carolina, Charlotte, NC 28223. (Subscr. to: c/o Charles McKelvey, Department of Sociology, Presbyterian College, Clinton, SC 29325) Ed. Judy Aulette. adv.; bk.rev.; abstr.; index; circ. 600. (also avail. in microfiche) **Indexed:** Lang.& Lang.Behav.Abstr., Sociol.Abstr. (1977-).
 Description: Provides a forum for sociologists and other scholars whose work addresses the problem of understanding social issues and creating a more humane and egalitarian society.

HUMOR; international journal of humor research. see *SOCIAL SCIENCES: COMPREHENSIVE WORKS*

300 BO ISSN 0018-8581
I B E A S.* 1966. m. free. Instituto Boliviano de Estudio y Accion Social, Casilla 3277, La Paz, Bolivia. bibl. (processed)

I D S BULLETIN. (Institute of Development Studies) see *BUSINESS AND ECONOMICS — International Development And Assistance*

I D S DISCUSSION PAPER. (Institute of Development Studies) see *BUSINESS AND ECONOMICS — International Development And Assistance*

I D S RESEARCH REPORTS. (Institute of Development Studies) see *BUSINESS AND ECONOMICS — International Development And Assistance*

301 DK ISSN 0105-0532
HN371
I E F INFORMATION.* no.18, 1981. irreg. Koebenhavns Universitet, Institut for Europaeisk Folkeforskning, Frue Plads, 1168 Copenhagen K, Denmark. illus.

I L P E S CUADERNOS. (Instituto Latinamericano y del Caribe de Planificacion Economica y Social) see *BUSINESS AND ECONOMICS — Macroeconomics*

301.2 991.4 PH ISSN 0073-9537
I P C MONOGRAPHS. (Text in English) irreg. price varies. Ateneo de Manila University, Institute of Philippine Culture, Box 154, Manila, Philippines. Ed. Alfonso De Guzman II.

301.2 991.4 PH ISSN 0073-9545
I P C PAPERS. (Text in English) irreg., latest no.15. price varies. Ateneo de Manila University, Institute of Philippine Culture, Box 154, Manila, Philippines.
 —BLDSC shelfmark: 4567.275500.

309 PH
I P C POVERTY RESEARCH SERIES. irreg. Ateneo de Manila University, Institute of Philippine Culture, Box 154, Manila, Philippines.

301 PH
I P C REPRINTS. (Text in English) irreg., latest no.23. Ateneo de Manila University, Institute of Philippine Culture, Box 154, Manila, Philippines.

301 330.9 BL
I P E A RELATORIOS DE PESQUISA. 1971. irreg. price varies. Instituto de Planejamento Economico e Social, Caixa Postal 2672, Rio de Janeiro, Brazil.
 Description: Presents applied research carried out by the IPEA staff covering Brazilian economic problems.

301 AT
I R S A ITEMS. (Text in English; occasionally summaries in Spanish) 1977. a. membership. International Rural Sociology Association, c/o Dept. of Sociology, Michigan State University, East Lansing, MI 48824. Ed. Harry Schwarzweller. bk.rev.; circ. 1,700. (tabloid format)

301 US
I S A G A NEWSLETTER. 1974. q. membership. International Simulation and Gaming Association, c/o Dr. S. Underwood, 4110 EECS bldg., University of Michigan, Ann Arbor, MI 48109-2122. TEL 313-936-2999. FAX 313-763-1674. bk.rev.; circ. 1,000.
 Description: Provides a forum for the exchange of ideas and knowledge on the design, applications, and use of games and simulation throughout the world.

301 CN ISSN 0828-6868
I S E R RESEARCH AND POLICY PAPERS. 1985. irreg. price varies. Institute of Social and Economic Research, Memorial University, St. John's, Newfoundland A1C 5S7, Canada. TEL 709-737-8156. FAX 709-737-2041. adv.; bk.rev.; circ. 250. (tabloid format; back issues avail.)
 —BLDSC shelfmark: 4582.842800.
 Description: Features article length papers. These papers vary from basic social scientific research to various forms of applied research, to policy analysis and recommendations. Draws mainly on research conducted under the auspices and focuses on Newfoundland and North Atlantic studies.

301 320 US
I S H I OCCASIONAL PAPERS IN SOCIAL CHANGE.* 1976. irreg., no.6, 1982. price varies. (Institute for the Study of Human Issues) I S H I Publications, 1530 Locust St., Ste. 80, Philadelphia, PA 19102. TEL 215-732-9729. Ed. J.M. Jutkowitz. circ. 1,000. (also avail. in microform from UMI)

IDEAS & ACTION. see *BUSINESS AND ECONOMICS — Labor And Industrial Relations*

IMMIGRATION JOURNAL. see *LAW — Civil Law*

IMPACT OF SCIENCE ON SOCIETY. see *SCIENCES: COMPREHENSIVE WORKS*

IN SUMMARY. see *SOCIAL SCIENCES: COMPREHENSIVE WORKS*

IN THE MAKING; directory of radical cooperation. see *BUSINESS AND ECONOMICS — Cooperatives*

SOCIOLOGY

INDAGINI E PROSPETTIVE. see *POLITICAL SCIENCE*

301.2 294.5   II
INDIA CULTURES. (Text in English) vol.22, 1965. q. Rs.10($5) Leonard Theological College, School of Research, Jabalpur 482001, Madhya Pradesh, India. Ed. Rev. Jacob Paul. bk.rev.; illus.; circ. 500.
Formerly: India Cultures Quarterly (ISSN 0019-4166)

301   II   ISSN 0019-5642
HM1
INDIAN JOURNAL OF SOCIOLOGY. (Text and summaries in English) 1970. q. Rs.100($25) Indian Academy of Social Sciences, c/o Sociology House, K21, Hauz Khas Enclave, New Delhi 110016, India. Ed. Keshav Dev Sharma. adv.; bk.rev.; abstr.; stat.; index; circ. 600. (tabloid format) **Indexed:** Lang.& Lang.Behav.Abstr., Sociol.Abstr.

INDIVIDUALIST. see *PHILOSOPHY*

301   DK   ISSN 0109-2421
▼**INDVANDREREN.** (Text in Danish; summaries in Arabic, Farsi, Greek, Kurdish, Serbo-Croatian, Tamil, Turkish, Urdu) 1983. 5/yr. DKK 75. Indvandrerforeningernes Sammenslutning (IND-sam), Blegdamsvej 4, st., DK-2200 Copenhagen N, Denmark. TEL 31-39-21-43. Eds. Jannis Gavalias, Anne Liveng. adv.; illus.; circ. 5,000.

301   AT   ISSN 1033-6273
▼**INFORMATION, THEORY AND SOCIETY.** 1992. s-a. Aus.$60. James Nicholas Publishers, P.O. Box 244, Albert Park, Vic. 3206, Australia. TEL 03-696-5545. FAX 613-699-2040. Ed. Rea Zajda. adv.; bk.rev.; index. **Indexed:** Aus.Educ.Ind., Cont.Pg.Educ., Sociol.Abstr., Sociol.Educ.Abstr.
Description: Major and current issues in information research, focusing on contemporary cultural studies and problems pertaining to the information age, post-industrialism, individualism, commodities and post-modernity.

301.4   GW   ISSN 0938-0124
▼**INFORMATIONEN FUER EINELTERNFAMILIEN.** 1990. 9/yr. Verband alleinstehender Muetter und Vaeter e.V., Von-Groote-Platz 20, 5300 Bonn 2, Germany. TEL 0228-352995. FAX 0228-358350. Ed. Gunhild Gutschmidt. circ. 1,350.

INSIDE M S; the magazine of the National Multiple Sclerosis Society. see *MEDICAL SCIENCES — Psychiatry And Neurology*

INSTITUT ZA KRIMINOLOSKA I SOCIOLOSKA ISTRAZIVANJA. ZBORNIK. see *CRIMINOLOGY AND LAW ENFORCEMENT*

INSTITUTE FOR CONTEMPORARY STUDIES. LETTER. see *SOCIAL SERVICES AND WELFARE*

951.9   II   ISSN 0970-2814
DS1
INSTITUTE OF ASIAN STUDIES. JOURNAL. (Text in English) 1983. s-a. Rs.60($12) Institute of Asian Studies, 377, 10th East St., Thiruvanmiyur, Madras 600 041, India. TEL 416728. Ed. Shu Hikosaka. adv.; bk.rev.; bibl.; illus.; stat.; circ. 500.
—BLDSC shelfmark: 4769.955500.
Description: Cross-cultural and comparative studies of Asian languages, literatures, religions, and other disciplines of Asian perspective.

INSTITUTE OF DEVELOPMENT STUDIES. ANNUAL REPORT. see *BUSINESS AND ECONOMICS — International Development And Assistance*

INSTITUTE OF DEVELOPMENT STUDIES. COMMISSIONED STUDIES. see *BUSINESS AND ECONOMICS — International Development And Assistance*

INSTITUTE OF MODERN RUSSIAN CULTURE NEWSLETTER. see *ETHNIC INTERESTS*

301.45   UK
INSTITUTE OF RACE RELATIONS. ANNUAL REPORT. 1974. a. Institute of Race Relations, 2-6 Leeke St., King's Cross Rd., London WC1X 9HS, England. TEL 071-837-0041. FAX 071-278-0623.

301.35   PE
INSTITUTO DE ESTUDIOS ANDINOS. CUADERNOS. 1978. irreg. Instituto de Estudios Andinos, Apartado 289, Huancayo, Peru. illus.

309   PE
INSTITUTO DE ESTUDIOS PERUANOS. COLECCION MINIMA. 1973. irreg., no.24, 1991. price varies. I E P Ediciones, Horacio Urteaga 694 (Campo de Marte), Lima 11, Peru. TEL 323070. FAX 324981.

INSTITUTO DE ESTUDIOS PERUANOS. DOCUMENTOS DE TRABAJO. see *ANTHROPOLOGY*

309   PE
INSTITUTO DE ESTUDIOS PERUANOS. ESTUDIOS DE LA SOCIEDAD RURAL. 1967. irreg., no.11, 1989. price varies. I E P Ediciones, Horacio Urteaga 694 (Campo de Marte), Lima 11, Peru. TEL 323070. FAX 324981.

301 340   UY
INSTITUTO INTERAMERICANO DEL NINO. JURIDICO SOCIAL. INFORMES TECNICOS. irreg. Instituto Interamericano del Nino, Avda. 8 de Octubre No. 2904, Montevideo, Uruguay.

301.2   US   ISSN 1057-7769
▼**INTERCULTURAL COMMUNICATION STUDIES.** 1991. 2/yr. $35 to individuals; institutions $88. Trinity University, Trinitonian Office, 715 Stadium Dr., San Antonio, TX 78212. Ed. Bates L. Hoffer. adv.; bk.rev.; circ. 200. (back issues avail.)
Description: Offers a multidisciplinary approach to the study of culture - language problems across cultures, whether major culutral groups or ethnic - socioeconometric subgroups within a larger group.
Refereed Serial

INTERCULTURAL STUDIES. see *LINGUISTICS*

362.7   FR   ISSN 0538-5490
HV703
INTERNATIONAL CHILDREN'S CENTRE. PARIS. REPORT OF THE DIRECTOR-GENERAL TO THE EXECUTIVE BOARD. irreg. Centre International de l'Enfance - International Children's Center, Chateau de Longchamp, Bois de Boulogne, 75016 Paris, France. TEL 1-45-20-79-92. FAX 1-45-25-73-67.
Description: Focuses on child health, with contributions from all disciplines relevant to the development of children's health services and activities.

INTERNATIONAL JOURNAL OF BIOSOCIAL AND MEDICAL RESEARCH; bridging the gap between the natural and social sciences to better understand human behavior. see *NUTRITION AND DIETETICS*

301   NE   ISSN 0020-7152
HM1
INTERNATIONAL JOURNAL OF COMPARATIVE SOCIOLOGY. 1960. q. fl.157($89.75) (effective 1992). (York University, Department of Sociology, CN) E.J. Brill, P.O. Box 9000, 2300 PA Leiden, Netherlands. TEL 071-312624. FAX 071-317532. TELEX 39296 BRILL NL. (In N. America: E.J. Brill, 24 Hudson St., Kinderhook, NY 12106. TEL 800-962-4406) Eds. K. Ishwaran, D. Vajpeyi. adv.; bk.rev.; charts. (also avail. in microform from SWZ; reprint service avail. from SWZ) **Indexed:** A.B.C.Pol.Sci., Curr.Cont., Lang.& Lang.Behav.Abstr., Mid.East: Abstr.& Ind., Soc.Sci.Ind., Sociol.Abstr. (1960-), SSCI, Stud.Wom.Abstr.
—BLDSC shelfmark: 4542.173000.
Description: Studies in different cultures on a comparative basis with view to reach a common level of abstraction.

301   FI   ISSN 0019-6398
INTERNATIONAL JOURNAL OF CONTEMPORARY SOCIOLOGY. 1963. s-a. $20 to individuals; institutions $40. c/o Dr. M'hammed Sabour, Dept. of Sociology, University of Joensuu, P.O. Box 111, SF-80101 Joensuu, Finland. TEL 358-73-1511. FAX 358-73-151-4528. adv.; bk.rev.; charts; illus.; cum.index. (also avail. in microfilm from UMI; reprint service avail. from UMI) **Indexed:** Amer.Hist.& Life, ASSIA, Crim.Just.Abstr., Curr.Cont., Hist.Abstr., Lang.& Lang.Behav.Abstr., Sociol.Abstr. (1971-), Sociol.Educ.Abstr., SSCI.
Formerly: Indian Sociological Bulletin.
Description: Discussion of contemporary ideas and research in sociology.

301   II   ISSN 0377-0141
HM1
INTERNATIONAL JOURNAL OF CRITICAL SOCIOLOGY. 1973. s-a. $12. Jaipur Institute of Sociology, II , C-168A, Bajaj Nagar, Jaipur 302 017, India. Ed. R.C. Gupta. bk.rev.; bibl.; charts. **Indexed:** Lang.& Lang.Behav.Abstr.

INTERNATIONAL JOURNAL OF GROUP TENSIONS. see *PSYCHOLOGY*

301   US   ISSN 0147-1767
GN496
INTERNATIONAL JOURNAL OF INTERCULTURAL RELATIONS. 1977. 4/yr. £150 (effective 1992). (Society for International Education, Training and Research) Pergamon Press, Inc., Journals Division, 660 White Plains Rd., Tarrytown, NY 10591-5153. TEL 914-524-9200. FAX 914-333-2444. (And: Headington Hill Hall, Oxford OX3 0BW, England. TEL 0865-794141) Ed. Dan Landis. adv.; bk.rev.; circ. 2,500. (also avail. in microform from MIM,UMI) **Indexed:** Adol.Ment.Hlth.Abstr., Amer.Bibl.Slavic & E.Eur.Stud., ASCA, ASSIA, Chic.Per.Ind., Crim.Just.Abstr., Lang.& Lang.Behav.Abstr., Psychol.Abstr., SSCI.
—BLDSC shelfmark: 4542.311000.
Description: Dedicated to advancing knowledge and understanding of theory, practice and research in inter-group relations.
Refereed Serial

361 614   US
INTERNATIONAL JOURNAL OF MASS EMERGENCIES AND DISASTERS. 1983. 3/yr. $48 membership. International Sociological Association, Research Committee on Disasters, Disaster Research Center, University of Delaware, Newark, DE 19716. TEL 302-451-6618. FAX 302-451-2828. Eds. Neil Britton, Ron Perry. bk.rev. (back issues avail.) **Indexed:** Sociol.Abstr. (1983-).

INTERNATIONAL JOURNAL OF SOCIAL ECONOMICS. see *BUSINESS AND ECONOMICS*

301   US   ISSN 0020-7659
HM1
INTERNATIONAL JOURNAL OF SOCIOLOGY. 1971. q. $260 to institutions. M. E. Sharpe, Inc., 80 Business Park Dr., Armonk, NY 10504. TEL 914-273-1800. FAX 914-273-2106. Ed. Michael Weber. **Indexed:** ASSIA, Lang.& Lang.Behav.Abstr., Mid.East: Abstr.& Ind., P.A.I.S., Stud.Wom.Abstr.
—BLDSC shelfmark: 4542.570000.
Formerly: Eastern. European Studies in Sociology and Anthropology.
Description: English translations from international sources.
Refereed Serial

301 300   UK   ISSN 0144-333X
HM1
INTERNATIONAL JOURNAL OF SOCIOLOGY AND SOCIAL POLICY. 1981. 8/yr. £229.95($699.95) Barmarick Publications, Enholmes Hall, Patrington, Hull HU12 0PR, England. TEL 0964-630033. Ed. Barrie O. Pettman. circ. 200. (back issues avail.; reprint service avail. from SWZ) **Indexed:** ABI Inform., ASSIA, Lang.& Lang.Behav.Abstr., Sociol.Abstr. (1976-).
—BLDSC shelfmark: 4542.571000.
Description: Seeks to provide research and exchange of ideas and new concepts in sociology and social policy as well as evaluating the effects of the implementation of past approaches and strategies.

301.4   II
INTERNATIONAL JOURNAL OF SOCIOLOGY OF THE FAMILY. 1971. s-a. $60. Prints India, 11 Darya Ganj, New Delhi 110 002, India. TEL 3268645. FAX 91-11-3275542. Ed. Man Singh Das. adv.; bk.rev.; circ. 1,200. (also avail. in microform; back issues avail.) **Indexed:** ASSIA, Lang.& Lang.Behav.Abstr., Popul.Ind., Sociol.Abstr. (1971-), SSCI.

INTERNATIONAL JOURNAL OF THE SOCIOLOGY OF LANGUAGE. see *LINGUISTICS*

INTERNATIONAL JOURNAL OF THE SOCIOLOGY OF LAW. see *LAW*

301　　　　　　　UN
INTERNATIONAL REVIEW FOR THE SOCIOLOGY OF SPORT. (Text English of French) 1966. 3/yr. DM.138. (Unesco, International Committee for Sociology of Sport (ICSS)) R. Oldenbourg Verlag GmbH, Box 801360, D-8000 Munich, Germany. FAX 1-4273-0521. TELEX 529296. Ed. Nigel Walk. adv.; bk.rev.; abstr.; bibl.; illus.; circ. 1,000. (back issues avail.) **Indexed:** Lang.& Lang.Behav.Abstr., Sociol.Abstr. (1968-), Sportsearch (1984-).
　Formerly: International Review of Sport Sociology (ISSN 0074-7769)
　Description: Forum for sports sociology, including related interdisciplinary topics such as social psychology, history and economics of sports, and philosophy.

301.4　　　　　　　II
INTERNATIONAL REVIEW OF MODERN SOCIOLOGY. 1971. s-a. $60. 11 Darya Ganj, New Delhi 110 002, India. TEL 3268645. FAX 91-11-3275542. TELEX 31-61087 PRIN IN. Ed. Man Singh Das. adv.; bk.rev.; circ. 1,200. (also avail. in microform from UMI; back issues avail.) **Indexed:** ASSIA, Lang.& Lang.Behav.Abstr., Sociol.Abstr. (1972-), SSCI.

INTERNATIONAL SOCIETY FOR THE SOCIOLOGY OF RELIGION. see RELIGIONS AND THEOLOGY

301　　　　　　　US
INTERNATIONAL SOCIOLOGICAL REVIEW. 1984. q. $10. Harvest Publishers, 1521 Shattuck Ave., Box 9503, N. Berkeley Sta., Berkeley, CA 94709. Ed. Richard Krooth.
　Description: Sociological dimensions of race, class and ethnicity in the global milieu.

301　　　　UK　　ISSN 0268-5809
HM1
INTERNATIONAL SOCIOLOGY. 1986. q. £27($45) to individuals; institutions £68($112). (International Sociological Association) Sage Publications Ltd., 6 Bonhill St., London EC2A 4PU, England. TEL 071-374-0645. FAX 071-374-8741. Ed. Richard Grathoff. adv.; color page #190; trim 193 x 114; adv. contact: Bernie Folan. **Indexed:** Curr.Cont., Int.Polit.Sci.Abstr., Sci.Cit.Ind., Sociol.Abstr. (1986-), SSCI.
　—BLDSC shelfmark: 4549.574200.
　Description: Draws together work of cross-cultural relevance from the international community of sociologists, focusing on fundamental issues of theory and method and on new directions in empirical research.

301　　　　NE　　ISSN 0074-8684
INTERNATIONAL STUDIES IN SOCIOLOGY AND SOCIAL ANTHROPOLOGY. 1963. irreg., vol.57, 1991. price varies. E.J. Brill, P.O. Box 9000, 2300 PA Leiden, Netherlands. TEL 071-39296. FAX 071-317532. TELEX 39296 BRILL NL. (In N. America: E.J. Brill, 24 Hudson St., Kinderhook, NY 12106. TEL 800-962-4406) Ed. K. Ishwaran.
　—BLDSC shelfmark: 4549.820000.

INTERPRETIVE PERSPECTIVES ON EDUCATION AND POLICY. see EDUCATION

INTERRACIAL BOOKS FOR CHILDREN BULLETIN. see PUBLISHING AND BOOK TRADE

INTERSECTIONS; a journal of urban and environmental studies. see ENVIRONMENTAL STUDIES

301　　　　　　　PO
INTERVENCAO SOCIAL. 1985. 3/yr. Esc.1200 to institutions; individuals Esc.950. Instituto Superior de Servico Social, Largo do Mitelo, 1, Lisbon 1000, Portugal. (Co-sponsors: Fundacao Calouste Gulbenkian; Junta Nacional de Investigacao Cientifica) Eds. Luisa Ferreira, Pedro Loff. circ. 1,000.

301 574　　　GL　　ISSN 0906-5504
INUIT TUSAATAAT. (Text in Danish, English and Inuit) 1982. m. Inuit Issittormiut Kattufiat (ICC) - Inuit Circumpolar Conference, P.O. Box 204, 3900 Nuuk, Greenland. FAX 011-299-23001. Ed.Bd. **Indexed:** HR Rep.
　Formerly (until 1990): Inuit (ISSN 0108-6898)
　Description: Focuses on subjects of concern to the indigenous arctic peoples and the nations of the arctic states: Canada, Denmark, Finland, Iceland, Norway, Sweden, USSR and USA.

INVANDRARRAPPORT; Invandrarnas debatt- och kulturtidskrift. see POPULATION STUDIES

301　　　　AG　　ISSN 0020-9961
INVESTIGACIONES EN SOCIOLOGIA.* (Summaries in English, French and Spanish) 1962. s-a. P.600($3) Universidad Nacional de Cuyo, Instituto de Sociologia, Patricias Mendocinas 1327, Mendoza, Argentina. bk.rev.; abstr.; charts; illus.; tr.lit.; index.

IRISH AMERICA MAGAZINE. see ETHNIC INTERESTS

ITALIA COOPERATIVA. see BUSINESS AND ECONOMICS — Cooperatives

261　　　　GW　　ISSN 0075-2584
HN30
JAHRBUCH FUER CHRISTLICHE SOZIALWISSENSCHAFTEN. 1960. a. price varies. (Universitaet Muenster, Institut fuer Christliche Sozialwissenschaften) Verlag Regensberg, Daimlerweg 58, Postfach 6748-6749, 4400 Muenster, Germany. TEL 0251-717061. FAX 0251-717725. **Indexed:** CERDIC.

301　　　　GW　　ISSN 0138-435X
JAHRBUCH FUER SOZIOLOGIE UND SOZIALPOLITIK. (Text in German; summaries English, French and Russian) 1980. a. (Akademie der Wissenschaften der DDR) Akademie-Verlag Berlin, Leipziger Str. 3-4, 1086 Berlin, Germany.

301　　　　GW　　ISSN 0177-4093
JAHRBUCH FUER VERGLEICHENDE SOZIALFORSCHUNG. 1984. a. DM.48. (Berliner Institut fuer Vergleichende Sozialforschung) Edition Parabolis, Potsdamerstr. 91, 1000 Berlin 30, Germany. TEL 030-262-3084. FAX 030-2629503. Eds. Jochen Blaschke, Jutta Aumueller.
　Formerly: Jahrbuch zur Geschichte und Gesellschaft des Vorderen und Mittleren Orients.
　Description: Covers ethnic relations, social comparative research, migration and refugees.

JAMES NICHOLAS EDUCATION NEWSLETTER; education publishing news. see EDUCATION — School Organization And Administration

301　　　　JA　　ISSN 0021-5414
JAPANESE SOCIOLOGICAL REVIEW/SHAKAIGAKU HYORON. (Text in Japanese; title and contents page in English) 1950. q. (Japanese Sociological Society - Nippon Shakai Gakkai) Yuhikaku Publishing Co. Ltd., 2-17 Kanda Jimbocho, Chiyoda-ku, Tokyo 101, Japano-ku. adv.; index; circ. 1,200. **Indexed:** Lang.& Lang.Behav.Abstr., Sociol.Abstr. (1955-).
　—BLDSC shelfmark: 4662.080000.

JARLIBRO. see LINGUISTICS

JASZKUNSAG; social and artistic journal. see LITERATURE

301　　　　　　　GW
JEDEFRAU & JEDERMANN; Zeitung fuer soziale Dreigliederung, Umweltfragen, neue Lebensformen. 1958. m. DM.2.50. Jedermann Verlag, Hauptstr. 99, D-8992 Wasserburg 1B, Germany. Ed. Peter Schilinski. circ. 1,200.
　Formerly: Jedermann.

301.3　　　　　　　IS
JERUSALEM URBAN STUDIES. (Text in English) 1970. irreg. $2. Hebrew University of Jerusalem, Institute of Urban & Regional Studies, Jerusalem, Israel. Eds. Arieh Shahar, Erik Cohen. charts; circ. 1,000.

301　　　　UK　　ISSN 0021-6534
DS101
JEWISH JOURNAL OF SOCIOLOGY. 1959. s-a. £10($20) to individuals; institutions £12($24). 187 Gloucester Place, London NW1 6BU, England. TEL 071-262-8939. Ed. Judith Freedman. adv.; bk.rev.; bibl.; index. **Indexed:** A.I.C.P., ASSIA, Curr.Cont., Ind.Jew.Per., Lang.& Lang.Behav.Abstr., Mid.East: Abstr.& Ind., P.A.I.S., Psychol.Abstr., Sociol.Abstr. (1959-), SSCI.
　—BLDSC shelfmark: 4668.355000.

JOURNAL FOR THE SCIENTIFIC STUDY OF RELIGION. see RELIGIONS AND THEOLOGY

301　　　　AU　　ISSN 0025-8822
JOURNAL FUER SOZIALFORSCHUNG. 1961. q. S.520 to individuals; institutions S.675. European Centre for Social Welfare Policy and Research, Berggasse 17, A-1090 Vienna, Austria. Ed. Bernd Marin. adv.; bk.rev.; abstr.; stat.; cum.index every 5 yrs.; circ. 600. (tabloid format)
　—BLDSC shelfmark: 5066.085000.
　Formerly: Die Meinung.

JOURNAL OF AGING & SOCIAL POLICY; a journal devoted to aging & social policy. see GERONTOLOGY AND GERIATRICS

JOURNAL OF APPLIED BEHAVIORAL SCIENCE. see PSYCHOLOGY

950 960　　　NE　　ISSN 0021-9096
DT1
JOURNAL OF ASIAN AND AFRICAN STUDIES. 1966. q. fl.140 (effective 1992). E.J. Brill, P.O. Box 9000, 2300 PA Leiden, Netherlands. TEL 071-312624. FAX 071-317532. TELEX 39296 BRILL NL. (In N. America: E.J. Brill, 24 Hudson St., Kinderhook, NY 12106. TEL 800-962-4406) Ed. K. Ishwaran. bk.rev. (reprint service avail. from SWZ) **Indexed:** A.B.C.Pol.Sci., A.I.C.P., Abstr.Anthropol., Amer.Hist.& Life, ASSIA, Curr.Cont., Curr.Cont.Africa, E.I., Geo.Abstr., Hist.Abstr., I D A, Lang.& Lang.Behav.Abstr., Mid.East: Abstr.& Ind., Rural Devel.Abstr., Rural Ext.Educ.& Tr.Abstr., Soc.Sci.Ind., SSCI.
　—BLDSC shelfmark: 4947.230000.
　Description: Scholarly accounts of man and society in the developing nations of Asia and Africa.

JOURNAL OF BIOSOCIAL SCIENCE. see BIOLOGY — Genetics

JOURNAL OF BUSINESS & SOCIAL STUDIES. see BUSINESS AND ECONOMICS

JOURNAL OF COMMUNITY AND APPLIED SOCIAL PSYCHOLOGY; an international journal of applied social psychology. see PSYCHOLOGY

JOURNAL OF COMMUNITY PSYCHOLOGY. see PSYCHOLOGY

301.4　　　　CN　　ISSN 0047-2328
HQ1　　　　　　　　　CODEN: JCFSAO
JOURNAL OF COMPARATIVE FAMILY STUDIES. 1970. 3/yr. Can.$55. University of Calgary, Department of Sociology, 2500 University Dr. N.W., Calgary, Alta. T2N 1N4, Canada. TEL 403-220-7317. FAX 403-282-8289. Ed. George Kurian. adv.; bk.rev.; abstr.; charts; stat.; cum.index; circ. 800. (processed; also avail. in microform from MIM,UMI; reprint service avail. from UMI) **Indexed:** Abstr.Pop.Cult, ASSIA, Curr.Cont., Curr.Lit.Fam.Plan., E.I., Excerp.Med., Lang.& Lang.Behav.Abstr., Mid.East: Abstr.& Ind., Popul.Ind., Psychol.Abstr, Rural Recreat.Tour.Abstr., Sage Fam.Stud.Abstr., Sociol.Abstr. (1970-), Sp.Ed.Needs Abstr., SSCI, Stud.Wom.Abstr., World Agri.Econ.& Rural Sociol.Abstr.
　—BLDSC shelfmark: 4961.930000.

301 200　　　CN
BL60
JOURNAL OF COMPARATIVE SOCIOLOGY AND ETHICS. Abbreviated title: J C S E. 1973. a. $50. (Industrial Relations Institute) M R W Limited, P.O. Box 7305, Ottawa K1L 8E4, Canada. TEL 613-831-1052. FAX 613-831-8452. Ed. Amarjit S. Sethi. adv.; bk.rev.; circ. 1,000. (back issues avail.) **Indexed:** Rel.Ind.One, Sociol.Abstr. (1973-).
　Formerly (until 1990): Journal of Comparative Sociology and Religion (ISSN 0709-3519)
　Description: Covers social themes, the issue of ethics in an information society, religion as a source of information for comparative values in post-industrial societies and developing economies.

| 301.34 | US | ISSN 0891-2416 |

HT101

JOURNAL OF CONTEMPORARY ETHNOGRAPHY; a journal of ethnographic research. 1972. q. $42 to individuals; institutions $125. Sage Publications, Inc., 2455 Teller Rd., Newbury Park, CA 91320. TEL 805-499-0721. FAX 805-499-0871. (And: Sage Publications, Ltd., 6 Bonhill Rd., London EC2A 4PU, England) Eds. Peter and Patricia Adler. adv.; bk.rev.; charts; illus.; index; circ. 1,200. (also avail. in microfilm from UMI) **Indexed:** A.I.C.P., Abstr.Anthropol., Abstr.Pop.Cult., ASSIA, C.I.J.E., Curr.Cont., E.I., Lang.& Lang.Behav.Abstr., Mid.East: Abstr.& Ind., P.A.I.S., Sage Pub.Admin.Abstr., Sage Urb.Stud.Abstr., Soc.Sci.Ind., Sociol.Abstr., SSCI, Stud.Wom.Abstr.
—BLDSC shelfmark: 4965.228000.
  Former titles: Urban Life (ISSN 0098-3039); (until vol.15): Urban Life and Culture (ISSN 0049-5662)

JOURNAL OF CROSS-CULTURAL PSYCHOLOGY. see *PSYCHOLOGY*

JOURNAL OF DEVELOPING AREAS. see *BUSINESS AND ECONOMICS — International Development And Assistance*

JOURNAL OF DEVELOPMENT STUDIES. see *BUSINESS AND ECONOMICS — International Development And Assistance*

JOURNAL OF DIVORCE & REMARRIAGE; clinical studies and research in family therapy, family mediation, family studies and family law. see *MATRIMONY*

JOURNAL OF EARLY ADOLESCENCE. see *CHILDREN AND YOUTH — About*

JOURNAL OF EXPERIMENTAL SOCIAL PSYCHOLOGY. see *PSYCHOLOGY*

| 301.4 | US | ISSN 0363-1990 |

HQ1

JOURNAL OF FAMILY HISTORY; studies in family, kinship and demography. 1976. q. $45 to individuals (foreign $55); institutions $90 (foreign $100). (National Council on Family Relations) J A I Press Inc., 55 Old Post Rd., No. 2, Box 1678, Greenwich, CT 06836-1678. TEL 203-661-7602. FAX 612-781-9348. Ed. Tamara Hareven. adv.; bk.rev.; charts; illus.; circ. 1,400. **Indexed:** Amer.Bibl.Slavic & E.Eur.Stud., Amer.Hist.& Life, Curr.Cont., E.I., Hist.Abstr., Hum.Ind., Mid.East: Abstr.& Ind., Popul.Ind., Psychol.Abstr., Sage Fam.Stud.Abstr., Sage Urb.Stud.Abstr., SSCI, Stud.Wom.Abstr.
●Also available online. Vendor(s): BRS.
—BLDSC shelfmark: 4983.680000.
  Supersedes: Family in Historical Perspective (ISSN 0360-3598)

| 301 | US | ISSN 0192-513X |

HQ1

JOURNAL OF FAMILY ISSUES. 1980. q. $42 to individuals; institutions $118. (National Council on Family Relations) Sage Publications, Inc., 2455 Teller Rd., Newbury Park, CA 91320. TEL 805-499-0721. FAX 805-499-0871. (And: Sage Publicatons, Ltd., 6 Bonhill St., London EC2A 4PU, England) Ed. Patricia A. Voydanoff. adv. (also avail. in microfilm from WSH) **Indexed:** C.I.J.E., Curr.Cont., Curr.Lit.Fam.Plan., Sage Fam.Stud.Abstr., Soc.Work Res.& Abstr., Sociol.Abstr., SSCI.
●Also available online. Vendor(s): BRS.
—BLDSC shelfmark: 4983.690000.
  Description: Covers contemporary social issues and problems of marriage and family life.

JOURNAL OF FAMILY LAW. see *LAW — Family And Matrimonial Law*

JOURNAL OF FAMILY THERAPY. see *MEDICAL SCIENCES — Psychiatry And Neurology*

JOURNAL OF FAMILY VIOLENCE. see *CRIMINOLOGY AND LAW ENFORCEMENT*

JOURNAL OF FLUENCY DISORDERS. see *PSYCHOLOGY*

JOURNAL OF FORECASTING; an international journal. see *BUSINESS AND ECONOMICS — Management*

JOURNAL OF GROUP PSYCHOTHERAPY, PSYCHODRAMA & SOCIOMETRY. see *PSYCHOLOGY*

| 301 | US | ISSN 0022-1465 |
| | | CODEN: JHSBA5 |

R11

JOURNAL OF HEALTH AND SOCIAL BEHAVIOR. 1960. q. $34 to individuals (foreign $40); institutions $63 (foreign $69); effective 1992. American Sociological Association, 1722 N St., N.W., Washington, DC 20036. TEL 202-833-3410. FAX 202-785-0146. Ed. Mary Fennell. adv.; bk.rev.; charts; illus.; index; circ. 5,000. (also avail. in microform from MIM,UMI; reprint service avail. from SWZ,UMI) **Indexed:** Abstr.Anthropol., Abstr.Health Care Manage.Stud., Abstr.Hyg., Adol.Ment.Hlth.Abstr., ASSIA, Biol.Abstr., CINAHL, Crim.Just.Abstr., Curr.Cont., Excerp.Med., FAMLI, Hosp.Lit.Ind., Ind.Med., Int.Nurs.Ind., Lang.& Lang.Behav.Abstr., Mid.East: Abstr.& Ind., Psychol.Abstr., Sage Fam.Stud.Abstr., Sage Pub.Admin.Abstr., Soc.Sci.Ind., Soc.Work Res.& Abstr., Sociol.Abstr. (1961-), Sp.Ed.Needs Abstr., SSCI, Stud.Wom.Abstr., Trop.Dis.Bull.
—BLDSC shelfmark: 4996.730000.
  Formerly: Journal of Health and Human Behavior (ISSN 0095-9006)
  Description: Publishes reports of empirical studies, theoretical analyses, and synthesizing reviews that employ a sociological perspective to clarify aspects of social life bearing on human health and illness, both physical and mental.
  Refereed Serial

| 301 | UK | ISSN 0952-1909 |

HM104

JOURNAL OF HISTORICAL SOCIOLOGY. 1988. q. £32.50($60) to individuals; institutions £72($125). Basil Blackwell Ltd., 108 Cowley Rd., Oxford OX4 1JF, England. TEL 0865-791100. FAX 0865-791347. TELEX 837022-OXBOOK-G. (US addr.: Basil Blackwell, Journals Dept., Three Cambridge Center, Cambridge, MA 02142, US) Ed.Bd. (reprint service avail. from UMI) **Indexed:** Sociol.Abstr. (1981-).
—BLDSC shelfmark: 5000.493000.
  Description: Provides an international forum for historically-informed reflection on human society.

JOURNAL OF HOMOSEXUALITY. see *HOMOSEXUALITY*

JOURNAL OF INTERNATIONAL STUDENT PERSONNEL. see *EDUCATION — International Education Programs*

JOURNAL OF INTERPERSONAL VIOLENCE; concerned with the study and treatment of victims and perpetrators of physical and sexual violence. see *CRIMINOLOGY AND LAW ENFORCEMENT*

| 354 | US | ISSN 0022-2089 |

HV1

JOURNAL OF JEWISH COMMUNAL SERVICE. 1923. q. $24 to individuals; organizations $30. Jewish Communal Service Association, 3084 State Hwy. 27, Ste. 9, Kendall Park, NJ 08824-1657. TEL 201-821-1871. Ed. Gail Naron Chalew. adv.; bk.rev.; charts; index, cum.index every 10 yrs.; circ. 2,800. (also avail. in microform from UMI; reprint service avail. from UMI) **Indexed:** ASSIA, Ind.Jew.Per., Mid.East: Abstr.& Ind., P.A.I.S., Psychol.Abstr., Soc.Work Res.& Abstr.
—BLDSC shelfmark: 5009.500000.

JOURNAL OF LANGUAGE AND SOCIAL PSYCHOLOGY. see *PSYCHOLOGY*

JOURNAL OF MARITAL AND FAMILY THERAPY. see *PSYCHOLOGY*

| 301.42 | US | ISSN 0022-2445 |
| | | CODEN: JMFAA6 |

JOURNAL OF MARRIAGE AND THE FAMILY. 1939. q. $50 to individuals; institutions $85. National Council on Family Relations, 3989 Central Ave., N.E., Ste. 550, Minneapolis, MN 55421-3921. TEL 612-781-9331. FAX 612-781-9348. Ed. Marilyn Coleman. adv.; bk.rev.; charts; index; circ. 7,400. (also avail. in microfilm from UMI; reprint service avail. from UMI) **Indexed:** Abstr.Hyg., Abstr.Soc.Work., Acad.Ind., Adol.Ment.Hlth.Abstr., ASSIA, Biog.Ind., Biol.Abstr., Bk.Rev.Ind. (1965-), C.I.J.E., CERDIC, Child.Bk.Rev.Ind. (1965-), Child Devel.Abstr., Commun.Abstr., Crim.Just.Abstr., Curr.Cont., Curr.Lit.Fam.Plan., Except.Child.Educ.Abstr., Excerp.Med., FAMLI, G.Soc.Sci.& Rel.Per.Lit., Hum.Ind., Lang.& Lang.Behav.Abstr., Mag.Ind., Mid.East: Abstr.& Ind., Past.Care & Couns.Abstr., Popul.Ind., Psychol.Abstr., Rehabil.Lit., Rel.Ind.One, Sage Fam.Stud.Abstr., Soc.Sci.Ind., Soc.Work Res.& Abstr., Sociol.Abstr. (1953-), SSCI, Stud.Wom.Abstr., Trop.Dis.Bull.
●Also available online. Vendor(s): BRS.
  Formerly: Marriage and Family Living.
  Description: Forum covering theory, research interpretation and critical discussion on subjects related to marriage and the family.

| 301 | US | ISSN 0022-250X |

HM1

JOURNAL OF MATHEMATICAL SOCIOLOGY. 1971. 4/yr. (1 vol., 4 nos./vol.). $206. Gordon and Breach Science Publishers, 270 Eighth Ave., New York, NY 10011. TEL 212-206-8900. FAX 212-645-2459. TELEX 236735 GOPUB UR. (Subscr. to: Box 786, Cooper Sta., New York, NY 10276. TEL 800-545-8398; UK subscr. to: P.O. Box 90, Reading, Berkshire RG1 8JL, England. TEL 0734-560-080) Ed. Patrick Doreian. adv.; index. (also avail. in microform) **Indexed:** Compumath, Curr.Cont., Lang.& Lang.Behav.Abstr., Math.R., Psychol.Abstr., Sci.Abstr., SSCI.
—BLDSC shelfmark: 5012.450000.
  Refereed Serial

| 301 | US | ISSN 1042-8224 |
| | | CODEN: JMSWE5 |

HV3176

▼**JOURNAL OF MULTICULTURAL SOCIAL WORK.** 1991. q. $28 to individuals; institutions $32; libraries $48. Haworth Press, Inc., 10 Alice St., Binghamton, NY 13904. TEL 607-722-1695. FAX 607-722-1424. TELEX 4932599. Ed. Paul R. Keys. (also avail. in microform from HAW; reprint service avail. from HAW) **Indexed:** Soc.Work Res.& Abstr.
  Description: Develops knowledge and promotes understanding of the impact of culture, ethnicity, race, and class on the individual, group, organization, and community on the delivery of human services.
  Refereed Serial

JOURNAL OF MULTILINGUAL & MULTICULTURAL DEVELOPMENT. see *LINGUISTICS*

| 300 572 370 900 | PH | ISSN 0115-2408 |

LA1290

JOURNAL OF NORTHERN LUZON; a semi-annual research forum. 1970. s-a. $15. Saint Mary's College of Bayombong, Nueva Vizcaya 1501, Philippines. Ed. Bonifacio V. Ramos. adv.; bk.rev.; bibl.; circ. 500. **Indexed:** Ind.Phil.Per.
  Description: Contains articles on ethnic groups of northern Luzon, including the Bontoc, Gaddang and Ifugao.

JOURNAL OF ORGANIZATIONAL BEHAVIOUR. see *PSYCHOLOGY*

| 301 | UK | ISSN 0306-6150 |

HD1513.A3

JOURNAL OF PEASANT STUDIES. 1973. q. £38($65) to individuals; institutions £90($135). Frank Cass & Co. Ltd., Gainsborough House, 11 Gainsborough Rd., London E11 1RS, England. TEL 081-530-4226. FAX 081-530-7795. Ed.Bd. adv.; bk.rev.; index. (also avail. in microfilm from UMI; back issues avail.) **Indexed:** A.I.C.P., Amer.Hist.& Life, ASSIA, Cott.& Trop.Fibr.Abstr., Curr.Cont., E.I., Geo.Abstr., Hist.Abstr., I D A, Int.Lab.Doc., Lang.& Lang.Behav.Abstr., Mid.East: Abstr.& Ind., P.A.I.S., Rural Devel.Abstr., Rural Recreat.Tour.Abstr., SSCI, Stud.Wom.Abstr., World Agri.Econ.& Rural Sociol.Abstr.
—BLDSC shelfmark: 5030.150000.
  Description: Examines the role of peasants in political, economic and social change worldwide.

SOCIOLOGY

JOURNAL OF RURAL DEVELOPMENT. see *POLITICAL SCIENCE*

JOURNAL OF RURAL HEALTH. see *MEDICAL SCIENCES*

301.35 US ISSN 0743-0167
HT401
JOURNAL OF RURAL STUDIES. 1985. q. £155 (effective 1992). Pergamon Press, Inc., Journals Division, 660 White Plains Rd., Tarrytown, NY 10591-5153. TEL 914-524-9200. FAX 914-333-2444. (And: Headington Hill Hall, Oxford OX3 0BW, England. TEL 0865-794141) Ed. Paul Cloke. adv. (also avail. in microform from MIM,UMI) **Indexed:** Cott.& Trop.Fibr.Abstr., Curr.Adv.Ecol.Sci., Curr.Cont, Environ.Per.Bibl., I D A, Risk Abstr., Rural Devel.Abstr., Soils & Fert, Triticale Abstr., World Agri.Econ.& Rural Sociol.Abstr.
—BLDSC shelfmark: 5052.128900.
Description: Forum for research in the broad spectrum of rural issues, including society, demography, housing, employment, transport, land-use, recreation, agriculture and conservation.
Refereed Serial

301 UK
JOURNAL OF SEX. 1976. m. £12. G.S.P. Ltd., Gadoline House, Whyteleafe, Surrey, England. Ed. James Hughes. adv.; bk.rev.; circ. 50,000.

JOURNAL OF SEX RESEARCH. see *PSYCHOLOGY*

301 900 US ISSN 0022-4529
HN1
JOURNAL OF SOCIAL HISTORY. 1967. q. $25 to individuals; institutions $55; students $17(effective Sep. 1991). Carnegie - Mellon University Press, Schenley Park, Pittsburgh, PA 15213. FAX 412-268-5288. Ed. Peter N. Stearns. adv.; bk.rev.; charts; stat.; index; circ. 1,900. (also avail. in microform from MIM,UMI; reprint service avail. from UMI) **Indexed:** Amer.Bibl.Slavic & E.Eur.Stud., Amer.Hist.& Life, Arts & Hum.Cit.Ind., Bk.Rev.Ind. (1984-), Child.Bk.Rev.Ind. (1984-), Crim.Just.Abstr., Curr.Cont., Hist.Abstr., Lang.& Lang.Behav.Abstr., Mid.East: Abstr.& Ind., Sage Fam.Stud.Abstr., Soc.Sci.Ind., Sociol.Abstr., SSCI, Stud.Wom.Abstr.
—BLDSC shelfmark: 5064.754000.
Description: Covers all aspects of social history, including all time periods and geographical areas. Focuses on new topics, methodologies and comparisons.

JOURNAL OF SOCIAL ISSUES. see *PSYCHOLOGY*

301 UK ISSN 0047-2794
HV1
JOURNAL OF SOCIAL POLICY. 1972. q. $65 to individuals; institutions $122. (Social Administration Association) Cambridge University Press, Edinburgh Bldg., Shaftesbury Rd., Cambridge CB2 2RU, England. TEL 0223-312393. FAX 0223-315052. TELEX 851817256. (North American addr.: Cambridge University Press, 40 W. 20th St., New York, NY 10011) Ed. Alan Deacon. adv.; bk.rev.; index. (also avail. in microform from UMI; reprint service avail. from SWZ) **Indexed:** A.B.C.Pol.Sci., Abstr.Hyg., ASSIA, Curr.Cont., Int.Lab.Doc., Lang.& Lang.Behav.Abstr., Med.Care Rev., Mid.East: Abstr.& Ind., P.A.I.S., PHRA, PSI, Psychol.Abstr., Soc.Sci.Ind., Sociol.Abstr, SSCI, Stud.Wom.Abstr., Trop.Dis.Bull., World Bibl.Soc.Sec.
—BLDSC shelfmark: 5064.780000.
Description: Theoretical, historical analysis of social policy worldwide, and investigation of processes and obstacles to implementing social policy at local and national levels.

360 301 US ISSN 0191-5096
HN1
JOURNAL OF SOCIOLOGY AND SOCIAL WELFARE. 1973. q. $28 to individuals (foreign $34); institutions $59 (foreign $67). Western Michigan University, School of Social Work, c/o Gary Mathews, Assoc. Ed., Kalamazoo, MI 49008-5034. TEL 616-387-3198. FAX 616-387-0958. Ed. Robert D. Leighninger, Jr. adv.; bk.rev.; index, cum.index; circ. 650. (also avail. in microform from UMI; back issues avail.; reprint service avail. from UMI) **Indexed:** Adol.Ment.Hlth.Abstr., ASSIA, Lang.& Lang.Behav.Abstr., Mid.East: Abstr.& Ind., PSI, Psychol.Abstr., Soc.Work. Res.& Abstr., Sociol.Abstr. (1973-).
—BLDSC shelfmark: 5064.935000.
Description: Articles on the analysis of social welfare institutions, policies and problems. Attempts to bridge the gap between social science theory and social work practice.

JOURNAL OF SPORT AND SOCIAL ISSUES. see *SPORTS AND GAMES*

301 US ISSN 1043-4070
HQ12 CODEN: JHSEEI
▼**JOURNAL OF THE HISTORY OF SEXUALITY.** 1990. q. $29 to individuals; institutions $50; students $20. University of Chicago Press, 5720 S. Woodlawn Ave., Chicago, IL 60637. TEL 312-753-3347. FAX 312-702-0694. TELEX 25-4603. (Subscr. to: Box 37005, Chicago, IL 60637) Ed. John C. Fout.
—BLDSC shelfmark: 5002.050000.
Description: Examines the history of sexuality in all its expressions, recognizing various differneces of class, culture, gender, race, and sexual preference. Provides a forum for historical, critical and theoretical research in the field. Presents original articles and critical reviews from historians and social scientists worldwide.
Refereed Serial

301 US ISSN 1054-1802
▼**JOURNAL OF URBAN AND CULTURAL STUDIES.** 1990. bi-a. $16 to individuals; institutions $32 (typically set in June). University of Massachusetts, Department of English, Wheatly Hall, Harbor Campus, Boston, MA 02126-3393. TEL 617-287-5760. FAX 617-265-7173. Ed.Bd. adv.; bk.rev. (back issues avail.) **Indexed:** Sociol.Educ.Abstr.

JUNGE KIRCHE; eine Zeitschrift Europaeischer Christen. see *RELIGIONS AND THEOLOGY*

301 572 MY ISSN 0126-9518
JURNAL ANTROPOLOGI DAN SOSIOLOGI. (Text in English and Malay) 1972. a. M.$10. (National University of Malaysia, Department of Anthropology and Sociology - Universiti Kebangsaan Malaysia) Penerbit Universiti Kebangsaan Malaysia, 43600 UKM Bangi, Selangor, Malaysia. TELEX UNIKEB MA 31496. Ed. Hock-Tong Cheu. bk.rev.; bibl.; circ. 500.
Formerly (until 1974): Jernal Antropoloji dan Sosioloji.

KAILASH; journal of Himalayan studies. see *HISTORY — History Of Asia*

KAN ANDERS. see *POLITICAL SCIENCE — International Relations*

301 PH ISSN 0115-6292
KAYA TAO. (Text in English) 1980. s-a. P.85($10.50) (De La Salle University, Behavioral Sciences Department) De La Salle University Press, 2401 Taft Ave., Manila, Philippines. TEL 2-595177. Ed. Jonathan Y. Okamura. adv.; bk.rev.; circ. 500.
Description: Publishes scholarly articles reflecting significant quantitative or qualitative research. Includes speeches, research reports, and "state of the art" papers.

950 US
KHOSANA. 1976. 2/yr. $10 to individuals; institutions $15 (effective Jan. 1990). Association for Asian Studies, Thailand - Laos - Cambodia Studies Group, Program for Southeast Asian Studies, Arizona State University, Tempe, AZ 85287-3101. TEL 602-965-4232. FAX 602-965-1608. (Subscr. to: Arlene B. Neher, Subscr. Mgr., Continuing Ed., Northern Illinois Univ., DeKalb, IL 60115-2845. TEL 815-753-1458) Ed. Jacqueline Butler-Diaz. bk.rev.; abstr.; bibl.; circ. 300. (back issues avail.)
Description: Contains academic news of Thai, Laotian and Cambodian studies. Includes information on conferences.

334 IS ISSN 0334-2182
KIBBUTZ (TEL AVIV); interdisciplinary research review. (Text in English, Hebrew) 1973. a. price varies. Federation of Kibbutz Movements, Box 303, Tel Aviv 61-000, Israel. Eds. Shimon Shur, Henry Near. circ. 1,250. **Indexed:** Lang.& Lang.Behav.Abstr.

KINDERSCHUTZ AKTUELL. see *SOCIAL SERVICES AND WELFARE*

301 US ISSN 0278-1557
BD175
KNOWLEDGE AND SOCIETY; studies in the sociology of culture past and present. 1978. irreg., vol.8, 1989. $58.50 to institutions. J A I Press Inc., 55 Old Post Rd., No. 2, Box 1678, Greenwich, CT 06836-1678. TEL 203-661-7602. Eds. Henrika Kuklick, Elizabeth Long. **Indexed:** Lang.& Lang.Behav.Abstr., Sociol.Abstr. (1978-).
—BLDSC shelfmark: 5100.441000.
Formerly: Research in Sociology of Knowledge, Science and Art (ISSN 0163-0180)

301 DK ISSN 0900-9922
KOBENHAVNS UNIVERSITET. SOCIOLOGISK INSTITUT. AFHANDLING. 1981. irreg. DKK 35. University of Copenhagen, Department of Sociology, Linnesgade 22, 1361 Copenhagen K, Denmark. TEL 33-150520. Ed. Birthe Hove.

KODO KEIRYOGAKU/JAPANESE JOURNAL OF BEHAVIORMETRICS. see *PSYCHOLOGY*

301 DK ISSN 0900-9876
KOEBENHAVNS UNIVERSITET. SOCIOLOGISK INSTITUT. ARBEJDSPAPIR. 1979. irreg. DKK 15. Koebenhavns Universitet, Sociologisk Institut, Linnesgade 22, 1361 Copenhagen K, Denmark. TEL 33-150520. FAX 33-150520. Ed. Birthe Hove.

301 150 GW ISSN 0023-2653
KOELNER ZEITSCHRIFT FUER SOZIOLOGIE UND SOZIALPSYCHOLOGIE. 1927. 4/yr. DM.139. Westdeutscher Verlag GmbH, Postfach 5829, 6200 Wiesbaden 1, Germany. TEL 0611-160230. FAX 0611-160229. TELEX 4186-928-VWV-D. Ed.Bd. adv.; bk.rev.; charts; illus.; index, cum.index; circ. 3,500. (reprint service avail. from SCH) **Indexed:** Curr.Cont., Ger.J.Psych., P.A.I.S.For.Lang.Ind., Phil.Ind., Psychol.Abstr., Sociol.Abstr. (1952-53), SSCI.

KOMMA; tijdschrift voor politiek en sociaal onderzoek. see *POLITICAL SCIENCE*

301 410 NE ISSN 0168-6682
KONTEKSTEN; publikatiereeks over taal, tekst en vertoog. (Text in Dutch, English) 1984. irreg. price varies. Erasmus Universiteit Rotterdam, Afdeling Medische Sociologie, P.O. Box 1738, 3000 DR Rotterdam, Netherlands. TEL 010-634100. (Co-sponser: Vakgroep Verzorgingssociologie van het Sociologisch Instituut van de Universiteit van Amsterdam) (back issues avail.)
—BLDSC shelfmark: 5112.565000.
Description: Studies of text and conservation analysis in the fields of medicine, social service and education.

301 PL ISSN 0860-2220
DK4185.R9
KRAJE SOCJALISTYCZNE. (Text in Polish; summaries in English, Russian) q. $28. (Polish Academy of Sciences, Institute of Socialist Countries) Ossolineum, Publishing House of the Polish Academy of Sciences, Rynek 9, 50-106 Wroclaw, Poland. TEL 386-25. (Dist. by: Ars Polona, Krakowskie Przedmiescie 7, 00-068 Warsaw) Ed. Ryszard Stemplowski.
Description: Papers on different aspects of the development of social and economic life in socialist countries.

301 320 GW
KRIEGSOPFER- UND BEHINDERTEN. RUNDSCHAU; Zeitschrift fuer Kriegsopfer und Behindertenfragen, Sozialpolitik Versorgungsbrecht und Gesellschaftspolitik. bi-m. DM.60. (Bund Deutscher Kriegs- und Wehrdienstopfer e.V.) Siegrfried Krach, Ed. & Pub., Hallplatz 15, D-8500 Nuremberg, Germany. illus.
Description: For disabled victims of war. Covers social politics, support, rights and sociology.

SOCIOLOGY

300   YU   ISSN 0023-5164
AP56
KULTURA; casopis za teoriju i sociologiju kulture i kulturnu politiku. (Text in Serbo-Croatian; summaries and contents in English) 1968. q. $15. Zavod za Proucavanje Kulturnog Razvitka, Rige od Fere 4, 11000 Belgrade, Yugoslavia. Ed. Branimir Stojkovic. bk.rev.; bibl.; charts; illus.; stat.; circ. 1,000.

301   DK   ISSN 0904-0919
L O - UNGDOMS BLAD. (Lands Organisation) 1988. s-m. free. L O i Danmark, Rosenoernsalle 12, 1634 Copenhagen V, Denmark. TEL 31 35 35 41. FAX 35-37-03-12. Ed. Ib Wistisen. circ. 10,000.

301   IT
LABORATORIO DI SCIENZE DELL'UOMO. 1984. q. L.30000. Casa Editrice Fratelli Palombi, Via Gracchi 181-185, 00192 Rome, Italy. Dir. Giancarlo Quaranta.
  Description: Forum covering debates on the role of social sciences.

LAND REFORM, LAND SETTLEMENT AND COOPERATIVES/REFORME AGRAIRE, COLONISATION ET COOPERATIVES AGRICOLES/REFORMA AGRARIA, COLONIZACION Y COOPERATIVAS. see AGRICULTURE — Agricultural Economics

301 410   FR   ISSN 0181-4095
P40
LANGAGE ET SOCIETE. 1977. q. 180 F. to individuals (foreign 220 F.); institutions 250 F. (foreign 290 F.). Maison des Sciences de l'Homme, 54 bd. Raspail, 75270 Paris Cedex 06, France. TEL 49-54-20-13. FAX 45-48-83-53. TELEX MSH 203 104 F. (Co-Sponsor: Centre National de la Recherche Scientific) Ed. Pierre Achard. bk.rev.; circ. 500. (back issues avail.)
—BLDSC shelfmark: 5155.669000.
  Description: Concerned with studies of sociolinguistics, sociology of language, discourse, history of language.

LANGUAGE AND SOCIETY/LANGUE ET SOCIETE. see PUBLIC ADMINISTRATION

LANGUAGE, CULTURE AND CURRICULUM. see LINGUISTICS

LANGUAGE SCIENCES; a world journal of the sciences of language. see LINGUISTICS

301   GW   ISSN 0458-7944
F1401
LATEINAMERIKA. (Text in English, German, Portuguese or Spanish) 1965. s-a. DM.10. Rostock Universitaet, Abt. Wissenschaftspublizistik, Vogelsang 13-14, 2500 Rostock 1, Germany. adv.; bk.rev.; circ. 800.
Indexed: Amer.Hist.& Life, Hisp.Amer.Per.Ind., Hist.Abstr., I D A, P.A.I.S.For.Lang.Ind.
  Description: Covers various aspects of Latin America: sociology, economy, history, ethnography, literature and politics.

LAVORO E SOCIETA; economia-cultura-politica-sociologia. see BUSINESS AND ECONOMICS

LAW & SOCIETY REVIEW. see LAW

LEADERSHIP QUARTERLY; an international journal of political, social and behavioral science. see BUSINESS AND ECONOMICS — Management

334   US   ISSN 0023-9836
LEAVES OF TWIN OAKS. 1967. q. $3 to individuals; institutions $6. Twin Oaks Community, Rt. 4, Box 169, Louisa, VA 23093. TEL 703-894-5126. Ed.Bd. illus.; circ. 800. (also avail. in microform from UMI; reprint service avail. from UMI)

LEISURE INFORMATION QUARTERLY. see LEISURE AND RECREATION

LEISURE STUDIES. see LEISURE AND RECREATION

LENDEMAINS; etudes comparees sur la France - vergleichende Frankreichforschung. see LITERARY AND POLITICAL REVIEWS

LESBIAN AND GAY COUNSELLING NEWS. see HOMOSEXUALITY

301.2 700   IT
LETTERA INTERNAZIONALE. 1984. q. L.30000. Ediesse S.R.L., Via Goito 39, 00185 Rome, Italy. circ. 5,000. (back issues avail.)

301   UK   ISSN 0267-7113
LIBERTARIAN ALLIANCE. SOCIOLOGICAL NOTES. 1985. irreg. £10($20) Libertarian Alliance, 1 Russell Chambers, Covent Garden, London WC2E 8AA, England. TEL 071-821-5502. FAX 071-834-2031.

LIES OF OUR TIMES; a magazine to correct the record. see JOURNALISM

350.865   FR
LOGEMENT ET FAMILLE; le reveil des locataires. m. Confederation Nationale du Logement, 8 rue Meriel, 93100 Montreuil, France. Ed. Claude Massu. circ. 199,360.

LOISIR ET SOCIETE/SOCIETY AND LEISURE. see LEISURE AND RECREATION

LONDON JOURNAL. see HISTORY — History Of Europe

306.84   US
LOVING MORE. 1984. q. $25. Paradise Educational Partnership, Box 6306, Captain Cook, HI 96704-6306. TEL 808-929-9691. Ed. Ryam Nearing. adv.; bk.rev.
  Formerly (until 1991): P E P Talk - Group Marriage News.
  Description: Focuses on topics relating to group marriage.

301 320   BL   ISSN 0102-6445
LUA NOVA; cultura e politica. 1984. 3/yr. $30. CEDEC, Rua Airosa Galvao, 64, 05002 Sao Paulo, SP, Brazil. TEL 871-2966. FAX 871-2123. Ed. Gabriel Cohn. circ. 2,000.
  Description: Provides theoretical studies, research, and contemporary debates in political science and sociology.

301   YU   ISSN 0352-4973
LUCA; casopis za filozofiju i sociologiju. 1984. 2/yr. Centar za Informativnu Djelatnost, Novice Cerovica 30, 81400 Niksic, Montenegro, Yugoslavia. (Co-sponsor: O.S.I.Z. Kulture i Naucnih Djelatnosti) circ. 1,000.

301.2   PL   ISSN 0076-1435
GR1
LUD. (Text in Polish; summaries in English and German) 1895. a. price varies. Polskie Towarzystwo Ludoznawcze, Ul. Szewska 36, 50-139 Wroclaw, Poland. (Dist. by: Ars Polona, Krakowskie Przedmiescie 7, Warsaw, Poland) Ed. Zbigniew Jasiewicz. bk.rev.; index; circ. 800. **Indexed:** A.I.C.P.

301.4 612   US
LUZ (MIAMI). 1953. m. $15. International Publishing Company, Inc., 10100 N.W. 25th St., Miami, FL 33172. Ed. Alberto Piccione. adv.; bk.rev.; film rev.; charts; illus.; circ. 100,000.

300   NE   ISSN 0165-1722
HD28
M & O; tijdschrift voor organisatiekunde en sociaal beleid. (Text in Dutch; summaries in English) 1947. bi-m. fl.91.50. Samsom BedrijfsInformatie, Box 4, 2400 MA Alphen aan den Rijn, Netherlands. TEL 01720-66800. FAX 01720-75933. TELEX 39682. Ed. P.W.M. van Haaren. adv.; bk.rev.; bibl.; charts; illus.; stat.; index; circ. 4,400. **Indexed:** Abstr.Hyg., C.I.S. Abstr., Psychol.Abstr., Trop.Dis.Bull.
—BLDSC shelfmark: 5313.920000.
  Former titles: Mens en Organisatie; Mens en Onderneming (ISSN 0025-9470)

309   NE   ISSN 0168-2857
MAANDBLAD AKTIVITEITENSEKTOR. 1980. a. fl.79. Vuga Uitgeverij BV, Box 16400, 2500 BK The Hague, Netherlands. Ed. Rene Wagemaker. adv.; bk.rev.; circ. 5,500.
  Incorporates: Ligament.

MAINE PROGRESSIVE. see POLITICAL SCIENCE

MALE - FEMALE ROLES; opposing viewpoints sources. see ANTHROPOLOGY

301   II
MAN AND LIFE. (Text in English) 1975. s-a. Rs.25($10) Institute of Social Research and Applied Anthropology, 35 Ballygunge Circular Rd., New Science Bldg., Calcutta University, Calcutta 700019, India. (Subscr. to: Indian Publicity Society, 21 Balaram Ghose St., Calcutta 700004, India) Eds. P.K. Bhowmick, R.K. Gupta. adv.; bk.rev.; circ. 600.

MANUSIA DAN MASYARAKAT/MAN AND SOCIETY. see ANTHROPOLOGY

301   IT
LE MAPPE - CULTURA E SOCIETA. 1982. irreg., no.6, 1988. price varies. Liguori Editore s.r.l., Via Mezzocannone, 19, 80134 Naples, Italy. TEL 081-5227139. Eds. G. Bechelloni, G. Pagliano.

309 614.7   IT
▼**MARCHETERRITORIO.** 1990. s-a. L.43000 (foreign L.55000)(effective 1992). Franco Angeli Editore, Viale Monza, 106, 20127 Milan, Italy. Ed.Bd.
  Description: Covers culture and environment of life in a city.

MARRIAGE AND FAMILY LAW AGREEMENTS. see LAW — Family And Matrimonial Law

301.4   US   ISSN 0149-4929
HQ536   CODEN: MFARDJ
MARRIAGE & FAMILY REVIEW. 1978. q. $40 to individuals; institutions $90; libraries $180. Haworth Press, Inc., 10 Alice St., Binghamton, NY 13904. TEL 800-342-9678. FAX 607-722-1424. TELEX 4932599. Ed. Marvin B. Sussman. adv.; bk.rev.; abstr.; index; circ. 437. (also avail. in microfiche from HAW; back issues avail.; reprint service avail. from HAW) **Indexed:** Adol.Ment.Hlth.Abstr., Bull.Signal, Chicago Psychoanal.Lit.Ind., Past.Care & Couns.Abstr., PSI, Psychol.Abstr., Sage Fam.Stud.Abstr., Soc.Work Res.& Abstr., Sociol.Abstr., Stud.Wom.Abstr.
—BLDSC shelfmark: 5382.860000.
  Description: Covers marriage, family planning, and crisis counseling.
  Refereed Serial

301 410   GW   ISSN 0438-4385
MARTIN-LUTHER-UNIVERSITAET HALLE-WITTENBERG. WISSENSCHAFTLICHE ZEITSCHRIFT; Gesellschafts- und Sprachwissenschaftliche Reihe. 6/yr. DM.148.50. Martin-Luther-Universitaet Halle-Wittenberg, Abteilung Wissenschaftspublizistik, August-Bebel-Str. 13, 4010 Halle, Germany. (Orders to: Buchexport, Leninstr. 16, 7010 Leipzig, Germany) **Indexed:** Hist.Abstr.

MASARYKOVA UNIVERZITA. FILOZOFICKA FAKULTA. SBORNIK PRACI. G: RADA SOCIALNEVEDNA. see BUSINESS AND ECONOMICS — Economic Systems And Theories, Economic History

301   US   ISSN 0743-7528
MATERIAL CULTURE DIRECTORIES. 1988. irreg. price varies. Greenwood Press, Inc. (Subsidiary of: Greenwood Publishing Group Inc.), 88 Post Rd. W., Box 5007, Westport, CT 06881-5007. TEL 203-226-3571. FAX 203-222-1502.

MEDIA CULTURE AND SOCIETY. see COMMUNICATIONS — Television And Cable

MEDIENPSYCHOLOGIE; Zeitschrift fuer Individual- und Massenkommunikation. see PSYCHOLOGY

301   IS   ISSN 0025-8679
MEGAMOT; behavioural sciences quarterly. (Text in Hebrew; summaries in English) 1949. q. $38. Henrietta Szold Institute, 9 Columbia St., Kiryat Menachem, Jerusalem 96583, Israel. FAX 2-437698. Ed. K. Binyamini. adv.; bk.rev.; abstr.; bibl.; charts; illus.; stat.; cum.index; circ. 1,000. **Indexed:** Ind.Heb.Per., Psychol.Abstr., SSCI.
  Formerly: Child Welfare Research Quarterly.

301   US
MELLEN STUDIES IN SOCIOLOGY. irreg., latest no.10. Edwin Mellen Press, 240 Portage Rd., Box 450, Lewiston, NY 14092. TEL 800-753-2788. FAX 754-4335.

300   NE   ISSN 0025-9454
MENS EN MAATSCHAPPIJ; tijdschrift voor sociale wetenschappen. 1925. 4/yr. (plus special issue). fl.105 to individuals; students fl.59; institutions fl.195(effective 1992). (Stichting Mens en Maatschappij) Bohn Stafleu Van Loghum B.V., P.O. Box 246, 3990 GA Houten, Netherlands. TEL 3403-95711. FAX 3403-50903. adv.; bk.rev.; bibl.; index; circ. 2,500. **Indexed**: A.I.C.P., E.I., Key to Econ.Sci., Sociol.Abstr. (1954-).

301.2   GW   ISSN 0543-4726
DER MENSCH ALS SOZIALES UND PERSONALES WESEN. 1963. irreg., vol.11, 1991. price varies. Ferdinand Enke Verlag, Postfach 101254, 7000 Stuttgart 10, Germany. TEL 0711-8931-0. FAX 0711-8931-419. TELEX 07252275-GTV-D. Ed.Bd.

301   FR
MENTALITES; histoire des cultures et des societes. s-a. 180 F. (foreign 230 F.). Presses Universitaires de France, Departement des Revues, 14 av. du Bois-de-l'Epine, 91003 Evry Cedex, France. TEL 1-60-77-82-05. FAX 1-60-79-20-45. TELEX PUF 600 474 F. Dir. Robert Muchembled.

MICHAEL'S THING. see *LITERARY AND POLITICAL REVIEWS*

301   DK   ISSN 0901-0025
MICRO PUBLICATIONS. SOCIAL SCIENCE SERIES; a Danish sociological journal. (Text in Scandinavian languages; summaries in English) 1952. 2/yr. $6. Institute for Longitudinal Studies, Peder Hvitfeldts straede 10, 1173 Copenhagen K, Denmark. Ed. Erik Hoegh. bk.rev.; index, cum.index; circ. 500. (also avail. in microfiche) **Indexed**: Hist.Abstr., Lang.& Lang.Behav.Abstr., Sociol.Abstr.
  Formerly: Sociologiske Meddeleiser (ISSN 0038-0350)

301   US   ISSN 0732-913X
HM1
MID-AMERICAN REVIEW OF SOCIOLOGY. 1976. s-a. $8 to individuals; institutions $20; students $6. Mid-American Review of Sociology Consortium, Department of Sociology, University of Kansas, Lawrence, KS 66045. TEL 913-864-4111. Ed. Colleen Greer. adv.; bk.rev.; circ. 300. (also avail. in microform from UMI; reprint service avail. from UMI) **Indexed**: Curr.Cont., Psychol.Abstr., Sociol.Abstr. (1976-), SSCI.
—BLDSC shelfmark: 5761.313500.
  Supersedes (as of vol.11): Kansas Journal of Sociology (ISSN 0022-8648)

301 949.7   CI   ISSN 0352-5600
DR1231   CODEN: MIGTE9
MIGRACIJSKE TEME/MIGRATION THEMES; casopis za istrazivanje migracija i narodnosti. (Text in Croatian and English; summaries in English) 1985. q. $20 to individuals; institutions $30. Sveuciliste u Zagrebu, Institut za Migracije i Narodnosti - University of Zagreb, Institute for Migration and Nationalities Studies, Trnjanska b.b., P.O. 88, 41001 Zagreb, Croatia. TEL 041 539-777. Ed. Emil Hersak. bk.rev.; circ. 800.
  Description: Covers historical and present perspectives of migration and nationalities. Includes socio-economical and political aspects of the studies.

MIGRANTI-PRESS. see *POLITICAL SCIENCE*

301.15   GW   ISSN 0721-2887
JV6004
MIGRATION; a European journal of international migration and ethnic relations. 1987. 4/yr. DM.72. Edition Parabolis, Potsdamerstr. 91, 1000 Berlin 30, Germany. TEL 030-2623085. FAX 030-2629503.

301 360   AT   ISSN 0311-3760
MIGRATION ACTION. (Text and summaries in English) 1974. 3/yr. Aus.$40 to indiviudals; institutions Aus.$40; foreign Aus.$50 (effective 1992). Ecumenical Migration Centre, 125 Leicester St., Fitzroy, Vic. 3065, Australia. TEL 03-426-0044. FAX 03-416-1827. Ed.Bd. adv.; bk.rev.; illus.; circ. 1,000. (back issues avail.) **Indexed**: P.A.I.S.
  Description: Covers news, views and debates on immigration, ethnic affairs, multiculturalism and community relations.

MIGRATIONS; revue des possibilites d'emploi-outre-mer, etranger. see *OCCUPATIONS AND CAREERS*

MINORITY RIGHTS GROUP. REPORTS. see *POLITICAL SCIENCE — Civil Rights*

301   US
MISSISSIPPI STATE UNIVERSITY. SOCIAL RESEARCH REPORT SERIES. 1983. bi-m. free. Mississippi State University, Social Science Research Center, Box 5287, Mississippi State, MS 39762. TEL 601-325-2495. Ed. J. Gipson Wells. circ. 400. **Indexed**: Sociol.Abstr.
  Formerly: Mississippi State University. Sociology Research Report Series.

325   GW   ISSN 0722-4516
MITTELDEUTSCHER KURIER. vol.18, 1971. m. DM.28. Bund der Mitteldeutschen, Poppelsdorfer Allee 82, 5300 Bonn 1, Germany. FAX 0228-654872. adv.; bk.rev.; abstr.; charts; film rev.; illus.; stat.; circ. 20,000. (newspaper)
  Formerly: Fluechtlings Anzeiger.

301   BO
MONOGRAFIAS DE POBLACION Y DESARROLLO. 1974. irreg., no.23, 1985. price varies. Centro de Investigaciones Sociales, Casilla 6931 - C.C., La Paz, Bolivia.

301   BO
MONOGRAFIAS DE RECURSOS HUMANOS. 1978. irreg., no.4, 1985. price varies. Centro de Investigaciones Sociales, Casilla 6931 - C.C., La Paz, Bolivia.

301.4   BO
MONOGRAFIAS DE SOCIOLOGIA FAMILIAR. 1974. irreg., no.9, 1984. price varies. Centro de Investigaciones Sociales, Casilla 6931 - C.C., La Paz, Bolivia.

301 572   NE   ISSN 0169-9202
MONOGRAPHS AND THEORETICAL STUDIES IN SOCIOLOGY AND ANTHROPOLOGY IN HONOUR OF NELS ANDERSON. 1972. irreg., vol.28, 1989. price varies. E.J. Brill, P.O. Box 9000, 2300 PA Leiden, Netherlands. TEL 071-312624. FAX 071-317532. TELEX 39296 BRILL NL. (In N. America: E.J. Brill, 24 Hudson St., Kinderhook, NY 12106. TEL 800-962-4406) Ed. K. Ishwaran.
—BLDSC shelfmark: 5915.130000.

301   AT
MORGAN GALLUP POLLS. 1941. w. Aus.$195. Roy Morgan Research Centre Pty. Ltd., G.P.O. Box 2282U, Melbourne, Vic. 3001, Australia. FAX 03-629-1250.
  Formerly: Australian Gallup Polls.

301   US   ISSN 0027-1535
AP2
MOTHER EARTH NEWS; the original country magazine. 1970-1990; resumed 1991. bi-m. $17.95. Sussex Publishers Inc., 24 E. 23rd St., 5th Fl., New York, NY 10010. TEL 212-260-7210. Ed. Owen Lipstein. adv.; bk.rev.; charts; illus.; tr.lit.; circ. 350,000. (also avail. in microform from UMI) **Indexed**: Acad.Ind., Access, Consum.Ind., Gard.Lit. (1992-), Hlth.Ind., Ind.How To Do It (1978-), Mag.Ind., MELSA, New Per.Ind., PMR, R.G., TOM.

301 917.306   US   ISSN 1058-9236
▼**MULTICULTURAL REVIEW**; dedicated to a better understanding of ethnic, racial and religious diversity. 1992. q. $59 (foreign $79). G P Subscription Publications (Subsidiary of: Greenwood Publishing Group Inc.), 88 Post Rd. W., Box 5007, Westport, CT 06881. TEL 203-226-3571. FAX 203-222-1502. Ed. Brenda Mitchell-Powell. adv.; bk.rev. (reprint service avail.)
  Incorporates (in 1992): Journal of Multicultural Librarianship.

MUSIK UND GESELLSCHAFT. see *MUSIC*

301   US   ISSN 0077-3212
N A A C P ANNUAL REPORT. 1910. a. $5. National Association for the Advancement of Colored People, 4805 Mt. Hope Dr., Baltimore, MD 21215-3297. circ. 5,000. (also avail. in microform from UMI)

309.1   US   ISSN 0147-0124
HM261.A1
N O R C REPORTER. 1967. 3/yr. free. National Opinion Research Center, 1155 E. 60th St., Chicago, IL 60637. TEL 312-702-1200. Ed. Jeff Hackett. circ. 2,500.
  Formerly (until 1986): National Opinion Research Center. Newsletter (ISSN 0077-5266)

301   US
NATIONAL COUNCIL ON FAMILY RELATIONS. REPORT. 1955. q. $12. National Council on Family Relations, 3989 Central Ave., N.E., Ste. 550, Minneapolis, MN 55421-3921. TEL 612-781-9331. FAX 612-781-9348. Ed. Kathy Collins Royce. circ. 4,500. (processed)
●Also available online. Vendor(s): BRS.
  Formerly: National Council on Family Relations Newsletter.
  Description: Features updates on national, international and NCFR Association of councils affairs, broad family field news and current issues in marriage and family life.

NATIONAL REVIEW OF CRIMINAL SCIENCES. see *CRIMINOLOGY AND LAW ENFORCEMENT*

301   CH   ISSN 0077-5851
NATIONAL TAIWAN UNIVERSITY JOURNAL OF SOCIOLOGY. (Text in Chinese and English) 1963. a. $5. National Taiwan University, Department of Sociology, 21 Hsuchow Rd., Taipei, Taiwan 10020, Republic of China. TEL 02-351-4239. Ed. Cheng-han Chang. bk.rev.; circ. 500. **Indexed**: Lang.& Lang.Behav.Abstr., Sociol.Abstr. (1978-). Key Title: Guoli Taiwan Daxue Shehui Xuekan.
—BLDSC shelfmark: 5064.931000.

301.4 613.9   AT   ISSN 0312-7567
NATURAL FAMILY PLANNING COUNCIL OF VICTORIA. BULLETIN. 1974. q. Aus.$10($10) Ovulation Method Research and Reference Centre of Australia, Family Life Centre, 27 Alexandra Parade, N. Fitzroy, Melbourne, Vic. 3068, Australia. TEL 61-3-481-1722. FAX 61-3-482-4208. Ed. John J. Billings. bk.rev.; cum.index every 2 yrs.; circ. 3,000. (tabloid format; back issues avail.)
  Description: Covers philosophy and theology of marriage, scientific research into reproductive biology pertaining to natural family planning, and the teaching of natural family planning.

301.2   NE   ISSN 0028-2383
NEERLANDIA. 1896. 5/yr. fl.40. Algemeen Nederlands Verbond, J. van Nassaustraat 109, 2596 BS The Hague, Netherlands. TEL 070-3245514. FAX 070-3246186. Ed.Bd. adv.; bk.rev.; bibl.; index; circ. 3,000 (controlled).
  Description: Information and documentation promoting Dutch culture and language, with focus on Dutch-Flemish cooperation in a united Europe.

NELEN YUBU. see *RELIGIONS AND THEOLOGY*

572 301.2   HU   ISSN 0541-9522
NEPI KULTURA - NEPI TARSADALOM. (Text in Hungarian; summaries in German) 1968. irreg., vol.14, 1987. (Magyar Tudomanyos Akademia, Neprajzi Kutato Csoport) Akademiai Kiado, Publishing House of the Hungarian Academy of Sciences, Box 24, H-1363 Budapest, Hungary. abstr.; bibl.; illus.

301   NE
NETHERLANDS. SOCIAAL EN CULTUREEL PLANBUREAU. CAHIERS. (Text in Dutch) 1974. irreg., latest no.87, 1991. price varies. Sociaal en Cultureel Planbureau - Netherlands Social and Cultural Planning Office, Postbus 37, 2280 AA Rijswijk, Netherlands. TEL 070-3198700. FAX 070-3963000. (Subscr. to: VUGA, Postbus 16400, 2500 BK The Hague, Netherlands. TEL 070-361-4011) Ed. M. de Rooij.

301   NE
NETHERLANDS. SOCIAAL EN CULTUREEL PLANBUREAU. SOCIALE AND CULTURELE RAPPORTEN/SOCIAL AND CULTURAL REPORTS. (Text in Dutch, English) 1975. biennial. price varies. Sociaal en Cultureel Planbureau - Social and Cultural Planning Office, Postbus 37, 2280AA Rijswijk, Netherlands. TEL 070-3198700. FAX 070-3963000. (Subscr. to: VUGA, Postbus 16400, 2500 BK, The Hague, Netherlands. TEL 070-361-4011) charts; stat.; circ. 1,400.

301   NE
NETHERLANDS. SOCIAAL EN CULTUREEL PLANBUREAU. STUDIES. 1977. irreg., latest no.14, 1991. price varies. Sociaal en Cultureel Planbureau, Postbus 37, 2280 AA Rijswijk, Netherlands. TEL 070-3198700. FAX 070-3963000. (Subscr. to: VUGA, Postbus 16400, 2500 BK The Hague, Netherlands. TEL 070-361-4011)

SOCIOLOGY

301   NE
NETHERLANDS JOURNAL OF SOCIAL SCIENCES. 1963. s-a. fl.87. (Netherlands Sociological and Anthropological Society) Van Gorcum en Co. B.V., P.O. Box 43, 9400 AA Assen, Netherlands. TEL 05920-46864. FAX 05920-72064. Ed. B. van Heerikhuizen. adv.; bk.rev.; index; circ. 3,500. **Indexed:** ASSIA, Curr.Cont., E.I., Lang.& Lang.Behav.Abstr., Mid.East: Abstr.& Ind., Risk Abstr., Rural Recreat.Tour.Abstr., Sociol.Abstr., Sociol.Educ.Abstr., SSCI, Stud.Wom.Abstr., World Agri.Econ.& Rural Sociol.Abstr.
    Former titles: Netherlands' Journal of Sociology; Sociologia Neerlandica (ISSN 0038-0172)

300   GW   ISSN 0028-3304
DIE NEUE ORDNUNG. 1946. 6/yr. DM.49. (Institut fuer Gesellschaftswissenschaften Walberberg e.V.) I.F.G. Verlag GmbH, Simrockstr. 19, 5300 Bonn 1, Germany. TEL 0228-216852. FAX 0228-220244. Ed. B. Streithofen. adv.; bk.rev.; index; circ. 2,400. (back issues avail.) **Indexed:** P.A.I.S.For.Lang.Ind.
  —BLDSC shelfmark: 6077.635000.
    Description: Discussion of current history, social issues and changes in society.

NEW DOCTOR. see MEDICAL SCIENCES

NEW ENVIRONMENT BULLETIN. see NEW AGE PUBLICATIONS

NEW GERMAN-AMERICAN STUDIES/NEUE DEUTSCHE-AMERIKANISCHE STUDIEN. see HUMANITIES: COMPREHENSIVE WORKS

NEW LIFE (LONDON, 1965). see RELIGIONS AND THEOLOGY — Roman Catholic

301.45   II   ISSN 0028-6532
NEW RACE.* 1966. q. Rs.10($5) Institute of Human Study, Hyderabad 7, India. Ed. V. Madhusudan Reddy. adv.; bk.rev.

309 360   UK
NEW REVIEW. 1989. bi-m. £15. Low Pay Unit, 9 Upper Berkeley St., London W1H 8BY, England. TEL 071-262-7278. Ed. Peta Lunberg. adv.; bk.rev.; circ. 1,000. (back issues avail.)
    Description: Carries reviews of research into causes, cures and the extent of poverty. Includes case histories and advice on individiual rights.

NEW SCHOOL OBSERVER. see COLLEGE AND ALUMNI

NEW ZEALAND RATIONALIST AND HUMANIST; a journal on philosophy, science, religion, literature & society. see PHILOSOPHY

301   NZ
NEW ZEALAND TOURISM DEPARTMENT. SOCIAL RESEARCH SERIES. 1981. irreg., latest 1988. price varies. Tourism Department, Research Services, P.O. Box 95, Wellington, New Zealand. TEL 04-4728-860. FAX 04-4781-736.
    Formerly: N Z T P Social Research Series (ISSN 0112-9740)

NIGERIAN JOURNAL OF ECONOMIC & SOCIAL STUDIES. see BUSINESS AND ECONOMICS

301 320   US   ISSN 1052-0384
NONVIOLENT SANCTIONS; news from the Albert Einstein Institute. 1989. q. $5. Albert Einstein Institute, 1430 Massachusetts Ave., Cambridge, MA 02138. TEL 617-876-0311. FAX 617-876-0837. Ed. Roger S. Powers. circ. 1,200. (back issues avail.)
    Description: Covers news and information about the strategic use of nonviolent action in group conflicts.

309   BE
NOORD - ZUID CAHIER. 1974. q. 600 BEF. V.Z.W. Wereldwijd, Arthur Goemaerelei 69, B-2018 Antwerp, Belgium. Ed. A.F. Peeters. circ. 2,000.
    Formerly: Tijdschrift voor Ontwikkelingssamenwerken.

NORTH AMERICAN CULTURE. see GEOGRAPHY

NORTH AMERICAN FARMER. see AGRICULTURE

NORTH-EAST INDIA COUNCIL FOR SOCIAL SCIENCE RESEARCH. JOURNAL. see POLITICAL SCIENCE

NOTES AFRICAINES. see POLITICAL SCIENCE

NOUVELLE REVUE D'ETHNOPSYCHIATRIE. see MEDICAL SCIENCES — Psychiatry And Neurology

NOUVELLES PRATIQUES SOCIALES. see SOCIAL SERVICES AND WELFARE

NURTURING TODAY; for self and family growth. see CHILDREN AND YOUTH — About

O P T: ONE PARENT TIMES. see CHILDREN AND YOUTH — About

OCCITANIA PASSAT E PRESENT. see POLITICAL SCIENCE

OESTERREICHISCHE OSTHEFTE. see POLITICAL SCIENCE

301   AU
OESTERREICHISCHE ZEITSCHRIFT FUER SOZIOLOGIE. q. $52. Verband der Wissenschaftlichen Gesellschaften Oesterreichs, Lindengasse 37, A-1070 Vienna, Austria. TEL 932166.

OMEGA (AMITYVILLE); journal of death and dying. see PSYCHOLOGY

ONTARIO FAMILY LAW QUANTUM SERVICE. see LAW — Family And Matrimonial Law

ONTARIO SYMPOSIA ON PERSONALITY AND SOCIAL COGNITION SERIES. see PSYCHOLOGY

OPINION; the way I see it. see PHILOSOPHY

341.1 320   CN   ISSN 0030-686X
OUR GENERATION. 1961. s-a. Can.$35 to individuals; institutions Can.$48; students Can.$25. 3981 St. Laurent Blvd., No.444, Montreal, Que. H2W 1Y5, Canada. TEL 514-844-4076. (Subscr. to: P.O. Box 1258, Succ. Place du Parc, Montreal, Que. H2W 2R3, Canada) Ed. Dimitrios Roussopoulos. adv.; bk.rev.; film rev.; bibl.; illus.; index; circ. 8,500. (also avail. in microform from UMI,MML; reprint service avail. from UMI) **Indexed:** Alt.Press Ind., Can.B.P.I., Can.Per.Ind., CMI, Fut.Surv., Peace Res.Abstr., Polit.Sci.Abstr.
  —BLDSC shelfmark: 6314.326000.
    Formerly: Our Generation Against Nuclear War.
    Description: An international journal of critical social theory.

P D S. (Perspektiven des Demokratishen Sozialismus) see POLITICAL SCIENCE

301 572   CN
P.E.I. COMMUNITY STUDIES. (Prince Edward Island) 1974. irreg. price varies. University of Prince Edward Island, Department of Sociology and Anthropology, Charlottetown, P.E.I. C1A 4P3, Canada. Ed. Satadal Das Gupta. circ. controlled.

PARENTING STUDIES. see PSYCHOLOGY

301.4 362.7   GW   ISSN 0176-2982
PATEN; Mitteilung der Vereinigung der Pflege- und Adoptiveltern im Lande Nordrhein-Westfalen. 1984. q. DM.13. Vereinigung der Pflege- und Adoptiveltern im Lande Nordrhein-Westfalen e.V., Bochumer Landstr. 215, D-4300 Essen 14, Germany. TEL 0201-501440. circ. 700. (back issues avail)
    Description: Provides reports and information for the parents of adopted and fostercare children and professionals in related fields.

301.45   UK   ISSN 0031-322X
DS145
PATTERNS OF PREJUDICE. 1967. s-a. £18($30) to individuals; institutions £25($40). Institute of Jewish Affairs, 11 Hertford St., London W1Y 7DX, England. TEL 01-491-3517. FAX 01-493-5883. (Co-sponsor: World Jewish Congress) Ed. A. Lerman. adv.; bk.rev.; bibl.; index; circ. 1,750. (also avail. in microform from UMI; reprint service avail. from UMI) **Indexed:** CERDIC, Hist.Abstr., HR Rep., Ind.Jew.Per., Mid.East: Abstr.& Ind.
  —BLDSC shelfmark: 6412.985000.
    Description: Studies national and international conditions, causes and manifestation of racial, religious and ethnic discrimination and prejudice, with particular reference to Jews.

PEACE & CHANGE; a journal of peace research. see POLITICAL SCIENCE — International Relations

PENSIERO POLITICO; rivista di storia delle idee politiche e sociali. see POLITICAL SCIENCE

PENSIERO POLITICO. BIBLIOTECA. see POLITICAL SCIENCE

PEOPLE. see BIRTH CONTROL

PEOPLE SEARCHING NEWS. see GENEALOGY AND HERALDRY

PERIPHERIE; Zeitschrift fuer Politik und Oekonomie in der dritten Welt. see BUSINESS AND ECONOMICS — International Development And Assistance

PERSPECTIVES IN URBAN GEOGRAPHY. see GEOGRAPHY

PERSPECTIVES ON THE AMERICAN SOUTH. see HISTORY — History Of North And South America

301   PE   ISSN 0079-1075
PERU - PROBLEMA. 1969. irreg., no.21, 1984. price varies. (Instituto de Estudios Peruanos) I E P Ediciones, Horacio Urteaga 694 (Campo de Marte), Lima 11, Peru. TEL 323070. FAX 324981. bk.rev.

301   PH   ISSN 0031-7810
HM1
PHILIPPINE SOCIOLOGICAL REVIEW. 1953. s-a. P.120($20) Philippine Sociological Society, Box 154, Manila 2801, Philippines. FAX 02-632-921-6159. TELEX INPHILCUL MANILA. Ed. Ricardo G. Abad. adv.; bk.rev.; bibl.; charts; stat.; index, cum.index: 1953-1987; circ. 500. (also avail. in microfilm; microfiche) **Indexed:** A.I.C.P., Abstr.Anthropol., Ind.Phil.Per., Lang.& Lang.Behav.Abstr., M.L.A., Sociol.Abstr. (1953-), SSCI.
  —BLDSC shelfmark: 6456.350000.

PHILOSOPHY OF HISTORY AND CULTURE. see PHILOSOPHY

301   US   ISSN 0031-8906
E185.5
PHYLON; the Atlanta University review of race and culture. 1940. q. $14 to individuals; institutions $24. Atlanta University, 223 James P. Brawley Dr., S.W., Atlanta, GA 30314. TEL 404-681-0251. Ed. Wilbur Watson. adv.; bk.rev.; index; circ. 2,200. (also avail. in microform from UMI,MIM; reprint service avail. from UMI,KTO) **Indexed:** Acad.Ind., Bk.Rev.Ind. (1976-), C.I.J.E., Child.Bk.Rev.Ind. (1976-), Commun.Abstr., Curr.Cont., G.Soc.Sci.& Rel.Per.Lit., Hist.Abstr. (until 1987), Ind.Sel.Per., M.L.A., Mag.Ind., Mid.East: Abstr.& Ind., P.A.I.S., Psychol.Abstr., Sage Fam.Stud.Abstr., Sage Urb.Stud.Abstr., Soc.Sci.Ind., SSCI.
  —BLDSC shelfmark: 6474.800000.
    Formerly: Phylon Quarterly.
    Description: Examines issues of race and culture as they relate to social and political behaviors and to literary analysis.

PHYSICS AND SOCIETY. see PHYSICS

PITTSBURGH STUDIES IN THEATRE AND CULTURE. see THEATER

301 330   UK   ISSN 0141-2779
PLANNING FOR SOCIAL CHANGE. 1976. a. $6500. Henley Centre for Forecasting Ltd., 2 Tudor St., Blackfriars, London EC4Y 0AA, England. TEL 071-353-9961. Ed. Michael Willmott.
    Description: Analysis and forecasts of consumer attitudes, motivations and behavior in the UK.

301.2   US   ISSN 0894-4253
                          CODEN: PLCUEC
PLAY & CULTURE. 1988. q. $40 to individuals (foreign $44); institutions $90 (foreign $94); students $24 (foreign $28). (Association for the Study of Play) Human Kinetics Publishers, Inc., Box 5076, Champaign, IL 61825-5076. TEL 217-351-5076. FAX 217-351-2674. Ed. Dr. Margaret Carlisle Duncan. bk.rev.; circ. 510. **Indexed:** Commun.Abstr., Curr.Cont., Psychol.Abstr., Soc.Sci.Ind., Sportsearch (1988-).
  —BLDSC shelfmark: 6539.105200.
    Description: Stimulates and communicates research, critical thought and theory in all areas related to the topic of play.
    Refereed Serial

301 320   AG   ISSN 0326-677X
PLURAL.* 1984. 4/yr. $50. Fundacion Plural, Avda. de Caseros 701, 1084 Buenos Aires, Argentina. TEL 30-3225. Ed.Bd. adv.; circ. 3,000.

301   NE   ISSN 0048-4482
HM73
PLURAL SOCIETIES. 1970. 3/yr. fl.50($25) to individuals; institutions fl.100($50). Stichting Plurale Samenlevingen - Foundation for the Study of Plural Societies, Box 13566, 2501 EN The Hague, Netherlands. Ed. A. Stam. adv.; bk.rev.; bibl.; charts; index; circ. 1,000. (back issues avail.) Indexed: A.B.C.Pol.Sci., Chic.Per.Ind., E.I., Geo.Abstr., Hist.Abstr., Mid.East: Abstr.& Ind., Rural Recreat.Tour.Abstr., World Agri.Econ.& Rural Sociol.Abstr.
—BLDSC shelfmark: 6541.013000.
     Description: Inter-ethnic relations are covered.

POLICING AND SOCIETY. see *CRIMINOLOGY AND LAW ENFORCEMENT*

POLICY SCIENCES; an international journal devoted to the improvement of policy making. see *POLITICAL SCIENCE*

POLIS; ricerche e studi su societa e politica in Italia. see *POLITICAL SCIENCE*

POLISH HISTORICAL LIBRARY. ANTHOLOGIES. MONOGRAPHS. OPERA MINORA. see *HISTORY — History Of Europe*

301   PL   ISSN 0032-2997
HM1
POLISH SOCIOLOGICAL BULLETIN. (Text in English) 1961. q. $36. (Polskie Towarzystwo Socjologiczne - Polish Sociological Association) Ossolineum, Publishing House of the Polish Academy of Sciences, Rynek 9, 50-106 Wroclaw, Poland. TELEX 0712771 OSS PL. (Dist. by: Ars Polona, Krakowskie Przedmiescie 7, 00-068 Warsaw, Poland) Ed. Jerzy Szacki. adv.; bk.rev.; index. Indexed: ASSIA, Lang.& Lang.Behav.Abstr., Sociol.Abstr. (1961-), SSCI, SSCI.
     Description: Papers and reports on various aspects of sociological research and its practical application.

320   US   ISSN 0732-1228
GN492
POLITICAL AND LEGAL ANTHROPOLOGY. 1980. a. $29.95 cloth; paper $19.95. (Association for Political and Legal Anthropology) Transaction Publishers, Transaction Periodicals Consortium, Department 3092, Rutgers University, New Brunswick, NJ 08903. TEL 908-932-2280. FAX 908-932-3138. Ed. Myron J. Aronoff.
—BLDSC shelfmark: 6543.872100.
     Description: Original analyses of political man. Articles cover a wide range of theoretical, conceptual, and methodological approaches to interrelationships among socioeconomic, cultural, and political phenomena.

POLITICAL POWER AND SOCIAL THEORY; a research annual. see *POLITICAL SCIENCE*

POLITICS AND SOCIETY. see *POLITICAL SCIENCE*

POLITICS AND THE INDIVIDUAL; international journal of political socialization and political psychology. see *POLITICAL SCIENCE*

301   PL   ISSN 0079-3442
POLSKA AKADEMIA NAUK. ODDZIAL W KRAKOWIE. KOMISJA SOCJOLOGICZNA. PRACE. (Text in Polish; summaries in English, French, Russian) 1963. irreg., no.48, 1984. price varies. Ossolineum, Publishing House of the Polish Academy of Sciences, Rynek 9, 50-106 Wroclaw, Poland. TELEX 0712771 OSS PL. (Dist. by: Ars Polona-Ruch, Krakowskie Przedmiescie 7, Warsaw, Poland)

301   PL   ISSN 0079-3620
CB161
POLSKA 2000. 1970. irreg. (3-4/yr.). price varies. (Polska Akademia Nauk, Komitet Badan i Prognoz "Polska 2000") Ossolineum, Publishing House of the Polish Academy of Sciences, Rynek 9, Wroclaw, Poland. TELEX 0712771 OSS PL. (Dist. by: Ars Polona-Ruch, Krakowskie Przedmiescie 7, Warsaw, Poland) Ed. Antoni Rajkiewicz. circ. 2,000.
—BLDSC shelfmark: 6545.740000.

301.4   FR
POMME D'API. 1966. m. 297 F. Bayard Presse, 5 rue Bayard, 75380 Paris Cedex 08, France. adv.; circ. 220,000.

301   US
POPULAR CULTURE ASSOCIATION. NEWSLETTER AND POPULAR CULTURE METHODS. 1971. irreg. membership. (Popular Culture Association) Bowling Green State University, Popular Culture Center, Bowling Green, OH 43403. TEL 409-372-2981. Ed. Michael T. Marsden. adv.; circ. 2,500. (also avail. in microform from UMI; reprint service avail. from UMI)
     Incorporates: Popular Culture Association Newsletter (ISSN 0048-4822)

POPULAR MUSIC & SOCIETY. see *MUSIC*

POPULATION RESEARCH LABORATORY. RESEARCH DISCUSSION PAPER SERIES. see *POPULATION STUDIES*

POPULATION TODAY. see *POPULATION STUDIES*

301   PO   ISSN 0870-4406
HD7209
PORTUGAL. INSTITUTO NACIONAL DE ESTATISTICA. ESTATISTICAS DE PROTECCAO SOCIAL, ASSOCIACOES SINDICAIS E PATRONAIS. 1938. a. Esc.2400. Instituto Nacional de Estatistica, Av. Antonio Jose de Almeida, 1078 Lisbon Codex, Portugal. (Orders to: Imprensa Nacional, Casa da Moeda, Direccao Comercial, rua D. Francisco Manuel de Melo 5, 1000 Lisbon, Portugal)
     Former titles (until 1985): Portugal. Instituto Nacional de Estatistica. Estatisticas de Seguranca Social, Associacoes Sindicais e Patronais. Continente, Acores e Madeira (ISSN 0870-6506); (until 1978): Portugal. Instituto Nacional de Estatistica. Estatisticas des Associqcoes Sindicais Patronais e Previdencia (ISSN 0377-211X); (until 1974): Portugal. Instituto Nacional de Estatistica. Estatisticas das Organizacoes Sindicais (ISSN 0079-4163)

POUR LA VIE; revue d'etudes familiales. see *POPULATION STUDIES*

PRACTICE (NEW YORK); the magazine of psychology and political economy. see *POLITICAL SCIENCE*

300   YU   ISSN 0032-6704
PRAKSA; casopis za drustvena pitanja. (Text in Serbo-Croatian) 1970. bi-m. 120 din. (Marksisticki Centar, Titograd) Pobjeda, Bulevar Revolucije, 81000 Titograd, Yugoslavia. Ed. Milija Komatina.

300   PL   ISSN 0137-3609
PREZENTACJE; miesiecznik teoretyczno-polityczny materialy z prasy zagranicznej. 1978. m. 600 Zl.($14.40) Wydawnictwo Wspolczesne R S W "Prasa-Ksiazka-Ruch", Ul. Wiejska 12, 00-420 Warsaw, Poland. (Dist. by: Ars Polona-Ruch, Krakowskie Przedmiescie 7, 00-068 Warsaw, Poland) circ. 15,000.
     Formerly (until 1978): Zeszyty Teoretyczno-Polityczne (ISSN 0044-443X)

301   US
PRIME OF LIFE. 1963. m. (except Jul., Aug.). $10. Lutheran Community Services, Inc., 27 Park Pl., New York, NY 10007-2502. Ed. Lucretia Dix. circ. 8,500.

PRIMO MAGGIO; saggi e documenti per una storia di classe. see *POLITICAL SCIENCE*

301   ZR
PROBLEMES SOCIAUX ZAIROIS. (Text in French) 1946. q. Centre d'Execution de Programmes Communautaires, 208 av. Kasa-Vubu, Box 1873, Lubumbashi, Zaire. Ed.Bd. bk.rev.; abstr.; charts; illus. Indexed: Trop.Dis.Bull.
     Formerly: Problemes Sociaux Congolais (ISSN 0032-9312)

PROBLEMI DELL'INFORMAZIONE. see *COMMUNICATIONS*

309   GP
PROGRES SOCIAL. w. Rue Toussaint l'Ouverture, 97100 Basse-Terre, Guadeloupe. TEL 81-1041. Ed. Henri Rodes. circ. 5,000.

SOCIOLOGY   4445

301   PL   ISSN 0033-2356
HM7
PRZEGLAD SOCJOLOGICZNY. (Summaries in English) 1930. s-a. price varies. (Lodzkie Towarzystwo Naukowe) Ossolineum, Publishing House of the Polish Academy of Sciences, Rynek 9, Wroclaw, Poland. TELEX 0712771 OSS PL. (Dist. by: Ars Polona-Ruch, Krakowskie Przedmiescie 7, Warsaw, Poland) Ed. Jan Lutynski. bk.rev.; bibl.; charts; index. Indexed: Hist.Abstr. (until 1990), Lang.& Lang.Behav.Abstr., Sociol.Abstr. (1957-).
     Description: Methodological aspects of Polish modern sociology and related sciences.

PSYCHOLOGY AND SOCIOLOGY OF SPORT: CURRENT SELECTED RESEARCH. see *PSYCHOLOGY*

PSYCHOSOCIAL REHABILITATION JOURNAL. see *PSYCHOLOGY*

301   US   ISSN 1050-5067
HM261
▼**PUBLIC PERSPECTIVE**; a review of public opinion and polling. 1990. bi-m. $105. Roper Center, Box 440, Storrs, CT 06268. Ed. Everett C. Ladd.

309   US   ISSN 1053-9751
PUBLIC PULSE. 1986. m. $247 (foreign $347). Roper Organization, Inc., 205 E. 42nd St., New York, NY 10017. TEL 212-599-0700. FAX 212-867-7008. Ed. Thomas Miller.
     Description: Evaluates what people are thinking, doing and buying, through survey data.

PUBLIK-FORUM. see *RELIGIONS AND THEOLOGY*

301   IT   ISSN 0033-4952
HM7
QUADERNI DI SOCIOLOGIA. 1951. 3/yr. L.60000 (foreign L.75000). Arnoldo Mondadori Editore, Casella Postale 17135, 20170 Milan, Italy. TEL 3199345. adv.; bk.rev.; bibl.; index; circ. 1,000. Indexed: Hist.Abstr., Lang.& Lang.Behav.Abstr., P.A.I.S.For.Lang.Ind., Sociol.Abstr. (1952-), SSCI.
—BLDSC shelfmark: 7166.900000.

QUADERNI STORICI. see *HISTORY*

QUALESOCIETA; rivista bimestrale di dialogo. see *POLITICAL SCIENCE*

301   IT   ISSN 0391-8521
QUALITA DELLA VITA. 1978. irreg., latest no.15. price varies. Edizioni Studium, Via Cassiodoro 14, 00193 Rome, Italy.

301   US   ISSN 0162-0436
HM1
QUALITATIVE SOCIOLOGY. 1978. q. $175 (foreign $205). Human Sciences Press, Inc. (Subsidiary of: Plenum Publishing Corp.), 233 Spring St., New York, NY 10013-1578. TEL 212-620-8000. FAX 212-463-0742. Eds. Jonathan B. Imber, Rosanna Hertz. adv. (also avail. in microform from UMI; reprint service avail. from UMI; back issues avail.) Indexed: Adol.Ment.Hlth.Abstr., Lang.& Lang.Behav.Abstr., Psychol.Abstr., Soc.Work Res.& Abstr., Sociol.Abstr. (1973-), Sociol.Abstr., Sp.Ed.Needs Abstr., Stud.Wom.Abstr.
—BLDSC shelfmark: 7168.124500.
     Description: Covers research based on the qualitative interpretation of social life, including theory, fieldwork and ethnography, historical and comparative analyses, and photographic studies.
     Refereed Serial

301   NE   ISSN 0033-5177
H61   CODEN: QQEJAV
QUALITY AND QUANTITY; international journal methodology. (Text in English and French) q. $179.50. Kluwer Academic Publishers, Postbus 17, 3300 AA Dordrecht, Netherlands. TEL 078-334911. FAX 078-334254. TELEX 29245. (Dist. by: Kluwer Academic Publishers Group, P.O. Box 322, 3300 AH Dordrecht; N. America dist. addr.: Box 358, Accord Station, Hingham, MA 02018-0358. TEL 617-871-6600) Ed. Vittorio Capecchi. bk.rev.; bibl.; charts; index. (back issues avail.; reprint service avail. from SWZ) Indexed: ASSIA, Compumath, Curr.Cont., J.Cont.Quant.Meth., Lang.& Lang.Behav.Abstr., Sociol.Abstr. (1967-), SSCI.
—BLDSC shelfmark: 7168.135000.

S

SOCIOLOGY

301   CN
QUEBEC (PROVINCE). CONSEIL DES AFFAIRES SOCIALES ET DE LA FAMILLE. RAPPORT ANNUEL. a. Can.$2. (Conseil des Affaires Sociales et de la Famille) Ministere des Communications, Direction Generale des Publications Gouvernementales, 2e etage, 1279 bd. Charest Ouest, Quebec, Que. G1N 4K7, Canada. TEL 413-643-3895.
   Formerly: Quebec (Province). Family and Social Affairs Council. Annual Report.

300   US   ISSN 0033-6742
R A P. 1969. m. $10. Radicals Against Poverty, 42 Melrose Pl., Montclair, NJ 07042. Ed. Arnie Korotkin. bk.rev.; circ. 1,500. (microfilm)
   Formerly: Vista R A P.

R D P. (Rural Development Perspectives) see *AGRICULTURE*

R N D. (Revue Notre-Dame) see *RELIGIONS AND THEOLOGY — Roman Catholic*

301.45   UK   ISSN 0306-3968
HT1501
RACE AND CLASS; a journal for Black and Third World liberation. 1959. q. £16($40) Institute of Race Relations, 2-6 Leeke St., King's Cross Rd., London WC1X 9HS, England. TEL 071-837-0041. FAX 071-278-0623. Eds. A. Sivanandan, E. Ahmad. adv.; bk.rev.; charts; index; circ. 4,000. **Indexed:** A.I.C.P., Alt.Press Ind., ASSIA, Br.Hum.Ind., CERDIC, Chic.Per.Ind., Curr.Cont.Africa, HR Rep., I D A, Lang.& Lang.Behav.Abstr., Left Ind. (1986-), Mid.East: Abstr.& Ind., SSCI.
   —BLDSC shelfmark: 7225.883000.
   Formerly: Race (ISSN 0033-7277)
   Description: Covers race and group relations.

301.45   UK   ISSN 0033-7358
HT1501
RACE TODAY. 1968. bi-m. £3. Race Today Collective, 165 Railton Rd., Brixton, London SE24 0LU, England. Ed. Leila Hassan. adv.; bk.rev.; index; circ. 5,000. **Indexed:** Curr.Cont.Africa.

RADIX. see *RELIGIONS AND THEOLOGY*

301.4   US
RAPPORT. bi-m. 12 Imbrie Pl., Sea Bright, NJ 07760. Ed. Michael S. Turback.

301   IT   ISSN 0486-0349
RASSEGNA ITALIANA DI SOCIOLOGIA. 1960. q. L.120000. Societa Editrice Il Mulino, Strada Maggiore, 37, 40125 Bologna, Italy. TEL 051-256011. FAX 051-256034. Ed. Pier Paolo Giglioli. adv.; index; circ. 1,800. (back issues avail.) **Indexed:** Hist.Abstr., Lang.& Lang.Behav.Abstr., P.A.I.S.For.Lang.Ind., Psychol.Abstr., Sociol.Abstr. (1960-), Stud.Wom.Abstr.

LA RAZA LAW JOURNAL. see *LAW*

READINGS IN SOCIAL AND POLITICAL THEORY. see *POLITICAL SCIENCE*

301   CN   ISSN 0034-1282
RECHERCHES SOCIOGRAPHIQUES. (Text in French) 1960. 3/yr. Can.$12. Universite Laval, Departement de Sociologie, Cite universitaire, Quebec, Que. G1K 7P4, Canada. TEL 418-656-2320. Ed. Marc-Andre Lessard. adv.; bk.rev.; abstr.; bibl.; charts; stat.; index, cum.index: 1960-1964; circ. 1,500. (also avail. in microform from UMI) **Indexed:** Hist.Abstr., Lang.& Lang.Behav.Abstr., Pt.de Rep. (1978-), Sociol.Abstr. (1960-).
   —BLDSC shelfmark: 7309.200000.

301   BE   ISSN 0771-677X
RECHERCHES SOCIOLOGIQUES. (Text in French; summaries in English) 1970. 3/yr. 1100 F. Universite Catholique de Louvain, Recherches Sociologiques, Place Montesquieu 1-10, B-1348 Louvain-la-Neuve, Belgium. TEL 010-47-42-04. FAX 010-47-29-97. Ed. Cecile Wery. bk.rev.; circ. 500. **Indexed:** Lang.& Lang.Behav.Abstr., Sociol.Abstr. (1970-).
   Description: Sociological analysis of social, methodological and theoretical problems.

301   US   ISSN 0894-4830
GV14.5
RECREATION: CURRENT SELECTED RESEARCH. 1988. a. $47.50. A M S Press, Inc., 56 E. 13th St., New York, NY 10003. TEL 212-777-4700. FAX 212-995-5413. Eds. James H. Humphrey, Fred Humphrey. index.
   Description: Research articles which address societal challenges across the domains of leisure behavior.

REINO; de deus no mundo dos homens. see *RELIGIONS AND THEOLOGY*

RELACIONES; estudios de historia y sociedad. see *HISTORY — History Of North And South America*

649 301   US   ISSN 0887-5480
RELATIONSHIP & FAMILY COMMUNICATIONS;* a unique guide for successful relationships. 1988. m. $16.80 to individuals; institutions $34. Relationship and Family Communications Company, c/o Gloria J. Gordon, Ed., 3409 E. Paris, Tampa, FL 33610. TEL 202-282-1979. (Subscr. to: RAFCOM Magazine, Box 1554, Washington, DC 20013-1554) adv.; circ. 100,000.
   Description: Discusses important issues in forming and maintaining loving relationships.

RELIGION AND AMERICAN CULTURE; a journal of interpretation. see *RELIGIONS AND THEOLOGY*

RELIGIONE E SOCIETA; storia della chiesa e dei movimenti cattolici. see *RELIGIONS AND THEOLOGY*

RELIGIONI E SOCIETA; rivista di scienze sociali della religione. see *RELIGIONS AND THEOLOGY*

REPRESENTATIVE RESEARCH IN SOCIAL PSYCHOLOGY. see *PSYCHOLOGY*

RESEARCH IN MELANESIA; a newsletter of anthropological and sociological research in Papua & New Guinea. see *ANTHROPOLOGY*

301 350   US   ISSN 0732-1317
H97
RESEARCH IN PUBLIC POLICY ANALYSIS AND MANAGEMENT. 1978. a. $63.50 to institutions. (Association for Public Policy Analysis Management) J A I Press Inc., 55 Old Post Rd., No. 2, Box 1678, Greenwich, CT 06836-1678. TEL 203-661-7602. Ed. Stuart Nagel.

305.8   US   ISSN 0195-7449
GN495.4
RESEARCH IN RACE AND ETHNIC RELATIONS; a research annual. 1979. a. $58.50 to institutions. J A I Press Inc., 55 Old Post Rd., No. 2, Box 1678, Greenwich, CT 06836-2678. TEL 203-661-7602. Eds. Cora Bagley Marrett, Cheryl B. Leggon. adv.; bk.rev. **Indexed:** Lang.& Lang.Behav.Abstr., Psychol.Abstr., Sociol.Abstr. (1988-).
   —BLDSC shelfmark: 7759.175000.

RESEARCH IN RELIGION AND FAMILY: BLACK PERSPECTIVES. see *RELIGIONS AND THEOLOGY*

301   US
RESEARCH IN RURAL SOCIOLOGY AND DEVELOPMENT. 1984. a. $58.50 to institutions. J A I Press Inc., 55 Old Post Rd., No. 2, Box 1678, Greenwich, CT 06836-1678. TEL 203-661-7602. Ed. Harry K. Schwarzweller. **Indexed:** Sociol.Abstr. (1979-).

301.24   US   ISSN 0163-786X
HN1
RESEARCH IN SOCIAL MOVEMENTS, CONFLICTS AND CHANGE. 1978. a. $58.50 to institutions. J A I Press Inc., 55 Old Post Rd., No. 2, Box 1678, Greenwich, CT 06836-1678. TEL 203-661-7602. Ed. Louis Kriesberg. **Indexed:** Lang.& Lang.Behav.Abstr., Sociol.Abstr. (1984-).
   —BLDSC shelfmark: 7770.570000.

301.07   US   ISSN 0196-1152
HM1
RESEARCH IN SOCIAL PROBLEMS AND PUBLIC POLICY; a research annual. 1979. a. $58.50 to institutions. J A I Press Inc., 55 Old Post Rd., No. 2, Box 1678, Greenwich, CT 06836-1678. TEL 203-661-7602. Eds. Michael Lewis, JoAnn L. Miller. **Indexed:** Lang.& Lang.Behav.Abstr., Psychol.Abstr., Sociol.Abstr. (1978-).
   —BLDSC shelfmark: 7770.580000.

305.5   US   ISSN 0276-5624
HT601
RESEARCH IN SOCIAL STRATIFICATION AND MOBILITY; a research annual. 1981. a. $63.50 to institutions. J A I Press Inc., 55 Old Post Rd., No. 2, Box 1678, Greenwich, CT 06836-1678. TEL 203-661-7602. Ed. Robert V. Robinson. **Indexed:** Lang.& Lang.Behav.Abstr., Sociol.Abstr. (1978-).

301   US   ISSN 0272-2801
HQ1075
RESEARCH IN THE INTERWEAVE OF SOCIAL ROLES; a research annual. 1980. a. $58.50 to institutions. J A I Press Inc., 55 Old Post Rd., No. 2, Box 1678, Greenwich, CT 06836-1678. TEL 203-661-7602. Ed. Helen Z. Lopata. **Indexed:** Lang.& Lang.Behav.Abstr., Psychol.Abstr.

RESEARCH IN THE SOCIOLOGY OF HEALTH CARE; a research annual. see *MEDICAL SCIENCES*

301.34   US   ISSN 0733-558X
HM131
RESEARCH IN THE SOCIOLOGY OF ORGANIZATIONS. 1982. a. $63.50 to institutions. J A I Press Inc., 55 Old Post Rd., No. 2, Box 1678, Greenwich, CT 06836-1678. TEL 203-661-7602. Ed. Samuel B. Bacharach. **Indexed:** Lang.& Lang.Behav.Abstr., Sociol.Abstr. (1982-).

301.1   US   ISSN 0277-2833
HD6951
RESEARCH IN THE SOCIOLOGY OF WORK. 1981. irreg. $63.50 to institutions. J A I Press Inc., 55 Old Post Rd., No. 2, Box 1678, Greenwich, CT 06836-1678. TEL 203-661-7602. Eds. Ida Harper Simpson, Richard L. Simpson. **Indexed:** Lang.& Lang.Behav.Abstr., Sociol.Abstr. (1981-).

301   US   ISSN 1049-7315
HV1   CODEN: RSWPEW
▼**RESEARCH ON SOCIAL WORK PRACTICE.** 1990. q. $39 to individuals; institutions $85. Sage Publications, Inc., 2455 Teller Rd., Newbury Park, CA 91320. TEL 805-499-0721. FAX 805-499-0871. Ed. Bruce Thyer. circ. 1,000. **Indexed:** Soc.Work Res.& Abstr.
   —BLDSC shelfmark: 7770.680000.
   Description: Devoted to the publication of empirical research concerning the methods and outcomes of social work practice.

REVELATION; social, political, economic and cultural monthly. see *LITERARY AND POLITICAL REVIEWS*

REVIEW OF RELIGIOUS RESEARCH. see *RELIGIONS AND THEOLOGY*

REVIEW OF SOCIAL ECONOMY. see *BUSINESS AND ECONOMICS*

301   UK   ISSN 0261-0272
REVIEWING SOCIOLOGY. 1979. 3/yr. £8 to individuals; institutions £20. City of Birmingham Polytechnic, Department of Sociololgy and Applied Social Studies, C Block, Perry Barr, Birmingham B42 2SU, England. Ed.Bd. adv.; cum.index; circ. 800. **Indexed:** Sociol.Abstr. (1972-).
   —BLDSC shelfmark: 7798.700000.
   Description: Book review journal in the social sciences.

301   CI   ISSN 0350-154X
HM7
REVIJA ZA SOCIOLOGIJU/SOCIOLOGICAL REVIEW. (Text in Serbo-Croatian; summaries in English) 1971. s-a. 150 din.($12.99) Sociolosko Drustvo Hrvatske - Croatian Sociological Association, Filozofski fakultet, Odsjek za Sociologiju, Djure Salaja 3, 41000 Zagreb, Croatia. TEL 041-513-155. Ed. Vjekoslav Afric. adv.; bk.rev.; bibl.; circ. 1,000. **Indexed:** Lang.& Lang.Behav.Abstr., Sociol.Abstr. (1971-).
   Description: Covers all aspects of sociology.

301   UY
REVISTA DE CIENCIAS SOCIALES. 1986. a. Fundacion de Cultura Universitaria, 25 de Mayo No. 568, 11000 Montevideo, Uruguay. TEL 96-11-52. (Subscr. to: I D E M, Casilla de Correo 1155)

301   PE
REVISTA DE DEBATES: DEBATES EN SOCIOLOGIA. 1977. a. $6.40. Pontificia Universidad Catolica del Peru, Departamento de Ciencias Sociales, Fondo Editorial, Apdo. 1761, Lima 100, Peru. FAX 51-14-611785. Eds. Gonzalo Portocarrero, Ana Ponce.

301   SP   ISSN 0425-3485
REVISTA DE ESTUDIOS COOPERATIVOS; revesco. 1963. a. 700 ptas. Asociacion de Estudios Cooperativos, Salustiano Olozaga 5, 4 dcha., 28001 Madrid, Spain. TEL 91-435-05-98. (Co-sponsor: Universidad de Madrid. Catedra Libre de Cooperacion) Ed. Jose Luis de Arco Alvarez. (also avail. in cards)

301   SP   ISSN 0303-9889
H8
REVISTA DE ESTUDIOS SOCIALES. 1960. 3/yr. 400 ptas.($11) Centro de Estudios Sociales de la Santa Cruz del Valle de los Caidos, Palacio Real, Bailen s-n, Apdo. de Correas 14158, Madrid 15, Spain. (Subscr. to: Libreria Editorial Augustinus, Gaztambide 75-77, Madrid 15) Ed. Luis Gonzalez Seara. bk.rev.; bibl.; circ. 2,000 (controlled). **Indexed:** Lang.& Lang.Behav.Abstr.
  Former titles (until 1971): Centro de Estudios Sociales del Valle de los Caidos. Boletin (ISSN 0008-9966); Centro de Estudios Sociales de la Santa Cruz del Valle de los Caidos. Boletin (ISSN 0429-8764)

301   SP   ISSN 0015-6043
REVISTA DE FOMENTO SOCIAL; ciencias sociales. 1946. q. 4180 ptas.($38) Centro Loyola de Estudios y Comunicacion Social, Pablo Aranda 3, Madrid-6, Spain. FAX 563-40-73. Ed. Javier Gorosquieta. adv.; bk.rev.; abstr.; index; circ. 3,000.
—BLDSC shelfmark: 7856.020000.
  Formerly (1946-1963): Fomento Social (ISSN 0210-4113)

301   CK
REVISTA DE SOCIOLOGIA. 1968. s-a. Universidad Pontificia Bolivariana, Facultad de Sociologia, Avda. La Playa 40-88, Apdo. 1178, Medellin, Colombia. bk.rev.; charts; bibl.; stat.

301   SP   ISSN 0210-5233
HM7
REVISTA ESPANOLA DE INVESTIGACIONES SOCIOLOGICAS. 1978. q. $45. Centro de Investigaciones Sociologicas, Calle Montalban, 8, 28014 Madrid, Spain. Dir. Joaquin Arango Vila-Belda. adv.; bk.rev.; cum.index; circ. 3,000. **Indexed:** Hist.Abstr., Lang.& Lang.Behav.Abstr., Psychol.Abstr., SCIMP (1989-), Sociol.Abstr. (1965-).
  Supersedes (1965-1977): Revista Espanola de la Opinion Publica (ISSN 0034-9429)

301   MX   ISSN 0557-8558
REVISTA INTERAMERICANA DE SOCIOLOGIA. 1966. 3/yr. $1.60 per no. Instituto Mexicano de Cultura, Providencia 330, Col. del Valle, Mexico 12, D.F., Mexico. Ed. Lucio Mendieta y Nunez. bk.rev.

301   SP   ISSN 0034-9712
H8
REVISTA INTERNACIONAL DE SOCIOLOGIA. 1941. q. 3300 ptas. (foreign 4950 ptas.). Consejo Superior de Investigaciones Cientificas (C.S.I.C.), Instituto "J. Balmes" de Sociologia, Vitruvio, 8, 28006 Madrid, Spain. Ed. Carmelo Vinas Y Mey. circ. 600. **Indexed:** Hist.Abstr., Sociol.Abstr. (1953-).
—BLDSC shelfmark: 7861.800000.
  Description: Covers sociology, demographics, population problems and social thought.

301 630   VE   ISSN 0798-1759
▼**REVISTA INTERNACIONAL DE SOCIOLOGIA SOBRE AGRICULTURA Y ALIMENTOS/INTERNATIONAL JOURNAL OF SOCIOLOGY OF AGRICULTURE AND FOOD**. (Text in English, Spanish) 1991. a. Bs.750($15) to individuals; institutions Bs.1500($25)(includes s-a. newsletter)(effective 1992). Universidad Central de Venezuela, Centro de Estudios del Desarrollo, Apto. Postal 6622, Caracas 1010-A, Venezuela. TEL 7523266. FAX 582-7512691. (U.S. subscr. addr.: Poba International, No. 151, Box 02-5255, Miami, FL 33102-5255) (Co-sponsor: Asociacion Internacional de Sociologia, Comite de Investigaciones de Sociologia sobre Agricultura y Alimentos) Eds. Alessandro Bonanno, Nelson Prato Barbosa. adv.; circ. 500.
  Description: Covers themes such as: social relationships, the market, work, technology and production in agricultural and food industries.

REVISTA INTERNACIONAL DEL TRABAJO. see *BUSINESS AND ECONOMICS — Labor And Industrial Relations*

301   MX   ISSN 0188-2503
H8
REVISTA MEXICANA DE SOCIOLOGIA. 1939. q. Mex.$55000($60) Universidad Nacional Autonoma de Mexico, Instituto de Investigaciones Sociales, Villa Obregon, Ciudad Universitaria, 04510 Mexico D.F., Mexico. TEL 5-550-04-79. FAX 5-548-43-15. Ed. Sara Gordon. adv.; bk.rev.; abstr.; bibl.; charts; index, cum.index; circ. 2,000. (also avail. in microform from UMI; reprint service avail. from SWZ,UMI) **Indexed:** Hisp.Amer.Per.Ind., Int.Lab.Doc., Lang.& Lang.Behav.Abstr., P.A.I.S.For.Lang.Ind., Psychol.Abstr., Sage Urb.Stud.Abstr., Sociol.Abstr. (1952-).

301   PY   ISSN 0035-0354
HM7
REVISTA PARAGUAYA DE SOCIOLOGIA. 1964. 3/yr. $40. Centro Paraguayo de Estudios Sociologicos, Eligio Ayala 973, Asuncion, Paraguay. FAX 595-21-447-128. Ed. Graziella Corvalan. bk.rev.; bibl.; charts; stat.; circ. 1,000. (also avail. in microform from UMI; reprint service avail. from UMI) **Indexed:** Hisp.Amer.Per.Ind., Int.Lab.Doc., Lang.& Lang.Behav.Abstr., Sociol.Abstr. (1964-).

REVISTA THEOBROMA. see *AGRICULTURE*

301.34   AE   ISSN 0568-9848
REVUE ALGERIENNE DU TRAVAIL. 1964. q. Ministere des Affaires Sociales, Rue Farid Zouieoueche, Kouba, Algiers, Algeria. TEL 2-77-91-33. TELEX 53447. bibl.

REVUE CANADIENNE DE PSYCHO-EDUCATION. see *PSYCHOLOGY*

301 100   FR
REVUE DU M A U S S. (Mouvement Anti-Utilitariste dans les Science Sociales) 1982. q. 195 F. Editions La Decouverte, 1, Place Paul Painleve, 75005 Paris, France. TEL 46-33-41-16. FAX 46-33-46-77.

REVUE ECONOMIQUE ET SOCIALE. see *BUSINESS AND ECONOMICS*

301   FR   ISSN 0397-7870
E169.1
REVUE FRANCAISE D'ETUDES AMERICAINES. (Text in English or French) 1976. 4/yr. 290 F. to individuals (foreign 350 F.); institutions 500 F. (Association Francaise d'Etudes Americaines) Presses Universitaires de Nancy, 25 rue Baron-Louis, B.P. 454, 54001 Nancy Cedex, France. TEL 337-37-65. Ed. Marc Chenetier. adv.; bk.rev.; bibl.; circ. 900. (back issues avail.) **Indexed:** Arts & Hum.Cit.Ind., Hist.Abstr., M.L.A.
  Description: Reference journal for American studies in France.

301   FR   ISSN 0035-2969
HM3
REVUE FRANCAISE DE SOCIOLOGIE. (Summaries in English, German, Russian, Spanish) 1960. q. (Centre National de La Recherche Scientifique) Editions du C N R S, 1 Place Aristide Briand, 92195 Meudon Cedex, France. TEL 1-45-34-75-50. FAX 1-46-26-28-49. TELEX LABOBEL 204 135 F. (Subscr. to: Presses du C N R S, 20-22, rue Saint Amand, 75015 Paris, France. TEL 1-45-33-16-00) Dir. J.D. Reynaud. adv.; bk.rev.; bibl.; charts; circ. 3,000. **Indexed:** Curr.Cont., E.I., Int.Lab.Doc., Lang.& Lang.Behav.Abstr., P.A.I.S.For.Lang.Ind., Pt.de Rep. (1979-), Rural Recreat.Tour.Abstr., Sociol.Abstr. (1960-), SSCI, World Agri.Econ.& Rural Sociol.Abstr.
—BLDSC shelfmark: 7904.430000.
  Description: Includes theoretical and methodological articles recording fundamental research, trends and developments, discussions of new developments in the field of sociology, and identifying new areas for sociological research.

300 331   FR   ISSN 0035-2985
HD4807
REVUE FRANCAISE DES AFFAIRES SOCIALES. 1946. q. 80 ECU($95) (typically set in Jan.). (Ministere des Affaires Sociales et de la Solidarite Nationale) Masson, 120 bd. Saint-Germain, 75005 Paris Cedex 06, France. TEL 1-46-34-21-60. FAX 1-45-87-29-99. TELEX 202 671 F. adv.; bibl.; charts; stat.; index; circ. 3,800. (also avail. in microfiche) **Indexed:** Abstr.Hyg., C.I.S. Abstr., Int.Lab.Doc., Lang.& Lang.Behav.Abstr., P.A.I.S.For.Lang.Ind., Trop.Dis.Bull.
—BLDSC shelfmark: 7902.250000.
  Formerly (until 1967): Revue Francaise du Travail.

301 500   FR   ISSN 0242-5149
AS161
REVUE IMPREVUE. 2/yr. Universite de Montpellier (Universite Paul Valery), B.P. 5043, 34032 Montpellier Cedex 1, France. TEL 67-14-20-00.
—BLDSC shelfmark: 4371.476500.

301.4   CN   ISSN 0707-9699
REVUE INTERNATIONALE D'ACTION COMMUNAUTAIRE; international review of community development. (Text in French; abstracts in English, French and Spanish) 1958. s-a. Can.$22 to individuals; institutions Can.$30. Forum International d'Action Communautaire, Ecole de Service Social, c/o Universite de Montreal, Ecole de Service Social, C.P. 6128, Succ. A, Montreal, Que. H3C 3J7, Canada. TEL 514-343-7222. FAX 514-343-2493. (Subscr. to: RIAC - Periodica, C.P. 444, Outremont, Quebec H2V 4R6, Canada) Ed. Frederic Lesemann. adv.; bk.rev.; abstr.; charts; stat.; cum.index every 2 yrs.; circ. 2,000. (back issues avail.) **Indexed:** Int.Polit.Sci.Abstr., Lang.& Lang.Behav.Abstr., Pt.de Rep. (1984-), Sociol.Abstr.
  Description: Critical debate on new trends in social policy: studies relationships in the social sector.

REVUE INTERNATIONALE DU TRAVAIL. see *BUSINESS AND ECONOMICS — Labor And Industrial Relations*

291.17   IT
RICERCHE DI STORIA SOCIALE E RELIGIOSA. 1972. s-a. price varies. (Centro Studi per le Fonti della Storia della Chiesa nel Veneto) Edizioni di Storia e Letteratura s.r.l., Via Lancellotti, 18, 00186 Rome, Italy. TEL 6540556. (Co-Sponsor: Centro Studi di Storia Sociale e Religiosa nel Mezzogiorno) Ed. Gabriele De Rosa. bk.rev.; illus. **Indexed:** CERDIC.

RIJKSUNIVERSITEIT TE LEIDEN. INSTITUUT VOOR CULTURELE ANTROPOLOGIE EN SOCIOLOGIE DER NIET-WESTERSE SAMENLEVINGEN. PUBLICATIE. see *ANTHROPOLOGY*

301.2   IT   ISSN 0085-5731
RIVISTA DI ETNOGRAFIA.* 1946. a. L.5000. Via Alfrado Rocco No. 98, Naples, Italy. Ed. Giovanni Tucci.

301.4   PL   ISSN 0239-5568
HD8039.S4
ROCZNIKI SOCJOLOGII MORSKIEJ. (Text in Polish; summaries in English) a. price varies. (Polish Academy of Sciences, Section Gdansk, Commission of Maritime Sociology) Ossolineum, Publishing House of the Polish Academy of Sciences, Rynek 9, 50-106 Wroclaw, Poland. TEL 386-25. (Dist. by: Ars Polona, Krakowskie Przedmiescie 7, 00-068 Warsaw, Poland) Ed. Ludwik Janiszewski.
  Formerly (until 1987): Socjologia Morska.
  Description: Studies and monographs on sociological phenomena occurring in the social groups connected, through their professional activity, with the sea.

301   PL   ISSN 0080-3731
ROCZNIKI SOCJOLOGII WSI. STUDIA I MATERIALY. (Text in Polish; summaries in English and Russian) 1962. a. price varies. (Polska Akademia Nauk, Instytut Filozofii i Socjologii) Ossolineum, Publishing House of the Polish Academy of Sciences, Rynek 9, Wroclaw, Poland. TELEX 0712771 OSS PL. (Dist. by: Ars Polona-Ruch, Krakowskie Przedmiescie 7, Warsaw, Poland) Ed. F. Mleczko. bk.rev.; circ. 500.
—BLDSC shelfmark: 8015.770000.
  Description: Papers on sociological research into problems of rural communities.

301   DK   ISSN 0108-2205
ROSKILDE UNIVERSITETSCENTER. INSTITUT FOR SAMFUNDSOEKONOMI OG PLANLAEGNING. ARBEJDSPAPIR. 1981. irreg., no.2, 1987. free. Roskilde Universitetscenter, Institut for Samfundsoekonomi og Planlaegning, Institut VIII, Postbox 260, 4000 Roskilde, Denmark.

301   RM
ROUMANIAN JOURNAL OF SOCIOLOGY. 1956. s-a. 70 lei($45) (Academia Romana) Editura Academiei Romane, Calea Victoriei 125, 79717 Bucharest, Rumania. (Dist. by: Rompresfilatelia, Calea Grivitei 64-66, P.O. Box 12-201, 78104 Bucharest, Rumania) bk.rev.
  Formerly: Revue Roumaine des Sciences Sociales. Serie de Sociologie (ISSN 0080-2646)

RUCH PRAWNICZY, EKONOMICZNY I SOCJOLOGICZNY. see *LAW*

SOCIOLOGY

301 IT
RUE MORGUE. 1989. 3/yr. L.30000. Bulzoni Editore, Via dei Liburni 14, 00185 Rome, Italy. TEL 06-4455207. FAX 06-4450355. Ed. Alberto Abruzzese.

RUNNYMEDE BULLETIN. see *POLITICAL SCIENCE — Civil Rights*

301.35   US   ISSN 0279-5957
HT401
RURAL SOCIOLOGIST. 1981. q. $18. Rural Sociological Society, c/o Patrick C. Jobes, Treasurer, Dept. of Sociology, Wilson Hall, Montana State University, Bozeman, MT 59717. TEL 406-994-5248. Ed. Rusty Brooks. index; circ. 1,000. (back issues avail.) **Indexed:** Agri.Eng.Abstr., ASSIA, Curr.Cont., Poult.Abstr., Triticale Abstr., World Agri.Econ.& Rural Sociol.Abstr.
—BLDSC shelfmark: 8052.629000.

301.35   US   ISSN 0036-0112
HT401   CODEN: RUSCA
RURAL SOCIOLOGY; devoted to scientific study of rural and small-town life. 1936. q. $63. Rural Sociological Society, c/o Patrick C. Jobes, Treasurer, Department of Sociology, Wilson Hall, Montana State University, Bozeman, MT 59717. Ed. Willis Goudy. adv.; bk.rev.; abstr.; bibl.; charts; stat.; index, cum.index: vols.1-20, 21-30, 31-40; circ. 3,000. (also avail. in microform from MIM,UMI; reprint service avail. from SCH) **Indexed:** Abstr.Anthropol., Abstr.Health Care Manage.Stud., Amer.Bibl.Slavic & E.Eur.Stud., ASSIA, Bibl.Agri., Biol.& Agr.Ind., C.I.J.E., Crim.Just.Abstr., E.I., Energy Ind., Energy Info.Abstr., Geo.Abstr., Hist.Abstr., I D A, Int.Lab.Doc., Lang.& Lang.Behav.Abstr., Mid.East: Abstr.& Ind., P.A.I.S., PHRA, Popul.Ind., Popul.Info., Psychol.Abstr., Rural Devel.Abstr., Rural Recreat.Tour.Abstr., Sage Urb.Stud.Abstr., Sci.Cit.Ind., Soc.Sci.Ind., Soc.Work Res.& Abstr., Sociol.Abstr. (1952-), Soils & Fert., SSCI, Stud.Wom.Abstr., World Agri.Econ.& Rural Sociol.Abstr.
—BLDSC shelfmark: 8052.630000.

360   UK   ISSN 0264-4002
RURAL VIEWPOINT. 1932. 6/yr. £7.50. A C R E (Action with Communities in Rural England), Somerford Court, Somerford Rd., Circencester, Glos. GL7 1TW, England. FAX 0285-654537. Ed. Fiona Eadie. adv.; bk.rev.; illus.; index; circ. 2,000. (back issues avail.) **Indexed:** ASSIA, Geo.Abstr.
—BLDSC shelfmark: 8052.640700.
Formerly: Village (ISSN 0042-6172)
Description: Covers rural community issues in Britain.

301   US   ISSN 0038-0210
JN51
S A. (Sociological Analysis); a journal in the sociology of religion. 1940. q. $50. Association for the Sociology of Religion, Marist Hall, Rm. 108, Catholic University of America, Washington, DC 20064. TEL 202-319-5447. adv.; bk.rev.; charts; stat.; index, cum.index: vols.1-24; circ. 1,325. (also avail. in microform from JAI,MIM,UMI; reprint service avail. from UMI) **Indexed:** ASSIA, Cath.Ind., Curr.Cont., Curr.Lit.Fam.Plan., Hist.Abstr. (until 1990), Lang.& Lang.Behav.Abstr., Rel.& Theol.Abstr. (1989-), Rel.Ind.One, Rel.Per., Sociol.Abstr., SSCI.
—BLDSC shelfmark: 8319.623000.
Formerly: American Catholic Sociological Review.

301   US   ISSN 0885-6729
S I N E T; social indicators network news. 1973. q. $16 (foreign $18). Abbott L. Ferriss, Ed. & Pub., Box 24064, Emory University Sta., Atlanta, GA 30322. TEL 404-373-4756. FAX 404-727-7532. adv.; bk.rev.; bibl.; circ. 300.
Former titles (until 1984): Social Indicators Newsletter (ISSN 0363-3195); Social Indicators.
Description: Brings together information on social indicator developments from Asia, the Pacific, Europe, and the Americas.

301 840   SZ
S K M.* (Schweizer Kontakt) (Text in German) bi-m. ($40) Exakt-Verlag, 8280 Kreuzlingen TG, Switzerland. illus.; tr.lit.

S P R C NEWSLETTER. (Social Policy Research Centre) see *SOCIAL SERVICES AND WELFARE*

S P R C REPORTS AND PROCEEDINGS. (Social Policy Research Centre) see *SOCIAL SERVICES AND WELFARE*

S P W. (Sozialistische Politik und Wirtschaft) see *POLITICAL SCIENCE*

S W S - RUNDSCHAU. (Sozialwissenschaftliche Studiengesellschaft) see *SOCIAL SCIENCES: COMPREHENSIVE WORKS*

301   US
SAGE STUDIES IN INTERNATIONAL SOCIOLOGY. 1976. irreg. price varies. (International Sociological Association) Sage Publications, Inc., 2455 Teller Rd., Newbury Park, CA 91320. TEL 805-499-0721. FAX 805-499-0871. (And Sage Publications, Ltd., 6 Bonhill St., London EC2A 4PU, England) bibl.; charts; stat.

261 301 100   US   ISSN 0093-2582
AS30
ST. CROIX REVIEW. 1968. bi-m. $25. Religion and Society Inc., Box 244, Stillwater, MN 55082. Ed. Angus MacDonald. bk.rev.; charts; illus.; circ. 3,400. (also avail. in microform from UMI,KTO; reprint service avail. from UMI; back issues avail.) **Indexed:** CERDIC.
Formerly: Religion and Society (ISSN 0034-396X)
Description: Social criticism of controversial subjects, from a traditional point of view.

301   DK   ISSN 0903-7543
SAMFUNDSFORSKNING. 1983. 4/yr. DKK 90. Statens Samfundsvidenskabelige Forskningsraad - Danish Social Science Research Council, Ministry of Education and Research, Department of Research, H.C. Andersens Boulevard 40, DK-1553 Copenhagen V, Denmark. TEL 45-33-114300. FAX 45-33-323501. TELEX 15652 FS. Ed. Inge M. Bryderup. bk.rev.; circ. 1,500.
Formerly: Nyt fra S S F (ISSN 0108-7924)
Description: Directed to Nordic scholars and researchers in social science. Presents information about new projects funded by the Council, lists new sponsored publications, and also focuses on research policy.

SAMISKE SAMLINGER. see *ANTHROPOLOGY*

LE SAUVEUR. see *RELIGIONS AND THEOLOGY*

300   SZ   ISSN 0036-7826
SCHWEIZERISCHE ZEITSCHRIFT FUER GEMEINNUETZIGKEIT. (Text in French and German) 1862. bi-m. 20 Fr. (Schweizerische Gemeinnuetzige Gesellschaft) Schulthess Polygraphischer Verlag AG, Zwingliplatz 2, 8001 Zurich, Switzerland. adv.; bk.rev.; bibl.; charts; illus.; index; circ. 8,000.
—BLDSC shelfmark: 8122.060000.

301   SZ
SCHWEIZERISCHE ZEITSCHRIFT FUER SOZIALVERSICHERUNG UND BERUFLICHE VORSORGE. 1957. bi-m. 108 Fr. Staempfli und Cie AG, Postfach, CH-3001 Berne, Switzerland. FAX 031-276699. TELEX 911987. Ed.Bd. adv.; bk.rev.; bibl.; charts; index; circ. 1,200. **Indexed:** ASCA, Curr.Cont., P.A.I.S.For.Lang.Ind., SSCI, World Bibl.Soc.Sec.
Formerly: Schweizerische Zeitschrift fuer Sozialversicherung (ISSN 0036-7877)

301   SZ   ISSN 0379-3664
HM5
SCHWEIZERISCHE ZEITSCHRIFT FUER SOZIOLOGIE/REVUE SUISSE DE SOCIOLOGIE. (Text in English, French or German; summaries in all 3 languages) 1975. 3/yr. 105 Fr. (Societe Suisse de Sociologie) Seismo Press, P.O. Box 313, CH-8028 Zurich, Switzerland. TEL 01-2611094. FAX 01-2521054. Ed. J. Coenen-Huther. adv.; bk.rev.; circ. 800. **Indexed:** Lang.& Lang.Behav.Abstr., Sage Fam.Stud.Abstr., Sociol.Abstr. (1976-).
—BLDSC shelfmark: 7953.394000.

SCOTTISH WOMEN'S TEMPERANCE NEWS. see *DRUG ABUSE AND ALCOHOLISM*

301.4   NE   ISSN 0037-3087
SEKSTANT. vol.58, 1978. m. (9/yr.). fl.37.50. Nederlandse Vereniging voor Sexuele Hervorming, Nieuwe Molstraat 6, Box 64, 2501 CB The Hague, Netherlands. adv.; bk.rev.; illus.; circ. 200,000.
Formerly: Verstandig Ouderschap.

301.41   US
SELECT.* 1962. q. $20 for 5 nos. Swing Select Ltd., 4111 Lincoln Blvd., Ste. 655, Marina Delrey, CA 90292. Ed. Dennis Worth. adv.; bk.rev.; tr.lit.

SERVIZIO MIGRANTI. see *POLITICAL SCIENCE*

SEX ROLES; a journal of research. see *PSYCHOLOGY*

301   JA
SHAKAIGAKU NENSHI. 1956. Waseda Daigaku, Shakai Gakkai, c/o Waseda Daigaku Bungakubu, 42 Toyama-cho, Shinjuku-ku, Tokyo, Japan. illus.

SHAREDEBATE INTERNATIONAL; a ShareWare diskette magazine. see *SOCIAL SCIENCES: COMPREHENSIVE WORKS*

820   IS
SHDEMOT; cultural forum of the kibbutz movement. (Text in English) 1974. 3/yr. IS.15($12) Federation of Kibbutz Movements, 10 Dubnov St., Tel Aviv, Israel. Ed. David Twersky. bk.rev.; illus.; circ. 2,500. **Indexed:** Ind.Heb.Per.

301   US
SHEHUIXUE YANJIU/SOCIOLOGICAL STUDIES. (Text in Chinese) bi-m. $33.80. China Books & Periodicals, Inc., 2929 24th St., San Francisco, CA 94110. TEL 415-282-2994. FAX 415-282-0994.

SIDEWINDER STUDIES IN HISTORY & SOCIOLOGY. see *HISTORY*

300   US   ISSN 1046-8781
H62   CODEN: SIGAEI
SIMULATION & GAMING; an international journal of theory, design and research. 1970. q. $42 to individuals; institutions $125. (Association for Business Simulation and Experiential Learning) Sage Publications, Inc., 2455 Teller Rd., Newbury Park, CA 91320. TEL 805-499-0721. FAX 805-499-0871. (And: Sage Publications, Ltd., 6 Bonhill St., London EC2A 4PU, England) (Co-sponsors: North American Simulation and Gaming Association; International Simulation and Gaming Association) Ed. David Crookall. adv.; bk.rev.; charts; index; circ. 3,000. (also avail. in microform from UMI; back issues avail.; reprint service avail. from UMI) **Indexed:** A.B.C.Pol.Sci., Abstr.Mil.Bibl., Adol.Ment.Hlth.Abstr., ASCA, Bk.Rev.Ind., C.I.J.E., Commun.Abstr., Comput.Cont., Comput.Rev., Curr.Cont., Educ.Admin.Abstr., Int.Polit.Sci.Abstr., J.Cont.Quant.Meth., LAMP, Lang.& Lang.Behav.Abstr., M.M.R.I., Media Rev.Dig., Mid.East: Abstr.& Ind., P.A.I.S., PHRA, Psychol.Abstr. Sci.Abstr., Soc.Sci.Ind., Sociol.Abstr., SSCI.
—BLDSC shelfmark: 8285.161000.
Formerly: Simulation and Games (ISSN 0037-5500)

300 323.4   UK   ISSN 0144-039X
HT851
SLAVERY & ABOLITION; a journal of comparative studies. 1980. 3/yr. £30($45) to individuals; institutions £70($110). Frank Cass & Co. Ltd., Gainsborough House, 11 Gainsborough Rd., London El1 1RS, England. TEL 081-530-4226. FAX 081-530-7795. Eds. Gad Heuman, James Walvin. adv.; bk.rev.; index. (also avail. in microfilm from UMI; back issues avail.) **Indexed:** Hist.Abstr.
—BLDSC shelfmark: 8309.373000.
Description: Discusses all aspects of human bondage throughout the ages.

300 943.72 943.85   CS   ISSN 0037-6833
SLEZSKY SBORNIK/ACTA SILESIACA; ctvrtletnik pro vedy o spolecnosti. (Text in Czech; summaries in English, French, German, Russian) 1878. q. DM.133. (Czechoslovak Academy of Sciences, Silesian Institute) Academia, Publishing House of the Czechoslovak Academy of Sciences, Vodickova 40, 112 29 Prague 1, Czechoslovakia. TEL 21-47-64. (Dist. in Western countries by: Kubon & Sagner, P.O. Box 34 01 08, 8000 Munich 34, Germany) Ed. Dan Gawrecki. bk.rev.; illus.; maps; cum.index: 1878-1952, 1953-1962; circ. 1,050. **Indexed:** Hist.Abstr.
Formerly (until 1935): Matice Opavska. Vestnik.
Description: Devoted to social scientific research in Silesia and the Ostrava industrial districts, Czech-Polish relations, and the nationality problem in this area.

SLOVANSKE STUDIE. see *HISTORY — History Of Europe*

SLOVANSKY PREHLED/SLAVONIC REVIEW. see *POLITICAL SCIENCE*

SLOVENSKA AKADEMIJA ZNANOSTI IN UMETNOSTI. FILOZOFSKI VESTNIK. see *PHILOSOPHY*

SMALL GROUP RESEARCH; an international journal of theory, investigation and application. see *PSYCHOLOGY*

301 320   AT   ISSN 0155-0306
HN841
SOCIAL ALTERNATIVES. 1977. q. Aus.$24 to individuals; institutions Aus.$34. c/o Department of Government, University of Queensland, St. Lucia, Qld. 4072, Australia. TEL 365-2324. FAX 365-1388. Ed.Bd. adv.; bk.rev.; film rev.; circ. 2,000. Indexed: ASCA, Aus.P.A.I.S., Curr.Cont., HR Rep., Lang.& Lang.Behav.Abstr., Sociol.Abstr., SSCI.
—BLDSC shelfmark: 8318.041300.
    Description: Covers a range of concerns relating to social, political, economic and cultural issues.

SOCIAL ANALYSIS; journal of cultural and social practice. see *ANTHROPOLOGY*

301 340   UK   ISSN 0964-6639
▼**SOCIAL AND LEGAL STUDIES**. 1992. q. £29($48) to individuals; institutions £79($130). Sage Publications Ltd., 6 Bonhill St., London EC2A 4PU, England. TEL 071-374-0645. FAX 071-374-8741. Eds. Sol Picciotto, Carol Smart. adv.: color page #150; trim 193 x 114; adv. contact: Bernie Folan. bk.rev.
    Description: Dedicated to critical work in law, jurisprudence, penality and the criminal justice system. Offers an interdisciplinary perspective that draws upon sociology, feminism, political economy, history and philosophy.

SOCIAL AND POLICY ISSUES IN EDUCATION. see *EDUCATION*

301   II   ISSN 0049-0857
HN681
SOCIAL CHANGE. 1971. q. Rs.40($22) to individuals; institutions Rs.60($30). Council for Social Development - Sangha Rachana, 53 Lodi Estate, New Delhi 110 003, India. Ed. O.P. Misra. adv.; bk.rev.; bibl.; circ. 1,100. (back issues avail.) Indexed: Geo.Abstr., I D A.
—BLDSC shelfmark: 8318.070500.
    Description: Promotes the studies and undertaking of social development, including: national and regional policies, planning processes, social and economic interaction in national growth, studies, research and survey techniques.

300 261   UK   ISSN 0037-7686
BL60
SOCIAL COMPASS; international review of sociology of religion. (Text in English, French) 1953. q. £26($43) to individuals; institutions £66($109). (Groupe de Sciences Sociales des Religions, BE) Sage Publications Ltd., 6 Bonhill St., London EC2A 4PU, England. TEL 071-374-0645. FAX 071-374-8741. Ed. A. Bastenier. adv.: color page #150; trim 193 x 114; adv. contact: Bernie Folan. bk.rev.; bibl.; charts; stat.; index, cum.index: 1953-1973. Indexed: Arts & Hum.Cit.Ind., ASCA, CERDIC, Curr.Cont., E.I., Lang.& Lang.Behav.Abstr., Mid.East: Abstr.& Ind., Rel.& Theol.Abstr. (1968-), Rel.Ind.One, Rel.Per., Sociol.Abstr. (1954-), SSCI.
—BLDSC shelfmark: 8318.075000.
    Description: Forum for all scholars in sociology, anthropology, religious studies and theology concerned with the sociology of religion. Individual issues focus on a particular topic in current social scientific research on religion in society.

SOCIAL DEBATT. see *POLITICAL SCIENCE*

330.9 301.3   UN
SOCIAL DEVELOPMENT NEWSLETTER. 1971. 2/yr. free. United Nations Centre for Social Development and Humanitarian Affairs, Social Development Division, Vienna International Centre, A-1400 Vienna, Austria. TEL 26 310. circ. 6,000. Indexed: HR Rep.

301   US   ISSN 0037-7732
HN51   CODEN: SOFOAP
SOCIAL FORCES. 1922. 4/yr. $28 to individuals (foreign $36); institutions $48 (foreign $56). (University of North Carolina at Chapel Hill, Departmnet of English) University of North Carolina Press, Box 2288, Chapel Hill, NC 27515-2288. TEL 919-966-3561. FAX 919-966-3829. Ed. Richard L. Simpson. adv.; bk.rev.; bibl.; index, cum.index: 1922-1972; circ. 4,300. (also avail. in microform from UMI,MIM; reprint service avail. from UMI) Indexed: A.B.C.Pol.Sci., Abstr.Anthropol., Acad.Ind., Adol.Ment.Hlth.Abstr., Amer.Bibl.Slavic & E.Eur.Stud., ASCA, ASSIA, Bk.Rev.Ind. (1965-), Chic.Per.Ind., Child.Bk.Rev.Ind. (1965-), Commun.Abstr., Crim.Just.Abstr., Curr.Cont., Curr.Lit.Fam.Plan., E.I., Educ.Admin.Abstr., Geo.Abstr., Hist.Abstr., Lang.& Lang.Behav.Abstr., Mid.East: Abstr.& Ind., P.A.I.S., Popul.Ind., Psychol.Abstr., Rural Recreat.Tour.Abstr., Sage Urb.Stud.Abstr., Soc.Sci.Ind., Soc.Work Res.& Abstr., Sociol.Abstr. (1952-), Sociol.Abstr., SSCI, Stud.Wom.Abstr.
—BLDSC shelfmark: 8318.089000.
    Refereed Serial

301   US
SOCIAL INDICATORS. 1977. bi-m. $5. American Institutes for Research, Social Indicators Research Program, 1791 Arastradero Rd., Box 1113, Palo Alto, CA 94302. TEL 415-493-3550. Eds. Robert J. Rossi, Kevin J. Gilmartin. adv.; bk.rev.; circ. 300. (looseleaf format)

301   NE   ISSN 0303-8300
HN25   CODEN: SINRDZ
SOCIAL INDICATORS RESEARCH; an international and interdisciplinary journal for quality-of-life measurement. 16/yr. (in 2 vols., 8 nos./vol.). $290. Kluwer Academic Publishers, Postbus 17, 3300 AA Dordrecht, Netherlands. TEL 078-334911. FAX 078-334254. TELEX 29245. (Dist. by: Kluwer Academic Publishers Group, P.O. Box 322, 3300 AH Dordrecht, Netherlands; N. America dist. addr.: Box 358, Accord Station, Hingham, MA 02018-0358. TEL 617-871-6600) Ed. Alex C. Michalos. adv.; bk.rev.; index. reprint service avail. from SWZ) Indexed: ASCA, ASSIA, CERDIC, Curr.Cont., E.I., Fut.Surv., Lang.& Lang.Behav.Abstr., Mid.East: Abstr.& Ind., P.A.I.S., P.I.R.A., Phil.Ind., Psychol.Abstr., Rural Recreat.Tour.Abstr., Sage Pub.Admin.Abstr., Sage Urb.Stud.Abstr., Soc.Work Res.& Abstr., Sociol.Abstr., SSCI, World Agri.Econ.& Rural Sociol.Abstr., World Bibl.Soc.Sec.
—BLDSC shelfmark: 8318.116000.

301   UK   ISSN 0954-206X
SOCIAL INVENTIONS. 1985. 3/yr. £15($40) Institute for Social Inventions, 20 Heber Rd., London NW2 6AA, England. TEL 081-208-2853. FAX 081-452-6434. Ed. Nicholas Albery. bk.rev.; circ. 650. (back issues avail.)
—BLDSC shelfmark: 8318.116900.
    Description: Covers non-technical social innovations for improving the quality of life; tackles social problems.

301   SI
SOCIAL ISSUES IN SOUTHEAST ASIA. (Text in English) 1985. irreg. price varies. Institute of Southeast Asian Studies, Heng Mui Keng Terrace, Pasir Panjang Rd., Singapore 0511, Singapore. TEL 778-0955. FAX 778-1735. TELEX RS 37068 ISEAS.
    Description: Publishes studies on the nature and dynamics of ethnicity, religions, urbanism, and population change in Southeast Asia.

301   US   ISSN 0885-7466
JC578   CODEN: SJREEO
SOCIAL JUSTICE RESEARCH. 1986. q. $125 (foreign $145)(effective 1992). Plenum Publishing Corp., 233 Spring St., New York, NY 10013-1578. TEL 212-620-8000. FAX 212-463-0742. TELEX 23-421139. Ed. Melvin J. Lerner. adv.; bk.rev. (also avail. in microform from JSC; back issues avail.) Indexed: Curr.Cont.
—BLDSC shelfmark: 8318.121500.
    Description: Covers the areas of sociology, anthropology, law, psychology and political science. *Refereed Serial*

SOCIAL JUSTICE REVIEW; pioneer American journal of Catholic social action. see *SOCIAL SCIENCES: COMPREHENSIVE WORKS*

301   II
SOCIAL LIFE.* (Text in English) 1972. m. Rs.8. 1184 Bahadur Garh Rd., Delhi 6, India. Ed. Attar Chand. adv.; charts; stat.

301   US   ISSN 0275-7524
SOCIAL ORDERS SERIES. irreg. Harwood Academic Publishers, 270 Eighth Ave., New York, NY 10011. TEL 212-206-8900. FAX 212-645-2459. TELEX 236735 GOPUB UR. (Subscr. to: Box 786, Cooper Sta., New York, NY 10276. TEL 800-545-8398; UK subscr. to: Box 90, Reading, Berkshire RG1 8JL, England. TEL 0734-560-080) Eds. J. Revel, M. Auge. (also avail. in microform)
—BLDSC shelfmark: 8318.127000.
    Refereed Serial

301.2   KE
SOCIAL PERSPECTIVES. irreg. Central Bureau of Statistics, Social Statistics Section, Ministry of Planning and National Development, Box 30266, Nairobi, Kenya. (Orders to: Central Bureau of Statistics, Box 30266, Nairobi, Kenya) charts; stat.

301   US   ISSN 0037-7783
HN51
SOCIAL POLICY. 1970. 4/yr. $20 to individuals; institutions $35. (Social Policy Corporation) Union Institute, 25 W. 43rd St., New York, NY 10036. TEL 212-642-2929. FAX 212-719-2488. Eds. Frank Riessman, Alan Gartner. adv.; bk.rev.; film rev.; illus.; circ. 4,000. (also avail. in microform from UMI,JAI; reprint service avail. from UMI) Indexed: A.B.C.Pol.Sci., Acad.Ind., Alt.Press Ind., ASCA, ASSIA, C.I.J.E., Curr.Cont., Film Lit.Ind. (1990-), Fut.Surv., Hist.Abstr. (until 1991), Lang.& Lang.Behav.Abstr., Left Ind. (1982-), Med.Care Rev., MEDSOC, Mid.East: Abstr.& Ind., Pers.Lit., Sage Pub.Admin.Abstr., Soc.Sci.Ind., Soc.Work Res.& Abstr., SSCI.
—BLDSC shelfmark: 8318.130100.
    Description: Contemporary social thought on policy issues and action.

350 658   UK   ISSN 0144-5596
H1
SOCIAL POLICY AND ADMINISTRATION. 1967. 4/yr. £30($65) to individuals; institutions £72.50($151). Basil Blackwell Ltd., 108 Cowley Rd., Oxford OX4 1JF, England. TEL 0865-791100. FAX 0865-791347. TELEX 837022-OXBOOK-G. Ed. R.A.B. Leaper. adv.; bk.rev.; bibl.; charts; illus.; stat.; index; circ. 900. (reprint service avail. from SWZ) Indexed: Abstr.Hyg., Adol.Ment.Hlth.Abstr., ASCA, ASSIA, Curr.Cont., Lang.& Lang.Behav.Abstr., Med. Care Rev., Res.High.Educ.Abstr., Rural Recreat.Tour.Abstr., SSCI, Stud.Wom.Abstr., World Agri.Econ.& Rural Sociol.Abstr., World Bank.Abstr., World Bibl.Soc.Sec.
—BLDSC shelfmark: 8318.130400.
    Formerly: Social and Economic Administration (ISSN 0037-7643)

301   US   ISSN 0037-7791
HN1   CODEN: SOPRAG
SOCIAL PROBLEMS. 1953. q. $69 (foreign $75). (Society for the Study of Social Problems, Inc.) University of California Press, Journals Division, 2120 Berkeley Way, Berkeley, CA 94720. TEL 510-642-4191. FAX 510-643-7127. Ed. Joseph W. Schneider. adv.; bk.rev.; bibl.; charts; index, cum.index: vols.1-17, 1952-1970; vols.18-28, 1970-1981; circ. 3,900. (also avail. in microform from MIM,UMI; back issues avail.; reprints avail. from UMI) Indexed: Abstr.Soc.Work, Acad.Ind., Amer.Hist.& Life, ASCA, ASSIA, C.I.J.E., Commun.Abstr., Crim.Just.Abstr., Curr.Cont., Excerp.Med., Fut.Surv., Hist.Abstr., Mid.East: Abstr.& Ind., P.A.I.S., Psychol.Abstr., Res.High.Educ.Abstr., Soc.Sci.Ind., Soc.Work Res.& Abstr., Sociol.Abstr. (1953-), SSCI, Stud.Wom.Abstr.
—BLDSC shelfmark: 8318.136000.
    Description: Provides a major forum for critical theoretical discussion and dialogue regarding controversial social issues and programs. *Refereed Serial*

SOCIAL PSYCHOLOGICAL APPLICATIONS TO SOCIAL ISSUES. see *PSYCHOLOGY*

SOCIOLOGY

301.1 US ISSN 0190-2725
HM1
SOCIAL PSYCHOLOGY QUARTERLY. 1937. q. $34 to individuals (foreign $40); institutions $63 (foreign $69); effective 1992. American Sociological Association, 1722 N St., N.W., Washington, DC 20036. TEL 202-833-3410. FAX 202-785-0146. Ed. Karen S. Cook. adv.; bibl.; index; circ. 5,000. (also avail. in microform from MIM,UMI; reprint service avail. from UMI) **Indexed:** Adol.Ment.Hlth.Abstr., ASCA, ASSIA, Crim.Just.Abstr., Curr.Cont., Educ.Admin.Abstr., Lang.& Lang.Behav.Abstr., M.L.A., Mid.East: Abstr.& Ind., Psychol.Abstr., Soc.Sci.Ind., Sociol.Abstr. (1953-), SSCI, Stud.Wom.Abstr.
—BLDSC shelfmark: 8318.146300.
Former titles (until 1978): Social Psychology (ISSN 0147-829X); (until 1977): Sociometry (ISSN 0038-0431)
Description: Publishes papers pertaining to the processes and products of social interaction. Includes the study of the primary relations of individuals to one another or to groups, collectives, or institutions, and also the study of intra-individual processes insofar as they substantially influence, or are influenced by, social forces.

SOCIAL QUESTIONS BULLETIN. see *RELIGIONS AND THEOLOGY — Protestant*

SOCIAL SCIENCE & MEDICINE. see *MEDICAL SCIENCES*

SOCIAL SCIENCE INFORMATION. see *SOCIAL SCIENCES: COMPREHENSIVE WORKS*

301.15 SZ
SOCIAL STRATEGIES; monographs on sociology and social policy-monographien zur Soziologie und Gesellschaftspolitik. (Text in English, French and German) 1975. irreg., no.17, 1985. price varies. Social Strategies Publishers Co-Operative Society, Petersgraben 27, CH-4051 Basel, Switzerland. TEL 061-258881. Ed. Paul Trappe. adv.; bk.rev.; circ. 2,000.

301 IE
SOCIAL STUDIES; Irish journal of sociology. 1947. q. £2.50($8) Christus Rex Society, c/o Department of Sociology, St. Patrick's College, Maynooth, County Kildare, Ireland. Ed. Liam Ryan. adv.; bk.rev.; charts; illus.; stat.; index; circ. 2,450. **Indexed:** Acad.Ind., Cath.Ind., CERDIC, Educ.Ind., P.A.I.S., SSCI.
Formerly: Christus Rex (ISSN 0009-5877)

SOCIAL STUDIES OF SCIENCE; an international review of research in the social dimensions of science and technology. see *SCIENCES: COMPREHENSIVE WORKS*

301 US ISSN 0164-2472
HN1
SOCIAL TEXT;* theory, culture, ideology. 1979. 4/yr. $8. Coda Press, Inc., Box 1474, Old Chelsea Sta., New York, NY 10011. **Indexed:** Alt.Press Ind., Lang.& Lang.Behav.Abstr., Left Ind. (1984-).
—BLDSC shelfmark: 8318.217700.

300 US ISSN 0037-802X
H1
SOCIAL THEORY AND PRACTICE; an international and interdisciplinary journal of social philosophy. 1970. 3/yr. $12 to individuals; libraries $33. Florida State University, Department of Philosophy, 919 W. College Ave., No. 5, Tallahassee, FL 32306-1054. TEL 904-644-0224. FAX 904-644-3832. Ed. Peter Dalton. adv.; bk.rev.; circ. 600. (also avail. in microfilm from UMI; reprint service avail. from UMI) **Indexed:** A.B.C.Pol.Sci., Abstr.Crim.& Pen., ASSIA, Hist.Abstr., Lang.& Lang.Behav.Abstr., Mid.East: Abstr.& Ind., Phil.Ind., Soc.Sci.Ind., Sociol.Abstr., SSCI.
—BLDSC shelfmark: 8318.217800.

301.2 DK
SOCIAL TIDSSKRIFT. 1925. m. Sankt Peters Straede 45, Copenhagen, Denmark. Ed. F. Nielsen.

SOCIALNI POLITIKA. see *POLITICAL SCIENCE*

301 UY ISSN 0081-0649
SOCIEDAD URUGUAYA.* irreg. Editorial Arca, Colonia 1263, Montevideo, Uruguay.

309 360 BL ISSN 0102-6992
HN281 CODEN: SOESE2
SOCIEDADE E ESTADO. 1986. s-a. Editora Universidade de Brasilia, Caixa Postal 04551, 70919 Brasilia D.F., Brazil. TELEX 611083 UNBS BR.

301.34 914.603 PO
SOCIEDADE E TERRITORIO. 1984. irreg., no.14, 1991. price varies. Edicoes Afrontamento, Lda., Rua de Costa Cabral, 859, Apdo. 2009, 4201 Porto, Portugal. TEL 489271. FAX 491777. Ed. Antonio Fonseca Ferreira.

301 IT
LE SOCIETA.* m. L.140000 (foreign L.280000). I P S O A S.p.A., Viale Milano Fiori, Strada 1, 20090 Assago (Milan), Italy. TEL 02-824761. Ed. Francesco Zuzic.

301 IT
▼**SOCIETA E AMBIENTE.** 1991. irreg. price varies. Liguori Editrice s.r.l., Via Mezzocannone 19, 80134 Naples, Italy. TEL 081-5527139. Ed. Franco Martinelli.

301 320.531 FR
SOCIETE FRANCAISE. 1981. 4/yr. 250 F. (foreign 500 F.). Institut des Recherches Marxistes, 64 bd. Auguste Blanqui, 75013 Paris, France. Ed. Alain Bertho. adv.; bk.rev.; cum.index; circ. 2,500.

301 CN ISSN 0537-6211
SOCIETE SAINT-JEAN-BAPTISTE DE MONTREAL. INFORMATION NATIONALE. 1962. m. Can.$5. Societe de Publication l'Information Nationale Inc., 82 rue Sherbrooke, W., Montreal, Que. H2x 1X3, Canada. TEL 514-843-8851. Ed. Pierre Lussier. adv.; bk.rev.; illus.; circ. 15,000.
Formerly: Societe Saint-Jean-Baptiste de Montreal Bulletin.

301 FR ISSN 0765-3697
SOCIETES; revue des sciences humaines et sociales. 1984. 4/yr. 520 F. Dunod, 15 rue Gossin, 92543 Montrouge Cedex, France. TEL 33-1-40-92-65-00. FAX 33-1-40-92-65-97. TELEX 270 004. (Subscr. to: Centrale des Revues, 11 rue Gossin, 92543 Montrouge Cedex, France. TEL 33-1-46-56-52-66) Ed. M. Maffesoli.
—BLDSC shelfmark: 8319.181500.
Description: Brings all the necessary information about research, about the different activities published in sociology, and the ways of integrating specialized knowledge in a large reflection.

301 572 CN ISSN 0381-1794
SOCIETY/SOCIETE. (Text in English, French) 1977. 3/yr. membership (Can.$10 to institutions). Canadian Sociology and Anthropology Association, Concordia University, 1455 bd. de Maisonneuve W., Montreal, Que. H3G 1M8, Canada. TEL 514-848-8780. FAX 514-848-3494. Ed. Arlene McLaren. circ. 1,300. (reprint service avail. from UMI) **Indexed:** Amer.Bibl.Slavic & E.Eur.Stud, Sociol.Abstr. (1978-).
Description: Internal publication of offical documents of the Society.

SOCIETY FOR THE SCIENTIFIC STUDY OF RELIGION. MONOGRAPH SERIES. see *RELIGIONS AND THEOLOGY*

SOCIETY NEWSLETTER. see *PSYCHOLOGY*

SOCIO-ECONOMIC PLANNING SCIENCES; an international journal of public sector decision-making. see *PUBLIC ADMINISTRATION*

SOCIO-ECONOMIC REVIEW OF PUNJAB. see *BUSINESS AND ECONOMICS — Economic Situation And Conditions*

SOCIOCRITICISM: LITERATURE, SOCIETY, AND HISTORY. see *LITERATURE*

301 NE ISSN 0165-1676
SOCIODROME; platform voor sociale wetenschappers. 5/yr. fl.57.50. Uitgeverij Boom, P.O. Box 1058, 7940 KB Meppel, Netherlands. TEL 05220-66111. FAX 05220-66198. Ed.Bd. circ. 1,700.

309 US
SOCIOECONOMIC NEWSLETTER. 1976. 6/yr. free. Institute for Socioeconomic Studies, Airport Rd., White Plains, NY 10604. TEL 914-428-7400. Ed. B.A. Rittersporn, Jr. charts; illus.; circ. 17,500 (controlled). (also avail. in microfiche from WSH) **Indexed:** Lang.& Lang.Behav.Abstr.

301 CS ISSN 0049-1225
SOCIOLOGIA/SOCIOLOGY. (Text in Slovak; summaries in English and Russian) 1969. bi-m. 84 Kcs.($22) (Slovenska Akademia Vied, Ustav Filozofie a Sociologie) Veda, Publishing House of the Slovak Academy of Sciences, Klemensova 19, 814 30 Bratislava, Czechoslovakia. (Dist. in Western countries by: John Benjamins B.V., Amsteldijk 44, Amsterdam (Z.), Netherlands) Ed. V. Bauch.
—BLDSC shelfmark: 8319.593000.
Description: Publishes original contributions from the theory, history and methodology of sociology and scientific communism, methods and techniques of sociologic research, critics of non-Marxist theories, problems of social development from capitalism to communism.

301 IT
SOCIOLOGIA (NAPLES). no.4, 1975. irreg. Societa Editrice Napoletana s.r.l., Corso Umberto I 34, 80138 Naples, Italy. Ed. Aurelio Paolinelli. **Indexed:** Lang.& Lang.Behav.Abstr., Sociol.Abstr. (1957-).

301 IT ISSN 0038-0156
SOCIOLOGIA (ROME); rivista di scienze sociali. 1967. 3/yr. L.50000. Istituto Luigi Sturzo, Via delle Coppelle 35, 00186 Rome, Italy. FAX 6564704. Ed. Gabriele DeRosa. adv.; bibl.
—BLDSC shelfmark: 8319.598000.

301 IT
SOCIOLOGIA DEI MEDIA. 1988. irreg., no.3, 1990. price varies. Liguori Editore s.r.l., Via Mezzocannone, 19, 80134 Naples, Italy. TEL 081-5227139. Eds. Giovanni Bechelloni, Milly Buonanno.

301.2 IT
SOCIOLOGIA DEI PROGRESSI CULTURALI. 1989. irreg., no.2, 1990. price varies. Liguori Editore s.r.l., Via Mezzocannone, 19, 80134 Naples, Italy. TEL 081-206077. Ed. Giovanni Bechelloni.

301 IT
SOCIOLOGIA E RICERCA SOCIALE. 1980. 3/yr. L.65000 (foreign L.80000)(effective 1992). Franco Angeli Editore, Viale Monza, 106, Casella Postale 17175, 20100 Milan, Italy. TEL 02-2895762. Ed. G. Statera. **Indexed:** Sociol.Abstr. (1981-).

301.15 II
SOCIOLOGIA INDICA. (Text in English) 1977. s-a? (Indian Institute of Sociology) Pearl Publishers, 206, Bidhan Sarani, Calcutta 6, India. Ed. Swapn Kumar Bhattacharyya. adv.; bk.rev.

SOCIOLOGIA RURALIS. see *AGRICULTURE*

301 IT
SOCIOLOGIA URBANA E RURALE. 1979. 3/yr. L.68000 (foreign L.80000)(effective 1992). Franco Angeli Editore, Viale Monza 106, 20127 Milan, Italy. TEL 02-28-27-651. Ed. Paolo Guidicini.

301 II ISSN 0038-0229
HN681
SOCIOLOGICAL BULLETIN. (Text in English) 1951. s-a. Rs.30($9) Indian Sociological Society, Centre for the Study of Social Systems, Jawaharlal Nehru University, New Delhi 110057, India. Ed.Bd. adv.; bk.rev.; bibl.; stat.; index, cum.index; circ. 1,500. (also avail. in microform) **Indexed:** ASSIA, Hist.Abstr., Lang.& Lang.Behav.Abstr., Sociol.Abstr. (1953-), SSCI.

301 US ISSN 0038-0237
HM1
SOCIOLOGICAL FOCUS. 1967. q. membership. North Central Sociological Association, c/o Dept. of Sociology, Western Michigan University, Kalamazoo, MI 49008. TEL 616-387-3607. Ed. Stanley Robbin. adv.; bk.rev.; bibl.; charts; index; circ. 900. (also avail. in microform from UMI; microfilm from WSH; reprint service avail. from UMI,WSH) **Indexed:** ASCA, ASSIA, C.L.I., Curr.Cont., Lang.& Lang.Behav.Abstr., Leg.Per., Mid.East: Abstr.& Ind., Sociol.Abstr. (1967-), Sp.Ed.Needs Abstr., SSCI, Stud.Wom.Abstr.
—BLDSC shelfmark: 8319.624500.

SOCIOLOGY

301 US ISSN 0884-8971
HM1
SOCIOLOGICAL FORUM. 1986. q. $110 (foreign $130)(effective 1992). (Eastern Sociological Society) Plenum Publishing Corp., 233 Spring St., New York, NY 10013-1578. TEL 212-620-8000. FAX 212-463-0742. TELEX 23-421139. Ed. Robin M. Williams, Jr. adv. (also avail. in microfilm from JSC) **Indexed:** Psychol.Abstr., Sociol.Abstr.
—BLDSC shelfmark: 8319.624600.
Description: Examines and presents the central interests of sociology in social organization and change as generic phenomena.
Refereed Serial

301 US ISSN 0038-0245
HM1
SOCIOLOGICAL INQUIRY. 1930. q. $18 to individuals; institutions $30. (Alpha Kappa Delta - International Sociology Honor Society) University of Texas Press, Box 7819, Austin, TX 78713. TEL 512-471-4531. Ed. Dennis L. Peck. adv.; bk.rev.; abstr.; index; circ. 2,600. (also avail. in microfilm from UMI; reprint service avail. from UMI) **Indexed:** A.B.C.Pol.Sci., Adol.Ment.Hlth.Abstr., ASCA, ASSIA, Commun.Abstr., Crim.Just.Abstr., Curr.Cont., Educ.Admin.Abstr., Hist.Abstr., Lang.& Lang.Behav.Abstr., Mid.East: Abstr.& Ind., Peace Res.Abstr., Soc.Sci.Ind., Sociol.Abstr. (1959-), Sp.Ed.Needs Abstr., SSCI, Stud.Wom.Abstr.
—BLDSC shelfmark: 8319.625000.
Description: Publishes the work of researchers and theorists in sociology.

301.01 UK ISSN 0081-1750
HM24
SOCIOLOGICAL METHODOLOGY. 1969. a. £34($55) to individuals; institutions £48.50($60). (American Sociological Association, US) Basil Blackwell Ltd., 108 Cowley Rd., Oxford OX4 1JF. TEL 0865-791100. Ed. Clifford C. Clogg. circ. 1,100. (also avail. in microfilm from UMI; back issues avail.; reprint service avail. from UMI) **Indexed:** Lang.& Lang.Behav.Abstr., Sociol.Abstr. (1978-).
—BLDSC shelfmark: 8319.629000.
Description: Contains material of interest to a wide variety of researchers.

301 US ISSN 0049-1241
HM1
SOCIOLOGICAL METHODS & RESEARCH. Abbreviated title: S M R. 1972. q. $48 to individuals; institutions $128. Sage Publications, Inc., 2455 Teller Rd., Newbury Park, CA 91320. TEL 805-499-0721. FAX 805-499-0871. (And Sage Publications, Ltd., 6 Bonhill St., London EC2A 4PU, England) Ed. J. Scott Long. adv.; bk.rev.; charts; illus.; index; circ. 1,300. (also avail. in microfilm from UMI; back issues avail.; reprint service avail. from UMI) **Indexed:** ASCA, ASSIA, Commun.Abstr., Curr.Cont., J.Cont.Quant.Meth., Lang.& Lang.Behav.Abstr., Mid.East: Abstr.& Ind., P.A.I.S., Pers.Lit., Sage Pub.Admin.Abstr., Soc.Work Res.& Abstr., Sociol.Abstr. (1975-), SSCI.
—BLDSC shelfmark: 8319.629500.

301 DK
SOCIOLOGICAL MICROJOURNAL. (Text in English, French and German) 1967. a. DKK 55($8) Erik Manniche and Kaare Svalastoga, Eds. & Pubs., 22 Linnegade, 1361 Copenhagen K, Denmark. (back issues avail.)

301 572 US
SOCIOLOGICAL OBSERVATIONS. 1977. irreg., vol.20, 1988. Sage Publications, Inc., 2455 Teller Rd., Newbury Park, CA 91320. TEL 805-499-0721. FAX 805-499-0871. (And Sage Publications, Ltd., 6 Bonhill St., London EC2A 4PU, England) Ed. John M. Johnson. (back issues avail.)

301 US ISSN 0731-1214
HM1
SOCIOLOGICAL PERSPECTIVES. 1958. q. $45 to individuals; institutions $90. (Pacific Sociological Association) J A I Press Inc., 55 Old Post Rd., Box 1678, Greenwich, CT 06836. Ed. John Pock. adv.; charts; stat.; index, cum.index every 5 yrs. (also avail. in microfilm from UMI; back issues avail.; reprint service avail. from UMI) **Indexed:** A.B.C.Pol.Sci., Abstr.Soc.Work., ASCA, CERDIC, Curr.Cont., Hist.Abstr., Lang.& Lang.Behav.Abstr., Mid.East: Abstr.& Ind., P.A.I.S., Sage Urb.Stud.Abstr., Soc.Work Res.& Abstr., Sociol.Abstr. (1958-), Sociol.Abstr., SSCI, Stud.Wom.Abstr.
—BLDSC shelfmark: 8319.629860.
Formerly (until 1982): Pacific Sociological Review (ISSN 0030-8919)

301 US ISSN 0163-8505
HM1
SOCIOLOGICAL PRACTICE. 1976. a. $18. (Sociological Practice Association) Michigan State University Press, 25 Manly Miles Bldg., 1405 S. Harrison Rd., East Lansing, MI 48823-5202. TEL 517-355-9543. Eds. Jan Fritz, Elizabeth Clark. bk.rev.; stat.; circ. 500. (also avail. in microform from UMI; reprint service avail. from UMI) **Indexed:** Lang.& Lang.Behav.Abstr., Sociol.Abstr. (1976-).
—BLDSC shelfmark: 8319.629900.
Formerly (1976-1977): S P: Sociological Practice (ISSN 0360-845X)

301 US ISSN 1050-6306
HM1 CODEN: SPRRE3
▼**SOCIOLOGICAL PRACTICE REVIEW.** 1990. s-a. $34 to individuals (foreign $40); institutions $63 (foreign $69); effective 1992. American Sociological Association, 1722 N St., N.W., Washington, DC 20036. TEL 202-833-3410. FAX 202-785-0146.
—BLDSC shelfmark: 8319.629950.
Description: Publishes research by and about sociologists in practice settings, including articles, case materials, and news, notes, and announcements.

301 US ISSN 0038-0253
HM1 CODEN: SOLQAR
SOCIOLOGICAL QUARTERLY. 1960. q. $35 to individuals; institutions $70. Midwest Sociological Society, Department of Sociology, Southern Illinois University, Carbondale, IL 62901. TEL 618-453-2494. Ed. Thomas G. Eynon. adv.; bk.rev.; charts; illus.; index, cum.index: 1953-1973, 1974-1983; circ. 2,550. (also avail. in microform from AMS,UMI; microfilm from WSH; back issues avail.; reprint service avail. from UMI,WSH) **Indexed:** A.B.C.Pol.Sci., Abstr.Soc.Work, Adol.Ment.Hlth.Abstr., Amer.Bibl.Slavic & E.Eur.Stud, Amer.Hist.& Life, ASCA, ASSIA, CERDIC, Commun.Abstr., Cont.Pg.Manage., Crim.Just.Abstr., Curr.Cont., E.I., Hist.Abstr., Lang.& Lang.Behav.Abstr., Mid.East: Abstr.& Ind., PSI, Psychol.Abstr., Soc.Sci.Ind., Soc.Work Res.& Abstr., Sociol.Abstr. (1960-), SSCI, Stud.Wom.Abstr.
—BLDSC shelfmark: 8319.630000.
Formerly: Midwest Sociologist.

301 US
HX542
SOCIOLOGICAL RECORD; a journal of translations from scholarly Soviet sources. 1962. bi-m. $330 to institutions. M.E. Sharpe, Inc., 80 Business Park Dr., Armonk, NY 10504. TEL 914-273-1800. FAX 914-273-2106. Ed. Murray Yanowitch. adv.; index. **Indexed:** Adol.Ment.Hlth.Abstr., Curr.Cont., P.A.I.S., Sage.Fam.Stud.Abstr., SSCI.
Formerly: Soviet Sociology (ISSN 0038-5824)
Refereed Serial

301 UK ISSN 0038-0261
HM1
SOCIOLOGICAL REVIEW. 1908; N.S. 1953. 5/yr. (University of Keele) Basil Blackwell Ltd., 108 Cowley Rd., Oxford OX4 1JF, England. TEL 0865-791100. FAX 0865-791347. TELEX 837022-OXBOOK-G. Ed.Bd. adv.; bk.rev.; bibl.; charts; index, cum.index; circ. 2,000. (also avail. in microform from UMI; reprint service avail. from UMI,KTO) **Indexed:** A.I.C.P., Adol.Ment.Hlth.Abstr., ASCA, ASSIA, Bk.Rev.Ind. (1965-), Br.Hum.Ind., Child.Bk.Rev.Ind. (1965-), Cont.Pg.Manage., Curr.Cont., Geo.Abstr., Hist.Abstr., Lang.& Lang.Behav.Abstr., Mid.East: Abstr.& Ind., Psychol.Abstr., Res.High.Educ.Abstr., Risk Abstr., Soc.Sci.Ind., Sociol.Abstr. (1962-), Sp.Ed.Needs Abstr., SSCI, Stud.Wom.Abstr.
—BLDSC shelfmark: 8319.640000.
Description: Subjects and discussions related to sociology, with topical essays on health and work, job training, equal opportunities and skills, social attitudes to family relationships, and more.

301 US ISSN 0273-2173
HM1
SOCIOLOGICAL SPECTRUM. 1980. q. $105. (Mid-South Sociological Association) Hemisphere Publishing Corporation (Subsidiary of: Taylor & Francis Group), 1900 Frost Rd., Ste. 101, Bristol, PA 19007-1598. TEL 215-785-5800. FAX 215-785-5515. Ed. Donald R. South. adv.; bk.rev.; abstr.; bibl.; illus.; stat.; index; circ. 600. (back issues avail.; reprint service avail. from UMI) **Indexed:** ASCA, Curr.Cont., Lang.& Lang.Behav.Abstr., Mid.East: Abstr.& Ind., Sociol.Abstr. (1981-), SSCI.
—BLDSC shelfmark: 8319.647800.
Formed by the merger of: Sociological Symposium (ISSN 0038-027X) & Sociological Forum (ISSN 0160-3469)
Description: Current thoughts in theoretical and applied psychology, education, social psychology, political science and anthropology.
Refereed Serial

301 UK ISSN 0735-2751
SOCIOLOGICAL THEORY. s-a. £21 to individuals; institutions £27.50. (American Sociological Association, US) Basil Blackwell Ltd., 108 Cowley Rd., Oxford OX4 1JF. TEL 0865-791100. Ed. Alan Sica. circ. 1,900. **Indexed:** Sociol.Abstr. (1983-).
—BLDSC shelfmark: 8319.650150.

301 US ISSN 1060-0876
SOCIOLOGICAL VIEWPOINTS. 1984. a. $5 to individuals; institutions $10. Pennsylvania Sociological Society, c/o M.Y. Rynn, Man. Ed., University of Scranton, Scranton, PA 18510-4605. TEL 717-941-6137. FAX 717-941-6369. Ed. Lawrence Rosen. bk.rev.; bibl. (back issues avail.) **Indexed:** Sociol.Abstr. (1987-).
Description: Publishes articles and critical essays on topics in sociology, including recent empirical research, methodological and theoretical issues, and critiques of social events.
Refereed Serial

301 BU ISSN 0324-1572
SOCIOLOGICESKI PROBLEMI. (Contents page and summaries in English and Russian) 1969. 6/yr. 1.50 lv. per no. (Bulgarska Akademiia na Naukite, Institut po Sotsiologiia) Publishing House of the Bulgarian Academy of Sciences, Acad. G. Bonchev St., Bldg. 6, 1113 Sofia, Bulgaria. (Dist. by: Hemus, 6, Rouski Blvd., 1000 Sofia, Bulgaria) (Co-sponsor: Bulgarska Sotsiologicheska Asotsiatsiia) Ed. Niko Jahiel. bk.rev.; circ. 470.

301 CS ISSN 0038-0288
HM7 CODEN: SLCSB2
SOCIOLOGICKY CASOPIS/SOCIOLOGICAL REVIEW. (Text in Czech; contents page in English, French, German and Russian; summaries in English, Russian) 1965. bi-m. DM.136. (Czechoslovak Academy of Sciences, Institute for Philosophy and Sociology) Academia, Publishing House of the Czechoslovak Academy of Sciences, Vodickova 40, 112 29 Prague 1, Czechoslovakia. TEL 231-91-15. (Dist. in Western countries by: Kubon & Sagner, P.O. Box 34 01 08, 8000 Munich 34, Germany) Ed. Karel Rychtarik. adv.; bk.rev.; abstr.; bibl. **Indexed:** ASCA, Bull.Signal., Lang.& Lang.Behav.Abstr., Psychol.Abstr., Sociol.Abstr. (1965-), SSCI.
Description: Covers studies devoted to general sociology and methodology, and to specialized sociological fields in Czechoslovakia and abroad.

SOCIOLOGIE DU TRAVAIL. see *BUSINESS AND ECONOMICS — Labor And Industrial Relations*

301 CN ISSN 0038-030X
HM3
SOCIOLOGIE ET SOCIETES. (Text in French; summaries in English, French, Spanish) 1969. s-a. Can.$26 to individuals; institutions Can.$45. Presses de l'Universite de Montreal, C.P. 6128, Succ. A, Montreal, Que. H3C 3J7, Canada. TEL 514-343-6933. Ed. Louis Maheu. adv.; bibl.; charts; stat.; circ. 2,500. (also avail. in microform from MIM; reprint service avail. from UMI) **Indexed:** Can.Wom.Per.Ind., Curr.Cont., Int.Lab.Doc., Lang.& Lang.Behav.Abstr., P.A.I.S.For.Lang.Ind., Psychol.Abstr., Pt.de Rep. (1979-), RAPRA, Sociol.Abstr. (1969-), SSCI.
—BLDSC shelfmark: 8319.650800.

301 FR
SOCIOLOGIE PERMANENTE. 1978. irreg. Editions du Seuil, 27 rue Jacob, 75261 Paris Cedex 6, France. Dir. Alain Touraine.

SOCIOLOGY

301   RM
SOCIOLOGIE ROMANEASCA. (Text in Rumanian; summaries in English, French and Russian) 1972. 6/yr. 102 lei. (Academia Romana) Editura Academiei Romane, Calea Victoriei 125, 79717 Bucharest, Rumania. (Dist. by: Rompresfilatelia, Calea Grivitei 64-66, P.O. Box 12-201, 78104 Bucharest, Rumania) Ed. Sorin Radulescu. bk.rev.; bibl. **Indexed:** Lang.& Lang.Behav.Abstr.
    Formerly (until 1990): Viitorul Social.

301 572   YU   ISSN 0038-0318
SOCIOLOGIJA; casopis za sociologiju, socijalnu, psihologiju i socijalnu antropologiju. (Text in Serbo-Croatian) 1959. q. 20000 din. Jugoslovensko Udruzenje za Sociologiju, Studentski trg 1, 11000 Belgrade, Yugoslavia. Ed. Esad Cimic. adv.; bk.rev.; circ. 1,000. **Indexed:** Lang.& Lang.Behav.Abstr., Sociol.Abstr. (1959-).

301   CI   ISSN 0038-0326
HT401
SOCIOLOGIJA SELA. (Text in Croatian; summaries in English and Russian) 1962. q. 500 din.($20) (effective 1992). Sveuciliste u Zagrebu, Institut za Drustvena Istrazivanja - University of Zagrab, Institut for Social Research, P.O. Box 280, Amruseva 8-III, 41000 Zagreb, Croatia. TEL 041 430-675. FAX 41-433-298. (Subscr. to: Mladost, Vanjska trgovina, Ilica 30, 41000 Zagreb, Croatia) Ed. Maja Stambuk. bk.rev.; cum.index; circ. 800. **Indexed:** Geo.Abstr., Lang.& Lang.Behav.Abstr., Rural Recreat.Tour.Abstr., Sociol.Abstr., Sociol.Abstr. (1963-), World Agri.Econ.& Rural Sociol.Abstr.
    Description: Publishes articles, research papers on rural sociology, rural economics, history and demography.

301   NE
SOCIOLOGISCH TIJDSCHRIFT. 1974. q. fl.62 to individuals; institutions fl.90; students fl.45. Wolters-Noordhoff B.V., Damsport 157, 9728 PS Groningen, Netherlands. TEL 050 226922. (Or Box 58, 9700 MB Groningen, Netherlands) **Indexed:** Sociol.Abstr. (1987-).
    Formerly: Amsterdams Sociologisch Tijdschrift.

301   NE   ISSN 0038-0334
SOCIOLOGISCHE GIDS; tijdschrift voor sociologie en sociaal onderzoek. (Text in Dutch, English, French or German; summaries in English) 1953. bi-m. fl.75.50 to individuals (foreign fl.114); institutions fl.134.50 (foreign fl.145)(effective 1992). Uitgeverij Boom, P.O. Box 1058, 7940 KB Meppel, Netherlands. TEL 05220-66111. FAX 05220-66198. adv.; bk.rev.; index; circ. 1,200. **Indexed:** E.I., Excerp.Med., Geo.Abstr., Lang.& Lang.Behav.Abstr., Sociol.Abstr. (1953-).
    —BLDSC shelfmark: 8319.653000.

301   BE
SOCIOLOGISCHE VERKENNINGEN. no.2, 1972. irreg., no.10, 1986. Leuven University Press, Krakenstraat 3, B-3000 Leuven, Belgium. TEL 016-284175. FAX 016-284176.

301   SW   ISSN 0038-0342
SOCIOLOGISK FORSKNING. 1964. q. SEK 150 to individuals; institutions Kr.300. Swedish Sociological Association, Umeaa Universitet, S-901 87 Umea, Sweden. FAX 090-166694. Ed.Bd. adv.; bk.rev.; cum.index: 1964-74; circ. 1,500. **Indexed:** ASCA, Lang.& Lang.Behav.Abstr., Sociol.Abstr. (1976-), SSCI.
    —BLDSC shelfmark: 8319.654000.

301   NR   ISSN 0081-1807
SOCIOLOGIST.* 1968. a. University of Ibadan, Sociological Society, Ibadan, Nigeria.

301   GW   ISSN 0038-0377
HM3
SOCIOLOGUS; Zeitschrift fuer empirische Ethnosoziologie und Ethnopsychologie. (Text in English and German) 1951. s-a. DM.82. Duncker und Humblot GmbH, Postfach 410329, 1000 Berlin 41, Germany. TEL 030-7900060. FAX 030-79000631. Ed. Juergen Jensen. bk.rev.; abstr.; illus.; index. (reprint service avail. from KTO) **Indexed:** A.I.C.P., Cott.&Trop.Fibr.Abstr., E.I., P.A.I.S.For.Lang.Ind., Rural Devel.Abstr., World Agri.Econ.& Rural Sociol.Abstr.
    —BLDSC shelfmark: 8319.660000.

301   UK   ISSN 0038-0385
HM1
SOCIOLOGY. 1967. 4/yr. £20.75 to individuals (foreign £25); insitutions £52 (foreign £57). (British Sociological Association) B S A Publications, Ltd., 351 Station Rd., Dorridge, Solihull, West Midlands B93 8EY, England. Eds. Liz Stanley, David Morgan. adv.; bk.rev.; charts; index; circ. 2,900. (also avail. in microform from UMI; reprint service avail. from UMI) **Indexed:** Abstr.Crim.& Pen., ASSIA, Br.Hum.Ind., Commun.Abstr., Crim.Just.Abstr., Curr.Cont., High.Educ.Curr.Aware.Bull., Hist.Abstr., Lang.& Lang.Behav.Abstr., Mid.East: Abstr.& Ind., Res.High.Educ.Abstr., Rural Recreat.Tour.Abstr., SCIMP (1979-), Soc.Sci.Ind., Sociol.Abstr. (1967-), Sociol.Educ.Abstr., Sp.Ed.Needs Abstr., SSCI, Stud.Wom.Abstr., World Agri.Econ.& Rural Sociol.Abstr.
    —BLDSC shelfmark: 8319.670000.
    Description: Provides debates, progress reports, and news regarding sociology.

301   US   ISSN 0038-0393
                       CODEN: SSORA5
SOCIOLOGY AND SOCIAL RESEARCH; an international journal. 1916. q. $60 to individuals (foreign $70); libraries $40 (foreign $50). University of Southern California, Los Angeles, CA 90089-2539. TEL 213-743-3533. Ed. Marcus Felson. adv.; charts; index; circ. 2,750. (also avail. in microform from UMI; back issues avail.; reprint service avail. from UMI) **Indexed:** Acad.Ind., Adol.Ment.Hlth.Abstr., Amer.Bibl.Slavic & E.Eur.Stud, ASCA, ASSIA, C.I.J.E., Cont.Pg.Manage., Crim.Just.Abstr., Curr.Cont., Curr.Lit.Fam.Plan., E.I., Geo.Abstr., Hist.Abstr., Int.Lab.Doc., Lang.& Lang.Behav.Abstr., Mid.East: Abstr.& Ind., P.A.I.S., Popul.Ind., Psychol.Abstr., Soc.Sci.Ind., Sociol.Abstr. (1952-), SSCI, Stud.Wom.Abstr.
    —BLDSC shelfmark: 8319.675000.

301   AT   ISSN 0156-4943
SOCIOLOGY OCCASIONAL PUBLICATIONS. 1978. irreg. University of New England, Department of Sociology, Armidale, N.S.W. 2351, Australia. TEL 067 73-2300. FAX 067-73-3122. (back issues avail.)

301 370   US   ISSN 0038-0407
L11   CODEN: SCYEB7
SOCIOLOGY OF EDUCATION; a journal of research in socialization and social structure. 1927. q. $34 to individuals (foreign $40); institutions $63 (foreign $69); effective 1992. American Sociological Association, 1722 N St., N.W., Washington, DC 20036. TEL 202-833-3410. FAX 202-785-0146. Ed. Julia Wrigley. adv.; charts; index; circ. 5,000. (also avail. in microform from UMI,MIM; reprint service avail. from UMI,KTO) **Indexed:** Adol.Ment.Hlth.Abstr., ASCA, ASSIA, C.I.J.E., Cont.Pg.Educ., Curr.Cont., Educ.Admin.Abstr., Educ.Ind., Educ.Tech.Abstr., High.Educ.Curr.Aware.Bull., Lang.& Lang.Behav.Abstr., Mid.East: Abstr.& Ind., P.A.I.S., Psychol.Abstr., Soc.Sci.Ind., Sociol.Abstr. (1952-), SSCI, SSCI, Stud.Wom.Abstr.
    —BLDSC shelfmark: 8319.678000.
    Formerly: Journal of Educational Sociology.
    Description: Publishes papers on educational processes and on human development. The research may focus on the individual, institutions, and structural arrangements among institutions bearing on education and human development.

301 616.8   UK   ISSN 0141-9889
RA418
SOCIOLOGY OF HEALTH AND ILLNESS. 1979. q. £34($72.50) to individuals; institutions £64.50($149). Basil Blackwell Ltd., 108 Cowley Rd., Oxford OX4 1JF, England. TEL 0865-791100. FAX 0865-791347. TELEX 837022-OXBOOK-G. Ed. Mildred Blaxter. adv.; bk.rev.; index; circ. 950. (also avail. in microform) **Indexed:** Abstr.Health Care Manage.Stud., Abstr.Hyg., ASCA, ASSIA, Excerp.Med., I.P.A., Lang.& Lang.Behav.Abstr., Med.Care Rev., Mid.East: Abstr.& Ind., Psychol.Abstr., Sociol.Abstr. (1979-), SSCI, Stud.Wom.Abstr.
    ●Also available online.
    —BLDSC shelfmark: 8319.692000.

301   US
SOCIOLOGY OF MUSIC SERIES. 1983. irreg., no.7, 1989. Pendragon Press, Rt. 1, Box 159, Stuyvesant, NY 12173-9720. TEL 518-828-3008. FAX 518-828-2368.

790   US   ISSN 0741-1235
SOCIOLOGY OF SPORT JOURNAL. Short title: S S J. 1984. q. $36 to individuals (foreign $40); institutions $80 (foreign $84); students $24 (foreign $28). (North American Society for the Sociology of Sport) Human Kinetics Publishers, Inc., Box 5076, Champaign, IL 61825-5076. TEL 217-351-5076. FAX 217-351-2674. Ed. Peter Donnelly. adv.; bk.rev.; bibl.; charts; stat.; index; circ. 850. (back issues avail.) **Indexed:** Curr.Cont., Lang.& Lang.Behav.Abstr., Phys.Ed.Ind., Sociol.Abstr. (1984-), Sportsearch (1984-), SSCI.
    —BLDSC shelfmark: 8319.696830.
    Description: Focuses on the relationship between sport, society, and social institutions from the perspectives of social psychology, sociology and anthropology. Designed to communicate research, critical thought, and theory development.
    Refereed Serial

SOCIOLOGY OF THE SCIENCES. YEARBOOK. see *SCIENCES: COMPREHENSIVE WORKS*

301 500   NE
SOCIOLOGY OF THE SCIENCES MONOGRAPHS. 1982. irreg. price varies. Kluwer Academic Publishers, Spuiboulevard 50, P.O. Box 17, 3300 AA Dordrecht, Netherlands. TEL 078-334911. FAX 078-334254. TELEX 29245. (Dist. by: Kluwer Academic Publishers Group, P.O. Box 322, 3300 AH Dordrecht, Netherlands; U.S. addr.: P.O. Box 358, Accord Sta., Hingham, MA 02018-0358)

301   AT
SOCIOLOGY RESEARCH MONOGRAPHS. 1978. irreg. University of New England, Department of Sociology, Armidale, N.S.W. 2351, Australia. TEL 067 73-2300. FAX 067-73-3122. (back issues avail.)

301   UK   ISSN 0959-8499
▼**SOCIOLOGY REVIEW.** 1991. q. £15.50 (foreign £24.50). Philip Allan Publishers Ltd., Deddington, Oxfordshire OX15 OSE, England. TEL 0869-38652. FAX 0869-38803.

301 572   SI
SOCIOLOGY WORKING PAPERS. (Text in English) 1972. irreg. price varies. (University of Singapore, Department of Sociology) Chopmen Publishers, Katong Shopping Centre, Mountbatten Rd., No. 05-28, Singapore 1543, Singapore. TEL 3441495. FAX 3440180. Ed. Peter S.J. Chen. circ. 500.

301   SI   ISSN 0217-9520
HN690.8
SOJOURN; social issues in Southeast Asia. (Text in English) 1986. s-a. S.$22($14) to individuals; institutions S.$29($20). Institute of Southeast Asian Studies, Heng Mui Keng Terrace, Off Pasir Panjang Rd., Singapore 0511, Singapore. TEL 7780955. FAX 7781735. TELEX RS 37068 ISEAS. Ed.Bd. adv.; bk.rev.; abstr.; bibl.; index. (back issues avail.) **Indexed:** Rural Devel.Abstr., World Agri.Econ.& Rural Sociol.Abstr.
    —BLDSC shelfmark: 8327.118750.
    Description: Deals with issues of ethnicity, religion, urbanism, and population change. Includes articles, research notes, and occasional English translations of pivotal research first published in Southeast Asian languages.

301   RU
SOTSIOLOGIYA KUL'TURY. 1974. a. 1.40 Rub. (Nauchno-Issledovatel'skii Institut Kul'tury, Otdel Sotsiologicheskikh Issledovanii) Izdatel'stvo Sovetskaya Rossiya, Proezd Sapunova 13/15, Moscow K-12, Russia.
    Formerly: Nauchno-Issledovatel'skii Institut Kul'tury. Trudy.

SOURCE (SEATTLE). see *RELIGIONS AND THEOLOGY*

301   SA   ISSN 0258-0144
HM1
SOUTH AFRICAN JOURNAL OF SOCIOLOGY. (Text in Afrikaans, English) 1970. q. R.48($35) Bureau for Scientific Publications, P.O. Box 1758, Pretoria 0001, South Africa. TEL 012-322-6422. Ed. Anna F. Steyn. bk.rev.; circ. 500. **Indexed:** Anim.Breed.Abstr., Ind.S.A.Per., Lang.& Lang.Behav.Abstr., Sociol.Abstr. (1970-), Sp.Ed.Needs Abstr., Stud.Wom.Abstr.
    —BLDSC shelfmark: 8340.200000.

SOUTH AFRICAN OUTLOOK; a journal dealing with ecumenical and racial affairs. see *RELIGIONS AND THEOLOGY*

301　　　　　　SA　　ISSN 1015-1370
SOUTH AFRICAN SOCIOLOGICAL REVIEW. 1973. s-a. $12. Association for Sociology in South Africa, Dept. of Sociology, University of Cape Town, Rondebosch 7700, South Africa. FAX 021-650-3726. Ed. Wilmot James. bk.rev.; circ. 400. (also avail. in microfiche)
　Formerly (until 1988): A S S A Proceedings.

SOUTH ASIA BULLETIN. see *HISTORY — History Of Asia*

SOUTH ASIA: JOURNAL OF SOUTH ASIAN STUDIES. see *HISTORY — History Of Asia*

SOUTHEAST ASIAN JOURNAL OF SOCIAL SCIENCES. see *SOCIAL SCIENCES: COMPREHENSIVE WORKS*

301　　　　　　US　　ISSN 0038-4577
HM1
SOUTHERN SOCIOLOGIST. 1968. 3/yr. $15 to non-members. Southern Sociological Society, Department of Sociology and Anthropology, Mississippi State University, MS 39762. TEL 601-325-8602. Eds. George S. Rent, James D. Jones. adv.; circ. 2,000. (also avail. in microform from UMI; reprint service avail. from UMI) **Indexed:** Lang.& Lang.Behav.Abstr., Sociol.Abstr.

SOVIET SOCIETY; international review of Soviet studies. see *POLITICAL SCIENCE — International Relations*

SOVIET STUDIES. see *BUSINESS AND ECONOMICS*

301 320.532　　US　　ISSN 1046-1809
SOVIET STUDIES. irreg. Harwood Academic Publishers, 270 Eighth Ave., New York, NY 10011. TEL 212-206-8900. FAX 212-645-2459. TELEX 236735 GOPUB UR. (Subscr. to: Box 786, Cooper Sta., New York, NY 10276. TEL 800-545-8398; UK subscr. to: Box 90, Reading, Berkshire RG1 8JL, England. TEL 0734-560-080) (also avail. in microform)
　—BLDSC shelfmark: 8359.919800.
　Refereed Serial

301　　　　　　GW　　ISSN 0038-6073
H5
SOZIALE WELT; Zeitschrift fuer sozialwissenschaftliche Forschung und Praxis. 1949. q. DM.80. (Arbeitsgemeinschaft Sozialwissenschaftlicher Institute e.V.) Verlag Otto Schwartz und Co., Annastr. 7, 3400 Goettingen, Germany. TEL 0551-31051. FAX 0551-372812. Ed. Ulrich Beck. adv.; bk.rev.; charts; index; circ. 1,500. **Indexed:** Lang.& Lang.Behav.Abstr., P.A.I.S.For.Lang.Ind., Phil.Ind., Sociol.Abstr. (1953-), World Bibl.Soc.Sec.
　—BLDSC shelfmark: 8361.070000.

301 360　　　　　GW　　ISSN 0724-3464
SOZIALWISSENSCHAFTEN UND BERUFSPRAXIS. 1978. q. DM.36($15) Berufsverband Deutscher Soziologen e.V., Postfach 1040, D-4800 Bielefeld 1, Germany. Ed.Bd. adv.; bk.rev.; circ. 400. (back issues avail.)

301　　　　　　GW　　ISSN 0340-918X
HM5
SOZIOLOGIE. s-a. DM.48. (Deutsche Gesellschaft fuer Soziologie) Ferdinand Enke Verlag, Postfach 101254, 7000 Stuttgart 10, Germany. TEL 0711-8931-0. FAX 0711-8931-419. TELEX 07252275-GTV-D. Ed. B. Schaefers. **Indexed:** Lang.& Lang.Behav.Abstr., Sociol.Abstr. (1975-).
　—BLDSC shelfmark: 8361.216200.

301　　　　　　GW　　ISSN 0081-3265
SOZIOLOGISCHE GEGENWARTSFRAGEN. NEUE FOLGE. 1957. irreg., no.51, 1991. price varies. Ferdinand Enke Verlag, Postfach 101254, 7000 Stuttgart 10, Germany. TEL 0711-8931-0. FAX 0711-8931-419. TELEX 07252275-GTV-D. Ed.Bd.

300　　　　　　GW　　ISSN 0343-4109
SOZIOLOGISCHE REVUE; Besprechungen neuer Literatur. 1978. q. DM.126. R. Oldenbourg Verlag GmbH, Rosenheimstr. 145, 8000 Munich 80, Germany. Ed.Bd. adv.; bk.rev.; index; circ. 1,500. (back issues avail.) **Indexed:** Lang.& Lang.Behav.Abstr., Sociol.Abstr. (1984-).
　—BLDSC shelfmark: 8361.217500.
　Description: Contains critical reviews of newly published books in all fields of sociology, and the sociological aspects of law, politics, medicine, and religion.

301 333.7　　　　AT
SPEAK. 1969. a. Aus.$0.10. c/o Audrey Windram, Ed., Conrad St., Longwood, S.A. 5153, Australia.

301　　　　　　UK　　ISSN 0955-0690
STAFFORDSHIRE POLYTECHNIC. DEPARTMENT OF SOCIOLOGY. OCCASIONAL PAPERS. 1984. irreg. free. Staffordshire Polytechnic, Department of Sociology, Leek Road, Stoke-On-Trent, Staffs ST4 2DF, England. TEL 0782-412515. FAX 0782-744035. Ed. Alan Sillitoe. (back issues avail.)
　—BLDSC shelfmark: 6221.335000.
　Formerly: North Staffordshire Polytechnic. Department of Sociology. Occasional Papers.

STATE, GOVERNMENT AND INTERNATIONAL RELATIONS. see *POLITICAL SCIENCE — International Relations*

STATION RELAY; facts and views on daily life in the Soviet Union. see *ANTHROPOLOGY*

STATO E MERCATO. see *POLITICAL SCIENCE*

301　　　　　　US
HQ759.92
STEPFAMILIES. 1980. q. $14 to individuals; institutions $22. Stepfamily Association of America, 215 Centennial Mall S., Ste. 212, Lincoln, NE 68508. TEL 402-477-7837. FAX 503-325-1454. Eds. Jan & Charlie Fletcher. adv.; bk.rev.; cum.index 1980-1987; circ. 1,500. (also avail. in microform from UMI; back issues avail.; reprint service avail. from UMI)
　Formerly (until 1989): Stepfamily Bulletin (ISSN 0195-5969)
　Description: Covers issues and concerns of stepparenting.

301　　　　　　US　　ISSN 0884-870X
STRESS IN MODERN SOCIETY. 1984. irreg., no.19, 1989. $32.50. A M S Press, Inc., 56 E. 13th St., New York, NY 10003. TEL 212-777-4700. FAX 212-995-5413. index. (back issues avail.)
　—BLDSC shelfmark: 8474.129700.
　Description: Monographs covering a broad range of topics from specific causes of stress to intervention methods.

301　　　　　　IT　　ISSN 0039-291X
HM7
STUDI DI SOCIOLOGIA. (Text in English, French and Italian) 1963. q. L.93000($71) (effective 1992). (Universita Cattolica del Sacro Cuore, Istituto di Sociologia) Vita e Pensiero, Largo Gemelli 1, 20123 Milan, Italy. TEL 02-8856310. FAX 02-8856260. TELEX 321033 UCATMI 1. Ed. Vincenzo Cesareo. adv.; bk.rev.; bibl.; charts; index. **Indexed:** Lang.& Lang.Behav.Abstr., Sociol.Abstr. (1963-).
　Description: Covers current issues in sociology.

STUDI EMIGRAZIONE/ETUDES MIGRATIONS. see *POPULATION STUDIES*

301 309　　　　　IT
STUDI SULLA MODERNIZZAZIONE E LO SVILUPPO. 1985. irreg., no.7, 1991. price varies. (Centro Gino Germani) Liguori Editore s.r.l., Via Mezzocannone, 19, 80134 Naples, Italy. TEL 081-5227139.

STUDIA ANTHROPONYMICA SCANDINAVICA; tidskrift foer nordisk personnamnsforskning. see *LINGUISTICS*

301　　　　　　PL　　ISSN 0039-3371
　　　　　　　　　　　　CODEN: STSOCP
STUDIA SOCJOLOGICZNE. q. $68. (Polska Akademia Nauk, Instytut Filozofii i Socjologii) Ossolineum, Publishing House of the Polish Academy of Sciences, Rynek 9, Wroclaw, Poland. TELEX 0712771 OSS PL. (Dist. by: Ars Polona-Ruch, Krakowskie Przedmiescie 7, Warsaw, Poland) (Co-sponsor: Komitet Nauk Socjologicznych) Ed. Wladyslaw Markiewicz. bk.rev.; bibl.; charts; index. **Indexed:** Lang.& Lang.Behav.Abstr., Psychol.Abstr.( ), Sociol.Abstr. (1961-).
　Description: Treatises on theoretical and methodological aspects of sociology.

301 320　　　　　RM
▼**STUDIA UNIVERSITATIS "BABES-BOLYAI". SOCIOLOGIA - POLITOLOGIA.** (Text in English, French, German, Rumanian) 1990. s-a. exchange basis. Universitatea "Babes-Bolyai", Biblioteca Centrala Universitara, Str. Clinicilor Nr. 2, Cluj-Napoca, Rumania.

STUDIEN ZUR LITERATUR- UND SOZIALGESCHICHTE SPANIENS UND LATEINAMERIKAS. see *LITERATURE*

STUDIES IN AFRICAN AND AFRO-AMERICAN CULTURE. see *HISTORY — History Of Africa*

STUDIES IN AFRICAN ECONOMIC & SOCIAL DEVELOPMENT. see *BUSINESS AND ECONOMICS — Economic Systems And Theories, Economic History*

STUDIES IN FAMILY PLANNING. see *POPULATION STUDIES*

301　　　　　　US　　ISSN 0889-3128
STUDIES IN GENDER AND CULTURE. 1988. s-a. Gordon & Breach Science Publishers, 270 Eighth Ave., New York, NY 10011. TEL 212-206-8900. FAX 212-645-2459. TELEX 236735 GOPUB UR. (Subscr. to: Box 786, Cooper Sta., New York, NY 10276. TEL 800-545-8398; UK subscr. to: P.O. Box 90, Reading, Berkshire RG1 8JL, England. TEL 0734-560-080) Ed. W. Martin.
　Refereed Serial

301　　　　　　NE
STUDIES IN HUMAN SOCIETY. 1986. irreg., vol.4, 1991. price varies. E.J. Brill, P.O. Box 9000, 2300 PA Leiden, Netherlands. TEL 071-312624. FAX 071-317532. TELEX 39296 BRILL NL. (In N. America: E.J. Brill, 24 Hudson St., Kinderhook, NY 12106. TEL 800-962-4406) Ed. P.J.M. Nas.

301　　　　　　US　　ISSN 0730-9139
NX501.5
STUDIES IN LATIN AMERICAN POPULAR CULTURE. 1982. a. $15 to individuals; institutions $45. c/o Charles M. Tatum, Department of Spanish & Portuguese, Univ. of Arizona, Tucson, AZ 85721. TEL 602-621-7347. Eds. Harold E. Hinds, Jr., Charles M. Tatum. adv.; bk.rev.; circ. 500. (back issues avail.) **Indexed:** Chic.Per.Ind., Hisp.Amer.Per.Ind., M.L.A.
　—BLDSC shelfmark: 8490.831000.

STUDIES IN LAW, POLITICS, AND SOCIETY; a research annual. see *LAW*

301.2　　　　　　US　　ISSN 0888-5753
E169.1
STUDIES IN POPULAR CULTURE. 1977. s-a. $15. Popular Culture Association in the South, c/o Dennis Hall, Ed., University of Louisville, Department of English, Louisville, KY 40292. (Subscr. to: Diane Calhoun-French, Academic Dean, Jefferson Community College, SW, Louisville, KY 40272) bk.rev.; circ. 500. (back issues avail.) **Indexed:** Film Lit.Ind. (1989-).
　Description: Publishes articles on film, literature, radio, television, music, graphics, the print media, and other aspects of popular culture from a sociological perspective.
　Refereed Serial

301　　　　　　US
STUDIES IN SOCIAL DISCONTINUITY. 1974. irreg., no.51, 1985. Academic Press, Inc., 1250 Sixth Ave., San Diego, CA 92101. TEL 619-231-0926. FAX 619-699-6715. Eds. C. Tilly, E. Shorter. (reprint service avail. from ISI)

STUDIES IN SOCIAL ECONOMICS. see *BUSINESS AND ECONOMICS*

300 301　　　　　US
STUDIES IN SOCIAL EXPERIMENTATION. 1975. irreg. price varies. Brookings Institution, 1775 Massachusetts Ave., N.W., Washington, DC 20036-2188. TEL 202-797-6255. FAX 202-797-6004.

301　　　　　　AT　　ISSN 0156-4420
STUDIES IN SOCIETY. 1978. irreg. price varies. Allen & Unwin Australia Pty. Ltd., 12th Fl., 8 Napier St, N. Sydney, N.S.W. 2059, Australia. FAX 02-922-4317. bibl.

301　　　　　　II
STUDIES IN SOCIOLOGY AND SOCIAL ANTHROPOLOGY. (Text in English) 1978. irreg. price varies. Hindustan Publishing Corp., 6-U.B. Jawahar Nagar, Delhi 110007, India. FAX 6863511. Ed. M.N. Srinivas.

SOCIOLOGY

301   **US**
STUDIES IN SOUTHERN ITALIAN AND ITALIAN-AMERICAN CULTURE/STUDI SULLA CULTURE DELL'ITALIA MERIDIONALE E ITALO-AMERICANA. irreg. Peter Lang Publishing, Inc., 62 W. 45th St., 4th Fl., New York, NY 10036. TEL 212-302-6740.
FAX 212-302-7574. Eds. Giose Rimanelli and Francis X. Femminella.
  Description: Publishes studies of the literature, arts, spoken modes and socio-historical life of Southern Italian society, as well as studies of the culture of Italian-Americans whose ancestry stems from Southern Italy.

301.1   **US**   **ISSN 0163-2396**
HM1
STUDIES IN SYMBOLIC INTERACTION; an annual compilation of research. 1978. a. $63.50 to institutions. J A I Press Inc., 55 Old Post Rd., No. 2, Box 1678, Greenwich, CT 06836-1678.
TEL 203-661-7602. Ed. Norman K. Denzin. illus.
Indexed: Lang.& Lang.Behav.Abstr., Psychol.Abstr., Sociol.Abstr. (1978-).
—BLDSC shelfmark: 8491.788000.

309 960   **ZA**
STUDIES IN ZAMBIAN SOCIETY. 1978. irreg., no.3, 1978. price varies. University of Zambia, School of Humanities and Social Sciences, Committee on Student Publications, Box 2379, Lusaka, Zambia. Ed. L.M. van den Berg. circ. 1,000.

301   **NE**   **ISSN 0081-8771**
STUDIES OF DEVELOPING COUNTRIES. (Text mainly in English) 1963. irreg., no.25, 1979. price varies. Van Gorcum en Co. B.V., P.O. Box 43, 9400 AA Assen, Netherlands. TEL 05920-46864.
FAX 05920-72064. (Dist. by: Longwood Publishing Group Inc., 27 S. Main Street, Wolfeboro, N.H. 03894)
  Formerly: Non-European Societies.

STUDIES OF ISRAELI SOCIETY. see *ETHNIC INTERESTS*

301   **US**   **ISSN 0039-4394**
SUBTERRANEAN SOCIOLOGY NEWSLETTER.
1967-1980; resumed 1987; N.S. 1990. irreg. $3. Subterranean Sociological Association, Dept. of Sociology, Eastern Michigan University, Ypsilanti, MI 48197. TEL 313-487-1849. Ed. Marcello Truzzi. bk.rev.; bibl.; circ. 600 (controlled). (processed)

301   **US**   **ISSN 0273-2017**
SURVIVAL TOMORROW;* resources for troubled times. (Includes Supplements) 1981. m. $60. c/o Nancy Tappan, Box 1050, Rogue River, OR 97537. Ed. Karl Hess. bk.rev.; circ. 15,000. (back issues avail.)

309   **US**
SURVIVORS.* 1980. bi-m. $10. Survivors Inc., Box 3564, Springfield, IL 62708-3564. Ed. D.L. Giles-Doering. adv.; bk.rev.; circ. 100,000.

301.4   **US**
SURVIVORS OUTREACH SERIES. 1980. 8/yr. $24 in US; Canada $27; elsewhere $30. Theos Foundation, 717 Liberty Ave., No. 1301, Pittsburgh, PA 15222-3510. bk.rev.; circ. 25.
  Description: An aid to coping with grief for widows and widowers.

301   **HU**   **ISSN 0133-3461**
HM7
SZOCIOLOGIA. (Text in Hungarian; summaries in English, Russian) 1972. q. $28. (Magyar Tudomanyos Akademia, Szoziologiai Intezet) Akademiai Kiado, Publishing House of the Hungarian Academy of Sciences, P.O. Box 24, H-1363 Budapest, Hungary. Ed. L. Cseh-Szombathy. bk.rev.; bibl.; index. **Indexed:** Lang.& Lang.Behav.Abstr., Sociol.Abstr. (1972-), World Agri.Econ.& Rural Sociol.Abstr.

301   **HU**   **ISSN 0082-1322**
SZOCIOLOGIAI TANULMANYOK. 1966. irreg., vol.29, 1987. price varies. (Magyar Tudomanyos Akademia) Akademiai Kiado, Publishing House of the Hungarian Academy of Sciences, P.O. Box 24, H-1363 Budapest, Hungary.

301.4   **US**
T F P NEWSLETTER. 1979. bi-m. free. American Society for the Defense of Tradition, Family and Property, Box 121, Pleasantville, NY 10570.
TEL 914-241-7015. Ed. David Mattingly.

301   **US**
▼**TAKING SIDES: CLASHING VIEWS ON CONTROVERSIAL ISSUES IN FAMILY AND PERSONAL RELATIONSHIPS**. 1991. irreg., 1st ed., 1992. $11.95. Dushkin Publishing Group, Inc., Sluice Dock, Guilford, CT 06437-9989. TEL 203-453-4351.
FAX 203-453-6000. Eds. Gloria W. Bird, Michael Sporakowski. illus.

301   **US**
▼**TAKING SIDES: CLASHING VIEWS ON CONTROVERSIAL ISSUES IN MASS MEDIA AND SOCIETY**. 1991. irreg., 1st ed., 1991. $11.95. Dushkin Publishing Group, Inc., Sluice Dock, Guilford, CT 06437-9989.
TEL 203-543-4351. FAX 203-453-6000. Eds. Alison Alexander, Jarice Hanson. illus.

301   **US**
TAKING SIDES: CLASHING VIEWS ON CONTROVERSIAL SOCIAL ISSUES. irreg., 6th ed., 1990. $11.95. Dushkin Publishing Group, Inc., Sluice Dock, Guilford, CT 06437-9989. TEL 203-453-4351.
FAX 203-453-6000. Eds. Kurt Finsterbusch, George McKenna. illus.

TAMBARA. see *ANTHROPOLOGY*

301   **HU**   **ISSN 0039-971X**
HX8
TARSADALMI SZEMLE. (Text in Hungarian; summaries in English, French, German and Russian) 1931-1933; resumed 1946. m. 708 Ft.($26) (Foundation of Taisaddini Szemle) Kossuth Konyvkiado, Steindl I. Utca 6, 1366 Budapest 5, Hungary. (Subscr. to: Kultura, Box 149, H-1389 Budapest, Hungary) Ed. Mihaly Bihari. bk.rev.; circ. 6,000. **Indexed:** Hist.Abstr., Rural Recreat.Tour.Abstr., World Agri.Econ.& Rural Sociol.Abstr.

301   **US**   **ISSN 0092-055X**
HM1
TEACHING SOCIOLOGY. 1973. q. $34 to individuals (foreign $40); institutions $63 (foreign $69); effective 1992. American Sociological Association, 1722 N St., N.W., Washington, DC 20036.
TEL 202-833-3410. FAX 202-785-0146. Ed. Dean Dorn. adv.; bk.rev.; index. (back issues avail.)
Indexed: ASCA, ASSIA, C.I.J.E., Cont.Pg.Educ., Curr.Cont., Educ.Ind., Educ.Tech.Abstr., High.Educ.Curr.Aware.Bull., Lang.& Lang.Behav.Abstr., Mid.East: Abstr.& Ind., Res.High.Educ.Abstr., Sociol.Abstr. (1973-), SSCI, Stud.Wom.Abstr.
—BLDSC shelfmark: 8614.340000.
  Description: Publishes research articles, teaching tips, and reports on teaching sociology.

TECHNIK UND GESELLSCHAFT. see *TECHNOLOGY: COMPREHENSIVE WORKS*

TECHNOLOGICAL FORECASTING AND SOCIAL CHANGE. see *TECHNOLOGY: COMPREHENSIVE WORKS*

301   **US**   **ISSN 0160-791X**
T14.5
TECHNOLOGY IN SOCIETY; an international journal. Previously announced as: Sociotechnology. 1979. q. £205 (effective 1992). Pergamon Press, Inc., Journals Division, 660 White Plains Rd., Tarrytown, NY 10591-5153. TEL 914-524-9200.
FAX 914-333-2444. (And: Headington Hill Hall, Oxford OX3 0BW, England. TEL 0865-794141) Ed. George Bugliarello. adv.; bk.rev.; charts; illus.; stat.; index; circ. 2,000. (also avail. in microform from MIM,UMI) **Indexed:** Amer.Bibl.Slavic & E.Eur.Stud., ASCA, Biostat., Curr.Cont., Educ.Tech.Abstr., Excerp.Med., Fut.Surv., Lang.& Lang.Behav.Abstr., Oper.Res.Manage.Sci., Psychol.Abstr., Qual.Contr.Appl.Stat., Sociol.Abstr.
—BLDSC shelfmark: 8761.023000.
  Refereed Serial

301   **IS**   **ISSN 0792-0601**
TEL AVIV - YAFO. CENTER FOR ECONOMIC AND SOCIAL RESEARCH. RESEARCH AND SURVEYS SERIES/TEL AVIV - YAFO. HA-MERKAZ LE-MEKHKAR KALKALI VE-KHEVRATI. MEKHKARIM VE-SEKARIM. (Text in Hebrew) no.12, 1963. irreg. Center for Economic and Social Research, Tel Aviv - Yafo Municipality, Malkhei Israel Square, Tel Aviv 64162, Israel.
TEL 03-262156. Ed. M. Hadad. circ. 600.
  Formerly: Tel Aviv - Yafo. Research and Statistical Department. Special Surveys (ISSN 0082-2639)
  Description: Contains research reports on various social and urban topics concerning Tel Aviv - Yafo.

TEMAS AMERICANISTAS. see *HISTORY — History Of North And South America*

300   **BO**   **ISSN 0040-2915**
TEMAS SOCIALES. 1968. q. $8. Universidad Mayor de San Andres, Facultad de Derecho, Casilla 1925, La Paz, Bolivia. Ed. Mario Diez. charts.

301 100 320   **YU**
TEME. (Text in Serbo-Croatian; contents in English, French, German and Russian) 1977. q. 10000 din. Univerzitet u Nisu, Trg Bratstva i Jedinstva, Nis, Yugoslavia. TEL 018 25-868. FAX 18-24488. TELEX 16362 UNIUNI YU. Ed. Marko Sekulovic. bk.rev.; circ. 500.
  Formerly (until Jun., 1990): Marksisticke Teme (ISSN 0351-1685)

301   **BL**   **ISSN 0103-2070**
HM22.B8
TEMPO SOCIAL. 1989. s-a. $30. Universidade de Sao Paulo, Faculdade de Filosofia, Letras e Ciencias Humanas, Secao de Publicacoes, CP. 8105, 05508 Sao Paulo, Brazil. TEL 011-813-3222.

TEXT; an interdisciplinary journal for the study of discourse. see *HUMANITIES: COMPREHENSIVE WORKS*

THEORETICAL POPULATION BIOLOGY; an international journal. see *BIOLOGY*

301   **NE**   **ISSN 0304-2421**
HM1   **CODEN: THSODL**
THEORY AND SOCIETY; renewal and critique in social theory. 1974. bi-m. $53 to individuals; institutions $180.50. Kluwer Academic Publishers, Postbus 17, 3300 AA Dordrecht, Netherlands.
TEL 078-334911. FAX 078-334254. TELEX 29245. (Dist. by: Kluwer Academic Publishers Group, P.O. Box 322, 3300 AH Dordrecht, Netherlands; N. America dist. addr.: Box 358, Accord Station, Hingham, MA 02018-0358.
TEL 617-871-6600) Ed. K. Lucas. bk.rev.; index; circ. 1,500. (reprint service avail. from SWZ)
Indexed: ASCA, ASSIA, Commun.Abstr., Curr.Cont., Lang.& Lang.Behav.Abstr., Left Ind. (1982-), P.A.I.S., Sociol.Abstr. (1974-), SSCI.
—BLDSC shelfmark: 8814.630000.

301   **UK**   **ISSN 0263-2764**
THEORY CULTURE & SOCIETY; explorations in critical social science. 1982. q. £28($46) to individuals; institutions £75($124). Sage Publications Ltd., 6 Bonhill St., London EC2A 4PU, England.
TEL 071-374-0645. FAX 071-374-8741. Ed. Mike Featherstone. adv.: color page £190; trim 177 x 101; adv. contact: Bernie Folan. bk.rev. **Indexed:** Alt.Press Ind, Curr.Cont., Sociol.Abstr. (1982-), SSCI.
—BLDSC shelfmark: 8814.631500.
  Description: Publishes papers by modern social and cultural theorists.

TIDSKRIFT FOER RAETTSSOCIOLOGI. see *LAW*

301   **CK**
TIERRA NUEVA. 1972. q. $32. Centro de Estudios para el Desarrollo e Integracion de America Latina, Carrera 90, No. 47-54, Apdo. Aereo 100572, Bogota, D.E. 10, Colombia. Ed. Maria B. Cabezas de Gonzalez. cum.index; circ. 1,000. **Indexed:** CERDIC.

301   **NE**   **ISSN 0168-8626**
TIJDSCHRIFT VOOR AGOLOGIE. bi-m. fl.116. Uitgeverij Boom, P.O. Box 1058, 7940 KB Meppel, Netherlands. TEL 05220-66111.
FAX 05220-66198. circ. 1,200.

301   **BE**   **ISSN 0040-7615**
H8
TIJDSCHRIFT VOOR SOCIALE WETENSCHAPPEN. (Text and summaries in English, French or German) 1956. 4/yr. 1000 Fr. to individuals; institutions 1450 Fr.; students 550 Fr. Rijksuniversiteit te Gent, Universiteitstraat 4, B-9000 Ghent, Belgium. Ed. Marthe Versichelen. bk.rev.; charts; index; circ. 700. **Indexed:** Key to Econ.Sci., Lang.& Lang.Behav.Abstr., Sociol.Abstr. (1958-).
—BLDSC shelfmark: 8844.600000.

TIKKUN MAGAZINE; a bi-monthly Jewish critique of politics, culture and society. see *ETHNIC INTERESTS*

301   UK   ISSN 0961-463X
▼**TIME AND SOCIETY.** 1992. 3/yr. £25($39) to individuals; institutions £55($89). Sage Publicatons Ltd., 6 Bonhill St., London EC2A 4PU, England. TEL 071-374-0645. FAX 071-374-8741. Ed. Barbara Adam. adv.: color page £150; trim 175 x 112; adv. contact: Bernie Folan. bk.rev. **Indexed:** Int.Polit.Sci.Abstr.
  Description: Publishes empirical and theoretical analyses on the subject of time, relating it to society and culture, and to theories of individual and social behavior and action.

TODAY (KENT). see *CHILDREN AND YOUTH — For*

IL TORCHIO ARTISTICO E LETTERARIO; organo ufficiale di stampa dell'Accademia Culturale d'Europa. see *ART*

301   US   ISSN 1052-5017
▼**TRANSFORMATIONS.** 1990. s-a. $20. New Jersey Project, c/o Sylvia Baer, Ed., Gloucester County College, Sewell, NJ 08080-9518.
  Description: Aims to integrate issues of women and gender, race-ethnicity, class, and sexuality into the curriculum of two- and four-year colleges.

TRANSILVANIA. see *HISTORY — History Of Europe*

301.4   CN   ISSN 0049-4429
TRANSITION. (Text in English, French) 1970. 4/yr. Can.$25 membership to individuals; institutions Can.$60. Vanier Institute of the Family, 120 Holland Ave., Ste.300, Ottawa, Ont. K1Y 0X6, Canada. TEL 613-722-4007. FAX 613-729-5249. Ed. Ish Theilheimer. bk.rev.; film rev.; bibl.; stat.; circ. 8,000. **Indexed:** Avery Ind.Archit.Per., Bank.Lit.Ind.
  Description: Articles on family issues.

TRANSPORTATION PLANNING AND TECHNOLOGY; reviews and communications. see *TRANSPORTATION*

TRAVAIL HUMAIN. see *PSYCHOLOGY*

301   AT
LA TROBE SOCIOLOGY PAPERS. 1973. irreg. La Trobe University, Department of Sociology, School of Social Sciences, Bundoora, Vic. 3083, Australia. circ. 300.

301   GW   ISSN 0722-494X
          CODEN: TUEXDZ
TUEXENIA. 1928. irreg. price varies. Floristisch - Soziologische Arbeitsgemeinschaft, Wilhelm-Weber-Str. 2, 3400 Goettingen, Germany. TEL 0551-395700. Ed. H. Dierschke. bk.rev.; circ. 1,500. **Indexed:** Biol.Abstr., Fababean Abstr., Forest.Abstr., Irr.& Drain.Abstr., Soils & Fert., Triticale Abstr., Weed Abstr.
  —BLDSC shelfmark: 9068.584000.
  Formerly (until 1980): Floristisch - Soziologische Arbeitsgemeinschaft. Mitteilungen (ISSN 0373-7632)

301.451   TU   ISSN 0082-6898
TURKISH REVIEW OF ETHNOGRAPHY/TURK ETNOGRAFYA DERGISI. 1956. a. price varies. Ministry of Culture, General Directorate of Monuments and Museums - Kultur Bakanligi, Anitlar ve Muzeler Genel Mudurlugu, Ankara, Turkey. FAX 4-31111417. (Orders to: Kultur Bakanligi, Doner Sermaye Isletmesi Merkez Mudurlugu, Akdale Sok. No. 18-1, Yenisehir - Ankara, Turkey)
  Formerly: Turk Tarih-Arkeologya ve Etnografya Dergisi.

TWENTIETH CENTURY FUND. NEWSLETTER. see *POLITICAL SCIENCE — International Relations*

301.45   SA   ISSN 0041-4794
DT763
TYDSKRIF VIR RASSE - AANGELEENTHEDE/JOURNAL OF RACIAL AFFAIRS. (Text in Afrikaans and English) 1949. q. R.40 (free to members). South African Bureau of Racial Affairs, Box 2768, Pretoria, South Africa. Ed. A.D. Pont. adv.; bk.rev.; stat.; circ. 5,000. **Indexed:** CERDIC, Ind.S.A.Per.
  —BLDSC shelfmark: 5043.780000.

U.I.A.M.S. INFORMATIONS. (International Union for Moral and Social Action) see *POLITICAL SCIENCE*

U K ALCOHOL ALERT. see *DRUG ABUSE AND ALCOHOLISM*

U S S R REPORT: LIFE SCIENCES. see *MEDICAL SCIENCES*

U S S R REPORT: POLITICAL AND SOCIOLOGICAL AFFAIRS. see *POLITICAL SCIENCE*

U S S R SERIAL REPORTS: SOCIOLOGICAL STUDIES. see *POLITICAL SCIENCE — International Relations*

301   GW   ISSN 0170-2416
UEBERSEE-MUSEUM, BREMEN. VEROEFFENTLICHUNGEN. REIHE E: HUMAN-OEKOLOGIE. 1978. irreg., vol.3, 1980. price varies. Uebersee-Museum, Bremen, Bahnhofsplatz 13, 2800 Bremen, Germany. **Indexed:** Biol.Abstr.

UNE VILLE, UN PAYS. see *HISTORY — History Of Europe*

UNION SIGNAL. see *DRUG ABUSE AND ALCOHOLISM*

301   VE   ISSN 1012-2508
UNIVERSIDAD CENTRAL DE VENEZUELA. CENTRO DE ESTUDIOS DEL DESARROLLO. CUADERNOS DEL C E N D E S. (Text in Spanish; abstracts in English) 1983. 3/yr. Bs.600($35) (foreign $40) to individuals; institutions Bs.1200($75) (foreign $80). Universidad Central de Venezuela, Centro de Estudios del Desarrollo, Apartado Postal 6622, Caracas 1010-A, Venezuela. TEL 7523266. FAX 582-7512691. (U.S. subscr. addr.: Poba International, No. 151, Box 02-5255, Miami, FL 33102-5255) Dir. Ramon Casanova. adv.; bk.rev.; circ. 2,000. (back issues avail.)
  Description: Covers Venezuelan development problems and those of the Third World in general.

301   PR
UNIVERSIDAD DE PUERTO RICO. CENTRO DE INVESTIGACIONES SOCIALES. INFORME ANUAL. (Text in Spanish) 1974. a. free. Universidad de Puerto Rico, Centro de Investigaciones Sociales, Rio Piedras, PR 00931. Ed. Wenceslao Serra Deliz. bk.rev.; bibl.; circ. 1,000.

301   PE
UNIVERSIDAD NACIONAL MAYOR DE SAN MARCOS. DEPARTAMENTO DE SOCIOLOGIA. REVISTA.* 1964. s-a. Universidad Nacional Mayor de San Marcos, Departamento de Sociologia, Avda. Republica de Chile 295, Casilla 454, Lima, Peru.

UNIVERSIDADE DE SAO PAULO. INSTITUTO DE ESTUDOS BRASILEIROS. REVISTA. see *GEOGRAPHY*

572 301   FR   ISSN 0249-5635
UNIVERSITE DE BORDEAUX II. CAHIERS ETHNOLOGIQUES. 1972. a. 100 F. (effective 1992). (Universite de Bordeaux II, Departement d'Anthropologie Sociale - Ethnologie) Presses Universitaires de Bordeaux, 3 place de la Victoire, 33000 Bordeaux, France. FAX 56-99-03-80. Ed. Christian Meriot. bk.rev.; circ. 400. **Indexed:** A.I.C.P.
  Formerly: Universite de Bordeaux II. Centre d'Etudes et de Rechercher Ethnologiques. Cahiers.

301   BE   ISSN 0066-2380
HN501
UNIVERSITE LIBRE DE BRUXELLES. INSTITUT DE SOCIOLOGIE. ANNEE SOCIALE. 1960. a. 1300 Fr. Universite Libre de Bruxelles, Institute de Sociologie, Av. Jeanne 44, B-1050 Brussels, Belgium. TEL 650-3359. FAX 650-3521. bk.rev.

301   BE   ISSN 0770-1055
UNIVERSITE LIBRE DE BRUXELLES. INSTITUT DE SOCIOLOGIE. REVUE. 1920. q. 1800 Fr. Ave. Jeanne 44, B-1050 Brussels, Belgium. adv.; bk.rev.; abstr.; bibl.; charts; index; circ. 1,150. **Indexed:** SSCI.

UNIVERSITE NATIONALE DE COTE D'IVOIRE. ANNALES. SERIE F: ETHNOSOCIOLOGIE. see *ANTHROPOLOGY*

330   US
UNIVERSITY OF ALASKA. INSTITUTE OF SOCIAL AND ECONOMIC RESEARCH. RESEARCH SUMMARY. 1980. irreg., no.52, 1991. free. University of Alaska, Institute of Social and Economic Research, 3211 Providence Dr., Anchorage, AK 99508. TEL 907-786-7710. Ed. Linda Leask. bk.rev.; charts; stat.; circ. 1,900. (also avail. in microfiche; back issues avail.)

301   NZ
UNIVERSITY OF AUCKLAND. DEPARTMENT OF SOCIOLOGY. PAPERS IN COMPARATIVE SOCIOLOGY. 1974. irreg., no.20, 1990. price varies. University of Auckland, Department of Sociology, Private Bag, Auckland, New Zealand. FAX 09-733-429. Ed. Ian Carter. circ. 100.

UNIVERSITY OF BIRMINGHAM. CENTRE FOR URBAN AND REGIONAL STUDIES. OCCASIONAL PAPERS. see *HOUSING AND URBAN PLANNING*

UNIVERSITY OF BIRMINGHAM. CENTRE FOR URBAN AND REGIONAL STUDIES. RESEARCH MEMORANDUM. see *HOUSING AND URBAN PLANNING*

UNIVERSITY OF BIRMINGHAM. CENTRE FOR URBAN AND REGIONAL STUDIES. URBAN AND REGIONAL STUDIES. see *HOUSING AND URBAN PLANNING*

UNIVERSITY OF BIRMINGHAM. CENTRE FOR URBAN AND REGIONAL STUDIES. WORKING PAPER. see *HOUSING AND URBAN PLANNING*

301   II
UNIVERSITY OF CALCUTTA. DEPARTMENT OF SOCIOLOGY. JOURNAL. (Supplement avail.) (Text in English) a. Rs.12. Dilip Kumar Mukherjee, Asutosh Building, Calcutta 700 073, India. Ed. Krishna Chakrabarty. bk.rev.; circ. 1,000.

UNIVERSITY OF CALIFORNIA, BERKELEY. INSTITUTE OF INTERNATIONAL STUDIES. RESEARCH SERIES. see *POLITICAL SCIENCE*

UNIVERSITY OF CANTERBURY. DEPARTMENT OF PSYCHOLOGY AND SOCIOLOGY. RESEARCH PROJECTS. see *PSYCHOLOGY*

301   GH
UNIVERSITY OF GHANA. DEPARTMENT OF SOCIOLOGY. CURRENT RESEARCH REPORT SERIES. no.2, 1972. irreg. University of Ghana, Department of Sociology, Legon, Ghana.

UNIVERSITY OF LAGOS. HUMAN RESOURCES RESEARCH UNIT. MONOGRAPH. see *POPULATION STUDIES*

309.1   US
UNIVERSITY OF MINNESOTA. CENTER FOR YOUTH DEVELOPMENT AND RESEARCH. CENTER QUARTERLY FOCUS. 1972. q. $0.25 per no. University of Minnesota, Center for Youth Development and Research, 48 McNeal Hall, 1985 Buford, St. Paul, MN 55108. TEL 612-373-2851. Ed. Miriam Seltzer.

301 330   JM
UNIVERSITY OF THE WEST INDIES. INSTITUTE OF SOCIAL AND ECONOMIC RESEARCH. WORKING PAPERS. no.7, 1975. irreg., latest no.35. University of the West Indies, Institute of Social and Economic Research, Mona Campus, Kingston 7, Jamaica, W.I. TEL 809-927-1020. FAX 809-927-2409. TELEX 2123 JA.

UNIVERZITET U ZAGREBU. PRAVNI FAKULTET. ZBORNIK. see *LAW*

UNIWERSYTET SLASKI W KATOWICACH. PRACE NAUKOWE. Z PROBLEMATYKI PRAWA PRACY I POLITYKI SOCJALNEJ. see *LAW*

361   US   ISSN 0042-0468
UNSCHEDULED EVENTS; research committee on disasters newsletter. 1967. q. $22 membership. International Sociological Association, Research Committee on Disasters, Colorado State University, Hazards Assessment Laboratory, Fort Collins, CO 80523. TEL 303-491-7347. FAX 303-491-2191. Ed. Dennis S. Mileti. adv.; bk.rev.; abstr.; circ. 250. (back issues avail.)

301   SW   ISSN 0502-7527
UPPSALA UNIVERSITY. DEPARTMENT OF SOCIOLOGY. RESEARCH REPORTS. (Text in English, Swedish) 1985. irreg. (4-6/yr.). SEK 200 for 5 nos. Uppsala University, Department of Sociology, Box 513, S-75120 Uppsala, Sweden. TEL 018-1825-00. FAX 46-18-181170. TELEX UNIVUP-S-76024. (back issues avail.)
  —BLDSC shelfmark: 7761.477700.
  Description: Covers research carried out in the department.

URBAN ANTHROPOLOGY AND STUDIES OF CULTURAL SYSTEMS AND WORLD ECONOMIC DEVELOPMENT. see *ANTHROPOLOGY*

URBAN LEAGUE REVIEW. see *ETHNIC INTERESTS*

URBAN PSYCHIATRY. JOURNAL. see *MEDICAL SCIENCES — Psychiatry And Neurology*

THE URBAN REVIEW; issues and ideas in public education. see *EDUCATION*

URBAN STUDIES. see *HOUSING AND URBAN PLANNING*

URBANIZACION, MIGRACIONES Y CAMBIOS EN LA SOCIEDAD PERUANA. see *ANTHROPOLOGY*

301   FR
UTOPIE.* 1967. s-a. Editions Economica, 49 rue Hericart, 75011 Paris, France. Dir. H. Tonka. bibl.
   Description: Covers urban and industrial sociology.

301   UK
V E S NEWSLETTER. no.12, 1981. irreg. (3-4/yr.). Voluntary Euthanasia Society, 13 Prince of Wales Terrace, London W8 5PG, England.
   Former titles: Exit; Exit News; Right to Die.

301   HU   ISSN 0324-7228
AP82
VALOSAG. 1957. m. $28.50. (Tudomanyos Ismaretterjexato Tarsulat) Hirlapkiado Vallalat, Blaha Lujza ter 3, 1959 Budapest 8, Hungary. TEL 1-382-399. TELEX 22-5554. (Subscr. to: Kultura, P.O. Box 149, H-1389 Budapest, Hungary) Ed. Istvan Lazari. adv.; bk.rev.; circ. 9,000. **Indexed:** Rural Recreat.Tour.Abstr., World Agri.Econ. & Rural Sociol.Abstr.

301   PO
VANDOMA. 1985. 2/yr. Apdo. 214, 4703 Braga Codex, Portugal. (Subscr. to: Movilibro, Rua do Bonfim, 98 r-c, Porto, Portugal) circ. 1,120.

301   US   ISSN 0361-5170
HV6250
VICTIMOLOGY; an international journal. 1976. q. $85. (National Institute of Victimology) Victimology, Inc., 2333 N. Vernon St., Arlington, VA 22207. TEL 703-528-3387. Ed. Emilio C. Viano. adv.; bk.rev.; circ. 2,000. (back issues avail.) **Indexed:** Abstr.Crim.& Pen., Adol.Ment.Hlth.Abstr., C.L.I., Chicago Psychoanal.Lit.Ind., CJPI, Crim.Just.Abstr., Hlth.Ind., L.R.I., Leg.Cont., Mid.East: Abstr.& Ind., Past.Care & Couns.Abstr., Psychol.Abstr., Sociol.Abstr., Stud.Wom.Abstr.
   —BLDSC shelfmark: 9232.420000.

VICTIMS OF VIOLENCE REPORT. see *LAW — Criminal Law*

301   FR   ISSN 0042-5605
H3
VIE SOCIALE. 1964. bi-m. 260 F. (foreign 310 F.). Centre d'Etudes, de Documentation, d'Information et d'Action Sociales (CEDIAS), 5 rue Las-Cases, 75007 Paris, France. TEL 45-51-66-10. Ed.Bd. bk.rev.; circ. 1,750 (controlled). (back issues avail.)
   —BLDSC shelfmark: 9235.420000.
   Description: A collection of stories, reflections, information and documentation.

VIOLENCE AND VICTIMS. see *PSYCHOLOGY*

301   IT
VITTORIO BACCELLI MAGAZINE. biennial. L.10000. Vittorio Baccelli, Ed. & Pub., C.P. 132, 55100 Lucca, Italy.

301 374 301.412   UK   ISSN 0260-3993
VIVE LA DIFFERENCE. 1979. q. £1.50 for 3 issues. C F W - Concern for Family & Womanhood, Campaign for the Feminine Woman, Springfield House, Chedworth, Cheltenham GL54 4AH, England. TEL 0285-720454. Ed. David W. Stayt. circ. 5,000.
   Description: Promotes and advances education in relations between men and women, including topics such as masculinity, femininity, sexual roles, marriage and the family unit.

309   UK   ISSN 0957-8765
HD62.6   CODEN: VOLUE8
▼**VOLUNTAS;** international journal of voluntary and non-profit organizations. 1990. s-a. £20($35) to individuals; institutions £45($80). (Charities Aid Foundation) Manchester University Press, Oxford Rd., Manchester M13 9PL, England. TEL 061-273-5539. FAX 061-274-3346. TELEX 666517-UNIMAN. Eds. H. Anheier, M. Knapp. **Indexed:** Soc.Work Res.& Abstr.
   —BLDSC shelfmark: 9254.577800.

301   GW
VON MANN ZU MANN. 1980. irreg. DM.3($30) Stiftung Aktiv Gegen Sexismus, Marburgerstr. 9, D-6000 Frankfurt 90, Germany. Ed. Rudi Gerharz.

200 301   US   ISSN 1059-6216
WALK AWAY; the newsletter for ex-fundamentalists. 1989. q. $12 (effective 1992). Institute for First Amendment Studies, Inc., Box 589, Great Barrington, MA 01230. TEL 413-274-3786. FAX 413-274-0245. Ed. Skipp Porteous. circ. 2,500. (also avail. in microfiche; back issues avail.)

WARSAW AGRICULTURAL UNIVERSITY. S G G W. ANNALS. AGRICULTURAL ECONOMICS AND RURAL SOCIOLOGY. see *AGRICULTURE — Agricultural Economics*

WEEKLY PROBES. see *POLITICAL SCIENCE*

WELLNESS PERSPECTIVES: RESEARCH, THEORY AND PRACTICE. see *PHYSICAL FITNESS AND HYGIENE*

301 320   NR   ISSN 0308-4450
HN820
WEST AFRICAN JOURNAL OF SOCIOLOGY AND POLITICAL SCIENCE. q. £20($40) University of Ibadan, Sociology Department, Ibadan, Nigeria. Ed. Justin Labinjon. adv.; bk.rev.; bibl.; circ. 1,000. (back issues avail.) **Indexed:** Curr.Cont.Africa, Lang.& Lang.Behav.Abstr.

THE WHITE RIBBON. see *DRUG ABUSE AND ALCOHOLISM*

301   US
WINGED MERCURY MISSIVE.* 1981. irreg. $5. Winged Mercury Networking, Box 5010, Dept. 244, Asheville, NC 28813-5010. Ed. Gary Smith. bk.rev.; circ. 288.

301   US   ISSN 0043-6666
HM1   CODEN: WSSCA
WISCONSIN SOCIOLOGIST. 1960. q. $14.50 to individuals; libraries $19. Wisconsin Sociological Association, Marquette University, Department of Social and Cultural Sciences, Milwaukee, WI 53233. TEL 414-288-6846. FAX 414-288-3300. Ed. Richard D. Knudten. adv.; bk.rev.; circ. 500. (processed) **Indexed:** Lang.& Lang.Behav.Abstr., Sociol.Abstr. (1962-).
   —BLDSC shelfmark: 9325.900000.

301   GW   ISSN 0138-5755
WISSENSCHAFT UND GESELLSCHAFT. 1973. irreg., vol.26, 1988. (Akademie der Wissenschaften der DDR) Akademie-Verlag Berlin, Leipziger Str. 3-4, 1086 Berlin, Germany. TELEX 114420-AVERL-DD.

WISSENSCHAFTLICHE PAPERBACKS; Sozial- und Wirtschaftsgeschichte. see *BUSINESS AND ECONOMICS — Economic Systems And Theories, Economic History*

301   AU
DER WOHLFAHRTSDIENST; Monatsschrift fuer Fragen der Wirtschaft und des Sozialen Lebens. 1952. m. free. Oesterreichischer Wohlfahrtsdienst, Kaerntnerstr. 51-1, A-1010 Vienna, Austria. TEL 5127823. Ed. Gretl Pilz. adv.; bk.rev.; bibl.

WOMEN IN CULTURE AND SOCIETY. see *WOMEN'S INTERESTS*

301 150   US   ISSN 0730-8884
HT675
WORK AND OCCUPATIONS; an international sociological journal. 1974. q. $40 to individuals; institutions $108. Sage Publications, Inc., 2455 Teller Rd., Newbury Park, CA 91320. TEL 805-499-0721. FAX 805-499-0871. (And: Sage Publications, Ltd., 6 Bonhill St., London EC2A 4PU, England) Ed. Curt Tausky. adv.; bk.rev.; index; circ. 1,000. (also avail. in microform from UMI; back issues avail.; reprint service avail. from UMI) **Indexed:** ABI Inform, ASSIA, BPIA, C.I.J.E., Curr.Cont., Ergon.Abstr., Int.Lab.Doc., Lang.& Lang.Behav.Abstr., Mid.East: Abstr.& Ind., Pers.Lit., Psychol.Abstr., Sage Fam.Stud.Abstr., Sage Pub.Admin.Abstr., Sociol.Abstr. (1976-), SSCI, Stud.Wom.Abstr.
   Formerly (until 1982): Sociology of Work and Occupations (ISSN 0093-9285)

301   UK   ISSN 0950-0170
HD6951
WORK, EMPLOYMENT & SOCIETY. 1987. q. £25 to non-member individuals; institutions £52. (British Sociological Association) B.S.A. Publications Ltd., 351 Station Rd., Dorridge, Solihull, W. Midlands B93 8EY, England. TEL 05645-2402. Ed. H.F. Moorhouse. bk.rev. (also avail. in microform from UMI) **Indexed:** ASSIA, Int.Lab.Doc., Sociol.Abstr. (1987-).
   —BLDSC shelfmark: 9348.149000.
   Description: Articles on all aspects of work, employment and unemployment.

WORK IN PROGRESS. see *POLITICAL SCIENCE — Civil Rights*

301.34   TR
WORKING PAPERS ON CARIBBEAN SOCIETY. SERIES A: NEW PERSPECTIVES IN THEORY AND ANALYSIS. 1978. irreg. $2. University of the West Indies, Department of Sociology, St. Augustine, Trinidad and Tobago.

301.34   TR
WORKING PAPERS ON CARIBBEAN SOCIETY. SERIES C: RESEARCH FINDINGS. irreg. University of the West Indies, Department of Sociology, St. Augustine, Trinidad and Tobago.

WORKING PAPERS ON WOMEN IN INTERNATIONAL DEVELOPMENT. see *BUSINESS AND ECONOMICS — International Development And Assistance*

WORLD LEISURE AND RECREATION. see *LEISURE AND RECREATION*

WORLD UNION. see *POLITICAL SCIENCE — International Relations*

WORLD WATCH. see *ENVIRONMENTAL STUDIES*

WORLDWATCH PAPERS. see *ENVIRONMENTAL STUDIES*

301   CC
XIANGGANG FENGQING/HONG KONG CUSTOMS. (Text in Chinese) bi-m. Guangdong Renmin Chubanshe, Qikan Bu, No. 10, 4 Malu, Dashatou, Guangzhou, Guangdong 510102, People's Republic of China. TEL 335210. Ed. Liu Bansheng.

XIN WENHUA SHILIAO/HISTORICAL RECORDS OF THE NEW CULTURE. see *HISTORY — History Of Asia*

301 320   II   ISSN 0049-8351
YOUNG AGE;* social and cultural fortnightly. (Text in English and Hindi) 1965. s-m. Rs.5($5) 3968 Rasta M. S. B., Jaipur 302003, India. Ed. Surendra Kumar. adv.; bk.rev.; circ. 2,500.

YOUTH & SOCIETY. see *CHILDREN AND YOUTH — About*

YUNNAN MINZU XUEYUAN XUEBAO/YUNNAN INSTITUTE OF NATIONALITIES. JOURNAL. see *ORIENTAL STUDIES*

301   GW   ISSN 0723-5607
Z A INFORMATION. 1977. s-a. free. Universitaet zu Koeln, Zentralarchiv fuer Empirische Sozialforschung, Bachemerstr. 40, 5000 Cologne 41, Germany. TEL 0221-47694-0. FAX 0221-4769444. Ed. Franz Bauske. adv.; bk.rev.; circ. 3,500. (back issues avail.)
   Description: Information and studies in social science, covering methodological research and comparative analysis. Includes reports of events.

301 310   GW   ISSN 0721-8516
Z U M A - NACHRICHTEN. 1977. s-a. free. Z U M A e.V., Postfach 122155, 6800 Mannheim 1, Germany. TEL 0621-180040. FAX 0621-18004-49. bk.rev.; circ. 3,000.

ZADOK CENTRE. SERIES NO.1. see *RELIGIONS AND THEOLOGY*

ZADOK CENTRE. SERIES NO.2. see *RELIGIONS AND THEOLOGY*

ZADOK CENTRE READING GUIDES. see *RELIGIONS AND THEOLOGY*

ZADOK PERSPECTIVES. see *RELIGIONS AND THEOLOGY*

ZEITSCHRIFT FUER AGRARGESCHICHTE UND AGRARSOZIOLOGIE. see *AGRICULTURE*

ZEITSCHRIFT FUER GANZHEITSFORSCHUNG. see *PHILOSOPHY*

301 340   GW   ISSN 0174-0202
ZEITSCHRIFT FUER RECHTSSOZIOLOGIE. s-a. DM.66 (students DM.51). Westdeutscher Verlag GmbH, Postfach 5829, 6200 Wiesbaden 1, Germany. TEL 0611-160230. FAX 0611-160229. TELEX 4186-928-VWV-D. Ed. Erhard Blankenburg. (back issues avail.) **Indexed:** Lang.& Lang.Behav.Abstr., Sociol.Abstr. (1980-).

301   GW   ISSN 0720-4361
ZEITSCHRIFT FUER SOZIALISATIONSFORSCHUNG UND ERZIEHUNGSSOZIOLOGIE. (Articles in English) 1980. q. DM.72. Juventa Verlag GmbH, Ehretstr. 3, 6940 Weinheim, Germany. TEL 06201-61035. FAX 06201-13135. Ed. Rosemarie Nave-Herz. adv.; bk.rev.; index; circ. 800. **Indexed:** Lang.& Lang.Behav.Abstr., Sociol.Abstr. (1983-).
—BLDSC shelfmark: 9486.375000.

ZEITSCHRIFT FUER SOZIALPSYCHOLOGIE. see *PSYCHOLOGY*

301   GW   ISSN 0340-1804
HM5
ZEITSCHRIFT FUER SOZIOLOGIE. 1972. bi-m. DM.132. Ferdinand Enke Verlag, Postfach 101254, 7000 Stuttgart 10, Germany. TEL 0711-8931-0. FAX 0711-8931-419. TELEX 07252275-GTV-D. Ed.Bd. adv.; bibl.; circ. 1,400. **Indexed:** Curr.Cont., P.A.I.S.For.Lang.Ind., Sociol.Abstr. (1972-), SSCI, Stud.Wom.Abstr.
—BLDSC shelfmark: 9486.393000.

ZEITSCHRIFT FUER WIRTSCHAFTS- UND SOZIALWISSENSCHAFTEN. see *BUSINESS AND ECONOMICS*

301   UY
ZETA. 1985. 2/yr. Zeta Ltda., Cuareim 1473, Montevideo, Uruguay.

301   FR
200 GROUPES FRANÇAIS D'AFRIQUE NOIRE. 1980. a. 1190 F. I C Publications, 10 rue Vineuse, 75116 Paris Cedex 16, France. TEL 1-45-27-30-82. FAX 1-45-20-81-74.

SOCIOLOGY — Abstracting, Bibliographies, Statistics

301 500 011   UK   ISSN 0260-0552
ALTERNATIVE ALTERNATIVE. 1980. every 4 weeks. free to qualified personnel. Dave Parry, Ed. & Pub., 3 Mason Lodge, Skene, Aberdeenshire AB32 6XR, Scotland. Ed. Dave Parry. bk.rev.; circ. 120.
Description: Covers relationship between science, politics, and religion.

301 011   US   ISSN 0740-8978
HM261
AMERICAN PUBLIC OPINION INDEX. 1983 (for 1981). a. $174.50. Opinion Research Service, 1342 Timberlane Rd., Ste. 201A, Tallahassee, FL 32312-1775. Ed. D.A. Gilbert.
Description: Topical listings of questions asked in national, state and local surveys and public opinion polls.

ARCHIVES DE SCIENCES SOCIALES DES RELIGIONS. see *SOCIAL SCIENCES: COMPREHENSIVE WORKS — Abstracting, Bibliographies, Statistics*

301 312   AT   ISSN 1032-4003
HQ705
AUSTRALIAN FAMILY AND SOCIETY ABSTRACTS. 1984. a. Aus.$85. Australian Institute of Family Studies, 300 Queen St., Melbourne, Vic. 3000, Australia. TEL 03-608-6888. FAX 03-600-0886. Eds. Deborah Whithear, Belinda Stonehouse.
●Also available online.
●Also available on CD-ROM.
Formerly: Family. Australian Family Studies Database.
Description: A computer-based bibliographic system containing references to the literature on families and family life in Australia.

301   US   ISSN 0742-6895
BIBLIOGRAPHIES AND INDEXES IN SOCIOLOGY. 1984. irreg. price varies. Greenwood Press, Inc. (Subsidiary of: Greenwood Publishing Group Inc.), 88 Post Rd. W., Box 5007, Westport, CT 06881-5007. TEL 203-226-3571. FAX 203-222-1502.
—BLDSC shelfmark: 1993.097540.

301.15   GW
BIBLIOGRAPHISCHE INFORMATIONEN ZU MIGRATION UND ETHNIZITAET. 1986. 4/yr. DM.48. Edition Parabolis, Potsdamerstr. 91, 1000 Berlin 30, Germany. TEL 030-2623085. FAX 030-2629503.
Formerly: Migration und Ethnizitaet (ISSN 0177-526X)

310   US   ISSN 0893-8504
BIO-BIBLIOGRAPHIES IN SOCIOLOGY. 1987. irreg. price varies. Greenwood Press, Inc. (Subsidiary of: Greenwood Publishing Group Inc.), 88 Post Rd. W., Box 5007, Westport, CT 06881-5007. TEL 203-226-3571. FAX 203-222-1502.
—BLDSC shelfmark: 2066.804420.

301 016   FR
BULLETIN SIGNALETIQUE. PART 529: SOCIOLOGIE. 1947. q. 355 F. Centre National de la Recherche Scientifique, Institut de l'Information Scientifique et Technique, 54 bd. Raspail, 75270 Paris cedex 06, France. FAX 45487015. TELEX MSH 203104 F. cum.index. **Indexed:** A.I.C.P., E.I., Popul.Ind.
●Also available online. Vendor(s): Telesystemes - Questel.
Formerly: Bulletin Signaletique. Part 529: Sociologie - Ethnologie (ISSN 0007-5566)

011 301   US   ISSN 0887-3569
CONTEMPORARY SOCIAL ISSUES: A BIBLIOGRAPHIC SERIES. 1986. q. $45. Reference and Research Services, 511 Lincoln St., Santa Cruz, CA 95060. TEL 408-426-4479. Ed. Joan Nordquist. (back issues avail.)
—BLDSC shelfmark: 3425.302700.
Description: Series of bibliographies on current social issues and problems.

301 016   US   ISSN 0094-3061
HM1
CONTEMPORARY SOCIOLOGY; a journal of reviews. 1972. bi-m. $39 to individuals (foreign $45); institutions $87 (foreign $93); effective 1992. American Sociological Association, 1722 N St., N.W., Washington, DC 20036. TEL 202-833-3410. FAX 202-785-0146. Ed. Walter Powell. adv.; bk.rev.; circ. 10,000. (also avail. in microform from UMI; reprint service avail. from SWZ,UMI) **Indexed:** Acad.Ind., Adol.Ment.Hlth.Abstr., Amer.Bibl.Slavic & E.Eur.Stud., Bk.Rev.Ind. (1965-), Chic.Per.Ind., Child.Bk.Rev.Ind. (1965-), E.I., Lang.& Lang.Behav.Abstr., Mid.East: Abstr.& Ind., Ref.Sour., Sociol.Abstr. (1980-), SSCI.
—BLDSC shelfmark: 3425.305000.
Description: Publishes reviews and critical discussions of recent works in sociology and in related disciplines which merit the attention of sociologists.

300 150 370   US   ISSN 0092-6361
CURRENT CONTENTS: SOCIAL & BEHAVIORAL SCIENCES. Short title: C C: S & B S. (Includes Author Index and Address Directory, Current Book Contents and Title Word Index) 1969. w. $390. Institute for Scientific Information, 3501 Market St., Philadelphia, PA 19104. TEL 215-386-0100. FAX 215-386-2291. (And: 132 High St., Uxbridge, Middlesex, UB8 1DP, England) (also avail. in magnetic tape; also avail. on diskette) **Indexed:** Compumath, E.I., Ind.Sci.Rev., Popul.Ind., SSCI.
●Also available online. Vendor(s): BRS (CCON,BEHA), DIALOG (File no.440).
—BLDSC shelfmark: 3496.209500.
Formerly: C C B S E (Current Contents, Behavioral, Social and Educational Sciences) (ISSN 0011-3387)
Description: Tables of contents of the world's leading publications covering social and behavioral sciences.

300   IS   ISSN 0334-7303
CURRENT RESEARCH IN THE SOCIAL SCIENCES IN ISRAEL. (Text in Hebrew; titles and subject index in English) 1977. q. $52. Henrietta Szold Institute, 9 Columbia St, Kiryat Menachem, Jerusalem 96583, Israel. FAX 2-437698. Ed. Shoshanna Langerman. abstr.; index; circ. 250.
Formerly: Current Research in Behavioral Sciences in Israel (ISSN 0334-2468)
Description: Contains bibliographies of scientific publications by Israeli social science researchers.

ECONOMIC AND SOCIAL STATISTICS OF SRI LANKA. see *BUSINESS AND ECONOMICS — Abstracting, Bibliographies, Statistics*

301 016   GR   ISSN 0013-2934
EKISTIC INDEX. 1968. s-a. $150. Athens Center of Ekistics, 24, Strat. Syndesmou St., Box 3471, Athens 10210, Greece. Ed. P. Psomopoulos. (back issues avail.)

318   PN   ISSN 0378-6765
ESTADISTICA PANAMENA. SITUACION SOCIAL. SECCION 451. ACCIDENTES DE TRANSITO. 1958. a. Bl.0.75. Direccion de Estadistica y Censo, Contraloria General, Apartado 5213, Panama 5, Panama. FAX 63-9322. circ. 850.

309 310   FI
FINLAND. STATISTIKCENTRALEN. STATISTISKA MEDDELANDEN. LEVNADSFOERHAALLANDEN I FINLAND/FINLAND. CENTRAL STATISTICAL OFFICE. LIVING CONDITIONS IN FINLAND. 1977. irreg. FIM 89. Tilastokeskus, Annankatu 44, SF-00100 Helsinki 10, Finland.

310   US   ISSN 0273-1037
HARRIS POLL. 1963. w. $325. (Tribune Media Services, Inc.) Louis Harris and Associates, Inc., 630 Fifth Ave., New York, NY 10020. TEL 212-698-9600. FAX 212-698-9669. TELEX 148383. stat.; index; circ. 400. (looseleaf format)
Formerly: A B C News - Harris Survey; Supersedes (1963-1978): Harris Survey Column Subscription (ISSN 0046-6875)
Description: Discusses current political issues. Contains tables with questions from national cross-section of population.

301 016   US   ISSN 0099-2453
Z7165.U5
HUMAN RESOURCES ABSTRACTS; an international information service. 1966. q. $74 to individuals; institutions $215. Sage Publications, Inc., 2455 Teller Rd., Newbury Park, CA 91320. TEL 805-499-0721. FAX 805-499-0871. (And Sage Publications, Ltd., 6 Bonhill Rd., London EC2A 4PU, England) Ed. Paul McDowell. adv.; index; circ. 600. (also avail. in microfilm from UMI; back issues avail.; reprint service avail. from UMI) **Indexed:** Curr.Lit.Fam.Plan.
—BLDSC shelfmark: 4336.435000.
Formerly: Poverty and Human Resources Abstracts (ISSN 0032-5864)

I C S S R JOURNAL OF ABSTRACTS AND REVIEWS: SOCIOLOGY & SOCIAL ANTHROPOLOGY. (Indian Council of Social Science Research) see *ANTHROPOLOGY — Abstracting, Bibliographies, Statistics*

INDICE ESPANOL DE CIENCIAS SOCIALES. SERIES B: ECONOMICS, SOCIOLOGY AND POLITICAL SCIENCE. see *BUSINESS AND ECONOMICS — Abstracting, Bibliographies, Statistics*

301 016.3   UK   ISSN 0085-2066
Z7161
INTERNATIONAL BIBLIOGRAPHY OF THE SOCIAL SCIENCES. SOCIOLOGY. Title page also reads: International Bibliography of Sociology. a. £95($170) in U.K. and Europe. British Library of Poltical and Economic Science, Lionel Robbins Building, 10 Portugal St., London WC2A 2HD, England. TEL 071-955-7144. (Co-Sponsor: Routledge, 11 New Fetter Lane, London EC4P 4EE) **Indexed:** A.I.C.P.
●Also available online. Vendor(s): QL Systems Ltd..
Description: A selective bibliography indexing monographs and the contents of over 2000 journals in the social sciences. Indexed by subject, geographical terms and author.

SOCIOLOGY — COMPUTER APPLICATIONS

301 016   UK   ISSN 0960-1546
▼**INTERNATIONAL CURRENT AWARENESS SERVICES. SOCIOLOGY.** 1990. m. £150($295) in U.K. and Europe; elsewhere £175. British Library of Political and Economic Science, Lionel Robbins Building, 10 Portugal St., London WC2A 2HD, England. TEL 071-955-7144. (Co Sponsor: Routledge, 11 New Fetter Lane, London EC4P 4EE)
Description: Lists tables of contents of sociology journals, book reviews and contents of selected multi-authored monographs. Indexed by subject keyword, and geographical placenames.

301.4 016   US   ISSN 0094-7814
Z7164.M2
INVENTORY OF MARRIAGE AND FAMILY LITERATURE. 1974. a. $99.95 hardcover; paper $49.95. National Council on Family Relations, 3989 Central Ave., N.E., Ste. 550, Minneapolis, MN 55421-3921. TEL 612-781-9331. FAX 612-781-9331. Eds. David H. Olson, Roxanne Markoff. (back issues avail.)
● Also available online. Vendor(s): BRS.
Formerly: International Bibliography of Research in Marriage and the Family (ISSN 0095-4551)

301.4 322.4 016   US
JOURNALS OF DISSENT AND SOCIAL CHANGE; a bibliography of titles in the California State University, Sacramento, library. 1969. irreg., 6th ed., 1986. $20. California State University, Sacramento, Library, 2000 Jed Smith Dr., Sacramento, CA 95819. TEL 916-278-6634. (Subscr. to: University Bookstore, California State Univ., Sacramento, 6000 J St., Sacramento, CA 95819) Ed. John Liberty. circ. controlled. (processed)

301 016   MX
MEXICO. CENTRO DE INFORMACION TECNICA Y DOCUMENTACION. INDICE DE REVISTAS. SECCION DE HUMANIDADES Y CIENCIAS SOCIALES. 1973. w. Mex.$312.50($16) Mexico. Servicio Nacional de Adiestramiento Rapido de la Mano de Obra en la Industria, Calzada Atzcapotzalco-la Villa 209, Mexico 16, D.F., Mexico. Ed. Gilberto Diaz Santana. circ. 156.

301.15 016   US
N T I S ALERTS: BEHAVIOR AND SOCIETY. w. $125 (foreign $175). U.S. National Technical Information Service, 5285 Port Royal Rd., Springfield, VA 22161. TEL 703-487-4929. cum.index. (back issues avail.)
Former titles: Abstract Newsletter: Behavior and Society (ISSN 0145-0034); Weekly Abstract Newsletter: Behavior and Society; Weekly Government Abstracts. Behavior and Society.

NIHON KODO KEIRYO GAKKAI TAIKAI HAPPYO RONBUN SHOROKUSHU. see PSYCHOLOGY — Abstracting, Bibliographies, Statistics

314 330.9   NO   ISSN 0085-4344
JV8212.Z5
NORWAY. STATISTISK SENTRALBYRAA. SOCIAL AND ECONOMIC STUDIES. (Text in Norwegian; summaries in English) 1954. irreg. price varies. Statistisk Sentralbyraa, Box 8131 Dep., 0033 Oslo 1, Norway. TEL 02-864500. FAX 02-864973. circ. 2,000.
NOTE US: news from Sociological Abstracts, Linguistics and Language Behavior Abstracts, and Social Planning-Policy & Development Abstracts. see ABSTRACTING AND INDEXING SERVICES

NOTES AND ABSTRACTS IN AMERICAN AND INTERNATIONAL EDUCATION. see EDUCATION — Abstracting, Bibliographies, Statistics

NOVAYA INOSTRANNAYA LITERATURA PO OBSHCHESTVENNYM NAUKAM. FILOSOFIYA I SOTSIOLOGIYA; bibliograficheskii ukazatel' see PHILOSOPHY — Abstracting, Bibliographies, Statistics

301   RU   ISSN 0868-4448
OBSHCHESTVENNYE NAUKI ZA RUBEZHOM. SOTSIOLOGIYA; referativnyi zhurnal. 1972. q. 2.80 Rub. Akademiya Nauk S.S.S.R., Institut Nauchoi Informatsii po Obshchestvennym Naukam, Ul. Krasikova 28-21, 117418 Moscow V-418, Russia. Ed. N.B. Polyakova.
Supersedes in part: Obshchestvennye Nauki za Rubezhom. Filosofiya i Sotsiologiya (ISSN 0132-7356)

310   US   ISSN 0193-2713
OPERANT SUBJECTIVITY; the Q methodology newsletter. 1977. q. $5 to individuals; institutions $7. Kent State University, Department of Political Science, Kent, OH 44242-0001. TEL 216-672-2060. (Ed. addr.: School of Education, University of Leicester, 21 University Rd., Leicester LE1 7RF) Ed. Steven R. Brown. bk.rev.; bibl.; circ. 100. **Indexed:** Psychol.Abstr.
—BLDSC shelfmark: 6267.550000.

301   AT   ISSN 0158-5789
PACIFIC AFFAIRS CURRENT AWARENESS BULLETIN. 1980. q. National Library of Australia, Publications Section, Public Programs, Parkes Place, Canberra, A.C.T. 2600, Australia. TEL 06-262-1365. FAX 06-273-4493. TELEX AA62100. circ. 600.
Description: Provides citations of mostly journal articles.

PEACE RESEARCH ABSTRACTS JOURNAL. see POLITICAL SCIENCE — Abstracting, Bibliographies, Statistics

309 330.9 016   JM
S E C I N ABSTRACTS. JOURNAL. 1982. biennial. $20. (Socio-Economic Information Network, Planning Institute of Jamaica) Documentation Center, 39-41 Barbados Ave., Kingston 5, Jamaica. circ. 150.
Formerly: S E C I N Abstracts.

301 016   US   ISSN 0164-0283
HQ536
SAGE FAMILY STUDIES ABSTRACTS. 1979. q. $72 to individuals; institutions $210. Sage Publications, Inc., 2455 Teller Rd., Newbury Park, CA 91320. TEL 805-499-0721. FAX 805-499-0871. (And: Sage Publications, Ltd., 6 Bonhill St., London EC2A 4PU, England) Ed. Paul McDowell. circ. 500.

SAGE RACE RELATIONS ABSTRACTS. see POLITICAL SCIENCE — Abstracting, Bibliographies, Statistics

011   US   ISSN 0887-3577
SOCIAL THEORY: A BIBLIOGRAPHIC SERIES. 1986. q. $45. Reference and Research Services, 511 Lincoln St., Santa Cruz, CA 95060. TEL 408-426-4479. Ed. Joan Nordquist. (back issues avail.)
Description: Series of bibliographies on and about the work of social theorists.

312 301   NZ
SOCIAL TRENDS IN NEW ZEALAND. 1977. irreg. NZ.$30.65. Department of Statistics, P.O. Box 2922, Wellington, New Zealand.

301 016   US   ISSN 0038-0202
HM1   CODEN: SOABA
SOCIOLOGICAL ABSTRACTS. 1953. 5/yr. $475 (subscr. includes a. index). Sociological Abstracts, Inc., Box 22206, San Diego, CA 92192. TEL 619-695-8803. FAX 619-695-0416. (Co-sponsor: International Sociological Association) Ed. Leo P. Chall. adv.; abstr.; index, cum.index: vols.1-10, 11-15; circ. 1,900. (back issues avail.) **Indexed:** A.I.C.P.
● Also available online. Vendor(s): BRS (SOCA), DIMDI (SA63), Data-Star (SOCA), DIALOG (File no.37). Also available on CD-ROM. Producer(s): SilverPlatter, Sociological Abstracts, Inc. (SocioFile).
—BLDSC shelfmark: 8319.622000.

SOCIOLOGY OF EDUCATION ABSTRACTS. see EDUCATION — Abstracting, Bibliographies, Statistics

301 015   HU   ISSN 0133-2074
SZOCIOLOGIAI INFORMACIO/SOCIOLOGICAL INFORMATION; a magyar nyelvu es magyar vonatkozasu szakirodalom valogatott bibliografiaja. 1972. a. 473 Ft. Fovarosi Szabo Ervin Konyvtar, Szociologiai Dokumentacios Osztaly, Szabo Ervin ter 1, 1088 Budapest, Hungary. FAX 36-1-1185-914. (Co-sponsor: Budapest Fovaros Onkormanyzata) Ed. Maria Vagh. adv.; bk.rev.; index; circ. 300.
Description: Current national bibliography of books and articles on Hungarian sociology written by Hungarian sociologists in the country or abroad.

301   IS   ISSN 0792-0598
TEL AVIV - YAFO. CENTER FOR ECONOMIC AND SOCIAL RESEARCH. STATISTICAL YEARBOOK. (Text in English and Hebrew) 1961. a. Center for Economic and Social Research, Tel Aviv - Yafo Municipality, Malkhei Israel Square, Tel Aviv 64162, Israel. TEL 03-262156. illus.
Former titles: Tel Aviv - Yafo. Research and Statistics Department. Yearbook; Tel Aviv Yearbook.
Description: Current statistical data on demographic, economic and social aspects of Tel Aviv - Yafo.

WORLD AGRICULTURAL ECONOMICS AND RURAL SOCIOLOGY ABSTRACTS; abstracts of world literature. see AGRICULTURE — Abstracting, Bibliographies, Statistics

SOCIOLOGY — Computer Applications

BEHAVIOR AND INFORMATION TECHNOLOGY. see PSYCHOLOGY

301   US
COMPUTER STUDIES: COMPUTERS IN SOCIETY. irreg., 3rd ed., 1990. $10.95. Dushkin Publishing Group, Inc., Sluice Dock, Guilford, CT 06437-9989. TEL 203-453-4351. FAX 203-453-6000. Ed. Kathryn Schellenberg. illus.

651.8   US   ISSN 0095-2737
QA76   CODEN: CMSCD3
COMPUTERS & SOCIETY. 1968. q. $24. Association for Computing Machinery, Special Interest Group on Computers and Society, 1515 Broadway, 17th Fl., New York, NY 10036. TEL 212-869-7440. FAX 604-822-5485. Ed. Richard S. Rosenberg. bk.rev.; circ. 1,500. **Indexed:** Comput.Cont., Sci.Abstr.
Formerly: S I G C A S Newsletter.

301   ISSN 0747-5632
BF39.5   CODEN: CHBEEQ
COMPUTERS IN HUMAN BEHAVIOR. 1985. q. £145 (effective 1992). Pergamon Press, Inc., Journals Division, 660 White Plains Rd., Tarrytown, NY 10591-5153. TEL 914-524-9200. FAX 914-333-2444. (And: Headington Hill Hall, Oxford OX3 0BW, England. TEL 0865-794141) Ed. Robert D. Tennyson. adv.; bk.rev. **Indexed:** Curr.Cont, Excerp.Med., Psychol.Abstr.
—BLDSC shelfmark: 3394.921600.
Description: Scholarly journal dedicated to examining the use of computers from a psychological perspective.
Refereed Serial

301   US   ISSN 0740-445X
HV41
COMPUTERS IN HUMAN SERVICES. 1985. q. $35 to individuals; institutions $60; libraries $105. Haworth Press, Inc., 10 Alice St., Binghamton, NY 13904. TEL 800-342-8678. FAX 607-722-1424. Ed. Dick Schoech. adv.; bk.rev.; circ. 503. (also avail. in microfiche from HAW; reprint service avail. from HAW) **Indexed:** Abstr.Health Care Manage.Stud., Excerp.Med., Psychol.Abstr., Sci.Abstr., Soc.Work Res.& Abstr.
—BLDSC shelfmark: 3394.922000.
Incorporates (in 1991): Computer Use in Social Services Network. Newsletter (ISSN 0889-6194)
Description: Explores the potentials of computer and related technologies in mental health.
Refereed Serial

INFORMATIQUE ET SCIENCES JURIDIQUES. see LAW — Computer Applications

310   US   ISSN 1044-7318
QA76.9.H85   CODEN: IJHIEC
INTERNATIONAL JOURNAL OF HUMAN-COMPUTER INTERACTION. 1989. q. $45 to individuals; institutions $105. Ablex Publishing Corporation, 355 Chestnut St., Norwood, NJ 07648. TEL 201-767-8450. FAX 201-767-6717. TELEX 135-393. Eds. Michael Smith, Gavriel Salvendy. index; circ. 400. **Indexed:** A.I.Abstr.
—BLDSC shelfmark: 4542.288000.
Description: Provides a forum for advancing the body of knowledge in cognitive and social sciences, ergonomics, and health as they relate to the use of computers.

301 621.381 UK ISSN 0959-0684
NEW TECHNOLOGY IN THE HUMAN SERVICES. 1985. q. £10($20) to individuals; institutions £30($60). C T I Centre for Human Services, Dept. of Social Work Studies, University of Southampton, Southampton S09 5NH, England. TEL 0703-593536. FAX 0703-581156. Ed. Bryan Glastonbury. adv.; bk.rev.; circ. 1,000. **Indexed:** Soc.Work Res.& Abstr.
  Formerly (until 1988): Computer Applications in Social Work and Allied Professions (ISSN 0267-1980)
  Description: Details use of computer applications, telecommunications & interactive video within social services & allied professions.

001.64 301 US ISSN 0736-6906
H61.3 CODEN: SGBUD4
S I G C H I BULLETIN. q. $45 to non-members. Association for Computing Machinery, Special Interest Group on Computer and Human Interaction, 1515 Broadway, 17th Fl., New York, NY 10036. TEL 212-869-7440. FAX 212-302-5826. Ed. William Hefley. bk.rev.; circ. 5,700. **Indexed:** Comput.Abstr., Sci.Abstr.
  Formerly: S I G S O C Bulletin.

SOFTWARE

see Computers–Software

SOLAR ENERGY

see Energy–Solar Energy

SOUND

see Physics–Sound

SOUND RECORDING AND REPRODUCTION

see also Music

789.9 US ISSN 0004-5438
ML1
A R S C JOURNAL. 1968. 2/yr. membership (includes A R S C Newsletter). Association for Recorded Sound Collections. Inc., c/o Phillip Rochlin, Exec. Dir., Box 10162, Silver Spring, MD 20914. TEL 301-593-6552. Ed. Ted P. Sheldon. adv.; bk.rev.; rec rev.; circ. 1,100. **Indexed:** Arts & Hum.Cit.Ind., Curr.Cont., M.L.A., Music Artic.Guide, Music Ind., RILM.
  Incorporates (in 1989): A R S C Bulletin (ISSN 0587-1956)
  Description: Devoted to the results of research, technical developments, unusual discoveries, discographies, and articles of general interest in the field.
  Refereed Serial

621.389 US
A R S C NEWSLETTER. 1977. q. membership. Association for Recorded Sound Collections, Inc., c/o Phillip Rochlin, Exec. Dir., Box 10162, Silver Spring, MD 20914. TEL 301-593-6552. Ed. David Sommerfield. adv.; circ. 1,100.
  Description: Provides coverage of ARSC activities, free brief notices of information desired and items offered or wanted.

780 US ISSN 0097-1138
TK7881.4
ABSOLUTE SOUND. 1973. bi-m. $38. Pearson Publishing Enterprises, Box 115, Sea Cliff, NY 11579. TEL 516-671-6342. FAX 516-676-5469. (Subscr. to: Box L, Dept. A, Sea Cliff, NY 11579) Ed. Harry Pearson, Jr. adv.; bk.rev.; rec.; rev.; index; circ. 27,500. (also avail. in microform from UMI) **Indexed:** Music Artic.Guide.

ALLIGATOR. see *MUSIC*

ALMANACCO DI STEREO. see *COMMUNICATIONS — Television And Cable*

621.389 780 IT ISSN 0393-0882
ALTA FEDELTA. 1957. m. L.60000 (foreign L.95000). Edisport S.p.A., Via Boccaccio 47, 20123 Milan, Italy. FAX 48008359. Ed. Massimo Bacchetti. adv.; bk.rev.; charts; illus.; index; circ. 73,500.
  Description: Consumer's electronic guide to audio, video and hi-fi equipment.

ANNUAIRE O.G.M.. (Office General de la Musique) see *MUSIC*

621.389 384.55 IT
ANNUARIO AUDIO & VIDEO. 1977. a. L.20000. Media Edizioni srl., Via Gaffurio 4, 20124 Milan, Italy. Ed. Edoardo Fleischner. adv.; circ. 40,000.

621.389 IT
ANNUARIO SUONO.* 1972. q. L.5300($10) per no. Gruppo Editoriale Suono s.r.l., Via Capo Peloro, 30, 00141 Rome, Italy. TEL 893608. adv.; illus.; circ. 95,000.

ANTENNA; rassegna mensile di tecnica elettronica. see *COMMUNICATIONS — Television And Cable*

AUDIO. see *MUSIC*

789.9 US ISSN 0004-7546
TK7881.7
AUDIO AMATEUR. 1970. 4/yr. $20. Audio Amateur Publications, Box 576, Peterborough, NH 03458. TEL 603-924-9464. FAX 603-924-9467. Ed. Edward T. Dell, Jr. adv.; bk.rev.; charts, illus.; index; circ. 7,000. (also avail. in microform from UMI) **Indexed:** Ind.How To Do It (1970-).
  —BLDSC shelfmark: 1787.870000.

621.389 US ISSN 0146-4701
TK7881.4
AUDIO CRITIC. 1977. q. $24. Audio Critic, Box 978, Quakertown, PA 18951. TEL 215-536-8884. Ed. Peter Aczel. adv.; record rev.

621.389 US ISSN 0004-7554
TK5981 CODEN: ADIOA3
AUDIO ENGINEERING SOCIETY. JOURNAL. 1953. 10/yr. $100 to non-members. Audio Engineering Society, 60 E. 42nd St., New York, NY 10165. TEL 212-661-2355. Ed. Daniel R. von Recklinghauren. adv.; bk.rev.; abstr.; bibl.; charts; illus.; index; cum.index: 1953-1980; circ. 10,786. (also avail. in microfilm from UMI; reprint service avail. from UMI) **Indexed:** A.S.& T.Ind., Curr.Cont., Eng.Ind., Sci.Abstr.
  —BLDSC shelfmark: 4706.000000.

621.389 IT
AUDIO GIORNALE.* 1977. m. (10/yr. plus supplement). L.25000($43) Gruppo Editoriale Suono s.r.l., Via Capo Peloro, 30, 00141 Rome, Italy. TEL 893608. adv.; illus.

621.389 IT
AUDIO REVIEW. Variant title: Audioreview. 1981. m. (11/yr.). L.70000 (foreign L.220000). Technimedia s.r.l., Via Carlo Perrier, 9, 00157 Rome, Italy. TEL 06-4180300. FAX 06-4512524. Ed. Paolo Nuti. adv.; circ. 45,000.

621.389 AG
AUDIO UNIVERSAL. m. $25. Editorial Fotografia Universal, Muniz 1327-49, Buenos Aires, Argentina.

621.38 FR ISSN 0246-2958
AUDIO VIDEO MAGAZINE. 1975. m. 477 F. Publications Georges Ventillard, 2 a 12, rue de Bellevue, 75019 Paris, France. FAX 42-41-89-40. TELEX PGV 230472F. Ed. Jean Pierre Ventillard. adv.; circ. 13,500.
  Formerly: Audio Magazine.

621.389 US
AUDIO WEEK. w. Warren Publishing, Inc., 475 5th Ave., No. 1202, New York, NY 10017-6223. TEL 212-686-5410. FAX 212-889-5097. Ed. Paul Gluckman.
  ●Also available online. Vendor(s): Data-Star, DIALOG, NewsNet.
  Description: Covers the consumer audio industry.

620.2 US
AUDIOCRAFT; an introduction to the tools and techniques of audio production. irreg., 2nd ed., 1989. $30 (members $22). National Federation of Community Broadcasters, 666 11th St. N.W., Ste. 805, Washington, DC 20001. TEL 202-393-2355. Ed. Randy Thom.
  Description: Practical, results-oriented guide covering topics from the basic concept of sound to the production of full-scale documentaries and concert recordings.

621.389 UK ISSN 0959-7697
AUDIOPHILE. Variant title: Audiophile with Hi-Fi Answers. m. $70. Haymarket Magazines Ltd., 38-42 Hampton Rd., Teddington, Middx. TW11 0JE, England. TEL 081-943-5000. FAX 081-943-5098. TELEX 895-2440-HAYMRT-G. illus.
  Formerly (until 1990): Hi-Fi Answers (ISSN 0269-9451)

621.389 AT ISSN 0816-9330
AUDIOVISION & PROSOUND. 1981. 10/yr. Aus.$40 (foreign Aus.$49). Horwitz Grahame Pty. Ltd., 506 Miller St., Cammeray, N.S.W. 2062, Australia. TEL 02-929-6144. FAX 02-957-1814. (Subscr. to: P.O. Box 306, Cammeray, N.S.W. 2062, Australia) Ed. Roger Harrison. circ. 8,000. (back issues avail.)
  Description: Effective uses of photography, video and sound in commerce and education.

620.2 AT
AUSTRALIAN HI-FI AND MUSIC REVIEW. 1970. m. Horwitz Grahame Pty. Ltd., 506 Miller St., Cammeray, N.S.W. 2062, Australia. TEL 02-929-6144. FAX 02-957-1814. (Subscr. addr: P.O. Box 306, Cammeray, N.S.W. 2062, Australia) Ed. Greg Borrowman. adv.; bk.rev.; charts; illus. **Indexed:** Pinpointer.
  Formerly: Australian Hi-Fi (ISSN 0159-0030)
  Description: Covers hi-fidelity systems and components.

534 AT ISSN 0310-8902
AUSTRALIAN HI-FI ANNUAL. 1971. a. Horwitz Grahame Pty. Ltd., 506 Miller St., Cammeray, N.S.W. 2062, Australia. TEL 02-929-6144. FAX 02-957-1814. (Subscr. addr.: P.O. Box 306, Cammeray, N.S.W. 2062, Australia) Ed. Greg Borrowman. **Indexed:** Pinpointer.
  Description: Hi-fidelity systems and components; technical advice.

621.389 US
B.A.S. SPEAKER. 1972. bi-m. $22. Boston Audio Society, Box 211, Mattapan, MA 02126-0002. TEL 617-282-8335. Ed. Mark Fishman. bk.rev.; circ. 1,500.
  Description: Hi-Fi consumer network.

B M - E. (Broadcast Management - Engineering) see *COMMUNICATIONS — Television And Cable*

BILLBOARD (NEW YORK). see *MUSIC*

621.389 US ISSN 0160-7790
TK7881.4
BILLBOARD'S INTERNATIONAL RECORDING EQUIPMENT & STUDIO DIRECTORY. a. $37. B P I Communications, Inc. (New York) (Subsidiary of: Affiliated Publications, Inc.), 1515 Broadway, 39th Fl., New York, NY 10036. TEL 212-764-7300. FAX 212-944-1719. (And: 9000 Sunset Blvd., Los Angeles, CA 90069. TEL 800-344-7119)
  Formerly: Billboard International Directory of Recording Studios.
  Description: Statistics on professional recording equipment, recording studios, recording studio equipment and usage.

BILLBOARD'S TAPE - DISC DIRECTORY. see *BUSINESS AND ECONOMICS — Trade And Industrial Directories*

SOUND RECORDING AND REPRODUCTION

620.2 UK
BROADCAST SYSTEMS INTERNATIONAL. 1982. m. £14($40) Spotlight Publications Ltd., Ludgate house 245 Blackfriars Rd., London SE1 9UR, England. Ed. Chris Spalding. adv.; charts; circ. 9,472. **Indexed:** Br.Tech.Ind.
 Formerly: Broadcast Systems Engineering (ISSN 0267-565X); Incorporates: Broadcast Sound.
 Description: Information for engineers and equipment operators on technological developments in cable and satellite transmission, video, studio facilities, and equipment, with product reviews, technical analysis, lists of exhibitions, and business commentary.

621.389 US
C D GUIDE. (Compact Disc) s-a. $5.95 per no. Connell Communications (Subsidiary of: International Data Group), Forest Rd., Hancock, NH 03449.

621 US ISSN 1044-1700
ML156.9
C D REVIEW. (Compact Disc) 1984. m. $29.94 (effective Jan. 1991). Connell Communications (Subsidiary of: International Data Group), Forest Rd., Hancock, NH 03449. TEL 603-525-4201. FAX 603-525-4423. (Subscr. to: P.O. Box 58835, Boulder, CO 80322-8835) Ed. Dick Lewis. adv.; circ. 125,000. (also avail. in microfilm from UMI)
 Formerly: Digital Audio and Compact Disc Review (ISSN 0743-619X)
 Description: A multi-category music magazine covering pop, rock, classical, jazz, folk, blues, world, country and new age styles. Offers reviews, reports on new stereo equipment and interviews with recording artists.

621.389 CN ISSN 0840-6154
C I R P A NEWSLETTER. 1975. 4/yr. Can.$40($40) to non-members. Canadian Independent Record Production Association, 144 Front St. W., Ste. 202, Toronto, Ont. M5J 2L7, Canada. TEL 416-593-1665. FAX 416-593-7563. Ed. Richard Sutherland. circ. 550.

621.38 388.3 US ISSN 0898-3720
CAR AUDIO & ELECTRONICS. 1988. m. $18.96. A V C O M Publishing, 21700 Oxnard St., Ste. 1600, Woodland Hills, CA 91367. TEL 818-593-3900. FAX 818-593-2274. Ed. William Neill. adv.; circ. 110,000.

CHRISTIAN MUSIC DIRECTORIES: RECORDED MUSIC. see MUSIC

COMPUTER MUSIC JOURNAL. see MUSIC — Computer Applications

621.389 US
CRUTCHFIELD'S CAR STEREO MAGAZINE. 1978. m. free. Crutchfield Corp., One Crutchfield Pk., P.O. Caller One, Charlottesville, VA 22906. TEL 804-973-1811. Ed. Bill Crutchfield. adv.; circ. 25,000.

621.389 US ISSN 0011-7145
 CODEN: DBSEDB
DB, THE SOUND ENGINEERING MAGAZINE. 1967. bi-m. $15. 203 Commack Rd., Ste. 1010, Commack, NY 11725. TEL 516-586-6530. Ed. Larry Zide. adv.; bk.rev.; charts; illus.; tr.lit.; circ. 20,000. (also avail. in microfilm from UMI; reprints avail. from UMI) **Indexed:** A.S.& T.Ind., A.S.& T.Ind., Comput.Cont., Curr.Cont., Sci.Abstr.
 —BLDSC shelfmark: 3535.868150.

DIANYING YISHU/FILM ART. see MOTION PICTURES

DISC COLLECTOR. see MUSIC

253 US ISSN 0192-334X
DISCOGRAPHIES. 1979. irreg., no. 48, 1992. price varies. Greenwood Press, Inc. (Subsidiary of: Greenwood Publishing Group Inc.), 88 Post Rd. W., Box 5007, Westport, CT 06881-5007. TEL 203-226-3571. FAX 203-222-1502. Ed. Michael Gray.
 —BLDSC shelfmark: 3595.543000.

DOWN HOME MUSIC NEWSLETTER. see MUSIC

621.389 US ISSN 1050-7868
E Q. 1990. 6/yr. $19.97. P S N Publications (Subsidiary of: United Newspapers Publications Ltd.), 2 Park Ave., 18th Fl., New York, CA 10016. TEL 212-213-3444. FAX 212-213-3484. Ed. Martin Porter. circ. 49,350.
 Description: Covers projects recording and sound studio techniques for the professional audio market.

EIKONOS; revista de la imagen y el sonido. see MOTION PICTURES

621.3 UK
FEDERATION OF BRITISH TAPE RECORDISTS. RECORDING NEWS. 1965. bi-m. membership. Federation of British Tape Recordists, 6 Borradale Court, Steeple Bumpstead, Haverhill, Essex CB9 7ES, England. Ed. Robin Elmore. adv.; bk.rev.; circ. 100.
 Formerly: Federation of British Tape Recordists. News and Views.

FONOFORUM. see MUSIC

FOTO-FILM-VIDEO-TIP; Magazin fuer Foto, Film und Tonaufzeichnung. see PHOTOGRAPHY

FOTOMUNDO. see PHOTOGRAPHY

FUNKSCHAU; Zeitschrift fuer Telekommunikationen und Unterhaltungselektronik. see COMMUNICATIONS — Telephone And Telegraph

GLASS AUDIO. see MUSIC

789.91 UK ISSN 0017-310X
ML5
GRAMOPHONE. 1923. m. £22($75) General Gramophone Publications, Ltd., 177-179 Kenton Rd., Harrow, Middlesex HA3 OHA, England. TEL 081-907-4476. FAX 081-907-0073. Ed. James Jolly. adv.; bk.rev.; rec.rev.; illus.; index; circ. 71,077. (also avail. in microfilm from UMI; back issues avail.; reprint service avail. from UMI) **Indexed:** Music Ind.
 —BLDSC shelfmark: 4209.000000.
 Description: Review of all major classical recordings released in the UK, plus audio-equipment news.

621.389 UK
GRAMOPHONE SPOKEN WORD CATALOGUE. 1960. a. £6($14.40) General Gramophone Publications Ltd., 177-179 Kenton Rd., Harrow, Middlesex HA3 OHA, England. circ. 3,000.
 Formerly: Gramophone Spoken Word and Miscellaneous Catalogue (ISSN 0262-0812)
 Description: Lists recordings on cassettes, LPs & CDs generally available in the UK.

621.389 AG
GUIA DE AUDIO. a. $2.50. Editorial Fotografia Universal, Muniz 1327-49, Buenos Aires, Argentina.

GUIDE TO RECORDING IN THE UK. see BUSINESS AND ECONOMICS — Trade And Industrial Directories

H.M. HEAVY METAL & HARD ROCK; quindicinale di musica specializzata. see MUSIC

621.389 DK
HI-FI & ELEKTRONIK. 1980. m. DKK 34.50. Bonniers Specialmagasiner A-S, Strandboulevarden 130, 2100 Copenhagen OE, Denmark. Ed. Aksel Brinck Jensen.
 Description: All about Hi-Fi equipment and consumer electronics.

621.38 DK ISSN 0108-4658
HI-FI AND VIDEO REVYEN. a. DKK 114.50. Bonniers Specialmagasiner A-S, Strandboulevarden 130, 2100 Copenhagen OE, Denmark. Ed. Dan Melchior. adv.; circ. 30,000.
 Formerly: Hi-Fi Revyen.
 Description: Catalogue of hi-fi products, TV sets and video equipment.

621.389 US
HI FI BUYERS' REVIEW. m. $15. Hampton International Communications, Inc., 211 E. 43rd St., Ste. 1306, New York, NY 10017. adv.

621.389 UK
HI-FI CHOICE. 1975. 12/yr. £24.95 (Europe £29.95; elsewhere £39.95). Dennis Publishing Ltd., 14 Rathbone Place, London W1P 1DE, England. TEL 01-631 1433. FAX 01-436-0350. Ed. John Bamford. adv.; circ. 35,000.
 Description: News and features on all hi-fi related topics, plus in-depth technical tests on hi-fi products.

621.389 IT
HI-FI STEREO; la rivista di musica e alta fedelta. 1988. m. L.72000 (foreign L.250000). Editore Progest s.r.l., Via Rovereto, 6, 00198 Rome, Italy. TEL 06-8441131. Ed. Giovanni B. Rodinis.

621.389 537.5 SZ
HI-FI VISION; das schweizer Monatsmagazin fuer Unterhaltungselektronik und Musik. (Text in German) 1968. 10/yr. 75 SFr. Fachpresse Goldach, CH-9403 Goldach, Switzerland. TEL 071-416611. FAX 071-413881. Ed. Konrad Kuenzler. adv.; illus.; circ. 11,000.
 Former titles: U E - Hi-Fi Vision; Unterhaltungs-Elektronik (ISSN 0379-2528)

621.38 FI ISSN 0357-0738
HIFI. m. Erikoislehdet Oy, Tecnopress, P.O. Box 16, SF-00381 Helsinki, Finland. TEL 358-0-120-5911. FAX 358-0-120-5999. Ed. Pekka Koistinen. circ. 14,210.
 Description: Directed to hi-fi hobbyists.

621.38 GW
HIFI & VIDEO MARKT; das Fachmagazin der Unterhaltungselektronik. 1977. m. S Z V KG, Schellingstr. 39-43, 8000 Munich 40, Germany. TEL 089-23726-0. FAX 089-23726-125. Ed. Wolfram Bangert. adv.; circ. 8,900 (controlled).
 Formerly: HiFi-Markt.

621.389 GW
HIFI EXKLUSIV. 1978. 5/yr. S Z V KG, Schellingstr. 39-43, 8000 Munich 40, Germany. TEL 089-23726-0. FAX 23726-125. Ed. Peter Nagy. adv.; circ. 24,000.

621.389 780 SW ISSN 0346-0576
HIFI & MUSIK. 1970. m. (10/yr.). SEK 260. Tidningen HiFi Musik AB, Frejgatan 18, S-113 49 Stockholm, Sweden. TEL 8-15-01-05. FAX 46-8612-04-26. adv.; circ. 15,000.

789.7 FR ISSN 0337-1891
ML5
HIFI STEREO; video - loisirs. 1969. m. 208 F. (foreign 304 F.). (Publications Radio-Electroniques et Scientifiques (PRES)) Publications Ventillard, 2 a 12 rue de Bellevue, 75940 Paris Cedex 19, France. Ed. Yves Marzio. adv.; bk.rev.; illus.; circ. 150,000.

621.389 UK
HIGH FIDELITY. 1977. m. £65. Haymarket Magazines Ltd., 38-42 Hampton Rd., Teddington, Middx. TW11 OJE, England. TEL 081-943-5000. FAX 081-943-5098. TELEX 895-2440-HAYMRT-G. Ed. Elizabeth Hughes. adv.; illus.; circ. 25,262.
 Former titles: New Hi-Fi Sound; Popular Hi-Fi; Popular Hi-Fi and Sound (ISSN 0309-5355)

621.389 JA
HIVI. (Text in Japanese) m. Stereo Sound Publishing Inc., Torikatsu Bldg. 7F, 5-2-5 Roppongi, Minato-ku, Tokyo 106, Japan. Ed. Katsuhiko Odakane. adv.
 Formerly: Sound Boy.

621.389 UK
TK7881.4
HOME & STUDIO RECORDING; the magazine for the recording musician. (UK Edition) 1983. m. £16.50 (foreign £19). Music Maker Publications Ltd., Alexander House, Forehill, Ely, Cambs CB7 4AF, England. TEL 0353-665577. FAX 0353-662489. (U.S. addr.: Music Maker Publications Inc., 22024 Lassen St., Ste. 118, Chatsworth, CA 91311) Ed. Paul White. adv.; bk.rev.; illus.; circ. 20,000.
 Formerly: Home Studio Recording.
 Description: Focuses on recording for the home studio, with reviews of the latest recording equipment used in the home or project studio environment.

SOUND RECORDING AND REPRODUCTION   4461

621.389 US ISSN 0896-7172
TK7881.4
HOME & STUDIO RECORDING; the magazine for the recording musician. (U.S. Edition) 1987. m. $20. Music Maker Publications Inc., 21601 Devonshire St., Ste. 212, Chatsworth, CA 91311. TEL 818-407-0744. FAX 818-407-0882. (UK addr.: Music Maker Publications Ltd., Alexander House, Forehill, Ely, Cambs CB7 4AF, England) Ed. Nick Bratzdorf. circ. 42,000.
  Incorporates (1986-1990): Music Technology (ISSN 0896-2480)
  Description: Focuses on recording in the home and studio environment. Features reviews of the latest available recording equipment and articles on techniques and applications.

HORN SPEAKER; the newspaper for the hobbyist of vintage electronics and sound. see ANTIQUES

016.789 II ISSN 0302-6744
ML156.4.N3
INDIAN RECORDS; film, classical, popular. (Text in English) m. price varies. Gramophone Company of India Ltd., 33 Jessore Rd., Calcutta 770 028, India. FAX 9133-280140. TELEX 021-5242. Ed. G. Vijayakumar. bibl.; circ. 28,000.
  Description: Lists releases of titles available on record, audio cassette, and CD; 40 per issue.

INTERNATIONAL MUSICIAN & RECORDING WORLD. see MUSIC

IRIS. see PHOTOGRAPHY

JOCKS. see MUSIC

621.389 GW ISSN 0933-0097
KLANG & TON. 1986. s-m. Michael E. Brieden Verlag, Ruhrorter Str. 9, 4200 Oberhausen, Germany. TEL 0208-20099. FAX 0208-803429.

LANGUAGE LEARNING JOURNAL. see LINGUISTICS

789.9 NE ISSN 0024-7286
LUISTER. 1952. m. fl.61. Wegener Tijl Tijdschriften Groep B.V., Postbus 9943, 1006 AP Amsterdam, Netherlands. TEL 020-5182828. FAX 020-5182843. Ed. Paul Korenhof. adv.; bk.rev.; rec.rev.; circ. 20,000.

MIX ANNUAL DIRECTORY OF RECORDING INDUSTRY FACILITIES AND SERVICES. see BUSINESS AND ECONOMICS — Trade And Industrial Directories

620.2 US ISSN 0164-9957
HD9697.P563
MIX MAGAZINE; professional recording, sound & music production. 1977. m. $46 (foreign $61). Act III Publishing, 6400 Hollis, Ste.12, Emeryville, CA 94608. TEL 510-653-3307. FAX 510-653-5142. (Subscr. to: Box 41094, Nashville, TN 37204. TEL 800-888-5139) Ed. David M. Schwartz. adv.; bk.rev.; illus.; software rev.; circ. 50,063. (back issues avail.) Indexed: Music Artic.Guide.

MUSIC AND SOUND RETAILER; the newsmagazine for musical instrument and sound product merchandisers. see MUSIC

MUSIC TECHNOLOGY. see MUSIC

621.389 AT ISSN 0814-6888
NATIONAL FILM AND SOUND ARCHIVE NEWSLETTER. 1984. q. free. National Film and Sound Archive, McCoy Circuit, Acton, A.C.T. 2601, Australia. TEL 06-267-1711. FAX 06-247-4651. TELEX 61930. Ed. Michele Parsons. circ. 3,000.
  Description: News of the activities and issues involving the National Film and Sound Archive.

NEWSFOR; moda, modi, tecnologie, spettacolo professionale per discoteche, meeting, American bar. see MUSIC

620.2 UK
NOSTALGIA. 1969. q. £2. c/o Charlie Wilson, 39 Leicester Rd., New Barnet, Herts ENS SEW, England. adv.; bk.rev.; charts; illus.
  Incorporates: Street Singer.

789.9 FR
NOUVELLE REVUE DU SON. 1953. 11/yr. 210 F. Editions Frequences, 1 bd. Ney, 75018 Paris, France. adv.; bk.rev.; rec rev.; abstr.; bibl.; charts; illus.; tr.lit.; index; circ. 35,000. Indexed: Pt.de Rep.
  Formerly (until 1976): Revue du Son (ISSN 0035-2675)

789.913 US ISSN 1047-2355
ML156.2
OPUS. 1949. q. $29.95. Schwann Publications (Subsidiary of: Stereophile), 535 Boylston St., Boston, MA 02116. TEL 617-437-1350. (Subscr. to: Box 55442, Boulder, CO 80322. TEL 800-234-3373) Ed. Paul Crapo. adv.; bk.rev.; circ. 30,000.
  Former titles (until 1990): Schwann-1 Record and Tape Guide (ISSN 0160-1571); Schwann-1, Records and Tapes (ISSN 0098-356X); Schwann Record and Tape Guide (ISSN 0036-715X)

PAUL'S RECORD MAGAZINE. see MUSIC

621.389 SZ ISSN 0253-004X
ML5
PHONOGRAPHIC BULLETIN. 1971. 2/yr. International Association of Sound Archives, Secretariat, c/o Sven Allerstrand, ALB, Box 7371, S-10391 Stockholm, Sweden. FAX 08-206968. Ed. Grace Koch. bk.rev.; bibl.; circ. 450. Indexed: LISA.
  —BLDSC shelfmark: 6465.156000.

POST (PORT WASHINGTON); the magazine for animation, audio, film and video professionals. see COMMUNICATIONS

621.389 JA
PRO SOUND. (Text in Japanese) bi-m. Stereo Sound Publishing Inc., Torikatsu Bldg. 7F, 5-2-5 Roppongi, Minato-ku, Tokyo 106, Japan. Ed. Katsuhiko Odakane. adv.
  Formerly: Tape Sound.

621.389 US ISSN 0164-6338
PRO SOUND NEWS; the international newsmagazine for the professional recording & sound production industry. 1979. m. $30. P S N Publications (Subsidiary of: United Newspapers Publications Ltd.), 2 Park Ave., 18th Fl., New York, NY 10016. TEL 212-213-3444. FAX 212-213-3484. Ed. Debra A. Pagan. adv.; circ. 19,538. (tabloid format)

621.389 UK ISSN 0269-4735
PRO SOUND NEWS (EUROPE). 1986. m. £25($50) Pro Sound News Publications, Link House, Dingwall Ave., Croydon CR9 2TA, England. FAX 01-760-0973. TELEX 947709. Ed. Joe Hosken. adv.; bk.rev.; charts; illus.
  Description: News items and features on the technological, marketing and operational aspects of the European sound production industry, focusing on tour and studio equipment and production, technical developments by country, and product surveys.

621.389 780 GW
PRODUCTIV'S HANDBUCH FUER MUSIKER. 1982. biennial. Musik Productiv, Gildestr. 60, 4530 Ibbenbueren, Germany. TEL 05451-5001-0. FAX 05451-5001-40. circ. 45,000.
  Description: Full listing of music equipment.

621.389 780 GW
PRODUCTIV'S SOLO. 1987. q. Musik Productiv, Gildestr. 60, 4530 Ibbenbueren, Germany. TEL 05451-5001-0. FAX 05451-5001-40. Ed. Heinz Rebellius. circ. 45,000. (back issues avail.)
  Description: Tests of music equipment, stories and interviews.

789.9 UK ISSN 0034-155X
ML156.9
RECORD COLLECTOR (LEICESTER). 1970. m. 35s. Heanor Record Centre Ltd., 6 Empire Rd., Leicester LE3 5HE, England. adv.; rec.rev.; illus.
  Supersedes: Record Buyer.

RECORD EXCHANGER. see MUSIC

621.389 US
TK7881.6
RECORDING ENGINEERING PRODUCTION; the pro audio applications magazine. Short title: R E P. 1970. m. $26 to qualified personnel; non-qualified $30. Intertec Publishing Corp., 9221 Quivira Rd., Overland Park, KS 66212-9981. TEL 913-888-4664. FAX 913-541-6697. TELEX 424156-INTERTEC-OLPK. Ed. Mike Joseph. adv.; bk.rev.; circ. 20,000.
  Formerly: Recording Engineer Producer (ISSN 0034-1673)
  Description: Technical and creative articles for engineers and producers of professional audio.

621.389 780 US ISSN 0199-4654
SENSIBLE SOUND. 1977. q. $20. 403 Darwin Dr., Snyder, NY 14226. TEL 716-839-2199. Ed. Karl A. Nehring. adv.; bk.rev.; tr.; lit.; circ. 7,800. (back issues avail.)
  Description: For the hobbyist and collector of audio equipment and recording paraphernalia. Also of interest to the music loving collector of records and CDs.

SHOW MEETING. see COMMUNICATIONS

SON HI-FI VIDEO. see COMMUNICATIONS — Radio

621.389 AT
SONICS YEARBOOK; Australia music industry reference yearbook. 1980. a. Aus.$1250($20) Federal Publishing Company, 180 Bourke Rd., Alexandria N.S.W. 2015, Australia. TEL 61-02-693-6666. FAX 02-693-9935. Ed. Greg Simmons. circ. 10,000. (back issues avail.)
  Description: Comprehensive listing of equipment and services available to the Australian sound, lighting, music and entertainment industries.

621.389 FR
SONO. m. (except Aug.). 45 F. Publications Georges Ventillard, 2a 12 rue de Bellevue, 75019 Paris, France.

620.2 681 US ISSN 0038-1845
SOUND & COMMUNICATIONS. 1955. m. $15. Testa Communications, Inc., 25 Willowdale Ave., Port Washington, NY 11050. TEL 516-767-2500. FAX 516-767-9335. Ed. Judith Morrison. adv.; bk.rev.; circ. 18,000.
  Description: Covers contracting, engineering, design and construction in the sound, video, and communications fields.

SOUND & HI FI/IHOS. see MUSIC

789.9 US
▼**SOUND & IMAGE**. 1990. s-a. Hachette Magazines, Inc., 1633 Broadway, New York, NY 10009. TEL 212-767-6000. (Subscr. to: Box 55627, Boulder, CO 80322-5627) Ed. Michael Riggs. circ. 150,000.
  Description: Covers videos and recordings; includes performer profiles and articles on custom installations.

621.3 778.59 US ISSN 0741-1715
SOUND & VIDEO CONTRACTOR; the international management and engineering journal for sound and video contractors. 1983. m. $27 (free to qualified personnel). Intertec Publishing Corp., 9221 Quivira Rd., Box 12901, Overland Park, KS 66212. TEL 913-888-4664. FAX 913-541-6697. Ed. Fred Ampel. adv.; tr.lit.; circ. 20,943.
  —BLDSC shelfmark: 8330.395000.

SOUND CHOICE. see MUSIC

621.389 UK ISSN 0957-9508
SOUND ENGINEER AND PRODUCER. 1987. m. $136. International Thomson Business Publishing, 7 Swallow Pl., 249-259 Regent St., London W1, England. TEL 01-491-9484. Ed. Simon Croft. circ. 8,966.
  Description: For senior audio professionals and buyers of equipment for recording studios worldwide.

SOUND ON SOUND. see MUSIC

SOUNDTRACK. see MUSIC

S

SOUND RECORDING AND REPRODUCTION — ABSTRACTING, BIBLIOGRAPHIES, STATISTICS

620.2   US   ISSN 0199-7920
TK5983
SPEAKER BUILDER. 1980. bi-m. $25. Audio Amateur Publications, Box 494, Peterborough, NH 03458. TEL 603-924-9464. FAX 603-924-9467. Ed. E.T. Dell. adv.; bk.rev.; circ. 9,000. (also avail. in microfilm from UMI; microfiche from UMI; back issues avail.) Indexed: Ind.How To Do It (1980-).
—BLDSC shelfmark: 8361.870400.

SPECTRUM (BOSTON). see *MUSIC — Abstracting, Bibliographies, Statistics*

SPIN. see *MUSIC*

780.5   GW   ISSN 0340-0778
STEREO; Hi-Fi- und Musikmagazin. 1974. m. DM.81.60. S Z V KG, Schellingstr. 39-43, 8000 Munich 40, Germany. TEL 089-23726-0. FAX 089-23726-125. Ed. Peter Nagy. adv.; illus.; circ. 113,000.

621.389 798.91   JA   ISSN 0289-3622
STEREO. (Text in Japanese) 1963. m. 770 Yen. Ongaku no Tomo Sha Corp., Kagurazaka 6-30, Shinjuku-ku, Tokyo 162, Japan. TEL 03-3235-2111. FAX 03-3235-2129. TELEX J23718 ONTOA. adv.; B&W page 336,000 Yen; color page 624,000 Yen; trim 257 x 182. circ. 150,000.
    Description: Aimed at lovers of record playing and audio techniques.

621.389   AT   ISSN 0819-0216
STEREO BUYER'S GUIDE. AUDIO YEARBOOK. 1971. a. Horwitz Grahame Pty. Ltd., 506 Miller St., Cammeray, N.S.W. 2062, Australia. TEL 02-929-6144. FAX 02-947-1814. (Subscr. addr.: P.O. Box 306, Cammeray, N.S.W. 2062, Australia) Ed. Greg Borrowman.
    Formerly: Stereo Buyer's Guide. Manual (ISSN 0312-0058)
    Description: Hi-fidelity component product reviews and buying advice.

621.389   AT   ISSN 0819-0208
STEREO BUYER'S GUIDE. C D PLAYERS, TURNTABLES AND CASSETTES DECKS. 1971. a. Horwitz Grahame Pty. Ltd., 506 Miller St., Cammeray, N.S.W. 2062, Australia. TEL 20-929-6144. FAX 20-957-1814. (Subscr. addr.: P.O. Box 306, Cammeray, N.S.W. 2062, Australia) Ed. Greg Borrowman.
    Former titles: Stereo Buyer's Guide. Turntables and Compact Disc Players; Stereo Buyer's Guide. Turntables (ISSN 0312-0066)
    Description: Compact disc, turntable and cassette-deck product-reviews and buying advice.

621.387   AT   ISSN 0819-0194
STEREO BUYER'S GUIDE. LOUDSPEAKERS, AMPLIFIERS AND TUNERS. 1971. a. Horwitz Grahame Pty. Ltd., 506 Miller St., Cammeray, N.S.W. 2062, Australia. TEL 02-929-6144. FAX 02-957-1814. (Subscr. addr.: P.O. Box 306, Cammeray, N.S.W. 2062, Australia) Ed. Greg Borrowman.
    Former titles: Stereo Buyer's Guide. Amplifiers, FM Tuners and Receivers (ISSN 0727-4459); Stereo Buyer's Guide. Amplifiers.
    Description: Loudspeaker, amplifier and tuner reviews, and buying advice.

789.9   US   ISSN 0039-1220
ML1
STEREO REVIEW. 1958. m. $13.94 (foreign $21.94). Hachette Magazines, Inc., 1633 Broadway, New York, NY 10009. TEL 212-767-6000. (Subscr. to: Box 55627, Boulder, CO 80322-5627. TEL 800-876-9011) Ed. Louise Boundas. adv.; bk.rev.; rec.; rev.; charts; illus.; index; circ. 557,640. (also avail. in microform from UMI; microfiche from MIM) Indexed: Acad.Ind., Bk.Rev.Ind. (1977-), Child.Bk.Rev.Ind. (1977-), Consum.Ind., Mag.Ind., Music Artic.Guide, Music Ind., PMR, R.G., RILM, TOM. ●Also available online. Vendor(s): DIALOG.
    Incorporates (in 1989): High Fidelity (ISSN 0018-1455); **Formerly**: HiFi Stereo Review.
    Description: Reviews and compares new audio components, reviews records: both classical and pop-rock releases.

338.4   US
STEREO REVIEW COMPACT DISC BUYERS' GUIDE. s-a. $3.95 per no. Hachette Magazines, Inc., 1633 Broadway, New York, NY 10009. TEL 212-767-6000. (Subscr. to: Box 55627, Boulder, CO 80322-5627)
    Description: Information on compact discs and players.

338.4   US
STEREO REVIEW'S STEREO BUYERS' GUIDE. 1957. a. $3.95. Hachette Magazines, Inc., 1633 Broadway, New York, NY 10009. TEL 212-767-6000. (Subscr. to: Box 55627, Boulder, CO 80322-5627) Ed. William Burton. adv.; circ. 200,000.
    Former titles: Stereo Directory and Buying Guide (ISSN 0090-6786); Stereo Hi-Fi Directory (ISSN 0081-5470)

STEREO REVIEW'S VIDEO BUYERS' GUIDE. see *COMMUNICATIONS — Video*

621.389   JA
STEREO SOUND. (Text in Japanese) q. Stereo Sound Publishing Co., Torikatsu Bldg. 7F, 5-2-5 Roppongi, Minato-ku, Tokyo 106, Japan. Ed. Katsuhiko Odakane. adv.

621.389   JA
STEREO TECHNIC/MUSEN TO JIKKEN. (Text in Japanese) 1924. m. 17140 Yen. Seibundo Shinkosha Publishing Co. Ltd., 1-5-5 Kanada Nishiki-cho, Chiyoda-Ku, Tokyo 101, Japan. Ed. Hiromitsu Nakazawa.

621.389 884.55   CN   ISSN 0833-9570
STEREO - VIDEO GUIDE.* 1972. 6/yr. Can.$10($7) Infracom Ltd., 238 Davenport Rd., No.252, Toronto, Ont. M5R 1J6, Canada. TEL 416-451-8395. Ed. Maurice Holtham. adv.; circ. 25,000.
    Former titles (until 1986): Stereo Guide (ISSN 0318-2592); Canadian Stereo Guide (ISSN 0705-1530)

621.389   IT
STEREOGUIDA.* 1976. bi-m. (plus special issue). L.19000($36) Gruppo Editoriale Suono s.r.l., Via Capo Peloro, 30, 00141 Rome, Italy. TEL 893608. Eds. G.M. Binari, D. Caimi. adv.; circ. 63,000.

STEREOPHILE; for the high-fidelity stereo perfectionist. see *MUSIC*

STEREOPHONY AND MUSIC. see *MUSIC*

780   IT
STEREOPLAY. 1972. m. L.65000. Gruppo Editoriale Suono s.r.l., Via Capo Peloro, 30, 00141 Rome, Italy. TEL 893608. FAX 896981. TELEX 621348 EDSUON I. Ed. Daniel Caimi. adv.; circ. 145,000.

620.2   UK   ISSN 0144-5944
TK7881.4
STUDIO SOUND & BROADCAST ENGINEERING. 1959. m. £24($70) Spotlight Publications Ltd., Ludgate House, 245 Blackfriars Rd., London SE1 9UR, England. TEL 01-686-2599. FAX 01-760-0973. TELEX 947709. Ed. Keith Spencer-Allen. adv.; bk.rev.; charts; illus.; index; circ. 16,666.
—BLDSC shelfmark: 8500.629500.
    Incorporates: Sound International (ISSN 0144-6037); **Former titles**: Studio Sound and Broadcasting; Studio Sound (ISSN 0039-954X)
    Description: News and feature articles on the technological state of sound engineering, with profiles, product reviews, and business analysis.

780   IT
SUONO STEREO HI-FI. 1971. m. L.60000. Gruppo Editoriale Suono s.r.l., Via Capo Peloro, 30, 00141 Rome, Italy. TEL 896977. FAX 896981. TELEX 621348 EDSUON I. Ed. Gianfranco Maria Binari. adv.; circ. 114,000.

SUPER VIDEO & AUDIO. see *COMMUNICATIONS — Video*

621.389   IT
SUPERSTEREO AUDIO MAGAZINE. 1979. m. (11/yr.). L.32000 for 12 nos. Phono Publishing Company, Via Gaffurio 2, 20124 Milan, Italy. Ed. Piero Dametti Bonetti. adv.; circ. 90,000.

621.389   UK
TALKING MACHINE REVIEW, INTERNATIONAL. 1962. q. £15. International Talking Machine Review, 105 Sturdee Ave., Gillingham, Kent ME7 2HG, England. TEL 0634-851-823. Ed. John W. Booth. adv.; bk.rev.; rec.rev.; charts; illus.; pat.; index; circ. 1,000 (controlled). (back issues avail.)
    Formerly: Talking Machine Review (ISSN 0039-9191)
    Description: Covers the history of sound recordings, discographies, artists, techniques and developments in archival-retrieval systems of disc, cylinder and other pre-CD-digital recordings. Provides histories of people and companies in the recording industry.

621.389   GW
TON - REPORT. 1957. bi-m. DM.30. Ring der Tonbandfreunde e.V., Wallfriedsweg 35, 4330 Muelheim-Ruhr 1, Germany. TEL 0208-426444. Ed. Lutz Koester. adv.; bk.rev.; circ. 1,500.

621.389   GW
TONMEISTER INFORMATIONEN. 1985. bi-m. Verband Deutscher Tonmeister, Wallensteinstr. 121, 8500 Nuernberg 80, Germany. TEL 0911-6590-482. FAX 0911-6590-199. bk.rev.

TUTTO STRUMENTI. see *MUSIC*

620.2   UK
VINTAGE RECORD MART. 1970. bi-m. £3.60. 16 London Hill, Rayleigh, Essex SS6 7HP, England. Ed. Frank K. Bailey. adv.; charts; circ. 400.

789.9   US   ISSN 0042-8299
VOICESPONDENT. 1953. q. $5. Voicespondence Club, 1711 Bellevue Ave., Richmond, VA 23227. Ed. Charles Owen. adv.; circ. 400. (audio cassette)

621.389   UK   ISSN 0309-3336
WHAT HI-FI?. vol.5, 1975. m. $65. Haymarket Magazines Ltd., 38-42 Hampton Rd., Teddington, Middx. TW11 0JE, England. TEL 081-943-5000. FAX 081-943-5098. TELEX 895-2440-HAYMRT-G. Ed. Mark Payton. adv.; charts; illus.; tr.lit.; circ. 63,100.
—BLDSC shelfmark: 9309.737000.
    Description: Hi-fi buyer's guide.

621.389   UK
WHICH COMPACT DISC & HI-FI FOR PLEASURE. m. $35. Spotlight Publications Ltd., Greater London House, Hampstead Rd., London NW1 7QZ, England. TEL 01-387 6611. Ed. Trevor Preece. adv.; circ. 25,341.
    Formerly: Hi-Fi for Pleasure.
    Description: Monthly news and review of the latest compact disc releases and compact disc players.

YINGYONG SHENGXUE/APPLIED ACOUSTICS. see *PHYSICS — Sound*

SOUND RECORDING AND REPRODUCTION — Abstracting, Bibliographies, Statistics

621.389 770 370   UK
BRITISH CATALOGUE OF AUDIO-VISUAL MATERIALS. Variant title: A V M A R C. 1979. irreg., latest 1983. £15 (foreign £18). British Library, Bibliographic Services, 2 Sheraton St., London W1V 4BH, England. TEL 01-323 7077. (back issues avail.)
●Also available online.

015 789.91   GW
DEUTSCHE NATIONALBIBLIOGRAPHIE. MUSIKTONTRAEGER-VERZEICHNIS. 1974. m. DM.720. (Deutsche Bibliothek, Abteilung Deutsches Musikarchiv) Buchhaendler-Vereinigung GmbH, Grosser Hirschgraben 17-21, 6000 Frankfurt a.M. 1, Germany. bibl.; index.
    Former titles: Deutsche Bibliographie. Musiktontraeger-Verzeichnis (ISSN 0170-1029) & Deutsche Bibliographie. Schallplatten-Verzeichnis.

MUSIC, BOOKS ON MUSIC AND SOUND RECORDINGS. see *MUSIC — Abstracting, Bibliographies, Statistics*

U.S. COPYRIGHT OFFICE. CATALOG OF COPYRIGHT ENTRIES. FOURTH SERIES. PART 7: SOUND RECORDINGS. see *PATENTS, TRADEMARKS AND COPYRIGHTS — Abstracting, Bibliographies, Statistics*

SPECIAL EDUCATION AND REHABILITATION

see Education–Special Education and Rehabilitation

SPORTS AND GAMES

see also Medical Sciences–Sports Medicine; Sports and Games–Ball Games; Sports and Games–Bicycles and Motorcycles; Sports and Games–Boats and Boating; Sports and Games–Horses and Horsemanship; Sports and Games–Outdoor Life

796.42 US ISSN 0361-347X
GV1060.67
A A U OFFICIAL TRACK AND FIELD HANDBOOK, RULES AND RECORDS. biennial. $3.50. Amateur Athletic Union of the United States, 3400 W. 86th St., Box 68207, Indianapolis, IN 46268. TEL 317-872-2900.

790.1 US
A BOLA. 1945. 4/wk. Sociedade Vicra Desportiva Lda., Travessa da Queimada 23, R-c E. 2o D., 1294 Lisbon, Portugal. TEL 01-3463981. FAX 01-3464503. Eds. Vitor Serpa, Joaquim Rita. circ. 180,000.

794.2 790.13 US
A C F BULLETIN. 1952. bi-m. $15. American Checker Federation, Box 365, Petal, MS 39465. TEL 601-582-7090. Ed. Charles C. Walker. circ. 1,000.
Description: Covers news of checker events worldwide, and includes annotated games of national tournament.

A C H P E R NATIONAL JOURNAL. (Australian Council for Health, Physical Education and Recreation) see EDUCATION

794.1 US
A P C T NEWS BULLETIN. 1967. 6/yr. $16 (foreign $30). American Postal Chess Tournaments, Box 305, Western Springs, IL 60558. Ed. Helen Warren. adv.; bk.rev.; circ. 800.
Description: Reports on annotated and not annotated games. Includes "how-to-improve" articles, computer chess, and theory.

790.1 SP
A S; diario grafico deportivo. 1968. d. Semana, S.A., Paseo de Onesimo Redondo, 26, Apdo. 383, Madrid 8, Spain. Ed. Luis G. de Linares. adv.; circ. 200,000.

796 SW ISSN 0567-4573
AARETS IDROTT. a. SEK 639. Stroembergs Idrottsboecker, Box 65, 16211 Vaellingby, Sweden.

796.9 SW ISSN 0282-860X
AARETS ISHOCKEY. a. SEK 639. (Svenska Ishockeyfoerbundet) Stroembergs Idrottsboecker, Box 65, 16211 Vaellingby, Sweden. illus.

796 FR ISSN 0065-0579
ACADEMIE DES SPORTS, PARIS. ANNUAIRE. 1965. irreg. (Academie des Sports, Paris) Editions Person, 34 rue de Penthievre, 75008 Paris, France. FAX 43-59-35-62. adv.

790.1 US
ACTION PURSUIT GAMES. 1988. m. $24.50. C F W Enterprises, Inc., 4201 W. Van Owen Pl., Burbank, CA 91505. TEL 818-845-2656. FAX 818-845-7761. (Subscr. to: Box 404, Mt. Morris, IL 61054) Ed. Brian Imada. adv.
Description: Covers the sport of paintball. Includes games, strategies, personalities, and equipment.

688.76 US ISSN 0199-4972
ACTION SPORTS RETAILER. 1980. m. $15. Pacifica Publishing Corporation, Box 348, South Laguna, CA 92677. TEL 714-499-5374. Ed. Brad Bonhall. adv.; circ. 15,900.

ACTIVEWEAR BUSINESS MAGAZINE. see CLOTHING TRADE

ADSUM. see MILITARY

790.1 IV
AFRIQUE - SPORTS. w. Abidjan, Ivory Coast.

AL-AHLY. see CLUBS

790.1 UA
▼**AL-AHRAM AL-RIYADI.** 1990. w. Mu'assasat al-Ahram, Sharia al-Galaa, Cairo, Egypt. TEL 02-758333. FAX 02-745888. TELEX 20185 AHRAM UN. adv.; illus.

796.815 JA ISSN 0915-9517
AIKI NEWS/AIKI NYUSU. (Text in English) 1974. q. $45. K.K. Aiki News, Lions Mansion No. 204, Tamagawa Gakuen 5-11-25, Machida-shi, Tokyo 194, Japan. TEL 0427-24-8675. Ed. Diane Bauerle. adv.; illus.; circ. 6,000. (back issues avail.) **Indexed:** Sportsearch (1990-).
Description: Aimed at serious practitioners of aikido, daito-ryu aikijutjutsu, and related martial arts. Includes articles on history, philosophy, and techniques of these arts.

799.202 CN ISSN 0382-4373
AIM. (Text in English, French) 1968. 4/yr. Can.$25. Shooting Federation of Canada - Federation de Tir au Canada, 1600 James Naismith Dr., Gloucester, Ont. K1B 5N4, Canada. TEL 613-748-5659. FAX 613-748-5706. TELEX 053-3660. Ed. Patrick F. Courtemanche. adv.; bk.rev.; circ. 4,000. (also avail. in microform from MML) **Indexed:** Sportsearch (1962-).

790.1 UK
AIR GUNNER. 1984. m. £18($35) Romsey Publishing Co. Ltd., 2 The Courtyard, Denmark St., Wokingham, Berkshire, England. TEL 0734-771677. FAX 0734-772903. Ed. Paul Dobson. circ. 20,000.
Description: Covers all aspects of air gun shooting.

AIRBORNE MAGAZINE; comprehensive coverage of Australian and New Zealand radio control modelling sports. see HOBBIES

799.202 UK
AIRGUN WORLD. 1977. m. £15.60 (foreign £21). Burlington Publishing Co. Ltd., 10 Sheet St, Windsor, Berks. SL4 1BG, England. Ed. Mark Bastin.

794.1 AG
AJEDREZ DE ESTILO. 1982. 24/yr. $119. Ajedrez Integral, Casilla de Correo 51, Sucursal 49, 1449 Buenos Aires, Argentina. TEL 331-6988. FAX 331-6988. Ed. Juan S. Morgado. adv.; bk.rev.; circ. 2,000.
Description: Contains almost 2000 annotated national and international games each year, theory and combinations.

794.1 CK
AJEDREZ UNIVERSAL. 1988. 12/yr. $45. Carrera 7a No. 34-61 oficina, 401 Bogota, D.E., Colombia. TEL 571-2452231. (U.S. addr.: Luis Bdo. Hoyos-Millon., 10 Bay St. Landing Apt. 6l, Staten Island, New York 10301) Dir. Jaime Lombana Ordonez. adv.; bk.rev.; circ. 30,000.
Description: Includes games, articles, news, theory, and combinations.

ALASKA'S WILDLIFE. see FISH AND FISHERIES

790 CS
ALBUM SLAVNYCH SPORTOVCOV. irreg, vol.4, 1976. price varies. Sport, Vajnorska Cesta 100-a, 892 58 Bratislava, Czechoslovakia. illus.

794.1 CK
ALFIL DAMA; revista colombiana de ajedrez. 6/yr. $25. Liga de Ajedrez de Antioquia, c/o Juan Gonzalo Arboleda, Exec. Dir., Carrera 50 No. 59-06, Medellin, Colombia. Ed.Bd.
Description: Contains selections of national and international games, "how-to-improve" articles, scholastic chess, and problems.

790.1 UK
▼**ALL SPORT WEEKLY.** 1990. w. Gallean Printers Ltd., Graphic House, 3 High St., Ickenham, Middlesex UB108LE, England. TEL 0895-679-333. FAX 0895-677-830. adv.; circ. 35,000.
Description: Covers local and national sports around the London area.

ALLIANCE UPDATE. see PHYSICAL FITNESS AND HYGIENE

790.1 GW
ALTDORFER SPORTSPIEGEL. 1972. q. DM.675. Turnverein Altdorf e.v., Ernhofen 12, 8566 Leinburg, Germany. Ed. Horst Topp. (back issues avail.)

790.1 US
AMATEUR ATHLETE. 1987. a. $2. Eliot Wineberg, Ed. & Pub., 7842 N. Lincoln Ave., Skokie, IL 60077. TEL 708-676-1900. FAX 708-676-0063. adv.; circ. 35,000.
Description: Lists over 800 running, bicycling and triathalon events in the midwest.

796 UK ISSN 0065-6690
AMATEUR ATHLETIC ASSOCIATION. HANDBOOK. 1925. a. £4. Amateur Athletic Association, 3 Duchess Place, Hagley Rd., Edgbaston, Birmingham B16 8NM, England. TEL 021-456-4050. Ed. Barry Willis. adv.; circ. 5,000.

796 US ISSN 0091-3405
GV563
AMATEUR ATHLETIC UNION OF THE UNITED STATES. OFFICIAL HANDBOOK OF THE A A U CODE. Cover title: A A U Code. 1888. a. $10. Amateur Athletic Union of the United States, 3400 W. 86th St., Box 68207, Indianapolis, IN 46268. TEL 317-872-2900. illus. Key Title: Official Handbook of the A.A.U. Code.

796.962 US
AMATEUR SPEEDSKATING UNION OF THE UNITED STATES. OFFICIAL HANDBOOK. 1930. biennial. $5. Amateur Speedskating Union of the United States, 1033 Shady Ln., Glen Ellyn, IL 60137. TEL 708-790-3230. Ed. Robert R. Vehe. adv.; circ. 3,000.
Formerly: Amateur Skating Union of the United States. Official Handbook (ISSN 0516-866X)

797.21 UK
AMATEUR SWIMMING ASSOCIATION HANDBOOK. 1905. a. £4. Amateur Swimming Association, Harold Fern House, Derby Square, Loughborough, Leics. LE11 OAL, England. TEL 0590 230431. Ed. A. Williams. circ. 3,700.

796 US ISSN 0569-1796
AMATEUR WRESTLING NEWS. 1955. 12/yr. (Sep.-Jul.). $24. Amateur Wrestling News, Box 60387, Oklahoma City, OK 73146. TEL 405-524-8551. FAX 405-524-8193. Ed. Ron Good. adv.; circ. 10,000. **Indexed:** Sports Per.Ind., Sportsearch.

799.202 US ISSN 0899-5192
AMERICAN AIRGUNNER. q. $15. Box 1459, Abilene, TX 79604-1459. TEL 915-673-6538. FAX 915-673-0404. adv.; bk.rev.
Description: Covers precision airguns; features new products, provides test reports, and reviews on air rifles.

796.86 US ISSN 0002-8436
U860
AMERICAN FENCING. 1949. q. $12 to non-members (foreign $18). United States Fencing Association, Inc., 1750 E. Boulder St., Colorado Springs, CO 80909. TEL 719-578-4511. FAX 719-632-5737. Ed. Bruce Milligan. adv.; illus.; index; circ. 8,000. (also avail. in microform from UMI) **Indexed:** Sports Per.Ind., Sportsearch (1980-).

658.8 338.476 US ISSN 0164-8136
AMERICAN FIREARMS INDUSTRY. 1973. m. $29.5. (A F I Communications Group Inc.) National Association of Federally Licensed Firearms Dealers, 2455 E. Sunrise Blvd., 9th Fl., Ft. Lauderdale, FL 33304-3118. TEL 305-561-3505. FAX 305-561-4129. Ed. R.A. Lesmeister. adv.; bk.rev.; charts; illus.; stat.; tr.lit.; circ. 27,000. (back issues avail.)
Description: Provides business and product information for licensed firearms dealers.

793 US ISSN 0148-0243
GV1459
AMERICAN GO JOURNAL. (News supplement avail. entitled: American Go Newsletter) 1948. q. $25 membership. American Go Association, Box 397, Old Chelsea Sta., New York, NY 10113. FAX 212-477-2812. Ed. Roy J. Laird. adv.; bk.rev.; circ. 1,000.
Description: Contains news and instructions on the ancient oriental game of Go (Paduk, Weigi).

AMERICAN HANDGUNNER. see HOBBIES

SPORTS AND GAMES

799.202 US
AMERICAN HANDGUNNER BOOK OF COMBAT. a. $6.95. Publishers Development Corp., 591 Camino de la Reina, Ste. 200, San Diego, CA 92108. TEL 619-297-8520. FAX 619-297-5353. TELEX 695-478.

799.202 US
AMERICAN HANDGUNNER BOOK OF THE 10MM. a. $6.95. Publishers Development Corp., 591 Camino de la Reina, Ste. 200, San Diego, CA 92108. TEL 619-297-8520. FAX 619-297-5353. TELEX 695-478.

796.962 US ISSN 8756-3789
GV848.4.U6
AMERICAN HOCKEY MAGAZINE. 1972. 10/yr. $12. (U S A Hockey) Publishing Group (Bloomington), 1022 W. 80th St., Bloomington, MN 55420. TEL 612-881-3183. FAX 612-881-2172. Ed. Tom Douglis. adv.; circ. 253,241 (controlled). (back issues avail.) **Indexed:** Sportsearch.
   Former titles: American Hockey and Arena; United States Hockey and Arena Biz (ISSN 0162-654X); Hockey and Arena Biz; U S Hockey Biz.
   Description: Covers amateur hockey: rules, profiles, referees and rink management.

794.2 US
AMERICAN INTERNATIONAL CHECKERS SOCIETY NEWSLETTER. 1970. m. $25. American International Checkers Society, 11010 Horde St., Wheaton, MD 20902. TEL 301-949-5920. Ed. Jack Birnman. bk.rev.; circ. 110. (back issues avail.)
   Description: News, game analyses, and problems devoted to 100-square checkers.

AMERICAN KENNEL CLUB AWARDS; new titles, shows, obedience trials, tracking tests, field trials and hunting tests. see PETS

AMERICAN PIGEON JOURNAL; devoted to all branches of pigeon raising--fancy, utility and racing. see PETS

636.596 US ISSN 0003-0686
SF481
AMERICAN RACING PIGEON NEWS. 1885. m. (Sep.-Jul.). $25. Wayne A. & Nancy L. Reinke, Eds. & Pubs., 34 E. Franklin St., Bellbrook, OH 45305. TEL 513-848-4972. adv.; bk.rev.; illus.; circ. 5,000.
   Description: Provides "how-to" articles, news and opinions on the sport of pigeon breeding, training, racing and showing on an international basis.

799.2 US ISSN 0003-083X
SK1
AMERICAN RIFLEMAN. 1885. m. $25 (membership). (National Rifle Association of America) N R A Publications, 470 Spring Park Pl., Ste.1000, Herndon, VA 22070. TEL 703-481-3340. FAX 703-481-3376. Ed. William F. Parkerson. adv.; bk.rev.; charts; illus.; pat.; stat.; circ. 1,453,410. (also avail. in microform from UMI) **Indexed:** Consum.Ind., Mag.Ind., PMR, Sports Per.Ind., Sportsearch.
   Description: Membership publication covering hunting, target shooting, gunsmithing, and gun collecting.

799.202 US ISSN 0734-5801
AMERICAN SINGLE SHOT RIFLE NEWS. 1948. bi-m. $20. American Single Shot Rifle Association, 625 Pine St., Marquette, MI 49855. TEL 906-225-1828. Ed. Rudi Prusok. adv.; bk.rev.; circ. 1,800.

796.91 US
AMERICAN SKATING WORLD. m. Business Communications, Inc. (Pittsburgh), 2545-47 Brownsville Rd., Pittsburgh, PA 15210-4514. TEL 412-885-7600. Ed. Robert A. Mock. adv.; circ. 15,000.

790.1 US
AMERICAN WOMAN MOTORSPORTS. 1989. bi-m. $10. Ladylike Enterprises, Inc., Box 826, Santa Monica, CA 90406. TEL 213-395-1171. FAX 213-394-5677. Ed. Jamie Elvidge. adv.; B&W page $836, color page $1810; trim 8 3/8 x 10 7/8. circ. 25,000.
   Former titles: American Woman Magazine; American Woman Road Riding; American Woman Road Rider.
   Description: Geared towards women riders of all types of motorcycles and female participants in other adventure and motor sports.

797 910.09 US
▼**AMERICA'S CUP DEFENSE.*** 1986. s-a. C D M Communications, Inc., 100 Fifth Ave., New York, NY 10011. TEL 212-243-0773. Ed. Paul Larsen.
   Formerly: America's Cup Challenge and Guide to Australia.

790 GW ISSN 0171-7243
AMUSEMENT-INDUSTRIE; Fachrevue fuer Freizeittechnologie. (Text in German; summaries in English) 1970. q. DM.40. Junfermann Verlag, Imadstr. 40, Postfach 1840, 4790 Paderborn, Germany. TEL 05251-34034. FAX 05251-36371. adv.; bk.rev.; abstr.; illus.; pat.; stat.; tr.lit.; index, cum.index; circ. 6,000.

790.1 FR
ANIMER; le magazine rural. 1966. bi-m. 180 F. Federation Nationale des Foyers Ruraux de France, 1 rue Ste. Lucie, 75015 Paris, France. TEL 45-78-01-78. FAX 45-75-68-94. Ed. Philippe G. Cahen. adv.; bk.rev.
   Former titles: Animer mon Pays, mon Village (ISSN 0244-4046); Federation Nationale des Foyers Ruraux de France. Bulletin d'Information (ISSN 0180-2410); (until 1972): Federation Nationale des Foyers Ruraux de France. Informations et Liaisons (ISSN 0071-4364)

790.1 FR
ANNEE SPORTIVE U.S.M.T.. a. membership. Union Sportive Metropolitaine des Transports, 159 Bd de la Villette, Paris 10, France. adv.

ANREGUNG; Zeitschrift fuer Gymnasialpaedagogik. see EDUCATION — Teaching Methods And Curriculum

797.21 658 US
AQUATICS INTERNATIONAL; design, management, maintenance, programming of public and semi-public facilities. 1989. 6/yr. $35 (foreign $105). Communication Channels, Inc., 6255 Barfield Rd., Atlanta, GA 30328-4369. TEL 404-256-9800. FAX 404-256-3116. TELEX 4611075 COMCHANI. Ed. Terri Simmons. circ. 30,000 (controlled). (also avail. in microform from UMI; reprint service avail. from UMI)
   Formerly (until 1991): Aquatics (ISSN 1042-9697); Incorporates (1989-1991): Aquatics Buyers' Guide.
   Description: Covers design, management, maintenance and programming of public and semi-public swimming pools, waterparks, beaches and other water-oriented facilities.

799.32 FR ISSN 1148-3652
L'ARCHER. 1848. w. (Apr.-Oct.). 130 F. (Associations d'Archers du Nord de la France) Independant du Pas-de-Calais, 14 rue des Clouteries, 62500 Saint Omer, France. TEL 21-93-73-65. FAX 21-39-72-50. adv.; circ. 750.

796 US
ARCHERY BUSINESS. 1975. 6/yr. free to qualified personnel. Ehlert Publishing Group, Inc., 319 Barry Ave. S., No. 101, Wayzata, MN 55391-1603. TEL 612-476-2200. Ed. Tim Dehn. adv.; bk.rev.; circ. 16,000. (reprint service avail. from UMI) **Indexed:** Sportsearch (1985-).
   Formerly: Archery Retailer (ISSN 0191-8427)

796.72 US
AREA AUTO RACING NEWS. 1963. w. $32. Area Auto Racing News, Inc., 2829 S. Broad St., Trenton, NJ 08610. TEL 609-888-3618. FAX 609-888-2538. Ed. Len Sammons. adv.; bk.rev.; circ. 29,000. (tabloid format)
   Description: Covers all northeast circle track auto races and all national series.

790.1 UK
ARENA (EDINBURGH). 1979. q. free. Scottish Sports Council, Caledonia House, South Gyle, Edinburgh EH12 9DQ, Scotland. TEL 031-317-7200. FAX 031-317-7202. Ed. Anita Hible. illus.; circ. 2,000 (controlled).
   Formerly (until 1989): Scottish Sports Council. Bulletin (ISSN 0142-6761)

790.1 US ISSN 1043-3120
ARM BENDER. 1971. q. $22. (American Armwrestling Association) Boss Publications, Box 132, Scranton, PA 18504-0132. TEL 717-342-4984. FAX 717-342-1368. (Co-sponsors: World Armwrestling Federation, Bob O'Leary Sports Supplements) Ed. Janne Haduck. adv.; circ. 1,500. (back issues avail.)
   Description: Promotes arm wrestling as a sport. Includes competition results, tips and tales of arm wrestlers.

799.32 UK ISSN 0144-7424
ARROWHEAD. 1958. 3/yr. membership. Society of Archer-Antiquaries, c/o Alf Webb, 5 Park Court, Bathhurst Park Rd., Lydney, Glos. GL15 5HG, England. TEL 0594-843548. bk.rev.; circ. controlled. (processed) **Indexed:** Sportsearch (1981-).
   Formerly: Society of Archer-Antiquaries. Newsletter (ISSN 0049-1187)
   Description: Contains items on archery.

ASSOCIATION FOR THE STUDY OF PLAY NEWSLETTER. see PSYCHOLOGY

796 FR
ATHLERAMA. 1962. a. 80 F. Federation Francaise d'Athletisme, 10 rue Faubourg Poissonniere, 75480 Paris Cedex 10, France. TEL 47-70-80-81. FAX 48-00-00-39. TELEX 642554. adv.; circ. 5,000.
   Formerly (until 1982): Athletisme Francais (ISSN 0067-012X)

790.1 US
ATHLETES IN ACTION. 1988. q. $6. 9815 Mason Montgomery Rd., Mason, OH 45040. TEL 513-459-9597. circ. 12,300. (tabloid format)

796 US ISSN 0044-9873
ATHLETIC ADMINISTRATION. 1966. q. $15 to non-members. National Association of Collegiate Directors of Athletics, Box 16428, Cleveland, OH 44116. TEL 800-527-8999. FAX 216-892-4007. Ed. M.J. Cleary. adv.; bk.rev.; charts; illus.; tr.lit.; circ. 3,800. **Indexed:** Phys.Ed.Ind., Sports Per.Ind., Sportsearch (1978-).

790.1 US ISSN 0747-315X
ATHLETIC BUSINESS. 1977. m. $36. Athletic Business Publications, Inc., 1842 Hoffman St., Ste. 201, Madison, WI 53704. TEL 608-249-0186. FAX 608-249-1153. Ed. Sue Schmid. adv.; bk.rev.; circ. 45,000. (back issues avail.) **Indexed:** Phys.Ed.Ind., Sportsearch (1985-).
   Formerly: Athletic Purchasing and Facilities (ISSN 0192-5482)

ATHLETIC DIRECTORY. see BUSINESS AND ECONOMICS — Trade And Industrial Directories

796 AT ISSN 0300-4600
ATHLETIC ECHO. (Text in Greek) 1961. w. Aus.$35. Petranis Press, 8 Atkin St., North Melbourne, Vic. 3051, Australia. TEL 329-6581. Ed. Jim Bakatsoulas. adv.; bk.rev.; circ. 5,000.

796 JA
ATHLETIC SPORTS MAGAZINE/RIKUJO-KYOGI MAGAZINE. (Text in Japanese) 1951. m. 8040 Yen. Baseball Magazine Sha, 3-10-10 Misaki-cho, Chiyoda-ku, Tokyo, Japan. Ed. Tadashi Otokawa.

796 CN ISSN 0229-4966
ATHLETICS; the Canadian track & field running magazine. 1976. 9/yr. Can.$16.50($19.50) Athletics Inc., 1220 Sheppard Ave.E., Willowdale, Ont. M2K 2X1, Canada. FAX 416-495-4052. Ed. Greg Lockhart. adv.; bk.rev.; illus.; circ. 8,000. (also avail. in microform from MML) **Indexed:** Can.Per.Ind., CMI, Sportsearch (1981-).
   Formerly: Ontario Athletics.

796 UK
ATHLETICS ARENA INTERNATIONAL; the international track & field athletics magazine. 1963. m. £5.50($10) Arena Publications Ltd., 325 Streatham High Rd., London SW16 3NS, England. Ed. Charles Elliott. adv.; bk.rev.; abstr.; charts; illus.; stat.; tr.lit.; cum.index; circ. 9,000.
   Formerly: Athletics Arena (ISSN 0004-6663)

SPORTS AND GAMES 4465

796 UK ISSN 0267-0267
ATHLETICS COACH. 1964. q. £9 (foreign £10). British Amateur Athletic Board, Edgbaston Hse., 3 Duchess Place, Hagley Place, Birmingham B16 8NM, England. Ed. Norman Brook. adv.; bk.rev.; circ. 1,200. **Indexed:** Phys.Ed.Ind., Sportsearch (1976-). —BLDSC shelfmark: 1765.881200.
   Formerly: British Athletics (ISSN 0068-1326)

ATHLETICS EMPLOYMENT WEEKLY. see OCCUPATIONS AND CAREERS

796 UK
ATHLETICS TODAY; the magazine that gets results. 1978. w. £39.50 (Europe £49; elsewhere £60.32). Athletics Today Publications Ltd., P.O. Box 272, 2-6 High St., 3rd Fl., Kingston-upon-Thames, Surrey KT1 1EA, England. TEL 071-547-3922. FAX 071-547-2271. TELEX 265451-MONREF-G. Ed. Randall Northam. adv.; bk.rev.; charts; illus.; circ. 37,000. **Indexed:** Sportsearch.
   Incorporates: Veteris; **Formerly:** Athlete's World; **Incorporates:** R.A.C.E; Marathon Runner; Athlete's Monthly. **Formerly:** Athlete's Today.

796 UK ISSN 0004-6671
ATHLETICS WEEKLY. 1945. w. £23.50. World Athletics & Sporting Publications Ltd., 344 High St., Rochester, Kent, England. Ed. M.F. Watman. adv.; bk.rev.; illus.; circ. 22,192. **Indexed:** Sportsearch (1976-).
   Incorporates: Modern Athletics & Womens Athletics.

796 GW ISSN 0004-6698
ATHLETIK;* illustrierte Fachzeitschrift fuer Schwerathletik. 1948. m. DM.35. (Deutscher Ringer-Bund) Athletik-Verlag, Gustav-Binz-Str. 8, D-7500 Karlsruhe 1, Germany. Ed. Werner Artmann. circ. 3,900.

ATLANTIC CITY ACTION. see BUSINESS AND ECONOMICS — Investments

796 IT
ATLETICA. 1933. m. L.30000($20) (Europe L.75000). Federazione Nazionale di Atletica Leggera, Via della Camilluccia, 703, 00135 Rome, Italy. TEL 06-326831. FAX 06-3294323. TELEX 611294. Ed. Gianni Gola. adv.; bk.rev.; circ. 17,000.

796 IT
ATLETICASTUDI; ricerca scientifica & technica applicata all'atletica leggera. 1970. m. L.30000. Federazione Italiana di Atletica Leggera (FIDAL), Via Della Camizzuccia 703, 00135 Rome, Italy. Ed. Gianni Gola. circ. 14,000. **Indexed:** Sportsearch (1983-).

796 NE ISSN 0004-668X
ATLETIEKWERELD. 1934. 18/yr. fl.117.60. Koninklijke Nederlandse Atletiek Unie, P.O.B. 567, 3430 AN Nieuwegein, Netherlands. TEL 03402-32920. FAX 03402-43044. Ed. Ria Staalman. adv.; bk.rev.; charts; illus.; stat.; index; circ. 7,000.

790.1 IT
ATTIVITA DOPOLAVORISTICHE. 1956. m. Dopolavoro Ferroviario di Torino, Via Sacchi 63, 10125 Turin, Italy. Ed. Settimo Todisco. adv.; circ. 7,000.

793 US ISSN 0092-6256
GV1570
AURORA A F X ROAD RACING HANDBOOK. 1973. a. $9.95. Auto World, 10 Green Ridge St., Scranton, PA 18509. TEL 717-346-7495. Ed. Oscar Koveleski. circ. 40,000.

AUSTRALIAN AIRSPORT. see AERONAUTICS AND SPACE FLIGHT

795.415 AT ISSN 0045-0332
AUSTRALIAN BRIDGE. 1970. bi-m. Aus.$25($29.50) (effective since Dec. 1990). Bridge Shop, P.O. Box 654, Spit Junction, N.S.W. 2088, Australia. TEL 02-960-2909. Ed. Stephen Lester. adv.; bk.rev.; circ. 2,500.

793 AT
AUSTRALIAN CHESS LORE. 1981. irreg. price varies. A.C.L. Partnership, 3 Roger Pitt St., Modbury Heights, S.A. 5092, Australia. Ed. J. van Manen. circ. 200. (back issues avail.)

799.2 AT
AUSTRALIAN CLAY TARGET SHOOTING NEWS. 1947. m. Aus.$25. Australian Clay Target Association Inc., P.O. Box 557, Mtn. Waverley, Vic. 3149, Australia. FAX 61-3-8072716. Ed. Alan J. Maher. adv.; bk.rev.; circ. 8,000.

793 AT ISSN 0819-7806
AUSTRALIAN CORRESPONDENCE CHESS QUARTERLY. 1948. q. Aus.$12 per copy. Correspondence Chess League of Australia, G.P.O. Box 2360, Sydney, N.S.W. 2001, Australia. Ed. A.O. Holloway. adv.; bk.rev.; circ. 1,500.
   Formerly: C C L A Record.

AUSTRALIAN GLIDING. see AERONAUTICS AND SPACE FLIGHT

796.41 AT
AUSTRALIAN GYMNAST. q. Aus.$21. Australian Gymnastic Federation, 2-6 Redwood Dr., Dingley, Vic. 3172, Australia. TEL 03-551-3833. Ed. Peggy Browne. adv.; bk.rev.; circ. 2,000. (back issues avail.) **Indexed:** Sportsearch (1980-).

AUSTRALIAN MOTORING YEAR. see TRANSPORTATION — Automobiles

796.355 AT
AUSTRALIAN RUNNER. 1980. bi-m. Aus.$46. 71A Burwood Rd., Hawthorn, Vic. 3122, Australia. TEL 03-819-9225. FAX 03-891-6418. (Subscr. to: P.O. Box 396, South Yarra, Vic. 3141, Australia) Ed. Terry O'Halloran. adv.; bk.rev.; circ. 15,000. (back issues avail.)
   Description: Covers track and field, road running, marathons, diet and nutrition, and training.

794.1 AT ISSN 0155-7831
AUSTRALIAN WOMEN'S CHESS BULLETIN. 1976. 4/yr. $13 for 2 yrs. Australian Women's Chess League, 139 Fisher St., Malvern, S.A. 5061, Australia. TEL 618-271-8009. FAX 618-271-3472. Ed. Evelyn Koshnitsky. adv.; circ. 300.
   Description: Devoted primarily to women's chess. Includes annotated games, biographies, interviews, and articles.

AUTO MOTOR UND SPORT. see TRANSPORTATION — Automobiles

AUTO MOTOR UND SPORT SPEZIAL. see TRANSPORTATIQN — Automobiles

AUTO MOTOR UND SPORT TESTJAHRBUCH. see TRANSPORTATION — Automobiles

796.72 US ISSN 0090-8029
GV1029
AUTO RACING DIGEST. 1973. bi-m. $22 (foreign $30). Century Publishing Co., 990 Grove St., Evanston, IL 60201-4370. TEL 708-491-6440. (Subscr. to: Box 568, Mt. Morris, IL 61054-0568. TEL 800-877-5893) Ed. Michael K. Herbert. adv.; charts; illus.; stat.; circ. 60,000. (also avail. in microform from UMI; back issues avail.; reprint service avail. from UMI) **Indexed:** Sports Per.Ind., Sportsearch.
   Description: For serious racing fans. Presents statistics and features on motorsports.

AUTO SPORT. see TRANSPORTATION — Automobiles

796.72 MX
AUTOMUNDO DEPORTIVO;* sports. 1969. m. $60. Editorial Mex-Ameris, S.A., Av. Morelos 16, Mexico D.F. Ed. Jesus Gonzalez Diaz. adv.; illus.; circ. 100,000.
   Formerly: Automondo.

796.72 US
AUTORACER'S MONTHLY. m. N L P Inc., Box 21447, Reno, NV 89515. TEL 415-848-1334. FAX 415-858-0727. Ed. Jim Crockett.

796.72 YU ISSN 0005-173X
AUTOSPORT;* specijalizovano nedeljno izdanje jugoslavenskog sportskog lista "Sport". (Text in Serbo-Croatian) 1966. w. 88 din. Borba, Trg Marksa i Engelsa 7, Belgrade, Yugoslavia. Ed. Ljubomir Lovric.

AUTOSPORT. see TRANSPORTATION — Automobiles

AUTOSPORT. see TRANSPORTATION — Automobiles

796.72 UK ISSN 0005-2647
B A R C NEWS. 1922. m. membership. British Automobile Racing Club, Thruxton Circuit, Nr. Andover, Hampshire, England. Ed. Mark Cole. adv.; bk.rev.; illus.; circ. 6,000.

794.1 UK
B C F NEWSLETTER. 12/yr. £12. British Chess Federation, 9a Grand Parade, St. Leonards-on-Sea, E. Sussex TN38 0DD, England.

B INTERNATIONAL. see GENERAL INTEREST PERIODICALS — Hong Kong

790.1 GW
B T V SPEIGEL. 1960. q. membership. Bremer Turnvereinigung von 1877 e.V., Gruenen Str. 19-21, 2800 Bremen 1, Germany. illus.; stat.; circ. 1,400.

790.1 GW
BAD AACHEN SPORT; die grosse Aachener Sportillustrierte. 1986. m. DM.30. Buero fuer Publizistik und Werbung, Juelicherstr. 317, 5100 Aachen, Germany. TEL 0241-164026-7. FAX 0241-163123. Ed. Achim Kaiser. adv.; bk.rev.; circ. 20,000. (looseleaf format; back issues avail.)

794.1 US
BADGER CHESS. 1982. 6/yr. $11. 4216 W. St. Paul Ave., Milwaukee, WI 53208. adv.; bk.rev.; circ. 450.
   Description: Covers primarily local news and games; includes theory.

796.345 DK ISSN 0005-3791
BADMINTON. (Text in Danish) 1949. 12/yr. DKK 40. Dansk Badminton Forbund, Idraettens Hus, Broendby Station 20, 2600 Glostrup, Denmark. Ed. Frede Kruse-Christiansen. adv.; circ. 6,000.

796.345 UK ISSN 0262-1940
BADMINTON ASSOCIATION OF ENGLAND. ANNUAL HANDBOOK. 1900. a. £2.50. Badminton Association of England, National Badminton Centre, Bradwell Rd., Loughton Lodge, Milton Keynes MK8 9LA, England. Ed. Geoffrey Snowdon. adv.; index; circ. 8,000.
   Formerly: Badminton Association of England. Official Handbook (ISSN 0067-2882)

796.342 JA
BADMINTON MAGAZINE. (Text in Japanese) 1980. m. 6600 Yen. Baseball Magazine Sha, 3-10-10 Misaki-cho, Chiyoda-ku, Tokyo, Japan. Ed. Keiko Miyazawa.

796.345 UK
BADMINTON NOW. 1982. 10/yr. £1.50. Badminton Association of England, National Badminton Centre, Bradwell Rd., Loughton Lodge, Milton Keynes MK8 9LA, England. Ed. Sue Ashton. adv.; bk.rev.; illus.; circ. 7,000. **Indexed:** Sportsearch (1985-).
   Supersedes: Badminton Gazette (ISSN 0005-3805)

796.345 GW ISSN 0175-825X
BADMINTON - REPORT. 1981. m. DM.30. Helmut Ruppert, Ed. & Pub., Scheffelstr. 5, Postfach 5028, 6200 Wiesbaden, Germany. TEL 0611-841194. Ed. Helmut Ruppert. adv.; bk.rev.; illus.; stat.; circ. 1,000. (back issues avail.)
   Description: Covers regional and international news. Features championships, coaching, events, and results of matches.

796.345 AT ISSN 0813-006X
BADMINTON SIDELINES. 1976. q. Aus.$12 (foreign Aus.$25). Victorian Badminton Association, P.O. Box 28, S. Melbourne, Vic. 3205, Australia. TEL 03-867-4245. FAX 03-820-9975. (Subscr. to: Badminton Sidelines, P.O. Box 28, S. Melbourne, Vic. 3205, Australia) Ed. Paul Kiteley. circ. 2,500.

796.345 UK
BADMINTON SPORTING DIARY. 1954. a. Frank Smythson Ltd., 44 New Bond St., London W1Y 0DE, England. TEL 01-629-8558. FAX 01-495-6111. Ed. R. O'Connell. circ. 3,000 (controlled).

797 US ISSN 0887-6061
BALLOON LIFE. 1986. m. $30. Balloon Life Magazine, Inc., 2145 Dale Ave., Sacramento, CA 95815. TEL 916-922-9648. FAX 916-922-4730. adv.; bk.rev.; circ. 3,950.
   Description: Covers the sport of hot air ballooning. Covers events, issues and people.

BALLOONING. see AERONAUTICS AND SPACE FLIGHT

SPORTS AND GAMES

797.21 MX
BALNEARIOS; donde ir a nadar. 1972. 3/yr. Agustin Melgar, 44-5, Col. Condesa, Mexico 11, DF, Mexico. Ed. Juan Flores Sedano. adv.; circ. 30,000.

794.1 LV
BALTIISKIE SHAKHMATY. Latvian edition: Sahs Baltija. (Text in Russian) 1960-1990 (Dec.); resumed May 1991. m. $32 (typically set in Jan.). (Latvijas Saha Savienibas) Sahs Baltija, P.O. Box 241, 226050 Riga, Latvia. TEL 0132-286-864. Ed. Nikolai Zhuravlev. circ. 10,000.
Formerly (until Dec. 1990): Shakhmaty (ISSN 0201-7822)
Description: Covers national and international chess games, opening theory, correspondence chess, "how-to-improve" articles, combinations, studies-problems and interviews.

790.1 617.1
▼**BALTIMORE SPORTS FOCUS**. 1990. m. $15.95. Capital Sports Focus, Inc., 1432 Fenwick Ln., Silver Spring, MD 20910-3323. TEL 301-587-9351. FAX 301-587-6347. Ed. Manny Rosenberg. bk.rev.; circ. 30,000 (controlled).
Description: Covers "lifestyle" sports in the Baltimore metro area.

799 CN ISSN 0045-155X
BARNET MARKSMAN. 1967. q. free. Barnet Rifle Club, 8550 Barnet Hwy, Barnet P.O., B.C. V0M 1E0, Canada. TEL 604-936-1965. Ed. Gladys E. Ball. circ. 1,000.

790.1 US
▼**BAY SPORTS REVIEW**. 1991. m. $20. Bay Sports Review, Box 4520, Berkeley, CA 94704. TEL 510-845-2062. FAX 510-444-6698. Ed. Keith Manson.
Supersedes: San Francisco Sports Review.
Description: Contains fans' responses to and opinions on sports questions and topics. Lists wagering odds on NFL, Super Bowl, NL, AL, World Series, NBA, Stanley Cup and more.

790.1 GW
BAYERNSPORT. 1970. w. DM.48. Bayerischer Landessportverband e.V., Georg-Brauchle-Ring 93, D-8000 Munich 50, Germany. TEL 089-15702-633. Ed. Rolf Hofmann. adv.; bk.rev.; film rev.; circ. 25,000. (back issues avail)

790 GW ISSN 0005-7231
BAYERNTURNER. 1953. s-m. DM.37.50. Bayerischer Turnverband e.V., c/o Georg Brauchle, Haus des Sports, 8000 Munich 2, Germany. Ed. A.D. Bauchinger. circ. 5,000.

BECKETT FOCUS ON FUTURE STARS. see *HOBBIES*

BECKETT HOCKEY MONTHLY. see *HOBBIES*

BEGA DISTRICT NEWS. see *GENERAL INTEREST PERIODICALS — Australia*

794.18 CC ISSN 1000-7679
BEIFANG QIYI/NORTHERN CHESS. (Text in Chinese) 1979. m. $28.70. Heilongjiang Qiyuan - Heilongjiang Chess Institute, 19 Heping Lu, Harbin, Heilongjiang 150040, People's Republic of China. TEL 229342. (Dist. in US by: China Books & Periodicals, Inc., 2929 24th St., San Francisco, CA 94110. TEL 415-282-2994) Ed. Wang Jialiang.

796.41 GW ISSN 0005-9358
BERLINER TURNZEITUNG. 1950. m. DM.10. Berliner Turnerbund e.V., Vorarlberger Damm 39, 1000 Berlin 41, Germany. TEL 030-7849017. adv.; bk.rev.; circ. 3,000.
Description: Information of the Berlin Gymnast Society. Contains coming events, past happenings, instructional material, and photos.

**796.082 US ISSN 0067-6292
GV741**
BEST SPORTS STORIES. 1944. a. $10.95. Sporting News Publishing Co., Attn: Tom Osenton, 1212 N. Lindbergh Blvd., St. Louis, MO 63132. TEL 314-997-7111. FAX 314-993-7726.

790.1 ZR
BETO NA BETO. w. 75 ave Tatamena, B.P. 757, Matadi, Zaire. Ed. Bia Zanda ne Nanga.

BILEN. see *TRANSPORTATION — Automobiles*

793 GW ISSN 0936-2665
BILLARD-SPORT MAGAZIN. 1923. m. DM.35. (Deutscher Billard-Bund e.V. - German Billiard-Federation) Sport-Media und Veranstaltungs GmbH, Hopfenweg 33b, 2900 Oldenburg, Germany. TEL 0441-3046051. FAX 0441-3046053. Ed. Harald Bauerbach. adv.; circ. 5,000.

790.1 US
BINGO BUGLE. (62 eds. nationwide) 1980. m. Bingo Bugle, Inc., Box 527, Vashon, WA 98070. TEL 800-327-6437. FAX 206-463-5630. circ. 938,000.
Description: Reports on the fundraising and entertainment aspects of bingo. Contains articles, photographs, stories and graphics.

051 CN
BINGO CALLER NEWS. bi-m. Can.$50. Nielsens' Publications Corporation, 19607 88th Ave., Langley, B.C. V3A 6Y3, Canada. TEL 604-888-7477. FAX 604-888-7489. Ed. Egon Nielsen. circ. 11,500.

790.1 ZR
BINGWA. w. Ave du 30 juin, Zone Lubumbashi no. 4334, Shaba, Zaire. Ed. Mateke Wa Mulamba.

796.815 US ISSN 0006-4106
BLACK BELT MAGAZINE. (Yearbook) 1960. m. $21. Rainbow Publications, Inc., 24715 Ave. Rockefeller, Box 918, Santa Clarita, CA 91380-9018. TEL 805-257-4066. FAX 805-257-3028. (Subscr. to: Box 16298, N. Hollywood, CA 91615-6298. TEL 800-266-4066) Ed. M. Uyehara. adv.; bk.rev.; charts; illus.; index; circ. 100,000. **Indexed:** Phys.Ed.Ind., Sports Per.Ind., Sportsearch (1977-).
Description: Covers judo and karate.

790.1 US
BLACK COLLEGE SPORTS REVIEW. 1979. m. $15. Black Sports, Inc., 617 N. Liberty St., Winston-Salem, NC 27102. TEL 919-723-9026. adv.; circ. 150,000.
Description: Contains sports profiles and features on Black college sports in division II and predominantly Black colleges and universities.

799.202 US ISSN 0745-1385
BLACK POWDER TIMES. 1974. m. $15 in U.S.; Canada $17; elsewhere $20. Fred Holder, Ed. & Pub., Box 842, Mt. Vernon, WA 98273. TEL 206-336-3351. FAX 206-424-9609. adv.; bk.rev.; illus.; tr.lit.; circ. 2,000. (tabloid format)
Formerly (until 1989): Then and Now (ISSN 8750-5886); Which was formed by the 1988 merger of: Blacksmith's Gazette; Then and Now; Which was formerly: Black Powder Times.
Description: Covers shooting, history and blacksmithing.

793 510 US
BLACKJACK FORUM. 1981. q. $30. R G E Publishing, 414 Santa Clara Ave., Oakland, CA 94610. TEL 510-465-6452. FAX 510-652-4330. Ed. Arnold Snyder. adv.; bk.rev.; charts; stat.; circ. controlled. (back issues avail.)

790.1 GW
BLAU GELB. 1975. bi-m. Sportgemeinde Weiterstadt 1886 e.V., Am Aulenberg 2, 6108 Weiterstadt, Germany. TEL 06150-3886. circ. 2,000. (looseleaf format)

790 FR ISSN 0045-2289
BLEU ET ROUGE;* le sport a Paris. 1902. 2/yr. 60 F. Edisport, 2 rue du Commandant-Guilband, 75016 Paris, France. Ed. Didier Dorsemaine. adv.; bk.rev.; film rev.; play rev.; circ. 15,000.

794.1 US
BLITZ CHESS. 1988. 4/yr. $25 (membership). World Blitz Chess Association, 8 Parnassus Rd., Berkeley, CA 94707. TEL 510-549-1169. FAX 510-486-8078. Ed. Walter S. Browne. adv.
Description: Features blitz (5-minute) games, crosstables, historical articles and quarterly rating list, upcoming events.

371.7 US
BLUE BOOK OF COLLEGE ATHLETICS OF SENIOR, JUNIOR AND COMMUNITY COLLEGES. 1930. a. $24.95. Athletic Publishing Co., Box 931, Montgomery, AL 36101-0931. FAX 205-263-4436. Ed. Allen Dees. adv.; circ. 5,000.
Formerly: Blue Book of College Athletics; Incorporates (1958-1988): Blue Book of Junior and Community College Athletics.

BLUE LIFE. see *GERONTOLOGY AND GERIATRICS*

796.8 CC
BO JI/TECHNIQUE OF SELF-DEFENSE. (Text in Chinese) m. $36.80. Shanxi Sheng Tiyu Yundong Weiyuanhui, 7, Tiyu Lu, Dayingpan, Taiyuan, Shanxi 030012, People's Republic of China. TEL 775310. (Dist. in US by: China Books & Periodicals, Inc., 2929 24th St., San Frnacisco, CA 94110. TEL 415-282-2994) Zhang Dakang.

790.1 US
BOB WATKINS SPORTS 24 MAGAZINE. 1989. m. $2 per no. Bob Watkins, Ed. & Pub., Box 124, Glendale, KY 42740. TEL 502-737-5585.
Description: Feature articles on people in sports, short features on local, regional and state athletic events, as well as opinion pieces.

790.1 IO
BOLA. w. Jalan Palmerah Selatan 17, Jakarta 10270, Indonesia. TEL 021-5483008. Ed. Hikmat Kusumaningrat. circ. 407,850.

790.1 BO
BOLIVIA EN EL DEPORTE.* q. Secretaria General de Deportes, La Paz, Bolivia. Ed. Enrique Sanchez. charts; illus.; stat.

796.72 US
BONNEVILLE RACING NEWS. m. 35549 W. Stetson, Hemet, CA 92343. TEL 714-926-2277. FAX 714-926-4619. Ed. Wendy Jeffries. circ. 20,000.

790.1 US
BOSTON BRUINS YEARBOOK. a. $7.50. Phoenix Media - Communications Group, c/o Stephen M. Mindich, 126 Brookline Ave, Boston, MA 02215. TEL 617-536-5390. FAX 617-536-1463. Ed. Christopher Young. circ. 75,000.

790 US
BOSTON MARATHON. 1979. a. $4. Phoenix Media - Communications Group, c/o Stephen M. Mindich, 126 Brookline Ave., Boston, MA 02215. TEL 617-536-5390. FAX 617-536-1463. Ed. Peter Kadais. adv.; circ. 116,800.

799.32 CN ISSN 0827-2638
BOWBENDER; Canada's archery magazine. 1984. 6/yr. Can.$15($20) Consolidated Communications, 807 Manning Rd., N.E., Ste. 200, Calgary, Alta. T2E 7M8, Canada. TEL 403-569-9520. FAX 403-569-9590. Ed. Kathleen Windsor. adv.; bk.rev.; stat.; tr.lit.; circ. 44,792. (back issues avail.)

794 US ISSN 0164-9183
BOWLERS JOURNAL.* 1913. m. $18. (Billiards and Bowling Institute of America) National Bowlers Journal, Inc., 200 S. Michigan Ave., Ste. 1430, Chicago, IL 60604. Ed. Mort Luby, Jr. adv.; bk.rev.; charts; illus.; stat.; circ. 20,000. **Indexed:** Phys.Ed.Ind., Sports Per.Ind., Sportsearch (1978-).
Former titles: National Bowlers Journal and Billiard Revue (ISSN 0027-8793); Bowlers Journal and Billiard Revue (ISSN 0006-8411)

790.1 US ISSN 8750-3603
BOWLING DIGEST. 1983. bi-m. $18 (foreign $30). Century Publishing Co., 990 Grove St., Evanston, IL 60201. TEL 708-491-6440. (Subscr. to: Box 570, Mt. Morris, IL 61054-0570. TEL 800-877-5893) Ed. Michael K. Herbert. adv.; charts; illus.; stat.; tr.lit.; circ. 110,000. (also avail. in microfilm; microfiche; back issues avail.) **Indexed:** Sports Per.Ind., Sportsearch (1985-).
Description: For serious bowling fans and participants. Presents statistics, features, and instructional tips behind the sport.

796.3 MX ISSN 0006-8470
BOX Y LUCHA; el mundo del ring. 1951. w. Mex.$832($29.29) Periodismo Especializado, S. A., Presidentes 187, Col. Portales, Mexico 13 D.F., Mexico. Ed. Antonio Elizarraras Corona. illus.

**796.83 IT ISSN 0006-8497
TS1200.A1**
BOXE RING. 1952. m. $70 (foreign $90). Flaminia Editrice, Via A. Pollaiolo, 3, 00197 Rome, Italy. illus.; circ. 30,000.

790.1 SW
BOXING. 6/yr. (Svenska Boxningsfoerbundet) Cewe Foerlaget, Box 77, 890 10 Bjaesta, Sweden. adv.; circ. 4,100.

SPORTS AND GAMES

796.332   GH
BOXING AND FOOTBALL ILLUSTRATED. 1976. m. POB 8392, Accra, Ghana. Ed. Nana O. Ampomah. circ. 10,000.

796.83   JA
BOXING MAGAZINE. (Text in Japanese) 1956. m. 8040 Yen. Baseball Magazine Sha, 3-10-10 Misaki-cho, Chiyoda-ku, Tokyo, Japan. Ed. Isao Hara.

796.83   UK
BOXING MONTHLY. m. £24($38) Greenflex Association, 24 Nottinghill Gate, London, England. FAX 81-727-5442. adv.; circ. 20,763.
   Description: Focuses on big American and British personalities and up and coming prospects.

796.83   UK   ISSN 0006-8519
BOXING NEWS. 1909. w. £60. R & D Publications Ltd., 30-34 Langham St., London W1N 5LB, England. TEL 071-580-9257. FAX 071-436-8268. Ed. Harry Mullan. adv.; bk.rev.; circ. 75,000. (tabloid format)
   Indexed: Sportsearch.

796.83   US
BOXING U S A. 1981. bi-m. $20. U S A Amateur Boxing Federation, 1750 E. Boulder St., Colorado Springs, CO 80909. TEL 719-578-4506. circ. 23,000. (tabloid format)

796.41   US   ISSN 0160-3280
GV461
BOYS GYMNASTICS RULEBOOK. a. $3.00. National Federation of State High School Associations, 11724 N.W. Plaza Circle, Box 20626, Kansas City, MO 64195-0626. TEL 816-464-5400. FAX 816-464-5571.

BRAILLE CHESS MAGAZINE. see *HANDICAPPED — Visually Impaired*

794.1   IC
BREFSKAKTIDINDI. 1979. irreg. (3-4/yr.). $16. Icelandic Correspondence Chess Federation, Grettisgata 42 B, IS-101 Reykjavik, Iceland. (Subscr. to: c/o Haimes Olafsson, Gen. Sec., Austvadsholti, 851 Hella, Iceland) Ed. Gunnar Hannesson. adv.; circ. 200.

790.1   GW   ISSN 0932-8823
GV428
BRENNPUNKTE DER SPORTWISSENSCHAFT. s-a. DM.39.50. (Deutsche Sport Hochschule Koeln) Academia Verlag GmbH, Postfach 1663, 5205 St. Augustin 1, Germany. TEL 02241-333349. FAX 02241-341528.
   Formerly: Jahrbuecher der Deutschen Sporthochschule Koeln.
   Description: Aimed at sports scientists, coaches and students.

795.414   NE   ISSN 0006-9825
BRIDGE. 1930. m. fl.63. Nederlandse Bridge Bond, c/o A. Boekhorst, Ed., Willem Dreeslaan 55, 3515 GB Utrecht, Netherlands. TEL 030-712644. FAX 030-711482. adv.; bk.rev.; charts; illus.; circ. 85,000.

795.414   UK
BRIDGE. 1926. m. $44.95. Maxwell Macmillan Chess & Bridge, London Rd., Wheatley, Oxford OX9 1YR, England. TEL 08677-4111. FAX 08677-5383. Ed. Paul Lamford. adv.; bk.rev.; illus.; index; circ. 10,000.
   Former titles: Bridge International; Bridge Magazine (ISSN 0006-9868); Incorporates: British Bridge World.
   Description: Contains articles on bidding and play, instruction competitions, tournament reports and humour.

795.414   SA
BRIDGE S A. 1954. 4/yr. R.30($30) to non-members. South African Bridge Federation, P.O. Box 890347, Lyndhurst 2106, South Africa. FAX 011-4406435. Ed. Julius Butkow. adv.; bk.rev.; circ. 2,500 (controlled). (tabloid format)
   Former titles (until 1989): South African Bridge Bulletin; (until 1979): Bridge Bulletin (ISSN 0006-9841)

795.414   US   ISSN 1043-6383
BRIDGE TODAY; the magazine for people who love to play bridge. 1988. 6/yr. $21 (foreign $29). Granovetter Books, 18 Village View Bluff, Ballston Lake, NY 12019. TEL 518-899-6670. FAX 518-899-7254. Eds. Pamela and Matthew Granovetter. circ. 5,000.

795.414   US   ISSN 0006-9876
BRIDGE WORLD. 1929. m. $36. Bridge World Magazine Inc., 39 W. 94th St., New York, NY 10025. TEL 212-866-5860. Eds. Edgar Kaplan, Jeff Rubens. adv.; bk.rev.; illus.; circ. 9,500. (back issues avail.)

795.414   FR   ISSN 0006-9914
BRIDGEUR. 1959. m. 410 F. Editions de Presse Specialisee, 28 Rue de Richelieu, 75001 Paris, France. TEL 1-42-96-25-00. FAX 1-40-20-92-34. Ed. J.P. Meyer. adv.; bk.rev.; illus.; circ. 30,000.

799.32   UK   ISSN 0007-0289
BRITISH ARCHER; devoted to the fast growing sport of archery. 1949. 6/yr. £8.80. B.A. Publishing Co. Ltd., 43-45 Milford Rd., Reading RG1 8LG, England. FAX 0734-583899. Ed. John Histead. adv.; bk.rev.; illus.; circ. 3,000. **Indexed:** Sportsearch (1977-).
   Incorporates: British Field Archer.

794.1   UK   ISSN 0007-0440
GV1313
BRITISH CHESS MAGAZINE. 1881. m. £46.50. British Chess Magazine Ltd., 9 Market St., St. Leonards on Sea, E. Sussex TN38 0DQ, England. FAX 0424-435439. Ed. Bernard Cafferty. adv.; bk.rev.; illus.; index; circ. 4,000.

796   UK   ISSN 0068-1938
GV1049
BRITISH CYCLING FEDERATION. HANDBOOK. 1959. a. £3. British Cycling Federation, 36 Rockingham Rd., Kettering, Northants NN16 8HG, England. TEL 0536-412211. FAX 0536-412142. Ed. James D. Hendry. adv.; circ. 10,000.
   Formerly: British Cycling Federation. Racing Handbook.

BRITISH HEALTH & FITNESS CLUB DIRECTORY. see *BUSINESS AND ECONOMICS — Trade And Industrial Directories*

598.2   UK   ISSN 0007-0777
BRITISH HOMING WORLD. 1933. w. £26.50. Royal Pigeon Racing Association, Severn Farm Industrial Estate, Severn Rd., Welshpool, Powys SY21 7DF, Wales. TEL 0938-552360. Ed. D.D. Glover. adv.; bk.rev.

BRITISH LEISURE & SWIMMING POOL DIRECTORY. see *BUSINESS AND ECONOMICS — Trade And Industrial Directories*

BRITISH LEISURE CENTRE DIRECTORY. see *BUSINESS AND ECONOMICS — Trade And Industrial Directories*

790.1   UK
BRITISH OLYMPIC ASSOCIATION DIARY. a. £8.50. British Olympic Association, Wandsworth Plain, London SW18 1EH, England. TEL 081-871-2677. FAX 081-871-9104. TELEX 932312-BOA-G. circ. 1,000.
   Formerly: British Olympic Association Year Book and Diary.

BRITISH OUTDOOR AMENITIES DIRECTORY. see *BUSINESS AND ECONOMICS — Trade And Industrial Directories*

796.72   UK   ISSN 0045-3137
BRITISH RACING NEWS. 1970. bi-m. membership. British Racing & Sports Car Club, Brands Hatch Circuit, Fawkham, Dartford, Kent DA3 8NH, England. Ed. John Nicol. adv.; bk.rev.; charts; illus.; stat.; circ. 4,000 (controlled). (tabloid format)

BROKEN SPOKE. see *TRANSPORTATION — Automobiles*

790.1   SW
BROTTNING. m. (8/yr.). SEK 371. (Svenska Brottningsfoerbundet) Cewe Foerlaget, Box 77, 890 10 Bjaesta, Sweden. (Subscr. to: PK-Banken. Box 365, 891 01 Oernskoeldsvik, Sweden) adv.; circ. 6,600.

796.41   DK   ISSN 0903-5524
BRYDNING/WRESTLING. 1972. 4/yr. DKK 75. Dansk Atlet Union, P.O. Box 183, DK-3520 Farum, Denmark. FAX 45-42-123951. TELEX 33 111 IDRAET DK. Ed. B. Elberg. adv.; bk.rev.; illus.; circ. 1,500.
   Former titles: D A U Bladet (ISSN 0108-9013); Dansk Atlet Union, Landdsorganisation for Brydning (ISSN 0108-8998)

796.815   NE
BUDO KOERIER. 1952. bi-m. fl.10. Nederlandse Judo Ju-Jitsu Associatie, Boomstraat 153, Tilburg, Netherlands. Ed. P.F. Beljaars.
   Formerly (until 1975): Judo-Koerier (ISSN 0047-2980)

790.1   GW   ISSN 0723-9297
BUDO UND TRANSKULTURELLE BEWEGUNGSFORSCHUNG. 1983. irreg., vol.11, 1987. price varies. Verlag Ingrid Czwalina, Reesenbuettler Redder 75, 2070 Ahrensburg, Germany. TEL 04102-59190. FAX 04102-50992. Ed. Horst Tiwald.

796   SP
BUDOKA Y SU REVISTA DE LAS ARTES MARCIALES. 1972. 11/yr. 2475 ptas.($30) Editorial Alas, Valencia 234, P.O. Box 36274, 08007 Barcelona, Spain. FAX 3-4537506. adv.; bk.rev.; circ. 12,000.
   Formerly: Revista de las Artes Marciales.

LA BUSCA. see *BIBLIOGRAPHIES*

790.1 330   US
BUSINESS OF SPORTS.* 1989. m. $4. 722 Ounwoodie Dr., Cincinnati, OH 45230-3905. TEL 513-241-3741. Ed. Bill Dorsey. circ. 50,000 (controlled).
   Description: For corporate Americans who are sports enthusiasts. Focuses on sports aspects of law, medicine and finance.

790.1   CN
C A B A NEWS BULLETIN. bi-m. Canadian Amateur Boxing Association, 333 River Road, Vanier, Ont. K1L 8H9, Canada. TEL 613-748-5608.

790.1   AT   ISSN 1033-0526
C A M S MANUAL OF MOTOR SPORT. 1959. a. Aus.$20. Confederation of Australian Motor Sport, P.O. Box 441, 382 Burke Rd., Camberwell, Vic. 3124, Australia. TEL 61-3-889-3746. FAX 61-3-809-1862. Ed. John A. Keeffe. adv.; circ. 12,500. (back issues avail.)
   Description: Motor sport rules and policy for Australia. Covers rallies, race and club sport. Historical record of championships for reference and contemporary use.

790.1   AT
C A M S REPORT. 1966. q. Aus.$10. Confederation of Australian Motor Sport, 382 Burke Rd., Camberwell, Vic. 3124, Australia. TEL 61-3-889-3746. FAX 61-3-809-1862. Ed. J.A. Keeffe. adv.; bk.rev.; circ. 14,000. (back issues avail.)

794.1   AT
C Q CHESS NEWS. 4/yr. $8. Rockhampton Chess Club, P.O. Box 1361, Rockhampton, Qld. 4700, Australia. Ed. Ian Murray. adv.
   Description: Includes regional news and games, articles.

790.1   US
C S S S DIGEST. 1989. q. Center for the Study of Sport in Society, Northeastern University, 271 Huntington Ave., Ste. 244, Boston, MA 02115. TEL 617-437-5815. FAX 617-437-5830.

790.1 384.554   US
CABLESPORTS NEWSLETTER. 1983. w. $325. Q V Publishing, Inc., Meadowbrook Office Park, Box 2000, York, ME 03909. TEL 207-363-6222. FAX 207-363-6182. Ed. Dantia Gould. adv. (back issues avail.)
   Former titles: Cable - Television Sports Newsletter; Cablesports Newsletter.
   Description: Covers trends in the televising of sports.

796.5   UK   ISSN 0068-5267
CAIRNGORM CLUB JOURNAL. 1889. biennial, no.101, 1988. £2.50. Cairngorm Club, c/o Secretary R.C. Shirreffs, 18 Bon-Accord Square, Aberdeen AB9 1YE, Scotland. Ed. A.D. Chessell. adv.; bk.rev.; index; circ. 450.

4468 SPORTS AND GAMES

794.1 US
CAISSA'S CHESS NEWS. 1983. 6/yr. $10. Box 09091, Cleveland, OH 44109-0091. Ed. E.A. Furst.
  Description: Devoted to chess combinations featuring tactical themes and check-mates.

794.1 US
CALIFORNIA CHESS JOURNAL. 1987. 6/yr. $15. 2724 Channing Way, Ste. 103, Berkeley, CA 94704. Ed. Peter Yu. adv.; bk.rev. (avail. on diskette)
  Description: Includes "how-to-improve" articles, endgame and opening theory, and master games and analysis; provides local, national and international chess coverage.

790.1 US
CALIFORNIA CITYSPORTS MAGAZINE. 1974. m. CitySports, Inc. of California, Box 3695, San Francisco, CA 94119. TEL 415-546-6150.
  Supersedes in part (in 1988): CitySports Magazine.
  Description: Covers all aspects of the California active lifestyle and participant (not professional) sports, including travel, recreation, nutrition and health, and profiles.

CAMPING-CAR. see TRANSPORTATION

796.5 AU
CAMPING REVUE; Magazin des Oesterreichischen Camping Clubs. 1967. 6/yr. membership. Oesterreichischer Camping Club, Johannesgasse 20, 1010 Vienna, Austria. FAX 7131807. TELEX 133907B-AUTO-A. Ed. Guenter Wiesinger. adv.; bk.rev.; abstr.; charts; illus.; stat.; circ. 10,000.
  Former titles: Sport Review; Oesterreichische Camping Revue; Oesterreichische Camping and Caravaning Revue (ISSN 0029-8972); Camping und Sport Revue.

799.32 CN
CANADIAN ARCHER. (Text in English and French) 1955. m. Can.$25($35) Federation of Canadian Archers, 1600 James Naismith Dr., Gloucester, Ont. K1B 5N4, Canada. TEL 613-748-5604. FAX 613-748-5785. TELEX 053-3660. Ed. Andrew Martin. adv.; bk.rev.; circ. 1,000. (processed)
  Indexed: Sportsearch.
  Former titles: F C A Official Newsletter; Canadian Archer (ISSN 0319-2571); (until March 1974): Federation of Canadian Archers. Official Bulletin (ISSN 0014-9454)

796 CN ISSN 0045-4427
CANADIAN ATHLETIC DIRECTOR AND COACH.* 1970. 6/yr. Can.$6. William B. Prentice & Associates, 30 Longwood Dr., Don Mills, Ont., Canada.

794.1 CN ISSN 0045-4540
CANADIAN CHESS CHAT. 1946. 6/yr. Can.$16. Glenquaich Press Limited, 51 Osborne Ave., Toronto, Ont. M4E 3A8, Canada. Ed. Michael D. Sharpe. bk.rev.; circ. 5,000.
  Description: Covers national and international games, correspondence chess, endgame studies and opening theory.

613.7 796 370 CN
CANADIAN JOURNAL OF HISTORY OF SPORT/REVUE CANADIENNE DE L'HISTOIRE DES SPORTS. (Text in English, French) 1970. s-a. Can.$12. University of Windsor, Faculty of Human Kinetics, Windsor, Ont. N9B 3P4, Canada. Eds. A. Metcalfe, M.A. Salter. bk.rev.; bibl.; circ. 500. Indexed: Amer.Hist.& Life, Can.Wom.Per.Ind., Hist.Abstr., Phys.Ed.Ind., Sp.Ed.Needs Abstr., Sportsearch (1981-).
  Formerly (until Dec. 1981): Canadian Journal of History of Sport and Physical Education (ISSN 0008-4115)

796 617.1 US ISSN 0833-1235 CODEN: CJSSEV
CANADIAN JOURNAL OF SPORT SCIENCES/REVUE CANADIENNE DES SCIENCES DU SPORT. Short title: C J S S - R C S S. (Text in English, French) 1976. q. $40 to individuals (foreign $45); institutions $80 (foreign $85); students $24 (foreign $28). (Canadian Association of Sport Sciences, CN) Human Kinetics Publishers, Inc., Box 5076, Champaign, IL 61825-5076. TEL 217-351-5076. FAX 217-351-2674. Ed. Dr. David Cunningham. adv.; bk.rev.; abstr.; bibl.; charts; stat.; index; circ. 900. Indexed: Biol.Abstr., Chem.Abstr., CMI, Ergon.Abstr., Excerp.Med., Ind.Med., Psychol.Abstr., Sportsearch (1987-).
  —BLDSC shelfmark: 3035.755000.
  Formerly: Canadian Journal of Applied Sport Science (ISSN 0700-3978)
  Description: Offers multidisciplinary forum for pure and applied scientific topics contributing to understanding of sport, exercise.
  Refereed Serial

790.1 CN ISSN 0227-3330
CANADIAN POOL & SPA MARKETING. 1976. bi-m. Can.$20($20) Hubbard Marketing & Publishing Ltd., 46 Crockford Blvd., Scarborough, Ont. M1R 3C3, Canada. TEL 416-752-2500. FAX 416-752-2748. Ed. Richard I. Hubbard. adv.; bk.rev.; circ. 3,000.

CANADIAN SPORTING GOODS & PLAYTHINGS. DIRECTORY. see BUSINESS AND ECONOMICS — Trade And Industrial Directories

CANADIAN SPORTSCARD COLLECTOR. see HOBBIES

796.8 CN ISSN 0705-176X
CANADIAN WRESTLER/LUTTEUR CANADIEN. 1977. 4/yr. Can.$16. Canadian Amateur Wrestling Association - Association Canadienne de Lutte Amateur, 1600 James Naismith, Gloucester, Ont., Canada. TEL 613-748-5686. FAX 613-748-5756. TELEX 053-3660. Ed. Toni Stokes. adv.; bk.rev.; circ. 7,500. **Indexed:** Sportsearch (1977-).

790.1 617.1 US ISSN 1041-5742
CAPITAL SPORTS FOCUS. 1989. m. $15.95. Capital Sports Focus, Inc., 1432 Fenwick Ln., Silver Spring, MD 20910-3328. TEL 301-587-9351. FAX 301-587-6347. Ed. Manny Rosenberg. adv.; bk.rev.; circ. 100,000. (controlled)
  Description: Covers lifestyle, sports, health and fitness for residents of Washington D.C. and the Baltimore metro area.

CAR CRAFT; the complete performance magazine. see TRANSPORTATION — Automobiles

793 US
CARD PLAYER; the magazine for those who play to win. 1988. fortn. $59. 1455 E. Tropicana Ave., No. 450, Las Vegas, NV 89119. TEL 702-798-5170. FAX 702-798-5577. Ed. June Field. adv.; bk.rev.; illus.
  Description: Covers casino and sports gambling, poker, and gambling industry news.

790.1 US
CARIBBEAN SPORTS & TRAVEL. 1992. q. $5. Graphcom Publishing Co., Inc., 1995 N.E. 150 St., Ste. 107, N. Miami, FL 33181. TEL 305-945-7403. FAX 305-947-6410. Ed. V.C. Hanna. adv.: B&W page $1580, color page $2330; trim size 8 x 10 3/4. bk.rev.; illus.; circ. 40,000.
  Incorporates (1971-1990): Pleasure Boating.
  Description: Covers diving, cruising, fishing, charters, and golf packages in the Caribbean islands.

790.1 647.94 US ISSN 0889-9797
CASINO CHRONICLE. 1983. w. (48/yr.) $155 (Canada $165; Mexico $170; elsewhere $205). Casino Chronicle Inc., 1412 Chanticleer, Cherry Hill, NJ 08003. TEL 609-751-8620. FAX 609-751-8620. Ed. Ben A. Borowsky. adv.; bk.rev.; film rev.; play rev.; pat.; stat.; tr.lit.; circ. 1,500. (back issues avail.)
  Description: Focuses on the gaming industry in New Jersey.

790.1 910.09 US ISSN 8755-6103
CASINO DIGEST. 1984. m. $47. Casino Digest, Inc., 1901-G Ashwood Ct., Ste. 123, Greensboro, NC 27408. TEL 919-375-6358. Ed. Joe Lawless. adv.; circ. 40,000. (tabloid format; back issues avail.; reprint service avail.)
  Description: Consumer news on casino gaming; informs consumer on all aspects of casino gaming and its related products and services.

793 US
CASINO GAMING INTERNATIONAL. m. Public Gaming Research Institute, 15825 Shady Grove Rd., No. 130, Rockville, MD 20850-4008. TEL 301-330-7600. FAX 301-330-7608. Ed. Duane Burke. circ. 11,000.

CASUS BELLI. see HOBBIES

796.72 US
CAVALCADE OF AUTO RACING. 1964. w. $15. Racing News, Inc., Box 668728, Charlotte, NC 28266. TEL 704-399-8395. Ed. Ernie Elkins. adv.; bk.rev.; circ. 23,000.

790.1 US ISSN 0747-6817
CENTER FOR SPORTS SPONSORSHIP'S SPONSOR QUEST.* 1984. m. $30. Center for Sports Sponsorship, Box 280, Plainsboro, NJ 08536. Ed. Vicki Edwards.

790.1 FR ISSN 0181-9224
CHAMPION D'AFRIQUE.* (Text in English, French, Spanish) 1973. q. free. (Association of National Olympic Committees - Association des Comites Naitonaux Olympiques) Editions Sport International, 21 rue d'Artois, 75008 Paris, France. TEL 33-1-42-86-01-94. FAX 33-1-42-86-01-32. Ed. Hassine Hamouda. adv.; bk.rev.; illus.; circ. 3,000. Indexed: Sportsearch.
  Former titles (until 1989): Champion d'Afrique; (until 1977): Champion d'Afrique - Afrique Olympique.

790.1 ZR
CHAMPION DU ZAIRE. w. Cite de la Voix du Zaire, B.P. 9365, Kinshasa I, Zaire. Ed. Kasonga Tshilunde Boya Yawumwe.

796.41 UK
CHASEFORM JUMPING ANNUAL. a. £15. Raceform Ltd., 2 York Rd., London SW11 3PZ, England.

790.1 613.7 IS
CHAYIM YAFIM. bi-m. Rehov Hanatzev 14, Tel Aviv 67 018, Israel. TEL 03-339115.

794.1 CN
CHECK!. (Editions in English, French) 1928. 6/yr. Can.$19 (US $24; elsewhere $28). Canadian Correspondence Chess Association, 37 Bemersyde Dr., Etobicoke, Ont. M9A 2S9, Canada. TEL 416-236-4136. Eds. J. Ken Macdonald, William Roach. adv.; bk.rev.; index; circ. 600. (back issues avail.)
  Description: Reports on national and international games and news; includes problems and studies.

790.7 371.893 US ISSN 0893-8091
CHEER NEWS TODAY. 1987. q. $4.99. Sky Publishing Inc., Box 72004, Marietta, GA 30007. TEL 404-993-7571. FAX 404-993-7571. Ed. Tamara Lindley. adv.; bk.rev.; tr.lit.; circ. 35,000. (back issues avail.)
  Description: News and information on high school and college cheerleading.

794.1 UK
CHESS. 1935. m. $44.95. Maxwell Macmillan Chess & Bridge, London Rd., Wheatley, Oxford OX9 1YR, England. TEL 08677-411136. FAX 08677-5383. (Dist. by: Odham Distrubution, 4-12 Dorrington St., London EC1N 7TL, England) Ed. Paul Lamford. adv.; bk.rev.; charts; illus.; stat.; index; circ. 10,000. (tabloid format)
  Former titles: Pergamon Chess; (until vol.53, 1988): Chess (ISSN 0009-3319).
  Description: Provides reports on international events, features on players, instructional articles and competitions.

SPORTS AND GAMES

794.1 PH
CHESS ASIA. 4/yr. $20. c/o Manalito M. Ferrer, Mgr. Ed., P.O. Box 1497, Makati Central P.O., Makati, Metro Manila, Philippines. Ed. Eugeno Torre.
  Description: Contains national and international games, "how-to-improve" articles, endgame and opening theory, studies and problems, and FIDE ratings.

794.1 US
CHESS CHOW. m. 115 W. 75th St., Apt. 2B, New York, NY 10023. TEL 212-580-0343. FAX 212-592-7382. Ed. Joel Bengamin. circ. 800.

794.1 UK
CHESS COLLECTOR. 1988. 2-3/yr. $50 to non-members. Chess Collectors International, 35 Shepherds Hill, London N6 5QJ, England. (U.S. subscr. addr.: c/o Marylin Exxes, 875 Fifth Ave. New York, NY 10021) Ed. Michael Mark.
  Description: Information about chess collectables, especially chess sets, chess art and history.

794.1 UK
CHESS COMPUTER WORLD. 4/yr. $20. Bryan Whitby, Ed. & Pub., 16 Manse Field Rd., Kingsley, Warrington, Cheshire WA6 8BZ, England. adv.
  Description: Provides players with independent information about computerized chess. Contains articles, results, games and assessment of computer playing strength.

794.1 US ISSN 0009-3327
CHESS CORRESPONDENT. 1926. 6/yr. $16. C C L A, Box 3481, Barrington, IL 60011-3481. Ed. Jerry Honn. bk.rev.; circ. 1,000.
  Description: Includes "how-to-improve" articles, theory, rating list, large annotated game section, and international news.

794.1 US ISSN 0147-2569
CHESS HORIZONS. 1969. 6/yr. $10 (Canada and Mexico $16). Massachusetts Chess Association, c/o Steve Frymer, 64 Asbury St., Lexington, MA 02173-6521. Ed. Erik Zoltan. adv.; bk.rev.; circ. 2,000.
  Description: New England coverage emphasized but offers national and international news, games and theory.

794.1 AT ISSN 0009-3343
CHESS IN AUSTRALIA. 1966. 6/yr. Aus.$20. (Australian Chess Federation) Peter Parr, Ed. & Pub., P.O. Box C274, Clarence St., Sydney, N.S.W. 2000, Australia. Ed. Peter Parr. adv.; bk.rev.; charts; index; circ. 1,800.

794.1 US ISSN 1044-8888
CHESS IN INDIANA. 1988. 5/yr. $10. Indiana State Chess Association, 1146 Strong Ave., Elkhart, IN 46514-2407. TEL 219-293-2241. Ed. Roger E. Blaine. adv.; charts; illus.; stats.; index; circ. 300. (back issues avail.)
  Description: News and history of chess tournaments, champions, and clubs in the state of Indiana.

794.1 SA
CHESS IN THE R S A. 12/yr. $15. c/o Charles van der Werthuizen, Co-Ed., P.O. Box 83694, South Hills, 2136 Johannesburg, South Africa. Ed. Darryl Accone.
  Description: Covers local and national games; includes articles, and studies-problems.

794.1 IT
CHESS IN U S S R. (Text in English) 4/yr. $40. S V E R, Via Serchio, 9-11, 00198 Rome, Italy. Ed. Juri Averbach.

CHESS JOURNALIST. see *JOURNALISM*

794.1 US ISSN 0197-260X
GV1263
CHESS LIFE. 1933. m. $33. United States Chess Federation, 186 Route 9W, New Windsor, NY 12553. TEL 914-562-8350. FAX 914-561-2437. Ed. Glen Petersen. adv.; bk.rev.; charts; illus.; stat.; tr.lit.; index; circ. 55,000. (also avail. in microform from UMI; back issues avail.)
  Formerly (until 1980): Chess Life and Review (ISSN 0009-3351); **Incorporates:** Chess Review.

794.1 II ISSN 0970-9142
CHESS MATE. 1983. 12/yr. $20. 18 I Main Rd., Shastringar, Madras 600 200, India. TEL 044-411607. FAX 91-44-2350305. TELEX 41-21060 PCO IN. Eds. Manuel Aaron, Arvind Aaron. adv.; bk.rev.; bibl.; circ. 2,500.
  Description: Covers the Asian chess scene. Includes "how-to-improve" articles, theory, combinations, and interviews.

794.1 UK ISSN 0960-1422
CHESS POST. 6/yr. £9 for 2 years. British Correspondence Chess Society, 85 Hillyard Rd., London W7 1BJ, England. Ed. R. Gillman. adv.; bk.rev.

794.1 GW
CHESSBASE MAGAZIN. 6/yr. DM.195. ChessBase GmbH, Hauptstrasse 28b, 2114 Hollenstedt, Germany. FAX 040-6301282. Ed. Gisbert Jacoby.
  Description: Covers current games, opening theory, endgame analyses, and includes articles.

CHESSTAMP REVIEW. see *PHILATELY*

CHI SONO. see *BIOGRAPHY*

790.1 US
CHICAGO SPORTS PROFILES. 1986. m. $10. Sports Profiles, 4711 Golf, Ste. 900, Skokie, IL 60076. TEL 708-673-0592. FAX 708-673-0633. adv.; circ. 75,000.
  Description: Covers local professional and college sports teams.

790.1 CC ISSN 0577-8948
CHINA SPORTS/ZHONGGUO TIYU. Variant title: China Sport. (Text in English) 1957. m. $39. (State Physical Culture and Sports Commission) Renmin Tiyu Chubanshe, 8 Tiyuguan Lu, Chongwen Qu, Beijing, People's Republic of China. FAX 5113105. (Dist. in US by: China Books & Periodicals, Inc., 2929 24th St., San Francisco, CA 94110) adv.; illus.; circ. 50,000. Indexed: Sportsearch (1980-).
  Formerly (until 1980): China's Sports.
  Description: Covers athletic events, sports training, traditional Chinese sports and martial arts.

CIBLES. see *HOBBIES*

796.91 CN ISSN 0227-2091
CIRCLE. 1979. bi-m. Can.$5 to non-members. Figure Skating Coaches of Canada, Box 93, Agincourt, Ont. M1S 3B4, Canada. TEL 416-438-2871. illus.
  Formerly: Professional Circle (ISSN 0227-2083)

796.72 US ISSN 0734-5437
TL236
CIRCLE TRACK. 1982. m. $19.95. Petersen Publishing Co., 8490 Sunset Blvd., Los Angeles, CA 90069. TEL 213-854-2222. Ed. C.J. Baker. adv.; circ. 100,000.

CITY FITNESS. see *PHYSICAL FITNESS AND HYGIENE*

794.1 US
CLEVELAND CHESS BULLETIN. irreg. (5 or 6/yr.). $10. Cleveland Chess Association, c/o James Thelen, Treas., 14326 Washington Blvd., University Heights, OH 44118. Ed. Robert W. Basalla. adv.; bk.rev.

CLINICAS DE MEDICINA DEPORTIVA DE NORTEAMERICA. see *MEDICAL SCIENCES*

790.1 US ISSN 0160-6166
CLUB LIVING.* 1977. 10/yr. Club Living, Inc., 16 Copper Beech Cir., White Plains, NY 10605-4702. Ed. Diana Davis Lyons. adv.; circ. 51,000 (controlled).

796.72 US
CLUB MOTORSPORT NEWS. bi-m. Box 5907, Daytona Beach, FL 32118. TEL 904-676-2424. FAX 904-673-6040. Ed. Marjorie Suddard.

796.21 US
▼**COACHING CONNECTION.** 1990. m. membership only. Roller Skating Associations, 7700 "A" St., Box 81846, Lincoln, NE 68501. TEL 402-489-8811.
  Description: For roller skating coaches and teachers.

796.077 AT ISSN 0814-7752
COACHING DIRECTOR. 1984. 2/yr. Australian Coaching Council Inc., P.O. Box 176, Belconnen, A.C.T. 2616, Australia. Indexed: Sportsearch (1984-).
  —BLDSC shelfmark: 3287.743000.

790.1 CN
COAST TO COAST. (Text in English, French) 1986. q. membership. Sport Federation of Canada, 1600 James Naismith Dr., Gloucester, Ont. K1B 5NA, Canada. TEL 613-748-5670. FAX 613-748-5706. Ed. M.J. Barber. circ. 1,000.
  Description: Covers issues in national sport, government actions in sport.

COLLECTION PSYCHOLOGIE ET PEDAGOGIE DU SPORT. see *PSYCHOLOGY*

797.21 US
COLLEGE SWIMMING COACHES ASSOCIATION OF AMERICA NEWSLETTER. 1958. 5/yr. membership. College Swimming Coaches Association of America, c/o Penny Lee Dean, Ed., 698 Birch Ave., Upland, CA 91786. adv.; circ. 650 (controlled). Indexed: Sportsearch.

799.202 623.4 US
COMBAT HANDGUNS. 1980. bi-m. Harris Publications, Inc., 1115 Broadway, 8th Fl., New York, NY 10010. TEL 212-807-7100.

793 US
COMEDY U S A NEWSWIRE. 10/yr. Laughs Unlimited, Inc., Box 20214, New York, NY 10028-0051. TEL 212-628-2850. Ed. Donna Coe.

790.1 US
COMMUNITY SPORTS NEWS; basketball, hockey, running, outdoors. 1983. s-m. free. Community Sports News Inc., 123 Barclay Rd., Chapel Hill, NC 27516. TEL 919-968-8741. Ed. Joel S. Bulkley. adv.; circ. 5,000. (tabloid format)
  Description: Local sports and commentary.

790.1 UK ISSN 0263-6697
COMPASS SPORT - ORIENTEER. 1980. 8/yr £13.95 (foreign £15). (British Orienteering Federation) Compass Sport Publications, 37 Sandycoombe Rd., Twickenham, Middx. TW1 2LR, England. TEL (081) 892-9429. Ed. Ned Paul. adv.; bk.rev.; circ. 5,500. (back issues avail.) Indexed: Sportsearch (1982-).
  Formed by the merger of: Compass Sport; Orienteer.

COMPUTER CHESS NEWS SHEET. see *COMPUTERS — Computer Games*

794.1 001.61 US
621.381
COMPUTER CHESS REPORTS. 1983. 2/yr. $10.99 (Canada $15.99; elsewhere $22.99). Computer Chess Digest Inc., c/o I C D Corp., 21 Walt Whitman Rd., Huntington Sta., NY 11746. TEL 516-424-3300. Ed. Larry Kaufman.

COMPUTERSCHAAK. see *COMPUTERS — Computer Games*

COMUNITA SPORTIVA; settimanale di informazione e orientamento delle attivita CSI. see *CHILDREN AND YOUTH — For*

790.1 613.7 GW ISSN 0340-2991
CONDITION; die Zeitschrift fuer Lauf- und Ausdauersport. 1970. m. DM.50. Interessengemeinschaft aelter Langstreckenlaeufer e.V., Schillerstr. 30, D-5620 Velbert 15, Germany. TEL 02053-5235. circ. 2,700.
  Description: Magazine about distance running and other endurance sports for senior citizens.

382 BL
CONFEDERACAO BRASILEIRA DE FUTEBOL. RELATORIO. a. Confederacao Brasileira de Desportos, Rua da Alfandega, 70, Rio de Janeiro, Brazil. illus.
  Formerly (after 1983): Confederacao Brasileira de Desportos. Relatorio.

790.1 ZR
CONGO SPORTS. w. 99 rue de Tshela Com., Kinshasa, Zaire. adv.

CONSTRUCTIONS EQUIPEMENTS POUR LES LOISIRS. see *BUILDING AND CONSTRUCTION*

SPORTS AND GAMES

795.414 US ISSN 0010-7840
CONTRACT BRIDGE BULLETIN. 1935. m. $12 to non-members. American Contract Bridge League, 2990 Airways Blvd., Memphis, TN 38116-3847. TEL 901-332-5586. FAX 901-398-7754. Ed. Henry G. Francis. adv.; bk.rev.; charts; illus.; circ. 175,000 (controlled).
Description: Covers in-depth all contract bridge activity in North America and reports on foreign tournaments. Includes results, schedules, features and instructional material.

790.1 NE ISSN 0045-8406
CONTRACTSPELER. 1961. bi-m. fl.17.50. Professional Players Union of Holland, Harderwijkweg 5, 2803 PW Gouda, Netherlands. TEL 01820-71172. FAX 01820-32732. (Co-sponsors: Professional Trotter and Jockey Union of Holland; Professional Cyclists Union of Holland) Ed. K. Jansen. adv.; bk.rev.; tr.; lit.; circ. 2,000. (tabloid format)

790.1 CN
CO-OPERATIVE GAME CATALOG; family pastimes, games, puzzles & books. 1970. 2/yr. Can.$1. Family Pastimes, RR 4, Perth, Ont. K7H 3C6, Canada. Ed. Jim Deacove. adv.; bk.rev.; illus.; circ. 40,000.

794.1 UK
CORRESPONDENCE CHESS. 1963. q. £4 to non-members. British Correspondence Chess Association, c/o J.M. Allain, Esq., 86 Mortimer Rd., London N1 4LH, England. TEL 071-254-7912. (Subscr. to: T. Paterson, Whitestones, Maddox Lane, Little Bookham, Leatherhead, Surrey KT23 3BS, England) (Affiliate: British Postal Chess Federation) Ed. Adam Raoof. adv.; bk.rev.; circ. 650.

COSMOS TOU TENNIS/WORLD OF TENNIS. see *SPORTS AND GAMES — Ball Games*

COST OF DOING BUSINESS FOR RETAIL SPORTING GOODS STORES. see *BUSINESS AND ECONOMICS — Domestic Commerce*

794.1 CN ISSN 0832-0136
COUNTERPLAY. 1984. 6/yr. $16. Counterplay Publishing Association, P.O. Box 4422, Vancouver, B.C. V6B 3Z8, Canada. adv.; bk.rev.; circ. 450.
Description: Covers local chess games and news; includes occasional theory, "how-to-improve" articles, and interviews.

794.1 FR ISSN 0011-0507
COURRIER DES ECHECS; revue mensuelle d'echecs par correspondance. 1947. m. 175 F. (typically set in Sep.). (Association des Joueurs d'Echecs Par Correspondance) Marcel Bert, Esc. 1, 5 place Maurice Berteaux, 78400 Chatou, France. adv.; illus.

790.1 CM
COURRIER SPORTIF DU BENIN. w. B.P. 17, Douala, Cameroun. Ed. Henri Jong. adv.

D J I F FRITID. (Danske Jernbaner Idraets og Fritidsforbund) see *HOBBIES*

790.1 GW
D J K - AKTIV. 1950. bi-m. free. Deutsche Jugendkraft e.V., Deutschhoeferstr. 17, 8720 Schweinfurt, Germany. TEL 09721-24163. Ed. Georg Loesch. adv.; circ. 2,500 (controlled). (back issues avail.)

797.21 GW
D L R G - AKTUELL. 1984. q. DM.6. D L R G - Kreisverband Kaufbeuren Ostallgau, P.O. Box 741, 8950 Kaufbeuren, Germany. FAX 049-834162876. Ed.Bd. circ. 550.

790.1 GW
D L V - VOLKSSPORT-KALENDER. 1969. a. free to qualified personnel. Deutsch Leichtathletik-Verband, Wertachstr. 11, D-8903 Bobingen 1, Germany. TEL 08234-2444. (Co-sponsor: Oesterreichischer Leichtathletik-Verband) Ed. Otto Hosse. (back issues avail.)
Description: List of popular races in Germany and Austria for participants.

797 GW
D S W '12 NACHRICHTEN. 1955. m. Darmstaedter Schwimm- und Wassersportclub 1912 e.V., Alsfelderstr. 31, 6100 Darmstadt, Germany. TEL 06151-713077. adv.; circ. 1,300.

794.2 NE ISSN 0011-5959
HET DAMSPEL. 1911. 6/yr. fl.25. Koninklijke Nederlandse Dambond - Royal Dutch Draughts Association, Postbus 294, 6880 AG Velp, Netherlands. TEL 085-640306. FAX 085-616840. bk.rev.; bibl.; charts; circ. 9,200.

790.1 CC
DANGDAI TIYU/CONTEMPORARY SPORTS. (Text in Chinese) m. (Heilongjiang Sheng Tiyu Yundong Weiyuanhui) Dangdai Tiyu Zazhishe, 20, Xuanxin Jie, Nangang-qu, Harbin, Heilongjiang 150001, People's Republic of China. TEL 223578. Ed. Yu Jitao.

795.414 DK ISSN 0011-6238
DANSK BRIDGE. 1941. m. DKK 120. Danmarks Bridgeforbund - Danish Bridge League, Skovledet 95 A, 3400 Hilleroed, Denmark. FAX 45-2-266789. (Subscr. to: Postboks 121, DK-3400 Hillerod, Denmark) Ed. Ib Lundby. adv.; bk.rev.; circ. 14,000.

790.1 DK ISSN 0109-5536
DANSK IDRAET. 1930. s-m. DKK 130. Danske Skytte-, Gymnastik- og Idraetsforeninger, Englandsvej 270, 2770 Kastrup, Denmark. Ed. Erling Madsen. circ. 10,000.

796 DK ISSN 0109-8705
DANSK KARATE FORBUND. MEDLEMSBLAD. 1984. q. membership. Dansk Karate Forbund, Idraettens Hus, Broenby Stadion 20, 2605 Broendby, Denmark. Ed. Joergen Nielsen. adv.; bk.rev.; illus.
Formerly: Dansk Karate Forbund (ISSN 0109-8691)

790.1 UK ISSN 0267-2286
DARTS PLAYER. 1985. a. £3.50($5) World Magazines Ltd., 2 Park Lane, Croydon, Surrey CR9 1Ha, England. TEL 081-681-2837. Ed. A.J. Wood. circ. 22,000. (back issues avail.)

799.32 UK ISSN 0140-6000
DARTS WORLD. 1972. m. £16($27) World Magazines Ltd., 2 Park Lane, Croydon, Surrey CR9 1HA, England. TEL 081-681-2837. Ed. A.J. Wood. adv.; bk.rev.; circ. 33,075. *Indexed:* Sportsearch.

790 QA
AL-DAWRI. 1978. w. A.H. al- Atiyah and Partners, P.O. Box 310, Doha, Qatar. TEL 328782. Ed. Rashid bin Owaid al-Thani. circ. 6,000.

797.21 GW ISSN 0011-796X
DELPHIN; Revue der Unterwasserwelt. 1954. m. DM.46.80. (Verband Deutscher Sporttaucher e.V.) Schmidt-Roemhild Verlag, Mengstr. 16, 2400 Luebeck 1, Germany. TEL 0451-1605-0. FAX 0451-1605224. Ed. J.-P. Berkemann. adv.; bk.rev.; charts; illus.; circ. 8,500. (also avail. in microfiche)
Incorporates: Neptun.

790.1 CU
DEPORTE, DERECHO DEL PUBLICO. 1968. m. Via Blanca y Boyeros, Havana, Cuba. TEL 7-40-6838. TELEX 511583. Dir. Manuel Vaillant Carpente. circ. 15,000.

790.1 CU ISSN 0138-6611
DEPORTE-DERECHO DEL PUEBLO. m. $22. (Instituto Nacional de Deportes, Educacion Fisica y Recreacion) Ediciones Cubanas, Obispo No. 527, Apdo. 605, Havana, Cuba. illus.
Description: Presents articles, interviews and photo features on current national and international events, including information on the military, cultural, sports and recreational activities of the Armed Forces.

790.1 CL
DEPORTE TOTAL. 1981. w. Luis Thayer Ojeda 1626, Casilla 3092, Providencia, Santiago, Chile. TEL 2-74-9421. TELEX 341194. Dir. Dario Rojas Morales. illus.; circ. 25,000.

796 SP
DEPORTE 2000. 1969. m. 420 ptas.($7.24) Instituto Nacional de Educacion Fisica y Deportes, Martin Fierro, Madrid-3, Spain. adv.; charts; illus.; stat.; index. (back issues avail.)

790.1 VE
DEPORTES. 1978. fortn. C.A. Editorial Hipodromo, Torre de la Prensa, Plaza del Panteon, Apartado 2976, Caracas 101, Venezuela. Dir. Raul Hernandez. circ. 71,927.

790.1 DR
DEPORTES. 1967. fortn. Publicaciones Ahora, San Martin 236, Apdo. Postal 1402, Santo Domingo, Dominican Republic. Dir. L.R. Cordero. circ. 5,000.

DEUTSCHE GEHOERLOSEN-ZEITUNG. see *HANDICAPPED — Hearing Impaired*

796 GW
DEUTSCHE HOCKEY ZEITUNG. 1947. 42/yr. DM.182.45. Sportverlag Schmidt & Dreisilker GmbH & Co., Postfach 260, 7032 Sindelfingen, Germany.

794.1 GW ISSN 0012-0650
DEUTSCHE SCHACHBLAETTER. 1962. m. DM.36. (Bayerischer Schachbund e.V.) Verlag Deutsche Schachblaetter, Wodanstr. 78, D-8500 Nuremberg 40, Germany. Ed. A. Diel. adv.; bk.rev.; index; circ. 6,000.

799.3 GW ISSN 0012-0707
DEUTSCHE SCHUETZENZEITUNG. 1954. m. DM.54. Deutscher Schuetzenbund e.V., Schiesssportschule, 6200 Wiesbaden-Klarenthal, Germany. TEL 0611-468070. FAX 0611-4680749. TELEX 4186-309. Ed. Dieter Nobbe. adv.; bk.rev.; circ. 9,000.

796 GW ISSN 0075-2401
GV204.G4
DEUTSCHER TURNER-BUND. JAHRBUCH DER TURNKUNST. 1906. a. DM.17. Deutscher Turner-Bund, Otto-Fleck-Schneise 8, 6000 Frankfurt a.M. 71, Germany. adv.

793 GW
DEUTSCHES BRIDGE-VERBANDSBLATT. (Text in English, German) 1951. m. (Deutscher Bridge-Verband e.V.) Topp & Moeller Druck und Verlag, Postfach 28 54, D-4930 Detmold, Germany. TEL 05231-68121. Ed. Volker Borho. circ. 22,000.

790.1 GW ISSN 0343-5318
DEUTSCHES TURNEN. 1856. m. DM.57. (Deutscher Turner-Bund) Pohl-Verlag, Herzog-Ernst-Ring 1, 3100 Celle, Germany. TEL 05141-7504-0. (Subscr. to: Deutscher Turner-Bund, Zentralredaktion, Otto-Fleck-Schneise 8, 6000 Frankfurt-M., Germany) Ed. M. Senftleben. adv.; circ. 6,000.

790.1 TS
AL-DHAID. 1985. m. Nadi al-Dhaid al-Riyadi - Al-Dhaid Sporting Club, P.O. Box 12532, Al-Dhaid, United Arab Emirates. TEL 0822750. FAX 822631. Ed. Muhammad bin Salim al-Qasimi. circ. 1,000.
Description: Covers local sports and cultural events.

DHANDHA. see *MATHEMATICS*

790.1 SP
DIA CUATRO QUE FUERA.... 1970. m. free. Junta Central de Fiestas de Moros y Cristianos, Palacio Municipal, Villena, Alicante, Spain. circ. controlled.

DIESEL; mensile di cultura, attualita, tecnica che tratta di tutte le motorizzazioni diesel per usi industriali, agricoli, nautici. see *ENGINEERING — Mechanical Engineering*

DIFFERENT WORLDS; the magazine for adventurers. see *LITERATURE — Adventure And Romance*

793 US
DIPLOMACY WORLD. 1974. q. $400. Pandemonium Press, 1273 Crest Dr., Encinitas, CA 92024. Ed. R. C. Walker. circ. 400.

790.1 DK ISSN 0107-9042
DISCINFORM. 1982. q. DKK 25. Dansk Frisbee Disc Forbund, Box 140, 3520 Farum, Denmark. illus.

797.21 CN
DIVE. (Text in English, French) q. free. Canadian Amateur Diving Association, 1600 James Naismith Dr., Ste.705, Gloucester, Ont. K1B 5N4, Canada. TEL 613-748-5631. Ed. Don Adams. circ. 1,500.
Formerly: Platformance.

DIVE BOAT CALENDAR & TRAVEL GUIDE: INTERNATIONAL EDITION. see *SPORTS AND GAMES — Boats And Boating*

SPORTS AND GAMES

797.21   US
▼**DIVE TRAINING.** 1991. m. $16.95. Dive Training, Ltd., 405 Main St., Parkville, MO 64152. TEL 816-741-5155. Ed. Scott M. Spangler. adv.; circ. 60,000.
   Description: Contains how-to information for new divers and their instructors. Offers safety information and promotes the diving experience.

797.23   UK
DIVER; dealing with undersea exploration, diving, marine research. 1955. m. £24. Eaton Publications, 55 High Street, Teddington, Middlesex TN34 1JY. TEL 081-943-4288. FAX 081-943-4312. Ed. B. Eaton. adv.; bk.rev.; charts; illus.; circ. 50,084. **Indexed:** Sportsearch.
   Formerly: Triton (ISSN 0041-3119)

797.21   US   ISSN 0273-8589
DIVER. 1980. 6/yr. $15. Taylor Publishing, Box 313, Portland, CT 06480. TEL 203-342-4730. Ed. Bob Taylor. circ. 2,000. **Indexed:** Sportsearch (1981-).
   Description: Covers everything relating to springboard and platform diving.

797 910   CN   ISSN 0706-5132
DIVER MAGAZINE. 1975. 9/yr. Can.$26.75. Seagraphic Publications Ltd., No. 295, 10991 Shellbridge Way, Richmond, B.C. V6X 3C6, Canada. TEL 604-273-4333. FAX 604-273-0813. Ed. Peter Vassilopoulos. adv.; bk.rev.; illus.; circ. 30,000. (back issues avail.)
   Formerly: Pacific Diver and Underwater Adventure.
   Description: Covers Canadian and North American regional dive destination articles and travel features.

790.1   US
DIVERSION (NEW YORK). 1973. m. $48. Hearst Professional Magazines, Inc., 60 E. 42nd St., Ste. 2424, New York, NY 10065. TEL 212-297-9600. FAX 212-808-9079. Ed. Tom Passavant. adv.; bk.rev.; illus.; circ. 176,000 (controlled).

797.23   AT
DIVING DOWN UNDER. 1978. q. Aus.$25. Australian Underwater Federation Inc., P.O. Box 1006, Civic Square, A.C.T. 2608, Australia. FAX 062-573018. Ed. M. Sheehan. adv.; bk.rev.; circ. 4,500.
   Formerly: A U F Dive News.

DOG SPORTS. see *PETS*

796   GW   ISSN 0173-0843
DOKUMENTE ZUM HOCHSCHULSPORT. 1976. irreg., vol.25, 1990. price varies. (Freie Universitaet Berlin, Zentraleinrichtung Hochschulsport) Verlag Ingrid Czwalina, Reesenbuettler Redder 75, 2070 Ahrensburg, Germany. TEL 04102-59190. FAX 04102-50992.

797   US
DOLPHIN DIGEST. w. Dolphin Publishing Company, 8033 N.W. 36th St., Miami, FL 33166-6609. TEL 305-594-0508. FAX 305-594-0518. Ed. Andrew Cohen. adv.; circ. 40,000.

793   IT
DOMENICA QUIZ. 1951. w. L.31200. Rizzoli Editore-Corriere della Sera, Via A. Rizzoli 2, 20100 Milan, Italy. Ed. E. Balduzzi.

790.1   IR
DONYAYE VARZESH. 1970. w. Ettela'at Publications, Khayyam Ave., Teheran 11144, Iran. TEL 021-311071. TELEX 212336. Ed. M. Samimi. adv.; circ. 100,000.

790.1   DK   ISSN 0109-5595
DRAGESPORT. 1984. bi-m. membership; libraries KR.200. Danske Drageflyver Union, Oestre Parkvej 5A, 4100 Ringsted, Denmark. illus.
   Formerly: Dansk Dragesport (ISSN 0105-1245)

794.1   IT
DUE ALFIERI. 1974. bi-m. L.6000. Circolo A. Gramsci, Via Toschi 25, 42100 Reggio Emilia, Italy. Ed. Benati Alessandro. adv.; charts; illus.; circ. 1,000.
   Formerly: Cronac Viva.

DUNE BUGGIES & HOT VWS; the fun car journal. see *TRANSPORTATION — Automobiles*

790.1   US
DURHAM COMMUNITY SPORTS NEWS. 1985. m. free. Durham Community Sports News Inc., 123 Barclay Rd., Chapel Hill, NC 27516. TEL 919-968-8741. Ed. Joel S. Bulkley. adv.; circ. 6,000. (tabloid format)
   Description: Local sports and commentary.

794.1   BE   ISSN 0012-7671
E G. (End Game) 1965. q. fl.35. Chess Endgame Consultants & Publishers, c/o W. Stoffelen, Ed., Henrilei 59, B-2930 Brasschaat, Belgium. TEL 032-365-15860. bk.rev.; illus.; circ. 450.

794.1   NZ
E P MAGAZINE. 1978. irreg., 3-4/yr. $12. (New Zealand Correspondence Chess Association) N Z C C A, P.O. Box 3278, Wellington, New Zealand. TEL 04-237-4753. Ed. J.W. Maxwell. circ. 250.
   Description: Reports on national and international news, games, and studies on problems.

794.1   CN   ISSN 0825-0049
ECHEC PLUS. 1978. bi-m. Can.$25 (US Can.$33). (Federation Quebecoise des Echecs) Editions Echec Plus, C.P. 640, Succ. "C", Montreal, Que. H2L 4L5, Canada. TEL 514-252-3034. FAX 514-251-8038. TELEX 0582647. Ed. Louis Morin. adv.; bk.rev.; index; circ. 3,000. (back issues avail.)
   Description: News and events: game analysis, problems, combinations.

794.1   BE
ECHIQUIER BELGE. (Test in Flemish, French) 1942. m. (except July-Aug. combined). $30 (foreign $33). Rue Van Waeyenberg 12, B-1140 Brussels, Belgium. Ed. Henri Muller. adv.; bk.rev.
   Description: Includes annotated games, combinations, results, and studies on problems.

794.1   FR
ECHIQUIER ISSEN. 1987. 6/yr. 160 F.($30) Bruno San Marco, Ed. & Pub., 43 rue de Normandie, 92 240 Clamart, France. Ed. Bruno Marco.
   Description: Features annotated games, articles and theory.

790.1   UA
L'ECHO SPORTIF. (Text in French) w. Michel Bittar, Ed. & Pub., 7 Sharia de l'Archeveche, Alexandria, Egypt.

ECO DELLA RIVIERA. see *TRAVEL AND TOURISM*

790.1   CK   ISSN 0120-677X
EDUCACION FISICA Y DEPORTE. 1979. s-a. Col.500($10) Instituto Universitario de Educacion Fisica y Deporte, Apdo. Aereo 1226, Medellin, Colombia. Ed. Francisco Garcia. bk.rev.; circ. 1,000.

EDUCATION PHYSIQUE ET SPORT. see *EDUCATION — Teaching Methods And Curriculum*

790.1   FR   ISSN 0245-8977
EDUCATION PHYSIQUE ET SPORTIVE AU 1ER DEGRE. Abbreviated title: E P S 1. 5/yr. 95 (foreign 120 F.). (Comite d'Etudes et d'Informations Pedagogiques de l'Education Physique et du Sport) Editions Revue E P S, 11 av. du Tremblay, 75012 Paris, France. TEL 1-48-08-30-87. FAX 1-43-98-37-38. Ed. Jean Vives. adv.

790.1 778   UA
EGYPTE - SPORTS - CINEMA. (Text in French) w. 7 av. Hourriya, Alexandria, Egypt. Ed. Emile Assaad. adv.

790.1   GW
DER EISSTOCKSCHUETZE. 1976. s-m. DM.40($10) Deutsche Eisschuetzen Vereinigung e.V., Menzingerstr. 68, 8000 Munich 60, Germany. TEL 089-8111055. FAX 089-8144477. TELEX 5213199-DEV-D. Ed. Hermann Binder. adv.; bk.rev.; circ. 1,950.

EMPLOYEE SERVICES MANAGEMENT; the journal of employee services, recreation, health and education. see *BUSINESS AND ECONOMICS — Management*

794.1   CN   ISSN 0822-5672
EN PASSANT. (Text in English and French) 1973. 6/yr. Can.$15 (foreign $18). En Passant Publishers Ltd., 2212 Gladwin Cres. E-1, Ottawa, Ont. K1B 5N1, Canada. TEL 613-733-2844. FAX 613-733-2844. Ed. Gordon Taylor. adv.; bk.rev.; circ. 3,000.
   Former titles: Chess Canada Echecs (ISSN 0225-7351); Chess Federation of Canada. Bulletin (ISSN 0317-8064)

794.1   US
EN PASSANT. 1946. 6/yr. $7. Chess Enterprises, 107 Crosstree Rd., Coraopolis, PA 15108. Ed. Bobby Dudley. adv.; bk.rev.
   Description: News and results of the club's events.

797.21   UK
ENGLISH SCHOOLS SWIMMING ASSOCIATION HANDBOOK. 1950. a. £1. English Schools Swimming Association, Beech Hurst, Forest Rd., East Horsley, Surrey KT24 5BL, England. TEL 04865-5488. Ed. M.J. Bracey. adv.; circ. 3,000.

790   YU   ISSN 0013-8436
ENIGMA; zabavni casopis: ukrstene reci, rebusi. 1952. w. 150 din.($13.90) Enigmatski Klub, Bulevar Vojvode Misica 67, Box 219, Belgrade, Yugoslavia. Ed. Vlasta Pavlovic.

ENTERTAINMENT AND SPORTS LAWYER. see *LAW*

790.1   GW   ISSN 0932-7797
ENTWICKLUNGSZUSAMMENARBEIT IM SPORT; Analysen - Dokumentationen - Lehrmaterialen. 1988. irreg., vol.8, 1990. price varies. Verlag Ingrid Czwalina, Reesenbuettler Redder 75, 2070 Ahrensburg, Germany. TEL 04102-59190. FAX 04102-50992. Eds. Rolf Andresen, Christian Kroeger.

790.1   FR
L'EQUIPE. 1946. w. 2650 F. S N C L'Equipe, 10 rue du Fbg. Montmartre, 75009 Paris, France. Ed.Bd. adv.; circ. 200,000. **Indexed:** Sportsearch (1980-).

790.1   SY
ESBOU AL-RIADI. 1955. w. Firdoisse Ave., Tibi Bldg., Damascus, Syria. Ed. Kamel El Bounni. adv.

790.1   EC
ESTADIO. 1962. fortn. $73. Editores Nacionales, Aguirre 730 y Boyaca, Casilla 1239, Guayaquil, Ecuador. TEL 4-327-200. FAX 4-320-499. TELEX 3423. Ed. Jose Calderon. circ. 70,000.

794.1   GW   ISSN 0179-3934
EUROPA-ROCHADE; die vielseitig-informative Schachzeitung. 1966. m. DM.42. Vogelsbergstr. 21, 6457 Maintal, Germany. TEL 06181-941001. FAX 06181-941005. Ed. C. Koehler. adv.; bk.rev.; bibl.; charts; illus.; circ. 17,000.
   Formerly: Rochade.

794.1   FR   ISSN 0014-2794
EUROPE-ECHECS. 1959. m. (except Jul.-Aug. combined). 285 F.($55) (foreign 315 F.). Raoul Bertolo, Ed. & Pub., 4C1 rue X. Marmier, 25000 Besancon, France. TEL 81-51-01-26. adv.; bk.rev.; play rev.; circ. 30,000.
   Description: Contains annotated games, national and international news, interviews, combinations, correspondence chess, and computer chess.

790.1   IT
EUROSKI. 1967. a. L.4500. Ideapiu S.r.l., Via Durini 3, 20122 Milan, Italy. Ed. Paolo De Michele. adv.; circ. 26,000.

EXPLORE; Canada's magazine of adventure travel. see *SPORTS AND GAMES — Outdoor Life*

794.1   RU
EXPRESS - SHAKHMATY. 1955. s-m. 12 Rub.($36.90) Fizkul'tura i Sport, Kalyaevskaya 27, 103006 Moscow, Russia. Ed. Yurii Averbakh. illus.; circ. 25,000. (also avail. in microform from MIM)
   Formerly: Shakhmatnyi Byulleten' (ISSN 0037-3230)

FACTS ON FILE. YEARBOOK. see *HISTORY — History Of North And South America*

FACTS ON FILE WORLD NEWS DIGEST WITH INDEX. see *HISTORY*

AL-FAEZ/WINNER. see *MEN'S INTERESTS*

790.1   IE
FAIR PLAY; journal of the amusement industry in Ireland. 1985. m. I£15. Enterprise Centre, Melitta Rd., Kildare, Ireland. TEL 0353-4521190. FAX 0353-4521438. Ed. Martin Dempsey. adv.: color page I#600; trim 15 x 7; adv. contact: Susan Feery. circ. 2,000.

SPORTS AND GAMES

790.1 659.152 US
▼**FANS.** 1992. q. free. Virgo Publishing, Inc., 4141 N. Scottsdale Rd., Ste. 316, Scottsdale, AZ 85251. TEL 602-990-1101. FAX 602-990-0819. Ed. Alisa Klemm.
Description: Covers the latest in licensed sports fashion. Includes apparel previews for NFL, NBA, MLB and NHL teams; articles on issues of interest surrounding your favorite teams; interviews with top athletes.

793 GW ISSN 0935-0721
FANTASYWELT; das Fachmagazin fur Rollenspieler. 1985. bi-m. DM.40. Katharinenstr. 15, 5205 St. Augustin 3, Germany. TEL 02241-31-13-13. Ed. Uwe Korner. adv.; bk.rev.; film rev.; play rev.; illus.; circ. 6,000. (back issues avail.)
Description: Role playing games, games for adults, fantasy and science fiction novels.

794 SP
FEBOX-BOXEO. no.19, 1975. m. 250 ptas.($6) Federacion Espanola Boxeo, Ferraz 16, Madrid-8, Spain.

796.86 SZ
FECHTEN/ESCRIME/SCHERMA.* 1978. q. (Schweizerischer Fechtverband - Federation Suisse d'Escrime (Federatione Svizzera di Scherma)) G. Buechi Verlag, Schaffhauserstr. 439, Postfach 236, CH-8052 Zuerich, Switzerland. circ. 7,000. **Indexed:** Sportsearch.

796.86 GW
FECHTSPORT. 1980. 8/yr. DM.84. Schluetersche Verlagsanstalt GmbH und Co., Postfach 5440, 3000 Hannover 1, Germany. TEL 0511-1236-0. Ed. Andreas Schirmer. circ. 16,989. (back issues avail.)

796 371.17 SZ ISSN 0428-1659
FEDERATION INTERNATIONALE DE GYMNASTIQUE. BULLETIN. 1950. q. 30 Fr. International Gymnastic Federation, c/o Norbert Bueche, Secretary, Rue des Oeuches 10, Case Postale 333, CH-2740 Moutier 1, Switzerland. TEL 032-936666. FAX 032-936671. TELEX 934961-FIG-CH. adv. **Indexed:** Sportsearch (1981-).

799.3 CN ISSN 0226-773X
FEDERATION OF CANADIAN ARCHERS. RULES BOOK. (Editions in English and French) 1984. irreg. Can.$10. Federation of Canadian Archers, 1600 James Naismith Dr., Gloucester, Ont. K1B 5N4, Canada. TEL 613-748-5604. FAX 613-748-5785. TELEX 053-3660.

FEELING SPORTS MAGAZINE. see HANDICAPPED — Visually Impaired

FELD WALD WASSER; schweizerische Jagdzeitung. see CONSERVATION

796.86 SA
FENCER/SKERMER. (Text in Afrikaans and English) 1954-1978; resumed 1980. q. R.1 to non-members. South African Amateur Fencing Association, Box 9261, Johannesburg 2000, South Africa. illus.

794.1 GW
FERNSCHACH DER D D R. 6/yr. Doebritscher Strasse 57B, Grosswabhausen, 5301, Germany. Ed. Hans Rabold.

FERRARI ITALIAN STYLE; periodico internazionale d'immagine, automobilismo e cultura. see TRANSPORTATION — Automobiles

796.355 US
FIELD HOCKEY RULEBOOK. a. $2.75. National Federation of State High School Associations, 11724 N.W. Plaza Circle, Box 20626, Kansas City, MO 64195-0626. TEL 816-464-5400. FAX 816-464-5571. Ed. Susan True.

796.815 US
FIGHTER INTERNATIONAL.* (Editions in English, Swedish) 1987. bi-m. $15.95. I P I Magazines, Box 1441, Largo, FL 34649-1441. TEL 813-584-0054. FAX 813-584-0592. Ed. John Corcoran. adv.; circ. 150,000.
Description: Includes investigative reports on the industry, martial arts sports and film coverage, and hard news pieces.

796.815 UK
FIGHTERS; the martial arts magazine. 1978. m. £18 (foreign $36). Peterson Publications Ltd., Peterson House, Northbank, Berryhill Industrial Estate, Droitwich, Worcs. WR9 9BL, England. TEL 0905-795564. FAX 0905-795905. Ed. Bruce P. Ayling. adv.; illus.; circ. 26,000. (back issues avail.)
Formerly: Fighters Monthly (ISSN 0260-4965)
Description: Presents all martial arts styles and techniques, including reports on all major championships.

796.8 US ISSN 0146-8812
FIGHTING WOMAN NEWS. 1975. q. $10 to individuals; institutions $15. 6741 Tung Ave. W., Theodore, AL 36582-6233. Ed. Debra Pettis. adv.; bk.rev.; charts; illus.; circ. 4,100. **Indexed:** Wom.Stud.Abstr.
Description: Communications medium for women in martial arts, self-defense and combative sports.

797 US
FISHEYE VIEW SCUBA MAGAZINE. 1987. q. $8. Quantum Leap Technologies, 1399 S.E. Ninth Ave., Ste. 4, Hialeah, FL 33010-5999. TEL 305-885-9985. FAX 305-885-9986. Ed. Robin V. Burr. adv.; circ. 25,000.
Description: Covers scuba-related topics from planning dive adventures and evaluating dive equipment to ocean conservation and diver safety.

796.2 658 US
FITNESS EQUIPMENT DEALER. bi-m. Virgo Publishing, Inc., 4141 N. Scottsdale, No. 316, Scottsdale, AZ 85251. TEL 602-990-1101. FAX 602-990-0819. Ed. Michael A. Nichols.

797.21 613.7 US
▼**FITNESS SWIMMER.** 1991. q. $9.95. Fitness Swimmer, Inc., 318 E. 39th St., 3rd Fl., New York, NY 10016. TEL 212-808-0111. FAX 212-679-8157. adv.: B&W page $1900, color page $2500; trim 8 1/8 x 10 3/4; adv. contact: Mike Gilmore. circ. 20,000.
Description: Covers the aquatic lifestyle of year-round swimmers, cross trainers and water exercise enthusiasts.

796 RU ISSN 0015-332X
FIZKUL'TURA I SPORT. 1922. m. 4.80 Rub. (Komitet po Fizicheskoi Kul'ture i Sportu pri Sovete Ministrov) Izdatel'stvo Fizkul'tura i Sport, Kalyaevskaya ul., 27, 101421 Moscow K-6, Russia. FAX 2001217. (Subscr. to: Sport Books, Ul. Sretenka 9, Moscow, Russia) Ed. A.M. Chaikovksii. bibl.; illus.; index; circ. 900,000.

FLIEGER-REVUE; Segelfluf - Motorflug - Fallschirmsport. see AERONAUTICS AND SPACE FLIGHT

FLORAL UNDERAWL & GAZETTE TIMES. see HOBBIES

779.202 US
FOULING SHOT. 1977. bi-m. $14. Cast Bullet Association, Inc., No. 1 Nantucket Lane, St. Louis, MO 63132. TEL 314-425-2466. (Subscr. to: c/o L. Fortier, 4103 Foxcraft Dr., Traverse City, MI 49684) Ed. Glenn Latham. adv.; bk.rev.; cum.index: 1977-1988; circ. 1,600. (back issues avail.)
Description: Disseminates technology of cast lead bullets for target shooting and hunting.

796 FR ISSN 0071-9102
FRANCE - SPORTS. (Text in French; summaries in English, German, Italian and Spanish) 1954. biennial. 232 F. Creations, Editions et Productions Publicitaires, 1 Place d'Estienne d'Orves, 75009 Paris, France. TEL 42-80-67-62. FAX 42-82-99-30. Ed. Martine Clauel. adv.; circ. 8,500.

790.1 NO ISSN 0332-9666
FRIIDRETT; journal of Norwegian athletics. m. $43. (Norwegian Athletics Association) Universitetsforlaget, P.O. Box 2959, N-9698 Oslo 6, Norway. Ed. Rolf Nordberg. adv.; circ. 7,500.

796 SW ISSN 0046-5135
FRIIDROTT. 1972. 16/yr. SEK 496. (Svenska Fri-ldrottsfoerbundet) Cewe-Foerlaget, Box 77, 2890 10 Bjaesta, Sweden. (Subscr. to: PK-Banken, Box 365, 891 01 Oernskoeldsvik, Sweden) Ed. Charlie Wedin. adv.; bk.rev.

FRITIDSHANDLAREN CYKEL OCH SPORT. see SPORTS AND GAMES — Bicycles And Motorcycles

790.1 617.1 CC
FUJIAN TIYU KEJI/FUJIAN SPORTS SCIENCE AND TECHNOLOGY. (Text in Chinese) q. Y3. Fujiansheng Tiyu Kexue Yanjiusuo - Fujian Sports Science Institute, No. 17, Zhuangyuan Xiang, Wusi Lu, Fuzhou, Fujian 350005, People's Republic of China. TEL 554963. (Dist. overseas by: Jiangsu Publications Import & Export Corp., 56 Gao Yun Ling, Nanjing, Jiangsu, P.R.C.) (Co-sponsor: Fujian Tiyu Kexue Xuehui) Ed. He Fangsheng.
Description: Covers sports theory, training, psychology, medicine as well as sports biophysics and biochemistry.

796 AT ISSN 0157-5295
FUN RUNNER. 1979. bi-m. Aus.$15. Vaucluse Press, P.O. Box 109, Rose Bay, N.S.W. 2029, Australia. Ed. Mike Agostini. adv.; bk.rev.; circ. 17,500. **Indexed:** Sportsearch (1980-).
Incorporates: Australasian Track and Field.

790.1 GW
FUNBOARD; Surf Spezial. 1983. irreg. (1-2/yr.). DM.8 per no. Verlag Delius Klasing und Co., Siekerwall 21, Postfach 48 09, 4800 Bielefeld 1, Germany. TEL 0521-559280. FAX 0521-559113. TELEX 932934-DEKLA. Ed. Ulrich Stanciu. bk.rev.; circ. 800 (controlled).

FUSSBALLTRAINING. see SPORTS AND GAMES — Ball Games

790.1 US
G L O W. (Gorgeous Ladies of Wrestling) 8/yr. $2.95 per no. Tempo Publishing Company, Inc., 475 Park Ave. S., New York, NY 10016. TEL 212-213-8620.

790.1 IE
GAELIC SPORT. 1958. m. 80p. per no. Holyrood Publications Ltd., 139a Lower Drumcondra Rd., Dublin 9, Ireland. Ed. Thomas McQuaid. adv.; bk.rev.; circ. 42,650. **Indexed:** Sportsearch.

790.1 059.916 IE ISSN 0332-1274
GAELIC WORLD; iris oifigiuil Cumann Luthchleas Gael. 1979. m. I£18 (foreign I£40). Costar Associates, 10 Burgh Quay, Dublin 2, Ireland. TEL 679-2011. FAX 679-2016. Ed. Owen McCann. adv.; illus.

798.8 SP
GALGOS. vol.29, 1977. bi-m. 1500 ptas. (effective Apr. 1991). Federacion Espanola de Galgos, Barquillo 19, 28004 Madrid, Spain. FAX 522-43-44. adv.; circ. 2,500.
Formerly (until Oct. 1979): Federacion Espanola Galguera. Boletin Mensual Informativo.

794.1 GW ISSN 0937-5457
GAMBIT REVUE. (Text in English and German) 1987. 4/yr. $20. Schachverlag Manfred Maedler, Lilienthalstr. 52, 4000 Duesseldorf 30, Germany. TEL 0211-0211-453186. Ed. Volker Drueke.
Description: Includes over 450 gambits by white and black, opening theory, and information articles.

791.8 US ISSN 0016-4313
GAMECOCK. 1935. m. (Aug.-Sep. combined). $20. Marburger Publishing Co., Inc., Box 158, Hartford, AR 72938-0158. Ed. Faye Leverett. adv.; circ. 13,250.

GAMEPRO. see COMPUTERS — Computer Games

790.1 US ISSN 0199-9788
GV1199
GAMES; puzzles, games, tests, contests, features. 1977-1990; resumed 1991. bi-m. $17.97 (foreign $27.97). B & P Publishing Company, Inc., 2000 Commonwealth Ave., Boston, MA 02166. TEL 617-332-7191. (Subscr. to: Box 55481, Boulder, CO 80322-5481. TEL 800-950-6339) Ed. Will S. Hortz. adv.; bk.rev.; illus. **Indexed:** Jun.High.Mag.Abstr.
Description: For persons who enjoy solving puzzles.

796 US
GAMES & LEISURE INC.. m. Sports Publications Ltd., 109 Fairfield Way, No. 207, Bloomingdale, IL 60108-1500. TEL 708-893-0999. FAX 708-893-9219. Ed. Shari J. Stauch. adv.; circ. 30,000.

SPORTS AND GAMES

790.1 330   US
GAMING & WAGERING BUSINESS. m. $40. B M T Publications, Inc., 7 Penn Plaza, New York, NY 10001-3900. TEL 212-594-4120. FAX 212-714-0514. Ed. Paul Dworin. circ. 10,817.
    Formerly: Gaming Business (ISSN 0196-2213)

GAMING SYSTEMS SOURCE DIRECTORY. see BUSINESS AND ECONOMICS — Trade And Industrial Directories

794.1   GW
GARDEZ. 1981. 3/yr. DM.10. Seidenbenderstr. 74, 6520 Worms, Germany. TEL 06241-54488. Eds. Achim Berkes, Joerg Berkes. adv.; circ. 150.

790.1   PO
GAZETA DOS DESPORTOS. 3/wk. Rua Poco dos Negros 163-1o, 1200 Lisbon, Portugal. TEL 01-609523. Dir. Joaquim Queiros. (newspaper)

790.1   BL
GAZETA ESPORTIVA. d. Fundacao Casper Libero, Av. Paulisto 900, Sao Paulo, SP, Brazil. Ed. Olimioda Silva e Sa. adv.

796   GW
GERMANY. BUNDESINSTITUT FUER SPORTWISSENSCHAFT. BIENNIAL REPORTS. 1973. biennial. free. Bundesinstitut fuer Sportwissenschaft - Federal Institute of Sport Science, Carl-Diem-Weg 4, 5000 Cologne 41, Germany. TEL 0221-4979-0. FAX 0221-495164. TELEX 8881178-BISP-D; illus.; circ. 2,000.
    Formerly: Bundesinstitut fuer Sportwissenschaft. Berichte und Aspekte (Year).
    Description: Provides information on the structure and functions of the institute.

790.1   GW   ISSN 0343-6586
GERMANY, FEDERAL REPUBLIC (1949-). BUNDESINSTITUT FUER SPORTWISSENSCHAFT. SPORTWISSENSCHAFTLICHE FORSCHUNGSPROJEKTE ERHEBUNG (YEAR). 1974. a. free. Bundesinstitut fuer Sportwissenschaft - Federal Institute of Sport Science, Carl-Diem-Weg 4, 5000 Cologne 41, Germany. TEL 0221-4979126. FAX 0221-495164. TELEX 8881178-BISP-D. Eds. H. Fleischer, L. Muelfarth. circ. 400. (back issues avail.)

793.732   UK
GIANT WORD GAMES.* 1979. m. £4.80. B E A P Ltd., Glenthorne House, Hammersmith Grove, London W6 0LG, England. Ed. Patricia Townsend.

796.41   IT   ISSN 0017-0046
GINNASTA. (Supplement avail.: Gymnica) 1895. m. L.15000 (foreign L.20000). Federazione Ginnastica d'Italia, Palazzo delle Federazioni Sportive, Viale Tiziano 70, 00196 Rome, Italy. TEL 06-36858175. Ed. Bruno Grandi. adv.; charts; illus.; circ. 1,500.
    Description: Covers gymnastics with speical focus on the Italians in international competitiion, as well as profiles of the athletes and coaches.

688.76   IT
GIORNALE DEGLI ARTICOLI SPORTIVI. 1966. m. Edizioni Miglio, Via Garibaldi 18, 40011 Anzola dell'Emilia (Bologna), Italy. adv.; circ. 10,500.

796.41   US
GIRLS GYMNASTICS RULES AND MANUAL. a. $3.00. National Federation of State High School Associations, 11724 N.W. Plaza Circle, Box 20626, Kansas City, MO 64195-0626. TEL 816-464-5400. FAX 816-464-5571.
    Former titles: Girls Gymnastics Rules (ISSN 0270-2029); Incorporates: Girls Gymnastics Manual.

797.55 796.522   SZ
GLEITSCHIRM; Zeitschrift fuer Gleitschirm. (Text in German) 10/yr. 72 Fr. (foreign 96 Fr.). Gasser AG, Kasernstr. 1, CH-7007 Chur, Switzerland. TEL 081-235241. FAX 081-221452. Ed. Peter Dontasch. adv.; circ. 20,000.
    Description: Explores paragliding.

793   JA
GO/IGO. (Text in Japanese) 1951. m. 12470 Yen. Seibundo Shinkosha Publishing Co. Ltd., 1-5-5 Kanada Nishiki-cho, Chiyoda-ku, Tokyo 101, Japan. Ed. Yuzaburo Takeda.

790.1   JA   ISSN 0286-0376
**GV1459
GO WORLD.** (Text in English) 1977. q. $20 (Europe £20). Ishi Press, Inc., C.P.O. Box 2126, Tokyo, Japan. TEL 0467-83-4369. FAX 0467-83-4710. (Subscr. in US to: Ishi Presss International, 76 Bonaventura Dr., San Jose, CA 95134. TEL 408-944-9900; Alt. addr.: 20 Bruges Pl., London NW1 0TE, UK) Ed. John Power. adv.; bk.rev.; index; circ. 10,500.

796.962   US
GOAL. 1948. fortn. (Oct. - Apr.). $12.97. (National Hockey League) Sports Media, Inc., 101 E. 52nd St., New York, NY 10022. TEL 212-308-6666. FAX 212-308-6685. adv.; circ. 260,000.
    Description: Contains articles on great players, coaching strategy, and playing tips. Includes interviews.

796   US
GOAL LINE. 1965. q. $35. National Art Museum of Sport, Bank One Center Tower, Ste. 200, Indianapolis, IN 46204-5186. TEL 317-687-1715. FAX 317-687-1718. Ed.Bd. circ. 4,500. (back issues avail.)
    Formerly (until 1990): National Art Museum of Sport Newsletter.

GOL. see SPORTS AND GAMES — Ball Games

796.352   US   ISSN 0072-4955
GOLF GUIDE. 1963. a. $2.50. Kwik-Fax Books (Subsidiary of: Martin Frederick, Inc.), Box 14613, Surfside Beach, SC 29587. TEL 803-238-3513. Ed. Joseph Gambatese.

790.1   GW
GOLF TENNIS POLO; magazine for sports, journeys, pastime, society and fashion. (Text in German) 1986. 3/yr. DM.32. Reinhold Sommerfeld GmbH, Kaiserstr. 9, 8000 Munich 40, Germany. TEL 089-399012. TELEX 5215031. circ. 30,000. (back issues avail.)

796.72   US
GOODGUYS GOODTIMES GAZETTE. m. 1451 Danville Blvd., Ste. 203, Alamo, CA 94507. TEL 415-838-9876. FAX 415-820-8241. Ed. Dan Danner.

790   AG   ISSN 0017-291X
GRAFICO. 1919. w. Editorial Atlantida, S. A., Azopardo 579, 1307 Buenos Aires, Argentina. TEL 33-4591. TELEX 21163. Ed. Constancio C. Vigil. illus.; circ. 127,000.

790.1   UK
GRASP. m. Main St., Bruntinthorpe, Nr. Lutterworth, Leicestershire, England. Indexed: Sportsearch (1983-).

796.72   AT   ISSN 0811-546X
THE GREAT RACE; official book of the Bathurst 1000. 1981. a. Aus.$39.95($39.95) Chevron Publishing Group Pty. Ltd., P.O. Box 206, Hornsby, N.S.W. 2077, Australia. TEL 02-476-3199. FAX 02-476-5739. Ed. Thomas B. Floyd. circ. 20,000.
    Formerly: James Hardie 1000.
    Description: Describes a week in the event of a single motor race.

798.8   UK   ISSN 0017-4157
GREYHOUND. 1968. m. £15($25) Greyhound Star Ltd., Spirella Bldg., Bridge Rd., Letchworth, Herts SG6 4ET, England. TEL 0462-679439. Ed. Floyd Amphlett. adv.; bk.rev.; bibl.; charts; illus.; mkt.; stat.; circ. 14,760.
    Description: Highlights dog racing.

GREYHOUND ADVISER. see PETS

798.8 798.8   IE
GREYHOUND NEWS. (Text in English) 1982. m. £15($33) Meath Chronicle Ltd., Market Sq., Navan, Co. Meath, Ireland. TEL 046-21442. FAX 046-23565. Ed. John Davis. circ. 6,767. (tabloid format)

GREYHOUND RECORDER. see PETS

798.8   US
GREYHOUND REVIEW. 1911. m. $20. National Greyhound Association, Box 543, Abilene, KS 67410. TEL 913-263-4660. FAX 913-263-4689. Ed. Gary Guccione. adv.; bk.rev.; illus.; stat.; circ. 7,200. (tabloid format)
    Formerly: Coursing News (ISSN 0045-8929)
    Description: Highlights greyhound racing.

791.8   US   ISSN 0017-4297
GRIT AND STEEL. 1899. m. $15. De Camp Publishing Co., Gaffney, SC 29342. TEL 803-489-2324. Ed. Mary M. Hodge. adv.; illus.; circ. 6,000.
    Description: Highlights cock fighting.

794.1   GW
GROB ANGRIFF. 15. 6/yr. DM.20. Koernerstrasse 15, 3500 Kassel, Germany. Ed. Peter Elger.
    Description: Devoted exclusively to chess games and theory of the opening that was popularized by the Swiss I M, Henri Grob.

GROUNDSMAN. see SPORTS AND GAMES — Outdoor Life

790.1   IT
GUERIN SPORTIVO; il settimanale di critica e politica sportiva. 1912. w. (50/yr.). L.200000. Conti Editore S.p.A., Via del Lavoro, 7, 40068 San Lazzaro di Savena (BO), Italy. TEL 051-6422111. FAX 051-6255418. adv.; circ. 200,000.

GUN REPORT; dedicated to the interests of gun enthusiasts everywhere. see HOBBIES

799.202   US
GUN TRADERS GUIDE. 1953. biennial. $18.95. Stoeger Publishing Co., 55 Ruta Ct., S. Hackensack, NJ 07606. TEL 201-440-2700.

799.3   US   ISSN 0017-5641
GUN WORLD; for the firearms & hunting enthusiast. 1960. 13/yr. $20. Gallant - Charger Publishing, Inc., 34249 Camino Capistrano, Box HH, Capistrano Beach, CA 92624. TEL 714-493-2101. Ed. Dean A. Grennell. adv.; bk.rev.; illus.; circ. 130,000. (also avail. in microform from UMI; reprint service avail. from UMI)
    Description: Covers all facets of shooting, with emphasis on new firearms.

799.3   US   ISSN 0017-5676
GUNS; finest in the firearms field. (Annual supplement avail.) 1955. m. $19.95. Publishers' Development Corp., 591 Camino de la Reina, Ste. 200, San Diego, CA 92108. TEL 619-297-5350. FAX 619-297-5353. TELEX 695-478. Ed. Jerry Lee. adv.; bk.rev.; circ. 160,000.
    Formerly: Guns Magazine.

799.202   AT   ISSN 0157-1729
GUNS AUSTRALIA. bi-m. Aus.$23 (foreign Aus.$58)(effective Apr. 1992). Yaffa Publishing Group, 17-21 Bellevue St., Surry Hills, N.S.W. 2010, Australia. TEL 02-281-2333. FAX 02-281-2750. adv.: B&W page Aus.$1050, color page Aus.$1465; trim 273 x 210. circ. 11,320.
    Description: Firearm enthusiasts' magazine which concentrates on hardware, ammunition, as well as shooting techniques.

GUNS REVIEW. see HOBBIES

799.202   US
GUNSITE GOSSIP. 1981. irreg. (approx. 18/yr.). $15. Gunsite Press, Box 401, Paulden, AZ 86334. TEL 602-636-4565. FAX 602-636-1236. Ed. Jeff Cooper. circ. 1,100. (looseleaf format; back issues avail.)

790.1   CC
GUOJI XIANGQI/CHESS. (Text in Chinese) bi-m. Shu-Rong Qiyi Chubanshe, 9, Qinglong Xiang, Chengdu, Sichuan 610031, People's Republic of China. TEL 28479. Ed. Liu Shancheng.

790.1   US
GUTMANN KNIFE JOURNAL. 1985. a. $2.50. (Gutmann Cutlery) Aqua-Field Publishing Co., Inc., 66 W. Gilbert St., Shrewsbury, NJ 07702. TEL 201-842-8300. Ed. Stephen Ferber. adv.; circ. 105,000.

SPORTS AND GAMES

796.41   UK
GYMNAST MAGAZINE. q. £9.50 (foreign £10.50). British Amateur Gymnastics Association, Holiday Inn London-Heathrow, Ste. 035-037, Stockley Rd., W. Drayton, Middlesex UB7 9NA, England. TEL 0895-446683. FAX 0895-444130. (Subscr. to: Worldwide Subscriptions, Unit 4, Gibbs Reed Farm, Ticehurst, Wadhurst, East Sussex, TN5 7HE, England) Ed. Trevor Low. adv.; bk.rev.; illus.; stat.; tr.lit.; circ. 9,000.
Description: Official journal of the British Amateur Gymnastics Association. Covers European events, gymnastic and acrobatic techniques and club news.

796.41   DK   ISSN 0108-3678
GYMNASTIK. 1982. m. DKK 110. Dansk Gymnastik Forbund, Idraettens Hus, 2605 Broendby, Denmark. FAX 45-42-45-55-02. TELEX 33 111 (IDRAET DK). Ed. Karl-Henrik Boersting. adv.; bk.rev.; illus.; circ. 3,000.
Formerly (until 1982): Vidar (ISSN 0108-366X)

796.41   NO   ISSN 0017-596X
GYMNASTIKK OG TURN. 1948. 10/yr. NOK 75. Norges Gymnastikk- og Turnforbund, Hauger Skolevei 1, 1351 Run, Norway. Ed. Thorf E. Thoresen. adv.; illus.

796.41   IT
GYMNICA. (Supplement to: Il Ginnasta) vol.4, 1987. m. L.10000 (foreign L.15000). Federazione Ginnastica d'Italia, Palazzo delle Federazioni Sportive, 00196 Rome, Italy. TEL (06)36858175. Ed. Bruno Grandi. charts; illus.; stat.
Description: Covers gymnastics with diagrams and illustrations of the various movements and gestures.

790.1   US   ISSN 0898-6894
H P V NEWS. bi-m. $25 (foreign $30) includes Human Power. International Human-Powered-Vehicle Association, Box 51255, Indianapolis, IN 46251-0255. TEL 317-876-9478. Ed. Jean Seay. illus. *Indexed:* Sportsearch (1983-).

790   GW
H S V - JOURNAL. 1959. s-m. avail. upon request. Hamburger Sport - Verein e.V., Rothenbaumchaussee 125, 2000 Hamburg 13, Germany. TEL 040-4155-0. FAX 040-4155109. Ed.Bd. adv.; circ. 20,000.
Formerly: H S V - Post (ISSN 0017-6257)

AL-HADAF. see SPORTS AND GAMES — Horses And Horsemanship

790.1   US
HALL OF FAME NEWS. 1979. q. International Tennis Hall of Fame, 100 Park Ave., New York, NY 10017. TEL 212-880-4179. Ed. David B. Fine. circ. 10,000.
Description: Discusses Hall of Fame activities and reports.

790   GW   ISSN 0017-6982
HAMBURGER SPORT - MITTEILUNGEN. 1949. w. DM.60. (Hamburger SportBund e.V.) Sport- und Jugend-Verlag GmbH und Co. KG, Laemmersieth 21, Postfach 600609, 2000 Hamburg 60, Germany. Ed. Anne Heitmann. adv.; bk.rev.; circ. 5,500.

796   AU   ISSN 0072-9698
HANDBALL UND FAUSTBALL IN OESTERREICH. irreg. Oesterreichischer Handball-und Faustball-Bund, Hauslabgasse 24, A-1050 Vienna, Austria. Ed. Friedrich Duschka.

790.1   GW   ISSN 0174-1209
HANDBUCH DES BERLINER SPORTS. 1976. a. DM.24.60. (Landessportbund Berlin e.V.) Schors-Verlags-Gesellschaft mbH, Postfach 1280, 6272 Niedernhausen, Germany. TEL 06127-8029. FAX 06127-8812. Ed. Dietrich Dolgner. circ. 19,000.

790.1   GW   ISSN 0174-1217
HANDBUCH DES BREMER SPORTS; fuer Sportler und Sportinteressierte. 1975. a. DM.24.60. (Landessportbund Bremen e.V.) Schors-Verlags-Gesellschaft mbH, Postfach 1280, 6272 Niedernhausen, Germany. TEL 06127-8029. FAX 06127-8812. Ed. Rudolf Kauer. circ. 14,000.

790.1   GW   ISSN 0174-1195
HANDBUCH DES HAMBURGER SPORTS. 1976. a. DM.24.60. (Hamburger Sport-Bund e.V.) Schors-Verlags-Gesellschaft mbH, Postfach 1280, 6272 Niedernhausen, Germany. TEL 06127-8029. FAX 06127-8812. Eds. Dirk Dieckwisch, Andreas Ohlrogge. circ. 15,000.

790.1   GW   ISSN 0174-1187
HANDBUCH DES SPORTS IN HESSEN; fuer alle Sportler und Sportinteressierte. 1977. a. DM.24.60. (Landessportbund Hessen e.V.) Schors-Verlags-Gesellschaft mbH, Postfach 1280, 6272 Niedernhausen, Germany. TEL 06127-8029. FAX 06127-8812. circ. 39,000.

799.202   US
HANDGUN ILLUSTRATED. bi-m. McMullen Publishing, 2145 W. La Palma Ave., Anaheim, CA 92801. TEL 714-635-9040.

799.202   UK   ISSN 0260-8693
HANDGUNNER: BRITAIN'S FOREMOST FIREARMS JOURNAL. 1980. 6/yr. $25. Handgunner, Seychelles House, Brightlingsea, Essex CO7 0NN, England. TEL 0206-305204. Ed. Jan A. Stevenson. adv.; bk.rev.; illus.; circ. 27,500.
Description: Covers all aspects of modern small arms for a high level professional readership worldwide.

796   UK   ISSN 0073-0416
HARPERS GUIDE TO SPORTS TRADE. 1948. a. £68($102) includes Harpers Sport & Leisure. Harpers Publishing, 47A High St., Bushey, Watford, Herts WD2 1BD, England. TEL 081-950-9522. FAX 081-950-7998. Ed. M. Johnson. adv.; circ. 3,600.
Description: Directory of sports goods manufacturers and distributors in the UK.

790.1 301.412   US   ISSN 1044-7377
HEADWAY. 1985. q. membership. Women's Sports Foundation, 342 Madison Ave., Ste. 728, New York, NY 10173. TEL 212-972-9170. FAX 212-949-8024. Ed. Kathryn Reith. adv.; circ. 9,000. (back issues avail.)
Description: Covers all areas of women in sports, with emphasis on issues which affect women's participation in or leadership of sports.

790.1   VE
HIPODROMO. m. Apdo. 1192, Caracas, Venezuela. circ. 98,140.

790.1   US   ISSN 0896-1379
GV859
HISTORICAL ROLLER SKATING OVERVIEW. 1982. q. membership. National Museum of Roller Skating, 4730 South St., Box 6759, Lincoln, NE 68506. TEL 402-483-7551. Ed. Barbara E. Sorenson. illus.; circ. 450. (back issues avail.)
Description: Covers skating in the history of American popular culture.

790.1 613.7 378.198   GW
HOCHSCHULSPORT. 1953. s-a. Technische Universitaet Muenchen, Sportzentrum, Abteilung Hochschulsport, Connollystr. 32, 8000 Munich 40, Germany. TEL 089-35491-1. Ed. Julius Bohus. adv.; circ. 70,000.

796.962   SW   ISSN 0345-4347
HOCKEY. vol.4, 1973. 12/yr. SEK 438. (Svenska Ishockeyfoerbundet) Cewe-Foerlaget, Box 77, 890 10 Bjaesta, Sweden. (Subscr. to: PK-Banken, Box 365, 891 01 Oernskoeldsvik, Sweden) Ed. Charlie Wedin. adv.; bk.rev.
Formerly (until 1975): Svensk Ishockeymagasin (ISSN 0049-2698)

796.355   AT   ISSN 0018-2982
HOCKEY CIRCLE.* 1933. q. Aus.$4. Australian Hockey Association, G.P.O. Box 363, Brisbane, Qld. 4001, Australia. Ed. Hec Cormie. adv.; illus.; circ. 5,000. *Indexed:* Sportsearch.

796.962   US   ISSN 0046-7693
GV846
HOCKEY DIGEST. 1972. m. (8/yr.). $22 (foreign $30). Century Publishing Co., 990 Grove St., Evanston, IL 60201-4370. TEL 708-491-6440. (Subscr. to: Box 572, Mt. Morris, IL 61054-0572. TEL 800-877-5893) Ed. Michael K. Herbert. adv.; charts; illus.; stat.; circ. 110,000. (also avail. in microform from UMI; back issues avail.; reprint service avail. from UMI) *Indexed:* Sports Per.Ind., Sportsearch.
Description: For serious NHL Hockey fans who want the statistics, features and excitement behind the action of the sport.

796   US   ISSN 0278-4955
GV846
HOCKEY GUIDE. Variant title: Sporting News Hockey Guide. 1967. a. $10.95. Sporting News Publishing Co., 1212 N. Lindbergh Blvd., St. Louis, MO 63132. TEL 314-997-7111. (Subscr. to: Box 44, St. Louis, MO 63166) Ed. Larry Wigge. illus.; stat.; circ. 4,000. (back issues avail.)
Former titles: Pro and Amateur Hockey Guide (ISSN 0090-0818); Pro and Senior Hockey Guide (ISSN 0079-550X)

796   US
HOCKEY ILLUSTRATED. vol.13, 1973. 3/yr. Lexington Library, Inc., 355 Lexington Ave., New York, NY 10017. TEL 212-973-3200. FAX 212-986-5926. Ed. Stephen Ciacciarelli. adv.; charts; illus. *Indexed:* Sports Per.Ind.
Formerly: Sport Heroes (ISSN 0049-190X)

796.962   CN   ISSN 0018-3016
HOCKEY NEWS; the international hockey weekly. 1947. w. (m. Jun.-Sep.). $32.95. 85 Scarsdale Rd., Ste. 100, Don Mills, Ont. M3B 2R2, Canada. TEL 416-445-5702. FAX 416-445-0753. (Subscr. to: P.O. Box 904, Buffalo, NY 14240, U.S.A.) Ed. Bob McKenzie. adv.; illus.; circ. 114,000. *Indexed:* CMI, Sports Per.Ind., Sportsearch.

796   UK   ISSN 0073-3164
HOMING WORLD STUD BOOK. 1938. a. £2.50. Royal Pigeon Racing Association, Severn Farm Industrial Estate, Severn Rd., Welshool, Powys SY21 7DF, Wales. TEL 0938-2360. Ed. D.D. Glover. adv.

HORIZONTE; revista de educacao fisica e desporto. see PHYSICAL FITNESS AND HYGIENE

798   UK
HORSESHOE. 1985. 2/yr. membership. British Horse Society, British Equestrian Centre, Kenilworth, Warwickshire CV8 2LR, England. TEL 0203-696697. FAX 0203-692351. TELEX BEFKEN 311152. Ed. Ceri Jenkins. adv.; circ. 50,000.
Description: To further the art of riding and driving and to encourage horsemastership and the welfare of horses and ponies.

HOT ROD. see TRANSPORTATION — Automobiles

790   CI   ISSN 0354-0650
HRVATSKI PLANINAR/CROATIAN MOUNTAINEER. 1898. bi-m. $15. Hrvatski Planinarski Savez - Croation Mountaineering Association, Kozarceva 22, 41000 Zagreb, Croatia. TEL 041-448-774. TELEX 041-441-088. Ed. Dr. Zeljko Poljak. adv.; bk.rev.; charts; illus.; index; cum.index; circ. 2,300.
Former titles (until Mar. 1991): Nase Planine (ISSN 0027-819X); (until 1944): Hrvatski Planinar.

790.1   US   ISSN 0898-6908
HUMAN POWER. 4/yr. $25 (foreign $30) includes H P V News. International Human-Powered-Vehicle Association, Box 51255, Indianapolis, IN 46251-0255. TEL 317-876-9478. Ed. David Gordon Wilson. illus. *Indexed:* Sportsearch (1981-). —BLDSC shelfmark: 4336.363000.

790.1   HU
HUNGARIAN UNIVERSITY OF PHYSICAL EDUCATION. REVIEW. Hungarian edition: A Testnevelesi Foiskola Kozlemenyei. (Text in English) 1986. a. 100 Ft. Magyar Testnevelesi Egyetem - Hungarian University of Physical Education, Alkotas u.44, 1123 Budapest, Hungary. TEL 36-1-564-444. Ed. Marta Makkar. illus.

790   IT   ISSN 0018-7933
HURRA JUVENTUS. 1963. m. L.4000. Juventus F.C. S.p.A., Galleria San Federico 54, 10121 Turin, Italy. Ed. Vitaliano de Gennaro. adv.; illus.

SPORTS AND GAMES   4475

I A S M H F NEWSLETTER. (International Association of Sports Museums and Halls of Fame) see MUSEUMS AND ART GALLERIES

796.72   US
I M S A ARROW. 1985. m. $40. International Motorsports Association, 3502 Henderson Blvd., Tampa, FL 33609. TEL 813-877-4672. FAX 813-876-4604. Ed. Ken Breslauer. adv.; bk.rev.; stat.; circ. 5,000.

796.72   US
I M S A YEARBOOK.* 1972. a. $12. International Motor Sports Association, Box 10709, Tampa, FL 33679. TEL 203-336-2116. FAX 203-335-8473. adv.; circ. 10,000.
  Description: Includes a photographic and statistical review of the past season, descriptions of five racing series, historical data, race track data, market information, driver biographies, and membership and license information.

796   SZ
I S U CONSTITUTION. (Text in English) biennial; latest 1990. 8 Fr. International Skating Union, Postfach, CH-7270 Davos-Platz, Switzerland. TEL 081-437577. FAX 081-436671. TELEX 853123-ISU-CH.

796   SZ
I S U REGULATIONS. (Text in English) biennial; latest 1990. 20 Fr. International Skating Union, Postfach, CH-7270 Davos-Platz, Switzerland. TEL 081-437577. FAX 081-436671. TELEX 853123-ISU-CH.

796.962   JA
ICE HOCKEY MAGAZINE. (Text in Japanese) 5/yr. 1950 Yen. Baseball Magazine Sha, 3-10-10 Misaki-cho, Chiyoda-ku, Tokyo, Japan. Ed. Kunihiro Otake.

796.962   US   ISSN 0732-8117
GV847.5
ICE HOCKEY RULE BOOK. a. $2.75. National Federation of State High School Associations, 11724 N.W. Plaza Circle, Box 20626, Kansas City, MO 64195-0626. TEL 816-464-5400. FAX 816-464-5571. Ed. Richard G. Fawcett.

790.1   US
ICE SKATING INSTITUTE OF AMERICA. NEWSLETTER. 1961. bi-m. $36. Ice Skating Institute of America, 355 W. Dundee Rd., Buffalo Grove, IL 60089-3500. TEL 708-808-7528. FAX 708-808-8319. Ed. Justine Townsend Smith. adv.; circ. 3,000. (back issues avail.)

IDEA TODAY. see PHYSICAL FITNESS AND HYGIENE

790.1   DK   ISSN 0900-8632
IDRAETSHISTORISK AARBOG. a. DKK 162.30. (Dansk Idraetshistorisk Forening) Odense University Press, Campusvej 55, DK-5230 Odense M, Denmark.

790.1   DK   ISSN 0109-3835
IDRAETSLIV. m. (11/yr.) Dansk Idraets-Forbund, Idraettens Hus, 2605 Broendby, Denmark. TEL 42-45-55-55. FAX 42-456245. adv.; circ. 13,800.

790.1   SW
IDROTTSBLADET. 1908. w. Idrottsbladet Trychon AB, Box 309, 151 24 Soedertaelje, Sweden. adv.; circ. 250,000.

796.42   US
ILLINOIS RUNNER. 10/yr. Midwest Sports Publications, Inc., Box 53, Fairbury, IL 61739-0053. TEL 815-692-4636. FAX 815-692-4537. Ed. Glenn Latimer. adv.; circ. 10,000.

688.76   IT
IMPIANTI SPORT; verde, ricreazione, piscine, attrezzature, turismo. 1976. 3/yr. $46. Edizioni Publipam s.r.l., Via Andrea Costa 2, 20131 Milan, Italy. TEL 02-2893517. FAX 02-2610875. adv.; circ. 4,500.

793   US
IMPOSSIBILITY - CHALLENGER. 1981. q. (Sri Chinmoy Centre) Aum Publications, Box 32433, Jamaica, NY 11431. TEL 718-523-1166. Ed. David Burke.

796.72   US
IN GEAR. m. California Association of 4 W D Clubs, Inc., 7700 Quinby Way, Sacramento, CA 95823-4110. TEL 916-391-9595. Ed. Linda L. Meusling.

790.1   US
IN MOTION (EUREKA). 1987. m. Compuset Desktop Publishing Services, 517 3rd St., Ste. 40, Eureka, CA 95501-0453. TEL 707-443-8602. Ed. Ted Silanpaa. adv.; circ. 50,000.

796.42   US
INDIANA RUNNER. 10/yr. 503 E. Main St., Hartford City, IN 47348-2222. TEL 317-348-4739. Ed. Doug Osborn. circ. 7,000.

796   US   ISSN 0279-9863
INFO A A U. 1929. bi-m. $12. Amateur Athletic Union of the United States, 3400 W. 86th St., Box 68207, Indianapolis, IN 46268. TEL 317-872-2900. Ed. David Morton. **Indexed:** Sports Per.Ind.
  Formerly: A A U News (ISSN 0199-6991)
  Description: Highlights events, athletes, individuals and news of the organization.

790.1   US   ISSN 1046-4980
GV741
INFORMATION PLEASE SPORTS ALMANAC (YEAR). a. $7.95. Houghton Mifflin Co., One Beacon St., Boston, MA 02107. Ed. Mike Mserole.

790.1   GW
INFORMATIONEN FUER MITARBEITER UND VEREINE. m. DM.20. Hessischer Leicht-Athletik-Verband, Otto-Fleck-Schneise 4, 6000 Frankfurt am Main 71, Germany. TEL 069-6789-213.

794.1   US   ISSN 0896-8195
INSIDE CHESS. 1988. fortn. $45. International Chess Enterprises, Inc., 120 Bellevue Ave. E (98102), Box 19457, Seattle, WA 98109. TEL 206-325-9838. FAX 206-325-9838. Ed. Yasser Seirawan. adv.; bk.rev.; index. cum.index; circ. 4,700. (back issues avail.)
  Description: Covers amateur to international level player interest in the game of chess.

796   CN
INSIDE HOCKEY. 6/yr. Publications Transcontinental (Don Mills), 85 Scarsdale Rd., Ste. 100, Don Mills, Ont. M3B 2R2, Canada. TEL 416-445-5702. FAX 416-445-0753. Ed. Bob McKenzie. circ. 50,000.

796.815   US
INSIDE KARATE. 1980. m. $18. C F W Enterprises, Inc., 4201 W. Van Owen Pl., Burbank, CA 91505. TEL 818-845-2656. FAX 818-845-7761. (Subscr. to: Box 404, Mt. Morris, IL 61054) Ed. John Soet. circ. 100,000. **Indexed:** Sportsearch (1984-).
  Formerly: Kick Illustrated (ISSN 0273-7574)
  Description: For the serious martial artist. Spotlighting on self-defense, personalities and fitness.

790.1   US   ISSN 0199-8501
INSIDE KUNG FU. 1973. m. $20. C F W Enterprises, Inc., 4201 W. Van Owen Pl., Burbank, CA 91505. TEL 818-845-2656. FAX 818-845-7761. (Subscr. to: Box 404, Mt. Morris, IL 61054) Ed. Dave Cater. adv.; bk.rev.; charts; illus.; circ. 100,000. (also avail. in video cassette) **Indexed:** Sportsearch (1976-).
  Description: Martial arts coverage.

790.1   US
INSIDE KUNG FU PRESENTS TAE KWON DO. 1986. m. $22. C F W Enterprises, Inc., 4201 W. Van Owen Pl., Burbank, CA 91505. TEL 815-734-4151. FAX 818-818-845-7761. (Subscr. to: Box 404, Mt. Morris, IL 61054) Eds. Dave Cater, John Soet. adv.; bk.rev.; charts; illus. (also avail. in video cassette)
  Description: Guide to all types of martial arts. Spotlights different aspects of the martial arts world.

790.1   US   ISSN 0195-3478
GV561
INSIDE SPORTS. 1979-1982; resumed 1983. m. $22 (foreign $34). Inside Sports, Inc., (Subsidiary of: Century Publishing Co.), 990 Grove St., Evanston, IL 60201-4370. TEL 708-491-6440. (Subscr. to: Box 346, Mt. Morris, IL 61054-0346) Ed. Michael K. Herbert. adv.; charts; illus.; stat.; circ. 675,000. (also avail. in microform from UMI; reprint service avail. from UMI; back issues avail.) **Indexed:** Access (1981-), Sports Per.Ind., Sportsearch (1984-).
  Description: For serious sports fans. Presents statistics, stories, and excitement behind pro and college baseball, football, basketball, hockey, boxing, and auto racing.

796.812   US
INSIDE WRESTLING. 1968. m. $17 (foreign $22). G C London Publishing Associates, Box 48, Rockville Centre, NY 11571. TEL 516-764-0300. FAX 516-764-4370. Ed. Stu Saks. adv.; charts; illus.; tr.lit.

790.1 384.554   US
INSIDERS SPORTSLETTER. 1981. bi-m. membership. American Sportscasters Association Inc., 5 Beekman St., Ste. 814, New York, NY 10038. TEL 212-227-8080. FAX 212-571-0556. Ed. Louis O. Schwartz. adv.; bk.rev.; circ. 2,500. (back issues avail.)

799.2   US   ISSN 0747-007X
INSIGHTS (HERNDON); N R A news for young shooters. 1980. m. $8. (National Rifle Association of America) N R A Publications, 470 Spring Park Pl., Ste. 1000, Herndon, VA 22070. TEL 703-481-3383. Ed. Brenda K. Dalessandro. adv.; circ. 45,000. (back issues avail.)
  Description: Educational articles on shooting sports. Includes information on competition and hunting for readers aged 7-20.

797   US
INSTITUTE OF DIVING. NEWSLETTER. 1977. q. membership. Institute of Diving, 17314 Back Beach Rd., Panama City Beach, FL 32413. Ed. Dorothy Parkinson. adv.; bk.rev.; circ. 500.

INSTITUTE OF SWIMMING TEACHERS & COACHES DIRECTORY OF MEMBERSHIP. see BUSINESS AND ECONOMICS — Trade And Industrial Directories

371.7   RM
INSTITUTUL DE SUBINGINERI ORADEA. LUCRARI STIINTIFICE SERIA EDUCATIE FIZICA SI SPORT. (Text in Rumanian, occasionally in English or French; summaries in Rumanian, English or German) 1967. a. Institutul de Subingineri Oradea, Calea Armatei Rosii Nr. 5, 3700 Oradea, Rumania.
  Formerly: Institutul Pedagogic Oradea. Lucrari Stiintifice Seria Educatie Fizica si Sport; which continues in part (in 1973): Institutul Pedagogic Oradea. Lucrari Stiintifice: Seria Educatie Fizica, Biologie, Stiinte Medicale; which superseded in part (in 1971): Institutul Pedagogic Oradea. Lucrari Stiintifice: Seria A and Seria B; which was formerly (until 1969): Institutul Pedagogic Oradea. Lucrari Stiintifice.

796   UK   ISSN 0074-137X
INTERNATIONAL ARCHERY FEDERATION. BULLETIN OFFICIEL. (Text in English and French) biennial., no.26, 1974. price varies. International Archery Federation, 46 The Balk, Walton, Wakefield, England. Ed. Mrs. I.K. Frith. adv.

796 371   JA   ISSN 0074-1728
INTERNATIONAL ASSOCIATION OF PHYSICAL EDUCATION AND SPORTS FOR GIRLS AND WOMEN. PROCEEDINGS OF THE INTERNATIONAL CONGRESS. (Proceedings published by host countries) irreg., 6th, 1969, Tokyo. Japan Association of Physical Education for Women and Girls, 6-102 O.M.Y.C., 3-1 Jinen-cho Yoyogi, Shibuya-ku, Tokyo, Japan. circ. controlled.

796.345   UK   ISSN 0255-4437
INTERNATIONAL BADMINTON FEDERATION. ANNUAL STATUTE BOOK. 1935. a. £10. International Badminton Federation, 4 Manor Park, Mackenzie Way, Cheltenham, Glos. GL51 9TX, England. TEL 0242-234904. FAX 0242-221030. index; circ. 2,000.
  Formerly: International Badminton Federation. Annual Handbook (ISSN 0074-1981)
  Description: Rules and regulations of the International Badminton Federation.

S

SPORTS AND GAMES

790.1   NE   ISSN 0378-4037
INTERNATIONAL BULLETIN OF SPORTS INFORMATION. 1977. q. $25. International Association for Sports Associations, P.O. Box 85558, 2508 CG The Hague, Netherlands. Ed.Bd. adv.; bk.rev.; circ. 400. **Indexed:** Sportsearch (1977-).
—BLDSC shelfmark: 4538.261000.
Description: News bulletin for library and documentation centers in the field of sports and physical education.

790.1   CN
INTERNATIONAL GAMBLERS CLUB NEWSLETTER. 1974. q. $24. International Gaming Inc., P.O. Box 73, Thornhill, Ont. L3T 3N1, Canada. TEL 416-731-5457. Ed. I. Kusyszyn. circ. 2,000. (back issues avail.)

796.41   US   ISSN 0276-1041
GV461
INTERNATIONAL GYMNAST MAGAZINE. 1956. 10/yr. $20. SundbySports, Inc., 225 Brooks, Box 2450, Oceanside, CA 92051. TEL 619-722-0030. Ed.Bd. adv.; bk.rev.; bibl.; illus.; index; circ. 30,000. (also avail. in microform from UMI; reprint service avail. from UMI) **Indexed:** Mid.East: Abstr.& Ind., Phys.Ed.Ind., Sports Per.Ind., Sportsearch (1976-). **Former titles (until 1980):** International Gymnast (ISSN 0162-9867); (until 1976): Gymnast (ISSN 0046-6670); Incorporates: Gymnastics World & Mademoiselle Gymnast (ISSN 0024-9408) & Modern Gymnast (ISSN 0026-7813)
Description: Covers gymnastics with in-depth competition reports, personalities and photos.

795.4   US
INTERNATIONAL HOME AND PRIVATE POKER PLAYERS NEWSLETTER. 1988. bi-m. $7. International Home & Private Poker Players' Association, Rte. 2, Box 2845, Manistique, MI 49854. TEL 906-341-5468. Ed. Tony Wuehle. circ. 300. (looseleaf format; back issues avail.)
Description: News of members and poker tournament results.

INTERNATIONAL JOURNAL OF PHYSICAL EDUCATION/INTERNATIONALE ZEITSCHRIFT FUER SPORTPAEDAGOGIK. see *EDUCATION — Teaching Methods And Curriculum*

790.1 612   US   ISSN 0740-2082
INTERNATIONAL JOURNAL OF SPORT BIOMECHANICS. Abbreviated title: I J S B. 1985. q. $36 to individuals (foreign $40); institutions $80 (foreign $84); students $24 (foreign $28). (International Society of Biomechanics) Human Kinetics Publishers, Inc., Box 5076, Champaign, IL 61825-5076. TEL 217-351-5076. FAX 217-351-2674. (International Society for the Biomechanics of Sport) Ed. Robert J. Gregor. adv.; bk.rev.; bibl.; charts; stat.; index; circ. 900. (back issues avail.) **Indexed:** Curr.Cont., Phys.Ed.Ind., Sportsearch (1985-).
—BLDSC shelfmark: 4542.680500.
Description: Designed to stimulate and communicate research and theory on the forces affecting human movement in sports and exercise.
Refereed Serial

616.8   IT   ISSN 0047-0767
GV706.4   CODEN: ISPYAN
INTERNATIONAL JOURNAL OF SPORT PSYCHOLOGY. (Text in English and French) 1970. q. L.90000($80) (International Society of Sports Psychology) Edizioni Luigi Pozzi s.r.l., Via Panama 68, 00198 Rome, Italy. TEL 06-8553548. FAX 06-8554105. Ed. Ferruccio Antonelli. adv.; bk.rev.; circ. 1,500. (also avail. in microform from SWZ; reprint service avail. from SWZ) **Indexed:** Curr.Cont., Phys.Ed.Ind., Psychol.Abstr., Sportsearch (1974-), SSCI.
—BLDSC shelfmark: 4542.681000.
Description: Covers sports medicine.

INTERNATIONAL JOURNAL OF SPORTS MEDICINE. see *MEDICAL SCIENCES — Sports Medicine*

790.1   UK   ISSN 0952-3367
GV571
INTERNATIONAL JOURNAL OF THE HISTORY OF SPORT. 1984. 3/yr. £28($45) to individuals; institutions £75($115). Frank Cass & Co. Ltd., Gainsborough House, 11 Gainsborough Rd., London E11 1RS, England. TEL 081-530-4226. FAX 081-530-7795. Ed. J.A. Mangan. adv.; index. (back issues avail.) **Indexed:** Phys.Ed.Ind., Sportsearch (1987-).
—BLDSC shelfmark: 4542.282000.
Formerly: British Journal of Sports History (ISSN 0264-9373)
Description: Presents research on the social history, sociology and anthropology of sport, recreation and leisure.

796   GR   ISSN 0074-7181
INTERNATIONAL OLYMPIC ACADEMY. REPORT OF THE SESSIONS. (Since 1968 issued in separate English, French and Greek vols.) 1961. a. $10 (free to qualified personnel). Hellenic Olympic Committee, 4 Kapsali St., Athens 10764, Greece. FAX 7242150. TELEX 219494. cum.index: 1961-69.; circ. 9,000. **Indexed:** Sportsearch.
Description: Covers profiles, results, statistics, training information and news, reports, text and photos.

790.1   US
INTERNATIONAL OLYMPIC LIFTER. 1974. bi-m. $25. I O L Publications, Box 65855, Los Angeles, CA 90065. TEL 800-328-8762. Ed. Bob Hise. adv.; bk.rev.; illus.; stat. (back issues avail.)
Description: Devoted to weight lifting, contains profiles, training information, and news reports.

795.414   UK   ISSN 0951-1555
INTERNATIONAL POPULAR BRIDGE MONTHLY. 1974. m. $40. Probray Press Ltd., 455 Alfreton Rd., Nottingham NG7 5LX, England. FAX 889-565939. Ed. Tony Sowter. adv.; bk.rev.; circ. 3,000.
Formerly: Popular Bridge Monthly.
Description: Publication dealing with entertainment and instruction. Concentrates on top level bridge worldwide.

796   FR   ISSN 0074-7645
INTERNATIONAL REFERENCE ANNUAL FOR BUILDING AND EQUIPMENT OF SPORTS, TOURISM, RECREATION INSTALLATIONS. 1970. a. price varies. Techno-Loisirs, 3 rue Sivel, Paris 14, France. adv.; circ. 10,000.

796   SZ   ISSN 0539-0168
INTERNATIONAL SKATING UNION. ICE DANCING REGULATIONS. biennial; latest 1990. 15 Fr. International Skating Union, Postfach, CH-7270 Davos-Platz, Switzerland. TEL 081-437577. FAX 081-436671. TELEX 853123-ISU-CH.

796   SZ   ISSN 0535-2479
INTERNATIONAL SKATING UNION. MINUTES OF CONGRESS. (Text in English) biennial; latest 1990. Davos. 10 Fr. International Skating Union, Postfach, CH-7270 Davos-Platz, Switzerland. TEL 081-437577. FAX 081-436671. TELEX 353123-ISU-CH.

797.21 069   US
INTERNATIONAL SWIMMING HALL OF FAME HEADLINES. 1965. q. membership. International Swimming Hall of Fame, One Hall of Fame Dr., Ft. Lauderdale, FL 33316. TEL 305-462-6536. FAX 305-525-4031. Ed. Laura Hatfield. adv.; circ. 2,500.
Formerly: International Swimming Hall of Fame News.
Description: Covers aquatics, news and events on the Swimming Hall of Fame.

796.355 790.1   US
INTERNATIONAL TRACK & FIELD ANNUAL. a. $15.95. (Association of Track & Field Statisticians) Prentice Hall Press, One Gulf & Western Plaza, New York, NY 10023. TEL 212-373-8500. Ed. Peter Matthews.

790 371.8   CS   ISSN 0038-7789
GV561
INTERNATIONAL UNION OF STUDENTS. SPORT BULLETIN. (Text in English, French and Spanish) 1957. bi-m. free. International Union of Students, Physical Education and Sports Department, 17th November St., 110 01 Prague 1, Czechoslovakia. Ed. Ivan Vejlupek. charts; illus.

790.1   US   ISSN 0748-9668
INTERNATIONAL UNIVERSITY COLLEGIATE SPORTS REPORT. 1973. q. $200. International University Press, 1301 S. Noland Rd., Independence, MO 64055. TEL 816-461-3633. Ed. John Wayne Johnston. circ. 1,000. (looseleaf format)

799.202   SZ
INTERNATIONALES WAFFEN-MAGAZIN. (Text in German; summary of contents in English) 1982. 10/yr. 88.50 SFr. Habegger Verlag Zuerich, Dietzingerstr. 3, Postfach, CH-8036 Zuerich, Switzerland. TEL 01-4667289. FAX 01-4667903. Ed. Peter Ernst Grimm. adv.; bk.rev.; charts; illus.; index; circ. 55,000.
Formerly (until Dec. 1989): Schweizer Waffen-Magazin (ISSN 0253-4878)
Description: Modern and antique firearms, shooting sports, self-defense.

IRONMAN. see *PHYSICAL FITNESS AND HYGIENE*

794.1   IT   ISSN 0021-2849
L'ITALIA SCACCHISTICA. 1911. m. L.60000 (foreign L.70000). Via Passeroni 6, 20135 Milan, Italy. Ed. Giovanni Ferrantes. adv.; bk.rev.; charts; illus.; index.
Description: Covers every aspect of the game of chess including national and international news.

790.1   IC   ISSN 1017-3579
ITHROTTABLADID. 8/yr. ISK 386 per no. Frodi Ltd., Armuli 18, 108 Reykjavik, Iceland. TEL 354-1-812300. FAX 1-812946. Ed. Thorgrimur Thrainsson. circ. 8,000.

790.1 320   US
JACK HUTSLAR'S WEEKLY NEWS. 1985. w. $52. North American Youth Sport Institute, 4985 Oak Garden Dr., Kernersville, NC 27284-9520. TEL 919-784-4926. Ed. Jack Hutslar. adv.; bk.rev.
Formerly: Jack Hutslar's Sport Scene.
Description: News and information, new products and research about tots, children and teens, covering sports, recreation, education, fitness and health.

DER JAGDSPANIEL. see *PETS*

790.1   GW   ISSN 0448-1445
JAHRBUCH DES SPORTS. 1977. a. DM.24.60. (Deutscher Sportbund) Schors-Verlags-Gesellschaft mbH, Postfach 1280, 6272 Niedernhausen, Germany. TEL 06127-8029. FAX 06127-8812. circ. 32,000.

799   NO
JAKT-FISKE. 1871. m. NOK 215. Norges Jeger- og Fiskerforbund, Hvalstadaasen 5, Box 94, 1364 Hvalstaad, Norway. Ed. Viggo Kristiansen. adv.; circ. 72,000.
Formerly: Jakt-Fiske-Friluftsliv (ISSN 0021-4051)

794.1   SP
JAQUE. 22/yr. $51. Centro de Ajedrez Internacional, S.A., C-Reina, 39, 28004 Madrid, Spain. Ed. D. Pablo Aguilera.
Description: Includes annotated games, combinations, articles, and studies on problems.

790.1   TS
AL-JAZIRAH. 1980. m. Nadi al-Jazirah, Al-Lajna al-Thiqafiyyah - Al-Jazirah Club, Cultural Group, P.O. Box 2750, Abu Dhabi, United Arab Emirates. TEL 464455. Ed. Saif Ahmad al-Hamili. circ. 1,000.
Description: Covers club sporting activities.

790   FR   ISSN 0021-6135
JEUNES. 1898. m. 220 F.($40) Federation Sportive et Culturelle de France, 22 rue Oberkampf, 75011 Paris, France. TEL 1-43-38-50-57. FAX 1-40-21-87-17. Ed. Jean-Marie Jouaret. bk.rev.; film rev.; play rev.; illus.; stat.; circ. 11,000. **Indexed:** Sportsearch.

790.1   CN
JIM RENNIE'S SPORTS LETTER. 1977. w. Rennie Publications Inc., P.O. Box 1000, Collingwood, Ont. L9Y 4L4, Canada. TEL 705-445-7161. FAX 705-445-8650. Ed. Jim Rennie. circ. 1,600. **Indexed:** Sportsearch (1980-).

790.1   CC
JINGJI YU JIANMEI. (Text in Chinese) bi-m. Shanghai Tiyu Xueyuan - Shanghai Sports Institute, 650 Qingyuan Huanlu, Shanghai 200433, People's Republic of China. TEL 5485546. Ed. Zhou Xiumu.

SPORTS AND GAMES

790.1   CC
JINGWU. (Text in Chinese) bi-m. Dangdai Tiyu Zazhishe, 20, Xuanxin Jie, Nangang-qu, Harbin, Heilongjiang 150001, People's Republic of China. TEL 223578. Ed. Yu Jitao.

794.1   BL
JOGO ABERTO; a revista brasileira de xadrez. 1985. 6/yr. Cr.$50,00($15) Editora Jogo Aberto, Ltda., Rua Treze de Maio, 21, Bela Vista, 01327 Sao Paulo, Brazil. TEL 011-258-6506. Ed. Isabel Sampaio. adv.; bk.rev.; bibl.; index; circ. 3,000. (tabloid format; back issues avail.)
    Description: Covers the game of chess, emphasis is placed on the female players of the game.

790.1   SP
JORNADA DEPORTIVA. d. $1979. Avda. de Buenos Aires 71, Apdo. 714, Santa Cruz de Tenerife, Canary Islands. adv.

790.1   CN
JOURNAL DU SPORT. m. Can.$7. Publications Nabec Inc., 903 Belanger E., Montreal, Que. H2S 1G9, Canada. Ed. Richard Milo. adv.; circ. 35,000.

790.1   GW   ISSN 1010-8262
GV201
JOURNAL OF COMPARATIVE PHYSICAL AND EDUCATION SPORT. s-a. DM.30($13.50) (foreign DM.28). (International Society on Comparative Physical Education and Sport (ISCPES)) Verlag Karl Hofmann, Steinwasenstr. 6-8, Postfach 1360, 7060 Schorndorf, Germany. TEL 07181-7811.
    —BLDSC shelfmark: 4963.100000.
    Refereed Serial

JOURNAL OF GAMBLING STUDIES. see *MEDICAL SCIENCES — Psychiatry And Neurology*

JOURNAL OF ORTHOPAEDIC AND SPORTS PHYSICAL THERAPY. see *MEDICAL SCIENCES — Sports Medicine*

613   US   ISSN 0730-3084
GV201
JOURNAL OF PHYSICAL EDUCATION, RECREATION AND DANCE. 1896. m. (Aug.-May). $65 to institutions. American Alliance for Health, Physical Education, Recreation, and Dance, 1900 Association Dr., Reston, VA 22091. TEL 703-476-3400. FAX 703-476-9527. Ed. Frances Rowan. adv.; bk.rev.; film rev.; bibl.; illus.; index; circ. 40,000. (also avail. in microform from UMI; reprint service avail. from ISI,UMI) **Indexed:** C.I.J.E., Educ.Ind., Phys.Ed.Ind., Rehabil.Lit., Sportsearch (1981-).
    Former titles (until May 1981): Journal of Physical Education and Recreation (ISSN 0097-1170); (until 1975): Journal of Health, Physical Education, Recreation.
    Description: Covers current issues, new methods, trends and materials in physical education, athletics, sports, recreation, and dance.

JOURNAL OF RECREATIONAL MATHEMATICS. see *MATHEMATICS*

JOURNAL OF SPORT AND EXERCISE PSYCHOLOGY. see *PSYCHOLOGY*

301.15   US   ISSN 0193-7235
GV561
JOURNAL OF SPORT AND SOCIAL ISSUES. 1977. s-a. $24 to individuals; institutions $48; senior citizens $16; includes C S S S Digest. Center for the Study of Sport in Society, Northeastern University, 271 Huntington Ave., Ste. 244, Boston, MA 02115. TEL 617-437-5815. FAX 617-437-5830. adv.; bk.rev.; circ. 550. (back issues avail.) **Indexed:** Alt.Press Ind., Amer.Bibl.Slavic & E.Eur.Stud, Lang.& Lang.Behav.Abstr., Phys.Ed.Ind, Rural Recreat.Tour.Abstr., Sociol.Abstr. (1977-), Sportsearch (1976-).

790.1 150   US   ISSN 0162-7341
GV561
JOURNAL OF SPORT BEHAVIOR. (Summaries in English and French) 1978. q. $20 (foreign $45). University of South Alabama, Department of Health, Physical Education and Leisure Services, Mobile, AL 36688. TEL 205-460-7131. FAX 205-460-7830. Ed. William G. Gilley. bk.rev.; circ. 400. **Indexed:** Phys.Ed.Ind., Psychol.Abstr., Sportsearch (1978-), Sportsearch.
    —BLDSC shelfmark: 5066.186000.
    Description: Deals with the sociological, psychological, anthropological and related applications to the science of sport.

790.1   US   ISSN 0094-1700
GV571
JOURNAL OF SPORT HISTORY. 1974. 3/yr. $30 to individuals (foreign $35); institutions $40 (foreign $45). North American Society for Sport History, 101 White Bldg., Pennsylvania State University, University Park, PA 16802. TEL 814-865-2416. Ed. Steven Riess. adv.; bk.rev.; illus.; circ. 1,000. **Indexed:** Amer.Hist.& Life, Chic.Per.Ind., Curr.Cont., Hist.Abstr., Phys.Ed.Ind., Sportsearch (1974-), SSCI.
    —BLDSC shelfmark: 5066.188000.

790.1 658   US   ISSN 0888-4773
JOURNAL OF SPORT MANAGEMENT. Abbreviated title: J S M. 1987. 3/yr. $30 to individuals (foreign $33); institutions $64 (foreign $67); students $18 (foreign $21). (North American Society for Sport Management) Human Kinetics Publishers, Inc., Box 5076, Champaign, IL 61825-5076. TEL 217-351-5076. FAX 217-351-2674. Eds. Drs. P. Chellandurai, Joy DeSensi. adv.; bk.rev.; bibl.; circ. 720. (back issues avail.) **Indexed:** Phys.Ed.Ind., Sportsearch (1987-).
    —BLDSC shelfmark: 5066.188300.
    Description: To foster exchange of theory and application of management to sport, exercise, dance, and play.
    Refereed Serial

790.1   UK   ISSN 0264-0414
GV561   CODEN: JSSCEL
JOURNAL OF SPORTS SCIENCES. 1983. 6/yr. £165($295) (foreign £180). (British Association of Sports Sciences) E. & F.N. Spon, 2-6 Boundary Row, London SE1 8HN, England. TEL 071-865-0066. FAX 071-522-9623. Ed. Thomas Reilly. **Indexed:** Excerp.Med. (1992-), Phys.Ed.Ind., Sportsearch (1983-).
    —BLDSC shelfmark: 5066.350000.
    Description: Provides a contact point between the separate disciplines in sports sciences. Includes contributions from the human sciences: anatomy, anthropology, behavioural sciences, physiology and psychology. Papers cover technologies such as design of playing equipment and sports facilities as well as applied research in training, team selection, performance prediction or modification and stress reduction.

797   US   ISSN 0747-5993
JOURNAL OF SWIMMING RESEARCH. 1984. a. $35 (Canada & Mexico $45; institutions and foreign $55). American Swimming Coaches Association, 304 S.E. 20th St., Fort Lauderdale, FL 33316. FAX 305-462-6280. (Co-sponsor: U.S. Swimming Sports Medicine) Ed. Rick Sharp. adv. **Indexed:** Sportsearch (1985-).
    —BLDSC shelfmark: 5067.820000.
    Description: Examines applied swimming science and research.
    Refereed Serial

796   US   ISSN 0094-8705
GV706
JOURNAL OF THE PHILOSOPHY OF SPORT. Abbreviated title: J P S. 1974. a. $18 to individuals (foreign $19); institutions $30 (foreign $31); students $12 (foreign $13). (Philosophic Society for the Study of Sport) Human Kinetics Publishers, Inc., Box 5076, Champaign, IL 61825-5076. TEL 217-351-5076. FAX 217-351-2674. Ed. Dr. Klaus V. Meier. bk.rev.; bibl.; circ. 525. (back issues avail.) **Indexed:** Curr.Cont., Phil.Ind., Sportsearch (1978-).
    —BLDSC shelfmark: 5034.520000.
    Description: Aims to foster philosophic interchange among scholars interested in better understanding sport.
    Refereed Serial

796   US   ISSN 0047-2956
JUCO REVIEW. 1948. 9/yr. $15. National Junior College Athletic Association, Box 7305, Colorado Springs, CO 80933-7305. TEL 719-590-9788. FAX 719-590-7324. Ed. George E. Killian. adv.; bk.rev.; stat.; circ. 3,700. (processed; also avail. in microform from UMI; reprint service avail. from UMI) **Indexed:** Phys.Ed.Ind., Sports Per.Ind., Sportsearch (1977-).

796.815   NE
JUDO. 1939. 5/yr. membership. Judo Bond Nederland, Blokhoeve 5, 3438 LC Nieuwegein, Netherlands. TEL 03402-38114. FAX 3402-44323. Ed.Bd. adv.; bk.rev.; illus.; circ. 70,000.
    Former titles: Budo Echo; Judo Echo (ISSN 0022-5827)

796.815   UK   ISSN 0022-5819
GV475.J9
JUDO. 1956. m. £9. Judo Ltd., Candem House, 717 Manchester Old Rd., Rhodes, Middleton, Manchester M24 4GF, England. Ed. John Drogan. adv.; bk.rev.; charts; illus.; circ. 8,000.

796.815   FR
JUDO. 1950. m. 100 F. Federation Francaise de Judo et Disciplines Associees (F.F.J.D.A.), 43, rue des Plantes, 75014 Paris, France. adv.; circ. 120,000. **Indexed:** Sportsearch (1980-).

796.815   US
JUDO JOURNAL. m. Judo Journal Publications, Box 18485, Irvine, CA 92713. **Indexed:** Sportsearch (1980-).

796.815   IT
JUDO REGIONALE. 1972. m. L.3000. c/o Cesare Violino, Ed., Via Mentana 5, 33100 Udine, Italy. adv.; bk.rev.; circ. 10,000.

JUGGLER'S WORLD MAGAZINE. see *HOBBIES*

793   UK   ISSN 0267-9442
JUMBO CROSS. 1985. m. Mirror Publications, Athene House, 66-73 Shoe Lane, London EC4P 4AB, England. TEL 01 377 4801. Ed. Alison MacKonochie. circ. 45,000.

794.1   AT
JUNIOR CHESS. 4/yr. $12. 31-114 Crimea Rd., Marsfield, Australia. Eds. Jonathan Mandel, Ben Price.

790.1   US
K O. (Knock Out) m. G C London Publishing Associates, Box 48, Rockville Centre, NY 11571. TEL 516-764-0300. FAX 516-764-4370.

796.815   FR
KARATE. 1974. m. 261 F. Societe Europeene de Magazines, 2 bis, rue Mercoeur, 75011 Paris, France. FAX 43-67-85-50. Ed. G. Barissat. circ. 117,000.

796.815   UK   ISSN 0022-9008
KARATE AND ORIENTAL ARTS. 1966. bi-m. £6($12) Paul H. Crompton Ltd., 102 Felsham Rd., London SW15 1DQ, England. Ed. Paul H. Crompton. adv.; bk.rev.; film rev.; bibl.; charts; illus.; circ. 20,000. **Indexed:** Sportsearch.

796.815   US
KARATE INTERNATIONAL. 9/yr. $3.95 per no. DoJo Publishing, 519 Eighth Ave., New York, NY 10018. TEL 212-976-6262. FAX 212-967-6288.

796.8   US   ISSN 0888-031X
GV1114.3
KARATE - KUNG FU ILLUSTRATED. 1969. bi-m. $8.50. Rainbow Publications, Inc., 24715 Ave. Rockefeller, Box 918, Santa Clarita, CA 91380-9018. TEL 805-257-4066. FAX 805-257-3018. (Subscr. to: Box 16298, N. Hollywood, CA 91615-6298. TEL 800-266-4066) Ed. Bill Beaver. adv. contact: Barbara Lessard. circ. 75,000. **Indexed:** Sportsearch.
    Formerly (until 1991): Karate Illustrated (ISSN 0022-9016)

790.1   IR
KAYHAN VARZESHI. w. Kayhan Publications, Ferdowsi Ave., P.O. Box 11365-9631, Teheran, Iran. TEL 021-310251. TELEX 212467. adv.; circ. 125,000.

4478 SPORTS AND GAMES

790.1 — Il
KHEL BHARATI. (Text in Hindi) 1982. fortn. Rs.300. Bennett, Coleman & Coleman & Co. Ltd. (New Delhi), Times House 7, Bahadur Shah Zafar Marg, New Delhi 110002, India. (U.S. subscr. addr.: Ms. Kalpana, 42-75 Main St., Flushing, NY 11355)

790.1 — PK
KHEL KI DUNYA. (Text in Urdu) s-m. Jamil Ahmad, 6-13 al-Yusuf Chambers, Hayat Bros., Box 340, Karachi, Pakistan.

790.1 — Il
KHELA. (Text in Bengali) 1981. w. 96 Raja Rammohan Sarani, Calcutta 700 009, India. TEL 33-355302. TELEX 212216. Ed. Asoke Dasgupta. circ. 18,900.

796 — GW — ISSN 0023-1290
KICKER - SPORTMAGAZIN. 1968. 2/wk. DM.290.80. Olympia-Verlag GmbH, Badstr. 4-6, 8500 Nuremberg, Germany. TEL (0911)2160. FAX 0911-2162641. Ed. Karl-Heinz Heimann. adv.; bk.rev.; abstr.; illus.; circ. 340,000.

KIDSPORTS. see *CHILDREN AND YOUTH — For*

796.812 — JA
KINDAI JUDO. (Text in Japanese; with summaries in English, French) 1979. m. 7200 Yen. Baseball Magazine Sha, 3-10-10 Misaki-cho, Chiyoda-ku, Tokyo, Japan. Ed. Yoshinori Nagase.

794.1 — UK
KINGPIN. 1986. 3/yr. £8 (foreign £12). 6 St. George's Rd., Ilford, Essex IG1 3PQ, England. TEL 081-554-6219. Ed. Jonathan Manley. adv.; bk.rev.; circ. 2,000.
Description: Includes games, news, "how-to-improve" articles, opening theory, endgame studies, and correspondence chess.

790.1 — BG
KIRAJAGAT. (Text in Bengali) 1977. w. National Sports Control Board, 62-63 Purana Paltan, Dhaka, Bangladesh. Ed. Ali Muzzaman Chowdhury. circ. 7,000.

794.1 — FI — ISSN 0358-1071
KIRJESHAKKI. 1961. 12/yr. FIM 180($52) Esko Nuutilainen, Ed. & Pub., PL 61, 04401 Jarvenpaa, Finland. FAX 0-2918336. adv.; bk.rev.; circ. 1,300.

790.1 — SP
KIROLAK; revista deportiva del pais Vasco. (Text in Basque and Spanish) 1971. m. 600 ptas.($15) c/o Jose Acosta Montoro, Ed., Villa Cord, Miraconcha, San Sebastian, Spain. Eds. Jose Acosta Montoro, Jose Maria Ferrer. adv.; bk.rev.; abstr.; bibl.; charts; illus.; stat.; tr.lit.; index; circ. 18,500 (controlled). (back issues avail.)

790.1 — GW
KLUBB NACHRICHTEN. 1950. bi-m. DM.20($20) Turn-Klubb zu Hannover, Maschstr. 16, 3000 Hannover 1, Germany. TEL 0511-8093483. adv.; circ. 3,500. (back issues avail.)

790.1 — GW
KLUBNACHRICHTEN. 1925. m. membership. Klubnachrichten - R R T K, Schillerstr. 39, 8400 Regensburg, Germany. TEL 0941-21400. Ed. Ham Richter.

796.86 — NE — ISSN 0047-3561
KONINKLIJKE OFFICIERS SCHERMBOND. KOS-GEBEUREN. fl.1.50($3). W.P.P. Hartman, Rembrandtkade 260, Rijswijk (Z.H.), Netherlands. adv.; circ. 800.

796 — NE — ISSN 0023-3501
KONKREET. 1969. bi-m. fl.10. Federatie van Bevoegde Nederlandse Sportleiders, Carmenstraat 9, Apeldoorn, Netherlands. Ed. Th.J. Van Son. adv.; bk.rev.; circ. 1,500.

790.1 — UA
AL-KORA WAL-MALAEB/SOCCER AND PLAYGROUNDS. (Text in Arabic) 1976. w. Dar al-Tahrir, 24 Sharia Zakaria Ahmed, Cairo, Egypt. TEL 02-741611. FAX 02-749949. TELEX 92475 TAHRIR UN. circ. 95,000. (newspaper)

790 — Il — ISSN 0023-4621
KRIDANGAN. (Text in Marathi) 1970. fortn. Rs.70. Prestige Publications, 461-1 Sadashiv Peth, Tilak Rd., Poona 411030, Maharashtra, India. Ed. C.S. Ghorpade. adv.; bk.rev.; illus.; circ. 30,000.

KULISY SPORTU. see *ETHNIC INTERESTS*

794.1 — US — ISSN 0148-057X
KXE6S VEREIN CHESS SOCIETY. ADVISORY BOARD RECORD. 1976. bi-m. Kxe6s Verein Chess Society, Box 2066, Chapel Hill, NC 27514. Ed. Steven Buntin. adv.; bk.rev.; abstr.; bibl.; charts; illus.; stat.; index, cum.index; circ. 500. (tabloid format; back issues avail.)

794.1 — US — ISSN 0148-0561
KXE6S VEREIN NEWSLETTER. 1975. bi-m. $10. Kxe6s Verein Chess Society, Box 2066, Chapel Hill, NC 27514. Eds. Steven Buntin, Jerry Clark. adv.; bk.rev.; bibl.; charts; illus.; stat.; index. (tabloid format; back issues avail.)

790.1 — US
L A SPORTS PROFILES. (Los Angeles) 1986. bi-m. $10. Sports Profiles, 4711 Golf, Ste. 900, Skokie, IL 60076. TEL 708-673-0592. FAX 708-673-0633. adv.; circ. 75,000.
Description: Covers local professional and college sports teams.

L S A NEWSLETTER. (Leisure Studies Association) see *LEISURE AND RECREATION*

793 — IT
LABIRINTO. 1948. m. (11/yr.). L.10000. Piazza del Parlamento 3, 00186 Rome, Italy. Ed. Luigi Bernabei. adv.; circ. 1,000.

790.1 — US — ISSN 0194-7893
GV989
LACROSSE. 1978. 6/yr. $30 to individuals; students $20. Lacrosse Foundation, Inc., 113 W. University Parkway, Baltimore, MD 21210. TEL 301-235-6882. FAX 301-366-6735. Ed. Janie Hurt. adv.; illus.stat.tr.lit.; circ. 8,000. (back issues avail.)
Description: Covers Lacrosse games. Includes action photographs and news on the Lacrosse foundation.

LAKELAND BOATING; the Great Lakes boating magazine. see *SPORTS AND GAMES — Boats And Boating*

790.1 — IT
LANCILLOTTO E NAUSICA; quadrimestrale di critica e storia dello sport. 1984. 3/yr. L.20000($15) La Meridiana Editore, Via Selci in Sabina, 14, I-00199 Rome, Italy. Ed.Bd. adv.; bk.rev.; circ. 10,000.

797.21 — US
LANELINES; the coaches' newsletter of United States swimming. vol.6, 1992. bi-m. $18 to non-members; members $8. United States Swimming, 1750 E. Boulder St., Colorado Springs, CO 80909. TEL 719-578-4578. (looseleaf format)

LAS VEGAS INSIDER. see *TRAVEL AND TOURISM*

796.72 — US
LATE MODEL DIGEST. fortn. Back Porch Publications, Box 69, Marble, NC 28905-0069. TEL 704-837-9539. FAX 704-837-7718. Ed. Brian McLeod. adv.

796 — RU — ISSN 0024-4155
GV1060.5
LEGKAYA ATLETIKA. 1955. m. 4.80 Rub. (Soyuz Sportivnykh Obshchestv i Organizatsii S.S.S.R.) Izdatel'stvo Fizkul'tura i Sport, Legkaya Atletika, Roshdestvensky b-r 10-7, 103031 Moscow K-31, Russia. FAX 2001217. Ed. V.S. Kayurov. illus.; index; circ. 75,000.

790.1 — GW — ISSN 0323-4134
LEICHTATHLET. 52/yr. DM.27.60 (foreign DM.37.80). Deutscher Verband fuer Leichtathletik, Dimitroffstr. 157, 1055 Berlin, Germany. (Subscr. to: Buchexport, Postfach 160, Germany)

613.7 790.1 — GW
LEIPZIGER SPORTWISSENSCHAFTLICHE BEITRAEGE. (Text in German; summaries in English, French, German and Russian) 1959. a. DM.84. (Fakultaet fuer Sportwissenschaft, Universitaet Leipzig) Academia Verlag GmbH, Postfach 1165, 5205 St. Augustin 1, Germany. TEL 2241-333349. FAX 2241-341528. Ed. H. Kirchgaessner. bk.rev.; illus.; index; circ. 400. (tabloid format)
Formerly: Deutsche Hochschule fuer Koerperkultur. Wissenschaftliche Zeitschrift (ISSN 0457-3919)

790.1 — GW — ISSN 0341-7387
LEISTUNGSSPORT. 1970. bi-m. DM.48 (foreign DM.54). Philippka-Verlag, Postfach 6540, 4400 Muenster, Germany. TEL 0251-23005-0. FAX 0251-23005-99. circ. 3,500. (back issues avail.) Indexed: Sportsearch (1972-).
— BLDSC shelfmark: 5182.205000.

LEISURE AND FITNESS. see *LEISURE AND RECREATION*

LEISURE INDUSTRY REPORT. see *LEISURE AND RECREATION*

LEISURE MANAGEMENT. see *LEISURE AND RECREATION*

LEISURE SCIENCES; an interdisciplinary journal. see *LEISURE AND RECREATION*

LEISURE STUDIES. see *LEISURE AND RECREATION*

790.1 — US
LET'S MAKE IT OFFICIAL. a. $2. National Federation of State High School Associations, 11724 N.W. Plaza Circle, Box 20626, Kansas City, MO 64195-0626. TEL 816-464-5400. FAX 816-464-5571.

796 — US
LET'S PLAY HOCKEY. 1972. 26/yr. $24. Let's Play, Inc., 2721 E. 42nd St., Minneapolis, MN 55406. TEL 612-729-0023. FAX 612-729-0259. adv.; circ. 18,000.
Description: For youth and amateur players, parents, coaches and fans.

794.1 — HU — ISSN 0230-5151
LEVELEZESI SAKKHIRADO. 1967. 6/yr. $4. Hungarian Chess Association, Correspondence Committee, H-1072 Budapest, Klauzal ter.5.II.30, Hungary. TEL 361-1213-832. Ed. Dezso Solt. adv.; bk.rev.; circ. 1,000.
Description: Covers national and international chess games and news, tables and results.

LICHAMELIJKE OPVOEDING. see *EDUCATION — Teaching Methods And Curriculum*

LOISIR ET SOCIETE/SOCIETY AND LEISURE. see *LEISURE AND RECREATION*

790.1 — FR
LOISIRS JEUNES. 1950. w. (44/yr.). 265 F. 36 rue de Ponthieu, 75008 Paris, France. Dir. J.M. Despinette.

793 745.1 — US — ISSN 0278-4114
TJ1557
LOOSE CHANGE. 1977. 10/yr. $39. Mead Publishing Company, 1515 S. Commerce St., Las Vegas, NV 89102-2703. TEL 702-387-8750. Ed. Daniel R. Mead. adv.; bk.rev.; circ. 3,600. (back issues avail.)
Description: Covers collecting slot machines, gambling memorabilia and coin operated amusement devices.

791 — Il — ISSN 0024-6654
LOTTERY GAZETTE. (Text in English and Hindi) 1969. w. Rs.11($2) J.C. Gupta, Ed. & Pub., 157-E Kamla Nagar, Delhi 7, India. adv.; film rev.; play rev.; circ. 12,000.

790.1 — US — ISSN 0277-5565
LOTTERY PLAYER'S MAGAZINE. 1981. m. $23.97. Regal Publishing Corporation, 321 New Albany Rd., Moorestown, NJ 08057. FAX 609-273-6350. Ed. Samuel W. Valenza, Jr. adv.; bk.rev.; play rev.; stat.; index; circ. 200,000. (back issues avail.)

795 — IT — ISSN 0024-6662
LOTTOROSCOPO; periodico mensile di previsioni sul lotto. 1957. m. L.25000. Lottoroscopo, Casella Postale 94, Via S. Nicolo 7, 43100 Parma, Italy. TEL 0521-206076. Ed. Giovanni Gatti. circ. 5,000.

799.2 — CI — ISSN 0024-6999
LOVACKI VJESNIK. 1892. m. 50 din.($8.55) (typically set in Jan.). (Savjet "Lovacki Vjesnik") Lovacki Savez Hrvatske, V. Nazora 61, Zagreb, Croatia. TEL 041-433 310. Ed. Tihomir Kovacevic. adv.; bk.rev.; circ. 82,000.

796 — US — ISSN 0024-7898
M A C GOPHER. 1915. m. $18. Minneapolis Athletic Club, 615 Second Ave. S., Minneapolis, MN 55402. TEL 612-339-3655. FAX 612-339-7923. Ed. Marilyn A. Siebert. adv.; circ. 4,400.

SPORTS AND GAMES 4479

796.215 US ISSN 0898-4786
GV1102.7.T7
M A TRAINING. (Martial Arts) 1973. bi-m. $16. Rainbow Publications, Inc., 24715 Ave. Rockefeller, Box 918, Santa Clarita, CA 91380-9018. TEL 805-257-4066. FAX 805-257-3018. (Subscr. to: Box 16298, N. Hollywood, CA 91615-6298. TEL 800-266-4066) Ed. Ian C. Blair. adv.; charts; illus.; circ. 20,000.
  Former titles: M A Weapons (ISSN 0893-2514); Fighting Stars - Ninja; Fighting Stars (ISSN 0274-5178)
  Description: Covers training for the martial artist in all styles and product reviews.

796 IS
MACCABI WORLD UNION. NEWSLETTER. (Text in English; Spanish edition also available) 1951. m. free. Maccabi World Union, Kfar Hamaccabiah, Israel. Ed. Zvi Eyal. adv.; circ. 500 (controlled). (processed)
  Formerly: Maccabi News Bulletin (ISSN 0541-5896)

MAGNUM. see SPORTS AND GAMES — Outdoor Life

796.42 US
MAINELY RUNNING. 10/yr. Lincoln County Publishing Co., 2 Howards Hill Rd., Brunswick, ME 04011. TEL 207-725-8680. Ed. John W. LeRoy. circ. 1,000.

354 CN
MANITOBA LOTTERIES FOUNDATION. ANNUAL REPORT. (Report year ends Mar. 31) 1971. a. Manitoba Lotteries Foundation, 830 Empress St., Winnipeg, Man. R3G 3H3, Canada. TEL 204-957-2500. FAX 204-957-2621. illus.; stat.; circ. 500.
  Formerly: Manitoba. Lotteries Commission. Annual Report (ISSN 0703-0827)

796 IE ISSN 0047-5874
MARATHON; Ireland's international athletics magazine. 1967. m. £5($10) Marathon Publications, Aghadark, Ballinamore, Co. Leitrim, Ireland. Ed. Padraig Griffin. adv.; bk.rev.; illus.; stat.; circ. 3,500. **Indexed:** Sportsearch.

796 US
MARIN SPORTS. m. Opportune Press, Inc., Box 848, Mill Valley, CA 94942. TEL 510-388-3211. FAX 510-388-1824. Ed. Peter Seidman.

790.1 340 US ISSN 1057-6029
▼**MARQUETTE SPORTS LAW JOURNAL.** 1990. s-a. $100. (National Sports Law Institute) Marquette University, Law School, 1103 W. Wisconsin Ave., Milwaukee, WI 53233. TEL 414-224-5143. Ed. James T. Gray.
  Description: Covers the scholarly treatment of sports and law issues.

799.202 IS
MATARAH. m. 18 Misilat Hachashmonaim, Tel Aviv, Israel.

794.1 SP
MATE POSTAL. (Editions in English and Spanish) 1974. q. $15. Comision Permanente Ajedrez Postal, Santa Eulalia, 28, torre, 08921 Santa Coloma de Gramanet, Barcelona, Spain. (Subscr. to: c/o Valentin Torra, Calle Aneto, 3, 08251 Santpedor (Barcelona), Spain) (Affiliate: International Correspondence Chess Federation) Ed. Carlos Ros Miro.

790.1 SY
MAUKEF AL-RIADI. w. Ouehda Organization, Damascus, Syria. adv.

794.1 NE
MAX EUWE-CENTRUM. NIEUWSBRIEF. 1987. 4/yr. $22. Stichting Max Euwe-Centrum, Postbus 11513, 1001 GM Amsterdam, Netherlands. TEL 020-6257017. FAX 020-6392077. Ed. L.C.M. Diepstraten. bk.rev.
  Description: News about chess activities at the Max Euwe-Centrum.

794.1 UK
MAXWELL MACMILLAN CHESS BOOKS. 1960. a. free. Maxwell Macmillan Chess & Bridge, London Rd., Wheatley, Oxford OX9 1YR, England. TEL 08677-4111. FAX 08677-5383. Ed. Jimmy Adams.
  Former titles: Pergamon Chess Books; Chess Book List (ISSN 0069-3197)

MEDIA SPORTS BUSINESS. see COMMUNICATIONS — Television And Cable

MEN'S FITNESS; the healthy man's guide to living. see PHYSICAL FITNESS AND HYGIENE

MERCURY (LOS ANGELES). see CLUBS

790.1 VE
MERIDIANO. d. Meridiario, C.A., Bloque DeArmas, Final Av. San Martin, Esq. La Quebradita 34-2, Edificio Berlioz, Piso 2, Apdo. 475, Caracas, Venezuela. adv.; circ. 300,000.

790.1 SZ
MESSAGE OLYMPIQUE/OLYMPIC MESSAGE. irreg. International Olympic Committee - Comite International Olympique, Chateau De Vidy, CH-1007 Lausanne, Switzerland. TEL 021-253271. FAX 021-241552. **Indexed:** Sportsearch (1982-).

790.1 US
METROSPORTS MAGAZINE. (In 2 eds.: New York Tri-State, Greater Boston) 1974. 11/yr. $18. Tate House Enterprises, Inc., 695 Washington St., New York, NY 10014. TEL 212-627-7040. FAX 212-242-3293. Eds. Miles & Julie Jaffe. adv.; bk.rev.; circ. 185,000 (controlled). (tabloid format; back issues avail.)
  Supersedes in part (in 1988): CitySports Magazine.
  Description: Covers all aspects of the New York Tri-State and Greater Boston active lifestyle and participant (not professional) sports, including travel, recreation, nutrition and health, and profiles.

794.1 US
MICHIGAN CHESS. 1971. 6/yr. $12. 7500 Anthony, Dearborn, MI 48126. Ed. David Moody. adv.; bk.rev.; circ. 1,000.

MICHIGAN OUT-OF-DOORS. see CONSERVATION

796.72 US ISSN 0047-732X
MIDWEST RACING NEWS. 1959. w. (Apr.-Sep.); m. (Oct.-Dec.) $15. Midwest Racing News, Inc., 6646 W. Fairview Ave., Milwaukee, WI 53213. TEL 414-778-4700. FAX 414-778-4688. Ed. Phil Hall. adv.; bk.rev.; illus.; circ. 8,000. (tabloid format)
  Description: Discusses regional and national automobile races and drivers.

790.1 FR
MINISTERE DE LA JEUNESSE ET DES SPORT. BULLETIN OFFICIEL. 22/yr. 215 F. (foreign 264 F.). Centre National de Documentation Pedagogique, 26, rue d'Ulm, 75230 Paris Cedex 05, France. TEL 46-34-90-00. (Subscr. to: CNDP-Abonnements, B.P. 107 - 05, 75224 Paris Cedex 05, France)
  Formerly: Secretariat a la Jeunesse et aux Sport. Bulletin Officiel.

794.1 US
MINNESOTA CHESS JOURNAL. 1963. 4/yr. $10. Minnesota Chess Association, 4744 Chicago Ave. S., Minneapolis, MN 55407. Ed. Keith Hayward. adv.; bk.rev.; circ. 800.
  Description: Reports on national events with local participants, and computer programs.

796 US
MINNESOTA HOCKEY. 1988. 8/yr. $17.95. Publishing Group (Bloomington), 1022 W. 80th St., Bloomington, MN 55420. TEL 612-881-3183. FAX 612-881-2172. adv.; circ. 9,877.
  Description: Covers the NHL, plus collegiate, high school and amateur hockey, as well as history and controversial topics.

796 US
MINNESOTA SPORTS. 11/yr. Skyway News, 33 S. Fifth St., Minneapolis, MN 55402-1050. TEL 612-375-9222. FAX 612-375-9208. Ed. Joe Oberle. adv.; circ. 40,000.

790.1 US
THE MISSOURI FOX TROTTER MAGAZINE. 1975. m. $10. John Tranbarger, RR1, Box 393, Pleasant Hope, MO 65725. TEL 417-759-7432. Ed. Linda Tranbarger. adv.; bk.rev.; circ. 675. (back issues avail.)
  Formerly: Missouri Fox Trotter.

790.1 GW
MITGLIEDERRUNDSCHREIBEN. 1953. m. Deutscher Sportbund, Otto-Fleck-Schneise 12, 6000 Frankfurt a.M. 71, Germany. TEL 069-6700-254. FAX 069-674906. circ. 1,400.

MODERN MOTOR. see TRANSPORTATION — Automobiles

MODUL: SCHACH-COMPUTER-SCHACH. see COMPUTERS — Computer Games

MONDO SOMMERSO; international magazine on sea diving activities, ecology and travels. see EARTH SCIENCES — Oceanography

794.1 IT
MONDOSCACCHI. irreg. (4-5/yr.) A M I S, C.P. 306, 00100 Rome, Italy. Ed. A. Zichichi.
  Description: Contains annotated games, "how-to-improve" articles, and national news. Some issues may be devoted exclusively to a particular technical or chess cultural theme.

796.522 SP ISSN 0027-0032
MONTANEROS DE ARAGON. 1949. q. free. Montaneros de Aragon, Calvo Sotelo 11, Zaragoza, Spain. Ed. Miguel - Angel Garcia Lopez. adv.; bibl.; charts; illus.

796.86 JA
MONTHLY JAPANESE FENCING/GEKKAN KENDO NIPPON. (Text in Japanese) 1976. m. 8160 Yen. Ski Journal Co. Ltd., 3-11, Yotsuya, Shinjuku-ku, Tokyo, Japan. Ed. Ryuka Nakano.

790.1 DK ISSN 0107-8976
MOTIONSGANG. 1982. bi-m. DKK 40. Sjaellandske Gangsport Foreninger, Mogens Aistrup, Baunevej 14, DK-2650 Hvidovre, Denmark.

790.1 CN
MOTONEIGISTE CANADIEN. (Text in French) 1975. 2/yr. C R V Publishing Co. Ltd., 3580 Poirier Blvd., Ville St-Laurent, Que. H4R 2J5, Canada. TEL 514-856-0788. Ed. Claude Leonard. adv.; illus.; circ. 100,000. **Indexed:** Sportsearch.

388.3 UK ISSN 0027-2019
MOTOR SPORT. 1924. m. £42. Teesdale Publishing Company Ltd., Standard House, Bonhill St., London EC2A 4DA, England. TEL 071-628 4741. FAX 071-638-8497. TELEX 888602 MONEWS G. Ed. W. Boddy. adv.; bk.rev.; charts; illus.; index; circ. 60,000.

796.72 UK
MOTORSCOT. 1949. m. £3. Scottish Clubman Ltd., 12 Evan St., Stonehaven, Kincardinshire, Scotland. Ed. A.J. Stephen. adv.; bk.rev.; bibl.; illus.; circ. 10,000.
  Formerly: Scottish Clubman (ISSN 0036-9152)
  Description: Covers automobile, motorcycle and kart racing.

796.72 US
MOTORSPORTS. bi-m. J.L. Quinn & Assoc. Inc., Box 8389, Fresno, CA 93747-8389. TEL 209-875-0434. Ed. Jim Quinn. circ. 5,000.

MOTORSPORTS MARKETING NEWS; the latest marketing & sponsorship news in motorsports. see BUSINESS AND ECONOMICS — Marketing And Purchasing

MUENZAUTOMAT; Fachzeitschrift fuer die Automatenbranche. see BUSINESS AND ECONOMICS — Management

MUSCLE CARS. see TRANSPORTATION — Automobiles

790.1 CN
MUSCLE MAG INTERNATIONAL. 1974. m. $45. Health Culture Inc., 52 Bramsteele Rd., Unit 2, Brampton, Ont. L6W 3M5, Canada. FAX 416-791-4292. Ed. Robert Kennedy. adv.; bk.rev.; charts; illus.; circ. 230,000. **Indexed:** Sportsearch.

MUSCLE TRAINING ILLUSTRATED. see PHYSICAL FITNESS AND HYGIENE

MUSCULAR DEVELOPMENT. see PHYSICAL FITNESS AND HYGIENE

790.1 US
N A A NEWSLETTER. 1985. q. membership. National Archery Association, 1750 E. Boulder St., Colorado Springs, CO 80909. TEL 719-578-4576. FAX 719-632-4733. Ed. Christine McCartney. adv.; circ. 3,800.
  Description: Covers the sport of archery in the US. Provides tournament dates with application forms.

S

SPORTS AND GAMES

796 US ISSN 0077-3336
N A I A HANDBOOK. 1959. biennial. $25. National Association of Intercollegiate Athletics, 1221 Baltimore Ave., Kansas City, MO 64105. TEL 816-842-5050. FAX 816-421-4471. Ed. Wallace Schwartz. (reprint service avail. from UMI)

796 US ISSN 0740-5995
N A I A NEWS. 1950. 12/yr. $25. National Association of Intercollegiate Athletics, 1221 Baltimore Ave., Kansas City, MO 64105. TEL 816-842-5050. FAX 816-421-4471. Ed. Tim Staley. bk.rev.; stat.; circ. 8,000. (also avail. in microform from UMI; reprint service avail. from UMI) Indexed: Sportsearch (1976-).
Former titles: N A I A News and Coach; N A I A News.

796 US
GV741
N A I A OFFICIAL RECORDS BOOK AND CHAMPIONSHIP SUMMARIES. 1958. a. $20. National Association of Intercollegiate Athletics, 1221 Baltimore Ave., Kansas City, MO 64105. TEL 816-842-5050. Ed. Charles Eppler. index; circ. 2,500. (reprint service avail. from UMI)
Formerly: N A I A Official Records Book (ISSN 0077-3344)

796.72 US
N A S C A R NEWS. 1949. fortn. $35 to non-members. National Association for Stock Car Auto Racing, Inc., 1801 Volusia Ave., Daytona Beach, FL 32114-1243. TEL 904-253-0611. FAX 904-252-8804. Ed. Paul C. Schaefer. adv.; bk.rev.; charts; illus.; tr.lit.; index; circ. 40,000.
Formerly: N A S C A R Newsletter (ISSN 0027-5999)

790.1 US
N A Y S I RESOURCE LIST. irreg. free. North American Youth Sport Institute, 4985 Oak Garden Dr., Kernersville, NC 27284-9520. TEL 919-784-4926. Ed. Dr. Jack Hutslar.
Description: Covers books and materials for persons working with children in sports, recreation, education, fitness and health.

790.1 US ISSN 0162-1467
GV347
N C A A DIRECTORY. 1976. a. $6. National Collegiate Athletic Association, Circulation Department, Box 7347, Overland Park, KS 66207-0347. TEL 913-339-1900. circ. 2,500.
Description: Includes membership roster, with district and division listing, and provides information on NCAA committees and organizational structure.

790.1 616.86
N C A A DRUG TESTING PROGRAM. a. $1.50. National Collegiate Athletic Association, Circulation Department, Box 7347, Overland Park, KS 66207-0347. TEL 913-339-1900.
Description: Establishes NCAA procedures and regulations for drug testing of student athletes, and includes a list of banned drugs.

799.202 US
N C A A MEN'S AND WOMEN'S RIFLE RULES. a. $4. National Collegiate Athletic Association, Circulation Department, Box 7347, Overland Park, KS 66207-0347. TEL 913-339-1900. illus.
Description: Covers official signals, interpretations, and rulings.

797.21 US ISSN 0736-5128
N C A A MEN'S AND WOMEN'S SWIMMING AND DIVING RULES. 1925. a. $3. National Collegiate Athletic Association, Circulation Department, Box 7347, Overland Park, KS 66207-0347. TEL 913-339-1900. illus.; circ. 8,200.
Former titles: N C A A Swimming (ISSN 0272-8095); Official National Collegiate Athletic Association Swimming Guide.
Description: Covers official signals, interpretations, and rulings.

796 US ISSN 0735-9195
GV847
N C A A MEN'S ICE HOCKEY RULES AND INTERPRETATIONS. 1926. a. $3. National Collegiate Athletic Association, Circulation Department, Box 7347, Overland Park, KS 66207-0347. TEL 913-339-1900. illus.; circ. 10,000.
Formerly: Official National Collegiate Athletic Association Ice Hockey Guide.
Description: Covers official signals, interpretations, and rulings.

790.1 US ISSN 0734-0508
GV839
N C A A MEN'S WATER POLO RULES. 1970. a. $3. National Collegiate Athletic Association, Circulation Department, Box 7347, Overland Park, KS 66207-0347. TEL 913-339-1900. illus.
Former titles: N C A A Water Polo Rules (ISSN 0271-860X); Official National Collegiate Athletic Association Water Polo Rules.
Description: Covers official signals, interpretations, and rulings.

796 US ISSN 0027-6170
N C A A NEWS. 1964. 46/yr. $24. National Collegiate Athletic Association, Circulation Department, Box 7347, Overland Park, KS 66207-0347. TEL 913-339-1906. FAX 913-339-1950. Ed. David Pickle. adv.; bk.rev.; circ. 20,000. (tabloid format)
Indexed: Sports Per.Ind., Sportsearch (1977-).
Incorporates: Football Statistics Rankings.

790.1 US ISSN 0736-511X
GV1195
N C A A WRESTLING RULES. 1927. a. $3. National Collegiate Athletic Association, Circulation Department, Box 7347, Overland Park, KS 66207-0347. TEL 913-339-1900. illus.; circ. 10,000.
Formerly: Official National Collegiate Athletic Association Wrestling Guide.
Description: Covers official signals, interpretations, and rulings.

796 US ISSN 0744-1347
N C G A NEWS. 1961. q. $17.50 to non-members; members $1. Northern California Golf Association, 3200 Lopez Rd., Box NCGA, Pebble Beach, CA 93953. TEL 408-625-4653. FAX 408-625-0150. Ed. Ted Blofsky, Jr. adv.; circ. 133,000.
Formerly: Northern California Golf Association. Blue Book.
Description: Provides news, articles, information on tournaments, courses and golfers, including association news.

790.1 US
N I R S A JOURNAL. 1977. 3/yr. $40. National Intramural Recreational Sports Association, 850 S.W. 15th St., Corvallis, OR 97333-4145. TEL 503-737-2088. FAX 503-737-2026. Ed. Gary L. Miller. adv.; bk.rev.; index; circ. 3,000. (back issues avail.) Indexed: Phys.Ed.Ind., Sportsearch (1979-).

N R A ACTION. (National Rifle Association of America) see LAW

796.93 US
N S A A NEWS.* 1965. 6/yr. membership. National Ski Areas Association, 8377B Greensboro Dr., McLean, VA 22102-3529. Ed. Kathe Dillmann. bk.rev.; circ. 2,500. (tabloid format)
Formerly: N S A A Newsletter (ISSN 0300-6670)

N S G A RETAIL FOCUS. (National Sporting Goods Association) see BUSINESS AND ECONOMICS — Marketing And Purchasing

N.S.W. SKINDIVER. (New South Wales) see SPORTS AND GAMES — Outdoor Life

NADI ABU DHABI AL-SIYAHI/ABU DHABI TOURIST CLUB. see CLUBS

NADI AL-WASL. see CLUBS

797.21 FR
NAGER SAUVER.* 1928. q. 80 F. Federation Francaise des Maitres-Nageurs Sauveteurs, 23, rue de la Sourdiere, B.P. 179, 75001 Paris, France. adv.; circ. 5,000.

790.1 JA
NANBA/SPORTS GRAPHIC NUMBER. (Text in Japanese) 1980. fortn. 11760 Yen. Bungei-Shunju Ltd., 3 Kioi-cho, Chiyoda-ku, Tokyo, Japan. FAX 03-264-4180. Ed. Atsuo Shitara.

AL-NASR. see CLUBS

797 FR
NATATION. m. 320 F. (foreign 560 F.). Federation Francaise de Natation, 148 av. Gambetta, 75020 Paris, France. TEL 40-31-17-70. FAX 40-31-19-90. TELEX 215249. adv.; illus. Indexed: Sportsearch.

790.1 NE
NATIONAAL SPORT MAGAZINE.* 1980. bi-m. fl.45. (Nederlandse Sport Federatie) Drukkerij G.J. van Amerongen B.V., Postbus 205, 3800 AE Amersfoort, Netherlands.
Formerly: Sport Intermedium.

796 US ISSN 0077-3794
GV563
NATIONAL COLLEGIATE ATHLETIC ASSOCIATION. ANNUAL REPORTS.. 1966. a. $12. National Collegiate Athletic Association, Circulation Department, Box 7347, Overland Park, KS 66207-0347. TEL 913-339-1900. circ. 2,500.

796 US ISSN 0077-3808
NATIONAL COLLEGIATE ATHLETIC ASSOCIATION. CONVENTION PROCEEDINGS. 1906; 1967 as independent title. a. $12. National Collegiate Athletic Association, Circulation Department, Box 7347, Overland Park, KS 66207-0347. TEL 913-339-1900. circ. 2,500.

796 US ISSN 0077-3816
GV563
NATIONAL COLLEGIATE ATHLETIC ASSOCIATION. MANUAL. Cover title: N C A A Manual. (Also published in editions for individual Divisions 1, 2, and 3.) 1906; 1966 as independent title. a. $11. National Collegiate Athletic Association, Circulation Department, Box 7347, Overland Park, KS 66207-0347. TEL 913-339-1900. circ. 7,500.
Description: Contains all NCAA legislation applicable to the three divisions, including constitution, operating and administrative by-laws.

796.06 US ISSN 0094-4459
GV563
NATIONAL COLLEGIATE ATHLETIC ASSOCIATION. PROCEEDINGS OF THE SPECIAL CONVENTION. 1973. irreg., latest 1987. National Collegiate Athletic Association, Circulation Department, Box 7347, Overland Park, KS 66207-0347. TEL 913-339-1900. Key Title: Proceedings of the Special Convention of the National Collegiate Athletic Association.

796 US ISSN 0190-4329
GV741
NATIONAL COLLEGIATE CHAMPIONSHIPS. 1954. a. $9.95. National Collegiate Athletic Association, Circulation Department, Box 7347, Overland Park, KS 66207-0347. TEL 913-339-1900. circ. 2,700.
Formerly: National Collegiate Championships Record Book (ISSN 0148-9798)
Description: Contains detailed summaries of championships of the preceding year, for both men's and women's athletics, with additional historical information.

796 US ISSN 0547-616X
NATIONAL DIRECTORY OF COLLEGE ATHLETICS (MEN'S EDITION). 1968. a. $17.50. (National Association of Collegiate Directors of Athletics) Collegiate Directories, Inc., Box 450640, Cleveland, OH 44145. TEL 216-835-1172. FAX 216-835-8835. Ed. Kevin Cleary. circ. 16,500.
Description: Lists 2,100 senior and junior colleges and vital information about each athletic department. Covers men's intercollegiate athletics in the U.S. and Canada, NCAA, NAIA and NJCAA and other collegiate information.

796 US ISSN 0739-1226
GV439
NATIONAL DIRECTORY OF COLLEGE ATHLETICS (WOMEN'S EDITION). 1973. a. $12.50. Collegiate Directories, Inc., Box 450640, Cleveland, OH 44145. TEL 216-835-1172. FAX 216-835-8835. Ed. Kevin Cleary. illus.; circ. 9,000.
Formerly: National Directory of Women's Athletics (ISSN 0092-5489)

SPORTS AND GAMES

790.1   US
NATIONAL FEDERATION HANDBOOK. a. $2.25. National Federation of State High School Associations, 11724 N.W. Plaza Circle, Box 20626, Kansas City, MO 64195-0626. TEL 816-464-5400. FAX 816-464-5571. **Indexed:** SRI.

796 636   AT   ISSN 0310-589X
NATIONAL GREYHOUND NEWS. 1971. m. Aus.$17($37.20) (New South Wales Greyhound Breeders, Owners and Trainers Association) Greyhound News Pty. Ltd., Box 72, Waverly, N.S.W. 2024, Australia. Ed. Noel C. Christensen. adv.; bk.rev.; circ. 20,000.
   Description: Covers dog racing.

798   US
NATIONAL GREYHOUND UPDATE. 11/yr. Hobson Publishing, 21684 Grand Ave., Cupertino, CA 95014. TEL 408-446-0551. Ed. Pres Hobson.

790.1   US
NATIONAL HIGH SCHOOL SPORTS RECORD BOOK. a. $3.95. National Federation of State High School Associations, 11724 N.W. Plaza Circle, Box 20626, Kansas City, MO 64195-0626. TEL 816-464-5400. FAX 816-464-5571. Ed. Fred Mares. **Indexed:** SRI.

796.9   CN
NATIONAL HOCKEY LEAGUE. OFFICIAL RULE BOOK. 1931. a. $3.50. National Hockey League Publishing, 75 International Blvd., Ste. 300, Toronto, Ont. M9W 6L9, Canada. TEL 416-798-0809. Ed. Phil Schener. illus.
   Description: Official rules governing play in the NHL, featuring referee's signals rink diagram and new rules.

NATIONAL P A L UPDATE. (National Police Athletic League) see *CHILDREN AND YOUTH — For*

796.72   US   ISSN 0028-0208
NATIONAL SPEED SPORT NEWS. 1932. w. $32. Kay Publishing Co., Inc., 79 Chestnut St., Box 608, Ridgewood, NJ 07451. TEL 201-445-3117. FAX 201-445-7677. Ed. Chris Economaki. adv.; bk.rev.; charts; illus.; circ. 76,000. (tabloid format; also avail. in microfiche)
   Description: Covers automobile racing.

796.72   US
NATIONAL SPEEDWAY DIRECTORY. 1975. a. $9. Slideways Publications, Box 448, Comstock Park, MI 49321. TEL 616-361-6229. Ed. Allan E. Brown. adv.; stat.; circ. 12,000.
   Formerly: Midwest Auto Racing Guide.
   Description: Lists every oval track, dragstrip and road course in the U.S. and Canada.

688.76   US
NATIONAL SPORTING GOODS ASSOCIATION BUYING GUIDE. 1967. a. membership. National Sporting Goods Association, 1699 Wall St., Mt. Prospect, IL 60056-5780. TEL 708-439-4000. FAX 708-439-0111. adv.; circ. 20,000.

790.1   US   ISSN 1054-2205
THE NATIONAL SPORTS REVIEW. a. $6.95. Preview Publishing, 100 W. Harrison, N. Tower, 5th Fl., Seattle, WA 98119. TEL 206-282-2322. FAX 206-284-2083.
   Description: Review of the year in sports.

790.1   US   ISSN 0739-6074
HD9992.U5
NATIONWIDE DIRECTORY OF SPORTING GOODS BUYERS. 1978. a. $147. Salesman's Guide, Inc., A Reed Reference Publishing Company, Division of Reed Publishing (USA) Inc., 121 Chanlon Rd., New Providence, NJ 07974. TEL 800-521-8110. FAX 908-665-6688. TELEX 138 755. (Subscr. to: Order Dept., Box 31, New Providence, NJ 07974) Ed. Carlton A. Dyce. index; circ. 2,000.
   Description: Lists 13,000 buyers and executives of 7,500 sporting goods retailers.

796.323   NE   ISSN 0028-2073
NEDERLANDS KORFBALBLAD. 1935. fortn. fl.35. Koninklijk Nederlands Korfbalverbond - Royal Dutch Basketball Association, Postbus 1000, 3980 DA Bunnik, Netherlands. TEL 3405-70655. FAX 3405-67025. Ed. Joop Bloemheuvel. adv.; bk.rev.; illus.; circ. 6,300.

636.6   NE   ISSN 0028-2391
NEERLANDS POSTDUIVEN ORGAAN. 1948. w. fl.58. Postbus 256, Nieuwe Fellenoord 12, 5612 KC Eindhoven, Netherlands. TEL 040-437003. Ed. J.M.A.M. deZeeuw. adv.; illus.

799.3   US   ISSN 0195-1599
NEW GUN WEEK. 1967. w. $32. Second Amendment Foundation, Box 488, Station C, Buffalo, NY 14209. FAX 716-884-4471. Ed. Joseph P. Tartaro. adv.; bk.rev.; illus.; circ. 30,000. (newspaper; reprint service avail.)
   Formerly: Gun Week (ISSN 0017-5633)

794.1   US   ISSN 0168-8782
NEW IN CHESS MAGAZINE; international chess information system. 1984. 8/yr. $68. Chess Combination, Inc., 2423 Noble Sta., Bridgeport, CT 06608-0423. TEL 203-367-1555. Ed. J.H. Timman. adv.; bk.rev.; bibl.; charts; illus.; index. (back issues avail.)
   Description: Articles on new developments in world chess tournament play.

794.1   US   ISSN 0168-7697
GV1449.5
NEW IN CHESS YEARBOOK. 1984. q. $148 (includes data diskettes) (NICBASE). Chess Combination, Inc., 2423 Noble Sta., Bridgeport, CT 06608-0423. TEL 203-367-1555.
   Description: Covers all major international chess tournaments, reproduces over 5,000 selected games annually, with many annotations and theoretical analyses.

790.1   US
NEW JERSEY. CASINO CONTROL COMMISSION. ANNUAL REPORT. 1979. a. free. Casino Control Commission, Attn: Carol Kokotajlo, Public Information Assistant, Arcade Bldg., Tennessee Ave. & Boardwalk, Atlantic City, NJ 08401. TEL 609-441-3749. Ed. Thomas P. Flynn. circ. 1,500. **Indexed:** SRI.

793   US
NEW JERSEY CASINO JOURNAL. m. Casino Journal Publishing Group, 2524 Arctic Ave., Atlantic City, NJ 08401. TEL 609-345-3239. FAX 609-345-3469. Ed. Glenn Fine. adv.; circ. 20,000.

796   UK
NEW STUDIES IN ATHLETICS. (Text in English; summaries in French) 1986. q. $20. International Amateur Athletic Federation (IAAF), Three Hans Crescent, Knightsbridge, London SW1X 0LN, England. TEL 071-581-8771. FAX 071-584-5907. (Co-sponsors: Fidal-Centro Studi & Ricerche; Bundesinstitut fur Sportwissenschaft) Ed.Bd. bk.rev.; bibl.; circ. 4,500. **Indexed:** Sportsearch (1987-).

796.962   US
NEW YORK RANGERS YEARBOOK; official guide and records. 1926. a. $6. New York Rangers Hockey Club, Madison Square Garden, 4 Pennsylvania Plaza, New York, NY 10001. TEL 212-563-8000. FAX 212-563-8101. Ed. Barry Watkins. adv.; illus.; stat.
   Formerly: New York Rangers Blue Book.

796.42   US   ISSN 0161-7338
NEW YORK RUNNING NEWS. 1958. bi-m. membership. New York Road Runners Club, 9 E. 89th St., New York, NY 10128. TEL 212-860-4455. FAX 212-860-9754. TELEX 238-093-NYRRUR. Ed. Raleigh Mayer. adv.; bk.rev.; stat.; circ. 30,000. (back issues avail.) **Indexed:** Sports Per.Ind., Sportsearch.
   Supersedes: New York Runners Club Newsletter.

790.1   US
NEW YORK SPORTS (DEER PARK).* 1989. m. $15. M J C Publishers, 770 Grand Blvd., K 10, NY 11729-5725. TEL 516-792-0250. Ed. Fred Goodman. circ. 60,000.
   Description: For residents who watch and participate in sports. Covers collegiate teams and nonprofessional sports as well.

NEW ZEALAND CAR. see *TRANSPORTATION — Automobiles*

794.1   NZ
NEW ZEALAND CHESS. 1974. 6/yr. NZ.$18($20) New Zealand Chess Federation, P.O. Box 3130, Wellington, New Zealand. Ed. Bill Ramsay. adv.; bk.rev.; circ. 380.
   Description: Reports on local, national and international games.

796.345   NZ   ISSN 0110-0297
NEW ZEALAND GYMNAST. 8/yr. New Zealand Gymnast, 8 Bideford St., New Plymouth, New Zealand. **Indexed:** Sportsearch (1980-).

NEW ZEALAND JOURNAL OF HEALTH, PHYSICAL EDUCATION AND RECREATION. see *EDUCATION — Teaching Methods And Curriculum*

790.1   GW
NIEDERSACHSENTURNER. 1950. m. DM.39.60. Pohl-Verlag, Herzog-Ernst-Ring 1, 3100 Celle, Germany. TEL 05141-7504-0. Ed. Manfred Senftleben. circ. 3,000. (back issues avail.)

794.2   NE
NIEUWE DAMSPEL. 1973. q. fl.45. G. Bakker, Ed. & Pub., Mozartlaan 30, 3533 GB Utrecht, Netherlands. bk.rev.; circ. 200.

790.1   BE
NIEUWSBRIEF SPORTSECRETARIAAT. (Supplement avail.) (Text in Flemish) w. 6059 (Subsidiary of: Wolters Samson Belgie n.v.), Louizalaan 485, B-1050 Brussels, Belgium. TEL 02-7231111. FAX 02-6498480. TELEX CEDSAM 64130.
   Description: Provides advice of administrative and fiscal nature on how to run a sports organization.

NIKEPHOROS; Zeitschrift fuer Sport und Kultur im Altertum. see *HISTORY*

796.41   MX
NOCAUT; solo Box. 1972. w. Mex.$6 per no. Anuar Maccise Dib, Ed. & Pub., Paseo Tollocan Km. 57.5, Toluca-Mexico, Mexico. adv.; circ. 75,000.

790.1   DK   ISSN 0900-0283
NORMTALSUNDERSOEGELSE FOR SPORTSBRANCHEN. 1983. a. DKK 305. Danmarks Sportshandler-Forening, Konsulenttjeneste, Naverland 34, 2600 Glosrup, Denmark. illus.

790.1   NO   ISSN 0029-1994
NORSK IDRETT; Norwegian magazine on all kinds of sports. 1933. 8/yr. $32. (Norwegian Confederation of Sports) Universitetsforlaget, P.O. Box 2959-Toyen, N-0608 Oslo 6, Norway. Ed. Tor K. Karlsen. adv.; bk.rev.; circ. 6,000.

794.1   NO
NORSK SJAKKBLAD. 1906. 8/yr. $35. Frenningsvei 3, 0558 Oslo 5, Norway. FAX 02-710007. Ed. Geir Arne Drangeid. adv.; bk.rev.

790.1 973   US
NORTH AMERICAN SOCIETY FOR SPORT HISTORY. NEWSLETTER. 1973. a. membership. North American Society for Sport History, 101 White Bldg., Penn State University, University Park, PA 16802. TEL 814-865-2416. Ed. Ronald A. Smith. bk.rev.; bibl. **Indexed:** Sportsearch.

796 970 980   US   ISSN 0093-6235
GV571
NORTH AMERICAN SOCIETY FOR SPORT HISTORY. PROCEEDINGS. 1973. a. membership. North American Society for Sport History, 101 White Bldg., Penn State University, University Park, PA 16802. TEL 814-865-2416. adv.; circ. 1,000. **Indexed:** Phys.Ed.Ind., Popul.Ind.

790.1   US
NORTHERN CALIFORNIA SCHEDULE. 1982. m. $12. Schedule Publication, 80 Mitchell Blvd., San Rafael, CA 94903. TEL 415-472-7223. FAX 415-472-7233. Ed. Kees Tuinzing. adv.; circ. 50,000.
   Description: Lists sports events for the coming 12 months. Includes running, bicycling, swimming, triathlons, biathlons, corporate fun runs and family orientated events.

794.1   US   ISSN 0146-6941
NORTHWEST CHESS. 1947. m. $12.50. Box 84746, Seattle, WA 98124-6046. Ed. Ralph Dubisch. adv.; bk.rev.; circ. 700.

NORTH WEST MAGAZINE. see *ADVERTISING AND PUBLIC RELATIONS*

796.42   US
NORTHWEST RUNNER. m. 1231 N.E. 94th, Seattle, WA 98115-3136. TEL 206-526-9000. Ed. Jim Whiting. adv.; circ. 7,000.

SPORTS AND GAMES

794.1 US
NOST-ALGIA. 1960. bi-m. $13 (foreign $16). Knights of the Square Table, 111 Amber St., Buffalo, NY 14220-1861. TEL 716-825-8281. Ed. Les Roselle. adv.; circ. 350.
  Description: Chess by mail.

790.1 IT
NUOVO TOTOGUIDA SPORT. 1974. w. L.650 per no. Giroal s.r.l., Casella Postale 6125, 00100 Roma-Prati, Italy. adv.; circ. 100,000.

790.1 IT
NUOVO VAI. 1977. m. (11/yr.). L.21000. Jet Sport s.a.s., Via Spalato 5, 20124 Milan, Italy. FAX 0392-66800391. Dir. Giustino Del Vecchio. adv.; circ. 40,000.

790.1 SW
NYA KRAFTSPORT. m. (8/yr.). SEK 273. (Svenska samt Nordiska Tyngdlyftningsfoerbunden) Cewe Foerlaget, Box 77, 890 10 Bjaesta, Sweden. (Subscr. to: PK-Banken, Box 365, 891 01 Oernskoeldsvik, Sweden) adv.; circ. 4,500.

790.1 CN
O H A HOCKEY NEWS. 1983. 4/yr. N C C Publishing, 222 Argyle Ave., Delhi, Ont. N4B 2Y2, Canada. TEL 519-582-2510. FAX 519-582-4040. Ed. D.G. Glendinning. adv.; circ. 40,000.

O N S - MITTEILUNGEN. (Obersten Nationalen Sportkommission fuer den Automobil in Deutschland GmbH) see *TRANSPORTATION — Automobiles*

790.1 DK ISSN 0107-4202
O - POSTEN. 1951. 8/yr. DKK 105 to non-members; members DKK 75. Dansk Orienterings Forbund - Danish Orienteering Federation, Broendby-Stadion 20, DK-2605 Broendby, Denmark. Ed. Mads Nedergaard. adv.; bk.rev.; charts; illus.; stat.; circ. 5,000. (back issues avail.)

790.1 FR ISSN 0475-171X
OCEANS. (Text in French) 1970. m. (9/yr.). 243 F. 2 rue Saint-Simon, 75007 Paris, France. Ed. J.P. de Kerraoul. adv.; bk.rev.; circ. 52,000. Indexed: So.Pac.Per.Ind.

794.1 SP
OCHO X OCHO; revista practica de ajedrez. m. $65. Zugarto Ediciones, S.A., Pablo Aranda, 3, 28006 Madrid, Spain. TEL 411-42-64. FAX 262-26-77. Ed. Roman Toran.
  Description: Contains annotated games, "how-to-improve" articles, and combinations.

797.23 US
ODYSSEY (DALY CITY). 1976. bi-m. Central California Diving Council, Box 779, Daly City, CA 94080. TEL 415-583-8492. Ed. Carol Rose. adv.; circ. 1,500.
  Description: Covers marine ecology, access, and legislation and underwater sports for Northern and Central Californian skin and scuba divers.

799.2 AU ISSN 0030-0012
OESTERREICHS WEIDWERK. 1928. m. S.438. (Niederoesterreichischer Landesjagdverband) Oesterreichischer Jagd- und Fischereiverlag des N. Oe. Landesjagdverbandes, Wickenburggasse 3, A-1080 Vienna, Austria. TEL 0043-2224216360. FAX 0043-22242163636. Ed. K. Ladstaetter. adv.; bk.rev.; circ. 41,000. Indexed: Biol.Abstr.
  Description: Covers hunting, fishing, environment and nature conservation. Includes news from Austrian hunting associations.

790.1 US
OFFICIAL INTERNATIONAL WRESTLING INSIDER. bi-m. Scott Magazines, 519 Eighth Ave., New York, NY 10018. TEL 212-967-6262. FAX 212-967-6288.

796.72 US
OFFROAD AMERICA.* vol.3, 1979. m. $18. R A V Publishing Group, 7140 Beneva Rd. No. D, Sarasota, FL 34238-2804. TEL 813-921-5687. Ed. George J. Haborak. adv.; illus.; circ. controlled.
  Formerly: Offroad East.

794.1 US ISSN 0885-6583
OHIO CHESS BULLETIN. 1946. bi-m. $10. Ohio Chess Association, 621 Hal-Bar Dr., Cambridge, OH 43725. (Subscr. to: James Pechac, 7722 Lucerne Dr., Apt. N-35, Middleburg Hts., OH 44130) Ed. Parley C. Long. adv.; bk.rev.; charts; illus.; stat.; index; circ. 500.

790.1 US ISSN 0279-9634
OHIO RUNNER. 1979. m. (Apr.-Nov.); bi-m. (Dec.-Mar.). $14 (Alaska, Canada, Hawaii & U.S. Possessions $15; elsewhere $18). Barbara St. George, Inc., Box 586, Hilliard, OH 43026. TEL 614-224-7500. Ed. Mark Hemman. adv.; circ. 11,000.
  Description: Covers the sport of road racing, track and field, biathlon and triathlon in Ohio, West Virginia, Western Pennsylvania, and Northern Kentucky.

790 RU ISSN 0131-2596
SK1
OKHOTA I OKHOTNICH'E KHOZYAISTVO. 1955. m. $21. Agropromizdat, Sadovo-Spasskaya, 18, 107807 Moscow, Russia. (Subscr. to: Mezhdunarodnaya Kniga, Moscow, G-200, Russia) Ed. O.K. Gusev. bk.rev.; index. Indexed: Biol.Abstr.

796.9 CN
OLDTIMERS' HOCKEY NEWS. 1975. m. (Sep.-Apr.). Can.$10($12) Tatham Publications Inc., Box 951, Peterborough, Ont. K9J 7A5, Canada. TEL 705-743-2679. FAX 705-748-3470. Ed. Dave Tatham. adv.; bk.rev.; illus.; circ. 15,000. (tabloid format)
  Former titles: Oldtimers' Sports News (ISSN 0711-5539); Canadian Oldtimers' Sports News; Canadian Oldtimers' Hockey News (ISSN 0381-5013)

790.1 UK
OLEANDER GAMES AND PASTIMES SERIES. a. Oleander Press, 17 Stansgate Ave., Cambridge CB2 2QZ, England. (U.S. address: 80 Eighth Ave., Ste. 303, New York, NY 10011)

790.1 RU ISSN 0204-2177
OLIMPIISKAYA PANORAMA. English edition: Olympic Panorama (ISSN 0204-2592); French edition: Panorama Olympique (ISSN 0204-2606); German edition: Olympisches Panorama (ISSN 0204-2614); Spanish edition: Panorama Olimpico (ISSN 0204-241X) (Text in Russian) 1976-1990; resumed 1981. q. National Olympic Committee of the U.S.S.R., 5-7 Zhdanov St., Moscow 103031, Russia. TEL 924 65 23. TELEX 411287. Ed. Viacheslav Gavrilin.
  Description: Covers international competitions, interviews with championship athletes, forthcoming 1992 Olympic games, new sporting events and more.

796 AU
OLYMPIA AKTUELL. 1973. bi-m. S.10 per no. Oesterreichisches Olympisches Comite, Prinz-Eugen-Str. 12, A-1040 Vienna, Austria. TEL 0222-653365. Ed. Heinz Jungwirth. adv.; bk.rev.; circ. 750.
  Former titles: Olympische Sport; Olympische Blaetter.

796 US ISSN 0094-9787
GV721.5
OLYMPIAN (COLORADO SPRINGS). 1974. 10/yr. $19.92. United States Olympic Committee, 1750 E. Boulder St., Colorado Springs, CO 80909. TEL 719-632-5551. FAX 719-578-4677. Ed. Frank Zang. adv.; charts; illus.; circ. 115,000. Indexed: Sports Per.Ind., Sportsearch (1977-).

OLYMPIAN (SAN FRANCISCO). see *CLUBS*

796.48 SZ ISSN 0010-2431
OLYMPIC REVIEW (YEAR). French edition: Revue Olympique (ISSN 0251-3498); Spanish edition: Revista Olimpica (ISSN 1018-1008) (Quarterly supplement avail.: Olympic Encyclopedia) (Editions in English, French and Spanish) 1967. m. 60 Fr. International Olympic Committee, Chateau De Vidy, CH-1007 Lausanne, Switzerland. TEL 021-253271. FAX 021-241552. TELEX 454024-ACIO-CH. Ed. Denis Echard. adv.; bk.rev.; illus.; index; circ. 6,000. Indexed: Phys.Ed.Ind., Sportsearch (1972-).
  —BLDSC shelfmark: 6256.405000.
  Description: News and information concerning the Olympics and the Olympic Movement. Articles cover future games, sporting life, Olympic host cities and countries, news of National Olympic Committees.

790.06 BE
OLYMPICS. (Text in French) q. 200 Fr. Comite Olympique et Interfederal Belge, Avenue de Bouchout 9, B-1040 Brussels, Belgium. TEL 02-4791940. TELEX 61760. Ed. Adrien van den Eede.

790.1 GW ISSN 0343-0235
OLYMPISCHE JUGEND. 1955. m. DM.20. (Deutschen Sportjugend) Limpert Verlag GmbH, Luisenplatz 2, 6200 Wiesbaden, Germany. TEL 0611-373072. FAX 0611-374351. Ed. Harald Pieper. bk.rev.; circ. 3,500.
  Description: Information for young athletes.

790.1 GW
OLYMPISCHES FEUER. bi-m. DM.28. (Deutschen Olympischen Gesellschaft) Pohl-Verlag, Herzog-Ernst-Ring 1, 3100 Celle, Germany. TEL 05141-7504-0. Ed. Harald Pieper. circ. 8,000. (back issues avail.)

796.815 IS
OMANUYOT HALICHIMA. m. P.O. Box 6112, Herziliya 46 101, Israel. TEL 03-9656239. Ed.Bd.

790.1 US
ON-DIRT MAGAZINE; the off-road and dirt racing news-magazine. 1984. m. $35. Alta Publishing, Inc., Box 6246, Woodland Hills, CA 91365. TEL 818-340-5750. Ed. Lori Peralta. circ. 200,000.

796.962 CN
ON ICE. 1989. q. Can.$11.97. On Ice Magazine Inc., P.O. Box 10, Sta. F, Toronto, Ont. M4Y 2L4, Canada. TEL 416-469-4367. FAX 416-360-4348. Ed. Jerry Amernic. adv.; bk.rev.; circ. 25,000.
  Description: Aimed at adult recreational hockey players aged 20 plus. Keeps readers informed with tournament listings, health reports and tips for improving their game.

794.1 AT
ON THE MOVE. 6/yr. $25. Victorian Chess Association, G.P.O. Box 2690X, Melbourne, Vic. 3001, Australia. Ed. I.J. Laurie.
  Description: Covers local news (Victorian), tournament details and results, and games.

797.23 NE
ONDERWATERWERELD.* 1960. 11/yr. fl.45. Rosier B.V., Postbus 78, 1610 AB Grootebroek, Netherlands. adv.; circ. 5,500.
  Former titles (until 1980): Duiksport; (until 1979): Sportduiker.

790.1 CN ISSN 0702-7842
GV56.06
ONTARIO. MINISTERE DES AFFAIRES CULTURELLES ET DES LOIS DE L'ONTARIO. RAPPORT ANNUEL. 1983. a. Ministry of Tourism and Recreation, Parliament Bldgs., Toronto, Ont. M7A 2R9, Canada. TEL 416-965-2506. circ. 10,000.

790.1 305.3 CN
ONTARIO WRESTLER MAGAZINE. 1981. bi-m. Can.$20($25) (effective 1991). Ontario Amateur Wrestling Association, 1220 Sheppard Ave. E., Willowdale, Ont. M2K 2X1, Canada. TEL 416-495-4165. FAX 416-495-4310. Ed. Bruno Colavecchia. adv.; illus.; stat.; circ. 2,500. Indexed: Sportsearch (1980-).

794.1 GW
ORANG-UTAN (SOKOLSKY OR POLISH OPENING). 1987. 3/yr. $10. Azaleenweg 16, 6000 Frankfurt a.M. 50, Germany. Ed. Wilhelm Gross.

796.426 US
OREGON DISTANCE RUNNER. q. $20 membership. Oregon Road Runners Club, Box 549, Beaverton, OR 97075-0549. TEL 503-626-2348. Ed. Melinda Pyrch. adv.; circ. 3,400.
  Description: Covers road and track running and walking, with a calendar of events, news articles and features, awards coverage.

ORTHOPEDIC AND SPORTS MEDICINE NEWS. see *MEDICAL SCIENCES — Sports Medicine*

796.5 US ISSN 0030-7025
SH11
OUTDOOR CALIFORNIA. 1953. bi-m. $6.50. Department of Fish and Game, 1416 Ninth St., Sacramento, CA 95814. TEL 916-445-7613. (Subscr. to: Box 15087, Sacramento, CA 95851-0087) Ed. Dave Dick. illus.; index; circ. 47,000. Indexed: Cal.Per.Ind. (1978-).

SPORTS AND GAMES

793 US
P B A TOUR OFFICIAL PROGRAM (YEAR). a. $2. Professional Bowlers Association of America, 1720 Merriman Rd., Box 5118, Akron, OH 44313. TEL 216-836-5568. FAX 216-836-2107. adv.; illus.; circ. 110,000.

790 333.7 US
P I N. 1989. q. $30 to non-members; members $18. National Recreation and Park Association, Northeast Service Center, 1800 Silas Deane Hwy., Ste. 1, Rocky Hill, CT 06067. TEL 203-721-1055. FAX 203-529-7518. Ed. Ellen O'Sullivan.
Description: Resource information and ideas for park and recreation activities organizers.

790.1 II
▼**P T - SPORTS SCIENCE.** 1990. m. Rs.430($30) K.K. Roy (Private) Ltd., 55 Gariahat Road, P.O. Box 10210, Calcutta 700 019, India. Ed. K.K. Roy. adv.; abstr.; bibl.; index; circ. 2,160.

796
PACIFIC SPORT. m. G C Publishing, 12021 Wilshire Blvd., Ste. 7063, Los Angeles, CA 90025-1200. TEL 213-478-2188. FAX 213-394-7501. Ed. Andre Sapp.

790.1 US
PAINT CHECK. 1989. m. $24. C B Publications, Inc., Box 347, Ossining, NY 10562. TEL 914-923-3543. Ed. Len Canter. circ. 55,000.
Description: For paintball enthusiasts (teams of well-camouflaged combatants who shoot at one another with paintball guns); covers strategy tips for first-timers and veterans of the sport - with an eye towards tournament coverage.

790.1 US
PAINTBALL; the complete guide to airgun pursuit games. 1988. m. $19.95 (effective Oct. 1990). C F W Enterprises, Inc., 4201 W. Van Owen Pl., Burbank, CA 91505. TEL 818-845-2656. FAX 818-845-7761. (Subscr. to: Box 404, Mt. Morris, IL 61054) adv.; bk.rev.; circ. 50,000. (back issues avail.)
Description: Presents coverage of the airgun pursuit games.

790.1 UK
PAINTBALL GAMES MAGAZINE. m. £14.40 (foreign £40). Aceville Publications Ltd., 89 East Hill, Colchester, Essex CO1 2QN, England. TEL 0206-871139. FAX 0206-871537. Ed. Matthew Tudor. adv.

794.1 PK
PAKISTAN CHESS MAGAZINE. (Text in English) 1987. 4/yr. $25. Mohammad Aejaz Ali Tahir, Ed. & Pub., Post Box 179, Karachi 74200, Pakistan. TEL 92-21-215459. TELEX 24083 DEBAL PK. adv.; bk.rev.; circ. 7,000.
Description: Reports on national and international games and news, opening theory, endgame studies, problems studies, interviews, and "how to improve" articles.

PALAESTRA; the forum of sport, physical education and recreation for the disabled. see HANDICAPPED

797.56 US ISSN 0031-1588
GV770
PARACHUTIST. 1956. m. $21.50. United States Parachute Association, 1440 Duke St., Alexandria, VA 22314. TEL 703-836-3497. FAX 703-836-3495. Ed. Kevin Gibson. adv.; bk.rev.; charts; illus.; circ. 20,000. **Indexed:** Sportsearch (1973-).

794.1 GW
PATT. 1971. m. Schachverein Bottrop 21, Am Quellenbusch 45, 4250 Bottrop, Germany. TEL 201-29999. Ed. Gerhard Sklarz. play rev.; charts; illus.; stat.; circ. 100. (looseleaf format; back issues avail.)

PENNSYLVANIA JOURNAL OF HEALTH, PHYSICAL EDUCATION, RECREATION AND DANCE. see EDUCATION — Teaching Methods And Curriculum

PERCHANCE. see LITERATURE — Science Fiction, Fantasy, Horror

797 US
PERFORMANCE SAILING.* 1987. q. $14.95. C D M Communications, Inc., 100 Fifth Ave., New York, NY 10011. TEL 212-243-0773. circ. 20,000.

799.1 IT ISSN 0031-6091
PESCARE; la rivista dei pescatori. 1962. m. L.65000 (foreign L.91000). Editoriale Olimpia, Viale Milton 7, 50129 Florence, Italy. TEL 055-473843. FAX 055-499195. TELEX 573084 EDOL I. Dir. Alessandro Menchi. adv.; charts; illus.; index; circ. 40,200.

796.41 GW
PFAELZER TURNER; Amtliches Organ des Pfaelzer Turnerbundes. bi-w. DM.35. Pfaelzer Turnerbund e.V., Am Schlagbaum 5, 6750 Kaiserslautern, Germany. TEL 0631-42115. FAX 0631-42868. (back issues avail.)

790.1 617.1 US
▼**PHILADELPHIA SPORTS FOCUS.** 1991. m. $15.95. Capital Sports Focus, Inc., 1432 Fenwick Ln., Silver Spring, MD 20910-3323. TEL 301-587-9351. FAX 301-587-6347. Ed. Manny Rosenberg.

PHILEMAT. see PHILATELY

790.1 613.7 CN ISSN 0843-2635
PHYSICAL EDUCATION DIGEST. 1985. 4/yr. $24. 111 Kingsmount Blvd., Sudbury, Ont. P3E 1K8, Canada. TEL 705-675-7055. FAX 705-675-5539. Ed. Dick Moss. adv.; circ. 3,050.
Formerly: Coaching Digest.
Description: Helps physical educators and scholastic coaches stay up-to-date. Covers up to 35 different topics including new games, drills, coaching cues, teaching techniques, P.E. research and specific sports tips.

636.596 UK
PIGEON RACING GAZETTE. 1946. m. £16.80($34) All-British Pigeon Racing Publishing Co. Ltd., 23 Torbay Rd., Paignton, Devon TQ4 6AA, England. TEL 0803-663759. FAX 0803-664303. Ed. W. Cowell. adv.; bk.rev.
Formerly: Pigeon Racing News and Gazette (ISSN 0048-4164)

PIONYRSKA STEZKA; mesicnik pro sport, turistiku, brannost. see CHILDREN AND YOUTH — For

796 IT
PISCINE OGGI. 1973. q. L.27000 (foreign L.50000). Editrice Il Campo, Via G. Amendola 11, 40121 Bologna, Italy. TEL 051-255360. Dir. Franco Maestrami. adv.; bk.rev.; circ. 15,000.

790.1 BL
PLACAR. 1970. m. Editora Abril, S.A., Rua Geraldo Flausino Gomes, 61, 14o andar, CEP 04575, Sao Paulo, Brazil. TEL 5345344. FAX 5221504. TELEX 1124134. (Subscr. to: Rua do Curtume 769, CEP 05065, Sao Paulo, Brazil) Ed. Victor Civita. adv.; illus.; stat.; charts; circ. 110,000.

PLAY & CULTURE. see SOCIOLOGY

793 US ISSN 0162-1343
HD9993.E453
PLAY METER. 1974. m. $50. Skybird Publishing Co., Inc., Box 24170, New Orleans, LA 70184. TEL 504-488-7003. adv.; charts; illus.; tr.lit.; index; circ. 5,000.

790 US ISSN 1047-5303
PLAYER. 1988. m. $20. Casino Journal Publishing Group, 2524 Arctic Ave., Atlantic City, NJ 08401. TEL 609-344-9000. FAX 609-345-3469. Ed. Glenn Fine. adv.; circ. 210,000.
Description: Statistics and inside information on all forms of legalized gambling, including casinos, horse racing, sports betting, and state lotteries. Includes interviews and feature stories.

PLY: SVENSKA SCHACKDATORFOERINGEN. see COMPUTERS — Computer Games

613.7 370 796 CS
POHYB A MY. (Text in Czech or Slovak) vol.29, 1984. m. 68 Kcs.($47.10) (Cesky Scaz Z R T V) Olympia a.s., Klimentska 1, 115 88 Prague 1, Czechoslovakia. (Dist. by: Artia, Ve Smeckach 30, 111 27 Prague 1, Czechoslovakia) Ed. Marta Ballingova. illus.
Former titles (until vol.36, 1991): Zakladni a Rekreacni Telesna Vychova (ISSN 0139-7915); Zakladni Telesna Vychova (ISSN Zakladni a Rekreacni Telesna Vychova.

790.1 US
POKER TIPS. Variant title: I H 3 P A Newsletter. 1984. bi-m. $7. International Home & Private Poker Players' Association, Rt. 2, Box 2845, Manistique, MI 49854. TEL 906-341-5468. Ed. Edwin "Tony" Wuehle. bk.rev.; circ. 300. (looseleaf format; back issues avail.)
Description: For the home and private club poker player, with emphasis on poker tournaments.

796 NO ISSN 0032-3357
POLITIIDRETT.* 1963. bi-m. Norwegian Police Athletic and Sports Association, Box 6384, Etlerstad., 0604 Oslo 6, Norway. Ed. Leif Orehagen. adv.; circ. 6,000.

797.21 US
POOLIFE. 1970. s-a. Olin Corporation, 120 Long Ridge Rd., Stamford, CT 06904. TEL 203-356-2000. Ed. Aleene Nask. adv.; circ. 750,000.
Formerly: H T H Poolife.

797.21 613.7 US
▼**POOLWAYS;** the magazine of outdoor living (year). 1990. a. free to swimming pool owners. Coastal Industries, 225 Passaic St., Box 8600, Passaic, NJ 07055. TEL 201-473-8600. Ed. Pamela Art.
Description: Articles on all aspcts of poolside living. Includes information on pool maintenance, new products, safety, health and beauty, and poolside entertainment.

POPULAR HOT RODDING. see TRANSPORTATION — Automobiles

796 US
POPULAR SPORTS. 1974. 8/yr. C B S Publications, Popular Magazine Group, 1515 Broadway, New York, NY 10036. TEL 212-719-6000. Ed. John Devaney. adv.; bk.rev.; illus. (also avail. in microfilm from UMI; reprint service avail. from UMI)

PORSCHE PANORAMA. see TRANSPORTATION — Automobiles

797.21 AT
PORTSEA BOOMER. 1949. m. Aus.$20. Portsea Surf Life Saving Club Ltd., 48 Rothesay Ave., East Malvern, Vic. 3145, Australia. TEL 03-571-2395. FAX 03-347-3453. Eds. Brian Eva, Ian Cambell. adv.; illus.; circ. 1,100. (also avail. in microform)
Description: Articles on surf lifesaving.

797.21 GW ISSN 0032-5198
POSEIDON; die maritime Zeitschrift der G S T. 1962. 6/yr. DM.42.60. Militaerverlag der Deutschen Demokratischen Republik, Storkower Str. 158, 1055 Berlin, Germany. TEL 4300618. Ed. Lutz Strobel. adv.; bk.rev.; charts; illus.

795.414 US ISSN 0032-5279
POST MORTEM.* 1952. 6/yr. 1.50. Greater New York Bridge Association, 401 E. 74th St., New York, NY 10021. Ed. Thomas M. Smith. adv.; bk.rev.; illus.; circ. 20,000.

794.1 NO
POSTSJAKK. 1945. 6/yr. NOK 200($30) Norges Postsjakkforbund - Norwegian Correspondence Chess Federation, Unni Kvil Nordal, Tangenveien 101, 1450 Nesoddtangen, Norway. Ed. Oeystein Sande. adv.; bk.rev.
Description: Includes annotated correspondence chess games, theory, national and international correspondence chess news.

790.1 CI ISSN 0350-9419
POVIJEST SPORTA. 1970. 4/yr. 260 din.($12) Hrvatski Sportski Savez, Ilica 7, 41000 Zagreb, Croatia. TEL 041 423-900. Ed. Franjo Frntic. adv.; bk.rev.; bibl.; index; circ. 2,000.
Description: Deals with the history of sports and sportsmen in Croatia and other countries and persons who have influenced the Croatian sports scene.

796.72 SW
POWER. bi-m. Broederna Linstroems Foerlags, Box 35, 443 00 Lerum, Sweden. adv.; circ. 31,170.

790.1 US
POWER HOTLINE. 1981. s-m. $28. Powerlifting U S A, Box 467, Camarillo, CA 93011. TEL 805-482-2378. Ed. M. Lambert. circ. 500.

4484 SPORTS AND GAMES

790.1 613.7   GW
POWER SPORT. 1985. 6/yr. DM.50 (foreign DM.72). Postfach 1151, 8011 Vaterstetten, Germany. TEL 08106-31675. FAX 08106-34605. Ed. Heinz Vierthaler. circ. 3,500.

790.1   US
POWEREDGE MAGAZINE. m. $2.95 per no. Power Edge Group, 4201 W. Van Owen Pl., Burbank, CA 91505. TEL 213-769-6777. (Subscr. to: Box 404, Mt. Morris, IL 61504)
    Description: Features the tops in the field of skateboarding.

790.1   US   ISSN 0199-8536
POWERLIFTING U S A. 1977. m. $26.95. Powerlifting U S A, Box 467, Camarillo, CA 93011. TEL 805-482-2378. Ed. Mike Lambert. adv.; bk.rev.; circ. 16,200. **Indexed:** Sportsearch (1983-).

793   UK   ISSN 0953-0592
PRACTICAL WARGAMER. 1987. q. £11.70 (foreign £10.10). Argus Specialist Publications Ltd., Argus House, Boundary Way, Hemels, Hampstead, Herts HP2 7ST, England. (Dist. by: Infonet Ltd., 5 River Park Estate, Berithamsted, Herts HP4 1HL, England) Ed. Ken Jones. adv.; bk.rev. (back issues avail.)
    Description: For wargamers of all ages and experience from fantasy to Napoleonic wargaming.

PRAIRIE CLUB BULLETIN; organized for the promotion of outdoor recreation in the form of walks, outings, camping and canoeing. see *CONSERVATION*

799   US   ISSN 0048-5144
PRECISION SHOOTING. 1940. m. $22 (Canada $24; others $28). Precision Shooting, Inc., 37 Burnham St., E. Hartford, CT 06108. TEL 203-643-1157. (Subscr. to.: 5735 Sherwood Forest Dr., Akron, OH 44319) Ed. David D. Brennan. adv.; bk.rev.; charts; illus.; tr.lit.; circ. 5,000. (back issues avail.) **Indexed:** Sportsearch.
    Description: Focuses on the subject of extreme rifle accuracy in the target shooting disciplines.

795   US
PREDICAMENT.* 1970. 10/yr. $5.50. Predicament, Inc., 8470 W. Zero, Casper, WY 82601. Eds. Tom and Julie Bishop. adv.; bk.rev.; illus.; tr.lit.; circ. 2,600. (tabloid format; back issues avail.)

PRESS MAGAZINE. see *CLOTHING TRADE*

794.1   BL
PRETO & BRANCO/BRAZILIAN CHESS MAGAZINE. 6/yr. $21. Promochess Ltda., XCX Postal 2730, 80001 Curitiba, Brazil. Ed. Rubens A. Filguth.
    Description: Includes national and international news and game theory.

790.1 658.3   SW
PRIMA LIV. 1953. 10/yr. SEK 120. L M P Forlagsgruppen, Box 630, 101 28 Stockholm, Sweden. TEL 08-21 50 54. FAX 08-21-50-54. Ed. Christina Brinnen. adv.; circ. 43,592.
    Formerly: Korp-Motion.
    Description: Focuses on intercompany athletics.

PRINTWEAR MAGAZINE. see *CLOTHING TRADE — Fashions*

790.1   US
PRO WRESTLING ILLUSTRATED. m. $22 (foreign $27). G C London Publishing Associates, Box 48, Rockville Centre, NY 11571. TEL 516-764-0300. FAX 516-764-4370. Ed. Stu Saks.

794.1   SP   ISSN 0032-9223
PROBLEMAS. 1935; 3rd series 1978. q. 2000 ptas. to individuals; institutions 1800 ptas. Sociedad Espanola de Problemistas de Ajedrez, Av. Principe Asturias 35, 4, 2a, 08012 Barcelona, Spain. (Co-sponsor: Federacion Espanola de Ajedrez) Ed. A.F. Arguelles. bk.rev.; bibl.; charts; illus.; circ. 500.

794.1   UK   ISSN 0032-9398
PROBLEMIST. 1926. bi-m. £12. British Chess Problem Society, c/o Paul Valois, Ed., 14 Newton Park Drive, Leeds LS7 4HH, England. bk.rev.; illus.; cum index every 4 yrs.; circ. 700.

796.812   JA
PROFESSIONAL WRESTLING/SHU-KAN. (Text in Japanese) 1972. w. 15300 Yen. Baseball Magazine Sha, 3-10-10 Misaki-cho, Chiyoda-ku, Tokyo, Japan. Ed. Takashi Yamamoto.

PROGRAMMING TRENDS IN THERAPEUTIC RECREATION. see *EDUCATION — Special Education And Rehabilitation*

791.8   US   ISSN 0161-5815
PRORODEO SPORTS NEWS. (Annual number avail.) 1952. fortn. $21. Professional Rodeo Cowboys Association Properties, Inc., 101 Pro Rodeo Dr., Colorado Springs, CO 80919. TEL 303-593-8840. FAX 719-593-8840. Ed. Kendra Santos. adv.; bk.rev.; illus.; stat.; circ. 31,500.
    Formerly (until vol.26, no.11, Apr. 1978): Rodeo Sports News (ISSN 0035-7758)

793
PUBLIC GAMING.* 1974. m. $65. Public Gaming Research Institute, 015825 Shady Grove, No. 130, Rockville, MD 20850. circ. 15,000.

790.1   US
PULL. 1978. a. World Pulling International, Inc., 6969 Worthington-Galena Rd., Ste. L-1000, Worthington, OH 43085. TEL 614-436-1761. FAX 614-436-0964. Ed. Rhdawnda L. Bliss. circ. 40,000.

790.1   US   ISSN 8750-4219
PULLER. 1971. m. $24.95 (foreign $34.95). World Pulling International, Inc., 6969 Worhtington-Galena Rd., Ste. L-1000, Worthington, OH 43085. TEL 614-436-1761. FAX 614-436-0964. Ed. Rhdawnda L. Bliss. circ. 8,000. (tabloid format; back issues avail.)

PURE-BRED DOGS, AMERICAN KENNEL GAZETTE. see *PETS*

793   UK
PUZZLE MONTHLY. 1974. 13/yr. I P C Magazine Ltd., King's Reach Tower, Stamford St., London SE1 9LS, England. Ed. Dennis Winston. adv.; circ. 164,824.

795.414   CC   ISSN 1000-3479
QIAOPAI/BRIDGE. (Text in Chinese) 1985. q. $12.30. (Zhongguo Qiaopai Xiehui - China Bridge Society) Renmin Tiyu Chubanshe, 8 Tiyuguan Lu, Chongwen Qu, Beijing 100061, People's Republic of China. TEL 757161. (Dist. in US by: China Books & Periodicals, Inc., 2929 24th St., San Francisco, CA 94110.. TEL 415-282-2994)
    Description: Covers the game of bridge.

QIGONG. see *PHYSICAL FITNESS AND HYGIENE*

794.1   UK
QUEEN'S FILE. 1983. 2/yr. $20. Women's Chess Association, Flat 19-17 Broad Court, London WC2B 2QN, England. Ed. Malena Griffiths. adv.; bk.rev.

794.1   AT
QUEENSLAND CHESS. 4/yr. $10. Chess Association of Queensland, Inc., P.O. Box 1361, Rockhampton, Qld. 4700, Australia. Ed. Ian Murray.
    Description: Contains state news, historical and "how-to-improve" articles.

QUONDAM MAGAZINE. see *CLUBS*

790.1   IT
QUOTASPORT. 1980. 3/yr. L.10000. Tecnico S.r.l., Via S. Calimero 11, 20122 Milan, Italy. Ed. Renato O. Foni. adv.; circ. 4,000.

796.77   UK
R A C MOTOR SPORT YEAR BOOK. 1956. a. £16. R A C Motor Sport Association Ltd., Motor Sports House, Riverside Park, Colnbrook, Slough SL3 0HG, England. TEL 0753-681736. FAX 0753-682938. TELEX 847796 RACING G. adv.; circ. 42,000.

R & R SHOPPERS NEWS. (Rest & Relaxation) see *COMMUNICATIONS — Television And Cable*

613.7 370   NE
R S G RICHTING - SPORT-GERICHT; vakblad voor training, onderwijs en wetenschap. 1946. m. fl.69.90. Stichting Sport-Gericht, Scheltuslaan 53, 2273 DM Voorburg, Netherlands. FAX 070-3864430. Ed. Annemiek Min. adv.; bk.rev.; abstr.; charts; illus.; circ. 60,000.
    Formed by the 1991 merger of: Richting (ISSN 0035-5135); (1979-1991): Sport-Gericht.
    Description: Covers training theory, physical education, sport and sports sciences.

R V NEWS. (Recreational Vehicle) see *TRANSPORTATION*

797   UK   ISSN 0557-661X
R Y A NEWS. 1968. 4/yr. membership. Royal Yachting Association, RYA House, Romsey Road, Eastleigh, Hants. S05 4YA, England. TEL 0703-629962. FAX 0703-629924. TELEX 47393-BOATIN-G. Ed. Carol Baker. adv.; circ. 70,000. **Indexed:** Sportsearch (1977-).

796   UK
RACEFORM FLAT ANNUAL. 1899. a. £16. Raceform Ltd., 2 York Road, London SW11 3PZ, England. Ed. D. Corbett. adv.; circ. 11,000.
    Formerly: Raceform Up-to-Date Form Book Annual (ISSN 0081-377X)

796   UK
RACEFORM WEEKLY. 1936. w. Raceform Ltd., Raceform House, 2 York Rd., London SW11 3PZ, England.
    Formerly: Raceform Up-to-Date (ISSN 0079-9394)

796.72   NO   ISSN 0802-7293
RACING. 44/yr. NOK 430. (Norsk Motor Klubb) Motor Media AS, P.O. Box 96, N-1801 Askim, Norway. TEL 9-886311. FAX 9-886332. Ed. Hallgeir Raknerud. adv.
    Formerly: Racing - Revyen.

796   UK   ISSN 0033-7366
RACING & FOOTBALL OUTLOOK. 1909. w. £17. Websters Publications Ltd., Onslow House, 60-66 Saffron Hill, London EC1N 8AY, England. Ed. F. Carter. circ. 57,059.

796   UK
RACING AND FOOTBALL OUTLOOK: FOOTBALL ANNUAL. 1935. a. £1.20. Webster's Publications Ltd., Onslow House, 60-66 Saffron Hill, London EC1N 8AY, England. circ. 75,000.

796   UK
RACING AND FOOTBALL OUTLOOK: JUMPING ANNUAL. 1968. a. £1. Webster's Publications Ltd., Onslow House, 60-66 Saffron Hill, London EC1N 8AY, England. circ. 28,000.

796   UK   ISSN 0079-9424
RACING AND FOOTBALL OUTLOOK: RACING ANNUAL. 1909. a. £1. Webster's Publications Ltd., Onslow House, 60-66 Saffron Hill, London EC1N 8AY, England. circ. 40,000.
    Formerly: Racing and Football Racing Annual.

796.72   AT   ISSN 0033-7374
RACING CAR NEWS. 1960. m. Aus.$48. Chevron Publishing Group Pty. Ltd., P.O. Box 206, Hornsby, N.S.W. 2077, Australia. TEL 02-476-3199. FAX 02-476-5739. Ed. Thomas B. Floyd. adv.; bk.rev.; illus.; circ. 18,000.
    Description: Covers automobile racing and rallies worldwide.

790.1   SI
RACING GUIDE. (Text in Chinese, English) 1987. s-w. 1 New Industrial Rd., Times Centre, Singapore 1953, Singapore. TEL 2848844. FAX 2881186. TELEX 25713. Eds. Benny Ortega, Kuek Chiew Teong. circ. 20,000.

796.72   US
RACING PICTORIAL MAGAZINE. 1959. q. $7. Racing Pictorial Magazine, Inc., Ed. Ray Mann, Box 500 B, Indianapolis, IN 46206. TEL 317-291-7900. adv.

636.596   SA
RACING PIGEON/WEDVLUGDUIF. (Text in Afrikaans and English) 1962. m. R.5.50. (S.A. Duiwesport) Duiwe Benodigdhede (Edms). Bpk., Posbus 594, Pietersburg 0700, South Africa. Ed. H.J. Van Waveren. adv.; charts; illus.; index; circ. 4,000.
    Formerly: Reisiesduif (ISSN 0030-2759)

636.596   UK   ISSN 0033-7390
RACING PIGEON; the British pigeon racing weekly. 1898. w. £36.40($69.50) Racing Pigeon Publishing Co. Ltd., Unit 13, 21 Wren St., London WC1X 0HF, England. TEL 071-833-5959. FAX 071-833-3151. Ed. Colin Osman. adv.; bk.rev.; circ. 30,000.

SPORTS AND GAMES

636.96 US ISSN 0146-8383
RACING PIGEON BULLETIN. w. $25. Wayne A. & Nancy L. Reinke, Eds. & Pubs., 34 E. Franklin St., Bellbrook, OH 45305. TEL 513-848-4972. adv.; bk.rev.; circ. 6,300. (tabloid format; back issues avail.)
 Description: Provides "how-to" articles, news, and opinions on the sport of pigeon breeding, training and racing.

796.72 US
RACING TIMES. m. Sports Weekly Publications, Box 300, North Easton, MA 02356. TEL 508-238-7016. FAX 508-230-2381. Ed. Mike Calinoff. circ. 60,642.

796.72 US
RACING WHEELS. 1962. w. 40/yr. $25. Gary's Enterprises, 7502 N.E. 133rd Ave., Box 1555, Vancouver, WA 98668. TEL 206-892-5590. Ed. G.S. Sterner. adv.; bk.rev.; illus.; stat.; circ. 11,450. (tabloid format)

793 GW
RAETSEL IN GROSSER SCHRIFT. 1979. bi-w. DM.2.50. Martin Kelter Verlag, Muehlenstieg 16-22, D-2000 Hamburg 70, Germany. TEL 6828950. Ed. Bodo Gohr. circ. 40,000.

793 AU
RAETSEL KRONE. m. S.240. Zeitungsverlag Dichand & Falk Gesellschaft MbH & Co., Muthg. 2, 1190 Vienna, Austria. Ed. Hans Dichand. circ. 127,500.

793 GW
RAETSEL SCHULE; fuer Jungen und Maedchen. 1983. m. DM.3. Martin Kelter Verlag, Muehlenstieg 16-22, D-2000 Hamburg 70, Germany. TEL 6828950. circ. 60,000.

793 GW
RAETSELFREUND. 1975. w. DM.2. Martin Kelter Verlag, Muehlenstieg 16-22, D-2000 Hamburg 70, Germany. TEL 6828950. Ed. Bodo Gohr. circ. 45,000.

793 GW
RAETSELFREUND DOPPELBAND. 1976. irreg. DM.3. Martin Kelter Verlag, Muehlenstieg 16-22, D-2000 Hamburg, Germany. TEL 6828950. Ed. Bodo Gohr. circ. 50,000.

796.72 UK ISSN 0140-542X
RALLY SPORT. 1972. m. £11.75. Goodhead Publications Ltd., 27 Murdock Rd., Bicester, Oxon. OX6 7RG, England. Ed. Colin Wilson. adv.; bk.rev.; circ. 25,000.

794.1 GW
RANDSPRINGER. 1982. 6/yr. DM.25($17) Erich Muenster Verlag, Heimstaetten Strasse 53, 8500 Nuremberg, Germany. TEL 0911-528442. FAX 0911-522755. Ed. Rainer Schlenker. adv.; bk.rev.
 Description: Presents usual and unusual chess openings.

793.73 YU ISSN 0034-0243
RAZONODA MILIONA; ukrstene reci, rebusi, zagonetke. 1958. q. 80 din.($1.70) Enigmatski Klub, Bulevar Vojvode Misica 67, Box 219, Belgrade, Yugoslavia. Ed. Vlasta Pavlovic.

RECOGNITION & PROMOTIONS BUSINESS. see GENEALOGY AND HERALDRY

790.1 MX
RECORD; revista deportiva. 1955. fortn. Mex.$10 per no. Nicolas Sanchez, Ed. & Pub., Avda. Juarez 127-12, Mexico 1, D.F., Mexico. adv.; circ. 15,000.

790.1 PO
RECORD. 1949. 3/wk. Travessa dos Inglesinhos 3-1o, 1200 Lisbon, Portugal. TEL 1-3455675. FAX 1-3476279. Ed. Joao Marcelino. circ. 120,000.

797.2 UK
RECREATION. 1931. 9/yr. £25. Institute of Baths and Recreation Management Inc., Giffard House, 36-38 Sherrard St., Melton Mowbray, Leicestershire LE13 1XJ, England. TEL 0664-65531. FAX 0664-501155. Ed. Jeremy Harrison. adv.; bk.rev.; index; circ. 3,000. Indexed: Sportsearch, W.R.C.Inf.
 Former titles: Baths Service and Recreation Management; (until Jan. 1978): Baths Service (ISSN 0005-626X)
 Description: Pool equipment, mechanical and electrical services, chemicals and water treatment equipment, lockers, management systems, sports hall and gymnastic equipment.

RECREATION - ACCESS IN THE '90'S. see HANDICAPPED

RECREATION ADVISOR. see TRAVEL AND TOURISM

RECREATION CANADA. see LEISURE AND RECREATION

RECREATION: CURRENT SELECTED RESEARCH. see SOCIOLOGY

790.1 US
RECREATIONAL ICE SKATING; the magazine for all skaters. 1976. 4/yr. $8. Ice Skating Institute of America, 355 W. Dundee Rd., Buffalo Grove, IL 60089-3500. TEL 708-808-7528. FAX 708-808-8329. Ed. Justine T. Smith. adv.; circ. 60,000.

796 US ISSN 0733-1436
REFEREE; magazine of sports officiating. 1976. m. $47.40. Referee Enterprises, Inc., Box 161, Franksville, WI 53126. TEL 414-632-8855. FAX 414-632-5460. Ed. Tom Hammill. adv.; bk.rev.; charts; illus.; index; circ. 35,000. Indexed: Phys.Ed.Ind., Sports Per.Ind., Sportsearch (1976-).

RESEARCH QUARTERLY FOR EXERCISE AND SPORT. see PHYSICAL FITNESS AND HYGIENE

790.1 BL ISSN 0101-3289
REVISTA BRASILEIRA DE CIENCIAS DO ESPORTE. 3/yr. Colegio Brasileiro de Ciencias do Esporte, Caixa Postal 20383, 01000 Sao Paulo SP, Brazil. Indexed: Sportsearch (1982-).

794.1 BL
REVISTA BRASILEIRA DE XADREZ POSTAL. 6/yr. free to qualified personnel. Clube de Xadrez Epistolar Brasileiro, Caixa Postal 317, 40001 Salvador (BA), Brazil. Ed. Paulo Gonclaves Guimaraes. circ. controlled.
 Description: Reports on national and international games and news, crosstables, results, and studies-problems.

REVISTA DE DERECHO DEPORTIVO. see EDUCATION

794.1 SP ISSN 0214-8900
REVISTA INTERNACIONAL DE AJEDREZ. 1987. 12/yr. $75. Ediciones Eseuve, S.A., Sebastian Elcano, 30, 28012 Madrid, Spain. FAX 4675513. Ed. Antonio Gude. adv.; bk.rev.
 Description: Contains annotated games, articles, correspondence chess, and studies-problems, interviews and computer chess information.

794.1 RM
REVISTA ROMANA DE SAH. 12/yr. $35. Interprinderea Rompresfilatelia, Sector Export-Import Press, Cales Grivitei 64-66, Bucaresti 12, Casuta Postala 200, Rumania. Ed. Florin Gheorghiu.
 Description: Contains national and international news and games, theory, correspondence chess, and studies-problems.

794.1 AG ISSN 0326-0011
EL REY; revista Argentina de ajedrez. 1980. m. Arg.$36($40) Hector Ricardo Liso Ed. & Pub., Casilla de Correo 7, 1653 Villa Ballester, Argentina. adv.; bk.rev.; play rev.; bibl.; charts; illus.; index; circ. 2,000. (back issues avail.)

790.1 SY
RIADA. (Text in Arabic) w. B.P. 292, Damascus, Syria. Ed. Noureddine Rial. adv.

790.1 IT
RIETI-SPORT. 1973. m. L.10000. Edizioni Sportive Reatine s.m.c., Via Centigliano, 15, 02100 Rieti, Italy. Ed. Zeno Fioritoni. adv.; circ. 3,500. (back issues avail.)

799.202 US ISSN 0162-3583
SK274
RIFLE; the sporting firearms journal. 1968. bi-m. $19. Wolfe Publishing Co., 6471 Airpark Dr., Prescott, AZ 86301. TEL 800-899-7810. FAX 602-778-5124. Ed. Dave Scovill. adv.; bk.rev.; charts; illus.; mkt.; pat.; stat.; index, cum.index every 2 yrs.; circ. 26,000.
 Formerly: Rifle Magazine (ISSN 0035-5216)

799.3 UK ISSN 0035-5224
RIFLEMAN. 1906. bi-m. £12.50 (foreign £23). National Small-Bore Rifle Association, Lord Roberts House, Bisley Camp, Brookwood, Woking, Surrey GU24 ONP, England. TEL 048347-6969. FAX 048347-6392. Ed. D. King. adv.; bk.rev.; charts; illus.; stat.; circ. 7,500. Indexed: Sportsearch (1978-).
 Description: Official journal of the U.K. governing body for .22 and airgun shooting.

790.1 JA
RIKUJO KYOGI. (Text in Japanese) 1967. m. Kodansha Ltd., International Division, 12-21 Otowa 2-chome, Bunkyo-Ku, Tokyo 112, Japan. TEL 03-3945-1111. FAX 03-3943-7815. TELEX J34509 KODANSHA. Ed. Yutaka Hirose. circ. 50,000.
 Description: Track & field magazine for sports lovers.

796.83 US ISSN 0035-5410
GV1115
RING; world's official boxing magazine. 1922. m. $12. G C London Publishing Associates, Box 48, Rockville Center, NY 11571. TEL 516-764-0300. FAX 516-764-4370. Ed. Nat Loubet. adv.; bk.rev.; bibl.; illus.; stat.; circ. 200,000. Indexed: Sports Per.Ind., Sportsearch (1977-).

790.1 US
RING RHETORIC. 1971. q. membership. America Association for the Improvement of Boxing, Inc., 86 Fletcher Ave., Mt. Vernon, NY 10552. TEL 914-664-4571. Ed. Stephen H. Acunto. adv.; circ. 300. (looseleaf format; back issues avail.)
 Description: To educate the public on the improvement of boxing and advancing the sport.

796 CN
RINGETTE CANADA. OFFICIAL RULES (YEARS). (Text in English, French) 1965. every 3/yrs. Can.$5. Ringette Canada Publications, 1600 James Naismith Drive, Gloucester, Ont. K1B 5N4, Canada. TEL 613-748-5655. Ed. L. McQuaid. adv.; circ. 10,000.
 Formerly: Ontario Ringette Association. Official Rules.

796.35 CN
RINGETTE REVIEW. (Annual special edition avail. since 1990: Gillette "Soft and Dri" Special Edition of Ringette) (Text in English, French) 1979. 3/yr. plus a. Can.$8. Ringette Canada Publications, 1600 James Naismith Drive, Gloucester, Ont. K1B 5N4, Canada. TEL 613-748-5655. Ed. Amy Elliot. adv.; bk.rev.; circ. 3,000. Indexed: Sportsearch (1982-).

790.1 US
RINGSIDE. bi-m. O'Quinn Studios, Inc., 475 Park Ave. S., New York, NY 10016. TEL 212-689-2830.

796.83 UK ISSN 0037-6310
RINGSPORT. 1959. bi-m. $10. Ringsport Publications, 5 Stockland St., Caerphilly, Glam., Wales. Ed. Evan R. Treharne. adv.; bk.rev.; illus.; circ. 15,000. Indexed: Sportsearch.
 Supersedes: Skill.

796.21 US
RINK DIGEST. 1989. m. membership. Roller Skating Associations, 7700 "A" St., Box 81846, Lincoln, NE 68501. TEL 402-489-8811.
 Description: For roller skating center operators and owners.

RINKSIDER. see BUSINESS AND ECONOMICS — Management

796 IT ISSN 0048-8372
RIVISTA DI DIRITTO SPORTIVO. 1949. q. L.50000 (foreign L.75000). (Comitato Olimpico Nazionale Italiano) Casa Editrice Dott. A. Giuffre, Via Busto Arsizio 40, 20151 Milan, Italy. TEL 02-38000905. FAX 02-38009582. Ed. A. Gattai. circ. 5,600.

SPORTS AND GAMES

790.1 059.927   TS
AL-RIYADAH WAL-SHABAB. (Text in Arabic) 1981. w. Mu'assasat al-Bayan lil-Sahafah wal-Tiba'a wal-Nashr, P.O. Box 8837, Dubai, United Arab Emirates. TEL 444400. FAX 449820. TELEX 47707 PRESS EM. Ed. Khalid Muhammad Ahmad.
Description: Covers sports news and youth activities.

790 059.927   UK
AL-RIYADIYYAH. (Text in Arabic) d. Saudi Research and Marketing Co., Arab Press House, 182-184 High Holborn, London WC1V 7AP, England. TEL 071-831-8181. FAX 071-831-2310. TELEX 889272. (And: P.O. Box 4556, Jeddah 21412, Saudi Arabia. TEL 02-669-1888) adv.

796.75
ROADRACING WORLD & MOTORCYCLE TECHNOLOGY. 9/yr. 29015 Avocado Way, Lake Elsinore, CA 92530. TEL 714-674-0552. FAX 714-674-8304. Ed. John D. Ulrich. adv.; circ. 10,000.

796   US
ROCKY MOUNTAIN SPORTS & FITNESS. m. 1919 14th St., No. 421, Boulder, CO 80302-5323. TEL 303-440-5111. FAX 303-440-3313. Ed. Diane French. adv.; circ. 42,000.

796.72   US
RODDER'S DIGEST. bi-m. Target Publications Inc., 1001 S. Marshall St., Ste. 57, Winston-Salem, NC 27101-5858. TEL 919-777-3619. FAX 919-724-0539. Ed. Steve Hendrickson. adv.

790.1   GW
ROLLSPORT. 1976. m. DM.48. Deutscher Rollsport-Bund e.V., Thomas-Mann-Strasse 6c, 6000 Frankfurt a.M. 50, Germany. TEL 069-581084. FAX 069-572507. adv.; circ. 1,000.
Description: News about roller skating.

790.1   GW
ROLLSTUHLSPORT. 1982. m. DM.40. (Deutscher Rollstuhl Sportverband e.V.) Reha-Verlag GmbH, Roonstr. 30, 5300 Bonn 2, Germany. TEL 0228-352328. (Subscr. to: Deutscher Rollstuhl Sportverband e.V., Friedrich-Alfred-Str. 15, 4100 Duisburg 1, Germany) Eds. Ralf Harperath, Herbert Krah. adv.; illus.; circ. 4,500. (back issues avail.)

790.1   IT
ROMAGNA PUNTO SPORT. 1979. m. L.50000. Romagna Sera, Via Paolo Bonoli,32, 47100 Forli, Italy. TEL (0543) 33596. Ed. Enzo Fasoli. adv.; circ. 7,000.

796.72   IT
ROMBO; settimanale a tutto motore. 1981. w. L.32000. Edizioni Sportive s.r.l., Corso Italia 15, Milan, Italy. Ed. Marcello Sabbatini. adv.; circ. 130,000.

790.1   UK
ROTHMANS SNOOKER YEARBOOK. 1985. a. £12.95. Queen Anne Press, 165 Great Dover St., London SE1 4YA, England. TEL 071-334-4800. FAX 071-334-4905. Ed. Janice Hale. stat.; circ. 6,000. (back issues avail.)

796.815   CC
ROUDAO YU SHUAIJIAO/JUDO & WRESTLING. (Text in Chinese) 1983. bi-m. $18.50. Shanxi Sheng Tiyu Yundong Weiyuanhui, 7, Tiyu Lu, Dayingpan, Taiyuan, Shanxi 030012, People's Republic of China. TEL 775310. (Dist. in US by: China Books & Periodicals, Inc., 2929 24th St., San Francisco, CA 94110. TEL 415-282-2994) Ed. Zhang Dakang.
Description: Covers contemporary judo and wrestling in China.

790.1   GW
ROVER BLATT; Journal fuer Freunde gelaendegaengiger Fahrzeuge. 1975. bi-m. membership. Deutscher Rover Club e.V., Markwinkel 3, 3401 Waake, Germany. TEL 05507-847. FAX 05507-1565. TELEX 965216. adv.; circ. 600. (back issues avail.)

797.123   UK
ROWING MAGAZINE MONTHLY; the independent magazine for enthusiasts everywhere. 1949. m. £28. Ayling Publications, P.O. Box 125C, Esher, Surrey KT10 OHE, England. TEL 0372-467098. FAX 0372-469967. Ed. Richard Ayling. adv.; bk.rev.; film rev.; circ. 5,000. **Indexed:** Sportsearch (1974-).
Formerly: Rowing Magazine (ISSN 0035-8584)

796   UK   ISSN 0080-4282
ROYAL CALEDONIAN CURLING CLUB. ANNUAL. 1838. a. £4. Royal Caledonian Curling Club, 2 Coates Crescent, Edinburgh EH3 7AN, Scotland. TEL 031-225-7083. FAX 031-220-6191. Ed. A.C.B. Guild. adv.; circ. 3,000.

796.72   UK
ROYAL SCOTTISH AUTOMOBILE CLUB OFFICIAL HANDBOOK. 1907. a. £2.25. Royal Scottish Automobile Club, 11 Blythswood Sq., Glasgow G2 4AG, Scotland. TEL 041-221 3850. FAX 041-221-3805. TELEX 779745-RSAC-G. Ed. Jonathan Lord. adv.; circ. 5,000.
Description: Motoring and touring guide.

796.35   US
RULES OF THE GAME OF FIELD HOCKEY. a. $3. International Hockey Federation, USFHA National Office, 1750 E. Boulder, Colorado Springs, CO 80909. TEL 719-578-4567. TELEX 452424. Ed.Bd.
Former titles: International Field Hockey Rules; Official Field Hockey Rules for School Girls (ISSN 0362-3270)

796.42   US   ISSN 0897-1706
GV1061
RUNNER'S WORLD. 1966. m. $15.97. Rodale Press, Inc., 33 E. Minor St., Emmaus, PA 18098. TEL 215-967-5171. TELEX 847338. Ed. Amby Burfoot. adv.; illus.; circ. 345,132. (processed; also avail. in microform from UMI; reprint service avail. from UMI) **Indexed:** Acad.Ind., Hlth.Ind., Mag.Ind., Phys.Ed.Ind., PMR, Sports Per.Ind., Sportsearch (1973-). Key Title: Runner's World (1987).
Incorporates (1978-1987): Runner (ISSN 0149-7316); Former titles (until 1987): Rodale's Runner's World (ISSN 0892-3744); (until 1985): Runner's World (ISSN 0035-9939); Distance Running News.
Description: Provides runners at any skill level with current training techniques, nutritional breakthroughs, equipment reviews, and race information in the United States and around the world.

RUNNING. see PHYSICAL FITNESS AND HYGIENE

RUNNING & FITNEWS. see PHYSICAL FITNESS AND HYGIENE

790.1   US   ISSN 0147-2968
GV1061
RUNNING TIMES; the national calendar magazine for runners. 1977. m. $25 (foreign $39.95). Air Age Fitness Group, Rt. 7, 251 Danbury Rd., Wilton, CT 06897. TEL 203-834-2900. FAX 203-762-9803. (Subscr. to: Box 511, Mt. Morris, IL 61054. TEL 800-877-5402) Ed. Bob Cooper. adv.; bk.rev.; illus.; stat.; circ. 80,000. (back issues avail.) **Indexed:** Sports Per.Ind., Sportsearch (1979-).

796   SA   ISSN 0049-1381
S A ATHLETE/S A ATLEET; track and field news. Variant title: South African Athlete. (Text in Afrikaans, English) 1968. m. R.12. South African Amateur Athletics Union, Box 1261, Pretoria 0001, South Africa. TEL 012-435-995. FAX 012-432244. Ed. Chris Botes. adv.; bk.rev.; circ. 7,000.

799.202   SA
S.A. MARKSMAN/S.A. SKERPSKUTTER. (Text in Afrikaans, English) 1959. q. membership only. South African Pistol Association - Suid-Afrikaanse Pistoolvereniging, MacKay Chambers, 11 Mackay Ave., Blairgowrie, Randburg 2194, South Africa. TEL 011-787-6915. FAX 0171-32427. (Editorial addr.: P.O. Box 1027, Welkom 9460, South Africa. TEL 0171-71304) Ed. Hans Steyl. adv.; circ. 2,000 (controlled).

S A SPORTS TRADER. see BUSINESS AND ECONOMICS — Marketing And Purchasing

797.21   SA
S A SWIMMER. 1972. 5/yr. free to qualified personnel. South African Amateur Swimming Federation, Box 48178, Qualbert 4078, Durban, South Africa. Ed. Morgan Naidoo. adv.; circ. 1,500.

S A Z; the leading trade newspaper. (Sport Artikel Zeitung Verlag) see BUSINESS AND ECONOMICS — Marketing And Purchasing

S B. (Sportstaettenbau und Baederanlagen - Sports Facilities and Swimming Pools) see BUILDING AND CONSTRUCTION

790.1
S D S - RIVISTA DI CULTURA SPORTIVA. (Scuola Dello Sport) (Text in Italian; summaries in English, French, Spanish) 1982. q. L.16,000. Comitato Olimpico Nazionale Italiano, Foro Italico, 00190 Rome, Italy. TEL 02-3685-9173. circ. 8,000.

S G M A COMPREHENSIVE QUARTERLY SALES TRENDS REPORT. (Sporting Goods Manufacturers Association) see BUSINESS AND ECONOMICS — Marketing And Purchasing

790.1   US
S G M A TODAY - ACTION UPDATE. bi-m. free. Sporting Goods Manufacturers Association, 200 Castlewood Dr., N. Palm Beach, FL 33408. TEL 407-842-4100. Ed. Michael May. circ. 5,000. (back issues avail.)
Formerly: Action Update.

790.1   CN
S P O R T S. (Science Periodical on Research and Technology in Sport) 12/yr. $12. Coaching Association of Canada, 333 River Rd., Ottawa, Ont. K1L 8H9, Canada. TEL 613-746-5624.

794.1   CI   ISSN 0350-2570
SAHOVKI GLASNIK; organ Sahovskog saveza Hrvatske. (Text in Croatian) 1925. m. $20. (Sahovki Savez Hrvatske) Sahovska Naklada, Bogoviceva 7, 41000 Zagreb, Croatia. TEL 041 273-692. Ed. Drazen Marovic. adv.; bk.rev.; circ. 5,500.

794.1   YU   ISSN 0352-115X
SAHOVSKA KOMPOZICIJA; magazine for chess problem popularization. (Text in Serbo-Croatian) 1981. m. $5. Chess Problems Section "Student", P.O. Box 132, 32 102 Cacak, Yugoslavia. Ed. Ljubisa Papic. circ. 300. (back issues avail.)

794.1   YU   ISSN 0351-1375
GV1313
SAHOVSKI INFORMATOR/CHESS INFORMANT/SAHMATNYJ INFORMATOR. 1966. 3/yr. $29. Francuska 31, 11001 Belgrade, Yugoslavia. TEL 630-109. FAX 11-626-583. TELEX 72677 CH INF YU. (Co-sponsor: World Chess Federation - F.I.D.E.) Ed. Aleksandar Matanovic. circ. 30,000.
Description: Includes a selection to the best games played by the world's greatest.

794.1   LV
SAHS BALTIJA. Russian edition: Baltiiskie Shakhmaty. (Text in Latvian) 1959-1990 (Dec.); resumed Apr. 1991. m. $32 (typically set in Jan.). (Latvijas Saha Savienibas) Sahs Baltija, P.O. Box 241, 226050 Riga, Latvia. TEL 0132-286-864. Ed. Nikolai Zhuravlev. bk.rev.; circ. 1,500.
Formerly (until Dec. 1990): Sahs (ISSN 0201-8101)
Description: Covers national and international chess games, opening theory, correspondence chess, "how-to-improve" articles, combinations, studies-problems, and interviews.

794.1   HU
SAKKELET. 1889. 12/yr. $36 (effective 1992). Nemzeti Sport Kft., c/o Andras Ozsvath, Ed., Nephadsereg u.10, 1005 Budapest 5, Hungary. TEL 0036-1-1312790. FAX 0036-1-1319738. (U.S. subscr. addr.: Center for Hungarian Literature, 4418 16th Ave., Brooklyn, NY 11204) adv.; illus. (avail. on disk)
Description: Includes annotated games, computer and correspondence chess, studies-problems, and combinations. Covers chess events in Hungary.

796.815   IT
SAMURAI - BUSHIDO E SUPER BANZI - PUGILATO. m. L.30000 (foreign L.120000). Sport Promotion s.r.l., Via Natale Battaglia 27, 20127 Milan, Italy. TEL 02-2856994.

794.1   IT
SCACCO; rivista mensile di tecnica e informazione sacchistica. 1970. 11/yr. $66. Edizione Scacco S.a.s., Corso Diaz 3, 12084 Mondovi (CN), Italy. TEL 0174-551054. Ed. Gallitto Salvatore. adv.; bk.rev.

SPORTS AND GAMES 4487

794.1 NE
SCHAAK. 1985. 22/yr. price varies. Karel de Stoutestraat 4, NL-3222 CP Hellevoetsluis, Netherlands. (US subscr. to: Chessco, 301 Union Arcade Bldg., Davenport, IA 52901) Ed. Jaap van der Kooij.
Description: Each issue is devoted to a particular opening variation and includes over 70 correspondence chess games.

794.1 NE
SCHAAKNIEUWS. 1986. 48/yr. fl.79.50 (foreign fl. 144). Visserstraat 16B, 5611 BT Eindhoven, Netherlands. TEL 040-457832. FAX 040-439355. Ed. H. Grooten. adv.; circ. 1,800.
Description: Includes current chess news and games, interviews, and articles of general interest.

794.1 NE
SCHAAKSCHAKERINGEN. 1966. 12/yr. $24. Bestuur Nederlandse Bond van Correspondentieschakers, c/o L.C.M. Diepstraten, Pres., Heideveldweg 20, 1251 XN Laren (NH), Netherlands. Ed. R. Feytens. bk.rev.; circ. 1,800.
Description: Includes annotated games, results, theory and articles.

794.1 GW ISSN 0048-9328
SCHACH. 1947. m. DM.53.40. Sportverlag GmbH, Neustaedtische Kirchstr. 15, 1086 Berlin, Germany. TEL 030-2212-215. FAX 030-2292920. adv.; bk.rev.

794.1 AU
SCHACH AKTIV. 12/yr. $25. Austrian Chess Federation, Herrengasse 16, A-8010 Graz, Austria. Ed. Lothar Karrer. adv.
Description: Contains national and international chess news and games, opening theory, correspondence chess, studies and problems.

794.1 GW
SCHACH-ARCHIV. 1951. 12/yr. $30. Schachzentrale Caissa, Weidenbaumsweg 80, 2050 Hamburg 80, Germany. TEL 040-7244282. FAX 040-7214647. adv.; bk.rev.; circ. 3,000.
Description: Deals with theoretical opening questions.

794.1 GW
SCHACH IN BADEN. 1977. 6/yr. $15. Badischen Schachverband, c/o Frank Schmidt, Ed., Froehlichstr. 12, 6800 Mannheim, Germany. adv.; bk.rev.
Description: Newsletter for chessplayers.

794.1 GW
SCHACH INFORMATIONEN. 1973. q. DM.20($15) Krefelder Schachklub Turm 1851 e.V., Johansenaue 1, 4150 Krefeld 1, Germany. TEL 2151-542233. FAX 2151-736389. adv.; circ. 250. (back issues avail.)
Description: Features club news, reports and results of events, and championships.

794.1 AU
SCHACHKLUB HIETZING MEMPHIS NACHRICHTENBLATT. 1946. q. free. Schachklub Hietzing Memphis, Cafe Frey, Favoritenstr. 44, A-1040 Vienna, Austria. Ed. Peter Linnert.
Formerly: Schacklub Hietzing Nachrichtenblatt (ISSN 0036-584X)

794.1 GW
SCHACHMAGAZIN 64 - SCHACH-ECHO. s.m. DM.66. Carl Ed. Schuenemann KG, Zweite Schlachtpforte 7, Postfach 106067, 2800 Bremen 1, Germany. TEL 0421-36903-72. FAX 0421-36903-39. circ. 9,700.
Formed by the 1992 merger of: Schachmagazin 64 (ISSN 0721-9539); (1953-1992): Schach-Echo (ISSN 0036-5831)
Description: Contains articles on chess tournaments, theory and strategy. Includes calendar of events.

794.1 SZ ISSN 0176-2257
DIE SCHACHWOCHE; aktuelle Schachnachrichten aus aller Welt. 1982. 50/yr. 140 Fr.($108) Schachagentur Caissa AG, Postfach 76, CH-5614 Sarmendorf, Switzerland. FAX 57-273181. TELEX 827922. Ed. Werner Widmer. adv.; circ. 8,700.
Description: Includes current international tournament information and over 2,400 games per year.

794.1 SW
SCHACKNYTT. 1970. 10/yr. $45. Harry Schuessler, Ed. & Pub., P.O. Box 15098, S-750 15, Uppsala, Sweden. FAX 46-18-555-444. adv.; bk.rev.

794.1 NE ISSN 0036-5890
SCHAKEND NEDERLAND. 1893. m. fl.50. Koninklijke Nederlandse Schaakbond - Royal Dutch Chess Federation, Postbus 22739, 1100 DE Amsterdam, Netherlands. TEL 020-6228520. Ed. Minze bij de Weg. adv.; bk.rev.; charts; illus.; index; circ. 31,000.
Description: Covers chess.

796.86 IT ISSN 0036-6005
SCHERMA. 1961. m. Via I. Pettinengo 39, Rome, Italy. adv.; bk.rev.
Description: Covers fencing.

799 NE ISSN 0048-9344
SCHIETSPORT. 1890. m. fl.35($12) Koninklijke Nederlandse Schutters Associatie - Royal Dutch Shooting Association, Burg. de Widtstraat 2, 3811 LV Amersfoort, Netherlands. TEL 033-622388. FAX 033-650626. Ed. B.D.U. Barneveld. adv.; bk.rev.; circ. 21,500.
Description: Covers shooting.

790.1 GW
SCHLITTENPOST. 1971. s-a. Deutscher Bob- und Schlittensportverband e.V., An der Schiessstaette 6, 8240 Berchtesgaden, Germany. TEL 08652-4096. FAX 08652-63707. adv.; charts; illus.; stat.; circ. 1,000.

794.1 US ISSN 1040-7707
SCHOOL MATES. 1987. bi-m. $7.50. United States Chess Federation, 186 Rt. 9W, New Windsor, NY 12553. TEL 914-562-6350. Ed. Jennie L. Simon. circ. 10,850.
Description: Presents chess on a beginner's level for young chess players. Includes profiles, analyses, instructions and puzzles.

799.202 GW
DER SCHUETZE. 1965. q. Schuetzengesellschaft Pforzheim 1450 e.V., Kirschenpfad 1, 7530 Pforzheim, Germany. TEL 07231-63310. Ed. Frank Herholz. circ. 1,000.

794.1 SZ
SCHWEIZER SCHACH-MAGAZIN/MAGAZINE SUISSE D'ECHECS. (Text mainly in German; occasionally in French, Italian) 1930. 11/yr. $25. Schindelacher, CH-3128 Ruemligen, Switzerland. FAX 31599217. Ed. Matthias Burkhalter. adv.; bk.rev.
Description: Covers national and international news and games, computer and correspondence chess, opening theory, studies, and problems.

790.1 SZ
SCHWEIZER SPORT & MODE. (Text in German) m. 82 Fr. (foreign 106Fr.). (Schweizer Sporthaendler Verband) Schweizer Sport & Mode, Muensterhof 14, CH-8022 Zurich, Switzerland. TEL 01-212-11-20. FAX 01-221-38-80. Ed. Beat Ladner.
Description: Trade paper for retailers of sporting goods.

796 SZ
SCHWEIZER VOLKSPORT/SPORT POPULAIRE SUISSE.* (Text in French and German) 1974. 6/yr. 12 Fr. Federation Suisse-Liechtenstein des Sports Populaires, 2733 Pontenet, Switzerland. Ed. Marco Roth. adv.; illus.; circ. 2,500.

794.1 SZ ISSN 0036-7745
SCHWEIZERISCHE SCHACHZEITUNG; revue Suisse des echecs, revista scacchistica Svizzera. (Text in French, German, Italian) 1900. m. 55 Fr. Schweizerischer Schachverband, c/o Robert Spoerri, Ed., Postfach 8214, CH-3001 Bern, Switzerland. TEL 031-225540. FAX 031-221983. (Subscr. to: c/o Paul Steinacher, Foehrlibuckstrasse 11, CH-8304 Wallisellen, Switzerland) adv.; bk.rev.; charts; illus.; circ. 10,000.
Description: Includes game analyses, theory, correspondence and computer chess, problems and studies.

797.21 GW
SCHWIMMSPORTVEREIN ESSLINGEN. VEREINSNACHRICHTEN. 1956. q. Schwimmsportverein Esslingen, c/o Helmut Weiss, Abt-Fulrad-Str. 4, 7300 Esslingen, Germany. TEL 0711-353867. adv.; circ. 1,200.

794.1 UK
SCOTTISH CHESS. 1960. 4/yr. $20. P.O. Box 67, 15 Hope St., Glasgow G2 6AQ, Scotland. FAX 041-204-4373. Ed. A.J. Shaw. adv.; bk.rev.; circ. 750.
Description: Covers national and international games, articles, and combinations.

796.96 UK ISSN 0036-9160
SCOTTISH CURLER. 1954. m. (Sep.-May). £9($27) Dunfermline Press, Pitreavie Business Park, Dunfermline, Fife KY11 5QS, Scotland. TEL 0383-728201. Ed. Robin Welsh. adv.; bk.rev.; illus.; circ. 10,000. **Indexed:** Sportsearch (1977-).
Description: Covers the sport of curling.

797.23 UK ISSN 0308-7379
SCOTTISH DIVER. 1960. bi-m. £8($27) Scottish Sub-Aqua Club, 40 Bogmoor Place, Glasgow G51 4TQ, Scotland. TEL 41-425-1021. FAX 41-330-4501. Ed. M. McGowan. adv.; bk.rev.; illus.; cum.index; circ. 2,500. **Indexed:** Sportsearch.
Description: Articles on sport-diving practices, dive sites worldwide, history of diving.

797 AT ISSN 0729-5529
SCUBA DIVER. bi-m. Aus.$27 (foreign Aus.$68)(effective Apr. 1992). Yaffa Publishing Group, 17-21 Bellevue St., Surry Hills, N.S.W. 2010, Australia. TEL 02-281-2333. FAX 02-281-2750. adv.: B&W page Aus.$1415, color page Aus.$1655; trim 273 x 210. circ. 8,193.
Description: Provides comprehensive coverage of the recreational diving filed.

790.1 US
SCUBA TIMES.* 1979. bi-m. $13. Poseidon Publishing Co., Box 2409, Pensacola, FL 32513-2409. TEL 904-478-5288. Ed. Cethie Cush. adv.; circ. 50,000.

797.23 US
SCUBAPRO DIVING AND SNORKELING. 1986. q. $10. (Scubapro) Aqua-Field Publishing Co., Inc., 66 W. Gilbert St., Shrewsbury, NJ 07702. TEL 908-842-8300. (Subscr. to: 3105 E. Harcourt, Rancho Dominguez, CA 90221) Ed. Stephen Ferber. adv.; circ. 95,000.

790.1 GW ISSN 0930-3308
SEITENWECHSEL. 1986. s-a. free. Georg August Universitaet - Goettingen, Zentrale Einrichtung fuer den Allgemeiner Hochschulsport, Sprangerweg 2, 3400 Goettingen, Germany. circ. 7,500.
Description: Covers university sports and past times.

790.1 BL
▼**SEMANA EM ACAO.** 1990. w. Editora Abril, S.A., R. Geraldo Flausino Gomez, 61, 04575 Sao Paulo, Brazil. TEL 534-5344. FAX 552-1504. TELEX 1124134. circ. 30,500.

790.1 US ISSN 0196-6243
SENIOR SPORTS NEWS. 1979. m. $2.50. National Senior Sports Association (NSSA), 10560 Main St., Ste. 250, Fairfax, VA 22030. TEL 703-385-7540. Ed. Lloyd Wright. circ. 5,000.

790.1 IT
SFINGE. m. Edizioni Poker di Coccia Marcella, Via Gentile da Mogliano 146, 00176 Rome, Italy. TEL 2715277. Ed. Eraclite Corbi.

794.1 BU
SHAKHMATNA MISL. 12/yr. $30. Sofia - 1504, ul., Rakitin 2, Bulgaria. (Subscr. to: British Chess Magazine, 9 Market St., St. Leonards-on-Sea, E. Sussex TN38 ODQ, England) Ed. P. Petkov.
Description: Contains national and international chess game analyses, theory, combinations, studies and problems.

794.1 RU ISSN 0037-3249
SHAKHMATY V S.S.S.R.. 1921. m. 12 Rub. Fiskultura i Sport, Kalyaevskaya 27, 103006 Moscow, Russia. Ed. Yuri Averbakh. bk.rev.; bibl.; circ. 25,000. (also avail. in microform from MIM)

790.1 LV ISSN 0558-1613
SHAKHS/SHAKHMATY.* (Editions in Latvian and Russian) 1959. s-m. $9.60. Ministerstvo Kultury, Riga, Latvia. charts; illus. (also avail. in microform from MIM)

SPORTS AND GAMES

790.1 CC
SHANGHAI XIANGQI/SHANGHAI CHESS. (Text in Chinese) bi-m. Shanghai Wenhua Chubanshe, 74 Shaoxing Lu, Shanghai 200020, People's Republic of China. TEL 372608. Ed. Hu Ronghua.

790.1 613.7 CC
SHAOLIN YU TAIJI. (Text in Chinese) bi-m. Henan Tiyu Baokan She, No. 3, Jiankang Lu, Zhengzhou, Henan 450053, People's Republic of China. TEL 331520. Ed. Gu Youyi.
Description: Covers traditional Chinese martial arts including shadow boxing practiced in the Shaolin Buddhist Temple.

SHARING THE VICTORY. see *RELIGIONS AND THEOLOGY*

794.1 II
SHATRANJ SAMARAT. 12/yr. $12. Chappa Nivas, Kambal Kendra Rd., Mandsaur, M.P., India. Ed. Nandkishor Joshi.

794.1 TS
AL-SHIRAH. (Text in Arabic, English) 1983. 3/yr. $30. Dubai Chess and Culture Club, P.O. Box 11354, Dubai, United Arab Emirates. TEL 281362. Ed. Khalid Ali bin Zayed. adv.; illus.; circ. 2,000.
Description: National and international coverage of games, and junior chess.

799.202 UK
SHOOT!. w. I P C Magazines Ltd., Holborn Group (Subsidiary of: Reed Business Publishing Ltd.), Commonwealth House, 1-19 New Oxford St., London WC1 1NG, England. TEL 01-404-0700. adv.; circ. 155,246.

799.202 US ISSN 0080-9365
TS535
SHOOTER'S BIBLE. 1925. a. $19.95. Stoeger Publishing Co., 55 Ruta Ct., S. Hackensack, NJ 07606. TEL 201-440-2700.
—BLDSC shelfmark: 8268.240000.

799.3 US ISSN 0037-4148
SHOOTING INDUSTRY. 1956. m. $25. Publishers' Development Corp., 591 Camino de la Reina, Ste. 200, San Diego, CA 92108. TEL 619-297-5350. FAX 619-297-5353. TELEX 695-478. Ed. Bruce Hillman. adv.; bk.rev.; charts; illus.; pat.; stat.; tr.lit.; circ. 22,500. **Indexed:** Bus.Ind., Tr.& Indus.Ind.

799.32 AT
SHOOTING LINES. 1962. bi-m. Aus.$5.50. Archery Association of Australia, 25 Albert St., Prospect, S.A. 5082, Australia. Ed. Alex J. Barter. adv.; bk.rev.; circ. 600.

799.202 UK
SHOOTING MAGAZINE. 1973. m. £16.80 (foreign £22.50). Burlington Publishing Co. Ltd., 10 Sheet St., Windsor, Berkshire SL4 1BG, England. Ed. Philip Upton. adv.; bk.rev.; circ. 16,955.

SHOOTING NEWS AND COUNTRY WEEKLY. see *SPORTS AND GAMES — Outdoor Life*

799.202 658.8 US ISSN 0887-9397
SHOOTING SPORTS RETAILER. 1983. 6/yr. $30. Box 25, Cuba, NY 14727-0025. TEL 212-840-0660. Ed. John E. Bartimole. adv.; tr.lit.; circ. 22,500.

799.2 US ISSN 0038-8084
GV1151
SHOOTING TIMES. 1960. m. $19.97. P J S Publications, Inc., News Plaza, Box 1790, Peoria, IL 61656. TEL 309-682-6626. Ed. James W. Bequette. circ. 200,000. **Indexed:** Consum.Ind., Sports Per.Ind., Sportsearch.

799 UK ISSN 0037-4164
SHOOTING TIMES AND COUNTRY MAGAZINE. 1882. w. Burlington Publishing Co. Ltd., Sheet St., Windsor, Berks SL4 1BG, England. Ed. Jonathan Young. adv.; bk.rev.; illus.; circ. 42,873. **Indexed:** Geo.Abstr.
Formerly: Shooting Times.

799 US ISSN 0049-0415
SHOTGUN NEWS; trading post for anything that shoots. 1946. 3/mo. $20. Snell Publishing Co., Box 669, Hastings, NE 68901. TEL 402-463-4589. FAX 402-463-3893. Ed. Robert M. Snell. adv.; illus.; tr.; lit.; circ. 170,000. (tabloid format)

790.5 613.7 US ISSN 0882-9640
SILENT SPORTS; Mid-America's aerobic recreational sports magazine. 1984. m. $14. Waupaca Publishing Co., 717 Tenth St., Box 152, Waupaca, WI 54981. TEL 715-258-5546. FAX 715-258-8162. Ed. Greg Marr. adv.; circ. 11,500. (back issues avail.)
Formerly: Wisconsin Silent Sports.
Description: Covers recreational fitness activities in the upper Midwest: bicycling, cross country skiing, running, canoeing, and backpacking.

797.21 SW
SIMFRAEMJAREN-LIVRAEDDAREN. 1935. q. SEK 50. Svenska Livraeddningssaellskapet-Simfraemjandet, Box 8346, 402 79 Goeteborg, Sweden. FAX 31-223234. Ed. Anders Werneten. adv.; circ. 14,000.

794.1 IT ISSN 0037-5608
SINFONIE SCACCHISTICHE. (Text in English, French and Italian) 1965. q. L.15000($12) Associazione Problemistica Italiana, Via della Camilluccia 145, 00135 Rome, Italy. Ed. Marco Bonavoglia. bk.rev.; bibl.; charts; index; circ. 6,000.

794.1 IC
SKAK. 12/yr. $40. Johann Jonsson, Ed. & Pub., P.O. Box 1179, Reykjavik - Silmar 31391-31975, Iceland. TEL 31391.

794.1 DK ISSN 0037-6043
SKAKBLADET. 1904. m. DKK 164. Dansk Skak Union, Tulipanvej 22, DK-6705 Esbjerg Oe, Denmark. Ed. Thorbjoern Rosenlund. adv.; bk.rev.; charts; illus.; index; circ. 10,000.

796.21 US ISSN 0037-6132
GV849.A1
SKATING. 1923. 10/yr. $15. United States Figure Skating Association, 20 First St., Colorado Springs, CO 80906. TEL 719-635-5200. FAX 719-635-9548. Ed. Kim Mutchler. adv.; bk.rev.; illus.; circ. 32,000. **Indexed:** Sports Per.Ind., Sportsearch (1975-).

799.313 US ISSN 0037-6140
GV1181
SKEET SHOOTING REVIEW; covering the sport of skeet shooting world wide. 1947. m. $15 or membership. National Skeet Shooting Association, Box 680007, San Antonio, TX 78268. TEL 512-688-3371. Ed. Susie Fluckiger. adv.; illus.; circ. 18,000. **Indexed:** Sportsearch (1974-).
Description: Contains information on new product and techniques.

790.1 CN
LE SKI (TORONTO, 1988). (Text in French) 1988. 4/yr. Can.$9.50. Solstice Publishing Inc., 19 Albany Ave., Toronto, Ont. M5R 3C2, Canada. TEL 416-535-0607. FAX 416-535-3419. circ. 18,000.

790.1 US
SKI DIRECTORY. 1976. a. membership. American Ski Association (Denver), 1675 Larimer St., Denver, CO 80202. TEL 303-825-0944. adv.; index; circ. 140,000. (back issues avail.)
Description: Discusses skiing, ski area information, and vacations.

790.1 US ISSN 0890-6076
SKI PATROL MAGAZINE. 1984. q. $15. National Ski Patrol System, Inc., Ski Patrol Bldg., Ste. 100, 133 S. Van Gordon St., Lakewood, CO 80228. TEL 303-988-1111. FAX 303-988-3005. Ed. Rebecca W. Ayers. adv.; bk.rev.; charts; illus.; cum.index; circ. 25,000.
Description: Discusses avalanche statistics, ski mountaineering, equipment, medical training, winter emergency care, fitness, risk management for ski patrollers. Includes ski area profiles.

796.93 US ISSN 0037-6213
SKI RACING. 1968. 20/yr. $12. Ski Racing International, Box 1125, Waitsfield, VT 05673-1125. TEL 802-496-7700. FAX 802-496-7704. adv.; bk.rev.; charts; illus.; stat.; circ. 25,000. (tabloid format) **Indexed:** Sports Per.Ind., Sportsearch (1976-).

797.23 US ISSN 0037-6345
SH458
SKIN DIVER MAGAZINE; devoted to the underwater world. 1951. m. $21.94. Petersen Publishing Co., 8490 Sunset Blvd., Los Angeles, CA 90069. TEL 213-854-2222. Ed. Bill Gleason. adv.; illus.; index; circ. 224,786. (also avail. in microform from UMI) **Indexed:** Cal.Per.Ind. (1990), Hlth.Ind., Mag.Ind., PMR, Sports Per.Ind., Sportsearch.
●Also available online. Vendor(s): DIALOG.

796 US
SKYBOX. q. Dorsey Publishing, 1328 Elam Ave., Cincinnati, OH 45225-1808. TEL 513-541-0269. FAX 513-541-0057. Ed. Bill Dorsey. adv.; circ. 100,275.

790.1 US ISSN 0192-7361
SKYDIVING. 1979. m. $16. Aerographics, Box 1520, DeLand, FL 32721. TEL 904-736-9779. FAX 904-736-9786. Ed. Michael F. Truffer. adv.; bk.rev.; circ. 8,400. (tabloid format; also avail. in microform from UMI; back issues avail.) **Indexed:** Sportsearch (1980-).
Description: Presents news and information about the equipment, events, techniques, people and places of sport parachuting.

799.3 DK ISSN 0037-6663
SKYTTE-BLADET. 1937. 10/yr. DKK 125. Dansk Skytte Union, Broendby Stadion 20, DK-2605 Broendby, Denmark. Ed. Svend Aage Rasmussen. adv.; bk.rev.; circ. 4,000.

790.1 UK
SMALL SIDE TEAM GAMES AND POTTED SPORTS. 1935. irreg. £0.55 per no. Ministry of Defense, Army Sport Control Board, Clayton Barracks, Aldershot, England.

790.1 US
SNO TIMES. 1976. 9/yr. $30 W. Division St., Box 1929, Eagle River, WI 54521. TEL 715-479-4421. Ed. Kurt Krueger. adv.; circ. 15,000.

794.735 UK ISSN 0269-0756
SNOOKER SCENE. 1972. m. £13.20. Everton's News Agency, Cavalier House, 202 Hagley Rd., Edgbaston, Birmingham B16 9PQ, England. FAX 021-452-1822. Ed. Clive Everton. adv.; bk.rev.; circ. 18,000.

SOARING. see *AERONAUTICS AND SPACE FLIGHT*

796.334 FR ISSN 0015-9557
SOCIETE D'EDITION DE PERIODIQUES SPORTIFS. 1955. w. 185 F. Sopusi, 10 rue du Faubourg Montmartre, 75009 Paris, France. (Subscr. to: 13 rue d'Enghien, 75010 Paris, France) Ed.Bd. adv.; circ. 175,000 (controlled). (looseleaf format)

790.1 UK ISSN 0560-6152
GV1183
SOCIETY OF ARCHER-ANTIQUARIES. JOURNAL. 1958. a. membership. Society of Archer-Antiquaries, c/o Alf Webb, 5 Park Court, Bathurst Park Rd., Lydney, Glos. Gl15 5HG, England. TEL 0594-843548. Ed. E. McEwen. bk.rev.; charts; illus.; circ. controlled.

SOCIOLOGY OF SPORT JOURNAL. see *SOCIOLOGY*

796 US
SOONERS ILLUSTRATED. 17/yr. Sports Magazines of America, Inc., Box 837, Tulsa, OK 74101-0837. TEL 918-496-7405. FAX 918-496-7485. Ed. M.C. Ross. adv.; circ. 18,900.

797.23 US
SOURCES (MONTCLAIR); the journal of underwater education. 1960. bi-m. $35. National Association of Underwater Instructors, Diving Association, Box 14650, Montclair, CA 91763-1150. TEL 714-621-5801. FAX 714-621-6405. Ed. Mike Williams. adv.; bk.rev.; circ. 12,000. **Indexed:** Sportsearch.
Formerly: N A U I News.

SOUTH AFRICAN AERONEWS. see *AERONAUTICS AND SPACE FLIGHT*

790.1 SA
SOUTH AFRICAN BOXING WORLD. 1976. bi-m. R.16($21) 805 Barclays Bank Bldg., Foreshore, Box 6288, Roggebaai 8012, Cape Town, South Africa. Ed. Bert Blewett. adv.; circ. 11,500. (back issues avail.)

SPORTS AND GAMES

796.346 SA ISSN 0038-2744
SOUTH AFRICAN TABLE TENNIS NEWS. 1953. 3/yr. R.12. South African Table Tennis Union, P.O. Box 14170, Farrarmere 1518, South Africa. TEL 011-849-0431. Ed. A.J. Williams. circ. 3,000.

SOUTH AFRICAN YACHTING. see SPORTS AND GAMES — Boats And Boating

798.4 AT ISSN 0038-2981
SOUTH AUSTRALIAN RACING CALENDAR. 1902. m. Aus.$45. South Australian Jockey Club Inc., G.P.O. Box 1695, Adelaide, S.A. 5001, Australia. FAX 08-295-1830. TELEX AA89404. Ed. F.P. Fox. adv.; cum.index; circ. 1,300.

790.1 US
SOUTHERN GAMEPLAN.* 1989. 9/yr. $17. SportsMedia, Inc., P.O. Box 59721, Birmingham, AL 35259-9721. TEL 205-324-0460. Ed. Ben Cook. adv.; circ. 100,000.
    Description: Features stories on national sports events affecting the southern U.S. and rising high school athletic stars, with emphasis on collegiate sports.

796.72 US ISSN 0049-1616
SOUTHERN MOTORACING. 1964. fortn. $12.50. Universal Services, Inc., Box 500, Winston-Salem, NC 27102. TEL 919-723-5227. Ed. Hank Schoolfield. adv.; bk.rev.; stat.; circ. 20,500. (tabloid format)

796.42 US
SOUTHERN RUNNER. bi-m. Dixie Web Graphics Co., Box 6524, Metairie, LA 70009-6524. TEL 504-454-8247. Ed. Valerie D. Andrews. circ. 10,000.

790.1 GW ISSN 0723-6174
SOUVENIR & GESCHENK. 1963. q. DM.50($13) (Bundesverband der Reiseandenken-Branche) Mauritius Verlags-Messe- und Werbe GmbH, Wittelsbacherstr. 10, Postfach 4129, 6200 Wiesbaden, Germany. TEL 06121/791285. Ed. Juergen Schreiber. adv.; bk.rev.; circ. 4,500.

SOVIET SPORTS REVIEW; specializing in track and field, weightlifting (weight training) and sports medicine. see MEDICAL SCIENCES — Sports Medicine

790.1 US
SPECIAL REPORT: SPORTS. (In 3 eds.: Health, Living, Sports) 1988. q. $60. Whittle Communications L.P., 333 Main Ave., Knoxville, TN 37902. TEL 615-595-5300. FAX 15-595-5670.
    Description: Covers health, lifestyle, sports, personalities and family. Each edition provides comprehensive coverage of a specific topic.

790.1 NE
SPECIAL SPORTS. 1981. 6/yr. fl.54. Postbus 12, 6200 AA Maastricht, Netherlands. FAX 045-227359. Ed. Hanco Naninck. adv.; bk.rev.; circ. 60,000.
    Formerly: Tennisrevue.
    Description: Covers tennis, golf, sailing, polo, skiing and sport sponsoring.

796.72 US ISSN 0747-5403
SPEEDWAY SCENE. 1971. w. $35 (foreign $52). Hockomock Publishing, 50 Washington St., Box 300, N. Easton, MA 02356. TEL 508-238-7016. FAX 508-230-2381. Ed. Val LeSieur. circ. 54,900. (tabloid format)
    Description: Covers circle track racing from Winston Cup to local tracks.

796.75 UK ISSN 0038-724X
SPEEDWAY STAR. vol.19, 1970. w. £22.50. Websters Publications Ltd., Onslow House, 60-66 Saffron Hill, London EC1N 8AY, England. Ed. P. Rising. adv.; illus.; circ. 28,500.
    Description: Concerns motorcycle racing.

796 AU
SPIEL-SPORT-FREIZEIT-MODE. vol.13, 1964. m. S.592. Oesterreichischer Wirtschaftsverlag, Nikolsdorfer Gasse 7-11, A-1051 Vienna, Austria. TEL 0222-555585. TELEX 1-11669. Ed. Erhard Zagler. adv.; illus.; circ. 2,600.
    Former titles: Sport-Spiel-Freizeit; Sportartikel-Sportmode (ISSN 0038-7959); Oesterreichische Sportartikel.

793 GW
SPIELCASINO; Spielzeitung fuer Schueler, Eltern und Lehrer. 1979. s-a. DM.4. Adolf Reichwein Schule, Uchteweg 26, 4800 Bielefeld 11, Germany. Ed. Dirk Hannethorth. circ. 650.

790.1 659.1 UK ISSN 0263-3809
SPONSORSHIP NEWS. 1982. m. £84 (foreign £94). Charterhouse Business Publications, P.O. Box 66, Wokingham, Berkshire RG11 4RQ, England. TEL 0734-772770. FAX 0734-774522. Ed. Jonathan Gee. adv.; bk.rev. (back issues avail.)

790.1 613.7 ER
SPORDIILM. 1920. m. $30. Kirjastust Perioodika, Parnu mnt. 8, 200090 Tallinn, Estonia. TEL 44-12-62. (Subscr. to: Akateeminen Kifjakauppa, 128 SF, 00101 Helsinki, Finland) Ed. Roland Hurt. adv.; bk.rev.; stat.; index; circ. 5,000.
    Formerly (until 1990): Kehakultuur (ISSN 0134-3270)

613.7 790 BE ISSN 0038-7770
SPORT. 1958. 4/yr. 450 Fr. Ministere de la Communaute Francaise, Direction Generale du Sport et du Tourisme, Bd. Leopold II, 44, B-1080 Brussels, Belgium. FAX 02-4132825. Ed. R. Hamaite. adv.; bk.rev.; circ. 2,500. **Indexed:** Acad.Ind., Sportsearch (1974-).

790 NO
SPORT. 1919. 8/yr. NOK 250. Norges Sportshandleres Forbund - Norwegian Sport Association, Drammensvn. 30, Oslo 2, Norway. Ed. Odd Frydenberg. adv.; circ. 2,400.
    Formerly (until 1974): Sportshandleren (ISSN 0049-1993)

790 US ISSN 0038-7797
GV561
SPORT. 1946. m. $17.94. Petersen Publishing Co., 8490 Sunset Blvd., Los Angeles, CA 90069. TEL 213-854-2222. Ed. Kelly Garrett. adv.; bk.rev.; illus.; circ. 931,517. (also avail. in microform from UMI; reprint service avail. from UMI) **Indexed:** Acad.Ind., Mag.Ind., PMR, Sports Per.Ind., Sportsearch (1977-), TOM.

790.1 IT
SPORT. 1966. w. L.20000. Gruppo Editoriale Sigma s.r.l., Via Due Macelli 23, 00187 Rome, Italy. adv.; circ. 128,800.

790.1 PL
SPORT. 1945. 5/w. Ul. Mlynska 1, 40-953 Katowice, Poland. TEL 48-32-637325. Ed. Adam Barteczko. circ. 80,000.

790.1 ZR
SPORT AFRICAIN. m. 13e niveau Tour adm, Cite de la Voix du Zaire, B.P. 3356, Kinshasa-Gombe, Zaire. Ed. Tshimpumpu Wa Tshimpumpu.

THE SPORT AMERICANA HOCKEY CARD PRICE GUIDE. see HOBBIES

SPORT & FITNESS. see PHYSICAL FITNESS AND HYGIENE

790.1 UK
SPORT & LEISURE (CARDIFF). 1984. 6/yr. free. Sports Council for Wales, National Sports Centre for Wales, Sophia Gardens, Cardiff CF1 9SW, Wales. FAX 0222-222431. adv.; bk.rev.; circ. 210,000. (tabloid format) **Indexed:** Sportsearch.
    Former titles: Sport Wales; Welsh Sports Review.

790 UK ISSN 0144-7181
SPORT AND LEISURE (LONDON). 1949. 6/yr. £15.20. Sports Council, 16 Upper Woburn Place, London WC1H 0QP, England. TEL 071-388-1277. FAX 071-383-5740. Ed. Louise Fyfe. adv.; bk.rev.; illus.; circ. 8,500. **Indexed:** ASSIA, Phys.Ed.Ind., Sportsearch (1990-).
    —BLDSC shelfmark: 8419.365000.
    Formerly: Sport and Recreation (ISSN 0038-7819)
    Description: Covers developments and new initiatives in recreation at elite and grass roots levels, sports politics and policies.

790.1 613.7 UK ISSN 0267-3304
SPORT AND RECREATION INFORMATION GROUP BULLETIN. 1984. 2/yr. £6 to individuals; institutions £15. Sheffield Libraries and Information Services, Sports Library and Information Centre, Surrey Street, Sheffield, England. TEL 0742-735929. Ed. Lesley Gunter. adv.; bk.rev.; circ. 100.

796.72 FR ISSN 0038-7827
SPORT-AUTO;* le magazine du sport automobile et de l'automobile sportive. 1962. m. 290 F. Gerpresse, 78 rue Jules Gesde, 92300 Levallois-Perret, France. TEL 672-018-280. Ed. Gerard Crombac. adv.; bk.rev.; charts; illus.; circ. 150,000. (tabloid format)

797.21 GW ISSN 0344-6492
SPORT- BAEDER- FREIZEITBAUTEN; internationale Fachzeitschrift fuer Planung, Bau, Einrichtung, Betrieb und Forschung. (Text in German; summaries in English, French and Italian) 1961. 6/yr. DM.69. Krammer Verlag, Hermannstr. 3, 4000 Duesseldorf 1, Germany. TEL 0211-67972-0. FAX 0211-6797231. TELEX 8586639-KRVG-D. Ed. D. Fabian. adv. contact: adv. contact: Heinz Martin. bk.rev.; charts; illus.; tr.lit.; circ. 4,500. **Indexed:** Br.Tech.Ind., Eng.Ind.
    —BLDSC shelfmark: 8419.675000.
    Formerly: Sport- und Baederbauten (ISSN 0038-7924)
    Description: International trade publication for the aquatic sport and recreation building industry. Covers various aspects of the construction and design of swimming pools and other sports facilities.

790.1 IT
SPORT CLUB. m. (11/yr.) L.110000 in Europe; America L.155000. Publimedia Societa Editrice, Corso Venezia 18, 20121 Milan, Italy. TEL 02-77521. FAX 02-781068.

790.1 658.7 US
SPORT CONSTRUCTION BUYER'S GUIDE. 1988. a. International Sport Summit, 372 Fifth Ave., Ste. 2G, New York, NY 10018. TEL 212-502-5306. TELEX RCA 261239. adv.; circ. 7,000.
    Description: For buyers of sport construction services.

796 IT
SPORT DEL MEZZOGIORNO. w. L.4750. Compagnia Editrice Napoletano, Via Chiatamone 65, 80121 Naples, Italy. Ed. Riccardo Cassero. adv.; circ. 50,490.

790.1 PL
SPORT DLA KAZDEGO; rekreacja fizyczna. m. 6 Zl. per no. Plac Dabrowskiego 8, IV p., 00-055 Warsaw, Poland. Ed. Tadeusz Golabek. circ. 50,000.

790.1 IT
SPORT E CITTA. 1968. q. L.30000 (foreign L.40000). R I M A s.r.l., Via Vincenzo da Filicaia 7, 20162 Milan, Italy. TEL 02-66103539. FAX 02-66103558. Ed. Renato O. Foni. adv.; circ. 13,000.
    Formerly: Impianti Attrezzature Sportive e Ricreative (ISSN 0393-4322)

SPORT & MEDICINA. see MEDICAL SCIENCES — Sports Medicine

790.1 FR
SPORT ET VIE. 6/yr. 30 F. (foreign 198 F.). Archeologia S.A., 25 rue Berbisey, 2100 Dijon, France. (Subscr. to: 1 rue des Artisans, B.P. 90, 21803 Quetigny Cedex, France. TEL 80-70-93-47)

790.1 IT
SPORT GIOVANE; giochi della gioventu. Short title: S G. (Special editions avail.) 1969. m. L.14000. Coni Servizio Promozione Sportiva, Foro Italico, 00194 Rome. TEL 36857467. FAX 36857116. Ed. Mario Pescante. adv.; illus.
    Formerly (until 1977): Giochi della Gioventu.
    Description: Forum for young people covering the world of sports in Italy. Includes articles on the politics of sport, sport techniques, medicine and the role sports play in public schools.

790.1 GW
SPORT HANDBUCH WUERTTEMBERG; fuer alle Sportler und Sportinteressierte. 1979. a. DM.24.60. (Wuerttembergischer Landessportbund e.V.) Schors-Verlags-Gesellschaft mbH, Postfach 1280, 6272 Niederhausen, Germany. TEL 06127-8029. FAX 06127-8812. Eds. Hans-Eberhard Rutzen, Eva-Maria Huebner. circ. 24,000.

SPORTS AND GAMES

790.1   GW
SPORT IN NIEDERSACHSEN. m. Landessportbund Niedersachsen e.V., Ferdinand-Wilhelm-Fricke-Weg 10, 3000 Hannover 1, Germany. TEL 0511-12680. FAX 0511-889862.

790.1   GW   ISSN 0178-1014
SPORT INFORM. 1969. bi-m. DM.54. Landessportbund Rheinland - Pfalz, Rheinallee 1, 6500 Mainz 1, Germany. TEL 06131-2814-0. FAX 06131-222379. Ed.Bd. adv.; bk.rev.; circ. 8,100. (back issues avail.)

790.1   BE
SPORT INTERNATIONAL. (Text in Arabic, French, German, Spanish) 1959. q. 480 Fr. International Military Sports Council - Conseil International du Sport Militaire, Rue Jacques Jordaens 26, 1050 Brussels, Belgium. TEL 02-647-6852. FAX 02-647-5387. TELEX 29416 CISM B. Ed. J. Wanderstein. circ. 5,000. **Indexed:** Sportsearch.
Formerly: Sport International Yearbook.
Description: Contains case reports, activities of the executive committee, sports medicine section, and results of sport events fostering good will among nations.

798.4   IT   ISSN 0038-7916
SPORT ITALIA.* 1948. w. L.250 per no. Sport Italia, Largo Toscanini 1, 20122 Milan, Italy. Ed. Sisal. adv.; bk.rev.; circ. 20,000.
Description: Covers horseracing.

790.1 659.1   US
SPORT MEDIA BUYER'S GUIDE. 1988. a. International Sport Summit, 372 Fifth Ave., Ste. 2G, New York, NY 10018. TEL 212-502-5306. TELEX RCA 261239. adv.; circ. 7,000.
Description: For sport media buyers at advertising agencies, and sport media buyers and sponsors at corporations with directory information.

790.1   GW
SPORT - OVERSEAS MILITARY EDITION. (Text in English) 1980. 6/yr. DM.60($30) International Publications GmbH, Waechtersbacher Str. 89, 6000 Frankfurt 61, Germany. TEL 069-4209600. Ed. Mark Vaughn. circ. 80,000.
Description: Season previews and sports news from the U.S., and military sports information for Americans in Europe.

SPORT PILOT; the magazine of recreational flying. see AERONAUTICS AND SPACE FLIGHT

790.1   US   ISSN 0888-9589
GV561
SPORT PLACE INTERNATIONAL; an international journal of sports geography. 1987. 3/yr. $20 to individuals (foreign $30); institutions $55 (foreign $65). Black Oak Press, 2624 Black Oak Dr., Stillwater, OK 74074. FAX 405-744-7673. Ed. Richard Pillsbury. adv.; charts; illus.; circ. 200. **Indexed:** Sportsearch (1987-).
—BLDSC shelfmark: 8419.635000.
Description: Explores the connections between people, their sports, and their places.

790.1   CN
SPORT PLUS. (Text in French) 1981. m. $20. 1028 Marie Victorin, Laval, Que. H7E 3C1, Canada. TEL 514-661-5586. Ed. Charles Andre Marchand. adv.; circ. 40,000.

THE SPORT PSYCHOLOGIST. see PSYCHOLOGY

790.1 320 613.7   US   ISSN 0270-1812
SPORT SCENE; focus on youth programs. 1979. q. $16 (foreign $25). North American Youth Sport Institute, 4985 Oak Garden Dr., Kernersville, NC 27284-9520. TEL 919-784-4926. Ed. Dr. Jack Hutslar. adv.; bk.rev.; circ. 15,000. **Indexed:** Sportsearch.
Description: Provides current information about children and sports. Contains articles to help leaders be more effective, parents become more effective teachers and coaches, increase participation, decrease drop-outs and injuries, and show how sports can be made more fun for children.

790.1   CN
SPORT SCIENCE FORUM/FORUM SCIENCES DES SPORTS. 1986. irreg. Shooting Federation of Canada - Federation de Tir du Canada, 1600 James Naismith Dr., Gloucester, Ont. K1B 5N4, Canada. TEL 613-748-5659. FAX 613-748-5706. **Indexed:** Sportsearch (1986-).

790.1 378.198   FR   ISSN 0221-0142
SPORT SCOLAIRE. 1978. bi-m. 160 F. Union Nationale du Sport Scolaire, 13 rue Saint Lazare, 75009 Paris, France. TEL 42-81-55-11. adv.; circ. 80,000.
Formerly (1971-1978): A S S U (Association du Sport Scolaire et Universitaire) (ISSN 0184-3540)

796   US
SPORT SHOP NEWS. m. 53 Sterling Rd., Trumbull, CT 06611. TEL 203-268-1921. Ed. Greg Martone. circ. 23,409.

790.1   IT
SPORT SUD. w. L.4750. Compagnia Editrice Napoletano, Via Chiatamone 65, Naples 80121, Itlay. Ed. Enrico Marucci. adv.

790.1   CN
SPORT - TALK. q. F.S. Productions, Box 10, Site 329, R.R. 3, Collingwood, Ont. L9Y 3Z2, Canada. **Indexed:** Sportsearch (1974-).

SPORT TRUCK. see TRANSPORTATION — Trucks And Trucking

790 658.8   GW   ISSN 0049-1926
SPORT UND MODE. (Text in French and German) 1948. m. DM.156. (Verband Deutscher Sportgeschaefte e.V.) Verlag Chmielorz GmbH und Co, Wilhelmstr. 42, 6200 Wiesbaden, Germany. Ed. Juergen B. Wamser. adv.; bk.rev.; abstr.; charts; illus.; pat.; stat.; circ. 5,000.

796   GW   ISSN 0038-7932
SPORT UND TECHNIK; das wehrpolitische Jugendmagazin der G S T. (Includes: Motorsport) 1952. m. DM.12.60. Zentralvorstand of Technical Sports in the GDR) Militaerverlag der Deutschen Demokratischen Republik, Storkower Str. 158, 1055 Berlin, Germany. TEL 2-4300618. Ed. Ulrich Berger. adv.; bk.rev.; film rev.; play rev.; charts; illus. (newspaper)
Formerly: Sport und Technik in Wort und Bild.

796   IT   ISSN 0490-5113
SPORT UNIVERSITARIO. 1951; N.S. 1969. q. free. Centro Universitario Sportivo Italiano, Via Angelo Brofferio 7, 00195 Rome, Italy. FAX 6-3724479. TELEX 6-620074 CUSI I. Ed. Ruggero Cornini. adv.; bk.rev.; circ. 5,000.

790.1 796.77   IS
SPORT VE RECHEV. w. Hamakome Publishing House, 34 Yitzak Sadeh St., Tel Aviv, Israel. TEL 03-337192.

790.1   GW   ISSN 0342-1724
SPORT-VORSCHAU/SPORTS PREVIEW. international. m. DM.27.50 per no. Verlag Horst Deike KG, Robert-Bosch-Str. 18, Postfach 100452, 7750 Konstanz, Germany. TEL 07531-65061. FAX 07531-65063.

796   NE   ISSN 0922-4270
SPORTACCOM; magazine voor realisatie, beheer en onderhoud van sportsaccomodaties. 1963. bi-m. fl.55. (Nederlandse Sport Federatie) Arko Uitgeverij b.v., Essenkade 4, 3992 AA Houten, Netherlands. TEL 03403-76933. FAX 03403-80600. Ed. T. van Zetten. adv.; charts; illus.; stat.
Former titles: Nederlandse Sport Federatie. Technische Mededelingen; Nederlandse Sport Federatie. Technische Bulletin (ISSN 0028-2308)
Description: Covers all sports played indoors in the Netherlands and the maintenance of facilities necessary.

793   NE   ISSN 0077-6777
SPORTACCOMMODATIE IN NEDERLAND/SPORTS: PUBLIC ACCOMMODATION. (Text in Dutch and English) 1959. irreg. price varies. Centraal Bureau voor de Statistiek, Prinses Beatrixlaan 428, Voorburg, Netherlands. (Orders to: SDU - Publishers, Christoffel Plantijnstraat, The Hague).

790.1   MF
SPORTAMO; magazine-hebdomadaire tele-sport. (Text in French) w. Rs.65. Nouvelle Imprimerie Mauricienne, 5, rue Jemmapes, Port Louis, Mauritius.

688.76 658   GW   ISSN 0720-1516
SPORTARTIKEL WIRTSCHAFT. 1980. m. DM.146. Verlag Chmielorz GmbH und Co., Wilhelmstr. 42, 6200 Wiesbaden, Germany. TEL 0611-39671. FAX 0611-301303. Ed. Juergen Wamser. adv.; bk.rev.; circ. 6,400.

790.1   LI
SPORTAS. 1956. 2/wk. Gedimino pr. 37, Vilnius 232600, Lithuania. TEL (0122) 616-757. Ed. Aleksandras Krukauskas. circ. 25,500. (newspaper)

790.1   US
SPORTBIL. 1978. a. International Sport Summit, 372 Fifth Ave., Ste. 2G, New York, NY 10018. TEL 212-502-5306. adv.; circ. 7,500.
Description: Opinion papers and data on the business of sport, sport events, and sport facilities.

SPORTCARE & FITNESS. see MEDICAL SCIENCES — Sports Medicine

797.21   SW   ISSN 0038-7967
SPORTDYKAREN. 1960. 5/yr. SEK 125. Swedish Sportdivers Federation, Idrottens Hus, S-12387 Farsta, Sweden. FAX 46-8-605-6372. Ed. Lennart Haak. adv.; bk.rev.; circ. 13,500.

790.1   GW   ISSN 0174-1152
SPORTHANDBUCH NIEDERSACHSEN; fuer alle Verbaende, Vereine und Sportinteressierte. 1979. a. DM.24.60. (Landessportbund Niedersachsen e.V.) Schors-Verlags-Gesellschaft mbH, Postfach 1280, 6272 Niedersachsen, Germany. TEL 06127-8029. FAX 06127-8812. Ed.Bd. circ. 35,000.

790.1   GW   ISSN 0174-1144
SPORTHANDBUCH NORDRHEIN-WESTFALEN. 1976. a. DM.24.60. (Landessportbund Nordrhein-Westfalen e.V.) Schors-Verlags-Gesellschaft mbH, Postfach 1280, 6272 Niedernhausen, Germany. TEL 06127-8029. FAX 06127-8812. Ed. Karl Hoffmann. circ. 85,000.

796   AA
SPORTI POPULLOR. w. $13.34. Ministere de l'Enseignement et de la Culture, Tirana, Albania.

790   PK   ISSN 0038-7991
SPORTIMES;* the magazine for sportsmen. (Text in English) 1956. m. Rs.160($16) Progressive Papers Limited, Progressive Papers Bldg., Rattan Chand Rd., Lahore 7, Pakistan. Ed. Sultan F. Husain. charts; illus.; stat. **Indexed:** Sportsearch.

790.1   AT
SPORTING GLOBE. 1922. w. Herald & Weekly Times Ltd., 44-74 Flinders St., Melbourne, Vic. 3000, Australia. TEL 03-652-1111. FAX 03-654-3133. TELEX 30104. Ed. Neville Willmott. circ. 43,049.
Description: Contains team sporting results, race results, previews, interviews, comments etc.

790.1   US
SPORTING GOODS AGENTS ASSOCIATION. NEWSLETTER. m. Sporting Goods Agents Association, Box 998, Morton Grove, IL 60053. TEL 708-296-3670. FAX 708-827-0196.

658.8 790   US   ISSN 0146-0889
SPORTING GOODS BUSINESS; the national newsmagazine of the sporting goods industry. 1967. m. $65 (free to qualified personnel). Miller Freeman Inc. (New York) (Subsidiary of: United Newspapers Group), 1515 Broadway, New York, NY 10036. TEL 212-869-1300. FAX 212-302-6273. Ed. Robert Carr. adv.; bibl.; charts; illus.; tr.lit. **Indexed:** Bus.Ind., Sportsearch (1977-), Tr.& Indus.Ind.

658.8 790   US   ISSN 0038-8017
GV743
SPORTING GOODS DEALER; national magazine of the sporting goods trade. 1899. m. free to qualified personnel. Sporting News Publishing Co., 1212 N. Lindbergh Blvd., St. Louis, MO 63132. TEL 314-997-7111. Ed. Steve Fechter. adv.; illus.; mkt.; tr.lit.; circ. 27,410. (reprint service avail. from UMI)

SPORTING GOODS MANUFACTURERS ASSOCIATION. EXECUTIVE COMPENSATION STUDY. see BUSINESS AND ECONOMICS — Labor And Industrial Relations

SPORTING GOODS MANUFACTURERS ASSOCIATION. FINANCIAL PERFORMANCE STUDY. see BUSINESS AND ECONOMICS — Labor And Industrial Relations

688.76   US
SPORTING GOODS WHOLESALER. bi-m. membership only. National Association of Sporting Goods Wholesalers, Box 1134, Chicago, IL 60611. TEL 312-565-0233.

SPORTS AND GAMES

796 US ISSN 0038-805X
SPORTING NEWS; the nation's oldest and finest sports publication. 1886. w. $82.80. Sporting News Publishing Co. (Subsidiary of: Times Mirror Company), 1212 N. Lindbergh Blvd., St. Louis, MO 63132. TEL 800-669-5700. Ed. John Rawlings. adv.; bk.rev.; illus.; stat.; circ. 725,000. (tabloid format; also avail. in microfilm from UMI,BHP,KTO; reprint service avail. from UMI.) **Indexed**: Access, Hlth.Ind., Mag.Ind., Sports Per.Ind., Sportsearch (1977-).
●Also available online. Vendor(s): Mead Data Central.

796.355 US
SPORTING NEWS HOCKEY DIRECTORY. 1982. a. $4.95. Sporting News Publishing Co. (Subsidiary of: Times Mirror Company), 1212 N. Lindbergh Blvd., St. Louis, MO 63132. TEL 314-997-7111. FAX 314-993-7726. adv.; circ. 200,000.

790.1 US
SPORTING NEWS SPORTS. a. Sporting News Publishing Co., 1212 N. Lindbergh Blvd., St. Louis, MO 63132. TEL 314-997-7111. (Subscr. to: Box 56, St. Louis, MO 63166)

798.8 IE ISSN 0049-1942
SPORTING PRESS. 1923. w. 80p. per no. (Irish Coursing Club) Greyhound & Sporting Press Ltd., Davis Rd., Clonmel County, Tipperary, Ireland. FAX 052-25018. Ed. J.L. Desmond. adv.; illus.; circ. 9,000. (newspaper) **Indexed**: Sportsearch.
Description: News about dog racing.

790.1 GH
SPORTING RECORD. w. P.O. Box 7962, Accra, Ghana. Ed. L.O. Addy. adv.

790.1 NR
SPORTING RECORDS. w. £N52. Daily Times of Nigeria Ltd., Publications Division, New Isheri Rd., Agidingbi - Ikeja, P.M.B. 21340, Lagos, Nigeria. TEL 900850-9. Ed. Cyril Kappo. adv.; circ. 222,975.
Description: Presents sporting reports and forecasts.

790.1 CN
SPORTING SCENE. 1980. m. Can.$20 (in US Can.$25). Sporting Scene, 22 Maberley Cres., West Hill, Ont. M1C 3K8, Canada. TEL 416-284-0304. FAX 416-284-1299. Ed. Peter Martens. adv.; circ. 19,800 (controlled). (tabloid format)

790.1 CN ISSN 1181-8808
SPORTING TIMES (CALGARY); voice of Alberta amateur sport. m. Can.$15 (foreign Can.$20). Casablanca Publishing, Box 101, 339 - 10 Ave. S.E., Calgary, Alta. T2N 0W2, Canada. TEL 403-289-3265. Ed. Geoffrey W. White. adv.; illus.; circ. 10,000. (tabloid format)

796 RU ISSN 0038-8092
SPORTIVNAYA ZHIZN' ROSSII. 1957. m. 9.60 Rub. (Soyuz Sportivnykh Obshchestv i Organizatsii Rossiiskoi S.F.S.R.) Soviet Russia, Armyanskii pereulok 13, 101000 Moscow, Russia. TEL 928-02-62. (Co-sponsor: Komitet po Fizkul'ture i Sportu) Ed. I.B. Maslennikov. adv.; illus.; index; circ. 488,992.

796 RU ISSN 0038-8106
SPORTIVNYE IGRY. 1955. m. 6 Rub. (Soyuz Sportivnykh Obshchestv i Organizatsii S.S.S.R.) Izdatel'stvo Fizkul'tura i Sport, Kalyaevskaya ul., 27, Moscow K-6, Russia. TEL 258-06-56. Ed. D.L. Rishkov. illus.; index; circ. 15,000.

796 GW ISSN 0014-6145
DER SPORTJOURNALIST. 1950. m. DM.60. (Verband Deutsche Sportpresse e.V.) Verlag Rommerskirchen, Rolandshof, 5480 Remagen-Rolandseck, Germany. TEL 02228-60010. FAX 02228-600149. TELEX 886912-ROKI-D. Ed. Thomas Rommerskirchen. adv.; bk.rev.; illus.; circ. 3,000.

SPORTMANAGEMENT. see *BUSINESS AND ECONOMICS — Management*

790 PL ISSN 0038-8122
SPORTOWIEC. 1949. w. $28. Ul. Mokotowska 25, 00-640 Warsaw, Poland. TEL 48-22-216208. (Dist. by: Ars Polona-Ruch, Krakowskie Przedmiescie 7, Warsaw, Poland) Ed. Jacek Zemantowski. bk.rev.; illus.; circ. 100,000.

SPORTPAEDAGOGIK; zeitschrift fuer Sport- Spiel- und Bewegungserziehung. see *EDUCATION — Teaching Methods And Curriculum*

790.1 GW ISSN 0173-2528
SPORTPRAXIS; die Fachzeitschrift fuer den Sportlehrer und Uebungsleiter. 1959. bi-m. DM.54. (Deutscher Sportbund) Limpert Verlag GmbH, Luisenplatz 2, Postfach 4027, 6200 Wiesbaden, Germany. TEL 0611-373072. FAX 0611-374351. TELEX 4064187-LIMP. Eds. H.-J. Langen, H. Meusel. adv.; bk.rev.; circ. 10,000. (back issues avail.)
Description: For sport teachers and trainers.

796 SI
SPORTS. (Text in English) 1972. 10/yr. S.$9. Singapore Sports Council, National Stadium, Kallang, Singapore 1439, Singapore. FAX 3409537. TELEX RG 35467-NASTAD. Ed. Mrs. Ong Poh. adv.; charts; illus.; stat.; circ. 17,000. **Indexed**: Sportsearch.

790.1 US
GV583
SPORTS ADDRESS BIBLE; the comprehensive directory of sports addresses. 1980. a. $24.95. Global Sports Productions Ltd., Box 3026, Santa Monica, CA 90408-3026. TEL 213-395-6533. Ed. Edward T. Kobak, Jr. adv.; bk.rev.; circ. 25,000. (also avail. in Braille; back issues avail.)
Formerly: Comprehensive Directory of Sports Addresses (ISSN 0743-4561)
Description: Lists addresses, telephone and fax numbers and contact persons from international, collegiate, professional and amateur sports.

790.1 658 US
▼**SPORTS ADVANTAGE**. 1991. s-a. $169. Standard Rate and Data Service, Inc., 3004 Glenview Rd., Wilmette, IL 60091. TEL 708-256-8333. FAX 708-441-2252.
Description: Contains over 2000 standardized listings ranging from special events and sponsorship opportunities, to team promotions for marketing executives.

796 US ISSN 0038-8149
SPORTS AFIELD. 1887. m. $13.97. Hearst Magazines, Sports Afield, 250 W. 55th St., New York, NY 10019. TEL 212-649-4000. Ed. Tom Paugh. adv.; bk.rev.; charts; illus.; circ. 511,314. (also avail. in microform from UMI) **Indexed**: Access (1975-), Consum.Ind., Mag.Ind., PMR, Sports Per.Ind.
Former titles: Sports Afield with Rod and Gun; Sports Afield.
Description: Hands-on magazine for outdoor enthusiasts.

790.1 UK ISSN 0961-5822
SPORTS & LEISURE NEWS. 1982. m. £18($36) Peterson Publications Ltd., Peterson House, Berryhill Industrial Estate, Droitwich, Worcs. WR9 9BL, England. TEL 0905-795564. Ed. Alan Turner. adv.; charts; illus.; circ. 12,500.
Formerly: Sports and Leisure Equipment News.

658.8 790 AT ISSN 1035-915X
SPORTS & LEISURE RETAILER. 1937. m. Aus.$44 (foreign Aus.$110)(effective Apr. 1992). Yaffa Publishing Group, 17-21 Bellevue St., Surry Hills, N.S.W. 2010, Australia. FAX 02-281-2750. (Subscr. to: GPO Box 606, Sydney, N.S.W. 2001, Australia) Ed. Liza Cruz. adv.; B&W page Aus.$1255, color page Aus.$1900; trim 297 x 210. illus.; stat.; circ. 4,018 (controlled).
Formerly: Australasian Sportsgoods and Toy Retailer (ISSN 0004-8488)
Description: Features new products and general news of interest to sportsgoods retailers.

SPORTS & LIFESTYLE MARKETING. see *BUSINESS AND ECONOMICS — Marketing And Purchasing*

790.1 US
SPORTS AND RECREATIONAL PROGRAMS OF THE NATION'S UNIVERSITIES AND COLLEGES. 1958. quinquennial. $4. National Collegiate Athletic Association, Circulation Department, Box 7347, Overland Park, KS 66207-0347. TEL 913-339-1900. circ. 3,000.

790.1 340 US
SPORTS AND THE COURTS; physical education and sports law newsletter. 1980. q. $40. Box 2836, Winston-Salem, NC 27102. TEL 919-725-0583. Ed. C. Thomas Ross. **Indexed**: Sportsearch (1981-).

790.1 629.132 US
SPORTS AVIATION. 1953. m. $35. Wittman Airfield, Box 3086, Oshkosh, WI 54903-3086. TEL 414-426-4800. Ed. Jack Cox. adv.; circ. 125,000.

688.76 CN ISSN 0829-3716
SPORTS BUSINESS. 1973. 8/yr. Can.$53.50($95) Laurentian Media Inc., 501 Oakdale Rd., Downsview, Ont. M3N 1W7, Canada. TEL 416-746-7360. FAX 416-746-1421. illus.; circ. 9,200. **Indexed**: Can.B.P.I.
Former titles: Sports Trade Canada & Sporting Trade Canada; Sporting Goods Trade (ISSN 0381-9280)

790.1 US
SPORTS BUSINESS. m. Center for Sports Sponsorship, Box 280, Plainsboro, NJ 08536. TEL 609-799-4722.

790.1 AT ISSN 0314-5468
SPORTS COACH; Australian coaching magazine. 1976. q. Aus.$15 (foreign Aus.$20). (Australian Sports Commission) Australian Coaching Council Inc., P.O. Box 176, Belconnen, A.C.T. 2616, Australia. TEL 06-2521550. FAX 06-2521200. TELEX AA62400 AUSIS. Ed. Lawrie Woodman. adv.; bk.rev.; circ. 8,500. (back issues avail.) **Indexed**: Phys.Ed.Ind., Sportsearch (1978-).
—BLDSC shelfmark: 8419.832000.

790 FR
SPORTS DANS LA CITE. 1962. q. 110 Fr. Federation Nationale des Offices Municipaux des Sports (F N O M S), 40 rue Piat, 75020 Paris, France. adv.; circ. 18,000.

790.1 KO
SPORTS DONG-A. 1978. w. Dong-A Ilbo, 139 Sejongno, Chongno-gu, Seoul, S. Korea. TEL 02-721-7114. Ed. Kwon O-Kie. circ. 184,902.

790.1 US
SPORTS EYE. d. $1 per no. Sports Eye, Inc., 18 Industrial Park Dr., Port Washington, NY 11050. TEL 516-484-3300. Ed. Jay Bergman.
Description: Covers thouroughbred racing.

790.1 JM
▼**SPORTS FOCUS**; the Jamaican quarterly sports magazine. 1990. q. M R C Services Ltd., 2 Easton Ave., Kingston 5, Jamaica, W.I. TEL 809-978-0650.

796 US ISSN 0038-822X
GV561
SPORTS ILLUSTRATED. 1954. w. $69.66. The Time Inc. Magazine Company (Subsidiary of: Time Warner, Inc.), Time & Life Bldg., Rockefeller Center, 1271 Ave. of the Americas, New York, NY 10020-1393. TEL 212-522-1212. (Subscr. to: Sports Illustrated, Box 61292, Tampa, FL 33661-1292) Ed. John Paranek. adv.; bk.rev.; illus.; index; circ. 3,150,000. (also avail. in microform from UMI; avail. in talking book ed.) **Indexed**: Abr.R.G., Acad.Ind., Biog.Ind., Bk.Rev.Ind. (1980-), Child.Bk.Rev.Ind. (1980-), CMI, Hlth.Ind., Jun.High.Mag.Abstr., Mag.Ind., PMR, R.G., Sports Per.Ind., Sportsearch (1974-), TOM.
●Also available online. Vendor(s): DIALOG, Mead Data Central, VU/TEXT Information Services, Inc..

790.1 US
▼**SPORTS ILLUSTRATED CLASSIC**. 1991. a. The Time Inc. Magazine Company (Subsidiary of: Time Warner - Magazines), Time & Life Bldg., Rockefeller Center, 1271 Ave. of the Americas, New York, NY 10020-1393. TEL 212-522-1212.

790.1 028.5 US
SPORTS ILLUSTRATED FOR KIDS. 1989. m. $17.95. The Time Inc. Magazine Company (Subsidiary of: Time Warner, Inc.), Time & Life Bldg., Rockefeller Center, New York, NY 10020-1393. TEL 212-522-1212. (Subscr. to: Box 830609, Birmingham, AL 35283-0609) Ed. Craig Neff. circ. 864,606. **Indexed**: Ind.Child.Mag.

790.1 US
SPORTS INC.; the sports business weekly. 1987. w. $69.95. Times Mirror Magazines, Inc., 2 Park Ave., New York, NY 10016. TEL 212-779-5000. Ed. Craig Reiss. circ. 2,500.

SPORTS AND GAMES

790.1   UK   ISSN 0261-5665
SPORTS INDUSTRY. 1981. m. £25 (foreign £34). B & M Publications (London) Ltd., P.O. Box 13, Hereford House, Bridle Path, Croydon, Surrey CR9 4NL, England. TEL 081-680-4200. FAX 081-681-5049. Ed. Richard Sutton. adv.; circ. 11,779.

790.1 330   US
SPORTS INDUSTRY NEWS; management & finance, regulation & litigation, media & marketing. 1983. w. $244. Game Point Publishing, Box 946, Camden, ME 04843. TEL 207-236-8346. Ed. Ray Swan. bk.rev.; stat. (looseleaf format)
    Formerly: Industry News (ISSN 0742-2024)
    Description: News items and briefs on management and finance, regulations and litigation, and media and marketing in amateur and professional sports, with news on negotiations and arbitration decisions on individual contracts.

790.1   CN
SPORTS JOURNAL. 1976. m. Can.$20($25) National Sports Journal Ltd., 7 Glenbrook Place S.W., Calgary, Alta. T3E TWU, Canada. TEL 403-287-2060. FAX 403-246-4464. Ed. Barry Whetstone. adv.; circ. 29,000. (newspaper; back issues avail.) Indexed: Sportsearch.
    Formerly: National Sports Journal.

796   JA
SPORTS MAGAZINE. 1972. 5/yr. 6480 Yen. Baseball Magazine Sha, 3-10-10 Misaki-cho, Chiyoda-ku, Tokyo, Japan. Ed. Ryusuke Takahashi. Indexed: R.G.

790.1 658.8   US
SPORTS MARKET PLACE. 1980. a. $165 (including updates $225). Sportsguide, Inc., Box 1417, Princeton, NJ 08542. TEL 609-921-8599. Ed. Richard A. Lipsey. adv.; index; circ. 1,500. (avail. on disc)
    Formerly: Sportsguide (ISSN 0277-0296)
    Description: Comprehensive listing of sports teams, leagues, governing bodies, TV and print media, sports marketing firms, sports information sources, and equipment, apparel and footwear suppliers.

SPORTS MARKETING PROFILES. see BUSINESS AND ECONOMICS — Marketing And Purchasing

790.1   US
SPORTS MEDIA NEWS. m. Center for Sports Sponsorship, Box 280, Plainsboro, NJ 08536. TEL 609-799-4722.

SPORTS MEDICINE DIGEST. see MEDICAL SCIENCES — Sports Medicine

790.1   US   ISSN 0161-6706
GV709.3
SPORTS 'N SPOKES. 1975. bi-m. $12 (foreign $16). (Paralyzed Veterans of America, Inc.) P V A Publications, 5201 N. 19th Ave., Ste. 111, Phoenix, AZ 85015. TEL 602-246-9426. FAX 602-242-6862. Ed. Cliff Crase. adv.; bk.rev.; circ. 9,000. (back issues avail.) Indexed: Phys.Ed.Ind., Sports Per.Ind., Sportsearch (1978-).
    Description: Covers wheelchair sports and recreation.

SPORTS - NUTRITION NEWS; incorporating the latest in health and fitness. see NUTRITION AND DIETETICS

796   CN
SPORTS PAGE. 11/yr. Dave White Assocaites Ltd., Box 61145, Kensington P.O., Calgary, Alta. T2N 4S6, Canada. TEL 403-254-2364. Ed. Dave White. circ. 20,000.

SPORTS, PARKS AND RECREATION LAW REPORTER. see LAW

790.1   US
▼**SPORTS PULSE.** 1990. bi-m. $9. Pulse Publications, Inc. (Bellingham), 339 Telegraph Rd., Bellingham, WA 98226. TEL 206-671-3933. adv.
    Description: Covers sporting, recreation and fitness related activities, news, and people in Whatcom County.

658.8 790   UK
SPORTS RETAILING.* 1917. m. £41 (foreign £58). Benn Publications Ltd., Sovereign Way, Tonbridge, Kent TN9 1RW, England. TEL 0732-364422. Ed. Geoffrey Manners. adv.; bk.rev.; index; circ. 4,000. (back issues avail.)
    Formerly: Sports Trader (ISSN 0038-8254)

796   US
SPORTS REVIEW SERIES. 15/yr. T.V. Sports, Inc., Box 48, Rockville Centre, NY 11571. Ed. Bob Gutowski. adv.; illus.

790.1   US
SPORTS REVIEW WRESTLING. m. $17 (foreign $22). G C London Publishing Associates, Box 48, Rockville Centre, NY 11571. TEL 516-764-0300. FAX 516-764-4370. Ed. Stu Saks.

790.1   US
SPORTS SOUTH. 1988. bi-m. $15. Regional Sports Publications, 7001 Peachtree Industrial Blvd., Ste. 404, Norcross, GA 30092. TEL 404-448-6226. FAX 404-368-2444. adv.; circ. 40,000.
    Formerly: Atlanta Sports South.

790.1   US
SPORTS SPONSOR. m. Center for Sports Sponsorship, Box 280, Plainsboro, NJ 08536. TEL 609-799-4722.

790.1   US
SPORTS SPONSORSHIP MANUAL SERIES. irreg. Center for Sports Sponsorship, Box 280, Plainsboro, NJ 08536. TEL 609-799-4722.

796.077   AT
SPORTS TRAINERS DIGEST. 1987. q. Aus.$11 (foreign Aus.$17). Australian Sports Medicine Federation, P.O. Box 897, Belconnen, A.C.T. 2616, Australia. TEL 062-51-6944. FAX 06-2531489. TELEX AUSIS 62400. Ed. Matt Reid.

658.8 790   US   ISSN 0890-8745
SPORTS TREND. 1969. m. $55. Shore Communications, Inc., 180 Allen Rd., N.E., Ste. 300 N, Atlanta, GA 30328. TEL 404-252-8831. FAX 404-252-4436. Ed. Jeff Atkinson. adv.; bk.rev.; circ. 29,102 (controlled).
    Formerly: Sports Merchandiser (ISSN 0049-1985)
    Description: Discusses the newest products and the latest trends and techniques for merchandising sporting goods.

797   DK
SPORTSDYKKEREN.* bi-m. Dansk Sportsdykker Forbund, c/o Ole Galthen, Vesterled 22, DK-6400 Soenderborg, Denmark. Ed. Henning Olsen. adv.; circ. 6,300.
    Description: Covers the sport of diving.

658.8 790   GW   ISSN 0931-5381
SPORTSHOP; international trade magazine for the sporting goods trade. (Supplement for ISPO Sportshop Hotline) (Text in English and German) 1949. m. DM.98 (foreign DM.102). (Bundesverband der Deutschen Sportartikel-Industrie e.V. - World Federation of the Sporting Goods Industry) Meisenbach GmbH, Hainstr. 18, Postfach 2069, 8600 Bamberg, Germany. TEL 0951-861-114. FAX 0951-861-164. TELEX 662844-MEIBA-D. Ed. Carolina Barksdale. adv.; bk.rev.; abstr.; illus.; stat.; circ. 8,000.
    Formerly (until 1987): Eurosport and Freizeitmode (ISSN 0340-739X); Formed by the merger of: Eurosport (ISSN 0014-259X); Freizeit-Mode (ISSN 0016-0938)

SPORTSTAETTEN UND SCHWIMMBAEDER; Zeitschrift fuer Einrichtung und Betrieb von Sport-, Baeder- und Freizeitanlagen. see BUILDING AND CONSTRUCTION

790.1   II
SPORTSTAR. (Text in English) 1978. w. 859-860 Anna Salai, Madras 600 002, India. TEL 44-835067. FAX 44-835325. TELEX 416655. Ed. N. Ram. circ. 86,600.

687.1   US   ISSN 0162-2242
TT649
SPORTSTYLE.* 1979. s-m.(except m. in Jun., Nov. and Dec.) $20. Fairchild Publications, Inc., SportStyle, 7 W. 34th St., New York, NY 10001. TEL 212-630-4000. FAX 212-337-3247. adv.; circ. 29,700. (tabloid format)
    ●Also available online. Vendor(s): DIALOG.
    Description: Merchandising publication for sports retailers. Coverage includes business information, as well as product and fashion trends.

790.1   XK   ISSN 1010-5743
SPORTSWATCH. 1985. q. $10. A L K I M Communication Production Company, Box MA 020, Marchand Post Office, Castries, St. Lucia, W.I. Ed. Albert De Terville. adv.; circ. 5,000.

790.1   II
SPORTSWORLD. (Text in English) 1978. w. Rs.310. Ananda Bazar Patrika Ltd., 6 Prafulla Sarkar St., Calcutta 700 001, West Bengal, India. TEL 28-4800. Ed. Mansur Ali Khan Pataudi. circ. 50,000. (back issues avail.)

797.21   GW
SPORTTAUCHER. m. DM.45.20. (Verband Deutscher Sporttaucher e.V.) Schmidt-Roemhild Verlag, Mengstr. 16, 2400 Luebeck 1, Germany. TEL 0451-1605-0. FAX 0451-1605224. TELEX 26536-MSRD.

790.1   RM
SPORTUL ILUSTRAT. 1947. m. $25. Editura Sportrom, Str. Vasile Conta 16, Bucharest, Rumania. TEL 113288. FAX 113459. Ed. Constantin Macovei. adv.; bk.rev.; illus.; circ. 50,000.

SPORTVERLETZUNG - SPORTSCHADEN. see MEDICAL SCIENCES

790.1   NE
SPORTWETENSCHAPPELIJKE ONDERZOEKINGEN. 1978. irreg. price varies. Uitgeverij de Vriesborch, P.O. Box 5229, 2000 LE Haarlem, Netherlands. TEL 023-325620. illus.; circ. 1,500.

796 371.7 613   GW   ISSN 0342-2380
SPORTWISSENSCHAFT. (Text in German; summaries in English, French, German) 1971. q. DM.64 (students DM.52). Verlag Karl Hofmann, Steinwasenstr. 6-8, Postfach 1360, 7060 Schorndorf, Germany. TEL 07181-7811. Ed. Ommo Grupe. bk.rev.; index; circ. 3,000. Indexed: Sportsearch (1976-).
    —BLDSC shelfmark: 8419.860800.
    Description: Deals with the science and theory of sports.

796   GW   ISSN 0342-457X
SPORTWISSENSCHAFT UND SPORTPRAXIS. 1970. irreg., vol.82, 1991. price varies. Verlag Ingrid Czwalina, Reesenbuettler Redder 75, 2070 Ahrensburg, Germany. TEL 04102-59190. FAX 04102-50992. Ed. Clemens Czwalina.
    Formerly: Schriftenreihe fuer Sportwissenschaft und Sportpraxis (ISSN 0080-7141)

796   KR   ISSN 0038-8300
SPORTYVNA GAZETA. 1934. 156/yr. 4.68 Rub. Komitet po Fizkul'ture i Sportu - State Committee of Physical Culture and Sports, 13 Cheljuskintsev St., Kiev, Ukraine. TEL 228-09-63. Ed. Yuri Peresunjko. illus.
    Formerly (until 1966): Radjanski Sport.

796 790.019   US   ISSN 0740-0802
SPOTLIGHT ON YOUTH SPORTS. 1979. q. $3. Michigan State University, Institute for the Study of Youth Sports, 213 I.M. Sports Circle Bldg., East Lansing, MI 48824. TEL 517-353-6689. bk.rev.; charts; illus.; circ. 7,000. (looseleaf format; back issues avail.) Indexed: Sportsearch 91980-).

796.72   US
SPRINT CAR. fortn. Griggs Publishing Co., Inc., Box 500, Concord, NH 28026-0500. TEL 704-786-7132. FAX 704-786-7162. Ed. Wayne Kindness. adv.; circ. 5,000.

790.1   GW
SQUASH ETC.; nimm eins Publikation fuer Sport Mode Freizeit. 1980. m. DM.54. Werbung & Marketing, Stahlstr. 19, 4156 Willich 1, Germany. TEL 02154-3055. Ed. Peter Tekook. adv.; circ. 6,150. (back issues avail.)

636.596   UK   ISSN 0952-4541
SQUILLS INTERNATIONAL PIGEON RACING YEAR BOOK. 1898. a. £5.70 hardcover; £3.50 softcover. Racing Pigeon Publishing Co. Ltd., Unit 13, 21 Wren St., London WC1X OHF, England. TEL 071-833-5959. FAX 071-833-3151. adv.

794.1   SW   ISSN 0347-5867
SSKK BULLETINEN. 6/yr. $32. P.O. Box 127, S-221 00 Lund, Sweden. FAX 46-46118343. Ed. Allan Jonasson. adv.; bk.rev.; circ. 2,300.
    Description: Reports on annotated games, combinations, and includes theoretical articles.

790.1   CF
STADE. 1985. w. B.P. 114, Brazzaville, Congo. TEL 81-47-18. TELEX 5285. Ed. Louis Ngami. circ. 12,000.

SPORTS AND GAMES

796 CS ISSN 0038-8920
STADION. 1953. w. 462.80 Kcs.($98) (Ceskoslovensky Svaz Telesne Vychovy, Cesky Ustredni Vybor) Olympia a.s., Klimentska 1, 115 88 Prague 1, Czechoslovakia. (Dist. by: Artia, Ve Smeckach 30, 111 27 Prague 1, Czechoslovakia) Ed. Milan Macho. adv.; bk.rev.; charts; illus.; stat.; circ. 50,000. (also avail. in microform)

790.1 613.7 GW ISSN 0172-4029
GV561
STADION; Internationale Zeitschrift fuer Geschichte des Sports. (Text in English, French, German) 1975. irreg. (1-2/yr.). DM.88. Academia Verlag GmbH, Postfach 1663, 5205 St. Augustin, Germany. Ed. Manfred Laemmer. adv.; bk.rev.; circ. 400. (back issues avail.) Indexed: Hist.Abstr, Sportsearch (1975-).
—BLDSC shelfmark: 8425.930000.
Incorporates: Arena.

796 IT
STADIUM; problemi dello sport. 1906. s-m. Centro Sportivo Italiano, Via delle Conciliazione 3, 00193 Rome, Italy. Ed. Aldo Notario. adv.

790.1 GW
STADTHANDBUCH NORDBADEN; fuer alle Sportler und Sportinteressierte. 1980. a. DM.24.60. (Badischer Sportbund e.V.) Schors-Verlags-Gesellschaft mbH, Postfach 1280, 6272 Niederhausen, Germany. TEL 06127-8029. FAX 06127-8812. Ed. Rudi Arnold. circ. 12,000.

STAR GUIDE; where to contact movie, TV stars and other celebrities. see MOTION PICTURES

793 US
STAR INTERNATIONAL.* (Text in English, Spanish) 1969. m. $18. Resorts Casino Publishing, 5330 Cameron St., No. 23, Las Vegas, NV 89118-2235. Ed. Ricardo Villasenor. circ. 38,500. (back issues avail.)
Description: Covers gaming resorts.

796 KR ISSN 0038-9935
START. 1922. m. $6. (Soyuz Sportivnykh Obshchestv i Organizatsii Ukrainskoi S.S.R.) Izdatel'stvo Molod, 38-42 Parkhomenko St., Kiev, Ukraine. TEL 224-222. Ed. A. Chaly.

START. see PHYSICAL FITNESS AND HYGIENE

796 US
STARTING LINE. q. Offshore Data Services, Inc., Box 19909, Houston, TX 77224-9909. TEL 713-781-2713. FAX 713-781-9594. Ed. Karissa G. Strong. circ. 3,500.

STELUTIS ALPINIS. see TRAVEL AND TOURISM

790.1 US
STING. 1986. 13/yr. $17.95. Coman Publishing Company, Inc., Box 2331, Durham, NC 27702. TEL 919-688-0218. FAX 919-682-1532. Ed. Bill Ballew. circ. 7,500.
Description: For Georgia Tech University sports fans.

796.7 UK ISSN 0049-2272
STOCK CAR.* 1967. m. British Stock Car Association, 101 Mountain Rd., Densbury, West Yorks. WF12 OBS, England. Ed. Deidre Nevett. adv.; circ. 6,500.

796.72 US
STOCK CAR RACING. 1966. m. $10. Four Wheeler Publishing (Subsidiary of: General Media Publishing Group), 27 S. Main St., Ipswich, MA 01938. TEL 508-356-7030. FAX 508-356-2492. Ed. Dick Berggren. adv.; illus.; circ. 105,500.

796.72 US
STREET RODDER. 1972. m. $15. McMullen Publishing, 2145 W. La Palma Ave., Anaheim, CA 92801. TEL 714-635-9040. Ed. Pat Ganahl. adv.; bk.rev.; circ. 97,078.

STUDIES IN SPORT, PHYSICAL EDUCATION AND HEALTH. see PHYSICAL FITNESS AND HYGIENE

SUGEI PAZURU. see MATHEMATICS

790.1 JA
SUMO WORLD. (Text and summaries in English) 1973. bi-m. 4500 Yen($28) c/o Foreign Press Club, 1-7-1 Yuraku-cho, Chiyoda-ku, Tokyo 100, Japan. TEL 03-3211-3168. FAX 0422-47-5715. Ed. Andy Adams. adv.; bk.rev.; circ. 10,000. (back issues avail.)
Description: Covers sumo wrestling in Japan.

796.812
SUMO WRESTLING (TOKYO, 1949)/SUMO. (Text in Japanese) 1949. m. 8040 Yen. Baseball Magazine Sha, 3-10-10 Misaki-cho, Chiyoda-cho, Tokyo, Japan. Ed. Tatsuhiko Fukudome.

796.812
SUMO WRESTLING (TOKYO, 1954). (Text in Japanese) 1954. bi-m. 670 Yen. Yomiuri Shinbun, Publication Dept., 7-1, 1-chome, Ote-machi, Chiyoda-ku, Tokyo, Japan. FAX 03-246-4904. Ed. Harunobu Kasai. adv.

SUN GUIDE TO THE FLAT. see SPORTS AND GAMES — Horses And Horsemanship

790.1 CN
SUNSPORTS. a. Solstice Publishing Inc., 19 Albany Ave., Toronto, Ont. M5R 3C2, Canada. TEL 416-535-0607. FAX 416-535-3419. Ed. Cathy Carl. circ. 50,000.

794.1 FI ISSN 0355-8096
SUOMEN SHAKKI. 1924. 12/yr. FIM 230($45) Esko Nuutilainen, Ed. & Pub., PL 61, 04401 Jarvenpaa, Finland. FAX 0-2918336. adv.; bk.rev.; circ. 2,100.
Description: Includes national and international games, interviews, "how-to-improve" articles, theory, combinations, and studies-problems.

SUPER KNOBEL KNIFFLIG. see CHILDREN AND YOUTH — For

790 IT ISSN 0039-5706
SUPERBA. vol.10, 1977. m. L.5000. Dopolavoro Ferroviario di Genova, Via A. Doria 13, 16126 Genoa, Italy. Ed. Millo Balduzzi. adv.; bk.rev.; charts; illus.

790 US
SUPERSTAR WRESTLER. 1986. 9/yr. Starlog Group, Inc., 475 Park Ave. S., New York, NY 10016.

797 BE ISSN 0775-8553
SURF AND FUN. 1969. 3/yr. 400 BEF per no. L W F, Voskenslaan 228, 9000 Ghent, Belgium. TEL 091-22-91-58. FAX 091-223789. Ed.Bd. bk.rev.; circ. 30,000.
Formerly: De Windsurfer.
Description: Covers all aspects of windsurfing, speedsail, speedtrials, regatta's and sports-fashion, surf-life style.

790.1 GR
SURF & SKI. (Text and summaries in Greek) 1981. bi-m. Dr.1000. Liberis Publications Ltd., 49 Pericleous St., 154 51 N. Psychico, Athens, Greece. Ed. Dimitri Kanellopoulos. circ. 12,000. (back issues avail.)

797 US ISSN 0276-6582
GV840.S8
SURFBOARD. (Text in English, French and Spanish) 1963. a. $12.95. Box 9024, La Jolla, CA 92038. Ed. Stephen M. Shaw. adv.; circ. 10,000.
Formerly: Surfboard Builder's Yearbook (ISSN 0081-9611)

799.202 UK
SURVIVAL WEAPONRY AND TECHNIQUES. m. £15.60 (foreign £38.50) Aceville Publications Ltd., 89 East Hill, Colchester, Essex CO1 2QN, England. TEL 0206-871139. FAX 0206-871537. Ed. Matthew Tudor. adv.

796.41 SW ISSN 0281-5443
SVENSK GYMNASTIK. 1942. 8/yr. SEK 180. Svenska Gymnastikfoerbundet - Swedish Gymnastic Federation, Idrottens Hus, 123 87 Farsta, Sweden. Ed. C-H Segerfeldt. adv.; bk.rev.; illus.; stat.; circ. 8,000.
Formerly: Gymnastikledaren (ISSN 0017-5978)

790 SW ISSN 0049-2663
SVENSK IDROTT. 1928. m. SEK 220. (Sveriges Riksidrottsfoerbund - Swedish Sports Confederation) Riksidrottsfoerbundet, Idrottens Hus, S-123 87 Farsta, Sweden. TEL 08-713-6000. FAX 08-94-81-89. Ed. Lars Roehne. adv.; bk.rev.; circ. 37,000.

796.86 US ISSN 1042-7880
SWASHBUCKLER. m. $22. Luna Ventures, Box 398, Suisun, CA 94585. Ed. Paul Doerr. (also avail. in microfiche; back issues avail.)
Description: Covers fencing, swashbuckling, Renaissance faires and related subjects.

793 US
▼**SWEEPSTAKES MAGAZINE**. 1992. m J and C USA Publications, Inc., 8000 Sagebrook Rd., Columbia, SC 29223. TEL 803-736-2836. adv.
Description: Contains information for participants in sweepstakes, games promotion giveaways and contests of all varieties, except lotteries.

797.21 CN ISSN 0319-0560
SWIM CANADA. 10/yr. 402 King St. E., Toronto, Ont. M5A 1L3, Canada. TEL 416-368-2606. Ed. N.J. Thierry. circ. 3,900. Indexed: Sportsearch (1974-).

797.21 US ISSN 8755-2027
SWIM MAGAZINE. 1984. bi-m. $15. Sports Publications, Inc., Box 45497, Los Angeles, CA 90045. TEL 213-674-2120. Ed. Kim Hansen. adv.: B&W page $1610, color page $2405; trim 8 1/4 x 10 3/4. circ. 7,000.

797.21 US ISSN 0195-6760
SWIM SWIM;* for fitness and masters swimmers. 1978. s-a? $12. Swim Swim, Inc., 1415 Third St., No. 303, Santa Monica, CA 90401-2321. Ed. Terry Mulgannon. adv.; charts; illus.; stat.; circ. 25,000. (back issues avail.)

797.21 US
SWIMMING AND DIVING AND WATER POLO RULEBOOK. a. $2.75. National Federation of State High School Associations, 11724 N.W. Plaza Circle, Box 20626, Kansas City, MO 64195-0626. TEL 816-464-5400. FAX 816-464-5571.
Former titles: Swimming and Diving Rules (ISSN 0163-2884); Swimming and Diving Case Book (ISSN 0145-3831); Supersedes: Swimming Rules.

797.21 JA
SWIMMING MAGAZINE. (Text in Japanese) 1977. m. 6240 Yen. Baseball Magazine Sha, 3-10-10 Misaki-cho, Chiyoda-ku, Tokyo, Japan. Ed. Tomohei Tsukide.

797.21 UK
SWIMMING POOL. 1960. bi-m. £27. M G S Publishing House Ltd., Rear of Penmark House, Woodbridge Meadows, Guildford, Surrey GU11 BL5, England. TEL 0483-306304. Ed. Alan Guthrie. adv.; bk.rev.; charts; illus.; index; circ. 10,000. Indexed: Br.Ceram.Abstr., Sportsearch.
Formerly: Swimming Pool Review (ISSN 0039-7385)

797.31 US
SWIMMING POOL AND SPA DEALER NEWS. 1982. m. Creative Media, Inc., 10244 Best Dr., Dallas, TX 75229. Ed. Alice Pies. adv.; circ. 13,000.

SWIMMING POOL - SPA AGE. see BUILDING AND CONSTRUCTION

SWIMMING POOL - SPA AGE DATA & REFERENCE ANNUAL. see BUILDING AND CONSTRUCTION

797.21 US ISSN 0039-7415
SWIMMING TECHNIQUE. 1964. q. $13 (foreign $19). Sports Publications, Inc., Box 45497, Los Angeles, CA 90045. TEL 213-674-2120. Ed. Brady Bingham. bk.rev.; film rev.; charts; illus.; index; circ. 8,500. (also avail. in microform from UMI; reprint service avail. from UMI) Indexed: Phys.Ed.Ind., Sports Per.Ind., Sportsearch (1965-).
—BLDSC shelfmark: 8576.400000.

SPORTS AND GAMES

797.21 UK ISSN 0039-7423
SWIMMING TIMES. 1923. m. £13.50 (foreign £15.50). (Amateur Swimming Association) Swimming Times Ltd., Harold Fern House, Derby Square, Loughborough, Leics. LE11 0AL, England. TEL 0509-234433. FAX 0509-235049. (Co-sponsor: Institute of Swimming Teachers and Coaches) Ed. Karren T. Glendenning. adv.; bk.rev.; charts; illus.; circ. 16,750. **Indexed:** Sportsearch (1977-).
  Incorporates: Swim.

797.21 US ISSN 0039-7431
GV837
SWIMMING WORLD. 1960. m. $19 (foreign $29). Sports Publications, Inc., Box 45497, Los Angeles, CA 90045. TEL 213-674-2120. Ed. Bob Ingram. adv.; bk.rev.; film rev.; charts; illus.; stat.; index; circ. 28,000. (also avail. in microform from UMI; reprint service avail. from UMI) **Indexed:** Sports Per.Ind., Sportsearch (1973-).
  Formerly: Junior Swimmer - Swimming World.

796.86 UK
SWORD. 1948. q. £18. Amateur Fencing Association, 83 Perham Rd., West Kensington, London W14, England. TEL 01-261-8652. Ed. Malcolm Fare. adv.; bk.rev.; illus.; stat.; circ. 3,500. **Indexed:** Sportsearch (1976-).

796.86 US
SWORDMASTER. 1976. q. $6. U S Academy of Arms, 279 E. Northfield Rd., Livingston, NJ 07039. TEL 201-992-0202. Ed. A. John Geraci. bk.rev.; abstr.; bibl.; charts; illus.; stat.; tr.lit.; circ. 1,000. (back issues avail.) **Indexed:** Sportsearch.

797.21 US ISSN 0746-5726
SYNCHRO. 1963. bi-m. $20 (foreign $24). Dawn P. Bean, Ed. & Pub., 11902 Red Hill Ave., Santa Ana, CA 92705. TEL 714-544-6699. adv.; circ. 1,850. **Indexed:** Sportsearch (1979-).
  Formerly (until Apr. 1979): Synchro - Info.
  Description: Provides news and articles on technique and competitive synchronized swimming results from around the world.

797.21 US
SYNCHRO U S A - NEWS. 1982. bi-m. membership. United States Synchronized Swimming, 201 S. Capitol, Ste. 510, Indianapolis, IN 46225. FAX 317-237-5705. Ed. Laura LaMarca. adv.; circ. 750.
  Description: Provides information on synchronized swimming on both competitive and recreational levels in the U.S.

794.1 PL
▼**SZACHISTA.** 1991. m. $25. Res Publica Press International, Ul. Walbrzyska 3-5, 02-739 Warsaw, Poland. TEL 48-22-45095056. Ed. Andrzej Filipowicz. adv.; bk.rev.; chart.; illus.
  Description: Contains chess news, chess history, annotated chess games, theory, combinations, studies and problems.

790.1 US
T D M A TODAY; representing the awards and engraving industry. 1979. m. (Trophy Dealers and Manufacturers Association) T D M A, 4325 N. Golden State Blvd., Ste. 102, Fresno, CA 93722. TEL 209-275-5100. FAX 209-275-8023. Ed. Ann Haws. adv.; tr.lit.; circ. 9,000. (tabloid format)
  Former titles: Trophy Dealer; T D M A Newsletter.

790.1 GW
T G M ECHO. 1975. q. Turngemeinde 1861 e.V., Kirchstr. 45, 6500 Mainz - Gonsenheim, Germany. TEL 06131-41106. Ed. Jochen Dietz. circ. 1,500.

790.1 GW ISSN 0179-0153
T U S INFO; Informationen aus dem Vereinsleben. 1985. q. DM.12($10) (T U S Stockum 1945 e.V.). Information about local sports, Postfach 7052, 5810 Witten 7, Germany. TEL 02302-49043. Ed. Rolf Korfmann. illus.; circ. 1,250. (back issues avail.)

790 GW ISSN 0344-4023
T U S - TURNEN UND SPORT. 1949. m. DM.41.40 (foreign DM.52.20). Pohl-Verlag, Herzog-Ernst-Ring 1, Postfach 103, 3100 Celle, Germany. TEL 05141-7504-0. FAX 05141-750475. Ed. Wolfram Herold. adv.; bk.rev.; illus.; index; circ. 16,100. (back issues avail.)
  —BLDSC shelfmark: 9074.700000.
  Incorporates: Leibesuebungen (ISSN 0024-0613)

790.1 GW
T U S VEREINSNACHRICHTEN. 1907. bi-m. membership. Turn- und Sportvereinigung Gaarden von 1875 e.V., Roentgenstr. 5, 2300 Kiel 14, Germany. TEL 0431-731176. Ed. Dieter Buenning. adv.; circ. 2,000.

796.41 GW
T V K 1877 ECHO. 1984. q. DM.20. Turnverein 1877 e.V. Essen-Kupferdreh, Kampmann Bruecke 1, 4300 Essen 15, Germany. TEL 0201-56305-20. FAX 0201-5630555. Ed. Bodo F. Schmischke. adv.; circ. 2,000. (back issues avail.)
  Description: Magazine for members of the Turnverein.

796.815 US ISSN 0741-028X
TAE KWAN DO TIMES; martial arts, fitness & health. 1981. bi-m. $10.99. Tri - Mount Publications, 1423 18th St., Bettendorf, IA 52722. TEL 319-359-7202. FAX 319-355-7299. Ed. Rod Speidel. adv.; bk.rev.; circ. 38,000. (back issues avail.)
  Description: Features interviews, articles and information about the martial arts.

790 KO
TAEHAN CHEYKHOE. CHEYUK CHONGSO.* 1973. irreg. Korea Amateur Sports Association, 19 Mugyo-dong, Seoul, S. Korea. Ed.Bd. illus.

790.1 GW
TAEKWONDO AKTUELL. 1977. m. DM.36($20) (Deutsche Taekwondo Union) Heinz Marx, Pub., Maximiliansplatz 12-I, 8000 Munich 2, Germany. TEL 089-222710. Ed.Bd. (back issues avail.)
  Description: Information on all aspects of Tae Kwon Do.

796.815 US ISSN 1043-1047
TAEKWONDO WORLD. 1983. q. $7. (American Taekwondo Association) A T A Publications, Box 289, Rapid City, SD 57709-0289. TEL 605-341-0402. Ed. Milo Dailey. adv.; illus.; circ. 26,000.
  Formerly: Martial Arts and Fitness.
  Description: Features martial arts, history and human interest stories.

790.1 CH
TAIWAN SPORTING GOODS BUYER'S GUIDE. (Text in English) a. $30. Trade Winds, Inc., No. 7, Lane 75, Yungkang St., Taipei, Taiwan 10602, Republic of China. TEL 02-393-2718. FAX 02-396-4022. TELEX 24177-FCTRADE.
  Description: Covers Taiwan's production of sportswear and goods for export.

TANZ UND GYMNASTIK. see *DANCE*

799.202 UK ISSN 0143-8751
TARGET GUN. m. £20 (foreign $40). Peterson Publications Ltd., Peterson House, Northbank, Berryhill Industrial Estate, Droitwich, Worcs. WR9 9BL, England. TEL 0905-795564. FAX 0905-795905. Ed. Richard Adkins. adv.; bk.rev.; illus.; circ. 24,500.

794.1 AT
TASMANIAN CHESS MAGAZINE. 1976. 4/yr. Aus.$8 (foreign Aus.$10). Neville Ledger Chess Centre, P.O. Box 837, Burnie, Tas. 7320, Australia. Ed. Neville Ledger. adv.; bk.rev.; circ. 400.
  Description: Reports on local and national games, computer and correspondence chess, endgame theory, historical and "how-to-improve" articles.

797.23 GW
TAUCH-BRILLE. 1986. m. DM.12. (Saarlaendischer Tauchsportbund) Kurt Huwig Druckerei, Goethestr. 50, 6601 Riegelsberg, Germany. TEL 06806-4001. Ed. Hannelore Huwig. circ. 800. (back issues avail.)
  Description: News about diving.

790.1 574 770
910.09 GW
TAUCHEN; internationales Unterwasser-Magazin. 1978. m. DM.84.20. Jahr-Verlag GmbH & Co., Burchardstr. 14, Postfach 103346, D-2000 Hamburg 1, Germany. TEL 040-339660. FAX 40-33966208. TELEX 2163485. Ed. Joerg Keller. adv.; bk.rev.; charts; illus.; index; circ. 25,000. (back issues avail.)

790.1 346.066 US
TEAM LICENSING BUSINESS. m. Virgo Publishing, Inc., 4141 N. Scottsdale Rd., Ste. 316, Scottsdale, AZ 85251. TEL 602-990-1101. FAX 602-990-0819.

688.76 US
TEAM LINE-UP. Variant title: Team Line-Up Newsletter. 1970. 4/yr. membership. National Sporting Goods Association, 1699 Wall St., Mt. Prospect, IL 60056-5780. TEL 708-439-4000. FAX 708-439-0111. Ed. Thomas B. Doyle. circ. 1,800.

688.76 FR
TECHNO-LOISIRS; guide international annuel de la construction et de l'equipment pour le sport et les loisirs. (Text in various European languages and Esperanto) 1971. biennial. 50 F.($10) Editions Techno-Loisirs, 3 rue Sivel, 75014 Paris, France. Ed. Georges Caille. adv.; bk.rev.; play rev.; bibl.; illus.; pat.; stat.; tr.lit.; index; circ. 10,000. (also avail. in magnetic tape)

794.1 IT
TELESCACCO NUOVO. 1983. 11/yr. $15. c/o Dr. Renato Incelli, Via A. D'Achiardi, 31, 00158 Rome, Italy. Ed. Angelo Bruni. bk.rev.; charts; illus.; circ. 2,100.
  Description: Covers annotated games, "how-to-improve" articles, combinations, theory, and news.

TELOVYCHOVNY PRACOVNIK. see *EDUCATION — Teaching Methods And Curriculum*

796 YU ISSN 0040-3024
TEMPO; ilustrovani nedelnji sportski list. (Text in Serbo-Croatian) 1966. w. 17664 din.($43) Politika, Cetinjska 1, 11000 Belgrade, Yugoslavia. TEL 11-321-075. Ed. Tomislav Markovic. circ. 180,000. (back issues avail.) **Indexed:** Music Ind.

794.1 AG
TEORIA AL DIA. 1984. 6/yr. $39. Ajedrez Integral, Casilla de Correo 51, Sucursal 49, 1449 Buenos Aires, Argentina. TEL 331-6988. FAX 331-6988. Ed. Juan S. Morgado.
  Description: Articles include latest novelties on chess theory, also articles by Svetozar Gligoric in each issue.

796 HU ISSN 0230-3337
GV201
A TESTNEVELESI FOISKOLA KOZLEMENYEI. English edition: Hungarian University of Physical Education. Review. (Text in Hungarian; summaries in English and Russian) 1954. 3/yr. 80 Ft. Magyar Testnevelesi Egyetem, Alkotas u. 44, Budapest H-1123, Hungary. TEL 36-1-564-444. Ed. Marta Makkar. illus.; circ. 500.
  Formerly: Magyar Testnevelesi Foiskola. Tudomanyos Kozlemenyek.

796 US ISSN 0040-4241
TEXAS COACH. 1957. m. (except June, July & Dec.). $13. Texas High School Coaches Association, Drawer 14627, Austin, TX 78761. TEL 512-454-6709. Ed. Yulandal McCarty. adv.; bk.rev.; illus.; circ. 10,600. **Indexed:** Phys.Ed.Ind., Sports Per.Ind., Sportsearch (1977-).

790.1 VN
THE THAO VAN HOA/SPORTS AND CULTURE. 1982. w. 5 Ly Thuong Kiet, Hanoi, Socialist Republic of Vietnam.

790.1 VN
THE THAO VIET-NAM/VIET-NAM SPORTS. 1968. w. 5 Trinh Hoai Duc St., Hanoi, Socialist Republic of Vietnam. Ed. Tran Can.

THERAPEUTIC RECREATION JOURNAL. see *PHYSICAL FITNESS AND HYGIENE*

790.1 US ISSN 0889-0692
THRASHER MAGAZINE. 1980. m. $18.50. High Speed Productions, Inc., Box 884570, San Francisco, CA 94188-4570. TEL 415-822-3083. FAX 415-822-8359. Ed. Kevin Thatcher. adv.; bk.rev.; circ. 250,000.
  Description: Covers skateboarding, snowboarding, music, video, and aggressive youth-oriented lifestyle.

SPORTS AND GAMES 4495

796.41 CC ISSN 1000-3444
TICAO/GYMNASTICS. (Text in Chinese) 1982. q. $16.80. (Zhongguo Ticao Xiehui - China Gymnastics Society) Renmin Tiyu Chubanshe, 8 Tiyuguan Lu, Chongwen Qu, Beijing 100061, People's Republic of China. TEL 757161. (Dist. in US by: China Books & Periodicals, Inc., 2929 24th St., San Francisco, CA 94110. TEL 415-282-2994) Ed. Jiang Youzhen.

TIDINGS. see SPORTS AND GAMES — Outdoor Life

794.1 SW ISSN 0040-6848
TIDSKRIFT FOER SCHACK. 1895. 10/yr. SEK 295. Sveriges Schackfoerbund - Swedish Chess Federation, Gethornskroken 21, S-281 49 Haesslehoim, Sweden. TEL 451-12850. FAX 451-14790. Ed. Bo Plato. adv.; bk.rev.; index; circ. 2,500.

TIEWELT. see BIOLOGY — Ornithology

790.1 US
TIGHT LINES. 1981. m. $15. (Greater Delaware Valley Kite Society, Inc.) Dirt Cheap Press, Box 888, Newfield, NJ 08344. FAX 609-697-2285. Ed. Leonard M. Conover. adv.; bk.rev.; charts; illus.; pat.; stat.; tr.lit.; circ. 500.
  Description: Humorous but technical information on kite-flying, and announcements on competitions and other activities pertaining to the members of the society, which was founded on Ben Franklin's birthday.

796 SZ ISSN 0040-8018
TIP; Sportmagazin. 1944. w. 69 Fr. Tip Verlag, Kirschgartenstr. 7, CH-4010 Basel, Switzerland. TEL 2725090. FAX 2725087. Ed. Max Pusterla. adv.; bk.rev.; film rev.; play rev.; illus.; circ. 35,000.

796 796.332 CS
TIP.* w. (Czechoslovak Union of Physical Education) Sport, Vajnorska Cesta 100-a, 832-58 Bratislava, Czechoslovakia.

790.1 CC
TIYU AIHAOZHE/SPORTS LOVERS. (Text in Chinese) m. $41.30. Sichuan Sheng Tiyu Weiyuanhui, 1, Tiyuchang Lu, Chengdu, Sichuan 610015, People's Republic of China. TEL 662574. (Dist. in US by: China Books & Periodicals, Inc., 2929 24th St., San Francisco, CA 94110. TEL 415-282-2994) Ed. Tang Ziliang.

790.1 CC
TIYU BOLAN. (Text in Chinese) m. Beijing Shi Tiyu Yundong Weiyuanhui, 2, Luchang Jie Toutiao, Xuanwu-qu, Beijing 100050, People's Republic of China. TEL 3012785. Ed. Liu Xingzhong.

790.1 US
TIYU HUABAO/SPORTS PICTORIAL. (Text in Chinese) bi-m. $25.20. China Books & Periodicals, Inc., 2929 24th St., San Francisco, CA 94110. TEL 415-282-2994. FAX 415-282-0994.

790.1 CC ISSN 1000-677X
TIYU KEXUE/SPORTS SCIENCE. (Text in Chinese; abstracts in English) 1981. bi-m. $27. (China Sports Science Society) Renmin Tiyu Chubanshe, 8 Tiyuguan Lu, Chongwen Qu, Beijing 100061, People's Republic of China. TEL 757161. (Dist. in US by: China Books & Periodicals, 2929 24th St., San Francisco, CA 94110. TEL 415-282-2994) Ed. Zhang Caizhen. circ. 20,000. **Indexed:** Sportsearch (1985-).

790.1 US
TODAY'S COACH.* 1975. q. $5. MacGregor Sports Education, 7001 Orchard Lake Rd., K, Ste. 420C, West Bloomfield, WI 48322-3608. TEL 414-786-0366. circ. 81,062.
  Description: Deals with coaching techniques and strategies in a variety of competitive sports; includes interviews, sports medicine, physical training and sports administration.

794.1 US
TOM PURSER'S B D G WORLD. (Blackmar-Diemer Gambit) 1983. 6/yr. $24. Blackmar Press, c/o Tom V. Purser, Ed., Box 7363, Warner Robins, GA 31095-0023. bk.rev.
  Description: Devoted to the games, analyses and stories about the Gambit.

794.1 FR ISSN 0990-1930
TOP ECHECS. 1988. 6/yr. $70. Top Echecs, s.a.r.l., 3 Centre Administratif des 7 Mares, 78990 Elancourt, France. Ed. Laurent Verat. adv.; circ. 2,000.
  Description: Contains annotated "super-tournament" games, interviews and articles on computer chess.

794.1 UK ISSN 0276-7090
GV1455
TOURNAMENT CHESS.* 1982. 6/yr. Tui Enterprises Ltd., 35 Ceres Rd., Plumstead, London SE18, England. Ed. M. Chandler. adv. (also avail. in microfilm; microfiche).

794.1 CN ISSN 0226-2630
TRACK & FIELD JOURNAL. irreg. Athletics Canada, 1600 James Naismith Dr., Gloucester, Ont. K1B 5N4, Canada. **Indexed:** Sportsearch (1980-). —BLDSC shelfmark: 8877.190000.

796.72
TRACKSIDE. fortn. Trackside Publications, 30 Main St., West Springfield, MA 01089. TEL 413-781-0500. FAX 413-781-1387. Ed. Bones Bourcier.

790.1 GW
TRAMPOLINTURNEN; Deutsche Trampolinzeitung. 1984. q. DM.15. Hermann Seifert, Ed.& Pub., Pasemannweg 20, 3000 Hannover 51, Germany. TEL 0511-6479209. circ. 500.

790.1 CS
TRENER;* the methodical magazine. 1957. m. 272 Kcs. (Slovak Physical Culture Organization, Central Committee) Sport, Vajnorska Cesta 100-a, 832 58 Bratislava, Czechoslovakia. Ed. Milan Perdoch. adv.; bk.rev.; bibl.; illus.; index.

790.1 US ISSN 0898-3410
TRIATHLETE; triathlons, duathlons, multi-sport events. 1986. 11/yr. $23.95. Winning International, Inc., 744 Roble Rd., Ste. 190, Allentown, PA 18103-9100. TEL 215-266-6893. FAX 215-266-7196. Ed. Harald Johnson. adv.; bk.rev.; circ. 105,000. **Indexed:** Sports Per.Ind.; Sportsearch (1986-).
  Formed by the merger of (1984-1986): Tri-Athlete; (1983-1986): Triathlon (ISSN 0745-5917)

790.1 AT
TRIATHLON SPORTS MAGAZINE. 1984. 9/yr. (6 m. issues and 3 bi-m. issues). Aus.$35. Triathlon Sports Pty. Ltd., P.O. Box 590, Miranda, N.S.W. 2228, Australia. TEL 2-528-2399. FAX 2-528-2367. Ed. Paul Oliver. adv.; circ. 16,000.
  Description: For health-conscious adults and serious athletes who swim, bicycle and run for fitness.

790.1 US
TRIATHLON TIMES; the official magazine of the national governing body for triathlon and related multi-sport events in the U.S. 1985. m. $32 (foreign $42). Triathlon Federation - USA, Box 15820, Colorado Springs, CO 80935-5820. TEL 719-597-9090. FAX 719-597-2121. Ed. Erika Hooker. adv.; circ. 40,000.

TRIBUNA DELL'IRPINIA; settimanale di attualita. see BUSINESS AND ECONOMICS

790.1 RM
▼**TRIBUNA SPORTURILOR.** 1990. w. Str. George Cosbuc 38, 2400 Sibiu, Rumania. TEL 924-12810. FAX 924-12026. Ed. Mircea Bitu. circ. 20,000.

790 IT ISSN 0041-4441
TUTTOSPORT. 1945. d. L.46500. Societa Editrice Sportiva, Via Villar 2, 10147 Torino, Italy. Ed. Gian Paolo Ormezzano. adv.; bk.rev.; circ. 200,000.

790.1 IT
TWIRLING. 1979. q. L.15000. Federazione Italiana Sportiva Twirling, Via Marconi, I-28047 Oleggio (No), Italy.

799.3 GW
U I T JOURNAL. (Text in English, French, German and Spanish) 1961. 6/yr. DM.44 (outside Europe DM.50). Union International de Tir, Bavariaring 21, 8000 Munich 2, Germany. FAX 089-5309481. TELEX 5216792-UIT-D. Ed. Wolfgang Schreiber. adv.; bk.rev.; charts; illus.; circ. 4,000.
  Formerly: Shooting Sport-Tir Sportif-Tiro Deportivo-Schiess-Sport (ISSN 0037-4156)

796.83 US
U S A AMATEUR BOXING FEDERATION. MEDIA GUIDE. 1981. a. free to qualified personnel. U S A Amateur Boxing Federation, 1750 E. Boulder St., Colorado Springs, CO 80909. TEL 719-578-4506. circ. controlled.
  Description: Biographies of boxers distributed only to the media.

796.83 US
U S A AMATEUR BOXING FEDERATION. OFFICIAL RULES. 1981. s-a. $10. U S A Amateur Boxing Federation, 1750 E. Boulder St., Colorado Springs, CO 80909. TEL 719-578-4506. circ. 10,000. (looseleaf format; back issues avail.)

790.1 052 US
U S A B A AGENDA. 1976. 12/yr. free. United States Association for Blind Athletes, 33 N. Institute, Colorado Springs, CO 80903. TEL 719-630-0422. FAX 719-578-4654. Ed. Charlie Huebner. bk.rev.; circ. 4,500. (also avail. in talking book)
  Former titles: SportsScoop; U S A B A Newsletter.

796.72 US
U S A C NEWS. 1956. fortn. membership. United States Auto Club, 4910 W. 16th St., Indianapolis, IN 46224. TEL 317-247-5151. Ed. Dick Jordan. illus.; stat.; circ. 7,500. (tabloid format)
  Description: Covers auto racing.

796.41 US ISSN 0748-6006
U S A GYMNASTICS. 1960. bi-m. $15. United States Gymnastics Federation, 201 S. Capitol Ave., Ste. 300, Pan American Plaza, Indianapolis, IN 46225. FAX 317-237-5069. TELEX 272385 USGYM IND. Ed. Luan Peszek. adv.; circ. 65,000.
  Description: Covers national and international gymnastics leading to and including the Olympics. Covers men's, women's and rythmic gymnastics.

796 US
GV847.5
U S A HOCKEY. a. $5. U S A Hockey, c/o Tom Douglis, 2997 Broadmoor Valley Rd., Colorado Springs, CO 80906. TEL 719-576-4990. FAX 719-576-4975.
  Formerly: Amateur Hockey Association of the United States. Official Guide (ISSN 0516-8635)

796 US
U S A HOCKEY. RULE BOOK. biennial. $5. U S A Hockey, c/o Tom Douglas, 2997 Broadmoor Valley Rd., Colorado Springs, CO 80906. TEL 719-576-4990. FAX 719-576-4975.
  Formerly: Amateur Hockey Association of the United States. Rule Book.

796.86 US
U S F A RULE BOOK: U S & INTERNATIONAL RULES. (Supplement avail.: Update) a. $15 with binder; without $8. United States Fencing Association, Inc., 1750 E. Boulder St., Colorado Springs, CO 80909. TEL 719-578-4511. FAX 719-632-5737.
  Formerly: Fencing Rules for Competitions.

796.21 US ISSN 1044-0801
▼**U S ROLLER SKATING.** 1991. m. (except Aug.) $10 per no. U S Amateur Confederation of Roller Skating, Box 6579, 4730 South St., Lincoln, NE 68506. TEL 402-483-7551. FAX 402-483-1465. adv.; circ. 65,000. **Indexed:** Sportsearch (1989-).
  Description: Contains news on American competitive roller skating. Covers events, training tips, sports medicine and clinics.

790.1 US
U S S A NEWS. 1978. q. free. United States Sports Academy, One Academy Dr., Daphne, AL 36526. TEL 205-626-3303. FAX 205-626-3874. TELEX 6821201 SPACO UW. circ. 10,000.
  Description: Provides news about educational programs and activities of the U.S. Sports Academy.

790 910.03 US
U S SPORTS. 1988. bi-m. National Publications Sales Agency, Inc., National Plaza, 1610 E. 79th St., Chicago, IL 60649. TEL 312-375-6800. adv.; circ. 200,000.
  Description: Focuses on blacks in sports, covering achievements, families, and business interests.

S

SPORTS AND GAMES

790.1 613.7 US ISSN 0883-0347
U S SWIMMING NEWS. 1976. m. $19.95 to non-members; members $10. United States Swimming, Inc., 1750 E. Boulder St., Colorado Springs, CO 80909. TEL 719-578-4578. FAX 719-578-4578. Ed. Jeff Dimond. circ. 3,900. (tabloid format)

796.342 US
U S T A COLLEGE TENNIS GUIDE. 1976. biennial. $7. United States Tennis Association, 707 Alexander Rd., Princeton, NJ 08540. TEL 609-452-2580. FAX 609-452-2265. TELEX 62879058. circ. 5,000.
   Description: Lists colleges and junior colleges in the U.S. that provide scholarships.

U S TEAM SPOTLIGHT. see *HANDICAPPED — Hearing Impaired*

790.1 GW ISSN 0342-8419
DER UEBUNGSLEITER; Arbeitshilfen fuer Uebungsleiter im Deutschen Sportbund. 1967. m. DM.38.50. Limpert Verlag GmbH, Luisenplatz 2, Postfach 4027, 6200 Wiesbanden, Germany. TEL 0611-373072. FAX 0611-374351. TELEX 4064187-LIMP. Ed. Friedhelm Kreiss. circ. 78,000. (looseleaf format; back issues avail.)
   Description: Practical help, tips and exercises for trainers.

797 US ISSN 0192-0871
GV840.S78
UNDERCURRENT. 1975. m. $58. Atcom, Inc., Atcom Bldg., 2315 Broadway, New York, NY 10024-4397. TEL 212-873-5900. FAX 212-799-1728. Ed. Ben Davison. adv.; circ. 13,000. (reprint service avail. from UMI)
   Description: For the sport diver featuring resort and equipment reviews, safety tips and ways to have more fun underwater.

797.23 551.46 US ISSN 0749-1794
UNDERWATER U S A. 1983. m. $11.95. Underwater U S A, Inc., 3185 Lackawanna Ave., Bloomsburg, PA 17815. TEL 717-784-6081. FAX 717-784-9226. Ed. Timothy J. Pelton. adv.; circ. 47,000. Indexed: Biol.Dig.

790 DK
UNGDOM OG IDRAET. 1897. w. DKK 325. Danske Gymnastik- og Ungdomsforeninger - Danish Gymnastic and Youth Organizations, P.O. Box 569, DK-7100 Vejle, Denmark. TEL 45-75-858177. FAX 45-75858190. Ed. Jens Sejer Andersen. adv.; bk.rev.; circ. 7,700.
   Formerly: Dansk Ungdom og Idraet (ISSN 0045-9631)

796.42 US
UNITED STATES CROSS-COUNTRY COACHES ASSOCIATION. ANNUAL BUSINESS MEETING. MINUTES. a. free. United States Cross-Country Coaches Association, c/o Ken O'Brien, Sec., Boyden Gym, University of Massachusetts, Amherst, MA 01003. TEL 413-545-2759.
   Supersedes: United States Cross-Country Coaches Association. Proceedings; Which was formerly: United States Cross-Country and Distance Running Coaches Association. Proceedings (ISSN 0082-9706)

790.1 GW
UNSER WANDERBOTE. 1972. q. DM.24 to non-members. Volkssportverein Wanderfreunde Mainz 1971 e.V., Kapellenstr. 44, Karl-Geib-Haus, 6500 Mainz-Gosenheim, Germany. TEL 06131-45562. (Subscr. to: Irmgard May, Ed., Hegelstrasse 27, 6500 Mainz Germany) circ. 1,200. (back issues avail.)
   Description: Covers swimming, bicycles and walking.

797 IT ISSN 1120-7752
UOMO MARE. 10/yr. L.6400 (foreign L.128000). Edizioni Conde Nast S.p.A., Piazza Castello 27, 20121 Milan, Italy. TEL 02-85611. FAX 02-870686. Ed. R. Franzoni. adv.; circ. 40,000.

V A H P E R D JOURNAL. (Virginia Association for Health, Physical Education and Dance) see *PHYSICAL FITNESS AND HYGIENE*

799.202 NO ISSN 0800-6016
VAAPENJOURNALEN. 1973. 8/yr. NOK 250. A-S Vaapenslitteratur, Box 1, N-1364 Hvalstad, Norway. Ed. Erik Braathen. adv.; bk.rev.; circ. 10,000.
   Formerly: Vaapen.

VEREINS PRAXIS; Arbeitshilfen fuer Fuehrungskraefte und Organisationsleiter. see *CLUBS*

796 US
VERMONT SPORTS TODAY. m. Box 496, Waterbury, VT 05676-0496. TEL 802-244-5796. FAX 802-224-8156. Ed. Kathryn Carter. adv.; circ. 10,000.

VI BILAEGARE. see *TRANSPORTATION — Automobiles*

790.1 US
VICTORY. 1983. 8/yr. $14.47. Titan Sports, Inc., 1055 Summer St., Box 3857, Stamford, CT 06905. TEL 203-352-2894. Ed. Edward D. Helinski.

VISABILITY. see *EARTH SCIENCES — Oceanography*

VOILA - RENAULT REVUE; Autos zum Leben. see *TRANSPORTATION — Automobiles*

796.8 US
W C W MAGAZINE. m. G.C. Londo Publishing Enterprises Inc., 55 Maple Ave., Rockville Centre, NY 11570. TEL 516-764-0300. Ed. Craig Peters.

790.1 US
W W F MAGAZINE. m. (World Wrestling Federation) Titan Sports, Inc., 1055 Summer St., Box 3857, Stamford, CT 06905. TEL 203-352-8600.

790.1 US
W W F WRESTLING SPOTLIGHT. 1988. q. $2.25 per no. (World Wrestling Federation) Titan Sports, Inc., 1055 Summer St., Box 3857, Stamford, CT 06905. TEL 203-352-8600. Ed. Thomas Emanuel. adv.; circ. 76,000.
   Description: Each issue focuses on a superstar of the WWF.

WALKWAYS. see *PHYSICAL FITNESS AND HYGIENE*

790.1 LE
WATAN AL RIYADI. (Text in Arabic) 1979. m. P.O. Box 615, Beirut, Lebanon. Ed. Antoine Chouery. adv.; circ. 150,000.

797 US
WATER SAFETY JOURNAL. 1978. q. $4. National Water Safety Congress, 96 Sheila Dr., Oxford, MS 38655. FAX 601-234-1828. Ed. Eugene L. Gathright. circ. 4,500.
   Former titles: National Water Safety Congress Journal; Water Safety Journal.

790.1 US ISSN 0894-0606
WATERBURY CHESS CLUB BULLETIN. 1976. s-a. $2. Rob Roy, Ed. & Pub., 54 Calumet St., Waterbury, CT 06710-1201. TEL 203-755-9749. adv.; bk.rev.; circ. 500.
   Formerly: Connecticut Backgammon Magazine.

WEIGHTLIFTING U S A. see *PHYSICAL FITNESS AND HYGIENE*

794.2 CC
WEIQI/GAME OF GO. (Text in Chinese) m. $32.30. Shanghai Shi Tiyu Yundong Weiyuanhui, 190, Huangpo Beilu, Shanghai 200003, People's Republic of China. TEL 3272716. (Dist. in US by: China Books & Periodicals, Inc., 2929 24th St., San Francisco, CA 94110. TEL 415-282-2994) Ed. Cao Zhilin.
   Description: Covers the board game of weiqi.

794.2 CC
WEIQI TIANDI. (Text in Chinese) m. $36.80. Xin Tiyu Zazhishe - New Sports Journal Publishing, 8 Tiyuguan Lu, Beijing 100061, People's Republic of China. TEL 415-282-2994, 7012603. FAX 415-282-0994. (Dist. in US by: China Books & Periodicals, Inc., 2929 24th St., San Francisco, CA 94110. TEL 415-282-2994) Ed. Hao Keqiang.
   Description: Covers the Chinese board game of weiqi.

790.1 UK
WELSH AMATEUR SWIMMING ASSOCIATION. HANDBOOK. 1897. every 4 yrs. £4. Welsh Amateur Swimming Association, Wales Empire Pool, Wood St., Cardiff, S. Glam CF1 1PP, Wales. FAX 0222-666131. adv.; circ. 500. (looseleaf format)

796.815 US
WHO'S WHO IN KARATE AND THE OTHER MARTIAL ARTS AND DIRECTORY OF BLACK BELTS.* a. Who's Who in Karate, Box 490, Grimesland, NC 27837-0490. Ed. Jerri Harris.

WILD WEST. see *MEN'S INTERESTS*

793 US ISSN 1047-854X
GV1301
WIN (VAN NUYS). 1977. m. $44 (foreign $51). Gambling Times, Inc., 16760 Stagg St., Ste. 213, Van Nuys, CA 91406. TEL 818-781-9355. FAX 818-781-3125. adv.; bk.rev.; charts; illus.; stat.; circ. 50,000. (also avail. in microfiche from UMI; back issues avail.)
   Formerly: Gambling Times (ISSN 0149-0214)
   Description: Offers news, views, advice, strategy, and statistics on gaming. Includes betting guides, reviews on casino conditions, and information on the casino and hotel entertainment scene.

790.1 US
WINDY CITY SPORTS. 1987. 11/yr. $15. Chicago Sports Resources, Inc., 1450 W. Randolph, Chicago, IL 60607. TEL 708-492-1080. Ed. Maryclaire Collins. adv.; bk.rev.; circ. 100,000. (tabloid format)

WINGED FOOT. see *PHYSICAL FITNESS AND HYGIENE*

796.72 US ISSN 0744-4869
WINSTON CUP ILLUSTRATED. 1982. bi-m. $40 (effective Jan. 1992). Griggs Publishing Co., 431 Copperfield Blvd. N.E., Concord, NH 28025-5011. TEL 704-786-7134. FAX 704-782-8122. Ed. Steve Waid. adv.; circ. 15,000. (back issues avail.)
   Description: Contains interviews and stories about the people in the NASCAR Winston Cup Series.

790.1 US
WOLFPACKER. 1980. 20/yr. $24.95. Coman Publishing Company, Inc., Box 2331, Durham, NC 27702. TEL 919-688-0218. FAX 919-682-1532. Ed. Bruce Winkworth. circ. 13,500.
   Description: For N C State University sports fans.

790.1 US ISSN 1048-9940
WOLVERINE. 1989. $32.95. Coman Publishing Company, Inc. (Ann Arbor), Box 1304, Ann Arbor, MI 48106. TEL 313-996-9092. FAX 313-996-8196. Eds. John Borton, Paul Dodd. adv.; circ. 9,500.
   Description: For University of Michigan sports fans.

799.3 US ISSN 1045-7704
WOMEN & GUNS. 1989. m. $24.95. Second Amendment Foundation, Box 488, Sta. C, Buffalo, NY 14209. TEL 205-454-7012. circ. 5,000.
   Description: For female gun owners who want to learn more about pleasure shooting and self-defense. Provides information on legislative issues, competition shooting and differences between types of guns.

790.1 US ISSN 8750-653X
GV709
WOMEN'S SPORTS AND FITNESS. 1974. 8/yr. $19.97. 1919 14th St., Ste. 421, Boulder, CO 80302. TEL 303-440-5111. FAX 303-440-3313. (Subscr. to: Box 472, Mt. Morris, IL 61054) Ed. Jane McConnell. adv.; bk.rev.; illus.; circ. 125,000. (also avail. in microform from UMI; back issues avail.) Indexed: Acad.Ind., Hlth.Ind., Jun.High.Mag.Abstr., Mag.Ind., PMR, Sports Per.Ind., Sportsearch (1985-).
   —BLDSC shelfmark: 9343.545000.
   Formerly (until 1984): Women's Sports (ISSN 0163-7428)
   Description: Provides profiles, how-to articles, equipment reviews, travel articles and reporting on controversial issues in women's sports.

796.47 AT
WORLD ACROBATICS. 1954. m. Aus.$18($24) Association of Acrobats, 6 Walworth Ave., Newport, N.S.W. 2106, Australia. Ed. R.P.H. Samuels. adv.; bk.rev.; dance rev.; play rev.; charts; illus.; circ. 1,500. Indexed: Sportsearch.
   Supersedes: Acrobatic.

SPORTS AND GAMES 4497

796.9 US ISSN 0095-7240
GV847.5
WORLD ALMANAC GUIDE TO PRO HOCKEY. irreg. $1.95. Bantam Books, Inc., 666 Fifth Ave., New York, NY 10019. TEL 212-765-6500. illus.

737 UK ISSN 0255-4429
WORLD BADMINTON. 1970. q. £6. International Badminton Federation, 4 Manor Park, Mackenzie Way, Cheltenham, Glos. GL51 9TX, England. TEL 0242-234904. FAX 0242-221030. Ed. R. Ward. adv.; circ. 9,000. **Indexed:** Sportsearch.
Description: Articles on the world of badminton; news, international events, tournaments and results.

796 US
WORLD BOXING. bi-m. $6. G C London Publishing Associates, Box 48, Rockville Centre, NY 11571. TEL 516-764-0300. FAX 516-764-4370. adv.; illus. **Indexed:** Sports Per.Ind.

796.86 US
WORLD FENCE NEWS. m. World Fence News, 6301 Manchaca Rd., Ste. M, Austin, TX 78745. TEL 512-445-3388. Ed. Rodger D. Duke.

790.1 US
WORLD GAMING REPORT. 18/yr. $60. 2265 Westwood Blvd., Ste. B214, Los Angeles, CA 90064.

796.355 UK
WORLD HOCKEY. (Text in English) 1969. q. £7 (foreign £10). (International Hockey Federation, BE) Harrow Press, Unit E6, Aladdin Workspace, 426 Long Dr., Greenford, Middx. UB6 8UH, England. TEL 081-575-3121. FAX 081-575-1320. TELEX 63393 FIH B. Ed. Chris Moore. adv.; bk.rev.; illus.; circ. 3,500. **Indexed:** Sportsearch (1975-).
Description: Color photographs, full reports on all major world events, results, fixtures, and features.

WORLD LEISURE AND RECREATION. see *LEISURE AND RECREATION*

790.1 613.7 US
THE WORLD OF A S P. q. membership. American Self-Protection Association, 825 Greengate Oval, Sagamore Hills, OH 44067. TEL 216-467-1750. Ed. Gary A. Cook. bk.rev.; circ. 200. (looseleaf format)
Description: Covers self-defense, combative sports, body-mind coordination, wellness, and fitness.
Refereed Serial

790.1 GW
WORLD OF SPORT. 3/yr. Strebel Zielgruppen Verlag GmbH, Hoehenstr. 17, Postfach 1329, 7012 Fellbach, Germany. TEL 0711-5206-1. FAX 0711-5281424. Ed. Guenter Bayer. adv.; illus.
Formerly (until 1990): Sport und Freizeit.

796.812 US
THE WRESTLER. 1968. m. $17 (foreign $22). G C London Publishing Associates, Box 48, Rockville Centre, NY 11571. TEL 516-764-0300. FAX 516-764-4370. Ed. Stu Saks. adv.; charts; illus.; tr.lit.

790.1 US
WRESTLING ALL STARS HEROES AND VILLAINS. 1982. bi-m. Mag Mania, 475 Park Ave. S., New York, NY 10016. TEL 212-689-2830. FAX 212-889-7933. Ed. George Napolitano. adv.; bk.rev.

790.1 US
WRESTLING EYE. m. $2.50 per no. Jems, Inc., 55 Ave of the Americas No. 309, New York, NY 10013. TEL 212-925-3377.

790.1 US
WRESTLING FURY. bi-m. $1.95 per no. Jems, Inc., 55 Ave. of the Americas No. 309, New York, NY 10013. TEL 212-925-3377.

790.1 US
WRESTLING MANUAL AND CASE BOOK. biennial. $2.75. National Federation of State High School Associations, 11724 N.W. Plaza Circle, Box 20626, Kansas City, MO 64195-0626. TEL 816-464-5400. FAX 816-464-5571.
Supersedes: Wrestling Officials Manual.

790.1 US ISSN 0891-0707
THE WRESTLING NEWS. 1972. q. $16 (foreign $20). (Pro Wrestling Enterprises) Norman Kietzer, Ed. & Pub., Rt. 1, Box 103, Vernon Center, MN 56090. adv.; circ. 9,000.

790.1 US ISSN 0743-2720
WRESTLING RINGSIDE. 8/yr. $11.99. O'Quinn Studios, Inc., 475 Park Ave. S., New York, NY 10016. TEL 212-689-2830. Ed. Michael Benson.

790.1 US
WRESTLING RULEBOOK. a. $2.75. National Federation of State High School Associations, 11724 N.W. Plaza Circle, Box 20626, Kansas City, MO 64195-0626. TEL 816-464-5400. FAX 816-454-5571.

790.1 US
WRESTLING SCENE. 1982. 8/yr. $16.98. O'Quinn Studios, Inc., 475 Park Ave. So., New York, NY 10016. Ed. Jacqueline Quartarano. adv.; circ. 110,000.

790.1 US ISSN 0199-6258
WRESTLING U.S.A. MAGAZINE. 1964. 12/yr. $25 (foreign $30). 1924 Baxter Dr., Bozeman, MT 59715. Ed. Lanny Bryant. adv.; circ. 13,000. (also avail. in microform)
Formerly: Scholastic Wrestling News.
Description: Geared to wrestling coaches and their students.

790.1 US
WRESTLING U S A. m. G C London Publishing Associates, Box 48, Rockville Centre, NY 11571. TEL 516-764-0300. FAX 516-764-4370. (Subscr. to: 1924 Baxter Dr., Bozeman, MT 59715) **Indexed:** Sportsearch (1983-).

796.812 US
WRESTLING WORLD. 6/yr. Lexington Library, Inc., 355 Lexington Ave., New York, NY 10017. TEL 212-973-3200. FAX 212-986-5926. Ed. Stephen Ciacciarelli. adv.; illus.

790.1 US ISSN 0278-9612
WRESTLING'S MAIN EVENT. 1982. m. $16. Pumpkin Press, Inc., 350 Fifth Ave., Ste. 8216, New York, NY 10118. TEL 212-947-4322. Ed. George Napolitano. adv.; bk.rev.; circ. 100,000.

796.8 CC
WUHUN/SOUL OF MARTIAL ARTS. (Text in Chinese) bi-m. $18.50. (Beijing Tiyu Yundong Weiyuanhui - Beijing Sports Society) Wuhun Zazhishe, 2 Luchangjie Toutiao, BeiweiLu, Xuanwuqu, Beijing 100050, People's Republic of China. TEL 3012785. (Dist. in US by: China Books & Periodicals, Inc., 2929 24th St., San Francisco, CA 94110. TEL 415-282-2994) Ed. Liu Xingzhong.

796.8 CC ISSN 1000-7318
WULIN/MARTIAL ARTS. (Text in Chinese) 1980. m. $35.90. (Guangdong Sheng Wushu Xuehui - Guangdong Martial Arts Society) Kexue Puji Chubanshe, Guangzhou Fenshe - Guangzhou Branch, 3 Xingping Li, Dahua Jie, Yingyuan Lu, Guangzhou, Guangdong 510047, People's Republic of China. (Dist. in US by: China Books & Periodicals, Inc., 2929 24th St., San Francisco, CA 94110. TEL 415-282-2994)

796.8 613.7 CC
WUSHU JIANSHEN/HEALTH THROUGH MARTIAL ARTS. (Text in Chinese) bi-m. $20.70. Xin Tiyu Zazhishe - New Sports Journal Publishing, 8 Tiyuguan Lu, Beijing 100061, People's Republic of China. TEL 751761. (Dist. in US by: China Books & Periodicals, Inc., 2929 24th St., San Francisco, CA 94110. TEL 415-282-2994) Ed. Yang Dingxin.

794.18 US
XIANG QI/CHINESE CHESS. (Text in Chinese) m. $17. China Books & Periodicals, 2929 24th St., San Francisco, CA 94110. TEL 415-282-2994. FAX 415-282-0994.

794.18 CC ISSN 1002-1906
XIANGQI YANJIU/STUDIES IN CHINESE CHESS. (Text in Chinese) 1977. bi-m. $18.50. (Harbin Tiyu Yundong Weiyuanhui - Harbin Sports Commission) Xiangqi Yanjiu Bianjibu, Renmin Tiyuchang - People's Stadium, Harbin, Heilongjiang 150020, People's Republic of China. TEL 487911. (Dist. in US by: China Books & Periodicals, Inc., 2929 24th St., San Francisco, CA 94110. TEL 415-282-2994)

796 CC ISSN 0441-3679
XIN TIYU/NEW SPORTS. (Text in Chinese) 1950. m. $41.30. Xin Tiyu Zazhishe - New Sports Journal Publishing, 8 Tiyuguan Lu, Beijing 100061, People's Republic of China. TEL 751402. (Dist. in US by: China Books & Periodicals, Inc., 2929 24th St., San Francisco, CA 94110. TEL 415-282-2994) Ed. Hao Keqiang.

Y M C A WEEKLY NEWS (VANCOUVER, BC). (Vancouver Downtown Young Men's Christian Association) see *PHYSICAL FITNESS AND HYGIENE*

794.1 UK
YEAR BOOK OF CHESS. 1919. a. £6. British Chess Federation, 9A Grand Parade, St. Leonards-on-Sea, East Sussex TN38 0DD, England. TEL 0424-442500. Ed. B. Concannon. adv.; stat.; index; circ. 2,500.
Description: Covers historical records and results. Includes club directory.

790.1 MP
▼**YERTONTSIYN SPORT/WORLD OF SPORT.** (Text in Mongolian) 1990. bi-m. Ulan Bator, Mongolia.

797.21 CC ISSN 1000-3495
YOUYONG/SWIMMING. (Text in Chinese) 1983. bi-m. $25.20. (Zhongguo Youyong Xiehui - China Swimming Society) Renmin Tiyu Chubanshe, 8 Tiyuguan Lu, Chongwen Qu, Beijing 100061, People's Republic of China. TEL 757161. (Dist. in US by: China Books & Periodicals, Inc., 2929 24th St., San Francisco, CA 94110. TEL 415-282-2994)

ZAJI YU MOSHU/ACROBATICS AND MAGIC. see *HOBBIES*

ZAMBIA. MINISTRY OF YOUTH AND SPORT. DEPARTMENT OF YOUTH DEVELOPMENT. ANNUAL REPORT. see *CHILDREN AND YOUTH — About*

796 ZA
ZAMBIA. MINISTRY OF YOUTH AND SPORT. REPORT. 1968. a., latest 1973. 35 n. Government Printer, P.O. Box 136, Lusaka, Zambia.
Formerly: Zambia. Sports Directorate. Report (ISSN 0084-506X)

799.2 GW ISSN 0044-2887
CODEN: ZEJAAA
ZEITSCHRIFT FUER JAGDWISSENSCHAFT. (Text in German; summaries in English, French and German) 1955. q. $108. Verlag Paul Parey (Hamburg), Spitalerstr. 12, Postfach 106304, 2000 Hamburg 1, Germany. TEL 040-33969-0. FAX 040-33969-199. TELEX 2161-391-PARV-D. (U.S. addr.: Paul Parey Scientific Publishers, 35 West 38th St., No.3W, New York, NY 10018) Ed. E. Ueckermann. adv.; bk.rev.; illus.; index. (reprint service avail. from ISI; back issues avail.) **Indexed:** Biol.Abstr., Chem.Abstr., Curr.Adv.Ecol.Sci., Curr.Cont., Excerp.Med., Forest.Abstr., Forest Prod.Abstr., Geo.Abstr., Helminthol.Abstr., Ind.Vet., Protozool.Abstr., Vet.Bull.
—BLDSC shelfmark; 9467.400000.

790.1 US
ZHONGGUO TIYU BAO/CHINA'S SPORTS NEWS. (Text in Chinese) d. $364.50. China Books & Periodicals, Inc., 2929 24th St., San Francisco, CA 94110. TEL 415-282-2994. FAX 415-282-0994. (newspaper)

796.8 CC ISSN 1000-3525
GV1100.7.A2
ZHONGHUA WUSHU/CHINESE MARTIAL ARTS. (Text in Chinese) 1982. m. $41.30. (Zhongguo Wushu Xiehui - China Martial Arts Society) Renmin Tiyu Chubanshe, 8 Tiyuguan Lu, Chongwen Qu, Beijing 100061, People's Republic of China. TEL 757161. (Dist. in US by: China Books & Periodicals, Inc., 2929 24th St., San Francisco, CA 94110. TEL 415-282-2994)

794.1 RU
64; shakhmatnoe obozrenie. 24/yr. $35. Kalinina Prospect, d 7-6, Moscow 121019, Russia. Ed. A.E. Karpov.
Description: Provides current chess news and includes articles.

SPORTS AND GAMES — Abstracting, Bibliographies, Statistics

796.323 US
BASKETBALL STATISTICIANS' MANUAL. a. $2.75. National Collegiate Athletic Association, Circulation Department, Box 7347, Overland Park, KS 66207-0347. TEL 913-339-1900. stat.
  Description: Provides official statistics rules, interpretations, and special rulings.

796.93 US
BIBLIOGRAPHY OF SKIING STUDIES. irreg. $25. University of Colorado, Business Research Division, Campus Box 420, Boulder, CO 80309. TEL 303-492-8227. FAX 303-492-3620. Ed. C.R. Goeldner. circ. 200.

797 FR ISSN 0067-8260
BIBLIOTHEQUE DE LA MER. 1970. irreg. price varies. Tchou Editeur, 6 rue du Mail, 75002 Paris, France.

796.95 310 US ISSN 0163-7207
GV776.A2
BOATING REGISTRATION STATISTICS. a. $20. National Marine Manufacturers Association, 401 N. Michigan Ave., Chicago, IL 60611. TEL 312-836-4747. stat.
  Description: State-by-state analysis of registered pleasure boats by length, hull material and propulsion system.

796.95 US
BOATING STATISTICS. 1960. a. free. U.S. Coast Guard, Commandant G-NAB, 2100 Second St., S.W., Washington, DC 20593-0001. TEL 202-267-0955. stat.; circ. 7,000.
  Formerly: U.S. Coast Guard Boating Statistics (ISSN 0565-1530)

796 CN
C F L FACTS, FIGURES AND RECORDS. 1985. a. Can.$16.95. (Canadian Football League) McClelland & Stewart, 481 University Ave., Ste. 900, Toronto, Ont. M5G 2E9, Canada. TEL 416-598-1114. FAX 416-598-7764. Eds. Diane Cote, Norm Miller. stat.; circ. 9,000. (back issues avail.)
  Description: Contains information, statistics, records, rules, and facts about the League.

797.122 US
CANOEIST BOOKLIST. a. American Canoe Manufacturers Association, 439 E. 51st St., New York, NY 10022. TEL 212-421-5220.

790.1 UK ISSN 0142-1484
CHARTERED INSTITUTE OF PUBLIC FINANCE AND ACCOUNTANCY. CHARGES FOR LEISURE SERVICES. ACTUALS. 1979. a. £40. Chartered Institute of Public Finance and Accountancy, 3 Robert St., London WC2N 6BH, England. TEL 071-895-8823. FAX 071-895-8825. (back issues avail.)
  —BLDSC shelfmark: 3129.913000.

790.1 UK ISSN 0141-187X
CHARTERED INSTITUTE OF PUBLIC FINANCE AND ACCOUNTANCY. LEISURE AND RECREATION STATISTICS. ESTIMATES. 1977. a. £55. Chartered Institute of Public Finance and Accountancy, 3 Robert St., London WC2N 6BH, England. TEL 071-895-8823. FAX 071-895-8825. stat. (back issues avail.)
  Formerly: Chartered Institute of Public Finance and Accountancy. Leisure Estimate Statistics.

790.1 UK ISSN 0266-9560
GV433.G72
CHARTERED INSTITUTE OF PUBLIC FINANCE AND ACCOUNTANCY. LEISURE USAGE. ACTUALS. 1983. a. £35. Chartered Institute of Public Finance and Accountancy, 3 Robert St., London WC2N 6BH, England. TEL 071-895-8823. FAX 071-895-8825. (back issues avail.)
  —BLDSC shelfmark: 5182.278500.

796 US ISSN 0084-8891
COLORADO SKI AND WINTER RECREATION STATISTICS. 1968. a. $25. University of Colorado, Business Research Division, Campus Box 420, Boulder, CO 80309. TEL 303-492-8227. Ed. Karen Duea. circ. 200.

790 US
GV53
CONGRESS FOR RECREATION AND PARKS. SYMPOSIUM FOR LEISURE RESEARCH. ABSTRACTS. a. $15. National Recreation and Park Association, 3101 Park Center Dr., Alexandria, VA 22302. TEL 703-820-4940. FAX 703-671-6772. index.
  Supersedes in part: Congress for Recreation and Parks. Proceedings (ISSN 0069-8903)

796.358 UK
CRICKET STATISTICIAN. 1973. q. £11. Association of Cricket Statisticians, 3 Radcliffe Rd., West Bridgford, Nottingham NG2 5FF, England. TEL 0602-455407. Ed. Philip J. Bailey. adv.; bk.rev.; circ. 1,500. (back issues avail.)
  Description: Covers historical research articles and cricket statistical analyses.

796.41 DK ISSN 0107-4547
D A F I TAL. 1977. a. DKK 65. Dansk Atletik Forbund, Idraettens Hus, Broendby Stadion 20, 2605 Broendby, Denmark. TEL 45-42-45-55-55. FAX 45-42-45-62-45. illus.
  Formerly: Dansk Atletik Forbund. Statistik.

796.397 US
DAGUERREOTYPES. 1934. irreg., latest 1981. $14.95 hardcover; paperback $9.95. Sporting News Publishing Co., 1212 N. Lindbergh, St. Louis, MO 63132. TEL 314-997-7111.

688.76 US
FITNESS IN AMERICA. 1987. biennial. $65. National Sporting Goods Association, 1699 Wall St., Mt. Prospect, IL 60056-5780. TEL 708-439-4000. FAX 708-439-0111. Ed. Thomas B. Doyle.
  Description: Analysis of adult participation in 7 fitness activities, with geographical and demographic information.

796.332 US
FOOTBALL STATISTICIAN'S MANUAL. a. $2.75. National Collegiate Athletic Association, Circulation Department, Box 7347, Overland Park, KS 66207-0347. TEL 913-339-1900. stat.
  Description: Provides official statistics rules, interpretations, and special rulings.

HEALTH, PHYSICAL EDUCATION AND RECREATION MICROFORM PUBLICATIONS BULLETIN. see PHYSICAL FITNESS AND HYGIENE — Abstracting, Bibliographies, Statistics

790.1 011 US
▼**INDEX TO THE SPORTING NEWS.** (Coverage starts from 1975) 1991. triennial. John Gordon Burke Publisher, Inc., Box 1492, Evanston, IL 60204-1492. TEL 708-866-8625.
  ●Also available online.
  Description: Subject index to the Sporting News.

688.76 US
LIFESTYLE CHARACTERISTICS OF SPORTING GOODS CONSUMERS. a. $165. National Sporting Goods Association, 1699 Wall St., Mt. Prospect, IL 60056-5780. TEL 708-439-4000. FAX 708-439-0111. Ed. Thomas B. Doyle.
  Description: Provides geographical and demographic analysis of sporting goods consumers.

623.82 796.95 US ISSN 1052-4282
▼**MARINEFACTS;** topical directory of marine information. 1990. q. $75 (effective 1992). Running End Ltd., Box 257, Crownsville, MD 21032-0257. TEL 410-923-1325. Ed. Charles Tuten. bk.rev.; abstr.; bibl. (back issues avail.)
  Description: Comprehensive bibliographic reference for marine business and mariners, from books, videos, periodicals, computer software and government publications.

N C A A BASEBALL. (National Collegiate Athletic Association) see SPORTS AND GAMES — Ball Games

N C A A BASKETBALL. (National Collegiate Athletic Association) see SPORTS AND GAMES — Ball Games

N C A A FOOTBALL. (National Collegiate Athletic Association) see SPORTS AND GAMES — Ball Games

N C A A SOFTBALL. (National Collegiate Athletic Association) see SPORTS AND GAMES — Ball Games

688.76 US
▼**N S G A SPORTS APPAREL DIARY.** 1991. a. $1000 to non-members. National Sporting Goods Association, 1699 Wall St., Mt. Prospect, IL 60056-5780. TEL 708-439-4000. FAX 708-439-0111. Ed. Thomas B. Doyle.
  Description: Analysis of sport and non-sport apparel purchases, with demographic and financial data for different product categories.

796.9 CN
NATIONAL HOCKEY LEAGUE. GUIDE & RECORD BOOK. 1932. a. $19.95. National Hockey League Publishing, 75 International Blvd., Ste. 300, Toronto, Ont. M9W 6L9, Canada. TEL 416-798-0809. Ed. Gary Meagher.
  Formerly: National Hockey League. Guide.
  Description: Statistics of contemporary and historic achievements in the National Hockey League. Contains a complete register of all professional players and prospects.

629.227 NE ISSN 0168-5864
NETHERLANDS. CENTRAAL BUREAU VOOR DE STATISTIEK. PRODUKTIESTATISTIEKEN: RIJWIEL- EN MOTORRIJWIELINDUSTRIE. (Text in Dutch; summaries in English) a. Centraal Bureau voor de Statistiek, Prinses Beatrixlaan 428, Voorburg, Netherlands. (Subscr. to: SDU - Publishers, Christoffel Plantijnstraat, The Hague)

790 314 NE ISSN 0168-4248
NETHERLANDS. CENTRAAL BUREAU VOOR DE STATISTIEK. STATISTIEK VAN DE INKOMSTEN EN UITGAVEN DER OVERHEID VOOR CULTUUR EN RECREATIE/STATISTICS OF GOVERNMENT EXPENDITURE ON CULTURE AND RECREATION. (Text in Dutch and English) 1964. a. Centraal Bureau voor de Statistiek, Prinses Beatrixlaan 428, Voorburg, Netherlands. (Dist. by: SDU - Publishers, Christoffel Plantijnstraat, The Hague, Netherllands)
  Formerly: Netherlands. Centraal Bureau voor de Statistiek. Statistiek van de Uitgaven der Overheid voor Cultuur en Recreatie (ISSN 0077-7196)

PHYSICAL FITNESS - SPORTS MEDICINE; a bibliographic service encompassing exercise physiology, sports injuries, physical conditioning and the medical aspects of exercise. see MEDICAL SCIENCES — Abstracting, Bibliographies, Statistics

PINPOINTER; the Australian index to leisure activities and consumer reports. see CONSUMER EDUCATION AND PROTECTION — Abstracting, Bibliographies, Statistics

796.5 388.344 US
R V BUSINESS. (Recreational Vehicle) 1972. m. (plus a. directory). $48. T L Enterprises, Inc., 29901 Agoura Rd., Agoura, CA 91301. TEL 818-991-4980. Ed. Mike Schneider. adv.; charts; tr.lit.; circ. 17,000 (controlled). Indexed: Bus.Ind., SRI, Tr.& Indus.Ind.
  Formerly: Recreational Vehicle Dealer; Incorporates: Recreational Vehicle Retailer (ISSN 0090-3841)
  Description: Provides statistics about the economical and business aspects ofthe industry.

REFERATOVY VYBER ZE SPORTOVNI MEDICINY A LECEBNE REHABILITACE/ABSTRACTS OF SPORTS MEDICINE AND REHABILITATION. see MEDICAL SCIENCES — Abstracting, Bibliographies, Statistics

380 796 310 CN ISSN 0318-9422
SANFORD EVANS GOLD BOOK OF SNOWMOBILE DATA AND USED PRICES. 1972. a. Can.$15.50. Sanford Evans Communications Ltd., 1700 Church Ave., Box 6900, Winnipeg, Man. R3C 3B1, Canada. TEL 204-694-2022. FAX 204-694-3040. Ed. Gary Henry.
  Description: Current model year and previous thirteen model years listed with weight, length, track width and engine statistics. Factory suggested price and current resale values are featured.

790.1 IT
LO SPETTACOLO IN ITALIA; annuario statistico. 1936. a. L.20000. Societa Italiana degli Autori ed Editori, Viale della Letteratura 30, 00144 Rome, Italy. TEL 06 59901. FAX 06-5923351. TELEX 611423. bk.rev. (back issues avail.)

SPORTS AND GAMES — BALL GAMES

688.76 US
SPORT CLOTHING EXPENDITURES IN (YEAR). a. $165. National Sporting Goods Association, 1699 Wall St., Mt. Prospect, IL 60056-5780. TEL 708-439-4000. FAX 708-439-0111. Ed. Thomas B. Doyle.
 Description: Demographic and financial analysis of clothing purchases related to sports participation.

688.76 US ISSN 0193-8401
SPORTING GOODS MARKET. 1973. a. $165. National Sporting Goods Association, 1699 Wall St., Mt. Prospect, IL 60056-5780. TEL 708-439-4000. FAX 708-439-0111. Ed. Thomas B. Doyle. (also avail. in microform; back issues avail.) **Indexed:** SRI.

SPORTS DOCUMENTATION CENTRE. SERIAL HOLDINGS. see EDUCATION — *Abstracting, Bibliographies, Statistics*

SPORTS DOCUMENTATION MONTHLY BULLETIN. see EDUCATION — *Abstracting, Bibliographies, Statistics*

688.76 US
SPORTS PARTICIPATION IN (YEAR): LIFECYCLE DEMOGRAPHICS. a. $175. National Sporting Goods Association, 1699 Wall St., Mt. Prospect, IL 60056-5780. TEL 708-439-4000. FAX 708-439-0111. Ed. Thomas B. Doyle.
 Description: Analyzes sports participation by economic status of the participants.

688.76 US ISSN 0882-8210
SPORTS PARTICIPATION IN (YEAR): SERIES 1. a. $175. National Sporting Goods Association, 1699 Wall St., Mt. Prospect, IL 60056-5780. TEL 708-439-4000. FAX 708-439-0111. Ed. Thomas B. Doyle.
 Description: Publishes results of research studies on participation in 26 sports from aerobics to wilderness camping.

688.76 US
SPORTS PARTICIPATION IN (YEAR): SERIES 2. a. $175. National Sporting Goods Association, 1699 Wall St., Mt. Prospect, IL 60056-5780. TEL 708-439-4000. FAX 708-439-0111. Ed. Thomas B. Doyle.
 Description: Publishes results of research studies on participation in 25 activities from archery to waterskiing.

688.76 US
SPORTS PARTICIPATION IN (YEAR): STATE BY STATE. a. $310. National Sporting Goods Association, 1699 Wall St., Mt. Prospect, IL 60056-5780. TEL 708-439-4000. FAX 708-439-0111. Ed. Thomas B. Doyle.
 Description: Projects sports participation on a state by state basis for 34 sports ranging from aerobics and bowling to skiing, tennis and volleyball.

790.1 016 GV561 US ISSN 0883-1580
SPORTS PERIODICALS INDEX.* 1985. m. (plus a. cum.). $245. National Reproductions, 535 E. Liberty St., Ann Arbor, MI 48104-2209. Ed. Grant Elderidge.

790.1 016 613.7 GV561 CN ISSN 0882-553X
SPORTSEARCH. (Text in English, French) 1974. m. $130 to individuals; institutions $240. Sport Information Resource Centre (SIRC) - Centre de Documentation pour le Sport, 1600 James Naismith Drive, Gloucester, Ont. K1B 5N4, Canada. TEL 613-748-5658. FAX 613-748-5701. Ed.Bd.
 ●Also available online. Vendor(s): BRS (SFDB), BRS/Saunders Colleague, Data-Star, DIALOG. Also available on CD-ROM. Producer(s): SilverPlatter.
 Former titles (until 1985): Sport and Fitness Index (ISSN 0826-7537); (until 1984): Sport and Recreation Index - Index de la Litterature des Sports et des Loisirs (ISSN 0705-6095); (until 1977): Sport Articles.

798.4 UK
STATISTICAL RECORD. 1971. q. (plus annual no.). Weatherbys, Sanders Rd., Wellingborough, Northants. NN8 4BX, England. TEL 0933-440077. FAX 0933-440807. TELEX 311582-ODECS. adv.; stat.; circ. 1,000.

799 310 US
U.S. FISH AND WILDLIFE SERVICE. NATIONAL SURVEY OF HUNTING, FISHING AND WILDLIFE-ASSOCIATED RECREATION. 1955. irreg., 6th, 1982. U.S. Fish and Wildlife Service, Washington, DC 20240. TEL 303-226-9403. charts; illus.; stat.

WILDLIFE REVIEW (FORT COLLINS); an indexing service for wildlife management. see CONSERVATION — *Abstracting, Bibliographies, Statistics*

SPORTS AND GAMES — Ball Games

796.323 US ISSN 0733-0448
A C C BASKETBALL HANDBOOK. (Atlantic Coast Conference) 1974. a. $6. U M I Publications, Inc., 1135 N. Tryon St., Box 30036, Charlotte, NC 28230. TEL 704-374-0420. FAX 704-374-0729. Ed. Ivan Mothershead. adv.; circ. 100,000. (back issues avail.)

796.332 AT
A C T A F L FOOTBALL RECORD. 1946. w. Aus.$18. A C T Australian Football League, P.O. Box 417, Woden, A.C.T. 2606, Australia. TEL 062-824608. FAX 062-816136. adv.; circ. 400.

794.6 GV909 US ISSN 0001-1754
A L B A BOWLS. 1962. q. $3. American Lawn Bowls Association, 445 Surfview Dr., Pacific Palisades, CA 90272. Ed. Ferrell Burton, Jr. adv.; illus.; index; circ. 6,000. **Indexed:** Sportsearch (1977-).

796.3 US ISSN 0890-5649
A P B A JOURNAL. 1967. m. $20.75. Howard Ahlskog, Ed. & Pub., 65 Norwood St., Greenfield, MA 01301-1919. TEL 413-772-0907. adv.; charts; stat.; circ. 3,200. (processed)

796 SW ISSN 0567-4565
AARETS FOTBOLL. a. SEK 639. Stroembergs Idrottsboecker, Box 65, 16211 Vaellingby, Sweden.

796.342 US
ADDVANTAGE MAGAZINE. m. free. United States Professional Tennis Association, 1 USPTA Centre, 3535 Briarpark Dr., Houston, TX 77042. TEL 713-978-7782. FAX 713-978-7780. adv.; circ. 9,000. (back issues avail.) **Indexed:** Sportsearch (1981-).

796.334 IT
AGENDA DELLO SPORT. 1975. a. L.15000. Longega Maurizio, Ed. & Pub., Via Cesare De Fabritiis, 133, 00136 Rome, Italy. TEL 63-82-797. adv.; bk.rev.; circ. 1,986.

796.352 CN
 CODEN: D8350430
ALBATROS; le seul magazine de golf en Francais. 1983. 6/yr. Can.$19.50. 5253 av. du Parc, Bureau 404, Montreal, Que. H2V 4P2, Canada. TEL 514-272-1358. FAX 514-272-1569. Ed. Russel Miller. adv.; bk.rev.; circ. 60,000. (back issues avail.)
 Description: Features news on golf tournaments, profiles of golfers, tips on technique, information on golf equipment, resorts and clubs.

796.3 SZ
ALMANACCO CALCISTICO SVIZZERO. (Text in Italian) 1950. a. 20 Fr. (Giornale del Popolo) Armando Libotte, Casella Postale, CH-6976 Castagnola, Switzerland. Ed.Bd. adv.; stat.; circ. 2,000.

796.357 US ISSN 0002-6816
AMATEUR BASEBALL NEWS. 1958. 7/yr. $5. American Amateur Baseball Congress Inc., Box 467, 118-119 Redfield Plaza, Marshall, MI 49068. TEL 616-781-2002. FAX 616-781-2060. Ed. Joseph P. Cooper, adv.; bk.rev.; film rev.; illus.; circ. 10,000. (tabloid format) **Indexed:** Sportsearch.

796.352 US
AMATEUR GOLF REGISTER. 1983. m. $12. Amateur Golfers' Association of America, Inc., 5555 Hollywood Blvd., Hollywood, FL 33021. TEL 800-327-9789. Ed. Davis Lundy. adv.; circ. 25,000.

796.357 US ISSN 0065-6739
AMATEUR SOFTBALL ASSOCIATION OF AMERICA. OFFICIAL GUIDE AND RULE BOOK. 1933. a. $3. Amateur Softball Association of America, 2801 N.E. 50th St., Oklahoma City, OK 73111. TEL 405-424-5266. FAX 405-424-3855.

796.33 FR
ANNEE DU FOOTBALL. 1973. a. price varies. Editions Calmann-Levy, 3 rue Auber, 75009 Paris, France. Ed. Jacques Thibert. illus.

796.33 FR
ANNEE DU RUGBY. 1973. a. price varies. Editions Calmann-Levy, 3 rue Auber, 75009 Paris, France. Ed. Christian Montaignac. illus.

796.342 FR
ANNEE DU TENNIS. 1979. a. price varies. Editions Calmann-Levy, 3 rue Auber, 75009 Paris, France. Ed.Bd. illus.

796.342 IT
ANNUARIO ILLUSTRATO DEL TENNIS. 1979. a. L.6000($15.50) D M K Editrice s.r.l., Via Boscovich 14, 20124 Milan, Italy. adv.; illus.; circ. 70,000.

796.334 IT ISSN 0003-7907
ARBITRO. 1967. m. free to qualified personnel. Federazione Italiana Giuoco Calcio, Via Gregorio Allegri 14, 00198 Rome, Italy. Ed. Giuseppe Adami. charts; illus.; circ. 20,000 (controlled).
 Description: For football referees.

796.352 US
ARIZONA GOLF JOURNAL.* 1984. bi-m. $10. Arizona Golf House, Inc., 5050 N 40th St., Ste. 200, Phoenix, AZ 85018-2139. TEL 602-949-8899. Ed. David Hubbard. adv.; circ. 30,000.

796.332 UK
AROUND FOOTBALL. 1982. m. £4.05. Corvus Publishing, King St., Royston, Herts. SG8 9BD, England. Ed. T.M. Grote. adv.; circ. 20,000.

796.352 UK
ARTISAN GOLFER. 1947. q. 10 Brooklands Gardens, Potters Bar, Herts., England. Ed. Peter Ellis.

796.334 UK ISSN 0263-0354
ASSOCIATION OF FOOTBALL STATISTICIANS. ANNUAL. 1981. a. £13.50. Association of Football Statisticians, c/o R.J. Spiller, Ed., 22 Bretons, Basildon, Essex, England. adv.; bk.rev.; circ. 1,600.

796.358 AT
AUSTRALIAN CRICKET. 1968. 6/yr. Aus.$31.62. Mason Stewart Publishing Pty. Ltd., P.O. Box 746, Darlinghurst, N.S.W. 2010, Australia. TEL 02-282-8450. FAX 02-360-5367. Ed. Philip Mason. bk.rev.; circ. 21,500. **Indexed:** Sportsearch (1977-).
 Former titles: Australian Cricket Newspaper; (until Oct. 1980): Australian Cricket (ISSN 0004-895X)

796.3 AT ISSN 0816-651X
AUSTRALIAN CRICKET JOURNAL. 1985. q. Aus.$11. College Press, G.P.O. Box 696, Adelaide, SA 5001, Australia. TEL 08-267-5418. Ed. Chris Harte. bk.rev.; bibl.; circ. 7,450. **Indexed:** Sportsearch (1989-).
 Description: Historical and sociological essays on cricket.

796 AT
AUSTRALIAN CRICKET TOUR GUIDE. 1970. a. Aus.$4.95. Mason Stewart Publishing Pty. Ltd., P.O. Box 747, Darlinghurst, N.S.W. 2010, Australia.
 Formerly: Australian Cricket Yearbook (ISSN 0084-7291)

796.354 AT ISSN 0817-6604
AUSTRALIAN CROQUET GAZETTE. 1951. q. Aus.$11 (typically set in Mar.). Australian Croquet Association, P.O. Box 296, Rosny Park, Tas. 7018, Australia. FAX 08-223-3390. Ed. Carolyn Spooner. adv.; bk.rev.; circ. 1,250. **Indexed:** Sportsearch (1980-).
 Description: Provides news on Australian croquet; general articles on coaching and history.

796.352 AT
AUSTRALIAN GOLF DIGEST. 1970. m. Aus.$15. Federal Publishing Company, 140 Joynton Ave., Waterloo, Sydney, N.S.W. 2017, Australia. Ed. Phil Tresidder. **Indexed:** Sportsearch (1985-).
 Former titles: Australian Golf (Year); Australian Golf Instructional (ISSN 0311-0400); Australian Golf (ISSN 0004-9212)

796.342 AT
AUSTRALIAN TENNIS MAGAZINE; Asia and the Pacific. 1976. m. Aus.$40 (foreign Aus.$45). Sports Publications Pty. Ltd., 230 Toorak Rd., Ste. 3, South Yarra, Vic. 3141, Australia. TEL 03-826-8448. FAX 03-827-8808. Ed. Suzi Petkovski. adv.; circ. 23,000. (back issues avail.)
 Formerly: Tennis Australia.

4500 SPORTS AND GAMES — BALL GAMES

796.334 UK
B & Q SCOTTISH FOOTBALL LEAGUE REVIEW. 1980. a. £3. Scottish Football League, 188 West Regent St., Glasgow G2 4RY, Scotland. TEL 041-248-3844. FAX 041-221-7450. TELEX 779312. Ed. David C. Thomson. adv.; illus.; circ. 25,000.
Formerly: Clydesdale Bank Scottish Football League Review (ISSN 0260-8804)

794.6 381 US
B B I A FLASHES. q. free. Billiard and Bowling Institute of America, 200 Castlewood Dr., N. Palm Beach, FL 33408. TEL 305-842-4100. Ed. J. Alden Briggs, Jr. stat.

B B I A MEMBERSHIP AND PRODUCT INFORMATION GUIDE. (Billiard and Bowling Institute of America) see BUSINESS AND ECONOMICS — Trade And Industrial Directories

794.72 US
B C A BREAK. q. membership. Billiard Congress of America, 1700 1st Ave. S., Ste. 25A, Iowa City, IA 52240-7049. TEL 319-351-2112. FAX 319-351-7767. circ. 2,500.
Formerly: Billiard Congress of America Bulletin.

B T V SPEIGEL. (Bremer Turnvereinigung von 1877 e.V.) see SPORTS AND GAMES

796.352 US
BACK NINE; northwest golf magazine. 1987. every 6 wks. $9. Back Nine Publishing Co., Inc., 1826 N.E. Serpentine Pl., Box 55427, Seattle, WA 98155. TEL 206-367-8094. Ed. Alan A. Wentzel. adv.; circ. 8,000.
Description: Covers golf courses, players and tournaments in the Pacific Northwest.

796.345 CN ISSN 0711-124X
BADMINTON CANADA. 1981-1986; N.S. 1988. 6/yr. Can.$6($8) Badminton Canada, 1600 Prof. James Naismith Dr., Gloucester, Ont. K1B 5N4, Canada. TEL 613-748-5605. FAX 613-748-5695. Ed. Roy Roberts. adv.; circ. 3,000.
Description: Covers badminton in Canada.

796.352 GW ISSN 0178-2436
BAHNENGOLFER. 1973. 6/yr. DM.20.50 (foreign DM.23). Deutscher Bahnengolf-Verband, Postfach 1213, 2000 Schenefeld, Germany. TEL 04101-41861. Ed. Britta Heinrichs. adv.; bk.rev.; circ. 1,300 (controlled).
Description: Information about competition in mini-golfing.

796.35 US
BALLS & STRIKES. 1933. 8/yr. (Mar.-Oct.). $10. Amateur Softball Association of America, 2801 N.E. 50th St., Oklahoma City, OK 73111. TEL 405-424-5266. FAX 405-424-3855. Ed. Bill Plummer, III. adv.; illus.; stat. Indexed: Sports Per.Ind., Sportsearch.

796.334 MX ISSN 0005-4410
BALON; futbol mundial. 1963. w. Mex.$832($34.84) Periodismo Especializado, S.A., Presidentes 187, Col. Portales, Mexico, 13, D.F., Mexico. Ed. Antonio Elizarraras Corona.
Description: Covers world soccer news.

796.357 US ISSN 0228-6033
GV863.A1
BASEBALL AMERICA. 1981. s-m. $35.95. Baseball America, Inc., Box 2089, Durham, NC 27702. TEL 919-682-9635. FAX 919-682-2880. Ed. adv.; circ. 70,000.
Formerly (until 1982): All-America Baseball News.

796.357 US ISSN 0199-0128
BASEBALL BULLETIN. 1974. bi-m. $15 (foreign $23). L N Publishing, Inc., Box 370, Rochester, MI 48308. FAX 313-897-1977. Ed. Larry Donald. adv.; bk.rev.; charts; illus.; stat.; circ. 20,000. (tabloid format) Indexed: Sportsearch.

BASEBALL CARD NEWS. see HOBBIES

BASEBALL CARD PRICE GUIDE MONTHLY. see HOBBIES

BASEBALL CARDS. see HOBBIES

796.357 US ISSN 0270-4218
GV877
BASEBALL CASE BOOK. a. $2.75. National Federation of State High School Associations, 11724 N.W. Plaza Circle, Box 20626, Kansas City, MO 64195-0626. TEL 816-464-5400. FAX 816-464-5571.

796.357 US ISSN 0005-609X
GV862
BASEBALL DIGEST. 1941. m. $22 (foreign $30). Century Publishing Co., 990 Grove St., Evanston, IL 60201-4370. TEL 708-491-6440. (Subscr. to: Box 360, Mt. Morris, IL 61054-0360. TEL 800-877-5893) Ed. John Kuenster. adv.; charts; illus.; stat.; circ. 350,000. (also avail. in microform from UMI; back issues avail.; reprint service avail. from UMI) Indexed: Cath.Ind., Sports Per.Ind., Sportsearch.
Description: For serious baseball fans. Provides statistics and stories behind the sport.

796.323 039 US
BASEBALL ENCYCLOPEDIA UPDATE. a. $13.95. Macmillan Publishing Company, 866 Third Ave., New York, NY 10022. Ed. Rick Wolff.

796.357 US
BASEBALL FORECAST (YEAR). a. Lexington Library, Inc., 355 Lexington Ave., New York, NY 10017. TEL 212-973-3200. FAX 212-986-5926. Ed. Stephen Ciacciarelli. adv.; charts; illus.

796.357 US ISSN 0067-4273
BASEBALL GUIDE. 1965. a. $2.50. Kwik-Fax Books (Subsidiary of: Martin Frederick, Inc.), Box 14613, Surfside Beach, SC 29587. TEL 803-238-4074. FAX 803-238-3513. Ed. Malcolm DeWitt. circ. 500,000.

796.357 US ISSN 0199-946X
BASEBALL HOBBY NEWS. 1979. m. $19.95. 4540 Kearny Villa Rd., Ste. 215, San Diego, CA 92123. TEL 619-565-2848. FAX 619-565-6608. Ed. Frank Barning. adv.; bk.rev.; circ. 91,000 (controlled).

796.357 US
BASEBALL ILLUSTRATED (YEAR). a. Lexington Library, Inc., 355 Lexington Ave., New York, NY 10017. TEL 212-973-3200. FAX 212-986-5926. Ed. Stephen Ciacciarelli. adv.; charts; illus.

796.31 US
BASEBALL INSIGHT; inside stats for serious fans. 1982. 27/yr. (w. Apr.-Oct.). $139 (includes a. Pitcher and Team Report). Parrish Publications, Box 23205, Portland, OR 97223. TEL 503-244-8975. Ed. Phil Erwin. bk.rev.; charts; stat.; circ. 600. (looseleaf format; back issues avail.)

796.357 JA
BASEBALL MAGAZINE. (Text in Japanese) 1946. w. 14070 Yen. Baseball Magazine Sha, 3-10-10 Misaki-cho, Chiyoda-ku, Tokyo, Japan. Ed. Takao Ouchi.

796.357 US
BASEBALL PREVIEW (YEAR). a. Lexington Library, Inc., 355 Lexington Ave., New York, NY 10017. TEL 212-973-3200. FAX 212-986-5926. Ed. Stephen Ciacciarelli. adv.; charts; illus.
Formerly: Saga's Baseball Special.

796.357 US ISSN 0734-6891
GV862
BASEBALL RESEARCH JOURNAL. 1972. a. $35 membership. Society for American Baseball Research, Inc., Box 93183, Cleveland, OH 44101. TEL 216-575-0500. FAX 216-575-0502. adv.; circ. 6,500. (back issues avail.) Indexed: Amer.Hist.& Life, Hist.Abstr., Phys.Ed.Ind., Sportsearch (1981-).

796.357 US
BASEBALL RULEBOOK. a. $2.75. National Federation of State High School Associations, 11724 N.W. Plaza Circle, Box 20626, Kansas City, MO 64195-0626. TEL 816-464-5400. FAX 816-464-5571.

796.357 US
BASEBALL UMPIRES MANUAL. biennial. $2.75. National Federation of State High School Associations, 11724 N.W. Plaza Circle, Box 20626, Kansas City, MO 64195-0626. TEL 816-464-5400. FAX 816-464-5571.

796.357 US
BASEBALL UPDATE. bi-m. 405 Tarrytown Rd., Ste. 405, White Plains, NY 10607. TEL 914-337-4796. Ed. Greg Goldstein.

796.323 GW ISSN 0178-9279
BASKETBALL. 1962. s-m. DM.69.40. Goettinger Tageblatt, Maschmuehlenweg 8-10, 3400 Goettingen, Germany. TEL 0551-4990520. FAX 0551-4990530. Ed. Alexander Gutowski. adv.; bk.rev.; circ. 9,000.

796.323 US
BASKETBALL ANNUAL (YEAR). a. Lexington Library, Inc., 355 Lexington Ave., New York, NY 10017. TEL 212-973-3200. FAX 212-986-5926. Ed. Stephen Ciacciarelli. adv.; charts; illus.

796.32 US ISSN 0525-4663
GV885.45
BASKETBALL CASE BOOK. a. $2.75. National Federation of State High School Associations, 11724 N.W. Plaza Circle, Box 20626, Kansas City, MO 64195-0626. TEL 816-464-5400. FAX 816-464-5571. adv.; illus.; circ. 300,000.

796.323 US ISSN 0098-5988
GV885.5
BASKETBALL DIGEST. 1973. 8/yr. $22 (foreign $30). Century Publishing Co., 990 Grove St., Evanston, IL 60201-4370. TEL 708-491-6440. (Subscr. to: Box 569, Mt. Morris, IL 61054-0569. TEL 800-877-5893) Ed. Michael K. Herbert. adv.; bibl.; charts; illus.; stat.; circ. 132,000. (also avail. in microform from UMI; reprint service avail. from UMI) Indexed: Sports Per.Ind.
Description: For serious basketball fans who want the statistics, features, and excitement behind the action of pro and college basketball.

796.323 US
BASKETBALL FORECAST (YEAR). a. Lexington Library, Inc., 355 Lexington Ave., New York, NY 10017. TEL 212-973-3200. FAX 212-986-5926. Ed. Stephen Ciacciarelli. adv.; charts; illus.

796.323 US
BASKETBALL GUIDE. 1971. a. $2.50. Kwik-Fax Books (Subsidiary of: Martin Frederick, Inc.), Box 14613, Surfside Beach, SC 29587. TEL 803-238-3513. Ed. Malcolm Dewitt. circ. 300,000.
Formerly: Pro Basketball Guide (ISSN 0079-5518)

796.323 US
BASKETBALL HALL OF FAME NEWSLETTER. 1979. q. Basketball Hall of Fame, 1150 W. Columbus Ave., Box 179, Springfield, MA 01101-0179. TEL 413-781-6500. FAX 413-781-1939. Ed. Robin Deutsch. circ. 4,500.

796.323 US
BASKETBALL HALL OF FAME YEARBOOK. 1972. irreg. $10. Basketball Hall of Fame, 1150 W. Columbus Ave., Box 179, Springfield, MA 01101-0179. TEL 413-781-6500. FAX 413-781-1939. Ed. Robin Deutsch.

796.323 US
BASKETBALL HANDBOOK. biennial. $2.75. National Federation of State High School Associations, 11724 N.W. Plaza Circle, Box 20626, Kansas City, MO 64195-0626. TEL 816-464-5400. FAX 816-464-5571.

796.323 UK
BASKETBALL MONTHLY. 1960. m. £9. (English Basketball Association) Basketball Publishing Ltd., Calomax House, Lupton Ave., Leeds LS9 6EE, England. Ed. Richard Taylor. adv.; bk.rev.; stat.; circ. 12,000. Indexed: Sportsearch.
Formerly: Basketball (ISSN 0005-6162)

796.323 US ISSN 0270-4226
GV885.2
BASKETBALL OFFICIALS MANUAL. biennial. $2.75. National Federation of State High School Associations, 11724 N.W. Plaza Circle, Box 20626, Kansas City, MO 64195-0626. TEL 816-464-5400. FAX 816-464-5571.

796.323 US
BASKETBALL RULEBOOK. a. $2.75. National Federation of State High School Associations, 11724 N.W. Plaza Circle, Box 20626, Kansas City, MO 64195-0626. TEL 816-464-5400. FAX 816-464-5571.

SPORTS AND GAMES — BALL GAMES 4501

796.323   US
BASKETBALL - SIMPLIFIED & ILLUSTRATED RULES. a. $2.75. National Federation of State High School Associations, 11724 N.W. Plaza Circle, Box 20626, Kansas City, MO 64195-0626. TEL 816-464-5400. FAX 816-464-5571.

796.323   US   ISSN 0005-6170
BASKETBALL WEEKLY. 1967. w. (during season). $34.95 for 20 nos. Football News Co., 17820 E. Warren, Detroit, MI 48224. TEL 313-881-9554. Ed. Matt Marsom. adv.; bk.rev.; illus.; stat.; circ. 55,000. (tabloid format) Indexed: Sports Per.Ind., Sportsearch.

796.357   US   ISSN 0731-812X
BATTER PERFORMANCE HANDBOOK. 1980. a. $5. Research Analysis Publications, Box 49213, Los Angeles, CA 90049. Ed. Ronald H. Lewis. adv.; charts; stat.; circ. 5,500.

796.342   GW   ISSN 0342-8915
BAYERN TENNIS. 1977. m. DM.55. Elsenheinmerstr. 59, 8000 Munich 21, Germany. TEL 089-573277. Ed. Ludwig Rembold. circ. 15,000.

796.332   US
BEAR REPORT. 26/yr. $24.95. Royle Publishing Co., Inc. (Subsidiary of: Royle Publishing Co., Inc.) 112 Market St., Sun Prairie, WI 53590. TEL 608-837-5161. FAX 608-837-3946. Ed. Mike Polzin. adv.; illus.; circ. 19,682.
   Description: Covers the Chicago Bears and the NFL. Includes game stories, statistics, coaches' comments and player profiles.

BECKETT BASEBALL CARD MONTHLY. see HOBBIES

BECKETT BASKETBALL MONTHLY. see HOBBIES

BECKETT FOOTBALL CARD MONTHLY. see HOBBIES

794.6   UK
BEDFORDSHIRE COUNTY BOWLING ASSOCIATION. HANDBOOK. 1914. a. £1 (typically set in Apr.). F.G. Pedder, 6 Greenacre Park, Clayhall Road, Kensworth, Beds. LU6 3RE, England. TEL 0582-872675. adv.; circ. 1,900.

796.352   JA
BEIJING GOLF CLUB NEWS. a. Pan Asia Corporation, 17-3 Ueno 1-chome, Taito-ku, Tokyo 110, Japan. TEL 03-8374140. FAX 03-8374217.

796.342   GW   ISSN 0723-1407
BEITRAEGE ZUR THEORIE UND PRAXIS DES TENNISUNTERRICHTS UND -TRAININGS. irreg., vol.14, 1990. price varies. (Deutscher Tennis Bund Sportwissenschaftlicher Beirat) Verlag Ingrid Czwalina, Reesenbuettler Redder 75, 2070 Ahrensburg, Germany. TEL 04102-59190. FAX 04102-50992.

796.357   UK
BENSON AND HEDGES CRICKET YEAR. 1981. a. £18.99. Pelham Books Ltd., 27 Wrights Lane, London W8 5TZ, England. TEL 071-416-3200. FAX 071-416-3293. Ed. David Lemmon.
   Description: Illustrated record of first-class games played world-wide.

796.357   UK
BENSON & HEDGES WEST INDIES CRICKET ANNUAL (YEAR). 1971. a. £3.75($15) (Benson & Hedges (Overseas) Ltd.) Caribbean Communications, 116 Queens Rd., Hersham, Walton-on-Thames, Surrey KT12 5LL, England. FAX 0932-232001. (And: P.O. Box 40W, Worthing, Christ Church, Barbados, W.I.) Ed. Tony Cozier. circ. 20,000.

769.323   US
BETWEEN THE LINES (SYRACUSE);* for the year round baseball enthusiast. 1989. 12/yr. (plus 2 special eds.). $15. 247 Arlington Ave., Syracuse, NY 13207-1603.
   Description: Provides a forum for the exchange of ideas between fans.

796.333   AT   ISSN 0311-175X
BIG LEAGUE.* 1957? w. Aus.$10($30) New South Wales Rugby League, 165 Phillip St., Sydney, N.S.W. 2000, Australia. Ed. G. Lester.
   Formerly: Rugby League News.

796.332 378.198   US
BIG TEN FOOTBALL MEDIA GUIDE. 1982. a. $12. Big Ten Conference, 1500 Higgins Rd., Park Ridge, IL 60068-5742. TEL 708-696-1010. FAX 708-696-1110. charts; illus.; stat.; circ. 4,000.
   Formerly: Big Ten Football Yearbook.

796.357   US   ISSN 1054-2248
GV863.A1
BILL MAZEROSKI'S BASEBALL. a. $7.95. Preview Publishing, 100 W. Harrison, N. Tower, 5th Fl., Seattle, WA 98119. TEL 206-282-2322. FAX 206-284-2083.
   Description: Preview of the upcoming season from insiders in the game.

794.6   US   ISSN 0164-761X
BILLIARDS DIGEST.* 1978. bi-m. $13. (National Bowlers Journal, Inc.) Luby Publishing, 200 S. Michigan Ave., K, Ste. 1430, Chicago, IL 60604-2404. TEL 312-266-7179. FAX 312-266-7215. Ed. Michael Panozzo. adv.; illus.; circ. 18,000.
   Description: Dedicated to the fine art of billiards.

794.72   US   ISSN 1047-2444
GV891.A1
BILLIARDS: THE (YEAR) OFFICIAL B C A RULES & RECORDS BOOK. 1948. a. $5.95. Billiard Congress of America, c/o Mark Cord, Ed., 1700 First Ave., Ste. 25A, Iowa City, IA 52240-7049. TEL 319-351-2112. FAX 319-351-7767. charts; illus.; stat.; circ. 100,000.
   Description: Contains rules for games of billiards, competition records, instruction, Hall of Fame listings, and history.

796.342   US
BLACK TENNIS. 1977. m. $10. Black Tennis Magazine, Inc., Box 210767, Dallas, TX 75211. Ed. Marcus A. Freeman, Jr. adv.; bk.rev.; circ. 15,000. (back issues avail.)

796.342   US
BOB LARSON'S JUNIOR AND COLLEGIATE TENNIS. 1988. m. $24. Bob Larson Ed. & Pub., Box 24379, Edina, MN 55424-0379. TEL 612-920-8947. FAX 612-927-7155. adv.; bk.rev.; circ. 4,500.
   Formerly: Bob Larson's Tennis Junior.
   Description: Focuses on the junior tennis player (12-18 years old) and collegiate tennis players. Includes tournament results, profiles, player development articles, and college recruitment tips.

796.357   US
BOOK OF BASEBALL RECORDS. a. $11.95. Seymour Siwoff, Ed. & Pub., 500 Fifth Ave., New York, NY 10036. TEL 212-869-1530.

796.357   US   ISSN 0739-4667
BOOK ON STARTING PITCHERS. 1983. a. $37.50. Research Analysis Publications, Box 49213, Los Angeles, CA 90049. Ed. Ronald H. Lewis. circ. 6,000.

796.342   DK   ISSN 0109-6761
BORDTENNIS AARBOGEN. 1982. a. DKK 45. Dansk Bord-Tennis Union, Idraettens Hus, Broendby Stadion 20, DK-2605 Broendby, Denmark. TEL 02-455555. FAX 43-63-43-50. TELEX 000945. Ed. Karl A. Soeltoft. adv.; illus.; circ. 3,000.

796.323   US
BOSTON CELTICS YEARBOOK. a. $7.50. Phoenix Media - Communications Group, c/o Stephen M. Mindich, 126 Brookline Ave., Boston, MA 02215. TEL 617-536-5390. FAX 617-536-1463. Eds. Joyce Kosofsky, Tod Rosenweig. adv.; circ. 75,000.

794.6   SW
BOWLAREN.* s-m. Svenska Bowlingfoerbundet, Box 4033, 203 11 Malmoe, Sweden. adv.; circ. 32,000.

794.6   UK
BOWLER.* 1973. m. £4.50. Academy Organisation (Magazines) Ltd., 57 Blythe St., Belfast BT12 5HX, N. Ireland. Ed. Bert Graham. adv.

794.6   UK
BOWLERS' WORLD. 1977. m. £8.50. South Lancashire Newspapers Ltd., 164 College St., St. Helens WA10 1TT, England. TEL 0744-22285. FAX 0744-27586. Ed. Terry Magee. adv.; bk.rev.; circ. 13,000.

794.6   US   ISSN 0162-0274
GV901
BOWLING MAGAZINE. 1934. 6/yr. $10. American Bowling Congress, 5301 S. 76th St., Greendale, WI 53129. TEL 414-421-6400. FAX 414-421-1194. Ed. Bill Vint. adv.; bk.rev.; illus.; circ. 130,000.
   Indexed: Sports Per.Ind., Sportsearch (1977-).

794.6   US
BOWLING NEWS. 1940. w. $25. Bowling News, Inc., 2606 W. Burbank Blvd., Burbank, CA 91505. TEL 818-849-4664. FAX 818-845-6321. adv.; bk.rev.; circ. 14,000. (tabloid format)
   Formerly: California Bowling News (ISSN 0008-0918)

794.6   IT   ISSN 0006-8438
BOWLING NOTIZIE;* mensile dello sport del bowling. 1966. m. L.3000 to non-members. Federazione Bowling Italiana, Via Marco d'Agrate No. 23, 20139 Milan, Italy.

794.6   US   ISSN 0006-8446
BOWLING PROPRIETOR. 1954. m. (June & July combined). membership. Bowling Proprietors' Association of America, Box 5802, Arlington, TX 76005. TEL 817-649-5105. FAX 817-633-2940. Ed. Daniel W. Burgess. adv.; bk.rev.; illus.; circ. 4,500. (controlled). (also avail. in microform from UMI; reprint service avail. fromn UMI) Indexed: Sportsearch (1978-).

796.31   AT
BOWLS. (Supplement avail.: N.S.W. Bowls News) 1936. m. Aus.$20. Royal New South Wales Bowling Association, Inc., P.O. Box E186, St. James, N.S.W. 2000, Australia. TEL 02-283-4555. FAX 02-283-4252. Ed. Rex Davies. adv.; bk.rev.; circ. 141,044. Indexed: Sportsearch.
   Formerly: Bowls in N.S.W. (ISSN 0006-8454)
   Description: Covers lawn bowling.

796.3   UK   ISSN 0262-6942
BOWLS INTERNATIONAL. 1981. m. £17 (foreign £18). Key Publishing Ltd., P.O. Box 100, Stamford, Lincs. PE9 1QX, England. TEL 0780-55131. FAX 0780-57261. TELEX 265871-MONREF-G. Ed. Chris Mills. adv.; bk.rev.; charts; illus.; circ. 12,767.

796.3   AT
BOWLS - NEWS AND VIEWS. 1954. 9/yr. $1. Victorian Ladies' Bowling Association, 109 Commercial Rd., South Yarra 3141, Australia. Ed. E. McLean. adv.; illus.; circ. 15,800.

796.334   AT   ISSN 0817-1203
BRITISH SOCCER WEEK. 1986. w. Aus.$85. Westways Publishing Co., 103 Gt. Eastern Hwy., Rivervale, W.A. 6103, Australia. TEL 09-362-4344. FAX 09-470-3162. (Subscr. to: P.O. Box 609, Cloverdale, W.A. 6105, Australia) Ed. Bill Cranny. circ. 13,500. (hard copy avail.)
   Description: Match reports and news of players and clubs in UK. Detailed results and league standings published in Australia five days after matches are played.

796.357   US
BULLPEN. q. Babe Ruth League, 1770 Brunswick Ave., Box 5000, Trenton, NJ 09638. TEL 609-695-1434. FAX 609-695-2505. adv.; circ. 32,000. (controlled).
   Description: Regulation amateur youth baseball and softball program.

796.352 658.7   US
▼**BUYING HABITS OF GOLF COURSE SUPERINTENDENTS.** 1990. a. $945. Golf Course Superintendents Association of America, 1421 Research Park Dr., Lawrence, KS 66049. TEL 913-841-2240. FAX 913-832-4433. Ed. Robert Shively. circ. 4,500.

796.323   US
C B A MEDIA GUIDE YEARBOOK. 1978. a. $15. Continental Basketball Association, 425 S. Cherry St., Ste. 230, Denver, CO 80222. TEL 303-331-0404. Ed. Greg Anderson. adv.; circ. 5,000.

796.323   US
C B A NEWSLETTER. 1978. w. (Nov.-Apr.) $40 for 20 nos. Continental Basketball Association, 425 S. Cherry St., Ste. 230, Denver, CO 80222. TEL 303-331-0404. Ed. Greg Anderson. adv.; circ. 1,200.
   Former titles: C B A Update; C B A Newsweekly.

SPORTS AND GAMES — BALL GAMES

796.352 CN
CADILLAC GOLF CLASSIC. 1988. a. Media Enterprises, 3 Ainsley Gardens, Islington, Ont. M9A 1M5, Canada. TEL 416-233-2171. FAX 416-233-2171. Ed. Julie Cohen. adv.: B&W page Can.$4950; trim 8 1/8 x 10 3/4. circ. 9,000.

796.323 US
CALIFORNIA BASKETBALL.* 1988. 3/yr. $8. California Football Magazine, Inc., 1330 E. 223rd St., Carson, CA 90745-4313. adv.; circ. 100,000.
  Description: Covers high school, junior college, university and pro basketball programs in the Golden State.

796.332 US
CALIFORNIA FOOTBALL.* 1986. 3/yr. $8. California Football Magazine, Inc., 1330 E. 223rd St., Carson, CA 90745-4313. Ed. David Raatz. adv.; circ. 100,000.

796.352 CN ISSN 0316-8131
CANADIAN AND PROVINCIAL GOLF RECORDS. 1972. a. Royal Canadian Golf Association, Golf House, R.R. 2, Oakville, Ont. L6J 4Z3, Canada. TEL 416-844-1800. FAX 416-845-7040. circ. 1,500.
  Formerly: Royal Canadian Golf Association. National Tournament Records (ISSN 0316-8212)
  Description: Complete records for all provincial and national golf tournaments in Canada since the 1880's.

796.352 CN ISSN 0084-8565
CANADIAN LADIES' GOLF ASSOCIATION. YEAR BOOK. (Text in English, French) 1947. a. Can.$3. Canadian Ladies' Golf Association, 1600 James Naismith Dr., 2nd Fl., Gloucester, Ontario K1B 5N4, Canada. TEL 613-748-5642. FAX 613-748-5720. Ed. Leonard Murphy. adv.; bk.rev.; illus.; stat.; index; circ. 10,000.

796.325 CN
CANADIAN VOLLEYBALL ANNUAL AND RULE BOOK. a. Can.$8. Canadian Volleyball Association, 1600 James Naismith Dr., Gloucester, Ont. K1B 5N4, Canada. TEL 613-748-5681. FAX 613-748-5727. TELEX 053-3660 SPORTREC. adv.; circ. 12,000.

796 VE
CANCHA. 1971. m. Urbanization Horizonte, 2da Traversal, Qta. Mabel, Caracas, Venezuela. adv.

CARD COLLECTOR'S PRICE GUIDE. see *HOBBIES*

796.352 US ISSN 0008-6770
CAROLINA GOLFER.* 1960. bi-m. $5. Wing Publications, Inc., Box 11268, Columbia, SC 29211. Ed. Sidney L. Wise. adv.; bk.rev.; charts; illus.; stat.; circ. controlled.

796.332 UK
CELTIC VIEW. 1965. w. £27 (£37 for US). Celtic Football Club, 18 Kerrydale St., Glasgow G40 3RW, Scotland. TEL 041-551-8103. FAX 041-554-2376. Ed. Donald Cowey. adv.; bk.rev.; circ. 27,000.

794.6 US ISSN 0009-3513
CHICAGO BOWLER; bowling weekly. 1934. w. $10. Chicago Bowler Inc., c/o John Weglarz, Pub., 350 W. 22nd St., Ste. 109, Lombard, IL 60148-4805. TEL 708-629-7665. Ed. Terri M. Weglarz. adv.; circ. 5,700. (tabloid format)

796.352 US
▼**CHICAGO DISTRICT GOLFER.** 1990. q. $12. (Chicago District Golf Association) P & C Publications, 2333 Waukegan Rd., Ste. S-280, Bannockburn, IL 60015. TEL 708-940-8333. Ed. Adam Ritt. adv.; circ. 70,000.
  Description: Includes news and trends, local courses and private clubs, previews of tournaments, personalities and history.

796.352 US
CHICAGO METRO GOLFER. 6/yr. Golf Publishing Inc., 516 N. York Rd., Bensonville, IL 60106-1607. TEL 708-860-5444. Ed. Gary Holaway. circ. 20,000.

796.352 US
CHICAGOLAND GOLF. 1989. 10/yr. Chicagoland Golf Publishing Co., Box 567, Lagrange, IL 60525. TEL 708-579-3860. adv.; circ. 25,000.
  Description: Provides information, previews, photographs and reporting on the PGA events in the area. Covers area courses, travel, teaching techniques and interviews.

796.357 UK
CLUB CRICKET CONFERENCE OFFICIAL HANDBOOK. 1915. a. £25. Club Cricket Conference, 361 West Barnes Lane, New Malden, Surrey KT3 6JF, England. TEL 081-949-4001. Ed. A.E.F. Stevens. circ. 3,500.

796.323 US ISSN 0009-9880
GV711
COACHING CLINIC. 1962. 10/yr. $35. Princeton Educational Publishers, Box 280, Plainsboro, NJ 08536. TEL 609-924-0319. Ed. Barry Pavalec. charts; illus.; circ. 7,000. Indexed: Phys.Ed.Ind., Sports Per.Ind., Sportsearch (1974-).
  Incorporates: Basketball Clinic (ISSN 0146-5007) & Women's Coaching Clinic (ISSN 0146-1133)

796.342 US ISSN 0279-1153
COLLEGE AND JUNIOR TENNIS. 1972. s-a. $15. Junior Tennis, Inc., 100 Harbor Rd., Port Washington, NY 11050. TEL 516-883-6601. FAX 516-883-5241. TELEX 293185. Ed. Wendy Peterson. adv.; bk.rev.; illus.; circ. 5,000. (back issues avail.)
  Description: Covers college and junior tennis, coverage, draw sheets, schedules, stories, photos, rankings, and results.

796.323 US
COLLEGE & PRO BASKETBALL ACTION. a. $4.95. Sports Eye, Inc., 18 Industrial Park Dr., Port Washington, NY 11050. TEL 516-484-3300.

796.31 US ISSN 0530-9751
COLLEGIATE BASEBALL. 1957. 14/yr. $18. Collegiate Baseball Newspaper Inc., c/o Lou Pavlovich, Ed., Box 50566, Tucson, AZ 85703. FAX 602-624-5501. adv.; illus.; circ. 9,500.
  Description: For baseball players, coaches, students. Covers the latest baseball products, innovative instructional clinics, and provides feature stories on baseball personalities.

796.357 US
COMPLETE BASEBALL RECORD BOOK. Variant title: Sporting News Official Baseball Record Book. 1949. a. $12.95. Sporting News Publishing Co., 1212 N. Lindbergh Blvd., St. Louis, MO 63132. TEL 314-997-7111. Ed. Craig Carter. (processed)
  Former titles (until 1985): Official Baseball Record Book (ISSN 0078-4605); One for the Book.

796.342 GR
COSMOS TOU TENNIS/WORLD OF TENNIS. 1982. bi-m. Dr.800. Liberis Publications Ltd., 49 Pericleous St., 154 51 N. Psychico, Athens, Greece. Ed. Dimitri Kanellopoulos. adv.; circ. 10,000. (back issues avail.)

796.352 SP
COSTAGOLF; Spain's magazine for golf and leisure. (Text in English; Spanish ed. avail.) 1975. m. 4000 ptas. Golf Area, S.A., Loma de los Riscos, 1, Apdo. 358, Torremolinos, Malaga, Spain. TEL 952-381-542. FAX 952-381-569. Ed. Peter Leonard. adv.; bk.rev.; illus.; stat.; tr.lit.; circ. 18,000. (back issues avail.)

796.352 US
COUNTRY CLUB. 1986. bi-m. Golf Club Publications, 16 Forest St., New Canaan, CT 06840. TEL 203-972-3892. Ed. E. MacFarlan Moore. adv.; circ. 150,275.
  Formerly: Golf Club.
  Description: Conveys the beauty, grandeur, history and pleasures of golf. Includes profiles of country clubs.

796.358 NE ISSN 0011-1236
CRICKET. 1930. 19/yr. (w. during summer). fl.55. Koninklijke Nederlandse Cricket Bond, Nieuwe Kalfjeslaan 21B, 1182 AA Amstelveen, Netherlands. TEL 020-451705. FAX 020-451715. Ed. G. de Grooth. adv.; bk.rev.; illus.; stat.; circ. 1,600.

796.358 AT ISSN 0310-9356
CRICKET QUADRANT. 1973. irreg. Aus.$0.40 per no. Australian Cricket Society, A.C.T. Branch, 91 Gouger St., Torrens, A.C.T. 2607, Australia. Ed. Julian Oakley.

796.358 II
CRICKET SAMRAT. (Text in Hindi) 1978. m. L-1 & 2, Kanchan House, Najafgarh Rd., Commercial Complex, New Delhi 110 015, India. TEL 11-591175. Ed. Anand Dewan. circ. 84,600.

796.358 PK
CRICKETER. (Text in English) 1973. m. Rs.24($7) Al-Abbas International Agencies, G.P.O. Box 3721, 3rd Fl., Spencer's Bldg., II Chundrigar Rd., Karachi 1, Pakistan. Ed. Hanif Mohammed. charts; illus.; stat. Indexed: Sportsearch (1981-).

796.3 AT
CRICKETER. 1973. 7/yr. Aus.$22.40 (foreign Aus.$49.70). Syme Magazines (Subsidiary of: Syme Media Pty. Ltd.), G.P.O. Box 628E, Melbourne, Vic. 3000, Australia. TEL 03-601-4222. FAX 03-670-9096. Ed. Ken Piesse. (back issues avail.)
  Description: Covers cricket at the international and local level.

796.358 UK ISSN 0266-7398
CRICKETER INTERNATIONAL. 1921. m. £22.25($48.89) Cricketer Ltd., Beech Hanger, Ashurst, Nr. Tunbridge Wells, Kent TN3 9ST, England. TEL 089-2740256. Ed. Christopher Martin-Jenkins. adv.; illus. Indexed: Sportsearch (1977-).
  Formerly: Cricketer (ISSN 0011-1260)
  Description: Covers all aspects of the game of cricket including techniques, player profiles, reports on series.

790.1 UK ISSN 0266-7401
CRICKETER QUARTERLY FACTS AND FIGURES. 1973. q. £9.50($21.09) Cricketer Ltd., Beech Hanger, Ashurst, Tunbridge Wells, Kent TN3 9ST, England. TEL 089-2740256. adv.
  Description: Facts and figures of cricket in England including international match results.

796.354 UK ISSN 0011-1880
CROQUET GAZETTE. 1901. 6/yr. £15. Croquet Association, Hurlingham Club, London SW6 3PR, England. TEL 071-736-3148. Ed. John Walters. adv.; bk.rev.; illus.; circ. 2,200. Indexed: Sportsearch.

796 US ISSN 1047-3084
CUBS VINE LINE. 1986. m. $19.95. Chicago National League Ball Club, Inc., Box 1159, Skokie, IL 60076-8159. FAX 312-404-4129. Ed. Ned Colletti. adv.; bk.rev.; circ. 30,000.

796.332 US
DALLAS COWBOYS OUTLOOK. 1967. a. $4.21. Sports Communications, Inc., P.O. Box 95, Waco, TX 76703. TEL 817-752-4351. Ed. Dave Campbell. adv.; circ. 55,622.

796.342 DK ISSN 0107-2242
DANSK SQUASH. 1980. 4/yr. membership. Dansk Squash Forbund, Idraettus Hus, Broendby Stadion 20, 2600 Glostrup, Denmark. illus.

794.6 GW
DELMENHORSTER KEGLER ZEITUNG. 1968. q. (Sportkegler Vereins Delmenhorst) Fink Druck GmbH, Brandenburgerstr. 4, Postfach 1219, 2870 Delmenhorst, Germany. TEL 04221-2768. circ. 1,300.

796.342 GW ISSN 0176-0599
DEUTSCHE TENNIS ZEITUNG. 1946. s-m. DM.103.60. Sportverlag Schmidt & Dreisilker GmbH & Co., Postfach 260, 7032 Sindelfingen, Germany. Ed. Rolf Stotz. adv.; bk.rev.; charts; illus.; circ. 50,000. (back issues avail.)
  Formerly (until 1981): Tennis.

790 GW ISSN 0170-1509
DEUTSCHE VOLLEYBALL ZEITSCHRIFT. 1977. m. DM.62.40 (foreign DM.67.80). Philippka-Verlag, Postfach 6540, 4400 Muenster, Germany. TEL 0251-23005-0. FAX 0251-23005-99. Ed. Konrad Honig. circ. 19,000. (back issues avail.)

796.334 GW
DEUTSCHER FUSSBALL-BUND. AMTLICHE MITTEILUNGEN. 1952. m. DM.5. Deutscher Fussball-Bund (DFB) - German Soccer Association, Otto-Fleck-Schneise 6, 6000 Frankfurt 71, Germany. FAX 069-6788266. TELEX 416815. circ. 1,300.
  Description: Covers the official announcements of the West German Soccer Association.

SPORTS AND GAMES — BALL GAMES 4503

790　　　　　GW　　ISSN 0930-0791
DEUTSCHER TISCHTENNIS SPORT. 1946. m. DM.67.20 (foreign DM.72). Philippka-Verlag, Postfach 6540, 4400 Muenster, Germany. TEL 0251-23005-0. FAX 0251-23005-99. Ed. Konrad Honig. circ. 17,500. (back issues avail.)

796.323　　　　US　　ISSN 1054-2213
DICK VITALE'S BASKETBALL. a. $7.95. Preview Publishing, 100 W. Harrison, N. Tower, 5th Fl., Seattle, WA 98119. TEL 206-282-2322. FAX 206-284-2083.
  Description: Preview of the upcoming college and professional basketball season from insiders in the game.

796.357　　　　US　　ISSN 0896-7970
DIEHARD. 1986. m. $21.95. Coman Publishing Company, Inc. (Boston), 167 Milk St., Ste. 402, Boston, MA 02109-9605. TEL 919-688-0218. FAX 919-682-1532. Ed. George Whitney. adv.; circ. 13,500.
  Description: For Boston Red Sox fans.

796.352　　　　US　　ISSN 1055-4785
▼**DISC GOLF JOURNAL**; the magazine for disc golfers everywhere. 1991. bi-m. $18. 1801 Richardson Dr., Ste. 6, Urbana, IL 61801. TEL 217-344-3552. Ed. Kathleen Ignowski.

DISCOVERY Y M C A. see *SOCIAL SERVICES AND WELFARE*

790.3　　　　　SP
DON BALON. 1975. w. Avda. Diagonal 435, 1o, 2A, 08036 Barcelona, Spain. TEL 93-2092000. FAX 93-2092611. Dir. Juan Pedro Martinez.

796.332　　　　US　　ISSN 1054-2191
DON HEINRICH'S COLLEGE FOOTBALL. a. $7.95. Preview Publishing, 100 W. Harrison, N. Tower, 5th Fl., Seattle, WA 98119. TEL 206-282-2322. FAX 206-284-2083.

796.332　　　　US　　ISSN 1054-2221
DON HEINRICH'S PRO PREVIEW. a. $7.95. Preview Publishing, 100 W. Harrison, N. Tower, 5th Fl., Seattle, WA 98119. TEL 206-282-2322. FAX 206-284-2083.
  Description: Previews the upcoming NFL season from an insider's viewpoint; includes statistics, analyses, strategies.

796.355　　　　US
EAGLE (COLORADO SPRINGS). 1932. 4/yr. $15. United States Field Hockey Association, Inc., USFHA National Office, 1750 E. Boulder St., Colorado Springs, CO 80909. TEL 719-578-4567. FAX 719-632-0979. Ed. Linda Asher. adv.; charts; illus.; circ. 5,000. **Indexed:** Sportsearch.
  Description: Information on field hockey and on the activities of the association.

796.323　　　　US　　ISSN 0195-0223
EASTERN BASKETBALL MAGAZINE. 1976. fortn. $37. Eastern Basketball Publishers, 7 May Ct., W. Hempstead, NY 11552. TEL 516-483-9495. Ed. Ralph T. Pollio. circ. 52,000.

796.332　　　　UK
EASTERN FOOTBALL NEWS. 1913. w. £0.17. Eastern Counties Newspaper Ltd., Prospect House, Rouen Rd., Norwich NR1 1RE, England. Ed. K. Peel. adv.
  Description: Covers soccer teams and matches.

796.334　　　　JA
ELEVEN/IREBUN. (Text in Japanese) 1971. m. 6240 Yen. Nihon Sports Publishing Co. Ltd., 2-6, 2-chome, Hakusan, Bunkyo-ku, Tokyo, Japan. Ed. Noritake Tezuka.
  Description: Discusses soccer teams and matches.

796.334　　　　DK　　ISSN 0109-1417
ENGELSK FODBOLD. 1982. m. membership. Supporters of English Football, c/o Kim Madsen, Faegangsvej 3, Boennerup Strand, 8585 Glaesborg, Denmark. illus.

796.352　　　　UK
ENGLISH AMATEUR GOLF. 11/yr. £20. (English Golf Union) Fore Golf Publications Ltd., c/o the Secretary, 1-3 Upper King St., Leicester LE1 6XF, England. FAX 0533-471322. Ed. K. Wricht. adv.; bk.rev.; circ. 10,000.
  Incorporates: Golf Course (ISSN 0953-6043); **Supersedes:** Golf News and Fixtures; English Golf Union. News and Fixtures (ISSN 0300-4260) Formerly (until 1987): Greenkeeper; Incorporates: Golf Greenkeeping; Which was formerly: Golf Greenkeeping and Course Maintenance; British Golf Greenkeeper (ISSN 0007-0742).

796.334　　　　UK
EUROPEAN CUPS; who won, which, when, where. 1988. a. £12.95. Kenneth Mason Publications Ltd., 12 North St., Emsworth, Hants PO10 7DQ, England. TEL 0243-377977. FAX 0243-379136. Ed. Ron Hockings.

796.3　　　　　GW
EUROVOLLEY MAGAZINE. (Text in English and French) 1984. q. DM.35($20) European Volleyball Confederation, Stiftung Deutscher Volleyball, Carl-Zeiss-Ring 17, 8045 Ismaning, Germany. TEL 089-965086. FAX 089-963831. circ. 10,000.

796.3　　　　　UK
EVENING TIMES WEE RED BOOK; the football annual. 1920. a. 80p. George Outram & Co. Ltd., 195 Albion St., Glasgow G1 1HP, Scotland. TEL 041-552-6255. FAX 041-553-1355. TELEX 779818. Ed. George McKechnie. adv.; circ. 40,000.

796.352　　　　US　　ISSN 0194-2387
EXECUTIVE GOLFER. 1972. bi-m. $27.50. Pazdur Publishing Co., 2171 Campus Dr., Irvine, CA 92715. TEL 714-752-6474. FAX 714-752-0398. Ed. Edward F. Pazdur. adv.; bk.rev.; illus.; circ. 125,000. **Indexed:** Sportsearch.
  Formerly: Country Club Golfer.

796.334　　　　SZ
F I F A. HANDBOOK. a. 40 Fr. Federation Internationale de Football Association, P.O. Box 85, CH-8030 Zurich, Switzerland. TEL 01-555400. FAX 01-556239. TELEX 817240 FIF CH. Ed.Bd.
  Description: Contains directory of committees and international referees as well as laws, association and competitions regulations plus guides for referees. Focuses on football (soccer).

796.334　　　　SZ
F I F A. OLYMPIC FOOTBALL TOURNAMENT. (Subseries of: F I F A. Technical Studies) (Text in English, French, German, Spanish) 1980. quadrennial. 20 Fr. Federation Internationale de Football Association, P.O. Box 85, CH-8030 Zurich, Switzerland. TEL 01-555400. FAX 01-556239. TELEX 817240 FIF CH. Ed.Bd.

764.334　　　　SZ
F I F A. TECHNICAL REPORTS. (Series of: World Cup, World Youth Championship, U-17 World Tournament and Olympic World Tournament) (Text in English, French, German, Spanish) irreg. price varies. Federation Internationale de Football Association, P.O. Box 85, CH-8030 Zurich, Switzerland. TEL 01-555400. FAX 01-556239. TELEX 817240 FIF CH. Ed.Bd.
  Formerly: F I F A. Technical Notes.

796.334　　　　SZ
F I F A. U-17 WORLD TOURNAMENT. (Subseries of: F I F A. Technical Studies) (Text in English, French, German, Spanish) 1985. biennial. 20 Fr. Federation Internationale de Football Association, P.O. Box 85, CH-8030 Zurich, Switzerland. TEL 01-555400. FAX 01-556239. TELEX 817240 FIF CH. Ed.Bd.

796.334　　　　SZ
F I F A. WORLD CUP. (Text in English, French, German, Spanish) 1978. quadrennial. 80 Fr. Federation Internationale de Football Association, P.O. Box 85, CH-8030 Zurich, Swizerland. TEL 01-555400. FAX 01-556239. TELEX 817240 FIF CH. Ed.Bd.
  Description: Includes official reports of matches.

796.334　　　　SZ
F I F A. WORLD YOUTH CHAMPIONSHIP. Variant title: F I F A Coca-Cola Cup. (Subseries of: F I F A. Technical Studies) (Text in English, French, German, Spanish) 1981. biennial. price varies. Federation Internationale de Football Association, P.O. Box 85, CH-8030 Zurich, Switzerland. TEL 01-555400. FAX 01-556239. TELEX 817240 FIF CH. Ed.Bd.

746.334　　　　SZ
F I F A MAGAZINE. (Text in English, French, German, Spanish) irreg. 3-4/yr. 50 Fr. for Europe (foreign 80 Fr.). Federation Internationale de Football Association, P.O. Box 85, CH-8030 Zurich, Switzerland. TEL 01-555400. FAX 01-556239. TELEX 817240 FIF CH. (Co-publisher: Unesco) Ed.Bd. **Indexed:** Sportsearch (1986-).
  Description: Provides information on federation activities.

796.334　　　　SZ
F I F A NEWS. (Editions in English, French, German, Spanish) 1963. m. 50 Fr. for Europe (foreign 80 Fr.). Federation Internationale de Football Association, P.O. Box 85, CH-8030 Zurich, Switzerland. TEL 01-555400. FAX 01-556239. TELEX 817240. bk.rev.; circ. 12,000.
  Supersedes: F I F A Official Bulletin (ISSN 0427-8321)

FANTASY BASEBALL. see *HOBBIES*

796.332　　　　US
FANTASY FOOTBALL. 1987. a. $4.95 ($5.95 in Canada). Preview Publishing, 100 W. Harrison, N. Tower, 5th Fl., Seattle, WA 98119. TEL 206-282-2322. FAX 206-284-2083.

796.357　　　　US
FASTPITCH SOFTBALL NEWS BULLETIN. 8/yr. $10 in U.S.; Canada and Mexico $20. Box 5331, Bethlehem, PA 18015.

796　　　　　　GW
FAUSTBALL. 1956. m. DM.7.20 (foreign DM.13.80). Deutscher Faustball-Verband, Grosse Plauensche Str. 17, 8010 Dresden, Germany. (Subscr. to: Buchexport, Postfach 160, 7010 Leipzig, Germany) Ed. Frank Stein.

796　　　　　　FR　　ISSN 0071-4267
FEDERATION INTERNATIONALE DE RUGBY AMATEUR. ANNUAIRE. 1965. a. free. International Amateur Rugby Federation, 7 Cite d'Antin, 75009 Paris, France. FAX 45-26-19-19. TELEX 660787. adv.; circ. 700 (controlled).

796　　　　　　GW　　ISSN 0323-3189
FEDERBALL.* m. DM.13.80. Saarlaendischer Badminton Verband, Saarufestr. 16, 6600 Saarbruecken, Germany.

796.332　　　　UK
FIRST DOWN. w. Mediawatch Ltd., Spendlove Centre, Charlbury, Oxford OX7 3PQ, England. TEL 011-44-608-811266. FAX 011-44-608-811830. adv.; circ. 502,084.
  Description: Covers American football, including detailed game reviews and previews, player and team profiles and news from the USA, the UK and Europe.

796.334　　　　US
FLAG & TOUCH FOOTBALL RULEBOOK AND OFFICIAL'S MANUAL. 1983. biennial. $5. National Intramural Recreational Sports Association, 850 S.W. 15th St., Corvallis, OR 97333-4145. TEL 503-737-2088. FAX 503-737-2026. Eds. Bruce L. Maurer, Jim Potter.
  Description: Provides football rules and information manual for game officials.

796.352　　　　US
FLORIDA GOLF. bi-m. Intermountain Publishing Corp., 1750 S. Brentwood Blvd., Ste. 801, St. Louis, MO 63144. TEL 314-961-1504. FAX 314-961-6249. Ed. James Achenbach.

796.352　　　　US
FLORIDA GOLF REPORTER. 1989. 6/yr. $9.95. Golf Reporter Enterprises Inc., Box 951422, Lake Mary, FL 32795-1422. FAX 407-767-5748. Ed. Mike Jamison. adv.; circ. 20,000 (controlled).
  Description: Covers all state amateur and all PGA section golf events in Florida. Includes travel tips and updates on new courses and real estate instruction.

796.352　　　　US
FLORIDA GOLFER. 1987. m. $17.50. Florida Golfer, Inc., 201 S. Airport Rd., Naples, FL 33942. TEL 813-643-4994. FAX 813-643-6581. adv.
  Description: Covers current and upcoming events. Profiles amateur and professional golfers.

SPORTS AND GAMES — BALL GAMES

796.334   US
FOOTBAG WORLD. 1983. q. $5 (foreign $15). World Footbag Association, 1317 Washington Ave., Ste. 7, Golden, CO 80401. TEL 303-278-9797. FAX 303-278-9841. Ed. Bruce Guettich. adv.; bk.rev.; circ. 5,000. (back issues avail.) Indexed: Sportsearch (1986-).
Description: Covers footbag games and its players. Includes a calendar of events, tournament results, stories, coaching advice and health tips.

796.332   US
FOOTBALL ACTION. 1975. s-a. $4.95. Sports Eye, Inc., 18 Industrial Park Dr., Port Washington, NY 11050. TEL 800-247-2923. Ed. Craig Ellenport. adv.
Description: Covers sports betting.

796.332   UK   ISSN 0071-724X
FOOTBALL ASSOCIATION YEAR BOOK. 1979. a. £5.99. Pelham Books Ltd., 27 Wrights Lane, London W8 5TZ, England. TEL 071-416-3200. FAX 071-416-3293. adv. Indexed: Br.Hum.Ind.
Description: Reviews of the English season plus fixtures for the forthcoming one.

FOOTBALL BASKETBALL & HOCKEY COLLECTOR. see *HOBBIES*

796.332   US   ISSN 0163-6200
GV955
FOOTBALL CASE BOOK. a. $2.75. National Federation of State High School Associations, 11724 N.W. Plaza Circle, Box 20626, Kansas City, MO 64195-0626. TEL 816-464-5400. FAX 816-464-5571.

796.334   US   ISSN 0015-6760
FOOTBALL DIGEST. 1971. 10/yr. $22 (foreign $30). Century Publishing Co., 990 Grove St., Evanston, IL 60201-4370. TEL 708-491-6440. (Subscr. to: Box 571, Mt. Morris, IL 61054-0571. TEL 800-877-5893) Ed. Michael K. Herbert. adv.; bk.rev.; illus.; circ. 200,000. (also avail. in microform from UMI; reprint service avail. from UMI) Indexed: Sports Per.Ind., Sportsearch.
Description: For serious adult football fans who want the statistics, features and excitement behind pro and college football.

796.332   US   ISSN 0364-8273
GV955.5.N35
FOOTBALL FORECAST (YEAR). a. Lexington Library, Inc., 355 Lexington Ave., New York, NY 10017. TEL 212-973-3200. FAX 212-986-5926. Ed. Stephen Ciacciarelli. adv.; charts; illus.

796.332   US   ISSN 0069-5548
FOOTBALL GUIDE. 1963. a. $2.50. Kwik-Fax Books (Subsidiary of: Martin Frederick, Inc.), Box 14613, Surfside Beach, SC 29587. TEL 803-238-3513. Ed. Malcolm DeWitt. circ. 1,000,0000.
Formerly: College and Pro Football Guide.

796.332   US
FOOTBALL HANDBOOK. biennial. $2.75. National Federation of State High School Associations, 11724 N.W. Plaza Circle, Box 20626, Kansas City, MO 64195-0626. TEL 816-464-5400. FAX 816-464-5571.

796.332   US
FOOTBALL NEWS. 1939. w. (during season). $34.95 for 20 nos. Football News Co., 17820 E. Warren, Detroit, MI 48224. TEL 313-881-9554. Ed. Matt Marsom. adv.; bk.rev.; stat.; circ. 86,000. (tabloid format)

796.332   US
FOOTBALL OFFICIALS HANDBOOK. biennial. $2.75. National Federation of State High School Associations, 11724 N.W. Plaza Circle, Box 20626, Kansas City, MO 64195-0626. TEL 816-464-5400. FAX 816-464-5571.

796.332   US
FOOTBALL OFFICIALS MANUAL. biennial. $2.75. National Federation of State High School Associations, 11724 N.W. Plaza Circle, Box 20626, Kansas City, MO 64195-0626. TEL 816-464-5400. FAX 816-464-5571.

796.332   US   ISSN 1054-0164
FOOTBALL PREVIEW (YEAR). a. Lexington Library, Inc., 355 Lexington Ave., New York, NY 10017. TEL 212-973-3200. FAX 212-986-5926. Ed. Stephen Ciacciarelli. adv.; charts; illus.
Formerly: N F L Preview (Year).

796.334   AT   ISSN 0015-6795
FOOTBALL RECORD. 1912. w. (30/yr., Apr.-Sep.). Aus.$60. Australian Football League, MCG, Jarra Park, Jolimont, Vic. 3002, Australia. Ed. Greg Hobbs. adv.; bk.rev.; charts; stat.; circ. 100,000.

796.334   UK
FOOTBALL REFEREE. 1974. 8/yr. £0.40 per no. Referees' Association, Westhill Rd., Coundon, Coventry, West Midlands CV6 2AD, England. TEL 0203-601701. FAX 0203-601556. Ed. Paul Gresty. adv.; bk.rev.; circ. 8,000 (controlled). (tabloid format)
Description: Discusses soccer matches and teams, and refereeing matters.

796.332   US   ISSN 0071-7258
GV939.A1
FOOTBALL REGISTER. 1966. a. $10.95. Sporting News Publishing Co., 1212 N. Lindbergh Blvd., St. Louis, MO 63132. TEL 314-997-7111. Eds. Howard M. Balzer, Barry Siegel.

796.332   US
FOOTBALL RULEBOOK. a. $2.75. National Federation of State High School Associations, 11724 N.W. Plaza Circle, Box 20626, Kansas City, MO 64195-0626. TEL 816-464-5400. FAX 816-464-5571.

796.332   US
FOOTBALL RULES - SIMPLIFIED AND ILLUSTRATED. a. $2.75. National Federation of State High School Associations, 11724 N.W. Plaza Circle, Box 20626, Kansas City, MO 64195-0626. TEL 816-464-5400. FAX 816-464-5571.

796.332   AT
FOOTBALL TIMES. 1976. w. (Mar.-Oct.). Aus.$55. Messenger Press, 1 Baynes Pl., Port Adelaide, S.A. 5015, Australia. TEL 08-475722. FAX 08-475267. (Subscr. to: P.O. Box 197, Port Adelaide, SA, Australia) Ed. Ashley Hornsey. adv.; bk.rev.; circ. 12,000. (back issues avail.)

796.334   UK
FOOTBALL WEEKLY NEWS. 1979. w. £25. Websters Publications Ltd., Onslow House, 60-66 Saffron Hill, London EC1N 8AY, England. Ed. Paul Parish. circ. 60,000.
Description: Discusses soccer matches and teams.

796.352   US   ISSN 0300-8509
FORE. 1968. bi-m. $1. Southern California Golf Association, 3740 Cahuenga Blvd., North Hollywood, CA 91604. TEL 818-980-3630. FAX 818-980-1808. Ed. Robert D. Thomas. adv.; bk.rev.; illus.; stat.; circ. 130,000. Indexed: Sportsearch.

796.332   US
▼**FOREST DAVIS' SOUTHERN FOOTBALL RECRUITING.** 1990. a. Box 94428, Birmingham, AL 35220. TEL 205-854-4785.

796.333   FR
FRANCE FOOTBALL. 12/yr. 415 F. Amaury Group, 4 rue Rouget-de-Lisle, 92137 Issy-les-Moulineaux Cedex, France. TEL 1-40-93-20-20. FAX 1-40-93-20-08. TELEX 203 004. illus.; circ. 158,553. Indexed: Sportsearch.
Formerly: Football Magazine.

796.3   FR
FRANCE TENNIS DE TABLE. 1944. m. 255 F. Federation Francaise de Tennis de Table, 4 rue Guillot, 92120 Montrouge, France. FAX 42-53-85-96. Ed. Jean Devys. adv.; circ. 5,000. Indexed: Sportsearch (1977-).

796   GW   ISSN 0009-9600
FUSSBALL CLUB PFORZHEIM. CLUB-NACHRICHTEN. 1952. m. membership. J. Esslinger Druckerei und Verlag, Poststr. 5, 7530 Pforzheim, Germany. adv.; circ. 1,500.

796.334   GW
FUSSBALL-WELTZEITSCHRIFT. 1986. 4/yr. DM.80 (foreign DM.98). International Federation of Football History and Statistics, Graf-von-Galen-Str. 72, 6200 Wiesbaden, Germany.
Formerly: 11 - Zeitschrift fuer Internationale Fussball-Geschichte und -Statistik.

796.07   GW   ISSN 0016-3228
DER FUSSBALLTRAINER. 1950. m. DM.55.80. Achalm-Verlag, Postfach 1642, 7410 Reutlingen, Germany. TEL 07121-302590. adv.; bk.rev.; illus.; index; circ. 3,500.
Description: Devoted to news and information for soccer trainers and coaches. Articles cover various aspects of soccer, tips for training, tactics, personal stories.

796.334   GW   ISSN 0174-6227
FUSSBALLTRAINING. 1983. m. DM.64.80 (foreign DM.69.60). Philippka-Verlag, Postfach 6540, 4400 Muenster, Germany. TEL 0251-23005-0. FAX 0251-23005-99. circ. 17,000. (back issues avail.)

796.332   FI
FUTARI. 8/yr. Erikoislehedt Oy Business Publications, P.O. Box 16, SF-00381 Helsinki, Finland. Ed. Matti Sovijaervi. circ. 58,697.

796.334   GW   ISSN 0323-8407
FUWO. 1949. 2/w. DM.78. Sportverlag GmbH, Neustaedtische Kirchstr. 15, 1086 Berlin, Germany. TEL 030-2212-215. FAX 030-2292920.

796.352   US
G C A NEWSLETTER. 10/yr. membership. Golf Course Association, 8030 Cedar, Ste. 228, Minneapolis, MN 55425. TEL 612-854-8482.

796.332   US
GIANTS EXTRA. 30/yr. $29.95. Giants Extra, 927 Washington Ave., N., Green Brook, NJ 08812. TEL 908-968-0033. Eds. Bobby Duhon, Chuck Mercein. illus.; stat.
Description: Features previews of games, player interviews, statistics of the team.

796.332   US
THE GIANTS NEWSWEEKLY. Short title: T G N. 1981. w. (Aug.-Jan.), m. (Feb.-July). $27.95. Pro Publishing, Inc., Box 816, Red Bank, NJ 07701. TEL 800-562-2198. Ed. Rick Maddock. adv.; illus.; stat.; circ. 66,000.
Description: News of the Giants from training camp through regular season.

796.323   IT
GIGANTI DEL BASKET. 1966. bi-m. L.100000. Conti Editore S.p.A., Via del Lavoro 7, 40068 San Lazzaro di Savena (Bologna), Italy. Ed. Dario Colombo. adv.; bk.rev.; circ. 97,000.
Description: Discusses various aspects of basketball.

796.334 796.962   CS
GOL. 1968. w. 130 Kcs.($78) Olympia a.s., Klimentska 1, 115 88 Prague 1, Czechoslovakia. (Dist. by: Artia, Ve Smeckach 30, 111 27 Prague 1, Czechoslovakia) Ed. Jiri Malej. illus.; index; circ. 55,000.
Description: Focuses on soccer and hockey.

796.352   NE
GOLF. 1936. m. fl.47.50. Media Bloemendaal B.V., P.B. 135, 2060 AC Bloemendaal, Netherlands. TEL 028-270044. FAX 028-274084. Ed. J.K. Kokke. adv.; charts; illus.; circ. 7,000. Indexed: Sportsearch.
Former titles: Golf Benelux; Golf (ISSN 0017-1727)

796.352   US   ISSN 0017-1808
GV961
GOLF. 1959. m. $19.94. Times Mirror Magazines, Inc., 2 Park Ave., New York, NY 10016. TEL 212-779-5000. (Subscr. to: Box 2786, Boulder, CO 80302) Ed. George Peper. adv.; illus.; circ. 878,869. (also avail. in microform from UMI; reprint service avail. from UMI) Indexed: Access, Mag.Ind., Phys.Ed.Ind., PMR, Sports Per.Ind., Sportsearch (1974-). Key Title: Golf Magazine (New York).

796.352   DK   ISSN 0902-8927
GOLF. 1943. 8/yr. DKK 215. Dansk Golf Union, Golfsvinget 12, 2625 Vallensbaek, Denmark. TEL 45-42-64-06-66. FAX 45-43-62-9193. Ed. Poul Bjerrum. adv.; bk.rev.; illus.; circ. 25,000. Indexed: Sportsearch.

796.352   US
GOLF BOOK OF RECORDS. a. Billian Publishing, Inc., 2100 Powers Ferry Rd., Ste. 300, Atlanta, GA 30339. TEL 404-955-5656. FAX 404-952-0669.

SPORTS AND GAMES — BALL GAMES

796.352 658   UK   ISSN 0267-1166
GOLF CLUB MANAGEMENT & EQUIPMENT NEWS.* 1933. bi-m. £30. Association of Golf Club Secretaries, Woodbury House, Jouldings Lane, Farley Hill, Reading, Berks RG1 1UR, England. Ed. N.G. Osman. adv.; bk.rev.; circ. 2,500. **Indexed:** Sportsearch.

796.352   US
GOLF CLUBMAKER. q. membership only. Professional Golf Club Repairmen's Association, 2053 Harvard Ave., Dunedin, FL 34698. TEL 813-733-4348. adv.; illus.; pat.; stat.; circ. 1,000. **Indexed:** Sportsearch (1984-).
Description: Provides information on repair and maintenance. Includes developments in the industry and association as well as research results.

GOLF COURSE BUILDERS OF AMERICA DIRECTORY. see *BUILDING AND CONSTRUCTION*

796.352   US   ISSN 0192-3048
GV975   CODEN: GCMAEA
GOLF COURSE MANAGEMENT. 1926. m. $30 (foreign $42). Golf Course Superintendents Association of America, 1421 Research Park Dr., Lawrence, KS 66049. TEL 913-841-2240. FAX 913-832-4466. Ed. Clay Loyd. adv.; illus.; circ. 24,000. **Indexed:** Sportsearch (1979-).
Former titles: Golf Superintendent (ISSN 0017-1840); Golf Course Reporter.

796.352   US
GOLF COURSE MANAGEMENT LETTER. irreg. membership. Golf Course Association, 8030 Cedar, Ste. 228, Minneapolis, MN 55425. TEL 612-854-8482.

796.352   US
GOLF COURSE NEWS. 1989. 9/yr. United Publications, Inc. (St. Petersburg), 7901 Fourth St., Ste. 311, St. Petersburg, FL 33702. TEL 813-576-7077. adv.; circ. 20,000.
Description: Provides information on golf course management and maintenance for supervisors, golf directors, architects, developers and builders.

658   US   ISSN 0436-1474
GV975
GOLF COURSE SUPERINTENDENTS ASSOCIATION OF AMERICA. MEMBERSHIP DIRECTORY; who's who in golf course management. Spine title: G C S A A Membership Directory. a. Golf Course Superintendents Association of America, 1421 Research Park Dr., Lawrence, KS 66049. TEL 913-841-2240. FAX 913-832-4466. Ed. Clay Loyd. circ. 10,300. Key Title: Membership Directory of the Golf Course Superintendents Association of America.

796.352   US   ISSN 0072-4947
GOLF COURSE SUPERINTENDENTS ASSOCIATION OF AMERICA. PROCEEDINGS OF THE INTERNATIONAL GOLF COURSE CONFERENCE AND SHOW. a. $50 to non-members. Golf Course Superintendents Association of America, 1421 Research Park Dr., Lawrence, KS 66049. TEL 913-841-2240. FAX 913-832-4466. Ed. Clay Loyd. circ. 4,500.

796.352   US
▼**GOLF DEVELOPMENT MAGAZINE.** 1991. m. $24. Crittenden Research, Inc., Box 1150, Novato, CA 94948. TEL 415-382-2406. FAX 415-382-2416. Ed. Casey Elston. adv.: B&W page $1695, color page $2295; trim 8 1/2 x 11. circ. 15,000.
Description: For owners, developers, investors and architects involved in the building of golf courses and resorts.

796.352   US   ISSN 0017-176X
GOLF DIGEST. (Editions in various languages) 1950. m. $23.94. New York Times Company Magazine Group, Sports - Leisure Division, 5520 Park Ave., Box 395, Trumbull, CT 06611-0395. TEL 203-373-7000. Ed. Jerry Tarde. adv.; bk.rev.; charts; illus.; tr.lit.; circ. 1,400,000. (also avail. in microfilm from UMI; back issues avail). **Indexed:** Consum.Ind., Phys.Ed.Ind., PMR, Sports Per.Ind., Sportsearch (1974-).
Description: Gives advice from players and experienced teachers.

796.352   IT
GOLF DIGEST ITALIA. 1981. 8/yr. L.63000 (typically set in Oct.). Casa Editrice Scode S.p.A., Corso Monforte 36, 20122 Milan, Italy. TEL 02-76006973. FAX 02-76004905. TELEX 324685 SCODE I. Ed. Carlo Gandini. adv.; bk.rev.; illus.; circ. 15,000.

796.352   FR
GOLF EN FRANCE; guide des terrains de golf francais. 1969. a. 90 F. Éditions Person, 34 rue de Penthievre, 75008 Paris, France.

796.352   FR   ISSN 0040-3458
GOLF EUROPEEN. 1914. 12/yr. 360 F. Golf European Publications, 5 rue Bellini, 92800 Puteaux, France. FAX 47-76-45-23. Ed. Andre J. Lafaurie. adv.; bk.rev.; illus.; circ. 29,000. **Indexed:** Sportsearch.
Formerly: Tennis et Golf.

796.352   US
GOLF FOR WOMEN. 1988. bi-m. $14.97. Meredith Corporation, 1716 Locust St., Des Moines, IA 50336. TEL 515-284-2484. FAX 515-284-2700. adv.; circ. 241,000.
Description: For women interested in learning more about and improving in golf. Covers instruction, equipment, LPGA tournaments, fashion and professional advice.

796.352   US
GOLF GEORGIA.* 1988. q. Seventy Two, Inc., 3702 Stonewall Dr. N.W., Atlanta, GA 30339-3311. TEL 404-953-3998. adv.; circ. 57,812.
Description: Features resorts, travel, golf course real estate projects and country club news.

794.6   CN
GOLF GUIDE. 1984. a. Can.$4.95. Sylvester Publications Ltd., Postal Bag 5022, Red Deer, Alta. T4N 6A1, Canada. TEL 403-347-4660. Ed. Donald C. Sylvester. adv.; illus.; circ. 40,000. (back issues avail.)
Former titles: Golf Courses of Alberta; Alberta Golf Guide; Incorporates: British Columbia Golf Guide.
Description: Directory of more than 600 golf courses in British Columbia, Alberta and Saskatchewan.

796.352   UK   ISSN 0263-4066
GOLF GUIDE - WHERE TO PLAY AND WHERE TO STAY. 1977. a. £6.99. F.H.G. Publications Ltd., Abbey Mill Business Centre, Seedhill, Paisley PA1 1JN, Scotland. TEL 041-887 0428. adv.; stat.; index; circ. 12,000.

796.352   US
GOLF ILLUSTRATED. 1914. 10/yr. $15. V P International, 5050 N. 40th St., Phoenix, AZ 85018. TEL 602-957-4646. Ed. Al Barkow. adv.; bk.rev.; illus.; circ. 450,000. **Indexed:** Sports Per.Ind.
Description: Covers all aspects of the game of golf including equipment, instruction, travel, fashion, fitness, etc.

796.352   AT
GOLF IN VICTORIA. 1959. 10/yr. Aus.$14. (Victorian Golf Association) V I P Printing Pty. Ltd., 43 De Haviland Rd., Mordialloc, Vic. 3195, Australia. TEL 03-8896731. (Subscr. to: Victorian Golf Association, 15 Bardolph St., Burwood, Vic. 3125, Australia) Ed. Garry Mansfield. adv.; circ. 15,000.

796.352   US
GV962
GOLF INDEX. 1980. s-a. $40. Ingledue Travel Publications, 444 Burchett St., Glendale, CA 91203. TEL 818-247-5530. FAX 818-247-5535. Ed. Ronald Ingledue. adv.; circ. 10,000.
Formerly (until 1992): International Golf Directory (ISSN 0272-1775)

796   US   ISSN 0160-6824
HD9993.G65
GOLF INDUSTRY.* 1975. 9/yr. $27. Sterling Southeast Inc., 3230 W. Commercial Blvd., No. 250, Fort Lauderdale, FL 33309-3451. TEL 305-893-8771. FAX 305-893-8783. TELEX 510-6009280. Ed. Jerry Renninger. adv.; circ. 16,692 (controlled). **Indexed:** Sportsearch (1979-).

796.352   US
▼**GOLF INTERNATIONAL MAGAZINE.*** 1990. bi-m. $19.95. Golf International, Inc., 2796 Quail St., Lakewood, CO 80215-7138. TEL 303-779-4803. FAX 303-779-9431. Ed. Jennifer C. Phillips. adv.; circ. 55,000.
Description: For the golf industry, from the novice to the professional. Features include PGA and LPGA player profiles, instruction, apparel and equipment reviews, and the best courses and resorts worldwide.

796.352   IT
GOLF ITALIANO. m. $90. Flaminia Editrice, Via A. Pollaiolo, 3, 00197 Rome, Italy.

796.352   US   ISSN 0017-1794
GV961
GOLF JOURNAL. 1947. 8/yr. $8. United States Golf Association, Golf House, Far Hills, NJ 07931. TEL 908-234-2300. Ed. David Earl. bk.rev.; illus.; index; circ. 285,000. (also avail. in microform from UMI; reprint service avail. from UMI) **Indexed:** Sports Per.Ind., Sportsearch.
Formerly: U S G A Golf Journal.

796.352   GW
GOLF JOURNAL. m. DM.67.20. Atlas Verlag und Werbung GmbH, Sonnenstr. 29, 8000 Munich 2, Germany. TEL 089-552142-0. FAX 089-553114. Ed. Ulrich Kaiser. adv.; bk.rev.; charts; illus.; circ. 9,350.
Incorporates (1972-1988): Golf - Contact.

796.352   JA
GOLF MAGAZINE. 1952. m. 10920 Yen. Golf Magazine Sha, 1-63 Kanda-Jimbo Cho, Chiyoda-ku, Tokyo, Japan. Ed. Shingo Hama.

796.352   IT
GOLF NEWS. (Text in Italian) 1982. 10/yr. L.75000 (foreign L.150000). Nuove Edizioni Internazionali, Via Pergolesi 29, 20124 Milan, Italy. TEL 02-66987700. FAX 02-6709167. (Dist by: Parrini Distribuzione, Piazza Indipendenza, 11B Rome, Italy) Ed. Pat Nesi. adv.; circ. 22,000.
Formerly (until 1989): Golf Magazine.

796.352   KE
GOLF NEWS. bi-m. free. Golf Publications, P.O. Box 31283, Nairobi, Kenya.

796.352   US
GOLF NEWS MAGAZINE. 1984. m. Dan & Joan Poppers, Eds. & Pubs., Box 1040, Rancho Mirage, CA 92270. TEL 619-324-8333. FAX 619-324-8011. adv.; circ. 28,000.
Description: Covers golf in Southern California. Provides news of events, tournaments, and courses.

GOLF PRO MERCHANDISER. see *BUSINESS AND ECONOMICS — Marketing And Purchasing*

796.352   US
GOLF PRODUCT NEWS. 6/yr. 15-22 Fair Lawn Ave., Fair Lawn, NJ 07410. TEL 201-796-6031. FAX 201-796-4562. Ed. Steven Witt. adv.; circ. 17,000.

GOLF PROPERTY. see *REAL ESTATE*

796.352   US
GOLF REPORTER. 6/yr. Box 370, Cornelius, NC 28301-0370. TEL 704-892-7272. Ed. Richard M. Sink, Jr. adv.; circ. 40,000.

796.352   US
GOLF SCENE MAGAZINE. 1987. 5/yr. $9.95. ADmore, Inc., 9701 Gravois Ave., St. Louis, MO 63123. TEL 800-451-0914. FAX 314-638-3880. Ed. Brian Hays. adv.; circ. 10,141.
Description: Local interest items for golfers at private clubs and public courses.

796.352   US   ISSN 0017-1824
GOLF SHOP OPERATIONS. 1963. 10/yr. $72. New York Times Company Magazine Group, Sports - Leisure Division, 5520 Park Ave., Box 395, Trumbull, CT 06611-0395. TEL 203-373-7000. Ed. Lew Fishman. illus.; stat.; circ. 16,000. (tabloid format) **Indexed:** Sportsearch.
Formerly: Pro Shop Operations.

796.352   SI   ISSN 0017-1832
GOLF SINGAPORE REVIEW. 1960. q. S.$4($3) F.G. Salaysay, Ed.& Pub., 455-a East Coast Rd., Singapore, 1542 Singapore. adv.; bk.rev.; circ. 5,000. **Indexed:** Sportsearch.

SPORTS AND GAMES — BALL GAMES

796.352 US
GOLF TIPS. 6/yr. $9.95. Werner Publishing Corporation, 12121 Wilshire Blvd., No.1220, Los Angeles, CA 90025-1175. circ. 125,000. **Indexed:** Sports Per.Ind.

796.352 US ISSN 0191-717X
GV975
GOLF TRAVELER. 1976. bi-m. $12. Golf Card International, Corp., 1137 E. 2100 South, Box 526439, Salt Lake City, UT 84152-6439. TEL 800-453-4260. FAX 801-484-0160. Ed. Annette Holyoak. adv.; bk.rev.; tr.lit.; circ. 72,300. (reprint service avail.)
Description: News about golf activities.

796.352 IT
GOLF WEEK. 1980. 18/yr. 20000. Via Friuli 1, 20090 Buccinasco, Italy. Ed. Enrico Magatti. adv.; circ. 15,000.

796.352 UK ISSN 0017-1883
GOLF WORLD. 1962. m. £38.90. Golf World Ltd., Advance House, 37 Mill Harbour, Isle of Dogs, London E14 9TX, England. FAX 01-538-4106. Ed. Robert Green. adv.; bk.rev.; charts; illus.; stat.; tr.lit.; circ. 106,457. **Indexed:** Sportsearch.

796.352 US ISSN 0017-1891
GV961
GOLF WORLD. 1947. w. (Jan.-Sep.), bi-w. (Oct.-Dec.) $29.94. New York Times Company Magazine Group (Subsidiary of: Sports - Leisure Division), 5520 Park Ave., Box 395, Trumbull, CT 06611-0395. TEL 203-373-7000. Ed. Terry Galvin. adv.; illus.; circ. 128,000. **Indexed:** Sports Per.Ind., Sportsearch (1977-).
Description: Contains news of the game and business of golf.

796.352 GW
GOLF ZEITUNG; Informationen fuer Entscheidungstraeger. 1988. m. DM.120. Verlag Egon Stengl, Triesterstr. 79, 8000 Munich 80, Germany. TEL 089-492097. FAX 089-492727. circ. 1,000. (back issues avail.)

796.352 GW ISSN 0931-573X
GOLFCLUB MAGAZIN. 1972. m. DM.50. Kopp Public, Hohenzollernstr. 33, 3000 Hannover 1, Germany. TEL 511-311041. FAX 511-311043. Ed. Hubert Kopp. adv.: adv.: B&W page DM.5460, color page DM.9960; trim 183 x 250. bk.rev.; circ. 21,009.

796.352 SA ISSN 0017-1913
GOLFER. (Text in Afrikaans, English) 1958. q. R.1.75 for 3 yrs. Transvaal Provincial Golf Association, Box 4645, Johannesburg, South Africa. Eds. Reg Marks, Ken Marks. adv.; bk.rev.; charts; illus.; stat.; circ. 5,000.
Incorporates: Transvaal Golfer.

610 IE
GOLFER'S COMPANION. 1973. 4/yr. £5. Sports Enterprises Ltd., Box 14, Dun Laoghaire, Dublin, Ireland. Ed. Pat Ruddy. adv.; bk.rev.; circ. 20,000.

796 UK ISSN 0072-498X
GOLFER'S HANDBOOK. 1897. a. £21.95. Macmillan Press Ltd., Houndmills, Basingstoke, Hampshire RG21 2XS, England. Ed. Laurence Viney. adv.; circ. 10,000.

796.352 910.2 US
GOLFER'S TRAVEL GUIDE. 1986. s-a. $12.95 per no. R S G Publishing, Inc., Box 612, Plymouth, MI 48170-0612. TEL 313-582-8860. FAX 313-582-3585. Ed. Betty Rasmussen. adv.; circ. 50,000.
Description: Reference to golf courses in the Great Lakes states (Michigan, Ohio, Indiana, Illinois, Wisconsin). Includes information on holes, par, yards and fees of both private and public golf courses.

796.352 CN
GOLFEXPERT. 1989. a. free. Edition Golfex Inc., 16312 boul. Govin West, Montreal, Quebec, Canada. TEL 514-696-7568. FAX 514-696-9779. Ed. Pierre Toupin. adv.; circ. 250,000.

796.352 UK
GOLFING YEAR. 1948. a. £5. (English Golf Union) Creative Press (Reading) Ltd., Portman Rd., Reading, Berks., England. Ed. K. Wright. adv.; bk.rev.; circ. 2,500.

796 GW ISSN 0017-1735
GOLFMAGAZIN. 1961. m. DM.96. Jahr-Verlag GmbH & Co., Burchardstr. 14, 2000 Hamburg 1, Germany. TEL 040-339660. FAX 040-33966208. TELEX 2163485. Ed. Gunther Marks. adv.; bk.rev.; circ. 16,500.
Formerly: Where to Golf in Europe (ISSN 0083-9213)

796.352 US
GOLFWEEK. 1975. w. Turnstile Publications, 220 E. 42nd St., New York, NY 10017. TEL 212-210-0777. Ed. Bob Feeman. adv.; circ. 39,522.
Description: Focuses on golf course real estate, golf travel and other aspects of golf course living.

796.352 US
GOVERNMENT RELATIONS BRIEFING. 1989. m. free. Golf Course Superintendents Association of America, 1421 Research Park Dr., Lawrence, KS 66049. TEL 913-841-2240. FAX 913-832-4466. Ed. Don Bretthauer. circ. 12,000. (back issues avail.)

796.352 635 CN ISSN 0380-3333
GREENMASTER. 1966. 6/yr. Can.$48. (Canadian Golf Superintendents Association - Association Canadienne des Surintendants de Golf) Kenilworth Publishing Inc., 80 W. Beaver Creek, Ste. 18, Richmond Hill, Ont. L4B 1H3, Canada. TEL 416-771-7333. FAX 416-771-7336. Ed. Dennis Mellersh. adv.; bk.rev.; circ. 2,000. **Indexed:** Sportsearch (1981-).

796.332 UK ISSN 0269-0675
GRIDIRON; for the best in american football. 1984. m. £21.95. Mediawatch Ltd., Spendlove Centre, Charlbry, Oxon OX7 3PQ, England. TEL 0608-811266. FAX 0608-811380. Ed. Alan Lees. circ. 20,000. (back issues avail.)

796.352 US
GULF COAST GOLFER. 1984. m. $27. Golfer Magazines, Inc., 9182 Old Katy Rd., Ste. 212, Houston, TX 77055-7432. TEL 713-464-0308. FAX 713-464-0129. Ed. Bob Gray. adv.; bk.rev.; circ. 30,000 (controlled).
Description: Provides information to golfers in South Texas on quality of courses, better playing techniques, upcoming tournaments, and area tournament results. Includes an alphabetical list of golf courses in that region.

796.31 NE ISSN 0017-7180
HANDBAL.* 1942. fortn. fl.7.50($2.50) (Dutch Handball Federation) G.U.Z., St. Jansstraat 1-3, Groningen, Netherlands. Ed. J. Notermans. adv.; circ. 3,500.

796.3 US ISSN 0046-6778
HANDBALL. 1951. bi-m. $22. U S Handball Association, c/o Bob Peters, 930 N. Benton Ave., Tucson, AZ 85711. FAX 602-745-8114. Ed.Bd. adv.; bk.rev.; charts; illus.; circ. 10,000. (also avail. in microform from UMI; reprint service avail. from UMI) **Indexed:** Phys.Ed.Ind., Sports Per.Ind., Sportsearch (1977-).
Formerly: Ace.

796.31 GW
HANDBALL (DORTMUND); Amtliches Jahrbuch des Deutscher Handball-Bundes. 1987. a. DM.7.80. Deutscher Handball-Bund Verlags und Vertriebs GmbH, Westfalendamm 77, 4600 Dortmund 1, Germany. TEL 0231-94248-0.

796 GW ISSN 0138-1296
HANDBALL (RAUGSDORF). m. DM.15.20 (foreign DM.22). Deutscher Handball-Verband, Kurparkallee 114, 1634 Raugsdorf, Germany. (Subscr. to: Buchexport, Postfach 160, 7010 Leipzig, Germany)

790 GW ISSN 0178-2983
HANDBALL MAGAZIN. 1984. m. DM.61.80 (foreign DM.68.40). Philippka-Verlag, Postfach 6540, 4400 Muenster, Germany. TEL 0251-23005-0. FAX 0251-23005-99. Ed. Konrad Honig. circ. 15,000.

790.1 GW ISSN 0172-2476
HANDBALLTRAINING. 1979. m. DM.63.60 (foreign DM.68.40). Philippka-Verlag, Postfach 6540, 4400 Muenster, Germany. TEL 0251-23005-0. FAX 0251-23005-99. Ed. Konrad Honig. circ. 115,000. (back issues avail.)
Formerly: Lehre und Praxis des Handballspiels.

796.325 SW
HANDBOLL. m. (10/yr.). SEK 398. (Svenska Hanbollfoerlaget) Cewe Foerlaget, Box 77, 890 10 Bjaesta, Sweden. (Subscr. to: PK-Banken, Box 365, 891 01 Oernskoelsdvik, Sweden) adv.; circ. 11,700.

796.3 UK ISSN 0085-1566
HOCKEY ASSOCIATION. OFFICIAL HANDBOOK. 1900. a. £5. Hockey Association, 16 Northdown Street, London N1 9BG, England. FAX 071-837-8163. TELEX 8814328-HOCKEY-G. Ed. S. Baines. adv.; index, cum.index; circ. 4,000.

796.3 UK ISSN 0950-9550
HOCKEY DIGEST. 1975. 10/yr. £17. Harrow Press - J N & H Lock & Co Ltd., Unit E6, Aladdin Workspace, 426 Long Dr., Greenford, Middx. UB6 8UH, England. TEL 081-575 3121. FAX 081-575-1320. Ed. Peter J. Luck. adv.; bk.rev.; circ. 6,500. **Indexed:** Sportsearch (1980-).
Incorporates: Hockey Field (ISSN 0018-3008); Indoor Hockey News.
Description: Includes articles, features, club and international news of topical interest to field hockey enthusiasts in Great Britain.

796 920 US ISSN 0090-2292
GV848.5.A1
HOCKEY REGISTER. 1972. a. $10.95. Sporting News Publishing Co., 1212 N. Lindbergh Blvd., St. Louis, MO 63132. TEL 314-997-7111. Ed. Larry Wigge. illus.; stat.

796.323 US ISSN 0749-5285
HOOP - N B A TODAY. 1984. 8/yr. $17.95. (National Basketball Association) Hoop Magazine, Box Hoop, Lowell, MA 01852. TEL 508-452-6310.
Formerly: N B A Today (ISSN 0279-1935)

796.332 378.198 US
HUSKERS ILLUSTRATED. 1981. m. (Jan.-Apr., Aug.); w. (Sep.-Nov.) $39.90. Sports Magazines of America, Inc., 7130 S. Lewis, Ste.210, Tulsa, OK 74136. TEL 918-496-7405. FAX 918-496-7485. (Subscr. to: Box 83222, Lincoln, NE 68501) Ed. M.C. Ross. adv.; circ. 12,000. (back issues avail.)
Description: Carries stories and information on athletics at the University of Nebraska, with special emphasis on football.

796.357 US
I B A REPORT. 1989. bi-m. International Baseball Association, Pan Am Plaza, Ste. 490, 201 S. Capitol Ave., Indianapolis, IN 46225. TEL 317-237-5757. FAX 317-237-5758. TELEX 981853 IBA HEAD UQ.

796.352 917.704 US
▼**ILLINOIS GOLFER'S TRAVEL GUIDE.** 1991. a. $5.95. R S G Publishing, Inc., Box 612, Plymouth, MI 48170-0612. TEL 313-582-8860. FAX 313-582-3585. Ed. Betty Rasmussen.
Description: Presents information on public and private golf courses in Illinois, including address and telephone, course description, facilities, and more.

796.352 917.704 US
▼**INDIANA GOLFER'S TRAVEL GUIDE.** 1991. a. $5.95. R S G Publishing, Inc., Box 612, Plymouth, MI 48170-0612. TEL 313-582-8860. FAX 313-582-3585. Ed. Betty Rasmussen.
Description: Presents information on public and private golf courses in Indiana, including address and telephone, course description, facilities, and more.

796.342 US
INSIDE TENNIS. 1981. m. $12. Inside Tennis, 3561 Lakeshore Ave., Oakland, CA 94610. Ed.Bd. adv.

796.325 US ISSN 1059-8227
INSIDE U S A VOLLEYBALL. 1972. q. $10 (foreign $20). U S A Volleyball, Inc., 2655 Camino del Rio N., Ste. 200, San Diego, CA 92108. FAX 619-299-5522. Ed. Richard Wanninger. adv.; bk.rev.; circ. 60,000.
Formerly: Volleyball U S A.
Description: Reviews activities of the association, U.S. Olympic teams and volleyball in general.

796 US ISSN 0731-8162
GV877
INSIDERS BASEBALL FACT-BOOK. 1976. a. $15. Research Analysis Publications, Box 49213, Los Angeles, CA 90049. Ed. Ronald H. Lewis. charts; stat.; circ. 3,700.

SPORTS AND GAMES — BALL GAMES

793   GW
INTERNATIONAL BASKETBALL FEDERATION. OFFICIAL REPORT OF THE WORLD CONGRESS. 1932. irreg., 14th, 1990, Buenos Aires. International Basketball Federation, Postfach 700607, 8000 Munich 70, Germany. FAX 089-785-3596. circ. 300 (controlled).
   Formerly: International Amateur Basketball Federation. Official Report of the World Congress (ISSN 0534-6622)

796.332   UK   ISSN 0074-610X
INTERNATIONAL FOOTBALL BOOK. 1959. a. £7.95. Souvenir Press Ltd., 43 Great Russell St., London WC1B 3PA, England. TEL 01-580 9307. Ed. Gordon Hallam. circ. 7,000.

INTERNATIONAL JOURNAL OF THERAPEUTIC COMMUNITIES. see *MEDICAL SCIENCES — Psychiatry And Neurology*

796.357   US
INTERNATIONAL SOFTBALL CONGRESS (YEAR) WORLD CHAMPIONSHIP GUIDE. 1953. a. $3. International Softball Congress, 6007 E. Hillcrest Circle, Anaheim Hills, CA 92807. TEL 714-998-5694. FAX 714-921-9327. TELEX 710-111-5864. Ed. Milt Stark. adv.; circ. 10,000.
   Formerly: International Softball Congress (Year) Official Yearbook and Guide.

796.342   US
INTERNATIONAL TENNIS WEEKLY.* 1976. w. $32. Association of Tennis Professionals, 4 Sawgrass Village, Ste. 240, Ponte Vedra, FL 32082. (European office: 4 Ave. Gordon Bennett, 76016, Paris, France) Ed. Temple Pouncey. adv.; circ. 3,400. **Indexed:** Sportsearch (1981-).

796.332 332.6   US
INVESTOR'S GUIDE TO FOOTBALL CARDS. 6/yr. Krause Publications, Inc., 700 E. State St., Iola, WI 54990. TEL 715-445-2214. Ed. Kit Kiefer.

IO. see *ANTHROPOLOGY*

796.332   US
IRON GAME HISTORY. 6/yr. University of Texas at Austin, Todd-McLean Collection, Rm. 217, Gergory Gymnasium, Austin, TX 78712. Eds. Terry & Jan Todd. **Indexed:** Sportsearch (1990-).

794   CN
JOURNAL QUEBEC QUILLES. (Text in French) 1988. 6/yr. Quebec Quilles Enr., C.P. 145, Succ. Longueuil, Quebec, Que. J4K 4Y3, Canada. TEL 514-468-9448. FAX 514-647-6389. Ed. Yves Larocque. adv.; circ. 17,000. (tabloid format)

796.352   US
KANSAS GOLF. q. Intermountain Publishing Corp., 1750 S. Brentwood Blvd., Ste. 801, St. Louis, MO 63144. TEL 314-961-1504. FAX 314-961-6249. Ed. Brad Catt. adv.

794.6   GW
KEGELN UND BOWLING. 1946. m. DM.44. Verlag Wolfgang Wildner, Kaulbachstr. 29, 3548 Arolsen, Germany. TEL 05691-1379. FAX 05691-6587. Ed. Wolfgang Wildner. adv.; bk.rev.; circ. 7,100. (back issues avail.)

796.332   CN
KICK OFF. m. $25. Kick Off Publications, 28-88 South Park Dr., Winnipeg, Man. R3T 2M1, Canada. TEL 204-269-5724. Ed. Will Oliver. adv.; circ. 50,000.

796.334   US
KICKOFF. m. members only. Major Indoor Soccer League Players Association, 2021 L St., N.W., Washington, DC 20036. Ed. Will Bray. circ. 220.
   Description: Covers collective bargaining of the league, player benefits, and soccer news.

796.357   US   ISSN 0075-6385
KNOTTY PROBLEMS OF BASEBALL. 1950. irreg. $6.95. Sporting News Publishing Co., 1212 N. Lindbergh Blvd., St. Louis, MO 63132. TEL 314-997-7111. Ed. Larry Wigge. (reprint service avail. from UMI)

796.342   UK
L T A HANDBOOK. 1980. a. £4.50. Lawn Tennis Association, W. Kensington, Queen's Club, London W14 9EG, England. FAX 01-381-6656. Ed. James Nicholls. adv.; circ. 6,000.
   Former titles: Tennis Great Britain; Lawn Tennis Association Handbook.

796.347   UK   ISSN 0023-7086
LACROSSETALK. 1948. 8/yr. £7.80. All England Women's Lacrosse Association, 4 Western Ct., Bromley St., Digbeth, Birmingham 9, England. TEL 021-7734422. Ed. G. Wilkerson. adv.; illus.; circ. 1,500. **Indexed:** Sports Per.Ind., Sportsearch.
● Also available online.
   Formerly (until 1989): Lacrosse.
   Description: Includes articles and comment on both women's and men's lacrosse in the UK.

796.352   UK
LADY GOLFER'S HANDBOOK. 1894. a. £4.50. Ladies Golf Union, The Scores, St. Andrews, Fife KY16 9AT, Scotland. TEL 0334-75811. FAX 0334-72818. adv.; circ. 3,500.

LANDSCAPE MANAGEMENT GOLF DAILY. see *GARDENING AND HORTICULTURE*

796.323   CC   ISSN 1000-3460
LANQIU/BASKETBALL. (Text in Chinese) 1981. bi-m. $18.50. (Zhongguo Lanqiu Xiehui - China Basketball Society) Renmin Tiyu Chubanshe, 8 Tiyuguan Lu, Chongwen Qu, Beijing 100061, People's Republic of China. TEL 757161. (Dist. in US by: China Books & Periodicals, Inc., 2929 24th St., San Francisco, CA 94110. TEL 415-282-2994) Ed. Mou Zuoyun.

796.3   US
LEGENDS SPORTS MEMORABILIA. bi-m. 2778-J Sweetwater Springs Blvd., Ste. 301, Rancho San Diego, CA 92078. TEL 619-460-9219. FAX 619-464-4353. Ed. Michael Godfrey.

796.3   US
LET'S PLAY SOFTBALL. 1986. 12/yr. $12. Let's Play, Inc., 2721 E. 42nd St., Minneapolis, MN 55406. TEL 612-729-0023. FAX 612-729-0259. adv.; circ. 12,000.
   Description: For players, parents, coaches, fans and officials.

796.332   US
LINDY'S A C C FOOTBALL ANNUAL. (Atlantic Coast Conference) 1987. a. $4.95. D M D Publications, Inc., 2700 Highway 280, Ste. 108, Birmingham, AL 35223. TEL 205-871-1182. Ed. Lindy Davis, Jr. adv.; circ. 25,000.

796.332   US
LINDY'S BIG 8 FOOTBALL ANNUAL. 1987. a. $4.95. D M D Publications, Inc., 2700 Highway 280, Ste. 108, Birmingham, AL 35223. TEL 205-871-1182. Ed. Lindy Davis, Jr. adv.; circ. 20,000.

796.332   US
LINDY'S BIG 10 FOOTBALL ANNUAL. 1987. a. $4.95. D M D Publications, Inc., 2700 Highway 280, Ste. 108, Birmingham, AL 35223. TEL 205-871-1182. Ed. Lindy Davis, Jr. circ. 40,000.

796.332   US
LINDY'S PAC 10 FOOTBALL ANNUAL. 1987. a. $4.95. D M D Publications, Inc., 2700 Highway 280, Ste. 108, Birmingham, AL 35223. TEL 205-871-1182. Ed. Don Borst. adv.; circ. 20,000.

796.332   US
LINDY'S PRO EDITION FOOTBALL ANNUAL. 1987. a. $4.95. D M D Publications, Inc., 2700 Highway 280, Ste. 108, Birmingham, AL 35223. TEL 205-871-1227. Ed. John Delcos. circ. 178,000.

796.332   US
LINDY'S S E C FOOTBALL ANNUAL. (Southeast Conference) 1982. a. $4.95. D M D Publications, Inc., 2700 Highway 280, Ste. 108, Birmingham, AL 35223. TEL 205-871-1182. Ed. Ben Cook. adv.; circ. 100,000.

796.332   US
LINDY'S SOUTHWEST FOOTBALL ANNUAL. a. $4.95. D M D Publications, Inc., 2700 Highway 280, Ste. 108, Birmingham, AL 35223. TEL 205-871-1182. Ed. Robert Cessna. adv.; circ. 20,000.

796.31   US
LOGBOOK (YEAR). a. $12.95. Parrish Publications, Box 23205, Portland, OR 97223. TEL 503-244-8975. Ed. Phil Erwin.

796.352   US
LYNX PLAY GOLF!. 1989. a. $2.50. (Lynx Golf, Inc.) Aqua-Field Publishing Co., Inc., 66 W. Gilbert St., Shrewsbury, NJ 07702. TEL 908-842-8300. Ed. Stephen Ferber. adv.; circ. 135,000.

796.357   US
▼**MAJOR LEAGUE BASEBALL OFFICIAL (YEAR) PREVIEW.** (In 3 regional editions and 1 national edition.) 1990. a. $4.95 per no. Hachette Magazines, Inc., 1633 Broadway, 45th Fl., New York, NY 10009. TEL 212-767-6000. Ed. Barry Shapiro. circ. 250,000.
   Description: Features interviews and profiles and includes complete batting and statistical averages. Each regional issue features a local star on the cover.

796.352   US
▼**MARKET INSIGHT.** 1991. m. membership. Golf Course Superintendents Association of America, Center for Golf Course Management, 1421 Research Park Dr., Lawrence, KS 66049. TEL 913-841-2240. FAX 913-841-2240.

796.352   US
MASSACHUSETTS GOLFER. q. Dunfey Publishing, 190 Park Rd., Weston, MA 02193. TEL 617-891-4300. Ed. Rick Dunfey. circ. 50,000.

796.334   UK
MATCH FOOTBALL. 1979. w. E M A P Pursuit Publications Ltd., Bretton Court, Bretton, Peterborough PE3 8DZ, England. Ed. Paul Stratton. adv.; illus.; circ. 130,170.
   Formerly: Match Weekly.
   Description: World Soccer round-up, "MatchFacts," - all the weekend's results and star ratings; full color posters, star player interviews, competitions; facts and figures.

796.352   US
MET GOLFER. 1983. q. Times Mirror Magazines, Inc., Sports Marketing Group, 2 Park Ave., No.6, New York, NY 10016-5691. TEL 212-779-5000. adv.; circ. 100,000.
   Description: For amateur and professional golfers in the New York metropolitan area. Covers events, tournaments, travel, fashion and personalities.

796.352   US
METRO GOLF. 7/yr. 6926 Willow St., N.W., Washington, DC 20012. TEL 202-882-4653. Ed. Lou DeSabla. circ. 40,000.

796.352   US
MICHIGAN GOLFER. 1980. 6/yr. $9. Great Lakes Sports Publications, Inc., 7990 W. Grand River, Ste. C, Brighton, MI 48116. TEL 313-227-4200. Ed. Terry Moore. circ. 16,000.
   Description: Covers golf events and news; includes calendar of events, technical advice, new products, and travel information.

796.352 917.704   US
MICHIGAN GOLFER'S MAP & GUIDE. 1981. a. $15.95. R S G Publishing, Inc., Box 612, Plymouth, MI 48170-0612. TEL 313-582-8860. FAX 313-582-3585. Ed. Betty Rasmussen. circ. 25,000.
   Description: Presents information on public golf courses in Michigan, N.W. Ohio, and S.W. Ontario, Canada, including address and telephone, course description, facilities, fees, and more.

796.352 917.704   US
▼**MICHIGAN GOLFER'S TRAVEL GUIDE.** 1991. a. $5.95. R S G Publishing, Inc., Box 612, Plymouth, MI 48170-0612. TEL 313-582-8860. FAX 313-582-3585. Ed. Betty Rasmussen. circ. 10,000.
   Description: Presents information on public and private golf courses in Michigan, including address and telephone, course description, facilities, and more.

796.352   US
MIDWEST GOLF NEWS. m. Box 529, Anna, IL 62906. TEL 618-833-2158. Ed. Mike Fitzgerald.

SPORTS AND GAMES — BALL GAMES

796.334 US
▼**MINNESOTA SOCCER TIMES**. 1991. 9/yr. $18. (Minnesota Youth Soccer Association) Publishing Group (Bloomington), 1022 W. 80th St., Bloomington, MN 55420. TEL 612-881-3183. FAX 612-881-2172. adv.; circ. 27,431.
   Description: Covers tournament rules and profiles outstanding players.

796.352 917.704 US
▼**MINNESOTA - WISCONSIN GOLFER'S TRAVEL GUIDE**. 1991. a. $5.95. R S G Publishing, Inc., Box 612, Plymouth, MI 48170-0612. TEL 313-582-8860. FAX 313-582-3585. Ed. Betty Rasmussen.
   Description: Presents information on public and private golf courses in Minnesota and Wisconsin, including address and telephone, course description, facilities, and more.

796.352 US
MISSOURI GOLF. q. Intermountain Publishing Corp., 1750 S. Brentwood Blvd., Ste. 801, St. Louis, MO 63144. TEL 314-961-1504. FAX 314-961-6249. Ed. Warren Mayes.

796.4 US ISSN 0363-2504
GV881
N A G W S GUIDE. SOFTBALL. 1938-1990. a. (American Alliance for Health, Physical Education, Recreation, and Dance, National Association for Girls and Women in Sport) Kendall - Hunt Publishing Co., 2460 Kerber Blvd., Dubuque, IA 52001. TEL 800-338-5578. circ. 8,000. **Indexed:** ERIC.
   Description: Current rules and articles on sport.

796.325 US ISSN 0065-7050
N A G W S GUIDE. VOLLEYBALL. 1938. a. (National Association for Girls and Women in Sport) Kendall - Hunt Publishing Co., 2460 Kerber Blvd., Dubuque, IA 52001. TEL 800-338-5578. circ. 17,000. **Indexed:** ERIC.
   Description: Rules and officiating techniques.

794.6 US
N A I R NEWS. q. membership only. National Association of Independent Resurfacers, c/o Nancy Suprenant, 5806 W. 127th St., Alsip, IL 60658. TEL 708-371-6384.
   Description: Provides association and industry developments for those who resurface bowling lanes.

796.357 US
N C A A BASEBALL. a. $5. National Collegiate Athletic Association, Circulation Department, Box 7347, Overland Park, KS 66207-0347. TEL 913-339-1900. stat.
   Description: Contains individual and team records, and statistical leaders.

796 US ISSN 0736-5209
GV877
N C A A BASEBALL RULES. 1974. a. $3. National Collegiate Athletic Association, Circulation Department, Box 7347, Overland Park, KS 66207-0347. TEL 913-339-1900. illus.
   Former titles: N C A A Baseball Annual Guide; Official National Collegiate Athletic Association Baseball Guide (ISSN 0466-1478)
   Description: Covers official signals, interpretations, and rulings.

796.323 US ISSN 0276-1017
GV885.45
N C A A BASKETBALL. 1923. a. $7.95. National Collegiate Athletic Association, Circulation Department, Box 7347, Overland Park, KS 66207-0347. TEL 913-339-1900. stat.; circ. 12,000.
   Incorporates: N C A A Basketball Records; Formerly (until 1980): Official National Collegiate Athletic Association Basketball Guide.
   Description: Contains individual and team records, statistical leaders, all-America teams, game results from the preceding year, with schedules for the current year.

796.33 US ISSN 0735-5475
GV937
N C A A FOOTBALL. 1969. a. $7.95. National Collegiate Athletic Association, Circulation Department, Box 7347, Overland Park, KS 66207-0347. TEL 913-339-1900. stat.; circ. 4,000.
   Incorporates: N C A A Football Guide; Former titles: N C A A Football Records; College Football Modern Record Book (ISSN 0092-881X)
   Description: Contains individual and team records, statistical leaders, all-America teams, game results from the preceding year, with schedules for the current year.

796.33 US ISSN 0736-5160
GV956.8
N C A A FOOTBALL RULES AND INTERPRETATIONS. 1961. a. $3. National Collegiate Athletic Association, Circulation Department, Box 7347, Overland Park, KS 66207-0347. TEL 913-339-1900. illus.; circ. 24,000.
   Formerly: Official National Collegiate Athletic Association Football Rules and Interpretations (ISSN 0094-5226)
   Description: Covers official signals, interpretations, and rulings.

796.32 US
GV885.45
N C A A MEN'S AND WOMEN'S BASKETBALL RULES AND INTERPRETATIONS. 1967. a. $3. National Collegiate Athletic Association, Circulation Department, Box 7347, Overland Park, KS 66207-0347. TEL 913-339-1900. illus.; circ. 25,000.
   Supersedes: N C A A Men's Basketball Rules and Interpretations (ISSN 0736-5187); Formerly: N C A A Basketball Rules and Interpretations; Official National Collegiate Athletic Association Basketball Rules and Interpretations (ISSN 0163-2817); Official National Collegiate Athletic Association Basketball Rules (ISSN 0094-5234)
   Description: Covers official signals, interpretations, and rulings.

796.32 US
N C A A MEN'S AND WOMEN'S ILLUSTRATED BASKETBALL RULES. a. $3. National Collegiate Athletic Association, Circulation Department, Box 7347, Overland Park, KS 66207-0347. TEL 913-339-1900. illus.
   Former titles: N C A A Men's Illustrated Basketball Rules; N C A A Illustrated Men's Rules (ISSN 0736-5179) & N C A A Illustrated Basketball Rules (ISSN 0272-5754)
   Description: Covers official signals, interpretations, and rulings.

796.334 US
GV943.4
N C A A MEN'S AND WOMEN'S SOCCER RULES. 1927. a. $3. National Collegiate Athletic Association, Circulation Department, Box 7347, Overland Park, KS 66207-0347. TEL 913-339-1900. illus.; circ. 11,700.
   Supersedes: N C A A Men's Soccer Rules (ISSN 0735-0368); Formerly: Official National Collegiate Athletic Association Soccer Guide.
   Description: Covers official signals, interpretations, and rulings.

796 US ISSN 0736-7775
N C A A MEN'S LACROSSE RULES. a. $3. National Collegiate Athletic Association, Circulation Department, Box 7347, Overland Park, KS 66207-0347. TEL 913-339-1900. illus.
   Former titles: N C A A Lacrosse Guide (ISSN 0732-9059); Official N C A A Lacrosse Guide.
   Description: Covers official signals, interpretations, and rulings.

796.323 US ISSN 0736-5195
GV885.45
N C A A MEN'S READ-EASY BASKETBALL RULES. 1973. a. $1.50. National Collegiate Athletic Association, Circulation Department, Box 7347, Overland Park, KS 66207-0347. TEL 913-339-1900. illus.; circ. 5,200.
   Formerly: Official Read-Easy Basketball Rules (ISSN 0277-559X)
   Description: Contains a popularized version of the official NCAA rules.

796.332 US
N C A A READ-EASY FOOTBALL RULES. a. $1.50. National Collegiate Athletic Association, Circulation Department, Box 7347, Overland Park, KS 66207-0347. TEL 913-339-1900.
   Description: Contains a popularized version of the official NCAA rules.

796.357 US
N C A A SOFTBALL. a. $5. National Collegiate Athletic Association, Circulation Department, Box 7347, Overland Park, KS 66207-0347. TEL 913-339-1900. stat.
   Description: Contains individual and team records, and statistical leaders.

794.6 AT
▼**N.S.W. BOWLS NEWS**. (Supplement to: Bowls) 1991. m. Royal New South Wales Bowling Association, Inc., P.O. Box E186, St. James, N.S.W. 2000, Australia. TEL 02-283-4555. FAX 02-283-4252. Ed. Rex Davies.

796.352 AT
N.S.W. GOLF. 1961. m. Aus.$3 per issue. New South Wales Golf Association, 17 Brisbane St., Darlinghurst, N.S.W. 2010, Australia. TEL 02-264-8433. FAX 02-261-4750. adv.; bk.rev.; circ. 12,000. (reprint service avail.)
   Description: Contains golf news, instructions, results, golf feature articles.

796.357 US
NATIONAL BASEBALL HALL OF FAME & MUSEUM YEARBOOK. 1981. a. National Baseball Hall of Fame, Main St., Box 590, Cooperstown, NY 13326. TEL 607-547-9988. Ed. William J. Guilfoile. circ. 30,000.

794.7 US
NATIONAL BILLIARD NEWS. m. Box 807, Northville, MI 48167. TEL 313-348-0053. FAX 313-348-7828. Ed. Conrad J. Burkman. circ. 14,500.

796.35 US ISSN 1047-6474
NATIONAL CROQUET CALENDAR. 1988. bi-m. $30 (foreign $45)(effective 1992). Garth Eliassen, Ed. & Pub., Box 208, Monmouth, OR 97361. TEL 503-838-5697. FAX 503-838-2633. adv.; circ. 400.
   Description: Covers championship croquet. Features national and international news, strategy articles, product information, and tournament schedules and results.

796.352 US
▼**NATIONAL GOLF MAGAZINE**. 1992. 10/yr. Bouclin and Glass, Eds. & Pubs., 175 Metro Center Blvd., Warwick, RI 02886. TEL 401-738-1265. FAX 401-739-0390. adv.: B&W page $1440, color page $1900; trim 8 3/8 x 10 7/8. circ. 15,000.
   Description: Covers men's and women's pro and amateur tour information, fashion, club profiles, tips and nostalgia.

NATIONAL HOCKEY LEAGUE. GUIDE & RECORD BOOK. see SPORTS AND GAMES — Abstracting, Bibliographies, Statistics

796.357 US ISSN 0734-6905
GV863.A1
NATIONAL PASTIME. 1982. a. membership. Society for American Baseball Research, Inc., Box 98183, Cleveland, OH 44101. TEL 914-246-9241. FAX 216-575-0502. adv.; circ. 6,500. **Indexed:** Sportsearch (1982-).

796.333 CN
NATIONAL RUGBY POST. 1985. 6/yr. Can.$25 (in US Can.$27; elsewhere Can.$39). (Canadian Rugby Union) National Rugby Post, 13228-76 St., Edmonton, Alta. T5C 1B6, Canada. TEL 403-476-0268. FAX 403-473-1066. adv.; circ. 6,000. (tabloid format)

796.334 US
NATIONAL SOCCER HALL OF FAME NEWSLETTER. m. National Soccer Hall of Fame, 11 Ford Ave., Oneonta, NY 13820.

796.323 US
NATIONAL WHEELCHAIR BASKETBALL ASSOCIATION. DIRECTORY. 1960. a. $50. National Wheelchair Basketball Association, 110 Seaton Bldg., University of Kentucky, Lexington, KY 40506. Ed. Stan Labanowich. circ. 350.

SPORTS AND GAMES — BALL GAMES

796.323 US
NATIONAL WHEELCHAIR BASKETBALL ASSOCIATION. NEWSLETTER. s-w. (Nov.-Mar.). membership only. National Wheelchair Basketball Association, 110 Seaton Bldg., University of Kentucky, Lexington, KY 40506.

796.342 US
NET FRIEND NEWS. 1978. bi-m. membership. American Tennis Federation, 200 Castlewood Dr., North Palm Beach, FL 33408. TEL 407-848-1026. FAX 407-863-8984.

796.32 UK ISSN 0144-0810
NETBALL. 1933-1937; resumed 1944. q. £6 (foreign £11). All England Netball Association, Francis House, Francis St., London SW1P 1DE, England. TEL 071-828-2176. Ed. G. Harrold. adv.; bk.rev.; circ. 5,000. **Indexed:** Sportsearch (1977-).

796.352 US
NEW ENGLAND GOLF MAGAZINE. 1989. bi-m. $11.70. New England Golf Magazine, Inc., 350 Main St., Nashua, NH 03060. TEL 800-627-7012. FAX 603-883-0997. adv.; circ. 50,000.
Description: Focuses on local events, tournaments, courses and players.

796.332 US
NEW YORK GIANTS OFFICIAL YEARBOOK (YEAR). 1986. a. $7. Woodford Publishing, 660 Market St., K No. 206, San Francisco, CA 94104-5011. TEL 415-397-1853. FAX 415-399-0942. adv.; illus.
Formerly: New York Giants Yearbook (Year).

796.332 US
NEW YORK JETS OFFICIAL YEARBOOK. 1971. a. $5 per copy. (New York Jets Football Club Inc.) New York Jets, 1000 Fulton Ave., Hempstead, NY 11550. Ed. Frank Ramos. charts; illus.; stat.; circ. 60,000.

796.323 US
NEW YORK KNICKS YEARBOOK; official guide and record book. 1947. a. $7 per no. (New York Knickerbockers Basketball Club) Madison Square Garden Corporation (Subsidiary of: Paramount Communications), 4 Pennsylvania Plaza, New York, NY 10001. TEL 212-465-6000. FAX 212-465-6498. Ed. John Cirillo. adv.; charts; illus.; stat.; circ. 13,000. (reprint service avail.)

796.357 US ISSN 0887-5863
NEW YORK METS INSIDE PITCH. 1985. m. $21.95. Coman Publishing Company, Inc., 505 S. Duke St., Ste. 504, Durham, NC 27701. TEL 919-688-0218. FAX 919-682-1532. (Subscr. to: Box 2331, Durham, NC 27702) Ed. Brent Belvin. adv.; circ. 26,000.

796.334 UK
NEWS OF THE WORLD FOOTBALL ANNUAL. 1887. a. £3.75. Invincible Press, 77-78 Fulham Palace Rd., London W6 8JB, England. TEL 081-741-7070. Eds. Bill Bateson, Albert Sewell. circ. 80,000.
Description: Teams, leagues, results of games and other football information for the season.

796.352 US
NORTH TEXAS GOLFER. 1986. 12/yr. $27. Golfer Magazines, Inc., 9182 Old Katy Rd., Ste. 212, Houston, TX 77055. TEL 713-464-0308. FAX 713-464-0129. Ed. Bob Gray, Sr. adv.; circ. 28,000 (controlled).
Description: Provides information to golfers in Texas above the 31st parallel on quality of courses, better playing techniques, upcoming tournaments, and tournament results. Includes an alphabetical list of golf courses in that area.

796.357 US ISSN 0078-3838
GV877
OFFICIAL BASEBALL GUIDE. 1942. a. $10.95. Sporting News Publishing Co., 1212 N. Lindbergh Blvd., St. Louis, MO 63132. TEL 314-997-7111. Ed. Dave Sloan.

796.357 US ISSN 0162-542X
OFFICIAL BASEBALL REGISTER. 1940. a. $10.95. Sporting News Publishing Co., 1212 N. Lindbergh Blvd., St. Louis, MO 63132. TEL 314-997-7111. Ed. Barry Siegel. cum.index: 1940-1973.
Formerly: Baseball Register (ISSN 0067-4281)

796.357 US ISSN 0078-3846
OFFICIAL BASEBALL RULES. 1950. a. $2.95. Sporting News Publishing Co., 1212 N. Lindbergh Blvd., St. Louis, MO 63132. TEL 314-997-7111.

796.3 US
OFFICIAL LAWN BOWLS ALMANAC. 1964. irreg. $1.50 to non-members. American Lawn Bowls Association, 445 Surfview Dr., Pacific Palisades, CA 90272. TEL 213-454-2775.
Former titles (until 1984): Official Lawn Bowls Handbook (ISSN 0065-9053); Lawn Bowler's Handbook.

796.3 US ISSN 0078-3862
GV885
OFFICIAL N B A GUIDE. 1958. a. $10.95. (National Basketball Association) Sporting News Publishing Co., 1212 N. Lindbergh Blvd., St. Louis, MO 63132. TEL 314-997-7111. Eds. Alex Sachare, Dave Sloan.
Formerly: Official National Basketball Association Guide.

796.323 US
OFFICIAL OHIO STATE UNIVERSITY MEN'S BASKETBALL PROGRAM. irreg. (published for each men's home basketball game). (Ohio State University) Zimmerman Publishing Company, Inc., 929 Harrison Ave., Ste. 202, Columbus, OH 43215. TEL 614-294-8878. FAX 614-294-4831. adv. (back issues avail.)
Description: The official game day program for the Ohio State University men's basketball team. Includes player and coach profiles, alumni news etc.

796.352 917.704 US
▼OHIO GOLFER'S TRAVEL GUIDE. 1990. a. $5.95. R S G Publishing, Inc., Box 612, Plymouth, MI 48170-0612. TEL 313-582-8860. FAX 313-582-3585. Ed. Betty Rasmussen. circ. 10,000.
Description: Presents information on public and private golf courses in Ohio, including address and telephone, course description, facilities, and more.

796.342 CN
ON COURT. 1982. 8/yr. Can.$12. Fourhand II, Inc., 1200 Sheppard Ave. E., Ste. 400, Willowdale, Ont. M2K 2S5, Canada. TEL 416-497-1370. FAX 416-494-5343. Ed. Tom Mayenknecht. adv.; bk.rev.; circ. 50,000 (controlled).

796.352 CN
ONTARIO GOLF NEWS. 1980. 5/yr. Can.$8. Ontario Golf News Inc., 2 Billingham Rd., Ste. 400, Toronto, Ont. M9B 6E1, Canada. TEL 416-232-2380. Ed. Ken McKenzie. adv.; bk.rev.; circ. 40,000 (controlled).
Description: Contains coverage of all the major tournaments played in Ontario and golf highlights across Canada. Lists all golf courses in Ontario plus instructional articles and golf rules.

796.342 CN
ONTARIO TENNIS. 1969. bi-m. Can.$9.95. Ontario Tennis Association, 1220 Sheppard Ave. E., Willowdale, Ont. M2K 2X1, Canada. TEL 416-495-4215. FAX 416-495-4222. Ed. David Dunkelman. adv.; bk.rev.; stat.; circ. 10,000. (tabloid format; back issues avail.)

796.352 US ISSN 0161-1259
GV961
P G A MAGAZINE. 1920. m. $23.95 to non-members. (Professional Golfers' Association of America) Quarton Group Publishers, Inc., 2155 Butterfield, Ste. 200, Troy, MI 48084. TEL 313-649-1110. FAX 313-649-2306. Ed. Lynn Henning. adv.; bk.rev.; illus.; circ. 35,000. **Indexed:** Sports Per.Ind., Sportsearch.
Formerly (until Oct. 1977): Professional Golfer (ISSN 0033-0132)

796.332 US
PACKER REPORT. 1973. 26/yr. (w. during football season). $27.95. Royle Publishing Co., Inc., 112 Market St., Sun Prairie, WI 53590. TEL 608-837-5161. FAX 608-837-3946. Ed. Al Pahl. adv.; circ. 26,342.
Description: Devoted to coverage of the Green Bay Packers and the NFL. Contains game stories, statistics, coaches' comments, player profiles, photos and line-ups.

796.358 PK
PAKISTAN BOOK OF CRICKET. (Text in English) 1976. a. Rs.10. Q. Ahmed, Pub., Spencers Bldg., 3rd Fl., I.I. Chundrigar Rd., G.P.O. Box 3721, Karachi, Pakistan. charts; illus.

796.352 JA
PAR GOLF. (Text in Japanese) 1969. m. 8160 Yen. Gakken Co. Ltd., 40-5, 4-chome, Kamiikedai, Ohta-ku, Tokyo 145, Japan. Ed. Kenichi Shiono.

796.352 IT
PARLIAMO DI GOLF. 1980. m. (9/yr.). membership. Editoriale Country and Sport, Via Washington, 27, 20146 Milan, Italy. TEL 39-2-4817447. FAX 39-2-4697893. Ed. Lio Selva. adv.; charts; illus.; stat.; circ. 26,700.
Description: Covers the sport of golf, includes list of competitions throughout Italy and worldwide.

790.1 US
PETANQUE NEWS. 1968. s-a. membership. Petanque News, U.S.A., Inc., 505 W. Broadway, New York, NY 10012. Ed. Alfred Levitt. adv.; bk.rev.; circ. 5,000.

796.323 US
▼PETERSEN'S COLLEGE BASKETBALL. 1991. a. $3.95. Petersen Publishing Co., 8490 Sunset Blvd., Los Angeles, CA 90069. TEL 213-854-2222. FAX 213-854-2718. adv.
Description: Previews the upcoming season, including predictions, schedules, ratings, and stats.

796.332 US ISSN 0276-2129
GV937
PETERSEN'S COLLEGE FOOTBALL. Running title: College Football. N.S. 1991. a. $3.95. Petersen Publishing Co., 8490 Sunset Blvd., Los Angeles, CA 90069. TEL 213-854-2222. FAX 213-854-2718. adv.; circ. 180,000.

796.357 US
PETERSEN'S PRO BASEBALL. 1977. a. $3.95. Petersen Publishing Co., 8490 Sunset Blvd., Los Angeles, CA 90069. TEL 213-854-2222. FAX 213-854-2718. adv.; circ. 196,000.
Description: Includes predictions, ratings, draft review, schedules and stats. Reviews the past season.

792.323 US ISSN 0192-2238
GV885.7
PETERSEN'S PRO BASKETBALL. 1977. a. $3.95. Petersen Publishing Co., 8490 Sunset Blvd., Los Angeles, CA 90069. TEL 213-854-2222. FAX 213-854-2718. Ed. Al Hall. circ. 157,486.

796.352 US
PHILADELPHIA GOLF MAGAZINE. 1986. 5/yr. $8. Philadelphia Golf Publishing Co., Box 96, Berwyn, PA 19312. TEL 215-647-4692. adv.; circ. 70,000.
Description: Provides news, entertainment and information about Philadelphia area golf. Covers pro and amateur tournaments.

796.357 US ISSN 8750-4278
PHILLIES REPORT; the exclusive Philadelphia Phillies newspaper. fortn. $19.95. Sports Press, Inc., P.O. Box 157, Springfield, PA 19064. TEL 215-543-4077. Ed. Richard N. Westcott. circ. 12,000. (tabloid format; back issues avail.)
Description: Contains features and news about Philadelphia's home team.

796.346 CC ISSN 1000-3452
PINGPANG SHIJIE/TABLE TENNIS WORLD. (Text in Chinese) 1982. q. $12.30. (Zhongguo Pingpang Xiehui - China Table Tennis Society) Renmin Tiyu Chubanshe, 8 Tiyuguan Lu, Chongwen Qu, Beijing 100061, People's Republic of China. TEL 757161. (Dist. in US by: China Books & Periodicals, Inc., 2929 24th St., San Francisco, CA 94110. TEL 415-282-2994)

796.31 US
PITCHER AND TEAM REPORT (YEAR). a. $10.95 (free with subscr. to: Baseball Insight). Parrish Publications, Box 23205, Portland, OR 97223. TEL 503-244-8975. Ed. Phil Erwin.

796.357 US ISSN 0731-8138
PITCHER PERFORMANCE HANDBOOK. 1965. a. $7.50. Research Analysis Publications, Box 49123, Los Angeles, CA 90049. Ed. Ronald H. Lewis. adv.; charts; stat.; circ. 9,000.

SPORTS AND GAMES — BALL GAMES

796.342 US
PLATFORM TENNIS NEWS. bi-m. American Platform Tennis Association, 251 Park St., Apt. 4, Upper Montclair, NJ 07043-1732. Ed. James McCready. circ. 3,000. (back issues avail.)

796.358 UK ISSN 0079-2314
PLAYFAIR CRICKET ANNUAL. a. £2.50. Queen Anne Press, 165 Great Dover St., London SE1 4YA, England. TEL 071-334-4800. FAX 071-334-4905. Ed. Bill Frindall. circ. 70,000.

796.3 UK ISSN 0079-2322
PLAYFAIR FOOTBALL ANNUAL. 1948. a. £2.99. Queen Anne Press, 165 Great Dover St., London SE1 4YA, England. TEL 071-334-4800. FAX 071-334-4905. Ed. J. Rollin. circ. 40,000.

796.352 CN
POCKET PRO GOLF MAGAZINE. 1978. 17/yr. Two St. Clair Ave., E., Toronto, Ont. M4T 2T5, Canada. TEL 416-961-8647. Ed. B.A. Longhurst.

796.353 US ISSN 0146-4574
GV1010
POLO. 1975. 10/yr. $30. Polo Publications, Inc., 656 Quince Orchard Rd., Gaithersburg, MD 20878-1472. TEL 301-977-0200. FAX 301-990-9015. Ed. Martha LeGrand. adv.; bk.rev.; illus.; circ. 7,500. **Indexed:** Sports Per.Ind., Sportsearch (1977-).
Formerly: Polo News.

796.357 US
PONY BASEBALL. BLUE BOOK. 1959. triennial. $4. Pony Baseball, Inc., Box 225, Washington, PA 15301. TEL 412-225-1060. Ed.Bd. circ. 20,000.
Formerly: Boys Baseball. Blue Book (ISSN 0068-0575)
Description: Guide for operating a youth baseball or softball program for the entire community.

796.357 US
PONY BASEBALL RULES AND REGULATIONS. (In 2 editions: Shetland, Pinto & Mustang Rules; Bronco, Pony, Colt & Palomino Rules) 1951. a. $0.50. Pony Baseball, Inc., Box 225, Washington, PA 15301. TEL 412-225-1060. Ed. Abraham L. Key. circ. 120,000.
Description: Rulebooks for different age level baseball leagues.

796.357 US
PONY BASEBALL - SOFTBALL EXPRESS. 1952. q. $1. Pony Baseball, Inc., Box 225, Washington, PA 15301. TEL 412-225-1060. Ed.Bd. adv.; illus.; circ. 26,000. (tabloid format)
Former titles: Pony Baseball Express; Pony Baseball Newsletter; Boys Baseball Newsletter; Boys Baseball Bulletin (ISSN 0006-856X)
Description: Covers current news in baseball.

794.7 US
POOL & BILLIARD MAGAZINE. m. Sports Publications Ltd., 109 Fairfield Way, No. 207, Bloomingdale, IL 60108-1500. TEL 708-893-0999. FAX 708-893-9219. Ed. Shari J. Stauch. adv.

796.332 US
POST-SEASON FOOTBALL HANDBOOK. 1989. a. Kwik-Fax Books (Subsidiary of: Martin Frederick, Inc.), Box 14613, Surfside Beach, SC 29587. TEL 803-238-3513. Ed. Martin Frederick.

796.352 US
PRIVATE COUNTRY CLUB GUEST POLICY DIRECTORY. 1976. a. $25. Pazdur Publishing Co., 2171 Campus Dr., Irvine, CA 92715. TEL 714-752-6474. FAX 714-752-0398. Ed. Edward F. Pazdur. adv.; circ. 125,000.
Supersedes (1976-1979): Golf and Country Club Guest Policy Directory.

796.322 US
PRO BASKETBALL ILLUSTRATED (YEAR). a. Lexington Library, Inc., 355 Lexington Ave., New York, NY 10017. TEL 212-973-3200. FAX 212-986-5926. Ed. Stephen Ciaccicarelli. charts; illus.

796.3305 US ISSN 0079-5526
PRO FOOTBALL (LOS ANGELES). 1960. a. $4.50. Petersen Publishing Co., 8490 Sunset Blvd., Los Angeles, CA 90069. TEL 213-854-2222.
Formerly: Petersen's Pro Football Annual (ISSN 0079-1156)

796.332 US ISSN 1054-0156
GV954
PRO FOOTBALL ILLUSTRATED (YEAR). a. Lexington Library, Inc., 355 Lexington Ave., New York, NY 10017. TEL 212-973-3200. FAX 212-986-5926. Ed. Stephen Ciaccicarelli. adv.

796.332 US ISSN 0032-9053
PRO FOOTBALL WEEKLY. 1968. 28/yr. (w. during football season, m. off-season). $55. Turnstile Publications, 220 E. 42nd St., New York, NY 10017. TEL 212-210-0777. Ed. Hub Arkush. adv.; bk.rev.; charts; illus.; stat.; circ. 100,000.

796.352 US ISSN 1041-5785
PUTT-PUTT WORLD; forthefunofit! 1958. 3/yr. free. Putt-Putt Golf Courses of America, Inc., 3007 Ft. Bragg Rd., Box 35237, Fayetteville, NC 20303. TEL 919-485-7131. FAX 919-485-1122. Ed. Donna Clayton Lloyd. adv.; circ. 70,000.
Description: Deals with accomplishments in the sport of putting and developments in miniature golf.

796.335 CN
QUEBEC SOCCER. m. Promotions Soccer Inc., Box 1000, Sta. M, Montreal, Que. H1V 3R2, Canada. TEL 514-252-3070. FAX 514-252-3162. Ed. Pascal Cifarelli. circ. 10,000.

RACING AND FOOTBALL OUTLOOK: FOOTBALL ANNUAL.
see SPORTS AND GAMES

RACING AND FOOTBALL OUTLOOK: JUMPING ANNUAL.
see SPORTS AND GAMES

RACING AND FOOTBALL OUTLOOK: RACING ANNUAL.
see SPORTS AND GAMES

796.342 US ISSN 0273-9194
RACQUET (NEW YORK). 1980. 6/yr. $18. Heather & Pine International, 42 W. 38 St., Ste. 1202, New York, NY 10018. TEL 212-768-8360. adv.; circ. 112,918.
Description: Concentrates on people, travel, fashion, humor, and equipment.

796.343 US
RACQUETBALL AROUND OHIO. 1982. bi-m. $10. Ohio Racquetball Association, 374 Slate Run Dr., Powell, OH 43065. TEL 614-548-4188. FAX 614-548-5079. Ed. Steve Lerner. adv.; circ. 2,500.
Description: Features events, schedules and rankings. Includes national and professional news and event coverage.

796.343 US ISSN 1060-877X
▼**RACQUETBALL MAGAZINE.** 1990. bi-m. $15. American Amateur Racquetball Association, 815 N. Weber, Colorado Springs, CO 80903. TEL 719-635-5396. FAX 719-635-0685. adv.; circ. 35,000.
Description: Covers international events, national championships, state and regional news, industry reports, schedules and rankings.

796.357 US
REDS REPORT. 1988. m. $21.95. Coman Publishing Company, Inc. (Cincinnati), 9785 Montgomery Rd., Ste. 301, Cincinnati, OH 45242. TEL 919-688-0218. FAX 919-682-1532. Ed. Mark Schmetzer. adv.; circ. 12,500.
Description: For Cincinnati Reds fans.

796.352 US
ROCHESTER GOLF WEEK & SPORTS LEDGER. 1989. w. $17.50. George Morgenstern, Ed. & Pub., 2535 Brighton-Henrietta Town Line Rd., Rochester, NY 14623-2711. TEL 716-427-2468. FAX 716-271-6014. adv.; bk.rev.; illus.; circ. 25,000. (reprint service avail.)
Description: Serves the golf sport market.

796.3 UK ISSN 0080-4088
ROTHMANS FOOTBALL YEARBOOK. 1970. a. £12.95 for paperback; hardcover £17.95. (Rothmans (U.K.) Ltd.) Queen Anne Press, 165 Great Dover St., London SE1 4YA, England. TEL 071-334-4800. FAX 071-334-4905. Ed. Jack Rollin. adv.; circ. 40,000.

796.333 UK ISSN 0262-4745
ROTHMANS RUGBY LEAGUE YEARBOOK. 1981. a. £12.95. (Rothmans (U.K.) Ltd.) Queen Anne Press, 165 Great Dover St., London SE1 4YA, England. TEL 071-334-4800. FAX 071-334-4905. Eds. David Howes, Raymond Fletcher. illus.; circ. 9,000.

796.333 US ISSN 0162-1297
RUGBY. 1975. m. (exc. Jan.). $27 (foreign $40). Rugby Press, Ltd., 2350 Broadway, Ste. 220, New York, NY 10024. TEL 212-787-1160. FAX 212-595-0934. Ed. Edward Hagerty. adv.; bk.rev.; circ. 10,500. (back issues avail.) **Indexed:** Sportsearch (1979-).
Description: Covers U.S. and Canadian match action. Provides club and personality profiles, details on tournaments and worldwide rugby news.

796.333 UK
RUGBY ANNUAL FOR WALES. 1968. a. £3.99. Welsh Brewers Ltd., Maesycoed Rd., Cardiff CF4 4UW, Wales. Ed. Arwyn Owen. adv.

796.3 UK ISSN 0080-4827
RUGBY FOOTBALL LEAGUE OFFICIAL GUIDE. a. £7. Rugby Football League, 180 Chapeltown Road, Leeds LS7 4HT, England. TEL 0532-624637. FAX 0532-623386.

796.333 PP
RUGBY LEAGUE NEWS. 1979. 28/yr. (during season). Word Publishing Co. Pty. Ltd., Box 1982, Boroko, Papua New Guinea. Ed. Sikio Oyassi. adv.; illus.; circ. 6,000.

796.333 AT ISSN 0035-9742
RUGBY LEAGUE WEEK. 1970. 33/yr. Aus.$51. Federal Publishing Company, 180 Bourke Rd., Alexandria, N.S.W. 2015, Australia. Ed. Geoff Prenter. circ. 62,389. (tabloid format)

796.333 JA
RUGBY MAGAZINE. (Text in Japanese) 1972. m. 7440 Yen. Baseball Magazine Sha, 3-10-10 Misaki-cho, Chiyoda-ku, Tokyo, Japan. Ed. Yoshinori Hamabe.

796.333 NE
RUGBY NIEUWS. 1977. bi-m. (per season). fl.25 (foreign fl.30). Dutch Rugby Union, Brinklaan 74C, 1404 GL Bussum, Netherlands. TEL 02159-38087. FAX 02159-18145. Ed.Bd. adv.; bk.rev.; circ. 6,000.
Description: Covers national and international matches.

796.333 UK
RUGBY WORLD AND POST. 1960. m. £25 (foreign £32)(typically set in Aug.). Rugby Publishing Ltd., Chiltern House, 17 College Avenue, Maidenhead SL6 6BX, England. TEL 0734-723319. FAX 0734-724447. (Subscr. to: P.O. Box 142, Reading RG4 9DX, England) Ed. Nigel Starmer-Smith. adv.; bk.rev.; illus.; circ. 52,000. **Indexed:** Sportsearch (1985-).
Incorporates: Rugby Post & Rugby World (ISSN 0035-9777) & Rugby Wales.

796.357 US
S A B R BULLETIN. 1971. 12/yr. Society for American Baseball Research, Inc., Box 93183, Cleveland, OH 44101. TEL 216-575-0500. FAX 216-575-0502. Ed. Morris Eckhouse. adv.; circ. 6,000.

796.352 SA ISSN 1013-3356
S A GOLF JOURNAL. 1926. m. R.40 (foreign R.160). S A Golf Journal (Pty) Ltd., P.O. Box 72464, Lynnwood Ridge 0040, South Africa. TEL 012-803-8006. FAX 012-803-8698. Ed. Seef Le Roux. adv.; bk.rev.; circ. 6,500.
Formed by the Nov. 1988 merger of: South African Golf & Golf Journal.
Description: Covers golf in South Africa and worldwide. Includes articles on tournaments, personalities, courses, holiday golf, world score cards, and instruction.

794.6 US ISSN 0193-5321
ST. LOUIS BOWLING REVIEW. 1970. s-m. $5. Red Bud Media Group, 431 Chez Paree, Hazelwood, MO 63042. TEL 314-731-4040. FAX 314-831-3610. adv.; circ. 30,000.

796 QA
AL-SAQR AL-RIYADI. 1977. m. $20 to individuals; institutions $25. Al- Saqr Magazine, P.O. Box 4925, Doha, Qatar. TEL 320476. Ed. M. Kazem. adv.; bk.rev.; illus.; circ. 120,000. (back isues avail.)
Formerly: Saqer - Falcon.

SPORTS AND GAMES — BALL GAMES

796.352   CN   ISSN 0711-3226
SCORE; Canada's golf magazine. (Text in English) 1981. 5/yr. Can.$16. Canadian Controlled Media Communications, 287 MacPherson Ave., Toronto, Ont. M4V 1A4, Canada. TEL 416-928-2909. FAX 416-966-1181. Ed. Bob Weeks. adv.; bk.rev.; illus.; circ. 111,572. (back issues avail.)

796.352   UK
SCOTLAND HOME OF GOLF. 1970. a. £2.95. Pastime Publications Ltd., 15 Dublin Street Lane South, Edinburgh EH1 3PX, Scotland. TEL 031-556-1105. FAX 031-556-1129. adv.; circ. 30,000.

796.352   US
▼**SENIOR GOLF WORLD**. 1991. m. S G W, Inc., Box 2508, Mission Viejo, CA 92690. TEL 714-733-9246. circ. 575,000.
    Description: Covers golf from the point of view of getting more enjoyment out of playing; includes travel information, golf related real estate, clothing and equipment.

796.352 301.435   US   ISSN 0037-2218
THE SENIOR GOLFER. 1986. 6/yr. $18.55 for 2 yrs. Senior Golfer, Inc., 1323 S.E. 17th St., Ste. 179, Ft. Lauderdale, FL 33316-1778. TEL 305-527-0778. FAX 305-525-5301. Ed. Oscar Fraley. adv.; bk.rev.; illus.; circ. 100,000.
    Description: Publication for the professional and amateur senior golfer. Covers senior tour members and outstanding senior amateurs, health, travel suggestions, product instruction. Includes list of events and results nationwide.

796.357   US   ISSN 1054-2183
GV863.A1
▼**THE SHOW**. 1990. a. Preview Publishing, 100 W. Harrison, N. Tower, 5th Fl., Seattle, WA 98119. TEL 206-282-2322. FAX 206-284-2083.
    Description: Includes profiles of players, managers and owners, as well as strategy, scouting, prospects, statistics and history.

796.3   US
SLO-PITCH NEWS. 1985. m. $9. Varsity Publications, 6506 23rd Ave. N.E., Seattle, WA 98115. TEL 206-524-8985. FAX 206-524-3710. Ed. Dennis Pauley. adv.; circ. 26,000. (tabloid format; back issues avail.)
    Description: Covers slo-pitch softball; reports statistics and rankings on a national level.

796.325   CN
SMASH. (Text in French) 1970. 4/yr. Can.$15. Federation de Volley-Ball du Quebec, 4545 ave. Pierre de Coubertin, C.P. 1000, Sta. M, Montreal, Que. H1V 3R2, Canada. TEL 514-252-3065. FAX 514-252-3176. Ed. Claude Pelletier. adv.; bk.rev.; circ. 2,100. (looseleaf format)

796.342   SZ
SMASH-TENNIS-MAGAZIN. m. 35 Fr. (Swiss Tennis Association) Smash Verlag AG, Ruedigerstrasse 12, 8021 Zurich, Switzerland. (Subscr. to: Zollikofer AG, Fuerstenlandstr. 122, 9001 St. Gallen, Switzerland) circ. 18,000. (back issues avail.)
    Formerly (until 1977): Tennis.

796.334   US   ISSN 0163-4070
SOCCER AMERICA. 1971. 50/yr. $46.94. Berling Communications, Inc., Box 23704, Oakland, CA 94623. TEL 415-528-5000. FAX 415-528-5177. Ed. Lynn Berling-Manuel. adv.; bk.rev.; illus.; circ. 25,000. (also avail. in microform from UMI; reprint service avail. from UMI) **Indexed**: Sports Per.Ind., Sportsearch (1976-).
    Formerly: Soccer West.
    Description: Delivers comprehensive, national soccer news and information to the sophisticated soccer fan. Covers the national team, the pros and college action. Also features international soccer, a monthly soccer events calendar, information and tips for adults working in youth soccer.

796.334
SOCCER CALIFORNIA. 1980. 5/yr. $4. California Youth Soccer Association, 5673 W. Las Positas Blvd., Ste. 202, Pleasanton, CA 94566. TEL 415-847-9111. adv.; circ. 98,000.
    Description: Contains news of tournaments and events, standings and scores, playing techniques and news of world soccer.

796.334   US   ISSN 0149-2365
GV942
SOCCER DIGEST. 1978. bi-m. $11.95 (foreign $30). Century Publishing Co., 990 Grove St., Evanston, IL 60201-1440. TEL 708-491-6440. (Subscr. to: Box 349, Mt. Morris, IL 61054-0349. TEL 800-877-5893) Ed. Michael K. Herbert. adv.; bk.rev.; charts; illus.; stat.; circ. 65,000. (also avail. in microform from UMI; reprint service avail. from UMI) **Indexed**: Sports Per.Ind.
    Description: Presents statistics and features on the sport for serious soccer fans.

796.334   US   ISSN 0560-3617
SOCCER JOURNAL. vol.25, 1980. 6/yr. $40 membership. National Soccer Coaches Association of America, West Gymnasium, S U N Y - Binghamton, Binghamton, NY 13902-6000. TEL 607-777-2133. FAX 607-777-4597. Ed. Tim Schum. adv.; bk.rev.; illus.; circ. 8,500. **Indexed**: Phys.Ed.Ind., Sports Per.Ind., Sportsearch (1979-).

796.334   JA
SOCCER MAGAZINE. (Text in Japanese) 1966. m. 6360 yen. Baseball Magazine Sha, 3-10-10 Misaki-cho, Chiyoda-ku, Tokyo, Japan. Ed. Keiichi Chino.

796.334   CN
SOCCER NEWS. 1982. q. Can.$5.95($6.95) Ontario Soccer Association, 1220 Sheppard Ave. E., Willowdale, Ont. M2K 2X1, Canada. TEL 416-495-4251. Ed. Bernacki. adv.; bk.rev.; circ. 20,000. (back issues avail.)

796.357   UK
SOCCER PRODUCTS & SERVICES. 1985. q. Soccer Products & Services, 66 High St., Henley in Arden, Solihull, W. Midlands B95 5BX, England. TEL 0564-79-3232. Ed. Chris Rodman. circ. 32,000.

796.334   US   ISSN 0731-9541
GV943.4
SOCCER RULEBOOK. a. $2.75. National Federation of State High School Associations, 11724 N.W. Plaza Circle, Box 20626, Kansas City, MO 64195. TEL 816-464-5400. FAX 816-464-5571.
    Formerly: National Federation of State High School Associations. Soccer Rules (ISSN 0163-4763)

796.3   UK   ISSN 0081-038X
SOCCER YEAR BOOK FOR NORTHERN IRELAND. 1966. a. £1.50. Howard Publications, 39 Boucher Rd., Belfast BT12 6UT, Northern Ireland. Ed. Malcolm Brodie.

796.3   CN
SOFTBALL B.C. MAGAZINE; the voice of the British Columbia Amateur Softball Association. 1980. q. Can.$7 (effective Jan. 1992). Softball British Columbia, P.O. Box 45570 Sunnyside Mall, Surrey, B.C. V4A 9N3, Canada. FAX 604-531-8831. Ed. Penny Gardner. adv.; circ. 7,000. (back issues avail.)
    Description: Contains membership information and articles of sport related interest.

796.323
SOFTBALL ILLUSTRATED; slowpitch softball instructional series. 1981. q. $19.95. G E D Publications, Box 304, Lima, OH 45805. Ed. Glen Eley.
    Description: Provides how-to-info on improving your game in the second largest team sport in America.

796.357   US   ISSN 0732-2844
GV881
SOFTBALL RULE BOOK. a. $2.75. National Federation of State High School Associations, 11724 N.W. Plaza Circle, Box 20626, Kansas City, MO 64195-0626. TEL 816-464-5400. FAX 816-464-5571. Ed. Bradley A. Rumble.
    Formerly: National Federation of State High School Associations. Softball Rules (ISSN 0146-8286)

796.357   US
SOFTBALL WORLD. 1977. m. $16.25. Sporting World, Box 10151, Grand Lake Station, Oakland, CA 94610. TEL 510-428-2000. Ed. George Epstein. adv.; bk.rev.

796.332   AT
SOUTH AUSTRALIAN FOOTBALL BUDGET. 1914. w. Aus.$70. South Australian National Football League, P.O. Box One, West Lakes, S.A. 5021, Australia. TEL 08-268-2088. FAX 08-45-7385. adv.; bk.rev.; circ. 7,000. (back issues avail.)

796.342   AT
SOUTH AUSTRALIAN TENNIS NEWS. 1948. m. Aus.$7. South Australia Hard Court Tennis League, P.O. Box 202, Goodwood, S.A. 5034, Australia. Ed. L. Tapp. adv.; bk.rev.; illus.; circ. 2,000. (back issues avail.)

796   SA
SOUTHERN AFRICA SQUASH SCENE. 1980. irreg. R.7.20. Cotswold Publications, 208 Gale St., P.O. Box 1925, Durban 4000, South Africa. TEL 031-3055974. FAX 031-3015926. Ed. Sue Miles. circ. 7,000.

796.352   US   ISSN 1043-6375
SOUTHERN LINKS. 1988. bi-m. $17.95. Southern Links Magazine Publishing Associates, 1040 William Hilton Parkway, Hilton Head Island, SC 29928. TEL 803-842-6200. FAX 803-842-6233. (Subscr. to: Box 1907, Marion, OH 43305) adv.; circ. 150,000. (back issues avail.)
    Description: Directed to golfers who are interested in travel oppourtunities in the Southeast.

794.6   US
SPARES AND STRIKES. 1957. w. $25. Box 226, Buffalo, NY 14225. TEL 716-684-5218. FAX 716-683-2952. Ed. Allen Appleford. adv.; circ. 4,000.
    Description: Bowling newspaper.

SPITBALL; the literary baseball magazines. see *LITERATURE*

THE SPORT AMERICANA BASEBALL ADDRESS LIST. see *HOBBIES*

THE SPORT AMERICANA BASEBALL CARD PRICE GUIDE. see *HOBBIES*

THE SPORT AMERICANA BASKETBALL CARD PRICE GUIDE AND ALPHABETICAL CHECKLIST. see *HOBBIES*

THE SPORT AMERICANA FOOTBALL CARD PRICE GUIDE. see *HOBBIES*

THE SPORT AMERICANA PRICE GUIDE TO BASEBALL COLLECTIBLES. see *HOBBIES*

THE SPORT AMERICANA TEAM BASEBALL CARD CHECKLIST. see *HOBBIES*

THE SPORT AMERICANA TEAM FOOTBALL AND BASKETBALL CARD CHECKLIST. see *HOBBIES*

794.6   FR   ISSN 0398-8341
SPORT BOWLING.* 1963. 9/yr. 80 F.($18) Bowling de Paris, Jardin d'Acclimation, 75116 Paris, France. Eds. Michel Chollet & Bernard Mora. adv.; illus.; circ. 3,000. **Indexed**: Sportsearch (1976-1983).

796.357   US   ISSN 0275-0732
GV863.A1
SPORTING NEWS BASEBALL YEARBOOK. a. $4.95. Sporting News Publishing Co., 1212 N. Lindbergh Blvd., St. Louis, MO 63132. TEL 314-997-7111. Eds. Gary Levy, Mike Nahrstedt. adv.

796.323   US
SPORTING NEWS COLLEGE BASKETBALL. a. Sporting News Publishing Co., 1212 N. Lindbergh Blvd., St. Louis, MO 63132. TEL 314-997-7111. (Subscr. to: Box 56, St. Louis, MO 63166)

796.332   US   ISSN 0733-2823
SPORTING NEWS COLLEGE FOOTBALL YEARBOOK. a. $4.95. Sporting News Publishing Co., 1212 N. Lindbergh Blvd., St. Louis, MO 63132. TEL 314-997-7111. Eds. Gary Levy, Mike Nahrstedt. adv.

796.357   US
▼**SPORTING NEWS FANTASY BASEBALL YEARBOOK**. 1991. a. $4.95. Sporting News Publishing Co., 1212 N. Lindbergh Blvd., St. Louis, MO 63132. TEL 314-997-7111. FAX 314-993-7726. adv.; circ. 157,000.

SPORTS AND GAMES — BALL GAMES

796.323 US ISSN 0739-3067
GV885.515.N37
SPORTING NEWS OFFICIAL N B A REGISTER. a. $10.95. Sporting News Publishing Co., 1212 N. Lindbergh Blvd., St. Louis, MO 63132. TEL 314-997-7111. Eds. Alex Sachare, Dave Sloan. (back issues avail.)
Formerly: Sporting News National Basketball Association Register (ISSN 0271-8170)

796.323 US ISSN 0895-0601
GV885.7
SPORTING NEWS PRO BASKETBALL YEARBOOK. a. $4.95. Sporting News Publishing Co., 1212 N. Lindbergh Blvd., St. Louis, MO 63132. TEL 314-997-7111. (Subscr. to: Box 56, St. Louis, MO 63166) Eds. Gary Levy, Mike Nahrstedt. adv.
Formerly: Sporting News Pro College Basketball Yearbook (ISSN 0733-6047)

796.332 US ISSN 0732-1902
GV937
SPORTING NEWS PRO FOOTBALL GUIDE. 1970. a. $10.95. Sporting News Publishing Co., 1212 N. Lindbergh Blvd., St. Louis, MO 63132. TEL 314-997-7111. Ed. Dave Sloan. (back issues avail.)
Formerly: Sporting News' National Football Guide (ISSN 0081-3788)

796.332 US ISSN 0276-2307
GV937
SPORTING NEWS PRO FOOTBALL YEARBOOK. a. $4.95. Sporting News Publishing Co., 1212 N. Lindbergh Blvd., St. Louis, MO 63132. TEL 314-997-7111. (Subscr. to: Box 44, St. Louis, MO 63166) Eds. Gary Levy, Mike Nahrstedt. adv.

796.332 US ISSN 0275-4487
GV956.2.S8
SPORTING NEWS SUPER BOWL BOOK. a. $10.95. Sporting News Publishing Co., 1212 N. Lindbergh Blvd., St. Louis, MO 63132. TEL 314-997-7111. Ed. Bob McCoy. (back issues avail.)

796.3 US
▼**SPORTS CARD TRADER.** 1990. m. $29.95 (foreign $41.95). Century Publishing Co., 990 Grove St., Evanston, IL 60201-4370. TEL 708-491-6440. (Subscr. to: Box 443, Mt. Morris, IL 61054-0443. TEL 800-877-5893) Ed. Douglas Kale.
Description: Features a "buy and sell" guide for baseball, football, basketball and hockey cards from 1933 to present; plus articles on how to make money in collecting sports cards.

SPORTS COLLECTORS DIGEST. see *HOBBIES*

796.357 US
SPORTS COLLECTORS DIGEST - BASEBALL CARD PRICE GUIDE. 1988. a. $18.95. Krause Publications, Inc., 700 E. State St., Iola, WI 54990. TEL 715-445-2214. Ed. Jeff Kurowski. circ. 284,000.

794.6 US
SPORTS REPORTER. 1940. w. $20. Pat McDonough, Ed. & Pub., 466 Highland Ave., Kearny, NJ 07032. TEL 201-955-0016. FAX 201-991-8941. adv. (tabloid format)
Description: Covers bowling in the metropolitan New York region, with tournament results and announcements of upcoming competitions.

796.323 US
▼**SPORTS VIEW COLLEGE BASKETBALL PREVIEW.** 1991. a. Sports View Publications, Inc., Box 310148, 640 Timbergrove Dr., Atlanta, GA 30331. TEL 404-239-6524. adv.; circ. 175,000.
Description: Covers the nation's historically black colleges and universities. Focuses on team analyses, profiles, and previews.

796.332 US
SPORTS VIEW COLLEGE FOOTBALL PREVIEW. 1989. a. $3.95. Sports View Publications, Inc., Box 310148, 640 Timbergrove Dr., Atlanta, GA 30331. TEL 404-239-6524. adv.; circ. 200,000.
Description: Covers the nation's historically black colleges and universities. Contains pre-season team analyses, player and team profiles, and tradition and history.

796.332 US
SPORTS WEEKLY NEWSLETTER. FOOTBALL ANALYST.* 1968. w. $100. R.W. Livingston, Ed. & Pub., Box 60008, N. Charleston, SC 29419-0008. TEL 803-797-6173. charts; stat.; circ. 3,000.

796.357 US
SPORTS WEEKLY NEWSLETTER - BASEBALL.* 1968. w. $120. R.W. Livingston, Ed. & Pub., Box 60008, N. Charleston, SC 29419-0008. TEL 803-797-6173.

796.323 US
SPORTS WEEKLY NEWSLETTER - BASKETBALL.* w. $100. R.W. Livingston, Ed. & Pub., Box 60008, N. Charleston, SC 29419-0008. TEL 803-797-6173.

631 796.357 US
SPORTSTURF. 1985. m. $33. Gold Trade Publications, Inc., Box 8420, Van Nuys, CA 91409. TEL 818-781-8300. Ed. Bruce Shank. adv.; circ. 21,371.
Former titles: Golf and Sportsturf (ISSN 1049-0000); Sportsturf (ISSN 0890-0167)

796.357 US
SPRING TRAINING; guide to the grapefruit and cactus leagues. 1988. a. $4. Spring Training, Inc., 606-B Cameron Ave., Box 667, Chapel Hill, NC 27514. TEL 919-967-2420. Ed. Myles Friedman. adv.; circ. 100,000.
Description: Focuses on Major League Baseball's exhibition season in Florida and Arizona. Offers team and schedule information.

796.345 CN
SQUASH LIFE. 1977. 5/yr. Can.$10. Squash Ontario, 1220 Sheppard Ave. E., Willowdale, Ont. M2K 2X1, Canada. TEL 416-495-4140. FAX 416-495-4130. Ed. Sherry Funston. adv.; bk.rev.; charts; illus.; circ. 7,500. (back issues avail.) **Indexed:** Sportsearch (1982-).
Description: News about squash tournaments and clubs, playing tips.

796 UK
SQUASH NEWS. q. £0.90. Squash Rackets Association Ltd., Westpoint, 33-34 Warple Way, Acton, London W3 0RQ, England. TEL 01-746-1616. circ. 10,000.

796.31 US ISSN 0164-7148
SQUASH NEWS. 1978. m. (exc. Jul./Aug.) $15. Squash News, Inc., 186 Arcadia Rd., Hope Valley, RI 02832. TEL 401-539-2381. FAX 401-539-2490. Ed. Hazel White Jones. adv.; bk.rev.; circ. 16,000. (tabloid format; back issues avail.)
Description: Full coverage of the game on both the amateur and professional level; includes features, instruction, personalities and upcoming events.

796 UK ISSN 0262-4338
SQUASH PLAYER INTERNATIONAL. 1971. 10/yr. £20.85. Stonehart Leisure Magazines, 67-71 Goswell Rd., London EC1V 7EN, England. TEL 03727-41411. FAX 03727-44493. Ed. Nick Troop. adv.; circ. 9,476. **Indexed:** Sportsearch (1977-).
Description: Articles and comment for squash players plus reports of important competitions.

796 UK
SQUASH RACKETS ASSOCIATION. ANNUAL. 1930. a. £7.45. Squash Rackets Association Ltd., West Point, 33-34 Warple Way, Acton, London W3 0RQ, England. TEL 01-746-1616. Ed. Katie Warburg. adv.; circ. 10,000.
Formerly: Squash Rackets Association. Handbook (ISSN 0081-3885)

796.34 UK ISSN 0952-8512
SQUASH WORLD.* 1986. 9/yr. £15 (foreign £21). Stonehart Leisure Magazines, 67-71 Goswell Rd., London EC1V 7EN, England. TEL 03727-41411. FAX 03727-44493. Ed. Larry Halpin. circ. 10,000. (back issues avail.)
Description: Articles on coaching, fitness, diet, and injuries. Includes tournament reports and previews.

796.257 US ISSN 0161-2018
GV877
STREET & SMITH'S BASEBALL. Variant title: Sport's Official Baseball Yearbook. 1941. a. $3.95. Street & Smith's Sports Group (Subsidiary of: Conde Nast Publications, Inc.), 304 E. 45th St., New York, NY 10017. TEL 212-880-8698. FAX 212-490-7927. Ed. Gerard Kavanagh. adv.; circ. 300,198.
Formerly: Street and Smith's Baseball Yearbook (ISSN 0491-1520)
Description: Provides information regarding teams representing the National, American, and Minor Leagues. Includes official National and American League schedules - official statistics, rosters, recap of league championship series, World Series, and individual records of hitters and pitchers. Player and team profiles, historical and topical features, and a review of the past season and a preview of the coming season.

796.33 US ISSN 0091-9977
GV956.8
STREET & SMITH'S COLLEGE FOOTBALL. Variant title: Sport's Official College Football Yearbook. a. $3.95. Street & Smith's Sports Group, 304 E. 45th St., New York, NY 10017. TEL 212-880-8698. FAX 212-490-7927. Ed. Gerard Kavanagh. adv.; illus.; circ. 273,559.
Description: Furnishes analyses of over 270 college football teams. Schedules include teams from each major conference. Player and team profiles, historical and topical features, review of past season and preview of coming season.

796.323 US
STREET & SMITH'S COLLEGE - PREP BASKETBALL. a. $3.95. Street & Smith's Sports Group (Subsidiary of: Conde Nast Publications, Inc.), 304 E. 45th St., New York, NY 10017. TEL 212-880-8698. FAX 212-490-7972. circ. 279,351.
Description: Covers major college teams, conferences, independents with over 450 scouting reports, team and conference schedules, team and individual statistics, TV-radio listings, as well as pre-season ratings. Includes All America teams on the collegiate and scholastic level.

796.32 US ISSN 0149-7103
GV885.7
STREET & SMITH'S PRO BASKETBALL. Variant title: Sport's Official Pro Basketball Yearbook. a. $3.95. Street & Smith's Sports Group (Subsidiary of: Conde Nast Publications, Inc.), 304 E. 45th St., New York, NY 10017. TEL 212-880-8698. FAX 212-490-7927. Ed. Jim O'Brien. adv.; illus.; circ. 241,810.
Formerly: Street and Smith's College and Pro Official Basketball Yearbook (ISSN 0092-511X)
Description: For coaches, players and avid basketball enthusiasts. Covers scouting reports, team and conference schedules, individual statistics, TV-radio listings as well as pre-season ratings.

796.33 US ISSN 0092-3214
GV937
STREET & SMITH'S PRO FOOTBALL. Variant title: Sport's Official Pro Football Yearbook. a. $3.95. Street & Smith's Sports Group (Subsidiary of: Conde Nast Publications, Inc.), 304 E. 45th St., New York, NY 10017. TEL 212-880-8698. FAX 212-490-7927. Ed. Gerard Kavanagh. adv.; illus.; circ. 311,484. (reprint service avail. from UMI)
Description: Provides information regarding teams representing the National Football conference, American Football conference, and Canadian Football League. Includes NFL rosters, schedules, individual player records, review of past season and preview of coming season.

796.342 US
STRINGER'S ASSISTANT. 1975. m. $54. United States Racquet Stringers Association, Box 40, Del Mar, CA 92104. TEL 619-481-3545. FAX 619-481-0624. adv.; circ. 6,622. **Indexed:** Sportsearch (1984-).
Description: Covers new products, industry trends, technical product information, and stringing techniques.

796.352 GW
STROKESAVER. 1988. 5/yr. H und K Sportmarketing GmbH, Am Schlosspark 3-5, 6200 Wiesbaden, Germany. TEL 0611-609070. adv. (back issues avail.)
Description: Provides information on various golf courses throughout Germany.

SPORTS AND GAMES — BALL GAMES

796.334   UK
SUN SOCCER ANNUAL. a. £3.75. Invincible Press Ltd., 77-85 Fulham Palace Rd., London W6 8JB, England. TEL 081-741-7070. circ. 40,000.
    Description: Previews the soccer season, player profiles, and club news.

796.323   IT
SUPERBASKET. 1978. 45/yr., (plus suppl.). L.108000. Rusconi Editori Associati S.p.A., Via Oldofredi 23, 20124 Milan, Italy. Ed.Aldo Giordani. circ. 80,000.

796.334   SW
SVENSK FOTBOLL. m. (10/yr.). SEK 399. (Svenska Fotbollfoerbundet) Cewe Foerlaget, P.O. Box 77, 890 10 Bjaesta, Sweden. (Subscr. to: PK-Banken, Box 365, 891 01 Oernskoeldsvik, Sweden) adv.; circ. 36,500.

796.352   SW
SVENSK GOLF. 1946. 12/yr. SEK 275. Swedish Golf Federation, P.O. Box 84, 182 11 Danderyd, Sweden. FAX 8-622-6930. Ed. Anders Janson. adv.; circ. 180,000.

796.342   SW
▼**SVENSK TENNIS/SWEDISH TENNIS.** (Text in Swedish) 1991. 9/yr. SEK 198 (foreign SEK 248). I C A - foerlaget, S-721 85 Vaesteraas, Sweden. TEL 46-21-19-40-00. FAX 46-21-19-42-21. Hans Mejdevi. adv.; circ. 98,000.
    Description: Covers tennis in Sweden and worldwide.

796.357   JA
SYUKAN BASEBALL. (Text in Japanese) 1958. w. 13770 Yen. Baseball Magazine Sha, 3-10-10 Misaki-cho, Chiyoda-ku, Tokyo, Japan. Ed. Takao Ouchi.

796.346   UK   ISSN 0039-8799
TABLE TENNIS NEWS. 1966. 8/yr. £10. English Table Tennis Association, 3rd Fl., Queensbury House, Havelock Rd., Hastings, E. Sussex TN34 1HF, England. TEL 0424-722525. FAX 0424-422103. Ed. John Wood. adv.; bk.rev.; illus.; circ. 3,000.
    Description: Gives up-to-date information on national and international events and activities.

796.346   US   ISSN 0887-6576
    CODEN: USPS 9420
TABLE TENNIS TOPICS. 1933. 6/yr. $15. United States Table Tennis Association, U.S. Olympic Complex, 1750 E. Boulder St., Colorado Springs, CO 80909. TEL 719-578-4583. FAX 719-632-6071. TELEX 187258. Ed. Tim Boggan. adv.; bk.rev.; charts; illus.; circ. 7,000. (processed) **Indexed:** Sportsearch.
    Former titles: Spin Magazine; (until 1983): Table Tennis News.
    Description: Contains feature articles, player profiles, coaching tips, club profiles and soft news.

371.3   US
TEACHER'S COURT;* where pros meet pros. 1979. q. membership. American Professional Racquetball Organization, 9259 E. Raintree Dr., Ste. 1027, Scottsdale, AZ 85260-7521. TEL 602-945-0143. Ed. Mort Leve. circ. 400.

796.342   CS
▼**TENIS.** (Text in Czech or Slovak) 1990. m. 120 Kcs.($41.50) (Ceskoslovensky Svaz Telesne Vychovy) Olympia, Klimentska 1, 115 88 Praque 1, Czechoslovakia. TEL 231-5583. (Dist. by: Artia, Ve Smeckach 30, 111 27 Praque 1, Czechoslovakia) Ed. Karel Blaha.

796.342   US   ISSN 0040-3423
    GV991
TENNIS. 1965. m. $19.94. New York Times Company Magazine Group, Sports - Leisure Division, 5520 Park Ave., Box 395, Trumbull, CT 06611-0395. TEL 203-373-7000. Ed. Donna Doherty. adv.; bk.rev.; charts; illus.; circ. 755,000. (also avail. in microfilm from UMI) **Indexed:** Consum.Ind., Mag.Ind., Phys.Ed.Ind., PMR, Sports Per.Ind., Sportsearch (1977-).

796.342   IT
TENNIS. 1978. m. L.12000. Federazione Italiana Tennis, V.le Tiziano 70, 00196 Rome, Italy. Ed. Stefano Balducci. adv.; circ. 15,000.

796.342   DK   ISSN 0900-7105
TENNIS AVISEN. 1920. 7/yr. DKK 75. Dansk Tennis Forbund, Broendby-Stadion 20, 2605 Broendby, Denmark. FAX 45-02-456245. TELEX 33111. Ed. Chr. Weide Larsen. adv.; bk.rev.; circ. 5,000.
    Indexed: Consum.Ind.
    Formerly: Tennis.

796.342   US
TENNIS BUYERS GUIDE. 1984. 6/yr. $36. New York Times Company Magazine Group, Sports - Leisure Division, 5520 Park Ave., Box 395, Trumbull, CT 06611-0395. TEL 203-373-7000. adv.; bk.rev.; illus.; stat.; circ. 10,000. (tabloid format)

796.342   US   ISSN 0191-5851
TENNIS INDUSTRY. 1972. m. (except Jan.). $22. Sterling Southeast Inc., 1450 N.E. 123rd St., N. Miami, FL 33161-6051. TEL 305-893-8771. FAX 305-893-8783. TELEX 510-6009280. Ed. Jeff Williams. adv.; circ. 20,707 (controlled). **Indexed:** Sportsearch (1977-).

796   IT   ISSN 0393-0890
TENNIS ITALIANO. 1929. m. L.59500($72) (foreign L.93500). Edisport S.p.A., Via Boccaccio 47, 20123 Milan, Italy. Ed. Piero Bacchetti. adv.; bk.rev.; illus.; index; circ. 72,000.
    Description: Covers news about tennis, international and regional sports news, tests of rackets and shoes.

796.342   GW
TENNIS-JAHRBUCH. 1952. a. DM.25. Deutscher Tennis Bund e.V., Hallerstr. 89, 2000 Hamburg 13, Germany. TEL 040-411780. FAX 040-41178222. (Subscr. to: Buch- und Offsetdruckerei Sass und Co., Reinhard-Rube-Str. 7, 3400 Goettingen, Germany) circ. 4,500.

796.342   JA
TENNIS JOURNAL. (Text in Japanese) 1982. m. 8640 Yen. Ski Journal Co., Ltd., 3-11, Yotsuya, Shinjuku-Ku, Tokyo, Japan. Ed. Seiji Miyashita.

796.342   JA
TENNIS MAGAZINE. (Text in Japanese) 1970. bi-w. 9360 Yen. Baseball Magazine Sha, 3-10-10 Misaki-cho, Chiyoda-ku, Tokyo, Japan. Ed. Koishi Nemoto. **Indexed:** Mag.Ind.

796.342   FR
TENNIS MAGAZINE.* 1976. m. (11/yr.). 388 F. Disney Hachette Presse, 23-25 rue de Berri, 75388 Paris Cedex 08, France. TEL 16-1-44-89-44-89. (Subscr. to: 90 rue de Flandre, 75947 Paris Cedex 19. TEL 16-1-40-34-35-00) Ed. P. Zagdoun. adv.; illus.; circ. 158,000.

796.342   UK   ISSN 0262-9224
TENNIS MAGAZINE. 1981. m. £34. South of England Newspaper, 85 Castle Lane W., Bournemouth, Dorset BH9 3LH, England. TEL 0202-517555. FAX 0202-536439. Ed. C. Elder. adv.; circ. 15,000.
    Description: Provides coverage of tournaments in the UK and abroad, product reviews and tests, player profiles and coaching articles.

796.342   US
TENNIS MIDWEST. bi-m. Box 24379, Edina, MN 55424-0379. TEL 612-920-8947. FAX 612-927-7155. Ed. Geoff Gorvin. adv.; circ. 12,000.

796.342   US
TENNIS NEWS OF FLORIDA. m. 1710 E. Tiffany Dr., Ste. 102, W. Palm Beach, FL 33407. TEL 407-845-7181. FAX 407-845-7282. Ed. Nellie Wiggins. circ. 44,000.

796.342   US
TENNIS NORTHEAST. 1988. 8/yr. Regional Sports Publications, 7001 Peachtree Industrial Blvd., Ste. 404, Norcross, GA 30092. TEL 404-448-6226. FAX 404-368-2444. adv.; circ. 30,000.

796.342   US
TENNIS SOUTH. 1986. 8/yr. $12. Regional Sports Publications, 7001 Peachtree Industrial Blvd., Ste. 404, Norcross, GA 30092. TEL 404-448-6226. FAX 404-368-2444. adv.; circ. 40,000.

796.342   SZ
TENNIS TICINESE. 1975. m. 25 Fr. Federazione Ticinese Tennis, Casella Postale 88, 6906 Lugano 6, Switzerland. Ed. O. Mellini.

796.342   US
▼**TENNIS U S T A.** (In 4 regional eds.) 1990. m. membership. (U S Tennis Association) New York Times Magazine Group, Sports - Leisure Division, 5520 Park Ave., Box 395, Trumbull, CT 06611. TEL 203-373-7155. FAX 203-371-2199. Ed. Bob Moseley. circ. 450,000 (controlled).
    Description: Includes news of the association's events on the national, regional and sectional level, with feature stories.

796.342   US   ISSN 0194-9098
TENNIS WEEK. 1974. 20/yr. $40. Tennis News, Inc., 124 E. 40th St., Ste. 1101, New York, NY 10016. TEL 212-808-4750. FAX 212-983-6302. Ed.Bd. adv.; bk.rev.; illus.; circ. 62,901. (tabloid format)
    Formerly: Tennis News.

796.342   US
TENNIS WEST. 1983. 8/yr. $12. Regional Sports Publications, 7001 Peachtree Industrial Blvd., Ste. 404, Norcross, GA 30092. TEL 404-448-6226. FAX 404-368-2444. adv.; circ. 80,000.

796.346   UK   ISSN 0040-3474
TENNIS WORLD. 1969. 10/yr. £18 (foreign £25). Presswatch Ltd., Spendlove Centre, Enstone Rd., Charlbury, Oxford OX7 3PQ, England. TEL 0608-811446. FAX 0608-811380. Ed. Alastair McIver. adv.; bk.rev.; illus.; circ. 13,104. **Indexed:** Sportsearch (1976-).
    Description: Features interviews, profiles, tournament reports and previews.

796.342   FI
TENNISMAAILMA. 4/yr. Erikoislehdet Oy, Tecnopress, P.O. Box 61, 00381 Helsinki, Finland. TEL 358-0-120-5911. FAX 358-0-120-5959. Ed. Harri Roschier. circ. 12,000.

793.342 613.7   US
TENNISPRO. 1988. 5/yr. free to qualified personnel. U S Professional Tennis Registry Foundation, Box 6754, Hilton Head Island, SC 29938. TEL 803-686-8733. FAX 803-785-7032. Ed. Jennifer Gberlein. adv.; bk.rev.; circ. 9,600. (back issues avail.)
    Description: Educational trade publication for tennis teachers worldwide. Includes sport science, programming, sports medicine, new drills and product reviews.

796.342   IT
TENNISTA. 1979. m. (11/yr.). L.25000. Cuba S.p.A., Via Orti della Farnesina 137, 00194 Rome, Italy. adv.; circ. 105,000.

796.332   US
TEXAS FOOTBALL MAGAZINE. 1960. a. $7.50. (Sports Communications, Inc.) Host Creative Communications, Inc., 904 N. Broadway, Lexington, KY 40505-8162. TEL 606-252-6681. (Subscr. to: Box 3071, Lexington, KY 40596) Ed. Dave Campbell. adv.; circ. 199,562. (back issues avail.)

796.342   US
TEXAS TENNIS. 1987. 8/yr. $12. Regional Sports Publications, 7001 Peachtree Industrial Blvd., Ste. 404, Norcross, GA 30092. TEL 404-448-6226. FAX 404-368-2444. adv.; circ. 30,000.

TIP. see SPORTS AND GAMES

796.342   GW   ISSN 0938-1910
TISCHTENNIS LEHRE. 1986. 6/yr. DM.27.30. B U G Verlag, Steppenbergallee 41, 5100 Aachen, Germany. TEL 02421-15568. FAX 02421-15285. Ed. Bernd Ulrich Gross. circ. 2,000. (back issues avail.)

796.346   AU   ISSN 0040-814X
TISCHTENNIS-SCHAU. 1965. 6/yr. S.75. Verein zur Foerderung des Tischtennissports in Oesterreich, Neulerchenfelderstr. 5-7, A-1160 Vienna, Austria. adv.; bk.rev.; circ. 800.

796.332   UK
TOPICAL TIMES FOOTBALL BOOK. 1959. a. £2.05. D.C. Thomson & Co. Ltd., 185 Fleet St., London EC4A 2HS, England.

SPORTS AND GAMES — BALL GAMES

796.357 US
▼**TOPPS.** 1990. q. $9.97. Topps Co., 245 36th St., Brooklyn, NY 11232. TEL 718-768-8900. Ed. Bob Woods. circ. 300,000.
  Description: For baseball card collectors between the ages of 9 and 16. Covers baseball and other sports stars and includes information about Topps and other brand-name cards.

TRADING CARDS. see *HOBBIES*

796.333 SA
TRANSVAAL RUGBY. (Text in Afrikaans and English) 1972. s-a. R.5. (Transvaal Rugby Football Union) Pieter Coetzee Promotions, P.O. Box 6842, Brackendowns 1454, South Africa. TEL 011-902-4656. Ed. P.H. Coetzee. adv.; bk.rev.; circ. 15,000.

796.334 SZ
▼**U E F A FLASH.** (Editions in English, French and German) 1991. m. free. Union of European Football Associations, Jupiterstr. 33, CH-3000 Bern 16, Switzerland. TEL 31-321735. FAX 31-321838. TELEX 912037-UEF-CH.

796.323 US
U M I'S SOUTHEASTERN BASKETBALL HANDBOOK. 1987. a. $5. U M I Publications, Inc., 1135 N. Tryon St., Box 30036, Charlotte, NC 28230. TEL 704-374-0420. FAX 704-374-0729. adv.; circ. 50,000.
  Description: Includes schedules, rosters and player profiles on S.E. college teams.

796.357 US
▼**U S A TODAY BASEBALL WEEKLY.** 1991. w. $35. 1000 Wilson Blvd., Arlington, VA 22229. TEL 800-USA-1415.

796.325 US
U S A VOLLEYBALL. 1986. a. $10 (effective Jun. 1991). Hagen Marketing and Communications, Box 707, Custer, SD 57730-0707. TEL 605-673-4100. FAX 605-673-4020. Ed. Ron Hagen. adv.; circ. 50,000. (back issues avail.)
  Description: Covers the activities, schedules, players and olympic information of the U S A team.

796.323 US ISSN 0041-5472
U S B W A TIP-OFF. 1959. m. (Nov.-Apr.). membership. United States Basketball Writers Association, c/o Joe Mitch, Ed., 803 Wildview Lane, St. Louis, MO 63011. TEL 703-780-8577. circ. 1,000. (processed)

796.35 US
U S CROQUET GAZETTE. 2/yr. Farsight Communications, Inc., 7100-24 Fairway Dr., Palm Beach Gardens, FL 33418-3763. TEL 407-627-4077. FAX 407-624-3040. Ed. Jack R. Osborn. circ. 10,000.

796.352 US ISSN 0041-5502
GV975
U S G A GREEN SECTION RECORD. 1963. 6/yr. $12. United States Golf Association, Far Hills, NJ 07931. TEL 908-234-2300. Ed. James T. Snow. bk.rev.; illus.; index; circ. 12,000. **Indexed:** Sportsearch (1977-).
  Formerly: Turf Management Affairs Section of USGA Journal and Turf Management.

796.352 US
U S OPEN MAGAZINE. a. Times Mirror Magazines, Inc., Sports Marketing Group, 2 Park Ave., No. 6, New York, NY 10016-5691. TEL 203-849-5040. Ed. George Peper. adv.; circ. 300,000.

796.352 US
▼**U S SENIOR OPEN MAGAZINE.** 1991. a. $5. (United States Golf Association) Times Mirror Magazines, Inc., Sports Marketing Group, 2 Park Ave., 5th fl., New York, NY 10016. TEL 212-779-5000. Ed. George Peper. adv.; circ. 350,000.
  Description: Covers the U S G A event, its history and past champions, and its present course and players.

796.357 US
U S Y S A NATIONAL DIRECTORY.* 1988. s-a. free. United States Youth Soccer Association, Inc., 2050 N. Plano Rd., No. 100, Richardson, TX 75082-4404. TEL 901-278-7972. Ed. Larry D. Austin. circ. 300.

796.334 US
U S Y S A NETWORK.* 1987. q. free to qualified personnel. United States Youth Soccer Association, Inc., 2050 N. Plano Rd., No. 100, Richardson, TX 75082-4404. TEL 918-584-1593. Ed. Gayl Wilson. adv.; bk.rev.; illus.; stat.; circ. 150,000. (tabloid format)
  Description: National and regional news of and for young players, their referees, coaches and parents.

796 SZ ISSN 0501-1590
UNION OF EUROPEAN FOOTBALL ASSOCIATIONS. BULLETIN. q. 50 Fr. includes its Press Releases. Union of European Football Associations - Union des Associations Europeenes de Football, 33 Jupiter Strasse, Case Postale 16, CH-3000 Berne 15, Switzerland. TEL 031-321735. FAX 031-321838. TELEX 912037-UEF-CH.
  Description: Includes association news, reports and results of events, championships, tournaments, international news, coming events, meetings, and new books.

796 SZ ISSN 0570-2070
UNION OF EUROPEAN FOOTBALL ASSOCIATIONS. HANDBOOK OF U E F A. (Text in English, French and German) 1959. base vol. (plus updates 3/yr.). 100 Fr. for base vol., updates 30 Fr. Union of European Football Associations - Union des Associations Europeennes de Football, 33 Jupiter Strasse, Case Postale 16, CH-3000 Berne 15, Switzerland. TEL 031-321735. FAX 031-321838. TELEX 912037-UEF-CH. Ed. U. Rudolph Rothenbuehler. bk.rev.; circ. 2,500.

796.352 US
U.S. WOMEN'S OPEN MAGAZINE. a. (United States Golf Association) Times Mirror Magazines, Inc., Sports Marketing Group, 2 Park Ave., 5th Fl., New York, NY 10016. TEL 212-779-5000. Ed. George Peper. adv.; circ. 200,000.
  Description: Covers the history of the event and the site, profiles of past champions, and analysis of the golf course.

796.353 US ISSN 0083-3118
UNITED STATES POLO ASSOCIATION. YEARBOOK. 1890. a. $25. United States Polo Association, 4059 Iron Works Pike, Lexington, KY 40511. FAX 606-231-9738. adv.; circ. 3,000.

796.343 US ISSN 0083-3398
UNITED STATES SQUASH RACQUETS ASSOCIATION. OFFICIAL YEAR BOOK. 1925. a. $6. United States Squash Racquets Association, Box 1216, Bala-Cynwyd, PA 19004. TEL 215-667-4006. FAX 215-667-6539. Ed. Darwin P. Kingsley, III. adv.; index; circ. 10,000.

796.342 US
UNITED STATES TENNIS ASSOCIATION. YEARBOOK. 1937. a. $16. H.O. Zimman, Inc., 152 Lynnway Seaport Landing, Lynn, MA 01902-3419. Ed. Adam Scharff. adv.; circ. 15,000.
  Formerly: United States Lawn Tennis Association. Yearbook (ISSN 0083-1557)

796.325 US
GV1017.V6
UNITED STATES VOLLEYBALL ASSOCIATION. OFFICIAL VOLLEYBALL RULE BOOK. 1920. a. $4. United States Volleyball Association, 8700 W. Bradley Rd., Milwaukee, WI 53224. TEL 800-638-1502. TELEX 719-635-0426. adv.; bk.rev.; index; circ. 41,000. (also avail. in microfiche)
  Formerly: United States Volleyball Association. Official Volleyball Guide (ISSN 0083-3592)

796.352 US
UTAH GOLF. q. Intermountain Publishing Corp. (Salt Lake City), 2319 Foothill Dr., No. 280, Salt Lake City, UT 84109. TEL 801-487-4653. FAX 801-467-7746. Ed. James F. Bailey. adv.; circ. 20,000.

796.334 NE ISSN 0042-7977
VOETBAL INTERNATIONAL. 1965. w. fl.3.35 per no. Postbus 817, 2900 AV Capelle aan den Yssel, Netherlands. Ed. C. van Cuilenborg. adv.; circ. 200,000. (tabloid format)

796.334 NE
VOETBAL TOTAAL. 1972. m. fl.47.50. Koninklijke Nederlandsche Voetbalbond - Royal Dutch Football Federation, P.O. Box 515, 3700 AM Zeist, Netherlands. TEL 03439-9211. FAX 03439-1397. (U.S. subscr. addr.: IPC Business Press Inc., 205 E. 42nd St., New York, NY 10017) adv.; illus.; stat.; circ. 30,500 (controlled).
  Former titles: K N V Ber; Nederlands Voetbal (ISSN 0047-9284)
  Description: Soccer teams and matches.

796.325 NE ISSN 0167-0247
VOLLEYBAL. 1952. m. fl.32.50 (foreign fl.47.50). Nederlandse Volleybal Bond - Dutch Vollyeball Association, Postbus 70, 3440 AB Woerden, Netherlands. TEL 03480-11994. FAX 03480-20809. TELEX 70421 NEVOB NL. Ed. Chr. Mast. adv.; bk.rev.; illus.; stat.; circ. 10,500.
  Formerly: Volley Kroniek (ISSN 0049-6731)
  Description: Technical and general coverage of national and international volleyball affairs.

796.325 US
▼**VOLLEYBALL.** 1990. bi-m. $12.95. Western Empire Publications, Box 3010, San Clemente, CA 92672. TEL 714-492-7873. FAX 714-498-6485. Ed. David Gilovich. circ. 30,000.
  Description: Contains instruction from coaches, players and pros. Covers competition including high school, Olympic and pro beach tours and profiles top talent and equipment.

796.325 US
VOLLEYBALL CASE BOOK. biennial. $2.75. National Federation of State High School Associations, 11724 N.W. Plaza Circle, Box 20626, Kansas City, MO 64195-0626. TEL 816-464-5400. FAX 816-464-5571.

796.325 US
VOLLEYBALL MONTHLY. 1982. m. $19.95. Straight Down, Inc., 1880 Santa Barbara St., Ste. F, San Luis Obispo, CA 93401. TEL 805-541-2294. FAX 805-541-2438. (Subscr. to: Box 3137, San Luis Obispo, CA 93403) Ed. Dennis Steers. adv.; bk.rev.; circ. 60,000. (back issues avail.) **Indexed:** Sports Per.Ind., Sportsearch (1984-).

796.325 US
VOLLEYBALL RULEBOOK. a. $2.75. National Federation of State High School Associations, 11724 N.W. Plaza Circle, Box 20626, Kansas City, MO 64195-0626. TEL 816-464-5400. FAX 816-464-5571.

796.352 US
▼**WESTERN LINKS.** 1991. bi-m. $17.95. Southern Links Magazine Publishing Associates, Box 76289, Hilton Head Island, SC 29938. TEL 803-842-6200. FAX 803-842-6233. Ed. Mark Brown. adv.; circ. 60,000 (controlled).
  Description: Includes travel information on golf locations in 13 Western states, interviews with golf legends and leaders; covers emerging trends and controversial issues.

796.352 US
WESTERN OPEN (YEAR). a. $4. Western Golf Association, 1 Briar Rd., Golf, IL 60029. TEL 708-724-4600. FAX 708-724-7133. adv.; circ. 20,000.
  Description: Covers Chicago's own golf tournament.

796.342 GW
WESTFALEN TENNIS. 1982. m. DM.50. Borgsmuller, Weseler Str. 54, 4400 Munster, Germany. circ. 10,000.

794.6 US
WINDY CITY BOWLING NEWS. bi-m. 2871 Klovar Ln., E. Troy, WI 53120. TEL 414-642-3989. FAX 414-642-5138. Ed. Lisa Vint.

796.332 US
WINNING POINTS.* 1972. 19/yr. $30. Starpoint Publishing Corporation, 438 W. 37th St., New York, NY 10018. TEL 212-749-4619. adv.; charts; stat.; circ. 20,000.

SPORTS AND GAMES — BICYCLES AND MOTORCYCLES

796.352 US
WISCONSIN GOLF. 1989. 8/yr. $12.95. Killarney Press, 2317 International Lane, Ste. 204, Madison, WI 53704. TEL 608-224-2600. FAX 608-224-2603. adv.; circ. 10,000.
Description: Features local golf personalities, tournaments, and courses. Covers travel, environmental issues, equipment and apparel, and instruction.

WISCONSIN GOLF DIRECTORY. see *BUSINESS AND ECONOMICS — Trade And Industrial Directories*

796.35 UK ISSN 0263-9041
WISDEN CRICKET MONTHLY. 1979. m. £33.50. Wisden Cricket Magazines Ltd., 6 Beech Lane, Guildford, Surrey GU2 5ES, England. FAX 0483-33153. (Subscr. to: First Floor, Stephenson House, Brunel Centre, Bletchley, Milton Keynes MK2 2EW) Ed. David Frith. adv.; bk.rev.; illus.; stat.; circ. 42,000.

794.6 US ISSN 0043-7255
GV901
WOMAN BOWLER. 1936. 8/yr. $6 (typically set in Aug.). Women's International Bowling Congress, Inc., 5301 S. 76th St., Greendale, WI 53129. TEL 414-421-9000. FAX 414-421-3013. Ed. Karen Sytsma. adv.; illus.; circ. 140,000. **Indexed:** Sports Per.Ind., Sportsearch (1977-).

796.357 US ISSN 0899-5508
WOMEN'S FASTPITCH WORLD. 1988. m. $35.99. Windmill Publishers, Box 326, St. Charles, IL 60174. TEL 708-377-7917. FAX 708-377-5330. circ. 6,000.
Description: News about women's and girls' fast pitch softball, with emphasis on coaching material.

796.352 US
WORLD AMATEUR GOLF COUNCIL. RECORD BOOK. 1958. biennial. membership. World Amateur Golf Council, Golf House, Box 708, Far Hills, NJ 07931-0708. TEL 908-234-2300. TELEX 710-986-2521. circ. 1,000.
Description: Covers world amateur team championships in golf.

796.31 US ISSN 1040-5216
WORLD BASEBALL. (Text in English, Spanish) 1983. 3/yr. $10. International Baseball Association, 201 S. Capitol Ave., Pan American Plaza, Ste. 490, Indianapolis, IN 46225. TEL 317-237-5757. FAX 317-237-5758. TELEX 981853 IBA HEAD UQ. Ed. E. David Osinski. adv.; charts; stat.; circ. 6,500. (back issues avail.)
Description: News on baseball around the world. Includes coverage of world tournaments and developments in the association's 71 member countries.

794.6 UK ISSN 0043-8278
WORLD BOWLS MAGAZINE. 1954. m. £14($40) Donald Newby Publications, Ltd., P.O. Box 17, East Horsley, Surrey KT24 5JU, England. TEL 0372-59319. Eds. Geoffrey Browne, Patrick Sullivan. adv.; bk.rev.; charts; illus.; tr.lit.; circ. 10,000. (also avail. in microform from UMI) **Indexed:** Sportsearch (1973-).
Incorporates: Bowling Times; British Bowls.

796.342 UK
WORLD OF TENNIS. 1969. a. £9.99. (International Tennis Federation) Harper Collins Publishers, 77-85 Fulham Palace Rd., London W6 8JB, England. FAX 081-307-4558. Ed. John Barrett. adv.; index; circ. 4,500.

796.334 UK ISSN 0043-9037
GV942
WORLD SOCCER. 1960. m. $30. Websters Publications Ltd., Onslow House, 60-66 Saffron Hill, London EC1N 8AY, England. Ed. Philip Rising. adv.; illus.; circ. 25,000. **Indexed:** Sportsearch (1973-).

794.6 028.5 US
Y A B A FRAMEWORK. 1964. 6/yr. free. Young American Bowling Alliance, 5301 S. 76th St., Greendale, WI 53129. TEL 414-421-4700. FAX 414-421-1194. Ed. Laura Plizka. adv.; circ. 25,000 (controlled). (tabloid format) **Indexed:** Sportsearch.
Former titles (until 1990): Y A B A World & Junior Bowler.
Description: Provides information, guidelines and recognition for sanctioned YABA coaches, association secretaries and sanctioned YABA bowling centers.

796.357 JA
YAKYO-TO/BASEBALL FANS.* (Text in Japanese) 1977. m. 6600 Yen. Nihon Sports Publishing Co. Ltd., 2-6, 2-chome, Hakusan, Bunkyo-ku, Tokyo, Japan. Ed. Yukio Koyanagi.

796.334 US
YOUTH SOCCER NEWS. 1985. m. Varsity Publications, 6506 23rd Ave. N.E., Seattle, WA 98115. TEL 203-524-8985. FAX 206-524-3710. adv.; circ. 28,600.
Description: Covers tournaments and leagues, youth soccer throughout Southern California, Washington, Nevada and Arizona. Includes coaching information and player profiles.

796.325 CC
ZHONGGUO PAIQIU/CHINA'S VOLLEYBALL. (Text in Chinese) q. $13.80. Xin Tiyu Zazhishe - New Sports Journal Publishing, 8 Tiyuguan Lu, Beijing 100061, People's Republic of China. TEL 751402. (Dist. in US by: China Books & Periodicals, Inc., 2929 24th St., San Francisco, CA 94110. TEL 415-282-2994) Ed. Yuan Weimin.

796.33 CC ISSN 1000-3517
ZUQIU SHIJIE/FOOTBALL WORLD. (Text in Chinese) 1981. m. $35. (Zhongguo Zuqiu Xiehui - China Football Society) Renmin Tiyu Chubanshe, 8 Tiyuguan Lu, Chongwen Qu, Beijing 100061, People's Republic of China. TEL 757161. (Dist. in US by: China Books & Periodicals, Inc., 2929 24th St., San Francisco, CA 94110. TEL 415-282-2994) Ed. Nian Weisi.

796 CN
20 - 20. 6/yr. Can.$15. Canadian Table Tennis Association, 1600 James Naismith Dr., Gloucester, Ont. K1B 5N4, Canada. TEL 613-748-5675. FAX 613-748-5705. illus.; circ. 5,000.
Description: Contains articles on and results of Canadians involved in table tennis.

SPORTS AND GAMES — Bicycles And Motorcycles

796.75 SW ISSN 0345-0813
ALLT OM M C. (MotorCyclar) 1965. 6/yr. SEK 165 (typically set in Jan.). Albinsson & Sjoebring Foerlags AB, Box 529, S-371 23 Karlskrona, Sweden. TEL 45-455-196-85. FAX 46-455-117-15. Ed. Peter Toernqvist. adv.; bk.rev.; circ. 22,065 (controlled). (back issues avail.)

388.347 796.7 IT
ALMANACCO LA MOTO. 1976. a. Edigamma s.r.l., Piazza dei Sanniti 9, 00185 Rome, Italy. TEL 06-4928412. FAX 06-4940719. Ed. Renato Circi. adv.; circ. 90,000.

388.47 US
AMERICAN ASSOCIATION OF BICYCLE IMPORTERS. NEWSLETTER. q. American Association of Bicycle Importers, c/o Philip Kamler, 234 Schuyler Ave., Kearney, NJ 07032. TEL 201-991-8200.

629.227 US ISSN 0002-7677
AMERICAN BICYCLIST & MOTORCYCLIST. 1879. m. $34 to qualified personnel; others $75 (effective Nov. 1990). Cycling Press, Inc., 80 Eighth Ave., New York, NY 10011. TEL 212-206-7230. FAX 212-633-0079. TELEX 220378 ABM. Ed. Chris Peterson. adv.; bk.rev.; illus.; tr.lit.; circ. 11,500. **Indexed:** Sportsearch (1976-).
Description: Trade publication for the bicycle industry: dealers, wholesale distributors, importers, and manufacturers.

796.7 US
AMERICAN BIG TWIN DEALER. q. Edgell Communications (Santa Ana), 1700 E. Dyer Rd., Ste. 250, Santa Ana, CA 92705-5716. TEL 714-252-5300. FAX 714-261-9790. Ed. Robin Handfield.

796.6 US
AMERICAN FREESTYLER. m. $17.95. Hi-Torque Publications, Inc., 10600 Sepulveda Blvd., Mission Hills, CA 91345. TEL 818-365-6831.

796.6 US
AMERICAN IRON MAGAZINE. m. $2.95 per no. T A M Communications Inc., 6 Prowitt St., Norwalk, CT 06855. TEL 203-855-0008. FAX 203-854-5962.

796.7 US
AMERICAN MOTORCYCLIST. 1947. m. $10. American Motorcyclist Association, Box 6114, Westerville, OH 43081-6114. TEL 614-891-2425. Ed. Greg Harrison. adv.; bk.rev.; illus.; index; circ. 165,312.
Former titles (until Sep. 1977): A M A News (ISSN 0003-0074); American Motorcycling.
Description: Focuses on the races and roadriding events sanctioned by the AMA each year, as well as motorcycle-related legislation at the various levels of government.

796.75 US
AMERICAN RACING MOTORCYCLES. 12/yr. Can.$20. 141 N. Meridian Rd., Youngstown, OH 44509.

796.6 FR
ANNEE DU CYCLISME. 1974. a. price varies. Editions Calmann-Levy, 3 rue Auber, 75009 Paris, France. illus.

796.6 AT ISSN 0819-3363
AUSTRALASIAN CYCLING & TRIATHOLON NEWS. 1985. m. Aus.$42. Jenbra Pty. Ltd., P.O. Box 4, Enmore 2042, Australia. TEL 02-361-4481. Ed. John Sheed. adv. (back issues avail.)

796.7 659.1 AT
AUSTRALASIAN DIRT BIKE. 1977. m. Aus.$45. A D B Holdings Pty. Ltd., P.O. Box 696, Brookvale, N.S.W. 2100, Australia. TEL 02-938-4155. FAX 02-939-2235. Ed. Geoff Eldridge. adv.; circ. 25,000. **Indexed:** Pinpointer.
Formerly: Cycle Australia.

796.6 AT ISSN 1034-3016
AUSTRALIAN CYCLIST. 1976. bi-m. Aus.$20 (foreign Aus.$30). Bicycle Federation of Australia, c/o P.O. Box 869, Artarmon, N.S.W. 2064, Australia. TEL 02-419-5419. FAX 02-412-1041. Ed. Neil Irvine. adv.; bk.rev.; circ. 117,400. (back issues avail.)
Formerly: Push On (ISSN 0157-0994)
Description: Covers all aspects of cycling, emphasising recreation and transportation.

796.75 AT ISSN 0158-4138
AUSTRALIAN MOTOR RACING YEAR. 1971. a. Aus.$39.95. Chevron Publishing Group Pty. Ltd., P.O. Box 206, Hornsby, N.S.W. 2077, Australia. FAX 02-476-5739. Ed. Thomas B. Floyd. circ. 15,000. (back issues avail.)
Description: Reviews Australian and major overseas motor sport championships.

796 AT
AUSTRALIAN RACING DRIVERS CLUB NEWSLETTER. 1971. 6/yr. Aus.$7. Australian Racing Drivers Club, Amaroo Park Raceway, Annangrove, N.S.W. 2156, Australia. FAX 61-2-679-1184. Ed. H. Ivan Stibbard. adv.; bk.rev.; circ. 2,000.
Formerly: Australian Racing Drivers Club Journal (ISSN 0311-0346)

796.7 AT
AUSTRALIAN TRAIL & TRACK MONTHLY. 1973. m. Aus.$22. L.W. & T.S. Nominees, Tootal Park, Tootal Rd., Dingley, Vic. 3172, Australia. Ed. Les Swallow. adv.; bk.rev.; circ. 24,000.
Formerly: Australian Trail and Track.

AUTOMARQUES; revue francaise du marche des automobiles neuves et d'occasion. see *TRANSPORTATION — Automobiles*

AUTORAMA; panoramica mensile delle attivita motoristiche. see *TRANSPORTATION — Automobiles*

AUTOREVUU. see *TRANSPORTATION — Automobiles*

796.6 UK
B M X ACTION BIKE.* 1981. m. £28. Muddy Fox Publications, 331 Athlon Rd., Wembley, Middx. HA0 1BY, England. Eds. Richard Grant, Nigel Thomas. adv.; circ. 69,000.

796.7 US
B M X PLUS. (Bicycle Motocross) m. $15.98. Hi-Torque Publications, Inc., 10600 Sepulveda Blvd., Mission Hills, CA 91345. TEL 818-365-6831.

BACK STREET HEROES. see *TRANSPORTATION — Automobiles*

SPORTS AND GAMES — BICYCLES AND MOTORCYCLES

796.75   GW
BAHNSPORT AKTUELL; Sandtrack - Speedway - Long Track - Ice Speedway. 1971. m. DM.70($12) Verlag Bahnsport Aktuell HG, Industriestr. 8, 6451 Rodenbach, Germany. TEL 06184-51051. FAX 06184-51004. Ed. Christian Kalabis. adv.; illus.; stat.; circ. 15,000. (back issues avail.)
    Description: International sports magazine for motorcycle racing. Features racing on sand courses, grass courses, on ice and speedways. Includes reports and results of events and championships, news, letters from readers, and future events.

BEST MOTORING. see *HOBBIES*

796.6   UK
BICYCLE ACTION.* 1984. m. £0.85 per no. Muddy Fox Publications, 331 Athlon Rd., Wembley. Middx. HA0 1BY, England. circ. 20,000.

796.6   US   ISSN 0745-8126
BICYCLE BUSINESS JOURNAL. 1947. m. $14. Quinn Publications, Inc. (Ft. Worth), 1904 Wenneca, Fort Worth, TX 76102. FAX 817-332-1619. adv.; charts; illus.; stat.; tr.lit.; index; circ. 10,000. **Indexed:** Sportsearch (1983-).
    Formerly: Bicycle Journal (ISSN 0006-2065)

380.1   US   ISSN 0361-381X
HD9999.B43
BICYCLE DEALER SHOWCASE. 1971. m. $35. Miramar Publishing Co., Box 3640, Culver City, CA 90231-3640. TEL 213-337-9717. Ed. Walt Jarvis. adv.; bk.rev.; illus.; circ. 10,661. **Indexed:** Sportsearch (1983-).
    Description: For bicycle and moped dealers with articles on selling and merchandizing.

796.6   US   ISSN 0361-381X
BICYCLE DEALER SHOWCASE BUYERS GUIDE. 1971. a. $35. Miramar Publishing Co., Box 3640, Culver City, CA 90231-3640. TEL 213-337-9717. (Subscr. to: 1 E. First St., Duluth, MN 55802) Ed. Walt Jarvis. adv.; circ. 10,148.
    Description: Annual guide for bicycle dealers.

796.6   US
BICYCLE FORUM. 1978. q. $20 to individuals; institutions $25. Bikecentennial, 150 E. Pine St., Missoula, MT 59802-4515. TEL 406-721-1776. (Subscr. to: Box 8308, Missoula, MT 59807-8308) index.
    Description: Offers a forum for readers and gives advice and information on issues of bicycle safety, education and facility design.

796.6   US   ISSN 0889-289X
GV1040
BICYCLE GUIDE. 1984. 9/yr. $12.95 (foreign $19.90). Raben Publishing Company, 545 Boylston St., 12th Fl., Boston, MA 02116-3606. TEL 617-236-1885. FAX 617-267-1849. (Subscr. to: Box 55729, Boulder, CO 80322-5729) Ed. Theodore Constantino. adv.; bk.rev.; circ. 165,000. **Indexed:** Sportsearch (1987-).
    Incorporates (in 1987): Bicycle Rider (Boston).

796.6   CN
BICYCLE HANDBOOK. 1977. a. Can.$3. Bicycling Association of British Columbia, 332-1367 West Broadway, Vancouver, B.C. V6H 4A9, Canada. Ed. Danelle Laidlaw. adv.; circ. 6,000.

796.6   US   ISSN 0742-8308
BICYCLE PAPER; the voice of Northwest cycling. 1972. m. (Mar.-Sep.); plus winter issue. $8. Northwest Classics, 7901 168th Ave., N.E., Ste. 103, Redmond, WA 98052. TEL 206-882-0706. Ed. Dave Shaw. adv.; bk.rev.; illus.; circ. 7,500. (tabloid format)
    Formerly: Great Bicycle Conspiracy.
    Description: Touring, racing, personality features. Includes calendar of events in the Northwest for bicycle enthusiasts.

796.6 658   US
▼**BICYCLE RETAILER AND INDUSTRY NEWS**. 1992. m. $24. JayWalker Publication, 1444-C S. St. Francis Dr., Santa Fe, NM 87501. TEL 505-988-5099. Ed. Marc Sani. adv.; B&W page $2520, color page $3150. (tabloid format)
    Description: Keeps retailers current on industry trends, new technology and marketing strategies.

796.6   US
BICYCLE RIDER (AGOURA). m. $15.98 (foreign $23.98). T L Enterprises, Inc., 29901 Agoura Rd., Agoura, CA 91301. TEL 818-991-4980. Ed. Bob Mendel. adv.

796.6   US   ISSN 0199-2139
GV1045
BICYCLE U S A. (Includes special ed.: Bicycle U S A Almanac) 1965. 8/yr. $25 to individuals; libraries $15. League of American Wheelmen, 190 W. Ostend St., Ste. 120, Baltimore, MD 21230. TEL 301-539-3399. FAX 301-539-3496. Ed. John W. Duvall. adv.; bk.rev.; circ. 21,000. **Indexed:** Sportsearch (1984-).
    Former titles: American Wheelmen; (until) 1979: L A W Bulletin.

796.6   UK
BICYCLES. 5th ed., 1987. every 18 mos. £155 per no. Key Note Publications Ltd., Filed House, Old Field Rd., Hampton TW12 2HQ, England. TEL 01-783-0755. FAX 01-250-3084. TELEX 23678.
    Description: Overview of the bicycle industry including industry structure, market size and trends, developments, future prospects, major company profiles.

796.6   US   ISSN 0006-2073
GV1040
BICYCLING. 1962. 10/yr. $15.97. Rodale Press, Inc., 33 E. Minor St., Emmaus, PA 18098. TEL 215-967-5171. TELEX 847338. Ed. Ed Pavelka. adv.; bk.rev.; illus.; index; circ. 266,465. (also avail. in microform from UMI; reprint service avail. from UMI) **Indexed:** Acad.Ind., Access, Consum.Ind., Hlth.Ind., Ind.How To Do It (1990-), Mag.Ind., Phys.Ed.Ind., PMR, Sports Per.Ind., Sportsearch (1974-).
    Formerly: American Cycling Magazine; Which incorporates (in 1981): American Cyclist.
    Description: Features fitness, training, nutrition, touring, racing, equipment, clothing, bike maintenance and new-product review.

796.6   UK   ISSN 0140-4547
BIKE. 1971. m. £22.20. E M A P National Publications Ltd., 20-22 Station Rd., Kettering, Northants NN15 7HH, England. TEL 0536-416416. FAX 0536-415748. Ed. Martyn Moore. adv.; bk.rev.; circ. 63,691.

796.6   GW
BIKE. 10/yr. DM.63 (foreign DM.74). Verlag Delius, Klasing und Co., Siekerwall 21, Postfach 4809, 4800 Bielefeld, Germany. TEL 0521-559283. FAX 0521-559113.

796.6   AT   ISSN 0810-2872
BIKE AUSTRALIA. bi-m. Aus.$60. Mason Stewart Publishing, 15-19 Boundary St., Rushcutters Bay, N.S.W. 2011, Australia. FAX 02-360-5357. adv.; circ. 7,516.

796.6   UK
BIKE BUYER. bi-m. £1.25. E M A P Pursuit Publications Ltd., Bretton Court, Bretton, Peterborough PE3 0UW, England. Ed. Dave Calderwood. adv.

796.6   US
BIKE JOURNAL. 9/yr. T A M Communications Inc., 6 Prowitt St., Norwalk, CT 06855. TEL 203-855-0008. FAX 203-854-5962.

796.6   SA
BIKE S.A.. 1975. m. R.26 (foreign R.41). Bike Promotions (Pty) Ltd., P.O. Box 894, Johannesburg 2000, South Africa. TEL 011-782-5521. FAX 011-888-3431. Ed. Simon Fourie. adv.; bk.rev.; illus.; circ. 24,000.
    Description: Information on motor bikes, bike gear and maintenance, courses and competitions.

388.347
BIKER; lifestyle magazine of events, news and bikes. bi-m. $3.50 per no. Paisano Publications, Inc., 28210 Dorothy Dr., Box 3075, Agoura Hills, CA 91301. TEL 818-889-8740. FAX 818-889-4726.

796.6 910.09   US
BIKEREPORT. 1975. 9/yr. $22 includes membership. Bikecentennial, Box 8308, Missoula, MT 59807-8308. TEL 406-721-1776. Ed. Daniel D'Ambrosio. adv.; bk.rev.; circ. 25,000. **Indexed:** Sportsearch.
    Description: Includes technical information, product news, articles concerning nutrition and training, and bicycling regulations.

BIROMBO. see *GENERAL INTEREST PERIODICALS — Italy*

796.7   AT
BORN TO DIE; the abominators bike magazine. 1989. 4/yr. Aus.$30. Bronson Family Publishing Group (Subsidiary of: U C P Publishing Pty. Ltd.), P.O. Box 604, Gladesville, N.S.W 2111, Australia. TEL 02-797-6387. FAX 920799-2125. Ed. Rod Bronson. circ. 40,000.
    Description: Covers custom motorcycles and Australian biker lifestyle.

388.347 640.73   US
BOSTON CYCLIST. 1979. bi-m. $15. Boston Area Bicycle Coalition, Box 1015, Kendall Square Branch, Cambridge, MA 02142-0008. TEL 617-491-RIDE. Ed. Scott Stevens. bk.rev.; charts; illus.; tr.lit.; circ. 425. (back issues avail.)
    Formerly: Spoke 'n Word.
    Description: Newsletter of the Coalition, a bicycle advocacy group working to promote the safe and practical use of the bicycle.

BRITISH CAR. see *TRANSPORTATION — Automobiles*

796.6   US
CALIFORNIA BICYCLIST. 1983. m. (11/yr.). $12. 490 2nd St., Ste. 304, San Francisco, CA 94107. TEL 415-546-7291. FAX 415-546-9106. Ed. Kimberly Grob. adv.; bk.rev.; circ. 175,000.

796.7   CN   ISSN 0820-8344
CANADIAN BIKER MAGAZINE. 1980. 8/yr. Can.$19.95($19.95) for 12 nos. Western Biker Publications Ltd., 2750 Rock Bay Ave., Victoria, B.C. V8X 3X4, Canada. TEL 604-384-0333. FAX 604-384-1832. (Subscr. to: P.O. Box 4122, Sta. "A", Victoria, B.C., V8X 3X4, Canada) Ed. W.L. Creed. adv.; bk.rev.; circ. 16,000. (back issues avail.)
    Description: Covers touring, off-road cycling, and news for motorcycle enthusiasts.

796.6   CN   ISSN 1180-1352
▼**CANADIAN CYCLIST**. 1990. 4/yr. Can.$14.35. Editions Tricycle, 3575 boul. Saint-Laurent, Bur. 310, Montreal, Que. H2X 2T7, Canada. TEL 514-847-1990. FAX 514-847-0242. Ed. Lyse Savard. adv.; circ. 30,000.

796.6   AT
CANBERRA CYCLIST. 1975. bi-m. Aus.$18. Pedal Power A.C.T., Inc., G.P.O. Box 581, Canberra, A.C.T. 2601, Australia. TEL 06-248-7995. FAX 06-207-3199. Ed. Neville Reece. adv.; bk.rev.; illus.; circ. 300. (back issues avail.)
    Formerly: Pedal Power (ISSN 0313-4334)
    Description: Includes rides calendar, ride reports, discounters list, new designs, letters to the editor, policy and planning reports.

796   AT
CAT-A-LOG. 1970. m. Aus.$1. Jaguar Car Club of Victoria, P.O. Box 161, Ringwood, Vic. 3134, Australia. Ed. John Howard Jones. adv.; bk.rev.; circ. 750.

629.227 796.7   US
CHILTON'S MOTORCYCLE AND A T V REPAIR MANUAL. (All-Terrain Vehicle) 1974. irreg. price varies. Chilton Co., Automotive Editorial Department, Chilton Way, Radnor, PA 19089.
    Incorporates: Chilton's Motorcycle Repair Manual.

796.6   US
CITY CYCLIST.* 1974. 6/yr. $20. Transportation Alternatives, 92 St. Marks. Pl., New York, NY 10009-5840. TEL 212-941-4600. FAX 212-274-8712. Ed.Bd. adv.; bk.rev.; circ. 8,000. **Indexed:** Sportsearch.
    Description: Covers bicycle transportation and environmental issues in New York City.

SPORTS AND GAMES — BICYCLES AND MOTORCYCLES

796   UK
CLASSIC BIKE. 1978. m. £21.60. E M A P National Publications Ltd., 20-22 Station Rd., Kettering, Northants NN15 7HH, England. TEL 0536-416416. FAX 0536-415748. Ed. John Pearson. adv.; circ. 59,428.

COMMERCE-REPARATION AUTOMOBILE. see TRANSPORTATION — Automobiles

CONTRACTSPELER. see SPORTS AND GAMES

796.7   GW   ISSN 0933-7792
CROSS MAGAZIN. 1986. m. DM.4. Suedwestdeutsche Verlagsanstalt Mannheim, R 1, Pressehaus am Marktplatz, 6800 Mannheim 1, Germany. TEL 0711-7200597. FAX 0621-1702-462. (Subscr. to: Zenit Pressevertrieb GmbH, Postfach 810640, 7000 Stuttgart 80, Germany) Ed. Juergen Tietze. adv.; circ. 15,343.

388.347   FR
LE CYCLE. m. 400 F. Societe EDI 92, 83 rue de Villiers, 92523 Neuilly sur Seine Cedex, France. TEL 47-38-64-64. FAX 47-47-53-16. TELEX 613448F. Ed. Dennis Jacob. circ. 60,000. **Indexed:** Acad.Ind.

796   CN   ISSN 0319-2822
CYCLE CANADA. French edition: Moto Journal (ISSN 0319-2865) 1971. m. Can.$24. Brave Beaver Pressworks Ltd., 86 Parliament St., Ste. 3B, Toronto, Ont. M5A 246, Canada. TEL 416-362-7966. FAX 416-362-3950. Ed. Bruce Reeve. adv.; bk.rev.; circ. 40,000. **Indexed:** CMI.

796.7   US
CYCLE NEWS; America's weekly motorcycle newspaper. w. $35. C N Publishing Group, 2201 Cherry Ave., Box 498, Long Beach, CA 90801. TEL 310-427-7433. FAX 310-427-6685. Ed. Jack Mangus. adv.; bk.rev.; film rev.; charts; illus.; circ. 38,000.
    Formed by the merger of: Cycle News - West and Cycle News - East; Cycle News - Central Edition.
    Description: Provides news on all aspects of motorcycling.

796.6   CN
CYCLE ONTARIO. m. Can.$14($21) (effective Jan. 1991). (Ontario Cycling Association) Pedal, Canadian Cycling News, 710 Spadina Ave., Ste. 709, Toronto, Ont. M5S 2J3, Canada. TEL 416-927-9681. FAX 416-495-4038. Ed. Dwight Yachuk. adv.; bk.rev.; circ. 5,000. (looseleaf format; back issues avail.)
    Formerly: Bicycle Ontario.
    Description: Coverage of all forms of cycling; racing, MTB, BMX and R&T. Includes a full calendar of events.

629.2   US   ISSN 0272-8923
TL440
CYCLE STREET AND TOURING GUIDE. 1980. a. $2.95. C B S, Inc. Publishing Co., Cycle (Subsidiary of: C B S, Inc.), 1515 Broadway, New York, NY 10036. TEL 212-719-6000. illus.

796.6   UK
CYCLE TOURING & CAMPAIGNING. 1878. bi-m. £15. Cyclists' Touring Club, 69 Meadrow, Godalming, Surrey GU7 3HS, England. TEL 0483-417217. FAX 0483-426994. Ed. Tim Hughes. adv.; bk.rev.; illus.; circ. 33,000. **Indexed:** Sportsearch.
    Formerly: Cycletouring.

796.6   UK
CYCLE TRADER. 1982. m. $62. Turret Group Plc., Turret House, 171 High St., Rickmansworth, Herts WD3 1SN, England. TEL 0923-777000. FAX 0923-221346. TELEX 9419706. Ed. Andrew Sutcliffe. adv.

796 016   US   ISSN 0011-4286
TL440
CYCLE WORLD. 1961. m. $19.94 (Europe $27.95; Canada $26.94). Hachette Magazines, Inc., 1499 Monrovia Ave., Newport Beach, CA 92663. TEL 800-456-3084. FAX 714-631-0651. (Subscr. to: Box 2776, Boulder, CO 80323) Ed. David Edward. adv.; bk.rev.; circ. 372,398. (also avail. in microform from UMI,MIM; reprint service avail. from UMI; back issues avail.) **Indexed:** Acad.Ind., Consum.Ind., Mag.Ind., PMR, R.G., Sportsearch. —BLDSC shelfmark: 3506.412000.
    Incorporates (in Oct. 1991): Cycle (New York, 1952) (ISSN 0574-8135)

796.7   US
CYCLE WORLD BUYER'S GUIDE. a. $3.95. Hachette Magazines, Inc. (Subsidiary of: Diamandis Communications, Inc.), 1499 Monrovia Ave., Newport Beach, CA 92663. TEL 714-720-5300. (Subscr. to: Cycle World, Box 51222, Boulder, CO 80321-1222) adv.; stat. (back issues avail.)
    Description: Covers riding impressions and previews of new motorcycles, scooters, ATV's and watercraft.

796   US   ISSN 0270-2746
TL440
CYCLE WORLD TEST ANNUAL AND BUYERS GUIDE. 1971. a. $3.50. C B S Magazines (Subsidiary of: C B S, Inc.), 1515 Broadway, New York, NY 10036. TEL 212-719-6000. Ed. Paul Dean. adv.; bk.rev.; charts; illus.; tr.lit.
    Formerly: Cycle World Road Test Annual.

796.75   CN
CYCLE 1. French edition: Motocycliste. 8/yr. Jevco Publishing Co., 2021 Union St., Ste. 1150, Montreal, Que. H3A 2S9, Canada. TEL 514-284-1732. FAX 514-289-9257.

796.6   JA
CYCLERACE MAGAZINE. (Text in Japanese) 1978. m. 6240 Yen. Baseball Magazine Sha, 3-10-10 Misaki-cho, Chiyoda-ku, Tokyo, Japan. Ed. Yoshihiro Shimotori.

796.6   CN
CYCLING: B.C.. m. membership. Bicycling Association of British Columbia, 332-1367 W. Broadway, Vancouver, B.C. V6H 4A9, Canada. Ed. Betty Third.

796.6   US
CYCLING U.S.A. 1980. m. $10. U.S. Cycling Federation, 1750 E. Boulder, Colorado Springs, CO 80909. FAX 719-578-4628. Ed. Steve Penny. adv.; illus.; circ. 30,000.
    Description: Offers federation-related news reports and releases, feature articles on all aspects of bicycle racing, profiles of coaches and cyclists, and information on events and programs of interest to federation members.

796.6   UK   ISSN 0011-4316
CYCLING WEEKLY. 1891. w. £45. I P C Magazines Ltd., Kings Reach Tower, Stamford Sd., London SE1 9LS, England. TEL 071-261-5849. FAX 071-261-7851. (Subscr. to: Reed Business Publishing Ltd.: 205 E. 42nd St., New York, NY 10017, U.S.A.) Ed. Martin Ayres. adv.; bk.rev.; illus.; circ. 38,970. **Indexed:** Sportsearch.
    Formerly: Cycling and Mopeds.
    Description: Covers all aspects of competitive cycle racing in the UK and abroad.

796   UK   ISSN 0143-0238
CYCLING WORLD. 1979. m. £30. Stone Leisure Group Ltd., Andrew House, 2a Granville Rd., Sidcup, Kent DA14 4BN, England. TEL 081-302-6150. FAX 081-302-1813. Ed. Robert Griffiths. adv.; circ. 35,000.
    Description: Cycling magazine for touring in Europe.

388.347   AT
CYCLING WORLD; the Australian bicycling magazine. 1977. bi-m. (with 2 special issues). Aus.$19.98. Mason Stewart Publishing Pty. Ltd., P.O. Box 746, Darlingurst, N.S.W. 2010, Australia. FAX 02-360-5367. Ed. Chuck Smeeton. adv.; bk.rev.; circ. 16,000. (back issues avail.) **Indexed:** Aus.Rd.Ind., Pinpointer, Sportsearch (1990-).
    Formerly (until 1990): Freewheeling (ISSN 0156-4579)

796.6   US
CYCLIST.* vol.3, 1986. 9/yr. $14.97. Cyclist Magazine Publishing Corp., 234 E. 46th St., Ste. 18-B, New York, NY 10017-2934. TEL 213-328-5700. (Subscr. to: Cyclist Reader Service, Box 993, Farmingdale, NY 11737-0001) Ed. John Francis.

796.6   US
CYCLISTS' YELLOW PAGES. a. membership only. Bikecentennial, 150 E. Pine St., Missoula, MT 59802-4515. TEL 406-721-1776. (Subscr. to: Box 8308, Missoula, MT 59807-8308) maps.
    Description: Information resource for bicyclists covering all 50 states, all Canadian provinces and territories, and 58 foreign countries; includes listings of hostels, bike shops, tour operators, cycling books and videos; tips on transporting bicycles (including airline regulations), getting in shape, and places to go mountain biking.

796.6   FR
CYCLO 2000. 1926. 7/yr. 170 F. Cyclo 2000, 19 rue de Boeuf, 69005 Lyon, France. TEL 78-42-44-08. adv.; illus.

796.6   FR
CYCLOTOURISME. 1929. m. 250 F. Federation Francaise de Cyclotourisme, 8 rue Jean Marie Jego, 75013 Paris, France. Ed.Bd. adv.; bk.rev.; circ. 25,000.

796.6   FR
CYCLOTOURISTE; le magazine des passionnes du velo. Cover title: Cyclo 2000. 1926. 7/yr. 170 F. Cyclo 2000, 19 rue de Boeuf, 69005 Paris, France. TEL 78-42-44-08. adv.; bk.rev.; illus.; circ. 5,000.

796.6   DK
CYKELBRANCHEN; fagblad for cykel-og krallertbranchen. 1899. fortn. membership. Cykelhandlernes Centralforening, Ny Kongensgade 20, 1557 Copenhagen V, Denmark. Ed. Erik Svebolle. adv.; bibl.; mkt.; index; circ. 1,500.
    Former titles (until Jan. 1978): Styret (ISSN 0039-4319); Cykelhandleren.

796.6   DK   ISSN 0107-7805
CYKLE-JUL. 1936. a. DKK 48. Joergen Beyerholm, Ed. & Pub., Vestervang 35, DK-3450 Blovstroed, Denmark. illus.
    Formerly: Cyclen.
    Description: Cycling magazine with Scandinavian championship results. Photos and stories of recent bicycling developments and racing history.

796.6   DK   ISSN 0109-4211
CYKLEN. 1982. 6/yr. DKK 58.50. Ole Jensen, Gothersgade 157-159, 1123 Copenhagen K, Denmark. Ed. Jan Marker. adv.; bk.rev.; illus.; circ. 15,000.

796   SW   ISSN 0280-3038
CYKLING.* 1935. 4/yr. SEK 50. Cykelfraemjandet - Swedish Cycling Promotion Institute, Box 6027, S-102 31 Stockholm, Sweden. TEL 8-101086. Ed. Lars Thoerngren. adv.; bk.rev.; illus.; circ. 11,000.
    Formerly (until 1981): Cykel- och Mopednytt (ISSN 0011-4391)

796.7   DK   ISSN 0109-3649
D M C - BLADET. 1982. bi-m. membership. Danske Motorcyklisters Raad, 54 Regstrupparken, P.O. Box 10, DK-4420 Regstrup, Denmark. Ed. Rolf Skovhoekke. adv.; bk.rev.; illus.
    Formerly (until Nov. 1983): D M C (ISSN 0107-8984)

629.227   US   ISSN 0888-4234
TL440
DEALERNEWS; the voice of the power sports vehicle industry. 1965. m. $25 (free to qualified personnel). Avanstar Communications, Inc., 7500 Old Oak Blvd., Cleveland, OH 44130. (Subscr. to: Box 6050, Duluth, MN 55806) Ed. Jay Koblenz. adv.; circ. 14,203. **Indexed:** Bus.Ind., Tr.& Indus.Ind.
    Former titles: Motorcycle DealerNews (ISSN 0192-0219); M D N Motorcycle Dealer News (ISSN 0887-0950)
    Description: News about merchandising and sales techniques, national trends, business conditions.

796.7   US   ISSN 0364-1546
TL440
DIRT BIKE. 1971. m. $14.98. Hi-Torque Publications, Inc., 10600 Sepulveda Blvd., Mission Hills, CA 91345. TEL 818-365-6831. Ed. Rick Sieman. adv.; circ. 176,062. **Indexed:** Jun.High.Mag.Abstr., Sportsearch.

796.6   US
DIRT BIKE CRASH AND BURN. 3/yr. $2.50 per no. Daisy - Hi-Torque Publications, Inc., 10600 Sepulveda Blvd., Mission Hill, CA 91345. TEL 818-365-6831.

SPORTS AND GAMES — BICYCLES AND MOTORCYCLES

796.7   US   ISSN 0735-4355
DIRT RIDER MAGAZINE. 1982. m. $17.94. Petersen Publishing Co., 8490 Sunset Blvd., Los Angeles, CA 90069. TEL 213-854-2222. Ed. Charlie Morey. adv.; illus.; circ. 159,900. (also avail. in microfilm from UMI) **Indexed:** Ind.How To Do It (1990-).

796.6   US
DIRT WHEELS. m. $14.98. Hi-Torque Publications, Inc., 10600 Sepulveda Blvd., Mission Hills, CA 91345. TEL 818-365-6831.

796.7   US
EAST COAST IRON BIKER NEWS. m. Steel Publications, Box 201, Landisville, NJ 08326. TEL 609-697-1335. FAX 609-697-8387.

796   US   ISSN 0046-0990
GV1059.5
EASYRIDERS. 1971. m. $34.95. Paisano Publications, Inc., 28210 Dorothy Dr., Box 3075, Agoura Hills, CA 91301. TEL 818-889-8740. FAX 818-889-4726. Ed. Keith Ball. adv.; bk.rev.; charts; illus.; tr.lit.; circ. 315,069.

796.7   US   ISSN 0027-2167
ENTHUSIAST. Title varies: Motorcycle Enthusiast. 1916. q. free. Harley-Davidson Motor Co., Inc., Box 653, Milwaukee, WI 53201. TEL 414-342-4680. Ed. Steve Piehl. adv.; illus.; circ. 300,000.

796   US
EXPLORE MINNESOTA BIKING. a. Office of Tourism, 375 Jackson St., Ste. 250, St. Paul, MN 55101. circ. 25,000.

796   SZ   ISSN 0071-4283
FEDERATION INTERNATIONALE MOTOCYCLISTE. ANNUAIRE. (Including International Motorcycle Sporting Calendar) (Text in English and French) 1912. a. 22 Fr. International Motorcycle Federation, 19 Chemin William-Barbey, 1292 Chambesy-Geneva, Switzerland. FAX 022-7582180. TELEX 419111. adv.; bk.rev.; circ. 10,000.

796.6   NE
FIETS. (Text in Dutch) 1982. 9/yr. fl.49.50. Uitgeverij Fiets b.v., Postbus 937, 1000 AA Amsterdam, Netherlands. FAX 020-221608. Ed. G.V.D. Beek. adv.; bk.rev.; circ. 43,000. (back issues avail.)
Description: Bicycle magazine with buyer's guide.

796.6   910.202   US
FODOR'S SPORTS: CYCLING. irreg. $12. Fodor's Travel Publications, Inc. (Subsidiary of: Random House, Inc.), 201 E. 50th St., New York, NY 10022. TEL 800-733-3000. (Dist. by: Random House, Inc., 400 Hahn Rd., Westminster, MD 21577) Eds. Arlene Plevin, Michael Spring.

796.6   FR
FRANCE CYCLISTE. m. 60 F. Federation Francaise de Cyclisme, 43 rue de Dunkerque, 75010 Paris, France. adv.

796   SW   ISSN 1100-052X
FRITIDSHANDLAREN CYKEL OCH SPORT. 1935. m. (11/yr.). SEK 225. Cykel- och Sporthandlarnes Riksfoerbund, Kungsgatan 19, 105 61 Stockholm 2, Sweden. FAX 46-8-249616. Ed. Roland Nordlander. adv.; charts; illus.; stat.; tr.lit.; circ. 1,611.
Formerly: Cykel- och Sporthandlaren (ISSN 0011-4383)

G V A MITGLIEDERVERZEICHNIS. (Gesamtverband Autoteile-Handel e.V.) see *TRANSPORTATION — Automobiles*

796.7   GW
GEBRAUCHT MOTORRAD UND ZUBEHOER KATALOG. 1981. a. DM.9.80. Motor Technik Verlag, Straussstaffel 3, 7000 Stuttgart 1, Germany. TEL 0711-16850-0. FAX 0711-1685054. (back issues avail.)

GENTE MOTORI. see *TRANSPORTATION — Automobiles*

338.476
GLASS'S GUIDE TO MOTOR CYCLE VALUES. 1950. m. £45. Glass's Guide Service Ltd., Elgin House, St. George's Ave., Weybridge, Surrey KT13 0BX, England. TEL 0932-853211. FAX 0932-849299. adv.
Formerly: Glass's Guide to Used Motor Cycle Values.

388.347   UK
GLASS'S MOTOR CYCLE CHECK BOOK. a. £12. Glass's Guide Service Ltd., Elgin House, St. George's Ave., Weybridge, Surrey KT13 0BX, England. TEL 0932-853211. FAX 0932-849299. adv.

796.6   US   ISSN 1048-8758
GO: THE RIDER'S MANUAL. 1976. m. $16.50. Wizard Publications, Inc., 3870 Del Amo Blvd., No. 504, Torrance, CA 90503-2119. (Dist. by: Kable News Company, Box 111, Mt. Morris, IL 61054) Ed. Mike Daily. adv.; illus.; stat.; circ. 80,000.
Formed by the merger of: Freestylin; B M X Action Magazine; Which was formerly: Bicycle Motocross Action.

388.347   396.7
388.3   IT
GUERIN SPORTIVO MESE. 1982. m. L.40000. Editoriale Master s.r.l., Via dell'Industria 6, 40068 San Lazzaro di Savena (Bologna), Italy. Ed. Italo Cucci. adv.; bk.rev.; circ. 95,000.
Formerly: Master.

796.7   US
HACK'D; the magazine for and about sidecarists. 1984. q. $15. J & C Enterprises, Box 813, Buckhannon, WV 26201. TEL 307-472-6146. Ed. Jim Dodson. adv.; bk.rev.; index; circ. 3,000. (back issues avail.)
Description: Covers motorcycle sidecars.

796.7   US   ISSN 0893-6447
HARLEY WOMEN; dedicated to all women motorcycle enthusiasts. 1985. bi-m. $12 (foreign $17). Asphalt Angels Publications, Inc., Box 374, Steamwood, IL 60107. TEL 708-888-2645. Ed. Linda Jo Giovannoni. adv.; circ. 20,000.
Description: Features male and female riders, and motorcycle events nationwide. Includes new products and clothing, fiction and poetry.

HORSELESS CARRIAGE GAZETTE. see *ANTIQUES*

796   US   ISSN 0046-8045
HOT BIKE. 1969. m. $20.95. McMullen Publishing, 2145 W. La Palma Ave., Anaheim, CA 92801. TEL 714-635-9040. FAX 714-533-9979. Ed. Buck Lovell. illus.; circ. 62,552.
Description: Covers high-performance motorcycles.

338.347   US
I B F NEWS. 1986. s-a. free. International Bicycle Fund, 4887 Columbia Dr. S., Seattle, WA 98108-1919. TEL 206-628-9314. Ed. David Mozer. circ. 7,000.
Description: News on bicycle transportation policy, programs and philosophy.

796.7   IT
IN MOTO. m. L.80000. Conti Editore S.p.A., Via del Lavoro 7, 40068 S. Lazzoro di Savena, Bologna, Italy. TEL 051-6227111. FAX 051-6255418. circ. 75,000.
Description: Covers production and racing bikes.

796.7   UK   ISSN 0020-6504
INTERNATIONAL CYCLE SPORT. 1968. m. $60. Kennedy Brothers (Publishing) Ltd., Goulbourne St., Keighley, West Yorkshire, England. Ed. J.D. Fretwell. adv.; charts; illus.; tr.lit. **Indexed:** Sportsearch.
Supersedes: Sporting Cyclist.

796.6   US
IRON HORSE. 9/yr. $3.95 per no. Scott Magazines, 519 Eighth Ave., New York, NY 10018. TEL 212-967-6262. FAX 212-967-6288.

796.6   US
IRON HORSE YEARBOOK. a. $4.95. Scott Magazines, 519 Eighth Ave., New York, NY 10018. TEL 212-967-6262. FAX 212-967-6288.

796   JA   ISSN 0446-6667
JAPAN'S BICYCLE GUIDE. (Text in English) 1951. a. exchange basis. Japan Bicycle Industry Association, 1-9-3 Akasaka, Tokyo 107, Japan. adv.; stat.

796.76   UK
KART AND SUPERKART MAGAZINE. 1979. m. £15.50. Kart and Superkart Ltd., Pindar Rd., Hoddesdon, Hertfordshire EN11 ODE, England. TEL 0992-444 201. FAX 0992-447327. TELEX 266343 G ZIP. Ed. Ed. McCormick. adv.; bk.rev.; circ. 6,000. (back issues avail.)

796.7   GW
KURVE. m. Syburger Verlag GmbH, Hertingerstr. 60, 4750 Unna, Germany. TEL 02303-86281. FAX 02303-86529. circ. 15,000.

796.6   SA
LIFE CYCLE. 1989. 6/yr. (South African Pedal Power Association) W.J. Flesch & Partners (Pty) Ltd., P.O. Box 3473, Cape Town 8000, South Africa. TEL 021-461-7472. FAX 021-4613758. Ed. Karin Engelbrecht-Pohl. adv.; circ. 18,000.

796   SW   ISSN 0024-7995
M C - NYTT. 1959. m. SEK 105. Broederna Lindstroms Foerlags, Box 35, 44300 Lerum, 443 01 Lerum 1, Sweden. Ed. Thommy Bernguist. adv.; bk.rev.; illus.; stat.; circ. 39,896.

796.7   DK   ISSN 0107-0606
M C REVYEN. (Text in Danish) a. DKK 114.50. Bonniers Specialmagasiner A-S, Strandboulevarden 130, 2100 Copenhagen OE, Denmark. Ed. Dan Melchior. circ. 25,000.
Description: Catalogue of all motorbikes sold on the Danish market.

796.7   CN
MASTERLINK. 8/yr. Can.$19.95($19.95) for 12 nos. Western Biker Publications Ltd., 2750 Rock Bay Ave., Victoria, B.C. V8X 3X4, Canada. TEL 604-384-0333. FAX 604-384-1832. (Subscr. to: P.O. Box 4122, Stn. A, Victoria, B.C. V8X 3X4, Canada) Ed. Len Creed. adv.; illus.

388.347   796.7   IT
MOTITALIA. 1947. m. L.18000. Federazione Motociclistica Italiana, Piazza dei Carracci, 1, 00196 Rome, Italy. TEL 06-3960091. Ed. F. Zerbi. adv.; bk.rev.; circ. 110,000.
Description: Deals with motorcycle racing in Italy; includes biographies of racers, activities of racing groups, and details of competitions.

388.347   796.7   IT
MOTO. 1976. m. L.75000. Edigamma s.r.l., Piazza dei Sanniti 9, 00185 Rome, Italy. TEL 06-4928412. FAX 06-4940719. Ed. Claudio Porrozzi. adv.; circ. 210,000.

796.7   GW   ISSN 0724-7206
MOTO CROSS & ENDURO. 1971. m. DM.88.60. Verlag Bahnsport Aktuell HG, Industristr. 8, 6458 Rodenbach 1, Germany. TEL 06184-51051. FAX 06184-51004. Ed. Christian Kalabis. adv.; bk.rev.; circ. 39,000.
Description: Sports magazine for all motorcross enthusiasts. Features reports, results and announcements of events, championships, national and international news, and new products.

796   CN   ISSN 0319-2865
MOTO JOURNAL. English edition: Cycle Canada (ISSN 0319-2822) (Editions in English, French) 1972. m. Can.$24. Brave Beaver Presworks Ltd., 86 Parliament St., Ste. 3B, Toronto, Ont. M5A 246, Canada. TEL 514-738-9439. FAX 738-4929. (Or: 5000 Rue Bachan, Bureau 600A, Montreal, PQ H4P 1T2) Ed. Jean-Pierre Belmonte. adv.; circ. 13,000.

796   FR   ISSN 0047-8180
MOTO REVUE. 1913. 48/yr. 520 F. (foreign 837 F.). Editions Lariviere, 15-17 Quai de l'Oise, 75166 Paris Cedex 19, France. TEL 1-40-34-22-07. FAX 1-40-35-84-41. TELEX 211 678 F. Ed. Eric Breton. adv.; abstr.; illus.; stat.; circ. 100,000.

796.75   FR
MOTO VERTE. m. 230 F. (foreign 270 F.). Editions Lariviere, 15-17 Quai de l'Oise, 75166 Paris Cedex 19, France. TEL 1-40-34-22-07. FAX 1-40-35-84-41. TELEX 211 678 F. Ed. Gilles Mallet. adv.

796.7   IT   ISSN 0027-1691
MOTOCICLISMO. 1914. m. L.55000 (foreign L.90000). Edisport S.p.A., Via Boccaccio 47, 20123 Milan, Italy. Ed. Massimo Bacchetti. adv.; bk.rev.; charts; illus.; mkt.; index; circ. 212,000.
Description: News about two and three-wheel motor vehicles including test results, industrial information, prices.

796.7   SP
MOTOCICLISMO. 1957. w. 16000 ptas. Luike - Motorpress, C. Ancora 40, 28045 Madrid, Spain. TEL 91-3470100. FAX 91-3470119. Dir. Javier Herrero. adv.; circ. 95,000.

388.347 UK
MOTOCOURSE. 1976. a. £24.95. Hazleton Publishing, 3 Richmond Hill, Richmond, Surrey TW10 6RE, England. Ed. Michael Scottd. adv.

388.347 796.7 IT
MOTOCROSS. 1971. m. L.60000 (foreign L.82000)(effective 1991). Nuova Editoriale Octopus s.r.l., Piazza Cadorna 2, 20123 Milan, Italy. FAX 02-809609. Ed. Ruggero Upiglio. adv.; circ. 200,000.

796.77 US ISSN 0146-3292
GV1060
MOTOCROSS ACTION. 1973. m. $17.98. Daisy - Hi-Torque Publications, Inc., 10600 Sepulveda Blvd., Mission Hills, CA 91345. TEL 818-365-6831. Ed. Jody Weisel. adv.; circ. 90,734. (back issues avail.)
Indexed: Sportsearch.

796.75 FR ISSN 0077-1570
MOTOCYCLO CATALOGUE; guide technique du cycle et du motocycle. 1951. a. 190 F. Editions S.O.S.P., 83 rue de Villiers, 92523 Neuilly Cedex, France. Ed. C. L. Lavaud. index.

796.7 NE ISSN 0027-1721
MOTOR. 1913. w. fl.107.50. (Royal Dutch Motorcycle Union (KNMV)) Wegener Tijl Tijdschriften Groep B.V., Postbus 9943, 1006 AP Amsterdam, Netherlands. TEL 020-5182828. FAX 020-177143. TELEX 15230. Ed. D.J. Evers. adv.; bk.rev.; circ. 51,000.

MOTOR. see TRANSPORTATION — Air Transport

796.7 796.6 DK ISSN 0107-7554
MOTOR - BLADET. 1928. m. (11/yr.). DKK 150. Danmarks Motor Union, Vejrmosegaards Alle 80, 7000 Fredericia, Denmark. Ed. Joergen Dorscheus. adv.; circ. 8,300.

796.7 UK ISSN 0027-1853
MOTOR CYCLE NEWS. 1952. w. £54. Frontline Ltd. (Subsidiary of: E M A P - Haymarket Ltd.), Park House, 117 Park Rd., Peterborough PE1 2TR, England. TEL 0733-55161. FAX 62788. TELEX 329292 FRONT G. Ed. Malcolm Gough. adv.; illus.; tr.lit.; circ. 131,870. (tabloid format)

380.1 US ISSN 0091-3774
HD9710.5.U5
MOTORCYCLE BLUE BOOK. Variant title: Hap Jones Motorcycle Blue Book. 1952. s-a. $18. Hap Jones, Ed. & Pub., Box 32368, San Jose, CA 95152. FAX 408-432-1926.

796.7 CN ISSN 0705-2030
MOTORCYCLE DEALER AND TRADE. m. avail. only to dealers, distributors and manufacturers in the motorcycling industry. Brave Beaver Pressworks Ltd., 86 Parliament St., Ste. 3B, Toronto, Ont. M5A 246, Canada. TEL 416-362-7966. FAX 416-362-3950. Ed. John Cooper. adv.

388.347 640.73 US
MOTORCYCLE DEALERNEWS BUYERS GUIDE. a. $12. Avanstar Communications, Inc., 7500 Old Oak Blvd., Cleveland, OH 44130. TEL 216-826-2839. FAX 216-891-2726. (Subscr. to: 1 E. First St., Duluth, MN 55802) Ed. Leslie Frohoff. circ. 14,201.

796.75 SA
MOTORCYCLE DEALERS' GUIDE. 1979. q. R.57.60. Mead & McGrouther (Pty) Ltd., 327 Surrey Ave., Box 1240, Ferndale, Randburg 2125, South Africa. Ed. O. Peruch. circ. 300.

796 UK ISSN 0265-7759
MOTORCYCLE ENTHUSIAST.* 1882. m. £12. Advanced Media Services, 32 Paul St., London W1N 6AB, England. Ed. M. Walker. adv.; bk.rev.; circ. 10,000. (back issues avail.)

796.7 US ISSN 0884-626X
MOTORCYCLE INDUSTRY MAGAZINE. 1980. m. free to qualified personnel. Industry Shopper Publishing, Inc., 31194 La Baya Dr., Ste. 200, Westlake Village, CA 91362. TEL 818-991-2070. FAX 818-991-9427. Ed. Rick Campbell. adv.; bk.rev.; circ. 12,000 (controlled).
Former titles: Motorcycle Industry Shopper (ISSN 0274-5437); Motorcycle Industry Magazine.

796.7 JA
MOTORCYCLE JAPAN; annual guide to Japan's motorcycle industry. (Text in English) 1983. a. 6080 Yen. Jan Corporation, Stork Bell Hamamatsucho, Rm.402, 2-17, Hamamatsu-cho 1-chome, Minato-ku, Tokyo 105, Japan. TEL 03-3438-0362. FAX 03-3438-0362. Ed. M. Sakurazawa. circ. 8,000.

796.7 US ISSN 0164-8349
MOTORCYCLE PRODUCT NEWS. 1974. m. $18. M H West, Inc. (Subsidiary of: Maclean Hunter Publishing Co.), 6633 Odessa Ave., Van Nuys, CA 91406. TEL 818-997-0664. FAX 818-997-1058. (29 N. Wacker Dr., Chicago, IL 60606) Ed. Bob Jackson. adv.; illus.; circ. 12,951 (controlled).
Description: Serves the trade selling, servicing, manufacturing, distributing, importing and exporting of motorcycles, motorscooters, mopeds, ATV's, personal watercraft, and parts and accessories.

MOTORCYCLE PRODUCT NEWS TRADE DIRECTORY. see BUSINESS AND ECONOMICS — Trade And Industrial Directories

796.7 US
MOTORCYCLE RED BOOK. 2/yr. $54.50. Maclean Hunter Market Reports, Inc., 29 N. Wacker Dr., Chicago, IL 60606-3297. TEL 312-726-2802. FAX 312-726-2574. (back issues avail.)

796.7 UK ISSN 0306-1647
MOTORCYCLE RIDER. 1964. 6/yr. £13. British Motorcyclists Federation (Enterprises) Ltd., Box 1149, Maidenhead, Berkshire SL6 8XR, England. TEL 0628-28753. FAX 081-949-6215. Ed. Jeremy Irwin. adv.; bk.rev.; circ. 12,000.
Description: Explores all aspects of motorcycling, including politics, touring, roadtests, product reviews and owners' reports.

796.7 US
MOTORCYCLE ROAD RACER ILLUSTRATED; the high performance racing and riding magazine. 1988. a. $3.95. C N Publishing Group, 2201 Cherry Ave., Long Beach, CA 90806. TEL 310-427-7433. FAX 310-427-6685. Ed. Paul Carruthers. circ. 130,000.
Description: Covers both motorcycle racing and championship competitions internationally, and national road racing competitions.

796.7 UK ISSN 0955-9116
MOTORCYCLE SPORT. m. £14.50 (foreign £16.50). Ravenhill Publishing Ltd., Standard House, Bonhill St., London EC2A 4DA, England. TEL 071-628-4741. FAX 071-638-8497. TELEX 888602-MONEWS-G. Ed. C.J. Ayton. adv.; circ. 17,428.

796.7 US ISSN 0027-2205
TL1
MOTORCYCLIST. 1912. m. $19.94. Petersen Publishing Co., 8490 Sunset Blvd., Los Angeles, CA 90069. TEL 213-854-2222. Ed. Art Friedman. adv.; bk.rev.; circ. 213,500. (also avail. in microform from UMI) **Indexed:** Consum.Ind., Ind.How To Do It (1990-), Sportsearch.
Incorporates (1970-1988): Motorcycle Buyer's Guide (ISSN 0077-1678)

796.7 US ISSN 0164-9256
MOTORCYCLIST'S POST. 1967. m. $15. (New England Motorcycle Dealers Association) Motorcyclists Post Publishing Co., Box 154, Rochdale, MA 01542. TEL 508-885-5221. FAX 508-752-5733. Ed. Robert F. Frink. adv.; bk.rev.; circ. 9,895. (tabloid format; back issues avail.)

796.75 SI
MOTORING. (Text in English) 1982. bi-m. 190 Middle Road, 14-07 Fortune Centre, Singapore 0718, Singapore. TEL 337055. FAX 3394857. TELEX 51088. Ed. Guy Coh. circ. 20,000.

388.3 GW ISSN 0027-237X
DAS MOTORRAD. 1920. fortn. DM.142 (foreign DM.181). Motor-Presse Stuttgart, Leuschnerstr. 1, Postfach 106036, 7000 Stuttgart 10, Germany. TEL 0711-18201. FAX 0711-1821669. Ed. Friedhelm Fiedler. adv.; illus.; circ. 255,995.

796.7 GW
MOTORRAD CLASSIC. 1987. bi-m. DM.45.90 (foreign DM.55.20). Motor-Presse Stuttgart, Leuschnerstr. 1, Postfach 106036, 7000 Stuttgart 10, Germany. TEL 0711-18201. FAX 0711-1821669. illus.; circ. 60,000.

796.7 GW
MOTORRAD KATALOG. 1970. a. DM.15. Motor-Presse Stuttgart, Leuschnerstr. 1, Postfach 106036, 7000 Stuttgart 10, Germany. TEL 0711-18201. FAX 0711-1821669. illus.; circ. 200,000.

796.7 GW
MOTORRAD MAGAZIN M O. 1978. m. DM.6. Motor Technik Verlag, Strausssstaffel 3, 7000 Stuttgart 1, Germany. TEL 0711-16850-0. FAX 0711-1685054. (back issues avail.)

796.7 GW
MOTORRAD NEWS; das Magazin fuer Sachsen-Anhalt und Thueringen. m. Syburger Verlag GmbH, Hertingerstr. 60, 4750 Unna, Germany. TEL 02303-86281. FAX 02303-86529. circ. 8,000.

796.7 GW
MOTORRAD OLDTIMER KATALOG; Marktuebersicht fuer klassische Motorraeder. a. DM.29.80. Heel-Verlag GmbH, Hauptstr. 354, 5330 Koenigswinter 1, Germany. FAX 02223-23028. Ed. Stefan Knittel. circ. 25,000.

796.7 GW
MOTORRAD, REISEN UND SPORT. 1983. m. DM.66. Heinrich Bauer Spezialzeitschriften, Industriestr. 16, 5000 Cologne 60, Germany. TEL 0221-7709148. FAX 0221-714153. TELEX 8882133. (Subscr. to: Postfach 300545, 2000 Hamburg 36, Germany) Ed. Knut Briel. adv.; circ. 63,748. (back issues avail.)
Description: Features on motorcycle tests, touring reports, motorcycles sports, classic motors.

796.7 GW
MOTORRAD SPIEGEL; das Baden-Wuerttemberger Motorrad Magazin. m. Syburger Verlag GmbH, Hertingerstr. 60, 4750 Unna, Germany. TEL 02303-86281. FAX 02303-86529. circ. 20,000.

796.7 GW
MOTORRAD SZENE; das Magazin der Motorradfahrer. m. Syburger Verlag GmbH, Hertingerstr. 60, 4750 Unna, Germany. TEL 02303-86281. FAX 02303-86529. circ. 20,000.

796.75 GW
MOTORRAD TEST (YEAR); Katalog. 1983. a. DM.12. Motor Technik Verlag GmbH, Strausssstaffel 3, 7000 Stuttgart 1, Germany. TEL 0711-16850-0. FAX 0711-16850-54. Ed. Franz Josef Schermer. circ. 100,000.

796.7 GW
MOTORRAD TEST KATALOG. 1983. biennial. DM.12. Motor Technik Verlag, Strausssstaffel 3, 7000 Stuttgart 1, Germany. TEL 0711-16850-0. FAX 0711-1685054. (back issues avail.)

796.7 GW
MOTORRADSZENE BAYERN. m. Syburger Verlag GmbH, Hertingerstr. 60, 4750 Unna, Germany. TEL 02303-86281. FAX 02303-86529. circ. 17,000.

796.7 GW
MOTORRADTREFF SPINNER; das Motorradmagazin fuer Berlin, Brandenburg und Mecklenburg. m. Syburger Verlag GmbH, Hertingerstr. 60, 4750 Unna, Germany. TEL 02303-86281. FAX 02303-86529. circ. 10,000.

388.347 396.7 IT
MOTOSPRINT. 1976. w. (51/yr.). L.190000. Conti Editore S.p.A., Via del Lavoro 7, 40068 S. Lazzaro di Savena (Bologna), Italy. TEL (051) 6227111. FAX 6256191. Ed. Tommaso Valentinetti. adv.; bk.rev.; circ. 85,000.

796.7 IT
MOTOTRENTINO; mototre, motolombardia, mototoscano. m. L.30000 (foreign L.40000). Mototrentino S.n.c., Loc. Centochiavi, 33-1, 38100 Trento, Italy. TEL 0461-820711. Ed. Mario Facchini.

SPORTS AND GAMES — BICYCLES AND MOTORCYCLES

796.7   IT
MOTOTURISMO; il piacere di andare in moto. 1987. bi-m. L.30000 (foreign L.60000). Editore L' Isola, Piazza Roma, 1, Lurago Marinone (CO), Italy. TEL 031-937736. FAX 031-937362. Ed. Tiziano Cantatore. adv.; bk.rev.; circ. 40,000.
   Description: Covers footage on motorcycle trips, history of motorbikes and includes information on organized tours for motorcyclists.

796.7   CC
MOTUO CHE/MOTORCYCLE. (Text in Chinese) m. Renmin Youdian Chubanshe - People's Posts and Telecommunications Publishers, 27 Dongchang'anjie, Beijing 100740, People's Republic of China. TEL 5138139. Ed. Yu Xiaochuan.

796.6   US
MOUNTAIN AND CITY BIKING. 9/yr. Challenge Publications, Inc., 7950 Deering Ave., Canoga Park, CA 91304-5007. TEL 818-887-0550. FAX 818-883-3019. Ed. Steve Giberson. circ. 103,000.

796.6   US
MOUNTAIN BIKE. bi-m. $11.97. Rodale Press, Inc., 33 E. Minor St., Emmaus, PA 18098. TEL 215-967-5171. TELEX 847338.
   Description: Adventure travel magazine for all-terrain cyclists featuring new products, riding techniques, event reports and previews.

796   US
MOUNTAIN BIKE ACTION. bi-m. $17.95. Hi-Torque Publications, Inc., 10600 Sepulveda Blvd., Mission Hills, CA 91345. TEL 818-365-6831. Ed. Jody Weisel. adv.

388.347 796.95   US
N.A.D.A. MOTORCYCLE - SNOWMOBILE - A T V - PERSONAL WATERCRAFT APPRAISAL GUIDE. 3/yr. $45. (National Automobile Dealers Association) N.A.D.A. Appraisal Guides, Box 7800, Costa Mesa, CA 92628-7800.
   Supersedes: N.A.D.A. Motorcycle Appraisal Guide (ISSN 0095-6953)

NESTEKIDE. see *TRANSPORTATION — Automobiles*

796.6   UK
NEW CYCLIST. 1988. m. £29.50. Stonehart Leisure Magazines, 67-71 Goswell Rd., London EC1V 7EN, England. TEL 071-410-9410. FAX 071-410-9440. Ed. Jim McGurn. circ. 31,041.

796.7   US
NORTHEAST RIDING.* 1983. 12/yr. $18. Northeast Riding, Inc., 19 Palisado Ave., Windsor, CT 06095-2527. Ed. Daniel Hatch. adv.
   Description: Covers area events, good roads, and club activities for motorcyclists who ride for recreation and for commuting.

796   SW   ISSN 0048-1211
NYA CYKLISTEN. vol.4, 1973. 9/yr. SEK 386. (Cykelfoerbundet) Cewe-Foerlaget, Box 77, 890 10 Bjaesta, Sweden. (Subscr. to: PK-Banken, Box 365, 891 01 Oernskeoldsvik, Sweden) Ed. Charlie Wedin. adv.; bk.rev.

796   FR   ISSN 0751-994X
OFFICIEL DU CYCLE ET DU MOTOCYCLE; seule revue de la profession. 1890. m. 700 F. (typically set in Nov.). (Federation Nationale du Commerce et de la Reparation du Cycle & Motocycle) Societe EDI 92, 83 rue de Villiers, 92523 Neuilly sur Seine Cedex, France. TEL 47-38-64-64. FAX 47-47-53-16. TELEX 613 448 F. Ed. Dennis Jacob. adv.; bk.rev.; charts; stat.; circ. 13,500.
   Formerly: Officiel du Cycle, du Motocycle et de la Motoculture (ISSN 0030-0519)
   Description: Monthly publication for motorcycle professionals in France.

796.6   US
ON ONE WHEEL. 1974. q. $10 (foreign $15). Unicycling Society of America, Inc., Box 40534, Redford, MI 48240. TEL 313-661-0334. Ed. Carol Brichford. adv.; circ. 400. (back issues avail.)
   Description: Information on all phases of unicycling: building techniques, tricks, meets.

796.6   US
ON THE ROAD (NEW YORK). q. $3.95 per no. Outlaw Biker Enterprises, Inc., 450 Seventh Ave., Ste. 2305, New York, NY 10001. TEL 212-564-0112. FAX 212-465-8350.

796   US   ISSN 0885-2030
OUTLAW BIKER. 1985. m. $29.95. Outlaw Biker Enterprises, Inc., 450 Seventh Ave., Ste. 2305, New York, NY 10001. TEL 212-564-0112. FAX 212-465-8350. Ed. Casey Exton. adv.; circ. 150,000. (back issues avail.)

796.7   AT   ISSN 0155-4360
OZBIKE; thunder Down Under. 1981. 12/yr. Aus.$60. U C P Publishing Pty. Ltd., 49 Ramsay St., Haberfield, N.S.W. 2045, Australia. TEL 02-797-6777. FAX 02-799-2125. (Subscr. to: P.O. Box 35, Haberfield, N.S.W. 2045) Ed. Boris Mihailovic. adv.; circ. 46,000. (back issues avail.)
   Description: Covers custom motorcycles and Australian biker lifestyle.

796.7   NO   ISSN 0801-0986
PAA HJUL. (Text in Norwegian) 1980. 6/yr. NOK 150. Norges Cykelforbund, Hanger Skolevei 1, N-1351 Rud, Norway. FAX 02-132989. TELEX 78586 NIF. Ed. Per Furseth. adv.; bk.rev.; circ. 8,500.

796.7   IT   ISSN 0031-3866
PEDALE D'ORO.* 1968. w. Perna Editore, Via Mario Papano 41, I-20145 Milan, Italy. Ed. Bruno Raschi. charts; illus.

796.7   US   ISSN 0162-3214
TL235.6
PETERSEN'S 4 WHEEL & OFF-ROAD. 1977. m. $19.94. Petersen Publishing Co., 8490 Sunset Blvd., Los Angeles, CA 90069. TEL 213-854-2222. Ed. Drew Hardin. adv.; circ. 325,000. (also avail. in microfiche)
   Formerly: Hot Rod Magazine's 4 Wheel and Off-Road.

796   CN
PRAIRIE PEDALER. 1985. q. Saskatchewan Cycling Association, 2205 Victoria Ave., Regina, Sask. S4P 0S4, Canada. TEL 306-780-8289. FAX 306-525-4009. adv.; circ. 400.

796.6   US
(YEAR) PRO BIKE DIRECTORY. irreg., latest 1990. $17. Bicycle Federation of America, 1818 R St. N.W., Washington, DC 20009. TEL 202-332-6986. FAX 202-332-6989.
   Description: Provides contact and program information for individuals, organizations, and government agencies involved in bicycling.

796.7   US
PRO BIKE NEWS. 1980. m. $18 in US; Canada $22; elsewhere $25. Bicycle Federation of America, 1818 R St., N.W., Washington, DC 20009. TEL 202-332-6986. FAX 202-332-6989. Ed. Jim Fremont. bk.rev.; circ. 600. (tabloid format; back issues avail.)

796.6   US
RACE ACROSS AMERICA PROGRAM. 1984. a. $3. (Race Across America - Ultra-Marathon Cycling Association) Info Net Publishing, Box 3789, San Clemente, CA 92672. TEL 714-492-7219. Ed. Herb Wetenkamp. adv.; circ. 117,500. (tabloid format; back issues avail.)
   Description: Covers the 3,000-mile trans-continental, annual, ultra-marathon bicycle race.

796.6   GW   ISSN 0720-8545
RADFAHREN; Zeitschrift fuer die Freunde des Fahrrads. 1980. bi-m. DM.52.40. Bielefelder Verlagsanstalt KG, Niederwall 53, 4800 Bielefeld 1, Germany. circ. 60,000.

629.227   GW   ISSN 0033-8540
RADMARKT; deutsche Fachzeitschrift der Zweiradwirtschaft. 1879. m. DM.114. Bielefelder Verlagsanstalt GmbH & Co. KG, Niederwall 53, Postfach 1140, 4800 Bielefeld, Germany. TEL 0521-595-520. adv.; bk.rev.; charts; illus.; mkt.; pat.; tr.lit.; tr.mk.; index; circ. 6,000.
   Description: Trade publication for the bicycle market. Covers the latest information concerning bicycles, motorcycles, scooters, and foreign trade. Includes letters to the editor and list of advertisers.

796.6   GW   ISSN 0138-1393
RADSPORTLER. 1949. w. DM.26.40. Deutscher Radsport-Verband der DDR, Muelenweg 12, 1635 Wuensdorf, Germany. Ed. Lothar Branzke. (tabloid format)

796.7   GW
▼**REISE MOTORRAD.** 1991. s-a. DM.9.80. Motor Technik Verlag, Strausssstaffel 3, 7000 Stuttgart 1, Germany. TEL 0711-16850-0. FAX 0711-1685054.

796.7   AT   ISSN 0027-2175
REVS MOTORCYCLE NEWS (REVS).* 1967. fortn. Aus.$50.70. Federal Publishing Company, 180 Bourke Rd., Alexandria, N.S.W. 2015, Australia. Ed. Mike Esdaile. circ. 18,016.

629.227   FR   ISSN 0150-7214
REVUE MOTO TECHNIQUE. 1969. q. 315 F. (foreign 350 F.). Editions Techniques pour l'Automobile et l'Industrie (ETAI), 20-22 rue de la Saussiere, 92100 Boulogne Billancourt, France. TEL 46-04-81-13. FAX 48-25-56-92. TELEX ETAIRTA 204850 F. Ed. Christian Rey. charts; illus.; circ. 16,500.
   Description: Each issue deals with 2 motorcycles and explains how to dismantle and repair them.

796.7   US   ISSN 0095-1625
GV1059.5
RIDER; motorcycle touring & commuting. 1974. m. $15.98 (foreign $25.98). T L Enterprises, Inc., 29901 Agoura Rd., Agoura, CA 91301. TEL 818-991-4980. Ed. Tash Matsuoka. illus.
   Description: Devoted to the motorcycle touring enthusiast. Bike test, new product evaluations, touring adventures, buyer's guides and more.

796.7   US   ISSN 0035-7243
TL440.5
ROAD RIDER; America's first motorcycle touring magazine. 1969. m. $19.97. Fancy Publications, Inc., Box 6050, Mission Viejo, CA 92690. TEL 714-855-8822. FAX 714-855-3045. (Subscr. to: Box 488, Mt. Morris, IL 61054) Ed. Bob Carpenter. adv.; bk.rev.; illus.; index; circ. 50,000. (back issues avail.)
   Description: For the traveling motorcyclists in search of two-wheeled adventure. Focuses on various aspects of motorcycle touring; foreign or domestic journeys, long distances or short weekenders.

ROADRACING WORLD & MOTORCYCLE TECHNOLOGY. see *SPORTS AND GAMES*

796.75   IT
RUOTE IN PISTA INTERNATIONAL. m.(10/yr.). L.115000. Milano Sole Editoriale S.r.l., Viale Cirene 1, 20135 Milan, Italy. TEL 02-5516117. FAX 02-5454790. Ed. Claudio Casaroli.

796.75   SA
S A MOTOR SPORT BULLETIN. (Text in English) 1983. bi-m. (South Africa Motor Sport Control) Camera Press, P.O. Box 260593, Excom 2023, South Africa. Ed. Chris Moss. adv.; bk.rev.; circ. 7,000.

796.7   US   ISSN 1051-0613
SAFE CYCLING. 1980. q. $15 per no. Motorcycle Safety Foundation, 2 Jenner St., Ste. 150, Irvine, CA 92718-3812. TEL 714-727-3227. FAX 714-727-4217. Ed. Julie Filatoff. bk.rev.; charts; illus.; stat.; tr.lit.; circ. 6,500 (controlled).
   Description: Motorcycle safety information for instructors and individuals.

388   CN   ISSN 0705-1840
SANFORD EVANS GOLD BOOK OF MOTORCYCLE DATA & USED PRICES. 1977. a. Can.$15.50. Sanford Evans Communications Group, 1700 Church Ave., Box 6900, Winnipeg, Man. R3C 3B1, Canada. TEL 204-694-2022. FAX 204-694-3040. Ed. G.B. Henry.
   Description: Valuation guide features trade-in value of motorcycles, vehicle identification numbers, weight, over-all length.

796.7   GW
SCHERMER'S MOTORRAD KATALOG. 1989. a. DM.12. Motor Technik Verlag, Strausssstaffel 3, 7000 Stuttgart 1, Germany. TEL 0711-16850-0. FAX 0711-1685054. (back issues avail.)

SPORTS AND GAMES — BOATS AND BOATING 4521

796.7 IT
▼SCOOTER MAGAZINE. 1991. q. L.20000 (foreign L.40000)(effective 1992). Editore L' Isola, Piazza Roma, 1, Lurago Marinone (CO), Italy. TEL 031-937736. FAX 031-937362. Ed. Tiziano Cantatore. adv.; circ. 30,000.
 Description: Covers new, vintage, and custom scooters, accessories, trips, technical tips, and news from clubs.

796.5 UK
SCOTTISH HOSTELLER. 1976. s-a. free. Scottish Youth Hostels Association, 7 Glebe Crescent, Stirling FK8 2JA, Scotland. TEL 0786-51181. FAX 0786-50198. TELEX 779689. Ed. E. Gardiner. adv.; bk.rev.; circ. 45,000.

796.65 US
SOUTHWEST CYCLING. 1982. m. $18. Southwest Cycling, 422 S. Pasadena Ave., Pasadena, CA 91105. TEL 818-793-3661. FAX 818-799-7254. circ. 60,000.
 Description: Covers racing, commuting and mountain biking. Includes a calendar of events.

SPEEDWAY STAR. see SPORTS AND GAMES

796.7 GW
SPORT MOTORRAD KATALOG. 1989. a. DM.9.80. Motor Technik Verlag, Strausstaffel 3, 7000 Stuttgart 1, Germany. TEL 0711-16850-0. FAX 0711-1685054. (back issues avail.)

796.6 US
SPORTBIKES. a. $3.95. Hachette Magazines, Inc., 1633 Broadway, 45th Fl., New York, NY 10009. TEL 212-767-6000.

629.227 IT
SUPER MOTOTECNICA. m. L.43000 (foreign L.90000). N.P.M. s.r.l., Via Molise, 3, 20085 Locate Triulzi (MI), Italy. TEL 02-90780478. FAX 02-9077862. Ed. Sandro Colombo.

796 UK ISSN 0262-8457
SUPERBIKE. m. £28.60. Link House Magazines Ltd., Link House, Dingwall Ave., Croydon, Surrey CR9 2TA, England. TEL 01-686 2599. FAX 01-760-0973. TELEX 947709. (Subscr. to: U M S, Stephenson House, 1st Fl., Brunel Centre, Bletchley, Milton Keynes, MK2 2EW) Ed. John Cutts. adv.
 Description: Information and feature articles on street motorcycling touring, drag racing, tuning features, reviews of machinery and equipment and profiles of enthusiasts.

388.347 US ISSN 0162-3923
SUPERCYCLE. m. $24.95 (foreign $34.95). Larry Flynt Publications, Inc., 9171 Wilshire Blvd., Ste. 300, Beverly Hills, CA 90210. TEL 310-858-7100. FAX 310-275-3857. Ed. Elliot Borin. adv.
 Description: Covers American motorcycles and their riders.

796.7 GW
DER SYBURGER; das nordrheinwestfaelische Motorrad-Magazin. 1980. m. DM.25. Syburger Verlag GmbH, Hertingerstr. 60, 4750 Unna, Germany. TEL 02303-86281. FAX 02303-86529. Eds. V. Heimann, G. Wagner. adv.; bk.rev.; circ. 30,000.

796.6 US
TEXAS BICYCLIST. 1989. m. $12. Yellow Jersey Enterprises, 3600 Jeanetta Dr., Ste. 1604, Houston, TX 77063. TEL 713-782-1661. FAX 713-782-7666. (Subscr. to: Box 49788, Austin, TX 78765) Ed. Kim Grob. adv.; bk.rev.; circ. 50,000 (controlled).
 Description: Provides information on local cycling tours, equipment and safety.

796.75 GW ISSN 0933-4440
TOUREN-FAHRER; Reportagen - Test - Technik. 1981. 6/yr. DM.39 (foreign DM.48). Reiner H. Nitschke Verlags GmbH, Pastor-Berg-Str. 4, 5489 Duempelfeld, Germany. TEL 02695-1009. FAX 02695-1400. Ed. Reiner H. Nitschke.

796.7 DK ISSN 0106-1925
TOURING NYT. 1966. 8/yr. DKK 190. M C Touring Club, Oddervej 79, DK-8270 Hojbjerg, Denmark. TEL 86-272515. FAX 86-27-31-19. Ed. Gunnar Skrydstrup. adv.; bk.rev.; circ. 9,800.

796.7 UK
TRAIL RIDERS FELLOWSHIP BULLETIN. 1970. q. £10($18) Trail Riders Fellowship, c/o Mrs. Rosemary Marsoton, Ed., 4 Surrey Rd., Woolston, Southampton SO1 9ED, England. TEL 0703 420813. adv.; bk.rev.; circ. 2,000. (back issues avail.)
 Description: Newsletter of the National Club for the encouragement of non-competitive green roads motorcycling and maintenance of rights of way, in England and Wales.

796.7 UK
TRIALS AND MOTOCROSS NEWS. 1977. w. 55p. per no. Lancaster and Morecambe Newspapers Ltd., Victoria St., Morecambe, Lancs. LA4 4AG, England. Ed. Bill Lawless. adv.; bk.rev.; circ. 30,000.

796 IT
TUTTOCICLISMO.* w. L.10000. F C I e U C I P, Via dei Mille 6, 00185 Rome, Italy. Ed. Mario de Angelis. adv.; circ. 15,000.

338.347 796.7 IT
TUTTOMOTO. 1978. m. L.38400 (foreign L.60000). Rusconi Editori Associati S.p.A., Servizio Abbonamenti, Via Vitruvio 43, 20124 Milan, Italy. TEL 02-67561. FAX 67562732. Ed. Gianni Marin. circ. 180,000.

629.227 IT
TUTTORALLY.* m. L.50000 (foreign L.80000). Barbero Editori S.r.l., Strada S. Felice 151-e, 10025 Pino Torinese, Italy. TEL 011-5611914. FAX 011-518476. Ed. Nanni Barbero.

629.227 NE ISSN 0165-1943
TWEEWIELER; maandblad voor de tweewielerbranche. 1921. m. Audet Tijdschriften bv, Postbus 16, 6500 AA Nijmegen, Netherlands. TEL 080-228316. FAX 080-239561. TELEX 48633. Ed. Jack Oortwijn. adv.; B&W page fl.2734; trim 215 x 285; adv. contact: Cor van Nek. abstr.; illus.; mkt.; stat.; circ. 5,010. **Indexed:** Key to Econ.Sci.
 Description: Supplies information about current developments of interest to bicycle, scooter and motorcycle retailers.

796 AT ISSN 0041-4700
TWO WHEELS. m. Aus.$33. Federal Publishing Company, 180 Bourke Rd., Alexandria, N.S.W. 2015, Australia. Ed. Bill McKinnon. circ. 19,818. **Indexed:** Aus.Rd.Ind., Pinpointer.

UNSER WANDERBOTE. see SPORTS AND GAMES

796.6 CN ISSN 1180-1360
VELO MAG. 6/yr. Can.$21.50. Editions Tricycle, 3575 boul. Saint-Laurent, Bur. 310, Montreal, Que. H2X 2T7, Canada. TEL 514-847-1990. FAX 514-847-0242. Ed. Lyse Savard. adv. **Indexed:** Pt.de Rep. (1989-).

796.6 FR
VELO MAGAZINE. 1979. m. 215 F. S N C L'Equipe, 10 rue du Fg. Montmartre, 75009 Paris, France. Ed. J.M. Leblanc. adv.; bk.rev.
 Formerly: Cyclisme.

796.6 US ISSN 0161-1798
VELONEWS; the journal of competitive cycling. 1972. 18/yr. $29.95. Inside Communications, 1830 N. 55th St., Boulder, CO 80301-2700. TEL 303-440-0601. FAX 303-444-6788. Ed. John Wilcockson. adv.; bk.rev.; film rev.; charts; illus.; stat.; index; circ. 45,000. (tabloid format; also avail. in microfilm from UMI; back issues avail.; reprint service avail. from UMI) **Indexed:** Sports Per.Ind., Sportsearch (1977-).
 Former titles (until 1974): Cyclenews; **(until 1972):** Northeast Bicycle News.
 Description: Reports on major bicycle races in U.S. and Europe and includes a complete calendar of U.S.-Canada races. Provides articles on training, products, physiology and mountain biking.

796.7 UK
VINTAGE MOTOR CYCLE. 1948. m. £18. Vintage Motor Cycle Club Ltd., 24 De Verdun Ave., Belton, Loughborough LE12 9TY, England. TEL 0530-223569. Ed. David Styles. adv.; bk.rev.; circ. 10,000.
 Formerly: Vintage Motor Cycle Club Magazine.

796.7 US
WALNECK'S CLASSIC CYCLE TRADER. m. $24. Walneck's Inc., 7923 Janes Ave., Woodridge, IL 60517. TEL 708-985-4995.

796.6 US
WINNING BICYCLING ILLUSTRATED. 1983. 11/yr. $23.95. Winning International, Inc., 744 Roble Rd., Ste. 190, Allentown, PA 18103-9100. TEL 215-266-6893. FAX 215-266-7196. Ed. Richard G. Carlson. adv.; circ. 59,264.
 Formerly: Winning Bicycle Racing Illustrated.
 Description: Features various forms of competitive bicycle racing.

629.227 CC ISSN 1000-999X
ZHONGGUO ZIXINGCHE/CHINESE BICYCLES. (Text in Chinese) bi-m. (Quanguo Zixingche Gongye Keji Qingbaozhan - National Bicycle Industry Science and Technology Station) Zhongguo Zixingche Bianjibu, No.6, Alley 360, Anyuan Road, Shanghai 200060, People's Republic of China. TEL 2584696. (Co-sponsor: Zhongguo Zixingche Xiehui) Ed. Song Xiandun.

796.7 GR ISSN 1105-1299
2 TROCHI/2 WHEELS. (Text in Greek) 1988. bi-m. Dr.2,400($22) Technical Press, S.A., 6 Gorgiou St., 11636 Athens, Greece. TEL 01-92-30-832. FAX 01-92-30-836. TELEX 222189 TECH GR. Ed. Costas Cavathas. circ. 20,000.
 Description: Covers motorcycles in general.

3 & 4 WHEEL ACTION. see TRANSPORTATION — Automobiles

SPORTS AND GAMES — Boats And Boating

796 UK ISSN 0144-1396
A Y R S AIRS. 1956. irreg. £15($30) Amateur Yacht Research Society, Pengelly House, Wilcove, Torpoint, Cornwall PL11 2PG, England. TEL 0752-812003. (U.S. addr.: Mr. M. Badham, Amateur Yacht Research Society, R F D No. 2, Box 180, Bath, ME 04530) Ed. R.M. Ellison. bk.rev.; circ. 1,400.

796.95 UK ISSN 0964-0932
ADMARINE. 1983. m. £12. Nigel Gearing Ltd., No.4 Red Barn Mews, High St., Battle, E. Sussex TN33 0AG, England. TEL 04246-4982. FAX 04246-4321. adv.; bk.rev.; circ. 20,000 (controlled). (tabloid format)
 Description: Reports on all aspects of the marine leisure industry.

797.14 AT
AHOY!. q. (Mooloolaba Yacht Club) National Publications Pty. Ltd., P.O. Box 297, Homebush West, N.S.W. 2140, Australia. TEL 02-764-1111. FAX 02-763-1699. circ. 2,000.
 Description: Covers all MYC events plus major yachting news.

797.14 AT
THE ALFRED'S YACHTSMAN. q. (Royal Prince Alfred Yacht Club) National Publications Pty. Ltd., P.O. Box 297, Homebush West, N.S.W. 2140, Australia. TEL 02-764-1111. FAX 02-763-1699. circ. 3,000.
 Description: Covers all club events plus major yachting and sailing news.

797.1 US
AMERICAN POWER BOAT ASSOCIATION. A P B A RULE - REFERENCE BOOK. (In 4 vols; Parts 1-3: Racing Rules; Part 4: Racing Records, Commissions, Membership Directory) 1903. a. $5 for each part to non-members. American Power Boat Association, 17640 E. Nine Mile Rd., Box 377, E. Detroit, MI 48021. TEL 313-773-9700. FAX 313-773-6490. index.
 Formerly: American Power Boat Association. A P B A Rule Book (ISSN 0065-9797)

797.123 US ISSN 0888-1154
GV790.6
AMERICAN ROWING. 1969. 6/yr. $30 (effective 1992). United States Rowing Association, 201 S. Capitol Ave., Ste. 400, Indianapolis, IN 46225-1054. TEL 317-237-5656. FAX 317-237-5646. Ed. Mo Merhoff. adv.; bk.rev.; illus.; index; circ. 30,000. **Indexed:** Phys.Ed.Ind., Sports Per.Ind., Sportsearch (1986-).
 Former titles: Rowing U S A (ISSN 0744-4788); Oarsman.

SPORTS AND GAMES — BOATS AND BOATING

797.1　　　　US　　ISSN 0279-9553
AMERICAN SAILOR. 1980. m. membership. U S Yacht Racing Union, Box 843, Franklin, TN 37064. TEL 615-791-1780. adv.; circ. 28,000. **Indexed:** Sportsearch (1981-).

797.1　　　　US　　ISSN 0300-7626
AMERICAN WHITE WATER. 1967. bi-m. $20. American Whitewater Affiliation, Box 85, Phoenicia, NY 12464. Ed. Chris Koll. adv.; bk.rev.; circ. 4,000. **Indexed:** Sportsearch (1978-).

797　　　　FR　　ISSN 0758-6639
ANNUAIRE NAUTISME. 1963. a. 160 F.($27) Editions de Chabassol, 30 rue de Gramont, 75002 Paris, France. TEL 42-97-50-30. FAX 42-86-02-81. Ed. B. Laloup. adv.

797.1　　　　IT
ANNUARIO DELLA NAUTICA. a. Nautica Editrice, Via Tevere 44, 00198 Rome, Italy. TEL 06-862050. FAX 853653. TELEX 611613 NAUTIC I. adv.; illus.

797.1　　　　US　　ISSN 0003-5904
ANTIQUE OUTBOARDER. 1966. q. $20 (foreign $24). Antique Outboard Motor Club, Inc., Box 09293, Milwaukee, WI 53209-0293. adv.; illus.; stat.; circ. 1,000. (tabloid format)
Description: Covers history, restoration, technical reports, antique outboard racing, special features, and chapter news.

796.95
ARGUS DU BATEAU. 1963. q. Editions Kerfan, 97-101 av. Semeria, B.P. 5, 06290 St. Jean Cap Ferrat, France. adv.; circ. 40,000.

796.95　　　　FR
ARGUS DU BATEAU ET DE TOUT LE MATERIEL NAUTIQUE. 1963. q. 35 F. per no. Editions Kerfan, 97-101 ave. Semeria, B.P. 5, 06290 St. Jean Cap Ferrat, France. Ed. G. Gouguenheim. adv.; stat.; tr.lit.; index; circ. 35,000.

791.95　　　　AT
AUSTRALIAN CHARTER GUIDE. a. A.B. Organisation Pty. Ltd., P.O. Box 319, Avalon Beach, N.S.W. 2107, Australia. TEL 02-918-8322. FAX 02-918-8884. (Dist. by: Gordon & Gotch, 25-37 Huntingdale Rd., Burwood, Vic. 3125, Australia) circ. 24,000.
Description: Includes wide-ranging feature articles with an annual survey of charter fleets, their rates, season factors and booking information.

796.95　　　　AT　　ISSN 0313-766X
AUSTRALIAN POWERBOAT. 1976. 6/yr. Aus.$25 (foreign Aus.$63)(effective 1992). Yaffa Publishing Group, 17-21 Bellevue St., Surry Hills, N.S.W. 2010, Australia. TEL 02-281-2333. FAX 02-281-2750. Ed. Ron Calcutt. adv.; B&W page Aus.$1400, color page Aus.$1780; trim 273 x 210. circ. 7,794.
Description: For the informed enthusiast who owns a power boat or intends to acquire one.

797.123　　　　AT
AUSTRALIAN ROWING. 1978. q. Aus.$10. Australian Rowing Council Inc., 6 Tarwhine Pl., Golden Bay, W.A. 6174, Australia. Ed. K.I. Matts. adv.; B&W page Aus.$250; adv. contact: K.I. Matts. bk.rev.; circ. 2,000. **Indexed:** Sportsearch (1983-).

797.1　　　　AT
AUSTRALIAN SAILING. m. Aus.$52 (foreign Aus.$130)(effective Apr. 1992). Yaffa Publishing Group, 17-21 Bellevue St., Surry Hills, N.S.W. 2010, Australia. TEL 02-281-2333. FAX 02-281-2750. adv.; B&W page Aus.$1405, color page Aus.$1910; trim 273 x 210. circ. 7,794.
Description: Covers the whole spectrum of sailing from dinghies to maxi yachts - for racing or pleasure. Includes coverage of major yachting events from around the world.

797.1　　　　AT　　ISSN 0311-7839
AUSTRALIAN SEA SPRAY. 1969. fortn. Aus.$22. (Sea Spray) Paper and Ink Publishing Co., Box 662, Manly, N.S.W. 2095, Australia. Ed. Bill Rowlings. adv.; bk.rev.; circ. 10,000.
Formerly: Australian Sea Spray Weekly (ISSN 0045-0863)

797.1　　　　AT　　ISSN 0005-0237
AUSTRALIAN SEACRAFT. 1947. m. Aus.$18. Federal Publishing Company, 180 Bourke Rd., Alexandria, N.S.W. 2015, Australia. Ed. G. Andrews. adv.; bk.rev.; charts; illus.; circ. 16,000.
Formerly: Seacraft (ISSN 0037-0061)

796.95　　　　AT　　ISSN 1035-3852
AUSTRALIAN YACHTING. 1983. m. Aus.$24. Baird Publications Pty. Ltd., 10 Oxford St., South Yarra, Vic. 3141, Australia. TEL 03-826-87411. FAX 03-827-0704. Ed. Neil Baird. adv.; bk.rev.; circ. 5,000.
Former titles: Nautical News & Australian Nautical News (ISSN 0812-163X)
Description: Includes boat reviews, news on yacht races, product information and feature articles.

797.1　　　　FR　　ISSN 0988-1956
AVIRON. 1886. irreg. (10-12/yr.). 120 F. (foreign 170 F.). Federation Francaise des Societes d'Aviron, c/o M. Dominique Roudy, 7 rue Lafayette, 75009 Paris, France. TEL 48-74-43-77. Ed. J.P. Bremer. adv.; bk.rev.; illus.; circ. 5,500. **Indexed:** Sportsearch (1977-).

796.95　　　　US
B O A T - U S REPORTS. 1966. bi-m. $6. Boat Owners Association of the United States, 880 S. Pickett St., Alexandria, VA 22304. TEL 703-823-9550. FAX 703-461-2845. Ed. Michael G. Sciulla. bk.rev.; circ. 400,000.
Description: Covers legislative, regulatory and consumer issues of interest to recreational boat owners.

796.95 640.73　　　　US
B U C NEW BOAT PRICE GUIDE. 1961. a. $19.95. B U C International Corp., 1314 N.E. 17th Court, Fort Lauderdale, FL 33305. TEL 305-565-6715. Ed. Walter J. Sullivan, III.
Description: Listing of boat and engine manufacturers. Includes complete specification and list prices.

797.1　　　　DK　　ISSN 0525-4515
BAAD-REVYEN. a. DKK 114.50. Bonniers Specialmagasiner A-S, Strandboulevarden 130, 2100 Copenhagen OE, Denmark. adv.; circ. 25,000.
Description: Full color catalogue of more than 500 sailboats and motorboats for private use available on the Scandinavian market.

796.95　　　　DK
BAADNYT. m. DKK 34.50. Bonniers Specialmagasiner A-S, Strandboulevarden 130, 2100 Copenhagen OE, Denmark. Ed. Torry Lindstroem. circ. 445,500.
Description: Tests, cruising articles and do-it-yourself material on boats in Denmark.

797.1　　　　SW　　ISSN 0005-6308
BAATNYTT/BOATING NEWS. 1961. 14/yr. SEK 87.50. Specialtidningsfoerlaget AB, Sveavaegen 53, 105 44 Stockholm, Sweden. Ed. Kurt Henningsson. adv.; bk.rev.; illus.; mkt.; index; circ. 50,700.

796.95　　　　IT
BARCHE E CATALOGO. 1980. m (10/yr.). L.63000. Gruppo Editoriale Commerciale, Via G. Galilei, 6, 20124 Milan, Italy. TEL 02-29002410. FAX 02-6552271. TELEX 330326 GECVAL I. Ed. Giorgia Gessner. adv.; bk.rev.; circ. 35,000 (controlled).

796.95　　　　AG
BARCOS. 1976. m. $48. Editorial Barcos S.R.L., Avda. Santa Fe 676, 1640 Acassusu, Buenos Aires, Argentina. TEL 54-1-7475572. Ed. Roberto Garcia Guevara. adv.; bk.rev.; circ. 10,500.

BASSMASTER CLASSIC REPORT. see *SPORTS AND GAMES — Outdoor Life*

797.1　　　　FR　　ISSN 0005-6235
BATEAUX. 1958. m. 250 F. Ami Des Jardins, S.A., 8-10 rue Pierre Brossolette, 92300 Levallois Perret, France. Ed. Philippe Simon. adv.; bk.rev.; bibl.; charts; illus.; mkt.; tr.lit.; index. cum.index; circ. 74,081.
Description: Features true stories from the high seas, navigation guides, nautical instruction, marine charts, etc.

796.95　　　　FR
BATO LOC INTERNATIONAL. 1964. 4/yr. 70 F. Editions Kerfan, 97-103 ave. Semeria, B.P. 18, 06230 St. Jean Cap Ferrat, France. TEL 93-011-037. adv.; stat.; tr.lit.; index; circ. 12,000.
Formerly: Marche Europeen du Bateau d'Occasion.

797.1　　　　US
BAY AND DELTA YACHTSMAN. 1965. m. $12. Recreation Publications, 2019 Clement Ave., Alameda, CA 94501. TEL 415-865-7500. FAX 415-865-0186. Ed. Bill Parks. adv.; circ. 20,000.
Description: For boating and yachting enthusiasts.

BERICHTEN AAN ZEEVARENDEN. see *GEOGRAPHY*

BLAKES BOATING ABROAD. see *TRAVEL AND TOURISM*

796.95　　　　UK
BLAKES BOATING HOLIDAY BOOKS. a. free. Blakes Holidays Ltd., Wroxham, Norwich NR12 8DH, England. TEL 0603-782141. TELEX 97114. Ed. T.E. Howes. adv.; circ. 30,000.

BLAKES BOATING IN BRITAIN. see *TRAVEL AND TOURISM*

797.1　　　　GW　　ISSN 0006-4637
DER BLAUE PETER; Zeitschrift fuer Segeln und Seefahrt. 1925. 4/yr. (Deutscher Hochseesportverband Hansa e.V.) Verlag Delius, Klasing und Co., Siekerwall 21, Postfach 4809, 4800 Bielefeld, Germany. TEL 0521-559-0. FAX 0521-559113. TELEX 932934-DEKLA. adv.; illus.; circ. 15,000.

796.95　　　　US　　ISSN 0163-7452
GV811.63.W56
BOARD & SAIL MAGAZINE. 1978. bi-m. $10. 5109 Esmeralda St., Sacramento, CA 95820. TEL 916-456-2130. (Subscr. to: Box 8108, Sacramento, CA 95818) Ed. David M. Yost. adv.; bk.rev.; circ. 10,000.

796.95　　　　UK
BOARDS. 1982. m. £23 (foreign £28.50). Yachting Press Ltd., 196 Eastern Esplanade, Southend-on-Sea, Essex SS1 3AB, England. Ed. Jeremy Evans. adv.; bk.rev.; circ. 21,490.

387.2 380.1　　　　ISSN 0006-5366
HF6201.B3
BOAT & MOTOR DEALER. (Annual supplement avail.: Boat & Motor Dealer's Market Manual) 1959. m. $20. Van Zevern Publications, Inc., 3949 Oakton St., Skokie, IL 60076. TEL 708-982-1810. FAX 708-675-7402. Ed. George P. Van Zevern. adv.; bk.rev.; circ. 32,000.

796.95　　　　US
BOAT & MOTOR DEALER'S MARKET MANUAL. (Supplement to: Boat & Motor Dealer) 1969. a. $35. Van Zevern Publications, Inc., 3949 Oakton St., Skokie, IL 60076. TEL 708-982-1810. Ed. George Van Zevern. adv.; bk.rev.; circ. 32,000.
Formerly: Boat and Motor Dealer's Market.

796.95 380.1　　　　CN
BOAT GUIDE. s-a. Outdoor Canada Publishing Ltd., 447 Speers Rd., Ste. 4, Oakville, Ont. L6K 3L7, Canada. TEL 416-695-0382. FAX 416-695-0382. Ed. Jan Mundy.
Description: Official program for Hamilton and London boat show. Lists Canadian prices, photos, specifications on all new power boats and engines. Includes editorials covering sport fishing, boating trends, electronics and an index of manufacturers.

796.95　　　　UK
BOAT MART INTERNATIONAL. 1986. m. £13.20 (foreign £34.50). Aceville Publications Ltd., 89 East Hill, Colchester, Essex CO1 2QN, England. TEL 0206-871450. FAX 0206-871537. Ed. David Bridle. (back isseus avail.)
Description: For budget and small craft enthusiasts; also covers accessories.

796.95　　　　US
BOAT PENNSYLVANIA. bi-m. Pennsylvania Fish Commission, Box 1673, Harrisburg, PA 17105-1673. Ed. Art Michaels.

796.95　　　　CN
BOAT WORLD. m. 10991 Shellbridge Way, Ste. 205, Richmond, B.C. V6X 3C6, Canada. TEL 604-669-8554. Ed. Gerry Kidd. circ. 13,500.

SPORTS AND GAMES — BOATS AND BOATING

623.82 US
BOATBUILDER; the journal of boat design and construction. vol.6, 1988. bi-m. $24 (foreign $30). Belvoir Publications, Inc., 75 Holly Hill Lane, Box 2626, Greenwich, CT 06836-2626. TEL 203-661-6111. FAX 203-661-4802. (Subscr. to: Box 333, Dept. TT, Denville, NJ 07834) Ed. Keith E. Lawrence.

623.82 US
BOATBUILDER'S INTERNATIONAL DIRECTORY; the boatbuilder's source book of designers, kit makers and suppliers. 1980. a. $7.50. Saffron Publishing, 1001 Bridgeway, Dept. 621, Sausalito, CA 94965. Ed. Peter Whyte. adv.; bk.rev.; circ. 10,000.

797.1 US ISSN 0006-5374
GV771
BOATING. 1956. m. $21.94. Hachette Magazines, Inc., 1633 Broadway, 45th Fl., New York, NY 10009. TEL 212-767-6000. (Subscr. to: Box 2886, Boulder, CO 80322) Ed. John Owens. adv.; bk.rev.; charts; illus.; index; circ. 191,934. (also avail. in microform from UMI,MIM) **Indexed:** Access (1975-), Consum.Ind., Mag.Ind., Sports Per.Ind.
●Also available online. Vendor(s): DIALOG.
Incorporates (1973-1980): Motorboat (ISSN 0093-6782); which incorporates in 1975: Family Houseboating (ISSN 0014-7273); **Formerly:** Popular Boating.

796.95 US
BOATING ALMANAC, VOLUME 1: RHODE ISLAND, MASSACHUSETTS, MAINE, NEW HAMPSHIRE. 1961. a. $10.50. Boating Almanac Co., Inc., 203 McKinsey Rd., Severna Park, MD 21146. TEL 301-647-0084. Ed. Peter A. Geis. adv.; charts.

796.95 US
BOATING ALMANAC, VOLUME 2: LONG ISLAND, CONNECTICUT, RHODE ISLAND, SOUTHERN MASSACHUSETTS. 1961. a. $10.50. Boating Almanac Co., Inc., 203 McKinsey Rd., Severna Park, MD 21146. TEL 301-647-0084. Ed. Peter A. Geis. adv.; charts.

796.95 US
BOATING ALMANAC, VOLUME 3: NEW JERSEY, DELAWARE BAY, HUDSON RIVER, LAKE CHAMPLAIN, ERIE CANAL. 1961. a. $10.50. Boating Almanac Co., Inc., 203 McKinsey Rd., Severna Park, MD 21146. TEL 301-647-0084. Ed. Peter A. Geis. adv.; charts.

796.95 US
BOATING ALMANAC, VOLUME 4: CHESAPEAKE BAY, DELAWARE, MARYLAND, DISTRICT OF COLUMBIA, VIRGINIA. 1961. a. $10.50. Boating Almanac Co., Inc., 203 McKinsey Rd., Severna Park, MD 21146. TEL 301-647-0084. Ed. Peter A. Geis. adv.; charts.

796.95 CN
BOATING BUSINESS. 1976. 6/yr. Outdoor Canada Publishing Ltd., 703 Evans Ave., Ste. 202, Toronto, Ont. M9C 5E9, Canada. TEL 416-695-0311. FAX 416-695-0382. Ed. Jan Mundy. adv.; circ. 4,008.

796.95 UK ISSN 0260-9452
BOATING BUSINESS AND MARINE TRADE NEWS. 1976. m. £12. Rushton Marine Press Ltd., Woodside, Burnhams Rd., Leatherhead, Surrey KT23 3BA, England. TEL 0372-453316. FAX 0372-459974. Ed. Lizzie Wright. adv.; illus.; circ. 7,000 (controlled).
Formerly (until 1981): Boating Business (ISSN 0702-7524)

796.95 910.09 US
BOATING IN THE SAN JUAN ISLANDS. a. free. Islands' Sounder, Box 758, Eastsound, WA 98245. circ. 75,000.
Description: Provides boating and tourist information on the San Juan islands.

387.2 US ISSN 0006-5404
HD9993.B633
BOATING INDUSTRY; the management magazine of the boating industry. 1937. m. $30 (foreign $100) includes Boating Industry's OEM Business. Communication Channels, Inc., 6255 Barfield Rd., Atlanta, GA 30328-4369. TEL 404-256-9800. FAX 404-256-3116. TELEX 4611075 COMCHANI. (And: 390 Fifth Ave., New York, NY 10018-8104. TEL 212-613-9700) Ed. Richard W. Porter. adv.; charts; illus.; tr.lit.; circ. 30,800. (also avail. in microform from UMI; reprint service avail. from UMI) **Indexed:** Bus.Ind., SRI, Tr.& Indus.Ind.
●Also available online. Vendor(s): DIALOG.
Incorporates: Marine Business (ISSN 0147-8923)
Description: Presents ideas, role models, and guidance for boat retailers to operate their businesses more effectively and profitably. Includes information on marine management, merchandising and selling, market analysis, and industry trends.

BOATING INDUSTRY MARINE BUYERS' GUIDE. see BUSINESS AND ECONOMICS — Trade And Industrial Directories

387.2 US
BOATING INDUSTRY'S O E M BUSINESS. Issued with: Boating Industry. 6/yr. (included in subscr. to Boating Industry). Communication Channels, Inc., 6255 Barfield Rd., Atlanta, GA 30328-4369. TEL 404-256-9800. FAX 404-256-3116. TELEX 4611075 COMCHANI. Ed. Richard W. Porter. adv.; circ. 8,000.
Description: Addresses concerns of boat manufacturers and their vendors, exclusive of marine retailers. Highlights OEM companies, personnel, facilities, manufacturing methods, product applications and technical advances in styling and engineering.

796.95 CN ISSN 0700-7388
BOATING NEWS. 1970. m. Can.$9. Tyrell Publishing, 26 Coal Harbour Wharf, 566 Cardero St., Vancouver, B.C. V6G 2W6, Canada. TEL 604-684-1643. Ed. Don Tyrell. adv.; bk.rev.; circ. 20,000.
Description: Covers commercial and pleasure boating.

796.95 NZ
BOATING SAFETY. 1971. q. free. Ministry of Transport, Maritime Transport Division, P.O. Box 27-006, Wellington, New Zealand. TEL 828-198. FAX 829-065. Ed. Helen Becker. illus.; circ. 6,450.
Formerly: Blue Water (ISSN 0110-7011)

797 US ISSN 1059-5155
VM320
BOATING WORLD. 1979. bi-m. $11.95 (foreign $17.95). Trans World Publishing, Inc., 2100 Powers Ferry Rd., Atlanta, GA 30339. TEL 404-955-5656. FAX 404-952-0669. Ed. Richard Lebovitz. adv.; bk.rev.; charts; index; circ. 159,900. (back issues avail.) **Indexed:** Ind.How To Do It (1986-).
Former titles: Boat Journal; Small Boat Journal (ISSN 0192-7596)

796.95 US
BOATS & HARBORS. 1971. 36/yr. $4. Crossville, TN 38555. TEL 615-484-6100. Ed. Edwin Donnelly. adv.; charts; illus.; tr.lit.

797.1 GW ISSN 0006-7636
BOOTE; das Wassersportmagazin. 1965. m. DM.66 (foreign DM.77.40). Verlag Delius, Klasing und Co., Siekerwall 21, Postfach 4809, 4800 Bielefeld, Germany. TEL 0521-559-283. FAX 0521-559113. TELEX 932934-DEKLA. Ed.Bd. adv.; illus.; circ. 88,000.

623.82 GW ISSN 0006-7644
BOOTSWIRTSCHAFT. 1964. bi-m. DM.30. (Deutscher Boots- und Schiffbauer-Verband) Verlag fuer Bootswirtschaft, Jungiusstr. 13, 2000 Hamburg 36, Germany. FAX 040-344227. TELEX 212609-MESSE-D. Ed. Fritz Hartz. adv.; bk.rev.; charts; illus.; index; circ. 1,000.

797.14 AT
THE BRISBANE TO GLADSTONE YACHT RACE PROGRAMME ANNUAL. a. (Annual Brisbane to Gladstone Race Classic) National Publications Pty. Ltd., P.O. Box 297, Homebush West, N.S.W. 2140, Australia. TEL 02-764-1111. FAX 02-763-1699. adv.; circ. 7,500.
Description: Contains the full entry list, historical notes on previous races and other information.

797 UK ISSN 0309-1252
BRISTOW'S BOOK OF YACHTS. 1963. a. £3.95. Navigator Publishing Ltd., Moorhouse Farmhouse, Lower Kingston, Ringwood, Hants, England. Ed. Philip Bristow. circ. 5,000.
Formed by the merger of: Bristow's Book of Motor Cruisers & Bristow's Book of Sailing Cruisers.

796.95 UK
BRITAIN & HOLLAND MARINA GUIDE. a. £5. Benn Business Information Services Ltd, P.O. Box 20, Sovereign Way, Tonbridge, Kent TN9 1RQ, England. TEL 0732-362666. FAX 0732-770483. TELEX 95162-BENTON-G.

797.123 UK
BRITISH ROWING ALMANACK. A R A YEARBOOK. 1861. a. £9 to non-members. Amateur Rowing Association, 6 Lower Mall, London W6 9DJ, England. TEL 081-748-3632. FAX 081-741-4658. Ed. Keith L. Osborne. bk.rev.; index.
Formerly: British Rowing Almanack (ISSN 0068-2446)

797 UK ISSN 0068-290X
BROWN'S NAUTICAL ALMANAC. 1858. a. £30. Brown, Son and Ferguson Ltd., 4-10 Darnley St., Glasgow G41 2SD, Scotland. FAX 041-420-1694. Eds. T. Nigel Brown, Capt. A.N. Cockroft. adv.; circ. 15,000.

797.124 CN ISSN 0045-4494
CANADIAN BOATING. 1926. 9/yr. Can.$19. Arthurs Publications Ltd., 5805 Whittle Rd., Ste. 208, Mississauga, Ont. L4Z 2J1, Canada. TEL 416-568-4131. FAX 416-568-4133. Ed. Gary Arthurs. adv.; bk.rev.; circ. 17,000. **Indexed:** CMI, CS Ind., Sportsearch.
Incorporates: Canadian Power and Sail.

797.14 CN
CANADIAN POWER ILLUSTRATED. 1989. 6/yr. Kerrwil Publications Ltd., 395 Matheson Blvd. E., Mississauga, Ont. L4Z 2H2, Canada. TEL 416-890-1846. FAX 416-890-5769. Ed. Mike Milne.

197.124 CN
CANADIAN SAILING REVIEW/REVUE CANADIENNE DE VOILE. 1983. irreg. Canadian Yachting Association - Association Canadienne de Yachting, 333 River Rd., Ottawa, Ont. K1L 8B9, Canada. **Indexed:** Sportsearch (1985-).

796.95 CN ISSN 0384-0999
CANADIAN YACHTING. 1976. 6/yr. Can.$45. Kerrwil Publications Ltd., 395 Matheson Blvd. E., Mississauga, Ont. L4Z 2H2, Canada. TEL 416-890-1846. FAX 416-890-5769. Ed. Barry Redmayne. adv.; bk.rev.; circ. 24,447. **Indexed:** Can.Per.Ind., Sportsearch (1986-).

797.1 UK
CANAL & RIVERBOAT MONTHLY. 1978. m. £18 (foreign £22.59). A.E. Morgan Publications Ltd., Stanley House, 9 West St., Epsom, Surrey KT18 7RL, England. TEL 0372-741411. FAX 0372-744493. Ed. C.J. Beadsmoore. adv.; bk.rev.; circ. 15,000.

797.122 IT
CANOA FLUVIALE. 1977. 4/yr. L.30000 (foreign L.35000). Federazione Italiana Canoa Fluviale, Via Ernesto Breda 19-c, 20126 Milan, Italy. TEL 02-257-6638. adv.; bk.rev.; circ. 5,000.

797.122 US ISSN 0360-7496
GV781
CANOE; America's resource for canoeing and kayaking. 1973. bi-m. $14.97. Canoe America Associates, Box 3146, Kirkland, WA 98083. TEL 206-827-6363. Ed. David Harrison. adv.; bk.rev.; charts; illus.; tr.lit.; circ. 63,300. **Indexed:** Phys.Ed.Ind., Sportsearch (1977-).
Supersedes (in 1978): American Canoeist.

797.122 US
CANOE AND KAYAK RACING NEWS. 1989. bi-m. $8. Canoe America Associates, Box 3146, Kirkland, WA 98083. TEL 206-827-6363. Ed. David Harrison. circ. 12,000.
Description: Covers every paddle-sport discipline, including slalom and down river, marathon, flat-water sprint, outrigger, and white-water rodeo, as well as open-water racing, triathlons, poling and wave ski.

SPORTS AND GAMES — BOATS AND BOATING

797.122   UK   ISSN 0008-5626
CANOE - CAMPER. 1938. 3/yr. £4.50 to non-members. Canoe Camping Club, 25 Waverly Road, South Norwood, London SE25 4HT, England. TEL 01-654-1835. Ed. Jill Griffin. adv.; bk.rev.; abstr.; charts; illus.; circ. 700.

797.122   UK
CANOE FOCUS. 1976. bi-m. £2 to non-members. British Canoe Union, Adbolton Lane, West Bridgford, Nottingham NG2 5AS, England. TEL 0602-821100. FAX 0602-821797. Ed. Caroline Tombs. adv.; bk.rev.; circ. 16,000 (controlled).
    Description: Covers canoeing news, events, expeditions, equipment and books.

797.122   FR
CANOE KAYAK MAGAZINE. 6/yr. 150 F. (foreign 180 F.). Archeologia S.A., 25 rue Berbisey, 21000 Dijon, France. (Subscr. to: 1 rue des Artisans, B.P. 90, 21803 Quetigny Cedex, France. TEL 80-70-93-48)

797.122   UK   ISSN 0269-9982
CANOEIST. 1953. m. £23.40 (in U.S. £31.08). S.T. & R.J. Fisher, 4 Sinodun Row, Appleford, Oxon OX14 4PE, England. TEL 0235-847270. FAX 0235-847520. Ed. S. Fisher. adv.; bk.rev.; index.
    Description: Covers all aspects of canoes and kayaks, competitive and recreational.

917 796.95   US   ISSN 0045-656X
CHESAPEAKE BAY MAGAZINE. 1971. m. $19.95. Chesapeake Bay Communications, Inc., 1819 Bay Ridge Ave., Annapolis, MD 21403. TEL 301-263-2662. Ed. Jean Weller. adv.; bk.rev.; charts; illus.; circ. 38,000. (also avail. in microfiche)
    Description: Covers boating, history, environment, ecology and the culture of the bay from the C-and-D Canal to Norfolk, VA.

796.95   US
CLASSIC BOATING.* 1984. bi-m. $20 (foreign $27). Norm Wangard, Pub., 280 Lac la Belle Dr., Oconomowoc, WI 53066-1648. TEL 714-973-6091. Ed. Jim Wangard. adv.; bk.rev.; circ. 5,200.
    Formerly (until 1987): Antique and Classic Boat.

796.95   AT   ISSN 0817-8585
CLUB MARINE. 1982. bi-m. Aus.$50($25) Club Marine Ltd., 40 The Esplanade, Brighton, Vic. 3186, Australia. TEL 03-593-1144. FAX 03-592-7783. Ed. Andrew J. Woodley. adv.; bk.rev.; circ. 37,000. (back issues avail.)

796.95 910.202   US
COASTAL CRUISING. 1985. 6/yr. $16.50. Nautilus Publishing, Inc., 108 Middle Ln., Beaufort, NC 28516. TEL 919-728-2233. FAX 919-726-6715. Ed. Ted Jones. adv.; bk.rev.; circ. 25,000.
    Formerly: Carolina Cruising.

623.82   FR
COTE INTER-EUROPE DU BATEAU D'OCCASION. 1966. 4/yr. 50 F. Editions Kerfan, 115 Ave. Semeria, B.P.5, 06290 St. Jean Cap Ferrat, France. Ed. D. Garnier-Gougenheim. adv.; circ. 25,000.

796.95   UK
CRUISING ASSOCIATION. MAGAZINE. 1910. 4/yr. membership. Cruising Association, Ivory House, St. Katharine Dock, London E1 9AT, England. TEL 071-481-0881. FAX 071-702-3989. Ed. Charles Ford. adv.; bk.rev.; circ. 5,000.
    Formerly: Cruising Association. Bulletin.

796.95   UK
CRUISING ASSOCIATION YEARBOOK. 1909. a. membership. Cruising Association, Ivory House, St. Katharine Dock, London E1 9AT, England. TEL 071-481-0881. FAX 071-702-3989. circ. 5,000.

797.14   AT
CRUISING HELMSMAN. 1982. m. Aus.$51 (foreign Aus.$128)(effective Apr. 1992). Yaffa Publishing Group, 17-21 Bellevue St., Surry Hills, N.S.W. 21010, Australia. TEL 02-281-2333. FAX 02-281-2750. Ed. Linda Wayman. adv.: B&W page Aus.$1260, color page Aus.$1600; trim 273 x 210. circ. 7,219. (back issues avail.)

797.124   US   ISSN 0098-3519
GV771
CRUISING WORLD. 1974. m. $24. Cruising World Publications, Inc., 5 John Clarke Rd., Newport, RI 02840. TEL 401-847-1588. FAX 401-848-5048. (Subscr. to: Box 3045, Harlan, IA 51537-3045) Ed. Bernadette Brennan Bernon. adv.; bk.rev.; charts; illus.; tr.lit.; index; circ. 146,183. (also avail. in microform from UMI; back issues avail.; reprint service avail. from UMI) **Indexed:** Mag.Ind.

796.95   US
DIRECTORY OF AMERICAN SAILING SCHOOLS AND CHARTER OPERATORS. 1982. irreg. $250. National Association of Sailing Instructors and Sailing Schools, 15 Renier Ct., Middletown, NJ 07748. TEL 908-671-6190. Ed. Richard Herbst.
    Description: Information on how to locate and select a sailing school or charter operator.

797.1   US
DIVE BOAT CALENDAR & TRAVEL GUIDE: INTERNATIONAL EDITION. 1985. bi-m. $15. Total Marketing, 17612 Beach Blvd., Ste. 20, Huntington Beach, CA 92647-6811. TEL 714-375-7529. Ed. Cheri Boone. adv.; circ. 6,000.
    Formed by the merger of: Dive Boat Calendar and Travel Guide: Pacific Coast Edition (ISSN 1044-9159); Dive Boat Calendar and Travel Guide: Florida - Caribbean Edition.
    Description: Provides current boat diving and travel information for scuba divers.

796.95   US   ISSN 1045-8131
EASTERN, SOUTHEAST BOATING NEWSPAPER (EASTERN EDITION). 1977. m. $9.97. Z Dock Publications Inc., 1091 General Knox, Box 603, Washington Crossing, PA 18977-0603. TEL 215-493-7416. FAX 215-493-7523. Ed. Alex Zidock, Jr. adv.; bk.rev.; circ. 25,000. (tabloid format; back issues avail.)
    Supersedes in part: Eastern Boating (ISSN 0743-8133); Which incorporated: Bow Waves Boating (ISSN 0743-8125)

796.95   US   ISSN 1045-814X
EASTERN, SOUTHEAST BOATING NEWSPAPER (SOUTHEAST EDITION). 1977. m. $9.97. Z Dock Publications Inc., 1091 General Knox, Box 603, Washington Crossing, PA 18977-0603. TEL 215-493-7416. FAX 215-493-7523. Ed. Alex Zidock, Jr. adv.; bk.rev.; circ. 25,000. (back issues avail.)
    Supersedes in part: Eastern Boating (ISSN 0743-8133); Which incorporated: Bow Waves Boating (ISSN 0743-8125)

796.95   US
▼**EMBASSY'S COMPLETE BOATING GUIDE TO FLORIDA'S EAST COAST.** 1991. a. $39.95. Embassy Imprint Inc., 142 Ferry Rd., Ste. 16, Old Saybrook, CT 06475. TEL 203-395-0188. FAX 203-395-0410. adv.; circ. 10,000.
    Description: Includes navigational charts, color photographs of every harbor, yacht club, marina and boat yard listings, sightseeing ideas and fishing tips.

796.95   US
EMBASSY'S COMPLETE BOATING GUIDE TO LONG ISLAND SOUND. a. Embassy Imprint Inc., 142 Ferry Rd., Ste. 16, Old Saybrook, CT 06475. TEL 203-395-0188. FAX 203-395-0410. adv.; circ. 10,000.

796.95   US
EMBASSY'S COMPLETE BOATING GUIDE TO RHODE ISLAND AND MASSACHUSETTS. 1989. q. $34.95. Embassy Imprint Inc., 142 Ferry Rd., Ste. 16, Old Saybrook, CT 06475. TEL 203-395-0188. FAX 203-395-0410. adv.; circ. 10,000.

797   FR   ISSN 0071-4194
FEDERATION FRANCAISE DE NATATION. ANNUAIRE. 1921. a. 250 F. Federation Francaise de Natation, 148 Ave. Gambetta, 75020 Paris, France. TEL 40-31-17-70. FAX 40-31-19-90. TELEX 215429.

623.8   FI   ISSN 0356-7753
FINNISH BOATBUILDING INDUSTRY. (Text in English, German, French) 1971. irreg. free. Suomen Vene- ja Moottoriyhdistys - Finnish Boat and Motor Association, Mariankatu 26 B 19, 00170 Helsinki 17, Finland.

FISHING BUSINESS INTERNATIONAL. see FISH AND FISHERIES

797.124 910.202   US
FODOR'S SPORTS: SAILING. irreg. $12. Fodor's Travel Publications, Inc. (Subsidiary of: Random House, Inc.), 201 E. 50th St., New York, NY 10022. TEL 800-733-3000. (Dist. by: Random House, Inc., 400 Hahn Rd., Westminster, MD 21157) Eds. Michael B. McPhee, Michael Spring.

623.82   IT   ISSN 0015-8666
FORZA 7; revista mensile di nautica. 1968. m. (10/yr.). L.100000 in Europe; America L.140000. Publimedia Societa Editrice, Corso Venezia 18, 20121 Milan, Italy. TEL 02-77521. FAX 02-781068. Ed. Giorgia Gessner. adv.; bk.rev.; charts; illus.; tr.lit.; circ. 35,000.

796.95   IT
FUORIBORDO. m. L.30500 (foreign L.58000). Editoriale Olimpia S.p.A., Viale Milton 1, 50129 Florence, Italy. TEL 055-473843. FAX 055-499195. TELEX 573084 EDOL.1. Ed. Alessandro Menchi.

797.1   CN   ISSN 0016-4259
GAM ON YACHTING.* 1957. 10/yr. Can.$12 (foreign $20). Gam on Yachting Inc., 401 Richmond St. W., Ste. 242, Toronto, Ont. M5V 3A8, Canada. TEL 416-599-4261. Ed. Karin Larson. adv.; bk.rev.; illus.; circ. 22,000. **Indexed:** Sportsearch.

GENTE MOTORI. see TRANSPORTATION — Automobiles

797.124   IT
GIORNALE DELLA VELA. 1975. m. L.110000. Editrice Portoria S.r.l., Via Chiosetto, 1, 20122 Milan, Italy. TEL 02-783-541. FAX 02-782601. Ed. Luca Oriani. adv.; bk.rev.; circ. 50,000.

796.95   IT   ISSN 1120-2262
GOMMONE E LA NAUTICA PER TUTTI. 1977. 10/yr. L.48000($83) (foreign L.96000). Stammer S.p.A., Centro Commerciale Milano San Felice, 20090 Segrate-Milan, Italy. TEL 02 7530651. FAX 027530587. TELEX 321083 STAMMER. Ed. Girolamo Bellina. adv.; circ. 30,000.
    Former titles: Gommone; Gommone e le Piccole Barche.

796.95   US
GORGE GUIDE. a. $3.95. Gorge Publishing, Inc., 500 Morton Rd., Box 918, Hood River, OR 97031. TEL 503-386-7440. FAX 503-386-7480. circ. 30,000.

796.95   US
GREAT LAKES BOATING MAGAZINE.* 1981. m. free. Chicago Boating Publications, Inc., 5029 Sixth Ave., Kenosha, WI 53140-3401. TEL 312-266-8400. Ed. Ron Schlachter. adv.; bk.rev.; circ. 42,000.
    Description: Covers boating news, racing events, adventures, and ecology.

796.95   US   ISSN 0194-4622
GREAT LAKES SAILING SCANNER.* 1971. 10/yr. $10. Scanner Publications, Inc., 3195 Edgewater Dr., Muskegon, MI 49441. TEL 616-722-4215. Ed. Sheila M. Cullen. adv.; bk.rev.; circ. 18,000.

797.124   US
GREAT LAKES SAILOR. 1987. m. (except Jan.-Feb. combined). $17.95 (Canada $25.95). Great Lakes Sailor, Inc., 2132 E Ninth St., Ste. 310, Cleveland, OH 44115-1245. TEL 216-861-1777. FAX 216-861-1790. Ed. Thomas Gibbons. adv.; circ. 22,000.

797   US
GROSSE POINTER. 1939. m. $25. Kelvin Publishing, Inc., 27421 Harper, St. Clair Shores, MI 48081. TEL 313-774-3530. Ed. Arthur Schulenburg. circ. 1,100. (back issues avail.)

910.202   US
GUIDE TO CRUISING THE CHESAPEAKE BAY. 1974. a. $27.95. Chesapeake Bay Communications, Inc., 1819 Bay Ridge Ave., Annapolis, MD 21403. TEL 301-263-2662. Ed. Dick Goertemiller.
    Description: Contains photographs, drawings and narratives to guide yachtsman to anchorages and ports of call along the bay from the C&D Canal to Norfolk, VA.

SPORTS AND GAMES — BOATS AND BOATING

797.1   US   ISSN 1042-1009
HEARTLAND BOATING. 1989. 6/yr. $12.95. Inland Publications, Inc., Box 1067, Martin, TN 38237. TEL 901-587-6791. FAX 901-587-6893. Ed. Molly Lightfoot Blom. adv.; bk.rev.; circ. 14,000.
Description: Provides stories about boating on the Tennessee, Ohio, Cumberland and Mississippi Rivers, the inland lakes and the Tenn-Tom waterway. Includes houseboating, sailing and cruising features, and marina profiles.

797   AT
HERON NEWSLETTER. 1964. q. Aus.$2.80. National Heron Sailing Association of Australia, 1 Ethel St., Balgowlah, N.S.W. 2093, Australia. Ed. Bruce Morrissey. adv.; circ. 1,750.

910.2   UK
HOSEASONS BOATING HOLIDAYS. 1946. a. free. Hoseasons Holidays, Sunway House, Oulton Broad, Lowestoft, Suffolk NR32 3LT, England. TEL 0502-501010. FAX 0502-500532. TELEX 975189-HOSEAS-G.
Formerly: Hoseasons Holiday Boats and Bungalows Hire (ISSN 0073-3431)

796.95   US   ISSN 0892-8320
HOT BOAT. vol.7, 1985. m. $19.95 (foreign $29.95). Larry Flynt Publications, Inc., 9171 Wilshire Blvd., Ste. 300, Beverly Hills, CA 90210. TEL 310-858-7100. FAX 310-275-3857. Ed. Kevin Spouse. adv.
Formerly: Hot Boat Magazine (ISSN 0745-6077)
Description: Focuses on motorized family water sporting events, personalities, "how-to" and technical data.

796.95   US
HOUSEBOAT ASSOCIATION OF AMERICA. NEWSLETTER. 1971. bi-m. $15. Houseboat Association of America, 4940 N. Rhett Ave., Charleston, SC 29406. TEL 803-744-6581. Ed. Robert E. Perkins. adv.; circ. 500. (looseleaf format; back issues avail.)
Description: News about houseboating and new products.

797.1   US
HOUSEBOAT MAGAZINE. 6/yr. Harris Publishing, Inc., 520 Park Ave., Idaho Falls, ID 83402. TEL 208-524-7000. Ed. Steve Janes. circ. 35,000.

623.82   GW   ISSN 0020-921X
I B N. (Internationale Bodensee & Boot Nachrichten); internationales Bodensee Wassersport Magazin. 1964. s-m. DM.84.90. Druck und Verlagshaus Hermann Daniel & Co. KG, Gruenewaldstr. 15, 7460 Balingen, Germany. FAX 07433-15000. TELEX 763644. Ed. Christoph F. Riedl. adv.; bk.rev.; illus.; index; circ. 8,000.

797.14   US
I C Y R A N A DIRECTORY.* a. free. Intercollegiate Yacht Racing Association of North America, Box 6597, San Antonio, TX 78209-0597. Ed. George H. Griswold. circ. 400.

623.82   FR   ISSN 0019-9389
INDUSTRIES NAUTIQUES. 1965. q. 160 F.($27) (Federation des Industries Nautiques) Editions de Chabassol, 30 rue de Gramont, 75002 Paris, France. TEL 42-97-50-30. FAX 42-86-02-81. Ed. B. Laloup. adv.; bk.rev.; illus.; stat.; index; circ. 2,500.

387.2   UK   ISSN 0020-6172
HD9999.B5
INTERNATIONAL BOAT INDUSTRY. 1968. bi-m. £33($66) Boating Publications, Ltd, Link House, Dingwall Ave., Croydon, Surrey CR9 T2A, England. TEL 081-686-2599. FAX 081-781-6065. Ed. Robert Greenwood. adv.; bk.rev.; circ. 9,827.
Formerly: International Boating.

797.124   US
INTERNATIONAL ETCHELLS CLASS NEWSLETTER. 1970. q. membership. International Etchells Class Association, Box 534, Wall Street Sta., New York, NY 10268. TEL 212-943-5757. Ed. Pamela P. Smith. adv.; circ. 1,400.
Formerly: International E-22 Class Newsletter.
Description: For owners of Etchells class yachts in fleets worldwide.

797.124   US
INTERNATIONAL ETCHELLS CLASS YEARBOOK. 1970. biennial. membership. International Etchells Class Association, Box 534, Wall Street Sta., New York, NY 11268. TEL 212-943-5757. Ed. Pamela P. Smith. adv.; circ. 4,000.
Formerly: International E-22 Class Yearbook.
Description: For owners of Etchells class yachts.

797.124   UK
INTERNATIONAL FIREBALL. 1970. 2/yr. membership. Fireball International, 47 Chiswick Quay, London W4 3UR, England. FAX 0392-410432. Ed. Richard Hughes. adv.; circ. 2,500.

796.95 330   US
INTERNATIONAL MARINE BUSINESS JOURNAL; the voice of the marine industries worldwide. 1989. 2/yr. Marine Business Journal, 1766, Bay Rd., Miami Beach, FL 33139. TEL 305-538-0700. Ed. Dean Clarke. circ. 26,000. (tabloid format; back issues avail.)
Description: Trade magazine about the U.S. marine industry. Covers products and services.

796.95   GW
INTERNATIONALES BODENSEE-JAHRBUCH DER SPORTSCHIFFAHRT. 1959. a. DM.18. (Bodensee Segler Verband) Druck & Verlagshaus Hermann Daniel GmbH & Co. KG, Gruenewaldstr. 15, 7460 Balingen 1, Germany. (Co-sponsor: Bodensee Motorboot Verband) circ. 10,000.

796.95   GW
INTERNATIONALES BODENSEE REGATTA PROGRAMM. 1959. a. DM.15. (Bodensee-Segler-Verband) Druck & Verlagshaus Hermann Daniel GmbH & Co. KG, Gruenewaldstr. 15, 7460 Balingen 1, Germany. TEL 07433-266-100. FAX 07433-15000. TELEX 763644. adv.; circ. 8,000.

797.1   IT   ISSN 0021-2857
ITALIA SUL MARE; mensile internazionale di nautica e di turismo marinaro. (Includes: 5 annual supplements) 1955. m. L.55000. (Salone Nautico Internazionale di Genoa) Vito Bianco, Ed. & Pub., Via Messina, 31, 00198 Rome, Italy. adv.; bk.rev.; charts; illus.; cum.index; circ. 20,000.
Description: Covers boating, tourism, sea sports and sea fashion.

797.124   US
J - 22 MAGAZINE. 1985. a. $25 includes membership. (J - 22 Class Association) Freeman Publishing Co., First & Main, P.O. Box 843, Franklin, TN 37064. TEL 615-791-1780. FAX 615-791-1788. Ed. Carolyn Freeman. adv.; circ. 3,000. (back issues avail.)
Description: National organ for the J-22 Class Sailboat Association; includes championship reports, skills, repairs, and rules.

796.95   US
JAVELIN CLASS ASSOCIATION YEARBOOK. (Supplement avail.) 1976. quinquennial (plus a. supplement). membership. Javelin Class Association, 874 Beecher's Brook Rd., Mayfield Village, OH 44143. TEL 216-461-8511. Ed. G.T. Reiber. circ. 250.

796.95   US
JAVELIN CLASS ASSOCIATION YEARBOOK. SUPPLEMENT. (Supplement to: Javelin Class Association Yearbook) 1977. a. membership. Javelin Class Association, 874 Beecher's Brook Rd., Mayfield Village, OH 44143. TEL 216-461-8511. Ed. G.T. Reiber.

797.1   US
JETSPORTS MAGAZINE. 1982. 5/yr. $10. Pfanner Communications, Inc., 1371 E. Warner Ave., Ste. E, Tustin, CA 92680-6442. TEL 714-259-8240. FAX 714-259-9377. adv.; circ. 40,515.
Formerly: JetSkier Magazine.
Description: Includes reports and photo stories on competitions, personalities, safety articles and a directory to products and services.

797.122   NE
KANO-SPORT. 1980. bi-m. fl.42. Nederlandse Kano Bond, Postbus 1160, 3800 BD Amersfoort, Netherlands. TEL 033-622341. FAX 033-612714. Ed. Jan Eggens. adv.; bk.rev.; circ. 10,000.
Formerly: Kano-Bulletin.

797.122   SW   ISSN 0022-8397
KANOT-NYTT. 1948. m. SEK 60. Svenska Kanotfoerbundet - Swedish Canoe Federation, Skeppsbron 11, 611 35 Nykoeping, Sweden. TEL 0155-69808. FAX 0155-18780. TELEX 14179-SPORT-S. Ed. K. Loefgen. adv.; bk.rev.; illus.; circ. 4,000.

797.122   GW   ISSN 0022-8923
KANU SPORT. 1919. m. DM.56. Deutscher Kanu-Verband - Wirtschafts- und Verlags GmbH, Bertallee 8, 4100 Duisburg, Germany. TEL 0203-721066. FAX 0203-341924. TELEX 17203389-KANU. Ed. Karl Ernst Pikelj. adv.; bk.rev.; illus.; circ. 10,000.

797.1   RU   ISSN 0022-930X
KATERA I YAKHTY. 1963. bi-m. 6 Rub. Izdatel'stvo Shipbuilding, Ul. Gogola 8, 191065 St. Petersburg, Russia. Ed. V.V. Ermolin.

797   GW   ISSN 0075-627X
KLASINGS BOOTSMARKT INTERNATIONAL; YACHTEN UND BOOTE ZUBEHOER, AUSRUESTUNG, MOTOREN. 1968. a. DM.22. Verlag Delius, Klasing und Co., Siekerwall 21, Postfach 4809, 4800 Bielefeld, Germany. TEL 0521-559-280. FAX 0521-559-113. TELEX 932934-DEKLA. Ed. Hans Donath. adv.

796.95   US
LAKE LIFE MAGAZINE. q. Box 43390, Atlanta, GA 30336. TEL 404-691-3024. FAX 404-691-7249. Ed. Allison Andrews. circ. 52,700.

796.95   US   ISSN 0744-9194
LAKELAND BOATING; the Great Lakes boating magazine. 1946. 11/yr. $18.94. O'Meara - Brown Publications, 1560 Sherman Ave., Ste. 1220, Evanston, IL 60201. TEL 708-869-5400. FAX 708-869-5989. Ed. Sarah Wortham. adv.; bk.rev.; illus.; circ. 36,133. (also avail. in microform from UMI) Indexed: Consum.Ind., Mich.Mag.Ind., Sportsearch.
Former titles (until 1983): Lakeland Boating Incorporating Sea (ISSN 0274-9076); (until 1980): Lakeland Boating (ISSN 0023-7345); Lakeland Yachting.

797   UK   ISSN 0075-8272
LAZY MAN'S GUIDE TO HOLIDAYS AFLOAT. 1966. a. $4. Archway Nicholas Publications Ltd., Faber House 6, Eastern Rd., Romford, Essex RM1 3PJ, England. TEL 0708-20011. FAX 0708-48759. TELEX 83507. Ed. Michael Faulkner. adv.; bk.rev.; circ. 120,000.
Description: Information on all aspects of boating vacations in the U.K. Information on fleets, waterways and cruising areas.

797.122   US
LEARN CANOEING!. a. American Canoe Manufacturers Association, 439 E. 51st St., New York, NY 10022. TEL 212-421-5220.

623.829   UK   ISSN 0024-3086
VK1300
LIFEBOAT. 1852. q. £3. Royal National Lifeboat Institution, West Quay Rd., Poole, Dorset BH15 1HZ, England. Ed. Norman Hicks. adv.; bk.rev.; illus.; circ. 145,000. (also avail. in microfilm from UMI)

797.1   UK   ISSN 0024-5062
LITTLE SHIP. 1928. q. membership. Little Ship Club, 38 Hill St., London W1X 8DP, England. Ed. M.I.P. Wise. adv.; bk.rev.; charts; illus.; circ. 4,000.

796.95   US
THE LOG AND SAN DIEGO LOG.* 1971. fortn. $13.75. Log Newspapers, Inc., 1025 Rosecrans St., San Diego, CA 92106. TEL 619-226-1608. FAX 619-226-0573. Ed. Louis Gerlinger III. adv.; bk.rev.; circ. 56,000.
Formerly: San Diego Log.
Description: Covers boating in Southern California and Western Arizona.

LOG OF MYSTIC SEAPORT. see *MUSEUMS AND ART GALLERIES*

797.14   US   ISSN 0076-0455
LOG OF THE STAR CLASS; official rule book. 1921. a. membership. International Star Class Yacht Racing Association, 1545 Waukegan Rd., Glenview, IL 60025. TEL 312-729-0630. FAX 312-729-0718. Ed. Richard L. Munson. adv.; circ. 3,970.

SPORTS AND GAMES — BOATS AND BOATING

797.124 FR ISSN 0047-5017
LOISIRS NAUTIQUES; architecture et construction navales. 1967. m. 295 F. (foreign 355 F.) 71 rue Amedee St. Germain, 33800 Bordeaux, France. Ed. Manon Baraille. adv.; circ. 56,000. (also avail. in microform)

797.1 US
LONG ISLAND POWER & SAIL. bi-m. Box 1128, Port Washington, NY 11050-0300. TEL 516-944-8654. FAX 516-944-8663. Ed. Kathleen M. Yasas. circ. 35,000.

797.1 US
M R A A NEWSLETTER. 1972. m. membership. Marine Retailers Association of America, 150 E. Huron, Ste. 802, Chicago, IL 60611. TEL 312-938-0359. FAX 312-938-9035. Ed. Kermit Small. adv.; circ. 16,000.
 Description: For members who are experienced professional marine dealers, with up-to-date information on industry trends.

796.95 CN
MAGAZINE NAUTIQUE. bi-m. Productions Tel-Art, 7905 St. Denis, Montreal, Que. H2R 2G2, Canada. TEL 514-383-6124. FAX 514-382-5939. Ed. Yvon Pedneault. circ. 12,000.

796.95 BL
MAR: VELA E MOTOR. 1976. m. $60. Editora Groupo 1 Ltda., Avda. Marechal Camara, 271-603, CEP 20020, Rio de Janeiro, Brazil. TEL (021) 533-1415. TELEX 02137398 RYCB. Ed. Roberto Falcao. adv.; bk.rev.; circ. 40,000.
 Formed by the merger of: Vela e Motor & Mar.

796.95 US
MARINA DOCK AGE. 1988. 6/yr. $20. Van Zevern Publications, Inc., 3949 Oakton St., Skokie, IL 60076. TEL 312-982-1810. circ. 18,000.
 Description: Magazine for the marina, boatyard business.

797.1 US ISSN 0025-312X
MARINE & RECREATION NEWS.* 1962. w. $10. Michigan Marine Dealers Association, 33150 Schollcraft, Livonia, MI 48150. TEL 313-777-8866. Ed. Arthur Kamm. adv.; bk.rev.; tr.mk.; circ. 86,000. (tabloid format)
 Formerly: Marina News.

796.95 677 ISSN 1051-5100
▼**MARINE STORES MERCHANDISING**; magazine of boating accessory, parts & service merchandising. 1990. 7/yr. $18. R C M Enterprises, Inc., Twelve Oaks Center, Ste. 922, Wayzata, MN 55391. TEL 612-473-5088. FAX 612-473-7068. Ed. Scott Hermes. adv.; index; circ. 15,000. (back issues avail.)

797.124 CN ISSN 0705-8993
MARINE TRADES. 1955. q. Can.$19. Arthurs Publications Ltd., 5805 Whittle Rd., Ste.208, Mississauga, Ont. L4Z 2J1, Canada. TEL 416-568-4131. Ed. Gary Arthurs.
 Formerly: Marine and Outdoor Trades (ISSN 0047-5939)

MARINEFACTS; topical directory of marine information. see SPORTS AND GAMES — Abstracting, Bibliographies, Statistics

797.1 US
THE MARINER. 1981. bi-w. $23.95. Chesapeake Publishing Corp. (Elkton), Box 429, Elkton, MD 21922-0429. TEL 301-398-3311. FAX 301-398-4044. Ed. Ira Black. adv.; circ. 14,500. (tabloid format)
 Description: Recreational boating on the Chesapeake Bay.

MARITIME STUDIES. see TRANSPORTATION — Ships And Shipping

796.95 US ISSN 0749-2006
MARLIN; the international sportfishing magazine. 1982. bi-m. $24.95. Ebsco Industries Inc., Box 12902, Pensacola, FL 32576. TEL 904-434-5571. FAX 904-433-6303. Ed. David Lear. adv.; bk.rev.; circ. 30,000. (back issues avail.)
 Description: International coverage of the sport of offshore fishing.

796.95 FR
MER & BATEAUX. 1977. m. 280 F. Edimer, 107, rue du Point du Jour, 92100 Boulogne, France. TEL 49-10-30-60. FAX 49-10-30-61. Dir. Patrick Teboul. adv.; bk.rev.; illus.; index; circ. 35,000.
 Formerly (until 1989): Annee Bateaux Magazine (ISSN 0184-5055)

796.95 US
MESSING ABOUT IN BOATS. 1983. bi-w. $20. Cycle Sport Publishing, 29 Burley St., Wenham, MA 01984. TEL 508-774-0906. Ed. Bob Hicks. adv.; bk.rev.; circ. 3,500. (back issues avail.)
 Description: Small boat owner news.

797 AT
MIRROR CLASS ASSOCIATION OF AUSTRALIA. YEARBOOK. 1969. a. Aus.$20. Mirror Class Association of Australia, 47 Gowrie St., South Oakleigh, Vic. 3167, Australia. Ed. W. Dooley. adv.; circ. 400.
 Supersedes in part: Mirror Class Association of Australia. Constitution-Rules of Measurement.

623.82 UK ISSN 0144-2910
MODEL BOATS. 1951. m. £19.80. Argus Specialist Publications Ltd., Argus House, Boundary Way, Hemels, Hampstead, Herts HP2 7ST, England. TEL 0442-876661. Ed. J. Cundell. adv.; charts; illus.; index; circ. 12,399. **Indexed**: Ind.How To Do It (1979-).
 Formerly: Model Maker and Model Boats (ISSN 0026-7333)

797.1 AT ISSN 0026-752X
MODERN BOATING. 1965. m. Aus.$39. Federal Publishing Company, 180 Bourke Rd., Alexandria, N.S.W. 2015, Australia. Ed. Mark Rothfield. adv.; bk.rev.; illus.; index; circ. 14,700. (processed) **Indexed**: Pinpointer.
 Description: Covers sail and power boats, basic hints to electronic navigation and all types of boating throughout Australia and New Zealand.

797.1 IT
MONDO BARCA; navigazione di porto. (Text in English, Italian) 1988. m. L.120000($92.30) Media Sea Communication S.r.l., Via Coni Zugna 6, 20144 Milan, Italy. TEL 02-4813695. FAX 02-4985912. Ed. Fabrizio de Checchi. adv.; circ. 38,500. (back issues avail.)
 Description: Deals with sail and motor boats, yachts, new products, equipment and sports events.

797 FR
MOTEUR BOAT MAGAZINE. 11/yr. 240 F. (foreign 295 F.). Editions Lariviere, 15-17 Quai de l'Oise, 75166 Paris Cedex 16, France. TEL 1-40-34-22-07. FAX 1-40-35-84-41. TELEX 211 678 F.

796.95 IT
MOTONAUTICA. m. L.70000($80) Renoma, Via Ippolito Nievo 33, Milan, Italy. TEL 312303. FAX 3493558. TELEX 330555.

MOTOR. see TRANSPORTATION — Automobiles

797.1 UK ISSN 0027-1780
MOTOR BOAT & YACHTING. 1904. m. $44. I P C Magazines Ltd., Kings Reach Tower, Stamford St., London SE1 9LS, England. TEL 071-261-5849. FAX 071-261-7851554. (Subscr. to: Reed Business Publishing Ltd., 205 E. 42nd St., New York, NY 10017, U.S.A.) Ed. Tom Willis. adv.; bk.rev.; charts; illus.; tr.lit.; index every 6 mos.; circ. 35,315. (also avail. in microform from UMI) **Indexed**: Br.Tech.Ind.
 Description: Boat tests, cruising guides, advice on seamanship and navigation for the committed boater.

797.1 US ISSN 0027-1799
VM320
MOTOR BOATING & SAILING. (Annual Show issues Jan., Sept.) 1907. m. $15.97. Hearst Magazines, Motor Boating & Sailing, 224 W. 57th St., New York, NY 10019. TEL 212-649-3068. FAX 212-649-3065. Ed. Peter Janssen. adv.; bk.rev.; charts; illus.; stat.; index; circ. 137,293. (also avail. in microform from UMI; back issues avail.) **Indexed**: Consum.Ind., Mag.Ind., PMR, R.G., Sports Per.Ind., Sportsearch.
 Formerly: Motor Boating.

797.1 DK
MOTOR - SOESPORT.* 1960. m. free. (Danmarks Motorbaads Union) DMV, danske fritidssejlere, Hjulmagervej 13D, DK-7100 Vejle, Denmark. Ed. Mogens Jensen. adv.; illus.; circ. 7,000.

796.95 US
MOTORBOAT. 1989. a. $14.98 (foreign $23.98). (Power and Motoryacht Association) Cahners Publishing Company (New York) (Subsidiary of: Reed International PLC), Division of Reed Publishing (USA) Inc., 475 Park Ave S., New York, NY 10016-6901. TEL 212-779-1999. FAX 212-545-5400. (Subscr. to: 44 Cook St., Denver, CO 80206. TEL 800-388-4511) Ed. Richard Thiel. adv.; circ. 110,000.
 Description: Aimed at first-time buyers and owners of powerboats 15 to 26 feet long. Contains reviews of boats, engines and accessories.

623.82 UK ISSN 0027-3155
MULTIHULL INTERNATIONAL. 1964. m. £18($50) (foreign £25)(effective 1991). Chandler Publications Ltd., 10 South St., Totnes, Devon TQ9 5DZ, England. TEL 0803-864668. FAX 0803-865649. Ed. Jack R.D. Heming. adv.; charts; illus.; tr.lit.; circ. 6,500.
 Incorporating (in 1968): Marine Product Guide.
 Description: Provides news and views on catamarans, trimarans and proas.

796.95 US ISSN 0749-4122
MULTIHULLS. 1975. bi-m. $18. Chiodi Advertising & Publishing, Inc., 421 Hancock St., N. Quincy, MA 02171. TEL 617-328-8181. FAX 617-471-0118. Ed. Charles K. Chiodi. adv.; bk.rev.; film rev.; charts; tr.lit.; circ. 49,000. (back issues avail.)

797.122 US
N A C L O NEWS. 1979. m. membership. National Association of Canoe Liveries and Outfitters, R.R. 2, Box 249, Butler, KY 41006-9674. TEL 606-472-2205. FAX 606-472-2030. circ. 350 (controlled).
 Description: Promotes safety, protection of waterways, and public rights of access and use of waterways.

796.95 US ISSN 1055-1972
HD9993.B63
N.A.D.A. LARGE BOAT APPRAISAL GUIDE. 3/yr. $60. (National Automobile Dealers Association) N.A.D.A. Appraisal Guides, Box 7800, Costa Mesa, CA 92628-7800.
 Supersedes in part: N.A.D.A. Boat Appraisal Guide.

N.A.D.A. MOTORCYCLE - SNOWMOBILE - A T V - PERSONAL WATERCRAFT APPRAISAL GUIDE. (National Automobile Dealers Association) see SPORTS AND GAMES — Bicycles And Motorcycles

796.95 US ISSN 1055-1964
HD9993.B63
N.A.D.A. SMALL BOAT APPRAISAL GUIDE. 3/yr. $85. (National Automobile Dealers Association) N.A.D.A. Appraisal Guides, Box 7800, Costa Mesa, CA 92628-7800.
 Supersedes in part: N.A.D.A. Boat Appraisal Guide.

796.95 US
N A S I S S NEWSLETTER. 1981. q. $10. National Association of Sailing Instructors and Sailing Schools, 15 Renier Ct., Middletown, NJ 07748. TEL 908-671-6190. Ed. Richard Herbst. (looseleaf format; back issues avail.)
 Description: Covers subjects dealing with the operation of sailing schools, charters, and the training of its customers to sail or charter boats.

797.1 US
N M M A CERTIFICATION HANDBOOK. 1956. a. National Marine Manufacturers Association, 401 N. Michigan Ave., Chicago, IL 60611. TEL 312-836-4747. index.
 Former titles: B I A Certification Handbook (ISSN 0067-9402); Boating Industry Associations Engineering Manual of Recommended Practices.

796.95 US ISSN 0363-1354
VM361
NATIONAL BOAT BOOK. a. $110. Maclean Hunter Market Reports, Inc., 29 N. Wacker Dr., Chicago, IL 60606-3297. TEL 312-726-2802. FAX 312-726-2574. (back issues avail.)

797.1 US
NATIONAL CIRCLE BOAT. m. Pierce Publications, Box 617, Sun City, CA 92586-9984. TEL 714-244-1104. FAX 714-244-1892. Ed. Gerry Kurz.

SPORTS AND GAMES — BOATS AND BOATING

797.1 US
NATIONAL DRAG BOAT. m. Pierce Publications, Box 617, Sun City, CA 92586-9984. TEL 714-244-1104. FAX 714-244-1892. Ed. Kelly Harper. circ. 40,000.

796.95 AT ISSN 1030-2425
NATIONAL MARINA SURVEY. 1987. a. A.B. Organisation Pty. Ltd., P.O. Box 319, Avalon Beach, N.S.W. 2107, Australia. TEL 02-918-8322. FAX 02-918-8884. adv.
   Description: Catalogues the cost and facilities of marinas throughout Australia and New Zealand.

NATIONAL MARINE BANKERS ASSOCIATION. SUMMARY ANNUAL REPORT. see BUSINESS AND ECONOMICS — Banking And Finance

796.95 330 US
NATIONAL MARINE BUSINESS JOURNAL; the voice of the marine industries nationwide. 1986. 6/yr. $15. Marine Business Journal, 1766 Bay Rd., Miami Beach, FL 33139. TEL 305-538-0700. Ed. Dean Clarke. circ. 26,000. (tabloid format; back issues avail.)
   Former titles: Southern Marine Business Journal; Florida Marine Business Journal.
   Description: Trade magazine about the marine industry. Covers political issues, new technologies and products. Includes export, management and insurance.

797.1 US
NATIONAL ORGANIZATION FOR RIVER SPORTS. CURRENTS. 1979. q. $15. National Organization for River Sports, 314 N. 20th St., Box 6847, Colorado Springs, CO 80934. TEL 719-473-2466. Ed. Greg Moore. adv.; bk.rev.; circ. 10,000. (back issues avail.)
   Description: Covers whitewater rivers and river running internationally, with emphasis on the United States.

796.95 FR
NAUT ARGUS. 1977. q. 245 F. Disney Hachette Presse, 23-25 rue de Berri, 75008 Paris Cedex 08, France. TEL 16-1-44-89-44-89. (Subscr. to: 90 rue de Flandre, 75947 Paris Cedex 19, France. TEL 16-1-40-34-35-00) Ed. Michel Koutsikides. adv.; illus.; circ. 2,500.

797.1 SP
NAUTIC PRESS; nautica deportiva. 1982. m. 3500 ptas. Diario Maritimas, S.A., Paseo de Colon 24, 08002 Barcelona, Spain. TEL 93-301-5646. FAX 93-318-6645. Ed. Juan Cardona. circ. 32,000.

797.1 IT
NAUTICA. 1962. m. L.100000. Nautica Editrice, Via Tevere 44, 00198 Rome, Italy. TEL 06-867026. FAX 853653. TELEX 611613 NAUTIC I. Ed. Mario Sonnino Sorisio. adv.; bk.rev.; charts; illus.

NAUTICAL RESEARCH JOURNAL. see TRANSPORTATION — Ships And Shipping

796.95 US
NAUTIQUE NEWS. 1961. 3/yr. free. Correct Craft, Inc., 6100 S. Orange Ave., Orlando, FL 32809. TEL 407-855-4141. FAX 407-851-7844. TELEX 56-7424 CORRCRAFT. Ed. Teresa "Terry" Dunagin. adv.; circ. 80,000.
   Formerly: Correct Craft Tribune.
   Description: News for boating and water sports enthusiasts, with special emphasis on Correct Craft boats.

797.1 SW
NAVIGATIONSSAELLSKAPETS MEDLEMSBLAD. 1926. 6/yr. SEK 60 to non-members. Navigationssaellskapet, Af Pontins Vaeg 6, S-115 21 Stockholm, Sweden. Ed. Sture Gaerdshagen. illus.; circ. 1,000.
   Formerly: Navis (ISSN 0028-1603)

796.95 FR ISSN 0762-7378
NEPTUNE YACHTING. 1962. 11/yr. 219 F. Disney Hachette Presse, 23-25 rue de Berri, 75008 Paris, France. TEL 16-1-44-89-44-89. (Subscr. to: 90 rue de Flandre, 75947 Paris Cedex 19, France. TEL 16-1-40-34-35-00) Ed. Christian Leveneur. adv.; illus.; circ. 50,000. **Indexed:** Sportsearch.
   Former titles: Neptune Nautisme; Cahiers du Yatching; Helice (ISSN 0037-6205)

797.124 US
NEW ENGLAND SAILBOARD JOURNAL. 1983. m. $12. North Shore Weeklies, Box 468, Marblehead, MA 01945-0468. TEL 617-639-2838.

NEW ZEALAND FISHERMAN. see SPORTS AND GAMES — Outdoor Life

797.1 799.1 NZ ISSN 0112-4412
NEW ZEALAND POWERBOAT. 1984. m. NZ.$49.50 (foreign NZ.$110). Vantage Publishing Limited, Cnr. Halsey & Madden Streets, Freemons Bay, Auckland, New Zealand. TEL 09-3098-292. FAX 09-3096-361. Ed. Barry Thompson. circ. 16,500. (back issues avail.)
   Description: Covers motor boating, boat racing, boat tests and evaluations, new designs, waterskiing and fishing.

796.95 US
NEWSWAVE.* 1986. s-a. Marine Challenge, Inc., 6418 U.S Highway 41 N., Ste. 266, Apollo Beach, FL 33572-1803. TEL 813-822-4749. FAX 813-822-0972. Ed. Ardith Bonnar. bk.rev.; tr.lit.; circ. 150,000. (tabloid format; back issues avail.)
   Description: Contains information on marine safety and survival.

NORSK BAATINDUSTRI. see TRANSPORTATION — Ships And Shipping

796.95 US
NORTHWEST SAILBOARD. 7/yr. $9.97. Gorge Publishing, Inc., 500 Morton Rd., Box 918, Hood River, OR 97031. TEL 503-386-7440. FAX 503-386-7480. circ. 25,000.

796.95 US ISSN 0739-747X
NOR'WESTING. 1965. m. $15. Nor'westing Inc., Box 1027, Edmonds, WA 98020. TEL 206-776-3138. FAX 206-776-3139. Ed. Thomas F. Kincaid. adv.; bk.rev.; charts; illus.; tr.lit.; circ. 10,600.
   Description: Covers recreational boating in the Pacific Northwest, British Columbia, Canada and Alaska.

796.95 US ISSN 0886-0149 VK555
OCEAN NAVIGATOR; marine navigation and ocean voyaging. 1985. 8/yr. $21. Navigator Publishing Corp., Box 569, Portland, ME 04112-0569. TEL 207-772-2466. Ed. Gregory Walsh. adv.; bk.rev.; circ. 35,000.
   Formerly (until Dec. 1985): Navigator.

769.95 US
O'DAY TODAY.* 1985. 3/yr. membership. O'Day Corporation, 100 Franklin St., Boston, MA 02110-1515. TEL 508-678-5291. FAX 508-674-6555. Ed. Paulie Rebello. circ. 6,000.
   Description: For owners of O'Day boats.

797.1 AU
OESTERREICHS KANUSPORT. 1948. 5/yr. S.100. Oesterreichischer Kanu-Verband, Berggasse 16, A-1090 Vienna, Austria. TEL (0222)93645. Ed. Guenter Goldbach. adv.; bk.rev.; abstr.; bibl.; charts; illus.; stat; tr.lit.; circ. 5,000.
   Formerly: Oesterreichs Paddelsport (ISSN 0029-9995)
   Description: News on canoes, sports events, canoe associations and canoe trips.

796.95 US
OFFSHORE (NEEDHAM). 1976. m. $19.97. Offshore Publications, Inc., Box 817, Needham, MA 02194. TEL 617-449-6204. FAX 617-449-9702. Ed. Martha M. Lostrom. adv.; bk.rev.; illus.; circ. 38,000.
   Formerly: New England Offshore (ISSN 0274-9394)

797 AT
OFFSHORE AUSTRALIAN YACHTING. 1969. bi-m. Aus.$30.70. (Cruising Yacht Club of Australia) National Publications Pty. Ltd., P.O. Box 297, Homebush, N.S.W. 2140, Australia. TEL 02-764-1111. FAX 02-763-1699. Ed. Peter Campbell. adv.; bk.rev.; charts;illus; circ. 7,500. (back issues avail.) **Indexed:** Tr.& Indus.Ind.
   Former titles: Offshore Yacht Racing and Cruising (ISSN 0819-7458); (until 1987): Offshore.
   Description: Covers all local, national and international offshore and inshore yachting; yacht racing, yacht tests and reviews, boats and boating.

797.14 US
▼**OFFSHORE WORLDWIDE.** 1991. 10/yr. $40. Offshore Worldwide, Inc., 2000 S. Dixie Hwy., Ste. 206-C, Miami, FL 33133. TEL 305-858-0970. Ed. J.D. Berg.
   Description: Covers international offshore powerboat racing.

797.1 SW
PAA KRYSS OCH TILL RORS. 1930. 11/yr. SEK 160. Svenska Kryssarklubben - Swedish Cruising Association, Karlavagen 67, 114 49 Stockholm, Sweden. TEL 8-6615872. FAX 8-6629518. Ed. Anders N. Johansson. adv.; bk.rev.; circ. 40,000.
   Formed by the merger of: Paa Kryss & Till Rors (Med Segel och Motor) (ISSN 0040-7682)

797.1 US ISSN 0193-3515 GV776.C2
PACIFIC BOATING ALMANAC. NORTHERN CALIFORNIA & NEVADA. 1965. a. $16.95. Pacific Boating Almanac, Box 341668, Los Angeles, CA 90034-1668. TEL 213-287-2831. Ed. Peter L. Griffes. illus.
   Formerly: Sea Boating Almanac. Northern California and Nevada (ISSN 0363-7700)

797.9 US ISSN 0276-8771 GV776.N76
PACIFIC BOATING ALMANAC. OREGON, WASHINGTON, BRITISH COLUMBIA & SOUTHEASTERN ALASKA. a. $16.95. Pacific Boating Alamanc, Box 341668, Los Angeles, CA 90034-1668. TEL 213-287-2830. Ed. Peter L. Griffes. illus.
   Former titles: Pacific Almanac. Pacific Northwest and Alaska (ISSN 0148-1177); Sea Boating Almanac. Pacific Northwest and Alaska (ISSN 0363-7999)

797.1 US ISSN 0193-3507 GV776.C22
PACIFIC BOATING ALMANAC. SOUTHERN CALIFORNIA, ARIZONA, BAJA. a. $16.95. Pacific Boating Almanac, Box 341668, Los Angeles, CA 90034-1668. TEL 213-287-2830. Ed. Peter L. Griffes. illus.
   Formerly: Sea Boating Almanac. Southern California, Arizona, Baja (ISSN 0363-6712)

797.1 CN ISSN 0030-8986
PACIFIC YACHTING. 1968. m. Can.$30. O P Publishing Ltd., Suite 202, 1132 Hamilton St., Vancouver, B.C. V6B 2S2, Canada. TEL 604-687-1581. FAX 604-687-1925. Ed. John Shinnick. adv.; bk.rev.; charts; illus.; circ. 16,000. **Indexed:** Can.Per.Ind.
   Formerly: Pacific Yachting Journal.

797.122 US
PADDLER. 1981. 6/yr. $15. Paddling Group, 4061 Oceanside Blvd., No. M, Oceanside, CA 92056. TEL 619-633-2293. FAX 619-630-1270. Ed. Eugene Buchanan. adv.; bk.rev.; circ. 100,000. **Indexed:** Sportsearch (1984-).
   Formerly: River Runner (ISSN 0886-9197)
   Description: Covers whitewater canoeing, rafting, and kayaking within the U.S. and internationally. Provides information on equipment, technique, conservation and other related sports, destinations, activities and issues.

796.95 US
PADDLING MAGAZINE. bi-m. Tanis Group, Inc., Box 635, Oscoda, MI 48750. TEL 517-739-9997. FAX 517-739-4122. Ed. Harry Roberts. circ. 200,000.

796.95 GW ISSN 0936-5877
PALSTEK; Technisches Wassersport Journal. 1985. bi-m. DM.24. Verlags-Agentur Schramm, Bismarckstr. 84, 2000 Hamburg 20, Germany. TEL 040-4208725. circ. 20,500.

PENNSYLVANIA ANGLER. see SPORTS AND GAMES — Outdoor Life

797.14 CN ISSN 0834-809X
PERFORMANCE RACING NEWS. m. Can.$21.15. Buy & Sell - Bargain Hunter Newspaper Ltd., 593 Yonge St., Toronto, Ont. M4Y 124, Canada. TEL 416-964-8700. FAX 416-964-8403. Ed. John Hopkins. adv.; B&W page Can.$2100; trim 10 1/2 x 15 3/4. illus.; circ. 30,000. (tabloid format; back issues avail.)
   Description: Provides coverage of many forms of motorsports racing.

SPORTS AND GAMES — BOATS AND BOATING

797.124   AT
PERFORMANCE SAILING. m. Aus.$3.98 per issue. A.B. Organisation Pty. Ltd., P.O. Box 319, Avalon Beach, N.S.W. 2107, Australia. TEL 02-918-8322. FAX 02-918-8884. (Dist. by: Network Distribution Company, 54-58 Park St., Sydney, N.S.W. 2000, Australia) circ. 10,000.
Description: Directed at the performance sailing community.

797.1   US
PERSONAL WATERCRAFT ILLUSTRATED; the personal watercraft recreation magazine. 1987. m. $18.95. C N Publishing Group, 2201 Cherry Ave., Long Beach, CA 90806. TEL 310-427-7433. FAX 310-427-6685. Ed. Paul Carruthers. circ. 68,115.
Description: Covers all aspects of the sport and recreational use of personal watercraft.

796.95   CN
PLAISANCIERS. 1986. 5/yr. C R V Publishing Co. Ltd., 3580 Poirier Blvd., Ville St-Laurent, Que. H4R 2J5, Canada. TEL 514-856-0788. Ed. Claude Leonard. circ. 25,000.

796.95
PORT HOLE. (Text in English or French) q. Canadian Power & Sail Squadrons, 26 Golden Gate Crt., Scarborough, Ont. M1P 3A5, Canada. TEL 416-293-2438. FAX 416-293-2445. Ed. Neville Barnett.
Description: Promotes safe boating through education. Keeps members informed of CPS activities, legal and legislative matters, new products and equipment. Entertains with amusing cruising yarns, timely marine maintenance, safety articles. Serves as a forum for lively exchange of opinions and ideas.

796.95   US   ISSN 0886-4411
POWER AND MOTORYACHT. 1985. m. $29.97 (Canada $47.97; elsewhere $44.97). (Power and Motoryacht Association) Cahners Publishing Company (New York), Consumer and Entertainment Division (Subsidiary of: Reed International PLC), Division of Reed Publishing (USA) Inc., 475 Park Ave. S., New York, NY 10016-6901. TEL 212-779-1999. FAX 212-545-5400. (Subscr. to: 44 Cook St., Denver, CO 80206. TEL 800-388-4511) Ed. Richard Thiel. adv.; circ. 160,000. (back issues avail.)
Description: For owners of powerboats 24 feet or larger. Articles covers engines, electronics, financing, fishing and operation.

797.14   CN
POWER BOATING CANADA. 6/yr. C R V Publications Canada Ltd., 2077 Dundas St. E., Ste. 202, Mississauga, Ont. L4X 1M2, Canada. TEL 416-624-8218. FAX 416-624-6764. Ed. Darryl Simmons. adv.; circ. 55,351.

797.122   CN
POWER STROKE. irreg. (3-5/yr.). membership. Saskatoon Canoe Club, Box 7764, Saskatoon, Sask. S7K 4J1, Canada. TEL 306-933-4460. Ed. Grant Cheston. circ. 150. (looseleaf format)
Description: Covers upcoming events and reports on completed events. Relates to recreational canoeing, marathon canoe racing and whitewater kayaking.

797.1   US   ISSN 0032-6089
GV835.9
POWERBOAT. 1968. m. (11/yr.) $27 (foreign $38). Nordco Publishing, Inc. (Subsidiary of: Nordskog Industries, Inc.), 15917 Strathern St., Van Nuys, CA 91406. TEL 818-989-1820. FAX 818-989-1823. (Subscr. to: Powerboat, c/o Kable News Co., Box 556, Mt. Morris, IL 61054. TEL 800-545-9364) Ed. Tosh Arimura. adv.; illus.; circ. 82,575. **Indexed:** Sportsearch.

623.82   US   ISSN 1040-3663
POWERBOAT REPORTS; the consumer resource for the powercraft owner. vol.3, no.20, 1990. s-m. $72. Belvoir Publications, Inc., 75 Holly Hill Lane, Box 2626, Greenwich, CT 06836-2626. TEL 203-661-6111. FAX 203-661-4802. (Subscr. to: Box 420234, Palm Coast, FL 32142) Ed. Timothy H. Cole.

797.1   UK   ISSN 0032-6348
VM320
PRACTICAL BOAT OWNER. 1967. m. $35.20. I P C Magazines Ltd., Specialist & Leisure Group (Subsidiary of: Reed International PLC), Westover House, West Quay Rd., Poole, Dorset BH15 1JG, England. TEL 0202-680603. FAX 0202-674335. Ed. George Taylor. bk.rev.; index; circ. 66,830.
—BLDSC shelfmark: 6593.964000.

796.95   US   ISSN 0161-8059
PRACTICAL SAILOR. 1970. s-m. $57. Belvoir Publications, Inc., 75 Holly Hill Lane, Box 2626, Greenwich, CT 06836-2626. TEL 203-661-6111. FAX 203-661-4802. (Subscr. to: 11 Commerce Blvd., Palm Ceast, FL 32137) Ed. Dan Spurr. circ. 40,000. **Indexed:** Sportsearch (1984-).

623.82   US
PROFESSIONAL BOATBUILDER. 1989. bi-m. free to qualified personnel. WoodenBoat Publications, Inc., Box 78, Brooklin, ME 04616. TEL 207-359-4651. FAX 207-359-8920. Ed. Chris Cornell. circ. 20,000 (controlled).
Description: For boat construction, repair, design and surveying company executives.

796.95   US   ISSN 0194-6218
PROPELLER. m. membership. American Power Boat Association, 17640 E. Nine Mile Rd., Box 377, E. Detroit, MI 48021. TEL 313-773-9700. FAX 313-773-6490. Eds. Holli Hagerstrom, Renee J. Mahn.
Description: Features accounts of racing events, technology, safety and racing accomplishments.

797.14 797.124   FI   ISSN 0355-6980
PURJEHTIJA/SEGLAREN. (Text in Finnish and Swedish) 1974. bi-m. Fmk.80($25) Finnish Yachting Association - Suomen Purjehtijiliitto, Radiokatu 20, SF-00240 Helsinki, Finland. TEL 358-0-1582350. FAX 358-0-1582369. TELEX 121797-SVUL. Ed. Raimo Raekikkoenen. adv.; bk.rev.; circ. 31,000 (controlled). (back issues avail.)

797.1   ISSN 0833-918X
QUEBEC YACHTING, VOILE ET MOTEUR. (Text in French) 1978. 8/yr. Can.$21. Publications Transcontinental Inc., 465 St. Jean St., 9th Fl., Montreal, Que. H2Y 3S4, Canada. TEL 514-842-6491. FAX 514-842-8557. Ed. Henri Rene de Cotret. adv.; bk.rev.; charts; illus.; circ. 7,897. **Indexed:** Can.Per.Ind., Pt.de Rep. (1985-), Sportsearch.
Former titles: Quebec Yachting et Voile (ISSN 0829-3198); Quebec Yachting (ISSN 0705-243X)

RADIO CONTROL BOAT MODELER. see HOBBIES

RADIO CONTROL BOAT MODELLER. see HOBBIES

797   UK
REGATTA. 1978. m. £20. Amateur Rowing Association, 6 Lower Mall, London W6 9DJ, England. TEL 081-748-3632. FAX 081-741-4658. Ed. C.J. Dodd. **Indexed:** Sportsearch (1987-).
Formerly (until 1987): A.R.A. Club News.

REVISTA MAR - VELA E MOTOR. see TRANSPORTATION — Automobiles

797.1   FR   ISSN 0035-5720
RIVIERE. q. 10 F. Canoe Kayak Club de France, 47 Quai Fuber, 94360 Bry sur Marne, France. bk.rev.

797.123   NE   ISSN 0048-8518
ROEIEN. 1939. m. fl.32.50 (effective Jan. 1991). Koninklijke Nederlandsche Roeibond, Bosbaan 6, 1182 AC Amstelveen, Netherlands. TEL 020-462740. FAX 020-463881. adv.; illus.; index; circ. 5,000.

796.95   UK   ISSN 0485-5175
ROVING COMMISSIONS; anthology of cruising logs. 1960. a. price request. Royal Cruising Club, c/o Sue Kimber, 34 Holmbush Rd., London SW15 3LE, England. TEL 081-788-5497. Ed. Trevor Wilkinson. bk.rev.; circ. 1,000.

797.1   US
ROW. 1989. bi-m. $24.95. F M I Publications Inc., 4390 Bodega Ave., Petaluma, CA 94952. TEL 707-762-6297. Ed. Greg Sabourin. circ. 35,000.
Description: Covers local, national and international news. Features people, races, rowing events, equipment, technique and medicine.

ROWING MAGAZINE MONTHLY; the independent magazine for enthusiasts everywhere. see SPORTS AND GAMES

797.1   UK   ISSN 0035-9041
ROYAL NAVAL SAILING ASSOCIATION JOURNAL. 1936. s-a. membership. Royal Naval Sailing Association, c/o Royal Naval Club & Royal Albert Yacht Platz, 17 Pembroke Rd., Portsmouth, Hants PO1 2NT, England. Ed. Lt. Col. P.R. Thomas. adv.; bk.rev.; illus.; circ. 6,800.

796.95   GW   ISSN 0342-8281
RUDERSPORT. 1883. every 8 days (May-Sept.), every 14 days (Oct.-Apr.). DM.130. (German Rowing Association) Limpert Verlag GmbH, Luisenplatz 2, Postfach 4027, 6200 Wiesbaden, Germany. TEL 0611-373072. FAX 0611-374351. Ed. Rolf Ziel. adv.; circ. 5,600.

797.124   US   ISSN 0036-2700
GV811
SAIL. 1970. m. $21.75 (Canada $26.45; Mexico $24.75; elsewhere $29.95). Cahners Publishing Company (Newton), Consumer and Entertainmant Division (Subsidiary of: Reed International PLC), Division of Reed Publishing (USA) Inc., 275 Washington St., Newton, MA 02158-1630. TEL 617-964-3030. FAX 617-558-4506. (Dist. by: Neodata Services, Box 2971, Boulder, CO 80329) Ed. Patience Wales. adv.; bk.rev.; charts; illus.; tr.lit.; circ. 175,000. (also avail. in microform from UMI; back issues avail.; reprint service avail. from UMI) **Indexed:** Consum.Ind., Mag.Ind., PMR, R.G., Sports Per.Ind., Sportsearch (1976-).
Description: For sailors at various levels: cruisers and racers, from novices to experts, actively involved in the development of their sailing skills.

796.95   US
SAILBOARD RETAILER. 1989. 8/yr. $20. Gorge Publishing, Inc., 500 Morton Rd., Box 918, Hood River, OR 97031. TEL 503-386-7440. FAX 503-386-7480. Ed. Carol York. circ. 4,500 (controlled).
Description: Includes retail selling tips and industry and product news.

797.124   US   ISSN 0148-8732
SAILBOAT & EQUIPMENT DIRECTORY. 1967. a. $3.95. Cahners Publishing Company (Newton) (Subsidiary of: Reed International PLC), Division of Reed Publishing (USA) Inc., 275 Washington St., Newton, MA 02158-1630. TEL 617-964-3030. FAX 617-558-4402. (Subscr. to: 44 Cook St., Denver, CO 80206. TEL 800-662-7776) (Co-publisher: Sail Publications) Ed. Patience Wales. adv.; bk.rev.; illus.; circ. 85,000.
Formerly (until 1970): Sailboat Directory (ISSN 0581-3115)
Description: Provides the sailing community, the public and the trade with a reference guide to the sailboats and sailboat products available in the US and Canada.

797.124   US   ISSN 0036-2719
SAILING; the beauty of sail. 1966. m. $24.95. Port Publications, Inc., 125 E. Main St., Port Washington, WI 53074. TEL 414-284-3494. FAX 414-284-0067. Ed. Wm. F. Schanen 3rd. adv.; bk.rev.; illus.; circ. 35,000. (also avail. in microform from UMI; reprint service avail. from UMI)
Formerly: Lake Michigan Sailing.

797.124   CN
SAILING BEAT. 17/yr. Sporting Beat Publishing Inc., 67 Mowat Ave., Ste. 132, Toronto, Ont. M6K 3E3, Canada. TEL 416-516-8205. FAX 416-516-8205. Ed. Iain MacMillan. circ. 12,000.

797.124   CN
SAILING CANADA. 11/yr. Sailing Canada Magazine, Ltd., 136 Walton St., Port Hope, Ont. L1A 1N5, Canada. TEL 416-444-3633. FAX 416-444-3931. Ed. Donna Fairey Carter. adv.

797.124   US
SAILING SCENE. m. New York Times Company, 5 John Clarke Rd., Newport, RI 02840-5641. TEL 401-847-1588. FAX 401-848-5048. Ed. Jane Tracy.

797.1   US   ISSN 0889-4094
GV811.8
SAILING WORLD; the authority on performance sailing. 1962. m. $24. Cruising World Publications, Inc. (Subsidiary of: New York Times Co.), 5 John Clarke Rd., Newport, RI 02840. TEL 401-847-1588. FAX 401-848-5048. (Subscr. to: Box 3213, Harlan, IA 51537) Ed. John Burnham. adv.; bk.rev.; illus.; circ. 61,000. (also avail. in microform from UMI; back issues avail.; reprint service avail. from UMI) **Indexed:** Sportsearch (1990-).
  Former titles: Yacht Racing and Cruising (ISSN 0190-7956); Yacht Racing (ISSN 0276-2935); One-Design and Offshore Yachtsman (ISSN 0030-2511)
  Description: For the active sailor who races or cruises. Covers sailboat design, sailing technique and equipment, charter cruising, seamanship, racing events and news.

796.95   US   ISSN 1051-063X
SAILORMAN STAR MAGAZINE. 1985. bi-m. $6. 350 E. State Rd. 84, Ft. Lauderdale, FL 33316. TEL 305-522-6716. Ed. Al Plant. adv.; bk.rev.; circ. 29,000. (reprint service avail.)
  Description: Covers boating life, equipment, regulations. Includes sailing stories.

797.1   US
SANTANA.* 1987. m. $12. Santana Publications, Inc., 4911 Warner Ave., No. 11, Huntington Beach, CA 92649-4474. TEL 714-893-3432. adv.; circ. 22,000.
  Description: Emphasizes manual sailing including racing and cruising.

797.1   US   ISSN 0746-8601
GV771
SEA; best of boating in the west. Variant title: Sea Magazine. (Covers the 13 Western United States; southern British Columbia, Canada, and coastal Mexico.) 1908. m. $19.94 (foreign $29.94). Duncan McIntosh Co. Inc., 17782 Cowan, Irvine, CA 92714-6012. TEL 714-660-6150. FAX 714-660-6172. Ed. Linda Yuskaitis. adv.; bk.rev.; charts; illus.; tr.lit. (also avail. in microform from UMI; reprint service avail. from UMI) **Indexed:** PMR, Sportsearch.
  Formerly (until 1984): Sea and Pacific Skipper (ISSN 0274-905X); Incorporates (in 1977): Rudder (ISSN 0274-9068); Which supersedes: Sea, Eastern Edition (ISSN 0163-7533); Sea and Pacific Motor Boat (ISSN 0036-9969)
  Description: Profiles boating personalities, cruise destinations, analysis of marine environmental issues, technical information, seamanship, and news from western harbors.

796.5   GR
SEA & YACHTING; the Greek monthly yachting magazine. (Text in Greek) 1977. m. Dr.9000($70) Valef Yachts S.A., 22 Akti Themistokleous, GR 185 36 Piraeus, Greece. TEL 45 29 571. FAX 41-37-805. TELEX 21-2000 VAL GR. Ed. Maro Paletsaki. adv.; circ. 20,000. (back issues avail.)

796.95 900   US   ISSN 0270-5524
SEA HERITAGE NEWS. 1980. q. $25. Sea Heritage Foundation, 254-26 75 Ave., Glen Oaks, NY 11004. TEL 718-343-9575. Ed. Bernie Klay. adv.; bk.rev.; circ. 50,000.
  Description: Covers all aspects of sea history and culture.

796.95   US   ISSN 0829-3279
SEA KAYAKER. 1984. q. $13. 6329 Seaview Ave. N.W., Seattle, WA 98107. TEL 206-789-6413. FAX 206-789-6392. (Subscr. to: Sea Kayaker, Inc., 6327 Seaview Ave. N.W., Seattle, WA 98107) Ed. Chris Cunningham. adv.; bk.rev.; circ. 10,000. (back issues avail.) **Indexed:** Sportsearch (1987-).
  Description: Explores kayak touring on sea and lakes, safety techniques, health, destinations, history and much more.

SEA RESCUE. see TRANSPORTATION — Ships And Shipping

797.1   NZ   ISSN 0037-0037
SEA SPRAY. 1945. m. NZ.$49.50 (foreign NZ$110)(typically set in Sep.). Vantage Publishing Limited, Cnr. Halsey & Madden Streets, Freemans Bay, Auckland, New Zealand. FAX 03-642-003. Ed. Shane Kelly. adv.; bk.rev.; charts; illus.; index; circ. 14,000. (back issues avail.)
  Incorporates: Boating World.
  Description: Covers general boating, cruising, yachting, amateur boat building, race reports, test reports.

797.14   UK
SEAHORSE. 1969. bi-m. £12($25) c/o The Observer, Chelsea Bridge House, Queenstown Rd., London SW8 4NN, England. Ed. Jason Holtam. adv. (back issues avail.) **Indexed:** Abstr.Engl.Stud.

796.95   US
▼**SEA'S INDUSTRY WEST**; western marine industry magazine. 1991. 5/yr. $25 (foreign $35). Duncan McIntosh Co. Inc., 17782 Cowan, Irvine, CA 92714. TEL 714-660-6150. FAX 714-660-6172. adv.; circ. 12,735.
  Description: Covers the western pleasure boat market for manufacturers, dealers, distributors and retailers.

797.124   GW
SEGELN; internationales Segler Magazin. 1979. m. DM.66.60. Jahr-Verlag GmbH & Co KG, Burchardstr. 14, Postfach 103344, 2000 Hamburg 1, Germany. TEL 040-339660. Ed. Thomas Dieck. circ. 24,000.

796   GW   ISSN 0175-1344
SEGELSPORT; Informationen und amtliche Mitteilungen des Deutschen Segler-Verbandes. 1974. m. DM.67.80. (Deutscher Segler-Verband) Westdeutsche Verlagsanstalt GmbH, Ahmser Str. 190, 4900 Herford, Germany. TEL 05221-775252. FAX 05221-775215. TELEX 17-5221855. Ed.Bd. adv.; bk.rev.; illus.; circ. 100,000.

797.1   SW   ISSN 0037-0916
SEGLARBLADET. 1911. m. SEK 125 (effective 1991). Goeteborgs Kungliga Segelsaellskap, P.O. Box 5039, S-421 05 Vaestra Froelunda, Sweden. Ed. Malin Schroeder. adv.; bk.rev.; charts; illus.; circ. 5,000.

797.124   GW
SEGLER ZEITUNG; Informationen fuer Sport Skipper. 1981. m. Segler Zeitung Verlag GmbH, Birkenallee 36, 2408 Timmendorfer Strand, Germany. TEL 04503-5071. FAX 04503-3701. Ed. Horst Schlichting.

797.124   NO
SEILSPORT. 1968. 6/yr. $55. (Norges Seilforbund) Seilsport Maritimt Forlag AS, Box 24 Voksenskogen, N-0708 Oslo 7, Norway. Ed. Tore Thjomoe. adv.; circ. 23,139.

SELF-CATERING AND FURNISHED HOLIDAYS. see TRAVEL AND TOURISM

623.82   UK   ISSN 0143-1153
SELL'S MARINE MARKET. 1979. a. £20. Benn Business Information Services Ltd., P.O. Box 20, Sovereign Way, Tonbridge, Kent TN9 1RQ, England. TEL 0732-362666. FAX 0732-770483. TELEX 95162-BENTON-G.
  Description: Annual directory of marine products and services.

623.82   US   ISSN 0734-0680
VM320
SHAVINGS. 1979. bi-m. $25 to individuals; students $10. Center For Wooden Boats, 1010 Valley St., Seattle, WA 98109. TEL 206-382-2628. adv.; bk.rev.; circ. 3,000. (back issues avail.)

796.95   US   ISSN 0749-9361
SHOWBOAT CENTENNIALS NEWSLETTER. 1979. irreg., no.28, 1991. free. Showboat Centennials, 76 Glen Dr., Worthington, OH 43085. TEL 614-431-9422. Ed. Donald T. McDaniel. circ. 150 (controlled). (looseleaf format; back issues avail.)
  Description: Monographs on the history of floating theaters and related river history.

796.95   US
SHOWBOATS INTERNATIONAL. bi-m. Hachette Magazines, Inc., 1633 Broadway, 45th Fl., New York, NY 10009. TEL 212-767-6000.

797.14   US   ISSN 0895-6332
SITE SAN DIEGO. 1987. irreg. (approx. 24/yr.) $160 (foreign $200). Box 3830, San Diego, CA 92103. TEL 619-679-1130. Ed. Vern Griffin. bk.rev.; circ. 100. (looseleaf format; back issues avail.)

797.1   NO   ISSN 0037-6000
SJOESPORT. 1961. 10/yr. NOK 155. Sjoesport A-S, P.O. Box 576, 5001 Bergen, Norway. adv.; bk.rev.; circ. 21,000 (controlled).

797.1   UK
SOLENT YEARBOOK; solent cruising & racing association year book. 1910. a. £4.50. (Solent Cruising & Racing Association) Isle of Wight County Press Ltd., Brannon House, 123 Pyle St., Newport, Isle of Wight PO30 1ST. FAX 0983-527204. Ed. R.L. Bradbeer. adv.; charts; circ. 5,000.
  Description: Provides information to all yachting and boating users of the Solent Cruising & Racing Association; includes classes, programme of events, navigational information.

796.95   US
SOUNDINGS (ESSEX); the nation's boating newspaper. 1963. m. $18.97. Soundings Publications, Inc., Pratt St., Essex, CT 06426-1122. TEL 203-767-3200. FAX 203-767-1048. Ed. Marleah Ross. adv.; bk.rev.; illus.; circ. 90,000. (tabloid format) **Indexed:** Amer.Hum.Ind., CERDIC.

796.95   US   ISSN 0194-8369
SOUNDINGS TRADE ONLY. 1981. m. $22. Soundings Publications, Inc., Pratt St., Essex, CT 06426-1122. TEL 203-767-3200. FAX 203-767-1048. Ed. David Eastman. circ. 35,000. (tabloid format)
  Formerly: Trade Only.
  Description: The boating business newspaper.

797.1   SA
SOUTH AFRICAN YACHTING. 1957. m. R.56($20) Yachting News (Pty) Ltd., P.O. Box 3473, Cape Town 8000, South Africa. TEL 021-4617472. FAX 021-4613758. Ed. Neil Rusch. adv.; bk.rev.; illus.; circ. 7,500.
  Former titles: South African Yachting, Sail, Power and Waterski (ISSN 0256-7431); South African Yachting, Powerboats, Sailing, Waterski (ISSN 0038-2817); South African Yachting, Power and Sail.
  Description: News, features and technical articles on dinghy and keelboat sailing.

796.95   US
SOUTHERN BOATING. 1972. m. $15. Southern Boating and Yachting, Inc., c/o Skip Allen, 1766 Bay Rd., Miami Beach, FL 33139-1414. TEL 305-538-0700. FAX 305-532-8657. adv.; bk.rev.; illus.; circ. 26,000.
  Description: Provides general boating information for the Southern U.S. and Caribbean.

797.124   US
SPEARHEAD (MAYFIELD). 1970. bi-m. membership. Javelin Class Association, 874 Beecher's Rd., Mayfield Village, OH 44143. TEL 216-461-8511. Ed. G.T. Reiber. illus.; circ. 250. (tabloid format)
  Description: Covers education and information about Javelin sailboats: accepted and approved modifications, social activities as well as racing.

797.124   NE
SPIEGEL DER ZEILVAART. vol.1, no.2, 1977. 10/yr. fl.60 (foreign fl.75) (effective 1992). Stichting Spiegel der Zeilvaart, Van Oosten de Bruijnstr. 13, 2014 VL Haarlem, Netherlands. TEL 023-317399. FAX 023-317399. (Subscr. to: Abo, Postbus 653, 2003 RR Haarlem, Netherlands) Ed. Wim de Bruijn. adv.; bk.rev.; illus.; circ. 10,000.

796.95   US
SPLASH (ANAHEIM). 1987. m. $39. McMullen and Yee Publishing, 2145 W. La Palma Ave., Anaheim, CA 92801. TEL 714-635-9040. FAX 714-533-9979. adv.; circ. 78,121.

797.124   IT
SPORT VELA. m. Organo Ufficiale della Federazione Italiana Vela, Viale Brigata Bisagno 2-17, Genoa, Italy. TEL 010-565723. Ed. Stefano Modonesi.

4530 SPORTS AND GAMES — BOATS AND BOATING

796.95 US
STANDARDS AND RECOMMENDED PRACTICES FOR SMALL CRAFT. 1965. base vol. plus a. supplement. $100 for base vol.; supplements $50 (effective Jan. 1990). American Boat & Yacht Council, Inc., Box 747, Millersville, MD 21108. TEL 301-923-3932. FAX 301-923-3988. Ed. Lysle B. Gray. circ. 3,000. (looseleaf format)

797.1 GW ISSN 0038-9706
STANDER; Boot und Motor und Wassersport. 1959. m. DM.73.80. (Deutscher Motoryachtverband e.V.) Westdeutsche Verlagsanstalt GmbH, Ahmser Str. 190, Postfach 3054, 4900 Herford, Germany. TEL 05221-775-0. FAX 05221-775215. TELEX 17-5221-855. Ed. Claus Breitenfeld. adv.; bk.rev.; charts; illus.; index; circ. 22,400.
Description: Information about navigation techniques and accessories.

797.1 US ISSN 0038-9927
STARLIGHTS. 1921. m. $8. International Star Class Yacht Racing Association, 1545 Waukegan Rd., Glenview, IL 60025. TEL 312-729-0630. FAX 312-729-0718. Ed. Richard L. Munson. adv.; bk.rev.; charts; stat.; tr.lit.; circ. 3,970.

STATION LOG. see *MUSEUMS AND ART GALLERIES*

796.95 US
STEAMBOATING. 1985. bi-m. $18. (International Steamboat Society) Bill Warren Mueller, Ed. & Pub., Rt. 1, Box 262, Middlebourne, WI 26149. TEL 304-386-4434. FAX 304-386-4868. adv.; bk.rev.; charts; illus.; circ. 1,500. (back issues avail.) **Indexed:** Ind.How To Do It (1990-).
Formerly: Steamboat News.
Description: For owners and operators of boats powered by steam engines and boilers.

797.1 IT
SUB. m. L.60000 (foreign L.90000). Adventures s.r.l., Via A. Anfossi 20, Milan, Italy.

797.14 AT
SYDNEY TO HOBART YACHT RACE PROGRAMME. a. National Publications Pty. Ltd., P.O. Box 297, Homebush West, N.S.W. 2140, Australia. TEL 02-764-1111. FAX 02-763-1699. circ. 7,500.
Description: Contains the full details of previous Sydney to Hobart races including the list of entries.

796.95 CN
TANZER TALK; newsletter of the Tanzer 22 class. 1971. bi-m. $25. Tanzer 22 Class Association, P.O. Box 22, Ste. Anne de Bellevue, Que. H9X 3L4, Canada. TEL 514-457-3929. Ed. John G. Charters. circ. 500. (back issues avail.)
Formerly: Tanzer 22 Newsletter.
Description: All news and information related to yachts and yachting.

THAMES BOOK. see *TRAVEL AND TOURISM*

797.1 US ISSN 0300-6557
GV776.A2
TRAILER BOATS. 1971. m. $19.97. Poole Publications, Inc., 20700 Belshaw Ave., Carson, CA 90746. TEL 310-537-6322. FAX 310-537-8735. Ed. Wiley Poole. adv.; bk.rev.; index; circ. 87,000. **Indexed:** Consum.Ind., Mag.Ind.
Description: Covers recreational boating topics, including boat and trailer tests, marine electronics, waterskiing, product evaluations, and boating destinations.

791.95 AT
TRAILERS TOWING & 4WD. 1980. a. A.B. Organisation Pty. Ltd., P.O. Box 319, Avalon Beach, N.S.W. 2107, Australia. TEL 02-918-8322. FAX 02-918-8884. (Dist. by: Gordon & Gotch, 25-37 Huntingdale Rd., Burwood, Vic. 3125, Australia) circ. 20,000.
Description: For trailerboat owners. Deals with the problems of launching and retrieving, trailer maintenance, state rules and regulations and evaluates four wheel drives in relation to the trailer owner.

797.124 GW
TRANS-OCEAN. 1968. q. DM.36. Verein zur Foerderung des Hochseesegelns e.V., Strichweg 48A, Postfach 728, 2190 Cuxhaven 1, Germany. TEL 04721-51800. FAX 04721-51874. Ed. Helmut Bellmer. adv.; bk.rev.; circ. 2,200. (back issues avail.)

623.82 GW
TRAUMBOOT REAL. 1987. bi-m. DM.15. Heinz Hueffel Verlag, Mittelstr. 2, 5468 St. Katharinen, Germany. TEL 02645-3959. FAX 02645-4827. circ. 5,000.

797.1 US
U S SAILING DIRECTORY. a. membership. United States Sailing Association, Box 209, Newport, RI 02840. TEL 401-849-5200. FAX 401-849-5208. TELEX 704592 USYRU NORT UD. Ed. Allison Peter. adv.; circ. 25,000.
Former titles: U S Y R U Directory; U S Y R U Yearbook.
Description: Provides reference material and results of each year's championships; contains reference list of race management contacts.

797.124 GW
UNSERE ALTE LIEBE. 1926. q. DM.120. Segler Vereinigung Cuxhaven, Postfach 672, 2190 Cuxhaven 1, Germany. TEL 04721-51800. Ed. Helmut Bellmer. circ. 1,000.

796.95 US
USED BOAT PRICE GUIDE. Spine title: B U C Used Boat Price Guide. 1961. s-a. $160 per 3-vol. set. B U C International Corp., 1314 N.E. 17th Ct., Fort Lauderdale, FL 33305. TEL 305-565-6715. Ed. Walter J. Sullivan III. stat.
Former titles: Older Boat Price Guide (ISSN 0197-212X); Used Boat Directory.

796.95 US
VAPOR TRAIL'S BOATING NEWS & INTERNATIONAL YACHTING & CRUISER AND MANUFACTURERS REPORT. 1966. m. $24. Gemini Productions, Ltd., 8962 Bainford Drive, Huntington Beach, CA 92646. TEL 714-833-8003. Ed. Patricia Collins. circ. 25,000.
Formed by the merger of: Vapor Trail's Yachting and Cruiser News; Vapor Trail's Boating News and Manufacturing Report; Which was formerly titled: Vapor Trail's Competition News and Manufacturing Report (ISSN 0042-2630)

796.95 BE
VAREN. 1969. m. 1000 Fr. Aco, Lierszestwg. 237, 2547 Lint, Belgium. TEL 03-489-20-72. circ. 18,500.
Description: Covers all aspects of yachting, sailing and motorboating.

797.124 CN
LA VELA. (Text in Italian) m. Can.$10. 6675 B Wilderton Ave., Montreal, Que. H3S 1L8, Canada. TEL 514-739-4213. Ed. Tony Vellone. circ. 11,965. (back issues avail.)

797.1 IT ISSN 0042-3181
VELA E MOTORE. 1923. m. L.65500($85) (foreign L.111000). Edisport S.p.A., Via Boccaccio 47, 20123 Milan, Italy. Ed. Piero Bacchetti. adv.; bk.rev.; charts; illus.; index; circ. 55,200.
Description: News about sailboats and powerboats, instruments, regattas, marinas and ports.

797.1 FI ISSN 0042-3343
VENE. (Text in Finnish) 1966. 10/yr. Fmk.314. Yhtyneet Kuvalehdet Oy, Maistraatinportti 1, 00240 Helsinki, Finland. TEL 0-15661. FAX 0-1566505. TELEX 121364. Ed. Matti Murto. adv.; illus.; index; circ. 35,000.

797.1 FI
VENEMAAILMA. 9/yr. Erikoislehdet Oy, Tecnopress, P.O. Box 16, 00381 Helsinki, Finland. TEL 358-0-120-5911. FAX 358-0-120-5959. Ed. Markku Vento. circ. 20,000.

797.124 FR ISSN 0751-5405
VOILES ET VOILIERS. m. 409 F. Societe d'Edition de Revues Nationales Specialisees, 21 rue du Faubourg St. Antoine, 75550 Paris Cedex 11, France. TEL 1-40-02-62-62. Ed. Pierre Lavialle. adv.; illus.

796.95 GW
WASSERSKI MAGAZIN. 1975. bi-m. DM.33. Westdeutsche Verlagsanstalt GmbH, Ahmser Str. 190, 4900 Herford, Germany. TEL 05221-775-252. FAX 05221-775-215. TELEX 17-5221-885. Ed. Claus D. Breitenfeld. circ. 10,000. (back issues avail.)
Description: News about waterskiing.

797.1 US ISSN 0899-9775
WATER SCOOTER. 1987. 6/yr. $21. Ehlert Publishing Group, Inc., 319 Barry Ave. S., Ste. 101, Wayzata, MN 55391-1603. TEL 612-476-2200. Ed. Michael Dapper. adv.; circ. 100,000.

797.1 US
▼**WATER SCOOTER BUSINESS.** 1990. q. $10. Ehlert Publishing Group, Inc., 319 Barry Ave. S., Ste. 101, Wayzata, MN 55391-1603. TEL 612-962-0598. Ed. Michael Dapper. circ. 5,000 (controlled).
Description: Discusses serving the personal water vehicle industry and includes industry and product news.

WATER SKIER. see *SPORTS AND GAMES — Outdoor Life*

WATER SKIER & POWERCRAFT. see *SPORTS AND GAMES — Outdoor Life*

797 US
WATERCRAFT DEALER. q. 1700 E. Dyer Rd., No. 250, Santa Ana, CA 92705-5716. TEL 714-252-5300. FAX 714-261-9700. Ed. Paul Smith. adv.

796.95 917.504 US ISSN 8756-0038
WATERFRONT NEWS; South Florida's nautical newspaper. 1984. m. $10. Ziegler Publishing Co., Inc., 1523 South Andrews Ave., Ft. Lauderdale, FL 33316. TEL 305-524-9450. FAX 305-524-9464. Ed. John Ziegler. adv.; bk.rev.; circ. 42,000. (tabloid format; back issues avail.)
Description: Covers South Florida's sailing, power boating, diving, fishing and waterfront community news.

797.1 NE ISSN 0043-1451
WATERKAMPIOEN. 1927. fortn. fl.108 to non-members. Koninklijke Nederlandse Toeristenbond ANWB - Royal Dutch Touring Club, Wassenaarseweg 220, Postbus 93200, 2509 BA The Hague, Netherlands. Ed. Robert Olieroock. adv.; bk.rev.; charts; illus.; index; circ. 62,000. **Indexed:** Key to Econ.Sci., Rural Recreat.Tour.Abstr., World Agri.Econ. & Rural Sociol.Abstr.

796.9 US
WATERWAY GUIDE - GREAT LAKES. 1982. a. $32.95. Communication Channels, Inc., 6255 Barfield Rd., Atlanta, GA 30328-4369. TEL 404-256-9800. FAX 404-256-3116. TELEX 4611075 COMCHANI. Ed. Judith Powers. adv.; charts.
Description: Navigation and travel guide for recreational boaters who cruise the U.S. and Canadian waters of the Erie, Ontario, Huron and Michigan lakes, the Hudson river, and Erie canal.

387.2 US
WATERWAY GUIDE - MID-ATLANTIC. a. $30.95. Communication Channels, Inc., 6255 Barfield Rd., Atlanta, GA 30328-4369. TEL 404-256-9800. FAX 404-256-3116. TELEX 4611075 COMCHANI. Ed. Judith Powers. adv.; charts.
Description: Navigation and travel guide for recreational boaters who cruise the Chesapeake Bay, Delmarve Coast, and the inter-coastal waterway from Norfolk to the Georgia - Florida boarder.

387.2 US
WATERWAY GUIDE - NORTHERN. a. $30.95. Communication Channels, Inc., 6255 Barfield Rd., Atlanta, GA 30328-4369. TEL 404-256-9800. FAX 404-256-3116. TELEX 4611075 COMCHANI. Ed. Judith Powers. adv.; charts.
Description: Navigation and travel guide for recreational boaters who cruise the waters of the Delaware Bay, New Jersey coast, Long Island Sound, and the coasts of Connecticut, Massachusetts and Maine.

387.2 US
WATERWAY GUIDE - SOUTHERN. a. $32.95. Communication Channels, Inc., 6255 Barfield Rd., Atlanta, GA 30328-4369. TEL 404-256-9800. FAX 404-256-3116. TELEX 4611075 COMCHANI. Ed. Judith Powers. adv.; charts.
Description: Navigation and travel guide for recreational boaters who cruise the east and west coast of Florida, Bahamas, Gulf Coast to Mexico and the Tenn-Tom Waterway.

796.95 UK
WATERWAYS. 1946. 3/yr. membership. Inland Waterways Association, 26 Chaseview Rd., Alrewas, Burton-on-Trent, Staffordshire DE13 7EL, England. Ed. Harry Arnold. adv.; bk.rev.; circ. 14,500.

796.95 US ISSN 0273-4699
WEST COAST SAILORS. m. Sailors' Union of the Pacific, 450 Harrison St., San Francisco, CA 94105. TEL 415-362-8363.

796.95 CN
WESTCOAST MARINER. 1986. m. $27 (foreign $33). Westcoast Publishing Ltd., 1496 W. 72nd Ave., Vancouver, B.C. V6P 3C8, Canada. TEL 604-266-7433. FAX 604-263-8620. Ed. Rob Morris. adv.; circ. 11,000.
  Description: For skippers and crews who work the Pacific Coast.

797.1 CN ISSN 0826-5003
WINDSPORT. 1982. 7/yr. Can.$16.50($19.50) 2255 B Queen St. E., Ste. 3266, Toronto, Ont. M4E 1G3, Canada. TEL 416-827-5462. FAX 416-827-0728. Ed. Steve Jarrett. adv.; bk.rev.; charts; illus.; stat.; circ. 15,500. (back issues avail.) **Indexed:** Sportsearch (1984-).

797.1 UK
WINDSURF. 1980. 10/yr. £42. c/o Coach House, Medcroft Rd., Tackley, Oxford OX5 3AH, England. FAX 086-983-733. adv.; illus.; circ. 25,000.
  Former titles: Windsurf and Boardsailing & Come Board Sailing.

797.1 IT
WINDSURF ITALIA. m. L.60000. Gruppo B. Editore, Via N. Bixio 40, 20129 Milan, Italy. TEL 02-29400. Ed. Angelo Berto.

976.95 US
▼**WINDSURFING CALIFORNIA.** 1990. 7/yr. $9.97. Gorge Publishing, Inc., 500 Morton Rd., Box 918, Hood River, OR 97031. TEL 503-386-7440. FAX 503-386-7480. circ. 25,000.

623.82 US ISSN 0095-067X
VM320
WOODENBOAT; the magazine for wooden boat owners, builders and designers. 1974. bi-m. $22.95. WoodenBoat Publications, Inc., Box 78, Brooklin, ME 04616. TEL 207-359-4651. FAX 207-359-8920. Ed. Jonathan A. Wilson. adv.; bk.rev.; illus.; index; circ. 105,000. **Indexed:** Ind.How To Do It (1981-).

WORKBOAT. see TRANSPORTATION — Ships And Shipping

797.1 GW ISSN 0043-9932
YACHT; Deutschlands fuehrende Yacht-Zeitschrift. 1904. fortn. DM.126.50 (foreign DM.149.50). Verlag Delius, Klasing und Co., Siekerwall 21, Postfach 4809, 4800 Bielefeld, Germany. TEL 0521-559-280. FAX 0521-559113. TELEX 932934-DEKLA. Ed. Harald Schwarzlose. adv.; illus.; circ. 140,000.

797.1 IT
YACHT DIGEST; la rivista dell'armatore da diporto. 1987. 6/yr. L.40000. Casa Editrice Scode S.p.A., Corso Monforte 36, 20122 Milan, Italy. TEL 02-76006973. FAX 02-76404905. TELEX 324685 SCODE I. Ed. Riccardo Villarosa. adv.; bk.rev.; illus.

797.1 US ISSN 0043-9940
GV771
YACHTING; power and sail. 1907. m. $19.98. Times Mirror Magazines, Inc., 2 Park Ave., New York, NY 10016. TEL 212-779-5000. Ed. Olive Moore. adv.; bk.rev.; charts; illus.; tr.lit.; circ. 147,489. (also avail. in microform from UMI) **Indexed:** Access, Bk.Rev.Ind. (1965-), Child.Bk.Rev.Ind. (1965-), Consum.Ind., Mag.Ind., PMR, R.G., Sports Per.Ind.

797.1 IT
YACHTING ITALIANO; mensile di nautica e cultura marinaresca. 1948. m. (11/yr.). L.22000. Nautilus s.r.l., Via Tadino 29, 20124 Milan, Italy. Ed. Sandro Pellegrini. adv.; charts; illus.; circ. 50,000.
  Formerly: Yachting Italiano-Atomare (ISSN 0043-9975)

796.95 UK
YACHTING LIFE. 1977. m. £12. K.A.V. Publicity (Glasgow) Ltd., 113 West Regent St., Glasgow G2 2RU, Scotland. Ed. Alistair M. Vallance. adv.; bk.rev.; circ. 8,000.

797.1 UK ISSN 0043-9983
YACHTING MONTHLY. 1906. m. $32. I P C Magazines Ltd., Specialist, & Leisure Group (Subsidiary of: Reed International PLC), King's Reach Tower, Stamford St., London SE1 9LS, England. TEL 01-261 5000. Ed. Andrew Bray. adv.; bk.rev.; charts; illus.; tr.lit.; index; circ. 49,141.

797.1 SZ
YACHTING NEWS. (Text in French and German) 1945. m. 82 SFr. Phyllomedusa AG, Seftigenstr. 310, CH-3084 Wabern, Switzerland. TEL 031-9608333. FAX 031-9612282. Ed. Urs Bretscher. adv.; bk.rev.; illus.; mkt.; stat.; tr.lit.; tr.mk.; circ. 25,000. **Indexed:** Access, Consum.Ind., Sportsearch.
  Formerly: Yachting (ISSN 0043-9959)

796.95 797.124 BE
YACHTING SUD - SUR L'EAU. (Text in French) 1923. m. (10/yr.). 700 Fr. (Europe 1000 Fr.; elsewhere 1100 Fr.). (Ligue Regionale du Yachting Belge) Editions Bertels, Rue Caroly 37, B-1040 Brussels, Belgium. TEL 02-5131104. FAX 02-513-11-04. Ed.Bd. adv.; bk.rev.; circ. 8,000.
  Formerly: Sur l'Eau.
  Description: Covers regional, national and international yachting developments.

797.1 UK ISSN 0043-9991
YACHTING WORLD. 1894. m. $44. I P C Magazines Ltd., Kings Reach Tower, Stamford St., London SE1 9LS, England. TEL 071-261-5849. FAX 071-261-7851. (Subscr. to: Reed Business Publishing Ltd., 205 E. 42nd St., New York, NY 10017, U.S.A.) Ed. Dick Johnson. adv.; bk.rev.; illus.; circ. 41,028. (also avail. in microform from UMI) **Indexed:** Sportsearch.

797.1 US ISSN 0094-8136
GV825
YACHTING YEAR BOOK OF NORTHERN CALIFORNIA. 1922. a. $7.95. Pacific Inter-Club Yacht Association of Northern California, Publication Office, 391 Miller Ave., Ste. 102, Mill Valley, CA 94941. TEL 415-388-8327. Ed. Burnett Tregoning. adv.; illus.; circ. 10,000.

796.95 AU
YACHTREVUE. 1976. m. S.350. O R A C Zeitschriftenverlag GmbH, Schoenbrunnerstr. 59-61, A-1050 Vienna, Austria. TEL 0222-551621. Ed. Luis Gazzari. adv.; bk.rev.; circ. 51,500. (back issues avail.)

797.1 UK ISSN 0044-0000
YACHTS AND YACHTING. 1947. fortn. £44 (foreign £49). Yachting Press Ltd., 196 Eastern Esplanade, Southend-on-Sea, Essex SS1 3AB, England. Ed. Frazer Clark. adv.; bk.rev.; charts; illus.; circ. 21,500. **Indexed:** Sportsearch (1973-).

769.95 910.202 US
YACHTSMAN'S GUIDE TO THE BAHAMAS. 1950. a. $24.95. Tropic Isle Publishers, Inc., Box 610938, N. Miami, FL 33261-0938. TEL 305-893-4277. FAX 305-893-4278. Ed. Meredith Helleberg Fields. adv.; circ. 15,000.
  Description: Cruising guide with sketch charts, charter planning, resort, restaurant, diving and marina information. Covers the history of the islands.

797.14 US ISSN 0084-3261
YACHTSMAN'S GUIDE TO THE CARIBBEAN. 1964. irreg., latest issue 1975. $6.75. Seaport Publishing Co., c/o Ed. Clifford M. Montague, 843 Delray Ave., Grand Rapids, MI 49506. TEL 616-949-0048. index.

797.14 US ISSN 0084-327X
YACHTSMAN'S GUIDE TO THE GREAT LAKES. 1956. a. $15. Seaway Publishing Co., 18-22 S. Elm St., Zeeland, MI 49464. TEL 616-772-2132. Ed. Paul Evan Koevering. adv.; index; circ. 5,000.
  Description: Guide to Great Lakes harbors.

796.95 US ISSN 0735-9020
GV817.V5
YACHTSMAN'S GUIDE TO THE VIRGIN ISLANDS & PUERTO RICO. 1968. a. $14.95. Tropic Isle Publishers, Inc., Box 610938, N. Miami, FL 33261-0938. TEL 305-893-4277. FAX 305-893-4278. Ed. Meredith Fields.
  Supersedes (in 1987): Yachtsman's Guide to the Greater Antilles (ISSN 0162-7635)
  Description: Cruising guide with sketch charts, charter planning, resorts, diving, restaurants, and marina information; also covers the history of the islands.

796.95 SP ISSN 0210-0320
YATE Y MOTONAUTICA; revista espanola de la mar. 1965. m. 4580 ptas.($46) Haymarket, S.A., Aribau, 168-170, 08036 Barcelona, Spain. TEL (93) 238 17 42. Dir. Luis Bosch. adv.; bk.rev.; bibl.; charts; illus.; circ. 20,000. (back issues avail.)

797.1 PL
ZAGLE; magazyn sportow wodnych. m. 9000 Zl. per no. Warszawskie Towarzystwo Wioslarskie, Ul. Mariusza Zaruskiego 12, 00468 Warsaw, Poland. Ed. Jerzy Piesniewski.

797.1 US
48 DEGREES NORTH. 1981. m. $15. Boundless Enterprises, Inc., 6327 Seaview Ave., N.W., Seattle, WA 98107. TEL 206-789-7359. FAX 206-789-6392. adv.; circ. 27,500.
  Description: Reports boating activities and racing for the Northwest.

796 UK
505 GREAT BRITAIN.* 1972. s-a. £6. International 505 Class, British Association, 3 the Embankment, Wraysbury, Staines, Middlesex, England. (Subscr. to: 3 The Embankment, Wraysbury, Staines, Middlesex TW19 5SL, England) Ed. Terry Lawton. adv.; bk.rev.; circ. 1,250. (back issues avail.)

SPORTS AND GAMES — Horses And Horsemanship

636.1 US
A H C NEWS. 1969. bi-m. membership only. American Horse Council, Inc., 1700 K St., N.W., Ste. 300, Washington, DC 20006. TEL 202-296-4031. FAX 202-296-1970. Ed. Mark Bernhard. circ. 3,200.

636.1 MX
ALAZAN. 1984. bi-m. Mex.$36000($40) Editorial Oso, S.A. de C.V., Zaragoza No. 11, San Juan Tepepan, Mexico 23, DF, Mexico. Ed. Jorge Ruben Ocampo. adv.; circ. 5,000.

798 CN ISSN 0227-0579
ALBERTA WILD ROSE QUARTER HORSE JOURNAL. 1966. m. Can.$13. Quarter Horse Association of Alberta, P.O. Box 9, Hwy. 800, Hill Spring, Alta. T0K 1E0, Canada. TEL 403-626-3613. FAX 403-626-3600. Ed. Jacki French. adv.; bk.rev.; circ. 9,500. (tabloid format)
  Formerly: Wild Rose Quarter Horse Country (ISSN 0228-0760)
  Description: Readership comprised mostly of horse show people.

798.2 UK
AMATEUR RIDER. 1989. m. £27($43) E.P.G. Publications Ltd., Finlay House, 6 Southfields Rd., Kinteon Road Industrial Estate, Southam, Warwickshire CV33 0JH, England. Ed. Francesca Bullock.
  Formerly (until 1990): Competition Rider.
  Description: Directed to those interested in amateur race riding.

636.1 US ISSN 0274-6565
AMERICAN FARRIERS JOURNAL. 7/yr. $37. Lessiter Publications, Box 624, Brookfield, WI 53008. TEL 414-782-4480. FAX 414-782-1252. circ. 7,000.
—BLDSC shelfmark: 0814.780000.
  Description: Articles on horse anatomy and physiology, leg pathology and therapy, shoeing, blacksmithing and horse handling.

SPORTS AND GAMES — HORSES AND HORSEMANSHIP

636.1   US
AMERICAN HORSE PROTECTION ASSOCIATION NEWSLETTER. 1966. s-a. $15. American Horse Protection Association, Inc., 1000 29th St., N.W., Ste. T100, Washington, DC 20007. TEL 202-965-0500. Ed. Robin C. Lohnes. circ. 15,000.

636.1   US
AMERICAN INDIAN HORSE NEWS. 1979. q. $15. Rte. 3, Box 64, Lockhart, TX 78644. TEL 512-398-6642. Ed. N. Falley. adv.; bk.rev.; circ. 500.

798.4   US   ISSN 0003-1445
AMERICAN TURF MONTHLY. 1946. m. $16. Star Publishing Corporation, 438 W. 37th St., New York, NY 10018. TEL 212-279-4619. Ed. Howard Rowe. adv.; bk.rev.; illus.; circ. 30,000.

798.2   US
AMERICA'S EQUESTRIAN. 1978. 7/yr. $18. Garri Publications Associates, Inc., 114 W. Hills Rd., Box 249, Huntington Station, NY 11746. TEL 516-423-0620. FAX 516-423-0567. adv.; bk.rev.; video rev.; circ. 16,500.
    Former titles: Garri's Horse World U S A; Eastern Horse World (ISSN 0745-9416)
    Description: Provides news on nutrition, veterinary findings, stable management, equine TV programs, as well as spotlights on experts in the field of horses. Includes calendar of horse events and features on major events.

636.1   US
APPALOOSA JOURNAL. 1946. m. $20 to non-members; members $15. Appaloosa Horse Club, Box 8403, Moscow, ID 83843. TEL 208-882-5578. FAX 208-882-8150. Ed. Debbie Pitner Moors. adv.; illus.; circ. 16,000. (also avail. in microform from UMI)
    Formerly: Appaloosa News (ISSN 0003-665X)

791.8   US   ISSN 0273-6519
APPALOOSA WORLD. 1980. m. Drawer 291310, Dayton Beach, FL 32029. TEL 904-767-6284. Ed. Gerald A. Matacale. index. (back issues avail.)

798.2   UK   ISSN 0402-7493
ARAB HORSE SOCIETY NEWS. 1935. 2/yr. Arab Horse Society, Windsor House, Ramsbury, N. Marlborough, Wilts SN8 2PE, England. TEL 0672-20782. FAX 0672-20880. Ed. Mrs. E. Bennett. adv.; illus.; circ. 3,400. (tabloid format)

798   UK
ARAB HORSE STUD BOOK. 1919. a. price varies. Arab Horse Society, Windsor House, Ramsbury, N. Marlborough, Wilts SN8 2PE, England. TEL 0672-20782. FAX 0672-20880. circ. 1,000. (tabloid format)

636.1   US
ARABIAN HORSE COUNTRY. 1981. m. $20. BeAnCa Publications, Box 4607, Portland, OR 97208. bk.rev.; circ. 39,504. (back issues avail.; reprint service avail.)

636.121   US   ISSN 0194-6803
ARABIAN HORSE EXPRESS. m. 8th and Maple Sts., Box 845, Coffeyville, KS 67337. TEL 316-251-7340. Eds. Anna Lechliter, Elton Weeks. bk.rev.; circ. 7,500.

798.4   US
ARABIAN HORSE TIMES. 1970. m. $25. Adams Corp., R.R. 3, Waseca, MN 56093. TEL 507-835-3204. FAX 507-835-5138. Ed. Joyce Denn. adv.; bk.rev.; circ. 20,000.

636.1   US   ISSN 0003-7494
ARABIAN HORSE WORLD; the magazine for owners, breeders and admirers of fine horses. (Annual Directories) 1960. m. $36 (foreign $70). Jay Shuler Co., Inc., 824 San Antonio Ave., Palo Alto, CA 94303. TEL 415-856-0500. FAX 415-856-2831. Ed. Jan Shuler. adv.; bk.rev.; illus.; index; circ. 12,000.

798.2   AT
ARABIAN STUDS AND STALLIONS MAGAZINE; Australia's leading Arabian magazine. 1974. a. Aus.$15. (Horse World Publications) H.C. Vink Publishers, P.O. Box 402, Cleveland, Qld. 4163, Australia. Ed. Pat Slater. adv.; bk.rev.; circ. 12,000. (back issues avail.)

798.2   GW   ISSN 0721-5169
ARABISCHE PFERDE. (Summaries in English) 1981. 4/yr. DM.42. Jahr-Verlag GmbH & Co., Burchardstr. 14, 2000 Hamburg 1, Germany. TEL 040-339660. FAX 040-33966208. TELEX 2163485. Ed. H.L. Britze. adv.; bk.rev.; circ. 6,800. (back issues avail.)

798   US   ISSN 0164-8047
ARENA NEWS;* a Texas journal of horse events. 1977. m. $15. Box 16229, Austin, TX 78761-6229. TEL 512-328-3266. Ed. Ruth Dawson. adv.; circ. 2,000.

798.2   US
ARIZONA HORSE CONNECTION. 1987. m. $12. Arizona Horse Connection, Inc., 301 W. Marlboro Dr., Chandler, AZ 85224. TEL 602-988-2111. Ed. Patti E. Trueba. adv.; circ. 10,000. (back issues avail.)
    Description: For all horse enthusiasts; features articles on ranches, trainers, horses of notable interest, and all types of riding disciplines.

798.2   CN
ATLANTIC HORSE & PONY. bi-m. Can.$11.75 (foreign Can.$16). P.O. Box 1509, Liverpool, N.S. BOT 1K0, Canada. TEL 902-683-2763. Ed.Bd. adv.; circ. 4,000.
    Description: For horse and pony owners, trainers and enthusiasts in the Atlantic region.

798.4   CN
ATLANTIC POST CALLS. 1979. 40/yr. Can.$40. Cumberland Publishing Ltd., 14 Lawrence St., Amherst, N.S. B4H 3G5, Canada. TEL 902-667-3469. FAX 902-667-0377. Ed. Doug Harkness. adv. contact: Dorothy Brown. circ. 2,400.

798.2   AT
AUSTRALIAN ARABIAN HORSE NEWS. 1974. q. Aus.$25. Horse World Publications, Australian Arabian Horse Society, P.O. Box 402, Cleveland, Qld. 4163, Australia. Ed. Pat Slater. adv.; bk.rev.; circ. 10,000 525 Ed. Ms. Pat Slater. (back issues avail.)

798.4   AT   ISSN 0084-7402
AUSTRALIAN HORSE RACING ANNUAL.* 1969. a. $7. Playfair Publishing Group, Box 52, Northbridge, N.S.W. 2063, Australia.

798.2   AT
AUSTRALIAN STOCK HORSE JOURNAL. 1975. bi-m. Aus.$18($20) P.O. Box 288, Scone, NSW 2337, Australia. TEL 065-451122. circ. 6,539.

636.1   AT   ISSN 0005-0350
AUSTRALIAN THOROUGHBREDS; Australia's only national magazine devoted to the breeding of thoroughbred horses. 1950. bi-m. Aus.$56. Australian Thoroughbreds Magazine, Box 561, Liverpool, N.S.W. 2170, Australia. Ed. Mike Davis. adv.; bk.rev.; stat.; circ. 12,000. (tabloid format)

798.4   AT   ISSN 0005-0407
AUSTRALIAN TROTTING REGISTER. 1960. m. Aus.$42 (foreign Aus.$100). (Australian Harness Racing Council) Cabon Publishing Co. Pty Ltd., 107 The Boulevard, Ivanhoe, Vic. 3079, Australia. Ed. Bruce Skeggs. adv.; bk.rev.; circ. 9,500. (back issues avail.)
    Description: Emphasis is on harness racing.

636.1   US   ISSN 0005-366X
BACKSTRETCH. 1962. bi-m. $14. United Thoroughbred Trainers of America Inc., 19899 W. Nine Mile Rd., Southfield, MI 48075. TEL 313-354-3232. FAX 313-354-3157. Ed. Harriet Randall. adv.; bk.rev.; illus.; circ. 12,000.

798.2   GW   ISSN 0174-0512
BAYERNS PFERDE ZUCHT UND SPORT; Reiten - Pferdepraxis - Fahren. 1980. m. DM.93.40. B L V Verlagsgesellschaft mbH, Lothstrasse 29, 8000 Munich, Germany. TEL 089-127050. Ed. Juergen Kemmler. circ. 16,000.

798.4   NZ
BEST BETS. w. News Media Ltd., Glenside Crescent, P.O. Box 1327, Auckland, New Zealand. Ed. Bob Lovett. circ. 45,000.

636.1   US   ISSN 1050-5741
BIT AND BRIDLE. 1964. m. $15 (foreign $22). Box 156, Wynot, NE 68792. TEL 402-357-3504. FAX 402-357-2497. Ed. Lori Knutson. adv.; bk.rev.; charts; circ. 4,000.
    Formerly (until Mar. 1989): Midwest Bridle and Bit (ISSN 0006-3851); Incorporates: Separator.

636.1 798.4   US   ISSN 0006-4998
SF277
THE BLOOD-HORSE. 1916. w. $75.50. (Thoroughbred Owners and Breeders Association) The Blood-Horse, Inc., 1736 Alexandria Dr., Box 4038, Lexington, KY 40544-4038. TEL 606-278-2361. FAX 606-276-4450. Ed. Edward L. Bowen. adv.; bk.rev.; charts; illus.; stat.; index; circ. 20,519. (also avail. in microform from UMI) Indexed: Sports Per.Ind.
    Description: Covers thoroughbred horse breeding and racing.

798.4 636.1   UK   ISSN 0067-9224
BLOODSTOCK BREEDERS' REVIEW. 1912. a. £65. Sagittarius Bloodstock Associates Ltd., 44 Conway Rd., London N15 3BA, England. TEL 081-800-0858. FAX 081-809-2830. Ed. Susan Cameron. bk.rev.; circ. 1,400.
    Description: Contains a review of thoroughbred racing in approximately 38 countries with editorial, photographic, and statistical coverage.

636.1   UK
BLOODSTOCK SALES REVIEW AND STUD REGISTER. 1966. a. £25. Hobson Publishing Plc., Bateman St., Cambridge CB2 1LZ, England. TEL 0223-354551. FAX 0223-323154. adv.

798   US
BRAYER; voice of the donkey & mule world. 1968. q. $15. American Donkey and Mule Society, Inc., 2901 N. Elm St., Denton, TX 76201-7631. Ed. Betsy Hutchins. adv.; bk.rev.; tr.lit.; circ. 5,000. (back issues avail.)

636   CN   ISSN 1184-2164
▼**BRITISH COLUMBIA AGRI DIGEST: HORSE ISSUE.** 1991. a. Can.$15. DoMac Publications Ltd., 207 W. Hastings St., Ste. 810, Vancouver, B.C. V6B 1J8, Canada. TEL 604-684-8255. FAX 604-684-1928. Ed. Barb Schmidt. adv.: B&W page Can.$895. circ. 3,800 (controlled).

798   UK   ISSN 0144-7203
BRITISH EQUESTRIAN DIRECTORY. (Supplement avail.) 1979. a. £13.95($36) Equestrian Management Consultants Ltd., Wothersome Grange, Bramham, Wetherby, Yorks LS23 6LY, England. TEL 0532-892267. FAX 0532-893352. Ed. Antony Wakeham. adv.; circ. 5,000.
    Description: Lists 17,000 breeders, retailers, riding schools, vets, farriers, trainers and holidays in Great Britain.

798   UK
BRITISH HORSE SOCIETY YEAR BOOK & EVENT GUIDE. 1983. a. £2.50 to non-members. British Horse Society, British Equestrian Centre, Stoneleigh, Kenilworth, Warks CV8 2LR, England. TEL 0203-696697. FAX 0203-692351. TELEX BEFKEN 311152. adv.; circ. 50,000.

798.4   US
CAL-WESTERN APPALOOSA. 1966. m. (9/yr.). $12 (effective Jan. 1990). 3097 Willow, Ste. 15, Clovis, CA 93612. TEL 209-291-0103. circ. 600.
    Description: Promotes Appaloosa horses; covers racing, showing, and breeding.

798.46   US
CALIFORNIA HORSE REVIEW.* 1963. m. $30. Related Industries Corp., c/o Jaqueline Hester, Ed., 2280 Grass Valley Hwy. No.236, Auburn, CA 95603-2536. adv.; circ. 7,322.

636.1   CN   ISSN 0008-2864
CANADIAN ARABIAN NEWS. 1960. 10/yr. Can.$20($25) Canadian Arabian Horse Registry, c/o Sandy Fischer, Editor, P.O. Box 600, Bowden, Alberta TOM OK0, Canada. TEL 403-224-3411. Ed. Sandra L. Fischer. adv.; bk.rev.; charts; circ. 3,000. **Indexed:** Sportsearch.

636.1   CN   ISSN 0382-5795
CANADIAN HACKNEY STUD BOOK. 1905. irreg. Canadian Hackney Society, c/o Canadian Livestock Records Corporation, Ottawa, Ont. K1V 0M7, Canada. TEL 613-731-7110. adv.; illus.

SPORTS AND GAMES — HORSES AND HORSEMANSHIP

636.1   CN   ISSN 0840-6200
CANADIAN HORSEMAN. (Includes annual supplement: Directory of Canadian Horse Industry and Buyers Guide) 1982. bi-m. Can.$18.95. Horse Publications Group, 225 Industrial Pkwy. S., P.O. Box 670, Aurora, Ont. L4G 4J9, Canada. TEL 416-727-0107. FAX 416-841-1530. Ed. Pamela Fraser. adv.; bk.rev.; circ. 10,000. **Indexed:** Sportsearch (1989-).
   Formerly (until 1988): Horse Sense (ISSN 0821-5073)

791.8   CN   ISSN 0317-7785
CANADIAN RODEO NEWS. 1964. m. Can.$17. (Canadian Professional Rodeo Association) Canadian Rodeo News Ltd., 223, 2116 27th Ave. N.E., Calgary, Alta. T2E 7A6, Canada. TEL 403-250-7292. FAX 403-250-6926. Ed. P. Kirby Watt. adv.; bk.rev.; circ. 4,000. **Indexed:** Sportsearch.
   Description: Promotion of professional rodeo in Canada.

791.8   CN   ISSN 0008-5073
CANADIAN SPORTSMAN. 1870. w. (June-Oct.); bi-m. (Nov.-May). Can.$43($55) Canadian Sportsman, 25 Old Plank Rd., P.O. Box 129, Straffordville, Ont. N0J 1Y0, Canada. TEL 519-866-5558. FAX 519-866-5596. Ed. Gary Foerster. circ. 6,500. (back issues avail.)

798.4   CN   ISSN 0830-0593
CODEN: IRCCEP
CANADIAN THOROUGHBRED; journal of racing and breeding. (Includes annual supplement: Directory of the Canadian Horse Industry (ISSN 0831-5183)) 1961. m. Can.$39.95($55) Horse Publications Group, 225 Industrial Pkwy. S., P.O. Box 670, Aurora, Ont. L4G 4J9, Canada. TEL 416-727-0107. FAX 416-841-1530. Ed. Jennifer Morrison. adv.; bk.rev.; charts; pat.; stat.; tr.lit.; index; circ. 4,000. (back issues avail.) **Indexed:** Sportsearch.
   Former titles: Thoroughbred Review; Canadian Horse (ISSN 0008-378X)
   Description: Covers Canadian racing and breeding statistics, major races and profiles.

798   UK   ISSN 0958-1820
CARRIAGE DRIVING. 1986. bi-m. £15($36) E.P.G. Publications Ltd., Finlay House, 6 Southfields Rd., Kineton Road Industrial Estate, Southam, Warwickshire CV33 0JH, England. FAX 0926-817214. Ed. John Bullock. adv.; bk.rev.; charts; illus. (back issues avail.)
   Description: Covers all types of carriage driving and related subjects.

798.2   US
CASCADE HORSEMAN. m. $12. Klamath Publishing, Box 788, Klamath Falls, OR 97601. TEL 503-883-4000. circ. 8,000.
   Description: West Coast horse industry publication.

CAVALLO MAGAZINE; mensile di natura, politica e cultura. see *ANIMAL WELFARE*

798   AG   ISSN 0008-8986
CENTAUROS; revista de polo, turf, equitacion, pato y troto. 1955. irreg., vol.40, 1978. Arg.$15. San Martin 66, Buenos Aires, Argentina. Eds. Jorge Oliva & Manuel Caramelo Gomex. **Indexed:** SSCI.

798   CN
CHARGER. 1986. m. Can.$16.95. Leprechaun Press Ltd., Alcomdale, Alta. T0G 0A0, Canada. TEL 403-892-3262. Ed. Margaret Hamilton. adv.; circ. 8,604.

798.4   UK
CHASEFORM NOTE-BOOK. w. £70. Raceform Ltd., 2 York Rd., London SW11 3PZ, England. Ed. Dan Corbett. circ. 4,000.
   Description: Covers jump racing in UK.

796.42   UK
CHASERS AND HURDLERS. 1975. a. £52. Portway Press Ltd., Timeform House, Northgate, Halifax, West Yorkshire HX1 1XE, England.
   Description: Essays and notes on the performances of horses.

798.2   FR   ISSN 0245-3614
CHEVAL MAGAZINE. 1971. m. 380 F. Optipress, B.P. 60, 78490 Montfort l'Amaury, France. TEL 34-86-29-00. FAX 34-86-78-79. adv.

798.2   FR
CHEVAL STAR. 1987. m. 140 F. Optipress, B.P. 60, 78490 Montfort l'Amaury, France. TEL 34-86-29-09. FAX 34-86-78-79. adv.
   Former titles: Cheveaux de Penny & Cheval Infos.
   Description: Illustrated stories on horses and ponies for kids and adolescents.

798.4   US   ISSN 0009-5990
SF321
CHRONICLE OF THE HORSE; the horse in sport--steeplechasing, horse shows, foxhunting, etc. 1937. w. $42. Chronicle of the Horses, Inc., Box 46, Middleburg, VA 22117. TEL 703-687-6341. FAX 703-687-3937. Ed. John Strassburger. adv.; bk.rev.; illus.; index s-a; circ. 24,000. (also avail. in microform from UMI) **Indexed:** Sports Per.Ind.
   Description: Sporting magazine covering the major English equestrian disciplines on a regional, national and international basis; also includes feature and training articles.

636.1   UK
CLYDESDALE STUD BOOK. 1877. a. £5. Clydesdale Society of Great Britain and Ireland, 24 Beresford Terrace, Ayr, Ayrshire, Scotland. FAX 0292-611295. Ed. Robert S. Gilmour. circ. 300.

CONTRACTSPELER. see *SPORTS AND GAMES*

798.2   CN   ISSN 0829-2930
CORINTHIAN HORSE SPORT. (Includes annual supplement: Directory of the Canadian Horse Industry (ISSN 0831-5183)) 1968. m. Can.$27.95($42.95) Horse Publications Group, 225 Industrial Pkwy. S., P.O. Box 670, Aurora, Ont. L4G 4J9, Canada. TEL 416-727-0107. FAX 416-841-1530. Ed. Susan Jane Anstey. adv.; bk.rev.; charts; pat.; stat.; tr.lit.; circ. 10,000. (back issues avail.) **Indexed:** Sportsearch.
   Former titles: Corinthian Horse Sport in Canada; Corinthian: Horse Sport; Corinthian (ISSN 0319-7581)
   Description: Features show results, training techniques, profiles, international news.

798.2   UK
▼**COUNTRY AND DISTANCE RIDER.** 1990. bi-m. £12.95. Champions International, May Garland Farm, Chiddingly Road, Horam, E. Sussex TN21 0JJ, England. TEL 04353-2703. FAX 0959-62015. Eds. A.G and D.J. Ferrige. adv.; bk.rev.
   Description: Covers long distance and endurance riding, pleasure riding.

798   CN
COURRIER HIPPIQUE. 1983. 6/yr. Can.$15. Sportam Inc., 4545 Pierre-de-Coubertin, Box 1000, Sta. M, Montreal, Que. H1V 3R2, Canada. TEL 514-252-3053. FAX 514-252-3165. adv.

636.1   FR   ISSN 0300-5607
COURSES ET ELEVAGE. 1954. 10/yr. 660 F. Union Nationale Interprofessionnelle du Cheval (UNIC), 22, rue de Penthievre, 75008 Paris, France. TEL 45-62-00-52. FAX 42-25-96-75. TELEX 650 913F EQUUS. adv.; bk.rev.; illus.; circ. 9,300.

798   US   ISSN 0887-2406
CURLY CUES. 1975. s-a. membership. American Bashkir Curly Registry, Box 453, Ely, NV 89301. TEL 702-289-4999. Ed. Sunny Martin. circ. 1,500.
   Description: Promotes the rare curly-coated horse, near to extinction in the U.S.

798   US   ISSN 0090-8711
CUTTIN' HOSS CHATTER. 1948. m. membership. National Cutting Horse Association, 4704 Hwy. 377, S., Ft. Worth, TX 76116-8805. TEL 817-244-6188. FAX 817-244-2015. Ed. Karl R. Little. adv.; bk.rev.; charts; illus.; tr.lit.; circ. 12,000. (back issues avail.)

798.2   GW
DEUTSCHE REITERLICHE VEREINIGUNG. REPORT. 1920. w. DM.150. F N - Verlag, Freiherr-von-Langenstr. 13, Postfach 110363, 4410 Warendorf 1, Germany. TEL 02581-7696. FAX 02581-633146. circ. 2,300.
   Description: Reports and articles on horses and riding.

798.2   CN   ISSN 0831-5183
DIRECTORY OF THE CANADIAN HORSE INDUSTRY. (Supplement to: Corinthian Horse Sport (ISSN 0829-2930); Canadian Thoroughbred (ISSN 0830-0593); Canadian Horseman (ISSN 0840-6200)) 1968. m. Can.$27.95($42.95) (effective Jan. 1991). Horse Publications Group, 225 Industrial Pkwy. S., Box 670, Aurora, Ont. L4G 4J9, Canada. TEL 416-727-0107. FAX 416-841-1530. Ed. Susan Jane Anstey. circ. 10,000. (back issues avail.)

DONKEY DIGEST. see *ANIMAL WELFARE*

DRAFT HORSE JOURNAL. see *AGRICULTURE — Poultry And Livestock*

798.2   US   ISSN 0147-796X
SF309.5
DRESSAGE & C T; dressage, eventing and the sport horse. 1971. 12/yr. $22. Sport Horse Publishing, Inc., 211 W. Main St., New London, OH 44851. TEL 419-929-3800. Ed. Ivan I. Bezugloff, Jr. adv.; bk.rev.; bibl.; charts; illus.; tr.lit.; cum.index vols. 1-5; circ. 9,800. (back issues avail.) **Indexed:** Sportsearch (1977-).
   Former titles: Dressage and Combined Training (ISSN 0147-7951); Dressage (ISSN 0046-0680)
   Description: Technical articles on the Olympic equestrian disciplines of dressage and combined training. Covers major national and international competitions, profiles and interviews.

798.2   UK   ISSN 0958-1804
DRESSAGE MAGAZINE; the key to good riding. 1987. m. £27($53) E.P.G. Publications Ltd., Finlay House, 6 Southfields Rd., Kineton Road Industrial Estate, Southam, Warwickshire CV33 0JH, England. TEL 0926-817848. FAX 0926-817214. Ed. John Bullock. adv.; bk.rev.; charts; illus. (back issues avail.)
   Formerly: Dressage Review.
   Description: Magazine devoted entirely to dressage.

798.2   US   ISSN 0276-7074
DRIVING DIGEST MAGAZINE; driving for every equine. bi-m. $13.50. Box 467, Brooklyn, CT 06234. Ed. Catherine Taylor.

798   US   ISSN 0191-7714
EASTERN-WESTERN QUARTER HORSE JOURNAL. 1967. 9/yr. $14. Eastern-Western Publishing Inc., 150 W. Grove St., Drawer 690, Middleboro, MA 02346. adv.; illus.; circ. 6,000.
   Formerly: Eastern Quarter Horse Journal.

798.2   CN
▼**ENGLISH RIDER.** 1990. bi-m. Can.$17.50 (foreign Can.$19). Golden Arc Publishing and Typesetting Ltd., 491 Book Rd. W., Ancaster, Ont. L9G 3L1, Canada. TEL 416-648-2035. FAX 416-648-6977. Ed. A.W. Finn. adv.; circ. 6,597. (tabloid format)

798   UK
EQUESTRIAN TRADE NEWS. 1978. m. £56($100) Equestrian Management Consultants Ltd., Wothersome Grange, Bramham, Wetherby, Yorks LS23 6LY, England. TEL 0532-892267. FAX 0532-893352. Ed. A.C. Wakeham. adv.; bk.rev.; circ. 3,500.
   Description: News on trade matters relating to saddlery, riding, clothing, feedstuffs and equipment, both overseas and in the U.K.

798   US   ISSN 0013-9831
EQUESTRIAN TRAILS. vol.24, 1970. m. membership. Equestrian Trails, Inc., 13741 Foothill Blvd., Ste. 220, Sylmar, CA 91342-3105. FAX 818-362-9443. Ed. Holly E. Carson. adv.; bk.rev.; charts; illus.; tr.lit.; circ. 5,000.

798   CN
EQUILIFE. (Text in English, French) s-m. P.O. Box 164, Dalkeith, Ont. K0B 1E0, Canada. TEL 613-874-2219. Ed. Diane Coombs. circ. 7,000.

EQUINE ATHLETE; the equine sportsmedicine news journal for trainers and veterinarians. see *VETERINARY SCIENCE*

SPORTS AND GAMES — HORSES AND HORSEMANSHIP

798 UK
EQUINE BEHAVIOUR. 1978. 2/yr. £6. Equine Behaviour Study Circle, Leyland Farm, Gawcott, Buckingham, Bucks, England. Ed. Moyra Williams. bk.rev.; abstr.; bibl.; charts; illus.; circ. 150. (back issues avail.)
Description: Includes observations, reports and analyses on all aspects of equine behavior from worldwide sources.

798 330 US
EQUINE BUSINESS JOURNAL. 1959. m. free to qualified personnel. Rich Publications, Box 72001, San Clemente, CA 92672-9201. TEL 714-361-1955. FAX 714-361-0333. Ed. Rene Riley. adv.; circ. 13,000. (controlled).
Former titles (until Oct. 1990): Western and English Fashions; (until Feb. 1984): Western Wear and Equipment (ISSN 0043-4280)
Description: For manufacturers, wholesalers, and retailers in the horse industry.

798.2 CN ISSN 0836-1355
EQUINE EMPLOYMENT AND EDUCATION GUIDE. 1988. a. Can.$29.95. Whitehouse Publishing, Inc., P.O. Box 1778, Vernon, B.C. V1T 8C3, Canada. TEL 604-545-9896. Ed. B.J. White. bk.rev.; circ. 1,000. (back issues avail.)
Description: For those looking for a career with horses.

EQUINE RESEARCH CENTRE NEWSLETTER. see *VETERINARY SCIENCE*

636.1 US
EQUINE TIMES. 1980. m. $8.50. Farmers' Advance News, Inc., 130 S. Main St., Box 8, Camden, MI 49232-0008. TEL 517-368-5201. FAX 517-368-5131. Ed. John Snyder. adv.; bk.rev.; circ. 3,000. (tabloid format)
Description: Serves the horse enthusiast in Michigan, Indiana and Ohio.

636.1 UK
▼**EQUINE WELFARE.** 1990. q. £8($18) E.P.G. Publications Ltd., Finlay House, 6 Southfields Rd., Kineton Road Industrial Estate, Southam, Warwickshire CV33 0JH, England. TEL 0926-817848. FAX 0926-817214. Ed. John Bullock.
Description: Covers all aspects of equine welfare activities on behalf of horses, ponies, donkeys and mules.

798 636.089 CN ISSN 0828-864X
EQUINEWS; serving the horse industry - all breeds, all disciplines. 1980. m. Can.$15 (foreign $20). John Whittle, Ed. & Pub. (Subsidiary of: Westview Publications), Site 15, C.5, R.R.6, Vernon, B.C. V1T 6Y5, Canada. TEL 604-542-2002. FAX 604-542-5576. Ed. B.J. White. adv.; bk.rev.; circ. 17,492. (tabloid format; back issues avail.)
Formerly (until 1984): Hoof Beats.

798.2 501 US ISSN 0149-0672
SF277
EQUUS. 1977. m. $24. Fleet Street Publishing Corp., 656 Quince Orchard Rd., Gaithersburg, MD 20878. TEL 301-977-3900. (Subscr. to: Neodata, Box 57919, Boulder, CO 80322-7919) Ed. Ami Shinitzky. adv.; bk.rev.; index; circ. 126,229. (also avail. in microform from UMI; reprint service avail. from UMI) **Indexed:** Farm & Garden Ind., Sports Per.Ind., Sportsearch (1978-).

636.1 798.4 UK ISSN 0260-7468
EUROPEAN RACEHORSE. 1949. 4/yr. £24($48) Turf Newspapers Ltd., 19 Clarges St., London W1Y 7PG, England. Ed. Richard Onslow. adv.; bk.rev.; illus.; index.
Incorporates: British Racehorse (ISSN 0007-1706)

636.1 DK ISSN 0108-7738
FJORDHESTEN. 1982. q. membership. Fjordhesteavlen, Landskontoret for Heste, Udkaervej 15, Skejby, 8200 Aarhus N, Denmark. illus.

636.1 US
FLORIDA THOROUGHBRED. Issued with: Thoroughbred Times. 1989. m. $18. Thoroughbred Publications Inc., 801 Corporate Dr., Ste. 101, Box 8237, Lexington, KY 40503. TEL 606-223-9800. FAX 800-231-5210. Ed. Mark Simon. circ. 6,700 (controlled).
Description: For horse owners and breeders in Florida, Alabama, Georgia, Mississippi and the Carolinas. Provides news and features on Florida racing and breeding, with an emphasis on statistics.

798.2 GW ISSN 0342-4758
FREIZEIT IM SATTEL. 1958. m. DM.55.20. Bruns & Muller OHG, Venusbergweg 10, 5300 Bonn 1, Germany. TEL 0228-217280. FAX 0228-261586. Ed. Erika Mueller. adv.; bk.rev.; circ. 22,000.

798.4 VE ISSN 0016-3775
GACETA HIPICA. 1950. w. Bs.156. Editora de Revistas, C.A., Avda. Principal los Ruices, Adpo. 2935, Caracas 101, Venezuela. Eds. Benigno Martin Pinedo, Jaime Martin Pinedo. adv.; circ. 158,600.

798 UK ISSN 0072-078X
GENERAL STUD BOOK. 1773. 4/yr. £128. Weatherbys, Sanders Rd., Wellingborough, Northants. NN8 48X, England. TEL 0933-440077. FAX 0933-440807. TELEX 311582-ODECS. adv.; stat.; circ. 1,000.

791.8 US
GIRLS' RODEO ASSOCIATION NEWS.* 1964. m. $5. Girls' Rodeo Association, c/o Ed. Lydia Moore, Rt. 5, Box 698, Blanchard, OK 73010-9805. illus.

GOLF TENNIS POLO; magazine for sports, journeys, pastime, society and fashion. see *SPORTS AND GAMES*

798.46 UK
GOODWOOD YEAR BOOK. 1986. a. Kingsclere Publications Ltd., Highfield House, 2 Highfield Ave., Newbury, Berkshire RG14 5DS, England. TEL 0635-38888. FAX 0635-528638. Ed. Hilary Armfield. circ. 5,000.
Description: Horse racing yearbook distributed to members of and visitors to Goodwood Racecourse.

636.1 SP ISSN 0085-1337
GUIA DE LOS CABALLOS VERIFICADOS EN ESPANA. 1875. a. 4500 ptas. Sociedad de Fomento de la Cria Caballar de Espana, Hipodromo de la Zarzuela, Aravaca, 28023 Madrid, Spain. TEL 207 07 51. TELEX 48 260 SFCCE. circ. 2,000.

798 FR
GUIDE DU CHEVAL ARABE EN FRANCE. 1964. a. 120 F. price varies. Guides Equestres, 5 rue Alexandre Cabanel, 75015 Paris, France. Eds. Caroline Elgosi, William de Choisey. adv.; circ. 8,000.
Formerly: Ou Monter a Cheval (ISSN 0078-7035)

636.1 UK
HACKNEY HORSE SOCIETY YEAR BOOK. a. £7 to non-members. Hackney Horse Society, Clump Cottage, Chitterne, Nr. Warminster, Wiltshire BA12 0LL, England. TEL 0985-50906.

636.1 US ISSN 0046-6700
HACKNEY JOURNAL.* 1970. bi-m. $9. Hackney Publications Inc., 56 Seventh Ave., Apt.10-A, New York, NY 10011-6672. Ed. Paul E. Bolton, Jr. adv.; bk.rev.; circ. 1,500. (tabloid format)

636.1 UK
HACKNEY STUD BOOK. quadrennial. £25. Hackney Horse Society, Clump Cottage, Chitterne, Nr. Warminster, Wiltshire BA12 0LL, England. TEL 0985-50906.

636.295 798.4 TS
AL-HADAF. (Text in Arabic) 1988. w. Mu'assasat Kaladari lil-Tiba'ah wal-Nashr, P.O. Box 11243, Dubai, United Arab Emirates. TEL 582400. FAX 582238. TELEX 46832. Ed. Abd al-Latif Kaladari. circ. 20,000.
Description: Covers all sporting activities within the U.A.E., with a focus on traditional Arab pursuits such as camel racing and horse racing.

636.1 SW ISSN 0345-486X
HAESTEN/HORSE; foer avel och sport. (Text in Swedish) 1920. m. SEK 350. Tidskriften Haesten, Pl 566 Kampavall, S-540 17 Lerdala, Sweden. Ed. Maria Cidh. adv.; B&W page SEK 4950, color page SEK 7750. circ. 10,000.

636.1 GW
DER HANNOVERANER. 1922. bi-m. membership. Verband Hannoverscher Warmblutzuechter e.V., Lindhooperstr. 92, 2810 Verden, Germany. TEL 04231-6730. FAX 04231-67312. Ed. Ludwig Christmann. adv.; bk.rev.; bibl.; charts; illus.; stat.; circ. 18,000.
Formerly: Hannoversches Pferd (ISSN 0017-7474)

798.46 AT
HARNESS RACER. 1948. m. Aus.$48. Harness Racing Board, 740 Mt. Alexander Rd., Moonee Ponds, Vic. 3039, Australia. TEL 03-375 4255. FAX 02-370-4299. Ed. Robert Pangho. adv.; circ. 5,500. (back issues avail.)
Formerly (until 1986): Gazette (Melbourne).
Description: Promotion and information guide for harness racing.

636.1 UK ISSN 0951-2640
HEAVY HORSE WORLD; the only magazine for heavy horse owners and enthusiasts in the U.K. 1987. q. £17.50($34) Christopher & Diana Zeuner, Park Cottage, West Dean, Chichester, West Sussex PO18 ORX, England. TEL 0243-63-364. Ed. Diana Zeuner. adv.; bk.rev.; circ. 2,500. (back issues avail.)
Formerly: Heavy Horse.

636.1 NE
HENGSTENBOEK. s-a. fl.50. Uitgeversmaatschappij C. Misset B.V., Hanzestr. 1, 7006 RH Doetinchem, Netherlands. TEL 08340-49911. FAX 08340-43839. TELEX 45481. (Subscr. to: Postbus 4, 7000 BA Doetinchem, Netherlands) circ. 2,000.
Description: Details about all the stallions approved for breeding in the Netherlands.

636.1 798 DK ISSN 0018-201X
HIPPOLOGISK TIDSSKRIFT. 1888. m. DKK 210. (Dansk Rideforbund) Landsbladet, V. Farimagsgade 6, 1606 Copenhagen, Denmark. TEL 33-112222. FAX 33-323046. (Co-sponsors: Sportsrideklubben i Koebenhavn, Danish Equestrian Federation) Ed. I.C. Christensen. adv.; bk.rev.; circ. 15,100.

798.4 NE ISSN 0046-7715
HOEFSLAG; geillustreerd weekblad voor paardenvrienden. 1949. w. fl.171. (Zuidgroep B.V. Uitgevers) Stichting de Hoefslag, Pb. 245, 5680 AE Best, Netherlands. FAX 31-4998-90923. Ed. M.C.M. Jurgens. adv.; bk.rev.; circ. 21,000.

798.4 US ISSN 0018-4683
HOOF BEATS. 1933. m. $10 to members; non-members $18. United States Trotting Association, 750 Michigan Ave., Columbus, OH 43215. TEL 614-224-2291. Ed. Dean A. Hoffman. adv.; illus.; circ. 27,000.
Description: Features horse racing.

798 US
HOOF PRINT. 1975. bi-m. $10. North American Trail Ride Conference, Box 20315, El Cajon, CA 92021. TEL 619-588-7245. Ed. Ruth Bourgeois. adv.; circ. 2,500.

798 US ISSN 0094-3355
HORSE AND HORSEMAN; the nation's finest horse magazine. 1971. m. $18. Gallant - Charger Publishing, Inc., 34249 Camino Capistrano, Box HH, Capistrano Beach, CA 92624. TEL 714-493-2101. Ed. Jack Lewis. adv.; bk.rev.; illus.; tr.lit.; circ. 96,000. (reprint service avail.) **Indexed:** Farm & Garden Ind.
Incorporating: International Rider and Driver (ISSN 0044-1090)
Description: Covers all facets of horsemanship with emphasis on breeds and training.

636.1 798 UK ISSN 0018-5140
HORSE AND HOUND. 1884. w. $119. I P C Magazines Ltd., Specialist, & Leisure Group (Subsidiary of: Reed International PLC), King's Reach Tower, Stamford St., London SE1 9LS, England. TEL 01-661-5000. Ed. Michael Clayton. adv.; bk.rev.; illus.; circ. 75,491.

798 UK
HORSE AND PONY (PETERBOROUGH). 1971. fortn. £30.50. E M A P Pursuit Publications Ltd., Bretton Court, Bretton, Peterborough PE3 8DZ, England. Ed. Sarah Haw. adv.; bk.rev.; circ. 50,028.

SPORTS AND GAMES — HORSES AND HORSEMANSHIP

636.1 UK
HORSE & RIDER. 1950. m. £22. D.J. Murphy (Publishers) Ltd., 296 Ewell Rd., Surbiton, Surrey KT6 7AQ, England. TEL 01-641-4911. Ed. Alison Bridge. adv.; bk.rev.; illus.; circ. 35,000. **Indexed:** Farm & Garden Ind., Jun.High.Mag.Abstr., Sportsearch.
Formerly: Light Horse (ISSN 0024-3329)

798 636.1 US ISSN 0018-5159
SF277
HORSE & RIDER. 1968. m. $18. Rich Publications (Subsidiary of: Cowles Media Company), 941 Calle Negocio, San Clemente, CA 92672-6202. TEL 714-361-1955. FAX 714-361-0333. Ed. Sue Copeland. adv.; bk.rev.; charts; illus.; tr.lit.; circ. 100,000. **Indexed:** PMR, Sportsearch (1984-).
Incorporates (1981-1991): Performance Horseman (ISSN 0744-3633)
Description: For the competitive horse owner, breeder and trainer. Covers training tips, techniques, feeding, Western fashion and lifestyle, riding equipment, medical reports, and special events.

798.2 CN ISSN 0847-9984
HORSE CHRONICLE. 1989. bi-m. Can.$10.70. Kennedy Publishing Inc., R.R. 2, Huntsville, Ont. P0H 1K0, Canada. TEL 705-789-6972. Ed. Leslie A. Kennedy. adv.; circ. 4,000.

636.1 US ISSN 0145-9791
SF277
HORSE ILLUSTRATED. 1976. m. $21.97. Fancy Publications, Inc., Box 6050, Mission Viejo, CA 92690. TEL 714-855-8822. (Subscr. to: Box 57549, Boulder, CO 80322-7549) Ed. Sharon Lemon Ralls. adv.; bk.rev.; illus.; circ. 90,000.
Description: For families caring for one or more pleasure horses and who ride both English and Western (all breeds). Covers the care, health and performance of the horse plus regular features on training, conditioning, feeding and showing.

636.1 US ISSN 0890-233X
SF278.5 CODEN: AESSE8
HORSE INDUSTRY DIRECTORY. 1972. a. $15. American Horse Council, Inc., 1700 K St, N.W., Ste. 300, Washington, DC 20006. TEL 202-296-4031. FAX 202-296-1970. Ed. Mark Bernhard.

HORSE INDUSTRY DIRECTORY OF CANADA. see
BUSINESS AND ECONOMICS — Trade And Industrial Directories

798 US
HORSE LOVER'S. 1936-1985. a. $3.95. Rich Publications (Subsidiary of: Cowles Media Company), 941 Calle Negocio, San Clemente, CA 92672-6202. TEL 714-361-1955. FAX 714-361-0333. adv.; circ. 65,000.

798 336 US
HORSE OWNERS AND BREEDERS TAX MANUAL. 1975. a. $90. American Horse Council, Inc., 1700 K St., N.W., Ste. 300, Washington, DC 20006. TEL 202-296-4031. FAX 202-296-1970. circ. 4,300. (looseleaf format; back issues avail.)

798 US
HORSE RACING QUIZ BOOK. a. £1.50. Raceform Ltd., 2 York Rd., London SW11 3PZ, England.

636.1 US
HORSE SHEETS. 1966. m. $15. Green Isle Publishing, Box 376, Orgeon, IL 61061. TEL 800-462-4827. Ed. Judith L. Knilans. adv.; bk.rev.; illus.; circ. (tabloid format)
Formerly (until Feb. 1990): Record Horseman; Incorporates: Capital Horseman; Straight from the Horse's Mouth.
Description: General interest, all-breed publication for the Rocky Mountain area horse enthusiast.

798 US
HORSE SHOW. 1937. m. $25. American Horse Shows Association, Inc., 220 E. 42nd St., 4th Fl., New York, NY 10017-5806. TEL 212-972-2472. FAX 212-983-7286. TELEX 7105813811 AMHORSE NYK. Ed. Kathleen Fallon. adv.; bk.rev.; circ. 54,000.
Description: Provides information on ruling, policies and officials and profiles top horsemen and horsewomen who compete at AHSA-recognized events.

636.1 US ISSN 0018-5191
HORSE WORLD; feature-oriented show-horse specialty publication. 1933. m. $35. Dabora, Inc., Box 1007, Shelbyville, TN 37160. TEL 615-684-8123. Ed. David L. Howard. adv.; bk.rev.; circ. 5,000. **Indexed:** Sportsearch.

798.2 US ISSN 0018-523X
HORSEMAN AND FAIR WORLD; devoted to the trotting and pacing horse. 1877. w. $40. Horseman Publishing Co. Inc., Box 11688, Lexington, KY 40577. TEL 606-254-4026. Ed. Harold Monaghan. adv.; illus.; stat.; circ. 10,000.
Description: Discusses harness horse racing and breeding.

636.1 798.4 US ISSN 0018-5256
HORSEMEN'S JOURNAL. 1949. m. $24. (Horsemen's Benevolent and Protective Association) Horsemen's Journal, Inc., 2800 Grand Rte. St. John St., New Orleans, LA 70119-3023. Ed. William Anderson. adv.; bk.rev.; bibl.; charts; illus.; stat.; index; circ. 45,000. (also avail. in microform from UMI; back issues avail.)
Description: Discusses horse breeding and racing.

798 US ISSN 0092-6353
HORSEPLAY. 1973. m. $22. H P Partnership, 11 Park Ave., Box 545, Gaithersburg, MD 20877. Ed. Cordelia Doucet. adv.; bk.rev.; circ. 48,000.

798.2 CN ISSN 0840-6715
HORSEPOWER; magazine for young horse lovers. 1988. bi-m. Can.$15.95($19.95) (effective 1991). Horse Publications Group, 225 Industrial Pkwy. S., Box 670, Aurora, Ont. L4G 4J9, Canada. TEL 416-727-0101. FAX 416-841-1530. Ed. Susan Stafford. circ. 4,500. (newspaper)
Description: Presents short stories, horse care information, caption contests.

636.1 US ISSN 0046-7936
HORSES. 1962. bi-m. $39.95 (foreign $59.95). Horses Magazine & Horses U.S.A., 21 Greenview, Carlsbad, CA 92008. TEL 619-931-9958. FAX 619-931-0450. Ed. John Quirk. adv.; bk.rev.; film rev.; stat.; circ. 10,000. **Indexed:** Sportsearch.
Description: Covers international equestrian events.

798.2 CN ISSN 0225-4913
HORSES ALL. 1977. m. Can.$13. Quarter Horse Association of Alberta, P.O. Box 9, Hwy. 800, Hill Spring, Alta T0K 1E0, Canada. TEL 403-626-3613. FAX 403-626-3600. Ed. Jacki French. adv.; bk.rev.; film rev.; illus.; circ. 9,962.
Description: Official publication of 42 national and regional associations including light horse, heavy horse, rodeo, and jumping. Includes veterinarian and health news.

798 CN
HORSES MAGAZINE; all breed news for a growing industry. 1983. bi-m. Can.$10. Ventura Publishing, Box 4381, Aldergrove, B.C. V0X 1A0, Canada. TEL 604-534-0039. (U.S. addr.: Ste., 4381, 177 Telegraph Rd., Bellingham, WA 98226) Ed. Linda Richards. circ. 5,300. (back issues avail.)
Description: Breed news and articles on the horse industry in Western Canada and the Northwest United States.

798 UK
HORSES TO FOLLOW. 1969. s-a. £5. Portway Press Ltd., Timeform House, Halifax HX1 1XE, England.
Description: Notes on fifty of the horses most likely to succeed in the coming season.

636.1 US ISSN 0018-5264
HORSETRADER. (Consists of all advertising; contains no editorial matter) 1960. m. $15. Horsetrader, Inc., Box 728, Middlefield, OH 44062. TEL 216-632-5266. FAX 216-632-5631. Ed. Jerry Goldberg. adv.; illus.; circ. 34,224.

798 UK
HOUNDS. 1984. 8/yr. £20($40) Ravensworld Ltd., Rose Cottage, Hughley, Shrewsbury, Shropshire SY5 6HX, England. TEL 074-636-637. Ed. Michael Sagar. adv.; bk.rev.; illus.; circ. 4,000.

798 US ISSN 1057-8501
HUNTER & SPORT HORSE. 1989. bi-m. $15.99. Midwest Hunter, Inc., 12204 Covington Rd., Fort Wayne, IN 46804. TEL 219-625-4030. FAX 219-625-3480. Ed. Laura Allen. adv.; circ. 25,500.
Former titles: Midwest Hunter & Sport Horse & Midwest Hunter.
Description: Covers dressage, combined training, hunter-jumper, foxhunting, pleasure, and related equestrian sports.

798.4 US
ILLINOIS RACING NEWS. 1972. m. $24. (Illinois Thoroughbred Breeders and Owners Foundation) Midwest Outdoors Ltd., 111 Shore Dr., Hinsdale, IL 60521. TEL 708-887-7722. FAX 708-887-1958. Ed. Joan Colby. adv.; bk.rev.
Description: Covers thoroughbred horse racing and breeding.

798 US
IN STRIDE. 1981. m. $12. 12675 S.W. First St., Beaverton, OR 97005. TEL 503-643-0271. FAX 503-644-2213. Ed. Barbara Zellner. adv.; bk.rev.; circ. 2,500. (back issues avail.)

798 FR
INFORMATION HIPPIQUE. 1957. m. (11/yr.). 150 F. 174 av. Charles de Gaulle, Neuilly-sur-Seine, France. Ed. Roger-Louis Thomas. adv.; illus.; circ. 16,000.

636.1 US
INSIDE INTERNATIONAL; the official publication of the Arabian breeds. 1979. bi-m. $18. International Arabian Horse Association, Box 33696, Denver, CO 80233. TEL 303-450-4774. FAX 303-450-5127. Ed. Shelley Bowling. adv.; circ. 28,000.

INTERNATIONAL GAMBLERS CLUB NEWSLETTER. see
SPORTS AND GAMES

798.2 US
INTERNATIONAL SADDLERY AND APPAREL JOURNAL. 1983. m. $36 to individuals; qualified personnel $24. Equine Excellence Management Group, Inc., Box 3039, Berea, KY 40403-3039. FAX 606-986-1770. adv.; circ. 14,000 (controlled).
Formerly (until Jan. 1992): Horse Digest (ISSN 0733-1339)

636.1 798.4 IE ISSN 0021-1184
IRISH FIELD. 1870. w. £61.28. Irish Times Ltd., 11-15 D'Olier St., Dublin 2, Ireland. Ed. Valentine Lamb. adv.; bk.rev.; illus.; circ. 10,553. (newspaper; also avail. in microfilm)
Description: Covers horse breeding, racing and show jumping.

798.2 GW
JAHRBUCH ZUCHT; Leistungen und Daten der Deutschen Pferdezucht. 1911. a. DM.60. (Deutsche Reiterliche Vereinigung e.V.) F N - Verlag, Freiherr-von-Langen-Str. 13, Postfach 110363, 4410 Warendorf 1, Germany. TEL 02581-7696. FAX 02581-633146. circ. 3,000.
Description: German stallion data, including lists of breeders.

798 CS
JAZDECTVO.* (Text in Czech, Slovak) 1953. m. 36 Kcs. (Slovak Technical University, Physical Education Organization) Sport, Vajnorska Cesta 100-a, 832-58 Bratislava, Czechoslovakia. (back issues avail.)

798.4 AG ISSN 0021-7115
JOCKEY CLUB.* (Text in English, Spanish) 1966. q. Arg.$35($12) Jockey Club of Buenos Aires, Cerrito 1353, 2 Piso, Buenos Aires, Argentina. (U.S. subscr. to: Franklin Square Subscription Agency, 545 Cedar Ln., Teaneck, NJ 07666) Ed. Eduardo Botta. adv.; illus.

798.2 CN ISSN 0380-3554
JR. RIDER. 1977. q. Can.$3($3.25) National Sport and Recreation Centre, Inc., c/o Jan Fewster, Ed., R.R. 1, Kemptville, Ont. K0G 1J0, Canada. TEL 613-746-0060. adv.; illus.

SPORTS AND GAMES — HORSES AND HORSEMANSHIP

798.2 US
JUST HORSIN' AROUND; news and advice for the Tennessee horseman. 1988. m. $25. Jordan Hills Enterprises, Jordan Hills Farm, Rt. 10 Jordan Rd., Franklin, TN 37064. TEL 615-791-5656. Ed. Margo Isom. circ. 12,000. (tabloid format; back issues avail.)

798 US
KANSAS HORSEMAN. 1980. m. $15. Kansas Horseman, Box 28, Lindsborg, KS 67456. TEL 913-227-3339. Ed. Terry Galloway. adv.; bk.rev.; circ. 2,000. (tabloid format; back issues avail.)

636.1 798 RU ISSN 0023-3285
KONEVODSTVO I KONNYI SPORT. 1842. m. $13.80. Agropromizdat, Sadovo-Spasskaya, 18, 107807 Moscow, Russia. (Subscr. to: Mezhdunarodnaya Kniga, Moscow, G-200, Russia) Ed. E.V. Kozhevunkov. bk.rev.; index. **Indexed:** Anim.Breed.Abstr., Nutr.Abstr.
—BLDSC shelfmark: 0092.100000.

798.2 US ISSN 0047-4088
LARIAT. 1949. m. $14. Lariat Company, 12675 S.W. First St., Beaverton, OR 97005. TEL 503-644-2233. FAX 503-644-2213. Ed. Barbara Zellner. adv.; bk.rev.; illus.; circ. 7,500. (tabloid format; back issues avail.)

636.1 798 US ISSN 0892-6271
LONE STAR HORSE REPORT. 1983. m. $10. Lone Star Horse Report, 5129 E. Belknap, Box 14767, Fort Worth, TX 76117. TEL 817-838-8642. Ed. Henry L. King. adv.; bk.rev.; circ. 7,000. (back issues avail.)
Description: Dedicated to the distribution of information about horses, horsemen, events and places in the North Texas-Southern Oklahoma horse market.

354 CN ISSN 0317-7262
SF335.C2
MANITOBA. HORSE RACING COMMISSION. ANNUAL REPORT. a. free. Horse Racing Commission, P.O. Box 40, Sta. A, Winnipeg, Man. R3K 1Z9, Canada. TEL 204-885-7770. FAX 204-831-0942. stat.; circ. 200.

636.1 US ISSN 0025-4274
SF277
MARYLAND HORSE. 1936. m. $42 (foreign $39). Maryland Horse Breeders Association, Box 427, Timonium, MD 21093. TEL 410-252-2100. FAX 400-560-0503. Ed. Richard W. Wilcke. adv.; bk.rev.; charts; illus.; stat.; circ. 5,000. **Indexed:** Sportsearch.
Description: Aims to promote thoroughbred racing and breeding in Maryland, as well as steeplechasing, eventing, hunting, showing, and polo. For thoroughbred breeders, trainers, owners, and enthusiasts in six states: Maryland, Delaware, Pennsylvania, New Jersey, Virginia, and West Virginia.

798 US
MICHIGAN QUARTER HORSE JOURNAL. 1955. m. $35 membership. Michigan Quarter Horse Association, 1640 Haslett Rd., No. 9, Haslett, MI 48840-8438. TEL 616-781-5766. Ed. Diane Graves. adv.; illus.; circ. 2,500. (back issues avail.)
Description: Articles on the advancement and improvement of the breeding and performance of the quarter horse.

MIN HEST. see CHILDREN AND YOUTH — For

798.2 US ISSN 0747-1424
MODERN HORSE BREEDING; the leading advisory resource for the breeding industry. 1984. m. (10/yr.). $29.95. Round Table Publishing, Inc., 656 Quince Orchard Rd., Gaithersburg, MD 20878. TEL 301-977-3900. Ed. Bobbie Lieberman. adv.; bk.rev.; circ. 6,000. **Indexed:** Farm & Garden Ind.

636.1 US ISSN 0027-1098
SF293.M8
THE MORGAN HORSE. 1941. m. $27.50 (effective Sep. 1991). American Morgan Horse Association, Box 960, Shelburne, VT 05482-0960. TEL 802-985-4944. FAX 802-985-8897. Ed. Suzy Lucine. adv.; bk.rev.; illus.; circ. 10,500.

798 US
MOUNTAIN RIDERS. 1989. m. $15. South By Southwest Ranch, 15190 Tierra Rejada, Moor Park, CA 93021. TEL 805-523-9334. Ed. Kate Poss. circ. 5,000 (controlled).
Description: For all horse owners, breeders and riders, with information on equestrian events, politics and personalities.

798.2 362.4 US
N A R H A NEWS. 1970. 6/yr. $18 membership. North American Riding for the Handicapped Association, Inc., Box 33150, Denver, CO 80233. TEL 303-452-1212. Ed. William Scebbi. adv.; bk.rev.; circ. 1,200. (tabloid format; back issues avail.) **Indexed:** Sportsearch (1983-).
Description: Provides news and technical information for people who assist the physically and mentally disabled to ride horses for therapy and recreation.

798.4 AT
NATIONAL BUCKSKIN SOCIETY. NEWSLETTER. 1973. q. membership. National Buckskin Society Inc., 35 Hall Rd., Carrum Downs, Vic. 3201, Australia. TEL 03-782-1234. Ed. J. Laszuk. circ. 170. (back issues avail.)
Description: Provides information on dressage, turnout, showing, and caring for horses.

798 US
NATIONAL CUTTING HORSE ASSOCIATION. RULE BOOK. 1946. a. membership. National Cutting Horse Association, 4704 Hwy. 377, S., Fort Worth, TX 76116-8805. TEL 817-244-6188. FAX 817-244-2015. Ed. Karl R. Little. circ. 12,000.

636.1 US ISSN 0027-9455
NATIONAL HORSEMAN.* 1865. m. $12. Box 43397, Louisville, KY 40243. Ed. Raymond E. Sheffield. adv.; illus.
Description: Focuses on show horses.

798.2 AT
NATIONAL TROTTING WEEKLY. 1975. w. Aus.$114.40. Syme Magazines (Subsidiary of: Syme Media Pty. Ltd.), G.P.O. Box 628E, Melbourne, Vic. 3000, Australia. TEL 03-601-4222. Ed. Richard Trembath. adv.; circ. 15,000. (back issues avail.)
Description: Harness racing in the eastern states of Australia.

798.2 910.202 US
SF285.35
NATIONWIDE OVERNIGHT STABLING DIRECTORY & EQUESTRIAN VACATION GUIDE. 1982. a. $24.95. Equine Travelers of America, Inc., 1026 W. Ash, Box 322, Arkansas City, KS 67005-0322. TEL 316-442-8131. Eds. James L. McDaniel, Janice J. Nelson. adv.; circ. 5,000.
Formerly (until 1990): Nationwide Overnight Stabling Directory (ISSN 0886-5647)

636.1 NZ ISSN 0028-8209
NEW ZEALAND HORSE & PONY. 1959. m. NZ.$40. (New Zealand Pony Clubs Association) News Media (Auckland) Ltd., P.O. Box 1327, Auckland, New Zealand. FAX 64-9-358-3003. Ed. Joan Gilchrist. adv.; bk.rev.; circ. 6,900.

636.1 US
NORTHEAST EQUINE JOURNAL. 1988. m. $14. Turley Publications, 312 Marlboro St., Keene, NH 03431. TEL 603-357-4271. FAX 603-357-7851. Ed. Natalee S. Roberts. adv.; bk.rev.; circ. 10,000.
Description: Feature articles on horses and horse people, including personality profiles, calendar of equestrian events, teaching and training techniques, equine healthcare and notes from around the region.

798.2 AU
OESTERREICHISCHE REITER - ZEITUNG. 8/yr. S.150. Steiger-Werbung Verlags- und Werbegesellschaft mbH, Hermanngasse 25, A-1070 Vienna, Austria. Ed. Hedwig Giesser. adv.; circ. 5,000.

636.1 798 GW ISSN 0030-2066
DAS OLDENBURGER SPORTPFERD. 1969. 4/yr. DM.30. Verband der Zuechter des Oldenburger Pferdes, Haarenfeld 52c, 2900 Oldenburg, Germany. TEL 0441-74061. FAX 0441-75412. Ed. Wolfgang Schulze-Schleppinghoff. adv.; bk.rev.; illus.; stat.; circ. 4,000.

798.4 UK
OWNERS TRAINERS & BREEDERS. 1980. bi-m. £18($40) Arrowhead Ltd., Nr. Borden, Hants., England. (Subscr. to: 50 High St., Eton, Berkshire SL4 6BL, England) Ed. David Watkinson. circ. 12,000.
Formerly (until Jan. 1983): Owners.

798 US
P O A. 1956. m. $22. Pony of the Americas Club Inc., 5240 Elmwood Ave., Indianapolis, IN 46203. TEL 317-788-0107. Ed. Becky Lohman. adv.; bk.rev.; circ. 1,300.
Formerly (until 1985): Pony of the Americas.
Description: Covers horse care, training, show results, and club events.

798.4 NE ISSN 0039-1387
PAARDESPORT IN REN EN DRAF. 1880. s-w. fl.255. Publico B.V., Nieuwe Parklaan 25, 2597 The Hague, Netherlands. TEL 70-351-4901. FAX 70-351-2786. Ed. John Brandsen. adv.; bk.rev.; charts; circ. 12,500.
Formed by the merger of: Stichting Nederlandse Draf- en Rensport. Officieel Bulletin; Draver en Volbloed.

798 US
PACIFIC COAST JOURNAL. 1963. m. $20. Pacific Coast Quarter Horse Association, Box 254822, Sacramento, CA 95865. TEL 916-924-7265. Ed. Kate Riordan. adv.; circ. 5,082.
Description: Focuses on equine breeding, taxes and laws, coverage of upcoming events and championship standings.

636.1 798 US ISSN 0164-5706
PAINT HORSE JOURNAL. 1962. m. $23 to non-members; members $18. American Paint Horse Association, Box 961023, Ft. Worth, TX 76161-0023. TEL 817-439-3412. FAX 817-439-1509. Ed. Bill Shepard. adv.; bk.rev.; circ. 13,500. (back issues avail.)

636.1 US ISSN 0031-045X
PALOMINO HORSES. 1942. m. $17.50. Palomino Horse Breeders of America, Inc., 15253 E. Skelly Dr., Tulsa, OK 74116-2620. TEL 800-647-6672. Ed. Tracy Thompson. adv.; bk.rev.; circ. 4,700.

798.4 FR
PANORAMA TIERCE.* 1960. w. Editions en Direct, Chemin Blague, 13290 Les Milles, France. Ed. Jean Maizoue. adv.; illus.

636.1 GW
PFERDE; Zucht und Sport in Schleswig-Holstein und Hamburg. 1960. m. DM.42.60. (Verband der Zuechter des Holsteiner Pferdes) Verlag Wartenberg und Soehne GmbH, Theodorstr. 41, 2000 Hamburg 50, Germany. adv.; bk.rev.; illus.; stat.; circ. 3,000.
Formerly: Holsteiner Pferd (ISSN 0018-3709)
Description: Covers all aspects of horse breeding.

798.2 GW ISSN 0176-490X
PFERDE HEUTE. 1978. m. DM.68 (foreign DM.78). Symposion Verlag, Wagnerstr. 12, 7300 Esslingen, Germany. TEL 0711-350001. FAX 0711-386766. Ed. H.A. Siegler. adv.; bk.rev.; circ. 70,000. (back issues avail.)

798.2 AU
▼**PFERDEREVUE.** 1990. m. S.420. O R A C Zeitschriftenverlag GmbH, Schoenbrunnerstr. 59-61, A-1050 Vienna, Austria. TEL 0222-551621-0. Ed. Werner Meisinger. circ. 37,000. (back issues avail.)

636.1 US ISSN 0031-9791
PIGGIN STRING.* 1960. m. $7. Lu Kibler, Ed. & Pub., 12631 Hinton Way, Santa Ana, CA 92705. adv.; bk.rev.; illus.; circ. 3,500.

636.1 US ISSN 0031-9937
PINTO HORSE. 1985. q. $20 to non-members; members $15. Pinto Horse Association of America Inc., 1900 Samuels Ave., Fort Worth, TX 76102. TEL 817-336-7842. FAX 817-336-7416. adv.; charts; illus.; stat.; circ. 2,500.
Supersedes: Pinto Horse International.

POLO. see SPORTS AND GAMES — Ball Games

636.1 798.2 UK ISSN 0032-4256
PONY; horses and horsemastership for children. 1949. m. £17. D.J. Murphy (Publishers) Ltd., 296 Ewell Rd., Surbiton, Surrey KT6 7AQ, England. Ed. Kate Austin. adv.; bk.rev.; illus.; circ. 35,000.

798.2　　　　　UK　ISSN 0958-1812
PONY CLUB MONTHLY; the magazine for all young riders. 1987. m. £23($43) E.P.G. Publications Ltd., Finlay House, 6 Southfields Rd., Kineton Road Industrial Estate, Southam, Warwickshire CV33 OJH, England. TEL 0926-817848. FAX 0926-817214. Ed. Rachel Lambert. adv.; bk.rev.; charts; illus. (back issues avail.)
   Formerly: Pony Club Magazine.
   Description: Covers all areas of riding and horsemanship for the young rider.

791.8　　　　　US
PONY JOURNAL. 1948. bi-m. $15. American Shetland Pony Club, Box 3415, Peoria, IL 61612-3415. TEL 309-691-9661. Ed. Barbara A. Stockwell. adv.; circ. 1,600. (back issues avail.)

798.2　　　　　US　ISSN 0090-8762
PRACTICAL HORSEMAN. 1973. m. $24.95. Gum Tree Store Press (Subsidiary of: Cowles Media Company), Gum Tree Corner, Unionville, PA 19375. TEL 215-857-1101. adv.; illus.; circ. 61,000.
   Indexed: Sports Per.Ind., Sportsearch (1977-).

798.4　　　　　SI
PUNTERS' WAY - SINGAPORE EDITION. (Malaysia edition avail.) (Text in Chinese, English) 1977. fortn. 42 MacTaggart Road, 06-02 MacTaggart Bldg., Singapore 1336, Singapore. TEL 2866733. FAX 02895413. Ed. T.S. Phan. adv.; circ. 60,000.
   Description: Provides information required by racegoers for reference in punting on horses, including photo-finish and computerised speed rating. Also publishes regular racing news from Australia and New Zealand.

636.1　　　　　US　ISSN 0164-6656
SF293.Q3
QUARTER HORSE JOURNAL. 1948. m. $17 (foreign $34). American Quarter Horse Association, 2701 I 40 E., Amarillo, TX 79120. FAX 806-376-8364. (Subscr. to: Box 32470, Amarillo, TX 79120) Ed. Audie Rackley. adv.; bk.rev.; illus.; circ. 63,000. (also avail. in microfiche from UMI) **Indexed:** PMR.
   Description: Covers horse show results, business opportunities, and all other news of interest related to the association.

636.1　　　　　US
QUARTER HORSE NEWS. 1978. s-m. $19.95. Quarter Horse News Inc., Morris Communications Corp., Box 9707, Ft. Worth, TX 76107. TEL 817-335-5128. FAX 817-335-2062. Ed. Glory Ann Kurtz. circ. 12,700. (tabloid format; back issues avail.)
   Description: Covers all facets and interests of the Quarter Horse industry, includes both professional and amateur aspects.

798.2　　　　　US
QUARTER HORSE TRACK. 1975. m. Quarter Horse Track Publishing, Inc., Box 9648, Ft. Worth, TX 76107. TEL 817-332-3801. Eds. Jerry McAdams, Ben Hudson. adv.; bk.rev.; circ. 8,611.

798.4　　　　　US　ISSN 0899-3130
THE QUARTER RACING JOURNAL. 1988. m. $17 (foreign $34). American Quarter Horse Association, 2701 I 40 E., Amarillo, TX 79120. TEL 806-376-4811. FAX 806-376-8364. (Subscr. to: Box 32470, Amarillo, TX 79120) Ed. Audice Rackley. adv.; bk.rev.; circ. 10,500. (back issues avail.)
   Description: Records and preserves the pedigree of the American Quarter horse. Covers the American Quarter horse racing industry.

636.1 798.4　US　ISSN 0091-7516
SF357.3
QUARTER RACING RECORD;* the magazine of quarter horse racing. 1961. m. $18. Quarter Racing Publishers, Inc., 2033 Heritage Park Dr., Oklahoma City, OK 73120-7502. Ed. H. David Smith. adv.; bk.rev.; charts; stat.; circ. 9,000.

798.4　　　　　UK
RACEFORM HANDICAP BOOK. 1944. w. £0.85 per issue. Raceform Ltd., 2 York Rd., London SW11 3PZ, England. Ed. Len Bell. adv.; bk.rev.; circ. 43,000. (tabloid format)
   Incorporates: Racehorse (ISSN 0048-6523)

798　　　　　UK　ISSN 0081-3761
RACEFORM "HORSES IN TRAINING". 1891. a. £9. Raceform Ltd., 2 York Rd., London SW11 3PZ, England. Ed. L. Bell. adv.; circ. 13,000.
   Formerly: Sporting Chronicle "Horses in Training".

798　　　　　UK　ISSN 0079-9408
RACEHORSES. 1948. a. £55. Portway Press Ltd., Timeform House, Northgate, Halifax, Yorkshire HX1 1XE, England. Ed. J.D. Newton. adv.; circ. 9,000.
   Description: Essays and notes on the performances of horses in the flat racing category.

798.2　　　　　FR
RACING. 1946. m. (Racing Club de France) Editions Arcadiennes, 5 rue Eble, 75007 Paris, France. adv.; illus.

798.46　　　　　US
RACING ACTION. 1987. w. $75. Sports Eye, Inc., 18 Industrial Park Dr., Port Washington, NY 11050. TEL 516-484-4300. Ed. Jim Joule. circ. 20,000. (tabloid format)

798.4　　　　　UK　ISSN 0033-7420
RACING SPECIALIST. 1909. w. £19. Websters Publications Ltd., Onslow House, 60-66 Saffron Hill, London EC1N 8AY, England. Ed. R. Cox. circ. 18,500.

798.4　　　　　US　ISSN 0033-7439
RACING STAR WEEKLY. 1932. w. $45. Star Publishing Corporation, 438 W. 37th st., New York, NY 10018. TEL 212-279-4619. Ed. Bob Smith. adv.; bk.rev.; stat.; circ. 12,000. (tabloid format)

798.2　　　　　US
RACING UPDATE. 1977. s-m. $200. Racing Update, Inc., Box 11052, Lexington, KY 40512. TEL 606-231-7966. Ed. William J. Oppenheim. circ. 1,500. (back issues avail.)

636.1　　　　　US
RACKING REVIEW. 1975. s-m. $20. c/o Ann O. Yeiser, Box 777, Waynesboro, TN 38485. illus.

636.1　　　　　UK
REGISTER OF NON-THOROUGHBRED MARES. 1974. a. £13.50. Weatherby's, Sanders Rd., Wellingborough, Northants. NN8 4BX, England. TEL 0933-440077. FAX 0933-440807. TELEX 311582-ODECS.

798.4　　　　　UK
REGISTERED NAMES OF HORSES. 1967. s-a. £35. Weatherbys, Sanders Rd., Wellingborough, Northants. NN8 4BX, England. TEL 0933-440077. FAX 0933-440807. TELEX 311582-ODECS. adv.; stat.

791.8 658　　　　　US
REGISTRY NEWS. 1968. q. membership only. Arabian Horse Registry of America, Inc., 12000 Zuni St., Westminster, CO 80234. TEL 303-450-4748. tr.lit.; circ. 25,000.
   Description: Updates the members of rules and policy changes related to registration and transfer records of purebred Arabian horses as well as activities of the registry.

798.4　　　　　GW
REITEN - ST. GEORG; Magazin fuer Pferdesport und Pferdezucht. 1899. m. DM.85.20. Jahr-Verlag GmbH & Co., Burchardstr. 14, D-2000 Hamburg 1, Germany. TEL 040-339660. FAX 040-33966208. TELEX 2163485. Ed. Hermann Kothe. circ. 33,000. (back issues avail.)

798.2　　　　　GW　ISSN 0720-5104
REITEN UND FAHREN. 1980. bi-m. DM.56($34) Verlag Paul Parey (Berlin), Seelbuschring 9-17, 1000 Berlin 42, Germany. TEL 030-70784-0. FAX 030-70784199. (U.S. addr.: Paul Parey Scientific Publishers, 150 E. 27th St., No.1A, New York, NY 10016) (back issues avail.)

798　　　　　GW　ISSN 0034-3692
REITER REVUE INTERNATIONAL. 1958. m. DM.90.60. Zeitschriftenverlag R B D V Rheinisch-Bergische Druckerei- und Verlagsgesellschaft mbH, Postfach 1135, D-4000 Duesseldorf 1, Germany. Ed. Gerhard Schroeder. adv.; bk.rev.; tr.lit.; index; circ. 48,000.

636.1　　　　　GW
REITER UND PFERDE IN WESTFALEN. 1976. m. DM.53.40 (foreign DM.74.40). Landwirtschaftsverlag GmbH, Huelsebrockstr. 2, 4400 Muenster-Hiltrup, Germany. TEL 02051-80-10. FAX 02501-801-204. TELEX 8-92665-LANDV-D. adv.; circ. 26,200.
   Description: Horse breeding and riding information.

798.2　　　　　GW　ISSN 0173-2404
REITERJOURNAL; Fachmagazin fuer Pferdzucht und Reitsport in Baden-Wuerttemberg. 1980. m. DM.91.20. Matthaes Verlag GmbH, Olgastr. 87, 7000 Stuttgart 1, Germany. TEL 0711-2133-0. Ed. Hugo Matthaes. index; circ. 18,000. (back issues avail.)

798.2　　　　　GW
REITSPORT IN WESER - EMS. 1975. m. DM.5. Hindenburgstr. 29, D-2900 Oldenbourg, Germany. TEL 0441-75055. Ed. Bernd Keine. circ. 6,400.

798.2　　　　　UK　ISSN 0035-516X
RIDING. 1936. m. I P C Magazines Ltd., King's Reach Tower, Stamford St., London SE1 9LS, England. Ed. Peter Churchill. adv.; bk.rev.; illus.; circ. 36,918.
   Indexed: Sportsearch.

798.2　　　　　US　ISSN 0738-8381
ROCKY MOUNTAIN QUARTER HORSE MAGAZINE. 1963. m. $15. Rocky Mountain Quarter Horse Association, 318 Livestock Exchange Bldg., Denver, CO 80216. TEL 303-296-1143. Eds. Darlene Goodwin, Ann McLarty. circ. 1,500. (back issues avail.)

796　　　　　US　ISSN 0149-6425
RODEO NEWS; the voice of the Professional International Rodeo Association. 1961. m. (11/yr.). $15. (International Professional Rodeo Association) Rodeo News, Inc., 721 North Cedar, Box 587, Pauls Valley, OK 73075. TEL 405-238-3310. Ed. Chuck Smith. adv.; bk.rev.; illus.; stat.; circ. 14,000.

798.4　　　　　UK　ISSN 0080-4819
RUFF'S GUIDE TO THE TURF AND THE SPORTING LIFE ANNUAL. 1842. a. £50. Sporting Life, Orbit House, 1 New Fetter Lane, London EC4A 1AR, England. TEL 071-822-3577. FAX 071-583-3885. Ed. Martin Pickering. adv.

636　　　　　US　ISSN 0889-2970
RURAL HERITAGE. 1976. q. $14 (effective Jan. 1991). Evener Enterprises, Box 516, Albia, IA 52531-0516. Ed. Allan Young. adv.; bk.rev.; illus.; circ. 10,000. (back issues avail.; reprint service avail.)
   Formerly: Evener (ISSN 0164-6613)

636.1　　　　　US　ISSN 0036-2271
SF277
SADDLE AND BRIDLE. 1927. m. $36. Saddle and Bridle, Inc., 375 N. Jackson Ave., St. Louis, MO 63130. TEL 314-725-9115. FAX 314-725-6440. Ed. Jeffrey Thompson. adv.; bk.rev.; illus.; circ. 6,500.
   Description: For owners and trainers of various breeds of English show horses. Provides information on training, management, veterinary care and horse show history.

798　　　　　US
SADDLE HORSE REPORT. 1976. w. $50. Dabora, Inc., Box 1007, Shelbyville, TN 37160. TEL 615-684-8123. Ed. David Howard. circ. 4,000.

798　　　　　SZ　ISSN 0036-7389
SCHWEIZER KAVALLERIST; Zeitschrift fuer Pferdesport und Pferdezucht. (Text in German) 1911. 19/yr. 88 Fr. Verlag Schweizer Kavallerist, Postfach, CH-8330 Pfaeffikon ZH, Switzerland. Ed. Georges Zehnder. adv.; bk.rev.; illus.; circ. 16,000.

636.1　　　　　SZ
SCHWEIZER PFERDE. (Text in German) bi-m. 5.50 Fr. per no. Roro-Press Verlag, Schwarnendingenstr. 80, CH-8050 Zurich, Switzerland. Ed.Bd. illus.

636.1　　　　　UK
SHETLAND PONY STUD-BOOK SOCIETY MAGAZINE. 1968. a. £5. Barbara M. McDonald, Ed. & Pub., 6 King's Pl., Perth PH2 8AD, Scotland. FAX 0738-36436. adv.; circ. 1,500.

798　　　　　UK
SHIRE HORSE SHOW CATALOGUE. 1897. a. £2. Shire Horse Society, East of England Showground, Peterborough PE2 OXE, England. TEL 0733-370038. FAX 0733-370038. TELEX 329155-EASTOF. Ed. Roy W. Bird. adv.; circ. 3,000.

636.1　　　　　UK
SHIRE HORSE STUD BOOK. a. £5. Shire Horse Society, East of England Showground, Peterborough PE2 OXE, England. TEL 0733-234451. FAX 0733-370038. TELEX 329155-EASTOF. circ. 3,000.

SPORTS AND GAMES — HORSES AND HORSEMANSHIP

798.2   US   ISSN 0744-3056
SIDE-SADDLE NEWS. 1974. 6/yr. $35. International Side-Saddle Organization, Box 282, Alton Bay, NH 03810. TEL 603-875-4000. FAX 603-875-7771. Ed. Charlotte B. Kneeland. adv.; bk.rev.; index; circ. 750. **Indexed:** Sportsearch.

636.1 798.4   SA
SOUTH AFRICAN RACEHORSE. 1953. bi-m. R.35. Horseman Publications (Pty) Ltd., P.O. Box 78220, Sandton, 2146 Transvaal, South Africa. TEL 011-444-4566. FAX 011-444-7888. Ed. Alison MacKenzie. adv.; bk.rev.; stat.; circ. 7,000.
    Former titles: South African Racehorse and Horseman; Which was formed by the 1981 merger of: South African Racehorse (ISSN 0038-2590); South African Horseman.
    Description: Offers authoritative and balanced coverage of racing and breeding.

798   SA   ISSN 0038-2655
SOUTH AFRICAN RIDER; a journal for horsemen. 1968. m. R.2.50($4.50) Blesston Printers & Publishers, Box 39387, Bramley, Johannesburg, South Africa. Ed. I. Finlay. adv.; bk.rev.; charts; illus.; circ. 2,500.

798   US   ISSN 0093-3929
SOUTHERN HORSEMAN. 1962. m. $15. Southern Publishing, 3839 Business Hwy., 45 N., Box 71, Meridian, MS 39302-0071. TEL 601-693-6607. Ed. Thelma Thompson. adv.; circ. 26,000.

798.4   US
SF321
SPEEDHORSE - RACING REPORT. 1969. m. $20. Speedhorse, Inc., Box 1000, Norman, OK 73070-1000. TEL 405-364-0831. adv.; bk.rev.; circ. 9,100.
    Incorporates (in 1990): Racing Report; Which was formerly: Speedhorse Tabloid; Incorporates (in 1990): Speedhorse (ISSN 0364-9237); Which was formerly: Quarter Racing World (ISSN 0048-6124).

798.2   IT
SPORT EQUESTRI. 1960. bi-m. L.6000($10) Atena S.p.A., Via di Val Tellina, 47-00151 Rome, Italy. Ed. Romelo Renolini. adv.; illus.; index; circ. 5,000.

798   AT
SPORTSMAN. 1900. s-w. Aus.$150. News Ltd., 2 Holt St., Surry Hills, N.S.W. 2010, Australia. TEL 02-2882433. FAX 2882300. Ed. Wayne Hickson. adv.; bk.rev.; circ. 30,000.

798.4   US   ISSN 0098-5422
SF277
SPUR; the magazine of thoroughbred and country life. 1965. bi-m. $24. Spur Publications, Inc., 13 W. Federal St., Box 85, Middleburg, VA 22117. TEL 703-687-6314. FAX 703-687-3925. Ed. Cathy Laws. adv.; bk.rev.; charts; illus.; circ. 15,000. **Indexed:** Sportsearch.
    Formerly (until 1974): Spur of Virginia (ISSN 0038-8688)
    Description: For owners, breeders, riders, trainers and enthusiasts of racing, steeplechasing, polo, fox hunting and jumping and the country lifestyle that surrounds these spots.

636.1   DK   ISSN 0107-3818
STAMBOG. a. DKK 73.20. (Dansk Varmblod, Dansk Rideheste Avlsforbund) Landsudvalget for Hesteavl, Vesterbrogade 6D, 1620 Copenhagen V, Denmark. illus.
    Formerly: Dansk Sportsheste Avlsforbunds Stambog.

636.1   DK   ISSN 0900-5846
STAMBOG OVER SHETLAND PONYER. a. DKK 65. Avlsforeningen for Shetlandsponyer, c/o John Lassen, Brunhoejvej 8, DK-8585 Glansborg, Denmark.

798   CN   ISSN 0834-0110
STANDARDBRED NEWS. 1971. fortn. Can.$35($50) Wicklow Hills Publishing Co. Inc., Box 150, Acton, Ont. L7J 2M3, Canada. TEL 519-856-9524. FAX 519-856-2347. Ed. Paul Nolan. adv.; bk.rev.; illus.; circ. 5,000. **Indexed:** Sportsearch.
    Former titles: Standardbred (ISSN 0705-2553); Standardbred Magazine.
    Description: For serious standardbred horse owners and breeders: features Canadian race results and industry news and comment.

798   AT   ISSN 0311-8215
STUD AND STABLE. 1971. irreg. Aus.$0.10. Percival Publishing Co. Pty. Ltd., 862 Elizabeth St., Waterloo, NSW 2017, Australia.
    Formerly: Australasian Stud and Stable (ISSN 0310-6403)

636.1   UK
SUFFOLK STUD BOOK. 1880. a. £10. Suffolk Horse Society, Market Hill, Woodbridge, Suffolk IP12 4LU, England. Ed. Philip Ryder-Davies. adv.; circ. 500.

798   UK
SUN GUIDE TO THE FLAT. a. £3.25. Invincible Press, 78-85 Fulham Palace Rd., London W6 8JB, England. TEL 081-437-9602. Ed. Ben Newton. circ. 40,000.
    Description: News on jockeys, tracks, races and horses for thoroughbred racing in the U.K.

798   US
T E A M CLUB NEWSLETTER. (Tellington-Jones Equine Awareness Method) 1981. 4/yr. membership. T.E.A.M News International, Box 3793, Santa Fe, NM 87501-0793. TEL 505-455-2945. Ed. Robin Hood. circ. 4,000.

798.2   US
TACK 'N TOGS BOOK; directory for retailers of apparel, equipment and supplies for horse and rider. 1971. a. $15. Miller Publishing Co., 12400 Whitewater Dr., Ste. 160, Box 2400, Minnetonka, MN 55343-2524. TEL 612-931-0211. FAX 612-931-0910. Ed. Dan DeWeese. adv.; charts; stat.; tr.lit.; circ. 22,023 (controlled). (reprint service avail. from UMI)

688.76   US   ISSN 0149-3442
TACK 'N TOGS MERCHANDISING; for retailers of apparel, equipment and supplies for horse and rider. 1970. m. $25 (free to qualified personnel). Miller Publishing Co., 12400 Whitewater Dr., Ste. 160, Box 2400, Minnetonka, MN 55343-2524. TEL 612-931-0211. FAX 612-931-0910. Ed. Dan DeWeese. adv.; charts; illus.; stat.; tr.lit.; circ. 22,023 (controlled). (also avail. in microform from UMI; reprint service avail. from UMI)

798.4   US   ISSN 0164-6168
TEXAS THOROUGHBRED. vol.4, 1979. q. $20. Texas Thoroughbred Breeders Association, Box 14967, Austin, TX 78761. TEL 512-458-6133. FAX 512-453-5919. adv.; illus.; circ. 2,800.

798.46   US
THOROUGHBRED & HARNESS RACING ACTION. w. $2 per no. Sports Eye, Inc., 18 Industrial Park Dr., Port Washington, NY 11050. TEL 516-484-3300.

636.1   AT   ISSN 0311-8347
THOROUGHBRED BREEDERS' HANDBOOK; stallion pedigrees for Australia and New Zealand. 1975. irreg. (3-4/yr.), 4th ed., 1988. Aus.$19.95. Libra Books Pty. Ltd., G.P.O. Box 10, Hobart, Tas. 7001, Australia. TEL 61-02-311754. FAX 61-02-341426. Ed. B.M. Wicks. circ. 2,000. (back issues avail.)

636.1 798   US   ISSN 0049-3821
SF293.T5
THOROUGHBRED OF CALIFORNIA. 1941. m. $42. California Thoroughbred Breeders Association, 201 Colorado Place, Arcadia, CA 91007. TEL 818-445-7800. FAX 818-574-0852. Ed. Nat Wess. adv.; bk.rev.; charts; illus.; index; circ. 7,000. (also avail. in microform from UMI; reprint service avail. from UMI)

798   US   ISSN 0082-4240
THOROUGHBRED RACING ASSOCIATIONS. DIRECTORY AND RECORD BOOK. 1955. a. $15 to non-members. Thoroughbred Racing Associations, 420 Fair Hill Dr., No.1, Elkton, MD 21921-2573. FAX 516-328-8137. Ed. Ken Kelly. circ. 3,000 (controlled).

798.4   US   ISSN 0887-2244
SF293.T5
THOROUGHBRED TIMES. 1985. w. $49.95. Thoroughbred Publications Inc., 801 Corporate Dr., Ste. 101, Box 8237, Lexington, KY 40503. TEL 606-223-9800. FAX 606-223-3966. Ed. Mark Simon. adv.; bk.rev.; circ. 25,000. (tabloid format; also avail. in microform; back issues avail.)
    Description: Covers breeding, racing and public auction news of the thoroughbred industry.

798   UK
TIMEFORM BLACK BOOK. 1940. w. price varies. Portway Press Ltd., Timeform House, Halifax HX1 1XE, England. Ed. J.D. Newton.
    Formerly: Timeform.
    Description: Contains individual dossiers of facts and opinions for every racer.

798.46   US   ISSN 1046-9974
TIMES: IN HARNESS. 1989. fortn. $65. Times: standard inc., 8125 Jonestown Rd., Harrisburg, PA 17112. TEL 717-469-2000. FAX 717-469-2005. Ed. David M. Polezal. adv.; circ. 7,000. (tabloid format)
    Description: Covers national and international harness racing; includes major harness racing events, race previews, and personality profiles.

798   UK
TODAY'S HORSE. m. £15.60 (foreign £34). Aceville Publications Ltd., 89 East Hill, Colchester, Essex CO1 2QN, England. TEL 0206-871450. FAX 0206-871537. Ed. Kate Finlayson. adv.

798.2   CN
TRAIL RIDERS OF THE CANADIAN ROCKIES NEWSLETTER. 1962. 3/yr. membership. Trail Riders of the Canadian Rockies, P.O. Box 6742, Station "D", Calgary, Alta. T2P 2E6, Canada. TEL 403-263-6963. Ed. Marlene Lea. adv.; circ. 230. (looseleaf format)

798.2   GW   ISSN 0720-9150
TRAKEHNER HEFTE. 1982. 4/yr. DM.42. Jahr-Verlag GmbH & Co., Burchardstr. 14, D-2000 Hamburg 1, Germany. TEL 040-339660. FAX 040-33966208. TELEX 2163485. Ed. H.L. Britze. circ. 7,000.

798.4   DK   ISSN 0109-2308
TRAVSPORT FOR FAGFOLK. 1983. q. DKK 78.40. Bent Kim Jepsen, Ed. & Pub., Faarupvej 102, 8381 Mundelstrup, Denmark. adv.; illus.

798.4   CN   ISSN 0704-0733
TROT. (Text in English and French) 1975. m. Can.$18 to non-members. Canadian Trotting Association, 233 Evans Ave., Toronto, Ont. M8Z 1J6, Canada. TEL 416-252-3565. Ed. Robert Megens. adv.; bk.rev.; circ. 25,000. **Indexed:** Sportsearch.
    Former titles: Maple Leaf Trot; Canadian Trot Canadien (ISSN 0045-5504)

798   IT
TROTTATORE. 1953. bi-m. L.50000. Associazione Nazionale Allevatori del Cavallo Trottatore (ANACT), Viale del Policlinico 131, I-00161 Rome, Italy. TEL 06 844-24-21. charts; illus.; stat.; circ. 2,300. (back issues avail.)

798   US   ISSN 0083-3509
TROTTING AND PACING GUIDE; official handbook of harness racing. 1947. a. $7.50. United States Trotting Association, 750 Michigan Ave, Columbus, OH 43215. TEL 614-224-2291. Ed. John Pawlak. index; circ. 7,000.

798   IT
TROTTO SPORTSMAN. 1946. 3/wk. L.250000. Editrice Trotto Italiano, Piazza Cavour 2, 20121 Milan, Italy. FAX 76002795. TELEX 323511. Ed. Ugo Berti. adv.; bk.rev.; circ. 65,000.
    Description: Offers starting lists and results of all official horse races in Italy. Includes the concerns of the horse racing world.

796   UK
THE TURF DIRECTORY. 1961. a. £39.50($88) Kilijaro Ltd., Douglas Lodge, 9 Cheveley Rd., Newmarket, Suffolk CB8 8AD, England. TEL 0638-662745. FAX 0638-662764. Ed. Virginia Fisher. adv.; circ. 3,000.
    Formerly: Directory of the Turf (ISSN 0419-3806)

798.4   AT   ISSN 0726-8254
TURF MONTHLY. 1952. m. Aus.$95. Turf Monthly Pty. Ltd., P.O. Box 210, Beecroft, N.S.W. 2119, Australia. TEL 02-634-4400. FAX 02-899-2947. Ed. Warwick Hobson. adv.; bk.rev.; circ. 34,000. (back issues avail.)
    Description: Covers all aspects of horse racing: breeding, punting, personalities and topicalities.

SPORTS AND GAMES — OUTDOOR LIFE

798.2 AU
TURF SPORT;* die Wochenzeitung fuer den Pferderennsport. 1979. s-w. S.1380. Walter Zwierschuelz, Ed. & Pub., Stroheckgane 1, A-1090 Vienna, Austria. TEL 2/88 inf. from Carol: Found only - "Turf Aktuell (Wochenzeitung fouer den Pferderennsport)". Previous add. for this rec.: Webgsse 43-23, A-1060 Vienna, Austria. circ. 2,500. (back issues avail.)
Formerly: Turf Aktuell.

798 US
U S E T NEWS.* 1956. irreg. (5-6/yr.). membership. United States Equestrian Team, c/o Bill Landsman Associates, 77 7th Ave. 10 Fl., New York, NY 10011-6626. TEL 212-370-4160. Ed. Bill Landsman. circ. 15,000.

798 US
U S T A SIRES AND DAMS; the register. 1948. a. $60. United States Trotting Association, 750 Michigan Ave, Columbus, OH 43215. TEL 614-224-2291. Ed. David Carr. index; circ. 9,000.
Formerly: Sires and Dams (ISSN 0083-3495)

798 US ISSN 0083-3517
SF325
U S T A YEAR BOOK. 1939. a. $15. United States Trotting Association, 750 Michigan Ave., Columbus, OH 43215. TEL 614-224-2291. Ed. David Carr. index; circ. 8,000.

798.2 US
UNITED STATES DRESSAGE FEDERATION BULLETIN. 1974. q. $40 includes membership; libraries $8. United States Dressage Federation, Inc., Box 80668, Lincoln, NE 68501. FAX 403-434-8545. Ed. Martha Worcester. adv.; illus.; circ. 22,000. **Indexed:** Sportsearch (1981-).
Description: Covers the art of riding and horse training. Includes competition results, articles, and news columns.

798.2 636.1 GW
UNSER PFERD. Fachzeitschrift fuer Pferdesport und Pferdezucht in Hessen. m. DM.28. Verlag G. Grandpierre, Obergasse 16, Postfach 1360, 6270 Idstein, Germany. Ed. W. Blum. circ. 4,500.

636.1 SW ISSN 0346-4687
VAAR PONNY. 1959. q. SEK 65. Svenska Ponnyavelsforbundet - Swedish Pony Breeding Society, Tjaerbyhus, S-312 00 Laholm, Sweden. TEL 430-10633. Ed. Birgitta Dyrsch. adv.; bk.rev.; illus.; circ. 4,100.
Formerly: Ponny (ISSN 0032-4213)
Description: Stud books for all pony breeds in Sweden, articles about pony breeding and shows.

630 798 US
VIRGINIA HORSE COUNCIL NEWS. 1973. m. (11/yr.). $10 includes membership. Virginia Horse Council, Box 72, Riner, VA 24149. TEL 703-382-3071. Ed. Alice Alley. adv.; circ. 550. (looseleaf format)
Formerly: Virginia Horse.
Description: Features articles on horse health; includes updates, 4-H recognitions, and industry events in Virginia.

798.4 US ISSN 0505-8813
VOICE OF THE TENNESSEE WALKING HORSE; a national publication devoted exclusively to the breed. 1962. m. (except Sep.) $18. Tennessee Walking Horse Breeders' & Exhibitors' Association, Box 286, Lewisburg, TN 37091. TEL 615-359-1567. FAX 615-359-2539. Ed. P.J. Wamble. adv.; circ. 8,500.
Description: Provides information for those who own, breed, train, or ride Tennessee Walking Horses, whether for show or pleasure. Covers industry events, personality profiles, health care, and farm management and includes training-related articles.

798 US
WALKING HORSE REPORT. 1971. w. $50. Dabora, Inc., Box 1007, Shelbyville, TN 37160. TEL 615-684-8123. Ed. David Howard. circ. 5,500.

798 US
WEEKLY TRACK TOPICS. 1963. w. Harness Tracks of America, Inc., 35 Airport Rd., Morristown, NJ 07960. TEL 201-285-9090. FAX 201-285-0867. Ed. Stanley F. Bergstein. circ. 2,000.

636.1 US
WELARA JOURNAL. 1982. s-a. $4 (foreign $5). Welara Pony Society, Box 401, Yucca Valley, CA 92286. TEL 619-364-2048. Ed. John H. Collins. circ. 1,200.

798 UK
WELSH PONY AND COB SOCIETY JOURNAL. 1962. a. membership. (Welsh Pony and Cob Society) Cambrian News Ltd., Queen St., Aberystwyth, Dyfed, Wales. adv.; circ. 6,000.

798 US
▼**WESTERN ENGLISH WORLD MAGAZINE**. 1990. m. $8. (Western and English Manufacturers Association) Bell Publications, 2403 Champa St., Denver, CO 80205. TEL 303-831-9161. FAX 303-295-2159. (Alt. ed. addr.: 789 Sherman St., Ste.160, Denver, CO 80203. TEL 303-837-1280) Ed. Kimber Green. circ. 12,000.

798 US
WESTERN HORSE. 1980. q. US $15.97. Frontier Publishing Co., Box FF, Sun City, CA 92381. Ed. Richard Gibson. adv.; circ. 70,000.

798.2 GW ISSN 0933-9345
WESTERN HORSE; Zucht - Haltung - Western Reiten. 1988. m. DM.70 (foreign DM.80). Verlag Ute Kierdorf, Gut Dohrgaul, 5272 Wipperfuerth, Germany. TEL 02267-4495. FAX 02267-4458. Ed. Hardy Oelke. adv.; bk.rev.; circ. 20,000. (back issues avail.)

636.1 US ISSN 0043-3837
SF277
WESTERN HORSEMAN; devoted mainly to Western or stock horse. 1936. m. $18 (foreign $25). Western Horseman, Inc., Box 7980, Colorado Springs, CO 80933-7980. (Subscr. to: Box 542, Mt. Morris, IL 61054-0542) Ed. Pat Close. adv.; bk.rev.; charts; illus.; index; circ. 194,000. (also avail. in microform from UMI; reprint service avail. from UMI) **Indexed:** Access, Biol.& Agr.Ind., PMR, Sports Per.Ind., Sportsearch, 800-545-9364.
Description: Covers Western riding, training, veterinary care, saddles and equipment, endurance riding, reining, rodeo, cowboy history and poetry, working ranches, Western art, packing and outfitting.

798.2 CN ISSN 0702-9071
WESTERN RIDER. 1970. m. Can.$17.50. Golden Arc Publishing and Typesetting Ltd., 491 Book Rd. W., Ancaster, Ont. L9G 3L1, Canada. TEL 416-648-2035. (Alt. addr.: Box 7065 Ancaster, Ont) Ed. A.W. Finn. adv.; bk.rev.; circ. 5,537.
Indexed: Sportsearch.
Formerly: Canadian Rider; Incorporates: Canadian Quarter Horse Journal (ISSN 0319-6348)

798.2 US
WHIP. 1974. q. $35. American Driving Society, Box 160, Metamora, MI 48455. TEL 313-678-2497. Ed. Ann L. Pringle. adv.; circ. 1,500. (back issues avail.)

798 US ISSN 0192-5210
YANKEE HORSETRADER;* voice of the eastern horseman. 1978. m. $10. Yankee Horsetrader Inc., Old West Rd., RR 1 Box 425, Arlington, VT 05250-9709. Ed. David E. Scribner. adv.; bk.rev.; illus.; circ. 8,500.

051 US
▼**YIPPY YI YEA MAGAZINE**; western style, coast to coast. 1992. q. $3.25 per no. Long Publications, Inc., 8393 E. Holly Rd., Holly, MI 48442. TEL 313-634-9675. FAX 313-634-0301. adv.: color page $795; adv. contact: Karen Brace. circ. 300,000.

636.1 UK
YOUR HORSE. 1983. m. £21. E M A P Pursuit Publications Ltd., Bretton Court, Bretton, Peterborough PE3 8DZ, England. Ed. Lesley Becks. adv.; circ. 38,216.

SPORTS AND GAMES — Outdoor Life

796.5 910 GW ISSN 0179-6089
A D A C CAMPINGFUEHRER. BAND 1: SUEDEUROPA. 1951. a. DM.24.80. (Allgemeiner Deutscher Automobil-Club e.V.) A D A C Verlag GmbH, Am Westpark 8, Postfach 700126, 8000 Munich 70, Germany. TEL 089-7676-0. Ed. H. Nitschke. adv.; circ. 185,000.
Supersedes in part: Internationaler Campingfuehrer (ISSN 0074-9753)

796.5 910 GW
A D A C CAMPINGFUEHRER. BAND 2: DEUTSCHLAND, MITTEL- UND NORDEUROPA. 1952. a. DM.24.80. (Allgemeiner Deutscher Automobil-Club e.V.) A D A C Verlag GmbH, Am Westpark 8, Postfach 700126, 8000 Munich 70, Germany. TEL 089-7676-0. adv.; circ. 150,000.

A D A C SKIATLAS. see TRAVEL AND TOURISM

796.93 US
A S F WASHINGTON LETTER. 1982. m. $200. American Ski Federation, 207 Constitution Ave., N.E., Washington, DC 20002. TEL 202-543-1595.

799.1 799.2 IC ISSN 1017-3625
A VEIDUM. 2/yr. ISK 455. Frodi Ltd., Armuli 18, 108 Reykjavik, Iceland. TEL 354-1-812300. FAX 1-812946. Ed. Eirikur S. Eiriksson. circ. 6,000.
Description: Focuses on sport fishing, hunting and shooting.

A Z U R CAMPING MAGAZIN. see TRAVEL AND TOURISM

796.52 US ISSN 0065-082X
GV199.8
ACCIDENTS IN NORTH AMERICAN MOUNTAINEERING. 1948. a. $6. American Alpine Club, 113 E. 90th St., New York, NY 10128. TEL 212-722-1628. Ed. John E. Williamson. circ. 8,000. (reprint service avail. from UMI)
Formerly: Accidents in American Mountaineering.

799 IT
ACQUASPORT. m. Organo Ufficiale della Federazione Italiana Pesca Sportiva e Attivita Subacquee, Viale Milton 7, Florence, Italy. TEL 055-473843. FAX 055-499195. Ed. Alessandro Menchi.

796.552 796.5 AT
ACTION OUTDOOR. 1983. bi-m. Aus.$22. Australian Sport Publications, 54 Schutt St., Newport, Vic. 3015, Australia. Ed. Ron Moon. adv.; bk.rev.; circ. 33,000. (back issues avail.)

796.522 US ISSN 0001-8236
F127.A2
ADIRONDAC. 1945. 10/yr. $20 to non-members. Adirondack Mountain Club, Inc., RR 3, Box 3055, Lake George, NY 12845. TEL 518-668-4447. Ed. Neal Burdick. adv.; illus.; index; circ. 11,000. **Indexed:** Acid Pre.Dig., Energy Ind., Energy Info.Abstr., Environ.Abstr.
Description: Features articles on conservation, nature, history, wilderness trips, use of equipment, places to go, club-sponsored outings and workshops.

917 US ISSN 0001-8252
F127.A2
ADIRONDACK LIFE. 1970. 7/yr. $17.95. Box 97, Jay, NY 12941. TEL 518-946-2191. FAX 518-946-7461. Ed. Tom Hughes. adv.; bk.rev.; bibl.; charts; illus.; circ. 50,000. **Indexed:** Acid Pre.Dig., Amer.Hist.& Life, Hist.Abstr.
Description: Provides news and information about the Adirondack region.

ADVENTURE EDUCATION AND OUTDOOR LEADERSHIP. see CHILDREN AND YOUTH — For

ADVENTURE ROAD. see TRAVEL AND TOURISM

AERONOVUM. see AERONAUTICS AND SPACE FLIGHT

796.552 910.09 IC ISSN 1017-3501
AFANGAR; outdoor living and Icelandic nature. 3/yr. ISK 455 per no. Farvegur, Bolholti 6, Reykjavik, Iceland. Ed. Valthor Hloedversson. circ. 6,000.
Description: Focuses on outdoor living and traveling in Iceland and abroad.

AIRFLOW. see AERONAUTICS AND SPACE FLIGHT

SPORTS AND GAMES — OUTDOOR LIFE

ALABAMA CONSERVATION. see *CONSERVATION*

799.3   US
ALABAMA GAME & FISH. m. Game & Fish Publications, Inc., 2250 Newmarket Pkwy., Ste. 110, Box 741, Marietta, GA 30061-0741. TEL 404-953-9222. Ed. Jimmy Jacobs. circ. 18,600.

354.9   US   ISSN 0362-6962
SK367
ALASKA. DIVISION OF WILDLIFE CONSERVATION. ANNUAL REPORT OF SURVEY - INVENTORY ACTIVITIES. 1970. a. Department of Fish and Game, Division of Wildlife Conservation, Box 22526, Juneau, AK 99802-2526. TEL 907-465-4190. Ed. Susan Abbott. illus.; circ. 250. Key Title: Annual Report of Survey - Inventory Activities.
  Formerly (until 1991): Alaska. Division of Game. Annual Report of Survey - Inventory Activities.

796.5 979.8   US   ISSN 0274-8282
ALASKA OUTDOORS. 1978. m. $23.95. Alaska Outdoors Development Corp., 400 D St., Ste. 200, Anchorage, AK 99501. TEL 907-278-7004. FAX 907-258-6027. Ed. Evan Swensen. adv.; bk.rev.; illus.; circ. 105,000. (back issues avail.)

799   CN   ISSN 0318-4943
ALBERTA FISHING GUIDE. 1972. a. Can.$4.95. Barry Mitchell Publications Ltd., 6C, 5571-45 St., Red Deer, Alta. T4N 1L2, Canada. TEL 403-347-5079. FAX 403-342-2280. Ed. Ann Mitchell. adv.; illus.; circ. 30,000.
  Description: Includes a comprehensive guide to 1300 sportfishing waters in Alberta, comes with current and detailed directions, species, size of fish, and facilities.

799   CN   ISSN 0833-0867
ALBERTA'S FISHING & HUNTING MAGAZINE. 1985. 10/yr. Can.$21.95 (foreign Can.$31.95). A F & H Publications, 12425 Jasper Ave., Edmonton, Alta. T5N 3K9, Canada. TEL 403-482-1777. FAX 403-488-5427. Ed. Dianne Proulx. adv.; circ. 14,000. (back issues avail.)
  Description: Teaches how-to, where-to, when-to and rules governing fishing and hunting.

796.5   US
ALLSTATE MOTOR CLUB R V PARK AND CAMPGROUND DIRECTORY.* 1960. a. $14.95. Prentice Hall Travel Directories, 15 Columbus Cir., New York, NY 10023-7706. TEL 708-945-3737. FAX 708-945-3786. adv.; circ. 290,000.
  Description: Contains information on public and private campgrounds in the US, Canada and Mexico.

796.5   SW   ISSN 0346-9190
ALLT OM HUSVAGN OCH CAMPING. 1976. 10/yr. SEK 210. Caravan Press AB, P.O. Box 1263, 171 24 Solna, Sweden. TEL 08-7305485. FAX 08-7355710. Ed. Lars-Erik Paulsson. adv.; bk.rev.; circ. 30,242 (controlled).

796.5   IT
ALMANACCO CARAVAN & CAMPER. a. Edigamma s.r.l., Piazza dei Sanniti, 9, 00185 Rome, Italy. TEL 06-4928412. FAX 06-4940719. Ed. Renato Circi.

796.5   IT
ALMANACCO ROULOTTE. 1977. a. Edigamma s.r.l., Piazza dei Sanniti 9, 00185 Rome, Italy. TEL 06-4928412. FAX 06-4940719. Ed. Renato Circi.

796.522   SZ   ISSN 0002-6336
ALPEN/ALPES. (Text in French, German) 1892. m. 58 Fr. (Club Alpin Suisse - Swiss Alpine Club) Staempfli und Cie AG, Postfach, CH-3001 Berne, Switzerland. FAX 031-276699. TELEX 911987. adv.; bk.rev.; charts; illus.; circ. 75,000.
  Description: Contains articles on mountaineering and maps.

796.522   IT   ISSN 0002-6468
ALPI VENETE. 1947. s-a. L.8000. Club Alpino Italiano Sezioni Trivenete, C.P. 514, 30170 Mestre PT (Venice), Italy. Ed. Armando Scandellari. adv.; bk.rev.; bibl.; charts; illus.

796.522 796.93   GW   ISSN 0177-3542
ALPIN-MAGAZIN. 1963. m. DM.76.80. Ringier Verlag GmbH, Gustav-Heinemann-Ring 212, 8000 Munich 83, Germany. TEL 089-638180. FAX 089-63818100.
  Formerly: Alpinismus (ISSN 0002-6484)

799.31   US   ISSN 0065-6747
AMATEUR TRAPSHOOTING ASSOCIATION. OFFICIAL TRAPSHOOTING RULES. 1923. a. membership. Amateur Trapshooting Association, 601 W. National Rd., Vandalia, OH 45377-0458. TEL 513-898-4638. FAX 513-898-5472. index; circ. 100,000.

796.52   US   ISSN 0065-6925
AMERICAN ALPINE JOURNAL. 1929. a. $20. American Alpine Club, 113 E. 90th St., New York, NY 10128. TEL 212-722-1628. Ed. H. Adams Carter. bk.rev.; index; circ. 6,000. (also avail. in microform from UMI; reprint service avail. from UMI) **Indexed:** GeoRef.
  —BLDSC shelfmark: 0809.995000.

796.552   US   ISSN 0147-9288
AMERICAN ALPINE NEWS. 1950. 4/yr. $4. American Alpine Club, 113 E. 90th St., New York, NY 10128. TEL 212-722-1628. adv.; bk.rev.; circ. 2,000. (reprint service avail. from UMI) **Indexed:** Sportsearch.
  Formerly: A A C News.
  Description: Contains articles on mountaineering and maps.

799.1   US
AMERICAN ANGLER. 1978. bi-m. $20. Northland Press, Inc., Box 280, Intervale, NH 03845. Ed. Jack Russell. adv.; bk.rev.; stat.; tr.lit.; circ. 30,000. (back issues avail.)
  Former titles: American Angler and Fly Tyer; American Fly Tyer; Fly Tyer (ISSN 0164-730X)

799.2   US   ISSN 0002-807X
AMERICAN COONER. 1970. m. $9. George O. Slankard, Ed. & Pub., 16 E. Franklin, Sesser, IL 62884. TEL 618-625-2711. adv.; illus.; circ. 22,000.

799.2   US   ISSN 0002-8452
SK1
AMERICAN FIELD; the sportsman's newspaper of America. 1874. w. $30. American Field Publishing Co., 542 S. Dearborn St., Chicago, IL 60605-1508. TEL 312-663-9797. FAX 312-663-5557. Ed. B.J. Matthys. adv.; bk.rev.; illus.; circ. 11,000. (tabloid format)

799   US
AMERICAN HANDGUNNER'S ANNUAL BOOK OF HANDGUNS. a. Publisher's Development Corp., 591 Camino de la Reina, Ste. 200, San Diego, CA 92108. TEL 619-297-8520. FAX 609-297-5353. TELEX 695-478. Ed. Cameron Hopkins. adv.; illus.; circ. 90,000.
  Description: Contains detailed specifications, photos, catalog guides, prices and editorial descriptions and information on firearms that qualify as handguns.

796.5   US   ISSN 0279-9472
AMERICAN HIKER. 1977. q. $10. American Hiking Society, Box 20160, Washington, DC 20041-2160. TEL 703-385-3252. Ed. Wayne Curtis. circ. 5,000.

796.5   US   ISSN 0164-5722
AMERICAN HIKER NEWSLETTER. 8/yr. membership. American Hiking Society, Box 20160, Washington, DC 20041-2160. TEL 703-385-3252.

799.2   US   ISSN 0092-1068
SK1
AMERICAN HUNTER. 1973. m. $25 (membership). (National Rifle Association of America) N R A Publications, 470 Spring Park Pl., Ste. 1000, Herndon, VA 22070. TEL 703-481-3383. FAX 703-481-3374. Ed. Tom Fulghan. adv.; bk.rev.; illus.; circ. 1,359,643. (back issues avail.)

796.93 640.73   US
AMERICAN SKIER. 1976. 4/yr. $1 per no. American Ski Association, 64 Inverness Dr., E., Englewood, CO 80112-5101. TEL 303-397-7676. adv.; circ. 83,000.
  Formerly (until 1990): Skiers Advocate.

388.3   US
AMERICAN SNOWMOBILER. 6/yr. Recreational Publications, Inc., 7582 Currell Blvd., St. Paul, MN 55125-2220. TEL 612-738-1953. FAX 612-738-2302. Ed. Jerry Bassett. adv.; circ. 40,000.

---

799   US
AMERICAN SURVIVAL GUIDE. 1980. m. $26.95. McMullen Publishing, 2145 W. La Palma Ave., Anaheim, CA 92801. TEL 714-635-9040. Ed. Jim Benson.
  Former titles: Shooter's Journal Survival Guide; Shooter's Journal.
  Description: For independent people interested in the protection of individual life and property, and the preservation of the U.S. Includes articles on medical and first aid tips, wilderness skills, self defense, and more.

AMUSEMENT BUSINESS; international newsweekly for live and amusement industry. see *THEATER*

790.1   US
AMUSEMENT INDUSTRY BUYERS GUIDE. 1986. a. $28. B P I Communications, Inc., Amusement Business Division, Box 24970, Nashville, TN 37202. TEL 615-321-4250. FAX 615-327-1575. Ed. Tom Powell. circ. 8,000.
  Formerly: Amusement Rides and Game Buyers Guide.
  Description: Contains comprehensive listings of manufacturers, importers and suppliers of all types of rides, games and merchandise as well as food and drink equipment and suppliers.

799   AU   ISSN 0003-2824
ANBLICK; Zeitschrift fuer Jagd, Fischerei, Jagdhundwesen und Naturschutz. 1946. m. S.426. Steirische Landesjaegerschaft, Heinrichstr. 125-4, A-8010 Graz, Austria. TEL 0316-31248. Ed. Hannes Kollar. adv.; bk.rev.; index; circ. 14,700. **Indexed:** Key Word Ind.Wildl.Res.
  Description: Focuses on fishing and hunting.

799.1   US
ANGLER.* 1974. bi-m. $9. Angler Publications, Box 12155, Oakland, CA 94604. TEL 415-658-9788.
  Description: Covers various fishing methods.

799   CN
ANGLER AND HUNTER; Ontario's wildlife magazine. 1976. 10/yr. Can.$19.95. (Ontario Federation of Anglers and Hunters, Inc.) Ontario Outdoors Publishing Ltd., P.O. Box 1541, Peterborough, Ont. K9J 7H7, Canada. TEL 705-748-3891. FAX 705-748-9577. Ed. Gary Ball. adv.; bk.rev.; circ. 72,000.
  Formerly: Angler and Hunter in Ontario (ISSN 0700-5032)

799.1   UK   ISSN 0003-3243
ANGLER'S MAIL. 1964. w. £34. I P C Magazines Ltd., Specialist, & Leisure Group (Subsidiary of: Reed International PLC), King's Reach Tower, Stamford St., London SE1 9LS, England. TEL 01-261-5000. Ed. Roy Westwood. adv.; bk.rev.; illus.; circ. 55,343.
  Description: Aimed at the avid fisherman.

799.1   UK
ANGLERS MAIL ANNUAL. 1975. a. £3.25. I P C Magazines Ltd., Fleetway Annuals, Kings Reach Tower, Stamford St., London SE1, England. Ed. J. Ingham. circ. 30,000.

799.1   US
ANGLING AMERICA MAGAZINE; the official freshwater tournament angling publication of America. 1987. bi-m. $12.95. Angling America, Inc., 635 Green Rd., Box 961, Madison, IN 47250. TEL 812-273-1612. Ed. Tonia Gordon. adv.; circ. 20,000.
  Description: Multi-species publication featuring bass, crappie, bluegill, walleye and catfish. Covers significant freshwater tournament events in America.

799.1   UK   ISSN 0956-5477
ANGLING GUIDE. 1970. irreg. £1.30. Department of Agriculture, Press Office, Upper Newtownards Rd., Belfast BT4 3SB, N. Ireland. TEL 650111. FAX 659856. adv.; circ. 12,000.

799.1   US   ISSN 1045-3539
THE ANGLING REPORT. 1988. m. $39 (Canada and Mexico $45; elsewhere $60). Oxpecker Enterprises, Inc., 12515 N. Kendall Dr., Ste. 302, Miami, FL 33186-1830. TEL 305-598-0735. FAX 305-598-0196. Ed. Don Causey. adv. contact: Robin G. Powell. circ. 3,200. (looseleaf format; back issues avail.)
  Description: Serves the angler who travels.

SPORTS AND GAMES — OUTDOOR LIFE

799.1 UK ISSN 0003-3308
ANGLING TIMES. 1953. w. £43.50. E M A P Pursuit Publications Ltd., Bretton Court, Bretton, Peterborough PE3 8DZ, England. Ed. Neil Pope. adv.; bk.rev.; illus.; tr.lit.; circ. 125,087.
  Description: News about game and sea fishing.

796.42 AT
ANNUAL ALMANAC OF RECORDS AND RESULTS. 1958. a. Aus.$4. Athletics Australia, P.O. Box 254, Moonee Ponds, Vic. 3039, Australia. TEL 03-370-7555. FAX 03-370-9739. TELEX AA151673 COBBER. adv.; circ. 4,000.
  Description: Covers records and results of the previous seasons Track and Field performances in Australia.

799 CN
ANNUEL DE CHASSE OU ANNUEL DE PECHE. 1987. a. Can.$4.95. Groupe Polygone Editeurs Inc., 11450 Albert-Hudon, Montreal, Que. H1G 3J9, Canada. TEL 514-327-4464. FAX 514-327-0514. Ed. Luc Lemay. adv.; circ. 50,000. (back issues avail.)
  Description: Articles on fishing, hunting, outdoor life and the environment.

799.1 745.1 US ISSN 0744-3749
ANTIQUE ANGLER; a quarterly newsletter-history of fishing-collectible tackle, etc. 1979. q. $7.50. Antique Angler, Inc., Box K, Stockton, NJ 08559. TEL 609-397-1577. Ed. Paul J. Webber. adv.; bk.rev.; circ. 2,000.

796.552 US
APPALACHIA BULLETIN. 1907. 10/yr. membership only. Appalachian Mountain Club, 5 Joy St., Boston, MA 02108. TEL 617-523-0636. FAX 617-523-0722. Ed. Catherine Buni. adv.; circ. 50,000.
  Supersedes: A M C Times.

796.522 US ISSN 0003-6587
G505
APPALACHIA JOURNAL. 1876. s-a. $10. Appalachian Mountain Club, 5 Joy St., Boston, MA 02108. TEL 617-523-0636. FAX 617-523-0722. Ed. Sandy Stott. adv.; bk.rev.; abstr.; bibl.; illus.; stat.; index. cum.index; circ. 11,000. *Indexed:* Biol.Abstr., Curr.Cont., GeoRef, Hist.Abstr.

796.5 US ISSN 0003-6641
F106
APPALACHIAN TRAILWAY NEWS. 1939. 5/yr. $15. Appalachian Trail Conference, Box 807, Harpers Ferry, WV 25425. TEL 304-535-6331. FAX 304-535-2667. Ed. Judith Jenner. bk.rev.; circ. 25,000. *Indexed:* GeoRef.
  Description: Features Appalachian trail news and features.

ARIZONA GAME AND FISH DEPARTMENT WILDLIFE BULLETIN. see *FISH AND FISHERIES*

796 799 US
ARIZONA GREAT OUTDOORS. 1989. q. $4. Interpersonal Enterprises, Inc., Box 6243, Scottsdale, AZ 85261. TEL 602-998-5868. Ed. Janet Jacobsen. adv.; circ. 25,000. (tabloid format; back issues avail.)
  Description: Reports on hiking, camping and other self-propelled outdoor recreation activities in the state of Arizona.

799 US
ARIZONA HUNTER AND ANGLER. 1984. m. $18. S & S Publications, Inc., 532 W. University, Mesa, AZ 85201. TEL 602-890-2547. Ed. Tom Stiles. adv.; circ. 18,810.
  Description: Features where-to-go and how-to-do-it articles on fishing and hunting in the state.

ARKANSAS GAME & FISH MAGAZINE. see *CONSERVATION*

ARKANSAS OUTDOORS. see *CONSERVATION*

799.3 US
ARKANSAS SPORTSMAN. m. Game & Fish Publications, Inc., 2250 Newmarket Pkwy., Ste. 110, Box 741, Marietta, GA 30061-0741. TEL 404-953-9222. Ed. Bob Browgat. circ. 10,500.

799 IT
ARMI E PESCA. 1955. m. L.35000 (foreign L.60000). (Italian Association of Traders and Dealers of Arms, Hunting and Fishing) Gest. Ed. di Daniele Paolucci, Via Redi, 22, 20129 Milan, Italy. TEL 02-29512541. FAX 02-294049500. adv.; bk.rev.; circ. 5,000.
  Formerly: Armieri (ISSN 0004-2412)
  Description: Focuses on firearms and other weapons.

799 IT
ARMI E TIRO; rivista di armi tiro, caccia e turismo. 1988. m. L.77000($92) (foreign L.121000). Edisport S.p.A., Via Boccaccio 47, 20123 Milan, Italy. adv.; bk.rev.; charts; illus.; index; circ. 79,500.
  Description: Covers weapon tests and archery used in hunting.

ARMY - NAVY STORE & OUTDOOR MERCHANDISER. see *CLOTHING TRADE*

796.5 296 US
ASSOCIATION OF JEWISH SPONSORED CAMPS. CAMP DIRECTORY. a. free. Association of Jewish Sponsored Camps, 130 E. 59th St., New York, NY 10022. TEL 212-751-0477.

ATHLETICS TODAY; the magazine that gets results. see *SPORTS AND GAMES*

796.93 US ISSN 0199-1574
ATLANTA SKIER.* 1967. q. $10 to nonmembers; members $5. Atlanta Ski Club, Inc., 6303 Barfield Rd., Ste. 120, Atlanta, GA 30328-4236. Ed. Joe Hatchell.

ATLANTIC SALMON JOURNAL. see *FISH AND FISHERIES*

799.1 AT ISSN 0158-572X
THE AUSTRALIAN ANGLER'S FISHING WORLD. 1969. m. Aus.$51 (foreign Aus.$128)(effective Apr. 1992). Yaffa Publishing Group, 17-21 Bellevue St., Surry Hills, N.S.W. 2010, Australia. FAX 02-281-2750. Ed. G. Schott. adv.: B&W page Aus.$1645, color page Aus.$1825; trim 273 x 210. charts; illus.; tr.lit.; circ. 17,439.
  Formerly: Australian Angler (ISSN 0045-0235)
  Description: Highlights various fishing methods.

796 AT
AUSTRALIAN LADIES GOLF UNION. OFFICIAL YEARBOOK. 1932. a. Aus.$7.50. Australian Ladies Golf Union, c/o Miss M.C. Mooney, Executive Director, P.O. Box 573, Ballarat, Vic. 3353, Australia. Ed. Maisie Mooney. adv.; circ. 16,000.

796 AT ISSN 0818-6510
AUSTRALIAN ORIENTEER. 1979. bi-m. Aus.$26. Orienteering Federation of Australia Inc., P.O. Box 263, Jamison Centre, A.C.T. 2614, Australia. TEL 06-251-3885. FAX 06-253-1574. Ed. David Hogg. adv.; circ. 2,000. (back issues avail.)
  Description: Covers the sport of orienteering in Australia.

799 AT ISSN 0004-9905
AUSTRALIAN OUTDOORS. 1948. q. Aus.$8.95. Federal Publishing Company, 180 Bourke Rd., Alexandria, N.S.W. 2015, Australia. Ed. L.A. Drake. adv.; bk.rev.; charts; illus.; circ. 22,000.
  Formerly: Outdoors Magazine (ISSN 0030-7173)
  Description: Focuses on fishing and hunting.

AUSTRALIAN PARKS & RECREATION. see *CONSERVATION*

796.93 AT ISSN 0084-7593
AUSTRALIAN SKI YEARBOOK. 1928. a. Aus.$5 per no. Yaffa Publishing Group, 17-21 Bellevue St., Surrey Hills, N.S.W. 2010, Australia. FAX 02-2812750. Ed. Teresa Curman. adv.; B&W page Aus.$1515, color page Aus.$1945; trim 273 x 210. bk.rev.; circ. 8,100.
  Description: Equipment guide and the year's round up.

799.2 AT
AUSTRALIAN SPORTING SHOOTER. 1963. m. Aus.$46 (foreign Aus.$115)(effective Apr. 1992). (Sporting Shooters Association of Australia) Yaffa Publishing Group, 17-21 Bellevue St., Surry Hills, N.S.W. 2010, Australia. TEL 02-281-2333. FAX 02-281-2750. adv.; B&W page Aus.$1646, color Aus.$2190; trim 273 x 210. bk.rev.; illus.; circ. 21,021. *Indexed:* Sportsearch (1978-), Sportsearch.
  Formerly: Australian Shooters Journal (ISSN 0810-5928)
  Description: Explores the world of guns and hunting.

AUTO CARAVAN NOTIZIE. see *TRAVEL AND TOURISM*

796.5 CN ISSN 0045-3013
B C OUTDOORS. (British Columbia) 1945. 7/yr. Can.$19.95. O P Publishing Ltd., Ste 202, 1132 Hamilton St., Vancouver, B.C. V6B 2S2, Canada. TEL 604-687-1581. FAX 604-687-1925. Ed. George Will. adv.; bk.rev.; circ. 42,000. *Indexed:* Can.Per.Ind., CMI, Key Word Ind.Wildl.Res., Sportsearch.
  Formerly: B.C. Digest.

799.1 CN ISSN 0827-2042
B.C. SPORT FISHING MAGAZINE. 1981. bi-m. Can.$14.50($15.50) P.M. Marketing Ltd., 909 Jackson Crescent, New Westminister, B.C. V3L 4S1, Canada. TEL 604-521-4901. Ed. Rikk Taylor. adv.; circ. 20,500.

796.5 US ISSN 0277-867X
GV199.6
BACKPACKER; the magazine of wilderness adventure. 1973. bi-m. $15. Rodale Press, Inc., 33 E. Minor St., Emmaus, PA 18098. TEL 215-967-5171. TELEX 847338. (Subscr. to: Box 2784, Boulder, CO 80322) Ed. John Delves. adv.; bk.rev.; circ. 175,000. (also avail. in microform from UMI) *Indexed:* Acad.Ind., Access, Consum.Ind., Mag.Ind., Phys.Ed.Ind., PMR, Sportsearch (1976-).
  ●Also available online. Vendor(s): DIALOG.
  Former titles (until 1980): Backpacker Including Wilderness Camping (ISSN 0199-3097); (until 1979): Backpacker (1973) (ISSN 0160-3329); Incorporates (1971-19??): Wilderness Camping (ISSN 0043-5430)
  Description: Includes articles on the latest equipment, destinations and how to get the most out of your trips.

769.552 US
BACKPACKING NEWSLETTER. 1976. m. $20. Frank Ashley, Ed. & Pub., Box 3818, Downey, CA 90242-0818. TEL 213-633-7821. bk.rev. (looseleaf format)

799 US ISSN 0005-3775
BADGER SPORTSMAN. 1943. m. $8. Vercauteren Publishing Inc., 19 E. Main St., Chilton, WI 53014. TEL 414-849-7036. FAX 414-849-4651. adv.; circ. 26,800. (tabloid format)

BAILY'S HUNTING DIRECTORY. see *BUSINESS AND ECONOMICS — Trade And Industrial Directories*

799.1 US
BASS AND FRESHWATER FISHING. 1979. a. $2.70. Times Mirror Magazines, Inc., 2 Park Ave., New York, NY 10016. TEL 212-779-5000. Ed. Vin T. Sparano. circ. 150,000. (reprint service avail. from UMI)
  Former titles: Southern Fishing by Outdoor Life & Outdoor Life's Guide to Fishing the South.

BASSIN'; official magazine of the weekend angler. see *FISH AND FISHERIES*

799.1 796.95 US
BASSMASTER CLASSIC REPORT. a. $2.95. (Bass Anglers Sportsman Society) B.A.S.S., Inc., Box 17900, Montgomery, AL 36141-0900. TEL 205-272-9530. FAX 205-279-7148. Ed. Dave Precht. adv.; circ. 125,000.
  Description: Press guide and program of the Bass Masters Classic.

779.1 US
BASSMASTER MAGAZINE. 1968. 10/yr. $15. (Bass Anglers Sportsman Society) B.A.S.S., Inc., Box 17900, Montgomery, AL 36141-0900. TEL 205-272-9530. FAX 205-279-7148. Ed. Dave Precht. adv.; bk.rev.; charts; illus.; circ. 526,060.
  Description: How-to, where-to and when-to information for bass fishermen.

SPORTS AND GAMES — OUTDOOR LIFE

797.3   US
BEACH 'N WAVES. 12/yr. Southern California Surf Magazine, Box 90175, San Diego, CA 92169. TEL 619-272-5599. Ed. Frank Manlove.

799.2   US
BEARDS & SPURS. s-a. $295 per no. Buckmasters, Box 235006, Montgomery, AL 36123-5006. TEL 205-269-3337. FAX 205-244-5523.

796.5   GW   ISSN 0179-1419
BERG (YEAR); Alpenvereins-Jahrbuch. 1869. a. DM.21.80. Deutscher Alpenverein, Praterinsel 5, 8000 Munich 22, Germany. (Co-sponsor: Oesterreichischer Alpenverein) index. **Indexed:** GeoRef.

796   GW   ISSN 0005-8963
DER BERGSTEIGER. 1932. m. DM.66. F. Bruckmann Munich, Verlag und Druck GmbH, Nymphenburgerstr. 86, 8000 Munich 2, Germany. TEL 089-1257332. adv.; bk.rev.
    Description: Covers mountaineering and skiing.

796.522   NE   ISSN 0005-898X
BERGVRIEND. 1952. bi-m. membership. Nederlandse Bergsportvereniging, Van Aerssenstraat 178, 2582 JT The Hague, Netherlands. Ed. C. Tamminga. adv.; bk.rev.; illus.; circ. 13,500.

799.1   JA
BEST FISHING. (Text in Japanese) 1977. m. 3970 Yen. Nihon Journal Press, 11-8, 2-chome, Higashi-Shimbashi, Minato-ku, Tokyo, Japan. Ed. Ichitaro Midorigawa.

796.93   US
▼**THE BEST OF CROSS COUNTRY SKIING.** 1990. a. $8.95. Cross Country Ski Areas Association, 259 Bolton Rd., Winchester, NH 03470. TEL 603-239-4341. FAX 603-239-6387. circ. 10,000.
    Description: Lists over 500 cross country ski areas in the US and selected areas in Canada. Includes information on groomed kilometers, ski services, lodging, and ski areas amenities and programs.

BICYCLING. see *SPORTS AND GAMES — Bicycles And Motorcycles*

799.1   CN
BIG FIN OUTDOOR REPORT. 1978. m. Group Quebecor Inc., 1700 Church Ave., Winnipeg, Man. R2X 3A2, Canada. TEL 204-694-3255. FAX 204-632-8709. Ed. Ron Miller. adv.; circ. 54,694. (also avail. in tabloid format)

799.2   US
▼**BIG GAME GUIDE.** 1991. a. Ehlert Publishing Group, Inc., 319 Barry Ave., S., Ste. 101, Wayzata, MN 55391-1603. TEL 612-962-0598.
    Description: Features bowhunting adventure stories.

799.2   US
SK301
BIG GAME HUNTING. Cover title: Petersen's Complete Guide to Hunting. 1977. a. $6.95. Petersen Publishing Co., 8490 Sunset Blvd., Los Angeles, CA 90069. TEL 213-854-2222.
    Formerly: Deer Hunting (Los Angeles) (ISSN 0270-0069)

796.93   CC
BINGXUE YUNDONG. (Text in Chinese) bi-m. Heilongjiang Sheng Tiyu Kexue Yanjiusuo - Heilongjiang Institute of Sport Science, 21, Xuanxi Jie, Nangang-qu, Harbin, Heilongjiang 141, People's Republic of China. TEL 221683. Ed. Sun Jingguo.

DER BLAUE PETER; Zeitschrift fuer Segeln und Seefahrt. see *SPORTS AND GAMES — Boats and Boating*

799.1   GW   ISSN 0720-4116
BLINKER; internationale Sportfischerzeitschrift. 1969. m. DM.72. Jahr-Verlag GmbH & Co., Burchardstr. 14, D-2000 Hamburg 1, Germany. TEL 040-33966220. FAX 040-33966208. TELEX 2163485. Ed. Karl Koch. circ. 80,000. (back issues avail.)

799   US
BOB ELLSBERG'S HUNTER & FISHERMAN'S PLANNING YEARBOOK; a complete guidebook, calendar & journal for the outdoorsman. a. $12.95. Outdoor Enterprises, 1048 Valley St., Astoria, OR 97103. TEL 503-325-5573. Ed. Paul F. Barnum. illus.

799.2   US
BOONE AND CROCKETT CLUB ASSOCIATES NEWSLETTER. 1986. q. $20. Boone and Crockett Club, 241 S. Fraley Blvd., Dumfries, VA 22026. TEL 703-221-1888. Ed. William H. Nesbitt.
    Description: Promotes the wise use of natural resources with emphasis on the concept of sportsmanship while afield; includes hunting, big game measuring and related articles.

799.32   US   ISSN 0006-8403
GV1183
BOW AND ARROW HUNTING; the world's leading archery magazine. 1963. bi-m. $18. Gallant - Charger Publishing, Inc., 34249 Camino Capistrano, Box HH, Capistrano Beach, CA 92624. TEL 714-493-2101. Ed. Jack Lewis. adv.; bk.rev.; illus.; circ. 98,000. (back issues avail.) **Indexed:** Sportsearch.
    Description: Concentrates on bowhunting with emphasis on North American species.

799.2   US
BOW & ARROW MAGAZINE'S BOWHUNTER'S ANNUAL. Spine title: Bowhunter's Annual. 1975. a. $3.95. Gallant - Charger Publishing, Inc., 34249 Camino Capistrano, Box HH, Capistrano Beach, CA 92624. TEL 714-493-2101. Ed. Jack Lewis. adv.; bk.rev.; circ. 108,000.

799.32   US   ISSN 0273-7434
BOWHUNTER; the magazine for the hunting archer. 1971. 8/yr. $24. Cowles Magazines, Inc. (Subsidiary of: Cowles Media Company), 6405 Flank Dr., Box 8200, Harrisburg, PA 17105-8200. TEL 717-540-8192. FAX 717-657-9526. Ed. M.R. James. adv.; bk.rev.; circ. 169,998. (also avail. in microform from UMI; reprint service avail. from UMI) **Indexed:** Sportsearch.
    Description: Features bow and arrow hunting adventure, how-to, safety and ethics.

799.32   US   ISSN 1049-9768
BOWHUNTING. 7/yr. $13.95. Petersen Publishing Co., 8490 Sunset Blvd., Los Angeles, CA 90069. TEL 213-854-2222. Ed. Bob Robb. adv.; illus.; circ. 85,000.

799.32   US   ISSN 1043-5492
BOWHUNTING WORLD. 1952. 8/yr. $20. Ehlert Publishing Group, Inc., 319 Barry Ave., S., Wayzata, MN 55391-1603. TEL 612-476-2200. Ed. Tim Dehn. adv.; bk.rev.; charts; illus.; mkt.; pat.; tr.lit.; tr.mk.; index; circ. 200,000. (also avail. in microform from UMI; reprint service avail. from UMI) **Indexed:** Consum.Ind., Mag.Ind., Phys.Ed.Ind., Sports Per.Ind., Sportsearch.
    Formerly (until 1989): Archery World (ISSN 0003-827X)

796.522   CN   ISSN 0045-2998
BRITISH COLUMBIA MOUNTAINEER. 1917. biennial. Can.$10. British Columbia Mountaineering Club, P.O. Box 2674, Vancouver, B.C. V6B 3W8, Canada. TEL 604-737-3000. Ed. M.C. Feller. adv.; bk.rev.; circ. 500.

799.2   US
BROWNING DEER HUNTING. 1986. a. $2.50. (Browning Arms) Aqua-Field Publishing Co., Inc., 66 W. Gilbert St., Shrewsbury, NJ 07702. TEL 201-842-8300. Ed. Stephen Ferber. adv.; circ. 100,000.

796.5   CN   ISSN 0383-9249
BRUCE TRAIL NEWS. 1963. q. Can.$12($12) (Bruce Trail Association) Trail News Inc., 17 Marlborough Avenue, Toronto, Ont. M5R 1X5, Canada. TEL 416-964-7281. Ed. Norman Day. adv.; bk.rev.; illus.; circ. 10,000 (controlled). (back issues avail.)
    Description: News about outdoor life, camping and the environment.

799.2   US
BUCKMASTERS WHITETAIL. bi-m. $3.95 per no. Buckmasters, Box 235006, Montgomery, AL 36123-5006. TEL 205-269-3337. FAX 205-244-5523.

799.2   US   ISSN 0889-6445
BUGLE (MISSOULA). 1984. q. $25. Rocky Mountain Elk Foundation, Box 8249, Missoula, MT 59807-8249. TEL 406-721-0010. FAX 406-549-4325. Ed. Dan Crockett. adv.; circ. 200,000 (controlled).
    Description: Focuses on conserving elk, other wildlife and their habitat, from the viewpoints of hunters, naturalists and all those who care about elk.

796 910.2   NE   ISSN 0007-3768
BUITENSPOOR. 1918. m. membership. Nederlandse Toeristen Kampeerclub, Kerkstraat 58, 5301 EJ Zaltbommel, Netherlands. Ed. J.H. Sanders. adv.; bk.rev.; charts; illus.; index; circ. 5,000.

796.5   UK   ISSN 0008-2406
C S E NEWS. 1962. m. £29. Camping & Sports Equipment Ltd., 4 Spring St., London W2 3RB, England. TEL 071-262-2886. FAX 071-706-0360. Ed. P. Moloney. adv.; bk.rev.; abstr.; illus.; mkt.; pat.; stat.; tr.lit.; circ. 6,011.
    Incorporating: Camping and Sports Equipment.
    Description: Trade journal for the camping and outdoor leisure sector: camping, caravaning, outdoor equipment and accessories.

C T P A NEWS. (California Travel Parks Association, Inc.) see *TRAVEL AND TOURISM*

799   IT
CACCIA E PESCA. 1967. m. L.35000. Editoriale Bertacchi s.r.l., Via Bertacchi 2, Milan, Italy. Ed. Giuseppe Negri. adv.; circ. 65,000.
    Description: Covers fishing and hunting, sports and outdoor games.

799.2   IT
CACCIATORE ITALIANO. m. Federazione Italiana Caccia, Viale Tiziano 70, 00196 Rome, Italy. Ed. Riccardo Todeschini. adv.; circ. 918,000.

799.1   US   ISSN 8750-8907
SH473
CALIFORNIA ANGLER. 1981. m. $18. 1921 E. Carnegie Way, No. 3N, Santa Ana, CA 92705-5510. TEL 714-261-9779. FAX 714-261-9853. Ed. John Skrabo. adv.; circ. 33,500.
    Formerly: Western Saltwater Fisherman.
    Description: Focuses on primarily fresh and saltwater fishing in California, the Baja Peninsula, Mexico mainland and the Pacific Basin.

CALIFORNIA FISH AND GAME. see *CONSERVATION*

CALIFORNIA - NEVADA CAMPBOOK. see *TRAVEL AND TOURISM*

796.5   GW
CAMP; Magazin fuer Caravan und Reisemobil. 1977. m. DM.61. Top Special Verlag, Valentinskamp 24, D-2000 Hamburg 36, Germany. TEL 040-347-3901. Ed. Manfred Ruopp. circ. 40,000.

796.5 670   US
CAMP DIRECTORS PURCHASING GUIDE. 1964. a. $22.50. Klevens Publications, Inc., 7600 Ave. H, Littlerock, CA 93543. TEL 805-944-4111. Ed. John Keller. adv.; bk.rev.; circ. 14,736. (back issues avail.)
    Description: Provides sources of material used in construction and operation of childrens' summer camps.

796.5   IT   ISSN 0008-2325
CAMPEGGIO ITALIANO. 1958. m. L.25000. Federazione Italiana del Campeggio e del Caravanning, Casella Postale 23, 50041 Calenzano (Florence), Italy. Ed. Lamberto Ariani. adv.; circ. 25,000. (back issues avail. 800)

CAMPERWAYS; the Middle Atlantic campers' newspaper. see *TRAVEL AND TOURISM*

796.5   US   ISSN 0162-3796
CAMPGROUND MANAGEMENT; business publication for profitable outdoor recreation. Variant title: Woodall's Campground Management. 1969. m. $24.95. Woodall Publishing Co., 28167 N. Keith Dr., Lake Forest, IL 60045. TEL 708-362-6700. FAX 708-362-8776. Ed. Mike Byrnes. adv.; bk.rev.; charts; illus.; stat.; tr.; lit.; circ. 16,900 (controlled). (tabloid format; back issues avail.)
    Description: Information for the development, rehabilitation, maintenance, operation and management of a campground.

796.5   DK   ISSN 0045-4125
CAMPING. 1926. m. membership. Dansk Camping Union - Danish Camping Union, Gl. Kongevej 74 D, DK-1850 Frederiksberg C, Denmark. FAX 31-210108. TELEX 22611-DCU-DK. Ed. Joergen Froehlich. adv.; bk.rev.; film rev.; charts; illus.; circ. 50,000.

SPORTS AND GAMES — OUTDOOR LIFE

796.5 **GW**
CAMPING; illustrierte Zeitschrift fuer Caravan-, Zelt-, Motor-Touristik und Wassersport. m. (Deutscher Camping Club e.V.) D C C-Wirtschaftsdienst und Verlag GmbH, Postfach 400428, 8000 Munich 40, Germany. TEL 089-334021. FAX 089-334737. TELEX 5215974. adv.; circ. 40,000.

796.5 **UK**
CAMPING & CARAVANNING. 1907. m. membership. Camping and Caravanning Club, Greenfields House, Westwood Way, Coventry CV4 8JH, England. TEL 0203-694995. FAX 0203-694886. Ed. Peter Frost. adv.; bk.rev.; illus.; circ. 96,528.
Formerly: Camping and Outdoor Life.

796.5 **UK**
CAMPING AND CARAVANNING IN BRITAIN. a. £7.99. Automobile Association, Fanum House, Basingstoke, Hants RG21 2EA, England. TEL 0256-20123. FAX 0256-22575. adv.
Formerly: Camping and Caravanning U.K.

796.5 **UK**
CAMPING & OUTDOOR LEISURE TRADER. Short title: C O L T. 1984. bi-m. £5. 97 Front St., Whickham, Newcastle-upon-Tyne NE16 4JL, England. Ed. Peter Lumley. adv.; circ. controlled.

796.5 **US** **ISSN 0896-5706**
CAMPING AND R V MAGAZINE. 1985. m. $17.95. Box 337, Iola, WI 54945. TEL 715-445-3235. FAX 715-445-4053. Ed. Barbara Case. adv.; circ. 20,000.

796.5 **UK** **ISSN 0952-5106**
CAMPING & WALKING. 1961. m. £27.70. Link House Magazines Ltd., Link House, Dingwall Ave., Croydon CR9 2TA, England. TEL 01-686-2599. FAX 01-760-0973. TELEX 947709. (Subscr. addr.: U M S, Stephenson House, 1st Fl. Brunel Centre, Bletchley, Milton Keynes, MK2 2EW) Ed. Philip Pond. adv.; charts. (back issues avail.)
Former titles (until 1986): Camping and Trailer (ISSN 0266-7878); Camping (ISSN 0032-4469)
Description: Family-oriented information about camping and walking.

796.5 **CN** **ISSN 0384-9856**
CAMPING CANADA. 1971. 7/yr. Can.$18. Camping Canada Magazine, 2585 Skymark Ave., Unit 306, Mississauga, Ont. L4W 4L5, Canada. TEL 416-624-8218. FAX 416-624-6764. Ed. Norm Rosen. adv.; bk.rev.; circ. 50,000. Indexed: Sportsearch.

CAMPING CARAVANNING AND SPORTS EQUIPMENT TRADES DIRECTORY. see BUSINESS AND ECONOMICS — Trade And Industrial Directories

796.5 **SZ** **ISSN 0008-2414**
CAMPING-CARAVANNING-REVUE. (Text in French, German, Italian) 1937. 10/yr. 19 Fr. Federation Suisse de Camping et de Caravanning - Swiss Federation of Camping and Caravanning, Case Postale 24, CH-6000 Lucerne 4, Switzerland. Ed.Bd. adv.; bk.rev.; circ. 11,093.

796.5 **CN**
CAMPING IN ONTARIO. a. Ontario Private Campground Association, 55 Nugget Ave., Ste. 230, Scarborough, Ont. M1S 3L1, Canada. TEL 416-293-2090. FAX 416-293-0934. Dir. Frances Craig. adv.; circ. 120,000.

796.54 **US** **ISSN 0008-2376**
CAMPING MAGAZINE. 1926. 6/yr. $18.95 (foreign $31.50). American Camping Association, Inc., 5000 State Rd. 67 N., Martinsville, IN 46151-7902. TEL 317-342-8456. FAX 317-342-2065. Ed. Nancy LaMarca. adv.; charts; illus.; stat.; tr.lit.; index; circ. 8,000. (also avail. in microform from UMI; back issues avail.; reprint service avail. from UMI) Indexed: Mag.Ind., R.G., Rehabil.Lit., Sports.Per.Ind., Sportsearch.

796.5 910.202 **IT**
CAMPITUR: CAMPING, CARAVANING, VILLAGGI TURISTICI. 1973. a. L.4000. C P M Editrice s.a.s., Via Carducci 21, 20123 Milan, Italy. Ed. Ernesto Cavallini. adv.; circ. 30,000.

796.52 **CN** **ISSN 0068-8207**
F1090 CODEN: CNAJA6
CANADIAN ALPINE JOURNAL. 1907. a. Can.$24.95. Alpine Club of Canada, Box 2040, Canmore, Alta. T0L 0M0, Canada. TEL 403-678-3200. FAX 403-678-3224. bk.rev.; illus.; index, cum.index: 1907-1987; circ. 3,500. (back issues avail.) Indexed: GeoRef., Sportsearch.
—BLDSC shelfmark: 3017.000000.

796.5 **CN** **ISSN 0316-280X**
CANADIAN CAMPER. 1968. 6/yr. membership. Canadian Family Camping Federation, P.O. Box 397, Rexdale, Ont. M9W 5L4, Canada. Ed. Carol Nagel. adv.; bk.rev.; circ. 300 (controlled). Indexed: Sportsearch.
Formerly: C.F.C.F. News for the Canadian Camper (ISSN 0045-4729)

796.96 **CN** **ISSN 0045-4648**
CANADIAN CURLING NEWS. 1957. m. Can.$20. Maxcurl Publications, 90 Dutch Myrtleway, Don Mills, Ont. M3B 3K8, Canada. TEL 416-495-4310. FAX 416-495-4310. Ed. Douglas D. Maxwell. adv.; bk.rev.; circ. 10,000. Indexed: Sportsearch.

799 **CN**
CANADIAN FISHING ANNUAL. a. Ontario Outdoors Publishing Ltd., Box 1541, Peterborough, Ont. K9J 7H7, Canada. TEL 705-748-3891. FAX 705-748-9577. Ed. Gary Ball.
Description: Contains fishing oriented articles stressing how-to, where-to, when-to and why-to conservation type articles.

796 **CN** **ISSN 0710-9326**
CANADIAN R V DEALER. 1975. bi-m. Can.$11. C R V Publications Canada Ltd., 2077 Dundas St. E., Ste. 202, Mississagua, Ont. L4X 1M2, Canada. TEL 416-624-8218. FAX 416-624-6764. Ed. Tim Stover. adv.; tr.; lit. Indexed: Sportsearch, Tr.& Indus.Ind.
Formerly: Canadian Camping and R V Dealer.

796.93 **CN**
CANADIAN SKI PRO CANADIEN. (Text in English and French) 1983. 4/yr. membership. Canadian Ski Instructors' Alliance, 774 Decarie Blvd., Ste. 310, Ville St.-Laurant, Que., Canada. TEL 514-748-2648. FAX 514-748-2476. Ed. Carolyn Paquette. adv.; circ. 16,000.
Formerly: Profile (ISSN 0835-4375)

799.1 **CN**
CANADIAN SPORTFISHING. 5/yr. 937 Centre Rd., No. 2020, Waterdown, Ont. N0J 1Y0, Canada. TEL 416-689-1112. FAX 416-689-2065. Ed. Wolf Seefeld. circ. 85,000.

797.56 **CN** **ISSN 0319-3896**
CANPARA. 1961. 5/yr. Can.$26.75 (foreign Can.$35) (typically set in Jan.). Canadian Sport Parachuting Association, 4185 Dunning Rd., Navan, Ont. K4B 1J1, Canada. TEL 613-835-3731. FAX 613-835-3731. Ed. P. Perdue. adv.; bk.rev.; circ. 4,500. Indexed: Sportsearch.
Former titles: Canadian Parachutist (ISSN 0045-5245); Parachute Club of Canada. Newsletter.

796.5 **IT**
CARA CARAVAN CAMPER. 1978. s-a. L.6500 per no. Di Baio Editore s.r.l., Via Settembrini 11, 20124 Milan, Italy. Ed. G.M. Jonghi Lavarini. adv.

796 **SA** **ISSN 0379-4636**
CARAVAN AND OUTDOOR LIFE. 1960. m. R.40 (foreign R.55). Caravan Publications (Pty) Ltd., P.O. Box 751, Cape Town 8000, South Africa. TEL 027-21-24-1457. FAX 027-21-261-809. Ed. Godfrey Castle. adv.; bk.rev.
Formerly: Caravan.
Description: Includes product tests, travel and touring features, and other articles - ranging from vehicle maintenance, to towing and 4-wheel drive tests, and outdoor cooking tips.

796.5 **SW** **ISSN 0008-6169**
CARAVAN BLADET. 1958. bi-m. SEK 100. Caravan Club of Sweden, Traengkaarsvaegen 39, 703 57 Oerebro, Sweden. TEL 19-137668. FAX 19-116082. Ed. Rune Petterson. adv.; circ. 13,000.

CARAVAN CAMPING DIRECTORY. see BUSINESS AND ECONOMICS — Trade And Industrial Directories

796.5 **GW**
CARAVAN CAMPING-JOURNAL; Zeitschrift fuer Camper, Caravaner, Touristen. 1957. m. DM.60. Westdeutsche Verlagsanstalt GmbH, Ahmser Str. 190, Postfach 3054, 4900 Herford, Germany. TEL 05221-775-0. FAX 05221-775215. TELEX 17-5221-855. Ed. Norbert M. Hoyer. adv.; illus.
Formerly: Camping Journal (ISSN 0008-2449)
Description: Information about travelling, new accessories and techniques.

CARAVAN INDUSTRY SUPPLIES & SERVICES DIRECTORY. see BUSINESS AND ECONOMICS — Trade And Industrial Directories

796.5 **UK**
CARAVAN MOTORCARAVAN & CAMPING. m. £13.20 (foreign £35.50). Aceville Publications Ltd., 89 East Hill, Colchester, Essex CO1 2QN, England. TEL 0206-871450. FAX 0206-871537. Ed. David Bridle. adv.

796.5 **SA**
CARAVAN PARK, CAMPING & BACKPACKING GUIDE TO SOUTHERN AFRICA/WOONWAPARK, KAMPER AND VOETSLAANGIDS VIR SUIDER-AFRIKA. (Text in Afrikaans and English) a. Erudita Publications (Pty) Ltd., Cnr. 11th Ave. & Main Rd., P.O. Box 29159, Melville, Johannesburg 2109, South Africa.

680 796 **FR** **ISSN 0399-7715**
CARAVANIER. 1965. 7/yr. 176 F. Ediregie, B.P. 86, 94420 Le Plessis Trevise, France. FAX 45-93-25-93. TELEX EDIGIE 262 572. Dir. Jean Rousseau. adv.; illus.; circ. 100,000.

CARAVANING; vacanze turismo auto. see TRAVEL AND TOURISM

799.1 **US**
CAROLINA FISH FINDER MAGAZINE. m. Fish Finder Industries, Inc., 810 Travelers Blvd., Summerville, SC 29485-8258. TEL 803-875-2490. FAX 803-875-9301. Ed. Ed Wiley. adv.; circ. 25,000.

799 **US** **ISSN 0008-6800**
CAROLINA SPORTSMAN.* 1960. bi-m. $5. Wing Publications, Inc., Box 11268, Columbia, SC 29211. Ed. Sidney L. Wise. adv.; bk.rev.; abstr.; charts; illus.; circ. controlled.

CATALOGUE OF CANADIAN RECREATION AND LEISURE RESEARCH. see LEISURE AND RECREATION

799 **SP** **ISSN 0212-5625**
CAZA Y PESCA; revista mensual de caza, pesca, tiro, armas y guarderia. 1943. m. 5500 ptas.($65) (foreign 7500 ptas.). Joaquin Espana Paya, Jose Abascal, 24, 1 Izda., 28003 Madrid, Spain. TEL 34-14473484. FAX 34-14474163. adv.; bk.rev.; charts; illus.; circ. 37,000. (back issues avail.)

799 **VE**
CAZA Y PESCA NAUTICA. 1954. m. $25. P.O. Box 60.764, Caracas 1060 A, Venezuela. Ed. Heinz R. Doebbel. adv.; circ. 25,500.
Description: Cover fishing, hunting and water sports.

799.2 **US** **ISSN 0009-1952**
CHASE; a full cry of hunting. 1920. m. $20. Chase Publishing Co., Inc., 1150 Industry Rd., Box 55090, Lexington, KY 40555. TEL 606-254-4262. Ed. Jo Ann Stone. adv.; bk.rev.; illus.; circ. 3,200.

CHATAR. see ARCHITECTURE

790 **US** **ISSN 0893-2778**
GV191.4
CHEVY OUTDOORS. Short title: Outdoors. 1986. q. $8. Aegis Group - Publishers (Subsidiary of: Lintas - Ceco Communications), 30400 Van Dyke Ave., Warren, MI 48093. TEL 313-574-9100. Ed. Michael Brudenell. adv.; circ. 1,000,000.
Formerly: Chevy Camper.
Description: Features, information, and events pertaining to all forms of outdoor recreation and leisure, with tips on fishing, cooking, boating recreational vehicles and personality profiles.

SPORTS AND GAMES — OUTDOOR LIFE

796.552 US
CHICAGO MOUNTAINEER. 1945. s-a. $10. (Chicago Mountaineering Club) Data Base Management Services, 998 Lake Country Ct., Oconomowoc, WI 53066. TEL 414-567-1110. (Subscr. to: Chicago Mountaineering Club, 22 S. Thurlow St., Hinsdale, IL 60921) Ed. David L. Harrison. bk.rev.; bibl.; circ. 350.
   Description: Covers technical rock climbing. Includes reports on expeditions and personal experiences.

796.42 JA
CITY RUNNER. (Text in Japanese) 1983. m. 4560 Yen. Gakken Co., Ltd., 40-5, 4 chome, Kamiikedai, Ohta-ku, Tokyo 145, Japan. Ed. Masahiro Onuma.

796.522 UK ISSN 0955-3045
CLIMBER AND HILLWALKER. 1961. m. £27. George Outram & Co. Ltd., The Plaza Tower, East Kilbride, Glasgow G74 1LW, Scotland. Ed. Peter Evans. adv.; bk.rev.; charts; illus.; tr.lit.; circ. 15,549. **Indexed:** Geo.Abstr., Sportsearch.
   —BLDSC shelfmark: 3286.096000.
   Former titles: Climber; Climber and Rambler (ISSN 0009-8973); Climber.

796.522 US ISSN 0045-7159
GV199.4
CLIMBING. 1970. 6/yr. $24. (Climbing, Ltd.) Elk Mountain Press, Inc., Box 339, Carbondale, CO 81623. TEL 303-963-9449. FAX 303-963-9442. Ed. Michael Kennedy. adv.; bk.rev.; charts; illus.; circ. 28,000. **Indexed:** Sportsearch.
   Description: Discusses rock-climbing and mountaineering.

796.552 US
CLIMBING ART. 1986. q. $12 (foreign $20). Fairfield Communications, 5620 S. 49th St., Lincoln, NE 68516. TEL 800-755-0024. FAX 402-421-1268. Ed. Pat Ament. adv.; bk.rev.; circ. 1,800. (back issues avail.)
   Description: Covers mountaineering and rock climbing, and examines the cultures of different mountain areas of the world.

799 UK
COARSE ANGLER. 1977. m. £16.80. (National Federation of Angler) N.F.A. Publications Ltd., 8 Stumperlowe Close, Sheffield S10 3PP, England. FAX 0742-306640. Ed. Colin Dyson. adv.; bk.rev.; circ. 21,000.
   Description: Presents various fishing techniques.

799.1 US
COLORADO HUNTING, FISHING & OUTDOOR GUIDE; official Colorado-Wyoming fishing guide. 1954. biennial. $12.95. Hart Publications, Inc., 1900 Grant St., Ste. 400, Box 1917, Denver, CO 80201. TEL 303-837-1917.
   Former titles: Tim Kelley's Fishing Guide; Official Colorado-Wyoming Fishing Guide.

799 US ISSN 0010-1699
SK351
COLORADO OUTDOORS. 1952. bi-m. $8.50. Division of Wildlife, 6060 Broadway, Denver, CO 80216. TEL 303-291-7469. Ed. Russell C. Bromby. charts; illus.; index; circ. 60,000. **Indexed:** Key Word Ind.Wildl.Res.

799.2 US
COLUMBIA DUCK & GOOSE SHOOTING. 1985. a. $2.50. (Columbia Sportswear) Aqua-Field Publishing Co., Inc., 66 W. Gilbert St., Shrewsbury, NJ 07702. TEL 201-842-8300. Ed. Stephen Ferber. adv.; circ. 115,000.

796.5 PO ISSN 0010-3969
COMPANHEIROS. 6/yr. free. Clube de Campismo de Lisboa, Rua de Misericordia 137, 2 Andar, Lisbon, Portugal. Ed. Armando Almeida Henriques. bk.rev.; illus.

796.5 US ISSN 1047-1669
COMPETITION ANGLER. 1989. m. $13. 2160 Renwick Dr., Poland, OH 44514. TEL 216-757-8171. FAX 216-533-3865. Ed. Jack Wollitz. adv.; bk.rev.; circ. 500 (controlled).
   Description: For tournament-style bass fishermen, primarily in Ohio. Covers bass tournaments, schedules and related bass fishing news.

799.3 US
COMPLETE SPORTSMAN: GUNS & HUNTING. bi-m. Harris Publications, Inc., 1115 Broadway, 8th Fl., New York, NY 10010. TEL 212-807-7100. FAX 212-627-4678. Ed. Lamar Underwood.

711 UK
CONGRESS IN PARK AND RECREATION ADMINISTRATION. REPORTS. triennial. International Federation of Park and Recreation Administration, General Secretary, The Grotto, Lower Basildon, Reading, Berkshire RG8 9NE, England. TEL 0491-874222. FAX 0491-874079.
   Formerly: World Congress in Public Park Administration. Reports (ISSN 0510-8225)

799.2 FR
CONNAISSANCE DE LA CHASSE. m. 300 F. (foreign 395 F.). Editions Lariviere, 15-17 Quai de l'Oise, 75166 Paris Cedex 19, France. TEL 1-40-34-22-07. FAX 1-40-35-84-41. TELEX 211 678 F. Ed. Jean Capiod. adv.

333.7 US ISSN 0092-5764
SD1
CONNECTICUT WALK BOOK. 1937. irreg., 16th ed., 1990. $14. Connecticut Forest and Park Association, Inc., Middlefield, 16 Meriden Rd., Rockfall, CT 06481-2961. TEL 203-346-2372. illus.
   Description: Guide to hiking trails in Connecticut.

796 SP
CONSEJO SUPERIOR DE INVESTIGACIONES CIENTIFICAS. GRUPOS DE MONTANA DE ACCION CULTURAL. BOLETIN INFORMATIVO.* (Text in Spanish; summaries in English, French, Spanish) 1972. s-a. 200 ptas. per no. Consejo Superior de Investigaciones Cientificas (C.S.I.C.), Grupos de Montana de Accion Cultura, Seranno, 117, 28006 Madrid, Spain. adv.; bk.rev.; abstr.; bibl.; illus.; stat.; tr.lit.; index, cum.index; circ. 500.

CONSERVATIONIST. see *CONSERVATION*

799.3 US
COON-HOUND CORNER. bi-m. 2298 S. Elliott Rd., S.W., Stockport, OH 43787. TEL 614-557-3248. FAX 614-557-3253. Ed. Katherine A. Janson. circ. 9,000.

COUNTRY SPORTS DIRECTORY. see *BUSINESS AND ECONOMICS — Trade And Industrial Directories*

COUNTRYSIDE COMMISSION NEWS. see *CONSERVATION*

799.1 US
CRAPPIE. 1989. 4/yr. $13.95 for 6 nos. NatCom, Inc., 15115 S. 76th E. Ave., Bixby, OK 74008. TEL 918-366-4441. FAX 918-366-4441. Ed. Gordon Sprouse. adv.

796.93 US
CROSS COUNTRY SKI AREA OPERATIONS SURVEY. 1985. a. $100. Cross Country Ski Areas Association, 259 Bolton Rd., Winchester, NH 03470. TEL 603-239-4341. FAX 603-239-6387. circ. 250. (back issues avail.)
   Description: For the industry covering revenue, skier visits, growth, and grooming patterns.

796.93 US ISSN 0278-9213
GV854.4
CROSS COUNTRY SKIER. 1981. 5/yr. $14.97. Collins Chase Publications, Inc., 1823 Fremont Ave. S., Minneapolis, MN 55403. TEL 612-377-0312. Ed. Jim Chase. adv.; bk.rev.; circ. 35,000. **Indexed:** Sports Per.Ind., Sportsearch (1981-).
   Formerly: Nordic Skiing.
   Description: Devoted to cross country skiing. Provides information for both novice and expert skiers in tuning up techniques, buying equipment, and finding new places to ski.

CYCLE TOURING & CAMPAIGNING. see *SPORTS AND GAMES — Bicycles And Motorcycles*

D C C - CARAVAN UND MOTORCARAVAN MODELLFUEHRER. (Deutscher Camping Club e.V.) see *TRANSPORTATION — Automobiles*

D C C - TOURISTIK SERVICE. (Deutscher Camping Club e.V.) see *TRAVEL AND TOURISM*

796 GW
D V V - KURIER. 1971. m. DM.15. Deutscher Volkssportverband, Fabrikstr. 8, 8262 Altoetting, Germany. TEL 08671-8071. FAX 08671-8377. adv.; circ. 12,000. (back issues avail.)

D W J - INFO; Mitteilungen des Bundesverbandes. (Deutsche Waldjugend) see *FORESTS AND FORESTRY*

799 US ISSN 0194-5769
DAKOTA COUNTRY. 1979. m. $13.95. Mitzel Outdoor Publications, Inc., Box 2714, Bismarck, ND 58502. TEL 701-255-3031. FAX 701-224-1412. Ed. William A. Mitzel. adv.; circ. 10,456.
   Description: Focuses on fishing and hunting in the Dakotas.

799 US ISSN 0891-902X
DAKOTA OUTDOORS. 1976. m. $10. Hipple Publishing Co., Inc., 333 W. Dakota, Box 669, Pierre, SD 57501-0669. TEL 605-224-7301. FAX 605-224-9210. Ed. Kevin Hipple. adv.; bk.rev.; tr.lit.; circ. 6,597. (back issues avail.)
   Formerly (until 1986): Dakota Fisherman.
   Description: Articles on South Dakota outdoor news, including legislative, governmental, and regulatory concerns.

779.2 US
DEER AND BIG GAME. 1977. a. $2.75. Times Mirror Magazines, Inc., 2 Park Ave., New York, NY 10016. TEL 212-779-5000. Ed. Vin T. Sparano. adv.; illus.; circ. 150,000. (reprint service avail. from UMI)
   Former titles: Midwest Fishing by Outdoor Life; Outdoor Life's Guide to Fishing the Midwest.

799.2 US ISSN 0164-7318
DEER & DEER HUNTING; practical & comprehensive information for white-tailed deer hunters. 1977. 8/yr. $17.95. Krause Publications, Inc., 700 E. State St., Iola, WI 54990. TEL 715-445-2214. FAX 715-445-4087. TELEX 556461 KRAUSE PUB UD. Ed. Al Hofacker. adv. contact: Debbie Knauer. bk.rev.; circ. 225,000.

799.2 US
DEER TRAIL. 1983. 5/yr. $17 includes membership. Whitetails Unlimited, Inc., Box 422, Sturgeon Bay, WI 54235. TEL 414-743-6777. adv.; circ. 35,000.

799.2 US
DEER UNLIMITED MAGAZINE.* 1978. bi-m. $7. Deer Unlimited of America, Inc., Box 1129, Abbeville, SC 29620-1129. Ed. Jim Edens. adv.; circ. 9,000.
   Description: Gives hunting tips.

DEL-MAR-VA HEARTLAND. see *AGRICULTURE*

DESIGN. see *ARCHITECTURE*

799.2 GW ISSN 0724-2654
DEUTSCHE JAGD-ZEITUNG; Forum fuer Jaeger und Naturfreunde. 1983. m. DM.48. Mittelrhein Verlag GmbH, Feldstr. 6, D-5408 Nassau, Germany. Ed. Walterpeter Twer. circ. 50,000.

799.1 US
DEUTSCHE SPORTFISCHER-ZEITUNG; Forum fuer den engagierten Angler und Naturfreund. 1983. m. DM.29. Mittelrhein Verlag GmbH, Feldstr. 6, D-5408 Nassau, Germany. Ed. Peter Sauer. adv.; bk.rev.; circ. 56,815.

796.522 GW ISSN 0012-1088
DEUTSCHER ALPENVEREIN; Mitteilungen-Jugend am Berg. 1948. bi-m. DM.6 membership. Deutscher Alpenverein, Praterinsel 5, 8000 Munich 22, Germany. Ed. Elmar Landes. adv.; bk.rev.; illus.; index. **Indexed:** GeoRef.
   Description: Covers mountaineering in the Alps.

799 AG ISSN 0012-2327
DIANA.* 1935. m. Tacuari 237, Buenos Aires, Argentina. Ed. Dir. Francisco Jose Cabrera. adv.; charts; illus.; mkt.
   Description: Focuses on fishing and hunting.

799.2 IT ISSN 0012-2343
DIANA (FLORENCE); rivista del cacciatore. 1906. fortn. L.103000 (L.137000). Editoriale Olimpia, Viale Milton 7, 50129 Florence, Italy. TEL 055-473843. FAX 055-499195. TELEX 573084 EDOL I. Ed. Dir. Giuliano Incerpi. adv.; illus.; index; circ. 92,000.

SPORTS AND GAMES — OUTDOOR LIFE

796   US
DIRECTIONS (CHICAGO). 1976. m. $20 (foreign $25). Live Free, Inc., 11123 St. Lawrence Ave., Chicago, IL 60628. TEL 312-928-5830. (Subscr. to: Box 1743, Harvey, IL 60426) Eds. James C. Jones, Joe Wieser. adv.; bk.rev.; illus.; circ. 3,800. (back issues avail.)
 Description: Articles, classified advertisements, and announcements on family and self-survival tactics and products.

796.54   CN   ISSN 0316-1226
DIRECTORY OF ACCREDITED CAMPS. (Text in English, French) 1963. a. Can.$3.41. Quebec Camping Association, 4545 Ave. Pierre-de-Coubertin, Montreal, Que. H1V 3R2, Canada. FAX 514-251-8038. adv.

790.1 551.44   UK
DIRECTORY OF BRITISH CAVING CLUBS (YEAR). 1982. a. £5. Rhychydwr, Crymych, Dyfed SA41 3RB, Wales. TEL 023 973 371. Ed. Tony Oldham. adv.; circ. 3,000. (back issues avail.)

796.5 296   US
DIRECTORY OF JEWISH RESIDENT SUMMER CAMPS. irreg. J W B Jewish Book Council, 15 E. 26th St., New York, NY 10010. TEL 212-532-4949.

792   US   ISSN 0361-4255
T391
DIRECTORY OF NORTH AMERICAN FAIRS, FESTIVALS AND EXPOSITIONS. Variant title: Amusement Business's Directory North American Fairs. 1888. a. $45. B P I Communications, Inc., Amusement Business Division, Box 24970, Nashville, TN 37202. TEL 615-321-4250. FAX 615-327-1575. Ed. Tom Powell. circ. 1,500.
 Formerly (until 1972): Cavalcade and Directory of Fairs (ISSN 0069-1291)
 Description: Lists over 6,000 state and county fairs, festivals and public expositions in the U.S. and Canada that run three days or more. Contains general and statistical data plus chronological cross references.

796 362.4   US
DISABLED OUTDOORS MAGAZINE. q. 5223 S. Lorel Ave., Chicago, IL 60638-1605. TEL 312-284-2206. Ed. John Kopchik, Jr. adv.; circ. 5,000.

796.352   US   ISSN 0892-2357
DISC GOLF WORLD NEWS. 1984. q. $12 in U.S.; Canada $16; Europe $18; elsewhere $20. Disc Golf World, 815 W. Rollins, Columbia, MO 65203. TEL 314-874-2981. (Subscr. to: Box 30011, Columbia, MO 65205) Eds. Lynne & Rick Rothstein. adv.; bk.rev.; charts; illus.; stat.; circ. 800.
 Formerly: Columbia Disc Golf News.
 Description: Review and preview of disc golf events, equipment and promotions, results, interviews and cartoons.

799.2   US
DIXIE GUN WORKS BLACKPOWDER ANNUAL. a. $2.95. Dixie Gun Works, Box 684, Union City, TN 38261. TEL 901-885-0374. FAX 901-885-0440. Ed. Butch Winter. adv.; circ. 100,000. (back issues avail.)
 Description: Covers hunting, history, modern uses of black powder, and topics relating to the black powder era.

796.93   UK   ISSN 0070-718X
DOWNHILL ONLY JOURNAL. 1936. a. membership. Downhill Only Club, c/o D.F. Ryan, Brigadier, Lodwick, Monxton, Hants SP11 8AW, England. adv.; bk.rev.; index; circ. 1,700.

DRACHENFLIEGER MAGAZIN; Offizielles Organ fuer Haengegleiter-Piloten, -Verbaende und Hersteller. see AERONAUTICS AND SPACE FLIGHT

DUCK STAMP DATA. see PHILATELY

796.93   US
E S R. NEWSLETTER. irreg. Eastern Ski Representatives Association, H.C.R. 1, Box 7, White Haven, PA 18661. TEL 717-443-7180.

769.93   US
E S R BUYERS' GUIDE. a. Eastern Ski Representatives Association, H.C.R. 1, Box 7, White Haven, PA 18661. TEL 717-443-7180.

799.1   US
EAST COAST ANGLER.* 1987. w. $15. East Coast Angler, Inc., P.O. Box 280, Somerville, NJ 08876-0280. TEL 800-333-4744. FAX 201-295-2008. Ed. Mickey Cooper. adv.; bk.rev.; circ. 10,000. (back issues avail.)
 Description: Reports on fresh and saltwater fishing.

799.32   US
EASTERN BOWHUNTING. 1989. m. $15. Eastern Publishing & Distributing, Inc., 8 Landing Ln., Hopedale, MA 01747. TEL 508-478-4754. FAX 508-478-3541. Ed. Roy Goodwin. adv.: B&W page $660, color page $960; trim 10 x 15 1/4. circ. 15,000.
 Description: Contains stories by bowhunters relating actual hunting experiences. Attempts to keep the sportsman informed of industry news, hunting programs, and new organizations, as well as updates on pending legislation.

EASTERN CANADA CAMPBOOK. see TRAVEL AND TOURISM

799   CN   ISSN 0827-8911
EASTERN WOODS & WATERS. 1985. 6/yr. Can.$16.95($23) J P L Publishers Ltd., P.O. Box 428, Dartmouth, N.S. B2Y 3Y5, Canada. TEL 902-468-2682. FAX 902-468-3996. Ed. James Gourlay. circ. 27,000. (back issues avail.)
 Description: Hunting and fishing news for Atlantic Canada.

796.93 330   US   ISSN 0147-4243
GV854.8.N58
ECONOMIC ANALYSIS OF NORTH AMERICAN SKI AREAS. Variant title: U S I A Economic Analysis of North American Ski Areas. 1971. a. $100. University of Colorado, Business Research Division, Campus Box 420, Boulder, CO 80309. TEL 303-492-8227. (Co-sponsor: United Ski Industries Association) Indexed: SRI.
 Supersedes (1971): N S A A Economics of the Skiing Industry.

EMPLOY. see OCCUPATIONS AND CAREERS

796.5   UK
EN ROUTE. 1963. 7/yr. membership. Caravan Club, East Grinstead House, East Grinstead, West Sussex RH19 1UA, England. Ed. David Hunter. adv.; bk.rev.; circ. 190,000.

796.93 330   US
END OF SEASON NATIONAL BUSINESS SURVEY.* a. $15. National Ski Areas Association, 8377B Greensboro Dr., McLean, VA 22102-3529.
 Description: Examines changes and trends in the domestic ski industry. Analyzes influence of season length, lift capacity, night skiing, and snow-making on business volume.

796 799   FI   ISSN 0356-3464
ERA. 1977. m. FIM 338. Yhtyneet Kuvalehdet Oy, Maistraatinportti 1, 00240 Helsinki, Finland. TEL 0-15661. FAX 0-1566505. TELEX 121364. Ed. Seppo Suuronen. adv.; circ. 40,623.

799   FI
ERAMIES. 1946. bi-m. FIM 60. Suomen Metsastaja ja Kalastajaliitto r.y., Heikkakuja 1C, 33230 Tampere, Finland. TEL 35831-126543. FAX 35831-233566. Ed. Kalervo Saarinen. adv.; bk.rev.; circ. 12,000.
 Description: Includes stories, technical reports, hunting and fishing tips.

ESCAPEES. see TRANSPORTATION — Automobiles

ESCAPEES CLUB. ANNUAL DIRECTORY. see TRANSPORTATION — Automobiles

797.173   VE
ESQUI ACUATICO Y OTROS DEPORTES. 1975. 6/yr. Av. Lisboa, Ota La Caromotana 5-01-19-28, Calif. Norte, Caracas 1070, Venezuela. adv.; circ. 10,000.

796.5   GW   ISSN 0071-2272
EUROPA CAMPING UND CARAVANING. INTERNATIONALER FUEHRER. (Text in English, French and German) 1959. a. DM.22.80. Drei Brunnen Verlag und Co., Postfach 101154, 7000 Stuttgart 10, Germany. FAX 0711-2576217. Ed. Ursel Wunder-Gessler.

790.1   CN   ISSN 0714-816X
EXPLORE; Canada's magazine of adventure travel. 1981. 4/yr. Can.$15($19) Thompson & Gordon Publishing Co. Ltd., 301 14th Street N.W., No. 470, Calgary, Alta. T2N 2A1, Canada. FAX 403-270-7922. Ed. Marion Harrison. adv.; bk.rev.; circ. 25,000. (also avail. in microfiche; reprint service avail. from MML; back issues avail.) Indexed: Can.Per.Ind., CMI.
 Description: Focuses on backpacking, bicycling, canoeing and skiing featuring Canadian and international destinations. Covers ecotourism, the environment, outdoor photography, sports medicine, equipment and new products for the outdoor recreationist.

EXPLORE MINNESOTA CAMPGROUND GUIDE. see TRAVEL AND TOURISM

796.95 796.42   US
EXPLORE MINNESOTA CROSS-COUNTRY SKIING. a. free. Office of Tourism, 375 Jackson St., Ste. 205, St. Paul, MN 55101. circ. 20,000.

796   US
EXPLORE MINNESOTA DOWNHILL SKIING. a. free. Office of Tourism, 375 Jackson St., Ste. 205, St. Paul, MN 55101. circ. 20,000.

EXPLORE MINNESOTA HIKING. see TRAVEL AND TOURISM

796.93   SZ   ISSN 0425-5291
F I S BULLETIN. (Text in English, French, German) q. 32 Fr. (International Ski Federation) Hallwag AG, Nordring 4, CH-3000 Berne, Switzerland. TEL 031-423131. FAX 031-414133. TELEX 912 661 CH. circ. 1,709. (back issues avail.) Indexed: Sportsearch (1973-).

FAIRS AND FESTIVALS (YEAR): NORTHEAST AND SOUTHEAST. see ARTS AND HANDICRAFTS

910.2   UK   ISSN 0957-7327
FAMILY SITES GUIDE. 1966. a. £3. Haymarket Magazines Ltd., 38-42 Hampton Rd., Teddington, Middx. TW11 0JE, England. TEL 081-943-5000. TELEX 895-2440-HAYMRT-G.
 Former titles: Camper Sites Guide; Practical Camper's Sites Guide; Camping Sites in Britain and France (ISSN 0068-6980)
 Description: Lists and evaluates over 1500 camper sites.

FANG; Fuehrungszeitschrift. see FORESTS AND FORESTRY

796   UK   ISSN 0015-0649
FIELD. 1853. m. £35. Burlington Publications, 10 Sheet St., Windsor, Berkshire SL4 1BG, England. TEL 753-856061. FAX 753-859652. Ed. Jonathan Young. adv.; bk.rev.; illus. Indexed: Geo.Abstr.
 —BLDSC shelfmark: 3918.900000.

799   US   ISSN 0015-0673
SK1
FIELD & STREAM. 1895. m. $15.94. Times Mirror Magazines, Inc., 2 Park Ave., New York, NY 10016. TEL 212-779-5000. FAX 212-725-3836. Ed. Duncan Barnes. adv.; bk.rev.; charts; illus.; circ. 2,000,000. (also avail. in microform from UMI,MIM; reprint service avail. from UMI) Indexed: Abr.R.G., Biog.Ind., Consum.Ind., Jun.High.Mag.Abstr., Mag.Ind., PMR, R.G., Sports Per.Ind., TOM.
 Description: Gives hunting and fishing tips.

799.17   US   ISSN 0163-5468
SH681
FIELD & STREAM BASS FISHING ANNUAL. Short title: Bass Fishing. 1977. a. $2.50 (newstand sales only). C B S Magazines, Consumer Publishing Group, 1515 Broadway, New York, NY 10036. TEL 212-719-6000. Ed. Glenn Sapir. circ. 200,000.

799   US
FIELD & STREAM DEER HUNTER'S GUIDE ANNUAL. Short title: Deer Hunting. 1978. a. $2.50 (newstand sales only). C B S Magazines, Consumer Publishing Group, 1515 Broadway, New York, NY 10036. TEL 212-719-6000. Ed. Glenn Sapir. circ. 250,000.
 Formerly: Field & Stream Deer Hunting Annual.

SPORTS AND GAMES — OUTDOOR LIFE

799.1   US   ISSN 0362-6385
SH401
FIELD & STREAM FISHING ANNUAL. Short title: Fishing. 1976. a. $2.50 (newstand sales only). C B S Magazines, Consumer Publishing Group, 1515 Broadway, New York, NY 10036. TEL 212-719-6000. Ed. Glenn Sapir. illus.; circ. 250,000.

799.2   US   ISSN 0361-3011
SK1
FIELD & STREAM HUNTING ANNUAL. Short title: Hunting Annual (New York). 1975. a. $2.50 (newstand sales only). C B S Magazines, Consumer Publishing Group, 1515 Broadway, New York, NY 10036. TEL 212-719-6000. Ed. Glenn Sapir. illus.; circ. 250,000.

799.2   US
FIGHTING KNIVES. 1989. 4/yr. $9.95. Larry Flynt Publications, Inc., 9171 Wilshire Blvd., Ste. 300, Beverly Hills, CA 90210. TEL 310-858-7100. FAX 310-275-3857. Ed. Gregory A. Walker. adv.; bk.rev.
  Description: Contains complete reviews of custom knives and their makers, combat and field use evaluations of custom and commercial knives, and coverage of knife accessories and related areas.

796.42   SW
FINAL SKOLIDROTT. 4/yr. (Svenska Skolidrottsfoerbundet) Cewe Foerlaget, P.O. Box 77, 890 10 Bjaesta, Sweden. adv.; circ. 6,000.

799.1   GW   ISSN 0015-2838
FISCH UND FANG; Zeitschrift fuer alle Angler und Freunde des Fischwassers. 1960. m. DM.64($34) (Verband Deutscher Sportfischer e.V.) Verlag Paul Parey (Hamburg), Spitalerstr. 12, 2000 Hamburg 1, Germany. TEL 040-33969-0. FAX 040-33969-198. TELEX 2161291-PARV-D. (US addr.: Paul Parey Scientific Publishers, 35 W. 38th St., Ste. 3W, New York, NY 10018. TEL 212-730-0518) Ed. W. Duever. adv.; bk.rev.; illus.; index; circ. 85,000. (reprint service avail. from ISI)
  Formerly: Fischwaid (ISSN 0722-706X)

799.1   US
FISH AND GAME FINDER. (In 22 regional editions.) 1973. m. free. Fish and Game Finder Magazines, 1233 W. Jackson St., Orlando, FL 32805. TEL 407-425-0045. FAX 407-425-1529. circ. 300,000 (controlled).
  Formerly: Fish Finder.
  Description: Promotes the various types of fishing and hunting for the active outdoorsman.

799.1   US   ISSN 0747-3397
THE FISH SNIFFER; for the northern California, Nevada, and Oregon angler. (Includes bi-monthly feature supplement Gamefishing West.) 1982. bi-w. $25. Northern California Angler Publications, Inc., Box 994, Elk Grove, CA 95759-0994. TEL 916-685-2245. FAX 916-685-1498. Ed. Harold A. Bonslett. adv.; circ. 21,500 approx. (tabloid format; back issues avail.)
  Description: Up-to-date news and features covering recreational fishing and conservation in the West.

FISHERIES AND WILDLIFE RESEARCH. see FISH AND FISHERIES

799.1   US
FISHERMAN. (In 5 regional editions: Florida; Long Island & Metro New York; Mid-Atlantic; New England; New Jersey) 1966. w. $20. L I F Publishing Corp., 14 Ramsey Rd., Shirley, NY 11967. TEL 516-345-5200. Ed. Fred Golofaro. adv.; bk.rev.; bibl.; illus.; tr.lit.
  Formerly: Long Island Fisherman.
  Description: Provides regional coverage of recreational fishing.

799   UK
FISHERMAN & LEISURE LIFE. 1973. m. £4. Pickering Hill Publishing Ltd., 92 Trinity Rd., Wimbledon, London SW19, England. Ed. Frank Godsman.

799   US   ISSN 0015-301X
FISHING AND HUNTING NEWS. (Ten editions avail. covering 13 Western states) 1944. bi-w. $49.95. Outdoor Empire Publishing, Inc., 511 Eastlake Ave. E., Box C 19000, Seattle, WA 98109. TEL 206-624-3845. FAX 206-340-9816. Ed. Vence Malernee. adv.; bk.rev.; charts; illus.; stat.; circ. 145,000. (tabloid format)

799.1   US
FISHING ANNUAL. a. $11.95. Prentice Hall Press, One Gulf & Western Plaza, New York, NY 10023. TEL 212-373-8500.

799.1   US
FISHING FACTS. 1963. 7/yr. $14.97. Fishing Facts, Inc., 312 E. Buffalo St., Milwaukee, WI 53202. TEL 414-287-4333. Eds. Spencer Petros, Carl Malz. adv.; charts; stat.; illus.; index; circ. 125,000.
  Indexed: Sports Per.Ind.
  Formerly: Fishing News.

799.1   US   ISSN 0164-0941
SH505
FISHING IN MARYLAND. 1953. a. $6.95. Fishing in Maryland, Inc., Box 201, Phoenix, MD 21131. TEL 301-243-3413. Ed. W. Cary de Russy. adv.; illus.; circ. 29,000.
  Supersedes in part: Fishing in the Mid-Atlantic; Fishing in Maryland and Virginia (ISSN 0363-8898)

FISHING MAGAZINE FOR YOUNG BOY. see CHILDREN AND YOUTH — For

799.1   AT   ISSN 0816-7885
FISHING NEWS; the newsmagazine of Australian angling. 1970. bi-m. Aus.$45($75) for 2 yrs. Mason Stewart Publishing Pty. Ltd., Darlinghust, N.S.W. 2010, Darlinghust, N.S.W. 2010, Australia. FAX 02-360-5367. Ed. Paul B. Kidd. circ. 14,500. (back issues avail.)
  Description: For amateur anglers. Advises where and how to catch fish in Australia.

799.1   US
FISHING SMART. 1987. a. $2.50. (Mercury Marine) Aqua-Field Publishing Co., Inc., 66 W. Gilbert St., Shrewsbury, NJ 07702. TEL 201-842-8300. Ed. Stephen Ferber. adv.; circ. 110,000.

799.1   US
FISHING TACKLE RETAILER. 1980. 11/yr. free to qualified personnel. B.A.S.S., Inc., Box 17900, Montgomery, AL 36117-0900. TEL 205-272-9530. FAX 205-279-7148. Ed. Dave Ellison. adv.; circ. 21,500.

799.1   US   ISSN 0015-3060
FISHING TACKLE TRADE NEWS. 1952. m. $45. Fishing Tackle Trade News, Inc., Div. Vickers Communications, Box 2669, Vancouver, WA 98668-2669. TEL 206-693-4721. FAX 206-693-3997. adv.; bk.rev.; illus.; circ. 21,500 (controlled).
  Description: Serves retailers of tackle and fishing products; wholesalers, jobbers, distributors, buying groups; importers and exporters of fishing products and sporting goods.

799.1   US   ISSN 0015-3079
SH401
FISHING WORLD. 1954. 6/yr. $9.97. (Fishing Club of America) Allsport Publishing Corp., 51 Atlantic Ave., Floral Park, NY 11001. TEL 516-352-9700. FAX 516-437-6841. Ed. Keith Gardner. adv.; bk.rev.; illus.; index; circ. 300,000. (back issues avail.)
  Description: Devoted to sportfishing.

799   CN
FISH'N CANADA NEWS. 1988. 4/yr. Can.$9.95 (US $9.95 elsewhere Can.$20). Fish'n Canada News Ltd., 1240 Phillip Murray Ave., Ste. 1, Oshawa, Ont. L1J 6Z9, Canada. TEL 416-571-3223. FAX 416-571-3328. Ed. Mary-Anne King. adv.; circ. 127,000. (tabloid format)

799.1   DK   ISSN 0109-1581
FISK & FRI; alt om lystfiskeri. 1983. m. DKK 270. Kronprinsessegade 42, 1306 Copenhagen K, Denmark. Ed. Svend Erik Vardrup. adv.; illus.; circ. 20,000.

799.1   SW
FISKEJOURNALEN. 9/yr. SEK 175. Sveriges Sportfiske och Fiskevaardsfoerbund, P.O. Box 11501, 100 61 Stockholm, Sweden. adv.; circ. 60,000.

FISKERIBLADET. see FISH AND FISHERIES

796.552   NO
FJELL OG VIDDE. q. Norske Turistforening, Stortingsgate 28, N., Oslo 1, Norway. adv.; bk.rev.; circ. 115,000.

799.1   GW   ISSN 0178-0409
FLIEGENFISCHEN; internationales Magazin fuer Flugangler. 1984. 6/yr. DM.72. Jahr-Verlag GmbH & Co., Burchardstr. 14, D-2000 Hamburg 1, Germany. TEL 040-339660. FAX 040-33966208. TELEX 2163485. Ed. Bernd Kuleisa. circ. 10,000. (back issues avail.)

799.1   GW
DER FLIEGENFISCHER. 1975. bi-m. DM.76($42) Verlag J. Schueck, Lohhofer Str. 11, 8500 Nuernberg 60, Germany. (Subscr. addr.: P.O. Box 1170, 8504 Stein, Germany) adv.; bk.rev.; index; circ. 5,000. (back issues avail.)
  Description: Covers fly fishing.

799   US   ISSN 0889-3322
FLORIDA GAME & FISH. 1986. m. $14.95. Game & Fish Publications, Inc., 2250 Newmarket Pkwy., Ste. 110, Box 741, Marietta, GA 30061-0741. Ed. Jimmy Jacobs. circ. 11,000. (back issues avail.)
  Description: Covers hunting and fishing in Florida.

799   US   ISSN 0015-3885
FLORIDA SPORTSMAN. 1969. m. $16.95. Wickstrom Publishers, Inc., 5901 S.W. 74th St., Ste. 310, Miami, FL 33143. TEL 305-661-4222. FAX 305-284-0277. Ed. Vic Dunaway. adv.; bk.rev.; charts; illus.; circ. 103-938. **Indexed:** Acid Rain Abstr., Acid Rain Ind.
  Formerly (until 1971): Florida and Tropic Sportsman.
  Description: For fisherman both visiting and residing in Florida, the Bahamas, and the American tropics. Covers fishing, hunting, boating.

FLORIDA WILDLIFE. see CONSERVATION

799.3   US
FLORIDA WOODS & WATERS MAGAZINE. 8/yr. New Tech Publications, Box 2531, Winter Park, FL 32790-2531. TEL 407-629-2393. Ed. Paul Andrea. adv.; circ. 21,000.

799.1   US   ISSN 0015-4741
SH401
FLY FISHERMAN; the magazine for the complete angler. 1969. 6/yr. $22. Cowles Magazines, Inc. (Subsidiary of: Cowles Media Company), 6405 Flank Dr., Box 8200, Harrisburg, PA 17105-8200. TEL 717-657-9555. FAX 717-657-9526. Ed. John Randolph. adv.; bk.rev.; cum.index vols. 1-16; circ. 130,000. (reprint service avail. from UMI)

799.1   US
FLY FISHING MADE EASY. 1984. a. $2.95. (Scientific Anglers) Aqua-Field Publishing Co., Inc., 66 W. Gilbert St., Shrewsbury, NJ 07702. TEL 201-842-8300. Ed. Stephen Ferber. adv.; circ. 130,000.

799.1   US
FLY ROD & REEL. 1979. 6/yr. $14.97. Down East Enterprise, Inc., Box 370, Camden, ME 04843. TEL 207-594-9544. FAX 207-594-7215. adv.; circ. 32,771.
  Formerly: Rod and Reel.
  Description: Covers conservation and fly-fishing how-to, equipment reviews and travel.

799.1   US
FLYFISHER. 1968. q. membership. Federation of Fly Fishers, Box 1088, W. Yellowstone, MT 59758. TEL 208-523-7300. FAX 406-646-9728. Ed. Dennis G. Bitton. adv.; tr.lit.; circ. 12,500. (back issues avail.)
  Description: Covers articles on fly fishing, where, how, why, and news from what's happening in the Federation.

799.1   UK   ISSN 0046-4228
FLYFISHERS JOURNAL. 1911. s-a. £14. Flyfishers' Club, 24A Old Burlington St., London W.1., England. Ed. Kenneth Robson. adv.; illus.; index; circ. 1,400.
—BLDSC shelfmark: 4754.230000.

799.1   US
FLYFISHING. 1978. 5/yr. $16. Frank Amato Publications, Box 02112, Portland, OR 97202. TEL 503-653-8151. adv.
  Description: Covers casting, fly tying, knots, best places to fish, conservation, new product services and domestic and foreign news.

SPORTS AND GAMES — OUTDOOR LIFE

797.5   CN   ISSN 0317-2481
FLYPAPER. 1974. q. membership. Alberta Hang Glider Association, P.O. Box 2011, Sta. M, Calgary, Alta. T2P 2M2, Canada. Ed. Doug Keller. illus.; circ. 250.

799.3   US
FOCUS (INDIANAPOLIS). M. Department of Natural Resources, 402 W. Washington, No. W273, Indianapolis, IN 46204. TEL 317-232-4080. FAX 317-232-8036. Ed. Hannah Kirchner. circ. 19,000.

FODOR'S SKIING IN THE U S A & CANADA. see *TRAVEL AND TOURISM*

796.5 910.202   US
FODOR'S SPORTS: HIKING. irreg. $12. Fodor's Travel Publications, Inc. (Subsidiary of: Random House, Inc.), 201 E. 50th St., New York, NY 10022. TEL 800-733-3000. (Dist. by: Random House, Inc., 400 Hahn Rd., Westminster, MD 21157) Eds. Cindy Ross, Michael Spring.

796.42 910.202   US
FODOR'S SPORTS: RUNNING. irreg. $12. Fodor's Travel Publications, Inc. (Subsidiary of: Random House, Inc.), 201 E. 50th St., New York, NY 10022. TEL 800-733-3000. (Dist. by: Random House, Inc., 400 Hahn Rd., Westminster, MD 21157) Eds. John Schubert, Michael Spring.

796.5   GW   ISSN 0071-7711
FORSCHUNGSSTELLE FUER JAGDKUNDE UND WILDSCHADENVERHUETUNG. SCHRIFTENREIHE. 1960. irreg., no.9, 1986. price varies. Verlag Paul Parey (Hamburg), Spitalerstr. 12, 2000 Hamburg 1, Germany. TEL 040-33969-0. FAX 040-33969199. TELEX 2161391-PARV-D. Ed.Bd. bibl.; illus.; index. (reprint service avail. from ISI)

FRANCE - SPORTS. see *SPORTS AND GAMES*

797   NZ
FREE FALL KIWI.* 1972. bi-m. NZ.$7. New Zealand Federation of Parachute Clubs, Inc., 30a Grange Rd., Honick, Auckland, New Zealand. adv.; charts; illus.

FREE FLIGHT/VOL LIBRE. see *AERONAUTICS AND SPACE FLIGHT*

796.5   GW
FREIZEIT - CARAVAN - CAMPING MAGAZIN. 1976. m. DM.20. F C C Verlag, Blumenweg 13, 3002 Wedemark 2, Germany. adv.; bk.rev.; illus.; circ. 209,000.

FRIENDS OF PARKS & RECREATION. see *CONSERVATION*

796   SW
FRILUFTSLIV. bi-m. SEK 75. Friluftsfraemjandet, P.O. Box 708, 101 30 Stockholm 1, Sweden. TEL 08-23-43-50. FAX 08-241903. Ed. Per Goethlin. adv.; bk.rev.; circ. 80,000.
    Formerly: I Aller Vaeder.

799.2   US   ISSN 0016-2620
FULL CRY; published exclusively for the American coon hound and trail hound enthusiast. 1939. m. $15. Gault Publications, Inc., Box 10, Boody, IL 62514. TEL 217-865-2332. FAX 217-865-2334. Ed. Seth Gault. adv.; bk.rev.; circ. 25,754.
    Description: For coon, bear, lion, bobcat and squirrel hunters.

799   US   ISSN 0016-2922
FUR - FISH - GAME. HARDING'S MAGAZINE. 1925. m. $15.95. A.R. Harding Publishing Co., 2878 E. Main St., Columbus, OH 43209. TEL 614-231-9585. Ed. Mitch Cox. adv.; bk.rev.; tr.lit.; circ. 110,000.
    Description: Presents hunting, trapping and fishing advice for practical outdoorsmen.

796.552   JA
GAKUJIN/ALPINIST. (Text in Japanese) 1947. m. Tokyo Shimbun Publications Dept., 2-3-13, Konan, Minato-ku, Tokyo 108, Japan. Ed. Takao Nakazono. circ. 150,000.

799   US
GAME & FISH. m. $2.50 per no. Game & Fish Publications, Inc., 2550 Newmarket Pkwy., Ste.110, Marietta, GA 30061-0741. TEL 404-953-9222. FAX 404-933-9510.

799.2   FR
GAZETTE OFFICIELLE DE LA CHASSE. every 10 days. 890 F. Office des Nouvelles Internationales, 18 rue de Folin, 64200 Biarritz, France. TEL 59-41-08-78. FAX 59-41-03-36. TELEX 570061. Ed. Jacques Darrigrand.

639.2   FR   ISSN 0046-5542
GAZETTE OFFICIELLE DE LA PECHE. Variant title: Gazette Officielle de la Peche et Environnement. 1959. every 10 days. 800 F. Office des Nouvelles Internationales, 18 rue de Folin, 64200 Biarritz, France. TEL 59-41-08-78. FAX 59-41-03-36. TELEX 570061. Ed. Jacques Darrigrand. (processed)

799   US   ISSN 0199-6517
GEORGIA SPORTSMAN. 1976. m. $14.95. Game & Fish Publications, Inc., 2250 Newmarket Pkwy., Ste. 110, Box 741, Marietta, GA 30061-0741. TEL 404-953-9222. Ed. J. Jacobs. circ. 50,000.

796.5   SA
GETAWAY. 1989. m. R.73 overseas. Ramsay, Son & Parker (Pty) Ltd., P.O. Box 180, Howard Place 7450, South Africa. TEL 021-5311391. FAX 021-5313333. TELEX 526931 SA. Ed. D. Steele. adv.; circ. 38,046.
    Description: Publishes articles on outdoor places of interest, game parks, nature conservation, photography, trailing and caravaning.

799.2   IT
GIORNALE DEL CACCIATORE. 1951. bi-m. free. Federazione Italiana della Caccia, Associazione Cacciatori Alto Adige, Via Manci 25, 39100 Bolzano, Italy. TEL 471-280626. FAX 471-281322. Ed. Ferrari Auer. adv.; bk.rev.; circ. 1,100.

GLEITSCHIRM; Zeitschrift fuer Gleitschirm. see *SPORTS AND GAMES*

GOLD PROSPECTOR. see *MINES AND MINING INDUSTRY*

799   CN
GONE FISHIN'. 1987. q. $15. 8 Wales Ave., Markham, Ont. L3P 2C1, Canada. Ed. Kelly Shankland. circ. 20,000.
    Description: Provides all the fishing and tourist information needed for a given area, such as what lakes hold what fish, what lures to bring, where to get bait, launching, servicing, where to stay, eat and other interests in the area.

GOOD BEACH GUIDE; indicates which beaches are likely to be polluted and which are believed to be free from sewage pollution. see *ENVIRONMENTAL STUDIES*

GOOD CAMPS GUIDE BRITAIN (YEAR). see *TRAVEL AND TOURISM*

GOOD CAMPS GUIDE EUROPE (YEAR). see *TRAVEL AND TOURISM*

GOOD CAMPS GUIDE FRANCE (YEAR). see *TRAVEL AND TOURISM*

796.93   UK
GOOD SKI GUIDE. 1981. irreg. £20. Hill Publications, 1-2 Dawes Court, 93 High St., Esher, Surrey KT10 9QD, England. Ed. John Hill. adv.; charts; illus.; stat.; tr.lit.; circ. 200,000. (back issues avail.)

796.93   UK
GOOD SKI RESORTS GUIDE. 1983. a. £2.50. Hill Publications, 1-2 Dawes Court, 93 High St., Esher, Surrey KT10 8AQ, England. TEL 0372-69799. adv.; charts; illus.; stat.; tr.lit.; circ. 40,000. (back issues avail.)

799   US   ISSN 0273-6691
GV191.2
GRAY'S SPORTING JOURNAL. 1975. 6/yr. $34.95 (effective Jan. 1992). Box 1207, Augusta, GA 30903-1207. TEL 800-458-4010. FAX 404-722-6060. Ed. Edward E. Gray. adv.; bk.rev.; circ. 30,000.
    Description: Hunting and fishing oriented literary magazine.

GREAT LAKES CAMPBOOK. see *TRAVEL AND TOURISM*

796.5   UK   ISSN 0140-7570
THE GREAT OUTDOORS. 1978. m. £27. George Outram & Co. Ltd., The Plaza Tower, East Kildride, Glasgow G74 1LW, Scotland. Ed. Cameron McNeish. circ. 27,112.

796.93   GW
DER GROSSE A D A C SKI ATLAS (YEAR). a. DM.44.80. (Allgemeiner Deutscher Automobil-Club e.V.) A D A C GmbH, Am Westpark 8, Postfach 70 01 26, D-8000 Munich, Germany. TEL 089-7676-0.

333.78   UK   ISSN 0017-4696
GROUNDSMAN. 1947. m. £30. (Institute of Groundsmanship) Adam Publishing Ltd., 42 West End Avenue, Pinner, Middlesex HA5 1BJ, England. TEL 081-868-3600. FAX 081-429-2374. Ed. Gene Price. adv.; bk.rev.; illus.; circ. 6,000 (controlled).
    Indexed: Sportsearch (1979-).
    —BLDSC shelfmark: 4220.150000.

GUIA QUATRO RODAS. CAMPING. see *TRAVEL AND TOURISM*

796 914.5   IT   ISSN 0072-792X
GUIDA CAMPING D'ITALIA. 1958. a. L.11000. Federazione Italiana del Campeggio e del Caravanning, Casella Postale 23, 50041 Calenzano (Florence), Italy. adv.

796.5   FR
GUIDE OFFICIEL CAMPING - CARAVANING. a. 62 F. (Federation Francaise de Camping et de Caravaning) Ediregie, B.P. 86, 94420 Le Plessis Trevise, France. FAX 45-93-25-93. TELEX EDIGIE 262572. adv.; circ. 135,000.

796.54   US   ISSN 1046-5774
GUIDE TO ACCREDITED CAMPS (YEAR). 1952. a. $10.95 (free with subscr. to Camping Magazine). American Camping Association, Inc., 5000 State Rd. 67 N., Martinsville, IN 46151-7902. TEL 317-342-8456. FAX 317-342-2065. index; circ. 14,000.
    Formerly: Parents' Guide to Accredited Camps; Which was formed by the merger of: Parents' Guide to Accredited Camps. West Edition; Parents' Guide to Accredited Camps. South Edition; Parents' Guide to Accredited Camps. Northeast Edition; Parents' Guide to Accredited Camps. Midwest Edition.
    Description: Lists over 2,000 camps accredited by the American Camping Association throughout the United States (and some abroad).

GUIDE TO CARAVAN AND CAMPING HOLIDAYS. see *TRAVEL AND TOURISM*

799.1   US   ISSN 0164-3746
GULF COAST FISHERMAN. Variant title: Harold Wells Gulf Coast Fisherman. 1976. q. $11.75. Harold Wells Gulf Coast Fisherman, Inc., Drawer P, Port Lavaca, TX 77979. FAX 512-552-8864. adv.; bk.rev.; circ. 10,500.
    Description: Covers all aspects of salt-water fishing from Florida to Texas.

799.2 636.7   US   ISSN 0279-5086
GUN DOG; upland bird and waterfowl dogs. 1981. bi-m. $17.97. Stover Publishing Co., Inc., 1901 Bell Ave., Ste. 4, Des Moines, IA 50315-1030. TEL 515-243-2472. FAX 515-243-0233. (Subscr. to: Box 343, Mt. Morris, IL 61054) Ed. Bob Wilbanks. adv.; bk.rev.; illus.
    Description: Gives hunting tips.

GUN SHOW CALENDAR. see *ANTIQUES*

799.202   US   ISSN 1042-6450
TS534.5
GUN TESTS; the consumer resource for the serious shooter. vol.3, no.3, 1991. m. $72 (foreign $80). Belvoir Publications, Inc., 75 Holly Hill Lane, Box 2626, Greenwich, CT 06836-2626. TEL 203-661-6111. FAX 203-661-4802. (Subscr. to: Box 420234, Palm Coast, FL 32142) Ed. Dave Tinker.

799.2   US
GUN WORLD ANNUAL. 1973. a. $3.95. Gallant - Charger Publishing, Inc., 34249 Camino Capistrano, Box HH, Capistrano Beach, CA 92624. TEL 714-493-2101. Ed. Jack Lewis. adv.; bk.rev.; illus.; circ. 126,000. (also avail. in microfilm from UMI)
    Formerly: Gun World Hunting Guide (ISSN 0362-4749)

SPORTS AND GAMES — OUTDOOR LIFE

799.3 US ISSN 0017-5684
TS535
GUNS & AMMO. 1958. m. $21.94. Petersen Publishing Co., 8490 Sunset Blvd., Los Angeles, CA 90069. TEL 213-854-2222. Ed. E. Bell, Jr. adv.; bk.rev.; charts; illus.; index; circ. 575,000. (also avail. in microform from UMI; reprint service avail. from UMI) **Indexed:** Consum.Ind., Mag.Ind., PMR, Sports Per.Ind. ●Also available online. Vendor(s): DIALOG.

797 US
HANG GLIDING.* 1970. m. membership. U S Hang Gliding Association, Box 8300, Colorado Springs, CO 80933. TEL 719-632-8300. Ed.Bd. adv.; bk.rev.; bibl.; charts; illus.; circ. 10,000. **Indexed:** Sportsearch (1978-).
Formerly (until 1976): Ground Skimmer.

796.5 790.01 UK ISSN 0263-8134
HARPERS SPORTS & LEISURE. 1930. every 3 wks. £68($102) includes Harpers Guide to Sports Trade. Harpers Publishing, 47A High St., Bushey, Watford, Herts WD2 1BD, England. TEL 081-950-9522. FAX 081-950-7998. Ed. S. Tomkinson. adv.; bk.rev.; film rev.; circ. 3,900.
Former titles: Harpers Sports; Harpers Sports and Camping (ISSN 0141-142X)
Description: Business magazine for the UK sports trade.

HELPING OUT IN THE OUTDOORS; a directory of volunteer jobs and internships in parks and forests nationwide. see BUSINESS AND ECONOMICS — Trade And Industrial Directories

799.1 NE
HENGELSPORT NIEUWS. 1977. bi-m. membership. Stichting Public Relations Hengelsport Friesland, Postbus 350, 8600 AJ Sneek, Netherlands. TEL 05154-9876. FAX 05154-9899. Ed. F. Meijer. adv.; bk.rev.; circ. 14,000.

919.4 796.74 AT ISSN 0085-1477
HERALD CARAVANNING GUIDE. 1931. a. Aus.$1. Herald Travel Bureau, Newspaper House, 247 Collins St., Melbourne, Vic. 3000, Australia. Ed. D. H. Day.

HIGH ADVENTURE; a Royal Rangers magazine for boys. see CHILDREN AND YOUTH — For

796.552 UK ISSN 0962-2667
HIGH MOUNTAIN SPORTS. 1982. m. $60. (British Mountaineering Council) High Magazine Ltd., 164 Barkby Rd., Leicester LE4 7LF, England. TEL 0533-460722. FAX 0533-460748. Ed. Geoff Birtles. adv.; bk.rev.; circ. 14,533. (back issues avail.)
Formerly: High Magazine (ISSN 0951-8940)
Description: Features on the climbing scene worldwide for hill walkers, mountaineers and rock climbers.

796 US
HIGHWAYS. 1966. m. (Good Sam Club) T L Enterprises, Inc., 29901 Agoura Rd., Agoura, CA 91301. TEL 818-991-4980. FAX 818-889-0750. Ed. David Griffith. adv.; circ. 550,000.
Formerly: Good Sam's Hi-Way Herald.
Description: For campers and recreational vehicle owners.

796.552 II
HIMALAYAN JOURNAL. (Text in English) 1928. a. Rs.200. Himalayan Club, P.O. Box 1905, Bombay 400 001, India. FAX 91-22-261-5977. Ed. Harish Kapadia. adv.; bk.rev.; charts; illus.; index; circ. 1,500. (tabloid format) **Indexed:** Helminthol.Abstr.

796.522 II ISSN 0018-1897
HIMAVANTA; India's only mountaineering monthly. (Text in English) 1969. m. Rs.35($12) Himalayan Federation, 63E Mohanirban Rd., Calcutta 700 029, India. TEL 74-1424. Ed. Kamal K. Guha. adv.; bk.rev.; circ. 11,000. (looseleaf format)
Description: Covers climbs, high altitude treks, explorations, glaciology, meteorology, climatology, environment, communications, archeology, sociology and anthropology of the Himalayas.

799.2 GW
HIRSCHMANNBRIEF. 1961. a. $5. Verein Hirschmann e.V., Schriftführer, Dr. Wolf-Eberhard Barth, 3424 Oderhaus Post St. Andreasberg, Germany. circ. 550.

796.5 NE
HOLLAND CAMPING. 1965. a. fl.14. Camping Media BV, Postbus 234, 6710 AH Arnhem, Netherlands. adv.; circ. 15,000.
Formerly: Camping Benelux.

799.1 US
HOOKED ON FISHING. bi-m. Southeast Outdoors, Inc., Box 682, Cape Girardeau, MO 63702-0682. TEL 314-651-3638. Ed. Sheri Robertson. circ. 10,500.

799.1 US
HOOKS AND LINES. bi-m. membership. International Women's Fishing Association, Drawer 3125, Palm Beach, FL 33480. Ed. Joan Willmott.

796 US ISSN 0018-4780
SK75
HOOSIER OUTDOORS. 1967. bi-m. $7.50. High Point Communications, Box 447, Cloverdale, IN 46120. TEL 317-795-6312. Ed. Philip E. Junker. adv.; bk.rev.; circ. 8,000. (back issues avail.)
Description: Outdoor activities in Indiana such as hunting, camping, fishing, boating and skiing.

796 US
HOT SPRINGS GAZETTE. 1977. q. $20. Silvertip Publishing Company, 12 S. Benton, Helena, MT 59601. Ed. Roger Phillips. adv.; bk.rev.; bibl.; charts; illus.; circ. 1,800. (back issues avail.)

HOUNDS. see SPORTS AND GAMES — Horses And Horsemanship

796.95 US
HUMMER TRAIL AND TOURING GUIDE. 1973. 5/yr. $7.95. Royal Printing, 112 Market St., Sun Prairie, WI 53590. TEL 608-837-5161. FAX 608-837-3946. Ed. Tom Anderson. adv.; circ. 20,000.
Description: Covers travel, trails, new products, events and personalities for snowmobilers in the Midwest.

799.2 US
HUNT; action hunting for action hunters. 1988. bi-m. $19.97. Timberline-B, Inc., Box 58069, Renton, WA 98058. TEL 206-226-4534. FAX 206-255-0320. Ed. Bill Boylon. adv.; circ. 87,500.

799.2 US
HUNT MAGAZINE. a. $2.95. Hunt Magazine, Box 58069, Renton, WA 98058. TEL 206-226-4534. FAX 206-255-0320.

799.2 US
HUNTER EDUCATION INSTRUCTOR. 1973. 8/yr. $12. Outdoor Empire Publishing, Inc., 511 Eastlake Ave. E., Box C 19000, Seattle, WA 98109. TEL 206-624-3845. Ed. Maureen Dolan. adv.; film rev.; charts; illus.; stat.; tr.lit.; index; circ. 10,000 (controlled). (tabloid format)
Former titles: Hunter Safety Instructor (ISSN 0737-6227); Hunter Safety News.

796.93 US
HUNTER MOUNTAIN NEWS. 1970. 12/yr. $15. (Hunter Mountain Ski Bowl) Hunter Mt. News Corp., Box 110, Syosset, NY 11791. TEL 516-496-4588. Ed. Paul E. Pepe. adv.; bk.rev.; charts; illus.; circ. 25,000.

799.2 US ISSN 0018-7860
HUNTER'S HORN. 1921. m. $10. Hunter's Horn, 114-120 E. Franklin Ave., Box 707, Sesser, IL 62884. TEL 618-625-2711. Ed. George Slankard. adv.; bk.rev.; illus.; circ. 9,800.
Description: Describes fox and wolf hunting.

799.2 US
HUNTING ANNUAL (LOS ANGELES). 1980. a. $6.95. Petersen Publishing Co., 8490 Sunset Blvd., Los Angeles, CA 90069. TEL 213-854-2222. Ed. Todd Smith. adv.; circ. 110,000.

799.2 US
HUNTING GUNS BY OUTDOOR LIFE & JIM CARMICHEL. 1984. a. $2.75. Times Mirror Magazines, Inc., 2 Park Ave., New York, NY 10016. TEL 212-779-5000. Ed. Vin T. Sparano. adv.

799 US
HUNTING RANCH BUSINESS. m. Fred King, Ed. & Pub., 5214 Starkridge, Houston, TX 77035. TEL 713-721-5919.

799.2 US ISSN 1053-4466
HUNTING REPORT: EDITION II - FOR BIRDSHOOTERS AND WATERFOWLERS. 1989. m. $45 (Canada and Mexico $51; elsewhere $66). Hunting Report, Inc., 12515 N. Kendall Dr., Ste. 302, Miami, FL 33186. TEL 305-598-0158. FAX 305-598-0916. Ed. Don Causey. adv. contact: Robin G. Powell. circ. 1,000. (looseleaf format; back issues avail.)

799.2 US ISSN 1052-4746
THE HUNTING REPORT FOR BIG GAME HUNTERS; serving the hunter who travels. 1981. m. $60 (Canada and Mexico $66; elsewhere $81). Oxpecker Enterprises, Inc., 12515 N. Kendall Dr., Ste. 302, Miami, FL 33186-1830. TEL 305-598-0735. FAX 305-598-0196. Ed. Don Causey. adv. contact: Robin G. Powell. bk.rev.; circ. 3,500. (looseleaf format; back issues avail.)

711 UK ISSN 1012-7720
I F P R A BULLETIN. q. International Federation of Park and Recreation Administration, General Secretary, The Grotto, Lower Basildon, Reading, Berkshire RG8 9NE, England. TEL (0491)-874222. FAX 0491-874059.

796.93 US
I LOVE NEW YORK SKIING AND WINTER ADVENTURES. a. free. Department of Economic Development, 1 Commerce Plaza, Albany, NY 12245. TEL 518-474-4116. FAX 518-486-6416. Ed. Joanne Thompson.
Description: Lists downhill and cross-country skiing centers and facilities.

799.1 US
I W F A YEARBOOK. 1955. a. membership. International Women's Fishing Association, Drawer 3125, Palm Beach, FL 33480. adv.; circ. 300.

333.78 US ISSN 0019-2155
ILLINOIS PARKS & RECREATION. 1970. bi-m. $20. Illinois Association of Park Districts, 211 E. Monroe, Springfield, IL 62701. TEL 217-523-4554. (Co-sponsor: Illinois Park and Recreation Association) Ed. Ted Flickinger. adv.; bk.rev.; illus.; stat.; circ. 4,000.
Formerly: Illinois Park and Recreation Quarterly.

799.1 US ISSN 0276-9905
SH401
IN-FISHERMAN; the journal of freshwater fishing. 1975. 7/yr. $16. In-Fisherman Communications Network, 651 Edgewood Dr., Box 999, Brainerd, MN 56401-0999. TEL 218-829-1648. FAX 218-829-3091. Ed. Doug Stange. adv.; circ. 336,400. **Indexed:** Access (1981-), Sports Per.Ind.

799.1 US ISSN 1048-4892
IN-FISHERMAN ANGLING ADVENTURES TRAVEL GUIDE; your travel and adventure guide to the world's best fishing, where, when, how. 1988. q. $12. In-Fisherman Communications Network, 651 Edgewood Dr., Box 999, Brainerd, MN 56401-0999. TEL 218-829-1648. FAX 218-289-3091.
Formerly (until 1989): In-Fisherman Angling Adventures (ISSN 1044-6826)

799.1 US
IN-FISHERMAN - WALLEYE GUIDE. 1983. a. In-Fisherman Communications Network, 651 Edgewood Dr., Box 999, Brainerd, MN 56401-0999. TEL 218-829-1648. FAX 218-829-3091. Ed. Doug Stange. adv.; circ. 197,000.

796.552 II
INDIAN MOUNTAINEER. (Text in English) 1978. s-a. Rs.10. Indian Mountaineering Foundation, Headquarters Complex, Benito Juarez Road, Anand Niketan, New Delhi 110021, India. Ed. M.C. Motwani. adv.; bk.rev.; circ. 2,000.

636.7 US
INFO (NORDMAN).* 1966. m. $20. International Sled Dog Racing Association, Box 5018, Woodland Park, CO 80866-5018. Ed. Pat Faherty. adv.; bk.rev.; circ. 2,000.

790.1 US
▼**INLINE.** 1991. bi-m. $14.97. InLine, Inc., 1919 14th St., Boulder, CO 80302. TEL 303-440-5111. Ed. Diane French. adv.; B&W page $2525, color page $3020. circ. 22,500 (paid); 26,000 (controlled).
Description: For in-line roller skating enthusiasts.

SPORTS AND GAMES — OUTDOOR LIFE

796.42   US
INSIDE TEXAS RUNNING. m. $12.50 (foreign $25). Joanne Schmidt, Ed. & Pub., 9514 Bristlebrook, Houston, TX 77083. TEL 713-498-3208. adv.; circ. 10,000.
  Description: Covers running, cycling, bi- and triathlon.

796.93   US
INSIDERS SKI LETTER. 1989. 10/yr. $33. Skiletter, Inc., 115 Lilly Pond Ln., Katonah, NY 10536. TEL 914-232-5094. Ed. I. William Berry.
  Description: Covers skiing for serious skiers.

799.1   US   ISSN 0257-1420
INTERNATIONAL ANGLER. 1973. bi-m. membership. International Game Fish Association, 1301 E. Atlantic Blvd., Pompano Beach, FL 33060-6744. TEL 305-467-0161. Ed. Ray Crawford. bk.rev.; illus.; stat.; circ. 25,000.
  Formerly: International Marine Angler.
  Description: Game fish world records, articles relating to recreational fishing, conservation and statistics on fishing.

799.32   US   ISSN 0739-0696
INTERNATIONAL BOWHUNTER. 1983. 6/yr. $12 (Canada and Mexico $19; elsewhere $29). (International Bowhunting Organization) International Bowhunting Publications, Inc., Rte.1, Box 41E, Box 67, Pillager, MN 56473-0067. TEL 218-746-3333. FAX 218-746-3333. Ed. Johnny E. Boatner. adv.: B&W page $849, color page $1099; adv. contact: Johnny Boatner. bk.rev.; film rev.; bibl.; charts; illus.; stat.; tr.lit.; circ. 57,000. (back issues avail.)

INTERNATIONAL CYCLE SPORT. see *SPORTS AND GAMES — Bicycles And Motorcycles*

796.5   GW   ISSN 0074-7122
INTERNATIONAL NATURIST GUIDE/INTERNATIONALER FKK-REISEFUEHRER/GUIDE NATURISTE INTERNATIONALE. a. DM.6.80. (International Naturist Federation) Richard Danehl's Verlag, Postfach 500344, 2000 Hamburg 50, Germany. adv.

796.91   IT
INTERNATIONAL SKATING. 8/yr. International Skating, Via Marco Polo, 3, 65100 Pescara, Italy. **Indexed:** Sportsearch (1984-).

INTERNATIONAL UNION OF ALPINE ASSOCIATIONS. BULLETIN/UNION INTERNATIONALE DES ASSOCIATIONS D'ALPINISME. BULLETIN. see *TRAVEL AND TOURISM*

796   AT
INTO THE BLUE. m. Coast and Mountain Walkers of New South Wales, Box 2449, G.P.O., Sydney, N.S.W. 2001, Australia. Ed. R. Nivison-Smith.

IOWA PARKS & RECREATION. see *CONSERVATION*

IOWA SIERRAN. see *CLUBS*

797   AT
IT. 1968. irreg. Aus.$0.10 per no. Canberra Bushwalking Club, Box 160, Canberra City, A.C.T. 2601, Australia.

796.552   JA
IWA-TO-YUKI/ROCK AND SNOW. (Text in Japanese) 1958. bi-m. Yama-kei Publishers Company, 1-1-33, Shiba-Daimon, Minato-ku, Tokyo 103, Japan. TEL 03-3436-4026. FAX 03-5472-4430. Ed. Tsunemichi Ikeda. circ. 50,000.

JACHT EN NATUURBEHEER. see *CONSERVATION*

799.2   DK
JAEGER. 1884. m. DKK 350 (typically set in July). Danmarks Jaegerforbund, Einer-Jensens Vaenge 1, 2000 Frederiksberg, Denmark. TEL 38 33 29 11. FAX 31-19-02-41. Ed. Martin Dahl-Hansen. adv.; bk.rev.; charts; illus.; stat.; index; circ. controlled.
  Formerly (until 1992): Dansk Jagt (ISSN 0011-6327)

799.2   GW   ISSN 0720-4523
JAEGER; Zeitschrift fuer die Jagdrevier. 1883. fortn. DM.11.60. Jahr-Verlag GmbH & Co., Burchardstr. 14, 2000 Hamburg 1, Germany. TEL 040-339660. FAX 040-33966208. TELEX 2163485. Ed. M. Kleymann. adv.; illus.; circ. 22,700.
  Formerly: Deutsche Jaeger-Zeitung (ISSN 0012-0324)
  Description: Discusses all aspects of hunting.

379.2   IT
JAEGERZEITUNG. (Text in German) 1951. bi-m. free. Sudtiroler Jagverband, Via Manci 25, 39100 Bolzano, Italy. TEL 471-280626. FAX 471-281322. adv.; bk.rev.; circ. 4,700.

799.2   GW
JAGD IN BAYERN. 1952. m. Landesjagdverband Bayern e.V., Implerstr. 25, D-8000 Munich 70, Germany. Ed. Alfred Preisser. circ. 43,000.
  Description: Examines wild animal welfare, guns, and pistols for the hunter.

799.2   GW   ISSN 0021-3926
JAGD UND JAEGER IN RHEINLAND-PFALZ. 1964. m. membership. (Landesjagdverband Rheinland-Pfalz) Verlag Dieter Hoffmann (Mainz), Senefelder Str. 25, 6500 Mainz 41, Germany. Ed. Nis Wagner. adv.; bk.rev.; circ. 17,500.
  Description: Emphasis is on hunting.

799.2   GW   ISSN 0021-3942
DER JAGDGEBRAUCHSHUND. 1965. m. DM.72.40. (Jagdgebrauchshundverband) B L V Verlagsgesellschaft mbH, Lothstr. 29, 8000 Munich 40, Germany. Ed. Karl Walch. adv.; bk.rev.; abstr.; illus.

799   DK   ISSN 0021-3977
JAGT OG FISKERI. 1923. m. DKK 120. Landsjagtforeningen, Frydendalsvej 20, 1809 Copenhagen K, Denmark. Ed. Villy Andersen. adv.; bk.rev.; illus.; circ. 50,000.
  Description: Covers hunting and fishing.

799.2   DK
JAGTHUNDEN. 1942. 10/yr. membership. Skovbjergvej 35, 7280 S. Felding, Denmark. adv.; circ. 6,000.

799   SW
JAKT OCH JAEGARE. 1940. m. SEK 140. Jaegarnas Riksfoerbund-Landsbygdens Jaegare, Saltsjoegatan 15, S-151 32 Soedertaelje, Sweden. Ed. Ulf Granstroem. adv.; bk.rev.; circ. 15,600.
  Description: Focuses on fishing and hunting.

799.2   SW
JAKTJOURNALEN. (Text in Swedish) 1970. 11/yr. SEK 325. AB Jaktjournalen, Box 10184, 434 44 Kungsbacka, Sweden. FAX 0300-16310. Ed. John Duff. adv.; bk.rev.; circ. 46,900.
  Description: Covers all aspects of hunting.

799   SW   ISSN 0021-406X
JAKTMAKER OCH FISKEVATTEN. 1913. m. SEK 69.50. B.O. Jahnsson, Ed. & Pub., Jakobsbergsplatsen 1, 724 61 Vaesteraas, Sweden. adv.; bk.rev.; circ. 60,642.
  Description: Looks at all aspects of fishing and hunting.

JERSEY SIERRAN. see *CONSERVATION*

799   FR
JOURNAL DU CHASSEUR. 1950. m. 75 F. Federation Departementementale des Chasseurs de la Gironde, Rue du petit Barail - B.P. 231, 33028 Bordeaux Cedex, France. TEL 56-39-88-23. Ed. Claude Businelli. adv.; bk.rev.; circ. 14,000.

JOURNAL OF APPLIED RECREATION RESEARCH. see *TRAVEL AND TOURISM*

796.5   US   ISSN 0021-9649
JOURNAL OF CHRISTIAN CAMPING. 1969. bi-m. $19.95 (foreign $21.95). Christian Camping International, Box 646, Wheaton, IL 60189. TEL 708-462-0300. FAX 708-462-0499. Ed. Skip Stogsdill. adv.; bk.rev.; illus.; stat.; index.
  Formerly: Camps and Conferences Magazine.
  Description: For camping professionals whose camps, conference and retreat centers are part of the Association.

JOURNAL OF LEISURE RESEARCH. see *LEISURE AND RECREATION*

333.7 658   US   ISSN 0735-1968
GV181.5
JOURNAL OF PARK AND RECREATION ADMINISTRATION. vol.4, 1986. q. $35 to individuals; institutions $40; foreign $45. Sagamore Publishing Inc., 302 W. Hill St., Box 673, Champaign, IL 61824-0673. TEL 217-359-5940. FAX 217-359-5979. **Indexed:** Sportsearch (1986-).
  —BLDSC shelfmark: 5029.145000.
  Description: Scholarly articles for the leisure service practitioner, focusing on planning, finance, organizational practice, personnel evaluation, programming, and marketing and promotion.

JOURNAL OF WILDERNESS MEDICINE. see *MEDICAL SCIENCES — Sports Medicine*

K O A DIRECTORY ROAD ATLAS AND CAMPING GUIDE. (Kampgrounds of America, Inc.) see *BUSINESS AND ECONOMICS — Trade And Industrial Directories*

799   AU
KAERNTNER JAEGER. 1971. q. membership. Kaerntner Jaegerschaft, Bahnhofstr. 38B, A-9020 Klagenfurt, Austria. Ed. G. Anderluh. adv.; bk.rev.; illus.
  Description: Covers all aspects of hunting.

796.5   BE   ISSN 0775-8545
KAMPEERTOERIST. 1952. m. (11/yr.) 795 Fr. (Vlaamse Kampeertoeristen) Making Magazines Media-Consultants, Koning Albertlaan 90, B-9000 Ghent, Belgium. TEL 091-200800. FAX 091-200886. adv.; bk.rev.; circ. 12,000.

KANSAS WILDLIFE & PARKS. see *CONSERVATION*

KASHSHAFAT AL-IMARAT/EMIRATES BOY SCOUTS. see *CLUBS*

790   US   ISSN 0192-3439
TL759.A1
KITELINES; quarterly journal of the worldwide kite community. 1977. q. $14 (foreign $18). Aeolus Press, Inc., Box 466, Randallstown, MD 21133-0466. TEL 410-922-1212. FAX 410-922-4262. Ed. Valerie Govig. adv.; bk.rev.; charts; illus.; index; circ. 13,000. (also avail. in microfiche; back issues avail.) **Indexed:** Ind.How To Do It.
  Supersedes: Kite Tales (ISSN 0192-3420)
  Description: Comprehensive international journal of kiting.

LAND AND WATER CONSERVATION FUND GRANTS MANUAL. see *CONSERVATION*

796.42   GW   ISSN 0047-4355
LEICHTATHLETIK. 1926. w. DM.224. B & W Bartels & Wernitz Sportverlag GmbH, Am Eichgarten 15, 1000 Berlin 41, Germany. Ed. Heinz Vogel. adv.; bk.rev.; index; circ. 10,000.

LEISURE MANAGER. see *LEISURE AND RECREATION*

LIVING AMONG NATURE DARINGLY!; how to for trappers, farmers, and homesteaders. see *GARDENING AND HORTICULTURE*

796.93   US
LONG ISLAND SKI. 1981. irreg. free. Leah S. Dunaief, Ed. & Pub., Box V.T., Setauket, NY 11733. TEL 516-751-1550. adv.; circ. 60,000.

796   US
LONG TRAIL NEWS. 1922. q. membership and exchange basis. Green Mountain Club, Inc., Box 889, Montpelier, VT 05601. TEL 802-223-3463. Ed. Katherine Borchert. adv.; bk.rev.; circ. 5,000.
  Formerly (until 1925): Green Mountain News.
  Description: News, information, letters, and announcements pertaining to the members and activities of the Green Mountain Club, which promotes hiking and conservation activities in this Vermont mountain range.

LOUISIANA CONSERVATIONIST. see *CONSERVATION*

799.2   US   ISSN 0744-3692
LOUISIANA GAME AND FISH. 1981. m. $14.95. Game & Fish Publications, Inc., 2250 Newmarket Pkwy., Ste. 110, Box 741, Marietta, GA 30061-0741. TEL 404-953-9222. Ed. Bob Borgwat. circ. 15,000.

SPORTS AND GAMES — OUTDOOR LIFE

799.2   XV   ISSN 0024-7014
LOVEC. (Text in Slovenian) 1918. m. 200 din.($10.45) Lovska Zveza Slovenije, Zupanciceva 9, Ljubljana, Slovenia. Eds. Tone Svetina, France Cvenkel.
    Description: Discusses hunting.

799.2 891.87 641.5 CS   ISSN 0541-8836
MAGAZIN POLOVNIKA. a. 25 Kcs. Priroda, Krizkova 9, 815 34 Bratislava, Czechoslovakia. TEL 472-41-45. illus.

799.2   SA
MAGNUM. (Text mainly in English; occasionally in Afrikaans) 1976. m. R.55 (foreign R.66)(effective 1991). South Africa Man 1982 Pty. Ltd., P.O. Box 35204, Northway 4065, South Africa. TEL 031-526-551. FAX 031-526566. Ed. Ronald K. Anger. adv.; bk.rev.; index; circ. 24,826. (back issues avail.)
    Formerly: Man.

799   US
MAINE SPORTSMAN. 1977. m. $12. All Outdoors, Box 365, Augusta, ME 04330. (Subscr. to: Box 507, Yarmouth, ME 04096) Ed. Harry Vanderweide. circ. 30,000.

799   FR
MAISON DE LA CHASSE ET DE LA NATURE. REVUE. 1969. a. per no. to non-members. (Maison de la Chasse et de la Nature) Editions Person, 34 rue de Penthievre, 75008 Paris, France. Ed. J.H. Person. adv.; bk.rev.; circ. 2,500.
    Formerly: Maison de la Chasse et de la Nature. Bulletin d'Information (ISSN 0987-741X)

MANITOBA NATURALISTS SOCIETY BULLETIN. see *CONSERVATION*

796.42   GW
MARATHON AKTUELL. 1981. m. DM.48($25) Sportverlag, Derfflinger Str. 34, D-4000 Duesseldorf 30, Germany. Ed. Burkhard Swara. adv.; bk.rev.; circ. 6,000. (back issues avail.)

MARINE & RECREATION NEWS. see *SPORTS AND GAMES — Boats And Boating*

MARINE PARKS JOURNAL. see *BIOLOGY*

MATKAILU/TOURISM. see *TRAVEL AND TOURISM*

799.2   IT
IL MESE DI CACCIA. m. (10/yr.). Associazione Nazionale Libera Caccia, Via Cavour 183-B, 00184 Rome, Italy. Ed. Mario Pagnoncelli. adv.; circ. 150,000.

352.7 799   US
MESSAGE POST; portable dwelling info-letter. 1980. 3/yr. $1 per no. Light Living Library, P.O. Box 190-F, Philomath, OR 97370. adv.; bk.rev.; circ. 1,000. (also avail. in microfiche; back issues avail.)
    Description: Emphasis on long-period backpack camping.

METSASTAJA. see *CONSERVATION*

799   FI   ISSN 0026-1629
METSASTYS JA KALASTUS. m. Fmk.373. Yhtyneet Kuvalehdet Oy, Maistraatinportti 1, 00240 Helsinki, Finland. TEL 0-15661. FAX 0-1566505. TELEX 121364. Ed. Mauri Soikkanen. adv.; illus.; circ. 33,548.
    Description: Concerns hunting and fishing.

799.1   US
MICHIGAN FISHERMAN. bi-m. Box 977, E. Lansing, MI 48826-0977. TEL 517-351-3074. Ed. Ken Darwin. adv.; circ. 40,000.

MICHIGAN NATURAL RESOURCES. see *CONSERVATION*

796.42   US
MICHIGAN RUNNER. 1979. 9/yr. $12.50. Great Lakes Sports Publications, Inc., 7990 W. Grand River, Ste. C, Brighton, MI 48116. TEL 313-227-4200. Ed. Dave Foley. circ. 12,000. (tabloid format)
    Description: Includes medical advice, calendar of running events and news.

796.94   US
MICHIGAN SNOWMOBILER. 6/yr. Box 417, E. Jordan, MI 49727-0417. TEL 616-536-2371. Ed. Lyle Shipe. adv.; circ. 38,500.

799 614   US   ISSN 0539-8908
SK91
MICHIGAN SPORTSMAN. 1976. m. $14.95. Game & Fish Publications, Inc., 2250 Newmarket Pkwy., Ste. 110, Box 741, Marietta, GA 30061-0741. TEL 404-953-9222. Ed. Ken Dunwoody. circ. 37,000. **Indexed:** Mich.Mag.Ind.

MIDEASTERN CAMPBOOK. see *TRAVEL AND TOURISM*

799.2   US
MIDWEST BOWHUNTER. 1985. bi-m. $7.95 (foreign $13.95). 413 Pearl St., Sioux City, IA 51101. TEL 712-255-5132. Ed. Ritch A. Stolpe. adv.; bk.rev.; circ. 5,000.
    Description: For the hunting archer. Provides hunter success stories and photos, conservation news and information on new products.

799   US
MIDWEST OUTDOORS. 1967. m. $11.95. Midwest Outdoors Ltd., 111 Shore Drive, Hinsdale, IL 60521. TEL 708-887-7722. FAX 708-887-1958. Ed. Eugene M. Laulunen. adv.; bk.rev.; charts; illus.; circ. 44,300. (tabloid format)

799.2   IT
MIGRATORI ALATI. 78. q. L.10000. Associazione Cacciatori Migratori Acquatici, Via Cascine, 4, 21027 Ispra (Va), Italy. Ed. Gianfranco Realini. adv.; bk.rev.; circ. 6,500.
    Formerly: Migratori Acquatici.
    Description: Covers hunting and ornithology.

799   US   ISSN 0274-8622
MINNESOTA SPORTSMAN. 1977. m. $14.95. Game & Fish Publications, Inc., 2250 Newmarket Pkwy., Ste. 110, Box 741, Marietta, GA 30061-0741. TEL 404-953-9222. Ed. Ken Dunwoody. adv.; illus.; circ. 40,000.

799   US
MISSISSIPPI GAME & FISH. m. Game & Fish Publications, Inc., 2250 Newmarket Pkwy., Ste. 110, Box 741, Marietta, GA 30061-0741. TEL 404-953-9222. FAX 404-933-9510. Ed. Bob Borgwat. adv.; circ. 11,800.

MISSISSIPPI OUTDOORS. see *CONSERVATION*

MISSOURI CONSERVATIONIST. see *CONSERVATION*

796.552   GW
MITTEILUNGSBLATT DER SEKTION LUDWIGSBURG DES D A V. 1972. a. D A V Ludwigsburg, Deutscher Alpenverein, Sektion Ludwigsburg, Postfach 304, 7140 Ludwigsburg, Germany. TEL 07141-927893. circ. 2,500. (back issues avail.)
    Description: Covers mountaineering and hiking.

796.42   AT   ISSN 0047-7672
MODERN ATHLETE AND COACH. 1962. q. Aus.$25. Australian Track & Field Coaches Association, 1 Fox Ave., Athelstone, S.A. 5076, Australia. TEL 08-337-4510. Ed. Jess Jarver. adv.; bk.rev.; circ. 2,500. **Indexed:** Phys.Ed.Ind., Sportsearch (1974-).
—BLDSC shelfmark: 5883.690000.
    Description: Covers coaching on all track and field events, and related subjects such as nutrition, psychology, and bio-mechanics.

796.522   FR   ISSN 0047-7923
MONTAGNE ET ALPINISME. 1955. 4/yr. 155 F. Club Alpin Francais, 24, av. de Laumiere, 75019 Paris, France. Ed. Annie Bertholet. adv.; illus.; charts; circ. 75,000.
    Description: Covers all aspects of mountaineering.

799   US
MONTANA OUTDOORS. 1970. bi-m. $7. Department of Fish, Wildlife and Parks, 1420 E. Sixth, Helena, MT 59620. TEL 406-444-2474. Ed. Dave Books. bk.rev.; illus.; circ. 40,000. (back issues avail.)

MOTOR CARAVAN WORLD. see *TRANSPORTATION*

796.5   UK
MOTOR CARAVANNER. 1960. m. membership. Motor Caravanners' Club, 71 Cricklewood Broadway, London NW2 3JR, England. Ed. Bill Brooks. adv.; bk.rev.; circ. controlled.

796.5   UK
MOTORCARAVAN & MOTORHOME MONTHLY. 1966. m. £35. Sanglier Publications Ltd., The Maltings, Manor Ln., Bourne, Lincs. PE10 9PH, England. TEL 0778-393313. FAX 0778-425437. Ed. Penny Smith. adv.; bk.rev.; circ. 23,000.
    Incorporating: Motor Caravan and Camping (ISSN 0027-1829)

796.5 388.346   US   ISSN 0744-074X
TX1100
MOTORHOME. 1968. 12/yr. $20. T L Enterprises, Inc., 29901 Agoura Rd., Agoura, CA 91301. TEL 818-991-4980. Ed. Bill Estes. adv.; illus.; mkt.; tr.mk.; circ. 120,000. **Indexed:** Consum.Ind.
    Former titles: Motorhome Life (ISSN 0164-503X) & Motorhome Life and Camper Coachman (ISSN 0361-1043); Which was formed by the merger of: Motorhome Life (ISSN 0027-2221) & Camper Coachman; Incorporating: Van Life and Family Trucking (ISSN 0160-6107)
    Description: Devoted exclusively to the motorhome enthusiast's lifestyle. Vehicle test, travel features, buyer's guides, new product previews, technical tips.

MOUNT BULLER NEWS. see *TRAVEL AND TOURISM*

796.552   UK   ISSN 0964-3427
MOUNTAIN. 1968. bi-m. $33. Mountain Magazine Ltd., Globe Works, Penistone Rd., Sheffield S6 3AE, England. TEL 0742-822-340. FAX 0742-820016. Ed. B.C. Newman. adv.; bk.rev.; index; circ. 15,000. (back issues avail.)
    Description: Features the leading edge of the sport with new developments in related technology an equipment for mountaineers and rock climbers.

796.552   SA
MOUNTAIN CLUB OF SOUTH AFRICA. JOURNAL. (Text in Afrikaans, English) 1894. a. R.18. Mountain Club of South Africa, 97 Hatfield St., Cape Town 8001, South Africa. TEL 021-453-412. Ed. P.D. Attenborough. adv.; bk.rev.; circ. 2,800.

MOUNTAIN VISITOR. see *TRAVEL AND TOURISM*

796.522   US   ISSN 0027-2620
F886
MOUNTAINEER (SEATTLE); to explore, study, preserve and enjoy the natural beauty of Northwest America. 1907. m. (plus special issues). $15. Mountaineers, Inc., 300 Third Ave., W., Seattle, WA 98119-4117. FAX 206-284-4977. Ed. Ken Lans. adv.; bk.rev.; circ. 13,000. **Indexed:** GeoRef.

799.3   US
MUSKY HUNTER MAGAZINE. bi-m. Esox Publishing, Inc., 959 W. Mason St., Green Bay, WI 54303-1762. TEL 414-496-0334. Ed. Joe Bucher. circ. 6,000.

799.3   US   ISSN 0027-5360
MUZZLE BLASTS. 1939. m. $30. National Muzzle Loading Rifle Association, Box 67, Friendship, IN 47021. TEL 812-667-5131. FAX 812-667-5137. Ed. Sharon Cunningham. adv.; bk.rev.; bibl.; charts; illus.; index; circ. 27,000.

796.552   US   ISSN 0274-5720
TS536.6.M8
MUZZLELOADER. 1974. bi-m. $14. Rebel Publishing Co., Inc., Route 5, Box 347M, Texarkana, TX 75501. TEL 903-832-4726. Ed. Bill Scurlock. adv.; bk.rev.; index; circ. 18,000. (back issues avail.)
    Description: Focuses on building, shooting, and hunting with muzzleloading guns, and on the history of muzzleloading guns in North America.

MYSLIVOST. see *CONSERVATION*

796.42   US   ISSN 0736-7783
GV1060.6
N C A A MEN'S AND WOMEN'S CROSS COUNTRY AND TRACK & FIELD RULES. 1922. a. $3. National Collegiate Athletic Association, Circulation Department, Box 7347, Overland Park, KS 66207-0347. TEL 913-339-1900. illus.; circ. 10,000.
    Formerly: Official National Collegiate Athletic Association Track and Field Guide (ISSN 0196-9358)
    Description: Covers official signals, interpretations, and rulings.

SPORTS AND GAMES — OUTDOOR LIFE

796.93   US   ISSN 0741-9279
GV854.A1
N C A A MEN'S AND WOMEN'S SKIING RULES. 1963. a. $4. National Collegiate Athletic Association, Circulation Department, Box 7347, Overland Park, KS 66207-0347. TEL 913-339-1900. illus.; circ. 1,000.
    Former titles: N C A A Skiing Rules; (until 1980): Official National Collegiate Athletic Association Skiing Rules; National Collegiate Athletic Association Official Skiing Rules (ISSN 0469-8592)
    Description: Covers official signals, interpretations, and rulings.

776.5 658   US
N C O A NEWS. 1981. m. membership. National Campground Owners Association, 11307 Sunset Hills Rd., Suite B-7, Reston, VA 22090. TEL 703-471-0143. Ed. Dawn M. Mancuso. adv.; bk.rev.; circ. 3,300.
    Description: Covers news in the commercial campground and resort park industry.

799   UK
N R A JOURNAL. 1860. q. National Rifle Association, Bisley Camp, Brookwood, Woking, Surrey GU24 OPB, England. TEL 0483-797777. FAX 0483-797285. Ed. R.F. Constant. adv.; circ. 6,000. Indexed: Sportsearch.
    Description: News and informational articles pertaining to the activities and membership of the NRA with results of competitions, personal profiles, agendas of meetings, and announcements of events.

797   AT
N.S.W. SKINDIVER. (New South Wales) 1950. 4/mo. Aus.$10. Australian Underwater Federation, N.S.W. Branch Sydney Metropolitan Zone, P.O. Box 44, Sans Souci, N.S.W. 2219, Australia. Ed. M.V. Sheehan. adv.; bk.rev.; illus.; circ. 4,500.
    Former titles: Skin Diving News from New South Wales; Australian Skindivers (ISSN 0005-0253); N.S.W. Skindiver.

796.42   US   ISSN 0744-2416
NATIONAL MASTERS NEWS. 1977. m. $25. National Masters News, Box 2372, Van Nuys, CA 91404. TEL 818-785-1895. FAX 818-782-1135. Ed. Al Sheahan. adv.; bk.rev.; stat.; circ. 5,500. (tabloid format; back issues avail.)
    Description: Covers running and track and field for athletes forty and over.

796.5   US
NATIONAL PARK GUIDE. 1966. a. $12.95. Prentice Hall Travel Directories (Subsidiary of: Simon & Schuster), 108 Wilmot Rd., Ste. 300, Deerfield, IL 60015. TEL 708-945-3737. FAX 708-945-3786. adv.: B&W page $1350, color page $1620; trim 8 x 10 3/4. circ. 25,000.
    Former titles: Allstate Motor Club National Park Guide; Rand McNally National Park Guide (ISSN 0079-9629)

799.31   US   ISSN 0077-5738
NATIONAL SKEET SHOOTING ASSOCIATION. RECORDS ANNUAL. 1947. a. $12. National Skeet Shooting Association, Box 680007, San Antonio, TX 78268. TEL 512-688-3371. Ed. Susie Fluckiger. adv.; index; circ. 18,000.

796   US
NATIONAL TRAILS COUNCIL. NEWSLETTER. 1971. q. $50. American Trails, 1400 16th St., N.W. Ste. 300, Washington, DC 20036. TEL 202-797-5418. FAX 202-797-5411. Ed. Nancy Levine. bk.rev.; circ. 1,000.
    Description: Provides information on trail issues.

NATIONAL WILDLIFE; dedicated to the wise use of our natural resources. see CONSERVATION

799   IT
NATURA OGGI. m. L.72000. Rizzoli Editore-Corriere della Sera, Via A. Rizzoli 2, 20132 Milan, Italy. Ed. L. Grandori.

NEBRASKALAND. see CONSERVATION

796.93   IT   ISSN 0028-4114
TD868
NEVE INTERNATIONAL. 1959. q. L.24000 (foreign L.35000). Publitec, Corso Massimo d'Azeglio 60, 10126 Turin, Italy. TEL 011-687093. FAX 011-6509801. Ed. Carlo G. Bertolotti. adv.; circ. 10,000.
    Description: Covers maintenance and management of wintersport resorts, snowmaking and ski slopes and lifts.

796   IT   ISSN 0028-4122
NEVESPORT ILLUSTRATO. 1965. w. (Oct.-Mar.). m. (Apr.-Sep.). L.15000. Guido Pietroni, Ed. & Pub., Via Bergamo 12a, 20135 Milan, Italy. adv.; bk.rev. (tabloid format)

796   US
NEW ALASKA OUTDOORS. m. Swensen's Alaska Outdoors Corp., 400 D St., Anchorage, AK 99501-2326. TEL 907-278-7004. Ed. Evan Swensen. adv.; circ. 52,800.

796   US
NEW ENGLAND OUT-OF-DOORS. m. 510 King St., Littleton, MA 01460-1250. TEL 508-486-4785. Ed. Bryant Chaplin. circ. 23,000.

796.42   US
NEW ENGLAND RUNNER. 1983. 8/yr. $18.95. New England Sports Publications, Box 252, Boston, MA 02113. TEL 617-891-1844. FAX 617-899-0481. adv.; circ. 14,575.
    Description: Covers running, triathalons, and track and field events in the six New England States and New York.

NEW ENGLAND SIERRAN. see CONSERVATION

796.93   US
NEW ENGLAND SKIERS' GUIDE. 1983. a. $2.95. Ski Racing International, Box 1125, Waitsfield, VT 05673-1125. TEL 802-496-7700. FAX 802-496-7704. Ed. Gary Black, Jr. adv.; circ. 90,000 (controlled).

796.93   US
▼**NEW ENGLAND SNOWBOARDER**. 1990. 7/yr. $7. North Shore Weeklies, Box 468, Marblehead, MA 01945-0468. TEL 617-639-2838. Ed. H. Brent Wilbur. circ. 15,000 (controlled).
    Description: Provides how-to instructions for snowboarders of all ages. Includes regional news of snowboarding events.

NEW HAMPSHIRE FISH AND GAME LAWS. see LAW

799.1   US   ISSN 1054-4623
NEW JERSEY LAKE SURVEY FISHING MAPS GUIDE. 1989. a. $8.95. New Jersey Sportsmen's Guides, Box 100, Somerdale, NJ 08083. TEL 609-665-8350. FAX 609-665-8656. Ed. Steve Perrone. adv.; circ. 6,000.
    Formerly (until 1991): New Jersey Lake Survey Map Guide (ISSN 1043-6405)
    Description: Covers fishing and exploring New Jersey lakes, with information on fish species, lake depths, and more.

796.42   US
NEW MEXICO SKIERS' GUIDE. a. Ski Racing International, Box 1125, Waitsfield, VT 05673-1125. TEL 802-496-7700. FAX 802-496-7704.

799   US
NEW YORK SPORTSMAN. 1972. 8/yr. $14.97. Northwoods Publications, Inc., 430 N. Front St., Lemoyne, PA 17043. TEL 717-761-1400. adv.; circ. 44,798.
    Description: Editorial features include hunting, fishing and trapping articles, as well as where-to and how-to within the regional scene. Includes news items and conservation.

799.1 797.1   NZ   ISSN 0113-9606
NEW ZEALAND FISHERMAN. 1988. m. NZ.$27.50 (foreign NZ.$110). Vantage Publishing Limited, Cnr. Halsey & Madden Streets, Freemans Bay, Auckland, New Zealand. TEL 09-3098-292. FAX 09-3096-361. Ed. William B. Kirk. circ. 25,000. (tabloid format; back issues avail.)
    Description: Covers sport fishing, boat and landbased, inland fresh water and ocean fishing, and conservation.

NEW ZEALAND POWERBOAT. see SPORTS AND GAMES — Boats And Boating

799.2   NZ   ISSN 0028-8802
NEW ZEALAND WILDLIFE. 1962. q. NZ.$20. New Zealand Deerstalkers' Association Inc., Box 6514, Te Aro, Wellington, New Zealand. FAX 0064-4-891-280. Ed. B.H. MacKrell. adv.; bk.rev.; charts; illus.; cum.index; circ. 4,500.
    Description: Provides hunting tips.

799   GW   ISSN 0048-0339
NIEDERSAECHSISCHER JAEGER. 1950. s-m. DM.85.80. (Landesjagdverband Niedersachsen) Landbuch-Verlag GmbH, Kabelkamp 6, Postfach 160, 3000 Hannover 1, Germany. adv.; bk.rev.
    Description: Covers cultural, historical, social, economical and ecological aspects of the region. Includes list of events and exhibitions.

799.2   US
NIKON HUNTER'S WORLD. 1987. a. $2.50. (Nikon, Inc.) Aqua-Field Publishing Co., Inc., 66 W. Gilbert St., Shrewsbury, NJ 07702. TEL 201-842-8300. Ed. Stephen Ferber. adv.; circ. 110,000.
    Formerly: Nikon's Big Game Hunting.

796.93 910.09 380   US
NORDIC NETWORK. 1976. bi-m. $25. Cross Country Ski Areas Association, 259 Bolton Rd., Winchester, NH 03470. TEL 603-239-4341. FAX 603-239-6387. Dir. Chris Frado. adv.; bk.rev.; circ. 450.
    Formerly: Cross Country Ski Areas of America Newsletter.

NORSK FISKARALMANAKK. see FISH AND FISHERIES

799.1   US   ISSN 1043-2450
NORTH AMERICAN FISHERMAN. 1988. bi-m. $18. North American Outdoor Group, Inc., 12301 Whitewater Dr., Box 3403, Minnetonka, MN 55343. TEL 612-936-0555. FAX 612-936-9755. Ed. Mark LaBarbara. adv.; bk.rev.; circ. 100,000.
    Description: A forum for avid and affluent fishermen.

799.2   US   ISSN 0194-4320
SK40
NORTH AMERICAN HUNTER. 1979. 7/yr. $18. North American Outdoor Group, Inc., 12301 Whitewater Dr., Box 3401, Minnetonka, MN 55343. TEL 612-936-9333. FAX 612-936-9755. Ed. Bill Miller. adv.; bk.rev.; circ. 225,000.
    Description: A forum for avid and affluent fishermen.

NORTH AMERICAN PYLON; dedicated to sports car autocrossing. see TRANSPORTATION — Automobiles

799.2   US   ISSN 0746-6250
NORTH AMERICAN WHITETAIL. 8/yr. $14.95. Game & Fish Publications, Inc., 2250 Newmarket Pkwy., Ste. 110, Box 741, Marietta, GA 30061-0741. TEL 404-953-9222. Ed. Gordon Wittington. adv.; circ. 125,000.

799   US
NORTH CAROLINA GAME & FISH. m. Game & Fish Publications, Inc., 2250 Newmarket Pkwy., Ste. 110, Box 741, Marietta, GA 30061-0741. TEL 404-953-9222. FAX 404-933-9510. Ed. Jeff Samsel.

NORTH CENTRAL CAMPBOOK. see TRAVEL AND TOURISM

NORTH DAKOTA OUTDOORS. see CONSERVATION

790 333.7   US
NORTHEAST MEMO.* 1966. q. free. U.S. Heritage Conservation and Recreation Service, Northeast Regional Office, c/o National Park Service, 2nd Chestnut St, No. 260 Custom House, Philadelphia, PA 19106. Ed. Roslyn H. Brewer. circ. 4,300. (processed; back issues avail.)
    Formerly: Northeast Outdoor Memo.

796.5   US   ISSN 0199-8463
NORTHEAST OUTDOORS. 1968. m. $8. Northeast Outdoors, Inc., 70 Edwin Ave., Box 2180, Waterbury, CT 06722. TEL 203-755-0158. FAX 203-755-3480. Ed. John Florian. bk.rev.; circ. 20,000. (tabloid format)
    Description: Describes campgrounds and tourist regions in the Northeastern U.S for family campers or those with RV's.

SPORTS AND GAMES — OUTDOOR LIFE

796.96   CN   ISSN 0011-3115
NORTHERN CURLING REVIEW. 1964. m. (Oct.-Apr.). Riegel Publications, 10623 Kingsway Ave., Edmonton, Alta. T5G 2Z6, Canada. TEL 403-426-1719. adv.; illus.; circ. 13,000. **Indexed:** Sportsearch.
Formerly: Curling Review.

NORTHWEST LIVING!; Washington, Oregon, Idaho, Western Canada, Alaska. see GENERAL INTEREST PERIODICALS — United States

769.93   US
NORTHWEST SKIER. 1958. m. $7.95. Cascade Communications, Inc., Box 99666, Seattle, WA 98199. TEL 206-329-4795. (Subscr. to: Box 23070, Seattle, WA 98102-0370) Ed. Jenny Peterson. adv.; bk.rev.; circ. 30,000. (back issues avail.) **Indexed:** Sportsearch.
Former titles: Northwest Skier and Northwest Sports (ISSN 0274-9149); Northwest Skier (ISSN 0029-3458)
Description: Covers skiing in Alaska, Idaho, Montana, Oregon, Washington and British Columbia.

796.93   US
NORTHWEST SKIING. 1984. 4/yr. $4. Western Ski Professionals, 12006 N.E. Glisan, Portland, OR 97220. TEL 503-254-3279. Ed. John Hoefling. adv.; bk.rev.; film rev.; stat.; tr.lit.; circ. 12,500. (back issues avail.)
Formerly: Northwest Ski News.

NORTHWESTERN CAMPBOOK; including location maps. see TRAVEL AND TOURISM

799   FR   ISSN 0048-0835
NOS CHASSES. 1958. m. 20 F.($5) Editions Chasse Sports, 28 rue de l'Ermitage, 75020 Paris, France. Ed. Marc Lambert. adv.; circ. 32,000. (controlled)

799.2   IT   ISSN 0029-4365
NOTIZIARIO DI CACCIA E PESCA-TIRO A VOLO. 1947. w. L.120000. Greentime s.r.l., Via Barberia 11, 40123 Bologna, Italy. Ed. Olga Misley. adv.; bk.rev.; illus.; circ. 50,000.
Description: Covers hunting, fishing and clay pigeon shooting.

797   US
OCEAN SPORTS INTERNATIONAL. q. Ocean Sports International Publishing, 1509 Seabright, Ste. B1, Santa Cruz, CA 95062. TEL 408-459-0425. FAX 408-462-0452. Ed. Susan Watrous. circ. 45,625.

OESTERREICHISCHE TOURISTENZEITUNG. see TRAVEL AND TOURISM

796   AU   ISSN 0029-8840
OESTERREICHISCHER ALPENVEREIN. AKADEMISCHE SEKTION GRAZ. MITTEILUNGEN. 1892. a. membership. Oesterreichischer Alpenverein, Akademische Sektion Graz, Rechbauerstr. 12, A-8010 Graz, Austria. adv.; bk.rev.; illus.; circ. 1,000.

796.522   AU   ISSN 0029-9715
OESTERREICHISCHER ALPENVEREIN. MITTEILUNGEN. 1863. bi-m. membership. Oesterreichischer Alpenverein, Wilhelm Greilstr. 15, A-6020 Innsbruck, Austria. TEL 0512-59547-11. FAX 0512-575528. Ed. Gerold Benedikter. adv.; bk.rev.; index; circ. 120,000. **Indexed:** Bibl.Cart.
Description: Covers mountain climbing and hiking, tourism, travel reports, expeditons, skiing, forestry, environmental planning and protection, history, and new publications. Includes readers' letters.

796 680   FR
L'OFFICIEL DES TERRAINS DE CAMPING ET DE CARAVANING. 1972. 9/yr. 270 F. Ediregie, B.P. 86, 94420 Le Plessis Trevise, France. FAX 45-93-25-93. TELEX EDIGIE 262572. Ed. Jacques Gout. adv.; circ. 11,000.

799.1   US
OHIO FISHERMAN. m. 1432 Parsons Ave., Columbus, OH 43207. TEL 614-445-7506. Ed. Dan Armitage.

799   US   ISSN 0746-6013
OKLAHOMA GAME & FISH. 1982. m. $14.95. Game & Fish Publications, Inc., 2250 Newmarket Pkwy., Ste. 110, Box 741, Marietta, GA 30061-0741. TEL 404-953-9222. Ed. Nick Gilmore. adv.; circ. 7,200.

797.172   UK   ISSN 0269-9575
ON BOARD INTERNATIONAL. 9/yr. £30. Stone Leisure Group Ltd., Andrew House, 2a Granville Rd., Sidcup, Kent DA14 4BN, England. TEL 081-302-6150. FAX 081-300-2315. Ed. Robert Griffiths. circ. 25,000.
Description: Covers all aspects of windsurfing.

796.172   UK   ISSN 0956-019X
ON BOARD SURF MAGAZINE. 1989. bi-m. £10 (foreign £15). Stone Leisure Group Ltd., Andrew House, 2A Granville Rd., Sidcup, Kent DA14 4BN, England. TEL 081-302-6150. FAX 081-300-2315. Ed. Mark Griffiths. adv.; circ. 15,000. (back issues avail.)
Description: Covers the best of European and international surfing.

796   US
ON THE TRAIL. m. Box 456, E. Syracuse, NY 13057-0456. TEL 315-437-9296. Ed. Dana S. Brown.

797   NE   ISSN 0048-1696
ONDERWATERSPORT. 1970. m. fl.40($20) Nederlandse Onderwatersport Bond - Netherlands Underwatersport Federation, De Kievit 2, 2751 CR Moerkapelle, Netherlands. Ed. G.G.M. van Oosterhout. adv.; bk.rev.; charts; illus.; tr.lit.; circ. 12,000. (processed)

799.1   CN
ONTARIO FISHERMAN. 1979. bi-m. Can.$13 (foreign Can.$16). Fishing Ontario Publications Ltd., R.R. 2, Wiarton, Ont. N0H 2T0, Canada. TEL 519-534-2889. FAX 519-534-2770. Ed. Darryl Choronzey. adv.; circ. 28,230.

799   CN   ISSN 0707-3178
ONTARIO OUT OF DOORS. 1969. 10/yr. Can.$24.95. MacLean Hunter Ltd., Special Interest Division, 227 Front St. E., Toronto, Ont. M5A 1E8. TEL 416-368-0185. FAX 416-941-9113. Ed. Burt Myers. adv.; bk.rev.; illus.; circ. 60,000. **Indexed:** Can.Per.Ind., CMI.
Description: Directed to the Ontario outdoor enthusiasts of with information about fishing, hunting, and camping activities. Includes where-to and how-to articles, and examines conservation of natural resources.

796.93   CN
▼**ONTARIO SKI GUIDE.** 1990. a. Can.$3.50 (typically set in Jan.). Charles Marketing Inc., 240 Westwood Rd., Ste. 9B, P.O. Box 1590, Guelph, Ont. N1H 7W9, Canada. TEL 519-821-5326. FAX 519-821-5326. Ed. Ted Charles. adv.; circ. 200,000.
Description: Guide to all alpine and cross country trails, hills, and resorts in Ontario.

796.95   CN
ONTARIO SNOWMOBILER. 1986. 5/yr. Can $17($22) (Ontario Federation of Snowmobile Clubs) Ontario Snowmobiler Publishing Ltd., RR 3, Centre Road, Mount Albert, Ont. L0G 1M0, Canada. TEL 416-473-7009. FAX 416-473-5217. Ed. Mark Lester. adv.; maps; circ. 51,500. (back issues avail.)
Description: News about snowmobiling and the snowmobile industry.

797.1   CN   ISSN 0226-5702
ONTARIO WATER SKIER. 1974. 4/yr. Can.$10. Ontario Water Ski Association, 1220 Sheppard Ave. E., Willowdale, Ont. M2K 2X1, Canada. TEL 416-495-4201. FAX 416-495-4310. TELEX 06-986157. Ed. Walter Sokolowski. adv.; B&W page Can.$240; trim 7 1/2 x 10. bk.rev.; illus.; circ. 1,500. **Indexed:** Sportsearch (1978-).
Description: Articles on water skiing, equipment, technique, events and activities in recreational and competitive forms of the sport.

333.78   UK
OPEN SPACES. 1927. 3/yr. £7.50 (Europe £10; elsewhere £15). Commons Open Spaces and Footpaths Preservation Society, 25A Bell St., Henley-on-Thames, Oxon RG9 2BA, England. TEL 0491-573535. Ed. K. Ashbrook. adv.; bk.rev.; circ. 3,000. **Indexed:** Rural Recreat.Tour.Abstr., World Agri.Econ.& Rural Sociol.Abstr.
Former titles: Commons, Open Spaces and Footpaths Preservation Society. Journal (ISSN 0010-3322); Commons, Open Spaces and Footpaths Preservation Society. Annual Report (ISSN 0265-8445)
Description: Journal of general interest to environmentalists concerned with land and public recreational access especially commons, village greens and rights of way.

790.1   US   ISSN 0886-1080
GV200.4
ORIENTEERING NORTH AMERICA. 1985. m. $20. (United States Orienteering Federation) S M & L Berman Publishing Co., 23 Fayette St., Cambridge, MA 02139-1111. TEL 617-868-7416. FAX 617-876-8186. (Alt. addr.: Box 1444, Forest Park, GA 30051) Eds. Sara Mae Berman, Lawrence J. Berman. adv.; bk.rev.; circ. 1,850. (back issues avail.)
Description: Covers all aspects of the sport of orienteering. Geared towards all levels of interest.

OUT AND ABOUT SMITH MOUNTAIN LAKE. see TRAVEL AND TOURISM

OUT WEST. see TRAVEL AND TOURISM

796.5   GW   ISSN 0935-3356
OUTDOOR; das andere Reisemagazin. 1988. bi-m. DM.45.90 (foreign DM.51.90). Rotpunkt Verlag, Ziegeleistr. 16, 7056 Weinstadt, Germany. TEL 07151-65042. FAX 07151-660571. (Subscr. to: Zenit Pressevertrieb GmbH, Postfach 810640, 7000 Stuttgart, Germany) Eds. Stephan Glocker, Robert Bartscher. adv.; bk.rev.; index; circ. 45,000. (back issues avail.)

796.5   UK
OUTDOOR ACTION.* 1961. m. £18. Hawker Consumer Publishing Ltd., 13 Park House, 140 Battersea Park Rd., London SW11 4NB, England. TEL 081-943-5000. FAX 081-943-5684. TELEX 895-2440-HAYMRT-G. Ed. Laura McCaffrey. adv.; bk.rev.; charts; illus.
Former titles: Camper; Practical Camper (ISSN 0032-6356)
Description: Information for the backpacker and the family camper.

796 917.1 333.7   CN   ISSN 0315-0542
OUTDOOR CANADA. 1972. 9/yr. Can.$24. Outdoor Canada Publishing Ltd., 703 Evans Ave., Ste. 202, Toronto, Ont. M9C 5E9, Canada. TEL 416-695-0311. FAX 416-695-0382. Ed. Teddi Brown. adv.; illus.; tr.lit.; circ. 124,525. (also avail. in microform from MIM) **Indexed:** Can.Per.Ind., CMI, Sportsearch.
Description: For active, outdoor Canadians and their families. Covers fishing, paddling, hiking, hunting, exploring, conservation and other natural interest topics.

799.06   CN   ISSN 0700-9909
OUTDOOR CREST. 1975. irreg. free. Toronto Sportsmen's Association, 17 Mill St., Willowdale, Ont. M2P 1B3, Canada. TEL 416-487-4477. Ed. Peter Edwards. illus.; circ. 1,200.
Formerly: Outdoor Crest Newsletter (ISSN 0700-9895)

799   US   ISSN 0030-7076
SK1
OUTDOOR LIFE. 1898. m. $13.94 (effective 1992). Times Mirror Magazines, Inc., 2 Park Ave., New York, NY 10016. TEL 212-779-5000. (Subscr. to: Box 54733, Boulder, CO 80322. TEL 800-365-1580) Ed. Vin. T. Sparano. adv.; illus.; circ. 1,500,000. (also avail. in microform from UMI; reprint service avail. from UMI) **Indexed:** Consum.Ind., Jun.High.Mag.Abstr., Mag.Ind., PMR, R.G., Sports Per.Ind., TOM.
●Also available online. Vendor(s): DIALOG.
Description: Concentrates on hunting and fishing.

796.5   US
OUTDOOR LIFE GUIDES. q. $2.75 per no. Times Mirror Magazines, Inc., 2 Park Ave., New York, NY 10016. TEL 212-779-5000.

SPORTS AND GAMES — OUTDOOR LIFE

688.76　　　　SA　　ISSN 1015-1451
OUTDOOR LIVING AND SPORTS GOODS (YEAR). a. South African Foreign Trade Organisation, Publishing Division, P.O. Box 782706, Sandton 2146, South Africa. TEL 011-883-3737. FAX 011-883-6569. TELEX 4-24111 SA. adv.

OUTDOOR NEWS. see *CONSERVATION*

OUTDOOR NEWS BULLETIN. see *CONSERVATION*

OUTDOOR OKLAHOMA. see *CONSERVATION*

799　　　　US
OUTDOOR PRESS. 1966. w. $40. Outdoor Press, N. 2012 Ruby St., Spokane, WA 99207. TEL 509-328-9292. FAX 509-327-9861. Ed. Fred C. Peterson II. adv.; bk.rev.; circ. 6,000. (tabloid format)
Description: Reports on hunting and fishing in the Pacific Northwest.

796　　　　US
OUTDOOR RETAILER. 1980. m. Pacifica Publishing Corporation, 31652 Second Ave., Box 348, South Laguna, CA 92677-0348. TEL 714-499-4591. FAX 714-499-5092. Ed. Pam Montgomery. circ. 12,154.

790.1　　　　AT
OUTDOOR SHOWMAN. 1949. bi-m. Aus.$20. Victorian Showmen's Guild, Box 36, Ascot Vale, Vic. 3032, Australia. TEL 61-3-376-8544. Ed. N. Herbst. adv.; circ. 1,000.

OUTDOOR SINGLES NETWORK. see *SINGLES' INTERESTS AND LIFESTYLES*

790.1　　　　US
OUTDOOR SPORTS AND RECREATION;* bringing the Minnesota and Wisconsin outdoors to the nation. 1946. bi-m. $9.95. Sport Publications Inc., 2700 Darling Dr., Alexandria, MN 56308-8608. FAX 612-944-1230. Ed. John Hall. adv.; bk.rev.; circ. 30,000.
Formerly: Sports and Recreation (ISSN 0892-8355)

796　　　　US
OUTDOORS ILLUSTRATED. q. Market Focus Publications, 904 Eighth Ave. S., Nashville, TN 37203. TEL 615-256-8844. Ed. Bill Hudgins. circ. 250,000.

051　　　　US　　ISSN 0893-195X
OUTDOORS, RECREATION & LEISURE. q. $2.95 per no. Aegis Group - Publishers (Subsidiary of: Lintas - Ceco Communications), 30400 Van Dyke Ave., Warren, MI 48093. TEL 313-574-9100.

OUTDOORS UNLIMITED. see *CONSERVATION*

796　　　　US　　ISSN 0278-1433
GV191.2
OUTSIDE (CHICAGO, 1980). 1976. 12/yr. $18. Mariah Publications Corporation, 1165 N. Clark St., Chicago, IL 60610. TEL 312-951-0990. FAX 312-664-5397. (Subscr. to: Box 51733, Boulder, CO 80321-1733) Ed. Mark Bryant. adv.; bk.rev.; illus.; circ. 375,000. (also avail. in microfilm from UMI; reprint service avail. from UMI) **Indexed:** Access (1980-), Sportsearch (1980-)
Former titles (until 1980): Mariah - Outside (ISSN 0194-4371); (until 1979) Mariah (ISSN 0149-7790)
Description: Inspires people to enjoy fuller, more rewarding lives through year-round participation in sports, travel, events, photography, and politics of the world.

797.2　　　　US
PACIFIC DIVER. 1988. bi-m. $14.95. Western Outdoors Publications, 3197-E Airport Loop Dr., Costa Mesa, CA 92626. TEL 714-546-4370. FAX 714-662-3486. Ed. John Brumm. adv.; bk.rev.; circ. 25,000.
Description: For Pacific Coast sports divers, features dive boat schedules and other information.

796.552　　　　FR
PARIS-CHAMONIX. 5/yr. 25 F.($5) Club Alpin Francais, Section de Paris, 7 rue la Boetie, 75008 Paris, France. Ed. Monique Rebiffe. adv.; bk.rev.; illus.; circ. 10,000. (back issues avail.)

PARKS AND RECREATION; journal of park and recreation management. see *CONSERVATION*

333.78　　　　UK
PARKS, GOLF COURSES AND SPORTS GROUNDS. 1935. m. £27. Clarke & Hunter (London) Ltd., 61 London Rd., Staines, Middx. TW18 4BN, England. TEL 0784-461326. FAX 0784-462073. Ed. Alan Guthrie. adv.; bk.rev.; abstr.; bibl.; charts; illus.; stat.; index; circ. 6,580. **Indexed:** Hort.Abstr., Sportsearch (1976-).
Formerly: Parks and Sports Grounds (ISSN 0031-224X)
Description: Concentrates on design, construction and maintenance of turf areas in parks, recreation areas and sports grounds.

799　　　　CN
▼**PARLONS PLEIN AIR CHASSE & PECHE.** 1991. 11/yr. Can.$32.95. Quebecor Ventes Media, 801 Sherbrooke St. E., 2nd Fl., Montreal, Que. H2L 4X9, Canada. TEL 514-597-2231. FAX 514-597-1932. Ed. Jean Page. adv.; Pierre/Tremblay. circ. 100,000. (tabloid format)

PEAK AND PRAIRIE. see *CONSERVATION*

799　　　　SZ
PECHEUR ROMAND. 1936. m. 42 Fr. (foreign 52 Fr.). Presses Centrales Lausanne SA, Rue de Geneve 7, 1003 Lausanne, Switzerland. Ed. A. Quartier. adv.; bk.rev.; charts; illus.; tr.lit.; index; cum.index; circ. 6,500.
Former titles: Nature Information; Pecheur et Chasseur Suisses (ISSN 0031-3734)
Description: Covers fishing and hunting.

796.5　　　　US　　ISSN 0031-434X
SH1
PENNSYLVANIA ANGLER. 1931. m. $5. Fish Commission, Box 1673, Harrisburg, PA 17105-1673. Ed. Art Michaels. bk.rev.; circ. 65,000.
Description: Covers fishing, boating and camping.

799　　　　US
PENNSYLVANIA GAME & FISH. 1982. m. $14.95. Game & Fish Publications, Inc., 2250 Newmarket Pkwy., Ste. 110, Box 741, Marietta, GA 30061-0741. TEL 404-953-9222. Ed. Kim Reighton. adv.; circ. 28,000.
Formerly: Pennsylvania Outdoors (ISSN 0745-225X)

799.2　　　　US　　ISSN 0031-451X
SK351
PENNSYLVANIA GAME NEWS. 1931. m. $9. Game Commission, 2001 Elmerton Ave., Harrisburg, PA 17110-9797. TEL 717-787-3745. FAX 717-772-2411. Ed. Bob Mitchell. bk.rev.; illus.; index; circ. 200,000. (also avail. in microform from UMI; reprint service avail. from UMI) **Indexed:** Biol.Abstr., Biol.Dig.

799　　　　US
PENNSYLVANIA SPORTSMAN. 8/yr. Northwoods Publications, Inc., 430 N. Front St., Lemoyne, PA 17043. TEL 717-761-1400. adv.
Description: Covers hunting, fishing, and trapping, as well as conservation for the outdoorsman.

799.1 614.7　　　　IT
PESCA IN. m. L.65000 (Europe L.95000; elsewhere L.100000). Ed.A.I. s.r.l. (Edizioni Aeronautiche Italiane), V. Guinicelli 4, 50133 Florence, Italy. TEL 055-574774. FAX 055-5740103. TELEX 580217 EDAI I. Ed. Riccardo Galigani. adv.; circ. 64,500.
Description: Covers freshwater fishing. Contains competition reports, scientific articles and environmental issues.

799.1　　　　IT
PESCA IN MARE. m. L.65000 (Europe L.95000; elsewhere L.100000). Ed.A.I. s.r.l. (Edizioni Aeronautiche Italiane), V. Guinicelli 4, 50133 Florence, Italy. TEL 055-574774. FAX 055-570103. TELEX 580217 EDAI I. adv.; circ. 81,000.
Description: Covers fishing, fishing boats, nautical environmental issues.

799.1　　　　IT
PESCARE MARE. q. L.16000 (foreign L.24000). Editoriale Olimpia S.p.A., Viale Milton 7, 50129 Florence, Italy. TEL 055-473843. FAX 055-499195. Ed. Alessandro Menchi.

799.1　　　　BL
PESCATUR. 1969. 6/yr. Grupo Editorial Proper, Rua Jose Clemente, 69 e 162, CEP 24000, Niteroi, RJ, Brazil. Ed. Iolande T. Marcier. adv.; circ. 30,000.

739.7　　　　US　　ISSN 1040-1865
PETERSEN'S HANDGUNS. m. $23.94. Petersen Publishing Co., 8490 Sunset Blvd., Los Angeles, CA 90069. TEL 213-854-2222. Ed. J. Libourel. circ. 150,800.

799.2　　　　US　　ISSN 0146-4671
SK1
PETERSEN'S HUNTING. 1973. m. $19.94. Petersen Publishing Co., 8490 Sunset Blvd., Los Angeles, CA 90069. TEL 213-854-2222. Ed. Craig Boddington. adv.; bk.rev.; illus.; circ. 343,900. (also avail. in microform from UMI)

799.1　　　　SZ　　ISSN 0031-6318
PETRI-HEIL; unabhaengige Sportfischerzeitung. 1950. m. 52.50 Fr. Graf und Neuhaus A.G., Moehrlistr. 69, CH-8033 Zurich, Switzerland. Ed. H. Dietiker. circ. 20,500.

799.2　　　　US
PHEASANTS FOREVER. 1982. 5/yr. $20. Pheasants Forever Inc., Box 75473, St. Paul, MN 55175. TEL 612-481-7142. FAX 612-481-0715. adv.; circ. 44,014.
Description: For pheasant hunters and enthusiasts. Focuses on conservation and the importance of wildlife, specifically upland birds.

PIONYRSKA STEZKA; mesicnik pro sport, turistiku, brannost. see *CHILDREN AND YOUTH — For*

799.2　　　　GW　　ISSN 0340-7829
DIE PIRSCH; Magazin fuer Jagd, Wild, Natur. 1948. fortn. DM.154. B L V Verlagsgesellschaft mbH, Lothstr. 29, 8000 Munich 40, Germany. FAX 1270534. TELEX 5215087. Ed. Michael Lewicki. adv.; bk.rev.; illus.
Formed by merger of: Pirsch (ISSN 0032-0269); Deutscher Jaeger (ISSN 0012-1118)

796.5　　　　FR　　ISSN 0048-427X
PLAISIRS DE LA CHASSE. 1952. 12/yr. 300 F. Imprimerie de Champagne, 14, rue du Patronage Laique, 52003 Chaumont Cedex, France. Ed. Antoine Cohen-Potin. adv.; circ. 55,000.

799.1　　　　FR　　ISSN 0032-0501
PLAISIRS DE LA PECHE. (Not published 1987-1988) 1953. bi-m. 149 F. (foreign 209 F.). Editions du Cameleon, 11 rue Vauthier, 92100 Boulogne Billancourt, France. TEL 1-46-04-48-84. FAX 1-46-04-26-48. Ed. Jean Tesseyre. adv.; bk.rev.; circ. 35,000.
Description: Covers fly fishing, ecology, and freshwater management.

796　　　　FR
PLANCHE A VOILE. q. Editions de l'Angle Aigu, 5 rue de Commandant Pilot, 92522 Neuilly-sur-Seine, France. **Indexed:** Sportsearch (1984-).

796　　　　FR
PLANCHE MAGAZINE. m. Editions de l'Angle Aigu, 5 rue du Commandant Pilot, 92522 Neuilly-sur-Seine, France. **Indexed:** Sportsearch (1988-).

799　　　　CN　　ISSN 0228-3530
LA PLONGEE; le magazine Francais des plongeurs d'Amerique. (Text in French) 1973. 6/yr. Can.$18($12) Federation Quebecoise des Activites Subaquatiques (F.Q.A.S.), 4545 Ave. Pierre-de-Coubertin, C.P. 1000, Succursale M, Montreal, Que. H1V 3R2, Canada. TEL 514-252-3009. FAX 514-252-3162. Ed. P. Couture. adv.; bk.rev.; circ. 7,000.

799　　　　CS
POL'OVNICTVO A RYBARSTVO/HUNTING AND FISHING. m. $51. (Slovak Hunters' Union) Obzor, Ceskoslovenskej Armady 35, 815 85 Bratislava, Czechoslovakia. (Co-sponsor: Slovak Fishermen's Union) **Indexed:** Ind.Vet., Poult.Abstr.

SPORTS AND GAMES — OUTDOOR LIFE

796   US
POLYHEDRON NEWSZINE. 1981. m. $20 membership. (Role Playing Game Association Network) T S R, Inc., Box 509, Lake Geneva, WI 53147. (Subscr. to: Box 5695, Boston, MA 02206) Ed. Jean Rabe. circ. 12,000.
 Description: Features articles on role-playing games, news about network activities and the game industry, previews of upcoming releases, and convention reports.

POOLWAYS; the magazine of outdoor living (year). see *SPORTS AND GAMES*

796.522   US   ISSN 0092-2226
F217.B6
POTOMAC APPALACHIAN.* 1932. m. $6. Potomac Appalachian Trail Club, Inc., 118 Park St., S.E., Vienna, VA 22180-4609. Ed.Bd. adv.; bk.rev.; illus.; circ. 3,800. **Indexed:** Sportsearch.
 Incorporates (in 1972): Potomac Appalachian Forecast; Formerly (until 1971): Potomac Appalachian Trail Club. Bulletin (ISSN 0032-5635)
 Description: Covers hiking and mountaineering.

796.93   US   ISSN 0145-4471
GV854.A1
POWDER. 1971. 7/yr. $12.95. Surfer Publications, Inc., 33046 Calle Aviador, San Juan Capistrano, CA 92675. TEL 714-496-5922. FAX 714-496-7849. Ed. Steve Casimiro. adv.; illus.; circ. 115,000.
 Indexed: Sports Per.Ind., Sportsearch (1979-).

796.93   SA   ISSN 1018-1385
POWER BOAT AND SKI. 1988. bi-m. R.24($12) Yachting News (Pty) Ltd., P.O. Box 3473, Cape Town 8000, South Africa. TEL 021-4617472. FAX 021-4613758. Ed. Geoff Dekenah. circ. 4,500.
 Formerly (until Nov. 1991): Power and Ski (ISSN 1012-3288)

POWER STROKE. see *SPORTS AND GAMES — Boats And Boating*

796   UK
PRACTICAL CARAVAN. 1966. m. £55. Haymarket Magazines Ltd., 38-42 Hampton Rd., Teddington, Middx. TW11 0JE, England. TEL 081-943-5000. TELEX 895-2440-HAYMRT-G. Ed. Bruce Black. circ. 51,529.
 Description: Product tests and tips about caravans.

796.5   US
▼**PRACTICAL SURVIVAL;** the voice of natural living and self-reliance. 1991. bi-m. $18 ($23 to Canada; elsewhere $28). Mountain Star International, Inc., 1750 30th St., Ste. 498, Boulder, CO 80301. TEL 303-449-4128. Ed. Tom Slizewski. adv.; illus.; circ. 125,000.
 Description: Covers all aspects of survival, including alternative lifestyles, technical reviews of equipment, self-reliance, edible plants, and more.

PSYCHOLOGY AND SOCIOLOGY OF SPORT: CURRENT SELECTED RESEARCH. see *PSYCHOLOGY*

799   CN   ISSN 0229-3811
GV585.3.Q4
QUEBEC (PROVINCE) DEPARTMENT OF RECREATION, FISH AND GAME. ANNUAL REPORT/MINISTERE DU LOISIR DE LA CHASSE ET DE LA PECHE. RAPPORT ANNUEL. (Editions in English, French) 1980. a. Can.$4. Publications du Quebec, C.P. 1005, Quebec, Que. G1K 7B5, Canada. TEL 418-643-5150.
 Formerly: Quebec (Province) Department of Tourism, Fish and Game. Annual Report (ISSN 0481-2786)

QUINNEHTUKQUT. see *CONSERVATION*

796.95   US
RACE & RALLY. 1968. 3/yr. $6.50. Snowmobiler Publications, Inc., c/o James E. Beilke, Ed., Box 993, Alexandria, MN 56308. TEL 612-763-5411. FAX 612-763-5411. adv.; circ. 100,000. **Indexed:** Sportsearch.
 Formerly: Snowmobiler's Race and Rally.

796.42   UK
RACE WALKING RECORD. 1941. m. £3.50. Race Walking Association, 65 Lordship Lane, London SE22, England. Ed. John Hedgethorne. circ. 1,000.

796.42   US
RACETIME.* 1989. m. $11.95. 15073 Keswick St., Van Nuys, CA 91405-1133. TEL 408-773-9699. Ed. Karl Laucher. circ. 5,000.
 Description: Covers racing events shown on the three major networks and cable stations.

RAMBLING TODAY. see *CONSERVATION*

796.54   US   ISSN 0733-8309
GV191.35
RAND MCNALLY CAMPGROUND AND TRAILER PARK GUIDE. EASTERN.. a. Prentice Hall Press (Subsidiary of: Simon & Schuster), One Gulf & Western Plaza, New York, NY 10023. TEL 212-373-8500.
 Supersedes in part: Rand McNally Campground and Trailer Park Guide (ISSN 0079-9610); Which was formerly: Rand McNally Guidebook to Campgrounds; Rand McNally Travel Trailer Guide (ISSN 0079-9645)

799 917.704   US
RAND MCNALLY FISHING HOTSPOTS: MIDWEST. 1987. a. $7.95. Prentice Hall Press (Subsidiary of: Simon & Schuster), One Gulf & Western Plaza, New York, NY 10023. TEL 212-373-8500. Ed. Jean Postlewaite. adv.; circ. 35,855.

796.5   CN
RATHERBY. 9/yr. Can.$10. Keeper Publications, 28 Fairy Ave., Box 2849, Huntsville, Ont. P0A 1K0, Canada. TEL 705-789-6600. FAX 705-789-6600. adv.; circ. 14,000.
 Description: Calendar, folklore and nature magazine for Muskoka Cottagers.

333.78   NE
RECREATIE EN TOERISME. 1968. m (11/yr.). fl.112 to non-members. Koninklijke Nederlandse Toeristenbond ANWB - Royal Dutch Touring Club, Wassenaarseweg 220, Postbus 93200, 2509 BA The Hague, Netherlands. Ed. Joop Janssen. adv.; bk.rev.; illus.; circ. 2,500. **Indexed:** Dok.Str., HRIS, Rural Recreat.Tour.Abstr., World Agri.Econ.& Rural Sociol.Abstr.
 Formerly: Recreatievoorzieningen.

RECREATION AND OUTDOOR LIFE DIRECTORY; a guide to national and international organizations. see *BUSINESS AND ECONOMICS — Trade And Industrial Directories*

RECREATION EXECUTIVE REPORT. see *LEISURE AND RECREATION*

796   US
RECREATION NEWS. m. Icarus Publishers, Inc., Box 32335, Washington, DC 20007. TEL 202-965-6960. Ed. Sam E. Polson. adv.; circ. 104,000.

796.93   US   ISSN 0746-4541
RECREATIONAL SKIER. 1969. 5/yr. membership. Skier Education Foundation, c/o U.S. Rec. Ski Association, Box 25469, Anaheim, CA 92825-5469. TEL 714-634-1050. FAX 714-634-2305. Ed. Howard Lee. adv.; bk.rev.; illus.; circ. 32,000. (tabloid format)
 Former titles: U S Ski News; Far West Ski News; Far West News (ISSN 0014-7648)

796.552   GW
REUTLINGER ALPINIST; Magazin der Sektion Reutlingen im Deutschen Alpenverein. 1984. q. Werbe-Design-Service GmbH, Tuebingerstr. 96, 7410 Reutlingen, Germany. TEL 07121-320987. bibl.; charts; stat.; index.
 Description: Description of adventures in the mountains, climbing and tourist excursions.

796.9   FR
REVUE ALPINE. q. 60 F. (Club Alpin Francais, Section Rhone-Alpes) Publications Periodiques Specialisees, 11, rue d'Algerie, 69001 Lyon, France. adv.; circ. 6,000.

799.2   FR   ISSN 0035-3752
REVUE NATIONALE DE LA CHASSE.* m. 230 F. Gerpresse, 78 rue Jules Gesde, 92300 Levallois-Perret, France. TEL 672-018-280. Ed. Jacques Simeon. adv.; bibl.; illus.; circ. 135,000.

799.2   GW   ISSN 0171-0796
RHEINISCHE-WESTFAELISCHER JAEGER. 1947. m. DM.46.80 (foreign DM.61.20). (Landesjagdverband Nordrhein-Westfalen e.V.) Landwirtschaftsverlag GmbH, Huelsbrockstr. 2, 4400 Muenster-Hiltrup, Germany. TEL 02501-80-10. FAX 0251-801-204. adv.; circ. 63,700. (back issues avail.)

799.1   BN   ISSN 0035-4953
RIBARSKI LIST. 1926. q. 200 din. per no. Sportsko-Ribovolovni Savez Bosne i Hercegovine, Stevana Sindelica 1-II, 71000 Sarajevo, Bosnia Hercegovina. Ed. Mustafa Lagumdzija. adv.; bk.rev.; circ. 35,000.

799.1   CI   ISSN 0350-6789
RIBOLOV. (Text in Serbo-Croatian) 1953. bi-m. free. Hrvatski Sportsko Ribolovni Savez - Croatian Sports Fishing Association, Trg Sportova 11, Zagreb, Croatia. FAX 041-325864. Ed. Damir Valdgoni. adv.; circ. 35,000.
 Formerly: Sportski Ribolov (ISSN 0038-8289)

RING JUNGER BUENDE. MITTEILUNGEN. see *CHILDREN AND YOUTH — About*

796.42   US   ISSN 0739-3784
ROAD RACE MANAGEMENT NEWSLETTER. 1982. m. $84. Road Race Management, Inc., 2101 Wilson Blvd., Ste. 437, Arlington, VA 22201. TEL 703-276-0093. Ed. Phil Stewart. adv.; circ. 600. (back issues avail.) **Indexed:** Sportsearch (1985-).
 Description: For sponsors, directors and organizers of long-distance running events.

796.522   AT   ISSN 0816-2425
ROCK (PRAHRAN). 1978-1980; resumed 1983. biennial. Aus.$6.95. Wild Publications Pty. Ltd., P.O. Box 415, Prahran, Vic. 3181, Australia. Ed. Chris Baxter. adv.; circ. 3,000.

796.552   US   ISSN 0885-5722
ROCK & ICE. 1984. bi-m. $24 (Canada and Mexico $36; elsewhere $44). Eldorado Publishing, Box 3595, Boulder, CO 80307. TEL 303-499-8410. Ed. George Bracksieck. adv.; bk.rev.; charts; illus.; circ. 18,500. (back issues avail.)
 Description: Covers America's climbing and other related outdoor adventures.

797.2   US
▼**RODALE'S SCUBA DIVING.** 1992. bi-m. Rodale Press, Inc., 33 Minor St., Emmaus, PA 18098. TEL 215-967-5171. adv.; illus.; circ. 125,000.
 Description: Covers all aspects of scuba diving for both enthusiasts and professionals.

796.552   GW   ISSN 0935-3372
ROTPUNKT; das Klettermagazin. 1985. bi-m. DM.45.90 (foreign DM.51.90). Rotpunkt Verlag, Ziegeleistr. 16, 7056 Weinstadt, Germany. TEL 07151-65042. FAX 07151-660571. (Subscr. to: Rotpunkt Leserservice, Postfach 810640, 7000 Stuttgart 80, Germany) Eds. Peter Schindler, Gunar Homan. adv.; bk.rev.; bibl.; stat.; circ. 30,000. (back issues avail.)
 Description: Focuses on climbing and mountaineering.

796.42   US   ISSN 0892-5038
RUNNING JOURNAL. 1984. m. $20. Carolina Runner, Inc., Box 157, Greeneville, TN 37744. FAX 615-638-3328. adv.; bk.rev.; circ. 12,000.
 Formerly: Racing South.
 Description: Covers running in the Southeast, along with race walking, bi- and triathloning. Includes a calendar of events covering 13 states.

799.1   GW
RUTE UND ROLLE. 1949. m. DM.58.20. Top Special Verlag, Gaensemarkt 24, 2000 Hamburg 36, Germany.
 Formerly: Deutscher Angelsport (ISSN 0323-3472)

RYBARSTVI. see *FISH AND FISHERIES*

796   US   ISSN 0085-6592
S F I BULLETIN. 1951. 10/yr. $10. Sport Fishing Institute, 1010 Massachusetts Ave., N.W., Ste.320, Washington, DC 20001. TEL 202-898-0770. Ed. Volfuer. adv.; bibl.; charts; illus.; circ. 15,000.
 Indexed: Environ.Abstr.
 Formerly: Sport Fishing Institute. Bulletin (ISSN 0097-0492)

SPORTS AND GAMES — OUTDOOR LIFE   4555

799.2 US
SAFARI; the journal of big game hunting. 1971. bi-m. $30 in U.S., Can, & Mex.; elsewhere $55. Safari Club International, 4800 W. Gates Pass Rd., Tucson, AZ 85745. TEL 602-620-1220. Ed. William R. Quimby. adv.; bk.rev.; illus.; circ. 17,000.

799.2 FR ISSN 0036-2867
SAINT HUBERT. 1901. m. 280 F. (foreign 380 F.). M.T.E., 17, place de General de Gaulle, 93100 Montreuil, France. Ed. J. Sire. adv.; bk.rev.; bibl.; illus.

SALAR. see *FISH AND FISHERIES*

799.1 CN
SALMO SALAR. 1976. bi-m. Association des Pecheurs Sportifs de Saumons du Quebec, 7525 Place Martin, Charlesbourg, Que., Canada.

799.1 UK ISSN 0036-3545
SALMON AND TROUT MAGAZINE. 1903. 3/yr. £2.25. John Sherratt & Son Ltd., Park Rd., Altrincham, Cheshire, England. Ed. P. Turing. adv.; bk.rev.; circ. 5,500. **Indexed:** Biol.Abstr.
—BLDSC shelfmark: 8071.000000.

799.1 US ISSN 0029-3431
SALMON - TROUT STEELHEADER. 1967. bi-m. $14.95. Frank Amato Publications, Box 02112, Portland, OR 97202. TEL 503-653-8108. FAX 503-653-2766. Ed. Frank W. Amato. adv.; bk.rev.; illus.; circ. 29,000.
Formerly: Northwest Salmon - Trout Steelheader.

799.1 US
SALT WATER FISHING. a. Times Mirror Magazines, Inc., 2 Park Ave., New York, NY 10016. TEL 212-779-5000.

799.1 US ISSN 0036-3618
SALT WATER SPORTSMAN. 1939. m. $19.95. (Salt Water Sportsman, Inc.) Times Mirror Magazines, Inc., 280 Summer St., Boston, MA 02210. TEL 617-439-9977. FAX 617-439-9357. (Subscr. to: Box 54358, Boulder, CO 80322) Ed. Barry Gibson. adv.; bk.rev.; illus.; index; circ. 137,000. (also avail. in microfilm from UMI; avail. in floppy disk) **Indexed:** Consum.Ind., PMR, Sportsearch.
Description: Covers marine fishing.

SANFORD EVANS GOLD BOOK OF SNOWMOBILE DATA AND USED PRICES. see *SPORTS AND GAMES — Abstracting, Bibliographies, Statistics*

799 FR ISSN 0751-9907
SAUVAGINE ET SA CHASSE. 1935. m. 200 F. Association Nationale des Chasseurs de Gibier d'Eau, 124 av. du Wagram, 75017 Paris, France. TEL 47-63-02-32. FAX 46-22-82-53. Ed. Raymond Pouget. adv.; bk.rev.; circ. 30,000.

DER SCHUETZE. see *SPORTS AND GAMES*

799 SZ ISSN 0036-8016
SCHWEIZER JAEGER/CHASSEUR SUISSE/CACCIATTORE SVIZZERO. 1915. 18/yr. 68 Fr. (Schweizerischer Patentjaeger- und Wildschutzverband) Druckerei Marcel Kuerzi AG, Werner-Kaelin-Str. 11, CH-8840 Einsiedeln, Switzerland. Ed. W. Fuchs. adv.; illus.; stat.; index; circ. 9,000.

796.93 IT ISSN 0036-8040
SCI; rivista degli sport invernali. 1957. 10/yr. L.60000. Casa Editrice Scode S.p.A., C.so Monforte 36, 20121 Milan, Italy. TEL 02-76006973. FAX 02-76004905. TELEX 324685 SCODE I. Ed. Gianni Bianco. adv.; bk.rev.; illus.; circ. 40,000.

796.93 IT
SCI FONDO. 1957. 5/yr. L.20000. Casa Editrice Scode S.p.A., Corso Monforte 36, 20122 Milan, Italy. TEL 02-76006973. FAX 02-76004905. TELEX 324685 SCODE I. Ed. Cesare Cerise. adv.; illus.; circ. 10,000.

796.93 IT
SCIARE. 1966. s-m. L.30000($20) D M K Editrice s.r.l., Via Boscovich 14, Milan, Italy. Ed. Massimo di Marco. adv.; circ. 85,000.

797.173 IT
SCINAUTICO. 1978. 4/yr. Federazione Italiana Scinautico, Via Piranesi 44-B, Milan, Italy. adv.; circ. 15,000.

917.1 CN
SCOPE CAMPING NEWS. 1965. 6/yr. Can.$15. Merton Publications Ltd., Box 39, Hyde Park, Ont. NOM 1ZO, Canada. Ed. Harold Merton. adv.; illus.; circ. 30,000.
Formerly: Scope: Recreational Vehicle and Camping News (ISSN 0048-9743)

799.1 UK
SCOTLAND FOR FISHING. 1970. a. £2.95. Pastime Publications Ltd., 15 Dublin Street Lane South, Edinburgh EH1 3PX, Scotland. TEL 031-556-1105. FAX 031-556-1129. adv.; circ. 30,000.

796.522 UK ISSN 0080-813X
G505
SCOTTISH MOUNTAINEERING CLUB. JOURNAL. 1890. a. £6.95. (Scottish Mountaineering Club) Cordee, 3a De Montfort St., Leicester LE1 7HD, England. TEL 0533-543579. FAX 0533-471176. Ed. W.D. Brooker. adv.; bk.rev.
—BLDSC shelfmark: 8210.930000.

796.5 GW ISSN 0176-4624
SCOUTING; Zeitschrift fuer Pfadfinderinnen und Pfadfinder. 1984. q. DM.19.20($10) Deutscher Spurbuchverlag, Hemmerleinsleite 46, Postfach 20, 8611 Baunach, Germany. TEL 09544-1561. FAX 09544-809. adv.; bk.rev.; circ. 2,500. (back issues avail.)

799.1 UK ISSN 0306-6568
SEA ANGLER. 1972. m. E M A P Pursuit Publications Ltd., Bretton Court, Bretton, Peterborough PE3 8DZ, England. Ed. Mel Russ. adv.; charts; illus.; stat.; tr.lit.; circ. 53,125.

799.1 UK ISSN 0265-024X
SEA FISHING TODAY. 1983. q. Goodhead Publications, 27 Murdock Rd., Bicester, Oxon. OX6 7RG, England. Ed. Russell Fisher. adv.

SEGELSPORT; Informationen und amtliche Mitteilungen des Deutschen Segler-Verbandes. see *SPORTS AND GAMES — Boats And Boating*

797.17 US
SELLING SCUBA. bi-m. Diving Equipment Manufacturers Association, Box 217, Tustin, CA 92681. TEL 714-744-5284.
Formerly (until Feb. 1989): D E M A Newsletter.

799 CN ISSN 0711-7957
SENTIER CHASSE - PECHE. 1971. m. (11/yr.). Can.$31.50 (foreign Can.$50). Groupe Polygone Editeurs Inc., 11450 Albert-Hudon, Montreal, Que. H1G 3J9, Canada. TEL 514-327-4464. FAX 514-327-0514. Ed. Jeannot Ruel. adv.; circ. 79,281. (back issues avail.) **Indexed:** Pt.de Rep. (1979-).
Formerly: Quebec Chasse et Peche (ISSN 0315-260X)
Description: Articles on fishing, hunting, outdoor life and the environment.

799.1 US
SHIMANO SPORT FISHING. 1984. a. $2.50. (Shimano American Corp.) Aqua-Field Publishing Co., Inc., 66 W. Gilbert St., Shrewsbury, NJ 07702. TEL 201-842-8300. Ed. Stephen Ferber. adv.; circ. 120,000.

799.2 UK
SHOOTING NEWS AND COUNTRY WEEKLY. 1983. w. £49.40. Press & Television Ltd., Yelverton, Devon PL20 7DE, England. Ed. J. Willcocks. adv.; bk.rev.; circ. 12,500. (back issues avail.)
Formerly: Shooting News and Weekly (ISSN 0954-8718)

799.2 US ISSN 0744-3773
SHOTGUN SPORTS. 1976. 10/yr. $26. Box 6810, Auburn, CA 95604. TEL 916-889-2220. FAX 916-889-9106. Ed. Frank Kodl. adv.; circ. 108,000.

796.93 AU
SICHERHEIT IM BERGLAND. 1972. a. S.180. Oesterreichisches Kuratorium fuer Alpine Sicherheit, Prinz Eugen Str. 12, A-1040 Vienna, Austria. Eds. Peter Baumgartner, Eduard Rabofsky. circ. 2,000.
Formerly: Fuer die Sicherheit im Bergland.

SIERRA ATLANTIC. see *CONSERVATION*

SIERRA REPORT. see *CONSERVATION*

796.5 917.9 US ISSN 8750-1600
SIGNPOST FOR NORTHWEST TRAILS. 1966. 12/yr. $25. Washington Trails Association, 1305 4th Ave., No. 512, Seattle, WA 98101-2401. TEL 206-625-1367. adv.; bk.rev.; index; circ. 3,000.
Formerly: Signpost for Northwest Hikers (ISSN 0583-2594)

796.93 US ISSN 0037-6159
GV854
SKI. 1936. 8/yr. $11.94. Times Mirror Magazines, Inc., 2 Park Ave., New York, NY 10016. TEL 212-779-5000. Ed. Richard Needham. adv.; illus.; circ. 436,058. (also avail. in microform from UMI; reprint service avail. from UMI) **Indexed:** Consum.Ind., Phys.Ed.Ind., PMR, Sports Per.Ind., Sportsearch (1974-).
Incorporates: Ski Life.

796.93 CN
LE SKI (TORONTO, 1987). (Text in French) 1987. s-a. Maclean-Hunter Ltd., Maclean-Hunter Bldg., 777 Bay St., Toronto, Ont. M5W 1A7, Canada. TEL 416-596-5029. Eds. Clive Hobson, Guy Thibadeau. circ. 15,000.

796.93 US
SKI AMERICA. 1973. q. Ski America Enterprises, Inc., Box 737, Riverview Rd., Lenox, MA 01240. TEL 413-637-9810. Ed. Joseph B. Hollister. adv.; bk.rev.; charts; illus.; circ. 300,000.

796.93 US ISSN 0037-6175
GV854.A1
SKI AREA MANAGEMENT. 1962. bi-m. $26. Beardsley Publishing Corp., Box 644, Woodbury, CT 06798. FAX 203-266-0452. Ed. David Rowan. adv.; bk.rev.; index; circ. 4,010. **Indexed:** Sportsearch (1974-).

796.93 CN ISSN 0702-701X
SKI CANADA. 1972. 6/yr. Can.$16.45. Solstice Publishing Inc., 19 Albany Ave., Toronto, Ont. M5R 3C2, Canada. TEL 416-535-0607. FAX 416-535-3419. Ed. Cathy Carl. adv.; circ. 53,337. **Indexed:** CMI, Sportsearch (1979-).
Formerly: Ski Canada Journal.

796.93 FR
SKI-FLASH MAGAZINE. 1967. m. 75 F. Edimonde Loisir, 25, rue de Berri, 75008 Paris, France. adv.; circ. 57,246.
Formed by the 1972 merger of: Ski Magazine; Niege et Glace (ISSN 0028-2545)

796.93 US ISSN 0197-3479
SKI INDUSTRY LETTER. 1979. fortn. $197 (FAX edition $296). Skiletter, Inc., 115 Lilly Pond Lane, Katonah, NY 10536. TEL 914-232-5094. Ed. I. William Berry. bk.rev.
Description: Covers the ski trade.

796.93 UK
SKI INTERNATIONAL.* 1981. bi-m. Exhibition House, Lordswood Industrial Estate, Chatham, Kent ME5 8UB, England. Ed. Peter Anslow. adv.; circ. 45,000.

796.93 JA
SKI JOURNAL. (Text in Japanese) 1966. m. 8640 Yen. Ski Journal Co. Ltd., 3-11, Yotsuya, Shinjuku-KU, Tokyo, Japan. Ed. Seiji Miyashita.

796.93 CN ISSN 0037-6221
SKI RUNNER. 1926. 4/yr. membership. (Toronto Ski Club) Frank McNulty Publishing, 100 Mountain Road, Unit 3, Collingwood, Ont. L9Y 3Z8, Canada. TEL 705-445-5024. Ed. Deena Dolan. adv.; bk.rev.; circ. 400. **Indexed:** Sportsearch.

796.93 SA
SKI-SCENE INCLUDING SOUTH AFRICAN FISHING. bi-m. R.15. Cotswold Publications, 208 Gale St., P.O. Box 1925, Durban 4000, South Africa. TEL 031-3055974. FAX 031-3015926. Eds. Shirley Bell, Denis Mercer. adv.
Incorporates: South African Fishing.

796.93 SZ ISSN 0037-623X
SKI - SCHWEIZER SKISPORT/SKI SUISSE/SCI SVIZZERO. (Text in French, German and Italian) 1968. 7/yr. 24 Fr. (Schweizerischer Ski-Verbandes) Habegger AG Druck und Verlag, Gutenbergstr. 1, CH-4552 Derendingen, Switzerland. TEL 065-411151. FAX 065-422632. TELEX 934744. Ed. Peter Kuster. adv.; bk.rev.; circ. 114,000 (controlled).

S

SPORTS AND GAMES — OUTDOOR LIFE

796.93 914.2 UK
SKI SCOTLAND. 1983. a. free. Highlands and Islands Enterprise, Hi-Line House, Station Rd., Dingwall, IV15 9JE, Scotland. circ. 200,000.
   Formerly: Ski Holidays Scotland.

796.93 UK ISSN 0954-9765
SKI SPECIAL. 1975. 4/yr. £10. Activity Magazines Ltd., 27 Belsize Lane, London NW3 5AS, England. TEL 071-435-5472. FAX 071-431-3742. TELEX 295441-BUSY-BG. Ed. Christopher Thomas. adv.; bk.rev.; circ. 60,000. (back issues avail.)
   Description: Information on skiing holidays worldwide, equipment and clothing.

796.93 UK ISSN 0955-8225
SKI SURVEY. 1972. 5/yr. £10. Ski Club of Great Britain, 118 Eaton Sq., London SW1W 9AF, England. FAX 071-245-1258. TELEX 291608 SKIDOM G. (Dist. by: Seymour Press Ltd., 1270 London Rd., Norbury, London SW16 4DA, England) Ed. Elisabeth Hussey. adv.; bk.rev.; cum.index every 3 yrs.; circ. 28,504. Indexed: Sportsearch.

796.93 US
SKI TECH. 1986. 6/yr. $16. Ski Racing International, Box 1125, Waitsfield, VT 05673-1125. TEL 802-496-7700. FAX 802-496-7704. adv.; circ. 13,421.
   Description: Provides product information on ski equipment, ski wear and accessories for owners, managers, buyers, sales and service personnel of ski shops, instructors, and consumers.

796.93 CN
SKI THE WEST. 1987. a. Can.$5. Kootenay Advertiser Ltd., 1510 2nd St. N., Cranbrook, B.C. V1C 3L2, Canada. FAX 604-489-3743. Ed. Daryl Shellborn. circ. 40,450.
   Description: For visitors who wish to ski in Southeast B.C., Northwest Montana and Northern Idaho.

796.42 US
SKI TRAVEL. 6/yr. Ski Racing International, Box 1125, Waitsfield, VT 05673-1125. TEL 802-496-7700. FAX 802-496-7704.

SKI WRITERS BULLETIN. see *JOURNALISM*

796.93 US ISSN 0161-1054
GV855
SKI X - C. (Cross - Country) 1978. a. $3.95. Rodale Press, Inc., 33 E. Minor St., Emmaus, PA 18098. TEL 215-967-5171. adv.; circ. 160,000.

796.93 US
SKIER.* 1964. 10/yr. $6. US - Ski Association., 8 John Brown Rd., Lake Placid, NY 12946-1807. Ed. Elmar Baxter. adv.; bk.rev.; film rev.; circ. 37,000. (tabloid format) Indexed: Sportsearch.
   Former titles: Southwest Skier (ISSN 0049-1667); Southern California Skier.

796.93 UK ISSN 0951-5941
SKIER. 1983. 7/yr. £12.25. Second Edition Ltd., Alpha House, Laser Quay, Medway City Estate, Rochester, Kent ME2 4HU, England. TEL 0634-720202. FAX 0634-720188. Ed. Frank Baldwin. adv.; bk.rev.; circ. 30,000. Indexed: Sportsearch (1978-).
   Incorporates: British Ski Magazine.
   Description: All aspects of ski related subjects: racing, equipment and travel.

796.93 US
SKIER'S POCKET GUIDE. (13 regional editions avail.) 1983. a. free. Pocket Guide Publications, Inc., 8530 Delmar, Ste., 215, St. Louis, MO 63124. TEL 314-991-5222. FAX 314-991-8911. Ed. Jackson D. Waterbury. adv.; circ. 1,000,000 (controlled).
   Description: Provides tips and advice on skiing, maps and local information on ski areas.

796.93 US ISSN 0037-6264
GV854.A1
SKIING. 1948. 7/yr. $11.94. Times Mirror Magazines, Inc., 2 Park Ave., New York, NY 10016. TEL 212-779-5000. Ed. William Grout. adv.; bk.rev.; illus.; index; circ. 441,106. (also avail. in microform from UMI; microfiche from MIM) Indexed: Acad.Ind., Mag.Ind., PMR, R.G., Sports Per.Ind., Sportsearch (1976-), TOM.

796.93 US ISSN 0037-6299
GV854.A1
SKIING TRADE NEWS. 1964. 8/yr. $15. C B S Magazines, Skiing Magazine Department (Subsidiary of: Times Mirror Magazines, Inc.), Two Park Ave., New York, NY 10016. TEL 212-719-6600. Ed. William Grout. adv.; charts; illus.; mkt.; stat.; tr.lit.; circ. 11,529. (reprint service avail.) Indexed: Bus.Ind., Tr.& Indus.Ind.
   ●Also available online. Vendor(s): DIALOG.
   Former titles: Skiing Trade Monthly News; Wintersports Trade Magazine.

796.93 GW
SKILEHRER MAGAZIN. 1980. bi-m. Deutscher Skilehrerverband e.V., Briennerstr. 50, 8000 Munich 2, Germany. TEL 089-529225. illus.; circ. 8,000.

796.93 FI
SKIMBAAJA. 8/yr. Erikoislehdet Oy, Sport, P.O. Box 16, 00381 Helsinki, Finland. TEL 358-0-120-5911. FAX 358-0-120-5959. Ed. Tatu Lehmuskallio. circ. 15,066.

796.93 CN
SKITRAX. 3/yr. 710 Spadina Ave., Ste. 709, Toronto, Ont. M5S 2J3, Canada. TEL 416-927-9681. FAX 416-963-8978. Ed. Benjamin A. Sadavoy. circ. 20,000.

796 US
SNO WEST. 4/yr. Harris Publications, Inc. (Idaho Falls), 520 Park Ave., Idaho Falls, ID 83402-3516. TEL 208-524-7000. FAX 208-522-5241. Ed. Steve Janes. adv.; circ. 125,000.

796 US
SNOW ACTION. 5/yr. Harris Publications, Inc. (Idaho Falls), 520 Park Ave., Idaho Falls, ID 83402-3516. TEL 208-524-7000. FAX 208-522-5241. Ed. Steve Janes.

796.93 US ISSN 0896-758X
GV191.4
SNOW COUNTRY; alpine skiing, freestyle, cross-country, snowboarding, apres-ski. 1988. 8/yr. $13.97. New York Times Company Magazine Group, Sports - Leisure Division, 5520 Park Ave., Box 395, Trumbull, CT 06611-0395. TEL 203-373-7000. (Subscr. to: P.O. Box 2071, Harlan, IA 51593-2270) circ. 350,000.
   Description: Provides travel advice for skiing, mountain climbing, golf, tennis, backpacking, white water rafting, biking, hang gliding, hiking, sailboarding and flyfishing.

796.95 CN ISSN 0711-6454
SNOW GOER; snowmobiling. 1979. 4/yr. Camar Publications Ltd., 130 Spy Court, Markham, Ont. L3R 5H6, Canada. TEL 416-485-8440. FAX 416-475-9246. Ed. Chris Knowles. adv.; circ. 170,000 (controlled).

796.95 US
▼**SNOW GOER.** 1990. 4/yr. $11.97 (foreign $21.97; Canada $17.97). Ehlert Publishing Group, Inc., 319 Barry Ave., S., Wayzata, MN 55391-1603. TEL 612-476-2200. FAX 612-476-8065. Ed. Dick Hendricks. adv.; circ. 104,000.
   Description: Provides information on new machines, travel, new products, performance, personalities, do-it-yourself projects and events.

796.93 US
SNOWBOARDER. 1989. q. $11.95. Surfer Publications, Inc., Box 1028, Dana Point, CA 92629. TEL 714-496-5922. Ed. Doug Paladini. adv.; circ. 75,000.
   Description: Provides technique and equipment tips, equipment reviews, as well as profiles of ski areas that allow snowboarding.

796.9 US ISSN 0274-8363
SNOWMOBILE. 1980. 4/yr. (during winter) $10. Ehlert Publishing Group, Inc., 319 Barry Ave., S., Wayzata, MN 55391-1603. TEL 612-476-2200. Ed. Dick Hendricks. adv.; circ. 475,000. (reprint service avail. from UMI)
   Incorporates (1966-1985): Snow Goer (ISSN 0191-8095); Formed by the 1980 merger of: SnoTrack (ISSN 0049-0822); Midwest Snowmobiler.

796.95 US ISSN 0883-8259
SNOWMOBILE BUSINESS. 1967. 4/yr. Ehlert Publishing Group, Inc., 319 Barry Ave., S., Wayzata, MN 55391-1603. TEL 612-476-2200. Ed. Dick Hendricks. adv.; charts; illus.; stat.; circ. 7,600.
   Formerly (until 1985): Snow Goer Trade.

796.95 CN
SNOWMOBILE CANADA. 2/yr. Can.$10($19) C R V Publishing Co. Ltd., 3580 Poirier Blvd., Ville St-Laurent, Que. H4R 2J5, Canada. TEL 514-856-0788. Ed. Norm Rosen. adv.; circ. 70,000.

790.1 US ISSN 0164-6540
SNOWMOBILE WEST MAGAZINE. Short title: Snowest. 1974. 4/yr. (Sep.-Dec.) $8. Harris Publishing, Inc. (Idaho Falls), 520 Park Ave., Idaho Falls, ID 83402. TEL 208-524-5890. FAX 208-522-5241. Ed. Steve Janes. circ. 135,000. (back issues avail.)
   Description: Contains articles on the sport of snowmobiling in the Western United States. Includes areas of trail riding, snowmobile previews, industry updates, some aspects of racing and other items related to snowmobiling.

796.93 US
SNOWSHOE. 1983. 12/yr. $6. United States Snowshoe Association, Corinth, NY 12822. Ed. Candice Bowen Bosworth.

796 US
SOBEK. 1976. q. $5. 6267 Robin Hood Way, Oakland, CA 94611. TEL 209-736-0226. FAX 415-834-1166. TELEX 3775709 SOBEK. Ed. Richard Bangs. adv.; bk.rev.; circ. 5,000.
   Formerly: Bush League.

799 US
SOUTH CAROLINA GAME & FISH. m. Game & Fish Publications, Inc., 2250 Newmarket Pkwy., Ste. 110, Box 741, Marietta, GA 30061-0741. TEL 404-953-9222. FAX 404-933-9510. Ed. Jeff Samsel. circ. 23,856.

SOUTH CAROLINA OUT-OF-DOORS. see *CONSERVATION*

799 US
▼**SOUTH CAROLINA RULES AND REGULATIONS FOR HUNTING AND FISHING LICENSES.** 1992. a. Atlantic Publication Group, Inc., Box 10343, Charleston, SC 29411. TEL 803-747-0025. FAX 803-744-0816. adv.; circ. 500,000.
   Description: Covers regulations for hunting, wildlife management areas, freshwater and saltwater fishing for purchasers of licenses.

SOUTH CAROLINA WILDLIFE. see *CONSERVATION*

SOUTH CENTRAL CAMPBOOK. see *TRAVEL AND TOURISM*

799.1 US
SOUTH COAST SPORTFISHING. m. $2.95 per no. Publishers Development Corp., 591 Camino de la Reina, Ste. 200, San Diego, CA 92108. TEL 619-297-5350. FAX 619-297-5350.

799.1 US
SOUTH FLORIDA'S ANGLER'S GUIDE. 1983. bi-m. $10. Don Simunek Enterprises, Inc., Box 6170, Lake Worth, FL 33466. TEL 407-968-2004. FAX 407-969-7943. adv.; circ. 25,000.
   Description: Covers freshwater and saltwater fishing.

799 US
SOUTHEASTERN ASSOCIATION OF FISH AND WILDLIFE AGENCIES. PROCEEDINGS. 1947. a. $16. Southeastern Association of Fish and Wildlife Agencies, c/o Joe L. Herring, Exec. Sec.-Treas., 1021 Rodney Dr., Baton Rouge, LA 70808. cum.index: vols. 1-39 (1947-1985). Indexed: Biol.Abstr.
   Formerly: Southeastern Association of Game and Fish Commissioners. Proceedings of the Annual Conference (ISSN 0081-2943).

SOUTHEASTERN CAMPBOOK. see *TRAVEL AND TOURISM*

SPORTS AND GAMES — OUTDOOR LIFE

799.1   US   ISSN 0199-3372
SK1
SOUTHERN OUTDOORS. 1946. 9/yr. $14.97. (Bass Anglers Sportsman Society) B.A.S.S., Inc., Box 17900, Montgomery, AL 36141. TEL 205-272-9530. FAX 205-279-7148. Ed. Larry Teague. adv.; bk.rev.; illus.; circ. 229,898. **Indexed:** PMR.
    Formerly: Southern Outdoors - Gulf Coast Fisherman (ISSN 0038-4399)
    Description: How-to, when-to and where-to information on fishing, hunting, boating and travel for southern sportsmen.

799.1   US
SOUTHERN SALTWATER. 1987. m. (8/yr.). free to qualified personnel. (Bass Anglers Sportsman Society) B.A.S.S., Inc., Box 17900, Montgomery, AL 36141. TEL 205-272-9530. FAX 205-279-7148. Ed. Colin Moore. adv.; bk.rev.; circ. 105,000.
    Formerly: Southern Outdoors' Saltwater.

SOUTHERN SIERRAN. see *CONSERVATION*

SOUTHWESTERN CAMPBOOK. see *TRAVEL AND TOURISM*

799   US
SOUTHWESTERN SPORTSMAN MAGAZINE. 1989. q. $11. Hetrick Publishing, Box H, Winkelman, AZ 85292. TEL 602-356-6049. Ed. Lee Hetrick. adv.; circ. controlled.
    Description: Features hunting and fishing excursions.

796.552   US   ISSN 0734-5895
SPELEONEWS. 1953. bi-m. $12. (National Speleological Society, Nashville and Chattanooga Grottoes) Nashville Grotto, c/o Barbara Munson, Rte. 9, Box 106, McMinnville, TN 37110. Eds. Chuck Mangelsdorf, Rodger Ling. bk.rev.; illus.; circ. 200.
    Description: News articles and historical notes on explorations of and expeditions to grottoes and caves.

SPORT AVIATION. see *AERONAUTICS AND SPACE FLIGHT*

796.5   FR
SPORT ET PLEIN AIR. 1952. m. (11/yr.). 150 F. Federation Sportive et Gymnique du Travail, 14-16 rue Scandicci, 93508 Pantin Cedex, France. Ed.Bd. adv.; circ. 70,000. **Indexed:** Sportsearch.

799.1   US
SPORT FISHING. 1986. 8/yr. $18.97. World Publications, Inc., 330 W. Canton, Box 2456, Winter Park, FL 32789. TEL 407-628-4802. FAX 407-628-7061. Ed. Dean Travis-Clarke. adv.; circ. 93,426.
    Description: Includes how-to and product information relating to offshore sport fishing.

797   UK   ISSN 0584-9217
SPORT PARACHUTIST.* 1964. bi-m. $18.40. British Parachute Association, Wahre Way, Glen Parva, Leicester LE2 9TF, England. Ed. D. Waterman. adv.; bk.rev.; illus.; circ. 6,500. **Indexed:** Sportsearch (1976-).

799   AT
SPORTDIVING IN AUSTRALIA AND THE SOUTH PACIFIC. 1968. bi-m. Aus.$34.50 (foreign Aus.$67). Mountain, Ocean & Travel Publications Pty. Ltd., P.O. Box 167, Narre Warren, Vic. 3805, Australia. TEL 059-443-774. FAX 059-444-024. Ed. Barry Andrewartha. adv.; bk.rev.; index; circ. 16,000. (back issues avail.)
    Formerly: Skindiving in Australia and the South Pacific (ISSN 0313-4954)

799.1   SW
SPORTFISKAREN. 1955. m. SEK 155. Sveriges Sportfiske och Fiskevaardsfoerbund, Box 11501, 100 61 Stockholm, Sweden. Ed. Olof Johanson. adv.; bk.rev.; abstr.; charts; illus.; index; circ. 60,000 (controlled).
    Former titles: Svenskt Fiske (ISSN 0039-694X); Svenskt Fiske Sportfiskaren.

799.1   SW
SPORTFISKAREN (YEAR). a. SEK 155. Sveriges Sportfiske och Fiskevaardsfoerbund, Box 11501, 100 61 Stockholm, Sweden. adv.; bk.rev.; illus.; circ. 44,000.
    Former titles: Svenskt Fiske; Fiske.

799.2   UK
SPORTING GUN. 1978. m. E M A P Pursuit Publications Ltd., Bretton Court, Bretton, Peterborough PE3 8DZ, England. Ed. Robin Scott. adv.; bk.rev.; illus.; tr.lit.; circ. 41,683.

797.56 629.132   NE   ISSN 0921-8017
SPORTPARACHUTIST. (Text in Dutch) 1959. bi-m. fl.45 to non-members. Koninklijke Nederlandse Vereniging voor Luchtvaart, Afdeling Parachutespringen - Netherlands Aeronautical Association, Department of Parachuting, Jozef Israelsplein 8, 2596 AS The Hague, Netherlands. TEL 070-3245457. FAX 070-3240230. Ed. N. Chudiak. adv.; bk.rev.; illus.; circ. 3,500.
    Formerly: Swing Through the Air (ISSN 0039-7458)
    Description: Covers technical (equipment, instruction, regulations) and social (competitions, shows, clubs and people) aspects of skydiving.

799.1   US
SPORTS FISHING. 8/yr. $18.97. World Publications, Inc., Box 2456, Winter Park, FL 32790. TEL 407-628-4802.

796.522   NO   ISSN 0049-2248
STI OG VARDE. 1970. q. NOK 70 to non-members. Bergen Turlag, C. Sundtsgt. 3, 5004 Bergen, Norway. FAX 02-83-1552. Ed. Oeivind Oevrebotten. adv.; illus.; circ. 10,000.

797   FR
SUBAQUA. 1958. bi-m. 150 Fr. (foreign 250 F.). Federation Francaise d'Etudes et de Sports Sous-Marins, 24 quai de Rive Neuve, 13007 Marseille, France. TEL 91-33-99-31. FAX 42-25-93-43. Ed. Bernard Dargaud. adv.; bk.rev.; charts; film rev.; illus.; index; circ. 45,000. **Indexed:** Sportsearch.
    Formerly: Etudes et Sports Sous-Marins (ISSN 0425-5054); Incorporates (in 1981): Aventure Sous-Marine (ISSN 0005-1977)

SUMMERTIME; Garten und Freizeitmoebel. see *INTERIOR DESIGN AND DECORATION — Furniture And House Furnishings*

796.522   US   ISSN 0039-5056
G505
SUMMIT: THE MOUNTAIN JOURNAL. 1955. q. $20. Summit Publications, Inc., 111 Schweitz Rd., Fleetwood, PA 19522. TEL 215-682-1701. FAX 215-682-1708. Ed. John Harlin, III. adv.; bk.rev.; illus.; index; circ. 20,000. **Indexed:** Sportsearch.
    Description: Covers international and U.S. mountain culture, environment, sport, history, photography, literature and travel.

799.1   FI
SUOMEN KALAPAIKKAOPAS. 1966. irreg., approx. biennial. Fmk.45. Kalatalouden Keskusliitto - Federation of Finnish Fisheries Associations (Centralfoerbundet foer Fiskerihushaallning), Koydenpurtojankatu 7 B 23, 00180 Helsinki 18, Finland. TEL 358-0-640-126. FAX 358-0-608-309. Ed.Bd. adv.; index; circ. 10,000.
    Former titles: Kalapaikkaopas; Kalapaikat; Kalastuspaikkaopas (ISSN 0075-4684)
    Description: Guide to angling in Finland.

796.72   US   ISSN 0039-5692
SUPER STOCK & DRAG ILLUSTRATED. 1964. m. $17.95. Four Wheeler Publishing (Subsidiary of: General Media Publishing Group), 6728 Eton Ave., Canoga Park, CA 91303. TEL 818-992-4777. FAX 818-992-4979. Ed. Dave Epperson. adv.; bk.rev.; illus.; stat.; circ. 118,109. (processed)

796.95   CN
SUPERTRAX. 1989. 4/yr. Can.$12.95. (Canadian Council of Snowmobile Organizations) Supertrax Publishing Inc., 74 Kenilworth Ave. N., Hamilton, Ont. L8H 4R5, Canada. TEL 416-549-1370. FAX 416-473-5217. Ed. Kent Lester. adv.; circ. 130,000.
    Description: News, tests and specifications about snowmobiles and the industry across Canada.

796.172   GW
SURF; windsurfing magazin. 1977. m. DM.60.50 (foreign DM.73). Verlag Delius, Klasing und Co., Siekerwall 21, 4800 Bielefeld 1, Germany. TEL 0521-559-280. FAX 0521-559-113. TELEX 932934-DEKLA. Ed. Gerd Kloos. adv.; illus.; circ. 135,000.

796.172   IT
SURF. 1980. L.22500. Nautilus s.r.l., Via Tadino 29, 20124 Milan, Italy. Ed. Silvio Mursia. adv.; circ. 50,000.

797.172   US
SURF REPORT. 1980. m. $35. Box 1028, Dana Point, CA 92629. TEL 714-496-5922. FAX 714-496-7849. Ed. Donna Oakley. adv.

796.172   GW   ISSN 0930-9195
SURFEN; internationales Windsurf-Magazin. 1982. 10/yr. DM.59. Jahr-Verlag GmbH & Co., Burchardstr. 14, D-2000 Hamburg 1, Germany. TEL 040-339660. FAX 040-33966208. TELEX 2163485. Ed. Martin Gebhardt. circ. 40,000. (back issues avail.)

797.172   US   ISSN 0039-6036
GV840.S8
SURFER; the international surfing magazine. 1960. m. $19.95. Surfer Publications, Inc., 33046 Calle Aviador, San Juan Capistrano, CA 92675. TEL 714-496-5922. FAX 714-496-7849. Ed. Steve Hawk. adv.; illus. **Indexed:** Mag.Ind., Sports Per.Ind., Sportsearch (1977-).

797.172   US   ISSN 0194-9314
SURFING. 1964. m. $18.95. Western Empire Publications, 950 Calle Amanecer, Ste. C, Box 3010, San Clemente, CA 92672. TEL 714-492-7873. FAX 714-498-6485. Ed. Bill Sharp. adv.; bk.rev.; illus.; circ. 92,000. **Indexed:** Cal.Per.Ind. (1990), Sportsearch (1978-).
    Incorporates (1985-1991): Body Boarding.

799   SW   ISSN 0039-6583
SVENSK JAKT. 1863. m. SEK 285. Svenska Jaegarefoerbundet, Box 26091, 10041 Stockholm, Sweden. FAX 08-7912303. Ed. Bertil Lundvik. adv.; bk.rev.; charts; illus.; circ. 146,000 (controlled).
    Description: Covers hunting, shooting and dog-breeding.

796.93   SW   ISSN 0049-2671
SVENSK SKIDSPORT. vol.5, 1973. 15/yr. SEK 399. (Svenska Skidfoerbundet) Cewe Foerlaget, Box 77, 890 10 Bjaesta, Sweden. (Subscr. to: PK-Banken, Box 365, 891 01 Oernskoeldsvik, Sweden) Ed. Sigge Bergman. adv.; bk.rev.

797.21 613.7   US
SWIMMING POOLS TODAY. 1985. q. $5. National Swimming Pool Owner's Association (NSPOA), 1213 Ridgecrest Circle, Denton, TX 76205. Ed. Tom A. Doron. bk.rev.; circ. 100,000. (looseleaf format)
    Description: Featuring the swimming pool: safety, chemistry, cleaning, repair, and new products; swimming for fitness and health; entertainment at the poolside.

SYLVANIAN. see *CONSERVATION*

796.42   JA
T. TENNIS; tennis magazine. (Text in Japanese) 1983. m. 4200 Yen. Gakken Co., Ltd., 40-5, 4 chome, Kamiikedai, Ohta-ku, Tokyo 145, Japan. Ed. Kunio Suganuma.

799.2   IT
TACARMI; tiro, armi, caccia. 1964. m. L.120000. Editrice Leone s.r.l., Via E. DeAmicis 25, 20123 Milan, Italy. FAX 02-89403518. Ed. P. Tagini. adv.; bk.rev.; circ. 30,000.

688.7   UK   ISSN 0015-3052
TACKLE & GUNS. 1957. m. £13.50. Frontline Ltd. (Subsidiary of: E M A P - Haymarket Ltd.), Park House, 117 Park Rd., Peterborough PE1 2TR, England. TEL 0733-555161. FAX 62788. TELEX 329292 FRONTG. Ed. Cyril Holbrook. adv.; bk.rev.; illus.; stat.; tr.lit.
    Formerly: Fishing Tackle Dealer.

799.1   US   ISSN 1048-9215
TACKLE TEST; the consumer resource for the serious angler. vol.11, no.2, 1991. m. $60 (foreign $68). Belvoir Publications, Inc., 75 Holly Hill Lane, Box 2626, Greenwich, CT 06836-2626. TEL 203-661-6111. FAX 203-661-4802. (Subscr. to: Box 2076, Knoxville, IA 50138) Ed. W. Todd Woodard.

SPORTS AND GAMES — OUTDOOR LIFE

799.1   US
TACKLE TIMES (BARRINGTON). 1979. 6/yr. membership. American Fishing Tackle Manufacturers Association, 1250 Grove Ave., Barrington, IL 60010. TEL 708-381-9490. FAX 708-381-9518. bk.rev.; circ. 2,000 (controlled).
Formerly: Top of the Week.

797   AT   ISSN 0157-2938
TASMANIAN TRAMP. 1933. biennial. price varies. Hobart Walking Club, G.P.O. Box 753H, Hobart, Tas. 7001, Australia. Ed.Bd. adv.; cum.index: 1933-1963; 1966-1979; circ. 1,000.

TENNESSEE CONSERVATIONIST; nature, environmental issues. see *CONSERVATION*

790.1   US   ISSN 0161-3871
TENNESSEE SPORTSMAN. 1980. m. $14.95. Game & Fish Publications, Inc., 2250 Newmarket Pkwy., Ste. 110, Box 741, Marietta, GA 30061-0741. TEL 404-953-9222. Ed. Bill Hartlay.

796.5   ISSN 0049-3481
TETON. 1969. a. $1.95. Teton Magazine, Box 1903, Jackson Hole, WY 83001. TEL 307-733-9220. Ed. Gene Downer. adv.; bk.rev.; illus.; circ. 20,000.

799   US
TEXAS FISH & GAME. 10/yr. $15. Highland Publishing Co., Drawer 1000, Marble Falls, TX 78654. TEL 512-693-5725. (Subscr. to: 4550 Post Oak Place Rd., Ste. 150, Houston TX 77027. TEL 713-626-3474)
Incorporates (1973-1991): Texas Fisherman.
Description: Covers hunting and fishing activities.

799 796.5   US
TEXAS OUTDOOR GUIDE MAGAZINE. 1968. bi-m. $12. Smith Publishing Co., Inc., Box 55573, Houston, TX 77055. Ed. Linda Peek Smith. adv.; bk.rev.; charts; illus.; stat.; tr.lit.; circ. 100,000. (back issues avail.)

799   US
TEXAS SPORTSMAN. m. Game & Fish Publications, Inc., 2250 Newmarket Pkwy., Ste. 110, Box 741, Marietta, GA 30061-0741. TEL 404-953-9222. FAX 404-933-9510. Ed. Nick Gilmore. circ. 38,300.

796.552   JA
THE-YAMA-TO-KEIKOKU/MOUNTAIN AND VALLEY. (Text in Japanese) 1930. m. Yama-Kei Publishers Co., 1-1-33, Shiba-Daimon, Minato-ku, Tokyo 105, Japan. TEL 03-3436-4023. Ed. Akira Yamaguchi. circ. 230,000.

796.42   UK
THROWER. q. National Athletics Coach, 152 Longdon Rd., Knowle, Solihull, W. Midlands B93 9HU, England. Ed. Max Jones. **Indexed:** Sportsearch (1984-).
Formerly: Circle.

796.42   CC   ISSN 1000-3509
TIANJING/TRACK & FIELD. (Text in Chinese) 1981. bi-m. $18.50. (Zhongguo Tianjing Xiehui - China Society of Track and Field) Renmin Tiyu Chubanshe, 8 Tiyuguan Lu, Chongwen Qu, Beijing 100061, People's Republic of China. (Dist. in US by: China Books & Periodicals, Inc., 2929 24th St., San Francisco, CA 94110)

TIDE. see *CONSERVATION*

790 352   CN
TIDINGS. 1979. q. Can.$15($20) (typically set Jan.). Recreation Association of Nova Scotia, P.O. Box 3010 S., Halifax, N.S. B3J 3G6, Canada. TEL 902-425-1128. FAX 902-425-5606. Ed. Scott Bullerwell. adv.; bk.rev.; circ. 3,500. (back issues avail.)

799   SP
TIRADORES; revista de caza, tiro y pesca. 1967. m. 675 ptas.($7) Calle Oruro 8, esc.Izqda. 1 C, 28016 Madrid, Spain. TEL 255-36-02-01. Ed. G. Romero-Requejo. adv.; illus.; charts.

796.5   GW
TOPMOBIL; Magazin fuer Caravan und Reisemobil. (Text in English, German) 1989. q. Top Special Verlag, Valentinskamp 24, D-2000 Hamburg 36, Germany. TEL 040-347-3901. Ed. Manfred Ruopp. circ. 50,000.

796.93 910.4   IT
TOURIST MAGAZINE. q. Editoriale Eurocamp s.r.l, Via Durini, No.3, 20122 Milan, Italy. TEL 02-76022377. FAX 02-76022430. Ed. Maria Paola Canegrati.

799.1   AT
TOURNAMENT FISHERMAN. q. Aus.$5.95. A.B. Organisation Pty. Ltd., P.O. Box 319, Avalon Beach, N.S.W. 2107, Australia. TEL 02-918-8322. FAX 02-918-8884. (Dist. by: Network Distribution Company, 54-58 Park St., Sydney, N.S.W. 2000, Australia) adv.

TRACES (JACKSON). see *CLUBS*

796.42   US
TRACK AND FIELD CASE BOOK. biennial. $2.75. National Federation of State High School Associations, 11724 N.W. Plaza Circle, Box 20626, Kansas City, MO 64195-0626. TEL 816-464-5400. FAX 816-464-5571. Ed. Thomas E. Frederick.

796.42   US   ISSN 0041-0284
TRACK & FIELD NEWS. 1948. m. $31 (foreign $39). Track & Field News, Inc., 2570 El Camino Real, No. 606, Mountain View, CA 94040. TEL 415-948-8188. FAX 415-948-9445. Ed. Bert Nelson. adv.; bk.rev.; illus.; mkt.; circ. 31,000. (also avail. in microform from UMI) **Indexed:** Sports Per.Ind., Sportsearch (1974-).
Description: Focuses on complete coverage of the sport from high school to the Olympic level. Includes news, features, interviews, and action photos.

796.42   US
TRACK AND FIELD OFFICIALS MANUAL. biennial. $2.75. National Federation of State High School Associations, 11724 N.W. Plaza Circle, Box 20626, Kansas City, MO 64195-0626. TEL 816-464-5400. FAX 816-464-5571. Ed. Frank Kovaleski.

796.42   US   ISSN 0041-0292
GV1060.6
TRACK AND FIELD QUARTERLY REVIEW. 1927. q. $20 (foreign $25)(effective 1992). National Collegiate Athletic Association, Division 1 Track Coaches Association, 1705 Evanston, Kalamazoo, MI 49008. TEL 616-349-1008. FAX 616-387-4461. Ed. George Dales. adv.; bk.rev.; charts; illus.; index. cum.index; circ. 2,200. (also avail. in microform from UMI; reprint service avail. from UMI) **Indexed:** Phys.Ed.Ind., Sportsearch (1976-).
—BLDSC shelfmark: 8877.350000.
Formerly (until 1964): Clinic Notes.
Description: Includes educational and technical articles by and for track and field coaches and athletes.

796.42   US
TRACK AND FIELD RULEBOOK. a. $2.75. National Federation of State High School Associations, 11724 N.W. Plaza Circle, Box 20626, Kansas City, MO 64195-0626. TEL 816-464-5400. FAX 816-464-5571.
Formerly: Track and Field Rules and Records.

796.42   US   ISSN 0041-0306
TRACK NEWSLETTER. 1955. 26/yr. $38 (foreign $57). Track & Field News, Inc., 2570 El Camino Real, No. 606, Mountain View, CA 94040. TEL 415-948-8188. FAX 415-949-9445. Ed. Garry Hill. circ. 600. **Indexed:** Sportsearch.
Description: Latest track and field, results and summaries.

796.42   US   ISSN 0742-3918
GV561
TRACK TECHNIQUE: OFFICIAL TECHNICAL PUBLICATION. 1960-1981; resumed 1983. q. $15 (foreign $16). (Athletics Congress - U S A) Track & Field News, Inc., 2570 El Camino Real, No. 606, Mountain View, CA 94040. TEL 415-948-8188. FAX 415-948-9445. Ed. Jed Goldfried. bk.rev.; bibl.; charts; illus.; circ. 3,500. (also avail. in microform from UMI) **Indexed:** Phys.Ed.Ind., Sports Per.Ind., Sportsearch.
Formerly (until 1981): Track Technique (ISSN 0041-0314).
Description: Covers technique and training for all events, injury care and prevention, biomechanics and physiology, motivation and coaching psychology, diet and nutrition, strength training, racing tactics.

797.172   AT
TRACKS. 1970. m. Aus.$30($53) Mason Stewart Publishing Pty. Ltd., P.O. Box 746, Darlinghurst, N.S.W. 2010, Australia. TEL 02-331-5006. FAX 02-360-5367. Ed. Gary Dunne. adv.; circ. 35,000.

796.15   US
TRADEWINDS. q. membership only. Kite Trade Association International, 50 First St., No.310, San Francisco, CA 94105. TEL 415-764-4908. FAX 415-764-4915.
Description: For those involved in various aspects of the kite industry.

796.522   US   ISSN 0041-0756
F782.R6
TRAIL AND TIMBERLINE. 1918. m. $8 to non-members (foreign $11). Colorado Mountain Club, 2530 W. Alameda Ave., Denver, CO 80219. TEL 303-922-8976. FAX 303-922-7680. Ed. Sally Ross. adv.; bk.rev.; charts; illus.; maps; index. cum.index every 10 yrs.; circ. 6,800.
Description: Membership magazine for the Colorado Mountain Club with news on mountain sports and conservation.

796   US
TRAIL BLAZER'S ALMANAC AND PIONEER GUIDE BOOK. 1934. a. $1.50. Trail Blazer's Publishing Co., 206 W. Fourth St., Kewanee, IL 61443. TEL 309-852-2602. adv.; circ. 1,100,000.
Formerly: Trail Blazer's Almanac.

799.3   US
TRAIL TALK. q. Whitetails Unlimited, Inc., Box 422, Sturgeon Bay, WI 54235. TEL 414-743-6777. Ed. Dale G. Deckman.

796 333.7   US   ISSN 0749-1352
TRAIL WALKER; news of hiking and conservation. 1963. bi-m. $15 to non-members. New York - New Jersey Trail Conference, Inc., 232 Madison Ave., No. 908, New York, NY 10016. TEL 212-685-9699. adv.; bk.rev.; circ. 5,500.

796.5   DK   ISSN 0108-6758
TRAILER. (Text in Danish and Swedish) 1983. m. DKK 19.75. Fut & Fart, Vejlevej 49, 7330 Brande, Denmark.

796.5 388.344   US   ISSN 0041-0780
TX1100
TRAILER LIFE. 1941. m. $18. T L Enterprises, Inc., 29901 Agoura Rd., Agoura, CA 91301. TEL 818-991-4980. Ed. Bill Estes. illus.; mkt.; circ. 306,512. (processed; also avail. in microform from UMI) **Indexed:** Consum.Ind., Mag.Ind., PMR.
Description: RV magazine for travel trailers, motorhome and truck campers. Travelogues, buyer's guides, vehicle tests, technical tips and more.

796.5 917.004   US
TRAILER LIFE CAMPGROUND AND R V SERVICES DIRECTORY. 1972. a. T L Enterprises, Inc., 29901 Agoura Rd., Agoura, CA 91301. TEL 818-991-4980. FAX 818-991-8102. adv.; circ. 300,250.
Description: Lists private RV parks, public campgrounds, tourist attractions, and RV service centers throughout the US, Canada and Mexico.

TRAILER LIFE'S RECREATIONAL VEHICLE CAMPGROUND AND SERVICES DIRECTORY. see *BUSINESS AND ECONOMICS — Trade And Industrial Directories*

799.1   AT
TRAILERBOATS AND FISHERMAN. m. Aus.$48. A.B. Organisation Pty. Ltd., P.O. Box 319, Avalon Beach, N.S.W. 2107, Australia. TEL 02-918-8322. FAX 02-918-8884. (Dist. by: Gordon & Gotch, 25-37 Huntingdale Rd., Burwood, Vic. 3125, Australia) circ. 12,000.
Description: For professional trailerboat fishermen.

796.5 917.704   US
TRAILS-A-WAY.* 1970. 12/yr. $8. T A W Publishing, Co., 9425 Greenville Rd., Greenville, MI 48838. TEL 616-754-2251. Ed. Martha Higbie. adv.; bk.rev.; circ. 62,000. (tabloid format)

SPORTS AND GAMES — OUTDOOR LIFE

796 US ISSN 0748-7401
TRANSWORLD SKATEBOARDING. 1983. m. $19.95 to individuals (foreign $38.55); libraries $14.97 (foreign $33.77). Transworld Publications, Inc., Box 6, Cardiff, CA 92033. TEL 619-722-7777. FAX 619-722-0653. (Subscr. to: Box 3712, Escondido, CA, 92025; Alt. addr.: 353 Airport Rd., Oceanside, CA 92054) adv.
   Description: Contains interviews with the leading skaters, contest coverage, features on local scenes, worldwide travel stories, and columns about how to improve skating skills, and how to choose a board.

796.93 US ISSN 1046-4611
TRANSWORLD SNOWBOARDING. 7/yr (Oct.-Apr.). $13.95 to individuals (foreign $24.80); libraries $10.47 (foreign $21.37). Transworld Publications, Inc., Box 6, Cardiff, CA 92007. TEL 619-722-7777. FAX 619-722-0653. (Subscr. to: Box 3774, Escondido, CA 92033; Alt. addr.: 353 Airport Rd., Oceanside, CA 92054) adv.

799 US ISSN 0041-1760
TRAP & FIELD. 1890. m. $22. Curtis Publishing Company (Indianapolis), 1200 Waterway Blvd., Indianapolis, IN 46202. TEL 317-633-2075. FAX 317-634-2192. Ed. Bonnie Nash. adv.; illus.; circ. 16,500. **Indexed:** Sportsearch (1977-).

799.2 US ISSN 8750-233X
SK283
TRAPPER AND PREDATOR CALLER. 1974. m. $16.95. Krause Publications, Inc., 700 E. State St., Iola, WI 54990. TEL 715-445-2214. FAX 715-445-4087. TELEX 556461 KRAUSE PUB UD. Ed. Gordy Krahn. circ. 48,924. (tabloid format)
   Description: Focuses on the newest trapping and calling techniques, equipment, and animal lures. Includes reports on activities state by state. Includes information on products helpful to outdoorsmen and on muzzle loading.

TRAVELLER. see *TRAVEL AND TOURISM*

TRENDS (ALEXANDRIA). see *CONSERVATION*

796 US
TRIATHLON TODAY. 9/yr. K A Z Publications, Inc., Box 1587, Ann Arbor, MI 48106-1587. TEL 313-662-1000. FAX 313-662-3388. Ed. Andrew Tilin. adv.; circ. 18,000.

796.42 GW ISSN 0931-3850
TRIATHLON UND SPORTWISSENSCHAFT. 1987. irreg., vol.5, 1991. price varies. (Sportwissenschaftlicher Beirat der Deutschen Triathlon Union) Verlag Ingrid Czwalina, Reesenbuettler Redder 75, 2070 Ahrensburg, Germany. TEL 04102-59190. FAX 04102-50992.

796 910.09 US
TRILOGY. 1989. bi-m. $14.95 (Canada & elsewhere $19.95). Trilogy Publishing, Inc, 310 Old E. Vine St., Lexington, KY 40507. TEL 800-274-8522. FAX 606-443-3453. adv.; circ. 100,000.
   Description: Focuses on outdoor adventures, travel and travails on land, sea and river.

799 333.7 SP
TROFEO. 1970. m. Telemaco 37, 28027 Madrid, Spain. TEL 91-300818. FAX 91-3203557. Dir. J. Delibes. circ. 35,000.
   Description: Covers hunting, fishing and nature conservation.

799.1 UK ISSN 0041-3372
TROUT AND SALMON; a journal for game fishermen. 1955. m. £26. E M A P Pursuit Publications Ltd., Bretton Court, Bretton, Peterborough PE3 8DZ, England. Ed. Sandy Leventon. adv.; illus.; circ. 52,727.

799.1 UK
TROUT FISHERMAN. m. £24. E M A P Pursuit Publications Ltd., Bretton Court, Bretton, Peterborough PE3 8DZ, England. Ed. Chris Dawn. adv.; bk.rev.; illus.; circ. 41,920.
   Description: For stillwater game fishermen.

799.2 US
▼**TURKEY & TURKEY HUNTING.** 1991. q. $2.95 per no. Krause Publications, Inc., 700 E. State St., Iola, WI 54990. TEL 715-445-2214. FAX 715-445-4087. TELEX 556461 KRAUSE PUB UD. adv.: B&W page $1290, color page $1680; trim 8 1/8 x 10 1/2; adv. contact: Debbie Knauer. circ. 90,000.
   Description: For serious, technical turkey hunters in the U.S. Includes how-to for both gun and bow hunters.

799.2 US ISSN 8750-0205
TURKEY HUNTER. 1983. 8/yr. $14.95. Krause Publications, Inc., 700 E. State St., Iola, WI 54990. TEL 715-445-2214. FAX 715-445-4087. TELEX 556461. Ed. Gerry Blair. adv.; circ. 54,798.
   Description: Guide to U.S. turkey hunting. Includes calling tips, first-hand hunting experiences, contest results, calendar of events and bow and gun techniques.

799.1 US
U S A OUTDOORS. 1975. bi-m. membership. Bassing America Corp., 4398 Sunbelt Dr., Dallas, TX 75248. TEL 214-380-2656. FAX 214-380-2659. Ed. John Brett. adv.; bk.rev.; circ. 46,000. (back issues avail.)
   Description: For tournament bass fishermen.

U S SKI WRITERS ASSOCIATION NEWSLETTER. see *JOURNALISM*

ULTRALIGHT FLYING; international magazine of ultralight aviation. see *AERONAUTICS AND SPACE FLIGHT*

796.42 US ISSN 0744-3609
ULTRARUNNING. 10/yr. 300 N. Main St., Box 481, Sunderland, MA 01375. **Indexed:** Sportsearch (1987-).

U.S. FISH AND WILDLIFE SERVICE. NATIONAL SURVEY OF HUNTING, FISHING AND WILDLIFE-ASSOCIATED RECREATION. see *SPORTS AND GAMES — Abstracting, Bibliographies, Statistics*

719.32 333.7 US
U.S. NATIONAL PARK SERVICE. RESEARCH REPORTS BY SERVICE PERSONNEL. 5-10/yr. U.S. National Park Service, Interior Bldg., Washington, DC 20240. TEL 202-343-1100. (Orders to: NTIS, Springfield, VA 22161)

796 SW ISSN 0281-2932
UTE-MAGASINET.* 1980. bi-m. SEK 175. Milvus Forlags AB, P.O. Box 147, S-83005 Jaerpen, Sweden. FAX 0642-11411. Ed. Marion Areng. adv.; bk.rev.; circ. 24,000.

VERMONT FISH AND WILDLIFE REGULATIONS. see *LAW*

796.522 SP ISSN 0042-4420
VERTEX.* (Text in Catalan; summaries in French, Spanish) 1966. bi-m. 195 ptas. Federacion Catalana de Montanismo, Ramblas 61, 1-2, Barcelona 12, Spain. adv.; bk.rev.; bibl.; charts; illus.; index; cum.index; circ. 4,000.

796.42 AT
VETERAN ATHLETE. 1986. m. Aus.$24($40) Mipen Enterprises Pl., McInnes Rd., Tynong North, Vic. 3813, Australia. TEL 059-428344. Ed. Mike Hall. adv.; circ. 1,000. (back issues avail.)

796.5 CN
VIE EN PLEIN AIR. (Text in French) 1970. q. C R V Publishing Co. Ltd., 3580 Poirier Blvd., Ville St-Laurent, Que. H4R 2J5, Canada. TEL 514-856-0788. Ed. Helene Trudeau.

796.5 CN
VIE ET CAMPING. (Text in French) 1976. 2/yr. C R V Publishing Co. Ltd., 3580 Poirier Blvd., Ville St-Laurent, Que. H4R 2J5, Canada. TEL 514-856-0788. adv. **Indexed:** Sportsearch.

796.5 NO
VILLMARKSLIV. 1972. m. NOK 216. Naturforlaget A-S, Bygdoe Alle 7, Oslo 2, Norway. Eds. Bjoern Holm-Hansen, Thorbjoern Tufte. adv.; circ. 52,000.

799 RM
VINATORUL SI PESCARUL ROMAN. 1948. m. 360 lei($6) Association of Hunters and Anglers, Calea Mosilor 128, Bucharest, Rumania. FAX 136804. Ed. Victor Tarus. adv.; bk.rev.; circ. 25,000.

790.1 US
VIRGINIA OUTDOORS PLAN (YEAR). 1965. quinquennial. $10. Department of Conservation & Recreation, Division of Planning and Recreation Resources, 203 Governor St., Ste. 326, Richmond, VA 23219. TEL 804-786-2556. FAX 804-786-6141. illus.; tr.lit.
   Formerly (1965 report): Virginia's Common Wealth.
   Description: Attempts to project to project future needs and identify emerging trends and issues that may effect open space, natural resources and recreation resources planning and management.

VIRGINIA WILDLIFE. see *CONSERVATION*

VIRGINIA WILDLIFE FEDERATION. FEDERATION RECORD. see *CONSERVATION*

796 US
VISIBILITY. 1984. q. $15 membership. Underwater Society of America, Box 628, Daly City, CA 94017. Eds. Carol Rose, Glenn Pollock. bk.rev.; circ. 2,500.

799 GW ISSN 0138-1601
VISIER; Zeitschrift fuer der G S T Sportschiessen und Waffenkunde. 1975. m. DM.65. (Gesellschaft fuer Sport und Technik) Militaerverlag der Deutschen Demokratischen Republik, Storkower Str. 158, 1055 Berlin, Germany. TEL 4300618. Ed.Bd.

796.5 CN
VOYAGEUR TRAIL NEWS. 3/yr. Can.$10. Voyageur Trail Association, Box 66, Sault Ste. Marie, Ont. P6B 3L7, Canada. Eds. Peter Frederick, Pim Delfgou. adv.; circ. 400.
   Description: News concerning hiking and camping activities of the Club.

796 AT
THE WALKER. 1929. a. Aus.$3.60. Melbourne Walking Club, Inc., G.P.O. Box 2446v, Melbourne, Vic. 3001, Australia. Ed. Laurie Bell. adv.; bk.rev.; circ. 3,000.
   Formerly: Melbourne Walker.

796.552 613.7 US ISSN 0739-4497
WALKING! JOURNAL;* the art, science and sport of walking. 1983. q. $8. Walking Journal, Inc., c/o Walkways Ctr., Box 1335, Concord, NH 03302-1335. Ed. Kevin Kelly. adv.; bk.rev.; charts; illus.; circ. 4,000. (back issues avail.)

799.1 US
WALLEYE. 1980. 6/yr. $12.50. Walleye International, Box 40210, Cleveland, OH 44140. TEL 216-333-9494. FAX 216-777-7803. Ed. H.B. Riser. adv.; circ. 48,066.
   Description: Covers fishing techniques, conditions, uses of new tackle, boats, equipment, new books, cooking and environmental issues.

796.5 GW ISSN 0178-1677
WANDERMAGAZIN. 1985. bi-m. DM.38.50. Verlag Andrea Saenger, Moltkestr. 95, 5300 Bonn 2, Germany. TEL 0228-351259. FAX 0228-353207. Ed. Michael Saenger. adv.; bk.rev.; circ. 70,000. (back issues avail.)

799.1 US
WASHINGTON FISHING HOLES. 1974. m. 807 Metcalf, Sedro Woolley, WA 98284-1422. TEL 206-855-1641.

797.173 US
WATER SKI. 1976. 10/yr. $18.97. World Publications, Inc., 330 W. Canton, Box 2456, Winter Park, FL 32790. TEL 407-628-4802. FAX 407-628-7601. Ed. Erik Calonius. adv.; illus.; circ. 114,775.
   Incorporates: Spray's Water Ski Magazine (ISSN 0273-7892); Which was formerly (until vol.4, no.7, 1980): Spray (ISSN 0164-9922)

797.173 US ISSN 0049-7002
GV840.S5
WATER SKIER. 1951. 7/yr. $20. American Water Ski Association, 799 Overlook Dr., Winter Haven, FL 33884. TEL 813-324-4341. FAX 813-325-8259. Ed. John Baker. adv.; charts; illus.; tr.lit.; circ. 25,000. (also avail. in microfiche) **Indexed:** Mag.Ind., Sportsearch (1974-).

797 UK
WATER SKIER & POWERCRAFT. m. £6. MDS Ltd., 55 Shelton St., London W.C.2., England. Ed. Bill Berry. adv.

4560 STATISTICS

797 639.9   AT
WAYSIDER. 1953. bi-m. Aus.$6. Catholic Bushwalking Club, c/o Environment Centre, 176 Cumberland St., the Rocks, Sydney, N.S.W. 2000, Australia. TEL 02-520-7081. Ed. Thomas Carroll. adv.; bk.rev.; circ. 350.

799   US
WEST VIRGINIA GAME & FISH. m. Game & Fish Publications, Inc., 2250 Newmarket Pkwy., Ste. 110, Box 741, Marietta, GA 30061-0741. TEL 404-953-9222. Ed. Aaron Pass.

799   US   ISSN 0049-7479
WESTERN OUTDOOR NEWS. 1954. w. $34.95. Western Outdoors Publications, 3197E Airport Loop Dr., Costa Mesa, CA 92626. TEL 714-546-4370. (Or: Box 2027, Newport Beach, CA 92659-1027) Ed. Pat McDonell. adv.; circ. 75,000. (tabloid format)

796.5   US   ISSN 0043-4000
SK1
WESTERN OUTDOORS. 1960. 9/yr. $14.95. Western Outdoors Publications, 3197E Airport Loop Dr., Costa Mesa, CA 92626. TEL 714-546-4370. (Or: Box 2027, Newport Beach, CA 92659-1027) Ed. Jack Brown. adv.; bk.rev.; illus.; circ. 143,000.
Indexed: Cal.Per.Ind. (1978-), PMR.

796.93   CN
WESTERN SKIER. 1972. 6/yr. Can.$10($15) McIntosh Publishing Co. Ltd., Box 430, North Battleford, Sask. S9A 2Y5, Canada. TEL 306-445-4401. FAX 306-445-1977. Ed. Rod McDonald. circ. 38,100.
Former titles: Saskatchewan Skier; (until 1989): Saskatchewan Ski Journal.
Description: Covers skiing in western Canada and the US, resort features, fashions, technique improvement, club news, and press releases.

799   CN   ISSN 0709-1532
WESTERN SPORTSMAN. 1969. bi-m. Can.$15.95. Western Sportsman Ltd., Box 737, Regina, Sask. S4P 3A8, Canada. TEL 306-352-2773. FAX 306-565-2440. Ed. Roger Francis. adv.; bk.rev.; charts; illus.; stat.; circ. 28,000.
Formerly: Fish and Game Sportsman (ISSN 0015-2897); Which was formed by the merger of: Fish and Game of Alberta; Saskatchewan Sportsman.

WHEELERS R V RESORT AND CAMPGROUND GUIDE: NORTH AMERICAN EDITION. see *TRAVEL AND TOURISM*

WHERE TO FISH. see *BUSINESS AND ECONOMICS — Trade And Industrial Directories*

WHITE BOOK OF SKI AREAS. U S AND CANADA. see *BUSINESS AND ECONOMICS — Trade And Industrial Directories*

790   CN   ISSN 0043-5015
WHITESHELL ECHO.* 1956. m. Can.$2($3) (Whiteshell District Association) Lance Publishing Co. Ltd., 56 Elm Park, Winnipeg, Man., Canada. Ed. Wes Rowson. circ. 4,000. (tabloid format)

796   AT   ISSN 0726-2809
WILD; Australia's wilderness adventure magazine. 1981. q. Aus.$25.96($32.95) Wild Publications Pty. Ltd., P.O. Box 415, Prahran, Vic. 3181, Australia. TEL 03-826-8482. Ed. Chris Baxter. charts; illus.; film rev.; index; circ. 18,286. (back issues avail.)
Description: Covers hiking, cross-country skiing, canoeing, mountaineering and caving in Australia.

799.1   GW   ISSN 0043-5422
WILD UND HUND; Zeitschrift fuer Jaeger und andere Naturfreunde. 1895. fortn. DM.124($65) Verlag Paul Parey (Hamburg), Spitalerstr. 12, 2000 Hamburg 1, Germany. TEL 040-33969-0. FAX 040-33969-199. TELEX 2161391-PARV-D. (U.S. address: Paul Parey Scientific Publishers, 35 West 38th St., No.3W, New York, NY 10018) Ed. Horst Reetz. adv.; bk.rev.; illus.; circ. 88,000. (reprint service avail. from ISI) **Indexed:** Ind.Vet., Vet.Bull.

799.2   US   ISSN 0886-0637
WILDFOWL; the magazine for duck & goose hunters. 1985. bi-m. $17.97. Stover Publishing Co., Inc., 1901 Bell Ave., Ste. 4, Des Moines, IA 50315. TEL 515-243-2472. FAX 515-243-0233. (Subscr. to: Box 372, Mt. Morris, IL 61054) Ed. Roger Sparks. (back issues avail.)
Description: For waterfowl hunters.

799   CN   ISSN 0043-5457
WILDLIFE CRUSADER. 1944. 6/yr. Can.$10. Manitoba Wildlife Federation, 1770 Notre Dame Ave., Winnipeg, Man., Canada. TEL 204-633-5967. FAX 204-632-5200. Ed. Denis Corneau. adv.; bk.rev.; charts; illus.; stat.; circ. 32,468.

799.2   US   ISSN 0886-3458
WILDLIFE HARVEST. 1970. m. $25. (North American Gamebird Association, Inc.) John M. Mullin, Ed. & Pub., Box 96, Goose Lake, IA 52750. TEL 319-242-3046. adv.; bk.rev.; circ. 2,943.
Description: Covers the market for shooting and hunting supplies, clothing and equipment, shotguns, shotshells, clay-targets and sporting clay traps.

797.173   US   ISSN 0279-9359
GV811.63.W56
WIND SURF.* 1971. m. $21. 2030 E. Gladwick St., Compton, CA 90220-6202. TEL 714-661-4888. FAX 714-661-0487. Ed. Drew Kampion. adv.; bk.rev.; tr.lit.; circ. 56,750. (reprint service avail.)
Indexed: Sports Per.Ind., Sportsearch (1984-).

790   US   ISSN 0049-7681
WINDSOR SPORTSMEN'S NEWS.* m. Windsor Sportsmen's Club, 2401 Dougall Rd., Box 452, Windsor, Ont., Canada. **Indexed:** Sportsearch.

796.172   US
GV811.63.W56
WINDSURFING; the nation's leading windsurfing magazine. 1981. $18.97. World Publications, Inc., 330 W. Canton, Box 2456, Winter Park, FL 32790. TEL 407-628-4802. FAX 407-628-7601. (Subscr. to: Box 183, Mt. Morris, IL 61054. TEL 800-394-6006) Ed. Debbie Z. Snow. circ. 75,000.
Formerly: Windrider (ISSN 0279-4659)

799.2   US
WING & SHOT; the magazine for upland bird hunters. 1986. bi-m. $17.97. Stover Publishing Co., Inc., 1901 Bell Ave., Ste. 4, Des Moines, IA 50315. TEL 515-243-2472. FAX 515-243-0233. Ed. Bob Wilbanks.
Description: For upland bird hunters.

799.2   US
WISCONSIN DEER REPORT. q. $3.95. Krause Publications, Inc., 700 E. State St., Iola, WI 54990. TEL 715-445-2214. FAX 715-445-4087. TELEX 556461 KRAUSE PUB UD. adv. contact: Debbie Knauer.
Description: Regional hunting magazine.

WISCONSIN NATURAL RESOURCES. see *CONSERVATION*

796   US   ISSN 0893-5769
WISCONSIN OUTDOOR JOURNAL. 1987. 8/yr. $14.95. Krause Publications, Inc., 700 E. State St., Iola, WI 54990. TEL 715-445-2214. FAX 715-445-4087. adv.; circ. 37,246.
Description: Offers information on hunting, fishing, camping and the sporting life in the state of Wisconsin. Covers natural resource management, natural history, outdoor-related news and legislation.

796.95   US
WISCONSIN SNOWMOBILE NEWS. 1987. 7/yr. $7. Royle Group, 112 Market St., Sun Prairie, WI 53590. TEL 608-837-3946. FAX 608-837-3946. Ed. Tom Anderson. adv.; circ. 23,966.
Description: Contains association news, legislative actions, and travel articles. Covers new products and personalities.

796   US   ISSN 0361-9451
SK143
WISCONSIN SPORTSMAN. 1972. m. $14.95. Game & Fish Publications, Inc., 2250 Newmarket Pkwy., Ste. 110, Box 741, Marietta, GA 30061-0741. TEL 404-953-9222. Ed. Ken Dunwoody. adv.; bk.rev.; circ. 72,000.

796.5   US
WOMEN OUTDOORS. 1980. q. $20. Woman Outdoors, Inc., 55 Talbot Ave., Medford, MA 02155. adv.; bk.rev.; circ. 1,000.

796   US
WOMEN'S OUTDOOR JOURNAL. Abbreviated title: W O J. 6/yr. Liberty Ridge Publishing, R.R.3, Box 72, Rockport, IN 47635. TEL 812-359-5293. Ed. Rebecca A. Hinton. circ. 4,000.

WONDERFUL WEST VIRGINIA. see *CONSERVATION*

WOODALL'S CAMPGROUND DIRECTORY. EASTERN EDITION. see *BUSINESS AND ECONOMICS — Trade And Industrial Directories*

WOODALL'S CAMPGROUND DIRECTORY. NORTH AMERICAN EDITION. see *BUSINESS AND ECONOMICS — Trade And Industrial Directories*

WOODALL'S CAMPGROUND DIRECTORY. WESTERN EDITION. see *BUSINESS AND ECONOMICS — Trade And Industrial Directories*

WOODALL'S TENT CAMPING GUIDE. see *BUSINESS AND ECONOMICS — Trade And Industrial Directories*

799.2   US
WORLD BOWHUNTERS. bi-m. 4008 W. Michigan Ave., Jackson, MI 49202. TEL 517-570-9060. Ed. Ted Nugent. circ. 15,000.

WORLD RECORD GAME FISHES. see *FISH AND FISHERIES*

WYOMING SIERRAN. see *CONSERVATION*

796.54   UK
YOUR BIG SITES LIST: CAMPING AND CARAVANNING CLUB SITES LIST; camping sites yearbook. 1920. biennial. membership. Camping and Caravanning Club, Greenfields House, Westwood Way, Coventry CV4 8JH, England. TEL 0203-694995. FAX 0203-694886. Ed. Peter Frost. circ. 96,528.
Supersedes in part (in 1989): Camping and Caravanning Club Handbook and Sites List; Which was formerly: Camping Club Handbook and Sites List; Camping Club of Great Britain and Ireland. Year Book with List of Camp Sites (ISSN 0068-6956)

796.54   UK
YOUR PLACE IN THE COUNTRY: A GUIDE TO CAMPING AND CARAVANNING CLUB SITES. 1920. a. membership. Camping and Caravanning Club, Greenfields House, Westwood Way, Coventry CV4 8JH, England. TEL 0203-694995. FAX 0203-694886. Ed. Peter Frost.
Supersedes in part (in 1989): Camping and Caravanning Club Handbook and Sites List; Which was formerly: Camping Club Handbook and Sites List; Camping Club of Great Britain and Ireland. Year Book with List of Camp Sites (ISSN 0068-6956)

799.1   CC   ISSN 1000-3487
ZHONGGUO DIAOYU/ANGLING IN CHINA. (Text in Chinese) 1984. bi-m. $12.60. (Zhongguo Diaoyu Xiehui - China Angling Society) Renmin Tiyu Chubanshe, 8 Tiyuguan Lu, Chongwen Qu, Beijing 100061, People's Republic of China. TEL 757176. (Dist. in US by: China Books & Periodicals, Inc., 2929 24th St., San Francisco, CA 94110. TEL 415-282-2994) Zhang Qian. adv.; circ. 200,000.

796.5 910.202   IT
2 C PLEIN AIR. 1971. m. (11/yr.) L.50000. Edizioni Plein Air Inc., Largo San Pio V, 16, 00165 Rome, Italy. FAX 06-6237266. Ed. Raffaele Jannucci. adv.; bk.rev.; circ. 56,000.
Former titles: 2 C Caravan Camping Camper; 2 C Caravan e Camping.

STATISTICS
see also specific subjects

A A M A INDUSTRY STATISTICAL REVIEW AND FORECAST. (American Architectural Manufacturers Association) see *BUILDING AND CONSTRUCTION — Abstracting, Bibliographies, Statistics*

A H A HOSPITAL STATISTICS (YEAR). see *HOSPITALS — Abstracting, Bibliographies, Statistics*

A M P S BLACK RADIO AND TELEVISION DIARY. (All Media and Product Survey) see *ADVERTISING AND PUBLIC RELATIONS — Abstracting, Bibliographies, Statistics*

A M P S METER WEEKLY REPORTS. (All Media and Product Survey) see *ADVERTISING AND PUBLIC RELATIONS — Abstracting, Bibliographies, Statistics*

A M P S WHITE - COLOURED - ASIAN RADIO DIARY. (All Media and Product Survey) see *COMMUNICATIONS — Abstracting, Bibliographies, Statistics*

310 001.64 US
A P D U NEWSLETTER. 1976. m. $250 membership. Association of Public Data Users, Princeton University Computing Center, 87 Prospect Ave., Princeton, NJ 08544. TEL 609-258-6025. FAX 609-258-3943. Ed. Susan Anderson. cum.index: 1976-1986; circ. 500. (back issues avail.)
   Description: Designed to inform readers of issues and policies that affect the collection and dissemination of public data by the federal government, and availability of data products in various media formats (print, CD-ROM).

310 GW
AACHEN. STATISTISCHES AMT. STATISTISCHE KURZINFORMATION. 1982. irreg. DM.2 per no. Statistisches Amt, Roemerstr. 10, 5100 Aachen, Germany. TEL 0241-4321235. circ. 350. (back issues avail.)
   Description: Each issue devoted to one area of statistics. Covers vital statistics, election statistics, and population statistics.

310 DK ISSN 0107-7120
AARHUS KOMMUNES STATISTISKE KONTOR. INFORMATION. 1970. irreg. (approx. 50/yr.). free. Aarhus Kommunes Statistiske Kontor, Raadhuset, 8100 Aarhus C, Denmark. (looseleaf format)

310 II
ABSTRACT OF STATISTICS FOR TAMIL NADU. (Text in English) 1956. q. Rs.4 per no. Director of Statistics, Madras 600006, India. (Subscr. to: Government Publication Dpot, 166 Anna Rd., Madras 600002, India) circ. controlled. (back issues avail.)

ACTUARIAL REVIEW. see *INSURANCE — Abstracting, Bibliographies, Statistics*

ADVANCES IN RISK ANALYSIS. see *PUBLIC HEALTH AND SAFETY — Abstracting, Bibliographies, Statistics*

ADVANCES IN STATISTICAL ANALYSIS AND STATISTICAL COMPUTING. see *COMPUTERS*

AEROSPACE FACTS AND FIGURES. see *AERONAUTICS AND SPACE FLIGHT — Abstracting, Bibliographies, Statistics*

318 MX ISSN 0186-0453
AGENDA ESTADISTICA. a. Mex.$85000. Instituto Nacional de Estadistica, Geografia e Informatica, Secretaria de Programacion y Presupuesto, Prol. Heroe de Nacozari 2301 Sur, Puerta 11, Planta Baja, Aguascalientes, 20290 Ags., Mexico. TEL 49-18-22-32. FAX 491-807-39. circ. 11,000.

AGRICULTURAL STATISTICS OF GREECE. see *AGRICULTURE — Abstracting, Bibliographies, Statistics*

AGRICULTURAL STATISTICS SERIES NO.3: EUROPEAN COMMUNITIES INDEX OF AGRICULTURAL PRICES. see *AGRICULTURE — Abstracting, Bibliographies, Statistics*

AIR CARRIER OPERATIONS IN CANADA/OPERATIONS DES TRANSPORTEURS AERIENS AU CANADA. see *AERONAUTICS AND SPACE FLIGHT — Abstracting, Bibliographies, Statistics*

AIR CARRIER TRAFFIC AT CANADIAN AIRPORTS. see *TRANSPORTATION — Abstracting, Bibliographies, Statistics*

310 DK ISSN 0109-8047
HA1461
AKTUELL NORDISK STATISTIK. (Text in Scandinavian languages) 1984. s-a. free. Nordisk Statistisk Sekretariat, Sejroegade 11, Dk-2100 Copenhagen OE, Denmark. circ. 750.

ALABAMA LABOR MARKET NEWS. see *BUSINESS AND ECONOMICS — Abstracting, Bibliographies, Statistics*

ALABAMA'S VITAL EVENTS. see *PUBLIC ADMINISTRATION — Abstracting, Bibliographies, Statistics*

ALASKA. AGRICULTURAL STATISTICS SERVICE. AGRICULTURAL STATISTICS. see *AGRICULTURE — Abstracting, Bibliographies, Statistics*

ALASKA FARM REPORTER. see *AGRICULTURE — Abstracting, Bibliographies, Statistics*

ALBERTA ECONOMIC ACCOUNTS. see *BUSINESS AND ECONOMICS — Abstracting, Bibliographies, Statistics*

338 CN ISSN 0317-3925
HA747.A79
ALBERTA STATISTICAL REVIEW; a quarterly statistical summary. 1970. q. free. Bureau of Statistics, Alberta Treasury, 600 Park Plaza, 10611-98 Avenue, Edmonton, Alta. T5K 2R7, Canada. TEL 403-427-3058. FAX 403-427-0409. circ. 1,300. **Indexed:** CS Ind.
   Formerly: Alberta Business Trends (ISSN 0002-4724)

316 AE
ALGERIA. DIRECTION DES STATISTIQUES ET DE LA COMPTABILITE NATIONALE. BULLETIN TRIMESTRIEL DE STATISTIQUES. 1949. q. 12 din. Direction des Statistiques et de la Comptabilite Nationale, Chemin Ibn-Badis al-Mouiz, El-Biar, Algiers, Algeria. (Dist. in US by: African Imprint Library Service, Box 350, West Falmouth, MA 02574. TEL 508-540-5378)
   Former titles: Algeria. Direction des Statistiques. Bulletin Trimestriel de Statistiques; Algeria. Sous-Direction des Statistiques. Bulletin de Statistiques Generales (ISSN 0002-5305); Algeria. Service de Statistique Generale. Bulletin Mensual.

311 II ISSN 0971-0388
ALIGARH JOURNAL OF STATISTICS. 1981. a. Rs.35($15) to individuals; institutions Rs.50 ($20). Aligarh Muslim University, Department of Statistics, Aligarh 202002, India. TELEX 564-230 AMU IN. circ. 300. **Indexed:** Biostat., Oper.Res.Manage.Sci., Qual.Contr.Appl.Stat.

ALL MEDIA & PRODUCT SURVEY. see *ADVERTISING AND PUBLIC RELATIONS — Abstracting, Bibliographies, Statistics*

314 GW ISSN 0002-6018
HA1 CODEN: ALSAAX
ALLGEMEINES STATISTISCHES ARCHIV. (Text in German; summaries in English) 1890. q. DM.128. (Vorstand der Deutschen Statistischen Gesellschaft) Vandenhoeck und Ruprecht, Theaterstr. 13, Postfach 3753, 3400 Goettingen, Germany. TEL 0551-6959-22. FAX 0551-695917. Ed. Horst Rinne. adv.; bk.rev.; bibl.; charts; index; circ. 620. (reprint service avail. from KTO) **Indexed:** Biol.Abstr., J.Cont.Quant.Meth., P.A.I.S.For.Lang.Ind.

AMERICAN JOURNAL OF MATHEMATICAL AND MANAGEMENT SCIENCES. see *MATHEMATICS*

AMERICAN PETROLEUM INSTITUTE. MONTHLY STATISTICAL REPORT. see *PETROLEUM AND GAS — Abstracting, Bibliographies, Statistics*

AMERICAN RADIO. see *COMMUNICATIONS — Abstracting, Bibliographies, Statistics*

AMERICAN SALARIES AND WAGES SURVEY. see *BUSINESS AND ECONOMICS — Abstracting, Bibliographies, Statistics*

AMERICAN STATISTICAL ASSOCIATION. SECTION ON STATISTICAL EDUCATION. PROCEEDINGS.. see *EDUCATION — Abstracting, Bibliographies, Statistics*

310 US
AMERICAN STATISTICAL ASSOCIATION. SECTION ON STATISTICAL GRAPHICS. PROCEEDINGS. (San Francisco, CA, August 17-20, 1987) a. American Statistical Association, Section on Statistical Graphics, 1429 Duke St., Alexandria, VA 22314. TEL 202-393-3253.

310 US ISSN 0149-9963
QA276.4
AMERICAN STATISTICAL ASSOCIATION. STATISTICAL COMPUTING SECTION. PROCEEDINGS (OF THE ANNUAL MEETING). 1976. a. $45 to non-members; members $30. American Statistical Association, 1429 Duke St., Alexandria, VA 22314-3402. TEL 703-684-1221. FAX 703-684-2037. stat.

311 US
AMERICAN STATISTICAL ASSOCIATION. SURVEY RESEARCH METHODS. PROCEEDINGS. 1978. a. $64 to non-members; members $43. American Statistical Association, 1429 Duke St., Alexandria, VA 22314-3402. TEL 703-684-1221. FAX 703-684-2037.
   Formerly: American Statistical Association. Statistical Section. Proceedings.

311 US ISSN 0003-1305
HA1 CODEN: ASTAAJ
AMERICAN STATISTICIAN. 1947. q. $40. American Statistical Association, 1429 Duke St., Alexandria, VA 22314-3402. TEL 703-684-1221. FAX 703-684-2037. (also avail. in microform from KTO,MIM,UMI,PMC; reprint service avail. from SWZ) **Indexed:** Biostat., Chem.Abstr., Child Devel.Abstr., Compumath, Comput.Abstr., Curr.Cont., Deep Sea Res.& Oceanogr.Abstr., Ind.Sci.Rev., J.Cont.Quant.Meth., Math.R., Oper.Res.Manage.Sci., P.A.I.S., Qual.Contr.Appl.Stat., Risk Abstr., Sci.Abstr., Sci.Cit.Ind., Soc.Sci.Ind., SSCI.
   —BLDSC shelfmark: 0857.650000.

016 US ISSN 0091-1658
Z7554.U5
AMERICAN STATISTICS INDEX; a comprehensive guide and index to the statistical publications of the U.S. Government. 1974. m. (with q. and a. cumulations). price varies. Congressional Information Service, 4520 East-West Hwy., Bethesda, MD 20814-3389. TEL 301-654-1550. FAX 301-654-4033. TELEX 292386 CIS UR. Ed. Daniel Coyle. abstr.; stat.; index; cum.index: 1974-79; 1980-84; 1985-88. **Indexed:** Mid.East: Abstr.& Ind., Noise Pollut.Publ.Abstr., Popul.Ind.
   ●Also available online. Vendor(s): DIALOG (File no.102).
   Also available on CD-ROM.
   —BLDSC shelfmark: 0857.655000.
   Description: Abstracts of U.S. government publications by subject, name, type of data breakdown, title and report number.

310 519.54 US ISSN 0163-9617
AMSTAT NEWS. 1974. 12/yr. $35. American Statistical Association, 1429 Duke St., Alexandria, VA 22314-3402. TEL 703-684-1221. FAX 703-684-2037. Ed. Marilyn J. Humm. adv.; circ. 15,000. (also avail. in microform from UMI; back issues avail.)

ANGOLA. DIRECCAO DOS SERVICOS DE ESTATISTICA. ANUARIO ESTATISTICO. see *PUBLIC ADMINISTRATION — Abstracting, Bibliographies, Statistics*

316 AO ISSN 0003-3413
ANGOLA. DIRECCAO DOS SERVICOS DE ESTATISTICA. BOLETIM MENSAL.* (Text in Portuguese) N.S. 1942. m. Esc.180. Direccao dos Servicos de Estatistica, Caixa Postal 1215, Luanda, Angola. adv.; stat.; circ. 15,200.

ANGOLA. DIRECCAO DOS SERVICOS DE ESTATISTICA. INFORMACOES ESTATISTICAS. see *PUBLIC ADMINISTRATION — Abstracting, Bibliographies, Statistics*

519.5 US ISSN 0090-5364
HA1 CODEN: ASTSC7
ANNALS OF STATISTICS. 1973. q. $130. Institute of Mathematical Statistics, Business Office, 3401 Investment Blvd., Ste. 7, Hayward, CA 94545. TEL 510-783-8141. circ. 4,600. (also avail. in microform from UMI) **Indexed:** Biostat., Compumath, Curr.Cont., Curr.Ind.Stat., Ind.Sci.Rev., J.Cont.Quant.Meth., Math.R., Oper.Res.Manage.Sci., Qual.Contr.Appl.Stat., Risk Abstr., Sci.Cit.Ind., SSCI.
   —BLDSC shelfmark: 1044.400000.
   Supersedes in part: Annals of Mathematical Statistics (ISSN 0003-4851)

ANNUAIRE DES STATISTIQUES DU COMMERCE EXTERIEUR DU TOGO. see *BUSINESS AND ECONOMICS — Abstracting, Bibliographies, Statistics*

317 CN
ANNUAIRE DU QUEBEC STATISTIQUES. 1914. a. Can.$39.95. (Bureau of Statistics) Ministere des Communications, Direction Generale des Publications Gouvernementales, 2e Etage, 1279 bd. Charest Ouest, Quebec, Que. G1N 4K7, Canada. TEL 418-643-3895. index; circ. 6,000.
   Formerly: Annuaire du Quebec (ISSN 0066-3018)

STATISTICS

316.6   DM
ANNUAIRE STATISTIQUE DE BENIN. a., latest 1975. 2000 Fr.CFA. Institut National de la Statistique et de l'Analyse Economique, B.P. 323, Cotonou, Benin.
    Formerly: Annuaire Statistique du Dahomey.

314   BE   ISSN 0770-0415
HA1393
ANNUAIRE STATISTIQUE DE LA BELGIQUE. (Text in Dutch, French) 1870. a. 1035 Fr. (foreign 1235 Fr.). Institut National de Statistique, 44 rue de Louvain, B-1000 Brussels, Belgium. TEL 02-513-96-50.
    —BLDSC shelfmark: 1073.482500.
    Formerly (until 1960): Annuaire Statistique de la Belgique et du Congo Belge.

314   FR   ISSN 0066-3654
HA1213
ANNUAIRE STATISTIQUE DE LA FRANCE. 1876. a. 550 F.($96) Institut National de la Statistique et des Etudes Economiques, 18 bd. Adolphe Pinard, 75675 Paris Cedex 14, France. TEL 41-17-50-50. TELEX 204924F INSEE. circ. 3,000.
    —BLDSC shelfmark: 1073.483000.

316   TI   ISSN 0066-3689
HA4684
ANNUAIRE STATISTIQUE DE LA TUNISIE. a. Institut National de la Statistique, 70 rue Echcham, Tunis, Tunisia.

316   MR   ISSN 0851-089X
ANNUAIRE STATISTIQUE DU MAROC. (Editions in Arabic, French) 1957. a. DH.165. Direction de la Statistique, B.P. 178, Rabat, Morocco. (also avail. in microfiche)
    Incorporates: Morocco. Direction de la Statistique. Statistiques Retrospectives; Parc Automobile du Maroc.

316.6   TG
ANNUAIRE STATISTIQUE DU TOGO. 1966. a., latest 1987. 4000 Fr.CFA. Direction de la Statistique, Boite Postale 118, Lome, Togo. illus.; stat.

ANNUAL BULLETIN OF STEEL STATISTICS FOR EUROPE. see *METALLURGY — Abstracting, Bibliographies, Statistics*

310   UK
ANNUAL REGISTRARS SERVICE. 1953. a. including cum.supplements. Extel Financial Ltd., Fitzroy House, 13-17 Epworth St., London EC2A 4DL, England. TEL 01-251-3333. FAX 01-608-3514. TELEX 884319.
    Formerly: Register of Registrars (ISSN 0482-1319)

ANNUAL REPORT ON THE CONSUMER PRICE INDEX. see *CONSUMER EDUCATION AND PROTECTION — Abstracting, Bibliographies, Statistics*

ANNUARIO DI STATISTICHE GIUDIZIARIE - TOMO 2. see *LAW — Abstracting, Bibliographies, Statistics*

314   IT   ISSN 0066-4545
HA1367
ANNUARIO STATISTICO ITALIANO. a. L.45000. Istituto Centrale di Statistica, Via Cesare Balbo 16, 00100 Rome, Italy. circ. 4,700.

ANNUARIUM STATISTICUM ECCLESIAE/STATISTIQUE DE L'EGLISE/STATISTICAL YEARBOOK OF THE CHURCH.. see *RELIGIONS AND THEOLOGY — Abstracting, Bibliographies, Statistics*

ANUARIO DE ESTADISTICAS ESTATALES. see *GEOGRAPHY — Abstracting, Bibliographies, Statistics*

318   UN   ISSN 1014-0697
ANUARIO ESTADISTICO DE AMERICA LATINA Y EL CARIBE/STATISTICAL YEARBOOK FOR LATIN AMERICA AND THE CARIBBEAN. (Text in English and Spanish) 1969. a. $65. Comision Economica para America Latina y el Caribe, Casilla 179-D, Santiago, Chile. (Subscr. to: United Nations Publications, Sales Section, Rm. DC2-0853, New York, NY 10017 (212-754-8302); or Distribution and Sales Section, Palais des Nations, 1211 Geneva 10, Switzerland) charts. (back issues avail.) **Indexed:** P.A.I.S.
    Former titles (until 1985): Anuario Estadistico de America Latina; (until 1973): Boletin Estadistico de America Latina (ISSN 0251-9445)

312   MX
ANUARIO ESTADISTICO DE CHIAPAS. a. $22. Instituto Nacional de Estadistica, Geografia e Informatica, Secretaria de Programacion y Presupuesto, Prol. Hereo de Nacozari, 2301, Acceso 10, C.P. 20290, Aguascalientes, Ags., Mexico. TEL 91-491-81968. FAX 91-491-80739.

317   CU   ISSN 0574-6132
ANUARIO ESTADISTICO DE CUBA. English edition: Statistical Yearbook Compendium of the Republic of Cuba. 1952. a. $15 in N. America; S. America $17; Europe $18; others $20. Comite Estatal de Estadisticas, Centro de Informacion Cientifico-Tecnica, Almendares No. 156, esq. a Desague, Gaveta Postal 6016, Havana, Cuba. (Dist. by: Ediciones Cubanas, Obispo No. 527, Apdo. 605, Havana, Cuba) circ. 1,000.

312   MX
ANUARIO ESTADISTICO DE ESTADO DE CHIHUAHUA. (In 2 vols.) a. $28.50. Instituto Nacional de Estadistica, Geografia e Informatica, Secretaria de Programacion y Presupuesto, Prol. Heroe de Nacozari, 2301, Acceso 10, C.P. 20290, Aguascalientes Ags., Mexico. TEL 91-491-81968. FAX 91-491-80739.

310   MX
ANUARIO ESTADISTICO DE LOS ESTADOS UNIDOS MEXICANOS. 1938. a. Mex.$29500($10) Instituto Nacional de Estadistica, Geografia e Informatica, Secretaria de Programacion y Presupuesto, Prol. Heroe de Nacozari 2301 Sur, Puerta 11, planta baja, Aguascalientes 20290 Ags., Mexico. TEL 49-18-22-32. FAX 491-807-39. circ. 5,000.

312   MX
ANUARIO ESTADISTICO DE OAXACA. a. Instituto Nacional de Estadistica, Geografia e Informatica, Secretaria de Programacion y Presupuesto, Patriotismo 711 Torr "A" P.H., Col. San Juan Mixcoac, Deleg. Benito Juarez, 03910 Mexico, D.F., Mexico.

318   PY
ANUARIO ESTADISTICO DEL PARAGUAY. 1886. a. exchange basis. Direccion General de Estadistica y Censos, Humaita 463, Asuncion, Paraguay. (Subscr. to: Casilla de Correo 1118, Asuncion, Paraguay) Ed. Jose Diaz de Bedoya. circ. 1,500.

318   BL   ISSN 0100-1299
HA971
ANUARIO ESTADISTICO DO BRASIL/STATISTICAL YEARBOOK OF BRAZIL. 1916. a. $100. Fundacao Instituto Brasileiro de Geografia e Estatistica, Av. Franklin Roosevelt, 166, Centro, CEP 20021 Rio de Janeiro, Brazil. TEL 021-284-7690. FAX 21-228-9575. TELEX 2139128. (Subscr. to: Divisao de Comercializacao e Promocao, Rua General Canabarro, 666, Bloco B 2o andar, Maracana, CEP 20271 Rio de Janeiro, Brazil) bk.rev.; charts; circ. 10,000. (back issues avail.)
    —BLDSC shelfmark: 1563.700000.

318   BL   ISSN 0100-8730
HA988.S2
ANUARIO ESTADISTICO DO ESTADO DE SAO PAULO. 1979. a. $69.10. Fundacao Sistema Estadual de Analise de Dados, Av. Casper Libero, 464, 01033 Sao Paulo, Brazil. charts; circ. 1,000.
    Description: Characterizes the social, economic, demographic and physical aspects of the state.

318   BL   ISSN 0102-0226
HC188.R4
ANUARIO ESTADISTICO DO RIO GRANDE DO SUL. 1972. a. Cr.$10000. Fundacao de Economia e Estatistica, Rua Duque de Caxias, No. 1691, CEP 90010 Porto Alegre, Rio Grande do Sul, Brazil. TEL 0512-259455. TELEX 0515042.
    Description: Covers information and statistics on the municipal level. Looks at physical, demographic, and socio-economic aspects of the state of Brazil.

310   GW   ISSN 0066-5673
ARBEITEN ZUR ANGEWANDTEN STATISTIK. 1967. irreg., vol.33,1990. price varies. Physica-Verlag GmbH und Co., Tiergartenstr. 17, Postfach 105280, 6900 Heidelberg 1, Germany. TEL 030-8207-424. FAX 030-8207-448. Ed.Bd. **Indexed:** Math.R.
    Formerly: Berlin. Freie Universitaet. Institut fuer Statistik und Versicherungsmathematik. Berichte (ISSN 0067-5865)

318   AG
ARGENTINA. CENTRAL DE ESTADISTICAS NACIONALES. INFORME. 1976. irreg. $110. Central de Estadisticas Nacionales, Av. De Mayo 953, 1084 Buenos Aires, Argentina. Ed. Carlos A. Canto Yoy. circ. 500.

ARGENTINA. INSTITUTO NACIONAL DE ESTADISTICA Y CENSOS. ANUARIO ESTADISTICO. see *POPULATION STUDIES — Abstracting, Bibliographies, Statistics*

310   AG   ISSN 0325-1969
HA943
ARGENTINA. INSTITUTO NACIONAL DE ESTADISTICA Y CENSOS. BOLETIN ESTADISTICO TRIMESTRAL. 1973. q. $42. Instituto Nacional de Estadistica y Censos, Hipolito Yrigoyen 250, piso 12 of. 1209, 1310 Buenos Aires, Argentina. Ed.Bd. **Indexed:** P.A.I.S.For.Lang.Ind.
    Formerly: Argentina. Direccion Nacional de Estadistica y Censos. Boletin de Estadistica (ISSN 0004-1017)

318   AG   ISSN 0326-6214
HB235.A7
ARGENTINA. INSTITUTO NACIONAL DE ESTADISTICA Y CENSOS. ESTADISTICA MENSUAL. m. $72 for 6 months. Instituto Nacional de Estadistica y Censos, Hipolito Yrigoyen 250, piso 12 of. 1209, 1310 Buenos Aires, Argentina.
    Former titles (until 1984): Argentina. Instituto Nacional de Estadistica y Censos. Boletin de Estadistica y Censos (ISSN 0325-1950); Argentina. Direccion Nacional de Estadistica y Censos. Boletin Mensual de Estadistica (ISSN 0518-4673)

ARKANSAS. DEPARTMENT OF LABOR. EMPLOYMENT SECURITY DIVISION. STATISTICAL REVIEW. see *BUSINESS AND ECONOMICS — Abstracting, Bibliographies, Statistics*

315   UN
ASIA - PACIFIC IN FIGURES. 1987. a. United Nations Economic and Social Commission for Asia and the Pacific (ESCAP), United Nations Bldg., Rajadamnern Ave., Bangkok 10200, Thailand.

AUDIT BUREAU OF CIRCULATIONS. ANNUAL REPORT. see *ADVERTISING AND PUBLIC RELATIONS — Abstracting, Bibliographies, Statistics*

AUDIT BUREAU OF CIRCULATIONS. SUPPLEMENTAL DATA REPORTS. see *ADVERTISING AND PUBLIC RELATIONS — Abstracting, Bibliographies, Statistics*

314   GW   ISSN 0004-7953
AUGSBURG IN ZAHLEN. 1946. q. DM.16. Amt fuer Stadtentwicklung und Statistik, Schmiedberg 6, 8900 Augsburg 22, Germany. stat.; circ. 500. (also avail. in microform)

AUSTRALIA. AIR TRANSPORT STATISTICS. AIRPORT TRAFFIC DATA. see *TRANSPORTATION — Abstracting, Bibliographies, Statistics*

AUSTRALIA. AIR TRANSPORT STATISTICS. COMMUTER AIRLINES. see *TRANSPORTATION — Abstracting, Bibliographies, Statistics*

AUSTRALIA. AIR TRANSPORT STATISTICS. DOMESTIC AIRLINES (ANNUAL). see *TRANSPORTATION — Abstracting, Bibliographies, Statistics*

AUSTRALIA. AIR TRANSPORT STATISTICS. DOMESTIC AIRLINES (QUARTERLY). see *TRANSPORTATION — Abstracting, Bibliographies, Statistics*

AUSTRALIA. AIR TRANSPORT STATISTICS. INTERNATIONAL SCHEDULED AIR TRANSPORT. see *TRANSPORTATION — Abstracting, Bibliographies, Statistics*

AUSTRALIA. AIR TRANSPORT STATISTICS. MONTHLY PROVISIONAL STATISTICS OF INTERNATIONAL SCHEDULED AIR TRANSPORT. see *TRANSPORTATION — Abstracting, Bibliographies, Statistics*

AUSTRALIA. AIR TRANSPORT STATISTICS. SURVEY OF HOURS FLOWN. see *TRANSPORTATION — Abstracting, Bibliographies, Statistics*

AUSTRALIA. BUREAU OF AGRICULTURAL AND RESOURCE ECONOMICS. MONTHLY FOREST PRODUCTS TRADE STATISTICS. see *FORESTS AND FORESTRY — Abstracting, Bibliographies, Statistics*

AUSTRALIA. BUREAU OF STATISTICS. APPARENT CONSUMPTION OF SELECTED FOODSTUFFS, AUSTRALIA, PRELIMINARY. see *PUBLIC ADMINISTRATION — Abstracting, Bibliographies, Statistics*

AUSTRALIA. BUREAU OF STATISTICS. BALANCE OF PAYMENTS, AUSTRALIA (ANNUAL). see *BUSINESS AND ECONOMICS — Abstracting, Bibliographies, Statistics*

AUSTRALIA. BUREAU OF STATISTICS. BALANCE OF PAYMENTS, AUSTRALIA (QUARTERLY). see *BUSINESS AND ECONOMICS — Abstracting, Bibliographies, Statistics*

AUSTRALIA. BUREAU OF STATISTICS. BALANCE OF PAYMENTS (CANBERRA, 1976). see *BUSINESS AND ECONOMICS — Abstracting, Bibliographies, Statistics*

350 319   AT   ISSN 0813-1317
AUSTRALIA. BUREAU OF STATISTICS. CATALOGUE OF SMALL AREA STATISTICS. 1983. s-a. Aus.$17.50 (foreign Aus.$22.50)(effective 1991). Australian Bureau of Statistics, P.O. Box 10, Belconnen, A.C.T. 2616, Australia. TEL 062-527911. FAX 062-51009. circ. 10.
   Description: Contains a subject index, an area index and a list of ABS publications containing small-area data. Also includes data on those small areas not covered in the data released on magnetic tape and microfiche formats.

AUSTRALIA. BUREAU OF STATISTICS. DISTRIBUTION AND COMPOSITION OF EMPLOYEE EARNINGS AND HOURS, AUSTRALIA, PRELIMINARY. see *BUSINESS AND ECONOMICS — Abstracting, Bibliographies, Statistics*

310   AT   ISSN 0727-1689
AUSTRALIA. BUREAU OF STATISTICS. MONTHLY SUMMARY OF STATISTICS, AUSTRALIA. 1937. m. Aus.$228 (foreign Aus.$313.20)(effective 1991). Australian Bureau of Statistics, P.O. Box 10, Belconnen, A.C.T. 2616, Australia. TEL 062-527911. FAX 062-516009. stat.; circ. 935.
   Formerly: Australia. Bureau of Statistics. Monthly Review of Business Statistics (ISSN 0027-0539)
   Description: Includes statisticsl data on population and vital statistics, employment and unemployment, wages and price, production, building, national accounts, finance, internal trade, foreign trade, balance of payments and transport.

319   AT   ISSN 0067-0855
HA3052
AUSTRALIA. BUREAU OF STATISTICS. NORTHERN TERRITORY STATISTICAL SUMMARY. 1960. a. Aus.$15 (foreign Aus.$22.10)(effective 1991). Australian Bureau of Statistics, P.O. Box 10, Belconnen, A.C.T. 2616, Australia. TEL 062-527911. FAX 516009. circ. 277.
   Description: Detailed information about the Territory including chronological table of important events, list of representatives and officials; population and vital statistics, occupied dwellings, employment, wages, trade unions, industrial disputes and more.

319   AT   ISSN 0726-2019
AUSTRALIA. BUREAU OF STATISTICS. QUEENSLAND OFFICE. BRISBANE CITY STATISTICAL SUMMARY. 1980. a. Aus.$8.50 (foreign Aus.$11.80). Australian Bureau of Statistics, Queensland Office, 313 Adelaide St., Brisbane, Qld. 4000, Australia. TEL 07-222-6022. FAX 07-229-6171. TELEX AA 40271.
   Description: Summary of information for statistical local areas of Brisbane City on area, population, dwellings, births, deaths, infant deaths, natural increase, building, manufacturing, road traffic accidents, pre-schools and child care centers and schools.

AUSTRALIA. BUREAU OF STATISTICS. QUEENSLAND OFFICE. DEMOGRAPHY, QUEENSLAND. see *POPULATION STUDIES — Abstracting, Bibliographies, Statistics*

AUSTRALIA. BUREAU OF STATISTICS. QUEENSLAND OFFICE. ESTIMATED RESIDENT POPULATION AND AREA, QUEENSLAND, PRELIMINARY. see *POPULATION STUDIES — Abstracting, Bibliographies, Statistics*

AUSTRALIA. BUREAU OF STATISTICS. QUEENSLAND OFFICE. ESTIMATED RESIDENT POPULATION, QUEENSLAND. see *POPULATION STUDIES — Abstracting, Bibliographies, Statistics*

319   AT   ISSN 1030-4789
AUSTRALIA. BUREAU OF STATISTICS. QUEENSLAND OFFICE. LOCAL GOVERNMENT AREAS STATISTICAL SUMMARY, QUEENSLAND. 1963. a. Aus.$16.50 (foreign Aus.$25.50). Australian Bureau of Statistics, Queensland Office, 313 Adelaide St., Brisbane, Qld. 4000, Australia. TEL 07-222-6022. FAX 07-229-6171. TELEX AA 40271.
   Formerly (until 1987): Australia. Bureau of Statistics. Queensland Office. Local Authority Areas Statistical Summary, Queensland (ISSN 0727-1808)
   Description: Summary of information for each legal local government area, statistical division and statistical district: area, population, births, deaths, building, manufacturing establishments, pre-school and child care centers, schools, agricultural industry and production, acute public hospitals, motor vehicles registered and road traffic accidents.

319   AT   ISSN 0048-6396
AUSTRALIA. BUREAU OF STATISTICS. QUEENSLAND OFFICE. MONTHLY SUMMARY OF STATISTICS, QUEENSLAND. 1961. m. Aus.$108 (foreign Aus.$147.60). Australian Bureau of Statistics, Queensland Office, 313 Adelaide St., Brisbane, Qld. 4000, Australia. circ. 700.
   Description: Summary of up-to-date statistics on a wide range of subjects.

319   AT   ISSN 1030-7389
AUSTRALIA. BUREAU OF STATISTICS. QUEENSLAND OFFICE. QUEENSLAND YEAR BOOK. a. Aus.$36.95 (foreign Aus.$47.95). Australian Bureau of Statistics, Queensland Office, 313 Adelaide St., Brisbane, Qld. 4000, Australia. index; circ. 2,500.
   Former titles (until 1965): Queensland Government Statistician. Official Year Book of Queensland (ISSN 1030-7370); (until 1957): Queensland Government Statistician. Queensland Year Book (ISSN 0085-5359); (until 1937): Queensland Government Statistician. Queensland Official Year Book (ISSN 0810-719X) Which was formerly (until 1901): Year Book of Queensland (ISSN 0810-7203).

319   AT   ISSN 0047-8032
HA3091
AUSTRALIA. BUREAU OF STATISTICS. SOUTH AUSTRALIAN OFFICE. MONTHLY SUMMARY OF STATISTICS, SOUTH AUSTRALIA. 1952. m. Aus.$108 (foreign Aus.$151.20). Australian Bureau of Statistics, South Australian Office, Box 2272, Adelaide, S.A. 5001, Australia. FAX 08-237-7566.
   Description: Current major statistical series on population, vital statistics, employment, unemployment, industrial disputes, earnings, production of selected items, building approvals, commencements and completions, foreign trade, retail sales, transport, state government finance, banking, new fixed capital expenditure, housing finance, and price indexes. Some series are seasonally adjusted.

AUSTRALIA. BUREAU OF STATISTICS. TASMANIAN OFFICE. MINING TASMANIA. see *MINES AND MINING INDUSTRY — Abstracting, Bibliographies, Statistics*

319.4   AT
AUSTRALIA. BUREAU OF STATISTICS. TASMANIAN OFFICE. TASMANIAN STATISTICAL INDICATORS. 1945. m. Aus.$108. Australian Bureau of Statistics, Tasmanian Office, G.P.O. Box 66A, Hobart, Tas. 7001, Australia. stat.; circ. 600.
   Former titles: Australia. Bureau of Statistics. Tasmanian Office. Monthly Summary of Statistics Tasmania (ISSN 0314-2094); Australia. Bureau of Statistics. Tasmanian Office. Monthly Summary of Statistics (ISSN 0039-9833)
   Description: Contains tables dealing with: population and vital statistics, employment and unemployment, wages and prices, production statistics, building, finance, trade, retail sales, tourism, motor vehicle registrations and road traffic accidents.

AUSTRALIA. BUREAU OF STATISTICS. VICTORIAN OFFICE. ESTIMATED RESIDENT POPULATION IN STATISTICAL LOCAL AREAS, VICTORIA. see *POPULATION STUDIES — Abstracting, Bibliographies, Statistics*

AUSTRALIA. BUREAU OF STATISTICS. VICTORIAN OFFICE. LOCAL GOVERNMENT FINANCE, VICTORIA. see *BUSINESS AND ECONOMICS — Abstracting, Bibliographies, Statistics*

319   AT   ISSN 0158-202X
AUSTRALIA. BUREAU OF STATISTICS. VICTORIAN OFFICE. MONTHLY SUMMARY OF STATISTICS, VICTORIA. 1960. m. Aus.$120. Australian Bureau of Statistics, Victorian Office, Box 2796Y, G.P.O., Melbourne, Vic. 3001, Australia. circ. 800.
   Formerly: Australia. Bureau of Statistics. Victorian Office. Victorian Monthly Statistical Review (ISSN 0049-6162)
   Description: Major monthly and quarterly statistical series covering population and vital statistics, employment and unemployment, wages and prices, production, building, public and private finance, trade, transport and communications and a list of Victorian publications released in that month.

994 319   AT   ISSN 1033-3665
AUSTRALIA. BUREAU OF STATISTICS. VICTORIAN OFFICE. SUMMARY OF STATISTICS (YEAR). 1956. a. Aus.$9. Australian Bureau of Statistics, Victorian Office, Box 2796Y, G.P.O., Melbourne, Vic. 3001, Australia. adv.; bk.rev.; index; circ. 1,200.
   Formerly: Victorian Pocket Yearbook (ISSN 0067-1207)
   Description: Compact tables covering most fields of statistics collected by the bureau relating to Victoria.

AUSTRALIA. BUREAU OF STATISTICS. VICTORIAN OFFICE. VALUE OF AGRICULTURAL PRODUCTION, VICTORIA. see *AGRICULTURE — Abstracting, Bibliographies, Statistics*

994 319   AT   ISSN 0067-1223
AUSTRALIA. BUREAU OF STATISTICS. VICTORIAN OFFICE. VICTORIAN YEARBOOK. 1873. a. Aus.$31. Australian Bureau of Statistics, Victorian Office, Box 2796Y, G.P.O., Melbourne, Vic. 3001, Australia. adv.; bk.rev.; bibl.; index; circ. 1,200.
   —BLDSC shelfmark: 9232.720000.
   Description: Provides comprehensive collection of statistical information about Victoria.

AUSTRALIA. BUREAU OF STATISTICS. WESTERN AUSTRALIAN OFFICE. FISHERIES, WESTERN AUSTRALIA. see *FISH AND FISHERIES — Abstracting, Bibliographies, Statistics*

319.4   AT   ISSN 0727-2367
AUSTRALIA. BUREAU OF STATISTICS. WESTERN AUSTRALIAN OFFICE. MONTHLY SUMMARY OF STATISTICS. 1958. m. Aus.$120 (foreign Aus.$147)(effective 1991). Australian Bureau of Statistics, Western Australian Office, 1-3 St. George's Terrace, Perth, W.A. 6000, Australia. circ. 312. (processed)
   Formerly: Australia. Bureau of Statistics. Western Australian Office. Monthly Statistical Summary (ISSN 0004-8542)
   Description: Indicators of business activity, population and vital statistics, employment and unemployment, wages and prices, production and building, finance, trade and transport.

319   AT   ISSN 0810-8633
HA3001
AUSTRALIA. BUREAU OF STATISTICS. YEAR BOOK AUSTRALIA. 1908. a. Aus.$69 (foreign Aus.$95)(effective 1991). Australian Bureau of Statistics, P.O. Box 10, Belconnen, A.C.T. 2616, Australia. TEL 062-527911. FAX 062-516009. circ. 1,861.
   Former titles (until 1975): Australia. Bureau of Statistics. Official Year Book of Australia (ISSN 0312-4746); (until 1973): Official Year Book of the Commonwealth of Australia (ISSN 0078-3927)
   Description: General statistical reference work, containing comprehensive information on demography, prices and household expenditures, labor and industry, social welfare, public health, law and order, education, agriculture and rural industry, and more.

STATISTICS

319.4 AT ISSN 1031-0541
AUSTRALIA AT A GLANCE. 1971. a. Aus.$1 (foreign Aus.$1.90)(effective 1991). Australian Bureau of Statistics, P.O. Box 10, Belconnen, A.C.T. 2616, Australia. circ. 2,409.
  Description: Condensed information about demography and manpower; finance; production and retail sales; price indexes; national accounts, overseas transactions; transport and building. Some international comparisons, state and capital cities information is also shown as are the principal exchange rates of the Australian dollar.

319 AT ISSN 1032-0512
AUSTRALIAN BUREAU OF STATISTICS. PUBLICATIONS TO BE RELEASED IN (YEAR). 1982. a. free. Australian Bureau of Statistics, P.O. Box 10, Belconnen, A.C.T. 2616, Australia. FAX 06-253-1404. stat.; circ. 40,000.
  Formerly (until 1988): Australian Bureau of Statistics. List of Publications to be Released in (Year).
  Description: Lists all ABS publications to be released by central and state offices in each year.

319.4 AT ISSN 0815-3523
AUSTRALIAN CAPITAL TERRITORY AT A GLANCE. 1984. a. Aus.$1 (foreign Aus.$1.90)(effective 1991). Australian Bureau of Statistics, P.O. Box 10, Belconnen, A.C.T. 2616, Australia.
  Description: Condensed information about population, vital statistics, education, health, welfare, crime and justice, earnings and income, labour force, prices, retail, trade, building, agriculture, tourist accommodation, finance, manufacturing, transport and climate.

319 AT ISSN 0067-1754
HA3008.A9
AUSTRALIAN CAPITAL TERRITORY STATISTICAL SUMMARY. 1963. a. Aus.$17 (foreign Aus.$24.10)(effective 1991). Australian Bureau of Statistics, P.O. Box 10, Belconnen, A.C.T. 2616, Australia. circ. 194.
  Description: Information for A.C.T. on climate, demography, social matters, education, employment, earnings, prices, household expenditure, agriculture, manufacturing, retail trade, construction, transport, finance and tourism.

AUSTRALIAN ENERGY STATISTICS. see *ENERGY — Abstracting, Bibliographies, Statistics*

310 AT ISSN 0004-9581
HA1 CODEN: AUJSA3
AUSTRALIAN JOURNAL OF STATISTICS. 1959. 3/yr. Aus.$60($55) (Statistical Society of Australia) Australian Statistical Publishing Association, Inc., G.P.O. Box 573, Canberra, A.C.T. 2601, Australia. Ed. I.R. James. adv.; bk.rev.; charts; index; circ. 1,500. (also avail. in microform from SWZ; back issues avail.; reprint service avail. from SWZ)
  Indexed: Biostat., J.Cont.Quant.Meth., Math.R., Oper.Res.Manage.Sci., Qual.Contr.Appl.Stat., SSCI. —BLDSC shelfmark: 1812.700000.

AUSTRALIAN NON-GOVERNMENT RAILWAYS OPERATING STATISTICS (YEARS). see *TRANSPORTATION — Abstracting, Bibliographies, Statistics*

AUSTRALIAN WOOL SALE STATISTICS. STATISTICAL ANALYSIS. PART A & B & C. see *TEXTILE INDUSTRIES AND FABRICS — Abstracting, Bibliographies, Statistics*

AUSTRIA. STATISTISCHES ZENTRALAMT. INDUSTRIE UND GEWERBESTATISTIK PART 1. see *BUSINESS AND ECONOMICS — Abstracting, Bibliographies, Statistics*

310 AU
AUSTRIA. STATISTISCHES ZENTRALAMT. MIKROZENSUS; JAHRESERGEBNISSE. (Subseries of its Beitraege zur Oesterreichischen Statistik) 1969. a. S.250. Oesterreichisches Statistisches Zentralamt, Hintere Zollamtsstr. 2b, 1033 Vienna, Austria. stat.; circ. 340.
  Description: Information on population, employment and stock of dwellings.

310 AU
AUSTRIA. STATISTISCHES ZENTRALAMT. PUBLIKATIONSANGEBOT. 1978. s-a. free. Oesterreichisches Statistisches Zentralamt, Hintere Zollamtsstr. 2b, 1033 Vienna, Austria. (back issues avail.)
  Description: Publications list and prices.

310 AU
AUSTRIA. STATISTISCHES ZENTRALAMT. STATISTISCHE NACHRICHTEN. 1923. a. S.1250. Oesterreichisches Statistisches Zentralamt, Hintere Zollamtsstr. 2b, 1033 Vienna, Austria. **Indexed:** P.A.I.S.For.Lang.Ind.
  Description: Data on all censuses in Austria.

B S R I A STATISTICS BULLETIN. (Building Services Research and Information Association) see *HEATING, PLUMBING AND REFRIGERATION — Abstracting, Bibliographies, Statistics*

314 GW ISSN 0408-1714
HA1320.B2
BADEN - WUERTTEMBERG. STATISTISCHES LANDESAMT. STATISTISCH-PROGNOSTISCHER BERICHT; Daten - Analysen - Perspektiven. 1973. a. Statistisches Landesamt, Boeblinger Str. 68, Postfach 106033, 7000 Stuttgart 10, Germany. TEL 0711-6410. TELEX 722815-STALA-D. Ed. Max Wingen. circ. 1,200.

314 GW
BADEN - WUERTTEMBERG. STATISTISCHES LANDESAMT. STATISTISCHE BERICHTE. m. Statistisches Landesamt, Boeblinger Str. 68, Postfach 106030, 7000 Stuttgart 10, Germany. TEL 0711-6410. FAX 0711-6412440. TELEX 722815-STALA-D. Ed. Max Wingen. circ. 1,000. (back issues avail.)

314 GW ISSN 0721-1821
BADEN - WUERTTEMBERG IN WORT UND ZAHL. 1953. m. DM.50.40. Statistisches Landesamt, Boeblinger Str. 68, Postfach 106033, 7000 Stuttgart 10, Germany. TEL 0711-641-0. TELEX 722815-STALA-D. Ed. Max Wingen. bk.rev.; circ. 1,100.

318 BF
BAHAMAS. DEPARTMENT OF STATISTICS. STATISTICAL ABSTRACT. 1969. a. $5. Department of Statistics, P.O. Box N 3904, Nassau, Bahamas.

318 BF
BAHAMAS. DEPARTMENT OF STATISTICS. STATISTICAL SUMMARY. 1971. q. $2. Department of Statistics, P.O. Box N 3904, Nassau, Bahamas.

BAHIA, BRAZIL (STATE). CENTRO DE ESTATISTICA E INFORMACOES. INDICE DE PRECO AO CONSUMIDOR. see *BUSINESS AND ECONOMICS — Abstracting, Bibliographies, Statistics*

BAHRAIN. MONETARY AGENCY. QUARTERLY STATISTICAL BULLETIN. see *BUSINESS AND ECONOMICS — Abstracting, Bibliographies, Statistics*

BALANCE OF PAYMENTS STATISTICAL YEARBOOK. see *BUSINESS AND ECONOMICS — Abstracting, Bibliographies, Statistics*

BALANCE SHEETS. see *BUSINESS AND ECONOMICS — Abstracting, Bibliographies, Statistics*

BANCO CENTRAL DE COSTA RICA. ANUARIO ESTADISTICO DE LAS CUENTAS MONETARIAS. see *BUSINESS AND ECONOMICS — Abstracting, Bibliographies, Statistics*

BANCO DE PORTUGAL. ESTATISTICA E ESTUDOS ECONOMICOS. see *BUSINESS AND ECONOMICS — Abstracting, Bibliographies, Statistics*

BANGLADESH BANK. STATISTICS DEPARTMENT. ANNUAL BALANCE OF PAYMENTS. see *BUSINESS AND ECONOMICS — Abstracting, Bibliographies, Statistics*

BANK OF GREECE. MONTHLY STATISTICAL BULLETIN. see *BUSINESS AND ECONOMICS — Banking And Finance*

BARBADOS. STATISTICAL SERVICE. BULLETIN. OVERSEAS TRADE. see *BUSINESS AND ECONOMICS — Abstracting, Bibliographies, Statistics*

317.29 BB ISSN 0378-8873
HA865
BARBADOS. STATISTICAL SERVICE. MONTHLY DIGEST OF STATISTICS. 1974. m. B.$0.50. Statistical Service, National Insurance Bldg., 3rd Fl., Fairchild St., Bridgetown, Barbados, W.I. illus.

310 BB
BARBADOS. STATISTICAL SERVICE. SURVEY OF ACCOMMODATION ESTABLISHMENTS. irreg. Statistical Service, National Insurance Bldg., 3rd Fl., Fairchild St., Bridgetown, Barbados, W.I.

BASIC AND CLINICAL BIOSTATISTICS. see *MATHEMATICS*

314 GW
BAYERISCHES LANDESAMT FUER STATISTIK UND DATENVERARBEITUNG. ZEITSCHRIFT - BAYERN IN ZAHLEN.. 1869. m. DM.88. Bayerisches Landsamt fuer Statistik und Datenverarbeitung, Neuhauserstr. 51, Postfach 200303, 8000 Munich 2, Germany. TEL 089-2119205. Ed. K. Witte. adv.; charts; tr.lit.; index; index; circ. 1,000. (back issues avail.)
  Formerly: Bayern in Zahlen (ISSN 0005-7215)

BEER STATISTICS NEWS. see *BEVERAGES*

310 DK ISSN 0107-5071
BEFOLKNINGEN I KOEBENHAVN I JANUAR. (Subseries: Tal fra Koebenhavns Statistiske Kontor) 1977. a. DKK 20. Koebenhavns Kommune, Oekonomidirektoratet, Statistisk Kontor, Vester Voldgade 87, 1552 Copenhagen V, Denmark. (Dist. by: Danske Boghandleres Kommissionsanstalt, Siljangade 6-8, 2300 Copenhagen S, Denmark)
  Formerly: Befolkningen i Januar.

314 AU ISSN 0067-2319
BEITRAEGE ZUR OESTERREICHISCHEN STATISTIK. 1953. irreg. price varies. Oesterreichisches Statistisches Zentralamt, Hintere Zollamtsstr. 2b, 1033 Vienna, Austria.
  Description: Publications from all branches of statistics collection.

314.93 BE ISSN 0770-0369
HA1393
BELGIUM. INSTITUT NATIONAL DE STATISTIQUE. ANNUAIRE DE STATISTIQUES REGIONALES. 1976. a. 415 Fr. (foreign 560 Fr.). Institut National de Statistique, 44 rue de Louvain, B-1000 Brussels, Belgium. charts; stat.

314 BE ISSN 0067-5431
BELGIUM. INSTITUT NATIONAL DE STATISTIQUE. ANNUAIRE STATISTIQUE DE POCHE. (Text in Dutch, French) 1965. a. 145 Fr. (foreign 190 Fr.). Institut National de Statistique, 44 rue de Louvain, B-1000 Brussels, Belgium.

314 BE ISSN 0045-1703
BELGIUM. INSTITUT NATIONAL DE STATISTIQUE. BULLETIN DE STATISTIQUE. (Supplement avail.: Communique Hebdomadaire) (Text in Dutch, French) 1909. m. 1035 Fr. (foreign 2035 Fr.). Institut National de Statistique, 44 rue de Louvain, B-1000 Brussels, Belgium. TEL 02-513-96-50. charts.
  Indexed: P.A.I.S.For.Lang.Ind.

310 BE ISSN 0069-8075
BELGIUM. INSTITUT NATIONAL DE STATISTIQUE. ETUDES STATISTIQUES. (Includes: Belgium. Institut National de Statistique. Comptes Nationaux de la Belgique) irreg. 175 Fr. (foreign 275 Fr.). Institut National de Statistique, 44 rue de Louvain, B-1000 Brussels, Belgium. TEL 02-513-96-50. **Indexed:** P.A.I.S.For.Lang.Ind.

BELGIUM. INSTITUT NATIONAL DE STATISTIQUE. STATISTIQUE DE LA NAVIGATION INTERIEURE. see *TRANSPORTATION — Abstracting, Bibliographies, Statistics*

BELGIUM. INSTITUT NATIONAL DE STATISTIQUE. STATISTIQUE DES ACCIDENTS DE LA CIRCULATION SUR LA VOIE PUBLIQUE AVEC TUES ET BLESSES. see *PUBLIC HEALTH AND SAFETY — Abstracting, Bibliographies, Statistics*

BELGIUM. INSTITUT NATIONAL DE STATISTIQUE. STATISTIQUE DES VEHICULES A MOTEUR NEUFS MIS EN CIRCULATION. see *TRANSPORTATION — Abstracting, Bibliographies, Statistics*

BELGIUM. INSTITUT NATIONAL DE STATISTIQUE. STATISTIQUE DU TOURISME ET DE L'HOTELLERIE. see *TRAVEL AND TOURISM — Abstracting, Bibliographies, Statistics*

BELGIUM. INSTITUT NATIONAL DE STATISTIQUE. STATISTIQUE DU TRAFIC INTERNATIONAL DES PORTS. see *TRANSPORTATION — Abstracting, Bibliographies, Statistics*

STATISTICS   4565

BELGIUM. INSTITUT NATIONAL DE STATISTIQUE. STATISTIQUES AGRICOLES. see AGRICULTURE — Abstracting, Bibliographies, Statistics

BELGIUM. INSTITUT NATIONAL DE STATISTIQUE. STATISTIQUES DE LA CONSTRUCTION ET DU LOGEMENT. see BUILDING AND CONSTRUCTION — Abstracting, Bibliographies, Statistics

BELGIUM. INSTITUT NATIONAL DE STATISTIQUE. STATISTIQUES DEMOGRAPHIQUES. see POPULATION STUDIES — Abstracting, Bibliographies, Statistics

BELGIUM. INSTITUT NATIONAL DE STATISTIQUE. STATISTIQUES DU COMMERCE INTERIEUR ET DES TRANSPORTS. see TRANSPORTATION — Abstracting, Bibliographies, Statistics

BELGIUM. INSTITUT NATIONAL DE STATISTIQUE. STATISTIQUES INDUSTRIELLES. see BUSINESS AND ECONOMICS — Abstracting, Bibliographies, Statistics

BELGIUM. MINISTERE DE L'EDUCATION NATIONALE. ETUDES ET DOCUMENTS. see EDUCATION — Abstracting, Bibliographies, Statistics

BELGIUM. MINISTERE DE LA SANTE PUBLIQUE ET DE L'ENVIRONNEMENT. ADMINISTRATION DES ETABLISSEMENTS DE SOINS. SERVICE D'ETUDES. ANNUAIRE STATISTIQUE DES ETABLISSEMENTS DE SOINS/BELGIUM. MINISTERIE VAN VOLKSGEZONDHEID EN LEEFMILIEU. BESTUUR VOOR DE VERZORGINGSINSTELLINGEN. STUDIEDIENST. STATISTISCH JAARBOEK VAN DE VERZORGININGSINSTELLINGEN.. see PUBLIC HEALTH AND SAFETY — Abstracting, Bibliographies, Statistics

310   GW   ISSN 0005-9331
BERLINER STATISTIK. (Supplements avail.) 1947. m. DM.54($18) (Statistisches Landesamt) Kulturbuch Verlag GmbH, Passauerstr. 4, 1000 Berlin 30, Germany. TEL 213-6071. FAX 213-4449. bk.rev.; charts; mkt.; stat.; circ. 1,500. **Indexed:** P.A.I.S.For.Lang.Ind.

BERUFSBILDUNGSBERICHT DUISBURG (YEAR). see EDUCATION — School Organization And Administration

BIBLIOGRAPHY OF ECONOMIC AND STATISTICAL PUBLICATIONS ON TANZANIA. see BUSINESS AND ECONOMICS — Abstracting, Bibliographies, Statistics

310   US   ISSN 8750-0434
BIOMETRIC BULLETIN. 1984. q. $10. Biometric Society, 1429 Duke St., Ste. 401, Alexandria, VA 22314-3402. TEL 703-836-8311. Ed. J.N. Perry. abstr.; circ. 6,000. (back issues avail.)

310 574   US   ISSN 0006-341X
                 CODEN: BIOMB6
BIOMETRICS. (Text in English, French, German) 1945. q. $80 to non-members. Biometric Society, 1429 Duke St., Ste. 401, Alexandria, VA 22314-3402. TEL 703-836-8311. adv.; bk.rev.; charts; illus.; stat.; index. cum.index: vols.1-20, 1945-1964; circ. 7,800. (also avail. in microform from UMI,PMC; microfiche from BHP; reprint service avail. from UMI) **Indexed:** Abstr.Anthropol., Agri.Eng.Abstr., Anim.Breed.Abstr., Appl.Mech.Rev., Biol.Abstr., Biol.& Agr.Ind., Biostat., C.I.S. Abstr., Chem.Abstr., Compumath, Comput.Cont., Curr.Adv.Ecol.Sci., Curr.Cont., Dairy Sci.Abstr., Deep Sea Res.& Oceanogr.Abstr., Dent.Ind., Excerp.Med., Food Sci.& Tech.Abstr., Forest.Abstr., Forest Prod.Abstr., Geo.Abstr., Helminthol.Abstr., Herb.Abstr., Hort.Abstr., I D A, Ind.Med., Ind.Sci.Rev., Ind.Vet., INIS Atomind., J.Cont.Quant.Meth., Math.R., Nutr.Abstr., Oper.Res.Manage.Sci., Plant Breed.Abstr., Qual.Contr.Appl.Stat., Risk Abstr., S.Abstr., Sci.Cit.Ind., Soils & Fert., Sorghum & Millets Abstr., Triticale Abstr., Vet.Bull., W.R.C.Inf.
—BLDSC shelfmark: 2088.000000.
Refereed Serial

310   BE   ISSN 0006-3436
BIOMETRIE-PRAXIMETRIE. (Text in Dutch, English, French) 1960. 4/yr. 1100 BEF($30) Societe Adolphe Quetelet, Bureau d'Informatique et de Statistique Appliquees, 22 Av. de la Faculte, B-5030 Gembloux, Belgium. FAX 081-614-941. TELEX 59165 CRAGX. Ed.Bd. adv.; bk.rev.; bibl.; charts; illus.; index; circ. 500. **Indexed:** Anim.Breed.Abstr., Biol.Abstr.
—BLDSC shelfmark: 2088.300000.
Description: Journal of quantitative biology and applications of statistical methods in the biological sciences.

BIOMETRIKA. see BIOLOGY — Abstracting, Bibliographies, Statistics

BLUE BOOK OF FOOD STORE OPERATORS & WHOLESALERS. see FOOD AND FOOD INDUSTRIES — Abstracting, Bibliographies, Statistics

310   SP   ISSN 0210-1580
BOLETIN DE ESTADISTICA Y COYUNTURA. bi-m. 3500 ptas. Camara Oficial de Comercio, Industria y Navegacion de Barcelona, Diagonal, 452, 08006 Barcelona, Spain. stat. **Indexed:** P.A.I.S.For.Lang.Ind.
Formerly: Boletin Estadistico Coyuntural (ISSN 0522-3806)

BOLIVIA. INSTITUTO NACIONAL DE ESTADISTICA. ANUARIO DE COMERCIO EXTERIOR. see BUSINESS AND ECONOMICS — Abstracting, Bibliographies, Statistics

BOLIVIA. INSTITUTO NACIONAL DE ESTADISTICA. ANUARIO DE ESTADISTICAS INDUSTRIALES. see BUSINESS AND ECONOMICS — Abstracting, Bibliographies, Statistics

BOLIVIA. INSTITUTO NACIONAL DE ESTADISTICA. ESTADISTICAS REGIONALES DEPARTAMENTALES. see PUBLIC ADMINISTRATION — Abstracting, Bibliographies, Statistics

318   BO
BOLIVIA EN CIFRAS. 1972. a. Instituto Nacional de Estadistica, Casilla de Correo No. 6129, La Paz, Bolivia.

310   GW
BONNER MONATSZAHLEN; Statistik aktuell. 1981. m. Einwohner- und Standesamt, Statistikstelle, Bottlerplatz, 5300 Bonn 1, Germany. TEL 0228-771-3480. FAX 0228-774216. TELEX 886861-SKBN-D. circ. 1,000. (back issues avail.)

BOOK OF THE STATES. see PUBLIC ADMINISTRATION

BOTSWANA. CENTRAL STATISTICS OFFICE. STATISTICAL BULLETIN. see BUSINESS AND ECONOMICS — Abstracting, Bibliographies, Statistics

BRAZIL. COMISSAO DE FINANCIAMENTO DA PRODUCAO. ANUARIO ESTATISTICO. see BUSINESS AND ECONOMICS — Abstracting, Bibliographies, Statistics

BRAZIL. FUNDACAO INSTITUTO BRASILEIRO DE GEOGRAFIA E ESTATISTICA. BOLETIM BIBLIOGRAFICO. see GEOGRAPHY — Abstracting, Bibliographies, Statistics

BRAZIL. SERVICO SOCIAL DO COMERCIO. ANUARIO ESTATISTICO. see PUBLIC ADMINISTRATION — Abstracting, Bibliographies, Statistics

317   CN
BRITISH COLUMBIA. MINISTRY OF FINANCE AND CORPORATE RELATIONS. CURRENT STATISTICS. 24/yr. Can.$75. Ministry of Finance and Corporate Relations, 1405 Douglas St., 2nd Fl., Victoria, B.C. V8V 1X4, Canada. TEL 604-387-0327. FAX 604-387-0329.
Description: Lists the latest monthly and annual data on the labour force, consumer price index and production.

BRITISH VIRGIN ISLANDS. STATISTICS OFFICE. BALANCE OF PAYMENTS. see BUSINESS AND ECONOMICS — Abstracting, Bibliographies, Statistics

BRITISH VIRGIN ISLANDS. STATISTICS OFFICE. NATIONAL INCOME AND EXPENDITURE. see BUSINESS AND ECONOMICS — Abstracting, Bibliographies, Statistics

947 314   HU   ISSN 0521-4882
BUDAPEST STATISZTIKAI EVKONYVE. a. 325 Ft. (Kozponti Statisztikai Hivatal) Statisztikai Kiado Vallalat, Kaszasdulo u. 2, Box 99, 1300 Budapest 3, Hungary. TEL 688-635. TELEX 22-6699. (Subscr. to: Kultura, Box 149, H-1389 Budapest, Hungary) circ. 800.

947 314   HU   ISSN 0438-2242
HA1208
BUDAPEST STATISZTIKAI ZSEBKONYVE. a. 99 Ft. (Kozponti Statisztikai Hivatal) Statiqum Kiado es Nyomda Kft., Kaszasdulo u. 2, Box 99, 1300 Budapest 3, Hungary. TEL 361-180-3311. FAX 361-168-8635. TELEX 22-6699. (Subscr. to: Kultura, Box 149, 1389 Budapest, Hungary) circ. 1,000.

314   HU   ISSN 0133-2449
BUDAPESTI STATISZTIKAI TAJEKOZTATO. q. (Kozponti Statisztikai Hivatal) Statisztikai Kiado Vallalat, Kaszasdulo u. 2, P.O. Box 99, 1300 Budapest 3, Hungary. TEL 688-635. TELEX 22-6699. (Subscr. to: Kultura, Box 149, H-1389 Budapest, Hungary)

316 316   BD
BURUNDI. DEPARTEMENT DES ETUDES ET STATISTIQUES. BULLETIN ANNUAIRE. a. 1100 Fr.CFA. Departement des Etudes et Statistiques, B.P. 156, Bujumbura, Burundi.

316   BD
BURUNDI. DEPARTEMENT DES ETUDES ET STATISTIQUES. BULLETIN TRIMESTRIEL. Title varies slightly. (Supplement avail.) 1965. q. 800 Fr. Departement des Etudes et Statistiques, B.P. 1156, Bujumbura, Burundi. stat. **Indexed:** P.A.I.S.For.Lang.Ind.
Supersedes: Burundi. Ministere du Plan. Departement des Statistiques. Bulletin de Statistique (ISSN 0525-2539)

316   BD
BURUNDI. DEPARTEMENT DES ETUDES ET STATISTIQUES. INFORMATIONS STATISTIQUES MENSUELLES. m. 1100 Fr.CFA. Departement des Etudes et Statistiques, B.P. 1156, Bujumbura, Burundi.

319   TR
C.S.O. STATISTICAL BULLETINS. 1972. irreg. price varies. Central Statistical Office, 23 Park St., P.O. Box 98, Port-of-Spain, Trinidad & Tobago, W.I. TEL 809-62-53705. (Dist. by: Government Printing Office, 110 Henry St., Port-of-Spain, Trinidad & Tobago, W.I.)

310   II   ISSN 0008-0683
HA1   CODEN: CSTBAA
CALCUTTA STATISTICAL ASSOCIATION. BULLETIN. (Text in English) 1947. q. Rs.60($16) Calcutta Statistical Association, Calcutta University, New Science Bldg., 35 B.C. Rd., Calcutta 19, India. Ed. S.K. Chatterjee. adv.; bk.rev.; charts; stat.; index; circ. 400. (reprint service avail. from SWZ) **Indexed:** J.Cont.Quant.Meth., Math.R., Stat.Theor.Meth.Abstr.

CALIFORNIA. AGRICULTURAL STATISTICS SERVICE. EXPORTS OF AGRICULTURAL PRODUCTS. see AGRICULTURE — Abstracting, Bibliographies, Statistics

312   US
CALIFORNIA COUNTY FACT BOOK.* 1960. a. $10.60. County Supervisors Association of California, 1100 K St., Ste. 101, Sacramento, CA 95814. TEL 916-441-4011. charts; stat.; circ. 1,000.

CALIFORNIA WORK INJURIES AND ILLNESSES. see OCCUPATIONAL HEALTH AND SAFETY — Abstracting, Bibliographies, Statistics

310   CM
CAMEROON. DIRECTION DE LA STATISTIQUE ET DE LA COMPTABILITE NATIONALE. BULLETIN MENSUEL DE STATISTIQUE. 1974. m. 12000 Fr.CFA. Direction de la Statistique et de la Comptabilite Nationale, B.P. 660, Yaounde, Cameroon. TEL 220-445. circ. 500.

CAMEROON. DIRECTION DE LA STATISTIQUE ET DE LA COMPTABILITE NATIONALE. NOTE ANNUELLE DE STATISTIQUE. see BUSINESS AND ECONOMICS — Abstracting, Bibliographies, Statistics

S

STATISTICS

316   CM
CAMEROON. PROVINCIAL STATISTICAL SERVICE OF THE SOUTH WEST. ANNUAL STATISTICAL REPORT, SOUTH WEST PROVINCE. a. Service Provincial de la Statistique du Sud-Ouest, Box 93, Buea, Cameroon.

CANADA. STATISTICS CANADA. AGGREGATE PRODUCTIVITY MEASURES. see *BUSINESS AND ECONOMICS — Abstracting, Bibliographies, Statistics*

CANADA. STATISTICS CANADA. AIR CHARTER STATISTICS. see *TRANSPORTATION — Abstracting, Bibliographies, Statistics*

CANADA. STATISTICS CANADA. AIR PASSENGER ORIGIN AND DESTINATION. CANADA - UNITED STATES REPORT. see *TRANSPORTATION — Abstracting, Bibliographies, Statistics*

354.71   CN   ISSN 0703-2633
HA742
CANADA. STATISTICS CANADA. ANNUAL REPORT. (Catalogue 11-201) (Text in English and French) 1919. a. free. Statistics Canada, Publications Sales and Services, Ottawa, Ont. K1A 0T6, Canada. TEL 613-951-7277. FAX 613-951-1584. (also avail. in microform from MML)
Description: Reviews the accomplishments of the Agency in the fiscal year, featuring an overview and introduction to Statistics Canada.

CANADA. STATISTICS CANADA. AVIATION STATISTICS CENTRE. SERVICE BULLETIN/CANADA. CENTRE DES STATISTIQUES DE L'AVIATION. BULLETIN DE SERVICE. see *TRANSPORTATION — Abstracting, Bibliographies, Statistics*

CANADA. STATISTICS CANADA. BEVERAGE AND TOBACCO PRODUCTS INDUSTRIES. see *TOBACCO — Abstracting, Bibliographies, Statistics*

CANADA. STATISTICS CANADA. BUILDING PERMITS. see *BUILDING AND CONSTRUCTION — Abstracting, Bibliographies, Statistics*

CANADA. STATISTICS CANADA. BUILDING PERMITS. ANNUAL SUMMARY. see *BUILDING AND CONSTRUCTION — Abstracting, Bibliographies, Statistics*

CANADA. STATISTICS CANADA. CABLE TELEVISION. see *COMMUNICATIONS — Abstracting, Bibliographies, Statistics*

CANADA. STATISTICS CANADA. CANADA'S MINERAL PRODUCTION: PRELIMINARY ESTIMATES. see *MINES AND MINING INDUSTRY — Abstracting, Bibliographies, Statistics*

CANADA. STATISTICS CANADA. CANADIAN ECONOMIC OBSERVER. see *BUSINESS AND ECONOMICS — Abstracting, Bibliographies, Statistics*

CANADA. STATISTICS CANADA. CLOTHING INDUSTRIES. see *CLOTHING TRADE — Abstracting, Bibliographies, Statistics*

CANADA. STATISTICS CANADA. COAL AND COKE STATISTICS. see *MINES AND MINING INDUSTRY — Abstracting, Bibliographies, Statistics*

CANADA. STATISTICS CANADA. COAL MINES. see *MINES AND MINING INDUSTRY — Abstracting, Bibliographies, Statistics*

CANADA. STATISTICS CANADA. COMMUNICATIONS SERVICE BULLETIN. see *COMMUNICATIONS — Abstracting, Bibliographies, Statistics*

CANADA. STATISTICS CANADA. COMMUNITY COLLEGES AND RELATED INSTITUTIONS, POSTSECONDARY ENROLLMENT AND GRADUATES. see *EDUCATION — Abstracting, Bibliographies, Statistics*

CANADA. STATISTICS CANADA. CONSTRUCTION IN CANADA. see *BUILDING AND CONSTRUCTION — Abstracting, Bibliographies, Statistics*

CANADA. STATISTICS CANADA. CONSUMER PRICES AND PRICE INDEXES. see *BUSINESS AND ECONOMICS — Abstracting, Bibliographies, Statistics*

CANADA. STATISTICS CANADA. CORPORATION FINANCIAL STATISTICS. see *BUSINESS AND ECONOMICS — Abstracting, Bibliographies, Statistics*

CANADA. STATISTICS CANADA. CORPORATION TAXATION STATISTICS. see *BUSINESS AND ECONOMICS — Abstracting, Bibliographies, Statistics*

CANADA. STATISTICS CANADA. CREDIT UNIONS. see *BUSINESS AND ECONOMICS — Abstracting, Bibliographies, Statistics*

CANADA. STATISTICS CANADA. CRUDE PETROLEUM AND NATURAL GAS INDUSTRY. see *PETROLEUM AND GAS — Abstracting, Bibliographies, Statistics*

CANADA. STATISTICS CANADA. DIRECT SELLING IN CANADA. see *BUSINESS AND ECONOMICS — Abstracting, Bibliographies, Statistics*

CANADA. STATISTICS CANADA. EDUCATION IN CANADA; a statistical review. see *EDUCATION — Abstracting, Bibliographies, Statistics*

CANADA. STATISTICS CANADA. ELEMENTARY - SECONDARY SCHOOL ENROLMENT. see *EDUCATION — Abstracting, Bibliographies, Statistics*

CANADA. STATISTICS CANADA. EMPLOYMENT, EARNINGS AND HOURS. see *BUSINESS AND ECONOMICS — Abstracting, Bibliographies, Statistics*

CANADA. STATISTICS CANADA. ESTIMATES OF LABOUR INCOME. see *BUSINESS AND ECONOMICS — Abstracting, Bibliographies, Statistics*

CANADA. STATISTICS CANADA. EXPORTS, MERCHANDISE TRADE H S BASED. see *BUSINESS AND ECONOMICS — Abstracting, Bibliographies, Statistics*

CANADA. STATISTICS CANADA. FABRICATED METAL PRODUCTS INDUSTRIES. see *METALLURGY — Abstracting, Bibliographies, Statistics*

CANADA. STATISTICS CANADA. FAMILY INCOMES, CENSUS FAMILIES. see *BUSINESS AND ECONOMICS — Abstracting, Bibliographies, Statistics*

CANADA. STATISTICS CANADA. FARM PRODUCTS PRICE INDEX. see *AGRICULTURE — Abstracting, Bibliographies, Statistics*

CANADA. STATISTICS CANADA. FIELD CROP REPORTING SERIES. see *AGRICULTURE — Abstracting, Bibliographies, Statistics*

CANADA. STATISTICS CANADA. FINANCIAL STATISTICS OF EDUCATION. see *EDUCATION — Abstracting, Bibliographies, Statistics*

CANADA. STATISTICS CANADA. FOOD INDUSTRIES. see *FOOD AND FOOD INDUSTRIES — Abstracting, Bibliographies, Statistics*

CANADA. STATISTICS CANADA. FRUIT AND VEGETABLE PRODUCTION. see *AGRICULTURE — Abstracting, Bibliographies, Statistics*

CANADA. STATISTICS CANADA. GAS UTILITIES, TRANSPORT AND DISTRIBUTION SYSTEMS. see *PETROLEUM AND GAS — Abstracting, Bibliographies, Statistics*

CANADA. STATISTICS CANADA. GENERAL REVIEW OF THE MINERAL INDUSTRIES, MINES, QUARRIES AND OIL WELLS. see *MINES AND MINING INDUSTRY — Abstracting, Bibliographies, Statistics*

CANADA. STATISTICS CANADA. GYPSUM PRODUCTS. see *BUILDING AND CONSTRUCTION — Abstracting, Bibliographies, Statistics*

CANADA. STATISTICS CANADA. HIGHWAY, ROAD, STREET AND BRIDGE CONTRACTORS. see *ENGINEERING — Abstracting, Bibliographies, Statistics*

CANADA. STATISTICS CANADA. HISTORICAL LABOUR FORCE STATISTICS, ACTUAL DATA, SEASONAL FACTORS, SEASONALLY ADJUSTED DATA. see *BUSINESS AND ECONOMICS — Abstracting, Bibliographies, Statistics*

CANADA. STATISTICS CANADA. HOUSEHOLD FACILITIES AND EQUIPMENT. see *HOME ECONOMICS — Abstracting, Bibliographies, Statistics*

CANADA. STATISTICS CANADA. IMPORTS, MERCHANDISE TRADE H S BASED. see *BUSINESS AND ECONOMICS — Abstracting, Bibliographies, Statistics*

CANADA. STATISTICS CANADA. INDUSTRIAL CORPORATIONS, FINANCIAL STATISTICS. see *BUSINESS AND ECONOMICS — Abstracting, Bibliographies, Statistics*

310   CN   ISSN 0380-0547
HA741
CANADA. STATISTICS CANADA. INFOMAT. French edition (ISSN 0380-0563) (Catalogue 11-002) (Editions in English and French) 1932. w. Statistics Canada, Publications Sales and Services, Ottawa, Ont. K1A 0T6, Canada. TEL 613-951-7277. FAX 613-951-1584. (also avail. in microform from MML)
Formerly: Statistics Canada Weekly (ISSN 0380-0555)
Description: Highlights major Statistics Canada reports, reference papers and other releases.

CANADA. STATISTICS CANADA. INTERNATIONAL TRAVEL. see *TRAVEL AND TOURISM — Abstracting, Bibliographies, Statistics*

310   CN   ISSN 0228-5134
Z7554.C2
CANADA. STATISTICS CANADA. LISTING OF SUPPLEMENTARY DOCUMENTS. (Catalogue 11-207) (Text in English and French) 1980. a. Can.$32($38) (foreign $45). Statistics Canada, Communications Division, 3rd Floor, R.H. Coats Bldg., Ottawa, Ont. K1A 0T6, Canada. TEL 613-951-7277. FAX 613-951-1584. (Subscr. to: Publications Sales and Services, Ottawa, Ont. K1A 0T6, Canada)
Description: Systematic inventory of supplementary Statistics Canada documents available to the public, includes technical papers, memoranda, discussions and working papers.

CANADA. STATISTICS CANADA. LIVESTOCK AND ANIMAL PRODUCTS STATISTICS. see *AGRICULTURE — Abstracting, Bibliographies, Statistics*

CANADA. STATISTICS CANADA. MANUFACTURING INDUSTRIES OF CANADA: SUB-PROVINCIAL AREAS. see *BUSINESS AND ECONOMICS — Abstracting, Bibliographies, Statistics*

CANADA. STATISTICS CANADA. MARKET RESEARCH HANDBOOK. see *BUSINESS AND ECONOMICS — Abstracting, Bibliographies, Statistics*

CANADA. STATISTICS CANADA. MECHANICAL TRADE CONTRACTORS. see *ENGINEERING — Abstracting, Bibliographies, Statistics*

CANADA. STATISTICS CANADA. MERCHANDISING INVENTORIES. see *BUSINESS AND ECONOMICS — Abstracting, Bibliographies, Statistics*

CANADA. STATISTICS CANADA. MINERAL WOOL INCLUDING FIBROUS GLASS INSULATION. see *BUILDING AND CONSTRUCTION — Abstracting, Bibliographies, Statistics*

CANADA. STATISTICS CANADA. MOTION PICTURE THEATRES AND FILM DISTRIBUTORS. see *MOTION PICTURES — Abstracting, Bibliographies, Statistics*

CANADA. STATISTICS CANADA. NATIONAL INCOME AND EXPENDITURE ACCOUNTS. see *BUSINESS AND ECONOMICS — Abstracting, Bibliographies, Statistics*

CANADA. STATISTICS CANADA. NON-METALLIC MINERAL PRODUCTS INDUSTRIES. see *CERAMICS, GLASS AND POTTERY — Abstracting, Bibliographies, Statistics*

CANADA. STATISTICS CANADA. NON-RESIDENTIAL GENERAL CONTRACTORS AND DEVELOPERS. see *BUILDING AND CONSTRUCTION — Abstracting, Bibliographies, Statistics*

CANADA. STATISTICS CANADA. OILS AND FATS. see *FOOD AND FOOD INDUSTRIES — Abstracting, Bibliographies, Statistics*

CANADA. STATISTICS CANADA. OTHER MANUFACTURING INDUSTRIES. see *BUSINESS AND ECONOMICS — Abstracting, Bibliographies, Statistics*

CANADA. STATISTICS CANADA. PASSENGER BUS AND URBAN TRANSIT STATISTICS. see *TRANSPORTATION — Abstracting, Bibliographies, Statistics*

CANADA. STATISTICS CANADA. PASSENGER BUS AND URBAN TRANSIT STATISTICS. see *TRANSPORTATION — Abstracting, Bibliographies, Statistics*

CANADA. STATISTICS CANADA. PENSION PLANS IN CANADA. see *INSURANCE — Abstracting, Bibliographies, Statistics*

CANADA. STATISTICS CANADA. PRIMARY IRON AND STEEL. see *METALLURGY — Abstracting, Bibliographies, Statistics*

CANADA. STATISTICS CANADA. PRINTING, PUBLISHING AND ALLIED INDUSTRIES. see *PRINTING — Abstracting, Bibliographies, Statistics*

CANADA. STATISTICS CANADA. PRIVATE AND PUBLIC INVESTMENT IN CANADA, INTENTIONS. see *BUSINESS AND ECONOMICS — Abstracting, Bibliographies, Statistics*

CANADA. STATISTICS CANADA. PRIVATE AND PUBLIC INVESTMENT IN CANADA. REVISED INTENTIONS. see *BUSINESS AND ECONOMICS — Abstracting, Bibliographies, Statistics*

CANADA. STATISTICS CANADA. PRODUCTION OF POULTRY AND EGGS. see *AGRICULTURE — Abstracting, Bibliographies, Statistics*

CANADA. STATISTICS CANADA. PRODUCTS SHIPPED BY CANADIAN MANUFACTURERS. see *BUSINESS AND ECONOMICS — Abstracting, Bibliographies, Statistics*

CANADA. STATISTICS CANADA. PROVINCIAL GOVERNMENT ENTERPRISE FINANCE: INCOME AND EXPENDITURE, ASSETS, LIABILITIES AND NET WORTH. see *BUSINESS AND ECONOMICS — Abstracting, Bibliographies, Statistics*

CANADA. STATISTICS CANADA. QUARTERLY ESTIMATES OF TRUSTEED PENSION FUNDS. see *BUSINESS AND ECONOMICS — Abstracting, Bibliographies, Statistics*

CANADA. STATISTICS CANADA. QUARTERLY REPORT ON ENERGY SUPPLY. DEMAND IN CANADA. see *ENERGY — Abstracting, Bibliographies, Statistics*

CANADA. STATISTICS CANADA. RADIO AND TELEVISION BROADCASTING. see *COMMUNICATIONS — Abstracting, Bibliographies, Statistics*

CANADA. STATISTICS CANADA. RAILWAY CARLOADINGS. see *TRANSPORTATION — Abstracting, Bibliographies, Statistics*

CANADA. STATISTICS CANADA. RAILWAY OPERATING STATISTICS. see *TRANSPORTATION — Abstracting, Bibliographies, Statistics*

CANADA. STATISTICS CANADA. REPORT ON FUR FARMS. see *LEATHER AND FUR INDUSTRIES — Abstracting, Bibliographies, Statistics*

CANADA. STATISTICS CANADA. RESTAURANT, CATERER AND TAVERN STATISTICS. see *HOTELS AND RESTAURANTS — Abstracting, Bibliographies, Statistics*

CANADA. STATISTICS CANADA. RETAIL CHAIN AND DEPARTMENT STORES. see *BUSINESS AND ECONOMICS — Abstracting, Bibliographies, Statistics*

CANADA. STATISTICS CANADA. ROAD MOTOR VEHICLES, FUEL SALES. see *TRANSPORTATION — Abstracting, Bibliographies, Statistics*

CANADA. STATISTICS CANADA. ROAD MOTOR VEHICLES, REGISTRATIONS. see *TRANSPORTATION — Abstracting, Bibliographies, Statistics*

CANADA. STATISTICS CANADA. RUBBER AND PLASTIC PRODUCTS INDUSTRIES. see *RUBBER — Abstracting, Bibliographies, Statistics*

CANADA. STATISTICS CANADA. SECURITY TRANSACTIONS WITH NON-RESIDENTS. see *BUSINESS AND ECONOMICS — Abstracting, Bibliographies, Statistics*

CANADA. STATISTICS CANADA. SHIPPING IN CANADA. see *TRANSPORTATION — Abstracting, Bibliographies, Statistics*

CANADA. STATISTICS CANADA. SURFACE AND MARINE TRANSPORT.. see *TRANSPORTATION — Abstracting, Bibliographies, Statistics*

CANADA. STATISTICS CANADA. SURVEY OF CANADIAN NURSERY TRADES INDUSTRY. see *GARDENING AND HORTICULTURE — Abstracting, Bibliographies, Statistics*

CANADA. STATISTICS CANADA. SYSTEM OF NATIONAL ACCOUNTS, CANADA'S INTERNATIONAL INVESTMENT POSITION. see *BUSINESS AND ECONOMICS — Abstracting, Bibliographies, Statistics*

CANADA. STATISTICS CANADA. TELECOMMUNICATIONS STATISTICS. see *COMMUNICATIONS — Abstracting, Bibliographies, Statistics*

CANADA. STATISTICS CANADA. TELEPHONE STATISTICS. see *COMMUNICATIONS — Abstracting, Bibliographies, Statistics*

CANADA. STATISTICS CANADA. TEXTILE PRODUCTS INDUSTRIES. see *TEXTILE INDUSTRIES AND FABRICS — Abstracting, Bibliographies, Statistics*

CANADA. STATISTICS CANADA. THE LABOUR FORCE. see *BUSINESS AND ECONOMICS — Abstracting, Bibliographies, Statistics*

CANADA. STATISTICS CANADA. TRUSTEED PENSION FUNDS - FINANCIAL STATISTICS. see *BUSINESS AND ECONOMICS — Abstracting, Bibliographies, Statistics*

CANADA. STATISTICS CANADA. VENDING MACHINE OPERATORS. see *BUSINESS AND ECONOMICS — Abstracting, Bibliographies, Statistics*

CANADA. STATISTICS CANADA. WHOLESALE TRADE. see *BUSINESS AND ECONOMICS — Abstracting, Bibliographies, Statistics*

CANADA. STATISTICS CANADA. WOOD INDUSTRIES. see *FORESTS AND FORESTRY — Abstracting, Bibliographies, Statistics*

317   CN   ISSN 0840-6014
HC115
CANADA, A PORTRAIT. 1980. biennial. Can.$25($29.95) (effective Apr. 1991). Statistics Canada, Publications Division, Ottawa, Ont. K1A 0T6, Canada. TEL 613-951-7277. FAX 613-951-1584.
Description: Presents current and historical information to form a portrait of Canada.

310   CN   ISSN 0319-5724
CANADIAN JOURNAL OF STATISTICS/REVUE CANADIENNE DE STATISTIQUE. (Text in English, French) 1973. q. Can.$80. Statistical Society of Canada, c/o David F. Bray, Managing Editor, 679 Denbury Avenue, Ottawa, Ont. K2A 2P2, Canada. TEL 613-722-7310. Ed. Marc Moore. adv.; bk.rev.; stat.; index; circ. 1,200. (back issues avail.) **Indexed:** Biostat., Compumath, Curr.Ind.Stat., J.Cont.Quant.Meth., Math.R., Oper.Res.Manage.Sci., Qual.Contr.Appl.Stat., Qual.Contr.Appl.Stat., Ref.Zh., Risk Abstr., Stat.Theor.Meth.Abstr.
—BLDSC shelfmark: 3035.760000.

310   CN   ISSN 0831-5698
HN101
CANADIAN SOCIAL TRENDS. French edition: Tendances Sociales Canadiennes (ISSN 0831-5701) (Catalogue 11-008) (Editions in English and French) 1982. q. Can.$34($40) (foreign $48). Statistics Canada, Publications Sales and Services, Ottawa, Ont. K1A 0T6, Canada. TEL 613-951-7277. FAX 613-951-1584. Ed. Craig McKie. adv.; charts; illus.; stat. **Indexed:** Amer.Hist.& Life, Can.Per.Ind., CMI, Hist.Abstr., Pt.de Rep. (1991-).
Description: Discusses the social, economic and demographic changes affecting the lives of Canadians and contains the latest figures for major social indicators.

310   CN   ISSN 0832-655X
CANADIAN STATISTICS INDEX. (Text in English, French) 1985. a. (plus semi-annual supplement). Can.$275. Micromedia Ltd., 20 Victoria St., Toronto, Ont. M5C 2N8, Canada. TEL 416-362-5211. FAX 416-362-6161. (also avail. in microfiche from MML; back issues avail.)

CASUALTY ACTUARIAL SOCIETY. DISCUSSION PAPER PROGRAM. see *INSURANCE — Abstracting, Bibliographies, Statistics*

CASUALTY ACTUARIAL SOCIETY. FORUM. see *INSURANCE — Abstracting, Bibliographies, Statistics*

CASUALTY ACTUARIAL SOCIETY. PROCEEDINGS. see *INSURANCE — Abstracting, Bibliographies, Statistics*

CASUALTY ACTUARIAL SOCIETY. YEARBOOK. see *INSURANCE — Abstracting, Bibliographies, Statistics*

310   338.9   JA
CATALOGUE OF STATISTICAL MATERIALS OF DEVELOPING COUNTRIES. (Text in English, Japanese) biennial. 4000 Yen: Institute of Developing Economies - Ajia Keizai Kenkyusho, 42 Ichigaya-Hommura-cho, Shinjuku-ku, Tokyo 162, Japan.

CENSO DE POBLACION Y VIVIENDAS. see *POPULATION STUDIES — Abstracting, Bibliographies, Statistics*

CENSUS OF AGRICULTURE (YEAR). see *AGRICULTURE — Abstracting, Bibliographies, Statistics*

CENSUS OF PRIVATE NON-PROFIT MAKING INSTITUTIONS IN FIJI. A REPORT. see *BUSINESS AND ECONOMICS — Abstracting, Bibliographies, Statistics*

CENTRAL BANK OF ICELAND. ECONOMIC STATISTICS. see *BUSINESS AND ECONOMICS — Abstracting, Bibliographies, Statistics*

CENTRAL BANK OF SOMALIA. BULLETIN/BANKIGA DHEXE EE SOOMAALIYA. FAAFIN. see *BUSINESS AND ECONOMICS — Abstracting, Bibliographies, Statistics*

CENTRAL BANK OF TRINIDAD AND TOBAGO. MONTHLY STATISTICAL DIGEST. see *BUSINESS AND ECONOMICS — Abstracting, Bibliographies, Statistics*

CENTRAL BANK OF TRINIDAD AND TOBAGO. QUARTERLY STATISTICAL DIGEST. see *BUSINESS AND ECONOMICS — Abstracting, Bibliographies, Statistics*

CENTRE D'ENQUETES STATISTIQUES DE CAEN. ENQUETE ANNUELLE D'ENTREPRISE: INDUSTRIES DIVERSES. see *BUSINESS AND ECONOMICS — Abstracting, Bibliographies, Statistics*

310   001.6   US   ISSN 0933-2480
QA276.A1   CODEN: CNDCE4
CHANCE; new directions for statistics and computers. 1988. 4/yr. $55. Springer-Verlag, Journals, 175 Fifth Ave., New York, NY 10010. TEL 212-460-1612. Eds. William F. Eddy, Stephen E. Fienberg. **Indexed:** Biostat.
—BLDSC shelfmark: 3129.632370.
Description: For those using statistical methods and approaches in market research, demographics, social sciences, and medicine.

CHARITY TRENDS. see *SOCIAL SERVICES AND WELFARE — Abstracting, Bibliographies, Statistics*

CHARTERED INSTITUTE OF PUBLIC FINANCE AND ACCOUNTANCY. CAPITAL EXPENDITURE AND DEBT FINANCING STATISTICS. ACTUALS. see *BUSINESS AND ECONOMICS — Abstracting, Bibliographies, Statistics*

CHARTERED INSTITUTE OF PUBLIC FINANCE AND ACCOUNTANCY. CEMETERIES & CREMATORIA STATISTICS. ACTUALS. see *PUBLIC HEALTH AND SAFETY — Abstracting, Bibliographies, Statistics*

CHARTERED INSTITUTE OF PUBLIC FINANCE AND ACCOUNTANCY. CHARGES FOR LEISURE SERVICES. ACTUALS. see *SPORTS AND GAMES — Abstracting, Bibliographies, Statistics*

4568 STATISTICS

CHARTERED INSTITUTE OF PUBLIC FINANCE AND ACCOUNTANCY. CHARGES FOR WATER SERVICES. see WATER RESOURCES — Abstracting, Bibliographies, Statistics

CHARTERED INSTITUTE OF PUBLIC FINANCE AND ACCOUNTANCY. COSTS OF WATER SERVICES. see WATER RESOURCES — Abstracting, Bibliographies, Statistics

CHARTERED INSTITUTE OF PUBLIC FINANCE AND ACCOUNTANCY. EDUCATION STATISTICS. ACTUALS. see EDUCATION — Abstracting, Bibliographies, Statistics

CHARTERED INSTITUTE OF PUBLIC FINANCE AND ACCOUNTANCY. FINANCE AND GENERAL STATISTICS. ESTIMATES. see BUSINESS AND ECONOMICS — Abstracting, Bibliographies, Statistics

CHARTERED INSTITUTE OF PUBLIC FINANCE AND ACCOUNTANCY. FIRE SERVICE STATISTICS. ACTUALS. see FIRE PREVENTION — Abstracting, Bibliographies, Statistics

CHARTERED INSTITUTE OF PUBLIC FINANCE AND ACCOUNTANCY. FIRE SERVICE STATISTICS. ESTIMATES. see FIRE PREVENTION — Abstracting, Bibliographies, Statistics

CHARTERED INSTITUTE OF PUBLIC FINANCE AND ACCOUNTANCY. HIGHWAYS AND TRANSPORTATION STATISTICS. ESTIMATES. see TRANSPORTATION — Abstracting, Bibliographies, Statistics

CHARTERED INSTITUTE OF PUBLIC FINANCE AND ACCOUNTANCY. HOMELESSNESS STATISTICS. see HOUSING AND URBAN PLANNING — Abstracting, Bibliographies, Statistics

CHARTERED INSTITUTE OF PUBLIC FINANCE AND ACCOUNTANCY. HOUSING REVENUE ACCOUNT STATISTICS. ESTIMATES. see HOUSING AND URBAN PLANNING — Abstracting, Bibliographies, Statistics

CHARTERED INSTITUTE OF PUBLIC FINANCE AND ACCOUNTANCY. HOUSING RENTS STATISTICS. ACTUALS. see HOUSING AND URBAN PLANNING — Abstracting, Bibliographies, Statistics

CHARTERED INSTITUTE OF PUBLIC FINANCE AND ACCOUNTANCY. LEISURE AND RECREATION STATISTICS. ESTIMATES. see SPORTS AND GAMES — Abstracting, Bibliographies, Statistics

CHARTERED INSTITUTE OF PUBLIC FINANCE AND ACCOUNTANCY. LEISURE USAGE. ACTUALS. see SPORTS AND GAMES — Abstracting, Bibliographies, Statistics

CHARTERED INSTITUTE OF PUBLIC FINANCE AND ACCOUNTANCY. LOCAL AUTHORITY AIRPORTS. ACCOUNTS AND STATISTICS. ACTUALS. see TRANSPORTATION — Abstracting, Bibliographies, Statistics

CHARTERED INSTITUTE OF PUBLIC FINANCE AND ACCOUNTANCY. LOCAL GOVERNMENT COMPARATIVE STATISTICS. ESTIMATES. see PUBLIC ADMINISTRATION — Abstracting, Bibliographies, Statistics

CHARTERED INSTITUTE OF PUBLIC FINANCE AND ACCOUNTANCY. PERSONAL SOCIAL SERVICES STATISTICS. ACTUALS. see SOCIAL SERVICES AND WELFARE — Abstracting, Bibliographies, Statistics

CHARTERED INSTITUTE OF PUBLIC FINANCE AND ACCOUNTANCY. PERSONAL SOCIAL SERVICES STATISTICS. ESTIMATES. see SOCIAL SERVICES AND WELFARE — Abstracting, Bibliographies, Statistics

CHARTERED INSTITUTE OF PUBLIC FINANCE AND ACCOUNTANCY. PLANNING AND DEVELOPMENT STATISTICS. ESTIMATES. see HOUSING AND URBAN PLANNING — Abstracting, Bibliographies, Statistics

CHARTERED INSTITUTE OF PUBLIC FINANCE AND ACCOUNTANCY. POLICE STATISTICS. ESTIMATES. see CRIMINOLOGY AND LAW ENFORCEMENT — Abstracting, Bibliographies, Statistics

CHARTERED INSTITUTE OF PUBLIC FINANCE AND ACCOUNTANCY. PROBATION STATISTICS. ACTUALS. see SOCIAL SERVICES AND WELFARE — Abstracting, Bibliographies, Statistics

CHARTERED INSTITUTE OF PUBLIC FINANCE AND ACCOUNTANCY. PUBLIC LIBRARY STATISTICS. ACTUALS. see LIBRARY AND INFORMATION SCIENCES — Abstracting, Bibliographies, Statistics

CHARTERED INSTITUTE OF PUBLIC FINANCE AND ACCOUNTANCY. PUBLIC LIBRARY STATISTICS. ESTIMATES. see LIBRARY AND INFORMATION SCIENCES — Abstracting, Bibliographies, Statistics

CHARTERED INSTITUTE OF PUBLIC FINANCE AND ACCOUNTANCY. REVENUE COLLECTION STATISTICS. ACTUALS. see BUSINESS AND ECONOMICS — Abstracting, Bibliographies, Statistics

CHARTERED INSTITUTE OF PUBLIC FINANCE AND ACCOUNTANCY. TRADING STANDARDS STATISTICS. ACTUALS. see BUSINESS AND ECONOMICS — Abstracting, Bibliographies, Statistics

CHARTERED INSTITUTE OF PUBLIC FINANCE AND ACCOUNTANCY. WASTE COLLECTION STATISTICS. ACTUALS. see PUBLIC ADMINISTRATION — Abstracting, Bibliographies, Statistics

CHARTERED INSTITUTE OF PUBLIC FINANCE AND ACCOUNTANCY. WASTE DISPOSAL STATISTICS. ACTUALS. see PUBLIC ADMINISTRATION — Abstracting, Bibliographies, Statistics

CHARTERED INSTITUTE OF PUBLIC FINANCE AND ACCOUNTANCY. WASTE DISPOSAL STATISTICS. ESTIMATES. see PUBLIC ADMINISTRATION — Abstracting, Bibliographies, Statistics

318   CL
CHILE. INSTITUTO NACIONAL DE ESTADISTICAS. BOLETIN DE EDIFICACION. 1962. m. $9. Instituto Nacional de Estadisticas, Av. Bulnes 418, Casilla 498, Correo 3-Santiago, Chile.

318   CL
CHILE. INSTITUTO NACIONAL DE ESTADISTICAS. COMPENDIO ESTADISTICO. 1971. a. $10. Instituto Nacional de Estadisticas, Av. Bulnes 418, Casilla 498, Correo 3-Santiago, Chile. stat.

318   CL
CHILE. INSTITUTO NACIONAL DE ESTADISTICAS. INFORMATIVO ESTADISTICO. q. $10. Instituto Nacional de Estadisticas, Av. Bulnes 418, Casilla 498, Correo 3-Santiago, Chile. **Indexed:** P.A.I.S.For.Lang.Ind.
Formerly (until 1975): Chile. Instituto Nacional de Estadisticas. Sintesis Estadistica (ISSN 0577-800X)

318   CL
CHILE. INSTITUTO NACIONAL DE ESTADISTICAS. SERIES ESTADISTICAS. 1981. quinquiennial. $20. Instituto Nacional de Estadisticas, Av. Bulnes 418, Casilla 498, Correo 3-Santiago, Chile.
Formerly: Chile. Instituto Nacional de Estadisticas. Anuario Estadistico.

CHILE. SERVICIO NACIONAL DE PESCA. ANUARIO ESTADISTICO DE PESCA. see FISH AND FISHERIES

CHINA FACTS AND FIGURES ANNUAL. see POLITICAL SCIENCE

315   CH
CHINA, REPUBLIC. EXECUTIVE YUAN. DIRECTORATE-GENERAL OF BUDGET, ACCOUNTING & STATISTICS. MONTHLY BULLETIN OF STATISTICS. (Text in English) 1975. m. NT.$121. Executive Yuan, Directorate-General of Budget, Accounting & Statistics, 2 Kwang-Chow Street, Taipei, Taiwan, Republic of China. TEL 02-363-6140. FAX 02-362-6029. (Subscr. to: China Culture Service, No. 5, Lane 333, Roosevelt Rd. Sec. 3, Taipei, Taiwan, R.O.C.) stat.; circ. 1,452.

310 011   CH   ISSN 0257-5736
CHINA, REPUBLIC. EXECUTIVE YUAN. DIRECTORATE-GENERAL OF BUDGET, ACCOUNTING & STATISTICS. SOCIAL INDICATORS (YEAR). (Text in Chinese, English; summaries in Chinese) 1979. a. NT.$350. Executive Yuan, Directorate-General of Budget, Accounting & Statistics, 2, Kwang-Chow St., Taipei, Taiwan, Republic of China.
TEL 02-381-4910. (Subscr. to: China Cultural Service, No. 5, Lane 333, Sec. 3, Roosevelt Rd., Taiwan, R.O.C.) circ. 800.

CHINA, REPUBLIC. MINISTRY OF FINANCE. DEPARTMENT OF STATISTICS. MONTHLY STATISTICS OF EXPORTS AND IMPORTS/CHIN CH'U K'OU MAO I T'UNG CHI YUEH PAO. see BUSINESS AND ECONOMICS — Abstracting, Bibliographies, Statistics

CHINA, REPUBLIC OF. REPORT ON TOURISM. STATISTICS (YEAR). see TRAVEL AND TOURISM — Abstracting, Bibliographies, Statistics

315   HK   ISSN 1052-9225
HA4631
CHINA STATISTICAL YEARBOOK. Chinese edition: Zhongguo Tongji Nianjian. (Text in English) 1981. a. HK.$550($110) for English ed.; Chinese ed. HK.$350 ($67). Economic Information & Agency, 342 Hennessy Rd., 10-16 Fl., Wanchai, Hong Kong. TEL 5738217. FAX 852-8388304. TELEX 60647 EICC HX. (U.S. and Europe subscr. to: Oxford University Press, 200 Madison Ave., New York, NY 10016) (back issues avail.)
Formerly: Statistical Yearbook of China (ISSN 0255-6766)

315.1   US
CHINA STATISTICS SERIES. 1989. irreg. price varies. Praeger Publishers (Subsidiary of: Greenwood Publishing Group Inc.), 88 Post Rd. W., Box 5007, Westport, CT 06881-5007. TEL 203-226-3571. FAX 203-222-1502.

339 318   CR
CIFRAS DE CUENTAS NACIONALES. 1968. a. free. Banco Central de Costa Rica, Departamento de Investigaciones y Estadistica, Apdo. 10058, San Jose, Costa Rica. charts; stat.; circ. 300.

CLASIFICACION MEXICANA DE OCUPACIONES. see OCCUPATIONS AND CAREERS — Abstracting, Bibliographies, Statistics

COAL STATISTICS INTERNATIONAL. see MINES AND MINING INDUSTRY — Abstracting, Bibliographies, Statistics

COLOMBIA. DEPARTAMENTO ADMINISTRATIVO NACIONAL DE ESTADISTICA. ANUARIO DE ESTADISTICAS INDUSTRIALES. see BUSINESS AND ECONOMICS — Abstracting, Bibliographies, Statistics

318   CK
COLOMBIA. DEPARTAMENTO ADMINISTRATIVO NACIONAL DE ESTADISTICA. ANUARIO DE JUSTICIA.* a. Departamento Administrativo Nacional de Estadistica, Banco Nacional de Datos, Centro Administrativo Nacional-Avda. El Dorado, Apdo. Aereo 80043, Bogota, Colombia.
Formerly: Colombia. Departamento Administrativo Nacional de Estadistica. Anuario General de Estadistica - Justicia.

COLOMBIA. DEPARTAMENTO ADMINISTRATIVO NACIONAL DE ESTADISTICA. ANUARIO GENERAL DE ESTADISTICA - TRANSPORTES Y COMUNICACIONES. see TRANSPORTATION — Abstracting, Bibliographies, Statistics

318   CK   ISSN 0120-6281
COLOMBIA. DEPARTAMENTO ADMINISTRATIVO NACIONAL DE ESTADISTICA. BOLETIN DE ESTADISTICA. (Includes supplement) 1951. q. Col.$4000($200) Departamento Administrativo Nacional de Estadistica, Banco Nacional de Datos, Centro Administrativo Nacional, Avda. El Dorado, Apdo. Aereo 80043, Bogota D.E., Colombia. Ed. Saul Ojeda Gomez. charts; illus.; stat.; index; circ. 3,000. **Indexed:** P.A.I.S.For.Lang.Ind.
Formerly (until Dec. 1984): Colombia. Direccion General de Estadistica. Boletin Mensual de Estadistica (ISSN 0010-1370)

310   CK   ISSN 0120-6745
HA1017.C47
COLOMBIA. DEPARTAMENTO ADMINISTRATIVO NACIONAL DE ESTADISTICA. CHOCO ESTADISTICO. a. Departamento Administrativo Nacional de Estadistica, Banco Nacional de Datos, Avda Eldorado, Apdo. Aereo No. 80043, Bogota, Colombia. TEL 2691100. Ed. Diego Martinez Arango.

318 CK
COLOMBIA. DEPARTAMENTO ADMINISTRATIVO NACIONAL DE ESTADISTICA. ESTADISTICAS HISTORICAS. irreg. Departamento Administrativo Nacional de Estadistica, Banco Nacional de Datos, Apartado Aereo 80043, Avda. Eldovado, Bogota, Colombia.

COMMODITY PRICE STATISTICS MONTHLY. see *BUSINESS AND ECONOMICS — Abstracting, Bibliographies, Statistics*

COMMODITY TRADE STATISTICS; according to the Standard International Trade Classification. see *BUSINESS AND ECONOMICS — Abstracting, Bibliographies, Statistics*

314 IT
COMMUNE DI GENOVA. NOTIZIARIO STATISTICO MENSILE. 1928. m. free. Comune di Genova, Via Garibaldi, 9, Genova, Italy. stat.; circ. 700.
Formerly: Genova Statistica (ISSN 0016-691X)

310 IO
COMMUNICATION STATISTICS. (Text in Indonesian) 1965. a. Rps.3000($1.50) Central Bureau of Statistics - Biro Pusat Statistik, Jalan Dr. Sutomo No. 8, Box 3, Jakarta Pusat, Indonesia. TEL 21-372808. circ. 300.

310 US ISSN 0361-0926
QA276.A1 CODEN: CSTMDC
COMMUNICATIONS IN STATISTICS. PART A: THEORY AND METHODS. 1973. 12/yr. $1085. Marcel Dekker Journals, 270 Madison Ave., New York, NY 10016. TEL 212-696-9000. FAX 212-685-4540. TELEX 421419. (Subscr. to: Box 10018, Church St. Sta., New York, NY 10249) Ed. W.B. Smith. adv.; charts. (also avail. in microform from RPI) **Indexed:** Biostat., Compumath, Curr.Cont., Ind.Sci.Rev., J.Cont.Quant.Meth., Math.R., Oper.Res.Manage.Sci., Qual.Contr.Appl.Stat., Risk Abstr., Sci.Abstr., Sci.Cit.Ind.
—BLDSC shelfmark: 3363.432000.
Supersedes in part (with vol.5, 1976): Communications in Statistics (ISSN 0090-3272)
Refereed Serial

310 621.319 US ISSN 0361-0918
QA276.A1 CODEN: CSSCDB
COMMUNICATIONS IN STATISTICS. PART B: SIMULATION AND COMPUTATION. 1976. 4/yr. $410. Marcel Dekker Journals, 270 Madison Ave., New York, NY 10016. TEL 212-696-9000. FAX 212-685-4540. TELEX 421419. (Subscr. to: Box 10018, Church St. Sta., New York, NY 10249) Ed. W.B. Smith. (also avail. in microform from RPI) **Indexed:** Biostat., Compumath, Curr.Cont., Ind.Sci.Rev., J.Cont.Quant.Meth., Math.R., Oper.Res.Manage.Sci., Qual.Contr.Appl.Stat., Sci.Abstr., Sci.Cit.Ind.
—BLDSC shelfmark: 3363.431000.
Supersedes in part (with vol.5, 1976): Communications in Statistics (ISSN 0090-3272)
Refereed Serial

310 US ISSN 0882-0287
QA274.A1 CODEN: CSSME8
COMMUNICATIONS IN STATISTICS. PART C: STOCHASTIC MODELS. 1985. 4/yr. $285 (or $1,691 for 3 Communications in Statistics publications). Marcel Dekker Journals, 270 Madison Ave., New York, NY 10016. TEL 212-696-9000. FAX 212-685-4540. TELEX 421419. (Subscr. to: Box 10018, Church St. Sta., New York, NY 10249) (Co-publisher: Operations Research Society of America (ORSA)) Ed. Marcel Neuts. (also avail. in microform from RPI) **Indexed:** Biostat.
—BLDSC shelfmark: 3363.431500.

COMMUNITY SERVICE STATISTICS: SCOTLAND. see *SOCIAL SERVICES AND WELFARE — Abstracting, Bibliographies, Statistics*

COMPANHIA PARANAENSE DE ENERGIA. INFORME ESTATISTICO ANUAL. see *ENERGY — Abstracting, Bibliographies, Statistics*

314 IT ISSN 0069-7958
COMPENDIO STATISTICO ITALIANO (YEAR). a. L.20000. Istituto Centrale di Statistica, Via Cesare Balbo 16, 00100 Rome, Italy. circ. 12,250.
Formerly: Compendio Statistico (ISSN 0390-640X)

310.6 NE
COMPSTAT SYMPOSIUM. PROCEEDINGS. (Computational Statistics) (Text in English) 1974. biennial. DM.120. (International Association for Statistical Computing, European Section) International Statistical Institute, Prinses Beatrixlaan 428, Postbus 950, 2270 AZ Voorburg, Netherlands. TEL 070-3375737. TELEX 32260 ISI NL. (Orders to: Physica-Verlag, c/o Springer GmbH, Auslieferungs-Gesellschaft, Haberstr. 7, 6900 Heidelberg-Rohrbach, Germany) Ed.Bd. abstr.
Description: Publishes papers reflecting current interests in computational statistics.

310 GW
QA276.4
COMPUTATIONAL STATISTICS. (Text in English) 1982. q. DM.198($128) Physica-Verlag GmbH und Co., Tiergartenstr. 17, Postfach 105280, 6900 Heidelberg 1, Germany. TEL 06221-345168. FAX 06221-300186. TELEX 461723-SPHDB-D. (Subscr. to: Springer Verlag GmbH, Postfach 311340, 1000 Berlin 31, Germany; Dist. in North America by: Springer-Verlag New York Inc., 175 Fifth Ave., New York, NY 10010, U.S.A.. TEL 212-460-1500) Ed. W. Haerdle. **Indexed:** Cyb.Abstr.
Formerly: C S Q - Computational Statistics Quarterly (ISSN 0723-712X)
Description: Covers computational aspects of new and existing statistical techniques.

314 GR ISSN 0069-8245
CONCISE STATISTICAL YEARBOOK OF GREECE. (Text in English and Greek) 1954. a. $7. National Statistical Service of Greece, Statistical Information and Publications Division, 14-16 Lycourgou St., 101 66 Athens, Greece. TEL 3244-748. FAX 3222205. TELEX 216734 ESYE GR.

CONCRETE PIPE INDUSTRY STATISTICS. see *ENGINEERING — Abstracting, Bibliographies, Statistics*

316 CF ISSN 0010-5805
CONGO. CENTRE NATIONAL DE LA STATISTIQUE ET DES ETUDES ECONOMIQUES. BULLETIN MENSUEL DE LA STATISTIQUE. 1958. m. 12000 Fr.CFA. Centre National de la Statistique et des Etudes Economiques, B.P. 2031, Brazzaville, Congo. charts; mkt.; circ. 500. (processed)

COST AND PRODUCTION SURVEY REPORT. see *MEDICAL SCIENCES*

310 CR ISSN 0589-8544
COSTA RICA. DIRECCION GENERAL DE ESTADISTICA Y CENSOS. INVENTARIO DE LAS ESTADISTICAS NACIONALES. 1964. irreg., latest 1970. exchange basis. Direccion General de Estadistica y Censos, San Jose, Costa Rica.

COUNTY PENETRATION REPORTS; a tabulation of county circulation data for daily and weekly newspapers. see *ADVERTISING AND PUBLIC RELATIONS — Abstracting, Bibliographies, Statistics*

CRIME AND DELINQUENCY IN CALIFORNIA. see *CRIMINOLOGY AND LAW ENFORCEMENT — Abstracting, Bibliographies, Statistics*

317.28 CU
CUBA. COMITE ESTATAL DE ESTADISTICAS. REVISTA ESTADISTICA. (Text in Spanish; summaries in English and Russian) 1979. s-a. Comite Estatal de Estadisticas, Centro de Informacion Cientifico-Tecnica, Almendares No. 156, esq. a Desague, Gaveta Postal 6016, Havana, Cuba. Ed. Ramon Sabadi Rodriquez. bk.rev.; bibl.; charts.

CUBA EN CIFRAS. see *BUSINESS AND ECONOMICS — Abstracting, Bibliographies, Statistics*

CUBA QUARTERLY ECONOMIC REPORT. see *BUSINESS AND ECONOMICS — Abstracting, Bibliographies, Statistics*

CURRENT INDEX TO STATISTICS; applications-methods-theory. see *MATHEMATICS — Abstracting, Bibliographies, Statistics*

CURRENT INDUSTRIAL REPORTS: BROADWOVEN FABRICS (GRAY). see *TEXTILE INDUSTRIES AND FABRICS — Abstracting, Bibliographies, Statistics*

CURRENT INDUSTRIAL REPORTS: FATS AND OILS. OILSEED CRUSHINGS. see *FOOD AND FOOD INDUSTRIES — Abstracting, Bibliographies, Statistics*

CURRENT INDUSTRIAL REPORTS: FATS AND OILS. PRODUCTION, CONSUMPTION, AND STOCKS. see *FOOD AND FOOD INDUSTRIES — Abstracting, Bibliographies, Statistics*

CYPRUS. DEPARTMENT OF STATISTICS AND RESEARCH. AGRICULTURAL STATISTICS. see *AGRICULTURE — Abstracting, Bibliographies, Statistics*

310 CY
CYPRUS. DEPARTMENT OF STATISTICS AND RESEARCH. CENSUS OF COTTAGE INDUSTRY. (Text in English) 1967. irreg. £C2. Ministry of Finance, Department of Statistics and Research, Nicosia, Cyprus.
Description: Data on establishments, employment, output, investments, structure and regional distribution of cottage industry.

CYPRUS. DEPARTMENT OF STATISTICS AND RESEARCH. CENSUS OF INDUSTRIAL PRODUCTION.. see *BUSINESS AND ECONOMICS — Abstracting, Bibliographies, Statistics*

CYPRUS. DEPARTMENT OF STATISTICS AND RESEARCH. CENSUS OF POULTRY. see *AGRICULTURE — Abstracting, Bibliographies, Statistics*

CYPRUS. DEPARTMENT OF STATISTICS AND RESEARCH. CRIMINAL STATISTICS. see *CRIMINOLOGY AND LAW ENFORCEMENT — Abstracting, Bibliographies, Statistics*

CYPRUS. DEPARTMENT OF STATISTICS AND RESEARCH. DEMOGRAPHIC SURVEY. (YEAR). see *POPULATION STUDIES — Abstracting, Bibliographies, Statistics*

310 CY
CYPRUS. DEPARTMENT OF STATISTICS AND RESEARCH. FUNCTIONS AND SERVICES. (Text in English) 1981. irreg. free. Ministry of Finance, Department of Statistics and Research, Nicosia, Cyprus.
Description: Information about the function and services of the Cyprus Department of Statistics and Research.

CYPRUS. DEPARTMENT OF STATISTICS AND RESEARCH. MULTI-ROUND DEMOGRAPHIC SURVEY. MIGRATION IN CYPRUS. see *POPULATION STUDIES — Abstracting, Bibliographies, Statistics*

310 CY
CYPRUS. DEPARTMENT OF STATISTICS AND RESEARCH. QUESTIONNAIRES FOR CENSUSES AND SURVEYS. (Text in English, Greek) 1982. irreg. EC$3. Ministry of Finance, Department of Statistics and Research, Nicosia, Cyprus.
Description: Summary of all questionnaires used by the Department of Statistics and Research in conducting censuses, surveys and other statistical inquiries.

CYPRUS. DEPARTMENT OF STATISTICS AND RESEARCH. STATISTICAL ABSTRACT. see *SOCIAL SCIENCES: COMPREHENSIVE WORKS — Abstracting, Bibliographies, Statistics*

314.37 947 CS ISSN 0070-248X
CZECHOSLOVAKIA. FEDERALNI STATISTICKY URAD. STATISTICKA ROCENKA. (Text in Czech; summaries in English and Russian) 1957. approx. a. $20 per no. Nakladatelstvi Technicke Literatury, Spalena 51, 113 02 Prague 1, Czechoslovakia. circ. 13,300.

314.37 947 CS
CZECHOSLOVAKIA. FEDERALNI STATISTICKY URAD. STATISTICKE PREHLEDY. 1967. m. $70.50. Federalni Statisticky Urad, Sokolovska 142, 186 13 Prague 8, Czechoslovakia. TELEX 121084. (Dist. by: Postal Press Service - Postovni Novinova Sluzba, Kafkova 19, Prague 6, Czechoslovakia) Ed. Hana Sekyrova.
Description: Regular as well as irregular statistical information on various fields of economic, social and cultural development of Czechoslovakia.

4570 STATISTICS

317   CN   ISSN 0827-0465
HC111
THE DAILY. 1932. d. Can.$120($144) (foreign $168). Statistics Canada, Publications Division, Ottawa, Ont. K1A 0T6, Ontario. TEL 613-951-7277. FAX 613-951-1584.
Description: Contains news summaries and announcements of reports, reference papers and a list of titles of the publications released.

314.8   DK   ISSN 0107-7139
HA1473
DANMARK I TAL. English edition: Data on Denmark. 1981. a. free. Danmarks Statistik, Sejroegade 11, 2100 Copenhagen OE, Denmark. TEL 01-29 82 22. illus.

310   DK   ISSN 0417-0164
DENMARK. DANMARKS STATISTIK. DETAILPRISER. 1963. q. DKK 64.75. Danmarks Statistik, Sejroegade 11, 2100 Copenhagen OE, Denmark. TEL 31-298222. FAX 31-184801. TELEX 16236. (back issues avail.)

314   DK   ISSN 0070-3567
HA1477
DENMARK. DANMARKS STATISTIK. STATISTISK AARBOG. (Text in Danish; notes in English) 1896. a. DKK 159.84. Danmarks Statistik, Sejroegade 11, 2100 Copenhagen OE, Denmark. TEL 31-298222. FAX 31-184801. TELEX 16236. cum.index: 1769-1972.
Description: Consists of tables (without explanatory text) with principal results of most censuses and surveys conducted by Danmarks Statistik

314   DK   ISSN 0070-3583
HA1472
DENMARK. DANMARKS STATISTIK. STATISTISK TIARS-OVERSIGT/DENMARKS STATISTICS. STATISTICAL TEN-YEAR REVIEW. 1961. a. DKK 80.33. Danmarks Statistik, Sejroegade 11, 2100 Copenhagen OE, Denmark. TEL 31-298222. FAX 31-184801.
Description: Presents comparable annual statistics for the past ten years, thus revealing both trends and structural changes. Adapted to the educational sector.

310   DK   ISSN 0106-6439
DENMARK. DANMARKS STATISTIK. STATISTISKE MEDDELELSER. 1852. irreg. price varies. Danmarks Statistik, Sejroegade 11, 2100 Copenhagen OE, Denmark. TEL 31-298222. FAX 31-184801. TELEX 16236.

314   DK   ISSN 0039-0682
DENMARK. DANMARKS STATISTIK. STATISTISKE UNDERSOGELSER. 1958. irreg. price varies. Danmarks Statistik, Sejroegade 11, 2100 Copenhagen OE, Denmark. TEL 31-298222. FAX 31-184801. TELEX 16236.

310   DK   ISSN 0109-8314
Z7554.D3
DENMARK. DANMARKS STATISTIK. VEJVISER I STATISTIKEN. 1984. irreg. DKK 65. Danmarks Statistik, Sejroegade 11, 2100 Copenhagen OE, Denmark. TEL 31-298222. FAX 31-184801. TELEX 16236.

310   UK   ISSN 0262-8295
DIGEST OF WELSH STATISTICS. 1954. a. £6. Welsh Office, Economic and Statistical Services Division, New Crown Bldg., Cathays Park, Cardiff CF1 3NQ, Wales. TEL 0222-825044. FAX 0222-825350. TELEX 487228. Ed. E. Swires-Hennessy. stat.; circ. 800.
—BLDSC shelfmark: 3588.335000.
Description: Specifics on social conditions, labor, education, production, distribution, transport and finance.

319   AT   ISSN 1032-8408
DIRECTORY OF SMALL AREA STATISTICS, QUEENSLAND. 1988. irreg., latest 1991. Aus.$5. Australian Bureau of Statistics, Queensland Office, 313 Adelaide St., Brisbane, Qld. 4000, Australia. TEL 07-222-6022. FAX 07-229-6171. TELEX AA 40271.
Description: A comprehensive listing of ABS publications that contain statistics for small geographic areas in Queensland.

310   US   ISSN 0278-405X
HA1
DIRECTORY OF STATISTICIANS. triennial. $125. American Statistical Association, 1429 Duke St., Alexandria, VA 22314-3402. TEL 703-684-1221. FAX 703-684-2037.
Formerly: Statisticians and Others in Allied Professions (ISSN 0081-508X)

DJIBOUTI. DIRECTION NATIONALE DE LA STATISTIQUE. BULLETIN DE STATISTIQUE ET DE DOCUMENTATION. see *PUBLIC ADMINISTRATION — Abstracting, Bibliographies, Statistics*

314   GW   ISSN 0418-1263
DUESSELDORF IN ZAHLEN. 1902. a. DM.20. Landeshauptstadt, Amt fuer Statistik und Wahlen, Postfach 1120, D-4000 Dusseldorf 1, Germany. stat.; circ. 570. (looseleaf format)

EARNINGS - INDUSTRY AND SERVICES. see *BUSINESS AND ECONOMICS — Abstracting, Bibliographies, Statistics*

310   US
EAST TENNESSEE DEVELOPMENT DISTRICT ECONOMIC STATISTICS. 1981. q. $1 per county ($10 per book). East Tennessee Development District, 5616 Kingston Pike, Box 19806, Knoxville, TN 37939-2806. TEL 615-584-8553. FAX 615-584-5159.
Description: Summarizes various federal, state and local sources which provide economic data for East Tennessee Development District region.

ECONOMIC AND SOCIAL STATISTICS OF SRI LANKA. see *BUSINESS AND ECONOMICS — Abstracting, Bibliographies, Statistics*

EDUCATION STATISTICS, NEW YORK STATE; prepared especially for members of the Legislature. see *EDUCATION — Abstracting, Bibliographies, Statistics*

315.6   UA
EGYPT. CENTRAL AGENCY FOR PUBLIC MOBILISATION AND STATISTICS. STATISTICAL YEARBOOK. (Text in Arabic and English) 1961. a. £E14. Central Agency for Public Mobilisation and Statistics, Box 2086, Nasr City, Cairo, Egypt.
Formerly: Statistical Handbook of Egypt.

318   ES   ISSN 0080-5661
EL SALVADOR. DIRECCION GENERAL DE ESTADISTICA Y CENSOS. ANUARIO ESTADISTICO. a. free or exchange basis. Direccion General de Estadistica y Censos, 1 Calle Poniente y 43 Avenida Norte, San Salvador, El Salvador.

317.284   ES   ISSN 0013-404X
EL SALVADOR. DIRECCION GENERAL DE ESTADISTICA Y CENSOS. BOLETIN ESTADISTICO. 1951. q. free or exchange basis. Direccion General de Estadistica y Censos, 1 Calle Poniente y 43 Avenida Norte, San Salvador, El Salvador. mkt.; stat.

318   ES   ISSN 0581-4111
EL SALVADOR. MINISTERIO DE PLANIFICACION Y COORDINACION DEL DESARROLLO ECONOMICO Y SOCIAL. INDICADORES ECONOMICOS Y SOCIALES. 1962. irreg., latest 1987-89. Ministerio de Planificacion y Coordinacion del Desarrollo Economico y Social, Seccion de Investigaciones Estadisticas, Casa Presidential, San Salvador, El Salvador. Ed.Bd. stat.; charts. **Indexed:** P.A.I.S.For.Lang.Ind.
Description: Covers El Salvador's public health, education, social security, employment, commerce, banking, public finance, construction, transportation, communication, agriculture and manufacture.

317.2   MX
ENCUESTA NACIONAL DE INGRESOS Y GASTOS DE LOS HOGARES. irreg. Instituto Nacional de Estadistica, Geografia e Informatica, Secretariado de Programacion e Presupuesto, Av. Prol. Hereo de Nacozari 2301 S., Puerta 11, planta baja, Aguascalientes 20290, Ags., Mexico.

ENERGIEVERSORGUNG OESTERREICHS. see *ENERGY — Abstracting, Bibliographies, Statistics*

314   GW
ENTWICKLUNGEN IN NORDRHEIN-WESTFALEN IM JAHRE (YEAR). 1972. a. Landesamt fuer Datenverarbeitung und Statistik Nordrhein-Westfalen, Mauerstr. 51, Postfach 101105, 4000 Duesseldorf 1, Germany. TEL 0211-9449-01. circ. 7,000.
Description: Statistics of all areas of life in Nordrhein-Westfalen: employment, industry, agriculture, schools, traffic, etc.

ESTABLECIMIENTOS MANUFACTURERAS EN PUERTO RICO. see *BUSINESS AND ECONOMICS — Abstracting, Bibliographies, Statistics*

310   US   ISSN 0014-1135
HA1   CODEN: ESTDA4
ESTADISTICA. (Text in English, French, Portuguese and Spanish) 1943. s-a. $7. Organization of American States, Department of Publications, 1889 F St., N.W., Washington, DC 20006. TEL 703-941-1617. Ed. M. Alicia Monzon De Madariaga. bibl.; charts; index, cum.index: 1943-1953; circ. 2,300. (also avail. in microfilm from UMI; reprint service avail. from UMI) **Indexed:** Geo.Abstr., Math.R., Popul.Ind.
—BLDSC shelfmark: 3812.530000.

319   PN
ESTADISTICA PANAMENA. BOLETIN. 1963. irreg. free. Direccion de Estadistica y Censo, Apdo. 5213, Panama 5, Panama. FAX 63-9322.

ESTADISTICA PANAMENA. SITUACION CULTURAL. SECCION 511. EDUCACION. see *EDUCATION — Abstracting, Bibliographies, Statistics*

ESTADISTICA PANAMENA. SITUACION DEMOGRAFICA. SECCION 221. ESTADISTICAS VITALES. see *POPULATION STUDIES — Abstracting, Bibliographies, Statistics*

ESTADISTICA PANAMENA. SITUACION ECONOMICA. SECCION 312. PRODUCCION PECUARIA. see *AGRICULTURE — Abstracting, Bibliographies, Statistics*

ESTADISTICA PANAMENA. SITUACION ECONOMICA. SECCION 312. SUPERFICIE SEMBRADA Y COSECHA DE ARROZ, MAIZ Y FRIJOL DE BEJUCO. see *AGRICULTURE — Abstracting, Bibliographies, Statistics*

ESTADISTICA PANAMENA. SITUACION ECONOMICA. SECCION 312. SUPERFICIE SEMBRADA Y COSECHA DE CAFE, TABACO Y CANA DE AZUCAR. see *AGRICULTURE — Abstracting, Bibliographies, Statistics*

ESTADISTICA PANAMENA. SITUACION ECONOMICA. SECCION 323. INDICE DE PRODUCCION FISICA DE LA INDUSTRIA MANUFACTURERA. see *BUSINESS AND ECONOMICS — Abstracting, Bibliographies, Statistics*

ESTADISTICA PANAMENA. SITUACION ECONOMICA. SECCION 331-COMERCIO. ANUARIO DE COMERCIO EXTERIOR. see *BUSINESS AND ECONOMICS — Abstracting, Bibliographies, Statistics*

ESTADISTICA PANAMENA. SITUACION ECONOMICA. SECCION 331. COMERCIO EXTERIOR (PRELIMINARY REPORT). see *BUSINESS AND ECONOMICS — Abstracting, Bibliographies, Statistics*

ESTADISTICA PANAMENA. SITUACION ECONOMICA. SECCION 351. INDICE DE PRECIOS AL POR MAYOR Y AL CONSUMIDOR. see *BUSINESS AND ECONOMICS — Abstracting, Bibliographies, Statistics*

ESTADISTICA PANAMENA. SITUACION ECONOMICA. SECCION 351. PRECIOS PAGADOS POR EL PRODUCTOR AGROPECUARIO. see *AGRICULTURE — Abstracting, Bibliographies, Statistics*

ESTADISTICA PANAMENA. SITUACION ECONOMICA. SECCION 352. HOJA DE BALANCE DE ALIMENTOS. see *BUSINESS AND ECONOMICS — Abstracting, Bibliographies, Statistics*

ESTADISTICA PANAMENA. SITUACION POLITICA, ADMINISTRATIVA Y JUSTICIA. SECCION 631. JUSTICIA. see *LAW — Abstracting, Bibliographies, Statistics*

STATISTICS 4571

ESTADISTICA PANAMENA. SITUACION SOCIAL. SECCION 431. SERVICIOS DE SALUD. see *SOCIAL SERVICES AND WELFARE* — *Abstracting, Bibliographies, Statistics*

ESTADISTICA PANAMENA. SITUACION SOCIAL. SECCION 451. ACCIDENTES DE TRANSITO. see *SOCIOLOGY* — *Abstracting, Bibliographies, Statistics*

ESTADISTICAS DEL COMERCIO EXTERIOR DE MEXICO. INFORMACION PRELIMINAR. see *BUSINESS AND ECONOMICS* — *Abstracting, Bibliographies, Statistics*

ESTIMATED RESIDENT POPULATIONS BY AGE AND SEX IN STATISTICAL LOCAL AREAS, VICTORIA. see *POPULATION STUDIES* — *Abstracting, Bibliographies, Statistics*

ETESIA STATISTIKE. EREVNA TOU KARKINOU/ANNUAL STATISTICAL SURVEY OF CANCER. see *MEDICAL SCIENCES* — *Abstracting, Bibliographies, Statistics*

311 MR ISSN 0851-9722
ETUDES DE CONJONCTURE: EVOLUTIONS ET TENDANCES. q. DH.66. Direction de la Statistique, B.P. 178, Rabat, Morocco. **Indexed:** P.A.I.S.For.Lang.Ind.
Former titles (until 1991): Conjoncture Economique (ISSN 0851-5921); (until 1988): Conjoncture Economique au Maroc (ISSN 0851-0989); Morocco. Direction de la Statistique. Etude de Conjoncture.

EXPORT STATISTICS OF AFGHANISTAN/IHSA'IYAH-I AMUAL-I SADIRATI-I AFGHANISTAN. see *BUSINESS AND ECONOMICS* — *Abstracting, Bibliographies, Statistics*

315.4 II
FACTS ABOUT HARYANA. 1967. irreg. Director of Public Relations, Chandigarh, India. stat.; circ. 3,000.

315 IS
FAMILY EXPENDITURE SURVEY. (Text in English and Hebrew) 1969. irreg. price varies. Central Bureau of Statistics, Box 13015, Hakirya Romema, Jerusalem 91 130, Israel. TEL 02-553400. stat. (back issues avail.)
Description: Research on consumption patterns, income and savings levels of urban families.

FAMILY SAVING SURVEY (YEAR). see *BUSINESS AND ECONOMICS* — *Abstracting, Bibliographies, Statistics*

FARM BUSINESS STATISTICS FOR SOUTH EAST ENGLAND. see *AGRICULTURE* — *Abstracting, Bibliographies, Statistics*

FERTILISER ASSOCIATION OF INDIA. FERTILISER STATISTICS. see *AGRICULTURE* — *Abstracting, Bibliographies, Statistics*

FIJI. BUREAU OF STATISTICS. AIRCRAFT STATISTICS. see *AERONAUTICS AND SPACE FLIGHT* — *Abstracting, Bibliographies, Statistics*

FIJI. BUREAU OF STATISTICS. CENSUS OF BUILDING AND CONSTRUCTION. see *BUILDING AND CONSTRUCTION* — *Abstracting, Bibliographies, Statistics*

FIJI. BUREAU OF STATISTICS. CENSUS OF DISTRIBUTION AND SERVICES. see *BUSINESS AND ECONOMICS* — *Abstracting, Bibliographies, Statistics*

FIJI. BUREAU OF STATISTICS. CENSUS OF INDUSTRIES. see *BUSINESS AND ECONOMICS* — *Abstracting, Bibliographies, Statistics*

FIJI. BUREAU OF STATISTICS. CONSUMER PRICE INDEX. see *BUSINESS AND ECONOMICS* — *Abstracting, Bibliographies, Statistics*

FIJI. BUREAU OF STATISTICS. CURRENT ECONOMIC STATISTICS. see *BUSINESS AND ECONOMICS* — *Abstracting, Bibliographies, Statistics*

FIJI. BUREAU OF STATISTICS. ECONOMIC AND FUNCTIONAL CLASSIFICATION OF GOVERNMENT ACCOUNTS. see *BUSINESS AND ECONOMICS* — *Abstracting, Bibliographies, Statistics*

FIJI. BUREAU OF STATISTICS. EMPLOYMENT SURVEY OF FIJI. see *BUSINESS AND ECONOMICS* — *Abstracting, Bibliographies, Statistics*

FIJI. BUREAU OF STATISTICS. FIJI FERTILITY SURVEY. see *POPULATION STUDIES* — *Abstracting, Bibliographies, Statistics*

FIJI. BUREAU OF STATISTICS. FIJI HOUSEHOLD INCOME AND EXPENDITURE SURVEY. see *BUSINESS AND ECONOMICS* — *Abstracting, Bibliographies, Statistics*

FIJI. BUREAU OF STATISTICS. NATIONWIDE UNEMPLOYMENT SURVEY. see *BUSINESS AND ECONOMICS* — *Abstracting, Bibliographies, Statistics*

FIJI. BUREAU OF STATISTICS. POPULATION OF FIJI; monograph for the U N World population. see *POPULATION STUDIES* — *Abstracting, Bibliographies, Statistics*

FIJI. BUREAU OF STATISTICS. QUARTERLY SURVEY OF EMPLOYMENT. see *BUSINESS AND ECONOMICS* — *Abstracting, Bibliographies, Statistics*

310 FJ
FIJI. BUREAU OF STATISTICS. STATISTICAL NEWS. 1979. m. $33 (foreign $33) (effective Jan. 1991). Bureau of Statistics, P.O. Box 2221, Suva, Fiji.

FIJI. BUREAU OF STATISTICS. SURVEY OF DISTRIBUTIVE TRADE. see *BUSINESS AND ECONOMICS* — *Abstracting, Bibliographies, Statistics*

FIJI. BUREAU OF STATISTICS. TOURISM AND MIGRATION STATISTICS. see *TRAVEL AND TOURISM* — *Abstracting, Bibliographies, Statistics*

FIJI. BUREAU OF STATISTICS. TRADE REPORT. see *BUSINESS AND ECONOMICS* — *Abstracting, Bibliographies, Statistics*

FIJI. BUREAU OF STATISTICS. VITAL STATISTICS. see *BUSINESS AND ECONOMICS* — *Abstracting, Bibliographies, Statistics*

FIJI FACTS AND FIGURES. see *BUSINESS AND ECONOMICS* — *Abstracting, Bibliographies, Statistics*

FINANCES OF PUBLIC SCHOOL SYSTEMS. see *EDUCATION* — *Abstracting, Bibliographies, Statistics*

FINANZAS PUBLICAS ESTATALES Y MUNICIPALES DE MEXICO. see *BUSINESS AND ECONOMICS* — *Abstracting, Bibliographies, Statistics*

FINLAND. STATISTIKCENTRALEN. STATISTISKA MEDDELANDEN. LEVNADSFOERHAALLANDEN I FINLAND/FINLAND. CENTRAL STATISTICAL OFFICE. LIVING CONDITIONS IN FINLAND. see *SOCIOLOGY* — *Abstracting, Bibliographies, Statistics*

311 FI ISSN 0355-2063
HA1
FINLAND. TILASTOKESKUS. KAESIKIRJOJA/FINLAND. STATISTIKCENTRALEN. HANDBOECKER/FINLAND. CENTRAL STATISTICAL OFFICE. HANDBOOKS. (Text in Finnish and sometimes in English and Swedish) 1971. irreg. price varies. Tilastokeskus, Annankatu 44, SF-00100 Helsinki 10, Finland.

314.71 FI ISSN 0015-2390
HA1450.5
FINLAND. TILASTOKESKUS. TILASTOKATSAUKSIA/FINLAND. STATISTIKCENTRALEN. STATISTISKA OEVERSIKTER/FINLAND. CENTRAL STATISTICAL OFFICE. BULLETIN OF STATISTICS. (Text in English, Finnish and Swedish) 1924. q. FIM 110. Tilastokeskus, Annankatu 44, SF-00100 Helsinki 10, Finland. (Subscr. to: Government Printing Centre, Box 516, SF-00100 Helsinki 10, Finland) charts; stat.; circ. 2,350.

FINLAND. TILASTOKESKUS. TILASTOTIEDOTUS. PALKAT LONER/WAGES AND SALARIES. see *BUSINESS AND ECONOMICS* — *Abstracting, Bibliographies, Statistics*

310 FI ISSN 0784-8463
HD9715.F5
FINLAND. TILASTOKESKUS. TILASTOTIEDOTUS. YRITYKSET FORETAG. (Text in English, Finnish, Swedish) a. FIM 335. (Central Statistical Office) Government Printing Centre, P.O. Box 516, SF-00101, Helsinki, Finland. TEL 358-0-17341. FAX 358-01734-2279. TELEX 1002111 TILASTO SF.
Formerly: Tilastotiedotus YR (ISSN 0355-2373)

314 FI ISSN 0357-0614
Z7554.F5
FINLAND. TILASTOKESKUS. VALTION TILASTOJULKAISUT/FINLAND. STATISTIKCENTRALEN. STATENS STATISTISKA PUBLIKATIONER/FINLAND. CENTRAL STATISTICAL OFFICE. GOVERNMENT STATISTICS. (Text in English, Finnish and Swedish) 1978. a. FIM 60. Tilastokeskus, Annankatu 44, SF-00100 Helsinki 10, Finland.

310 GW
FLENSBURGER ZAHLENSPIEGEL (YEAR). 1951. a. DM.7.50. Stadt Flensburg, Der Magistrat, Amt fuer Stadtentwicklung, Postfach 2742, 2390 Flensburg, Germany. circ. 500.

318 US ISSN 0071-6022
HA311
FLORIDA STATISTICAL ABSTRACT. Variant title: Florida Statistical Abstracts Annual. 1967. a. price varies. (University of Florida, Bureau of Economic and Business Research) University Presses of Florida, 15 N.W. 15th St., Gainesville, FL 32603. TEL 904-392-1351. Ed. Anne Shoemyen. circ. 3,700. (also avail. in microfiche from BHP) **Indexed:** SRI.

FLORIDA VITAL STATISTICS. see *POPULATION STUDIES* — *Abstracting, Bibliographies, Statistics*

FOOD INDUSTRY STATISTICS DIGEST. see *FOOD AND FOOD INDUSTRIES* — *Abstracting, Bibliographies, Statistics*

FRANCE. CONSEIL NATIONAL DU CREDIT. STATISTIQUES MENSUELLES. see *BUSINESS AND ECONOMICS* — *Abstracting, Bibliographies, Statistics*

FRANCE. CONSEIL NATIONAL DU CREDIT. STATISTIQUES TRIMESTRIELLES. see *BUSINESS AND ECONOMICS* — *Abstracting, Bibliographies, Statistics*

314 FR ISSN 0007-4713
FRANCE. INSTITUT NATIONAL DE LA STATISTIQUE ET DES ETUDES ECONOMIQUES. BULLETIN MENSUEL DE STATISTIQUE. 1911. m. 319 F. (foreign 399 F.); microfiche 162 F. (foreign 203 F.). Institut National de la Statistique et des Etudes Economiques, 18 bd. Adolphe Pinard, 75675 Paris Cedex 14, France. stat.; circ. 7,600. (also avail. in microfiche) **Indexed:** P.A.I.S.For.Lang.Ind.
—BLDSC shelfmark: 2877.730000.
Formerly (until 1949): Statistique Generale de la France. Bulletin.
Description: Statistics on employment, industry, business, prices and finance in France and other countries.

311.2 FR ISSN 0151-9514
FRANCE. INSTITUT NATIONAL DE LA STATISTIQUE ET DES ETUDES ECONOMIQUES. COURRIER DES STATISTIQUES. 4/yr. 125 F. Institut National de la Statistique et des Etudes Economiques, 18 bd. Adolphe Pinard, 75675 Paris Cedex 14, France.
Description: Presents a global image of the life of the public statistical system.

FRANCE. MINISTERE DE L'AGRICULTURE ET DE LA FORET. ANALYSES ET ETUDES. CAHIERS. see *AGRICULTURE* — *Abstracting, Bibliographies, Statistics*

FRANCE. MINISTERE DE L'URBANISME ET DU LOGEMENT. STATISTIQUES ET ETUDES GENERALES. see *HOUSING AND URBAN PLANNING* — *Abstracting, Bibliographies, Statistics*

FRANCE. SERVICE D'ETUDE DES STRATEGIES ET DES STATISTIQUES INDUSTRIELLES. LA SITUATION DE L'INDUSTRIE. PREMIERS RESULTATS. see *BUSINESS AND ECONOMICS* — *Abstracting, Bibliographies, Statistics*

STATISTICS

314 GW
FRANKFURT AM MAIN. AMT FUER STATISTIK, WAHLEN UND EINWOHNERWESEN. STATISTISCHES JAHRBUCH. 1951. a. DM.28. Amt fuer Statistik, Wahlen und Einwohnerwesen, Postfach 102121, 6000 Frankfurt a.M. 1, Germany. TEL 069-212-33667. FAX 069-212-37888. circ. 1,400.
Formerly: Frankfurt am Main. Statistisches Amt und Wahlamt. Statistisches Jahrbuch (ISSN 0071-9218)
Description: Covers complete statistical information of the town. Includes population, economy, housing, public health, finance, culture and elections.

310 GW ISSN 0177-7351
FRANKFURTER STATISTISCHE BERICHTE. 1936. q. DM.16. Amt fuer Statistik, Wahlen und Einwohnerwesen, Postfach 102121, 6000 Frankfurt a.M., Germany. TEL 069-212-33667. FAX 069-212-37888. circ. 800.
Description: Covers complete statistics of the town: vital, population, economical, financial, public health, cultural, housing and more.

FROZEN FISHERY PRODUCTS. ANNUAL SUMMARY. see FISH AND FISHERIES — Abstracting, Bibliographies, Statistics

310 GW
FULDA. STATISTISCHER BERICHT. 1974. a. free. Magistrat der Stadt Fulda, Abt. 103, Postfach 1020, 6400 Fulda, Germany. TEL 0661-102198. FAX 0661-79153. TELEX 6619707-STDFD. circ. 1,000.

310 GO
GABON. DIRECTION GENERALE DE L'ECONOMIE. BULLETIN MENSUEL DE STATISTIQUE. m. Direction de la Statistique et des Etudes Economiques, B.P. 179, Libreville, Gabon.
Former titles: Gabon. Direction de la Statistique et des Etudes Economique. Bulletin Mensuel de Statistique; Gabon. Service National de la Statistique. Bulletin Mensuel de Statistique.

GAMBIA. CENTRAL STATISTICS DEPARTMENT. EDUCATION STATISTICS. see EDUCATION — Abstracting, Bibliographies, Statistics

GAMBIA. CENTRAL STATISTICS DEPARTMENT. SUMMARY OF TOURIST STATISTICS. see TRAVEL AND TOURISM — Abstracting, Bibliographies, Statistics

GAMBIA. CENTRAL STATISTICS DEPARTMENT. TOURIST STATISTICS. see TRAVEL AND TOURISM — Abstracting, Bibliographies, Statistics

GAS INDUSTRY STATISTICS (YEAR). see PETROLEUM AND GAS — Abstracting, Bibliographies, Statistics

314 GW
GEMEINDEN NORDRHEIN-WESTFALENS; Informationen aus der amtlichen Statistik. 1976. a. DM.15. Landesamt fuer Datenverarbeitung und Statistik Nordrhein-Westfalen, Mauerstr. 51, Postfach 101105, 4000 Duesseldorf 1, Germany. TEL 0211-9449-01. circ. 1,200. (back issues avail.)

DIE GENOSSENSCHAFTEN IN DER BUNDESREPUBLIK DEUTSCHLAND. STATISTIK. see BUSINESS AND ECONOMICS — Cooperatives

GEORGIA DESCRIPTIONS IN DATA. see POPULATION STUDIES — Abstracting, Bibliographies, Statistics

GEORGIA STATISTICAL ABSTRACT. see BUSINESS AND ECONOMICS — Abstracting, Bibliographies, Statistics

GERMANY (FEDERAL REPUBLIC, 1949-). BUNDESANSTALT FUER ARBEIT. BERUFSBERATUNG. ERGEBNISSE DER BERUFSBERATUNGSSTATISTIK. see BUSINESS AND ECONOMICS — Abstracting, Bibliographies, Statistics

310 GW ISSN 0433-7344
GERMANY (FEDERAL REPUBLIC, 1949-). BUNDESMINISTERIUM FUER ERNAEHRUNG, LANDWIRTSCHAFT UND FORSTEN. STATISTISCHER MONATSBERICHT. 1949. m. DM.190. Bundesministerium fuer Ernaehrung, Landwirtschaft und Forsten, Planungskoordination und -grundlagen, Rochnsstr. 1, 5300 Bonn, Germany. TEL 0228-529-1. FAX 0228-4262. TELEX 886844-BML-D. (Subscr. to: Bundesamt fuer Ernaehrung und Forstwirtschaft, Adickesallee 40, 6000 Frankfurt a.M., Germany) Eds. M. Hesse, I. Gnilka. circ. 1,050.

GHANA. STATISTICAL SERVICE. ECONOMIC SURVEY. see BUSINESS AND ECONOMICS — Abstracting, Bibliographies, Statistics

316 GH
GHANA. STATISTICAL SERVICE. QUARTERLY DIGEST OF STATISTICS. 1952. q. $15 per issue. Statistical Service, Box 1098, Accra, Ghana.
Formerly: Ghana. Central Bureau of Statistics. Quarterly Digest of Statistics (ISSN 0435-8864)

GHANA. TOURIST CONTROL BOARD. BI-ANNUAL STATISTICS ON TOURISM. see TRAVEL AND TOURISM — Abstracting, Bibliographies, Statistics

310 SW ISSN 0072-5110
GOETEBORGS UNIVERSITET. STATISTISKA INSTITUTIONEN. SKRIFTSERIE. PUBLICATIONS. (Text in English or Swedish) 1954. irreg., no.20, 1987. price varies. Almqvist & Wiksell International, Box 638, S-101 28 Stockholm, Sweden. Ed. Sture Holm.

318.1 BL
GOIAS, BRAZIL. SECRETARIA DO PLANEJAMENTO E COORDENACAO. BOLETIM ESTADISTICO. (Includes comparative data for previous years) irreg? Secretaria do Planejamento e Coordenacao, Goiania, Brazil.
Continues: Goias, Brazil. Departamento Estadual de Estatistica. Boletim Estatistico.

314 UK ISSN 0072-5730
GREAT BRITAIN. CENTRAL STATISTICAL OFFICE. ANNUAL ABSTRACT OF STATISTICS. 1948. a. price varies. (Central Statistical Office) H.M.S.O., Publications Centre, 51 Nine Elms Lane, London SW8 5DR, England. TEL 01-873-9090. FAX 01-873-8463. TELEX 297138. circ. 5,500. (reprint service avail. from KTO,SCH)

GREAT BRITAIN. CENTRAL STATISTICAL OFFICE. FINANCIAL STATISTICS. see BUSINESS AND ECONOMICS — Abstracting, Bibliographies, Statistics

314 UK ISSN 0261-1791
GREAT BRITAIN. CENTRAL STATISTICAL OFFICE. GUIDE TO OFFICIAL STATISTICS. 1976. biennial. (Central Statistical Office) H.M.S.O., Publications Centre, 51 Nine Elms Lane, London SW8 5DR, England. TEL 01-873-9090. FAX 01-873-8463.

314 UK ISSN 0308-6666
GREAT BRITAIN. CENTRAL STATISTICAL OFFICE. MONTHLY DIGEST OF STATISTICS. 1946. m. £60. (Central Statistical Office) H.M.S.O., Publication Centre, 51 Nine Elms Lane, London SW8 5DR, England. TEL 01-873-9090. FAX 01-873-8463. TELEX 297138. stat.
—BLDSC shelfmark: 5937.400000.

314 UK ISSN 0261-1783
GREAT BRITAIN. CENTRAL STATISTICAL OFFICE. REGIONAL TRENDS. 1965. a. (Central Statistical Office) H.M.S.O., Publications Centre, 51 Nine Elms Lane, London SW8 5DR, England. TEL 01-873-9090. FAX 01-873-8463. TELEX 297138. (Avail. from: Open University Educational Enterprises Ltd., 12 Cofferidge Close, Stony Stratford, Milton Keynes MK11 1BY England) charts; stat.
Former titles: Great Britain. Central Statistical Office. Regional Statistics (ISSN 0308-146X); Great Britain. Central Statistical Office Abstracts of Regional Statistics (ISSN 0072-5749)

311 UK ISSN 0072-5757
GREAT BRITAIN. CENTRAL STATISTICAL OFFICE. RESEARCH SERIES. 1968. irreg. price varies. Central Statistical Office, Great George St., London SW1P 3AQ, England. (Dist. by: Open University Educational Enterprises Ltd., 12 Cofferidge Close, Stony Stratford, Milton Keynes MK11 1BY, England)

314 UK ISSN 0017-3630
CODEN: STANE2
GREAT BRITAIN. CENTRAL STATISTICAL OFFICE. STATISTICAL NEWS; developments in British official statistics. 1968. q. £15. (Central Statistical Office) H.M.S.O., Publications Centre, 51 Nine Elms Lane, London SW8 5DR, England. TEL 01-873-9090. FAX 01-873-8463. TELEX 297138. (also avail. in microform from UMI; reprint service avail. from UMI)
—BLDSC shelfmark: 8448.575000.

311 UK ISSN 0081-8313
GREAT BRITAIN. CENTRAL STATISTICAL OFFICE. STUDIES IN OFFICIAL STATISTICS. irreg. price varies. (Central Statistical Office) H.M.S.O., Publications Centre, 51 Nine Elms Lane, London SW8 5DR, England. TEL 01-873-9090. FAX 01-873-8463. TELEX 297138.

GREECE. NATIONAL STATISTICAL SERVICE. ANNUAL STATISTICAL SURVEY ON MINES, QUARRIES AND SALTERNS. see MINES AND MINING INDUSTRY — Abstracting, Bibliographies, Statistics

GREECE. NATIONAL STATISTICAL SERVICE. LABOUR FORCE SURVEY. see BUSINESS AND ECONOMICS — Abstracting, Bibliographies, Statistics

314 GR
GREECE. NATIONAL STATISTICAL SERVICE. MONTHLY STATISTICAL BULLETIN. (Text in English, Greek) m. $60. National Statistical Service of Greece, Statistical Information and Publications Division, 14-16 Lycourgou St., 10166 Athens, Greece. TEL 3244-748. FAX 3222205. TELEX 216734 ESYE GR.

GREECE. NATIONAL STATISTICAL SERVICE. RESULTS OF SEA FISHERY SURVEY BY MOTOR VESSELS. see FISH AND FISHERIES — Abstracting, Bibliographies, Statistics

GREECE. NATIONAL STATISTICAL SERVICE. SHIPPING STATISTICS. see TRANSPORTATION — Abstracting, Bibliographies, Statistics

GREECE. NATIONAL STATISTICAL SERVICE. SOCIAL WELFARE AND HEALTH STATISTICS. see SOCIAL SERVICES AND WELFARE — Abstracting, Bibliographies, Statistics

GREECE. NATIONAL STATISTICAL SERVICE. STATISTICS OF THE DECLARED INCOME OF LEGAL ENTITIES AND ITS TAXATION. see BUSINESS AND ECONOMICS — Abstracting, Bibliographies, Statistics

GREECE. NATIONAL STATISTICAL SERVICE. STATISTICS ON CIVIL, CRIMINAL AND REFORMATORY JUSTICE. see CRIMINOLOGY AND LAW ENFORCEMENT — Abstracting, Bibliographies, Statistics

GREECE. NATIONAL STATISTICAL SERVICE. STATISTICS ON THE DECLARED INCOME OF PHYSICAL PERSONS AND ITS TAXATION. see BUSINESS AND ECONOMICS — Abstracting, Bibliographies, Statistics

GREECE. NATIONAL STATISTICAL SERVICE. TRANSPORT AND COMMUNICATION STATISTICS. see TRANSPORTATION — Abstracting, Bibliographies, Statistics

GREEK ECONOMY IN FIGURES (YEAR). see BUSINESS AND ECONOMICS — Abstracting, Bibliographies, Statistics

310 DK ISSN 0106-228X
GROENLAND (COPENHAGEN)/KALAALLIT NUNAAT. (Text in Danish and English) 1968. a. DKK 70. Statsministeriet, Groenlandsafdelingen, Hausergade 3, 1128 Copenhagen K, Denmark. FAX 33-936815. TELEX 27125-MFG. circ. 3,800.

317 CN ISSN 0711-852X
HC120.I5
GROSS DOMESTIC PRODUCT BY INDUSTRY. 1987. m. Can.$127($152) (foreign $178). Statistics Canada, Publications Division, Ottawa, Ont. K1A 0T6, Canada. TEL 613-951-7277. FAX 613-951-1584.
Description: Contains monthly, quarterly, and annual estimates of GDP for 183 industries, including aggregates and special industry groupings.

GROUPEMENT DES INDUSTRIES ELECTRONIQUES. STATISTIQUES ANNUELLES. see ELECTRONICS

310   CC
GUANGXI TONGJI/GUANGXI STATISTICS. (Text in Chinese) bi-m. Guangxi Tongji Ju - Guangxi Bureau of Statistics, 22 Xinzhu Lu, Nanning, Guangxi 530022, People's Republic of China. TEL 22368. Ed. Su Xiaohan.

318   GT
GUATEMALA. DIRECCION GENERAL DE ESTADISTICA. ENCUESTA DE LA INDUSTRIA MANUFACTURERA FABRIL. Variant title: Encuesta Industrial. 1972. a. $15. Direccion General de Estadistica, Departamento de Estudios Especiales y Estadisticas Continuas, Ministerio de Economia, 8A Calle No. 9-55, Zona 1, Guatemala.
    Formerly: Guatemala. Direccion General de Estadistica. Departamento de Estudios Especiales y Estadisticas Continuas. Produccion, Venta y Otros Ingresos de la Encuesta Anual de la Industria Manufacturera Fabril.

318   GT
GUATEMALA. INSTITUTO NACIONAL DE ESTADISTICA. ANUARIO ESTADISTICO. 1970. a., latest 9187. Q.8($20) Instituto Nacional de Estadistica, Ministerio de Economia, 8A Calle no. 9-55, Zona 1, Guatemala, Guatemala. TEL 26136, 82587. charts; illus.
    Formerly: Guatemala en Cifras.

317.281   GT   ISSN 0017-5048
GUATEMALA. INSTITUTO NACIONAL DE ESTADISTICA. BOLETIN ESTADISTICO. (Former name of issuing body: Direccion General de Estadistica) 1967. a. $15. Instituto Nacional de Estadistica, Ministerio de Economia, 8A Calle no. 9-55, Zona 1, Guatemala, Guatemala. TEL 26136-82587. charts; mkt.; circ. 2,500.

310   US   ISSN 0434-9067
Z7554.U5
GUIDE TO U S GOVERNMENT STATISTICS. a. $195. Documents Index, Inc., Box 195, McLean, VA 22101. TEL 703-356-2434. Eds. Donna Andriot, Jay Andriot.
    Description: Entries include classification numbers, title, beginning and closing dates, frequency and annotations, as well as detailed bibliographic information, with an extensive index by title, subject, area and agency.

HACETTEPE BULLETIN OF NATURAL SCIENCES AND ENGINEERING. see MATHEMATICS

314   IC   ISSN 0254-4733
HAGSKYRSLUR ISLANDS/STATISTICS OF ICELAND. (Text in Icelandic; summaries in English) 1914. irreg. Hagstofa Islands - Statistical Bureau of Iceland, Skuggasund 3, IS-150 Reykjavik, Iceland. TEL 354-1-60-98-00. FAX 354-1-62-88-65. Dir. Hallgrimur Snorrason. (back issues avail.)

314.912   IC   ISSN 0019-1078
HAGTIDINDI. 1916. m. $40. Hagstofa Islands - Statistical Bureau of Iceland, Skuggasund 3, IS-150 Reykjavik, Iceland. TEL 354-1-60 98 00. FAX 354-1-62-88-65. Ed. Hallgrimur Snorrason. stat.; index; circ. 2,200.
    Description: Includes statistics on population, work force, foreign trade, prices and production.

HAIGUAN TONGJI/CUSTOMS STATISTICS. see BUSINESS AND ECONOMICS — Abstracting, Bibliographies, Statistics

317.29   HT   ISSN 0017-6788
HA881
HAITI. INSTITUT HAITIEN DE STATISTIQUE. BULLETIN TRIMESTRIEL DE STATISTIQUE. 1952. a. (with q. supplement) free. Institut Haitien de Statistique et d'Informatique, Departement des Finances et des Affaires Economique, Blvd. Harry Truman, Port-au-Prince, Haiti, W. Indies. Dir. Raymond Gardiner. charts; mkt.; stat.; circ. 500. **Indexed:** P.A.I.S.For.Lang.Ind.

314   GW   ISSN 0017-6877
HAMBURG IN ZAHLEN. 1947. m. DM.40. Statistisches Landesamt, Steckelhoern 12, 2000 Hamburg 11, Germany. charts; stat.; circ. 1,200.
    Formerly: Hamburger Monatszahlen.

315   II   ISSN 0072-9728
HANDBOOK OF BASIC STATISTICS OF MAHARASHTRA STATE. (Editions in English and Marathi) 1960. a. Rs.3.90. Directorate of Economics and Statistics, D.D. Bldg, Old Custom House, Bombay 400023, India. Ed. S.M. Vidwans.

HANDBOOK OF INDUSTRIAL STATISTICS. see BUSINESS AND ECONOMICS — Abstracting, Bibliographies, Statistics

HANDBUCH DER OESTERREICHISCHEN SOZIALVERSICHERUNG. see INSURANCE — Abstracting, Bibliographies, Statistics

HANDELSHOCHSCHULE LEIPZIG. WISSENSCHAFTLICHE ZEITSCHRIFT. see BUSINESS AND ECONOMICS

310   DK   ISSN 0106-8490
HANDELSHOEJSKOLEN I AARHUS. SKRIFTSERIE. no.3, 1982. irreg. price varies. Aarhus Graduate School of Management, Department of Information Science, Fuglesangsalle 4, 8210 Aarhus V, Denmark. TEL 06-155588. FAX 06-150188. Ed. Kai Kristensen. illus.

314   FI   ISSN 0357-3362
HELSINGIN KAUPUNGIN TILASTOKESKUKSEN NELJANNESVUOSIKATSAUS/HELSINGFORS STADS. STATISTIKCENTRAL KVARTALSOEVERSIKT. 1979. q. FIM 100. Tilastokeskus, Toolontorinkatu 2 B, 00260 Helsinki 26, Finland. FAX 358-0-4029-454. Ed. E. Holstila. circ. 950.
    Supersedes: Tilastollisia Kuukaustitietoja Helsingista (ISSN 0040-7658)

310   FI   ISSN 0785-8736
HELSINGIN KAUPUNGIN TILASTOLLINEN VUOSIKIRJA. (Text in Finnish and Swedish) 1908. a. FIM 110. Helsingin Kaupungin Tictokeskus, Helsingfors Stads Taktacentral - City of Helsinki, Information Management Centre, Toolontorinkatu 2 B, 00260 Helsinki, Finland. FAX 90-4029-454. Ed. Pirkko-Leena Tuovinen. stat.; circ. 1,300. (back issues avail.)
    Formerly (until 1988): Helsingin Kaupunki Tilastolunen Vuosikirja (ISSN 0356-9489)

314   GW
HESSISCHE KREISZAHLEN. 1956. s-a. DM.8. Hessisches Statistisches Landesamt, Rheinstr. 35-37, 6200 Wiesbaden, Germany. TEL 0611-3680. FAX 0611-378324.
    Description: Government publication covering extensive vital statistics.

HIGHER EDUCATION ABSTRACTS; abstracts of periodical literature, monographs and conference papers on college students, faculty and administration. see EDUCATION — Higher Education

317   US   ISSN 0073-2664
HISTORICAL STATISTICS OF THE UNITED STATES. 1949. irreg. price varies. U.S. Bureau of the Census, Data User Services Division, Washington, DC 20233. TEL 301-763-4100. (Dist. by: Supt. of Documents, Washington, DC 20402)

318   HO
HONDURAS EN CIFRAS. 1965. a. free. Banco Central de Honduras, Departamento de Estudios Economicos, 1a Calle, 6a y 7a avenida, Tegucigalpa, D.C., Honduras. TEL 37-2270. TELEX 1121. charts; stat.

315   HK
HONG KONG. ANNUAL DIGEST OF STATISTICS. (Text in English) 1978. a. HK.$98. Census and Statistics Department, Wanchai Tower 1, 12 Harbour Rd., Hong Kong. TEL 8428801. FAX 852537-1543. (Subscr. to: Director of Information Service, Information Services Department, 1 Battery Path, G-F, Central, Hong Kong) charts; stat.

310 330.9   HK
HONG KONG. CENSUS AND STATISTICS DEPARTMENT. CONSUMER PRICE INDEX. ANNUAL REPORT. (Text in English) a. price varies. (Census and Statistics Department) Government Publication Centre, G.P.O. Bldg, Ground Fl., Connaught Place, Hong Kong, Hong Kong. (Subscr. to: Director of Information Services, Information Services Dept., 1 Battery Path, G-F, Central, Hong Kong) Ed.Bd.

310 330.9   HK
HONG KONG. CENSUS AND STATISTICS DEPARTMENT. CONSUMER PRICE INDEX. REPORT. (Text in English) m. HK.$42. (Census and Statistics Department) Government Publication Centre, G.P.O. Bldg., Ground Fl., Connaught Place, Hong Kong, Hong Kong. (Subscr. to: Director of Information Services, Information Services Dept., 1 Battery Path, G-F, Hong Kong, Hong Kong) Ed.Bd. (back issues avail.)

310 657   HK
HONG KONG. CENSUS AND STATISTICS DEPARTMENT. DIRECTOR OF AUDITS. REPORT. (Editions in Chinese, English) irreg., latest 1988. price varies. Government Publication Centre, G.P.O. Building, Ground Fl., Connaught Place, Hong Kong, Hong Kong. (Subscr. to: Director of Information Services, Information Services Dept., 1 Battery Path, G-F, Central, Hong Kong) Ed.Bd.

HONG KONG. CENSUS AND STATISTICS DEPARTMENT. GENERAL HOUSEHOLD SURVEY LABOUR FORCE CHARACTERISTICS. see BUSINESS AND ECONOMICS — Abstracting, Bibliographies, Statistics

310 330.9   HK
HONG KONG. CENSUS AND STATISTICS DEPARTMENT. MONTHLY SURVEY OF RETAIL SALES. REPORT. (Text in English) m. HK.$12. (Census and Statistics Department) Government Publication Centre, G.P.O. Bldg., Ground Fl., Connaught Place, Hong Kong, Hong Kong. (Subscr. to: Director of Information Services, Information Services Dept., 1 Battery Path, G-F, Central, Hong Kong) Ed.Bd.

HONG KONG. CENSUS AND STATISTICS DEPARTMENT. REPORT ON HALF-YEARLY SURVEY OF WAGES, SALARIES AND EMPLOYEE BENEFITS. VOLUME I. see BUSINESS AND ECONOMICS — Abstracting, Bibliographies, Statistics

HONG KONG. CENSUS AND STATISTICS DEPARTMENT. SALARIES AND EMPLOYEE STATISTICS. REPORT. MANAGERIAL AND PROFESSIONAL EMPLOYEES (EXCLUDING TOP MANAGEMENT). see BUSINESS AND ECONOMICS — Abstracting, Bibliographies, Statistics

HONG KONG. CENSUS AND STATISTICS DEPARTMENT. SHIPPING STATISTICS. see TRANSPORTATION — Abstracting, Bibliographies, Statistics

HONG KONG. ESTIMATES OF GROSS DOMESTIC PRODUCT. see BUSINESS AND ECONOMICS — Abstracting, Bibliographies, Statistics

HONG KONG ECONOMIC TRENDS. see BUSINESS AND ECONOMICS — Abstracting, Bibliographies, Statistics

315   HK
HONG KONG IN FIGURES. 1976. a. free. Census and Statistics Department, Wanchai Tower 1, 12 Harbour Rd., Hong Kong. TEL 582-4661. FAX 8528651900.

315   HK   ISSN 0300-418X
HA1950.H6
HONG KONG MONTHLY DIGEST OF STATISTICS. 1970. m. HK.$576. Census and Statistics Department, Wanchai Tower 1, 12 Harbour Rd., Hong Kong. TEL 8428802. FAX 582-5371543. (Subscr. to: Director of Information Services, 1 Battery Path, G-F, Central, Hong Kong) Ed.Bd. stat.; circ. 2,000.

HOUSING MARKET STATISTICS. see BUSINESS AND ECONOMICS — Abstracting, Bibliographies, Statistics

HOUSING SURVEY OF JAPAN (YEAR). see HOUSING AND URBAN PLANNING — Abstracting, Bibliographies, Statistics

310   HU   ISSN 0441-4713
HUNGARY. KOZPONTI STATISZTIKAI HIVATAL. NEMZETKOZI STATISZTIKAI EVKONYV. quadrennial. 371 Ft. Statiqum Kiado es Nyomda Kft., Kaszasdulo u. 2, P.O. Box 99, 1300 Budapest 3, Hungary. TEL 361-180-3311. FAX 361-168-8635. TELEX 22-6699. (Subscr. to: Kultura, Box 149, 1389 Budapest, Hungary) circ. 3,000.

4574 STATISTICS

314   HU   ISSN 0073-4039
HA1201   CODEN: STEVEC
HUNGARY. KOZPONTI STATISZTIKAI HIVATAL. STATISZTIKAI EVKONYV. English edition (ISSN 0237-1901) 1871. a. 550 Ft. (English ed. 1100 Ft.). Statiqum Kiado es Nyomda Kft., Kaszasdulo u. 2, P.O. Box 99, 1300 Budapest 3, Hungary. TEL 361-168-8635. FAX 361-168-8635. TELEX 22-6699. (Subscr. to: Kultura, Box 149, 1389 Budapest, Hungary)

314   HU   ISSN 0018-781X
HUNGARY. KOZPONTI STATISZTIKAI HIVATAL. STATISZTIKAI HAVI KOZLEMENYEK. 1957. m. 1320 Ft.($48.50) Statiqum Kiando es Nyomda Kft., Kaszasdulo u. 2, P.O. Box 99, 1300 Budapest 3, Hungary. TEL 361-180-3311. FAX 361-168-8635. TELEX 22-6699. (Subscr. to: Kultura, Box 149, 1389 Budapest, Hungary) Ed. Lorinc Soos. charts; stat.; circ. 1,350.

314   HU   ISSN 0039-0690
HUNGARY. KOZPONTI STATISZTIKAI HIVATAL. STATISZTIKAI SZEMLE. 1923. m. 396 Ft.($52) Statisztikai Kiado Vallalat, Kaszasdulo u. 2, P.O.B.99, 1300 Budapest 3, Hungary. TEL 688-635. TELEX 22-6699. (Subscr. to: Kultura, Box 149, H-1389 Budapest, Hungary) Ed. Maria Visi Lakatos. cum.index 1923-1962; circ. 1,500.
Indexed: Popul.Ind.
Formerly: Magyar Statisztikai Szemle.

314.391   HU   ISSN 0018-7828
HUNGARY. KOZPONTI STATISZTIKAI HIVATAL. TERULETI STATISZTIKA. (Text in Hungarian; contents page in English & Russian) 1957. bi-m. 198 Ft.($21.50) Statisztikai Kiado Vallalat, Kaszasdulo u. 2, P.O.B.99, 1300 Budapest 3, Hungary. TEL 688-635. TELEX 22-6699. (Subscr. to: Kultura, Box 149, H-1389 Budapest, Hungary) Ed. Tibor Kordcs. bk.rev.; circ. 1,320.
—BLDSC shelfmark: 8796.170000.
Formerly: Megyei es Varosi Statisztikai Ertesito.

947 314   HU   ISSN 0303-5344
HUNGARY. KOZPONTI STATISZTIKAI HIVATAL. TERULETI STATISZTIKAI EVKONYV. a. 201 Ft. Statisztikai Kiado Vallalat, Kaszasdulo u. 2, P.O.B.99, 1300 Budapest 3, Hungary. TEL 688-635. TELEX 22-6699. (Subscr. to: Kultura, Box 149, H-1389 Budapest, Hungary)

319.4 333.91 330.9 AT   ISSN 0729-5030
HUNTER VALLEY RESEARCH FOUNDATION. WORKING PAPERS. 1969. irreg. Hunter Valley Research Foundation, P.O. Box 23, Tighes Hill, N.S.W. 2297, Australia. TEL 049-69-4566. FAX 049-614981. Ed. W.E.J. Paradice. charts. (back issues avail.)

I C E S FISHERIES STATISTICS/BULLETIN STATISTIQUE DES PECHES MARITIMES. see *FISH AND FISHERIES — Abstracting, Bibliographies, Statistics*

IDAHO. DEPARTMENT OF HEALTH AND WELFARE. ANNUAL SUMMARY OF VITAL STATISTICS. see *PUBLIC HEALTH AND SAFETY — Abstracting, Bibliographies, Statistics*

IMPORTED CRUDE OIL AND PETROLEUM PRODUCTS. see *PETROLEUM AND GAS*

IMPORTS STATISTICS OF AFGHANISTAN/IHSA'IYAH-I AMUAL-I VARIDATI-I AFGHANISTAN. see *BUSINESS AND ECONOMICS — Abstracting, Bibliographies, Statistics*

310   IT
INDAGINE STATISTICA NAZIONALE. biennial. (Associazione Nazionale dei Produttori di Piastrelle di Ceramica) Edi.Cer. S.p.A., Viale S. Giorgio, 2, 41049 Sassuolo (Modena), Italy. TEL 0536-804585. FAX 0536-807935. TELEX 511050.

INDEPENDENT SECTOR. UPDATE. see *EDUCATION*

310   US   ISSN 0737-4461
Z7552
INDEX TO INTERNATIONAL STATISTICS. 1983. m. (with q. and a. cumulations). $1,305. Congressional Information Service, 4520 East-West Hwy., Bethesda, MD 20814-3389. TEL 301-654-1550. FAX 301-654-4033. TELEX 292386 CIS UR. Ed. Polly A. Bosch. abstr.; index; cum.index: 1983-87. (back issues avail.)
●Also available on CD-ROM.
—BLDSC shelfmark: 4380.455200.
Description: Identifies, catalogues, describes and indexes publications of international, intergovernmental organizations.

317   CN   ISSN 0843-6142
Z7554.C2
INDEX TO STATISTICS CANADA SURVEYS AND QUESTIONNAIRES. (Text in English, French) 1981. a. Can.$26($31) (foreign $36). Statistics Canada, Publications Division, Ottawa, Ont. K1A 0T6, Canada. TEL 613-951-7277. FAX 613-951-1584.
Description: Lists all the questionnaire-based surveys of Statistics Canada and the questionnaires used in conducting the surveys, under the Division of Statistics Canada that is resonsible for the survey.

315   II
INDIA. CENTRAL STATISTICAL ORGANIZATION. ANNUAL REPORT. (Text in English) 1949. a. price varies. Central Statistical Organization, Sardar Patel Bhavan, Sansad Marg, New Delhi 110001, India. adv.; circ. 400.
Formerly: India. Central Statistical Organization. Sample Surveys of Current Interest in India. Report (ISSN 0073-6163)

315.4   II   ISSN 0019-4174
INDIA. CENTRAL STATISTICAL ORGANIZATION. MONTHLY ABSTRACT OF STATISTICS. (Text in English and Hindi) 1948. m. Rs.648($233.28) Central Statistical Organization, Sardar Patel Bhavan, Sansad Marg, New Delhi 1, India. bk.rev.; charts; circ. 650.

315   II   ISSN 0073-6155
HA1713
INDIA. CENTRAL STATISTICAL ORGANIZATION. STATISTICAL ABSTRACT. (Text in English) 1951. a. Rs.253.50($91.26) Central Statistical Organization, Sardar Patel Bhavan, Sansad Marg, New Delhi 110001, India.
—BLDSC shelfmark: 8447.412000.

INDIA. DEPARTMENT OF RURAL DEVELOPMENT. ADMINISTRATIVE INTELLIGENCE DIVISION. PROGRESS REPORT ON SMALL FARMERS DEVELOPMENT AGENCY PROGRAMME. see *AGRICULTURE — Abstracting, Bibliographies, Statistics*

INDIA. DEPARTMENT OF RURAL DEVELOPMENT. ADMINISTRATIVE INTELLIGENCE DIVISION. SOME SPECIAL PROGRAMMES OF RURAL DEVELOPMENT. STATISTICS. see *AGRICULTURE — Abstracting, Bibliographies, Statistics*

INDIA. MINISTRY OF AGRICULTURE. BULLETIN ON COMMERCIAL CROPS STATISTICS. see *AGRICULTURE — Abstracting, Bibliographies, Statistics*

INDIA. MINISTRY OF HOME AFFAIRS. VITAL STATISTICS DIVISION. SAMPLE REGISTRATION BULLETIN. see *POPULATION STUDIES — Abstracting, Bibliographies, Statistics*

INDIA. MINISTRY OF HOME AFFAIRS. VITAL STATISTICS DIVISION. SURVEY OF CAUSES OF DEATH (RURAL). see *POPULATION STUDIES — Abstracting, Bibliographies, Statistics*

INDIAN PETROLEUM AND NATURAL GAS STATISTICS. see *PETROLEUM AND GAS — Abstracting, Bibliographies, Statistics*

310 001.6   II   ISSN 0250-9636
INDIAN SOCIETY OF STATISTICS AND OPERATIONS RESEARCH. JOURNAL. (Text in English) 1980. a. Rs.70 to Indian libraries; $35 to foreign libraries. Indian Society of Statistics and Operations Research, M.S. College, Department of Mathematics, P.O. Box 65, Saharanpur 247001, India. TEL 25407. Eds. S.U. Khan, P.L. Maggu. adv.; bk.rev.; abstr.; bibl.; stat.; index. (back issues avail.) **Indexed:** Math.R., Zent.Math.
—BLDSC shelfmark: 4769.020000.

310   II   ISSN 0073-6686
INDIAN STATISTICAL INSTITUTE. ANNUAL REPORT. 1933. a. free. 203 Barrackpore Trunk Rd., Calcutta 700 035, India. TEL 52-6694. TELEX 21-2210 STAT IN. circ. 2,000.

310   II
INDIAN STATISTICAL INSTITUTE. LECTURE NOTES. 1961. irreg. price varies. Macmillan Company of India Ltd., c/o Indian Statistical Institute, 203 Barrackpore Trunk Rd., Calcutta 700035, India. (also avail. in microfilm)
Formerly: Indian Statistical Institute. Research and Training School. Publications.

310 519   II   ISSN 0073-6716
INDIAN STATISTICAL INSTITUTE. STATISTICS AND PROBABILITY SERIES. RESEARCH MONOGRAPHS. irreg. Statistical Publishing Society, 204-1 Barrackpore Trunk Rd., Calcutta 700035, India. Ed. R.R. Rao.

310   II   ISSN 0073-6724
INDIAN STATISTICAL SERIES. irreg., nos.24-25, 1970. price varies. Indian Statistical Institute, 203 Barrackpore Trunk Rd., Calcutta 700 035, India. TEL 52-6694. TELEX 21-2210 STAT IN.

314   FR
INDICATEURS TELEMATIQUES. 6/yr. 2400 F. A Jour, 11 rue du Marche St. Honore, 75001 Paris, France. TEL 42-96-67-22. FAX 40-20-07-75. TELEX 615887 AJOUR.

339   PR   ISSN 0019-7017
INDICE DE PRECIOS AL CONSUMIDOR PARA FAMILIAS OBRERAS EN PUERTO RICO. (Text in English and Spanish) 1966. m. free. Department of Labor, Bureau of Labor Statistics, 505 Munoz Rivera Ave., Hato Rey, PR 00918. charts; stat. (processed)

310   IO
INDONESIA. WELFARE INDICATORS. (Text in English, Indonesian) 1972. a. Rps.10000($7) Central Bureau of Statistics - Biro Pusat Statistik, Jalan Dr. Sutomo No. 8, Box 3, Jakarta Pusat, Indonesia. TEL 21-372808. circ. 200.
Formerly: Indonesia. Social Welfare Indicators.

INDONESIA OIL STATISTICS/STATISTIK PERMINYAKAN INDONESIA. see *PETROLEUM AND GAS — Abstracting, Bibliographies, Statistics*

INDONESIA STATISTICS. see *BUSINESS AND ECONOMICS — Abstracting, Bibliographies, Statistics*

INDUSTRIAL TRENDS. see *BUSINESS AND ECONOMICS — Abstracting, Bibliographies, Statistics*

INDUSTRY REVIEW. see *BUSINESS AND ECONOMICS — Abstracting, Bibliographies, Statistics*

310   CL
INFORME SOBRE CHILE. 1979. a. $152. Editorial Gestion, Rafael Canas 114, Casilla 16485, Correo 9 Santiago, Chile. TEL 562-491526. FAX 562-2361114. adv.; circ. 10,000.

314   AU
INNSBRUCK. STATISTISCHES JAHRBUCH. 1952. a. S.125. Stadtmagistrat Innsbruck, Innrain 10, A-6020 Innsbruck, Austria. TEL 05222-5360522. FAX 05222-5360521. index; circ. 500.
Description: Statistical yearbook of the city of Innsbruck.

INSTITUTE OF STATISTICAL MATHEMATICS. ANNALS. see *MATHEMATICS*

310   BL
INSTITUTO DO DESENVOLVIMENTO ECONOMICO-SOCIAL DO PARA. ANUARIO ESTATISTICO DO ESTADO DO PARA. 1977. a. $1. Instituto do Desenvolvimento Economico-Social do Para, Av. Nazare 871, Belem, Para, Brazil. bibl.; charts; stat.
Description: Discusses socio-economic issues of the state.

INSTITUTO INTERAMERICANO DEL NINO. ESTADISTICA E INFORMATICA. INFORMES TECNICOS. see *SOCIAL SERVICES AND WELFARE*

INSURANCE REGULATORY INFORMATION SYSTEM RATIO RESULTS. see *INSURANCE — Abstracting, Bibliographies, Statistics*

INTER - INDUSTRY STUDY OF THE NEW ZEALAND ECONOMY. see BUSINESS AND ECONOMICS — Abstracting, Bibliographies, Statistics

INTERNATIONAL COMMISSION FOR THE CONSERVATION OF ATLANTIC TUNAS. STATISTICAL BULLETIN. see FISH AND FISHERIES — Abstracting, Bibliographies, Statistics

INTERNATIONAL COMMISSION FOR THE SOUTHEAST ATLANTIC FISHERIES. STATISTICAL BULLETIN. see FISH AND FISHERIES — Abstracting, Bibliographies, Statistics

INTERNATIONAL COTTON INDUSTRY STATISTICS. see TEXTILE INDUSTRIES AND FABRICS — Abstracting, Bibliographies, Statistics

310   NE   ISSN 0074-8609
HA11   CODEN: BIISAR
INTERNATIONAL STATISTICAL INSTITUTE. BULLETIN. PROCEEDINGS OF THE BIENNIAL SESSIONS. (Edited by local organizing committees in the respective host country) (Text in English) 1885. biennial, 48th, 1991, Cairo. fl.150. International Statistical Institute, Prinses Beatrixlaan 428, Postbus 950, 2270 AZ Voorburg, Netherlands. TEL 070-3375737. TELEX 32260 ISI NL. **Indexed:** Math.R., Stat.Theor.Meth.Abstr.
   Description: Proceedings of the biennial sessions of the ISI, including the text of all invited papers covering the spectrum of the statistical profession: statistical theory and method, applied statistics, and other topics.

310   NE
INTERNATIONAL STATISTICAL INSTITUTE. COMPARATIVE STUDIES. CROSS-NATIONAL SUMMARIES AND E C E REPORTS. 1980. irreg., vol.45, 1985. free. International Statistical Institute, Prinses Beatrixlaan 428, Postbus 950, 22270 AZ Voorburg, Netherlands. TEL 070-3375737. TELEX 32260 ISI NL.
   Formerly: International Statistical Institute. Comparative Studies. Cross-National Summaries.

310   NE   ISSN 0306-7734
                      CODEN: ISTRDP
INTERNATIONAL STATISTICAL REVIEW. 1933. 3/yr. $58. International Statistical Institute, Prinses Beatrixlaan 428, Postbus 950, 22270 Voorburg, Netherlands. TEL 070-3375737. TELEX 32260 ISI NL. Eds. D.J. Trewin, B.W. Silverman. adv.; bk.rev.; charts; illus.; stat.; index; circ. 4,000. (reprint service avail. from SWZ) **Indexed:** Biostat., Compumath, Cont.Pg.Manage., Curr.Cont., Ind.Vet., J.Cont.Quant.Meth., Math.R., Oper.Res.Manage.Sci., Qual.Contr.Appl.Stat., Sci.Abstr., Sci.Cit.Ind., Stat.Theor.Meth.Abstr., Vet.Bull.
   —BLDSC shelfmark: 4549.660000.
   Formerly: International Statistical Institute Review (ISSN 0020-8779)
   Description: Provides a view of work in statistics, covering the spectrum of the statistical profession and including the most relevant aspects of probability.

INTERNATIONAL SUGAR ORGANIZATION STATISTICAL BULLETIN. see FOOD AND FOOD INDUSTRIES — Abstracting, Bibliographies, Statistics

INTERNATIONAL TEXTILE MACHINERY SHIPMENT STATISTICS. see TEXTILE INDUSTRIES AND FABRICS — Abstracting, Bibliographies, Statistics

INTERNATIONAL TRADE STATISTICS YEARBOOK. see BUSINESS AND ECONOMICS — Abstracting, Bibliographies, Statistics

IOWA OFFICIAL REGISTER. see POLITICAL SCIENCE — Abstracting, Bibliographies, Statistics

IOWA STATE UNIVERSITY. STATISTICAL LABORATORY. ANNUAL REPORT. see MATHEMATICS — Abstracting, Bibliographies, Statistics

315   IQ
IRAQ. CENTRAL STATISTICAL ORGANIZATION. ANNUAL ABSTRACT OF STATISTICS. (Text in Arabic and English) a. ID.2($6) Central Statistical Organization, Publication and Public Relations Department, Baghdad, Iraq. stat.; circ. 2,000.

319   IQ
IRAQ. CENTRAL STATISTICAL ORGANIZATION. STATISTICAL POCKET BOOK. a. ID.250. Central Statistical Organization, Baghdad, Iraq. stat.

IRELAND. CENTRAL STATISTICS OFFICE. CENSUS OF INDUSTRIAL PRODUCTION. see BUSINESS AND ECONOMICS — Abstracting, Bibliographies, Statistics

314   IE   ISSN 0075-062X
IRELAND (EIRE) CENTRAL STATISTICS OFFICE. TUARASCAIL AR STAIDREAMH BEATHA - REPORT ON VITAL STATISTICS. 1864. a. £8.45. Stationery Office, Dublin, Ireland. TEL 781666. FAX 972360. (Subscr. to: Government Publication Office, Trade and Postal Sales, Bishop St., Dublin 8, Ireland)
   Formerly: Detailed Annual Report of the Registrar General for Ireland.

314   IE   ISSN 0790-8970
IRELAND. STATIONERY OFFICE. STATISTICAL ABSTRACT. 1931. a. £25. Stationery Office, Bishop St., Dublin 8, Ireland. TEL 781666. (Subscr. to: Government Supplies Agency, Trade and Postal Sales, Bishop St., Dublin 8, Ireland) circ. 2,000.
   Formerly (until 1986): Statistical Abstract of Ireland (ISSN 0081-4660)

314   IE   ISSN 0790-8334
HF189
IRELAND. STATIONERY OFFICE. STATISTICAL BULLETIN. 1925. q. £27. Stationery Office, Bishop St., Dublin 8, Ireland. TEL 781666. (Subscr. to: Government Supplies Agency, Trade and Postal Sales, Bishop St., Dublin 8, Ireland) charts; mkt.; stat. **Indexed:** Curr.Lit.Fam.Plan., P.A.I.S., PROMT, Rehabil.Lit.
   —BLDSC shelfmark: 8447.458540.
   Former titles: Irish Statistical Bulletin (ISSN 0021-1370); Irish Trade Journal and Statistical Bulletin.
   Description: Presents detailed results of all short-term economic series with retrospection. Periodic articles on annual inquiries and methodology are also included.

IRON AND STEEL STATISTICAL YEARBOOK. see METALLURGY — Abstracting, Bibliographies, Statistics

ISRAEL. CENTRAL BUREAU OF STATISTICS. AGRICULTURAL STATISTICS QUARTERLY. see AGRICULTURE — Abstracting, Bibliographies, Statistics

ISRAEL. CENTRAL BUREAU OF STATISTICS. CAUSES OF DEATH. see POPULATION STUDIES — Abstracting, Bibliographies, Statistics

315   IS   ISSN 0021-1982
HA1931
ISRAEL. CENTRAL BUREAU OF STATISTICS. MONTHLY BULLETIN OF STATISTICS. (Text in English and Hebrew) 1949. m. $60 includes supplement. Central Bureau of Statistics, P.O.B. 13015, Jerusalem 91 130, Israel. TEL 02-21 12 11. stat.

310 016   IS   ISSN 0334-3278
ISRAEL. CENTRAL BUREAU OF STATISTICS. NEW STATISTICAL PROJECTS AND PUBLICATIONS IN ISRAEL. (Text in Hebrew; summaries in English) 1970. q. $20. Central Bureau of Statistics, Box 13015, Jerusalem 91 130, Israel. TEL 02-21 12 11. bibl.; index. (back issues avail)

312   IS
ISRAEL. CENTRAL BUREAU OF STATISTICS. QUARTERLY STATISTICS OF THE ADMINISTERED TERRITORIES. (Text mainly in Hebrew; occasionally in English) 1968. q. price varies. Central Bureau of Statistics, Box 13015, Jerusalem 91 130, Israel. TEL 02-21 12 11. stat. (back issues avail.)

ISRAEL. CENTRAL BUREAU OF STATISTICS. STAFF IN UNIVERSITIES. see EDUCATION — Abstracting, Bibliographies, Statistics

315.69   IS   ISSN 0081-4679
HA1931
ISRAEL. CENTRAL BUREAU OF STATISTICS. STATISTICAL ABSTRACT OF ISRAEL/SHENATON STATISTI LE-YISRAEL. (Text in English and Hebrew) 1949. a. $27. Central Bureau of Statistics, Box 13015, Jerusalem 91 130, Israel. TEL 02-21 12 11.
   —BLDSC shelfmark: 8447.414000.

ISRAEL. CENTRAL BUREAU OF STATISTICS. SUICIDES AND ATTEMPTED SUICIDES. see POPULATION STUDIES — Abstracting, Bibliographies, Statistics

ISRAEL. CENTRAL BUREAU OF STATISTICS. VITAL STATISTICS. see POPULATION STUDIES — Abstracting, Bibliographies, Statistics

ITALY. CENTRO PER LA STATISTICA AZIENDALE. INDEX. see BUSINESS AND ECONOMICS — Abstracting, Bibliographies, Statistics

314   IT   ISSN 0021-3136
HA1360
ITALY. ISTITUTO CENTRALE DI STATISTICA. BOLLETINO MENSILE DI STATISTICA. 1925. m. L.101000 (foreign L.124000). Istituto Centrale di Statistica, Via Cesare Balbo 16, 00100 Rome, Italy. charts; stat.; index; circ. 5,000. **Indexed:** P.A.I.S.For.Lang.Ind.
   Description: Detailed data of demographic, social, economic and financial phenomena.

314   IT   ISSN 0390-6620
HA1363
ITALY. ISTITUTO CENTRALE DI STATISTICA. INDICATORI MENSILI. m. L.27000. Istituto Centrale di Statistica, Via Cesare Balbo 16, 00100 Rome, Italy. circ. 3,200.

ITALY. ISTITUTO CENTRALE DI STATISTICA. STATISTICA ANNUALE DEL COMMERCIO CON L'ESTERO. PARTE 1-6 TOMO 2. see BUSINESS AND ECONOMICS — Abstracting, Bibliographies, Statistics

ITALY. ISTITUTO CENTRALE DI STATISTICA. STATISTICA ANNUALE DEL COMMERCIO CON L'ESTERO. TOMO 1. see BUSINESS AND ECONOMICS — Abstracting, Bibliographies, Statistics

ITALY. ISTITUTO CENTRALE DI STATISTICA. STATISTICA TRIMESTRALE DEL COMMERCIO CON L'ESTERO. see BUSINESS AND ECONOMICS — Abstracting, Bibliographies, Statistics

ITALY. ISTITUTO CENTRALE DI STATISTICA. STATISTICHE DEL COMMERCIO INTERNO. see BUSINESS AND ECONOMICS — Abstracting, Bibliographies, Statistics

ITALY. ISTITUTO CENTRALE DI STATISTICA. STATISTICHE DELLA NAVIGAZIONE MARITTIMA. see TRANSPORTATION — Abstracting, Bibliographies, Statistics

ITALY. ISTITUTO CENTRALE DI STATISTICA. STATISTICHE DEMOGRAFICHE. see POPULATION STUDIES — Abstracting, Bibliographies, Statistics

ITALY. ISTITUTO CENTRALE DI STATISTICA. STATISTICHE GIUDIZIARIE. see LAW — Abstracting, Bibliographies, Statistics

ITALY. ISTITUTO CENTRALE DI STATISTICA. STATISTICHE INDUSTRIALI. see BUSINESS AND ECONOMICS — Abstracting, Bibliographies, Statistics

ITALY. ISTITUTO CENTRALE DI STATISTICA. STATISTICHE METEOROLOGICHE. see METEOROLOGY — Abstracting, Bibliographies, Statistics

310   US   ISSN 0162-1459
HA1   CODEN: JSTNAL
J A S A JOURNAL OF THE AMERICAN STATISTICAL ASSOCIATION. 1888. q. $160. American Statistical Association, 1429 Duke St., Alexandria, VA 22314-3402. TEL 703-684-1221. FAX 703-684-2037. adv.; bk.rev.; bibl.; index; circ. 17,172. (also avail. in microform from MIM,UMI,KTO,PMC; reprint service avail. from SWZ,UMI) **Indexed:** Abstr.Hyg., B.P.I., Biol.Abstr., Biostat., Bus.Ind., Child Devel.Abstr., Compumath, Comput.Rev., Cont.Pg.Manage., Curr.Cont., Excerp.Med., Hort.Abstr., J.Cont.Quant.Meth., J.of Econ.Lit., Math.R., Oper.Res.Manage.Sci., Popul.Ind., Psychol.Abstr., Qual.Contr.Appl.Stat., Risk Abstr., SSCI, Tr.& Indus.Ind., Trop.Dis.Bull., World Bank.Abstr.
   —BLDSC shelfmark: 4694.000000.
   Formerly: American Statistical Association. Journal (ISSN 0003-1291)

314   NE
JAARBOEK EINDHOVEN. 1957. a. Gemeente Eindhoven, Afdeling Onderzoek en Statistiek, P.O. Box 90150, 5600 RB Eindhoven, Netherlands. FAX 040-433585. TELEX 51365 NL. Ed.Bd. stat.; illus.; index; circ. 500.

4576 STATISTICS

310   GW
JAHRBUECHER FUER STATISTIK UND LANDESKUNDE VON BADEN-WUERTTEMBERG. 1953. a. DM.16.10. Statistisches Landesamt, Boeblinger Str. 68, Postfach 106033, 7000 Stuttgart 10, Germany. Ed. Max Wingen. bibl.; charts; stat.; cum.index: 1977-1983; circ. 850. (back issues avail.)

315.4   II
JAMMU AND KASHMIR. DIRECTORATE OF ECONOMICS AND STATISTICS. DIGEST OF STATISTICS. (Text in English) q. Directorate of Economics and Statistics, Planning and Development Department, Jammu and Kashmir, India.

JAPAN. MANAGEMENT AND COORDINATION AGENCY. STATISTICS BUREAU. EMPLOYMENT STATUS SURVEY. see BUSINESS AND ECONOMICS — Abstracting, Bibliographies, Statistics

JAPAN. MINISTRY OF HEALTH AND WELFARE. STATISTICS AND INFORMATION DEPARTMENT. HANDBOOK OF HEALTH AND WELFARE STATISTICS. see PUBLIC HEALTH AND SAFETY — Abstracting, Bibliographies, Statistics

315   JA   ISSN 0385-969X
JAPAN. MINISTRY OF HEALTH AND WELFARE. STATISTICS AND INFORMATION DEPARTMENT. MONTHLY REPORT ON VITAL STATISTICS. m. 520 Yen. Ministry of Health and Welfare, Statistics and Information Department - Kosei-sho Daijin Kanbo Tokei Joho-bu, 7-3 Ichigaya Honmura-cho, Shinjuku-ku, Tokyo 162, Japan. TEL 03-586-3361. (Order from: Health and Welfare Statistics Association, 5-13-14 Roppongi, Minato-ku, Tokyo, Japan) Key Title: Jinko Dotai Tokei Geppo, Gaisu.
    Formerly (until 1970): Jinko Dotai Tokei Maigetsu Gaisu (ISSN 0385-9681)

JAPAN. MINISTRY OF HEALTH AND WELFARE. STATISTICS AND INFORMATION DEPARTMENT. REPORT ON ACTIVITIES OF PUBLIC HEALTH CENTERS. see MEDICAL SCIENCES — Abstracting, Bibliographies, Statistics

JAPAN. MINISTRY OF HEALTH AND WELFARE. STATISTICS AND INFORMATION DEPARTMENT. REPORT ON SURVEY OF NATIONAL MEDICAL CARE INSURANCE SERVICES. see INSURANCE — Abstracting, Bibliographies, Statistics

JAPAN. MINISTRY OF HEALTH AND WELFARE. STATISTICS AND INFORMATION DEPARTMENT. REPORT ON SURVEY OF OCCUPATIONAL STATISTICS ON VITAL EVENTS. see OCCUPATIONS AND CAREERS — Abstracting, Bibliographies, Statistics

JAPAN. MINISTRY OF HEALTH AND WELFARE. STATISTICS AND INFORMATION DEPARTMENT. REPORT ON SURVEY OF PUBLIC ASSISTANCE. see SOCIAL SERVICES AND WELFARE — Abstracting, Bibliographies, Statistics

JAPAN. MINISTRY OF HEALTH AND WELFARE. STATISTICS AND INFORMATION DEPARTMENT. REPORT ON SURVEY OF SOCIO-ECONOMIC ASPECTS ON VITAL EVENTS. see BUSINESS AND ECONOMICS — Abstracting, Bibliographies, Statistics

JAPAN. MINISTRY OF HEALTH AND WELFARE. STATISTICS AND INFORMATION DEPARTMENT. REPORT ON SURVEY OF SOCIAL WELFARE INSTITUTIONS. see SOCIAL SERVICES AND WELFARE — Abstracting, Bibliographies, Statistics

JAPAN. MINISTRY OF HEALTH AND WELFARE. STATISTICS AND INFORMATION DEPARTMENT. STATISTICAL REPORT ON COMMUNICABLE DISEASES. see MEDICAL SCIENCES — Abstracting, Bibliographies, Statistics

JAPAN. MINISTRY OF HEALTH AND WELFARE. STATISTICS AND INFORMATION DEPARTMENT. STATISTICAL REPORT ON FOOD POISONINGS. see MEDICAL SCIENCES — Abstracting, Bibliographies, Statistics

JAPAN. MINISTRY OF HEALTH AND WELFARE. STATISTICS AND INFORMATION DEPARTMENT. STATISTICAL REPORT ON PUBLIC HEALTH ADMINISTRATION AND SERVICES/EISEI GYOSEI GYOMU HOKOKU. see PUBLIC HEALTH AND SAFETY — Abstracting, Bibliographies, Statistics

JAPAN. MINISTRY OF HEALTH AND WELFARE. STATISTICS AND INFORMATION DEPARTMENT. STATISTICAL REPORT ON SOCIAL WELFARE ADMINISTRATION AND SERVICES. see SOCIAL SERVICES AND WELFARE — Abstracting, Bibliographies, Statistics

312   JA   ISSN 0075-3270
JAPAN. MINISTRY OF HEALTH AND WELFARE. STATISTICS AND INFORMATION DEPARTMENT. VITAL STATISTICS. Variant title: Vital Statistics Japan. 1899. a. (in 3 vols.). 7210 Yen for vol.1; vol.2 8800 Yen; vol.3 9800 Yen. Ministry of Health and Welfare, Statistics and Information Department - Kosei-sho Daijin Kanbo Tokei Joho-bu, 7-3 Ichigaya-Honmura cho, Shinjuku-ku, Tokyo 162, Japan. TEL 03-260-3181. (Order from: Health & Welfare Statistics Association, 5-13-14, Roppongi, Minato-ku, Tokyo, Japan) Key Title: Jinko Dotai Tokei.
    Formerly: Nihon Teikoku Jinko Dotai Tokei - Vital Statistics of the Japanese Empire.

JAPAN. POCKET SIZE STATISTICS OF SUGAR PRODUCTS. see FOOD AND FOOD INDUSTRIES — Abstracting, Bibliographies, Statistics

315   JA   ISSN 0389-3502
HC461
JAPAN: AN INTERNATIONAL COMPARISON. Variant title: Japan (Year). (Text in English) a. 900 Yen($7) Keizai Koho Center, Otemachi Bldg. 6-1, Ote-machi 1-chome, Chiyoda-ku, Tokyo 100, Japan. FAX 03-3201-1418. Ed. Nabeshima Michihisa.
    Description: Pocket-sized statistical profile of Japan in comparison with other nations. Covers population and area, national income, agriculture and food supply, industry and services, foreign trade, balance of payments, exchange rates, employment, wages, and productivity.

310   JA   ISSN 0910-9684
JIDOSHA HOYU SHARYOSU. 1973. m. 3708 Yen. Jidosha Kensa Toroku Kyoryokukai, Toranomon Kiyoshi Bldg., 3-10, 4-chome, Toranomon, Minato-ku, Tokyo 105, Japan. TEL 03-3432-5611. FAX 03-3432-1044. Ed. Isamu Seki. bk.rev.; circ. 1,500. (back issues avail.)

315   JO   ISSN 0075-4013
HA4561
JORDAN. DEPARTMENT OF STATISTICS. ANNUAL STATISTICAL YEARBOOK. (Text in Arabic and English) 1950. a. $30 includes External Trade Statistics. Department of Statistics, P.O. Box 2015, Amman, Jordan. TEL 842171. FAX 833518. TELEX 24117 STATIS JO.

JOURNAL CONTENTS IN QUANTITATIVE METHODS. see BUSINESS AND ECONOMICS — Abstracting, Bibliographies, Statistics

310 510   UK   ISSN 0266-4763
QA276.A1
JOURNAL OF APPLIED STATISTICS. 1975. 4/yr. $106 to individuals; institutions $264. Carfax Publishing Co., P.O. Box 25, Abingdon, Oxfordshire OX14 3UE, England. TEL 0235-555335. FAX 0235-553559. (U.S. subscr. addr.: Carfax Publishing Co., Box 2025, Dunnellon, FL 32630) Ed. Gopal K. Kanji. adv.; bk.rev. (also avail. in microfiche; back issues avail.) Indexed: Biostat., Comput.Abstr., Curr.Ind.Stat., J.Cont.Quant.Meth., Oper.Res.Manage.Sci., Qual.Contr.Manage.Sci.
—BLDSC shelfmark: 4947.110000.
    Formerly (until 1984): Bulletin in Applied Statistics.

JOURNAL OF BUSINESS AND ECONOMIC STATISTICS. see BUSINESS AND ECONOMICS — Abstracting, Bibliographies, Statistics

JOURNAL OF ECONOMIC & SOCIAL MEASUREMENT. see BUSINESS AND ECONOMICS — Abstracting, Bibliographies, Statistics

311   SW   ISSN 0282-423X
HA 1523   CODEN: JOFSEA
JOURNAL OF OFFICIAL STATISTICS; an international review. (Text in English) 1952-1963; N.S. 1985. q. SEK 300($50) Statistics Sweden, S-115 81 Stockholm, Sweden. TEL 08-7834000. FAX 08-7834288. TELEX 015261 SWESTAT S. (Subscr. to: Journal of Official Statistics, SCB-Distribution, S-701 89 Oerebro, Sweden) Ed. Lars Lyberg. adv.; bk.rev.; charts; illus.; stat.; index; circ. 1,100. (back issues avail.) Indexed: Biostat., Curr.Ind.Stat., J.Cont.Quant.Meth., Oper.Res.Manage.Sci., Popul.Ind., Qual.Contr.Appl.Stat., Stat.Theor.Meth.Abstr.
—BLDSC shelfmark: 5026.235000.
    Formerly (until 1985): Sweden. Statistiska Centralbyraan. Statistik Tidskrif (ISSN 0039-7261)
    Description: Specializes in issues pertinent to survey sampling with emphasis on the methodology and applications used by statistical agencies in the production of official statistics.

319.14   PH   ISSN 0022-3603
HA1821
JOURNAL OF PHILIPPINE STATISTICS. (Text in English) 1940. q. $8 per copy. National Statistics Office, Ramon Magsaysay Blvd., Box 779, Manila, Philippines. FAX 610794. Ed. Preciosa Astillero. charts; stat.; circ. 300. Indexed: Ind.Phil.Per., P.A.I.S.

JOURNAL OF STATISTICAL COMPUTATION AND SIMULATION. see COMPUTERS — Computer Simulation

311.2   NE   ISSN 0378-3758
QA276.A1   CODEN: JSPIDN
JOURNAL OF STATISTICAL PLANNING AND INFERENCE. (Text in English) 1977. 12/yr.(in 4 vols.; 3 nos./vol.). fl.1308 (effective 1992). North-Holland (Subsidiary of: Elsevier Science Publishers B.V.), P.O. Box 211, 1000 AE Amsterdam, Netherlands. TEL 020-5803911. FAX 020-5803598. TELEX 18582 ESPA NL. (Subscr. in U.S. and Canada to: Elsevier Science Publishing Co., Inc., Box 882, Madison Sq. Sta., New York, NY 10159. TEL 212-989-5800) Ed. S.S. Gupta. (also avail. in microform from RPI; back issues avail.; reprint service avail. from SWZ) Indexed: Biostat., BPIA, Bus.Ind., Compumath, Curr.Cont., Ind.Sci.Rev., J.Cont.Quant.Meth., Math.R., Oper.Res.Manage.Sci., Qual.Contr.Appl.Stat., Sci.Abstr.
—BLDSC shelfmark: 5066.842000.
    Description: Provides information on statistics, with special emphasis on statistical planning and the related areas of combinatorial mathematics and probability theory.
    Refereed Serial

311   BG
JOURNAL OF STATISTICAL RESEARCH. 1967. s-a. $6. University of Dhaka, Institute of Statistical Research and Training, Ramna, Dhaka 1000, Bangladesh. Ed.Bd. bk.rev.; charts; stat. Indexed: Math.R.
    Supersedes: University of Dhaka. Institute of Statistical Research and Training. Bulletin (ISSN 0020-3165)

JUSTIZ IN ZAHLEN. see LAW — Abstracting, Bibliographies, Statistics

316   NR
KADUNA STATE STATISTICAL YEARBOOK. 1975. a. Ministry of Economic Planning and Rural Development, Economic Planning Division, P.M. Bag 2032, Kaduna, Nigeria.
    Formerly: North Central State Statistical Yearbook.

316.69   NR
KANO STATE STATISTICAL YEAR BOOK. 1970. a. price varies. Statistics Division, P.M.B. 3291, Kano, Nigeria. Ed.Bd. bk.rev.; stat.
    Supersedes: Northern Nigeria. Ministry of Economic Planning. Statistical Year Book.

KAYHAN YEARBOOK; a complete directory and encyclopedia of facts, data and statistics on Iran. see HISTORY — History Of The Near East

311 510   JA   ISSN 0914-8930
KEISANKI TOKEIGAKU/BULLETIN OF THE COMPUTATIONAL STATISTICS OF JAPAN. (Text in Japanese; summaries in English and Japanese) 1988. a. Nihon Keisanki Tokei Gakkai - Japanese Society of Computational Statistics, c/o Okayama Daigaku Kyoyobu, Tokeigaku Kyoshitsu, 1-1, Tsushima 2-chome, Okayama-shi, Okayama-ken 700, Japan. abstr.

KENTUCKY. CABINET FOR HUMAN RESOURCES. VITAL STATISTICS REPORT. see *PUBLIC HEALTH AND SAFETY* — Abstracting, Bibliographies, Statistics

KENYA. CENTRAL BUREAU OF STATISTICS. AGRICULTURAL CENSUS (LARGE FARM AREAS). see *AGRICULTURE* — Abstracting, Bibliographies, Statistics

KENYA. CENTRAL BUREAU OF STATISTICS. DEVELOPMENT ESTIMATES. see *BUSINESS AND ECONOMICS* — Abstracting, Bibliographies, Statistics

KENYA. CENTRAL BUREAU OF STATISTICS. EMPLOYMENT AND EARNINGS IN THE MODERN SECTOR. see *BUSINESS AND ECONOMICS* — Abstracting, Bibliographies, Statistics

KENYA. CENTRAL BUREAU OF STATISTICS. ESTIMATES OF RECURRENT EXPENDITURES. see *BUSINESS AND ECONOMICS* — Abstracting, Bibliographies, Statistics

KENYA. CENTRAL BUREAU OF STATISTICS. ESTIMATES OF REVENUE EXPENDITURES. see *BUSINESS AND ECONOMICS* — Abstracting, Bibliographies, Statistics

KENYA. CENTRAL BUREAU OF STATISTICS. SURVEYS OF INDUSTRIAL PRODUCTION. see *BUSINESS AND ECONOMICS* — Abstracting, Bibliographies, Statistics

316.76   KE   ISSN 0453-6002
KENYA STATISTICAL DIGEST. 1963. q. price varies. Central Bureau of Statistics, Ministry of Planning and National Development, Box 30266, Nairobi, Kenya. (Orders to: Government Printing and Stationery Office, Box 30128, Nairobi, Kenya)

KNITSTATS; the yearly statistical bulletin for the hosiery and knitwear industry. see *TEXTILE INDUSTRIES AND FABRICS* — Abstracting, Bibliographies, Statistics

310   DK   ISSN 0106-3839
HA1489.C6
KOBENHAVNS STATISTISKE AARBOG; for Koebenhavn og Frederiksberg samt Hovedstadsregionen. (Text in Danish and English) 1919. a. DKK 200. Statistisk Kontor - Copenhagen Statistical Office, Vester Voldgade 87, 1552 Copenhagen V, Denmark. (Subscr. to: Danske Boghandleres Kommissionsanstalt, Siljangade 6-8, 2300 Copenhagen S, Denmark) circ. 2,400.

310   GW   ISSN 0933-632X
KOELNER STATISTISCHE NACHRICHTEN. 1979. q. DM.8. Amt fuer Statistik und Einwohnerwesen, Stadthaus Chorweiler, Athener Ring 4, 5000 Cologne 71, Germany. TEL 0221-221-1872. circ. 1,000.

KOREA (REPUBLIC). NATIONAL STATISTICAL OFFICE. ANNUAL REPORT ON THE INTERNAL MIGRATION STATISTICS. see *POPULATION STUDIES* — Abstracting, Bibliographies, Statistics

KOREA (REPUBLIC). NATIONAL STATISTICAL OFFICE. POPULATION & HOUSING CENSUS REPORT. see *POPULATION STUDIES* — Abstracting, Bibliographies, Statistics

315   KO   ISSN 0075-6873
HA4630.5
KOREA STATISTICAL YEARBOOK/HANGUK TONGGYE YONGAM. (Text in English, Korean) 1952. a. 16000 Won. National Statistical Office, 90, Gyongun-dong, Jongro-gu, Seoul 110-310, S. Korea. TEL 02-720-2788. (Subscr. to: the Korean Statistical Association, Room 302, Chungok Building, 561-30, Sinsa-dong, Gangnam-gu, Seoul 135-120, S. Korea) circ. 1,200.
   Formerly (until 1961): Daihan Minguk Tongyei Nyengam (ISSN 0253-3014)

KOREAN TRADERS ASSOCIATION. STATISTICAL YEARBOOK OF FOREIGN TRADE. see *BUSINESS AND ECONOMICS* — Abstracting, Bibliographies, Statistics

314   GW
KREFELD. AMT FUER STATISTIK UND STADTENTWICKLUNG. STATISTISCHES JAHRBUCH. 1926. a. DM.10. Amt fuer Statistik und Stadtentwicklung, Konrad-Adenauer-Platz 17, 4150 Krefeld, Germany. Ed.Bd. bk.rev.; circ. 450.

314   GW
KREISSTANDARDZAHLEN NORDRHEIN-WESTFALEN; statistische Angaben fuer kreisfreie Staedte und Kreise. 1951. a. DM.10. Landesamt fuer Datenverarbeitung und Statistik Nordrhein-Westfalen, Mauerstr. 51, Postfach 101105, 4000 Duesseldorf 1, Germany. TEL 0211-9449-01. circ. 1,300. (back issues avail.)

KULTUR- UND STADTNACHRICHTEN AUS WEITRA. see *HISTORY*

315.367   KU
KUWAIT. CENTRAL STATISTICAL OFFICE. ANNUAL STATISTICAL ABSTRACT. (Text in Arabic, English) 1965. a. Central Statistical Office, P.O. Box 26188, Safat 13122, Kuwait. TEL 242-8200. TELEX 22468. circ. 450.
   Supersedes (1980-198?): Kuwait. Central Statistical Office. Monthly Digest of Statistics (ISSN 0023-5768)

LABOR FORCE AND NONAGRICULTURAL EMPLOYMENT ESTIMATES. see *BUSINESS AND ECONOMICS* — Abstracting, Bibliographies, Statistics

LABOUR FORCE AND MIGRATION SURVEY. see *POPULATION STUDIES* — Abstracting, Bibliographies, Statistics

LABOUR FORCE SITUATION IN INDONESIA: PRELIMINARY FIGURES/KEADAAN ANGKATAN KERJA DI INDONESIA: ANGKA SEMENTARA. see *BUSINESS AND ECONOMICS* — Abstracting, Bibliographies, Statistics

THE LABOUR FORCE, VICTORIA. see *BUSINESS AND ECONOMICS* — Abstracting, Bibliographies, Statistics

314   AU
LANDESHAUPTSTADT INNSBRUCK. STATISTISCHER VIERTELJAHRESBERICHT. 1950. q. S.120. Stadtmagistrat Innsbruck, Innrain 10, A-6020 Innsbruck, Austria. TEL 06222-5360523. FAX 0512-5360521. index; circ. 500.
   Description: Statistical information on the Austrian city of Innsbruck.

315.692   LE   ISSN 0023-9860
LEBANON. DIRECTION CENTRALE DE LA STATISTIQUE. BULLETIN STATISTIQUE MENSUEL. (Text in Arabic and French) 1963. m. free. Direction Centrale de la Statistique, Ministere du Plan, Beirut, Lebanon. mkt.; stat.; circ. 1,900.
   Formerly: Lebanon. Service de Statistique Generale. Bulletin Statistique Mensuel.

315   LE   ISSN 0075-8388
LEBANON. DIRECTION CENTRALE DE LA STATISTIQUE. RECUEIL DE STATISTIQUES LIBANAISES.* (Text in Arabic and French) 1963. a. free. Direction Centrale de la Statistique, Ministere du Plan, Beirut, Lebanon.

310   US
LECTURE NOTES IN STATISTICS. 1980. irreg. price varies. Springer-Verlag, 175 Fifth Ave., New York, NY 10010. TEL 212-460-1500. (Also Berlin, Heidelberg, Tokyo and Vienna) Ed.Bd. (reprint service avail. from ISI)

311   MH
LEGISLACAO DO SISTEMA DE INFORMACAO ESTATISTICA DE MACAU/LAW OF MACAU STATISTICAL INFORMATION SYSTEM. (Text in Chinese, Portuguese) 1989. irreg. free. Direccao dos Servicos de Estatistica e Censos, P.O. Box 3022, Macau.

LENGTH OF STAY BY DIAGNOSIS & OPERATION, UNITED STATES. see *HOSPITALS* — Abstracting, Bibliographies, Statistics

LENGTH OF STAY BY DIAGNOSIS & OPERATION, UNITED STATES, NORTH CENTRAL REGION. see *HOSPITALS* — Abstracting, Bibliographies, Statistics

LENGTH OF STAY BY DIAGNOSIS & OPERATION, UNITED STATES, NORTHEASTERN REGION. see *HOSPITALS* — Abstracting, Bibliographies, Statistics

LENGTH OF STAY BY DIAGNOSIS & OPERATION, UNITED STATES, SOUTHERN REGION. see *HOSPITALS* — Abstracting, Bibliographies, Statistics

LENGTH OF STAY BY DIAGNOSIS & OPERATION, UNITED STATES, WESTERN REGION. see *HOSPITALS* — Abstracting, Bibliographies, Statistics

LETTERE D'AFFARI. see *BUSINESS AND ECONOMICS* — Abstracting, Bibliographies, Statistics

309   DK   ISSN 0900-2499
LEVEVILKAAR I DANMARK/LIVING CONDITIONS IN DENMARK; statistisk oversigt. (Text in Danish and English) 1976. quadrennial. DKK 143.44. Danmarks Statistik, Sejroegade 11, 2100 Copenhagen OE, Denmark. TEL 31-298222. FAX 31-184801. TELEX 16236. (Dist. by: Danske Boghendleres Kommissionsanstalt, Siljangade 6, 2300 Copenhagen S, Denmark)
   Description: Compendium of social statistics concerning main aspects of the Danish population's living conditions.

LIBRARY AND INFORMATION SCIENCE EDUCATION STATISTICAL REPORT. see *LIBRARY AND INFORMATION SCIENCES* — Abstracting, Bibliographies, Statistics

339.42   LY   ISSN 0023-1630
LIBYA. CENSUS AND STATISTICS DEPARTMENT. MONTHLY COST OF LIVING INDEX FOR TRIPOLI TOWN. (Text in Arabic and English) 1964. m. free. Secretariat of Planning, Census and Statistics Department, P.O. Box 600, Tripoli, Libya. charts; stat.

315   LY   ISSN 0075-9287
LIBYA. CENSUS AND STATISTICS DEPARTMENT. STATISTICAL ABSTRACT. (Text in Arabic and English) 1958. a. free. Secretariat of Planning, Census and Statistics Department, P.O. Box 600, Tripoli, Libya.

LUXEMBOURG. SERVICE CENTRAL DE LA STATISTIQUE ET DES ETUDES ECONOMIQUES. ANNUAIRE STATISTIQUE. see *BUSINESS AND ECONOMICS* — Abstracting, Bibliographies, Statistics

LUXEMBOURG. SERVICE CENTRAL DE LA STATISTIQUE ET DES ETUDES ECONOMIQUES. ANNUAIRE STATISTIQUE RETROSPECTIF. see *BUSINESS AND ECONOMICS* — Abstracting, Bibliographies, Statistics

LUXEMBOURG. SERVICE CENTRAL DE LA STATISTIQUE ET DES ETUDES ECONOMIQUES. COLLECTION D ET M: DEFINITIONS ET METHODES. see *BUSINESS AND ECONOMICS* — Abstracting, Bibliographies, Statistics

MACAO. DIRECCAO DOS SERVICOS DE ESTATISTICA E CENSOS. ANUARIO ESTATISTICO DO COMERCIO EXTERNO/MACAO. CENSUS AND STATISTICS DEPARTMENT. YEARBOOK OF EXTERNAL TRADE STATISTICS. see *BUSINESS AND ECONOMICS* — Abstracting, Bibliographies, Statistics

310   MH
MACAO. DIRECCAO DOS SERVICOS DE ESTATISTICA E CENSOS. ANUARIO ESTATISTICO/MACAO. CENSUS AND STATISTICS DEPARTMENT. YEARBOOK OF STATISTICS. (Text in Chinese, English and Portuguese) 1932. a. free. Direccao dos Servicos de Estatistica e Censos, Rua Inacio Baptista, No.4D-6, P.O. Box 3022, Macao. TEL 550935. FAX 561884. circ. 500.

MACAO. DIRECCAO DOS SERVICOS DE ESTATISTICA E CENSOS. BALANCO ENERGETICO (ANUAL)/MACAO. CENSUS AND STATISTICS DEPARTMENT. BALANCE OF ENERGY (ANNUAL). see *ENERGY* — Abstracting, Bibliographies, Statistics

MACAO. DIRECCAO DOS SERVICOS DE ESTATISTICA E CENSOS. BALANCO ENERGETICO/MACAO. CENSUS AND STATISTICS DEPARTMENT. BALANCE OF ENERGY. see *ENERGY* — Abstracting, Bibliographies, Statistics

MACAO. DIRECCAO DOS SERVICOS DE ESTATISTICA E CENSOS. BOLETIM MENSAL DO COMERCIO EXTERNO/MACAO. CENSUS AND STATISTICS DEPARTMENT. MONTHLY BULLETIN OF EXTERNAL TRADE. see *BUSINESS AND ECONOMICS* — Abstracting, Bibliographies, Statistics

4578 STATISTICS

314   MH
MACAO. DIRECCAO DOS SERVICOS DE ESTATISTICA E CENSOS. BOLETIM MENSAL DE ESTATISTICA/MACAO. CENSUS AND STATISTICS DEPARTMENT. MONTHLY DIGEST OF STATISTICS. (Text in Chinese, Portuguese) 1976. m. free. Direccao dos Servicos de Estatistica e Censos, Rua Inacio Baptista, No.4D-6, P.O. Box 3022, Macao. TEL 550935. FAX 561884. circ. 400.

MACAO. DIRECCAO DOS SERVICOS DE ESTATISTICA E CENSOS. CENSOS DA POPULACAO/MACAO. CENSUS AND STATISTICS DEPARTMENT. POPULATION CENSUS. see *POPULATION STUDIES* — *Abstracting, Bibliographies, Statistics*

MACAO. DIRECCAO DOS SERVICOS DE ESTATISTICA E CENSOS. ESTATISTICAS DA PESCA/MACAO. CENSUS AND STATISTICS DEPARTMENT. STATISTICS OF FISHERY. see *FISH AND FISHERIES* — *Abstracting, Bibliographies, Statistics*

MACAO. DIRECCAO DOS SERVICOS DE ESTATISTICA E CENSOS. ESTATISTICAS DEMOGRAFICAS/MACAO. CENSUS AND STATISTICS DEPARTMENT. DEMOGRAPHIC STATISTICS. see *POPULATION STUDIES* — *Abstracting, Bibliographies, Statistics*

MACAO. DIRECCAO DOS SERVICOS DE ESTATISTICA E CENSOS. ESTATISTICAS DA JUSTICA E DA CRIMINALIDADE/MACAO. CENSUS AND STATISTICS DEPARTMENT. STATISTICS OF JUSTICE AND CRIMINALITY. see *LAW* — *Abstracting, Bibliographies, Statistics*

MACAO. DIRECCAO DOS SERVICOS DE ESTATISTICA E CENSOS. ESTATISTICAS DO TURISMO/MACAO. CENSUS AND STATISTICS DEPARTMENT. TOURISM STATISTICS. see *TRAVEL AND TOURISM* — *Abstracting, Bibliographies, Statistics*

MACAO. DIRECCAO DOS SERVICOS DE ESTATISTICA E CENSOS. ESTATISTICAS DO TURISMO (RELATORIO ANUAL)/MACAO. CENSUS AND STATISTICS DEPARTMENT. TOURISM STATISTICS (ANNUAL REPORT). see *TRAVEL AND TOURISM* — *Abstracting, Bibliographies, Statistics*

MACAO. DIRECCAO DOS SERVICOS DE ESTATISTICA E CENSOS. ESTIMATIVAS DO PRODUTO INTERNO BRUTO/MACAO. CENSUS AND STATISTICS DEPARTMENT. GROSS DOMESTIC PRODUCT. see *BUSINESS AND ECONOMICS* — *Abstracting, Bibliographies, Statistics*

MACAO. DIRECCAO DOS SERVICOS DE ESTATISTICA E CENSOS. ESTIMATIVAS DA POPULACAO RESIDENTE EM MACAU/MACAO. CENSUS AND STATISTICS DEPARTMENT. ESTIMATION OF RESIDENT POPULATION IN MACAO. see *POPULATION STUDIES* — *Abstracting, Bibliographies, Statistics*

MACAO. DIRECCAO DOS SERVICOS DE ESTATISTICA E CENSOS. II RECENSEAMENTO GERAL A HABITCAO/MACAO. CENSUS AND STATISTICS DEPARTMENT. II GENERAL CENSUS OF HOUSING. see *HOUSING AND URBAN PLANNING* — *Abstracting, Bibliographies, Statistics*

MACAO. DIRECCAO DOS SERVICOS DE ESTATISTICA E CENSOS. IMPORTACAO DE MAO-DE-OBRA E RENOVACAO DE CONTRATOS DE TRABALHADORES NAO RESIDNETES/MACAO. CENSUS AND STATISTICS DEPARTMENT. STATISTICS OF NON RESIDENT WORKERS IMPORTATION. see *POPULATION STUDIES* — *Abstracting, Bibliographies, Statistics*

MACAO. DIRECCAO DOS SERVICOS DE ESTATISTICA E CENSOS. INDICADORES ESTATISTICOS - OPERACOES SOBRE IMOVEIS E SOCIEDADES/MACAO. CENSUS AND STATISTICS DEPARTMENT. STATISTICAL DATA - TRANSACTIONS CONCERNING REAL ESTATE AND COMPANIES. see *REAL ESTATE* — *Abstracting, Bibliographies, Statistics*

MACAO. DIRECCAO DOS SERVICOS DE ESTATISTICA E CENSOS. INDICE DE PRECOS NO CONSUMIDOR/MACAO. CENSUS AND STATISTICS DEPARTMENT. CONSUMER PRICE INDEX. see *BUSINESS AND ECONOMICS* — *Abstracting, Bibliographies, Statistics*

MACAO. DIRECCAO DOS SERVICOS DE ESTATISTICA E CENSOS. INDICE DE PRECOS NO CONSUMIDOR (RELATORIO ANUAL)/MACAO. CENSUS AND STATISTICS DEPARTMENT. CONSUMER PRICE INDEX (ANNUAL REPORT). see *BUSINESS AND ECONOMICS* — *Abstracting, Bibliographies, Statistics*

MACAO. DIRECCAO DOS SERVICOS DE ESTATISTICA E CENSOS. INQUERITO AO ENSINO/MACAO. CENSUS AND STATISTICS DEPARTMENT. EDUCATION SURVEY. see *EDUCATION* — *Abstracting, Bibliographies, Statistics*

MACAO. DIRECCAO DOS SERVICOS DE ESTATISTICA E CENSOS. INQUERITO AO EMPREGO E SALARIOS NA CONSTRUCAO CIVIL/MACAO. CENSUS AND STATISTICS DEPARTMENT. SURVEY OF EMPLOYMENT AND WAGES IN THE CONSTRUCTION INDUSTRY. see *BUSINESS AND ECONOMICS* — *Abstracting, Bibliographies, Statistics*

MACAO. DIRECCAO DOS SERVICOS DE ESTATISTICA E CENSOS. INQUERITO AOS RESTAURANTES, HOTEIS E ESTABELECIMENTOS SIMILARES/MACAO. CENSUS AND STATISTICS DEPARTMENT. CENSUS OF RESTAURANTS, HOTELS AND SIMILAR ESTABLISHMENTS. see *HOTELS AND RESTAURANTS* — *Abstracting, Bibliographies, Statistics*

MACAO. DIRECCAO DOS SERVICOS DE ESTATISTICA E CENSOS. INQUERITO AS EMBARCACOES DE PESCA/MACAO. CENSUS AND STATISTICS DEPARTMENT. SURVEY OF FISHING VESSELS. see *FISH AND FISHERIES* — *Abstracting, Bibliographies, Statistics*

MACAO. DIRECCAO DOS SERVICOS DE ESTATISTICA E CENSOS. INQUERITO INDUSTRIAL/MACAO. CENSUS AND STATISTICS DEPARTMENT. INDUSTRIAL SURVEY. see *BUSINESS AND ECONOMICS* — *Abstracting, Bibliographies, Statistics*

MACAO. DIRECCAO DOS SERVICOS DE ESTATISTICA E CENSOS. INQUERITO TRIMESTRAL AO COMERCIO A RETALHO/MACAO. CENSUS AND STATISTICS DEPARTMENT. QUARTERLY RETAIL SURVEY. see *BUSINESS AND ECONOMICS* — *Abstracting, Bibliographies, Statistics*

315   MH
MACAO. DIRECCAO DOS SERVICOS DE ESTATISTICA E CENSOS. PLANO DE ACTIVIDADES/MACAO. CENSUS AND STATISTICS DEPARTMENT. ACTIVITIES PLAN. (Text in Chinese, Portuguese) 1988. a. free. Direccao dos Servicos de Estatistica e Censos, P.O. Box 3022, Macao.

MACAO. DIRECCAO DOS SERVICOS DE ESTATISTICA E CENSOS. RECENSEAMENTO DOS ALOJAMENTOS INFORMAIS/MACAO. CENSUS AND STATISTICS DEPARTMENT. CENSUS OF INFORMAL ACCOMODATION. see *POPULATION STUDIES* — *Abstracting, Bibliographies, Statistics*

MACAO. DIRECCAO DOS SERVICOS DE ESTATISTICA E CENSOS. RELATORIO ANUAL DA CONSTRUCAO CIVIL/MACAO. CENSUS AND STATISTICS DEPARTMENT. CIVIL CONSTRUCTION IN MACAO (ANNUAL REPORT). see *REAL ESTATE* — *Abstracting, Bibliographies, Statistics*

315   MH
MACAO. DIRECCAO DOS SERVICOS DE ESTATISTICA E CENSOS. RELATORIO DE ACTIVIDADES/MACAO. CENSUS AND STATISTICS DEPARTMENT. ACTIVITIES REPORT. (Text in Chinese, Portuguese) 1986. a. free. Direccao dos Servicos de Estatistica e Censos, P.O. Box 3022, Macao.

MACAO. DIRECCAO DOS SERVICOS DE ESTATISTICA E CENSOS. SERIES RETROSPECTIVAS DO COMERCIO EXTERNO/MACAO. CENSUS AND STATISTICS DEPARTMENT. RETROSPECTIVE SERIES OF EXTERNAL TRADE. see *BUSINESS AND ECONOMICS* — *Abstracting, Bibliographies, Statistics*

MACAO. DIRECCAO DOS SERVICOS DE ESTATISTICA E CENSOS. TRANSPORTE DE MERCADORIAS POR VIAS DE UTILIZACAO. see *BUSINESS AND ECONOMICS* — *Abstracting, Bibliographies, Statistics*

310   MH
MACAO EM NUMEROS/MACAO IN FIGURES. (Text in Chinese, English, Portuguese) 1976. a. free. Direccao dos Servicos de Estatistica e Censos, P.O. Box 3022, Macao.

314.9   PO
MADEIRA. SERVICO REGIONAL DE ESTATISTICA. BOLETIM TRIMESTRAL DE ESTATISTICA. 1972. q. Esc.1800 (effective Jan. 1991). Servico Regional de Estatistica, Calcada de Santa Clara No. 38, 9000 Funchal, Madeira, Portugal. circ. 350.
Former titles: Portugal. Instituto Nacional de Estatistica. Delegacao do Funchal. Boletim Trimestral de Estatistica - Regio Autonoma de Madeira; Portugal. Instituto Nacional de Estatistica. Delegacao do Funchal. Boletim Trimestral de Estatistica - Arquipelago de Madeira (ISSN 0303-1705)

314   HU   ISSN 0133-5847
MAGYAR STATISZTIKAI ZSEBKONYV. English edition: Statistical Pocket Book of Hungary (ISSN 0441-473X); German edition: Statistisches Taschenbuch Ungarns (ISSN 0139-4231); Russian edition: Vengerski Statisticheski Spravochnik (ISSN 0505-1975) 1933. a. 48 Ft. (language editions 300 Ft.). (Kozponti Statisztikai Hivatal) Statiqum Kiado es Nyomda Kft., Kaszasdulo u. 2, P.O.B. 99, 1300 Budapest 3, Hungary. TEL 361-180-3311. FAX 361-168-8635. TELEX 22-6699. (Subscr. to: Kultura, Box 149, 1389 Budapest, Hungary) circ. 1,200 (Eng. ed.).

310   HU   ISSN 0230-5828
MAGYARORSZAG. English edition: Hungary (ISSN 0230-5755) German edition: Ungarn (ISSN 0230-5909); Russian edition: Vengria v Godu (ISSN 0230-5925) 1964. a. 80 Ft. (language editions 110 Ft.). (Kozponti Statisztikai Hivatal) Statiqum Kiado es Nyomda Kft., Kaszasdulo u. 2, Box 99, 1300 Budapest 3, Hungary. TEL 361-180-3311. FAX 361-168-8635. TELEX 22-6699. (Subscr. to: Kultura, Box 149, 1389 Budapest, Hungary) Ed. Jozsef Palfy. circ. 200,000. **Indexed:** PROMT.

311   UA   ISSN 0542-1748
AL-MAJALLAH AL-IHSA'IYYAH AL-MISRIYYAH/EGYPTIAN STATISTICAL JOURNAL. Abbreviated title: E S J. (Text and summaries in Arabic and English) 1957. s-a. $15. Cairo University, Institute of Statistical Studies and Research, Tharwat St., Orman, Giza, Cairo, Egypt. TELEX 94372. Ed. M.R. Mahmoud. (back issues avail.) **Indexed:** Math.R.

MALAGASY REPUBLIC. DIRECTION GENERALE DE LA BANQUE DES DONNEES DE L'ETAT. RECENSEMENT INDUSTRIEL. see *BUSINESS AND ECONOMICS* — *Abstracting, Bibliographies, Statistics*

MALAWI. NATIONAL STATISTICAL OFFICE. HOUSEHOLD INCOME AND EXPENDITURE SURVEY. see *POPULATION STUDIES* — *Abstracting, Bibliographies, Statistics*

316   MW
MALAWI. NATIONAL STATISTICAL OFFICE. MONTHLY STATISTICAL BULLETIN. m. K.1.25. National Statistical Office, Box 333, Zomba, Malawi.

310   MW   ISSN 0076-3284
MALAWI. NATIONAL STATISTICAL OFFICE. NATIONAL ACCOUNTS REPORT. 1967. a. K.5($3.90) National Statistical Office, P.O. Box 333, Zomba, Malawi.

316   MW
MALAWI STATISTICAL YEARBOOK. 1965. a. K.8. National Statistical Office, Box 333, Zomba, Malawi.
Supersedes: Malawi. National Statistical Office. Compendium of Statistics (ISSN 0076-3268)

MALAYSIA. DEPARTMENT OF MINES. STATISTICS RELATING TO THE MINING INDUSTRY OF MALAYSIA. see *MINES AND MINING INDUSTRY* — *Abstracting, Bibliographies, Statistics*

315   MY   ISSN 0080-5203
MALAYSIA. DEPARTMENT OF STATISTICS. ANNUAL BULLETIN OF STATISTICS SABAH. 1964. a. M.$10. Department of Statistics - Jabatan Perangkaan, Wisma Statistik, Block E, Jalan Cenderasari, 50514 Kuala Lumpur, Malaysia. TEL 088-232277. (Orders to: Department of Statistics, Malaysia (Sabah Branch), 1st Fl., Federal House, Jalan Mat Salleh, 88000 Kota Kinabalu, Sabah, Malaysia) circ. 465.

310　　　　　　　MY　　ISSN 0127-4732
MALAYSIA. DEPARTMENT OF STATISTICS. ANNUAL STATISTICAL BULLETIN SARAWAK. Variant title: Sarawak. Department of Statistics. Annual Statistical Bulletin. (Text in English) 1964. a. M.$8. Department of Statistics - Jabatan Perangkaan, Wisma Statistik, Block E, Jalan Cenderasari, 50514 Kuala Lumpur, Malaysia. (Orders to: Department of Statistics, Malaysia (Sarawak Branch), 5th Fl., Bangunan Tun Datuk, Patinggi Tuanku Hj. Bujang, 93514 Kuching, Sarawak, Malaysia)

315　　　　　　　MY
MALAYSIA. DEPARTMENT OF STATISTICS. MONTHLY BULLETIN OF STATISTICS, SABAH. (Text in English) m. M.$5 per no. Department of Statistics - Jalan Cenderasari, Wisma Statistik, Block E, Jalan Cenderasari, 50514 Kuala Lumpur, Malaysia. TEL 03-2922133. (Subscr. to: Department of Statistics (Sabah Branch), 1st Fl., Federal House, Jalan Mat Salleh, 88000 Kota Kinabalu, Sabah, Malaysia. TEL 088-232277)

310　　　　　　　MY
MALAYSIA. DEPARTMENT OF STATISTICS. MONTHLY STATISTICAL BULLETIN, MALAYSIA/SIARAN PERANGKAAN BULANAN SEMENANJUNG MALAYSIA. (Text in English, Malay) 1949. m. M.$6 per no. Department of Statistics - Jabatan Perangkaan, Wisma Statistik, Block E, Jalan Cenderasari, 50514 Kuala Lumpur, Malaysia. TEL 03-2922133.453.
　Former titles (until 1990): Monthly Statistical Bulletin, Peninsular Malaysia; (until 1977): Monthly Statistical Bulletin of West Malaysia (ISSN 0542-3686)

315　　　　　　　MY
MALAYSIA. DEPARTMENT OF STATISTICS. MONTHLY STATISTICAL BULLETIN, SARAWAK. (Text in English) m. M.$5 per no. Department of Statistics, Wisma Statistik, Block E, Jalan Cenderasari, 50514 Kuala Lumpur, Malaysia. TEL 03-2922133. (Subscr. to: Department of Statistics (Sarawak Branch), 5th Fl., Bangunan Tun Datuk, Patinggi Tuanku HJ. Bujang, 93514 Kuching, Sarawak, Malaysia. TEL 082-240287)

MALAYSIA. DEPARTMENT OF STATISTICS. MONTHLY TIN STATISTICS OF MALAYSIA. see *MINES AND MINING INDUSTRY* — *Abstracting, Bibliographies, Statistics*

315　　　　　　　MY
MALAYSIA. DEPARTMENT OF STATISTICS. NATIONAL ACCOUNTS STATISTICS, MALAYSIA. (Text in English) 1982. a. M.$5. Department of Statistics, Wisma Statistik, Block E, Jalan Cenderasari, 50514 Kuala Lumpur, Malaysia. TEL 03-2922133.

MALAYSIA. DEPARTMENT OF STATISTICS. VITAL STATISTICS, PENINSULAR MALAYSIA. see *POPULATION STUDIES* — *Abstracting, Bibliographies, Statistics*

315.95　　　　　MY　　ISSN 0127-2624
HA1791
MALAYSIA. DEPARTMENT OF STATISTICS. YEARBOOK OF STATISTICS. (Text in English) 1965. a. M.$12. Department of Statistics - Jabatan Perangkaan, Wisma Statistik, Block E, Jalan Cenderasari, 50514 Kuala Lumpur, Malaysia. TEL 03-2922133.
　Former titles (until 1989): Malaysia. Department of Statistics. Statistics Handbook Malaysia; (until 1984): Malaysia. Department of Statistics. Annual Bulletin of Statistics (ISSN 0542-3570)

316.6　　　　　　ML
MALI. SERVICE DE LA STATISTIQUE GENERALE, DE LA COMPTABILITE NATIONALE ET DE LA MECANOGRAPHIE. BULLETIN MENSUEL DE STATISTIQUE. m. 4000 F. Direction Nationale de la Statistique et de l'Information, B.P. 12, Bamako, Mali.

314　　　　　　　MM　　ISSN 0081-4733
MALTA. CENTRAL OFFICE OF STATISTICS. ANNUAL ABSTRACT OF STATISTICS. a. L.2. Central Office of Statistics, Auberge d'Italie, Valletta, Malta. (Subscr. to: Publication Bookshop, Auberge de Castille, Vallette, Malta)

314.585　　　　　MM　　ISSN 0025-1437
MALTA. CENTRAL OFFICE OF STATISTICS. QUARTERLY DIGEST OF STATISTICS. 1960. q. £1. Central Office of Statistics, Auberge d'Italie, Valletta, Malta. (Subscr. to: Publications Bookshop, Auberge de Castille, Vallette, Malta) (processed)

317.127　　　　　CN　　ISSN 0700-2971
MANITOBA STATISTICAL REVIEW. 1972. q. Can.$55. Bureau of Statistics, 155 Carlton St., 6th Fl., Winnipeg, Man. R3C 3H8, Canada. TEL 204-945-2995. FAX 204-957-1793. illus.; circ. 220. **Indexed:** CS Ind.
　Incorporates (in Jan. 1979): Manitoba Price Statistics; Formerly: Manitoba Digest of Statistics.

MARKETING RESEARCH STUDY OF THE HOUSEWARES INDUSTRY. see *BUSINESS AND ECONOMICS* — *Abstracting, Bibliographies, Statistics*

330.9 316　　　　MR　　ISSN 0076-4655
LE MAROC EN CHIFFRES. (Editions in Arabic, French) 1961. a. DH.33. Direction de la Statistique, B.P. 178, Rabat, Morocco. (Co-sponsor: Banque Marocaine du Commerce Exterieur, Direction du Developpement) circ. 20,000 (6,000 Arabic Ed., 14,000 French Ed.). (also avail. in microfiche)

MASSACHUSETTS TAXPAYERS FOUNDATION. STATE BUDGET TRENDS. see *BUSINESS AND ECONOMICS* — *Abstracting, Bibliographies, Statistics*

316.6　　　　　　MU　　ISSN 0543-1433
MAURITANIA. DIRECTION DE LA STATISTIQUE ET DES ETUDES ECONOMIQUES. BULLETIN MENSUEL STATISTIQUE. (Text in French) m. 20 Fr.CFA. Direction de la Statistique et des Etudes Economiques, B.P. 240, Nouakchott, Mauritania. illus.

316.982　　　　　MF
MAURITIUS. CENTRAL STATISTICAL OFFICE. BI-ANNUAL DIGEST OF STATISTICS. 1961. a. Rs.100. Central Statistical Office, Port-Louis, Mauritius. (Subscr. to: G.P.O., La Tour Koenig, Port Louis, Mauritius) stat.
　Former titles: Mauritius. Central Statistical Office. Quarterly Digest of Statistics; Mauritius. Central Statistical Office. Bi-Annual Digest of Statistics; Mauritius. Central Statistical Office. Quarterly Digest of Statistics (ISSN 0025-6056)

MAURITIUS. CENTRAL STATISTICAL OFFICE. DIGEST OF DEMOGRAPHIC STATISTICS. see *POPULATION STUDIES* — *Abstracting, Bibliographies, Statistics*

MAURITIUS. CENTRAL STATISTICAL OFFICE. INTERNATIONAL TRAVEL AND TOURISM STATISTICS. see *TRAVEL AND TOURISM* — *Abstracting, Bibliographies, Statistics*

316.982　　　　　MF
MAURITIUS. CENTRAL STATISTICAL OFFICE. STATISTICAL SUMMARY. 1978. a. Rs.30. Central Statistical Office, Port-Louis, Mauritius. (Subscr. to: G.P.O., La Tour Koenig, Port-Louis, Mauritius)

314　　　　　　　YU　　ISSN 0350-4247
MESECNI STATISTICKI PREGLED. (Text in Serbian) 1952. m. 120 din.($15) Republicki Zavod za Statistiku, Bulevar Lenjina 4, Titograd, Yugoslavia. Ed. Andreja Stokic. circ. 310.

METAL STATISTICS (YEARS). see *METALLURGY* — *Abstracting, Bibliographies, Statistics*

311　　　　　　　GW　　ISSN 0026-1335
QA276.A1　　　　　　　　　CODEN: MTRKA8
METRIKA; international journal for theoretical and applied statistics. (Text in English) 1953. bi-m. DM.330. Physica-Verlag GmbH und Co., Tiergarten 17, Postfach 105280, 6900 Heidelberg 1, Germany. TEL 030-8207-424. FAX 030-8207-448. (Subscr. to: Springer Verlag GmbH, Postfach 311540, 1000 Berlin 31, Germany; Dist. in North America by: Springer-Verlag New York Inc., 175 Fifth Ave., New York, NY 10010, U.S.A.. TEL 212-460-1500) Eds. W. Uhlmann, O. Krafft. adv.; bk.rev.; charts; index; circ. 1,000. (back issues avail.; reprint service avail. from SWZ) **Indexed:** Biostat., Curr.Cont., Int.Abstr.Oper.Res., J.Cont.Quant.Meth., Math.R., Sci.Abstr.
—BLDSC shelfmark: 5748.700000.
　Description: Covers statistical methods and mathematical statistics: statistical quality control, sampling control, sampling theory, design of experiments.
　Refereed Serial

310　　　　　　　IT　　ISSN 0026-1424
HA1　　　　　　　　　　　CODEN: MRONAM
METRON; rivista internazionale di statistica. (Text in various European languages) 1920. s-a. DM.190 (typically set in Dec.). Universita degli Studi di Roma, Facolta di Scienze Statistiche Demografiche ed Attuariali, Dipartimento di Statistica, Probabilita e Stat. Applicate, Citta Universitaria, 00185 Rome, Italy. FAX 00396-4747743. (Dist. by: E S I A Books and Journals, Via Palestro, 30, 00185 Rome, Italy) Ed. Carlo Benedetti. adv.; bk.rev.; abstr.; charts; stat.; index; cum.index; circ. 1,000. **Indexed:** Biol.Abstr., Curr.Cont., Math.R.
—BLDSC shelfmark: 5748.930000.
　Description: Articles by mathematicians, statisticians and economists in the topics of demography, physics, biology and medicine.

310　　　　　　　US　　ISSN 0741-9767
HG8963.M5
METROPOLITAN LIFE INSURANCE COMPANY. STATISTICAL BULLETIN S B. 1920. q. $50 to individuals (foreign $60); libraries $40. Metropolitan Life Insurance Company, 1 Madison Ave., New York, NY 10010. FAX 212-213-0577. Ed. Charles B. Arnold, M.D. charts; stat.; index; circ. 20,000. (also avail. in microfilm from UMI,BLH; reprint service avail. from UMI) **Indexed:** B.P.I., Biol.Abstr., BPIA, Bus.Ind., Curr.Cont., Nutr.Abstr., P.A.I.S., SRI.
　Former titles (1982-1983): Metropolitan Life Foundation. Statistical Bulletin (ISSN 0736-4822); (until 1981): Statistical Bulletin - Metropolitan Life (ISSN 0026-1513)
　Description: Demographic and medical care data on health care coverage, focusing on charges across the nation, mortality trends, life table analyses, and profiles of major population groups.

MEXICO. DIRECCION GENERAL DE ESTADISTICA. ESTADISTICA INDUSTRIAL ANUAL. see *BUSINESS AND ECONOMICS* — *Abstracting, Bibliographies, Statistics*

317　　　　　　　MX　　ISSN 0186-2707
MEXICO. INSTITUTO NACIONAL DE ESTADISTICA, GEOGRAFIA E INFORMATICA. REVISTA DE ESTADISTICA. 1938. irreg., vol.3, no.6, 1989. free. Instituto Nacional de Estadistica, Geografia e Informatica, Secretaria de Programacion e Presupuesto, Prol. Heroe de Nacozari 2301 Sur, Puerta 11, planta baja, Aguascalientes 20290 Ags., Mexico. TEL 49-18-22-32. FAX 491-807-39. (Subscr. to: Direccion General de Estudios del Territorio Nacional, Balderas 71, Col. Centro, Mexico 1, D.F., Mexico) mkt.; stat.; index; circ. 1,000.
—BLDSC shelfmark: 7854.440000.
　Formerly: Mexico. Direccion General de Estadistica. Revista de Estadistica (ISSN 0026-1769)

310　　　　　　　MX
MEXICO STATISTICAL DATA. (Text in English) 1980. irreg. Banco Nacional de Mexico, S.A., Department of Economic Research, Madero 21, Piso 2, 06000 Mexico, D.F., Mexico. FAX 761-90-44-79025.

MILLION DOLLAR PROJECT PLANNED LIST. see *ARCHITECTURE*

MINAS GERAIS, BRAZIL. DEPARTAMENTO DE ESTRADAS DE RODAGEM. SERVICO DE TRANSITO. ESTATISTICA DE TRAFEGO E ACIDENTES. see *TRANSPORTATION* — *Abstracting, Bibliographies, Statistics*

316　　　　　　　MZ
MOCAMBIQUE - INFORMACAO ESTATISTICA. 1982. m. (Comissao Nacional do Plano) Centro de Documentacao Economica, C.P. 2051, Maputo, Mozambique.

MONTANA. DEPARTMENT OF SOCIAL AND REHABILITATION SERVICES. STATISTICAL REPORT. see *SOCIAL SERVICES AND WELFARE* — *Abstracting, Bibliographies, Statistics*

MONTHLY ACTS TABLES & TABLE OF UNREPEALED PRINCIPAL ACTS. see *LAW* — *Abstracting, Bibliographies, Statistics*

MONTHLY REPORT ON TOURISM - REPUBLIC OF CHINA/KUAN KUANG TZU LIAO. see *TRAVEL AND TOURISM* — *Abstracting, Bibliographies, Statistics*

4580 STATISTICS

315 BG ISSN 0377-1555
HA1730.8
MONTHLY STATISTICAL BULLETIN OF BANGLADESH.
(Supplement avail.: annual data) (Text in English) 1972. m. Tk.600($144) (effective Jan. 1990). Bureau of Statistics, Secretariat, Dhaka 2, Bangladesh. TEL 409871. Ed. Md. Mohiuddin Ahamed. circ. 300.
Supersedes: Bangladesh. Bureau of Statistics. Monthly Bulletin of Statistics (ISSN 0012-849X)
Description: Presents current data on performance of family planning, labor and employment, wages, agriculture, meteorology, industrial production, transport and communication, foreign trade, national income accounts, as well as public finance and accounting.

315.19 KO ISSN 0027-0563
MONTHLY STATISTICS OF KOREA. (Text in English, Korean) 1958. m. 2700 Won. National Statistical Office, 90, Gyongun-dong, Jongro-gu, Seoul 110-310, S. Korea. TEL 02-720-2788. (Subscr. to: the Korean Statistical Association, Room 302, Chungok Building, 561-30, Sinsa-dong, Gangnam-gu, Seoul 135-120, S. Korea) stat.; index; circ. 1,300.

MONTHLY STATUTORY RULES TABLES & TABLE OF UNREVOKED PRINCIPAL STATUTORY RULES. see *LAW — Abstracting, Bibliographies, Statistics*

310 382 MJ
MONTSERRAT. STATISTICS OFFICE. OVERSEAS TRADE REPORT. irreg. Statistics Office, Plymouth, Monserrat.

312 MR ISSN 0256-9159
HC810.A1
MOROCCO. DIRECTION DE LA STATISTIQUE. BULLETIN MENSUEL DES STATISTIQUES. (Text in Arabic, French) q. DH.363. Direction de la Statistique, B.P. 178, Rabat, Morocco.

MOROCCO. DIRECTION DE LA STATISTIQUE. INDICE DES PRIX A LA PRODUCTION INDUSTRIELLE, ENERGETIQUE ET MINIERE. see *BUSINESS AND ECONOMICS — Abstracting, Bibliographies, Statistics*

MOROCCO. DIRECTION DE LA STATISTIQUE. INDICE DU COUT DE LA VIE. see *BUSINESS AND ECONOMICS — Abstracting, Bibliographies, Statistics*

MOROCCO. DIRECTION DE LA STATISTIQUE. POPULATION ACTIVE URBAINE, RAPPORT DE SYNTHESE. see *POPULATION STUDIES — Abstracting, Bibliographies, Statistics*

MOROCCO. DIRECTION DE LA STATISTIQUE. POPULATION ACTIVE URBAINE, RESULTATS DETAILLES. see *POPULATION STUDIES — Abstracting, Bibliographies, Statistics*

MUSIC U S A; annual statistical review of the musical instrument industry. see *MUSIC*

N M F S FISHERIES MARKET NEWS REPORT. (National Marines Fishery Service) see *FISH AND FISHERIES — Abstracting, Bibliographies, Statistics*

310 PH ISSN 0115-2092
N S O MONTHLY BULLETIN OF STATISTICS. (Text in English) m. $4 per no. National Statistics Office, Ramon Magsaysay blvd., P.O. Box 779, Manila, Philippines. FAX 610794.

310 RU
NARODNOE KHOZYAISTVO ALTAISKOGO KRAYA. 1967. every 5 yrs. (Tsentral'noe Statisticheskoe Upravlenie) Redaktsionno-Poligraficheskoe Proizvodstvennoe Ob'edinenie "Soyuzblankoizdat", Altaiskoe Redaktsionno-Proizvodstvennoe Otdelenie, B. Olonskaya 28, Barnaul, Russia. Ed. Olga Zamiatina. stat.; circ. 5,000.

314 BE ISSN 0771-0410
HA1393
NATIONAAL INSTITUUT VOOR DE STATISTIEK. WEEKBERICHT. French ed.: Institut National des Statistiques. Communique Hebdomadaire (ISSN 0771-0364) (Editions in Dutch, French) w. 750 Fr. (foreign 1425 Fr.). Ministerie van Economische Zaken, Nationaal Instituut voor de Statistiek, Leuvenseweg 44, B-1000 Brussels, Belgium.

NATIONAL NEWSPAPER INDEX. see *BUSINESS AND ECONOMICS — Abstracting, Bibliographies, Statistics*

NAVAL RESEARCH LOGISTICS: AN INTERNATIONAL JOURNAL. see *MILITARY — Abstracting, Bibliographies, Statistics*

NEBRASKA STATISTICAL HANDBOOK. see *PUBLIC ADMINISTRATION — Abstracting, Bibliographies, Statistics*

634.9 NE
NEDERLANDSE BOSSTATISTIEK. 1952. irreg., latest 1971 (covers 1964-68). Centraal Bureau voor de Statistiek, Prinses Beatrixlaan 428, Voorburg, Netherlands. (Dist. by: SDU - Publishers, Christoffel Plantijnstraat, The Hague, Netherlands) circ. 650.

315.49 NP
NEPAL. CENTRAL BUREAU OF STATISTICS. STATISTICAL POCKET BOOK. (Text in English) 1974. biennial. $1. Central Bureau of Statistics, Ramshah Path, Thapathali, Kathmandu, Nepal. TEL 2-29946. illus.; circ. 5,000.

NETHERLANDS. CENTRAAL BUREAU VOOR DE STATISTIEK. JUSTICIELE KINDERBESCHERMING. see *CHILDREN AND YOUTH — Abstracting, Bibliographies, Statistics*

314.92 NE ISSN 0166-0268
NETHERLANDS. CENTRAAL BUREAU VOOR DE STATISTIEK. MAANDSCHRIFT. (Title and contents page in Dutch and English) 1906. m. fl.100. Centraal Bureau voor de Statistiek, Prinses Beatrixlaan 428, Voorburg, Netherlands. (Dist. by: SDU - Publishers, Christoffel Plantijnstraat, The Hague, Netherlands)

NETHERLANDS. CENTRAAL BUREAU VOOR DE STATISTIEK. MAANDSTATISTIEK VAN DE BEVOLKING. see *POPULATION STUDIES — Abstracting, Bibliographies, Statistics*

NETHERLANDS. CENTRAAL BUREAU VOOR DE STATISTIEK. MAANDSTATISTIEK VAN DE LANDBOUW. see *AGRICULTURE — Abstracting, Bibliographies, Statistics*

314 NE
NETHERLANDS. CENTRAAL BUREAU VOOR DE STATISTIEK. REGIONAAL STATISTISCH ZAKBOEK. a. Centraal Bureau voor de Statistiek, Prinses Beatrixlaan 428, Voorburg, Netherlands. (Dist. by: SDU - Publishers, Christoffel Plantijnstraat, The Hague, Netherlands)

310 NE
NETHERLANDS. CENTRAAL BUREAU VOOR DE STATISTIEK. STATISTICAL STUDIES. 1953. irreg. price varies. Centraal Bureau voor de Statistiek, Prinses Beatrixlaan 428, Voorburg, Netherlands.

NETHERLANDS. CENTRAAL BUREAU VOOR DE STATISTIEK. STATISTIEK VAN DE INVESTERINGEN IN VASTE ACTIVA IN DE NIJVERHEID/STATISTICS ON FIXED CAPITAL FORMATION IN INDUSTRY. see *BUSINESS AND ECONOMICS — Abstracting, Bibliographies, Statistics*

310 NE ISSN 0166-9680
NETHERLANDS. CENTRAAL BUREAU VOOR DE STATISTIEK. STATISTISCH BULLETIN. irreg. Centraal Bureau voor de Statistiek, Prinses Beatrixlaan 428, Voorburg, Netherlands. (Dist. by: CBS, P.O. Box 959, 2270 AZ Voorburg, Netherlands) circ. 3,500.

310 NE ISSN 0168-3705
NETHERLANDS. CENTRAAL BUREAU VOOR DE STATISTIEK. STATISTISCH ZAKBOEK/POCKET YEARBOOK. (Text in Dutch, English) 1944. a. Centraal Bureau voor de Statistiek, Prinses Beatrixlaan 428, Voorburg, Netherlands. (Dist. by: SDU - Publishers, Christoffel Plantijnstraat, The Hague, Netherlands)

NETHERLANDS. CENTRAAL BUREAU VOOR DE STATISTIEK. STATISTISCHE ONDERZOEKINGEN. see *BUSINESS AND ECONOMICS — Abstracting, Bibliographies, Statistics*

314 NE
NETHERLANDS. CENTRALE COMMISSIE VOOR DE STATISTIEK. JAARVERSLAG. 1899. a. Centrale Commissie voor de Statistiek, The Hague, Netherlands. FAX 070-3877429. TELEX 32692-CBS-NL. Ed. W.J. de Wreede. circ. 900.
Description: Covers activities and meetings of the commission and its sub-commissions.

NEVADA LIBRARY DIRECTORY AND STATISTICS. see *BUSINESS AND ECONOMICS — Trade And Industrial Directories*

NEW BRUNSWICK. TOURISM RECREATION & HERITAGE. TECHNICAL SERVICES BRANCH. PROVINCIAL PARK STATISTICS. see *CONSERVATION — Abstracting, Bibliographies, Statistics*

NEW CALEDONIA. INSTITUT TERRITORIAL DE LA STATISTIQUE ET DES ETUDES ECONOMIQUES. BULLETIN DE CONJONCTURE. see *BUSINESS AND ECONOMICS — Abstracting, Bibliographies, Statistics*

NEW CALEDONIA. INSTITUT TERRITORIAL DE LA STATISTIQUE ET DES ETUDES ECONOMIQUES. INDICES DES PRIX LA CONSOMMATION. see *BUSINESS AND ECONOMICS — Abstracting, Bibliographies, Statistics*

330.9 319 NL ISSN 0336-3945
HA4007.N4
NEW CALEDONIA. INSTITUT TERRITORIAL DE LA STATISTIQUE ET DES ETUDES ECONOMIQUES. INFORMATIONS STATISTIQUES RAPIDES. 1972. m. CFPF2600 (foreign CFPF 4400). Institut Territorial de la Statistique et des Etudes Economiques, B.P. 823, Noumea, New Caledonia. TEL 27-54-81. Ed. Ph. Maesse. adv.; circ. 1,200.
Formerly: New Caledonia. Service de la Statistique. Informations Statiques Rapides.

NEW CALEDONIA. INSTITUT TERRITORIAL DE LA STATISTIQUE ET DES ETUDES ECONOMIQUES. TABLEAUX DE L'ECONOMIE CALEDONIENNE. see *BUSINESS AND ECONOMICS — Abstracting, Bibliographies, Statistics*

NEW HAMPSHIRE VITAL STATISTICS. see *POPULATION STUDIES — Abstracting, Bibliographies, Statistics*

310 UK ISSN 0028-601X
NEW JOURNAL OF STATISTICS AND OPERATIONAL RESEARCH.* 1965. 3/yr. £1($2.76) c/o Cornelius Mack, Ed., University of Bradford, Bradford 7, Yorkshire, England. (processed)

317 US ISSN 0077-8575
HA531
NEW MEXICO STATISTICAL ABSTRACT. 1970. irreg. $22.50. University of New Mexico, Bureau of Business and Economic Research, 1920 Lomas NE, Albuquerque, NM 87131-6021.
TEL 505-277-2216. FAX 505-277-7066. circ. 600.

NEW SOUTH WALES COAL YEARBOOK (YEAR). see *MINES AND MINING INDUSTRY — Abstracting, Bibliographies, Statistics*

319.4 AT ISSN 0725-5039
NEW SOUTH WALES IN BRIEF. 1977. a. free. Australian Bureau of Statistics, New South Wales Office, 3rd Fl., St. Andrews House, Sydney Square, Sydney, N.S.W. 2000, Australia.
Description: Condensed information about the population and its characteristics; welfare; health; education; law; labour; prices; building; transport; agriculture, mining, energy, manufacturing, overseas trade; retail trade; tourist accommodation; State and local government finances, banks, and other private finance; household income; private final consumption expenditure; and the position of N.S.W. relative to Australia.

319 AT ISSN 0810-9338
DU150
NEW SOUTH WALES YEAR BOOK. 1906. s-a. Aus.$26.95 soft cover (foreign Aus.$41.95). Australian Bureau of Statistics, New South Wales Office, St. Andrews House, Sydney Square, George St., Sydney, N.S.W. 2000, Australia.
Formerly: Official Year Book of New South Wales (ISSN 0085-4441)
Description: Provides extensive information about the state.

317 US
NEW YORK (STATE). ROCKEFELLER INSTITUTE OF GOVERNMENT. NEW YORK STATE STATISTICAL YEARBOOK. 1967. a. $50. Nelson A. Rockefeller Institute of Government, 411 State St., Albany, NY 12203. FAX 518-443-5788. Ed. Michael Cooper. index; circ. 5,000. (also avail. in microfiche) **Indexed:** SRI.
  Formerly: New York (State) Division of the Budget. New York State Statistical Yearbook (ISSN 0077-9334)
  Description: Contains statistical information on New York State, as well as select U.S. data. Gives complete descriptions of each state agency and the name and phone number of a contact at each agency.

NEW ZEALAND. DEPARTMENT OF STATISTICS. CONSUMER EXPENDITURE. see BUSINESS AND ECONOMICS — Abstracting, Bibliographies, Statistics

NEW ZEALAND. DEPARTMENT OF STATISTICS. DEMOGRAPHIC TRENDS. see POPULATION STUDIES — Abstracting, Bibliographies, Statistics

NEW ZEALAND. DEPARTMENT OF STATISTICS. INCOMES. see BUSINESS AND ECONOMICS — Abstracting, Bibliographies, Statistics

319 NZ ISSN 0114-2119
HA3032
NEW ZEALAND. DEPARTMENT OF STATISTICS. KEY STATISTICS; a monthly abstract of statistics. m. (except Jan.). NZ.$275. Department of Statistics, P.O. Box 2922, Wellington, New Zealand. charts; mkt.; stat.; circ. 2,400.
  Formerly: New Zealand. Department of Statistics. Monthly Abstract of Statistics (ISSN 0027-0180)

NEW ZEALAND. DEPARTMENT OF STATISTICS. POPULATION CENSUS: INTERNAL MIGRATION. see POPULATION STUDIES — Abstracting, Bibliographies, Statistics

NEW ZEALAND. DEPARTMENT OF STATISTICS. POPULATION CENSUS: TOTAL POPULATION STATISTICS. see POPULATION STUDIES — Abstracting, Bibliographies, Statistics

NEW ZEALAND. HEALTH STATISTICAL SERVICES. CLIENT SERVICES NEWSLETTER. see PUBLIC HEALTH AND SAFETY

NEW ZEALAND. HEALTH STATISTICAL SERVICES. FETAL AND INFANT DEATHS. see MEDICAL SCIENCES — Abstracting, Bibliographies, Statistics

311 NZ ISSN 0111-9176
NEW ZEALAND STATISTICIAN. 1966. 2/yr. NZ.$37 (foreign NZ$48). New Zealand Statistical Association (Inc.), P.O. Box 1731, Wellington, New Zealand. TEL 64-6-356-9099. FAX 64-6-350-5611. Ed. R.H. Morton. adv.; bk.rev.; abstr.; stat.; circ. 350. **Indexed:** Curr.Ind.Stat.
  —BLDSC shelfmark: 6099.425000.

NEW ZEALAND TOURISM DEPARTMENT. VISITOR STATISTICS RESEARCH SERIES. see TRAVEL AND TOURISM — Abstracting, Bibliographies, Statistics

316.6 NG
NIGER. DIRECTION DE LA STATISTIQUE ET DES COMPTES NATIONAUX. BULLETIN TRIMESTRIEL DE STATISTIQUE. q. 1200 F. Direction de la Statistique et des Comptes Nationaux, Ministere du Plan, Niamey, Niger. illus.
  Former titles: Niger. Ministere du Developpement et de la Cooperation. Direction de la Statistique. Bulletin de Statistique; Niger. Service de la Statistique. Bulletin Trimestriel de Statistique (ISSN 0545-9516)

316 NR ISSN 0078-0626
HA1977.N5
NIGERIA. FEDERAL OFFICE OF STATISTICS. ANNUAL ABSTRACT OF STATISTICS. (Text in English) a. $25. Federal Office of Statistics, P.M.B. 12528, Nigeria.

NIGERIA. FEDERAL OFFICE OF STATISTICS. BUILDING AND CONSTRUCTION SURVEY. see BUILDING AND CONSTRUCTION — Abstracting, Bibliographies, Statistics

316 NR ISSN 0029-0017
NIGERIA. FEDERAL OFFICE OF STATISTICS. DIGEST OF STATISTICS. 1952. q. £N15($15) Federal Office of Statistics, P.M.B. 12528, Nigeria. stat.

NIGERIA. FEDERAL OFFICE OF STATISTICS. INDUSTRIAL SURVEY. see BUSINESS AND ECONOMICS — Abstracting, Bibliographies, Statistics

NIGERIA. FEDERAL OFFICE OF STATISTICS. REPORT ON GENERAL CONSUMER SURVEY REPORT. see BUSINESS AND ECONOMICS — Abstracting, Bibliographies, Statistics

NIGERIA. FEDERAL OFFICE OF STATISTICS. REPORT ON GENERAL HOUSEHOLD. see BUSINESS AND ECONOMICS — Abstracting, Bibliographies, Statistics

NIGERIA. FEDERAL OFFICE OF STATISTICS. REPORT ON GENERAL HOUSEHOLD SURVEY. see HOUSING AND URBAN PLANNING — Abstracting, Bibliographies, Statistics

NIGERIA. FEDERAL OFFICE OF STATISTICS. REPORT ON NATIONAL CONSUMER SURVEY. see BUSINESS AND ECONOMICS — Abstracting, Bibliographies, Statistics

NIGERIA. FEDERAL OFFICE OF STATISTICS. REPORT ON URBAN HOUSEHOLD SURVEY. see HOUSING AND URBAN PLANNING — Abstracting, Bibliographies, Statistics

NIGERIA. FEDERAL OFFICE OF STATISTICS. SOCIAL STATISTICS IN NIGERIA. see SOCIAL SCIENCES: COMPREHENSIVE WORKS — Abstracting, Bibliographies, Statistics

NIHON SUGAKKAI KOEN ABUSUTORAKUTO. TOKEI SUGAKU BUNKAKAI. see MATHEMATICS — Abstracting, Bibliographies, Statistics

NONFERROUS CASTINGS. see METALLURGY — Abstracting, Bibliographies, Statistics

310 US ISSN 1048-5252
QA278.8 CODEN: NOSTEK
NONPARAMETRIC STATISTICS. 4/yr. $108. Gordon and Breach Science Publishers, 270 Eighth Ave., New York, NY 10011. TEL 212-206-8900. FAX 212-645-2459. TELEX 236735 GOPUB UR. (Subscr. to: Box 786, Cooper Sta., New York, NY 10276. TEL 800-545-8398; UK subscr. to: P.O. Box 90, Reading, Berkshire RG1 8JL, England. TEL 0734-560-080) Ed. Ibrahim A. Ahmad. (also avail. in microform)
  —BLDSC shelfmark: 5022.842200.
  Refereed Serial

314 DK ISSN 0078-1088
DL1
NORDISK STATISTISK AARSBOK/YEARBOOK OF NORDIC STATISTICS. (Subseries of: NORD) (Text in English and Swedish) 1962. a. DKK 248 (typically set in Feb.- Mar.). Nordic Council of Ministers, Store Strandstraede 18, DK-1255 Copenhagen Oe, Denmark. TEL 45-39-17-39-17. FAX 45-31-18-48-01. (Co-sponsor: Nordic Statistical Secretariat, Sejroegade 11, DK-2100, Copenhagen Oe, Denmark) Ed. Harry de Sharengrad. **Indexed:** IIS.
  —BLDSC shelfmark: 9414.643000.
  Description: Presents statistical information on the five Nordic countries; Denmark, Finland, Iceland, Norway and Sweden, including selected data for Greenland, the Faroe Islands and Aaland.

310 DK ISSN 0106-9039
HA1461
NORDISK STATISTISK SEKRETARIAT. TEKNISKE RAPPORTER/NORDIC STATISTICAL SECRETARIAT. TECHNICAL REPORTS. (Text in Scandinavian languages; summaries in English) 1968. irreg., no.56, 1991. Nordisk Statistisk Sekretariat - Nordic Statistical Secretariat, Sejroegade 11, DK-2100 Copenhagen OE, Denmark. FAX 45-31-18-48-01.

314 DK ISSN 0078-1096
NORDISK STATISTISK SKRIFTSERIE/STATISTICAL REPORTS OF THE NORDIC COUNTRIES. (Text in Scandinavian languages; editions occasionally in English) 1954. irreg., no.55, 1991. price varies. Nordisk Statistisk Sekretariat - Nordic Statistical Secretariat, P.O. Box 2550, DK-2100 Copenhagen OE, Denmark. TEL 45-39-17-39-17. FAX 45-31-18-48-01. circ. 3,000.
  —BLDSC shelfmark: 6123.200000.

NORDRHEIN - WESTFAELISCHEN INDUSTRIE- UND HANDELSKAMMER. STATISTISCHES JAHRBUCH. see BUSINESS AND ECONOMICS — Abstracting, Bibliographies, Statistics

310 GW ISSN 0468-656X
NORDRHEIN-WESTFALEN. STATISTISCHES JAHRBUCH. 1949. a. DM.45. Landesamt fuer Datenverarbeitung und Statistik NRW, Mauerstr. 51, Postfach 101105, 4000 Duesseldorf 1, Germany. TEL 0211-9449-01. TELEX 8586654-LDST-D. circ. 2,000.
  —BLDSC shelfmark: 8454.826000.
  Formerly: Duesseldorf. Statistisches Jahrbuch.

NORTH CAROLINA REPORTED PREGNANCIES. see BIRTH CONTROL — Abstracting, Bibliographies, Statistics

NORTH DAKOTA. JUDICIAL SYSTEM. ANNUAL REPORT. see LAW — Abstracting, Bibliographies, Statistics

319.4 AT ISSN 0815-3809
NORTHERN TERRITORY AT A GLANCE. 1983. a. Aus.$1. Australian Bureau of Statistics, Northern Territory Office, 6th Fl., MLC Building, 81 Smith Street, Darwin, N.T. 0800, Australia. circ. 9,000.
  Description: Contains a wide range of statistical information on the Northern Territory, including physical data, population, vitals, employment and wages, price indices, agriculture and fishing, mineral production, manufacturing, building, foreign trade and tourism.

NORWAY. STATISTISK SENTRALBYRAA. ARBEIDSMARKEDSSTATISTIKK - LABOUR MARKET STATISTICS. see BUSINESS AND ECONOMICS — Abstracting, Bibliographies, Statistics

NORWAY. STATISTISK SENTRALBYRAA. BEFOLKNINGS STATISTISK HEFTE 2/NORWAY. CENTRAL BUREAU OF STATISTICS. POPULATION STATISTICS VOL.2. see POPULATION STUDIES — Abstracting, Bibliographies, Statistics

NORWAY. STATISTISK SENTRALBYRAA. FISKERISTATISTIKK. see FISH AND FISHERIES — Abstracting, Bibliographies, Statistics

NORWAY. STATISTISK SENTRALBYRAA. HELSEPERSONELLSTATISTIKK. see MEDICAL SCIENCES — Abstracting, Bibliographies, Statistics

NORWAY. STATISTISK SENTRALBYRAA. HELSESTATISTIKK/HEALTH STATISTICS. see PUBLIC HEALTH AND SAFETY — Abstracting, Bibliographies, Statistics

NORWAY. STATISTISK SENTRALBYRAA. INDUSTRISTATISTIKK. VOL.1/INDUSTRIAL STATISTICS. VOL.1. see BUSINESS AND ECONOMICS — Abstracting, Bibliographies, Statistics

NORWAY. STATISTISK SENTRALBYRAA. INDUSTRISTATISTIKK. VOL.2/INDUSTRIAL STATISTICS. VOL.2. see BUSINESS AND ECONOMICS — Abstracting, Bibliographies, Statistics

NORWAY. STATISTISK SENTRALBYRAA. JORDBRUKSSTATISTIKK/AGRICULTURAL STATISTICS. see AGRICULTURE — Abstracting, Bibliographies, Statistics

NORWAY. STATISTISK SENTRALBYRAA. KOMMUNE OG FYLKESTINGS VALGET/NORWAY. CENTRAL BUREAU OF STATISTICS. MUNICIPAL AND COUNTY ELECTIONS. see PUBLIC ADMINISTRATION — Abstracting, Bibliographies, Statistics

NORWAY. STATISTISK SENTRALBYRAA. KREDITTMARKED STATISTIKK/CREDIT MARKET STATISTICS. see BUSINESS AND ECONOMICS — Abstracting, Bibliographies, Statistics

NORWAY. STATISTISK SENTRALBYRAA. KRIMINALSTATISTIKK/CRIMINAL STATISTICS. see CRIMINOLOGY AND LAW ENFORCEMENT — Abstracting, Bibliographies, Statistics

STATISTICS

NORWAY. STATISTISK SENTRALBYRAA. LOENNSSTATISTIKK/WAGE STATISTICS. see BUSINESS AND ECONOMICS — Abstracting, Bibliographies, Statistics

NORWAY. STATISTISK SENTRALBYRAA. NASJONALREGNSKAPSSTATISTIKK/NATIONAL ACCOUNTS STATISTICS. see BUSINESS AND ECONOMICS — Abstracting, Bibliographies, Statistics

NORWAY. STATISTISK SENTRALBYRAA. REISELIVSTATISKK/STATISTICS ON TRAVEL. see TRAVEL AND TOURISM — Abstracting, Bibliographies, Statistics

NORWAY. STATISTISK SENTRALBYRAA. SAMFERDSELSSTATISTIKK/NORWAY. CENTRAL BUREAU OF STATISTICS. TRANSPORT AND COMMUNICATION STATISTICS. see TRANSPORTATION — Abstracting, Bibliographies, Statistics

NORWAY. STATISTISK SENTRALBYRAA. SKOGSTATSTIKK. see FORESTS AND FORESTRY — Abstracting, Bibliographies, Statistics

314 NO ISSN 0377-8908
NORWAY. STATISTISK SENTRALBYRAA. STATISTISK AARBOK/STATISTICAL YEARBOOK. (Subseries of its Norges Offisielle Statistikk) (Text in English, Norwegian) 1880. a. NOK 95. Statistisk Sentralbyraa, Box 8131 Dep., 0033 Oslo 1, Norway. TEL 02-864500. FAX 02-864973. circ. 42,500.

314 NO ISSN 0029-3636
NORWAY. STATISTISK SENTRALBYRAA. STATISTISK MAANEDSHEFTE/MONTHLY BULLETIN OF STATISTICS. (Text in English, Norwegian) 1882. m. NOK 415. Statistisk Sentralbyraa, Box 8131 Dep., 0033 Oslo 1, Norway. TEL 02-864500. FAX 02-864973. stat.; circ. 4,500.

310 NO ISSN 0550-0567
NORWAY. STATISTISK SENTRALBYRAA. STATISTISK UKEHEFTE/WEEKLY BULLETIN OF STATISTICS. 1960. w. NOK 520. Statistisk Sentralbyraa, Box 8131-Dep., 0033 Oslo 1, Norway. TEL 02-864500. FAX 02-864973. stat.; circ. 2,100.

NORWAY. STATISTISK SENTRALBYRAA. STORTINGSVALG/NORWAY. CENTRAL BUREAU OF STATISTICS. PARLIAMENTARY ELECTIONS. see PUBLIC ADMINISTRATION — Abstracting, Bibliographies, Statistics

NORWAY. STATISTISK SENTRALBYRAA. UTDANNINGSSTATISTIKK. see EDUCATION — Abstracting, Bibliographies, Statistics

NORWAY. STATISTISK SENTRALBYRAA. UTENRIKSHANDEL/NORWAY. CENTRAL BUREAU OF STATISTICS. EXTERNAL TRADE. see BUSINESS AND ECONOMICS — Abstracting, Bibliographies, Statistics

NORWAY. STATISTISK SENTRALBYRAA. VAREHANDELSSTATISTIKK/WHOLESALE AND RETAIL TRADE STATISTICS. see BUSINESS AND ECONOMICS — Abstracting, Bibliographies, Statistics

310 NO
NORWAY. STATISTISK SENTRALBYRAA. VEJVISER I NORSK STATISTIKK/GUIDE TO NORWEGIAN STATISTICS. 1963. irreg. free. Statistisk Sentralbyraa - Central Bureau of Statistics, P.O. Box 8131 Dep., N-0033 Oslo 1, Norway. TEL 02-86-45-00. Eds. Elly Lie, Liv Argel. circ. 10,000.
  Description: Presents a survey of official Norwegian statistics, systematically arranged according to the classification by subject matters of the CBS. Covers statistics compiled by the CBS or by other government agencies.

O E C D. EXTERNAL DEBT STATISTICS. see BUSINESS AND ECONOMICS — Abstracting, Bibliographies, Statistics

310 330.9 AQ
O E C S ANNUAL DIGEST OF STATISTICS. 1984. irreg. EC$25($10) Organisation of Eastern Caribbean States, Economic Affairs Secretariat, P.O. Box 822, St. John's, Antigua, W.I. TEL 809-462-1530. FAX 809-462-1537. stat.; circ. 350.
  Description: Summarizes statistics in the member countries.

O E C S ENERGY BULLETIN. see ENERGY — Abstracting, Bibliographies, Statistics

310 330.9 AQ
O E C S NATIONAL ACCOUNT DIGEST. 1985. irreg. EC$25($10) Organisation of Eastern Caribbean States, Economic Affairs Secretariat, P.O. Box 822, St. John's, Antigua, W.I. TEL 809-462-1530. FAX 809-462-1537. charts; stat.; circ. 350.
  Description: Covers the national income and expenditure of OECS member countries.

310 330.9 AQ
O E C S STATISTICAL POCKET DIGEST. 1983. irreg. EC$5($2) Organisation of Eastern Caribbean States, Economic Affairs Secretariat, P.O. Box 822, St. John's, Antigua, W.I. TEL 809-462-1530. FAX 809-462-1537. stat.; circ. 1,500.
  Description: Reference guide to statistics and basic information about OECS member countries.

OCCUPATIONAL DISEASE IN CALIFORNIA. see OCCUPATIONAL HEALTH AND SAFETY — Abstracting, Bibliographies, Statistics

OHIO. DEPARTMENT OF HUMAN SERVICES. CHILD WELFARE STATISTICS. see SOCIAL SERVICES AND WELFARE — Abstracting, Bibliographies, Statistics

OKLAHOMA BUSINESS BULLETIN. see BUSINESS AND ECONOMICS — Abstracting, Bibliographies, Statistics

ONTARIO PUBLIC SECTOR; of official personnel in federal, provincial and municipal governments in the province of Ontario. see PUBLIC ADMINISTRATION — Abstracting, Bibliographies, Statistics

OPERANT SUBJECTIVITY; the Q methodology newsletter. see SOCIOLOGY — Abstracting, Bibliographies, Statistics

317 US ISSN 1050-0383
HN90.P8
OPINIONS (YEAR). a. $129. Gale Research Inc., 835 Penobscot Bldg., Detroit, MI 48226-4094. TEL 313-961-2242. FAX 313-961-6083. TELEX 810-221-7086. Eds. Chris John Miko, Edward Weilant.
  Description: Contains extracts from public opinion surveys and polls conducted by business, government, professional and news organizations.

OREGON PROPERTY TAX STATISTICS. see BUSINESS AND ECONOMICS — Abstracting, Bibliographies, Statistics

OREGON PUBLIC HEALTH STATISTICS REPORT. see PUBLIC HEALTH AND SAFETY — Abstracting, Bibliographies, Statistics

310 US ISSN 0250-6289
HA755
ORGANIZATION OF AMERICAN STATES. STATISTICAL BULLETIN. 1979. q. $12. Organization of American States, General Secretariat, 1889 F St., N.W., Washington, DC 20006. TEL 703-941-1617. charts; stat.; circ. 1,000. (back issues avail.)
  Indexed: IIS, P.A.I.S.

OXFORD BULLETIN OF ECONOMICS AND STATISTICS. see BUSINESS AND ECONOMICS

310 510 JA ISSN 0285-0370
OYO TOKEIGAKU/JAPANESE JOURNAL OF APPLIED STATISTICS. (Text and summaries in Japanese) 1971. 3/yr. 6000 Yen. Oyo Tokei Gakkai - Japanese Society of Applied Statistics, Dept. of Mathematics, Keio University, 14-1, Hiyoshi 3-chome, Kohoku-ku, Yokohama-shi, Kanagawa-ken 223, Japan. FAX 81-45-562-4442.

P M A STATISTICAL FACTBOOK; pharmaceuticals, in-vivo diagnostic. (Pharmaceutical Manufacturers Association) see PHARMACY AND PHARMACOLOGY — Abstracting, Bibliographies, Statistics

PAKISTAN. CENTRAL BUREAU OF EDUCATION. EDUCATIONAL STATISTICS BULLETIN SERIES. see EDUCATION — Abstracting, Bibliographies, Statistics

PAKISTAN INSTITUTE OF DEVELOPMENT ECONOMICS. STATISTICAL PAPERS SERIES. see BUSINESS AND ECONOMICS — Abstracting, Bibliographies, Statistics

315 PK ISSN 0078-8473
PAKISTAN STATISTICAL ASSOCIATION. PROCEEDINGS. (Text in English) a. Rs.2. Pakistan Statistical Association, Institute of Statistics, University of the Punjab, Lahore, Pakistan.

318 PN ISSN 0078-8996
PANAMA EN CIFRAS. 1953. a. BI.O.75. Direccion de Estadistica y Censo, Contraloria General, Apartado 5213, Panama 5, Panama. FAX 63-9322. circ. 8,000.

319 PP ISSN 0310-5377
PAPUA NEW GUINEA. NATIONAL STATISTICAL OFFICE. ABSTRACT OF STATISTICS. 1967. q. K.6 (foreign K.7). National Statistical Office, P.O. Wards Strip, Papua New Guinea. FAX 675-255057. TELEX FINANCE NE 22312-10. Ed. Nick Suvulo. tables.; circ. 560.
  Supersedes: Papua and New Guinea. Quarterly Summary of Statistics (ISSN 0031-1537)
  Description: Includes monthly or quarterly figures drawn from most of the economic statistical series compiled by the NSO and some by the Bank of Papua New Guinea.

PAPUA NEW GUINEA. NATIONAL STATISTICAL OFFICE. CENSUS OF EMPLOYMENT. see BUSINESS AND ECONOMICS — Abstracting, Bibliographies, Statistics

339 319 PP ISSN 1017-6500
PAPUA NEW GUINEA. NATIONAL STATISTICAL OFFICE. CONSUMER PRICE INDEX. 1964. q. K.6 (foreign K.7). National Statistical Office, P.O. Wards Strip, Papua New Guinea. FAX 657-255057. TELEX FINANCE NE 22312. Ed. Nick Suvulo. tables.; circ. 800.
  Supersedes: Papua New Guinea. Bureau of Statistics. Quarterly Retail Price Index (ISSN 0031-1529)
  Description: Covers six urban areas and contains price indexes, for groups and major sub-groups of household expenditures, and retail prices of major domestic commodities.

PAPUA NEW GUINEA. NATIONAL STATISTICAL OFFICE. DOMESTIC FACTOR INCOMES, BY REGION AND PROVINCE. see BUSINESS AND ECONOMICS — Abstracting, Bibliographies, Statistics

PAPUA NEW GUINEA. NATIONAL STATISTICAL OFFICE. ECONOMIC INDICATORS. see BUSINESS AND ECONOMICS — Abstracting, Bibliographies, Statistics

PAPUA NEW GUINEA. NATIONAL STATISTICAL OFFICE. GOVERNMENT FINANCE STATISTICS. see BUSINESS AND ECONOMICS — Abstracting, Bibliographies, Statistics

PAPUA NEW GUINEA. NATIONAL STATISTICAL OFFICE. GROSS DOMESTIC PRODUCT AND EXPENDITURE. see BUSINESS AND ECONOMICS — Abstracting, Bibliographies, Statistics

PAPUA NEW GUINEA. NATIONAL STATISTICAL OFFICE. IMPORT PRICE INDEXES. see BUSINESS AND ECONOMICS — Abstracting, Bibliographies, Statistics

PAPUA NEW GUINEA. NATIONAL STATISTICAL OFFICE. INTERNATIONAL TRADE - EXPORTS. see BUSINESS AND ECONOMICS — Abstracting, Bibliographies, Statistics

PAPUA NEW GUINEA. NATIONAL STATISTICAL OFFICE. INTERNATIONAL TRADE - IMPORTS. see BUSINESS AND ECONOMICS — Abstracting, Bibliographies, Statistics

PAPUA NEW GUINEA. NATIONAL STATISTICAL OFFICE. PRODUCTION STATISTICS. see BUSINESS AND ECONOMICS — Abstracting, Bibliographies, Statistics

STATISTICS   **4583**

PAPUA NEW GUINEA. NATIONAL STATISTICAL OFFICE. STATISTICAL BULLETIN: CENSUS OF RETAIL SALES AND SELECTED SERVICES. see *BUSINESS AND ECONOMICS — Abstracting, Bibliographies, Statistics*

PAPUA NEW GUINEA INTERNATIONAL ARRIVALS AND DEPARTURES. see *POPULATION STUDIES — Abstracting, Bibliographies, Statistics*

318.92   PY   ISSN 0031-1677
PARAGUAY. DIRECCION GENERAL DE ESTADISTICA Y CENSOS. BOLETIN ESTADISTICO. (Supplement to Anuario Estadistico de la Republica del Paraguay) 1957. s-a. free. Direccion General de Estadistica y Censos, Humaita 463, Casilla de Correo 1118, Asuncion, Paraguay. Ed. Jose Diaz de Bedoya. mkt.; stat.; circ. 1,000.

PEDIATRIC LENGTH OF STAY BY DIAGNOSIS AND OPERATION, UNITED STATES. see *HOSPITALS — Abstracting, Bibliographies, Statistics*

PENNSYLVANIA. BOARD OF PROBATION AND PAROLE. MONTHLY STATISTICAL REPORT. see *CRIMINOLOGY AND LAW ENFORCEMENT — Abstracting, Bibliographies, Statistics*

PERSONALE- OG OEKONOMIATISTIK FOR SYGEHUSVAESENET. see *HOSPITALS — Abstracting, Bibliographies, Statistics*

PETROLEUM MARKET INTELLIGENCE. see *PETROLEUM AND GAS — Abstracting, Bibliographies, Statistics*

PHILIPPINE STATISTICAL YEARBOOK. see *BUSINESS AND ECONOMICS — Abstracting, Bibliographies, Statistics*

311   PH   ISSN 0031-7829
PHILIPPINE STATISTICIAN. 1953. s-a. P.50($15) Philippine Statistical Association, Box 3223, Manila, Philippines. Ed. Ann Inez N. Gironella. charts; circ. 500. Indexed: Ind.Phil.Per., P.A.I.S.
—BLDSC shelfmark: 6456.375000.

PHILIPPINES. BUREAU OF LABOR AND EMPLOYMENT STATISTICS. OCCUPATIONAL WAGES SURVEY. see *BUSINESS AND ECONOMICS — Abstracting, Bibliographies, Statistics*

PHILIPPINES. NATIONAL STATISTICS OFFICE. ANNUAL SURVEY OF ESTABLISHMENTS. see *BUSINESS AND ECONOMICS — Abstracting, Bibliographies, Statistics*

PHILIPPINES. NATIONAL STATISTICS OFFICE. DIRECTORY OF LARGE ESTABLISHMENTS. see *BUSINESS AND ECONOMICS — Abstracting, Bibliographies, Statistics*

315   PH   ISSN 0116-2624
PHILIPPINES. NATIONAL STATISTICS OFFICE. INTEGRATED SURVEY OF HOUSEHOLDS BULLETIN.. q. $100. National Statistics Office, Ramon Magsaysay Blvd., Box 779, Manila, Philippines. FAX 610794. circ. 300.
Formerly: Philippines. National Census and Statistics Office. Sample Survey of Households Bulletin.

PHILIPPINES. NATIONAL STATISTICS OFFICE. VITAL STATISTICS REPORT. see *POPULATION STUDIES — Abstracting, Bibliographies, Statistics*

310   GW
PIRMASENS ZAHLEN UND FAKTEN: STATISTISCHE JAHRBUCH STADT PIRMASENS. 1979. a. Stadtplanungsamt, Bahnhofstr. 41, 6780 Pirmasens, Germany. TEL 06331-842433. FAX 06331-842540. TELEX 452286. circ. 200.

319   AT   ISSN 0727-145X
POCKET YEAR BOOK, AUSTRALIA. 1913. a. Aus.$7.40 (foreign Aus.$10)(effective 1991). Australian Bureau of Statistics, P.O. Box 10, Belconnen, A.C.T. 2616, Australia. TEL 062-527911. FAX 062-516009. circ. 1,141.
Formerly: Pocket Compendium of Australian Statistics (ISSN 0079-239X)
Description: Brief comprehensive summary of basic statistics of Australia.

319   AT   ISSN 0079-2446
POCKET YEAR BOOK OF SOUTH AUSTRALIA. 1917. a. Aus.$8.50 (foreign Aus.$11). Australian Bureau of Statistics, South Australian Office, Box 2272, G.P.O., Adelaide, S.A. 5001, Australia. FAX 08-237-7566.
Description: Compact tables covering most types of statistical information collected by the ABS; it also lists the State Government Ministry.

319   AT   ISSN 0159-9321
HA3012
POCKET YEARBOOK OF NEW SOUTH WALES. 1913. a. Aus.$9 (foreign Aus.$11.50). Australian Bureau of Statistics, New South Wales Office, St. Andrews House, Sydney Square, George St., Sydney, N.S.W. 2000, Australia.
Description: Provides basic statistical information on New South Wales.

310   PL   ISSN 0006-4025
HA1451
POLAND. GLOWNY URZAD STATYSTYCZNY. BIULETYN STATYSTYCZNY. (Contents page in English and Russian) 1957. m. $21. Glowny Urzad Statystyczny, Al. Niepodleglosci 208, 00-925 Warsaw, Poland. TEL 48 22 25-03-45. (Dist. by: Ars Polona Ruch, Krakowskie Przedmiescie 7, Warsaw, Poland) charts; stat.; index; circ. 2,500.

POLAND. GLOWNY URZAD STATYSTYCZNY. BUDZET PANSTWA/POLAND. CENTRAL STATISTICS OFFICE. STATE BUDGET. see *BUSINESS AND ECONOMICS — Abstracting, Bibliographies, Statistics*

314   PL   ISSN 0079-2608
HA1451
POLAND. GLOWNY URZAD STATYSTYCZNY. MALY ROCZNIK STATYSTYCZNY/POLAND. CENTRAL STATISTICS OFFICE. CONCISE STATISTICAL YEARBOOK. (Editions in English, French, German, Polish and Russian) 1958. a. 30 Zl. Glowny Urzad Statystyczny, Al. Niepodleglosci 208, 00-925 Warsaw, Poland. TEL 48 22 25-03-45.

314.38   PL
POLAND. GLOWNY URZAD STATYSTYCZNY. MALY ROCZNIK STATYSTYKI MIEDZYNARODOWEJ. (Subseries of its: Seria Statystyka Miedzynarodowa) 1972. irreg., latest 1986. 125 Zl. Glowny Urzad Statystyczny, Al. Niepodleglosci 208, 00-925 Warsaw, Poland. TEL 48 22 25-03-45. illus.; stat.

314   PL   ISSN 0079-2780
POLAND. GLOWNY URZAD STATYSTYCZNY. ROCZNIK STATYSTYCZNY/POLAND. CENTRAL STATISTICS OFFICE. STATISTICAL YEARBOOK. (Text in Polish; summaries in English and Russian) 1921. a. Glowny Urzad Statystyczny, Al. Niepodleglosci 208, 00-925 Warsaw, Poland. TEL 48 22 25-03-45.
—BLDSC shelfmark: 8005.600000.

310   PL   ISSN 0079-273X
POLAND. GLOWNY URZAD STATYSTYCZNY. ROCZNIK STATYSTYKI MIEDZYNARODOWEJ/POLAND. CENTRAL STATISTICS OFFICE. YEARBOOK OF INTERNATIONAL STATISTICS. irreg., latest 1987. Glowny Urzad Statystyczny, Al. Niepodleglosci 208, 00-925 Warsaw, Poland. TEL 48 22 25-03-45.

311   PL
POLAND. GLOWNY URZAD STATYSTYCZNY. STATYSTYKA POLSKI. STUDIA I PRACE STATYSTYCZNE. (Text in Polish; summaries in English and Russian) 1966. irreg., vol.16, 1988. Glowny Urzad Statystyczny, Al. Niepodleglosci 208, 00-925 Warsaw, Poland. TEL 48 22 25-03-45.
Formerly: Poland. Glowny Urzad Statystyczny. Studia i Prace Statystyczne (ISSN 0079-2845)

314   PL   ISSN 0043-518X
HA1451
POLAND. GLOWNY URZAD STATYSTYCZNY. WIADOMOSCI STATYSTYCZNE. (Text in Polish; contents page and summaries in English, Russian) 1985. m. $21. Glowny Urzad Statystyczny, Al. Niepodleglosci 208, 00-925 Warsaw, Poland. TEL 48 22 25-03-45. (Dist. by: Ars Polona - Ruch, Krakowskie Przedmiescie 7, Warsaw, Poland) charts; stat.; index; circ. 3,400.
—BLDSC shelfmark: 9315.450000.

310   PL   ISSN 0079-2829
POLAND. GLOWNY URZAD STATYSTYCZNY. ZESZYTY METODYCZNE. 1966. irreg., no.73, 1988. price varies. Glowny Urzad Statystyczny, Al. Niepodleglosci 208, 00-925 Warsaw, Poland. TEL 48 22 25-03-45. (Dist. by: Ars Polona-Ruch, Ul. Krakowskie Przedmiescie 7, Warsaw, Poland)

POLLING REPORT. see *POLITICAL SCIENCE — Abstracting, Bibliographies, Statistics*

310   US
POPULAR STATISTICS SERIES. 1983. irreg., vol.5, 1987. price varies. Marcel Dekker, Inc., 270 Madison Ave., New York, NY 10016. TEL 212-696-9000. FAX 212-658-4540. TELEX 421419.

314   PO   ISSN 0871-8741
PORTUGAL. INSTITUTO NACIONAL DE ESTATISTICA. ANUARIO ESTATISTICO. CONTINENTE, ACORES E MADEIRA. (Text in French and Portuguese) 1875. a. Esc.6700. Instituto Nacional de Estatistica, Av. Antonio Jose de Almeida, 1078 Lisbon Codex, Portugal. (Orders to: Imprensa Nacional, Casa da Moeda, Direccao Comercial, Rua D. Francisco Manuel de Melo 5, 1000 Lisbon, Portugal)
Formerly: Portugal. Instituto Nacional de Estatistica. Anuario Estatistico (ISSN 0079-4112)

314   PO
PORTUGAL. INSTITUTO NACIONAL DE ESTATISTICA. BOLETIM MENSAL DE ESTATISTICA: CONTINENTE, ACORES E MADEIRA. (Text in English, Portuguese) 1929. m. Esc.2500. Instituto Nacional de Estatistica, Av. Antonio Jose de Almeida, 1078 Lisbon Codex, Portugal. (Dist. by: Imprensa Nacional, Casa da Moeda, Direccao Comercial, rua D. Francisco Manuel de Melo 5, 1000 Lisbon, Portugal) bibl.; stat.; circ. 1,450. Indexed: P.A.I.S.For.Lang.Ind.
Formerly: Portugal. Instituto Nacional de Estatistica. Boletim Mensal (ISSN 0032-5082)

PORTUGAL. INSTITUTO NACIONAL DE ESTATISTICA. ESTATISTICAS DOS TRANSPORTES E COMMUNICACOES: CONTINENTE, ACORES E MADEIRA. see *TRANSPORTATION — Abstracting, Bibliographies, Statistics*

314   PO   ISSN 0378-3227
PORTUGAL. INSTITUTO NACIONAL DE ESTATISTICA. SERIE ESTATISTICAS REGIONAIS. 1970. irreg. Instituto Nacional de Estatistica, Av. Antonio Jose de Almeida, 1078 Lisbon Codex, Portugal. (Orders to: Imprensa Nacional, Casa da Moeda, Direccao Comercial, rua D. Francisco Manuel de Melo 5, 1000 Lisbon, Portugal) stat.; circ. controlled.

314   PO   ISSN 0871-8725
PORTUGAL EM NUMEROS. (Editions in English and Portuguese) 1969. a. Esc.120. Instituto Nacional de Estatistica, Av. Antonio Jose de Almeida, 1078 Lisbon Codex, Portugal.
Former titles: Portugal (Year) (ISSN 0377-2470); (until 1977): Portugal. Instituto Nacional de Estatistica. Sinopse de Dados Estatisticos: Continente Ilhas Adjacentes.

314.6   PO   ISSN 0871-4614
PORTUGAL EM NUMEROS; SITUACAO SOCIO-ECONOMICA. English edition: Portugal; Economic and Social Indicators (ISSN 0871-4622) 1987. a. free. Ministerio do Planeamento e Administracao Territorio, Departamento Central de Planeamento, Avda. D. Carlos I, 126, 1200 Lisbon, Portugal.

POULTRY MARKET STATISTICS. see *AGRICULTURE — Abstracting, Bibliographies, Statistics*

314.97   XV   ISSN 0032-8227
PRIKAZI IN STUDIJE. (Text in Slovenian) 1955. m. 18 din. per no. Zavod SR Slovenije za Statistiko, Vozarski Pot 12, Ljubljana, Slovenia. Ed. Branko Mlinar. charts; stat. (processed)

PROBABILITY AND MATHEMATICAL STATISTICS. see *MATHEMATICS — Abstracting, Bibliographies, Statistics*

PRODUCCION AGRICOLA - PERIODO DE VERANO. see *AGRICULTURE — Abstracting, Bibliographies, Statistics*

PRODUCTION OF CANADA'S LEADING MINERALS. see *MINES AND MINING INDUSTRY — Abstracting, Bibliographies, Statistics*

STATISTICS

PROFILES OF EARNINGS IN CYPRUS: BY EDUCATION, OCCUPATION, EXPERIENCE, AGE, SEX AND SECTOR. see *BUSINESS AND ECONOMICS — Abstracting, Bibliographies, Statistics*

PROPANE INDUSTRY PROFILE; statistical handbook of the LP-gas industry. see *PETROLEUM AND GAS — Abstracting, Bibliographies, Statistics*

310 PL ISSN 0033-2372
HA1 CODEN: PZSTAD
PRZEGLAD STATYSTYCZNY. 1954. q. $24. (Polska Akademia Nauk, Komitet Statystyki i Ekonometrii - Polish Economic Society) Panstwowe Wydawnictwo Naukowe, Miodowa 10, 00-251 Warsaw, Poland. (Dist. by: Ars Polona, Krakowskie Przedmiescie 7, 00-068 Warsaw, Poland) Ed. Z. Czerwinski. bk.rev.; charts; illus.; index; circ. 1,000. **Indexed:** Int.Abstr.Oper.Res., Math.R., Sci.Abstr.

PUERTO RICO. DEPARTMENT OF HEALTH. ANNUAL HEALTH SERVICES REPORT. see *PUBLIC HEALTH AND SAFETY — Abstracting, Bibliographies, Statistics*

PUERTO RICO. DEPARTMENT OF HEALTH. OFFICE OF PLANNING, EVALUATION AND REPORTS. DIVISION OF STATISTICS AND REPORTS. ANNUAL VITAL STATISTICS REPORT. see *POPULATION STUDIES — Abstracting, Bibliographies, Statistics*

QATAR YEARBOOK. see *PUBLIC ADMINISTRATION — Abstracting, Bibliographies, Statistics*

310 330.9 US
QUANTITY AND QUALITY IN ECONOMIC RESEARCH. 1985. a. $53. (International Society of Statistical Science in Economics) University Press of America, 4720 Boston Way, Ste. A, Lanham, MD 20706. TEL 707-585-0615. Ed. R.Ch. Brown.

310 AF
QUARTERLY REVIEW OF AFGHAN STATISTICS/SHMAYR SIRANAH-YI IHSA'IYAH. (Text in Persian) 1976. q. Central Statistical Office, Nader Shah Minah, Block No. 4, Box 2002, Kabul, Afghanistan. stat.

QUARTERLY TIMBER STATISTICS. see *FORESTS AND FORESTRY — Abstracting, Bibliographies, Statistics*

317 CN ISSN 0227-0668
QUEBEC (PROVINCE) BUREAU OF STATISTICS. STATISTIQUES. 1962. q. Can.$15. Ministere des Communications, Direction Generale des Publications Gouvernementales, 2e etage, 1279 Bd. Charest Ouest, Quebec, Que. G1N 4K7, Canada. TEL 413-643-3895. index; circ. 1,850. **Indexed:** Pt.de Rep. (1985-).
—BLDSC shelfmark: 8453.990000.
Formerly (until Apr. 1981): Revue Statistique du Quebec (ISSN 0039-0550)

319 AT ISSN 0157-3713
QUEENSLAND AT A GLANCE. 1978. a. free. Australian Bureau of Statistics, Queensland Office, 313 Adelaide St., Brisbane, Qld. 4000, Australia. TEL 07-222-6022. FAX 07-229-6171. TELEX AA 40271.
Description: Provides statistics on all aspects of Queensland life: population, labor, wages, health, welfare services, law and crime, education, agriculture, mining, construction, transportation, communication, tourism, prices and finance.

319 AT ISSN 0085-5316
QUEENSLAND POCKET YEAR BOOK. 1950. a. Aus.$7.50 (foreign Aus.$10.80). Australian Bureau of Statistics, Queensland Office, 313 Adelaide St., Brisbane, Qld. 4000, Australia. TEL 07-222-6022. FAX 07-229-6171. TELEX AA 40271. index; circ. 2,500.

R I A QUARTERLY STATISTICS REPORT - ROBOTICS. (Robotic Industries Association) see *COMPUTERS — Automation*

R V BUSINESS. (Recreational Vehicle) see *SPORTS AND GAMES — Abstracting, Bibliographies, Statistics*

310 UK ISSN 0268-6376
RADICAL STATISTICS. 1975. 3/yr. £10 to individuals; libraries £10. Radical Statistics Group, c/o London Hazards Centre, Headland House, 3rd Fl., 308 Grays Inn Rd., London WC1X 8DS, England. adv.; bk.rev.; circ. 300.
—BLDSC shelfmark: 7228.098900.
Description: A forum for radical ideas in the political development and exploitation of statistical methods and in the uses and abuses of statistics.

RAJASTHAN, INDIA. DIRECTORATE OF ECONOMICS AND STATISTICS. BASIC STATISTICS. see *BUSINESS AND ECONOMICS — Abstracting, Bibliographies, Statistics*

RAUMFORSCHUNG UND RAUMORDNUNG. see *HOUSING AND URBAN PLANNING — Abstracting, Bibliographies, Statistics*

314 FR ISSN 0990-2562
REGARDS SUR L'ILE-DE-FRANCE. 1979. q. 160 F. Institut National de la Statistique et des Etudes Economiques (INSEE), Direction Regionale de Paris, 12 rue Boulitte, 75675 Paris Cedex 14, France. TEL 40-44-10-10. FAX 40-44-13-75. TELEX 250 970 F. Ed. Alain Godinot. adv.; circ. 1,500.
Formerly (until 1988): Aspects Statistiques de l'Ile de France.

RELAIS - STATISTIQUES DE L'ECONOMIE PICARDE. see *BUSINESS AND ECONOMICS — Abstracting, Bibliographies, Statistics*

REPORT ON PASSENGER ROAD TRANSPORT IN ZAMBIA. see *TRANSPORTATION — Abstracting, Bibliographies, Statistics*

REPORT ON VITAL STATISTICS. see *POPULATION STUDIES — Abstracting, Bibliographies, Statistics*

RESEARCH AND STUDIES. see *EDUCATION — Abstracting, Bibliographies, Statistics*

318 BL
RESENHA ESTATISTICA DO RIO GRANDE DO SUL. 1977. a. Cr.$6000. Fundacao de Economia e Estatistica, Rua Duque de Casias, 1691, CEP 90010 Porto Alegre, Rio Grande do Sul, Brazil.

REVIEW OF ECONOMICS AND STATISTICS. see *BUSINESS AND ECONOMICS — Abstracting, Bibliographies, Statistics*

314 BL ISSN 0034-7175
HA984
REVISTA BRASILEIRA DE ESTATISTICA/BRAZILIAN STATISTICAL JOURNAL. (Text in Portuguese; summaries in English) 1940. s-a. $40. Fundacao Instituto Brasileiro de Geografia e Estatistica, Av. Franklin Roosevelt, 166 Centro, CEP 20021 Rio de Janeiro, Brazil. TEL 021-284-7690. FAX 21-228-9575. TELEX 2139128. (Subscr. to: Divisiao de Comercializacao e Promocao, Rua General Canabarro, 666, Bloco B 2o andar, Maracana, CEP 20271 Rio de Janeiro, Brazil) bk.rev.; bibl.; charts; illus.; stat.; index; circ. 1,000. (back issues avail.) **Indexed:** Popul.Ind.
—BLDSC shelfmark: 7844.600000.

REVISTA DE ECONOMIA Y ESTADISTICA. see *BUSINESS AND ECONOMICS*

314.98 RM ISSN 0035-8037
REVISTA DE STATISTICA. (Text in Rumanian; summaries in English and Russian) 1952. m. 1200 lei($80) (effective Nov. 1991). Comisia Nationala pentru Statistica - National Commission for Statistics, Str. Stavropoleos Nr. 6, Bucharest, Rumania. FAX 400-145560. TELEX 11153. (Dist. by: Rompresfilatelia, Calea Grivitei 64-66, Box 12201, Bucharest, Rumania) circ. 8,500. **Indexed:** Rural Recreat.Tour.Abstr., World Agri.Econ.& Rural Sociol.Abstr.
Description: Provides official figures from the commission.

318 BL
REVISTA DO SEITE. 1980. irreg. Cr.$15.00($5) Fundacao de Economia e Estatistica, Rua Gen. Vitorino 77, C.P. 2355, 90.000 Porto Alegre, Brazil. Ed. Roberto La Rocca. (also avail. in microform)
Formerly: Rio Grande do Sul, Brazil. Fundacao de Economia e Estatistica. Boletim Estatistico do Seite.

REVISTA ECONOMIA; nueva etapa. see *BUSINESS AND ECONOMICS*

310 FR ISSN 0035-175X
CODEN: RVSTA7
REVUE DE STATISTIQUE APPLIQUEE. 1953. q. 550 F. Centre d'Enseignement et de Recherche de Statistique Appliquée (CERESTA), 10 rue Bertin Poiree, 75001 Paris, France. TEL 42-33-97-14. FAX 42-33-81-29. Ed. Pierre Cazes. adv.; bk.rev.; bibl.; charts; stat.; index. cum.index: vols. 1-17; circ. 800. (reprint service avail. SWZ) **Indexed:** Biostat., Math.R., Oper.Res.Manage.Sci., Qaul.Contr.Appl.Stat., SSCI.

REVUE DROMOISE. see *ARCHAEOLOGY*

RHODE ISLAND. DEPARTMENT OF EDUCATION. (YEAR) STATISTICAL TABLES. see *EDUCATION — Abstracting, Bibliographies, Statistics*

314 IT ISSN 0035-7960
ROMA E PROVINCIA ATTRAVERSO LA STATISTICA; dati mensili e annuali. 1956. a. L.800. per no. Camera di Commercio Industria Artigianato e Agricoltura di Roma, Via De'Burro 147, 00186 Rome, Italy. Ed. Dr. Leonida Attili. bk.rev.; charts; stat.; index; cum.index; circ. controlled.

310 UK
HA1 CODEN: JSTAAG
ROYAL STATISTICAL SOCIETY. JOURNAL. SERIES A: STATISTICS IN SOCIETY. 1838. 3/yr. £37($73) Basil Blackwell Ltd., 108 Cowley Road, Oxford OX4 1JF, England. TEL 0865-791100. FAX 0865-791347. Eds. D. Holt, S.M. Gore. adv.; bk.rev.; bibl.; index; circ. 5,700. (also avail. in microfilm from BHP) **Indexed:** Abstr.Hyg., Appl.Mech.Rev., Biostat., Compumath, Curr.Cont., Deep Sea Res.& Oceanogr.Abstr., High.Educ.Curr.Aware.Bull., Ind.Vet., J.Cont.Quant.Meth., J.of Econ.Lit., Math.R., Oper.Res.Manage.Sci., P.A.I.S., Popul.Ind., Qual.Contr.Appl.Stat., Res.High.Educ.Abstr., Rural Recreat.Tour.Abstr., SSCI, Trop.Dis.Bull., Vet.Bull., World Agri.Econ.& Rural Sociol.Abstr., World Bank.Abstr.
Formerly: Royal Statistical Society. Journal. Series A: General (ISSN 0035-9238)
Description: Contains papers on economic, social and governmental issues, historical, biographical, philosophical, demographical and medical statistics.

311 UK ISSN 0035-9246
HA1 CODEN: JSTBAJ
ROYAL STATISTICAL SOCIETY. JOURNAL. SERIES B: METHODOLOGICAL. 1934. 3/yr. £37($73) Basil Blackwell Ltd., 108 Cowley Road, Oxford OX4 1JF, England. TEL 0865-791100. FAX 0865-791347. Eds. J.T. Kent, R.L. Smith. adv.; bibl.; index; circ. 4,500. **Indexed:** Abstr.Hyg., Appl.Mech.Rev., Biostat., Compumath, Curr.Cont., Hort.Abstr., J.Cont.Quant.Meth., Math.R., SSCI, Trop.Dis.Bull.
—BLDSC shelfmark: 4867.000000.
Description: Addresses theory and development of new statistical methods and applications of established methods.

310 UK ISSN 0035-9254
HA1 CODEN: APSTAG
ROYAL STATISTICAL SOCIETY. JOURNAL. SERIES C: APPLIED STATISTICS. 1952. 3/yr. £37($73) (Royal Statistical Society) Basil Blackwell Ltd., 108 Cowley Rd., Oxford OX4 1JF, England. TEL 0865-791100. FAX 0865-791347. (Subscr. to: Journals Subscription Department, Marston Book Services, P.O. Box 87, Oxford OX2 0DT, England) Eds. I.R. Dunsmore, D.J. Hand. adv.; bk.rev.; bibl.; index; circ. 5,400. (back issues avail.) **Indexed:** Biostat., Br.Archaeol.Abstr., Br.Tech.Ind., C.I.S. Abstr., Compumath, J.Cont.Quant.Meth., Math.R., Nutr.Abstr., Oper.Res.Manage.Sci., Qual.Contr.Appl.Stat., RAPRA, Risk Abstr., Sci.Abstr., SSCI, W.R.C.Inf.
Description: Discusses the application of statistical methods to practical problems including computer algorithms.

316.7 RW
RWANDA. DIRECTION GENERALE DE LA STATISTIQUE. BULLETIN DE STATISTIQUE. (Supplement avail.) 1964. q. 400 F. Direction Generale de la Statistique, B.P. 46, Kigali, Rwanda.
Formerly: Rwanda. Direction Generale de la Documentation et de la Statistique Generale. Bulletin de Statistique.

STATISTICS 4585

311.2   US   ISSN 0196-5204
QA297   CODEN: SIJCD4
S I A M JOURNAL ON SCIENTIFIC AND STATISTICAL COMPUTING. 1980. bi-m. $210 to non-members; members $48. Society for Industrial and Applied Mathematics, Attn: P. Clifford, 3600 University City Science Center, Philadelphia, PA 19104-2688. TEL 215-382-9800. FAX 215-386-7999. TELEX 446-715. Ed. Linda Petzold. charts; illus.; stat.; index; circ. 1,736. (also avail. in microform from IAM; back issues avail.) **Indexed:** ASCA, Biostat., Compumath, Cyb.Abstr., Int.Aerosp.Abstr., J.Cont.Quant.Meth., Math.R., Oper.Res.Manage.Sci., Qual.Contr.Appl.Stat., Sci.Abstr.
—BLDSC shelfmark: 8271.357200.
   Description: Contains research articles on those techniques of scientific computation concerned with the solution of continuous or statistical models (as opposed to discrete models).
Refereed Serial

310   XK
ST. LUCIA. STATISTICAL DEPARTMENT. ANNUAL STATISTICAL DIGEST. 1960. a. EC$15. Statistical Department, New Government Bldg., 2nd Fl., Castries, St. Lucia, W.I. TEL 809-45-22697. FAX 809-45-31648. TELEX 6394 FORAFF. Ed. Bryan Boxill.

310   XK
ST. LUCIA. STATISTICAL DEPARTMENT. STATISTICAL POCKET DIGEST. 1979. a. EC$2($2) Statistical Department, New Government Bldg., 2nd Fl., Castries, St. Lucia, W.I. TEL 809-45-22697. FAX 809-45-31648. TELEX 6394 FORAFF. Ed. Bryan Boxill.

311   II   ISSN 0581-4790
SAMVADADHVAM. (Text in Bengali, English and Hindi) 1956. irreg. Indian Statistical Institute, 203 Barrackpore Trunk Rd., Calcutta 700035, India. Ed. Bd. bk.rev.; bibl.; charts; illus.; stat.; circ. 2,500 (controlled).

SANFORD EVANS GOLD BOOK OF SNOWMOBILE DATA AND USED PRICES. see *SPORTS AND GAMES — Abstracting, Bibliographies, Statistics*

311   II   ISSN 0581-572X
    CODEN: SANABS
SANKHYA. SERIES A; Indian journal of statistics. (Text in English) 1933. q. Statistical Publishing Society, 204-1 Barrackpore Trunk Rd., Calcutta 700035, India. Ed.Bd. adv.; bibl.; index; circ. 1,500 (combined). (also avail. in microfilm; microfiche) **Indexed:** Biol.Abstr., Biostat., Chem.Abstr., J.Cont.Quant.Meth., Math.R., P.A.I.S., SSCI.

310   II   ISSN 0581-5738
    CODEN: SANBBV
SANKHYA. SERIES B; Indian journal of statistics. (Text in English) 1933. q. Statistical Publishing Society, 204-1 Barrackpore Trunk Rd., Calcutta 700035, India. Ed.Bd. adv.; bibl.; stat.; circ. 1,500 (combined). **Indexed:** Biol.Abstr., Biostat., Chem.Abstr., P.A.I.S., SSCI.
—BLDSC shelfmark: 8075.005000.

318   AG
SANTIAGO DEL ESTERO. DIRECCION GENERAL DE INVESTIGACIONES ESTADISTICA Y CENSOS. ESTADISTICAS SOCIALES. a. free. Direccion General de Investigaciones Estadistica y Censos, Palacio de los Tribunales, Santiago del Estero, Argentina. Dir. Jose Humberto Alegre. stat.

314   SF
SAO TOME E PRINCIPE. REPARTICAO PROVINCIAL DOS SERVICOS DE ESTATISTICA. BOLETIN TRIMESTRAL DE ESTATISTICA. 1971. q. Reparticao Provincial dos Servicos de Estatistica, Caixa Postal No. 256, Sao Tome, Sao Tome e Principe.

315   II
SARVEKSHANA. (Text in English and Hindi) 1977. q. Rs.100($36) National Sample Survey Organisation, Sardar Patel Bhavan, Parliament St., New Delhi 110001, India. (Subscr. to.: Controller of Publications, Civil Lines, Delhi 110 054, India) stat.; circ. 1,000. (back issues avail.)

319   SU
SAUDI ARABIA. CENTRAL DEPARTMENT OF STATISTICS. STATISTICAL YEARBOOK. (Text in Arabic, English) 1965. a. sR.30. Central Department of Statistics, Box 3735, Riyadh 11118, Saudi Arabia.
   Description: Presents a picture of economic and social development in the kingdom on the basis of scientifically organized studies.

SAUDI ARABIA. MINISTRY OF EDUCATION. EDUCATIONAL STATISTICS. see *EDUCATION — Abstracting, Bibliographies, Statistics*

310   UK   ISSN 0303-6898
QA276.A1   CODEN: SJSADG
SCANDINAVIAN JOURNAL OF STATISTICS; theory and applications. (Supplements avail.) (Text in English) 1974. 4/yr. Kr.670. Basil Blackwell Ltd., 108 Cowley Rd., Oxford OX4 1JF, England. TEL 0865-791100. FAX 0865-791347. TELEX 837022-OXBOOK-G. adv.; abstr.; illus.; index; circ. 700. **Indexed:** ASCA, Biostat., Compumath, Curr.Cont., J.Cont.Quant.Meth., Math.R., Oper.Res.Manage.Sci., Qual.Contr.Appl.Stat., Risk Abstr.
—BLDSC shelfmark: 8087.549000.

SCOTLAND. REGISTRAR GENERAL. ANNUAL REPORT. see *POPULATION STUDIES — Abstracting, Bibliographies, Statistics*

314   UK
SCOTTISH ABSTRACT OF STATISTICS. 1971. a. £18. Scottish Office, New St. Andrew's House, Rm. 5-52, Edinburgh EH1 3SX, Scotland. TEL 031-244-4987. FAX 031-244-4785. circ. 600.
   Supersedes (in 1971): Digest of Scottish Statistics.
   Description: Major reference volume of statistics of life in Scotland.

SELECTED VITAL STATISTICS AND HEALTH STATISTICS INDICATORS. ANNUAL REPORT. see *POPULATION STUDIES — Abstracting, Bibliographies, Statistics*

310   US   ISSN 0747-4946
QA279.7   CODEN: SEANEX
SEQUENTIAL ANALYSIS. 1982. 4/yr. $30 to individuals; institutions $255. Marcel Dekker Journals, 270 Madison Ave., New York, NY 10016. TEL 212-696-9000. FAX 212-685-4540. TELEX 421419 MARDEEK. (Subscr. to: Box 10018, Church St. Sta., New York, NY 10249) Eds. B.K. Ghosh, P.K. Sen. abstr. (also avail. in microform from RPI) **Indexed:** Biostat., Curr.Ind.Stat., J.Cont.Quant.Meth., Oper.Res.Manage.Sci., Qual.Contr.Appl.Stat., Stat.Theor.Meth.Abstr., Zent.Math.
—BLDSC shelfmark: 8242.279500.
   Formerly: Communications in Statistics. Part C: Sequential Analysis.

SEYCHELLES. DEPARTMENT OF FINANCE. ECONOMIC INDICATORS. see *BUSINESS AND ECONOMICS — Abstracting, Bibliographies, Statistics*

SEYCHELLES. DEPARTMENT OF FINANCE. NATIONAL ACCOUNTS. see *PUBLIC ADMINISTRATION — Abstracting, Bibliographies, Statistics*

310   SE
SEYCHELLES. DEPARTMENT OF FINANCE. STATISTICAL BULLETIN.. 1980. q. R.25. Department of Finance, Statistics Division, P.O. Box 206, Independence House, Victoria, Republic of Seychelles. stat. (back issues avail.)

310   SE
SEYCHELLES. DEPARTMENT OF FINANCE. STATISTICS DIVISION. STATISTICAL ABSTRACT. 1977. a. 60 Fr. Department of Finance, Statistics Division, P.O. Box 206, Victoria, Mahe, Seychelles. circ. 250.

SEYCHELLES. DEPARTMENT OF FINANCE. VISITOR SURVEY. see *TRAVEL AND TOURISM — Abstracting, Bibliographies, Statistics*

SEYCHELLES. PRESIDENT'S OFFICE. STATISTICS DIVISION. CENSUS. see *POPULATION STUDIES — Abstracting, Bibliographies, Statistics*

SEYCHELLES. PRESIDENT'S OFFICE. STATISTICS DIVISION. EMPLOYMENT & EARNINGS. see *BUSINESS AND ECONOMICS — Abstracting, Bibliographies, Statistics*

SEYCHELLES. PRESIDENT'S OFFICE. STATISTICS DIVISION. EXTERNAL TRADE. see *BUSINESS AND ECONOMICS — Abstracting, Bibliographies, Statistics*

SEYCHELLES. PRESIDENT'S OFFICE. STATISTICS DIVISION. MIGRATION AND TOURISM STATISTICS. see *TRAVEL AND TOURISM — Abstracting, Bibliographies, Statistics*

SEYCHELLES. PRESIDENT'S OFFICE. STATISTICS DIVISION. POPULATION AND VITAL STATISTICS. see *POPULATION STUDIES — Abstracting, Bibliographies, Statistics*

SEYCHELLES. PRESIDENT'S OFFICE. STATISTICS DIVISION. PRODUCTION INDICATORS. see *BUSINESS AND ECONOMICS — Abstracting, Bibliographies, Statistics*

SEYCHELLES. PRESIDENT'S OFFICE. STATISTICS DIVISION. RETAIL PRICES. see *BUSINESS AND ECONOMICS — Abstracting, Bibliographies, Statistics*

SEYCHELLES. PRESIDENT'S OFFICE. STATISTICS DIVISION. STATISTICAL ABSTRACT. see *BUSINESS AND ECONOMICS — Abstracting, Bibliographies, Statistics*

SEYCHELLES. PRESIDENT'S OFFICE. STATISTICS DIVISION. TOURISM. see *TRAVEL AND TOURISM — Abstracting, Bibliographies, Statistics*

310   HK
▼**SHANGHAI STATISTICAL YEARBOOK (YEAR).** (Text in English) 1990. a. HK.$50($10) Economic Information & Agency, 10 F Kuo Wah Bldg., 342 Hennessy Rd., Wanchai, Hong Kong. TEL 5738217. FAX 8388304.

310   CC
SHANGHAI TONGJI/SHANGHAI STATISTICS. (Text in Chinese) m. (Shanghai Shi Tongji-ju - Shanghai Municipal Bureau of Statistics) Shanghai Tongji Bianjibu, 1008 Dong Changzhi Road, Shanghai 200082, People's Republic of China. TEL 5458253. Ed. Yan Delun.

310   NE   ISSN 0254-7694
SHORT BOOK REVIEWS. (Text in English) 1980. 3/yr. $20. International Statistical Institute, Prinses Beatrixlaan 428, Postbus 950, 2270 AZ Voorburg, Netherlands. TEL 070-3375737. TELEX 32260 ISI NL. Ed. Dr. A.M. Herzberg. adv.; bk.rev.; circ. 4,300.
   Description: Provides a rapid book review service for statisticians covering books on statistics and related subjects published throughout the world.

316   SL
SIERRA LEONE. CENTRAL STATISTICS OFFICE. ANNUAL STATISTICAL DIGEST. 1969? a. Le.8. Central Statistics Office, Tower Hill, Freetown, Sierra Leone.

310   SL   ISSN 0080-9535
SIERRA LEONE IN FIGURES. a. free. Bank of Sierra Leone, P.O. Box 30, Freetown, Sierra Leone. TELEX 3232 FREETOWN.

SINGAPORE. DEPARTMENT OF STATISTICS. REPORT ON THE SURVEY OF SERVICES (YEAR). see *PUBLIC ADMINISTRATION — Abstracting, Bibliographies, Statistics*

SINGAPORE. DEPARTMENT OF STATISTICS. REPORT ON THE SURVEY OF WHOLESALE TRADE, RETAIL TRADE, RESTAURANTS & HOTELS (YEAR). see *HOTELS AND RESTAURANTS — Abstracting, Bibliographies, Statistics*

SINGAPORE MONTHLY TRADE STATISTICS: IMPORTS & EXPORTS. see *BUSINESS AND ECONOMICS — Abstracting, Bibliographies, Statistics*

315   SI   ISSN 0583-3655
HA1797.S5
SINGAPORE YEARBOOK OF STATISTICS. a. S.$13.40. Department of Statistics, 8 Shenton Way 10-01 Treasury Bldg., Singapore 0106, Singapore. TEL 3209702. FAX 3209689. TELEX RS-63001 STAT. charts.
   Description: Provides important data on the demographic, economic and social characteristics of Singapore.

STATISTICS

SOCIAL INDICATORS BY PREFECTURE (YEAR). see *SOCIAL SERVICES AND WELFARE — Abstracting, Bibliographies, Statistics*

SOCIAL TRENDS IN NEW ZEALAND. see *SOCIOLOGY — Abstracting, Bibliographies, Statistics*

310   FR
SOCIETE DE STATISTIQUE DE PARIS. JOURNAL; la revue internationale des statisticiens d'expression Francaise. 1859. q. 500 F. to individuals (foreign 600 F.); institutions 1,000 F.(foreign 1,200 F.). Societe de Statistiqtique de Paris, 18 bd. Pinard, 75675 Paris cedex 14, France. Ed. Philippe Tassi. bk.rev.; bibl.; charts; stat.; circ. 2,000. (also avail. in microfiche from BHP; reprint service avail. from KTO) **Indexed:** J.Cont.Quant.Meth., P.A.I.S.For.Lang.Ind.
     Former titles: Societe de Statistique de Paris et de France. Journal; Societe de Statistique de Paris. Journal (ISSN 0037-914X)

316   SO
SOMALIA IN FIGURES. triennial. free. Ministry of National Planning, Direction of Statistics, P.O. Box 1742, Mogadisho, Somalia.
     Description: Contains statistics on the population, livestock, agriculture, fishery, economy, transportation, education and health trends and conditions in Somalia.

310   JA   ISSN 0446-5849
SOMU-CHO. TOKEI-KYOKU KENKYU IHO/MANAGEMENT AND COORDINATION AGENCY. STATISTICS BUREAU. RESEARCH MEMOIR. (Text in Japanese; summaries in English) 1950. s-a. Somu-cho, Tokei-kyoku - Management and Coordination Agency, Statistics Bureau, 19-1, Wakamatsu-cho, Shinjuku-ku, Tokyo 160, Japan.

SOURCEBOOK OF CRIMINAL JUSTICE STATISTICS. see *CRIMINOLOGY AND LAW ENFORCEMENT — Abstracting, Bibliographies, Statistics*

SOUTH AFRICA. CENTRAL STATISTICAL SERVICE. BIRTHS - WHITES, COLOUREDS AND ASIANS. see *POPULATION STUDIES — Abstracting, Bibliographies, Statistics*

SOUTH AFRICA. CENTRAL STATISTICAL SERVICE. BUILDING PLANS PASSED AND BUILDINGS COMPLETED. see *BUILDING AND CONSTRUCTION — Abstracting, Bibliographies, Statistics*

316   SA
HA1991
SOUTH AFRICA. CENTRAL STATISTICAL SERVICE. BULLETIN OF STATISTICS. (Text in Afrikaans, English) 1967. q. R.8.75 per no. Central Statistical Service, Private Bag X44, Pretoria 0001, South Africa. TEL 012-310-8911. FAX 012-3108500. (Orders to: Government Printing Works, Private Bag X85, Pretoria 0001, South Africa) charts; mkt.; stat.; circ. 1,200.
     Former titles: South Africa. Department of Statistics. Bulletin of Statistics (ISSN 0034-5024); South Africa. Department of Statistics. Monthly Bulletin of Statistics.

SOUTH AFRICA. CENTRAL STATISTICAL SERVICE. CENSUS OF ELECTRICITY, GAS AND STEAM. see *ENERGY — Abstracting, Bibliographies, Statistics*

SOUTH AFRICA. CENTRAL STATISTICAL SERVICE. CENSUS OF MINING. see *MINES AND MINING INDUSTRY — Abstracting, Bibliographies, Statistics*

SOUTH AFRICA. CENTRAL STATISTICAL SERVICE. DEATHS OF BLACKS. see *POPULATION STUDIES — Abstracting, Bibliographies, Statistics*

SOUTH AFRICA. CENTRAL STATISTICAL SERVICE. LOCAL GOVERNMENT STATISTICS. see *PUBLIC ADMINISTRATION — Abstracting, Bibliographies, Statistics*

SOUTH AFRICA. CENTRAL STATISTICAL SERVICE. NEW VEHICLES REGISTERED. see *TRANSPORTATION — Abstracting, Bibliographies, Statistics*

SOUTH AFRICA. CENTRAL STATISTICAL SERVICE. REGISTERED VEHICLES AS AT 30 JUNE. see *TRANSPORTATION — Abstracting, Bibliographies, Statistics*

316   SA
SOUTH AFRICA. CENTRAL STATISTICAL SERVICE. STATISTICAL NEWS RELEASES. (Series of 135 news releases, P0002 - P9307) irreg. free. Central Statistical Service, Private Bag X44, Pretoria 0001, South Africa. TEL 012-310-8911. FAX 012-3108500.
     Formerly: South Africa. Department of Statistics. Statistical News Releases.

SOUTH AFRICA. CENTRAL STATISTICAL SERVICE. STATISTICAL NEWS RELEASE. RETAIL PRICES - ALL ITEMS. see *BUSINESS AND ECONOMICS — Abstracting, Bibliographies, Statistics*

SOUTH AFRICA. CENTRAL STATISTICAL SERVICE. STATISTICAL NEWS RELEASE. SURVEY OF HOUSES, SECTIONAL TITLE UNITS AND DOMESTIC WORKERS. see *HOUSING AND URBAN PLANNING — Abstracting, Bibliographies, Statistics*

SOUTH AFRICA. CENTRAL STATISTICAL SERVICE. STATISTICAL NEWS RELEASE. TRANSFERS OF RURAL IMMOVABLE PROPERTY. see *REAL ESTATE — Abstracting, Bibliographies, Statistics*

SOUTH AFRICA. CENTRAL STATISTICAL SERVICE. STATISTICS OF DEVELOPMENT BOARDS. see *PUBLIC ADMINISTRATION — Abstracting, Bibliographies, Statistics*

SOUTH AFRICA. CENTRAL STATISTICAL SERVICE. SURVEY OF THE ACCOUNTS OF COMPANIES.. see *BUSINESS AND ECONOMICS — Abstracting, Bibliographies, Statistics*

SOUTH AFRICA. CENTRAL STATISTICAL SERVICE. TOURISM AND MIGRATION. see *POPULATION STUDIES — Abstracting, Bibliographies, Statistics*

SOUTH AFRICA. DEPARTMENT OF AGRICULTURE AND FISHERIES. DIVISION OF ECONOMIC SERVICES. ABSTRACT OF AGRICULTURAL STATISTICS/KORTBEGRIP VAN LANDBOUSTATISTIEKE. see *AGRICULTURE — Abstracting, Bibliographies, Statistics*

310   SA
SOUTH AFRICA. DEPARTMENT OF HOME AFFAIRS. ANNUAL REPORT. a. price varies (typically set in Apr.). Department of Home Affairs, Private Bag X114, Pretoria 0001, South Africa. TEL 012-314-8911. FAX 012-3264571. TELEX 321358 SA. stat.; circ. 860.
     Incorporates: South Africa. Central Statistical Service and Government Printing Works & South Africa. Central Statistical Service. Annual Report; Formerly: South Africa. Department of Statistics. Annual Report of the Statistics Advisory Council and of the Secretary of Statistics.

SOUTH AFRICA. OFFICIAL YEARBOOK OF THE REPUBLIC OF SOUTH AFRICA. see *HISTORY — Abstracting, Bibliographies, Statistics*

316   SA   ISSN 0038-271X
QA276.A1   CODEN: SASSB5
SOUTH AFRICAN STATISTICAL JOURNAL/SUID-AFRIKAANSE STATISTIESE TYDSKRIF. (Text in Afrikaans, English; summaries in English) 1967. s-a. $50 (effective 1992). South African Statistical Association - Suid-Afrikaanse Statistiese Vereniging, P.O. Box 27321, Sunnyside 0132, South Africa. FAX 011-339-1697. Ed. J.S. Galpin. adv.; index; circ. 350. **Indexed:** ASCA, Biostat., Compumath, Ind.S.A.Per., J.Cont.Quant.Meth., Math.R., Oper.Res.Manage.Sci., Qual.Contr.Appl.Stat., SSCI, Stat.Theor.Meth.Abstr.
     —BLDSC shelfmark: 8346.450000.
     Description: Covers topics in theoretical mathematical statistics and applications.

316   SA   ISSN 0081-2544
HA1991
SOUTH AFRICAN STATISTICS. (Text in Afrikaans, English) 1968. biennial. latest 1990. R.25. Central Statistical Service, Private Bag X44, Pretoria 0001, South Africa. TEL 012-310-8911. FAX 012-3108500. (Orders to: Government Printing Works, Private Bag X85, Pretoria 0001, South Africa)
     Formerly (until 1966): South Africa. Department of Statistics. Statistical Year Book.

319   AT   ISSN 0085-6428
SOUTH AUSTRALIAN YEARBOOK. 1966. a. Aus.$29.50 (foreign Aus.$55). Australian Bureau of Statistics, South Australian Office, Box 2272, G.P.O., Adelaide, S.A. 5001, Australia. FAX 08-237-7566.

317.57   US
SOUTH CAROLINA STATISTICAL ABSTRACT. 1972. a. $20. Budget and Control Board, Division of Research & Statistical Services, Rembert C. Dennis Bldg., Rm. 425, 1000 Assembly St., Columbia, SC 29201. TEL 803-734-3788. FAX 803-734-3619. bk.rev.; stat.; circ. 1,400. (also avail. in microfiche)
     Description: Presents data on factors impacting on the state's social and economic development: manufacturing, wholesale and retail trade, construction, housing, business and industry employment, agriculture, banking and finance, income, education, tourism, and population.

SOUTH DAKOTA. STATE DEPARTMENT OF SOCIAL SERVICES. ANNUAL STATISTICAL REPORT. see *SOCIAL SERVICES AND WELFARE — Abstracting, Bibliographies, Statistics*

310   NL   ISSN 0377-2039
SOUTH PACIFIC COMMISSION. STATISTICAL BULLETIN. (Text in English and French) 1973. irreg., no.39, 1991. South Pacific Commission, B.P. D5, Noumea, Cedex, New Caledonia.
     —BLDSC shelfmark: 8447.971200.

SOUTH PACIFIC ECONOMIES: STATISTICAL SUMMARY. see *BUSINESS AND ECONOMICS — Abstracting, Bibliographies, Statistics*

SOUTH PACIFIC EPIDEMIOLOGICAL AND HEALTH INFORMATION SERVICE ANNUAL REPORT. see *PUBLIC HEALTH AND SAFETY — Abstracting, Bibliographies, Statistics*

SOVIET ARMED FORCES REVIEW ANNUAL. see *MILITARY*

314   SP   ISSN 0066-5177
SPAIN. INSTITUTO NACIONAL DE ESTADISTICA. ANUARIO ESTADISTICO: EDICION EXTENSA. 1912. a. Instituto Nacional de Estadistica, P de la Castellana, 183, 28071 Madrid, Spain.

314   SP
SPAIN. INSTITUTO NACIONAL DE ESTADISTICA. BOLETIN MENSUAL DE ESTADISTICA. 1918. m. Instituto Nacional de Estadistica, P. de la Castellana, 183, 28071 Madrid, Spain. charts; stat.; index; circ. 3,100. **Indexed:** P.A.I.S.For.Lang.Ind.
     Formerly: Spain. Instituto Nacional de Estadistica. Boletin de Estadistica (ISSN 0038-6391)

314   SP   ISSN 0014-1151
HA1   CODEN: ESTEA7
SPAIN. INSTITUTO NACIONAL DE ESTADISTICA. ESTADISTICA ESPANOLA. q. Instituto Nacional de Estadistica, P de la Castellana, 183, 28071 Madrid, Spain. bk.rev.; bibl.; charts; illus.; stat.; circ. 1,000. **Indexed:** Ind.SST.

314   SP   ISSN 0213-7410
SPAIN. INSTITUTO NACIONAL DE ESTADISTICA. INDICES DE PRECIOS DE CONSUMO. BOLETIN INFORMATIVO. 1971. q. Instituto Nacional de Estadistica, P de la Castellana, 183, 28071 Madrid, Spain.
     Formerly: Spain. Instituto Nacional de Estadistica. Indice del Coste de la Vida.

SPAIN. MINISTERIO DE AGRICULTURA, PESCA Y ALIMENTACION. BOLETIN MENSUAL DE PRECIOS. see *AGRICULTURE — Agricultural Economics*

310   SP
SPAIN. MINISTERIO DE ECONOMIA Y HACIENDA. MEMORIA ESTADISTICA. SEGUROS PRIVADOS. 1953. a. 9100 ptas. Ministerio de Economia y Hacienda, Direccion General de Seguros, Paseo de la Castellana 44, 28046 Madrid, Spain. TEL 91-575-48-00. FAX 91-431-44-35. circ. 500.

310   US   ISSN 0172-7397
SPRINGER SERIES IN STATISTICS. 1979. irreg. price varies. Springer-Verlag, 175 Fifth Ave., New York, NY 10010. TEL 212-460-1500. (Also Berlin, Heidelberg, Tokyo and Vienna) Ed.Bd. (reprint service avail. from ISI) **Indexed:** Math.R.

314 GW ISSN 0344-5550
HC287.H4
STAAT UND WIRTSCHAFT IN HESSEN. 1946. m. DM.35. Hessisches Statistisches Landesamt, Rheinstr. 35-37, 6200 Wiesbaden 1, Germany. TEL 0611-3680. FAX 0611-378324. bk.rev.; charts.
—BLDSC shelfmark: 8425.570000.
Description: Government publication including economic and vital statistics.

310 GW ISSN 0930-2034
STADT REMSCHEID STATISTISCHES JAHRBUCH. 1949. a. DM.25. Amt fuer Stadtentwicklung und Statistik, Hindenburgstr. 52-58, D-5630 Remscheid, Germany. Ed. Hoffmann. bk.rev.; circ. 450. (back issues avail.)

STATE AND LOCAL STATISTICS SOURCES. see *PUBLIC ADMINISTRATION*

310 IT ISSN 0039-0380
STATISTICA. 1941. q. L.12000. Cooperativa Libraria Universitaria, Piazza Verdi 2a, Bologna, Italy. Ed. P. Fortunati. adv.; bk.rev.; bibl.; index; circ. 2,500.
Indexed: J.Cont.Quant.Meth., Math.R., Popul.Ind.
—BLDSC shelfmark: 8447.350000.

314 NE ISSN 0039-0402
HA1
STATISTICA NEERLANDICA. (Text in English) 1952. q. fl.140 (foreign fl. 190)(effective 1992). Vereniging voor Statistiek - Netherlands Society for Statistics and Operations Research, Postbus 282, 1850 AG Heiloo, Netherlands. TEL 072-338311. FAX 072-333372. adv.; bk.rev.; stat.; index; circ. 1,300. (reprint service avail. from SWZ) **Indexed:** Biostat., Int.Abstr.Oper.Res., J.Cont.Quant.Meth., Key to Econ.Sci., Math.R., Oper.Res.Manage.Sci., Qual.Contr.Appl.Stat.
—BLDSC shelfmark: 8447.390000.

314 IC ISSN 1017-6683
STATISTICAL ABSTRACT OF ICELAND. 1930. irreg., latest 1991. $40. Hagstofa Islands - Statistical Bureau of Iceland, Skuggasund 3, IS-150 Reykjavik, Iceland. TEL 354-1-60-98-00. FAX 354-1-62-88-65. Ed. Hallgrimur Snorrason. circ. 2,500.

315 II ISSN 0081-4709
STATISTICAL ABSTRACT OF MAHARASHTRA STATE. (Text in English) a. Rs.20.50. Directorate of Economics and Statistics, D.D. Bldg., Old Custom House, Bombay 400023, India.

310 II ISSN 0081-4717
STATISTICAL ABSTRACT OF RAJASTHAN. (Text in English) 1958. a. Rs.65. Directorate of Economics and Statistics, Tilak Marg, Jaipur, Rajasthan, India.

319 CJ
STATISTICAL ABSTRACT OF THE CAYMAN ISLANDS. 1975. a. $20. Statistics Office, Government Administration Bldg., Grand Cayman, Cayman Islands, British W.I. TEL 809-94-9790. FAX 809-97544. TELEX 4260 CIGOVT.
Formerly: Statistical Abstract of the Government of the Cayman Islands.

315 CE
STATISTICAL ABSTRACT OF THE DEMOCRATIC SOCIALIST REPUBLIC OF SRI LANKA. (Text in English) 1949. irreg., latest 1989. Rs.203. Department of Census and Statistics, Ministry of Plan Implementation, P.O. Box 563, No. 6, Albert Crescent, Colombo 7, Sri Lanka. (Order from: Superintendent, Government Publications Bureau, Colombo, Sri Lanka) index; circ. 1,878.
Formerly: Statistical Abstract of Ceylon (ISSN 0081-4636)

317.3 US ISSN 0081-4741
HA202
STATISTICAL ABSTRACT OF THE UNITED STATES. 1878. a. price varies. U.S. Bureau of the Census, Data User Services Division, Washington, DC 20233. TEL 301-763-4100. (Dist. by: Supt. of Documents, Washington, DC 20402) (also avail. in microfiche; microfilm from UMI,BHP; reprint service avail. from UMI)
●Also available online. Vendor(s): CompuServe Consumer Information Service, DIALOG.
—BLDSC shelfmark: 8447.421000.

311 IE ISSN 0081-4776
STATISTICAL AND SOCIAL INQUIRY SOCIETY OF IRELAND. JOURNAL. 1846. a. £10. Statistical and Social Inquiry Society of Ireland, c/o Central Statistics Office, Ardee Rd., Rathmines, Dublin 6, Ireland. FAX 01-972360. Ed. William Keating. cum.index: 1847-1947, 1947-1979.; circ. 700.
Indexed: C.R.E.J., P.A.I.S., Rural Recreat.Tour.Abstr., World Agri.Econ.& Rural Sociol.Abstr.

310 TH ISSN 0858-1886
STATISTICAL BUDGET AND ACTIVITIES IN THAILAND. (Text in Thai) 1966. a. National Statistical Office, Statistical Techniques Division, Larn Luang Road, Bangkok Metropolis 10100, Thailand.
Description: List of statistical organizations and units under different ministries and departments having submitted their own budgets through the National Statistical Office each year.

315 II
STATISTICAL HANDBOOK OF TAMIL NADU. (Text in English) 1969. a. Rs.6. Director of Statistics, Madras 600006, India. (Subscr. to: Government Publication Depot, 166 Anna Rd., Madras 600002, India)

315 TH ISSN 0857-9466
STATISTICAL HANDBOOK OF THAILAND. (Text in English) 1964. a. price varies. National Statistical Office, Statistical Information Division, Larn Luang Rd., Bangkok 10100, Thailand. FAX 2813814. circ. 1,000.
—BLDSC shelfmark: 8448.522000.
Description: Area, geography, climate, population, public health and vital statistics, education, agriculture, forestry, mining, public finance and national income, money and banking.

310 PH
STATISTICAL HANDBOOK OF THE PHILIPPINES. (Text in English) a. $9. National Statistics Office, Ramon Magsaysay Blvd., P.O. Box 779, Manila, Philippines. FAX 610794.
Description: Reference book that contains all statistical information possible.

316.67 GH
STATISTICAL HANDBOOK OF THE REPUBLIC OF GHANA. a. NC.1.70. Information Services Department, Box 745, Accra, Ghana.

STATISTICAL INDICATOR REPORTS. see *BUSINESS AND ECONOMICS — Abstracting, Bibliographies, Statistics*

315 UN ISSN 0252-4457
STATISTICAL INDICATORS FOR ASIA AND THE PACIFIC. (Text in English) 1971. q. United Nations Economic and Social Commission for Asia and the Pacific (ESCAP), United Nations Bldg., Rajadamnern Ave., Bangkok 10200, Thailand. (Dist. by: United Nations Publications, Room DC2-0853, New York, NY 10017; or Distribution and Sales Section, Palais des Nations, CH-1211 Geneva 10, Switzerland) **Indexed:** IIS.
Former titles: Statistical Indicators in E S C A P Countries; Statistical Indicators in E C A F E Countries (ISSN 0049-2175)

310 AF
STATISTICAL INFORMATION OF AFGHANISTAN/MA'LUMAT-I IHSA'IVI-I AFGHANISTAN. (Text in Persian or Pushto) no. 3, 1975. irreg. Central Statistical Office, Nader Shah Minah, Block No. 4, Box 2002, Kabul, Afghanistan. stat.

STATISTICAL INSTITUTE OF JAMAICA. DEMOGRAPHIC STATISTICS. see *POPULATION STUDIES — Abstracting, Bibliographies, Statistics*

STATISTICAL INSTITUTE OF JAMAICA. MONETARY STATISTICS REPORT. see *BUSINESS AND ECONOMICS — Abstracting, Bibliographies, Statistics*

STATISTICAL INSTITUTE OF JAMAICA. NATIONAL INCOME AND PRODUCT. see *BUSINESS AND ECONOMICS — Abstracting, Bibliographies, Statistics*

319 JM
STATISTICAL INSTITUTE OF JAMAICA. POCKETBOOK OF STATISTICS. 1978. a. Jam.$11. Statistical Institute of Jamaica, 9 Swallowfield Rd., Kingston 5, Jamaica, W.I.
Formerly: Jamaica. Department of Statistics. Pocketbook of Statistics.

317 JM
STATISTICAL INSTITUTE OF JAMAICA. STATISTICAL ABSTRACT. 1972. a. (published 9 months after year to which it relates). Jam.$21. Statistical Institute of Jamaica, 9 Swallowfield Rd, Kingston 5, Jamaica, W.I. circ. 1,000.
Former titles: Jamaica. Department of Statistics. Statistical Abstract; Jamaica. Department of Statistics. Annual Abstract of Statistics (ISSN 0075-2983)

319 JM
STATISTICAL INSTITUTE OF JAMAICA. STATISTICAL REVIEW. m. Jam.$16.50 per no. Statistical Institute of Jamaica, 9 Swallowfield Rd., Kingston 5, Jamaica, W.I.
Formerly: Jamaica. Department of Statistics. Statistical Review.

315 IS
STATISTICAL MONTHLY OF ISRAEL. (Text in English and Hebrew) 1950. m. Central Bureau of Statistics, P.O. Box 13015, Jerusalem 91 130, Israel. TEL 02-21 12 11. (back issues avail.) **Indexed:** Ind.Heb.Per.

310 JA ISSN 0561-922X
STATISTICAL NOTES OF JAPAN. (Text in English) 1953. irreg., no.45, 1991. free. International Statistical Affairs Division, Statistical Standards Department, Statistics Bureau, Management and Coordination Agency, 19-1 Wakamatsu-cho, Shinjuku-ku, Tokyo, Japan. FAX 81-3-5273-1181. circ. 550 (controlled).

314 EI ISSN 0254-0649
HC241.2
STATISTICAL OFFICE OF THE EUROPEAN COMMUNITIES. INDUSTRIAL PRODUCTION. q. $56. Statistical Office of the European Communities, L-2985 Luxembourg, Luxembourg. (Subscr. in U.S. to: Unipub, 4611-F Assembly Dr., Lanham, MD 20706-4391)
—BLDSC shelfmark: 4459.697000.

310 GW ISSN 0932-5026
HA15 CODEN: STPAE4
STATISTICAL PAPERS/STATISTISCHE HEFTE. (Text in English and German) 1960. 4/yr. DM.178($94) Springer-Verlag, Heidelberger Platz 3, D-1000 Berlin 33, Germany. TEL 030-8207-1. (Also Heidelberg, Tokyo, Vienna, and New York) Ed. G. Bamberg. adv.; bk.rev.; charts; illus.; circ. 800. (also avail. in microform from UMI; reprint service avail. from ISI,SCH) **Indexed:** J.Cont.Quant.Meth., Math.R., P.A.I.S.For.Lang.Ind.
Formerly (until 1988): Statistische Hefte (ISSN 0039-0631)
Description: Forum for the presentation and critical assessment of statistical methods, particularly for discussion of their methodological foundations and potential applications.

315 II ISSN 0081-5012
STATISTICAL POCKET BOOK: INDIA. (Text in English) 1956. a. Rs.45($15.50) Central Statistical Organization, Sardar Patel Bhavan, Sansad Marg, New Delhi 110001, India.
Formerly: Statistical Pocket Book of the Indian Union.

315.8 AF
STATISTICAL POCKET-BOOK OF AFGHANISTAN. 1972. irreg. Department of Statistics, Kabul, Afghanistan. illus.

315 CE
STATISTICAL POCKET BOOK OF THE DEMOCRATIC SOCIALIST REPUBLIC OF SRI LANKA. (Editions in English, Sinhalese, Tamil) 1966. a. Rs.49 for English ed.; Rs. 53 for Sinhalese, Tamil eds. Department of Census and Statistics, Ministry of Plan Implementation, Box 563, Colombo 7, Sri Lanka. (Dist. by: Superintendent, Government Publications Bureau, Colombo, Sri Lanka) circ. 3,450. (back issues avail.)
Former titles: Statistical Pocket Book of Sri Lanka; Statistical Pocket Book of Ceylon (ISSN 0585-1777)

319 TU
STATISTICAL POCKET BOOK OF TURKEY/TURKIYE ISTATISTIK CEP YILLIGI. (Text in English, Turkish) 1938. biennial. State Institute of Statistics - Devlet Istatistik Enstitusu, Necatibey Caddesi 114, Ankara, Turkey.

STATISTICS

310 YU ISSN 0585-1815
STATISTICAL POCKET-BOOK OF YUGOSLAVIA. (Text in English) 1955. a. Savezni Zavod za Statistiku - Federal Statistical Office, Kneza Milosa 20, Belgrade, Yugoslavia.

310 BG
STATISTICAL POCKETBOOK OF BANGLADESH. (Text in English) 1978. a. Tk.60($14) Bureau of Statistics, Secretariat, Dhaka 2, Bangladesh. charts; stat.; circ. 5,000.
   Description: Information on Bangladesh's statistics for population, agriculture, industry and banking.

315.98 IO ISSN 0126-3595
STATISTICAL POCKETBOOK OF INDONESIA/BUKU SAKU STATISTIK INDONESIA. (Subseries of its Statistik Tahunan) (Text in English and Indonesian) 1940. a. Rps.7500($5) Central Bureau of Statistics - Biro Pusat Statistik, Jalan Dr. Sutomo 8, Box 3, Jakarta Pusat, Indonesia. TEL 21-372808. circ. 1,500.
   Supersedes: Statistik Indonesia.

317 US
STATISTICAL PROFILE OF IOWA. a. free. Iowa Department of Economic Development, 200 E. Grand Ave., Des Moines, IA 50309. TEL 515-242-4878. index.
   Description: Details on Iowa's business community.

310 011 US ISSN 0278-694X
Z7554.U5
STATISTICAL REFERENCE INDEX. 1980. m. (with q. and a. cumulations). price varies. Congressional Information Service, 4520 East-West Hwy., Bethesda, MD 20814-3389. TEL 301-654-1550. FAX 301-654-4033. TELEX 292386 CIS UR. Ed. Lynn K. Marble. abstr.; stat.; index, cum.index: 1980-85, 1986-89. (back issues avail.)
   ●Also available on CD-ROM.
   Description: Indexes and abstracts statistics contained in publications from more than 1,000 leading American sources.

319 IR ISSN 1010-9617
HA4570.2
STATISTICAL REFLECTION OF THE ISLAMIC REPUBLIC OF IRAN. Arabic edition: Iran al-Islam fi Mir'a al-Ihsa' (ISSN 1010-9625); Farsi edition: Iran Dar A'inah-i Amar (ISSN 1010-9633) (Text in English) 1981. a. Statistical Centre of Iran, Dr. Fatemi Ave., Tehran 14144, Iran. TEL 655061. FAX 653451. TELEX 213233 AMAR IR. charts stat.

STATISTICAL REPORT ON VISITOR ARRIVALS TO INDONESIA. see TRAVEL AND TOURISM — Abstracting, Bibliographies, Statistics

STATISTICAL REVIEW OF GOVERNMENT IN UTAH. see PUBLIC ADMINISTRATION — Abstracting, Bibliographies, Statistics

310 US ISSN 0883-4237
QA276.A1 CODEN: STSCEP
STATISTICAL SCIENCE; a review journal. 1986. q. $75. Institute of Mathematical Statistics, 3401 Investment Blvd., Ste. 7, Hayward, CA 94545. TEL 510-783-8141. Ed. Robert E. Kass. bk.rev.; circ. 3,500. (also avail. in microform from UMI) Indexed: Biostat., Oper.Res.Manage.Sci., Qual.Contr.Appl.Stat.
   —BLDSC shelfmark: 8448.953000.
   Refereed Serial

310 AT ISSN 0314-6820
STATISTICAL SOCIETY OF AUSTRALIA. NEWSLETTER. 4/yr. Aus.$8($10) (Statistical Society of Australia) Australian Statistical Publishing Association, Inc., G.P.O. Box 573, Canberra, A.C.T. 2601, Australia.

310 016 NE ISSN 0039-0518
HA1
STATISTICAL THEORY AND METHOD ABSTRACTS. 1959. 4/yr. $145. International Statistical Institute, Prinses Beatrixlaan 428, Postbus 950, 2270 AZ Voorburg, Netherlands. TEL 070-3375737. TELEX 32260 ISI NL. Eds. C. van Eeden, J.L. Mynheer. adv.; abstr.; index; circ. 1,400. (reprint service avail. from KTO)
   Indexed: Hort.Abstr., Math.R.
   Formerly: International Journal of Abstracts.
   Description: Provides international coverage of published articles on mathematical statistics and probability; contains almost 4,000 abstracts.

300.8 UN ISSN 0252-3655
STATISTICAL YEARBOOK FOR ASIA AND THE PACIFIC/ANNUAIRE STATISTIQUE POUR L'ASIE ET LE PACIFIQUE. (Text in English and French) 1968. a. price varies. United Nations Economic and Social Commission for Asia and the Pacific (ESCAP), United Nations Bldg., Rajadamnern Ave., Bangkok 10200, Thailand. (Dist. by: United Nations Publications, Room DC2-0853, New York, NY 10017; or Distribution and Sales Section, Palais des Nations, CH-1211 Geneva 10, Switzerland) Indexed: IIS.
   —BLDSC shelfmark: 8452.832000.
   Formerly: Statistical Yearbook for Asia and the Far East (ISSN 0085-6711)

315 BG ISSN 0302-2374
STATISTICAL YEARBOOK OF BANGLADESH. (Text in English) 1964. a. Tk.200($40) Bureau of Statistics, Secretariat, Dhaka 2, Bangladesh.
   Formerly: Statistical Digest of Bangladesh.
   Description: Data on population, agriculture, industry, foreign trade and banking in Bangladesh.

314 GR ISSN 0081-5071
STATISTICAL YEARBOOK OF GREECE. (Text in English and Greek) a. $20. National Statistical Service of Greece, Statistical Information and Publications Division, 14-16 Lycourgou St., 10166 Athens, Greece. TEL 3244-748. FAX 3222205. TELEX 216734 ESYE GR.

319 IR
STATISTICAL YEARBOOK OF IRAN. (Text in Farsi) 1967. a. Statistical Centre of Iran, Dr. Fatemi Ave., Teheran 14144, Iran. TEL 655061. FAX 653451. TELEX 213233 AMAR IR. charts; illus.; stat.

317.292 JM
STATISTICAL YEARBOOK OF JAMAICA. 1973. a. Jam.$72. Statistical Institute of Jamaica, 9 Swallowfield Rd, Kingston 5, Jamaica, W.I. illus.

310 LH
STATISTICAL YEARBOOK OF LIECHTENSTEIN/STATISTISCHES JAHRBUCH FUERSTENTUM LIECHTENSTEIN. 1977. a. free. Office of National Economy of the Principality of Liechtenstein, Vaduz FL-9490, Liechtenstein. FAX 41-75-66289. Ed.Bd. circ. 1,200. (back issues avail.)

315 TH ISSN 0857-9067
STATISTICAL YEARBOOK OF THAILAND. (Text in English and Thai) 1909. a. price varies. National Statistical Office, Statistical Information Division, Larn Luang Rd., Bangkok, Thailand. FAX 2813814. circ. 1,000.
   Description: Information on the geography, climate, population, public health and vital statistics of Thailand.

STATISTICAL YEARBOOK OF THE REPUBLIC OF CHINA. see BUSINESS AND ECONOMICS — Abstracting, Bibliographies, Statistics

314 BU
STATISTICHESKI GODISHNIK NA NARODNA REPUBLIKA BULGARIA. 1909. a. 7.28 lv. (Ministerstvo na Informatsiiata i Suobshteniiata, Komitet za Socialna Informacia v N.R. Bulgaria) Foreign Trade Co. "Hemus", 7 Levsky St., 1000 Sofia, Bulgaria. stat.; circ. 2,000.

311 UK ISSN 0039-0526
HA1 CODEN: STTNAP
THE STATISTICIAN. 1950. 5/yr. $128 to individuals; institutions $317. (Institute of Statisticians) Carfax Publishing Co., P.O. Box 25, Abingdon, Oxfordshire OX14 3UE, England. TEL 0235-555335. FAX 0235-553559. (U.S. subscr. addr.: Carfax Publishing Co., Box 2025, Dunnellon, FL 32630) Ed. Dr. A.P. Haws. adv.; bk.rev.; charts. (also avail. in microfiche; back issues avail.) Indexed: ASCA, Biostat., Compumath, Cont.Pg.Manage., Curr.Cont., Excerp.Med., J.Cont.Quant.Meth., Oper.Res.Manage.Sci., P.A.I.S., Qual.Contr.Appl.Stat., Sci.Abstr., SSCI.
   —BLDSC shelfmark: 8453.200000.

310 YU ISSN 0585-1920
HA1631 CODEN: SGJUEB
STATISTICKI GODISNJAK JUGOSLAVIJE. 1954. a. Savezni Zavod za Statistiku, Kneza Milosa 20, Belgrade, Yugoslavia.
   —BLDSC shelfmark: 8453.455000.

310 YU ISSN 0352-3349
STATISTICKI KALENDAR JUGOSLAVIJE. 1955. a. Savezni Zavod za Statistiku, Savremena Administracija, Kneza Milosa 20, Belgrade, Yugoslavia.

314.97 BN ISSN 0039-0542
STATISTICKI PREGLED SOCIJALISTICKE REPUBLIKE BOSNE I HERCEGOVINE. (Text in Serbo-Croatian) 1953. m. $10.45. Republicki Zavod za Statistiku, Jugoslavenske Narodne Armije 54, Sarajevo, Bosnia Hercegovina. Ed. Nedjo Kovacevic.

310 001.6 UK ISSN 0960-3174
QA276.4
STATISTICS AND COMPUTING. q. Chapman & Hall, 2-6 Boundary Row, London SE1 8HN, England. TEL 071-865-0066. FAX 071-522-9623. (Dist. by: International Thomson Publishing Services, Ltd., N. Way, Andover, Hampshire SP10 5BE, England. TEL 0264-33-2424; US addr.: Chapman & Hall, 29 W. 35th St., New York, NY 10001-2291. TEL 212-244-3336) Ed. David J. Hand. bk.rev.
   —BLDSC shelfmark: 8453.516500.
   Description: Covers the entire range of interaction between statistics and computing.
   Refereed Serial

310 NE ISSN 0167-7152
QA276.A1
STATISTICS & PROBABILITY LETTERS. (Text in English) 1982. 15/yr.(in 3 vols.; 6 nos./vol.) fl.939 (effective 1992). North-Holland (Subsidiary of: Elsevier Science Publishers B.V.), P.O. Box 211, 1000 AE Amsterdam, Netherlands. TEL 020-5803911. FAX 020-5803598. TELEX 18582 ESPA NL. (Subscr. in U.S. and Canada to: Elsevier Science Publishing Co., Inc., Box 882, Madison Sq. Sta., New York, NY 10159. TEL 212-989-5800) Ed. Richard A. Johnson. (back issues avail.) Indexed: ASCA, Compumath, J.Cont.Quant.Meth., Math.R.
   —BLDSC shelfmark: 8453.518000.
   Description: Covers all fields of statistics and probability, and provides an outlet for rapid publication of short communications in the field.
   Refereed Serial

STATISTICS FOR IRON AND STEEL INDUSTRY IN INDIA. see METALLURGY — Abstracting, Bibliographies, Statistics

STATISTICS IN MEDICINE. see MEDICAL SCIENCES — Abstracting, Bibliographies, Statistics

STATISTICS OF JAPANESE NON-LIFE INSURANCE BUSINESS. see INSURANCE — Abstracting, Bibliographies, Statistics

STATISTICS OF LIFE INSURANCE BUSINESS IN JAPAN. see INSURANCE — Abstracting, Bibliographies, Statistics

STATISTICS OF ROAD TRAFFIC ACCIDENTS IN JAPAN. see TRANSPORTATION — Abstracting, Bibliographies, Statistics

STATISTICS OF SOUTHERN COLLEGE AND UNIVERSITY LIBRARIES. see LIBRARY AND INFORMATION SCIENCES — Abstracting, Bibliographies, Statistics

STATISTICS OF THE MISUSE OF DRUGS IN THE UNITED KINGDOM: SEIZURES AND OFFENDERS DEALT WITH. see MEDICAL SCIENCES — Abstracting, Bibliographies, Statistics

STATISTICS OF WORLD TRADE IN STEEL. see METALLURGY — Abstracting, Bibliographies, Statistics

STATISTICS ON WORLD TRADE IN ENGINEERING PRODUCTS. BULLETIN. see METALLURGY — Abstracting, Bibliographies, Statistics

STATISTICS RELATING TO REGIONAL AND MUNICIPAL GOVERNMENTS IN BRITISH COLUMBIA. see PUBLIC ADMINISTRATION — Abstracting, Bibliographies, Statistics

310 016   US   ISSN 0585-198X
Z7551
STATISTICS SOURCES; a subject guide to data on industrial, business, social, educational, financial and other topics for the U.S. and selected foreign countries. 1960. irreg., 14th ed., 1990. $335 for set. Gale Research Inc., 835 Penobscot Bldg., Detroit, MI 48226. TEL 313-961-2242. FAX 313-961-6083. TELEX 810-221-7086. Eds. Jacqueline Wasserman O'Brien, Steven R. Wasserman.
Description: Irregularly updated guide to statistics data.

314   SW   ISSN 1100-9381
STATISTICS SWEDEN. QUARTERLY FOREIGN TRADE STATISTICS S I T C. (Contents page and summaries in English) 1954. q. SEK 500. Statistiska Centralbyraan, Distribution, S-701 89 Oerebro, Sweden. circ. 1,250.
Formerly (until 1990): Sweden. Statistiska Centralbyraan. Utrikeshandel. Maanadsstatistik (ISSN 0039-7288)

310   US
STATISTICS: TEXTBOOKS AND MONOGRAPHS SERIES. 1972. irreg., vol.126, 1992. price varies. Marcel Dekker, Inc., 270 Madison Ave., New York, NY 10016. TEL 212-696-9000. FAX 212-685-4540. TELEX 421419.

310   DK   ISSN 0106-2344
STATISTIK FOR HOVEDSTADSREGIONEN/STATISTICAL YEARBOOK FOR THE COPENHAGEN REGION. (Text in Danish and English) 1977. a. DKK 150. Hovedstadsregionens Statistikkontor, Gl. Koegelandevej 3, DK-2500 Valby, Denmark. TEL 45-36-44-29-29. FAX 45-36-44-11-44. Ed. P.J. Nielsen. illus.; circ. 2,500 (controlled).

STATISTIQUES FINANCIERES DES INSTITUTIONS DE DEPOT. see BUSINESS AND ECONOMICS — Abstracting, Bibliographies, Statistics

314.92   NE
STATISTISCH OVERZICHT HILVERSUM. 1954. s-a. fl.30. Bureau voor Onderzoek en Statistiek, Koninginneweg 5, Hilversum, Netherlands. Ed. R.W. de Jong. charts; circ. 250.
Former titles: Statistisch Jaaroverzicht Hilversum; Statistisch Kwartaaloverzicht Hilversum (ISSN 0028-291X); Incorporates: Population Statistics Hilversum (ISSN 0032-4736)

STATISTISCHE MONATSHEFTE SCHLESWIG-HOLSTEIN. see PUBLIC ADMINISTRATION — Abstracting, Bibliographies, Statistics

310   GW
STATISTISCHE RUNDSCHAU NORDRHEIN-WESTFALEN. 1949. m. DM.48. Landesamt fuer Datenverarbeitung und Statistik Nordrhein-Westfalen, Mauerstr. 51, Postfach 101105, 4000 Duesseldorf 1, Germany. TEL 0211-9449-01. circ. 720. (back issues avail.)

STATISTISCHE STUDIEN. see BUSINESS AND ECONOMICS — Abstracting, Bibliographies, Statistics

STATISTISCHER BERICHT DER STADT FRANKENTHAL. see PUBLIC ADMINISTRATION — Abstracting, Bibliographies, Statistics

STATISTISCHER VIERTELJAHRESBERICHT HANNOVER. see PUBLIC ADMINISTRATION — Abstracting, Bibliographies, Statistics

314   AU   ISSN 0081-5314
STATISTISCHES HANDBUCH FUER DIE REPUBLIK OESTERREICH. 1882. a. $69. (Oesterreichisches Statistisches Zentralamt) Oesterreichische Staatsdruckerei, Vienna, Austria. TEL 0222-787631. adv.; circ. 2,700.

314   GW   ISSN 0081-5322
STATISTISCHES JAHRBUCH BERLIN. 1945. a. DM.55. (Statistisches Landesamt) Kulturbuch Verlag GmbH, Passauerstr. 4, 1000 Berlin 30, Germany. TEL 213-6071. FAX 213-4449. (back issues avail.)
Supersedes: Berlin in Zahlen.

314   GW
STATISTISCHES JAHRBUCH DER D D R. 1956. a. DM.65. (Staatliche Zentralverwaltung fuer Statistik) Staatsverlag der DDR, Otto-Grotewohl-Str. 17, 1086 Berlin, Germany. stat.

314   SZ   ISSN 0081-5330
STATISTISCHES JAHRBUCH DER SCHWEIZ/ANNUAIRE STATISTIQUE DE LA SUISSE. 1891. a. price varies. (Statistisches Amt) Neue Zuercher Zeitung, Postfach, CH-8021 Zurich, Switzerland. TEL 01-2581505.
—BLDSC shelfmark: 1073.490500.

314   GW
STATISTISCHES JAHRBUCH DER STADT AUGSBURG. 1953. irreg. DM.28. Amt fuer Stadtentwicklung und Statistik, Schmiedberg 6, 8900 Augsburg 22, Germany. circ. 400.

STATISTISCHES JAHRBUCH DER STADT KOELN. see PUBLIC ADMINISTRATION — Abstracting, Bibliographies, Statistics

310   AU
STATISTISCHES JAHRBUCH DER STADT WIEN. 1883. a. S.400. Statistisches Amt der Stadt Wien, Volksgartenstr. 3, A-1016 Vienna, Austria. TEL 4000-88611. FAX 4000-9997910. (Subscr. to: Jugend und Volk Verlagsgesellschaft m.b.H., Tiefer Graben 7-9, A-1010 Vienna, Austria) adv.; charts; index; circ. 800. (back issues avail.)
Description: Statistical data on the city of Vienna, including statistics of city districts and suburban areas.

STATISTISCHES JAHRBUCH DEUTSCHER GEMEINDEN. see PUBLIC ADMINISTRATION — Abstracting, Bibliographies, Statistics

310   GW   ISSN 0077-2062
STATISTISCHES JAHRBUCH MUENCHEN. 1969. a. DM.25. Amt fuer Statistik und Datenanalyse, Tal 30, D-8000 Munich 2, Germany. Ed. Egon Dheus.

310   GW
STATISTISCHES LANDESAMT HAMBURG. DATEN UND INFORMATIONEN FALTBLATT. 1977. a. free. Statistisches Landesamt Hamburg, Steckelhorn 12, 2000 Hamburg 11, Germany. TEL 040-3681-0. FAX 040-36811700. TELEX 212121-SENATD. circ. 60,000.

314   GW   ISSN 0433-6844
HA1248.A2
STATISTISCHES TASCHENBUCH DER D D R. (Editions in Arabic, English, French, German, Russian, and Spanish) a. DM.6.50. (Staatliche Zentralverwaltung fuer Statistik) Staatsverlag der DDR, Otto-Grotewohl-Str. 17, 1086 Berlin, Germany.

310   AU
STATISTISCHES TASCHENBUCH DER STADT WIEN. 1884. a. S.70. Statistisches Amt der Stadt Wien, Volksgartenstr. 3, A-1016 Vienna, Austria. TEL 4000-88611. FAX 4000-9997910. (Subscr.to: Jugend und Volk Verlagsgesellschaft m.b.H., Tiefer Graben 7-9, A-1010 Vienna, Austria) adv.; charts; stat.; index; circ. 1,500. (back issues avail.)

310   SW   ISSN 0081-5381
HA1523
STATISTISK AARSBOK FOER SVERIGE/ABSTRACT OF SWEDISH STATISTICS. 1914. a. SEK 410. Statistiska Centralbyraan, Publishing Unit, S-701 89 Oerebro, Sweden. circ. 12,300.

STATISTISK TIAARS-OVERSIGT FOR KOEBENHAVNS KOMMUNE. see PUBLIC ADMINISTRATION — Abstracting, Bibliographies, Statistics

STATS - MONTHLY STATISTICAL AND MARKETING DIGEST. see BUSINESS AND ECONOMICS — Abstracting, Bibliographies, Statistics

314   AU   ISSN 0039-1093
HA1188.S8
STEIRISCHE STATISTIKEN. 1957. q. S.120. Amt der Steiermaerkischen Landesregierung, Praesidialabteilung - Referat Statistik, Burgring 4, A-8010 Graz, Austria. FAX 877-2339. TELEX 311838-LGRGZ-A. Ed. Ernst Burger. charts; stat.; index; circ. 500. (tabloid format)

310   GW
STOCHASTIK IN DER SCHULE. 1981. 3/yr. DM.20. Verein zur Foerderung des Schulischen Statistikunterrichts e.V., Kammannstr. 13, 5800 Hagen 1, Germany. Ed.Bd. adv.; bk.rev.; bibl.; cum.index: 1979-1989. (back issues avail.)
Refereed Serial

STUDIES IN BAYESIAN ECONOMETRICS AND STATISTICS. see BUSINESS AND ECONOMICS — Economic Systems And Theories, Economic History

STUDIES IN PSEPHOLOGY. see POPULATION STUDIES — Abstracting, Bibliographies, Statistics

SUDAN. DEPARTMENT OF STATISTICS. FOREIGN TRADE STATISTICS. see BUSINESS AND ECONOMICS — Abstracting, Bibliographies, Statistics

310   SJ
SUDAN. DEPARTMENT OF STATISTICS. STATISTICAL YEARBOOK. (Text in English) 1973. a. Department of Statistics, Box 700, Khartoum, Sudan.

SUMMARY OF RATE SCHEDULES OF NATURAL GAS PIPELINE COMPANIES. see ENERGY — Abstracting, Bibliographies, Statistics

314   FI   ISSN 0081-5063
SUOMEN TILASTOLLINEN VUOSIKIRJA/STATISTISK AARSBOK FOER FINLAND/STATISTICAL YEARBOOK OF FINLAND. (Text in English, Finnish, Swedish) 1879. a. Fmk.245. Tilastokeskus, Annankatu 44, SF-00100 Helsinki 10, Finland. (Subscr. to: Central Statistics Office of Finland, Box 504, SF-00100 Helsinki, Finland) circ. 5,000.
—BLDSC shelfmark: 8452.850000.

318   SR
SURINAME. ALGEMEEN BUREAU VOOR DE STATISTIEK. NATIONALE REKENINGEN. (Subseries of: Suriname in Cijfers) irreg. Algemeen Bureau voor de Statistiek, Paramaribo, Surinam.

317   CN   ISSN 0714-0045
HA31.2
SURVEY METHODOLOGY. 1975. s-a. Can.$30($36) (foreign $42). Statistics Canada, Publications Division, Ottawa, Ont. K1A 0T6, Canada. TEL 613-951-7277. FAX 613-951-1584. **Indexed**: Oper.Res.Manage.Sci., Qual.Contr.Appl.Stat.
—BLDSC shelfmark: 8550.560000.
Description: Presents articles dealing with various aspects of statistical development relevant to a statistical agency and evaluation of specific methodologies as applied to actual data collection or the data themselves.

SURVEY OF HOUSEHOLD ECONOMIC ACTIVITIES (YEAR). see BUSINESS AND ECONOMICS — Economic Situation And Conditions

SURVEY OF OPERATING PERFORMANCE FOR MUSIC DEALERS. see MUSIC

SURVEY ON GRADUATING STUDENTS ABROAD. see EDUCATION — Abstracting, Bibliographies, Statistics

316   SQ   ISSN 0586-1357
SWAZILAND. CENTRAL STATISTICAL OFFICE. ANNUAL STATISTICAL BULLETIN. 1966. a. E.2. Central Statistical Office, Box 456, Mbabane, Swaziland. illus.; circ. 800.

316   SQ
SWAZILAND. CENTRAL STATISTICAL OFFICE. ANNUAL SURVEY OF SWAZI NATION LAND. 1972. a., latest 1982. free. Central Statistical Office, Box 456, Mbabane, Swaziland. stat.; circ. 500.

SWAZILAND. CENTRAL STATISTICAL OFFICE. CENSUS OF INDUSTRIES. see BUSINESS AND ECONOMICS — Abstracting, Bibliographies, Statistics

SWAZILAND. CENTRAL STATISTICAL OFFICE. EDUCATION STATISTICS. see EDUCATION — Abstracting, Bibliographies, Statistics

SWAZILAND. CENTRAL STATISTICAL OFFICE. TIMBER STATISTICS. see FORESTS AND FORESTRY — Abstracting, Bibliographies, Statistics

SWEDEN. LUFTFARTSVERKET. AARSBOK. see TRANSPORTATION — Abstracting, Bibliographies, Statistics

SWEDEN. LUFTFARTSVERKET. CHARTERSTATISTIK. see TRANSPORTATION — Abstracting, Bibliographies, Statistics

SWEDEN. LUFTFARTSVERKET. FLYGPLATSSTATISTIK. see TRANSPORTATION — Abstracting, Bibliographies, Statistics

STATISTICS

314 SW ISSN 0039-7253
HA1523
SWEDEN. STATISTISKA CENTRALBYRAAN. ALLMAAN MAANADSSTATISTIK/MONTHLY DIGEST OF SWEDISH STATISTICS. (Contents page and summaries in English) 1963. m. SEK 500. Statistiska Centralbyraan, Distribution, S-701 89 Oerebro, Sweden. circ. 4,000.

309 SW ISSN 0347-7193
SWEDEN. STATISTISKA CENTRALBYRAAN. LEVNADSFOERHAALLANDEN. RAPPORT. (Text in English, Swedish) 1975. irreg. Statistiska Centralbyraan, Distribution, S-701 89 Oerebro, Sweden. illus.
Formerly: Sweden. Statistiska Centralbyraan. Living Conditions Reports.

314 SW ISSN 0082-0229
SWEDEN. STATISTISKA CENTRALBYRAAN. MEDDELANDEN I SAMORDNINGSFRAAGOR/REPORTS ON STATISTICAL CO-ORDINATION. 1966. irreg. price varies. Statistiska Centralbyraan, Publishing Unit, S-701 89 Oerebro, Sweden.

SWEDEN. STATISTISKA CENTRALBYRAAN. STATISTISKA MEDDELANDEN. SUBGROUP BO (HOUSING AND CONSTRUCTION). see *BUILDING AND CONSTRUCTION — Abstracting, Bibliographies, Statistics*

314 SW ISSN 0082-0350
SWEDEN. STATISTISKA CENTRALBYRAAN. URVAL SKRIFTSERIES - SELECTION SERIES. (Text in Swedish; summaries in English) 1969. irreg. price varies. Statistiska Centralbyraan, Publishing Unit, S-701 89 Oerebro, Sweden. circ. 750.

314 SW ISSN 0039-727X
SWEDEN. STATISTISKA CENTRALBYRAAN. UTRIKESHANDEL. KVARTALSSTATISTIK. (Contents page and summaries in English) 1961. q. SEK 950. Statistiska Centralbyraan, Distribution, S-701 89 Oerebro, Sweden. circ. 1,400.

SWITZERLAND. BUNDESAMT FUER STATISTIK. BILANZ DER WOHNBEVOLKERUNG IN DEN GEMEINDEN DER SCHWEIZ - BILAN DEMOGRAPHIQUE DES COMMUNES SUISSES. see *POPULATION STUDIES — Abstracting, Bibliographies, Statistics*

SWITZERLAND. BUNDESAMT FUER STATISTIK. SCHUELERINNEN, SCHUELER UND STUDIERENDE - ELEVES ET ETUDIANTS. see *EDUCATION — Abstracting, Bibliographies, Statistics*

SWITZERLAND. DIRECTORATE GENERAL OF CUSTOMS. ANNUAL REPORT. see *BUSINESS AND ECONOMICS — Abstracting, Bibliographies, Statistics*

SWITZERLAND. DIRECTORATE GENERAL OF CUSTOMS. ANNUAL STATISTICS. see *BUSINESS AND ECONOMICS — Abstracting, Bibliographies, Statistics*

SWITZERLAND. DIRECTORATE GENERAL OF CUSTOMS. MONTHLY STATISTICS. see *BUSINESS AND ECONOMICS — Abstracting, Bibliographies, Statistics*

315 SY ISSN 0081-4725
SYRIA. CENTRAL BUREAU OF STATISTICS. STATISTICAL ABSTRACT. (Text in Arabic, English) 1948. a. $75. Central Bureau of Statistics, Damascus, Syria.
Description: Various current statistics of different sectors.

310 II ISSN 0082-1578
TAMIL NADU. DEPARTMENT OF STATISTICS. ANNUAL STATISTICAL ABSTRACT. (Text in English) 1954. a. Rs.11. Director of Statistics, Madras 600006, India. (Subscr. to: Government Publication Depot, 166 Anna Rd., Madras 600002, India)

316.78 TZ ISSN 0039-9469
TANZANIA. BUREAU OF STATISTICS. QUARTERLY STATISTICAL BULLETIN. q. EAs.4 per no. Bureau of Statistics, Box 796, Dar es Salaam, Tanzania. (Orders to: Government Publications Agency, Box 1801, Dar es Salaam, Tanzania) mkt.

TANZANIA. BUREAU OF STATISTICS. SURVEY OF EMPLOYMENT. see *BUSINESS AND ECONOMICS — Abstracting, Bibliographies, Statistics*

TANZANIA. BUREAU OF STATISTICS. SURVEY OF INDUSTRIAL PRODUCTION. see *BUSINESS AND ECONOMICS — Abstracting, Bibliographies, Statistics*

314 SZ
TASCHENSTATISTIK (YEAR). (Text in English, French, German and Italian) a. Bundesamt fuer Statistik, Hallwylstr. 15, CH-3003 Bern, Switzerland. TEL 031-618836. FAX 031-617856.

319 AT ISSN 0314-1640
TASMANIAN POCKET YEARBOOK. 1913. a. Aus.$7.50. Australian Bureau of Statistics, Tasmanian Office, G.P.O. Box 66A, Hobart, Tas. 7001, Australia. circ. 3,300.
Description: Presents a basic statistical summary of Tasmania.

TAX BURDEN ON TOBACCO. see *TOBACCO — Abstracting, Bibliographies, Statistics*

TEACHING STATISTICS; an international journal for teachers of pupils aged 9 to 19. see *EDUCATION — Abstracting, Bibliographies, Statistics*

310 510 DK ISSN 0107-3826
TECHNICAL UNIVERSITY OF DENMARK. INSTITUTE OF MATHEMATICAL STATISTICS AND OPERATIONS RESEARCH. RESEARCH REPORTS. irreg. Technical University of Denmark, Institute of Mathematical Statistics and Operations Research, Bldg. 321, DK-2800 Lyngby, Denmark. FAX 45-42-88-13-97. illus.
Formerly: Instituttet for Matematisk Statistik og Operationsanalyse. Working Paper (ISSN 0107-5233)

TENNESSEE PUBLIC LIBRARY STATISTICS. see *LIBRARY AND INFORMATION SCIENCES — Abstracting, Bibliographies, Statistics*

317 US ISSN 0082-2760
HA641
TENNESSEE STATISTICAL ABSTRACT. 1969. a. $32. University of Tennessee, Center for Business and Economic Research, Knoxville, TN 37996-4170. TEL 615-974-5441. FAX 615-974-3100. TELEX 557461 UTSUPBLST. Ed. Betty B. Vickers. circ. 1,400. (also avail. in microfiche from BHP)

TEXAS BLUE BOOK OF LIFE INSURANCE STATISTICS. see *INSURANCE — Abstracting, Bibliographies, Statistics*

THAILAND. NATIONAL STATISTICAL OFFICE. ANNOTATED STATISTICAL BIBLIOGRAPHY. see *BIBLIOGRAPHIES*

310 TH ISSN 0858-2696
THAILAND. NATIONAL STATISTICAL OFFICE. ANNUAL REPORT. (Text in Thai) 1963. a. National Statistical Office, Statistical Information Division, Larn Luang Rd., Bangkok 10100, Thailand. FAX 2813814.
Description: Results of work following the program of the National Statistical Office administration in general for the reported year.

315.93 TH ISSN 0857-9482
THAILAND. NATIONAL STATISTICAL OFFICE. QUARTERLY BULLETIN OF STATISTICS. (Text in English and Thai) 1952. q. price varies. National Statistical Office, Statistical Information Division, Larn Luang Rd., Bangkok 10100, Thailand. FAX 2813814. charts; stat.; circ. 1,200.
Description: Statistical tables on climate, population and vital statistics, social statistics, production, transport and communication.

315 TH
THAILAND. NATIONAL STATISTICAL OFFICE. RESEARCH PAPER. 1975. irreg. National Statistical Office, Statistical Information Division, Larn Luang Rd., Bangkok, Thailand. FAX 2813814.

310 658.3 US
TIMING ANALYSIS PROJECTION. Short title: T A P. 1971. s-m. to clients only. Covato Research Corporation, Manor Oak II, Ste. 333, 1910 Cochran Rd., Pittsburgh, PA 15220. TEL 412-341-3700. FAX 412-341-5563. Ed. Phillip R. Covato. index; circ. 100. (back issues avail.)

316.6 TG
TOGO. DIRECTION DE LA STATISTIQUE. BULLETIN MENSUEL DE STATISTIQUE. m. 5600 Fr.CFA. Direction de la Statistique, Boite Postale 118, Lome, Togo.

TOGO. MINISTRY OF ECONOMY AND FINANCE. BULLETIN DE STATISTIQUES. see *BUSINESS AND ECONOMICS — Abstracting, Bibliographies, Statistics*

310 JA ISSN 0285-7677
TOKEI. (Text in Japanese) 1947. m. 4800 Yen. Nihon Tokei Kyokai - Japan Statistical Association, Crest 21, 6-21, Yocho-machi, Shinjuku-ku, Tokyo 162, Japan. TEL 03-5269-3051. FAX 03-5269-3058.

TOKEI SURI KENKYUJO KENKYU RIPOTO/JAPAN. INSTITUTE OF STATISTICAL MATHEMATICS. RESEARCH REPORTS, GENERAL SERIES. see *MATHEMATICS*

310 CC ISSN 0496-4225
TONGJI YANJIU/STATISTICS RESEARCH. (Text in Chinese) bi-m. Zhongguo Tongji Chubanshe, Gujia Tongji-ju, Sanchenhe, Beijing 100826, People's Republic of China. TEL 813226. Ed. Mo Rida.

310 JA
TOYO KEIZAI. STATISTICS MONTHLY. (Text in Japanese) 1939. m. Toyo Keizai Inc., 1-2-1, Nihonbashi Hongoku-cho, Chuo-ku, Tokyo 103, Japan. TEL 03-3246-5575. FAX 03-3242-4068. Ed. Masaki Hara. circ. 15,000.

311 TR ISSN 0082-6502
TRINIDAD AND TOBAGO. CENTRAL STATISTICAL OFFICE. ANNUAL STATISTICAL DIGEST. 1951. a. T.T.$10. Central Statistical Office, 23 Park St., P.O. Box 98, Port-of-Spain, Trinidad & Tobago, W.I. TEL 809-62-5370. (Dist. by: Government Printer, 110 Henry St., Port-of-Spain, Trinidad & Tobago, W.I.)

TRINIDAD AND TOBAGO. CENTRAL STATISTICAL OFFICE. BUSINESS SURVEYS. see *BUSINESS AND ECONOMICS — Abstracting, Bibliographies, Statistics*

317 TR
TRINIDAD AND TOBAGO. CENTRAL STATISTICAL OFFICE. POCKET DIGEST. 1973. a. T.T.$100. Central Statistical Office, 23 Park St., P.O. Box 98, Port-of-Spain, Trinidad & Tobago, W.I. TEL 809-62-53705. (Dist. by: Government Printing Office, 110 Henry St., Port-of-Spain, Trinidad & Tobago, W.I.)

TRINIDAD AND TOBAGO. CENTRAL STATISTICAL OFFICE. QUARTERLY TRAVEL. see *TRAVEL AND TOURISM — Abstracting, Bibliographies, Statistics*

310 TR
TRINIDAD AND TOBAGO. CENTRAL STATISTICAL OFFICE. STAFF PAPERS. 1967. irreg. free. Central Statistical Office, 23 Park St., P.O. Box 98, Port-of-Spain, Trinidad & Tobago, W.I. TEL 809-62-53705. (Dist. by: Government Printing Office, 110 Henry St., Port-of-Spain, Trinidad & Tobago, W.I.)

TUNGSTEN STATISTICS. see *METALLURGY — Abstracting, Bibliographies, Statistics*

316.11 TI ISSN 0041-4115
TUNISIA. INSTITUT NATIONAL DE LA STATISTIQUE. BULLETIN MENSUEL DE STATISTIQUE. (Text in Arabic, French) 1954. m. 22 din. Institut National de la Statistique, 70 rue Echcham, Tunis, Tunisia. stat. Indexed: P.A.I.S.For.Lang.Ind.

314.961 TU ISSN 0041-4263
TURKEY. DEVLET ISTATISTIK ENSTITUSU. AYLIK ISTATISTIK BULTENI/MONTHLY BULLETIN OF STATISTICS. (Text in English, Turkish) 1952. m. free. State Institute of Statistics, Necatibey Caddesi 114, Ankara, Turkey. charts; stat.
Description: Monthly statistical and evaluation bulletin.

TURKEY. DEVLET ISTATISTIK ENSTITUSU. MILLI EGITIM ISTATISTIKLERI: OGRETIM YILI BASI. see *EDUCATION — Abstracting, Bibliographies, Statistics*

315 TU ISSN 0082-691X
TURKIYE ISTATISTIK YILLIGI/STATISTICAL YEARBOOK OF TURKEY. 1929. biennial. exchange basis. State Institute of Statistics, Necatibey Caddesi 114, Ankara, Turkey.

U N C T A D COMMODITY YEARBOOK. (United Nations Conference on Trade and Development) see *BUSINESS AND ECONOMICS — Abstracting, Bibliographies, Statistics*

U S S R FACTS & FIGURES ANNUAL. see *POLITICAL SCIENCE — Abstracting, Bibliographies, Statistics*

310   US   ISSN 0888-7926
U S STATISTICS; America's leading newsletter on data for decisionmaking. 1986. m. $95 (foreign $110). U S Statistics, Inc., 1101 King St., Ste. 601, Alexandria, VA 22314. TEL 703-979-9699. (Subscr. to: Box 816, Alexandria, VA 22313) Ed. Cynthia Rosacker. stat. (back issues avail.)
●Also available online.

310 060   UN   ISSN 0082-7533
UNESCO STATISTICAL REPORTS AND STUDIES. (Editions in English and French) 1955. irreg., no.30, 1988. price varies. Unesco, 7-9 Place de Fonteney, 75700 Paris, France. TEL 577-16-10. (Dist. in U.S. by: Unipub, 4611-F Assembly Dr., Lanham, MD 20706-4391)

310   UN   ISSN 0082-7541
                CODEN: SYUNDY
UNESCO STATISTICAL YEARBOOK. (Text in English, French and Spanish) 1952. a. $95. Unesco, 7-9 Place de Fonteney, 75700 Paris, France. TEL 577-16-10. (Dist. in U.S. by: Unipub, 4611-F Assembly Dr., Lanham, MD 20706-4391) **Indexed:** IIS.
—BLDSC shelfmark: 9090.220000.

UNION LABOR IN CALIFORNIA. see *LABOR UNIONS — Abstracting, Bibliographies, Statistics*

310   IT
UNIONE REGIONALE CAMERE DI COMMERCIO DELL'EMILIA-ROMAGNA. STATISTICHE REGIONALI. 1970. q. L.30000. Unione Regionale Camere di Commercio dell'Emilia-Romagna (C.E.R.E.S.), Via Montegrappa 4-D, 40121 Bologna, Italy. TEL 051-223030. circ. 1,200.

UNITED ARAB EMIRATES. WIZARAT AL-SIHHAH. AL-KITAB AL-IHSA'I AL-SANAWI/UNITED ARAB EMIRATES. MINISTRY OF HEALTH. STATISTICAL YEARBOOK. see *MEDICAL SCIENCES — Abstracting, Bibliographies, Statistics*

UNITED MUTUAL FUND SELECTOR. see *BUSINESS AND ECONOMICS — Abstracting, Bibliographies, Statistics*

UNITED NATIONS. DEPARTMENT OF INTERNATIONAL ECONOMIC AND SOCIAL AFFAIRS. STATISTICAL OFFICE. CONSTRUCTION STATISTIC YEARBOOK. see *BUILDING AND CONSTRUCTION — Abstracting, Bibliographies, Statistics*

UNITED NATIONS. NATIONAL ACCOUNTS STATISTICS. ANALYSIS OF MAIN AGGREGATES. see *BUSINESS AND ECONOMICS — Abstracting, Bibliographies, Statistics*

UNITED NATIONS. NATIONAL ACCOUNTS STATISTICS. GOVERNMENT ACCOUNTS AND TABLES. see *BUSINESS AND ECONOMICS — Abstracting, Bibliographies, Statistics*

UNITED NATIONS. NATIONAL ACCOUNTS STATISTICS. MAIN AGGREGATES AND DETAILED TABLES. see *BUSINESS AND ECONOMICS — Abstracting, Bibliographies, Statistics*

310   UN   ISSN 0082-8459
HA12.5   CODEN: STYBDH
UNITED NATIONS. STATISTICAL YEARBOOK. (Text in English and French) 1949. a. price varies. (United Nations Statistical Office) United Nations Publications, Room DC2-853, New York, NY 10017. TEL 212-963-3802. FAX 212-963-3489. (Or: Distribution and Sales Section, Palais des Nations, CH-1211 Geneva 10, Switzerland) (also avail. in microfiche)

310   UN   ISSN 0041-7432
HC57
UNITED NATIONS STATISTICAL OFFICE. MONTHLY BULLETIN OF STATISTICS. (Supplement avail.) (Text in English, English and French, French and Spanish) 1947. m. $225. United Nations Publications, Rm. DC2-853, New York, NY 10017. TEL 212-963-8300. FAX 212-963-3489. charts; mkt. **Indexed:** Nutr.Abstr.
   Description: Provides monthly statistics on 74 subjects from over 200 countries and territories, including special tables that graphically portray important economic developments.

U.S. BUREAU OF LABOR STATISTICS. EMPLOYMENT SITUATION. see *BUSINESS AND ECONOMICS — Abstracting, Bibliographies, Statistics*

001.4   US
HA203
U.S. BUREAU OF THE CENSUS. CENSUS AND YOU. 1966. m. $18. U.S. Bureau of the Census, Data User Services Division, Washington, DC 20233. TEL 301-763-4100. (Dist. by: Supt. of Documents, Washington, DC 20402) Ed. Neil Tillman. circ. 8,000. (also avail. in microfiche) **Indexed:** Amer.Stat.Ind., Ind.U.S.Gov.Per., PROMT.
●Also available online. Vendor: CompuServe Consumer Information Service, DIALOG.
   Former titles: U.S. Bureau of the Census. Data User News (ISSN 0096-9877); U.S. Bureau of the Census. Small Area Data Activities; U.S. Bureau of the Census. Small Area Data Notes.

317   US   ISSN 0082-9455
HA202
U.S. BUREAU OF THE CENSUS. COUNTY AND CITY DATA BOOK. 1944. irreg. price varies. U.S. Bureau of the Census, Data User Services Division, Washington, DC 20233. TEL 301-763-4100. (Dist. by: Supt. of Documents, Washington, DC 20402) (also avail. in microfiche)
●Also available online. Vendor(s): CompuServe Consumer Information Service, DIALOG.

317.3   US   ISSN 0276-6566
HA202
U.S. BUREAU OF THE CENSUS. STATE AND METROPOLITAN AREA DATA BOOK. irreg. price varies. U.S. Bureau of the Census, Data User Services Division, Washington, DC 20233. TEL 301-763-4100. (Dist. by: Supt of Documents, Washington, DC 20402) (also avail. in microfiche)
●Also available online. Vendor(s): CompuServe Consumer Information Service, DIALOG.

310   US   ISSN 0082-9544
U.S. BUREAU OF THE CENSUS. TECHNICAL PAPERS. 1953. irreg. price varies. U.S. Bureau of the Census, Data User Services Division, Washington, DC 20233. TEL 301-763-4100. (Dist. by: Supt. of Documents, Washington, DC 20402) Key Title: Technical Papers - U.S. Department of Commerce, Bureau of the Census.

310   US   ISSN 0082-9552
U.S. BUREAU OF THE CENSUS. WORKING PAPERS. 1954. irreg. U.S. Bureau of the Census, Data User Services Division, Washington, DC 20233. TEL 301-763-4100.

U.S. DEPARTMENT OF EDUCATION. NATIONAL CENTER FOR EDUCATION STATISTICS. PUBLIC ELEMENTARY AND SECONDARY STATE AGGREGATE DATA, BY STATE. see *EDUCATION — Abstracting, Bibliographies, Statistics*

U.S. DEPARTMENT OF TRANSPORTATION. NATIONAL TRANSPORTATION STATISTICS. ANNUAL; a supplement to the summary of national transportation statistics. see *ENERGY — Abstracting, Bibliographies, Statistics*

U.S. FEDERAL HIGHWAY ADMINISTRATION. MONTHLY MOTOR GASOLINE REPORTED BY STATES. see *PETROLEUM AND GAS — Abstracting, Bibliographies, Statistics*

U.S. FISH AND WILDLIFE SERVICE. NATIONAL SURVEY OF HUNTING, FISHING AND WILDLIFE-ASSOCIATED RECREATION. see *SPORTS AND GAMES — Abstracting, Bibliographies, Statistics*

U.S. NATIONAL INSTITUTE ON DRUG ABUSE. STATISTICAL SERIES D. DATA FROM THE CLIENT ORIENTED DATA ACQUISITION PROCESS. QUARTERLY REPORT. PROVISIONAL DATA. see *PHYSICAL FITNESS AND HYGIENE — Abstracting, Bibliographies, Statistics*

339   UY   ISSN 0041-8439
UNIVERSIDAD DE LA REPUBLICA. FACULTAD DE CIENCIAS ECONOMICAS Y ADMINISTRACION. INSTITUTO DE ESTADISTICA. INDICE DE PRECIOS AL CONSUMIDOR. 1962. m. Urg.$3.40. Universidad de la Republica, Facultad de Ciencias Economicas y de Administracion, Instituto de Estadistica, Montevideo, Uruguay. stat. (processed)

UNIVERSIDADE FEDERAL DO RIO DE JANEIRO. INSTITUTO DE MATEMATICA. MEMORIAS DE MATEMATICA. see *MATHEMATICS — Abstracting, Bibliographies, Statistics*

314   DK   ISSN 0105-9645
UNIVERSITETETS STATISTISKE INSTITUT. RESEARCH REPORT. no.76, 1981. irreg. Universitetets Statistiske Institut, Studiestraede 6, DK-1455 Copenhagen K, Denmark.
   Formerly: Koebenhavns Universitet. Statistiske Institut. Afhandlinger. Graa Serie.

UNIVERSITY OF GHANA. INSTITUTE OF STATISTICAL, SOCIAL AND ECONOMIC RESEARCH. DISCUSSION PAPERS. see *SOCIAL SCIENCES: COMPREHENSIVE WORKS*

UNIVERSITY OF NEW ENGLAND. DEPARTMENT OF ECONOMETRICS. WORKING PAPERS IN ECONOMETRICS AND APPLIED STATISTICS. see *BUSINESS AND ECONOMICS — Abstracting, Bibliographies, Statistics*

310   US   ISSN 0078-1495
UNIVERSITY OF NORTH CAROLINA, CHAPEL HILL. INSTITUTE OF STATISTICS. MIMEO SERIES. 1947. irreg. (approx. 3/mo.). price varies. University of North Carolina at Chapel Hill, Department of Statistics, Chapel Hill, NC 27514. TEL 919-962-2307. cum.index.

URUGUAY. DIRECCION GENERAL DE ESTADISTICA Y CENSOS. INDICE MEDIO DE SALARIOS. see *BUSINESS AND ECONOMICS — Abstracting, Bibliographies, Statistics*

UTAH MARRIAGE AND DIVORCE ANNUAL REPORT. see *POPULATION STUDIES — Abstracting, Bibliographies, Statistics*

UTAH STATISTICAL ABSTRACT. see *BUSINESS AND ECONOMICS — Abstracting, Bibliographies, Statistics*

315.4   II   ISSN 0042-1626
UTTAR PRADESH. STATE PLANNING INSTITUTE. QUARTERLY BULLETIN OF STATISTICS. (Text in English and Hindi) 1966. q. Rs.35. State Planning Institute, Economic and Statistics Division, Uttar Pradesh, India. stat.; circ. controlled. (processed)
   Description: Statistics relating to industry, labor, prices, agriculture, transportation, population.

VENEZUELA. MINISTERIO DE ENERGIA Y MINAS. APENDICE ESTADISTICO. see *ENERGY — Abstracting, Bibliographies, Statistics*

VENEZUELA. MINISTERIO DE HACIENDA. BOLETIN ESTADISTICO. see *HOUSING AND URBAN PLANNING — Abstracting, Bibliographies, Statistics*

314   IC
VERSLUNARSKYRSLUR - EXTERNAL TRADE/EXTERNAL TRADE STATISTICS. (Text in Icelandic; summaries in English) 1914. a. $40. Hagstofa Islands - Statistical Bureau of Iceland, Skuggasund 3, IS-150 Reykjavik, Iceland. TEL 1-609800. FAX 1-628865. Dir. Hallgrimur Snorrason. (back issues avail.)
   Description: Presents external trade statistics of Iceland.

314.7   RU   ISSN 0042-4692
VESTNIK STATISTIKI. 1949. m. 31.80 Rub. (Tsentral'noe Statisticheskoe Upravlenie pri Sovete Ministrov) Izdatel'stvo Statistika, Ul. Kirova, 39, Moscow K-450, Russia. index; circ. 35,000. (reprint service avail. from KTO) **Indexed:** Curr.Dig.Sov.Press, Rural Recreat.Tour.Abstr., World Agri.Econ.& Rural Sociol.Abstr.

310   AU
VIENNA. STATISTISCHES AMT DER STADT WIEN. STATISTISCHE MITTEILUNGEN. 1876. q. S.200. Statistisches Amt der Stadt Wien, Volksgartenstr. 3, A-1016 Vienna, Austria. TEL 4000-88611. FAX 4000-9997910. Ed. Peter Pokay. bk.rev.; stat.; circ. 800.
   Formerly (until 1985): Mitteilungen aus Statistik und Verwaltung der Stadt Wien (ISSN 0026-6876)
   Description: Statistical tables and analyses concerning population, economy, social statistics and education in the city of Vienna.

VITAL STATISTICS OF IOWA. see *POPULATION STUDIES — Abstracting, Bibliographies, Statistics*

SURGERY

DIE WAEHRUNGEN DER WELT; Statistische Beihefte, Reihe 5, zu den Monatsberichten der Deutschen Bundesbank. see *BUSINESS AND ECONOMICS — Abstracting, Bibliographies, Statistics*

WASHINGTON (STATE). DEPARTMENT OF NATURAL RESOURCES. ANNUAL FIRE STATISTICS. see *FORESTS AND FORESTRY — Abstracting, Bibliographies, Statistics*

WEATHER AND FORECASTING. see *METEOROLOGY*

WEST BENGAL. ANNUAL FINANCIAL STATEMENT (BUDGET). see *BUSINESS AND ECONOMICS — Abstracting, Bibliographies, Statistics*

WEST BENGAL. BUREAU OF APPLIED ECONOMICS AND STATISTICS. STATISTICAL HANDBOOK. see *BUSINESS AND ECONOMICS — Abstracting, Bibliographies, Statistics*

310   AT
HA3753
WESTERN AUSTRALIA: FACTS AND FIGURES. 1919. a. Aus.$8.95 (foreign Aus.$11.45)(effective 1991). Australian Bureau of Statistics, Western Australian Office, 30 Terrace Rd., Perth, W.A. 6000, Australia. TEL 323-5323. circ. 536.
Formerly: Western Australian Pocket Yearbook (ISSN 0083-8756)
Description: Contains tables on climate, population, government, education, wages, employment, production, building, finance, prices, transport and tourism.

310   GW
WIRTSCHAFT UND VERKEHR NORDRHEIN-WESTFALENS IN ZAHLEN. 1984. m. DM.20. Landesamt fuer Datenverarbeitung und Statistik Nordrhein-Westfalen, Mauerstr. 51, Postfach 101105, 4000 Duesseldorf 1, Germany. TEL 0211-9449-01. circ. 400. (back issues avail.)

WISCONSIN. DIVISION OF CORRECTIONS. OFFICE OF INFORMATION MANAGEMENT. ADMISSIONS TO JUVENILE INSTITUTIONS. see *CRIMINOLOGY AND LAW ENFORCEMENT — Abstracting, Bibliographies, Statistics*

WORLD MINERAL STATISTICS; world production, exports and imports. see *MINES AND MINING INDUSTRY — Abstracting, Bibliographies, Statistics*

WORLD WROUGHT COPPER STATISTICS. see *METALLURGY — Abstracting, Bibliographies, Statistics*

379   US   ISSN 0093-5530
LB2826.W8
WYOMING. DIVISION OF PLANNING, EVALUATION AND INFORMATION SERVICES. STATISTICAL REPORT SERIES. 1973. a. free. Division of Planning, Evaluation and Information Services, Cheyenne, WY 82001. TEL 307-777-6267. stat. Key Title: Statistical Report Series (Cheyenne).

YAMAGUCHI-KEN EISEI KOGAI KENKYU SENTA NENPO. see *PUBLIC HEALTH AND SAFETY — Abstracting, Bibliographies, Statistics*

330 314.97   YU   ISSN 0019-3585
YOGOSLAVIA. SAVAZNI ZAVOD ZA STATISTIKU. INDEKS; mesecni pregled privredne statistike SFR Jugoslavije. (English and French translations of texts and terms avail. on request) 1952. m. 400 din.($23.33) Savezni Zavod za Statistiku, Kneza Milosa 20, Belgrade, Yugoslavia. TEL 681-999. Ed. Ibrahim Latific. mkt.; stat.; circ. 4,400.

310   YU   ISSN 0351-0603
YUGOSLAVIA. SAVEZNI ZAVOD ZA STATISTIKU. METODOLOSKE STUDIJE, RASPRAVE I DOKUMENTACIJA. 1973. irreg. Savezni Zavod za Statistiku, Kneza Milosa 20, Belgrade, Yugoslavia.

310   YU   ISSN 0513-6547
YUGOSLAVIA. SAVEZNI ZAVOD ZA STATISTIKU. METODOLOSKI MATERIJALI. irreg. Savezni Zavod za Statistiku, Kneza Milosa 20, Belgrade, Yugoslavia.

310   YU
YUGOSLAVIA. SAVEZNI ZAVOD ZA STATISTIKU. RADNE ORGANIZACIJE PREMA VISINI NAJNIZEG I NAJVISEG NETO LICNOG DOHOTKA. (Subseries of its Statisticki Bilten) s-a. 20 din. Savezni Zavod za Statistiku, Kneza Milosa 20, Belgrade, Yugoslavia. TEL 681-999. circ. 1,000.

314   YU   ISSN 0039-0534
YUGOSLAVIA. SAVEZNI ZAVOD ZA STATISTIKU. STATISTICKA REVIJA. (Summaries in English and French) 1954. q. 160 din.($8.88) Savezni Zavod za Statistiku, Kneza Milosa 20, Belgrade, Yugoslavia. TEL 681-999. (Co-sponsor: Jugoslovensko Statisticko Drustvo) Ed. Branislav Ivanovic. bk.rev.; bibl.; index; circ. 1,000.

314   YU   ISSN 0084-4365
HA1631
YUGOSLAVIA. SAVEZNI ZAVOD ZA STATISTIKU. STATISTICKI BILTEN. (Text in Serbian with English, French and Russian translation) 1950. w. 600 din.($66.67) Savezni Zavod za Statistiku, Kneza Milosa 20, Belgrade, Yugoslavia. TEL 681-999. Ed. Ibragim Catific.

310   YU   ISSN 0513-6555
HA37.Y8
YUGOSLAVIA. SAVEZNI ZAVOD ZA STATISTIKU. STUDIJE, ANALIZE I PRIKAZI. 1953. irreg. Savezni Zavod za Statistiku, Kneza Milosa 20, Belgrade, Yugoslavia.
Formerly (until 1960): Yugoslavia. Savezni Zavod za Statistiku. Studije i Analize.

Z U M A - NACHRICHTEN. see *SOCIOLOGY*

310   ZR
ZAIRE. INSTITUT NATIONAL DE LA STATISTIQUE. BULLETIN TRIMESTRIEL DES STATISTIQUES GENERALES. q. Institut National de la Statistique, Direction des Services Generaux, B.P. 20, Kinshasa, Zaire.

ZAMBIA. CENTRAL STATISTICAL OFFICE. AGRICULTURAL AND PASTORAL PRODUCTION (COMMERCIAL FARMS). see *AGRICULTURE — Abstracting, Bibliographies, Statistics*

ZAMBIA. CENTRAL STATISTICAL OFFICE. AGRICULTURAL AND PASTORAL PRODUCTION (NON-COMMERCIAL). see *AGRICULTURE — Abstracting, Bibliographies, Statistics*

ZAMBIA. CENTRAL STATISTICAL OFFICE. CONSUMER PRICE STATISTICS. see *BUSINESS AND ECONOMICS — Abstracting, Bibliographies, Statistics*

316   ZA   ISSN 0027-0377
ZAMBIA. CENTRAL STATISTICAL OFFICE. MONTHLY DIGEST OF STATISTICS. 1964. m. $32. Central Statistical Office, P.O. Box 31908, Lusaka, Zambia. TEL 211231. stat.
Description: For the study of social and economic conditions in Zambia.

ZAMBIA. CENTRAL STATISTICAL OFFICE. QUARTERLY AGRICULTURAL STATISTICAL BULLETIN. see *AGRICULTURE — Abstracting, Bibliographies, Statistics*

316   ZA   ISSN 0084-4551
HA1977.R48
ZAMBIA. CENTRAL STATISTICAL OFFICE. STATISTICAL YEAR BOOK. 1967. a. K.3. Central Statistical Office, P.O. Box 31908, Lusaka, Zambia. TEL 211-231.

ZAMBIA. CENTRAL STATISTICAL OFFICE. VITAL STATISTICS. see *POPULATION STUDIES — Abstracting, Bibliographies, Statistics*

ZHONGGUO NIANJIAN. see *GENERAL INTEREST PERIODICALS — China*

315   CC   ISSN 1002-4557
ZHONGGUO TONGJI/CHINA STATISTICS. (Text in Chinese) 1980. m. $15 (foreign $39.50). (State Statistical Bureau - Guojia Tongji Ju) China Statistics Publishing House - Zhongguo Tongji Chubanshe, 38 Yuetan Nanjie, Sanlihe, Beijing 100826, People's Republic of China. TEL 8217162. TELEX 22778-FASSB-CN. (Dist. in US by: China Books & Periodicals, Inc., 2929 24th St., San Francisco, CA 94110. TEL 415-282-2994) circ. 150,000. (back issues avail.)
Description: Covers government statistical organization, practice and research on statistics.

ZIMBABWE. CENTRAL STATISTICAL OFFICE. CENSUS OF PRODUCTION. see *BUSINESS AND ECONOMICS — Abstracting, Bibliographies, Statistics*

ZIMBABWE. CENTRAL STATISTICAL OFFICE. INCOME TAX STATISTICS; analysis of assessments and loss statements. see *BUSINESS AND ECONOMICS — Abstracting, Bibliographies, Statistics*

316   RH   ISSN 0556-8706
ZIMBABWE. CENTRAL STATISTICAL OFFICE. MONTHLY DIGEST OF STATISTICS. 1964. m. with q. supplements. Rhod.$10. Central Statistical Office, Box 8063, Causeway, Salisbury, Zimbabwe. circ. 1,100.

316   RH
ZIMBABWE. CENTRAL STATISTICAL OFFICE. QUARTERLY DIGEST OF STATISTICS. q. Central Statistical Office, P.O. Box 8063, Causeway, Harare, Zimbabwe.

ZIMBABWE. CENTRAL STATISTICAL OFFICE. QUARTERLY POULTRY CENSUS. see *AGRICULTURE — Abstracting, Bibliographies, Statistics*

SURGERY

see *Medical Sciences–Surgery*

TAXATION

see *Business and Economics–Public Finance, Taxation*

TEACHING METHODS AND CURRICULUM

see *Education–Teaching Methods and Curriculum*

TECHNOLOGY: COMPREHENSIVE WORKS

A F P SCIENCES; information scientifique, technique, medicale. (Agence France-Presse) see *MEDICAL SCIENCES*

A S T C NEWSLETTER. (Association of Science-Technology Centers) see *MUSEUMS AND ART GALLERIES*

A S T I S CURRENT AWARENESS BULLETIN. (Arctic Science & Technology Information System) see *TECHNOLOGY: COMPREHENSIVE WORKS — Abstracting, Bibliographies, Statistics*

600   US   ISSN 0740-2961
A S T M STANDARDS INFOBRIEFS. 1982. q. $12 to non-members. American Society for Testing and Materials, 1916 Race St., Philadelphia, PA 19103. TEL 215-299-5400. FAX 215-977-9679. Ed. B. Schindler. circ. 3,000. (reprint service avail. from UMI)

A T E A JOURNAL. (American Technical Education Association, Inc.) see *EDUCATION*

620   HU   ISSN 0001-7035
T4   CODEN: ATSHA8
ACADEMIA SCIENTIARUM HUNGARICA. ACTA TECHNICA. (Text in English, French, German, Russian) 1950. q. $56. (Magyar Tudomanyos Akademia) Akademiai Kiado, Publishing House of the Hungarian Academy of Sciences, P.O. Box 24, H-1363 Budapest, Hungary. Ed. P. Michelberger. adv.; bk.rev.; bibl.; charts; illus.; index. (back issues avail.) **Indexed:** Appl.Mech.Rev., Curr.Cont., GeoRef., Int.Aerosp.Abstr., ISMEC, Met.Abstr., Sci.Abstr., World Alum.Abstr.
—BLDSC shelfmark: 0664.000000.

600   MX   ISSN 0515-3085
T78   CODEN: APTMAY
ACTA POLITECNICA MEXICANA. (Text in Spanish; summaries in English, French, German) 1959. q. Mex.$150($10) Instituto Politecnico Nacional, Comision de Operacion y Fomento de Actividades Academicas, Apdo. Postal 42-161, Prolongacion de S. Diaz Miron y Plan de San Luis, Mexico 17, D.F., Mexico. Ed. Rafael Nevero Zuloaga. bibl.; charts; cum.index. **Indexed:** Biol.Abstr., Chem.Abstr., Sci.Abstr.

TECHNOLOGY: COMPREHENSIVE WORKS

600 CS
ACTA POLYTECHNICA. RADA 4: TECHNICKO-TEORETICKA; prace CVUT v Praze. 1967. q. 32 Kcs.($6) (Ceske Vysoke Uceni Technicke) Statni Pedagogicke Nakladatelstvi, Ostrovni 30, 113 01 Prague 1, Czechoslovakia. (Subscr. to: c/o Tamara Jedlicewa, Raktorot C V U T, Zikova 4, 166 35 Prague 6, Czechoslovakia) Ed. Lubomir Kalivoda. charts; illus.; circ. 600. **Indexed:** INIS Atomind.

600 CS
ACTA POLYTECHNICA. RADA 5: SPOLECENSKO-VEDNI; prace CVUT v Praze. 1967. q. 32 Kcs.($6) (Ceske Vysoke Uceni Technicke) Statni Pedagogicke Nakladatelstvi, Ostrovni 30, 113 01 Prague 1, Czechoslovakia. (Subscr. to: c/o Tamara Jedlicewa, Raktorot C V U T, Zikova 4, 166 35 Prague, Czechoslovakia) Ed. Lubomir Kalivoda. charts; illus.; circ. 600.

600 CS
ACTA POLYTECHNICA. RADA 6: VSEOBECNA; prace CVUT v Praze. 1967. q. 32 Kcs.($6) (Ceske Vysoke Uceni Technicke) Statni Pedagogicke Nakladatelstvi, Ostrovni 30, 113 01 Prague 1, Czechoslovakia. (Subscr.to: c/o Tamara Jedlicewa, Rektorot C V U T, Zikova 4, 166 35 Prague, Czechoslovakia) Ed. Lubomir Kalivoda. charts; illus.; circ. 600.

ADVANCES IN ENVIRONMENTAL SCIENCE AND ENGINEERING. see *ENVIRONMENTAL STUDIES*

669 620.1 US ISSN 0069-8490
ADVANCES IN X-RAY ANALYSIS. Represents: Annual Conference on Applications of X-Ray Analysis. Proceedings. 1960. a. price varies. (University of Denver, Denver Research Institute) Plenum Publishing Corp., 233 Spring St., New York, NY 10013-1578. TEL 212-620-8000. FAX 212-463-0742. TELEX 23-421139. Ed.Bd. **Indexed:** Biol.Abstr., Br.Ceram.Abstr., Chem.Abstr., GeoRef.
—BLDSC shelfmark: 0712.200000.
Refereed Serial

AEROSPACE TESTING SEMINAR. PROCEEDINGS. see *AERONAUTICS AND SPACE FLIGHT*

600 330 UK ISSN 0954-6782
T1
AFRICAN REVIEW OF BUSINESS AND TECHNOLOGY. 1964. m. £48($86) Alain Charles Publishing Ltd., 27 Wilfred St., London SW1E 6PR, England. TEL 071-834-7676. FAX 071-973-0076. TELEX 297165. Ed. Jonquil L. Phelan. adv.; circ. 17,330. (back issues avail.) **Indexed:** RICS.
Former titles: African Technical Review (ISSN 0266-6677); West African Technical Review ABC (ISSN 0043-3039)
Description: For personnel in executive and managerial capacities in government, industry and commerce operating in Africa.

AGRICULTURAL RESEARCH ORGANIZATION. SCIENTIFIC ACTIVITIES. see *AGRICULTURE*

600 300 PL ISSN 0454-4811
AKADEMIA GORNICZO-HUTNICZA IM. STANISLAWA STASZICA. ZESZYTY NAUKOWE. ZAGADNIENIA TECHNICZNO-EKONOMICZNE. (Text and summaries in English and Polish) irreg., no.44, 1990. price varies. Wydawnictwo A G H, Al. Mickiewicza 30, paw. B-5, 30-059 Krakow, Poland. (Dist. by: Ars Polona, Krakowskie Przedmiescie 7, 00-068 Warsaw, Poland)

620 AI ISSN 0002-306X
TA4.A35 CODEN: IATNAK
AKADEMIYA NAUK ARMYANSKOI S.S.R. IZVESTIYA. SERIYA TEKHNICHESKIKH NAUK. (Text in Russian; summaries in Armenian) 1957. bi-m. 11.10 Rub. Akademiya Nauk Armyanskoi S.S.R., Ul. Barekamutian, 24, Erevan, Armenia. charts; index. **Indexed:** INIS Atomind., Math.R., Sci.Abstr.
—BLDSC shelfmark: 0072.860000.

AKADEMIYA NAUK AZERBAIDZHANSKOI S.S.R. IZVESTIYA. SERIYA FIZIKO-TEKHNICHESKIKH I MATEMATICHESKIKH NAUK. see *PHYSICS*

AKADEMIYA NAUK LATVIISKOI S.S.R. IZVESTIYA. SERIYA FIZICHESKIKH I TEKHNICHESKIKH NAUK. see *PHYSICS*

AKADEMIYA NAUK MOLDAVSKOI S.S.R. IZVESTIYA. SERIYA FIZIKO-TEKHNICHESKIKH I MATEMATICHESKIKH NAUK. see *PHYSICS*

620 RU ISSN 0002-3434
CODEN: IZSTA4
AKADEMIYA NAUK S.S.S.R. SIBIRSKOE OTDELENIE. IZVESTIYA. SERIYA TEKHNICHESKIKH NAUK. 1963. 3/yr. 10.50 Rub. Akademiya Nauk S.S.S.R, Sibirskoe Otdelenie, Prospekt Nauki, 21, Novosibirsk, Russia. bk.rev.; charts; illus.; index. **Indexed:** Chem.Abstr., INIS Atomind., Math.R., Met.Abstr., World Alum.Abstr.

600 UZ
AKADEMIYA NAUK UZBEKSKOI S.S.R. IZVESTIYA. SERIYA TEKHNICHESKIKH NAUK. (Text in Russian) 1957. bi-m. 11.10 Rub. Akademiya Nauk Uzbekskoi S.S.R., Ul. Kuibysheva, 15, Tashkent, Uzbekistan. **Indexed:** Chem.Abstr., INIS Atomind., Met.Abstr., Sci.Abstr., World Alum.Abstr.

AKADEMIYA NAVUK BELARUSSKAI S.S.R. VESTSI. SERIYA FIZIKA-TEKHNICHNYKH NAVUK. see *PHYSICS*

600 CN ISSN 0080-1526
ALBERTA RESEARCH COUNCIL. ANNUAL REPORT. 1921. a. free. Alberta Research Council, Publications Department, P.O. Box 8330, Sta. F, Edmonton, Alta. T6H 5X2, Canada. TEL 403-450-5223. FAX 403-461-2651. TELEX 037-2147. **Indexed:** GeoRef.
Description: Current programs research of the Alberta Research Council.

600 CN ISSN 0080-1534
ALBERTA RESEARCH COUNCIL. CONTRIBUTION SERIES. 1931. irreg. Can.$3. Alberta Research Council, Publications Dept., P.O. Box 8330, Sta. F, Edmonton, Alta. T6H 5X2, Canada. TEL 403-450-5390. FAX 403-461-2651. TELEX 037-2147.
Description: Reprints papers published in professional journals by members of the Alberta Research Council.

600 CN ISSN 0034-5180
CODEN: RCAIAN
ALBERTA RESEARCH COUNCIL. INFORMATION SERIES. 1947. irreg. price varies. Alberta Research Council, Publications Dept., P.O. Box 8330, Sta. F, Edmonton, Alta. T6H 5X2, Canada. TEL 403-450-5390. FAX 403-461-2651. TELEX 037-2147. **Indexed:** Chem.Abstr, Eng.Ind.
Description: Covers indices, symposia proceedings and reports of applied studies.

600 CN
ALBERTA RESEARCH COUNCIL. REPORTS. 1919. irreg. price varies. Alberta Research Council, Publications Dept., P.O. Box 8330, Sta. F, Edmonton, Alta. T6H 5X2, Canada. TEL 403-450-5390. FAX 403-461-2651. TELEX 037-2147. **Indexed:** GeoRef.
Formerly: Research Council of Alberta. Report (ISSN 0080-1607)

ALGO 2000; revista de divulgacion cientifica, tecnica y cultural. see *SCIENCES: COMPREHENSIVE WORKS*

600 SP
ALTA TECNOLOGIA; ilustrada. 1986. m. 2750 ptas.($29) Tecnologia y Prensa S.A., Ctra. de Irun, Km. 12,400, 28049 Madrid, Spain. (Distr. in U.S. by: High Technology Publishing Corporation, 38 Commercial Wharf, Boston, MA 02110; Tel. 617-227-4700) Ed. Norberto Gallego. adv.; charts; illus.; stat.; circ. 20,000. (back issues avail.)

600 378 II ISSN 0065-6623
ALTECH. 1950. a. on exchange basis. (Anna University) Alagappa College of Technology, Madras 600 025, Tamil Nadu, India. Ed. C.M. Lakshmanan. circ. 1,000. **Indexed:** Chem.Abstr.
Description: Reports the research in various areas of technology carried out in the Alagappa College of Technology.

AMERICAN COUNCIL OF INDEPENDENT LABORATORIES. DIRECTORY; a guide to the leading independent testing, research and inspection firms of America. see *SCIENCES: COMPREHENSIVE WORKS*

600 970 500 US ISSN 8756-7296
T1
AMERICAN HERITAGE OF INVENTION & TECHNOLOGY. 1985. 3/yr. $12. Forbes, Inc., Forbes Bldg., 60 Fifth Ave., New York, NY 10011. TEL 212-206-5500. Ed. Frederick Allen. illus.; circ. 285,000.
—BLDSC shelfmark: 0817.734000.

AMERICAN PETROLEUM INSTITUTE. HEALTH AND ENVIRONMENTAL SCIENCES DEPARTMENT. REPORTS AND OTHER PUBLICATIONS, INDEX AND ABSTRACTS. see *PUBLIC HEALTH AND SAFETY — Abstracting, Bibliographies, Statistics*

AMERICAN POWER CONFERENCE. PROCEEDINGS.. see *ENERGY*

AMERICAN PUBLIC WORKS ASSOCIATION. DIRECTORY. see *PUBLIC ADMINISTRATION*

338 US
AMERON NEWS. 1970. q. Ameron, 4700 Ramona Blvd., Monterey Park, CA 91754. FAX 213-263-7690. Ed. S.D. Stracner. charts; illus.; circ. 10,000 (controlled).

ANIMAL FEED SCIENCE AND TECHNOLOGY; an international scientific journal. see *AGRICULTURE — Feed, Flour And Grain*

600 US
ANNUAL MEMBRANE TECHNOLOGY - PLANNING CONFERENCE PROCEEDINGS (YEAR). a. $350. Business Communications Co., Inc. (Norwalk), 25 Van Zant St., Ste. 13, Norwalk, CT 06855. TEL 203-853-4266. FAX 203-853-0348. TELEX 6502934929 WUI.

ANNUAL REVIEW OF GLOBAL EDUCATION. see *EDUCATION*

658.5 GW ISSN 0003-6099
ANTRIEBSTECHNIK. (Includes: Antriebstechnik-Handbuch) (Text in German; index in English and German) 1962. m. DM.198 (foreign DM.216). (Forschungsvereinigung Antriebstechnik e. V.) Vereinigte Fachverlage GmbH, Lise-Meitner-Str. 2, Postfach 2760, 6500 Mainz 1, Germany. TEL 06131-992-01. FAX 06131-992-100. TELEX 04-187752. Ed. Prof. Winter. adv.; bk.rev.; abstr.; charts; illus.; circ. 16,000. (back issues avail.) **Indexed:** Excerp.Med., Fluidex, ISMEC, Met.Abstr., World Alum.Abstr.
—BLDSC shelfmark: 1553.300000.

APPLIED ERGONOMICS; human factors in technology and society. see *ENGINEERING*

600 338.4 II
APPROPRIATE TECHNOLOGY DOCUMENTATION BULLETIN. (Text in English) 1974. bi-m. Rs.25($10) National Institute of Small Industry Extension Training, Yousufguda, Hyderabad 500045, India. TELEX 425-6381-SIET-IN. Ed. S. Pandurangam.

600 SA
APPROPRIATE TECHNOLOGY NEWSLETTER. irreg. Council for Scientific and Industrial Research, Division of Information Services, P.O. Box 395, Pretoria 0001, South Africa. TEL 012-841-4062.
Description: Review articles and announcements regarding appropriate technology.

600 NO
ARBEIDSLEDEREN. bi-m. NOK 40. Norges Arbeidslederforbund, Drammensveien 40, Postboks 2523 Solli, Oslo 2, Norway. Ed. Gunnar J. Larsen. adv.; circ. 11,114.

658.5 GW ISSN 0003-780X
ARBEITSVORBEREITUNG; Zeitschrift fuer Planung und Steuerung der Fertigung. 1964. bi-m. DM.85.80. Carl Hanser Verlag, Kolbergerstr. 22, Postfach 860420, 8000 Munich 80, Germany. TEL 089-926940. Ed.Bd. adv.; bk.rev.; circ. 5,000.

600 AG ISSN 0326-8101
ARGENTINA TECNOLOGICA. 1986. bi-m. free. Banco de la Provincia de Buenos Aires, San Martin 137, 1004 Buenos Aires, Argentina. TEL 331-8375-9 (Int. 1289). circ. 20,000.

ARQUEOLOGIA INDUSTRIAL. see *ARCHAEOLOGY*

ARTE. see *ART*

ARTS AND SCIENCES NEWSLETTER. see *SCIENCES: COMPREHENSIVE WORKS*

TECHNOLOGY: COMPREHENSIVE WORKS

658.5   FR   ISSN 0004-3990
T2
ARTS ET MANUFACTURES. 10/yr. 20 F. Association des Anciens Eleves de l'Ecole Centrale de Paris, 8 rue Jean-Goujon, 75008 Paris, France. circ. 13,000. **Indexed:** Met.Abstr., World Alum.Abstr.
—BLDSC shelfmark: 1736.301000.

600 500   AT   ISSN 0810-7688
ASCENT. 3/yr. (Federal Department of Industry, Technology and Commerce) Australian Government Publishing Service, G.P.O. 84, Canberra, A.C.T. 2601, Australia. TEL 761000. Ed. P.R. Section.
—BLDSC shelfmark: 1739.210000.

600   HK
ASIA TECHNOLOGY. 1989. 12/yr. $39. Review Publishing Co., Ltd., Centre Point 7F, G.P.O. Box 160, 181 Gloucester Rd., Wanchai, Hong Kong. TEL 5-832-8300. FAX 5-834-5571. Ed. Peter Gwynne. adv.; circ. 16,000.
Description: Introduces new technology from around the world.

600   TH
ASIAN INSTITUTE OF TECHNOLOGY. ANNUAL RESEARCH AND ACTIVITIES REPORT. 1962. a. free. Asian Institute of Technology, c/o Academic Secretary, P.O. Box 2754, Bangkok 10501, Thailand. FAX 66-2-516-2126. TELEX 84276 AIT TH. Ed. Roger A. Hawkey. circ. 1,000. (microfiche) **Indexed:** GeoRef.
Formerly: Asian Institute of Technology. Research Summary (ISSN 0572-4198)

600 330   UK   ISSN 0956-3784
ASIAN REVIEW OF BUSINESS AND TECHNOLOGY. 1979. m. £44($77) Alain Charles Publishing Ltd., 27 Wilfred St., London SW1E 6PR, England. TEL 071-834-7676. FAX 071-973-0076. TELEX 297165. Ed. David Clancy. (back issues avail.)
—BLDSC shelfmark: 1742.745050.
Formerly: Far Eastern Technical Review (ISSN 0144-8218)

ASSOCIATED SCIENTIFIC AND TECHNICAL SOCIETIES OF SOUTH AFRICA. ANNUAL PROCEEDINGS. see *SCIENCES: COMPREHENSIVE WORKS*

600   FR   ISSN 0066-9288
ASSOCIATION FRANCAISE DES EXPERTS DE LA COOPERATION TECHNIQUE INTERNATIONALE. ANNUAIRE. 1965. a. $2. Association Francaise des Experts de la Cooperation Technique Internationale, 12, rue Mesnil, 75116 Paris, France. TEL 45-53-41-16.

AUSTRALASIAN ARTS AND EDUCATIONS. see *EDUCATION*

AUSTRALASIAN SCIENCE MAGAZINE. see *SCIENCES: COMPREHENSIVE WORKS*

AUSTRALIAN SCIENCE AND TECHNOLOGY NEWSLETTER. see *SCIENCES: COMPREHENSIVE WORKS*

600   AU
AUSTRIA INNOVATIV. 1986. bi-m. S.88. Bohmann Druck und Verlag Gesellschaft mbH & Co. KG, Leberstr. 122, 1110 Vienna, Austria. Ed. Thurnher Harald. adv.; bk.rev.; circ. 17,000.
Description: Covers new technological research and experiments in industry and universities.

620   PL
CODEN: TCMYAH
AUTO-TECHNIKA MOTORYZACYJNA. m. $162. S I M A D Spolka z o.o., Wal Miedzyszynski 646, 03-994 Warsaw, Poland. (Subscr. to: Auto-Technika Motoryzacyjna, ul. Bartycka 20, 00-716 Warsaw, Poland) Ed. Marian Karwas. circ. 100,000. **Indexed:** Chem.Abstr., ISMEC.
Formerly: Technika Motoryzacyjna (ISSN 0040-1153)

AWISHKARA. see *SCIENCES: COMPREHENSIVE WORKS*

B B R; Wasser und Rohrbau. (Brunnenbau, Bau von Wasserwerk, Rohrleitungsbau) see *WATER RESOURCES*

607   CN
B C I T ANNUAL REPORT. 1975. a. British Columbia Institute of Technology, Marketing & Development, Communications Dept., 3700 Willingdon Ave., Burnaby, B.C. V5G 3H2, Canada. TEL 604-434-5734. Ed. Mary Bacon. illus.
Former titles: B C I T: The Career Campus (ISSN 0707-3291); British Columbia Institute of Technology. Annual Report (ISSN 0381-260X)

600 378   CN
B C I T UPDATE. w. free. British Columbia Institute of Technology, Marketing & Development, Communications Department, 3700 Willingdon Ave., Burnaby, B.C. V5G 3H2, Canada. TEL 604-434-5734. Ed. Mary Bacon.

600   GW   ISSN 0170-9615
B M F T JOURNAL. 1973. 6/yr. free. Bundesministerium fuer Forschung und Technologie, Postfach 200240, 5300 Bonn 2, Germany. Ed. Gert Scharrenberg. circ. 90,000.
Description: Government publication covering events, information on research and technology.

600 510   US
BALSKRISHNAN - NEUSTADT SERIES.* irreg. price varies. Holt, Rinehart and Winston, Inc., c/o Harcourt Brace Javonovich, Orlando, FL 32887. TEL 407-345-2500.

500 600   GW   ISSN 0932-7541
BATTELLE INFORMATION. 1967. 3/yr. free. Battelle Europe, Am Roemerhof 35, 6000 Frankfurt a.M., Germany. FAX 069-7908-80. TELEX 411966. (U.S. address: Battelle Memorial Institute, 505 King Ave., Columbus OH 43201) Ed. Doris Jessen. bk.rev.; cum.index; circ. 7,500. **Indexed:** Excerp.Med., Int.Packag.Abstr., Paper & Bd.Abstr.
Former titles (until April, 1987): Battelle Aktuell; (until 1978): Battelle Information.
Description: Features Battelle research centers in Europe, devoted to research and development in electronic systems, engineering, advanced materials, biological and environmental sciences, and technology management.

605   US   ISSN 0145-8477
CODEN: BATODH
BATTELLE TODAY. 1976. 4/yr. free to qualified personnel. Battelle Memorial Institute, Communications Office, Attn: Harry R. Templeton, Ed., 505 King Ave., Columbus, OH 43201. TEL 614-424-7818. bk.rev.; illus.; circ. 36,000 (controlled). (back issues avail.; reprint service avail. from UMI) **Indexed:** Biol.Abstr., CAD CAM Abstr., Chem.Abstr., Graph.Arts Lit.Abstr., Int.Packag.Abstr., Met.Abstr., Paper & Bd.Abstr., Print.Abstr., PROMT.
Supersedes (in 1976): Battelle Memorial Institute. Research Outlook (ISSN 0092-1122); Which was formerly: Battelle Research Outlook (ISSN 0522-4810)
Description: Highlights of Battelle's worldwide activity in innovative research, technology commercialization and management of large technical programs.

BEITRAEGE ZUR FORSCHUNGSTECHNOLOGIE; Schriftenreihe fuer Experimentalmethodik, Systemanalyse und Instrumentierung in der naturwissenschaftlichen, medizinischen und technischen Forschung. see *SCIENCES: COMPREHENSIVE WORKS*

BESSATSU SAIENSU. see *SCIENCES: COMPREHENSIVE WORKS*

BIBLIOGRAPHIC GUIDE TO TECHNOLOGY. see *BIBLIOGRAPHIES*

BIBLIOTECAS, ARQUIVOS E MUSEUS. see *LIBRARY AND INFORMATION SCIENCES*

BIO-TECHNOLOGY; the international monthly for industrial biology. see *BIOLOGY — Biotechnology*

BIOMEDICAL SCIENCE AND TECHNOLOGY; a review journal. see *MEDICAL SCIENCES*

BIOPROCESS TECHNOLOGY SERIES. see *BIOLOGY*

600   US   ISSN 0067-9127
T15.A1
BLAETTER FUER TECHNIKGESCHICHTE. 1932. irreg. (Technisches Museum fuer Industrie und Gewerbe, Forschungsinstitut fuer Technikgeschichte, AU) Springer-Verlag, 175 Fifth Ave., New York, NY 10010. **Indexed:** Amer.Hist.& Life, Hist.Abstr.

BOLETIN S I N I C Y T. (Sistema Nacional de Informacion Cientifica y Tecnologia) see *SCIENCES: COMPREHENSIVE WORKS*

BOMBAY TECHNOLOGIST. see *CHEMISTRY*

BRAZIL. CONSELHO NACIONAL DE DESENVOLVIMENTO CIENTIFICO E TECNOLOGICO. BOLETIM. see *SCIENCES: COMPREHENSIVE WORKS*

600   UK   ISSN 0140-766X
BRITISH ELECTROTECHNICAL APPROVALS BOARD. ANNUAL LIST OF APPROVED ELECTROTECHNICAL EQUIPMENT. 1966. a. free. B E A B, Mark House, the Green, 9-11 Queen's Rd., Hersham, Walton-on-Thames, Surrey KT12 5NA, England. circ. 10,000 (controlled).

620 658.5   UK   ISSN 0007-0823
BRITISH INDUSTRY AND ENGINEERING. 1926. q. British Industrial Publicity Overseas Ltd., 90 Moorsom St., Birmingham B6 4NT, England. TEL 021-359-0030. FAX 021-359-7441. circ. controlled.
Description: Promotes British and other products and services throughout the USSR.

BRITISH STANDARDS MICROFILE. see *ENGINEERING*

BUILDING SERVICES ENGINEERING RESEARCH & TECHNOLOGY. see *BUILDING AND CONSTRUCTION*

BULLETIN OF LAW, SCIENCE & TECHNOLOGY. see *LAW*

BULLETIN OF SCIENCE TECHNOLOGY AND SOCIETY. see *SCIENCES: COMPREHENSIVE WORKS*

600   PL   ISSN 0068-4597
BYDGOSKIE TOWARZYSTWO NAUKOWE. WYDZIAL NAUK TECHNICZNYCH. PRACE. SERIA Z: (PRACE ZBIOROWE). 1966. irreg. price varies. Bydgoskie Towarzystwo Naukowe, Jezuicka 4, Bydgoszcz, Poland. (Dist. by: Ars Polona-Ruch, Krakowskie Przedmiescie 7, Warsaw, Poland)

600 745.2   UK   ISSN 0261-6920
C A D - C A M INTERNATIONAL. no.5, 1978. m. £36 (Europe £49; elsewhere £59). E M A P Business & Computer Publications Ltd., Priory Court, 30-32 Farringdon Ln., London EC1R 3AU, England. TEL 071-251-6222. FAX 071-608-2696. TELEX 936566. Ed. Brian Davis. adv.; circ. 12,000. (back issues avail.) **Indexed:** BMT, Br.Ceram.Abstr., Comput.Dtbs., Int.Packag.Abstr., Sci.Abstr.

C A SERVICES TODAY. see *CHEMISTRY — Abstracting, Bibliographies, Statistics*

600 500 620   US
C I R A S NEWS. 1966. q. $10 (outside Iowa). Iowa State University, Center for Industrial Research and Service, I S U Research Park, Ste. 500, 2501 N. Loop Dr., Ames, IA 50010-8286. TEL 515-294-3420. FAX 515-294-4925. Ed. William R. Berkland. circ. 6,306. (tabloid format; back issues avail.)
Description: Provides Iowa manufacturing executives with information about methods for improving their management techniques and manufacturing and processing operations. Also describes services available to them from the CIRAS and other service agencies.

600   IT
C I S E NEWSLETTER. (Centro Informazioni Studi Esperienze) (Editions in English & Italian) 1980. q. free. C I S E - Tecnologie Innovative, Casella Postale 12081, 20134 Milan, Italy. FAX 02-21672620. TELEX 311643 CISE I. Ed. Paolo Civardi. circ. 15,000 (5,000 English ed.; 10,000 Italian ed.).
Description: Covering development and innovation in the industrial field with emphasis on electric power generation.

C I S T I NEWS/ACTUALITES I C I S T. (Canada Institute for Scientific and Technical Information) see *SCIENCES: COMPREHENSIVE WORKS — Computer Applications*

TECHNOLOGY: COMPREHENSIVE WORKS

600 UK
C I T E REPORTS. Open University, Institute of Educational Technology, Walton Hall, Milton Keynes MK7 6AA, England. Ed. Hansa Solanki.

C L S U SCIENTIFIC JOURNAL. (Central Luzon State University) see AGRICULTURE

C O D A T A BULLETIN. (Committee on Data for Science and Technology) see SCIENCES: COMPREHENSIVE WORKS

C O S T E D NEWSLETTER. (Committee on Science and Technology in Developing Countries) see SCIENCES: COMPREHENSIVE WORKS

C R I C RAPPORT DE RECHERCHE. see SCIENCES: COMPREHENSIVE WORKS

C S I R ANNUAL REPORT - TECHNOLOGY IMPACT. see SCIENCES: COMPREHENSIVE WORKS

C S I R O DIRECTORY. (Commonwealth Scientific and Industrial Research Organization) see SCIENCES: COMPREHENSIVE WORKS

CA M'INTERESSE. see SCIENCES: COMPREHENSIVE WORKS

CALENDAR OF SCIENTIFIC AND TECHNOLOGICAL MEETINGS IN ISRAEL. see MEETINGS AND CONGRESSES

CANADA. MINISTRY OF STATE FOR SCIENCE AND TECHNOLOGY. ANNUAL REPORT. see SCIENCES: COMPREHENSIVE WORKS

CANADIAN AREA DEVELOPMENT. see SCIENCES: COMPREHENSIVE WORKS

CANADIAN R & D DIRECTORY. see BUSINESS AND ECONOMICS — International Commerce

600 001.3 GW ISSN 0176-0629
CAROLO-WILHELMINA MITTEILUNGEN. 1966. s-a. Technische Universitaet Braunschweig, 3300 Braunschweig, Germany. Ed. Edgar Rosen. bibl.; charts; illus.
  Formerly (until 1986): Technische Universitaet Braunschweig. Mitteilungen.

CENTAURUS; international magazine of the history of mathematics, science and technology. see SCIENCES: COMPREHENSIVE WORKS

CENTRE DE RECHERCHES SCIENCE ET VIE. CAHIERS. see SCIENCES: COMPREHENSIVE WORKS

600 500 BE ISSN 0069-1968
T10.65.B4 CODEN: CDORBV
CENTRE NATIONAL DE DOCUMENTATION SCIENTIFIQUE ET TECHNIQUE. RAPPORT D'ACTIVITE. 1964. biennial. free. Centre National de Documentation Scientifique et Technique - National Center for Scientific and Technical Documentation, 4, Bd. de l'Empereur, B-1000 Brussels, Belgium. Dir. A. Cockx. index; circ. 1,000 (controlled). Indexed: Bull.Signal.
  Description: Offers a concise evaluation of activities and accomplishments of the year. Also reports on results of the previous years, to illuminate long-term projects.

600 IT ISSN 0392-8225
LA CERAMICA MODERNA; mensile di informazione tecnica. 1979. m. (11/yr.). L.39000 (foreign L.67000). Gruppo Editoriale Faenza Editrice s.p.a., Via Pier. de Crescenzi, 44, 48018 Faenza RA, Italy. TEL 0546-663488. FAX 0546-660440.

600 CS ISSN 0069-2301
CESKOSLOVENSKA AKADEMIE VED. ROZPRAVY. T V: RADA TECHNICKYCH VED. (Text in Czech, English; summaries in English, French, German, Russian) 1891. irreg., vol. 98, 1988. price varies. Academia, Publishing House of the Czechoslovak Academy of Sciences, Vodickova 40, 112 29 Prague 1, Czechoslovakia. TEL 23-63-065. circ. 500.

CEYLON INSTITUTE OF SCIENTIFIC & INDUSTRIAL RESEARCH. ANNUAL REPORT. see SCIENCES: COMPREHENSIVE WORKS

CHECKPOINT (WASHINGTON); newsletter from the frontiers of a future civilized world order. see SCIENCES: COMPREHENSIVE WORKS

CHEMICAL ENGINEERING WORLD; India's foremost technical journal. see ENGINEERING — Chemical Engineering

CHINA CENTER OF ADVANCED SCIENCE AND TECHNOLOGY SERIES. see SCIENCES: COMPREHENSIVE WORKS

CHINA REPORT: SCIENCE AND TECHNOLOGY. see SCIENCES: COMPREHENSIVE WORKS

CHONGQING KEJI/CHONGQING SCIENCE AND TECHNOLOGY. see SCIENCES: COMPREHENSIVE WORKS

CHUBU UNIVERSITY. COLLEGE OF ENGINEERING. MEMOIRS/CHUBU DAIGAKU KOGAKUBU KIYO. see ENGINEERING

CHUO DAIGAKU RIKOGAKUBU KIYO/CHUO UNIVERSITY. FACULTY OF SCIENCE AND ENGINEERING. BULLETIN. see SCIENCES: COMPREHENSIVE WORKS

CHURCH AND SOCIETY NEWSLETTER; Christian social thought in a future perspective. see RELIGIONS AND THEOLOGY

CIENCIA INTERAMERICANA. see SCIENCES: COMPREHENSIVE WORKS

CIENCIA PARA TODOS. see SCIENCES: COMPREHENSIVE WORKS

CIENCIA TECNOLOGIA Y DESARROLLO. see SCIENCES: COMPREHENSIVE WORKS

CIENCIA Y DESARROLLO. see SCIENCES: COMPREHENSIVE WORKS

600 500 CU ISSN 0253-7397
CIENCIAS TECNICAS FISICAS Y MATEMATICAS. 1981. irreg., no.6, 1986. exchange basis. Academia de Ciencias de Cuba, Apartado 2291, Zona 2, Havana, Cuba. (Dist. by: Ediciones Cubanas, Obispo No. 461, Apdo. 605, Havana, Cuba) Ed. Jose Altshuler. circ. 1,500. Indexed: Sci.Abstr.
—BLDSC shelfmark: 3198.205655.

600 UK
CIRCUIT WORLD. 1973. q. £44.80($90) (Institute of Interconnection Technology) Wela Publications Ltd., 8 Barns St., Ayr KA7 1XA, Scotland. TEL 0292-283186. FAX 0292-284719. (Co-sponsor: Printed Circuit Interconnection Federation) Ed. William Goldie. adv.; bk.rev. (back issues avail.) Indexed: Copper Abstr., Sci.Abstr.

600 US
CLOVERVIEW. q. Virginia Polytechnic Institute and State University, 202 Media Bldg., Blacksburg, VA 24061. TEL 703-961-7370.

600 NE ISSN 0165-232X
GB641 CODEN: CRSTDL
COLD REGIONS SCIENCE AND TECHNOLOGY. 1979. 3/yr. fl.366 (effective 1992). Elsevier Science Publishers B.V., P.O. Box 211, 1000 AE Amsterdam, Netherlands. TEL 020-5803911. FAX 020-5803598. TELEX 18582 ESPA NL. (Subscr. in U.S. and Canada to: Elsevier Science Publishing Co., Inc., Box 882, Madison Sq. Sta., New York, NY 10159. TEL 212-989-5800) Ed. M. Mellor. (also avail. in microform from RPI) Indexed: Appl.Mech.Rev., Chem.Abstr., Curr. Cont., Eng.Ind., Forest Prod.Abstr., Geo.Abstr., GeoRef., Geotech.Abstr., Irr.& Drain.Abstr., Soils & Fert.
—BLDSC shelfmark: 3295.760000.
  Description: Deals with the scientific and technical problems of cold environments, including both natural and artificial environments.
  Refereed Serial

600 SP
COLECCION TECNOLOGIA Y SOCIEDAD. 1978. irreg. price varies. Editorial Gustavo Gili, S.A., Rosellon 87-89, Barcelona 29, Spain.

600 AT ISSN 0069-7184
Q180.A8 CODEN: ASIRAF
COMMONWEALTH SCIENTIFIC AND INDUSTRIAL RESEARCH ORGANIZATION. ANNUAL REPORT. 1948. a. Aus.$5. C.S.I.R.O. (Dickson), P.O. Box 225, Dickson, A.C.T. 2602, Australia. Indexed: AESIS, Biol.Abstr., GeoRef.

677 600 UK ISSN 0266-3538
TA418.9.C6 CODEN: CSTCEH
COMPOSITES SCIENCE AND TECHNOLOGY. 1968. 12/yr.(in 3 vols.). £575 (effective 1992). Elsevier Science Publishers Ltd., Crown House, Linton Rd., Barking, Essex IG11 8JU, England. TEL 081-594-7272. FAX 081-594-5942. TELEX 896950 APPSCI G. (Subscr. in U.S. and Canada to: Elsevier Science Publishing Co., Inc., Box 882, Madison Sq. Sta., New York, NY 10159. TEL 212-989-5800) Eds. B. Harris, Tsu-Wei Chou. adv.; B&W page £345; 192 x 258; adv. contact: Claire Coakley. bk.rev.; illus.; index. (also avail. in microform from RPI; back issues avail.) Indexed: Abstr.Bull.Inst.Pap.Chem., Chem.Abstr., Curr.Cont., Eng.Ind., Excerp.Med., Int.Aerosp.Abstr., J.of Ferroc., Met.Abstr., Sci.Cit.Ind., Text.Tech.Dig., World Alum.Abstr., World Text.Abstr.
—BLDSC shelfmark: 3365.650000.
  Incorporates (in 1985): Fibre Science and Technology (ISSN 0015-0568)
  Description: Publishes original articles, occasional review papers, and letters, on all aspects of the fundamental and applied science of engineering composites.
  Refereed Serial

600 SA
COMPUTECH. (Text in English) m. R.15. Technews (Pty) Ltd., P.O. Box 626, Kloof 3640, South Africa. TEL 031-764-0593. FAX 031-864-0386. Ed. Mike Barker. circ. 12,500 (controlled). (tabloid format)
  Description: Covers advanced industrial technology: automation, computation, instrumentation.

600 PH
CON - SCIENCE. (Text in English and Pilipino; summaries in English) 1979. bi-m. P.1. Industrial Technology Development Institute, P. Gil, Taft Ave., P.O. Box 774, Manila, Philippines. FAX 632-592275. TELEX ITT 40404. Ed. Ronand Henson. bk.rev.; circ. 750.
  Formerly: N I S T Newsletter.

CONFERENCE ON SPACE SIMULATION. PROCEEDINGS. see AERONAUTICS AND SPACE FLIGHT

600 US
CONFERENCE ON U S TECHNOLOGY POLICY. PROCEEDINGS. Variant title: I E E E Conference on U S Technology Policy. Proceedings. 1977. biennial. price varies. (I E E E, Technical Activities Board) Institute of Electrical and Electronics Engineers, Inc., 345 E. 47th St., New York, NY 10017. TEL 212-705-7900. FAX 212-705-7682. (Subscr. to: IEEE Service Center, Box 1331, 445 Hoes Lane, Piscataway, NJ 08855-1331) (Co-sponsor: IEEE, United States Activities Board)
  Formerly (until 1979): Conference on U S Technological Policy. Proceedings.
  Description: Discusses policies in the areas of energy, national resources, information systems and public understanding.

600 CR ISSN 0253-2492
Q180.C75
CONSEJO NACIONAL PARA INVESTIGACIONES CIENTIFICAS Y TECNOLOGICAS, COSTA RICA. INFORME ANUAL. 1975. a. free. Consejo Nacional para Investigaciones Cientificas y Tecnologicas, Departamento de Informacion y Documentacion, Apdo. 10318, San Jose, Costa Rica. circ. 1,000.

CONSUMER INFORMATION APPLIANCE; the platform for enhanced services. see COMMUNICATIONS — Telephone And Telegraph

CONTRIBUTIONS TO THE HISTORY OF NATURAL SCIENCES AND TECHNOLOGY IN THE BALTIC/IZ ISTORII ESTESTVOZNANIYA I TEKHNIKI PRIBALTIKI. see SCIENCES: COMPREHENSIVE WORKS

600 US ISSN 0887-1930
HG4057
CORPORATE TECHNOLOGY DIRECTORY. (In 4 vols.) 1986. a. $425. Corporate Technology Information Services, Inc., 12 Alfred St., Ste. 200, Woburn, MA 01801. TEL 617-932-3939. FAX 617-932-6335. TELEX 497 2961 CRPTECH. Ed. Steven W. Parker. circ. 35,000. (back issues avail.)
  ●Also available online. Vendor(s): Orbit Information Technologies (CORP).
  Also available on CD-ROM. Producer(s): R.R. Bowker.
  Description: Provides information on America's 30,000 manufacturers of high-tech products.

TECHNOLOGY: COMPREHENSIVE WORKS

CORROSION PREVENTION AND CONTROL. see *METALLURGY*

COULEE CONTINUE. see *OCCUPATIONAL HEALTH AND SAFETY*

CROSSROADS; Halacha and the modern world. see *RELIGIONS AND THEOLOGY — Judaic*

CURRENT AWARENESS. S D I SERVICE. (Scientific Documentation Centre Ltd.) see *MEDICAL SCIENCES*

CYTOTECHNOLOGY; international journal of cell culture and biotechnology. see *BIOLOGY — Cytology And Histology*

600 340   GW
D I N. CATALOGUE OF TECHNICAL RULES. German edition: D I N - Katalog fuer Technische Regeln (ISSN 0722-9313) (Text in English, German) 1926. a. DM.280($90) (Deutsches Institut fuer Normung e.V. (D I N)) Beuth Verlag GmbH, Burggrafenstr. 6, 1000 Berlin 30, Germany. FAX 030-2601231. TELEX 183622-BVB-D. (Dist. in US by: Global Engineering Documents, 2805 McGaw Ave., P.O. Box 19539, Irvine, CA 92714) circ. 11,000.

DAEDALUS. see *MUSEUMS AND ART GALLERIES*

DANESHMAND. see *SCIENCES: COMPREHENSIVE WORKS*

600   DK   ISSN 0416-6981
DANSK TEKNISK LITTERATURSELSKAB. SKRIFTSERIE. a. DKK 100. Dansk Teknisk Litteraturselskab, Anker Engelunds Vej 1, DK-2800 Lyngby, Denmark.

600   SA
DATAWEEK. (Text in English) fortn. R.30. Technews (Pty) Ltd., P.O. Box 626, Kloof 3640, South Africa. TEL 031-764-0593. FAX 031-764-0386. Ed. R.K. Beaumont. circ. 7,800 (controlled). (tabloid format)
Description: Covers electronic technology: components, design, manufacture, testing and maintenance.

DAXUE KEJI/UNIVERSITY SCIENCE AND TECHNOLOGY. see *SCIENCES: COMPREHENSIVE WORKS*

DEFENCE SCIENCE JOURNAL. see *MILITARY*

DEFENSE TECHNOLOGY BUSINESS. see *MILITARY*

DEJINY VED A TECHNIKY/HISTORY OF SCIENCES AND TECHNOLOGY. see *SCIENCES: COMPREHENSIVE WORKS*

600   DK   ISSN 0906-5822
DENMARK. FORSKNINGSAFDELINGEN. FORSKNING. 1975. 10/yr. DKK 400. Forskningsafdelingen - Danish Research Administration, H.C. Andersens Boulevard 40, 1553 Copenhagen V, Denmark. FAX 01-323501. TELEX 15652-FS. Ed. Inge Berg Hansen. adv.; bk.rev.; bibl.; circ. 2,500.
Former titles: Denmark. Forskningsdirektoratet. Forskning og Samfund & Denmark. Forskningsafdelingen. Forskning og Samfund (ISSN 0106-4762)

600   DK   ISSN 0109-0070
DENMARK. TEKNOLOGISTYRELSEN. NYHEDSBREV. 1982. bi-m. free. Teknologistyrelsen, Tagensvej 135, 2200 Copenhagen N, Denmark.

600   US
DENTAL PRODUCTS REPORT INTERNATIONAL. 1980. 6/yr. $24. Medical Economics Company Inc., 680 Kinderkamack Rd., Oradell, NJ 07649. TEL 201-262-3030. FAX 201-262-5461. Ed. Jeanne K. Matson. adv.; circ. 35,000. (tabloid format)

DESIGN & DRAFTING NEWS. see *ENGINEERING*

745.2   US   ISSN 1042-8534
DESIGN MANAGEMENT. 1976. m. $42 (foreign $112). Communication Channels, Inc., 6255 Barfield Rd., Atlanta, GA 30328-4369. TEL 404-256-9800. FAX 404-256-3116. TELEX 4611075 COMCHANI. Ed. Tim Darnell. adv.; bk.rev.; index; circ. 41,500. (also avail. in microform from UMI; reprint service avail. from UMI)
Former titles (until 1988): Design Graphics World; (until Jan. 1979): Engineering Graphics; Supersedes (1961-1976): Drafting and Repro Digest (ISSN 0745-8754)
Description: For architects and engineers working within the CAD environment who are responsible for creating designs and for managing the design projects.

745.2   US   ISSN 0011-9407
TA175   CODEN: DIGNAO
DESIGN NEWS; news for OEM design engineers. 1946. 24/yr. $94.95 (Canada $149.75; Mexico $139.95; elsewhere $179.95). Cahners Publishing Company (Newton) (Subsidiary of: Reed International PLC), Division of Reed Publishing (USA) Inc., 275 Washington St., Newton, MA 02158-1630. TEL 617-964-3030. FAX 617-558-4402. (Subscr. to: 44 Cook St., Denver, CO 80206. TEL 800-662-7776) Ed. Lawrence D. Maloney. adv.; abstr.; charts; illus.; pat.; tr.lit.; index; circ. 170,193. (also avail. in microform from RPI; reprint service avail. from UMI) **Indexed:** A.I.Abstr., A.S.& T.Ind., Bus.Ind., CAD CAM Abstr., Chem.Abstr., DM & T, Energy Info.Abstr., Hlth.Ind., Ind.Sci.Rev., Mag.Ind., Met.Abstr., PMR, PROMT, Robomat., Sci.Abstr., Sh.& Vib.Dig., Tel.Abstr., Text.Tech.Dig., Tr.& Indus.Ind., World Alum.Abstr. —BLDSC shelfmark: 3560.000000.
Description: For design engineers and engineering management. Provides information on power transmission, fastening, computers and CAD-CAM, fluid power, electrical and electronic design, new materials, new processes and new patents. Emphasis is on both mechanical and electrical-electronic design.
Refereed Serial

DESIGN PRODUCTS AND APPLICATION. see *ENGINEERING*

745.2   GW   ISSN 0932-3724
DESIGN-REPORT. bi-m. Rat fuer Formgebung, Ludwig-Erhard-Anlage 1, 6000 Frankfurt a.M. 1, Germany. TEL 069-747919. FAX 069-7410911. circ. 1,200.

600   UK
DESIGN REVIEW. q. (Chartered Society of Designers) Tradevine Ltd., 26 Cramer St., London W1M 3HE, England. TEL 071-486-7419. FAX 071-486-1451. (Subscr. to: 29 Bedford Sq., London WC1B 3EG, England. TEL 071-631-1510) Ed. Deyan Sudjic. adv. contact: Craig Pearson.

DESIGN STUDIES. see *ARCHITECTURE*

600   GW
DER DEUTSCHE TECHNIKER. 1968. bi-m. DM.22. G. von Raison, Ed. & Pub., Postfach 1240, 3206 Lamspringe, Germany. TEL 05183-466. adv.; bk.rev.; circ. 11,000.

600   US   ISSN 0192-1312
HN980
DEVELOPMENT COMMUNICATION REPORT. 1972. q. $10 (free to qualified personnel). (Institute for International Research) Clearinghouse on Development Communication, 1815 N. Ft. Myer Dr., Ste. 600, Arlington, VA 22209. TEL 703-527-5546. FAX 703-527-4661. TELEX 710-833-0320 IIRINC VA. (Co-sponsor: U.S. Agency for International Development) Ed. Kathleen Selvaggio. bk.rev.; circ. 7,000 (controlled). **Indexed:** Educ.Tech.Abstr., ERIC, Rural Ext.Educ.& Tr.Abstr., Rural Recreat.Tour.Abstr., World Agri.Econ.& Rural Sociol.Abstr.
Formerly (until 1976): Instructional Technology Report.
Refereed Serial

600   US
DEVELOPNET NEWS; online news and views on technology transfer in international development. q. free. Volunteers in Technical Assistance, Inc., 1815 N. Lynn St., Ste.200, Arlington, VA 22209-2079. TEL 703-276-1800. FAX 703-243-1865. TELEX 440192 VITAUI. Ed. Patricia Mantey. bk.rev.
●Available only online.
Description: Specializes in information dissemination and communications technology; offers services in the areas of sustainable agriculture, food processing, renewable energy applications, water sanitation and supply, small enterprise development and information management.

007   US   ISSN 0886-0076
T176   CODEN: DARTEB
DIRECTORY OF AMERICAN RESEARCH AND TECHNOLOGY; organizations active in product development for business. a. $297. R.R. Bowker, A Reed Reference Publishing Company, Division of Reed Publishing (USA) Inc., 121 Chanlon Rd., New Providence, NJ 07974. TEL 800-521-8110. FAX 908-665-6688. TELEX 138 755. (Subscr. to: Order Dept., Box 31, New Providence, NJ 07974) (also avail. in magnetic tape) **Indexed:** Copper Abstr.
●Also available online. Vendor(s): Orbit Information Technologies (DART).
Also available on CD-ROM. Producer(s): R.R. Bowker.
Formerly (until 1986): Industrial Research Laboratories of the United States (ISSN 0073-7623)
Description: Profiles over 11,000 US and Canadian corporate and nonprofit, independent, and university research facilities. Lists key personnel, contact information, staff size, and research activities. Includes a Personnel Index and a Classification Index that cross-references organizations under 33 fields and 1,500 subfields.

DIRECTORY OF FEDERAL LABORATORIES. see *BUSINESS AND ECONOMICS — Trade And Industrial Directories*

DIRECTORY OF JAPANESE TECHNICAL RESOURCES IN THE UNITED STATES. see *BUSINESS AND ECONOMICS — Trade And Industrial Directories*

600   US
DIRECTORY OF MEMBRANE & HIGH TECH SEPARATIONS (YEAR). a. $300. Business Communications Co., Inc. (Norwalk), 25 Van Zant St., Ste. 13, Norwalk, CT 06855. TEL 203-853-4266. FAX 203-853-0348. TELEX 6502934929 UWI.
Formerly: Yearbook and Directory of Members and Separation Technology.

DIRECTORY OF RESEARCH ORGANISATIONS AND FACILITIES IN SOUTH AFRICA. see *SCIENCES: COMPREHENSIVE WORKS*

DIRECTORY OF SCIENTIFIC AND TECHNICAL ASSOCIATIONS IN ISRAEL. see *SCIENCES: COMPREHENSIVE WORKS*

DIRECTORY OF SOUTH AFRICAN ASSOCIATIONS/GIDS VAN SUID-AFRIKAANSE VERENIGINGS. see *SCIENCES: COMPREHENSIVE WORKS*

DIRECTORY OF THE SCIENTISTS, TECHNOLOGISTS, AND ENGINEERS OF THE P C S I R. (Pakistan Council of Scientific and Industrial Research) see *SCIENCES: COMPREHENSIVE WORKS*

DISCOVER (BURBANK). see *SCIENCES: COMPREHENSIVE WORKS*

600 500   CC   ISSN 0253-4258
DONGBEI GONGXUEYUAN XUEBAO/NORTHEAST INSTITUTE OF TECHNOLOGY. JOURNAL. (Text in Chinese) q. $1.50 per no. Dongbei Gongxueyuan - Northeast Institute of Technology, No.1, Wenhua Lu 1 Duan, Heping-qu, Shenyang, Liaoning 110006, People's Republic of China. (Dist. outside China by: China International Book Trading Corp., P.O. Box 399, Beijing, P.R.C.) **Indexed:** Chem.Abstr., Math.R.

600   DK   ISSN 0108-6707
DRIFTSTEKNIKERBOGEN. 1974. a. DKK 100. Danmarks Tekniske Hoejskole, Driftsteknisk Institut, Bygn. 423, DK-2800 Lyngby, Denmark. TEL 45-93-44-66. FAX 45-93-44-67. illus.; circ. 300.
Formerly: Driftsteknikerdag.

DZALUU DZOHION BUTEEGCH/YOUNG INVENTOR. see *SCIENCES: COMPREHENSIVE WORKS*

TECHNOLOGY: COMPREHENSIVE WORKS 4597

600 FR
E A O. (Enseignement Assiste par Ordinateur) m. 1200 F. A Jour, 11 rue du Marche St. Honore, 75001 Paris, France. TEL 42-96-67-22. FAX 40-20-07-75. TELEX TELEXEL 615887 F.

E D A. (Electronic Design Automation Ltd.) see *ELECTRONICS*

600 US ISSN 0278-4270
TK6553
E M C TECHNOLOGY & INTERFERENCE CONTROL NEWS. (Electro-Magnetic Compatibility) Running title: E M C Technology. 1982. bi-m. free to qualified personnel. Interference Control Tech, State Rt. 625, Box D, Gainesville, VA 22065. TEL 703-347-0030. FAX 703-347-5813. Ed. Don White. adv.; bk.rev.; charts; illus.; stat.; index; circ. 38,000. (back issues avail.)
—BLDSC shelfmark: 3733.156000.
  Description: For engineers in the electronics OEM. Provides news and expert tips on how to suppress electromagnetic and electrostatic interference in any commercial or military design in any industry.

E N E A NOTIZIARIO-ENERGIA E INNOVAZIONE; informazione sull'energia e sulle nuove tecnologie. see *ENERGY*

600 US
E O S - E S D TECHNOLOGY. (Electrical Overstress - Electrostatic Discharge); the magazine for ESD-control professionals in the electronics industry. European edition: E O S - E S D Technology Europe. 1989. bi-m. $65. Brinton Group Inc., 49 Eaton Rd., Framingham, MA 01701. TEL 508-877-7958. FAX 508-877-3457. (also avail. in microfiche; microfilm)

600 US
E O S - E S D TECHNOLOGY EUROPE. (Electrical Overstress - Electrostatic Discharge); the magazine for ESD control professionals in the electronics industry. American edition: E O S - E S D Technology. 1987. q. $65. Brinton Group Inc., 49 Eaton Road, Framingham, MA 01701. TEL 508-877-7958. FAX 508-877-3457. circ. controlled. (also avail. in microfiche; microfilm)

E R I C - I R UPDATE. (Educational Resources Information Center - Information Resources) see *LIBRARY AND INFORMATION SCIENCES — Computer Applications*

600 US
EAST ASIA HIGH TECH REVIEW. 1991. m. $295. Mead Ventures, Inc., Box 44952, Phoenix, AZ 85064. TEL 602-234-0044. FAX 602-234-0076. Ed. Christopher Mead.
  Formed by merger of: Japan High Tech Review (ISSN 0743-4871) & Southeast Asia High Tech Review (ISSN 0892-1938) & Korea High Tech Review (ISSN 0888-7373)
  Description: Contains information on East Asian high tech industries, including computer hardware and software, data communications, fiber optics, video technologies, robotics and semiconductors.

600 US ISSN 0145-1421
CODEN: EWTDDZ
EAST-WEST TECHNOLOGY DIGEST. 1976. m. $99. Welt Publishing Co., Ste. 800, 1413 K St., N.W., Washington, DC 20005. TEL 202-371-0555. Eds. Jerry Orvedahl, Larry Holland. bk.rev.; bibl.; charts. (back issues avail.) **Indexed:** Chem.Abstr.
  Formerly: Soviet Technology Digest.
  Description: Containing information on technological development from the formerly Soviet Union and Eastern Europe. Offers news about license offers, inventions, products available for purchasing and research in progress.

620 FR
ECOLE NATIONALE SUPERIEURE DE TECHNIQUES AVANCEES. RAPPORT D'ACTIVITE SUR LES RECHERCHES. 1972. biennial. free. Ecole Nationale Superieure de Techniques Avancees, Direction des Recherches, 32, Bd. Victor, 75015 Paris, France. TEL 45-52-55-87. FAX 45525587. bk.rev.; circ. 1,200.

600 US ISSN 1043-8599
HC79.T4 CODEN: EINTEO
▼**ECONOMICS OF INNOVATION AND NEW TECHNOLOGY.** 1991. 4/yr. $55. Harwood Academic Publishers, 270 Eighth Ave., New York, NY 10011. TEL 212-206-8900. FAX 212-645-2459. TELEX 236735 GOPUB UR. (Subscr. to: Box 786, Cooper Sta., New York, NY 01276. TEL 800-545-8398; UK subscr. to: P.O. Box 90, Reading, Berkshire RG1 8JL, England. TEL 0734-560-080) Eds. Peter Swann, W. Edward Steinmuller. (also avail. in microform)
—BLDSC shelfmark: 3657.021000.
  Refereed Serial

EDUCATION AND TRAINING. see *EDUCATION*

EDUCATIONAL TECHNOLOGY; the magazine for managers of change in education. see *EDUCATION*

600 JA ISSN 0387-7434
EDUCATIONAL TECHNOLOGY RESEARCH. s-a. $22. (Educational Technology Journal Association of Japan) Japan Scientific Societies Press, 6-2-10 Hongo, Bunkyo-ku, Tokyo 113, Japan. TEL 3814-2001. FAX 3814-2002. TELEX 2722268 BCJSP J. (Dist. by: Business Center for Academic Societies Japan, Koshin Bldg., 6-16-3 Hongo, Bunkyo-ku, Tokyo 113, Japan; Dist. in U.S. by: International Specialized Book Services, Inc., 5602 N.E. Hassalo St., Portland, OR 97213)

EMBASSY OF SWITZERLAND BULLETIN. see *SCIENCES: COMPREHENSIVE WORKS*

ENCYCLOPEDIA OF PHYSICAL SCIENCE & TECHNOLOGY YEARBOOK. see *SCIENCES: COMPREHENSIVE WORKS*

ENERGIE; das Magazin fuer Wirtschaft, Forschung, Technik, Umwelt. see *ENERGY*

ENERGY CONSERVATION AND UTILIZATION TECHNOLOGIES. see *CONSERVATION*

604.2 US ISSN 0046-2012
ENGINEERING DESIGN GRAPHICS JOURNAL. 1936. 3/yr. (in 1 vol.). $7.50 to non-members (foreign $25); members $6. American Society for Engineering Education, Engineering Design Graphics Division, c/o John B. Crittenden, Ed., Division of Engineering Fundamentals, Virginia Polytechnic Institute and State University, Blacksburg, VA 24061-0218. TEL 703-231-6555. adv.; bk.rev.; charts; illus.; circ. 800. (also avail. in microform from UMI; reprint service avail. from UMI; back issues avail.)
—BLDSC shelfmark: 3758.960000.
  Former titles (until vol.33, no.3, 1969): Journal of Engineering Graphics; (until vol.22, no.2, 1958): Journal of Engineering Drawing.
  Description: Articles devoted to the fundamentals of engineering graphics education and graphics technology. Topics include engineering graphics, computer graphics, descriptive geometry, geometric modeling, computer-aided drafting and design, graphic data processing, and graphics instruction.
  Refereed Serial

ENTREPRENEURS & INVESTORS ANNUAL. see *BUSINESS AND ECONOMICS — Small Business*

ENVIRONMENTAL SCIENCE AND TECHNOLOGY: A WILEY-INTERSCIENCE SERIES OF TEXTS AND MONOGRAPHS. see *ENVIRONMENTAL STUDIES*

600 CU
EQUIPOS Y PRODUCTOS. TECNOLOGIA. m. Academia de Ciencias, Instituto de Documentacion e Informacion Cientifico-Tecnica (I D I C T), Capitolio Nacional, Prado y San Jose, Habana 2, Havana, Cuba.

EUROPE - LATIN AMERICA REPORT: SCIENCE AND TECHNOLOGY. see *SCIENCES: COMPREHENSIVE WORKS*

600 SZ
EUROPEAN ORGANIZATION FOR QUALITY. CONFERENCE PROCEEDINGS. 1970. a. price varies. European Organization for Quality - Organisation Europeenne pour la Qualite, P.O. Box 5032, CH-3001 Bern, Switzerland. TEL 031-216166. FAX 031-216951. TELEX 913278-ATAG-CH.
  Formerly: European Organization for Quality Control. Conference Proceedings (ISSN 0071-2981)

EUROPEAN RESEARCH CENTRES; a directory of organizations in science, technology, agriculture and medicine. see *SCIENCES: COMPREHENSIVE WORKS*

EUROPEAN SOURCES OF SCIENTIFIC AND TECHNICAL INFORMATION. see *SCIENCES: COMPREHENSIVE WORKS*

658.5 SZ ISSN 0014-3243
EUROTEC; European technical news. (Text in English, French and German) 1941. bi-m. 70 Fr. Hugo Buchser S.A., Route de Acacias 25, P.O. Box 30, CH-1211 Geneva 24, Switzerland. TEL 022-3003737. FAX 022-3003748. adv.; bk.rev.; bibl.; charts; illus.; mkt.; pat.; stat.; tr.lit.; circ. 11,000.

600 500 BL
EVENTOS EM POLITICA CIENTIFICA E TECNOLOGICA. q. free. Instituto Brasileiro de Informacao em Ciencia e Tecnologia, SAS Quadra 2, Lote 6, Bloco H, 70070 Brasilia, D.F., Brazil. TEL 2176161. FAX 2262677.
  Formerly: Calendario de Eventos Tecnico-Cientificos Realizados no Brazil (ISSN 0100-3399)

EVERYMAN'S SCIENCE. see *SCIENCES: COMPREHENSIVE WORKS*

600 614.7 US ISSN 0192-7469
EXHAUST NEWS. 1977. m. $12. Heather Publishing Co., Box 120937, Arlington, TX 76012. TEL 817-860-2375. Ed. Lee Cruse. adv.; circ. 14,000.

EXPERIENTIA. SUPPLEMENTUM. see *BIOLOGY*

600 DK ISSN 0108-9048
F A T - BLADET. no.45, 1983. irreg. (2-4/yr.). membership. Foreningen af Teleteknikere, Rolfsvej 37-2, 2000 Copenhagen F, Denmark.
  Formerly: Foreningen af Teleteknikere.

600 FR ISSN 0985-2220
CODEN: FTSUE4
F T S. (French Technology Survey) (Text in English, French) 6/yr. 900 F.($150) Association pour la Diffusion de l'Information Technologique (ADITECH), 96 Bd Auguste Blanqui, 75013 Paris, France. TEL 33-1-47-07-14-41. FAX 33-1-45-35-43-45. Ed. Fabienne Huyghe. adv.
  Description: Presents high level information related to French technological innovation and European trends.

658.7 SW ISSN 0014-6234
FABRIKSARBETAREN. 1891. 19/yr. SEK 80. Svenska Fabriksarbetarefoerbundet, Box 1114, 111 81 Stockholm, Sweden. Ed. Tage Israelsson. adv.; bk.rev.; illus.; circ. 99,000.
  Description: Published by the Swedish Factory Worker's Union for the members of the Union. Articles vary from wage negotiations and political questions to environmental problems.

600 US ISSN 0172-5203
FACHBERICHTE MESSEN - STEUERN - REGELN. 1977. irreg. price varies. Springer-Verlag, 175 Fifth Ave., New York, NY 10010. TEL 212-460-1500. (Also Berlin, Heidelberg, Tokyo and Vienna) (reprint service avail. from ISI)

658.7 621 AT ISSN 0728-9413
FACTORY EQUIPMENT NEWS. 1966. m. Aus.$66. Thomson Publications Australia, 47 Chippen St., Chippendale, N.S.W. 2008, Australia. TEL 02-699-2411. FAX 02-698-3920. TELEX 122226. Ed. Jones Alpers. adv.; illus.; tr.lit.; circ. 16,500. **Indexed:** Br.Ceram.Abstr.
  Formerly: F E N: Australian Factory Equipment News (ISSN 0014-5807)

600 500 UK ISSN 0071-4097
FAWLEY FOUNDATION LECTURES. (Not published in 1985 and in 1988) 1954. a. £2. University of Southampton, Highfield, Southampton SO9 5NH, England. FAX 0703-593037. TELEX 47661. Ed. S.L. Headleand. circ. 3,500.

TECHNOLOGY: COMPREHENSIVE WORKS

600 US
FEDERAL APPLIED TECHNOLOGY DATABASE. Short title: F A T D. s-m. price varies. U.S. National Technical Information Service, 5285 Port Royal Rd., Springfield, VA 22161. TEL 703-487-4630.
●Available only online. Vendor(s): BRS.
Description: Includes information on federal laboratory resources, technology and inventions for licensing catalogs.

600 US
FEDERAL TECHNOLOGY CATALOG. Included with: N T I S Tech Notes (ISSN 0889-8464) a. $33 in US, Canada, Mexico; elsewhere $66 (free with NTIS Tech Notes). U.S. National Technical Information Service, 5285 Port Royal Rd., Springfield, VA 22161. TEL 703-487-4630. (back issues avail.)

600 US
FEDERAL TECHNOLOGY TRANSFER. 1981. bi-m. $90. National Technology Transfer Institute, 1200 Pennsylvania Ave., Box 7206, Washington, DC 20044. TEL 703-931-0511. Ed. Kurt Willinger. circ. 300. (back issues avail.)
Formerly (until 1985): Technology Utilization.
Description: Profiles Federal laboratories and their R & D technology transfers. to U.S. businesses.

FERRUM; Nachrichten aus der Eisenbibliothek. see METALLURGY

658.5 GW ISSN 0015-024X
CODEN: FTGBAJ
FERTIGUNGSTECHNIK UND BETRIEB; Fachzeitschrift fuer Vorbereitung und Durchfuehrung der Produktion in der metallverarbeitenden Industrie. (Text in German; summaries in English and Russian) 1951. m. DM.96. Verlag Technik GmbH, Oranienburger Str. 13-14, 1020 Berlin, Germany. TEL 030-2870-0. TELEX 0112228-TECHN-DD. Ed. Edelgard Wendorf. adv.; bk.rev.; bibl.; charts; illus.; pat.; stat.; index, cum.index; circ. 6,900. **Indexed:** C.I.S. Abstr., Chem.Abstr., Met.Abstr., Sci.Abstr., Sh.& Vib.Dig., World Alum.Abstr.
—BLDSC shelfmark: 3909.050000.
Description: Deals technically with problems of the metal-working industry: computer-aided design, automated manufacturing systems, robotics, modernization.

668.6 II
FERTILISER TECHNOLOGY. (Text in English) 1964. q. Rs.15($6) Fertilizer (Planning & Development) India Ltd., Sindri, Dhanbad 828122, Bihar, India. Ed. Benoy K. Banerjee. bk.rev.; abstr.; stat.; cum.index; circ. 800. **Indexed:** Anal.Abstr., Anal.Abstr., Biol.Abstr., Chem.Abstr., Fert.Abstr., Field Crop Abstr., Herb.Abstr., Hort.Abstr., Indian Sci.Abstr., PROMT, Ref.Zh., Sci.Abstr., Soils & Fert.
Formerly (until vol.12, no.3, 1975): Technology (ISSN 0040-1641)

FH-BO-JOURNAL. (Fachhochschule Bochum) see COLLEGE AND ALUMNI

FIBEROPTIC PRODUCT NEWS. see COMMUNICATIONS — Telephone And Telegraph

FINANCIAL TECHNOLOGY BULLETIN. see BUSINESS AND ECONOMICS — Banking And Finance

600 US ISSN 1058-0948
▼**FLAME RETARDANCY NEWS.** 1991. m. $295 (foreign $345). Business Communications Co., Inc. (Norwalk), 25 Van Zant St., Ste. 13, Norwalk, CT 06855. TEL 203-853-4266. FAX 203-853-0348. TELEX 6502934929 WUI. Ed. Norma Corbitt.
●Also available online. Vendor(s): NewsNet.

600 US ISSN 1043-6030
FLORIDA TECHNOLOGY REVIEW. 1989. m. $127 (effective Jan. 1992). Technology Transfer Specialists Inc, Box 03-4075, Indialantic, FL 32903-0975. TEL 407-777-6777. Ed. S. Carl Ahmed. adv.; bk.rev.; charts; illus.; stat.; circ. 4,600. (looseleaf format; back issues avail.)
Description: Examines on-going research, future trends, and the current prgrams that affect scientific and techonological findings in Florida's universities, state & federal governments, and private enterprise.

600 371.9 US
FOCUS ON TECHNOLOGY. q. free. TeleSensory, Inc., 455 N. Bernardo Ave., Box 7455, Mountain View, CA 94043. TEL 415-960-0920. FAX 415-969-9064. Ed. Anne Leahy-Jones. circ. 50,000. (back issues avail.)
Formerly (until 1989): R E News.
Description: Offers technological aids serving the low vision and blind community.

FORSKNING OCH FRAMSTEG. see SCIENCES: COMPREHENSIVE WORKS

FORUM WISSENSCHAFT; das kritische Wissenschaftsmagazine. see SCIENCES: COMPREHENSIVE WORKS

FRONTIERS OF POWER CONFERENCE. PROCEEDINGS. see ENERGY

600 GW ISSN 0071-9749
FUEHRER DURCH DIE TECHNISCHE LITERATUR; Katalog technischer Werke fuer Studium und Praxis. 1900. a. DM.36. Fr. Weidemanns Buchhandlung (H.Witt), Georgstr. 11, Postfach 6406, 3000 Hannover 1, Germany. TEL 0511-14014. FAX 0511-325971. Ed. K. Deichmann. adv.; circ. 20,000.

600 JA
FUKUI UNIVERSITY. FACULTY OF EDUCATION. MEMOIRS. SERIES 5: APPLIED SCIENCE AND TECHNOLOGY. (Text in Japanese; summaries in English and Japanese) 1964. a. Fukui University, Faculty of Education, 9-1, 3-chome, Bunkyo, Fukui 910, Japan.

FUKUOKA KYOIKU DAIGAKU KIYO. DAI-3-BUNSATSU. SUGAKU, RIKA, GIJUTSUKA HEN/FUKUOKA UNIVERSITY OF EDUCATION. BULLETIN. PART 3: MATHEMATICS, NATURAL SCIENCES AND TECHNOLOGY. see SCIENCES: COMPREHENSIVE WORKS

FUORISTRADA. see ENVIRONMENTAL STUDIES

338.5 UK ISSN 0016-3287
HB3730 CODEN: FUTUBD
FUTURES; the journal of forecasting, planning and policy. 1968. 10/yr. £215 in UK & Europe; elsewhere £230. Butterworth - Heinemann Ltd. (Subsidiary of: Reed International PLC), Linacre House, Jordan Hill, Oxford OX2 8DP, England. TEL 0865-310366. FAX 0865-310898. TELEX 83111 BHPOXF G. (Subscr. to: Turpin Transactions Ltd., Distribution Centre, Blackhorse Rd., Latchworth, Herts SG6 1HN, England. TEL 0462-672555) Ed. Clare Degenhardt. bk.rev.; charts; illus.; index. (also avail. in microform from UMI; back issues avail.) **Indexed:** ABC, ABI Inform, BPIA, C.I.S. Abstr., Curr.Cont., Eng.Ind., Field Crop Abstr., Fut.Surv., Herb.Abstr., INIS Atomind., Int.Lab.Doc., Rural Recreat.Tour.Abstr., SCIMP, Soc.Sci.Ind., SSCI, World Agri.Econ.& Rural Sociol.Abstr.
—BLDSC shelfmark: 4060.650000.
Description: Features studies, analyses and projections of the future, for those in business, industrial R & D, academic research, defense planning, international relations, and public affairs.
Refereed Serial

600 US
FUTURETECH. 1986. s-m. $1500 (foreign $1545). Technical Insights, Inc., 32 N. Dean St., Englewood, NJ 07631. TEL 201-568-4744. FAX 201-568-8247. TELEX 425900 SWIFT UI ATT. (Subscr. to: Box 1304, Fort Lee, NJ 07024-1304) Ed. Peter Finlay. bibl.; pat. (looseleaf format; back issues avail.)
●Also available online. Vendor(s): NewsNet.
Description: Presents strategic technologies judged capable of having an impact on broad industrial fronts.

FUTURETECH STRATEGIC MARKETS. see BUSINESS AND ECONOMICS — Marketing And Purchasing

FUTURICS; a quarterly journal of futures research. see SOCIOLOGY

600 US ISSN 0738-9264
FUTURIFIC; foundation for optimism. 1976. m. $60 to individuals; institutions $120; foreign $120. Futurific Inc., 280 Madison Ave., Ste. 1210, New York, NY 10016. TEL 212-684-4913. Ed. Balint Szent-Miklosy. adv.; bk.rev.; film rev.; play rev.; circ. 10,000.
Description: Newsmagazine of the future, focusing on solutions, not problems. Reviews current events and forecasts their most likely outcomes.

THE FUTURIST; a journal of forecasts, trends, and ideas about the future. see SCIENCES: COMPREHENSIVE WORKS

500 SZ
FUTUROLOGY. (Text in English) q. 60 Fr. International Creative Center - Rencontres Creatives Internationales, 20, Ch. Colladon, CH-1211 Geneva 28, Switzerland. Ed. Dali Schindler. adv.

600 US
G A T F SECOND SIGHT. 1967. irreg. $20 to non-members; members $10. Graphic Arts Technical Foundation, 4615 Forbes Ave., Pittsburgh, PA 15213-3796. TEL 412-621-6941. FAX 412-621-3049. TELEX 9103509221. circ. controlled. **Indexed:** Graph.Arts Lit.Abstr.
Formerly: G A T F Technical Services Report.

G A T F WORLD. (Graphic Arts Technical Foundation) see PRINTING

600 GW
GATE; contributions to technological cooperation. 1978. q. DM.88. Verlag Echo aus Deutschland, Koenigstr. 2, 7000 Stuttgart 1, Germany. Ed. Manfred H. Dehn. circ. 4,000.

GATEWAY ENGINEER. see ENGINEERING

620 UZ ISSN 0016-6022
GELIOTEKHNIKA. English translation: Applied Solar Energy (US ISSN 0003-701X) 1965. bi-m. 15.60 Rub. Akademiya Nauk Uzbekskoi S.S.R., Ul. Kuibysheva, 15, Tashkent, Uzbekistan. **Indexed:** Biol.Abstr., Chem.Abstr., INIS Atomind., Sci.Abstr.

GENETIC ENGINEERING NEWS; the information source of the biotechnology industry. see BIOLOGY — Genetics

GERMAN STANDARDS (DIN) ENGLISH LANGUAGE. see ENGINEERING

GERMANY (FEDERAL REPUBLIC, 1949-). BUNDESMINISTERIUM FUER FORSCHUNG UND TECHNOLOGIE. B M F T FOERDERUNGSKATALOG. see SCIENCES: COMPREHENSIVE WORKS

GLOBAL BIOGEOCHEMICAL CYCLES. see SCIENCES: COMPREHENSIVE WORKS

800 US
GLOBAL ELECTRONICS. 1980. m. $12. Pacific Studies Center, 222B View St., Mountain View, CA 94041. TEL 415-969-1545. FAX 415-968-1126. Ed. Lenny Siegel. bk.rev.; charts; stat.; circ. 350. (back issues avail.) **Indexed:** Alt.Press Ind.
Formerly (until 1985): Global Electronics Information Newsletter (ISSN 0739-0416)
Description: Covers current trends in the computer and semiconductor industries, emphasizing the impact on the workforce and environment.

600 IT
GOLEM. 1989. m. L.70000 (foreign L.105000)(effective 1992). Edizioni Dedalo s.r.l., Casella Postale 362, 70100 Bari, Italy. TEL 080-371555. FAX 080-371979. Ed. Danco Singer.
Description: Provides information to those who use or want to use new technologies.

600 CC
GONGYE ZHANWANG/INDUSTRIAL PROSPECT. (Text in Chinese) q. Shanghai Gongye Jishu Fazhan Jijinhui - Shanghai Industrial Technology Development Foundation, 75 Guangdong Lu, Shanghai 200002, People's Republic of China. TEL 3231618. Ed. Gan Cidi.

600 US ISSN 0882-3766
Q179.98
GOVERNMENT RESEARCH DIRECTORY. 1980. irreg., 6th ed., 1990. $390. Gale Research Inc., 835 Penobscot Bldg., Detroit, MI 48226. TEL 313-961-2242. FAX 313-961-6083. TELEX 810-221-7086. Ed. Annette Piccirelli.
● Also available online. Vendor(s): DIALOG.
 Formerly: Government Research Centers Directory (ISSN 0270-4811)

GRAM SHILP. see *SCIENCES: COMPREHENSIVE WORKS*

600 608.7 US
GUIDE TO AVAILABLE TECHNOLOGIES; an annual guide to business opportunities in technology. 1985. a. $150. Techni Research Associates, Inc., Willow Grove Plaza, York & Davisville Rds., Willow Grove, PA 19090. TEL 215-657-1753. Ed. L.F. Schiffman.

GUNMA UNIVERSITY, FACULTY OF EDUCATION. ANNUAL REPORT: ART, TECHNOLOGY, HEALTH & PHYSICAL EDUCATION, AND SCIENCE OF HUMAN LIVING SERIES. see *EDUCATION — Higher Education*

GUOJI KEJI JIAOLIU/INTERNATIONAL SCIENCE AND TECHNOLOGY EXCHANGE. see *SCIENCES: COMPREHENSIVE WORKS*

GUOWAI KEJI DONGTAI/FOREIGN SCIENCE AND TECHNOLOGY DEVELOPMENT. see *SCIENCES: COMPREHENSIVE WORKS*

658.5 GW ISSN 0018-3822
H O B - DIE HOLZBEARBEITUNG. 1954. 10/yr. DM.96.10. A.G.T. Verlag Thum GmbH, Teinacher Str. 34, Postfach 109, 7140 Ludwigsburg, Germany. TEL 07141-33046. FAX 07141-33828. TELEX 7264853. Ed. L. Friedrich. circ. 10,931.
 Description: Design and operation of machines, systems and tools for working and processing wood, wood materials, plastics and materials processed like wood.

600 JA
HAKODATE TECHNICAL COLLEGE. RESEARCH REPORTS/HAKODATE KOGYO KOTO SENMON GAKKO KIYO. (Text in Japanese; summaries in English) 1967. a. Hakodate Technical College - Hakodate Kogyo Koto Senmon Gakko, 226 Tokura-cho, 2 Hakodate 042, Japan. illus. **Indexed:** Chem.Abstr.

HANDBUCH DER DATENBANKEN FUER NATURWISSENSCHAFT, TECHNIK, PATENTE. see *COMPUTERS — Data Base Management*

658.5 GW
DAS HANDWERK. 1947. s-m. DM.1.20 per no. Verlag Die Wirtschaft Berlin GmbH, Am Friedrichshain 22, 1055 Berlin, Germany. Ed. Renate Morchutt. adv.; bk.rev.
 Formerly: Das Neue Handwerk (ISSN 0028-3193)
 Description: Trade publication for all craft trades. Includes news and information, features, reports of events and exhibitions.

600 US
HAWAII HIGH TECH JOURNAL.* 1984. q. $10. EastWest Magazine Company Ltd., 3660 Waialae Ave., Ste.209, Honolulu, HI 96816-3236. TEL 808-538-0934. FAX 808-531-9843. Ed. Barry Hampe. circ. 7,000.
 Description: Reports on high tech developments in the state of Hawaii.

HEALTH TECHNOLOGY MANAGEMENT. see *MEDICAL SCIENCES*

HEIDELBERGER ARBEITSBUECHER. see *SCIENCES: COMPREHENSIVE WORKS*

HEIDELBERGER JAHRBUECHER. see *SCIENCES: COMPREHENSIVE WORKS*

HEIDELBERGER TASCHENBUECHER. see *SCIENCES: COMPREHENSIVE WORKS*

HERION - INFORMATIONEN. see *ENGINEERING — Hydraulic Engineering*

HIGH TECH INVESTOR (BARRINGTON). see *BUSINESS AND ECONOMICS — Investments*

600 US ISSN 0741-0808
HIGH-TECH MATERIALS ALERT; advanced materials: their uses and manufacture. 1984. m. $535 (foreign $595). Technical Insights, Inc., 32 N. Dean St., Englewood, NJ 07631. TEL 201-568-4744. FAX 201-568-8247. TELEX 425900 SWIFT UI. (Subscr. to: Box 1304, Fort Lee, NJ 07024-1304) Ed. Alan Brown. bk.rev.; bibl.; charts; pat.; stat.; tr.lit. (back issues avail.)
● Also available online. Vendor(s): Mead Data Central.
 —BLDSC shelfmark: 4307.361070.
 Description: Details of significant developments in materials, alloys and metallic whiskers and ceramic and graphite fibers.

HIGH TECH SEPARATIONS NEWS. see *CHEMISTRY — Analytical Chemistry*

600 US
HIGH TECH TOMORROW. m. $95. 330 W. 42nd St., New York, NY 10036. TEL 212-239-9000. Ed. Laurie Meisler.

HIGH TECHNOLOGY LAW JOURNAL. see *LAW*

600 IT
HIGHTECH ITALIA; mensile di alta tecnologia applicata. bi-m. L.30000 (foreign L.120000)(effective 1992). Tecniche Nuove s.p.a., Via C. Menotti 14, 20129 Milan, Italy. TEL 02-75701. FAX 02-7570205.

HISTORICAL STUDIES IN IRISH SCIENCE AND TECHNOLOGY. see *SCIENCES: COMPREHENSIVE WORKS*

HISTORY AND TECHNOLOGY. see *HISTORY*

600 UK ISSN 0307-5451
T14.7
HISTORY OF TECHNOLOGY. 1976. a. price varies. Mansell Publishing Ltd., Villiers House, 41-47 Strand, London WC2N 5JE. TEL 071-839-4900. FAX 071-839-1804. TELEX 9413701-CASPUB-G. (Dist. in U.S. by: Publications Distribution Center, P.O. Box C831, Rutherford, NJ 07070) Eds. G. Hollister-Short, F.A.J.L. James. **Indexed:** Amer.Hist.& Life, Br.Archaeol.Abstr., Hist.Abstr.
 Description: Contains essays on the technical problems of different periods and societies and the measures taken to solve them.

600 PL ISSN 0137-8813
HORYZONTY TECHNIKI. 1948. m. $22. (Naczelna Organizacja Techniczna (NOT)) Wydawnictwo Czasopism i Ksiazek Technicznych SIGMA - NOT, Ul. Biala 4, P.O. Box 1004, 00-950 Warsaw, Poland. (Dist. by: Ars Polona-Ruch, Krakowskie Przedmiescie 7, Warsaw, Poland) (Co-sponsor: Towarzystwo Wiedzy Powszechnej) Ed. Jerzy Wierzbowski. circ. 100,000.

HOSPITAL TECHNOLOGY SERIES. see *HOSPITALS*

HUANAN LIGONG DAXUE XUEBAO (ZIRAN KEXUE BAN)/SOUTH-CHINA UNIVERSITY OF SCIENCE AND ENGINEERING. JOURNAL (NATURAL SCIENCE EDITION). see *SCIENCES: COMPREHENSIVE WORKS*

HUAZHONG LIGONG DAXUE XUEBAO/CENTRAL-CHINA UNIVERSITY OF SCIENCE AND ENGINEERING. JOURNAL. see *SCIENCES: COMPREHENSIVE WORKS*

HUMAN DESIGN. see *ART*

745.2 AU ISSN 0018-7224
HUMAN INDUSTRIAL DESIGN. (Text in German) 1968. irreg. Verlag Dr. Herta Ranner, Zeismannsbrunngasse 1, A-1070 Vienna, Austria. TEL 0222-935387. Ed. H. Ranner. adv.; bk.rev.

600 UK ISSN 0265-3028
 CODEN: HYCRD5
HYBRID CIRCUITS. 1982. 3/yr. £45.60($91.20) (International Hybrid Microelectronics Society - Europe) Wela Publications Ltd., 8 Barns St., Ayr KA7 1XA, Scotland. TEL 0292-283186. FAX 0292-284719. Ed. William Goldie.
 —BLDSC shelfmark: 4340.345000.

600 US ISSN 0160-1040
T37
I A. (Industrial Archeology) 1976. s-a. $25 to individuals; institutions $30; students $20 (subscr. includes S I A Newsletter). Society for Industrial Archeology, NMAH-5014, MRC 629, Smithsonian Institution, Washington, DC 20560. Ed. David R. Starbuck. adv.; bk.rev.; illus.; circ. 1,600. (back issues avail.) **Indexed:** Avery Ind.Archit.Per.
 —BLDSC shelfmark: 4357.850000.
 Description: Explores post-18th century technology and society.

I D: INTERNATIONAL DESIGN MAGAZINE; planning-design-marketing. see *INTERIOR DESIGN AND DECORATION*

600 US
I E E E CONFERENCE ON DECISION AND CONTROL. PROCEEDINGS. a. price varies. (I E E E, Control Systems Society) Institute of Electrical and Electronics Engineers, Inc., 345 E. 47th St., New York, NY 10017-2349. TEL 212-705-7900. FAX 212-705-7682. (Subscr. to: Box 1331, 445 Hoes Lane, Piscataway, NJ 08855-1331) **Indexed:** Comput.Cont.
 Formerly (until 1982): I E E E Conference on Decision and Control, Including the Symposium on Adaptive Processes. Proceedings (ISSN 0191-2216); *Incorporates (as of 1970):* Symposium on Adaptive Processes.

I E E E ENGINEERING IN MEDICINE AND BIOLOGY MAGAZINE. see *BIOLOGY — Bioengineering*

600 621.3 US ISSN 0278-0097
T14.5 CODEN: ITSMDC
I E E E TECHNOLOGY AND SOCIETY MAGAZINE. 1982. q. $64 to non-members. (I E E E, Society on Social Implications of Technology) Institute of Electrical and Electronics Engineers, Inc., 345 E. 47th St., New York, NY 10017-2394. TEL 212-705-7366. FAX 908-981-1855. (Subscr. to: Box 1331, 445 Hoes Ln., Piscataway, NJ 08855-1331. TEL 908-562-3948) Ed. Leon Zelby. (also avail. in microform from UMI,EEE)
 —BLDSC shelfmark: 4363.095000.
 Formerly: Technology and Society.

I E E E TRANSACTIONS ON INDUSTRY APPLICATIONS. see *ENGINEERING — Electrical Engineering*

600 US
I F U. (Text in German) vol.51, 1980. irreg. price varies. (Universitaet Stuttgart, Institut fuer Umformtechnik, GW) Springer-Verlag, 175 Fifth Ave., New York, NY 10010. TEL 212-460-1500. (Also Berlin, Heidelberg, Tokyo and Vienna) Ed. K. Lange. (reprint service avail. from ISI)

745.2 SA
I N F O P A K MANUFACTURING. w. Council for Scientific and Industrial Research, Division of Information Services, P.O. Box 395, Pretoria 0001, South Africa. TEL 012-841-4062.

I N T INFORMATIVO. (Instituto Nacional de Tecnologia) see *SCIENCES: COMPREHENSIVE WORKS*

600 US
I T E A JOURNAL OF TEST AND EVALUATION. 1983. q. $60 (foreign $80). International Test & Evaluation Association, 440 Fair Lakes Court, Fairfax, VA 22033. TEL 703-631-6220. adv.; circ. 2,000.
 Description: Articles on test and evaluation procedures, methods and philosophies used in testing both software and hardware.

I T E S T BULLETIN. (Institute for Theological Encounter with Science and Technology) see *RELIGIONS AND THEOLOGY*

I T E S T CONFERENCE PROCEEDINGS. (Institute for Theological Encounter with Science and Technology) see *RELIGIONS AND THEOLOGY*

I U E NEWS. (International Union of Electronic, Electrical, Salaried, Machine and Furniture Workers, A F L - C I O) see *LABOR UNIONS*

TECHNOLOGY: COMPREHENSIVE WORKS

600　　　　　　　　AG　　ISSN 0326-3878
N7
IDEAS EN ARTE Y TECNOLOGIA. 1984. 3/yr. $48. Universidad de Belgrano, Teodoro Garcia 2090, 1426 Buenos Aires, Argentina. TEL 774-2133. Ed. Avelino J. Porto. bk.rev.; bibl.; circ. 1,000. (back issues avail.)
　　Description: Covers architecture, engineering and computer science.

600 500　　　　　JA　　ISSN 0386-1163
　　　　　　　　　　　　　CODEN: IKDRDP
IKUTOKU KOGYO DAIGAKU KENKYU HOKOKU. B RIKOGAKU HEN/IKUTOKU TECHNICAL UNIVERSITY. RESEARCH REPORTS. PART B. SCIENCE AND TECHNOLOGY. (Text in English and Japanese; summaries in English) 1976. a. Ikutoku Technical University - Ikutoku Kogyo Daigaku, 1030 Shimoogino, Atsugi-shi, Kanagawa-ken 243-02, Japan. FAX 0462-42-6111. **Indexed:** Chem.Abstr., Jap.Per.Ind.

IMAGE PROCESSING; capture management and analysis. see BUSINESS AND ECONOMICS

600　　　　　　　　US　　ISSN 1041-4320
IMAGING TECHNOLOGY REPORT. 1987. m. $145 (foreign $160). Microfilm Publishing, Inc., Box 950, Larchmont, NY 10538-0950. TEL 914-834-3044. Ed. Mitchell Badler.
　　—BLDSC shelfmark: 4368.996600.
　　Description: Reviews optical disk and business imaging technologies.

600　　　　　　　　US
IMPACT ASSESSMENT BULLETIN. 1981. q. $40 to individuals; institutions $60. International Association for Impact Assessment, Box 70, Belhaven, NC 27810. TEL 919-964-2338. FAX 919-964-2340. Ed. A. Roper. bk.rev.; charts; circ. 700. (back issues avail.)
　　Formerly: I A I A Bulletin (ISSN 0734-9165)

IN TECHNOLOGY. see BUSINESS AND ECONOMICS

INDIA. DEPARTMENT OF SCIENCE & TECHNOLOGY. ANNUAL REPORT. see SCIENCES: COMPREHENSIVE WORKS

600　　　　　　　　II　　ISSN 0073-6511
INDIAN INSTITUTE OF TECHNOLOGY, MADRAS. ANNUAL REPORT. (Text in English) 1960. a. Indian Institute of Technology at Madras, c/o Central Library, Madras 600 036, India.

INDIAN JOURNAL OF HISTORY OF SCIENCE. see SCIENCES: COMPREHENSIVE WORKS

600 338.91　　　II　　ISSN 0970-7867
INDIAN JOURNAL OF RURAL TECHNOLOGY. (Text and summaries in English) 1989. s-a (2 nos. per vol.). Rs.100($25) Department of Rural Development, Council for Advancement of People's Action and Rural Technology (CAPART), Guru Nanak Foundation Bldg., New Mehrauli Rd., New Delhi 110 067, India. TEL 11-665107. TELEX 73290. Ed. Asha Joglekar. charts; stat.
　　Description: Publishes original papers, review articles, case studies, and communications on rural energy, water supply, health and medicare, industries, transport, housing, enviroment, and agricultural equipment.

607　　　　　　　　II
INDIAN JOURNAL OF TECHNICAL EDUCATION. (Text in English) 1971. 2/yr. membership. Indian Society for Technical Education, IIT Campus, New Delhi 110 016, India. TEL 653431. Ed. P.J. George. bk.rev.; illus.; circ. 12,000.

338 658.5　　　　BL　　ISSN 0019-7718
HC186
INDUSTRIA & PRODUTIVIDADE. 1968. m. Cr.$480($48) Confederacao Nacional da Industria, Rua Santa Luzia, 735, 10o andar, 20030 Rio de Janeiro, Brazil. TEL 220-3808. Ed. Francisco Santos Lopes. adv.; charts; illus.; pat.; stat; circ. 10,000.
　　Formerly: Desenvolvimento e Conjuntura.

600　　　　　　　　UK　　ISSN 0019-7971
INDUSTRIAL ARCHAEOLOGY; the journal of the history of industry and technology. 1964. a. £24($48) (foreign £26). Graphmitre Ltd., 1 West St., Tavistock, Devon PL19 8DS, England. adv.; bk.rev.; illus.; cum.index vols.1-16; circ. 2,000. (back issues avail.; reprint service avail. from SWZ) **Indexed:** Avery Ind.Archit.Per., Br.Archaeol.Abstr., Br.Hum.Ind, Br.Tech.Ind., Geo.Abstr., Hist.Abstr. (until 1984), Mid.East: Abstr.& Ind., RILA.
　　—BLDSC shelfmark: 4445.300000.
　　Formerly: Journal of Industrial History.

600　　　　　　　　II
INDUSTRIAL CONSULTANCY. 1978. m. Rs.250 (foreign $200). Industrial Consultancy, Post Bag no.8, Kalkaji, New Delhi 110 019, India. FAX 011-3324693. TELEX 63085 JNBR. Ed. R.C. Paliwal. adv.; bk.rev.; circ. 10,000. (reprint service avail. from ISI)

621.9　　　　　　UK　　ISSN 0019-8145
TJ1193　　　　　　　　CODEN: INDRA9
INDUSTRIAL DIAMOND REVIEW. 1940. bi-m. free to qualified personnel. De Beers Industrial Diamond Division Pty. Ltd., Charters, Sunninghill, Ascot, Berks SL5 9PX, England. FAX 0344-28188. TELEX 848021-DEBID-G. Ed. Paul Daniel. adv.; bk.rev.; abstr.; illus.; index; circ. 10,000. (also avail. in microfilm from UMI; reprint service avail. from UMI, ISI) **Indexed:** Br.Ceram.Abstr., Br.Tech.Ind., Chem.Abstr., Curr.Cont., Eng.Ind., Excerp.Med., ISMEC, Ref.Zh., Sci.Cit.Ind., World Alum.Abstr.
　　—BLDSC shelfmark: 4450.000000.
　　Incorporates: Industrial Diamond Abstracts.
　　Description: Reviews developments in the design and manufacture of diamond, CBN, PCD, and PCBN tooling; also provides applications in industry and science.

INDUSTRIAL EDUCATION. see EDUCATION — Higher Education

600　　　　　　　　UK　　ISSN 0264-8644
INDUSTRIAL JETTING REPORT. bi-m. $250 (foreign £140). S T I Ltd., 4 Kings Meadow, Ferry Hinksey Rd., Oxford OX2 0DU, England. TEL 0865-798898. FAX 0865-798788. (Dist. in U.S. by: Air Science Co., P.O. Box 143, Corning, NY 14830. TEL 607-962-5591)

616　　　　　　　　US　　ISSN 0019-8447
TA401　　　　　　　　CODEN: INDLAP
INDUSTRIAL LABORATORY. English translation of: Zavodskaya Laboratoriya. 1958. m. $1095 (foreign $1280)(effective 1992). (Ministerstvo Chernoi Metallurgii S.S.S.R., Tsentral'noe Upravlenie Nauchno-Tekhnicheskogo Obshchestvoi po Chernoi Metallurgii, UR) Plenum Publishing Corp., Consultants Bureau, 233 Spring St., New York, NY 10013-1578. TEL 212-620-8468. FAX 212-463-0742. TELEX 23-421139. Ed. N.P. Lyakishev. (also avail. in microfilm from JSC; back issues avail.) **Indexed:** Appl.Mech.Rev., Cadscan, Chem.Titles, Comput.& Info.Sys., Curr.Cont., Electron.& Communic.Abstr.J, Energy Res.Abstr., Eng.Ind., Excerp.Med., INIS Atomind., Lead Abstr., Pollut.Abstr., Solid.St.Abstr., Zincscan.
　　—BLDSC shelfmark: 0412.100000.
　　Refereed Serial

INDUSTRIAL MATHEMATICS. see MATHEMATICS

338 658.5　　　　　US
INDUSTRIAL PRODUCT BULLETIN. 1942. 10/yr. $12 (free to qualified personnel). Gordon Publications, Inc., 301 Gibraltar Dr., Morris Plains, NJ 07950. TEL 201-292-5100. FAX 201-898-9281. Ed. Anita LaFond Koronsky. adv.; illus.; tr.lit.; circ. 200,000. (tabloid format; also avail. in microform from UMI; reprint service avail. from UMI)
　　Formerly: Industrial Bulletin (ISSN 0019-8021)

INDUSTRIAL PRODUCTS FINDER. see BUSINESS AND ECONOMICS — Trade And Industrial Directories

658.7　　　　　　US　　ISSN 0019-8617
INDUSTRIAL PROGRESS;* a pictorial look at new industrial products and processes, plus features of interest to men. 1961. bi-m. free. (Goodyear Industrial Products Division) Donnelly Marketing (Subsidiary of: Reuben H. Donnelly Corp.), 1901 S. Meyers Rd., Ste. 700, Oakbrook Terrace, IL 60181. (Subscr. to: Goodyear Tire and Rubber Co., 1144 E. Market St., Akron, OH 44316) Ed. Frederick H. Kling. illus.; circ. 60,000 (controlled).

INDUSTRIAL TEACHER EDUCATION DIRECTORY. see EDUCATION — Higher Education

338 658.5　　　　II　　ISSN 0019-8803
HC431
INDUSTRIAL TIMES. (Text in English) 1958. fortn. Rs.235. Eve's Weekly Ltd., J.K. Somani Bldg., Bombay Samachar Marg, Bombay 400 023, India. Ed. Sushil Silvano.

600　　　　　　　　US　　ISSN 0743-3271
INDUSTRIAL WEST;* serving the machine tool & metal working industries. 1984. m. free to qualified personnel. Mitchell Publishing Co., Box 3974, Ontario, CA 91761-0990. TEL 818-442-8321. (Alt. addr.: Box 4909, El Monte, CA 91734-0909) Ed. Sid Crown. adv.; bk.rev.; tr.lit.; circ. 25,000.
　　Description: News, articles, announcements, and items of interest to the machine tool and metal-working industries.

338 658.5　　　　US　　ISSN 0019-8889
INDUSTRIAL WORLD; serving industrial management worldwide. Spanish edition: Industrial World en Espanol. (Supplements avail.) 1946. 6/yr. $50 (free to qualified personnel). Johnston International Publishing (Subsidiary of: Hunter Publishing Limited Partnership), 950 Lee St., Des Plaines, IL 60016. TEL 708-296-0770. FAX 708-803-3328. Ed. Jose Fuentecilla. adv.; bk.rev.; charts; illus.; index; circ. 80,000 (45,000 English ed.; 35,000 Spanish ed.) (controlled). **Indexed:** Excerp.Med.
　　Former titles: American Manufacturer (ISSN 0096-5278); American Manufacturer and Iron World.
　　Description: Reports on new production technologies for the manufacturing and process industries.

INDUSTRIAS PESQUERAS; revista maritima quincenal. see BUSINESS AND ECONOMICS

338 671　　　　　GW　　ISSN 0019-9036
　　　　　　　　　　　　　CODEN: IANZAQ
INDUSTRIE-ANZEIGER; polytechnische Zeitschrift fuer die technische Industrie. 1879. s-w. (plus special issues). DM.270.40 (foreign DM.327.60). (Wirtschaftsverband Eisen, Blech und Metall Verarbeitende Industrie) Konradin-Industrieverlag GmbH, Ernst-Mey-Str. 8, Postfach 100252, 7022 Leinfelden-Echterdingen, Germany. TEL 0711-7594-0. FAX 0711-7594-390. Ed. R. Langbein. adv.; bk.rev.; charts; illus.; mkt.; stat.; circ. 40,000. **Indexed:** C.I.S. Abstr., Chem.Abstr., Cyb.Abstr., Eng.Ind., Excerp.Med., Fluidex, INIS Atomind., Key to Econ.Sci., Met.Abstr., Packag.Sci.Tech., Sci.Abstr., World Alum.Abstr.
　　—BLDSC shelfmark: 4474.620000.
　　Description: For the machine industry. Provides news and information on manufacturing, technological research and new products.

600　　　　　　　　FR　　ISSN 0537-5819
INDUSTRIES ET TECHNIQUES FRANCAISES; le magazine de la performance industrielle. 1957. 22/yr. 440 F. (foreign 697 F.)(effective Jan. 1991). C E P Information Technologie, Immeuble Europais, 26 rue d'Oradour sur Glane, 75504 Paris Cedex 15, France. TEL 1-44-25-31-31. FAX 1-45-57-35-06. TELEX 270 589 F. adv.; illus.; mkt.; tr.lit.; circ. 41,000. **Indexed:** C.I.S. Abstr., Excerp.Med., Met.Abstr., World Alum.Abstr.
　　Former titles: Industries et Techniques (ISSN 0150-6617); Argus Manager (ISSN 0004-122X)

INFORMACION CIENTIFICA Y TECNOLOGICA. see SCIENCES: COMPREHENSIVE WORKS

INFRARED SOCIETY OF JAPAN. PROCEEDING. see PHYSICS — Heat

600　　　　　　　　FR
INNOVATION. fortn. 1980 F. A Jour, 11 rue du Marche St. Honore, 75001 Paris, France. TEL 42-96-67-22. FAX 40-20-07-75. TELEX 615887 AJOUR.

600 500　　　　　CN
INNOVATION. irreg. (every 3-4 mos.). Attn.: Technology Liaison Dir., 235 Queen St., 10th Fl., Ottawa, Ont. K1A 0H5, Canada. TEL 613-954-3458. FAX 613-954-1894.

INNOVATION. see SOCIAL SCIENCES: COMPREHENSIVE WORKS

TECHNOLOGY: COMPREHENSIVE WORKS

| 600 500 | GW |

INNOVATIONS-NACHRICHTEN. 1980. q. free. Arbeitsgemeinschaft der Industrie- und Handelskammern in Baden Wuerttemberg, Jaegerstr. 30, 7000 Stuttgart 10, Germany. TEL 0711-2005-0. FAX 0711-2005-354. circ. 4,000. (looseleaf format)

| 600 | US | ISSN 0300-757X |

INSIDE R & D; a weekly report on technical innovation. 1972. w. $740 (foreign $840). Technical Insights, Inc., 32 N. Dean St., Englewood, NJ 07631. TEL 201-568-4744. FAX 201-568-8247. TELEX 4259000 SWIFT UI. (Subscr. to: Box 1304, Fort Lee, NJ 07024) Ed. Charles Joslin. bk.rev.; bibl.; charts; pat.; stat.; tr.lit. (back issues avail.) **Indexed:** PROMT.
●Also available online. Vendor(s): DIALOG, Mead Data Central.
—BLDSC shelfmark: 4518.153000.
  Description: Covers new and significant developments in technology.

L'INSTALLATORE ITALIANO; la rivista mensile degli impianti tecnici. see *HEATING, PLUMBING AND REFRIGERATION*

| 620 | UK | ISSN 0020-3130 |

INSTITUTE OF SCIENCE TECHNOLOGY. BULLETIN. 1955. m. membership. Institute of Science Technology, Mansell House, 22 Bore St., Lichfield, Staffs. WS13 6LP, England. Ed. I. Gray. adv.; bk.rev.; abstr.; circ. 2,000. **Indexed:** Art & Archaeol.Tech.Abstr.

| 600 | DR |

INSTITUTO TECNOLOGICO DE SANTO DOMINGO. BIBLIOTECA. BOLETIN DE ANALITICAS. 1983. s-a. Instituto Tecnologico de Santo Domingo, Biblioteca, Apdo. 249-2, Santo Domingo, Dominican Republican. circ. 600.

| 600 | RM |

INSTITUTUL POLITEHNIC BUCURESTI. BULETIN STIINTIFIC/POLYTECHNICAL INSTITUTE OF BUCHAREST. SCIENTIFIC BULLETIN. (In 3 series: Mechanical Engineering (1220-3041), Electrical Engineering (1220-3033), Chemistry, Metallurgy and Materials Science (1220-305X)) (Text in English, Rumanian) 1929. 4/yr. $195 per series. Institutul Politehnic Bucuresti - Polytechnical Institute of Bucharest, Splaiul Independentei 313, 77206 Bucharest 16, Rumania. FAX 400-12-01-88. TELEX IPOLB R 10252. bk.rev.; abstr.; bibl.; charts; circ. 1,300. **Indexed:** Appl.Mech.Rev., B.C.I.R.A., Chem.Abstr., Eng.Ind., INIS Atomind., Math.R., Sci.Abstr.
  Former titles (until 1989): Institutul Politihnic Bucuresti. Buletin; (until 1983): Institutul Politehnic "Gheorghe Gheorghiu-Dej". Buletin (ISSN 0020-4242)

INTERNATIONAL CONGRESS ON TECHNOLOGY AND TECHNOLOGY EXCHANGE. PROCEEDINGS. see *ENGINEERING*

INTERNATIONAL FIBER SCIENCE AND TECHNOLOGY SERIES. see *CHEMISTRY — Organic Chemistry*

INTERNATIONAL JOURNAL OF ENERGY SYSTEMS. see *ENERGY*

INTERNATIONAL JOURNAL OF INSTRUCTIONAL MEDIA. see *EDUCATION — Teaching Methods And Curriculum*

| 600 | SZ | ISSN 0268-1900 |
| TA401 | | CODEN: IJMTE2 |

INTERNATIONAL JOURNAL OF MATERIALS & PRODUCT TECHNOLOGY; the journal of materials innovation, failure preventive technology, product liability and technical insurance. (Abstracts in English, German, French, Japanese) 1986. q. $155 in N. America; elsewhere £100. (Unesco, UN) Inderscience Enterprises Ltd., World Trade Centre Bldg., 110 Ave. Louis Casai, Case Postale 306, CH-1215 Geneva-Aeroport, Switzerland. FAX 22-7910885. TELEX 289950. Ed. M.A. Dorgham. adv.; bk.rev.; abstr.; illus.; charts; index; circ. 7,000. (back issues avail.)
—BLDSC shelfmark: 4542.335500.
  Description: Covers the technologies of oils and lubricants, steel, aluminum, plastics and composites, electronic (solid state) materials, ceramics, corrosion resistant and finishing materials, polymers, resins and rubber products.

INTERNATIONAL JOURNAL OF TECHNOLOGY AND DESIGN EDUCATION. see *EDUCATION — Teaching Methods And Curriculum*

| 600 658 | SZ | ISSN 0267-5730 |
| T1 | | CODEN: IJTMEG |

INTERNATIONAL JOURNAL OF TECHNOLOGY MANAGEMENT; journal of engineering and technology management, technology policy and strategy. (Text in English; abstracts in French, German, Japanese) 1986. 8/yr. $250. (Unesco, UN) Inderscience Enterprises Ltd., World Trade Centre Bldg., 110 Ave. Louis Casai, Case Postale 306, CH-1215 Geneva-Aeroport, Switzerland. Ed. M.A. Dorgham. adv.; bk.rev.; abstr.; charts; illus.; index; circ. 20,000. (back issues avail.) **Indexed:** A.I.Abstr., ABI Inform, B.P.I., CAD CAM Abstr., Energy Info.Abstr., Robomat., Tel.Abstr., Telegen.
—BLDSC shelfmark: 4542.693700.
  Description: Presents conference reports, company profiles, news about technology transfer and R & D management.

INTERNATIONAL JOURNAL OF VEHICLE DESIGN; journal of vehicle engineering, automotive technology and components. see *TRANSPORTATION*

| 600 | UK | ISSN 0020-7845 |

INTERNATIONAL LICENSING. 1964. m. £105 (typically set in Jan.). International Licensing Ltd., Portman House, George St., Aylesbury, Bucks HP20 2HU, England. TEL 0296-395737. FAX 0296-433199. Ed. Nicholas Bartman. adv.; bk.rev.; pat.; tr.mk.; circ. 11,000.
  Description: Covers over 2000 news products and technology opportunities available for import or license.

| 600 | II |

INTERNATIONAL PRESS CUTTING SERVICE: TECHNICAL NEWS REPORT. 1979. w. $85. International Press Cutting Service, Box 63, Allahabad 211001, India. Ed. Nandi Khanna. (looseleaf format)

| 658 | US |

INTERNATIONAL TRENDS IN MANUFACTURING TECHNOLOGY. 1983. irreg. price varies. Springer-Verlag, 175 Fifth Ave., New York, NY 10010. TEL 212-460-1500. (Co-publisher: I F S (Publications) Ltd.) Ed.Bd.

INTERNATIONAL UNDERWATER SYSTEM DESIGN. see *EARTH SCIENCES — Oceanography*

| 600 500 | US | ISSN 1040-3485 |

INVENT; an international publication for inventors, innovators, entrepreneurs, designers and engineers. 1972. bi-m. $35. Mindsight Corporation, 3201 Corte Malpaso, Ste. 304, Camarillo, CA 93010. TEL 805-388-3097. FAX 805-388-9040. Ed. David Alan Foster. adv.; bk.rev.; charts; illus.; circ. 12,000. (tabloid format)
  Formerly (until no.6, vol.15, 1987): Lightbulb.
  Description: Covers a broad range of the latest developments in practically all fields of human enterprise and technological advancement.

| 600 500 539.7 | IT |

INVENTIVA; periodico tecnico-scientifico-sociale. 1958. q. L.2000. Unione Italiana Inventori, Casella Postale 322, 80100 Naples, Italy. Ed. Emilio C. Oberdan Vicario. adv.; bk.rev.; circ. 4,000.

INVESTIGACION Y CIENCIA. see *SCIENCES: COMPREHENSIVE WORKS*

ISRAEL ACADEMY OF SCIENCES AND HUMANITIES. SECTION OF HUMANITIES. PROCEEDINGS. see *HUMANITIES: COMPREHENSIVE WORKS*

| 620 | IS | ISSN 0021-2202 |
| | | CODEN: ISJTAC |

ISRAEL JOURNAL OF TECHNOLOGY. (Text in English) 1951. irreg. $50. Weizmann Science Press of Israel, P.O. Box 801, Jerusalem 91007, Israel. TEL 783203. FAX 783784. TELEX 26144-BXJM-IL-7086. Ed. D. Abir. adv.; charts; illus.; index; circ. 425. **Indexed:** Appl.Mech.Rev., Biol.Abstr., Cadscan, Chem.Abstr., Curr.Cont., Energy Info.Abstr., Eng.Ind., Fluidex, Food Sci.& Tech.Abstr., Geo.Abstr., Herb.Abstr., Ind.Sci.Rev., INIS Atomind., Int.Aerosp.Abstr., Lead Abstr., Math.R., Met.Abstr., Nutr.Abstr., Robomat., Sci.Abstr., Sci.Cit.Ind., Sh.& Vib.Dig., Soils & Fert., World Alum.Abstr., World Surf.Coat., Zincscan.
—BLDSC shelfmark: 4583.815000.

ISSUES IN SCIENCE AND TECHNOLOGY. see *SCIENCES: COMPREHENSIVE WORKS*

| 600 | IT |

ITALIAN TECHNOLOGY; the journal of Italian engineering, machinery and technical products. 1975. q. $60 free. E R I S S.p.A., Via Tellini, 14, 20155 Milan, Italy. Ed. Andrea Carli. bk.rev.

I'91. see *LIBRARY AND INFORMATION SCIENCES*

JAHRBUCH ARBEIT UND TECHNIK. see *SCIENCES: COMPREHENSIVE WORKS*

| 600 | GW |

JAHRBUCH SCHWEISSTECHNIK. 1986. a. DM.38. Deutscher Verlag fuer Schweisstechnik, Aachener Str. 172, Postfach 101965, 4000 Duesseldorf 1, Germany. TEL 0211-15759-0. FAX 0211-1575950. TELEX 8582583. adv.; bk.rev.; circ. 7,000.

JANUS; revue internationale de l'histoire des sciences, de la medecine, de la pharmacie et de la technique. see *SCIENCES: COMPREHENSIVE WORKS*

| 607 | JA | ISSN 0441-0734 |
| T177.J3 | | CODEN: HKKHAG |

JAPAN. GOVERNMENT INDUSTRIAL DEVELOPMENT LABORATORY, HOKKAIDO. REPORTS/HOKKAIDO KOGYO KAIHATSU SHIKENJO HOKOKU. 1966. irreg. Government Industrial Development Laboratory, Hokkaido - Hokkaido Kogyo Kaihatsu Shikenjo, 2-17 Tsukisamu-higashi, Toyohira-ku, Sapporo 062, Hokkaido, Japan. **Indexed:** Chem.Abstr.

| 600 | JA |

JAPAN. GOVERNMENT INDUSTRIAL DEVELOPMENT LABORATORY, HOKKAIDO. TECHNICAL DATA/HOKKAIDO KOGYO KAIHATSU SHIKENJO GIJUTSU. 1961. irreg. Government Industrial Development Laboratory, Hokkaido - Hokkaido Kogyo Kaihatsu Shikenjo, 2-17 Tsukisamu-higashi, Toyohira-ku, Sapporo 062, Hokkaido, Japan. charts.

| 600 | JA | ISSN 0027-7614 |
| | | CODEN: NKGSAR |

JAPAN. GOVERNMENT INDUSTRIAL RESEARCH INSTITUTE, NAGOYA. TECHNICAL NEWS. (Text in Japanese) 1952. m. Government Industrial Research Institute, Nagoya, 1 Hirate-machi, Kita-ku, Nagoya, Japan. Ed. S. Suzuki. abstr.; bibl.; index, cum.index.
—BLDSC shelfmark: 7493.000000.

| 600 | JA | ISSN 0385-5236 |

JAPAN JOURNAL OF EDUCATIONAL TECHNOLOGY. q. $46. (Educational Technology Journal Association of Japan) Japan Scientific Societies Press, 6-2-10 Hongo, Bunkyo-ku, Tokyo 113, Japan. TEL 3814-2001. FAX 3814-2002. TELEX 2722268 BCJSP J. (Dist. by: Business Center for Academic Societies Japan, Koshin Bldg., 6-16-3 Hongo, Bunkyo-ku, Tokyo 113, Japan; Dist. in U.S. by: International Specialized Book Services, Inc., 5602 N.E. Hassalo St., Portland, OR 97213; in Asia by: Toppan Company Pvt. Ltd., 38 Liu Fang Rd., Box 22 Jurong Town, Jurong, Singapore 2262)

JAPAN REPORT: SCIENCE AND TECHNOLOGY. see *SCIENCES: COMPREHENSIVE WORKS*

| 620.1 | JA | ISSN 0038-1586 |
| | | CODEN: SOKAB9 |

JAPAN SOCIETY FOR TECHNOLOGY OF PLASTICITY. JOURNAL/SOSEI TO KAKO. (Text in Japanese; summaries in English) 1960. m. 10500 Yen($42) Japan Society for Technology of Plasticity - Nihon Sosei Kako Gakkai, Torikatsu Bldg., 5-2-5 Roppongi, Minato-ku, Tokyo 106, Japan. TEL 03-3402-0849. FAX 03-3402-0965. Ed. Hiromu Suzuki. adv.; bk.rev.; abstr.; charts; bibl.; index, cum.index; circ. 5,000. (back issues avail.) **Indexed:** Chem.Abstr., JTA, Met.Abstr., World Alum.Abstr.
—BLDSC shelfmark: 4808.150000.

| 600 | JA |

JAPANESE INDUSTRY AND TECHNOLOGY. DIGEST. (Text in English) 1978. m. 1500 Yen($10) (Trade Policy Research Institute) Japan Trade & Industry Publicity, Inc., Toranomon Kotohira Kaikan, 2-8 Toranomon 1-chome, Minato-ku, Tokyo 105, Japan. (U.S. addr.: Akiwa Information Access, 247 W. 72nd St., Ste. 1RE, New York, NY 10023) Ed. Isamu Yoshina. circ. 10,000. (back issues avail.) **Indexed:** CAD CAM Abstr., Energy Info.Abstr., Environ.Abstr., Key to Econ.Sci., Tel.Abstr.

TECHNOLOGY: COMPREHENSIVE WORKS

600   US   ISSN 1058-7314
JAPANESE TECHNOLOGY REVIEWS: NEW MATERIALS (SECTION C). 1989. 2/yr. (in 1 vol.) $60. Gordon and Breach Science Publishers, 270 Eighth Ave., New York, NY 10011. TEL 212-206-8900. FAX 212-645-2459. TELEX 236735 GOPUB UR. (Subscr. to: Box 786, Cooper Sta., New York, NY 10276. TEL 800-545-8398; UK subscr. to: P.O. Box 90, Reading, Berkshire RG1 8JL, England. TEL 0734-560-080) Ed. Toshiaki Ikoma. (also avail. in microform)
  Supersedes in part: Japanese Technology Review (ISSN 0898-5693)
  Refereed Serial

JAPANINFO; Fernost Berichte: Deutscher Dienst fuer Wirtschaft, Politik, Technologie und Gesellschaft. see BUSINESS AND ECONOMICS — International Commerce

600   FR   ISSN 0021-5554
LA JAUNE ET LA ROUGE. 1948. 10/yr. 280 F. (effective through 1991). Societe Amicale des Anciens Eleves de l'Ecole Polytechnique, 5 rue Descartes, 75005 Paris, France. TEL 33-1-46-33-74-25. FAX 44-07-01-69. adv.; bk.rev.; circ. 13,000.
  —BLDSC shelfmark: 4663.422000.
  Description: Publications of the former students of Ecole Polytechnique Association.

600   CC   ISSN 1000-5803
JIANGXI GONGYE DAXUE XUEBAO/JIANGXI INDUSTRIAL UNIVERSITY. JOURNAL. (Text in Chinese) q. Jiangxi Gongye Daxue, No.61, Beijing Donglu, Nanchang, Jiangxi 330029, People's Republic of China. TEL 333535. Ed. Liu Bingsheng.

JINRI KEJI/SCIENCE AND TECHNOLOGY TODAY. see SCIENCES: COMPREHENSIVE WORKS

JINZHAN: GUOJI MAOYI YU KEJI JIAOLIU/PROGRESS: INTERNATIONAL EXCHANGE IN TRADE, SCIENCE AND TECHNOLOGY. see BUSINESS AND ECONOMICS — International Commerce

600   CC   ISSN 1002-283X
JISHU KAIFA YU YINJIN/EXPLORATION AND IMPORT OF TECHNOLOGY. (Text in Chinese) 1985. bi-m. Y3.60. Fujiansheng Keji Qingbao Yanjiusuo - Fujian Institute of Scientific and Technological Information, 52 Hudong Lu, Fuzhou, Fujian 350003, People's Republic of China. TEL 0591-557288. FAX 0591-556468. (Dist. overseas by: Jiangsu Publications Import & Export Corp., 56 Gao Yun Ling, Nanjing, Jiangsu, P.R.C.) (Co-sponsor: Science and Technology Department of Fujian Economics Committee) Ed. Ye Zhonghua. circ. 3,000.
  Description: Focuses on technology and resource development, advanced and practical technology and the latest technological and economic information in Fujian, Taiwan and Hong Kong.

600   US
JOHNS HOPKINS STUDIES IN THE HISTORY OF TECHNOLOGY. 1967; N.S. 1978. irreg. price varies. Johns Hopkins University Press, 701 W. 40th St., Ste. 275, Baltimore, MD 21211. TEL 410-516-6900. FAX 410-516-6998. (reprint service avail. from UMI)
  Refereed Serial

600 900   US   ISSN 0147-8885
RB43   CODEN: JOHIDN
JOURNAL OF HISTOTECHNOLOGY.* 1977. q. $20. (National Society for Histotechnology) Mayo Publications, Inc., 5900 Princess Garden Parkway, Ste. 805, Lanham, MD 20706. TEL 708-969-3828. Ed. Jules Elias. adv.; bk.rev.; index; circ. 2,911. **Indexed:** Biol.Abstr., Chem.Abstr., Excerp.Med.
  —BLDSC shelfmark: 5002.400000.
  Refereed Serial

JOURNAL OF INDUSTRIAL TEACHER EDUCATION. see EDUCATION — Higher Education

JOURNAL OF PURE AND APPLIED SCIENCES/TEMEL VE UYGULAMALI BILMLER DERGISI. see SCIENCES: COMPREHENSIVE WORKS

JOURNAL OF SCIENCE AND TECHNOLOGY. see SCIENCES: COMPREHENSIVE WORKS

600   US   ISSN 0892-9912
JOURNAL OF TECHNOLOGY TRANSFER. 1976. q. $45. Technology Transfer Society, 611 N. Capitol Ave., Indianapolis, IN 46204. Ed. Ralph Segman. bk.rev.; circ. 800.
  ●Also available online. Vendor(s): BRS, DIALOG. Also available on CD-ROM.
  —BLDSC shelfmark: 5068.570000.
  Description: Articles describing methods, mechanisms, case studies and theories of technology transfer.
  Refereed Serial

600   UK   ISSN 0143-9782
QA280   CODEN: JTSADL
JOURNAL OF TIME SERIES ANALYSIS. 1980. 6/yr. £35($71) to individuals; institutions £131($237). Basil Blackwell Ltd, 108 Cowley Rd., Oxford OX4 1JF, England. Ed. M. Priestley. adv.; index; circ. 1,000. (back issues avail.; reprint service avail. from SWZ) **Indexed:** Agri.Eng.Abstr., Biostat., J.Cont.Quant.Meth., Math.R., Oper.Res.Manage.Sci., Qual.Contr.Appl.Stat., Sci.Abstr.
  —BLDSC shelfmark: 5069.400000.

600
JUNKAN ASU NO KAGAKU GIJUTSU/NEWS OF SCIENCE AND TECHNOLOGY OF TOMORROW. (Text in Japanese) 1973. 3/m. Kagaku Gijutsu Koho Zaidan - Japan Foundation for Scientific & Technical Information, Serada Bldg., 35-3 Nishi-shinbashi 2-chome, Minato-ku, Tokyo 105, Japan.

600   CU   ISSN 0449-4555
T4
JUVENTUD TECNICA. 1965. m. $20 in N. America; S. America $26; Europe $29; elsewhere $41. (Union de Jovenes Comunistas, Movimento de Brigadas Tecnicas) Ediciones Cubanas, Departamento de Exportacion, Obispo No. 527, Apdo. 605, Havana, Cuba. Dir. German Fernandez Burguet. bibl.; illus.; circ. 100,000.
  Description: Reflects the Technical Youth Brigades' participation in the multifaced economic development of the country. Covers articles, commentaries, photo features, and national and international sports events.

KAGAKU GIJUTSU BUNKEN SABISU/SCIENCE AND TECHNOLOGY INFORMATION SERVICE. see SCIENCES: COMPREHENSIVE WORKS

600   JA
KAGAKU GIJUTSU-CHO NENPO. (Text in Japanese) 1957. a. (Kagaku Gijutsu-cho - Science and Technology Agency) Okura-sho, Insatsu-kyoku, Ministry of Finance, Printing Bureau, 2-4 Toranomon 2-chome, Minato-ku, Tokyo 105, Japan. **Indexed:** INIS Atomind.
  Description: The annual report of the agency.

600 500   JA
KAGAKU GIJUTSU HAKUSHO/WHITE PAPER OF SCIENCE AND TECHNOLOGY IN JAPAN. (Text in Japanese) 1958. a. 1900 Yen effective 1990. Okura-sho, Insatsu-kyoku - Ministry of Finance, Printing Bureau, 2-4 Toranomon 2-chome, Minato-ku, Tokyo 105, Japan. bk.rev.; stat.

600   JA
KAGAKU GIJUTSU HAKUSHO NO ARAMASHI. (Text in Japanese) 1987. a. 260 Yen effective 1990. Okura-sho, Insatsu-kyoku - Ministry of Finance, Printing Bureau, 2-4 Toranomon 2-chome, Minato-ku, Tokyo 105, Japan.
  Description: Summary of Kagaku Gijutsu Hakusho.

600   JA
KAGAKU GIJUTSU KENKYU CHOSA HOKOKU/REPORT ON THE SURVEY OF RESEARCH AND DEVELOPMENT. (Text in English and Japanese) 1960. a. Somu-cho, Tokei-kyoku - Management and Coordination Agency, Statistics Bureau, 19-1 Wakamatsu-cho, Shinjuku-ku, Tokyo 162, Japan. stat.

600   JA
KAGAKU GIJUTSU KENKYU CHOSA KEKKA NO GAIYO. (Text in Japanese) a. Somu-cho, Tokei-kyoku - Management and Coordination Agency, Statistics Bureau, 19-1 Wakamatsu-cho, Shinjuku-ku, Tokyo 162, Japan. stat.
  Description: Contains an outline of the Kagaku Gijutsu Kenkyu Chosa Hokoku.

600   JA
KAGAKU GIJUTSU SHINKO CHOSEIHI NYUSU. (Text in Japanese) 1983. irreg. Kagaku Gijutsu-cho - Science and Technology Agency, 2-1 Kasumigaseki 2-chome, Chiyoda-ku, Tokyo 100, Japan.
  Description: Contains news of special coordination funds for promoting science and technology.

600   JA
KAGAKU GIJUTSU SHINKO CHOSEIHI SHIKEN KENKYU JISSHI KEIKAKU. (Text in Japanese) a. Kagaku Shinbunsha, 8-1 Hamamatsu-cho 1-chome, Minato-ku, Tokyo 105, Japan.
  Description: Contains planning papers of experimental studies by special coordination funds for promoting science and technology.

600   JA   ISSN 0368-5918
KAGAKU TO KOGYO (OSAKA)/SCIENCE AND INDUSTRY. (Text and summaries in Japanese and English) 1926. m. Osaka Koken Kyokai - Osaka Society of Industrial Research, Osaka-shiritsu Kogyo Kenkyujo, 6-50 Morinomiya 1-chome, Joto-ku, Osaka-shi, Osaka-fu 536, Japan. abstr.
  —BLDSC shelfmark: 5081.110000.
  Description: Contains original papers, reviews, commentary, and news.

620   JA   ISSN 0022-7730
KAIGAI GIJUTSU HAIRAITO/TECHNOLOGY HIGHLIGHT. (Text in Japanese) 1967. m. $155. Japan Information Center of Science and Technology - Nihon Kagaku Gijutsu Joho Senta, 5-2 Nagata-cho, 2-chome, Chiyoda-ku, Tokyo 100, Japan. TEL 03-3581-6411. FAX 03-3581-6446. TELEX 02223604-J. bk.rev.; abstr.; bibl.; index; circ. 1,300.
  Formerly: Technical Highlights from Overseas.

620   JA   ISSN 0022-832X
**   CODEN: KDKOAL**
KANAZAWA DAIGAKU KOGAKUBU KIYO/KANAZAWA UNIVERSITY. FACULTY OF TECHNOLOGY. MEMOIRS. (Text in English and Japanese) 1952. s-a. exchange basis. Kanazawa Daigaku, Kogakubu - Kanazawa University, Faculty of Technology, 40-20 Kodatsuno 2-chome, Kanazawa-shi, Ishikawa-ken 920, Japan. Ed. Genichi Yoshimura. charts; illus.; circ. 800. (also avail. in microfiche) **Indexed:** Chem.Abstr., INIS Atomind., JCT, Sci.Abstr.
  —BLDSC shelfmark: 5602.000000.

620   JA   ISSN 0453-2198
TA7   CODEN: TRKUAW
KANSAI UNIVERSITY TECHNOLOGY REPORTS/KANSAI DAIGAKU KOGAKU KENKYU HOKOKU. (Text in English) 1959. a. exchange basis. Kansai University, Faculty of Engineering - Kansai Daigaku Kogakubu, 3-3-35 Yamate-cho, Suita 564, Osaka, Japan. Ed. Katsutaro Katsuta. bk.rev. **Indexed:** Chem.Abstr., Geo.Ref., JCT, JTA, Math.R., Sci.Abstr.
  —BLDSC shelfmark: 8759.600000.

KE-JI RIBAO/SCIENCE & TECHNOLOGY DAILY. see SCIENCES: COMPREHENSIVE WORKS

KE XUE. see SCIENCES: COMPREHENSIVE WORKS

600 500   JA
KEIO GIJUKU DAIGAKU RIKOGAKUBUHO. (Text in Japanese) 1962. a. Keio Gijuku Daigaku, Rikogakubu - Keio University, Faculty of Science and Technology, 14-1, Hiyoshi 3-chome, Kohoku-ku, Yokohama-shi, Kanagawa-ken 223, Japan.
  Description: Contains news of the faculty.

KEJI DAOBAO/SCIENCE AND TECHNOLOGY HERALD. see SCIENCES: COMPREHENSIVE WORKS

KEJI JINBU YU DUICE. see SCIENCES: COMPREHENSIVE WORKS

KEJI KAIFA DONGTAI/SCIENCE AND TECHNOLOGY EXPLORATION TREND. see SCIENCES: COMPREHENSIVE WORKS

KEJI YINGYU XUEXI/LEARNING ENGLISH FOR SCIENCE & TECHNOLOGY. see LINGUISTICS

KEJI YU FAZHAN/SCIENCE, TECHNOLOGY AND DEVELOPMENT. see SCIENCES: COMPREHENSIVE WORKS

KELVIN NEWS/KELVINNUUS. see SCIENCES: COMPREHENSIVE WORKS

KENKYU GIJUTSU KEIKAKU/JOURNAL OF SCIENCE POLICY AND RESEARCH MANAGEMENT. see *BUSINESS AND ECONOMICS — Management*

KENYA JOURNAL OF SCIENCES. SERIES A: PHYSICAL AND CHEMICAL SCIENCES. see *SCIENCES: COMPREHENSIVE WORKS*

KENYA NATIONAL ACADEMY FOR ADVANCEMENT OF ARTS AND SCIENCES. NEWSLETTER. see *SCIENCES: COMPREHENSIVE WORKS*

KEXUE JISHU YANJIU CHENGGUO GONGBAO/BULLETIN OF SCIENTIFIC AND TECHNOLOGICAL ACHIEVEMENTS. see *SCIENCES: COMPREHENSIVE WORKS*

KEXUE JISHU YU BIANZHENGFA/SCIENCE, TECHNOLOGY, AND DIALECTICS. see *SCIENCES: COMPREHENSIVE WORKS*

KHOA HOC KY THUAT KINH TE THE GIOI/WORLD SCIENCE, TECHNOLOGY AND ECONOMY. see *SCIENCES: COMPREHENSIVE WORKS*

KINKI DAIGAKU RIKOGAKUBU KENKYU HOKOKU/KINKI UNIVERSITY. FACULTY OF SCIENCE AND TECHNOLOGY. JOURNAL. see *SCIENCES: COMPREHENSIVE WORKS*

KOBE DAIGAKU DAIGAKUIN SHIZEN KAGAKU KENKYUKA KIYO B/KOBE UNIVERSITY. GRADUATE SCHOOL OF SCIENCE AND TECHNOLOGY. MEMOIRS. SERIES B. see *SCIENCES: COMPREHENSIVE WORKS*

600   JA   ISSN 0287-6507
KOBE UNIVERSITY. GRADUATE SCHOOL OF SCIENCE AND TECHNOLOGY. MEMOIRS. SERIES A/KOBE DAIGAKU DAIGAKUIN SHIZEN KAGAKU KENKYUKA KIYO. A. (Text and summaries in English) 1983. a. Kobe Daigaku, Daigakuin Shizen Kagaku Kenkyuka - Kobe University, Graduate School of Science and Technology, 1-1, Rokkodai-cho, Nada-ku, Kobe-shi, Hyogo-ken 657, Japan. abstr.

KORUNK TUDOMANYA. see *SCIENCES: COMPREHENSIVE WORKS*

658.5   GW   ISSN 0023-4435
KRAFTHAND. 1927. bi-w. DM.94.50. Krafthand Verlag Walter Schulz, Gottlieb-Daimler-Str. 10, Postfach 1462, 8939 Bad Woerishofen, Germany. Ed. W. Schweizer. adv.; bk.rev.; charts; illus.; mkt.; tr.lit.; index; circ. 18,500.

KULTUR UND TECHNIK. see *MUSEUMS AND ART GALLERIES*

KULTURBERICHTE AUS NIEDEROESTERREICH. see *ART*

600   KO
KWAHAK KISUL YORAM/HANDBOOK OF SCIENCE AND TECHNOLOGY. 1970. a. Ministry of Science and Technology, Seoul, S. Korea. circ. 1,500.

KWARTALNIK HISTORII NAUKI I TECHNIKI/QUARTERLY JOURNAL OF THE HISTORY OF SCIENCE AND TECHNOLOGY. see *SCIENCES: COMPREHENSIVE WORKS*

KYOTO INSTITUTE OF TECHNOLOGY. FACULTY OF ENGINEERING AND DESIGN. MEMOIRS. see *SCIENCES: COMPREHENSIVE WORKS*

500 600   JA   ISSN 0453-0357
T4   CODEN: KKDKAN
KYUSHU INSTITUTE OF TECHNOLOGY. BULLETIN: SCIENCE AND TECHNOLOGY/KYUSHU KOGYO DAIGAKU KENKYU HOKOKU: KOGAKU. (Text in Japanese; abstracts in English) 1951. s-a. exchange basis. Kyushu Institute of Technology - Kyushu Kogyo Daigaku, 1-1 Sensui-cho, Tobata, Kitakyushu 804, Japan. abstr. **Indexed:** Chem.Abstr., GeoRef., JTA, Sci.Abstr.
—BLDSC shelfmark: 2601.540000.

LAMY DROIT DE L'INFORMATIQUE; Informatique, Telematique, Reseaux. see *LAW*

600   US   ISSN 0075-7926
LANDOLT-BOERNSTEIN, ZAHLENWERTE UND FUNKTIONEN AUS NATURWISSENSCHAFTEN UND TECHNIK. NEUE SERIE. GROUP 4: MACROSCOPIC AND TECHNICAL PROPERTIES OF MATTER. 1974. irreg. price varies. Springer-Verlag, 175 Fifth Ave., New York, NY 10010. TEL 212-460-1500. (Also Berlin, Heidelberg, Tokyo and Vienna) Ed. K.H. Hellwege. (reprint service avail. from ISI)

600   UK
LASER. 1966. irreg. £0.30 per no. 26 Selwood Rd., Addiscombe, Croydon CR0 7JR, Surrey, England. Ed.Bd. adv.; bk.rev.; bibl.; charts; illus.; circ. 100.

700   US   ISSN 0749-5250
LASER DISC NEWSLETTER. 1984. m. $35 (foreign $50). Box 420, East Rockaway, NY 11518. TEL 516-594-9304. Ed. Douglas Pratt. circ. 4,000.
Description: Covers consumer news on movie, cultural, and educational laser discs available in both the American and Japanese markets.

LICENSING LAW HANDBOOK. see *LAW*

LINDE BERICHTE AUS TECHNIK UND WISSENSCHAFT. see *SCIENCES: COMPREHENSIVE WORKS*

600   US   ISSN 0024-5852
U168
LOGISTICS SPECTRUM. 1967. q. $50 (foreign $60). Society of Logistics Engineers, 8100 Professional Pl., Ste. 211, New Carollton, MD 20785-2225. TEL 800-695-7653. FAX 301-459-1522. TELEX 469527. Ed. Elizabeth P. Crowe. bk.rev.; circ. 8,500. (reprint service avail. from UMI) **Indexed:** Abstr.Mil.Bibl., Air Un.Lib.Ind., D M & T, PROMT.
—BLDSC shelfmark: 5292.350000.

M P G SPIEGEL. (Max-Planck-Gesellschaft zur Foerderung der Wissenschaften) see *SCIENCES: COMPREHENSIVE WORKS*

M T DIALOG. (Medizin-Technischer) see *MEDICAL SCIENCES*

MCGRAW-HILL YEARBOOK OF SCIENCE AND TECHNOLOGY. see *SCIENCES: COMPREHENSIVE WORKS*

MACHINE VISION & APPLICATIONS. see *COMPUTERS — Cybernetics*

620   IS   ISSN 0024-9335
MADA; Hebrew bimonthly of popular science. 1956. bi-m. Weizmann Science Press of Israel, P.O. Box 801, Jerusalem 91007, Israel. TEL 783203. FAX 783784. TELEX 26144-BXJM-IL-7086. Ed. Y. Unna. adv.; bk.rev.; bibl.; charts; illus.; index; circ. 10,000. (processed) **Indexed:** Chem.Abstr., Ind.Heb.Per., INIS Atomind.
—BLDSC shelfmark: 5330.800000.

600   GW   ISSN 0723-7049
MAGAZIN FUER TECHNIK UND UNTERRICHT. q. DM.60. Verlag B. Franzbecker, Mozartstr. 3, 3202 Bad Salzdetfurth, Germany.

600   US   ISSN 0899-5729
MAINTENANCE TECHNOLOGY. 1988. m. $75 (foreign $95). Applied Technology Publications, Inc., 1300 S. Grove Ave., Barrington, IL 60010. TEL 708-382-8100. FAX 708-304-8603. Ed. Robert C. Baldwin. adv.; bk.rev.; circ. 80,000 (controlled).
—BLDSC shelfmark: 5352.631000.
Description: Provides practical technical and business information to maintenance professionals in four broad subject areas: Maintenance of electrical systems and instrumentation, maintenance of mechanical systems, maintenance of plant facilities, and management of maintenance operations.

600   IO   ISSN 0541-7406
MAJALAH PERUSAHAAN GULA. (Text in Indonesian; summaries in English) q. $25. Pusat Penelitian Perkebunan Gula Indonesia, Jl. Paulawan 25, Pasurnan 67126, Indonesia. TEL 0343-21086. FAX 0343-21178. TELEX 31008 SUGEXS IA. **Indexed:** Hort.Abstr.
—BLDSC shelfmark: 5352.893000.

600   MY   ISSN 0127-6441
MALAYSIAN TECHNOLOGIST. (Text in English) vol.24, 1974. bi-m. M.$7 per no. Technological Association of Malaysia, 46 Jalan 52-4, New Town Centre, 46200 Petaling Jaya, Selangor, Malaysia. FAX 03-756-9637. Ed. Ir. Chang Choong Kong. adv.; abstr.; charts; illus.; stat.; tr.lit.; index; circ. 1,500. (also avail. in record)
Formerly: Technical Association of Malaysia. Journal (ISSN 0040-0882)

600   SA
MANUFACTURING REVIEW. w. Council for Scientific and Industrial Research, Division of Information Services, P.O. Box 395, Pretoria 0001, South Africa. TEL 012-86-9211.
Formerly: M T R
Description: Brief summaries of selected articles and their sources.

531 338   US   ISSN 0896-1611
MANUFACTURING REVIEW. 1988. q. $100. American Society of Mechanical Engineers, 22 Law Dr., Box 2900, Fairfield, NJ 07007-2900. TEL 201-882-1170. FAX 201-882-5155. (Co-sponsor: Institute of Industrial Engineers) Ed. Philip H. Francis. adv.; bk.rev.; circ. 7,000. (back issues avail.) **Indexed:** Appl.Mech.Rev., CAD CAM Abstr., Eng.Ind., Robomat.
—BLDSC shelfmark: 5367.279000.
Description: To advance the science, technology, and practice of production.

600   US   ISSN 8750-2100
MASS HIGH TECH. 1982. fortn. $28. Mass Tech Times, Inc., 500 W. Cummings Pk., Ste. 3500, Woburn, MA 01801. TEL 617-935-1100. FAX 617-935-0308. Ed. Patrick L. Porter. adv.; bk.rev.; illus.; circ. 12,000. (also avail. in microfiche from UMI) **Indexed:** Tel.Abstr., Telegen.
● Also available online.

MATERIALS SCIENCE & ENGINEERING B: SOLID-STATE MATERIALS FOR ADVANCED TECHNOLOGY. see *ENGINEERING — Engineering Mechanics And Materials*

620   US   ISSN 0025-6420
MECANICA POPULAR. (Editions avail. for Central America, Argentina, Brazil, Colombia, Dominican Republic, Ecuador, Mexico, Peru, Puerto Rico, U.S., Venezuela) (Text in Spanish) m. $22.50. Editorial America, S.A., Vanidades Continental Bldg., 6355 N.W. 36th St., Virginia Gardens, FL 33166. TEL 305-871-6400. FAX 305-871-8769. Ed. Santiago Villazon. adv.; illus.; circ. 172,189.

MECHANICAL CONTRACTOR LITERATURE SHOWCASE. see *ENGINEERING — Mechanical Engineering*

600 500   JA   ISSN 0285-8258
MEIJI DAIGAKU KAGAKU GIJUTSU KENKYUJO HOKOKU. SOGO KENKYU/MEIJI UNIVERSITY. INSTITUTE OF SCIENCE AND TECHNOLOGY. REPORT. SPECIAL PROJECT. (Text and summaries in English and Japanese) 1981. a. Meiji Daigaku, Kagaku Gijutsu Kenkyujo - Meiji University, Institute of Science and Technology, 1-1 Higashi-mita 1-chome, Tama-ku, Kawasaki-shi, Kanagawa-ken 214, Japan.

600 500   JA   ISSN 0386-4944
Q4   CODEN: MDKKDY
MEIJI DAIGAKU KAGAKU GIJUTSU KENKYUJO KIYO/MEIJI UNIVERSITY. INSTITUTE OF SCIENCE AND TECHNOLOGY. MEMOIRS. (Text in English and Japanese; summaries in English) 1962. irreg. Meiji Daigaku, Kagaku Gijutsu Kenkyujo - Meiji University, Institute of Science and Technology, 1-1 Higashi-mita 1-chome, Tama-ku, Kawasaki-shi, Kanagawa-ken 214, Japan. **Indexed:** Chem.Abstr., Jap.Per.Ind.

600 500   JA   ISSN 0543-3916
Q4   CODEN: MDKGBK
MEIJI DAIGAKU KAGAKU GIJUTSU KENKYUJO NENPO/MEIJI UNIVERSITY. INSTITUTE OF SCIENCE AND TECHNOLOGY. ANNUAL REPORT. (Text in Japanese) 1959. a. Meiji Daigaku, Kagaku Gijutsu Kenkyujo - Meiji University, Institute of Science and Technology, 1-1 Higashi-mita 1-chome, Tama-ku, Kawasaki-shi, Kanagawa-ken 214, Japan. abstr. **Indexed:** Chem.Abstr.

600   JA   ISSN 0386-4952
                          CODEN: MDRKAW
MEIJO DAIGAKU RIKOGAKUBU KENKYU HOKOKU/MEIJO UNIVERSITY. FACULTY OF SCIENCE AND TECHNOLOGY. REPORTS. (Text in English and Japanese; summaries in English) 1957. a. Meijo Daigaku, Rikogakubu - Meijo University, Faculty of Science and Technology, 1-501 Shiogamaguchi, Tenpaku-ku, Nagoya-shi, Aichi-ken 468, Japan. abstr. **Indexed:** Chem.Abstr., Jap.Per.Ind., Sci.Abstr.
—BLDSC shelfmark: 7467.085000.

MESSTECHNISCHE BRIEFE; Zeitschrift fuer das Elektrische Messen Mechischer Groessen. see *ENGINEERING — Mechanical Engineering*

TECHNOLOGY: COMPREHENSIVE WORKS

MESTNYI PROIZVODSTVENNYI OPYT V PROMYSHLENNOSTI/LOCAL LEVEL EXPERIENCE IN THE MANUFACTURING INDUSTRY; nauchno-tekhnicheskii referativnyi sbornik. see *ENGINEERING — Mechanical Engineering*

MESTNYI PROIZVODSTVENNYI OPYT V STROITEL'STVE/LOCAL LEVEL EXPERIENCE IN THE CONSTRUCTION INDUSTRY; nauchno-tekhnicheskii referativnyi sbornik. see *BUILDING AND CONSTRUCTION*

METALLOBERFLAECHE; Zeitschrift fuer Oberflaechenbearbeitung metallischer und nichtmetallischer Werkstoffe. see *METALLURGY*

600 UK
MICRO TECHNOLOGY. 1981. m. M T Publications, 80 Highgate Rd., London NW5 1PB, England. FAX 071-485-9030. adv.; circ. 28,000.

MICROGRAVITY - SCIENCE AND TECHNOLOGY; international journal for microgravity research and applications. see *AERONAUTICS AND SPACE FLIGHT*

MILJOE & TEKNOLOGI. see *ENVIRONMENTAL STUDIES*

620 610 US ISSN 0739-5914
Z7403
MIND: THE MEETINGS INDEX. 1984. bi-m. $425 (foreign $450). InterDok Corp., 173 Halstead Ave., Box 326, Harrison, NY 10528. TEL 914-835-3506. FAX 914-835-6757. Ed. Yvette Roper.
—BLDSC shelfmark: 5775.498000.
Description: Lists future conferences, seminars, workshops, congresses, meetings, institutes and courses.

600 JA ISSN 0914-627X
MITO KAGAKU GIJUTSU/SOCIETY OF NON-TRADITIONAL TECHNOLOGY. JOURNAL. (Text in Japanese) 1973. m. Mito Kagaku Gijutsu Kyokai - Society of Non-Traditional Technology, Toranomon Kotohira Kaikan, 2-8 Toranomon 1-chome, Minato-ku, Tokyo 105, Japan.
Description: Contains reviews, commentary, and news of the organization.

MITSUBISHI ELECTRIC ADVANCE; a quarterly survey of new products, systems and technology. see *ENGINEERING — Electrical Engineering*

600 JA ISSN 0026-6817
CODEN: TRMHA3
MITSUBISHI HEAVY INDUSTRIES TECHNICAL REVIEW. (Text in English) 1964. 3/yr. 4500 Yen. Mitsubishi Heavy Industries, Ltd., Technical Administration Department, 2-5-1 Marunouchi, Chiyoda-ku, Tokyo 100, Japan. TEL 03-3212-3111. FAX 03-3201-6258. TELEX J-22282. (Subscr. to: The Ohm-sha, Ltd., 1, 3-chome Kanda-Nishiki-cho, Chiyoda-ku, Tokyo 101, Japan) circ. 4,000. **Indexed:** BMT, Chem.Abstr., Int.Aerosp.Abstr., JCT, JTA, Met.Abstr., Ocean.Abstr., Pollut.Abstr.
—BLDSC shelfmark: 8725.695000.

600 JA ISSN 0387-2432
CODEN: MIJGAF
MITSUBISHI JUKO GIHO. (Text in Japanese; summaries in English) 1964. 6/yr. 3000 Yen. Mitsubishi Heavy Industries, Ltd., 2-5-1 Marunouchi, Chiyoda-ku, Tokyo 100, Japan. TEL 03-3212-3111. FAX 03-3201-6258. TELEX J-22282. (Subscr. to: The Ohm-sha, Ltd., 1, 3-chome Kanda-Nishiki-cho, Chiyoda-ku, Tokyo 101, Japan) circ. 11,000. **Indexed:** Chem.Abstr., JCT.
—BLDSC shelfmark: 5829.806000.

670 JA ISSN 0540-469X
MITSUBISHI TECHNICAL BULLETIN. (Text in English) 1962. irreg. exchange basis. Mitsubishi Heavy Industries, Ltd., Technical Administration Dept., 2-5-1 Marunouchi, Chiyoda-ku, Tokyo 100, Japan. TEL 03-3212-3111. FAX 03-3201-6258. TELEX J-22282. circ. 1,600. **Indexed:** Sci.Abstr.
—BLDSC shelfmark: 5829.807000.

745.2 IT
MODO; mensile di informazione sul design. (Text in Italian; summaries in English) 1977. m. (10/yr.). L.120000. Ricerche Design Editrice s.r.l., Via Roma 21, 20094 Corsico (Milan), Italy. TEL 02-4491149. FAX 4405544. Ed. Cesare Secondi. adv.; bk.rev.; circ. 35,000. (back issues avail.) **Indexed:** Artbibl.Mod., Avery Ind.Archit.Per., Br.Tech.Ind.
Description: Discusses industrial design.

600 500 IR
MOKHTAREIN VA MOBTAKERIN. q. Soroush Press, 228 Mottahhari Ave., P.O. Box 15875-1163, Teheran, Iran. TEL 021-830771.

600 UK
MONITOR (LUTON); newspaper of A B B instrumentation. 1969. q. A B B Kent plc, Lea Rd., Luton, Beds. LU1 3AE, England. Ed. P.L. Culley. circ. 6,000. (tabloid format; back issues avail.)
Formerly (until 1990): Kent News.

MONOGRAFIE Z DZIEJOW NAUKI I TECHNIKI. see *SCIENCES: COMPREHENSIVE WORKS*

300 US
MONOGRAPHS ON SCIENCE, TECHNOLOGY, AND SOCIETY. irreg. price varies. Oxford University Press, 200 Madison Ave., New York, NY 10016. TEL 212-679-7300. Ed. Sir Alec Merrison.
Refereed Serial

600 LY
AL-MUNTIJUN. m. P.O. Box 734, Tripoli, Libya.

600 HU ISSN 0236-7408
MUSZAKI KONYV-MAGAZIN. 1965. 2/yr. free. Muszaki Konyvkiado Vallalat, Szentharomsag ter 1, 1014 Budapest, Hungary. TEL 557-122. Ed. Daniel Csabai. adv.; bk.rev.; illus.; circ. 30,000.
Former titles (until 1984): Muszaki Konyv Ujdonsagok Hiradoja & Muszaki Konyv Hirado.

N A T A NEWS. (National Association of Testing Authorities) see *SCIENCES: COMPREHENSIVE WORKS*

600 NE
N A T O ADVANCED SCIENCE INSTITUTES SERIES E: APPLIED SCIENCES. (Text in English) 1974. irreg., no.196, 1991. price varies. (North Atlantic Treaty Organization, Scientific Affairs Division, BE) Kluwer Academic Publishers, Postbus 17, 3300 AA Dordrecht, Netherlands. TEL 078-334911. FAX 078-334254. TELEX 29245. (Dist. by: Kluwer Academic Publishers Group, P.O. Box 322, 3300 AH Dordrecht, Netherlands; N. America dist. addr.: Box 358, Accord Sta., Hingham, MA 02018-0358. TEL 617-871-6600) **Indexed:** Biol.Abstr., Chem.Abstr., GeoRef., Math.R.
●Also available online. Vendor(s): European Space Agency (File no.128).
Formerly: N A T O Advanced Study Institute Series E: Applied Sciences.

N D T INTERNATIONAL; the independent journal of non-destructive testing. (Non Destructive Testing) see *ENGINEERING — Engineering Mechanics And Materials*

N I S S A T NEWSLETTER. (National Information System for Science and Technology) see *SCIENCES: COMPREHENSIVE WORKS*

600 FR
N T I. (Nouvelles Technologies de l'Information) 10/yr. 300 F. A Jour, 11 rue du Marche St. Honore, 75001 Paris, France. TEL 42-96-67-22. FAX 40-20-07-75. TELEX 615887 AJOUR.

600 US ISSN 0889-8464
N T I S TECH NOTES. Includes: Selected Technology for Licensing. 1977. m. $205 (foreign $410). U.S. National Technical Information Service, 5285 Port Royal Rd., Springfield, VA 22161. TEL 703-487-4630. FAX 703-321-8547. TELEX 64617. (Subscr. to: c/o Anita Weissman, Cir. Dir., Box 8757, Baltimore, MD 21240) Ed. Edward J. Lehmann. illus. (back issues avail.) **Indexed:** Abstr.Bull.Inst.Pap.Chem., Biol.Abstr., Ceram.Abstr., Curr.Pack.Abstr., MEDOC, Met.Abstr., Pollut.Abstr., PROMT, Rehabil.Lit., Tel.Abstr., World Alum.Abstr. **Incorporates:** N A S A Tech Briefs (ISSN 0145-319X)
Description: Bound publication of one page summaries of selected federal technology, reported by U.S. federal agencies. Divided in subject categories: agriculture and food, computers, electrotechnology, energy, engineering, medicine and biology, physical sciences, machinery, materials, manufacturing, testing and instrumentation.

600 KR ISSN 0206-3131
NADEZHNOST' I DOLGOVECHNOST' MASHIN I SOORUZHENNII; respublikanskii mezhvedomstvennyi sbornik nauchnykh trudov. (Text in Russian) 1982. s-a. (Akademiya Nauk Ukrainskoi S.S.R., Institut Problem Prochnosti) Izdatel'stvo Naukova Dumka, c/o Yu.A. Khramov, Dir, Ul. Repina, 3, Kiev 252 601, Ukraine. (Subscr. to: Mezhdunarodnaya Kniga, Moscow, G-200, Russia) Ed. V.T. Troshchenko.
—BLDSC shelfmark: 0119.131000.

NANJING DAXUE XUEBAO (ZIRAN KEXUE BAN)/NANJING UNIVERSITY. JOURNAL (NATURAL SCIENCE EDITION). see *SCIENCES: COMPREHENSIVE WORKS*

NARODNI TECHNICKE MUZEUM. CATALOGUES OF COLLECTIONS. see *MUSEUMS AND ART GALLERIES*

600 CS ISSN 0035-9378
NARODNI TECHNICKE MUZEUM. ROZPRAVY. (Text in Czech; summaries in English, German) 1962. irreg. (approx. 4/yr.). exchange basis only. Narodni Technicke Muzeum, Kostelni 42, 170 78 Prague 7, Czechoslovakia. bibl.; illus. **Indexed:** Numis.Lit.

NATIONAL DEFENSE ACADEMY. MEMOIRS. MATHEMATICS, PHYSICS, CHEMISTRY, AND ENGINEERING/BOEI DAIGAKKO KIYO. RIKOGAKU HEN. see *SCIENCES: COMPREHENSIVE WORKS*

600 620 KO
NATIONAL INDUSTRIAL RESEARCH INSTITUTE. REPORT. (Text in Korean; summaries in English) 1948. a. free. National Industrial Research Institute, 199 Dongsoong-dong, Chongno-ku, Seoul, S. Korea. illus.

600 CN ISSN 1183-9082
▼**NATIONAL RESEARCH COUNCIL OF CANADA. INSTITUTE FOR INFORMATION TECHNOLOGY. ANNUAL REPORT.** French edition: Conseil National de Recherches du Canada. Institut de Technologie de l'Information. Rapport Annuel (ISSN 1183-9090) 1991. a. free. National Research Council of Canada, Institute for Information Technology - Conseil National de Recherches du Canada, Institut de Technologie de l'Information, Rm. 310, M-50, Ottawa, Ont. K1A 0R6, Canada. TEL 613-993-1880. FAX 613-952-7998. Ed. Evelyn M. Kidd. circ. 2,200.
Description: Reports on current research projects, current publications and gives an Institute profile.

NATUUR EN TECHNIEK/NATURE AND TECHNOLOGY; natuurwetenschappelijk en technisch maandblad/scientific and technical monthly. see *SCIENCES: COMPREHENSIVE WORKS*

600 600 YU ISSN 0351-1030
NAUCNI PODMLADAK: TEHNICKE NAUKE; strucni casopis studenata Univerziteta u Nisu. (Text in Serbo-Croatian; summaries in English) 1969. q. 2500 din.($4) Univerzitet u Nisu, Strucno Udruzenje Studenata, Sumatovacka bb, 18000 Nis, Serbia, Yugoslavia. TEL 018 22-226. Ed. Milorad Pavlovic. adv.; circ. 500. **Indexed:** Lang.& Lang.Behav.Abstr.
Supersedes in part (in 1971): Naucni Podmladak: Tehnicke Nauke. Drustvene Nauke.

NAUKA I TEKHNIKA/ZINATNE UN TEKHNIKA. see *SCIENCES: COMPREHENSIVE WORKS*

NAUKA I ZHIZN'; nauchno-populyarnyi zhurnal. see *SCIENCES: COMPREHENSIVE WORKS*

NETSU SHORI/JAPAN SOCIETY FOR HEAT TREATMENT. JOURNAL. see *METALLURGY*

600 332.6 US ISSN 0882-6382
NEW & EMERGING TECHNOLOGY; executive newsreport and forecast on industrial innovation. 1983. m. $180. Box 1188, Bay City, MI 48706. TEL 517-893-7700. FAX 517-894-5390. Ed. David L. Rogers. adv.; bk.rev.; index; circ. 5,000. (back issues avail.)
Formerly (until 1985): Midwest Technology (ISSN 0740-8668)
Description: Reports on new technologically-based products and companies, especially in automated manufacturing, involving robotics, machine vision and artifical intelligence; also covers socio-technical developments affecting the economy, and investment and financial market opportunities.

TECHNOLOGY: COMPREHENSIVE WORKS 4605

658.7 US ISSN 0028-4963
TJ1
NEW EQUIPMENT DIGEST. 1936. m. $50 (free to qualified personnel). Penton Publishing (Subsidiary of: Pittway Company), 1100 Superior Ave., Cleveland, OH 44114-2543. TEL 216-696-7000. FAX 216-696-8765. (Subscr. to: Box 95759, Cleveland, OH 44101) Ed. Robert King. adv.; bk.rev.; illus.; tr.lit.; circ. 213,000 (controlled). (also avail. in microform from UMI; reprint service avail. from UMI)
Description: Descriptions of new or significantly improved industrial products.

658.7 CN ISSN 0028-4971
NEW EQUIPMENT NEWS. 1940. m. Can.$50. Canadian Engineering Publications Ltd., 5080 Timberlea Blvd., Ste. 8, Mississauga, Ont. L4W 5C1, Canada. TEL 416-602-0814. FAX 416-602-0818. Ed. B. Lehman. adv.; abstr.; charts; illus.; tr.lit.; circ. 28,024. (tabloid format)
Description: Provides in-plant buyers and specifiers with current information on industrial product developments.

658.7 SA ISSN 0028-498X
NEW EQUIPMENT NEWS. Abbreviated title: N E N. 1963. m. R.73 (foreign R.98)(effective 1992). Thomson Publications (Subsidiary of: Times Media Ltd.), P.O. Box 56182, Pinegowrie 2123, South Africa. TEL 011-789-2144. FAX 011-789-3196. Ed. Gill Marsden. adv.; abstr.; illus.; tr.lit.; circ. 9,036.

600 US ISSN 0740-3569
NEW FROM EUROPE; research advisory service on technological developments from Western Europe. 1979. m. $295. Prestwick Publications, Inc., 390 N. Federal Hwy., Ste. 401, Deerfield Beach, FL 33441-2209. Ed. Roy H. Roecker. bk.rev.

600 US ISSN 0740-3550
NEW FROM JAPAN; research advisory service on Japanese technological developments. 1974. m. $295. Prestwick Publications, Inc., 390 N. Federal Hwy., Ste. 401, Deerfield Beach, FL 33441-2209. Ed. Roy H. Roecker. bk.rev.

600 US ISSN 0740-3577
NEW FROM U S; research advisory service on U.S. technological developments. 1981. m. $295. Prestwick Publications, Inc., 390 N. Federal Hwy., Ste. 401, Deerfield Beach, FL 33441-2209. Ed. R.H. Roecker. bk.rev.

600 UK ISSN 0265-3443
CODEN: NMJAE6
NEW MATERIALS - JAPAN. 1980. m. £262 (effective 1992). Elsevier Science Publishers Ltd., Crown House, Linton Rd., Barking, Essex IG11 8JU, England. TEL 081-594-7272. FAX 081-594-5942. TELEX 896950 APPSCI G. (Subscr. in U.S. and Canada to: Elsevier Science Publishing Co., Inc., Box 882, Madison Sq. Sta., New York, NY 10159. TEL 212-989-5800) Ed. N. Butler. (back issues avail.) Indexed: Met.Abstr., World Alum.Abstr.
●Also available online. Vendor(s): Data-Star, DIALOG.
—BLDSC shelfmark: 6084.474590.
Description: Covers new materials, products, processes, manufacturing techniques, and commercial prospects originating in Japan.

600 SW ISSN 1100-956X
NEW SCANDINAVIAN TECHNOLOGY. (Text in English) 1989. q. $30. Bjare Information AB, Box 5173, S-102 44 Stockholm, Sweden. TEL 46-8-662-28-69. FAX 46-8-6628859. Ed. Torgny Bjare. adv.; circ. 25,000.
Formerly (until 1989): New Swedish Technology (ISSN 0280-378X)
Description: Presents accounts of occurrences on the technical R&D front in the Nordic countries.

600 US ISSN 0894-0789
T1
NEW TECHNOLOGY WEEK. 1987. w. $495. King Publishing Group, Inc., 627 National Press Bldg., Washington, DC 20045. TEL 202-638-4260. FAX 202-662-9744. Ed. Richard A. McCormack. bk.rev. Indexed: Comput.Lit.Ind.
●Also available online. Vendor(s): Data-Star, DIALOG.

600 UK
NEWCOMEN BULLETIN. 1939. 3/yr. membership. Newcomen Society for the Study of the History of Engineering and Technology, Science Museum, S. Kensington, London SW7 2DD, England. TEL 01-589-1793. bk.rev.; bibl.

NEWCOMEN SOCIETY FOR THE STUDY OF THE HISTORY OF ENGINEERING AND TECHNOLOGY. TRANSACTIONS. see *ENGINEERING*

NEWTON/NYUTON. see *SCIENCES: COMPREHENSIVE WORKS*

NICHI-FUTSU RIKOKA KAISHI/SOCIETE FRANCO-JAPONAISE DES SCIENCES PURES ET APPLIQUEES. BULLETIN. see *SCIENCES: COMPREHENSIVE WORKS*

600 500 JA ISSN 0369-4313
NIHON DAIGAKU RIKOGAKU KENKYUJO SHOHO/NIHON UNIVERSITY. RESEARCH INSTITUTE OF SCIENCE AND TECHNOLOGY. JOURNAL. (Text in Japanese) 1950. s-a. exchange basis. Nihon Daigaku, Rikogaku Kenkyujo - Nihon University, Research Institute of Science and Technology, 1-8 Kanda Surugadai, Chiyoda-ku, Tokyo 101, Japan. abstr.; circ. controlled. Indexed: Chem.Abstr., JCT, JTA, Sci.Abstr.
—BLDSC shelfmark: 4847.900000.

600 JA
NIHON DAIGAKU RIKOGAKUBU GAKUJUTSU KOENKAI KOEN RONBUNSHU. (Text in Japanese) a. Nihon Daigaku, Rikogakubu Rikogaku Kenkyujo - Nihon University, College of Science and Technology, Research Institute of Science and Technology, 1-8 Kanda Surugadai, Chiyoda-ku, Tokyo 101, Japan.
Description: Contains proceedings from the meetings of the institute.

NIHON NO KAGAKU TO GIJUTSU/JAPAN SCIENCE AND TECHNOLOGY. see *SCIENCES: COMPREHENSIVE WORKS*

NIHON UNIVERSITY. RESEARCH INSTITUTE OF SCIENCE AND TECHNOLOGY. REPORT. see *SCIENCES: COMPREHENSIVE WORKS*

600 JA ISSN 0913-7912
NIIGATA KOGYO TANKI DAIGAKU KENKYU KIYO/NIIGATA TECHNICAL JUNIOR COLLEGE. JOURNAL. (Text in Japanese; summaries in English) 1971. irreg. Niigata Kogyo Tanki Daigaku - Niigata Technical Junior College, 5827 Kamishin'ei-cho, Niigata-shi, Niigata-ken 950-21, Japan.
Description: Contains original papers.

600 620 500 JA ISSN 0286-2743
Q4 CODEN: NKHEDR
NIIHAMA KOGYO KOTO SENMON GAKKO KIYO. RIKOGAKU HEN/NIIHAMA NATIONAL COLLEGE OF TECHNOLOGY. MEMOIRS. SCIENCE AND ENGINEERING. (Text in English and Japanese; summaries in English) 1965. a. Niihama Kogyo Koto Senmon Gakko - Niihama National College of Technology, 7-1 Yakumo-cho, Niihama-shi, Ehime-ken 792, Japan. Indexed: Chem.Abstr., INIS Atomind., Jap.Per.Ind.
—BLDSC shelfmark: 5629.342000.

600 620 JA ISSN 0911-1018
NIKKEI NEW MATERIALS. (Text in Japanese) 1985. 17/yr. 16000 Yen. Nikkei Business Publications, Inc., 3-3-23, Misakicho, Chiyoda-ku, Tokyo 101, Japan. TEL 03-5210-8502. FAX 03-5210-8119. Ed. Yasutami Kuwahara. adv.; circ. 17,942. (back issues avail.)
—BLDSC shelfmark: 6113.178370.
Description: Contains information on new trends, technologies and materials, as well as development processes and applications.

600 JA ISSN 0910-6227
NISHINIPPON KOGYO DAIGAKU KIYO. RIKOGAKU HEN/NISHINIPPON INSTITUTE OF TECHNOLOGY. MEMOIRS. SCIENCE AND TECHNOLOGY. (Text in English and Japanese; summaries in English) 1969. a. Nishinippon Kogyo Daigaku - Nishinippon Institute of Technology, 1633 Aratsu, Kanda-machi, Miyako-gun, Fukuoka-ken 800-03, Japan.

NORGES TEKNISK-NATURVITENSKAPELIGE FORSKNINGSRAAD. AARSBERETNING/ROYAL NORWEGIAN COUNCIL FOR SCIENTIFIC AND INDUSTRIAL RESEARCH. ANNUAL REPORT. see *SCIENCES: COMPREHENSIVE WORKS*

338 FR ISSN 0029-1803
NORMANDIE INDUSTRIELLE. 1939. q. 120 F. (Societe Industrielle de Rouen) Editions Lecerf, 22 rue des Bons Enfants, Rouen, France. Ed. M. Lecerf. adv.; bk.rev.; bibl.; charts; illus.; tr.lit.; circ. 5,700. Indexed: C.I.S. Abstr.
—BLDSC shelfmark: 6133.000000.

NORTHERN PERSPECTIVES. see *ENVIRONMENTAL STUDIES*

600 CU
NOTICIERO CIENTIFICO. SERIE: TECNOLOGIA. fortn. Academia de Ciencias, Instituto de Documentacion e Informacion Cientifico-Tecnica (I D I C T), Capitolio Nacional, Prado y San Jose, Habana 2, Havana, Cuba.

NOTRE DAME TECHNICAL REVIEW. see *ENGINEERING*

600 CN
NOVA SCOTIA RESEARCH FOUNDATION CORPORATION. ANNUAL REPORT. a. Nova Scotia Research Foundation Corporation, 101 Research Dr., Woodside Industrial Park, Box 790, Dartmouth, N.S. B2Y 3Z7, Canada. TEL 902-424-8670. FAX 902-424-8670. Ed.Bd.

600 US
O C D DIAMOND. 1935. m. American Cyanamid Co., Organic Chemical Division, Bound Brook, NJ 08805. TEL 201-831-2000. Ed. Robert G. Meyer. circ. 6,500 (controlled).
Formerly (until 1976): Bound Brook Diamond.

600 FR ISSN 1011-792X
Q172.5.S34
O E C D. MAIN SCIENCE AND TECHNOLOGY INDICATORS/O C D E. PRINCIPAUX INDICATEURS DE LA SCIENCE ET DE LA TECHNOLOGIE. 1988. s-a. 170 F.($36) Organization for Economic Cooperation and Development, 2 rue Andre-Pascal, 75775 Paris Cedex 16, France. TEL 45-24-87-19. FAX 45-24-81-76. (U.S. orders to: O.E.C.D. Publications and Information Center, 2001 L St., N.W., Ste. 700, Washington, DC 20036-4910. TEL 202-785-6323) (also avail. in microfiche from OEC,UMI)
—BLDSC shelfmark: 5352.070000.

600 500 FR
O E C D. REVIEWS OF NATIONAL SCIENCE AND TECHNOLOGY POLICY. irreg. price varies. Organization for Economic Cooperation and Development, 2 rue Andre-Pascal, 75775 Paris Cedex 16, France. TEL 45-24-82-00. FAX 45-24-85-00. (U.S. orders to: O.E.C.D. Publications and Information Center, 2001 L St., N.W., Ste. 700, Washington, DC 20036-4910. TEL 202-785-6323) (also avail. in microfiche from OEC)

O R S T O M INSTITUT FRANCAIS DE RECHERCHE POUR LE DEVELOPEMENT EN COOPERATION. RAPPORT D'ACTIVITE. see *SCIENCES: COMPREHENSIVE WORKS*

O S A ANNUAL MEETING DIGEST. (Optical Society of America, Inc.) see *PHYSICS — Optics*

OAK RIDGE NATIONAL LABORATORY REVIEW. see *PHYSICS — Nuclear Physics*

OIL & GAS REPORT. see *BUSINESS AND ECONOMICS*

600 CN ISSN 0380-1969
ONTARIO TECHNOLOGIST. 1958. 6/yr. Can.$25 (foreign Can.$35)(effective Jan. 1991). Ontario Association of Certified Engineering Technicians & Technologists, 10 Four Seasons Pl., Ste. 404, Etobicoke, Ont. M9B 6H7, Canada. TEL 416-621-9621. FAX 416-621-8694. Ed. Ruth M. Klein. adv.; bk.rev.; circ. 18,840.

600 BL
OPEMA EM RITMO DE BRASIL JOVEM. 1968. irreg. free. (Ministerio dos Transportes, Operacao Maua) Assessoria de Relacoes Publicas, Editora, Promocoes e Publicidade Ltda., Av. Beira Mar 406, Grupo 906, Rio de Janeiro, Brazil. adv.; illus.; stat.; circ. 60,000.

ORGANIZATION OF AFRICAN UNITY. SCIENTIFIC TECHNICAL AND RESEARCH COMMISSION. PUBLICATION. see *SCIENCES: COMPREHENSIVE WORKS*

600 500 JA ISSN 0375-0191
CODEN: OKDRAK
OSAKA KOGYO DAIGAKU KIYO. RIKO HEN/OSAKA INSTITUTE OF TECHNOLOGY. MEMOIRS. SERIES A. SCIENCE AND TECHNOLOGY. (Text in English and Japanese; summaries in English) 1962. 2/yr. Osaka Kogyo Daigaku - Osaka Institute of Technology, 16-1 Omiya 5-chome, Asahi-ku, Osaka-shi, Osaka-fu 535, Japan. charts; illus. Indexed: Biol.Abstr., Chem.Abstr., INIS Atomind., Jap.Per.Ind., JCT, Math.R.

4606 TECHNOLOGY: COMPREHENSIVE WORKS

OSAKA KYOIKU DAIGAKU KIYO. DAI-3-BUMON. SHIZEN KAGAKU/OSAKA KYOIKU UNIVERSITY. MEMOIRS. SERIES 3: NATURAL SCIENCE AND APPLIED SCIENCE. see *SCIENCES: COMPREHENSIVE WORKS*

607   JA   ISSN 0369-0369
Q180.J3   CODEN: MISIAW
OSAKA UNIVERSITY. INSTITUTE OF SCIENTIFIC AND INDUSTRIAL RESEARCH. MEMOIRS/OSAKA DAIGAKU SANGYO KAGAKU KENKYUJO KIYO. (Text in European languages) 1941. a. exchange basis. Osaka Daigaku, Sangyo Kagaku Kenkyujo - Osaku University, Institute of Scientific and Industrial Research, Mihoga-oka, Ibaraki, Osaka 567, Japan. Ed.Bd. circ. 750. **Indexed:** Chem.Abstr., INIS Atomind.
—BLDSC shelfmark: 5620.000000.

OTTAWA R & D REPORT. see *ENGINEERING*

600   PK
P A S T I C TRANSLATIONS. 1957. irreg., latest 1982. Rs.10($4) Pakistan Scientific and Technological Information Centre, Quaid-i-Azam University Campus, Box No.1217, Islamabad, Pakistan. cum.index; circ. 500. (also avail. in microfilm)
Formerly: P A N S D O C Translations (ISSN 0078-8368)

600   US   ISSN 0478-9997
P - D NEWS; including captsule job listings. 1957. w. $51. Publications & Communications, Inc., 12416 Hymeadow Dr., Austin, TX 78750-1896. TEL 512-331-3918. FAX 512-331-3900. (Subscr. to: Box 399, Cedar Park, TX 78613-9987) Ed. Janiece Wade. adv.; circ. 5,000. (back issues avail.)
●Also available online.
Description: Covers the contract technical services industry.

P E D. (Production & Industrial Equipment Digest) see *ENGINEERING*

600   UK
P E R A NEWS. 1947. 6/yr. Production Engineering Research Association International, Melton Mowbray, Leicestershire LE13 OPB, England. FAX 0664-501264. **Indexed:** BMT.
Formerly: P E R A Bulletin.

600   GW   ISSN 0936-0492
P T B BERICHTE. irreg. Physikalisch Technische Bundesanstalt, Bundesallee 100, Postfach 3345, 3300 Braunschweig, Germany. TEL 0531-5920. FAX 0531-5924006. TELEX 0952822-PTB-D.
—BLDSC shelfmark: 1927.042000.

PAKISTAN JOURNAL OF SCIENTIFIC AND INDUSTRIAL RESEARCH. see *SCIENCES: COMPREHENSIVE WORKS*

PALEOCEANOGRAPHY. see *SCIENCES: COMPREHENSIVE WORKS*

PAPUA NEW GUINEA UNIVERSITY OF TECHNOLOGY. REPORTER. see *COLLEGE AND ALUMNI*

620   HU   ISSN 0031-3750
T4
PECSI MUSZAKI SZEMLE.* 1956. q. membership. Muszaki es Termeszettudomanyi Egyesuletek Szovetsege, Baranya Megyei Szervezet, P.F. 451, HU-1372 Budapest, Hungary. Ed. Zoltan Miklosvari. charts; illus.; cum.index every 5 yrs.; circ. 1,200. **Indexed:** Hung.Build.Bull.

600 001.642   US
▼**PENNSYLVANIA TECHNOLOGY.** 1990. q. $19.95. Pittsburgh High Technology Council, 4516 Henry St., Pittsburgh, PA 15213-9916. TEL 412-687-2700. FAX 412-687-2791. Ed. Betsy Momich. circ. 25,000.
Description: For all levels of managment, and professionals in engineering, computers, marketing and sales.

600   PH   ISSN 0116-7294
T1   CODEN: PTEJEB
PHILIPPINE TECHNOLOGY JOURNAL; a quarterly organ for Philippine technological researchers. 1976. q. P.60($25) Science and Technology Information Institute (DOST), Bicutan, Taguig, Metro Manila, P.O. Box 3596, Manila, Philippines. TEL 8220961. Ed. Ricardo M. Lantican. adv.; bk.rev.; cum.index every 5 yrs.; circ. 2,000. (back issues avail.) **Indexed:** Chem.Abstr., Excerp.Med., Food Sci.& Tech.Abstr., Forest.Abstr., Philip.Abstr., Rural Recreat.Tour.Abstr., Soils & Fert., World Agri.Econ.& Rural Sociol.Abstr.
Former titles: D O S T Technology Journal (ISSN 0115-2777); National Science and Technology Journal; N S D B Technology Journal.

600   GW   ISSN 0340-4366
PHYSIKALISCH-TECHNISCHEN BUNDESANSTALT BRAUNSCHWEIG UND BERLIN. JAHRESBERICHT. 1971. a. free. Physikalisch-Technische Bundesanstalt, Braunschweig und Berlin, Referat Schrifttum, Bundesallee 100, 3300 Braunschweig, Germany. TEL 0531-5920. FAX 0531-5924006. TELEX 952822-PTB-D. circ. 1,600.
—BLDSC shelfmark: 4636.360000.
Description: Describes activities of all laboratories of the PTB; includes a list of publications.

620   PL   ISSN 0239-7528
CODEN: BASSEP
POLISH ACADEMY OF SCIENCES. BULLETIN. TECHNICAL SCIENCES. (Text in English, French, German and Russian) 1953. q. $100. Polska Akademia Nauk, Centrum Upowszechniania Nauki, Palac Kultury i Nauki, Pietro XXIII, pok.23-10, 00-901 Warsaw, Poland. (Dist. by: Ars Polona, Krakowskie Przedmiescie 7, 00-068 Warsaw, Poland) Ed. T. Sliwinski. bibl.; charts; illus.; index; circ. 350. **Indexed:** Appl.Mech.Rev., Chem.Abstr., Eng.Ind., Geotech.Abstr., INIS Atomind., Key Word Ind.Wildl.Res., Math.R., Met.Abstr., Phys.Abstr., Sci.Abstr.
Formerly (until 1983): Academie Polonaise des Sciences. Bulletin. Serie des Sciences Techniques (ISSN 0001-4125)

POLISH TECHNICAL REVIEW. see *ENGINEERING*

600   PL   ISSN 0137-138X
POLITECHNIKA KRAKOWSKA. ZESZYTY NAUKOWE. PODSTAWOWE NAUKI TECHNICZNE. (Text in Polish; summaries in English, French, German and Russian) 1968. irreg. price varies. Politechnika Krakowska, Ul. Warszawska 24, 31-155 Krakow, Poland. TEL 48-12-374289. FAX 48-12-335773. TELEX 322468 PK PL. (Dist. by Ars Polona-Ruch, Krakowskie Przedmiescie 7, 00-068 Warsaw, Poland) bibl.; charts; illus.; circ. 200.

600   IT
POLITECNICO. 1988? q. L.23600($48) (students L.11800)(effective 1991). (Politecnico di Milano) Masson Italia Periodici, Via Statuto 2-4, 20120 Milan, Italy. TEL 02-6367-1. FAX 02-6367-211. Ed. Carlo Ortolani. circ. 4,000.

620   US   ISSN 0032-4558
T1
POPULAR MECHANICS. 1902. m. $15.94 (effective 1992). Hearst Magazines, Popular Mechanics, 224 W. 57th St., New York, NY 10019. TEL 212-649-3076. (Subscr. to: Box 7170, Red Oak, IA 51591. TEL 800-333-4948) Ed. Joe Oldham. adv.; illus.; circ. 1,688,784. (also avail. in microform from UMI) **Indexed:** Abr.R.G., Acad.Ind., Art & Archaeol.Tech.Abstr., Biog.Ind., Consum.Ind., Gdlns, HRIS, Ind.Child.Mag., Ind.How To Do It (1963-), Jun.High.Mag.Abstr., Mag.Ind., MELSA, PMR, R.G., TOM.
Description: Examines new products, techniques as well as scientific and technological developments. Covers the automobile, the home, shop, outdoors, and science and technology.

620   US   ISSN 0360-2273
TT155
POPULAR MECHANICS DO-IT-YOURSELF YEARBOOK. a. Hearst Magazines, Popular Mechanics, 224 W. 57th St., New York, NY 10019. illus.

620   US   ISSN 0161-7370
AP2   CODEN: PSCIEP
POPULAR SCIENCE; the what's new magazine. 1872. m. $13.94 (foreign $21.94)(effective 1992). Times Mirror Magazines, Inc., 2 Park Ave., New York, NY 10016. TEL 212-779-5000. (Subscr. to: Box 5100, Harlan, IA 51563. TEL 800-289-9399) Ed. C.P. Gilmore. adv.; bk.rev.; charts; illus.; pat.; tr.lit.; index; circ. 2,000,000. (also avail. in microform from UMI; reprint service avail. from UMI) **Indexed:** Abr.R.G., Acad.Ind., Acid Rain Ind., CAD CAM Abstr., Consum.Ind., Energy Info.Abstr., Environ.Abstr., Gdlns., GeoRef., Ind.Child.Mag., Ind.How To Do It (1963-), Jun.High.Mag.Abstr., Mag.Ind., MELSA, PMR, R.G., Robomat., Tel.Abstr., TOM.
●Also available online. Vendor(s): DIALOG.
Formerly: Popular Science Monthly (ISSN 0032-4647)
Description: Comprehensive coverage of a broad range of scientific and technological topics such as computers and electronics, energy, tools and techniques, new products and inventions as well as horticulture.

POPULAR SCIENCE AND TECHNOLOGY. see *SCIENCES: COMPREHENSIVE WORKS*

POSITIVE ALTERNATIVES. see *POLITICAL SCIENCE*

POST; a magazine for the promotion of science and technology. see *SCIENCES: COMPREHENSIVE WORKS*

POUR LA SCIENCE. see *SCIENCES: COMPREHENSIVE WORKS*

600   GW   ISSN 0934-7348
TS180
POWDER HANDLING & PROCESSING. 1989. q. 284 F. Trans Tech Publications, Postfach 1254, 3392 Clausthal-Zellerfeld, Germany. TEL 05323-40077. FAX 05323-40079. TELEX 953-713-TTP-D. Ed. Reinhard Woehlbier. circ. 10,000.
—BLDSC shelfmark: 6571.910000.
Description: Explores practical problems of processing, handling, storing, packaging powder and dry particles, as well as equipment design and engineering.

PRIMARY D A T A. (Design and Technology Association) see *EDUCATION — Teaching Methods And Curriculum*

PRISMA (KASSEL). see *SCIENCES: COMPREHENSIVE WORKS*

607   US
PROBABLE LEVELS OF R & D EXPENDITURES: FORECAST AND ANALYSIS. 1960? a. free. Battelle Memorial Institute, Columbus Operations, 505 King Ave., Columbus, OH 43201. TEL 614-424-6424. charts; stat.; circ. controlled. **Indexed:** SRI.

PROBLEME DE AUTOMATIZARE. see *ENGINEERING*

600   UK
PROCESS INSTRUMENTATION REVIEW. 1980. q. free. A B B Kent plc, Lea Rd., Luton, Beds. LU1 3AE, England. Ed. P.L. Culley. circ. 18,500. (tabloid format; back issues avail.) **Indexed:** Fluidex, World Text.Abstr.
Formerly (until 1990): Kent Review (ISSN 0143-8697)

PRODUCT & PROCESS INNOVATION. see *COMPUTERS — Electronic Data Processing*

670   UK   ISSN 0032-9762
TS200   CODEN: PRFIAT
PRODUCT FINISHING. 1948. m. $107. Sawell Publications Ltd., 127 Stanstead Rd., London SE23 1JE, England. Ed. J.E. Bean. adv.; bk.rev.; charts; illus.; pat.; tr.lit.; tr.mk.; index; circ. 4,380. **Indexed:** Art & Archaeol.Tech.Abstr., Br.Tech.Ind., Cadscan, Chem.Abstr., Eng.Ind., Excerp.Med., Int.Packag.Abstr., Lead Abstr., Met.Abstr., World Alum.Abstr., World Surf.Coat., Zincscan.
—BLDSC shelfmark: 6853.000000.

PRODUCTS FINISHING. see *PAINTS AND PROTECTIVE COATINGS*

PRODUCTS FINISHING DIRECTORY. see *PAINTS AND PROTECTIVE COATINGS*

TECHNOLOGY: COMPREHENSIVE WORKS

600   CN   ISSN 0701-1687
PRODUITS POUR L'INDUSTRIE QUEBECOISE. (Text in French) 1976. 6/yr. Can.$30. Action Communications Inc., 135 Spy Ct., Markham, Ont. L3R 5H6, Canada. TEL 416-477-3222. FAX 416-477-4320. Ed. David Terhune. adv.; circ. 15,725. (tabloid format; back issues avail.)

600 500   FR   ISSN 0397-8060
T175   CODEN: PRTCDG
PROGRES TECHNIQUE. 1974. 5/yr. 440 F. Association Nationale de la Recherche Technique, 101 av. Raymond Poincare, 75016 Paris, France. FAX 1-45-01-85-29. Ed. Christian Dambrine. adv.; bk.rev.; bibl.; circ. 3,000. **Indexed:** Met.Abstr.
●Also available online.
    Supersedes (since 1976): Recherche Technique.

PROJECT APPRAISAL. see *BUSINESS AND ECONOMICS* — *Investments*

600   PL   ISSN 0239-3174
PROJEKTOWANIE I SYSTEMY. (Text in Polish; summaries in English, Russian) a. price varies. (Polish Academy of Sciences, Committee of Science) Ossolineum, Publishing House of the Polish Academy of Sciences, Rynek 9, 50-106 Wroclaw, Poland. TEL 386-25. (Dist. by: Ars Polona, Krakowskie Przedmiescie 7, 00-068 Warsaw, Poland) Ed. Wojciech Gasparski.
    Description: Papers on designing process and system science.

600   PL   ISSN 0137-8783
HD8536
PRZEGLAD TECHNICZNY, INNOWACJE. 1875. w. $66. (Naczelna Organizacja Techniczna) Wydawnictwo Czasopism i Ksiazek Technicznych SIGMA - NOT, Ul. Biala 4, P.O. Box 1004, 00-950 Warsaw, Poland. (Dist. by: Zaklad Kolportazu SIGMA-NOT, ul. Bartycka 20, P.O. Box 1004, 00-950 Warsaw, Poland) (Co-sponsor: Polskie Towarzystwo Ekonomiczne) Ed. Ewa Mankiewicz-Cudny. circ. 30,000. **Indexed:** C.I.S.Abstr.
    Formerly (until 1977): Innowacje (ISSN 0208-5615); Which was formed by the 1974 merger of: Wektory; Przeglad Techniczny (ISSN 0033-2380)

PUBLIKATIONEN ZU WISSENSCHAFTLICHEN FILMEN. SEKTION TECHNISCHE WISSENSCHAFTEN, NATURWISSENSCHAFTEN. see *MOTION PICTURES*

PUROMETEUSU. see *SCIENCES: COMPREHENSIVE WORKS*

658.5   SZ   ISSN 0033-5169
             CODEN: EOQUDF
QUALITY. (Text in English; summaries in French, German, Russian and Spanish) 1958. 4/yr. 110 SFr. European Organization for Quality - Organisation Europeenne pour la Qualite, P.O. Box 5032, CH-3001 Bern, Switzerland. TEL 031-216166. FAX 031-263257. TELEX 913278-ATAG-CH. adv.; bk.rev.; abstr.; bibl.; charts; illus.; stat.; circ. 2,700. **Indexed:** Oper.Res.Manage.Sci., P.A.I.S., Qual.Contr.Appl.Stat., Robomat., Sci.Abstr.

QUEBEC SCIENCE. see *SCIENCES: COMPREHENSIVE WORKS*

QUIDDITY; polemical review of new developments in publishing. see *BUSINESS AND ECONOMICS — Marketing And Purchasing*

QUIPU; revista latinoamericana de historia de las ciencias y la tecnologia. see *SCIENCES: COMPREHENSIVE WORKS*

600   US
▼**R & D STRATEGIST.** 1990. q. $145. Auerbach Publishers (Subsidiary of: Warren, Gorham & Lamont), One Penn Plaza, New York, NY 10119. TEL 212-971-5000. FAX 617-423-2026. (Subscr. to: 210 South St., Boston, MA 02111-9990. TEL 800-950-1218)

RADIO KIT ELETTRONICA. see *HOBBIES*

THE RAND CORPORATION'S RESEARCH PUBLICATIONS. see *SCIENCES: COMPREHENSIVE WORKS*

620   IT
RASSEGNA DI MECCANICA; mensile di tecnica e organizzazione. (Text and summaries in English and Italian) 1967. m. L.96000 (foreign L.140000)(effective 1992). Franco Angeli Editore, Viale Monza 106, 20127 Milan, Italy. TEL 02-28-27-651. Ed. Franco Angeli. adv.; bk.rev.; circ. 10,000.
    Formerly: Rassegna Internazionale di Meccanica (ISSN 0033-9709)

600   GW
RATGEBER FORSCHUNG UND TECHNOLOGIE; Foerderungsmoeglichkeiten und Beratungshilfen. 1985. a. DM.42.80. Deutscher Wirtschaftsdienst, Marienburgerstr. 22, 5000 Cologne 51, Germany. TEL 0221-37695-0. Ed. Adolf Gaube.

RECHERCHE. see *SCIENCES: COMPREHENSIVE WORKS*

RELIABILITY ENGINEERING AND SYSTEM SAFETY. see *ENGINEERING*

REPORT TO S C A R ON SOUTH AFRICAN ANTARCTIC RESEARCH ACTIVITIES. (Scientific Committee for Antarctic Research) see *SCIENCES: COMPREHENSIVE WORKS*

REPORTERO INDUSTRIAL; new equipment, machinery and techniques for industry. see *MACHINERY*

REPUBLIC OF CHINA. NATIONAL SCIENCE COUNCIL. PROCEEDINGS. PART D: MATHEMATICS, SCIENCE, AND TECHNOLOGY EDUCATION. see *SCIENCES: COMPREHENSIVE WORKS*

600   US   ISSN 0746-9179
T175   CODEN: REDEEA
RESEARCH & DEVELOPMENT. 1959. m. $69.95 (Canada $118.95; Mexico $110.95; elsewhere $133.95). Cahners Publishing Company (Des Plaines) (Subsidiary of: Reed International PLC), Division Reed Publishing (USA) Inc., 1350 E. Touhy Ave., Box 5080, Des Plaines, IL 60017-5080. TEL 708-635-8800. FAX 908-390-2618. (Subscr. to: 44 Cook St., Denver, CO 80206. TEL 800-662-7776) Ed. Rob Cassidy. adv.; bk.rev.; charts; illus.; stat.; index; circ. 120,107 (controlled). (also avail. in microform from RPI) **Indexed:** Abstr.Bull.Inst.Pap.Chem., Anal.abstr., ASCA, B.P.I, BMT, Br.Ceram.Abstr., Bus.Ind., Cadscan, Ceram.Abstr., Chem.Abstr., Curr.Cont., Curr.Pack.Abstr., Energy Ind., Energy Info.Abstr., Eng.Ind., Excerp.Med., Fluidex, Graph.Arts Lit.Abstr., Ind.Sci.Rev., Int.Aerosp.Abstr., Lead Abstr., Mag.Ind., Met.Abstr., PROMT, Risk Abstr., Sci.Abstr., Sh.& Vib.Dig., SRI, Text.Tech.Dig., Tr.& Indus.Ind., World Alum.Abstr., Zincscan.
●Also available online. Vendor(s): DIALOG.
    Formerly (until 1984): Industrial Research and Development (ISSN 0160-4074); Which was formed by the merger of: Industrial Research (ISSN 0019-8722); Research - Development (ISSN 0034-5199)
    Description: Technical review of applied research and development with scientific data from all industrial areas.
    Refereed Serial

600   II
RESEARCH & DEVELOPMENT IN INDUSTRY. 1976. a. Rs.50. Department of Science and Technology, New Mehrauli Rd., New Delhi 110016, India. Ed. A.R. Rajeswari. circ. 1,000.

600 500   JA
RESEARCH AND DEVELOPMENT IN JAPAN AWARDED THE OKOCHI MEMORIAL PRIZE. (Text in English) 1970. a. Okochi Kinenkai - Okochi Memorial Foundation, 17-1 Toranomon 1-chome, Minato-ku, Tokyo 105, Japan. **Indexed:** Eng.Ind.

600   US
T175
RESEARCH & DEVELOPMENT PRODUCT SOURCE TELEPHONE DIRECTORY. (Published as an issue of Research & Development (ISSN 0746-9179)) a. $50. Cahners Publishing Company (Des Plaines) (Subsidiary of: Reed International PLC), Division of Reed Publishing (USA) Inc., 1350 E. Touhy Ave., Box 5080, Des Plaines, IL 60017-5080. TEL 708-635-8800. FAX 708-390-2618. (Subscr. to: 44 Cook St., Denver, CO 80206. TEL 800-662-7776) adv.; circ. 100,000 (controlled). (back issues avail.)
    Formerly (until 1992): Research and Development Telephone Directory (ISSN 0160-4074)

620   II   ISSN 0034-513X
T1   CODEN: RSIDAO
RESEARCH AND INDUSTRY; a journal for entrepreneurs and technologists. (Text in English) 1956. q. Rs.125($42) Council of Scientific and Industrial Research, Publications & Information Directorate, Hillside Rd., New Delhi 110 012, India. TEL 11-586301. Eds. V.K. Sharma, M.M.S. Karki. adv.; bk.rev.; abstr.; charts; illus.; tr.lit.; index; circ. 800. **Indexed:** CAD CAM Abstr., Cadscan, Chem.Abstr., Energy Info.Abstr., Environ.Abstr., Food Sci.& Tech.Abstr., ISMEC, Lead Abstr., Soils & Fert., Tel.Abstr., Zincscan.
    —BLDSC shelfmark: 7715.300000.

RESEARCH ENGINEERING MANUFACTURING. see *ENGINEERING*

RESEARCH IN PHILOSOPHY AND TECHNOLOGY. see *PHILOSOPHY*

600   US   ISSN 0737-1071
HD45
RESEARCH ON TECHNOLOGICAL INNOVATION, MANAGEMENT AND POLICY. 1983. a. $63.50 to institutions. J A I Press Inc., 55 Old Post Rd., No. 2, Box 1678, Greenwich, CT 06836-1678. TEL 203-661-7602. Ed. Richard S. Rosenbloom.
    Refereed Serial

667.2   UK   ISSN 0557-9325
TP890
REVIEW OF PROGRESS IN COLORATION AND RELATED TOPICS. 1970. a. £12. Society of Dyers and Colourists, Box 244, Perkin House, Bradford, Yorkshire BD1 2JB, England. TEL 0274-7215138. FAX 0274-392888. Ed. Paul Dinsdale. circ. 3,800. (also avail. in microfilm) **Indexed:** Abstr.Bull.Inst.Pap.Chem., Art & Archaeol.Tech.Abstr., Chem.Abstr., Text.Tech.Dig., World Surf.Coat., World Text.Abstr.
    Description: Review articles on coloration.

600   BL   ISSN 0048-7643
             CODEN: RBTNAO
REVISTA BRASILEIRA DE TECNOLOGIA. (Text in Portuguese; summaries in English) 1970. q. free. Conselho Nacional de Desenvolvimento Cientifico e Tecnologico, Av. W-3 Norte Q-509-D, Brasilia, Brazil. FAX 061-274-1950. Ed. Giulio Massarani. illus.; charts; bibl.; circ. 3,000. **Indexed:** Anal.Abstr., Chem.Abstr., Dairy Sci.Abstr., Nutr.Abstr., World Agri.Econ.& Rural Sociol.Abstr.
    —BLDSC shelfmark: 7845.780000.

REVISTA DE EGRESADOS. see *COLLEGE AND ALUMNI*

600   GT
REVISTA I C A I T I. 1985. q. free. Instituto Centroamericano de Investigacion y Tecnologia Industrial, Avenida la Reforma 4-47, Zona 10, Guatemala, C.A., Guatemala. Ed. Salvador Samayoa. bibl.; charts; illus.; circ. 4,500.

600 378   CK   ISSN 0120-1603
REVISTA UNIVERSIDAD TECNOLOGICA. 1977. s-a. free. Universidad Tecnologica de Pereira, La Julita, Apdo. Aereo 97, Pereira, Colombia. adv.; bk.rev.; circ. 2,000.

REVUE D'HISTOIRE DES SCIENCES ET DE LEURS APPLICATIONS. see *SCIENCES: COMPREHENSIVE WORKS*

REVUE DES INGENIEURS ET TECHNICIENS EUROPEENS. see *ENGINEERING*

600 620   SZ   ISSN 0374-4256
REVUE POLYTECHNIQUE. (Text in French) 1898. m. 70 SFr. (foreign 150 SFr.). Marcel Meichtry Editions, Chemin de la Caroline, 26, CH-1213 Petit-Lancy - Geneva, Switzerland. TEL 022-7921027. FAX 022-928834. TELEX 422098 HSPI CH. Ed. Marcel Meichtry. adv.; bk.rev.; bibl.; charts; illus.; tr.lit.; index. circ. 10,200. **Indexed:** Cyb.Abstr.
    —BLDSC shelfmark: 7942.560000.
    Description: Provides technical information of relevance to Swiss machine and information technology industries.

REVUE PRUMYSLU A OBCHODU. see *BUSINESS AND ECONOMICS — Production Of Goods And Services*

TECHNOLOGY: COMPREHENSIVE WORKS

620   LU   ISSN 0035-4260
CODEN: RTLXA4
REVUE TECHNIQUE LUXEMBOURGEOISE. (Text in English, French and German) 1908. q. 600 Fr. Association Luxembourgeoise des Ingenieurs et Industriels, 4 bd. Grande-Duchesse Charlotte, Luxembourg, Luxembourg. adv.; bk.rev.; bibl.; index; circ. 1,500. **Indexed:** Chem.Abstr., Eng.Ind., Met.Abstr., World Alum.Abstr.
—BLDSC shelfmark: 7955.000000.

RHEINISCH-WESTFAELISCHE AKADEMIE DER WISSENSCHAFTEN. VORTRAEGE NATUR-INGENIEUR-UND WIRTSCHAFTSWISSENSCHAFTEN. see *SCIENCES: COMPREHENSIVE WORKS*

RIVISTA DEL CONSULENTE TECNICO. see *LAW*

600   US   ISSN 0883-8046
T12.3.W47
ROCKY MOUNTAIN HIGH TECHNOLOGY DIRECTORY. 1985. a. $129 (typically set in Jan.). Leading Edge Communications, Inc., 2620 S. Parker Rd., Ste. 185, Aurora, CO 80014. Ed. Charles J. Koelsch. circ. 1,500.

679.9   GW   ISSN 0035-7863
ROHSTOFF RUNDSCHAU; Fachblatt des gesamten Handels mit Alt- und Abfallstoffen. 1938. s-m. DM.102. Werk-Verlag Dr. Edmund Banaschewski GmbH, Hans-Cornelius-Str. 4, 8032 Munich-Graefelfing, Germany. TEL 089-855021. FAX 089-853799. TELEX 522451. Ed. Edmund Banaschewski. adv.; illus.; stat.; index.

ROYAL SOCIETY NEWS. see *SCIENCES: COMPREHENSIVE WORKS*

S E R C BULLETIN. (Science and Engineering Research Council) see *SCIENCES: COMPREHENSIVE WORKS*

300 600   US
S H O T NEWSLETTER. 1969. q. $5 membership. Society for the History of Technology, c/o Bruce Seely, Ed., Dept. of Social Sciences, Michigan Technological Univ., Houghton, MI 49931-1295. TEL 906-487-2459. FAX 906-487-2468. circ. 1,750. (back issues avail.)
Description: Circulates news among members of the Society.

S I A M JOURNAL ON CONTROL AND OPTIMIZATION. (Society for Industrial and Applied Mathematics) see *MATHEMATICS*

S I A M JOURNAL ON NUMERICAL ANALYSIS. see *MATHEMATICS*

S I A M JOURNAL ON OPTIMIZATION. see *MATHEMATICS*

S I A M NEWS. (Society for Industrial and Applied Mathematics) see *MATHEMATICS*

S I A M REVIEW. (Society for Industrial and Applied Mathematics) see *MATHEMATICS*

S I D INTERNATIONAL SYMPOSIUM. DIGEST OF TECHNICAL PAPERS. (Society for Information Display) see *ENGINEERING*

600 629.3   US   ISSN 0747-623X
S O L ETTER. 1966. m. (11/yr.). $15 membership. Society of Logistics Engineers, 8100 Professional Pl., No. 211, New Carollton, MD 20785-2225. TEL 800-695-7653. FAX 301-459-1522. Ed. Marya B. Anderson. adv.; tr.lit.; circ. 8,500. (back issues avail.)
Description: Updates of topics and events for the society as well as the field of logistics.

600 500   JA
S T A: ITS ROLES AND ACTIVITIES. (Science and Technology Agency) (Text in English) a. free. Kagaku Gijutsu-cho, 1-2 Kasumigaseki 2-chome, Chiyoda-ku, Tokyo 100, Japan. FAX 81-3-3593-1370.

600   FR   ISSN 1010-5247
S T I REVIEW. (Science Technology Industry) French edition: S T I Revue (ISSN 1010-5239) 1986. s-a. 180 F.($40) Organization for Economic Cooperation and Development, 2 rue Andre-Pascal, 75775 Paris Cedex 16, France. (U.S. orders to: O.E.C.D. Publications and Information Center, 2001 L St., N.W., Ste. 700, Washington, DC 20036-4910. TEL 202-785-6323) (also avail. in microfiche from OEC)
Indexed: Environ.Abstr., Tel.Abstr.
—BLDSC shelfmark: 8464.758000.
Description: Contains reports and articles on science, technology and industry policy issues which are of current interest to the member countries of the organization.

600 500   JA   ISSN 0289-7016
S U T BULLETIN. (Text and summaries in Japanese) 1984. m. (Science University of Tokyo - Tokyo Rika Daigaku) Tokyo Rika Daigaku Shuppankai - Science University of Tokyo Press, 1-3 Kagurazaka, Shinjuku-ku, Tokyo 162, Japan.
Description: Contains reviews and commentary.

SAIENSU. see *SCIENCES: COMPREHENSIVE WORKS*

SAMUEL NEAMAN INSTITUTE FOR ADVANCED STUDIES IN SCIENCE AND TECHNOLOGY. ANNUAL REPORT. see *SCIENCES: COMPREHENSIVE WORKS*

SANG TAO/CREATIVITY. see *BUSINESS AND ECONOMICS*

658.5   JA   ISSN 0036-4371
SANGYO GIJUTSU JOHO YOKKAICHI/INDUSTRIAL AND TECHNOLOGICAL INFORMATION OF YOKKAICHI CITY. (Text in Japanese) 1961. m. free. Yokkaichi-shiritsu Toshokan - Yokkaichi City Library, 2-42 Kubota 1-chome, Yokkaichi-shi, Mie-ken 510, Japan. bk.rev.; charts; illus.; pat.; circ. controlled. (processed)

600   JA
SANGYO GIJUTSU NO REKISHITEKI TENKAI CHOSA KENKYU. (Text in Japanese) 1982. a. Nihon Kagaku Gijutsu Shinko Zaidan - Japan Science Foundation, 2-1 Kitanomaru Koen, Chiyoda-ku, Tokyo 102, Japan.
Description: Contains results of surveys on the development of industrial science.

SANTA CLARA COMPUTER AND HIGH-TECHNOLOGY LAW JOURNAL. see *LAW*

SASKATCHEWAN RESEARCH COUNCIL. ANNUAL REPORT. see *SCIENCES: COMPREHENSIVE WORKS*

SAUDI-ARABIAN SASO STANDARDS MICROFILE. see *ENGINEERING*

SCHOOL SCENE. see *EDUCATION*

SCIENCE AND ENGINEERING RESEARCH COUNCIL. REPORT. see *SCIENCES: COMPREHENSIVE WORKS*

SCIENCE AND PUBLIC POLICY. see *SCIENCES: COMPREHENSIVE WORKS*

SCIENCE AND TECHNOLOGY. see *SCIENCES: COMPREHENSIVE WORKS*

SCIENCE AND TECHNOLOGY (SAN DIEGO, 1987); opposing viewpoints sources. see *BIOLOGY*

SCIENCE AND TECHNOLOGY IN CHINA. see *SCIENCES: COMPREHENSIVE WORKS*

SCIENCE AND TECHNOLOGY IN JAPAN. see *SCIENCES: COMPREHENSIVE WORKS*

SCIENCE AND TECHNOLOGY IN JAPAN. see *SCIENCES: COMPREHENSIVE WORKS*

SCIENCE AND TECHNOLOGY IN LATIN AMERICA. see *SCIENCES: COMPREHENSIVE WORKS*

SCIENCE AND TECHNOLOGY IN THE MIDDLE EAST. see *SCIENCES: COMPREHENSIVE WORKS*

SCIENCE STUDIES; a Scandinavian journal. see *SCIENCES: COMPREHENSIVE WORKS*

SCIENTIFIC AND TECHNICAL INFORMATION IN FOREIGN COUNTRIES/KAIGAKI KAGAKU GIJUTSU JOHO SHIRYO. see *SCIENCES: COMPREHENSIVE WORKS*

SCIENTIFIC AND TECHNICAL SOCIETIES OF CANADA/SOCIETES SCIENTIFIQUES ET TECHNIQUES DU CANADA. see *SCIENCES: COMPREHENSIVE WORKS*

SCIENTIFIC OPINION. see *SCIENCES: COMPREHENSIVE WORKS*

600   AT   ISSN 0725-900X
SCITECH. 1981. m. Aus.$210 (foreign Aus.$240). Scitech Publication Pty. Ltd., G.P.O. Box 1915, Canberra, A.C.T. 2601, Australia. TEL 062-477-220. FAX 62 496648. Ed. Jane Ford. circ. 1,300. (back issues avail.)

621.9   UK   ISSN 0266-7428
SCOTTISH INDUSTRIAL HISTORY. 1969. a. £10. Business Archives Council of Scotland, c/o L.M. Richmond, The Archives, University of Glasgow, Glasgow G12 8QQ, Scotland. FAX 041-330-4808. TELEX 777070-UNIGLA. (Co-sponsor: Scottish Industrial Heritage Society) Ed.Bd. adv.; bk.rev.; illus.; circ. 400. (processed)
Formerly: S S I A and S S P H M Newsletter.

600 607   US   ISSN 0080-830X
SCRIPPS CLINIC AND RESEARCH FOUNDATION. ANNUAL REPORT. 1924. a. free. Scripps Clinic and Research Foundation, 10666 N. Torrey Pines Rd., La Jolla, CA 92037. TEL 619-455-9100. FAX 619-554-8841. circ. 5,000.

600   JA   ISSN 0037-105X
CODEN: SEKEAI
SEISAN KENKYU/PRODUCTION RESEARCH. (Text in English and Japanese) 1949. m. free. University of Tokyo, Institute Production Technology - Tokyo Daigaku Seisan Gijutsu Kenkyujo, 7-22-1 Roppongi, Minato-ku, Tokyo, Japan. TEL 03-3402-6231. TELEX 0242-3216 IISTYO J. charts; illus.; circ. 1,980. **Indexed:** Abstr.J.Earthq.Eng., Appl.Mech.Rev., Chem.Abstr., Robomat, Sci.Abstr.
—BLDSC shelfmark: 8219.800000.

SELSKOSTOPANSKA TEKHNIKA. see *AGRICULTURE — Agricultural Equipment*

SEMINAR REPORTEUR; journal of science and technology. see *SCIENCES: COMPREHENSIVE WORKS*

600   II
SENDOC BULLETIN. PART 1: INDUSTRY AND TECHNOLOGY. (Text in English) 1973. m. Rs.50($20) National Institute of Small Industry Extension Training, Yousufguda, Hyderabad 500045, India. TELEX 425-6381-SIET-IN. Ed. S. Pandurangam.

SENSOR BUSINESS DIGEST. see *BUSINESS AND ECONOMICS — Marketing And Purchasing*

600   RU   ISSN 0321-2653
T4   CODEN: ISSND8
SEVERO-KAVKAZSKII NAUCHNYI TSENTR VYSSHEI SHKOLY. TEKHNICHESKIE NAUKI. IZVIESTIYA/NORTH-CAUCASUS SCIENTIFIC CENTER OF HIGH SCHOOL. TECHNICAL SCIENCE. NEWS. 4/yr. 7.20 Rub. Rostovski Universitet, Ul. Pyshkinskaia 160, 344 700 Rostov-na-Donu, Russia. TEL 8-8630536411. TELEX 123520.
—BLDSC shelfmark: 0082.323000.

600 500   CC   ISSN 0253-9942
SHANGHAI JIAOTONG DAXUE XUEBAO/SHANGHAI JIAOTONG UNIVERSITY. BULLETIN. (Text in Chinese; summaries in Chinese and English) 1984. bi-m. Y1.5. Shanghai Jiaotong Daxue - Shanghai Jiaotong University, Library, 1954 Huashan Lu, Shanghai 200030, People's Republic of China. TEL 4310310. circ. 3,000. **Indexed:** Chem.Abstr, Math.R., Sci.Abstr.
Description: Covers education, research and alumni affairs in the university.

SHIJIE FAMING/WORLD INVENTIONS. see *SCIENCES: COMPREHENSIVE WORKS*

SHIJIE KEXUE JISHU/WORLD SCIENCE AND TECHNOLOGY. see *SCIENCES: COMPREHENSIVE WORKS*

600   JA
SHIZEN/NATURE. (Text in Japanese) 1946. m. 8450 Yen. Chuokoron-Sha, Inc., 8-7, Kyobashi 2-chome, Chuo-ku, Tokyo 104, Japan. Ed. Akihiko Okabe. **Indexed:** Chem.Abstr.

600 GW ISSN 0934-9391
SIEG TECH. 1985. 20/yr. DM.570. Sieg Tech Verlag, Gottfried-Claren-Str. 21, 5300 Bonn 3, Germany. TEL 0228-466034. FAX 0228-477418. circ. 15,000. (back issues avail.)

SMITHSONIAN. see *SOCIAL SCIENCES: COMPREHENSIVE WORKS*

SOCIEDAD LATINOAMERICANA DE HISTORIA DE LAS CIENCIAS Y LA TECNOLOGIA. BOLETIN INFORMATIVO. see *SCIENCES: COMPREHENSIVE WORKS*

338 FR ISSN 0037-9441
T2
SOCIETE INDUSTRIELLE DE MULHOUSE. BULLETIN. 1828. q. 285 F. Societe Industrielle de Mulhouse, 10 rue de la Bourse, B.P. 1329, 68056 Mulhouse cedex, France. FAX 89-45-46-47. Ed. Gerard Schmidt. adv.; bk.rev.; illus.; cum.index: 1946-1970; circ. 3,000.

600 US ISSN 0160-1067
T37
SOCIETY FOR INDUSTRIAL ARCHEOLOGY NEWSLETTER. 1972. q. $30 to individuals & institutions; students $20 (includes Industrial Archeology). Society for Industrial Archeology, NMAH 5014-MRC 629, Smithsonian Institution, Washington, DC 20560. Ed. Robert M. Frame, III. bk.rev.; bibl.; circ. 1,600. **Indexed:** Avery Ind.Archit.Per.
Description: Examines current activity in the preservation of post-18th century technologies and industries.

667.2 UK ISSN 0037-9859
TP890 CODEN: JSDCAA
SOCIETY OF DYERS AND COLOURISTS. JOURNAL. 1884. 10/yr. £120 to non-members (includes Review of Progress in Coloration and Related Topics). Society of Dyers and Colourists, Box 244, Perkin House, Grattan Rd., Bradford, Yorkshire BD1 2JB, England. TEL 0274-7215138. FAX 0274-392888. Ed. Paul Dinsdale. adv.; bk.rev.; abstr.; bibl.; charts; illus.; stat.; index; circ. 3,800. (also avail. in microform from UMI) **Indexed:** A.S.& T.Ind., Anal.Abstr., Art & Archaeol.Tech.Abstr., Br.Tech.Ind., Chem.Abstr., Chem.Eng.Abstr., Curr.Cont., Curr.Leather Lit., Excerp.Med., Text.Tech.Dig., W.R.C.Inf., World Surf.Coat., World Text.Abstr.
—BLDSC shelfmark: 7794.160000.
Description: Research and practical papers on coloration.

600 629.13 US ISSN 0885-3916
SOCIETY OF LOGISTICS ENGINEERS. ANNALS. 1986. a. $15 to non-members. Society of Logistics Engineers, 8100 Professional Pl., No. 211, New Carollton, MD 20785-2225. TEL 800-695-7653. FAX 301-459-1522. TELEX 469527. Ed. Benjamin Ostrofsky. circ. 2,500.
—BLDSC shelfmark: 1031.710000.
Description: Forum for the research and exchange of scholarly opinions in the disciplines identified with logistics.

600 US ISSN 0893-3499
SOCIETY OF LOGISTICS ENGINEERS. PROCEEDINGS. Variant title: International Logistics Symposium Proceedings. 1966. a. price varies. Society of Logistics Engineers, 8100 Professional Pl., No. 211, New Carollton, MD 20785-2225. TEL 800-695-7653. FAX 301-459-1522. (reprint service avail. from UMI)

SOFT TECHNOLOGY; alternative technology in Australia. see *CONSERVATION*

SOGO GAKUJUTSU KENKYU SHUKAI. see *SCIENCES: COMPREHENSIVE WORKS*

600 500 JA ISSN 0289-5560
SOGO KENKYUJO HOKOKU. (Text in Japanese) 1984. a. Tokyo Rika Daigaku, Sogo Kenkyujo - Science University of Tokyo, Research Institute for Science and Technology, 2641 Yamazaki, Noda-shi, Chiba-ken 278, Japan.
Description: Provides news of the institute.

600 747 FR ISSN 0339-1507
SOL ET MURS MAGAZINE. 1976. q. 70 F. S.E.P Edition, 194-196 rue Marcadet, 75018 Paris, France. Ed. Catherine Bouillon.

613.1 US
SOLAR MIND. bi-m. $25 to individuals; students and non-profit organizations $12. Joe Stephenson, Ed. & Pub., 759 S. State St., No. 81, Ukiah, CA 95482.
Description: Explores alternative approaches to technology and its relationship to the environment.

604.24 SA ISSN 0036-0643
SOUTH AFRICAN DRAUGHTSMAN/S A TEKENAAR. Variant title: S A Draughtsman. (Text in Afrikaans, English) vol.5, 1970. 3/yr. membership. South African Institute of Draughtsmen - Suid Afrikaanse Instituut van Tekenaars, P.O. Box 30, Bergvliet 7864, South Africa. TEL 021-72-3938. FAX 021-72-3938. Ed. W.H. Young. adv.; bk.rev.; charts; illus.; stat.; circ. 3,000 (controlled).
Description: News of interest to draughtsmen at the institute.

SOUTH AFRICAN JOURNAL OF AGRICULTURAL EXTENSION/SUID-AFRIKAANSE TYDSKRIF VIR LANDBOUVOORLIGTING. see *AGRICULTURE*

SOUTH AFRICAN JOURNAL OF ANTARCTIC RESEARCH. see *SCIENCES: COMPREHENSIVE WORKS*

600 NL ISSN 0081-2862
DU1 CODEN: SPCTAW
SOUTH PACIFIC COMMISSION. TECHNICAL PAPER. (Text in English or French) 1949. irreg., no.199, 1990. South Pacific Commission, B.P. D5, Noumea, Cedex, New Caledonia. **Indexed:** Rev.Plant Path.

600 US ISSN 0892-9270
TL787 CODEN: SPTEE8
SPACE TECHNOLOGY; industrial and commercial applications. 1981. 4/yr. £185 (effective 1992). Pergamon Press, Inc., Journals Division, 660 White Plains Rd., Tarrytown, NY 10591-5153. TEL 914-524-9200. FAX 914-333-2444. (And: Headington Hill Hall, Oxford OX3 0BW, England. TEL 0865-794141) Ed. R. Monti. adv.; pat.; circ. 2,000. (also avail. in microform from MIM,UMI) **Indexed:** Cadscan, Curr.Cont., Deep Sea Res.& Oceanogr.Abstr., Energy Ind., Energy Info.Abstr., Environ.Per.Bibl., Geo.Abstr., Int.Aerosp.Abstr., Intl.Civil Eng.Abstr., Lead Abstr., Risk Abstr., Robomat., Sci.Abstr., Soft.Abstr.Eng., Zincscan.
—BLDSC shelfmark: 8361.656000.
Former titles: Earth-Oriented Applications of Space Technology (ISSN 0277-4488); (until 1982): Advances in Earth-Oriented Applications of Space Technology (ISSN 0191-538X)
Refereed Serial

600 500 BL
SPECTRUM; jornal Brasileiro ciencias. bi-m. Cr.$3600($45) Editora Spectrum Ltda., Av. Santa Ines, 836 - sala 2, 02415 Sao Paulo SP, Brazil. Eds. Eduardo Subacius, Sandra Maria Rodrigues Subacius. circ. 10,000.

600 NE ISSN 0168-468X
SPEUR- EN ONTWIKKELINGSWERK IN NEDERLAND/RESEARCH AND DEVELOPMENT ACTIVITIES IN THE NETHERLANDS. (Text in Dutch and English) 1959. a. Centraal Bureau voor de Statistiek, Prinses Beatrixlaan 428, Voorburg, Netherlands. (Dist. by: SDU - Publishers, Christoffel Plantijnstraat, The Hague, Netherlands)

600 US ISSN 0148-2203
T1
SPINOFF. a. U.S. National Aeronautics and Space Administration, Office of Space and Terrestrial Applications, Box 8756, Baltimore-Washington International Airport, MD 21240. TEL 202-755-2320. (Orders to: Supt. of Documents, Washington, DC 20402) illus. **Indexed:** Ind.How To Do It.

745.2 US ISSN 0049-1888
SPOKESMAN. 1964. 5/yr. $6 to libraries and non-members. New York State Industrial Arts Association, c/o James D. Maxim, Ed., 9 Bristol St., Cuba, NY 14727. TEL 716-968-3734. adv.; bk.rev.; charts; illus.; circ. 3,500.
Incorporates: Spokesman Journal.

600 YU ISSN 0081-3974
SRPSKA AKADEMIJA NAUKA I UMETNOSTI. ODELJENJE TEHNICKIH NAUKA. GLAS. (Text in Serbo-Croatian; summaries in English, French, German or Russian) N.S. 1949. irreg. price varies. Srpska Akademija Nauka i Umetnosti, Knez Mihailova 35, 11001 Belgrade, Serbia, Yugoslavia. FAX 38-11-182-825. TELEX 72593 SANU YU. (Dist. by: Prosveta, Terazije 16, Belgrade, Serbia, Yugoslavia) circ. 500. **Indexed:** Art & Archaeol.Tech.Abstr., Chem.Abstr., Met.Abstr., Sci.Abstr., World Alum.Abstr.

600 YU ISSN 0081-4040
SRPSKA AKADEMIJA NAUKA I UMETNOSTI. ODELJENJE TEHNICKIH NAUKA. POSEBNA IZDANJA. (Text in Serbo-Croatian; summaries in English, French, German or Russian) 1950. irreg. price varies. Srpska Akademija Nauka i Umetnosti, Knez Mihailova 35, 11001 Belgrade, Serbia, Yugoslavia. FAX 38-11-182-825. TELEX 72593 SANU YU. (Dist. by: Prosveta, Terazije 16, Belgrade, Serbia, Yugoslavia) circ. 600. **Indexed:** Ref.Zh.

600 IT ISSN 1121-063X
STAMPI; progettazione e costruzione. bi-m. L.30000 (foreign L.120000)(effective 1992). Tecniche Nuove s.p.a., Via C. Menotti, 14, 20129 Milan, Italy. TEL 02-75701. FAX 02-7570205.

STEEL INDIA. see *METALLURGY*

621.86 UK ISSN 0039-1832
STORAGE HANDLING DISTRIBUTION; monthly journal of materials management. (Biennial supplement avail.) 1953. m. $73.80. Turret-Wheatland Ltd., 12 Greycaine Rd., Watford, Herts. WD2 4JP, England. adv.; illus.; tr.lit.; circ. 15,600. **Indexed:** BMT, Br.Tech.Ind., Int.Packag.Abstr., Packag.Sci.Tech., Sci.Abstr.
—BLDSC shelfmark: 8466.360000.

600 PL ISSN 0081-6604
STUDIA I MATERIALY Z DZIEJOW NAUKI POLSKIEJ. SERIA D. HISTORIA TECHNIKI I NAUK TECHNICZNYCH. (Text in Polish; summaries in English and French) 1958. irreg., no.9, 1978. price varies. (Polska Akademia Nauk, Zaklad Historii Nauki, Oswiaty i Techniki) Panstwowe Wydawnictwo Naukowe, Ul. Miodowa 10, 00-251 Warsaw, Poland. (Dist. by: Ars Polona, Krakowskie Przedmiescie 7, 00-068 Warsaw, Poland) Ed. E. Olszewski. circ. 240.

STUDIA I MATERIALY Z DZIEJOW NAUKI POLSKIEJ. SERIA E. ZAGADNIENIA OGOLNE. see *SCIENCES: COMPREHENSIVE WORKS*

600 CS ISSN 0862-3171
STUDIE Z DEJIN TECHNIKY. 1988. irreg. (1-2/yr.). exchange basis only. Ceskoslovenska Akademie Ved, Historicky Ustav, Vysehradska 49, 128 26 Prague 2, Czechoslovakia. Ed. Jan Janko.

600 IS
STUDIES IN TECHNOLOGY. (Text in Hebrew) q. Ort Israel Pedagogical Center, Derech Hatayasim 28, Tel Aviv 67299, Israel. TEL 03-395057. FAX 03-5160282. Ed. Rafi Nachmias.

620 RM ISSN 0039-4017
TA350 CODEN: SCMAA2
STUDII SI CERCETARI DE MECANICA APLICATA. 1950. 6/yr. 330 lei($69) (Academia Romana) Editura Academiei Romane, Calea Victoriei 125, 79717 Bucharest, Rumania. (Dist. by: Rompresfilatelia, Calea Grivitei 64-66, P.O. Box 12-201, 78104 Bucharest, Rumania) Ed. Ioan Anton. bk.rev.; charts; illus.; index; circ. 1,000. **Indexed:** Appl.Mech.Rev.., Chem.Abstr., Math.R., Met.Abstr.

600 500 JA
SUMMARY OF WHITE PAPER ON SCIENCE AND TECHNOLOGY. (Text in English) a. (Kagaku Gijutsu-cho - Science and Technology Agency) Foreign Press Center - Forin Puresu Senta, 2-1 Uchisaiwai-cho 2-chome, Chiyoda-ku, Tokyo 100, Japan. abstr.

SUPERCONDUCTIVITY: PHYSICS, CHEMISTRY, TECHNOLOGY. see *PHYSICS*

600 FR
SYSTEMES EXPERTS. m. 1650 F. A Jour, 11 rue du Marche St. Honore, 75001 Paris, France. TEL 42-96-67-22.

4610 TECHNOLOGY: COMPREHENSIVE WORKS

600 330 SA ISSN 0040-0955
T.I. (Technical Information for Industry) (Text in Afrikaans, English) 1963. irreg. free. Council for Scientific and Industrial Research, Division of Information Services, P.O. Box 395, Pretoria 0001, South Africa. TEL 2712-841-2013. Ed. A.G. Brount. charts; illus.; index; circ. 5,000. **Indexed:** Ind.S.A.Per.

600 US ISSN 1041-6587
▼**T I E S**. (Technology, Innovation and Entrepreneurship for Students) 1988. bi-m. $15. Drexel University, 3219 Arch St., Philadelphia, PA 19104. TEL 215-590-8623. FAX 215-895-4917. (Co-sponsors: American Honda Foundation, Sun Company, Inc., Bell Atlantic, DuPont Imaging) Ed. Patricia Hutchinson. adv.; bk.rev.; circ. 54,000.
Description: Explores inventive minds and new technology.

T I S T R RESEARCH NEWS. (Thailand Institute of Scientific and Technological Research) see *SCIENCES: COMPREHENSIVE WORKS*

600 DK
T L - TEKNIKEREN. 22/yr. Teknisk Landsforbund, Noerre Voldgade 12, 1358 Copenhagen K, Denmark. Ed. Hans Daugaard. adv.; circ. 21,193.

T N C - AKTUELLT. (Tekniska Nomenklaturcentralen) see *LINGUISTICS*

600 US
T SQUARED NEWSLETTER. m. $65. Technology Transfer Society, 611 N. Capitol Ave., Indianapolis, IN 46204. TEL 317-262-5022. Ed. K. Hayes. (tabloid format; back issues avail.)
Description: Methods, meetings, models, theories and results describing the management, diffusion and transfer of technology.

600 IS ISSN 0334-9527
TAGLIT. (Text in Hebrew) 1987. 8/m. free. P.O. Box 17255, Tel Aviv 61171, Israel. TEL 03-806122. FAX 03-7520698. Ed. David Butbul. circ. 10,000.

600 UK ISSN 0267-5307
TECHNICAL REVIEW. MIDDLE EAST. 1984. bi-m. £42($72) Alain Charles Publishing Ltd., 27 Wilfred St., London SW1E 6PR, England. TEL 071-834-7676. FAX 071-973-0076. TELEX 297165. Ed. Jonquil Phelan. (back issues avail.)

600 GW
TECHNICAL TRENDS. (Editions in Czech and Russian) 1987. q. Verlags- und Vertiebsgesellschaft mbH, Postfach 101555, 4040 Neuss 1, Germany. TEL 2101-5903-0. FAX 02101-547733. TELEX 8517506-PLAD-D. Ed. Jan de Vries. circ. 21,000.

600 CS
TECHNICKE NOVINY/TECHNICAL NEWS. (Text in Slovak) 1953. w. 104 Kcs. Praca, Publishing House of the Slovak Trade Unions Council, Stefanikova 19, 812 71 Bratislava, Czechoslovakia. TEL 7-333779. FAX 7-330046. Ed. Eduard Drobny. circ. 80,000.
Description: For new science, technology and innovation.

600 331.88 CS ISSN 0040-1064
TECHNICKY TYDENIK; casopis pro novou techniku a otazky zlepsovatelskeho a vynalezcovskeho hnuti. vol.21, 1973. w. 52 Kcs.($33) Ustredni Rada Odboru, Nam. Antonina Zapoteckeho 2, 113 59 Prague 3, Czechoslovakia. (Dist. by: Artia, Ve Smeckach 30, 111 27 Prague 1, Czechoslovakia) Ed. Jaroslav Kaspar. charts; illus.; circ. 40,000.

620 GW
TECHNIK HEUTE; Monatshefte fuer technische Berufe. 1940. m. DM.62.50. Verlag Dr. Ing. Paul Christiani, Hermann-Hesse-Weg 2, 7750 Konstanz, Germany. adv.; bk.rev.; charts; illus.; index; circ. 23,000.
Formerly: Ausbau (ISSN 0004-8097)

600 301 GW
TECHNIK UND GESELLSCHAFT. 1982. a. price varies. Campus Verlag, Heerstr. 149, 6000 Frankfurt a.M. 90, Germany. TEL 069-7682041. FAX 069-7682046. Ed. Gotthard Bechmann. circ. 1,500.

TECHNIKA CHRONIKA/ANNALES TECHNIQUES. see *SCIENCES: COMPREHENSIVE WORKS*

600 IS
TECHNION - ISRAEL INSTITUTE OF TECHNOLOGY. PRESIDENT'S REPORT. (Text in English) 1975. a. free to qualified personnel. Technion - Israel Institute of Technology, Division of Public Affairs, Haifa 3200, Israel. Ed. Harvey L. Brown. circ. 30,000 (controlled). **Indexed:** Sci.Abstr.
Formerly: Israel Institute of Technology. President's Report and Reports of Other Officers (ISSN 0072-9329)

620 IS ISSN 0792-3244
T173 CODEN: TCNNAN
TECHNION MAGAZINE. (Text in English; summaries in French, German and Spanish) 1965. s-a. free. Technion - Israel Institute of Technology, Public Affairs Division, Technion City, Haifa 32000, Israel. FAX 04-221581. Ed. Susan Rose. adv.; bk.rev.; illus.; circ. 35,000. **Indexed:** Avery Ind.Archit.Per.
Supersedes: Technion (ISSN 0040-1188)

600 FR ISSN 0040-1250
T2 CODEN: TEMDA2
TECHNIQUE MODERNE. 1908. bi-m. 945 F. S I R P E, 76 rue de Rivoli, 75004 Paris, France. TEL 33-1-42-78-52-20. FAX 33-1-42-74-40-48. Ed. R. Drouhin. adv.; bk.rev.; abstr.; bibl.; charts; illus.; mkt.; index; circ. 3,400. (also avail. in microfilm from UMI) **Indexed:** Chem.Abstr., Excerp.Med., Sci.Abstr., World Alum.Abstr.
—BLDSC shelfmark: 8741.000000.

600 FR ISSN 0082-2469
TECHNIQUES D'AUJOURD'HUI. 1970. irreg. price varies. Larousse, 17 rue du Montparnasse, 75280 Paris Cedex 06, France.

605 JA
TECHNIQUES INDUSTRIELLES DU JAPON. (Text in French) 1959. a. 2000 Yen. Societe-Franco-Japonaise des Techniques Industrielles - Nichifutsu Kogyo Gijutsukai, 2-3 Kanda Surugadai, Chiyoda-ku, Tokyo 101, Japan.

600 GW ISSN 0494-9390
CODEN: TMKWA3
TECHNISCHE MITTEILUNGEN KRUPP. (Editions in English and German) 1986. irreg. (2-4/yr.). free. Fried. Krupp GmbH, Postfach 10 19 52, 4300 Essen 1, Germany. charts; illus.; index; circ. 4,000. **Indexed:** Chem.Abstr., Eng.Ind., Met.Abstr., World Alum.Abstr.
Supersedes (1920-1985): Technische Mitteilungen Krupp. Forschungsberichte; Technische Mitteilungen Krupp. Werksberichte (ISSN 0040-1463)

600 NE
TECHNISCHE REVUE. 1972. fortn. free to qualified personnel. Uitgeversmaatschappij C. Misset B.V., Hanzestr. 1, 7006 RH Doetinchem, Netherlands. TEL 08340-49911. FAX 08340-43839. TELEX 45481. (Subscr. to: Postbus 4, 7000 BA Doetinchem) Ed. J. van Bruggen. adv.: B&W page fl.13167; trim 280 x 380; adv. contact: Cor van Nek. illus.; circ. 15,230 (controlled).
Description: For management in commercial enterprises.

600 GW
TECHNISCHE REVUE. 1981. m. free. Elsevier Thomas Fachverlag, Max-Hufschmidt-Str. 1, Postfach 1869, 6500 Mainz 1, Germany. TEL 06131-80110. FAX 06131-831193. Ed. Rainer Sauer. adv.; bk.rev.; circ. 50,500. (tabloid format)

600 SZ ISSN 0040-148X
TECHNISCHE RUNDSCHAU; Europaeische Industrie- und Handelszeitung. (Supplements avail.) 1908. w. 111 SFr. (foreign 201 SFr.). Hallwag AG, Nordring 4, CH-3001 Berne, Switzerland. TEL 031-423131. FAX 031-414133. TELEX 912 661 CH. Ed. Hannes Gysling. adv.; bk.rev.; bibl.; charts; illus.; tr.lit.; index; circ. 20,000. **Indexed:** C.I.S. Abstr., Chem.Abstr., Cyb.Abstr., Sci.Abstr.
—BLDSC shelfmark: 8753.300000.

620 GW ISSN 0043-6925
TA1001.D7 CODEN: WZTUAU
TECHNISCHE UNIVERSITAET DRESDEN. WISSENSCHAFTLICHE ZEITSCHRIFT. (Text in German; summaries in English, German, Russian) 1952. bi-m. DM.312($64) Technische Universitaet Dresden, Mommsenstr. 13, 8027 Dresden, Germany. TEL 463-2773. adv.; bk.rev.; bibl.; charts; illus.; index; circ. 1,400. (back issues avail.) **Indexed:** Bibl.Cart., Chem.Abstr, Dok.Str., Excerp.Med., Forest.Abstr., Forest Prod.Abstr., Geotech.Abstr., Math.R., VITIS.
—BLDSC shelfmark: 9339.110000.

600 380 GW ISSN 0077-2089
Q9
TECHNISCHE UNIVERSITAET MUENCHEN. JAHRBUCH. 1952. a. DM.50. Technische Universitaet Muenchen, Arcisstr. 21, 8000 Munich 2, Germany. TEL 089-2105-8601. FAX 089-21058622. circ. 1,100.
—BLDSC shelfmark: 4628.200000.

600 GW ISSN 0863-0925
TA4 CODEN: WZTMEA
TECHNISCHE UNIVERSITAET OTTO VON GUERICKE. WISSENSCHAFTLICHE ZEITSCHRIFT. 1957. 8/yr. DM.160. Technische Universitaet Otto von Guericke, Postfach 4120, 3010 Magdeburg, Germany. TEL 5922277. bk.rev.; bibl.; charts; illus. **Indexed:** Chem.Abstr., Math.R., Met.Abstr., World Alum.Abstr.
—BLDSC shelfmark: 9339.500000.
Description: Devoted to scientific studies conducted at the university, including mathematics and physics and mechanical engineering.

658.5 GW ISSN 0040-1552
TECHNISCHER HANDEL; Zentralblatt fuer den technischen Bedarf. 1913. m. DM.93.20. (Verband der Technischen Haendler) Curt R. Vincentz Verlag, Schiffgraben 41-43, Postfach 6247, 3000 Hannover, Germany. TEL 0511-990980. Ed. L. Vincentz. adv.; bk.rev.; abstr.; circ. 1,767. (tabloid format)

600 500 BE ISSN 0771-6826
TECHNOLOGIA; historical and social studies in science, technology and industry. 1978. q. 450 BEF to non-members. Association des Ingenieurs Industriels et Ingenieurs Techniciens de Bruxelles (AIIBr), 26 av. de l'Amarante, 1020 Brussels, Belgium. Ed. Jean C. Baudet. bk.rev.; circ. 1,000.
—BLDSC shelfmark: 8755.476000.
Incorporates (in 1983): Comite Belge d'Histoire des Sciences. Notes Bibliographiques - Belgisch Komitee voor de Geschiedis der Wetenschappen. Bibliograpische Notas (ISSN 0010-2415); **Formerly (until 1981):** Technologia Bruxellensis (ISSN 0771-7415)

600 301.24 US ISSN 0040-1625
T174 CODEN: TFSCB3
TECHNOLOGICAL FORECASTING AND SOCIAL CHANGE. 1969. 8/yr. (in 2 vols., 4 nos./vol.) $272 to institutions (foreign $306) (effective 1992). Elsevier Science Publishing Co., Inc. (New York), 655 Ave. of the Americas, New York, NY 10010. TEL 212-989-5800. FAX 212-633-3965. TELEX 420643 AEP UI. Ed. Harold A. Linstone. adv.; bk.rev. (also avail. in microform from RPI; reprint service avail. from SWZ) **Indexed:** ASCA, B.P.I., BPIA, Br.Tech.Ind., Bus.Ind., Cont.Pg.Manage., Curr.Cont., Econ.Abstr., Educ.Admin.Abstr., Educ.Tech.Abstr., Eng.Ind., Excerp.Med., Fut.Surv., Geo.Abstr., HRIS, I D A, INSPEC, Int.Abstr.Oper.Res., Int.Polit.Sci.Abstr., J.Cont.Quant.Meth., J.of Econ.Abstr., Key to Econ.Sci., Lang.& Lang.Behav.Abstr., Manage.Abstr., Mid.East: Abstr.& Ind., Risk Abstr., Sage Pub.Admin.Abstr., Sage Urb.Stud.Abstr., Sci.Abstr., SCIMP, Sociol.Abstr., SSCI, Tr.& Indus.Ind.
—BLDSC shelfmark: 8757.351000.
Formerly: Technological Forecasting.
Description: Deals directly with the methodology and practice of technological forecasting and future studies as planning tools as they interrelate social, environmental and technological factors.
Refereed Serial

TECHNOLOGIE-NACHRICHTEN - MANAGEMENT-INFORMATIONEN. see *BUSINESS AND ECONOMICS — Management*

TECHNOLOGY: COMPREHENSIVE WORKS 4611

600   GW   ISSN 0344-9750
TECHNOLOGIE-NACHRICHTEN - PROGRAMM-INFORMATIONEN. 1970. s-m. DM.360. T N V GmbH, An den Eichen, 5202 Hennef 1, Germany. TEL 02248-1881. FAX 02248-1796. Ed. Nicola Gasterstaedt. circ. 500.

600   GW   ISSN 0932-2558
TECHNOLOGIE UND MANAGEMENT. 1951. q. DM.60($25) D I E Verlag H. Schaefer GmbH, Postfach 2243, 6380 Bad Homburg, Germany. FAX 6172-71288. Ed. Mueller-Merbach. adv.; index; circ. 4,000. (back issues avail.)
   Formerly (until 1987): Technologie Manager.

600   IS   ISSN 0333-9521
T4
TECHNOLOGIES; Israel's magazine of high technology. 1983. m. $100 (effective 1992). Shukit Publishing Ltd., P.O. Box 39244, Tel Aviv 61392, Israel. TEL 052-581054. FAX 052-573628. Ed. Haim Amit. adv.; circ. 15,000.
   Description: Information on high-tech applicable to the Israeli market, both local and imported. Covers electronics, industry oriented computers, control and automation as well as tests.

745.2   FR
TECHNOLOGIES. (Supplement to: Usine Nouvelle) m. Groupe Usine Nouvelle, 59 rue du Rocher, 75008 Paris, France. circ. 68,000.

600   CN
TECHNOLOGIES DE L'INFORMATION ET SOCIETE. Abbreviated title: T.I.S. (Text in French) 1988. 3/yr. Universite du Quebec a Montreal, Service des Publications, C.P.8888, Succ. A, Montreal, Que. H3C 3P8, Canada. TEL 514-282-4511. **Indexed:** Pt.de Rep. (1988-).

600   FR
TECHNOLOGIES ET FORMATIONS. 1945. 6/yr. 364 F. (foreign 514 F.). P Y C Edition, 5 ave du Verdun, B.P. 105, 94208 Ivry-sur-Seine Cedex, France. TEL 1-49-94-01-04. FAX 1-46-72-41-85. TELEX 263 424. (Subscr. to: B.S.I. 49 rue de la Vanne, 92126 Montrouge Cedex, France) Ed. L. Donnadieu. adv.; bk.rev.; circ. 2,833.
   Formerly: Ingenieur et le Technicien de l'Enseignement Technique (ISSN 0046-9521)
   Description: Intended for vocational schools and training managers.

600   US
TECHNOLOGIST. 1987. m. $15 (effective Jan. 1992). (Technology Club of Syracuse) Cuthill Research Services, Inc., Box 430, Fayetteville, NY 13066. TEL 315-682-7455. Ed. Steve Karon. circ. 9,600.
   Description: For members of technical professional societies in 32 specialized fields.

500   US   ISSN 1054-4267
TECHNOLOGY ALERT. 6/yr. $89 (Canada $99; elsewhere $119). Merton Allen Associates, InfoTeam Inc., Box 15640, Plantation, FL 33318-5640. TEL 305-473-9560. FAX 305-473-0544. Ed. Merton Allen.
   Formerly: Technology Alert and Technology Alert Database Reports; Formed by the 1990 merger of: Technology Alert; Technology Alert Database Reports.
   Description: Presents on-line descriptions of available technical papers and reports abstracted from publishers' subscription newsletters. Contains summary and listings of available database searches on a variety of specific technological, management, marketing, and finance subjects.

600   UK   ISSN 0953-7325
HD45
TECHNOLOGY ANALYSIS & STRATEGIC MANAGEMENT. 1989. q. $96 to individuals; institutions $240. Carfax Publishing Co., P.O. Box 25, Abingdon, Oxfordshire OX14 3UE, England. TEL 0235-555335. FAX 0235-553559. (Subscr. addr. in U.S.: Carfax Publishing Co., Box 2025, Dunnellon, FL 32630) Ed. Harry Rothman. adv.; bk.rev. (also avail. in microfiche)
   —BLDSC shelfmark: 8758.543000.
   Description: International research linking the analysis of science and technology with the strategic needs of policy makers and management.

300 600   US   ISSN 0040-165X
T1
TECHNOLOGY AND CULTURE; devoted to the study of the development of technology and its relations with society and culture. 1960. q. $29 to individuals; institutions $60; students $20; emeritus $24. (Society for the History of Technology) University of Chicago Press, Journals Division, c/o Alex Roland, Secretary, Department of History, Duke University, Durham, NC 27706. TEL 312-753-3347. FAX 312-702-0694. TELEX 25-4603. (Subscr. to: University of Chicago Press, Journals Division, Box 37005, Chicago, IL 60637) Ed. Robert C. Post. adv.; bk.rev.; bibl.; charts; illus.; index, cum.index: vols.1-10, 1959-69; circ. 2,600. (also avail. in microform from KTO,MIM,UMI; reprint service avail. from ISI,KTO,UMI) **Indexed:** Acad.Ind., Amer.Bibl.Slavic & E.Eur.Stud., Amer.Hist.& Life, Art & Archaeol.Tech.Abstr., Arts & Hum.Cit.Ind., ASCA, ASSIA, Bk.Rev.Ind. (1989-), Br.Archaeol.Abstr., Child.Bk.Rev.Ind. (1989-), Curr.Cont., Excerp.Med., Hist.Abstr., Lang.& Lang.Behav.Abstr., Mid.East: Abstr.& Ind., Rural Recreat.Tour.Abstr., Soc.Sci.Ind., SSCI, World Agri.Econ.& Rural Sociol.Abstr.
   —BLDSC shelfmark: 8758.600000.
   Refereed Serial

600   US
TECHNOLOGY FORECASTS & TECHNOLOGY SURVEYS. 1969. m. $144. Technology Forecasts, 205 S. Beverly Dr., Ste. 208, Beverly Hills, CA 90212. TEL 213-273-3486. Ed. Irwin Stambler. bk.rev. (back issues avail.) **Indexed:** PROMT.
   Description: Discusses important trends or advances in science and technology likely to have major future impact.

620   IE   ISSN 0040-1676
T1   CODEN: TEIRDR
TECHNOLOGY IRELAND. 1969. 10/yr. £19. Eolas - the Irish Science and Technology Agency, Glasnevin, Dublin 9, Ireland. TEL 01-370101. FAX 01-379620. Eds. Tom Kennedy, Mary Mulvihill. adv.; bk.rev.; abstr.; index; circ. 6,000. **Indexed:** Bull.Signal., Excerp.Med., Food Sci.& Tech.Abstr., Fuel & Energy Abstr., Int.Packag.Abstr., Intl.Civil Eng.Abstr., Ocean.Abstr., Paper & Bd.Abstr., Pollut.Abstr., Soft.Abstr.Eng., W.R.C.Inf.

600   US   ISSN 1058-2282
TECHNOLOGY N Y REPORT. 1983. m. $87. Box 535, Troy, NY 12180. TEL 518-276-8769. Ed. Olga K. Anderson. adv.; bk.rev.; circ. 2,500.
   Formerly: Technology N Y Newsletter (ISSN 0732-7382)

TECHNOLOGY RESOURCE GUIDE. see BUSINESS AND ECONOMICS — Trade And Industrial Directories

TECHNOLOGY REVIEW. see SCIENCES: COMPREHENSIVE WORKS

745.2   US   ISSN 0746-3537
T61
TECHNOLOGY TEACHER. 1939. 8/yr. $55 to non-members and libraries (foreign $60). International Technology Education Association, 1914 Association Dr., Reston, VA 22091. TEL 703-860-2100. FAX 703-860-0353. Ed. Judy Miller. adv.; bk.rev.; abstr.; bibl.; charts; illus.; index; circ. 8,000. (also avail. in microform from UMI; back issues avail.) **Indexed:** C.I.J.E., Curr.Cont., Educ.Ind.
   Former titles (until 1983): Man - Society - Technology (ISSN 0022-1813); Journal of Industrial Arts Education.

620   CN   ISSN 0712-9467
   CODEN: TETOE6
TECHNOLOGY TODAY. 1958. q. free. ORTECH International, Department of Marketing, Mississauga, Ont. L5K 1B3, Canada. TEL 416-822-4111. Ed. T.E. Kingry. circ. 10,000. (looseleaf format) **Indexed:** World Text.Abstr.
   Formerly: Ontario Research Foundation. Newsletter (ISSN 0048-1831)

TECHNOLOGY TRANSFER SOCIETY. INTERNATIONAL SYMPOSIUM PROCEEDINGS. see BUSINESS AND ECONOMICS — Management

600   US   ISSN 0732-5533
T1
TECHNOLOGY UPDATE (CLEVELAND). w. $225 (foreign $250)(effective 1992). Predicasts, A Ziff Communications Company, 11001 Cedar Ave., Cleveland, OH 44106. TEL 800-321-6388. FAX 216-229-9944. (Or: Predicasts Europe, 8-10 Denman St., London W1V 7RF, England. TEL 071-494-3817)
   Formerly: Technology Survey.
   Description: Provides abstracts of current information in 32 high technology fields, including computers, lasers, genetic engineering, robotics, fiber optics, medicine.

600   HK
TECHNOVA; a technical journal for P.R. China. (Text in Chinese (simplified characters)) 1978. 2/yr. HK.$70($12) Adsale Publishing Company, 21st Fl., Tung Wai Commercial Bldg., 109-111 Gloucester Rd., Wanchai, Hong Kong. TEL 892-0511. FAX 838-4119. TELEX 63109-ADSAP-HX. Ed. Josephine Cheng. adv.; circ. 40,000. (back issues avail.)
   Description: News of various industries which the People's Republic of China finds necessary to import.

600   UK   ISSN 0166-4972
HD45
TECHNOVATION; an international journal of technical innovation and entrepreneurship. 1981. 8/yr. £179 (effective 1992). Elsevier Science Publishers Ltd., Crown House, Linton Rd., Barking, Essex IG11 8JU, England. TEL 081-594-7272. FAX 081-594-5942. TELEX 896950 APPSCI G. (Subscr. in U.S. and Canada to: Elsevier Science Publishing Co., Inc., Box 882, Madison Sq. Sta., New York, NY 10159. TEL 212-989-5800) Eds. G. Hayward, G. Rosegger. **Indexed:** ABI Inform, ASCA, Biostat., Comput.Cont., Cont.Pg.Manage., Curr.Cont., Eng.Ind., Manage.Cont., Risk Abstr.
   —BLDSC shelfmark: 8761.150000.
   Description: Covers all facets of the technical innovation process: from the development of a new product or process through commercial utilization.
   Refereed Serial

TECHUMIM. see RELIGIONS AND THEOLOGY — Judaic

620   AG   ISSN 0040-1781
TECNICA E INDUSTRIA. 1922. m. Arg.$35($120) c/o Dante R. Marchesotti, 694 Rodriguez Pena, 5o, 1020 Buenos Aires, Argentina. TEL 46-3193. Ed. E.R. Fedele. adv.; bk.rev.; charts; illus.; mkt.; pat.; tr.lit.; tr.mk.; circ. 5,000. **Indexed:** Chem.Abstr.

600   SP   ISSN 0213-7488
TECNO 2000; revista per a la innovacio tecnologica a l'empresa. (Supplement avail.: Kernixon Reporter) (Text in Catalan; summaries in English, French, Spanish) m. 4000 ptas. Fundacio Catalana per a la Recerca, Diagonal, 449, 7e, 08036 Barcelona, Spain. TEL 93-321-31-54. FAX 93-322-26-11. Ed. David Segarra. adv.; illus.
   —BLDSC shelfmark: 8762.728000.
   Description: Provides information on technological innovations in and for industry.

600   CR   ISSN 0379-3982
T4
TECNOLOGIA EN MARCHA. 1978. q. $20. Instituto Tecnologico de Costa Rica, Apdo. 159, Cartago, Costa Rica. FAX 51-5348. TELEX 8013-ITCR-CR. Ed. Mario Castillo Mendez. adv.; bk.rev.; bibl.; charts; circ. 1,500.

600   EC   ISSN 0257-1749
T4
TECNOLOGICA. 1976. q. $30. Escuela Superior Politecnica del Litoral, P.O. Box 5863, Guayaquil, Ecuador. Ed. Homero Ortiz. circ. 500. (microform)

TEHNICKE NOVINE. see CHILDREN AND YOUTH — About

620   RU   ISSN 0040-2257
TEKHNIKA MOLODEZHI. (Former name of issuing body: Vsesoyuznyi Leninskii Kommunisticheskii Soyuz Molodezhi, Tsentral'nyi Komitet) 1933. m. 18 Rub.($36.50) Izdatel'stvo Molodaya Gvardiya, Novodmitrovskaya ul. 5A, 125015 Moscow, Russia. TEL 095-285-8883. (Dist. by: Mezhdunarodnaya Kniga, ul. Dimitrova D.39, 113095 Moscow, Russia) Ed. S.V. Chumakov. adv.; bk.rev.; illus.; index; circ. 1,819,000. **Indexed:** Chem.Abstr.

TECHNOLOGY: COMPREHENSIVE WORKS

600   FI   ISSN 0355-4287
TEKNIIKAN MAAILMA. 21/yr. FIM 760. Yhtyneet Kuvalehdet Oy, Maistraatinportti 1, 00240 Helsinki, Finland. TEL 358-0-15661. FAX 358-0-1566505. TELEX 121364. Ed. Mauri Salo. adv.; circ. 124,105.
    Description: Covers automobiles, home electronics, videos and cameras for the prospective buyer.

620   FI   ISSN 0785-997X
TEKNIIKKA & TALOUS/INGENJOERSNYTT. (Text in Finnish and Swedish) 1961. w. FIM 713. Oy Talentum Ab, Ratavarjuvankatu 2, 00520 Helsinki, Finland. TEL 90-148-801. FAX 358-0-141-382. TELEX 123629 TALEN SF. Ed. Heikki Vuonamo. adv.; bk.rev.; circ. 97,045. (looseleaf format) **Indexed:** C.I.S. Abstr.
    Formerly: Insinooriuutiset (ISSN 0020-2010); Incorporates: Tekniikka (ISSN 0040-2303)

600   DK   ISSN 0108-3562
TEKNIK-SAMFUND; nyhedsbrev. 1982. 4/yr. DKK 125. (Statens Samfundsvidenskabelige Forskningsraad) Technology Assessment Unit, Technical University of Denmark, Building 208, DK-2800 Lyngby, Denmark. FAX 45-42-88-20-14. bk.rev.

600   MY
TEKNOLOGI. (Text in English and Malay) 1977. 2/yr. $10. University of Technology Malaysia, Academic Publishing Unit - Universiti Teknologi Malaysia, Gurney Rd., 54100 Kuala Lumpur, Malaysia. FAX 07-572555. TELEX UTM-MA-60205. Ed. Mohd Zali B. Shaari. circ. 500.

600   DK   ISSN 0107-3761
TEKNOLOGI OG EFFEKTIVITET; orientering og aarsberetning. 1981. a. free. Teknologistyrelsen, Tagensvej 135, 2200 Copenhagen N, Denmark.

TELECOMMUNICATIONS DIRECTORY; an international descriptive guide to approximately 2,300 telecommunications organizations, systems, and services. see *COMMUNICATIONS*

TENSOR. see *MATHEMATICS*

TEORIE VEDY/THEORY OF SCIENCE. see *SCIENCES: COMPREHENSIVE WORKS*

620   GW
THYSSEN EDELSTAHLWERKE. MITTEILUNGSBLATT. 1952. 8/yr. Thyssen Edelstahlwerke AG, Oberschlesienstr. 16, Postfach 730, 4150 Krefeld 1, Germany. TEL 02151-832073. FAX 02151-832022.

620   JA   ISSN 0040-9006
                CODEN: RIISAX
TOKYO DAIGAKU SEISAN GIJUTSU KENKYUJO HOKOKU/UNIVERSITY OF TOKYO. INSTITUTE OF INDUSTRIAL SCIENCE. REPORT. (Text mainly in Japanese, occasionally English, French or German) 1950. irreg. (6-8/yr.). free. University of Tokyo, Institute of Industrial Science - Tokyo Daigaku Seisan Gijutsu Kenkyujo, 22-1 Roppongi 7-chome, Minato-ku, Tokyo 106, Japan. Ed. Prof. Egami. charts; circ. 900. **Indexed:** Chem.Abstr., Eng.Ind., JCT, JTA, Met.Abstr., Sci.Abstr.
    —BLDSC shelfmark: 7520.350000.

605   JA   ISSN 0495-8055
TOKYO INSTITUTE OF TECHNOLOGY. RESEARCH LABORATORY OF RESOURCES UTILIZATION. REPORT/SHIGEN KAGAKU KENKYUJO. (Text in English) a. Tokyo Kogyo Daigaku, Shigen Kagaku Kenkyujo - Tokyo Institute of Technology, Research Laboratory of Resources Utilization, 2-1, Ookayama 2-chome, Meguro-ku, Tokyo 152, Japan. **Indexed:** Sci.Abstr.

600   JA   ISSN 0082-4747
TA7   CODEN: MTTMAO
TOKYO METROPOLITAN UNIVERSITY. FACULTY OF TECHNOLOGY. MEMOIRS/TOKYO-TORITSU DAIGAKU KOGAKUBU HOKOKU. (Text in English) 1951. a. free. Tokyo-toritsu Daigaku, Kogakubu - Tokyo Metropolitan University, Faculty of Technology, 1-1 Fukazawa 2-chome, Setagaya-ku, Tokyo 158, Japan. Ed. Yoichi Higashi. **Indexed:** Chem.Abstr., INIS Atomind., JCT, JTA, Met.Abstr., Sci.Abstr., World Alum.Abstr.
    —BLDSC shelfmark: 5603.000000.

TOKYO-TO SHIKEN KENKYU KIKAN NO KENKYU KEIKAKU. see *PUBLIC ADMINISTRATION — Municipal Government*

600   JA
TOKYO-TORITSU KOKA TANKI DAIGAKU KENKYU HOKOKU/METROPOLITAN COLLEGE OF TECHNOLOGY, TOKYO. MEMOIRS. (Text in English or Japanese) 1973. a. Tokyo-toritsu Koka Tanki Daigaku, Gakujutsu Kenkyu Un'eikai - Tokyo Metropolitan Technical College, 6-6 Asahigaoka Hino, Tokyo 191, Japan. Ed.Bd. circ. controlled.

TORONTO OFFICE GUIDE. see *SCIENCES: COMPREHENSIVE WORKS*

600   US   ISSN 0739-0971
TRANET; transnational network for appropriate/alternative technologies. 1976. bi-m. $30 to individuals; libraries $50; institutions $150. Tranet, Inc., Box 567 Pond St., Rangeley, ME 04970. TEL 207-864-2252. Ed. William N. Ellis. bk.rev.; circ. 1,500. (looseleaf format; back issues avail.)

600   GW   ISSN 0178-4099
TRANSFER; magazine for industrial processes, equipment and supplies. (Text in English) 1985. 8/yr. DM.120. Vogel-Verlag und Druck KG, Max-Plank-Str. 7-9, Postfach 67 40, 8700 Wuerzburg 1, Germany. TEL 0931-418-0. FAX 0931-416291. TELEX 680131. Ed. Arnold Metzner. adv.; circ. 20,000(controlled).

TRANSIZIONE. see *POLITICAL SCIENCE*

TREATISE ON MATERIALS SCIENCE & TECHNOLOGY. see *ENGINEERING — Engineering Mechanics And Materials*

605   PH   ISSN 0115-2157
TRENDS IN TECHNOLOGY. 1972. q. free. Economic Development Foundation, 6764 Ayala Ave., Box 370 MCC, Makati, Rizal, Philippines. illus.; circ. 500.

600   UK
TREVITHICK SOCIETY. OCCASIONAL PUBLICATION. 1974. irreg., no.3, 1984. £3. Trevithick Society, c/o Mr. E.W.A. Edmonds, Sec., Newlands, Tarrandean Ln., Perranwell Sta., Truro, Cornwall TR3 7NW, England. TEL 0872 863931. circ. 1,000.

600   JA
TRIGGER. (Text in Japanese) 1982. m. Nikkan Kogyo Shinbun, Ltd., 8-10, Kudan Kita, 1-chome, Chiyoda-ku, Tokyo 102, Japan. TEL 03-3263-2311. FAX 03-3262-4603. TELEX NIKKANKO-J29687. Ed. Mitsuo Lijima. circ. 100,000.
    Description: Offers general information on all industrial technology.

TUDOMANY. see *SCIENCES: COMPREHENSIVE WORKS*

TWO THIRDS. see *AGRICULTURE — Agricultural Economics*

600 614.7   US
U C A T NEWS AND VIEWS.* 4/yr. free. University of California, Davis, Appropriate Technology Program, 2043 Bainer Hall, Davis, CA 95616. TEL 916-752-1011. Ed. David Hills. illus.

U S S R REPORT: SCIENCE AND TECHNOLOGY POLICY. see *SCIENCES: COMPREHENSIVE WORKS*

U S SCI-TECH. see *BIOLOGY — Biological Chemistry*

600   HU
UJ TECHNIKA. 1967. q. $10. Szentharomsag ter 1, 1014 Budapest, Hungary. TEL 155-7122. TELEX 22-6490. circ. 35,000.

UNDERWATER TECHNOLOGY. see *EARTH SCIENCES — Oceanography*

600   UN
UNESCO. REGIONAL OFFICE FOR SCIENCE AND TECHNOLOGY FOR LATIN AMERICA AND THE CARIBBEAN. BOLETIN. (Text in Spanish) 1952. 2/yr. free. Unesco, Regional Office of Science and Technology for Latin America and the Caribbean, 1320 Bulevar Artigas, Casilla de Correo 859, Montevideo, Uruguay. bk.rev.; abstr.; bibl.; circ. 2,000.
    Formerly: Unesco. Field Science Office for Latin America. Boletin.

600   GW   ISSN 0171-2268
T3
UNI HANNOVER. 1974. s-a. exchange basis. Universitaet Hannover, Universitaetsbibliothek, Welfengarten 1 B, 3000 Hannover 1, Germany. FAX 0511-715936. Eds. K.H. Manegold, G. Schlitt. circ. 3,000.
    —BLDSC shelfmark: 9090.477000.
    Formerly (until 1978): T U Hannover.

UNI REPORT. see *SCIENCES: COMPREHENSIVE WORKS*

UNION LIST OF SCIENTIFIC AND TECHNICAL PERIODICALS IN ZAMBIA. see *BIBLIOGRAPHIES*

U.S. NATIONAL AERONAUTICS AND SPACE ADMINISTRATION. RESEARCH AND TECHNOLOGY OPERATING PLAN (RTOP) SUMMARY. see *AERONAUTICS AND SPACE FLIGHT*

338 600   US   ISSN 0083-2383
T176
U.S. NATIONAL SCIENCE FOUNDATION. RESEARCH AND DEVELOPMENT IN INDUSTRY. (Subseries of: U.S. National Science Foundation. Surveys of Science Resource Series) a. U.S. National Science Foundation, Science Resource Studies, Washington, DC 20550. TEL 202-634-4622.

600 378   CK
UNIVERSIDAD TECNOLOGICA DEL CHOCO. REVISTA. 1976. irreg. Universidad Tecnologica del Choco, Difusion Cultural, Carrera 2 no. 25-22, Quibdo, Choco, Colombia. Ed. Giorgio M. Manzini.

600   BL
UNIVERSIDADE FEDERAL DO CEARA. CENTRO DE TECNOLOGIA. BOLETIM TRIMESTRAL. q. Universidade Federal do Ceara, Centro de Tecnologia, Campus Universitario do Pici, Bl. 713, C.P. 2574, Fortaleza, Ceara, Brazil.

600   BE   ISSN 0075-9333
T2
UNIVERSITE DE LIEGE. FACULTE DES SCIENCES APPLIQUEES. COLLECTION DES PUBLICATIONS. (Text in French; summaries in English and German) 1966. bi-m. 1200 BEF. Universite de Liege, Faculte des Sciences Appliquees, 75 rue du Val-Benoit, 4000 Liege, Belgium.

600   AT   ISSN 1030-5947
UNIVERSITY OF TECHNOLOGY. SYDNEY CALENDAR. (In 2 vols.) 1965. a. Aus.$5 (foreign Aus.$10). University of Technology, Sydney - 02-330-1551, P.O. Box 123, City Campus, Broadway, N.S.W. 2007, Australia. TEL 02-330-1990. FAX 02-330-1551. circ. 3,000.
    Former titles (until 1989): New South Wales Institute of Technology Calendar (ISSN 0314-6057); (until 1970): New South Wales Institute of Technology Handbook.
    Description: Contains a wide range of information about courses, officers, and the staff of the university.

600 500   AT
UNIVERSITY OF TECHNOLOGY, SYDNEY. RESEARCH AND CONSULTANCY REPORT. 1974. a. free. University of Technology, Sydney, P.O. Box 123, City Campus, Broadway, N.S.W. 2007, Australia. TEL 02-330-1253. FAX 02-330-1244. Ed. P.P. Steenbergen. circ. 1,500.
    Formerly (until 1987): University of Technology, Sydney. Research Report (ISSN 0312-5378)
    Description: Compilation of graduate research projects.

600   CS
UROB - UDELEJ SI SAM. vol.9, 1974. q. 14 Kcs. per no. Alfa, Hurbanovo nam. 3, 815 89 Bratislava, Czechoslovakia. bibl.; charts; illus.
    Continues: Praktikus.

658.2   FR   ISSN 0042-126X
HC271
USINE NOUVELLE; technology and economics. 1896. w. (plus m. & a. supplements). 760 F. (foreign 1529 F.)(effective Jan. 1992). Groupe Usine Nouvelle, 59 rue du Rocher, 75008 Paris, France. TEL 43-87-37-88. FAX 43-87-42-65. TELEX 650-485 F. Ed. Jacques Monnier. adv.; charts; illus.; mkt.; pat.; stat.; tr.lit.; circ. 60,000. **Indexed:** C.I.S. Abstr., Chem.Abstr., Int.Lab.Doc., Key to Econ.Sci., Met.Abstr., PROMT, World Alum.Abstr.
    —BLDSC shelfmark: 9134.000000.

600　　　　　　　　　FI　　ISSN 1235-0613
V T T JULKAISUJA/V T T PUBLIKATIONER. (Text in Finnish, Swedish) 1981. irreg. Valtion Teknillinen Tutkimuskeskus, Information Service, P.O. Box 42, 02151 Espoo 15, Finland. FAX 358-0-4564374. (reprint service avail. from NTI) **Indexed:** Biol.Abstr., Chem.Abstr.
　Formerly (until 1992): Valtion Teknillinen Tutkimuskeskus. Tutkimuksia (ISSN 0358-5077)

600　　　　　　　　　FI　　ISSN 0357-9387
　　　　　　　　　　CODEN: VTTSE9
V T T SYMPOSIUM. (Text in official language of symposium) 1981. irreg. price varies. Valtion Teknillinen Tutkimuskeskus, Information Service - Technical Research Centre of Finland, P.O. Box 42, 02151 Espoo 15, Finland. FAX 358-0-4564374.

600　　　　　　　　　FI　　ISSN 1235-0605
V T T TIEDOTTEITA/V T T MEDDELANDEN/V T T RESEARCH NOTES. (Text in English, Finnish or Swedish) 1981. irreg. Valtion Teknillinen Tutkimuskeskus, Information Service, P.O. Box 42, 02151 Espoo 15, Finland. FAX 358-0-4564374. (reprint service avail. from NTI)
　Formerly (until 1992): Valtion Teknillinen Tutkimuskeskus. Tiedotteita (ISSN 0358-5085)

VADEMECUM DEUTSCHER LEHR- UND FORSCHUNGSSTAETTEN. STAETTEN DER FORSCHUNG. see *SCIENCES: COMPREHENSIVE WORKS*

VEDA, TECHNIKA A MY/SCIENCE, TECHNOLOGY AND WE. see *CHILDREN AND YOUTH — For*

VIGNANA BHARATHI. see *SCIENCES: COMPREHENSIVE WORKS*

600　　　　　　　　　US
VIRGINIA EXTENSION. q. Virginia Polytechnic Institute and State University, 202 Media Bldg, Blacksburg, VA 24061. TEL 703-961-7370.
　Description: Magazine concerning Virginia's extension activities.

VISHWAKARMA. see *ENGINEERING*

VISIONS (BEAVERTON). see *SCIENCES: COMPREHENSIVE WORKS*

658.5　　　　　　　GW　　ISSN 0340-4544
TJ3
W T - WERKSTATTSTECHNIK; Zeitschrift fuer industrielle Fertigung. 1907. 12/yr. DM.258($135) (Verein Deutscher Ingenieure, Fachgruppe Betriebstechnik) Springer-Verlag, Heidelberger Platz 3, 1000 Berlin 33, Germany. TEL 030-2807-1. (Also Heidelberg, Tokyo, Vienna, and New York) adv. (also avail. in microform from UMI; reprint service avail. from ISI) **Indexed:** Appl.Mech.Rev., C.I.S. Abstr., Curr.Cont., Met.Abstr., Risk Abstr., World Alum.Abstr.
　Formerly: Werkstattstechnik (ISSN 0043-2806)

600　　　　　　　　　US
WASHINGTON TECHNOLOGY. fortn. Tech News, Inc., 1953 Gallows Rd., Ste. 130, Vienna, VA 22182-3932. TEL 703-848-2800. FAX 703-848-2353. Ed. Esther T. Smith.

600 500　　　　　　GW　　ISSN 0172-1623
WECHSELWIRKUNG; Technik Naturwissenschaft Gesellschaft. 1979. bi-m. DM.48 (foreign DM.52). Remember e.G., Mariabrunnstr. 48, 5100 Aachen, Germany. TEL 0241-403249. FAX 0241-21424. Ed.Bd. adv.; bk.rev.; circ. 7,500. (back issues avail.)
　Description: New research and developments in science and technology and their social aspects. Includes list of events and exhibitions.

WEIZMANN INSTITUTE OF SCIENCE, REHOVOT, ISRAEL. SCIENTIFIC ACTIVITIES. see *SCIENCES: COMPREHENSIVE WORKS*

600　　　　　　　　　SZ
WERKMEISTER/CONTREMAITRE. (Text in French & German) 1894. fortn. 43 SFr. Schweizerischer Verband Technischer Betriebskader, Schaffhauserstr. 2-4, 8006 Zurich, Switzerland. Ed. Roger Erb. adv.; illus.; index. (tabloid format) **Indexed:** C.I.S. Abstr.
　Formerly: Werkmeister und Technische Arbeitsleiter - Contremaitre et Agent de Maitrise (ISSN 0043-2776)

WERKSTATT UND BETRIEB; Zeitschrift fuer Maschinenbau, Konstruktion und Fertigung. see *MACHINERY*

600　　　　　　　　　GW
WERKSTOFFE - IN DER FERTIGUNG. 1963. 6/yr. DM.84. Holz-Verlag GmbH und Co. K.G., VDK-Str. 25, Postfach 1320, 8901 Kissing, Germany. adv.; bk.rev.; illus.; pat.; tr.lit.; index.
　Former titles: Werkstoffe - Betriebsleitung Technik (ISSN 0176-6058); Werkstoffe und Technik; Werkstoffe (ISSN 0043-2814)

600 658　　　　　　US
WESTERN TECHNOLOGY & MANAGEMENT.* (Text in Chinese) 1980. m. free. (China Council for Promotion of International Trade) Western Technology & Management Inc., 235 E. 95th St. A, No. 176, New York, NY 10128-4019. Ed. Louis F. Sharpe. adv.; charts; illus.; stat.; circ. 50,000.

600　　　　　　　　　AT　　ISSN 1034-7658
WHAT'S NEW IN SCIENTIFIC & LABORATORY TECHNOLOGY. 1981. m. Aus.$30. Westwick-Farrow Pty. Ltd., Cnr. Fox Valley Rd. and Kiogle St., Wahroonga, N.S.W. 2076, Australia. Ed. Garry Hardie. circ. 8,200 (controlled). (back issues avail.)
　Description: Contains new product information for laboratory management.

WHO KNOWS: A GUIDE TO WASHINGTON EXPERTS. see *SCIENCES: COMPREHENSIVE WORKS*

WHO'S WHO IN INDIAN ENGINEERING AND INDUSTRY. see *BIOGRAPHY*

WHO'S WHO IN TECHNOLOGY. see *SCIENCES: COMPREHENSIVE WORKS*

WONDER: OBSERVING & CONFRONTING THE ENIGMAS THAT SURROUND US. see *SCIENCES: COMPREHENSIVE WORKS*

WORCESTER POLYTECHNIC INSTITUTE - STUDIES IN SCIENCE, TECHNOLOGY AND CULTURE. see *SCIENCES: COMPREHENSIVE WORKS*

600 608.7　　　　　US
WORLD TECHNOLOGY; patent licensing gazette. 1968. bi-m. $136 (foreign $148). Techni Research Associates, Inc., Willow Grove Plaza, York & Davisville Rds., Willow Grove, PA 19090. TEL 215-657-1753. Ed. Louis F. Schiffman. bk.rev.; pat. (looseleaf format; also avail. in microfilm from UMI; back issues avail.; reprint service avail. from UMI)
　Formerly (until 1975): Patent Licensing Gazette (ISSN 0031-2878)
　Description: Covers chemical, mechanical, electrical and general discovery.

891.7　　　　　　　PL　　ISSN 0860-276X
WYZSZA SZKOLA PEDAGOGICZNA IM. KOMISJI EDUKACJI NARODOWEJ W KRAKOWIE. ROCZNIK NAUKOWE-DYDAKTYCZNY. PRACE TECHNICZNE. 1973. irreg., no.5, 1992. price varies. Wydawnictwo Naukowe W S P, Ul. Karmelicka 41, 31-128 Krakow, Poland. TEL 33-78-20. (Co-sponsor: Ministerstwo Edukacji Narodowej)

339 600　　　　　　CC　　ISSN 1001-5396
XIANDAIHUA/MODERNIZATION. (Text in Chinese; table of contents in English) m. Y1($0.60) per no. (Zhongguo Kexue Jishu Xiehui - China Association for Science and Technology) Xiandaihua Zazhishe, 32, Baishiqiao Lu, Beijing 100081, People's Republic of China. TEL 896357. (Dist. outside China by: China International Book Trading Corp., P.O. Box 2820, Beijing, P.R.C.) Ed. Li Baoheng. adv.

605　　　　　　　　JA
YAMAGUCHI UNIVERSITY. FACULTY OF ENGINEERING. TECHNOLOGY REPORTS. (Text in English) 1972. a. exchange basis. Yamaguchi University, Kogakubu - Yamagachi University, Faculty of Engineering, Tokiwadai, Ube-shi 755, Japan. **Indexed:** Chem.Abstr., JCT, JTA, Sci.Abstr.

600 500　　　　　　JA　　ISSN 0388-8738
YOSHIDA KAGAKU GIJUTSU ZAIDAN NYUSU/YOSHIDA FOUNDATION FOR SCIENCE AND TECHNOLOGY. NEWS. (Text in Japanese) 1975. q. Yoshida Kagaku Gijutsu Zaidan - Yoshida Foundation for Science and Technology, Mezon Yonban-cho, 6, Yonban-cho, Chiyoda-ku, Tokyo 102, Japan.

Z W F - C I M. (Zeitschrift fuer Wirtschaftliche Fertigung und Automatisierung) see *MACHINERY*

ZAMBIA JOURNAL OF SCIENCE AND TECHNOLOGY. see *SCIENCES: COMPREHENSIVE WORKS*

ZENIT. see *SCIENCES: COMPREHENSIVE WORKS*

ZHONGGUO KE-JI SHILIAO/CHINA HISTORICAL MATERIALS OF SCIENCE AND TECHNOLOGY. see *SCIENCES: COMPREHENSIVE WORKS*

ZHONGGUO KEJI SHILIAO/HISTORICAL MATERIAL OF CHINESE SCIENCE AND TECHNOLOGY. see *SCIENCES: COMPREHENSIVE WORKS*

ZHONGGUO KEXUE JISHU DAXUE XUEBAO/CHINA UNIVERSITY OF SCIENCE AND TECHNOLOGY. JOURNAL. see *SCIENCES: COMPREHENSIVE WORKS*

ZHONGGUO ZIXINGCHE/CHINESE BICYCLES. see *SPORTS AND GAMES — Bicycles And Motorcycles*

ZHONGWAI JISHU QINGBAO/CHINESE AND FOREIGN TECHNOLOGY INFORMATION. see *SCIENCES: COMPREHENSIVE WORKS*

ZIRAN BIANZHENGFA TONGXUN/JOURNAL OF DIALECTICS OF NATURE. see *SCIENCES: COMPREHENSIVE WORKS*

TECHNOLOGY: COMPREHENSIVE WORKS — Abstracting, Bibliographies, Statistics

600　　　　　　　　　CN　　ISSN 0705-8454
A S T I S CURRENT AWARENESS BULLETIN. 1978. bi-m. Can.$80. Arctic Science & Technology Information System, Arctic Institute of North America, University of Calgary, 2500 University Dr. N.W., Calgary, Alta. T2N 1N4, Canada. TEL 403-284-7515. Ed. C. Ross Goodwin. circ. 130.
　●Also available online. Vendor(s): QL Systems Ltd.. Also available on CD-ROM.
　—BLDSC shelfmark: 1747.067500.
　Formerly: Arctic Institute of North America. Library. Accessions List.
　Description: Designed to get information about new arctic literature and research projects. Records are arranged by subject, with geographic and author indexes.

ABSTRACT NEWSLETTER: URBAN AND REGIONAL TECHNOLOGY AND DEVELOPMENT. see *HOUSING AND URBAN PLANNING — Abstracting, Bibliographies, Statistics*

ABSTRACTS IN BIOCOMMERCE. see *BUSINESS AND ECONOMICS — Abstracting, Bibliographies, Statistics*

ABSTRACTS OF ROMANIAN SCIENTIFIC AND TECHNICAL LITERATURE. see *SCIENCES: COMPREHENSIVE WORKS — Abstracting, Bibliographies, Statistics*

600 500　　　　　　JA　　ISSN 0914-4897
ABSTRACTS OF SCIENTIFIC AND TECHNOLOGICAL PUBLICATIONS. (Text in English) 1965. a. Ajinomoto K.K., Chuo Kenkyujo - Ajinomoto Co., Inc., Central Research Laboratories, 1-1 Suzuki-cho, Kawasaki-ku, Kawasaki-shi, Kanagawa-ken 210, Japan.

AGBIOTECH NEWS AND INFORMATION. see *BIOLOGY — Abstracting, Bibliographies, Statistics*

600　　　　　　　　　FR
ANNEE TECHNOLOGIQUE. (Supplement to: l'Usine Nouvelle) a. Groupe Usine Nouvelle, 59, rue du Rocher, 75008 Paris, France. TEL 43-87-37-88. TELEX 650 485 F. circ. 70,000.

600　　　　　　　　　FR
ANNUAIRE DES SERVEURS TEMPS PARTAGE. a. 110 F. A Jour, 11 rue du Marche St. Honore, 75001 Paris, France. TEL 42-96-67-22. FAX 40-20-07-75. TELEX 615887F AJOUR.

600　　　　　　　　　AT
APPROPRIATE TECHNOLOGY IN AUSTRALIA & NEW ZEALAND. 1986. irreg. (every 3-4/yrs.). Aus.$198. Noyce Publishing, G.P.O. Box 2222T, Melbourne, Vic. 3001, Australia. (back issues avail.)

600　　　　　　　　　AT
APPROPRIATE TECHNOLOGY IN INDIAN PERIODICALS. 1988. biennial. Noyce Publishing, G.P.O. Box 2222T, Melbourne, Vic. 3001, Australia. (back issues avail.)

T

TECHNOLOGY: COMPREHENSIVE WORKS — ABSTRACTING, BIBLIOGRAPHIES, STATISTICS

600 016   AT
APPROPRIATE TECHNOLOGY INDEX. Short title: A T Index. 1980. q. Aus.$245. Noyce Publishing, G.P.O. Box 2222T, Melbourne, Vic. 3001, Australia. (back issues avail.)
   Description: Bibliographical indexing service to literature on appropriate technology and related fields.

600 318   AG
ARGENTINA. INSTITUTO DE ASUNTOS TECNICOS. ESTADISTICAS. 1974. irreg. Instituto de Asuntos Tecnicos, Direccion de Estadistica, Palacio Municipal, Cordoba, Argentina. charts.

ASLIB BOOK GUIDE; a monthly list of recommended scientific and technical books. see BIBLIOGRAPHIES

BAHIA, BRAZIL (STATE). CENTRO DE PESQUISAS E DESENVOLVIMENTO. SUMARIOS DE PERIODICOS EM CIENCIA E TECNOLOGIA. see *SCIENCES: COMPREHENSIVE WORKS — Abstracting, Bibliographies, Statistics*

600 900   GW   ISSN 0323-4355
BIBLIOGRAPHIE GESCHICHTE DER TECHNIK. (Text in German) 1971. a. DM.90. Saechsische Landesbibliothek, Marienalle 12, 8060 Dresden, Germany. Eds. Michael Letocha, Peter Hesse. bk.rev.; circ. 200.

BIBLIOGRAPHIES ON THE HISTORY OF SCIENCE AND TECHNOLOGY. see *SCIENCES: COMPREHENSIVE WORKS — Abstracting, Bibliographies, Statistics*

BOLETIN DE TRADUCCIONES. see *SCIENCES: COMPREHENSIVE WORKS — Abstracting, Bibliographies, Statistics*

BRITISH REPORTS, TRANSLATIONS AND THESES. see *SCIENCES: COMPREHENSIVE WORKS — Abstracting, Bibliographies, Statistics*

BULLETIN ANALYTIQUE DE LA LITTERATURE SCIENTIFIQUE ET TECHNIQUE ROUMAINE. see *SCIENCES: COMPREHENSIVE WORKS — Abstracting, Bibliographies, Statistics*

CARINDEX: SCIENCE & TECHNOLOGY. see *SCIENCES: COMPREHENSIVE WORKS — Abstracting, Bibliographies, Statistics*

600 016   UK   ISSN 0261-0191
CATCHWORD AND TRADE NAME INDEX. Short title: C A T N I. (Supplement to: Current Technology Index (ISSN 0260-6593) 3/yr. (including a. cumulation). £128($241) in UK & EEC; rest of world £142. Bowker-Saur Ltd. (Subsidiary of: Reed International Books), 59-60 Grosvenor St., London W1X 9DA, England. TEL 071-493-5841. FAX 071-499-1590. (Subscr. to: Bailey Bros. and Swinfen Ltd., Warren House, Bowles Well Gardens, Folkestone, Kent CT19 6PH, England. TEL 0303-850501; N. American subscr. to: K.G. Saur, A Reed Reference Publishing Company, 121 Chanlon Rd., New Providence, NJ 07974. TEL 908-665-3576)

600   JA   ISSN 0577-9774
Q4
CHOSEN GAKUJUTSU TSUHO/KOREAN SCIENTIFIC INFORMATION. (Text in English and Japanese) 1964. s-a. Korean Association of Science and Technology in Japan - Zainihon Chosenjin Kagaku Gijutsu Kyokai, 33-14, Hakusan, 4-chome, Bunkyo-ku, Tokyo 112, Japan.

CIENCIA Y TECNICA; boletin bibliografico nacional y extranjero. see *SCIENCES: COMPREHENSIVE WORKS — Abstracting, Bibliographies, Statistics*

CURRENT BIBLIOGRAPHIES ON SCIENCE AND TECHNOLOGY: MECHANICAL ENGINEERING & CONSTRUCTION ENGINEERING. see *METALLURGY — Abstracting, Bibliographies, Statistics*

CURRENT LITERATURE ON SCIENCE OF SCIENCE. see *SCIENCES: COMPREHENSIVE WORKS — Abstracting, Bibliographies, Statistics*

CURRENT OPINION IN BIOTECHNOLOGY. see *BIOLOGY — Biotechnology*

600 011   CE
CURRENT TECHNICAL LITERATURE. (Text in English) 1966. q. exchange basis. Ceylon Institute of Scientific and Industrial Research, Information Service, 363 Bauddhaloka Mawatha, P.O. Box 787, Colombo 7, Sri Lanka. Ed. C.L.M. Nethsingha. circ. 200. (back issues avail.)

600 016   UK   ISSN 0260-6593
Z7913
CURRENT TECHNOLOGY INDEX. 1962. bi-m. plus a. cumulation. £423($808) in UK & EEC; elsewhere £469. Bowker-Saur Ltd. (Subsidiary of: Reed International Books), 59-60 Grosvenor St., London W1X 9DA, England. TEL 071-493-5841. FAX 071-499-1590. (Subscr. to: Bailey Bros. and Swinfen Ltd., Warner House, Bowles Well Gardens, Folkestone, Kent CT19 6PH, England. TEL 0303-850501; N. American subscr. to K.G. Saur, A Reed Reference Publishing Company, 121 Chanlon Rd., New Providence, NJ 07974. TEL 908-665-3576) Ed. T.J. Edwards. (also avail. in magnetic tape) Indexed: BMT, Fluidex.
● Also available online. Vendor(s): DIALOG (File no.142).
Also available on CD-ROM. Producer(s): R.R. Bowker. —BLDSC shelfmark: 3504.340000.
   Formerly: British Technology Index (ISSN 0007-1889)
   Description: Indexes British periodicals in all branches of engineering, chemical technology, instrumentation, building, transport, and computerization.

DIRECTORY OF PUBLISHED PROCEEDINGS. SERIES S E M T - SCIENCE, ENGINEERING, MEDICINE AND TECHNOLOGY. see *MEETINGS AND CONGRESSES — Abstracting, Bibliographies, Statistics*

DISSERTATION ABSTRACTS INTERNATIONAL. SECTION B: PHYSICAL SCIENCES AND ENGINEERING. see *SCIENCES: COMPREHENSIVE WORKS — Abstracting, Bibliographies, Statistics*

DOCUMENTATION - TECHNIQUE, SCIENTIFIQUE ET COMMERCIALE; revue d'information de l'edition francaise et etrangere. see *SCIENCES: COMPREHENSIVE WORKS — Abstracting, Bibliographies, Statistics*

FLUID SEALING ABSTRACTS. see *ENGINEERING — Abstracting, Bibliographies, Statistics*

600 016   GW   ISSN 0343-5520
Z7403
FORSCHUNGSBERICHTE AUS TECHNIK UND NATURWISSENSCHAFTEN/REPORTS IN THE FIELDS OF SCIENCE AND TECHNOLOGY. 1973. q. $410. (Technische Informationsbibliothek, Hannover) V C H Verlagsgesellschaft mbH, Postfach 101161, 6940 Weinheim, Germany. TEL 06201-602-0. FAX 06201-602328. TELEX 465516-VCHWH-D. (U.S. addr.: V C H Publishers, Inc., 220 E. 23rd St, New York, NY 10010-4606) (Co-sponsor: Fachinformationszentrum Energie Physik Mathematik) adv.; bk.rev.; index; circ. 550. (also avail. in microfilm; reprint service avail. from ISI) —BLDSC shelfmark: 7644.600000.
   Former titles (until 1979): Deutsche Forschungsberichte (ISSN 0340-0751); Deutsche Forschungsberichte. Neueingange.

600 500 016   US   ISSN 0094-4505
GUIDE TO AMERICAN SCIENTIFIC AND TECHNICAL DIRECTORIES. 1972. biennial. $75. Todd Publications, 18 N. Greenbush Rd., W. Nyack, NY 10994. TEL 914-358-6213. Ed. Barry T. Klein.

HUNGARIAN R AND D ABSTRACTS. SCIENCE AND TECHNOLOGY. see *SCIENCES: COMPREHENSIVE WORKS — Abstracting, Bibliographies, Statistics*

I N S D O C. RUSSIAN SCIENTIFIC AND TECHNICAL PUBLICATIONS. ACCESSIONS LIST. (Indian National Scientific Documentation Centre) see *SCIENCES: COMPREHENSIVE WORKS — Abstracting, Bibliographies, Statistics*

INDEX DOCUMENTATION - ECONOMIE - SCIENCE - TECHNIQUE. see *BUSINESS AND ECONOMICS — Abstracting, Bibliographies, Statistics*

INDEX TO SCIENTIFIC & TECHNICAL PROCEEDINGS. see *SCIENCES: COMPREHENSIVE WORKS — Abstracting, Bibliographies, Statistics*

INDIA. DEPARTMENT OF SCIENCE AND TECHNOLOGY. RESEARCH AND DEVELOPMENT STATISTICS. see *SCIENCES: COMPREHENSIVE WORKS — Abstracting, Bibliographies, Statistics*

600 016   II
INDIAN INSTITUTE OF TECHNOLOGY, MADRAS. PH.D. DISSERTATION ABSTRACTS. (Text in English) a. Indian Institute of Technology at Madras, Central Library, Madras 600 036, India.

500 600 016   II
INDIAN SCIENCE INDEX. SER.B CALCUTTA: PRE-MODERN PERIOD. a. Rs.80 (foreign Rs.350). Centre for Asian Dokumentation, K-15, Cit Bldg., Christopher Road, Calcutta 700 014, India. Ed. S. Chaudhuri.
   Description: Covers Indian scientific and technological journals.

INDICE ESPANOL DE CIENCIA Y TECNOLOGIA/INDEX TO SPANISH SCIENCE AND TECHNOLOGY. see *SCIENCES: COMPREHENSIVE WORKS — Abstracting, Bibliographies, Statistics*

600 016   TZ   ISSN 0251-2459
INDUSTRIAL ABSTRACTS FOR TANZANIA. 1981. s-a. $28. Library Services Board, National Documentation Centre, P.O. Box 9283, Dar es Salaam, Tanzania. Ed. D.A. Sekimang'a.

IPARI FORMATERVEZESI SZAKIRODALMI TAJEKOZTATO/INDUSTRIAL DESIGN ABSTRACTS. see *ENGINEERING — Abstracting, Bibliographies, Statistics*

JAPANESE PERIODICALS INDEX. SCIENCE AND TECHNOLOGY/ZASSHI KIJI SAKUIN. KAGAKU GIJUTSU HEN. see *SCIENCES: COMPREHENSIVE WORKS — Abstracting, Bibliographies, Statistics*

500 600 016   JA   ISSN 0022-765X
KAGAKU GIJUTSU BUNKEN TOYAMA/TOYAMA SCIENCE AND TECHNICAL DOCUMENTS. (Text in Japanese) 1959. bi-m. 200 Yen. Kagaku Gijutsu Bunken Riyo Shikokai - Promotive Association for Science and Technical Documents Utililization, c/o Toyama Prefectural Library, 206-3 Chayamachi, Toyama 930-01, Japan. bk.rev.; abstr.; bibl.; circ. 500 (controlled). (looseleaf format)

600 500   JA
KAGAKU GIJUTSU FORAMU HOKOKUSHO. (Text in English and Japanese) a. Kagaku Gijutsu-cho, Kagaku Gijutsu Seisaku-kyoku - Science and Technology Agency, Science and Technology Policy Bureau, 2-1 Kasumigaseki 2-chome, Chiyoda-ku, Tokyo 100, Japan. abstr.
   Description: Annual report of the forum on science and technology.

KOREAN SCIENTIFIC ABSTRACTS. see *SCIENCES: COMPREHENSIVE WORKS — Abstracting, Bibliographies, Statistics*

600 500   JA
KUNI NO SHIKEN KENKYU GYOMU KEIKAKU. (Text in Japanese) 1979. a. Kagaku Gijutsu-cho, Kagaku Gijutsu Seisaku-kyoku - Science and Technology Agency, Science and Technology Policy Bureau, 2-1 Kasumigaseki 2-chome, Chiyoda-ku, Tokyo 100, Japan. abstr.
   Description: Contains information on national research projects.

016 600   PK
LISTS OF P A S T I C BIBLIOGRAPHIES. (Text in English) 1957. a. (latest 1978). Rs.10($4) Pakistan Scientific and Technological Information Centre, Quaid-i-Azam University, Box 217, Islamabad, Pakistan. Ed. Mumtaz Begum. circ. 500. (also avail. in microfilm)
   Formerly: Lists of P A N S Doc Bibliographies (ISSN 0078-835X)

LUSO; journal of science and technology. see *SCIENCES: COMPREHENSIVE WORKS — Abstracting, Bibliographies, Statistics*

MEXICO. CENTRO DE INFORMACION TECNICA Y DOCUMENTACION. INDICE DE REVISTAS. SECCION DE CIENCIA Y TECNOLOGIA. see *SCIENCES: COMPREHENSIVE WORKS — Abstracting, Bibliographies, Statistics*

600 016 US
N T I S ALERTS: FOREIGN TECHNOLOGY. w. $165 (foreign $225). U.S. National Technical Information Service, 5285 Port Royal Rd., Springfield, VA 22161. TEL 703-487-4630. FAX 703-321-8547. TELEX 64617. index. (back issues avail.)
Formerly: Abstract Newsletter: Foreign Technology.

600 016 US
N T I S ALERTS: GOVERNMENT INVENTIONS FOR LICENSING. w. $250 (foreign $365). U.S. National Technical Information Service, 5285 Port Royal Rd., Springfield, VA 22161. TEL 703-487-4630. FAX 703-321-8547. TELEX 64617. Ed. Linda J. LaGarde. index. (back issues avail.)
Former titles: Abstract Newsletter: Government Inventions for Licensing; Weekly Abstract Newsletter: Government Inventions for Licensing; Weekly Government Abstracts. Government Inventions for Licensing (ISSN 0364-6491)

600 016 US
N T I S ALERTS: MANUFACTURING TECHNOLOGY. w. $165 (foreign $225). U.S. National Technical Information Service, 5285 Port Royal Rd., Springfield, VA 22161. TEL 703-487-4630. FAX 703-321-8547. TELEX 64617. index. (back issues avail.)
Formerly: Abstract Newsletter: Manufacturing Technology.

600 US
N T I S TITLE INDEX. q. $400 in US Canada, Mexico; elsewhere $800. U.S. National Technical Information Service, 5825 Port Royal Rd., Springfield, VA 22161. TEL 703-487-4630. index, cum.index. (microfiche; back issues avail.)

600 016 CS
NARODNI TECHNICKE MUZEUM. BIBLIOGRAFIE. PRAMENY. (Text in Czech and German) 1970. irreg. exchange basis. Narodni Technicke Muzeum, Kostelni 42, 170 78 Prague 7, Czechoslovakia.

500 600 016 JA ISSN 0454-1944
NATIONAL DIET LIBRARY. MONTHLY LIST OF FOREIGN SCIENTIFIC AND TECHNICAL PUBLICATIONS/KAIGAI KAGAKU GIJUTSU SHIRYO GEPPO. (Text in English and Japanese) 1956. m. 53148 Yen. National Diet Library - Kokuritsu Kokkai Toshokan, 1-10-1 Nagata-cho, Chiyoda-ku, Tokyo 100, Japan. TEL 03-3581-2331. TELEX 2225393. bibl.; circ. 315.
Formerly (until 1980): Monthly List of Selected Atomic Energy Publications (ISSN 0385-3330)

600 314.9 NE ISSN 0470-6684
HD9735.N2
NETHERLANDS. CENTRAAL BUREAU VOOR DE STATISTIEK. MAANDSTATISTIEK VAN DE INDUSTRIE. 1953. m. fl.112. Centraal Bureau voor de Statistiek, Prinses Beatrixlaan 428, Voorburg, Netherlands. (Orders to: SDU - Publishers, Christoffel Plantijnstraat, The Hague) circ. 925.

NEW TECHNICAL BOOKS; a selective list with descriptive annotations. see SCIENCES: COMPREHENSIVE WORKS — Abstracting, Bibliographies, Statistics

500 JA
NIHON KAGAKUSHI GAKKAI NENKAI KENKYU HAPPYO KOEN YOSHISHU. (Text in Japanese) a. Nihon Kagakushi Gakkai - History of Science Society of Japan, 16-3-91 Nihonbashi 2-chome, Chuo-ku, Tokyo 103, Japan. abstr.
Description: Contains abstracts of the annual meeting of the society.

600 JA
NIHON SANGYO GIJUTSUSHI GAKKAI NENKAI KOEN GAIYOSHU/JAPAN SOCIETY FOR THE HISTORY OF INDUSTRIAL TECHNOLOGY. ANNUAL CONFERENCE. PROCEEDINGS. (Text in Japanese) 1985. a. Nihon Sangyo Gijutsushi Gakkai - Japan Society for the History of Industrial Technology, Osaka Kogyokai Osaka Shoko Kaigisho Bldg. 5F, 58-7 Uchihon-machi, Hashizume-cho, Higashi-ku, Osaka-shi, Osaka-fu 540, Japan. abstr.

600 330 016 PL ISSN 0032-3004
TA4 CODEN: PTEAAE
POLISH TECHNICAL AND ECONOMIC ABSTRACTS. (Editions in English, French, German and Russian) 1951. q. $26. Instytut Informacji Naukowej, Technicznej i Ekonomicznej, Al. Niepodleglosci 188, 00-931 Warsaw, Poland. (Dist. by: Ars Polona - Ruch, Krakowskie Przedmiescie 7, Warsaw, Poland) Ed. E. Zwolanski. adv.; abstr.; index; circ. 1,500.
Indexed: Chem.Abstr., Concr.Abstr., Fluidex, Plant Breed.Abstr., RAPRA, World Surf.Coat.
Formerly: Polish Technical Abstracts.

745.2 016 GW ISSN 0024-4805
RAT FUER FORMGEBUNG. LITERATURHINWEISE. 1961. q. DM.40. Rat fuer Formgebung, Ludwig-Erhard-Anlage 1, 6000 Frankfurt a.M. 1, Germany. TEL 069-747919. FAX 069-7410911. bk.rev.; bibl.; circ. 700(combined).

600 RU
REFERATIVNYI ZHURNAL. TEKHNICHESKAYA ESTETIKA I ERGONOMIKA. 1987. q. 7.55 Rub. Vsesoyuznyi Institut Nauchno-Tekhnicheskoi Informatsii (VINITI), Ul. Usievicha 20a, 125 219 Moscow, Russia. FAX 943-0060. TELEX 411249. Ed. Yu.N. Sorokin. circ. 1,369.

REFERATIVNYJ BJULLETEN RUMYNSKOJ NAUCHNO-TEHNICHESKOJ LITERATURY. see SCIENCES: COMPREHENSIVE WORKS — Abstracting, Bibliographies, Statistics

600 CN
▼**SASKTECH DIRECTORY**; a directory of advanced technology capabilities in Saskatchewan. (Text in English) 1991. a. free. Saskatchewan Economic Diversification and Trade, Science and Technology Division, 206-15 Innovation Blvd., Saskatoon, Sask. S7N 2X8, Canada. TEL 306-933-7200. FAX 306-933-8244.
Description: Profiles over 200 companies in advanced technology industries, including microelectronics, automation, fiber optics, computer and software development, biotechnology, space, communication, and related research.

SCI-TECH NEWS. see SCIENCES: COMPREHENSIVE WORKS — Abstracting, Bibliographies, Statistics

SCIENCE BOOKS & FILMS. see SCIENCES: COMPREHENSIVE WORKS — Abstracting, Bibliographies, Statistics

SCIENTIFIC AND TECHNICAL BOOKS AND SERIALS IN PRINT; an index to literature in science and technology. see SCIENCES: COMPREHENSIVE WORKS — Abstracting, Bibliographies, Statistics

SCIENTIFIC SERIALS IN THAI LIBRARIES. see SCIENCES: COMPREHENSIVE WORKS — Abstracting, Bibliographies, Statistics

SCITECH BOOK NEWS; an annotated bibliography of new books in science, technology, & medicine. see BIBLIOGRAPHIES

SCITECH REFERENCE PLUS; complete bibliographic information on SciTech books and serials, bibliographical data on science professionals, and corporate profiles of research and business facilities. see SCIENCES: COMPREHENSIVE WORKS — Abstracting, Bibliographies, Statistics

600 AT
SCITECH TECHNOLOGY DIRECTORY. 1986. a. Aus.$125. Scitech Publication Pty. Ltd., G.P.O. Box 1915, Canberra, A.C.T. 2601, Australia. FAX 62-496648. Ed. Jane Ford.
Description: Covers government assistance, technology centers, venture capital and other technology support bodies.

SELECTED RAND ABSTRACTS; a quarterly guide to publications of the Rand Corporation. see SCIENCES: COMPREHENSIVE WORKS — Abstracting, Bibliographies, Statistics

620 016 AG
SERVICIOS ELECTRICOS DEL GRAN BUENOS AIRES S.A. BOLETIN BIBLIOGRAFICO. vol. 38, 1970. m. free. Servicios Electricos del Gran Buenos Aires S.A., Biblioteca y Hemeroteca, Balcare 184, Buenos Aires, Argentina. bk.rev.; abstr.; bibl.; circ. controlled.
Formerly: Biblioteca y Hemeroteca de Servicios Electricos del Gran Buenos Aires. Boletin Bibliografico (ISSN 0006-1751)

SHINKU TANKU NENPO/ABSTRACTS OF THINK TANK REPORTS. see SCIENCES: COMPREHENSIVE WORKS — Abstracting, Bibliographies, Statistics

620 016 US ISSN 0049-1209
SOCIETY OF MANUFACTURING ENGINEERS. TECHNICAL DIGEST; abstracts of technical papers on microfiche and hard copy. 1965. q. $26 to non-members; members $18. Society of Manufacturing Engineers, One SME Dr., Box 930, Dearborn, MI 48121-0930. TEL 313-271-1500. FAX 313-271-2861. TELEX 297742 SME UR (VIA RCA). circ. 1,000.
—BLDSC shelfmark: 8656.613000.

STANDARDS ACTION. see METROLOGY AND STANDARDIZATION — Abstracting, Bibliographies, Statistics

600 016 CS
STATNI VEDECKA KNIHOVNA. VYBER NOVINEK. SERIE G: TECHNIKA. 1974. 6/yr. 18 Kcs. Statni Vedecka Knihovna, Kounicova 5-7, 601 87 Brno, Czechoslovakia. circ. 300.

TECHNICAL EDUCATION ABSTRACTS. see EDUCATION — Abstracting, Bibliographies, Statistics

THAI ABSTRACTS, SERIES A. SCIENCE AND TECHNOLOGY. see SCIENCES: COMPREHENSIVE WORKS — Abstracting, Bibliographies, Statistics

TRIBOS - TRIBOLOGY ABSTRACTS. see ENGINEERING — Abstracting, Bibliographies, Statistics

VSESOYUZNYI INSTITUT NAUCHNO-TEKHNICHESKOI INFORMATSII. DEPONIROVANNYE NAUCHNYE RABOTY. see SCIENCES: COMPREHENSIVE WORKS — Abstracting, Bibliographies, Statistics

WASEDA DAIGAKU DAIGAKUIN RIKOGAKU KENKYU IHO/WASEDA UNIVERSITY. GRADUATE SCHOOL OF SCIENCE AND ENGINEERING. SYNOPSES OF SCIENCE AND ENGINEERING PAPERS. see ENGINEERING — Abstracting, Bibliographies, Statistics

600 AT
WOMEN AND APPROPRIATE TECHNOLOGIES; a bibliography. 1988. biennial. Noyce Publishing, G.P.O. Box 2222T, Melbourne, Vic. 3001, Australia.

600 016 II ISSN 0043-8944
WORLD REPORT ON TECHNICAL ADVANCEMENT. 1967. m. Rs.350($50) K.K. Roy (Private) Ltd., 55 Gariahat Rd., P.O. Box 10210, Calcutta 700 019, India. Ed. K.K. Roy. adv.; abstr.; pat.; stat.; index; circ. 1,000. (tabloid format)

TELEPHONE AND TELEGRAPH

see Communications–Telephone and Telegraph

TELEVISION AND CABLE

see Communications–Television and Cable

TEXTILE INDUSTRIES AND FABRICS

see also Cleaning and Dyeing; Clothing Trade

677 II
CODEN: ATTDD4
A C T. (A T I R A Communications on Textile) 1966. q. $20. Ahmedabad Textile Industry's Research Association, Polytechnic P.O., Ahmedabad 380015, India. TELEX 121-6571 ATRA IN. Indexed: Chem.Abstr., Text.Tech.Dig., World Text.Abstr.
Formerly: A T I R A Technical Digest (ISSN 0378-8148)

TEXTILE INDUSTRIES AND FABRICS

677   HK   ISSN 1015-8138
▼**A T A JOURNAL**; journal for Asia on textile & apparel. (Text in English; summaries in Chinese) 1990. bi-m. HK.$210($45) for Asia; elsewhere $51. Adsale Publishing Company, Tung Wai Commercial Bldg., 21st Fl., 109-111 Gloucester Rd., Wanchai, Hong Kong. TEL 892-0511. FAX 838-4119. TELEX 63109-ADSAP-HX. (Subscr. to: P.O. Box 20032, Hennessy Rd., Hong Kong) Ed. Linus Wu. adv.; circ. 12,300. (back issues avail.)
Formerly: Asia Textile and Apparel.
Description: For textile and apparel industry management in Asia.

338.4   GW   ISSN 0170-4060
A V R. (Allgemeiner Vliesstoff-Report) (Text in English and German) 1972. bi-m. DM.121.20. D P W Verlag GmbH, Postfach 1353, 6056 Heusenstamm, Germany. TEL 06104-6060. FAX 06104-606317. Ed. H. Osthus. adv.; bk.rev.; abstr.; bibl.; illus.; pat.; stat.; circ. 8,000. **Indexed:** Paper & Bd.Abstr., Text.Tech.Dig., World Text.Abstr.
—BLDSC shelfmark: 0792.380000.

677.3   AT
ABOUT WOOL. 1978. irreg. free. Australian Wool Corporation, G.P.O. Box 4867, Melbourne, Vic. 3001, Australia. TEL 03-341-9111. FAX 03-341-9273. TELEX AA 30548 HWOOL.
Description: Information sheets for school students.

ADVANCED COMPOSITES BULLETIN; an international newsletter. see PLASTICS

677   UK   ISSN 0144-7521
AFRICAN TEXTILES; for the African textile industry. (Text in English, French) 1980. bi-m. £36($65) Alain Charles Publishing Ltd., 27 Wilfred St., London SW1E 6PR, England. TEL 071-834-7676. FAX 071-973-0076. TELEX 297165. Ed. Zsa Tebbit. (back issues avail.) **Indexed:** Cott.& Trop.Fibr.Abstr., Text.Tech.Dig., World Text.Abstr.
—BLDSC shelfmark: 0734.931000.

677.7   US
AGENT. s-a. Halper Publishing Company, 600 Central Ave., Ste. 226, Highland Park, IL 60035. TEL 708-831-6678. adv.

667 338.4   II   ISSN 0075-4005
AHMEDABAD TEXTILE INDUSTRY'S RESEARCH ASSOCIATION. JOINT TECHNOLOGICAL CONFERENCES. PROCEEDINGS. (Text in English) 1960. a. $15. Ahmedabad Textile Industry's Research Association, Polytechnic P.O., Ahmedabad 380015, India. TELEX 121-6571 ATIRA IN. circ. 1,000. **Indexed:** Text.Tech.Dig, World Text.Abstr.

677   II
ALL INDIA HANDLOOM EXPORTERS GUIDE. irreg. $10 per no. c/o S. Narayanan, 11-B Ramachandra Iyer St., Madras 600017, India.

ALL INDIA TEXTILES DIRECTORY. see BUSINESS AND ECONOMICS — Trade And Industrial Directories

ALL PAKISTAN TEXTILE MILLS ASSOCIATION. CHAIRMAN'S REVIEW. see BUSINESS AND ECONOMICS — Production Of Goods And Services

677.028   US   ISSN 0040-490X
AMERICAN ASSOCIATION OF TEXTILE CHEMISTS AND COLORISTS. BUYER'S GUIDE. (Special (July) issue of: Textile Chemist and Colorist) 1969. a. $66 to non-members; members $34. American Association of Textile Chemists and Colorists, P.O. Box 12215, Research Triangle Park, NC 27709. TEL 919-549-8141. FAX 919-549-8933. Ed. Jack Kissiah. adv.; circ. 9,600.
Formerly: American Association of Textile Chemists and Colorists. Products Buyer's Guide (ISSN 0065-7352)

677.028   US   ISSN 0192-4699
TP890.5   CODEN: BPNADG
AMERICAN ASSOCIATION OF TEXTILE CHEMISTS AND COLORISTS. NATIONAL TECHNICAL CONFERENCE. BOOK OF PAPERS. 1974. a. $61 to non-members; members $34. American Association of Textile Chemists and Colorists, Box 12215, Research Triangle Park, NC 27709. TEL 919-549-8141. FAX 919-549-8933. (back issues avail.) **Indexed:** Chem.Abstr., Eng.Ind., Text.Tech.Dig., World Text.Abstr. Key Title: Book of Papers, National Technical Conference.

677.028   US
AMERICAN ASSOCIATION OF TEXTILE CHEMISTS AND COLORISTS. TECHNICAL MANUAL. 1924. a. $80 to non-members; members $42. American Association of Textile Chemists and Colorists, Box 12215, Research Triangle Park, NC 27709. TEL 919-549-8141. FAX 919-549-8933. circ. 2,000.

AMERICAN DYESTUFF REPORTER; devoted to textile wet-processing, dyeing, finishing, bleaching, etc., new product information, news of the industry. see CLEANING AND DYEING

677   US
AMERICAN TEXTILE DIRECTORY. Variant title: Textile Red Book. a. $74.50. Billian Publishing, Inc., 2100 Powers Ferry Rd., Ste. 300, Atlanta, GA 30339. TEL 404-955-5656. FAX 404-952-0669.
Formerly: Clark's Directory of Southern Textile Mills.

677   US   ISSN 0890-9970
TS1300   CODEN: ATINEE
AMERICA'S TEXTILES INTERNATIONAL. 1887. m. $43 (Canada $53; elsewhere $115). Billian Publishing, Inc., 2100 Powers Ferry Rd., Ste. 125, Atlanta, GA 30339. TEL 404-955-5656. FAX 404-952-0669. Ed. Monte G. Plott. adv.; bk.rev.; circ. 32,368. (also avail. in microfilm from PMC,UMI) **Indexed:** Art & Archaeol.Tech.Abstr., Chem.Abstr., Text.Tech.Dig., Tr.& Indus.Ind., World Text.Abstr.
—BLDSC shelfmark: 1765.882900.
Formerly: America's Textile (ISSN 0737-0040) Incorporates: Fiber World; (1899-1984): Textile Industries (ISSN 0040-4985); (1973-1984): Fiber Producer (ISSN 0361-4921); Which superseded: Fiber Producer Buyer's Guide (ISSN 0091-6617).

ANNUAL BOOK OF A S T M STANDARDS. VOLUME 07.01. TEXTILES - YARN, FABRICS, AND GENERAL TEST METHODS. see ENGINEERING — Engineering Mechanics And Materials

ANNUAL BOOK OF A S T M STANDARDS. VOLUME 07.02. TEXTILES - FIBERS, ZIPPERS. see ENGINEERING — Engineering Mechanics And Materials

677   NZ
APPAREL; to all clothing, textile and footwear manufacturers and retail clothing outlets. 1968. m. NZ.$48. Apparel Publishing Ltd., Box 56-071, Dominion Rd., Auckland 3, New Zealand. TEL 09-685-685. FAX 09-603706. Ed. Valerie Blomfield. adv.; circ. 4,000. **Indexed:** Text.Tech.Dig.

APPAREL BUYERS GUIDE YEAR BOOK. see BUSINESS AND ECONOMICS — Trade And Industrial Directories

677   US
APPAREL DIGEST. 1934. m. $75. Institute of Textile Technology, Box 391, Charlottesville, VA 22902-0391. TEL 804-296-5511. FAX 804-977-5400. Ed. Dennis Loy.
Former titles (until 1990): Apparel Needle Trades Digest; (until 1986): Apparel Digest.
Description: Contains summaries of the literature for the apparel and related industres.

646   US   ISSN 0275-8873
HD4966.C62
APPAREL PLANT WAGES SURVEY. a. $60 to non-members; members $25. American Apparel Manufacturers Association, 2500 Wilson Blvd., Ste. 301, Arlington, VA 22201. TEL 703-524-1864. FAX 703-522-6741. **Indexed:** SRI.
Supersedes in part: Apparel Plant Wages and Personnel Policies (ISSN 0084-6678)

677   IT
ARREDO TESSILI COMPLEMENTI - BIANCHERIA CASA. (Supplement avail.) (Text in English and Italian; summaries in Italian) 1977. bi-m. L.60000($100) Nuove Tecniche Editoriali S.r.l., Via San Siro 27, 20149 Milan, Italy. TEL 02-4812213. FAX 02-48193425. TELEX 325043 NTE ETP-I. Ed. Tosca Bartolini. adv.; illus.; circ. 20,000. (back issues avail.)
Formed by the 1990 merger of: Arredo Tessili Complementi (ISSN 0393-4462); Which was formerly (until 1984): 4T di Arredo Tessile & Arredo Biancheria Casa (ISSN 0393-4454); Which was formerly (until 1984): Arredo Tessile.
Description: Features articles on household linens; their fabrics, designs and manufacturing.

ART, CRAFT, DESIGN & TEXTILE TECHNOLOGY DIRECTORY. see EDUCATION — Guides To Schools And Colleges

677   BE   ISSN 0571-1924
ARTES TEXTILES: BIJRAGEN TOT DE GESCHIEDENIS VAN DE TAPIJT. (Text in Dutch) 1953. irreg. Vereniging voor de Geschiedenis van de Textiele Kunsten, Centrum Voor de Geschiedenis van de Tapijtkunst, Frans de Coninckstr. 17, 9218 Ledeberg, Belgium. bk.rev.; bibl. **Indexed:** RILA.

677   JA
ASIAN TEXTILE RECORD. 51/yr. $900. Intercontinental Marketing Corp., I.P.O. Box 5056, Tokyo 100-31, Japan. FAX 81-3-667-9646.

677   IT
ASSOCIAZIONE NOBILITAZIONE TESSILE. NOTIZIARIO. 1945. w. free. Istituto per l'Assistenza e Servizi alle Aziende Tessili s.r.l., V.le Sarca, 223, 20126 Milan, Italy. TEL 02-66103404. FAX 02-66103444. Ed. Giovanni Frangi. bk.rev.; bibl.; mkt.; pat.; stat. (looseleaf format)
Formerly (until 1985): Associazione Italiana Industriali Tintori, Stampatori e Finitori Tessili. Notiziario (ISSN 0004-5950)

677   AT   ISSN 0725-086X
AUSTRALASIAN TEXTILES. 1981. bi-m. Aus.$40 (foreign Aus.$90). (Society of Dyers & Colorists of Australia and New Zealand, Southern Australia Section of the Textile Institute) Australasian Textiles Publishers, Box 286, Belmont, Vic. 3216, Australia. TEL 052-552699. FAX 052-561668. Ed. S. Boston. adv.; bk.rev.; circ. 2,300. **Indexed:** Text.Tech.Dig., World Text.Abstr.
—BLDSC shelfmark: 1796.375000.

677   AT   ISSN 0816-3588
AUSTRALIAN APPAREL MANUFACTURER. 1926. bi-m. Aus.$36 (foreign Aus.$90)(effective Apr. 1992). Yaffa Publishing Group, 17-21 Bellevue St., Surry Hills, N.S.W. 2010, Australia. TEL 02-281-2333. FAX 02-281-2750. Ed. B. McBride. adv.; B&W page Aus.$1535, color page Aus.$2169; trim 297 x 210. bk.rev.; bibl.; charts; illus.; pat.; stat.; circ. 2,939 (controlled). **Indexed:** Chem.Abstr., World Text.Abstr.
Former titles: Textile and Apparel Manufacturer (ISSN 0810-574X); Textile Journal of Australia (ISSN 0040-5019)
Description: For key executives in every sector of the Australian apparel manufacturing industry.

677.3   AT
AUSTRALIAN WOOL COMPENDIUM. m. Aus.$25 (foreign Aus.$30). Australian Wool Corporation, Economics Dept., G.P.O. Box 4867, Melbourne, Vic. 3001, Australia. TEL 341 9111. Ed. P. Hanson. (looseleaf format)

677   AT
AUSTRALIAN WOOL CORPORATION. WOOL MARKET NEWS: MONTHLY PERSPECTIVE. 1975. m. free. Australian Wool Corporation, Economics Department, P.O. Box 4867, Melbourne, Vic. 3001, Australia. Ed. W. Watkins. circ. 3,600.
Formerly: Australian Wool Corporation. Bi-Monthly Market Report (ISSN 0310-1398)

677.76   GW   ISSN 0005-4925
BAND- UND FLECHTINDUSTRIE/NARROW FABRIC AND BRAIDING INDUSTRY. (Text in English and German) 1964. m. DM.72. (Industrieverband Deutscher Bandweber und Flechter e.V) Melliand Textilberichte GmbH, Rohrbacher Str. 76, 6900 Heidelberg, Germany. adv.; bk.rev.; bibl.; circ. 1,700. **Indexed:** Excerp.Med., Text.Tech.Dig., World Text.Abstr.
—BLDSC shelfmark: 1861.570000.

677   BG
BANGLADESH JOURNAL OF JUTE & FIBRE RESEARCH. 1976. s-a. $5 per no. Bangladesh Jute Research Institute, Sher-e-Banglanagar, Dhaka 7, Bangladesh. Ed. Md. Harun-Ur-Rashid.

TEXTILE INDUSTRIES AND FABRICS 4617

677 CC ISSN 1002-3348
BEIJING FANGZHI/BEIJING TEXTILE. (Text in Chinese) 1979. bi-m. Y10.80. Beijing Fangzhi Gongcheng Xuehui - Beijing Textile Engineering Society, 2 Shilipu, Chaoyangmenwai, Beijing 100025, People's Republic of China. TEL 5004477. FAX 5004271. TELEX 210362 FRHTL CN. Ed. Xu Xiaochun. adv.: B&W page Y3,500. circ. 12,000.
 Description: Covers new technical processes, development of machines and products, and research activities in dyeing and printing.

677 GW ISSN 0005-8270
BEKLEIDUNG UND MASCHENWARE; Fachzeitschrift fuer die industrielle Fertigung und fuer den Handel. (Text in German; contents page in Russian) 1962. 6/yr. DM.36 (foreign DM.46.20). Fachbuchverlag, Karl-Heine-Str. 16, 7031 Leipzig, Germany. adv.; bk.rev.; bibl.; charts; illus.; tr.lit.; index. Indexed: Text.Tech.Dig., World Text.Abstr.
 Description: Trade publication for the clothing industry, featuring manufacturing, trade, latest styles and fashions, industrial technology, industry news, reports and announcements of events.

677.3 636.3 US
BLACK SHEEP NEWSLETTER. 1974. q. $12 (foreign $16). Black Sheep Press, 25455 N.W. Dixie Mtn. Rd., Scappose, OR 97056. Ed. Peggy Lundquist. adv.; bk.rev.; circ. 2,500.
 Description: For growers, spinners and textile artists interested in colored and white sheep wool and other animal fibers.

LA BOBINA - NOTIVEST. see *CLOTHING TRADE*

677 JA
BOKEN REPORT. (Text in Japanese) 1951. a. 2000 Yen. Japan Spinners Inspecting Foundation, 18-15, 1-chome, Ue-machi, Chuo-ku, Osaka 540, Japan. TEL 06-762-5881. FAX 06-762-5889. Ed. Tadanori Inoko. adv.; circ. 1,000. (back issues avail.)
 Formerly (until vol.49, 1970): J S I F Report.

BUTTERICK HOME CATALOG. see *CLOTHING TRADE — Fashions*

BUYER. see *CLOTHING TRADE*

677 US
C L A GUIDELINES; management guidelines for C L A members. 1972. m. membership. Coin Laundry Association, 1315 Butterfield Rd., Ste. 212, Downers Grove, IL 60515. TEL 708-963-5547. FAX 708-963-5864. Ed. Frank J. Vitek. circ. 3,000. (back issues avail.)

677 US
C L A NEWS. 1972. m. membership. Coin Laundry Association, 1315 Butterfield Rd., Ste. 212, Downers Grove, IL 60515. TEL 708-963-5547. Ed. Frank J. Vitek. circ. 3,000. (tabloid format; back issues avail.)
 Description: Industry news and educational material for owners of coin laundry and dry cleaning retail stores.

677.3 AT ISSN 0312-5211
C S I R O WOOL TEXTILE NEWS. 1954. irreg. free. Commonwealth Scientific and Industrial Research Organization., Division of Wool Technology, P.O. Box 21, Belmont, Vic. 3216, Australia. TEL 052-47-2611. Ed. P.T. Naughtin. circ. 2,500. Indexed: World Text.Abstr.

677 II ISSN 0084-8859
C.T.T.S. ANNUAL. (Text and summaries in English) 1949. a. College of Textile Technology, Serampore, Students Union, Serampore, West Bengal, India. Ed. S.C. Ukil.

CANADIAN TEXTILE DIRECTORY. see *BUSINESS AND ECONOMICS — Trade And Industrial Directories*

CARBON & HIGH PERFORMANCE FIBRES DIRECTORY. see *PLASTICS*

677 747.4 US ISSN 0192-4486
HD9937.U6
CARPET & RUG INDUSTRY. 1973. m. $42. Rodman Publications, Inc., 17 S. Franklin Tpk., Box 555, Ramsey, NJ 07446. TEL 201-825-2552. FAX 201-825-0553. TELEX 550302. Ed. Frank O'Neill. adv.; bk.rev.; abstr.; charts; illus.; pat.; stat.; circ. 6,000. Indexed: Art & Archaeol.Tech.Abstr., Text.Tech.Dig., World Text.Abstr.

677 US
CARPET AND RUG INSTITUTE. DIRECTORY. 1950. a. $15. Carpet and Rug Institute, 310 Holiday Ave., S., Box 2048, Dalton, GA 30720-2048. TEL 404-278-3176. FAX 404-278-8835. Ed. Truett Lomax.
 Formerly: Carpet and Rug Institute. Directory and Report (ISSN 0069-0740)

677 UK ISSN 0069-0767
CARPET ANNUAL. 1931. a. £64 (foreign £79). Benn Business Information Services Ltd., P.O. Box 20, Sovereign Way, Tonbridge, Kent TN9 1RQ, England. TEL 0732-362666. FAX 0732-770483. TELEX 95162-BENTON-G. Ed. Cheryl Veal. adv.; circ. 1,500.
 Description: Guide to manufacturers, retailers and wholesalers in the floorcovering industry.

677 US ISSN 0095-6457
TS1772
CARPET SPECIFIER'S HANDBOOK. 1974. irreg., 4th ed., 1987. $20. Carpet and Rug Institute, 310 Holiday Ave., S., Box 2048, Dalton, GA 30720-2048. TEL 404-278-3176. FAX 404-278-8835. illus.

CATALOGUE BIENNALE INTERNATIONALE DE LAUSANNE. see *ART*

677 FR
CENTRE INTERNATIONAL D'ETUDE DES TEXTILES ANCIENS. BULLETIN. Short title: Bulletin du C I E T A. (Text and summaries in English, French) 1955. a. 250 F. to members; institutions 600 F. (effective 1992). Centre International d'Etude des Textiles Anciens, 34 rue de la Charite, 69002 Lyon, France. TEL 78-37-15-05. FAX 72-40-25-12. bk.rev.; bibl.; illus. (processed) Indexed: World Text.Abstr.
 Former titles (until 1989): Textiles Anciens; (until 1987): Centre International d'Etude des Textiles Anciens. Bulletin de Liaison (ISSN 0008-980X)

677.4 CS ISSN 0528-9432
CODEN: CMVLA8
CHEMICKE VLAKNA. (Text in English, Russian, Slovak) 1951. q. 5 Kcs. per no. Research Institute for Man-Made Fibres, 059 21 Svit, Okr. Poprad, Czechoslovakia. FAX 55663. TELEX 078217 SVIT. (Co-sponsor: Ministry of Industry) circ. 500. Indexed: Abstr.Bull.Inst.Pap.Chem., Chem.Abstr., Text.Tech.Dig., World Text.Abstr.
 —BLDSC shelfmark: 3154.500000.

677 GW ISSN 0340-3343
TS1300
CHEMIEFASERN - TEXTIL-INDUSTRIE; Zeitschrift fuer die gesamte Textilindustrie. (Text in German and English) 1919. m. DM.203.50. Deutscher Fachverlag GmbH, Mainzer Landstr. 251, Postfach 100606, 6000 Frankfurt a.M. 1, Germany. Ed. Hans Koslowski. adv.; bk.rev.; abstr.; charts; illus.; index; circ. 7,800. Indexed: Abstr.Bull.Inst.Pap.Chem., Art & Archaeol.Tech.Abstr., C.I.S. Abstr., Chem.Abstr., Cott.& Trop.Fibr.Abstr., Excerp.Med., Key to Econ.Sci., PROMT, Text.Tech.Dig., World Text.Abstr.
 —BLDSC shelfmark: 3157.750000.
 Former titles: Chemiefasern; Textil-Anwendungstechnik.

677 330.9 HK
CHINA TEXTILE/ZHONGGUO FAZHI; a bimonthly textile & apparel journal for P.R. China. (Text in Chinese; table of contents in Chinese, English) 1983. 7/yr. HK.$273($70) for Asia; elsewhere $77 (typically set in July). (Ministry of Textile Industry, Beijing Textile Research Institute, CC) Adsale Publishing Company, Tung Wai Commercial Bldg., 21st Fl., 109-111 Gloucester Rd., Wanchai, Hong Kong. TEL 892-0511. FAX 838-4119. TELEX 63109-ADSAP-HX. (Subscr. to: P.O. Box 20032, Hennessy Rd., Hong Kong) Ed. Linus Wu. adv.; circ. 35,000. (back issues avail.)
 Description: Introduces to China advanced foreign technology, machinery and processing materials in the textile industry.

CLEO EN LA MODA. see *LEATHER AND FUR INDUSTRIES*

CLOTHING & TEXTILES RESEARCH JOURNAL. see *CLOTHING TRADE*

677.1 II ISSN 0530-0495
COIR. (Text in English) 1956. s-a. Rs.30($12.50) Coir Board, c/o T. Devidas, Ed., Cochin 682016, India.
 Description: Articles on India's coir industry.

COLOURAGE. see *CLEANING AND DYEING*

677 IT
COMMERCIALE BOLLETTINO DELLA LANIERA. SUPPLEMENTO. 1924. w. L.20000. Editoriale Laniera s.r.l., Via Mure P. Castello 9, 36100 Vicenza, Italy. Ed. Felice Dall'Ara. adv.; circ. 1,100.

COMPOSITES SCIENCE AND TECHNOLOGY. see *TECHNOLOGY: COMPREHENSIVE WORKS*

CONFECCION INDUSTRIAL. see *CLOTHING TRADE*

CONFECTIE. see *CLOTHING TRADE*

677 BE
CONTACT. (Text in Flemish, French) 1950. 12/yr. 2000 BEF. Belgian Knitwear Association - Federation de la Maille, Rode Beukendreef 14, 9831 Deurle, Belgium. TEL 091-82-21-11. FAX 091-82-40-21. Ed.Bd. adv.; bk.rev.; charts; stat.; circ. 500. (back issues avail.)

677.2 PK
COTISTICS BI-ANNUAL COTTON STATISTICAL BULLETIN. (Text in English) 1972. q. free. Pakistan Central Cotton Committee, Marketing and Economic Research Section, Secretary, Moulvi Tamizuddin Khan Rd., Karachi 1, Pakistan. TEL 524104-6. charts; stat.
 Formerly: Cotistics Quarterly Cotton Statistical Bulletin.

677.21 US
COTTON. PART 1: BI-MONTHLY REVIEW OF THE WORLD SITUATION. (Editions in English, French, Spanish) 1947. bi-m. $45 (includes part 2). International Cotton Advisory Committee, 1901 Pennsylvania Ave., N.W., Ste. 201, Washington, DC 20006. TEL 202-463-6660. charts; stat.; circ. 3,200. Indexed: Key to Econ.Sci., PROMT, World Text.Abstr.
 Formerly: Cotton. Part 1: Monthly Review of the World Situation.

COTTON. PART 2: WORLD STATISTICS. see *TEXTILE INDUSTRIES AND FABRICS — Abstracting, Bibliographies, Statistics*

677.21 US
COTTON DIGEST INTERNATIONAL. 1928. m. $40. Cotton Digest Co., Inc., Box 820768, Houston, TX 77282-0768. TEL 713-977-1644. FAX 713-467-6935. Ed. Elizabeth Edwards Abbey. adv.; illus.; mkt.; circ. 5,500. Indexed: Text.Tech.Dig.
 Formerly: Cotton Digest (ISSN 0010-9797)

677.21 US ISSN 0010-9800
COTTON GIN AND OIL MILL PRESS; the magazine of the cotton ginning and oilseed processing industries. 1889. fortn. $7.50. Haughton Publishing Co. of Texas, Box 180218, Dallas, TX 75218. TEL 214-288-7511. Ed. Don Swanson. adv.; charts; illus.; stat.; circ. 3,000. (also avail. in microfilm from UMI) Indexed: Chem.Abstr., Text.Tech.Dig.

677.21 US ISSN 0070-0673
TS1550
COTTON INTERNATIONAL. 1914. a. $15. Meister Publishing Co., 37733 Euclid Ave., Willoughby, OH 44094. TEL 216-942-2000. Ed. William Spencer. circ. 10,856. Indexed: Text.Tech.Dig.
 Formerly: Cotton Trade Journal International.

677.21 UK
COTTON OUTLOOK. 1923. w. $715.82. Cotlook Ltd., Cotlook House, 458 New Chester Rd., Rock Ferry, Birkinhead, Merseyside L42 2AE, England. (Dist. in U.S. by: Cotlook Ltd., 5100 Poplar, Ste. 2520, Memphis, TN 38137) Ed. Ray Butler. adv.; charts; mkt.; stat. (processed)
 Formerly: Cotton and General Economic Review (ISSN 0010-9789)

D T V - INTERN. (Deutscher Textilreinigungs-Verband e.V.) see *CLEANING AND DYEING*

T

4618 TEXTILE INDUSTRIES AND FABRICS

677   US   ISSN 0011-5460
DAILY NEWS RECORD. 1892. 5/w. $62. Fairchild Publications, Inc., Daily News Record (Subsidiary of: Capital Cities Media, Inc.), 7 W. 34th St., New York, NY 10001. TEL 212-630-4000. Ed. Ed Nardoza. adv.; bk.rev.; illus.; mkt.; pat.; circ. 22,177. (also avail. in microform from FCM,MIM) **Indexed:** Bus.Ind., PROMT, Text.Tech.Dig., Tr.& Indus.Ind.
●Also available online. Vendor(s): DIALOG.
Description: Covers the men's and boy's apparel industry, includes articles from newspapers on textile manufacturers, clothing manufacturers, wholesalers, converters, and retailers.

667   US
DATATEXTILE. m. Industrial Fabrics Association International, 345 Cedar St., No. 800, St. Paul, MN 55101-1014. TEL 612-222-2508. FAX 612-222-8215. Ed. Kevin Jagielski. tr.lit.

DAVISON'S SALESMAN'S BOOK. see *BUSINESS AND ECONOMICS — Trade And Industrial Directories*

DAVISON'S TEXTILE BLUE BOOK. see *BUSINESS AND ECONOMICS — Trade And Industrial Directories*

677.76   GW   ISSN 0012-0758
DEUTSCHE SEILER-ZEITUNG. 1879. m. DM.62. (Bundesverband des Deutschen Seiler-, Segel- und Netzmacherhandwerks e.V.) Aegis-Verlag, Breite Gasse 2, 7900 Ulm, Germany. FAX 0731-6021276. (Co-sponsor: Bundesverband Verschnuerungs- und Verpackunngsmittel e. V. Sitz Frankfurt) Ed. Ernst Bauer. adv.; bk.rev.; illus.; circ. 1,000.

677.3   GW
DEUTSCHES WOLLFORSCHUNGSINSTITUT. VORTRAEGE. 1953. irreg. DM.10. Deutsches Wollforschungsinstitut, Technische Hochschule Aachen, Veltmanplatz 8, 5100 Aachen, Germany.

677   US
DIEMAKING DIECUTTING INTELLIGENCE NEWSLETTER. 1986. q. $40. Larson Associates, 95 Mt. Blue St., Norwell, MA 02061. TEL 617-659-2115. FAX 617-659-2411. adv.; circ. 6,000.
Description: Covers the diecutting industry.

677   II
DIRECT TEXTILE BULLETIN. q. $41.04. Ministry of Urban Development, Department of Publication, Civil Lines, Delhi 110 054, India. TEL 11-2512527.

677 620   SP
DIRECTORY OF THE SPANISH COTTON-SYSTEM TEXTILE ENTERPRISES/DIRECTORIO EMPRESAS TEXTILES DE PROCESO ALGODONERO/DIRECTORI EMPRESES TEXTILS DE PROCES COTONER/DIRECTOIRE ENTERPRISES TEXTILES DE PROCESSUS COTONNIER. (Text in English, French, Catalan, Spanish) 1986. a. 5000 ptas.($50) Asociacion Industrial Textil de Proceso Algodonero (A.I.T.P.A.), Gran Via de les Corts Catalanes, 670, 08010 Barcelona, Spain. TEL 34-3189200. FAX 34-33026235. circ. 3,000.

380.1
DIRECTORY OF WOOL, HOSIERY AND FABRICS. (Text in English) 1950. a. Rs.50. Commerce Publications Limited, NKM International House, 178 Backbay Reclamation, Bombay 400020, India. Ed. Subhash Chandra Sarker.
Formerly: India and Pakistan Wool, Hosiery and Fabrics.

677   UK   ISSN 0012-3811
TS1828
DISPOSABLES AND NONWOVENS. bi-m. £20($50) (foreign £30)(effective 1991). Chandler Publications Ltd., 10 South St., Totnes, Devon TQ9 5DZ, England. TEL 0803-864668. FAX 0803-865649. Ed. Jack Heming. adv.; bk.rev.; circ. 2,000. **Indexed:** World Text.Abstr.
—BLDSC shelfmark: 3598.730000.
Description: Provides news for manufacturers, converters and dealers in disposable and nonwoven materials.

677   AT
DOMESTIC TEXTILES & WALLCOVERINGS TRADE JOURNAL. a. Aus.$40. Furnishing Publications Pty. Ltd., 251 Hawthorn Rd., Caulfield, Vic. 3162, Australia. TEL 03-523-8444. FAX 03-523-0291. Ed. Keith Dunn. adv.; charts; illus.; tr.lit.; circ. 6,144.
Former titles: Furnishing Textiles and Wallcoverings Trade Journal; Domestic Textiles and Wallcoverings Trade Journal.

677   US
DRAFTS & DESIGNS. 1958. 10/yr. $10. Robin and Russ Handweavers, 533 N. Adams St., McMinnville, OR 97128. TEL 503-472-5760. Ed. Russell E. Groff. adv.; charts; illus.; circ. 800. (looseleaf format; back issues avail.)
Description: Covers multiple harness patterns; sample swatch included with each issue.

677   AU   ISSN 0012-6071
DREIHAMMER. 1939. 4/yr. free. F.M. Haemmerle Textilwerke AG, A-6850 Dornbirn, Austria. TEL 05572-64561. Ed. Michael Lins. circ. 2,800.

E N I ANNUAL REPORT. (Ente Nazionale Idrocarburi) see *ENERGY*

ECHO. see *HOME ECONOMICS*

677   IT   ISSN 0012-9526
ECO DELL'INDUSTRIA TESSILE. 1948. 2/w. L.100000. Eleonora Caselli, Via Tripoli 24, 13051 Biella, Italy. Ed. Germano Caselli. adv.

677.21   UA   ISSN 0013-2403
EGYPTIAN COTTON GAZETTE. 1947. 2/yr. £8 per no. Cotton Exporters Association, P.O. Box 433, Alexandria, Egypt. Eds. Ahmed H. Youssef, Mongui Hefni. adv.; illus.; mkt.; stat. **Indexed:** Chem.Abstr.

677   US   ISSN 0080-6811
EMBROIDERY DIRECTORY. 1947. a. $5. Schiffli Lace and Embroidery Manufacturers Association, Inc., 8555 Tonnelle Ave., N. Bergen, NJ 07047-4738. TEL 201-868-7200. Ed. I. Leonard Seiler. adv.; circ. 2,000.
Former titles: Schiffli Digest and Directory; Schiffli Directory.

677   US
EMBROIDERY NEWS. 1955. irreg. (6-8/yr.). free to qualified personnel. Schiffli Lace and Embroidery Manufacturers Association, Inc., 8555 Tonnelle Ave., N. Bergen, NJ 07047-4738. TEL 201-868-7200. Ed. I. Leonard Seiler. adv.; bk.rev.; circ. 850.

677   FR   ISSN 0181-8120
ENTRETIEN DES TEXTILES. 1969. m. 285 F. Centre Technique de la Teinture et du Nettoyage (CTTN), Chemin des Mouilles, B.P. 41, 69131 Ecully Cedex, France. FAX 78-43-34-12. TELEX 305 299 F. Ed. Marc Eglizeau. adv.; bk.rev.; circ. controlled.

677 382   DK
EXPORT GUIDE - DANSK TEXTIL OG BEKLAEDNING/EXPORT GUIDE - DANISH TEXTILE AND CLOTHING. 1956. biennial. free. Textilindustrien, Bredgade 410, P.O. Box 300, DK-7400 Herning, Denmark. TEL 97-12-13-66. FAX 97-12-23-50. TELEX 62 199 JYTEX DK.
Formerly: Dansk Textil Exportguide - Danish Textile Export Guide (ISSN 0109-8586)

F T B-HANDEL. (Farben-Tapeten-Bodenbelaege) see *BUSINESS AND ECONOMICS*

677   US
THE FABRIC & FIBER SOURCEBOOK; your one-and-only mail-order guide. 1989. irreg. $12.95. Taunton Press, Inc., 63 S. Main St., Box 5506, Newtown, CT 06470-5506. TEL 800-888-8286. FAX 203-426-3434. Ed. Bobbi McRae. illus.; index.
Description: Lists over 650 US sources for fibers, textiles, and related materials, giving address, phone number, catalog price, discount schedules, year established, and line of business. Also describes what is sold by each supplier, and gives name of personnel contact or owner. Includes geographical and subject indices.

677   US
FABRICNEWS. 1970. q. $24. Arthur J. Imparato Associates, 80 Park Ave., New York, NY 10016. TEL 213-274-6752. Ed. Shirley Jones. adv.; circ. 9,500 (controlled).
Incorporates (1975-1990): Trade (New York).
Description: Covers home sewing, needlearts and crafts.

FABRICS & ARCHITECTURE. see *ARCHITECTURE*

677   NO
FABRIKKABEIDEREN. 10/yr. Norsk Kjemisk Industriarbeider Forbund, Youngsgt 11, Oslo, Norway. TEL 401340.

677 687   US
FAIRCHILD'S TEXTILE & APPAREL FINANCIAL DIRECTORY. 1974. a. $60 (effective Oct. 1990). Fairchild Books (Subsidiary of: Fairchild Publications Inc.), 7 E. 12th St., New York, NY 10003. TEL 212-887-1866. FAX 212-887-1946. TELEX 232666 FAPB. Ed. Robert Benjamin. circ. 750. (back issues avail.) **Indexed:** SRI.

677   CC
FANGZHI XUEBAO/CHINA TEXTILE ENGINEERING ASSOCIATION. JOURNAL. (Text in Chinese) m. $1 per no. Zhongguo Fangzhi Gongcheng Xuehui - China Textile Engineering Association, 297 Wulumuqi Beilu, Shanghai 200040, People's Republic of China. TEL 2581667. (Dist. overseas by: China International Book Trading Corporation, P.O. Box 399, Beijing, P.R.C.) **Indexed:** Chem.Abstr, World Text.Abstr.

677   IT
FASHION. 1970. w. L.165000($170) (effective Jan. 1992). Edizioni Ecomarket S.p.A., Corso Venezia 26, 20121 Milan, Italy. TEL 02-76007371. FAX 02-783012. Ed. Gianni Bertasso. adv.; circ. 30,000.
Formerly: G T - Giornale Tessile.

677   US
HD9929.5.U6
FIBER ORGANON; featuring man-made fibers. 1930. m. $300 (foreign $400). Fiber Economics Bureau, Inc., 101 Eisenhower Pkwy, Roseland, NJ 07068. TEL 201-228-1107. FAX 201-228-7598. Ed. Rosemarie Frick. bk.rev.; charts; mkt.; stat.; index; circ. 3,500. **Indexed:** P.A.I.S., PROMT, SRI, Text.Tech.Dig., World Text.Abstr.
Formerly: Textile Organon (ISSN 0040-5132)
Description: Covers synthetic fibers.

677   US   ISSN 0071-4682
                     CODEN: FSCSDC
FIBER SCIENCE SERIES. 1970. irreg., vol.8, 1979. price varies. Marcel Dekker, Inc., 270 Madison Ave., New York, NY 10016. TEL 212-696-9000. FAX 212-685-4540. Ed. L. Rebenfeld.
Refereed Serial

547.85   US   ISSN 0015-0541
TS1548.5   CODEN: FICYAP
FIBRE CHEMISTRY. English translation of: Khimicheskie Volokna. 1969. bi-m. $860 (foreign $1005)(effective 1992). (Russian Academy of Sciences, RU) Plenum Publishing Corp., Consultants Bureau, 233 Spring St., New York, NY 10013-1578. TEL 212-620-8468. FAX 212-463-0742. TELEX 23-421139. Ed. G.I. Kudryavtsev. (also avail. in microfilm from JSC; back issues avail.) **Indexed:** Appl.Mech.Rev., Chem.Titles, Eng.Ind., Excerp.Med.
—BLDSC shelfmark: 0411.752000.
Refereed Serial

677   US   ISSN 0046-3728
FIBRE MARKET NEWS. 1963. w. $110 (effective Jan. 1992). (Group Interest Enterprises) G.I.E., Inc. Publishers, 4012 Bridge Ave., Cleveland, OH 44113. TEL 216-961-4130. FAX 216-961-0364. Ed. Daniel Sandoval. adv.; charts; stat.; circ. 2,700.
Description: Covers issues pertaining to the collection process and marketing of secondary fiber for recycling.

TEXTILE INDUSTRIES AND FABRICS

677   FR   ISSN 0750-4764
TS1300
FILIERE MAILLE. 1982. 6/yr. 300 F. (Federation Francaise des Industries de la Maille et de la Bonneterie) Editions de l' Industrie Textile, 16 rue Ballu, 75009 Paris, France. TEL 48-74-15-96. FAX 48-74-01-89. TELEX 283 438 F. Ed. Pierre S. Robin. adv.; bk.rev.; abstr.; bibl.; charts; illus.; pat.; stat.; index. Indexed: Text.Tech.Dig., World Text.Abstr.
—BLDSC shelfmark: 3925.644000.
   Formed by the merger of: Maille Informations (ISSN 0150-651X); Moniteur de la Maille.

677   UK
FINANCIAL SURVEY COMPANY DIRECTORY. a. I C C Financial Surveys Ltd., Field House, 72 Oldfield Rd., Hampton, Middlesex TW12 2HQ, England. TEL 01-783-0977. FAX 01-783-1940.

677   JA
FRATERNITY MONTHLY MAGAZINE. m. Zensen Japanese Federation of Textile, Garment, Chemical, Mercantile and Allied Industry Workers' Unions, 8-16 Kudan, Minami 4-chome, Chiyoda-ku, Tokyo 102, Japan. TEL 03-3265-5465. TELEX ZENSEN TOKYO.

FURNISHINGS RECORD. see *INTERIOR DESIGN AND DECORATION — Furniture And House Furnishings*

677   FR
G A P. (Groupe Avant-Premiere) 1969. m. 370 F. (Societe G A P) Liaisons Convergence, 14 rue Chapal, 92309 Levallois-Perret, France. Ed. Aline Laresse. circ. 17,000.

GAAF GOED; vakblad voor de interieur-textiel-branche. see *INTERIOR DESIGN AND DECORATION — Furniture And House Furnishings*

677   AG   ISSN 0046-5364
GACETA TEXTIL. 1934. m. Gaceta Editora Coop Ltda., 25 de Mayo no. 786, piso 12, Buenos Aires, Argentina. Ed. Emma P. Zappettini. adv.; abstr.; bibl.; illus.; stat.; circ. 15,000.

677   AG   ISSN 0016-3996
                      CODEN: GALAAL
GALAXIA. 1963. m. Asociacion Argentina de Quimicos y Coloristas Textiles, Bulnes 1425, 1176 Buenos Aires, Argentina. Ed. Oscar Decivo. adv.; bk.rev.; abstr.; bibl.; charts; illus.; stat.; circ. 1,500. Indexed: Chem.Abstr.
—BLDSC shelfmark: 4066.600000.

GARMENT MANUFACTURER'S INDEX. see *CLOTHING TRADE*

677.028   US   ISSN 0882-4983
GEOTECHNICAL FABRICS REPORT; engineer's guide to geosynthesis. 1983. 9/yr. $30 (foreign $42). Industrial Fabrics Association International, 345 Cedar St., Ste. 800, St. Paul, MN 55101. TEL 612-222-2508. Ed. Danette Fettig. adv.; tr.lit.; cum.index: 1983-87; circ. 12,000. (reprint service avail.) Indexed: World Text.Abstr.
—BLDSC shelfmark: 4158.934000.
   Description: Case histories, technical papers and industry news related to fabrics and geomembranes used in civil engineering.

677   IT   ISSN 0017-1964
GOMITOLO. (Text in Italian or Spanish) 1963. 5/yr. L.20000($35) Edizioni Moderne Internazionali, Via Burlamacchi, 11, 20135 Milan, Italy. Ed. Anna Maria Pietraccini. adv.; circ. 90,000.

677   IT
GUIDA ALL'INDUSTRIA ITALIANA DELLA MAGLIERIA E DELLA CALZETTERIA. (Text in English, French, German, Italian and Spanish) 1970. a. L.95000. (Italian Association of Knitwear Producers) Gesto s.r.l., Via Cesare Battisti 21, 20122 Milan, Italy. TEL 02-55187581. adv.
   Formerly: Annuario dell'Industria Italiana della Magliera e della Calzetteria.
   Description: Directory of Italian knitwear and hosiery producers and their suppliers.

677.39   CC
GUOWAI SICHOU/FOREIGN SILK. (Text in Chinese) bi-m. Suzhou Sichou Gongxueyuan - Suzhou Institute of Silk Engineering, 14 Xiangmen Lu, Suzhou, Jiangsu 215005, People's Republic of China. TEL 225614. Ed. Wu Rongru.

HABIT; herr- och dammodebranschen. see *CLOTHING TRADE — Fashions*

HALI; the international magazine of fine carpets and textiles. see *ARTS AND HANDICRAFTS*

338.4   II   ISSN 0436-7316
HD9886.I42
HANDBOOK OF THE INDIAN COTTON TEXTILE INDUSTRY. (Text in English) a. Rs.15. Cotton Textiles Export Promotion Council, Engineering Centre 9, 4 Mathew Rd., Bombay, India.

677   UK   ISSN 0144-5871
HIGH PERFORMANCE TEXTILES; an international newsletter. 1980. m. £219 (effective 1992). Elsevier Science Publishers Ltd., Crown House, Linton Rd., Barking, Essex IG11 8JU, England. TEL 081-594-7272. FAX 081-594-5942. TELEX 896950 APPSCI G. (Subscr. in U.S. and Canada to: Elsevier Science Publishing Co., Inc., Box 882, Madison Sq. Sta., New York, NY 10159) Ed. Peter Lennox-Kerr. bk.rev.; stat. (back issues avail.) Indexed: Art & Archaeol.Tech.Abstr., PROMT, Text.Tech.Dig., World Text.Abstr.
   ●Also available online. Vendor(s): DIALOG.
—BLDSC shelfmark: 4307.338700.
   Description: For directors and senior managers responsible for technology, research and development, design, new product development, new ventures or overall corporate strategy.

677   II
HISTORIC TEXTILES OF INDIA. (Text in English) 1972. irreg., vol.4, 1990. $80. Calico Museum of Textiles, Sarabhai Foundation, The Retreat, Shahibag, Ahmedabad 380 004, India. Ed. John Irwin. circ. 500.

HOME ECONOMICS ASSOCIATION OF VICTORIA. NEWSLETTER. see *HOME ECONOMICS*

HOME FASHIONS MAGAZINE. see *INTERIOR DESIGN AND DECORATION — Furniture And House Furnishings*

667   US
HOME TEXTILES INTERNATIONAL. q. Fairchild Publications, Inc., Home Textiles, 7 W. 34th St., 3rd Fl., New York, NY 10001. TEL 212-630-3689. FAX 212-630-3675. Ed. Donna Boyle Swartz. tr.lit.

677   US   ISSN 0195-3184
HOME TEXTILES TODAY; the business and fashion newspaper of the home textiles industry. 1979. 26/yr. $59.95. Cahners Business Newspapers (Subsidiary of: Reed International PLC), Division of Reed Publishing (USA) Inc., 200 S. Main St., Box 2754, High Point, NC 27261. TEL 919-889-0113. FAX 919-841-8256. (Subscr. to: Box 1424, Riverton, NJ 08077) Ed. Warren Shoulberg. adv.; charts; illus.; stat.; circ. 12,069. (tabloid format)
   Description: For the marketing, merchandising and retailing of home textile products.

677   HK
▼**HONG KONG GARMENTS AND ACCESSORIES.** (Text in English) 1990. s-a. $24 (free to qualified personnel). Hong Kong Trade Development Council, 36-39th Fl., Office Tower, Convention Plaza, 1 Harbour Rd., Hong Kong. TEL 584-4333. FAX 824-0249. Ed. Saul Lockhart. adv.; illus.; stat.; circ. 20,000.

HOSIERY AND TEXTILE JOURNAL; monthly review for manufacturers and merchants. see *CLOTHING TRADE*

677   US   ISSN 0018-5396
HD9940.A1
HOSIERY AND UNDERWEAR. (Section 2 of Body Fashions/Intimate Apparel) 1917. m. $25. Avanstar Communications, Inc., 7500 Old Oak Blvd., Cleveland, OH 44130. TEL 216-826-2839. FAX 216-891-2726. (Subscr. to: 1 E. First St., Duluth, MN 55802) Ed. Jill Gerson. adv.; charts; illus.; index; circ. 10,407. (reprint service avail. from UMI) Indexed: Text.Tech.Dig., World Text.Abstr.

677   II
HOSIERY REPORT WEEKLY. (Text in English and Hindi) 1966. 3/m. Rs.250 (foreign £40). Kuldip Kumar Mehan, F-21B, New Qutab Road, Sadar Bazar, Delhi 110 006, India. Shanti Saroup Mehan. adv.; circ. 5,000.
   Formerly: Hosiery (ISSN 0018-5418)

677   US
I N D A ASSOCIATION OF THE NONWOVEN FABRICS INDUSTRY. I N D A - TEC SYMPOSIUM PAPERS. (Former name of issuing body: International Nonwovens and Disposables Association) 1973. a. price varies. I N D A Association of the Nonwoven Fabrics Industry, 1001 Winstead Dr., Ste. 460, Cary, NC 27513. TEL 919-677-0060. FAX 919-677-0211.

677   SZ
I T M F. COUNTRY STATEMENTS. (Text in English) 1977. a. 100 SFr. International Textile Manufacturers Federation - Federation Internationale des Industries Textiles, Am Schanzengraben 29, Postfach, CH-8039 Zurich, Switzerland. TEL 01-2017080. FAX 01-2017134. TELEX 817578. charts; illus.; stat.
   Description: Provides information on the current state of the textile industry in each member country. Data relates general economic situation, textile manufacturing capacities, activities, and trade in textiles.

677   SZ
I T M F DIRECTORY. biennial. free. International Textile Manufacturers Federation, Am Schanzengraben 29, Postfach, CH-8039 Zurich, Switzerland. TEL 01-2017080. FAX 01-2017134. TELEX 817578. Ed. Herwig M. Strolz.
   Formerly: I F C A T I Directory (ISSN 0445-0698)

677   II   ISSN 0970-3497
INDIA. DIRECTORATE OF JUTE DEVELOPMENT. JUTE DEVELOPMENT JOURNAL. (Text and summaries in English) 1938. q. Rs.12. Directorate of Jute Development, c/o Dr. K. Chakravarty, Nizam Palace Campus, 234-4 Acharyya Jagadish Bose Rd., Calcutta 700 020, India. Ed. S. Nath. adv.; bk.rev.; abstr.; charts; illus.; stat.; index; circ. 200. (back issues avail.) Indexed: Abstr.Trop.Agri., Field Crop Abstr., Potato Abstr.
   Formerly: India. Directorate of Jute Development. Jute Bulletin (ISSN 0046-8940)

381   II   ISSN 0970-9800
INDIA. TEXTILES COMMITTEE. CONSUMER PURCHASES OF TEXTILES. (Text in English) 1969. q. Rs.500. Textiles Committee, Market Research Wing, Government of India, Ministry of Textile, Mahalaxmi Engineering Estate, 2nd Fl., Lady Jamshedji Cross Rd. No. 1, Mahlm, Bombay 400 016, India. TELEX 76338 TCI IN. charts; stat.; circ. 200.

677.21   II   ISSN 0019-459X
INDIAN COTTON MILLS FEDERATION JOURNAL. (Text and summaries in English) 1964. m. Rs.100($30) Indian Cotton Mills Federation, Textile Centre, 34 P. d'Mello Rd., Box 1449, Bombay 9, India. TEL 862043. TELEX 011-75426. Ed. C.V. Radhakrishnan. adv.; bk.rev.; stat.; index; circ. 1,300.
—BLDSC shelfmark: 4764.300000.

677   II
INDIAN JOURNAL OF FIBRE & TEXTILE RESEARCH. (Text in English) 1976. q. Rs.125($42) Council of Scientific and Industrial Research, Publications & Information Directorate, Hillside Rd., New Delhi 110 012, India. TEL 11-586301. Ed. R.N. Sharma. Indexed: Abstr.Bull.Inst.Pap.Chem., Art & Archaeol.Tech.Abstr., Chem.Abstr, Cott.& Trop.Fibr.Abstr., Text.Tech.Dig., World Text.Abstr.
   Formerly: Indian Journal of Textile Research (ISSN 0377-8436)

677.39 638   II   ISSN 0445-7722
SF541   CODEN: IJSEAH
INDIAN JOURNAL OF SERICULTURE. (Text in English) 1962. s-a. Rs.25($20) Central Sericultural Research & Training Institute, Srirampuram, Manandavadi Road, Mysore 570 008, India. TEL 568194. TELEX 0864-203-CSRI-IN. Indexed: Biol.Abstr., Curr.Adv.Ecol.Sci., Forest.Abstr., Trop.Oil Seeds Abstr., Weed Abstr.
—BLDSC shelfmark: 4421.150000.
   Description: Documents research findings and the latest innovations in the textile industry.

677.13 676.14   II   ISSN 0073-6562
INDIAN JUTE MILLS ASSOCIATION. ANNUAL SUMMARY OF JUTE AND GUNNY STATISTICS. (Annual supplement to "Monthly Summary") (Text in English) 1955. a. Rs.25. Indian Jute Mills Association, Royal Exchange, 6 Netaji Subhas Rd., Calcutta 1, India. circ. 400.

4620 TEXTILE INDUSTRIES AND FABRICS

677 676   II   ISSN 0073-6570
INDIAN JUTE MILLS ASSOCIATION. LOOM AND SPINDLE STATISTICS. 1941. biennial. Rs.5. Indian Jute Mills Association, Royal Exchange, 6 Netaji Subhas Rd., Calcutta 1, India. circ. 500.

677.39   II   ISSN 0019-6355
INDIAN SILK. (Text in English and Hindi) 1962. m. Rs.60. Central Silk Board, United Mansions, 2nd Fl., 39 M.G. Road, Bangalore 560 001, India. TEL 568194. Ed. V. Balasubramanian. adv.; charts; illus.; mkt.; stat.; tr.lit. **Indexed:** Text.Tech.Dig.

677
INDIAN SYNTHETIC & RAYON. Short title: I S R. (Text in English) 1956. s-a. Rs.100 (free to overseas buyers). Synthetic & Rayon Textiles Export Promotion Council, Resham Bhawan, 78 Veer Nariman Rd., Bombay 400 020, India. FAX 91-22-2048358. TELEX 011-83703 SEPC IN. Ed. O.P. Dhawan. adv.; charts; illus.; stat.; tr.lit.; circ. 3,000.
   Formerly: Indian Silk and Rayon (ISSN 0442-736X)

677   II   ISSN 0537-2666
TS1312
INDIAN TEXTILE ANNUAL & DIRECTORY. (Text in English) 1965. a. $15. Eastland Publications (Private) Ltd., 44 Chittaranjan Ave., Calcutta 700 012, India. TEL 27-3096. Ed. J.R. Dutta. adv.; bk.rev.; charts; illus.; pat.; circ. 5,000.

677   II   ISSN 0970-0870
INDIAN TEXTILE BULLETIN. (Text in English) 1964. q. Rs.41.20($14.85) Ministry of Urban Development, Department of Publication, Civil Lines, Delhi 110 054, India. TEL 11-2517409.

677   II   ISSN 0019-6436
TS1300   CODEN: INTJAV
INDIAN TEXTILE JOURNAL. 1890. m. Rs.120($34) Business Press Private Ltd., Surya Mahal, 5 Burjorji Bharucha Marg, Bombay 400 001, India. Ed. S. Laxminarain. adv.; bk.rev.; abstr.; charts; illus.; index; circ. 5,000. **Indexed:** Anim.Breed.Abstr., Chem.Abstr., Cott.& Trop.Fibr.Abstr., Text.Tech.Dig., World Text.Abstr.
   —BLDSC shelfmark: 4430.000000.

677.21   IT   ISSN 0019-7491
INDUSTRIA COTONIERA. (Supplement avail.: Rapporto sulla Industria Cotoniera Italiana) 1948. 8/yr. L.88000. Istituto per Assistenza e Servizi alle Aziende Tessili s.r.l. (I.A.S.A.T.), Viale Sarca, 223, 20126 Milan, Italy. TEL 02-66103838. FAX 02-66103863. adv.; bk.rev.; charts; illus.; stat.; index; circ. 2,000. **Indexed:** Art & Archaeol.Tech.Abstr., Chem.Abstr., Text.Tech.Dig., World Text.Abstr.

677   AG   ISSN 0019-7742
INDUSTRIA TEXTIL SUD AMERICANA. 1941. bi-m. Arg.$18($5) EDITESA S.A., Avda. Roque Saenz Pena 825, Buenos Aires, Argentina. Ed. Dr. Elio Gabellini. adv.; charts; illus.; mkt.; circ. 2,000. **Indexed:** Chem.Abstr.

677   US   ISSN 0019-8307
INDUSTRIAL FABRIC PRODUCTS REVIEW. 1915. m. $34 (Canada & Mexico $39; elsewhere $90). Industrial Fabrics Association International, 345 Cedar St., Ste. 800, St. Paul, MN 55101. TEL 612-222-2508. Ed. Sue Hagen. adv.; bk.rev.; illus.; tr.lit.; index; circ. 10,000. (back issues avail.) **Indexed:** Text.Tech.Dig., World Text.Abstr.
   —BLDSC shelfmark: 4450.600000.
   Formerly: Canvas Products Review.
   Description: Profiles, product news, how-to, industry news and other information of industrial and technical fabric product manufacturers.

677   US   ISSN 0019-8307
INDUSTRIAL FABRIC PRODUCTS REVIEW BUYER'S GUIDE; the encyclopedia of industrial fabrics. 1976. a. $20. Industrial Fabrics Association International, 345 Cedar St., Ste. 800, St. Paul, MN 55101. TEL 612-222-2508. adv.; circ. 10,000.
   Description: Supply reference for manufacturers of industrial-technical fabric products.

677   FR   ISSN 0019-9176
INDUSTRIE TEXTILE. 1883. 11/yr. 900 F. (includes supplement: Filiere Maille). Editions de l' Industrie Textile, 16 rue Ballu, 75009 Paris, France. TEL 48-74-15-96. FAX 48-74-01-89. TELEX 283 438 F. Ed. Pierre S. Robin. adv.; bk.rev.; abstr.; bibl.; charts; illus.; mkt.; pat.; stat.; index; circ. 6,000. **Indexed:** C.I.S. Abstr., Chem.Abstr., Excerp.Med., Key to Econ.Sci., PROMT, Text.Tech.Dig., World Text.Abstr.
   —BLDSC shelfmark: 4474.000000.
   Incorporates (1936-1982): Teintex (ISSN 0040-2192)

677   GR
INFANSIS - TEXTILE. (Editions in Arabic and Greek) 6/yr. 3 Vasiliou Papa Koropi, Attiki, Greece. Ed. Panagiotis Drakatos. adv.; circ. 8,000.

677   US   ISSN 0733-8244
INSIDE TEXTILES. 1980. s-m. $167 (foreign $197). Point Publishing Co., Inc., Box 1309, Point Pleasant Beach, NJ 08742. TEL 201-295-8258. Ed. Noreen C. Heimbold. bk.rev.

677   GW
INSTITUT FUER TEXTILTECHNIK DER RHEINISCH-WESTFAELISCHEN TECHNISCHEN HOCHSCHULE AACHEN. MITTEILUNGEN. (Text in English, German) 1953. a. DM.50. Institut fuer Textiltechnik der Rheinisch-Westfaelischen Technischen Hochschule Aachen, Eilfschornsteinstr. 18, 5100 Aachen, Germany. TEL 0241-805621. FAX 0241-805631. TELEX 832704. Ed. B. Wulfhorst. circ. 250.

677   II   ISSN 0257-4438
TS1300
INSTITUTION OF ENGINEERS (INDIA). TEXTILE ENGINEERING DIVISION. JOURNAL. (Text in English) 1978. s-a. Rs.40($5) Institution of Engineers (India), Textile Engineering Division, 8 Gokhale Rd., Calcutta 700 020, India. TEL 033-288334. FAX 033-288345. TELEX 0217885 IEIC IN. Ed. K.N. Majumdar. adv.; charts; illus.; index; circ. 2,000.

677   SP   ISSN 0212-6699
INSTITUTO DE INVESTIGACION TEXTIL Y DE COOPERACION INDUSTRIAL. BOLETIN INTEXTER. 1956. 2/yr. 1800 ptas. (foreign ptas. 2,250). Instituto de Investigacion Textil y de Cooperacion Industrial, Colon 15, 08222 Terrassa, Spain. FAX 3437-398272. TELEX 59437 EIDD. Ed. F.J. Carrion. adv.; bk.rev.; illus.; circ. 1,000. **Indexed:** Ind.SST, World Text.Abstr.
   —BLDSC shelfmark: 2207.411000.
   Formerly: Instituto de Investigacion Textil y de Cooperacion Industrial. Boletin (ISSN 0210-251X)

675   RM   ISSN 0253-1119
INSTITUTUL POLITEHNIC "GHEORGHE ASACHI" DIN IASI. BULETINUL. SECTIA VII: TEXTILE, PIELARIE. (Text in English, French, German and Russian) 1946. s-a. exchange basis. Institutul Politehnic "Gheorghe Asachi" din Iasi, Calea 23 August 11, 6600 Jassy, Rumania. TEL 46577. (Subscr. to: Rompresfilatelia, P.O. Box 12-201, Bucharest, Rumania) Ed. Dr. D. Mangeron. adv.; bk.rev.; bibl.; circ. 450. **Indexed:** Appl.Mech.Rev., Chem.Abstr., Math.R., Ref.Zh.
   Formerly: Institutul Politehnic Iasi. Buletinul. Sectia VII: Textile, Pielarie.

677   UK
INTERIOR. (Text in English, French, German) 1965. 3/yr. £86($170) International Textiles Benjamin Dent Ltd., 33 Bedford Pl., London WC1B 5JX, England. TEL 71-637-2211. FAX 71-637-2248. TELEX 8954884 BENDEN. Ed. Nina Hirst. circ. 9,000. (back issues avail.)
   Formerly: International Textiles Interior (ISSN 0954-1438)

667 338.4   US   ISSN 0095-683X
HD9869.N64
INTERNATIONAL DIRECTORY OF THE NONWOVEN FABRICS INDUSTRY. 1970. biennial. price varies. I N D A Association of the Nonwoven Fabrics Industry, 1001 Winstead Dr., Ste. 460, Cary, NC 27513. TEL 919-677-0060. FAX 919-677-0211. Ed. Peggy F. Blake.
   Formerly: Directory for the Nonwoven Fabrics and Disposable Soft Goods Industries (ISSN 0070-5020)

677 667   UK   ISSN 0020-658X
            CODEN: IDBFAT
INTERNATIONAL DYER, TEXTILE PRINTER, BLEACHER AND FINISHER. 1879. m. £45($98) World Textiles Publications, 76 Kirkgate, Bradford, W. Yorks. BD1 1TB, England. Ed. Phil Owen. adv.; bk.rev.; abstr.; illus.; pat.; tr.lit.; circ. 2,391. (also avail. in microform from UMI; reprint service avail. from UMI) **Indexed:** Br.Tech.Ind., Chem.Abstr, PROMT, Text.Tech.Dig., World Text.Abstr.
   —BLDSC shelfmark: 4539.753000.

667 677   IT   ISSN 0074-5898
INTERNATIONAL FEDERATION OF ASSOCIATIONS OF TEXTILE CHEMISTS AND COLORISTS. REPORTS OF CONGRESS. irreg., 11th, 1978, Italy. Associazione Italiana di Chimica Tessile e Coloristica, Via Borgonnovo 11, I-20121 Milan, Italy.

677 546   US   ISSN 1049-801X
INTERNATIONAL FIBER JOURNAL. 1986. bi-m. $20. McMickle Publications, Inc., 2919 Spalding Dr., Atlanta, GA 30350-4628. TEL 404-394-6098. FAX 404-393-0161. Ed. Wilbur Newcomb. circ. 8,000 (controlled).
   Description: For upper and middle management in polymerizers, fiber producers, texturers, nonwovens, and yarn spinning.

677   II   ISSN 0047-0961
INTERNATIONAL PRESS CUTTING SERVICE: JUTE, GUNNY, HESSIAN, BURLAP, COIR. 1967. w. $65. International Press Cutting Service, Box 63, Allahabad 211001, India. Ed. N. Khanna. bk.rev.; index; circ. 1,200. (looseleaf format; also avail. in processed)

677   II   ISSN 0047-1119
INTERNATIONAL PRESS CUTTING SERVICE: TEXTILE NEWS. 1957. w. $65. International Press Cutting Service, Box 63, Allahabad 211001, India. Ed. N. Khanna. bk.rev.; index; circ. 1,200. (looseleaf format; also avail. in processed)

677   SZ
INTERNATIONAL PRODUCTION COST COMPARISON. 1979. biennial. 100 SFr. International Textile Manufacturers Federation, Am Schanzengraben 29, Postfach, CH-8039 Zurich, Switzerland. TEL 01-2017080. FAX 01-2017134. TELEX 817578.
   Description: Focuses on costs of producing yarns as well as spinning and weaving in Brazil, Germany, India, Japan, Korea and the US.

677.39   FR   ISSN 0290-8271
INTERNATIONAL SILK ASSOCIATION. MONTHLY NEWSLETTER. (Text in English, French) 1975. m. membership only. International Silk Association - Association Internationale de la Soie, 34 rue de la Charite, 69002 Lyon, France. TEL 78-42-10-79. FAX 78-37-56-72. TELEX 330-949. bk.rev.; bibl.; illus.; mkt.; stat.; circ. 500.
   Supersedes: International Silk Association. Bulletin (ISSN 0020-8698)

677   SZ
INTERNATIONAL TEXTILE MANUFACTURING. 1960. a. 80 SFr. International Textile Manufacturers Federation, Am Schanzengraben 29, Postfach, CH-8039 Zurich, Switzerland. TEL 01-2017080. FAX 01-2017134. TELEX 817578. **Indexed:** World Text.Abstr.
   Supersedes: Cotton and Allied Textile Industries (ISSN 0574-2315)
   Description: Contains full text of papers presented at annual conference.

677   SP   ISSN 0302-5268
TS1300   CODEN: IITTCS
INVESTIGACION E INFORMACION TEXTIL Y DE TENSIOACTIVOS. (Text and summaries in Spanish; abstracts in English) 1958. q. 3500 ptas. (foreign 4000 ptas.). Consejo Superior de Investigaciones Cientificas (Barcelona), Instituto de Tecnologia Quimica y Textil, Jordi Girona 18-26, 08034 Barcelona, Spain. FAX 93-204-59-04. TELEX 979771 DEBE. Ed. Alberto Barella. adv.; bk.rev.; abstr.; bibl.; circ. 1,750. **Indexed:** Chem.Abstr., Ind.SST, Text.Tech.Dig., World Text.Abstr.

677 RU ISSN 0021-3497
CODEN: IVTTAF
IZVESTIYA VYSSHIKH UCHEBNYKH ZAVEDENII. SERIYA TEKHNOLOGIYA TEKSTIL'NOI PROMYSHLENNOSTI. 1957. bi-m. 26.70 Rub. Ivanovskii Tekstil'nyi Institut, Ivanovo, Russia. charts; index. (tabloid format) **Indexed:** Chem.Abstr., Cott.& Trop.Fibr.Abstr., World Text.Abstr.
—BLDSC shelfmark: 0077.860000.

677 687 US
JEANSFLASH. s-a. Jeanswear Communication, 240 Madison Ave., 12th Fl., New York, NY 10016. TEL 212-689-3462. FAX 212-545-1709.
Description: Covers industry and association developments.

677 SP
JERSEY. 1961. q. 2200 ptas. Prensa Tecnica, S.A., Caspe 118-120, Barcelona 13, Spain. Ed. F. Canet Thomas. adv.; illus.; circ. 5,000.

677 FR ISSN 0021-8197
JOURNAL DU TEXTILE. Abbreviated title: J T. 1964. w. 16 F. per no. Editions Hennessen, 61 rue de Malte, 75541 Paris Cedex 11, France. TEL 1-43-57-21-89. FAX 1-47-00-08-35. Dir. Lucien Abra. adv.; illus.; circ. 20,000. (tabloid format) **Indexed:** Key to Econ.Sci.
Description: Follows news of the textile trade from fabrics, home decoration and store management to fashion trends in ready-to-wear, menswear, childrenswear, sportswear and lingerie.

677.028 UK ISSN 0267-7806
JOURNAL FOR WEAVERS, SPINNERS & DYERS. 1952. q. £10.75 (foreign £13). Association of Guilds of Weavers, Spinners & Dyers, 38 Sandown Dr., Hereford HR4 9LU, England. TEL 0432-59066. Ed.Bd. adv.; bk.rev.; charts; illus.; mkt.; pat.; tr.mk.; circ. 3,000.
—BLDSC shelfmark: 5072.554500.
Former titles: Weavers Journal; Guilds of Weavers, Spinners and Dyers. Quarterly Journal (ISSN 0017-5439)
Description: Provides for interchange of information on the subject, includes technical notes and reviews.

677 698 US ISSN 0093-4658
TS1512 CODEN: JCTFAL
JOURNAL OF COATED FABRICS. 1971. q. $180. Technomic Publishing Co., Inc., 851 New Holland Ave., Box 3535, Lancaster, PA 17604. TEL 717-291-5609. FAX 717-295-4538. TELEX 230 753565 (TECHNOMIC UD). Ed. William C. Smith. bk.rev.; charts; illus.; index; circ. 400. (also avail. in microform from UMI; reprint service avail. from UMI) **Indexed:** Appl.Mech.Rev., Art & Archaeol.Tech.Abstr., Chem.Abstr., Curr.Cont., Eng.Ind., Excerp.Med., Text.Tech.Dig., World Text.Abstr.
—BLDSC shelfmark: 4958.794000.
Formerly: Journal of Coated Fibrous Materials (ISSN 0047-2298)
Refereed Serial

JOURNAL OF SERICULTURAL SCIENCE OF JAPAN/NIPPON SANSHIGAKU ZASSHI. see BIOLOGY — Entomology

JOURNAL OF THE COIN LAUNDRY AND DRYCLEANING INDUSTRY. see CLEANING AND DYEING

677.13 BG
JUTE AND JUTE FABRICS - BANGLADESH. (Text in English) 1975. m. Tk.30($5) Bangladesh Jute Research Institute, Sher-e-Banglanagar, Dhaka 7, Bangladesh. Ed. Harun-Ur-Rashid. adv.; charts; stat.; circ. 500. **Indexed:** Art & Archaeol.Tech.Abstr., Biol.Abstr., Chem.Abstr., Text.Tech.Dig.
Formerly (until Jan. 1975): Jute and Jute Fabrics - Pakistan (ISSN 0022-7099)

677 GW ISSN 0047-3405
KETTENWIRK-PRAXIS. English edition (ISSN 0170-401X) (Text in German; summaries in English, French) 1967. q. DM.55 (with English DM.88; with French DM.215). Karl Mayer GmbH, Postfach 1120, 6053 Obertshausen, Germany. TEL 06104-402-0. FAX 06104-43574. TELEX 0410-174. Ed. Rolf Hufschlaeger. adv.; bk.rev.; film rev.; abstr.; bibl.; illus.; pat.; cum.index; circ. 2,800. **Indexed:** Text.Tech.Dig., World Text.Abstr.
—BLDSC shelfmark: 5090.610000.

677.3 US ISSN 0084-1234
KNITOVATIONS. 1939. s-a. $20. Woolknit Associates, Inc., 267 Fifth Ave., Ste. 806, New York, NY 10016. TEL 212-683-7785. Ed. Mildred Faulk. adv.; circ. 5,660. **Indexed:** Text.Tech.Dig.
Formerly (until 1952): Woolknit Annual.

677 UK
KNITTING & HABERDASHERY: THE NEEDLECRAFTS REVIEW. 1959. bi-m. £18. Arthur S. Damery, Ed. & Pub., Marshalls Chambers, 80A South St., Romford, Essex RM1 1RX, England. FAX 0708-745795. adv.; bk.rev.; circ. 5,000. (back issues avail.)
Former titles: Knitting and Haberdashery Review; Knitting Wool Review.

677 UK ISSN 0266-8394
KNITTING INTERNATIONAL. 1894. m. £44 (foreign £48). Ferry Pickering Publishers Ltd., Eastern Boulevard, Leicester LE2 7BN, England. TEL 0533-548271. FAX 0533-470194. TELEX 341088. Ed. John Gibbon. adv.; bk.rev.; circ. 6,000. **Indexed:** Br.Tech.Ind., Text.Tech.Dig., World Text.Abstr.
—BLDSC shelfmark: 5100.364000.
Formerly: Hosiery Trade Journal.

677 746 GW ISSN 0177-4875
KNITTING TECHNIQUE. German edition: Wirkerei- und Strickerei-Technik (ISSN 0043-6097); Spanish edition: Punto Tecnica y Moda (ISSN 0724-3847) 1979. bi-m. DM.104. Meisenbach GmbH, Hainstr. 18, Postfach 2069, 8600 Bamberg, Germany. TEL 0951-861-134. FAX 0951-861-170. TELEX 662844-MEIBA-D. Ed. Lothar Rauscher. adv.; bk.rev.; abstr.; charts; illus.; pat.; index; circ. 4,000. **Indexed:** Text.Tech.Dig., World Text.Abstr.
Formerly: W S T Knitting Technik (ISSN 0173-4415)

KRUL'S MAANDBLAD VOOR STOOM- EN CHEMISCHE WASSERIJEN, VERVERIJEN EN WASSALONS. see CLEANING AND DYEING

677 IT
LANIERA. 1887. m. L.20000. Editoriale Laniera s.r.l., Via Contra Mure di Porta Castello 9, 36100 Vicenza, Italy. Ed. Felice Dall'Ara. adv.; bk.rev.; index; circ. 2,300. **Indexed:** Text.Tech.Dig.

677 US
LATIN AMERICAN TEXTILE INDUSTRY DIRECTORY. (Text in English, Portuguese, Spanish) 1985. a. $150. Aquino Productions, Box 15760, Stamford, CT 06901. TEL 203-325-3138. Ed. Andres C. Aquino. adv.

677 AU ISSN 0024-0907
TS1300 CODEN: LEBEAW
LENZINGER BERICHTE. (Text and summaries in English and German) 1953. s-a. S.300. Lenzing AG, A-4860 Lenzing, Austria. FAX 07672-7251175. TELEX 026-606-LENFA-A. Ed. Herbert Zdiarsky. adv.; charts; illus.; circ. 2,000. **Indexed:** Abstr.Bull.Inst.Pap.Chem., Chem.Abstr., INIS Atomind., Text.Tech.Dig., World Text.Abstr.
—BLDSC shelfmark: 5182.500000.

LIVESTOCK, MEAT AND WOOL MARKET NEWS. see AGRICULTURE — Poultry And Livestock

677 IT ISSN 0024-9947
MAGLIE CALZE INDUSTRIA. 1967. bi-m. L.90000. (Italian Association of Knitwear Producers) Gesto s.r.l., Via Cesare Battisti 21, 20122 Milan, Italy. TEL 02-55187581. Ed. Eugenio Faiella. adv.; bk.rev.; abstr.; bibl.; illus.; pat.; stat.; tr.lit.; index. **Indexed:** World Text.Abstr.
Description: Technical and economic news for the knitting industry.

677 HU ISSN 0025-0309
TS1300
MAGYAR TEXTILTECHNIKA. 1948. m. $97. (Textilipari Muszaki es Tudomanyos Egyesulet) Lapkiado Vallalat, Lenin korut 9-11, 1073 Budapest 7, Hungary. TEL 222-408. (Subscr. to: Kultura, P.O. Box 149, H-1389 Budapest, Hungary) Eds. Pal Fusti, Sandor Gonci. adv.; bk.rev.; charts; illus.; circ. 1,000. **Indexed:** Abstr.Bull.Inst.Pap.Chem., Art & Archaeol.Tech.Abstr., Chem.Abstr., Cott.& Trop.Fibr.Abstr., Text.Tech.Dig., World Text.Abstr.
—BLDSC shelfmark: 5345.600000.

677.39 II ISSN 0377-7537
TS1640 CODEN: MMTIBW
MAN-MADE TEXTILES IN INDIA. (Text in English) 1957. m. Rs.100($15) or £10. Silk and Art Silk Mills' Research Association, Sasmira, Sasmira Marg, Worli, Bombay 400 025, India. TEL 22-493-5351. Ed. V.V. Patki. adv.; bk.rev.; abstr.; charts; illus.; stat.; index; circ. 1,500. **Indexed:** Chem.Abstr., Indian Sci.Ind., Text.Tech.Dig., World Text.Abstr.
—BLDSC shelfmark: 5361.032000.
Formerly: Silk and Rayon Industries of India (ISSN 0037-525X)
Description: Trade magazine about silk and silk mills industry.

MARINE STORES MERCHANDISING; magazine of boating accessory, parts & service merchandising. see SPORTS AND GAMES — Boats And Boating

677 US ISSN 0885-9949
MARINE TEXTILES. 1986. 9/yr. $28. R C M Enterprises, Inc., Twelve Oaks Center, Ste. 922, Wayzata, MN 55391. TEL 612-473-5088. FAX 612-473-7068. Ed. Mara Sidney. adv.; index; circ. 5,500. (back issues avail.)
Description: Covers fabric products and furnishings used in boating.

677 US
MARINE TEXTILES BUYERS' GUIDE. 1986. a. $15. R C M Enterprises, Inc., Twelve Oaks Center, Ste. 922, Wayzata, MN 55391. TEL 612-473-5088. FAX 612-473-7068. Ed. Mara Sidney. adv.; bk.rev.; index; circ. 5,500.
Description: Covers marine textiles, provides information and ideas about textiles used in boating.

677 GW ISSN 0341-0781
TS1300 CODEN: MTIRDL
MELLIAND TEXTILBERICHTE/MELLIAND TEXTILE REPORTS. (Editions in English, German) 1920. m. DM.240 (with English supplement DM.480). Melliand Textilberichte GmbH, Rohrbacherstr. 76, 6900 Heidelberg, Germany. adv.; bk.rev.; abstr.bibl.; circ. 7,591. **Indexed:** Abstr.Bull.Inst.Pap.Chem., Art & Archaeol.Tech.Abstr., Chem.Abstr., Cott.& Trop.Fibr. Abstr., Curr.Cont., Excerp.Med., INIS Atomind., PROMT, Text.Tech.Dig., W.R.C.Inf., World Text.Abstr.
—BLDSC shelfmark: 5546.020050.
Former titles (until 1976): Melliand Textilberichte International (ISSN 0375-9350); (until 1969): Melliand Textilberichte (ISSN 0025-8989) And (until 1923): Textil uber Wissenschaft (ISSN 0936-5575).

677 US ISSN 0198-7275
TS1300
MELLIAND TEXTILBERICHTE (ENGLISH EDITION)/INTERNATIONAL TEXTILE REPORTS. 1972. m. $295. Ralph McElroy Co., Inc., Journals Division, Box 5776, Austin, TX 78763. charts; stat. **Indexed:** Text.Tech.Dig., W.R.C.Inf., World Text.Abstr.

MENSWEAR RETAILERS OF AMERICA. BULLETIN. see CLOTHING TRADE

MENSWEAR RETAILERS OF AMERICA. FINANCIAL AND OPERATIONS BULLETIN. see CLOTHING TRADE

677 US
MILL REPORT. 1976. irreg. Platt Saco Lowell, Drawer 2327, Greenville, SC 29602. TEL 803-859-3211. charts; illus.

677 US
MILLWORK MANUFACTURING.* 1985. bi-m. $15 per no. Associations Publications, Inc., Box 640, Collierville, TN 38027-9986. TEL 901-853-7470. Ed. Kimberly K. Ford. adv.; circ. 6,620.

677 SZ
MITTEX: MITTEILUNGEN UEBER TEXTILINDUSTRIE; Schweizerische Fachschrift fuer die gesamte Textilindustrie. vol. 80, 1973. m. 62 SFr. Schweizerische Vereinigung von Textilfachleuten, Lindenweg 7, 8122 Pfaffhausen-Zurich, Switzerland. Ed. Anthony U. Trinkler. adv.; bk.rev.; charts; illus.; mkt.; pat.; tr.lit.; index; circ. 3,000. **Indexed:** Chem.Abstr., Excerp.Med., Text.Tech.Dig.
Formerly: Mitteilungen ueber Textilindustrie (ISSN 0026-6949)

DER MODELLHUT. see CLOTHING TRADE

TEXTILE INDUSTRIES AND FABRICS

677.4   II   ISSN 0377-1490
HD9929.2.I5
MODERN FIBRES. (Text in English) vol. 4, 1973. q. Rs.20. Association of Man-Made Fibre Industry, Resham Bhavan, 78 Veer Nariman Rd., Bombay 400020, India. Ed. K.V. Ramaswamy. charts, stat.

677   BE
MODIS. (Editions in Dutch, French) 1949. 10/yr. 1800 BEF($24) (Nationaal Verbond der Textieldetaillisten - National Association of Tailors and Retailers) R. Soenens, Ed. & Pub., 8 Spastraat, 1040 Brussels, Belgium. TEL 02-2309354. adv.; charts; illus.; stat.; circ. 10,000.
Formerly: Navetex (ISSN 0028-1514)

677 630   AT
THE MOHAIR BULLETIN. (Supplement avail.) 1983. 5/yr. membership. Angora Mohair Breeders of Australia Ltd., P.O. Box 1104, Fyshwick, A.C.T. 2609, Australia. TEL 062-391-244. FAX 062-391-270. adv.; circ. 3,200.
Former titles (until Dec. 1991): Australian Angora Mohair Journal; Australasian Angora Mohair Journal.
Description: Disseminates current Angora goat and Mohair information to members.

MONTHLY COTTON LINTERS REVIEW. see
AGRICULTURE — Agricultural Economics

677   AG
MUNDO TEXTIL ARGENTINO. 1962. m. 25 de Mayo 267-218, Buenos Aires, Argentina. Ed. Leonor F. Breitman. adv.; circ. 2,800.

NATIONAL COTTONSEED PRODUCTS ASSOCIATION. TRADING RULES. see *AGRICULTURE — Feed, Flour And Grain*

677   AT
NATIONAL COUNCIL OF WOOL SELLING BROKERS OF AUSTRALIA. NEWS BULLETIN. 1956. m. free. National Council of Wool Selling Brokers of Australia, 1st Fl., Wool Exchange House, 530 Little Collins St., Melbourne, Vic. 3000, Australia.

677   TZ
NATIONAL TEXTILE CORPORATION. ANNUAL REPORT AND ACCOUNTS. (Text in English) 1974. a. National Textile Corporation, Directorate of Planning and Finance, Box 9531, Dar es Salaam, Tanzania. adv.; circ. 500.

338.4   JA   ISSN 0910-8505
NIHON BOSEKI GEPPO/JAPAN SPINNERS' ASSOCIATION. MONTHLY REPORT. (Text in Japanese) 1947. m. 10200 Yen. Japan Institute of Cotton Textile Technology and Economy, Mengyo Kaikan, 5-8, 2-chome, Bingo-machi, Chuo-ku, Osaka-shi, Japan. TEL 06-203-5161. FAX 06-229-1590. TELEX 06-522-2230-SPINAS-J. Ed. Shodo Okuda. adv.; circ. 5,000.
—BLDSC shelfmark: 5946.316000.

677 676   US   ISSN 0163-4429
HD9869.N64   CODEN: NOINDJ
NONWOVENS INDUSTRY; the international magazine for the nonwoven fabrics and disposable soft goods industry. 1970. m. $48. Rodman Publications, Inc., 17 S. Franklin Tpk., Box 555, Ramsey, NJ 07446. TEL 201-825-2552. FAX 201-825-0553. TELEX 550302. Ed. Michael Jacobsen. adv.; bk.rev.; charts; illus.; pat.; stat.; tr.lit.; index; circ. 11,000. Indexed: Abstr.Bull.Inst.Pap.Chem., Chem.Abstr., Paper & Bd.Abstr., PROMT, Text.Tech.Dig., World Text.Abstr.
—BLDSC shelfmark: 6117.343000.
Former titles (until 1977): Formed Fabrics Industry (ISSN 0163-4399); Nonwovens and Disposable Soft Goods; Disposable Soft Goods (ISSN 0046-0362)

677   US   ISSN 1053-9832
CODEN: NMFRE3
NONWOVENS MARKETS AND FIBER STRUCTURES REPORT. 1986. s-m. $439. Miller Freeman, Inc. (Subsidiary of: United Newspapers), 600 Harrison St., San Francisco, CA 94107. TEL 415-905-2200. FAX 415-905-2232. TELEX 278273. Ed. Lydia Cain.

677 608.7   US
▼**NONWOVENS PATENT NEWS.** 1990. m. $857. D.K. Smith, Ed. & Pub., 3112 E. Hampton Ave., Mesa, AZ 85204. TEL 602-924-0813. FAX 602-924-6966.
Description: Contains articles, patent abstracts, and diagrams of U.S., European and Japanese patents that affect the nonwoven textile industry. Includes polymers, films, tissues, processes, equipment, converted products, and related items.

677   UK
NONWOVENS REPORT INTERNATIONAL. 1971. m. plus a. supplement. $127. Texpress, Merridale House, Mauldeth Road, Stockport, Cheshire SK4 3NT, England. TEL 061-432-1005. Ed. Derek T. Ward. bk.rev.; charts; pat.; stat.

677   NO   ISSN 0029-2168
TS1300
NORSK TEKSTILTIDENDE. 1920. m. NOK 150($30) in Norway; elsewhere NOK 180. Norsk Tekoinstitutt - Norwegian Textile Institute, P.B.4298 Nygaardstangen, Lars Hillelsgt. 34, 5028 Bergen, Norway. TEL 05-32 72 40. FAX 05-310609. Ed. Eva Bjoemdal. adv.; bk.rev.; illus.; stat.; circ. 1,300. Indexed: World Text.Abstr.
Description: Prints information of interest to those concerned with the textile and clothing industries.

677   IT   ISSN 0391-6448
NUOVA SELEZIONE TESSILE; mensile di tecnologie e sviluppi di fibre filati filatura ritorcitura tessitura nontessuti. (Supplement avail.: Nuova Selezione Tessile News) (Text in Italian) 1961; N.S. 1989. m. L.70000($120) Nuove Tecniche Editoriali S.r.l., Via San Siro 27, 20149 Milan, Italy. TEL 02-4812213. FAX 02-48193425. TELEX 325043 NTEETP I. Ed. Tosca Bertolini. adv.; bk.rev.; bibl.; charts; illus.; index; circ. 6,500. (back issues avail.) Indexed: World Text.Abstr.
—BLDSC shelfmark: 6184.920000.
Formerly: Selezione Tessile (ISSN 0392-9809)
Description: Features articles on the textile industry. Includes articles on textile texture, color, machinery and production.

677   FI   ISSN 0029-6813
NYKYTEKSTIILI. 1954. m. FIM 510. Nykytekstiili Oy, Liisankatu 27 A 7, 00170 Helsinki 17, Finland. TEL 358-0-170028. FAX 358-0-135-5028. Ed. Monica Koskenranta. adv.; bk.rev.; illus.; mkt.; circ. 6,600. (back issues avail.)

677.028 658   US
NYLON FILAMENT & POLYESTER FILAMENT GROWTH. 1983. triennial. $9,800. Statistikon Corp., Box 246, E. Norwich, NY 11732. TEL 516-922-0882. FAX 516-624-3145. Ed. Jordan P. Yale.

677   UK   ISSN 0309-2097
O E REPORT. 1976. bi-m. £50($100) (foreign £55($110)). Technical Industrial Services, 1 London Pl., New Mills, Stockport SK12 4ER, England. TEL 0663-742005. FAX 0663-747657. Ed. Peter Lennox-Kerr. bk.rev.; charts; illus.; circ. 450.

677   AU   ISSN 0029-9545
OESTERREICHISCHE TEXTIL-MITTEILUNGEN;* Unabhaengige Fachzeitung fuer die gesamte Textilwirtschaft. 1965. w. S.240. Verlag fuer Wirtschaftspraxis, St.-Julien-Strasse 25, Postfach 255, 5021 Salzburg, Austria. Ed. Hans M. Wueschner. adv.; bk.rev.

677   AU
OESTERREICHISCHE TEXTIL ZEITUNG. w. S.440. Johann L. Bondi und Sohn, Industriestr. 2, A-2380 Perchtoldsdorf, Austria. Ed. Franz Bondi. adv.

677   BE
OFFICIEL DES TEXTILES. (Text in French) q. 38 rue de l'Autonomie, 1070 Brussels, Belgium. adv.; circ. 10,000.

646 677   FR
OFFICIEL DES TEXTILES (HABILLEMENT). s-a. 540 F. Publications Mandel, L'Edison, 43 bd. Vauban, 78182 St-Quentin-en-Yvelines Cedex, France. TEL 1-30-64-90-80. FAX 1-30-64-79-15. Ed. Charles Mandel. adv.; illus.

677   FR   ISSN 0040-5221
OFFICIEL DU PRET A PORTER. no. 82, 1976. q. 440 F. Publications Mandel, L'Edison, 43 bd. Vauban, France. TEL 1-30-64-90-80. FAX 1-30-64-79-15. Ed. Charles Mandel. adv.; illus.

PAKISTAN CENTRAL COTTON COMMITTEE. AGRICULTURAL SURVEY REPORT. see
AGRICULTURE — Crop Production And Soil

PAKISTAN CENTRAL COTTON COMMITTEE. TECHNOLOGICAL BULLETIN. SERIES A. see
AGRICULTURE — Crop Production And Soil

PAKISTAN CENTRAL COTTON COMMITTEE. TECHNOLOGICAL BULLETIN. SERIES B. see
AGRICULTURE — Crop Production And Soil

677   PK
PAKISTAN TEXTILE. (Text in English) 1977. q. Rs.40. All Pakistan Textile Mills Association, Mohammadi House, 3rd Fl., I.I. Chundrigar Rd., Karachi 2, Pakistan. Indexed: World Text.Abstr.

677   PK   ISSN 0048-2757
PAKISTAN TEXTILE JOURNAL. (Text in English) 1950. m. Rs.300($45) Mazhar Yusuf, 309, Shaheen Super Market, Kehkashan Clifton, Karachi, Pakistan. TELEX 25484-ITA-PK. Ed. S.M. Asim. adv.; bk.rev. Indexed: Art & Archaeol.Tech.Abstr., Chem.Abstr., Text.Tech.Dig.

PHILADELPHIA COLLEGE OF TEXTILES & SCIENCE. PORTFOLIO. see *COLLEGE AND ALUMNI*

677 746.92   SP
PINKER MODA. 1960. 11/yr. $120. Ediciones Tecnicas Doria, Avda. Puerta del Angel 7, Sobreat. A y B, 08002 Barcelona, Spain. FAX 3-3011105. Ed. Francisco Doria. adv.; bk.rev.; bibl.; illus.; stat.; tr.lit.; circ. 12,000 (controlled).

677.21   GR   ISSN 0032-0234
PIRAIKI-PATRAIKI. 1955. q. free. Piraiki-Patraiki Cotton Manufacturing Co. Inc., Dragatsaniou 8, 105 59 Athens, Greece. Ed. Haris Makrykostas. adv.; bk.rev.; charts; illus.; circ. 10,000.

677   US
PLATT SACO LOWELL REPLACEMENT PARTS NEWS.* vol.17, 1976. irreg. free to qualified personnel. Platt Saco Lowell, Replacement Parts Center, P.O. Drawer 2327, Greenville, SC 29602. TEL 803-859-3211. Ed. L.H. Irby. illus.; circ. 3,000. (tabloid format)

677   PL   ISSN 0076-0331
POLITECHNIKA LODZKA. ZESZYTY NAUKOWE. WLOKIENNICTWO. (Text in Polish; summaries in English and Russian) 1954. irreg. price varies. Wydawnictwo Politechniki Lodzkiej, Ul. Wolczanska 219, 93-085 Lodz, Poland. (Dist. by: Ars Polona-Ruch, Krakowskie Przedmiescie 7, Warsaw, Poland) Ed. Waldemar Kobza. circ. 186. Indexed: Chem.Abstr., Text.Tech.Dig, World Text.Abstr.
—BLDSC shelfmark: 9512.320900.
Description: Spinning technology, synthetic fibers technology, weaving technology and fiber science.

677   PL
PRZEGLAD WLOKIENNICZY PLUS TECHNIK WLOKIENNICZY. (Text in Polish; summaries in English) 1992. m. $61. (Stowarzyszenie Wlokiennikow Polskich) Wydawnictwo Czasopism i Ksiazek Technicznych SIGMA - NOT, Ul. Biala 4, P.O. Box 1004, 00-950 Warsaw, Poland. (Dist. by: SIGMA NOT Ltd., Ul. Bartycka 20, 00-716 Warsaw, Poland) Ed. Jerzy Zakrzewski. adv.; bk.rev.; charts; illus.; pat.; stat.; circ. 1,050. Indexed: Abstr.Bull.Inst.Pap.Chem., Chem.Abstr, Text.Tech.Dig., World Text.Abstr.
Formed by the merger of (1947-1992): Przeglad Wlokienniczy (ISSN 0033-2410); (1929-1992): Technik Wlokienniczy (ISSN 0492-4851)
Description: Covers textile industry, technology and machinery.

677.13   BG
QUARTERLY SUMMARY OF JUTE GOODS STATISTICS.* (Text in English) 1955. q. Tk.72. (Bangladesh Jute Industries Corp.) Bangladesh Jute Association, BJA Bldg., 137 Banga Bandhu Rd., P.O. Box 59, Narayanganj, Dhaka, Bangladesh.
Formerly: Pakistan Jute Association. Monthly Summary of Jute Goods Statistics (ISSN 0027-0601)

677.2   IT
RAPPORTO SULLA INDUSTRIA COTONIERA ITALIANA. (Supplement to: Industria Cotoniera) a. free. Istituto per Assistenza e Servizi alle Aziende Tessili s.r.l. (I.A.S.A.T.), Viale Sarca, 223, 20126 Milan, Italy. TEL 02-66103838. FAX 02-66103863.

677 SP ISSN 0300-9718
RM1 CODEN: IJCPB5
REVISTA DE QUIMICA TEXTIL. 1966. q. $4000.
Asociacion Espanola de Quimicos y Coloristas
Textiles, Gran Via, 670, 6, 08010 Barcelona, Spain.
Ed. C. Schneegluth. adv.; bk.rev.; charts; illus.; circ.
1,200. **Indexed:** Chem.Abstr., Ind.SST, World
Text.Abstr.
—BLDSC shelfmark: 7870.300000.

677 BL ISSN 0035-0524
REVISTA TEXTIL. 1930. 6/yr. $80. (Primeira Escola de
Tecelagem) R. da Silva Haydu & Cia. Ltda., Rua
Parana 136, P.O. Box 10 675, Sao Paulo, Brazil.
TEL 011-270-9066. FAX 011-2792409. TELEX
1124187. (Co-sponsor: Associacao de Tecnicos de
Tecido Brasileiros) Ed. Ricardo Haydu. adv.; bk.rev.;
circ. 25,000.

677 UA
SANAET EL-NASSIG/INDUSTRIE TEXTILE. (Text in Arabic,
English and French) m. 5 rue de l'Archeveche,
Alexandria, Egypt. Ed. Phillipe Colas.

667.028 IT ISSN 0393-652X
CODEN: SCTIEV
SELEZIONE CHIMICA TINTORIA; bimestrale di tecnologie
e sviluppi nella tintura stampa finissaggio di tessuti e
maglieria. (Text in English and Italian) 1986. 6/yr.
L.45000($75) Nuove Tecniche Editoriali S.r.l., Via
San Siro, 27, 20149 Milan, Italy. TEL 02-4812213.
FAX 02-48193425. TELEX 325043 NTEETP I. Eds.
Maria Grazia Guzzinati, Fabio Viviani. adv.; bk.rev.;
circ. 5,500. (back issues avail.)
Description: Covers the industry of dyeing and
textiles. Shows the various machinery on the market
today and also examines various fabrics, and the
market of these fabrics.

677 JA ISSN 0037-2064
SEN-I KOGYO ZASSHI/TEXTILE REVIEW; boshokukai.
(Text in Japanese) 1909. 5/yr. 1000 Yen per no.
Boshoku-Zasshisha - Textile Journal and Book Pub.
Co., 7-9, Ohnodai 1-chome, Osakasayama-si 589,
Japan. Ed. Ken-ichi Uno. adv.; bk.rev.; abstr.; bibl.;
charts; illus.; pat.; stat.; index; circ. 3,400. (also
avail. in microform) **Indexed:** Chem.Abstr.

677 JA ISSN 0371-0580
TS1300
SEN'I KIKAI GAKKAISHI. English edition: Textile
Machinery Society of Japan. Journal (ISSN
0040-5043) (Text in Japanese) 1948-1965; N.S.
1972. m. 22,590 Yen. Textile Machinery Society of
Japan - Nihon Sen'i Kikai Gakkai, Osaka Science &
Technology Center Bldg., Utsubo Koen, 8-4
Utsubo-Hon-machi 1-chome, Nishi-ku, Osaka 550,
Japan. TEL 06-443-4691. Ed. Z. Maekawa. circ.
8,000. **Indexed:** JTA, Text.Tech.Dig., World
Text.Abstr.
—BLDSC shelfmark: 4908.499000.
 First series (ISSN 0285-905X) was superseded
by: Sen'i Kikai Gakkai Ronbunshi (Textile Machinery
Society of Japan. Proceedings) (ISSN 0040-5051);
and Sen'i Kogaku (Textile Machinery Society of
Japan. Transactions) (ISSN 0040-506X); which
merged in 1972 to form new series.

677 JA ISSN 0037-2072
CODEN: SESKB9
**SEN'I SEIHIN SHOHI KAGAKU/JAPAN RESEARCH
ASSOCIATION FOR TEXTILE END-USES. JOURNAL.**
(Text in Japanese; summaries in English) 1960. m.
18460 Yen. Japan Research Association for Textile
End-Uses - Nihon Sen'i Seihin Shohi Kagakkai, Rm.
No. 201, Yoshin Ogimachi City Heights, 11-5,
Doshin 2-chome, Kita-ku, Osaka 530, Japan.
FAX 81-6-358-1442. Ed. Seiei Tajimi. adv.; bk.rev.;
charts; illus.; tr.lit.; index; circ. 6,000. **Indexed:** Art &
Archaeol.Tech.Abstr., Chem.Abstr., JTA,
Text.Tech.Dig., World Text.Abstr.
—BLDSC shelfmark: 4805.800000.

677.39 UK ISSN 0266-0822
SERICA. 1970. s-m. £35. Silk Association of Great
Britain, c/o Rheinbergs Ltd., Morley Rd., Tonbridge
TN9 1RN, England. TEL 0732-351357.
FAX 0732-770217. TELEX 95311. circ. 150
(controlled).
Description: Covers all aspects of silk and silk
production.

677.028 DK ISSN 0108-0458
SERIGRAFEN. 1978. q. Dansk Serigraf Forening,
Oesterbrogade 72, 2100 Copenhagen OE,
Denmark. illus.

677 IT
LA SETA. (Text in English or Italian; summaries in
English, French, Italian) 1931. 3/yr. L.60000
(foreign L.100000). Stazione Sperimentale per la
Seta, Via G. Colombo 81, 20133 Milan, Italy.
TEL 02 235047. FAX 02-235047. Ed. Bruno
Marcandalli. adv.; bk.rev.; abstr.; bibl.; charts; illus.;
stat.; circ. 1,000. (back issues avail.)
Description: Includes scientific and technological
reports concerned with silk, protein, synthetic fibers
and textiles.

677 CC ISSN 1001-2044
**SHANGHAI FANGZHI KEJI/SHANGHAI TEXTILE SCIENCE
AND TECHNOLOGY.** (Text in Chinese) bi-m. Shanghai
Fangzhi Kexue Yanjiuyuan - Shanghai Institute of
Textile Science and Technology, 545 Lanzhou Lu,
Shanghai 200082, People's Republic of China.
TEL 5461341. Ed. Gu Boyuan.

SHEEP! MAGAZINE; published for practical sheep
farmers and ranchers. see AGRICULTURE — Poultry
And Livestock

**SHINSHU UNIVERSITY. FACULTY OF TEXTILE SCIENCE
AND TECHNOLOGY. JOURNAL. SERIES A: BIOLOGY.**
see BIOLOGY

**SHINSHU UNIVERSITY. FACULTY OF TEXTILE SCIENCE
AND TECHNOLOGY. JOURNAL. SERIES C: CHEMISTRY.**
see ENGINEERING — Chemical Engineering

746 JA ISSN 0583-0664
**SHINSHU UNIVERSITY. FACULTY OF TEXTILE SCIENCE
AND TECHNOLOGY. JOURNAL. SERIES D: ARTS.** (Text
in Japanese and European languages; summaries in
English) 1956. irreg. exchange basis. Shinshu
University, Faculty of Textile Science and Technology
- Shinshu Daigaku Sen'i Gakubu, 3-15-1 Tokida,
Ueda, Nagano 386, Japan.

SHUTTLE CRAFT GUILD. MONOGRAPHS. see
NEEDLEWORK

677 667 US ISSN 0049-0423
TT848
SHUTTLE, SPINDLE & DYEPOT. 1969. q. $25.
Handweaver's Guild of America, 120 Mountain Ave.,
Bloomfield, CT 06002. TEL 203-242-3577. Ed.
Bobbi Miller. adv.; bk.rev.; illus.; circ. 13,000. (also
avail. in microform from UMI; reprint service avail.
from UMI) **Indexed:** Art & Archaeol.Tech.Abstr., Art
Ind., Ind.How To Do It (1978-), MELSA, Pinpointer,
Text.Tech.Dig.
—BLDSC shelfmark: 8271.000000.

677.39 CC ISSN 1001-7003
SICHOU/SILK. (Text in Chinese) m. Zhongguo Sichou
Xuehui, 121 Moganshan Lu, Hangzhou, Zhejiang
310011, People's Republic of China. TEL 881769.
Ed. Sun Jinhui.

677.39 CC ISSN 1004-1265
SICHUAN SICHOU/SICHUAN SILK. (Text in Chinese)
1979. q. $16. (Sichuansheng Sichou Gongye
Yanjiusuo - Sichuan Silk Manufacturing Research
Institute) Sichuan Sichou Bianjibu, 33 Jinxianqiao
Xiajie, Chengdu, Sichuan 610031, People's Republic
of China. TEL 668534.

677.39 382 II
SILK EXPORT BULLETIN. 1982. bi-m. (Central Silk
Board) Bangalore Printing and Publishing Co. Ltd.,
88 Mysore Rd., Bangalore 560 001, India. Ed. N.
Nataraja. charts; illus.; stat.

677 JA ISSN 0037-9875
CODEN: SENGA5
**SOCIETY OF FIBER SCIENCE AND TECHNOLOGY, JAPAN.
JOURNAL/SEN'I GAKKAISHI.*** (Text in Japanese;
summaries in English) 1944. m. $76. Society of
Fiber Science and Technology - Sen'i Gakkai, c/o
Japan Publications Trading Co., Box 5030, Tokyo
International, Tokyo 100-31, Japan. Ed. Toshiyuki
Uryu. adv.; abstr.; bibl.; illus.; circ. 5,000. **Indexed:**
Art & Archaeol.Tech.Abstr., ASCA, Chem.Abstr.,
Excerp.Med., JTA, Text.Tech.Dig., World Text.Abstr.
—BLDSC shelfmark: 3914.610000.

TEXTILE INDUSTRIES AND FABRICS 4623

677.3 SA
**SOUTH AFRICA. DIVISION OF TEXTILE TECHNOLOGY.
ANNUAL REPORT.** (Text in Afrikaans, English) 1954.
a. free. Division of Textile Technology, Box 1124,
Port Elizabeth 6000, South Africa.
FAX 041-53-2325. TELEX 24-5183. Ed. P. Horn.
bibl.; charts; illus.; circ. 1,200.
 Former titles: Textile and Fibre Programme.
Division of Processing and Chemical Manufacturing
Technology. Annual Report (ISSN 0560-9941) &
South African Wool and Textile Research Institute.
Annual Report.

677 US ISSN 0038-4607
SOUTHERN TEXTILE NEWS. 1945. w. $15. Mullen
Publications, Inc. (Charlotte), Box 668926,
Charlotte, NC 28266. TEL 704-394-5111. Ed.
Marjorie T. Richardson. adv.; illus.; mkt.; stat.; circ.
7,200. (tabloid format; also avail. in microfilm)
Indexed: Text.Tech.Dig.

677 UK ISSN 0950-5024
THE STOCKLISTS; for carpet and floorcovering buyers.
1975. m. £20.50. Mayville Publishing Co., Ltd.,
Mayville House, 142 Park Rd., Timperley,
Altrincham, Cheshire WA15 6QT, England. Ed. Roy
Spragg. adv.; circ. 13,000.
Description: For those who buy floor coverings
throughout Britain and Ireland.

STOCKLISTS COLOUR MAGAZINE. see INTERIOR DESIGN
AND DECORATION — Furniture And House
Furnishings

677.2 SJ ISSN 0562-5033
SUDAN COTTON BULLETIN. (Text in English) 1960. m.
Cotton Public Corporation, Department of Research
and Statistics, Box 1672, Khartoum, Sudan. Ed.Bd.
charts; stat.

677.39 CC ISSN 1000-1999
**SUZHOU SICHOU GONGXUEYUAN XUEBAO/SUZHOU
INSTITUTE OF SILK ENGINEERING.** (Text in
Chinese) q. Suzhou Sichou Gongxueyuan - Suzhou
Institute of Silk Engineering, 14 Xiangmen Lu,
Suzhou, Jiangsu 215005, People's Republic of
China. TEL 225614. Ed. Wu Rongru.

677 US
SWATCHES. 1984. s-a. National Association of
Decorative Fabric Distributors, 3008 Millwood Ave.,
Columbia, SC 29205. TEL 803-252-5646. adv.;
circ. 17,000 (controlled).

T-SHIRT BUSINESS INFO MAPPING NEWSLETTER. see
BUSINESS AND ECONOMICS — Small Business

677 FR
T U T. (Textiles et Usages Techniques); la revue des
utilisateurs. (Text in French; summaries in English)
q. 360 F. Editions de l' Industrie Textile, 16 rue
Ballu, 75009 Paris, France. TEL 48-74-15-96.
FAX 48-74-01-89. TELEX 283 438 F. illus.
Description: Directed to the end-users of technical
material.

677 JA
T W A R O NEWS. m. Asian Regional Organisation of the
International Textile, Garment and Leather Workers'
Federation, Zeusen Kaikan Bldg. 8-16, Kudan
Minami 4-chome, Chiyoda-ku, Tokyo, Japan.
TEL 03-2655465.

677 GW
TASCHENBUCH DER TEXTILEN RAUMAUSSTATTUNG. a.
DM.48. Fachverlag Schiele und Schoen GmbH,
Markgrafenstr. 11, 1000 Berlin 61, Germany.
TEL 030-251-6029. FAX 030-2517248. TELEX
181470-SUNDS-D. Ed. Dirk Artz.

677 GW ISSN 0082-1837
TASCHENBUCH DES TEXTILEINZELHANDELS. 1962. a.
Deutscher Fachverlag GmbH, Mainzer Landstr. 251,
Postfach 100606, 6000 Frankfurt a.M. 1,
Germany. TEL 069-7595-01.

677 GW ISSN 0082-1896
TASCHENBUCH FUER DIE TEXTIL-INDUSTRIE. 1951. a.
DM.52. Fachverlag Schiele und Schoen GmbH,
Markgrafenstr. 11, 1000 Berlin 61, Germany.
TEL 030-251-6029. FAX 030-2517248. TELEX
181470-SUNDS-D. Ed. W. Loy. adv.; circ. 5,000.
—BLDSC shelfmark: 8606.570000.

T

TEXTILE INDUSTRIES AND FABRICS

677 668.4 UK ISSN 0964-5993
▼**TECHNICAL TEXTILES INTERNATIONAL.** 1992. m. £85($137.50) (effective 1992). Elsevier Science Publishers Ltd., Crown House, Linton Rd., Barking, Essex IG11 8JU, England. TEL 081-594-7272. FAX 081-594-5942. TELEX 896950 APPSCI G. (Subscr. in U.S. and Canada to: Elsevier Science Publishing Co., Inc., Box 882, Madison Sq. Sta., New York, NY 10159. TEL 212-989-5800) Ed. N. Butler.
Description: Covers the latest developments in technical textiles and fiber-reinforced materials, from design to end-products, with analyses of industry trends and reports from major exhibitions and conferences.

677 GW
TECHNISCHES TEXTIL FORUM; internationale Fachzeitschrift fuer textiles Bauen. m. DM.72. Verlag F.H. Kleffmann GmbH, Rottstr. 1-3, 4630 Bochum 1, Germany. TEL 0234-14018. FAX 0234-683519. TELEX 825668-KLEFF. Ed. F. Kleffmann. circ. 2,500. (back issues avail.)
Formerly: Zelte Planen Markisen (ISSN 0724-5092)

677 SP ISSN 0040-1900
TECNICA TEXTIL INTERNACIONAL. 1957. m. 10000 ptas.($100) Ediciones Tecnicas Especializadas, Traversere de Gracia 15, 4, Barcelona 08021, Spain. TEL 3-2097933. FAX 3-2096918. Ed. Juan B. Puig. adv.; bk.rev.; abstr.; bibl.; illus.; stat.; circ. 7,500. (tabloid format; back issues avail.) **Indexed:** Ind.SST, Text.Tech.Dig.
Description: Covers the textile industry in Spain, Portugal and Latin America.

677 IT ISSN 0394-5413
TECNOLOGIE TESSILI. 1987. m. L.75000($130) (foreign L.150000). Stammer S.P.A., Centro Commerciale, Milano S. Felice, 20090 Segrate (Milan), Italy. TEL 02-7530651. Ed. Gerolamo Bellina. circ. 15,000.

677 746.92 FI ISSN 0355-7898
TEKSI. 1936. m. (9/yr.). FIM 530. Tekstiilikauppiaiden Liitto r.y. - Association of the Finnish Textile Retailers, Mariankatu 26 B, 00170 Helsinki, Finland. TEL 358-0-1351288. FAX 358-0-1351384. Ed. Aimo Virtanen. adv.; circ. 5,047.
Formerly: Tekstiilikauppias.
Description: Covers the retail business, wholesale trade and textile industry in Finland.

677 FI ISSN 0040-2370
TEKSTIILILEHTI. 1937. 6/yr. FIM 280. Suomen Tekstiiliteknillinen Liitto r. y. - Textile-technical Association of Finland, Suvantokatu 1A, 33100 Tampere, Finland. FAX 359-31-120714. Ed. Clas Rosenberg. adv.; bk.rev.; charts; illus.; circ. 2,000.

677 CI ISSN 0492-5882
TEKSTIL; savezni casopis za tekstilnu tehnologiju i konfekciju. (Text in Serbo-Croatian; abstracts in English and German) 1952. m. $30. Savez Inzenjera i Tehnicara Tekstilaca Hrvatske, Novakova 8-II, P.P. 829, Zagreb, Croatia. TEL 041 276-671. Eds. Dragutin Hoffer, Dinko Pezelj. **Indexed:** Art & Archaeol.Tech.Abstr., Bull.Signal., Chem.Abstr., Cott.& Trop.Fibr.Abstr., Ref.Zh., Text.Tech.Dig., World Text.Abstr.
—BLDSC shelfmark: 8779.000000.

677 TU
TEKSTIL VE MUHENDIS. (Text and summaries in English, French, German, Turkish) 1987. bi-m. TL.90000($60) Chamber of Mechanical Engineers - T M M O B Makina Muhendisleri Odasi, Elmasbahceler Mah., Sabunevi Sok., Muhendislar Ishani No. 19, Kat 1, 16230 Bursa, Turkey. TEL 24-121190. FAX 24-121194. Ed. Yusuf Unler. adv.; bk.rev.; charts; illus.; circ. 6,000. (back issues avail.)
Formerly (until 1991): Tekstil ve Makina.
Description: Covers raw material, spinning, preparing, weaving, knitting, dyeing, printing, finishing, testing and quality control, clothing, marketing and other subjects.

677 500 XV ISSN 0351-3386
TEKSTILEC; glasilo slovenskih tekstilcev. (Text in Slovenian; summaries in English and German) 1957. m. $40. (Splosno Zdruzenje Tekstilne Industrije Slovenije - General Association of Slovene Textile Industry) Urednistvo Tekstilec, Snezniska 5, p.p. 311, 61000 Ljubljana, Slovenia. TEL 61 224-417. Ed. Anica Levin. adv.; bk.rev.; abstr.; illus.; stat.; index; circ. 3,000. (back issues avail.) **Indexed:** World Text.Abstr.
●Also available online. Vendor(s): DIALOG.
—BLDSC shelfmark: 8779.050000.
Description: Publishes original reports on textile development and research, news from all textile mechanical and chemical technologies, trade in ready-made clothes and design, and information on the Slovenian textile industry.

677 659.152 NO
TEKSTILFORUM. 1931. 12/yr. NOK 460. Norges Tekstilforbund - Norwegian Textile Retailers Association, Box 2590, Solli, N-0203 Oslo 2, Norway. TEL 02-557430. FAX 02-552888. Ed. Live Nordby. adv.; bk.rev.; charts;.; illus.; circ. 6,000.
Former titles: Manufaktur (ISSN 0025-259X); Tekstilforum (ISSN 0332-5520)

677 YU ISSN 0040-2389
TEKSTILNA INDUSTRIJA. 1953. 6/yr. 1200 din. Savez Inzenjera i Tehnicara Tekstilaca SR Srbije, Kneza Milosa 7-II, 11000 Belgrade, Serbia, Yugoslavia. Ed. Branko Ilic. adv.; bk.rev.; index; circ. 2,600. **Indexed:** Chem.Abstr.

677 BU
TEKSTILNA PROMISHLENOST. 1952. 10/yr. $22. Ministerstvo na Lekata Promishlenost, Sofia, Bulgaria. (Dist. by: Hemus, 6, Rouski Blvd., 1000 Sofia, Bulgaria) (Co-sponsor: Nauchno- Tekhnicheski Suiuz po Tekstil i Obleklo) Ed. A. Chervendinev. circ. 3,700. **Indexed:** Chem.Abstr, Text.Tech.Dig., World Text.Abstr.

677 RU ISSN 0040-2397
TS1300 CODEN: TTLPA2
TEKSTIL'NAYA PROMYSHLENNOST'. 1941. m. 27 Rub. Ministerstvo Legkoi Promyshlennosti, Moscow, Russia. (Subscr. to: Mezhdunarodnaya Kniga, Moscow G-200, Russia) Ed. G.I. Pikovskii. adv.; bk.rev.; bibl.; charts; illus.; pat.; tr.lit.; circ. 11,500. **Indexed:** Abstr.Bull.Inst.Pap.Chem., Biol.Abstr., Chem.Abstr., Cott.&Trop.Fibr.Abstr., Text.Tech.Dig., World Text.Abstr.
—BLDSC shelfmark: 0177.000000.

667 IT
TESSUTO COLLEZIONI. q. L.360000 (foreign L.480000). Zanfi Editori s.r.l., Via Ganaceto 121, P.O. Box 433, 41100 Modena, Italy. TEL 059-222292. FAX 059-225718. TELEX 522272 ZANFI I. illus.
Description: Covers fabrics, yarns and accessories, the raw materials of fashion.

677 BE
TEX-TEXTILIS. (Text in Dutch and French) 1945. bi-m. 750 BEF. (National Organization for Textile Engineers and Directors) Drukkerij-Uitgeverij Vyncke, 92 Savaanstraat, B-9000 Ghent, Belgium. (Co-sponsor: Dutch Textile Institute) Ed. Daniel Vyncke. adv.; bk.rev.; bibl.; charts; illus.; stat.; index; circ. 2,500. **Indexed:** Chem.Abstr., Excerp.Med., Text.Tech.Dig., World Text.Abstr.
Formerly: Textilis (ISSN 0040-5280)

677 746.92 BE
TEXBEL. (Editions in Dutch, French) 1970. m. 1650 BEF. Diligentia Business Press, N.V., 42 av. du Houx, 1170 Brussels, Belgium. TEL 02-673-81-70. FAX 02-660-36-00. TELEX BELBUSS 23830. Ed. Chris Vermuyten. adv.; circ. 13,000.

677 II ISSN 0970-5686
TEXINCON. Variant title: Textile Information Condensed. (Text in English) 1989. q. Rs.300 (foreign $50 or £25). National Information Centre for Textile and Allied Subjects, 3rd Fl., Atira, Ahmedabad 380 015, India. TELEX 121-6571 ATRA IN. adv.; bk.rev.; abstr.; circ. 1,000. (also avail. on diskette)
Description: Specialized articles and reviews of recent developments and publications of interest to persons in the textile industry.

TEXINFORM; information index for the textile industry. see BUSINESS AND ECONOMICS — Trade And Industrial Directories

677 SA
TEXINFORM MONTHLY BULLETIN. (Text in English) m. Kenneth Rosenthal (Pty) Ltd., Ste. 304, Rosepark North, 8 Sturdee Ave., Rosebank 2196, South Africa. (Subscr. to: Box 52665, Saxonwold 2132, Johannesburg, South Africa) Ed. Kenneth Rosenthal. adv. (looseleaf format)
Formerly: Texinform Bulletin.

677.31 SA ISSN 0036-1003
TEXNEWS. 1967. q. free. Division of Textile Technology, Box 1124, Port Elizabeth 6000, South Africa. FAX 041-53-2325. TELEX 24-5183. Ed. P. Horn. **Indexed:** Text.Tech.Dig., World Text.Abstr.
—BLDSC shelfmark: 8077.295000.
Formerly: South African Wool and Textile Research Institute. Bulletin.
Description: Technical news for the textile industry.

677 NE ISSN 0040-4772
TEXPRESS; economic and technical weekly for Benelux textile and clothing industries and trade. 1957. w. fl.230 (foreign fl.310). V N U Business Publications B.V., Rijnsburgstr. 11, 1059 AT Amsterdam, Netherlands. Ed. J.G. Post. adv.; bk.rev.; charts; illus.; mkt.; tr.lit.; circ. 2,750. **Indexed:** Key to Econ.Sci.

677.3 SA
TEXREPORT. 1952. irreg. $20 per no. Division of Textile Technology, Box 1124, Port Elizabeth 6000, South Africa. FAX 041-532325. TELEX 24-5183. Ed. P. Horn. circ. 250. **Indexed:** Text.Tech.Dig., World Text.Abstr.
Formerly (until 1989): S A W T R I Technical Report (ISSN 0081-2560)

338.4 US ISSN 0092-3540
HD9853
TEXSCOPE: U S A TEXTILE INDUSTRY OVERVIEW. 1974. irreg., latest 1983. Werner Management Consultants, Inc., 111 W. 40th St., New York, NY 10018. TEL 212-730-1280. Ed. Mary Scannapield. stat.; circ. controlled. Key Title: Texscope (New York).

677 NE
TEXTIELHISTORISCHE BIJDRAGEN. 1959. a. fl.27.50. Stichting Textielgeschiedenis, Brassehorst 11, 7531 KH Enschede, Netherlands. Ed. E.J. Fischer. bk.rev.; circ. 600.

677 NE
TEXTIELVISIE; vakblad voor de textielbranche. 1963. 14/yr. fl.146. (Stichting Mitex) Audet Tijdschriften bv, Postbus 16, 6500 AA Nijmegen, Netherlands. TEL 080-228316. FAX 080-239561. TELEX 48633. Ed. Steffen van Beek. adv.; B&W page fl.2587; trim 210 x 297; adv. contact: Cor van Nek. circ. 10,630. **Indexed:** Key to Econ.Sci.
Formerly: Textiel-Visie - Weekly (Amsterdam) (ISSN 0040-4810).
Description: Covers all sectors of the retail fashion business in the Netherlands.

677 CS ISSN 0040-4829
TEXTIL/TEXTILE; technical monthly dealing with textile and clothing industry. (Text in Czech; summaries in English, German, Russian) 1945. m. $43.80. (U B O K) Nakladatelstvi Technicke Literatury, Spalena 51, 113 02 Prague 1, Czechoslovakia. (Dist. by: Artia, Ve Smeckach 30, 111 27 Prague 1, Czechoslovakia) Ed. Eva Prihodova. adv.; bk.rev.; illus.; pat.; index. cum.index; circ. 4,900. **Indexed:** C.I.S. Abstr.

677 VE
TEXTIL. 1976. q. Instituto de Capacitacion Textil, Avenida Urdaneta, Ibarra a Pilota, Edificio Karam, Piso 4, 403-406, Apdo. 2173, Caracas 101, Venezuela. **Indexed:** Text.Tech.Dig.

677 DK ISSN 0040-4837
TEXTIL. s-a. DKK 749. (Dansk Textilunion) Specialbladsforlaget, Finsensvej 80, DK-2000 Frederiksberg, Denmark. TEL 38-88-32-22. FAX 38-88-30-38. (Textil og Beklaedningsindustrien) Ed. Annette Suhr. circ. 6,880.

677 GW
TEXTIL-BEKLEIDUNG. m. Gewerkschaft Textile-Bekleidung, Rossstr. 94, 4000 Duesseldorf 30, Germany. TEL 43091. TELEX 584365.

TEXTILE INDUSTRIES AND FABRICS 4625

677 GW ISSN 0082-3627
TEXTIL-INDUSTRIE UND IHRE HELFER. 1957. a. DM. 38. Industrieschau-Verlagsgesellschaft, Berliner Allee 8, 6100 Darmstadt, Germany.

677 SW ISSN 0284-6152
TEXTIL MAGAZINE.* 1954. m. SEK 410. BasPress Forlags AB, Brunnsgatan 9, 17225 Sundbyberg, Sweden. FAX 08-98-42-69. Eds. Ulla Gabay, Kerstin Weyler. adv.; bk.rev.; charts; illus.; circ. 10,323.
Formerly: Textilbranschen (ISSN 0040-4888)

677 GW ISSN 0342-2224
TEXTIL MITTEILUNGEN; mit dem Wirtschaftsblatt Branche und Business. 1946. w. DM.277.50. Branche und Business Fachverlag, Koenigsallee 70, 4000 Duesseldorf 1, Germany. TEL 0211-132375. FAX 0211-324862. circ. 35,000. (looseleaf format)

677 GW ISSN 0040-4853
TS1300 CODEN: TXPIAT
TEXTIL PRAXIS INTERNATIONAL. Abbreviated title: T P I. 1946. m. DM.202.80 (with English supplement DM. 278.40). (Verein Deutscher Faerber e.V.) Konradin Verlag Robert Kohlhammer GmbH, Ernst-Mey-Str. 8, 7022 Leinfelden-Echterdingen, Germany. TEL 0711-7594-0. FAX 0711-7594-390. Ed. Horst Meyrahn. adv.; bk.rev.; charts; illus.; mkt.; pat.; tr.lit.; index, cum.index; circ. 7,154. (back issues avail.) **Indexed:** Art & Archaeol.Tech.Abstr., C.I.S. Abstr., Chem.Abstr., Excerp.Med., PROMT, Text.Tech.Dig., W.R.C.Inf., World Text.Abstr.
Formerly: Textil-Praxis.
Description: Covers research in textile technology and processing. Features chemistry, spinning, weaving, knitting, and dyeing. Includes industry news, events, and positions available.

677 SZ ISSN 0040-4861
TEXTIL-REVUE. (Text in German) 1921. 41/yr. 144 SFr. (foreign 188 SFr.). Zollikofer AG, Fuerstenlandstr. 122, CH-9001 St. Gallen, Switzerland. TEL 071-297777. FAX 071-257487. TELEX 77537. Ed.Bd. adv.; illus.; circ. 7,000.
Indexed: Key to Econ.Sci.
Formed by the merger of: Schweizer Textil-Zeitung & Schweizerische Textildetaillisten-Zeitung.

677 GW ISSN 0040-487X
TEXTIL-WIRTSCHAFT. 1946. w. DM.328 (foreign DM.414.80). Deutscher Fachverlag GmbH, Mainzer Landstr. 251, Postfach 100606, 6000 Frankfurt a.M. 1, Germany. Ed. Joerg Hintz. adv.; bk.rev.; charts; illus.; mkt.; pat.; tr.lit.; tr.mk.; index; circ. 42,800. **Indexed:** PROMT.

677 US
TEXTILE ARTISTS' NEWSLETTER; a journal of the textile arts & history. 1978. q. $9. Textile Artists' Supply, 3006 San Pablo Ave., Berkeley, CA 94702. TEL 415-548-9988. Ed. Susan C. Druding. adv.; bk.rev.; charts; illus.; stat.; circ. 1,500. (tabloid format)

677 HK ISSN 0049-3554
TS1399 CODEN: TASIDM
TEXTILE ASIA. 1970. m. HK.$302 in Hong Kong; Macao and China HK.$348; elsewhere $74. Business Press Ltd., California Tower, 11-F, 30-32 d'Aguilar St., P.O. Box 185, Central, Hong Kong. TEL 5233744. FAX 8106966. TELEX 60275-TEXIA-HX. Ed. Kayser Sung. adv.; bk.rev.; charts; illus.; stat.; index; circ. 15,700. **Indexed:** Cott.&Trop.Fibr.Abstr., Text.Tech.Dig., World Text.Abstr.
—BLDSC shelfmark: 8801.730000.

677 HK
TEXTILE ASIA INDEX. 1982. a. $15. Business Press Ltd., California Tower, 11-F, 30-32 D'Aguilar St., P.O. Box 185, Central, Hong Kong. TEL 5247467. FAX 8-106966. TELEX 60275-TEXIA-HX. Ed. Kayser Sung.

677 II ISSN 0368-4636
TS1300 CODEN: JTXAA9
TEXTILE ASSOCIATION (INDIA). JOURNAL. (Text in English) 1940. bi-m. Rs.75($60) Textile Association (India), Central Office, 72-A, Dr. M.B. Raut Rd., Shivaji Park, Dadar, Bombay 400 028, India. Ed. D.B. Ajgaonkar. adv.; bk.rev.; circ. 10,000. **Indexed:** Chem.Abstr., Cott.& Trop.Fibr.Abstr., Indian Sci.Abstr., Text.Tech.Dig., World Text.Abstr.
—BLDSC shelfmark: 4907.900000.
Formerly (until 1971): Textile Digest.

677 658 US ISSN 0739-0491
TEXTILE BUSINESS OUTLOOK; international textile forecasts. 1972. 2/yr. $985. Statistikon Corp., Box 246, E. Norwich, NY 11732. TEL 516-922-0882. FAX 516-624-3145. Ed. Jordan P. Yale. charts; pat.; stat.

677 667 US ISSN 0040-490X
TEXTILE CHEMIST AND COLORIST. (Annual Buyer's Guide avail.) 1969. m. $30 to non-members. American Association of Textile Chemists and Colorists, Box 12215, Research Triangle Park, NC 27709. TEL 919-549-8141. FAX 919-549-8933. Ed. Jack Kissiah. adv.; bk.rev.; bibl.; charts; illus.; index, cum.index; circ. 9,600. (also avail. in microform from UMI; reprint service avail. from UMI) **Indexed:** Abstr.Bull.Inst.Pap.Chem., ASCA, Chem.Abstr., Eng.Ind., Excerp.Med., Text.Tech.Dig., World Text.Abstr.

677 II ISSN 0040-4926
TP890 CODEN: TDYPAN
TEXTILE DYER AND PRINTER. (Text in English) 1967. fortn. Rs.50($35) Sevak Publications, 306 Shri Hanuman Industrial Estate, G.D. Ambekar Rd., Post Box No. 7110, Wadala, Bombay 400 031, India. Ed. Ravi Raghavan. adv.; charts; illus.; stat.; circ. 4,500. **Indexed:** Art & Archaeol.Tech.Abstr., Chem.Abstr., Text.Tech.Dig., World Text.Abstr.
—BLDSC shelfmark: 8801.930000.

677 700 AT ISSN 0818-6308
TEXTILE-FIBRE FORUM; the fibre magazine of the Australian region. 1981. 3/yr. Aus.$17($14) Australian Forum for Textile Arts Ltd., Sturt Crafts Centre, P.O. Box 192, Mittagong, N.S.W. 2575, Australia. TEL 048-60-2085. Ed. Janet De Boer. adv.; bk.rev.; index; circ. 6,000.
Formerly: Fibre Forum (ISSN 0725-9565)

677 658 US
TEXTILE FINANCIAL OUTLOOK. a. $3985. Statistikon Corp., 81 Peach Tree Dr., Box 246, E. Norwich, NY 11732. TEL 516-922-0882. FAX 516-624-3145. Ed. Jordan P. Yale.
Description: Provides evaluation, analysis and forecasts of the textile industry's quarterly balance sheet and income statement.

677 UK
TEXTILE FORECAST; British cloth for international menswear. 1973. 3/yr. $64. Benjamin Dent & Co. Ltd., 33 Bedford Pl., London WC1B 5JX, England. Ed. Stephen Higginson. adv.; circ. 5,000. **Indexed:** Text.Tech.Dig.

677 US
TEXTILE HI-LIGHTS. 1938. q. $50 (foreign $75). American Textile Manufacturers Institute, Inc., 1801 K St., N.W., Ste. 900, Washington, DC 20006. TEL 202-862-0500. FAX 202-862-0570. TELEX 710-822-9489. Ed.Bd. circ. 2,500. (also avail. in microform; back issues avail.)

677 660 600 UK ISSN 0260-6518
HD9850.1
TEXTILE HORIZONS. m. £65($130) Textile Institute, 10 Blackfriars St., Manchester M3 5DR, England. TEL 061-834-8457. FAX 061-835-3087. TELEX 668297-TEXINS-G. (Subscr. in U.S. and Canada to: Box 1897, Lawrence KS 66044-8897) Dir. Godfrey Hall. adv.; bk.rev.; bibl.; charts; illus.; stat.; index; circ. 9,000. **Indexed:** Abstr.Bull.Inst.Pap.Chem., Appl.Mech.Rev., Art & Archaeol.Tech.Abstr., Br.Tech.Ind., Chem.Abstr., Curr.Cont., Excerp.Med., PROMT, Text.Tech.Dig., World Text.Abstr.
—BLDSC shelfmark: 8801.994000.
Formerly: Textile Institute and Industry (ISSN 0039-8357)

677 II
TEXTILE INDIA PROGRESS; monthly devoted to entire textile sector. (Text in English) 1964. m. Rs.300. Eastern Press Services (India), Asheerwad, 3-49 East Sion, Bombay 400 022, India. TEL 472912. Ed. Raju V. Chandran. adv.; bk.rev.; illus.; circ. 20,000.
Formerly: Textile India (ISSN 0040-4977)

677 SA
TEXTILE INDUSTRIES BUYERS GUIDE FOR SOUTHERN AFRICA. (Text in English) 1985. biennial. R.100. George Warman Publications (Pty.) Ltd., P.O. Box 3847, Cape Town 8000, South Africa. TEL 021-24-5320. FAX 021-261-332. TELEX 521849. Ed. Desmond Varley.
Description: Guide for buyers of textiles, yarns, textile machinery, and consumables.

677 SA ISSN 0254-0533
CODEN: TIDADD
TEXTILE INDUSTRIES DYEGEST SOUTHERN AFRICA. (Text in English) 1977. m. R.96. (Textile Institute - South Africa) George Warman Publications (Pty.) Ltd., Box 3847, Cape Town 8000, South Africa. TEL 021-24-5320. FAX 021-26-1332. TELEX 5-21849 SA. Ed. Tony Walker. adv.; circ. 1,400. **Indexed:** Ind.S.A.Per., Text.Tech.Dig., World Text.Abstr.
—BLDSC shelfmark: 8802.105000.
Formed by the merger of: Dyers Dyegest (ISSN 0250-0019) & Textile Industries Southern Africa.
Description: Technical journal of spinning, weaving, knitting and yarn preparation, dyeing and textile finishing.

677 II ISSN 0040-4993
TS1300
TEXTILE INDUSTRY & TRADE JOURNAL. (Text in English) 1963. bi-m. $30. Praveen Corp., Sayajiganj, Baroda 390005, India. Ed. C.M. Pandit Amie. adv.; bk.rev.; bibl.; illus.; circ. 5,000. **Indexed:** Art & Archaeol.Tech.Abstr., Cott.&Trop.Fibr.Abstr., Text.Tech.Dig.

677 US ISSN 0094-9884
TK4035.T4 CODEN: IATTD7
TEXTILE INDUSTRY TECHNICAL CONFERENCE (PUBLICATION). Variant title: Annual Textile Industry Technical Conference (Publication). a. (I E E E, Industry Applications Society) Institute of Electrical and Electronics Engineers, Inc., 345 E. 47th St., New York, NY 10017-2394. TEL 212-705-7900. FAX 212-705-7682. (Subscr. to: Box 1331, 445 Hoes Lane, Piscataway, NJ 08855-1331)
Formerly: Textile Industry Technical Conference. Record (ISSN 0082-3651)

677 UK
TEXTILE INSTITUTE. ANNUAL CONFERENCE. a. Textile Institute, 10 Blackfriars St., Manchester M3 5DR, England. TEL 061-834-8457. FAX 061-835-3087. TELEX 668297-TEXIN-G. Ed. P.W. Harrison. bibl.; charts; illus.; stat. **Indexed:** World Text.Abstr.

677 UK ISSN 0040-5000
TS1300 CODEN: TXTIDA
TEXTILE INSTITUTE. JOURNAL. 1910. q. £74 (foreign £80). Textile Institute, 10 Blackfriars St., Manchester M3 5DR, England. TEL 061-834-8457. FAX 061-835-3087. TELEX 668297-TEXINS-G. (Subscr. in U.S. and Canada to: Box 1897, Lawrence KS 66044-8897) Ed. J.W.S. Hearle. abstr.; bibl.; illus.; index, cum.index; circ. 3,700. **Indexed:** Abstr.Bull.Inst.Pap.Chem., Appl.Mech.Rev., Art & Archaeol.Tech.Abstr., Biol.Abstr., Br.Tech.Ind., Chem.Abstr., Curr.Cont., Curr.Leather Lit., Eng.Ind., Excerp.Med., RAPRA, Text.Tech.Dig., World Text.Abstr.
—BLDSC shelfmark: 4908.000000.

677 II ISSN 0040-5035
TEXTILE MACHINERY; accessories & stores. (Text in English) 1965. bi-m. Rs.30. Chary Publications, 14 Sidh Prasad, Ghatkopar Mahul Rd., Tilak Nagar, Bombay 400089, India. Ed. S.T. Chary. adv.; charts; illus.; stat.; circ. 4,000. **Indexed:** Art & Archaeol.Tech.Abstr.

677 JA ISSN 0040-5043
TS1300 CODEN: JTMJAF
TEXTILE MACHINERY SOCIETY OF JAPAN. JOURNAL. Japanese edition: Sen'i Kikai Gakkaishi (ISSN 0371-0580) (Text in English) 1955. q. 8,070 Yen. Textile Machinery Society of Japan - Nihon Sen'i Kikai Gakkai, Osaka Science & Technology Center Bldg., Utsubo Koen, 8-4 Utsubo-Hon-machi, 1-chome, Nishi-ku, Osaka 550, Japan. TEL 06-443-4691. Ed. J. Hosokawa. adv.; bk.rev.; charts; illus.; circ. 4,000. **Indexed:** Art & Archaeol.Tech.Abstr., Chem.Abstr., Eng.Ind., JTA, Text.Tech.Dig., World Text.Abstr. Key Title: Journal of the Textile Machinery Society of Japan.
—BLDSC shelfmark: 4908.500000.

TEXTILE INDUSTRIES AND FABRICS

677 II ISSN 0040-5078
TEXTILE MAGAZINE. (Text in English) 1959. m. Rs.150. (Textile Mills and Manufacturing Association) Gopali & Co., 407-408 Mount Rd., Madras 600 035, India. Ed. M. Rajagopalan. bk.rev.; circ. 15,000. **Indexed:** Key to Econ.Sci., Text.Tech.Dig.

677 US
TEXTILE MANUFACTURING; the journal of manufacturing technology. 1988. bi-m. $30 (foreign $42). Merit Publications, Inc., 18 Perimeter Park Dr., Ste. 108, Atlanta, GA 30341. TEL 404-451-4990. Ed. Earl G. Whited. adv.; illus.; circ. 18,250.
Description: For textile plant managers, engineers and department managers.

677 UK ISSN 0040-5116
TS1300 CODEN: TXMOAW
TEXTILE MONTH. 1968. m. £55($156) World Textiles Publications, 76 Kirkgate, Bradford, W. Yorks. BD1 1TB, England. TEL 0274-726358. Ed. P. Owen. adv.; bk.rev.; illus.; mkt.; tr.lit.; index; circ. 8,016. **Indexed:** Art & Archaeol.Tech.Abstr., Br.Tech.Ind., Chem.Abstr., Cott.& Trop.Fibr.Abstr., Excerp.Med., Key to Econ.Sci., PROMT, Text.Tech.Dig., World Text.Abstr.
—BLDSC shelfmark: 8805.018000.
Incorporates: Skinner's Record of the Manmade Fibres Industry; Man-Made Textiles; Textile Recorder.

TEXTILE MUSEUM BULLETIN. see *MUSEUMS AND ART GALLERIES*

677 700 US ISSN 0083-7407
NK8802.W3
TEXTILE MUSEUM JOURNAL. 1962. a. $15. Textile Museum, 2320 "S" St., N.W., Washington, DC 20008. TEL 202-667-0441. FAX 202-483-0994. circ. 3,000. **Indexed:** Art & Archaeol.Tech.Abstr., Art Ind., Artbibl.Mod., World Text.Abstr.
—BLDSC shelfmark: 8805.300000.
Supersedes: Workshop Notes Washington, D.C. Textile Museum.
Description: Forum for original research on artistic and technical processes and the role of textiles in their historic and cultural contexts. Areas represented are: Near East, Central, South and Southeast Asia, and South and Central America.

677 US
TEXTILE NETWORK NEWS. q. Textile Network Marketing, Box 1072, Woodinville, WA 98072. TEL 206-487-0675. Ed. Dorothy Cope.

677 II ISSN 0040-5124
TEXTILE NEWS. (Text in English) 1968. m. Rs.40. L. K. Pandeya, Ed. & Pub., Block F, 105c New Alipore, Calcutta 700053, India. **Indexed:** PROMT.

TEXTILE NEWSLETTER. see *OCCUPATIONAL HEALTH AND SAFETY*

677 UK ISSN 0268-4764
HD9850.1 CODEN: TOINEI
TEXTILE OUTLOOK INTERNATIONAL. 6/yr. £335($675) (Economist Intelligence Unit) Business International Ltd., 4 Duke St., London W1A 1DW, England. TEL 71-493 6711. FAX 71-499-9767. TELEX 266353 EIUG. (US addr.: Business International Corp., 215 Park Ave. S., New York, NY 10003. TEL 212-460-0600)
—BLDSC shelfmark: 8805.605000.
Description: Aimed at senior textile executives, provides industry and market analysis and company profiles. Forecasts trends and developments.

677 658 US ISSN 0739-4144
TEXTILE PRICING OUTLOOK; textile petrochemicals, raw materials, fibers, yarns, fabrics, end uses: price forecasts. 2/yr. $985. Statistikon Corp., Box 246, E. Norwich, NY 11732. TEL 516-922-0882. FAX 516-624-3145. Ed. Jordan P. Yale. stat.

677 UK ISSN 0040-5167
TS1300 CODEN: TXPRAM
TEXTILE PROGRESS. 1969. q. £60($110) Textile Institute, 10 Blackfriars Street, Manchester M3 5DR, England. TEL 061-834-8457. FAX 061-835-3087. TELEX 668297-TEXINS-G. Ed. P.W. Harrison. bibl.; charts; illus.; index; circ. 2,300. **Indexed:** Abstr.Bull.Inst.Pap.Chem., Chem.Abstr., Text.Tech.Dig., World Text.Abstr.
—BLDSC shelfmark: 8805.700000.

677 US ISSN 0040-5175
TS1300 CODEN: TRJOA9
TEXTILE RESEARCH JOURNAL. 1930. m. $140 (typically set in Aug.). Textile Research Institute, 601 Prospect Ave., Box 625, Princeton, NJ 08542. TEL 609-924-3150. FAX 609-683-7836. Ed. Richard K. Toner. bk.rev.; bibl.; charts; illus.; index; circ. 2,500. (also avail. in microform from UMI) **Indexed:** A.S.& T.Ind., Anim.Breed.Abstr., Appl.Mech.Rev., Art & Archaeol.Tech.Abstr., ASCA, Biol.Abstr., Chem.Abstr., Cott.& Trop.Fibr.Abstr., Curr.Cont., Eng.Ind., Excerp.Med., PROMT, RAPRA, Sci.Abstr., Text.Tech.Dig., World Text.Abstr.
—BLDSC shelfmark: 8809.000000.
Description: Devoted to the dissemination of fundamental and applied scientific information in the physical, chemical, and engineering sciences related to the textile and allied industries.
Refereed Serial

677 GR
TEXTILE REVIEW; epitheorisis klostoifantourgias. (Supplement avail.: Directory: Textile Machinery, Equipments, Space Parts and Services) (Editions in Arabic, Greek) 1961. 6/yr. (Greek ed.) 4/yr. (Arabic ed.). Irinis Str., No. 9, 18547 N. Faliron, Athens, Greece. TEL 4813515. TELEX 213379 TEXR. Ed. Basil D. Loukaitis. adv.

677 NE
TEXTILE SCIENCE AND TECHNOLOGY. 1975. irreg., vol.10, 1991. price varies. Elsevier Science Publishers B.V., Books Division, P.O. Box 211, 1000 AE Amsterdam, Netherlands. TEL 020-5803911. FAX 020-5803705. TELEX 18582 ESPA NL. (Subscr. in U.S. and Canada to: Elsevier Science Publishing Co., Inc., Box 882, Madison Sq. Sta., New York, NY 10159. TEL 212-989-5800)
Refereed Serial

677 UK
TEXTILE TIMES INTERNATIONAL. 1852. m. £6. (Irish Linen Guild) Granite Publications, 62 Castlereagh St., Belfast BT5 4NJ, N. Ireland. Ed. George A.E. Roberts. adv.; bk.rev.; mkt.; tr.lit.; circ. 5,340.
Formerly: Textiles of Ireland and Linen Trade Circular (ISSN 0040-523X)

677 II ISSN 0040-5205
TEXTILE TRENDS. (Text in English) 1958. m. $100. Eastland Publications (Private) Ltd., 44 Chittaranjan Ave., Calcutta 700 012, India. TEL 27-3096. Ed. M. Chakraborti. adv.; bk.rev.; charts; illus.; mkt.; pat.; tr.lit.; tr.mk.; circ. 5,500. **Indexed:** Art & Archaeol.Tech.Abstr.

677 US ISSN 0040-5213
TS1300 CODEN: TEWOAH
TEXTILE WORLD. 1868. m. $42 (free to qualified personnel). MacLean Hunter Publishing Company, Textile Publications, 4170 Ashford-Dunwoody Rd., Ste. 420, Atlanta, GA 30319. TEL 404-847-2770. FAX 404-252-6150. (Subscr. to: 29 N. Wacker Dr., Chicago, IL 60606) McAllister Isaacs III. adv.; bk.rev.; charts; illus.; tr.lit.; circ. 28,142 (controlled). (also avail. in microform from UMI) **Indexed:** A.S.& T.Ind., ABI Inform., ASCA, B.P.I., Bus.Ind., C.I.S. Abstr., Chem.Abstr., Cott.& Trop.Fibr.Abstr., Eng.Ind., Excerp.Med., PROMT, RAPRA, SRI, Text.Tech.Dig., Tr.& Indus.Ind., World Text.Abstr.
—BLDSC shelfmark: 8811.000000.
Former titles (until 1931): Textile Advance News; (until 1924): Textiles; (until 1923): Posselt's Textile Journal; (until 1915): Textile World Journal.
Description: For executives, specialists and managers. Covers yarn manufacturing, knitting, weaving, nonwovens, dyeing, chemical treatment, and fibers.

677 US
TEXTILES: LATIN AMERICAN INDUSTRIAL REPORT. (Avail. for each of 22 Latin American countries) 1985. a. $435 per country report. Aquino Productions, Box 15760, Stamford, CT 06901. TEL 203-325-3138.

677 US ISSN 0040-5140
TEXTILES PANAMERICANOS; revista para la industria textile. (Text in Spanish) 1941. q. $40 (foreign $48). Billian Publishing, Inc., 2100 Powers Ferry Rd., Ste. 300, Atlanta, GA 30339. TEL 404-955-5656. FAX 404-952-0669. Ed. James Woodruffe. adv.; bk.rev.; charts; illus.; circ. 11,100. **Indexed:** Art & Archaeol.Tech.Abstr., Text.Tech.Dig.

677 SP ISSN 0211-7975
TEXTILES PARA EL HOGAR. 1967. 6/yr. 7100 ptas.($83) (effective 1992). Publica, S.A., Ecuador, 75, entlo., 08029 Barcelona, Spain. TEL 93-321-50-46. FAX 93-322-19-72. Ed. Balague Castella. adv.; illus.; circ. 4,000.

677 SZ ISSN 0040-5248
TEXTILES SUISSES. (Text in English, French and German) 1927. 4/yr. 84 SFr. Schweizerische Zentrale fuer Handelsfoerderung - Swiss Office for Trade Promotion, Case Postale 1128, CH-1001 Lausanne, Switzerland. TEL 021-231824. FAX 021-207337. TELEX 455425-OSEC-CH. Ed. Peter Pfister. adv.; illus.; circ. 13,000(controlled). **Indexed:** Key to Econ.Sci.
Description: Features Swiss clothing fabrics and their use in international fashion industry.

677 SZ ISSN 0082-3708
TEXTILES SUISSES: INTERIEUR. (Text in English, French, and German) 1970. a. 25 SFr. Schweizerische Zentrale fuer Handelsfoerderung - Swiss Office for Trade Promotion, Case Postale 1128, CH-1001 Lausanne, Switzerland. TEL 021-131824. FAX 021-207337. TELEX 455425-OSEC-CH. Ed. Peter Pfister. adv.; illus.; circ. 11,000.
Description: Deals with all home textiles such as drapes and net curtaining, upholstery fabrics, bed and bath linens, carpets, and others as well.

677 GW
TEXTILFORUM. 1982. 4/yr. DM.70. (Arbeitsgemeinschaft fuer Textil) Textil-Werkstatt Verlag, Postfach 5944, 3000 Hannover 1, Germany. TEL 0511-817007. FAX 0511-813108. Ed. Beatrijs Sterk. adv.; bk.rev.; circ. 6,000.
Formerly (until 1990): Deutsches Textilforum (ISSN 0722-1258)

677 NE ISSN 0040-5264
TEXTILIA. (Supplement avail.: Textilia Plus) 1921. w. (plus 8 special editions). fl.203 in Benelux (foreign fl. 335) includes Textilia Journaal and Textilia Plus). V N U Business Publications B.V., Rijnsburgstraat 11, Amsterdam, Netherlands. TEL 020-5102911. TELEX 14407 PUBLI NL. Ed. C.J.C. Keunen. adv.; bk.rev.; abstr.; bibl.; charts; illus.; mkt.; pat.; stat.; tr.lit.; circ. 10,434. **Indexed:** Key to Econ.Sci., Text.Tech.Dig.
Description: Trade publication for the business in textiles, fashions, and home textiles. Features trade news and information, fashion news and trends, and international news. Includes list of events, positions available.

677 GW ISSN 0934-3342
TEXTILKUNST; Informationen fuer kreatives Gestalten. 1973. 4/yr. DM.62 (foreign DM.70). Verlag M. und H. Schaper, Kalandstr. 4, Postfach 1642, 3220 Alfeld, Germany. Ed. B. Koch-Muenchmeyer. adv.; bk.rev.; illus.; circ. 7,000. **Indexed:** Art & Archaeol.Tech.Abstr., Text.Tech.Dig.

677 GW ISSN 0323-3804
TS1300 CODEN: TEXTC5
TEXTILTECHNIK; technisch-wissenschaftliche Zeitschrift fuer alle Zweige der Textilindustrie. (Text mainly in German; occasionally in English and Russian) 1951. m. DM.114 (foreign DM.134.40). Fachbuchverlag, Karl-Heine-Str. 16, 7031 Leipzig, Germany. Ed.Bd. adv.; bk.rev.; abstr.; bibl.; charts; illus. **Indexed:** Art & Archaeol.Tech.Abstr., C.I.S. Abstr., Chem.Abstr., Excerp.Med., Text.Tech.Dig., World Text.Abstr.
Formerly: Deutsche Textiltechnik (ISSN 0012-0839)
Description: Trade publication for the textile industry, featuring textile machinery and manufacture, computerization, production development, trade and industrial news, reports and announcements of events.

677.028 CC ISSN 1000-1557
TIANJIN FANGZHI GONGXUEYUAN XUEBAO/TIANJIN INSTITUTE OF TEXTILE SCIENCE AND TECHNOLOGY. JOURNAL. (Text in Chinese) 1982. q. $8. Tianjin Fangzhi Gongxueyuan - Tianjin Textile Engineering Institute, 63 Chenglinzhuang Dao, Tianjin 300160, People's Republic of China. TEL 021-413251. TELEX 234025 TJFY. Ed. Kong Fanchao. adv. contact: Jianguo Chen. circ. 2,000.

TEXTILE INDUSTRIES AND FABRICS 4627

677 667.3 IT ISSN 0040-7984
CODEN: TINCAW
TINCTORIA (MILAN); i progressi delle industrie della nobilitazione tessile. (Text mainly in Italian; occasionally in English) 1903. m. L.125000($115) (Textile Ennobling Association) Edizioni Ariminum, Via Negroli 51, 20133 Milan, Italy. TEL 02-73-00-91. FAX 02-717346. Ed. Giovanni Frangi. adv.; bk.rev.; abstr.; charts; illus.; pat.; tr.lit.; tr.mk.; index; circ. 3,000. (back issues avail.) **Indexed:** Art & Archaeol.Tech.Abstr., Chem.Abstr.
—BLDSC shelfmark: 8857.100000.
Description: Devoted to textile wet processing, dyeing, finishing, bleaching and more.

677 JA
TORAY INDUSTRIES. ANNUAL REPORT. a. Toray Industries Inc., Zaimubu Kokusai Zaimuka, 2-2-1 Muro-machi Nihonbashi, Chuo-ku, Tokyo 103, Japan. TEL 03-3245-5222. FAX 03-3245-5818.

UNCOVERINGS; research papers. see WOMEN'S INTERESTS

677 GW
UNFALLSCHIRM. q. Textil- und Bekleidungs-Berufsgenossenschaft, Oblatterwallstr. 18, Postfach 100095, 8900 Augsburg 1, Germany.

UNITED STATES: COTTON QUALITY REPORTS FOR GINNINGS. see AGRICULTURE — Agricultural Economics

UTSUKUSHII-KIMONO/BEAUTIFUL KIMONO. see CLOTHING TRADE — Fashions

V W D - LANDWIRTSCHAFT UND ERNAEHRUNG. (Vereinigte Wirtschaftsdienste GmbH) see BUSINESS AND ECONOMICS — Investments

V W D - TEXTIL. (Vereinigte Wirtschaftsdienste GmbH) see BUSINESS AND ECONOMICS — Investments

677 FR
VETIR; revue des industries de l'habillement. 1955. m. 7 ter, cours des Petites-Eauries, 75010 Paris, France. Ed. M. Thirou. adv.; circ. 2,700. **Indexed:** Text.Tech.Dig., World Text.Abstr.

677 GW ISSN 0935-6347
VLIESSTOFF NONWOVEN INTERNATIONAL. (Text in English and German) 1986. m. DM.160. V N I Verlag, Landwehrstr. 21, 6054 Rodgau 1, Germany. Ed. Ruth Beddies. circ. 8,000.
—BLDSC shelfmark: 9246.053000.

677 790.13 US
WARP & WEFT. 1949. m. (except July-Aug.). $12. Robin and Russ Handweavers, 533 N. Adams St., McMinnville, OR 97128. TEL 503-472-5760. Ed. Russell Groff. circ. 400.
Description: Covers four-harness patterns; sample swatch included with each issue.

677 GW ISSN 0043-1699
WEBE MIT; Zeitschrift fuer das Handweben. 1956. 4/yr. DM.23. Webe Mit-Verlag, 7005 Winterbach, 7065 Manolzweiler, Germany. Ed. S. Traub. adv.; bk.rev.; circ. 4,000.

WIADOMOSCI PRODUKCYJNE: WLOKNO, ODZIEZ, SKORA. see CLOTHING TRADE

677 GW ISSN 0043-6097
WIRKEREI - UND STRICKEREI - TECHNIK; Fachzeitschrift fuer die Maschenindustrie und -Veredelung sowie fuer Maschentrends. Spanish edition: Punto - Tecnica y Moda (ISSN 0724-3847); English edition: Knitting Technique (ISSN 0177-4875) 1951. m. (Spanish ed. q.). DM.149 (foreign DM.164; Spanish ed. DM.70). Meisenbach GmbH, Hainstr. 18, Postfach 2069, 8600 Bamberg 1, Germany. TEL 0951-861-134. FAX 0951-861-170. TELEX 662844-MEIBA-D. Ed. Lothar Rauscher. adv.; bk.rev.; abstr.; illus.; pat.; index; circ. 4,270. **Indexed:** Art & Archaeol.Tech.Abstr., Chem.Abstr., Text.Tech.Dig., World Text.Abstr.

677.3 SA ISSN 0259-0182
WOLNUUS/WOOL NEWS. (Text in Afrikaans, English) 1980. w. free. S.A. Wool Board, P.O. Box 2191, Port Elizabeth 6056, South Africa. TEL 041-544301. FAX 041-546760. Ed. J.W. Gieselbach. circ. 700.
Formed by the merger of: Wool News Service; Wolnuusdiens.

677.31 II ISSN 0043-7808
CODEN: WWIDA5
WOOL AND WOOLENS OF INDIA. (Text in English) vol. 7, 1970. q. Rs.100 (foreign Rs.200). Indian Woollen Mills' Federation, Churchgate Chambers 5, 7th Fl., 5 New Marine Lines, Bombay 400 020, India. TEL 2624675. TELEX 011-83067. Ed. K.V.A. Warrier. adv.; abstr.; charts; illus.; mkt.; stat.; circ. 450. **Indexed:** Chem.Abstr., Ind.Vet., Text.Tech.Dig., Vet.Bull., World Text.Abstr.

677.3 II
WOOL & WOOLLEN. (Text in English) 1964. m. Rs.120. Eastern Press Services (India), Asheerwad, 3-49 Sion East, Bombay 400 022, India. TEL 472912. Ed. Raju V. Chandran. adv.; bk.rev.; illus.; circ. 10,000.

677.3 AT
WOOL MARKET NEWS; weekly market summary. 1975. w. free. Australian Wool Corporation, Box 4867, Melbourne, Vic. 3001, Australia. Ed. M. Mc Donald.

677.31 II ISSN 0043-7824
WOOL NEWS. (Text in English) 1965. q. Rs.75($8) Wool & Woollens Export Promotion Council, 612-714 Ashoka Estate, 24 Barakhamba Rd., New Delhi 110001, India. TEL 011-3315512. FAX 91-011-3314626. TELEX 031-66673. Ed. Ashok K. Madhra. circ. 1,000 (controlled).

677.3 UK
WOOL QUARTERLY. 1979. q. £80. Commonwealth Secretariat, Publications Division, Marlborough House, Pall Mall, London SW1Y 5HX, England. Ed. Michael Godfrey. charts; illus.; stat. **Indexed:** IIS, World Text.Abstr.

677.31 UK
WOOL RECORD. 1909. m. £51 (foreign £91). Wool Record Ltd., 76 Kirkgate, Bradford, W. Yorkshire BD1 1TB, England. FAX 0274-735045. TELEX 517617 WOOLMN G. Ed. Mark Keighley. adv.; bk.rev.; mkt. **Indexed:** Art & Archaeol.Tech.Abstr., Chem.Abstr., Key to Econ.Sci., PROMT, Text.Tech.Dig., World Text.Abstr.
Formerly: Wool Record and Textile World (ISSN 0043-7832)

677.31 UK
WOOL RECORD WEEKLY MARKET REPORT. 1907. w. £91 (foreign £107). Wool Record Ltd., 76 Kirkgate, Bradford, W. Yorkshire BD1 1TB, England. FAX 0274-735045. TELEX 517617-WOOLMN-G. Ed. H.M.F. Mallett. adv.; charts; mkt.; index. **Indexed:** World Text.Abstr.
Incorporates (in Dec. 1977): Weekly Wool Chart (ISSN 0043-2008)

677.3 NZ ISSN 0112-2754
WOOL RESEARCH ORGANISATION OF NEW ZEALAND. SPECIAL PUBLICATIONS. 1976. irreg. price varies. Wool Research Organisation of New Zealand (Inc.), Private Bag, Christchurch, New Zealand. FAX 03-3252-717. G.H. Crawshaw. **Indexed:** Text.Tech.Dig., World Text.Abstr.
Description: Proceedings of meetings on New Zealand wool, including cellular, chemical and physical properties, appraisal, sale, scouring, processing, end-use performance and marketing.

677.3 NZ ISSN 0112-2908
WOOL RESEARCH ORGANISATION OF NEW ZEALAND COMMUNICATIONS. 1967. irreg. NZ.$100 per no. (typically set in July). Wool Research Organisation of New Zealand, Private Bag, Christchurch, New Zealand. TEL 03-3252-421. FAX 3-325-2717. circ. 300.
—BLDSC shelfmark: 3359.100000.
Description: Fundamental studies on New Zealand wool, including cellular, chemical and physical properties, appraisal, sale, scouring, processing, end-use performance and marketing.

677.3 NZ ISSN 0112-2851
WOOL RESEARCH ORGANISATION OF NEW ZEALAND REPORTS. 1970. irreg. NZ.$100 per no. (typically set in July). Wool Research Organisation of New Zealand, Private Bag, Christchurch, New Zealand. TEL 03-3252-421. FAX 3-325-2717. circ. 300.
—BLDSC shelfmark: 7634.730000.
Description: Practical research on New Zealand wool, including cellular, chemical and physical properties, appraisal, sale, scouring, processing, end-use performance and marketing.

677.3 AT ISSN 0084-1218
WOOL REVIEW. 1938. a. free. National Council of Wool Selling Brokers of Australia, 1st Fl., Wool Exchange House, 530 Little Collins St., Melbourne, Vic. 3000, Australia.

677.31 US ISSN 0043-7840
WOOL SACK. 1931. 6/yr. $4. North Central Wool Marketing Corp., Box 328, Brookings, SD 57006. TEL 605-692-2324. FAX 605-692-8182. Ed. Dick Boniface. adv.; bk.rev.; illus.; mkt.; circ. 10,000.

677.3 UK ISSN 0043-7859
CODEN: WOSRA7
WOOL SCIENCE REVIEW. 1948. irreg. free. International Wool Secretariat, Development Centre, Valley Dr., Ilkley, W. Yorks LS29 8PB, England. TEL 0943-601521. TELEX 51457. circ. 3,000. **Indexed:** Br.Tech.Ind., Chem.Abstr., World Text.Abstr.

WOOL TECHNOLOGY AND SHEEP BREEDING. see AGRICULTURE — Poultry And Livestock

677.3 AT
WOOLGROWER. q. Australian Wool Corporation, P.O. Box 4867, Melbourne, Vic. 3001, Australia. **Indexed:** Text.Tech.Dig.

677.31 II ISSN 0043-7883
WOOLLENS & WORSTEDS OF INDIA. (Text in English) vol.4, 1970. s-a. Rs.100($10) (free to qualified personnel). Wool & Woollens Export Promotion Council, 612-714 Ashoka Estate, Barakhamba Rd., New Delhi 110001, India. TEL 3315512. FAX 91-011-3314626. TELEX 031-66673. Ed. Ashok K. Madhra. adv.; illus.; mkt.; stat.; circ. 1,000.

677.2 PK
WORLD COTTON MARKETS REVIEW. (Text in English) 1972. m. Pakistan Central Cotton Committee, Marketing and Economic Research Section, Secretary, Moulvi Tamizuddin Khan Rd., Karachi 1, Pakistan. TEL 524104-6. charts; stat.

677 IS
YALKUT; central periodical of the textile industry in Israel. (Text in Hebrew) 1952. q. $30. Israel Textile Association, Shenkar Bldg., 12 Anna Frank St., Ramat Gan 52 526, Israel. TEL 03-7521133. Ed. S. Rozenzveig. adv.; bk.rev.; circ. 1,200.

677 UK ISSN 0084-411X
YEARBOOK ON JUTE.* (Text in English) 1967. a. Asian Trade Publications Lte., Garavi Gujarat House, 1-2 Silex St., London SE1 0DW, England.

677 CC ISSN 1000-4017
YIN RAN/PRINTING AND DYEING. (Text in Chinese) bi-m. Fangzhi Gongye-bu, Yinran Hangye Jishu Kaifa Zhongxin - Ministry of Textile Industry, Printing and Dyeing Technology Exploration Center, 545 Zhengzhou Lu, Shanghai 200082, People's Republic of China. TEL 5460011. (Co-sponsor: Quanguo Yinran Gongye Keji Qingbao Zhan) Ed. Wang Xiuling.

677 JA
ZENSEN MONTHLY JOURNAL. m. Zensen Japanese Federation of Textile, Garment, Chemical, Mercantile and Allied Industry Workers' Unions, 8-16 Kudan, Minami 4-chome, Chiyoda-ku, Japan. TEL 03-265-5465. TELEX ZENSEN TOKYO.

677 JA
ZENSEN NEWSPAPER. w. Japanese Federation of Textile, Garment, Chemical, Mercantile and Allied Industry Workers' Union, 8-16 Kudan, Minami 4-chome, Chiyoda-ku, Tokyo 102, Japan. TEL 03-3265-5465. TELEX ZENSEN TOKYO.

677.39 CC ISSN 1000-2103
ZHEJIANG SICHOU GONGXUEYUAN XUEBAO. (Text in Chinese) q. Zhejiang Sichou Gongxueyuan, 88 Wenyi Lu, Hangzhou, Zhejiang 310033, People's Republic of China. TEL 885814. Ed. Cao Qianlong.

677 ISSN 0529-6013
ZHONGGUO FANGZHI/CHINESE TEXTILE. (Text in Chinese) m. Fangzhi-bu Bangong-ting - General Office of the Ministry of Textile Industry, Room 302, 105 Jiangsi Zhonglu, Shanghai 200002, People's Republic of China. TEL 3233411. Ed. Wang Zhifu.

TEXTILE INDUSTRIES AND FABRICS — Abstracting, Bibliographies, Statistics

677 US
ZHONGGUO FANGZHI BAO/CHINA'S TEXTILES. (Text in Chinese) d. $138.50. China Books & Periodicals, Inc., 2929 24th St., San Francisco, CA 94110. TEL 415-282-2994. FAX 415-282-0994. (newspaper)

677 CC ISSN 1000-1476
ZHONGGUO FANGZHI DAXUE XUEBAO. English edition: China Textile University. Journal. (Text in Chinese) bi-m. Zhongguo Fangzhi Daxue, 1882 Yan'an Xilu, Shanghai 200051, People's Republic of China. TEL 2599800.
—BLDSC shelfmark: 4729.219300.

TEXTILE INDUSTRIES AND FABRICS — Abstracting, Bibliographies, Statistics

677 310 AT ISSN 0311-9882
AUSTRALIAN WOOL SALE STATISTICS. STATISTICAL ANALYSIS. PART A & B & C. (Issued in 3 parts) 1972. a. free. Australian Wool Corporation, P.O. Box 4867, Melbourne, Vic. 3001, Australia. Ed. M. McDonald. circ. 750.
—BLDSC shelfmark: 1824.750000.
Former titles: Australian Wool (ISSN 0067-222X); Australian Wool Corporation. Statistical Analysis (ISSN 0084-764X)

677 CN ISSN 0319-891X
HD9864.C2
CANADA. STATISTICS CANADA. TEXTILE PRODUCTS INDUSTRIES. (Catalogue 34-251) (Text in English and French) 1960. a. Can.$35($42) (foreign $49). Statistics Canada, Publications Sales and Services, Ottawa, Ont. K1A 0T6, Canada. TEL 613-951-7277. FAX 613-951-1584. (also avail. in microform from MML)
Formerly (until 1985): Canada. Statistics Canada. Carpet, Mat and Rug Industry (ISSN 0527-4893)
Description: Annual census of manufactures.

667.2 016 UK
COLOUR INDEX: ADDITIONS & AMENDMENTS. 1980. q. £66. Society of Dyers and Colourists, Box 244, Perkin House, Bradford, W. Yorks BD1 2JB, England. TEL 0274-7215138. FAX 0274-392888. (Co-sponsor: American Association of Textile Chemists & Colorists) Ed.Bd. circ. 1,000. (back issues avail.)

677.2 US
COTTON. PART 2: WORLD STATISTICS. Title varies: International Cotton Advisory Committee. Quarterly Statistical Bulletin. (Text in English, French, and Spanish) 1947. 2/yr. $45 (with Part 1). International Cotton Advisory Committee, 1901 Pennsylvania Ave., N.W., Ste. 201, Washington, DC 20006. TEL 202-463-6660. charts; stat.; circ. 3,200(combined). Indexed: PROMT, Text.Tech.Dig., World Text.Abstr.

677 310 US
HD9851
CURRENT INDUSTRIAL REPORTS: BROADWOVEN FABRICS (GRAY). (Series MQ22-T) q. (plus a. issue). $7. U.S. Bureau of the Census, Data User Services Division (DAUS), Washington, DC 20233. TEL 301-763-4100. (Dist. by: Supt. of Documents, Washington, DC 20402) Ed. Gary M. Young.
Indexed: Amer.Stat.Ind.
●Also available online. Vendor(s): CompuServe Consumer Information Service, DIALOG.
Former titles: Current Industrial Reports: Finished Fabrics. Production, Inventories, and Unfilled Orders (ISSN 0272-5509); Current Industrial Reports: Woven Fabrics. Production, Inventories, and Unfilled Orders (ISSN 0145-5028)

677.028 620 US ISSN 1049-1376
▼**C2C ABSTRACTS: JAPAN - TEXTILES.** 1990. m. $200. Scan C2C, 500 E St. S.W., Ste. 800, Washington, DC 20024. TEL 800-525-3865. FAX 202-863-3855.
●Also available online. Vendor(s): Data-Star (JPTC), DIALOG (File no.582), European Space Agency (File no.241), Orbit Information Technologies (JTEC). Also available on CD-ROM. Producer(s): Dialog Information Services.
Description: Contains abstracts of articles from Japanese scientific, business, and technical journals. Lists title, author, author affiliation, journal title, volume and number, date, page numbers, abstract, number of bibliographic references, and language.

677 US
▼**DAVISON'S TEXTILE BLUE BOOK EUROPE.** 1991. a. $125. Davison Publishing Co., Box 477, Ridgewood, NJ 07451. TEL 201-445-3135. FAX 201-445-4397.
Description: Comprehensive directory of Western European textile companies listing weavers, knitters, spinners, nonwowen mills, dyers and finishers, as well as hosiery and carpet mills. Arranged alphabetically by country and city.

677 US
DAVISON'S TEXTILE BUYER'S GUIDE. 1934. a. $60. Davison Publishing Co., Inc., Box 477, Ridgewood, NJ 07451. TEL 201-445-3135. FAX 201-445-4397. Ed. Bruce W. Nealy.
Description: Directory with separate classifications for suppliers of chemicals, equipment, machinery, services and supplies used in the textile industry.

677 687 GW
EXTRAKTE: TEXTILIEN UND BEKLEIDUNG. 1966. w. DM.498 (foreign DM.560). Extrakte-Team-Verlag GmbH, Postfach 180162, Wolfgang-Doering-Str. 2-4, 4000 Duesseldorf 13, Germany. TEL 0211-701011. FAX 0211-701013. Ed. Dietmar Cloos. adv.; charts; stat.; tr.lit.; circ. 4,000. (back issues avail.)

677 CC ISSN 1000-3916
FANGZHI WENZHAI/TEXTILE ABSTRACT. (Text in Chinese) bi-m. Shanghai Fangzhi Kexue Yanjiuyuan - Shanghai Institute of Textile Science, 545 Lanzhou Lu, Shanghai 200082, People's Republic of China. TEL 5641341. Ed. Gao Dequan.

338.4 677 II
INDIAN COTTON TEXTILE INDUSTRY; ANNUAL STATISTICAL BULLETIN. (Text in English) 1968. a. Southern India Mills' Association, Coimbatore, India. circ. 500.

677.2 SZ ISSN 0538-6829
HD9870.4
INTERNATIONAL COTTON INDUSTRY STATISTICS. 1958. a. 100 SFr. International Textile Manufacturers Federation, Am Schanzengraben 29, Postfach, CH-8039 Zurich, Switzerland. TEL 01-2017080. FAX 01-2017134. TELEX 817578. charts; stat. (also avail. in microform) Indexed: World Text.Abstr.
Description: Covers productive capacity, machinery utilization and raw material consumption in the short-staple sector.

677.2 SZ
INTERNATIONAL TEXTILE MACHINERY SHIPMENT STATISTICS. 1974. a. 150 SFr. International Textile Manufacturers Federation, Am Schanzengraben 29, Postfach, CH-8039 Zurich, Switzerland. TEL 01-2017080. FAX 01-2017134. TELEX 817578. charts; stat.
Formerly: International Cotton Industry Statistics. Supplement.
Description: Provides information on machinery capacities installed in almost the entire world. Also identifies investment trends.

677 338.1 JA ISSN 0447-5321
HD9086.J3
JAPAN COTTON STATISTICS AND RELATED DATA. 1953. a. $45. Japan Cotton Traders' Association, 2-9, Awaji-machi 3-chome, Chuo-ku, Osaka 541, Japan. TEL 6-201-2215. FAX 6-231-5122. TELEX 0524-2177-JCTA-J.

677.3 310 UK ISSN 0260-8855
KNITSTATS; the yearly statistical bulletin for the hosiery and knitwear industry. 1986. a. £45. Knitting Industries' Federation, 53 Oxford St., Leicester LE1 5XYD, England. TEL 0533-541608. FAX 0533-542273. Ed. J.P. Harrison. bk.rev.; index; circ. 700. (back issues avail.) Indexed: World Text.Abstr.

630 677.13 II ISSN 0027-0598
MONTHLY SUMMARY OF JUTE AND GUNNY STATISTICS. (Text in English) 1945. m. Rs.80. Indian Jute Mills Association, Royal Exchange, 6 Netaji Subhas Rd., Calcutta 1, India. stat.; circ. 300.

NEW ZEALAND WOOL BOARD. STATISTICAL HANDBOOK. see AGRICULTURE — Abstracting, Bibliographies, Statistics

SACHGUETERERZEUGUNG SCHNELLBERICHT. see CERAMICS, GLASS AND POTTERY — Abstracting, Bibliographies, Statistics

677 JA
SEN-I KOUGYO YORAN/JAPAN TEXTILE INDUSTRY. DIRECTORY. (Text in Japanese) 1910. a. 14,900 Yen. Boshoku-Zasshisha - Textile Journal and Book Pub. Co., 7-9, Ohnodai 1-chome, Osakasayama-si 589, Japan. TEL 81-06-633-7734. Ed. Ken-ichi Uno. circ. 3,200.
Description: Covers Japanese textile manufacturers, institutes and universities. Also lists inspection and testing institutes, textile associations, and textile machinery traders and dealers in Japan.

677.39 II
SILK IN INDIA. biennial. Central Silk Board, United Mansions, 2nd Fl., 39 M.G. Road, Bangalore 560 001, India. TEL 568194. stat.
Description: Statistical information on fabric production, market exports, foreign exchange earned, country output and comparison with world production.

677 AT
TEXTILE AND APPAREL INDEX OF AUSTRALASIA.* 1948. biennial. Aus.$59.95. Farmgate Press, 7 Havelock St., West Perth, W.A. 6005, Australia. TEL 09-388-2277. FAX 09-388-2211. Ed. Ross Dunkley. adv.; circ. 5,000.
Formerly: Textile and Apparel Index of Australia.
Description: Comprehensive listings of all companies associated with textile, clothing and apparel industries in Australia and New Zealand.

677 016.677 US ISSN 0040-5191
TS1300
TEXTILE TECHNOLOGY DIGEST. 1944. m. $415. Institute of Textile Technology, Charlottesville, VA 22902. TEL 804-296-5511. FAX 804-977-5400. Ed. Dennis Loy. bk.rev.; abstr.tr.lit.; tr.mk.; index. (also avail. in microform from UMI)
●Also available online. Vendor(s): DIALOG (File no.119).
Also available on CD-ROM.

677 011 US
TEXTILE TECHNOLOGY DIGEST: ABSTRACT ALERT. 1989. bi-m. $95. Institute of Textile Technology, Box 391, Charlottesville, VA 22902-0391. TEL 804-296-5511. FAX 804-977-5400. Ed. Dennis Loy.
Description: Abstracts from the parent publication "Textile Technology Digest."

677 US
▼**TEXTILE TECHNOLOGY DIGEST: SELECTED INFORMATION.** 1990. m. $95. Institute of Textile Technology, Box 391, Charlottesville, VA 22902-0391. TEL 804-296-5511. FAX 804-977-5400. Ed. Dennis Loy.
Description: Selective dissemination of information from the parent publication "Textile Technology Digest."

677 016 UK ISSN 0043-9118
TS1300 CODEN: WTXAA
WORLD TEXTILE ABSTRACTS. 1969. 12/yr. £320 (effective 1992). Elsevier Science Publishers Ltd., Crown House, Linton Rd., Barking, Essex IG11 8JU, England. TEL 081-594-7272. FAX 081-594-5942. TELEX 896950 APPSCI G. (Subscr. in U.S. and Canada to: Elsevier Science Publishing Co., Inc., Box 882, Madison Sq. Sta., New York, NY 10159. TEL 212-989-5800) bk.rev.; index. (reprint service avail.) Indexed: Abstr.Bull.Inst.Pap.Chem., Anal.Abstr., Anim.Breed.Abstr., Appl.Mech.Rev., Ergon.Abstr.
●Also available online. Vendor(s): DIALOG (File no.67), Orbit Information Technologies (WTA), Pergamon Infoline (WTA).
Supersedes: Shirley Institute Summary of Current Literature; Textile Abstracts.
Description: Provides abstracts of scientific, technical and technico-economic literature relevant to fibre-forming polymers, textile and related industries and the applications of fibrous and textile materials in conventional textile products.

THEATER

see also Dance

792 US
A A T E NEWSLETTER. 1987. q. $68 includes membership (foreign $75). American Alliance for Theatre & Education, Theatre Department, Arizona State University, Tempe, AZ 85287-3411. TEL 602-965-6064. FAX 602-965-9073. Ed. Gordon Hedahl. bk.rev.; circ. 1,400.
Description: Current information, jobs, events for educators and theater artists who work for or with youth.

792 GW
A K T. (Aktuelles Theater) 1969. m. membership. Frankfurter Bund fuer Volksbildung GmbH, Eschersheimer Landstr. 2, 6000 Frankfurt a.M. 1, Germany. TEL 069-1545146. FAX 069-1545138. Eds. J. Kessler, G. Holzapfel. adv.; bk.rev.; circ. 15,000.

A M S STUDIES IN THE RENAISSANCE. see *LITERATURE*

792 US ISSN 0044-7927
PN2000
A S T R NEWSLETTER. 1972. 2/yr. membership. American Society for Theatre Research, c/o P.T. Dircks, Ed., C.W. Post College, Dept. of English, Greenvale, NY 11548. TEL 516-299-2391. adv.; circ. 600 (controlled). (processed)

791.3 642.5 US
ABEL VALUE NEWS; panem et circenses/bread and circuses. 1969. m. $15. Abel News Agencies, 403 1st Ave. N., Estherville, IA 51334-2223. Ed. Peter M. Abel. adv.; bk.rev.; film rev.; play rev.; bibl.; charts; illus.; stat.; tr.lit.; circ. 25,000.
Formerly (until 1983): Abel (ISSN 0001-3153)

ACADEMY PLAYERS DIRECTORY. see *MOTION PICTURES*

792.028 FR ISSN 0991-949X
ACTEURS. 1982. 10/yr. 390 F. (foreign 450 F.). Actes Sud, 18, rue de Savoie, 75006 Paris, France. TEL 43-29-91-89. FAX 43-54-24-10. (Subscr. to: Teletrans, 99 rue d'Amsterdam, 75008 Paris, France. TEL 1-42-80-68-55) Ed. Pierre Laville. adv.
Formerly: Theatre Acteurs.

ADAM INTERNATIONAL REVIEW. see *LITERATURE*

AFRICAN ARTS. see *ART*

AGENCIES: WHAT THE ACTOR NEEDS TO KNOW. see *BUSINESS AND ECONOMICS — Trade And Industrial Directories*

792 NE
AGENDA. 1978. 7/yr. donation. Toneelgroep Amsterdam, Marnixstraat 427, 1017 PK Amsterdam, Netherlands. Ed.Bd. circ. 27,000.
Formerly (until 1987): Publiekstheaterkrant.

791 PL ISSN 0065-6526
ALMANACH SCENY POLSKIEJ. 1960. s-a. (Polska Akademia Nauk, Instytut Sztuki) Wydawnictwa Artystyczne i Filmowe, Ul. Pulawska 61, 02-595 Warsaw, Poland. TEL 48-22-455301. FAX 22-48-455584. (Dist. by: Ars Polona-Ruch, Krakowskie Przedmiescie 7, Warsaw, Poland) Ed. Kazimierz Andrzej Wysinski. circ. 1,500.

ALPHA. see *LITERATURE*

792 US
ALPHA PSI OMEGA: PLAYBILL. 1927. a. free. Alpha Psi Omega National Theatre Honorary, c/o Wabash College, Crawfordsville, IN 47933. TEL 217-581-2021. (Co-sponsor: Delta Psi Omega) Ed. James Fisher. bk.rev.; play rev.; illus.; stat.; circ. 7,000 (controlled).

780 790 US
ALTERNATE ROOTS NEWSLETTER. 1977. q. $15. Alternate Roots, Little Five Points Community Center, 1083 Austin Ave., Atlanta, GA 30307. TEL 404-577-1079. Ed. Josephine Grant. circ. 5,000.

792.0222 CS ISSN 0002-6786
AMATERSKA SCENA; ochotnicke divadlo. vol.2, 1965. m. 48 Kcs.($44.80) (Ministerstvo Kultury Ceske Republiky) Panorama, Halkova 1, 120 72 Prague 2, Czechoslovakia. TEL 2-2361391. (Dist. by: Artia, Ve Smeckach 30, 111 27 Prague 1, Czechoslovakia; Editorial addr.: Mrstikova 23, 100 00 Prague 10, Czechoslovakia) Ed. Tomas Cach. play rev.; abstr.; circ. 1,600.

792.022 UK ISSN 0002-6867
AMATEUR STAGE. 1946. m. £10($20) Stacey Publications, 1 Hawthorndene Rd., Hayes, Bromley, Kent, England. Ed. Roy Stacey. adv.; bk.rev.; illus.; music rev.; play rev.; index; circ. 7,000. (also avail. in microform from UMI)

792 US ISSN 8750-3255
PN2000
AMERICAN THEATRE; the monthly forum for news, features and opinion. 1984. m. $27 (foreign $45). Theatre Communications Group, Inc., 355 Lexington Ave., New York, NY 10017. TEL 212-697-5230. (Dist. by: Eastern News Distributors, Inc., 1130 Cleveland Rd., Sandusky, OH 44870) Ed. Jim O'Quinn. circ. 18,000. **Indexed**: Access (1984-), Bk.Rev.Ind. (1989-), Chic.Per.Ind., Child.Bk.Rev.Ind. (1989-).
—BLDSC shelfmark: 0857.860000.
Description: Each issue features reports on plays in print, performances, as well as theater season schedules around the country and internationally. Includes full-length play scripts six times a year.

792 US ISSN 0899-9880
▼**AMERICAN UNIVERSITY STUDIES. SERIES 26. THEATER ARTS**. 1990. irreg. Peter Lang Publishing, Inc., 62 W. 45th St., 4th Fl., New York, NY 10036. TEL 212-302-6740. Ed. Michael Flamini.

791 US ISSN 0003-2344
GV1851.A3
AMUSEMENT BUSINESS; international newsweekly for live and amusement industry. 1894. w. $79 (Canada $95; elsewhere $110). B P I Communications, Inc., Amusement Business Division, Box 24970, Nashville, TN 37202. TEL 615-321-4250. FAX 615-327-1575. (Subscr. to: Box 41489, Nashville, TN 37204-1489) Ed. Tom Powell. adv.; illus.; circ. 11,806. (also avail. in microform from UMI,MIM) **Indexed**: Bus.Ind., Tr.& Indus.Ind.
●Also available online. Vendor(s): DIALOG.

ANGLICA GERMANICA: SERIES 2. see *LINGUISTICS*

792 CC
ANHUI XIN XI. (Text in Chinese) bi-m. Y1.20 per no. Anhui Yishu Yanjiusuo - Anhui Art Institute, Hefei, Anhui 230001, People's Republic of China. TEL 255920. adv.

791 UK ISSN 0140-7740
ANIMATIONS; a review of puppets and related theatre. 1977. bi-m. £15 (Europe £25; elsewhere £30). Puppet Centre Trust, Battersea Arts Centre, Lavender Hill, London SW11 5TN, England. TEL 071-228-5335. Ed. Penny Francis. bk.rev.; circ. 800.

792 FR ISSN 0066-3026
ANNUAIRE DU SPECTACLE. 1956, 11th ed. a. 550 F. Publications Mandel, L'Edison, 43 bd. Vauban, 78182 St-Quentin-en-Yvelines Cedex, France. TEL 1-30-64-90-80. FAX 1-30-64-79-15.
Description: Lists names, addresses, telephone, fax and telex numbers for people in the entertainment industry.

APPLAUSE THEATRE BOOK REVIEW & CATALOG. see *LITERATURE*

792 CL ISSN 0716-4440
APUNTES. 1960. s-a. $30 in U.S.; Europe $36. Universidad Catolica de Chile, Escuela de Teatro, Diagonal Oriente 3300, Santiago, Chile. TEL 56-2-2744041. FAX 56-2-2232577. Ed. Maria de la Luz Hurtado. adv.; bk.rev.; bibl.; illus.; circ. 1,200. **Indexed**: Rel.Ind.One.
Description: Presents the founding philosophy and supporting respect for the theater. Contains a modern drama in its entirety and activites and news of the theater.

792 IT ISSN 0066-6661
ARCHIVIO DEL TEATRO ITALIANO. 1968. irreg; latest 1982. price varies. Edizioni II Polifilo, Via Borgonuovo 2, 20121 Milan, Italy. Ed. Giovanni Macchia.

792 IT
ARIEL. 1986. 3/yr. L.60000. (Istituto di Studi Pirandelliani) Bulzoni Editore, Via dei Liburni n.14, 00185 Rome, Italy. TEL 06-4455207. FAX 06-4450355. Ed. Alfredo Barbina.

ARISTOS; devoted to the preservation and advancement of traditional values (as opposed to modernism and post-modernism) in the arts. see *ART*

ART AND CULTURE. see *ART*

792 DK ISSN 0901-9901
ARTE NYT. 1958. 3/yr. DKK 35. Hvidkildevej 64, 2400 Copenhagen NV, Denmark. TEL 31-10-16-22. FAX 38-33-20-83. adv.; circ. 55,000.

ARTES. see *ART*

792 US ISSN 1051-9718
ARTISTS AND ISSUES IN THE THEATRE. irreg. Peter Lang Publishing, Inc., 62 W. 45th St., 4th Fl., New York, NY 10036. TEL 212-302-6740. FAX 212-302-7574. Ed. August W. Staub.
—BLDSC shelfmark: 1735.283660.

792 US
ARTS ALIVE!; a magazine promoting the Arts. 1977. m. $15. Admar Associates - Theatrical Faces Inc., 548 N. New St., Bethlehem, PA 18018. TEL 215-758-8211. FAX 215-691-0234. adv.; circ. 12,000 (controlled).
Former titles (until 1986): Lehigh Valley Arts Alive; (until 1982): Theatrical Faces.

792 CN
ARTS CLUB THEATRE ENCORE. 1984. bi-m. Arts Club Theatre, 1585 Johnston St., Vancouver, B.C. V6H 3R9, Canada. TEL 604-687-5315. Ed. Chris Tyrell.

792 US ISSN 0004-4067
ARTS MANAGEMENT. 1962. 5/yr. $18. Radius Group Inc., 408 W. 57th St., New York, NY 10019. TEL 212-245-3850. Ed. Alvin H. Reiss. bk.rev.; stat; index; circ. 12,000. (also avail. in microform from UMI; reprint service avail. from UMI)
Description: National news service for those who finance, manage and communicate the arts.

792 780 CN ISSN 0823-9746
ARTSBOARD. m. Can.$21.40. Professional Association of Canadian Theatres, PACT Communications Centre, 64 Charles St. E., Toronto, Ont. M4Y 1T1, Canada. TEL 416-968-3033. FAX 416-968-3035. Ed. Scott Walbridge. adv.; circ. 500. (looseleaf format)
Description: Employment bulletin for the arts in Canada.

ARTSEARCH; the national employment service bulletin for the performing arts. see *OCCUPATIONS AND CAREERS*

ARTSPACE (COLUMBUS). see *ART*

792 950 US ISSN 0742-5457
PN2860
ASIAN THEATRE JOURNAL. 1984. s-a. $15 to individuals (foreign $18); institutions $30 (foreign $35). (Association for Asian Performance) University of Hawaii Press, Journals Department, 2840 Kolowalu St., Honolulu, HI 96822. TEL 808-956-8833. FAX 808-988-6052. Ed. Samuel L. Leiter. adv.; bk.rev.; illus.; circ. 600. (back issues avail.; reprint service avail from UMI)
—BLDSC shelfmark: 1742.752300.
Supersedes: Asian Theatre Reports (ISSN 0161-4908)
Description: Focuses on the performing arts of Asia.
Refereed Serial

ASOCIACION ARGENTINA DE ACTORES. MEMORIA Y BALANCE. see *LABOR UNIONS*

4630 THEATER

792　　　　　　IS　ISSN 0334-5963
PN2001
ASSAPH. SECTION C. STUDIES IN THE THEATRE. (Text in English) 1984. a. $6 to individuals; institutions $10. Tel Aviv University, Faculty of Visual and Performing Arts, Department of Theatre Arts, Ramat Aviv, Tel Aviv 69978, Israel. FAX 03-414622. Ed. Eli Rozik. circ. 500. (back issues avail.)

ASSOCIACAO PORTUGUESA DE EMPRESAS CINEMATOGRAFICAS. JORNAL. see *MOTION PICTURES*

792　　　　　　　　CN
ASSOCIATION FOR CANADIAN THEATRE RESEARCH. NEWSLETTER. 1976. s-a. membership. Association for Canadian Theatre Research, c/o Department of Theatre and Film, University of British Columbia, Vancouver, B.C. V6T 1Z2, Canada. FAX 604-822-5985. Ed. Denis Johnston. circ. 250.
Formerly: Association for Canadian Theatre History. Newsletter (ISSN 0705-7989)
Description: Contains a range of news items of interest to members, including reports of association business, conferences in related disciplines, calls for papers, annual bibliography, progress reports on research projects, abstracts from annual conference.

700 780.65　　　　US
ASSOCIATION OF PERFORMING ARTS PRESENTERS BULLETIN. 1958. 10/yr. membership. Association of Performing Arts Presenters, 1112 16th St., N.W., Ste. 400, Washington, DC 20036. TEL 202-833-2787. FAX 202-833-1543. Ed. Arthur J. Johnson. bk.rev.; circ. 1,800. (processed)
Former titles: A C U C A A Bulletin; Association of College, University and Community Arts Administrators. Bulletin & Association of College and University Concert Managers. Bulletin (ISSN 0004-5640)
Description: Practical information on presentation of performing arts events, and on events and opportunities in the presenting field.

792 778.53　　　　US
ASSOCIATION OF TALENT AGENTS. NEWSLETTER. m. Association of Talent Agents, 9255 Sunset Blvd., Ste. 318, Los Angeles, CA 90069. TEL 213-274-0628. FAX 213-274-5063.

ATOKA; Yoruba photoplay series. see *LITERATURE*

792 150　　　　IT
ATTI DELLO PSICODRAMMA. (Text in Italian; summaries in English) 1975. a. L.35000 for 2 years. Astrolabio-Ubaldini, Via Lungara 3, 00165 Rome, Italy. (Co-sponsor: Associazione Ricerche sullo Psicodramma Analitico di Roma) Ed. Ottavio Rosati. adv.; illus.; circ. 5,000. **Indexed:** Psychol.Abstr.

792　　　　　　US
AUDARENA STADIUM INTERNATIONAL GUIDE. Variant title: AudArena Stadium Guide. 1959. a. $65. B P I Communications, Inc., Amusement Business Division, Box 24970, Nashville, TN 37202. TEL 615-321-4250. FAX 615-327-1575. Ed. Tom Powell. adv.; circ. 9,000. **Indexed:** Sportsearch (1973-).
Former titles: Audarena Stadium Guide and International Directory (ISSN 0067-0537); Arena, Auditorium, Stadium Guide (ISSN 0518-3979)
Description: Directory of over 6,500 arenas, auditoriums, stadiums, exhibit halls and amphitheatres in the US, Canada, and overseas. Complete data on facilities, including contracts, seating capacities, floor size and services offered.

AUSTIN CHRONICLE. see *MUSIC*

792　　　　AT　ISSN 0810-4123
PN3010
AUSTRALASIAN DRAMA STUDIES. 1982. s-a. Aus.$30 (foreign Aus.$40). University of Queensland, c/o Department of English, St. Lucia, Qld. 4072, Australia. TEL 61-703652135. FAX 61-7-3652799. Eds. V. Kelly, R. Fotheringham. adv.; bk.rev.; circ. 500.
Description: Theatre studies with an emphasis on Australian and New Zealand drama.

800 780.6　　　　PO
AUTORES. 1958. 4/yr. free. Sociedade Portuguesa de Autores, Av. Duque de Loule, 31, 1098 Lisbon Codex, Portugal. FAX 530257. TELEX 42563 SOPAUT P. Dir. Dr. Luiz Francisco Rebello. charts; illus.

792　　　　FR　ISSN 0045-1169
PN6113
AVANT SCENE THEATRE. 1949. 20/yr. 753 F. Editions de l' Avant Scene, 6 rue Git-le-Coeur, 75006 Paris, France. TEL 1-46-34-28-20. FAX 1-43-54-50-14. **Indexed:** Arts & Hum.Cit.Ind., Curr.Cont.
—BLDSC shelfmark: 1837.119000.

792　　　　　　US
BACKSTAGE; the performing arts weekly. 1960. w. $55. B P I Communications, Inc., 330 W. 42nd St., New York, NY 10036. TEL 212-947-0020. FAX 212-967-6786. Ed. Sherry Eaker. adv.; bk.rev.; play rev.; illus.; tr.lit.; circ. 36,000. (tabloid format; also avail. in microfiche from UMI; reprint service avail. from UMI) **Indexed:** Tr.& Indus.Ind.
Incorporates (in 1977): Business Screen (ISSN 0007-7046)
Description: Presents news stories, informative columns, reviews, previews of upcoming theatre seasons, listings of agents, casting directors, rehersal spaces, personal managers, acting coaches, and notices for stage, screen, television and cabaret performers and staff.

792.02　　　　BG
BAHUBACANA. (Text in Bengali) 1978. irreg. Tk.3. Bahubacana Natyagoshthi, 11-2 Jaynag Rd., Bakshi Bazar, Dhaka 1, Bangladesh. play rev.

BALLET-HOO. see *DANCE*

792　　　　IS　ISSN 0045-138X
BAMAH; educational theatre review. (Text in Hebrew; summaries in English) 1959. q. $35. Bamah Association, P.O. Box 7098, Jerusalem 91070, Israel. Eds. Ruth Blumert, Dwora Gilula. adv.; bk.rev.; index, cum.index. **Indexed:** Ind.Heb.Per.

791.3　　　　US　ISSN 0005-4968
BANDWAGON; the circusiana magazine. 1939. 6/yr. $19. Circus Historical Society, 2515 Dorset Rd., Columbus, OH 43221. TEL 614-294-5361. Ed. Fred D. Pfening, Jr. adv.; bk.rev.; illus.; circ. 1,800. (also avail. in microform)

792 821　　　　UK　ISSN 0264-6137
BARE NIBS. 1983. q. £2.60($5) Ware Arts Centre, 31 Richmond Close, Ware, Herts., England. (Subscr. addr.: 24 The Ridgeway, Ware, Herts., England) Ed. Steve Woollard. adv.; circ. 150. (back issues avail.)

792　　　　　　US
BI-MONTHLY THEATRICAL CALENDAR. 1939. bi-m. $100. Celebrity Service, Inc., 1780 Broadway, Ste. 300, New York, NY 10019. TEL 212-757-7979. FAX 212-397-4626. Ed. Frank Gehrecke.
Former titles: Bi-Weekly Theatrical Calendar; Weekly Theatrical Calendar.

792 793.32　　　　CU
BIBLIOTECA NACIONAL JOSE MARTI. DEPARTAMENTO DE INFORMACION Y DOCUMENTACION DE LA CULTURA. SERIE TEATRO Y DANZA. m. Biblioteca Nacional Jose Marti, Departamento de Informacion y Documentacion de la Cultura, Plaza de la Revolucion, Havana, Cuba.

792　　　　IT　ISSN 0045-1959
BIBLIOTECA TEATRALE; rivista di studi e ricerche sullo spettacolo. 1971-1979 (no. 23-24); resumed 1987. q. L.55000($12) (Istituto Internazionale per la Ricerca Teatrali) Bulzoni Editore, 14 via dei Liburni, 00185 Rome, Italy. TEL 06-4455207. FAX 06-4450355. Eds. Ferruccio Marotti, Cesare Molinari. adv.; bk.rev.; abstr.; bibl.; index, cum.index. (back issues avail.)

792　　　　GW　ISSN 0006-4378
BLAETTER DER FREIEN VOLKSBUEHNE BERLIN. 1947. bi-m. DM.7. Verlag der Freien Volksbuehne Berlin e.V., Ruhrstr. 6, 1000 Berlin 31, Germany. Ed. Guenter Schulz. adv.; bk.rev.; play rev.; illus.; stat.; index; circ. 24,000.

792　　　　　　DK
BOERNETEATERAVISEN. 1972. a. DKK 85. Teatercentrum i Danmark, Frederiksborggade 20, DK-1360 Copenhagen K, Denmark. TEL 33-156900. FAX 33-13-14-39. Ed. Jensen Carsten. bk.rev.; circ. 14,000 (controlled).
Formerly: Teater for Boern og Unge (ISSN 0901-0106)
Description: Focuses on professional theater for children and youth. Includes articles on cultural, political and economic matters relevant to the theater world. Features reviews of plays, interviews and biographical sketches of actors.

BOMB; artists, writers, actors, directors. see *ART*

BORDER CROSSINGS. see *ART*

792 380　　　　UK　ISSN 0142-5218
PN2595
BRITISH ALTERNATIVE THEATRE DIRECTORY. 1979. a. £10.95. French & Scott, Ivor House, Ste. 2, 1 Bridge St., Cardiff CF1 2TH, England. TEL 0222-2386131. Ed. David McGillivray.
—BLDSC shelfmark: 2287.250000.

BRITISH PERFORMING ARTS YEARBOOK. see *DANCE*

791.53　　　　UK
BRITISH PUPPET AND MODEL THEATRE GUILD. (NEWSLETTER). 1956. m. $20 membership. British Puppet and Model Theatre Guild, c/o Gordon Shapley, Ed., 18 Maple Rd., Yeading, Hayes, Middlesex UB4 9LP, England. bk.rev.; circ. 400.
Description: For amateur and professional puppeteers thoughout the UK and the world.

792　　　　US　ISSN 0068-2748
BROADSIDE (NEW YORK, 1940). (Supplement avail.: Performance Arts Resources (ISSN: 0360-3814)) 1940; N.S. 1973. q. $20 to individuals; institutions $25. Theatre Library Association, 111 Amsterdam Ave., New York, NY 10023. TEL 212-870-1670. Ed. Alan J. Pally. bk.rev.; circ. 500. (back issues avail.) **Indexed:** Lib.Lit.
Description: Includes information regarding TLA sponsored events, articles about exhibits and collections related to the performing arts, and other items of interest in the fields of theatre, film and dance worldwide.

792　　　　AU　ISSN 0007-3075
BUEHNE. 1958. 11/yr. S.620. O R A C Zeitschriftenverlag GmbH, Schoenbrunnerstr. 59, A-1050 Vienna, Austria. TEL 0222-551621-0. FAX 0222-551621-78. adv.; bk.rev.; play rev.; record rev.; illus.; circ. 126,000 (controlled). **Indexed:** Music Ind.

792　　　　GW　ISSN 0007-3083
DIE BUEHNENGENOSSENSCHAFT. 1949. 10/yr. DM.56. (Genossenschaft Deutscher Buehnenangehoeriger) Buehnenschriften-Vertriebs-Gesellschaft, Feldbrunnenstr. 74, 2000 Hamburg 13, Germany. TEL 040-445185. Ed. Hans Herdlein. adv.; bk.rev.; illus.

792　　　　GW　ISSN 0933-1263
PN2004
BUEHNENKUNST; Sprache - Musik - Bewegung. 1987. q. DM.58. Verlag Urachhaus, Urachstr. 41, 7000 Stuttgart 1, Germany. TEL 0711-260589. Ed. Else Klink. play rev.; illus.; circ. 4,000. (back issues avail.)

792　　　　SZ　ISSN 0007-3091
BUEHNENTECHNISCHE RUNDSCHAU; Zeitschrift fuer Theatertechnik, Buehnenbau und Buehnengestaltung. 1907. 6/yr. 70 SFr. (Deutsche Theatertechnische Gesellschaft) Orell Fuessli & Friedrich Verlag, Dietzingerstr. 3, CH-8036 Zurich, Switzerland. TEL 041-4667711. FAX 041-4667457. TELEX 813575. Ed. Prof. W. Unruh. adv.; bk.rev.; abstr.; bibl.; charts; illus.; cum.index every 2 yrs.; circ. 1,600. **Indexed:** Br.Tech.Ind.
—BLDSC shelfmark: 2357.700000.

792　　　　　　US
BURNS MANTLE BEST PLAY ANNUAL. 1919. a. $36.95 cloth; paper $18.95. Applause Theatre Book Publishers, 211 W. 71st St., New York, NY 10023. TEL 212-595-4735. FAX 212-721-2856. Eds. Otis L. Guernsey, Jeffrey Sweet. circ. 20,000.

792　　　　　FR　　ISSN 0295-9909
CAHIERS DU G I T A. 1985. a. 150 F. Universite de Montpellier (Universite Paul Valery), Groupe Interdisciplinaire du Theatre Antique, B.P. 5043, 34032 Montpellier Cedex 1, France. TEL 67-14-20-00. Dir. Paulette Ghiron-Bistagne. bk.rev.

792　　　　　BE　　ISSN 0771-4653
Z2174.D7
CAHIERS THEATRE LOUVAIN. (Text in French) 1968. q. 1450 BEF. Ferme de Blocry, Place de l'Hocaille, B-1348 Louvain-La-Neuve, Belgium. TEL 010-450500. FAX 010-453234. Ed. Armand Delcampe. adv.; bk.rev.; bibl.; circ. 1,000.
　　Formerly: Cahiers-Theatre (ISSN 0068-5232)
　　Description: Discusses a different theme in twentieth century theatre in each issue.

792　　　　　CN　　ISSN 0045-4044
CALLBOARD. 1951. 4/yr. Can.$15 (foreign Can.$20). Nova Scotia Drama League, 5516 Spring Garden Rd., Ste. 305, Halifax, N.S. B3J 1G6, Canada. TEL 902-425-3876. FAX 902-422-0881. Ed. Eva J. Moore. adv.; bk.rev.; circ. 1,100.

792　　　　　US
CALLBOARD (SAN FRANCISCO); monthly theatre news magazine. 1976. m. $32. Theatre Bay Area, 657 Mission St., Ste. 402, San Francisco, CA 94105-4116. TEL 415-957-1557. FAX 415-957-1556. Ed. Jean Schiffman. adv.; bk.rev.; circ. 10,000. (back issues avail.)
　　Description: Provides trade information for professionals in the Bay Area.

817　　　　　US
CALLIOPE (BALTIMORE). 1968. m. membership. Clowns of America, Inc, 1052 Foxwood Ln., Baltimore, MD 21221. Ed. Albert E. Sikorsky, Jr. adv.; bk.rev.; bibl.; circ. 6,000.
　　Supersedes: Joeygram (ISSN 0021-7158)

CAMPUS ACTIVITIES PROGRAMMING. see EDUCATION — Higher Education

CANADA COUNCIL ANNUAL REPORT AND SUPPLEMENT/RAPPORT ANNUEL DU CONSEIL DES ARTS DU CANADA ET SON SUPPLEMENT. see ART

792　　　　　CN
CANADA ON STAGE: THE NATIONAL THEATRE YEARBOOK. 1974. a. Professional Association of Canadian Theatres, PACT Communications Centre, 64 Charles St. E., Toronto, Ont. M4Y 1T1, Canada. TEL 416-968-3033. illus.; index.
　　Formerly: Canada on Stage: Canadian Theatre Review Yearbook (ISSN 0380-9455)

792　　　　　CN　　ISSN 1183-1243
▼**CANADIAN JOURNAL OF DRAMA AND THEATRE**. 1991. 2/yr. Can.$16($16) University of Calgary Press, 816 MacKimmie Library Tower, 2500 University Dr. N.W., Calgary, Alta. T2N 1N4, Canada. TEL 403-220-7578. FAX 403-282-0085. TELEX 03-821545. Ed. Roberta Bramwell. adv.; circ. 70.
　　Description: Publishes research on design, literary criticism, theater history, acting, dramaturgy, directing and developmental drama performance.
　　Refereed Serial

792　　　　　CN　　ISSN 0315-0836
PN2009
CANADIAN THEATRE REVIEW. 1,088. 1974. q. Can.$27.50 to individuals; institutions Can.$45; students Can.$22. University of Toronto Press, Journals Department, P.O. Box 1280, 1011 Sheppard Ave. W., Downsview, Ont. M3H 5V4, Canada. TEL 416-667-7781. FAX 416-667-7832. Ed. Alan Filewood. adv.; bk.rev.; illus.; play rev.; cum.index: nos.1-16. (also avail. in microform from MML; back issues avail.) **Indexed:** Arts & Hum.Cit.Ind., Can.Per.Ind., Can.Wom.Per.Ind., CMI, Curr.Cont., Ind.Bk.Rev.Hum., M.L.A., Mid.East: Abstr.& Ind.
　　—BLDSC shelfmark: 3045.281800.

792　　　　　IT
IL CASTELLO DI ELSINORE. 1988. 2/yr. L.53000 (Europe L.75000; elsewhere L.95000). Rosenberg and Sellier, Via Andrea Doria, 14, 10123 Turin, Italy. TEL 011-561-39-07. FAX 011-532188.

790.2　　　　US
CAVALCADE OF ACTS & ATTRACTIONS. 1973. a. $50. B P I Communications, Inc., Amusement Business Division, Box 24970, Nashville, TN 37202. TEL 615-321-4250. FAX 615-327-1575. Ed. Tom Powell. circ. 7,000.
　　Formerly: Cavalcade and Directory of Acts and Attractions (ISSN 0090-2993)
　　Description: Directory of personal appearance artists (musical and theatrical), touring shows, carnivals and other specialized entertainment such as fireworks firms, and rodeos. Also contains listings of booking agents, personal managers, promoters and producers.

792　　　　　US　　ISSN 0069-1372
GV54.N7
CELEBRITY SERVICE INTERNATIONAL CONTACT BOOK; trade directory/entertainment industry. a. $40. Celebrity Service, Inc., 1780 Broadway, Ste. 300, New York, NY 10019. TEL 212-757-7979. FAX 212-397-4626. Ed. Sara Wiener. adv.

CENTER FOR SOVIET AND EAST-EUROPEAN STUDIES IN THE PERFORMING ARTS. BULLETIN. see HUMANITIES: COMPREHENSIVE WORKS

CENTER MAGAZINE. see ART

792　301.4157　US
CENTER STAGE (NEW YORK). 1987. m. $25. Lesbian & Gay Community Services Center, Inc., 208 W. 13th St., New York, NY 10011. TEL 212-620-7310. Ed. Dino Georgiou. circ. 23,000.

CENTRE CULTUREL FRANCAIS DE YAOUNDE. PROGRAMME SAISON. see ART

CHIRICU. see LITERATURE

792　　　　　US　　ISSN 0891-6381
GV1580　　　　CODEN: CHDAEO
CHOREOGRAPHY AND DANCE; an international journal. 1988. 2/yr. $60. Harwood Academic Publishers, 270 Eighth Ave., New York, NY 10011. TEL 212-206-8900. FAX 212-645-2459. TELEX 236735 GOPUB UR. (Subscr. to: Box 786, Cooper Sta., New York, NY 10276. TEL 800-545-8398; UK addr.: P.O. Box 90, Reading, Berkshire RG1 8JL, England. TEL 0734-560-080) Ed. Robert P. Cohan. (also avail. in microform)
　　Description: Concerned with the ballet and related forms of dance performed on stage, including the techniques whereby choreographers are trained. Covers historical and social influences on dance.
　　Refereed Serial

CINEGUIA; annuario espanol del espectaculo y audiovisuales. see MOTION PICTURES

CINESCHEDARIO - LETTURE DRAMMATICHE. see MOTION PICTURES

792　　　　　NE
CIRCUS-GIDS NEDERLAND. m. fl.27.50. Piet de Jong, C.H. Petersstraat 10, 9714 CK Groningen, Netherlands. Ed. John de Vries. bk.rev.; circ. 700.

790　　　　　GW
CIRCUS-PARADE. 1976. m. DM.75. Circus-Club International, Klosterhof 10, 2308 Preetz, Germany. TEL 04342-83103. Ed. Friedel Zscharschuch. adv.; bk.rev.; circ. 4,000.

792　　　　　US　　ISSN 0889-5996
CIRCUS REPORT. 1972. w. $35 (Canada and Mexico $45; elsewhere $50). 525 Oak St., El Cerrito, CA 94530-3699. TEL 415-525-3332. Ed. Don Marcks. adv.; bk.rev.; circ. 2,400.

791.3　　　　FR　　ISSN 0009-7373
CIRQUE DANS L'UNIVERS. 1950. q. membership. Club du Cirque, 11 rue Ch-Silvestri, 94300 Vincennes, France. Ed. L.R. Dauven. bk.rev.; illus.; circ. 2,000.

CITY GUIDE - BROADWAY MAGAZINE. see TRAVEL AND TOURISM

792　800　　　US　　ISSN 0748-237X
CLIPPER STUDIES IN THE THEATER. 1985. irreg., no.14, 1992 (approx. 2/yr.). price varies. Borgo Press, Box 2845, San Bernardino, CA 92406. TEL 714-884-5813. Eds. Paul David Seldis, William L. Slout.
　　Description: Monographs and anthologies on American and European theatre, from its beginnings to modern times.

THEATER　　4631

792　　　　　BL
COLECAO TEATRO. no.2, 1974. irreg. Universidade Federal do Rio Grande do Sul, Porto Alegre, Brazil. bibl.

COLOQUIO: ARTES; revista de artes visuais musica e bailado. see ART

792　　　　　FR　　ISSN 0759-125X
COMEDIE FRANCAISE. 1971. 4/yr. 300 F. (foreign 350 F.). Place Colette, 75001 Paris, France. Ed. Jean-Loup Riviere. adv.; bk.rev.; illus.; circ. 25,000.
　　—BLDSC shelfmark: 3330.212930.

COMMUNICATION QUARTERLY. see EDUCATION

COMMUNICATIONS FROM THE INTERNATIONAL BRECHT SOCIETY. see LITERATURE

792　　　　　US
COMPLETE CATALOGUE OF PLAYS (YEAR). 1936. a. Dramatists Play Service, Inc., 440 Park Ave. S., New York, NY 10016. TEL 212-683-8960. FAX 212-213-1539. Ed. Bradley G. Kalos. adv.; bk.rev.; circ. 35,000.
　　Description: Lists all plays leased by the Dramatists Play Service, including title, author, quotes from reviews, cast and scenic requirements, and a description of the play.

792　　　　　CU　　ISSN 0010-5937
CONJUNTO. 1964. q. $10 in N. America; S. America $12; Europe $17. (Casa de las Americas, Departamento de Teatro) Ediciones Cubanas, Obispo No. 527, Aptdo. 605, Havana, Cuba. Dir. Manuel Galich. abstr.; bibl.; illus.; circ. 3,000. **Indexed:** Hisp.Amer.Per.Ind.

CONNECTICUT POETRY REVIEW. see LITERATURE — Poetry

792.028 791.4　　　UK
CONSORTIUM FOR DRAMA & MEDIA IN HIGHER EDUCATION. NEWSLETTER. 3/yr. membership. British Universities Film and Video Council, 55 Greek St., London W1V 5LR, England. TEL 071-734-3687. FAX 071-287-3914. Ed. Nick Wray. bk.rev.; film rev.; play rev.; circ. 5,500. (looseleaf format; back issues avail.)

CONTACTS. see PUBLISHING AND BOOK TRADE

792　780.65　　AT　　ISSN 1032-6456
CONTACTS & FACILITIES IN THE AUSTRALIAN ENTERTAINMENT INDUSTRY. 1963. a. Aus.$46 (foreign Aus.$80). Showcase Publications, P.O. Box 951, Crows Nest, N.S.W. 2065, Australia. TEL 02-4382144. FAX 02-438-2007.
　　Formerly: Contacts and Facilities in the Entertainment Industry.

CONTEMPORARY THEATRE, FILM & TELEVISION. see BIOGRAPHY

792　　　　　US　　ISSN 1048-6801
▼**CONTEMPORARY THEATRE REVIEW**; an international journal. 1991. 2/yr. (in 1 vol., 2 nos./vol.) $57. Harwood Academic Publishers, 270 Eighth Ave., New York, NY 10011. TEL 212-206-8900. FAX 212-645-2459. TELEX 236735 GOPUB UR. (Subscr. to: Box 786, Cooper Sta. New York, NY 10276. TEL 800-545-8398; UK subscr. to: P.O. Box 90, Reading, Berkshire RG1 8JL, England. TEL 0734-560-080) Eds. Franc Chamberlain, Rick Tavorian. (also avail. in microform)
　　Description: Covers research in the field of performance, including all aspects of the theatre event.
　　Refereed Serial

792　　　　　US　　ISSN 1049-6513
CONTEMPORARY THEATRE STUDIES. irreg. Harwood Academic Publishers, 270 Eighth Ave., New York, NY 10011. TEL 212-206-8900. FAX 212-645-2459. TELEX 236735 GOPUB UR. (Subscr. to: Box 786, Cooper Sta., New York, NY 10276. TEL 800-545-8398; UK subscr. to: Box 90, Reading, Berkshire RG1 8JL, England. TEL 0734-560-080) Ed. Rich Takvorian. (also avail. in microform)
　　Refereed Serial

THEATER

792   US   ISSN 0163-3821
CONTRIBUTIONS IN DRAMA AND THEATRE STUDIES. 1979. irreg., no.47, 1992. price varies. Greenwood Press, Inc. (Subsidiary of: Greenwood Publishing Group Inc.), 88 Post Rd. W., Box 5007, Westport, CT 06881-5007. TEL 203-226-3571. FAX 203-222-1502. Ed. Joseph Donohue.
—BLDSC shelfmark: 3458.310000.

792   IT
CRONACHE DEL TEATRO; settimanale di informazioni e rassegna stampa. 1981. w. L.190000. A G I S Lombarda, Piazza Luigi di Savoia, 24, 20124 Milan. TEL 02-6690241. film rev.; circ. 250. (looseleaf format; back issues avail.)
Description: Covers theater, critical theatrical study and Italian films viewed on Italian television.

792   US   ISSN 0011-2666
CUE OF THETA ALPHA PHI. 1928. a. $3.50. Theta Alpha Phi National Fraternity for the Performing Arts, c/o Betty Stockton, 242 E. Park St., Westerville, OH 43801. adv.; bk.rev.; illus.; tr.lit.; circ. 3,500. (reprint service avail. from UMI)

792.022   NE   ISSN 0038-7258
D O E. 1951. bi-m. fl.17.50. Stichting "Ons Leekenspel", Gudelalaan 2, Bussum, Netherlands. Ed.Bd. bk.rev.; bibl.; illus.; circ. 1,300.
Formerly: Speel.

DAILY VARIETY; news of the entertainment industry. see COMMUNICATIONS — Television And Cable

792   CC
DANGDAI XIJU/CONTEMPORARY DRAMA; xiju - dianshi shuangyuekan. (Text in Chinese) bi-m. $23.90. Zhongguo Xijujia Xiehui, Shaanxi Fenhui - China Dramatists Association, Shaanxi Chapter, 172, Dongmutou Jie, Xi'an, Shaanxi 710001, People's Republic of China. TEL 23171. (Dist. in US by: China Books & Periodicals, Inc, 2929 24th St., San Francisco, CA 94110. TEL 415-282-2994) Ed. Du Yaomin.

792   CC
DAWUTAI. (Text in Chinese) bi-m. Hebei Sheng Yishu Yanjiusuo - Hebei Art Research Institute, 41, Beima Lu, Shijiazhuang, Hebei 050071, People's Republic of China. TEL 743588. Ed. Feng Feng.

700   US
DENVER ARTS CENTER PROGRAMS. bi-m. Publishing House, Inc., P.O. Box 215, Westminster, CO 80030-4860. TEL 303-428-9529. FAX 303-430-1676. Ed. Melanie Simonete. circ. 680,000.

792   GW   ISSN 0011-975X
DIE DEUTSCHE BUEHNE; Theatermagazin. 1909. m. DM.72. Deutscher Buehnenverein, Quatermarkt 5, 5000 Cologne, Germany. TEL 0221-2081218. FAX 0221-2081228. TELEX 813575-CH-OREL. (Subscr. to: Orell Fuessli und Friedrich, Dietzinger 3, CH-8036 Zurich, Switzerland) Ed. Wolfgang Ruf. adv.; bk.rev.; charts; illus.; play rev.; index; circ. 3,500. (reprint service avail. from KTO)
—BLDSC shelfmark: 3564.103000.
Description: Covers German and international performing arts.

792   GW   ISSN 0070-4431
PN2640
DEUTSCHES BUEHNEN-JAHRBUCH; Theatergeschichtliches Jahr- und Adressbuch. 1889. a. DM.57.20. (Genossenschaft Deutscher Buehnenangehoeriger) Buehnenschriften-Vertriebs-Gesellschaft, Feldbrunnenstr. 74, 2000 Hamburg 13, Germany. TEL 040-445185. adv.

792   PL   ISSN 0012-2041
PN1607
DIALOG; miesiecznik poswiecony dramaturgii wspolczesnej teatralnej, filmowej, radiowej i telewizyjnej. 1956. m. $11. Wydawnictwo Wspolczesne R S W "Prasa-Ksiazka-Ruch", Ul. Wiejska 12, 00-420 Warsaw, Poland. TEL 48-22-285330. (Dist. by: Ars Polona-Ruch, Krakowskie Przedmiescie 7, Warsaw, Poland) Ed. Konstanty Puzyna. bk.rev.; circ. 7,500. **Indexed:** M.L.A.

DIRECTORY OF NORTH AMERICAN FAIRS, FESTIVALS AND EXPOSITIONS. see SPORTS AND GAMES — Outdoor Life

791.53   UK
DIRECTORY OF PROFESSIONAL PUPPETEERS. 1976. biennial. Puppet Centre Trust, Battersea Arts Centre, Lavender Hill, London SW11 5TN, England. TEL 071-228-5335. Ed.Bd. illus.; circ. 2,000. (back issues avail.)

DIRECTORY OF THE ARTS. see ART

792   CS   ISSN 0012-4141
DIVADELNI NOVINY.* vol. 14, 1970. fortn. 26 Kcs. Svaz Ceskoslovenskych Divadelnich a Rozhlasovych Umelcu, Valdstejnske nam. 3, Prague 1, Czechoslovakia. (Co-sponsor: Divadelni Ustav) Ed. Jaroslav Opavsky.
Formerly: Divadelni a Filmove Noviny.

DOCTOR WHO MAGAZINE. see COMMUNICATIONS — Television And Cable

792   YU   ISSN 0351-5494
DOKUMENTI - INFORMACIJE. (Text in Macedonian, Serbo-Croation, Slovenian) 1978. s-a. Sterijino Pozorje, Zmaj Jovina 22, 21000 Novi Sad, Voivodina, Yugoslavia. TEL 021-23-161. FAX 021-615-976.

792   GW
DOMSPATZ; Zeitschrift fuer Fulda. 1981. m. DM.25($30) Domspatz Verlag, Kanalstr. 14, 6400 Fulda, Germany. TEL 0661-75515. FAX 0661-78430. Ed. Johannes Guedelhoefer. adv.; film rev.; charts. (back issues avail.)
Description: News and articles about cultural events in Fulda.

792   UK   ISSN 0012-5946
PN2001
DRAMA;* the quarterly theatre review. 1919. q. $17 to individuals; institutions $21. British Theatre Association, Cranbourn Mansions, Cranbourn St., London WC2H 7AG, England. TEL 01-935-2571. FAX 01-224-2457. Ed. Christopher Edwards. adv.; bk.rev.; illus.; play rev.; index; circ. 6,500. (also avail. in microform from SWZ,UMI; reprint service avail. from UMI) **Indexed:** Abstr.Engl.Stud., Arts & Hum.Cit.Ind., Bk.Rev.Ind., Br.Hum.Ind., Curr.Cont., Hum.Ind., Ind.Bk.Rev.Hum.

792 800   US
▼**DRAMA CRITICISM.** 1991. a. $75. Gale Research Inc., 835 Penobscot Bldg., Detroit, MI 48226-4094. TEL 313-961-2242. FAX 313-961-6083. TELEX 810-221-7086. Ed. Lawrence J. Trudeau.
Description: Provides excerpts from significant commentary on 12-15 of the most widely studied dramatists from antiquity to contemporary times in each volume.

DRAMA-LOGUE. see MOTION PICTURES

792   UK
THE DRAMA MAGAZINE. 1973. 3/yr. £8 (foreign $10) to non-members; with membership £15. Holborn Centre for Performing Arts, Three Cups Yard, Sandland St., London WC1 4PZ, England. TEL 071-405-4519. Ed. David Shepperd. adv.; bk.rev.; illus.; circ. 1,500.
Incorporates (in 1990): London Drama Magazine.

792 375   US   ISSN 1046-5022
DRAMA - THEATRE TEACHER. 1988. 3/yr. $25 (foreign $30). American Alliance for Theatre & Education, Theatre Department, Arizona State University, Tempe, AZ 85287-3411. TEL 602-965-6064. FAX 602-965-9073. Ed. Phil Taylor. adv.; bk.rev.; circ. 1,100.
Description: Practical articles on theatre education with an emphasis on classroom instruction K-12.

792   US   ISSN 0012-5989
PN3175.A1
DRAMATICS; devoted to the advancement of theatre arts in the secondary schools. 1929. 9/yr. $18. Educational Theatre Association, 3368 Central Parkway, Cincinnati, OH 45225. TEL 513-559-1996. Ed. Don Corathers. adv.; bk.rev.; charts; illus.; index; circ. 35,500. (also avail. in microform from UMI; back issues avail.; reprint service avail. from UMI) **Indexed:** Curr.Cont.
Formerly: Dramatics-Dramatic Curtain.

792   US
DRAMATISTS GUILD NEWSLETTER. 1977. m. (except Jul., Aug.). membership. Dramatists Guild, Inc., 234 W. 44th St., New York, NY 10036. TEL 212-398-9366. Ed. Jason Milligan. circ. 7,500. (tabloid format; back issues avail.)

792   US   ISSN 0012-6004
PN2000
DRAMATISTS GUILD QUARTERLY. 1964. q. membership. Dramatists Guild, Inc., 234 W. 44th St., New York, NY 10036. TEL 212-398-9366. Ed. Otis L. Guernsey, Jr. adv.; bk.rev.; circ. 8,200.

800   US   ISSN 0733-1606
PN2289
DRAMATISTS SOURCEBOOK. 1982. a. $14.95. Theatre Communications Group, Inc., 355 Lexington Ave., New York, NY 10017. TEL 212-697-5230. Ed. Gillian Richards. index; circ. 5,000.
Description: Lists opportunities for playwrights, translations, composers, lyricists and librettists.

792   UK   ISSN 0141-1179
DRAMAU'R BYD. (Text in Welsh) 1969. irreg. price varies. (Welsh Arts Council) University of Wales Press, 6 Gwennyth St., Cathays, Cardiff CF2 4YD, Wales. TEL 0222-31919. FAX 0222-230908. Ed. William R. Lewis.
Description: Major European plays translated into Welsh.

800 700   US   ISSN 1048-9401
NX449
EARLY DRAMA, ART, AND MUSIC REVIEW. 1978. s-a. $6 to individuals; institutions $8. Medieval Institute Publications, Western Michigan University, Kalamazoo, MI 49008. TEL 616-387-4155. FAX 616-387-4150. Ed. Clifford Davidson. bk.rev.; circ. 250. (back issues avail.)
Incorporates: Medieval Music-Drama News;
Formerly: E D A M Newsletter (ISSN 0196-5816)
Description: Brief articles about, reviews of, and notes and announcements about activities of concern to the Early Drama, Art and Music project at the university.

792   US   ISSN 0013-1997
EDUCATIONAL THEATRE NEWS. 1952. 6/yr. $3. Southern California Educational Theatre Association, 9811 Pounds Ave., Whittier, CA 90603. TEL 310-947-6334. FAX 310-947-6333. Ed. Lee Korf. adv.; bk.rev.; film rev.; play rev.; illus.; circ. 3,100. (tabloid format)
Description: News coverage of secondary, youth, community, and college-university and international theatre activities, including conferences, legislation, and technical advances.

792   RU
EKRAN. 1957. 18/yr. 1.50 Rub. per no. Soyuz Kinematografistov S.S.S.R., Ul. Chasovaya 5, B, 125319 Moscow, Russia. TEL 152-88-21. Ed. V.P. Demin. illus.; index; circ. 700,000.
Formerly (until no.1, 1991): Sovetskii Ekran (ISSN 0038-5123)

792   US
EMERSON STUDIES IN THEATRE AND FILM. irreg. Peter Lang Publishing, Inc., 62 W. 45th St., 4th Fl., New York, NY 10036. TEL 212-302-6740. FAX 212-302-7574. Ed. Miles W. Coiner.
Description: Focuses on the art of performance, its history, criticism and theory, rather than in the verbal dramatic text.

792   II   ISSN 0013-6980
ENACT; monthly theatre magazine. (Text in English) 1967. m. Rs.35($12.50) Paul's Press, E44-11, Okhla Industrial Area, Phase II, New Delhi 110020, India. Ed. Rajinder Paul. adv.; bk.rev.; film rev.; play rev.; circ. 48,448.

ENCORE (BLACKSBURG). see LITERATURE

791.4   UK
ENGLISH NATIONAL OPERA PROGRAMME. m. £1 per no. English National Opera, London Coliseum, St. Martin's Lane, London WC2, England. FAX 01-836-8379. Ed. Nicholas John. adv.; circ. 25,000.
Description: Each opera has separate programme.

792   US
ENSEMBLE; the new variety arts review. 1987. q. $50. Corporeal Studio Ltd., One Hudson St., New York, NY 10013. TEL 212-619-0152. (Subscr. to: Box 227, Canal St. Sta., New York, NY 10013) Ed. J.R. Moore. adv.; bk.rev.; film rev.; play rev.; illus.; circ. 7,500. (tabloid format; back issues avail.)
 Description: Reviews and critism of mime, clown, juggling, variety acts, dance, performance art and film.

ENTERTAINMENT LAW & FINANCE. see LAW

ENTERTAINMENT MAGAZINE. see MUSIC

ENTERTAINMENT MAGAZINE. see MUSIC

ENTERTAINMENT, PUBLISHING AND THE ARTS HANDBOOK. see COMMUNICATIONS — Television And Cable

792   SW   ISSN 0345-2581
ENTRE; teatertidskrift. 1974. 4/yr. SEK 160. Svenska Riksteatern - Swedish National Theatre Centre, S-145 83 Norsborg, Sweden. TEL 0753-99352. FAX 0753-83012. Ed. Claes Englund. bk.rev.; circ. 5,000.
 Description: Contains theater and book reviews, general information and criticism, and a performance calendar for Sweden.

792   CN   ISSN 0319-8650
ENVERS DU DECOR; la vie du theatre. (Text in French) vol.5, 1973. bi-m. free. Theatre du Nouveau Monde, 84 Ouest, rue Ste-Catherine, Montreal, Que. H2X 1Z6, Canada. TEL 514-861-0563. Ed. Roch Carrier. adv.; illus. (tabloid format)

EPOCA; revista de cultura. see LITERATURE

792.028   UK
EQUITY JOURNAL. 1931. 5/yr. membership. British Actor's Equity Association, 8 Harley St., London W1N 2AB, England. TEL 071-636-6367. FAX 071-580-0970. adv.; circ. 45,000.

792   US   ISSN 0013-9890
EQUITY NEWS. 1915. m. $15 (free to qualified personnel). Actors Equity Association, 165 W. 46th St., New York, NY 10036. TEL 212-869-8530. Ed. Dick Moore. bk.rev.; illus.; circ. 36,000.

792   AG
ESPACIO DE CRITICA E INVESTIGACION TEATRAL. 1986. q. Arg.$60($28) Fundacion para el Desarrollo del Arte, Av. Coronel Diaz 2277, Piso 24, Depto. B, 1425 Buenos Aires, Argentina. TEL 824 6400. bk.rev.; circ. 3,000. (back issues avail.)
 Description: Critical reviews of theatre.

ESSAYS IN POETICS. see LITERATURE

792   CN   ISSN 0821-4425
ESSAYS IN THEATRE. 1982. s-a. Can.$15 to individuals (foreign $15); libraries Can.$20 (foreign $20). University of Guelph, Department of Drama, Guelph, Ont. N1G 2W1, Canada. TEL 519-824-4120. FAX 519-837-1315. Eds. H. Lane, A. Wilson. bk.rev.; circ. 300. **Indexed:** Arts & Hum.Cit.Ind.; M.L.A.
 —BLDSC shelfmark: 3811.789000.

792 780   US
ESSAYS ON ASIAN THEATER, MUSIC AND DANCE. vol.3, 1974. irreg. (approx. 1-2/yr.). price varies. Asia Society, 725 Park Ave., New York, NY 10021. TEL 212-288-6400. FAX 212-517-8315. TELEX 224953 ASIA UR.

792   AA
ESTRADA. bi-m. Central House of Popular Creativity, Tirana, Albania.

792 410 800 375.4 US   ISSN 0097-8663
ESTRENO; journal on the contemporary Spanish theater. (Text in Spanish) articles in English or Spanish) 1975. s-a. $14 to individuals; institutions $23. 350 N. Burrowes Bldg., University Park, PA 16802. Ed. Martha Halsey. adv.; bk.rev.; bibl.; index; circ. 1,000. **Indexed:** Arts & Hum.Cit.Ind.; Curr.Cont.; M.L.A.
 —BLDSC shelfmark: 3812.592000.

ETUDES CINEMATOGRAPHIQUES. see MOTION PICTURES

EUGENE O'NEILL REVIEW. see LITERATURE

800   IT
EVENTO TEATRALE. SEZIONE: AUTORI ITALIANI DEL NOVECENTO.* 1976. irreg. Edizioni Abete, Via Prenestina, 685, Rome, Italy.

792   US
EXPERIMENT THEATRE; "one minute" poetic drama. irreg. $5.50. Experiment Press, 6565 N.E. Windermere Rd., Seattle, WA 98105-2057. Ed. Carol Ely Harper.

792   NE
F I R T - I F T R - SIBMAS BULLETIN. 1977. s-a. membership. Federation Internationale pour la Recherche Theatrale - International Federation for Theatre Research, c/o Van Eeghenstraat 113ll, 1071 EZ Amsterdam, Netherlands. Eds. Eric Alexander, Liliana Alexandrescu. circ. 450.

FACE TO FACE WITH TALENT. see COMMUNICATIONS — Television And Cable

FACILITIES DIRECTORY/REPERTOIRE DES SALLES DE SPECTACLE. see DANCE

FAIRS AND FESTIVALS (YEAR): NORTHEAST AND SOUTHEAST. see ARTS AND HANDICRAFTS

792   AT
FANFARE. 1972. m. Aus.$20. Circus Fans Association of Australasia, 29 Elizabeth Pde., Charlestown, N.S.W. 2290, Australia. TEL 049-431504. Ed. Geoffrey A. Greaves. circ. 250. (back issues avail.)
 Description: Circus news in Australia and New Zealand.

792   CN   ISSN 0046-3256
PN2306.S77
FANFARES. 1967. q. membership. Stratford Shakespearean Festival Foundation of Canada, Festival Theatre, Box 520, Stratford, Ont. N5A 6V2, Canada. TEL 519-271-4040. circ. 20,000.

791.53   GW   ISSN 0430-3873
FIGURENTHEATER. 1923. s-a. DM.10($7) Deutsches Institut fuer Puppenspiel, Hattingerstr. 467, D-4630 Bochum, Germany. TEL 0234-47778. Ed. Juergen Kluender. circ. 1,500. (back issues avail.)
 Description: Covers international puppetry.

FILM A DIVADLO. see COMMUNICATIONS — Television And Cable

FILM, SZINHAZ, MUZSIKA. see MOTION PICTURES

792   AT
FIRST NIGHTERS' CURTAINCALL.* 1970. m. Aus.$3. Gallery First Nighters' Club, c/o Mrs. G. Fall, 33 Shirley Rd., Roseville, NSW 2069, Australia.

792   GW   ISSN 0930-5874
FORUM MODERNES THEATER. (Text in English, French and German) 2/yr. DM.78. Gunter Narr Verlag, Postfach 2567, 7400 Tubingen 1, Germany. TEL 07071-78091. FAX 07071-75288. Ed. Gunter Ahrends.
 —BLDSC shelfmark: 4024.093500.

792   FR   ISSN 0015-9433
FRANCE - THEATRE; la vie du spectacle. 1957. bi-m. 25 F. Syndicat National des Agences, 16 Av. l'Opera, Paris (1e), France. Ed. Henri Soupe. bk.rev.; play rev. (processed)

FREMANTLE ARTS REVIEW. see ART

FRIENDS FOCUS. see CLUBS

792   CC   ISSN 0257-0211
FUJIAN XIJU/FUJIAN THEATER. (Text in Chinese) 1979. bi-m. Y2.50($12.20) Fujiang Sheng Yishu Yanjiusuo, Fujian Xiju Bianjibu, 62 Yangqiao Lu, Fuzhou, Fujian 350001, People's Republic of China. TEL 31163. (Dist. overseas by: Jiangsu Publications Import & Export Corp., 56 Gao Yun Ling, Nanjing, P.R.C., in US by: China Books & Periodicals, Inc., 2929 24th St., San Francisco, CA 94110. TEL 415-282-2994) Ed. Yuan Rongsheng.
 Description: Focuses on local drama and theater in Fujian Province.

792   UK   ISSN 0016-4283
PN6111
GAMBIT; an international drama magazine. 1963. irreg. Calder Publications, 9-15 Neal St., London WC2H 9TU, England. TEL 071-497-1741. Ed. Tony Dunn. adv.; bk.rev.; illus.; play rev.; circ. 1,500. **Indexed:** Abstr.Engl.Stud.; Ind.Bk.Rev.Hum.

792 917.306
GESTOS; teoria y practica del teatro hispanico. (Text in English, Spanish) 1986. s-a. $18 to individuals (foreign $22); institutions $30 (foreign $34). University of California, Irvine, School of Humanities, Dept. of Spanish and Portuguese, Irvine, CA 92717. FAX 714-725-2803. Ed. Juan Villegas. adv.; bk.rev.; play rev.; circ. 700. (back issues avail.) **Indexed:** M.L.A.
 Description: Discusses theater theory, with emphasis on Hispanic theater. Includes essays, news and publication of plays on Hispanic theater for specialists.

GESTUS; a quarterly journal of Brechtian studies. see LITERATURE

792   VN
GIAO VIEN NHAN DAN/PEOPLE'S THEATRE. 1959. w. Ministry of Education and Training, Le Truc, Hanoi, Socialist Republic of Vietnam. TEL 52849. Ed. Nguyen Truong Thuy.

GIORNALE DELLO SPETTACOLO. see DANCE

792   US
GLOBE (MIAMI).* script opportunities for dramatists in all media. 1984. m. $26.50. International Society of Dramatists, Box 192012, Miami, FL 33119-2012. TEL 305-674-1831. Ed. A. Delaplaine. bk.rev.; circ. 8,000. (looseleaf format; back issues avail.)

792   YU   ISSN 0351-9120
PN2850
GODISNJAK JUGOSLOVENSKIH POZORISTA/YEARBOOK OF YUGOSLAV THEATERS. (Text in Albanian, Hungarian, Macedonian, Serbocroatian, Slovenian) 1978. a. $20. Sterijino Pozorje, Zmaj Jovina 22, 21000 Novi Sad, Vojvodina, Yugoslavia. TEL 021-23-161. Ed. Svetko Borovcanin.

GOETIKUSS. see EDUCATION

792 792.8   FR   ISSN 0982-9873
LE GRAND HUIT. (Text in French) 1986. 10/yr. 40 F. Le Grand Huit, B.P. 675, 35008 Rennes, France. Ed. Pierre Debauche. adv.; circ. 20,000.

792   FR   ISSN 0993-5835
GROUPE INTERDISCIPLINAIRE DU THEATRE ANTIQUE. TEXTES ET DOCUMENTS. 1984. irreg. price varies. Universite de Montpellier (Universite Paul Valery), Groupe Interdisciplinaire du Theatre Antique, B.P. 5043, 34032 Montpellier Cedex 1, France. TEL 67-14-22-43. (back issues avail.)

792   CN
GRYPHON THEATRE NEWS. 1979. q. Gryphon Theatre Foundation, Brock St., Barrie, Ont. L4N 2M2, Canada.

H D K INFO. (Hochschule der Kunste Berlin) see ART

HISPANIC AMERICAN ARTS; all you want or must know, about everything, in all the fields of Hispanic American arts. see ART

HOJAS LITERARIAS ILUSTRADAS. see LITERATURE

HOLLYWOOD ACTING COACHES AND TEACHERS DIRECTORY. see EDUCATION — Teaching Methods And Curriculum

HOLLYWOOD REPORTER. see MOTION PICTURES

HORISONT. see LITERATURE

HORIZONT; veszprem megyei kozmuvelodesi tajekoztato. see CLUBS

I C A MONTHLY BULLETIN. (Institute of Contemporary Arts) see ART

THEATER

792 790.13   GW
IN SACHEN SPIEL UND FEIER. 1949. s-m. DM.27.50. Hoefling Verlag Dr. V. Mayer, Koenigsbergerstr. 18-22, 6940 Weinheim, Germany. FAX 062101-14988. Ed. Rudolf Guder. adv.; bk.rev.; play rev.; illus.; index; circ. 4,000.
Formerly (until 1972): Bunte Wagen.

INDEPENDENT SHAVIAN. see *LITERATURE*

792   US
INSIDE THE BLACK HILLS. 1974. q. $12. Arts and Leisure Publications, Box 707, Custer, SD 57730. TEL 605-673-4100. FAX 605-673-4020. Ed. Ron Hagen. adv.; bk.rev.; circ. 50,000. (back issues avail.)
Former titles (until 1990): In Performance; San Francisco Ballet; A.C.T.

INSTITUTO BRASIL - ESTADOS UNIDOS. BOLETIM. see *EDUCATION*

792   US
INTERMISSION (ALEXANDRIA). 1988. s-m. $10. K Communications, 6205 Redwood Lane, Alexandria, VA 22310. TEL 703-971-7530. FAX 703-971-7520. (Subscr. to in Missouri area: 135 W. Rose, Webster Grove, MO 63119) Ed. Verna A. Kerans. adv.; bk.rev.; circ. 20,000.
Formerly (until 1989): Review (Alexandria).
Description: Covers theatre and related performing arts. Also reviews films and occasionally restaurants in the area.

792   US
INTERNATIONAL THEATRE INSTITUTE OF THE UNITED STATES. NEWSLETTER. 1989. q. International Theatre Institute of the United States, Inc., 220 W. 42nd St., Ste. 1710, New York, NY 10036. TEL 212-944-1490. FAX 212-944-1506. Ed. Louis A. Rachow. bk.rev.; circ. 1,500 (controlled). (back issues avail.)
Description: Reports on the activities of ITI Worldwide, ITI US and the theatre professionals who are served by ITI's international programs.

792   CS
INTERSCENA. (Summaries in English, French, German) s-a. 10 Kcs.($24.70) Divadelni Ustav, Prague 1, Celetna 17, Czechoslovakia. Ed. Jana Pleskacova. bibl.; charts; illus.; circ. 200. **Indexed:** C.I.S. Abstr.

800 792   UK   ISSN 0260-7964
IRISH DRAMA SELECTIONS. 1982. irreg. price varies. Colin Smythe Ltd., Box 6, Gerrards Cross, Buckinghamshire SL9 8XA, England. FAX 0753-886469. (Pub. in U.S. by: Catholic University of America Press, 620 Michigan Ave. N.E., Washington, DC 20064) Eds. Joseph Ronsley, Ann Saddlemyer. (reprint service avail. from ISI)
Description: Volumes of selected plays by Irish dramatists.

792   IT
ISTITUZIONI CULTURALI PIEMONTESI. PUBBLICAZIONI. 1976. irreg. (Istituzioni Culturali Piemontesi) Cassa di Risparmio di Torino, Via XX Settembre 31, Turin, Italy.

JAHRBUCH DER BAYERISCHEN STAATSOPER. see *MUSIC*

JAMAICA PICTORIAL. see *MUSIC*

792   CS
JAVISKO. m. $60. (Cultural Institute in Bratislava) Obzor, Ceskoslovenskej Armady 35, 815 85 Bratislava, Czechoslovakia.

792   CN   ISSN 0382-0335
PN2305.Q4
JEU; cahiers de theatre. 1976. q. Can.$36 to individuals, institutions Can.$45. Cahiers de Theatre Jeu Inc., 426 rue Sherbrooke Est, Bur. 102, Montreal, Que. H2L 1J6, Canada. TEL 514-288-2808. Ed. Lorraine Camerlain. adv.; bk.rev.; play rev.; illus.; circ. 1,400. (back issues avail.) **Indexed:** Pt.de Rep. (1983-).

792   GW   ISSN 0863-1611
JOURNAL FUER UNTERHALTUNGSKUNST. 1969. m. DM.48 (foreign DM.62.40). Henschelverlag Kunst und Gesellschaft, Oranienburger Str. 67-68, 104 Berlin, Germany. adv.; charts; illus.
Formerly (until 1989): Unterhaltungskunst (ISSN 0042-0565)

792   US   ISSN 1044-937X
PS332
JOURNAL OF AMERICAN DRAMA AND THEATRE. 1989. 3/yr. $12. C A S T A, City University of New York, Graduate School, 33 W. 42nd St., New York, NY 10036. TEL 212-642-2445. Eds. Vera Mowry Roberts, Walter J. Meserve.

JOURNAL OF BECKETT STUDIES. see *LITERATURE*

792   US
JOURNAL OF DRAMATIC THEORY AND CRITICISM. 1986. s-a. $10 to individuals (foreign $15); institutions $18 (foreign $24); students $8 (foreign $13). Hall Center for the Humanities, 211 Watkins Home, University of Kansas, Murphy Hall, Lawrence, KS 66045. TEL 913-864-4798. FAX 913-864-4120. Ed. John Gronbeck-Tedesco. adv. (back issues avail.)
Description: Addresses the theoretical issues associated with performance and performance texts.

792   CC   ISSN 0578-0659
JUBEN/PLAY SCRIPTS. (Text in Chinese) 1952. m. Y21.60($67.50) (Zhongguo Xijujia Xiehui - Chinese Theater Aartists' Association) Zhongguo Xiju Chubanshe, 52, Dongsi Ba(8) Tiao, Beijing 100700, People's Republic of China. TEL 443661. (Dist. outside China by: China International Book Trading Corp., P.O. Box 399, Beijing, P.R.C.; Dist. in US by: China Books & Periodicals, Inc., 2929 24th St., San Francisco, CA 94110. TEL 415-282-2994) Ed. Wei Min.

792 808   BF
JUNKANOO. m. $18. Junkanoo Publications, Box N 4923, Nassau, Bahamas. Eds. John Munnings, Melanie Pintard.

792   US
JUST FOR LAUGHS. 1983. 11/yr. $18. J F L Communications, Inc., 22 Miller Ave., Mill Valley, CA 94941. TEL 415-383-4746. FAX 415-383-0142. adv.: B&W page $1500, color page $2000; trim 10 x 14. circ. 50,000.
Description: Chronicles stand-up comedy. Profiles performers, lists locations and schedules, provides stories and gossip.

792 791.4   CC
JUYING YUEBAO/DRAMA & FILM MONTHLY. (Text in Chinese) m. $36.80. Jiangsu Sheng Wenhua Ting, 1, Qingdao Lu, Nanjing, Jiangsu 210008, People's Republic of China. TEL 635459. (Dist. in US by: China Books & Periodicals, Inc., 2929 24th St., San Francisco, CA 94110. TEL 415-282-2994) Ed. Wang Hong.

792   CC   ISSN 1001-3768
JUZUOJIA/PLAYWRIGHT. (Text in Chinese) bi-m. Heilongjiang Sheng Wenhuating - Heilongjiang Provincial Bureau of Culture, Qingming Sidao, Nangang-qu, Harbin, Heilongjiang 150080, People's Republic of China. TEL 30198. Ed. Liu Shuzhang.

K & C. see *ART*

KASSEL KULTURELL. see *ART*

792   CI
KAZALISTE; revija za scensku glazbu i kulturu. 1965. fortn. $5.20. Hrvatsko Narodno Kazaliste u Osijeku, Prolaz Radoslava Bacica 1, Osijek, Croatia. Ed. Ljubomir Standjevic. illus.

792   UK
KING POLE CIRCUS MAGAZINE. (Supplement avail.: Circus Directory of the British Isles) 1934. q. £17. Circus Friends' Association of Great Britain, c/o Membership Secretary, 20 Foot Wood Crescent, Shawclough, Rochdale, Lancs OL12 6PB. Ed. David Jamieson. adv.; bk.rev.; illus.; stat.; circ. 850. (back issues avail.)
Description: Articles and reviews on circus productions and personalities of past and present.

792   GW
KLAPPE AUF. 1987. m. DM.30. Belschner und Godulla GdbR, Adlerstr. 22, 7500 Karlsruhe 1, Germany. TEL 0721-606093. circ. 17,000. (back issues avail.)

792   GW
DAS KULISSENMAGAZIN. 1988. m. free. Ernst Waldau Theater, Waller Heerstr. 165, 2800 Bremen 1, Germany. TEL 0421-383031. FAX 0421-381947. Ed. Rolf B. Wessels.

792   GW
KURSPROGRAMM SPIEL UND THEATER. 1981. s-a. Rhein. AG Spiel und Theater in Regierungsbezirk Koeln e.V., Kurfuerstenstr. 18, 5000 Cologne 1, Germany. TEL 0221-323482. Ed. Josef Broich.

L H A T BULLETIN. (League of Historic American Theatres) see *ARCHITECTURE*

792   US   ISSN 0023-8813
PN2309
LATIN AMERICAN THEATRE REVIEW; a journal devoted to the theatre and drama of Spanish & Portuguese America. (Text in English, Portuguese, Spanish; summaries in English) 1967. s-a. $15 to individuals; institutions $30. University of Kansas, Center of Latin American Studies, 107 Lippincott Hall, Lawrence, KS 66045. TEL 913-864-4213. FAX 913-864-4555. Ed. George W. Woodyard. adv.; bk.rev.; bibl.; cum.index; circ. 1,200. **Indexed:** Arts & Hum.Cit.Ind., Chic.Per.Ind., Curr.Cont., Hisp.Amer.Per.Ind., Ind.Bk.Rev.Hum., M.L.A.
—BLDSC shelfmark: 5160.175000.
Description: Presents interviews; theatre history; international stories; profiles of fascinating individuals; theatre news; and articles about leading theatre companies and innovators.

LAUGH-MAKERS; variety arts for family entertainment. see *HOBBIES*

LEBENDIGES DARMSTADT; Veranstaltungsvorschau. see *MUSEUMS AND ART GALLERIES*

792 778.5   IT   ISSN 0024-144X
AS221
LETTURE; libro e spettacolo, mensile di studi e rassegne. 1946. 10/yr. L.40000. (Parrocchia di Santa Maria alla Scala in San Fedele) Edizioni Letture, Piazza San Fedele 4, 20121 Milan, Italy. Ed. Alessandro Scurani. adv.; bk.rev.; film rev.; music rev.; play rev.; bibl.; illus.; index, cum.index; circ. 5,000.
—BLDSC shelfmark: 5185.230000.

LIAISON; revue culturelle de l'Ontario francais. see *ART*

LIGHTING DIMENSIONS. see *ARCHITECTURE*

792   US
LINCOLN CENTER CALENDAR OF EVENTS. 6/yr. free. Lincoln Center, 70 Lincoln Center Plaza, New York, NY 10023. TEL 212-875-5000. Ed. Sunny Levine. circ. 100,000.
Description: Covers events at Lincoln Center.

792   AU   ISSN 0024-4139
LINZER THEATERZEITUNG. 1955. m. S.100. Landestheater Linz, Promenade 39, A-4010 Linz, Austria. Ed.Bd. adv.; bk.rev.; circ. 10,000. (tabloid format)

792   US   ISSN 1043-6650
▼**LONDON STAGE 1800-1900: A DOCUMENTARY RECORD AND CALENDAR OF PERFORMANCES.** 1990. irreg. price varies. Greenwood Press, Inc. (Subsidiary of: Greenwood Publishing Group Inc.), 88 Post Rd. W., Box 5007, Westport, CT 06881-5007. TEL 203-226-3571. FAX 203-222-1502.

792   UK   ISSN 0263-2322
LONDON THEATRE INDEX (YEAR). 1981. a. £10($20) London Theatre Record, 4 Cross Deep Gardens, Twickenham, Middx. TW1 4QU, England. TEL 081-892 6087. FAX 081-744-3002. Ed. Ian Herbert. adv.
Description: Annual critical review, with name index to who did what in the year's London productions.

792   US
LONDON THEATRE NEWS. 1988. m. $49. 12 E. 86th St., New York, NY 10028. FAX 212-249-9371. Ed. Roger B. Harris. bk.rev.; rec.rev.; circ. 1,900.
Description: Provides reviews of shows, new and old, recommendations, interviews, restaurant reviews and current show listings for London.

"MAGISCHE" WELT; Zeitschrift fuer angewandte Tricktechnik und Wahrnehmungstaeuschung. see *HOBBIES*

MAJOR ATTRACTIONS. ANNUAL DIARY. see *MUSIC*

THEATER 4635

792   CN
MANITOBA THEATRE CENTRE. HOUSE PROGRAMME.
1958. 6/yr. free. Manitoba Theatre Centre, 174 Market Ave., Winnipeg, Man. R3B 0P8, Canada. TEL 204-956-1340. FAX 204-947-3741. Ed. Blair Cosgrove. adv.; illus.; circ. 22,000.
Formerly: Stage Center.

792   US   ISSN 0025-3928
MARQUEE. 1968. base vol. (plus q. updates). $25. Theatre Historical Society of America, 624 Wynne Rd., Springfield, PA 19064. TEL 215-543-8378. (Subscr. to: 249 Grattan St., San Francisco, CA 94117) Ed. Irvin R. Glazer. bk.rev.; illus.; index, cum.index: 1970-1979; circ. 1,000. (also avail. in microform from UMI; back issues avail.) **Indexed:** Avery Ind.Archit.Per.
Description: Features theatre buildings.

MASK. see EDUCATION — *Teaching Methods And Curriculum*

792   AU   ISSN 0025-4606
PN2004
MASKE UND KOTHURN; Internationale Beitraege zur Theaterwissenschaft. (Text in English, French, German and Italian) 1955. 4/yr. DM.140. (Universitaet Wien, Institut fuer Theaterwissenschaft) Boehlau Verlag GmbH & Co.KG., Dr.-Karl-Lueger-Ring 12, Postfach 581, A-1011 Vienna, Austria. TEL 0222-63-87-35-0. FAX 63-81-58. TELEX 114-506-SPRIW-A. Ed. Wolfgang Greisenegger. adv.; bk.rev.; bibl.; illus.; index; circ. 800. **Indexed:** Arts & Hum.Cit.Ind., Curr.Cont., M.L.A.

792   AT   ISSN 0025-469X
MASQUE.* 1967. bi-m. Aus.$3.80. Masque Publications, G.P.O. Box 3504, Sydney, N.S.W., 2001, Australia. Ed. Rod Webb. adv.; film rev.; play rev.; illus.; circ. 10,000.

792.02   US   ISSN 0731-3403
PR621
MEDIEVAL AND RENAISSANCE DRAMA IN ENGLAND; an annual gathering of research, criticism, and reviews. 1984. a. $57.50 hardbound. A M S Press, Inc., 56 E. 13th St., New York, NY 10003. TEL 212-777-4700. FAX 212-995-5413. Ed. J. Leeds Barroll, III. bk.rev.; index. (back issues avail.)
—BLDSC shelfmark: 5534.262600.
Description: Collection of essays and reviews pertaining to English drama prior 1640, exclusive of Shakespeare.

792   UK   ISSN 0143-3784
PN2587
MEDIEVAL ENGLISH THEATRE. 1979. 2/yr. £5 (foreign £7). Medieval English Theatre, c/o Dept. of English, University of Lancaster, Lancaster LA1 4YT, England. FAX 0524-843-085. Ed.Bd. circ. 400. **Indexed:** M.L.A.
—BLDSC shelfmark: 5534.265850.
Description: Articles on all aspects of medieval and Tudor English and continental theatres.

791.53   GW   ISSN 0076-6216
MEISTER DES PUPPENSPIELS. 1959. irreg. price varies. Deutsches Institut fuer Puppenspiel, Hattingerstr. 467, 4630 Bochum, Germany. TEL 0234-47778. Ed. Dr. Juergen Kluender. (back issues avail.)

MEMPHIS STAR. see MUSIC

METRU. see MOTION PICTURES

MICROCRITICA; arte-musica-teatro-literatura. see MUSIC

792   SZ   ISSN 0026-4385
MIMOS. (Text in French and German) q. 10 SFr. to non-members. Schweizerische Gesellschaft fuer Theaterkultur - Swiss Association for Theatre Research, c/o Louis Naef, Postfach 180, CH-6130 Willisau, Switzerland. TEL 045-81-39-22.

MISSOURI SPEECH & THEATRE JOURNAL. see COMMUNICATIONS

MODERN DRAMA. see LITERATURE

792   US   ISSN 0026-7856
PN6111
MODERN INTERNATIONAL DRAMA; magazine for contemporary international drama in translation. 1967. s-a. $7 to individuals; institutions $12.50(effective 1992). State University of New York at Binghamton, Max Reinhardt Archive, Binghamton, NY 13901. TEL 607-777-2704. Eds. Anthony M. Pasquariello, George E. Wellwarth. adv.; cum.index: vols. 1-10 in vol.11, 1978; circ. 600. (tabloid format; also avail. in microform from UMI; reprint service avail. from UMI) **Indexed:** Amer.Bibl.Slavic & E.Eur.Stud, Arts & Hum.Cit.Ind., Curr.Cont., Mid.East: Abstr.& Ind.
Description: Devoted exclusively to the publication of previously untranslated plays.

MOLODEZHNAYA ESTRADA. see CHILDREN AND YOUTH — *For*

792   US
MOVEMENT THEATRE QUARTERLY. 1983. q. $20. National Movement Theatre Association, Box 1437, Portsmouth, NH 03802-1437. TEL 603-436-6660. Ed. M. Marguerite Mathews. adv.; bk.rev.; illus.; circ. 300.
Formerly: Mime News.

MUENCHENER KULTURFUEHRER MIT THEATERPLAN. see GENERAL INTEREST PERIODICALS — *Germany*

MUSICA, CINEMA, IMMAGINE, TEATRO. see MUSIC

792.022   US   ISSN 0027-4658
MUSICAL SHOW; devoted to the amateur presentation of Broadway musical shows on the stage. 1962. 4/yr. free to producers of musical shows. Tams-Witmark Music Library, Inc., 560 Lexington Ave., New York, NY 10022. TEL 212-688-2525. FAX 212-688-3232. Ed. Robert A. Hut. bk.rev.; circ. 175,000.

792 782.1   GW   ISSN 0932-7118
MUSICALS; das Musicalmagazin. 1986. bi-m. DM.50($22) Verlag Klaus-Dieter Kraft, Balanstr. 19, 8000 Munich 80, Germany. TEL 089-448-9895. FAX 089-448-2858. Ed. Klaus-Dieter Kraft. adv.; bk.rev.; play rev.; circ. 4,000. (back issues avail)
Description: Provides reports and reviews on musicals and musical comedies from all over the world.

MUSIK & THEATER; die aktuelle Kulturzeitschrift. see MUSIC

N A C CALENDAR OF EVENTS. (National Arts Centre) see DANCE

N A D S A ANNUAL CONFERENCE DIRECTORY. (National Association of Dramatic and Speech Arts) see ADVERTISING AND PUBLIC RELATIONS

N A T O NEWS & VIEWS. (National Association of Theatre Owners) see MOTION PICTURES

N E A GRANTMAKING PROGRAMS: CHALLENGE AND ADVANCEMENT. (National Endowment for the Arts) see LITERATURE

792 782   US
N E A GRANTMAKING PROGRAMS: OPERA - MUSICAL THEATER. a. free. National Endowment for the Arts, Public Information Office, 1100 Pennsylvania Ave., N.W., Washington, DC 20506. TEL 202-682-5400.
Description: Grant application guidelines.

792   US
N E A GRANTMAKING PROGRAMS: THEATER. a. free. National Endowment for the Arts, Public Information Office, 1100 Pennsylvania Ave., N.W., Washington, DC 20506. TEL 202-682-5400.
Description: Grant application guidelines.

NASHVILLE SCENE. see MUSIC

792 778.53   US
NATIONAL ASSOCIATION OF PERFORMING ARTS MANAGERS AND AGENTS. NEWSLETTER. q. National Association of Performing Arts Managers and Agents, c/o Pentacle, 104 Franklin St., New York, NY 10013. TEL 212-226-2000.

792.028   US
NATIONAL COSTUMERS MAGAZINE. 1923. 10/yr. National Costumers Association, Inc., c/o Mary Lau Landes, Ed., 811 N. Capitol Ave., Indianapolis, IN 46204. TEL 317-635-3655. adv.; bk.rev.; circ. 350.

792   UK
NATIONAL FEDERATION OF PLAYGOERS SOCIETIES. NEWSLETTER. 1957. q. free. National Federation of Playgoers Societies, 3 Gwenfo Dr., Wenvoe, Cardiff CF5 6ER, England. Ed. A. Morris-Janes. circ. 50 (controlled). (processed)

NATIONAL LIST OF HISTORIC THEATRE BUILDINGS. see ARCHITECTURE

792   JA   ISSN 0388-0648
NATIONAL THEATRE OF JAPAN. 6/yr. 4-1 Hayabusa-cho, Chiyoda-ku, Tokyo 102, Japan. TEL 03-3265-7411. FAX 03-3265-7402.

792   GW   ISSN 0934-9383
NATIONALTHEATER MANNHEIM THEATERZEITUNG. 1975. m. Nationaltheater Mannheim, Mozartstr. 9, 6800 Mannheim 1, Germany. TEL 0621-16800. FAX 0621-1680-385. Ed. Arnold Petersen. adv.; charts; illus.; circ. 15,000. (back issues avail.)

792   II   ISSN 0028-1115
NATYA.* (Text in English) vol.10, 1969. q. Rs.12.($3.50) Bharatiya Natya Sangh, 34 New Central Market, New Delhi, India. Ed. A.R. Krishna. adv.; bk.rev.; dance rev.; play rev.

NE SKENEN E FEMIJEVE. see CHILDREN AND YOUTH — *For*

792   NE   ISSN 0168-3519
NETHERLANDS. CENTRAAL BUREAU VOOR DE STATISTIEK. MUZIEK EN THEATER. irreg. Centraal Bureau voor de Statistiek, Prinses Beatrixlaan 428, Voorburg, Netherlands. (Orders to: SDU - Publishers, Christoffel Plantijnstraat, The Hague)
Formerly: Netherlands. Centraal Bureau voor de Statistiek. Statistiek van het Gesubsidieerde Toneel.

792   AU   ISSN 0028-3096
NEUE BLAETTER DES THEATERS IN DER JOSEFSTADT. (Text in German; occasionally in English, French) 1953. s-m. S.12. Theater in der Josefstadt, Direktion, Josefstaedterstr. 26, A-1082 Vienna, Austria. Ed. Gustav Kropatschek. adv.; bibl.; illus.; circ. 10,000. (tabloid format)

NEUE WEGE; Kulturzeitschrift junger Menschen. see CHILDREN AND YOUTH — *For*

791.33   US
NEW CALLIOPE. 1983? 6/yr. $25 includes membership. (Clowns of America International, Inc.) Olson Publishing, Box 570, Lake Jackson, TX 77566-0570. TEL 712-258-3075. Ed. Cal Olson. adv.; bk.rev.; illus.; circ. 5,150.
Description: Provides articles on clowning. Photos and illustrations include ideas for costuming and makeup design.

NEW CULTURE; a review of contemporary African arts. see ART

NEW DOG. see LITERARY AND POLITICAL REVIEWS

792   US   ISSN 1050-9720
▼**NEW ENGLAND THEATRE JOURNAL.** 1990. a. $10. New England Theatre Conference, 50 Exchange St., Waltham, MA 02154. Ed. Charles E. Combs.
Description: Covers a broad range of subjects, including traditional scholarship, performance theory, and pedagogy, as well as theatre performance, design, and technology.

792   UK   ISSN 0266-464X
PN2001
NEW THEATRE QUARTERLY. 1971. q. $29 to individuals; institutions $61. Cambridge University Press, Edinburgh Bldg., Shaftesbury Rd., Cambridge CB2 2RU, England. TEL 0223-312393. FAX 0223-315052. TELEX 851817256. (N. American addr.: Cambridge University Press, 40 W. 20th St., New York, NY 10011) Eds. Clive Barker, Simon Trussler. (also avail. in microform from UMI; reprint service avail. from SWZ)
—BLDSC shelfmark: 6088.870500.
Formerly (until 1985): Theatre Quarterly (ISSN 0049-3600)

4636 THEATER

792 384.55 US
NEW YORK CASTING - SURVIVAL GUIDE; and datebook. 1980. a. $15. Peter Glenn Publications, Inc., 17 E. 48th St., New York, NY 10017. TEL 212-688-7940. Ed. Chip Brill. adv.
Description: Resource tool for performing artists.

792 680 US
NEW YORK ON STAGE. a. c/o Theatre Development Fund, 1501 Broadway, Rm. 2110, New York, NY 10036. Ed. Eve Rodriguez.
Description: Contains listings of Broadway, off-Broadway, and off-off-Broadway theaters, and dance and music companies.

792 US ISSN 0028-7784
PN2000
NEW YORK THEATRE CRITICS' REVIEWS. 1940. irreg. (18-20/yr.). $122 (foreign $145). Critics Theatre Reviews, Inc., 52 Vanderbilt Ave., 11th Fl., New York, NY 10017. TEL 212-697-5802. FAX 212-682-2932. Eds. Norma Adler, Pat Willard. index, cum.index: 1940-1960, 1961-1972, 1973-1986; circ. 850. (looseleaf format) **Indexed:** Arts & Hum.Cit.Ind., Curr.Cont.

792 US ISSN 0160-0583
PN2266
NEW YORK TIMES THEATRE REVIEWS. 1870. biennial. Times Books (Subsidiary of: Random House, Inc.), 201 E. 50th St., New York, NY 10022-7703. TEL 212-751-2600. illus.

NEWSBANK REVIEW OF THE ARTS: FILM AND TELEVISION. see *MOTION PICTURES*

792 US ISSN 0737-3996
NEWSBANK REVIEW OF THE ARTS: PERFORMING ARTS. 1972. m. (q. and a. cumulations). price varies. NewsBank, Inc., 58 Pine St., New Canaan, CT 06840-5426. TEL 203-966-1100. FAX 203-966-6254. (paper index; articles on microfiche; CD ROM index)

792 820 US ISSN 0893-3766
PN1851
NINETEENTH CENTURY THEATRE. 1973. s-a. $12 to individuals (foreign $14); institutions $20 (foreign $22). University of Massachusetts, Nineteenth Century Theatre, c/o Dept. of English, Amherst, MA 01003. TEL 413-545-0498. Ed. Joseph Donohue. adv.; bk.rev.; bibl.; illus.; circ. 400. (also avail. in microform from UMI; back issues avail.; reprint service avail. from UMI) **Indexed:** Abstr.Engl.Stud., Amer.Hum.Ind., Arts & Hum.Cit.Ind., Curr.Cont., LCR, M.L.A.
—BLDSC shelfmark: 6113.231700.
Formerly: Nineteenth Century Theatre Research (ISSN 0316-5329)

NUOVA RASSEGNA; periodico di attualita-lettere-arti-cinema-teatro. see *LITERARY AND POLITICAL REVIEWS*

791.53 CN ISSN 0030-3062
O P A L (Ontario Puppetry Association Letter) 1962. 6/yr. Can.$20. Ontario Puppetry Association, 171 Avondale Ave., Willowdale, Ont. M2N 2V4, Canada. TEL 416-222-9029. Ed. Dorothy McKay. adv.; bk.rev.; play rev.; circ. 250.

792 793.32 US
OFF BROADWAY;* a guide to theater, dance, performances and other events off the beaten track. m. Off x Six, 277 W. 10th St., New York, NY 10011. Ed. Jimmey Johnson.

792 US
ON - STAGE STUDIES. 1976. a. $7. (Colorado Shakespeare Festival) University of Colorado, Department of Theatre and Dance, Box 261, Boulder, CO 80309-0261. TEL 303-492-1527. FAX 303-492-7722. Ed. Richard K. Knaub. circ. 500.
Formerly: Colorado Shakespeare Festival Annual (ISSN 0198-831X)

ON THE STREET. see *MUSIC*

OPERA AMERICA. REPERTOIRE SURVEY. see *MUSIC*

OPERA AMERICA NEWSLINE. see *MUSIC*

792 US
OUR GANG. 1973. irreg. (3-4/yr.). free. Hayes Registry, Actors' Exchange, Actors' Service, 701 Seventh Ave., Ste. 900, New York, NY 10036. TEL 212-757-6300. Ed. Enid Weicher. adv.; circ. 1,000. (back issues avail.)
Description: Information from Hayes for people in the theatrical and peripheral fields.

792 910.03 US
OVERTURE (NEW YORK); a Black theatre annual. 1981. a. $5. Audience Development Committee, Box 30, Manhattanville Sta., New York, NY 10027. Ed. A. Peter Bailey.

792 780 UK
OVERTURES; the magazine devoted to the musical on stage and record. no.9, 1980. bi-m. £2.50($10) 41 Eton Ave., Sudbury, Wembley, Middx. HAD 3AZ, England. Eds. Rexton S. Bunnett, John Muir.

800 792 UK ISSN 0141-1152
OXFORD THEATRE TEXTS. 1972. irreg. price varies. Colin Smythe Ltd., P.O. Box 6, Gerrards Cross, Buckinghamshire SL9 8XA, England. TEL 0753-886000. FAX 0753-886469. (Dist. in U.S. by: Dufour Editions, P.O. Box 449, Chester Springs, PA 19425) illus. (reprint service avail. from ISI)
Description: Plays by Francis Warner.

790 SA
P A C O F S NEWS/S U K O V S NUUS. (Text in Afrikaans and English) 1972. q. free. Performing Arts Council, Orange Free State, P.O. Box 1292, 9300 Bloemfontein, South Africa. FAX 51-305523. TELEX 267145 SA. Ed. Charmaine Ferreira. illus.; circ. 6,000.

792 784 US
PALACE PEEPER. 1937. m. $25 (typically set in Sep.). Gilbert and Sullivan Society of New York, 185 West End Ave., No. 20-F, New York, NY 10023. Ed. Marc Shepherd. circ. 350.
Description: Contains history, criticism, humor, and membership news.

792 PL ISSN 0031-0522
PN2859.P6
PAMIETNIK TEATRALNY; poswiecony historii i krytyce teatru. 1952. q. $36. (Polska Akademia Nauk, Instytut Sztuki) Ossolineum, Publishing House of the Polish Academy of Sciences, Rynek 9, Wroclaw, Poland. (Dist. by: Ars Polona-Ruch, Krakowskie Przedmiescie 7, Warsaw, Poland) Eds. Bohdan Korzeniewski, Zbigniew Raszewski. adv.; bk.rev.; bibl.; illus.; index; circ. 1,380.
Description: Devoted to the history of Polish theatre and theatrical criticism.

792 IT
PATALOGO; annuario dello spettacolo teatro. 1979. a. price varies. Ubulibri, Via B. Ramazzini, 8, 20129 Milan, Italy. TEL 02-221234. FAX 02-29510265. Ed. Franco Quadri.
Description: Yearbook which shows all the spectacles staged in Italy, includes reviews of theatrical critics.

792 US ISSN 0031-5222
PERFORMING ARTS; the theatre & music magazine. 1967. m. $30 (foreign $35). Performing Arts Network, 3539 Motor Ave., Los Angeles, CA 90034-4800. TEL 213-839-8000. Ed. Herbert Glass. adv.; bk.rev.; film rev.; play rev.; circ. 250,000.

PERFORMING ARTS BUYERS GUIDE: FOOTNOTES. see *DANCE*

792 CN ISSN 0031-5230
PN1582.C3
PERFORMING ARTS IN CANADA. 1961. q. Can.$8($16) Avanti Magazines Inc., 1100 Caledonia Rd., Toronto, Ont. M6A 2W5, Canada. TEL 416-785-4300. FAX 416-785-4329. Ed. Sarah B. Hood. adv.; bk.rev.; illus.; index; circ. 80,550. (also avail. in microfiche from UMI; reprint service avail. from MMI) **Indexed:** Arts & Hum.Cit.Ind., Can.Per.Ind., CMI, Curr.Cont., Mag.Ind., Music Ind.
Description: Covers performing arts in Canada: music, dance, theater and film.

792 US ISSN 0735-8393
PN1561
PERFORMING ARTS JOURNAL. 1976. 3/yr. $17 to individuals; institutions $35. (P A J Publications) Johns Hopkins University Press, Journals Publishing Division, 701 W. 40th St., Ste. 275, Baltimore, MD 21211-2190. TEL 410-516-6988. FAX 410-516-6998. Eds. Bonnie Marranca, Gautam Dasgupta. adv.; bk.rev.; play rev.; illus.; circ. 1,176. (also avail. in microfilm from UMI; back issues avail.) **Indexed:** Amer.Bibl.Slavic & E.Eur.Stud., Amer.Hum.Ind., Arts & Hum.Cit.Ind., Bk.Rev.Ind. (1981-), Child.Bk.Rev.Ind. (1981-), Curr.Cont., Hum.Ind.
—BLDSC shelfmark: 6423.893000.
Description: International critical coverage of contemporary theater, dance, music, and drama.

792 016 US ISSN 0360-3814
Z6935
PERFORMING ARTS RESOURCES. (Supplement to: Broadside (New York, 1940) (ISSN: 0068-2748)) 1974. a. $20 to individuals; institutions $25. Theatre Library Association, 111 Amsterdam Ave., New York, NY 10023. Ed. Barbara Naomi Cohen-Stratyner. circ. 500. (back issues avail.) **Indexed:** M.L.A.
Description: Gathers and disseminates articles on resources materials relating to theatre, popular entertainments, film, television and radio; descriptions of collections, and essays on conservation and management.

800 IT
PICCOLO TEATRO DI MILANO. 1977. 5/yr. L.100000. Piccolo Teatro di Milano, Via Rovello 2, 20121 Milan, Italy. FAX 2-874836. TELEX 316279. Ed. Giorgio Strehler. adv.; bk.rev.; circ. 60,000.

792 US ISSN 0895-9706
PR6066.I53
PINTER REVIEW: ANNUAL ESSAYS. 1987. a. $15 to individuals; institutions $25. University of Tampa, Box 11F, Tampa, FL 33606. Eds. Francis Gillen, Steven H. Gale.
Description: Publishes critical essays, notes, production reviews and commentaries on the plays, screenplays and other writings of Harold Pinter.

792 US
PITTSBURGH STUDIES IN THEATRE AND CULTURE. irreg. Peter Lang Publishing, Inc., 62 W. 45th St., 4th Fl., New York, NY 10036. TEL 212-302-6740. FAX 212-302-7574. Ed. Dennis Kennedy.
Description: Connects the study of theatre practice with larger issues in history, politics, art, social institutions, popular entertainment, or performance theory.

PLATEAU. see *ART*

800 US
PLAY SOURCE. 1980? irreg. (5-6/yr.). included in subscription to Plays in Process (ISSN 0736-0711). Theatre Communications Group, Inc., 355 Lexington Ave., New York, NY 10017. Ed. Regina Raiford.
Description: Gives brief descriptions of full-length, one-act, and musical theatre scripts. Includes addresses of where to write for permission to present, read, and learn about newer plays which are not yet licensed by the agencies that handle playscripts.

792 US ISSN 0032-146X
PLAYBILL; the national magazine of the theatre. 1884; N.S. 1982. m. $21 (effective 1992). Playbill Incorporated, 52 Vanderbilt Ave., 11th Fl., New York, NY 10017-3893. TEL 212-557-5757. Ed. Joan Alleman. adv.; illus.; circ. 1,015,000.
Description: Provides information necessary to the understanding and enjoyment of each Broadway play, certain Lincoln Center and Off-Broadway productions and regional attractions served. Includes articles by and about theatre personalities, fashion, and events.

792 CN ISSN 0048-4415
PLAYBOARD; professional stage magazine. 1967. m. Can.$15. Arch-Way Publishers Ltd., 7560 Lawrence Dr., Burnaby, B.C. V5A 1T6, Canada. TEL 604-420-6115. FAX 604-420-6115. Ed. Chuck Davis. adv.; circ. 600,000.

THEATER 4637

799.022 371.3 US ISSN 0032-1540
PN1601
PLAYS; the drama magazine for young people. 1941. m. (Oct-May; except Jan.-Feb. combined). $27. Plays, Inc., 120 Boylston St., Boston, MA 02116-4615. TEL 617-423-3157. Ed. Sylvia K. Burack. adv.; bk.rev.; index; circ. 18,000. (also avail. in microform from UMI; back issues avail.; reprint service avail. from UMI) **Indexed:** Biog.Ind., Ind.Child.Mag., Mag.Ind.
  Description: Provides a complete supply of royalty-free dramatic material for schools, young people's clubs and libraries.

822 UK ISSN 0554-3045
PLAYS. A CLASSIFIED GUIDE TO PLAY SELECTION. 1951. a. £2.20($6) Stacey Publications, 1 Hawthorndene Road, Hayes, Bromley, Kent, England. Ed. Roy Stacey. adv.; bibl.

800 US
PLAYS & PLAYWRIGHTS.* 1985. biennial. $29.95 free. International Society of Dramatists, Box 192012, Miami, FL 33119-2012. TEL 305-674-1831. Ed. A. Delaplaine. circ. 5,600.

800 US ISSN 0736-0711
PS634
PLAYS IN PROCESS. 1980. a. $60 (includes Playsource). Theatre Communications Group, Inc., 355 Lexington Ave., New York, NY 10017. TEL 212-697-5230. Ed. Gillian Richards. circ. 400. (back issues avail.)
  Description: Twelve playscripts selected from over 150 submissions annually. All plays have been performed in U.S. theatres.

700 NE ISSN 0032-1621
PLUG;* maandelijks informatieblad van het Cultureel Jongeren Paspoort. 1967. m. fl.15. Culturele Raad Noordholland, Postbus 163, 1970 AD Ijmuiden, Netherlands. Ed. Leo Veen. adv.; bk.rev.; film rev.; play rev.; abstr.; illus.; circ. 62,500 (controlled).

792 BN ISSN 0032-616X
PN2007
POZORISTE; casopis za pozorisnu umjetnost. (Text in Serbo-Croatian) 1959. bi-m. 60 din. Narodno Pozoriste, Tuzla, Bosnia Hercegovina. Ed. Mustafa Hadzialic. circ. 1,100.

PRAXIS; a journal of cultural criticism. see ART

792 780 AT ISSN 0819-1565
PRESS PRESS MAGAZINE; the Tasmanian quarterly on music and the performing arts. 1986. q. Aus.$8. Press Press Publications, Inc., P.O. Box 151, Sandy Bay, Tas. 7005, Australia. TEL 002-241487. FAX 002-240245. Ed. Tony Ryan. adv.; circ. 1,000. (back issues avail.)

PRODUCTION AND CASTING REPORT. see MOTION PICTURES

792 375 US
PROFESSIONAL THEATRE FOR YOUNG AUDIENCES. biennial. $10. American Alliance for Theatre & Education, Theatre Department, Arizona State Department, Arizona State University, Tempe, AZ 85287-3411. TEL 602-965-6064. FAX 602-965-9073.
  Description: Provides a profile of professional theatre organizations that produce work for young audiences.

PROFILE (WASHINGTON). see MUSIC

792 PO
PROGRAMA.* 1978. Esc.50 per no. Grupo de Teatro de Campolide, 43, 2o D. Cde. Antas, Lisbon, Portugal. Ed. Joaquim Benite. bk.rev.; play rev.; illus.; circ. 20,000.

792 US ISSN 0033-1007
PROLOGUE (MEDFORD). 1945. irreg. (3-4/yr.). free. Tufts University, Department of Drama & Dance, Medford, MA 02155. TEL 617-381-3524. Ed. Peter D. Arnott. play rev.; circ. 5,000. **Indexed:** Amer.Bibl.Slavic & E.Eur.Stud.

792 US
PROLOGUE (MILWAUKEE). every 6 wks. free to qualified personnel. Milwaukee Repertory Theater, 108 E. Wells St., Milwaukee, WI 53202. TEL 414-224-1761. FAX 414-224-9790. Ed. Fran Serlin-Cobb. circ. 10,000.
  Description: Articles on theater pieces produced by the Milwaukee Repertory Theater.

792 UK ISSN 0033-1147
PROMPT.* 1962. 3/yr. $2. University College London, Dramatic Society, Gower St., London WC1B 6BT, England. Ed. Richard Briffett. adv.; bk.rev.; illus.; play rev.; circ. 1,500.

792 SP
PUBLICO. 1983. bi-m. Capitan Haya 44, 28020 Madrid, Spain. TEL 91-5723311. FAX 91-2705199. circ. 7,000.

792 AU ISSN 0020-1642
PUBLICUM; Innsbrucker Theater- und Konzertspiegel. 1957. m. S.150. Tiroler Landestheater, Rennweg 2, Postfach 134, A-6010 Innsbruck, Austria. TEL 0512-81746. FAX 0512-81746. Ed. Jutta Hoepfel. adv.; bk.rev.; record rev.; illus.; circ. 10,000.
  Formerly: Innsbrucker Konzertspiegel.

PULSE. see MUSIC

PUNKT; kwartalnik gdanskich srodowisk tworczych. see LITERATURE

791.53 SZ ISSN 0033-4405
PUPPENSPIEL UND PUPPENSPIELER/MARIONNETTES ET MARIONNETTISTES; zeitschrift fuer das theater mit Figuren. (Text in French and German) 1960. 3/yr. 36 Fr. Schweizerische Vereinigung fuer Puppenspiel, c/o Gustav Gysin, Ed., Roggenstr. 1, CH-4125 Riehen, Switzerland. TEL 061-499264. adv.; bk.rev.; circ. 1,150.

791.53 US ISSN 0033-443X
PN1970
PUPPETRY JOURNAL. 1949. q. membership. Puppeteers of America, 8005 Swallow Dr., Macedonia, OH 44056. (Subscr. to: 5 Cricklewood Path, Pasadena, CA 91107-1002) Eds. George & Pat Latshaw. adv.; bk.rev.; play rev.; charts; illus.; circ. 2,500 (controlled). (also avail. in microform from UMI; reprint service avail. from UMI)

792 780 CC ISSN 0578-0608
QU YI/VARIETY SHOW. (Text in Chinese) m. Y15($42.20) Zhongguo Quyijia Xiehui, Wenlian Dalou, 10 Nongzhanguan Nanli, Beijing 100026, People's Republic of China. (Dist. outside China by: China International Book Trading Corp., P.O. Box 399, Beijing, P.R.C.; Dist. in US by: China Books & Periodicals, Inc., 2929 24th St., San Francisco, CA 94110. TEL 415-282-2994) Ed. Luo Yang.

792.02 AU ISSN 0259-0786
QUELLEN ZUR THEATERGESCHICHTE. 1975. irreg., no.3, 1981. price varies. Verband der Wissenschaftlichen Gesellschaften Oesterreichs, Lindengasse 37, A-1070 Vienna, Austria. TEL 932166. Ed. Otto Schindler.

792.2 US
RAVE;* the comedy performance magazine. 1986. m. $15. Rave Communications, Inc., 228 E. 45th St., New York, NY 10017. Ed. Ron Smith. circ. 250,000.

792 800 CN ISSN 0700-9283
PR641
RECORDS OF EARLY ENGLISH DRAMA NEWSLETTER. (Text in English) 1976. s-a. Can.$7.50. University of Toronto, Erindale College, English Department, Mississauga, Ont. L5L 1C6, Canada. TEL 416-828-3737. FAX 416-828-5328. Ed. J. Dutka. bk.rev.; circ. 500. **Indexed:** Hist.Abstr., M.L.A. —BLDSC shelfmark: 7325.650000.
  Description: Articles and notes on English drama, ceremony and minstrelsy to 1642.

792 809 US ISSN 0486-3739
PN1785
RENAISSANCE DRAMA. 1967. a. $45.95. Northwestern University Press, 625 Colfax St., Evanston, IL 60201. TEL 312-491-5313. Ed. Mary Beth Rose. circ. 2,000. **Indexed:** Arts & Hum.Cit.Ind., Curr.Cont., M.L.A.
—BLDSC shelfmark: 7356.865200.
  Description: Collection of essays on topics in Renaissance drama.

792 US ISSN 0098-647X
PR621
RESEARCH OPPORTUNITIES IN RENAISSANCE DRAMA. 1956. a. free. c/o David M. Bergeron, Ed., Department of English, University of Kansas, Lawrence, KS 66045. TEL 913-864-4520. adv.; bk.rev.; play rev.; bibl.; illus.; circ. 1,700. **Indexed:** M.L.A.

792 US ISSN 0034-5822
PN2592
RESTORATION & EIGHTEENTH CENTURY THEATRE RESEARCH. 1962; N.S. 1986. s-a. $8. Loyola University of Chicago, Department of English, 6525 N. Sheridan Rd., Chicago, IL 60626. Ed. Douglas H. White. bk.rev.; bibl.; illus.; circ. 1,000. **Indexed:** Abstr.Engl.Stud., Hist.Abstr., M.L.A.
—BLDSC shelfmark: 7777.830000.

792 BL ISSN 0102-7336
REVISTA DE TEATRO. 1955. q. $30 or membership. Sociedade Brasileira de Autores Teatrais, Av. Almte. Barroso 97, 3 Castelo, Rio de Janeiro, R.J., Brazil. FAX 55212407431. Ed. Aldo Calvet. adv.; circ. 5,000. (back issues avail.)

792 FR ISSN 0035-2373
PN2003
REVUE D'HISTOIRE DU THEATRE. (Text in English, French) 1948. q. $65. Societe d'Histoire du Theatre, 98 Bd. Kellermann, 75013 Paris, France. TEL 4588-4655. bk.rev.; charts; illus.; index, cum.index. (reprint service avail. from SWZ) **Indexed:** Arts & Hum.Cit.Ind., Curr.Cont., Hist.Abstr., M.L.A.
—BLDSC shelfmark: 7880.960000.

792 IT ISSN 0035-5186
RIDOTTO; rassegna mensile di teatro. 1951. m. L.2500. Societa Italiana Autori Drammatici, Via Po, 10, 00198 Rome, Italy. adv.; bk.rev.; bibl.; charts; illus.; index; circ. 5,000. **Indexed:** M.L.A.

RONDELL PROGRAMM. see MOTION PICTURES

RUCH MUZYCZNY; a musical review. see MUSIC

792 II
RUCHI. 1982. s-a. Rs.5. University of Calcutta, School of Drama, Aranattukara, Trichur, 680618. Kerala, India. circ. 500. (back issues avail.)

792.927 TS
AL-RUWALAH. (Text in Arabic) 1963. q. Sharjah National Theater, P.O. Box 5373, Sharjah, United Arab Emirates. TEL 354522. Ed. Ahmed bin Muhammad al-Qasimi. circ. 1,000.
  Description: Discusses the development and status of Arab theater in the Gulf region, and provides a forum for exchange of information and experience among persons connected with the theater.

RYTME; nyt om folkemusik, rock, jazz og teater i Nordjylland. see MUSIC

792.02 CN
S D A JOURNAL - NEWSLETTER. 4/yr. Can.$20 (foreign Can.$25). (Saskatchewan Drama Association) Saskatchewan Teachers' Federation, Box 1108, Saskatoon, Sask. S7K 3N3, Canada. Ed. Catherine Anderson. adv.

792 UK
SADLER'S WELLS THEATRE PROGRAMME. 1931. irreg. (approx. m.). £1. Sadler's Wells Trust Ltd., Rosebery Ave., London EC1R 4TN, England. TEL 071-278-6563. FAX 071-837-0965. TELEX 265871. Ed. Susanna Beaumont. adv.; bk.rev.; bibl.; illus.; circ. 9,000. (back issues avail.)
  Description: Details of performances, casts, synopsis, biographies and credits.

792 VN
SAN KHAU/THEATRE. 1976. m. 51 Tran Hung Dao St., Hanoi, Socialist Republic of Vietnam. TEL 64423. Ed. Xuan Trinh.

THEATER

SANGEET NATAK; journal of Indian music, dance, theatre. see *MUSIC*

SCANDINAVICA. see *LITERATURE*

792   GW   ISSN 0036-5726
NA6840.G35
SCENA.* (Supplement to "Theater der Zeit") 1962. q. included in subscription to "Theater der Zeit.". Institut fuer Technologie Kultureller Einrichtungen, Clara Zetkin- Str. 1205, 108 Berlin, Germany. Ed. Hans Gussmann. bk.rev.; abstr.; charts; illus.; stat.; tr.lit.; cum.index; circ. 12,000.

792   YU   ISSN 0036-5734
PN2007
SCENA; casopis za pozorisnu umetnost. 1965. bi-m. 50000 din. Sterijino Pozorje, Zmaj Jovina 22, 21000 Novi Sad, Yugoslavia. Ed. Radomir Putnik. bk.rev.; circ. 1,250.

792 780   SA   ISSN 0256-002X
SCENARIA. (Text in English) 1977. m. R.78($90) Seven Arts Publishers (Pty) Ltd., P.O. Box 72161, Pakview 2122, Johannesburg, South Africa. FAX 011-788-6313. Ed. Julius F. Eichbaum. adv.; bk.rev.; film rev.; play rev.; illus.; circ. 10,000. (back issues avail.) **Indexed:** Ind.S.A.Per.
  Incorporates: Arabesque.
  Description: Discusses the performing arts in South Africa and worldwide.

SCENERY, COSTUMES, AND MUSICAL MATERIALS DIRECTORY. see *MUSIC*

SCENES MAGAZINE; mesuel suisse d'information culturelle. see *ART*

792   GW   ISSN 0176-1188
DIE SCHAUBUEHNE; Quellen und Forschungen zur Theatergeschichte. irreg., vol.72, 1988. price varies. Franz Steiner Verlag Wiesbaden GmbH, Birkenwaldstr. 44, Postfach 101526, 7000 Stuttgart 1, Germany. TEL 0711-2582-0. FAX 0711-2582290. Ed. Carl Niessen.

729   GW   ISSN 0342-4553
SCHAUSPIELFUEHRER; der Inhalt der wichtigsten Theaterstuecke aus aller Welt. 1953. triennial, vol.15, 1992. DM.148 per vol. (Universitaet Wien, Institut fuer Theaterwissenschaft, AU) Anton Hiersemann Verlag, Rosenbergstr. 113, Postfach 140155, 7000 Stuttgart 1, Germany. TEL 0711-638265. FAX 0711-6369010. Ed. Wolfgang Greisenegger.

SCHWARZER FADEN; Vierteljahresschrift fuer Lust und Freiheit. see *POLITICAL SCIENCE*

792   SZ
SCHWEIZERISCHE GESELLSCHAFT FUER THEATERKULTUR. JAHRBUECHER. 1928. a. price varies. Schweizerische Gesellschaft fuer Theaterkultur - Swiss Association for Theatre Research, c/o Louis Naef, Postfach 180, CH-6130 Willisau, Switzerland. TEL 045-81-39-22.

792   SZ
SCHWEIZERISCHE GESELLSCHAFT FUER THEATERKULTUR. SCHRIFTEN. 1928. irreg., no.20, 1990. Schweizerische Gesellschaft fuer Theaterkultur - Swiss Association for Theatre Research, c/o Louis Naef, Postfach 180, CH-6130 Willisau, Switzerland. TEL 045-81-39-22.

800   US   ISSN 0748-2558
SHAKESPEARE BULLETIN. 1982. q. $10. Lafayette College, English Department, Easton, PA 18042. TEL 215-250-5248. Eds. James P. Lusardi, June Schlueter. adv.; bk.rev.; play rev.; circ. 400. (back issues avail.) **Indexed:** M.L.A.
  Formerly: New York Shakespeare Society Bulletin.
  Description: Covers performance criticism and scholarship. Provides commentary on Shakespeare and Renaissance drama. Covers the U.S., Canada, U.K. and elsewhere.

SHAKESPEARE NEWSLETTER. see *LITERATURE*

SHAKESPEARE OXFORD SOCIETY. NEWSLETTER. see *LITERATURE*

SHAKESPEARE QUARTERLY. see *LITERATURE*

SHAKESPEARE WORLDWIDE. see *LITERATURE*

792   CC   ISSN 0559-7277
SHANGHAI XIJU/SHANGHAI THEATER. (Text in Chinese) 1959. bi-m. Y9($24.30) (Shanghai Xijujia Xiehui) Shanghai Xiju Zazhishe, 238 Yan'an Xilu, Shanghai 200040, People's Republic of China. (Dist. outside China by: Guoji Shudian - China International Book Trading Corp., P.O. Box 399, Beijing, P.R.C.; Dist. in US by: China Books & Periodicals, Inc., 2929 24th St., San Francisco, CA 94110. TEL 415-282-2994) Ed. Zhao Laijing.

792   CC
SHANGHAI YISHUJIA/SHANGHAI ARTIST. (Text in Chinese) bi-m. $19.40. (Shanghai Yishu Yanjiusuo - Shanghai Art Institute) Shanghai Yishujia Bianjibu, No.2, Alley 112, Fenyang Lu, Shanghai 200031, People's Republic of China. TEL 4377362. (Dist. in US by: China Books & Periodicals, Inc., 2929 24th St., San Francisco, CA 94110. TEL 415-282-2994)

SHAVIAN. see *LITERATURE*

SHOW MUSIC; the musical theatre magazine. see *MUSIC*

SHOWCALL. see *MUSIC*

792   AT   ISSN 1032-6448
SHOWCAST CASTING DIRECTORY. 1963. a. Aus.$100 (foreign Aus.$175). Showcast Publications, P.O. Box 951, Crows Nest, N.S.W. 2065, Australia. TEL 02-438 2144. FAX 02-438-2007.
  Former titles: Showcast Directory; Showcast General Directory.
  Description: Directory of actors and actresses.

792 647.968   UK   ISSN 0265-9808
SIGHTLINE; journal of theatre technology and design. vol.24, no.4 1990. q. £12($24) to non-members. (Association of British Theatre Technicians) Theatrical Trading Ltd., 4 Great Pultneney St., London W1R 3DF, England. TEL 071-434-3901. Ed. Ian Herbert. adv.; bk.rev.
  Description: Covers all technical aspects of theatrical production, including design, technology, lighting, sound, training, planning, safety and regulations, and serves as a forum for issues of concern to technicians.

792   US
SIGHTLINES (NEW YORK).* 1965. m. membership. U S Institute for Theatre Technology, Inc., 10 W. 19th St., Ste. 5A, New York, NY 10011. TEL 212-924-9088. Eds. Eric Fielding, Cecelia Fielding. adv.; circ. 3,000.
  Formerly: U S I T T Newsletter (ISSN 0565-6311)

792   US
SIMON'S DIRECTORY OF THEATRICAL MATERIALS, SERVICES AND INFORMATION. 1955. irreg. price varies. Package Publicity Service, Inc., 27 W. 24th St., Rm. 402, New York, NY 10010. Ed. Avivah Simon. adv.; bk.rev.; circ. 10,000.

SINGER'S GUIDE TO THE PROFESSIONAL OPERA COMPANIES. see *MUSIC*

792   DK   ISSN 0106-665X
Z5781
SKUESPILREGISTER; supplement. 1979. a. DKK 234.35. Bibliotekscentralen, Tempovej 7-11, DK-2750 Ballerup, Denmark. TEL 2-974000. FAX 2-655310.

792   CS   ISSN 0037-699X
SLOVENSKE DIVADLO/SLOVAK THEATER. (Text in Slovak; summaries in English and Russian) 1952. q. 72 Kcs.($20) (Slovenska Akademia Vied) Veda, Publishing House of the Slovak Academy of Sciences, Klemensova 19, 814 30 Bratislava, Czechoslovakia. (Dist. in Western countries by: John Benjamins B.V., Amsteldijk 44, Amsterdam (Z.), Netherlands) Ed. Milos Mistrik. bk.rev.; film rev.; play rev.; illus. **Indexed:** M.L.A.
—BLDSC shelfmark: 8309.775000.
  Description: Deals with the history of film, theater, radio and television art.

792   US   ISSN 0584-4738
SOUTHERN THEATRE. 1964. q. $10. Southeastern Theatre Conference, 506 Stirling St., University of North Carolina, Greensboro, NC 27412. TEL 919-272-3645. Ed. Darwin Honeycutt. adv.; bk.rev.; play rev.; index; circ. 3,500. (back issues avail.)
  Description: Provides current articles on the theatre.

792 370   UK   ISSN 0038-7142
SPEECH AND DRAMA. 1951. 2/yr. £6.50. Society of Teachers of Speech and Drama, 4 Fane Rd., Oxford OX3 0SA, England. TEL 0865-728304. Ed. Paul Ranger. adv.; bk.rev.; play rev.; index; circ. 2,000. (also avail. in microform from UMI; reprint service avail. from UMI)
—BLDSC shelfmark: 8411.195000.

792   IT   ISSN 0038-738X
GV1
SPETTACOLO; rassegna economica e sociale degli spettacoli e delle attivita artistiche e culturali. (Text in Italian; summaries in English, French) 1951. q. L.14000 (foreign L.22000). Societa Italiana degli Autori ed Editori, Viale della Letteratura 30, 00100 Rome, Italy. TEL 06 59901. FAX 06-5923351. TELEX 611423. Ed.Bd. adv.; bk.rev.; abstr.; charts; mkt.; stat.; index; circ. 2,000. (back issues avail.) **Indexed:** Film Lit.Ind. (1990-).
—BLDSC shelfmark: 8413.520000.

791   IT
SPETTACOLO VIAGGIANTE. 1948. bi-m. L.10000. Associazione Nazionale Esercenti Spettacoli Vaggianti, Via di Villa Patrizi 10, 00161 Rome, Italy. Ed. Mario Faccio. adv.; circ. 4,000.

792.02   GW
SPIEL & BUEHNE. 1974. 3/yr. DM.20. Bund Deutscher Amateurtheater e.V., Steinheimerstr. 7-1, 7920 Heidenheim, Germany. TEL 07321-48300. FAX 07321-48341. adv.

792   GW   ISSN 0038-7509
SPIEL UND THEATER; Zeitschrift fuer Amateurtheater, Darstellendes Kinderspiel, Schul- und Jugendtheater, Theatererziehung und Medienkunde. 1949. 3/yr. DM.18. Deutscher Theaterverlag GmbH, Koenigsberger Str. 18-22, Postfach 100261, 6940 Weinheim, Germany. FAX 06201-14988. adv.; bk.rev.; play rev.; circ. controlled. (tabloid format)
  Formerly: Laienspieler.

792   GW   ISSN 0038-7517
DER SPIELPLAN; die monatliche Theatervorschau. 1954. m. (11/yr.). DM.60. Loewendruck Bertram GmbH, Postfach 3744, 3300 Braunschweig, Germany. TEL 0531-352246. adv.; illus.

792   GW
STAATSTHEATER STUTTGART. MONATSVORSCHAU. m. Staatstheater Stuttgart, Oberer Schlossgarten 6, Postfach 10 43 45, 7000 Stuttgart 1, Germany. TEL 0711-20320. FAX 0711-2032-389. TELEX 723777. adv.; circ. 50,000.

STAD ANTWERPEN. CULTUREEL JAARBOEK. see *MUSEUMS AND ART GALLERIES*

792   ZA
STAGE. (Text in English) 1956. irreg. price varies. Lusaka Theatre Club (Co-Op) Ltd., P.O. Box 30615, Lusaka, Zambia. Ed. Mase Mulondiwa. adv.; bk.rev.; play rev.; circ. 300 (controlled).

791 792   UK   ISSN 0038-9099
STAGE AND TELEVISION TODAY. 1880. w. £14. Carson and Comerford Ltd., Stage House, 47 Bermondsey St., London SE1 3XT, England. Eds. Peter Hepple, Edward Durham Taylor. adv.; bk.rev.; illus.; play rev.; tele.rev.; circ. 30,500. (tabloid format; also avail. in microform)

792   US
STAGE DIRECTIONS. 10/yr. S M W Communications, Inc., Beacon Bldg., 3020 Beacon Blvd., West Sacramento, CA 95691-3436. TEL 916-373-0201. FAX 916-373-0232. Ed. Stephen Peithman. circ. 1,400.

792 791.43   IE
STAGECAST-IRISH STAGE AND SCREEN DIRECTORY. 1962. biennial. $15. Stagecast Publications, 15 Eaton Square, Monkstown, Dublin County, Ireland. Ed. Derek Young. adv.; illus.; stat.; circ. 500. (back issues avail.)

792   US
STAGES; the national theatre magazine. 1984. m. $20. Curtains, Inc., 301 W. 45th St., 5A, New York, NY 10036. TEL 212-245-9186. FAX 201-836-4107. Ed. Frank Scheck. adv.; bk.rev.; play rev.; illus.; circ. 35,000. (tabloid format; back issues avail.)

THEATER

700 792   AT   ISSN 1033-3975
STAGES. 1982. m. Aus.$35. Victorian Arts Centre Trust, 100 St. Kilda Rd., Melbourne, Vic. 3004, Australia. TEL 03-684-8484. FAX 03-682-8282. Ed. Michael Kaye. adv.; bk.rev.; play rev.; circ. 5,000. (back issues avail.)
    Formerly: Victorian Arts Centre Magazine (ISSN 0811-5478)
    Description: Coverage of the performing arts at all levels.

STERZ; Zeitschrift fuer Literatur, Kunst und Kulturpolitik. see *LITERATURE*

792   UK   ISSN 0950-0634
PN2091.E4
STRANDLIGHT. (Text in English; summaries in French and German) 1937. 3/yr. free. Strand Lighting Ltd., Grant Way, Islewoth, Middlesex TW7 5QD, England. FAX 01-5682103. TELEX 27976. (Dist. in North America by: Bill Groener, V.P. Sales and Marketing Strand Lighting Inc., 18111 S. Santa Fe Ave., Box 9004, Rancho Dominguez, CA 90224, USA) Ed. Richard Harris. bk.rev.; charts; illus.; circ. 14,000. Indexed: Br.Tech.Ind.
    Formerly (until 1985): Tabs (ISSN 0306-9389)
    Description: Articles and product descriptions on theatre and television lighting with descriptions of projects from around the world.

792   CN   ISSN 0085-6770
PN2306.S77
STRATFORD FESTIVAL; souvenir book. (Includes: Stratford Festival Story) 1953. a. Can.$8. Stratford Shakespearean Festival Foundation of Canada, Box 520, Stratford, Ont. N5A 6V2, Canada. TEL 519-271-4040.

890   SW   ISSN 0282-8006
PT9816
STRINDBERGIANA. 1985. a. $200 (typically set in May). Strinbergssaellskapet - Strindberg Society, Drottninggatan 85, 11160 Stockholm, Sweden. bk.rev.

792   US   ISSN 0081-6051
PN2277.N5
STUBS (METRO NY); the seating plan guide for New York theatres, music halls, sports stadia. 1967. irreg. $9.95. Stubs Communications Co., 226 W. 47th St., New York, NY 10036. TEL 212-398-8370. FAX 212-398-8389. Ed. Ronald S. Lee. adv.; circ. 30,000.

792   PL   ISSN 0208-404X
STUDIA I MATERIALY DO DZIEJOW TEATRU POLSKIEGO. 1957. irreg., vol.18, 1986. price varies. (Polska Akademia Nauk, Instytut Sztuki) Ossolineum, Publishing House of the Polish Academy of Sciences, Rynek 9, Wroclaw, Poland. TELEX 0712771 OSS PL. (Dist. by: Ars Polona-Ruch, Krakowskie Przedmiescie 7, Warsaw, Poland)
    Formerly: Studia i Materialy z Dziejow Teatru Polskiego (ISSN 0081-6647)
    Description: Polish theatre life in Poland.

792 800   US   ISSN 0886-7097
PS352
STUDIES IN AMERICAN DRAMA, 1945 - PRESENT. 1986. s-a. $16 to individuals; institutions $32. Ohio State University Press, 1070 Carmack Rd., Columbus, OH 43210. TEL 614-292-6390. Eds. Philip C. Kolin, Colby H. Kullman. adv.; play rev.; bibl.; illus. (also avail. in microform from UMI; back issues avail.) Indexed: Amer.Hum.Ind.
—BLDSC shelfmark: 8489.057000.
    Description: Presents scholarly articles on theatre history, dramatic influences and technique, original interviews, theatre documents, useful bibliographies, and theatre reviews.

792   US
STUDIES IN FRENCH THEATRE. irreg. Peter Lang Publishing, Inc., 62 W. 45th St., 4th Fl., New York, NY 10036. TEL 212-302-6740. FAX 212-302-7574. Ed. Sharon Harwood-Gordon.
    Description: Provides a forum for critical interpretation and analysis of French theatrical works and authors from the Middle Ages to the present day.

792 917.306   US
STUDIES IN HISPANIC AMERICAN AND LATIN AMERICAN THEATRE. irreg. Peter Lang Publishing, Inc., 62 W. 45th St., 4th Fl., New York, NY 10036. TEL 212-302-6740. FAX 212-302-7574. Ed. Kirsten F. Nigro.

792.02   US
STUDIES IN RESTORATION AND EIGHTEENTH-CENTURY DRAMA. irreg. Peter Lang Publishing, Inc., 62 W. 45th St., 4th Fl., New York, NY 10036. TEL 212-302-6740. FAX 212-302-7574. Ed. Laura Morrow.
    Description: Presents various approaches to British drama from the Restoration through the eighteenth century.

792   US
STUDIES IN THEATRE ARTS. irreg. Edwin Mellen Press, 240 Portage Rd., Box 450, Lewiston, NY 14092. TEL 716-754-8566. FAX 716-754-4335.

792   RM   ISSN 0039-3991
PN1609.R6
STUDII SI CERCETARI DE ISTORIA ARTEI. SERIA TEATRU, MUZICA, CINEMATOGRAFIE/STUDIES AND RESEACH IN ART HISTORY. SERIES: THEATRE, MUSIC, CINEMATOGRAPHY. (Text in Rumanian; summaries in English, French, German and Russian) 1954. a. 35 lei($45) (Academia Romana) Editura Academiei Romane, Calea Victoriei 125, 79717 Bucharest, Rumania. (Dist. by: Rompresfilatelia, Calea Grivitei 64-66, P.O. Box 12-201, 78104 Bucharest, Rumania) bk.rev.; illus.; index. Indexed: RILM.

STUDIO; tjedni informativni list za televiziju, radio, film, teatar i muziku. see *COMMUNICATIONS — Television And Cable*

SUN BELT JOURNAL. see *BUSINESS AND ECONOMICS*

SYDNEY OPERA HOUSE. DIARY. see *MUSIC*

792   GW   ISSN 0039-811X
SZENE; Fachzeitschrift der DDR fuer Amateurtheater, -kabaret, -puppenspiel und -pantomime. 1966. 4/yr. DM.9. Zentralhaus-Publikationen, Dittriching 4, Postfach 1051, 7010 Leipzig, Germany. (Subscr. to: Buchexport, Leninstr. 16, 7010 Leipzig, Germany) Ed. Petra Moll. play rev.; charts; illus.
    Description: Covers amateur theater, cabaret, puppetry and pantomime in East Germany.

792   SZ
SZENE SCHWEIZ/SCENE SUISSE/SCENA SVIZZERA. 1973. a. 25 Fr. Schweizerische Gesellschaft fuer Theaterkultur - Swiss Association for Theatre Research, c/o Louis Naef, Postfach 180, CH-6130 Willisau, Switzerland. TEL 045-81-39-22.

792   HU   ISSN 0039-8136
SZINHAZ. 1968. m. $32. (Szinhazmuveszeti Szovetseg) Lapkiado Vallalat, Lenin korut 9-11, 1073 Budapest 7, Hungary. TEL 222-408. (Subscr. to: Kultura, P.O. Box 149, H-1389 Budapest, Hungary) Ed. Ivan Boldizsar. bk.rev.; index. Indexed: M.L.A.

792   US
T D F SIGHTLINES. 1986. q. free. Theatre Development Fund, 1501 Broadway, New York, NY 10036. TEL 212-221-0885. FAX 212-768-1563. Ed. Stuart W. Little. circ. 1,600.
    Description: Covers matters of general theater interest. Includes news of the fund.

792   US   ISSN 0012-5962
PN2000
T D R. (The Drama Review); a journal of performance studies. 1955. q. $30 to individuals (foreign $44); institutions $70 (foreign $84); students $20 (foreign $34). M I T Press, 55 Hayward St., Cambridge, MA 02142. TEL 617-253-2889. FAX 617-258-6779. TELEX 921473. (Editorial addr.: TDR, New York University - Tisch School of the Arts, 721 Broadway, 6th fl., New York, NY 10003) Ed. Richard Schechner. adv.; bk.rev.; index; circ. 4,750. (also avail. in microform from UMI,MIM; back issues avail.; reprint service avail. from UMI) Indexed: Abstr.Engl.Stud.; Acad.Ind.; Amer.Bibl.Slavic & E.Eur.Stud.; Arts & Hum.Cit.Ind.; Bk.Rev.Ind. (1975-), Child.Bk.Rev.Ind. (1975-), Curr.Cont., Hum.Ind., M.L.A., Mag.Ind., Mid.East: Abstr.& Ind.
● Also available online.
—BLDSC shelfmark: 3623.197000.
    Formerly: Tulane Drama Review.
    Description: Provides a forum for writing about performances and their social, economic, and political contexts.

T.G.I.F. CASTING NEWS. see *OCCUPATIONS AND CAREERS*

791   SA
T R U K P A C T INFO. (Text in Afrikaans, English) 1968. q. free. Transvaalse Raad vir die Uitvoerende Kunste - Performing Arts Council Transvaal, P.O. Box 566, Pretoria 0001, South Africa. FAX 012-322-3913. TELEX 3-20753 PACT SA. adv.; color page R.4600; adv. contact: Yvonne Eskell. circ. 40,000.
    Former titles (until 1991): Theatre Guide - Theatre Gids; (until 1990): T R U K - P A C T (ISSN 0085-7416)

792 028.5   US
T Y A TODAY. (Theatre for Young Audiences) 1985. s-a. $50 to individuals; libraries $30; students $25. International Association of Theatre for Children and Young People, United States Center, c/o Theatre Service, Box 15282, Evansville, IN 47716-0282. TEL 812-474-0549. FAX 212-595-0336. Ed. Amie Brockway. adv.; bk.rev.; play rev.; illus.; circ. 1,000. (back issues avail.)
    Description: Concerned with promotion and development of the professional theatre for young audiences in America and with the international inter-change of theatre artistry and research.

TANZAKTUELL; Zeitung fuer Tanz Theater Bewegung. see *DANCE*

TAPROOT. see *LITERATURE*

792   DK   ISSN 0900-0119
TEATERBLADET. m. DKK 152.50. Teaterfundet, Sankt Knuds Vej 26, 1903 Copenhagen V, Denmark.
    Formerly: Teater, Film og T V (ISSN 0108-6251)

792   SW   ISSN 0040-0750
TEATERN. 1934. 4/yr. free. Svenska Riksteatern - Swedish National Theatre Centre, S-145 83 Norsborg, Sweden. Ed. Eric Lindqvist. illus.

792   DK   ISSN 0107-248X
PN2044.D4
TEATERRAADETS INDSTILLING. 1976. a. free. Ministry of Culture, Danish Theater Council, Vesterbrogade 24, 4th, 1620 Copenhagen V, Denmark. TEL 45-1-247304.

792   DK   ISSN 0109-3363
TEATERSEMINAR. 1982. a. DKK 45. Danmarks Teaterforeninger, Frederiksborggade 20-3 m.f., 1360 Copenhagen K, Denmark. TEL 33-15-42-48. FAX 33-13-14-39.

792   PL   ISSN 0040-0769
TEATR. 1945. m. $11.70. Ul. Jakubowska 14, 03-902 Warsaw, Poland. TEL 48-22-175594. (Dist. by: Ars Polona-Ruch, Krakowskie Przedmiescie 7, Warsaw, Poland) Ed. Anrzej Wanat. bk.rev.; illus.; index; circ. 6,800.

792   RU   ISSN 0040-0777
PN2007
TEATR; zhurnal dramaturgii i teatra. 1937. m. 30 Rub. (Teatral'nyi Soyuz Rabochikh) Izdatel'stvo Izvestiya, Ul. Gertsena 49, Moscow 49, Russia. TEL (095) 291-5788. (Co-sponsor: Soyuz Pisatelei) Ed. A. Salinskii. bk.rev.; dance rev.; play rev.; illus.; circ. 32,600. Indexed: Curr.Dig.Sov.Press.

792   RU   ISSN 0040-0785
TEATRAL'NAYA ZHIZN'. 1958. s-m. 22.20 Rub. Vserossiiskoe Teatral'noe Obschestvo, Moscow, Russia. (Co-sponsors: Ministerstvo Kul'tury; Soyuz Pisatelei Rossiiskoi S.F.S.R.) Ed. Yu.A. Zubkov. illus.; index; circ. 50,000.

792   AG   ISSN 0040-0793
TEATRO.* 1964. m. Arg.$500.($6) Concepcion Arenal 3932, Buenos Aires, Argentina.

792   IT
TEATRO. irreg., latest no.4. price varies. Angelo Longo Editore, Via Paolo Costa 33, P.O. Box 431, 48100 Ravenna, Italy. TEL 0544-217026. circ. 2,000.

792   IT
TEATRO. STUDI E TESTI. 1985. irreg., no.7, 1989. price varies. Casa Editrice Leo S. Olschki, Casella Postale 66, 50100 Florence, Italy. TEL 055-6530684. FAX 055-6530214.

THEATER

792 — AG
TEATRO C E L C I T; revista de teatrologia, tecnicas y reflexion sobre la practica teatral iberoamericana. 1987. 2/yr. $50 in America; Europe $65; elsewhere $80(effective 1991). Centro Latinoamericano de Creacion e Investigacion Teatral, Bolivar 827, 1066 Buenos Aires, Argentina. TEL 541-361-8358. FAX 541-331-7353. Ed. Carlos A. Ianni. adv.; bk.rev.; circ. 1,000. (back issues avail.)
Supersedes: Teatro: Teoria y Practica.

792 780 945 — IT — ISSN 1120-9569
TEATRO E STORIA. 1986. s-a. L.80000. (Centro per la Sperimentazione e la Ricerca Teatrale di Pontedera) Societa Editrice Il Mulino, Strada Maggiore, 37, 40125 Bologna, Italy. TEL 051-256011. FAX 051-256034. Ed. Claudio Meldolesi. adv.; index; circ. 1,100. (back issues avail.)

792 — IT
TEATRO FESTIVAL. bi-m. Mucchi Editore, Casella Postale 64 Centro, 41100 Modena, Italy. Ed. Ugo Volli.

792 — RM
PN2844
TEATRULAZI. 1956. m. 300 lei($64) Ministerul Culturii, Piata Presei Libere 1, Sector 1, Bucharest, Rumania. (Subscr. to: Calea Grivitei 66-68, Box 12201, Bucharest, Rumania) Ed. Dumitro Solomon. adv.; bk.rev.; illus.; play rev.
Formerly: Teatrul (ISSN 0040-0815)

792 — BU — ISSN 0204-6253
TEATUR. 1946. m. 5 lv.($12) (Komitet za Izkustvo i Kultura) Foreign Trade Co. "Hemus", 7 Levsky St., 1000 Sofia, Bulgaria. (Co-sponsor: Suiuz na Artistite) Ed. Iu. Vuchkov. play rev.; circ. 4,046.

792 — US — ISSN 1053-8860
TECHNICAL BRIEF. 1982. 3/yr. $7 to individuals; institutions $10. Yale University, School of Drama, Technical Production Department, 222 York St., New Haven, CT 06520. TEL 203-432-9664. FAX 203-432-1550. Eds. Bronislaw Sammler, Don Harvey. illus.; index; circ. 1,000.
Description: Articles by and for technical theater practitioners complete with mechanical drawings representing solutions to technical theater problems.

792 — US — ISSN 0161-0775
PN2000
THEATER (NEW HAVEN). 1968. 3/yr. $20 to individuals; institutions $24. Yale University, School of Drama, Yale Repertory Theatre, 222 York St., New Haven, CT 06520. TEL 203-432-1568. FAX 203-432-1550. Ed. Joel Schechter. adv.; bk.rev.; illus.; play rev.; index; circ. 3,000. (also avail. in microform from UMI; reprint service avail.) **Indexed:** Curr.Cont., Film Lit.Ind. (1977-), Hum.Ind., Ind.Bk.Rev.Hum., M.L.A., Mid.East: Abstr.& Ind.
—BLDSC shelfmark: 8814.306000.
Formerly (until vol.8, no.2 & 3, 1976): Yale - Theatre (ISSN 0044-0167)
Description: Criticism, essays, reviews, translations, interviews. Each issue contains full text of a new play.

792 — GW — ISSN 0040-5418
PN2004
THEATER DER ZEIT. 1946. m. DM.120. Henschel Verlag GmbH, Oranienburger Str. 67-68, 1040 Berlin, Germany. adv.; bk.rev.; dance rev.; play rev.; bibl.; illus.; index. **Indexed:** Curr.Cont., RILM.
—BLDSC shelfmark: 8814.310000.
Description: Covers all areas of theatre in the Germany: dramatic art, opera, children's theatre, musicals, ballet and puppet theatre.

792 — SZ — ISSN 0040-5507
PN2004
THEATER HEUTE. 1960. m. 195 Fr. (Erhard Friedrich Verlag) Orell Fuessli & Friedrich Verlag, Dietzingerstr. 3, CH-8036 Zurich, Switzerland. TEL 041-4667711. FAX 041-4667457. TELEX 813575. Ed. Henning Rischbieter. adv.; bk.rev.; illus.; circ. 20,000 (controlled). **Indexed:** Curr.Cont.

792 — AU
THEATER IN GRAZ. 1952. w. S.220. Vereinigte Buehnen Graz, Burggasse 16, A-8010 Graz, Austria. Ed. Gernot Schoeppl. adv.; bk.rev.; play rev.; illus.; circ. 6,000.
Formerly: Theaternachrichten (ISSN 0040-5450)

792 — GW — ISSN 0040-5442
THEATER-RUNDSCHAU; Blaetter fuer Buehne, Film, Musik und Literatur. 1955. m. DM.33.60. (Bund der Theatergemeinden e.V.) Theater-Rundschau-Verlag GmbH, Bonner Talweg 10, 5300 Bonn 1, Germany. TEL 0228-915031. FAX 0228-9150350. adv.; bk.rev.; bibl.; illus.; circ. 56,000. (newspaper)

792 — GW
THEATER TELEGRAMM. 1952. irreg. DM.84. Hans D. Weiss Verlag, Wallbergstr. 9, 8150 Holzkirchen, Germany. TEL 08024-1090. bk.rev. (looseleaf format)

792 — US — ISSN 0896-1956
THEATER WEEK. 1987. w. $49 (foreign $74). That New Magazine, Inc., 28 W. 25th St., 4th Fl., New York, NY 10010. TEL 212-627-2120. FAX 212-727-9321. Ed. John Harris. adv.; bk.rev.; circ. 12,000. (back issues avail.)
Description: Covers broadway and regional theater.

792 — GW
THEATERMAGAZIN. 1978. m. DM.28. (Niedersaechsischen Staatstheater Hannover) Schluetersche Verlagsanstalt GmbH und Co., Postfach 5440, 3000 Hannover 1, Germany. TEL 0511-1236-445. FAX 0511-1236-400. Ed. Sabine Hammer. circ. 25,000. (back issues avail.)

792 — GW — ISSN 0175-5889
THEATERPAEDAGOGIK; Beitraege zur Praxis und Theorie der Theaterausbildung. 1981. s-a. DM.9. Hochschule der Kuenste Berlin, Pressestelle, Ernst-Reuter-Platz 10, 1000 Berlin 10, Germany. TEL 030-3185-2450. Ed. Rainer E. Klemke. circ. 300. (back issues avail.)

792 — GW
THEATERPAEDAGOGISCHE BIBLIOTHEK. 1983. irreg., vol. 6, 1987. Florian Noetzel Verlag, Heinrichshofen Buecher, Valoisstrasse 11, 2940 Wilhelmshaven, Germany. (Dist. in U.S. by: C.F. Peters Corp., 373 Park Ave. S., New York, NY 10016) Eds. Georg Immelmann, Rudolf Liechtenhan.

792 — US — ISSN 0735-1895
PN2000
THEATERWORK.* 1980. bi-m. $9. Box 8150, Santa Fe, NM 87504-8150. Ed.Bd. adv.; bk.rev.; circ. 2,000. **Indexed:** Alt.Press Ind.

792 — GW — ISSN 0723-1172
PN2004
THEATERZEITSCHRIFT. q. DM.51 (students DM.43.80). (Verein zur Erfoschung Theatraler Verkehrformen e.V.) Wochenschau Verlag, Adolf-Damaschke-Str. 103, 6231 Schwalbach, Germany. Ed.Bd. circ. 1,700.
Description: Theory and history of theatre, cinema and television.

792 — SZ — ISSN 0378-6935
THEATERZYTIG; Monatszeitschrift des Zentralverbandes Schweizer Volkstheater. 1973. 11/yr. 36 Fr. (members 30 Fr.). (Zentralverband Schweizer Volkstheater) Verlag Sauerlaender, Laurenzenvorstadt 89, CH-5001 Aarau, Switzerland. TEL 064-268626. FAX 064-245780. TELEX 981195 SAG CH. Ed. Erwin Kessler. adv.; bk.rev.; bibl.; illus.
Formerly: Dialog.
Description: Information and calendar of Swiss amateur and national theatre.

792 — US
THEATRE (NEW YORK). 1977. 8/yr. $12. 41 W. 72nd St., Apt. 14G, New York, NY 10023. TEL 212-221-6078. Eds. Ira J. Bilowit, Debbi Wasserman. circ. 10,000.

792 — US
THEATRE & EVENTS GUIDE. 1960. m. $24. Theatre & Events Guide, Inc., 111 W. 72nd St., New York, NY 10023. TEL 212-799-5901. Ed. Adele Gold. circ. 35,700.

792 — US — ISSN 0082-3821
PN2012
THEATRE ANNUAL. 1942. a. price varies. University of Akron, College of Fine Arts and Applied Arts, School of Theatre Arts, Akron, OH 44325-1005. TEL 216-972-6081. FAX 216-375-5101. Ed. Wallace Sterling. circ. 350. **Indexed:** Abstr.Engl.Stud., Arts & Hum.Cit.Ind., Curr.Cont., M.L.A.

792 — US
THEATRE CLASSICS. 1987. a. $45. League of Historic American Theatres, 1511 K St., N.W., Ste. 923, Washington, DC 20005. TEL 202-783-6966. Ed. Tara Schroeder. adv.; circ. 1,000. (back issues avail.)
Description: Offers an in depth look at 8 historic theatres across the nation which have been restored and are operating as performing arts facilities.

792 — US — ISSN 0040-5469
PN2000
THEATRE CRAFTS. (Includes annual directory) 1967. 10/yr. $36. Theatre Crafts Associates, 135 Fifth Ave., New York, NY 10010-7193. TEL 212-677-5997. FAX 212-677-3857. (Subscr. to: Theatre Crafts, P.O. Box 470, Mt. Morris, IL 61054) Ed. Patricia MacKay. adv.; bk.rev.; charts; illus.; circ. 27,500. (also avail. in microform from UMI) **Indexed:** Arts & Hum.Cit.Ind., Bk.Rev.Ind. (1978-), Child.Bk.Rev.Ind. (1978-), Curr.Cont., Educ.Ind., Film Lit.Ind. (1988-), Mag.Ind., PMR, R.G., TOM.
—BLDSC shelfmark: 8814.341400.
Description: Covers all aspects of the performing arts for theatre, film and video, including lighting, sound, and set and costume design.

792 — US
THEATRE CRAFTS INTERNATIONAL. 1979. 6/yr. $34.95. Theatre Crafts Associates, 135 Fifth Ave., New York, NY 10010. FAX 212-677-3857. (Subscr. to: Box 462, Mt. Morris, IL 61054) Ed. Patricia MacKay. adv.; bk.rev. **Indexed:** Br.Tech.Ind.
Incorporates: Cue International; **Formerly:** Cue Technical Theatre Review (ISSN 0144-6088)
Description: Covers the design, technology and business aspects of theatre, dance, opera, film, television, clubs and concerts on an internationl basis.

842 — FR
THEATRE D'AUJOURD'HUI. 1976. irreg. price varies. Editons Klincksieck, 11 rue de Lille, 75005 Paris, France. Dir. Paul Vernois.

792 — US — ISSN 0040-5477
NA1
THEATRE DESIGN AND TECHNOLOGY;* news on the construction of theatres, new technical developments, costume design, engineering, stage design, lighting, sound, health & safety, administration, and education. 1965. q. membership. U S Institute for Theatre Technology, Inc., 10 W. 19th St., Ste. 5A, New York, NY 10011. TEL 212-924-9088. FAX 212-924-9343. Eds. Eric Fielding, Cecelia Fielding. adv.; bk.rev.; play rev.; bibl.; charts; illus.; pat.; circ. 3,750. (also avail. in microform from UMI; reprint service avail. from UMI) **Indexed:** Avery Ind.Archit.Per., Br.Tech.Ind.
—BLDSC shelfmark: 8814.343000.

792 — US — ISSN 0271-3136
PN2289
THEATRE DIRECTORY; the annual contact resource of theatres and related organizations. 1972. a. $5.95. Theatre Communications Group, Inc., 355 Lexington Ave., New York, NY 10017. TEL 212-697-5230. Ed. David Boyce. circ. 5,000.

792 — US — ISSN 0737-0172
PN2275.C3
THEATRE DIRECTORY OF THE BAY AREA (YEAR). 1981. biennial. $18. Theatre Bay Area, 657 Mission St., No. 402, San Francisco, CA 94105-4116. FAX 415-957-1556. Ed. Jean Schiffman. adv.; circ. 1,400. (back issues avail.)
Description: Comprehensive guide to theater activities in the San Francisco Bay area for performers and theater lovers.

792 — PL — ISSN 0040-5493
PN2859.P6
THEATRE EN POLOGNE/THEATRE IN POLAND. (Text in English and French) 1958. q. $24 (effective Jan. 1990). Miedzynarodowy Instytut Teatralny, Polski Osrodek - International Theatre Institute, Polish Center, Pl. Pilsudskiego 9, 00-078 Warsaw, Poland. TEL 48-22-263027. Ed. August Grodzicki. adv.; bk.rev.; abstr.; bibl.; illus.; play rev.; tr.lit.; index; circ. 1,700. (tabloid format) **Indexed:** Arts & Hum.Cit.Ind., Curr.Cont.

| 792 | FR | ISSN 0049-3597 |

THEATRE ENFANCE ET JEUNESSE. (Text in English, French) 1963. s-a. $45. Association du Theatre pour l'Enfance et la Jeunesse, 98 Bd. Kellermann, 75013 Paris, France. illus.

| 792.02 | FR | ISSN 0398-0049 |

THEATRE ET ANIMATION; revue trimestrielle des spectacles non-professionnels et des techniques d'expression et d'animation. 1976. q. 160 F. Federation Nationale des Compagnies de Theatre et d'Animation, 12 Chaussee d'Antin, 75441 Paris Cedex 09, France. Ed. Dir. Bernard Goupil.
 Incorporating: Nos Spectacles; Theatre Amateur (ISSN 0029-3741); Theatre et Spectacles Non Professionnels, Techniques d'Expression et d'Animation.

| 840 | IT | |

THEATRE FRANCAIS DE LA RENAISSANCE; premiere serie. 1986. irreg., no.3, 1990. price varies. Casa Editrice Leo S. Olschki, Casella Postale 66, 50100 Florence, Italy. TEL 055-6530684. FAX 055-6530214.

| 792 | CN | ISSN 0226-5761 |
| PN2009 | | |

THEATRE HISTORY IN CANADA/HISTOIRE DU THEATRE AU CANADA. (Text in English, French) 1980. s-a. Can.$15 to individuals; students Can.$12; institutions Can.$22. University of Toronto, Graduate Centre for Study of Drama, 214 College St., Toronto, Ont. M5T 2Z9, Canada. TEL 416-586-7984. (Co-sponsor: Queen's University in Kingston) Eds. Richard Plant, L.E. Doucette. bk.rev.; circ. 490. **Indexed:** Arts & Hum.Cit.Ind., Can.Lit.Ind., Can.Per.Ind., Curr.Cont.
 —BLDSC shelfmark: 8814.347160.

| 792 | US | ISSN 0733-2033 |
| PN2000 | | |

THEATRE HISTORY STUDIES. 1981. a. $8 to individuals; libraries $13. Mid-America Theatre Association, c/o Ron Engle, Ed., Theatre Arts Department, University of North Dakota, Box 8182, Grand Forks, ND 58202. TEL 701-777-3446. (Co-sponsor: University of North Dakota) Ed. Ron Engle. adv.; bk.rev.; circ. 1,000. **Indexed:** Arts & Hum.Cit.Ind., M.L.A.
 —BLDSC shelfmark: 8814.347200.

| 792 | US | ISSN 0040-5515 |

THEATRE INFORMATION BULLETIN.* 1944. w. $100. Proscenium Publications, 71 Vanderbilt Ave., No. 320, New York, NY 10169-0005. TEL 212-532-2570. Eds. Joan Marlowe, Betty Blake. (processed)

| 792 | UK | ISSN 0263-6344 |

THEATRE IRELAND; the magazine which is for and about the theatre. 1982. q. £13. Theatre Ireland Ltd., 29 Main St., Castlerock, Co. Derry BT51 4RA, N. Ireland. TEL 0265-848130. FAX 0265-40903. Ed. Lynda Henderson. adv.; illus.
 —BLDSC shelfmark: 8814.347300.
 Description: Contains articles on Irish theatre, playwrights, student and other drama festivals, and theatre companies. Includes a theatre news column.

| 792 | US | ISSN 0192-2882 |
| PN3171 | | |

THEATRE JOURNAL (BALTIMORE). 1949. q. $20 to individuals (foreign $30.40); institutions $48 (foreign $57.40). Johns Hopkins University Press, Journals Publishing Division, 701 W. 40th St., Ste. 275, Baltimore, MD 21211. TEL 410-516-6987. FAX 410-516-6998. Eds. William B. Worthen, Janette Reinelt. adv.; bk.rev.; play rev.; bibl.; illus.; circ. 1,692. (also avail. in microfiche from UMI; reprint service avail. from UMI; back issues avail.) **Indexed:** Abstr.Engl.Stud., Arts & Hum.Cit.Ind., C.I.J.E., Chic.Per.Ind., Child.Bk.Rev.Ind. (1980-), Curr.Cont., Educ.Ind., Hum.Ind.
 Formerly (until 1979): Educational Theatre Journal (ISSN 0013-1989)
 Description: Covers a broad range of topics in the study and teaching of theater, including social and historical studies, production reviews, and theoretical inquiries that illuminate dramatic text and production.

| 792 | CN | |

THE THEATRE LISTING. 1986. a. Can.$12. Professional Association of Canadian Theatres, PACT Communications Centre, 64 Charles St. E., Toronto, Ont. M4Y 1T1, Canada. TEL 416-968-3033. FAX 416-968-3035. Ed. Beverley A.B. Sweeting. adv.; illus.
 Formerly: Behind the Scenes.
 Description: Directory of professional English language Canadian theatres from coast to coast. Also includes service organizations, artists associations, government departments and agencies.

| 792 | UK | ISSN 0040-5523 |

THEATRE NOTEBOOK; journal of the history and technique of the British theatre. 1946. 3/yr. $26. Society for Theatre Research, c/o The Theatre Museum, 1E Tavistock St., London WC2E 7PA, England. Ed.Bd. adv.; bk.rev.; illus.; index, cum.index: vols. 1-25, 26-40; circ. 1,050. (also avail. in microfilm) **Indexed:** Abstr.Engl.Stud., Arts & Hum.Cit.Ind., Br.Tech.Ind., Curr.Cont., Hum.Ind., M.L.A.

THEATRE ORGAN REVIEW. see *MUSIC*

| 792 | US | |

▼**THEATRE PATRON.** 1990. m. $12. J B & Me Publishing, Box 3879, Manhattan Beach, CA 90266. TEL 213-546-1255. Ed. Marilyn Elkind. play rev.; circ. 10,000.
 Description: Lists shows playing in small and large theaters in Los Angeles, New York and London.

| 792 | US | ISSN 0361-7947 |
| PN2266 | | |

THEATRE PROFILES; an illustrated reference guide to nonprofit professional theatres in the United States. 1973. biennial. $19.95. Theatre Communications Group, Inc., 355 Lexington Ave., New York, NY 10017. TEL 212-697-5230. Ed. Steven Samuels. illus. (back issues avail.)
 —BLDSC shelfmark: 8814.354500.

| 792 | FR | ISSN 0335-2927 |

THEATRE PUBLIC. 1974. bi-m. 250 F.($55) (foreign 275 F.). Theatre de Gennevilliers, 41 av. des Gresillons, 92230 Gennevilliers, France. FAX 40-86-17-44. Ed. Alain Girault. adv.; bk.rev.; circ. 2,000. (back issues avail.)

| 792 070 | UK | ISSN 0962-1792 |
| PN2596.L6 | | |

THEATRE RECORD. 1981. fortn. £90($180) 4 Cross Deep Gardens, Twickenham, Middx. TW1 4QU, England. TEL 081-892 6087. FAX 081-744-3002. Ed. Ian Herbert. adv.; bk.rev.; play rev.; cum.index. (looseleaf format; back issues avail.)
 Formerly (until 1991): London Theatre Record (ISSN 0261-5282)
 Description: Reprints unabridged critical reviews and cast lists of all London and most new British theatre.

| 792 | UK | ISSN 0307-8833 |
| PN2001 | | |

THEATRE RESEARCH INTERNATIONAL. (Text in English; summaries in French) 1958. 3/yr. £49($98) (International Federation for Theatre Research) Oxford University Press, Oxford Journals, Pinkhill House, Southfield Road, Eynsham, Oxford OX8 1JJ, England. TEL 0865-882283. FAX 0865-882890. TELEX 837330-OXPRES-G. Ed. C. Schumacher. adv.; bk.rev.; bibl.; illus.; index; circ. 1,050. (also avail. in microform from UMI) **Indexed:** Arts & Hum.Cit.Ind., Curr.Cont., Hist.Abstr., Hum.Ind., Ind.Bk.Rev.Hum., M.L.A., Mid.East: Abstr.& Ind.
 —BLDSC shelfmark: 8814.370300.
 Formerly: Theatre Research (ISSN 0040-5566)
 Description: Presents history and criticism of drama conceived and the art of the theatre, providing both a medium of communication for scholars and a service to students of art, architecture, design, music and drama literature.

| 792.02 | US | ISSN 0362-0964 |
| PN1620.045 | | |

THEATRE STUDIES. 1955. a. $8 to individuals; institutions $10. Ohio State University, Theatre Research Institute, 1430 Lincoln Tower, 1800 Cannon Dr., Columbus, OH 43210. TEL 614-292-8250. Ed. B. Rose. adv.; bk.rev.; bibl.; illus.; cum.index vols. 1-20 in vol. 20 (1973-74); circ. 1,200. (also avail. in microfilm; back issues avail.) **Indexed:** Abstr.Engl.Stud., Amer.Hum.Ind., Arts & Hum.Cit.Ind., Curr.Cont., G.Perf.Arts, M.L.A.

| 792 | US | ISSN 0040-5574 |
| PN2000 | | |

THEATRE SURVEY.* 1960. s-a. $15. American Society for Theatre Research, c/o Prof. Judith Milhons, Graduate Center, Ph.D. Program in Theatre, 33 W. 42nd St., New York, NY 10036. adv.; bk.rev.; illus.; circ. 1,250. (also avail. in microform from UMI; reprint service avail from UMI) **Indexed:** Abstr.Engl.Stud., Arts & Hum.Cit.Ind., Chic.Per.Ind., Curr.Cont., Hist.Abstr., Hum.Ind., M.L.A.
 —BLDSC shelfmark: 8814.375000.

| 792 | US | ISSN 1054-8378 |

▼**THEATRE TOPICS.** 1991. s-a. $14 to individuals; institutions $22. (Association for Theatre in Higher Education) Johns Hopkins University Press, Journals Publishing Division, 701 W. 40th St., Ste. 275, Baltimore, MD 21211. TEL 410-516-6987. FAX 410-516-6998. Ed. Beverley Byers-Pevitts.
 Description: Addresses the concerns of scholars and artists in the areas of performance studies, dramaturgy, and theatre pedagogy.
 Refereed Serial

| 792.0973 | US | ISSN 0082-3856 |

THEATRE WORLD. a. $25. Crown Publishers, Inc., 201 E. 50th St., New York, NY 10022. TEL 212-254-1600. Ed. John Willis.

| 792 | UK | ISSN 0265-2609 |
| PN2001 | | |

THEATREPHILE. q. £15($30) D.F. Cheshire, Sean McCarthy, Eds. & Pubs., 5 Dryden St., Covent Garden, London WC2E 9NW, England.
 —BLDSC shelfmark: 8814.387600.

| 792 | IT | ISSN 0040-5604 |

THEATRON; rivista quadrimestrale di cultura, documentazione e informazione teatrale. (Text in English, French, German, Italian) 1961. 3/yr. L.20000($16) Centro Teatrale Internazionale di Documentazione e di Collaborazione Tra Teatri di Ricerca e Universitari, Via Fabiola 1, 00152 Rome, Italy. Dir. Elda A. Vernara. adv.; bk.rev.; play rev.; bibl.; illus.; stat.; index, cum.index.

| 051 | CN | |

THEATRUM. 5/yr. Theatrum Publishing Inc., P.O. Box 688, Sta. C, Toronto, Ont. M6J 3S1, Canada. TEL 416-493-5740. Ed. Nigel Hunt. circ. 7,600.

| 792 | GW | |

THEMA; Essener Theater Magazin. 1988. m. Theater und Philharmonie Essen GmbH, Rolandstr. 10, 4300 Essen 1, Germany. TEL 0201-8122-0. FAX 0201-8122-105. Eds. Andreas Buechel, Gernot Wojnarowicz. adv.; play rev.; illus.; circ. 15,000. (back issues avail.)

| 792 | GW | |

THEMA - DAS THEATERMAGAZIN; Theatermagazin fuer Freunde und Foerderer des Badisches Staatstheaters Karlruhe. 1987. m. free. Badisches Staatstheater Karlsruhe, Postfach 1449, Baumeisterstr. 11, 7500 Karlsruhe 1, Germany. play rev.; illus.; circ. 12,000.
 Formerly (until 1989): Musengau.

| 792 | UK | ISSN 0263-676X |
| PN1601 | | |

THEMES IN DRAMA. 1979. a. $42 to individuals; institutions $69. Cambridge University Press, Edinburgh Bldg., Shaftesbury Rd., Cambridge CB2 2RU, England. TEL 0223-312393. FAX 0223-315052. TELEX 851817256. (North American addr.: Cambridge University Press, 40 W. 20th St., New York, NY 10011) Ed. James Redmond. (also avail. in microform from UMI)
 Description: Reviews the dramatic and theatrical activities of a wide range of cultures and periods.

TIAN WAI TIAN/SKY OUTSIDE SKY. see *MOTION PICTURES*

| 792 | NE | ISSN 0167-5516 |

TIJDSCHRIFT VOOR THEATERWETENSCHAP. 1979. q. fl.30 to individuals; institutions fl.40. Instituut voor Theaterwetenschap, Kromme Nieuwe Gracht 29, 3512 HD Utrecht, Netherlands. TEL 020-279709. Ed. H. Schoenmakers. adv.; bk.rev.; circ. 400.
 Description: Covers theater, theatrical dance, film, television with a historical and theoretical perspective.

THEATER

792 NE ISSN 0040-9170
PN2002
TONEEL TEATRAAL. 10/yr. fl.45. Nederlands Theaterinstituut, Herengracht 166-168, 1016 BP Amsterdam, Netherlands. Ed. Mieke Kolk. adv.; bk.rev.; play rev.; charts; illus.; circ. 5,300.
Formerly: Mickery Mouth and Toneel Teatraal.

TOURARTS. see BUSINESS AND ECONOMICS — Trade And Industrial Directories

792 MX
TRAMOYA; cuaderno de teatro. 1975. q. $25. Universidad Veracruzana, Zona Universitaria, Lomas del Estadio, Jalapa, Veracruz, Mexico. FAX 281-74461. (U.S. addr.: Rutgers University, Dept. of Spanish, Camden, NJ 08102) Ed. Joaquina Soto. circ. 1,500.

TUITION, ENTERTAINMENT, NEWS, VIEWS. see ART

792 US
U S OUTDOOR DRAMA. 1964. q. $12. Institute of Outdoor Drama, University of North Carolina at Chapel Hill, CB3240 NCNB Plaza, Chapel Hill, NC 27599-3240. TEL 919-962-1328. Ed. Judy Via. bk.rev.; circ. 1,000. (looseleaf format)
Formerly (until 1990): Institute of Outdoor Drama Newsletter (ISSN 0020-3017)
Description: Covers news, announcements, theatre literature citations, and information on all aspects of outdoor historical drama planning and production such as writing, directing, designing, staging, promotion, auditions, and management.

792 SP
UNIVERSIDAD DE MURCIA. CATEDRA DE TEATRO. CUADERNOS. 1978. irreg. Universidad de Murcia, Secretariado de Publicaciones y Intercambio Cientifico, Santo Cristo 1, 30001 Murcia, Spain. circ. 2,000.

792.07 TZ
UNIVERSITY OF DAR ES SALAAM. THEATRE ARTS DEPARTMENT. ANNUAL REPORT. a. University of Dar es Salaam, Theatre Arts Department, P.O. Box 35091, Dar es Salaam, Tanzania.

700 US ISSN 0042-2738
PN2000
VARIETY. 1905. w. $129 (Canada $155; Europe $250; Asia-Pacific Rim $450; elsewhere $350). (Variety, Inc.) Cahners Publishing Company (New York), Consumer and Entertainment Division (Subsidiary of: Reed International PLC), Division of Reed Publishing (USA) Inc., 475 Park Ave. S., New York, NY 10016-6901. TEL 212-779-1100. FAX 212-779-0026. (Subscr. to: 44 Cook St., Denver, CO 80206. TEL 800-662-7776) Ed. Peter Bart. adv.; bk.rev.; film rev.; music rev.; play rev.; rec.rev.; tele.rev.; circ. 30,102. (also avail. in microform from MIM,KTO,BHP) Indexed: Bus.Ind.; Film Lit.Ind. (1973-), Intl.Ind.TV, Mag.Ind., Music Ind., PMR, SRI, Tr.& Indus.Ind.
Description: Covers all of the entertainment business: film, TV, cable, homevideo, legitimate theater, music and personal appearance.

792 011 US
VARIETY'S DIRECTORY OF MAJOR U S SHOW BUSINESS AWARDS. irreg., latest 1989. $59.95. R.R. Bowker, A Reed Reference Publishing Company, Division of Reed Publishing (USA) Inc., 121 Chanlon Rd., New Providence, NJ 07974. TEL 800-521-8110. FAX 908-665-6688. TELEX 138 755. (Subscr. to: Order Dept., Box 31, New Providence, NJ 07974)
Description: Lists names of all nominees and winners for every Oscar, Emmy, Tony, Grammy, and Pulitzer Prize for drama ever awarded. Organized chronologically.

VARIETY'S WHO'S WHO IN SHOW BUSINESS. see BIBLIOGRAPHIES

792 700 UK
VENUE MAGAZINE. 1982. s-m. £20. House Grove Ltd., 37-39 Jamaica St., Bristol BS2 8JP, England. TEL 0272-428 491. Ed. D.A. Templeton. adv.; bk.rev.; film rev.; play rev.; illus.; circ. 15,000. (back issues avail.)

792 TH
VILLA WINA. (Text in Thai) m. Chalerm Ketr Theatre Bldg., 3rd Floor, Bangkok, Thailand. Ed. Bhongsakdi Piamlap.

VLAANDEREN; tijdschrift voor kunst en letteren. see ART

792 FR
VOIES DE LA CREATION THEATRALE. a. price varies. Editions du C N R S, 1 Place Aristide Briand, 92195 Meudon Cedex, France. TEL 1-45-34-75-50. FAX 1-46-26-28-49. TELEX LABOBEL 204 135 F. (Subscr. to: Presses du C N R S, 20-22, rue Saint Amand, 75015 Paris, France. TEL 1-45-33-16-00) adv.; bk.rev.; index; circ. 1,500 (controlled).

792 RU ISSN 0507-3952
VOPROSY TEATRA; sbornik statei i materialov. 1965. a. 1.45 Rub. Vserossiiskoe Teatral'noe Obshchestvo, Ul. Gorkogo, 16, Moscow, Russia. (Co-sponsor: Institut Istorii Iskusstv) bibl.; illus.

WASHINGTON OPERA MAGAZINE. see MUSIC

792 SA ISSN 0043-1036
WAT KAN ONS OPVOER/WHAT CAN WE STAGE. 1967. s-a. free. Dramatic Artistic & Literary Rights Organisation (Pty) Ltd., SAMRO House, Cor. de Beer & Juta Streets, Braamfontein, South Africa. Eds. G.D. Roos, P.J. Roos. circ. 2,000 (controlled).

792 US
WE REMEMBER DEAN INTERNATIONAL. 1978. bi-m. $12 (Canada $13; elsewhere $20). We Remember Dean International, c/o Sylvia Bongiovanni, Box 5025, Fullerton, CA 92635. adv.; bk.rev.; circ. 500.
Formerly: We Remember Dean International Newsletter.
Description: Dedicated to preserving the memory of James Dean.

DIE WERKSTATT. see DANCE

WESTERN JOURNAL OF COMMUNICATION. see LINGUISTICS

WHAT'S ON IN LONDON (LONDON, 1935). see TRAVEL AND TOURISM

WHAT'S ON IN LONDON (LONDON, 1966). see TRAVEL AND TOURISM

791.3 US ISSN 0043-499X
WHITE TOPS; devoted exclusively to the circus. 1927. bi-m. $22 to non-members. Circus Fans Association of America, Rt. 1, Box 6735, White Stone, VA 22578. TEL 804-435-2951. Ed. James E. Foster. adv.; bk.rev.; illus.; circ. 2,500.

792 US ISSN 1047-1715
PN2289
▼**WHO'S WHERE IN THE AMERICAN THEATRE;** a directory of affiliated theatre artists in the U.S.A. 1990. irreg., 3rd ed. 1992. $14.95. Feedback Theatrebooks, 305 Madison Ave., Ste. 1146, New York, NY 10165. TEL 207-359-2781. FAX 212-687-4185. Ed. Mollie Ann and Walter J. Meserve. adv. (back issues avail.)
Description: Provides job titles, affiliations, addresses and phone numbers for more than 3300 individuals working in theatre in America.

WHO'S WHO IN ENTERTAINMENT. see MOTION PICTURES

792 AU
WIENER FORSCHUNGEN ZUR THEATER UND MEDIENWISSENSCHAFT. 1972. irreg. price varies. (Universitaet Wien, Institut fuer Theaterwissenschaft) Universitaets Verlagsbuchhandlung GmbH, Servitengasse 5, A-1092 Vienna, Austria. TEL 0222-348124. FAX 0222-3102805. Ed. Margaret Dietrich. index; circ. 1,000.
Formerly: Vienna. Universitaet. Institut fuer Theaterwissenschaft. Wissenschaftliche Reihe (ISSN 0083-6176)

792 AU ISSN 0377-0745
HD8799.S9
WIENER GESELLSCHAFT FUER THEATERFORSCHUNG. JAHRBUCH. 1944. irreg., no.27, 1986. price varies. (Wiener Gesellschaft fuer Theaterforschung) Verband der Wissenschaftlichen Gesellschaften Oesterreichs, Lindengasse 37, A-1070 Vienna, Austria. TEL 932166. Ed. Otto G. Schindler. circ. 500.

796 301.412 US ISSN 0740-770X
WOMEN & PERFORMANCE: A JOURNAL OF FEMINIST THEORY. 1983. s-a. $14 to individuals; institutions $25. Women & Performance Project, 721 Broadway, 6th Fl., New York, NY 10003. TEL 212-998-1625. Ed. Judy Burns. adv.; bk.rev.; circ. 1,300. Indexed: Alt.Press Ind., Left Ind. (1984-).
—BLDSC shelfmark: 9343.273000.
Description: Publishes articles concerned with traditional and non-traditional performance, such as film, theater, music, dance and performing art.

792.02 CC
XIJU/DRAMA. Variant title: Zhongyang Xiju Xueyuan Xuebao. (Text in Chinese) q. $24. Zhongyang Xiju Xueyuan - Central Academy of Drama, 39 Dong Mianhua Lane, Jiaodaokou, Beijing, People's Republic of China. (Dist. outside China by: China International Book Trading Corp., P.O. Box 2820, Beijing, P.R.C.; Dist. in US by: China Books & Periodicals, Inc., 2929 24th St., San Francisco, CA 94110. TEL 415-282-2994)

XIJU WENXUE/DRAMA LITERATURE. see LITERATURE

792 CC ISSN 0257-943X
XIJU YISHU/THEATRE ARTS. (Text in Chinese) 1978. q. Y8($24) Shanghai Xiju Xueyuan - Shanghai Theatre Academy, 630 Huashan Lu, Shanghai 200040, People's Republic of China. TEL 021-521909. (Dist. outside China by: China International Book Trading Corp., P.O. Box 399, Beijing, P.R.C.; Dist. in US by: China Books & Periodicals, Inc., 2929 24th St., San Francisco, CA 94110. TEL 415-282-2994) circ. 5,000.

792 CC
XIJU YISHU/THEATRE ART. (Text in Chinese) q. Zhongguo Xiju Xueyuan, 3 Liren Jie, Xuanwu-qu, Beijing 100054, People's Republic of China. TEL 333931.

XPRESS. see ART

YEARBOOK OF INTERDISCIPLINARY STUDIES IN THE FINE ARTS. see ART

YINGJU XINZUO/NEW FILM AND PLAY SCRIPTS. see LITERATURE

YOUNG CINEMA AND THEATRE/JEUNE CINEMA ET THEATRE; cultural magazine of the IUS. see MOTION PICTURES

792 375 US ISSN 0892-9092
PN3157
YOUTH THEATRE JOURNAL. 1986. q. $25 (foreign $30). American Alliance for Theatre & Education, Theatre Department, Arizona State University, Tempe, AZ 85287-3411. TEL 602-965-6064. FAX 602-965-9073. Ed. Catherine Dezseran. adv.; bk.rev.; circ. 1,200.
—BLDSC shelfmark: 9421.582200.
Description: Includes articles concerning theatre for young audiences and theatre and drama education.

792 CC
ZHONGGUO XIJU/CHINA'S THEATER. (Text in Chinese) bi-m. $27.50. (Zhongguo Xijujia Xiehui - China Theatre Artists' Association) Zhongguo Xiju Chubanshe, 52, Dongsi Ba(8) Tiao, Beijing 100700, People's Republic of China. (Dist. in US by: China Books & Periodicals, Inc., 2929 24th St., San Francisco, CA 94110. TEL 415-282-2994) Ed. Huo Dashou.

792 UK ISSN 0261-6939
2D: DRAMA, DANCE. 1981. 2/yr. £6($10) (foreign £7)(effective 1992). 2D Publications, 33 Cannock St., Leicester LE4 7HR, England. Ed. Robert Staunton. adv.; bk.rev.; illus.; circ. 3,000. Indexed: Cont.Pg.Educ.
—BLDSC shelfmark: 3623.196450.

THEATER — Abstracting, Bibliographies, Statistics

792   US   ISSN 0360-2788
Z6935
BIBLIOGRAPHIC GUIDE TO THEATRE ARTS. a. $180 cloth (foreign $200). G.K. Hall & Co., 70 Lincoln St., Boston, MA 02111. TEL 617-423-3990. FAX 617-423-3999. TELEX 94-0037.
    Description: Covers all aspects of the theatre. Lists materials catalogued during the past year by the New York Public Library, Theatre and Drama Collection.

800 792.8   US   ISSN 0742-6933
BIBLIOGRAPHIES AND INDEXES IN THE PERFORMING ARTS. 1984. irreg. price varies. Greenwood Press, Inc. (Subsidiary of: Greenwood Publishing Group Inc.), 88 Post Rd. W., Box 5007, Westport, CT 06881-5007. TEL 203-226-3571. FAX 203-222-1502.

792 493.3 791.43   US   ISSN 0892-5550
BIO-BIBLIOGRAPHIES IN THE PERFORMING ARTS. 1987. irreg. price varies. Greenwood Press, Inc. (Subsidiary of: Greenwood Publishing Group Inc.), 88 Post Rd. W., Box 5007, Westport, CT 06881-5007. TEL 203-226-3571. FAX 203-222-1502.

BULLETIN SIGNALETIQUE. PART 523: HISTOIRE ET SCIENCES DE LA LITTERATURE. see *LITERATURE — Abstracting, Bibliographies, Statistics*

011   US
PERFORMING ARTS BIOGRAPHY MASTER INDEX. 1979. irreg., 2nd ed., 1982. $175. Gale Research Inc., 835 Penobscot Bldg., Detroit, MI 48226. TEL 313-961-2242. FAX 313-961-6083. TELEX 810-221-7086. Eds. Barbara McNeil, Miranda Herbert.
    Formerly: Theatre, Film, and Television Biographies Master Index.

792   IT
TEATRO ARCHIVIO; bolletino del Civico Museo Biblioteca dell'Attore. 1970. 3/yr. L.30000($26) (Civico Museo Biblioteca dell'Attore del Teatro di Genova) Bulzoni Editore, Via dei Liburni n.14, 00185 Rome, Italy. TEL 06-4455207. FAX 06-4450355. Ed. Alessandro d'Amico. illus.; cum.index. (back issues avail.)

THEORY OF COMPUTING

see Computers–Theory of Computing

TOBACCO

679.7   SP
ACTUALIDAD TABAQUERA; revista del tabaco. 1964. m. 2332 ptas.($85) (typically set in Jan.). Tabapress, S.A., Barquillo 38, 28004 Madrid, Spain. Ed. Raimundo de los Reyes-Garcia. adv.; illus.; charts. (back issues avail.)

ALCOHOL, TOBACCO AND FIREARMS BULLETIN. see *LAW*

658.8   IT   ISSN 0392-5773
AMICI DELLA PIPA; rivista bimestrale per la conoscenza e la diffusione della pipa. (Text in Italian; summaries in English) 1978. bi-m. L.20000($35) Amici della Pipa, C.P. 10734, 00100 Rome, Italy. TEL 513 2790. Ed. Giancarlo Fortunato. adv.; bk.rev.; circ. 7,000.

679.7   FR   ISSN 0399-0206
ANNALES DU TABAC SECTION 1. 1963. a. free to qualified personnel. Societe Nationale d'Exploitation Industrielle des Tabacs et Allumettes, 53 Quai d'Orsay, 75347 Paris, France. Ed. R. Geneve. bibl.; circ. 1,100. **Indexed:** Chem.Abstr., Crop Physiol.Abstr., Excerp.Med., Field Crop Abstr., Herb.Abstr., Plant Breed.Abstr., Soils & Fert., Weed Abstr.
—BLDSC shelfmark: 1001.710000.

679.7   FR   ISSN 0399-0354
ANNALES DU TABAC SECTION 2. 1977. a. free to qualified personnel. Societe Nationale d'Exploitation Industrielle des Tabacs et Allumettes, 53 Quai d'Orsay, 75340 Paris, France. FAX 1-45-56-63-29.

658.8 679.7   AT   ISSN 0045-0820
AUSTRALIAN RETAIL TOBACCONIST. 1940. m. Aus.$15. New South Wales Retail Tobacco Traders Association, Alexander House, 1st Fl., 107 Alexander St., Crows Nest, N.S.W. 2065, Australia.

679.73   GW   ISSN 0173-783X
TS2220   CODEN: BTAID3
BEITRAEGE ZUR TABAKFORSCHUNG INTERNATIONAL. (Text in English and German; summaries in English, French and German) 1961. irreg. free. Verband der Cigarettenindustrie, Koenigswintererstr. 550, 5300 Bonn 3, Germany. TEL 0228-4490641. FAX 0228-442582. Ed. Bd. charts; illus.; stat.; circ. 1,100. (also avail. in microfilm from UMI; reprint service avail. from UMI) **Indexed:** Anal.Abstr., Biol.Abstr., Chem.Abstr., Curr.Adv.Ecol.Sci., Curr.Cont., Excerp.Med., Field Crop Abstr., Helminthol.Abstr., Herb.Abstr., Sci.Cit.Ind.
—BLDSC shelfmark: 1887.451000.
    Formerly (until 1978): Beitraege zur Tabakforschung (ISSN 0005-819X)
    Description: Research on all aspects of tobacco plants, cultivation, manufacture of tobacco products, and the physical and chemical analysis of tobacco and tobacco smoke.

679.9 633.7   BU   ISSN 0521-6680
BULGARSKI TIUTIUN. 1956. m. 2.50 lv.($10) Izdatelstvo Profizdat, 82, Dondukov Blvd., Sofia, Bulgaria. (Dist. by: Hemus, 6, Rouski Blvd., 1000 Sofia, Bulgaria) circ. 4,800. **Indexed:** Soils & Fert., Weed Abstr.
—BLDSC shelfmark: 0018.636000.

C T N. (Confectioner, Tobacconist, Newsagent) see *FOOD AND FOOD INDUSTRIES — Bakers And Confectioners*

633.71   CN   ISSN 0008-5189
CANADIAN TOBACCO GROWER. 1952. 4/yr. Can.$7. N C C Publishing, 222 Argyle Ave., Delhi, Ont. N4B 2Y2, Canada. TEL 519-582-2510. FAX 519-582-4040. Ed. Ben Steidman. adv.: B&W page Can.$712; trim 8 x 11; adv. contact: W.H. Arts. charts; illus.; mkt.; circ. 3,920.
—BLDSC shelfmark: 3045.500000.

CANDY WORLD ILLUSTRATED. see *FOOD AND FOOD INDUSTRIES — Bakers And Confectioners*

679.7 658.8   FR
CAROTTE MODERNE. 1958. 4/yr. Societe Pym, 27 rue Hermel, 75018 Paris, France. TEL 42-64-86-11. FAX 42-64-08-09. adv.; circ. 20,000.

633.7   II
CENTRAL TOBACCO RESEARCH INSTITUTE AND ITS REGIONAL RESEARCH STATIONS. ANNUAL REPORT. (Text in English) 1967. a. exchange basis. Indian Council of Agricultural Research, Central Tobacco Research Institute, Rajahmundry 533 105, India. TEL 71871-4. TELEX 0474-205. Ed.Bd. charts; stat.; circ. 150.
    Incorporates: Tobacco Research Institute. Annual Report; Tobacco Research Station, Hunsur, Report; Wrapper and Hookah Tobacco Research Station Report.

633.71   CU   ISSN 0138-8185
CIENCIA Y TECNICA EN LA AGRICULTURA. SERIE: TABACO. (Table of contents and abstracts in English) 2/yr. $14 in N. and S. America; Europe $16; others $17; or exchange basis. Centro de Informacion y Documentacion Agropecuario, Gaveta Postal 4149, Havana 4, Cuba. (Dist. by: Ediciones Cubanas, Obispo No. 527, Apdo. 605, Havana, Cuba) **Indexed:** Agrindex, Field Crop Abstr., Herb.Abstr., Seed Abstr., Soils & Fert.
    Former titles (until 1978): Cuba. Centro de Informacion y Documentacion Agropecuario. Boletin de Resenas. Serie: Tabaco; Cuba. Centro de Informacion y Divulgacion Agropecuario. Boletin de Resenas. Serie: Tabaco.

658.8   US
COMPLEAT SMOKER. q. Compleat Smoker, Box 7036, Evanston, IL 60204. TEL 708-864-6016. FAX 708-864-1770. Ed.Bd. circ. 2,500.

COUNCIL FOR TOBACCO RESEARCH, U.S.A. REPORT. see *MEDICAL SCIENCES*

633.71   CU
CUBATABACO. (Text in English and Spanish) 1972. q. $10 in N. and S. America; Europe $12; elsewhere $14. (Ministerio de la Agricultura, Centro de Diseno de Envases y Divulgacion) Ediciones Cubanas, Obispo No. 527, Aptdo. 605, Havana, Cuba. TEL 7-61-8453. Dir. Zoila Couceyro. adv.; bk.rev.; circ. 8,000.

633.71   CU
CUBATABACO INTERNACIONAL. (Text in English) 1979. s-a. Instituto de la Demanda Interna, Amargura 103, San Ignacio, 10100 Havana, Cuba. TEL 7-61-8453. Dir. Zoila Couceyro. circ. 3,000.

679.7   FR
DEBITANT DE TABAC. 1904. 11/yr. Federation des Gerants de Debits de Tabac de l'Ile, 18 rue Leningrad, 75008 Paris, France. Ed. Yvette Mantion. adv.; circ. 6,500.

679.7   GW   ISSN 0012-0820
DER DEUTSCHE TABAKBAU. 1916. m. DM.52.50. Mainzer Verlagsanstalt und Druckerei, Postfach 3120, 6500 Mainz, Germany. Ed. Hans-Gerd Koenen. adv.; bk.rev.; charts; illus.; stat.; circ. 4,000. **Indexed:** Chem.Abstr.

679.7   HU   ISSN 0012-4931
    CODEN: DOHAAW
DOHANYIPAR. (Text in Hungarian; summaries in German) 1954. q. $14. (Magyar Elelmezesipari Tudomanyos Egyesulet) Lapkiado Vallalat, Lenin korut 9-11, 1073 Budapest 7, Hungary. TEL 222-409. (Subscr. to: Kultura, P.O. Box 149, H-1389 Budapest, Hungary) Ed. Istvan Bordacs. adv.; bk.rev.; charts; illus.; circ. 1,570. **Indexed:** Chem.Abstr.

DRUG ABUSE UPDATE. see *DRUG ABUSE AND ALCOHOLISM*

679.7   II   ISSN 0046-4031
FLAME AND FLAVOUR. 1968. m. Rs.18. Tapan Kumar Das, Ed. & Pub., 12B 4 Indra Roy Rd., Calcutta 25, India. adv.; illus.; circ. 1,900. (tabloid format)

633.71   US   ISSN 0015-4512
FLUE CURED TOBACCO FARMER; for commercial growers of flue-cured tobacco and related agribusiness. 1964. m. (Nov.-Jun.). $10 free to tobacco producers. Specialized Agricultural Publications, Inc., Box 95075, Raleigh, NC 27625. TEL 919-872-5040. FAX 919-872-6531. TELEX 802736. Ed. Dayton Matlick. adv.; charts; illus.; mkt.; pat.; tr.mk.; circ. 25,000 (controlled).
—BLDSC shelfmark: 3959.660000.

INDEPENDENT FOOD RETAILER. see *FOOD AND FOOD INDUSTRIES*

679.7   II
INDIA. TOBACCO BOARD. ANNUAL REPORT. 1975. a. Tobacco Board, Box 451, Lakshmipuram, Guntur 522007, India. TELEX 32434.

679.7   II   ISSN 0047-1135
INTERNATIONAL PRESS CUTTING SERVICE: TOBACCO NEWS; cigarettes - cigars - bidis. 1967. w. $65. International Press Cutting Service, P.O. Box 63, Allahabad 211001, India. Ed. N. Khanna. bk.rev.; index; circ. 1,200. (processed)

633.71   IT
ISTITUTO SPERIMENTALE PER IL TABACCO. ANNALI. (Summaries in English) 1973. a. free. Istituto Sperimentale per il Tabacco, Via P. Vitiello 66, 84018 Scafati, Italy. Ed. Emanuel Marcelli. circ. 1,000. (back issues avail.) **Indexed:** Biol.Abstr., Field Crop Abstr., Herb.Abstr., Plant Breed.Abstr., Tob.Abstr.

679.7 658.8   MF
MAURITIUS. TOBACCO BOARD. ANNUAL REPORT. 1932. a. free. Tobacco Board, Plaine Lauzun, Mauritius. Ed.Bd. charts; circ. 325. **Indexed:** Tob.Abstr.
    Description: Covers the operations and activities of the board.

MEALEY'S LITIGATION REPORT: TOBACCO. see *LAW — Civil Law*

TOBACCO

658.8 053.931   NE   ISSN 0925-8175
MIXTURE; magazine voor genieters. 1986. s-a. free. (N S O, Branche Organisatie tabaksdetailhandel) Stichting Promotie Tabaksdetailhandel (SPT), Koninginnegracht 135, 2514 AM The Hague, Netherlands. TEL 070-3553262. FAX 070-3556616. Ed. Dick van Vlaardingen. adv.: B&W page fl.10500; color page fl.12600; trim size 148 x 210. charts; illus.; tr.lit.; circ. 225,000.
Formerly (until 1990): Even Uitblazen.
Description: Consumer orientation as a vehicle for tobacco retailer promotion.

633.71   NR
NIGERIAN TOBACCO COMPANY. ANNUAL REPORT AND ACCOUNTS. 1961. a. free. Nigerian Tobacco Company (Plc), Corporate Affairs Department, Western House, 8-10 Broad St., P.O. Box 137, Lagos, Nigeria. TEL 600300-9. FAX 634715. TELEX 21561 TOBACCO NG. Ed. Irene Ubah. circ. 50,000.
Formerly: Nigerian Tobacco Company. Report (ISSN 0078-0820)

633.71   US
NORTH CAROLINA TOBACCO REPORT. 1950. a. free. Department of Agriculture, Box 27647, Raleigh, NC 27611. Ed. Carl W. Sofley. charts; stat.; circ. 6,000. (back issues avail.)
Description: Record of former sales, warehouse sales and quotas of tobacco growing in North Carolina.

679.7   AU   ISSN 0029-9561
OESTERREICHISCHE TRAFIKANTEN-ZEITUNG. m. S.552. Oesterreichischer Wirtschaftsverlag, Nikolsdorfer Gasse 7-11, A-1051 Vienna, Austria. TEL 0222-555585. TELEX 1-11669. (Affiliate: Tabaktrafikanten und -verleger) Ed. Josef Jerko. adv.; illus.; circ. 6,800. (tabloid format)

658.8 679.7   US
PHILIP MORRIS MAGAZINE. 1985. q. free. Philip Morris U S A, 120 Park Ave., New York, NY 10017. TEL 212-880-5000. Ed. Frank Gannon. adv.; circ. 12,000,000.
Description: News and features of interest to smokers.

658.8   GW
PIPE CLUB; Magazin fuer Tabakgeniesser. 1974. q. DM.17. Mainzer Verlagsanstalt und Druckerei, Grosse Bleiche 44-50, 6500 Mainz, Germany. TEL 06131-144220. FAX 06131-144415. TELEX 4187753. Ed. Hans-Gerd Koenen. adv.; bk.rev.; circ. 50,000. (back issues avail.)
Description: Magazine for pipe smokers.

658.8 679.7   US   ISSN 0032-0161
PIPE SMOKER'S EPHEMERIS. 1964. q. free. (Universal Coterie of Pipe Smokers) Tom Dunn, Ed.& Pub., 20-37 120th St., College Point, NY 11356. adv.; bk.rev.; abstr.; bibl.; illus.; tr.lit.; index; circ. 7,500 (controlled). (processed)

679.7   US   ISSN 0363-8480   CODEN: RATSDZ
RECENT ADVANCES IN TOBACCO SCIENCE; proceedings of the tobacco chemists' conference. 1975. a. $20 (outside N. America $30). (Tobacco Chemists' Research Conference Board) Tobacco Literature Service, 2314 D.H. Hill Library, Raleigh, NC 27695-7111. TEL 919-515-2836. **Indexed:** Chem.Abstr.

658.8 664.15   UK   ISSN 0961-5202
RETAIL NEWSAGENT TOBACCONIST CONFECTIONER. 1889. w. £50 (typically set in June). Newtrade Publishing Ltd., 11 Angel Gate, City Rd., London EC1V 2PT, England. FAX 071-837-0821. Ed. John G. Haylett. adv.; bk.rev.; circ. 20,063.
Formerly: Retail Newsagent, Bookseller and Stationer (ISSN 0034-6098)

679.7   US
RETAIL TOBACCONIST. 6/yr. $45 (Canada and Mexico $75; elsewhere $95). Leo Douglas, Inc., 9607 Gayton Rd., Richmond, VA 23233. TEL 804-741-6704. FAX 804-750-2399.

679.7   FR   ISSN 0035-225X
REVUE DES TABACS; organe international de la culture, de l'industrie et de la vente du tabac. 1925. m. 430 F. (foreign 550 F.). Editions Litteraire, Techniques et Artistiques, 9 rue Saint Fiacre, 75002 Paris, France. FAX 42-36-04-62. Ed. Michel Burton. adv.; charts; illus.; mkt.; pat.; tr.mk.; circ. 30,000.

658.8   US
SMOKERS PIPELINE; the journal of kapnismology. 1983. bi-m. $15 (foreign $40). American Pipe Collectors Club, Box 2089, Merrifield, VA 22116-2089. TEL 703-971-2627. FAX 703-971-3352. Ed. C. Bruce Spencer. adv.; bk.rev.; circ. 4,500. (tabloid format)
Former titles: Pipe Smoker and Tobacciana Trader; Pipe Smoker (ISSN 0746-1380)
Description: Contains articles on pipes, tobacco, events, history, and people; promotes pipe collecting as a hobby and for profit.

658.8   US
SMOKESHOP. 1976. m. $24. B M T Publications, Inc., 7 Penn Plaza, New York, NY 10001-3900. TEL 212-594-4120. FAX 212-714-0514. Ed. Paul Dworin. adv.; circ. 5,500.

658.8 679.7   AT
SMOKING HABITS OF AUSTRALIANS. 1973. a. Roy Morgan Research Centre Pty. Ltd., P.O. Box 2282U, Melbourne, Vic. 3001, Australia. FAX 03-629-1250.

338.1   SA
SOUTH AFRICA. TOBACCO BOARD. ANNUAL REPORT. 1939. a. Tobacco Board, P.O. Box 26100, Arcadia, Pretoria 0007, South Africa. FAX 284851-305. TELEX 323369. Ed.Bd. stat.; circ. 2,000.

679.7   US
T M A DIRECTORY OF CIGARETTE BRANDS. 1977. base vol. (plus a. update). $125 to members; non-members $225. Tobacco Merchants Association of the United States, Inc., Box 8019, Princeton, NJ 08543-8019. TEL 609-275-4900. FAX 609-275-8379.

658.8   US
T M A EXECUTIVE SUMMARY. w. membership only. Tobacco Merchants Association of the United States, Inc., 231 Clarksville Rd., Ste. 6, Box 8019, Princeton, NJ 08543-8019. TEL 609-275-4900. FAX 609-275-8379.
● Also available online.
Description: Summary of the principal industry developments occurring over the past week in the US and around the world. Serves as an index to the other TMA publications issued during the given week.

679.7   US
T M A GUIDE TO TOBACCO TAXES; summaries of key provisions of tobacco tax laws, all tobacco products, all states. 1962. base vol. (plus q. update). $795 to non-members; members $495. Tobacco Merchants Association of the United States, Inc., 231 Clarksville Rd., Ste. 6, Box 8019, Princeton, NJ 08543-8019. TEL 609-275-4900. FAX 609-275-8379. Eds. Farrell Delman, Sam Gen. circ. controlled. (looseleaf format)
Description: Compendium of federal and state tobacco tax law showing comparisons between states on all key tax variables such as excise tax rates, discount rates, sales prohibitions to minors, and other marketing related information.

658.8   US
T M A INTERNATIONAL TOBACCO GUIDE. 2 base vols. (plus a. update). $11500 to non-members; members $7500. Tobacco Merchants Association of the United States, Inc., 231 Clarksville Rd., Ste. 6, Box 8019, Princeton, NJ 08543-8019. TEL 609-275-4900. FAX 609-275-8379. illus.
Description: Volume I consists of country comparisons for the major economic and socio-political variables, as well as trade statistics for all manufactured and unmanufactred tobacco. Volume II provides a country-by-country breakdown of all the economic and socio-political variables describing the tobacco industry.

658.8   US
T M A ISSUES MONITOR. 1980. q. membership only. Tobacco Merchants Association of the United States, Inc., 231 Clarksville Rd., Ste. 6, Box 8019, Princeton, NJ 08543-8019. TEL 609-275-4900. FAX 609-275-8375. Ed. Farrell Delman.
Description: Tracks the principal tobacco issues in the US and worldwide and summarizes the principal economic, legislative, and regulatory developments.

679.7   US
T M A LEAF BULLETIN. 1950. bi-w. membership only. Tobacco Merchants Association of the United States, Inc., 231 Clarksville Rd., Ste. 6, Box 8019, Princeton, NJ 08543-8019. TEL 609-275-4900. FAX 609-275-8379. Ed. Thomas C. Slane. circ. controlled. (looseleaf format)
Description: Furnishes tobacco auction market statistics, for all leaf types, including stabilization inventories, and provides a brief legislative and regulatory rundown on matters impacting the leaf sector.

679.7 340   US
T M A LEGISLATIVE BULLETIN. bi-w. membership only. Tobacco Merchants Association of the United States, Inc., 231 Clarksville Rd., Ste. 6, Box 8019, Princeton, NJ 08543-8019. TEL 609-275-4900. FAX 609-275-8379. Ed. James Vari. stat.; circ. 350. (back issues avail.)
● Also available online.
Incorporates (1924-198?): T M A State Bulletin; (1924-198?): T M A National Bulletin.
Description: Analyzes congressional and state legislative activity on all issues affecting all tobacco products and summarizes key provisions of these bills and laws.

679.7   US
T M A TOBACCO BAROMETER. 1923. m. membership only. Tobacco Merchants Association of the United States, Inc., 231 Clarksville Rd., Ste. 6, Box 8019, Princeton, NJ 08543-8019. TEL 609-275-4900. FAX 609-275-8379. Ed. Thomas C. Slane. circ. controlled. (looseleaf format)
Description: Domestic industry guide to manufactured production, taxable removals, and tax-exempt removals for cigarettes, large cigars, little cigars, chewing tobacco, snuff, and pipe tobacco.

679.7   US
T M A TOBACCO BAROMETER: SMOKING, CHEWING, SNUFF. 1923. q. membership only. Tobacco Merchants Association of the United States, Inc., 231 Clarksville Rd., Ste. 6, Box 8019, Princeton, NJ 08543-8019. TEL 609-275-4900. FAX 609-275-8379. Ed. Thomas C. Slane. circ. controlled. (looseleaf format)
● Also available online.
Description: Domestic industry guide to manufactured production, invoiced domestic sales, imports, and exports for chewing tobacco, snuff, and all forms of smoking tobacco, including roll-your-own tobacco. Provides seasonal adjustments.

679.7   US   ISSN 0495-6753
T M A TOBACCO TRADE BAROMETER. (In 6 parts: Part 1: Balance of Trade Summary - all imports and all exports; Part 2: Exports of Leaf Tobacco - US exports by product & country; Part 3: Exports of Tobacco Products - US exports by product & country; Part 4: Imports of Leaf Tobacco - US imports by product & country; Part 5: Imports of Tobacco Products - US imports by products & country; Part 6: Imports of Smokers' Accessories - US imports by products & country) 1967. m. membership only. Tobacco Merchants Association of the United States, Inc., 231 Clarksville Rd., Ste. 6, Box 8019, Princeton, NJ 08543-8019. TEL 609-275-4900. FAX 609-275-8379. Ed. Thomas C. Slane. circ. controlled. (looseleaf format)
Description: Details all imports and all exports of all tobacco leaf and products, including tobacco sundries, by product and country providing values and quantities. Compares current data to the previous year.

658.8 336   US
T M A TOBACCO WEEKLY. w. membership only. Tobacco Merchants Association of the United States, Inc., 231 Clarksville Rd., Ste. 6, Box 8019, Princeton, NJ 08543-8019. TEL 609-275-4900. FAX 609-275-8379.
Description: Summary run-down on key domestic industry issues as they unfold at the Federal, State, and Local levels. Covers excise taxes, marketing and distribution issues, corporate finance, leaf and trade, health campaigns, and product liability.

TOBACCO

658.8 602.7   US
T M A TRADEMARK REPORT. m. membership only. Tobacco Merchants Association of the United States, Inc., 231 Clarksville Rd., Ste. 6, Box 8019, Princeton, NJ 08543-8019. TEL 609-275-4900. FAX 609-275-8379.
●Also available online.
Description: Tracks tobacco product and tobacco accessory trademarks and brand names from test markets through registration and covers renewals and cancellations.

679.7   US
T M A WORLD ALERT. w. membership only. Tobacco Merchants Association of the United States, Inc., 231 Clarksville Rd., Ste. 6, Box 8019, Princeton, NJ 08543-8019. TEL 609-275-4900. FAX 609-275-8379. Ed. F. Delman. circ. 375. (back issues avail.)
●Also available online.
Formerly: International Executive Summary.
Description: News-flash country by country description of key industry and corporate developments around the world including corporate finance, excise taxes, marketing and distribution issues, leaf and trade, and health campaigns.

658.8   US
T M A WORLD CONSUMPTION & PRODUCTION. a. membership only. Tobacco Merchants Association of the United States, Inc., 231 Clarksville Rd., Ste. 6, Box 8019, Princeton, NJ 08543-8019. TEL 609-275-4900. FAX 609-275-8379.
Description: Details country by country consumption and production of tobacco products over the previous 10 years.

679.7   SZ   ISSN 0039-8721
TABAK/TABAC. (Text in French, German) 1903. fortn. 33 Fr. Verband Schweizerischer Tabakhaendler - Federation Suisse des Marchands de Tabacs, Alte Landstr. 26, CH-4657 Dulliken, Switzerland. Ed. Leo Fuerer. adv.; illus.; stat. **Indexed:** Field Crop Abstr., Plant Grow.Reg.Abstr., Seed Abstr.

679.7   GW   ISSN 0039-8748
HD9130.1
TABAK JOURNAL INTERNATIONAL. (Text in Dutch, English, French, German, Italian, Spanish) 1963. bi-m. DM.134($76) Mainzer Verlagsanstalt und Druckerei Will und Rothe GmbH & Co., Grosse Bleiche 44-50, 6500 Mainz, Germany. Ed. Hans-Gerd Koenen. adv.; bk.rev.; charts; illus.; stat.; cum.index; circ. 4,000. **Indexed:** Excerp.Med.
—BLDSC shelfmark: 8859.577650.

658.8 338   NE   ISSN 0925-7543
TABAK PLUS BENELUX; vakblad voor de tabaksdetailhandel. 1939. 10/yr. fl.55. (N S O, Branche Organisatie Tabaksdetailhandel) Stichting Promotie Tabaksdetailhandel (SPT), Koninginnegracht 135, 2514AM The Hague, Netherlands. TEL 070-3553262. FAX 070-3556616. Ed. Dick van Vlaardingen. adv.: B&W page fl.2025 (37000 BEF); color page fl.2835 (51800 BEF); trim size 148 x 210. bk.rev.; charts; illus.; stat.; tr.lit.; circ. 13,500.

633.71   GW   ISSN 0049-2825
DIE TABAK ZEITUNG; Fachorgan der Tabakwirtschaft. 1891. w. DM.204.40. Mainzer Verlagsanstalt und Druckerei Will und Rothe GmbH & Co., Grosse Bleiche 44-50, 6500 Mainz, Germany. TEL 06131-144220. FAX 06131-144415. Ed. Hans-Gerd Koenen. adv.; bk.rev.; circ. 9,000. (tabloid format)

658.8 679.7   UK   ISSN 0040-8271
HD9130.1
TOBACCO; the management journal of tobacco trade distribution within the UK. 1881. bi-m. $90. International Trade Publications Ltd., Queensway House, 2 Queensway, Redhill, Surrey RH1 1QS, England. TEL 0737-768611. FAX 0737-761989. TELEX 948669-TOPJNL-G. Ed. Jaques Cole. adv.; abstr.; charts; illus.; stat.; tr.lit.; index; circ. 4,000. **Indexed:** Chem.Abstr., Excerp.Med.

658.8   US
TOBACCO AND NEW PRODUCTS WORLD. 1910. q. $8. Lott Publishing Co., Box 710, Santa Monica, CA 90406. TEL 213-397-4217. circ. 3,000.

679.7   US   ISSN 0082-4593
TOBACCO ASSOCIATES. ANNUAL REPORT. 1948. a. free. Tobacco Associates, Inc., 1306 Annapolis Dr., Ste. 102, Raleigh, NC 27605. TEL 919-821-7670. cum.index: 1948-1972.; circ. 7,500.

679.7   US   ISSN 0964-4563
▼**TOBACCO CONTROL: AN INTERNATIONAL JOURNAL.** 1992. q. £80($140) B M J Publishing Group, B.M.A. House, Tavistock Sq., London WC1H 9JR, England. TEL 071-387-4499. FAX 071-383-6402. Ed. Ronald Davis. adv.; bk.rev.; charts; illus.; index.
—BLDSC shelfmark: 8859.576550.

TOBACCO INDUSTRY LITIGATION REPORTER; the national journal of record of litigation affecting the tobacco industry. see *LAW*

679.7   US   ISSN 0049-3945
HD9130.1   CODEN: TBCIAE
TOBACCO INTERNATIONAL. 1886. fortn. $32. Lockwood Trade Journal Co., Inc., 130 W. 42nd St., New York, NY 10036-7802. TEL 212-391-2060. FAX 212-827-0945. Ed. Glen John. adv.; bk.rev.; illus.; tr.lit.; circ. 3,000. (reprint service avail. from UMI) **Indexed:** Biol.Abstr., Chem.Abstr., Field Crop Abstr., Herb.Abstr., Plant Grow.Reg.Abstr., Soils & Fert., Soyabean Abstr.
Formerly: Tobacco International Weekly.

658.8   AT
TOBACCO JOURNAL. 1931. m. Aus.$0.50 per no. Retail Tobacco Sellers Association of Victoria, Box 1780, Melbourne, Vic. 3001, Australia. (Co-sponsor: Retail Tobacco Traders' Association of Tasmania)

679 918   US
TOBACCO: LATIN AMERICAN INDUSTRIAL REPORT. (Avail. for each of 22 Latin American countries) 1985. a. $435 per country report. Aquino Productions, Box 15760, Stamford, CT 06901. TEL 203-325-3138. Ed. Andres C. Aquino.

338.1   II
TOBACCO NEWS. (Text in English) 1951. m. $7.50. Tobacco Board, P.O. Box 451, Lakshmipuram, Guntur 522007, India. **Indexed:** Field Crop Abstr.
Formerly: Indian Tobacco (ISSN 0445-8192)

679.7   US
TOBACCO REPORTER; devoted to all segments of the international tobacco industry: processing, trading, manufacturing. 1874. m. $30 in U.S (foreign $65). Specialized Agricultural Publications, Inc., Box 95075, Raleigh, NC 27625. TEL 919-872-5040. TELEX 802736. Ed. Dayton Matlick. adv.; bk.rev.; charts; illus.; mkt.; pat.; tr.lit.; circ. 5,000. **Indexed:** Field Crop Abstr.
Former titles: T R; Tobacco Reporter (ISSN 0040-8328); Supersedes: Western Tobacco Journal (ISSN 0361-5693)

633.71   II   ISSN 0379-055X
CODEN: TRESDX
TOBACCO RESEARCH. (Text and summaries in English) 1975. s-a. Rps.150($25) Indian Society of Tobacco Science, Central Tobacco Research Institute, Rajahmundry 533 105, Andhra Pradesh, India. Ed. P. Harishu Kumar. adv.; circ. 300. (back issues avail.) **Indexed:** Biol.Abstr., Field Crop Abstr., Plant Grow.Reg.Abstr., Soils & Fert., Weed Abstr.

679.7   US   ISSN 0082-4623
TOBACCO SCIENCE YEARBOOK. 1958. a. $26. Lockwood Trade Journal Co., Inc., 130 W. 42nd St., New York, NY 10036-7802. TEL 212-391-2060. index. (reprint service avail. from UMI)
—BLDSC shelfmark: 8859.579000.

332.6   US   ISSN 0360-439X
HD9134
TOBACCO STOCKS. q. $5 per no. U.S. Agricultural Marketing Service, Tobacco Division, U.S. Department of Agriculture, Washington, DC 20250. TEL 202-447-4976. **Indexed:** Amer.Stat.Ind.
Supersedes: Tobacco Stocks Report. T O B

658.8   UK
TOBACCO TRADE DIRECTORY AND DIARY. a. $63. International Trade Publications Ltd., Queensway House, 2 Queensway, Redhill, Surrey RH1 1QS, England. TEL 0737 768611. FAX 0737-761989. TELEX 948669-TOPJNL-G.
Formerly: Tobacco Trade Marketing Directory; **Incorporating:** Tobacco Directory and Diary (ISSN 0264-5394); Tobacco Trade Year Book and Diary (ISSN 0082-4631); Smoker's Handbook (ISSN 0081-0355)

658.8   US
TOBACCO WORLD ILLUSTRATED. 1962. q. $12. Lott Publishing Co., Box 710, Santa Monica, CA 90406-1107. TEL 310-397-4217. Ed. Dave Lott. circ. 2,000.

633.71 664.8   NO   ISSN 0049-3961
TOBAKK - FRUKT - SJOKOLADE. 1918. 6/yr. NOK 100($14) free. Tobakk- og Kioskhandelens Landsforbund, Torggt. 30, 0183 Oslo, Norway. TEL 02-20-64-28. Ed. Per-Tore Sliper. adv.; tr.lit.; circ. 2,000.

658.8 679.7   SW   ISSN 0346-2765
TOBAKSHANDLAREN/TOBACCONIST. (Text in Swedish) 1910. 8/yr. SEK 150($20) membership. Tobaks- & Servicehandelns Riksfoerbund - National Union of Retail Tobacconists, Instrumentvagen 10, Box 9025, 12609 Hagersten, Sweden. TEL 46-8-810160. FAX 46-8-7269090. Ed. Sture Niklasson. adv.; circ. 2,000.

679.7   AU
TRAFIK-JOURNAL. 1964. 10/yr. S.220. Fachvereinigung der Trafikanten im Freien Wirtschaftsverband, Schottenfeldgasse 28, A-1070 Vienna, Austria. TELEX 136048-FWV-Z-A. Ed. Rudolf Bernkopf. circ. 1,500.
Formerly: Tabakverschleisser Oesterreichs (ISSN 0039-8772)

U.S. DEPARTMENT OF AGRICULTURE. TOBACCO SITUATION AND OUTLOOK REPORT. see *AGRICULTURE — Agricultural Economics*

679.7   US
UNITED STATES DISTRIBUTION JOURNAL; the news publication of tobacco, confectionery, grocery distribution. 1874. m. $24. B M T Publications, Inc., 7 Penn Plaza, New York, NY 10001-3900. TEL 212-594-4120. FAX 212-714-0514. Ed. Kevin Francella. adv.; illus.; mkt.; stat.; circ. 7,267. **Indexed:** Bus.Ind., Tr.& Indus.Ind.
Former titles: United States Tobacco and Candy Journal (ISSN 0041-8137); United States Tobacco Journal.

658.8 679.7   US
UNITED STATES DISTRIBUTION JOURNAL SUPPLIER DIRECTORY. 1963. a. $10. B M T Publications, Inc., 7 Penn Plaza, New York, NY 10001-3900. TEL 212-594-4120. FAX 212-714-0514. Ed. Kevin Francella. adv.; index; circ. 5,000. **Indexed:** Tr.& Indus.Ind.
Former titles: United States Tobacco and Candy Journal Supplier Directory (ISSN 0083-3479); United States Tobacco Journal Supplier Directory.

UNIVERSITY OF SALAHADDIN. COLLEGE OF AGRICULTURE. SCIENTIFIC JOURNAL "ZANCO". see *AGRICULTURE*

679.7   IT   ISSN 0042-7829
LA VOCE DEL TABACCAIO. 1927. w. membership. Federazione Italiana Tabaccai, Via Leopoldo Serra 32, 00153 Rome, Italy. TEL 06-589-7151. FAX 06-5809826. TELEX 06-612223. Eds. Sergio Baronci, Ivo Tolu. adv.; illus.; circ. 48,000. (tabloid format)

679.7   UK   ISSN 0043-9126
SB273
WORLD TOBACCO. 1963. bi-m. $135. International Trade Publications Ltd., Queensway House, 2 Queensway, Redhill, Surrey RH1 1QS, England. TEL 0737-768611. FAX 0737-761989. TELEX 948669-TOPJNL-G. Ed. George Gay. adv.; bk.rev.; charts; illus.; mkt.; pat.; tr.lit.; tr.mk.; circ. 4,200. **Indexed:** PROMT.
—BLDSC shelfmark: 9360.100000.

TOBACCO — ABSTRACTING, BIBLIOGRAPHIES, STATISTICS

679.7   UK   ISSN 0084-2273
WORLD TOBACCO DIRECTORY. 1938. a. $139. International Trade Publications Ltd., Queensway House, 2 Queensway, Redhill, Surrey RH1 1QS, England. TEL 0737-768611. FAX 0737-761989. TELEX 948669-TOPJNL-G. adv.

679.7   RH
ZIMBABWE. TOBACCO RESEARCH BOARD. ANNUAL REPORT AND ACCOUNTS. 1954. a. free. Tobacco Research Board, Library, Kutsaga Station, P.O. Box 1909, Harare, Zimbabwe. TELEX 22618 ZW. circ. 660.
  Formerly: Zimbabwe - Rhodesia. Tobacco Research Board. Annual Report and Accounts (ISSN 0080-2875)

679.7   RH
ZIMBABWE TOBACCO TODAY. 1977. m. Z.$44 (foreign Z.$50). (Zimbabwe Tobacco Association) Thomson Publications Zimbabwe (Pvt) Ltd., Thomson House, P.O. Box 1683, Harare, Zimbabwe. TEL 736835. TELEX 24705 ZW. Ed. M. Van Hoffen. adv.; illus.; mkt.; pat.; tr.mk.
  Former titles: Rhodesia Tobacco Today; Rhodesian Tobacco Journal (ISSN 0035-4880); Incorporating: Tobacco Today; Stock and Crops (ISSN 0039-1557)

TOBACCO — Abstracting, Bibliographies, Statistics

679.7 016   FR   ISSN 0010-8723
C O R E S T A; bulletin d'information. (Text in English, French) 1957. q. membership. Centre de Cooperation pour les Recherches Scientifiques Relatives au Tabac (Coresta), 53 Quai d'Orsay, 75347 Paris Cedex 7, France. FAX 1-45-56-62-30. TELEX 250604. Ed. Francois Jacob. bk.rev.; abstr.; charts; illus.; circ. 1,000. **Indexed:** Field Crop Abstr.

338.4   CN   ISSN 0835-0019
HD9348.C3
CANADA. STATISTICS CANADA. BEVERAGE AND TOBACCO PRODUCTS INDUSTRIES. (Catalogue 32-251) (Text in English, French) 1918. a. Can.$35($42) (foreign $49). Statistics Canada, Publications Sales and Services, Ottawa, Ont. K1A 0T6, Canada. TEL 613-951-7277. FAX 613-951-1584. (also avail. in microform from MML)
  Formerly: Canada. Statistics Canada. Tobacco Products Industries (ISSN 0300-0249)

658.8 336 310   US   ISSN 0563-6191
HD9130.1
TAX BURDEN ON TOBACCO. 1966. a. Tobacco Institute, 1875 I St., N.W., Washington, DC 20006. TEL 202-457-4800. stat.; circ. 2,500. **Indexed:** SRI.
  Description: Annual tabulation of federal, state and local tobacco tax collections, rates.

633.71 016   US   ISSN 0040-8298
TOBACCO ABSTRACTS; world literature on Nicotiana. 1957. bi-m. $26 (foreign $42). Tobacco Literature Service, 2314 D.H. Hill Library, North Carolina State University, Raleigh, NC 27695-7111. TEL 919-515-2836. Ed. Pamela E. Puryear. abstr.; index; circ. 500. **Indexed:** Field Crop Abstr., Herb.Abstr., Plant Breed.Abstr.
  —BLDSC shelfmark: 8859.575000.
  Description: Covers tobacco culture, economics, genetics, chemistry, manufacture and distribution.

633.71 679.7 317   US
U.S. AGRICULTURAL MARKETING SERVICE. ANNUAL REPORT ON TOBACCO STATISTICS. (Subseries of: U.S.D.A. Statistical Bulletin) a. $3. U.S. Agricultural Marketing Service, Washington, DC 20250. TEL 202-447-3489. stat. (tabloid format)

TOXICOLOGY AND ENVIRONMENTAL SAFETY

see Environmental Studies–Toxicology and Environmental Safety

TRADE AND INDUSTRIAL DIRECTORIES

see Business and Economics–Trade and Industrial Directories

TRANSPORTATION

see also Transportation–Air Transport; Transportation–Automobiles; Transportation–Computer Applications; Transportation–Railroads; Transportation–Roads and Traffic; Transportation–Ships and Shipping; Transportation–Trucks and Trucking

380.5   US
A A S H T O REFERENCE BOOK OF MEMBER DEPARTMENT PERSONNEL AND COMMITTEES. a. $15. American Association of State Highway and Transportation Officials, 444 N. Capitol St., N.W., Ste. 225, Washington, DC 20001. TEL 202-624-5800.
  Formerly: Reference Book of Highway Personnel (ISSN 0516-9445)

A B C AIR CARGO GUIDE. see *TRANSPORTATION — Air Transport*

380.5   US
A B F BY-LINES. 1953. m. free to qualified personnel. A B F Freight System, Inc., 301 S. 11th St., Ft. Smith, AR 72901. Ed. Jan Cutsinger. adv.; charts; illus.; stat.; circ. 10,000 (controlled).

380.5   FR
ACTUALITES SOCIALES DES TRANSPORTS; routiers et des activities auxiliaires des transports. 1965. m. 150 F. Editions Celse, 68 rue Cardinet, 75017 Paris, France. Ed. Daniel Mace. adv.; circ. 2,000.

AIR TRANSPORT WORLD. see *AERONAUTICS AND SPACE FLIGHT*

AIRPORT SERVICES MANAGEMENT; the business magazine for managers of aviation services and airports. see *AERONAUTICS AND SPACE FLIGHT*

AIRPORTS INTERNATIONAL MAGAZINE. see *AERONAUTICS AND SPACE FLIGHT*

380.5   CN   ISSN 0836-1509
HE357.Z6
ALBERTA TRANSPORTATION AND UTILITIES. 1975. a. Alberta Transportation, Public Communications Office, Main floor, Twin Atria, 4999-98 Ave., Edmonton, Alta. T6B 2X3, Canada. TEL 403-427-7674. FAX 403-466-3166. Ed. Ms. Terry Lotzer. circ. 600. (also avail. in microfiche from MML)
  Incorporates: Alberta. Department of Utilities. Annual Report. *Former titles:* Alberta Transportation. Annual Report (ISSN 0702-7702); Alberta Department of Transportation. Annual Report (ISSN 0318-4757); Alberta. Department of Utilities and Telecommunications. Annual Report; Alberta. Department of Utilities and Telephones. Annual Report; Alberta. Utilities Division. Annual Report (ISSN 0381-2294).

388.346   US   ISSN 1043-5824
HD9710.37.U6
▼**ALLSTATE MOTOR CLUB R V SALES, RENTAL AND SERVICE DIRECTORY.*** 1990. a. Prentice Hall Travel Directories, 15 Columbus Cir., New York, NY 10023-7706. TEL 708-945-3737. FAX 708-945-3786. adv.; circ. 25,000.
  Description: Gives state-by-state listings of RV sales, rental and service facilities in chart format.

388.3 629.222   US
▼**ALTERNATIVE TRANSPORTATION NEWS.** 1991. bi-m. $20. Earthmind, Box 743, Mariposa, CA 95338-0743. TEL 213-396-1527. Ed. Michael Hackleman. adv.; bk.rev.; illus.
  Description: Discusses the technologies and global issues shaping the search for alternatives to gasoline-powered transportation, including electric and human-powered vehicles, alternative fuels, battery innovations, activities of researchers and enthusiasts, and environmental impact questions.

AMBULANCE INDUSTRY JOURNAL. see *BUSINESS AND ECONOMICS — Trade And Industrial Directories*

388.4   AT   ISSN 0003-1968
AMONG OURSELVES. 1946. q. free. State Transport Authority, P.O. Box 2351, Adelaide, S.A. 5001, Australia. FAX 08-231-2445. Ed. Cicely Findlay. illus.; circ. 4,000.

380.5   US
ANIMAL TRANSPORTATION ASSOCIATION. INTERNATIONAL CONFERENCE. PROCEEDINGS. 1978. a. price varies. Animal Tansportation Association, Inc., Box 797095, Dallas, TX 76379-7095. TEL 214-713-9954. FAX 214-713-9783. TELEX 203941 ACTD UR. adv.; bk.rev.; circ. 400.
  Formerly: Animal Air Transportation Association. International Conference. Proceedings (ISSN 8755-9447)
  Description: Covers all areas involved in the transport of animals worldwide.

380.5 614.7   FR
ANNALES DE LA VOIRIE ET DE L'ENVIRONNEMENT. (Supplements avail.: Droit de l'Environnement; Annales de la Voirie). m. (10/yr.). 650 F. (with supplements 1390 F.). Publications Paul Dupont, 38 rue Croix des Petits Champs, 75001 Paris, France.

ANNUAIRE F F C A T. (Federation Francaise des Commissionnaires et Auxiliares de Transport Commissionnaires en Douane, Transitaires et Agents Aeriens) see *BUSINESS AND ECONOMICS — Trade And Industrial Directories*

380.5   FR   ISSN 0066-3549
ANNUAIRE NATIONAL DES TRANSPORTS. 1948. a. 860 F. Editions Louis Johanet, 68 rue Boursault, 75017 Paris, France. adv.

380.5   SP
ANO DEL TRANSPORTE. 1976. a. 1000 ptas. Luike - Motorsport, C. Ancora, 40, 28045 Madrid, Spain. illus.

380.52   BL
ANUARIO ESTATISTICO DOS TRANSPORTES. 1970. a. free. Empresa Brasileira de Planejamento de Transportes, G E I P O T, San Quadro 3 Blocos n-o, CEP 70.061, Brazil. FAX 061-1316. TELEX 061-1316. circ. 1,000.

380.5   US
ASTRALOG. 1964. bi-m. membership only. American Society of Transportation and Logistics, Inc., 3600 Chamberlain Ln., No. 232, Louisville, KY 40241-1989. TEL 502-425-1780. circ. 2,000. (tabloid format)
  Formerly (until 1983): A S T L Newsletter.
  Description: News and information on the activities of the society.

380.5   CN   ISSN 0381-9345
ATLANTIC PROVINCES TRANSPORTATION COMMISSION. TIPS & TOPICS. 1961. m. free in North America; elsewhere Can.$15. Atlantic Provinces Transportation Commission, P.O. Box 577, Moncton, N.B. E1C 8L9, Canada. TEL 506-857-2820. Ed. Jack MacQuerrie. circ. 3,200. (back issues avail.)

380.5   CN
ATLANTIC TRANSPORTATION JOURNAL. 1988. q. $18 (foreign $30). N.S. Business Publishing Ltd., 2099 Gottingen St., Halifax, N.S. B3K 3B2, Canada. TEL 902-420-0437. FAX 902-423-8212. adv.; circ. 17,637. (tabloid format)

380.5 AT
AUSTRALASIAN BUS AND COACH; the management magazine for bus and coach operators. 1988. m. (except Jan.). Aus.$35($70) Publishing Services (Qld.) Pty. Ltd., 244 St. Paul's Terrace, Spring Hill, Brisbane, Qld. 4000, Australia. TEL 61-7-854-1286. Ed. Andrew Stewart. circ. 4,334. (back issues avail.)
  Description: Discusses transportation, travel and tourism.

AUSTRALIAN CARAVAN WORLD AND OUTDOOR LIFE. see *TRAVEL AND TOURISM*

388.322 IT
AUTOBUS. 1977. m. L.60000. Gesto s.r.l., Via Cesare Battisti 21, 20122 Milan, Italy. TEL 02-55187581. Ed. Elio Guaglio. adv.; bk.rev.; charts; illus.; circ. 15,000.
  Former titles (until 1990): Autocarri e Autobus-Trans; Autocarri e Autobus (ISSN 0393-8239)

388.322 SP
AUTOBUSES Y AUTOCARES. 1989. m. 5500 ptas. Tecnipublicaciones, S.A., Fernando VI, 27, 28004 Madrid, Spain. TEL 91-319-7889. FAX 91-410-1069. Ed. Armando Estrada. circ. 5,000.
  Description: Covers passenger transport and public transportation by bus.

388.322 NE
AUTOBUSKRONIEK. 1963. 11/yr. membership. Autobus Documentatie Vereniging, Penningmeester, Biterstraat 22, 8011 XL Zwolle, Netherlands. Ed. M.R.A. Velthuis. adv.; bk.rev.; circ. 1,200.

388 385 IT
AUTOFERROTRANVIERE. 1955. m. L.100 per no. Federazione Provinciale Autoferrotranvieri di Milano, Corso Porta Vittoria 43, Milan, Italy. Ed. Bruno di Pol. adv.; circ. 24,000.

388.322 AU ISSN 0005-0830
AUTOREVUE. 1965. m. S.420($12) O R A C Zeitschriftenverlag GmbH, Schoenbrunnerstr. 59-61, A-1050 Vienna, Austria. TEL 0222-551621-0. Ed. Herbert Voelker. adv.; illus.; circ. 121,500. (back issues avail.)

B I C - CODE. (Bureau International des Containers) see *PACKAGING*

380.52 GW
B V G AKTUELL. 10/yr. Berliner Verkehrs Betriebe, Potsdamerstr. 188, 1000 Berlin 30, Germany. TEL 030-2561. circ. 350,000.

380.5 KE
BANDARI; staff newspaper of Kenya Ports Authority. (Text in English) 1969. q. free. Kenya Ports Authority, P.O. Box 95009, Mombasa, Kenya. TELEX 21243 BANDARI. adv.; illus.; circ. 12,000 (controlled).
  Formerly (until 1979): Bandari Zetu.

380.5 US
BATTERY COUNCIL INTERNATIONAL. CONVENTION PROCEEDINGS. 1975. a. $20. Battery Council International, 401 N. Michigan Ave., Chicago, IL 60611. TEL 312-644-6610. abstr.; charts; illus.; stat.; circ. 750.
  Formerly: Battery Council International. Convention Minutes.
  Description: Contains transcript of the annual meeting.

380.5 GW ISSN 0722-9399
BERLINER VERKEHRSBLAETTER. 1954. m. DM.22.80. Arbeitskreis Berliner Nahverkehr e.V., Bingerstr. 88, 1000 Berlin 33, Germany. adv.; bk.rev.; charts; illus.; index; circ. 3,000. (back issues avail.)
  Description: Information magazine on public transportation in Berlin. Focus on traffic situation, roads, bus system and railroads.

380.5 NE
BESTELAUTO; Misset select. (Text in Dutch) a. C. Misset B.V., Hanzestr. 1, 7006 RH Doetinchem, Netherlands. TEL 08340-49911. FAX 08340-43839. TELEX 45481. Ed. P.C. Wieman. adv.: B&W page fl.19941; unit 187 x 257; adv. contact: Cor van Nek. circ. 370,000.

388.322 DK ISSN 0901-3229
BILRUTEN. 1925. m. DKK 184. Landsforeningen Danmarks Bilruter, P.O. Box 17, 7100 Vejle, Denmark. FAX 75834619. Ed. Povl Tiedemann. adv.; bk.rev.; circ. 2,500.

386 GW ISSN 0179-7743
BINNENSCHIFFAHRTS-NACHRICHTEN. 1946. s-m. DM.101.20. (Bundesverband der Deutschen Binnenschiffahrt E.V.) Schiffahrts-Verlag Hansa, Elbchaussee 277, D-2000 Hamburg 52, Germany. TEL 040-822807-0. FAX 040-822807-52. TELEX 213075-HANSA-D. (Co-sponsor: C.Schroedter & Co. (GmbH & Co. KG)) adv.; bk.rev.; bibl.; charts; illus.; stat.; circ. 4,500.

380.5 GW ISSN 0173-0290
BLICKPUNKT STRASSENBAHN. 1979. bi-m. DM.36. Arbeitsgemeinschaft Blickpunkt Strassenbahn e.V., Postfach 410167, 1000 Berlin 41, Germany. Ed. Thomas E. Fischer. adv.; bk.rev.; cum.index: 1979-1988; circ. 3,000. (back issues avail.)

380.5 IT ISSN 0006-7849
BORSA DEI NOLI; settimanale dei traffici marittimi, aerei e terrestri. 1962. w. L.45000. Publicrea Editrice Borsa dei Noli S.d.f., Corso Gastaldi 11, Genoa 16131, Italy. Ed. Novello Secondina. adv.; charts; illus.; stat.; circ. 14,500. (tabloid format)

380.52 UK
BRITAIN'S TOP 500 TRANSPORT COMPANIES. 1986. a. £145. Jordan & Sons Ltd., 21 St. Thomas St., Bristol BS1 6JS, England. TEL 0272-230600. FAX 0272-230063. TELEX 449119.
  Formerly: Britain's Freight-Forwarding Industry.

380.5 UK
BRITISH SHIPPER AND FORWARDER. 1980. m. £25. European Freight Publishing, Grenville House, 7 Church Rd., Teddington TW11 8PF, England. TEL 01-977-9284. FAX 01-977-1984. Ed. Simon Bottery. adv.; illus.; tr.lit.; circ. 12,311. (reprint service avail. from UMI)
  Formerly: British Shipper (ISSN 0260-0951)

380.5 CF
BULLETIN ANNUEL DES TRANSPORTS ET PARC AUTO. 1984. a. 3000 Fr.CFA. Centre National de la Statistique et des Etudes Economiques, B.P. 2031, Brazzaville, Congo. TEL 83-36-94.

380.5 LE
BULLETIN DES TRANSPORTS MARITIMES ET TERRESTRES. (Text in Arabic and French) 1972. s-a. Direction Generale des Transports, Beirut, Lebanon. Ed. Adel Harfouche. charts; illus.

BUS-FAHRT; internationale Fachzeitschrift fuer Omnibusverkehr. see *TRAVEL AND TOURISM*

388.322 UK ISSN 0143-9162
BUS FAYRE; the monthly magazine for everyone interested in buses. 1978. m. £20 (foreign £22). Autobus Review Publications Ltd., 42 Coniston Ave., Queensbury, Bradford, West Yorkshire BD13 2JD, England. Ed. K.A. Jenkinson. adv.; bk.rev.; circ. 18,000.
  Formerly (until Apr. 1982): Fare Stage (ISSN 0143-9170)

388.322 US
BUS GARAGE INDEX. 1967. a. $20 (effective 1991). Friendship Publications, Inc., Box 1472, Spokane, WA 99210-1472. TEL 509-328-9181. FAX 509-325-0405. Ed. William A. Luke. circ. 2,000. (reprint service avail.)

380.1 US ISSN 0739-7194
BUS INDUSTRY MAGAZINE. 1963. q. Can.$25($20) Bus History Association, Inc., Loring M. Lawrence, Ed., 195 Lancelot Dr., Manchester, NH 03104-1420. (Subscr. to: 965 McEwan, Windsor, Ont. N9B 2G1, Canada) bk.rev.; illus.; circ. 400. (back issues avail.)
  Former titles: Bus Review; Bus History.

388.322 US
BUS OPERATOR. 1985. bi-m. Tom Jackson & Associates, Inc., 1210 Eighth Ave. S., Nashville, TN 37203. TEL 615-242-7747. adv.; circ. 7,000.
  Description: Provides intercity bus operations professionals with technical and management information and regulatory and legislative news.

388.322 US ISSN 0192-8902
BUS RIDE. 1965. 8/yr. $25 (effective 1991). Friendship Publications, Inc., Box 1472, Spokane, WA 99210-1472. TEL 509-328-9181. FAX 509-325-0405. Ed. William A. Luke. adv.; bk.rev.; circ. 13,500. **Indexed:** HRIS.

338.3 US ISSN 0363-3764
HE5623.A45
BUS RIDE: BUS INDUSTRY DIRECTORY. Spine title: Bus Industry Directory. 1972. a. $65 (effective 1991). Friendship Publications, Inc., Box 1472, Spokane, WA 99210-1472. TEL 509-328-9181. FAX 509-325-0405. Ed. William A. Luke. circ. 1,500. (reprint service avail.)

388.322 US ISSN 0199-6096
BUS TOURS MAGAZINE. 1979. bi-m. $10 (foreign $15). National Bus Trader, Inc., 9698 Judson Rd., Polo, IL 61064. TEL 815-946-2341. FAX 815-946-2147. Ed. Larry Plachno. circ. 11,000. (back issues avail.)

385 388 GW
BUS UND BAHN. 1967. m. DM.12. (Verband Oeffentlicher Verkehrsbetriebe) Alba Publikation Alf Teloeken GmbH und Co. KG, Postfach 320 108, Roemerstr. 9, 4000 Duesseldorf 30, Germany. Ed.Bd. bk.rev.; circ. 5,600. (back issues avail.) **Indexed:** Dok.Str.

388.3 UK ISSN 0007-6392
BUSES. 1949. m. £24. Ian Allan Ltd., Terminal House, Station Approach, Shepperton, Surrey TW17 8AS, England. TEL 0932-228950. Ed. Stephen Morris. adv.; bk.rev.; charts; illus.; index; circ. 19,000. (reprint service avail. from UMI) **Indexed:** HRIS.
  Formerly: Buses Illustrated.
  Description: Relating to the road passenger transport industry in the UK.

388.322 UK ISSN 0141-9927
BUSES EXTRA. 1978. bi-m. £14. Ian Allan Ltd., Terminal House, Sta. Approach, Shepperton, Surrey TW17 8AS, England. TEL 0932-228950. Ed. Stephen Morris. adv.; bk.rev.; charts; illus.; circ. 13,000. (reprint service avail. from UMI)
  Description: In-depth views of historic and contemporary passenger road transport.

388.322 US
BUSES INTERNATIONAL. 1980. q. $25 membership. (Buses International Association) Friendship Publications, Inc., Box 1472, Spokane, WA 99210-1472. TEL 509-328-9181. FAX 509-325-0405. Ed. William A. Luke. circ. 100. (back issues avail.)
  Description: Focuses on bus transportation.

388.322 UK
HE5601
BUSES YEARBOOK. a. price varies. Ian Allan Ltd., Terminal House, Station Approach, Shepperton, Surrey TW17 8AS, England. TEL 0932-228950. circ. 8,500. (reprint service avail. from UMI)
  Formerly: Buses Annual (ISSN 0068-4376)
  Description: Historic and contemporary articles illustrating aspects of passenger road transport.

388.322 NO
BUSSEN. 1956. bi-m. NOK 100. Norsk Rutebilarbeiderforbund, Moellergt. 24, 0179 Oslo 1, Norway. FAX 02-115939. adv.; circ. 5,700.

380.5 GW ISSN 0720-4507
BUSVERKEHR. 1981. m. DM.63. Kirschbaum Verlag GmbH, Siegfriedstr. 28, Postfach 210209, 5300 Bonn 2, Germany. TEL 0228-343057. FAX 0228-857145. TELEX 889596-KIRVL-D. adv.; bk.rev.; bibl.; charts; illus.; index; circ. 7,000.

380.52 AG
C A T A C. 1954. 6/yr. Argentine Association of Freight Transport, Avda. Belgrano 1870, Piso 3, Buenos Aires, Argentina. Ed. Jorge Navas. adv.; circ. 3,500.

388.321 UK
CAB TRADE NEWS. 1972. fortn. £8. Drummond House, 203-209 N. Gower St., London NW1, England. FAX 01-630-5861. Ed.Bd.

TRANSPORTATION

381.41   US   ISSN 0270-384X
HE199.5.F3
CALIFORNIA FRESH FRUIT AND VEGETABLE SHIPMENTS BY RAIL, TRUCK, AND AIR. a. $10. (Department of Food & Agriculture) Federal-State Market News Service (Sacramento), Box 942871, Sacramento, CA 94271-0001. TEL 916-654-0298. FAX 916-654-1046. stat.
    Formerly: Movement of California Fruits and Vegetables by Rail, Truck, and Air (ISSN 0094-2790)

388.346   FR
CAMPING-CAR. 1978. 7/yr. 194 F. Ediregie, B.P. 86, 94420 Le Plessis Trevise, France. FAX 45-93-25-93. TELEX EDIGIE 262572. Ed. Svend Meyzonnier. adv.; illus.; circ. 70,000.
    Formerly: Van et le Camping-Car (ISSN 0183-0139)

380.5   CN
CANADA. NATIONAL TRANSPORTATION AGENCY. ANNUAL REPORT. (Text in English, French) 1988. a. free. National Transportation Agency, Ottawa, Ont. K1A 0N9, Canada. FAX 613-953-8353. (Subscr. to: Supply and Services Canada, Canadian Government Publishing Centre. Ottawa, Ont. K1A 0S9, Canada) circ. 7,500.
    Formerly: Canada. Transport Commission. Annual Report (ISSN 0068-9912)

380.5   CN
CANADIAN (TOTONTO). (Supplement avail.: Inter-Canadian) (Editions in English, French) m. Inside Guide Magazine Co. Ltd., 111 Avenue Rd., Ste. 807, Toronto, Ont. M5R 3J8, Canada. TEL 416-962-9184. FAX 416-962-2380. adv.; circ. 150,000.

380.5 384   CN
CANADIAN NATIONAL ANNUAL REPORT. (Editions in English, French) 1923. a. free. Canadian National Railways, 1 Rideau Street, Ottawa, Ont. K1N 8S7, Canada. TEL 613-560-0207. FAX 514-399-5344. Ed. Graham Dallas. circ. 35,000. (also avail. in microfiche)

CANADIAN RAIL/RAIL CANADIEN. see TRANSPORTATION — Railroads

621.1   CN   ISSN 0045-5393
CANADIAN STEAM. 1972. q. $1. Richard L. Coulton, Ed. & Pub., Bentley, Alta. T0C 0J0, Canada. adv.; bk.rev.; illus.; index; circ. 50. (processed)

385   CN   ISSN 0045-5466
CANADIAN TRANSPORT. (Text in English and French) 1909. m. Can.$8.40. Canadian Brotherhood of Railway, Transport and General Workers, 2300 Carling Ave., Ottawa, Ont., Canada. TEL 613-829-8764. FAX 613-824-6815. Ed. Russel Biggar. circ. 35,000. (also avail. in microfilm from UMI)

380.5 658.7   CN   ISSN 0008-5200
HE1
CANADIAN TRANSPORTATION AND DISTRIBUTION MANAGEMENT. 1898. m. Can.$44.89($52.95) (foreign $74). Southam Business Communications Inc. (Subsidiary of: Southam Inc.), 1450 Don Mills Rd., Don Mills, Ont. M3B 2X7, Canada. TEL 416-445-6641. FAX 416-442-2261. Ed. Michelle Ramsay. adv.; illus.; stat.; circ. 14,000. **Indexed:** BPIA, Can.B.P.I.
    Formerly: Canadian Transportation; Which incorporates: Traffic and Distribution Management.

CANADIAN TRANSPORTATION LAW REPORTER. see LAW

388.346   GW   ISSN 0008-6185
CARAVANING; illustrierte Wohnwagen-Spezialzeitschrift. 1959. m. DM.49. Drei Brunnen Verlag und Co., Postfach 101154, 7000 Stuttgart 10, Germany. FAX 0711-2576217. Ed. R. Eckl. adv.; bk.rev.; bibl.; charts; illus.; mkt.; stat.; tr.lit.; index; circ. 21,000. (processed)

380.5   CN   ISSN 0834-9797
CARGO EXPRESS. 1979. 10/yr. Can.$35. Baxter Publishing Co., 310 Dupont St., Toronto, Ont. M5R 1V9, Canada. TEL 416-968-7252. FAX 416-968-2377. Ed. Pat Cancilla. adv.; bk.rev.; charts; illus.; circ. 11,000.
    Former titles: Cargo Exchange; Air Cargo Canada; Incorporates (in 1991): Transportation Business; Which was formerly: Quarterly Report on Transportation (ISSN 0711-0049)

380.52   UK   ISSN 0306-0985
TA1215   CODEN: CSYIBN
CARGO SYSTEMS INTERNATIONAL. 1974. m. £47 (US $152; Europe $122). C S Publications Ltd., McMillan House, 54 Cheam Common Rd., Worcester Park, Surrey KT4 8RJ, England. FAX 44-81-330-5112. Ed. Vincent Champion. adv.; circ. 7,500. **Indexed:** BMT, Br.Rail.Bd., Excerp.Med., Fluidex.
—BLDSC shelfmark: 3052.400000.
    Formery: Cargo Systems.

CARGOVISION. see TRANSPORTATION — Air Transport

338   IT   ISSN 0008-6959
CARROZZIERE ITALIANO. 1962. m. L.120000. Edizioni Pubblire, Corso Garibaldi, 42, 20121 Milan, Italy. TEL 02-801529. FAX 02-801520. Ed. Maffeis Giuditta. adv.; bk.rev.; illus.; stat.; circ. 10,000.

380.5   NR
CHARTERED INSTITUTE OF TRANSPORT. ANNUAL. 1959. a. Chartered Institute of Transport, Nigerian Ports Authority, 51 Herbert Macauley St., Ebuke-metta, Lagos, Nigeria. adv.

380.5   US
CHICAGO AREA TRANSPORTATION STUDY. ANNUAL REPORT. irreg., latest 1981. $4.50. Chicago Area Transportation Study, 300 W. Adams St., Chicago, IL 60606. TEL 312-793-7433. FAX 312-793-3481. charts; illus.

658.8   US   ISSN 0273-6721
HF5487
CHILTON'S DISTRIBUTION MAGAZINE; the transportation and business logistics magazine. 1901. m. $55. Chilton Co., Chilton Way, Radnor, PA 19089. TEL 215-964-4379. Ed. Thomas A. Foster. adv.; bk.rev.; charts; illus.; stat.; tr.lit.; index; circ. 70,000. (also avail. in microform from UMI; back issues avail.; reprint service avail.) **Indexed:** B.P.I., Intl.Mgmt.Info., Manage.Cont., SRI, Tr.& Indus.Ind.
   ●Also available online. Vendor(s): DIALOG, Mead Data Central.
—BLDSC shelfmark: 3172.994580.
    Former titles: Chilton's Distribution (ISSN 0195-7244); Chilton's Distribution Worldwide (ISSN 0193-3248); Distribution Worldwide (ISSN 0012-3951); Distribution Manager.
    Description: Focuses on traffic management and inventory control.

380.5 915.1   HK   ISSN 0258-3259
CHINA TRANSPORT. 1985. q. $50. (China Communications and Transportation Association) China Transport Publications Ltd., 4306 China Resources Bldg., 43rd Fl., 26 Harbour Rd., Hong Kong, Hong Kong. TEL 5-8913831. TELEX 68444 HKTF HX. Ed. Oliver Wong. adv.; bk.rev.; circ. 6,000.

380.5   FR   ISSN 0755-1088
CHRONIQUE DU TRANSPORTEUR. 1947. m. 270 F. (foreign 290 F.). Bureau d'Etudes et de Recherches Theoriques, 80 rue Jules Ferry, 93177 Bagnolet Cedex, France. TEL 1-43-60-02-36. FAX 1-48-97-11-88. Ed. Arlette Jaron. adv.; circ. 13,000.

388.4   US   ISSN 0045-6985
CITY AND SUBURBAN TRAVEL. 1953. m. $15. Transit Research Foundation of Los Angeles Inc., Box 3542, Terminal Annex Sta., Los Angeles, CA 90051. TEL 312-454-2221. (And: 17350 Sunset Blvd., No. 204C, CA 90272) Ed. Jean Bennett. bk.rev.; charts; illus.; circ. 1,300.

CITY CYCLIST. see SPORTS AND GAMES — Bicycles And Motorcycles

380.5   US
CLIPS. 1986. bi-m. $275. Association for Commuter Transportation, 808 17th St. N.W., No. 200, Washington, DC 20006. TEL 202-223-9669. Ed. Mark Wright. circ. 1,000.
    Description: News clips from throughout U S on transportation and related topics.

388.322   UK
COACH AND BUS WEEK. 1978. w. £45. Response Publishing Ltd., Wentworth House, Wentworth St., Peterborough PE1 1DS, England. TEL 0733-63100. FAX 0733-62656. Ed. Mark Barton. adv.; bk.rev.; circ. 6,000.
    Formerly: Coachmart.

388.3   UK   ISSN 0009-9899
COACHING JOURNAL AND BUS REVIEW. 1932. m. £25 (foreign £40). Yandell Publishing Ltd., 9 Vermont Place, Tongwell, Milton Keynes MK15 8JA, England. TEL 0908-613323. FAX 0908-618529. Ed. Graham Yandell. adv.; bk.rev.; charts; illus.; stat.; tr.lit.; circ. 4,330. **Indexed:** HRIS.
    Description: Trade news for the coach and bus industry.

388.346   US
COAST TO COAST MAGAZINE. 8/yr. Coast to Coast Resorts, 64 Inverness Dr. E., Englewood, CO 80112. TEL 303-790-2267. FAX 303-397-7657. Ed. Valerie Rogers. circ. 362,992.

385   EI
COMMISSION OF THE EUROPEAN COMMUNITIES. EUROPA TRANSPORT. ANNUAL REPORT. (Supplement to: C E C Documentation Bulletin) 1980. a. price varies. Commission of the European Communities, Directorate-General for Transport, 200, rue de la Loi, 1049 Brussels, Belgium. FAX 02-236-8350. TELEX COMEU B 21877. circ. 3,500.
    Description: Contains a comprehensive review of recent developments in the international intra-Community goods transport market.

380.5 362.4   UK   ISSN 0263-9378
COMMUNITY TRANSPORT MAGAZINE; the journal for minibus & non-profit transport operators. 1982. s-m. £9($30) Community Transport Association, Highbank, Halton St., Hyde, Cheshire SK14 2NY, England. TEL 061-351-1475. FAX 061-367-8396. Ed. Alison Shore. adv.; bk.rev.; circ. 1,500. (back issues avail.)

380.5 630   US   ISSN 0895-4437
COMMUNITY TRANSPORTATION REPORTER; the magazine of the rural and specialized transit industry. 1984. m. $35. Community Transportation Association of America, 725 15th St., N.W., Ste. 900, Washington, DC 20005. TEL 202-628-1480. FAX 202-737-9197. Ed. Barbara-Rasin Price. adv.; bk.rev.; index, cum.index: 1983-1987; circ. 10,000 (controlled).
    Formerly (until Jun. 1987): Rural Transportation Reporter.
    Description: Funding, legislation, trends, and surveys in community transportation.

388   US   ISSN 0069-9039
HE28.C8
CONNECTICUT MASTER TRANSPORTATION PLAN. 1971. a. Department of Transportation (Conndot), c/o Director of Planning, Bureau of Planning, 24 Wolcott Hill Rd., Wethersfield, CT 06109. TEL 203-566-5114. circ. 1,000.
    Incorporates (in 1973): Connecticut Highway Needs Report.

380.5   JA   ISSN 0289-8322
CONTAINER AGE; the authoritative voice of intermodal transportation and distribution. (Text in Japanese) 1967. m. 6000 Yen. Container Age Ltd., 3F Ogihara Bldg., 1-13-2, Nishi-Shinbashi, Minato-ku, Tokyo 105, Japan. TEL 03-3501-0600. FAX 03-3501-0600. Ed. Eiji Niimoto. adv.; bk.rev.; circ. 18,700.
    Description: Serves intermodal transportation industry, specifically shippers, manufacturers, carriers, and freight forwarders.

380.52 380.1   GW
CONTAINER CONTACTS. 1971. a. DM.35.51. K.O. Storck Verlag, Stahltwiete 7, 2000 Hamburg 50, Germany. TEL 040-850-0071. FAX 040-850-7758. TELEX 17403448. Ed. H. Meder.

658.7   US   ISSN 0010-7360
TA1215
CONTAINER NEWS; serving the intermodal industry. 1965. m. $36 (foreign $106). Communication Channels, Inc., 6255 Barfield Rd., Atlanta, GA 30328-4369. TEL 404-256-9800. FAX 404-256-3116. TELEX 4611075 COMCHANI. Ed. Herb Schild. adv.; bk.rev.; charts; illus.; pat.; stat.; tr.lit.; circ. 22,000. (also avail. in microform from UMI; reprint service avail. from UMI) **Indexed:** Curr.Pack.Abstr., Int.Packag.Abstr., Key to Econ.Sci.
   ●Also available online.
    Description: Covers the worldwide container and intermodal shipping industry (transportation by ocean, rail, truck and air carriers).

658.7   UK   ISSN 0010-7379
CONTAINERISATION INTERNATIONAL. 1967. m. £150. National Magazine Co. Ltd., 72 Broadwick St., London W1V 2BP, England. TEL 071-439-5000. FAX 071-437-6886. Ed. Jane R.C. Boyes. adv.; illus.; tr.lit.; circ. 10,000. (reprint service avail. from UMI) **Indexed:** BMT, Fluidex, Int.Packag.Abstr.
—BLDSC shelfmark: 3425.080000.

658.7   UK   ISSN 0305-7402
CONTAINERISATION INTERNATIONAL YEARBOOK. 1968. a. £180. National Magazine Co. Ltd., 72 Broadwick St., London W1V 2BP, England. TEL 071-439-5000. FAX 071-437-6886. Ed. Mark Lambert. adv.; illus.; circ. 2,500.

CONTAINERIZATION AND MATERIAL HANDLING ANNUAL. see *PACKAGING*

CONTAINERS. see *PACKAGING*

380.5   IT
COOPERAZIONE E TRASPORTI. m. Via Puccini 5, 20121 Milan, Italy. Ed. Alessandro Pasquali.

388.322   UK
CRONER'S COACH AND BUS OPERATIONS. 1983. q. £61.30. Croner Publications Ltd., Croner House, London Rd., Kingston, Surrey KT2 6SR, England. TEL 081-547-3333. FAX 081-547-2637. Ed. Colin Clark. (looseleaf format)
Description: Covers the rules and regulations governing coach and bus operations in UK law.

380.5   US
D M W B E ACTION NEWSLETTER. 1988. q. (Metropolitan Transportation Authority, Disadvantaged Minority and Women Business Enterprises) New York City Transit Authority, Affirmative Action Department, 81 Willoughby St., Brooklyn, NY 11201.

380.5   US
D R I - McGRAW-HILL TRANSPORTATION REVIEW. a. D R I - McGraw-Hill, 24 Hartwell Ave., Lexington, MA 02173. TEL 617-863-5100. FAX 617-860-6332. TELEX 200 284.
Formerly: Data Resources Transportation Review.

388.1   DK   ISSN 0900-3665
D S B BLADET. 1943. m. DKK 150. Danske Statsbaner - Danish State Railways, Soelvgade 40, DK-1349 Copenhagen K, Denmark. FAX 33-32-62-54. Ed. Jesper Sejl. bk.rev.; circ. 33,500.
Formerly: Vingehjulet (ISSN 0042-6296)

629.2   DK
D V BOGEN. 1960. a. Danske Vognmaend Hovedorganisationen, Gammeltorv 18, 1457 Copenhagen K, Denmark. cum.index.
Formerly: L D V Bogen.

380.5   GW
D V Z BRIEF. (Deutsche Verkehrs - Zeitung) w. DM.46. Deutscher Verkehrs Verlag, Nordkanalstr. 36, 2000 Hamburg 1, Germany. TEL 040-2371401. Ed. Frank Schnell.

380.5   DK   ISSN 0106-0724
DANMARKS TRANSPORT-TIDENDE. 1978. 22/yr. DKK 250. Forlaget Erik Koch Larsen ApS, Hojvangen 6, 3480 Fredensborg, Denmark. FAX 42-281002. Ed. Erik Koch Larsen. adv.; circ. 11,473.

380.5 355   US   ISSN 0011-7625
U1
DEFENSE TRANSPORTATION JOURNAL; magazine of international defense transportation and logistics. 1945. bi-m. $35 to non-members (effective 1992). National Defense Transportation Association, 50 S. Pickett St., No. 220, Alexandria, VA 22304-3008. TEL 703-751-5011. FAX 703-823-8761. Eds. Joseph G. Mattingly, Jr., Dennis L. Edwards. adv.; bk.rev.; charts; illus.; index; circ. 8,100. (also avail. in microform from UMI; reprint service avail. from UMI) **Indexed:** Abstr.Mil.Bibl., Air.Un.Lib.Ind., DM & T, PROMT.
—BLDSC shelfmark: 3546.240000.
Formerly: National Defense Transportation Journal.

380.5   US
DELAWARE VALLEY PLANNING NEWS. (Includes: Regional Transportation & Planning News for the Delaware Valley) 1980. 4/yr. free. Delaware Valley Regional Planning Commission, Bourse Bldg., 21 S. Fifth St., Philadelphia, PA 19106. TEL 215-592-1800. Ed. Candace B. Snyder. circ. 2,500. (tabloid format; back issues avail.)

380.5   GW
DEUTSCHE VERKEHRSWISSENSCHAFTLICHE GESELLSCHAFT. SCHRIFTENREIHE. REIHE A. DOKUMENTATION. 1965. a. DM.39. Deutsche Verkehrswissenschaftliche Gesellschaft, Bruederstr. 53, 5060 Bergisch Gladbach 1, Germany. TEL 02204-60027. FAX 02204-67743. Ed. K. Thielen. bk.rev.; circ. 1,800. **Indexed:** Dok.Str.

380.5 338.01   UK
DEVELOPING WORLD TRANSPORT. 1987. a. £49.95($89.95) Grosvenor Press International Ltd., Holford Mews, Cruikshank St., London WC1X 9HD, England. TEL 01-278-3000. FAX 01-278-1674. Ed. Richard Parkes. circ. 10,000.
Description: Annual update on the transport industry in developing countries, and in conjunction with C.I.I.

DIESEL; mensile di cultura, attualita, tecnica che tratta di tutte le motorizzazioni diesel per usi industriali, agricoli, nautici. see *ENGINEERING — Mechanical Engineering*

380.5   US
DIRECTORY OF COMMON MOTOR CARRIER AGENCY TARIFFS. 1941? s-a. $45. Transportation Consulting & Service Corp., 1033 Graceland Ave., Des Plaines, IL 60016. TEL 708-298-1094. FAX 708-298-5877.
Description: Lists bureau name, tariff number, ICC or state number, effective dates, type of tariff and price of tariff.

380.5   UK   ISSN 0954-2094
DISTRIBUTION. 1988. bi-m. £48($100) Trinity Publishing Ltd., Times House, Station Approach, Ruislip, Middx. HA4 8NB, England. TEL 0895-677677. FAX 0895-676027. Ed. S. Goodall. circ. 15,000. (back issues avail.)

380 330   FR
DOCUMENTS TARIFAIRES TRANSPORT. (Supplements avail.) a. 1035 F. (with supplements 4584 F.)(effective 1990). Lamy S.A., 155, rue Legendre, 75850 Paris Cedex 17, France. TEL 1-46-27-28-90. FAX 42-29-86-81. TELEX 214 398. (looseleaf format)

380.5   CS   ISSN 0012-5520
DOPRAVA/TRANSPORT; odborna technicko-ekonomicka revue pro vsechna dopravni odvetvi. (Text in Czech; contents page and summaries also in French, German, Russian) 1959. q. $36.30. (Federalni Ministerstvo Dopravy) Nakladatelstvi Dopravy a Spoju, Hybernska 5, 115 78 Prague 1, Czechoslovakia. (Dist. by: Artia, Ve Smeckach 30, 111 27 Prague 1, Czechoslovakia) Ed. Pavla Opavova. adv.; bibl.; illus.; circ. 3,000.

629   US
DRIVER LETTER. bi-m $12.50 to non-members; members $10. National Safety Council, Motor Transportation Department, 444 N. Michigan Ave., Chicago, IL 60611. TEL 312-527-4800. circ. 130,000.
Description: Professional driver letter for trucking, bus, and school bus industries.

380.5   NE
E W SPECIAL; transport en verpakking. no.2, 1976. irreg. fl.1 per no. B.V. Uitgeversmaatschappij Bonaventura, Hoogoorddreef 60, 1101 BE Amsterdam, Netherlands. TEL 20-5674911. FAX 20-5674629. TELEX 14013 BONAV NL. Ed. J. Folkerstma.

380.5   US   ISSN 0190-4175
ELECTRIC VEHICLE PROGRESS. 1979. s-m. $337. Alexander Research & Communications, Inc., 215 Park Ave., S., Ste. 1301, New York, NY 10003. TEL 212-228-0246. FAX 212-228-0376. Ed. Laurence A. Alexander. charts; illus. **Indexed:** Cadscan, Lead Abstr., Zincscan.
Description: Newsletter of electric vehicle commercialization. Focuses on news and data on both technical and business aspects of the electric vehicle industry.

TRANSPORTATION   4649

629.229   UK
ELECTRIC VEHICLES.* 1914. q. Allens (Clerkenwell) Ltd., 177 Hagden Lane, Watford, Herts, England. Ed. Lloyd Arkill. adv.; bk.rev.; illus.; pat.; tr.lit.; circ. 3,000.
Former titles: Electric Vehicles for Industry (ISSN 0013-4171); Electric Vehicles.
Description: Covers battery electric vehicles.

388   IT   ISSN 1120-2289
ELEVATORI. 1972. bi-m. L.33000 (foreign L.53000). Volpe Editore, Via Pacinotti 4, 20090 Segrate, Italy. FAX 02-2139355. TELEX 313661. adv.; circ. 2,800.

EMPLO REVIEW/TYDSKRIF. see *LABOR UNIONS*

380.5   GR
EPITHEORESIS SYNKOINONIAKOU DIKAIOU. 1973. m. Dr.4000 to individuals; institutions Dr.8000. c/o Onoufrios Onouphriades, Ed., Metamorphoseos 3, 174 55 Kalamaki, Athens, Greece. TEL 98-20-336. bk.rev.; circ. 5,000.

380.5 001.5   PN   ISSN 1012-3555
HE222.A15
ESTADISTICA PANAMA. SITUACION ECONOMICA. SECCION 333. TRANSPORTE. 1958. a. Bl.0.75. Direccion de Estadistica y Censo, Contraloria General, Apartado 5213, Panama 5, Panama. FAX 63-9322. circ. 1,000.
Supersedes (in 1985): Estadistica Panamena. Situacion Economica. Seccion 333-334. Transporte y Comunicaciones (ISSN 0378-7389)

380.5   EI
EUROPA TRANSPORT. (Text in English, French, German) a. $12.50. Office for Official Publications of the European Communities, L-2985 Luxembourg, Luxembourg. (Dist. in the U.S. by: Unipub, 4611-F Assembly Dr., Lanham, MD 20706-4391)

347.7 385.1   BE   ISSN 0014-3154
K5
EUROPEAN TRANSPORT LAW/DROIT EUROPEEN DES TRANSPORTS/EUROPAEISCHES TRANSPORTRECHT/DIRITTO EUROPEO DEI TRASPORTI/EUROPEES VERVOERRECHT. (Text in Dutch, English, French, German, Italian, Spanish) 1966. bi-m. 5900 Fr. European Transport Law, Maria-Henriettalei 1, B-2018 Antwerp, Belgium. TEL 03-2313655. FAX 03-2342380. TELEX 32544 LAWY B. Ed. Robert Wijffels. bk.rev.; charts; illus.; stat.; index; circ. 5,200. (back issues avail.)
—BLDSC shelfmark: 3830.320000.

380.5   IT
EUROTRANSPORTS; mensile di tecnica ed economia del trasporto. 1961. m. L.40000. (New Euro Image Srl.) Edizione Andrea Latorre Sas, Via Giovanni Rotondi 3, 20145 Milan, Italy. TEL 02-4625381. FAX 02-4697561. Ed. Michele Latorre. adv.; bk.rev.; abstr.; bibl.; charts; illus.; mkt.; pat.; stat.; circ. 25,000.
Incorporates: Container in Italia e nel Mondo (ISSN 0010-7352) & Eurotransports Illustrato (ISSN 0014-3251)

380.5   CN   ISSN 0838-5416
EXPEDITEUR. 1988. 10/yr. Can.$35($45) Editions Bomart Ltee., 7493 TransCanada Hwy., Ste. 103, St. Laurent, Que. H4T 1T3, Canada. TEL 514-337-9043. FAX 514-337-1862. Ed. Martin Duclos. adv.; circ. 10,106.
Description: Covers the latest developments on the shipping scene, profiling their technical, economical or social dimensions.

380.52   UK
F T A YEARBOOK. 1963. a. £25. Freight Transport Association, Hermes House, St. Johns Rd., Tunbridge Wells TN4 9UZ, England. TEL 0892-26171. FAX 0892-34989. TELEX 957158. adv.; circ. 21,000.

320   CN
F Y I. (For Your Information) 1967. bi-m. Trans Mountain Pipe Line Company Ltd., 800-601 W. Broadway, Vancouver, B.C. V5Z 4C5, Canada. TEL 604-876-6711. FAX 604-873-3911. Ed. J. Hess. stat.; circ. 500. (back issues avail.)
Description: Provides description of company and employee activities and policies.

FAHR MIT UNS; Hamburger illustrierte Nahverkehrszeitschrift. see *TRANSPORTATION — Roads And Traffic*

TRANSPORTATION

388.346　　　US　ISSN 0360-3024
TL298
FAMILY MOTOR COACHING. 1963. m. $24. (Family Motor Coach Association) Famoco Corporation, 8291 Clough Pike, Cincinnati, OH 45244. TEL 513-474-3622. FAX 513-474-2332. Ed. Pamela Kay. adv.; bk.rev.; index; circ. 92,000.
　Description: Publishes travel articles of particular interest to motorhome travelers, along with technical information concerning mechanics, coach housekeeping, and the latest RV products and accessories.

380.5　　　US
FEDERAL CARRIERS REPORTS. 4 base vols. (plus fortn. updates). $935. Commerce Clearing House, Inc., 4025 W. Peterson Ave., Chicago, IL 60646. TEL 312-583-8500.

FEMNET. see WOMEN'S INTERESTS

FIETS. see SPORTS AND GAMES — Bicycles And Motorcycles

380.5　　　UK
FLEET NEWS. 1978. w. £60. Response Publishing (Subsidiary of: E M A P plc), Wentworth House, Wentworth St., Peterborough PE1 1DS, England. TEL 0733-63100. Ed. Mike Gunnell. adv.; bk.rev.; circ. 26,500.

380.5　　　US　ISSN 0547-888X
FLEET SAFETY NEWSLETTER. 1966. bi-m. $19 to non-members; members $15. National Safety Council, Motor Transportation Department, 444 N. Michigan Ave., Chicago, IL 60611. TEL 312-527-4800. Ed. Janet Hazlett.
　Former titles: Safety Newsletter: Fleet Safety; Safety Newsletter: Commercial Vehicle Section.

380.5 629.288　　　AT　ISSN 0312-4681
FLEETLINE. 1976. m. Aus.$48. Historic Commercial Vehicle Association Co-Op, G.P.O. Box 1010, Sydney, N.S.W. 2001, Australia. FAX 02-858-1137. Ed. L. Pascoe. adv.; bk.rev.; circ. 450.
　Description: Current news regarding buses in Australia.

388.3　　　US　ISSN 0092-0177
HE5633.F6
FLORIDA. DIVISION OF MOTOR VEHICLES. TAGS AND REVENUE. 1928. a. free. Department of Highway Safety and Motor Vehicles, Division of Administrative Services, Neil Kirkman Bldg., Tallahassee, FL 32304. TEL 904-488-6084. Ed.Bd. circ. 1,000.

FOERDERMITTEL-JOURNAL; Materialfluss, Lager, Transport und Verpackung. see MACHINERY

380　　　SZ
FOERDERTECHNIK. (Text in German) 9/yr. 95 Fr. Industrie-Verlag AG, Muehlebachstr. 43, CH-8032 Zurich, Switzerland. Ed. J. Kistler. adv.; charts; illus.; circ. 6,400.
　Formerly: Wirtschaft und Technik im Transport (ISSN 0049-6820)

FRACHT - DIENST. see TRANSPORTATION — Ships And Shipping

380.5 380.5　　　GW　ISSN 0342-3042
FRACHT MANAGEMENT. Abbreviated title: F M. m. (with 2 double issues/yr.). Konradin-Verlag Robert Kohlhammer GmbH, Postfach 100252, 7022 Leinfelden-Echterdingen KG, Germany. TEL 0711-7594-0. Ed. Peter Schaeuble. adv.; bk.rev.; circ. 15,051 (controlled). (back issues avail.)
　Description: Focuses on in-company and external transport, distribution, storage, transport packaging, materials handling, transshipment and logistics.

354.44　　　FR　ISSN 0399-0281
FRANCE. MINISTERE DE L'AMENAGEMENT DU TERRITOIRE, DE L'EQUIPEMENT, DU LOGEMENT ET DES TRANSPORTS. BULLETIN OFFICIEL. w. 111 F. Direction des Journaux Officiels, 26, rue Desaix, 75727 Paris Cedex 15, France. TEL 1-45-78-61-44.

380.5　　　UK　ISSN 0016-0849
FREIGHT. 1945. m. £25. Freight Transport Association, Hermes House, St. John's Rd., Tunbridge Wells, Kent TN4 9UZ, England. TEL 0892-26171. FAX 0892-34989. TELEX 957158. Ed. James Hookham. adv.; bk.rev.; circ. 14,989 (controlled). **Indexed:** BMT, HRIS.
　—BLDSC shelfmark: 4033.460000.
　Formerly: Industrial Road Transport.

380.52　　　UK
FREIGHT HANDLER. 1981. m. £15. K.A.V. Publicity (Glasgow) Ltd., 113 West Regent St., Glasgow G2, Scotland. TEL 041 226 3861. Ed. Alistair M. Vallance. adv.; circ. 9,500 (controlled).

388　　　UK　ISSN 0071-9471
FREIGHT INDUSTRY YEARBOOK; classified reference guide for transport vehicle manufacturers, operators and users. 1950. a. £100. Guardian Communications Ltd., Third Floor, Albany House, Hurst St., Birmingham B5 4BD, England. TEL 021-622 4011. FAX 021-625-3564. TELEX 948669-TOPJNL-G. Ed. W. Farnorth. adv.
　—BLDSC shelfmark: 4033.475000.
　Formerly: Goods Vehicle Year Book.
　Description: British guide to the U.K. freight industry, the yearbook contains over 20 specialist sections, and covers the spectrum of freighting services.

380.5　　　UK
FREIGHT MANAGEMENT & DISTRIBUTION TODAY. 1966. m. £20. Freight Management, 230-234 Longline, London SE1 4QE, England. TEL 071-403-4353. FAX 071-403-0233. TELEX 884595. Ed. Andy Holder. adv.; bk.rev.; circ. 10,948. (also avail. in microform from UMI)
　Formerly: Freight Management (ISSN 0016-0873)
　Description: Directed to senior executives in industry with distribution job functions.

380.5　　　US
FREIGHT MANAGEMENT REPORT; the independent monthly report on transportation cost reduction. 1983. m. $135. Transportation Research Associates, Box 4150, Toms River, NJ 08756-4150. TEL 908-505-0920. FAX 908-505-0970. Ed. Thomas F. Dillon. index; circ. 100. (back issues avail.)
　Formerly: Freight Marketing Report (ISSN 0892-3566)

380.5　　　UK
GARAGE & TRANSPORT SELECTOR. 1978. q. A.G.B. Hulton Ltd., Warwick House, Azalea Dr., Swanley, Kent BR8 8JF, England. circ. 48,120.

380.5　　　GW　ISSN 0016-5808
T55.3.H3
GEFAEHRLICHE LADUNG; See - Luft - Bahn - Strasse. 1956. m. DM.171.96. K.O. Storck Verlag, Stahltwiete 7, 2000 Hamburg 50, Germany. TEL 040-850-0071. FAX 040-850-7758. TELEX 17403448. Ed. Horst Meder. adv.; bk.rev.; bibl.; charts; illus.; index. **Indexed:** INIS Atomind.
　Formerly: Gefaehrliche Fracht.

388　　　UK
GLASS'S COMMERCIAL VEHICLE CHECK BOOK. a. £15. Glass's Guide Service Ltd., Elgin House, St. George's Ave., Weybridge, Surrey KT13 0BX, England. TEL 0932-853211. FAX 0932-849299. adv.

GO DEVIL. see PETROLEUM AND GAS

GOODS IN TRANSIT. see LAW — Corporate Law

380.5 633　　　US
GRAIN TRANSPORTATION SITUATION. 1981. w. $28. U.S. Department of Agriculture, Office of Transportation, 1405 Auditors Bldg., Washington, DC 20250. TEL 202-447-6793. Ed. William L. Dunton. **Indexed:** Amer.Stat.Ind.
　Description: Features current happenings within the university community.

GUIA AEREA Y MARITIMA. see TRAVEL AND TOURISM

380.5　　　VE
GUIA AEREA Y MARITIMA DE VENEZUELA C.A.; Aruba, Curacao y Bonaire. 1968. m. $90. Ministerio de Fomento - Ministry of Public Works, Apdo. 68121, Caracas 1062-A, Venezuela. (Dist. by: Target Group Communications Inc., 7225 N.W. 12th St., 2nd Fl., Miami, FL 33126) Ed. Gregorio Burgana. adv.; circ. 5,400.

629.28　　　MX
GUIA AUTOMOTRIZ. 1954. m. J. Rodriguez & Cia, S.A., Sur 51 No. 118, Col. Ermita, Mexico 13, Mexico. Ed. Juan Rodriquez. adv.; circ. 15,000.

380.5　　　CN
GUIDE DU TRANSPORT. (Text in English, French) 1938. a. Can.$65($75) Editions Bomart Ltee., 7493 TransCanada Hwy., Ste. 103, St. Laurent, Que. H4T 1T3, Canada. TEL 514-337-9043. FAX 514-337-1862. adv.; circ. 5,000.
　Description: For the person who wants to receive or ship material between Montreal and most Canadian, American and foreign cities. Lists companies offering products or services related to the transportation industry.

380.5 630　　　US
HANDBOOK OF LIVE ANIMAL TRANSPORT. 1984. q. (plus periodic suppl.). $150. Silesia Companies, Inc., 619 Broad Creek Dr., Box 441110, Ft. Washington, MD 20744-1110. TEL 301-292-1970. FAX 301-292-1787. Ed. Dale L. Anderson. index; circ. 160. (looseleaf format)
　Formerly: Handbook of Animal Transportation.
　Description: Compilation of articles, listings and information on all phases of transporting animals worldwide.

380.5　　　GW　ISSN 0073-019X
HANDBUCH OEFFENTLICHER VERKEHRSBETRIEBE. 1952. irreg. price varies. (Verband Oeffentlicher Verkehrsbetriebe) Erich Schmidt Verlag GmbH & Co. (Bielefeld), Viktoriastr. 44A, Postfach 7330, 4800 Bielefeld 1, Germany. TEL 0521-583080. adv.

380.5　　　UK　ISSN 0143-6864
HAZARDOUS CARGO BULLETIN. 1980. m. £75 (typically set in Jan.). Intapress Publishing Ltd., 38 Tavistock St., London WC2E 7PB, England. TEL 071-240-0837. FAX 071-836-9321. Ed. Michael Corkhill. adv.; bk.rev.; circ. 20,000. (back issues avail.) **Indexed:** Curr.Pack.Abstr., Fluidex, Int.Packag.Abstr., Packag.Sci.Tech.
　—BLDSC shelfmark: 4274.396000.
　Description: Covers the transport, storage and handling of hazardous materials worldwide.

HAZARDOUS MATERIALS TRANSPORTATION. see ENVIRONMENTAL STUDIES — Waste Management

HAZMAT TRANSPORT. see ENVIRONMENTAL STUDIES — Waste Management

380.52　　　US
HEREFORD'S AMERICAS; air freight handbook. 1979. s-a. $110 (free to qualified personnel). Hereford's Air Freight Handbooks, 1328 Broadway, Ste. 1125, New York, NY 10001. TEL 212-564-0068. FAX 212-594-3841. (Affiliate: Maclean Hunter Ltd.) adv.; circ. 10,723.
　Formerly: Hereford's North America (ISSN 0143-5906)
　Description: Lists all known airlines, freight forwarders, charter airlines, and brokers in the Americas region.

380.5　　　US　ISSN 0161-0325
HIGHWAY & VEHICLE - SAFETY REPORT. 1974. 26/yr. $297 (foreign $232). Stamler Publishing Co., 178 Thimble Islands Rd., Box 3367, Branford, CT 06405. TEL 203-488-9808. FAX 203-488-9898. Ed. S. Paul Stamler. bk.rev.; abstr.; bibl.; stat. (back issues avail.)
　Description: Covers new developments in transportation and vehicle safety.

I E E E TRANSACTIONS ON VEHICULAR TECHNOLOGY. see ENGINEERING — Electrical Engineering

I T F NEWS. (International Transport Workers' Federation) see LABOR UNIONS

625.7　　　US　ISSN 0192-3994
I T S REVIEW. 1977. 4/yr. free. University of California, Berkeley, Institute of Transportation Studies, 109 McLaughlin Hall, Berkeley, CA 94720. TEL 415-642-3593. FAX 415-642-1246. Ed. Laura Steinman. illus.; circ. 5,000.
　Supersedes: I T S Bulletin.

IN TRANSIT. see LABOR UNIONS

TRANSPORTATION 4651

380.5 US
INBOUND LOGISTICS. 1981. 12/yr. Thomas Publishing Company, Five Penn Plaza, 8th Fl., 250 W. 34th St., New York, NY 10001. TEL 212-290-7336. FAX 212-629-1584. Ed. Richard S. Sexton. adv.; circ. 43,000.
   Former titles (until July 1985): Inbound Traffic Guide; Thomas Register's Inbound Traffic Guide.
   Description: Controlling and buying inbound freight services and equipment.

388 II ISSN 0019-4956
INDIAN INSTITUTE OF ROAD TRANSPORT. MONTHLY BULLETIN. (Text in English) 1953. m. Rs.20($6) Indian Institute of Road Transport, Best House, P.O. Box 192, Bombay 400 039, India. Ed. C.D. Jeffereis. adv.; bk.rev.; charts; illus.; index; circ. 1,300.

INDUSTRIAL HANDLING & STORAGE. see *MACHINERY*

INDUSTRIAL HERITAGE MAGAZINE; industry - transport - people. see *MINES AND MINING INDUSTRY*

INFORMACION; imagen nacional e internacional de comunicaciones y transportes. see *COMMUNICATIONS*

380.5 FR ISSN 0020-0298
INFORMATION TRANSPORTS; periodique mensuel de documentation et d'information des transports ferroviaires, routiers, fluviaux et maritimes. 1933. m. 40 F. 57 rue de Soissons, 33000 Bordeaux (Gironde), France. Ed.Bd. adv.; charts; circ. 5,000. (tabloid format)

380.5 GW ISSN 0931-1688
INFORMATIONDIENST VERKEHR. 1980. q. DM.40. Arbeitskreis Verkehr und Umwelt e.V. (Umkehr), Kirchstr. 4, 1000 Berlin 21, Germany. TEL 030-392-61-46. adv.; bk.rev.; bibl.; illus.; stat.; circ. 1,200. (back issues avail.)

352.7 FR
INFOS FEDERALES. no.83, 1981. q. Federation des Travaux Publics et des Transports, 46 rue des Petites-Ecuries, 75010 Paris, France. Ed. Rene Valladon. bk.rev.; charts; illus.; stat.
   Formerly: Federation des Travaux Publics et des Transports. Revue (ISSN 0046-3523)

388 PL
INSTYTUT TRANSPORTU SAMOCHODOWEGO. ZESZYTY NAUKOWE. (Text in Polish; summaries in English and Russian) 1962. irreg. (approx. 2-3/yr.). free. Instytut Transportu Samochodowego, Stalingradzka 40, Warsaw, Poland. TEL 48 22 11-29-33. TELEX 813316 ITS PL. Ed. L. Stepniak. bk.rev.; illus.; stat.; pat.; circ. controlled.

INTERCHANGE (ROCKVILLE). see *LABOR UNIONS*

380.5 US
INTERMODAL AGE. 1985. bi-m. $20. Simmons-Boardman Publishing Corporation, 345 Hudson St., New York, NY 10014-4502. TEL 212-620-7200. FAX 212-633-1165. Ed. Douglas John Bower. adv.; circ. 20,000.

380.52 US
INTERMODAL REPORTER;* news and analysis of the intermodal industry. 1985. s-m. $230 in U.S.; Canada $235; elsewhere $240. K - III Press, Inc., 424 W. 33rd St., New York, NY 10001. TEL 800-221-5488. FAX 212-695-5025. Ed. Robert J. Kursar. adv.; circ. 1,100.
   Description: Specializes in news, trends and analysis of the industry. Contains insight on equipment usage, rail policy, legislation, court rulings, pricing, labor liability, service innovations and technology.

380.5 UK ISSN 0032-5007
INTERNATIONAL FREIGHTING WEEKLY; sea, air, rail, road. 1962. w. £50. Maclean Hunter Ltd., Maclean Hunter House, Chalk Lane, Cockfosters Rd., Barnet, Herts EN4 0BU, England. TEL 081-975-9759. FAX 081-440-1796. TELEX 299072 MACHUN G. Ed. Paul Berrill. adv.; bk.rev.; charts; illus.; stat.; tr.lit.; circ. 19,828. (tabloid format) Indexed: BMT, PROMT.
   Incorporating: Ports and Terminals - International Freighting.

380.52 658.788 UK ISSN 0957-476X
▼**INTERNATIONAL JOURNAL OF RADIOACTIVE MATERIALS TRANSPORT.** 1990. 4/yr. £75 (foreign $170). Nuclear Technology Publishing, P.O. Box 7, Ashford, Kent TN25 4NW, England. TEL 233-641683. FAX 233-610021. TELEX 966119-NTP-UKG. Ed. E.P. Goldfinch. circ. 1,000. (back issues avail.) Indexed: Energy Info.Abstr., Environ.Abstr.
   —BLDSC shelfmark: 4542.524800.
   Description: Covers all aspects of the transport of radioactive materials including regulations, package design, safety assessments, testing, accidents and experience in the transport of all forms of radioactive materials.

380.5 IT ISSN 0391-8440
INTERNATIONAL JOURNAL OF TRANSPORT ECONOMICS/RIVISTA INTERNAZIONALE DI ECONOMICA DEI TRASPORTI. (Text and summaries in English) 1974. 3/yr. L.70000($64) Via G.A. Guattani 8, 00161 Rome, Italy. Ed. Gianrocco Tucci. adv.; bk.rev.; index; circ. 1,000. (back issues avail.) Indexed: BPIA, C.R.E.J., Geo.Abstr., HRIS, J.of Econ.Lit.
   —BLDSC shelfmark: 4542.696000.

380.5 621 SZ ISSN 0143-3369
TL1   CODEN: IJVDDW
INTERNATIONAL JOURNAL OF VEHICLE DESIGN; journal of vehicle engineering, automotive technology and components. (Text in English) 1979. bi-m. $190. (International Association for Vehicle Design) Inderscience Enterprises Ltd., World Trade Centre Bldg., 110 Ave. Louis Casai, Case Postale 306, CH-1215 Geneva-Aeroport, Switzerland. (Co-sponsor: UNESCO) Ed. M.A. Dorgham. adv.; bk.rev.; abstr.; charts; illus.; keyword index; circ. 10,000. Indexed: Agri.Eng.Abstr., Appl.Mech.Rev., Br.Tech.Ind., CAD CAM Abstr., Cadscan, Curr.Cont., Energy Info.Abstr., Eng.Ind., Environ.Abstr., Ergon.Abstr., Excerp.Med., HRIS, Ind.Sci.Rev., Lead Abstr., Met.Abstr., Phys.Abstr., Robomat., Sci.Abstr., Sci.Cit.Ind., Sh.& Vib.Dig., World Alum.Abstr., Zincscan.
   —BLDSC shelfmark: 4542.697500.
   Description: Contains articles on the engineering design, research into and development of all types of self-propelled vehicles and their components. Includes reports of events, technical notes, and readers' letters.

INTERNATIONAL SYMPOSIUM ON THE AERODYNAMICS AND VENTILATION OF VEHICLE TUNNELS. PROCEEDINGS. see *ENGINEERING — Civil Engineering*

380.5 SZ
INTERNATIONAL TRANSPORT JOURNAL - OVERSEAS DIGEST. French edition: Journal pour le Transport International. German edition: Internationale Transport Zeitschrift. 1939. w. 170 SFr. Rittman Ltd., Spalentorweg 9, Postfach, CH-4003 Basel, Switzerland. TEL 061-2618830. FAX 061-2610878. TELEX 962217. adv.; adv.: B&W page 4500 SFr.; trim 184 x 268. circ. 27,900.

INTERNATIONAL TRANSPORT WORKERS' FEDERATION REPORT ON ACTIVITIES. see *LABOR UNIONS*

386 BE ISSN 0074-9311
INTERNATIONAL UNION FOR INLAND NAVIGATION. ANNUAL REPORT. (Editions in French, German) 1953. a. free. International Union for Inland Navigation - Union Internationale de la Navigation Fluviale, 19 rue de la Presse, 1000 Brussels, Belgium.

380.5 BE
INTERNATIONAL UNION OF PUBLIC TRANSPORT. TECHNICAL REPORTS OF THE CONGRESSES. French edition: Union Internationale des Transports Publics. Rapports Techniques des Congres Internationaux (ISSN 0378-1976); German edition: Internationaler Verband fuer Oeffentliches Verkehrswesen. Technische Berichte zu den Internationalen Kongressen. 1885. biennial. 650 BEF. International Union of Public Transport, Av. de l'Uruguay 19, B-1050 Brussels, Belgium. TEL 322-673-6100. FAX 322-660-1072. TELEX 63916 UITP B. Ed. P. Laconte. adv.; circ. 18,000.
   Description: Deals with all problems of the urban and regional public transport.

625.5 AU
INTERNATIONALE SEILBAHN-RUNDSCHAU/INTERNATIONAL AERIAL LIFT REVIEW. (Text in French and German) 8/yr. S.1039. (Organizzazione Internationale dei Trasporti a Fune) Bohmann Druck und Verlag GmbH & Co. KG, Leberstr. 122, A-1110 Vienna, Austria. TEL 0222-741595. FAX 0222-741595-183. TELEX 132312. Ed.Bd. adv.; abstr.; charts; illus.; circ. 3,300.
   Formerly: Internationale Berg- und Seilbahn-Rundschau (ISSN 0253-3715)

380.5 SZ ISSN 0020-9341
INTERNATIONALE TRANSPORT-ZEITSCHRIFT/JOURNAL POUR LE TRANSPORT INTERNATIONAL/INTERNATIONAL TRANSPORT JOURNAL-OVERSEAS DIGEST. (Editions in French, German; summaries in English) 1939. w. 200 Fr. Rittmann Ltd., Spalentorweg 9, Postfach, 4003 Basel, Switzerland. FAX 061-2610878. TELEX 962217-TRA-CH. adv.; bk.rev.; illus.; circ. 20,200. Indexed: PROMT.

380.5 SZ
INTERNATIONALE TRANSPORT ZEITSCHRIFT. French edition: Journal pour le Transport International. English edition: International Transport Journal - Overseas Digest. (Includes: Overseas Digest) 1939. w. 200 SFr. Rittman Ltd., Spalentorweg 9, Postfach, CH-4003 Basel, Switzerland. TEL 061-2618830. FAX 061-2610878. TELEX 962217. Ed. F. Rittman. adv.: adv.; B&W page 3600 SFr.; trim 184 x 268. circ. 20,200 (9,600 French ed.; 10,600 German ed.).

380.5 SP ISSN 0213-3091
INTER-TRANSPORT. 1970. w. 14800 ptas. Publicaciones Men-Car, S.A., Paseo de Colon, 24, 08002 Barcelona, Spain. TEL 93-301-5516. FAX 93-318-6645. Eds. Juan Cardona, Manuel Cardona. adv.; illus.; stat.; circ. 13,500. (back issues avail.)
   Formerly: Men-Car, Guia de Medios de Transporte Internacional.

ISTITUTO ITALIANO DI NAVIGAZIONE. ATTI. see *AERONAUTICS AND SPACE FLIGHT*

380.5 RU ISSN 0134-7799
ITOGI NAUKI I TEKHNIKI: ORGANIZATSIYA UPRAVLENIYA TRANSPORTOM. irreg., vol.8, 1989. 5.40 Rub. Vsesoyuznyi Institut Nauchno-Tekhnicheskoi Informatsii (VINITI), Baltiiskaya ul. 14, Moscow A-219, Russia.
   —BLDSC shelfmark: 0128.198500.

380.52 RU ISSN 0202-7909
ITOGI NAUKI I TEKHNIKI: PROMYSHLENNYI TRANSPORT. irreg., vol.12, 1988. 6.60 Rub. Vsesoyuznyi Institut Nauchno-Tekhnicheskoi Informatsii (VINITI), Baltiiskaya ul. 14, Moscow A-219, Russia. (Subscr. to: Mezhdunarodnaya Kniga, Dimitrova ul. 39, 113095 Moscow, Russia)
   —BLDSC shelfmark: 0134.425000.

380.5 UK
JANE'S URBAN TRANSPORT SYSTEMS. 1982. a. £135($210) Jane's Information Group, Sentinel House, 163 Brighton Rd., Coulsdon, Surrey CR5 2NH, England. TEL 081-763-1030. FAX 081-763-1005. TELEX 916907 JANES G. (U.S. & Can. order from: Dept. DSM, 1340 Braddock Pl., Ste. 300, Box 1436, Alexandria, VA 22314-1651) Ed. Chris Bushell. adv.; index.
   Description: Comprehensive survey of urban transport systems and equipment manufacturers worldwide.

JARMUVEK, MEZOGAZDASAGI GEPEK; motorok, vasuti jarmuvek, kozuti jarmuvek, hajok, mezogazdasagi gepek, epitoipari gepek, repulogepek. see *ENGINEERING — Mechanical Engineering*

380.5 BL
JORNAL DOS TRANSPORTES.* vol.4, 1974. bi-m. Ministerio dos Transportes, Esplanado dos Ministerios, Bloco 9, Brasilia, Brazil. Ed. Walter Duarte. adv.; illus.

TRANSPORTATION

388 629.04   US   ISSN 0197-6729
TF1300   CODEN: JATRDC
JOURNAL OF ADVANCED TRANSPORTATION. 1967. 3/yr. $60. (Advanced Transit Association) Institute for Transportation, Inc., Box 4670, Duke Sta., Durham, NC 27706. TEL 919-660-5312. FAX 919-660-8963. Eds. Charles M. Harman, S.C. Wirasinghe. abstr.; bibl.; charts; illus.; stat.; circ. 1,000. (also avail. in microform from MIM,UMI; reprint service avail. from UMI) **Indexed:** Appl.Mech.Rev., Br.Rail.Bd., Eng.Ind., Fluidex, HRIS, Hwy.Res.Abstr.
—BLDSC shelfmark: 4918.947800.
Formerly (until vol.12, 1979): High Speed Ground Transportation Journal (ISSN 0018-1501)
Description: Includes ariticles for practitioners and scholars principally on advances in engineering, operations and economics of mass transportation.

JOURNAL OF COMMERCE, INDUSTRY & TRANSPORTATION. see BUSINESS AND ECONOMICS — Domestic Commerce

JOURNAL OF MOTOR VEHICLE LAW. see LAW

614.8   US   ISSN 0022-4375
HV675.A1   CODEN: JSFRAV
JOURNAL OF SAFETY RESEARCH. 1982. q. £105 (effective 1992). (National Safety Council) Pergamon Press, Inc., Journals Division, 660 White Plains Rd., Tarrytown, NY 10591-5153. TEL 914-524-9200. FAX 914-333-2444. (And: Headington Hill Hall, Oxford OX3 0BW, England. TEL 0865-794141) Ed. Thomas Planek. adv.; bk.rev. (also avail. in microform from UMI) **Indexed:** ASCA, Biol.Abstr., C.I.S. Abstr., Curr.Cont, Psychol.Abstr., Psycscan, Risk Abstr.
—BLDSC shelfmark: 5052.130000.
Refereed Serial

JOURNAL OF SHIPPING, CUSTOMS, AND TRANSPORT LAW. see LAW — Military Law

380.5 330   UK   ISSN 0022-5258
HE1
JOURNAL OF TRANSPORT ECONOMICS AND POLICY. 1967. 3/yr. £41($90) University of Bath, Claverton Down, Bath BA2 7AY, England. TEL 0225-826302. FAX 0225-826767. TELEX 449097. (Co-sponsor: London School of Economics and Political Science) Ed. S. Glaister. adv.; bk.rev.; index; circ. 1,300. (back issues avail.) **Indexed:** ABI Inform, BMT, BPIA, Br.Rail.Bd., C.R.E.J., Curr.Cont., Geo.Abstr., HRIS, J.of Econ.Lit., P.A.I.S., Risk Abstr., Rural Recreat.Tour.Abstr., SSCI, World Agri.Econ.& Rural Sociol.Abstr.
—BLDSC shelfmark: 5069.900000.

380.5 900   UK   ISSN 0022-5266
HE1
JOURNAL OF TRANSPORT HISTORY. 1953; N.S.1971. s-a. £25($45) to individuals; institutions £60($110). Manchester University Press, Oxford Rd., Manchester M13 9PL, England. TEL 061-273-5539. FAX 061-274-3346. TELEX 666517-UNIMAN. Ed. John Armstrong. adv.; bk.rev.; bibl.; illus.; circ. 600. (back issues avail.) **Indexed:** Amer.Hist.& Life, Br.Hum.Ind., Geo.Abstr., Hist.Abstr.; Mid.East: Abstr.& Ind.
—BLDSC shelfmark: 5070.000000.
Description: History of transport from a social and economic perspective.

380.5   II   ISSN 0970-4736
JOURNAL OF TRANSPORT MANAGEMENT. 1966. m. Rs.72 (foreign £20 or $30). Association of State Road Transport Undertakings, C.I.R.T. Bldg., Bhosari, Poona 411 026, India. TEL 83477. FAX 0212-84426. TELEX 146-212 CIRT IN. Ed. M.K. Thomas. adv.; bk.rev.; charts; illus.; stat.; circ. 2,100.
Supersedes (in Aug. 1977): State Transport News (ISSN 0039-016X)
Description: Articles about highway conditions and maintenance of transport vehicles.

629.04   US   ISSN 0733-947X
TA1001   CODEN: JTPEDI
JOURNAL OF TRANSPORTATION ENGINEERING. 1969. bi-m. $88 to non-members (foreign $97); members $22 (foreign $31). American Society of Civil Engineers, Air Transport, Highway, Pipeline, Urban Transportation Divisions, 345 E. 47th St., New York, NY 10017-2398. TEL 212-705-7288. FAX 212-980-4681. Ed. Kumares C. Sinha. circ. 5,200. **Indexed:** A.S.& T.Ind., BMT, CAD CAM Abstr., Curr.Cont., Deep Sea Res.& Oceanogr.Abstr., Dok.Str., Energy Info.Abstr., Eng.Ind., Environ.Abstr., Environ.Per.Bibl., Excerp.Med., Fluidex, Gas Abstr., GeoRef., HRIS, I D A, Ind.Sci.Rev., Intl.Civil Eng.Abstr., Soft.Abstr.Eng., W.R.C.Inf.
—BLDSC shelfmark: 5070.350000.
Former titles: Journal of Transportation and Pipeline Engineering; Transportation Engineering Journal (ISSN 0569-7891); American Society of Civil Engineers. Transportation Engineering Division. Journal (ISSN 0044-801X)
Description: Technical and professional articles on planning, design, construction, maintenance and operation of air, highway, and urban transportation, as well as pipeline facilities for water, oil and gas.
Refereed Serial

380.5   PK   ISSN 0075-5109
HE560.K3
KARACHI PORT TRUST. YEAR BOOK OF INFORMATION, PORT OF KARACHI, PAKISTAN. (Text in English) 1961. a. Rs.50. Karachi Port Trust, Post Box 4725, Karachi, Pakistan. TEL 201305. FAX 2415567. TELEX 2739 KPT PK. Ed. Kafil Ahmed Khan.

380.5   KE
KENRAIL. (Text in English, Swahili) 1955. m. free. Kenya Railways Corporation, Box 30121, Nairobi, Kenya. FAX 2542340049. TELEX 22254 RAILKE. Ed. E. Muthui. adv.; bk.rev.; illus.; circ. 22,500. (tabloid format)
Supersedes in part: Sikio (ISSN 0037-5136)

380.5   HU   ISSN 0023-4362
TA1001   CODEN: KOSZAZ
KOZLEKEDESTUDOMANYI SZEMLE. (Summaries in English, French, German, Russian) 1951. m. $38. (Kozlekedestudomanyi Egyesulet) Lapkiado Vallalat, Lenin korut 9-11, 1073 Budapest 7. TEL 222-408. (Subscr. to: Kultura, Box 149, H-1389 Budapest, Hungary) Ed. Bela Czere. charts; illus. **Indexed:** Rural Recreat.Tour.Abstr., Sci.Abstr., World Agri.Econ.& Rural Sociol.Abstr.

380.5   GW
KRAFTVERKEHRS HANDBUCH. a. DM.28.04. Verlag Heinrich Vogel, Neumarkterstr. 18, 8000 Munich 80, Germany. TEL 089-43180-0. FAX 089-4312837.

380.52   DK   ISSN 0108-8335
KRAKS TRANSPORTKATALOG. 1973. a. DKK 210. Kraks Forlag AS, Virumgardsvej 21, DK-2830 Virum, Denmark. TEL 45-834583. FAX 45-831011. adv.; circ. 10,000.

380.5   FI   ISSN 0023-5091
KULJETUS. 1958. m. FIM 300. Finnish Society for Transport Economy, Katjanokankatu 5 D 14, SF 00160 Helsinki, Finland. TEL 90-179-566. FAX 90-177-675. (Co-sponsor: Finnish Pallet Association) Ed. Kari Litja. adv.; circ. 3,800.
Description: For professionals in the transport and materials handling fields.

380.5   UK
L T NEWS. 1973. m. £7 (free to qualified personnel). London Regional Transport, 55 Broadway, Westminster, London SW1H OBD, England. Ed. A.B. Russell. adv.; bk.rev.; illus.; circ. 42,000.
Former titles (until 1990): L R T News; (until 1984): L T News.

LAMY TRANSPORT TOME 1; route. see LAW — International Law

LAMY TRANSPORT TOME 2; douane, commissionnaires de transport, transports maritime, transports par chemin de fer, transports aeriens, lexique. see LAW — International Law

LAMY TRANSPORT TOME 3; marchandises dangereuses. see LAW — International Law

380.5   FR   ISSN 0180-7811
LIAISONS TRANSPORTS EQUIPEMENT. 1977. m. 50 F. Confederation Francaise Democratique du Travail, Federation Generale des Transports et de l'Equipement, 47-49 ave Simon Bolivar, 75950 Paris Cedex 19, France.

LIBERIA. MINISTRY OF COMMERCE, INDUSTRY AND TRANSPORTATION. ANNUAL REPORT. see BUSINESS AND ECONOMICS — Production Of Goods And Services

388.342   IT   ISSN 0024-3779
LINEA Z;* quindicinale d'attualita e politica dei trasporti. 1962. fortn. L.7200. Organizzazione Zeppieri, Viale Castro Preto Rio 82, Rome, Italy. Ed. Pietro Zeppieri. adv.; stat.; circ. 4,000.
Description: Discusses public transportation topics.

388.322   UK   ISSN 0076-0013
LITTLE RED BOOK, CLASSIFIED TO ALL PUBLIC TRANSPORT FLEET OWNERS AND OPERATORS AND VEHICLE MANUFACTURERS. 1899. a. price varies. Ian Allan Ltd., Terminal House, Station Approach, Shepperton, Surrey TW17 8AS, England. TEL 0932-228950. Ed. Gavin Booth. adv.; circ. 3,000. (reprint service avail. from UMI)
Formerly: Passenger Transport Year Book.
Description: Trade directory for the road passenger transport industry.

380.5 630   US   ISSN 1043-1039
LIVE ANIMAL TRADE & TRANSPORT MAGAZINE. q. $20 (foreign $26). Silesia Companies, Inc., 619 Broad Creek Dr., Box 441110, Fort Washington, MD 20744-1110. TEL 301-292-1970. FAX 301-292-1781. circ. 1,750.
Description: Stories on every aspect of animal trade and transport.

LOG TRUCKER. see FORESTS AND FORESTRY — Lumber And Wood

380.5   IT
LOGISTICA; organizzazione, metodi e sistemi. 1970. 10/yr. L.80000 (foreign L.200000)(effective 1992). Tecniche Nuove s.p.a., Via C. Menotti 14, 20129 Milan, Italy. TEL 02-75701. FAX 02-7570205. Ed. G. Nardella. adv.; bk.rev.; abstr.; charts; illus.; pat.; tr.lit.; circ. 5,300.
Former titles: Magazzini e Trasporti - Logistica; Magazzini e Trasporti (ISSN 0024-9874)
Description: Information for storage, lifting and material handling technicians.

380.5   CN   ISSN 0047-4991
U168   CODEN: LGTRA5
LOGISTICS AND TRANSPORTATION REVIEW. 1965. 4/yr. $31. University of British Columbia, Centre for Transportation Studies, Vancouver, B.C. V6T 1Z2, Canada. TEL 604-822-4510. FAX 604-822-8521. TELEX 04-51233. Ed. W.G. Waters. adv.; bk.rev.; charts; illus.; pat.; tr.mk.; index; circ. 1,000. (also avail. in microform; reprint service avail. from UMI) **Indexed:** ABI Inform., BPIA, Bus.Ind., Cont.Pg.Manage., Curr.Cont., Geo.Abstr., HRIS, J.of Econ.Lit., Maize Abstr., Manage.Cont., Sci.Abstr., Tr.& Indus.Ind., Triticale Abstr., World Agri.Econ.& Rural Sociol.Abstr.
—BLDSC shelfmark: 5292.315000.
Former titles: Logistics Review (ISSN 0024-5844); Logistics Review and Military Logistics Journal.

LOGISTICS TODAY. see ENGINEERING — Mechanical Engineering

MALAWAI. NATIONAL STATISTICAL OFFICE. TRANSPORT STATISTICS. see TRANSPORTATION — Abstracting, Bibliographies, Statistics

380.5   MX
MAS CAMINOS; por un sistema integral de transportes. 1970. m. free. Asociacion Mexicana de Caminos, Tiber 103, 06500 Mexico D.F., Mexico. TEL 207-46-60. adv.; charts; illus. **Indexed:** Dok.Str.
Formerly (until Dec. 1990): Caminos (ISSN 0008-2236)

TRANSPORTATION

380.5   US   ISSN 0364-3484
HE4201
MASS TRANSIT.* 1974. m. $30. P T N Publishing Corp., 445 Broad Hollow Rd., Ste. 21, Melville, NY 11747-4722. TEL 516-845-2700. FAX 516-845-7109. Ed. Patricia S. Brucato. adv.; bk.rev.; circ. 18,000. **Indexed:** A.S.& T.Ind., Avery Ind.Archit.Per., B.P.I., Br.Rail.Bd., Dok.Str., HRIS, Ind.Sci.Rev., Tr.& Indus.Ind.
   Description: Covers urban transportation worldwide, focusing on transit authorities, construction projects, products, suppliers and consultants.

621.86   GW   ISSN 0170-334X
MATERIALFLUSS; Zeitschrift fuer Logisitk-Management, Transport, Lager, Versand. 1969. m. DM.158. Verlag Moderne Industrie, Justus-von-Liebig-Str. 1, 8910 Landsberg, Germany. TEL 08191-125-0. FAX 08191-125-483. TELEX 527208. Ed. Reinhard Irrgang. adv.; bk.rev.; illus.; circ. 15,000.

658.7 380.5   CN   ISSN 0025-5343
MATERIALS MANAGEMENT & DISTRIBUTION. 1956. m. Can.$33. Maclean Hunter Ltd., Business Publication Division, Maclean-Hunter Bldg., 777 Bay St., Toronto, Ont. M5W 1A7, Canada. TEL 416-596-5709. Ed. Richard Rix. adv.; bk.rev.; charts; illus.; stat.; tr.lit.; index; circ. 19,500. **Indexed:** Can.B.P.I., Excerp.Med., ISMEC.
   Formerly: Materials Handling in Canada.

380.5   MF   ISSN 0076-5554
MAURITIUS. MINISTRY OF WORKS AND INTERNAL COMMUNICATIONS. REPORT. a. price varies. Government Printing Office, Elizabeth II Ave., Port Louis, Mauritius.

380.5   US   ISSN 0162-6221
HE5601
METRO (REDONDO BEACH). 1904. bi-m. plus Factbook (Oct.) $25 (Canada $30; elsewhere $38). Bobit Publishing Company, 2512 Artesia Blvd., Redondo Beach, CA 90278. TEL 310-376-8788. FAX 310-376-9043. Ed. Bill Paul. adv.; charts; illus.; stat.; circ. 18,000 (controlled). **Indexed:** HRIS.
   Formerly: Metropolitan (ISSN 0026-1467)
   Description: Management information for transit bus, charter motorcoach and rail transit operations.

380.5 330   UK
MIDDLE EAST TRANSPORT. 1977. 10/yr. £25($60) A.F. Productions Ltd., 4 Lindfield Close, Saltdean, Brishton BN2 8AP, England. Ed. Alan Freeman. adv.; bk.rev.; illus.; stat.; circ. 6,527. (also avail. in microfilm; back issues avail.) **Indexed:** Key to Econ.SCi.
   Former titles (until 1988): Middle East Transport and Telecommunications; Middle East Industry and Transport (ISSN 0261-1473); Middle East Transport (ISSN 0140-8313)
   Description: Provides freight handling tips.

MOBILE ROBOTS AND UNMANNED VEHICLES. see COMPUTERS — Artificial Intelligence

380.5   US
MODERN TIRE DEALER: TIRE, TOOLS & EQUIPMENT MERCHANDISING GUIDE. 1972. a. $25. Bill Communications, Inc. (Akron), 341 White Pond Dr., Box 3599, Akron, OH 44309-3599. TEL 216-867-4401. FAX 216-867-0019. Ed. Lloyd Stoyer. adv.; circ. 33,000 (controlled). (reprint service avail. from UMI)
   Formerly: Modern Tire Dealer Products Catalog (ISSN 0026-8496)
   Description: Provides listings of tire dealer products.

380.52   NO   ISSN 0802-5193
MODERNE TRANSPORT. 1968. 11/yr. NOK 280. Teknisk Presse A.S, Hovfaret 17, P.O. Box 335 Skoeyen, N-0212 Oslo 2, Norway. TEL 47-2-52-10-40. FAX 47-2-50-66-48. Ed. Christian Ryg. adv.; circ. 9,164.
   Former titles: Moderne Bil Transport (ISSN 0801-5384); Moderne Transport (ISSN 0332-6128)
   Description: Covers logistics and transport. Also focuses on forwarding, warehousing, materials handling and packaging.

645   GW   ISSN 0047-780X
DER MOEBELSPEDITEUR.* 1946. fortn. DM.61. (Arbeitsgemeinschaft Moebeltransport Bundesverband e.V.) Verlag der Moebelspediteur, Brandeis Offenbacher Str. 113a, Postfach 482, D-6078 Neu-Isenburg, Germany. Eds. Walter Beier, Erich Hebel. adv.; circ. 1,840.

380.5   SA   ISSN 0258-719X
MOMENTUM. (Text and summaries in Afrikaans, English) q. free. Transnet Limited, P.O. Box 72501, Parkview 2122, South Africa. TEL 011-488-7139. FAX 011-488-7127. Ed. Alrika Hefers. bk.rev.; abstr.; bibl.; charts; illus.; circ. 15,000.
   Description: Details the role that transport plays in the socio-economic structures of South Africa.

MONDE DU CAMPING CAR. see TRAVEL AND TOURISM

388.346   UK   ISSN 0142-0011
MOTOR CARAVAN WORLD. m. £30. Stone Leisure Group Ltd., Andrew House, 2a Granville Rd., Sidcup, Kent DA14 4BN, England. TEL 081-302-6150. FAX 081-302-1813. Ed. Bob Griffith. adv.; illus.; circ. 23,800.
   Formerly: Motor Caravan Monthly.
   Description: Magazine covering all aspects of recreational vehicles in Europe.

MOTOR CARAVANNER. see SPORTS AND GAMES — Outdoor Life

380.5   NZ
MOTOR INDUSTRY YEAR BOOK. 1947. a. NZ.$36. New Zealand Motor Trade Federation, P.O. Box 11755, Wellington, New Zealand. TEL 04-858-893. FAX 04-858-899. TELEX NZ 31222. Ed. R.C. Morpeth. adv.; circ. 1,000.
   Description: Statistics on the motor trade.

380.5 340   CN   ISSN 0709-5341
KE2112.A45
MOTOR VEHICLE REPORTS. 1979. 12/yr. (in 6 vols.). Can.$115. Carswell Publications, Corporate Plazae., 2075 Kennedy Rd., Scarborough, Ont. M1T 3V4, Canada. TEL 416-609-8000. FAX 416-298-5094. Ed. Murray Segal. **Indexed:** Ind.Can.L.P.L.

388.322   US
MOTORCOACH MARKETER. 1985. a. (American Bus Association) Tom Jackson & Associates, Inc., 1210 Eighth Ave., S., Nashville, TN 37203. TEL 615-242-7747. FAX 615-259-2042. adv.; circ. 5,500.
   Description: Lists bus and tour operators and suppliers of bus products and services.

MOTORHOME. see SPORTS AND GAMES — Outdoor Life

MUTUALISTE DU METRO. see LABOR UNIONS

380.5   US
N A F A FLEET EXECUTIVE; the magazine for vehicle management. 1957. m. membership. National Association of Fleet Administrators, Inc., 120 Wood Ave., S., Ste. 615, Iselin, NJ 08830-2709. TEL 908-494-8100. FAX 908-494-6789. Ed. Denise M. Rucci. adv.; bk.rev.; illus.stat.; index; circ. 4,000. (back issues avail.) **Indexed:** SRI.
   Formerly: N A F A Bulletin.
   Description: Covers government legislation and regulation, survey results, interviews with prominent industry personalities, technological developments and intra-association news pertaining to car, van and light truck fleet management in the US and Canada.

380.5   US
N A F A FLEET FOCUS. vol.15, no.10, Oct. 1989. m. National Association of Fleet Administrators, Inc., 120 Wood Ave. S., Ste. 615, Iselin, NJ 08830-2709. TEL 201-494-8100. FAX 201-494-6789.
   Formerly: N A F A Newsletter.
   Description: Features timely legislative and association news, meeting and conference notices, and technological innovations.

380.5   US
N F T A ANNUAL REPORT. 1967. a. free. Niagara Frontier Transportation Authority, Public Information Officer, 181 Ellicott St., Buffalo, NY 14203. TEL 716-855-7300. FAX 716-855-7657. circ. 500.
   Description: Defines aims and goals of the NFTA, which are to maintain a transportation network for the benefit of the people of Western New York State. Reports on the NFTA's financial position.

380.5   NE
N I W O MEDEDELINGEN. irreg. free to qualified personnel. Nederlandsche Internationale Wegvervoer Organisatie, Postbus 3004, 2280 MB Rijswijk, Netherlands. TEL 070-3992011. adv.; circ. 3,500 (controlled).

N O A C A NEWS. (Northeast Ohio Areawide Coordinating Agency) see HOUSING AND URBAN PLANNING

N S T A ANNUAL SAFE TRANSIT CONFERENCE. PROCEEDINGS. (National Safe Transit Association) see PACKAGING

385   US
N Y C T A FACTS & FIGURES.* 1970. a. $5. New York City Transit Authority, 370 Jay St., Box M, Brooklyn, NY 11201. TEL 718-330-3000. Ed. Ruth Fredericks.

380.5   GW
NAHVERKEHR. 1983. bi-m. DM.120. Alba Fachverlag GmbH & Co., Postfach 320 108, Roemerstr. 9, D-4000 Duesseldorf 30, Germany. Ed. A. Teloeken. adv.; bk.rev.; circ. 3,000. **Indexed:** Dok.Str.

380.5   GW
NAHVERKEHRS NACHRICHTEN. Cover title: NaNa. 1956. w. Alf Teloeken, Ed. & Pub., Postfach 320 108, Roemerstr. 9, 4000 Duesseldorf 30, Germany. adv.; bk.rev.

388.322   US   ISSN 0194-939X
TL232
NATIONAL BUS TRADER; the magazine of bus equipment for the United States and Canada. 1977. m. $20 (foreign $25). National Bus Trader, Inc., 9698 Judson Rd., Polo, IL 60614. TEL 815-946-2341. FAX 815-946-2347. Ed. Larry Plachno. adv.; bk.rev.; circ. 6,000. (back issues avail.)
   Description: Covers integral design bus vehicles, primarily inter-city coaches.

380.5   US
NATIONAL COOPERATIVE TRANSIT RESEARCH AND DEVELOPMENT PROGRAM. RESEARCH RESULTS DIGEST. irreg., no.177, 1990. price varies. National Research Council, Transportation Research Board, 2101 Constitution Ave., N.W., Washington, DC 20418. TEL 202-334-3214. FAX 202-334-2519. circ. 2,800.
   Description: Informal reports providing early awareness of results of NCTRP research projects.

380.5   US   ISSN 0732-4839
NATIONAL COOPERATIVE TRANSIT RESEARCH AND DEVELOPMENT PROGRAM REPORT. irreg., no.17, 1990. price varies. National Research Council, Transportation Research Board, 2101 Constitution Ave., N.W., Washington, DC 20418. TEL 202-334-3214. FAX 202-334-2519. circ. 2,100. (also avail. in microfiche) **Indexed:** Dok.Str. —BLDSC shelfmark: 6021.866200.
   Description: Formal reports issued at the conclusion of NCTRP research projects.

380.5   US   ISSN 0732-1856
NATIONAL COOPERATIVE TRANSIT RESEARCH AND DEVELOPMENT PROGRAM SYNTHESIS OF TRANSIT PRACTICE. irreg., no.14, 1990. price varies. National Research Council, Transportation Research Board, 2101 Constitution Ave., N.W., Washington, DC 20418. TEL 202-334-3214. FAX 202-334-2519. (Co-sponsor: Urban Mass Transit Administration) circ. 2,300. (also avail. in microfiche) **Indexed:** Dok.Str.
   Description: Studies current practices in the field of public transit.

380.5   US
NATIONAL INDUSTRIAL TRANSPORTATION LEAGUE. NOTICE. 1936. w. membership. National Industrial Transportation League, 1700 N. Moore St., Ste. 1900, Arlington, VA 22209-1904. TEL 703-524-5011. FAX 703-524-5017. circ. 1,500.
   Description: Comprehensive information on domestic and international issues.

TRANSPORTATION

380.5   US   ISSN 0148-849X
NATIONAL RESEARCH COUNCIL. TRANSPORTATION RESEARCH BOARD. BIBLIOGRAPHY. 1947. irreg., no.64, 1989. price varies. National Research Council, Transportation Research Board, 2101 Constitution Ave., N.W., Washington, DC 20418. TEL 202-334-3214. FAX 202-334-2519. bibl. (also avail. in microfiche)
    Description: Summaries of published research findings in various transportation-related disciplines.

388.322   US   ISSN 0889-0749
LB2864
NATIONAL SCHOOL BUS REPORT. 1971. a. price varies. National School Transportation Association, Box 2639, Springfield, VA 22152. TEL 703-644-0700. Ed. Karen Finkel. adv.; stat.; tr.lit.; circ. 1,700.

387 623.89   AT   ISSN 0077-6262
V1
NAVIGATION. 1959. a. $5. Australian Institute of Navigation, Box 2250 G.P.O, Sydney, N.S.W, Australia. Ed. S. Cohen. adv.; bk.rev.; circ. 600.
    Indexed: Int.Aerosp.Abstr.

388 387   NE   ISSN 0168-5074
NETHERLANDS. CENTRAAL BUREAU VOOR DE STATISTIEK. STATISTIEK VAN HET PERSONENVERVOER/STATISTICS OF PASSENGER TRANSPORT. (Text in Dutch and English) 1943. a. Centraal Bureau voor de Statistiek, Prinses Beatrixlaan 428, Voorburg, Netherlands. (Dist. by: SDU - Publishers, Christoffel Plantijnstraat, The Hague, Netherlands)

380.5   US
NETWORK (EAST PEORIA); the magazine for international material handling. 1980. m. Woodward Communications, 252 E. Washington, Box 2338, E. Peoria, IL 61611. TEL 309-669-4431. adv.; circ. 14,000.
    Description: Covers news, manufacturers, new products, feature stories and people profiles.

380.15   GW   ISSN 0934-1307
NEUE ZEITSCHRIFT FUER VERKEHRSRECHT. 1988. m. DM.185. C.H. Beck'sche Verlagsbuchhandlung, Wilhelmstr. 9, 8000 Munich 40, Germany. TEL 089-381890. Ed.Bd. adv.; bk.rev. (back issues avail.)

380   US
NEW ENGLAND JOURNAL OF TRANSPORTATION. 1918. w. $72. 31 Fargo St., Box 404, Boston, MA 02127. TEL 617-695-1660. FAX 617-695-1665. Ed. George Lauriat. adv.; charts; illus.; stat.; circ. 5,000. (back issues avail.)
    Formerly (until 1989): Boston Marine Guide.
    Description: Covers all modes of cargo transportation and relevant developments in international and domestic trade.

380.5   US
NEW JERSEY. DEPARTMENT OF TRANSPORTATION. ANNUAL REPORT. 1894. a. free. Department of Transportation, 1035 Parkway Ave., CN 600, Trenton, NJ 08625. charts; illus.
    Former titles (until 1977): New Jersey. Department of Transportation. Highlight of Activities; (until 1974): New Jersey. Department of Transportation. Report of Operations (ISSN 0085-395X); (until 1970): New Jersey. Department of Transportation. Annual Report.

380.5   US
NEWSLINE (EVANSTON). s-a. Northwestern University Transportation Center, 1936 Sheridan Rd., Evanston, IL 60208-4040. TEL 708-491-7287. circ. 10,000.
    Description: Newsletter covering research, executive education, graduate education and placement. Includes industry updates related to the transportation center.

380.52 658.788   NE
NIEUWSBLAD TRANSPORT. 1987. 3/w. fl.315 (foreign fl.775). Transportuitgaven BV, P.O. Box 30180, 3001 DD Rotterdam, Netherlands. TEL 010-4053133. Ed. A.M. Sanders. adv.; bk.rev.; circ. 10,000. (newspaper; back issues avail.)
    Description: Covers transportation, distribution, export, and logistics.

380.5 910.09   GW
NIX WIE WEG; Mitfahrzentralen in Deutschland und aller Welt. (Text in English, French, German) 1980. w. Prolix Verlag GmbH, Goehtestr. 23, 7800 Freiburg, Germany. Ed. Daniel Jaeger. circ. 30,000. (back issues avail.)

LE NORD. see *FORESTS AND FORESTRY*

380.5 330   NO   ISSN 0359-7601
NORDISK KOMITE FOR TRANSPORT FORSKNING. PUBLIKATION. (Text in Norwegian, Danish or Swedish) irreg., no.64, 1990. free. Nordisk Komite for Transport Forskning - Nordic Committee of Transport Research, c/o Institute of Transport Economics, P.O. Box 6110, Etterstad, N-Oslo 6, Norway. TELEX 47-02-570290. circ. 1,200.

380.5
NORTHWESTERN UNIVERSITY. TRANSPORTATION CENTER. PUBLICATIONS LIST. 1978. a. free. Northwestern University, Transportation Center, 1936 Sheridan Rd., Evanston, IL 60208. TEL 708-492-7287. circ. 2,500.

380.5   US   ISSN 0029-4039
NOTES FROM UNDERGROUND. 1970. m. $16 to individuals; institutions $25 (includes Task Force Reports). Committee for Better Transit, Inc., Box 3106, Long Island City, NY 11103. TEL 718-728-0091. Ed. Stephen Dobrow. bk.rev.; circ. 2,500. (also avail. in microform from UMI; reprint service avail. from UMI)
    Incorporating: Better Transit Bulletin (ISSN 0006-0240)
    Description: News and views on mass transit and related areas, with emphasis on the New York-New Jersey metropolitan area.

NOTTINGHAM LICENSED TAXI OWNERS & DRIVERS ASSOCIATION. NEWSLETTER. see *BUSINESS AND ECONOMICS — Small Business*

380.5   SZ
NUTZVERKEHR MAGAZIN T I R; Transport Werkverkehr Logistik Bus Touristik. 1970. m. 60 Fr. (foreign 80 Fr.). Neue T I R Verlag AG, Dorfstr. 5, CH-3550 Langnau, Switzerland. TEL 035-21915. FAX 035-24642. circ. 12,000.

380.5   MP
▼**ODTEY BICHIG/SPECIAL DELIVERY.** (Text in Mongolian) 1990. q. Ulan Bator Railway Administration, Ulan Bator, Mongolia. circ. 35,603.
    Description: Published for transport and communication workers.

380.5   AU   ISSN 0029-9790
OESTERREICHISCHER PERSONENVERKEHR. vol.10, 1970. m. S.568. (Fachverband und Fachgruppe fuer die Befoerderungsgewerbe mit Personenkraftwagen sowie Autobusunternehmungen Oesterreichs) Oesterreichischer Wirtschaftsverlag, Nikolsdorfer Gasse 7-11, A-1051 Vienna, Austria. TEL 0222-555585. TELEX 1-11669. Ed. Heinz Thomann. adv.; bk.rev.; stat.; circ. 10,800.

380.5   US   ISSN 0190-6690
OFFICIAL INTERMODAL EQUIPMENT REGISTER. 1969. q. $53. K - III Press, Inc., 424 W. 33rd St., New York, NY 10001. TEL 800-221-5488. FAX 212-695-5025. adv.; circ. 2,500. (also avail. in magnetic tape)
    Description: Contains dimensions and capacities for 3,000,000 containers, trailers, bogies and chassis used by the companies listed.

OFFICIAL INTERMODAL GUIDE; directory of intermodal services, facilities and personnel. see *BUSINESS AND ECONOMICS — Trade And Industrial Directories*

380   US
OFFICIAL SHIPPERS GUIDE - CHICAGO MOTOR FREIGHT DIRECTORY. 1872. s-a. $35. Official Motor Freight Guide, Inc., 1130 S. Canal St., Chicago, IL 60607. TEL 312-939-1434. Ed. E. Eric Robison. adv.; charts; stat.

388.322 658.1   IT
OMNIBUS. 1979. q. free. Azienda Municipalizzata Trasporti Genova, Via Montaldo 2, I-16137 Genoa, Italy. TEL 010-5997437. FAX 5997400. TELEX 271090. Ed. Riccardo Canepa. adv.; bk.rev.; charts; illus.; stat.; circ. 10,000.
    Description: Publishes articles on current news in the public transportation industry.

388.322   UK   ISSN 0305-9243
OMNIBUS MAGAZINE. 1931. bi-m. £10. Omnibus Society, 39 Lilyhill Terrace, Edinburgh EH8 7DR, Scotland. TEL 031-661-3813. FAX 031-553-3943. Ed. Gavin Booth. adv.; bk.rev.; bibl.; circ. 800.
    —BLDSC shelfmark: 6256.550000.
    Description: Covers history and development of road passenger transport.

388.322   GW   ISSN 0724-7664
OMNIBUSSPIEGEL. 1979. bi-m. DM.54. Verlag Dieter Hanke, Am Weitgarten 37, 5300 Bonn 3, Germany. TEL 0228-440953. adv.; bk.rev.; circ. 1,200.

380.5   NE
OPENBAAR VERVOER (AMSTERDAM, 1958). 1958. m. fl.15 in Benelux (elsewhere fl.24.50). P.H. Kiers, Ed. & Pub., Assumburg 94, 1081 GC Amsterdam, Netherlands. TEL 020-6422979. adv.; bk.rev.; circ. 1,325.
    Description: Examines trains, trams, and buses in the Netherlands and Belgium and urban rail worldwide.

PACKUNG UND TRANSPORT; Fachmagazin fuer Verpackung, Materialfluss und Logistik. see *PACKAGING*

380.5 658 690   US
▼**PARKING TECHNOLOGY.** 1991. m. Witter Publishing Co., Inc., 84 Park Ave., Flemington, NJ 08822. TEL 908-788-0343. FAX 908-788-3781. adv.; circ. 25,000.
    Description: Covers aspects of parking facilities and technology including: construction, facility operations, and management.

380.5   US   ISSN 0364-345X
HE4441
PASSENGER TRANSPORT. 1943. w. $65. American Public Transit Association, 1201 New York Ave., N.W., Ste. 400, Washington, DC 20005. TEL 202-898-4119. FAX 202-898-4095. Ed. Dennis Kouba. adv.; stat.; index; circ. 4,073.
    Indexed: HRIS.

380.5   HU
PERIODICA POLYTECHNICA. TRANSPORTATION. (Text in English, German) q. $12. (Budapesti Muszaki Egyetem) Akademiai Kiado, Publishing House of the Hungarian Academy of Sciences, P.O. Box 24, H-1363 Budapest, Hungary.

380.5   NE   ISSN 0376-6772
PERSONENVERVOER.* 1947. 11/yr. fl.85. (Nederlandse Organisatie voor het Personenvervoer) Autotrend B.V., P.O. Box 55, 2235 ZH Valkenburg, Netherlands. FAX 070-559413. Ed. R.J. Tanja. adv.; bk.rev.; illus.; circ. 3,000 (controlled). **Indexed:** Key to Econ.Sci.

380.5   PH   ISSN 0031-7888
PHILIPPINES TRANSPORTATION.* 1952. m. P.12.($12) Manuel Vijungco, Ed. & Pub., Box 998, Manila, Philippines. adv.; illus.; mkt.; tr.lit.; circ. 6,500.

POCKET BOOK OF TRANSPORT STATISTICS OF INDIA. see *TRANSPORTATION — Abstracting, Bibliographies, Statistics*

380.5   RU   ISSN 0235-5116
POD'EMNO-TRANSPORTNAYA TEKHNIKA I SKLADY. 1972. 6/yr. 1.20 Rub. per no. Izdatel'stvo Transport, Komsomol'skii prosp., 42, 119048 Moscow G-48, Russia. Ed. G.N. Shishkin. illus.
    Indexed: C.I.S. Abstr.
    —BLDSC shelfmark: 0129.830000.
    Formerly (until 1989): Promyshlennyi Transport (ISSN 0131-5560)

380.5   PL
POLITECHNIKA KRAKOWSKA. ZESZYTY NAUKOWE. INZYNIERIA TRANSPORTOWA I ELEKTRYCZNA. (Text in Polish; summaries in English, French, German, Russian) 1977. irreg. price varies. Politechnika Krakowska, Ul. Warszawska 24, 31-155 Krakow, Poland. TEL 48-12-374289. FAX 48-12-335773. TELEX 322468 PK PL. (Dist. by: Ars Polona-Ruch, Krakowskie Przedmiescie 7, 00-068 Warsaw, Poland) bibl.; charts; illus.; circ. 200.
    Formerly: Politechnika Krakowska. Zeszyty Naukowe. Transport (ISSN 0860-0783)

380.5   PL   ISSN 0209-3324
**POLITECHNIKA SLASKA. ZESZYTY NAUKOWE.
TRANSPORT.** 1983. irreg. Politechnika Slaska, Katowicka 7, 44-100 Gliwice, Poland. FAX 371655. TELEX 036304. (Dist. by: Ars Polona, Krakowskie Przedmiescie 7, 00-068 Warsaw, Poland) Ed. Barbara Maciejna. circ. 205.

380.5   US
PORT OF DETROIT LOG. 1984. 3/yr. $10. Fourth Seacoast Publishing Co., Inc., 25300 Little Mack, St. Clair Shores, MI 48081. TEL 313-779-5570. FAX 313-779-5547. (Subscr. to: Box 145, St. Clair Shores, MI 48080) Ed. Roger J. Buysse.

387   US   ISSN 0085-5030
HE554.N4
PORT OF NEW ORLEANS ANNUAL DIRECTORY. 1969. a. free to qualified personnel. Port of New Orleans, 2 Canal St., Box 60046, New Orleans, LA 70160. TEL 504-528-3249. FAX 504-524-4156. TELEX 58-7496. Ed. Paul S. McKelvey. adv.; bk.rev.; charts; illus.; stat.; circ. 20,000 (controlled).
    Description: Covers port administration, planned improvements, computer capabilities, intermodal connections, facilities and tariffs. Includes a listing of maritime businesses in the New Orleans area by services.

POWDER HANDLING & PROCESSING. see *TECHNOLOGY: COMPREHENSIVE WORKS*

POWER LETTER. see *ENERGY*

380.5   CS   ISSN 0032-7514
PREPRAVNI A TARIFNI VESTNIK/TRANSPORTATION AND TARIFF NEWS. 1945. fortn. 101.40 Kcs.($8.66) Federalni Ministerstvo Dopravy, c/o Editorial Office, Hybernska 5, 115 78 Prague 1, Czechoslovakia. (Subscr. to: PNS-Ustredni Expedice a Dovoz Tisku Prague, Administrava Vyvozu Tisku, Kovpakova 26, 16000 Prague 6, Czechoslovakia) Ed. Irena Hrabankova. bk.rev.; circ. 9,760.

PRESHIPMENT TESTING. see *PACKAGING*

PREVISIONS GLISSANTES DETAILLEES EN PERSPECTIVES SECTORIELLES (VOL.33): TRANSPORTS. see *BUSINESS AND ECONOMICS — Economic Situation And Conditions*

380.5   CN
PRIVILEGE. q. (Air Canada) Southam Printing Limited, Airmedia Division, 150 John St., Ste. 900, Toronto, Ont. M5V 3E3, Canada. TEL 416-591-1551. FAX 416-591-3511. Ed. Karen Hanley. adv.; circ. 90,000.

380.5   US
PRO-DEVELOPMENT LETTER. 1983. q. $25. American Society of Transportation and Logistics, Inc., 3600 Chamberlain Ln., No. 232, Louisville, KY 40241-1989. TEL 502-425-1780. Ed. Joseph Cavinato. circ. 2,000. (tabloid format; back issues avail.)
    Description: For professional development in transportation, logistics, and physical distribution management.

380.5   US
PROFESSIONAL BROKER. 1980. bi-m. $70. Transportation Brokers Conference of America, 60 Revere, Ste. 500, Northbrook, IL 60062. TEL 708-480-1046. FAX 708-480-9282. Ed. Lisa Richter-Matthews. adv.; circ. 2,865.
    Description: Covers the development and technical aspects of transportation brokerage.

380.5   PL   ISSN 0033-2232
PRZEGLAD KOMUNIKACYJNY; miesiecznik ekonomiczno-techniczny. 1945. m. $7.20. Stowarzyszenie Inzynierow i Technikow Komunikacji (SITK), Ul. Czackiego 3-5, Warsaw, Poland. (Dist. by: Ars Polona- Ruch, Krakowskie Przedmiescie 7, Warsaw, Poland) Ed. Tadeusz Basiewicz. bk.rev.; bibl.; charts; illus.; stat.; index, cum.index; circ. 3,600.

380.5   BE
HE4201
PUBLIC TRANSPORT INTERNATIONAL. (Text in English, French, German) 1952. q. 2000 BEF. International Union of Public Transport, Av. de l'Uruguay 19, B-1050 Brussels, Belgium. TEL 322-673-6100. FAX 322-660-1072. TELEX 63916 UITP B. Ed. Pierre Laconte. adv.; bk.rev.; abstr.; tr.lit.; index, cum.index: 1952-1984; circ. 19,500. **Indexed:** Dok.Str., HRIS.
    Formerly: U I T P Revue (ISSN 0041-5154); **Supersedes:** International Union of Tramways, Light Railways and Motor Omnibuses. Review.

380.5   CN   ISSN 0702-0996
HE30.Q4
QUEBEC (PROVINCE). COMMISSION DES TRANSPORTS DU QUEBEC. RAPPORT ANNUEL. a. Can.$2. (Commission des Transports du Quebec) Ministere des Communications, Direction Generale des Publications Gouvernementales, 2e etage, 1279 boul. Charest Ouest, Quebec, Que. G1N 4K7, Canada. TEL 413-643-3895.
    Formerly: Quebec (Province). Commission des Transports. Rapports des Activites de la Commission des Transports du Quebec (ISSN 0318-5303)

380.5 069   US
R.E. OLDS TRANSPORTATION MUSEUM NEWSLETTER. 1980. q. membership. R.E. Olds Transportation Museum Association, Inc., 240 Museum Dr., Lansing, MI 48933. TEL 517-372-0422. adv.; bk.rev.; circ. 1,200. (looseleaf format; back issues avail.)
    Description: Covers topics of interest to museum members, including Lansing-built transportation (cars, airplanes, bicycles and trucks).

R M F. (Rail Miniature Flash) see *HOBBIES*

796.5   US
R V BUYERS GUIDE. (Recreational Vehicle) 1982. a. $3.95. T L Enterprises, Inc., 29901 Agoura Rd., Agoura, CA 91301. TEL 818-991-4980. Ed. Bill Estes. adv.; circ. 100,000.
    Description: Advice on choosing an RV. Listings of more than 500 motorhomes, trailers and campers.

388.346   US
R V NEWS.* (Recreational Vehicle) 1975. m. $36. D & S Media Enterprises, Inc., 6125 S. Ash Ave, Ste. B8, Tempe, AZ 85283-5608. TEL 818-991-6043. Ed. Sherman Goldenberg. adv.; circ. 24,871.
    Description: Covers general news about the recreational vehicle industry.

380.5   MX
REALIDADES. 1955. m. Mex.$4 per no. Direccion General de Transito, Palma Norte 413-105, Mexico 1, D.F., Mexico. adv.; circ. 10,000.

380.5   FR   ISSN 0304-3320
HE192.5
RECHERCHE EN MATIERE D'ECONOMIE DES TRANSPORTS/RESEARCH ON TRANSPORT ECONOMICS. 1968. a. 400 F.($85) Organization for Economic Cooperation and Development, European Conference of Ministers of Transport, 19 rue de Franqueville, 75775 Paris Cedex 16, France. FAX 45-24-97-42. TELEX 611040. (Dist. by: O.E.C.D. Publication Service, 2 rue Andre-Pascal, 75775 Paris Cedex 16, France. TEL 45-24-82-00; U.S. orders to: O.E.C.D. Publications and Information Center, 2001 L St., N.W., Suite 700, Washington, D.C. 20036-4095) circ. 800. (also avail. in microfiche from OEC) **Indexed:** BMT.
●Also available online. Vendor(s): European Space Agency (File no.74/TRANSDOC Subfile: RESEARCH). —BLDSC shelfmark: 7773.780000.
    Description: Presents a general review of research activities undertaken in the ECMT member countries as well as a selection of American projects.

387 623.8   UK   ISSN 0080-0422
REED'S NAUTICAL ALMANAC. (In three editions: European, American East Coast & Mediteranean) 1931. a. $27.50. Thomas Reed Publications Ltd., Weir House, Hurst RD., E. Molesey, Surrey KT8 9AQ, England. TEL 081-941-8090. FAX 081-941-8046. TELEX 883526-REED-G. Ed. Jean Fowler. index.

380.5   FR
REGIE AUTONOME DES TRANSPORTS PARISIENS. BULLETIN DE DOCUMENTATION ET D'INFORMATION. Short title: Documentation, Information-R A T P. 5/yr. Regie Autonome des Transports Parisiens, Direction des Etudes Generales, 53 ter Quai des Grands Augustins, 75271 Paris Cedex 6, France. illus.
    Formerly: Regie Autonome des Transports Parisiens. Bulletin d'Information et de Documentation Generale.

380.5 658   UK   ISSN 0034-4265
REMOVALS AND STORAGE. 1924. m. membership. (British Association of Removers) Quarrington-Curtis Ltd., 15 Canute Rd., Southampton SO1 1FJ, England. TEL 0703 63438. FAX 0703-632198. TELEX 477704. Ed. Stephen J. Webb. adv.; bk.rev.; circ. 1,800 (controlled).

RESALE WEEKLY. see *BUILDING AND CONSTRUCTION*

380.5   US
RESEARCH IN TRANSPORTATION ECONOMICS. 1983. a. $63.50 to institutions. J A I Press Inc., 55 Old Post Rd., No. 2, Box 1678, CT 06836-1678. TEL 203-661-7602. Ed. Theodore E. Keeler.

380.5   BL
REVISTA O CARRETEIRO. m. Rua Palacete das Aguias 284, 04635 Sao Paulo SP, Brazil. TEL 11-533-5237. Dir. Jose A. de Castro. circ. 160,000.

380.5   RM
REVISTA TRANSPORTURILOR SI TELECOMUNICATIILOR; transport feroviar; auto, drumuri, navigatie; posta si telecomunicatii. (Text in Rumanian; summaries in English, French, German and Russian) 1974. m. $87. Ministerul Transporturilor si Telecomunicatiilor, Calea Grivitei 193b, 78141 Bucharest, Rumania. (Subscr. to: ROMPRESFILATELIA, Sectorul Export-Import Presa, P.O. Box 12-201, Galea Grivitei nr.64-66, 10376 Bucharest, Rumania) (Co-sponsor: Institutul de Cercetari si Proiectari Tehnologice in Transporturi) Ed. Sabin Petrean. adv.; bk.rev.; bibl.; charts; illus. **Indexed:** C.I.S. Abstr., Dok.Str.

388.3   SZ   ISSN 0005-1314
REVUE AUTOMOBILE; journal suisse de l'automobile. German ed.: Automobil Revue. (Text in French) 1906. w. 102 Fr. for German ed. (foreign 165 Fr.); French ed. 81 Fr. (foreign 129 Fr.). Hallwag AG, Nordring 4, CH-3001 Berne, Switzerland. TEL 031-423131. FAX 031-414133. TELEX 912 661 CH. adv.; bk.rev.; charts; illus.; mkt.; stat.; circ. 76,916 (French ed. 22,445; German ed. 54,261).

RIVISTA GIURIDICA DELLA CIRCOLAZIONE E DEI TRASPORTI. see *LAW*

380.5 388.31   UK
ROAD DOCUMENTATION FOR DEVELOPING COUNTRIES. a. free. Transport and Research Laboratory, Overseas Unit, Old Wokingham Rd., Crowthorne, Berkshire, England. Ed. S.G. Jobbins. circ. 500.

380.5   JA   ISSN 0917-0863
ROAD HOME. 1989. 6/yr. International Highway Construction Corporation, 37-13 Udagawa-cho, Shibuya-ku, Tokyo 150, Japan. TEL 03-3481-5733. FAX 03-3481-5994. Ed. Tateo Yamaoka.
    Description: Aims to promote world peace by proposing an international highway that links all nations of the world, including a highway through China and an undersea tunnel connecting Japan and Korea.

388   US   ISSN 0048-8542
ROLLING ALONG. 1949. q. free. North Dakota Motor Carriers Association, Box 874, Bismarck, ND 58502. (Affiliate: American Trucking Association) Ed. LeRoy H. Ernst. adv.; circ. 3,000.

384 380.52   UK
ROUTES; directory of International Freighting Services. (Supplement to: International Freighting Weekly) 1972. q. Maclean Hunter Ltd., Maclean Hunter House, Chalk Lane, Cockfosters Rd., Barnet, Hersts EN4 0BU, England. TEL 081-975-9759. FAX 081-440-1796. TELEX 299072 MACHUN G. Ed. Mike Banks. adv.; bk.rev.; circ. 19,118.

S C & R A NEWSLETTER. (Specialized Carriers & Rigging Association) see *TRANSPORTATION — Trucks And Trucking*

TRANSPORTATION

380.5 US ISSN 0486-8323
SAFE DRIVER. 1954. m. $19 to non-members; members $15. National Safety Council, Industrial Section, 444 N. Michigan Ave., Chicago, IL 60611. TEL 800-621-7619. Ed. Kathleen Knowles. circ. 190,000.

SAFETY, INDUSTRIAL RELATIONS, AND GOVERNMENT AFFAIRS SPECIAL REPORT. see *TRANSPORTATION — Trucks And Trucking*

SAMFERDSEL. see *TRANSPORTATION — Roads And Traffic*

380.5 US ISSN 0362-2800
SAN FRANCISCO BAY AREA RAPID TRANSIT DISTRICT. ANNUAL REPORT. 1958. a. San Francisco Bay Area Rapid Transit District, 800 Madison St., Oakland, CA 94607. TEL 415-464-6000. Ed. Michael Healy. illus.; circ. 5,000. Key Title: Annual Report - San Francisco Bay Area Rapid Transit District.

380.5 SZ ISSN 0080-6048
SANKT GALLER BEITRAEGE ZUM FREMDENVERKEHR UND ZUR VERKEHRSWIRTSCHAFT: REIHE VERKEHRSWIRTSCHAFT. 1970. irreg., no.14, 1991. price varies. (Hochschule St. Gallen fuer Wirtschafts- und Sozialwissenschaften, Institut fuer Fremdenverkehr und Verkehrswirtschaft) Paul Haupt AG, Falkenplatz 14, 3001 Berne, Switzerland. TEL 031-232425.

380.5 US
SCHOOL BUS BRIEFS. q. free. Department of Public Instruction, Pupil Transportation Service, 125 S. Webster St., Box 7841, Madison, WI 53707-7841. Ed. Kathleen J. Cole. circ. controlled.
Formerly: Chrome Yellow.

388.3 US ISSN 0036-6501
SCHOOL BUS FLEET. vol.15, 1970. bi-m. plus Factbook (Jan.). $25 (Canada $30; elsewhere $38). Bobit Publishing Company, 2512 Artesia Blvd., Redondo Beach, CA 90278. TEL 310-376-8788. FAX 310-376-9043. Ed. Jody Bush. adv.; charts; illus.; stat.; circ. 19,000 (controlled). Indexed: HRIS, SRI.
Description: Serving the universe of pupil transportation.

338.322 370 US
▼**SCHOOL TRANSPORTATION NEWS.** 1991. 11/yr. $24. B P Communications, 415 Paulina St., Redondo Beach, CA 90277. TEL 213-379-9949. FAX 213-379-7092. adv.; circ. 15,000. (tabloid format)
Description: Focuses on news developments in school transportation at all academic levels.

388 UK ISSN 0048-9808
SCOTTISH TRANSPORT. 1963. a. £11.25 for 3 nos. Scottish Tramway and Transport Society, P.O. Box 78, Glasgow G3 6ER, Scotland. Ed. Brian T. Deans. adv.; bk.rev.; circ. 1,500. (reprint service avail. from UMI)
—BLDSC shelfmark: 8211.270000.
Formerly: Scottish Tramlines.

380.5 SA ISSN 0038-2760
SOUTH AFRICAN TRANSPORT; the independent transport journal. 1969. m. R.48($20) Bolton Publications (Pty) Ltd., 49A Seventh Ave., Parktown North 2193, South Africa. TEL 011-880-3520. FAX 880-6574. Ed. Richard Proctor-Sims. adv.; bk.rev.; charts; illus.; index; circ. 3,500. (also avail. in microform from UMI; reprint service avail. from UMI) Indexed: Ind.S.A.Per.

380.5 US ISSN 0362-2843
SOUTHERN CALIFORNIA RAPID TRANSIT DISTRICT. ANNUAL REPORT. 1964. a. free. Southern California Rapid Transit District, Marketing Department, 425 S. Main, Los Angeles, CA 90013-1393. TEL 213-972-4660. FAX 213-972-4669. Eds. Anthony Fortuno, Mike Barnes. illus.; circ. 17,000. Key Title: Annual Report - Southern California Rapid Transit District.

380.5 SP ISSN 0210-9220
SPAIN. MINISTERIO DEL INTERIOR. DIRECCION GENERAL DE TRAFICO. BOLETIN INFORMATIVO. 1960. m. Ministerio del Interior, Direccion General de Trafico, Calle J. Valcarcel, 28, 28071 Madrid, Spain. illus.; stat.; circ. 2,600.

380.52 GW ISSN 0342-7749
DER SPEDITEUR. 1953. m. DM.45. Deutscher Verkehrs-Verlag GmbH, Nordkanalstr. 36, Postfach 101609, 2000 Hamburg 1, Germany. TEL 040-2371401. FAX 040-23714123. Ed. Bernhard Kaltz. adv.: B&W page DM.4100; trim 260 x 175; adv. contact: Werner Holders. circ. 5,877.

380.5 GW ISSN 0038-9013
STADTVERKEHR. 1956. 10/yr. DM.85. E K Verlag, Mercystr. 15, Postfach 5560, 7800 Freiburg, Germany. TEL 0761-75033. Ed. Eva Kunow. adv.; bk.rev.; charts; illus.; index; circ. 6,000.
Description: Discusses public transport facilities.

380.5 UK
STEAM HERITAGE YEARBOOK, PRESERVED TRANSPORT & INDUSTRIAL ARCHAEOLOGY GUIDE. 1968. a. £2.30. T E E Publishing, Edwards Centre, Regent St., Hinckley, Leics. LE10 0BB, England. Ed. C.L. Deith. adv.; circ. 25,000.
Former titles: Steam Year Book, Preserved Transport and Industrial Archaeology Guide; Steam and Organ Year Book and Preserved Transport Guide.

380.5 AU ISSN 0029-9073
DER STRASSENGUETERVERKEHR. m. S.592. (Gewerbliches Gueterbefoerderungswesen Oesterreichs) Oesterreichischer Wirtschaftsverlag, Nikolsdorfer Gasse 7-11, A-1051 Vienna 5, Austria. TEL 0222-555585. TELEX 1-11669. Ed. Heinz Thomann. circ. 9,200. Indexed: Sci.Abstr.
Formerly: Oesterreichische Fuhrwerker-Zeitung.

380.5 AT
STREET MACHINE. 1977. 8/yr. Aus.$36. Australian Consolidated Press, 54-58 Park St., Sydney, N.S.W. 2000, Australia. TEL 02-282-8000. FAX 02-267-2150. Ed. Tim Britten. circ. 71,500.
Formerly: Van Wheels.

STUDIEN ZUR VERKEHRSWIRTSCHAFT. see *BUSINESS AND ECONOMICS*

380.5 CN
SURFACE TRANSPORTATION R & D IN CANADA. 1963. a. Can.$10.50 to non-members; members Can.$7. Transportation Association of Canada, 2323 St. Laurent Blvd., Ottawa, Ont. K1G 4K6, Canada. TEL 613-736-1350. FAX 613-736-1395. Ed. C.J. Hedges. index.
Former titles: Transportation R and D in Canada (ISSN 0381-8284); Transportation Research in Canada; Road Research in Canada.
Description: Summarizes research and development projects carried out by federal and provincial transport ministries, universities and the private sector.

380.5 CN
T A C NEWS; executive digest - focus. French edition: Nouvelles de l'A T C. 1975. bi-m. Can.$54 to non-members. Transportation Association of Canada, 2323 St. Laurent Boulevard, Ottawa, Ont. K1G 4K6, Canada. TEL 613-736-1350. FAX 613-736-1395. Ed. Harvey F. Chartrand. circ. 2,000. (back issues avail.)
Formerly: R T A C News (ISSN 0317-1280)
Description: Reviews association activities and general developments and trends in transportation in Canada and abroad.

380.5 US
T B C A UPDATE. bi-m. Transportation Brokers Conference of America, 60 Revere Dr., Ste. 500, Northbrook, IL 60062-1577. TEL 708-480-1046. FAX 708-480-9282. Ed. Lisa Richter Matthews.

380.5 US ISSN 0738-6826
TE1
T R NEWS. 1963. bi-m. $38 to N. America; elsewhere $41. National Research Council, Transportation Research Board, 2101 Constitution Ave., N.W., Washington, DC 20418. TEL 292-334-3218. FAX 202-334-2519. Ed. Nancy A. Ackerman. bk.rev.; charts; illus.; circ. 10,000. Indexed: Br.Rail.Bd., Dok.Str., Geotech.Abstr., Intl.Civil Eng.Abstr., Noise Pollut.Publ.Abstr., Soft.Abstr.Eng.
Former titles: Transportation Research News (ISSN 0095-2656); Highway Research News (ISSN 0018-1749)
Description: Features articles on innovative practices and current research in all modes of transportation.

380.5 SZ
T T - REVUE. (Transport und Tourismus) 1945. m. 39 Fr. Verband Oeffentlicher Verkehr, Daehlhoelzliweg 12, CH-3000 Berne 6, Switzerland. Dir. Dr. C. Pfund. adv.; bk.rev.; abstr.; illus.; stat.; circ. controlled.
Formerly: V S T Revue (ISSN 0042-1928)

T W U EXPRESS. (Transport Workers Union of America) see *LABOR UNIONS*

380.5 CH
TAIWAN TRANSPORTATION EQUIPMENT GUIDE. 3/yr. NT.$1000($40) in Asia, Middle East, Oceania; elsewhere $50. China Economic News Service, 561 Chunghsiao E. Rd. Sec. 4, Taipei, Taiwan 10516, Republic of China. TEL 02-642-2629. FAX 02-642-7422. TELEX 27710-CENSPC.

380.5 FR
TARIF PIECES DETACHEES. 1969. q. 555 F. Editions Techniques pour l'Automobile et l'Industrie (ETAI), 20-22 rue de la Saussiere, 92100 Boulogne-Billancourt, France. TEL 46-04-81-13. FAX 48-25-56-92. TELEX ETAIRTA 204850F. Ed. Daniel Thallinger.
Description: Covers 120 domestic and import cars. Indicates prices of car parts (body as well as engine).

TASMANIAN TRANSPORT STATISTICS. see *TRANSPORTATION — Abstracting, Bibliographies, Statistics*

388.321 UK ISSN 0049-304X
TAXI; the newspaper of the taxi trade. 1968. fortn. £18. Licensed Taxi Drivers Association, 9-11 Woodfield Rd., London W9 2BA, England. FAX 071-286-2494. Ed. David Barnes. adv.; bk.rev.; illus.; tr.lit.; circ. 10,000.

388.321 NO
TAXI. m. (10/yr.). NOK 40. Norges Taxiforbund, Trondheimsvn. 100, Box 6538 R, Oslo 5, Norway. Ed. Kolbjoern Bekkelund.
Formerly: Norsk Drosjeeierblad (ISSN 0048-0584)

380.5 AT
TAXI. bi-m. members only. (N.S.W. Taxi Association) Associated Business Publications (Pty) Ltd., 104-3 Smail St., Ultimo, N.S.W. 2007, Australia. Ed. John Bowe. adv.; bk.rev.; circ. 4,000.

388.321 US
TAXI & LIVERY MANAGEMENT. q. International Taxicab Association, 3849 Farragut Ave., Kensington, MD 20895-2004. TEL 301-946-5701. FAX 301-946-4641. Ed. Irene Weiniger. adv.; circ. 5,800.

388.321 AT
TAXI NEWS. 1949. m. Aus.$1. (Taxi Council of Queensland) A. Webb & Sons Pty. Ltd., 60 Baxter St., Fortitude Valley 4006, Australia. Ed. C.H. Dwyer. adv.; circ. 2,000. (tabloid format)

388.321 CN
TAXI NEWS. 1985. m. Can.$12($30) Chedmount Investment Ltd., 38 Fairmount Cres., Toronto, Ont. M4L 2H4, Canada. TEL 416-468-2328. FAX 416-466-4220. Ed. John Duffy. adv.; bk.rev.; circ. 10,000. (back issues avail.)
Description: News and events affecting Canada's taxi industry.

388.321 UK ISSN 0040-0254
TAXINEWS. 1960. 6/yr. £4. Owner Drivers Society, 21 Buckingham Palace Road, London SW1W 0PN, England. TEL 01-834-3976. Ed. E.S. Perry. adv.; bk.rev.; illus.; circ. 12,000.

388.321 SW ISSN 0040-022X
TAXITRAFIKEN. m. Svenska Taxifoerbundet, Warfvinges Vaeg 29, 112 51 Stockholm, Sweden. Ed. Berndt Bryngelsson. adv.; charts; illus.; circ. 9,700.

TRANSPORTATION   4657

380.5   US   ISSN 0040-4748
CODEN: TXTRA8
TEXAS TRANSPORTATION RESEARCHER. 1965. q. in U.S. & Canada free (foreign $25). Texas Transportation Institute, Texas A & M Univ. System, College Sta., TX 77843-3135. TEL 409-845-1734. FAX 409-845-9848. Ed. Susan Lancaster. illus.; index; circ. 4,300. (also avail. in microform from UMI) **Indexed:** Eng.Ind.
Description: Showcases transportation research and professional activities of the Institute.

385.2   UK   ISSN 0266-9404
THOMAS COOK AIRPORTS GUIDE EUROPE. (Text in English; summaries in French, German, Italian, Spanish) 1984-1987; resumed 1990. biennial. Thomas Cook Publishing, P.O. Box 227, Peterborough PE3 6SB, England. Ed. S. York. adv.; index; circ. 17,000.
Formerly: Thomas Cook Airport Links (ISSN 0265-4415)

385.2 387.54   UK   ISSN 0952-620X
HE3004   CODEN: TCETEY
THOMAS COOK EUROPEAN TIMETABLE; railway and shipping services throughout Europe. (Text in English; summaries in French, German, Spanish) 1873. m. £95.40 (foreign £132). Thomas Cook Publishing, P.O. Box 227, Peterborough PE3 6SB, England. TEL 0733-268943. FAX 0733-505792. TELEX 32581. Ed. B.A. Fox. adv.; index; circ. 204,000.
—BLDSC shelfmark: 8820.230150.
Former titles (until 1980): Thomas Cook Continental Timetable (ISSN 0144-7467); Supersedes in part (in 1980): Thomas Cook International Timetable (ISSN 0141-2701); Thomas Cook Continental Timetable; Cooks Continental Timetable (ISSN 0010-8286)
Description: Comprehensive timetable for railway and shipping services throughout Europe, with maps, town plans, passport and visa regulations.

385.2 387.54   UK   ISSN 0144-7475
HE1805   CODEN: TCOTDF
THOMAS COOK OVERSEAS TIMETABLE; railway, road and shipping services outside Europe. (Text in English; summaries in French, German, Italian, Spanish) 1981. bi-m. £47.10 (foreign £63.60). Thomas Cook Publishing, P.O. Box 227, Peterborough PE3 6SB, England. TEL 0733-268943. FAX 0733-505792. TELEX 32581. Ed. P.I. Tremlett. adv.; index; circ. 24,000.
—BLDSC shelfmark: 8820.230300.
Supersedes in part (in 1980): Thomas Cook International Timetable (ISSN 0141-2701)
Description: Comprehensive timetables for rail, bus and shipping services for virtually all countries outside Europe, with maps and town plans. Includes useful Travel Information section and index of over 7000 places.

380.5   NE   ISSN 0040-7623
HE7   CODEN: TIVEDD
TIJDSCHRIFT VOOR VERVOERSWETENSCHAP/JOURNAL FOR TRANSPORT SCIENCE. (Text in Dutch, English) 1965. q. fl.145. Netherlands Centre for Transportation (NEA), Training and Consultancy, Polakweg 13, 2288 GG Rijswijk, Netherlands. TEL 70-3988375. FAX 70-3954186. TELEX 32556 NL. (Subscr. to: Postbus 1969, 2280 DZ Rijswijk, Netherlands) Ed. C.M.L. van der Velde. adv.; bk.rev.; abstr.; bibl.; charts; stat.; index; circ. 500. **Indexed:** Dok.Str., Excerp.Med., HRIS, Key to Econ.Sci.

380.5   SP
TODOTRANSPORTE; revista mensual del transporte. 1984. m. 5500 ptas. (foreign 10000 ptas.). Tecnipublicaciones S.A., Fernando VI, 27, 28004 Madrid, Spain. TEL 91-319-7889. FAX 91-319-7089. TELEX 43905 YEBE E. Ed. Armando Estrada. adv.; circ. 15,600.
Description: Covers the transportation industry, including travel, cargo, air, railroad, ship and highway.

TOURISPRESS ITALIA; giornale d'informazione turistica. see *TRAVEL AND TOURISM*

TOWING NEWS. see *ENGINEERING*

380.5   MW
TRAFFIC. (Text in English) q. Centraf Associates Ltd., Box 30462, Chichiri, Blantyre 3, Malawi.

388.31   US   ISSN 0041-0691
HE1   CODEN: TRMADJ
TRAFFIC MANAGEMENT; for buyers of transportation services and related equipment. 1962. m. $69.95 (Canada $131.95; Mexico $123.95; elsewhere $128.95). Cahners Publishing Company (Newton) (Subsidiary of: Reed International PLC), Division of Reed Publishing (USA) Inc., 275 Washington St., Newton, MA 02158-1630. TEL 617-964-3030. FAX 617-558-4470. (Subscr. to: 44 Cook St., Denver, CO 80206. TEL 800-662-7776) Ed. Francis J. Quinn. adv.; illus.; tr.lit.; circ. 73,434. **Indexed:** B.P.I, BPIA, Bus.Ind., Data Process.Dig., Manage.Cont., Sci.Abstr., Tr.& Indus.Ind.
—BLDSC shelfmark: 8882.140000.
Description: For operations traffic and corporate management. Covers transportation strategies, new products and services, cost reductions, regulations and the law.

388.31   US   ISSN 0041-073X
HE2714
TRAFFIC WORLD; the weekly newsmagazine of transportation and distribution. 1907. w. $159. Journal of Commerce, Inc. (Washington), 741 National Press Bldg., Washington, DC 20045. TEL 202-383-6140. FAX 202-737-3349. adv.; illus.; stat.; circ. 10,500. (also avail. in microform from UMI; reprint service avail. from UMI) **Indexed:** B.P.I., HRIS.

TRAILER LIFE. see *SPORTS AND GAMES — Outdoor Life*

388.4   UK   ISSN 0049-4372
TRAMWAY MUSEUM SOCIETY. JOURNAL. vol.2, 1961. q. membership. Tramway Museum Society, National Tramway Museum, Crich, Matlock, Derby OE4 5DP, England. Ed. E. Wright. adv.; bk.rev.; charts; illus.; circ. 1,800.

TRANSACTION. see *RELIGIONS AND THEOLOGY — Protestant*

TRANSIT TIMES (ATLANTA). see *TRANSPORTATION — Railroads*

388   US   ISSN 0049-4410
TRANSIT - TIMES (OAKLAND). 1958-1990; resumed 1991. q. free. Alameda - Contra Costa Transit District, 1600 Franklin St., Oakland, CA 94612. TEL 416-891-4777. FAX 415-891-7205. Ed. Michael B. Mills. charts; illus.; circ. 8,500.

380.5   US   ISSN 0748-7347
TRANSITPULSE; news of worldwide people mover developments. 1983. bi-m. $55 (foreign $70). Trans21, Box 249, Fields Corner Sta., Boston, MA 02122. TEL 617-825-2318. FAX 617-354-1542. Ed. Lawrence J. Fabian. bk.rev.; circ. 850. (tabloid format; back issues avail.)
Description: Covers worldwide developments in automated passenger transport systems for urban, suburban and airport travel.

380.5   SA
TRANSNET ANNUAL REPORT (YEAR). (Editions in Afrikaans and English) a. free. Transnet Limited, Public Relations Department, P.O. Box 72501, Parkview 2122, South Africa. TEL 011-488-7410. FAX 011-488-7129. TELEX 447224 SA. charts; illus.; stat.; index; circ. Afrikaans ed. 2,500; English ed. 4,500.
Formerly (until 1990): S A Transport Services Annual Report (Year).
Description: Reports on the activities of all Transnet divisions, including the railways, ports, petroleum pipelines, and South African Airways.

380.5   MX
TRANSPOR. 1978. m. San Francisco 224, piso 5, Col. del Valle, Apdo. Postal 12879, Mexico 12, D.F., Mexico. Ed. Enrique Landgrave Villanueva. adv.; circ. 5,000.

380.5   II   ISSN 0041-137X
HE1
TRANSPORT; automobile, aviation, railways, shipping, tourism. (Text in English) 1951. q. Rs.3 per no. Transport Publications, 20 Noble Chambers, S.A. Brelvi Rd., Bombay 400001, India. Ed. K.H. Rau. adv.; bk.rev.; illus.; circ. 5,000. (also avail. in microfilm from UMI)

380.5 910.09   EC   ISSN 1018-2179
TRANSPORT; guia ecuatoriana de transporte y turismo. 1963. m. S/32000($90) (effective 1992). Apartado de Correos 09-01-5603, Sucre 2204, Guayaquil, Ecuador. TEL 593-4-363848. FAX 593-4-374717. Ed. Pablo Cevallos. adv.; circ. 4,127. (back issues avail.)
Description: For travel agents and others in the Ecuadorian travel industry.

380.5   LU
TRANSPORT. fortn. 5 rue C.M. Spoo, 2546 Luxembourg, Luxembourg.

380.5   UK   ISSN 0144-3453
HE1
TRANSPORT (LONDON). 1980. 10/yr. £50 includes yearbook. Chartered Institute of Transport, 80 Portland Place, London W1N 4DP, England. TEL 10-636-9952. Ed. David Robinson. **Indexed:** Br.Rail.Bd., Br.Tech.Ind., Geo.Abstr., HRIS, P.A.I.S.
—BLDSC shelfmark: 9025.372000.
Supersedes: Chartered Institute of Transport. Journal (ISSN 0020-3181)

380.5   CN   ISSN 0227-3020
TRANSPORT - ACTION; the newsletter of public transport consumers. (Text in English and French) 1975. bi-m. Can.$22. Transport 2000 Canada, P.O. Box CP-858, Sta. B, Ottawa, Ont. K1P 5P9, Canada. TEL 613-594-3290. FAX 613-594-3271. Ed. Roy Jamieson. adv.; bk.rev.; circ. 2,100.
Formerly: Transport 2000 Canada. Bulletin.
Description: News and opinion on urban transit, passenger rail, airlines and intercity busses for users of public transport services in Canada.

380   II   ISSN 0041-1388
TRANSPORT AND COMMUNICATIONS. (Text in English) 1961. m. Rs.40. O.N. Pandeya, 105-C Block F, New Alipore, Calcutta 700053, India. Ed. L.K. Pandeya. circ. 6,787.

380   UN   ISSN 0252-4392
TRANSPORT & COMMUNICATIONS BULLETIN FOR ASIA & THE PACIFIC. 1950. a. price varies. United Nations Economic and Social Commission for Asia and the Pacific (ESCAP), United Nations Bldg., Rajadamnern Ave., Bangkok 10200, Thailand. (Dist. by: United Nations Publications, Room DC2-0853, New York, NY 10017; or Distribution and Sales Section, Palais des Nations, CH-1211 Geneva 10, Switzerland) bk.rev.; charts; illus.; stat. **Indexed:** IIS, P.A.I.S.
—BLDSC shelfmark: 9025.504200.
Formerly: Transport and Communications Bulletin for Asia and the Far East (ISSN 0041-1396)

380.5   II   ISSN 0300-449X
TRANSPORT AND TOURISM JOURNAL. (Text in English) 1967. q. Rs.15. 1969 Ganj Mearkhan, Daryaganj, New Delhi 110002, India. Ed. M.S. Gambhir. adv.; charts; illus.

380.52   US
TRANSPORT-DE-REGULATION REPORT. m. Freight Traffic Institute, 960 Broadway, Hicksville, NY 11801. TEL 516-822-1183. FAX 516-822-1126. Ed. Stephen Tinghitella. circ. 600.

380.5   BE   ISSN 0009-6083
TRANSPORT ECHO; magazine de logistique et management du transport. (Editions in Dutch, French) Dutch ed. 1945; French ed. 1987. m. (newsletter w.) 7000 Fr. (effective 1992). Transmedia N.V., Cuylitsstraat 39, B-2018 Antwerp, Belgium. TEL 03-238-58-36. FAX 03-216-44-88. Ed. Nicole Martinet. adv.; bk.rev.; illus.; stat.; circ. 22,418. **Indexed:** Key to Econ.Sci.
Description: Trade magazine for logistics and transport management.

380.52   NE
TRANSPORT EN OPSLAG. 1977. 12/yr. fl.189.50. Uitgeversmaatschappij C. Misset B.V., Box 4, 7000 BA Doetinchem, Netherlands. TEL 08340-49911. FAX 08340-43839. TELEX 45481. Ed. P.P. Roessel. adv.; B&W page fl.3213; unit 187 x 257; adv. contact: Cor van Nek. bk.rev.; charts; illus.; index; circ. 11,720. **Indexed:** Key to Econ.Sci.
Description: Information on materials handling, storage, distribution and warehousing.

TRANSPORTATION

380.5   UK   ISSN 0020-3122
TL230.A1
TRANSPORT ENGINEER. 1945. m. £18($30) Institute of Road Transport Engineers, Pegasus House, 116-120 Golden Lane, London EC1Y OTL, England. TEL 071-251-1227. FAX 071-253-1228. Ed. John Dickson-Simpson. adv.; bk.rev.; circ. 17,000.
Indexed: Br.Tech.Ind.
— BLDSC shelfmark: 9025.590000.

380.5   UK
TRANSPORT ENGINEER'S HANDBOOK. irreg., latest 1984. £12. Kogan Page Ltd., 120 Pentonville Rd., London N1 9JN, England. TEL 071-278-0433. FAX 071-837-6348. TELEX 263088 KOGAN G.

380 658.7   SZ
TRANSPORT, FOERDER- UND LAGERTECHNIK; Schweizerische Fachzeitschrift fuer rationellen Gueterumschlag, Logistik, Transport, Lagerhaltung und Foerdertechnik. 1945. m. 90 Fr. (foreign 110 Fr.). S H Z Fachverlag AG, Alte Landstr. 43, CH-8700 Kusnacht-Zurich, Switzerland. TEL 01-910 80 22. FAX 01-9105155. Ed. Rudolf Weber. adv.; bk.rev.; illus.; circ. 5,150. (processed)
Former titles: Transport und Lagertechnik (ISSN 0041-1574); Verpackung und Transport.
Description: Looks at freight transport and storage.

380.5 900   UK   ISSN 0041-1469
TRANSPORT HISTORY. 1968. a. £24($48) Graphmitre Ltd., 1 West St., Tavistock, Devon PL19 8DS, England. adv.; bk.rev.; illus.; index; circ. 2,000. (back issues avail.) **Indexed:** Br.Hum.Ind., Hist.Abstr.

380.5 658.7   SW
TRANSPORT I DAG. 1969. 10/yr. SEK 490. Fateco AB, P.O. Box 2078, S-183 02 Taeby, Sweden. FAX 46-8768-1492. Ed. Paul E. Branke. adv.; bk.rev.; circ. 3,200.
Former titles: Transport Teknik Scandinavia (ISSN 0284-074X); Transport Teknik (ISSN 0041-154X)

380.5   II
TRANSPORT INDUSTRY AND TRADE ANNUAL. 1963. a. $10. Praveen Corp., Sayajigani, Baroda 390005, India. Ed. C.M. Pandit. circ. 2,500.
Formerly: Transport Industry and Trade Journal (ISSN 0041-1477)

380.5   DK
TRANSPORT - MAGASINET (FREDENSBORG); the periodical rallying all transport interests. 1960. 22/yr. DKK 394. Dansk Auto Media A-S, Hoejvangen 23, Box 159, DK-3480 Fredensborg, Denmark. TEL 31-216801. FAX 31-212396. Ed. A.J.S. Dam. adv.; bk.rev.; circ. 17,342. **Indexed:** C.R.E.J.
Formerly: Transport (Fredensborg) (ISSN 0041-1361); Incorporates (in 1980): Emballage (ISSN 0013-6549)

380.5   UK
TRANSPORT MANAGEMENT. 1944. bi-m. £15 (foreign £18). Institute of Transport Administration, 32 Palmerston Rd., Southampton SO1 1LL, England. FAX 0703-634165. Ed. John Saunders. adv.; bk.rev.; circ. 4,000.

380.5   SA
TRANSPORT MANAGEMENT. 1980. m. R.73 (foreign R.98)(effective 1992). Thomson Publications (Subsidiary of: Times Media Ltd.), P.O. Box 56182, Pinegowrie 2123, South Africa. TEL 011-886-3720. FAX 011-789-3196. TELEX 4-22125. Ed. Jim Penrith. adv.; bk.rev.; circ. 4,857. **Indexed:** Ind.S.A.Per.

388   UK
TRANSPORT MANAGER'S AND OPERATOR'S HANDBOOK. 1970. a. £21. Kogan Page Ltd., 120 Pentonville Rd., London N1 9JN, England. TEL 071-278-0433. FAX 071-837-6348. TELEX 263088 KOGAN G. Ed. David Lowe. adv.; charts; illus.
Formerly: Transport Manager's Handbook (ISSN 0306-9435)
Description: UK and EEC transport legislation, major technical developments and significant changes within the transport industry.

380.5   UK
TRANSPORT MANAGERS JOURNAL. 1953. m. £25. Association of Transport Management Ltd., 16-20 George St., Birmingham B12 3RG, England. Ed. W. Gavin. adv.; bk.rev.; circ. 12,250.

380.5   PL   ISSN 0137-4435
TRANSPORT MUSEUMS. (Yearbook of the International Association of Transport Museums) (Text in English) irreg., vol.9, 1985. (Centralne Muzeum Morskie, Gdansk) Ossolineum, Publishing House of the Polish Academy of Sciences, Rynek 9, Wroclaw, Poland. TELEX 0712771 OSS PL. (Subscr. to: International Association of Transport Museums, Zeughaus Str. 1-5, Cologne, Germany) (Co-sponsor: International Association of Transport Museums) Ed. Przemyslaw Smolarek.

380.5   UK
TRANSPORT NEWS. 1977. m. £15. K.A.V. Publicity (Glasgow) Ltd., 113 West Regent St., Glasgow G2 2RU, Scotland. Ed. Alistair Vallance. adv.; circ. 9,500. **Indexed:** ASCA.

380.5   UK   ISSN 0306-2252
TRANSPORT NEWS DIGEST. 1968. m. £18. Transport Press Services, Pegasus House, 116-120 Golden Lane, London EC1Y OTL, England. FAX 071-253-1228. Ed. J. Dickson-Simpson. adv.; circ. 700.

380.5   NZ   ISSN 0110-6236
TRANSPORT NEWS OF NEW ZEALAND. 1934. m. NZ.$45. (New Zealand Road Transport Association) Transport News of New Zealand Ltd., 3rd Fl., Newspaper House, 93 Boulcott St., Wellington, New Zealand. TEL 04-731-032. FAX 04-712-649. Ed. Keith Richardson. adv.; bk.rev.; stat.; circ. 5,034. (back issues avail.)
Description: Keeps transport industry informed of current technical, legal and industrial issues and events.

380.5   SW   ISSN 0346-2773
TRANSPORT OCH HANTERING. 1971. m. SEK 545. T.H. Foerlag, Box 45056, S-104 30 Stockholm, Sweden. FAX 08-104618. Ed. John Murray. adv.; bk.rev.; circ. 4,000.
Incorporates: Bulkhantering; Formerly: Transport och Hanteringsekonomi (ISSN 0085-7327)

380.5   FR   ISSN 0397-474X
TRANSPORT PUBLIC. 1890. 11/yr. 470 F. Union des Transports Publics (UTP), 5 rue d'Aumale, 75009 Paris, France. TEL 1-48-74-63-51. FAX 44-91-94-60. Ed. Robert Viennet. adv.; bk.rev.; circ. 3,000. **Indexed:** HRIS.
Formerly (until 1982): Revue des Transports Publics Urbain et Regionaux.
Description: Covers news, facts, events and analyses of public transportation.

380.5   UK   ISSN 0144-1647
TRANSPORT REVIEWS. 1981. q. £96($167) Taylor & Francis Ltd., Rankine Rd., Basingstoke, Hants RG24 0PR, England. TEL 0256-840366. FAX 0256-479438. TELEX 858540. Ed. S.M.A. Banister. adv.; bk.rev. Indexed: HRIS, I D A.
—BLDSC shelfmark: 9025.933000.
Description: Covers all modes of transport. Describes transport organizations and policies in individual countries. Topics covered include major cities, modelling, education, public transport, research, and the use of computers.
Refereed Serial

TRANSPORT SALARIED STAFF JOURNAL. see *BUSINESS AND ECONOMICS — Labor And Industrial Relations*

380.5   UK
TRANSPORT TICKET SOCIETY. JOURNAL.* 1946. m. £4. Transport Ticket Society, 18 Villa Rd., Lutton LU2 7NT, England. illus.; index; circ. controlled. (processed)

TRANSPORT WORKERS OF THE WORLD. see *LABOR UNIONS*

331.88   MY
TRANSPORT WORKERS UNION. TRIENNIAL REPORT. (Text in English) triennial. Transport Workers Union, Transport Workers House, 21 Jalan Barat, Petaling Jaya, Malaysia. TEL 03-7566115. Ed. V. David.

380.52   US
TRANSPORT 2000 AND INTERMODAL WORLD.* vol.6, 1972. bi-m. $15. BuenaVentura Publishing Co., 965 Mission St., San Francisco, CA 94103-2921. adv.; bk.rev.; tr.lit.; circ. 11,000 (controlled). **Indexed:** BMT, PROMT.
Former titles: Transport 2000 (ISSN 0362-3815); (until 1976): Intermodal World; Brandon's Intermodal World; Container World.

380.5   SW   ISSN 0492-004X
TRANSPORTARBETAREN/TRANSPORTWORKER. 1899. m. (11/yr.). Kr.100. Svenska Transportarbetarefoerbundet - National Federation of Transportworkers Unions, Vasagatan 11, Box 714, 101 33 Stockholm 1, Sweden. TEL 08-7237700. Ed. Martin Viredius. adv.; bk.rev.; abstr.; illus.; index; circ. 61,961. (also avail. in microform)

388   NE   ISSN 0049-4488
HE7   CODEN: TRPOB6
TRANSPORTATION; an international journal devoted to the improvement of transportation planning and practice. (Text in English) 1972. q. $159. Kluwer Academic Publishers, Postbus 17, 3300 AA Dordrecht, Netherlands. TEL 078-334911. FAX 078-334254. TELEX 29245. (Dist. by: Kluwer Academic Publishers Group, P.O. Box 322, 3300 AH Dordrecht, Netherlands; N. America dist. addr.: Box 358, Accord Station, Hingham, MA 02018-0358. TEL 617-871-6600) Ed. Martin G. Richards. bk.rev.; index. (reprint service avail. from SWZ) **Indexed:** ASCA, Bibl.Ind., BMT, Curr.Cont., Dok.Str., Eng.Ind., Environ.Abstr., Excerp.Med., HRIS, Intl.Civil Eng.Abstr., Sage Urb.Stud.Abstr., Soft.Abstr.Eng., SSCI, Trans.Res.Abstr.
—BLDSC shelfmark: 9026.050000.
Supersedes (1980-198?): Developments in Transport Studies.

380.5   US
▼**TRANSPORTATION (SACRAMENTO);** a resource guide to who's doing what in California. 1990. irreg. $20. California Institute of Public Affairs, Box 189040, Sacramento, CA 95818. TEL 916-442-CIPA. FAX 916-442-2478. (Affiliate: The Claremont Graduate School) circ. 500.
Description: Detailed reference to governmental agencies at all levels, associations, institutes, academic programs, and transportation systems in California.

658.7 380.5   US   ISSN 0895-8548
TS149
TRANSPORTATION & DISTRIBUTION. 1960. m. $45 (free to qualified personnel). Penton Publishing (Subsidiary of: Pittway Company), 1100 Superior Ave., Cleveland, OH 44114-2543. TEL 216-696-7000. FAX 216-696-8765. (Subscr. to: Box 95759, Cleveland, OH 44101) Ed. Perry Trunick. adv.; bk.rev.; illus.; tr.lit.; circ. 74,138 (controlled). (also avail. in microform from UMI; reprint service avail. from UMI) **Indexed:** ABI Inform, B.P.I, BPIA, Bus.Ind., Curr.Pack.Abstr., Excerp.Med., Manage.Cont., PROMT, Tr.& Indus.Ind.
●Also available online. Vendor(s): DIALOG.
—BLDSC shelfmark: 9026.119800.
Former titles (until 1987): Handling and Shipping Management (ISSN 0194-603X); (until vol.19, no.10, Oct. 1978): Handling and Shipping (ISSN 0017-7385)
Description: Covers shipper-carrier relationships, new systems and technology in handling and warehousing products, and information processing systems applicable to inventory management and increased productivity and customer service.

380.5   US
TRANSPORTATION CONSUMER. 1978. 6/yr. free. U.S. Department of Transportation, Office of Public and Consumer Affairs, 400 Seventh St., S.W., Washington, DC 20590. TEL 202-655-4000. bibl.; illus.; circ. 6,000. **Indexed:** Ind.U.S.Gov.Per.
Supersedes (1976-1978): Consumer Transpotopics; (1972-1976): Transportation Topics for Consumers (ISSN 0364-6653)

380.5   US   ISSN 0889-0889
HE203
TRANSPORTATION IN AMERICA; a statistical analysis of transportation in the United States. 1983. 3/yr. $50 to individuals; libraries and bookstores $40. Eno Foundation for Transportation, Inc., 8150 Leesburg Pike, Vienna, Westport, VA 22182. TEL 703-883-8243. FAX 703-790-5933. Ed. Frank A. Smith. circ. 1,000. (back issues avail.) **Indexed:** SRI.
Description: Analysis of traffic and costs of commercial and private freight and passenger transport in US by all modes.

TRANSPORTATION

380.5   US   ISSN 0041-1612
HE1   CODEN: TRNJA
TRANSPORTATION JOURNAL. 1961. q. $50. American Society of Transportation and Logistics, Inc., 3600 Chamberlain Ln., No. 232, Louisville, KY 40241-1989. TEL 502-425-1780. Ed. John C. Spychalski. bk.rev.; charts; illus.; pat.; stat.; circ. 3,500. (also avail. in microfilm from UMI; reprint service avail. from UMI,WSH) **Indexed:** ABI Inform., ASCA, B.P.I, Bus.Ind., C.L.I., Curr.Cont., Energy Rev., Environ.Abstr., Environ.Per.Bibl., HRIS, Leg.Per., Mar.Aff.Bibl., Mid.East: Abstr.& Ind., P.A.I.S., SSCI, Tr.& Indus.Ind.
—BLDSC shelfmark: 9026.250000.

380 918   US
TRANSPORTATION: LATIN AMERICAN INDUSTRIAL REPORT. 1985. a. $235 per country report. Aquino Productions, Box 15760, Stamford, CT 06901. TEL 203-325-3138. Ed. Andres C. Aquino.

380.5   US   ISSN 0308-1060
  CODEN: TPLTAK
TRANSPORTATION PLANNING AND TECHNOLOGY; reviews and communications. 1972. 4/yr. (in 1 vol.). $199. Gordon and Breach Science Publishers, 270 Eighth Ave., New York, NY 10011. TEL 212-206-8900. FAX 212-645-2459. TELEX 236735 GOPUB UR. (Subscr. to: Box 786, Cooper Sta., New York, NY 10276. TEL 800-545-8398; UK subscr. to: P.O. Box 90, Reading, Berkshire RG1 8JL, England. TEL 0734-560-080) Ed. David Gillingwater. adv.; bk.rev. (also avail. in microform from MIM; back issues avail.) **Indexed:** Br.Rail.Bd., Eng.Ind., Geo.Abstr., HRIS.
—BLDSC shelfmark: 9026.265000.
  Formerly: Transportation Technology (ISSN 0041-1671)
  Refereed Serial

380.5   US   ISSN 0278-9434
HE331   CODEN: TRQUDV
TRANSPORTATION QUARTERLY. 1947. q. free to qualified personnel. Eno Foundation for Transportation, Inc., 270 Saugatuck Ave., Westport, CT 06880-0055. TEL 203-227-4852. FAX 203-227-3928. Ed. Robert S. Holmes. circ. 3,500. (also avail. in microfilm, reprint service avail. from UMI) **Indexed:** A.S.& T.Ind., ASCA, Avery Ind.Archit.Per., Curr.Cont., Dok.Str., Eng.Ind., Environ.Abstr., Fut.Surv., HRIS, I D A, Intl.Civil Eng.Abstr., Mid.East: Abstr.& Ind., P.A.I.S., Risk Abstr., Sage Urb.Stud.Abstr., Soft.Abstr.Eng., SSCI.
—BLDSC shelfmark: 9026.266000.
  Formerly (until 1982): Traffic Quarterly (ISSN 0041-0713)

380.5   US   ISSN 0191-2607
HE192.5   CODEN: TRAGDB
TRANSPORTATION RESEARCH. PART A: GENERAL; an international journal. 1967. 6/yr. £215 (with Part B: £390)(effective 1992). Pergamon Press, Inc., Journals Division, 660 White Plains Rd., Tarrytown, NY 10591-5153. TEL 914-524-9200. FAX 914-333-2444. (And: Headington Hill Hall, Oxford OX3 0BW, England. TEL 0865-794141) Ed. Frank A. Haight. adv.; bk.rev.; circ. 1,600. (also avail. in microform from MIM,UMI) **Indexed:** A.S.& T.Ind., BPIA, Bus.Ind., Cont.Pg.Manage., Curr.Cont., Dok.Str., Energy Rev., Eng.Ind., Environ.Abstr., Environ.Per.Bibl., Ergon.Abstr., Excerp.Med., Geo.Abstr., HRIS, I D A, Int.Abstr.Oper.Res., Manage.Cont., Sci.Abstr., SSCI.
—BLDSC shelfmark: 9026.274600.
  Supersedes in part: Transportation Research (ISSN 0041-1647)
  Description: General papers on all modes of passenger and freight transportation.
  Refereed Serial

380.5   US   ISSN 0191-2615
HE192.5   CODEN: TRBMDY
TRANSPORTATION RESEARCH. PART B: METHODOLOGICAL; an international journal. 1967. 6/yr. £215 (with Part A: £390)(effective 1992). Pergamon Press, Inc., Journals Division, 660 White Plains Rd., Tarrytown, NY 10591-5153. TEL 914-524-9200. FAX 914-333-2444. (And: Headington Hill Hall, Oxford OX3 0BW, England. TEL 0865-794141) Ed. Frank A. Haight. adv.; bk.rev. (also avail. in microform from MIM,UMI) **Indexed:** A.S.& T.Ind., ASCA, BPIA, Br.Rail.Bd., Energy Rev., Environ.Abstr., Environ.Per.Bibl., Ergon.Abstr., Geo.Abstr., HRIS, Int.Abstr.Oper.Res., Math.R., Sci.Abstr., SSCI.
  Supersedes in part: Transportation Research (ISSN 0041-1647)
  Description: Papers on all methodological aspects of transportation, with a particular focus on mathematical analysis.
  Refereed Serial

380.5   US   ISSN 0097-8515
TE1   CODEN: HWRCAI
TRANSPORTATION RESEARCH CIRCULAR. 1965. irreg., no.367, 1990. price varies. National Research Council, Transportation Research Board, 2101 Constitution Ave., N.W., Washington, DC 20418. TEL 202-334-3214. FAX 202-334-2519. circ. 3,600. (also avail. in microfiche) **Indexed:** Dok.Str.
  Description: Presents interim research findings and research problem statements.

TRANSPORTATION SAFETY LAW PRACTICE MANUAL. see *LAW*

TRANSPORTATION SAFETY RECOMMENDATIONS. see *PUBLIC HEALTH AND SAFETY*

380.5   US   ISSN 0041-1655
TA1001   CODEN: TRSCBJ
TRANSPORTATION SCIENCE. 1967. q. $30 to individuals; institutions $77 (foreign $82). Operations Research Society of America, Mount Royal and Guilford Aves., Baltimore, MD 21202. TEL 301-528-4146. Ed. Mark Daskin. charts; illus.; stat.; index; circ. 1,500. (also avail. in microform from KTO; back issues avail.) **Indexed:** A.S.& T.Ind., ASCA, BMT, Dok.Str., Eng.Ind., HRIS, Int.Abstr.Oper.Res., Intl.Civil Eng.Abstr., Math.R., Oper.Res.Manage.Sci., Qual.Contr.Appl.Stat., Sci.Abstr., Soft.Abstr.Eng.
—BLDSC shelfmark: 9026.280000.

380.5   UK   ISSN 0278-3819
TRANSPORTATION STUDIES. 1982. irreg., vol.14, 1990. Gordon & Breach Science Publishers, P.O. Box 90, Reading, Berkshire RG1 8JL, England. TEL 0734-560-080. FAX 0734-568-211. TELEX 849870 SCIPUB G. (US addr.: Box 786, Cooper Sta., New York, NY 10276. TEL 800-545-8398) Eds. Norman Ashford, William G. Bell. (also avail. in microform)
—BLDSC shelfmark: 9026.315000.
  Refereed Serial

TRANSPORTATION TELEPHONE TICKLER. see *BUSINESS AND ECONOMICS — Trade And Industrial Directories*

380   US   ISSN 0094-9922
HE17
TRANSPORTATION U S A. 1974. q. $3.10. U.S. Department of Transportation, 400 Seventh St. S.W., Washington, DC 20590. TEL 202-655-4000. (Dist. by: Supt. of Documents, Washington, DC 20402) (also avail. in microform from MIM) **Indexed:** Ind.U.S.Gov.Per.

380.5   CU
TRANSPORTE Y VIAS DE COMUNICACION. q. $25 in N. America; S. America $26; Europe $28. (Ministerio de Educacion Superior) Ediciones Cubanas, Obispo No. 527, Apdo. 605, Havana, Cuba.

380.5   CU   ISSN 0496-1021
TRANSPORTES.* 1962. bi-m. Ministerio del Transporte, Rancho Boyeros y Tulipan, Havana, Cuba. Ed. Sergio Farinas. illus.; pat.; tr.lit.; circ. 25,000.
  Incorporates: Proa y Puerto.

TRANSPORTEUR; au service du personnel dans le transport et les industries connexes. see *RELIGIONS AND THEOLOGY — Protestant*

388.3   NO
TRANSPORTFORUM-KOLLEKTIVTRAFIKK. (Text in English, Norwegian) 1929. m. NOK 230 to individuals; students NOK 130; other Nordic countries NOK 360; elsewhere NOK 410. Norske Transportbedrifters Landsforening, Soerkedalsveien 6, 0369 Oslo 3, Norway. TEL 02-96-50-20. FAX 02-60-14-94. Ed. Einar Spurkeland. adv.; bk.rev.; circ. 4,600.
  Formerly: Rutebiltidende (ISSN 0048-8836)
  Description: Directed to employees in coach service, bus line service and city transit, transport of goods, ferry boat service and coastal liners.

380.5   GW   ISSN 0176-358X
TRANSPORTMARKT. (Text in English and German) 1980. m. DM.60. Transportmarkt Verlag GmbH, Ehlersbergerweg 214, 2000 Tangstedt, Germany. TEL 040-6071445. FAX 040-6072343. Ed. Friedemann Bast. adv.; bk.rev.; bibl.; stat.; circ. 9,600. (back issues avail.)

380.52   GW   ISSN 0174-559X
K24   CODEN: TRSPER
TRANSPORTRECHT; Zeitschrift fuer das gesamte Recht der Gueterbefoerderung, der Spedition, der Versicherungen des Transports, der Personenbefoerderung und der Reiseverstaltung. 1979. 10/yr. DM.258. Alfred Metzner Verlag, Zeppelinallee 43, 6000 Frankfurt a.M. 97, Germany. TEL 069-793009-0. TELEX 4189621-KOMED. Ed. Christian Runge. adv.; bk.rev.; index; circ. 2,500. (back issues avail.)
  Formerly: Transportation Law and Legislation.

380.5   FR   ISSN 0564-1373
HE3
TRANSPORTS. 1956. bi-m. 701.27 F. (foreign 820 F.). Editions Techniques et Economiques, 3, rue Soufflot, 75005 Paris, France. TEL 46-34-10-30. FAX 46-34-55-83. TELEX 260-717 F. Ed. Genevieve Epstein. adv.; bk.rev.; bibl.; illus.; stat.; index; circ. 4,000. (back issues avail.) **Indexed:** HRIS, PROMT.
  Description: Covers the economies of all methods of transport.

380.5   FR
TRANSPORTS ACTUALITES. 39/yr. 330 F. (foreign 457 F.)(effective Jan. 1991). Groupe Usine Nouvelle, 1 cite Bergere, 75009 Paris, France. TEL 48-24-23-24. FAX 48-24-31-77. TELEX 650702. Eds. Philippe-Edouard Grardel, Jean-Pierre Maysonnave. circ. 10,336.

380.5   FR   ISSN 0397-6521
TRANSPORTS URBAINS; forum des transports publics. 1964. q. 260 F. Groupement pour l'Etude des Transports Urbains Modernes, 173 rue Armand Silvestre, 92400 Courbevoie, France. Ed. Alain Sutter. adv.; bk.rev.; circ. 2,000.
  Formerly (until 1974): Forum des Transports Publics (ISSN 0071-8033)

380.5   BL
TRANSROTAS - TRAVEL & CARGO BUSINESS GUIDE. m. $234. Panrotas Editora Ltda, Av. Jabaquara, 1761, CEP 04045 Sao Paulo, Brazil. TEL 011-275-0211. FAX 011-276-1602. TELEX 011-56693. Ed. Jose Guillermo Condomi Alcorta. circ. 5,000.

380.5   SA
▼**TRANSTALK.** (Text in Afrikaans, English) 1991. q. free. Transnet Limited, P.O. Box 72501, Parkview 2122, South Africa. TEL 011-488-7410. FAX 011-488-7129. Ed. Alrika Hefers. illus. (tabloid format)
  Description: General interest magazine for Transnet employees, with health, education, sports, and environmental news.

380.5   IT
TRASPORTI; diritto, economia, politica. 1973? 3/yr. L.15000. Casa Editrice Dott. Antonio Milani, Via Jappelli 5, 35100 Padua, Italy. Ed.Bd.

380.5   IT
TRASPORTI E TRAZIONE; rivista di tecnica, economia e pianificazione dei trasporti. 1988. bi-m. L.54000($92) to individuals; students L.20000 (effective 1991). Masson Italia Periodici, Via Statuto 2-4, 20120 Milan, Italy. TEL 02-6367-1. FAX 02-6367-211. Ed. Ernesto Stagni. circ. 2,000.

TRANSPORTATION

380.5   IT
TRASPORTI INDUSTRIALI E MOVIMENTAZIONE. 1955. m. L.96000 (foreign L.145000). Etas s.r.l., Via Mecenate, 91, 20138 Milan, Italy. TEL 02-580841. FAX 02-5064867. Ed. Alberto Russo Frattasi. circ. 5,454. (back issues avail.)
Formerly: Trasporti Industriali (ISSN 0041-1809)

380   NE
TRENDS IN TRANSPORT. a. fl.89.25. Delwel Uitgeverij B.V., Postbus 19110, 2500 CC The Hague, Netherlands. TEL 070-3624800. FAX 070-3605606. (Co-sponsor: Coopers & Lybrand Dijker Van Dien) Ed. J. Koekebakker.

388.4   AT   ISSN 0155-1264
TROLLEY WIRE. 1952. q. Aus.$19 (foreign Aus.$25). South Pacific Electric Railway Co-Operative Society Ltd., P.O. Box 103, Sutherland, N.S.W. 2232, Australia. TEL 02-542-3646. Ed.Bd. bk.rev.; stat.; circ. 1,200. (back issues avail.) **Indexed:** Aus.Rd.Ind.

388.322   UK   ISSN 0266-7452
TROLLEYBUS MAGAZINE. 1963. bi-m. £11.50 (foreign £12.50). National Trolleybus Association, 49 Alzey Gardens, Harpenden, Hertfordshire AL5 5SY, England. (Subscr. to: 10 Compton Close, Flitwick, Bedford MK45 1TA, England) Ed. Roland Box. adv.; bk.rev.; illus.; circ. 750. (tabloid format)
Description: Covers many facets of trolleybuses and their operation.

TRUCK AND BUS TRANSPORTATION; Australia's leading national road transport fleetowner monthly. see *TRANSPORTATION — Trucks And Trucking*

380.5   US   ISSN 0082-9404
U.S. BUREAU OF THE CENSUS. CENSUS OF TRANSPORTATION. (Consists of 1 survey: Truck Inventory and Use Survey) 1963. quinquennial. price varies. U.S. Bureau of the Census, Data User Services Division, Washington, DC 20233. TEL 301-763-4100. (Dist. by: Supt. of Documents, Washington, DC 20402) (also avail. in microfiche)

353.85   US   ISSN 0092-3117
HE206.3
U.S. DEPARTMENT OF TRANSPORTATION. FISCAL YEAR BUDGET IN BRIEF.* a. U.S. Department of Transportation, Office of Budget, 400 Seventh St., S.W., Washington, DC 20590. Key Title: Budget in Brief - Department of Transportation (Washington).

380.5   US   ISSN 0099-2267
HE192.5
U.S. DEPARTMENT OF TRANSPORTATION. OFFICE OF UNIVERSITY RESEARCH. AWARDS TO ACADEMIC INSTITUTIONS BY THE DEPARTMENT OF TRANSPORTATION. a. U.S. Department of Transportation, Office of University Research, 400 7th St., S.W., Washington, DC 20590. TEL 202-655-4000. Key Title: Awards to Academic Institutions by the Department of Transportation.

388.3   US
U.S. FEDERAL HIGHWAY ADMINISTRATION. HIGHWAY AND URBAN MASS TRANSPORTATION. 1970. irreg. (2-3/yr.). price varies. U.S. Federal Highway Administration, 400 Seventh St. S.W., Washington, DC 20590. TEL 202-426-0632. charts; illus.
Indexed: Ind.U.S.Gov.Per, Tr.& Indus.Ind.

625.7 016   US   ISSN 0068-6115
UNIVERSITY OF CALIFORNIA, BERKELEY. INSTITUTE OF TRANSPORTATION STUDIES. LIBRARY REFERENCES. 1955. irreg., no.78, 1978. price varies. University of California, Berkeley, Institute of Transportation Studies Library, 412 McLaughlin Hall, Berkeley, CA 94720. TEL 415-642-3604. FAX 415-642-1246. Ed. Michael Kleiber.

385.1   CN
UNIVERSITY OF MANITOBA. TRANSPORT INSTITUTE. OCCASIONAL PAPER. 1968. irreg., latest 1992. University of Manitoba, Transport Institute, 612-181 Freedman Crescent, Winnipeg, Man. R3T 2N2, Canada. TEL 204-474-9842. FAX 204-275-0831.
Formerly: University of Manitoba. Center for Transportation Studies. Occasional Paper. (ISSN 0076-3977)

380.5   CN   ISSN 0318-1251
UNIVERSITY OF TORONTO - YORK UNIVERSITY. JOINT PROGRAM IN TRANSPORTATION. ANNUAL REPORT. a. University of Toronto - York University Joint Program in Transportation, 42 St. George St., Toronto, Ont. M5S 2E4, Canada. TEL 416-978-7282.

380.5   PL   ISSN 0208-4821
UNIWERSYTET GDANSKI. WYDZIAL EKONOMIKI TRANSPORTU. ZESZYTY NAUKOWE. EKONOMIKA TRANSPORTU LADOWEGO. (Text in Polish; summaries in English and Russian) 1971. irreg. price varies. Uniwersytet Gdanski, Wydzial Ekonomiki Transportu, c/o Biblioteka Glowna, Ul. Armii Krajowej 110, 81-824 Sopot, Poland. TEL 51-0061. TELEX 051 2247 BMOR PL. (Dist. by: Ars Polona-Ruch, Krakowskie Przedmiecie 7, 00-680 Warsaw, Poland) circ. 250.
—BLDSC shelfmark: 9512.433500.
Description: Covers problems of inland transport economics, organization of transport and transport policy, economic problems of particular branches of transport, such as railway, road and inland water.

UNIWERSYTET SLASKI W KATOWICACH. PRACE NAUKOWE. PROBLEMY PRAWA PRZEWOZOWEGO. see *LAW*

380.5   US
URBAN TRANSPORT NEWS; management, funding, ridership, technology. 1973. fortn. $280.54 (effective Sep. 1992). Business Publishers, Inc., 951 Pershing Dr., Silver Spring, MD 20910-4464. TEL 301-587-6300. FAX 301-585-9075. Ed. Tom Ramstack. bk.rev. (looseleaf format)
●Also available online. Vendor(s): NewsNet (TS10).
Formerly: Public Transit Report (ISSN 0148-4087)
Description: Presents developments in urban transport that increase efficiency and safety, such as mass transit systems and battery-powered cars.

388.322   US   ISSN 1040-4880
URBAN TRANSPORTATION MONITOR. 1987. bi-w. $175 (foreign $195). Lawley Publications, 2701 C West 15th St., Ste. 501, Plano, TX 75075. TEL 214-596-6680. FAX 214-964-3785. Ed. Daniel B. Rathbone. adv.; bk.rev.; circ. 700.
Description: Presents news and information on all aspects of urban transportation, transit, and traffic engineering. Survey conducted for each issue.

380.5   SW
VAEGMAESTAREN. 1928. bi-m. SEK 50. Foereningen Sveriges Vaegmaestare, Skolgatan 5, S-15400 Gnesta, Sweden. Ed. Ivan Bratt. adv.; circ. 2,123.

380.5   US
VANNING NOW. 4/yr. Council of Councils, 589 Old Post Rd., Dept. TR, Virginia Beach, VA 23452-2914. TEL 804-340-2305. Ed. Brian Walker. adv.; circ. 600.

380.5 629.04   NE   ISSN 0042-3114
TL243   CODEN: VSDYA4
VEHICLE SYSTEM DYNAMICS; international journal of vehicle mechanics and mobility. (Text in English) 1972. bi-m. $297. Swets Publishing Service (Subsidiary of: Swets en Zeitlinger B.V.), Heereweg 347, 2161 CA Lisse, Netherlands. TEL 31-2521-35111. FAX 31-2521-15888. TELEX 41325. (Dist. in N. America by: Swets & Zeitlinger, Box 517, Berwyn, PA 19312. TEL 215-644-4944) Eds. P. Lugner, J. Karl Hedrick. adv.; bk.rev.; bibl.; charts; illus.; index; circ. 1,000. (also avail. in microform from SWZ) **Indexed:** Agri.Eng.Abstr., Appl.Mech.Rev., Br.Rail.Bd., Curr.Cont., Fluidex, HRIS, ISMEC, Sci.Abstr., Sh.& Vib.Dig.
—BLDSC shelfmark: 9153.670000.

380.52   GW
VERBUNDFAHRPLAN. (Text in English, French, German) 1972. a. DM.4. Muenchner Verkehrs- und Tarifverbund, Thierschstr. 2, 8000 Munich 22, Germany. TEL 089-23803-0. FAX 089-23803-282. circ. 120,000. (back issues avail.)

380.5 388.31   GW
VERKEHRS RUNDSCHAU. 1944. w. DM.197.40 (foreign DM.235). Heinrich Vogel Fachzeitschriften GmbH, Neumarkterstr. 18, Postfach 802020, 8000 Munich, Germany. TEL 089-431800. charts; stats.; circ. 114,420.

380.5   GW
DAS VERKEHRSGEWERBE WESTFALEN-LIPPE.* 1952. m. Verband fuer das Verkehrsgewerbe Westfalen-Lippe e.V., c/o Dr. E. Bauer, Hafenstr. 6, Postfach 7649, 4400 Muenster, Germany. circ. 2,500. (back issues avail.)

380.5 340   GW
VERKEHRSRECHTLICHE MITTEILUNGEN. m. DM.39. Kirschbaum Verlag GmbH, Siegfriedstr. 28, Postfach 210209, 5300 Bonn 2, Germany. TEL 0228-343057. FAX 0228-857145. TELEX 889596-KIRVL-D. **Indexed:** Dok.Str.

380.5   GW   ISSN 0723-6689
VERKEHRSWIRTSCHAFT. 1982. m. DM.138.70. Verlag VerkehrsWirtschaft Gerd Achilles, Spaldingstr. 210, Postfach 106104, 2000 Hamburg 1, Germany. TEL 040-230173. FAX 040-234613. Ed. Klaus Heims. adv.; bk.rev.; circ. 12,500. (back issues avail.)

380.5   AT
VICTORIAN ROAD TRANSPORT ASSOCIATION. ANNUAL REPORT. a. free. Victorian Road Transport Association, 17 Raglan St., South Melbourne, Vic. 3205, Australia. TEL 699-8833. FAX 03-669-7437. circ. 2,000.

380.5   IT   ISSN 0393-8077
TE4
VIE E TRASPORTI; rassegna di tecnica ed economia dei trasporti. 1929. bi-m. L.45000 (foreign L.54000). Casa Editrice la Fiaccola (Milan), Via Ravizza 62, 20149 Milan, Italy. TEL 02-4814355. FAX 02-4814834. TELEX 335512 COSTRU I. Dir. Giuseppe Saronni. adv.; abstr.; charts; illus.; stat.; index; circ. 8,000. (back issues avail.) **Indexed:** Chem.Abstr.
Former titles: Rivista della Strada (ISSN 0035-5992); Asfalti, Bitumi, Catrami.

380.5   DK   ISSN 0106-1666
VIRKSOMHEDS NYT. 1970. 15/yr. free. Christtreu, Strandlodsvei 48, DK-2300 Copenhagen S, Denmark. TEL 32-844848. FAX 31-582055. Ed. B. Remby. adv.; bk.rev.; illus.; charts; circ. 19,691 (controlled).
Former titles: Materialehaandtering og Transport Nyt (ISSN 0025-5297); Materiale Haandtering.
Description: Factory equipment, packing, storage and transportation.

380.5   DK
VIRKSOMHEDS NYTS; Leverandoerregister. 1984. a. Christtreu, Strandlodsvei 48, DK-2300 Copenhagen S, Denmark. TEL 32-844848. FAX 31-582055. circ. 19,691.

380.5   RU
VSESOYUZNYI NAUCHNO-ISSLEDOVATEL'SKII INSTITUT TRANSPORTNOGO STROITEL'STVA. TRUDY. vol.106, 1977. irreg. 0.83 Rub. per no. Izdatel'stvo Transport, Komsomol'skii prosp., 42, 119048 Moscow G-48, Russia. Ed.Bd. circ. 1,000. **Indexed:** Chem.Abstr.

W S S A GRAPEVINE. (Wine and Spirits Shippers Association) see *BEVERAGES*

354   AT
WESTERN AUSTRALIA. DEPARTMENT OF TRANSPORT. ANNUAL REPORT. 1934. a. free. Department of Transport, 136-138 Stirling Highway, Nedlands, W.A. 6009, Australia. FAX 09-386-5119. TELEX 94521. circ. 200 (controlled).
Formerly (until 1986): Western Australia. Transport Commission. Annual Report of the Commissioner of Transport.

380.5 388.324   AT   ISSN 0725-8895
WESTERN TRANSPORT. 1981. m. Aus.$50. Publishing Services (Qld.) Pty. Ltd., 244 St. Paul's Terrace, Spring Hill, Brisbane, Qld. 4000, Australia. Ed. Bill Cranny. adv.; circ. 4,141. (back issues avail.)
Description: Covers news and features on vehicle tests. Includes interviews, and product reviews for trucking firms.

380.5 630   US   ISSN 1042-2633
HE9788.4.A55
WHO'S WHO IN LIVE ANIMAL TRADE & TRANSPORT. 1985. biennial. $25. Silesia Companies, Inc., 619 Broad Creek Dr., Box 441110, Fort Washington, MD 20744-1110. TEL 301-292-1970. FAX 301-292-1787. Ed. Dale L. Anderson. adv. (back issues avail.)
Formerly: Who's Who in Animal Transportation (ISSN 8755-688X)
Description: Worldwide listing of personnel involved in the transporting of animals.

TRANSPORTATION — ABSTRACTING, BIBLIOGRAPHIES, STATISTICS

380.5   SA   ISSN 0257-5426
WIEL. (Text in Afrikaans) 1978. m. R.35 (foreign R.60)(effective 1992). Thomson Publications (Subsidiary of: Times Media Ltd.), P.O. Box 56182, Pinegowrie 2123, South Africa. TEL 011-789-2144. FAX 011-789-3196. Ed. J. Herbst. adv.; bk.rev.; circ. 21,925. (back issues avail.)

388.346   US
WOODALL'S R V BUYER'S GUIDE. 1978. a. $4.95. Woodall Publishing Co., 28167 N. Keith Dr., Box 5000, Lake Forest, IL 60045. TEL 708-362-6700. FAX 708-362-8776. adv.; circ. 85,000.
    Description: Helps consumers select a recreational vehicle and accessories.

ZHONGGUO JIAOTONG NIANJIAN/CHINA COMMUNICATIONS AND TRANSPORTATION YEARBOOK. see *COMMUNICATIONS*

TRANSPORTATION — Abstracting, Bibliographies, Statistics

629.2   IT   ISSN 0001-2033
A N F I A NOTIZIARIO STATISTICO. 1959. m. (11/yr.) L.350000($500) Associazione Nazionale fra le Industrie Automobilistiche - Italian Automobile Manufacturers Association, Corso G. Ferraris 61, 10128 Turin, Italy. TEL 561-3661. FAX 545986. stat.; circ. 500. (back issues avail.)
    Description: Covers statistics on the production, market and foreign trade of the Italian automobile industry.

387.7 317   US   ISSN 0002-2225
HE9803.A1
AIR CARRIER FINANCIAL STATISTICS. 1970. q. $16. U.S. Department of Transportation, Research & Special Programs Administration, Office of Aviation Information Management, 400 Seventh St., S.W., Washington, DC 20402. TEL 202-783-3238. stat.; circ. 500. **Indexed:** Amer.Stat.Ind.

387.7   CN   ISSN 0701-7928
HE 9815.A1
AIR CARRIER TRAFFIC AT CANADIAN AIRPORTS. (Catalogue 51-005) (Text in English, French) 1976. q. Can.$122($146) (outside Canada and US Can.$171). Statistics Canada, Transportation Division, Aviation Statistics Centre, Les Terrasses de la Chaudiere, 15 Eddy St., Hull, Que. K1A 0N9, Canada. TEL 613-951-7277. FAX 613-951-1584. (Subscr. to: Publications Sales and Services, Ottawa, Ont. K1A 0T6, Canada. TEL 819-997-1986)
    Description: Examines trends in traffic, volume of passengers, charter services, aircraft movements and regional and local schedules.

388.324   US   ISSN 1050-7671
▼**AMERICAN TRUCKING ASSOCIATIONS. CURRENT ECONOMIC BULLETIN.** 1990. w. $99. American Trucking Associations, Inc., Statistical Analysis Department, 2200 Mill Rd., Alexandria, VA 22314. TEL 703-838-1754. FAX 800-225-8382. Ed. Michael J. Arendes.
    Description: Compilation of economic trend data.

338   AO
ANGOLA. DIRECCAO DOS SERVICOS DE ESTATISTICA. ESTATISTICA DOS VEICULOS MOTORISADOS. 1967. a. Direccao dos Servicos de Estatistica, Ministerio do Planeamento e Coordenacao Economica, C.P. 1215, Luanda, Angola. circ. 750.

380.5   UN   ISSN 0066-3859
                             CODEN: ABTSEQ
ANNUAL BULLETIN OF TRANSPORT STATISTICS FOR EUROPE. (Text in English, French and Russian) 1950. a. price varies. Economic Commission for Europe (ECE), Palais des Nations, 1211 Geneva 10, Switzerland. TEL 22-740-0921. FAX 22-740-0931. TELEX 412962. (Or: United Nations Publications, Rm. DC2-853, New York, NY 10017) (also avail. in microfiche) **Indexed:** IIS.

ANNUAL SUMMARY OF MERCHANT SHIPS COMPLETED IN THE WORLD. see *TRANSPORTATION — Ships And Shipping*

387.7   SP
ANUARIO ESTADISTICO DEL TRANSPORTE AEREO ESPANA - (YEAR). (Comunidad Economica Europea edition avail.) a. free. Ministerio de Transportes, Turismo y Comunicaciones, Direccion General de Aviacion Civil, Gabinete de Planificacion, Jefe Administrador base de datos, C. Josefa Valcalcel 52, 28071 Madrid, Spain.

621.86 016   HU   ISSN 0230-5348
ANYAGMOZGATASI ES CSOMAGOLASI SZAKIRODALMI TAJEKOZTATO/ABSTRACT JOURNAL FOR MATERIALS HANDLING AND PACKAGING. 1982. m. 7000 Ft. Orszagos Muszaki Informacios Kozpont es Konyvtar (O.M.I.K.K.) - National Technical Information Centre and Library, Muzeum u. 17, Box 12, 1428 Budapest, Hungary. (Subscr. to: Kultura, Box 149, 1389 Budapest, Hungary) Eds. Felenc Hervai, Bela Kertesz. abstr.; index; circ. 350.
    Supersedes (1967-1982): Muszaki Lapszemle. Anyagmozatas, Csomagolas - Technical Abstracts. Materials Handling, Packaging (ISSN 0027-3023)

387.7   AT   ISSN 0729-6096
AUSTRALIA. AIR TRANSPORT STATISTICS. AIRPORT TRAFFIC DATA. 1980. a. free. Department of Transport & Communications, Domestic Aviation Information Section, P.O. Box 594, Canberra City, A.C.T. 2601, Australia. TEL 06-274-7720. FAX 06-274-7727. charts; circ. 400.

387.7   AT   ISSN 0727-6672
AUSTRALIA. AIR TRANSPORT STATISTICS. AUSTRALIAN AIR DISTANCES. 1982. irreg. free. Department of Transport & Communications, Domesitc Aviation Information Section, P.O. Box 594, Canberra City, A.C.T. 2601, Australia. TEL 06-274-7720. FAX 06-274-7727. charts; circ. 380. (back issues avail.)

387.7   AT   ISSN 1037-5937
AUSTRALIA. AIR TRANSPORT STATISTICS. COMMUTER AIRLINES. 1968. s-a. free. Department of Transport & Communications, Domestic Aviation Information Section, P.O. Box 594, Canberra City, A.C.T. 2601, Australia. TEL 06-274-7720. FAX 06-274-7727. circ. 470. (back issues avail.)
    Formerly: Australia. Air Transport Statistics. Commuter Air Transport (ISSN 0727-274X)

387.7   AT   ISSN 1037-1273
AUSTRALIA. AIR TRANSPORT STATISTICS. DOMESTIC AIRLINES (ANNUAL). 1922. a. free. Department of Transport & Communications, Domestic Aviation Information Section, P.O. Box 594, Canberra City, A.C.T. 2601, Australia. circ. 780. (back issues avail.)
    Formerly: Australia. Air Transport Statistics. Domestic Air Transport (ISSN 0159-396X)

387.7   AT   ISSN 0727-2782
AUSTRALIA. AIR TRANSPORT STATISTICS. DOMESTIC AIRLINES (QUARTERLY). 1967. q. free. Department of Transport & Communications, Domestic Aviation Information Section, P.O. Box 594, Canberra City, A.C.T. 2601, Australia. TEL 06-274-7720. FAX 06-274-7727. circ. 690. (back issues avail.)

387.7   AT
AUSTRALIA. AIR TRANSPORT STATISTICS. INTERNATIONAL SCHEDULED AIR TRANSPORT. 1934. s-a. free. Department of Transport & Communications, International Aviation Policy Division, P.O. Box 594, Canberra, A.C.T. 2601, Australia. circ. 400. (back issues avail.)
    Formerly: Australia. Air Transport Statistics. International Air Transpore (ISSN 0727-2723)

387.7   AT   ISSN 0727-2790
AUSTRALIA. AIR TRANSPORT STATISTICS. MONTHLY PROVISIONAL STATISTICS OF INTERNATIONAL SCHEDULED AIR TRANSPORT. 1981. m. free. Department of Transport & Communications, International Aviation Policy Division, P.O. Box 594, Canberra, A.C.T. 2601, Australia. Ed. I.M. Hunter. circ. 400. (back issues avail.)

387.7   AT   ISSN 0727-2766
AUSTRALIA. AIR TRANSPORT STATISTICS. SURVEY OF HOURS FLOWN. 1964. s-a. free. Department of Transport & Communications, Domestic Aviation Information Section, P.O. Box 594, Canberra, A.C.T. 2601, Australia. TEL 06-274-7720. FAX 06-274-7727. circ. 1,000. (back issues avail.)

388   AT   ISSN 0727-1638
AUSTRALIA. BUREAU OF STATISTICS. MOTOR VEHICLE REGISTRATIONS, AUSTRALIA. m. Aus.$120 (foreign Aus.$147)(effective 1991). Australian Bureau of Statistics, P.O. Box 10, Belconnen, A.C.T. 2616, Australia. TEL 062-527911. FAX 062-516009. circ. 462.
    Description: For each state and territory registrations of new motor cars and station wagons, utilities and panel vans. Details of registrations of new tractors, trailers, caravans and plant and equipment are also included.

380.5   AT   ISSN 1031-2730
AUSTRALIA. BUREAU OF STATISTICS. QUEENSLAND OFFICE. MOTOR VEHICLE REGISTRATIONS, QUEENSLAND. 1957. m. Aus.$120 (foreign Aus.$180). Australian Bureau of Statistics, Queensland Office, 313 Adelaide St., Brisbane, Qld. 4000, Australia. TEL 07-222-6022. FAX 07-229-6171. TELEX AA 40271.
    Description: Number of new motor vehicles, including motorcycles and trailers, and new mobile equipment registered by type, make, number of cylinders and weight.

387 382 319   AT   ISSN 0814-138X
AUSTRALIA. BUREAU OF STATISTICS. SHIPPING AND AIR CARGO COMMODITY STATISTICS, AUSTRALIA. 1974. q. Aus.$56 (foreign Aus.$70.40)(effective 1991). Australian Bureau of Statistics, P.O. Box 10, Belconnen, A.C.T. 10, Australia. TEL 062-527911. FAX 062-516009. circ. 211.
    Former titles: Australia. Bureau of Statistics. Shipping and Cargo, Australia; Australia. Bureau of Statistics. Overseas and Coastal Shipping; Australia. Bureau of Statistics. Overseas Shipping Cargo.
    Description: Provides information on gross weight and value of inward and outward cargo classified by: mode of transport; Australian State of loading or discharge; commodity classified by the Australian Transport Freight Commodity Classification.

385.264 310   AT
AUSTRALIAN NON-GOVERNMENT RAILWAYS OPERATING STATISTICS (YEARS). 1979. irreg. free. Bureau of Transport and Communicatons Economics, G.P.O. Box 501, Canberra, A.C.T. 2601, Australia. TEL 06-274-6067. FAX 06-274-6816. charts; circ. 100.
    Former titles: Australia. Non-Government Railways Statistics & Australia. Land Transport Statistics. Non-Government Railways (ISSN 0727-2804)

AUSTRALIAN ROAD RESEARCH IN PROGRESS. see *ENGINEERING — Abstracting, Bibliographies, Statistics*

388 016   US   ISSN 0145-6776
AUTO INDEX. (Includes year end cumulation issue) 1973. 6/yr. $6. 7 Clinton Pl., Suffern, NY 10901. Ed. David F. Plump. adv.; bibl.; circ. 300.
    Description: Index covers 14 automotive magazines for road tests, owner surveys and articles on maintenance and technical subjects.

629.283   FI   ISSN 0567-1795
AUTO JA TIE/AUTOMOBILES AND HIGHWAYS IN FINLAND (YEAR). (Text in English, Finnish) 1960. a. FIM 105. Finnish Road Association, P.O. Box 131, 00701 Helsinki, Finland. TEL 358-0-70010881. FAX 358-0-3511181. Ed. Jouko Perkkio. charts; illus.; stat.; index; circ. 1,700. (back issues avail.)

388.3   IT
AUTOMOBILE IN CIFRE. 1950? a. L.45000($80) (Associazione Nazionale fra le Industrie Automobilistiche) Giorgio Nada Editore, Via Claudio Treves, 15-17, 20090 Vimodrone MI, Italy. TEL 273011261. FAX 27301454. (Co-sponsor: Unione Italiana Costruttori Autoveicoli) stat. (back issues avail.)
    Description: Covers new registrations and import and export sales of used vehicles.

338.478   UK   ISSN 0951-158X
AUTOMOTIVE INDUSTRY DATA NEWSLETTER. Short title: A I D Newsletter. 1983. s-m. £320. Automotive Industry Data Ltd., City House, 2-4 Dam St., Lichfield, Staffs WS13 6AA, England. TEL 0543-257295. FAX 0543-256884. Ed. John May. s-a index. (back issues avail.)
    Description: Provides statistical analysis of motor industry.

4662 TRANSPORTATION — ABSTRACTING, BIBLIOGRAPHIES, STATISTICS

388　　　　　　　US
AUTOMOTIVE LITERATURE INDEX. 1981. quinquennial. $40. Wallace Publishing, 2307 Shoreland Ave., Toledo, OH 43611. TEL 419-729-9065. Ed. A. Wallace. bk.rev.; film rev.; play rev.; charts; illus.; cum.index; circ. 1,000. (back issues avail.)

380.5　　　　　　　IT
AUTOVEICOLI CIRCOLANTI IN ITALIA. a. L.35000($35) Associazione Nazionale fra le Industrie Automobilistiche, Corso G. Ferraris 61, 10128 Turin, Italy. TEL 561-3661. FAX 545956. stat. (back issues avail.)
Description: Covers vehicles in use. Includes make, model, engine type, body and loading capacity.

623.8 016　　　UK　　ISSN 0268-9650
VM1
B M T ABSTRACTS. 1946. m. £180($225) (British Maritime Technology Ltd.) B M T Cortec Ltd., Wallsend Research Stn., Wallsend, Tyne and Wear NE28 6UY, England. FAX 091-263-8754. Ed. G. Smith. abstr.; index; circ. 500. **Indexed:** World Surf.Coat.
●Also available online.
Formerly (until Jan. 1986): British Ship Research Association. Journal (ISSN 0007-1765)

387　　　　　　　II
BASIC PORT STATISTICS OF INDIA. 1970. a., latest edition in print 1977. $27.54. Ministry of Shipping and Transport, Transport Research Division, I D A Bldg., Jamnagar House, Shahjahan Rd., New Delhi 110011, India. (Orders to: Controller of Publications, Civil Lines, Delhi 110006, India)
Former titles: Port Transport Statistics of India; India Ports and Shipping Statistics.

388　　　　II　　ISSN 0067-6462
BASIC ROAD STATISTICS OF INDIA. Hindi edition: Mool Sarak Ankrey. 1948. a. Rs.79.40 for Hindi ed.; English ed. $3.78. Ministry of Shipping and Transport, Transport Research Division, I D A Bldg., Jamnagar House, Shahjahan Rd, New Delhi 110011, India. (Orders to: Controller of Publications, Civil Lines, New Delhi 110006, India)

386　　　　BE　　ISSN 0773-2805
BELGIUM. INSTITUT NATIONAL DE STATISTIQUE. STATISTIQUE DE LA NAVIGATION INTERIEURE. Dutch edition (ISSN 0773-2813) (Text in French) 1971. a. 230 Fr. (foreign 330 Fr.). Institut National de Statistique, 44 rue de Louvain, B-1000 Brussels, Belgium.
Incorporates (1949-1982): Belgium. Institut National de Statistique. Statistique de la Navigation du Rhin (ISSN 0067-5520)

338.4　　　　BE　　ISSN 0773-3070
BELGIUM. INSTITUT NATIONAL DE STATISTIQUE. STATISTIQUE DES VEHICULES A MOTEUR NEUFS MIS EN CIRCULATION. Dutch edition (ISSN 0773-3089) (Text in French) 1955. a. 290 Fr. (foreign 390 Fr.). Institut National de Statistique, 44 rue de Louvain, B-1000 Brussels, Belgium.

387.1　　　　BE　　ISSN 0772-7739
BELGIUM. INSTITUT NATIONAL DE STATISTIQUE. STATISTIQUE DU TRAFIC INTERNATIONAL DES PORTS. Dutch edition (ISSN 0772-800X) (Text in French) 1952. a. 690 Fr. (foreign 490 Fr.). Institut National de Statistique, 44 rue de Louvain, B-1000 Brussels, Belgium.
Formerly: Belgium. Institut National de Statistique. Statistique Annuelle du Trafic International des Ports (ISSN 0067-5482)

380.5 910.09　　　BE　　ISSN 0772-6694
HF3601
BELGIUM. INSTITUT NATIONAL DE STATISTIQUE. STATISTIQUES DU COMMERCE EXTER. Dutch Edition: Statistieken over de Buitenlandse Handel (ISSN 0772-6686) (Text in French) 1967. m. 3750 Fr. (foreign 6170 Fr.). Institut National de Statistique (I.N.S.), Rue de Louvain, 44, B-1000 Brussels, Belgium. TEL 02-513-9650. stat.; circ. 450. (also avail. in microfilm; back issues avail.)

271　　　　BE　　ISSN 0773-4255
BELGIUM. INSTITUT NATIONAL DE STATISTIQUE. STATISTIQUES DU COMMERCE INTERIEUR ET DES TRANSPORTS. (Text in Dutch, French) 1972. m. 1000 Fr. (foreign 2000 Fr.). Institut National de Statistique, Rue de Louvain 44, B-1000 Brussels, Belgium. charts; stat. **Indexed:** P.A.I.S.For.Lang.Ind.
Formed by the merger of: Belgium. Institut National de Statistique. Statistiques des Transports & Belgium. Institut National de Statistique. Statistique du Commerce; Incorporates: Activities des Aerodromes Belges (ISSN 0067-5415)

388 016　　　　YU　　ISSN 0352-6402
BILTEN DOKUMENTACIJE. SERIJA S1. SAOBRACAJ/BULLETIN OF DOCUMENTATION. SERIES S1. TRAFFIC. 1952. bi-m. $198. Jugoslovenski Centar za Tehnicku i Naucnu Dokumentaciju - Yugoslav Center for Technical and Scientific Documentation (YCTSD), Sl. Penezica-Krcuna 29-31, Box 724, 11000 Belgrade, Yugoslavia. Ed. Ljiljana Kojic-Bogdanovic.
Formerly (until 1984): Bilten Dokumentacije. Serija E2. Saobracaj (ISSN 0351-7586)

387
BOLETIN ESTADISTICO DE TRAFICO AEREO INTERNACIONAL. 1976. a. free. Direccion General de Aviacion Civil, Division de Transporte Aereo, Buenos Aires No. 149 y Avda. 10 de Agosto, Quito, Ecuador. TEL 552288. TELEX 22710 DACUIO ED. stat.
Formerly: Ecuador. Direccion de Aviacion Civil. Estadisticas de Trafico Aereo.

387.7　　　　CN　　ISSN 0828-8208
HE9815.Z7
CANADA. STATISTICS CANADA. AIR CHARTER STATISTICS. (Catalogue 51-207) 1970. q. Can.$36($43) (foreign Can.$50). Statistics Canada, Transportation Division, Aviation Statistics Centre, Les Terrasses de la Chaudiere, 15 Eddy St., Hull, Que K1A 0N9, Canada. TEL 613-951-7277. FAX 613-951-1584. (Subscr. to: Publications Sales and Services, Ottawa, Ont. K1A 0T6, Canada)
Formerly: Canada. Statistics Canada. International Air Charter Statistics (ISSN 0705-4297)
Description: Examines the domestic and international air charter operations of more than 80 carriers. Covers passenger, and cargo charter traffic.

387.7　　　　CN　　ISSN 0705-4343
HE9815.A1
CANADA. STATISTICS CANADA. AIR PASSENGER ORIGIN AND DESTINATION. CANADA - UNITED STATES REPORT. (Catalogue 51-205) (Text in English and French) 1968. a. Can.$42($50) (foreign Can.$59). Statistics Canada, Transportation Division, Aviation Statistics Centre, Les Terrasses de la Chaudiere, 15 Eddy St., Hull, Que K1A 0N9, Canada. TEL 613-951-7277. FAX 613-951-1584. (Subscr. to: Publications Sales and Services, Ottawa, Ont. K1A 0T6, Canada) (also avail. in microform from MML)

387.7　　　　CN　　ISSN 0703-2692
HE9815.A1
CANADA. STATISTICS CANADA. AIR PASSENGER ORIGIN AND DESTINATION. DOMESTIC REPORT. a. Can.$31. Statistics Canada, Transportation Division, Aviation Statistics Centre, Les Terrasses de la Chaudiere, 15 Eddy St., Hull, Que. K1A 0N9, Canada. TEL 819-951-6942. circ. 530.

387.7　　　　CN　　ISSN 0068-7057
CANADA. STATISTICS CANADA. AVIATION STATISTICS CENTRE. SERVICE BULLETIN/CANADA. CENTRE DES STATISTIQUES DE L'AVIATION. BULLETIN DE SERVICE. (Catalog 51-004) (Text in English, French) 1968. m. Can.$93($112) (outside Canada and US Can.$130). Statistics Canada, Transportation Division, Aviaition Statistics Centre, Les Terrasses de la Chaudiere, 15 Eddy St., Hull, Que. K1A 0N9, Canada. (Subscr. to: Publications Sales and Services, Ottawa, Ont. K1A 0T6, Canada. TEL 819-997-1986) (also avail. in microform from MML)
Description: Includes financial and operational advance statistics for Level I carriers. Covers the air transport industry, airports, fare basis statistics, passenger and cargo traffic.

388　　　　CN　　ISSN 0383-5766
HE5635
CANADA. STATISTICS CANADA. PASSENGER BUS AND URBAN TRANSIT STATISTICS. (Catalogue 53-215) (Text in English and French) 1956. a. Can.$36($43) (foreign $50). Statistics Canada, Publications Sales and Services, Ottawa, Ont. K1A 0T6, Canada. TEL 613-951-7277. FAX 613-951-1584. (also avail. in microform from MML)
Description: Shows investment, operating revenues, expenses on intercity and rural bus companies and urban transit systems.

380.5　　　　CN　　ISSN 0829-1756
CANADA. STATISTICS CANADA. PASSENGER BUS AND URBAN TRANSIT STATISTICS. (Catalogue 53-003) (Text in English, French) 1955. m. Can.$71($85) (foreign $99). Statistics Canada, Publications Sales and Services, Ottawa, Ont. K1A 0T6, Canada. TEL 613-951-7277. FAX 613-951-1584.
Formerly: Canada. Statistics Canada. Urban Transit; Canada. Statistics Canada. Urban Transport (ISSN 0380-5948)
Description: Outlines revenues, passengers carried and vehicle kilometers run on urban transit systems with gross operating revenues from urban transit operations exceeding $500,000.

385　　　　CN　　ISSN 0380-6308
CANADA. STATISTICS CANADA. RAILWAY CARLOADINGS. (Catalog 52-001) (Text in English, French) 1924. m. Can.$83($100) (foreign $116). Statistics Canada, Publications Sales and Services, Ottawa, Ont. K1A 0T6, Canada. TEL 613-951-7277. FAX 613-951-1584. (also avail. in microform from MML)
Description: Outlines 70 commodities by cars loaded and tonnes of revenue freight carried in eastern and western Canada by class I and II railways.

385　　　　CN　　ISSN 0380-5964
HE2801
CANADA. STATISTICS CANADA. RAILWAY OPERATING STATISTICS. (Catalogue 52-003) (Text in English, French) 1921. m. Can.$105($34) (foreign $147). Statistics Canada, Publications Sales and Services, Ottawa, Ont. K1A 0T6, Canada. TEL 613-951-7277. FAX 613-951-1584. (also avail. in microform from MML)
Description: Includes statistics on operating finances and traffic as well as information on seven railways.

388.3　　　　CN　　ISSN 0703-654X
HD9574.C2
CANADA. STATISTICS CANADA. ROAD MOTOR VEHICLES, FUEL SALES. (Catalogue 53-218) (Text in English, French) 1960. a. Can.$17($20) (foreign $24). Statistics Canada, Publications Sales and Services, Ottawa, Ont. K1A 0T6, Canada. TEL 613-951-7277. FAX 613-951-1584. (also avail. in microform from MML)
Formerly: Canada. Statistics Canada. Motor Vehicle. Part 2. Motive Fuel Sales (ISSN 0527-5830)
Description: Presents gross and net sales of gasolines and net fuel sales of diesel oil and liquefied petroleum gas used for automotive purposes by year and month, province and territory.

388.3　　　　CN　　ISSN 0706-067X
HE5635
CANADA. STATISTICS CANADA. ROAD MOTOR VEHICLES, REGISTRATIONS. (Catalogue 53-219) (Text in English, French) 1960. a. Can.$17($20) (foreign $24). Statistics Canada, Publications Sales and Services, Ottawa, Ont. K1A 0T6, Canada. TEL 613-951-7277. FAX 603-951-1584. (also avail. in microform from MML)
Description: Presents data on registrations of motor vehicles by type including passenger automobiles, trucks, motorcycles, buses and trailers.

TRANSPORTATION — ABSTRACTING, BIBLIOGRAPHIES, STATISTICS 4663

387   CN   ISSN 0835-5533
HE769
CANADA. STATISTICS CANADA. SHIPPING IN CANADA.
(Catalogue 54-205) (Text in English and French) 1946. a. Can.$41($49) (foreign $57). Statistics Canada, Publications Sales and Services, Ottawa, Ont. K1A 0T6, Canada. TEL 613-951-7277. FAX 613-951-1584. (also avail. in microform from MML)
Formerly: Canada. Statistics Canada. Water Transportation (ISSN 0380-0342)
Description: Presents domestic and international shipping activities at Canadian ports.

385   CN   ISSN 0828-2897
HE215.A15
CANADA. STATISTICS CANADA. SURFACE AND MARINE TRANSPORT.. (Catalogue 50-002) (Text in English, French) 1971. irreg. Can.$75($90) (foreign $105). Statistics Canada, Publications Sales and Services, Ottawa, Ont. K1A 0T6, Canada. TEL 613-951-7277. FAX 613-951-1584.
Formerly (until 1984): Canada. Statistics Canada. Railway Transport. Service Bulletin (ISSN 0700-2211)
Description: Presents analytical data, time series analysis and special tabulations covering trucking, rail, bus, urban, and marine transportation, and highway infrastructure.

380.5   CN   ISSN 0826-6026
HE9815.A1
CANADIAN CIVIL AVIATION. (Text in English, French) 1970. a. $43. Statistics Canada, Transportation Division, Aviation Statistics Centre, Les Terrasses de la Chaudiere, 15 Eddy St., Hull, Que. K1A 0N9, Canada. TEL 819-997-1986. FAX 819-953-8499. (Subscr. to: Publication Sales & Service, Ottawa K1A 0T6, Canada) circ. 390.
Formerly: Air Carrier Financial Statements.
Description: Reports on activities of over 250 air Canadian carriers operating in Canada. Includes operational and financial statistics on number of passengers carried, kilometers and hours flown, income statements and balance sheets.

387 971   CN   ISSN 0835-6963
Z6841.C2
CANADIAN MARITIME BIBLIOGRAPHY. (Text in English, French) 1986. a. Can.$10. Memorial University of Newfoundland, Maritime Studies Research Unit, St. John's, Nfld. A1C 5S7, Canada. TEL 709-737-8424. FAX 709-737-4569. TELEX 016-4677. (Subscr. to: Canadian Nautical Research Society, P.O. Box 7008, Sta. J, Ottawa, Ont. K2A 3Z6, Canada) Eds. Lewis R. Fischer, M. Stephen Salmon. adv.; circ. 300.
Description: Bibliography of published materials on Canadian maritime history.
Refereed Serial

385.1 332   US   ISSN 0008-6924
CARRIER REPORTS. 1960. q. $35. Box 39, Lubec, ME 04652. Ed. Richard W. Honer. adv.; stat.

380.5   UK   ISSN 0260-9894
HE243.A15
CHARTERED INSTITUTE OF PUBLIC FINANCE AND ACCOUNTANCY. HIGHWAYS AND TRANSPORTATION STATISTICS. ESTIMATES. 1982. a. £40. Chartered Institute of Public Finance and Accountancy, 3 Robert St., London WC2N 6BH, England. TEL 071-895-8823. FAX 071-895-8825. (back issues avail.)

387.7 310   UK
CHARTERED INSTITUTE OF PUBLIC FINANCE AND ACCOUNTANCY. LOCAL AUTHORITY AIRPORTS. ACCOUNTS AND STATISTICS. ACTUALS. 1979. a. £35. Chartered Institute of Public Finance and Accountancy, 3 Robert St., London WC2N 6BH, England. TEL 071-895-8823. FAX 071-895-8825. (back issues avail.)
Formerly: Chartered Institute of Public Finance and Accountancy. Local Authority Airports. Accounts and Statistics (ISSN 0260-9967)

318   CK
COLOMBIA. DEPARTAMENTO ADMINISTRATIVO NACIONAL DE ESTADISTICA. ANUARIO GENERAL DE ESTADISTICA - TRANSPORTES Y COMUNICACIONES. irreg.? Departamento Administrativo Nacional de Estadistica, Banco Nacional de Datos, Centro Administrativo Nacional, Avda. Eldorado, Bogota, Colombia.

380.5   FR
COMMENT EVALUER LA PART DU TRAFIC MARITIME DE NOTRE COMMERCE EXTERIEUR QUI ECHAPPE AUX PORTS FRANCAIS. 1975. a. 260 F. Ministere de Transport, Observatoire Economique et Statistique des Transports (OEST), 55 rue Brillat-Savarin, 75658 Paris Cedex 13, France.

380.5 016   US   ISSN 0011-3654
Z7164.T8
CURRENT LITERATURE IN TRAFFIC AND TRANSPORTATION. 1960. q. $15. Northwestern University, Transportation Library, Evanston, IL 60208-2300. TEL 708-491-5275. FAX 708-491-8306. bibl.; circ. 550. (also avail. in microfilm from UMI; reprint service avail. from UMI)

387 314   DK   ISSN 0070-3486
HE851
DANMARKS SKIBE OG SKIBSFART/DANISH SHIPS AND SHIPPING. (Text in Danish; notes in English) 1921. a. DKK 46.72. Danmarks Statistik, Sejroegade 11, 2100 Copenhagen OE, Denmark. TEL 31-298222. FAX 31-184801. TELEX 16236.

614 380.5   FR
E C M T STATISTICAL REPORT ON ROAD ACCIDENTS. a. price varies. Organization for Economic Cooperation and Development, European Council of Ministers of Transport, 2 rue Andre-Pascal, 75775 Paris Cedex 16, France. TEL 45-24-82-00. (U.S. orders to: O.E.C.D. Publications and Information Center, 2001 L St., N.W., Ste. 700, Washington, DC 20036-4910. TEL 202-785-6323) (also avail. in microfiche from OEC)

388.3   SZ
EINGEFUEHRTE MOTORFAHRZEUGE/VEHICULES A MOTEUR IMPORTES. (Text in French and German) 1929. a. 7.50 Fr. Bundesamt fuer Statistik, Hallwylstr. 15, CH-3003 Bern, Switzerland. TEL 031-618836. FAX 031-617856.

388 016   RU   ISSN 0131-7962
EKSPRESS-INFORMATSIYA. GORODSKOI TRANSPORT. 1961. 48/yr. 38.20 Rub. Vsesoyuznyi Institut Nauchno-Tekhnicheskoi Informatsii (VINITI), Baltiiskaya ul., 14, Moscow A-219, Russia. (Subscr. to: Mezhdunarodnaya Kniga, Dimitrova ul. 39, 113095 Moscow, Russia)

625.1 016   RU
EKSPRESS-INFORMATSIYA. ORGANIZATSIYA PEREVOZOK. AVTOMATIZIROVANNIE SISTEMY UPRAVLENIA TRANSPORTOM. 1962. 48/yr. 38 Rub. Vsesoyuznyi Institut Nauchno-Tekhnicheskoi Informatsii (VINITI), Baltiiskaya ul., 14, Moscow A-219, Russia. (Subscr. to: Mezhdunarodnaya Kniga, Dimitrova ul. 39, 113095 Moscow, Russia)
Formerly: Ekspress-Informatsiya. Organizatsiya Perevozok, Avtomatizirovanie, Telemekhanika i Svyaz' na Zheleznykh Dorogakh (ISSN 0207-5016)

380.5 016   RU   ISSN 0131-0402
EKSPRESS-INFORMATSIYA. PROMYSHLENNYI TRANSPORT. 1960. 48/yr. 38 Rub. Vsesoyuznyi Institut Nauchno-Tekhnicheskoi Informatsii (VINITI), Baltiiskaya ul., 14, Moscow A-219, Russia. (Subscr. to: Mezhdunarodnaya Kniga, Dimitrova ul. 39, 113095 Moscow, Russia)

380.5   FR
ENQUETE PERMANENTE SUR L'UTILISATION DES VEHICULES DE TRANSPORT EN COMMUN DE PERSONNES EN (YEAR). 1979. a. 80 Fr. Observatoire Economique et Statistique des Transports, 55 rue Brillat-Savarin, 75658 Paris Cedex 13, France. Ed. Yves Jacquin. circ. 13,000.

388.3   SZ
ENTWICKLUNG DES MOTORFAHRZEUGBESTANDES IN DER SCHWEIZ/EVOLUTION DE L'EFFECTIF DES VEHICULES A MOTEUR EN SUISSE. (Text in French and German) 1984. a. 7 Fr. Bundesamt fuer Statistik, Hallwylstr. 15, CH-3003 Bern, Switzerland. TEL 031-618836. FAX 031-617856.

388.3   US   ISSN 0160-4570
HE5623.A1
F & O S MOTOR CARRIER ANNUAL REPORT. (Financial and Operating Statistics); results of operations class I & II motor carriers of property; regulated by the Interstate Commerce Commission. a. $400 (including Motor Carrier Quarterly Report $495). American Trucking Associations, Inc., Statistical Analysis Department, 2200 Mill Rd., Alexandria, VA 22314. TEL 703-838-1792. FAX 800-838-1992. illus.
Supersedes: F and O S (ISSN 0098-2245)

388.3   US
F & O S MOTOR CARRIER QUARTERLY REPORT. (Financial and Operating Statistics) q. $400 (including Motor Carrier Annual Report $495). American Trucking Associations, Inc., Statistical Analysis Department, 2200 Mill Rd., Alexandria, VA 22314. TEL 203-838-1792. FAX 703-838-1992.
Description: Data and cumulative summaries based on quarterly reports filed with the ICC by Class I and II carriers.

380.5   FJ
FIJI. BUREAU OF STATISTICS. SHIPPING STATISTICS. 1971. a., latest 1984. $5 (effective Jan. 1991). Bureau of Statistics, P.O. Box 2221, Suva, Fiji.

385.1   FI   ISSN 0430-5272
FINLAND. TILASTOKESKUS. LIIKENNETILASTOLLINEN VUOSIKIRJA/FINLAND. STATISTIKCENTRALEN. SAMFAERDSELSTATISTISKAARSBOK/FINLAND. CENTRAL STATISTICAL OFFICE. YEARBOOK OF TRANSPORT STATISTICS. (Section XXXVI of Official Statistics of Finland) (Text in English, Finnish and Swedish) 1958. a. FIM 68. Tilastokeskus, Annankatu 44, SF-00100 Helsinki 10, Finland.

388.31   FI   ISSN 0355-2284
HE255.3.A15
FINLAND. TILASTOKESKUS. TIELIIKENNEONNETTOMUUDET/FINLAND. STATISTISKCENTRALEN. VAEGTRAFIKOLYCKOR/FINLAND. CENTRAL STATISTICAL OFFICE. ROAD TRAFFIC ACCIDENTS. (Text in English, Finnish and Swedish) 1967. a. FIM 90. Tilastokeskus, P.O. Box 504, SF-00101 Helsinki, Finland. (back issues avail.)

380.5   FR
FRANCE. OBSERVATOIRE ECONOMIQUE ET STATISTIQUE DES TRANSPORTS. MEMENTO DE STATISTIQUES DES TRANSPORTS. a. 100 F. Observatoire Economique et Statistiques des Transports, 55-57 rue-Brillat-Savarin, 75658 Paris Cedex 13, France.
Formerly: France. Departement des Statistiques de Transport. Memento de Statistiques des Transports.

380.5   FR   ISSN 0244-7819
FRANCE. OBSERVATOIRE ECONOMIQUE ET STATISTIQUE DES TRANSPORTS. NOTE DE CONJONCTURE. m. 600 Fr. Ministere de l'Equipement, du Logement, de l'Amenagement du Territoire et des Transports, Observatoire Economique et Statistique des Transports., 55 rue Brillat-Savarin, 75658 Paris Cedex 13, France. TEL 45.89.89.2.
Incorporating: Departement des Statistiques des Transports. Bulletin Mensuel de Statistiques.

387.74 310   UK
GREAT BRITAIN. CIVIL AVIATION AUTHORITY. U.K. AIRLINES MONTHLY OPERATING & TRAFFIC STATISTICS. 1973. m. price varies. Civil Aviation Authority, Greville House, 37 Gratton Rd., Cheltenham, Glos GL50 2BN, England.
Supersedes in part (as of 1983): Great Britain. Civil Aviation Authority. C A A Monthly Operating and Traffic Statistics (ISSN 0265-0266); Former titles (until 1983): Great Britain. Civil Aviation Board. C A A Monthly Statistics (ISSN 0306-3577); Business Monitor Civil Aviation Series.

387.74   UK
GREAT BRITAIN. CIVIL AVIATION AUTHORITY. U.K. AIRPORTS MONTHLY STATEMENTS OF MOVEMENTS, PASSENGERS AND CARGO. 1973. m. price varies. Civil Aviation Authority, Grevill House, 37 Gratton Rd., Cheltenham, Glos GL50 2BN, England.
Supersedes in part (as of 1983): Great Britain. Civil Aviation Authority. C A A Monthly Operating and Traffic Statistics (ISSN 0265-0266)

T

TRANSPORTATION — ABSTRACTING, BIBLIOGRAPHIES, STATISTICS

387 GR ISSN 0072-7423
GREECE. NATIONAL STATISTICAL SERVICE. SHIPPING STATISTICS. (Text in English and Greek) 1967. a. $10. National Statistical Service of Greece, Statistical Information and Publications Division, 14-16 Lycourgou St., 10166 Athens, Greece. TEL 3244-748. FAX 3222205. TELEX 216734 ESYE GR.

301.6 380.5 GR ISSN 0256-3657
GREECE. NATIONAL STATISTICAL SERVICE. TRANSPORT AND COMMUNICATION STATISTICS. (Text in Greek) 1967. a. $7. National Statistical Service of Greece, Statistical Information and Publications Division, 14-16 Lycourgou St., 10166 Athens, Greece. TEL 3244-748. FAX 3222205. TELEX 216734 ESYE GR.

388 016 HU ISSN 0231-1941
HAJOZASI SZAKIRODALMI TAJEKOZTATO/SHIPPING ABSTRACTS. 1949. bi-m. 2700 Ft. Orszagos Muszaki Informacios Kozpont es Konyvtar (O.M.I.K.K.) - National Technical Information Centre and Library, Muzeum u. 17, Box 12, 1428 Budapest, Hungary. (Subscr. to: Kultura, Box 149, 1389 Budapest, Hungary) Ed. Nandorne Raics. abstr.; index; circ. 350.
Supersedes in part (as of 1982): Muszaki Lapszemle. Kozlekedes - Technical Abstracts. Transportation (ISSN 0027-5042)

625 388.1 016 US
TE1
HIGHWAY RESEARCH ABSTRACTS. 1968. q. $85 to N. America; elsewhere $90. National Research Council, Transportation Research Board, Highway Research Information Service, 2101 Constitution Ave., N.W., Washington, DC 20418. TEL 202-334-3218. FAX 202-334-2519. TELEX 248664 NASWUR. Ed.Bd. abstr.; circ. 2,500.
●Also available online.
Formerly (until 1990): H R I S Abstracts (ISSN 0017-6222)
Description: Abstracts of research reports, technical papers in conference proceedings, and journal articles on highway research related topics.

623.89 JA ISSN 0389-7605
HOKKYOKUSEI HOIKAKUHYO/POLARIS ALMANAC FOR AZIMUTH DETERMINATION. (Text in Japanese) a. Kaijo Hoan-cho - Maritime Safety Agency, 1-3, Kasumigaseki 2-chome, Chiyoda-ku, Tokyo 100, Japan. charts; stat.

310 385.1 HK
HONG KONG. CENSUS AND STATISTICS DEPARTMENT. SHIPPING STATISTICS. (Text in English) 1984. a. HK.$21. Government Publication Centre, G.P.O. Bldg., Ground Fl., Connaught Place, Hong Kong, Hong Kong. (Subscr. to: Director of Information Services, Information Services Dept., 1 Battery Path, G-F, Central, Hong Kong) Ed.Bd.

388.31 HU ISSN 0237-8280
HE247.5.A15
HUNGARY. KOZPONTI STATISZTIKAI HIVATAL. KOZLEKEDESI EVKONYV. a. 310 Ft. Statisztikai Kiado Vallalat, Kaszasdulo u. 2, P.O.B.99, 1300 Budapest 3, Hungary. TEL 1-688-635. TELEX 22-6699. (Subscr. to: Kultura, Box 149, H-1389 Budapest, Hungary) circ. 650.
Former titles: Hungary. Kozponti Statisztikai Hivatal. Kozlekedesi Posta es Tavkozlesi; Hungary. Kozponti Statisztikai Hivatal. Kozlekedesi es Hirkozlesi Evkonyv (ISSN 0133-9133)

387 016 UK
I C H C A QUARTERLY BULLETIN. 1978. q. £30 to non-members. International Cargo Handling Coordination Association, 71 Bondway, London SW8 1SH, England. TEL 44-793-1022. FAX 44-820-1703. TELEX 261106-G. Ed. Dale Bryce. adv.; bk.rev.; circ. 2,000.
Formerly: Cargo Handling Abstracts (ISSN 0141-0687)
Description: Contains information bulletins and a comprehensive listing of upcoming international industry conferences, exhibitions and seminars.

385 II ISSN 0376-9909
HE3291
INDIAN RAILWAYS YEARBOOK. (Text in English) 1973. a. Railway Board, Directorate of Statistics and Economics, New Delhi 110001, India.

338.476 IT
INDUSTRIA AUTOMOBILISTICA MONDIALE. a. L.30000($40) Associazione Nazionale fra le Industrie Automobilistiche, Corso G. Ferraris 61, 10128 Turin, Italy. TEL 561-3661. FAX 545956. stat.
Description: Comments and information on the motor industry worldwide.

388.3 US
INDUSTRY STATISTICS (YEAR). 1982. biennial. $50. Battery Council International, 401 N. Michigan Ave., Chicago, IL 60611. TEL 312-644-6610. Ed.Bd. circ. 1,000.
Formerly: Statistics Annual.

385 016 GW
INFORMATION EISENBAHN;* Dokumentation des Fachschrifttums. 1953. m. DM.120. Deutsche Bundesbahn, Wallstr. 56, 6500 Mainz 1, Germany. adv.; bk.rev.; abstr.; stat.; tr.lit.; circ. 2,300.
Formerly: Kurzauszuege aus dem Schrifttum fuer das Eisenbahnwesen (ISSN 0023-5695)
Description: Documentation of specialized railway publications, including abstracts.

387.74 SZ
INTERNATIONAL AIR TRANSPORT ASSOCIATION. MONTHLY INTERNATIONAL STATISTICS. (Text in English) 1980. m. 1000 Fr.($750) International Air Transport Association, P.O. Box 160, CH-1216 Cointrin - Geneva, Switzerland. TEL 022-7983366. FAX 022-7983553. TELEX 415586. circ. 300.
Description: Report showing traffic, capacity and passenger load factor trends of international scheduled services.

387 UN ISSN 0074-2422
INTERNATIONAL CIVIL AVIATION ORGANIZATION. DIGESTS OF STATISTICS. SERIES AT. AIRPORT TRAFFIC. (Editions in English, French, Russian, Spanish) a. price varies. International Civil Aviation Organization, Attn: Document Sales Unit, 1000 Sherbrooke St. W., Montreal, Que. H3A 2R2, Canada. TEL 514-285-8219. FAX 514-288-4772. TELEX 05-24513.
Description: Statistics on airports open to international traffic.

387 UN ISSN 0074-2430
INTERNATIONAL CIVIL AVIATION ORGANIZATION. DIGESTS OF STATISTICS. SERIES F. FINANCIAL DATA. (Editions in English, French, Russian, Spanish) a. price varies. International Civil Aviation Organization, Attn: Document Sales Unit, 1000 Sherbrooke St. W., Montreal, Que. H3A 2R2, Canada. TEL 514-285-8219. FAX 514-288-4772. TELEX 05-24513.

387 UN
INTERNATIONAL CIVIL AVIATION ORGANIZATION. DIGESTS OF STATISTICS. SERIES FP. FLEET, PERSONNEL, COMMERCIAL AIR CARRIERS. (Classification of its Digest of Statistics, issued from 1947. Digest and Series numbering maintained separately) (Editions in English, French, Russian and Spanish) a. price varies. International Civil Aviation Organization, Attn: Document Sales Unit, 1000 Sherbrooke St. W., Montreal, Que. H3A 2R2, Canada. TEL 514-285-8219. FAX 514-288-4772. TELEX 05-24513.
Formerly: International Civil Aviation Organization. Digests of Statistics. Series FP. Fleet, Personnel (ISSN 0074-2449)

387 UN ISSN 0074-2457
INTERNATIONAL CIVIL AVIATION ORGANIZATION. DIGESTS OF STATISTICS. SERIES R. CIVIL AIRCRAFT ON REGISTER. (Editions in English, French, Russian, Spanish) 1961. a. price varies. International Civil Aviation Organization, Attn: Document Sales Unit, 1000 Sherbrooke St. W., Montreal, Que. H3A 2R2, Canada. TEL 514-285-8219. FAX 514-288-4772. TELEX 05-24513.

387 UN ISSN 1014-0093
INTERNATIONAL CIVIL AVIATION ORGANIZATION. DIGESTS OF STATISTICS. SERIES TF. TRAFFIC BY FLIGHT STAGE. (Text in English, French, Spanish, Russian) a. price varies. International Civil Aviation Organization, Attn: Document Sales Unit, 1000 Sherbrooke St. W., Montreal, Que. H3A 2R2, Canada. TEL 514-285-8219. FAX 514-288-4772. TELEX 05-24513.
Formerly: International Civil Aviation Organization. Digests of Statistics. Series TF. Traffic Flow (ISSN 0074-2473)

387 UN ISSN 1014-0077
INTERNATIONAL CIVIL AVIATION ORGANIZATION. DIGESTS OF STATISTICS. SERIES T. TRAFFIC, COMMERCIAL AIR TRAFFIC. (Editions in English, French, Russian, Spanish) 1947. a. price varies. International Civil Aviation Organization, Attn: Document Sales Unit, 1000 Sherbrooke St. W., Montreal, Que. H3A 2R2, Canada. TEL 514-285-8219. FAX 514-288-4772. TELEX 05-24513.
Former titles (until 1977): International Civil Aviation Organization. Digests of Statistics. Series T. Airline Traffic (ISSN 1014-0085); (until 1975): International Civil Aviation Organization. Digests of Statistics. Series T. Traffic (ISSN 0074-2465)
Description: Traffic statistics for scheduled airlines provided by country.

387 629.1 016 UN ISSN 0074-249X
Z5063.A1
INTERNATIONAL CIVIL AVIATION ORGANIZATION. INDEX OF I C A O PUBLICATIONS. ANNUAL CUMULATION. (Text in English) irreg. price varies. International Civil Aviation Organization, Attn: Document Sales Unit, 1000 Sherbrooke St. W., Montreal, Que. H3A 2R2, Canada. TEL 514-285-8219. FAX 514-288-4772. TELEX 05-24513.

INTERNATIONAL MEDIA GUIDE. CONSUMER MAGAZINES WORLDWIDE. see *ADVERTISING AND PUBLIC RELATIONS — Abstracting, Bibliographies, Statistics*

385 FR
INTERNATIONAL RAIL STATISTICS. a. Union Internationale des Chemins de Fer - Internationaler Eisenbahnverband, 14-16 Rue Jean Rey, 75015 Paris, France. TEL 2730120.

385 FR ISSN 0074-7580
INTERNATIONAL RAILWAY STATISTICS. STATISTICS OF INDIVIDUAL RAILWAYS. (Text in English, French, German) 1927. a. 520 F. International Union of Railways, 14 rue Jean Rey, 75015 Paris, France. TEL 42-73-01-40. FAX 42-73-01-40. TELEX 270835FUNINFER.
Description: Collection of statistics on lines, traction, rolling stock, personnel, traffic and finances.

380.5 US
INTERNATIONAL ROAD FEDERATION. WORLD ROAD STATISTICS. 1948. a. International Road Federation, 525 School St. N.W., Washington, DC 20024. TEL 202-554-2106. TELEX 44036.

385.1 BE ISSN 0378-1968
INTERNATIONAL STATISTICAL HANDBOOK OF URBAN PUBLIC TRANSPORT/RECUEIL INTERNATIONAL DE STATISTIQUES DES TRANSPORTS PUBLICS URBAINS/INTERNATIONALES STATISTIK-HANDBUCH FUER DEN OEFFENTLICHEN STADTVERKEHR. 1964. irreg. 4500 BEF. International Union of Public Transport, Av. de l'Uruguay 19, B-1050 Brussels, Belgium. TEL 322-673-6100. FAX 322-660-1072. TELEX 63916 UITP B.
Supersedes: International Union of Public Transport. Transports Publics dans les Principales Villes du Monde (ISSN 0539-113X)
Description: Contains statistical data on 1100 networks worldwide (urban public transport).

330 IE ISSN 0444-5147
IRELAND. CENTRAL STATISTICS OFFICE. PARTICULARS OF VEHICLES REGISTERED AND LICENSED FOR THE FIRST TIME. a. £1.50. Central Statistics Office, Earlsfort Terrace, Dublin 2, Ireland. TEL 01-767531. FAX 01-682221. (processed)

330 IE ISSN 0791-346X
IRELAND. CENTRAL STATISTICS OFFICE. STATISTICS OF PORT TRAFFIC. a. £1.50. Central Statistics Office, Earlsfort Terrace, Dublin 2, Ireland. TEL 01-767531. FAX 01-682221. (processed)
Description: Presents information for each harbour authority on the number of arrivals and net register tonnage of trading and passenger vessels. Includes the weight of goods and number of livestock handled and details on the type of traffic.

388.3 IS ISSN 0075-1057
ISRAEL. CENTRAL BUREAU OF STATISTICS. MOTOR VEHICLES. (Subseries of its Special Series) (Text in Hebrew; summaries in English) irreg., no.746, 1983. price varies. Central Bureau of Statistics, Box 13015, Jerusalem 91 130, Israel. TEL 02-21 12 11.

TRANSPORTATION — ABSTRACTING, BIBLIOGRAPHIES, STATISTICS

380.3 310   IS
ISRAEL. CENTRAL BUREAU OF STATISTICS. ROAD ACCIDENTS WITH CASUALTIES. (Text in English and Hebrew) 1950. a., no.761, 1984. price varies. Central Bureau of Statistics, Box 13015, Jerusalem 91 130, Israel.

387 314   IT
HE839
ITALY. ISTITUTO CENTRALE DI STATISTICA. STATISTICHE DELLA NAVIGAZIONE MARITTIMA. 1972. a. L.22000. Istituto Centrale di Statistica, Via Cesare Balbo 16, 00100 Rome, Italy.
    Formerly: Italy. Istituto Centrale di Statistica. Annuario Statistico della Navigazione Marittima (ISSN 0075-1898)

385   IT   ISSN 0021-3144
ITALY. MINISTERO DEI TRASPORTI E DELL'AVIAZIONE CIVILE. AZIENDA AUTONOMA DELLE FERROVIE DELLO STATO. BOLLETTINO STATISTICO MENSILE.* 1942. m. L.9000. (Azienda Autonoma delle Ferrovie dello Stato) Edizioni Richerche, Viale Ippocrate 85, Rome, Italy. charts; stat.

629.286   JA
JAPAN AUTO ABSTRACTS. (Text in English) w. 840000 Yen. Dodwell Marketing Consultants, Kowa no.35, Bldg., 14-14 Akasaka-ku, Tokyo 107, Japan. TEL 03-3589-0207. FAX 03-3589-0516. TELEX J22274 DODWELL.
    Description: English abstracts of Japanese-press articles related to the Japanese auto industry.

388   HU   ISSN 0231-0724
KOZUTI KOZLEKEDESI SZAKIRODALMI TAJEKOZTATO/ROAD TRANSPORT ABSTRACTS. 1949. m. 3200 Ft. Orszagos Muszaki Informacios Kozpont es Konyvtar (O.M.I.K.K.) - National Technical Information Centre and Library, Muzeum u. 17, P.O. Box 12, 1428 Budapest, Hungary. Ed. E. Vajda. circ. 510.
    Supersedes in part (as of 1982): Muszaki Lapszemle. Kozlekedes - Technical Abstracts. Transportation (ISSN 0027-5042)

629.2 016   UK   ISSN 0309-0817
TL1
M I R A AUTOMOBILE ABSTRACTS. 1955. m. £175($350) Motor Industry Research Association, Watling St., Nuneaton, Warwickshire CV10 OTU, England. FAX 0203-343772. TELEX 311277. Ed. J. Woodward. adv.; bk.rev.; abstr.; index; circ. 800. Indexed: Agri.Eng.Abstr., BMT, Fluidex.
●Also available online. Vendor(s): European Space Agency.
—BLDSC shelfmark: 1831.930000.
    Former titles: M I R A Abstracts (ISSN 0305-8972); Automobile Abstracts (ISSN 0005-1357)
    Description: Abstracts of technical papers relating to automotive engineering.

380.5   MW
MALAWI. NATIONAL STATISTICAL OFFICE. TRANSPORT STATISTICS. 1980. a. K.8. National Statistical Office, Box 333, Zomba, Malawi.

623.8 016   UK
MARINE MANAGEMENT HOLDINGS. TRANSACTIONS. 1889. 6/yr. £110. Marine Management Holdings Ltd., Memorial Bldg., 76 Mark Lane, London EC3R 7JN, England. (Subscr. addr. in U.S.: Learned Information, Inc, 143 Old Marlton Pike, Medford, NJ 08055. TEL 609-654-6266) Ed. Peter Yakimuik. adv.; abstr.; charts; illus.; index; circ. 5,000. (also avail. in microform from MIM) Indexed: API Catal., API Hlth.& Environ., API Oil., API Pet.Ref., API Pet.Subst., API Transport., BMT, Br.Tech.Ind., Chem.Abstr., Eng.Ind., Fluidex, ISMEC, Met.Abstr., Ocean.Abstr., Pollut.Abstr., Sh.& Vib.Dig., World Alum.Abstr.
    Former titles: Institute of Marine Engineers. Technical Reports (ISSN 0309-3948); Institute of Marine Engineers. Transactions (ISSN 0020-2924)

623.82 016   JA   ISSN 0286-7427
MARINE TECHNOLOGY RESEARCH ABSTRACTS & INDEX (MATRAX)/SENPAKU - KAIYO KOGAKU GIJUTSU BUNKEN SOKUHO. (Supplement avail.) (Text in English, Japanese) 1966. bi-m. 25000 Yen. Ship and Ocean Foundation, Library, 15-16 Toranomon 1-chome, Minato-ku, Tokyo 105, Japan. TEL 03-3502-2371. FAX 03-3502-2033. TELEX 2222652-JSIF-J. bibl.; circ. 400.
—BLDSC shelfmark: 5378.680000.
    Former titles (until 1982): J A F S A Library News (ISSN 0385-1176); (until Dec. 1975): N S S Library News.
    Description: Bibliographic guide covering information on shipbuilding and offshore engineering research and development. Includes related research reports and papers.

387 011   US
MARITIME ABSTRACTS. m. $300. National Maritime Research Center, Kings Point, NY 11024-1699.
    Description: Includes articles from major shipping and marine science journals as well as books, reports, conference papers, and government documents.

386 382   US
MARITIME RESEARCH. WEEKLY NEWSLETTER. 1953. w. $240. Maritime Research, Inc., 499 Ernston Rd., Box 805, Parlin, NJ 08859. TEL 908-727-8040. charts; stat.

388.314   MF
MAURITIUS. CENTRAL STATISTICAL OFFICE. DIGEST OF ROAD TRANSPORT STATISTICS. 1985. a. Rs.75. Central Statistical Office, Port-Louis, Mauritius. (Subscr. to: G.P.O., La Tour Koenig, Port-Louis, Mauritius)

318   BL
MINAS GERAIS, BRAZIL. DEPARTAMENTO DE ESTRADAS DE RODAGEM. SERVICO DE TRANSITO. ESTATISTICA DE TRAFEGO E ACIDENTES. 1969. a. free. Departamento de Estradas de Rodagem, Servico de Transito, Av. Andradas, 1120, 30000 Belo Horizonte, Brazil. stat.; circ. 1,000.
    Formerly: Minas Gerais, Brazil. Departamento de Estradas de Rodagem. Servico de Transito. Estatistica de Trafego.

385   II   ISSN 0027-0504
MONTHLY RAILWAY STATISTICS. (Text in English, Hindi) vol.16, 1967. m. Railway Board, Director, Statistics & Economics, Public Relations, New Delhi 110001, India. charts; stat.

629.2 016   UK
MOTOR INDUSTRY MANAGEMENT. 1946. m. £30 (foreign £36). Institute of the Motor Industry, Fanshaws, Brickendon, Herts. SG13 8PQ, England. TEL 099-286521. FAX 099-286521. Ed. Chris Phillips. adv.; bk.rev.; abstr.; bibl.; charts; illus.; index, cum.index; circ. 100,000.
    Incorporates (1988-1990): Motor Industry Engineer; **Former titles:** Motor Management (ISSN 0020-2746); Institute of the Motor Industry. Journal (ISSN 0020-3173)

MOTOR SPECIFICATIONS & PRICES. see TRANSPORTATION — *Automobiles*

388.3   SZ
MOTORFAHRZEUGBESTAND IN DER SCHWEIZ AM 30. SEPTEMBER (YEAR)/EFFECTIF DES VEHICULES A MOTEUR EN SUISSE AU 30 SEPTEMBRE (YEAR). (Text in French and German) 1951. a. 32 Fr. Bundesamt fuer Statistik, Hallwylstr. 15, CH-3003 Bern, Switzerland. TEL 031-618836. FAX 031-617856.

380.5 016   US
N T I S ALERTS: TRANSPORTATION. w. $125 (foreign $175). U.S. National Technical Information Service, 5285 Port Royal Rd., Springfield, VA 22161. TEL 703-487-4630. FAX 703-321-8547. TELEX 64617. index. (back issues avail.)
    Former titles: Abstract Newsletter: Transportation (ISSN 0163-1527); Weekly Abstract Newsletter: Transportation; Weekly Government Abstracts. Transportation.

387   JA   ISSN 0469-4783
NAGOYA PORT STATISTICS ANNUAL/NAGOYAKO TOKEI NENPO. (Text in Japanese) 1958. a. free. Nagoya Port Authority - Nagoyako Kanri Kumiai, 1-8-21 Irifune, Minato-ku, Nagoya 455, Japan. TEL 052-661-4111. FAX 052-661-0155. TELEX 4463816 NPA J. stat.; circ. 1,000.

387   JA   ISSN 0027-7592
NAGOYA PORT STATISTICS MONTHLY/NAGOYAKO TOKEI GEPPO. (Text in Japanese) 1949. m. free. Nagoya Port Authority - Nagoyako Kanri Kumiai, 1-8-21 Irifune, Minato-ku, Nagoya 455, Japan. TEL 052-661-4111. FAX 052-661-0155. TELEX 4463816 NPA J. bk.rev.; stat.; circ. 400.

388.1   US
NEBRASKA. DEPARTMENT OF ROADS. NEBRASKA SELECTED STATISTICS. a. Department of Roads, Transportation Planning Division, 1500 N.E. Hwy. 2, Box 94759, Lincoln, NE 68509-4759. TEL 402-479-4316. FAX 402-479-4325. illus.
    Former titles: Nebraska. Department of Roads. Highway Statistics: State and Local Road and Street Data for (Year); Nebraska Highway Statistics: State and Local Construction Mileage (ISSN 0099-0442)

331   NE   ISSN 0024-8770
NETHERLANDS. CENTRAAL BUREAU VOOR DE STATISTIEK. MAANDSTATISTIEK VERKEER EN VERVOER. 1937. m. fl.100. Centraal Bureau voor de Statistiek, Prinses Beatrixlaan 428, Voorburg, Netherlands. (Orders to: SDU - Publishers, Christoffel Plantijnstraat, The Hague, Netherlands) stat.; index; circ. 510.

388.3   NE   ISSN 0168-4973
NETHERLANDS. CENTRAAL BUREAU VOOR DE STATISTIEK. STATISTIEK DER MOTORVOERTUIGEN/STATISTICS OF MOTOR VEHICLES. (Text in Dutch and English) 1966. a. Centraal Bureau voor de Statistiek, Prinses Beatrixlaan 428, Voorburg, Netherlands. (Dist. by: SDU - Publishers, Christoffel Plantijnstraat, The Hague, Netherlands)
    Formerly: Netherlands. Centraal Bureau voor de Statistiek. Statistiek der Motorrijtuigen (ISSN 0077-698X)

387 314.9   NE   ISSN 0168-4825
NETHERLANDS. CENTRAAL BUREAU VOOR DE STATISTIEK. STATISTIEK VAN AAN-, AF- EN DOORVOER. GOEDERENVERVOER PER GOEDERENSOORT VAN EN NAAR DE ZEEHAVENS VAN ROTTERDAM EN AMSTERDAM. 1950. a. Centraal Bureau voor de Statistiek, Prinses Beatrixlaan 428, Voorburg, Netherlands. (Orders to: SDU - Publishers, Christoffel Plantijnstraat, The Hague, Netherlands) circ. 300.
    Formerly: Netherlands. Centraal Bureau voor de Statistiek. Statistiek van het Internationaal Zeehavenvervoer.

388.1   NE   ISSN 0168-5023
NETHERLANDS. CENTRAAL BUREAU VOOR DE STATISTIEK. STATISTIEK VAN DE VERKEERSONGEVALLEN OP DE OPENBARE WEG/STATISTICS OF ROAD-TRAFFIC ACCIDENTS. (Text in Dutch and English) 1947. a. Centraal Bureau voor de Statistiek, Prinses Beatrixlaan 428, Voorburg, Netherlands. (Dist. by: SDU - Publishers, Christoffel Plantijnstraat, The Hague, Netherlands)

388.3   SW
NEW CAR PRICE-LIST. bi-m. SEK 144. AB Bilstatistik, Box 5514, S-114 85, Stockholm, Sweden. TEL (08) 783-80-00. FAX 468-6619679. TELEX 119-23-BIL S.

388.3   CN   ISSN 0705-5595
NEW MOTOR VEHICLE SALES. (Text in English, French) 1932. m. Can.$144($173) (foreign $202). Statistics Canada, Publications Division, Ottawa, Ont. K1A 0T6, Canada. TEL 613-951-7277. FAX 613-951-1584.
    Description: Presents data on new motor vehicles: number and value of new passenger cars, trucks and buses sold, by month, as well as cumulatively, for both current and previous years.

388.3   SW
NEW REGISTRATIONS. m. SEK 868. AB Bilstatistik, Box 5514, S-114 85 Stockholm, Sweden. TEL (08) 783-80-00. FAX 468-6619679. TELEX 119-23 BIL S.

387.5   JA
NIHON SHOSEN SENPUKU TOKEI. 1972. a. free. Japanese Shipowners' Association, Research and Public Relations Division - Nihon Senshu Kyokai, c/o Kaiun Bldg., 6-4 Hirakawa-cho 2-chome, Chiyoda-ku, Tokyo 102, Japan. FAX 03-262-4760. TELEX J2322148. stat.; circ. 2,800.
    Description: Statistical summary of the Japanese merchant fleet.

T

TRANSPORTATION — ABSTRACTING, BIBLIOGRAPHIES, STATISTICS

380.5   NO   ISSN 0468-8147
NORWAY. STATISTISK SENTRALBYRAA. SAMFERDSELSSTATISTIKK/NORWAY. CENTRAL BUREAU OF STATISTICS. TRANSPORT AND COMMUNICATION STATISTICS. (Subseries of its Norges Offisielle Statistikk) (Text in English and Norwegian) 1958. a. NOK 60. Statistisk Sentralbyraa - Central Bureau of Statistics, Box 8131-Dep., 0033 Oslo 1, Norway. TEL 02-864500. FAX 02-864973. circ. 1,100.

388.31   SZ
OEFFENTLICHE VERKEHR/TRANSPORTS PUBLICS. (Text in French and German) 1985. a. 49 Fr. Bundesamt fuer Statistik, Hallwylstr. 15, CH-3003 Bern, Switzerland. TEL 031-618836. FAX 031-617856.

380.5 016   FR   ISSN 0761-1803
P A S C A L FOLIO. F 25: TRANSPORTS TERRESTRES ET MARITIMES. 1984. 10/yr. 645 F. Centre National de la Recherche Scientifique, Institut de l'Information Scientifique et Technique, B.P. 54, 54514 Vandoeuvre-Les-Nancy Cedex, France. TEL 83-50-46-00.
Formerly: P A S C A L Folio. Part 25: Transports Terrestres et Maritimes; Which supersedes in part (1980-1984): Bulletin Signaletique. Part 892: Batiment. Travaux Publics. Transports (ISSN 0223-4254)

388 310   PP
PAPUA NEW GUINEA. NATIONAL STATISTICAL OFFICE. STATISTICAL BULLETIN: REGISTERED MOTOR VEHICLES. (Text in English) 1962. a. £1.50. Department of Transport, Database Bureau Office, c/o Database Manager, P.O. Box 457, Konedoba, Papua New Guinea. circ. 100.
Description: Provides statistics on the total stock of motor vehicles in Papua New Guidea that have been registered or re-registered during the year. Registrations are broken down by vehicle type, ownership, province, make and capacity of vehicle.

380.5   II   ISSN 0079-2381
POCKET BOOK OF TRANSPORT STATISTICS OF INDIA. 1968. a. $12.96. Ministry of Shipping and Transport, Transport Research Division, I D A Bldg., Jamnagar House, Shahjahan Rd., New Delhi 110011, India. (Orders to: Controller of Publications, Civil Lines, Delhi 110006, India)
Formerly: India Transport Statistics.

314 387   PL   ISSN 0079-2667
POLAND. GLOWNY URZAD STATYSTYCZNY. ROCZNIK STATYSTYCZNY GOSPODARKI MORSKIEJ/POLAND. CENTRAL STATISTICS OFFICE. YEARBOOK OF SEA ECONOMY STATISTICS. (Subseries of its: Statystyka Polski) 1969. irreg., latest 1983. 65 Zl. Glowny Urzad Statystyczny, Al. Niepodleglosci 208, 00-925 Warsaw, Poland. TEL 48 22 25-03-45. stat.; illus.; charts; circ. 1,040.

380.5 314   PL   ISSN 0079-2802
POLAND. GLOWNY URZAD STATYSTYCZNY. ROCZNIK STATYSTYCZNY TRANSPORTU/POLAND. CENTRAL STATISTICS OFFICE. YEARBOOK OF TRANSPORT STATISTICS. (Subseries of its: Statystyka Polski) 1967. irreg., latest 1987. 77 Zl. Glowny Urzad Statystyczny, Al. Niepodleglosci 208, 00-925 Warsaw, Poland. TEL 48 22 25-03-45.

387 317   PL   ISSN 0079-2837
POLAND. GLOWNY URZAD STATYSTYCZNY. STATYSTYKA ZEGLUGI SRODLADOWEJ I DROG WODNYCH SRODLADOWYCH. (Subseries of Its Seria Statystyka Polski Materialy Statystyczne) a. 15 Zl. Glowny Urzad Statystyczny, Al. Niepodleglosci 208, 00-925 Warsaw, Poland. TEL 48 22 25-03-45.

315.2   JA
PORT OF YOKOHAMA. ANNUAL STATISTICS.. (Text in Japanese) no.212, Nov. 1969. a. free. Port and Harbor Bureau, Industry and Trade Center Bldg., 2 Yamashita-cho Nakaku, Yokohama, Japan. FAX 45-671-7158. (processed)
Formerly: Port of Yokohama. Monthly Statistics. (ISSN 0032-4876)

380.5 301.16 314   PO   ISSN 0377-2292
HE77
PORTUGAL. INSTITUTO NACIONAL DE ESTATISTICA. ESTATISTICAS DOS TRANSPORTES E COMMUNICACOES: CONTINENTE, ACORES E MADEIRA. 1970. a. Esc.4000. Instituto Nacional de Estatistica, Avda. Antonio Jose de Almeida 1, 1078 Lisbon Codex, Portugal.

388.324   US
QUARTERLY SURVEY OF GENERAL FREIGHT CARRIER OPERATING RESULTS. 1974. q. $10. Regular Common Carrier Conference, 2200 Mill Rd., Ste. 350, Alexandria, VA 22314-4467.
TEL 703-838-1967. FAX 703-684-4328. charts; stat.; circ. 1,000.
Description: Detailed financial and operating statistics for general freight trucking companies showing trends from 1967 to present.

385   BL   ISSN 0102-4930
R F F S A. ANUARIO ESTATISTICO. 1960. a. free. Rede Ferroviaria Federal, S.A., Departamento Geral de Estatistica, Rio de Janeiro, Brazil.
Description: Provides statistical information on the railway system of Brazil.

338 625 016   RU   ISSN 0486-2252
REFERATIVNYI ZHURNAL. AVTOMOBIL'NYE DOROGI. 1963. m. 45.80 Rub. (48 Rub. including index). Vsesoyuznyi Institut Nauchno-Tekhnicheskoi Informatsii (VINITI), Baltiiskaya ul., 14, Moscow A-219, Russia. (Subscr. to: Mezhdunarodnaya Kniga, Dimitrova ul. 39, 113095 Moscow, Russia)

388 016   RU   ISSN 0034-2297
REFERATIVNYI ZHURNAL. AVTOMOBIL'NYI I GORODSKOI TRANSPORT. 1961. m. 111 Rub. (120.20 Rub. including index). Vsesoyuznyi Institut Nauchno-Tekhnicheskoi Informatsii (VINITI), Baltiiskaya ul., 14, Moscow A-219, Russia. (Subscr. to: Mezhdunarodnaya Kniga, Dimitrova ul. 39, 113095 Moscow, Russia)

621.43 016   RU   ISSN 0486-2279
REFERATIVNYI ZHURNAL. DVIGATELI VNUTRENNEGO SGORANIYA. 1956. m. 48 Rub. (51 Rub. including index). Vsesoyuznyi Institut Nauchno-Tekhnicheskoi Informatsii (VINITI), Baltiiskaya ul., 14, Moscow A-219, Russia. (Subscr. to: Mezhdunarodnaya Kniga, Dimitrova ul. 39, 113095 Moscow, Russia)

388.3 614 016   RU   ISSN 0202-9952
REFERATIVNYI ZHURNAL. ORGANIZATSIYA I BEZOPASNOST' DOROZHNOGO DVIZHENIYA. 1973. m. 18 Rub. (19.40 Rub. including index). Vsesoyuznyi Institut Nauchno-Tekhnicheskoi Informatsii (VINITI), Baltiiskaya ul., 14, Moscow A-219, Russia. (Subscr. to: Mezhdunarodnaya Kniga, Dimitrova ul. 39, 113095 Moscow, Russia)

REFERATIVNYI ZHURNAL. TRUBOPROVODNYI TRANSPORT. see ENGINEERING — Abstracting, Bibliographies, Statistics

387 016   RU   ISSN 0484-2545
REFERATIVNYI ZHURNAL. VODNYI TRANSPORT. 1962. m. 92.40 Rub. (102.40 Rub. including index). Vsesoyuznyi Institut Nauchno-Tekhnicheskoi Informatsii (VINITI), Baltiiskaya ul., 14, Moscow A-219, Russia. (Subscr. to: Mezhdunarodnaya Kniga, Dimitrova ul. 39, 113095 Moscow, Russia)

387.7 016   RU   ISSN 0484-2561
REFERATIVNYI ZHURNAL. VOZDUSHNYI TRANSPORT. 1962. m. 77 Rub. (84.40 Rub. including index). Vsesoyuznyi Institut Nauchno-Tekhnicheskoi Informatsii (VINITI), Baltiiskaya ul., 14, Moscow A-219, Russia. (Subscr. to: Mezhdunarodnaya Kniga, Dimitrova ul. 39, 113095 Moscow, Russia)

385.1 016   RU   ISSN 0034-2645
REFERATIVNYI ZHURNAL. VZAIMODEISTVIE RAZNYKH VIDOV TRANSPORTA I KONTEINERNYE PEREVOZKI. 1961. m. 29.60 Rub. (30.60 Rub. including index). Vsesoyuznyi Institut Nauchno-Tekhnicheskoi Informatsii (VINITI), Baltiiskaya ul., 14, Moscow A-219, Russia. (Subscr. to: Mezhdunarodnaya Kniga, Dimitrova ul. 39, 113095 Moscow, Russia)

385 016   RU   ISSN 0484-2596
REFERATIVNYI ZHURNAL. ZHELEZNODOROZHNYI TRANSPORT. 1960. m. 67 Rub. (73.90 Rub. including index). Vsesoyuznyi Institut Nauchno-Tekhnicheskoi Informatsii (VINITI), Baltiiskaya ul., 14, Moscow A-219, Russia. (Subscr. to: Mezhdunarodnaya Kniga, Dimitrova ul. 39, 113095 Moscow, Russia)

388.1   ZA
REPORT ON PASSENGER ROAD TRANSPORT IN ZAMBIA. 1968. a. $4. Central Statistical Office, P.O. Box 31908, Lusaka, Zambia. TEL 211-231.

388   HU   ISSN 0231-3928
REPULESI SZAKIRODALMI TAJEKOZTATO/AVIATION AND AIR TRANSPORT ABSTRACTS. bi-m. 3000 Ft. Orszagos Muszaki Informacios Kozpont es Konyvtar (O.M.I.K.K.) - National Technical Information Centre and Library, Muzeum u. 17, P.O. Box 12, 1428 Budapest, Hungary. (Subscr. to: Kultura, P.O. Box 149, 1389 Budapest, Hungary) Ed. Ferenc Bardosi. circ. 200.
Supersedes in part (as of 1982): Muszaki Lapszemle. Kozlekedes - Technical Abstracts. Transportation (ISSN 0027-5042)

016 629.2 620   US   ISSN 0741-2029
S A E TECHNICAL LITERATURE ABSTRACTS. 1975. q. $100. Society of Automotive Engineers, 400 Commonwealth Dr., Warrendale, PA 15096-0001. TEL 412-776-4841. FAX 412-776-5760. cum.index: 1965-1989. (also avail. in magnetic tape; back issues avail.) **Indexed:** Corros.Abstr., Fluidex, Sh.& Vib.Dig.
●Also available online. Vendor(s): Orbit Information Technologies.
—BLDSC shelfmark: 8062.928500.
Supersedes (1965-1985): S A E Quarterly Abstracts.

359.97   US   ISSN 0163-2833
TL553.8
S A R STATISTICS. (Search and Rescue) a. U.S. Coast Guard, Office of Navigation Safety and Waterway Services, 2100 Second St., S.W., Washington, DC 20593-0001. TEL 202-267-1943.

380.5   FR
S I T R A M TRAFFIC INTERNATIONAL RESULTATS TRIMESTRIELS. 1979. q. 261 F. Ministere de Transport, Observatoire Economique et Statistique des Transports (OEST), 55 rue Brillat-Savarin, 75658 Paris Cedex 13, France.

388.31   SZ
SCHWEIZERISCHE STRASSENVERKEHRSZAEHLUNG/RECENSEMENT SUISSE DE LA CIRCULATION ROUTIERE. (Text in French and German) 1985. every 5 yrs. 19 Fr. Bundesamt fuer Statistik, Hallwylstr. 15, CH-3003 Bern, Switzerland. TEL 031-618836. FAX 031-617856.

388.31   SZ
SCHWEIZERISCHE VERKEHRSSTATISTIK/STATISTIQUE SUISSE DES TRANSPORTS. (Text in French and German) 1976. a. 37 Fr. Bundesamt fuer Statistik, Hallwylstr. 15, CH-3003 Bern, Switzerland. TEL 031-618836. FAX 031-617856.

387.7   MM   ISSN 0080-9268
SHIPPING AND AVIATION STATISTICS OF THE MALTESE ISLANDS. a. L.1. Central Office of Statistics, Auberge d'Italie, Valletta, Malta. (Subscr. to: Publications Bookshop, Auberge de Castille, Valletta, Malta)

387   UK
SHIPPING STATISTICS AND ECONOMICS. 1970. m. £460 (outside Europe £490). Drewry Shipping Consultants Ltd., 11 Heron Quay, London E14 4JF, England. TEL 071-538 0191. FAX 071-987-9396. TELEX 21167 HPDLDN G.
Description: Provides the shipping professional with numerous tables and charts supported by concise, well written commentary on worldwide trends.

387   SI
SINGAPORE SHIPPING & CARGO STATISTICS. (Text in English) 1979. m. S.$60 in Singapore; Malaysia - Brunei S$100; elsewhere S$180. Port of Singapore Authority, Cargo Systems Department, Research and Statistics Section, 13th Fl., PSA Building, 460 Alexandra Rd., Singapore 0511, Singapore. FAX 2795713. TELEX RS 21507. Ed. Mary Yeo. charts; circ. 190. (back issues avail.)
Formerly (until 1989): Singapore. Department of Statistics. Shipping and Cargo Statistics (ISSN 0129-6477)
Description: Covers vessel movements and cargo handled at the Port of Singapore.

629.222   UK
SOCIETY OF MOTOR MANUFACTURERS AND TRADERS. MONTHLY STATISTICAL REVIEW. m. $122 to non-members; members £82. Society of Motor Manufacturers and Traders Ltd., Forbes House, Halkin St., London SW1X 7DS, England. TEL 071-235-7000. FAX 071-235-7112. TELEX 21628.

TRANSPORTATION — ABSTRACTING, BIBLIOGRAPHIES, STATISTICS 4667

388   SA
SOUTH AFRICA. CENTRAL STATISTICAL SERVICE. NEW VEHICLES REGISTERED. (Report No. 71-51-01) a. Central Statistical Service, Private Bag X44, Pretoria 0001, South Africa. TEL 012-310-8911. FAX 012-3108500. (Orders to: Government Printing Works, Private Bag X85, Pretoria 0001, South Africa)
    Former titles: South Africa. Central Statistical Service. Statistics of New Vehicles Registered; South Africa. Department of Statistics. Statistics of New Vehicles Registered; South Africa. Department of Statistics. Statistics of New Vehicles Licensed.

388.3 310   SA
SOUTH AFRICA. CENTRAL STATISTICAL SERVICE. REGISTERED VEHICLES AS AT 30 JUNE. (Report No. 71-11-01) 1972. a. Central Statistical Service, Private Bag X44, Pretoria 0001, South Africa. TEL 012-310-8911. FAX 012-3108500. (Orders to: Government Printing Works, Private Bag X85, Pretoria 0001, South Africa)
    Former titles: South Africa. Central Statistical Service. Statistics of Motor and Other Vehicles; South Africa. Department of Statistics. Statistics of Motor and Other Vehicles.

312.44   SA
SOUTH AFRICA. CENTRAL STATISTICAL SERVICE. ROAD TRAFFIC COLLISIONS. (Report No. 71-61-01) a. Central Statistical Service, Private Bag X44, Pretoria 0001, South Africa. TEL 012-310-8911. FAX 012-3108500. (Orders to: Government Printer, Bosman St., Private Bag X85, Pretoria 0001, South Africa)
    Former titles: South Africa. Central Service. Road Traffic Accidents; South Africa. Department of Statistics. Road Traffic Accidents (ISSN 0584-195X)

388.314   SA
SOUTH AFRICA. DIVISION OF ROADS AND TRANSPORT TECHNOLOGY. TRANSPORT STATISTICS/DIVISIE VIR PAD- EN VERVOERTEGNOLOGIE. (Text in Afrikaans, English) 1969. a. R.45. Division of Roads and Transport Technology, Box 395, Pretoria 0001, South Africa. FAX 841-32-32. TELEX 3-21312SA. Ed. C.C. Hamilton. charts; illus.; circ. 1,000.
    Former titles: National Institute for Transport and Road Research. Transport Statistics & National Institute for Transport and Road Research. Road Statistics.

614.86   SP   ISSN 0085-655X
SPAIN. MINISTERIO DEL INTERIOR. DIRECCION GENERAL DE TRAFICO. BOLETIN INFORMATIVO: ACCIDENTES. 1962. a. Ministerio del Interior, Direccion General de Trafico, Gabinete de Estudios, Calle J. Valcarcel, 28, 28071 Madrid, Spain. circ. 2,000.

614.86   SP   ISSN 0304-9191
HE5081
SPAIN. MINISTERIO DEL INTERIOR. DIRECCION GENERAL DE TRAFICO. BOLETIN INFORMATIVO: ANUARIO ESTADISTICO GENERAL. 1960. a. Ministerio del Interior, Direccion General de Trafico, Gabinete de Estudios, Calle J. Valcarcel, 28, 28071 Madrid, Spain. circ. 2,500.

STATISTICA DEGLI INCIDENTI STRADALI. see *PUBLIC HEALTH AND SAFETY — Abstracting, Bibliographies, Statistics*

380.5   EI
STATISTICAL OFFICE OF THE EUROPEAN COMMUNITIES. TRANSPORT, COMMUNICATIONS, TOURISME - ANNUAIRE STATISTIQUE. (Text in Dutch, French, German, Italian) a. Office for Official Publications of the European Communities, L-2985 Luxembourg, Luxembourg. (Dist. in the U.S. by: European Community Information Service, 2100 M St., N.W., Ste. 707, Washington, DC 20037)
    Formerly: Statistical Office of the European Communities. Statistiques des Tranports. Annuaire (ISSN 0081-4962)

380.5   FR
STATISTICAL TRENDS IN TRANSPORT. (Text in English, French) 1965. a. 150 F.($32) Organization for Economic Cooperation and Development, European Conference of Ministers of Transport, 19 rue de Franqueville, 75775 Paris Cedex 16, France. FAX 45-24-97-42. TELEX 611 040. (Dist. by: O.E.C.D. Publications Service, 2 rue Andre-Pascal, 75775 Paris Cedex 16, France. TEL 45-24-82-00; U.S. orders to: O.E.C.D. Publications and Information Center, 2001 L St., N.W., Ste. 700, Washington, D.C. 20036-4095) (also avail. in microfiche)
    Description: Sets out the main statistical data concerning the transport sector in the 19 member countries of the ECMT.

388.1   UN   ISSN 0081-5160
STATISTICS OF ROAD TRAFFIC ACCIDENTS IN EUROPE. 1956. a. price varies. Economic Commission for Europe (ECE), Palais des Nations, 1211 Geneva 10, Switzerland. TEL 734-6011. FAX 733-9879. TELEX 412962. (Or: United Nations Publications, Rm. DC2-853, New York, NY 10017) (also avail. in microfiche) **Indexed:** IIS.

388.31 310   JA
STATISTICS OF ROAD TRAFFIC ACCIDENTS IN JAPAN. a. $7. International Association of Traffic and Safety Sciences, 6-20, 2-chome, Yaesu, Chuo-ku, Tokyo 104, Japan. TEL 03-273-7884. FAX 03-272-7054.

386   NE
STATISTIEK VAN DE SCHEEPVAARTBEWEGING IN NEDERLAND/CENSUS OF INLAND SHIPPING IN THE NETHERLANDS AT LOCKS AND BRIDGES. (Text in Dutch and English) 1946. a. Centraal Bureau voor de Statistiek, Prinses Beatrixlaan 428, Voorburg, Netherlands. (Orders to: SDU - Publishers, Christoffel Plantijnstraat, The Hague, Netherlands)

387   GW   ISSN 0073-0203
STATISTIK DES HAMBURGISCHEN STAATES; Handel und Schiffahrt des Hafens Hamburg. 1845. irreg. DM.26. Statistisches Landesamt, Steckelhoern 12, 2000 Hamburg 11, Germany.

387.7   SW   ISSN 0348-2251
SWEDEN. LUFTFARTSVERKET. AARSBOK. 1976. a. SEK 42. Luftfartsverket - Board of Civil Aviation, S-601 79 Norrkoeping, Sweden. stat.

387.7   SW
SWEDEN. LUFTFARTSVERKET. CHARTERSTATISTIK. 1970. s-a. SEK 84. Luftfartsverket - Board of Civil Aviation, S-601 79 Norrkoeping, Sweden.

387.7   SW
SWEDEN. LUFTFARTSVERKET. FLYGPLATSSTATISTIK. m. SEK 180. Luftfartsverket - Board of Civil Aviation, S-601 79 Norrkoeping, Sweden.

380   SW   ISSN 0082-0334
HE260.A15
SWEDEN. STATISTISKA CENTRALBYRAAN. STATISTISKA MEDDELANDEN. SUBGROUP T (TRANSPORT AND OTHER FORMS OF COMMUNICATION). (Text in Swedish; table heads and summaries in English) N.S. 1963. irreg. SEK 1200. Statistiska Centralbyraan, Publishing Unit, S-701 89 Oerebro, Sweden. circ. 1,000.

388   SZ
SWITZERLAND. BUNDESAMT FUER STATISTIK. IN VERKEHR GESETZTE NEUE MOTORFAHRZEUGE - VEHICULES A MOTEUR NEUFS MIS EN CIRCULATION. (Text in French and German) 1929. a. 22 Fr. Bundesamt fuer Statistik, Hallwylstr. 15, CH-3003 Berne, Switzerland. FAX 031-617856. TELEX 912871.
    Continues in part: Switzerland. Statistisches Amt. Eingefuehrte Motorfahrzeuge: In Verkehr Gesetzte Neue Motorfahrzeuge.

387.7   AU
TAETIGKEITSBERICHT DES VERKEHRS ARBEITSINSPEKTORATES FUER DAS JAHR (YEAR). 1952. quadrennial. free. Bundesministerium fuer oeffentliche Wirtschaft und Verkehr, Gruppe Verkehrs - Arbeitsinspektorat, Radetzskystr. 2, 1030 Vienna, Austria. circ. 850.

380.5 315   CH
TAIWAN ANNUAL STATISTICAL REPORT OF TRANSPORTATION/TAI-WAN SHENG CHIAO T'UNG T'UNG CHI NIEN PAO. (Text in Chinese and English) 1946. a. Taiwan Provincial Government, Department of Transportation - Tai-wan Sheng Cheng Fu Chiao T'ung Chu, Nantou Hsien, Taiwan, Republic of China. stat.

380.5   AT
TASMANIAN TRANSPORT STATISTICS. 1971. a. Aus.$10. Transport Department Tasmania, G.P.O. Box 1002 K, Hobart, Tas. 7001, Australia. FAX 002-310976. Ed.Bd. charts; stat.; circ. 300.
    Formerly: Tasmanian Transport Bulletin (ISSN 0310-7531)

315.2   JA
TETSUDO SHARYOTO SEISAN DOTAI TOKEI GEPPO/MONTHLY SURVEY ON CURRENT ROLLING STOCK PRODUCTION. (Text in Japanese) 1954. m. free. Ministry of Transport, Transport Policy Bureau - Un'Yu-sho Un'Yu-seisaku-kyoku, Information and Research Department, 2-1-3 Kasumigaseki, Chiyoda-ku, Tokyo 100, Japan.
    Formerly: Monthly Statistics of Actual Production of Railway Cars (ISSN 0040-4055)

315.2   JA
TETSUDO SHARYOTO SEISAN DOTAI TOKEI NENPO/ANNUAL SURVEY ON CURRENT ROLLING STOCK PRODUCTION. (Text in Japanese) 1954. a. free. Ministry of Transport, Transport Policy Bureau - Un'Yu-sho Un'Yu-seisaku-kyoku, Information and Research Department, 2-1-3 Kasumigaseki, Chiyoda-ku, Tokyo 100, Japan.
    Formerly: Annual Statistics of Actual Production of Railway Cars.

380.5   AT   ISSN 1033-9752
TRANSPORT AND COMMUNICATIONS INDICATORS. 1976. q. Aus.$15. (Bureau of Transport and Communications Economics) Australian Government Publishing Service, G.P.O. Box 84, Canberra, A.C.T. 2601, Australia. TEL 062 954861. FAX 062-957295. TELEX AA 62013. stat.; circ. 500. (back issues avail.)
    Formerly: Transport Indicators (ISSN 0812-0927)
    Description: Guide to Australian transport and communications trends. Covers freight, passenger modes, fuel prices, and some general economic indicators.

387.5   FR
TRANSPORT MARITIME: ETUDES ET STATISTIQUES. 1956. a. 140 F. Comite Central des Armateurs de France, 73 bld. Haussmann, 75008 Paris, France. FAX 42-65-71-89. circ. 4,500.
    Formerly: Marine Marchand: Etudes et Statistiques (ISSN 0069-6439)

388.1   UK
TRANSPORT STATISTICS GREAT BRITAIN. (Joint publication with the Scottish Development Department and Welsh Office) 1976. a. price varies. H.M.S.O., P.O. Box 276, London SW8 5DT, England. circ. 2,000.
    Incorporates: Great Britain. Department of the Environment. Highway Statistics (ISSN 0072-6893); Passenger Transport in Great Britain (ISSN 0079-0133)

380.5 016   US   ISSN 0091-1410
Z7295
TRANSPORTATION. CURRENT LITERATURE. 1921. fortn. free. U.S. Department of Transportation, Library Services Division, 400 Seventh St., S.W., Washington, DC 20590. TEL 202-655-4000. Ed. Eugene Beck. bibl.; circ. 950 (controlled). (processed)
    Formerly: Highways. Current Literature (ISSN 0018-1781)

380.5   US
TRANSPORTATION ACCIDENT BRIEFS. (Subseries of: Aviation, Highway, Marine, Pipeline, Railroad) irreg. price varies. (Department of Transportation, National Transportation Safety Board) U.S. National Technical Information Service, 5825 Port Royal Rd., Springfield, VA 22161. TEL 703-487-4630.
    Description: Presents basic facts, conditions, circumstances, and probable cause(s) in each instance. Additional statistical information is tabulated by types of accidents and casualties related to types of carriers involved, and causal factors.

TRANSPORTATION — ABSTRACTING, BIBLIOGRAPHIES, STATISTICS

387.7 US
TRANSPORTATION ACCIDENT BRIEFS. AVIATION. (Subseries of: Transportation Accident Briefs) irreg. (approx. 18/yr.). $225 in US, Canada, Mexico; elsewhere $450. (Department of Transportation, National Transportation Safety Board) U.S. National Technical Information Service, 5825 Port Royal Rd., Springfield, VA 22161. TEL 703-487-4630.

338.31 US
TRANSPORTATION ACCIDENT BRIEFS. HIGHWAYS. (Subseries of: Transportation Accident Briefs) irreg. (approx. 3/yr.). $16.50 per issue in US, Canada, Mexico; elsewhere $33. (Department of Transportation, National Transportation Safety Board) U.S. National Technical Information Service, 5825 Port Royal Rd., Springfield, VA 22161. TEL 703-487-4630.

387 US
TRANSPORTATION ACCIDENT BRIEFS. MARINE. (Subseries of: Transportation Accident Briefs) irreg. (approx. 4/yr.). $13.50 per issue in US, Canada, Mexico; elsewhere $27. (Department of Transportation, National Transportation Safety Board) U.S. National Technical Information Service, 5825 Port Royal Rd., Springfield, VA 22161. TEL 703-487-4630.

TRANSPORTATION ACCIDENT BRIEFS. PIPELINE. see PETROLEUM AND GAS — Abstracting, Bibliographies, Statistics

385 US
TRANSPORTATION ACCIDENT BRIEFS. RAILROADS. (Subseries of: Transportation Accident Briefs) irreg. (approx. 4/yr.). $13.50 per issue in US, Canada, Mexico; elsewhere $27. (Department of Transportation, National Transportation Safety Board) U.S. National Technical Information Service, 5825 Port Royal Rd., Springfield, VA 22161. TEL 703-487-4630.

380.5 US
TRANSPORTATION ACCIDENT REPORTS. (Subseries of: Aviation, Highway, Marine, Pipeline, Railroad) irreg. price varies. (Department of Transportation, Transportation Safety Board) U.S. National Technical Information Service, 5825 Port Royal Rd., Springfield, VA 22161. TEL 703-487-4630.
Description: Reviews investigations of selected accidents conducted by the NTSB. Contains, in narrative form, the board's factual findings and analysis leading to probable cause.

380.5 US
TRANSPORTATION ACCIDENT REPORTS. HIGHWAY. (Subseries of: Transportation Accident Reports) irreg. (approx. 7/yr.). $85 in US, Canada, Mexico; elsewhere $170. (Department of Transportation, National Transportation Safety Board) U.S. National Technical Information Service, 5825 Port Royal Rd., Springfield, VA 22161. TEL 703-487-4630.

387 US
TRANSPORTATION ACCIDENT REPORTS. MARINE. (Subseries of: Transportation Accident Reports) irreg. (approx. 10/yr.). $95 in US, Canada, Mexico; elsewhere $190. (Department of Transportation, National Transportation Safety Board) U.S. National Technical Information Service, 5825 Port Royal Rd., Springfield, VA 22161. TEL 703-487-4630.

TRANSPORTATION ACCIDENT REPORTS. PIPELINE. see PETROLEUM AND GAS — Abstracting, Bibliographies, Statistics

385 US
TRANSPORTATION ACCIDENT REPORTS. RAILROADS. (Subseries of: Transportation Accident Reports) irreg. (approx. 10/yr.). $85 in US, Canada, Mexico; elsewhere $170. (Department of Transportation, National Transportation Safety Board) U.S. National Technical Information Service, 5825 Port Royal Rd., Springfield, VA 22161. TEL 703-487-4630.

TRANSPORTATION ENERGY RESEARCH. see ENERGY — Abstracting, Bibliographies, Statistics

380.5 US ISSN 0082-5956
TRANSPORTATION STATISTICS IN THE UNITED STATES. 1954. irreg. price varies. U.S. Interstate Commerce Commission, 12th St. and Constitution Ave., N.W., Washington, DC 20423. TEL 202-655-4000. (Orders to: Supt. of Docs., Washington, DC 20402) (also avail. in microfilm from BHP)

380.5 FR
TRANSPORTS ROUTIERS DE MARCHANDISES EFFECTUES PAR DES TRANSPORTEURS ETRANGERS SUR LE TERRITOIRE FRANCAIS. 1973. quadrennial. 260 F. Ministere de Transport, Observatoire Economique et Statistique des Transports (OEST), 55 rue Brillat-Savarin, 75658 Paris Cedex 13, France.

387.1 TI
TUNISIA. OFFICE DES PORTS NATIONAUX. BULLETIN ANNUEL DES STATISTIQUES. Cover title: Tunisia. Office des Ports Nationaux. Trafic Maritime. a. Office des Ports Nationaux, Tunis, Tunisia.

388.4 016 BE
U I T P BIBLIO-EXPRESS. (Summaries in English, French, German) 1962. 10/yr. 3000 BEF. International Union of Public Transport, Av. de l'Uruguay 19, B-1050 Brussels, Belgium. TEL 322-673-6100. FAX 322-660-10-72. TELEX 63916 UITP B. circ. 3,000.
U I T P Biblio-Index (ISSN 0041-5146)
Description: Part of a computerized bibliographical database.

387.7 FR
UNION DES CHAMBRES DE COMMERCE ET ETABLISSENENTS GESTIONNAIRES D'AEROPORT. STATISTICS ON AIRPORT TRAFFIC. a. Union des Chambres de Commerce et Etablissenents Gestionnaires d'Aeroport, 45 Av. d'Iena, 75116 Paris, France. TEL 7206546. TELEX 610396.

380.5 016 US ISSN 0083-0380
U.S. DEPARTMENT OF TRANSPORTATION. BIBLIOGRAPHIC LISTS. 1969. irreg. U.S. Department of Transportation, Library Services Division, 400 Seventh St. N.W., Washington, DC 20590. TEL 202-655-4000. (Order from: National Technical Information Service, 5285 Port Royal Rd., Springfield, VA 22161)

388.3 US
U.S. FEDERAL HIGHWAY ADMINISTRATION. HIGHWAY STATISTICS. 1945. a. price varies. U.S. Federal Highway Administration, Highway Statistics Division, 400 Seventh St. S.W., DC 20590. TEL 202-426-0632. (Orders to: Supt. of Documents, U.S. Government Printing Office, Washington, DC 20402) Ed. A. French.

388.4 US ISSN 0090-8223
HE4441
URBAN MASS TRANSPORTATION ABSTRACTS. (Subseries of: Transit Research Information Center. Report) 1972. bi-m. U.S. Urban Mass Transportation Administration, 400 Seventh St. S.W., Washington, DC 20590. TEL 202-426-9157. index; circ. 2,000.

388.411 US ISSN 0734-0648
HE305
URBAN TRANSPORTATION ABSTRACTS. 1982. a. $65. National Research Council, Transportation Research Board, 2101 Constitution Ave., N.W., Washington, DC 20418. TEL 202-334-3218. FAX 202-334-2519. (Co-sponsor: Urban Mass Transportation Administration) Ed. S.D. Crowther. abstr.; bibl.; circ. 500. (back issues avail.)
Description: Abstracts of research reports, technical papers, journal articles, and on-going research in urban transportation and public transit.

388 HU ISSN 0231-0767
VASUTI KOZLEKEDESI SZAKIRODALMI TAJEKOZTATO/RAILWAY TRANSPORTATION ABSTRACTS. m. 4000 Ft. Orszagos Muszaki Informacios Kozpont es Konyvtar (O.M.I.K.K.) - National Technical Information Centre and Library, Muzeum u. 17, 1428 Budapest, Hungary. (Subscr. to: Kultura, P.O. Box 149, 1389 Budapest, Hungary) Ed. Raczne Agnes Kovacs. circ. 400.
Supersedes in part (as of 1982): Muszaki Lapszemle. Kozlekedes - Technical Abstracts. Transportation (ISSN 0027-5042)

387.7 FR
VENTILATION DU TRAFIC COMMERCIAL. m. 440 F. (effective 1992). Aeroports de Paris, Service Previsions et Statistiques, Orly Sud 103, 94396 Orly Aerogare Cedex, France.

012 380.5 SZ
VERKEHRSTECHNIK IN DER SCHWEIZ; Lieferantenkatalog der schweizerischer oeffentlicher Verkehrsbetriebe. 1965. a. 28 Fr.($19) Cicero Verlag AG, Postfach, CH-8021 Zurich, Switzerland. TEL 01-4888400. FAX 01-4888300. TELEX 812648-CH. Ed. P. Eggspuehler. adv.; circ. 5,000.

629.2 US ISSN 0083-7229
HD9710.U5
WARD'S AUTOMOTIVE YEARBOOK. 1938. a. $190 (or included with sub. to Ward's Automotive Reports). Ward's Communications (Subsidiary of: Intertec Publishing Corp.), 28 W. Adams St., Detroit, MI 48226. TEL 313-962-4433. FAX 313-962-5593. Ed. James W. Bush. adv.; bk.rev.; charts; illus.; stat.; index; circ. 5,087.
Description: Comprehensive reference work of vital industry statistics: U.S. and worldwide auto and truck production; sales by market segment, engine size, and model year; factory-installed equipment tables; vehicle registrations; supplier directory.

387 II
WATER TRANSPORT STATISTICS OF INDIA. 1969. a. $11.70. Ministry of Shipping and Transport, Transport Research Division, I D A Bldg., Jamnagar House, Shahjahan Rd., New Delhi 11001, India. (Orders to: Controller of Publications, Civil Lines, Delhi 110006, India)
Formerly: India (Republic) Ministry of Shipping and Transport. Statistics of Water Transport Industries (ISSN 0081-5144)

388 US ISSN 0084-0572
WISCONSIN. DEPARTMENT OF TRANSPORTATION. DIVISION OF PLANNING AND BUDGET. HIGHWAY MILEAGE DATA. (Former name of issuing body: Division of Planning) 1946. a. $12. Department of Transportation, Division of Planning, Box 7913, 4802 Sheboygan Ave., Madison, WI 53707. TEL 608-266-3661. circ. 200.

388 US ISSN 0084-0580
G1416.P21
WISCONSIN. DEPARTMENT OF TRANSPORTATION. DIVISION OF PLANNING. HIGHWAY TRAFFIC. Short title: Wisconsin Highway Traffic. 1968. a. $14.50. Department of Transportation, Division of Planning, Data Development Section, 4802 Sheboygan Ave., Box 7913, Madison, WI 53707. TEL 608-266-1466. circ. 300.
Formerly: Wisconsin. Division of Highways. System Planning Section. Highway Traffic in Wisconsin Cities (ISSN 0512-0624)

388 US ISSN 0098-0323
HE371.W6
WISCONSIN TRAFFIC DATA - AUTOMATIC TRAFFIC RECORDER; monthly average daily traffic. Short title: Wisconsin Traffic Data - A T R. 1970. a. $14.69. Department of Transportation, Division of Planning, Data Development Section, 4802 Sheboygan Ave., Box 7913, Madison, WI 53707. TEL 608-266-1466. circ. 125.
Former titles: Wisconsin. Department of Transportation. Automatic Traffic Recorder Data; Wisconsin. Department of Transportation. Traffic Planning Section. Automatic Recorder Station Traffic Data (ISSN 0091-6080)

387.7 SZ ISSN 0084-1366
TL720.A1
WORLD AIR TRANSPORT STATISTICS. 1956. a. $75. International Air Transport Association, Publications, 33 Route de L'Aeroport, P.O. Box 672, 1215 15 Airport, Switzerland. (back issues avail.)

387 016 UK ISSN 0264-0775
CODEN: WPHADD
WORLD PORTS AND HARBOURS ABSTRACTS. 1976. bi-m. $320 (foreign £170). S T I Ltd., 4 Kings Meadow, Ferry Hinksey Rd., Oxford OX2 0DU, England. TEL 0865-798898. FAX 0865-798788. (Dist. in U.S. by Air Science Co., Box 143, Corning, NY 14830. TEL 607-962-5591) Ed. Lindsay Gale. bk.rev.; abstr.; index, cum.index. (back issues avail.)
●Also available online. Vendor(s): DIALOG (File no.96/FLUIDEX, European Space Agency (File no.48/FLUIDEX).
Incorporates (with vol.7, Dec. 1982): International Dredging Abstracts (ISSN 0308-1400)
Description: Covers the hydraulics of inland and coastal waters in relation to docks and quay piers. Includes construction, maintenance and use of structures.

388.411   SZ   ISSN 0444-1419
WORLD ROAD STATISTICS. (Text in English, French and German.) a. 180 Fr. International Road Federation - Federation Routiere Internationale, 63 Rue de Lausanne, CH-1202 Geneva, Switzerland. TEL 22-7317150. FAX 22-7317158. TELEX 412479-IRF-CH.
   Formerly: Welt-Strassen-Statistik.
   Description: Presents statistical data on transport, road networks, traffic, accidents, taxation, etc.

380.5   SZ   ISSN 0302-7902
WORLD TRANSPORT DATA/STATISTIQUES MONDIALES DE TRANSPORT. (Text in English and French) 1973. irreg., latest 1990. 115 Fr. International Road Transport Union, 3 rue de Varembe, B.P. 44, CH-1211 Geneva 20, Switzerland. FAX 7330660. circ. 4,000.

384 314   YU   ISSN 0513-0794
YUGOSLAVIA. SAVEZNI ZAVOD ZA STATISTIKU. SAOBRACAJ I VEZE. (Subseries of its Statisticki Bilten) (Edition also in English) 100 din.($5.56) Savezni Zavod za Statistiku, Kneza Milosa 20, Belgrade, Yugoslavia. TEL 681-999. illus.; circ. 1,100.

380.5   ZA   ISSN 0514-5392
ZAMBIA. CENTRAL STATISTICAL OFFICE. TRANSPORT STATISTICS. q. $4. Central Statistical Office, P.O. Box 31908, Lusaka, Zambia. TEL 211-231.

TRANSPORTATION — Air Transport

387.744   UK   ISSN 0141-6529
A B C AIR CARGO GUIDE. 1958. m. £144. Reed Travel Group (Subsidiary of Reed International PLC), Church St., Dunstable, Bedfordshire LU5 4HB, England. TEL 0582-600111. TELEX 82168-AIRABC-G. Ed. D. Bird. adv.; circ. 10,500.
   Formerly: A B C Air Cargo Guide and Directory (ISSN 0001-0391)
   Description: Full listings of flight routines, world schedules and rates.

387.744   UK
A B C EXECUTIVE FLIGHT PLANNER: ASIA PLANNER. 1983. m. £69. Reed Travel Group (Subsidiary of: Reed International PLC), Church St., Dunstable, Bedfordshire LU5 4HB, England. TEL 0582-600111. TELEX 82168-AIRABC-G. Ed. R. Cooper. circ. 5,100.
   Former titles: A B C Executive Flight Planner - Asia Planner; A B C Air Asia (ISSN 0265-4024)
   Description: Regionalized guide to air schedules.

629.1 385   UK
A B C EXECUTIVE FLIGHT PLANNER: EUROPE, MIDDLE EAST & AFRICA. 1975. m. £69. Reed Travel Group (Subsidiary of: Reed International PLC), Church St., Dunstable, Bedfordshire LU5 4HB, England. circ. 9,500.
   Former titles: A B C Air Europe, Middle East and North Africa (ISSN 0951-6905); American Express SkyGuide Europe - Middle East; (until 1985): A B C Air - Rail Europe (ISSN 0305-8077)
   Description: Regionalized guide to air schedules.

387.7   UK
A B C EXECUTIVE FLIGHT PLANNER: NORTH AMERICA. 1988. m. £55. Reed Travel Group (Subsidiary of: Reed International PLC), Church St., Dunstable, Bedfordshire LU5 4HB, England. TEL 0582-600111. TELEX 82168-AIRABC-G. adv.
   Description: Regionalized guide to air schedules.

387.7   UK   ISSN 0309-6157
A B C WORLD AIRWAYS GUIDE. 1946. m. £306. Reed Travel Group (Subsidiary of: Reed International PLC), Church St., Dunstable, Bedfordshire LU5 4HB, England. TEL 0582-600111. TELEX 82168-AIRABC-G. (US addr.: 500 Plaza Dr., Secaucus, NJ 07096. TEL 201-902-2000) Dir. R.J.L. Speirs. adv.; circ. 86,637.
   Description: Covers worldwide fare schedules and fare information, plus ancillary air travel information.

387.7   US
A C C A EXPRESS. q. Air Courier Conference of America, 50 Church St., Montclair, NJ 07042-2745. TEL 201-744-5771. FAX 201-744-6353. Ed. Herb Lev. circ. 1,500.

629   US   ISSN 0194-8652
A C FLYER. (Air Craft) 1972. m. $24 (foreign $41). McGraw-Hill, Inc., 1221 Ave. of the Americas, New York, NY 10020. TEL 212-512-2000. (Subscr. to: Box 564, Hightstown, NJ 08520) adv.; circ. 80,174.
   Description: Lists used aircraft for sale.

629.13   GW   ISSN 0001-0987
A D V - INFORMATIONSDIENST. 1949. m. DM.58. Arbeitsgemeinschaft Deutscher Verkehrsflughaefen - German Airports' Association, Flughafen, 7000 Stuttgart 23, Germany. FAX 711-7901746. TELEX 7245658. Ed. Udo Wolffram. bk.rev.; stat.; index; circ. 350.
   Description: Summary of press publications on airports, air transportation and the aerospace industry.

387.7   US
A O C S NEWS.* 1976. q. $15. Airline Operational Control Society, 152 N. Jamestown Rd., Coraopolis, PA 15108-1015. TEL 412-741-5349. Ed. Steven M. Mineck. index; circ. 350. (looseleaf format; back issues avail.)
   Description: Published for the benefit of AOCS members, an organization of aviation professionals involved in the operational control of an airline.

A P A HOLIDAY. (Airline Passengers Association) see *TRAVEL AND TOURISM*

387.736   FR
A P A LA UNE. 1956. 11/yr. free. Aeroports de Paris, Service Communication Programme - Paris Airport Authority, 291 Bd. Raspail, 75675 Paris cedex 14, France. Ed. Anatole Rojinski. adv.; bk.rev.; illus.; stat.; circ. 6,000.
   Formerly: Propos en l'Air (ISSN 0033-1384)

A S U TRAVEL GUIDE; the airline employee's discount directory. (Airline Service Unlimited) see *TRAVEL AND TOURISM*

387.742   US
ACCENT (OGDEN). 1981. m. Meridian Publishing, Inc., Box 10010, Ogden, UT 84409. TEL 801-394-9446. Ed. Robyn C. Walker. adv.; tr.lit.; circ. 150,842.
   Formerly: Inflight.

387.7   UK   ISSN 0306-3550
ACCIDENTS TO AIRCRAFT ON THE BRITISH REGISTER. 1949. irreg. price varies. Civil Aviation Authority, Greville House, 37 Gratton Rd., Cheltenham, Glos GL50 2BN, England.

ADVANCED COMPOSITES MONTHLY. see *AERONAUTICS AND SPACE FLIGHT*

387.7   GW
AERO LLOYD; Bord Magazin. (Text in English and German) 1984. q. (Aero Lloyd Airlines) F U V Flugurlaub Verlag, Lessingstr. 7-9, D-6370 Oberursel, Germany. TEL 06171-6400. adv.; circ. 100,000. (back issues avail.)
   Formerly: Flugurlaub.

387.736   GW
AEROGUIDE; Nationale und Internationale Flugverbindungen von 140 deutschen Flughaefen. 1985. a. Verlag fuer Wirtschaftliche Informationen, Malvenweg 4, 5000 Cologne 80, Germany. TEL 0221-634091.

387.736   FR   ISSN 0245-8756
AEROPORTS DE PARIS. BULLETIN MENSUEL DE STATISTIQUES. 1960. m. 210 F. (effective 1992). Aeroports de Paris, Service Documentation et Statistiques, Orly Sud 103, 94396 Orly Aerogare, France.

387.7   FR   ISSN 0065-3721
AEROPORTS DE PARIS. RAPPORT DU CONSEIL D'ADMINISTRATION. (Editions in English and French) a. free. Aeroports de Paris - Paris Airport Authority, Service Relations Publiques et Editions, 291 Bd. Raspail, 75675 Paris, France.

387.7   FR   ISSN 0078-947X
AEROPORTS DE PARIS. SERVICE STATISTIQUE. STATISTIQUE DE TRAFIC. 1951. a. 210 F. (effective 1992). Aeroports de Paris - Paris Airport Authority, Service Previsions et Statistiques, Orly Sud 103, 94396 Orly Aerogare Cedex, France.

387.736   FR
AEROPORTS DE PARIS. TRAFIC DES PRINCIPAUX AEROPORTS MONDIAUX. (Text in English and French) a. 160 F. (effective 1992). Aeroports de Paris, Service Documentation et Statistiques, Orly Sud 103, 94396 Orly Aerogare, France.

387.736   FR   ISSN 0336-626X
AEROPORTS MAGAZINE. 1968. 10/yr. 250 F. Aeroports de Paris, Service Communication, 291 Bd. Raspail, 75675 Paris Cedex 14, France. adv.; circ. 8,000.

387.7   UK   ISSN 0261-2313
AFRICAN AIR TRANSPORT. 1980. q. free to qualified personnel. T C E Publications Ltd., 30 Queens Terrace, Southampton, Hampshire SO1 1BQ, England. FAX 703-333641. Ed. Brian Walters. adv.; bk.rev.; illus.; circ. 3,217.

AIR ALASKA; the northern aviator's news. see *AERONAUTICS AND SPACE FLIGHT*

387.7   UK
AIR & BUSINESS TRAVEL. 1965. s-m. £6($10) Interline News Ltd., 9-15 Neal St., London WC2H 9PF, England. Ed. John Pointer. adv.; bk.rev.; circ. 13,000.
   Former titles: Air Travel & Air Travel and Interline News (ISSN 0262-4249); Interline and Air Travel News; Interline News.

387.7   UK
AIR-BRITAIN AIRLINE FLEETS. 1980. a. £12. Air-Britain (Historians) Ltd., 1 East St., Tonbridge, Kent TN9 1HP, England.
   Former titles: Airline Fleets (ISSN 0262-1657) & World Airline Fleets Handbook.
   Description: Airline fleet data worldwide on over 1500 operators in 166 countries.

387.744   IT
AIR CARGO. (Text in Italian; summaries in English) 1968. s-m. L.205000 (foreign L.340000). Editoriale Aeronautica s.r.l., Via Nicolo Paganini 7, 00198 Rome, Italy. TEL 06-8414691. FAX 06-8443154. Ed. Oscar Dariz. adv.; circ. 1,000.

387.744   US
AIR CARGO NEWS. 1975. 12/yr. $36. Air Cargo News, Inc., Box 777, Jamaica, NY 11431. TEL 718-479-0176. Ed. Milton A. Caine. adv.; circ. 42,000.

387.7   US   ISSN 0745-5100
HE9788
AIR CARGO WORLD. 1910. m. $45 (foreign $115). Communication Channels, Inc., 6255 Barfield Rd., Atlanta, GA 30328-4369. TEL 404-256-9800. FAX 404-256-3116. TELEX 4611075 COMCHANI. Ed. David J. Premo. adv.; bk.rev.; illus.; tr.lit.; index; circ. 25,000. (also avail. in microform from UMI; reprint service avail. from UMI)
   ●Also available online.
   —BLDSC shelfmark: 0774.750000.
   Former titles (until 1982): Air Cargo Magazine (ISSN 0148-7469); (until 1976): Cargo Airlift; Air Transportation (ISSN 0002-2551)
   Description: International magazine devoted to the expeditious movement of goods and information. Serves the fields of transportation, physical distribution, courier and small package shipping, import-export and bulk freight traffic in industries utilizing air as a distribution vehicle.

387.7   US
AIR CARRIER, AIRCRAFT UTILIZATION AND PROPULSION RELIABILITY REPORT. m. U.S. Federal Aviation Administration, Department of Transportation (DOT), Aviation Standards National Field Office, National Safety Data Branch, AVN-120, Box 25082, Oklahoma City, OK 73125.

387.7   US
AIR CARRIER INDUSTRY SCHEDULE SERVICE TRAFFIC STATISTICS. MEDIUM REGIONAL CARRIERS. 1970. a. $12. U.S. Department of Transportation, Research & Special Programs Administration, Office of Aviation, 400 Seventh St., S.W., Washington, DC 20590. TEL 202-783-3238. stat.; circ. 700. (processed)
Indexed: Amer.Stat.Ind.
   Former titles: Air Carrier Industry Schedule Service Traffic Statistics & Commuter Air Carrier Traffic Statistics (ISSN 0270-448X)

4670 TRANSPORTATION — AIR TRANSPORT

387.7 US ISSN 0092-2870
HE9788.5.U5
AIR FREIGHT DIRECTORY. 1961. bi-m. $76.50. Air Cargo, Inc., 1819 Bay Ridge Ave., Annapolis, MD 21403. Ed. Stephanie Wilkins. adv.; circ. 7,500.
Supersedes: Air Freight Directory of Points in the United States Served Directly by Air and by Pick-up and Delivery Service and by Connecting Motor Carriers (ISSN 0515-8125)

341.46 NE ISSN 0165-2079
K1
AIR LAW. (Text in English) 1975. bi-m. fl.294($157) Kluwer Law and Taxation Publishers, P.O. Box 23, 7400 GA Deventer, Netherlands.
TEL 31-5700-47261. FAX 31-5700-22244. TELEX 49295 KLUDV NL. (Dist. by: Libresso Distribution Centre, P.O. Box 23, 7400 GA Deventer, Netherlands. TEL 31-5700-33155; N. America dist. addr.: 6 Bigelow St., Cambridge, MA 02139. TEL 617-354-0140) Ed.Bd. (back issues avail.)
Indexed: Abstr.Bk.Rev.Curr.Leg.Per., C.L.I., Int.Aerosp.Abstr., L.R.I., Leg.Per.
—BLDSC shelfmark: 0774.131000.

AIR LINE PILOT; the magazine of professional flight deck crews. see AERONAUTICS AND SPACE FLIGHT

387.7 NZ ISSN 0065-4817
AIR NEW ZEALAND. ANNUAL REPORT. 1965. a. free. Air New Zealand Ltd, 1 Queen St., Auckland, New Zealand. FAX 64-09-3662764. (U.S. addr: 1960 E. Grand Ave., Ste. 900, El Segundo, CA 90245) circ. 30,000.

387 AT ISSN 0727-338X
AIR PILOT. 1952. q. free to qualified personnel. Australian Federation of Air Pilots, 132 Albert Rd., South Melbourne, Vic. 3205, Australia. Ed. Terry O'Connell. adv.; bk.rev.; illus.; circ. 5,000.

341.46 US ISSN 0400-1915
AIR TRAFFIC CONTROL ASSOCIATION. BULLETIN. m. membership only. Air Traffic Control Association, Inc., 2300 Clarendon Blvd., Ste. 711, Arlington, VA 22201. TEL 703-522-5717.

387.7 US
AIR TRANSPORT. 1937. a. $10. Air Transport Association of America, 1709 New York Ave., N.W., Washington, DC 20006. TEL 202-626-4000. FAX 202-626-4181. Ed.Bd. **Indexed:** SRI.
Description: Report of the United States scheduled airline industry.

387.7 CN ISSN 0065-485X
AIR TRANSPORT ASSOCIATION OF CANADA. ANNUAL REPORT. 1960. a. Air Transport Association of Canada, 747 Metropolitan Life Bldg., 99 Bank St., Ottawa, Ont. K1P 6B9, Canada.
TEL 613-233-7727. Ed. Donald H. Watson. circ. 1,000.

387.7 II
AIR TRANSPORTATION ANNUAL (BOMBAY). (Text in English) 1980. a. Rs.20($5) Amalgamated Press, Narang House, 41 Ambalal Doshi Marg, Bombay 400023, India. Ed. Jeanette da Silva. circ. 2,000.
Description: Devoted to air travel, tourism, and the hotel industry in India.

387.7 RH
AIR ZIMBABWE ANNUAL REPORT. 1968. a. free. Air Zimbabwe Corporation, P.O. Box AP. 1, Harare Airport, Harare, Zimbabwe. circ. 2,000.
Formerly: Air Rhodesia Annual Report.

629.13 US ISSN 1044-8012
AIRCRAFT TECHNICIAN. 1989. bi-m. $65 (Canada and Mexico $80; elsewhere $120). Johnson Hill Press, Inc., 1233 Janesville Ave., Fort Atkinson, WI 53538. TEL 414-563-6388. FAX 414-563-1701. Ed. Greg Napert. adv.; circ. 25,000 (controlled). (tabloid format)
Description: Focuses on the technical and mechanical side of the 19-passenger and below airline industry.

387.7 332 UK ISSN 0143-2257
HE9782
AIRFINANCE JOURNAL. 1980. m. £138. Euromoney Publications PLC, Nestor House, Playhouse Yard, London EC4V 5EX, England. TEL 071-236-3288. FAX 071-248-8625. TELEX 886196 EURMON G. Ed. Chris Kjelgaard. adv.; circ. 4,500. (back issues avail.)
Description: Aviation and aerospace financing techniques.

387.7 658 UK ISSN 0268-7615
AIRLINE BUSINESS. 1985. m. $99. Reed Business Publishing Group (London) (Subsidiary of: Reed International PLC), 151 Wardour St., London W1V 4BN, England. TEL 081-661-3500. circ. 25,600.
●Also available online. Vendor(s): Data-Star, Mead Data Central.
—BLDSC shelfmark: 0784.505000.
Description: Covers politics, finance and trends in the air transport industry.

387.7 658 US ISSN 1051-631X
AIRLINE EXECUTIVE INTERNATIONAL; the management magazine for today's worldwide airline industry. 1976. m. $45 (foreign $115). Communication Channels, Inc., 6255 Barfield Rd., Atlanta, GA 30328-4369. TEL 404-256-9800.
FAX 404-256-3116. TELEX 4611075 COMCHANI. Ed. David J. Premo. adv.; bk.rev.; circ. 45,600. (also avail. in microform from UMI; reprint service avail. from UMI)
●Also available online.
Formerly (until 1990): Airline Executive (ISSN 0278-6702)
Description: Covers the U.S. and international airline and air transport industry, offering information about manufacturers, aircraft, airlines, airport, supporting elements and the personnel involved.

387.7 US ISSN 1040-5410
AIRLINE FINANCIAL NEWS. 1986. w. $450 (effective 1992). Phillips Publishing, Inc., Defense - Aviation Group, 1925 N. Lynn St., Ste. 1000, Arlington, VA 22209. TEL 703-522-8333. FAX 703-522-8334. TELEX 5101011287. adv.
●Also available online. Vendor(s): Data-Star, DIALOG, NewsNet.

629.13 UK ISSN 0002-2721
AIRLINE FLEET RECORD. 3/yr. $225. Aviation Studies International, Sussex House, Parkside, Wimbledon, London SW19 5NB, England. TEL 081-946-5082.
Description: Lists by continent the fleets of 1,500 airlines.

387.7 US ISSN 0095-4683
HE9768
AIRLINE HANDBOOK. 1972. a. $16. AeroTravel Research Publications, Box 3694, Cranston, RI 02910. TEL 401-941-6140. Ed. Paul K. Martin. illus.

387.7 US
AIRLINE INDUSTRIAL RELATIONS CONFERENCE. NEWSLETTER. bi-m. Airline Industrial Relations Conference, 1920 N St., N.W., Ste. 250, Washington, DC 20036. TEL 202-861-7550.

629.13 US ISSN 0002-2748
AIRLINE NEWSLETTER. 1967. s-m. $65. Roadcap Aviation Publications, 1030 S. Green Bay Rd., Lake Forest, IL 60045. TEL 708-234-4730. Ed. Roy R. Roadcap. cum.index. (looseleaf format)
Formerly: World Airline Record Newsletter (ISSN 0512-2368)
Description: News and analysis of trends in commercial air transportation.

387.7 SP
AIRLINE NINETY TWO; revista de aviacion comercial y aeropuertos. 10/yr. 3850 ptas. (Europe 5990 ptas.; America 10790 ptas.). Defensa Edefa, S.A., Editorial de Publicaciones, Jorge Juan, 98-2, 28009 Madrid, Spain. TEL 1-577-49-57. FAX 577-46-70. adv.: B&W page 201000 ptas., color page 350000 ptas.; trim 187 x 267. circ. 10,500.
Description: Covers commercial aviation and airports.

387.742 US ISSN 0892-4236
AIRLINE, SHIP & CATERING ONBOARD SERVICES MAGAZINE; the international trade publication for the passenger service and duty free markets. 1974. 8/yr. $25 (foreign $65). (Airline Inflight Food Service Association) International Publishing Company of America, 665 La Villa Dr., Miami Springs, FL 33166. TEL 305-887-1700.
FAX 305-885-1923. Ed. Jim O'Neal. adv.; circ. 9,000.
Former titles: Airline and Travel Food (ISSN 0161-1755); Airline Food and Flight Service; Airline News.
Description: Geared towards food service management of domestic and international airlines. Covers ships, railroads, catering firms and other suppliers to the travel industry.

387.7 US ISSN 0896-6575
HE9761.1
AIRLINERS. 1988. q. $15.95. World Transport Press, Inc., Box 52-1238, Miami, FL 33152-1238.
TEL 305-477-7163. FAX 305-599-1995. Ed. John Wegg. adv.; bk.rev.; circ. 16,000.
Description: Presents news, air transport trends, articles, and photography of the commercial aviation industry.

387.736 UK
AIRPORT; travelling in style. m. free. Inc. Publications, 38 St. John St., London EC1M 4AY, England.
TEL 01-251-8798. FAX 01-251-8801. Ed. Alison James. adv.

387.7 US
AIRPORT EXECUTIVE MAGAZINE. bi-m. American Association of Airport Executives, 4224 King St., Alexandria, VA 22302. TEL 703-824-0500.

387.71 GW ISSN 0174-3279
AIRPORT FORUM NEWS; airport business report. (Text in English) 1973. bi-w. DM.480($300) Momberger Airport Information, P.O. Box 1127, 7255 Rutesheim, Germany. TEL 07152-51640.
FAX 07152-55005. Ed. M. Momberger. bk.rev. (back issues avail.) **Indexed:** Key to Econ.Sci.

387.7 US
AIRPORT HIGHLIGHTS. 1964. 26/yr. $110 (foreign $150). Airports Association Council Inyernational, 1220 19th St., N.W., Ste. 200, Washington, DC 20036. TEL 202-293-8500. FAX 202-331-1362. Ed. Nancy Hasanian. bk.rev.; circ. 2,000.

387.736 US
AIRPORT JOURNAL. m. Box 273, Clarendon Hills, IL 60514-0273. TEL 708-318-6872. Ed. John S. Andrews. adv.; circ. 26,500.

614.85 387.7 US ISSN 0898-574X
AIRPORT OPERATIONS. bi-m. $50 (foreign $55). Flight Safety Foundation, Inc., 2200 Wilson Blvd., Ste. 500, Arlington, VA 22201-3306.
TEL 703-522-8300. FAX 703-525-6047. TELEX 901176 FSF INC AGTN. (reprint service avail. from UMI)
Formerly (until vol.13, no.5, 1987): Airport Operations Safety Bulletin; **Incorporates (in 1978):** Airport Operations Ground Safety Bulletin; Airport Ground Safety Bulletin.

AIRPORT POCKET GUIDE; a publication to aid air travelers. see TRAVEL AND TOURISM

387.7 US
AIRPORT PRESS. 1978. bi-m. $32. Box 879, JFK Sta., Jamaica, NY 11430. TEL 718-244-6788. Ed. Dick Eisley. circ. 29,000. (tabloid format)

387.7 US ISSN 0044-7021
AIRPORT REPORT. 1954. s-m. membership. American Association of Airport Executives, 4224 King St., Alexandria, VA 22302. FAX 703-820-1395. Ed. Craig J. Spencer. adv.; bk.rev.; illus.; circ. controlled. (looseleaf format)

387.736 UK
AIRPORT SUPPORT. 1982. m. £37. Camrus Airport Publishers Ltd., 320 High St., Sutton, Surrey SM1 1PR, England. FAX 1-642-9039. TELEX 916230-CAMRUS-G. Ed. Keith Magnay. adv.; bk.rev.; circ. 11,421.
Description: Covers news and features on aircraft ground support, airport construction, and air traffic control.

TRANSPORTATION — AIR TRANSPORT

387.7 US
AIRPORTS. w. $450 (foreign $500). McGraw-Hill, Inc., Aviation Week Group, 1156 15th St., N.W., Washington, DC 20005. TEL 202-822-4600. Ed. Avery Vise.
●Also available online. Vendor(s): DIALOG (File no.624/McGRAW-HILL PULICATIONS ONLINE), Dow Jones/News Retrieval, Mead Data Central, NewsNet.
  Description: Aimed at airport managers, users, and suppliers. Subjects covered include noise abatement, landing rights, curfews, franchise and rental fees, regulation, funding, FAA grants.

387.7 JM
AIRTEAM CIRCLE. s-a. Airports Authority of Jamaica, 64 Knutsford Blvd., Kingston 5, Jamaica, W.I. TEL 809-92-61622. Ed. Trevor Spence. adv.

387.7 UK ISSN 0306-0349
AIRTRADE. 1975. m. £50. Maclean Hunter Ltd., Maclean Hunter House, Chalk Lane, Cockfosters Rd., Barnet, Herts EN4 0BU, England. TEL 081-975-9759. FAX 081-440-1796. TELEX 299072 MACHUN G. Ed. Chris Pocock. circ. 8,332.

ALASKA AIRLINES MAGAZINE. see *TRAVEL AND TOURISM — Airline Inflight And Hotel Inroom*

387.7 CN
▼**ALASKA AREA AIRPORT BUSINESS DIRECTORY.** 1991. a. $7.50. Business Directories International, 107, 5621-11 St. N.E., Calgary, Alta. T2E 6Z7, Canada. TEL 403-295-9200. FAX 403-295-6335. Ed. Gary Gaudreau. adv.; circ. 7,000.
  Description: Lists services and personnel at Anchorage International, Merrill Field, Fairbanks International, Juneau International, Ketchikan International airports among others.

ANUARIO ESTADISTICO DEL TRANSPORTE AEREO ESPANA - (YEAR). see *TRANSPORTATION — Abstracting, Bibliographies, Statistics*

387.7 CN
▼**ATLANTIC REGION AVIATION BUSINESS DIRECTORY.** 1991. a. Can.$7.50. Consolidated Communications, 807 Manning Rd., N.E., Ste. 200, Calgary, Alta. T2E 7M8, Canada. TEL 403-569-9520. FAX 403-569-5950. Ed. Gary Guadreau. adv.; B&W page Can.$1550; trim 5 1/2 x 8 1/2; adv. contact: John Batuik. circ. 4,500.
  Description: Lists services and personnel at Halifax International, Moncton, Fredericton, Saint John, Charlottetown, St. John's and Gander Airports.

387.7 PO ISSN 0870-8924
ATLANTIS; inflight magazine. 1981. 6/yr. free. T A P Air Portugal, Bldg. 27, 7th fl., Lisbon Airport, 1704 Lisbon, Portugal. TEL 847-02-50. FAX 848-19-55. TELEX 12231 TAPLIS P. Ed. A. Campos Batista. adv.; circ. 120,000.

ATLAS - AIR FRANCE; geographie physique et humaine - decouverte de l'homme et de la nature. see *TRAVEL AND TOURISM*

919 AT
AUSTRALIAN WAY. 1947. m. not available on subscription. (Australian Airlines) P O L Concepts Pty. Ltd., 125-127 Little Eveleigh St., Redfern, N.S.W. 2016, Australia. Ed. Maggy Oehlbeck. adv.; bk.rev.; charts; illus.; circ. 60,000.
  Formerly (until Jul. 1986): Transair (ISSN 0041-1043)

387.71 629.132 BE ISSN 0772-876X
AVIANEWS INTERNATIONAL; Pan-European Aerospace and Defense Monthly. (Editions English, French) 1972. 11/yr. 2,500 Fr.($80) S.A. Frankie & Lette, 23 Chemin Sainte Anne, B-1380 Ohain, Belgium. TEL 2-653-15-43. FAX 2-653-16-29. Ed. Didier Daoust. adv.; bk.rev.; circ. 31,000.
  Formerly: Avianews.
  Description: Features commercial aviation, defense and space technology.

387.7 910.09 II ISSN 0970-3578
AVIATION & SPACE JOURNAL. (Text in English) 1977. q. Rs.110($25) V.J. Joseph, Ed. & Pub., 3 Radhe Nivas, 36th Rd., Bandra, Bombay 400 050, India. TEL 6427281-273193. adv.; charts; illus.; stat. (reprint service avail.)
  Description: Devoted to air transport, travel and tourism, as well as the trade fair and hotel industries.

THE AVIATION CONSUMER. see *AERONAUTICS AND SPACE FLIGHT*

AVIATION EDUCATION NEWS BULLETIN. see *AERONAUTICS AND SPACE FLIGHT*

629.132 FR
AVIATION ET PILOTE; revue des loisirs de l'air. 1973. m. 300 F. Societe d'Edition et d'Exploitation de Supports, Aerodrome de Lognes-Emerainville, 77322 Marne la Vallee Cedex 2, France. TEL 1-64-62-05-06. FAX 1-64-62-11-09. Ed. Jacques Callies. adv.; bk.rev.; circ. 25,000.
  Former titles: Aviation et Pilote Prive; Pilote Prive; Aero-Club et le Pilote Prive.

387.7 US
AVIATION INTERNATIONAL NEWS. bi-m. 21 Cross Ave., Midland Park, NJ 07432. TEL 201-444-5075. Ed. James Holahan. adv.; circ. 31,000.

341.46 US
AVIATION LAW REPORTS. 4 base vols. plus s-m. updates. $1460. Commerce Clearing House, Inc., 4025 W. Peterson Ave., Chicago, IL 60646. TEL 312-583-8500.

AVIATION LITIGATION REPORTER; the national journal of record of aviation litigation. see *LAW*

AVIATION MEDICINE. see *MEDICAL SCIENCES*

341.46 US
AVIATION REGULATORY DIGEST SERVICE. m. $250. Hawkins Publishing Co., Inc., Box 480, Mayo, MD 21106-0480. TEL 301-798-1677. Ed. Carl R. Eyler. circ. 90. (looseleaf format; back issues avail.)
  Formerly: Civil Aeronautics Board Service.

AVIATION SAFETY; the twice-monthly journal of accident prevention. see *AERONAUTICS AND SPACE FLIGHT*

387.7 CN
AVIATION TRADE. 1984. m. Omnicore Puclishing Inc., 34 Lakeshore Rd., E., Port Credit, Ont. L5G 1C8, Canada. TEL 416-497-9562. Ed. Mike Minnich. circ. 18,723.

629.1 II
AVION;* a monthly on aviation. 1971. m. Rs.32. 16-Park Area, New Delhi 5, India. Ed. J.K. Jain. adv.; charts; illus.

AVIONICS REVIEW. see *AERONAUTICS AND SPACE FLIGHT*

387.7 UK
B A A NEWS. 1975. m. free to BAA staff and pensioners. B A A plc., 130 Wilton Rd., London SW1V 1LQ, England. TEL 071-932-6736. FAX 071-932-6773. Ed. David Bland. adv.; circ. 12,000. (tabloid format)
  Formerly (until 1987): Airport News.

387.7 051 AQ
B W I A SUNJET. (British West Indies Airways) 1982. 4/yr. F T Caribbean, P.O. Box 1037, St. John's, Antigua, W.I. FAX 462-3492. Ed.Bd. circ. 75,000. (back issues avail.)

387.74 GW ISSN 0005-9242
BERLIN-FLUGPLAN. (Berlin Flight Schedule and Airport Information) 1952. m. free. Berliner Flughafen-GmbH, Flughafen Tegel, 1000 Berlin 51, Germany. TEL 030-41012131. FAX 030-41012111. TELEX 181708-BFGTGD. Ed. W.-D. Schultze. adv.; bk.rev.; abstr.; mkt.; circ. 40,000.
  Description: Contains schedules of flights of the Berlin-Tegel and Berlin Tempelhof Airports. Also includes airfares and airport information.

BEST FARES; Texas report. see *TRAVEL AND TOURISM*

BOLETIN ESTADISTICO DE TRAFICO AEREO INTERNACIONAL. see *TRANSPORTATION — Abstracting, Bibliographies, Statistics*

BOSTON SEA AND AIR PORT HANDBOOK. see *BUSINESS AND ECONOMICS — Trade And Industrial Directories*

387.7 UK ISSN 0306-7041
BRITISH AIRWAYS EXECUTIVE. 1967. bi-m. free. British Airways PLC., Box 10, Heathrow Airport, Middlesex TW6 2JA, England. Ed. G. Wall. adv.; circ. 110,000 (controlled).
  Incorporates: Incentive and Agenda.

387.7 UK
BRITISH AIRWAYS NEWS. 1940. w. free to staff and qualified personnel. British Airways PLC., P.O. Box 10, Heathrow Airport, Middlesex TW6 2JA, England. FAX 01-897-6230. TELEX 8813983-BAWYSC-G. Ed. Michael Blunt. adv.; bk.rev.; illus.; circ. 57,000.
  Former titles: B O A C News; B O A C Review (ISSN 0005-3252)

387.7 US
BUSINESS AVIATION WEEKLY; the weekly of business aviation. 1965. w. $420 (foreign $470). McGraw-Hill, Inc., Aviation Week Group, 1156 15th St., N.W., Washington, DC 20005. TEL 202-822-4600. Ed. David Collogan. adv.; bk.rev.; charts; illus.; stat.; tr.lit.; q. cum.index. (looseleaf format)
  ●Also available online. Vendor(s): DIALOG (File no.624/McGRAW-HILL PUBLICATIONS ONLINE), Dow Jones/News Retrieval, Mead Data Central (WBA).
  Formerly: Business Aviation (ISSN 0045-3617)

387.7 US
BUSINESS FLYER; the frequent travel newsletter. 1986. m. $50. Holcon, Box 276, Newton Center, MA 02159. TEL 800-359-3774. Ed. Jane Costello. adv.; bk.rev.; circ. 80,000. (back issues avail.)
  Description: Designed to enable business and leisure travelers to make the most of their travel.

387.7 UK
BUSINESS LIFE. 1986. 10/yr. £20. (British Airways) Headway Publications Ltd. (Subsidiary of: Maxwell Consumer Publishing and Communications Ltd.), Greater London House, Hampstead Rd., London NW1 7QQ, England. TEL 071-388-3171. FAX 071-383-7486. TELEX 269470. circ. 135,000.

BYWAYS (FAIRFAX). see *TRAVEL AND TOURISM*

387.7 JA
C A A C INFLIGHT MAGAZINE. (Text in Chinese, English and Japanese) 1982. bi-m. free. (Civil Aviation and Administration of China, Publicity and Advertising Corp.) Bi no Bi Publishing Co., Ltd., 103-28 Tanakamonzen-cho, Sakyo-ku, Kyoto 606, Japan. Ed. Zhang Baoxin. adv.; circ. 150,000.

387.71 CN
▼**C B A A MAGAZINE.** 1991. s-a. membership. Canadian Business Aircraft Association, 50 O'Connor St., Ste. 1317, Ottawa, Ont. K1P 6L2, Canada. TEL 613-236-5611. FAX 613-236-2361. adv.; illus.
  Description: Articles of business aviation interest.

387.7 US
C N S FOCUS. 4/yr. Cargo Network Services, 300 Garden City Plaza, Ste. 344, Garden City, NY 11530-3325. TEL 516-747-3312. FAX 516-747-3431. Ed. Tony Calabrese. adv.

387.7 CN
CALGARY AIRPORT BUSINESS DIRECTORY. 1977. a. Can.$7.50. Business Directories International, 107, 5621-11 St. N.E., Calgary, Alta. T2E 6Z7, Canada. TEL 403-295-9200. FAX 403-295-6335. Ed. Gary Gaudreau. adv.; circ. 5,000. (back issues avail.)
  Description: Lists services and personnel at Calgary International, Springbank, Medicine Hat, Lethbridge, Airdrie, Okotoks and High River Airports.

629.13 CN ISSN 0008-2848
CANADIAN AIRCRAFT OPERATOR; Canada's general aviation newspaper. 1964. s-m. Can.$22. Arthurs Publications Ltd., 5805 Whittle Rd., Ste. 208, Mississauga, Ont. L4Z 2J1, Canada. TEL 416-568-4131. Ed. R.G. Halford. adv.; bk.rev.; illus.; stat.; circ. 8,150. (tabloid format)

387.7 CN ISSN 0829-2132
CANADIAN AVIATION NEWS. 1976. bi-w. Can.$6($7.50) Canadian Aviation News Ltd., Suite 202, 1338 T - 36 Ave. N.E., Calgary, Alta. T2E 6T6, Canada. TEL 403-250-9833. Ed. R. Engel. adv.; circ. 10,000. (also avail. in microfiche)
  Formerly (until 1984): Canadian Western Aviation News.

TRANSPORTATION — AIR TRANSPORT

387.7   CN
CANADIAN BUSINESS AIRCRAFT ASSOCIATION. COMMUNIQUE. irreg. Canadian Business Aircraft Association, 50 O'Connor St., Ste. 1317, Ottawa, Ont. K1P 6L2, Canada. TEL 613-236-5611. FAX 613-236-2361.
Supersedes in part: Canadian Business Aircraft Association. Newsletter.
Description: Covers items of a general or technical interest such as the future of Canada's air navigation system.

387.7   CN
CANADIAN BUSINESS AIRCRAFT ASSOCIATION. MEMBERSHIP BULLETIN. irreg. Canadian Business Aircraft Association, 50 O'Connor St., St.1317, Ottawa, Ont. K1P 6L2, Canada. TEL 613-236-5611. FAX 613-236-2361.
Supersedes in part: Canadian Business Aircraft Association. Newsletter.
Description: Covers association news, excluding operations topics.

387.7   CN
CANADIAN BUSINESS AIRCRAFT ASSOCIATION. NEWS BRIEF. m. Canadian Business Aircraft Association, 50 O'Connor St., Ste. 1317, Ottawa, Ont. K1P 6L2, Canada. TEL 613-236-5611.
Supersedes in part: Canadian Business Aircraft Association. Newsletter.
Description: Provides items of general interest to CBAA membership.

387.7   CN
CANADIAN BUSINESS AIRCRAFT ASSOCIATION. OPERATIONS BULLETIN. irreg. Canadian Business Aircraft Association, 50 O'Connor St., Ste. 1317, Ottawa, Ont. K1P 6L2, Canada. TEL 613-236-5611. FAX 613-236-2361.
Supersedes in part: Canadian Business Aircraft Association. Newsletter.
Description: Deals specifically with matters pertaining to business aviation operations.

CANADIAN CIVIL AIRCRAFT REGISTER. see *AERONAUTICS AND SPACE FLIGHT*

CANADIAN CIVIL AVIATION. see *TRANSPORTATION — Abstracting, Bibliographies, Statistics*

CANADIAN GENERAL AVIATION NEWS. see *AERONAUTICS AND SPACE FLIGHT*

387.444   US   ISSN 0278-0801
CARGO FACTS. 1981. 12/yr. $195 (foreign $240). Laird Seattle Holdings, Inc., 1601 Fifth Ave., Westlake Center, No. 525, Seattle, WA 98101. TEL 206-587-6537. FAX 206-587-6540. Ed. Stefen B. Swedin. adv.; circ. 1,000. (back issues avail.)

387.7   NE
CARGOVISION. (Text in English) 1986. bi-m. free. (K.L.M. Royal Dutch Airlines) Multi Media International, P.O. Box 469, 1180 AL Amstelveen, Netherlands. TEL 20-5473550. FAX 20-6438581. Ed. Mairiona McInally Kier. charts; illus.; stat.; circ. 40,000 (controlled). (back issues avail.)
Description: Publication from KLM Cargo covering worldwide cargo news and information, company activities, international trade and freight market, airports, and profiles of cities served by KLM Cargo.

387.7   US   ISSN 0069-1437
HE9803.A1
CENSUS OF U.S. CIVIL AIRCRAFT. 1965. a. $8.50. U.S. Federal Aviation Administration., Office of Management Systems, 800 Independence Ave., S.w., Washington, DC 20591. TEL 202-655-4000. (Orders to: NTIS, Springfield, VA 22161)

CESTE I MOSTOVI/ROADS AND BRIDGES. see *ENGINEERING — Civil Engineering*

387.7   HK
CIVIL AIRCRAFT ACCIDENT REPORTS. (Text in English) irreg., latest 1979. price varies. (Civil Aviation Department) Government Publication Centre, G.P.O. Bldg., Ground Fl., Connaught Place, Hong Kong. Hong Kong. TEL 5-8428801. (Subscr. to: Director of Information Services, Information Services Dept., 1 Battery Path, G-F, Central, Hong Kong) Ed.Bd.

387.7   UK
CIVIL AIRCRAFT MARKINGS. a. price varies. Ian Allan Ltd., Terminal House, Station Approach, Shepperton, Surrey TW17 8AS, England. TEL 0932-228950. (reprint service avail. from UMI)
Description: Listing of civil aviation markings.

387.7 331.88   UK
CIVIL AVIATION NEWS; the paper that unites all aviation workers. 1978. bi-m. £2($5) Community Centre, F.C.A., Hanworth Rd., Feltham, Middx, England. Ed. Dave Howell. adv.; bk.rev.; circ. 10,000.

387.7   UK
▼**CIVIL AVIATION TRAINING.** Short title: C A T. 1990. q. £16($32) Monch UK Ltd., 84 Alexandra Rd., Farnborough, Hants GU14 6DD, England. TEL 0252-517974. FAX 0252-512714. Ed. David Saw. adv.; circ. 12,000 (controlled).
Description: Provides reports on training within air carriers for airlines, training centers, pilot schools, and trade bodies.

CIVIL TRANSPORT DATA SHEETS. see *AERONAUTICS AND SPACE FLIGHT*

387.7   GW
COCKPIT REPORT. (Text in German) 1972. bi-m. free. Vereinigung Cockpit e.V., Lerchesbergring 24, 6000 Frankfurt a.M. 70, Germany. TEL 069-681065. FAX 069-682678. circ. 800.

387.742   US   ISSN 1054-7436
TL726
COMMUTER AIR INTERNATIONAL; the international magazine for regional, commuter, and short haul airlines. 1978. m. $45 (foreign $115). Communication Channels, Inc., 6255 Barfield Rd., Atlanta, GA 30328-4369. TEL 404-256-9800. FAX 404-253-3116. TELEX 4611075 COMCHANI. Ed. David Premo. adv.; bk.rev.; circ. 29,500. (also avail. in microform from UMI; reprint service avail. from UMI)
●Also available online.
Formerly (until 1990): Commuter Air (ISSN 0199-2686)
Description: Reflects the interests of the regional-commuter airline industry, its carriers, service organizations, manufacturers and vendors. Focuses on the nuts and bolts of managing an airline, with emphasis on solving a variety of problems ranging from maintenance to labor disputes.

387.7   US   ISSN 1040-5402
COMMUTER - REGIONAL AIRLINE NEWS. w. $450 (effective 1992). Phillips Publishing, Inc., Defense - Aviation Group, 1925 N. Lynn St., Ste. 1000, Arlington, VA 22209. TEL 703-522-8333. FAX 703-522-8334. TELEX 5101011287. Ed. Kelly Q. Murphy. adv.
●Also available online. Vendor(s): Data-Star, DIALOG, NewsNet.

387.7   US
COMMUTER REGIONAL AIRLINE NEWS INTERNATIONAL. w. $450 (effective 1992). Phillips Publishing, Inc., Defense - Aviation Group, 1925 N. Lynn St., Ste. 1000, Arlington, VA 22209. TEL 703-522-8333. FAX 703-522-8334.

387.7   UK   ISSN 0265-4504
COMMUTER WORLD. 1984. 6/yr. $75. Shephard Press Ltd., 111 High St., Burnham, Bucks. SL1 7JZ, England. TEL 0628-604311. FAX 0628-664334. Ed. Ian Harbison. circ. 11,341.

387.7   UK
CONCORD INFLIGHT ENTERTAINMENT GUIDE. a. Headway Publications Ltd. (Subsidiary of: Maxwell Consumer Publishing and Communications Ltd.), Greater London House, Hampstead Rd., London NW1 7QQ, England. TEL 071-388-3171. FAX 071-387-9618. Ed. William Davis. circ. 180,000.

387   AT
CONTACT (SOUTH YORRA). 1945. q. free. Royal Australian Air Force Association, Victoria Division, Air Forces Memorial Centre, 4 Cromwell Rd., South Yorra, Vic. 3141, Australia. TEL 03-240 8573. EK. Watts. adv.; bk.rev.; circ. 3,500. **Indexed:** AESIS.

CONTINENTAL (DALLAS). see *GENERAL INTEREST PERIODICALS — United States*

387.736   FR   ISSN 1141-4804
CONTROL; magazine international de la navigation aerienne et des aeroports. 1972. q. 84 F. (foreign 104 F.)(typically set in Sep.). Association Professionnelle de la Circulation Aerienne, Aerogare Cidex 048, F-33700 Merignac, France. TEL 56-55-63-77. Ed. Michel Drobycheff. adv.; bk.rev.; circ. 4,000.
Description: Acts as a channel for the exchange of ideas and information related to air traffic, airports, communication, space, training.

387.7   US
CONTROLLER. 1981. fortn. Peed Corporation, Box 85310, Lincoln, NE 68501. TEL 402-477-8900. adv.; circ. 192,852. (tabloid format)

CORPORATE AVIATION SAFETY SEMINAR. PROCEEDINGS. see *AERONAUTICS AND SPACE FLIGHT*

387.7   US
D F W PEOPLE - THE AIRPORT NEWSPAPER. (Dallas - Fort Worth). w. $60. Wood Publications, Inc., 400 Fuller-Wiser, Ste. 125, Euless, TX 76039. TEL 817-540-4666. FAX 817-685-7562. adv.; circ. 12,000 (controlled).
Description: Directed to employees at DFW International, Alliance and Meacham airports.

387.7 910.22   US
DETROIT NEWSPAPER AGENCY. TRAVEL DIRECTORY. biennial. free. Detroit Newspaper Agency, Travel Advertising, 615 W. Lafayette, Detroit, MI 48226. TEL 313-222-2326. FAX 313-222-6015. TELEX 810-221-7448. circ. 6,000.
Formerly: Detroit News Travel Directory.

341.46   IT
DIRITTO E PRACTICA DELL'AVIAZIONE CIVILE. 1987. s-a. price varies. Casa Editrice Dott. A. Giuffre, Via Busto Arsizio 40, 20151 Milan, Italy. TEL 02-38009582. FAX 02-38009582.

E A A EXPERIMENTER; the "how to" magazine for the aircraft builder. (Experimental Aircraft Association) see *AERONAUTICS AND SPACE FLIGHT*

387.7   UN
ECONOMIC SITUATION OF AIR TRANSPORT. REVIEW AND OUTLOOK (YEARS). (Issued in ICAO Circular Series) (Editions in English, French, Russian, Spanish) triennial. price varies. International Civil Aviation Organization, Attn: Document Sales Unit, 1000 Sherbrooke St. W., Montreal, Que. H3A 2R2, Canada. TEL 514-285-8219. FAX 514-288-4772. TELEX 05-24513.
Formerly: Review of Economic Situation of Air Transport (ISSN 0085-5596)

387 510   EC
ECUADOR. DIRECCION DE AVIACION CIVIL. MATHEMATICS. m. Direccion de Aviacion Civil, P.O. Box 2077, Quito, Ecuador.

387.7   CN
EDMONTON AIRPORT BUSINESS DIRECTORY. 1977. a. Can.$7.50. Business Directories International, 107, 5621-11 St. N.E., Calgary, Alta. T2E 6Z7, Canada. TEL 403-295-9200. FAX 403-295-6335. Ed. Gary Gaudreau. adv.; circ. 5,000. (back issues avail.)
Description: Lists services and personnel at Edmonton Municipal and International, Cooking Lake, Ponoka, Red Deer, St. Albert, Villeneuve and Wetaskiwin Airports.

ENROUTE. see *TRAVEL AND TOURISM*

387   SP   ISSN 0421-4986
ESTADISTICAS DE LA AVIACION CIVIL EN ESPANA. a. Ministerio del Aire, Subsecretaria de Aviacion Civil, Princesa 88, Madrid, Spain.

387.7   UN   ISSN 0071-2558
EUROPEAN CIVIL AVIATION CONFERENCE (REPORT OF SESSION). (Issued as a subseries of Air Transport. Series D: Reports) (Editions in English, French) 1955. triennial since 1961 with intermediate sessions; triennial 14th, 1991; intermediate 19th 1990. free. European Civil Aviation Conference, 3 bis, Villa Emile-Bergerat, 92522 Neuilly sur Seine Cedex, France. FAX 46-24-18-18. (reprint service avail.)

TRANSPORTATION — AIR TRANSPORT

387.7 UK
EUROPEAN HELICOPTER ASSOCIATION HANDBOOK. 1972. a. $10. (European Helicopter Association) Shephard Press Ltd., 111 High St., Burnham, Bucks. SL1 7JZ, England. TEL 0628-604311. FAX 0628-664334. Ed. Capt. E.H. Brown. adv.; circ. 2,000.
  Formerly (until 1987): British Helicopter Advisory Board Handbook.

387.7 658 US ISSN 0893-3081
F B O (Fixed Base Operator) 1986. 9/yr. $65 in U.S.; Canada and Mexico $80; elsewhere $120. Johnson Hill Press, Inc., 1233 Janesville Ave., Ft. Atkinson, WI 53538. TEL 414-563-6388. FAX 414-563-1701. Ed. John Infanger. circ. 17,500 (controlled). (tabloid format)
  Description: For general aviation managers and executives.

387.74 614.86 US
FACTS AND ADVICE FOR AIRLINE PASSENGERS. 1979. biennial. $2. Aviation Consumer Action Project, Box 19029, Washington, DC 20036. TEL 202-785-3704. Ed.Bd.
  Description: Shows how to avoid or minimize the inconvenience of airline service problems.

387.73 US
FEDERAL AVIATION ADMINISTRATION: HIGH ALTITUDE POLLUTION PROGRAM. biennial. Federal Aviation Administration, Office of Environment and Energy, Washington, DC 20591.

FLAP INTERNACIONAL; revista latinoamericana de aviacao. see *AERONAUTICS AND SPACE FLIGHT*

387.82 UK
FLIGHT INTERNATIONAL DIRECTORY PART 1 - UNITED KINGDOM (YEAR). 1973. biennial. £36. Reed Business Publishing Group, Enterprise Division (Subsidiary of: Reed International PLC), Quadrant House, The Quadrant, Sutton, Surrey SM2 5AS, England. TEL 081-652-3882. FAX 081-652-8986. (Subscr. to: P.O. Box 1315, Potters Bar, Herts EN6 1PU, England. TEL 0707-54611) Ed. Malcolm Ginsberg.
  Incorporates: Who's Who in British Aviation; **Formerly:** Flight Directory of British Aviation.

387.7 UK
FLIGHT INTERNATIONAL DIRECTORY PART 2 - MAINLAND EUROPE AND IRELAND (YEAR). 1982. biennial. £35. Reed Business Publishing Group, Enterprise Division (Subsidiary of: Reed International PLC), Quadrant House, The Quadrant, Sutton, Surrey SM2 5AS, England. TEL 081-652-3882. FAX 081-652-8986. (Subscr. to: P.O. Box 1315, Potters Bar, Herts EN6 1PU, England. TEL 0707-54611) Ed. Malcolm Ginsberg. circ. 3,000.
  Incorporates: Who's Who in European Aviation; **Formerly:** Flight Directory of European Aviation.

387.7 614.8 US
FLIGHT SAFETY FOUNDATION. ANNUAL INDEX. a. Flight Safety Foundation, Inc., 2200 Wilson Blvd., Ste. 500, Arlington, VA 22201-3306. TEL 703-820-2777. FAX 703-820-9399. TELEX 901176 FSF INCAGTN.

387.7 629.132 US
FLIGHTLINE. 1965. q. $21.50. Pilots International Association, Inc., 4000 Olson Memorial Hwy., Minneapolis, MN 55422. TEL 612-588-5175. Ed. Jason Rasmussen. circ. 6,000. (tabloid format) back issues avail.
  Description: Covers general aviation topics. Provides membership information, safety tips.

387.7 GW
▼**FLUGBEGLEITER;** Bordbuch der Flugbereitschaft des Bundesministers der Verteidigung. 1991. q. free. ProPress Verlag GmbH, Am Buschhof 8, 5300 Bonn 3, Germany. TEL 0228-449090. FAX 0228-444296. circ. 15,000.

387.7 GW
FLUGBLATT; der aktuelle Report. 1969. s-a. Flughafen Stuttgart GmbH, Postfach 230461, 7000 Stuttgart 23 (Flughafen), Germany. TEL 0711-7901-1. circ. 5,500.

387.736 GW
FLUGHAFEN NACHRICHTEN DUESSELDORF. free. irreg. (6-8/yr.). Flughafen Duesseldorf GmbH, Public Relations Dept., Postfach 300363, 4000 Duesseldorf 30, Germany. TEL 0211-4212306. FAX 0211-421-6666. TELEX 8584818. Ed. Peter Zarth.
  Description: Reports about Dusseldorf Airport for airport staff.

387.7 GW ISSN 0015-4563
DER FLUGLEITER. 1954. q. DM.8. Verband Deutscher Flugleiter, Schorndorferstr. 81, 7300 Esslingen, Germany. Ed. Werner Fischbach. adv.; bk.rev.; bibl.; illus.; pat.; stat.; circ. 3,000. (looseleaf format)

387.7 GW
FLUGPLAN KOELN-BONN. 1952. 7/yr. Flughafen Koeln-Bonn GmbH, Postfach 980920, 5000 Cologne 90, Germany. FAX 02203-404079. adv.; circ. 750,000.

387.7 PK ISSN 0046-4236
FLYER INTERNATIONAL; aviation and tourism. (Text in English) 1964. m. $75. (Azam Ali) Manhattan International Ltd., 187-3B-2 P.E.C.H. Society, Karachi 29, Pakistan. Ed. Ms. Semeen Jaffery. adv.; bk.rev.; charts; illus.; tr.lit.; circ. 15,000.

387.72 SW ISSN 0015-4776
FLYGPOSTEN. 1954. q. SEK 45($8) Svensk Pilotfoerening - Swedish Air Line Pilots Association, Olofsgatan 10, 111 36 Stockholm, Sweden. FAX 46-760-55649. Ed. Michael Agelii. adv.; illus.; circ. 3,000.

FLYING DOCTOR YEARBOOK. see *HOSPITALS*

051 US
FLYING TIMES; a publication for NY-NJ travel agents. 1986. 6/yr. free. Port Authority of New York and New Jersey, Aviation Customer and Marketing Services Division, One World Trade Ctr., Rm. 65N, New York, NY 10048. TEL 212-435-4874. FAX 212-435-4838. Ed. Joann Breslin. circ. 10,000.

387.74 US ISSN 0887-7823
GENERAL AVIATION ACCIDENT REPORT; ongoing record of all general aviation accidents reported to the F A A. 1983. w. $1350. Andrews Publications, 1646 West Chester Pike, Box 1000, Westtown, PA 19395. TEL 215-399-6600. FAX 215-399-6610. Ed. Harry G. Armstrong. index. (looseleaf format; back issues avail.)

387.7 US
GENERAL AVIATION AIRCRAFT SHIPMENT REPORT. 1946. q. $3. General Aviation Manufacturers Association, 1400 K St., NW, Ste. 801, Washington, DC 20005. TEL 202-393-1500. FAX 202-842-4063. stat.; circ. 1,500. (back issues avail.) **Indexed:** SRI.
  Formerly: General Aviation Airplane Shipment Report.

387.7 US
GENERAL AVIATION STATISTICAL DATABOOK. 1980. a. $10. General Aviation Manufacturers Association, 1400 K St., N.W., Ste. 801, Washington, DC 20005. TEL 202-393-1500. FAX 202-842-4063. stat. **Indexed:** SRI.

629.13 RU ISSN 0017-3606 CODEN: GRAVAC
GRAZHDANSKAYA AVIATSIYA. (Text in Russian) 1930. m. 19.20 Rub. Ministerstvo Grazhdanskoi Aviatsii, Moscow, Russia. bk.rev.; illus.; index. **Indexed:** Chem.Abstr.
  —BLDSC shelfmark: 0052.000000.

387.7 UK
GREAT BRITAIN. AIR TRANSPORT USERS COMMITTEE ANNUAL REPORT. 1975. a. free. Air Transport Users Committee, Kingsway House, 2nd fl., 103 Kingsway, London WC2B 6QX, England. TEL 071-242-3882. FAX 071-831-4132. circ. 2,000.
  Formerly: Great Britain. Civil Aviation Authority. Air Transport Users Committee Annual Report.

387.7 UK
GREAT BRITAIN. B A A ANNUAL REPORT AND ACCOUNTS. 1966. a. B A A plc., Corporate Office, 130 Wilton Rd., London SW1V 1LQ, England. Ed. F. Gibson Smith. illus.; circ. 700,000.
  Formerly: Great Britain. British Airports Authority. Annual Report and Accounts (ISSN 0068-1229)

387.71 UK ISSN 0306-3569
HE9843.A1
GREAT BRITAIN. CIVIL AVIATION AUTHORITY. ANNUAL REPORT AND ACCOUNTS. 1949. a. price varies. Civil Aviation Authority, Greville House, 37 Gratton Rd., Cheltenham, Glos GL50 2BN, England.
  Formerly: Great Britain. Air Transport Licensing Board. Report (ISSN 0072-5617)

387.7 UK
GREAT BRITAIN. CIVIL AVIATION AUTHORITY. GENERAL AVIATION AIRMISS BULLETIN; a review of selected incidents. irreg. price varies. Civil Aviation Authority, Greville House, 37 Gratton Rd., Cheltenham, Glos GL50 2BN, England.
  Formerly: Great Britain. Civil Aviation Authority. General Aviation Airmisses (ISSN 0144-2481)

387.7 UK ISSN 0309-667X
GREAT BRITAIN. CIVIL AVIATION AUTHORITY. GENERAL AVIATION SAFETY INFORMATION LEAFLETS. m. price varies. Civil Aviation Authority, Greville House, 37 Gratton Rd., Cheltenham, Glos GL50 2BN, England.

387.7 UK
GREAT BRITAIN. CIVIL AVIATION AUTHORITY. INTERNATIONAL REGISTER OF CIVIL AIRCRAFT. (Supplements avail.) a. price varies. Civil Aviation Authority, Grevill House, 37 Gratton Rd., Cheltenham, Glos GL50 2BN, England. (also avail. in microfiche)

387.7 UK ISSN 0141-9498
GREAT BRITAIN. CIVIL AVIATION AUTHORITY. LIBRARY BULLETIN. 1978. m. price varies. Civil Aviation Authority, Greville House, 37 Gratton Rd., Cheltenham, Glos GL50 2BN, England.
  —BLDSC shelfmark: 5190.950000.

387.7 UK
GREAT BRITAIN. CIVIL AVIATION AUTHORITY. U.K. AIRLINES ANNUAL OPERATING, TRAFFIC & FINANCIAL STATISTICS. 1973. a. price varies. Civil Aviation Authority, Greville House, 37 Gratton Rd., Cheltenham, Glos GL50 2BN, England.
  Supersedes in part (as of 1983): Great Britain. Civil Aviation Authority. Annual Statistics.

387.7 UK
GREAT BRITAIN. CIVIL AVIATION AUTHORITY. U.K. AIRPORTS ANNUAL STATEMENTS OF MOVEMENTS, PASSENGERS AND CARGO. 1973. a. price varies. Civil Aviation Authority, Grevill House, 37 Gratton Rd., Cheltenham, Glos GL50 2BN, England.
  Supersedes in part (as of 1983): Great Britain. Civil Aviation Authority. Annual Statistics.

387.742 CC
GUANGZHOU MINHANG/GUANGZHOU CIVIL AVIATION. (Text in Chinese) bi-m. Guangzhou Minhang Baoshe, Baiyun Jichang (Airport), Guangzhou, Guangdong 510406, People's Republic of China. TEL 678901. Ed. Ma Tingwei.

387.72 MX
GUIA AEREA DE MEXICO Y CENTRO-AMERICA. 1968. m. Mex.$185000. Libros Especializados Editores, S.A., Schiller 108, Apdo. Postal 53-039, 11570 Mexico, D.F., Mexico. TEL 545-1628. FAX 525-52030712. Eds. Alex Silva, Simon Garcia Gabriela del Rio. adv.; illus.; circ. 7,500.

629.13 BL ISSN 0017-5145
GUIA AERONAUTICO. 1947. m. $120. Editora Guia Aeronautico Ltda., Rua Joao Alvares 27, 20220 Rio de Janeiro 14, RJ, Brazil. Ed. Ruy Costa Barros. adv.; charts; circ. 15,000.

387.74 AG
GUIA ARGENTINA DE TRAFICO AEREO. 1947. m. Arg.$950000($120) Peron 679-8-802, 1038 Buenos Aires, Argentina. TEL 49-2797. Ed. Kay Krum. adv.; circ. 8,000. (back issues avail.)

GUILD NEWS. see *AERONAUTICS AND SPACE FLIGHT*

H A C TECHLINE. (Historical Aircraft Corporation) see *AERONAUTICS AND SPACE FLIGHT*

HADASHOT SAPANUT VETEUFAH - YIDION; shipping and aviation news. see *TRANSPORTATION — Ships And Shipping*

HANGKONG ZHISHI/AEROSPACE KNOWLEDGE. see *AERONAUTICS AND SPACE FLIGHT*

TRANSPORTATION — AIR TRANSPORT

387.7 US ISSN 0739-5728
HD9711.25.A1
HELICOPTER ANNUAL. 1983. a. $40 to non-members. Helicopter Association International, 1619 Duke St., Alexandria, VA 22314-3406. TEL 703-683-4646. Ed. Daniel P. Warsley. adv.; circ. 20,000. **Indexed:** SRI.

387.7 US
HELICOPTER ASSOCIATION INTERNATIONAL. OPERATIONS UPDATE. m. $35 to non-members. Helicopter Association International, 1619 Duke St., Alexandria, VA 22314. TEL 703-683-4646. FAX 703-683-4745. TELEX 89-615. circ. 1,000. (looseleaf format)
Description: Reports related to government and industry activities which affect helicopter operators.

HELICOPTER ASSOCIATION INTERNATIONAL. PRELIMINARY ACCIDENT REPORTS AND TECHNICAL NOTES. see *AERONAUTICS AND SPACE FLIGHT*

387.7 UK ISSN 0262-0448
HELICOPTER WORLD. 1981. q. £30($60) Shephard Press Ltd., 111 High St., Burnham, Bucks. SL1 7JZ, England. TEL 0628-604311. FAX 0628-664334. Ed. Ian Harbison. circ. 11,943.

359 CN
HELICOPTERS MAGAZINE CANADA. 1980. q. Can.$22($40) Corvus Publishing Group Ltd., 158 1224 Aviation Park N.E., Calgary, Alta. T2E 7E2, Canada. TEL 403-275-9457. FAX 403-275-3925. Ed. Paul J. Skinner. adv.; bk.rev.; circ. 7,500.
Formerly: Helicopters in Canada (ISSN 0227-3160)

387.7 629.1 US
HELIPORT DEVELOPMENT GUIDE. biennial. $75 to non-members; members $45. Helicopter Association International, 1619 Duke St., Alexandria, VA 22314. TEL 703-683-4646. FAX 703-683-4745. TELEX 89-615.
Description: Includes copies of selected FAA publications and lists consultants.

387.7 UK ISSN 0951-9637
HEREFORD'S WORLDWIDE. 1986. a. £35($45) MacLean Hunter Ltd., MacLean Hunter House, Chalk Lane, Cockfosters Rd., Barnet, Herts EN4 0BU, England. TEL 081-975-9759. FAX 081-440-1796. TELEX 299072-MACHUN-G. adv.; circ. 11,371.

387.74 HK
HONG KONG. CIVIL AVIATION DEPARTMENT. DIRECTOR'S ANNUAL REPORT. (Text in English) 1984. a. HK.$25. Government Publication Centre, G.P.O. Bldg., Ground Fl., Connaught Place, Hong Kong, Hong Kong. TEL 5-8428801. (Subscr. to: Director of Information Services, Information Services Dept., 1 Battery Path, G-F, Central, Hong Kong) Ed.Bd.

387.74 HK
HONG KONG AIRLINE TIMETABLE. (Text in English) 1978. m. HK.$108($17.50) Thomson Press Hong Kong Ltd., 19-F, Tai Sang Commercial Bldg., 24-34 Hennessy Rd., Hong Kong. TEL 5-283351. FAX 8650825. Ed. Jyoti Dandwani. adv.; circ. 15,170. (back issues avail.)
Description: Contains airline flight schedules and information on hotels, consulates, holidays, events, currency conversion rates, airline codes, and airport taxes.

387.7 CN
I A T A ANNUAL REPORT. (Director General's report to the Annual General Meeting of the International Air Transport Association) (Text in English, French and Spanish) 1945. a. free; limited distribution. International Air Transport Association, 2000 Peel St., Montreal, Que. H3A 2R4, Canada. TEL 514-844-6311. circ. controlled.
Formerly: State of the Air Transport Industry (ISSN 0081-4571)

387.7 CN
I A T A DANGEROUS GOODS REGULATIONS. (Editions in English, French, German, Spanish) 1957. a. $47.50. International Air Transport Association, 2000 Peel St., Montreal, Que. H3A 2R4, Canada. TEL 514-844-6311. circ. 55,000.

341.46 CN
I A T A LIVE ANIMALS REGULATIONS. (Editions in English, French and Spanish) 1975. a. $40. International Air Transport Association, 2000 Peel St., Montreal, Que. H3A 2R4, Canada. TEL 514-844-6311.

387.7 SZ
I A T A PUBLICATIONS AND TRAINING MATERIAL AVAILABLE TO THE PUBLIC. (Text in English) 1979. a. free. International Air Transport Association, Publications, 33 Route de L'Aeroport, P.O. Box 672, 1215 Geneva 15 Airport, Switzerland.
Former titles: International Air Transport Association. Industry Automation and Finance Services Department. Publications; International Air Transport Association. Economics and Industry Finance Department. Bulletin; International Air Transport Association. Industry Research Division. Bulletin; International Air Transport Association. Industry Research Division. Service Information Bulletin.

387 CN ISSN 0376-642X
I A T A REVIEW. (Text in English) 1966. q. International Air Transport Association, 2000 Peel St., Montreal, Que. H3A 2R4, Canada. TEL 514-844-6311. circ. controlled.
Formerly: I A T A News Review (ISSN 0085-199X)

I B A C INTERNATIONAL UPDATE. (International Business Aviation Council) see *AERONAUTICS AND SPACE FLIGHT*

387 UN ISSN 0074-2481
I C A O CIRCULARS. (Editions in English, French, Spanish, Russian) no.18, 1951. irreg. price varies. International Civil Aviation Organization, Attn.: Document Sales Unit, 1000 Sherbrooke St. W., Montreal, Que. H3A 2R2, Canada. TEL 514-285-8219, 514-288-4772. TELEX 05-24513.

387.7 US
ILLINOIS AVIATION. 1950. bi-m. $5. Department of Transportation, Division of Aeronautics, Capital Airport, Springfield, IL 62706. TEL 217-753-4400. Ed. Richard M. Ware. circ. 25,000. (tabloid format)

INDIAN BRADSHAW. see *TRANSPORTATION — Railroads*

387.74 US
INITIAL DECISIONS AND BOARD OPINIONS AND ORDERS IN SAFETY. irreg. (approx. 12/yr.). $230 in U.S., Canada, Mexico; elsewhere $460. (Department of Transportation, National Transportation and S.A., Federal Aviation Administration) U.S. National Technical Information Service, 5825 Port Royal Rd., Springfield, VA 22161. TEL 703-487-4630.
Description: Decisions are made by the administrative law judges from the bench or in writing on whether the FAA had a right to suspend or revoke the airman certificate and whether the pilot violated regulations in a specific case.

INTAIR. see *CONSUMER EDUCATION AND PROTECTION*

387.7 US
INTERNATIONAL AIR REVIEW. 4/yr. Challenge Publications, Inc., 7950 Deering Ave., Canoga Park, CA 91304. TEL 818-887-0550. FAX 818-883-3019. Ed. Michael O'Leary. adv.

387.7 NE
INTERNATIONAL AIR SHOW GUIDE. (Text in English) 1981. a. fl.10. Flash Aviation, Postbus 855, 5600 AW Eindhoven, Netherlands. Ed. C. van den Heuvel. adv.; bk.rev.; circ. 10,000.
Formerly: Aviation Focus.

387.7 CN
INTERNATIONAL AIR TRANSPORT ASSOCIATION. ANNUAL GENERAL MEETING. REPORTS AND PROCEEDINGS. (Text in English, French and Spanish) 1945. a. free. International Air Transport Association, 2000 Peel St., Montreal, Que. H3A 2R4, Canada. TEL 514-844-6311.
Former titles: International Air Transport Association. Annual Report; Air Transport Association. Annual General Meeting Reports and Proceedings; International Air Transport Association. Bulletin (ISSN 0074-1329)

INTERNATIONAL AIR TRANSPORT NEWSLETTER. see *OCCUPATIONAL HEALTH AND SAFETY*

387.7 UK
INTERNATIONAL AVIATION NEWS. 1948. m. £20. Romac Associates, 12 Nymans Court, Crawley, W. Sussex RH10 6PP, England. TEL 0293-523554. FAX 0293-518886. Ed.Bd. bk.rev.; circ. 16,000.

387 UN ISSN 0074-221X
K4093
INTERNATIONAL CIVIL AVIATION ORGANIZATION. AERONAUTICAL AGREEMENTS AND ARRANGEMENTS. ANNUAL SUPPLEMENT. (Text in English, French) 1965. a. price varies. International Civil Aviation Organization, Attn: Document Sales Unit, 1000 Sherbrooke St. W., Montreal, Que. H3A 2R2, Canada. TEL 514-285-8219. FAX 514-288-4772. TELEX 05-24513.

387.7 UN ISSN 0074-2368
INTERNATIONAL CIVIL AVIATION ORGANIZATION. ASSEMBLY. REPORT AND MINUTES OF THE LEGAL COMMISSION. (Editions in Arabic, English, French, Russian, Spanish) irreg., 27th, Montreal, 1989. price varies. International Civil Aviation Organization, Attn: Document Sales Unit, 1000 Sherbrooke St. W., Montreal, Que. H3A 2R2, Canada. TEL 514-285-8219. FAX 514-288-4772. TELEX 05-24513.

387.7 UN ISSN 0074-2376
INTERNATIONAL CIVIL AVIATION ORGANIZATION. ASSEMBLY. REPORT OF THE ECONOMIC COMMISSION. irreg., 27th, 1989. price varies. International Civil Aviation Organization - Organisation de l'Aviation Civile Internationale, Attn: Document Sales Unit, Succursale: Place de l'Aviation Internationale, 1000 Sherbrooke Street West, Montreal, Quebec H3A 2R2, Canada. TEL 514-285-8219. FAX 514-288-4772. TELEX 05-24513.

387.7 UN ISSN 0074-235X
INTERNATIONAL CIVIL AVIATION ORGANIZATION. ASSEMBLY. RESOLUTIONS. (Editions in Arabic, English, French, Russian, Spanish) 1965, 15th. irreg., 27th, Montreal, 1989. price varies. International Civil Aviation Organization, Attn: Document Sales Unit, 1000 Sherbrooke St. W., Montreal, Que. H3A 2R2, Canada. TEL 514-285-8219. FAX 514-288-4772. TELEX 05-24513.

387 UN
INTERNATIONAL CIVIL AVIATION ORGANIZATION. COUNCIL. ANNUAL REPORT. (Editions in Arabic, English, French, Russian, Spanish) a. price varies. International Civil Aviation Organization, Attn: Document Sales Unit, 1000 Sherbrooke St. W., Montreal, Que. H3A 2R2, Canada. TEL 514-285-8219. FAX 514-288-4772. TELEX 05-24513. **Indexed:** IIS.

INTERNATIONAL CIVIL AVIATION ORGANIZATION. DIGESTS OF STATISTICS. SERIES AT. AIRPORT TRAFFIC. see *TRANSPORTATION — Abstracting, Bibliographies, Statistics*

INTERNATIONAL CIVIL AVIATION ORGANIZATION. DIGESTS OF STATISTICS. SERIES F. FINANCIAL DATA. see *TRANSPORTATION — Abstracting, Bibliographies, Statistics*

INTERNATIONAL CIVIL AVIATION ORGANIZATION. DIGESTS OF STATISTICS. SERIES FP. FLEET, PERSONNEL, COMMERCIAL AIR CARRIERS. see *TRANSPORTATION — Abstracting, Bibliographies, Statistics*

INTERNATIONAL CIVIL AVIATION ORGANIZATION. DIGESTS OF STATISTICS. SERIES R. CIVIL AIRCRAFT ON REGISTER. see *TRANSPORTATION — Abstracting, Bibliographies, Statistics*

INTERNATIONAL CIVIL AVIATION ORGANIZATION. DIGESTS OF STATISTICS. SERIES TF. TRAFFIC BY FLIGHT STAGE. see *TRANSPORTATION — Abstracting, Bibliographies, Statistics*

INTERNATIONAL CIVIL AVIATION ORGANIZATION. DIGESTS OF STATISTICS. SERIES T. TRAFFIC, COMMERCIAL AIR TRAFFIC. see *TRANSPORTATION — Abstracting, Bibliographies, Statistics*

TRANSPORTATION — AIR TRANSPORT 4675

387.7   UN   ISSN 0074-2503
INTERNATIONAL CIVIL AVIATION ORGANIZATION. LEGAL COMMITTEE. MINUTES AND DOCUMENTS (OF SESSIONS). (Editions in English, French and Spanish) 1948. triennial, 27th, Montreal, 1990. price varies. International Civil Aviation Organization, 1000 Sherbrooke St. W., Montreal, Que. H3A 2R2, Canada. TEL 514-285-8266.

658   US   ISSN 0538-7442
INTERNATIONAL FEDERATION OF OPERATIONAL RESEARCH SOCIETIES. AIRLINE GROUP (A G I F O R S) PROCEEDINGS. 1961. a. $260. International Federation of Operational Research Societies, Airline Group, c/o Joe D. Hinson, Federal Express, 2831 Airways, Memphis, TN 38132. FAX 901-395-7451. circ. 300. (processed; back issues avail.)

387.7   US
INTERNATIONAL FLIGHT ATTENDANTS ASSOCIATION NEWSLETTER. 3/yr. International Flight Attendants Association, c/o P.R. Miller, 2314 Old New Windsor Pike, New Windsor, MD 21776.

387.7 387   US
INTERNATIONAL OMEGA ASSOCIATION NEWSLETTER. 3/yr. $25. International Omega Association, Inc., Box 2324, Arlington, VA 22202-0324. Ed. Bob Revel. adv.; bk.rev.; circ. 350.
   Description: Technical, engineering and scientific interchange of information relating to Omega navigation.

387.7   RU   ISSN 0202-7887
TL552
ITOGI NAUKI I TEKHNIKI: VOZDUSHNYI TRANSPORT. (Text in Russian) 1969. irregr., latest vol.18-19, 1989. 6.60 Rub. Vsesoyuznyi Institut Nauchno-Tekhnicheskoi Informatsii (VINITI), Baltiiskaya ul. 14, Moscow A-219, Russia. (Subscr. to: Mezhdunarodnaya Kniga, Dimitrova ul. 39, 113095 Moscow, Russia)
  —BLDSC shelfmark: 0041.560000.

387.7   UK
JANE'S AIRPORT AND A T C EQUIPMENT. 1982. a. £135($225) Jane's Information Group, Sentinel House, 163 Brighton Rd., Coulsdon, Surrey CR5 2NH, England. TEL 081-763-1030. FAX 081-763-1005. TELEX 916907 JANES G. (U.S. & Canada order from: Dept. DSM, 1340 Braddock Pl., Ste. 300, Box 1436, Alexandria, VA 22314-1651) Ed. David Rider. adv.; index.
   Formerly: Jane's Airport Equipment.
   Description: International directory for the aviation ground support market, covering 1500 manufacturers of all categories of airport equipment with detailed product specifications.

387.736   UK   ISSN 0954-7649
HE9797.A1
JANE'S AIRPORT REVIEW. bi-m. £55($93) Jane's Information Group, Sentinel House, 163 Brighton Rd., Coulsdon, Surrey CR5 2NH, England. TEL 081-763-1030. FAX 081-763-1005. TELEX 916907 JANES G.
  ●Also available online. Vendor(s): DIALOG.
   Description: For senior executives in the airport management, airlines and air traffic control, and national and international regulatory authorities. Covers new products and services.

387.7   UK
JANE'S WORLD AIRLINES. binder (plus q. updates). £550($210) Jane's Information Group, Sentinel House, 163 Brighton Rd., Coulsdon, Surrey CR5 2NH, England. TEL 081-763-1030. FAX 081-763-1005. TELEX 916907 JANES G.
  ●Also available on CD-ROM.
   Description: Airline-by-airline reports covering airline structure and operations; includes fleet structure, routes operated, traffic statistics and financial data.

387.7 658.8   US   ISSN 0021-6003
JET CARGO NEWS; for air shipping decision makers. 1968. m. $30 (foreign $45). Hagall Publishing Co., Box 920952, Ste. 398, Houston, TX 77292-0952. TEL 713-681-4760. FAX 713-682-3871. Ed. Patricia Chandler. adv.; B&W page $3250; adv. contact: Regina Michael. bk.rev.; charts; illus.; circ. 27,187. (tabloid format)
   Description: Dedicated to providing the air shipping industry with timely, factual news related to domestic and international movement of goods by air and the purchase of shipping equipment, services and supplies.

387.7   US
JETRADER.* m. International Society of Transport Aircraft Traders, 1101 14th St. NW, Ste. 1100, Washington, DC 20005. TEL 202-371-1237. TELEX 5101011287 CRNEWS ISTAT.

387.7 910.09   SZ
JETSTREAM AIR NEWS; Swiss aviation magazine. 1961. m. 42 Fr. Postfach 1130, CH-8058 Zurich-Airport, Switzerland. Ed. Martin Hirzel. adv.; circ. 5,000. (back issues avail.)

341.46   AG
JORNADAS NACIONALES DE DERECHO AERONAUTICO Y ESPACIAL. TRABAJOS. irreg. $15 per no. Universidad Nacional de Cordoba, Instituto de Derecho Aeronautico y Espacial y de las Telecomunicaciones de Cordoba, Ituzaingo 87, piso 4, Local 10, 5000 Cordoba, Argentina. TEL 43138. TELEX 51.418 LOREN AR.

387.7 617.1   US   ISSN 1046-9095
JOURNAL OF AIR MEDICAL TRANSPORT. 1981. m. $28 (effective 1991). WordPerfect Publishing Corporation, 270 W. Center St., Orem, UT 84057. TEL 801-226-5555. FAX 801-226-8804. Ed. Bryan Larsen. adv.; abstr.; charts; illus.; stat.; cum.index: 1981-1989; circ. 4,000. (back issues avail.)
  —BLDSC shelfmark: 4926.430000.
   Formerly (until 1989): Hospital Aviation.
   Description: Focuses on the transport of patients by helicopter and airplane. Includes articles on medical research and program operation.

387.7   NE   ISSN 0022-7374
K L M NEWS. (Text in Dutch, English, French, Spanish) 1946. irreg. free. K.L.M. Royal Dutch Airlines, Pb 7700, 1117 ZL Schiphol, Netherlands. Ed.Bd.

387.7   GW
L B A INFO. 1988. q. Luftfahrt - Bundesamt, Lilienthalplatz 6, 3300 Braunschweig, Germany. TEL 0531-2355-0. circ. 2,000.

387.7   CS   ISSN 0457-5792
LETECKY OBZOR. (Text in Czech or Slovak) 1957. 6/yr. 18 Kcs.($27) Nakladatelstvi Dopravy a Spoju, Hybernska 5, 115 78 Prague 1, Czechoslovakia. (Dist. by: Artia, Ve Smeckach 30, 111 27 Prague 1, Czechoslovakia) Ed. Miluse Kristova. adv.; bk.rev.; charts; illus.; circ. 4,000.

387.7 385   FR   ISSN 0756-8037
LETTRE CONFIDENTIELLE DES TRANSPORTS. (Text in French) 1974. w. 2132 Fr. Societe Generale d'Editions Techniques (SOGETEC), 249 rue Lecourbe, 75015 Paris, France. TEL 48-28-73-14. Ed. Elie Le Du. bk.rev.; circ. 1,000.

387.7 051   AQ
LIAT ISLANDER. 1979. s-a. F T Caribbean, P.O. Box 1037, St. John's, Antigua, W.I. FAX 462-3492. Ed.Bd. circ. 50,000. (back issues avail.)

387.7   US
LIGHT AIRCRAFT MANUFACTURERS ASSOCIATION. NEWSLETTER. irreg. free. Light Aircraft Manufacturers Association, 22 Deer Oaks Ct., Pleasanton, CA 94566. TEL 415-449-5992. circ. 400.

LIGHT PLANE MAINTENANCE; the monthly maintenance report to pilots and aircraft owners. see *AERONAUTICS AND SPACE FLIGHT*

LOG. see *AERONAUTICS AND SPACE FLIGHT*

387.7   NE
LUCHTVAART. 1984. 11/yr. fl.63 (foreign fl.102.50). Ten Brink Meppel B.V., Postbus 1064, 7940 KB Meppel, Netherlands. TEL 05220-54646. FAX 05220-55517. Ed. Thijs Postma. adv.; bk.rev.; circ. 10,000.
   Formerly: Luchtvaartwereld.

387.7   GW
LUFTHANSEAT; Zeitung fuer die Mitarbeiter der Lufthansa. (Text in English, German) 1955. m. free. Deutsche Lufthansa AG, Von Gablenz Str. 2-6, 5000 Cologne, Germany. Ed. Gisela Zander. bk.rev.; circ. 40,000.

387.7   MW   ISSN 0076-3055
MALAWI. DEPARTMENT OF CIVIL AVIATION. ANNUAL REPORT. a. K.0.30. Government Printer, P.O. Box 37, Zomba, Malawi.

MASSACHUSETTS INSTITUTE OF TECHNOLOGY. FLIGHT TRANSPORTATION LABORATORY. F T L REPORTS AND MEMORANDA. see *AERONAUTICS AND SPACE FLIGHT*

MECHANIST. see *AERONAUTICS AND SPACE FLIGHT*

387.1   CN
▼**MID-CANADA AIRPORT BUSINESS DIRECTORY.** 1990. a. Can.$7.50. Business Directories International, 107, 5621-11 St. N.E., Calgary, Alta. T2E 6Z7, Canada. TEL 403-295-9200. FAX 403-295-6335. Ed. Gary Gaudreau. adv.; circ. 4,000.
   Description: Lists companies, services and personnel for the Winnipeg International, St. Andrews, Regina, Saskatoon and Thunder Bay Airports.

387.7   US   ISSN 0194-5068
MIDWEST FLYER MAGAZINE; serving the Upper Midwest. 1978. m. $15. Flyer Publications, Inc., Box 199, Oregon, WI 53575-0199. Ed. Dave Weiman. adv.; bk.rev.; circ. 15,000.

387.7   CN
MIRABEL AIRPORT DIRECTORY. 1975. a. Anchor Press, 1056 Chemin du Golf, Nun's Island, Verdun, Que. H3E 1H4, Canada. TEL 514-766-8650. FAX 514-766-5559.

266 387.7   US
MISSION AVIATION LIFE LINK. 1945. a. free or donation. Mission Aviation Fellowship, 1849 Wabash Ave., Box 3202, Redlands, CA 92373. TEL 714-794-1151. FAX 714-794-3016. Ed. Ghislaine Benney. circ. 40,000.
   Former titles: Mission Aviation; Missionary Aviation (ISSN 0026-6043)
   Description: Covers the activities of the organization, a Christian air service operating in the Third World.

387.7   GW
MONATSBERICHT ANGEZEIGTER FLUGUNFAELLE. bi-m. Flugunfall Untersuchungsstelle, Lilienthalplatz, Postfach 3054, 3300 Braunschweig, Germany. TEL 0531-39020.

387.7   GW   ISSN 0343-6594
MONATSBERICHT DER ANGEZEITEN FLUGUNFALLUNTERSUCHUNGSSTELLE. 1983. m. Luftfahrt-Bundesamt, Flugunfalluntersuchungsstelle, Lilienthalplatz 8, Postfach 37 40, D-3300 Braunschweig 1, Germany. TEL 0531-3902-1. circ. 100.

387.7   US
MONTANA AND THE SKY. 1961. m. $3. Department of Transportation, Aeronautics Division, Box 5178, Helena, MT 59604. TEL 406-444-2506. FAX 406-444-2519. Ed. Debbie Alke. circ. 2,000.

387.7   CN
MONTREAL AIRPORT BUSINESS DIRECTORY. 1977. a. Can.$7.50. Business Directories International, 107, 5621-11 St. N.E., Calagary, Alta. T2E 6Z7, Canada. TEL 403-295-9200. FAX 403-295-6335. Ed. Gary Gaudreau. circ. 7,000. (back issues avail.)
   Description: Lists services and personnel at Montreal International Airports of Dorval and Mirabel. Quebec, St-Hubert, St-Jean, Trois Rivieres and Ottawa Area Airports.

387.742   AT
MORGAN INDEX ON AIRLINE TRAVEL (AUSTRALIA). 1973. s-a. Roy Morgan Research Centre Pty. Ltd., Box 2282U, Melbourne, Vic. 3001, Australia. FAX 03-629-1250.

388.3   IT
MOTOR. 1944. m. L.75000. Societa Edizioni Tecniche, Piazza A. Mancini 4-G, 00196 Rome, Italy. TEL 06-390962. FAX 06-3965431. Ed. Sergio Favia del Core. adv.; bk.rev.; circ. 112,243.

387.7 630   US
N A A A NEWSLETTER. w. National Agricultural Aviation Association, 1005 E St. S.E., Washington, DC 20003-2847. TEL 202-546-5722. FAX 202-546-5726. Ed. Harold Collins.

4676 TRANSPORTATION — AIR TRANSPORT

387.7   US
N A T A NEWS. 1969. m. $20 to non-members. National Air Transportation Association, 4226 King St., Alexandria, VA 22302. TEL 703-845-9000. FAX 703-845-8176. Ed. Michele Daron. adv.; charts; illus.; stat.; tr.lit.; circ. 23,000. (back issues avail.)
Formerly: AirTran News.

387.7   US   ISSN 0745-9874
N T S B REPORTER. (National Transportation Safety Board) 1983. m. $36. Peter Katz Productions, Inc., 5 Odell Plaza, Yonkers, NY 10701. TEL 914-423-6000. Ed. Peter Katz. (back issues avail.)
Description: Reports on aviation accident investigations.

387.7   KE   ISSN 0077-2666
NAIROBI AIRPORT. ANNUAL REPORT.* 1958. a. Director of Aerodromes, P.O. Box 19001, Nairobi, Kenya.

387.7   US
NATIONAL AIR TRANSPORTATION ASSOCIATION. ANNUAL REPORT. a. National Air Transportation Association, 4226 King St., Alexandria, VA 22302. TEL 703-845-9000.

387.7 629.13   US
NATIONAL AIR TRANSPORTATION ASSOCIATION. GENERAL AVIATION OPERATIONS. q. National Air Transportation Association, 4226 King St., Alexandria, VA 22302. TEL 703-845-9000.

387.7   US
NATIONAL AIR TRANSPORTATION ASSOCIATION. INDUSTRY BAROMETER. a. National Air Transportation Association, 4226 King St., Alexandria, VA 22302. TEL 703-845-9000.

387.7   US
NATIONAL AIR TRANSPORTATION ASSOCIATION. WAGE AND SALARY HANDBOOK. a. National Air Transportation Association, 4226 King St., Alexandria, VA 22302. TEL 703-845-9000.

387.7   US
NATIONAL AIRSPACE SYSTEM PLAN: FACILITIES, EQUIPMENT AND ASSOCIATED DEVELOPMENT. a. U.S. Department of Transportation, Federal Aviation Administration, 800 Independence Ave., S.W., Washington, DC 20591.

629.1 387.7   US
NATIONAL BUSINESS AIRCRAFT ASSOCIATION. MAINTENANCE AND OPERATIONS BULLETIN. irreg. National Business Aircraft Association, 1200 18th St., N.W., 2nd fl., Washington, DC 20036-2598. TEL 202-783-9000. FAX 202-331-8364.

387.7   US
NATIONAL TRANSPORTATION SAFETY BOARD DIGEST SERVICE. 1972. m. $270. Hawkins Publishing Co., Inc., Box 480, Mayo, MD 21106-0480. TEL 410-798-1677. FAX 410-798-1098. Ed. Carl R. Eyler. circ. 150. (looseleaf format)

387.7   NE   ISSN 0168-552X
NETHERLANDS. CENTRAAL BUREAU VOOR DE STATISTIEK. STATISTIEK VAN DE LUCHTVAART/NETHERLANDS. CENTRAL BUREAU OF STATISTICS. CIVIL AVIATION STATISTICS. (Text in Dutch and English) 1949. a. fl.25. Centraal Bureau voor de Statistiek, Prinses Beatrixlaan 428, Voorburg, Netherlands. (Orders to: SDU - Publishers, Christoffel Plantijnstraat, The Hague, Netherlands)

NEW ENGLAND JOURNAL OF TRANSPORTATION. see *TRANSPORTATION*

387.7   US   ISSN 0091-6978
TL726.3.N5
NEW JERSEY AIRPORT DIRECTORY. 1968. irreg., latest 1981. $2. Department of Transportation, 1035 Parkway Ave., CN 600, Trenton, NJ 08625. illus.

387.7   US
NORTHWEST PASSAGES. s-m. free to qualified personnel. Northwest Airlines, Inc., 5101 Northwest Dr., St. Paul, MN 55111-3034. TEL 612-726-7357. Ed. Joan Palm. adv.; circ. 58,000 (controlled). (newspaper)
Description: Employee newspaper with articles on the aviatiation industry and specifically Northwest Airlines, covering corporate developments, employee news and concerns.

387.744   US
O A G AIR CARGO GUIDE. 1957. m. $97. Official Airline Guides, Inc., 2000 Clearwater Dr., Oak Brook, IL 60521. TEL 708-574-6000. FAX 708-574-6667. TELEX 21014211. adv.; circ. 10,100.
Formerly: Air Cargo Guide.
Description: Lists information on shipping freight by air, including direct and connecting cargo air services worldwide.

387.74   US   ISSN 0277-2108
HE9803.A2
O A G FREQUENT FLYER. Variant title: Frequent Flyer. m. $24 (effective 1992). Official Airline Guides, Inc. (New York), 1775 Broadway, 19th Fl., New York, NY 10019. TEL 800-323-3537. (Subscr. to: 2000 Clearwater Dr., Oak Brook, IL 60521) Ed. Joe Brancatelli. circ. 275,000.
●Also available online.

387.74   US
O A G POCKET FLIGHT GUIDE EUROPE, MIDDLE EAST, AFRICA EDITION. 1978. m. $65. Official Airline Guides, Inc., 2000 Clearwater Dr., Oak Brook, IL 60521. TEL 708-574-6000. FAX 708-574-6667. circ. 22,500.
Formerly: O A G Pocket Flight Guide Europe and Middle East Edition.
Description: Pocket-size guide to direct and connecting air services to and from Europe, the Middle East, and Africa, including travel within these regions.

387.74   US
O A G POCKET FLIGHT GUIDE NORTH AMERICAN EDITION. 1970. m. $65. Official Airline Guides, Inc., 2000 Clearwater Dr., Oak Brook, IL 60521. TEL 708-574-6000. FAX 708-574-6667. TELEX 2101421. circ. 333,857.
Formerly: O A G North American Pocket Flight Guide (ISSN 0191-1538)
Description: Pocket-size guide to direct and connecting air services for travel between the U.S., Canada, Mexico and the Caribbean.

387.74   US
O A G POCKET FLIGHT GUIDE PACIFIC ASIA EDITION. 1982. m. $65. Official Airline Guides, Inc., 2000 Clearwater Dr., Oak Brook, IL 60521. TEL 708-574-6000. FAX 708-574-6667. TELEX 2101421. circ. 11,100.
Formerly: O A G Pocket Flight Guide Pacific Area Edition.
Description: Pocket-size guide to direct and connecting air service for travel to and within all countries of the Pacific geographical region.

387.74   AU
OESTERREICHISCHE LUFTFAHRT PRESSE. 1953. s-m. S.1290. Seidengasse 32-17, A-1070 Vienna 7, Austria. FAX 5266116. Eds. Leo Froehlich, Helga Markowitsch. adv.; bk.rev.; circ. 2,000.
Formerly: Oesterreichischer Luftfahrt Pressedienst (ISSN 0029-9774)

387.74   US   ISSN 0191-1619
HE9802.A2   CODEN: ODFEEE
OFFICIAL AIRLINE GUIDE. NORTH AMERICAN EDITION. 1948. fortn. $245 without fares; $330 with fares. Official Airline Guides, Inc., 2000 Clearwater Dr., Oak Brook, IL 60521. TEL 708-574-6000. FAX 708-574-6667. TELEX 210144. adv.; circ. 153,277.
Description: Reference guide to direct and connecting air services within the U.S., Canada, Mexico and the Caribbean.

387.7   US   ISSN 0364-3875
HE9768
OFFICIAL AIRLINE GUIDE. WORLDWIDE EDITION. m. $220. Official Airline Guides, Inc., 2000 Clearwater Dr., Oak Brook, IL 60521. TEL 708-574-6000. FAX 708-574-6667. TELEX 2101421. circ. 45,800. **Indexed:** Rehabil.Lit.
Former titles: Official Airline Guide. International Edition (ISSN 0097-5192); Official Airline Guide. Quick Reference International Edition. Part 1.
Description: Reference guide to international direct and connecting air services for all scheduled airlines worldwide. Does not include air services within and between the U.S., Canada, Mexico and Caribbean.

OFFICIAL GUIDE TO FLIGHT ATTENDANTS CAREERS. see *OCCUPATIONS AND CAREERS*

OFFICIAL GUIDE TO TRAVEL AGENT & TRAVEL CAREERS. see *OCCUPATIONS AND CAREERS*

387.7   US
OFFSHORE DESIGN GUIDE: HELIPORTS. s-a. Helicopter Safety Advisory Conference, Box 60220, Houston, TX 77205. TEL 713-757-8107.

387.7   CN
THE ORIGINAL AIRPORT NEWS. 1989. bi-w. $25. Airport News, 7040 Torbram Rd., Unit 4, Mississauga, Ont. L4T 3Z4, Canada. TEL 416-672-0206. FAX 416-672-0244. circ. 20,000 (controlled).

387.7   GW   ISSN 0175-0143
PILOT UND FLUGZEUG. 1974. m. DM.113.40. Wiesbadener Str. 59b, D-6240 Koenigstein, Germany. Ed. Heiko Teegen. adv.; charts; illus.; circ. 15,000.
Formerly: Luftfahrt International.

387.7   US
PIPER'S MAGAZINE. m. Joe Jones Publishing, Inc., Box 337, Iola, WI 54945. TEL 715-445-5000. FAX 715-445-4053. Ed. David Sakrison. adv.; circ. 11,000.

307.71   US
PORT AUTHORITY OF NEW YORK AND NEW JERSEY. AVIATION DEPARTMENT. AIRPORT STATISTICS. a. Port Authority of New York and New Jersey, Aviation Department, Aviation Economics Division, One World Trade Ctr., New York, NY 10048. TEL 212-466-7000. stat.

387.736   US
PORT AUTHORITY OF NEW YORK AND NEW JERSEY. AVIATION DEPARTMENT. AVIATION ANNUAL REPORT. a. Port Authority of New York and New Jersey, Aviation Department, One World Trade Ctr., New York, NY 10048.

388.324   US   ISSN 0032-8901
TL721.4
PRIVATE PILOT. 1965. m. $21.97. Fancy Publications, Inc., Box 6050, Mission Viejo, CA 92690. TEL 714-855-8822. FAX 714-855-3045. (Subscr. addr.: Box 55064, Boulder, CO 80322-5064) Ed. Mary Silitch. adv.; bk.rev.; charts; illus.; stat.; circ. 100,000.
Description: For the owner-flyer. Focuses on those issues relevant to the serious owner and pilots of single engine and light twin engine aircraft. Emphasis is on new and used aircraft evaluation, new avionics products, travel, flying club activities and pilot training programs.

387.7   US   ISSN 0555-3407
PROFESSIONAL PILOT MAGAZINE. 1967. m. $36. Queensmith Communications Corporation, 3014 Colvin St., Alexandria, VA 22314. TEL 703-370-0606. FAX 703-370-7082. Ed. Clifton Stroud. adv.; bk.rev.; circ. 35,000.
Description: Presents information of interest to corporate, charter, and commuter airlines pilots and associated personnel.

387.7   GR   ISSN 1105-1310
PTISI/FLIGHT. 1979. m. $42.50. Technical Press S.A., 6 Gorgiou St., Athens 11636, Greece. TEL 01-92-30-832. FAX 01-92-30-836. TELEX 222189 TECH GR. Ed. Costas Cavathas. circ. 38,000.
Description: Aerospace technology and defense matters.

387.74 387   PR
PUERTO RICO. PORTS AUTHORITY. OFFICE OF ECONOMIC RESEARCH. STATISTICAL REPORT. (Text in English; summaries in English) 1955. m. free. Ports Authority, Office of Economic Research & Statistics, G.P.O. Box 362829, San Juan, PR 00936. stat.; circ. 500. (back issues avail.)

387.7   AT
QANTAS AIRWAYS. REPORT. (Subseries of: Australia. Parliament. Parliamentary Papers) a. price varies. Australian Government Publishing Service, G.P.O. Box 84, Canberra, A.C.T. 2601, Australia. illus.

387.744 388.324   US
QUICK CALLER: BOSTON AREA AIR CARGO DIRECTORY. 1976. a. $9.50. Fourth Seacoast Publishing Co., Inc., 25300 Little Mack, St. Clair Shores, MI 48081. TEL 313-779-5570. FAX 313-779-5547. (Subscr. to: Box 145, St. Clair Shores, MI 48080) Ed. Roger J. Buysse. circ. 10,000.

TRANSPORTATION — AIR TRANSPORT

387.7   388.324   US
QUICK CALLER: CHICAGO AREA AIR CARGO DIRECTORY. a. $9.50. Fourth Seacoast Publishing Co., Inc., 25300 Little Mack, St. Clair Shores, MI 48081. TEL 313-779-5570. FAX 313-779-5547. (Subscr. to: Box 145, St. Clair Shores, MI 48080) Ed. Roger J. Buysse.

387.744   388.324   US
QUICK CALLER: DETROIT AREA AIR CARGO DIRECTORY. 1973. a. $9.50. Fourth Seacoast Publishing Co., Inc., 25300 Little Mack, St. Clair Shores, MI 48081. TEL 313-779-5570. FAX 313-779-5547. (Subscr. to: Box 145, St. Clair Shores, MI 48080) Ed. Roger J. Buysse. circ. 10,000.

387.7   388.324   US
QUICK CALLER: LOS ANGELES AREA AIR CARGO DIRECTORY. a. $9.50. Fourth Seacoast Publishing Co., Inc., 25300 Little Mack, St. Clair Shores, MI 48081. TEL 313-779-5570. FAX 313-779-5547. (Subscr. to: Box 145, St. Clair Shores, MI 48080) Ed. Roger J. Buysse.

387.744   388.324   US
QUICK CALLER: MIAMI AREA AIR CARGO DIRECTORY. 1975. a. $9.50. Fourth Seacoast Publishing Co., Inc., 25300 Little Mack, St. Clair Shores, MI 48081. TEL 313-779-5570. FAX 313-779-5547. (Subscr. to: Box 145, St. Clair Shores, MI 48080) Ed. Roger J. Buysse. circ. 10,000.

387.744   388.324   US
QUICK CALLER: NEW YORK METRO AREA AIR CARGO DIRECTORY. 1989. a. $9.50. Fourth Seacoast Publishing Co., Inc., 25300 Little Mack, St. Clair Shores, MI 48081. TEL 313-779-5570. FAX 313-779-5547. (Subscr. to: Box 145, St. Clair Shores, MI 48080) Ed. Roger J. Buysse. circ. 10,000.

387.744   388.324   US
QUICK CALLER: SAN FRANCISCO BAY AREA AIR CARGO DIRECTORY. 1982. a. $9.50. Fourth Seacoast Publishing Co., Inc., 25300 Little Mack, St. Clair Shores, MI 48081. TEL 313-779-5570. FAX 313-779-5547. (Subscr. to: Box 145, St. Clair Shores, MI 48080) Ed. Roger J. Buysse. circ. 10,000.

387.7   UK
REDCOAT. 1989. q. Redcoat Express Ltd., 12 Gatwick Metro Centre, Balcombe Rd., Horley, Surrey RH6 9GA, England. TEL 0293-774141. FAX 0293-774080. TELEX 87337 REDAIR.
Description: Concerned with air communication specifically for the West African community in the diaspora.

387.7   US
REGIONAL AIRLINE ASSOCIATION. ANNUAL REPORT. 1974. a. $50 to non-members. Regional Airline Association, 1101 Connecticut Ave., N.W., Ste. 700, Washington, DC 20036. TEL 202-857-7170. FAX 202-223-4579. Ed. Deborah McElroy. adv.; illus.; stat.; circ. 2,700 (controlled).
Description: Provides comprehensive analysis of issues and trends affecting the US domestic regional airline industry, with company information for airlines and suppliers.

629   US
REGIONAL AVIATION WEEKLY. 1986. w. $450 (foreign $475). McGraw-Hill, Inc., Aviation Week Group, 1156 15th St., N.W., Washington, DC 20005. TEL 202-822-4600. Ed. Arnold Lewis. charts; stat. (looseleaf format)
● Also available online. Vendor(s): DIALOG (File no.624/McGRAW-HILL PUBLICATIONS ONLINE), Dow Jones/News Retrieval, Mead Data Central (RAWKEY).

387.7   FR   ISSN 0080-066X
REGISTRE AERONAUTIQUE INTERNATIONAL. 1966. a. (with q. suppl.). 1500 F. Bureau Veritas, Registre International de Classification de Navires et d'Aeronefs, 92077 Paris la Defense Cedex 44, France. FAX 42-91-52-95. TELEX 611183F BVAVO. bk.rev.; circ. 1,000. (also avail. in microfilm)

387.7   629.1   US
ROTOR ROSTER. 1987. a. $12.50. Air Track, Box 610, Hilliard, FL 32046. TEL 912-496-3504. FAX 912-496-7513. adv.; charts; illus.; circ. 10,000. (magnetic tape; back issues avail.)
Description: Provides worldwide listing of civil helicopter owners.

S P A WATER LANDING DIRECTORY. (Seaplane Pilots Association) see *AERONAUTICS AND SPACE FLIGHT*

S P I C; revista de turismo. see *TRAVEL AND TOURISM*

387.7   SZ
DIE SCHWEIZERISCHE ZIVILLUFTFAHRT; l'aviation civile Suisse. (Text in French, German) 1925. a. 12 Fr. Bundesamt fuer Zivilluftfahrt - Federal Office for Civil Aviation (Office Federal de l'Aviation Civile), Inselgasse, CH-3003 Berne, Switzerland. Ed. Daniel Ruhier. circ. 1,400.
Supersedes (from 1975): Schweizerische Luftverkehrsstatistik - Statistique du Trafic Aerien Suisse.

387.1   CN
▼**SEATTLE AIRPORT BUSINESS DIRECTORY.** 1990. a. $7.50. Business Directories International, 107, 5621-11 St. N.E., Calgary, Alta. T2E 6Z7, Canada. TEL 403-295-9200. FAX 403-295-6355. Ed. Gary Gaudreau. adv.; circ. 7,500.
Description: Lists companies, services and personnel at area airports.

341.46   UK
SHAWCROSS & BEAUMONT: AIR LAW. (In 3 volumes) 4/yr. $1,050. Butterworth & Co. (Publishers) Ltd. (Subsidiary of: Reed International PLC), 88 Kingsway, London WC2B 6AB, England. TEL 71-405-6900. FAX 71-405-1332. TELEX 95678. (US addr.: Butterworth Legal Publishers, 90 Stiles Rd., Salem, NH 03079. TEL 800-548-4001) (looseleaf format)

SHIPPING AND AVIATION STATISTICS OF THE MALTESE ISLANDS. see *TRANSPORTATION — Abstracting, Bibliographies, Statistics*

387.7   US
SIGHT LECTURE. a. Wings Club, 52 Vanderbilt Ave., 18th Fl., New York, NY 10017. TEL 212-867-1770.

387.7   SI
SINGAPORE CHANGI AIRPORT TIMETABLE. (Text in English) 1989. q. $8. Times Trade Directories Pte. Ltd., Times Centre, 1 New Industrial Road, Singapore 1953, Singapore. TEL 2848844. FAX 2881186. TELEX RS 25713 TIMESS.

387.7   US
SPEEDNEWS. w. Gil Speed & Associates, 1801 Ave. of the Stars, Ste. 210, Los Angeles, CA 90067-5904. TEL 213-203-9603. FAX 213-203-9352. Ed. Ann More. circ. 3,000.
● Also available online. Vendor(s): NewsNet.

387.7   US
STATION BREAK. m. 300 7th St., S.W., Ste. 110, Washington, DC 20024-2520. TEL 202-554-8677. FAX 202-863-0265. Ed. Lee Ann Landers. circ. 75,000.

387.7   910.09   US
STRATEGIC INFORMATION ON U S AIR TRAVEL. 1987. s-m. $350 (foreign $400). Nationwide Intelligence, Box 1922, Saginaw, MI 48605. TEL 517-752-6123. Ed. David W. Oppermann. bk.rev. (looseleaf format)
● Also available online.
Description: Travel planning reference service, with travel alerts, airline, airport and city briefings, and general reference information.

380.5   CI   ISSN 0351-1898
SUVREMENI PROMET. (Text in Croatian; summaries in English) 1979. bi-m. 2500 din.($42) to individuals; institutions 12000 din. University of Zagreb, Faculty of Transportation, Vukeliceva 4, 41000 Zagreb, Croatia. TEL 041 215 767. Ed. Franko Rotim. adv.; bk.rev.; circ. 1,400.

387.74   TH   ISSN 0125-1090
THAILAND AIRLINE TIMETABLE. (Text in English) 1976. m. Advertising and Media Consultants Ltd., Silom Condominium, 12th Fl., 52-38 Soi Saladaeng 2, Bangkok, Thailand. TEL 233-9111. FAX 236-6764. TELEX 82463-LOOKEAS-TH. circ. 20,000.

387.7   CN
TORONTO AIRPORT BUSINESS DIRECTORY. 1979. a. Can.$7.50. Business Directories International, 107, 5621-11 St. N.E., Calgary, Alta. T2E 6Z7, Canada. TEL 403-295-9200. FAX 403-295-6355. Ed. Gary Gaudreau. adv.; circ. 7,000. (back issues avail.)
Description: Lists services and personnel at area airports.

387.7   US   ISSN 0886-4217
U S AVIATION REPORTS. 1928. irreg. price varies. Oceana Publications, Inc., 75 Main St., Dobbs Ferry, NY 10522. TEL 914-693-1320. FAX 914-693-0402. Ed. Christopher Knauth. circ. 200.
Description: Reports on U.S. and Canadian aviation law.

387.7   US
U.S. FEDERAL AVIATION ADMINISTRATION. NATIONAL AVIATION SYSTEM: DEVELOPMENT AND CAPITAL NEEDS. 1969. irreg., latest 1980. free. U.S. Federal Aviation Administration, c/o Freda Johnson, 800 Independence Ave., S.W., Washington, DC 20591. TEL 202-655-4000. (Orders to: Supt. of Documents, Washington, DC 20402) illus.; circ. 3,000.
Former titles: U.S. Federal Aviation Administration. National Aviation System: Challenges of the Decade Ahead & U.S. Federal Aviation Administration. National Aviation System Policy Summary (ISSN 0092-4555)

387.74   US
U.S. NATIONAL TRANSPORTATION SAFETY BOARD. AIRCRAFT ACCIDENT REPORTS. (Formerly issued by Department of Transportation) irreg. $35 (brief format $40). U.S. National Transportation Safety Board, Department of Transportation, Washington, DC 20590. TEL 202-426-8787. FAX 703-321-8547. (Orders to: National Technical Information Service, 5285 Port Royal Rd., Springfield, VA 22151) Indexed: Amer.Stat.Ind.

387.7   CN
VANCOUVER AIRPORT BUSINESS DIRECTORY. 1978. a. Can.$7.50. Business Directories International, 107, 5621-11 St. N.E., Calgary, Alta. T2E 6Z7, Canada. TEL 403-295-9200. FAX 403-295-6355. Ed. Gary Gaudreau. adv.; circ. 7,000. (back issues avail.)
Description: Lists services and personnel at Vancouver International, Victoria International, Abbotsford, Boundary Bay, Chilliwack, Delta Air Park, Kamloops, Kelowna, Langley, Pitt Meadows and Vernon Airports.

387.7   II
VAYUYAN; air journal of the East. (Text in English) 1974. m. Rs.85($30) Vikrant Publications, 1 Todarmal Rd., Bengali Market, New Delhi 110001, India. Ed. Krishna Kumar. adv.; charts; illus.

WATER FLYING. see *AERONAUTICS AND SPACE FLIGHT*

WATER FLYING ANNUAL. see *AERONAUTICS AND SPACE FLIGHT*

WEEKLY REVIEW OF COLLECTIVE BARGAINING. see *BUSINESS AND ECONOMICS — Labor And Industrial Relations*

629.13   CN
WINGS. 1957. bi-m. Can.$25($45) (effective Jan. 1991). Corvus Publishing Group Ltd., 158, 1224 Aviation Park, N.E., Calgary, Alta. T2E 7E2, Canada. TEL 403-275-9457. FAX 403-275-3925. Ed. Paul J. Skinner. adv.; bk.rev.; illus.; index; circ. 11,500. (tabloid format; back issues avail.)
Former titles: Wings Magazine of Canada (ISSN 0701-1369); Canadian Wings (ISSN 0008-5367)
Description: Provides domestic and international coverage of corporate, commercial and military aviation.

910.09   US
WINGS OF ALOHA. (Text in Japanese) 1989. q. Honolulu Publishing Company, Ltd., 36 Merchant St., Honolulu, HI 96813. TEL 808-524-7400. FAX 808-531-2306. Ed. Pat Pitzer. circ. 20,000.
Description: In-flight magazine of Aloha Airlines and Aloha Island Air. Contains general information about Hawaii.

4678 TRANSPORTATION — AUTOMOBILES

387.1　　　　　US　　ISSN 1049-7781
WINGS WEST; the Western aviation magazine. 1985. q. $14.95 (foreign $35). Wings West Associates, 89 Sherman St., Denver, CO 80203. TEL 303-778-7145. FAX 303-837-0256. Ed. Babette Andre. adv.; bk.rev.; circ. 20,000. (back issues avail.)
  Description: Presents news and information for Western aircraft owners, pilots and their families.

WOLKENRIDDER. see *TRAVEL AND TOURISM*

WORLD AIR TRANSPORT STATISTICS. see *TRANSPORTATION — Abstracting, Bibliographies, Statistics*

287.7　　　　　CN
WORLD AIRLINE COOPERATION REVIEW. q. International Air Transport Association, 2000 Peel St., Montreal, Que. H3A 2R4, Canada. TEL 514-844-6311. Dir. Gunter Eser.

387.7　　　　　UK　　ISSN 0951-8673
WORLD AIRLINE FLEETS NEWS. 1977. m. £35($55) Browcom House, Browells Lane, Feltham, Middx. TW13 7EQ, England. TEL 01-890 8933. FAX 01-890-4971. (Dist. in U.S. by: Taylor & Francis Inc., 242 Cherry St., Philadelphia, PA 19106-1906) Ed. Ricky-Dene Hallidat. adv.; bk.rev.; circ. 5,000.
  Former titles (until 1987): Airline Data News (ISSN 0263-3272) & World Airline Fleets Monthly (ISSN 0140-6450)

629.1 387.7　　　US
▼**WORLD AIRLINE NEWS**. 1991. w. $495 (foreign $560)(effective 1992). Phillips Publishing, Inc., Defense - Aviation Group, 1925 N. Lynn St., Ste. 1000, Arlington, VA 22209. TEL 703-522-8333. FAX 703-522-8334. Ed. Joe Murphy.

387.7　　　　　US　　ISSN 0084-1374
WORLD AIRLINE RECORD. 1948. irreg., 7th ed.; 1972 (with q. supplements). $43.50. Roadcap Aviation Publications, 108 S. Green Bay Rd., Lake Forest, IL 60045. TEL 708-234-4730. Ed. Roy R. Roadcap.

WORLD METEOROLOGICAL ORGANIZATION. COMMISSION FOR AERONAUTICAL METEOROLOGY. ABRIDGED FINAL REPORT OF THE (NO.) SESSION. see *METEOROLOGY*

ZAKENREIS/BUSINESS TRAVEL. see *TRAVEL AND TOURISM*

387.7　　　　　ZA
ZAMBIA. DEPARTMENT OF CIVIL AVIATION. ANNUAL REPORT. (Text in English) a. Government Printer, Box 30136, Lusaka, Zambia.

387.7　　　　　CC
ZHONGGUO MINHANG/C A A C INFLIGHT MAGAZINE. (Text in Chinese, English, Japanese) no.45, 1990. bi-m. Zhongguo Minhuang Xuanchuan Guanggao Gongsi - Civil Aviation Administration of China Publicity & Advertising Corporation, No.4, Building No.47, Tongfu Jiadao, Dengshi Dongkou, Beijing 100006, People's Republic of China. TEL 5005964. Ed. An Shiqin. circ. 150,000.

ZHONGGUO MINHANG BAO/CIVIL AVIATION ADMINISTRATION OF CHINA. JOURNAL. see *TRAVEL AND TOURISM*

387.7　　　　　US
630 NEWS. 1978. bi-m. $39 to non-members. Independent Federation of Flight Attendants, 630 Third Ave., 5th fl., New York, NY 10017. TEL 212-818-1130. FAX 212-949-4058. adv.

TRANSPORTATION — Automobiles

796.72　　　　US　　ISSN 1056-2532
A A A MOTORIST. 1991. 6/yr. membership. (American Automobile Association) Lehigh Valley Motor Club, Box 1910, Allentown, PA 18105-1910. TEL 215-434-5141. FAX 215-434-7662. Ed. Judy Barberick. adv.; charts; illus.; stat.; circ. 74,000.
  Supersedes (1910-1987): Lehigh Valley Motor Club News.

A A A TODAY (CINCINNATI). (American Automobile Association) see *TRAVEL AND TOURISM*

388.3　　　　　US　　ISSN 0890-7471
A A A TODAY MAGAZINE. 1927. bi-m. membership. (American Automobile Association) Automobile Club Publications, 1380 Dublin Rd., Ste. 109, Columbus, OH 43215-1025. TEL 614-481-8088. Ed. Johanna Guzik. adv.; bk.rev.; circ. 1,900,000 (controlled). (reprint service avail.)
  Formed by the merger of: Motor Travel (ISSN 0027-2086); Motorist.

A A A TRAVELER (YORK). see *TRAVEL AND TOURISM*

388.3　　　　　US　　ISSN 0277-1403
A A A WORLD (HEATHROW). 1947. 6/yr. $4 to non-members; members $2. American Automobile Association, 1000 A A A Dr., Heathrow, FL 32746-5063. TEL 407-444-8544. Ed. Douglas H. Damerst. adv.; charts; illus.; circ. 2,875,000.
  Formerly (until 1981): Florida A A A Motorist (ISSN 0015-3842)
  Description: Devoted to travel and automotive concerns.

A A A WORLD: WISCONSIN EDITION. (American Automobile Association) see *TRAVEL AND TOURISM*

388.3　　　　　US　　ISSN 0001-0154
HE5623.A1
A A M V A BULLETIN. 1935. bi-m. $25 in U.S.; Canada $30; elsewhere $40. American Association of Motor Vehicle Administrators, 4200 Wilson Blvd., Ste. 600, Arlington, VA 22203. TEL 703-522-4200. FAX 703-522-1553. Ed. Jennifer Cagan Thompson. charts; illus.; circ. 2,500.

388.3 910.09　　　GW
A C E LENKRAD. 1954. m. membership. (Auto Club Europa e.V.) Ace Verlag GmbH, Schmidenerstr. 233, 7000 Stuttgart 50, Germany. TEL 0711-5303-200. FAX 0711-5303-210. TELEX 7254873-ACEP. Ed. Ernst Bauer. adv.; bk.rev.; circ. 640,000.
  Description: Automobile club magazine featuring the latest news on cars, parts and accessories. Articles also cover testing, road safety and travel. Includes readers' comments.

388.3　　　　　IT　　ISSN 0001-0715
A C I INFORMAZIONI. 1947. m. L.4000. Automobile Club d'Italia, Via Marsala 8, Rome, Italy. Ed. C. Storri. mkt.; stat.; index; circ. 3,000.

629.286　　　　SZ
A C S ZURICH. m. Swiss Motor Club, International Werbung, P.O. Box, CH-8032 Zurich 1, Switzerland. circ. 15,000.

388.3　　　　　GW　　ISSN 0007-2842
A D A C MOTORWELT. 1925. m. membership. (Allgemeiner Deutscher Automobil-Club e.V.) A D A C Verlag GmbH, Am Westpark 8, Postfach 700126, 8000 Munich 70, Germany. TEL 089-7676-0. Ed. Theodor Siepert. adv.; bibl.; charts; illus.; stat. (processed) **Indexed**: Dok.Str.

629.283　　　　GW
A D A C SIGNALE. 1988. s-a. free. (Allgemeiner Deutscher Automobil-Club e.V.) A D A C Verlag GmbH, Am Westpark 8, Postfach 700126, 8000 Munich 70, Germany. TEL 089-7676-0. circ. 3,000.

796.77　　　　GW
A D A C SPECIAL AUTO. a. DM.12.80. (Allgemeiner Deutscher Automobil-Club e.V.) A D A C Verlag GmbH, Am Westpark 8, Postfach 700126, 8000 Munich 70, Germany. TEL 089-7676-0.

308.3　　　　　US
A D R A NEWSLETTER. 1970. m. free to members only. Automotive Dismantlers & Recyclers Association, 10400 Eaton Pl., Ste. 203, Fairfax, VA 22030-2208. TEL 703-385-1001. Ed. Kristine L. Moore. circ. 2,000.

A F A S QUARTERLY. (Automotive Fine Arts Society) see *ART*

665.5 669 629.2　　FR
A F P - AUTO; bulletin quotidien d'informations. 1972. d. 16920 F. (foreign 18492 F.). Agence France-Presse, 13 Place de la Bourse, B.P. 20, 75061 Paris Cedex 2, France. TEL 40-41-46-46. TELEX 210064 AFPA.
  Formerly: Auto-Industries.

629.286　　　　AG
A G E S. 1925. 6/yr. Asociacion de Garajes y Estaciones de Servico, Hipolito Yrigoyen 2738, Buenos Aires, Argentina. adv.; circ. 1,000.

629.286　　　　US
A I A UPDATE. 1983. m. membership only. (Auto International Association) Sema Publications, Box 4910, Diamond Bar, CA 91765-0910. TEL 714-860-2961. FAX 714-860-1709. Ed. Eric Marsing. circ. 350.
  Formerly: A I A News.
  Description: Discusses imported auto parts for foreign built cars domiciled in the US.

629.2　　　　AT　　ISSN 0044-5681
A I M. 1967. 23/yr. Aus.$293 (foreign Aus.$493). Automotive Industry Matters Pty. Ltd., P.O. Box 184, Albert Park, Vic. 3206, Australia. FAX 059-898666. Ed. Trevor Dawson-Grove.

A L P C A NEWSLETTER. (Automobile License Plate Collectors Association) see *HOBBIES*

A M G B A OCTAGON. (American M G B Association) see *ANTIQUES*

796.77　　　　UK
A M MAGAZINE. 1948. 4/yr. membership. Aston Martin Owners' Club Ltd., 22 Bank St., Braintree, Essex, England. FAX 0376-551431. Ed. Brian Joscelyne. adv.; bk.rev.; circ. 4,000 (controlled).
  Formerly: A M Quarterly.

388.3　　　　　GW　　ISSN 0001-1983
A M Z. (Auto Motor Zubehoer); Fachzeitschrift fuer das gesamte Kraftfahrzeugwesen. 1912. m. DM.10. Verlagsgesellschaft Gruetter GmbH, Postfach 91 07 08, 3000 Hannover 91, Germany. TEL 0511-4609300. FAX 0511-4609320. TELEX 922979-DRUCK. Ed. Konrad Hofer. adv.; bk.rev.; illus.; stat.; tr.lit.; index; circ. 25,000.

629.2　　　　IT　　ISSN 0001-2661
A T A ASSOCIAZIONE TECNICA DELL'AUTOMOBILE.* (Text mainly in Italian; occasionally in English) 1948. m. $7.50. Associazione Tecnica dell'Automobile, Via Pettinati 20, 10126 Torino, Italy. adv.; bk.rev.; abstr.; bibl.; charts; illus.; pat.; index; circ. 3,000. **Indexed**: Appl.Mech.Rev.
  —BLDSC shelfmark: 1765.400000.

629.2　　　　GW　　ISSN 0001-2785
　　　　　　　　　　　CODEN: AUTZA6
A T Z. (Automobiltechnische Zeitschrift); fuer Forschung, Entwicklung, Konstruktion, Versuch und Fertigung. 1898. m. DM.239.40. Franckh-Kosmos Verlags-GmbH und Co., Pfizerstr. 5-7, Postfach 106011, 7000 Stuttgart 1, Germany. TEL 0711-2191-332. Ed. Richard van Basshuysen. adv.; bk.rev.; bibl.; charts; illus.; stat.; index, cum.index every 20 yrs.; circ. 4,500. **Indexed**: Appl.Mech.Rev., C.I.S. Abstr., Eng.Ind., Excerp.Med., Fluidex, INIS Atomind., ISMEC, Met.Abstr., Sh.& Vib.Dig.
  —BLDSC shelfmark: 1833.000000.
  Description: Trade publication for the automobile industry. Features construction, development, research, production engineering, and testing. Includes industry news, reports of meetings and events.

388.3 910.09　　　GW
A V D AUTO BORDBUCH. a. DM.6. A V D Verlag GmbH, Lyonerstr. 16, 6000 Frankfurt a.M. 71, Germany. TEL 069-66060. (back issues avail.)

796.7　　　　FR
ACTION AUTOMOBILE. 1934. m. (11/yr.). 198 F. (foreign 236 F.)(effective 1992). Excelsior Publications, 1 rue du Colonel Pierre Avia, 75503 Paris Cedex 15, France. TEL 46-48-48-48. FAX 46-48-48-09. TELEX 631 994 F. Ed. Michel Guegan. adv. contact: Gilles de Keranflech. bk.rev.; charts; illus.; circ. 306,181.
  Formerly: Action Automobile et Touristique (ISSN 0001-7418)

ACTION ERA VEHICLE. see *ANTIQUES*

388.3　　　　　US
ACTION WHEELS. 10/yr. $3.95 per no. Starlog Group, Inc., 475 Park Ave. S., New York, NY 10016. TEL 212-689-2830. FAX 212-689-7933.

TRANSPORTATION — AUTOMOBILES

629.2 　　　US　　ISSN 0065-2555
ADVANCES IN ENGINEERING. irreg. price varies. Society of Automotive Engineers, 400 Commonwealth Dr., Warrendale, PA 15096-0001. TEL 412-776-4841. FAX 412-776-5760.
Refereed Serial

388.3 　　　US
AFTERMARKET BUSINESS. 1936. 13/yr. $25. Avanstar Communications, Inc., 7500 Old Oak Blvd., Cleveland, OH 44130. TEL 216-826-2839. FAX 216-891-2726. (Subscr. to: 1 E. First St., Duluth, MN 55802) Ed. Richard Weinberg. adv.; charts; illus.; stat.; circ. 22,587. (tabloid format) **Indexed:** Bus.Ind., PROMT, Tr.& Indus.Ind.
● Also available online. Vendor(s): DIALOG.
Former titles: Home and Auto (ISSN 0162-8801); Home and Auto Retailer (ISSN 0018-3911)
Description: Previews of new products, industry news, merchandizing trends and company and business activities of automotive aftermarket retailers.

AFTERMARKET BUSINESS BUYER'S GUIDE. see BUSINESS AND ECONOMICS — Marketing And Purchasing

.338.476　　CN　　ISSN 0828-6116
AFTERMARKET CANADA. 1985. m. Can.$30 (free to qualified personnel). S G B Communications, 2050 Speers Rd., Unit 1, Oakville, Ont. L6L 2X8, Canada. TEL 416-847-0277. FAX 416-847-7752. Ed. Steve Manning. adv.; bk.rev.; circ. 11,600.
Description: Industry news on the automotive aftermarket. Includes information on wholesaling and replacement parts.

629.286　　　US
AIR CONDITIONING & HEATING SERVICE & REPAIR - DOMESTIC CARS, LIGHT TRUCKS & VANS. 1977. a. $37. Mitchell International, Inc., 9889 Willow Creek Rd., Box 26260, San Diego, CA 92196-0260. TEL 800-648-8010. FAX 619-578-4752. illus.; circ. 20,000. (also avail. in microform)
● Also available on CD-ROM.
Description: Auto service and repair manual for professional auto technicians.

629.286　　　US
AIR CONDITIONING & HEATING SERVICE & REPAIR - IMPORTED CARS & TRUCKS. 1977. a. $37. Mitchell International, Inc., 9889 Willow Creek Rd., Box 26260, San Diego, CA 92196-0260. TEL 800-878-6550. FAX 619-578-4752. illus. (also avail. in microform)
● Also available on CD-ROM.
Description: Auto service and repair manual for professional auto technicians.

629.2　　　FI　　ISSN 0355-9610
AJA. 4/yr. P.O. Box 16, SF-00381 Helsinki, Finland. Ed. Jukka Miettinen. adv.; circ. 100,000.

388　　　DK
AKTUEL BILSPORT. 1974. m. $19. Dansk Automobil Sports Union, Gersonsvej 25, 2900 Hellerup, Denmark. Ed. Sven Lautrup. adv.; circ. 10,000.
Formerly: Auto Orienting.

388　　　US　　ISSN 0364-930X
TL215.A35
ALFA OWNER. 1958. m. $35. (Alfa Romeo Owners Club) Pfanner Communications, Inc., 1371 E. Warner Ave., Ste. E, Tustin, CA 92680-6442. TEL 714-259-8240. FAX 714-259-9377. (Subscr. to: 2468 Gum Tree Ln., Fallbrook, CA 92028) Ed. Elyse Barrett. adv.; bk.rev.; illus.; circ. 5,800.

388.3　　　US
ALFA ROMEO WORLD. bi-m. $3.95 per no. Hyde Park Group, 2001 W. Main St., Stamford, CT 06902. TEL 203-969-2533. FAX 203-348-3555.

388.3　　　US
ALL CHEVY. q. $2.50 per no. McMullen Publishing, 2145 W. La Palma Ave., Anaheim, CA 92801. TEL 714-635-9040. FAX 714-533-9779.

796.77　　　CN
ALMANACH DE L'AUTO. 1984. a. Can.$11.95. Publicor Inc., 7 Chemin Bates, Outremont, Que. H2V 1A6, Canada. TEL 514-270-1100. FAX 514-270-6900. Ed. Claude Bedard. adv.; circ. 24,018.

ALSACE AUTOMOBILE. see TRAVEL AND TOURISM

ALTERNATIVE TRANSPORTATION NEWS. see TRANSPORTATION

343　　　US　　ISSN 0093-4062
KF2210.Z95
AMERICAN AUTOMOBILE ASSOCIATION. DIGEST OF MOTOR LAWS. (Vols. for 1965-79 compiled by its Legal Dept.; vols. for 1980-present compiled by its Traffic Safety Dept.) a. $6. American Automobile Association, 1000 AAA Dr., Heathrow, FL 32746-5063. TEL 407-444-7962. FAX 407-444-7380. Ed. Charles A. Butler. circ. 80,000. Key Title: Digest of Motor Laws.

388.3　　　US
AMERICAN CARWASH REVIEW. 1964. a. $8. Lott Publishing Co., Box 1107, Santa Monica, CA 90406. TEL 310-397-4217. Ed. Dave Lott. adv.; tr.lit.; circ. 3,031. (tabloid format)
Formerly: Car Wash Review (ISSN 0008-607X)

629.286　　　US　　ISSN 0095-1811
HD9999.C27
AMERICAN CLEAN CAR. 1972. bi-m. $33. Crain Associated Enterprises, 500 N. Dearborn St., Chicago, IL 60610. TEL 312-337-7700. Ed. Larry Ebert. adv.; circ. 18,000. (reprint service avail. from UMI)

388.3　　　US
▼ **AMERICAN DREAM CARS.** 1990. a. $8.95. Edmund Publications Corp., 200 Baker Ave., Ste.. 309, Concord, MA 01742. TEL 508-371-9788. FAX 508-371-9806.
Description: Pricing of current value of American dream cars manufactured from 1946-1972. Includes rating variations as well as buying tips and photos.

796.77　　　US
AMERICAN RODDER. 1987. m. $3.50 per no. Paisano Publications, Inc., 28010 Dorothy Dr., Box 3075, Agoura Hills, CA 91301. TEL 818-889-8740. FAX 818-889-4726. adv.; circ. 150,000.

ANTIQUE AUTOMOBILE. see ANTIQUES

388.3　　　AG　　ISSN 0004-0991
ARGENTINA AUTOMOTRIZ. vol.4, 1970. 6/yr. $20. Camara Argentina del Libro - Argentine Book Association, Av. Belgrano 1580, 6 Piso, 1093 Buenos Aires, Argentina. Ed. Hugo Brik. adv.; bk.rev.; charts; stat.; circ. 27,800.

388.3　　　FR
ARGUS DE L'AUTOMOBILE ET DES LOCOMOTIONS. w. 500 F. (foreign 760 F.). S.N.E.E.P., 1 Place Boieldieu, 75002 Paris, France. TEL 42-61-83-03. FAX 49-27-09-50. TELEX ARGAUTO 214633F. adv.

ARIZONA A A A HIGHROADS. see TRAVEL AND TOURISM

796.77　　　US
ARNOLT-BRISTOL REGISTRY. 1985. s-a. $10. Box 60, Brooklandville, MD 21022. Ed. Lee Raskin. adv.; circ. 275. (back issues avail.)

388　　　US
ARROW (ROCHESTER). 1957. q. $25 membership. Pierce-Arrow Society, Inc., 135 Edgerton St., Rochester, NY 14607. Ed. Bernard J. Weis. illus.; circ. 1,100. (processed)

388.3　　　NE　　ISSN 0004-3966
ARTS EN AUTO. 1934. fortn. membership. (Vereniging van Artsen) Wegener Tijl Tijdschriften Groep B.V., P.B. 9943, 1006 AP Amsterdam, Netherlands. TEL 020-5182828. FAX 020-5182843. Ed.Bd. adv.; bk.rev.; illus.; index; circ. 46,000 (controlled).

ARZT UND AUTO; der kraftfahrende Arzt. see MEDICAL SCIENCES

ASSOCIATION FOR THE ADVANCEMENT OF AUTOMOTIVE MEDICINE. PROCEEDINGS. see MEDICAL SCIENCES

629.2　　　US
ATLAS BULLETIN. 1933. bi-m. free to qualified personnel. Atlas Supply Co., 11 Diamond Rd., Springfield, NJ 07081. TEL 201-379-6550. Ed. Russell M. Eggert. index; circ. 45,000.
Description: Highlights automotive accessories.

388 629.286　　UK　　ISSN 0260-664X
AUSTIN HEALEY YEAR BOOK. 1978. a. Magpie Publishing Co., Holmerise, Seven Hills Rd., Cobham, Surrey, England. illus.

AUSTRALIA. BUREAU OF STATISTICS. MOTOR VEHICLE REGISTRATIONS, AUSTRALIA. see TRANSPORTATION — Abstracting, Bibliographies, Statistics

388.3　　　AT
AUSTRALIAN FLEET MAGAZINE. 1986. bi-m. Aus.$45. M P A Group, 20 Stokes St., Port Melbourne, Vic. 3207, Australia. TEL 03-646-5688. FAX 03-646-8330. Ed. Elisabeth Tuckey. adv.; circ. 6,500. (back issues avail.)
Description: Industry magazine for the automotive fleet of Australia.

796.77　　　AT
AUSTRALIAN JAGUAR DRIVER. m. Aus.$30. Jaguar Drivers Club of Australia, P.O. Box 2, Drummoyne, N.S.W. 2047, Australia. Ed. Owen Graham. adv.; circ. 700.

388.3　　　AT
AUSTRALIAN MOTOR MANUAL. 1946. m. Aus.$0.70 per no. David Syme & Co., P.O. Box 628 E, Melbourne, Vic. 3001, Australia. Ed. Paul Harrington. circ. 31,662. **Indexed:** Gdlns.
Formerly: Motor Manual (ISSN 0047-8210)

388　　　AT　　ISSN 0810-9958
AUSTRALIAN MOTORING YEAR. 1982. a. Aus.$39.95($39.95) Chevron Publishing Group Pty. Ltd., P.O. Box 206, Hornsby, N.S.W. 2077, Australia. TEL 02-476-3199. FAX 02-476-5739. Ed. Thomas B. Floyd. circ. 15,000. (back issues avail.)
Description: Australian automotive industry review.

629.286　　　SZ
AUTO. Variant title: A C S Auto. (Text in German) 1972. 10/yr. 50 Fr. (Swiss Automobile Club) Hallwag AG, Nordring 4, CH-3001 Berne, Switzerland. TEL 031-42-31-31. FAX 031-414133. TELEX 912 661 CH. Eds. Curt Schild, K. Martin Sip. adv.; circ. 70,538.

388 388.3　　BE　　ISSN 0774-1324
AUTO. 1986. fortn. 1250 F. Vlaamse Toeristenbond, Vlaamse Automobilistenbond, Sint-Jakobsmarkt 45-47, B-2000 Antwerp, Belgium. TEL 22-03-400. FAX 234-05-98. TELEX 31679. circ. 105,000.
Description: Car tests, consumer information, motor sport.

629.286　　　IT
AUTO; mensile di automobilismo e tecnica automobilistica. 1985. m. L.58000 (foreign L.100000)(typically set in Jan.). Conti Editore S.p.A., Via del Lavoro, 7, 40068 San Lazzaro di Savena (BO), Italy. TEL 051-6227111. FAX 051-6255418. TELEX 510212. Ed. Tommaso Valentinetti. adv.; bk.rev.; circ. 151,000.

388.3　　　II　　ISSN 0005-0709
AUTO AGE. (Text in English) 1953. bi-m. Rs.40. Agelong, B-1-440, Kalyani 741 235, India. Ed. Amalendu Syam. adv.; bk.rev.; charts; illus.; stat.; circ. 20,000. (tabloid format)

388.3　　　US　　ISSN 0894-1270
AUTO AGE; the news magazine of automotive sales & management. 1966. m. $36. M H West, Inc. (Subsidiary of: Maclean Hunter Publishing Co.), 6633 Odessa Ave., Van Nuys, CA 91406. TEL 818-997-0644. FAX 818-997-1058. (Subscr. to: 29 N. Wacker Dr., Chicago, IL 60606) Ed. C.D. Bohon. adv.; illus.; circ. 33,501 (controlled). **Indexed:** PROMT.
Former titles: Automotive Age (ISSN 0005-1470) & Automotive Age - Kelley Blue Book Reporter; Which was formed by the merger of: Automotive Age & Kelley Blue Book Reporter.
Description: Serves the new car and truck dealership industry, including manufacturers, distributors, finance and leasing companies, and repair and body shops.

388　　　NZ
AUTO AGE. bi-m. 33 Wyndham St., P.O. Box 5, Auckland, New Zealand. circ. 196,400.

TRANSPORTATION — AUTOMOBILES

388.3 380.1 US
AUTO AGE BUYER'S GUIDE. 1966. a. $10. M H West, Inc. (Subsidiary of: Maclean Hunter Publishing Co.), 6633 Odessa Ave., Van Nuys, CA 91406. TEL 818-997-0644. FAX 818-997-1058. (Subscr. to: 29 N. Wacker Dr., Chicago, IL 60606) adv.; circ. 35,000.

338 629.2 GW ISSN 0179-4078
AUTO AKTUELL. m. Verband der Automobilindustrie e.V., Westendstr. 61, 6000 Frankfurt a.M. 1, Germany. TEL 069-7570-0. FAX 069-7570-261. TELEX 411293.

AUTO AND FLAT GLASS JOURNAL. see *CERAMICS, GLASS AND POTTERY*

629.2 NE
AUTO & MOTOR TECHNIEK. 1940. 11/yr. fl.106. Uitgeversmaatschappij C. Misset B.V., Hanzestr. 1, 7006 RH Doetinchem, Netherlands. TEL 08340-49911. FAX 08340-43839. TELEX 45481. (Subscr. to: Postbus 4, 7000 BA Doetinchem, Netherlands) Ed. A. Cupedo. adv.: B&W page fl.2637; unit 187 x 257; adv. contact: Cor van Nek. bk.rev.; charts; illus.; circ. 23,590. Indexed: Excerp.Med.
Formerly: A M T - V A M Orgaan; Formed by the merger of: Auto Service; Auto en Motor Techniek.
Description: Technical magazine dealing with the maintenance and repair of cars.

388.3 US
AUTO & TRUCK INTERNATIONAL. Spanish edition: Auto y Camion Internacional. (Editions in English and Spanish) 1917. 6/yr. $50 (free to qualified personnel). Johnston International Publishing (Subsidiary of: Hunter Publishing Limited Partnership), 950 Lee St., Des Plaines, IL 60016-6588. TEL 708-296-0770. FAX 708-803-3328. (Subscr. to: Box 5050, Des Plaines, IL 60017) Ed. Jim Halloran. adv.; bk.rev.; charts; illus.; tr.lit.
Former titles: Automobile International - Automovil Internacional (ISSN 0005-1594); Automotive World.
Description: For vehicle repair shops, fleets, vehicle dealers, dealers of parts, accessories and equipment and automotive manufacturers in 183 countries and territories worldwide.

388.3 IT
AUTO ATTREZZATURE. s-a. L.120000. Edizioni Pubblire, Corso Garibaldi, 42, 20121 Milan, Italy. TEL 02-801529. FAX 02-801520. Ed. G. Maffeis. adv.; circ. 10,000.
Former titles: Attrezzature; Equip Auto - 3A.

388.3 629.2 DK
AUTO BLADET. 1936. m. DKK 110. Centralforeningen af Autoreparatorer i Danmark, Kirkevej 1-3, 2630 Taastrup, Denmark. FAX 45-44-53-13-10. Ed. Benny Kirkegaard. index; circ. 3,300. (reprint service avail.)
Formerly: Motor - Service og Auteknisk Tidsskrift (ISSN 0027-1993)

796.77 IT
AUTO CAPITAL. bi-m. L.36000. Rizzoli Editore-Corriere della Sera, Vai Angelo Rizzoli 2, 20132 Milan, Itlay.

629 SP
AUTO-CLUB. 1983. bi-m. Real Automovil Club de Espana, Jose Abascal 10, 28003 Madrid, Spain. TEL 447-92-00. TELEX 45411 CIJA E. Ed. Fernando Falco. adv.; bk.rev.; circ. 190,000.

388.3 US ISSN 0746-8504
AUTO CLUB NEWS. vol.62, 1970. bi-m. $1 to non-members; members free; foreign $1.50. Automobile Club of Southern California, Box 2890, Los Angeles, CA 90051. TEL 213-741-4880. FAX 213-741-3069. Ed. Jennifer Geller. charts; illus.; circ. 2,500,000.
Formerly: Auto Club News Pictorial (ISSN 0005-0725)

388.3 IT
AUTO D'EPOCA. m. L.45000 (foreign L.65000). Auto d'Epoca S.r.l., Viale Brigata Treviso, 21-C, 31100 Treviso, Italy. TEL 0422-66503. Ed. Guido DeMozzi.

629.2 SA
AUTO DATA DIGEST. 1974. a. R.37. Mead & McGrouther (Pty) Ltd., 327 Surrey Ave., PO Box 1240, Ferndale, Randburg 2125, South Africa. Eds. O. Peruch, W. Calcutt. circ. 4,500.

388.3 SA
AUTO DEALERS' GUIDE. 1960. m. R.76.20. Mead & McGrouther (Pty) Ltd., 327 Surrey Ave., P.O. Box 1240, Ferndale, Randburg 2125, South Africa. adv.; circ. 6,000.
Formerly: Auto Dealers' Digest (ISSN 0005-0733)

629.283 FR
AUTO DEFENSE. bi-m. 150 F. (foreign 180 F.). Societe d'Editions Modernes Parisienne, 83, rue Jean Mermoz, 75008 Paris, France. TEL 42-66-92-36. TELEX SEMP 650016F.

627.286 IT ISSN 0393-8387
AUTO E DESIGN. (Text in English and Italian) 1979. bi-m. L.79000($127) (foreign L.132500). Auto e Design s.r.l., Corso Francia 161, 10139 Turin, Italy. TEL 011-766628. FAX 011-758810. Ed. Fulvio Cinti. adv.; bk.rev.; circ. 13,000.
—BLDSC shelfmark: 1827.160000.
Description: Designed for auto industry's design centers, design studios, major designers and specialized schools.

388 SZ
AUTO EXKLUSIV. (Text in German) m. 79.80 Fr. (foreign 90 Fr.). Hallwag AG, Nordring 4, CH-3001 Berne, Switzerland. TEL 031-423131. FAX 031-414133. TELEX 912 661 CH. circ. 6,800.

796.77 US
AUTO EXOTICA. m. Fantasy Publications, 6034 S. Lindbergh Blvd., St. Louis, MO 63123-7041. TEL 314-487-0054. Ed. William Kemper. adv.; circ. 50,000.

388 FR ISSN 0150-7230
AUTO EXPERTISE. (Includes supplement: Tarif Pieces Detachees) 1966. bi-m. (with q. supplement). 615 F. (foreign 705 F.). Editions Techniques pour l'Automobile et l'Industrie (ETAI), 20 rue de la Saussiere, 92100 Boulogne Billancourt, France. TEL 46-04-81-13. FAX 48-25-56-92. TELEX ETAIRTA 204850 F. Ed. Jacques Dubroca. circ. 13,100.
Description: Provides repair estimates for cars in accidents.

796.77 HU ISSN 0864-9219
AUTO EXTRA. 1988. m. $45 (effective 1992). Axel Springer - Budapest Kft. (Budapest), P.O.B. 430, 1537 Budapest, Hungary. (Subscr. to: Kultura, P.O.B. 149, 1389 Budapest, Hungary) Ed. Bencze Szabo Peter.

388.3 US ISSN 1045-5760
AUTO FINANCE UPDATE. m. $275. Warren, Gorham and Lamont, One Penn Plaza, New York, NY 10119. TEL 800-950-1201. FAX 212-971-5240. TELEX 928-464.
Formerly: Automobile Finance Update.
Description: Provides information on managing an auto loan portfolio.

388.3 666.1 US
AUTO GLASS MAGAZINE. bi-m. National Glass Association, 8200 Greensboro Dr., Ste. 302, McLean, VA 22102-3881. TEL 703-442-4890. FAX 703-442-0630. Ed. Nicole Harris. circ. 6,000.

629.286 CN
AUTO HEBDO. (Text in English, French) 1976. w. 130 DeLiege St., Montreal, Que. H2P 1J2, Canada. Ed. Elio Vettes. adv.; circ. 28,000.

388.3 IT ISSN 1120-7655
AUTO IN. bi-m. L.48000 (foreign L.96000). Edizioni Conde Nast S.p.A., Piazza Castello, 27, 20121 Milan, Italy. TEL 02-85611. FAX 02-870686. Ed. Gino Rancati.

388.3 IT
AUTO IN FUORISTRADA. m. L.48000 (foreign L.68000). Rusconi Editori Associati S.p.A., Via Vitruvio, 43, 20124 Milan, Italy. TEL 02-67561. FAX 67562732. Ed. GianPiero Anselmi. circ. 120,000. (back issues avail.)

AUTO INDEX. see *TRANSPORTATION — Abstracting, Bibliographies, Statistics*

380.5 001.6 UK
AUTO INDUSTRY NEWSLETTER. 1979. m. $385. Industrial Newsletters Ltd., 42 Market Sq., Toddington, Dunstable, Beds LU5 6BS, England. FAX 05255-4759. TELEX 825489. Ed. John Mortimer.
Description: Provides international coverage of the car, truck and components industry for engineers and management-level professionals. Includes information about manufacturing routes, contracts placed, design ideas and technological developments.

629.2 GW ISSN 0175-9531
DAS AUTO-INTERNATIONAL-IN ZAHLEN/INTERNATIONAL AUTO STATISTICS. (Text in English, German) 1981. a. price varies. Verband der Automobilindustrie e.V., Westendstr. 61, Postfach 170563, 6000 Frankfurt a.M. 1, Germany. TEL 069-7570-0. FAX 069-7570-261. (back issues avail.)

388.3 FR ISSN 0005-0768
AUTO-JOURNAL. 1950. s-m. 360 F. Societe EDP, 8-10, rue Pierre Brossolette, 92300 Levallois Perret, France. TEL 40-87-42-37. TELEX 612 177. Dir. Jacques Hersant. adv.; bibl.; charts; illus.; circ. 400,000 (paid); 267,000 (controlled).

388.3 BE
AUTO JOURNAL; journal du XXe siecle. (Text in English, French) 26/yr. Diffusion et Publicite S.A., 318 rue Vanderkindere, B-1180 Brussels, Belgium. Ed. P. de Vanssay. adv.; circ. 20,000.

629.2 GW
AUTO-KATALOG. 1957. a. DM.14. Vereinigte Motor-Verlage GmbH und Co. KG, Leuschnerstr. 1, Postfach 106036, 7000 Stuttgart 10, Germany. TEL 0711-18201. FAX 0711-1821756. Ed. Rudolf Heitz. adv.; abstr.; index; circ. 330,000.
Formerly: Auto-Modelle.
Description: Presentation of text and pictures of new cars from around the world.

629.286 GW
AUTO KATALOG. 1956. a. DM.14. Motor-Presse Stuttgart, Leuschnerstr. 1, Postfach 106036, 7000 Stuttgart 10, Germany. TEL 0711-18201. FAX 0711-1821669. Ed. Rudolf Heitz. illus.

388.3 US ISSN 0005-0776
HD9999.C27
AUTO LAUNDRY NEWS. 1953. m. $15. Columbia Communications, Inc., 370 Lexington Ave., New York, NY 10017. TEL 212-532-9290. FAX 212-779-8345. Ed. Jean Daniel Noland. adv.; charts; illus.; stat.; tr.mk.; circ. 18,500.

AUTO MAGAZINE. see *MILITARY*

388 629.2 SP
AUTO MECANICA. 1969. m. 1200 ptas. Luike - Motorsport, C. Ancora, 402, 28045 Madrid, Spain. Eds. Carlos Hernandez Herrero, Luis de Madariaga. adv.; illus.; charts; stat.; circ. 16,000. (back issues avail.)

658.8 US
AUTO MERCHANDISING NEWS; the national business magazine for the volume aftermarket. 1971. m. $36 (free to qualified personnel). Mortimer Communications, Inc., Box 1185, Fairfield, CT 06430. TEL 203-384-9323. FAX 203-375-1463. Ed. Bill Mortimer. adv.; bk.rev.; circ. 23,224 (controlled).
Description: Designed to help retailers and distributors of auto parts and accessories run their businesses more efficiently.

629.2 BE
AUTO-MOTO-REVUE. (Text in Dutch, French) m. 2050 BEF. Chambre Syndicale du Commerce Automobile de Belgique, Bd. de la Woluwe 46, B-9, B-1200 Brussels, Belgium.

388.3 HU ISSN 0005-0792
AUTO-MOTOR. 1946. s-m. $43.50. Lapkiado Vallalat, Lenin korut 9-11, 1073 Budapest 7, Hungary. TEL 222-408. (Subscr. to: Kultura, P.O. Box 149, H-1389 Budapest, Hungary) Ed. Imre Kokai. adv.; bk.rev.; charts; illus.; circ. 280,000.

TRANSPORTATION — AUTOMOBILES

388.3 796.72 GW ISSN 0005-0806
AUTO MOTOR UND SPORT. 1946. 26/yr. DM.122.20 (foreign DM.146.90). Vereinigte Motor-Verlage GmbH und Co. KG, Leuschnerst. 1, Postfach 106036, 7000 Stuttgart 10, Germany. TEL 0711-18201. FAX 0711-1821756. adv.; charts; illus.; circ. 485,000.
Description: Articles, tests and reports on cars and everything relating to them.

388.3 796.72 GW
AUTO MOTOR UND SPORT SPEZIAL. 1976. a. Vereinigte Motor-Verlage GmbH und Co. KG, Leuschnerst. 1, Postfach 106036, 7000 Stuttgart 10, Germany. Ed. Helmut Luckner. adv.; charts; illus.; stat.; tr.; lit.

388.3 796.72 GW
AUTO MOTOR UND SPORT TESTJAHRBUCH. 1984. a. Vereinigte Motor-Verlage GmbH und Co. KG, Leuschnerst. 1, Postfach 106036, 7000 Stuttgart 10, Germany. TEL 0711-18201. FAX 0711-1821756. Ed. Helmut Luckner. adv.; charts; illus.; stat.; tr.lit.

388 629.286 GW
AUTO MOTORRAD UND FREIZEIT. 1986. m. DM.57.60 (foreign DM.62.40). Steinmetzstr. 1, D-2400 Luebeck, Germany. TEL 0451-89721. Ed. Juergen Koslowski. circ. 116,000.

629.286 IT
AUTO OGGI; settimanale di auto e consigli pratici sul mondo dei motori. 1986. w. L.78000 (foreign L.114400). Arnoldo Mondadori Editore S.p.A., Casella Postale 1833, 20101 Milan, Italy. TEL 3199345. Ed. Sandro Liberali. circ. 310,000.

796.77 FR
AUTO PASSION. bi-m. 150 F. (foreign 180 F.). Societe d'Editions Modernes Parisienne, 38, rue Jean Mermoz, 75008 Paris, France. TEL 42-66-92-36. TELEX SEMP 650016F.

388.3 US ISSN 1042-6205
AUTO PRICE ALMANAC. bi-m. \$26.95. Pace Publications (Milwaukee), 1020 N. Broadway, Ste. 111, Milwaukee, WI 53202. TEL 414-272-9977. FAX 414-272-9973.
Description: Dealer's cost and manufacturer's suggested list price for all new American and foreign cars, with used car prices covering the past ten years.

338.3 US ISSN 0743-7129
AUTO RACING MEMORIES. 1981. bi-m. \$25. A R M Publishing Co., Box 12226, St. Petersburg, FL 33733. TEL 813-895-3482. Ed. Ken Breslauer. circ. 6,221. (back issues avail.)
Description: Covers antique race cars and American auto racing history.

AUTO RENTAL FLEET. see *BUSINESS AND ECONOMICS — Marketing And Purchasing*

388.3 330 US
AUTO RENTAL NEWS. m. Bobit Publishing Company, 2512 Artesia Blvd., Redondo Beach, CA 90278-3210. TEL 213-376-8788. FAX 213-376-9043. Ed. Edward J. Bobit. circ. 16,500.

388.3 US
AUTO RETAIL REPORT; independent medium interpreting news of the automotive industry. 1989. bi-w. \$427. United Communications Group, 11300 Rockville Pike, Ste. 1100, Rockville, MD 20852-3030. TEL 301-816-8950. Ed. Donna Lawrence. bk.rev.; stat.; circ. 5,000. (processed)
Formed by the 1989 merger of: Autoservice Profit Report; (1945-1989): Motor News Analysis (ISSN 0027-1942)

388.3 SP ISSN 0005-1691
AUTO REVISTA; semanario del motor. 1959. w. 15000 ptas. (foreign 21000 ptas.). Tecnipublicaciones, S.A., Fernando VI, 27, 28004 Madrid, Spain. TEL 91-319-7889. FAX 91-319-7089. TELEX 43905 YEBE E. Ed. Raul del Hoyo. adv.; bk.rev.; bibl.; charts; illus.; mkt.; pat.; stat.; tr.lit.; circ. 38,000.
Description: Covers the automobile business and industry. Contains prices and test results.

388.3 US
AUTO REVISTA. (Text in English, Spanish) 1988. bi-w. 4444 Spring Valley Rd., Ste. 105, Dallas, TX 75244. TEL 214-386-0040. FAX 214-386-4255. adv.; circ. 27,040.
Description: Focuses on the auto market in Dallas and Fort Worth.

629.286 AU
AUTO REVUE. 1965. m. Verlag Orac GmbH, Graben 17, A-1010 Vienna, Austria. Ed. Herbert Voelker. adv.; circ. 112,300.

729.286 US
AUTO SERVICE INSIDER. fortn. Atcom, Inc., 2315 Broadway, New York, NY 10024-4332. TEL 212-873-5900. FAX 212-799-1728. Ed. Steve Byers.

388.3 US
AUTO SERVICE TODAY. 1988. bi-w. \$195. Atcom, Inc., Atcom Bldg., 2315 Broadway, New York, NY 10024. TEL 212-873-5900. FAX 212-799-1728. Ed. Stephen Byers. circ. 500. (back issues avail.)

388 IT
AUTO 70. m. L.500 per no. Via G. Verdi 53, 10124 Turin, Italy. Ed.Bd. adv.; circ. 80,000.

388.3 US
AUTO SOUND & SECURITY. bi-m. \$2.95 per no. McMullen Publishing, 2145 W. LaPalma Ave., Anaheim, CA 92801. TEL 714-635-9040. FAX 714-533-9979.

796.77 PO
AUTO SPORT. 1977. w. Esc.7700. Sociedade Editora de Publicacoes, Lda., Av. Sacadura Cabral 26, Dafundo, 1495 Lisbon, Portugal. TEL 01-4198065. FAX 01-4199082. Dir. Pedro Castelo. adv.; B&W page Esc.120000, color page Esc.150000; trim 155 x 215. circ. 24,600.

629.286 PL
AUTO SUKCES. m? Inter-Media, Ul. Nowy Swiat 27, 00-029 Warsaw, Poland. TEL 48-22-460383. (Subscr. to: Ksiegarnia Wysylkowa, P.O. Box 10, 00-273 Warsaw, Poland) Ed. Krzysztof Dabrowski.

629.2 SZ ISSN 0005-0857
AUTO-TECHNIK; der Automobil-Mechaniker. 1951. m. (10/yr.). 75 Fr. Verlag Aargauer Tagblatt AG, Bahnhofstrasse 39-43, 5001 Aarau, Switzerland. Ed. J. Pfyl. adv.; circ. 8,500.

388.3 AU ISSN 0001-2688
AUTO TOURING; die Oesterreichische Kraftfahrzeug-Zeitung. Abbreviated title: A.T. 1947. m. S.100. Oesterreichischer Automobil- Motorrad- und Touring-Club Betriebe Gmbh, Schubertring 1-3, A-1010 Vienna, Austria. Ed. Alfons Malushka. adv.; illus.; circ. 745,000.

388.3 US
TL1
AUTO TRIM & RESTYLING NEWS; maintenance and repair of auto upholstery, etc. 1953. 12/yr. \$25 (in Canada \$45; elsewhere \$90). National Association of Auto Trim Shops, 180 Allen Rd., N.E., No. 300N, Atlanta, GA 30328-4862. Ed. Gary Fong. adv.; bk.rev.; charts; illus.; circ. 9,400.
Formerly: Auto Trim News (ISSN 0005-0865)
Description: Covers automotive and marine soft goods, restoration and replacement, upholstery, convertible tops and carpets. Also contains a restyling segment covering sunroofs, pinstriping and aerodynamic altering.

614.86 GW
AUTO UND VERKEHR. 1966. bi-m. (Kraftfahrer Schutz e.V.) K S-Verlag GmbH, Uhlandstr. 7, D-8000 Munich, Germany. circ. 208,366.

388 AU
AUTO UND WIRTSCHAFT. 1988. m. S.300. E und W Zeitschriftenverlag GmbH, Wilhelminenstr. 91 IIC, A-1160 Vienna, Austria. FAX 0222-469032-30. circ. 21,000.

796.77 FR ISSN 0222-3996
AUTO VERTE. m. 250 F. (foreign 270 F.). Editions Lariviere, 15-17 Quai de l'Oise, 75166 Paris Cedex 19, France. TEL 1-40-34-22-07. FAX 1-40-35-84-41. TELEX 211 678 F. Ed. Richard Verdelet.

629.2 621.38 FR ISSN 0005-0881
AUTO-VOLT; Electrauto. 1929. m. 530 F. (foreign 645 F.). Editions Techniques pour l'Automobile et l'Industrie (ETAI), 20 rue de la Saussiere, 92100 Boulogne Billancourt, France. TEL 46-04-81-13. FAX 48-25-56-92. TELEX ETAIRTA 204850 F. Ed. Loic de Parcevaux. adv.; charts; illus.; index; circ. 7,560. **Indexed:** Sci.Abstr.
—BLDSC shelfmark: 1835.500000.
Description: Provides information on electronic equipment of cars and ways to uphold and regulate them.

388.3 GW
AUTO ZEITUNG. 1969. bi-w. DM.143. Heinrich Bauer Spezialzeitschriften Verlag, Industriestr. 16, 5000 Cologne 60, Germany. TEL 0221-7709157. FAX 0221-714153. Ed. G. Wiechmann. adv.; bk.rev.; charts; illus.; circ. 135,000.

629.286 338.476 GW
AUTO ZUBEHOER MARKT; Fachmagazin fuer Marketing, Trends und Technik. 1988. m. DM.120(\$85) Fachverlag Selisky GmbH, Obere Muensterstr. 18, D-4620 Castrop-Rauxel, Germany. TEL 02305-1711. Ed. Norbert Selisky. circ. 4,500.
Description: For car-accessory traders and producers, technical and marketing news.

629.286 IT
AUTO 70; mensile di informazione tecnica e commerciale sul motorismo. m. L.2000 per no. Via G. Verdi, 53, 10124 Turin, Italy. Ed. Giacomo Gaspardo Moro. circ. 32,000.

AUTOBUS. see *TRANSPORTATION*

388.3 UK ISSN 0955-5889
TL1
AUTOCAR & MOTOR. 1895. w. £75. Haymarket Magazines Ltd., 38-42 Hampton Rd., Teddington, Middx. TW11 OJE, England. TEL 081-943-5000. FAX 081-943-5653. TELEX 895-2440-HAYMRT-G. Ed. Bob Murray. adv.; bk.rev.; illus.; index; circ. 97,080. (also avail. in microform from UMI,PMC; microfilm from BHP) **Indexed:** Br.Tech.Ind., RAPRA.
—BLDSC shelfmark: 1828.010000.
Incorporates: Motor (ISSN 0143-6945); **Formerly:** Autocar (ISSN 0005-092X)

629.2 FR ISSN 0067-2424
AUTOCATALOGUE; guide technique de mecanique automobile. 1913. a. 220 F. Editions S.O.S.P., 83 rue de Villiers, 92523 Neuilly Cedex, France. Ed. C.L. Lavaud. index.

388.3 AG ISSN 0005-0946
AUTOCLUB; revista del automovilismo, turismo e informaciones. 1961. bi-m. Automovil Club Argentino, Av. del Libertador 1850, Buenos Aires, Argentina. Ed. Cesar C. Carman. adv.; bk.rev.; abstr.; charts; illus.; mkt.; stat.; tr.lit.; circ. 710,600.

388.3 GW
AUTOFACHMANN. (Includes instructional materials) 1952. m. DM.103. (Zentralverband des Kraftfahrzeughandwerks) Vogel-Verlag und Druck KG, Max-Planck-Str. 7-9, Postfach 6740, 8700 Wuerzburg 1, Germany. TEL 0931-418-0. Ed. Werner Degen. adv.; bk.rev.; abstr.; charts; illus.; stat.; cum.index; circ. 76,812 (controlled).
Formerly: Junghandwerker im Kraftfahrzeug Betrieb (ISSN 0022-6432)

388.3 IT
AUTOGIORNALE.* 1975. s-m. L.15000. Edistampa s.r.l., Via Donatello, Lotto 45, 71036 Lucera (Foggia), Italy. Ed. Edoardo Rossi. circ. 50,000.

AUTOGLASS. see *CERAMICS, GLASS AND POTTERY*

388.3 GW ISSN 0005-0989
AUTOHAUS; Fachmagazin fuer Unternehmensfuehrung und Werkstattpraxis. 1957. fortn. DM.256.80. (Zentralverband des Kraftfahrzeuggewerbes e.V.) Autohaus Verlag GmbH, Alte Landstr. 8-10, 8012 Ottobrunn B, Germany. TEL 089-60805-0. Ed. Hannes Brachat. adv.; bk.rev.; charts; illus.; tr.lit.; circ. 21,000.

629.2 US ISSN 0199-6908
AUTOINC.. 1952. m. \$20. Automotive Service Association, 1901 Airport Fwy., Ste. 100, Box 929, Beford, TX 76021. TEL 817-283-6205. FAX 817-685-0225. adv.; stat.; tr.lit.; circ. 14,000.
Former titles: Automotive Independent; Independent Garageman.

TRANSPORTATION — AUTOMOBILES

629.286   MX
AUTOINDUSTRIA. 1971. m. Queretaro 229-402, Apdo. 71339, 06700 Mexico D.F., Mexico. TEL 5-264-2848. Ed. Alfredo Villagran Arevalo. adv.; bk.rev.; circ. 30,384.

388.3   NE   ISSN 0005-0997
AUTOKAMPIOEN. 1908. 26/yr. fl.103.50 to non-members. Koninklijke Nederlandse Toeristenbond ANWB - Royal Dutch Touring Club, Wassenaarseweg 220, Postbus 93200, 2509 BA The Hague, Netherlands. Ed. W. Leniger. adv.; bibl.; charts; illus.; mkt.; stat.; circ. 80,000.

388.3   GW
AUTOKAUFMANN. 1983. m. DM.175. (Zentralverband des Kraftfahrzeuggewerbes) Vogel Verlag und Druck KG, Max-Planck-Str. 7-9, Postfach 67 40, 8700 Wuerzburg 1, Germany. TEL 0931-418-0. Ed. Juergen Rinn. adv.; abstr.; charts; illus.; stat.; index; circ. 6,000.

388.3   GW   ISSN 0937-3381
AUTOKOSTEN UND STEUERN AKTUELL; Kosten und Steuern. vol.11, 1977. a. DM.44. (Allgemeiner Deutscher Automobil-Club e.V.) A D A C Verlag GmbH, Am Westpark 8, Postfach 700126, 8000 Munich 70, Germany. TEL 089-7676-0. circ. 9,000.
Former titles: A D A C Handbuch - Geschaeftswagen (ISSN 0931-0053) & Was Kostet der Geschaeftswagen; (until vol.15, 1979-80): Was Kostet Mein Auto?

388.3   FR
AUTOMARQUES; revue francaise du marche des automobiles neuves et d'occasion. 1965. bi-m. 239 F. Editions S.O.S.P., 83 rue de Villiers, 92523 Neuilly Cedex, France. Dir. Claude Lavaud. adv.; circ. 10,000.

AUTOMOBIEL KLASSIEK. see ANTIQUES

388.3   SA   ISSN 0304-8721
HD9710.S7
AUTOMOBIL. (Text and summaries in Afrikaans, English) 1909. m. R.31.35. (Motor Industries' Federation) M & M Publications, P.O. Box 8859, Johannesburg 2000, South Africa. FAX 880-5790. Ed. R.W. Emslie. adv.; bk.rev.; circ. 9,045.
Formerly: Automobile in Southern Africa (ISSN 0005-139X)

629.2 796.7 388.34   CS   ISSN 0404-3529
AUTOMOBIL/AUTOMOBILE. (Quarterly supplement: Stavba Automobilu) (Text in Czech or Slovak; summaries in English, German, Russian) 1955. m. $51. (Federalni Ministerstvo Hutnictvi, Strojirenstvi a Elektrotechniky) Nakladatelstvi Technicke Literatury, Spalena 51, 113 02 Prague 1, Czechoslovakia. (Dist. by: Artia, Ve Smeckach 30, 111 27 Prague 1, Czechoslovakia) Ed. Milan Josif. charts; illus.; circ. 60,000.

629.2   GW   ISSN 0005-1306
AUTOMOBIL-INDUSTRIE; research, design, manufacturing. (Summaries in English, French) 1956. 6/yr. DM.150. Vogel-Verlag und Druck KG, Max-Planck-Str. 7-9, Postfach 6740, 8700 Wuerzburg 1, Germany. TEL 0931-418-0. Ed. Rolf Gnadler. adv.; bk.rev.; illus.; tr.lit.; circ. 4,389.
Indexed: Curr.Cont.

338.476   GW
AUTOMOBIL PRODUKTION. 1987. bi-m. DM.144. Verlag Moderne Industrie, Justus-von-Liebig-Str. 1, Postfach 1751, 8910 Landsberg, Germany. TEL 08191-125-0. FAX 08191-125-483. Ed.Bd. adv.: B&W page DM.5600; trim 257 x 178; adv. contact: Thomas Heringer. circ. 8,000.

629.222   GW
AUTOMOBIL- UND MOTORRAD-CHRONIK. (Includes English Supplement) 1972. m. DM.78. Motor-Presse Verlag GmbH, Postfach 10 42, Leuschnerstr. 1, D-7000 Stuttgart 1, Germany. Ed. Halwart Schrader. adv.; bk.rev.; illus.; pat.; stat.; tr.lit.; index; circ. 12,000. (back issues avail.)
Description: Looks at antique cars.

388.3   CN   ISSN 0005-1330
L'AUTOMOBILE; pour le grossiste. (Text in French) 1939. bi-m. Can.$13.91($21) (foreign $21). Southam Business Communications Inc., 1450 Don Mills Rd., Don Mills, Ont. M3B 2X7, Canada. TEL 416-445-6641. FAX 416-442-2261. Ed. J.M. Germain. adv.; bk.rev.; charts; illus.; stat.; tr.lit.; circ. 12,000. (back issues avail.) **Indexed:** Pt.de Rep. (1979-).

388.3   IT   ISSN 0005-1349
AUTOMOBILE. 1945. m. L.20000. (Automobile Club d'Italia) Editrice dell' Automobile s.r.l., Viale Regina Margherita 290, 00198 Rome, Italy. TEL 06-4402061. FAX 06-8840926. Ed. Carlo Luna. adv.; bk.rev.; film rev.; charts; illus.; stat.; tr.lit.; circ. 1,500,000.

629.2   UK   ISSN 0955-1328
AUTOMOBILE. 1982. m. £50. Enthusiast Publishing Ltd., c/o Peter Hart, Holmerise, Seven Hills Rd., Cobham, Surrey KT11 1ES, England. TEL 0932-64212. FAX 0932-862430. adv.; bk.rev.; circ. 15,000.
Description: Reports on pre-1950 cars and commercial vehicles.

388.3   US   ISSN 0894-3583
AUTOMOBILE (NEW YORK). m. $18 (foreign $22). K-III Magazines, 200 Madison Ave., New York, NY 10016. TEL 212-447-4700. FAX 212-447-4778. (Subscr. to: Box 7078, Red Oak, IA 51566. TEL 800-289-2886) Ed. Davis E. Davis, Jr. (reprint service avail. from UMI) **Indexed:** Access (1988-).
Description: Provides entertaining and informative coverage of automotive subjects, from road tests and new car reviews to vintage car collecting.

AUTOMOBILE & TRACTOR; ancillary & agri equipment. see AGRICULTURE — Agricultural Equipment

AUTOMOBILE ASSOCIATION MEMBERS HANDBOOK. see TRAVEL AND TOURISM

388   RH
AUTOMOBILE ASSOCIATION OF ZIMBABWE. MEMBERS' HANDBOOK. 1923. biennial. membership. Automobile Association of Zimbabwe, Fanum House, 57 Samora Machel Ave., Harare, P.O. Box 585, Zimbabwe. TELEX 22167 ZW. adv.; circ. 50,000.
Description: Information on services for members.

388.3   IT
AUTOMOBILE CLUB TORINO. 1949. bi-m. membership. Automobile Club Torino, Via Giolitti 15, 10123 Turin, Italy. Ed. Tancredi Savaro. adv.; circ. 129,000.

AUTOMOBILE DESIGN LIABILITY. see LAW

388.3   II   ISSN 0005-1403
AUTOMOBILE INDIA. 1952. m. Rs.40($25) Garg Publishing Co., 775 Nicholson Rd., Delhi 6, India. Ed. B. Das Garg. adv.; illus.; stat.; circ. 7,500. (tabloid format; avail. on records)

338.476   JA
AUTOMOBILE INDUSTRY - JAPAN AND TOYOTA. (Text in English) 1972. a. free. Toyota Motor Corporation, International Public Affairs Division, 1-4-18, Koraku, Bunkyo-ku, Tokyo 112, Japan. TEL 03-3817-9930. FAX 03-3817-9017. charts; illus.; stat.; circ. 15,000. **Indexed:** JCT.
Formerly: Motor Industry of Japan; Incorporates: Toyota in Brief.

AUTOMOBILE INSURANCE LOSSES, COLLISION COVERAGES, VARIATIONS BY MAKE AND SERIES. see INSURANCE

AUTOMOBILE MAGAZINE. see TRAVEL AND TOURISM

388.3   US   ISSN 0005-1438
TL1
AUTOMOBILE QUARTERLY. 1962. q. $69.95 for hardcover. Automobile Quarterly, Inc. (Subsidiary of: Kutztown Publishing Co.), Box 348, Kutztown, PA 19530. TEL 800-523-0236. FAX 215-683-3287. Ed. Jonathan A. Stein. charts; illus.; cum.index: 1962-1982; circ. 19,500. (back issues avail.) **Indexed:** A.S.& T.Ind., Ind.Sci.Rev.
Description: Contains articles on contemporary, modern, classic, collectibles, historic, special interest, sports, racing, postwar and pre-war cars.

629.2   SZ   ISSN 0084-7674
AUTOMOBILE YEAR/L'ANNEE AUTOMOBILE/AUTO-JAHR. (Editions in English, French, German) 1953. a. 82 Fr. Editions J R, P.O. Box 81, CH-1001 Lausanne, Switzerland. TEL 021-6178800. FAX 021-6178854. (Dist. in UK by: Motor Racing Publications Ltd., Unit 6, The Pilton Estate, 46 Pitlake, Croydon CR0 3RY, England) Ed. J.-R. Piccard. adv.; circ. 39,000.
—BLDSC shelfmark: 1832.700000.

388   US
AUTOMOBILER. 1923. m. $2. (Automobile Club of Hartford) Hartford Automobiler, 815 Farmington Ave., West Hartford, CT 06119. TEL 203-236-3261. Ed. Michael Klein. adv.; circ. 130,000.

388.3   FR   ISSN 0759-6065
AUTOMOBILES CLASSIQUES. 1977. bi-m. 240 F. Publications Conde Nast S.A., 4 place du Palais Bourbon, 75341 Paris Cedex 07, France. TEL 45-50-32-32. FAX 45-51-43-18. (Subscr. to: 60732 Sainte-Genevieve Cedex, France. TEL 16-44-03-44-00; In U.S. subscr. to: International Subscriptions Inc., 1305 Paterson Plank Rd., North Bergen, NJ 07047-1890. TEL 201-867-9381) Eds. Antoine Prunet, Rosine Bertrand. adv.; bk.rev.; circ. 35,000.
Formerly: Enthousiaste.

318   US
AUTOMOBILES: LATIN AMERICAN INDUSTRIAL REPORT. (Avail. for each of 22 Latin American countries) 1985. a. $435 per country report. Aquino Productions, Box 15760, Stamford, CT 06901. TEL 203-325-3138. Ed. Andres C. Aquino.

AUTOMOBILISME ARDENNAIS. see TRAVEL AND TOURISM

796.77   IT
AUTOMOBILISMO. 1985. m. L.55000($65) (foreign L.84000). Edisport S.p.A., Via Boccaccio, I-20123 Milan, Italy. FAX 48008359. Ed. Massimo Bacchetti. adv.; bk.rev.; charts; illus.; index; circ. 130,000.
Description: Provides information on cars, industrial news and results of tests. Includes technical and sport reports.

388   IT
AUTOMOBILISTA. 1983. m. L.20000. Edizioni Pubblire, Corso Garibaldi, 20121 Milan, Italy. adv.; circ. 28,000.

388   FR
AUTOMOBILISTE. 1966. bi-m. 60 F. 42, rue du Bac, 75007 Paris, France. Ed. Adrien Malght. adv.; bk.rev.; circ. 18,000.

388.3   IT
AUTOMONDO; mensile automobilistico di politica attualita e cultura. 1964. 11/yr. L.7000($15) Imprendinet Italiana s.r.l., Via L. Manara 15, 20122 Milan, Italy. Dir. Gianni Cancellieri. adv.; bk.rev. (back issues avail.)

629   US   ISSN 0192-0995
TL255
AUTOMOTIVE BODY REPAIR NEWS. 1962. m. $48. Chilton Co., Chilton Way, Radnor, PA 19089. TEL 215-964-4000. FAX 215-964-4981. Ed. Tony Molla. adv.; bk.rev.; circ. 60,503 (controlled). (tabloid format)
Description: For professional businesses engaged in automotive collision repair and paint-refinish.

629.286   US
AUTOMOTIVE BODY REPAIR NEWS (YEAR) BUYERS GUIDE AND FACT BOOK.* 1977. a. Stanley Publishing Co., S. Revere Dr., Ste. 202, Northbrook, IL 60064-1566. TEL 312-332-0210. FAX 312-332-0329. Ed. Neal E. Mann. adv.; tr.lit.; circ. 62,039.

388   US
AUTOMOTIVE BOOSTER OF CALIFORNIA. m. McAnally & Associates, Inc., Box 765, La Canada, CA 91012-0765. TEL 818-790-6554. Ed. Don McAnally. adv.; circ. 3,700.

338.3   US
AUTOMOTIVE CONTACT. 1945? m. Automotive Contact, Box 517, Terre Haute, IN 47808. TEL 812-232-2441. Ed. T.L. Spelman. adv.; bk.rev.; circ. 5,000.

TRANSPORTATION — AUTOMOBILES

338.3   US
AUTOMOTIVE CONTACT DIRECTORY. INDIANA. a. $27.95. Automotive Contact, Box 517, Terre Haute, IN 47808. TEL 812-232-2441. Ed. T.L. Spelman. adv.; circ. 3,250.
    Formerly: Indiana Automotive Directory.

388.3 629.2   US   ISSN 0005-1497
AUTOMOTIVE COOLING JOURNAL. 1956. m. $25. National Automotive Radiator Service Association, Box 97, E. Greenville, PA 18041. TEL 215-541-4500. FAX 215-679-4977. Ed. Wayne Juchno. adv.; bk.rev.; index; circ. 10,200.

629 330   US
AUTOMOTIVE DEALERS DIGEST. fortn. Davco, Inc., Box 1272, Ridgewood, NJ 07451-1272. TEL 908-583-2100. Ed. Raphael Cohen.

629.2   AT
AUTOMOTIVE ENGINEER. 1933. 6/yr. Aus.$54 to non-members. Institute of Automotive Mechanical Engineers (Inc.), 227 Great North Rd., Fivedock, N.S.W. 2046, Australia. TEL 02-713-4711. FAX 02-713-2671. Ed. Ralph Gross. adv.; bk.rev.; charts; illus.; tr.lit.; circ. 24,800 (controlled). **Indexed:** Agri.Eng.Abstr., Fluidex, HRIS.
    Formerly: Australian Automotive Engineering and Equipment (ISSN 0004-8720)

629.2   UK   ISSN 0307-6490
TL1
AUTOMOTIVE ENGINEER; for designers of cars, vans, trucks, etc. 1962. 6/yr. £55($99) (Institution of Mechanical Engineers) Mechanical Engineering Publications, Ltd., Northgate Ave., Bury St. Edmunds, Suffolk 1P32 6BW, England. TEL 0284-763277. FAX 0284-704006. TELEX 817376. Ed. John Fenton. adv.; bk.rev.; charts; illus.; pat.; tr.lit.; circ. 8,391. **Indexed:** API Abstr., API Catal., API Hlth.& Environ., API Oil., API Pet.Ref., API Pet.Subst., API Transport., Aus.Rd.Ind., BMT, Br.Tech.Ind., Eng.Ind., Excerp.Med., Fluidex, HRIS, ISMEC, Met.Abstr., Sh.& Vib.Dig., World Alum.Abstr.
    —BLDSC shelfmark: 1833.818000.
    Formed by the merger of: Automotive Design Engineering (ISSN 0005-1500) & Journal of Automotive Engineering.
    Description: News and informational briefs and research papers on technological, design, and product development pertaining to the mechanical, electronic, and operational aspects of on- and off-highway vehicles.

629.2   US   ISSN 0098-2571
TL1   CODEN: AUEGBB
AUTOMOTIVE ENGINEERING MAGAZINE. 1972. m. $72 (foreign $96). Society of Automotive Engineers, 400 Commonwealth Dr., Warrendale, PA 15096. TEL 412-776-4841. illus.; circ. 88,000. (also avail. in microfiche) **Indexed:** A.S.& T.Ind., Acad.Ind., Agri.Eng.Abstr., API Abstr., API Catal., API Hlth.& Environ., API Oil., API Pet.Ref., API Pet.Subst., API Transport., B.C.I.R.A., BMT, Cadscan, Ergon.Abstr., Excerp.Med., Fluidex, Geotech.Abstr., Ind.Sci.Rev., INIS Atomind., ISMEC, Lead Abstr., Met.Abstr., PROMT, Rural Recreat.Tour.Abstr., Sci.Abstr. Sh.& Vib.Dig., Tr.& Indus.Ind., World Alum.Abstr., Zincscan.
    —BLDSC shelfmark: 1833.820000.
    Formerly (until 1972): S A E Journal of Automotive Engineering (ISSN 0097-711X)

388.3   US   ISSN 0195-1564
HD9710.U5
AUTOMOTIVE EXECUTIVE. 1928. m. $24. National Automobile Dealers Association, 8400 Westpark Dr., McLean, VA 22102. TEL 703-821-7150. FAX 703-821-7234. Ed. Joe Phillips. adv.; illus.; index; circ. 23,000. (back issues avail.)
    Incorporates: N.A.D.A. Newsletter; (in 1979): Cars and Trucks (ISSN 0027-5778); *Formerly (until 1974):* N.A.D.A. Magazine.

388.3   US   ISSN 0005-1519
AUTOMOTIVE FLEET. 1961. m. plus Factbook (Apr.). $35 (Canada $24; elsewhere $53). Bobit Publishing Company, 2512 Artesia Blvd., Redondo Beach, CA 90278. TEL 310-376-8788. FAX 310-376-9043. Ed. Mike Antich. adv.; charts; illus.; stat.; circ. 24,000 (controlled). **Indexed:** SRI.
    Description: Covers the car and light truck fleet market.

629.2   US
AUTOMOTIVE INDUSTRIES. (Annual Statistical Number) 1895. m. $55. Chilton Co., Chilton Way, Radnor, PA 19089. TEL 215-964-4255. Ed. J. McElroy. adv.; bk.rev.; charts; illus.; tr.lit.; s-a. index; circ. 95,000. (also avail. in microfilm from UMI,PMC; microfiche from UMI; reprint service avail. from UMI) **Indexed:** A.S.& T.Ind., B.P.I., Bus.Ind., CAD CAM Abstr., Educ.Ind., Eng.Ind., Excerp.Med., Ind.Sci.Rev., ISMEC, Met.Abstr., PROMT, Robomat, SRI, Tr.& Indus.Ind., World Alum.Abstr.
    ●Also available online. Vendor(s): DIALOG, Mead Data Central.
    Former titles: Chilton's Automotive Industries (ISSN 0273-656X); (until 1976): Automotive Industries (ISSN 0005-1527)
    Description: Contains comprehensive information on all aspects of the automobile industry. Subjects covered may include new cars production scheduling, inventory control, materials development, personnel management techniques, robotics and automation applications and European manufacturing.

338.476   SA   ISSN 1018-8371
AUTOMOTIVE INDUSTRIES (YEAR). (Text in English) a. South African Foreign Trade Organisation, Publishing Division, P.O. Box 782706, Sandton 2146, South Africa. TEL 011-883-3737. FAX 011-883-6569. TELEX 4-24111 SA. adv.; index.
    Formerly: Automotive (Year).

380.5   II
AUTOMOTIVE INDUSTRY OF INDIA - FACTS & FIGURES. (Text in English) 1966. a. Rs.50. All-India Automobile and Ancillary Industries Association, 80 Dr. Annie Besant Rd., Worli, Bombay 400018, India. Ed. S. Panikar. circ. 1,000.
    Formerly: Automotive and Ancillary Industry.

629.222   US   ISSN 0898-2155
AUTOMOTIVE INVESTOR. m. $79 (foreign $137). Mary Ann Liebert, Inc., 1651 Third Ave., New York, NY 10128. TEL 212-289-2300. FAX 212-289-4697. Ed. Richard M. Langworth. charts; illus.; mkt.; tr.lit.
    Description: Financial newsletter for buyers, sellers, and collectors of vintage, classic, and special-interest cars, 1925 onwards. Provides contacts for technical information, analyzes market trends and investment opportunities.

AUTOMOTIVE LITIGATION REPORTER; the twice monthly national reporting service of litigation concerning common automotive defects. see *LAW*

388.3   US
AUTOMOTIVE MARKET REPORT. 1951. w. $68. Automotive Auction Publishing, Inc., 1200 Fulton Bldg., Pittsburgh, PA 15222. TEL 412-281-2338. Ed. Clyde K. Hillwig. adv.; mkt.; circ. 10,000. **Indexed:** PROMT.
    Formerly: Automotive Market Report and Auto Week (ISSN 0005-1543)

388.476 380.1   US
AUTOMOTIVE MARKETING WHO'S WHO A P A A SHOW DIRECTORY. 1976. a. (Automotive Parts and Accessories Association) Chilton Co., Chilton Way, Radnor, PA 19089. TEL 215-964-4226. adv.; circ. 15,000.

629.286   UK   ISSN 0963-7109
▼**AUTOMOTIVE MATERIALS.** 1991. 4/yr. Shephard Press Ltd., 111 High St., Burnham, Bucks SL1 7JZ, England. TEL 0628-604311. FAX 0628-664334. (In U.S.: 14 S. Hill Rd., Colonia, NJ 07067. TEL 908-388-4245) Ed. Peter Donaldson. adv.; circ. 12,500.
    Description: Covers the selection and buying of materials in the automotive industry.

388.3   US   ISSN 0045-1088
AUTOMOTIVE MESSENGER. 1957. m. $10. Hansen Publishing Inc., 431 Chez Paree, Hazelwood, MO 63042. FAX 314-831-3610. Ed. H. Hansen. adv.; bibl.; charts; illus.; pat.; tr.lit.; circ. 11,000. (tabloid format)

388.3 629.2   US   ISSN 0005-1551
TL1
AUTOMOTIVE NEWS; engineering, financial, manufacturing, sales, marketing, servicing. 1925. w. $75 (effective Jan. 1992). Crain Communications Inc., (Detroit), Automotive News, 1400 Woodbridge Ave., Detroit, MI 48207. TEL 313-446-6000. Ed. Peter Brown. adv.; bk.rev.; charts; illus.; mkt.; stat.; tr.lit.; circ. 79,000. (tabloid format; also avail. in microform from UMI,PMC) **Indexed:** Acad.Ind., B.P.I., Bus.Ind., PROMT, SRI, Tr.& Indus.Ind.
    —BLDSC shelfmark: 1834.100000.

629.2   US
AUTOMOTIVE NEWS MARKET DATA BOOK. 1933. a. $37.50 (effective Jan. 1992). Crain Communications, Inc. (Detroit), Automotive News, 1400 Woodbridge Ave., Detroit, MI 48207. TEL 313-446-6000. Ed. Peter Brown. adv.; circ. 79,000. (also avail. in microform from UMI; reprint service avail. from UMI)
    Formerly: Automotive News Almanac (ISSN 0067-2580)

388.3   US   ISSN 0005-156X
AUTOMOTIVE NEWS OF THE PACIFIC NORTHWEST. 1919. m. $10. 14789 S.E. 82nd Dr., Clackamas, OR 97015-9624. FAX 503-656-1547. Ed. William H. Boyer. adv.; bk.rev.; illus.; tr.lit.; circ. 4,800.

388.3   US   ISSN 0896-3614
AUTOMOTIVE PARTS INTERNATIONAL. 1986. s-m. $425. International Trade Services, Box 5950, Bethesda, MD 20824-5950. TEL 202-857-8454. FAX 301-229-2077. Ed. Ronald J. DeMarines. (back issues avail.)
    ●Also available online.
    Description: Reports on news and trends involving the auto parts industry worldwide.

629.288   US   ISSN 0567-2317
TL1
AUTOMOTIVE REBUILDER; the independent voice of the rebuilding industry. (Includes Purchasing Directory published in Jan.) 1964. 12/yr. $79. Babcox Publications, 11 S. Forge St., Box 1810, Akron, OH 44309-1810. TEL 216-535-6117. FAX 216-535-0874. Ed. Dave Wooldridge. adv.; circ. 476 (paid); 22,402 (controlled).
    Description: Serves engine and vehicle mechanical parts rebuilders.

629   US
AUTOMOTIVE RECYCLING. 1975. bi-m. $30. Automotive Dismantlers and Recyclers Association, 10400 Eaton Pl., Ste. 203, Fairfax, VA 22030-2208. TEL 703-385-1001. Ed. Kristine L. Moore. adv.; circ. 4,000.
    Former titles: Dismantlers Digest; Automotive Recycler and Merchandiser; Auto Wrecker.

388.324   UK
AUTOMOTIVE REPAIR & RE-MANUFACTURE. 1983. q. £15. E.R. Publicity Services, 112 Manor Rd., Chigwell, Essex 1G7 5PW, England. TEL 01-501-2377. Ed. Walter Reeves. circ. 1,100. (back issues avail.)
    Description: Automotive engine reconditioning and the parts, services, and machinery available in this market.

388.3   CN   ISSN 0005-1578
AUTOMOTIVE RETAILER. 1947. m. Can.$24. Automotive Retailers' Publishing Co. Ltd., 4281 Canada Way, Ste.120, Burnaby, V5G 4P1, Canada. TEL 604-432-7987. FAX 604-432-1756. Ed. Reg Romero. adv.; bk.rev.; circ. 5,000. **Indexed:** Can.B.P.I.

AUTOMOTIVE, TOOLING, METALWORKING, AND ASSOCIATED INDUSTRIES. NEWSLETTER. see *OCCUPATIONAL HEALTH AND SAFETY*

388.3 658   US   ISSN 0889-3918
AUTOMOTIVE WEEK. 1975. w. $110. Automotive Week Publishing Co., Box 3495, Wayne, NJ 07474-3495. TEL 201-694-7792. Ed. Chuck Laverty. adv.; s-a index. (back issues avail.)
    Formerly: Automotive Buyer.
    Description: Covers merchandise, marketing, trends and fast-breaking news reports of auto replacement market retailers, wholesalers and distributors.

388   IT
AUTOMOTO GIORNALE. 1970. m. L.2500. Club de Commone, c/o Lorenzo Janni, Ed., Via Cavour 38, 20094 Corsico (Milan), Italy. adv.; circ. 30,000.

TRANSPORTATION — AUTOMOBILES

388.3 AG ISSN 0005-1608
AUTOMOTOR.* 1960. m. Arg.$5.00($7.) Erwin Toppelberg, Santiago del Estero 643, Buenos Aires, Argentina. Ed. Diego Perez Cevallos. adv.; charts; illus.; index; circ. 13,500.

338.3 SP
AUTOMOVIL. m. Luike - Motorpress, Ancora 40, 28045 Madrid, Spain. TEL 91-3470100. FAX 91-3470143. Dir. Carlos Hernandez. circ. 75,000.

388.3 VE ISSN 0005-1616
AUTOMOVIL DE VENEZUELA. 1961. m. Bs.720($55) *Ortiz & Asociados s.r.l., Calle Sorbona, Edif. Marta, Piso 1, Ofic. 18, Colinas de Bello Monte, Caracas, Venezuela. TEL 58-2-751-1355. FAX 58-2-751-11-22. TELEX 27474 ORTIZ VC. Ed. Armando Ortiz P. adv.; circ. 7,500 (controlled).

388.3 SP
AUTOMOVILISMO EN ESPANA. (Includes special nos.) 1942. m. 2200 ptas. Editorial Borrmart, S.A., Ramon de la Cruz 68, Madrid 1, Spain. Ed. Ramon Borreda Garcia. adv.; bk.rev.; bibl.; illus.; stat.; index; circ. 17,500.

629.286 KE
AUTONEWS. (Text in English) 1930. m. EAs.300($30) membership. (Automobile Association of Kenya) News Publishers Ltd., 4th Fl., Norwich Union Bldg., Mama Ngina St., Nairobi, Kenya. Ed. Clive Mutiso. adv.; bk.rev.; charts; illus.; circ. 15,000 (controlled).

629.286 CN ISSN 0827-2808
AUTOPARTS DISTRIBUTOR. 1984. 9/yr. $24. A P D Publishing Inc., 491 Elinton Ave., W., Ste. 307, Toronto, Ont. M5N 1A8, Canada. TEL 415-480-1380. Ed. Edward Belitsky. adv.

388.3 US ISSN 1045-1978
▼**AUTOPARTS REPORT**; news and analysis of the changing autoparts industry. 1990. 24/yr. $297 (foreign $357). Cutter Information Corp., 37 Broadway, Arlington, MA 02174. TEL 617-648-8700. FAX 617-648-8707. TELEX 650 100 9891 MCI UW. Ed. Steven Weitzman.
● Also available online. Vendor(s): Data-Star, DIALOG, NewsNet.
Description: Provides analysis of new marketing techniques, tracks the forces of consolidation, and explains the effects of industry changes.

614.86 CN ISSN 0836-1630
AUTOPINION. 1981. a. Can.$4.95. Canadian Automobile Association, 1775 Courtwood Cres., Ottawa, Ont. K2C 3J2, Canada. TEL 613-226-7631. FAX 613-225-7383. TELEX 053-4440. Ed. David Steventon.
Description: Published for the consumer and automobile enthusiast. Contains specifications, editorial copy and feature articles on new and used automobiles.

629.2 SP ISSN 0567-2392
AUTOPISTA. 1957. w. 1200 ptas. Luike - Motorpress, Ancora 40, 28045 Madrid, Spain. TEL 91-3470100. FAX 91-3470135. Eds. Carlos Hernandez Herrero, Luis de Madariaga. adv.; circ. 90,000 (controlled). (back issues avail.)

388.3 IT ISSN 0005-1683
AUTORAMA; panoramica mensile delle attivita motoristiche. 1956. m. L.6000. Autorama s.r.l., Via Manzoni 38, 20121 Milan, Italy. Ed. Giovanni L. Cernuschi. adv.

629.2 LU
AUTOREVUE. 1948. m. B.P. 231, L-2012 Luxembourg, Luxembourg. TEL 22-99-3. Ed. Paul Neyens. illus.; circ. 10,000.

796.77 796.75 ER ISSN 0868-4405
▼**AUTOREVUU**. 1990. m. $30. Kirjastus Perioodika, Parnu mnt. 8, 200090 Tallinn, Estonia. TEL 0142-441-262. FAX 0142-442-484. (Subscr. to: Akateeminen Kirjakauppa, 128 SF, 00101 Helsinki, Finland) Ed. Roland Hurt. stat.; circ. 9,000.

629.286 IT
AUTORIPARATORE, IL GOMMISTA, ELETTRAUTO. bi-m. L.120000. Edizioni Pubblire, Corso Garibaldi, 42, 20121 Milan, Italy. TEL 02-801529. FAX 02-801520. adv.; circ. 10,000.
Formerly: Autoriparatore; Incorporates: Gommista.

388.3 IT
AUTORUOTE 4X4. 1986. m. (11/yr.). L.110000 in Europe; America L.150000. Publimedia Societa Editrice, Corso Venezia 18, 20121 Milan, Italy. TEL 02-77521. FAX 02-781068. Ed. Francesco Buffa di Perrero. (back issues avail.)

388.3 II ISSN 0005-0695
AUTOSPARK. 1949. m. Rs.300($25) 101 Vijay Apts., C.D. Barfiwala Marg, Andheri (West), Bombay 400058, India. TEL 6212733. Ed. Vijay Kumar Vats. adv.; bk.rev.; charts; illus.; mkt.; stat.; circ. 12,000.

AUTOSPORT; specializovano nedeljno izdanje jugoslavenskog sportskog lista "Sport". see *SPORTS AND GAMES*

796.72 UK
AUTOSPORT. 1950. w. £135($149) Haymarket Specialist Magazines Ltd., 60 Waldegrave Road, Teddington, Middx. TW11 8LG, England. TEL 081-943-5000. FAX 081-943-5922. TELEX 895-2440-HAYMRT-G. Ed. Peter Foubister. charts; illus.; stat. (processed; also avail. in microform from UMI)
Description: Details automobile racing.

796.77 IT
AUTOSPORT. 1975. m. L.10000. (Autosport) Edicentro S.r.l., Via Giuseppe Mantellini 18, Rome 00179, Italy. Ed. Anselmo Baffigi. adv.; circ. 110,000.

388.3 IT ISSN 0005-1748
AUTOSPRINT. 1961. w. L.190000. Conti Editore S.p.A., Via del Lavoro 7, 40068 San Lazzaro di Savena, Bologna, Italy. TEL (051) 6227111. FAX 6255418. TELEX 510272. Ed. Carlo Cavicchi. adv.; bk.rev.; circ. 113,564.
Description: Focuses on racing cars.

796.77 IT
AUTOSPRINT ANNO. 1970. a. L.8000. Conti Editore S.p.A., Via del Lavoro 7, 40068 S. Lazzaro di Savena (Bologna), Italy. TEL (051) 6227111. FAX 6255418. Ed. Carlo Cavicchi. adv.; circ. 60,000.
Description: Focuses on racing cars.

629.2 BE
AUTOTECHNICA; la revue du professionnel de l'automobile. (Editions in Dutch, French) m. 1800 BEF. Chambre Syndicale du Commerce Automobile de Belgique, Bd. de la Woluwe 46, B-9, B-1200 Brussels, Belgium.
Formerly: Chambre Syndicale du Commerce Automobile de Belgique. Bulletin Mensuel.

388.3 AG
AUTOTECNICA.* vol.37, 1972. m. Union Propietarios de Talleres Mecanicos de Automoviles, Alsina 2540, Buenos Aires, Argentina. Ed. Jose F. Vinotto. adv.; illus.

629.286 IT
AUTOTECNICA. m. (11/yr.). L.65000 (foreign L.130000). N.P.M. s.r.l., Via Molise 3, 20085 Locate Triulzi (MI), Italy. TEL 02-90780478. Ed. Sandro Colombo.

338.476 UK
AUTOTRADE. m. $140. Morgan-Grampian (Publishers) Ltd., Morgan-Grampian House, 30 Calderwood St., London SE18 6QH, England. TEL 01-855-7777. FAX 01-854-7476. Ed. Susan Gay. adv.; circ. 40,085.
Description: Covers all aspects of the automotive trades, including service garages, bodyshops, accessory retailers and distributors.

388.3 GW
DER AUTOVERMIETER. 1955. q. DM.59.35 (foreign DM.60.70). (Bundesverband der Automieter Deutschlands) Heinrich Vogel Fachzeitschriften GmbH, Neumarkter Str. 18, Postfach 802020, 8000 Munich 80, Germany. TEL 089-43180-0. Ed. Heinzmartin Nitsche. adv.; bk.rev.; illus.; index; circ. 1,600.
Formerly (until 1986): Kraftfahrzeugvermieter (ISSN 0023-4400)
Description: Discusses automobile rentals.

388.3 SW ISSN 0005-1799
AUTOVETERANEN. 1959. 6/yr. membership. Swedish Veteran Car Club, Dejefors, 66900 Deje, Sweden. Ed. Eric Lofberg. adv.; illus.

388.3 NE ISSN 0005-0873
AUTOVISIE;* independent automobile magazine. 1956. 26/yr. fl.112.50. B.V. Uitgeversmaatschappij Bonaventura, Hoogoorddreef 60, 1101 BE Amsterdam, Netherlands. TEL 20-5674911. FAX 20-5674629. TELEX 14013 BONAV NL. Ed. N. de Jong. adv.; bk.rev.; circ. 52,450. **Indexed**: Excerp.Med.

388.3 US ISSN 0005-1802
AUTOWEEK. 1958. w. $28. Crain Communications, Inc. (Detroit), 1400 Woodridge Ave., Detroit, MI 48207-3187. TEL 313-446-6000. FAX 313-446-1650. TELEX 810-221-5122. (Subscr. to: 965 E. Jefferson, Detroit, MI 48207) Ed. Matt DeLorenzo. adv.; bk.rev.; illus.; circ. 268,595.
● Also available online. Vendor(s): Mead Data Central.
Formerly: Autoweek and Competition Press.
Description: Covers new domestic and imported cars and trucks. Gives driving impressions, road tests and evaluations.

388.3 UK ISSN 0005-1829
AUTOWORLD. 1962. 4/yr. £6. Renault U.K. Ltd., Western Ave., London W3 ORZ, England. Ed. Marguerite Nudd. adv.; bk.rev.; charts; circ. 150,000.
Formerly: Ici Renault.

388.3 GW
AUTOZEITUNG. 1969. fortn. DM.143. Heinrich Bauer Verlag, Burchardstr. 11, 2000 Hamburg 1, Germany. TEL 040-3019-0. FAX 040-326589. Ed. Guenter Wiechmann. circ. 180,225.

629.22 US ISSN 0149-1911
TL215.A94
AVANTI OWNERS ASSOCIATION NEWSLETTER.* q. $7.50. Avanti Owners Association International, Box 322, Uxbridge, MA 01569. Key Title: Newsletter - Avanti Owners Association.

629.2 796.7 388.3 XV
AVTO; Jugoslovanska avtomobilisticna revija. 1967. fortn. Delo Revije p.o., Dunajska 5, 61000 Ljubljana, Slovenia. Ed. Ivan Vidic.

338.3 RU ISSN 0005-2337
AVTOMOBIL'NAYA PROMYSHLENNOST'. 1934. m. 7.20 Rub. Izdatel'stvo Mashinostroenie, 4, Stromynsky Lane, Moscow, 107076, Russia. Ed. V.P. Morozov. adv.; bk.rev.; bibl.; charts; illus.; index; circ. 13,000. **Indexed**: Agri.Eng.Abstr., Biol.Abstr., Chem.Abstr., Met.Abstr., World Alum.Abstr.
—BLDSC shelfmark: 0003.100000.

AVTOMOBIL'NYE DOROGI. see *ENGINEERING — Civil Engineering*

388.3 RU ISSN 0005-2345
TL4 CODEN: AVTRAN
AVTOMOBIL'NYI TRANSPORT. 1923. m. 6 Rub. (Ministerstvo Transporta) Concern " Rosavtotrans", Likhov per 3, 103051 Moscow, Russia. TEL 200-20-02. Ed. E.P. Kuprin. charts; illus. **Indexed**: Chem.Abstr.
—BLDSC shelfmark: 0005.000000.

B A R C NEWS. (British Automobile Racing Club) see *SPORTS AND GAMES*

388.3 US
B C I NEWS. q. free to members. Battery Council International, 401 N. Michigan Ave., Chicago, IL 60611. TEL 312-644-6610. Ed. Larry Fleischman. circ. 725.

388.3 GW
B M W CLUB JOURNAL. (Text in English and German) 1984. q. DM.14. B M W Club Europa e.V., Petuelring 130, 8000 Munich 40, Germany. TEL 089-3508281. FAX 089-38954209. adv.; bk.rev.; circ. 15,000.

796.77 157.61 UK ISSN 0267-9841
BACK STREET HEROES. 1983. m. £19.20. Myatt McFarlane plc, P.O. Box 28, Altrincham, Cheshire WA15 8SH, England. TEL 061-928-3480. FAX 061-941-6897. Ed. Ian Hodge. adv.; bk.rev.; circ. 50,000. (back issues avail.)
Description: Covers motorcycles with particular emphasis on customizing and performance.

388.3　　　　　　FR　ISSN 0005-6197
BASSE NORMANDIE AUTOMOBILE. 1949. m. free. Chambre Syndicale Nationale du Commerce et de la Reparation Automobile, Secteur Regional Basse-Normandie, 4 rue Pasteur, B.P. No. 7, 14011 Caen Cedex, France. Ed. Jean P. Pellan. adv.; circ. 1,000 (controlled).

BATTERIES INTERNATIONAL. see ENGINEERING — Electrical Engineering

629.2 621.38　　　US　ISSN 0005-6359
BATTERY MAN; international journal for starting, lighting, ignition & generating systems. 1921; N.S. 1959. m. $12. Independent Battery Manufacturers Association, Inc., 100 Larchwood Dr., Largo, FL 34640. TEL 813-586-1408. Ed. Celwyn E. Hopkins. adv.; bk.rev.; charts; illus.; tr.lit.; index; circ. 5,500. Indexed: Cadscan, Lead Abstr., PROMT, Zincscan. —BLDSC shelfmark: 1866.620000.
　　Description: Looks at automobile electrical system servicing.

388.3　　　　　　GW　ISSN 0005-7061
DAS BAYERISCHE KRAFTFAHRZEUGHANDWERK. 1955. a. Autohaus Verlag GmbH, Alte Landstr. 8-10, 8012 Ottobrunn B, Germany. TEL 089-60805-0. Ed. Klemens G. Lang. illus.; circ. 6,000.

388　　　　　　　　JA
BEST CAR. (Text in Japanese) 1978. s-m. Kodansha Ltd., International Division, 12-21 Otowa 2-chome, Bunkyo-ku, Tokyo 112, Japan. TEL 03-3945-1111. FAX 03-3943-7815. TELEX J34509 KODANSHA. Ed. Yu Katsumata. circ. 470,000.
　　Formerly: Best Car Guide.
　　Description: For car enthusiasts.

388 388.413　　　NO　ISSN 0800-5850
BIL. (Text in Norwegian) 1975. 10/yr. NOK 225. Fagbladforlaget AS, Urtegaten 9, P.O. Box 9247, Vaterland, 0134 Oslo 1, Norway. TEL 02-680313. FAX 02-682085. Ed. Jan Johansson. circ. 68,000.
　　Description: Includes results of testing of new cars and car related products. Covers technical features, in-car entertainment equipment.

629.222　　　　　DK　ISSN 0006-2332
BIL OG MOTOR. m. DKK 225 (typically set in Jan.). Danmarks Automobilforhandler Forening, Alhambravej 5, 1826 Frederiksberg C, Denmark. FAX 31-313075. adv.; circ. 2,700.

388.3　　　　　　DK　ISSN 0107-0924
BIL-REVYEN. a. DKK 114.50. Bonniers Specialmagasiner A-S, Strandboulevarden 130, 2100 Copenhagen OE, Denmark. adv.; circ. 80,000.
　　Description: Full color catalogue of more than 1000 cars from all over the world.

388.3　　　　　　NO　ISSN 0006-2367
BILBRANSJEN - BILTEKNISK FAGBLAD. 1929. m. $20. Norges Bilbransjeforbund, Drammensv. 97, Oslo 2, Norway. Ed. Oyvind Holmvik. adv.; charts; illus.; stat.; tr.lit.; circ. 5,000.
　　Formerly: Bilbransjen; Incorporates: Oljebladet (ISSN 0030-2120).

796.77　　　　　　DK
BILEN. 1967. m. DKK 34.50. Bonniers Specialmagasiner A-S, Strandboulevarden 130, 2100 Copenhagen OE, Denmark. Ed. Klaus Lyngfeldt.
　　Former titles: Bilen, Motor og Sport & Bilen og Baaden (ISSN 0006-2464)
　　Description: Car testing, special techniques and car racing.

388.3　　　　　　DK　ISSN 0901-6120
BILISMEN I DANMARK. 1967. a. free. Automobil-Importoerernes Sammenslutning, Ryvangs Alle 68, DK-2900 Hellerup, Denmark. Ed. Kai Noerrung.
　　Description: Lists new-registered vehicles and vehicles in use, by make.

388.3　　　　　　IC
BILLINN. bi-m. ISK 386 per no. Frodi Ltd., Armula 18, 105 Reykjavik, Iceland. TEL 354-1-812300. FAX 1-812946. Ed. Leo M. Jonsson. adv.; circ. 9,000.
　　Former titles: Bilabladid Billinn; Bilabladid Oekuthor.

796.77　　　　　　SW
BILSPORT. 1962. fortn. SEK 649. Stig L Sjoeberg, P.O. Box 529, 371 23 Karlskrona, Sweden. Ed. Gert Karlsson. adv.; circ. 75,100.

388.3　　　　　　US　ISSN 0897-9421
THE BLUE SEAL. 1984. s-a. free. National Institute for Automotive Service Excellence, 13505 Dulles Technology Dr., Herndon, VA 22071-3415. TEL 703-713-3800. FAX 703-713-0727. Ed. Martin Lawson. bk.rev.; stat.; circ. 425,000.
　　Description: For mechanics who have passed ASE certification exams, and their employers.

388.33 629.2　　UK　ISSN 0006-5501
BODY. 1919. m. £30 (Europe £46). Vehicle Builders and Repairers Association (VBRA), Belmont House, 102 Finkle Lane, Gildersome, Leeds LS27 7TW, England. TEL 0532-538333. FAX 0532-380496. Ed. Judi Barton. adv.; illus.; stat.; circ. 9,250.
　　—BLDSC shelfmark: 2117.200000.

629.286　　　　　US
BODY ENGINEERING. s-a. American Society of Body Engineers, 25875 Jefferson, St. Clair Shores, MI 48081. TEL 313-774-8180. Ed. Robert Szefi. adv.; tr.lit.; circ. 5,225. (reprint service avail.) Indexed: Met.Abstr., World Alum.Abstr.

629.286　　　　　US
BODY LANGUAGE. 1982. m. $70 includes Collision Parts Journal. (Aftermarket Body Parts Association) Sarco Management and Publications, 2500 Wilcrest Dr., Ste. 510, Houston, TX 77042-2752. TEL 800-323-5832. Ed. Stan Rodman. circ. 865.
　　Description: Covers automobile repair industry including updates on legislation, regulation and legal activities as they affect the state of collision repair and the use of aftermarket (non-OEM) replacement body parts.

388.3　　　　　　CN　ISSN 0045-2319
BODYSHOP. 1970. bi-m. Can.$13.91($21) (foreign $21). Southam Business Communications Inc., 1450 Don Mills Rd., Don Mills, Ont. M3B 2X7, Canada. TEL 416-445-6641. FAX 416-442-2261. Ed. Brian Harper. adv.; circ. 13,500.

629.286　　　　　US　ISSN 0730-7241
BODYSHOP BUSINESS; the Bobcox magazine for the body repair industry. (BodyShop Business Profit Handbook - April) 1982. 13/yr. $75. Babcox Publications, 11 S. Forge St., Box 1810, Akron, OH 44309-1810. TEL 216-535-6117. FAX 216-535-0874. Ed. John Norton. adv.; tr.lit.; circ. 709 (paid); 54,386 (controlled). (reprint service avail.)
　　Description: Edited for the owners and managers of collision repair shops. Features management and technical articles to help run a better business.

388.3　　　　　　NE　ISSN 0006-839X
BOVAGBLAD. 1938. 24/yr. fl.92. Stichting Bovag Orgaan - Motor Agents' Association, Postbus 1100, 3980 DC Bunnik, Netherlands. FAX 03405-67855. Ed. B.J. Th. de Bruijn. adv.; bk.rev.; circ. 18,500.

629.286　　　　　AT
BOYCE'S SERVICE STATION MANUAL. 1985. a. Aus.$60($70) David Boyce Publishing and Associates, 44 Regent Street, Redfern, N.S.W. 2016, Australia. circ. 2,500.
　　Description: For mechanics servicing the auto industry.

388.3　　　　　　US
BRACKET RACING, U S A. 1989. bi-m. $16. C S K Publishing Co., Inc., 299 Market St., Saddle Brook, NJ 07662. TEL 201-712-9300. FAX 201-712-9899. (Subscr. to: Box 1010, Denville, NJ 07834) Ed. Steve Collison. adv.; tr.lit.; circ. 24,500. (back issues avail.)
　　Description: Geared toward bracket racers, with information on staging, reaction time, rollout, finish line strategies, vehicle preparation, safety equipment, and coverage of all major events.

388.33　　　　　US　ISSN 0193-726X
TL275.A1
BRAKE AND FRONT END; for the undercar service merchandiser. (Includes Life Guide published in Mar.) 1931. 12/yr. $70. (Babcox Publications) Babcox Publications, 11 S. Forge St., Box 1810, Akron, OH 44309-1810. TEL 216-535-6117. FAX 216-535-0874. Ed. Mary DellaValle. adv.; bk.rev.; illus.; charts; index; circ. 27,500.
　　Formerly: Brake and Front End Service (ISSN 0006-9019)

388.3　　　　　　US
BRITISH CAR. 1985. bi-m. $16.95 (foreign $34.95). Box 9099, Canoga Park, CA 91309. TEL 818-710-1234. FAX 818-710-1877. Ed. Dave Destler. adv.; bk.rev.; circ. 35,000.
　　Formerly: British Car and Bike.

BRITISH RACING NEWS. see SPORTS AND GAMES

796.72　　　　　　CN　ISSN 0045-3226
BROKEN SPOKE. 1958. bi-m. Can.$8. Calgary Sports Car Club, P.O. Box 61143 Kensington Postal Stn., Calgary, Alta. T2N 4S6, Canada. TEL 403-285-1177. FAX 403-270-3525. Ed. Ross Farnham. adv.; circ. 200 (controlled).
　　Description: Covers club, regional motorsport news, coming events in the western Canada area and technical articles pertaining to racing automobiles.

388 910.09　　　US　ISSN 0162-9689
TL232
BUS WORLD; magazine of buses and bus systems. 1978. q. $14 (Canada $16; elsewhere $24). Stauss Publications, Box 39, Woodland Hills, CA 91365. TEL 818-710-0208. Ed. Julian Wolinsky. adv.; bk.rev.; charts; illus.; circ. 5,500.

796.77　　　　　　AT
BUSHDRIVER. 1977. bi-m. Aus.$23($29.10) Ric Williams and Associates Pty. Ltd., 25 Valley Park Cres., Turramurra, N.S.W. 2074, Australia. FAX 02-488-8550. Ed. Ric Williams. adv.; charts; illus.; tr.lit.; circ. 20,000. (back issues avail.)
　　Description: Contains articles on travel and vehicle tests. Provides a historical background and tips on four-wheel drive.

BUSINESS DRIVER. see BUSINESS AND ECONOMICS — Marketing And Purchasing

388.3　　　　　　GW　ISSN 0178-9988
BUSKURSBUCH. 1984. s-a. DM.34. Deutsche Bundesbahn Zentrale, Kaiserstr. 3, Postfach 1569, D-6500 Mainz 1, Germany. circ. 14,000.

388.3　　　　　　SW　ISSN 0282-7654
BUSS - SVENSK OMNIBUSTIDNING/SWEDISH BUS & COACH MAGAZINE. 1929. 10/yr. SEK 315. Bussfoerlaget AB, Gammelgaardsvaegen 21, 112 64 Stockholm, Sweden. TEL 08-130105. FAX 08-137600. Ed. Bjarne Wilmarsgaard. adv.; charts; illus.; stat.; index; circ. 4,122.
　　Formerly: Svensk Omnibustidning (ISSN 0039-6672)

388.3　　　　　　CN
▼**C A A NEWS AND VIEWS**. (Editions in English and French) 1991. bi-m. Canadian Automobile Association, 1775 Courtwood Cres., Ottawa, Ont. K2C 3J2, Canada. TEL 613-226-7631. FAX 613-225-7383. TELEX 053-4440. Ed. David Leonhardt. circ. 600.

C A M S REPORT. (Confederation of Australian Motor Sport) see SPORTS AND GAMES

629.286　　　　　FR
C R A; commerce reparation automobile. w. 320 F. Publi-Inter, 75 rue Voltaire, 92532 Levallois-Perret, France. Ed. Remy Thibault. adv.

388.3　　　　　　UK
CAB DRIVER. 1921. fortn. £8. (National Federation of Taxicab Associations) London Publishing Company, 15 Harewood Avenue, London NW1 GLX, England. adv.; bk.rev.; illus.; circ. 12,000.
　　Incorporates: Steering Wheel (ISSN 0039-0984)

796.77 910.09　　US
CALIFORNIA EVENTS ANNUAL. a. $7.95. Camaro Publishing Co., 90430 World Way Center, Los Angeles, CA 90009. TEL 213-837-7500.

TRANSPORTATION — AUTOMOBILES

796.77   US
CALIFORNIA SPORTS CAR. 1980. m. Pfanner Communications, Inc., 1371 E. Warner Ave., Ste. E, Tustin, CA 92680-6442. TEL 714-259-8240. FAX 714-259-9377. Ed. Jane Shaw. adv.; circ. 3,787.

796.77   US
CAMARO AMERICA NEWSLETTER.* 1981. m. $20. Camaro Owners of America, Inc., 10 Green Ridge St., Scranton, PA 18509-1828. circ. 2,500. (back issues avail.)

796.77   US
CAMARO CORRAL. 1984. bi-m. $20. United States Camaro Club, Inc., Box 608167, Orlando, FL 32860-8167. TEL 407-880-1967. FAX 407-880-1972. Ed. Ken Moorhead. adv.; bk.rev.; charts; illus.; stat.; circ. 15,000. (back issues avail.)
 Description: For the collector, restorer, driver and enthusiast of the Chevrolet Camaro car.

796.77   US
CAMARO TRANS-AM. a. $3.50 per no. McMullen Publishing, 2145 W. La Palma Ave., Anaheim, CA 92801. TEL 714-635-9040.

629.224   SP   ISSN 0211-2930
CAMBUS; actualidad tecnica del vehiculo industrial. 1970. 11/yr. 4000 ptas. Pedeca Sociedad Cooperativa, Ltda., Maria Auxiliadora 5, 28040 Madrid, Spain. TEL 459 60 00. Dir. Jose A. Rueda. circ. 10,000.

629   CN
CANADIAN AUTO REVIEW. Variant title: C A R. 8/yr. Can.$24.61($30) (foreign $30). Southam Communications, Inc., 1450 Don Mills Rd., Don Mills, Ont. M3B 2X7, Canada. TEL 416-445-6641. FAX 416-442-2213. Ed. Richard Jacobs. circ. 7,600.
 Description: For the new car and truck dealer industry. Includes product news and features.

388.3   CN   ISSN 0707-624X
CANADIAN AUTOMOBILE ASSOCIATION. ANNUAL REPORT. (Text in English, French) 1959. a. free. Canadian Automobile Association, 1775 Courtwood Cres., Ottawa, Ont. K2C 3J2, Canada. TEL 613-226-7631. FAX 613-225-7383. TELEX 053-4440.

388   CN
CANADIAN AUTOMOBILE ASSOCIATION. C A A PUBLIC POLICY. 1981. irreg. Canadian Automobile Association, 1775 Courtwood Cresc., Ottawa, Ont. K2C 3J2, Canada. TEL 613-226-7631. FAX 613-225-7383. TELEX 053-4440. Ed. David Leonhardt. circ. 3,000.
 Formerly: Canadian Automobile Association. Public Policy Newsletter (ISSN 0838-0007)

388   CN   ISSN 0702-2441
CANADIAN AUTOMOBILE ASSOCIATION. STATEMENT OF POLICY. 1975. a. Canadian Automobile Association, 1775 Courtwood Cresc., Ottawa, Ont. K2C 3J2, Canada. TEL 613-226-7631. FAX 613-225-7383. TELEX 053-4440. Ed. Michael S. McNeil. circ. 4,000.
 Formerly: Canadian Automobile Association. Policies and Resolutions.

629.286   CN
CANADIAN AUTOMOTIVE FLEET. (Supplement avail.) 1984. bi-m. Bobit Publishing (Canada) Ltd., 152 Parliament St., Toronto, Ont. M5A 2Z1, Canada. TEL 416-864-1700. FAX 416-864-1498. Ed. Michael Goetz. adv.; circ. 12,200.

629.286   CN   ISSN 1180-2065
CANADIAN AUTOMOTIVE TECHNICIAN. 1989. q. Can.$18($26) Southam Business Information & Communications Group Inc., 1450 Don Mills Rd., Don Mills, Ont. M3B 2X7, Canada. TEL 416-442-2000. FAX 416-442-2077. Ed. David Booth. circ. 30,600.
 Description: Discusses technological advances of interest to automotive service professionals.

388.3   CN   ISSN 0008-2945
       CODEN: CAUTAB
CANADIAN AUTOMOTIVE TRADE. 1920. 10/yr. Can.$31. Southam Business Communications, Inc., 1450 Don Mills Rd., Don Mills, Ont. M3B 2X7, Canada. TEL 416-445-6641. FAX 416-442-2213. Ed. David Booth. adv.; bk.rev.; bibl.; charts; illus.; tr.lit.; circ. 30,088. (reprint service avail.) **Indexed:** Can.B.P.I.
 Description: Service repair industry magazine. Provides news about running an automotive garage.

338.476 658   CN
CANADIAN AUTOPARTS MARKETING. 1986. 8/yr. Can.$27. Southam Business Communications, Inc., 1450 Don Mills Rd., Don Mills, Ont. M3B 2X7, Canada. TEL 416-445-6641. FAX 416-442-2213. Ed. Dennis Mellersh. adv.; circ. 10,921.

388.3   CN   ISSN 0045-527X
CANADIAN RED BOOK; official used car valuations. (Text in English, French) 1959. m. Can.$60. Maclean-Hunter Ltd., Business Publication Division, Maclean-Hunter Bldg., 777 Bay St., Toronto, Ont. M5W 1A7, Canada. TEL 416-596-5082. Ed. S.A. Whittaker. adv.; circ. 11,500. (back issues avail.)

388   SP
CANARIAS MOTOR. 1968. 24/yr. Edican S.L., Italia 23, Primero, Las Palmas de Gran Canaria, Canary Islands. Ed. Rafael Calvo Molina. adv.; circ. 20,000.

388.3   SA   ISSN 0008-5995
CAR; the motoring journal of Southern Africa. 1957. m. (foreign R.62). Ramsay, Son & Parker (Pty) Ltd., Box 180, Howard Place 7450, Cape Town, South Africa. TEL 021-5311391. FAX 021-5313333. TELEX 526933 SA. Ed. David Trebett. adv.; charts; illus.; mkt.; stat.; circ. 136,475.
 Incorporates: Technicar (ISSN 0040-1013)
 Description: Publishes articles on new cars, motor sport, exotic cars, do-it-youself repairs, technical articles and car prices.

388.3   UK   ISSN 0008-5987
CAR. 1962. m. £29.40. F.F. Publishing Ltd., PO Box 2, Diss, Norfolk IP22 3AP, England. TEL 0379-650077. Ed. Gavin Green. adv.; illus.; mkt.; circ. 581.

388.3   UK
CAR & ACCESSORY TRADER. Short title: C A T. 1979. m. £24 £35. Haymarket Specialist Motoring Publications, Ltd., 60 Waldegrave Rd., Teddington, Middx. TW11 8LG, England. TEL 081-943-5000. FAX 081-943-5927. TELEX 895 2440 HAYMART G. Ed. David Jenkinson. adv.; circ. 17,458.
 Description: Contains news, features on trends, and information about cars and car accesspries.

388.3   US   ISSN 0008-6002
TL236
CAR AND DRIVER. 1955. m. $19.94. Hachette Magazines, Inc., 1633 Broadway, New York, NY 10009. TEL 212-767-6000. Ed. William Jean. adv.; bk.rev.; circ. 900,951. (also avail. in microform from UMI; microfiche from MIM) **Indexed:** Acad.Ind., Consum.Ind., HRIS, Mag.Ind., PMR, R.G., Sports Per.Ind., TOM.
 •Also available online. Vendor(s): DIALOG.

629.2   US
CAR AND DRIVER BUYERS GUIDE. 1957. a. $4.95. Hachette Magazines, Inc., 1633 Broadway, New York, NY 10009. TEL 212-767-6000. Ed. Don Coulter. adv.; circ. 155,000.
 Formerly: Car and Driver Yearbook (ISSN 0069-0260)

629.222   US
CAR AND DRIVER ROAD TEST ANNUAL. a. $4.95. Hachette Magazines, Inc., 1633 Broadway, 45th Fl., New York, NY 10009. TEL 800-289-9464. (Subscr. to: Box 51133, Boulder, CO 80321-1133) Ed. William Jeanes. adv.; bk.rev.; illus.; stat.; circ. 250,000.
 Description: Compiles road test evaluations of the preceding year, with comparisons of the most popular models.

629.286   GW
▼**CAR & HIFI.** 1990. m. DM.7($50) Michael E. Brieden Verlag, Ruhrorter Str. 9, 4200 Oberhausen, Germany. TEL 0208-20099. FAX 0208-803429.

629.288   US   ISSN 0008-6975
CAR & PARTS ANNUAL. 1983. a. $4.95. Amos Press Inc., 911 Vandemark Rd., Box 482, Sidney, OH 45365. TEL 513-498-0803. FAX 513-498-0808. Ed. Robert Stevens.
 Description: Covers various aspects of automobile maintenance and collection for collectors and restorers of antique automobiles.

CAR AUDIO & ELECTRONICS. see SOUND RECORDING AND REPRODUCTION

CAR AUDIO & FM; la prima rivista di musica in auto. see MUSIC

CAR AUDIO ANNUARIO; la guida mercato del car stereo. see ENGINEERING — Electrical Engineering

CAR BOOK (YEAR); an indispensable guide to the safest, most economical new cars. see CONSUMER EDUCATION AND PROTECTION

388   UK
CAR BUYER. 1976. w. £48.88. Shaw's Car Buyer Ltd., 182 Pentonville Rd., London N1 9LB, England. TEL 071-278-4393. FAX 071-837-6286. adv.; circ. 33,000.
 Description: Concerns new and second hand cars sold in London and the southeast counties.

629.286   US
CAR CARE NEWS. 1983. m. $24. 4010 Airline Dr., Houston, TX 77022. Ed. Jay Hagins. adv.; illus.
 Description: For do-it-yourself enthusiasts and those who are mechanically inclined.

629.222   US   ISSN 0164-5552
TL1
CAR COLLECTOR AND CAR CLASSICS. 1966. m. $32 (foreign $42). Classic Publishing, Inc., Box 28571, Atlanta, GA 30328. TEL 404-998-4603. Ed. Westley D. Peterson. adv.; bk.rev.; illus.; circ. 40,000.
 Incorporates (1979-1988): Nostalgic Cars; Which was formerly (until 1987): Car Exchange (ISSN 0164-0836); Formed by the 1979 merger of: Car Classics (ISSN 0095-0556); Car Collector.
 Description: Features factual articles on car history, opinion articles on current trends.

614.86   CN   ISSN 0705-1298
CAR COSTS. (Text in English) 1972. a. Canadian Automobile Association, 1775 Courtwood Cres., Ottawa, Ont. K2C 3J2, Canada. TEL 613-226-7631. FAX 613-225-7383.
 Description: Describes how to calculate costs of owning and operating an automobile in Canada.

796.72   US   ISSN 0008-6010
CAR CRAFT; the complete performance magazine. 1953. m. $19.94. Petersen Publishing Co., 8490 Sunset Blvd., Los Angeles, CA 90069. TEL 213-854-2222. Ed. John Baechtel. adv.; illus.; circ. 427,000. (also avail. in microform from UMI)
 Description: Covers automobile racing.

388.3   US   ISSN 0148-6721
CAR DEALER INSIDER NEWSLETTER. 1965. w. $235. Atcom, Inc., Atcom Bldg., 2315 Broadway, New York, NY 10024-4397. TEL 212-873-5900. FAX 212-799-1728. Ed. James Koscs. bk.rev.; charts; tr.lit.; circ. 3,000. (back issues avail.; reprint service avail. from UMI)
 Incorporates (1965-1989): Truck Insider Newsletter (ISSN 0041-3399)
 Description: For automobile dealers in the new car retailing business.

388.3   US
CAR FACTS. bi-m. $3.95 per no. Pace Publications (Milwaukee), 1020 N. Broadway, Ste. 111, Milwaukee, WI 53202. TEL 414-272-9977. FAX 414-272-9973.

629.22   JA   ISSN 0915-1702
CAR GRAPHIC. (Text in Japanese) 1962. m. 20000 Yen. Nigensha Publishing Co., Ltd., 2-2 Kanda Jinbo-cho, Chiyoda-ku, Tokyo 101, Japan. TEL 03-3239-0145. FAX 03-3239-0336. Ed. S. Kumakura. adv.; bk.rev.; circ. 200,000. **Indexed:** JTA. **Key Title:** C G, Car Graphic.

629.286   UK
CAR HI FI. 1986. bi-m. £20. Evro Publishing Co. Ltd., 60 Waldegrave Rd., Teddington, Middx. TW11 8LG, England. TEL 081-943-5943. Ed. Naj Marcuard. circ. 40,000. (back issues avail.)

629.2 UK ISSN 0008-6037
CAR MECHANICS. 1958. m. £19.95. A G B Publications Ltd., Audit House, Field End Rd., Ruislip, Middx. HA4 9LT, England. TEL 01-767-4499. FAX 01-429-3117. TELEX 926726. Ed. Mike Penny. adv.; bk.rev.; illus.; circ. 55,051.
Description: Targeted at the do-it-yourself enthusiast and the secondhand car buyer.

629.222 UK
CAR NUMBERS MAGAZINE. 1979. bi-m. £10. Hartley Publications, P.O. Box, Bradford-on-Avon, Wilshore BA15 1YQ, England. TEL 0225-782390. Ed. Tony Hill. circ. 50,000. (back issues avail.)

388.3 US
CAR PAGES; the magazine for New York City car owners. 1989. m. Gator Publications, 601 W. 112th St., Ste. 6E, New York, NY 10025. TEL 212-865-1903. Ed.Bd. adv.

388 658.8 US
CAR PRICES. 1965. a. $3.50 per no. People's Publishing Co., Inc., 5440 Ericson Way, Arcata, CA 95521. TEL 707-822-8442. FAX 707-822-0973. Ed. Rosemary Anderson. adv.; stat.; circ. 50,000.
Formerly: American Car Prices.
Description: Listing of dealer and retail prices of new model cars and trucks, domestic and foreign.

388.3 US ISSN 0008-6053
CAR RENTAL & LEASING INSIDER NEWSLETTER. 1963. bi-w. £235. Atcom, Inc., Atcom Bldg., 2315 Broadway, New York, NY 10024-4397. TEL 212-873-5900. FAX 212-799-1728. Ed. John Kirk. circ. 1,000. (reprint service avail. from UMI)
Formerly: Car and Truck Rental and Leasing Insider Newsletter.
Description: For professionals in the automobile rental and leasing industry.

388 JA
CAR ROAD. (Text in Japanese) 1978. m. 2640 Yen. Kotsu Times Co. Ltd., 4-3 Uchi-kanda 2-chome, Chiyoda-ku, Tokyo 101, Japan. Ed. Takayoshi Yamada.

629.296 JA
CAR STYLING. (Text in English, Japanese) 1973. bi-m. 11400 Yen($89.75) San'ei Shobo Publishing Co., 4-8-16, Kita-Shinjuku, Shinjuku-ku, Tokyo 169, Japan. TEL 03-364-4819. FAX 03-364-4819. Ed. Akira Fujimoto. adv.; bk.rev.; circ. 30,000. (back issues avail.) Indexed: JTA.
Description: Primarily features automobile design, but also includes other design fields.

388 JA
CAR TOP. (Text in Japanese) 1968. m. 2640 Yen. Kotsu Times Co. Ltd., 4-3 Uchi-kanda 2-chome, Chiyoda-ku, Tokyo 101, Japan. Ed. Shuichi Miyasaka.

388.3 658 US ISSN 1047-4404
CAR TRADER. m. (plus w. regional suppl.). $41.95. Heartland Communications Group, Inc., 900 Central Ave., Box 916, Fort Dodge, IA 50501. TEL 515-955-1600. FAX 800-247-2000. circ. 35,000.
Description: Source for locating classic and antique cars nationwide.

CARAVAN & CHALET PARKS GUIDE. see TRAVEL AND TOURISM

796.77 CN
CARGUIDE. French edition: Magazine Carguide. (Supplement avail.: Toronto International Auto Show Program (ISSN 0704-7339)) 1971. q. Can.$12.99 (foreign Can.$20.99). Formula Publications Ltd., 447 Speers Rd., Ste. 4, Oakville, Ont. L6K 3S7, Canada. TEL 416-622-5150. FAX 416-622-1824. Ed. Alan E. McPhee. adv.; B&W page Can.$3800, color page Can.$4550; trim 8 1/8 x 10 7/8. circ. 229,259 (207,307 Eng.ed., 91,952 Fr.ed.)
Incorporates: Light Truck Guide.
Description: Official program for Toronto International Auto Show and Ottawa-Hull Auto Show. Lists complete mechanical specifications, photos, suggested retail price and fuel consumption of every new car available in Canada.

388.3 NE ISSN 0008-6940
CARROSSERIE. 1936. m. fl.84.50. Nederlandse Vereniging van Ondernemers in het Carrosseriebedrijf, Postbus 299, 2170 AG Sassenheim, Netherlands. FAX 02522-65255. Ed. Henk Barnhoorn. adv.; bk.rev.; circ. 2,700 (controlled). Indexed: Key to Econ.Sci.
Description: Magazine for car bodyshops and bodybuilders.

629.286 FR
CARROSSERIE. 10/yr. (French Body Work Federation) E S C, 35 rue des Renauldes, 75017 Paris, France. Eds. P. Gadas, J.S. Choppelon. adv.; circ. 4,500.

388.3 UK ISSN 0008-6967
CARS & CAR CONVERSIONS. 1965. m. £26.80. Link House Magazines Ltd., Link House, Dingwall Ave., Croydon, Surrey CR9 2TA, England. TEL 01-686-2599. FAX 01-760-0973. TELEX 947709. (Subscr. to: U M S, Stephenson House, 1st Fl., Brunel Centre, Bletchely, Milton keynes, MK2 2EW) Ed. Nigel Fryatt. adv.; bk.rev.; charts; illus.; tr.lit.; circ. 70,123.
Incorporates: Autoperformance.
Description: Profiles rallies, racing, road automobiles, drivers, and competitions with extensively detailed features on technical developments in "ion" equipment.

629.288 US ISSN 0008-6975
TL7.A1
CARS & PARTS; the magazine serving the car hobbyist. (Annual supplement avail.) 1957. m. $20 (foreign $22). Amos Press Inc., 911 Vandemark Rd., Box 482, Sidney, OH 45365. TEL 513-498-0803. FAX 513-498-0808. Ed. Robert Jay Stevens. adv.; bk.rev.; illus.; index; circ. 105,000.
Description: For car collectors and hobbyists.

796.77 UK
CARSPORT MAGAZINE. 1982. m. £17. Carsport Publications, Fairhill Rd., Cookstown BT80 8AG, Northern Ireland. FAX 66728. Ed. James Greer. adv.; bk.rev.; circ. 9,629.

388.3 US ISSN 0008-7092
CARWASH JOURNAL.* vol.6,1967. m. $10. Automatic Car Wash Association, 1 E. 22nd St., Ste. 400, Lombard, IL 60148-4915. Ed. Robin King. adv.; illus.

CATALOGO AUTOMOVILES TURISMOS. see TRAVEL AND TOURISM

629.28 SP
CATALOGO DE EQUIPATALLERES. a. 3500 ptas. Tecnipublicaciones, S.A., Fernando VI, 27, 28004 Madrid, Spain. TEL 91-319-7889. FAX 91-319-7089. TELEX 43905 YEBE E.

629.286 380 IT
CATALOGO MOTORISTICO. (Text in English, French, German, Italian) 1962. a. L.50000. Azienda Cataloghi Italiani s.a.s., Piazzale Lugano 9, 20158 Milan, Italy. TEL 02-39322181. FAX 02-6454786. Ed. Lucio Torella. adv.; circ. 35,000 (controlled).
Description: Contains information on Italian production of parts, accessories, equipment and machinery for different types of motor vehicles.

629 SP
CATALOGO RECAMBIOS Y ACCESORIOS. a. 4500 ptas. Tecnipublicaciones, S.A., Fernando VI, 27, 28004 Madrid, Spain. TEL 91-319-7889. FAX 91-319-7089. TELEX 49305 YEBE E.

388.3 BE
CATALOGUE GENERAL DE L'INDUSTRIE ET DU COMMERCE AUTOMOBILE DE BELGIQUE. (Text in Dutch, French) 1950. a. 2100 BEF. Chambre Syndicale du Commerce Automobile de Belgique, Bd. de la Woluwe 46, B-9, B-1200 Brussels, Belgium. adv.

388.3 US ISSN 0889-2504
CAVALLINO MAGAZINE; the magazine of Ferrari. 1978. s-m. $24. Cavallino Inc., Box 810719, Boca Raton, FL 33481-0819. TEL 407-994-1345. FAX 407-994-9473. Ed. John Barnes. adv.; bk.rev.; circ. 19,500.

388.3 918.904 UY
CENTUR. 1977. a. free. Centro Automovilista del Uruguay, Artigas 1773, Montevideo, Uruguay. Ed. Ever Cabrera Tornielli. adv.; circ. 10,000.

CHAMBRE SYNDICALE NATIONALE DES ELECTRICIENS ET SPECIALISTES DE L'AUTOMOBILE. ANNUAIRE. see ENGINEERING — Electrical Engineering

388.3 DK
CHAUFFOER NYT. 1973. bi-m. DKK 100. Skibhusvej 55, 5000 Odense C, Denmark. TEL 65-97-25-02. FAX 45-65-972407. Ed. Per S. Grove-Stephensen. adv.; circ. 25,000.

388 DK ISSN 0901-3946
CHAUFFOEREN.* 1911. m. free. Vibevej 31, 2400 Copenhagen, Denmark. adv.; bk.rev.; illus.; circ. 11,000.

388.3 SA
CHEQUERED FLAG. fortn. R.50. Titan Publications (Pty) Ltd., Rodland House, 382 Jan Smuts Av., Craighall 2196, South Africa. Ed. Justin Haler. adv.; circ. 25,000.
Formerly: S A Motorscene (ISSN 0256-0550)

388.3 US
CHEVY ACTION. 2/yr. $3.95 per no. Dobbs Publications, 3816 Industry Blvd., Lakeland, FL 33811. TEL 813-646-5743. FAX 813-644-8373.

796.77 US
CHEVY - CORVETTE BUYER'S GUIDE. 1984. m. $21.95. Buyer's Guide National Magazines, 2907 Gill St., Box 1800, Bloomington, IL 61702. TEL 309-829-5214. FAX 309-827-7595. (Subscr. to: Box 1953, Mt. Morris, IL 61054) adv.; circ. 40,000.
Formerly: Corvette - Chevy Buyer's Guide.
Description: Marketplace and news for car enthusiasts and restorers, includes new products, tech and club articles.

388.3 US
CHEVY HIGH PERFORMANCE. bi-m. $13.95. Petersen Publishing Co., 8490 Sunset Blvd., Los Angeles, CA 90069. TEL 213-854-2222. Ed. Mike Magda. adv.; illus.; circ. 100,000.
Formerly: Chevrolet High Performance.

388.3 US
CHEVY POWER. bi-m. $2.95 per no. Magazine Specialties, 153 Asharok Ave., Northport, NY 11768. TEL 516-261-5260.

629.2 US ISSN 0069-3634
TL152
CHILTON'S AUTO REPAIR MANUAL; American cars from 1979 to 1986. 1968. a. price varies. Chilton Co., Automotive Editorial Department, Chilton Way, Radnor, PA 19089.

388.3 US ISSN 0193-3264
CHILTON'S AUTOMOTIVE MARKETING; a monthly publication for the automotive aftermarket. 1971. m. $36. Chilton Co. (Subsidiary of: Capital Cities - A B C Publishing), Chilton Way, Radnor, PA 19089. TEL 215-964-4395. adv.; circ. 32,342. (also avail. in microfilm from UMI; microfiche from BLH,UMI; reprint service avail. from UMI) Indexed: Bus.Ind., Tr.& Indus.Ind.
●Also available online. Vendor(s): DIALOG, Mead Data Central.
Incorporates (1955-1991, May): Automotive Aftermarket News (ISSN 0192-0987); Former titles (1977): Chilton's A M. Automotive Marketing; (1972-1976): Automotive Marketing (ISSN 0045-107X); (1971): Chilton's A M. Automotive Marketing.

629.2 US
CHILTON'S IMPORT CAR REPAIR MANUAL; from 1979-1986. 1971. a. price varies. Chilton Co., Automotive Editorial Department, Chilton Way, Radnor, PA 19089. Ed.Bd.
Former titles: Chilton's Import Automotive Repair Manual; Chilton's Import Car Repair Manual (ISSN 0084-8743); Chilton's Foreign Car Repair Manual.

338.4 US ISSN 0749-5579
TL152
CHILTON'S LABOR GUIDE AND PARTS MANUAL. MOTOR AGE PROFESSIONAL MECHANICS EDITION. 1927. a. Chilton Co., Chilton Way, Radnor, PA 19089. TEL 215-964-4723. illus.
Former titles: Chilton's Motor-Age Professional Labor Guide and Parts Manual (ISSN 0361-9397); Chilton's Motor Age Labor Guide and Parts Manual.

TRANSPORTATION — AUTOMOBILES

388.3 US ISSN 0193-7022
CHILTON'S MOTOR AGE; for the professional automotive service industry. 1899. m. $20. Chilton Co., Chilton Way, Radnor, PA 19089. TEL 215-964-4390. Ed. Tony Molla. adv.; illus.; mkt.; stat.; tr.lit.; index; circ. 136,233. (also avail. in microfilm from UMI; microfiche from UMI; reprint service avail. from UMI) **Indexed:** Bus.Ind., Tr.& Indus.Ind.
● Also available online. Vendor(s): DIALOG, Mead Data Central.
Formerly: Motor Age (ISSN 0027-1772)

629.28
TL152 US ISSN 0363-2393
CHILTON'S MOTOR-AGE PROFESSIONAL AUTOMOTIVE SERVICE MANUAL. 1927. a. $85. Chilton Co., Chilton Way, Radnor, PA 19089.
TEL 215-964-4000. FAX 215-964-4745. illus.
Former titles: Chilton's Motor-Age Service Handbook (ISSN 0097-4773); Chilton's Automotive Service Manual.

629.224 US
CHILTON'S TRUCK AND VAN REPAIR MANUAL; gasoline and diesel engines, from 1977 to 1984. 1971. biennial. price varies. Chilton Co., Automotive Editorial Department, Chilton Way, Radnor, PA 19089.
Formerly: Chilton's Truck Repair Manual (ISSN 0045-6721)

388.3 HK
CHINA AUTOMOTIVE JOURNAL/XIANDAI QICHE; an automotive journal for P.R. China. (Text in Chinese; table of contents in Chinese, English) 1985. 2/yr. HK.$78($20) for Asia; elsewhere $22. (China Automotive Technology and Research Center, CC) Adsale Publishing Company, Tung Wai Commercial Bldg., 21st Fl., 109-111 Gloucester Rd., Wanchai, Hong Kong. TEL 892-0511. FAX 838-4119. TELEX 63109-ADSAP-HX. (Subscr. to P.O. Box 20032, Hennessy Rd., Hong Kong) (Co-sponsor: China National Automotive Industry Corporation) Ed. Josephine Cheng. adv.; circ. 15,000. (back issues avail.)
Description: Information on advanced technology development and market trends of the automotive industry for readers in the PRC.

796.77 US
CHRYSLER POWER. 1984. bi-m. $19.75. C P O Publishing, Box 1210, Azusa, CA 90702.
TEL 818-303-6220. adv.; circ. 78,861.
Description: Attempts to serve the needs of Chrysler car owners, with emphasis on high performance, restoration and technical information.

629.222 UK ISSN 0263-3183
CLASSIC & SPORTSCAR. 1963. m. £39.50. Haymarket Magazines Ltd., 60 Waldegrave Rd., Teddington, Middx. TW11 8LG, England. TEL 081-943-5000. FAX 081-943-5927. TELEX 895-2440-HAYMRT-G. Ed. Mick Walsh. circ. 101,054.
—BLDSC shelfmark: 3274.503200.
Formerly: Old Motor (Teddington).
Description: Devoted to classic cars, aimed at collectors and car enthusiasts.

796.77 US
▼**CLASSIC CARS NATIONAL BUYER'S GUIDE.** 1990. m. $34.95. Buyer's Guide National Magazines, 2907 Gill St., Box 1800, Bloomington, IL 61702. (Subscr. to: Box 335, Mt. Morris, IL 61054) adv.
Description: Marketplace, price guide and show coverage for car enthusiasts and restorers.

629.283 GW ISSN 0933-7075
CLUB MAGAZIN; Aktuelle Informationen des ADAC Nordbaden. 1988. q. D W S Werbeagentur und Verlag GmbH, Kriegsstr. 160, 7500 Karlsruhe, Germany.

388.3 SP
COCHE ACTUAL. fortn. Luike - Motorpress, C. Ancora 40, 28045 Madrid, Spain. TEL 91-3470100. FAX 91-3470119. Dir. Rafael Escamilla. circ. 150,000.

629.222 US ISSN 0742-812X
COLLECTIBLE AUTOMOBILE. 1984. bi-m. $28.50. Publications International, Ltd., 7373 N. Cicero Ave., Lincolnwood, IL 60646. TEL 708-676-3470. FAX 708-676-3671. adv.; bk.rev.; charts; illus.; circ. 100,000. (back issues avail.)
Formerly: Consumer Guide Elite Cars.

624.286 US ISSN 0739-7437
COLLISION; dedicated to the improvement of the auto body trade. Variant title: Collision-Tow-Age. 1960. 9/yr. $18.60. Kruza Kaleidoscopix, Inc., Box 389, Franklin, MA 02038. TEL 508-528-6211. Ed. Jay Kruza. adv.; bk.rev.; charts; illus.; stat.; tr.lit.; circ. 18,000.
Formerly (until 1974): Shop Talk.

388 US
COLLISION PARTS JOURNAL. 1983. q. $20. (Aftermarket Body Parts Association) Sarco Management and Publications, 2500 Wilcrest Dr., Ste. 510, Houston, TX 77042-2752.
TEL 800-323-5832. Ed. Stan Rodman. circ. 2,300.
Formerly: A B P D A Journal.
Description: Covers happenings in the collision parts industry as they pertain to members of the Aftermarket Body Parts Association.

629.2 US
COLLISION REPAIR SPECIALIST. 1985. q. $15. Society of Collision Repair Specialists (SCRS), 734 Videll St., San Lorenzo, CA 94580. TEL 714-838-3115. Ed. Chris Kemp. adv.; circ. 5,000.
Formerly: Collision Repair Digest.
Description: Covers SCRS news, technical updates, problem solving, and management skills for the collision repair industry.

388.3 FR
COMMERCE-REPARATION AUTOMOBILE. 1949. w. 320 F. (Chambre Syndicale Nationale du Commerce et de la Reparation Automobile) Publi-Inter, 75, rue Voltaire, 92532 Levallois-Perret, France. Ed. J.P. Thibault. adv.; circ. 39,700.

338 UK ISSN 0267-8519
COMPANY CAR (REDHILL). 1971. m. $116. International Trade Publications Ltd., Queensway House, 2 Queensway, Redhill, Surrey RH1 1QS, England. TEL 0737-768611. FAX 0737-761989. TELEX 948669-TOPJNL-G. Ed. John Blauth. adv.; bk.rev.; circ. 20,500. (back issues avail.)
Formerly (until 1984): Car Fleet Management.

629.22 US ISSN 0097-8337
TL5
CONSUMER GUIDE MAGAZINE. (Each issue is on a specific subject) 1966. irreg. (32-44/yr.). $99 for 34 nos. (effective 1992). Publications International, Ltd., 7373 N. Cicero Ave., Lincolnwood, IL 60646. TEL 708-676-3470. FAX 708-676-3671. Ed. Richard Popely. illus.; circ. 220,000. **Indexed:** Hlth.Ind., Mag.Ind.

629.286 US
CONTINENTAL COMMENTS. 1954. q. $20. (Lincoln Continental Owners Club) H H N Designs, 5005 Indiana St., Golden, CO 80403-1143. (Subscr. to: Lincoln Continental Owners Club, Box 549, Nogales, AZ 85621) Ed. Hugh H. Nutting. circ. 2,500.

CONTINENTAL MOTORING HOLIDAYS. see TRAVEL AND TOURISM

629.286 US
CONVENIENT AUTOMOTIVE SERVICES RETAILER. 1987. bi-m. Graphic Concepts, Inc., 1801 Rockville Pike, Ste. 330, Rockville, MD 20852.
TEL 301-984-4000. FAX 301-984-7340. Ed. Robert Silverstein. adv.; circ. 9,000 (controlled).
Description: For investors, franchise owners, and managers in the car care service industry.

629.2 621.38 US
CONVERGENCE: INTERNATIONAL CONGRESS ON TRANSPORTATION ELECTRONICS. PROCEEDINGS. biennial. Society of Automotive Engineers, 400 Commonwealth Dr., Warrendale, PA 15096-0001. TEL 412-776-4841. FAX 412-776-5760.
(Co-sponsor: Institute of Electrical and Electronics Engineers)
● Also available online. Vendor(s): European Space Agency, FIZ Technik, Orbit Information Technologies.
Formerly: Convergence: International Colloquium on Automotive Electronic Technology. Proceedings.

CORMORANT NEWS BULLETIN. see ANTIQUES

CORPORATE FLEET MANAGEMENT. see BUSINESS AND ECONOMICS — Management

629.286 IT
CORRERE DELL'AUTORIPARATORE. 1980. m. L.18000. Omicron, Via Susa 42, 10138 Turin, Italy. Ed. Gian Paolo Pecoraro. adv.; circ. 12,000.

388.3 AG
CORSA. 1966. w. Editorial Abril S.A., Leandro N. Alem 896, Buenos Aires, Argentina. adv.; illus.; tr.lit.; circ. 75,000.

796.77 US ISSN 0195-1661
CORVETTE FEVER. 1978. m. $19.97. Dobbs Publications, 3816 Industry Blvd., Lakeland, FL 33811. TEL 813-646-5743. Ed. Paul Zazarine. adv.; bk.rev.; illus.; tr.lit.; circ. 35,000. (back issues avail.)
Incorporates (1976-1991): Keepin' Track of Vettes (ISSN 0191-474X)

796.77 US
CORVETTE ILLUSTRATED. q. $3.50 per no. McMullen Publishing, 2145 W. La Palma Ave., Anaheim, CA 92801. TEL 714-635-9040.

388.3 US ISSN 0897-4179
CORVETTE QUARTERLY. 1988. q. $8. Aegis Group - Publishers (Subsidiary of: Lintas - Ceco Communications), 30400 Van Dyke Ave., Warren, MI 48093. TEL 313-574-9100. (Subscr. to: Box 40278, Redford, MI 48240) Ed. Jerry Burton. circ. 250,000. (back issues avail.)
Description: Covers the current and past model years of Corvettes. Geared towards the Corvette enthusiast for the purpose of selling new Corvettes.

658.8 US
COUNTERMAN; the magazine for professional men & women selling automotive products. (Includes Machine Shop Profit Planner published in Jan.) 1983. 12/yr. $70. Babcox Publications, 11 S. Forge St., Box 1810, Akron, OH 44309-1810. TEL 216-535-6617. FAX 216-535-0874. Ed. Gary Molinaro. adv.; tr.lit.; circ. 236 (paid); 52,500 (controlled).

CRUTCHFIELD'S CAR STEREO MAGAZINE. see SOUND RECORDING AND REPRODUCTION

388 UK ISSN 0591-2334
CUSTOM CAR. 1970. m. £28.95. Link House Magazines Ltd., Link House, Dingwall Avenue, Croydon, Surrey CR9 2TA, England.
TEL 01-686-2599. FAX 01-760-0973. TELEX 947709. (Subscr. to: U M S, Stephenson House, 1st Fl., Brunel Centre, Bletchely, Milton Keynes, MK2 2EW) Ed. Keith Seume. adv.; bk.rev.; circ. 37,183.
Incorporates: Hot Rod and Custom U.K.
Description: Contains feature articles and photography on automobile customizing, with profiles of models, owners, and customizers, technical advice, and announcements of events and competitions.

796.77 AT ISSN 0817-6795
CUSTOM RODDER. 1967. q. Aus.$23.50 (foreign Aus.$36) for 6 issues. Eddie Ford Publications, Private Bag, Newstead, Vic. 3462, Australia. TEL 61-054-762212. FAX 61-54-762592. Ed. Eddie Ford. (back issues avail.)
Description: Devoted to the modified car. Covers the field of street rods, custom cars, street machines, American cars and vans.

629.286 CN
CUSTOM TRUCK & TRAIL CANADA. 1989. 5/yr. Can.$12.50. Autotrack Communications Ltd., 895 Sandy Beach Rd., Ste. 12E, Pickering, Ont. L1W 3N6, Canada. TEL 416-420-0508.
FAX 416-420-2453. Ed. Bob English. adv.; circ. 30,000.
Formerly (until 1991): Off-Road Canada.

659.1 US ISSN 0070-2277
CYCLE BUYERS GUIDE. 1968. a. $2.98. Hachette Magazines, Inc., 1633 Broadway, 45th Fl., New York, NY 10009. TEL 212-767-6000. Ed. Phil Schilling. adv.; circ. 200,000.

388.3 US
CYLINDER HEAD & BLOCK IDENTIFICATION GUIDE. biennial. $60 to non-members; members $30. Automotive Engine Rebuilders Association, 330 Lexington Dr., Buffalo Grove, IL 60089-6998. TEL 708-541-6550. FAX 708-541-5808. circ. 4,300.

D A C - DIGITAL AUDIO CLUB. see ENGINEERING — Electrical Engineering

D A R. (Deutsches Autorecht) see LAW

TRANSPORTATION — AUTOMOBILES

796.5   GW
D C C - CARAVAN UND MOTORCARAVAN MODELLFUEHRER. a. DM.19.80. (Deutscher Camping Club e.V.) D C C - Wirtschaftsdienst und Verlag GmbH, Postfach 400428, 8000 Munich 40, Germany. TEL 089-334021. FAX 089-334737. TELEX 5215974. adv.; circ. 15,000.
  Formerly: D C C - Caravan Modellfuehrer.

388.3   US
D R I - McGRAW-HILL AUTOMOTIVE REVIEW. m. D R I - McGraw-Hill, 24 Hartwell Ave., Lexington, MA 02173. TEL 617-863-5100. FAX 617-860-6332. TELEX 200 284.

629.283 340   US   ISSN 0889-0234
D W I JOURNAL: LAW & SCIENCE. m. $237. Whitaker Newsletters Inc., 313 South Ave., Fanwood, NJ 07023. TEL 908-889-6339. FAX 908-889-6339. Ed. Kathie Levine.
  Description: Covers news and analysis pertaining to case law decisions on drunk driving defense.

629.2   UK
DAILY EXPRESS GUIDE TO WORLD CARS. 1954. a. Express Newspapers Plc., 245 Blackfriars Rd., London SW1 9UFT, England. TEL 01-928-8000. Ed. Sue Bailey. adv.; circ. 200,000.
  Description: Pictures and details of the latest automobiles from manufacturing companies around the world.

796.77   UK
DAILY MAIL MOTOR REVIEW. 1954. a. £2.10. Mail Newspapers Plc., Carmelite House, c/o Dir. Sally Cartwright, Carmelite House, England. TEL 01-353-6000. FAX 01-353-1866.
  Description: Guide to new cars available in the UK.

388.3   DK
DANSK TAXI TIDENDE. 1922. m. DKK 60. Dansk Taxi Forbund, Kildevaeldets Alle 12, 2600 Glostrup, Denmark. FAX 02-633503. Ed.Bd. adv.; charts; illus.; circ. 4,000.
  Formerly: Taxa Droske Tidende (ISSN 0040-0130)

629.1 629.2   FR
DE L'AUTOMOBILE ET DE L'AERONAUTIQUE.* 1951. q. (Association des Anciens Eleves de l'Ecole Technique d'Aeronautique et de Construction Automobile) E.T.A.C.A., 3 rue Pablo Neruda, 92300 Levallois-Perret, France. (Orders to: J. Argoud, 61 bis av. J.B. Clement, 92140 Clamart, France) Ed. Jacques Argoud.

388.32   AT
DE LUXE & RED CAB NEWS. 1959. m. Aus.$0.02 per no. De Luxe & Red Cabs Co-Operative Trading Society Ltd., 357 Glenmore Road, Paddington, New South Wales 2021, Australia. Ed. N.S. Lake. adv.; circ. 1,250.

388.3   US
DEALERS' CHOICE. 1961. q. $40 includes membership. Texas Automobile Dealers Association, 1108 Lavaca St., Box 1028, Austin, TX 78767-1028. TEL 512-476-2686. FAX 512-476-2179. Ed. John T. Devenport. adv.; bk.rev.; index; circ. 1,800 (controlled). (back issues avail.)
  Description: Provides automotive and business information for franchised new car and truck dealers in Texas.

DIASPORA - M I V A; Verkehrshilfe des Bonifatiuswerkes. see *RELIGIONS AND THEOLOGY — Roman Catholic*

629.22   US   ISSN 0160-7065
TL229.D5
DIESEL CAR DIGEST; the quarterly journal of the light-duty diesel. 1976. q. $8.50. Diesel Car Journals, Box 160253, Sacramento, CA 95816. Ed. Robert E. Flock. adv.; bk.rev.; circ. 10,000.

DIESEL - LEHTI. see *ENGINEERING — Mechanical Engineering*

388   UK
DISABLED DRIVER. 1948. bi-m. membership. 45 Castleton Ave., Bexleyheath, Kent, England. Ed. Ben H. Tinton. adv.; bk.rev.; circ. 13,000.

DISCOVERY (CHICAGO). see *TRAVEL AND TOURISM*

629.28   US
DOMESTIC CARS SERVICE & REPAIR; engine performance, electrical, mechanical. (In 2 vols.) 1967. a. $109. Mitchell International, Inc., 9889 Willow Creek Rd., Box 26260, San Diego, CA 92196-0260. TEL 800-648-8010. FAX 619-578-4752. illus.; circ. 27,000.
  ●Also available on CD-ROM.
  Formerly (until 1971): National Service Data: Domestic (ISSN 0272-8745)
  Description: Auto service and repair manual for professional auto technicians.

629.28   US
DOMESTIC LIGHT TRUCKS & VANS SERVICE & REPAIR. 1915. a. $89. Mitchell International, Inc., 9889 Willow Creek Rd., Box 26260, San Diego, CA 92196-0260. TEL 800-648-8010. FAX 619-578-4752. Ed. Tom Garrett. illus.; circ. 27,000. (also avail. in microform)
  ●Also available on CD-ROM.
  Formerly (until 1967): Domestic Cars. Tune-up, Mechanical Transmission Service & Repair.
  Description: Auto service and repair manual for professional auto technicians.

629   SP
DOSSIER - CATALOGO FRENOS. a. 1000 ptas. Tecnipublicaciones, S.A., Fernando VI, 27, 28004 Madrid, Spain. TEL 91-319-7889. FAX 091-319-7089. TELEX 43905 YEBE E.

614.86 340   US   ISSN 0730-2568
KF2231.A15
DRINKING DRIVING LAW LETTER. 1982. 26/yr. $127. Callaghan & Co., 155 Pfingsten Rd., Deerfield, IL 60015. TEL 800-323-1336. Ed. Donald H. Nichols. bk.rev.; index; circ. 2,000. (back issues avail.)
  Description: Contains the latest legal, technical and procedural information on the latest issues in drunk driving cases.

629.222   US
DRIVE! (PLEASANT HILL). 1986. m. $18. Bam Publications, Inc., 3470 Buskirk Ave., Pleasant Hill, CA 94523. TEL 510-934-3700. FAX 510-934-2417. Ed. Pete Biro. adv.; circ. 90,000.
  Formerly (until 1990): Swap Talk.
  Description: For California car and truck enthusiasts.

629.286   US
DRIVING. 1924. bi-m. $4. (American Automobile Association) New Jersey Automobile Club, One Hanover Rd., Florham Park, NY 07932. TEL 201-377-7200. Ed. Pamela S. Fischer. adv.; circ. 150,000. (back issues avail.)
  Formerly (until 1969): New Jersey Autoist.

629.283   US
DRIVING MAGAZINE. 1978. bi-m. £15($40) (Driving Instructors Association (D.I.A.)) D I A (International) Ltd., Safety House, Beddington Farm Rd., Cromdon CR0 4X2, England. TEL 081-665-5151. FAX 081-665-5565. Ed. Graham R.J. Fryer. bk.rev.; circ. 13,500. (back issues avail.)

388.3   US   ISSN 0012-7132
TL236.7
DUNE BUGGIES & HOT VWS; the fun car journal. 1967. m. $19.97. Wright Publishing Co., 2950 Airway A7, Box 2260, Costa Mesa, CA 92628. TEL 714-979-2560. FAX 714-979-3998. Ed. Bruce Simurda. adv.; bk.rev.; charts; illus.; stat.; index; circ. 110,000.

388.3   US
DUPONT REGISTRY. 1985. 12/yr. $39.95 (Canada $54.95; elsewhere $99.95). DuPont Publishing, Inc., 2502 N. Rocky Point Dr. Ste. 1095, Tampa, FL 33607-1443. TEL 813-281-5656. FAX 813-281-1215. (Subscr. to: 1802 Industrial Hwy., Harlan, IA 51537) adv.; circ. 100,000.

388.3   US   ISSN 0192-3595
EASTERN AFTERMARKET JOURNAL. 1957. bi-m. $24 for two yrs. Stan Hubsher, Ed. & Pub., Box 373, Cedarhurst, NY 11516. TEL 516-295-3680. FAX 516-569-5296. adv.; circ. 8,570 (controlled).
  Formerly: Eastern Automotive Journal.

629.2   IT   ISSN 0422-2628
ECO MOTORI. no.122, 1974. m. L.9000. Piazza Roma 33-a, 70122 Bari, Italy. Ed. Sebastianu Pugliese. adv.; illus.; stat.

796.77   GW
EDITION WEISS-BLAU; das Magazin der BMW-Freunde. 1985. m. DM.120. Krumdal 12, D-2000 Hamburg-Blankenese, Germany. TEL 040-860400. FAX 040-860647. Ed. Thomas Mueller. (back issues avail.)
  Formerly: Nullzwei.
  Description: Geared towards BMW collectors worldwide.

629.2   US
EDMUND'S CAR SAVVY. 1973. a. $4.95. Edmund Publications Corp., 200 Baker Ave., Ste. 309, Concord, MA 01742. TEL 508-371-9788. FAX 508-371-9806. charts; illus.; circ. 75,000.
  Formerly: Edmund's Auto-Pedia (ISSN 0270-5354)
  Description: Includes federal crash report, leasing facts and accident report forms.

388.3   US
EDMUND'S ECONOMY CAR BUYING GUIDE. 1980. a. $4.95. Edmund Publications Corp., 200 Baker Ave., Ste. 309, Concord, MA 01742. TEL 508-371-9788. FAX 508-371-9806. Ed. William Badnow. (back issues avail.)
  Description: Lists popular American and foreign cars whose EPA estimated mileage exceeds 24 miles per gallon. Includes prices, specs and photos.

338.4   US   ISSN 0531-7886
TL162
EDMUND'S FOREIGN CAR PRICES. 1969. 2/yr. $4.95 per no. Edmund Publications Corp., 200 Baker Ave., Ste. 309, Concord, MA 01742. TEL 508-371-9788. FAX 508-371-9806. Ed. William Badnow. charts; illus. (back issues avail.)
  Description: Includes wholesale and retail prices, optional equipment, specs, performance sheets, photos and warranty details.

388   US
EDMUND'S NEW CAR PRICES. 1969. 3/yr. $4.85 per no. Edmund Publications Corp., 200 Baker Ave., Ste. 309, Concord, MA 01742. TEL 508-371-9788. FAX 508-371-9806. Ed. William Badnow. illus.; stat. (back issues avail.)
  Description: Includes dealer and retail invoice prices of all new GM, Ford and Chrysler cars and their factory installed optional equipment.

388   US   ISSN 0424-5059
EDMUND'S USED CAR PRICES. 1968. 4/yr. $13.40. Edmund Publications Corp., 200 Baker Ave., Ste. 309, Concord, MA 01742. TEL 508-371-9788. FAX 508-371-9806. Ed. William Badnow. (back issues avail.)
  Description: Lists all American and popular foreign makes for the past 10 years. Includes price of each model and their current wholesale and retail evaluation.

629.2   US
EDMUND'S VAN, PICKUP, SPORT UTILITY BUYER'S GUIDE. 1978. s-a. $7.90 per no. Edmund Publications Corp., 200 Baker Ave., Ste. 309, Concord, MA 01742. TEL 508-371-9788. FAX 508-371-9806.
  Formerly: Edmund's Van, Pickup, Off Road Vehicles.
  Description: Includes dealer cost and suggested retail price, specs, gas mileage and photos of over 65 models with factory installed option prices.

796.7   US   ISSN 0046-1326
EDSELETTER. 1969. m. $15 (membership). International Edsel Club, 3240 Sitterly Rd. N.W., Canal Winchester, OH 43110. (Subscr. to: Box 371, Sully, IA 50251) Ed. Paula S. Perrault. adv.; bk.rev.; circ. 1,000. (processed)
  Description: Contains information on the repair and preservation of the Edsel, folklore and club events.

629.286   AT   ISSN 0818-8491
ELECTRIC VEHICLE NEWS. Short title: E V News. 1974. m. Aus.$30. Australian Electric Vehicle Association Inc., Melbourne Branch, P.O. Box 4622SS, Melbourne, Vic. 3001, Australia. TEL 03-691-4094. FAX 03-691-1362. Ed. Kerry Hill. circ. 430. (back issues avail.)
  Description: Covers electric road vehicle developments, solar and electric car racing news.

TRANSPORTATION — AUTOMOBILES

629.286 US
ELECTRICAL COMPONENT LOCATOR - DOMESTIC CARS, LIGHT TRUCKS & VANS. 1980. a. $37. Mitchell International, Inc., 9889 Willow Creek Rd., Box 26260, San Diego, CA 92196-0260. TEL 800-648-8010. FAX 619-578-4752. illus.; circ. 20,000.
● Also available on CD-ROM.
Description: Auto service and repair manual for professional auto technicians.

629.286 US
ELECTRICAL COMPONENT LOCATOR - IMPORTED CARS, LIGHT TRUCKS & VANS. 1980. a. $37. Mitchell International, Inc., 9889 Willow Creek Rd., Box 26260, San Diego, CA 92196-0260. TEL 800-648-8010. FAX 619-578-4752. circ. 15,000.
● Also available on CD-ROM.
Description: Auto service and repair manual for professional auto technicians.

ELECTRICITE AUTOMOBILE. see ENGINEERING — Electrical Engineering

EMERGENCY RESPONSE GUIDEBOOK. see PUBLIC HEALTH AND SAFETY

796.5 910.09 US
ESCAPEES. 1978. bi-m. $40. (Escapees Club) RoVing Press, 100 Rainbow Dr., Livingston, TX 77351. TEL 409-327-8873. FAX 409-327-4388. Ed. Kay Peterson. adv.; bk.rev.; circ. 30,000. (back issues avail.)
Description: Information on travel as it applies to extended travel in recreational vehicles.

388.3 US
ESCAPEES CLUB. ANNUAL DIRECTORY. a. membership only. RoVing Press, Rte. 5, Box 310, Livingston, TX 77351. TEL 409-327-8873. FAX 409-327-4388. Ed. Kay Peterson. adv.

338.3 FR ISSN 0153-906X
ETUDES ET DOCUMENTATION DE LA R T A. (Revue Technique Automobile) 1946. irreg. 102 F. Editions pour l'Automobile et l'Industrie, 20-22 rue de la Saussiere, 92100 Boulogne-Billancourt, France. TEL 46-04-81-13. FAX 48-25-56-92. TELEX 204850F. Ed. Pascal Cromback. adv.; charts; illus.; circ. 2,500.

388.3 US
EUROPEAN CAR. 1971. 12/yr. $18.80. Argus Publishers Corporation, Box 49659, Los Angeles, CA 90049. TEL 213-820-3601. FAX 213-207-9388. (Street addr.: 12100 Wilshire Blvd., Ste. 250, Los Angeles, CA 90025) Ed. Greg Brown. circ. 82,779.
Former titles (until 1991): V W and Porsche Etc (ISSN 0273-6748); V W and Porsche; Volkswagen Greats (ISSN 0049-6723)
Description: Covers European marques, aftermarket products, replacement parts, restorations, and how-to-do-it, where-to-get-it articles.

388 UK ISSN 0267-8233
HD9710.E8
EUROPEAN MOTOR BUSINESS. 4/yr. £425($845) (Economist Intelligence Unit) Business International Ltd., 40 Duke St., London W1A 1DW, England. TEL 71-499 2278. FAX 71-499-9767. TELEX 266353 EIUG. (US addr.: Business International Corp., 215 Park Ave. S., New York, NY 10003. TEL 212-460-0600)
—BLDSC shelfmark: 3829.764520.
Description: Analyzes the activity of the automotive industries of Western Europe and their national and international markets.

388.3 US
EXCELLENCE (ROSS). bi-m. $16 (effective Jan. 1992). Ross Periodicals, 33 Redwood Dr., Box 1529, Ross, CA 94957. TEL 415-382-0580. circ. 35,000.
Description: Provides current news and information about the Porsche and the people who drive it.

659.1 UK ISSN 0014-4460
EXCHANGE AND MART. 1868. w. £130 motoring section; Exchange and Mart Southern edition £218. Link House Advertising Periodicals Ltd., 25 West St., Poole, Dorset BH15 1LL, England. FAX 0202-671171. TELEX 417109. adv.; circ. 145,831.
Description: Advertisements of various products, special focus on automobiles.

796.77 US
EXOTIC CARS QUARTERLY. q. Diamandis Communications, 1499 Monrovia Ave., Newport Beach, CA 92663-2752. TEL 714-720-5300. FAX 714-631-2374. Ed. Ron Sessions. circ. 100,000.

388.3 FR ISSN 0755-110X
L'EXPERT AUTOMOBILE. (Supplements avail.) 1965. m. 1010 F. Societe d'Edition de l'Expertise Automobile et Materiel Industriel, 19 rue des Filles du Calvaire, 75140 Paris Cedex 03, France. TEL 16-1-42-77-32-50. FAX 16-1-40-27-02-63. Ed. J. Barataud. adv.; illus.; stat.; circ. 25,000.

796.77 FR
F I A YEAR BOOK OF AUTOMOBILE SPORT. a. Editions V.M., 116 bd. Malesherbes, 75017 Paris, France. TEL 42-27-25-44. FAX 47-66-57-74. circ. 6,500.

796.77 US ISSN 0885-4750
TL215.M8
FABULOUS MUSTANGS AND EXOTIC FORDS. bi-m. $15 (foreign $21). Argus Publishers Corporation, Box 49659, Los Angeles, CA 90049. TEL 213-820-3601. FAX 213-207-9388. (Street addr.: 12100 Wilshire Blvd., Ste. 250, Los Angeles, CA 90025) Ed. Kevin Boales. adv.; circ. 71,547. (back issues avail.)
Description: Features Mustangs, exotic Fords, Mach 1s, Shelbys and AC Cobras. Provides factory specs, aftermarket and new product information, previews, classic restoration and racing machinery information.

388.3 GW ISSN 0014-6838
FAHRSCHULE; Zeitschrift fuer die Kraftfahrlehrer. 1949. m. DM.96.90 (foreign DM.106.10). Heinrich Vogel Fachzeitschriften GmbH, Neumarkter Str. 18, Postfach 802020, 8000 Munich 80, Germany. TEL 089-43180-0. Ed. Heinzmartin Nitsche. adv.; bk.rev.; circ. 16,500 (controlled).

388.3 GW
▼**FAHRZEUG;** Aktuell - Historie - Modell. 1990. s-m. DM.45 (foreign DM.48). Flugzeug Publikations GmbH, Herbststr. 3, 7918 Illertissen, Germany. FAX 07303-7114. Ed. Willy Queissner. circ. 10,000. (back issues avail.)

629.2 GW ISSN 0014-6862
FAHRZEUG UND KAROSSERIE. 1947. m. DM.148.80 (foreign DM.167.40). (Zentralverband Karosserie und Fahrzeugtechnik) A.W. Gentner Verlag, Postfach 101742, 7000 Stuttgart 10, Germany. TEL 0711-63672-0. FAX 0711-63672-11. Eds. Peter Schulz, E. Reisch. circ. 6,500.

388.3 NO
FALKEN NYTT. q. NOK 12. Falken Redningskorps A-S, Stabburveien 1, 0873 Oslo 8, Norway. Ed. Arve Andreson. adv.; circ. 105,000.

FAMILY SITES GUIDE. see SPORTS AND GAMES — Outdoor Life

796.77 UK
FAST CAR. 1987. m. £38.40 (foreign £73.68). Security Publications Ltd., Argosy House, 161a-163a High St., Orpington, Kent BR6 0LW, England. TEL 0689-74025. Ed. Greg Emmerson. circ. 60,000. (back issues avail.)
Description: Covers engine modifications, body styling, and engine building.

796.77 UK ISSN 0266-5182
FAST LANE. 1984. m. $48. I P C Magazines Ltd., Kings Beach Tower, Stamford St., London SE1 9LS, England. TEL 071-261-5849. FAX 071-261-7851. (Subscr. to: Reed Business Publishing Ltd., 205 E. 42nd St., New York, NY 10017, U.S.A.) Ed. Peter Dron. bk.rev.; circ. 51,073.
Description: Covers supercars and performance varieties of production cars.

338.3 US
FAST TRACK NEWS. 5/mo. Integrated Automotive Resources, Inc., 656 E. Swedesford Rd., No. 206, Wayne, PA 19087-1606. TEL 215-688-4445. FAX 215-293-0451.

388.3 US
FAT FENDERED STREET RODS. q. $3.95 per no. Challenge Publications, Inc., 7950 Deering Ave., Canoga Park, CA 91304. TEL 818-887-0550. FAX 818-883-3019.

629.283 US
FEDERAL MOTOR VEHICLE SAFETY STANDARDS AND REGULATIONS; with amendments and interpretations. 1972. base vol. plus m. updates. $82. U.S. National Highway Traffic Safety Administration, Department of Transportation, 400 7th St., S.W., Washington, DC 20590. (Dist. by: Supt. of Docs., U.S. Government Printing Office, Washington, DC 20402)

629.286 BE ISSN 0014-9640
FEGARBEL REVUE. Dutch edition (ISSN 0774-1200) (Editions in Dutch, French) 1926. m. 1200 Fr. Wolters Kluwer (Subsidiary of: Kluwer Editorial), Louizalaan 485, B-1050 Brussels, Belgium. TEL 02-641-74-11. FAX 02-647-43-32. TELEX 62067 WOSABE. Ed. Mark DeBlock. adv.; bk.rev.; circ. 12,000.
Description: Keeps reader up-to-date with the automobile industry.

796.77 IT
FERRARI FORMULA 1 ANNUAL. (Text in English, French, Italian) 1989. a. Automobilia s.r.l., Via Ponte Seveso, 25, 20125 Milan, Italy. TEL 02-6884928. FAX 02-6886091. Ed. Enrico Benzing.

796.72 914 IT
FERRARI ITALIAN STYLE; periodico internazionale d'immagine, automobilismo e cultura. (Text in English, Italian) bi-m. L.35000 (foreign L.60000). Esseffe Editrice S.r.l., Via Dogana, 3, Milan, Italy. TEL 02-867141. TELEX 323827 ABSERV. Ed. Sergio Massaro.

796.77 UK
FERRARI WORLD MAGAZINE. bi-m. $40. Hyde Park Books Ltd., Hyde Park House, 5 Manfred Rd., London SW15 2RS, England. TEL 081-877-1080. FAX 081-874-1845.

629 IT ISSN 0393-3318
FERRARISSIMA. (Text in English, French, Italian) 1984. s-a. L.125000($140) Automobilia s.r.l., Via Ponte Seveso, 25, 20125 Milan, Italy. TEL 02-6884928. FAX 02-6886091. Eds. Bruno Alfieri, Piero Casucci. circ. 5,000. (back issues avail.)

338.3 FR
FICHES TECHNIQUES R T A. (Revue Technique Automobile) 1978. irreg. 910 F. Editions Techniques pour l'Automobile et l'Industrie (ETAI), 20-22 rue de la Saussiere, 92100 Boulogne-Billancourt, France. charts; illus. (looseleaf format)

338.3 FR
FICHES TECHNIQUES R T C. (Revue Technique Carrosserie) irreg. 410 F. Editions Techniques pour l'Automobile et l'Industrie (ETAI), 20-22 rue de la Saussiere, 92100 Boulogne-Billancourt, France. charts; illus. (looseleaf format)

338.3 FR
FICHES TECHNIQUES R T D. (Revue Technique Diesel) irreg. 405 F. Editions Techniques pour l'Automobile et l'Industrie (ETAI), 20-22 rue de la Saussiere, 92100 Boulogne-Billancourt, France.

FLEET ASSOCIATION DIRECTORY. see BUSINESS AND ECONOMICS — Marketing And Purchasing

FLEET FINANCIALS. see BUSINESS AND ECONOMICS — Marketing And Purchasing

388.3 UK ISSN 0953-9085
FLEET OPERATORS HANDBOOK; a unique reference book from the publishers of Fleet News. 1980. a. £30. Emap Response Ltd., Wentworth House, Wentworth St., Peterborough PE1 1DS, England. TEL 0733-63100. FAX 0733-67367. Ed. Rob Barrowman. stat.; index; circ. 10,000 (controlled). (back issues avail.)

FLORIDA MOTOR VEHICLE LIABILITY LAW. see LAW

388.3 US ISSN 0015-4830
FLYING LADY.* 1951. bi-m. membership. Rolls-Royce Owners' Club, Inc., c/o Green Oak Farm, 7404 Mt. Vista Rd., Kingsville, MD 21087. Eds. Ken and Marmie Karger. adv.; bk.rev.; charts; illus.; index; circ. 4,500.
Description: Includes historical and technical articles.

TRANSPORTATION — AUTOMOBILES 4691

796.77 US
FORD BUYER'S GUIDE. 1986. m. $18. Buyer's Guide National Magazines, 2907 Gill St., Box 1800, Bloomington, IL 61702. (Subscr. to: Box 1953, Mt. Morris, IL 61054) adv.; circ. 30,000.
  Former titles: Ford, Mustang Buyer's Guide; Ford, Mustang and Classic Thunderbird Buyer's Guide.
  Description: Marketplace and news for the car enthusiasts and restorers, includes new products, tech and club articles.

796.77 790.13 US
FORD ENTHUSIAST MAGAZINE. 1980. bi-m. $22 (Canada $30; foreign $40). Performance Ford Club of America Inc., 13155 U S R 23, Ashville, OH 43103. TEL 615-983-2273. Ed. France Crites. adv.; bk.rev.; circ. 6,000. (back issues avail.)
  Description: For those interested in Ford powered vehicles, especially models of the 1950's and later. Includes a sale-wanted section.

388.3 GW ISSN 0015-7007
FORD-NACHRICHTEN;* Zeitschrift fuer die Mitarbeiter der Ford-Werke AG. (Text in German, Italian, Turkish) 1958. m. free. Ford-Werke AG, Ottoplatz 2, Postfach 210369, 5000 Cologne, Germany. Ed. Heribert Schwinges. charts; illus.; stat.; tr.lit.; circ. 50,000. (tabloid format)

796.7 US ISSN 0015-7015
FORD TIMES; the Ford owner's magazine. 1908. m. $9 (free to qualified personnel). Ford Motor Co., One Illinois Center, 111 E. Wacker Dr., Ste. 1700, Chicago, IL 60601. TEL 312-819-1330. FAX 312-565-5923. Ed. Scott Powers. adv.; illus.; index; circ. 900,000. **Indexed:** Ind.Free Per.

FORD WORLD. see BUSINESS AND ECONOMICS — Labor And Industrial Relations

629.286 UK
FORECOURT TRADER.* m. £2 per no. William Reed Ltd., Crawley, Sussex, England. TEL 081-943-5000. TELEX 895-2440-HAYMART-G. Ed. Jo Kelly.
  Description: Covers the latest news and views in the industry, with product features and an independent look into market areas.

388.3 797.77 CN ISSN 0848-8630
FORMULA; the international autosport magazine. 1985. 10/yr. Can.$29.96($39.50) Kerrwil Publications Ltd., 395 Matheson Blvd. E., Mississauga, Ont. L4Z 2H2, Canada. TEL 416-890-1846. FAX 416-890-5769. Ed. Rene Fagnan. adv. contact: adv. contact: Malcolm Elston. bk.rev.; stat.; circ. 50,000. (back issues avail.)
  Formerly: Formula 2000 (ISSN 0827-6374)
  Description: Covers world of autosports, sportscar previews and roadtests.

629 CN
▼**FORMWORKS.** 1991. 6/yr. Can.$36 (foreign Can.$48). Groupe Culturel Prefontaine, 1463 rue Prefontaine, Montreal, Que. H1W 2N6, Canada. TEL 514-523-6832. FAX 514-523-2312. Ed. Terrance Galvin. adv.; circ. 5,300.

388.3 US ISSN 0015-9123
FOUR WHEELER MAGAZINE; world's leading four wheel drive magazine. 1962. m. $14.87. Four Wheeler Publishing Ltd., 1965 Broadway, New York, NY 10023. TEL 212-496-6100. FAX 818-992-4979. Ed. John Stewart. adv.; bk.rev.; charts; illus.; mkt.; tr.lit.; circ. 305,000.

388.3 US ISSN 0884-9889
FRIENDS (WARREN); travel and adventure in America. 1939. bi-m. $8.99. Aegis Group - Publishers (Subsidiary of: Lintas - Ceco Communications), 30400 Van Dyke, Warren, MI 48093. TEL 313-574-9100. Ed. Gerald Burton. adv.; circ. 7,000,000. (back issues avail.)
  Description: Covers the new Chevrolets and traveling.

388.3 US ISSN 0016-1810
FROM THE STATE CAPITALS. MOTOR VEHICLE REGULATION. 1946. w. $215 (foreign $235)(effective Dec. 1990). Wakeman-Walworth, Inc., 300 N. Washington St., Alexandria, VA 22314. TEL 703-549-8606. FAX 703-549-1372. (processed)
  Description: Covers highway safety, vehicle inspection and equipment requirements, driver licensing and education in the US.

629.2 796.77 GW ISSN 0171-5046
G V A MITGLIEDERVERZEICHNIS. 1969. a. DM.68. Gesamtverband Autoteile-Handel e.V., Postfach 1256, Oberstr. 36-42, 4030 Ratingen 1, Germany. TEL 02102-25041. FAX 02102-26113. TELEX 28526. adv.; stat.; circ. 1,500. (back issues avail.)

388.33 UK ISSN 0264-0163
GARAGE AND AUTOMOTIVE RETAILER. 1955. m. £30. A.G.B. Hulton Ltd., Warwick House, Azalea Dr., Swanley, Kent BR8 8JE, England. Ed. Mark Robinson. adv.; bk.rev.; circ. 36,000.
  Former titles: Garage and Transport Group; Garage and Transport (ISSN 0307-1154); Garage and Transport Equipment (ISSN 0046-5429)

388.33 IT ISSN 0016-4542
GARAGE & OFFICINA.* 1953. m. L.12000. (Associazione Nazionale Autoriparatori e Autoricambisti) Edistampa s.r.l., Via Donatello, Lotto 45, 71036 Lucera (Foggia), Italy. Ed. Edoardo Rossi. adv.; circ. 20,000.

629.286 CN
GARAGE & SERVICE STATION NEWS. 1934. m. $7. Garage & Service Station News Publishing Co., No. 204, 260 Raymur Ave., Vancouver 6, B.C., Canada. Ed. Theodore L. Coates. adv.; illus.; tr.lit.; circ. controlled.

GENERAL MOTORS PUBLIC INTEREST REPORT. see BUSINESS AND ECONOMICS — Production Of Goods And Services

388 629.2 US
GENERAL MOTORS SYMPOSIA SERIES. 1971. irreg. latest 1988. price varies. Plenum Publishing Corp., 233 Spring St., New York, NY 10013-1578. TEL 212-620-8000. FAX 212-463-0742. TELEX 23-421139.
  Refereed Serial

388.3 IT
GENTE MOTORI. 1972. m. L.57600 (foreign L.100000). Rusconi Editori Associati S.p.A., Servizio Abbonamenti, Via Vertruvio 43, 20124 Milan, Italy. TEL 02-67561. FAX 67562732. Ed. Gianni Marin. adv.; bk.rev.; circ. 342,120.

388.3 IT
GENTLEMAN AUTOMOBILI. m. P.C. Boggio 38, 10138 Turin, Italy. Ed. Giorgio Bellia.

629.286 US
GEORGIA AUTOMOTIVE BUSINESS. m. 1395 S. Marietta Pkwy., Ste. 114, Marietta, GA 30067. TEL 404-499-2128. FAX 404-421-1649. Ed. Keisha L. McCray. adv.; circ. 10,000.

629.2 GW ISSN 0072-145X
GERMAN MOTOR TRIBUNE. 1951. a. DM.30. (Export Service Gruenert) Broenner Verlag Breidenstein GmbH, Stuttgarter Str. 18-24, 6000 Frankfurt a.M. 1, Germany. FAX 069-2600509. TELEX 411964. Ed. Werner Siebeneicher. adv.; circ. 10,000.
  Description: Available free of charge to firms abroad interested in importing automotive goods from Germany.

629 GH
GHANA. STATISTICAL SERVICE. MOTOR VEHICLE REGISTRATION. q. $20. Statistical Service, P.O. Box 1098, Accra, Ghana.
  Formerly: Ghana. Central Bureau of Statistics. Motor Vehicle Registration.

388 UK
GLASS'S CAR CHECK BOOK. a. £12. Glass's Guide Service Ltd., Elgin House, St. George's Ave., Weybridge, Surrey KT13 0BX, England. TEL 0932-853211. FAX 0932-849299. adv.

338.476 UK
GLASS'S GUIDE TO CAR VALUES. 1933. m. £80. Glass's Guide Service Ltd., Elgin House, St. George's Avenue, Weybridge, Surrey KI13 0BX, England. TEL 0932-853211. FAX 0932-849299. adv.
  Formerly: Glass's Guide to Used Car Values.

338.476 UK
GLASS'S GUIDE TO COMMERCIAL VEHICLE VALUES. 1951. m. £75. Glass's Guide Service Ltd., Elgin House, St. George's Avenue, Weybridge, Surrey KT13 0BX, England. TEL 0932-853211. FAX 0932-849299. adv.
  Formerly: Glass's Guide to Used Commercial Vehicle Values.

388 UK
GLASS'S INDEX OF REGISTRATION MARKS. a. £15. Glass's Guide Service Ltd., Elgin House, St. George's Ave., Weybridge, Surrey KT13 0BX, England. TEL 0932-853211. FAX 0932-849299.

388.3 SA
GO!. (Text in English) 1963. 3/yr. free. (Public Affairs Department) Shell South Africa (Pty) Ltd., P.O. Box 2231, Cape Town 8000, South Africa. TEL 021-408-4911. FAX 021-253807. circ. 1,500 (controlled).
  Formerly (until 1985): Shell Dealer News (ISSN 0037-3532)

GO (CHARLOTTE). see TRAVEL AND TOURISM

614.86 CN
GOING PLACES MAGAZINE. 1975. 6/yr. Can.$2. Canada Wide Magazines Ltd., 4180 Lougheed Hwy., No. 401, Burnaby, B.C. V5C 6A7, Canada. TEL 604-299-7311. Ed. Robin Roberts. adv.; bk.rev.; illus.; index; circ. 85,000.
  Formerly: Westworld Magazine; **Supersedes:** B.C. Motorist (ISSN 0005-2884)
  Description: Features automotive-related tips, club news and national and international travel.

629.222 US
GOLD BOOK CLASSICS & ANTIQUES. s-a. $20. Gold Book, Inc., 430 Tenth St., N.W., Ste S-202, Atlanta, GA 30318. TEL 800-842-6848. FAX 404-872-8343. Ed. Ben Dyer. (looseleaf format)
  Description: Provides values in four condition categories for more than 6,000 antique vehicles manufactured between 1897 and 1942.

629.2 US ISSN 1057-0535
GOLD BOOK CONTEMPORARY VEHICLES. 6/yr. $60. Gold Book, Inc., 430 Tenth St., N.W., Ste. S-202, Atlanta, GA 30318. TEL 800-842-6848. FAX 404-872-8343. Ed. Ben Dyer. (looseleaf format)
  Supersedes in part: Gold Book Used Car Value Guide.
  Description: Provides values in three condition categories plus wholsale and loan values for more than 10,000 domestic and imported cars and trucks manufactured since 1976.

629.2 US ISSN 1057-0136
GOLD BOOK OLDER VEHICLES. q. $40. Gold Book, Inc., 430 Tenth St., N.W., Ste. S-202, Atlanta, GA 30318. TEL 800-842-6848. FAX 404-872-8343. Ed. Ben Dyer. (looseleaf format)
  Supersedes in part: Gold Book Used Car Value Guide.
  Description: Provides values in three condition categories plus loan value for more than 10,000 domestic and imported cars and truck manufactured between 1945 and 1975.

628.228 US
GOLD BOOK SPECIAL INTEREST VEHICLES. q. $20. Gold Book, Inc., 430 Tenth St., N.W., Ste. S-202, Atlanta, GA 30318. TEL 800-842-6848. FAX 404-872-8343. Ed. Ben Dyer.
  Description: Provides values in three condition categories for more than 3,000 domestic and imported performance and collectible vehicles manufactured since 1946.

388.3 UK ISSN 0017-2111
GOOD MOTORING. 1935. q. £2.80. Good Motoring (Publishers) Ltd., c/o Guild of Experienced Motorists, Station Rd., Forest Row, E. Sussex, RH18 5EN, England. TEL 034282-5676. Ed. Derek Hainge. adv.; bk.rev.; illus.; circ. 60,000.
  Description: General motoring journal published for the members of the Guild of Experienced Motorists.

388.3 UK
GOODS VEHICLE COSTING AND PRICING HANDBOOK. irreg. £18.95. Kogan Page Ltd., 120 Pentonville Rd., London N1 9JN, England. TEL 071-278-0433. FAX 071-837-6348. TELEX 263088 KOGAN G. Ed. David Lowe.
  Description: Practical ways to cost vehicles and calculate profitable haulage rates.

629 IT ISSN 0392-6796
LE GRANDI AUTOMOBILI/GREAT CARS. (Text in English, Italian) 1983. q. L.50000($60) Automobilia s.r.l., Via Ponte Seveso, 25, 20125 Milan, Italy. TEL 02-6884928. FAX 02-6886091. Ed. Bruno Alfieri. circ. 9,000. (back issues avail.)

T

TRANSPORTATION — AUTOMOBILES

388.3   US
GRASSROOTS MOTORSPORTS. 1984. bi-m. $14.97. Motorsport Marketing, Inc., 425 Parque Dr., Ormond Beach, FL 32174. TEL 904-673-4148. FAX 904-673-6040. Ed. Marjorie Suddard. adv.; bk.rev.; circ. 15,000.
    Former titles: Auto-X and Grassroots Motorsports; Auto-X.

GREATER WASHINGTON - MARYLAND SERVICE STATION AND AUTOMOTIVE REPAIR ASSOCIATION. MEMBERSHIP DIRECTORY & BUYER'S GUIDE. see *BUSINESS AND ECONOMICS — Trade And Industrial Directories*

GUERIN SPORTIVO MESE. see *SPORTS AND GAMES — Bicycles And Motorcycles*

629.286   VE
GUIA AUTOMOTRIZ DE VENEZUELA/VENEZUELAN AUTOMOTIVE GUIDE. 1970. a. $20. Promotrix, S.R.L., Calle Sorbona, Edif. Marta, Piso 1, Ofic. 18, Colinas de Bello Monte, Caracas, Venezuela. TEL 7511355. FAX 582-7511122. TELEX 27474 ORTIZ VC. Ed. Armando Ortiz P. adv.; circ. 8,000 (controlled).

629   MX
GUIA DE LA INDUSTRIA: AUTOMOTRIZ. 1968. a. Mex.$100000($50) Informatica Cosmos, S.A. de C.V., Fernandez Arrieta 5-101, Col. Los Cipreses, 04830 Mexico D.F., Mexico. TEL 677-48-68. FAX 679-35-75. Ed. Cesar Macazaga O. adv.; circ. 5,000.

629.286   FR
GUIDE DE L'EQUIPEMENT ET DE L'OUTILLAGE. 1989. a. 350 F. Editions Techniques pour l'Automobile et l'Industrie (ETAI), 20-22 rue de la Saussiere, 92100 Boulogne-Billancourt, France. TEL 46-04-81-13. FAX 48-25-56-92. TELEX ETAIRTA 204850F. Ed. Jean Graudens. adv.; circ. 55,000.
    Description: Supplies jobber store owners and managers with names of products and locations of suppliers of all equipment related to cars, vans and trucks.

388.3   UK
GUIDE TO HEAVY GOODS VEHICLE TEST AND LICENCES. 1976. a. £8.99. Kogan Page Ltd., 120 Pentonville Rd., London N1 9JN, England. TEL 071-278-0433. FAX 071-837-6348. TELEX 263088 KOGAN G. Ed. David P. Soye.
    Description: Complete instruction on qualifying for the HGV license, including sample questions and useful addresses.

629.286   US
GUIDE TO MUSCLE CARS. 1983. bi-m. $15. Argus Publishers Corporation, Box 49659, Los Angeles, CA 90049. TEL 213-820-3601. FAX 213-207-9388. (Street Addr.: 12100 Wilshire Blvd., Los Angeles, CA 90025) Ed. Chris Hemer. adv.; circ. 63,292.
    Description: Covers GTOs, Mopars, Chevys, Buicks, Javelin-GTXs, and Fords. Contains features on restorations, technical information, resource assistance, project cars and performance and new car tests.

338.476   JA
GUIDE TO THE MOTOR INDUSTRY OF JAPAN. (Text in English) 1960. q. 4000 Yen. Japan Motor Industrial Federation, Otemachi Bldg., 1-6-1 Otemachi, Chiyoda-ku, Tokyo 100, Japan. FAX 03-3211-5798. Ed. Kohki Fujimori. adv.; circ. 20,000. (back issues avail.)

388.3   GW   ISSN 0017-5765
GUTE FAHRT; Zeitschrift fuer Autofahrer, Volkswagen, Audi. 1950. m. DM.49.50 (foreign DM.64.50). Verlag Delius, Klasing und Co., Siekerwall 21, Postfach 4809, 4800 Bielefeld, Germany. TEL 0521-559-280. FAX 0521-559-113. TELEX 932934-DEKLA. Ed. Hermann Rest. adv.; illus.; circ. 240,000.

614.85   US
H L D I INJURY AND COLLISION LOSS EXPERIENCE; cars by make and model. a. free. Highway Loss Data Institute, c/o Stephen L. Oesch, General Counsel, Sec.-Treas., 1005 N. Glebe Rd., Ste. 800, Arlington, VA 22201. TEL 703-247-1600. FAX 703-247-1678.

388.3   GW
HALLO! TAXI; Das Magazin fuer Taxifahrer. 1982. m. DM.36. Hallo! Taxi Fachverlag, Raimund Cassalette, Ostertorsteinweg 42-43, 2800 Bremen 1, Germany. TEL 0421-321681. FAX 0421-324883. adv.

629.222   US
HEMMINGS MOTOR NEWS. 1954. m. $23.95. Watering, Inc., Box 256, Bennington, VT 05201. TEL 802-442-3101. FAX 802-447-1561. (Subscr. address: Box 100, Bennington, VT 05201) adv.; circ. 300,000.
    Description: Addresses antique automobiles.

629.286   US   ISSN 1040-0044
HIGH-PERFORMANCE MOPAR. 1986. bi-m. $16. C S K Publishing Co., Inc., 299 Market St., Saddle Brook, NJ 07662. TEL 201-712-9300. FAX 201-712-9899. (Subscr. to: Box 1010, Denville, NJ 07834) Ed. Jeff Bauer. adv.; bk.rev.; circ. 57,500. (back issues avail.)
    Description: Edited for the Chrysler activist who's into modifying, racing, collecting and restoring. New Chryslers featured and old Mopar retrospectives also covered.

796.77   US   ISSN 0745-5941
HIGH-PERFORMANCE PONTIAC. 1979. bi-m. $16. C S K Publishing Co., Inc., 299 Market St., Saddle Brook, NJ 07662. TEL 201-712-9300. FAX 201-712-9899. Ed. Sue Elliott. adv.; circ. 44,250. (back issues avail.)
    Description: For the dyed-in-the-wool Pontiac enthusiast covering all models from mid-'50s, with emphasis on stock musclecars.

629.2   SI   ISSN 0439-1292
HIGHWAY. (Text in English) 1955. bi-m. membership. (Automobile Association of Singapore) Triple A Pte Ltd, P.O. Box 152, Thomson Road Post Office, Singapore 9157, Singapore. Ed.Bd. adv.; bk.rev.; charts; illus.; circ. 32,000.

388.3   US
HILDY'S FORD BLUE BOOK.* 1926. a. Cummins Publishing Co., 6557 Forest Park Dr., Troy, MI 48098-1954. TEL 313-358-4900.

HOME & AWAY. see *TRAVEL AND TOURISM*

HORSELESS CARRIAGE GAZETTE. see *ANTIQUES*

796.72   US   ISSN 0018-6031
TL236
HOT ROD. 1948. m. $19.94. Petersen Publishing Co., 8490 Sunset Blvd., Los Angeles, CA 90069. TEL 213-854-2718. FAX 213-854-2865. Ed. Jeff Smith. adv.; bk.rev.; charts; illus.; circ. 850,000. (also avail. in microform from UMI; reprint service avail. from UMI) **Indexed:** Abr.R.G., Access, Consum.Ind., Jun.High.Mag.Abstr., Mag.Ind., PMR, R.G., Sports Per.Ind., TOM.
    ● Also available online. Vendor(s): DIALOG.
    Description: Covers racing events.

I A D A BULLETIN. (Independent Automotive Damage Appraisers Association) see *INSURANCE*

614.86 388   JA   ISSN 0386-1104
I A T S S RESEARCH. (Text in English) 1977. biennial. 9000 Yen($66) International Association of Traffic and Safety Sciences, 6-20, 2-chome, Yaesu, Chuo-Ku, Tokyo 104, Japan. TEL 03-273-7884. FAX 03-272-7054. TELEX J29358 HONDA FND. Ed. Masaki Koshi. stat.; tr.lit.; circ. 2,000. (back issues avail.) **Indexed:** HRIS, JTA.
    Description: For administrators, policy-makers, and scientists on traffic and its safety.

338 629.2   UK
I B C A M JOURNAL. 1974. m. membership only. Institute of British Carriage and Automobile Manufacturers, 31 Redstone Farm Rd., Hall Green, Birmingham B28 9NU, England. TEL 021-778-4354. FAX 021-702-2615. Ed. Loraine Clarke. adv.; bk.rev.; illus.; circ. 2,500.
    Former titles: News from I B C A M; I B C A M Journal (ISSN 0306-2910); **Supersedes:** Institute of British Carriage and Automobile Manufacturers. Institute Bulletin.

629.286 330   US
I C A LETTER. m. International Carwash Association, 1 E. 22nd St., Ste. 400, Lombard, IL 60148-4915. TEL 708-495-0144.

388.3   UK
I C M E (CARS). 1932. a. £35. Glass's Guide Service Ltd., Elgin House, St. Georges Avenue, Weybridge, Surrey KT13 0BX, England. TEL 0932-853211. FAX 0932-849299.

388   UK
I C M E (HEAVY COMMERCIAL VEHICLES). 1989. a. £35. Glass's Guide Service Ltd., Elgin House, St. Georges Avenue, Weybridge, Surrey KT13 0BX, England. TEL 0932-853211. FAX 0932-849299.

388   UK
I C M E (LIGHT COMMERCIAL VEHICLES). 1989. a. £15. Glass's Guide Service Ltd., Elgin House, St. Georges Avenue, Weybridge, Surrey KT13 0BX, England. TEL 0932-853211. FAX 0932-849299.

629.2   US   ISSN 0098-3551
TK6570.M6
I E E E VEHICULAR TECHNOLOGY CONFERENCE. RECORD. Title varies: Vehicular Technology Group Conference. Record; I E E E Vehicular Technology Group. Proceedings of the Annual Conference. a. Institute of Electrical and Electronics Engineers, Inc., 345 E. 47th St, New York, NY 10017-2394. TEL 212-705-7900. FAX 212-705-7682. (Subscr. to: Box 1331, 445 Hoes Ln., Piscataway, NJ 08855-1331) illus. **Key Title:** Record - Vehicular Technology Conference.

629.286 637   US
I M A C A DIRECTORY.* 1987. a. $35. International Mobile Air Conditioning Association, 2100 N. Highway 360, Ste. 1300, Grand Prairie, TX 75050-1034. TEL 214-484-5750. Ed. Paul M. Allen. circ. 500.
    Supersedes (as of 1981): International Buyer's Guide of Mobile Air Conditioning; (as of 1977): Mobile Air Conditioning.
    Description: Directory of motor vehicle air conditioning and installed accessory suppliers at manufacturer, wholesale, and jobber levels.

388.3   IT
ILLUSTRATOFIAT. 1952. m. Fiat, Corso Marconi 10, Turin, Italy. adv.; bk.rev.; illus.; circ. 245,000.

346 614.86   US   ISSN 0162-4989
KF1297.A8
IMPACT (WASHINGTON). 1975. bi-m. $75 (foreign $90). Center for Auto Safety, 2001 S St., N.W., Ste. 410, Washington, DC 20009. TEL 202-328-7700. Ed. Debra Barclay. bk.rev.; circ. 1,000. (back issues avail.)
    Description: Reports on the auto safety work of CAS. Covers safety legislation, auto defects, lemon laws, recalls and federal and state investigations.

629.286   US   ISSN 0199-4468
IMPORT AUTOMOTIVE PARTS & ACCESORIES. 1979. m. $30 (effective Jan. 1991). Meyers Publishing Corp., 6211 Van Nuys Blvd., Ste. 200, Van Nuys, CA 91401. TEL 818-785-3900. FAX 818-785-4397. TELEX 650-292-3000-MCI. Ed. Paul Dexler. adv.; circ. 35,000 (controlled).

388.3   US
IMPORT SERVICE. 1987. m. Gemini Communications, 306 N. Cleveland Massillon Rd., Akron, OH 44333-9302. TEL 216-666-9553. adv.; circ. 66,000.

629.28   US   ISSN 0735-7877
TL159
IMPORTCAR & TRUCK; parts and accessories for import vehicles. (Includes Machine Shop Profit Planner published in Jan.) 1979. 12/yr. $70. Babcox Publications, 11 S. Forge St., Box 1810, Akron, OH 44309-1810. TEL 216-535-6117. FAX 216-535-0874. Ed. Kathy O'Rouke. adv.; charts; illus.; stat.; tr.lit.; circ. 30,000. (back issues avail.)
    Former titles (until 1984?): ImportCar (Akron); Babcox's ImportCar (ISSN 0278-6532); (until 1980): Importcar (Akron) (ISSN 0271-6712); Babcox's Importcar (ISSN 0194-2492)
    Description: Serves the import car repair and service specialists as well as car dealers with import repair facilities, jobbers and warehouse distributors.

629.286 US
IMPORTED CARS, LIGHT TRUCKS & VANS SERVICE & REPAIR. (In 3 vols.: Engine Performance, Electrical, Mechanical) 1967. a. $123. Mitchell International, Inc., 9889 Willow Creek Rd., Box 26260, San Diego, CA 92196-0260. TEL 800-648-8010. FAX 619-578-4752. Ed. Tom Garrett. circ. 20,000. (also avail. in microform)
● Also available on CD-ROM.
Description: Auto service and repair manual for professional auto technicians.

629.2 CN ISSN 0702-5785
IN THE DRIVER'S SEAT.* m. free. Ontario Safety League, 21 Four Seasons Place, Etobicoke, Ont. M9B 6J8, Canada. TEL 416-593-2670. circ. controlled.

388.3 US
IN THE WIND. bi-m. $3.50 per no. Paisano Publications, Inc., 28210 Dorothy Dr., Box 3075, Agoura Hills, CA 91301. TEL 818-889-8740. FAX 818-889-4726.

629.2 IT ISSN 0073-7291
INDUSTRIA ITALIANA DEL CICLO E DEL MOTOCICLO. ANNUARIO. (Text in English, French, German, Italian and Spanish) 1960. a. free. Associazione Nazionale Ciclo, Motociclo e Accessori, Via Mauro Macchi, 32, Milan, Italy. TEL 02-66981818. TELEX 315694 ANCMA I 609 02-66982072. adv.; bk.rev.; index; circ. 12,000.
Description: Forum covering the production of motorcycles, bicycles, mopeds, motoscooters, component parts and accessories.

629.2 FR ISSN 0073-7747
INDUSTRIE FRANCAISE DES MOTEURS A COMBUSTION INTERNE; repertoire alphabetique des constructeurs. 1953. irreg. free. Syndicat des Constructeurs de Moteurs a Combustion Interne, 39-41 rue Louis Blanc, 92400 Courbevoie, France. TEL 47-17-62-81. FAX 47-17-62-82. (Subscr. to: Cedex 72, 92038 Paris la Defense, France)

INDUSTRY STATISTICS (YEAR). see TRANSPORTATION — Abstracting, Bibliographies, Statistics

629.2 FR ISSN 0020-1200
INGENIEURS DE L'AUTOMOBILE. 1927. m. 205 F. (Societe des Ingenieurs de l'Automobile) R.A.I.P., 22 rue de la Saussiere, 92100 Boulogne, France. Ed. Paul Bardez. adv.; bk.rev.; abstr.; illus.; circ. 5,500. **Indexed:** C.I.S. Abstr., Eng.Ind., Excerp.Med., World Alum.Abstr.

INSPECTED BED & BREAKFAST IN BRITAIN. see TRAVEL AND TOURISM

INSTALLATION NEWS. see COMMUNICATIONS

621 UK ISSN 0954-4070
TJ1 CODEN: PMDEEA
INSTITUTION OF MECHANICAL ENGINEERS. PROCEEDINGS. PART D: JOURNAL OF AUTOMOBILE ENGINEERING. 1984. q. £116($220) for part D; £748($1420) for parts A-I. Mechanical Engineering Publications Ltd., Northgate Ave., Bury St. Edmunds, Suffolk IP32 6BW, England. TEL 0284-763277. FAX 0284-704006. TELEX 817376. Ed. M. Lewis. bibl.; illus.; index, cum.index; circ. 1,294. **Indexed:** A.S.& T.Ind., Appl.Mech.Rev., B.C.I.R.A., BMT, Br.Rail.Bd., Br.Tech.Ind., Chem.Abstr., Curr.Cont., Eng.Ind., HRIS, Math.R., Met.Abstr., Sci.Abstr.
—BLDSC shelfmark: 6724.900770.
Formerly: Institution of Mechanical Engineers. Proceedings. Part D: Transport Engineering (ISSN 0265-1904); Supersedes in part: Institution of Mechanical Engineers. Proceedings (ISSN 0020-3483)
Description: Focuses on transport engineering.

629.283 UK
INSTRUCTOR. 1959. q. free to qualified personnel. Royal Automobile Club, R.A.C House, South Croydon, Surrey CR2 6XW, England. TEL 081-686-0088. FAX 081-680-0108. Ed. John Cowan. adv.; bk.rev.; circ. 1,500. (tabloid format; also avail. in microform from UMI; reprint service avail. from UMI) **Indexed:** Acad.Ind., Child.Bk.Rev.Ind., Ind.Child.Mag., Tr.& Indus.Ind.
Description: News items and commentary on current legislative and educational developments in automobile and commercial vehicle operator training.

INTER AUTO ECOLES DE FRANCE - INTER AUTO ROUTE. see EDUCATION

629.286 UK ISSN 0261-2267
HD9710..A1
INTERNATIONAL AUTOMOTIVE REVIEW. q. $1276. E M A P Response Publishing Ltd., Wentworth House, Wentworth St., Petersborough PE1 1DS, England. TEL 0274-499821. FAX 0274-547143. TELEX 51317 MCBUNI G. Ed. Mike Woodmansey. adv.; charts; stat. (back issues avail.; reprint service avail. from SWZ)
—BLDSC shelfmark: 4536.521000.
Description: Aims to provide international, in-depth coverage of topics of current and incoming strategic interest to the automotive industry worldwide. Presents specialist articles and country surveys.

629.286 US
INTERNATIONAL CONFERENCE ON VEHICLE STRUCTURAL MECHANICS. PROCEEDINGS. 1975. biennial. Society of Automotive Engineers, 400 Commonwealth Dr., Warrendale, PA 15096-0001. TEL 412-776-4841. FAX 412-776-5760.

388 UK ISSN 0267-8225
HD9710.A1
INTERNATIONAL MOTOR BUSINESS. q. £385($765) (Economist Intelligence Unit) Business International Ltd., 40 Duke St., London W1A 1DW, England. TEL 71-493-6711. FAX 71-499-9767. TELEX 266353 EIUG. (US addr.: Business International Corp., 215 Park Ave. S., New York, NY 10003. TEL 212-460-0600)
—BLDSC shelfmark: 4544.361000.
Description: Provides an analysis of trends and forecasts of international automotive industries and markets.

INTERSTANDOX; information for the world of the car repair painter. see PAINTS AND PROTECTIVE COATINGS

INTERSTANDOX EXTRA. see PAINTS AND PROTECTIVE COATINGS

388.3 IE ISSN 0376-7221
IRISH MOTOR INDUSTRY. 1968. m. £20 (foreign £35). (Society of the Irish Motor Industry) Jude Publications Ltd., 4 Tara St., Dublin 2, Ireland. TEL 713500. FAX 713074. Ed. Kate Tammemagi. adv.; bk.rev.; circ. 2,500. (controlled).

388.3 US
ITALIAN CARS - CLASSIC & SPORT. bi-m. $4.95 per no. Hyde Park Group, 2001 W. Main St., Stamford, CT 06902. TEL 203-969-2533. FAX 203-348-3555.

629.2 JA ISSN 0389-4304
TL240 CODEN: JREVDY
J S A E REVIEW. (Text in English) 1978. q. $15 per issue. Society of Automotive Engineers of Japan, Inc. - Jidosha Gijutsukai, 10-2, Goban-cho, Chiyoda-ku, Tokyo 102, Japan. **Indexed:** Chem.Abstr., Fluidex, HRIS, JTA, Met.Abstr., PROMT, World Alum.Abstr.
—BLDSC shelfmark: 5073.725000.

796.72 AT
JAGUARS WEST. m. Aus.$40 (typically set July). Jaguar Car Club of Western Australia, P.O. Box 6027, East Perth, W.A. 6004, Australia. circ. 400.
Formerly (until 1990): Jaguar Torque.

338.476 JA
JAN CORPORATION. FACTS & INFO; annual guide to Japan's auto industry. (Text in English) 1981. a. 10460 Yen. Jan Corporation, Stork Bell Hamamatsucho, Rm.402, 2-17, Hamamatsu-cho 1-chome, Minato-ku, Tokyo 105, Japan. TEL 03-3438-0361. FAX 03-3438-0362. Ed. Akira Shikakura. circ. 8,000.
Formerly (until 1991): Automotive Herald. Facts and Info.

JAPAN AUTO ABSTRACTS. see TRANSPORTATION — Abstracting, Bibliographies, Statistics

388.3 JA ISSN 0021-4329
JAPAN AUTOMOTIVE NEWS. (Text in English) 1959. m. 13500 Yen. Jan Corporation, Stork Bell Hamamatsucho, Rm.402, 2-17, Hamamatsu-cho 1-chome, Minato-ku, Tokyo 105, Japan. TEL 03-3438-0361. FAX 03-3438-0362. Akira Shikakura. adv.; bk.rev.; charts; illus.; stat.; circ. 21,000. (tabloid format) **Indexed:** JCT, JTA.

629.286 JA
JAPAN MOTOR INDUSTRY. 6/yr. $60. Intercontinental Marketing Corp., I.P.O. Box 5056, Tokyo 100-31, Japan. FAX 81-3-667-9646.

388 UK ISSN 0266-898X
JAPANESE MOTOR BUSINESS. 4/yr. £385($765) (Economist Intelligence Unit) Business International Ltd., 40 Duke St., London W1A 1DW, England. TEL 71-499-2278. FAX 71-499-9767. TELEX 266353 EIUG. (US addr.: Business International Corp., 215 Park Ave. S., New York, NY 10003. TEL 212-460-0600)
—BLDSC shelfmark: 4659.660000.
Description: Examines the impact of the Japanese market on the international automotive markets.

629.286 CC
JIASHI YUAN. (Text in Chinese) m. (Tianjin Qiche Zhizhao Chang - Tianjin Automobile Manufacturing Company) Jiashi Yuan Bianjibu, 201 Hongqi Nanlu, Tianjin 300191, People's Republic of China. TEL 341918. Ed. Zhao Pengwan.

629.286 JA ISSN 0385-7298
JIDOSHA GIJUTSU/SOCIETY OF AUTOMOTIVE ENGINEERS OF JAPAN. JOURNAL. (Text in Japanese) 1947. m. 21000 Yen. Society of Automotive Engineers of Japan, Inc. - Jidosha Gijutsukai, 10-2, Goban-cho, Chiyoda-ku, Tokyo 102, Japan. **Indexed:** JCT.
—BLDSC shelfmark: 4880.910000.
Formerly: Jidosha Gijutsu Kyokai Kaiho.

629.286 JA ISSN 0287-8321
JIDOSHA GIJUTSUKAI RONBUNSHU/SOCIETY OF AUTOMOTIVE ENGINEERS OF JAPAN. TRANSACTIONS. (Text in Japanese; summaries in English) 1970. q. price varies. Society of Automotive Engineers of Japan, Inc. - Jidosha Gijutsukai, 10-2, Goban-cho, Chiyoda-ku, Tokyo 102, Japan. **Indexed:** JCT.
—BLDSC shelfmark: 9005.600000.

629.286 621 JA
JIDOSHA KOGAKU/AUTOMOBILE ENGINEERING. 1952. m. 590 Yen. Tetsudo Nihon-sha, 1-4, 2-chome, Nishi-kanda, Chiyoda-ku, Tokyo, Japan. Ed. M. Okasawa. adv.; circ. 98,000. **Indexed:** A.S.& T.Ind., JCT, JTA.

388.3 CN ISSN 0021-7050
JOBBER NEWS; for Canadian automotive wholesalers and salesmen warehouse distributors and automotive rebuilders. 1931. m. Can.$42.80($59) (foreign $53.50). Southam Business Communications Inc., 1450 Don Mills Rd., Don Mills, Ont. M3B 2X7, Canada. TEL 416-445-6641. FAX 416-442-2261. Ed. S.S. Dixon. adv.; charts; illus.; tr.lit.; circ. 11,900.

629.2 US ISSN 0148-5792
HD9710.A1
JOBBER RETAILER; the publication for retailers and wholesalers of automotive parts and equipment. 1977. 13/yr. $60 (foreign $75); includes AfterMarket Manual. Bill Communications, Inc. (Akron), 341 White Pond Dr., Box 3599, Akron, OH 44309-3599. TEL 216-867-4401. FAX 216-867-0019. Ed. Mike Mavrigian. circ. 31,000. (tabloid format; also avail. in microform from UMI; reprint service avail. from UMI)
Description: Serves the owners and managers of automotive aftermarket part suppliers, specifically wholesale jobbers and warehouse distributors.

388.3 US
JOBBER TOPICS REPORTS. 1922. m. $50 (foreign $60). Irving-Cloud Publishing Co., 7300 N. Cicero Ave., Lincolnwood, IL 60646. TEL 708-674-7300. FAX 708-674-7015. Ed. Martin Schultz. bk.rev.; illus.; index; circ. 58,294. **Indexed:** Bus.Ind., SRI, Tr.& Indus.Ind.
Formerly (until 1992): Jobber Topics (ISSN 0021-7069); Incorporates: Automotive Distribution; Automotive Wholesaler.
Description: For wholesale distributors in the automotive aftermarket industry.

629.283 614.8 US
JOURNAL OF TRAFFIC SAFETY EDUCATION. 1953. q. $8. California Association for Safety Education, 5151 State University Dr., Los Angeles, CA 90032. TEL 213-343-4622. Ed. William Cole. adv.; bk.rev.; circ. 2,800. **Indexed:** Educ.Ind., HRIS.

629.28 GW
JURID-TIP. 1956. 3/yr. free. Jurid Werke GmbH, Postfach 1249, 2057 Reinbek, Germany. circ. 60,000.

TRANSPORTATION — AUTOMOBILES

388.3 GW
K F Z BETRIEB AKTUELLE WOCHENZEITUNG. w. DM.235. (Zentralverband des Kraftfahrzeughandwerks) Vogel Verlag und Druck KG, Max-Planck-Str. 7-9, Postfach 6740, 8700 Wuerzburg 1, Germany. TEL 0931-418-0. circ. 29,570 (controlled).

388.3 GW
K F Z BETRIEB UNTERNEHMERMAGAZIN. 1910. m. DM.235. (Zentralverband des Kraftfahrzeughandwerks) Vogel-Verlag und Druck KG, Max-Planck-Str. 7-9, Postfach 6740, 8700 Wuerzburg 1, Germany. TEL 0931-418-0. Ed. E. Haack. adv.; illus.; circ. 29,589 (controlled).
Former titles: K F Z Betrieb (ISSN 0722-7841); K F Z Betrieb und Automarkt (ISSN 0047-3049)

388.3 AU
K F Z WIRTSCHAFT. 1948. m. S.684. (Bundesinnung der Kraftfahrzeugmechaniker) Oesterreichischer Wirtschaftsverlag, Nikolsdorfer Gasse 7-11, 1051 Vienna 5, Austria. Ed. Fritz Wagenleiter. adv.; bk.rev.; charts; illus.; circ. 9,700.
Former titles: K F Z Werkstaette (ISSN 0022-7323); Kraftfahrzeug.

629.286 GW ISSN 0343-9011
K F Z ZEITSCHRIFT FUER DEN NACHWUCHS DES KRAFTFAHRZEUHANDWERKS. 1957. m. DM.64.80. Frankfurter Fachverlag, Michael Kohl GmbH & Co. KG, Emil-Sulzbach-Str. 12, 6000 Frankfurt a.M. 97, Germany. Ed. Siegfried Rauch. adv.; bk.rev.; circ. 20,000.

614.86 JA ISSN 0451-2006
KAGAKU KEISATSU KENKYUJO HOKOKU KOTSU KEN/NATIONAL RESEARCH INSTITUTE OF POLICE SCIENCE. REPORT. RESEARCH ON TRAFFIC SAFETY AND REGULATION. (Text in Japanese; summaries in English) 1960. s-a. Kagaku Keisatsu Kenkyujo - National Research Institute of Police Science, 6 Sanban-cho, Chiyoda-ku, Tokyo 102, Japan. circ. 900. Indexed: Psychol.Abstr.

629.286 DK
KARROSSERI BLADET.* 10/yr. Sammenslutningen af Karrosseribyggere og Autooprettere i Danmark, Bogesvinget 4, 2740 Skovlunde, Denmark. Ed. Sv. Aa. Nielsen. adv.; circ. 530.

796.77
KART SPORT. 1982. m. 5510 Ashborn Rd., Baltimore, MD 21227. Ed. Joe Xavier. adv.; illus.

796.7 US ISSN 0096-3216
GV1029.5
KARTER NEWS. 1957. m. $18. International Kart Federation, 4650 Arrow Hwy., Ste. B-4, Montclair, CA 91763. TEL 714-625-5497. FAX 714-621-6019. adv.; circ. 5,000.

388.3 UK ISSN 0022-913X
KARTING. 1960. m. £25($43) Lodgemark Press, Bank House, Summerhill, Chislehurst, Kent BR7 5RD, England. TEL 081-467-6533. FAX 081-468-7999. TELEX 9312110347-LP-G. Ed. M.C. Burgess. adv.; bk.rev.; charts; illus.; mkt.; tr.lit.; index; circ. 14,000. **Indexed:** Sportsearch.

388.3 NE ISSN 0022-9881
KEMPHAAN.* 1956. m. free. Automobiel Sport Club "de Kempenrijders", Helmerslaan 27, Eindhoven, Netherlands. adv.; bk.rev.; illus.

388.3 US
KEYSTONE A A A MOTORIST. 1911. bi-m. $2. A A A Mid-Atlantic, 2040 Market St., Philadelphia, PA 19103. TEL 215-864-5000. FAX 215-568-1153. Ed. John C. Moyer. adv.; illus.; circ. 310,000. (tabloid format)
Formerly: Keystone Motorist (ISSN 0023-0995)
Description: Covers automotive subjects, foreign and domestic travel.

KIT CAR. see HOBBIES

388.3 US
KIT CAR ILLUSTRATED. bi-m. $2.50 per no. McMullen Publishing, 2145 W. La Palma Ave., Anaheim, CA 92801. TEL 714-635-9040.

629.283 DK
KOERELAEREREN. m. (11/yr.). Dansk Koerelaerer Union, Ellested, 5853 Oerbaek, Denmark. adv.; circ. 2,500.

388.3 US ISSN 0890-9156
KOREA AUTOMOTIVE REVIEW. 1986. m. $295. Mead Ventures, Inc., Box 44952, Phoenix, AZ 85064. TEL 602-234-0044. FAX 602-234-0076. Ed. Christopher Mead.
●Also available online. Vendor(s): Data-Star, DIALOG, NewsNet.
Description: Provides articles on current doings of Korean automotive companies. Includes plans for any new automobiles, import and export activities; covers firms in the U.S. and in Korea.

388 678.2 US
KOVACH TIRE REPORT. 1984. m. $125 (foreign $250). Bill Communications, Inc. (Akron), 341 White Pond Dr., Box 3599, Akron, OH 44309-3599. TEL 216-867-4401. FAX 216-867-0019.
Description: For executives of tire manufacturers and tire dealers in North America.

629.2 GW
KRAFTFAHRT-BUNDESAMT. MITTEILUNGEN. ERGAENZUNGSHEFTE. 2/yr. DM.36.38. Kirschbaum Verlag GmbH, Siegfriedstr. 28, Postfach 210209, 5300 Bonn 2, Germany. TEL 0228-343057. FAX 0228-857145. TELEX 889596-KIRVL-D.

629.2 GW ISSN 0341-468X
HE5669
KRAFTFAHRT-BUNDESAMT. STATISTISCHE MITTEILUNGEN. 1954. m. DM.231.12. Kirschbaum Verlag GmbH, Siegfriedstr. 28, Postfach 210209, 5300 Bonn 2, Germany. TEL 0228-343057. FAX 0228-857145. TELEX 889596-KIRVL-D. charts; stat.; circ. 400.

388.3 GW ISSN 0023-4419
TL3
KRAFTFAHRZEUGTECHNIK; technische Zeitschrift des Kraftfahrwesens. Short title: K F T. 1951. m. DM.48 (foreign DM.62.40). Heinrich Bauer Spezialzeitschriftenverlag, Industriestr. 16, 5000 Cologne 60, Germany. Ed. Knut Boettcher. adv.; bk.rev.; charts; illus.; circ. 228,000. **Indexed:** Excerp.Med., INIS Atomind.
Description: Covers all aspects of automotive engineering.

388.3 JA ISSN 0286-4312
KURUMA NO TECHO/BIG CAR LIFE. 1949. m. 100 Yen per no. Nissan Motor Co. Ltd., Advertising Department - Nissan Jidosha Kabushiki Kaisha, 6-17-2 Ginza, Chuo-ku, Tokyo 104, Japan. Ed. M. Uchida. circ. 500,000.
Formerly (until 1964): Light-Car.

796.77 IT
LAMBORGHINI REVIEW. (Text in English, Italian) 1988. 3/m. L.175000($175) Automobilia s.r.l., Via Ponte Seveso, 25, 20125 Milan, Italy. TEL 02-6884928. FAX 02-6886091. Ed. Stefano Pasini.

796.77 US
LANCIA ENTHUSIAST. 1983. m. membership. American Lancia Club, c/o Armand Giglio, Turk Hill Rd., Brewster, NY 10509. (Subscr. to: Keith Goring, Rt. 1, Box 136, Norfolk, CT 06058) Ed. Neil Pering. adv.; circ. 1,000.

388.3 US ISSN 0023-7515
LANCIANA. 1954. q. membership. American Lancia Club, c/o Armand Giglio, Turk Hill Rd., Brewster, NY 10509. (Subscr. to: Keith Coring, Rt. 1, Box 136, Norfolk, CT 06058) Ed. Paul Feine. adv.; bk.rev.; circ. 1,000.

388 GW ISSN 0023-866X
LASTAUTO OMNIBUS. 1924. m. DM.72 (foreign DM.79.80). Vereinigte Motor-Verlage GmbH und Co. KG, Leuschnerstr. 1, Postfach 106036, 7000 Stuttgart 10, Germany. TEL 0711-18201. FAX 0711-1821756. Ed. Rainer Rex. adv.; charts; illus.; mkt.; pat.; tr.lit.; index; circ. 14,200. **Incorporates:** Kraftverkehr.
Description: Technical data and supply sources, company portraits and cost tables on cars and their manufacture.

629.222 TS
LEGEND. (Text in Arabic, English) 1987. q. free. Motivate Publishing, P.O. Box 2331, Dubai, United Arab Emirates. TEL 246060. FAX 245270. TELEX 48366 MAM EM. Ed. Chuck Grieve. circ. 18,000.
Description: Lifestyle magazine for Jaguar owners in the Middle East.

629.286 US ISSN 0898-5820
TL23
LEGEND SERIES: MUSCLE CARS OF THE '60S - '70S. 1988. bi-m. $19.95. Amos Press Inc., 911 Vandemark Rd., Box 482, Sidney, OH 45365. TEL 513-498-0803. (Subscr. to: Box 4251, Sidney, OH 45365) Ed. Robert J. Stevens. adv.; index; circ. 55,000. (back issues avail.)
Formerly: Legend Series Muscle Cars of the '60s.
Description: For collectors and restorers of muscle cars.

388.3 AT ISSN 0024-0451
LEGIONAIR. 1966. m. $10.15. Legion Cabs Trading Co-Operative Society Ltd., 77 Foveaux St., Surry Hills N.S.W. 2010, Australia. Ed. H.E. Barwell. adv.; circ. 2,000.

LEISURE WORLD. see LEISURE AND RECREATION

629.22 CN ISSN 0834-2423
LEMON AID MAGAZINE. French Edition: Roulez Sans Vous Faire Roulez (ISSN 0840-8475) (Editions in English, French) 1972. q. Can.$12.84. Automobile Protection Association Consumer Publications Co. Inc. - Association pour la Protection Automobile, 292 Ouest, bd. St. Joseph, Montreal, Que. H2V 2N7, Canada. TEL 514-273-1733. circ. 25,000.
Former titles: Lemon Aid Bulletin - Auto Conseils (ISSN 0821-3747); Consumer Bulletin - Bulletin aux Consommateurs (ISSN 0708-3963)

614.86 640.73 US
LEMON TIMES. 1979. q. $15. Center For Auto Safety, 2001 S St., N.W., Ste. 410, Washington, DC 20009. TEL 202-328-7700. Ed. Debra Barclay. circ. 13,000.
Description: Highlights important actions and findings, including such topics as airbags, tips for using small claims court and car defect.

338.3 SA
LEYKOR GUIDE TO BRIGHTER MOTORING. (Text in Afrikaans, English) 2/yr. Union Trades Directories (Pty) Ltd., 22-24 North Block, Mutual Square, Davenport Rd., P.O. Box 687, Durban 4000, South Africa. adv.

388.3 US ISSN 8750-7374
LIMOUSINE & CHAUFFEUR. (Includes a. Factbook) 1983. bi-m. $28 (Canada $38; elsewhere $50). Bobit Publishing Company, 2512 Artesia Blvd., Redondo Beach, CA 90278. TEL 310-376-8788. FAX 310-376-9043. circ. 12,000.
Description: Serves the information needs of the limousine service industry.

388.3 US
LION OF BELFORT. 1970. bi-m. $12. Peugeot Owners' Club, 6649 E. 65th St., Indianapolis, IN 46220-4301. TEL 317-845-5050. Ed. Marvin A. Needler. adv.; bk.rev.; circ. 650. (back issues avail.)

388.33 US
LOCATOR (WHITING). 1955. m. $29. John F. Holmes Publishing Co., Inc., Whiting, IA 51063. TEL 800-457-0660. FAX 712-458-2687. Ed. John F. Holmes. adv.
Formerly: Salvage Locator (ISSN 0048-9050)
Description: Magazine of used auto and truck parts.

796.77 US
LOWRIDER. 1978. m. $31. Park Avenue Publishing, Box 648, Walnut, CA 91788-0648. TEL 714-598-2300. FAX 714-598-3551. adv.; circ. 117,583.
Description: Focuses on customizing, lowering, hydraulics and accessories for cars and trucks.

388.3 LU
LUXEMBURGER AUTO REVUE. (Text in German) 1948. m. 950 Fr. Merfra, Sarl, 78 Grand Rue, Luxembourg, Luxembourg. Ed. Paul Meyers. adv.; bk.rev.; circ. 13,500.

629.286 US
M A C S SERVICE REPORTS. 1987. bi-m. $75 to non-members. Mobile Air Conditioning Society, 1709 N. Broad St., Box 1307, Lansdale, PA 19446. TEL 215-362-5800. Ed. Elvis Hoffpavir. circ. 400.
Formerly: R - 12.
Description: Information for members of the automobile air conditioning service and repair industry.

TRANSPORTATION — AUTOMOBILES

629.288 US ISSN 0888-4641
M AND M RAPPER.* 1986. q. $15. Microcar and Minicar Club, Box 1948, Vashon, WA 98070-1948. TEL 213-439-4148. Ed. Allan G.Y. Meyer. adv.; illus.; circ. 250. (back issues avail.)

629.283 UK
M S A NEWS JOURNAL. 1935. q. free to libraries. (Motor Schools Association of G.B.) Integral Publishing Co. Ltd., Hulton House, Chester Rd., Stockport SK7 5NU, England. Ed. John R. Lepine. adv.; bk.rev.; circ. 28,000. (back issues avail.)

388.3 AT ISSN 0047-5297
M T A JOURNAL. 1919. q. Aus.$15. Motor Traders' Association of New South Wales, P.O. Box 32, Potts Point, N.S.W. 2011, Australia. Ed. David Taylor. adv.; circ. 6,700. **Indexed:** Aus.Rd.Ind., Chem.Abstr.

388.3 629.2 GW ISSN 0024-8525
TJ751 CODEN: MOTZAS
M T Z. (Motortechnische Zeitschrift); Verbrennungsmotor und Gasturbine. 1939. m. DM.239.40. Franckh-Kosmos Verlags-GmbH und Co., Pfizerstr. 5-7, Postfach 106011, 7000 Stuttgart 1, Germany. TEL 0711-2191-332. FAX 0711-2191-350. Ed.Bd. adv.; bk.rev.; abstr.; bibl.; charts; illus.; stat.; index, cum.index every 20 yrs.; circ. 3,400. **Indexed:** Appl.Mech.Rev., BMT, Eng.Ind., Excerp.Med., Fluidex, Sh.& Vib.Dig. —BLDSC shelfmark: 5980.890000.
Description: Trade publication for the engine and turbine industry. Features research and development, product engineering, tests and measurement. Also includes events, news, and new products.

338.476 US ISSN 0146-9932
HD9710.U5
M V M A MOTOR VEHICLE FACTS AND FIGURES. 1976. a. $7.50. Motor Vehicle Manufacturers Association of the U.S. Inc., 7430 Second Ave., Suite 300, Detroit, MI 48202. TEL 313-872-4311. **Indexed:** SRI. Key Title: Motor Vehicle Facts & Figures.
Formed by the merger of: Automobile Facts and Figures (ISSN 0067-253X) & Motor Truck Facts (ISSN 0077-1643)

MANOVELLA; e route a raggi. see *HOBBIES*

388.3 US
MARKETPLACE. bi-m. membership. Nash Car Club of America, 4151 220 St., Clinton, IA 52732. (Subscr. to: c/o Bob Aaron, 635 Lloyd St., Hubbard OH 44425)
Description: For car enthusiasts dedicated to promoting the history, preservation and restoration of the Nash and related automobiles.

796.77 GW ISSN 0175-9698
MARKT FUER KLASSISCHE AUTOMOBILE UND MOTORRAEDER. 1980. m. V F Verlags GmbH, Huettenstr. 10, D-6200 Wiesbaden, Germany. FAX 06121-261633. (Subscr. to: Abo Abteilung, Postfach 1147, 6200 Wiesbaden, Germany) Ed. Otto Walenta. adv.; bk.rev.; circ. 310,500.
Description: For classic automobile and motorcycle enthusiasts. Includes new products, readers' comments, and large classified listings for automobiles and parts for sale.

MARYLAND MOTORIST. see *TRAVEL AND TOURISM*

388.3 IS
MICHERON RECHEV VEACHZAKATO. 1987. 10/yr. Cheshev Ltd., P.O. Box 40021, Tel Aviv 61 400, Israel. TEL (03)216291.

MICHIGAN LIVING. see *TRAVEL AND TOURISM*

388.3 US
MIDGETS & MINI-SPRINTS RACING NEWS.* bi-m. Victory Lane Publishing, Inc., 19766 State Rd. 279, Oak Hill, OH 45656-9735. Ed. Marlon R. Atkins.

388.3 US
MIDWEST AUTOMOTIVE & AUTOBODY NEWS. 1928. m. $10. Automotive Publishing Co., 2900 W. Peterson Ave., Chicago, IL 60659. TEL 312-764-1640. Ed. Warren B. Daemicke. circ. 11,562 (controlled).
Formerly: Midwest Automotive News (ISSN 0026-3338)

388.3 US ISSN 0026-3435
MIDWEST MOTORIST. 1915. bi-m. $3. American Automobile Association, Automobile Club of Missouri, 12901 North Forty Dr., St. Louis, MO 63141. TEL 314-523-7350. Ed. Michael J. Right. adv.; bk.rev.; charts; illus.; stat.; circ. 370,000.
Formerly: Auto Club News.

MIDWEST RACING NEWS. see *SPORTS AND GAMES*

388.3 US
MIDWESTERN STATE SALVAGE GUIDE; used auto and truck parts locator magazine. 1968. m. $12. Midwestern Salvage Guide Magazine Inc., 3700 Decker, Moore, OK 73160. TEL 405-787-0795. (Subscr. to: Box 1864, Bethany, OK 73008) Ed. Louanne Duckworth. circ. 9,000. (tabloid format)
Description: For bodyshop workers, adjusters, and auto salvagers. Covers used auto parts availability.

388 US
MID-WESTERN 4-WHEELER. 1979. 6/yr. $8. Midwest 4-Wheel Drive Association, 1517 Sunset Ln., New Holstein, WI 53061. TEL 414-898-4598. Ed. Linda Welch. adv.; circ. 1,300.
Description: Covers events and issues of special interest to owners of four-wheel drive vehicles.

MILE POST. see *HOBBIES*

388.3 UK ISSN 0026-380X
MILESTONES. 1946. 3/yr. £0.30 per no. (Institute of Advanced Motorists) Advanced Mile-Posts Publications Ltd., I.A.M. House, 359-365 Chiswick High Rd., London W4 4HS, England. Ed. Ian Webb. adv.; bk.rev.; charts; illus.; circ. 80,000.

MILITARY VEHICLES. see *MILITARY*

629.22 AT
MINOR MATTERS. 1980. m. free. Ballarat Morris Minor Club, P.O. Box 451, Ballarat, Vic. 3350, Australia. Ed. Bryan Snowden. adv.

MISS INFORMATION'S AUTOMOTIVE CALENDAR OF EVENTS. see *ANTIQUES*

796.7 US
MODEL A NEWS. 1953. bi-m. $15 (foreign & Canada $16). Model A Restorers Club, 24822 Michigan Ave., Dearborn, MI 48124. TEL 313-278-1455. Ed. Kenneth Keeley. adv.; index; circ. 9,000. (back issues avail.)

MODEL CARS. see *HOBBIES*

388.3 FR ISSN 0047-7648
MODELISME;* automobile internationel. (Text in English, French) bi-m. 26 F.($6.25) 94 bd. de Sebastopol, 75003 Paris, France. circ. 12,000.

388.3 796.72 AT ISSN 0026-8143
MODERN MOTOR. 1954. m. Aus.$59.40. Australian Consolidated Press, 54-58 Park St., Sydney, N.S.W. 2000, Australia. Ed. David Robertson. adv.; bk.rev.; illus.; pat.; index; circ. 40,700. (processed) **Indexed:** Gdlns.
—BLDSC shelfmark: 5890.300000.
Description: Provides with latest industry trends, correvit computer car testing, comprehensive coverage of international recing events.

MODERN TIRE DEALER; covering tire sales and car service. see *RUBBER*

388.3 CN
MONDE DE L'AUTO. 1985. 5/yr. Can.$6. World of Wheels Publishing, Inc., 2061 McCowan Rd., Ste. 207, Scarborough, Ont. M1S 3Y6, Canada. TEL 514-747-9121. FAX 514-747-9046. Ed. Max d'Orsonnes. bk.rev.; circ. 42,000.
Description: Includes articles of general interest to car owners and operators such as information and prices on new cars, maintenance information and tips.

629.2 BE
LE MONITEUR DE L'AUTOMOBILE. Dutch edition: Auto Gids. (Text in French) 1979. s-m. 1740 Fr. Editions Auto-Magazine S.A., Chaussee de la Hulpe 181, bte. 2, 1170 Brussels, Belgium. TEL 02-660-1920. FAX 02-643-2200. TELEX 26379. Ed. Etienne Visart. circ. 390,000.

796.7 FI ISSN 0359-7636
MOOTTORI (YEAR). (Text in Finnish; summaries in Swedish) 1925. 12/yr. FIM 180. Autoliitto r.y. - Automobile and Touring Club of Finland, Kansakoulukatu 10, 00100 Helsinki 10, Finland. FAX 90-5662360. Ed. Juha Partanen. adv.; bk.rev.; charts; illus.; circ. 55,000.
Former titles (1979-1982): Auto ja Liikenne (ISSN 0356-4827); (Until 1978): Moottori (ISSN 0027-0970)

796.77 790.13 US
MOPAR MUSCLE. 1988. q. Dobbs Publications, 3816 Industry Blvd., Lakeland, FL 33811. TEL 813-644-0449. Ed. Greg Rager. circ. 75,500. (back issues avail.)
Description: Provides "how-to" and technical information. Includes parts and service sources, restoration and repair data, buying tips, news on Mopar events nationwide.

388.3 GW
MOT; Auto Technik Zukunft. 1955. fortn. DM.110 (foreign DM.136). Vereinigte Motor-Verlage GmbH und Co. KG, Leuschnerstr. 1, Postfach 106036, 7000 Stuttgart 1, Germany. TEL 0711-18201. FAX 0711-1821756. Ed. K. Freund. adv.; illus.; circ. 136,000.
Formerly: Mot Auto-Kritik (ISSN 0027-1462)

338.3 FR
MOTEURS DIESEL. irreg. Editions Techniques pour l'Automobile et l'Industrie (ETAI), 20-22 rue de la Saussiere, 92100 Boulogne-Billancourt, France. charts; illus.

338.3 FR
MOTO CRAMPONS. (Supplements avail.) m. 240 F. (foreign 300 F.). Societe des Editions Techniques et Touristiques de France, 60-62 rue Danjou, 92100 Boulogne, France. TEL 46-09-95-96. FAX 46-09-99-85. TELEX 633 055 F.

338.3 FR
MOTO FLASH. 1975. bi-m. Societe Europeene d'Editions, 4 rue du Progres, 13005 Marseille, France. Ed. Serge Klutchinikoff.

388.3 FR
MOTO JOURNAL. (Supplements avail.) w. 558 F. (foreign 798 F.). Societe des Editions Techniques et Touristiques de France, 60-62 rue Danjou, 92100 Boulogne, France. TEL 46-09-95-96. FAX 46-09-99-85. TELEX 633 055 F.

796.72 914 DK ISSN 0047-8199
MOTOR. 1906. fortn. (22/yr.). membership. (Forenede Danske Motorejere - Federation of Danish Motorists) Forlaget Motor ApS, Firskovvej 32, P.O. Box 500, DK-2800, Lyngby. TEL 45-930800. FAX 45-933242. TELEX 15857. Ed. Bo Chr. Koch. adv.; charts; illus.; pat.; stat.; tr.lit.; index; circ. 205,000.

388.3 II ISSN 0027-1713
MOTOR; Tamil auto-two wheeler publication. (Text in Tamil) 1959. m. Rs.50. V. Krishnan, Ed. & Pub., 9 State Bank St., First Lane, Mount Road, Madras 600 002, India. TEL 849305. adv.; bk.rev.; circ. 18,000.

388.3 NO ISSN 0027-173X
MOTOR. 1933. m. NOK 220. Norges Automobil-Forbund - Norwegian Automobile Association, P.O. Box 494, 0105 Oslo 1, Norway. TEL 02-34-14-00. FAX 002-33-21-76. Ed. Svein Ola Hope. adv.; bk.rev.; circ. 470,703.

388.3 SW ISSN 0027-1764
MOTOR. 1943. m. SEK 290. Motormaennens Forlag, Sturegatan 32, P.O. Box 5855, 102 48 Stockholm, Sweden. FAX 8-666-01-29. Ed. Erik Friberg. adv.; bk.rev.; illus.; circ. 210,000.
Incorporates (in 1982): S M T (ISSN 0039-6664)

388.3 US ISSN 0027-1748
TL1
MOTOR; the magazine for the responsible automotive technician. 1903. m. $18. Hearst Business Publishing, 645 Stewart Ave., Garden City, NY 11530. TEL 516-227-1399. FAX 516-227-1405. Ed. Wade Hoyt. adv.; bk.rev.; illus.; mkt.; stat.; tr.lit.; index; circ. 127,000. (also avail. in microform from UMI)

TRANSPORTATION — AUTOMOBILES

388.3   BE
MOTOR; le magazine du moteur et des loisirs. (Text in French) 1922. 11/yr. 750 BEF membership. (Royal Motor Union) Miro Communication, 128 av. de l'Observatoire, 4000 Liege, Belgium. TEL 041-527684. FAX 041-525705. Ed. Michel Ernotte. adv.: B&W page 25000 BEF, color page 38000 BEF; bleed 295 x 208; adv. contact: Michel Ernotte. circ. 40,000.

388.3   PO
MOTOR. w. Rua das Chagas 16-4o Dto., Lisbon, Portugal. TEL 01-3470889. FAX 01-3470691. Dir. Fernando Bello.

629.2   US
MOTOR AUTO REPAIR MANUAL. (In 2 vols.) 1938. a. $106. Hearst Corporation, Motor Manuals Department, 5600 Crooks Rd., Troy, MI 48098. TEL 800-426-6867. index.
    Formerly: Motor's Auto Repair Manual (ISSN 0098-1745)
    Description: Mechanical repair procedures for American-made cars.

MOTOR CLUB NEWS. see *TRAVEL AND TOURISM*

629.28   US
MOTOR CRASH ESTIMATING GUIDE. 1955. 16/yr. $170. Hearst Corporation, Crash Books Department, 5600 Crooks Rd., Ste. 200, Troy, MI 48098. TEL 800-426-6867. (Subscr. to: Box 10115, Des Moines, IA 50350) Ed. Philip Cunningham. adv.; circ. 25,000.
    Description: Provides information necessary for assessing vehicle collision damage.

614.86   US   ISSN 0160-1644
TL152
MOTOR EARLY MODEL CRASH ESTIMATING GUIDE. q. $130. Hearst Corporation, Crash Books Department, 5600 Crooks Rd., Ste. 200, Troy, MI 48098. TEL 800-426-6867. (Subscr. to: Box 10115, Des Moines, IA 50350) Ed. Philip C. Cunningham.

388.3   AT
MOTOR EQUIPMENT NEWS. 1981. m. Aus.$25. Trade Press Australia, 54 Kellett St., Kings Corss, N.S.W. 2011, Australia. TEL 02-358-1155. FAX 02-356-3834. Ed. Neill Thomas. circ. 25,000.
    Description: Covers all aspects of the automotive industry trade including service and repair and parts and accessories.

338.4   US   ISSN 0164-6346
TL152
MOTOR IMPORTED CAR CRASH ESTIMATING GUIDE. m. $170. Motor Publications, Crash Books Department, 5600 Crooks Rd., Ste. 102, Troy, MI 48098. (Subscr. to: Box 10115, Des Moines, IA 50350) Ed. Philip C. Cunningham. illus.; circ. controlled.
    Description: Provides information necessary for assessing vehicle collision damage.

388.3   AT
MOTOR INDUSTRY JOURNAL. 1919. m. Aus.$40. Victorian Automobile Chamber of Commerce, 464 St. Kilda Rd., Melbourne, Vic. 3004, Australia. FAX 03-829-3401. Ed. Mitchell MacKey. adv.; bk.rev.; charts; stat.; index; circ. 5,500. (back issues avail.) Indexed: Aus.Rd.Ind.
    Former titles: V A C C Journal (ISSN 0004-8712); Australian Automobile Trade Journal.

388.3   NZ
MOTOR INDUSTRY NEWS. 1951. bi-m. NZ.$39. Automotive Institute of New Zealand Inc., P.O. Box 1503, Wellington, New Zealand. TEL 04-847-289. FAX 04-828-201. Ed. M.K.S. Sutherland. adv.; bk.rev.; illus.; stat.; index; circ. 2,000.
    Formerly: Service Side.

629.222   UK
MOTOR INDUSTRY OF GREAT BRITAIN (YEAR) WORLD AUTOMOTIVE STATISTICS. 1926. a. £75 to non-members; members £40. Society of Motor Manufacturers and Traders Ltd., Forbes House, Halkin St., London, SW1X 7DS, England. TEL 071-235-7000. FAX 071-235-7112. circ. 1,000.
    Formerly: Motor Industry of Great Britain (ISSN 0077-1597)

388.3   IT   ISSN 0027-1926
MOTOR ITALIA. 1926. a. $20. Motor Italia S.r.l., c/o Stamperia Artistica Nazionale, Corso Siracusa 37, 10136 Turin, Italy. FAX 0039-11-365593. TELEX 214134 SANTO I. Ed. G. Rogliatti. adv.; bk.rev.; bibl.; charts; illus.; pat.; index; circ. 5,000.

388   GW
MOTOR KLASSIK. 1984. m. DM.77 (foreign DM.89). Vereinigte Motor-Verlage GmbH und Co. KG, Leuschnerst. 1, Postfach 106036, 7000 Stuttgart 10, Germany. TEL 0711-18201. FAX 0711-1821756. Ed. Dirk-Michael Conradt. circ. 77,500.
    Description: Information for sports car fans.

629.28   US
MOTOR LIGHT TRUCK & VAN REPAIR MANUAL. a. $54. Hearst Corporation, Motor Manuals Department, 5600 Crooks Rd., Troy, MI 48098. TEL 800-426-6867. Ed. Louis C. Forier.
    Former titles: Motor Light Truck and Van Tuneup and Repair Manual; Motor Light Truck and Van Repair Manual; Motor Truck Repair Manual (ISSN 0098-3624); Motor Truck and Diesel Repair Manual (ISSN 0077-1724)

629.286   DK
MOTOR MAGASINET. 1969. 44/yr. DKK 374. Dansk Auto Media A-S, Hoejvangen 23, 3480 Fredensborg, Denmark. FAX 42-282015. Ed. Bo Christian Koch. adv.; bk.rev.; circ. 17,500.

388.3   AT   ISSN 0818-5549
MOTOR NEWS. 1956. bi-m. membership. Royal Automobile Club of Tasmania, Murray & Patrick Sts., Hobart, Tas. 7001, Australia. TEL 002-38220. FAX 002-348784. Ed. D.J. Rose. adv.; bk.rev.; circ. 100,000.
    Formerly: Tasmanian Motor News (ISSN 0039-9841)

629.2   US   ISSN 0077-1716
MOTOR PARTS & TIME GUIDE. 1910. a. $66. Hearst Corporation, Motor Manuals Department, 5600 Crooks Rd., Troy, MI 48098. TEL 800-426-6867. Ed. Philip Cunningham.
    Formerly: Motor's Flat Rate and Parts Manual.

388.3   UK   ISSN 0306-6274
MOTOR REPORT INTERNATIONAL. 1971. fortn. $330 (effective 1992). Circlemartin Ltd., Box 87, Dorking, Surrey RH4 2YS, England. TEL 0306-740042. Ed. A. Carding. circ. 500. Indexed: PROMT.
    Description: News and statistical data of the automotive industry worldwide.

388.3   UK
MOTOR RETAILER. 1960. m. £35 to non-members. Retail Motor Industry Federation, 201 Great Portland St., London W1N 6AB, England. TEL 071-580-9122. FAX 071-580-6376. Ed. Beverly Hicks. adv.; bk.rev.; tr.lit.; index; circ. 16,500.
    Formerly: Motor Trade Executive (ISSN 0027-2027)

629.286   GW
MOTOR REVUE. 1951. a. DM.15. Motor-Presse Stuttgart, Leuschnerstr. 1, Postfach 106036, 7000 Stuttgart 10, Germany. TEL 0711-18201. FAX 0711-1821669. Ed. Klaus Westrup. illus.; circ. 50,000.

388.3   US   ISSN 0027-1977
TL1
MOTOR SERVICE; the journal for professional automotive repairmen. 1921. m. $36 (Canada and Mexico $45; elsewhere $86). Hunter Publishing Limited Partnership, 950 Lee St., Des Plaines, IL 60016. TEL 708-296-0770. FAX 708-803-3328. Ed. James J. Halloran. adv.; circ. 134,000.

629.286 338.476   UK
MOTOR SPECIFICATIONS & PRICES. 1930. a. £10. Stone & Cox (Publications) Ltd., 44 Fleet St., London EC4Y 1BS, England. Ed. Ernest Holland. (back issues avail.)
    Description: List of prices and specifications of all motor vehicles in the UK and worldwide.

MOTOR SPORT. see *SPORTS AND GAMES*

338   AT
MOTOR TRADE ASSOCIATION OF WESTERN AUSTRALIA. JOURNAL. 1935. m. Aus.$50. Motor Trade Association of Western Australia, M T A House, 69 Walters Dr., Herasman, 6016, Australia. TEL 09-242-3300. FAX 09-242-3759. Ed. Graham Short. adv.; illus.; mkt.; circ. 2,000.
    Former titles: W A A C C S Motor Industry (Western Australian Automobile Chamber of Commerce) (ISSN 0042-9430); Service Station and Motor Trader.
    Description: Provides information on industrial and trade matters.

388.3   AT   ISSN 0027-2035
MOTOR TRADE JOURNAL. 1930. m. Aus.$48 plus postage. Motor Trade Association of S.A., Inc., 50-51 Greenhill Rd., Wayville, S.A. 5034, Australia. FAX 061-8-373-1724. Ed. Richard Flashman. adv.; bk.rev.; index; circ. 2,300. (tabloid format)

388.3   AT
MOTOR TRADER. 1933. m. $48. Motor Trades Association of Queensland, P.O. Box 359, South Brisbane, Brisbane, Qld. 4101, Australia. TEL 07-844-7555. FAX 07-844-4488. Ed. C.R. Jackson. adv.: B&W page $840, color page $1155. illus.; circ. 2,500.
    Former titles: Q A C C Motor Trader; Queensland Motor Industry (ISSN 0033-6203)

388.3   UK   ISSN 0027-2043
MOTOR TRADER. 1905. w. $217.10. Reed Business Publishing Group, Enterprise Division (Subsidiary of: Reed International PLC), Quadrant House, The Quadrant, Sutton, Surrey SM2 5AS, England. TEL 081-652-3276. FAX 081-652-8986. (Subscr. to: Oakfield House, Perrymount Rd., Haywards Heath, W. Sussex RH16 3DH, England. TEL 444-445566) Ed. David Raeside. adv.; charts; illus.; index; circ. 37,059 (controlled).

388.3   RH   ISSN 0027-2051
MOTOR TRADER AND FLEET OPERATOR. 1956. m. Z.$38 (foreign Z.$50). (Motor Trade Association) Thomson Publications Zimbabwe (Pvt) Ltd., Thomson House, P.O. Box 1683, Harare, Zimbabwe. TEL 736835. TELEX 24705 ZW. (Co-sponsor: Motor Industry Employers' Association) Ed. S. Orange. adv.; bk.rev.

388.3   SW   ISSN 0077-1619
HE5680
MOTOR TRAFFIC IN SWEDEN. Swedish edition: Bilismen i Sverige. 1948. a. SEK 57.50($35) (Bilindustri Foereningen - Association of Swedish Automobile Maufacturers and Wholesalers) AB Bilstatistik, Box 5514, S-114 85 Stockholm, Sweden. TEL (08) 783-80-00. FAX 468-6619679. TELEX 119 23 BILS. circ. 1,500.
    Description: Contains statistics on vehicles in use, production, export, import and other useful information.

388.3   US   ISSN 0027-2094
TL1
MOTOR TREND. 1949. m. $19.94. Petersen Publishing Co., 8490 Sunset Blvd., Los Angeles, CA 90069. TEL 213-854-2222. Ed. Jeff Karr. adv.; bk.rev.; charts; illus.; index; circ. 900,000. (also avail. in microfilm from UMI) Indexed: B.P.I., Consum.Ind., Jun.High.Mag.Abstr., Mag.Ind., PMR, R.G., Sports Per.Ind., TOM.
    ●Also available online. Vendor(s): DIALOG.
    Incorporates: Car Life; Sports Car Graphic (ISSN 0038-8165); Wheels Afield (ISSN 0043-4787)

629.28   US
MOTOR TREND'S NEW CAR BUYERS' GUIDE. 1976. a. $3.95. Petersen Publishing Co., 8490 Sunset Blvd., Los Angeles, CA 90069. TEL 213-854-2222. FAX 213-854-2866. adv.; circ. 250,000.
    Description: Highlights cars from the US, Japan and Europe.

388.3   US
MOTOR TREND'S ROAD TESTS. 1986. a. $3.95. Petersen Publishing Co., 8490 Sunset Blvd., Los Angeles, CA 90069. TEL 213-854-2222. FAX 213-854-2718. adv.; circ. 639.3.
    Description: Highlights domestic and imported vehicle road tests with subjective driving impressions, technical information, and comprehensive test results.

TRANSPORTATION — AUTOMOBILES

796.77   US
MOTOR TREND'S SPORTS CARS OF THE WORLD. 1985. a. $3.95. Petersen Publishing Co., 8490 Sunset Blvd., Los Angeles, CA 90069. TEL 213-854-2222. FAX 213-854-2866. adv.; circ. 200,000.
   Description: Showcases sports car classics. Analyzes current models.

629.28   US
MOTOR TREND'S TRUCK AND VAN BUYERS' GUIDE. 1977. a. $3.95. Petersen Publishing Co., 8490 Sunset Blvd., Los Angeles, CA 90069. TEL 213-854-2222. FAX 213-854-2866. adv.; circ. 200,000.
   Description: Contains descriptions and fact sheets for the buyer of a new truck or van.

388.3   AU
MOTOR UND ERDOEL. 1950. w. S.370 per month. Austria Presse Agentur (APA), Gunoldstr. 14, A-1199 Vienna, Austria. Ed. H. Jaros. (processed)
   Formerly: Motor - Dienst und Erdoel - Nachrichten (ISSN 0027-1888)

629.2   CN   ISSN 0316-6198
MOTOR VEHICLE DATA BOOK. 1947. a. Can.$34. Sanford Evans Communications Ltd., 1700 Church Ave., Box 6900, Winnipeg, Man. R3C 3B1, Canada. TEL 204-694-2022. FAX 204-694-3040. Ed. G.B. Henry.
   Description: Identification and registration guide, listing 9 years of statistics including: curb weight, wheelbase, vehicle identification number, engine statistics and M.S. retail price.

629.286   JA
MOTOR VEHICLE ENGINEERING SPECIFICATIONS - JAPAN. (Text in Japanese) a. 12000 Yen. Society of Automotive Engineers of Japan, Inc. - Jidosha Gijutsukai, 10-2, Goban-cho, Chiyoda-ku, Tokyo 102, Japan.

388.34 310   JA   ISSN 0463-6635
MOTOR VEHICLE STATISTICS OF JAPAN. 1958. a. free. Japan Automobile Manufacturers Association, Otemachi Bldg., 1-6-1 Otemachi, Chiyoda-ku, Tokyo 100, Japan. FAX 03-287-2072. stat.; circ. 7,500.

629.222   US   ISSN 1055-8233
▼**MOTOR WORLD.** (Supplement avail.) 1991. a. $23.99. Publishing & Business Consultants, 951 S. Oxford, No. 109, Los Angeles, CA 90006. TEL 213-732-3477. (Subscr. to: Box 75392, Los Angeles, CA 90075) Ed. Atia Napoleon. adv.; circ. 100,000.
   Previously announced as: Car Owners.
   Description: Covers automotive maintenance with news of industry trends.

388.3   SW   ISSN 0027-2140
MOTORBRANSCHEN; official journal of the motor trade and repair organization in Sweden. 1939. 10/yr. SEK 166. (Motorbranschens Riksfoerbund - Swedish National Association for Motor Trades; National Association of Tire Dealers and Repairers) Motorbranschens Foerlag, Karlvaegen 14 A, P.O. Box 5611, S-114 86 Stockholm, Sweden. FAX 08-206747. Ed. Hans Bister. adv.; charts; illus.; circ. 6,380.
   Incorporates: Motorbranschens Registeringsstatistik (ISSN 0027-2159)

388.3   NO   ISSN 0027-2213
MOTORFOEREREN.* 1939. m. NOK 100. Motorfoerernes Avholdsforbund, Esko Nor, Boks 144, 2001 Lillestroem, Norway. Ed. Per Wangen. adv.; bk.rev.; illus.; circ. 39,000.

388   UK   ISSN 0963-7338
MOTORHOME MAGAZINE. q. £10 (foreign £15). Stone Leisure Group, Andrew House, 2a Granville Rd., Sidcup, Kent DA14 4BN, England. TEL 081-302-6150. FAX 081-300-2315. Ed. Dave Randle. circ. 18,000.

388   IT   ISSN 0393-7666
MOTORI. 1950. bi-m. L.22000 (foreign L.65000)(effective 1992). Torino Motori s.r.l., Corso Galileo Ferraris 155, Cas. Post. 336, 10134 Turin, Italy. TEL 011-3181138. FAX 011-3181610. Ed. Raffaele Sanguineti. adv.; circ. 30,000.
   Formerly (until 1986): Torino Motori (ISSN 0493-5306)
   Description: Forum featuring articles on automobiles and trucks in their technical and commercial aspects. Includes articles on hi-fi in cars.

388.3   II   ISSN 0027-223X
MOTORINDIA. (Text in English) 1956. m. Rs.150. (Auto Dealers' & Fleet Operators' Associations) Gopali & Co., 407-408 Mount Rd., Madras 600 035, India. Ed. M. Rajagopalan. adv.; bk.rev.; circ. 25,000.

388.3   II   ISSN 0027-2248
MOTORING. (Text in English) 1964. m. rs.6 to non-members. Western India Automobile Association, 76 Veer Nariman Rd., Churchgate, Bombay 20, India. Ed. Lt.Col. L.C. Fonseca. adv.; circ. 30,000 (controlled). (tabloid format)

910.202 796.77   UK
MOTORING & LEISURE. 1924. m. £12 (effective Jan. 1991). Civil Service Motoring Association Ltd., Britannia House, 95 Queens Rd., Brighton BN1 3WY, England. TEL 0273-21921. FAX 0273-23990. Ed. David Arnold. adv.; bk.rev.; circ. 270,000 (controlled).
   Formerly: Civil Service Motoring.

388.3   UK   ISSN 0027-2264
MOTORING NEWS. 1955. w. £53. News Publications Ltd., Standard House, Bonhill St., London EC2A 4DA, England. FAX 071-638-8497. TELEX 888602-MONEWS-G. Ed. Mark Skewis. adv.; bk.rev.; charts; illus.; circ. 80,000. (tabloid format)

388.3   UK
MOTORIST. 1934. $20.80. I P C Magazines Ltd., Practical Group, Westover House, West Quay Rd., Poole, Dorset BH15 1JG, England. Ed. Charles Deane. adv.; bk.rev.; illus.; tr.lit.; circ. 67,316.
   Indexed: Pinpointer.
   Formerly: Practical Motorist (ISSN 0032-6437)

MOTORIST (SEATTLE). see TRAVEL AND TOURISM

388.3   UK   ISSN 0027-2302
MOTORISTS GUIDE TO NEW & USED CAR PRICES. 1962. m. £20.40. Foxpride Ltd., 67 Tyrrell St., Leicester LE3 5SB, England. TEL 0533-511393. FAX 0533-511335. Ed. L.J. Shoebridge. adv.; illus.; stat.; circ. 50,000.
   Description: Valuation guide for the general public when purchasing or selling a car, light commercial vehicle, or motor caravan.

MOTORLAND. see TRAVEL AND TOURISM

388.3   NO   ISSN 0027-2337
MOTORLIV; Norsk bilmagasin. 1921. 10/yr. NOK 200. Kongelig Norsk Automobilklub, P.O. Box 2425, Solli, 0202 Oslo 2, Norway. TEL 47-2-561900. FAX 47-2-552354. Ed. Petter R. Iversen. adv.; charts; illus.; circ. 25,000.

MOTORSCOT. see SPORTS AND GAMES

388.3   US   ISSN 0027-2396
MOTRIX; the Spanish-language automotive service magazine for Latin America. 1954. 6/yr. $30. Hunter Publishing Ltd., 950 Lee St., Des Plains, IL 60016-6588. Ed. Irv Lineal. adv.; bk.rev.; charts; illus.; tr.lit.; circ. 30,000. (reprint service avail. from UMI)

629.286   CC   ISSN 1001-7666
MOTUOCHE JISHU/JOURNAL OF MOTORCYCLE TECHNOLOGY. (Text in Chinese) 1988. bi-m. $2.5 per no. Zhongguo Qiche Jishu Yanjiu Zhongxin - China Automative Technology & Research Center, P.O. Box 59, Tianjin 300162, People's Republic of China. TEL 470547. FAX 470843. Ed. Shang Guohua.

388.3   US
MUSCLE CAR REVIEW. m. $2.95 per no. Dobbs Publications, 3816 Industry Blvd., Lakeland, FL 33811. TEL 813-646-5743.

796.7   US
MUSCLE CARS. bi-m. C S K Publishing Co., Inc., 299 Market St., Saddle Brook, NJ 07662-5312. TEL 201-712-9300. FAX 201-712-9899. Ed. Jim Campisano. adv.; circ. 44,000.

388.3   US   ISSN 1054-8912
MUSCLE MUSTANGS & FAST FORDS. 1988. 7/yr. $16. C S K Publishing Co., Inc., 299 Market St., Saddle Brook, NJ 07662. TEL 201-712-9300. FAX 201-712-9899. (Subscr. to: Box 1010, Danville, NJ 07834) Ed. Steve Collison. adv.; bk.rev.; circ. 41,000. (back issues avail.)
   Description: For the late model Ford enthusiast, featuring only late-model hop-ups, performance tips and guides, straight line and circle track coverage, tech features and how-tos to make 'Stang faster.

796.77   US   ISSN 0899-1421
MUSCLECAR CLASSICS. bi-m. $13.95. Petersen Publishing Co., 8490 Sunset Blvd., Los Angeles, CA 90069. TEL 213-854-2222. Ed. Jeff Tann. circ. 102,600.

629.286   US   ISSN 0897-0963
MUSCLECARS. 1983. bi-m. $15. C S K Publishing Co., Inc., 299 Market St., Saddle Brook, NJ 07662. TEL 201-712-9300. FAX 201-712-9899. (Subscr. to: Box 1010, Denville, NJ 07834) Ed. Jim Campisano. adv.; circ. 40,000. (back issues avail.)
   Description: Edited for car lovers of the late Fifties, Sixties and early Seventies (1958-1972) featuring all the musclecars such as GTO, Hemi, Mustang, Chevelle, Camaro.

MUSTANG & FORDS. see ANTIQUES

796.77   US
MUSTANG ILLUSTRATED. q. McMullen Publishing, 2145 W. La Palma Ave., Anaheim, CA 92801. TEL 714-635-9040.

796.77   US
MUSTANG MONTHLY. m. $24.97. Dobbs Publications, 3816 Industry Blvd., Lakeland, FL 33811. TEL 813-646-5743. FAX 813-644-8373.

388.3   US
N A D A OFFICIAL USED CAR GUIDE. Eastern Edition (ISSN 0193-2780) (Avail. in 9 Regional Editions) 1933. m. $43. National Automobile Dealers Association, Used Car Guide Co., 8400 Westpark Dr., McLean, VA 22102. TEL 703-821-7000. circ. 370,000.

388.3   US
N A D A OFFICIAL WHOLESALE USED CAR TRADE-IN GUIDE. fortn. $44. National Automobile Dealers Association, Used Car Guide Co., 8400 Westpark Dr., McLean, VA 22102. TEL 703-821-7000.
   Former titles: Official Used Car Trade-In Guide; N A D A Dealers Wholesale Auto Auction Report; N A D A Official Car and Truck Appraisal Guide; N A D A Auto Auction True Values Guide (ISSN 0027-5786)

388.3   US
N A D A OLDER USED CAR GUIDE. 3/yr. $40. (National Automobile Dealers Association) N.A.D.A. Appraisal Guides, Box 7800, Costa Mesa, CA 92628-7800.

381   US   ISSN 0092-4601
HD9715.7.U6
N A D A RECREATION VEHICLE APPRAISAL GUIDE. 3/yr. $85. (National Automobile Dealers Association) N.A.D.A. Appraisal Guides, Box 7800, Costa Mesa, CA 92628-7800.

388.3   US
N A F A ANNUAL REFERENCE BOOK. 1960. a. $45. National Association of Fleet Administrators, Inc., 120 Wood Ave., S., Ste. 615, Iselin, NJ 08830-2709. TEL 908-494-8100. FAX 908-494-6789. Ed. Denise M. Rucci. adv.; stat.; circ. 4,000.
   Formerly: N A F A Conference Brochure and Reference Book (ISSN 0550-8843)

796.77   US
N H R A SOUVENIR YEARBOOK. a. $5. National Hot Rod Association, 2035 Financial Way, Glendora, CA 91740. TEL 818-963-7695. circ. 100,000.
   Description: Drag racing year in review.

629.286   US
NASH TIMES. 1970. bi-m. $23 (foreign $24). Nash Car Club of America, 4151 220 St., Clinton, IA 52732. TEL 319-242-5490. (Subscr. to: c/o Bob Aaron, 635 Lloyd St., Hubbard, OH 44425) Eds. Charlie and Maggie Wilson. circ. 2,000. (back issues avail.)
   Description: For car enthusiasts dedicated to promoting the history, preservation, and restoration of the Nash and related automobiles.

388.3 US
NATIONAL AUTOMOTIVE PARTS ASSOCIATION.
OUTLOOK. 1967. 10/yr. National Automotive Parts Association, 2999 Circle 75 Parkway, Atlanta, GA 30339. TEL 404-956-2200. FAX 404-956-2211. Ed. Kathy Randall. adv.; circ. 16,500.
  Description: For owners and managers of NAPA auto parts stores only.

796.72 US
NATIONAL DRAGSTER. 1960. 48/yr. $45. National Hot Rod Association, 2035 Financial Way, Glendora, CA 91740. TEL 818-963-7695. Ed. Phil Burgess. adv.; stat.; circ. 80,000. (tabloid format)
  Description: Covers drag racing and NHRA events. Features technical articles, new product data, performance standards, race previews, interviews and official rule changes.

388 US
NATIONAL FOUR WHEEL DRIVE ASSOCIATION NEWS. m. National Four Wheel Drive Association, 3310 E. Shangrila Rd., Phoenix, AZ 85028. TEL 602-996-1124. bk.rev.; bibl.

658 US
NATIONAL LIMOUSINE EXCHANGE.* 1989. bi-w. Turnkey Publishing, Inc., 3420 Executive Center Dr., No. 250, Austin, TX 78731-1602. TEL 512-345-5316. adv.; circ. 9,000. (tabloid format)
  Description: Runs displays and provides information on new and used limousine and related products for sale.

629.222 UK
NATIONAL MOTOR MUSEUM PICTORIAL GUIDE. 1959. a. £1.95. (National Motor Museum Trust) Montagu Ventures Ltd., Beaulieu, Hampshire SO42 7ZN, England. TEL 0590-612345. FAX 0590-612624. Ed. M.E. Ware. adv.; illus.; stat.; circ. 120,000.

NATIONAL MOTORIST. see *TRAVEL AND TOURISM*

388.3 665.7 US
NATURAL GAS VEHICLE. 6/yr. $192 to non-members (foreign $240); members $96 (foreign $144). American Gas Association, 1515 Wilson Blvd., Arlington, VA 22209. TEL 703-841-8400. FAX 703-841-8406. (Subscr. to: Dept. 0765, McLean, VA 22109-0765)

629.222 796.7 FI ISSN 0472-8874
NESTEKIDE. 1961. q. free. Neste Oy, P.O. Box 20, 02151 Espoo, Finland. TEL 358-0-4504153. FAX 358-0-4504798. TELEX 124641. Ed. Helena Haapalinna. adv.; bk.rev.; illus.; circ. 57,000.
  Formerly (until 1990): Oljyposti.

388.3 US ISSN 1050-5423
NEW AND USED FOREIGN AND JAPANESE CAR PRICES. 1973. bi-m. $21.95. Pace Publications (Milwaukee), 1020 N. Broadway, Ste. 111, Milwaukee, WI 53202. TEL 414-272-9977. FAX 414-272-9973.
  Formerly (until 1992): Foreign Car Prices.
  Description: Lists dealer's cost and manufacturer's suggested list price for every price for every foreign automobile and every single option available for each, with previous ten year listings for used foreign cars.

388.3 US ISSN 1049-8583
NEW CAR PRICES - BUYER'S GUIDE REPORTS. bi-m. $21.95. Pace Publications (Milwaukee), 1020 N. Broadway, Ste. 111, Milwaukee, WI 53202. TEL 414-272-9977. FAX 414-272-9973.
  Description: Lists dealer's cost and manufacturer's suggested list price for every American automobile and every option available for each model.

629.286 JA
NEW DEVELOPMENTS IN AUTOMOBILE MATERIALS FOR THE 90'S. 1988. w. $3200. Toray Research Center, Inc., (Subsidiary of: Toray Industries, Ltd.) 3-1-8, Nihonbashi - Muromachi, Chuo-ku, Tokyo 103, Japan. TEL 81-3-3245-5895. FAX 81-3-3245-5789. TELEX J22623 TRC.

388.33 US ISSN 0028-713X
NEW YORK AUTO REPAIR NEWS. 1948. m. $12 (free to qualified personnel). Van Allen Publishing Co., Box 354, Hicksville, NY 11802. TEL 516-422-5521. Ed. Richard Van Allen. adv.; circ. 11,300 (controlled).

388.3 US ISSN 0028-7385
NEW YORK MOTORIST. 1926. m. $2. Automobile Club of New York, Inc., 1415 Kellum Pl., Garden City, NY 11530. TEL 516-873-2238. FAX 516-873-2355. Ed. Sy Oshinsky. adv.; illus.; circ. 680,000. (tabloid format; also avail. in microform)
  Description: Features legislative, governmental and traffic safety developments of significance to motorists, and information on travel and vacation opportunities.

629.286 796.72 NZ ISSN 0113-0196
NEW ZEALAND CAR. 1986. m. NZ.$44 (foreign NZ.$110). Vantage Publishing Limited, Cnr. Halsey & Madden Streets, Freemans Bay, Auckland, New Zealand. TEL 09-3098-292. FAX 09-3096-361. Ed. Donn Anderson. circ. 18,000. (back issues avail.)
  Description: Covers all automobile interests, new car tests, new car and product releases, and motor sports.

388.3 JA ISSN 0029-0734
NISSAN DIESEL TECHNICAL REVIEW. (Text in Japanese; table of contents also in English) 1950. s-a. free. Nissan Diesel Motor Co. Ltd. - Nihon Nissan Jizeru Kogyo K.K., 1-1 Ageo, Saitama-ken 362, Japan. Ed. Hisashi Ariga. bk.rev.; abstr.; bibl.; charts; illus.; circ. 4,000.

388.3 JA ISSN 0029-0742
NISSAN GRAPHIC/NISSAN GURAFU. (Text in Japanese) 1946. m. 100 Yen per no. Nissan Motor Co. Ltd., Advertising Department - Nissan Jidosha K.K., 6-17-2 Ginza, Chuo-ku, Tokyo 104, Japan. Ed. M. Uchida. adv.; bk.rev.; illus.; circ. 500,000.

388 GW
NISSAN LIFE. 1977. bi-m. DM.18. Nissan Motor Deutschland GmbH, Nissanstr. 1, 4040 Neuss, Germany. TEL 02131-388255. FAX 02131-37880. adv.; circ. 360,000.
  Description: Cars, motor sports, new product information.

388 FR
NORD-AUTOMOBILE. 10/yr. 140 F. Automobile-Club, B.P. 635, 59061 Roubaix Cedex, France. TEL 20-73-92-80. FAX 20-73-67-87. Ed. B. Morel. circ. 40,000.

796.72 US ISSN 1053-4881
NORTH AMERICAN PYLON; dedicated to sports car autocrossing. 1990. m. $24. Kelly Communications, Box 1203, Pleasanton, CA 94566-0120. TEL 510-846-7728. Ed. John F. Kelly Jr. adv. contact: John F. Kelly Jr. circ. 3,200. (tabloid format; back issues avail.)
  Description: Reports on autocross time trial events throughout the U.S. and Canada, with road tests of new cars and inteviews of prominent drivers and personalities in the sport.

629 US
NORTHERN AUTOMOTIVE NEWS. m. 13304 Stone Rd., Minnetonka, MN 55343-6147. TEL 612-544-6805. adv.; circ. 7,000.

388.3 US ISSN 0029-3148
NORTHERN LIGHTS (MINNEAPOLIS). 1954. 8/yr. membership. Antique Automobile Club of America, Minnesota Region, 621 E. 61st St., Minneapolis, MN 55417. TEL 612-869-1710. Ed. Paul M. Remfer. adv.; circ. 550.

338.476 UK ISSN 0958-4277
NORTH WEST AUTO TRADER. 1981. w. £2.25 per no. Maracomp Ltd., Unit 1, Catherine St., Bewsey Industrial Estate, Warrington, Cheshire WA5 5LH, England. TEL 0925-33000. FAX 0925-411181. Ed. John Harris Title. adv.; circ. 61,228. (back issues avail.)
  Formerly: North West Automart.
  Description: Advertising medium for buying and selling vehicles.

388.3 US ISSN 0029-3393
NORTHWEST MOTOR; journal for the automotive industry. 1909. m. $15. Northwest Motor Publishing Company, 811 First Ave., Ste. 600, Seattle, WA 98104. TEL 206-624-3470. FAX 206-624-3360. Ed. Peter D. duPre. adv.; bk.rev.; illus.; stat.; tr.lit.; circ. 5,800. (also avail. in microform from UMI)

388 388.324 IT
NOTIZIARIO MOTORISTICO/MOTOR NEWS/MOTOR - NACHRICHTEN/BULLETIN MOTORISTIQUE; autoattrezzature-impiantistica. (Text in English, French, German, Italian) 1966. fortn. L.50000. Azienda Cataloghi Italiani s.a.s., Piazzale Lugano 9, 20158 Milan, Italy. TEL 02-39322181. FAX 02-6454786. adv.; bk.rev.; circ. 60,000.
  Description: Covers technical, financial, and commercial news for the automotive industry, with special issues during international auto shows.

388.3 US ISSN 0029-5434
NOZZLE. 1970. m. Greater Washington-Maryland Service Station & Automotive Repair Association, 9420 Annapolis Rd., Ste. 307, Lanham, MD 20706-3021. TEL 301-577-2875. Ed. Roy Littlefield, III. adv.; charts; illus.; circ. 3,500.

629.286 SP
NUESTROS TALLERES; revista profesional de la reparacion, mantenimiento, venta y postventa de vehiculos. 1980. m. 6500 ptas. (foreign 10000 ptas.). Tecnipublicaciones, S.A., Fernando VI, 27, 28004 Madrid, Spain. TEL 91-319-7889. FAX 91-319-7089. TELEX 43905 YEBE E.
  Description: Covers the auto repair industry. Includes new equipment, legal articles and interviews.

797.77 GW
O N S - MITTEILUNGEN. m. DM.52. Obersten Nationalen Sportkommission fuer den Automobil in Deutschland GmbH, Haus des Motorsports, Waidmannstr. 47, D-6000 Frankfurt, Germany. TEL 069-633007-0. TELEX 04-13149.

338.476 CN ISSN 0835-1740
OCTANE. 1987. 4/yr. Can.$18. Maclean Hunter Ltd. (Calgary), 1015 Centre St. N., Ste. 200, Calgary, Alta. T2E 2P8, Canada. TEL 403-276-7881. FAX 403-276-5026. (Subscr. to: 777 Bay St., Toronto, Ont. M5W 1A7) Ed. David Coll. circ. 7,557.

796.7 US
OFF ROAD. 1969. m. $14.98. Argus Publishers Corporation, Box 49659, Los Angeles, CA 90049. TEL 213-820-3601. FAX 213-207-9388. (Street addr.: 12100 Wilshire Blvd., Ste. 250, Los Angeles, CA 90025) Ed. Duane Elliott. adv.; circ. 88,957. (also avail. in microform from UMI; reprint service avail. from UMI) Indexed: Mag.Ind.
  Former titles: Off Road Vehicles and Adventure; Off Road Vehicles.
  Description: Four-wheel vehicle adventure and mechanics.

796.77 US ISSN 1042-0819
OFF-ROAD ADVERTISER. 1967. m. $15. Two Trees Publishing, Inc., Box 1154, Arcata, CA 95521-1154. TEL 310-860-7007. Ed. Fred C. Horton. adv.; circ. 82,375.
  Description: Activities, races, and classifieds of interest to owners of four wheel drive vehicles.

388.3 621.9 UK ISSN 0953-203X
OFF ROAD AND 4 WHEEL DRIVE. 1984. m. £21 (foreign £29.55). Link House Magazines, Dingwall Ave., Croydon, Surrey CR9 2TA, England. TEL 081-686-2599. FAX 081-760-0973. Ed. John Beese. adv.; bk.rev.; charts; illus.; circ. 40,000. (back issues avail.)

629 US
OFFICIAL N A S C A R YEARBOOK AND PRESS GUIDE. 1986. a. $8. U M I Publications, Inc., Box 30036, Charlotte, NC 28230. TEL 703-374-0420. FAX 704-374-0729. Ed. Ivan Mothershead. adv.; circ. 180,000. (back issues avail.)

388.3 FR ISSN 0030-0454
OFFICIEL DE L'AUTOMOBILE; la premiere revue de la profession. 1891. bi-m. 650 F. (Federation Nationale du Commerce et de l'Artisanat Automobile) Societe EDI 92, 83 rue de Villiers, 92553 Neuilly-Seine Cedex, France. TEL 47-38-64-64. FAX 47-47-53-16. TELEX 613448F. Ed. Dennis Jacob. adv.; abstr.; charts; illus.; mkt.; index; circ. 21,000.
  Description: For automobile professionals in France.

TRANSPORTATION — AUTOMOBILES

629.286   330   US
OHIO & NORTHERN KENTUCKY GASOLINE DEALERS & GARAGE NEWS. bi-m. Greater Cincinnati Gasoline Dealers Association, 3410 Glenway Ave., Cincinnati, OH 45205-2902. TEL 513-921-3182. Ed. Virginia Kunnen. circ. 1,800.

OHIO MOTORIST. see *TRAVEL AND TOURISM*

629.2   CN
OLD AUTOS. 1987. s-m. Can.$22 (foreign Can.$42). Old Autos, 348 Main St., Box 419, Bothwell, Ont. N0P 1C0, Canada. TEL 519-695-2303. FAX 519-695-3716. Ed. Murray McEwan. adv.; circ. 8,143. (tabloid format)

629.222   US
OLD CARS WEEKLY; the newspaper of the hobby. 1973. w. $29.95. Krause Publications, Inc., 700 E. State St., Iola, WI 54990. TEL 715-445-2214. FAX 715-445-4087. TELEX 55 6461 KRAUSE PUB UD. Ed. Brad Bowling. adv.; bk.rev.; charts; illus.; tr.lit.; circ. 69,451. (tabloid format; also avail. in microform from UMI)
  Formerly: Old Cars (ISSN 0048-1637)
  Description: Directed to collectors of antique and collectible cars of the last 100 years. Contains news and features on collector cars, restoration tips, auction results, and car show information.

796.77   GW   ISSN 0932-0075
OLDTIMER ADRESSEN LEXIKON; alle Adressen rund um den Oldtimer. 1984. a. DM.19.80. Heel-Verlag GmbH, Hauptstr. 354, 5330 Koenigswinter 1, Germany. Ed. Peter Braun. circ. 20,000.

796.77   GW
OLDTIMER KATALOG; Marktuebersicht fuer klassische Automobile. a. DM.29.80. Heel-Verlag GmbH, Hauptstr. 354, 5330 Koenigswinter 1, Germany. Ed. Dieter Guenther. circ. 20,000.

388.3   GW
OMNIBUS-REVUE UND BUS AKTUELL. 1950. w. DM.122.60 (foreign DM.136.40). Heinrich Vogel Fachzeitschriften GmbH, Neumarkter Str. 18, Postfach 802020, 8000 Munich 80, Germany. TEL 089-43180-0. Ed. Heinzmartin Nitsche. adv.; charts; illus.; tr.lit.; index; circ. 6,300 (controlled).
  Formerly: Omnibus-Revue (ISSN 0030-2279)

796.77   US   ISSN 0279-2737
ON TRACK. 1981. fortn. $29.97. O T Publishing, Inc., 17165 Newhope, Unit M, Box 8509, Fountain Valley, CA 92708-0509. TEL 714-966-1131. FAX 714-556-9776. Ed. Andrew Crask. adv.; bk.rev.; circ. 39,000. (back issues avail.)

338.3   CN
ONTARIO. MINISTRY OF TRANSPORTATION. ONTARIO ROAD SAFETY ANNUAL REPORT. 1957. a. free. Ministry of Transportation, 1201 Wilson Ave., Downsview, Ont. M3M 1J8, Canada. TEL 416-248-3585. (Subscr. to: Publications Services Section, 5th Fl., 880 Bay St., Toronto, Ont. M7A 1N8, Canada. TEL 800-668-9938) illus.; stat.
  Former titles: Ontario. Ministry of Transportation and Communications. Ontario Road Safety Annual Report; (until 1985): Ontario. Ministry of Transportation and Communications. Motor Vehicle Accident Facts; Continues: Ontario. Ministry of Transportation and Communications. Highway Traffic Collisions.

388   AT   ISSN 0048-1947
OPEN ROAD. 1921. bi-m. membership. (National Roads and Motorists Association) Open Road Publishing Co., 151 Clarence St., Sydney, N.S.W. 2000, Australia. TEL 02-260 9222. FAX 02-260-8288. Ed. W. McKinnon. adv.; bk.rev.; circ. 1,445,000.
  Indexed: Aus.Rd.Ind.
  Description: Feature articles and news on motoring and leisure with reports on new and used cars.

388.3   US
OPEN WHEEL. 1981. m. $19.95. Four Wheeler Publishing (Subsidiary of: General Media Publishing Group), 27 S. Main St., Ipswich, MA 01938. TEL 508-356-7030. FAX 508-356-2492. Ed. Dick Berggren. circ. 150,000.
  Description: Covers sprint car, midget, supermodified and Indy car racing. Includes technical features, personality profiles, columns and race reports.

388.3   629.2   CN
OPPORTUNITIES UNLIMITED. biennial. free. Automotive Industries Association of Canada, 1272 Wellington St., Ottawa, Ont. K1Y 3A7, Canada. TEL 613-728-5821. FAX 613-728-6021. Ed. Mireille Schippers. circ. 40,000.

629.286   US
P & S A NEWS. (Performance & Specialty Automotive) 1988. m. free to qualified personnel. Sema Publications, Box 4910, Diamond Bar, CA 91765-0910. TEL 714-860-2961. FAX 714-860-1709. Ed. Tony Thacker. circ. 35,000 (controlled).
  Formerly: Performance Aftermarket Magazine (ISSN 1043-7991)
  Description: Covers specialty automotive product news.

629.286   US
P B E SPECTRUM. (Paint, Body, & Equipment) 1989. bi-m. Irving-Cloud Publishing Co., 7300 N. Cicero Ave., Lincolnwood, IL 60646. TEL 708-674-7300. FAX 708-674-7015. Ed. Martin Schultz.
  Description: Informs body shop personnel on procedures, products and trends.

388   GW
P S DIE MOTORRAD-ZEITUNG. 1976. m. DM.59.40 (foreign DM.78). Motor-Presse Stuttgart, Leuschnerstr. 1, Postfach 106036, 7000 Stuttgart 10, Germany. TEL 0711-18201. FAX 0711-1821669. Ed. Friedrich Fiedler. circ. 45,000.

629.2   US   ISSN 0744-8155
PACIFIC AUTOMOTIVE NEWS. 1973. bi-m. $15. Northwest Motor Publishing Company, 811 First Ave., Ste 600, Seattle, WA 98104. TEL 206-624-3470. FAX 206-624-3360. Ed. Peter D. duPre. adv.; circ. 17,000.
  Description: Independent publication serving the automotive trade of the Pacific Coast.

PACKARD CORMORANT. see *ANTIQUES*

796.77   US   ISSN 0887-9613
PANTERA INTERNATIONAL NEWS. Short title: P I News. 1975. q. $50 (foreign $60)(effective 1992). Pantera International, 18586 Main St., Ste. 100, Huntington Beach, CA 92648. Ed. David Adler. adv.; charts; illus.; index; circ. 500. (back issues avail.)
  Description: Features technical "how to" information on the repair, service and modification of the Pantera automobile. Includes reprints of out-of-print articles and want ads.

388   UK
PARKERS CAR PRICE GUIDE. 1972. m. $55. Parkers Price Guides Ltd., 45 St. Mary's Rd., Ealing, London W5 5RQ, England. Ed. Nicholas Barfield. adv.

388.3   US   ISSN 0031-2193   HE371.A2
PARKING; the magazine of the parking industry. 1952. 10/yr. $95 (foreign $125). National Parking Association, 1112 16th St. N.W., Ste. 300, Washington, DC 20036. TEL 202-296-4336. Ed. George Dragotta. adv.; bk.rev.; charts; illus.; circ. 6,000. Indexed: P.A.I.S.
  —BLDSC shelfmark: 6406.780000.
  Incorporates (1973-1990): N P A Government Affairs Report; (1972-1990): Parking World; Which was formerly (1963-1971): National Parking Association Newsletter (ISSN 0277-0970); Newsletter - National Parking Association (ISSN 0027-9862)

388.3   US
PARKING PROFESSIONAL. 1984. m. $48. Institutional and Municipal Parking Congress, Box 7167, Fredericksburg, VA 22404. TEL 703-371-7535. FAX 703-371-8022. Ed. Marie E. Witmer. adv.; circ. 2,000.

629.24   IT   ISSN 1120-1789
PARTS. 1979. m. L.60000($104) (foreign L.120000). Stammer S.p.A., Centro Commerciale Milano San Felice, 20090 Segrate-Milan, Italy. TEL 02 7530651. FAX 02-7530587. TELEX 321083 STAMMER. Ed. Girolamo Bellina. adv.; circ. 8,000.
  Formerly: Tutto Ricambi.

629.283   US
PARTS & PEOPLE. m. Automotive Counseling and Publishing Co., Inc., 837 Sherman, No. 2B, Denver, CO 80203-2913. TEL 303-860-0545. FAX 303-860-0532. Ed. Dave Lucia. adv.; circ. 10,000.

388.3   US
PERFORMANCE (BENSALEM). 1984. bi-m. $15. R H O Publications, 1580 Hampton Rd., Bensalem, PA 19020. TEL 215-639-4456. circ. 75,000.
  Formerly (until 1991): Morperformance.

796.77   UK   ISSN 0265-6183
PERFORMANCE CAR. 1968. 12/yr. $60. A G B Publications Ltd., Audit House, Field End Rd., Ruislip, Middx. HA4 9LT, England. TEL 01-868-4499. FAX 01-429-3117. TELEX 926726. Ed. Dav Calderwood. adv.; bk.rev.; charts; illus.; tr.mk.; circ. 66,440.
  Formerly: Hot Car (ISSN 0018-6007)

PETERSEN'S 4 WHEEL & OFF-ROAD. see *SPORTS AND GAMES — Bicycles And Motorcycles*

388.3   US
PIERCE-ARROW SERVICE BULLETIN. 1968. 6/yr. $25 membership. Pierce-Arrow Society, Inc., 135 Edgerton St., Rochester, NY 14607. Ed. Bernard J. Weis. circ. 1,100. (processed)

388   JA
PIT INN. (Text in Japanese) 1972. m. 2400 Yen. Geibunsha, 5, 3-chome, Kanda-Surugadai, Chiyoda-ku, Tokyo, Japan. Ed. Keizo Takanashi.
  Formerly: Pit Stop.

PLYMOUTH BULLETIN. see *ANTIQUES*

PNEUMATIQUE; publication d'education et de defense professionnelle. see *RUBBER*

796.77   US
POPULAR CARS. 1981. m. McMullen Publishing, 2145 W. La Palma Ave., Anaheim, CA 92801. TEL 714-635-9040. Ed. Bruce Hampson. adv.
  Formerly: Custom Rodder.

388.3   US   ISSN 0032-4523   TL236
POPULAR HOT RODDING. 1962. m. $16.94. Argus Publishers Corporation, Box 49659, Los Angeles, CA 90049. TEL 213-820-3601. FAX 213-207-9388. (Street addr.: 12100 Wilshire Blvd., Ste. 250, Los Angeles, CA 90025) Ed. Pete Pesterre. adv.; illus.; circ. 248,210.
  Description: Photos and features about hot rods on streets, at shows, and races.

388.3   UK   ISSN 0032-4574
POPULAR MOTORING; and practical car maintenance. 1962. m. £12. Frontline Ltd. (Subsidiary of: E M A P - Haymarket Ltd.), Park House, 117 Park Rd., Peterborough PE1 2TR, England. Ed. Dave Stirling. adv.; charts; illus.; mkt.; circ. 66,389.

796.77   US   ISSN 0147-3565   TL215.P75
PORSCHE PANORAMA. 1955. m. $36 membership. Porsche Club of America, Inc., Box 10402, Alexandria, VA 22310. TEL 703-922-9300. FAX 404-377-7041. (Subscr. to: 912 Lullwater Rd., Atlanta, GA 30307) Ed. Betty Jo Turner. adv.; bk.rev.; charts; illus.; stat.; circ. 31,000. (also avail. in microfilm; back issues avail.; reprint service avail. from UMI)

796.77   US   ISSN 0192-8481
PORSCHE UEBER ALLES. 10/yr. $5. Porsche Club of America, Western Michigan Region, 1503 43rd St., Wyoming, MI 49509. Ed. Charlie Richardson.

629.222   UK   ISSN 0260-2911
PRACTICAL CLASSICS; the do-it-yourself magazine for the older-car owner and enthusiast. 1980. m. $69. E M A P National Publications Ltd., 20-22 Station Rd., Kettering, Northants NN15 7HH, England. TEL 0536-416416. FAX 0536415748. Ed. Peter Simpson. adv.; bk.rev.; illus.; circ. 71,000. (back issues avail.)
  —BLDSC shelfmark: 6593.974330.

388.3   IT
PRESA DIRETTA; quadrimestrale di automobilismo. 3/yr. Via Tiburtina 1159, 00156 Rome, Italy. Ed. Antonio Ghini. adv.; circ. 460,000.

PREVENTION ROUTIERE. see *PUBLIC HEALTH AND SAFETY*

PREVISIONS GLISSANTES DETAILLEES EN PERSPECTIVES SECTORIELLES (VOL.12): CONSTRUCTION AUTOMOBILE. see *BUSINESS AND ECONOMICS — Economic Situation And Conditions*

388.324 796.77 US ISSN 1044-4629
TL230.A1
PRICE GUIDE PRESENTS. (Contains four Muscle Car issues.) 1989. q. $10.95. Krause Publications, Inc., 700 E. State St., Iola, WI 54990. TEL 715-445-2214. FAX 715-445-4087. TELEX 556461 KRAUSE PUB UD. Eds. Ken Buttolph, Jim Lenzke. adv.; circ. 60,000. (back issues avail.)
Supersedes: Truck Prices.
Description: Contains current data and pricing for collectible muscle cars.

629.286 US
PROFESSIONAL CAR WASHING & DETAILING. 1976. m. $39. National Trade Publications, Inc., 13 Century Hill, Latham, NY 12110-2197. TEL 518-783-1281. Ed. Suzanne Stansbury. adv.; circ. 16,932.
Formerly: Professional Car Washing (ISSN 0191-6823)

629.286 US
▼**PROFESSIONAL TOOL AND EQUIPMENT NEWS.** 1991. 6/yr. $14 (foreign $46). Professional Tool and Equipment News, Inc., Box 43078, Mission Viejo, CA 92690-9917. TEL 714-770-2799. FAX 714-830-7523. Ed. Tom Carruthers. adv.; circ. 104,703.
Description: Reports on new tools and equipment available for diagnosing and repairing vehicles properly and profitably.

388 GW
PROFI AM STEUER. 1971. bi-m. DM.30. (Vereingung der Technischen Ueberwachungs-Vereine e.V.) Verlag T Ue V Rheinland GmbH, Am Grauen Stein, 5000 Cologne 91, Germany. TEL 0221-83932653. adv.; illus.

388.3 910.202 GW
PROMOBIL. 1982. m. DM.56.40 (foreign DM.69). Motor-Presse Stuttgart, Leuschnerstr. 1, Postfach 106036, 7000 Stuttgart 10, Germany. TEL 0711-18201. FAX 0711-1821669. Ed. Adi Kemmer. adv.; circ. 42,000. (back issues avail.)
Description: Travel, touring and outfitting information for drivers of recreational vehicles.

629.286 CN
▼**PROMOBILE.** (Text in French) 1990. 4/yr. membership. (Conseil provincial des Comites paritaires de l'Automobile) Parson Communications Inc., 300 Leo-Pariseau, Ste.704, Box 953 Succ. Place du Parc, Montreal, Que. H2W 2N1, Canada. TEL 514-499-1141. FAX 514-499-0307. adv.; circ. 67,000. (tabloid format)

629.286 CC ISSN 1000-680X
QICHE GONGCHENG/AUTOMOTIVE ENGINEERING. (Text in Chinese; abstracts in English) 1979. q. Y11.20 (foreign Y40). Zhongguo Qiche Gongcheng Xuehui - Society of Automotive Engineers of China, 16 Fuxingmenwai Dajie, Beijing 100860, People's Republic of China. TEL 860262. TELEX 22656 CNAIC CN. (Dist. outside China by: Guoji Shudian - International Book Trading Corp., P.O. Box 399, Beijing, P.R.C.) Ed. Wu Huile. adv. contact: Zhenmin Zhong. circ. 4,000.

629.286 CC
QICHE GONGYI/AUTOMOTIVE TECHNOLOGY. (Text in Chinese) bi-m. Changchun Qiche Yanjiusuo - Changchun Automobile Research Institute, 42, Dongfeng Dajie, Changchun, Jilin 130011, People's Republic of China. TEL 504613. Ed. Chang Guangjia.

629.286 CC ISSN 1000-3703
QICHE JISHU/AUTOMOBILE TECHNOLOGY. (Text in Chinese) m. Changchun Qiche Yanjiusuo - Changchun Automobile Research Institute, 17, Chuangye Dajie, Changchun, Jilin 130011, People's Republic of China. TEL 73909. Ed. Han Xuechun.

629.283 CC ISSN 1000-6796
QICHE ZHI YOU/FRIENDS OF AUTOMOBILE. (Text in Chinese) bi-m. Zhongguo Qiche Gongcheng Xuehui - China Automobile Engineering Society, 16 Fuxingmenwai Dajie, Beijing 100860, People's Republic of China. TEL 860262. Ed. Jin Ruting.

QUATRO RODAS. see *TRAVEL AND TOURISM*

388.3 IT ISSN 0033-5916
QUATTRORUOTE. 1956. m. $90. Editoriale Domus, Via Achille Grandi 5-7, 20089 Rozzano (MI), Italy. TEL 02-824721. FAX 02-26863093. Ed. Raffaele Mastrostefano. adv.; bk.rev.; illus.; index; circ. 700,000.

QUE AUTOMOVIL COMPRO?; guia del comprador de coches. see *CONSUMER EDUCATION AND PROTECTION*

388.3 BE ISSN 0022-7242
R A C B ROYAL AUTO. (Editions in Dutch, French) 1905. m. (except Aug.). 750 Fr. Koninklijke Automobiel Club van Belgie - Royal Automobile Club of Belgium (R.A.C.B.), 53 rue d'Arlon, B-1040 Brussels, Belgium. Ed. Raoul Tuyttens. adv.; bk.rev.; charts; illus.; index; circ. 33,000. (controlled)

R A C EUROPEAN HOTEL GUIDE. (Royal Automobile Club) see *TRAVEL AND TOURISM*

R A C HOTEL GUIDE GREAT BRITAIN & IRELAND. (Royal Automobile Club) see *TRAVEL AND TOURISM*

R A C MOTOR SPORT YEAR BOOK. see *SPORTS AND GAMES*

388.3 NE ISSN 0166-1922
R A I ACTUEEL. 1945. w. fl.95($50) Nederlandse Vereniging "de Rijwiel- en Automobiel Industrie", Europaplein 2, 1078 GZ Amsterdam, Netherlands. TEL 020-5491212. FAX 020-463857. Ed. M.F. Timmer. bk.rev.; stat.; tr.mk.; circ. 2,500. **Indexed:** Key to Econ.Sci.
Formerly: R A I Orgaan (ISSN 0030-7785)

R V WEST. see *TRAVEL AND TOURISM*

RACING CAR NEWS. see *SPORTS AND GAMES*

RACING WHEELS. see *SPORTS AND GAMES*

629.286 US ISSN 0739-2060
RADIATOR REPORTER. 1973. m. $140. Runzheimer International, Runzheimer Park, Rochester, WI 53167. TEL 414-534-3121. (Subscr. to: 555 Skokie Blvd,,, Ste. 340, Northbrook, IL 60062. TEL 800-942-9949) Ed. Elliot Kravetz. (looseleaf format)

796.77 UK ISSN 0269-8315
RADIO CONTROL MODEL CARS. 1979. m. £19.20. Argus Specialist Publications Ltd., Argus House, Boundary Way, Hemels, Hampstead, Herts HP2 7ST, England. (Dist. by: Infonet Ltd., 5 River Park Estate, Berkhamsted, Herts HP4 1HL, England) Ed. Alan Harman. adv.; bk.rev.; circ. 14,674. (back issues avail.)
Description: Product news, reviews, race reports, letters and advice for model car enthusiasts.

RALLY SPORT. see *SPORTS AND GAMES*

388.3 796.72 GW ISSN 0033-9148
RALLYE RACING. 1966. m. DM.104 (foreign DM.117). Top Special Verlag, Valentinskamp 24, 2000 Hamburg, Germany. TEL 040-3474467. adv.; bk.rev.; charts; illus.; index; circ. 160,000.
Formerly: Automobil Sport-Zeitschrift.

RANCHERO COURIER. see *HOBBIES*

790.13 US ISSN 0733-4745
TL298
RECREATIONAL VEHICLE BLUE BOOK. 3/yr. $110. Maclean Hunter Market Reports, Inc., 29 N. Wacker Dr., Chicago, IL 60606-3297. TEL 312-726-2802. FAX 312-726-2574. (back issues avail.)

388.3 US ISSN 0736-7953
HD9710.U5
RED BOOK USED CAR GUIDE. 8/yr. $49.50. Maclean Hunter Market Reports, Inc., 29 N. Wacker Dr., Chicago, IL 60606-3297. TEL 312-726-2802. FAX 312-726-2574. (also avail. on diskette; back issues avail.)

629.288 AT
REFINERIEN. 1958. 6/yr. free. Dulux Australia, Box 60, Clayton, Vic. 3168, Australia. FAX 61-2-4765739. Ed. K. Virtue. adv.; circ. 16,000.

REISEN MIT DEM AUTO. see *TRAVEL AND TOURISM*

388.3 UK
RENAULT CONTACT. 1975. m. Renault U.K. Ltd., Western Ave., London W3 0RZ, England. Ed. Marguerite Nudd. circ. 9,500.
Description: Information magazine for Renault dealers in the UK.

629.286 AT ISSN 0311-4163
RESTORED CARS. 1973. q. Aus.$23.50 (foreign Aus.$36) for 6 issues. Eddie Ford Publications, Private Bag, Newstead, Vic. 3462, Australia. TEL 054-762212. FAX 054-762592. Ed. Eddie Ford. (back issues avail.)
Description: Devoted to the restored or original car. Includes veteran, vintage, classic and post-war period cars to cars of the 50's, 60's, and 70's, and muscle cars.

629.286 US
▼**RESTYLING AND ACCESSORIES MARKETING.** 1991. bi-m. $50. Shore Communications, Inc., 180 Allen Rd., Ste. 300N, Atlanta, GA 30328-4893. TEL 404-252-8831. FAX 404-252-4436. Ed. Karen Schaffner. adv.; circ. 11,000. (controlled)
Description: Focuses on the benefits of aftermarket restyling and accessorization of new automobiles.

629.28 796.77 PO ISSN 0870-273X
REVISTA A C P. 1929. m. $24. Automovel Club de Portugal, R. Rosa Araujo, 24, 1200 Lisbon, Portugal. TEL 3563931. FAX 3574732. Ed. Manuela Martins. adv.; illus.; circ. 160,000.

796 BL
REVISTA MAR - VELA E MOTOR. 1976. m. Editora Grupo 1 Ltda., Av. Mal Camara 271, Ste. 603, Rio de Janiero 20020. TEL 5521-533-1415. FAX 5521-533-1702. TELEX 2137398 RYCB BR. Ed. Roberto Falcao. circ. 50,000.

REVUE AUTOMOBILE; journal suisse de l'automobile. see *TRANSPORTATION*

388.3 629.2 FR ISSN 0017-307X
REVUE TECHNIQUE AUTOMOBILE. 1946. m. 810 F. (foreign 985 F.). Editions Techniques pour l'Automobile et l'Industrie (ETAI), 20 rue de la Saussiere, 92100 Boulogne Billancourt, France. TEL 46-04-81-13. FAX 48-25-56-92. TELEX ETAIRTA 204850 F. Ed. Benoit Perot. circ. 28,000.
Description: Aimed at jobbers and experienced amateurs; deals with a different car each month and explains how to repair it.

338.476 FR ISSN 0150-7206
REVUE TECHNIQUE CARROSSERIE. 1963. bi-m. 510 F. (foreign 585 F.). Editions Techniques pour l'Automobile et l'Industrie (ETAI), 20-22 rue de la Saussiere, 92100 Boulogne Billancourt, France. TEL 46-04-81-13. FAX 48-25-56-92. TELEX ETAIRTA 204850 F. Ed. Jean-Pierre Nicolas. charts; illus.; circ. 8,500.
Description: Aimed at car body-builders, steel-workers and painters, details how to repair the car body and describes the tools to be used.

629.2 FR ISSN 0037-2579
REVUE TECHNIQUE DIESEL. 1963. bi-m. 545 F. (foreign 640 F.). Editions Techniques pour l'Automobile et l'Industrie (ETAI), 20 rue de la Saussiere, 92100 Boulogne Billancourt, France. TEL 46-04-81-13. FAX 48-25-56-92. TELEX ETAIRTA 204850 F. Ed. Bernard Adam. circ. 9,200.
Formerly: Service Diesel.
Description: Deals with trucks, public works material and industrial engines. Describes a particular diesel oil truck and explains how to repair it.

388.3 AT ISSN 0035-7170
ROAD AHEAD. 1926. bi-m. free to members. (Royal Automobile Club of Queensland, Brisbane) Road Ahead Publishing Co. Pty Ltd., G.P.O. Box 1403, Brisbane, Qld. 4001, Australia. FAX 257-1863. Ed. G.J. Fites. adv.; bk.rev.; charts; illus.; circ. 580,000. (controlled)

TRANSPORTATION — AUTOMOBILES 4701

388.3 US ISSN 0035-7189
TL1
ROAD & TRACK. 1947. m. $19.94. Hachette Magazines, Inc., Road & Track, 1499 Monrovia Ave., Newport Beach, CA 92663. TEL 714-720-5300. FAX 714-631-2374. TELEX 910 596-1353. Ed. Tom Bryant. adv.; bk.rev.; charts; illus.; record rev.; index; circ. 700,000. (also avail. in microform from UMI; reprint service avail. from UMI) **Indexed:** Acad.Ind., Access, Consum.Ind., Mag.Ind., PMR, R.G., Sports Per.Ind., TOM.

796.77 US
ROAD & TRACK SPORTS & G T CARS. 1965. a. $4.95. Hachette Magazines, Inc. (Newport Beach), Road & Track Specials, 1499 Monrovia Ave., Newport Beach, CA 92663. TEL 714-720-5300. Ed. Ron Sessions. adv.; circ. 250,000. (also avail. in microform from UMI; back issues avail.) **Indexed:** R.G.

629.286 US
▼**ROAD SERVICE NEWS.** 1991. m. $24. Road Service News Corp., 629 Amboy Ave., 3rd. Fl., Edison, NJ 08837. TEL 908-738-5905. FAX 908-738-6116. adv.: B&W page $2250, color page $3250; trim 11 x 15; adv. contact: Mickey Kaplan. circ. 40,000.
Description: Includes news, marketing, business trends, new products, service tips and education.

614.8 SA ISSN 0035-7391
ROBOT. (Text in Afrikaans and English) 1962. 4/yr. free. National Road Safety Council - Nasionale Verkeersveiligheidsraad, N R S C Bldg., Beatrix St., Private Bag X147, Pretoria 0001, South Africa. TEL 012-28-5929. FAX 012-3232215. TELEX 320828. Ed. M. le Grange. adv.; bk.rev.; illus.; stat.; film rev.; circ. 50,000. **Indexed:** Robomat.
Description: General interest road and traffic safety information.

ROCKY MOUNTAIN MOTORIST. see *TRAVEL AND TOURISM*

388.3 US
ROD ACTION. 1972. m. $18.95. Challenge Publications, Inc., 7950 Deering Ave., Canoga Park, CA 91304. TEL 213-887-0550. Ed. Steve Anderson. adv.; bk.rev.; charts; illus.; circ. 95,000.
Description: Covers automobile racing.

629.28 US
ROD & CUSTOM MAGAZINE. 1989. bi-m. Petersen Publishing Co., 8490 Sunset Blvd., Los Angeles, CA 90069. TEL 213-854-2222. Ed. Pat Ganahl. adv.; circ. 100,000.
Description: Focuses on aspects of contemporary street rodding, including trends, racing and techniques.

388.3 UK ISSN 0035-7952
ROLLS ROYCE OWNER.* 1963. m. 42s.($6.25) Owner Publication, 6 The Lawn, St. Leonards on Sea, Sussex, England. Ed. Jeremy Bacon. adv.; bk.rev.; charts; illus.; index; circ. 500.

ROMBO; settimanale a tutto motore. see *SPORTS AND GAMES*

388.3 FR ISSN 0035-8568
ROUTE. no.33, 1970. q. 40 F. Comite National du Secours Routiers Francais, 50 quai Bleriot, 75016 Paris, France. Ed. Pierre Merard. adv.; charts; illus.; stat.; circ. 7,000.

388.3 AT ISSN 0035-9300
ROYALAUTO. 1925. m. (except Jan.). membership. (Royal Automobile Club of Victoria) Automobile Club Publishing Co., 550 Princes Highway, Noble Park, Vic. 3174, Australia. FAX 613-790-2628. Ed. Grant Roff. adv.; bk.rev.; circ. 1,100,000. **Indexed:** Aus.Rd.Ind.

629.221 CN ISSN 0048-8771
RUNNING BOARD. 1961. m. Can.$10. Edmonton Antique Car Club, P.O. Box 102, Edmonton 15, Alta., Canada. Ed. Murray Walkemeyer. adv.; circ. 150.
Formerly: Edmonton Antique Car Club. Bulletin.

388 330.9 US ISSN 0730-8647
RUNZHEIMER ON CARS & LIVING COSTS. 1963. q. Runzheimer International, Runzheimer Park, Rochester, WI 53167. TEL 414-534-3121. (Subscr. to: 555 Skokie Blvd., Ste. 340, Northbrook, IL 60062. TEL 800-942-9949) Ed. Peter D. Packer. circ. 98,000. (tabloid format; back issues avail.)

614.86 US ISSN 0894-492X
RUNZHEIMER REPORTS ON FLEET MAINTENANCE & SAFETY. 1987. m. $196. Runzheimer International, Runzheimer Park, Rochester, WI 53167. TEL 414-534-3121. (Subscr. to: 555 Skokie Blvd., Ste. 340, Northbrook, IL 60062. TEL 800-942-9949) Ed. Ralph McDarmont. (looseleaf format)

629.286 658 US
RUNZHEIMER REPORTS ON FLEET MANAGEMENT. 1981. m. $247. Runzheimer International, Runzheimer Park, Rochester, WI 53167. TEL 414-534-3121. (Subscr. to: 555 Skokie Blvd., Ste. 340, Northbrook, IL 60062. TEL 800-942-9949) Ed. Ralph McDarmont. (looseleaf format; back issues avail.)
Formerly: Runzheimer Reports on Transportation (ISSN 0730-8655)

RUOTECLASSICHE. see *ANTIQUES*

629.2 AT ISSN 0036-0651
S A E - AUSTRALASIA. 1940. bi-m. Aus.$48 (foreign Aus.$65). Society of Automotive Engineers, 191 Royal Parade, Parkville, Vic. 3052, Australia. TEL 03-347-2220. FAX 03-347-0464. Ed. Richard Skjellerup. adv.; bk.rev.; illus.; index; circ. 3,500. (back issues avail.) **Indexed:** Aus.Rd.Ind., Met.Abstr., World Alum.Abstr.
—BLDSC shelfmark: 8062.830000.
Formerly: I A A E Journal.
Description: Technical papers, development reports and membership activities: for professional auto engineers, technicians and enthusiasts.

629.28 US ISSN 0362-8205
TL151
S A E HANDBOOK. 1905. a. $250 4-vol. set. Society of Automotive Engineers, 400 Commonwealth Dr., Warrendale, PA 15096-0001. TEL 412-776-4841. FAX 412-776-5760.
●Also available online. Vendor(s): Orbit Information Technologies.

388 US ISSN 0148-7191
CODEN: STPSDN
S A E TECHNICAL PAPERS. irreg. $7 to non-members; members $4. Society of Automotive Engineers, 400 Commonwealth Dr., Warrendale, PA 15096-0001. TEL 412-776-4841. FAX 412-776-5760. index, cum.index: 1906-1964, 1965-1989. (back issues avail.) **Indexed:** Pollut.Abstr., Soils & Fert.
●Also available online. Vendor(s): European Space Agency, FIZ Technik, Orbit Information Technologies.

629.28 US ISSN 0096-736X
TL1
S A E TRANSACTIONS. a. $750. Society of Automotive Engineers, 400 Commonwealth Dr., Warrendale, PA 15096. TEL 412-776-4970. index. **Indexed:** Geotech.Abstr., Noise Pollut.Publ.Abstr.
●Also available online. Vendor(s): Orbit Information Technologies.

388.3 US
S C & O: SPECIALTY & CUSTOM DEALER; the business magazine for the specialty automotive market. (Includes Machine Shop Profit Planner published in Jan.) 1966. 12/yr. $70. Babcox Publications, 11 S. Forge St., Box 1810, Akron, OH 44309-1810. TEL 216-535-6117. FAX 216-535-0874. Ed. Steve Cole. circ. 26,000.
Formerly: Speed and Custom Dealer (ISSN 0038-7193)

629.286 US ISSN 0279-5051
S E M A NEWS.* 1968. m. membership. Specialty Equipment Market Association, PO Box 4910, Diamond Bar, CA 91765-0910. TEL 213-692-9402. FAX 213-695-3700. Ed. John Rader. adv.; circ. 3,500. (tabloid format)

629.222 UK
S M M T BUYERS GUIDE. a. £25 to non-members; members £15. Society of Motor Manufacturers and Traders Ltd., Forbes House, Halkin St., London SW1X 7DS, England. TEL 071-235-7112. FAX 071-235-7112. TELEX 21628. circ. 10,000.
Former titles: Buyers' Guide to the Automotive Industry of Great Britain for International Buyers; Buyers' Guide to the Motor Industry of Great Britain.

SACRED OCTAGON. see *ANTIQUES*

614.8 629.28 UK ISSN 0036-2387
SAFE DRIVER. 1929. 3/yr. membership. Order of the Road, 14 Churchfields, Nutley, Uckfield, E. Sussex TN22 3NA, England. TEL 0825-71-2271. Ed. John Taylor. adv.; bk.rev.; circ. 1,800 (controlled).
Description: News about road safety, members' services, motoring and travel.

388 US
ST. PAUL, MINNESOTA. TWIN CITIES AREA METROPOLITAN TRANSIT COMMISSION. ANNUAL REPORT. 1969. a. free. Twin Cities Area Metropolitan Transit Commission, 560 N. 6th St., Minneapolis, MN 55411-4398. TEL 612-349-7696. FAX 612-349-7612. Ed. Steve Beseke. circ. 7,000.
Formerly: St. Paul, Minnesota. Metropolitan Transit Commission. Annual Report (ISSN 0082-710X)
Description: Examines the activities of the organizations' previous year.

388 CN ISSN 0381-8179
SANFORD EVANS GOLD BOOK OF USED CAR PRICES. 1952. m. Can.$68. Sanford Evans Communications Ltd., 1700 Church Ave., Box 6900, Winnipeg, Man. R3C 3B1, Canada. TEL 204-694-2022. FAX 204-694-3040. Ed. Gary Henry.
Description: Lists previous eight models of cars and light duty trucks. Valuations for three major Canadian markets, factory suggested price, and current wholesale and retail values.

629.224 JA ISSN 0036-4398
SANGYO SHARYO/INDUSTRIAL VEHICLES. (Text in Japanese) 1964. m. 3600 Yen($12) Japan Industrial Vehicles Association - Nihon Sangyo Sharyo Kyokai, Tobu Bldg., 5-26, 1-chome, Moto-Akasaka, Minato-ku, Tokyo 107, Japan. TEL 03-403-5556. FAX 03-403-5057. Ed. Masaru Terada. adv.; circ. 1,000. **Indexed:** JTA.

388.3 380.5 YU
SAVREMENI VOZAC. (Text in Serbo-Croatian) 1975. bi-m. 600 din. Savez Vozaca Srbije, Pop Lukina 1, 11000 Belgrade, Yugoslavia. TEL 636-515. Ed. Zdravko Ilic. circ. 20,000. (back issues avail.)

629.222 TS
AL-SAYYARAH AL-ARABIYYAH. (Text in Arabic) 1989. m. Muhammad Rashid Amiri, Prop., P.O. Box 8790, Dubai, United Arab Emirates. TEL 211123. FAX 213080. TELEX 48906. Ed. Abu Bakr Amiri. circ. 2,000.
Description: Provides news and information on cars for enthusiasts in the Gulf region, including road tests and safety topics.

SCALE MODELS INTERNATIONAL. see *HOBBIES*

692.2 US
SECRETARY OF ENERGY ANNUAL REPORT TO CONGRESS. a. U.S. Department of Energy, Secretary of Energy, 1000 Independence Ave., S.W., Washington, DC 20585.

629.286 US ISSN 1043-7053
SERVICE QUARTERLY. 1929. q. $40. Service Station Dealers Association of Michigan, 200 N. Capitol, Ste. 420, Lansing, MI 48933. TEL 517-484-4096. Ed. Letitia A. Skeen. adv.; circ. 3,500. (back issues avail.)
Formerly: Service Station Dealers News.

388.3 AT ISSN 0818-2884
SERVICE STATION. 1961. m. Aus.$49. Berg Bennett & Associates Pty. Ltd., 73 Mullens St., Balmain, N.S.W. 2041, Australia. FAX 02-555-1434. Ed. B. Mark. adv.; circ. 9,500.
Formerly: Automotive Service (ISSN 0005-1586)
Description: Matters concerning government legislation, marketing and technical information, customer relations and more.

388.33 CN ISSN 0037-2668
SERVICE STATION & GARAGE MANAGEMENT. 1934. m. Can.$34.24($46) (foreign $46). Southam Business Communications Inc., 1450 Don Mills Rd., Don Mills, Ont. M3B 2X7, Canada. TEL 416-445-6641. FAX 416-442-2261. Ed. Gary Kenez. adv.; circ. 31,100. **Indexed:** Can.B.P.I.
Formerly: Service Station Management and Merchandising (ISSN 0037-2676)

TRANSPORTATION — AUTOMOBILES

388.33 US ISSN 0488-3896
TL153.A1
SERVICE STATION MANAGEMENT. 1958. 6/yr. $36 (Canada and Mexico $45; elsewhere $83). Hunter Publishing Limited Partnership, 950 Lee St., Des Plaines, IL 60016. TEL 708-296-0770. FAX 708-803-3328. Ed. Peggy Smedley. adv.; circ. 82,000.
Description: For retail gasoline stations involved in automotive repairs.

614.86 IT
SETTESTRADE; mensile automobile Club Roma. m. (10/yr.). Settestrade S.r.l., Via C. Colombo 261, Palazzo ACI, Rome, Italy. TEL 06-5106. Ed. Attilio Baglioni.

SHOP MANAGEMENT HANDBOOK. see *BUSINESS AND ECONOMICS — Management*

388 US
SHOP TALK.* 1979. m. $50. International Mobile Air Conditioning Association, 2100 N. Highway 360, Ste. 1300, Grand Prairie, TX 75050-1034. TEL 214-484-5750. Ed. Paul M. Allen. circ. 500. (back issues avail.)
Description: News and articles of interest to the motor vehicle air conditioning and the installed accessories industry.

629.286 IT
SICILIA MOTORI. 1982. m. (11/yr.). L.35000. RODA Informazione & Immagine S.r.l., Via L. Ariosto 16-C, 90144 Palermo, Italy. TEL 91-6254302. FAX 91-6259751. TELEX P.P. PA 911153. Ed. Dario Pennica. adv.; circ. 5,000.

388.3 CS ISSN 0322-7154
SILNICNI OBZOR; mesicnik pro technicke, technologicke a ekonomicke otazky automobilove a mestske dopravy a silnichniho hospodarstvi. (Text in Czech or Slovak; summaries in English, French, German, Russian) vol.13, 1965. m. 48 Kcs.($57.90) (Federalni Ministerstvo Vnitra) Nakladatelstvi Dopravy a Spoju, Hybernska 5, 115 78 Prague 1, Czechoslovakia. (Dist. by: Artia, Ve Smeckach 30, 111 27 Prague 1, Czechoslovakia) Ed. A.V. Novotny. adv. Indexed: Geotech.Abstr.
Formerly: Silnicni Doprava (ISSN 0037-5292)

SKOZI T A M. (Towarne Avtomobilov in Motorjev) see *ENGINEERING — Mechanical Engineering*

388.3 US
SKYLINER. 1971. m. $24. International Ford Retractable Club Inc., Box 92, Jerseyville, IL 62052. TEL 618-498-5485. adv.; charts; illus.; tr.lit.; circ. 1,350.
Description: Social and educational information on 1957-59 Ford Retractable cars.

SOCIEDAD ESPANOLA DE AUTOMOVILES DE TURISMO. MEMORIA Y BALANCE. see *TRAVEL AND TOURISM*

388.3 621.38 US
SOUND CHALLENGE. bi-m. $16.95 (Canada $24.95; elsewhere $34.95). Bobit Publishing Company, 2512 Artesia Blvd., Redondo Beach, CA 90278. TEL 310-376-8788. FAX 310-376-9043.
Description: For autosound enthusiasts and participants in the international Autosound Challenge Association events.

388.3 AT ISSN 0038-2957
SOUTH AUSTRALIAN MOTOR. 1913. bi-m. membership. Royal Automobile Association of South Australia Inc., 41 Hindmarsh Square, Adelaide, S.A. 5000, Australia. TEL 08-2234555. FAX 08-232-0904. Ed. Martin Chipperfield. circ. 330,000. Indexed: Aus.Rd.Ind., Pinpointer.

796.72 US
SOUTHEAST DRAGSTER. 1989. 10/yr. $15. National Hot Rod Association, 2035 Financial Way, Glendora, CA 91740. TEL 818-963-7695. Ed. Kevin McKenna. adv.; stat.; circ. 12,000. (tabloid format)
Description: Covers drag racing in the southeastern United States. Includes interviews and new product news.

SOUTHERN MOTORACING. see *SPORTS AND GAMES*

388.3 US ISSN 0049-1845
SPECIAL INTEREST AUTOS. 1970. bi-m. $19.95. Watering, Inc., Special Interest Publications, Box 904, Bennington, VT 05201. TEL 802-442-3101. FAX 802-447-1561. (Subscr. to: Box 196, Bennington, VT 05201) Ed. David Brownell. adv.; charts; illus.; index, cum.index: 1970-1986; circ. 33,600. (back issues avail.)
Description: Covers cars built from 1925-1970.

796.77 US ISSN 0894-7414
SPECIALTY AUTOMOTIVE MAGAZINE. 1983. q. $18 (free to qualified personnel). Meyers Publishing Corp., 6211 Van Nuys Blvd., Ste. 200, Van Nuys, CA 91401. TEL 818-785-3900. FAX 818-785-4397. TELEX 650-292-3000 MCI. Ed. Paul Dexler. adv.; tr.lit.; circ. 25,000. (reprint service avail.)
Formerly: Specialty Automotive Parts & Accessories.

SPORT-AUTO; le magazine du sport automobile et de l'automobile sportive. see *SPORTS AND GAMES*

796 GW
SPORT AUTO. 1969. m. DM.66 (foreign DM.79.20). Vereinigte Motor-Verlage GmbH and Co. KG, Leuschnerstr. 1, Postfach 106036, 7000 Stuttgart 10, Germany. TEL 0711-18201. FAX 0711-1821756. Ed. Heiner Buchinger. adv.; bk.rev.; index; circ. 81,005. (back issues avail.)
Description: Popular magazine for sportscar enthusiasts. Covers the latest trends and styles, technology, tests, racing, and events. Includes letters from readers.

796.77 LE
SPORT AUTO MAGAZINE. (Text in Arabic; Summaries in Arabic and English) 1973. m. $40. Barson Publications, Ltd., P.O. Box 113-5358, Beirut, Lebanon. TEL 01-361580. TELEX 23388 BARSON LE. Ed. Ibrahim M. Fakhri. adv.; charts; illus.; stat.; circ. 70,298. (back issues avail.)
Description: Includes new model reviews, road testing and evaluation, international and regional motor sports coverage.

388.3 US
SPORT COMPACT CAR. bi-m. $3.25 per no. McMullen Publishing, 2145 W. La Palma Ave., Anaheim, CA 92801. TEL 714-635-9040.

SPORT VE RECHEV. see *SPORTS AND GAMES*

796.77 GW
SPORTFAHRER. 1974. m. Top Special Verlag, Valentinskamp 24, P.O. Box 30 54 24, 2000 Hamburg 36, Germany. circ. 40,353.

388.3 US ISSN 1042-9662
TL236
SPORTS CAR INTERNATIONAL. 1985. m. $17.95. Continental Web Press, 1430 Industrial Dr., Box 366, Itasca, IL 60143. TEL 708-773-1903. Ed. Mark Ewing. adv.; bk.rev.; charts; illus.; circ. 90,000. (back issues avail.)
Formerly (until July 1989): Sports Car Illustrated.
Description: For performance car enthusiasts and those traditionalists who define cars as entertainment.

796.77 US
SPORTSCARS OF THE WORLD. a. $3.95. Petersen Publishing Co., 8490 Sunset Blvd., Los Angeles, CA 90069. TEL 213-854-2222.

388 US ISSN 0887-3453
SPOTLIGHT (ROBBINSVILLE). bi-m. membership. Automobile Club of Central New Jersey, 3 AAA Drive, Robbinsville, NJ 08691-1898. TEL 609-890-2220. Ed. Cecilia M. Downey.

629.28 US ISSN 0585-086X
TL6 CODEN: SCCCBR
STAPP CAR CRASH CONFERENCE PROCEEDINGS. 10th, 1967. a. Society of Automotive Engineers, 400 Commonwealth Dr., Warrendale, PA 15096-0001. TEL 412-776-4841. FAX 412-776-5760. Indexed: Biol.Abstr.
● Also available online. Vendor(s): European Space Agency, FIZ Technik, Orbit Information Technologies.

629.286 IT
STARTER. m. L.54000 (foreign L.91000). Casa Editrice Universo S.p.A., Via Margherita De Vizzi, 35, 20092 Cinisello Balsamo (MI), Italy. TEL 02-618331. Ed. Raffaele D'Argenzio.

388 DK ISSN 0901-6139
STATISTIK OVER REGISTRERING AF NYE AUTOMOBILER I DANMARK. (Text in Danish; summaries in English) 1949. m. DKK 1155. Automobil-Importoerernes Sammenslutning, Ryvangs Alle 68, 2900 Hellerup, Denmark. Ed. Kai Noerrung.
Description: Data on new registration of vehicles. Listed by make-model and county of owner-user.

338.475 US
STEAM AUTOMOBILE. 1958. q. $20. Steam Automobile Club of America, Inc., Box 285, Niles, MI 49120. TEL 616-683-4269. (Subscr. to: 1227 W. Voorhees, Danville, IL 61832) Ed. Karl A. Petersen. adv.; bk.rev.; illus.; pat.; circ. 915. (back issues avail.)

STOCK CAR. see *SPORTS AND GAMES*

796.77 US
STOCK CAR & MOTORSPORTS.* m. $2.95 per no. 4639 Apricot Rd., Simi Valley, CA 93063.

388.3 CS
STOP; auto-moto revue. 1971. fortn. 130 Kcs.($21) A R T T E P a.s., Martanovicova 25, 819-13 Bratislava, Czechoslovakia. FAX 42-7-231-829. (Subscr. to: Slovart, Gottwaldovo nam. 48, 805 32 Bratislava) Ed. Jan Korecky. adv.; illus.; circ. 115,000.
Description: Technical and sports motoring information.

STRASSEN. see *TRAVEL AND TOURISM*

796.72 FI
STREET & RACE. 9/yr. Erikoislehdet Oy, Sport, P.O. Box 16, 00381 Helsinki, Finland. TEL 358-0-120-5911. FAX 358-0-120-5959. Ed. Jarmo Markkanen. circ. 8,324.

796.77 UK ISSN 0143-5949
TL236.3
STREET MACHINE. 1979. m. $48. A G B Publications Ltd., Audit House, Field End Rd., Eastcote, Ruislip, Middlesex HA4 9LT, England. TEL 01-868-4499. (Subscr. in US: Expediters of the Printed Word, Dept St. Machine, P.O. Box 1305, Long Island City, NY 11101) Ed. Clive Househam. circ. 77,773. (back issues avail.)

388.3 US
STREET ROD ACTIONS. m. $2.95 per no. Challenge Publications, Inc., 7950 Deering Ave., Canoga Park, CA 91309. TEL 818-887-0550. FAX 818-883-3019.

STREET RODDER. see *SPORTS AND GAMES*

796.77 US
STREET RODDING ILLUSTRATED. bi-m. McMullen Publishing, 2145 W. La Palma Ave., Anaheim, CA 92801. TEL 714-635-9040.

STRUCTURE OF THE JAPANESE AUTO PARTS INDUSTRY. see *BUSINESS AND ECONOMICS — Economic Situation And Conditions*

388.3 SA ISSN 0039-4203
STUURWIEL.* (Text in Afrikaans) 1966. m. R.2.40. Res Publica (Pty) Ltd., Box 2045, Pretoria, South Africa. Ed. F.J. Joubert. adv.; circ. controlled. (processed)

388.3 629.2 IT ISSN 0039-4254
STYLE AUTO; architettura della carrozzeria. (Text in English or Italian) 1964. a. L.5000($10) softbound; hardbound L.8000($13). Style Auto Editrice, Corso Adriatico 26, 10129 Turin, Italy. Ed. Mario Dinarich. adv.; illus.

388 GW
SUCH & FIND KRAFTFAHRZEUG. 1983. w. DM.176. Kempen Verlag GmbH, Wilhelm-Stoppler-Platz 3, 5400 Koblenz, Germany. TEL 0261-89920. Ed. A. Kempen.

388.476 GW
SUEDHESSISCHES AUTO MAGAZIN. 1986. 10/yr. DM.30. Biber Druck und Satz, Justus-von-Liebig-Str. 7a, 6101 Gross-Bieberau, Germany. Ed. Bernd Ruths. bk.rev.; circ. 35,000. (back issues avail.)
Former titles: Auto Magazin (Gross-Bieberau); Auto Anzeiger.

388.3　　　　　　FI　　ISSN 0355-2691
SUOMEN AUTOLEHTI; the automotive magazine of Finland. 1933. m. Fmk.320. Kustannusliike Autotieto Oy, Koydenpunojankatu 8, SF-00180 Helsinki, Finland. FAX 358-0-6944027. Ed. Heikki Haapaniemi. adv.; bk.rev.; circ. 8,100.
　—BLDSC shelfmark: 8541.500000.

388.33　　　　　US　　ISSN 0896-0437
TL153.A1
SUPER AUTOMOTIVE SERVICE. 1929. m. $79. Irving-Cloud Publishing Co., 7300 N. Cicero Ave., Lincolnwood, IL 60646. TEL 708-674-7300. FAX 708-674-7015. Ed. Martin Schultz. adv.; illus.; mkt.; stat.; index. (processed) **Indexed:** Bus.Ind., Tr.& Indus.Ind.
　Formerly: Super Service Station (ISSN 0039-5676)
　Description: For service stations, independent repair shops and tire dealerships.

629.22　　　　　JA　　ISSN 0915-4116
SUPER C G; super car graphic. (Text in Japanese) 1989. q. 11,000 Yen. Nigensha Publishing Co. Ltd., 2-2 Kanda Jinbo-cho, Chiyoda-ku, Tokyo 101, Japan. TEL 03-3239-0371. FAX 03-5275-0192. Ed. Shizuo Takashima. adv.; bk.rev.; circ. 100,000.
　Description: Covers classic and "super" cars for enthusiasts and connoisseurs.

388.3　　　　　　US　　ISSN 0146-2628
TL215.C5
SUPER CHEVY. 1973. m. $16.94. Argus Publishers Corporation, Box 49659, Los Angeles, CA 90049. TEL 213-820-3601. FAX 213-207-9388. (Street addr.: 12100 Wilshire Blvd., Ste. 250, Los Angeles, CA 90025) Ed. Bruce Hampson. adv.; illus.; circ. 161,586.
　Formerly: Chevy Hi-Performance.
　Description: Contains hands-on and restoration articles, new product information, project cars and coverage of Chevy-powered events.

388.3　　　　　　US
SUPER FORD. m. $2.95 per no. Dobbs Publications, 3816 Industry Blvd., Lakeland, FL 33811. TEL 813-646-5743.

SUPER STOCK & DRAG ILLUSTRATED. see *SPORTS AND GAMES — Outdoor Life*

388　　　　　　US
▼**SUPER STREET TRUCK.** 1990. q. Argus Publishers Corporation, Box 49659, Los Angeles, CA 90049. TEL 213-820-3601. FAX 213-207-9388. (Street addr.: 12100 Wilshire Blvd., Ste. 250, Los Angeles, CA 90025) Ed. Bruce Hampson. adv.; circ. 40,000.
　Description: For the hands-on truck enthusiast interested in total performance and appearance for street trucks.

796.77　　　　　　FR
SUPER V W. q. 90 F. (foreign 120 F.). Societe d'Editions Modernes Parisienne, 38, rue Jean Mermoz, 75008 Paris, France. TEL 42-66-92-36. TELEX SEMP 650016F.

629.286　　　　　US
SUPERCHARGER. 1928. 8/yr. (Oct.-May). membership only. Society of Automotive Engineers, Detroit Section, 21000 W. Ten Mile Rd., Southfield, MI 48075. TEL 313-357-3340. Ed. Sandra Bouckley. adv.; circ. 9,819.

SUPPLY LINE. see *HOBBIES*

629.286　　　　　US
SURGEONS OF STEEL. 1982. m. $36 (effective Sep. 1990). (Nebraska Autobody Association, Inc.) Anderson Management Services, Inc., 1111 Lincoln Mall, Ste. 308, Lincoln, NE 68508-2882. TEL 402-476-1528. FAX 402-476-1259. Ed. Robert L. Anderson. circ. 1,200.
　Description: Covers automotive collision-repair.

629.286　　　　　SW　　ISSN 0348-3304
SVENSKA MOTOR-MAGASINET. 1978. fortn. SEK 250. Pro Motor AB, Florettgatan 5, P.O. Box 22148, S-250 22 Helsingborg, Sweden. FAX 42-114734. Ed. Olle Holm. adv.; illus.; circ. 22,000. (tabloid format)

388.3　　　　　　CS　　ISSN 0039-7016
SVET MOTORU. 1947. w. 156 Kcs.($44) Magnet Press, Vladislavova 26, 113 66 Prague 1, Czechoslovakia. (Subscr. to: Artia, Ve Smeckach 30, 111 27 Prague 1, Czechoslovakia) Ed. Miroslav Ebr. adv.; charts; illus.; index; circ. 350,000.

388　　　　　　SZ
SWITZERLAND. BUNDESAMT FUER STATISTIK. STRASSENVERKEHRSUNFAELLE - ACCIDENTS DE LA CIRCULATION ROUTIERE EN SUISSE. (Text in French, German) 1963. a. 22 Fr. Bundesamt fuer Statistik, Hallwylstr. 15, CH-3003 Berne, Switzerland. FAX 031-617856. TELEX 912871. stat.

388　　　　　　GW
T UE V AUTOREPORT; Sicherheitsanalyse, 78 Modelle des In- und Auslandes. 1976. a. DM.8. (Vereinigung der Technischen Ueberwachungs-Vereine e.V.) Verlag T Ue V Rheinland GmbH, Am Grauen Stein, 5000 Cologne 91, Germany.

388.3 388　　　　　ER
TALLINNA TEHNIKAULIKOOL. POVYSHENIE KACHESTVA PROEKTIROVANIYA, STROITEL'STVA I EKSPLUATATSII AVTODOROG I GORODSKIKH ULITS. (Subseries of: Toimetised) (Text in Russian; summaries in English or German) irreg. price varies. Tallinna Tehnikaulikool, Ehitajate tee 5, Tallinn, Estonia. TEL 53-72-58.
　Former titles: Polutehniline Instituut Tallinn. Povyshenie Kachestva Proektirovaniya, Storitel'stva i Ekspluatatsii Avtodorog i Gorodskih Ulits; Polutehniline Instituut Tallinn. Teoreticheskoe i Eksperimental'noe Issledovanie Avtomobil'nykh Dorog i Avtomobil'nogo Transporta Estonskoi S.S.R. v Usloviyakh Intensivnoi Avtomobilizatsii (ISSN 0320-3433)

629.286　　　　　GW
TANKSTELLE. 1954. m. DM.104.40. (National Association of the German Service Station and Garage Industry) Verlag Kirchheim und Co. GmbH, Kaiserstr. 41, Postfach 2524, 6500 Mainz, Germany. TEL 06131-671081. circ. 14,500.

388.33　　　　　AU
TANKSTELLE UND GARAGE. 1930. m. S.597. Bohmann Druck und Verlag GmbH & Co. KG, Leberstr. 122, A-1110 Vienna, Austria. TEL 0222-74095. FAX 0222-74095-183. TELEX 132312. circ. 5,600.
　Former title: Garage, Tankstelle und Servicestation (ISSN 0016-4550)

629.2　　　　　GW
TASCHENFACHBUCH DER KRAFTFAHRZEUGBETRIEBE. 1953. a. DM.13.50. Krafthand-Verlag Walter Schulz, St.-Anna-Str. 26, 8939 Bad Woerishofen, Germany. Ed. Walter Schulz.

338 629.2　　　　GW　　ISSN 0083-548X
TATSACHEN UND ZAHLEN AUS DER KRAFTVERKEHRSWIRTSCHAFT. 1927. a. price varies. Verband der Automobilindustrie e.V., Westendstr. 61, Postfach 170563, 6000 Frankfurt a.M. 1, Germany. TEL 069-7570-0. FAX 069-7570-261. (back issues avail.)

629.283　　　　　SA
TAXI TALK. 1987. m. free. Thomson Publications (Subsidiary of: Times Media Ltd.), P.O. Box 56182, Pinegowrie 2123, South Africa. TEL 011-789-2144. FAX 011-789-3196. Ed. Samkelo Kumalo. circ. 36,702 (controlled).
　Formerly: Drive On.

600　　　　　　UK
TECHNICAL SERVICE DATA (CARS). 1935. a. £25. Glass's Guide Service Ltd., Elgin House, St. George's Ave., Weybridge, Surrey KT13 0BX, England. TEL 0932-853211. FAX 0932-849299.
　Formerly: Technical Service Data (Automotive) (ISSN 0082-2329)

388　　　　　　UK
TECHNICAL SERVICE DATA (HEAVY COMMERCIAL VEHICLES). 1989. a. £25. Glass's Guide Service Ltd., Elgin House, St. Georges Avenue, Weybridge, Surrey KT13 0BX, England. TEL 0932-853211. FAX 0932-849299.

388　　　　　　UK
TECHNICAL SERVICE DATA (LIGHT COMMERCIAL VEHICLES). 1989. a. £15. Glass's Guide Service Ltd., Elgin House, St. Georges Avenue, Weybridge, Surrey KT13 0BX, England. TEL 0932-853211. FAX 0932-849299.

629.286　　　　　IT
TECNICA DELL'AUTOMOBILE.* 1948. m. (11/yr.). L.30000($50) Associazione Tecnica dell'Automobile, Via Pettinati 20, 10126 Torino, Italy. adv.; circ. 2,800.

629.222　　　　　UK
THOROUGHBRED AND CLASSIC CARS. 1973. m. £42.80. I P C Magazines Ltd., Kings Reach Tower, Stamford St., London SE1 9LS, England. TEL 071-261-5849. FAX 071-261-7851. (Subscr. to: Reed Business Publishing Ltd., 205 E. 42nd St., New York, NY 10017, U.S.A.) Ed. Tony Dron. adv.; bibl.; charts; illus.; tr.lit.; circ. 113,127. (also avail. in microform from UMI)
　Former titles: Classic Cars; Thoroughbred and Classic Cars (ISSN 0143-7267); (until 1974): Classic Car.
　Description: Covers classic cars past and present with an emphasis on those built 1950-1975.

388.3　　　　　　CN
THUNDER BAY CAR & TRUCK NEWS. m. North Superior Publishing Inc., 1145 Barton St., Thunder Bay, Ont. P7B 5N3, Canada. TEL 807-623-2348. FAX 807-623-7515. circ. 10,000.

629.286　　　　　SP
TIENDA DE RECAMBIOS Y ACCESORIOS. 1982. m. 6500 ptas.($45) (foreign 10000 ptas.). Tecnipublicaciones, S.A., Fernando VI, 27, 28004 Madrid, Spain. Ed. Miguel Angel F. Prieto.

388.3　　　　　　US
TIGER TALES. 1969. m. $25 includes membership. California Association of Tiger Owners, 5165 Slauson Ave., Culver City, CA 90230. TEL 213-391-8973. circ. 980.
　Description: Provides a medium through which Sunbeam Tiger owners may pool ideas and resources on the care and maintenance of their vehicles.

TIRE BUSINESS. see *RUBBER*

678.32　　　　　US　　ISSN 0040-8085
TS1870
TIRE REVIEW; the magazine for progressive tire dealers. (Includes C E O Report published in Jan.; Sourcebook and Purchasing Directory published in Sept.; NTDRA Show Issues published in Sept.) 1901. 13/yr. $75. Babcox Publications, 11 S. Forge St., Box 1810, Akron, OH 44309-1810. TEL 216-535-6117. FAX 216-535-0874. Ed. Jim Davis. adv.; circ. 32,455. **Indexed:** Chem.Abstr., RAPRA.
　—BLDSC shelfmark: 8858.401000.
　Formerly: Tire and T B A Review.

340　　　　　　US
TITLE AND REGISTRATION BOOK; summary of motor vehicle laws and regulations. 1977. a. $40. National Automobile Dealers Association (Costa Mesa), Box 7800, Costa Mesa, CA 92628. TEL 800-824-0259. Ed. Pat Phillips.

796.77　　　　　　CY
TO AFTOKINITO. 1972. m. £C9 (effective 1985). Vista Publications, P.O. Box 4890, Arsinois 86, Flat 4, Nicosia, Cyprus. Ed. Andrew Karmios. adv.; circ. 10,000. (back issues avail.)

629.283　　　　　UK
TOP CAR MAGAZINE. 1985. m. £15.80 (foreign £41). Security Publications Ltd., Argosy House, 161a-163a High St., Orpington, Kent BR6 0LW, England. TEL 0689-74025. Ed. Chris Wright. adv.; bk.rev.; circ. 60,000. (back issues avail.)
　Formerly (until Nov. 1990): Your Car Magazine (ISSN 0267-2952)

388.3　　　　　　FR
TOP'S CARS. s-m. 455 F. (foreign 685 F.). Societe des Publications Modernes Specialisees, 60-62 rue Danjou, 92100 Boulogne, France. TEL 46-09-95-96. (Subscr. to: 24 bd. Vauban, B.P. 137, 80103 Abbeville Cedex, France. TEL 22-31-31-12) adv.

TRANSPORTATION — AUTOMOBILES

796.77   CN   ISSN 0704-7339
TORONTO INTERNATIONAL AUTO SHOW PROGRAM. Issued with: Carguide. 1974. a. Can.$4. Formula Publications Ltd., 447 Speers Rd., Ste. 4, Oakville, Ont. L6K 3S7, Canada. TEL 416-622-5150. FAX 416-622-1824. Ed. Alan McPhee. adv.; circ. 50,000.

388.3   CN
TOURING. (Editions in English and French) 1922. 4/yr. membership. Canadian Automobile Association, Quebec Division, c/o Consultants C G E I, 3281 Jean-Beraud Ave., Chomedey, Laval, Que. H7T 2L2, Canada. TEL 514-334-5912. FAX 514-688-6269. TELEX 055-62411. Ed. Denis Duquette. adv.; B&W page Can.$5780, color page Can.$7205; trim 6 5/8 x 9 5/8; adv. contact: Christiane Parant. bk.rev.; film rev.; illus.; stat.; circ. 411,506.
Formerly: Autoclub (ISSN 0005-0954)

TOURING. see *TRAVEL AND TOURISM*

TOURING CLUB MAGAZINE. see *TRAVEL AND TOURISM*

388.3   FR
TOUT TERRAIN MAGAZINE. 1989. 11/yr. 286 F. Ediregie, B.P. 86, 94420 Le Plessis Trevise, France. FAX 45-93-25-93. TELEX EDIGIE 262572. Ed. Jean-Jacques Deverly. circ. 55,000.

629.286   JA
TOYOTA AND AUTOMOTIVE ELECTRONIC. (Text in English) 1987. irreg. free. Toyota Motor Corporation, International Public Affairs Division, 1-4-18, Koraku, Bunkyo-ku, Tokyo 112, Japan. TEL 03-3817-9936. FAX 03-3817-9017. circ. 10,000.

629.286   JA
▼**TOYOTA AND AUTOMOTIVE SAFETY.** (Text in English) 1991. irreg. free. Toyota Motor Corporation, International Public Affairs Division, 1-4-18, Koraku, Bunkyo-ku, Tokyo 112, Japan. TEL 03-3817-9930. FAX 03-3817-9017.

614.7   JA
▼**TOYOTA AND THE ENVIRONMENT.** (Text in English) 1991. irreg. free. Toyota Motor Corporation, International Affairs Division, 1-4-18, Koraku, Bunkyo-ku, Tokyo 112, Japan. TEL 03-381709930. FAX 03-3817-9017. circ. 10,000.

629.286   JA
▼**TOYOTA ENGINE TECHNOLOGY.** (Text in English) 1990. irreg. free. Toyota Motor Corporation, International Public Affairs Division, 1-4-18, Koraku, Bunkyo-ku, Tokyo 112, Japan. TEL 03-3817-9930. FAX 03-3817-9017. circ. 5,000.

629.286   JA
TOYOTA MOTOR CORPORATION. ANNUAL REPORT. (Text in English) 1965. a. free. Toyota Motor Corporation, International Public Affairs Division, 1-4-18, Koraku, Bunkyo-ku, Tokyo 112, Japan. TEL 03-3817-9930. FAX 03-3817-9017. circ. 40,000.

340
KF2226.A3   US   ISSN 0893-3030
TRAFFIC LAW REPORTS. 1987. m. $98. Knehans-Miller Publications, Box 88, Warrenburg, MO 64093. TEL 816-429-1102. Ed. Dane C. Miller. index. (looseleaf format)
Description: Summaries of all Federal and State Appellate Court decisions relating to traffic. Indexed by subject and jurisdiction.

629.286   US   ISSN 0277-8300
TRANSMISSION DIGEST. 1981. m. $28. M D Publications, Inc. (Springfield), 3057 E. Cairo, Box 2210, Springfield, MO 65801. TEL 417-866-3917. FAX 417-866-2781. Ed. Lola Miller. adv.; circ. 23,000.
Description: Covers the automatic and standard transmission repair and service aftermarket.

TRANSPORT-NYTT. see *TRANSPORTATION — Ships And Shipping*

388.3   UY
TRANSPORTE AUTOMOTOR. 1977. m. Confederacion Uruguay del Transporte Automotor, Lima 1423, Montevideo, Uruguay. Ed. Jose M. Camano Abal.

338   US
TREND SETTER. m. Kustom Kemps of America, 2548 Galcier Dr., Wichita, KS 67215-1502. TEL 316-721-4095. Ed. Denise Crane.

388.3   US   ISSN 1050-7272
TRUCK & VAN PRICES - BUYER'S GUIDE REPORTS. 1973. bi-m. $21.95. Pace Publications (Milwaukee), 1020 N. Broadway, Ste. 111, Milwaukee, WI 53202. TEL 414-272-9977. FAX 414-272-9973.
Description: Lists dealer's cost and manufacturer's suggested list price for every American small truck or van, with all options available, and prices for the preceding ten years.

629.283   UK
TRUCK DRIVER'S HANDBOOK. irreg. £6.99. Kogan Page Ltd., 120 Pentonville Rd., London N1 9JN, England. TEL 071-278-0433. FAX 071-837-6348. TELEX 263088 KOGAN G. Ed. David P. Soye.
Formerly: H G V Driver's Handbook.
Description: For truck drivers with sections on the law and the road.

388.3   US
TURBO & HIGH TECH PERFORMANCE. 1985. bi-m. $16.97. Mag-Tec Productions, 9582 Hamilton Ave., Huntington Beach, CA 92646. TEL 714-962-7795. FAX 714-965-2268. Ed. Kipp Kington. adv.
Formerly: Turbo.
Description: Covers late-model, high-performance vehicles.

388   DK   ISSN 0901-3032
TURIST- OG RUTEBILBLADET. 1941. 5/yr. DKK 50. Niels W. Gadesvej 1, DK-8000 Aarhus C, Denmark. TEL 86-118680. FAX 86-14-4452. Ed. Rene Wittendorff. adv.; circ. 4,600.
Formerly: Rutebil-Bladet.

TURNING WHEELS. see *ANTIQUES*

380.5   FI   ISSN 0041-4468
TUULILASI. 1963. m. FIM 423. A-Lehdet Oy, Hitsaajankatu 7, 00810 Helsinki 81, Finland. FAX 0-787-311. Ed. Erkki Raukko. adv.; bk.rev.; illus.; circ. 98,359.
Incorporates (in 1973): Moottoriviesti (ISSN 0027-0962)
Description: Motoring magazine for Finland.

TYRE AND RIM ASSOCIATION OF AUSTRALIA STANDARDS MANUAL. see *RUBBER*

388   II
TYRE SAMACHAR. 1973. m. Rs.50. S. Swaminthan, Ed. & Pub., No. 9, State Bank St., First Lane, Mount Road, Madras 600 002, India. TEL 849305. adv.; bk.rev.; circ. 17,000.

U I T - MAGAZINE. see *TRAVEL AND TOURISM*

614.85   US   ISSN 0739-7100
U M T R I RESEARCH REVIEW. (Former issuing body: Highway Safety Research Institute) 1970. bi-m. $20. University of Michigan, Transportation Research Institute, 2901 Baxter Rd., Ann Arbor, MI 48109-2150. TEL 313-764-2171. Ed. Robert E. Sweet. charts; illus.; circ. 2,100. (also avail. in microfilm; back issues avail.) **Indexed:** Eng.Ind., P.A.I.S., Psychol.Abstr., Psycscan.
—BLDSC shelfmark: 9083.200000.
Former titles (until 1982): H S R I Research Review (ISSN 0146-8545); (until 1977): H S R I Research (ISSN 0364-3476)

388.3   UK   ISSN 0041-6207
ULSTER MOTORIST. m. £1. c/o Ulster Bank Ltd., Waring St., Belfast 1, N. Ireland. adv.; illus.
Incorporates: Drive.

629.286   US
UNDERCAR DIGEST; the management journal for exhaust, brake and chassis specialists. 1976. m. $28. M D Publications, Inc. (Springfield), 3057 E. Cairo, Box 2210, Springfield, MO 65801. TEL 417-866-3917. FAX 417-866-2781. Ed. James R. Wilder. adv.; bk.rev.; charts; illus.; tr.lit.; circ. 30,000. (back issues avail.)
Formerly: Muffler Digest (ISSN 0893-6943)
Description: Covers the exhaust and undercar repair aftermarket.

338   US
UNDERCAR DIGEST SHORT LINE NEWSLETTER. 24/yr. M D Publications, Inc., Box 2210, Springfield, MO 65801-2210. TEL 417-866-3917. FAX 417-866-2781. Ed. James R. Wilder.

629.2   US   ISSN 0270-756X
TL1
U.S. DEPARTMENT OF ENERGY. ANNUAL REPORT TO CONGRESS ON THE AUTOMOTIVE TECHNOLOGY DEVELOPMENT PROGRAM. 1979. a. free. U.S. Department of Energy, Office of Transportation Technologies, Washington, DC 20585. TEL 202-586-8012. Ed. Saunders B. Kramer. circ. 200. **Key Title:** Annual Report to Congress on the Automotive Technology Development Program.

629.287   US   ISSN 0565-7717
TL242
U.S. NATIONAL HIGHWAY TRAFFIC SAFETY ADMINISTRATION. MOTOR VEHICLE SAFETY DEFECT RECALL CAMPAIGNS. Continues a publication with the same title issued by the administration under an earlier name: National Highway Safety Bureau. 1970. q. U.S. National Highway Traffic Safety Administration, 400 Seventh St., S.W., Washington, DC 20590. (Dist. by: Supt. of Documents, Washington, DC 20402) **Indexed:** Amer.Stat.Ind. **Key Title:** Motor Vehicle Safety Defect Recall Campaigns (Washington).

388   US
UNITED'S VOICE. q. California Association of 4 W D Clubs, Inc., 7700 Quinby, Sacramento, CA 95823-4110. TEL 916-391-9595. Ed. Linda L. Meusling.

388.3   II
UPPER INDIA MOTORIST. 1954. m. $25. Automobile Association of Upper India, C-8, Institutional Area, South of IIT, New Delhi 110 016, India. TEL 6553973. Ed. T.K. Malhotra. adv.; circ. 30,000.

388.3   US
USED CAR DEALER. 1981. m. $36. National Independent Automobile Dealers Association, 2521 Brown Blvd., Ste. 100, Arlington, TX 76006-5203. TEL 817-640-3838. FAX 817-649-5866. Ed. Don A. Harris. adv.; charts; illus.; stat.; circ. 16,033.
Description: Covers items of interest to the used car dealer industry, including profit centers and legislative issues.

388.3   US
▼**USED CAR MERCHANDISING.** 1990. bi-m. $14.85. Cherokee Publishing Company, 125 Edinburgh S., Cary, NC 27511-6441. TEL 919-469-9911. FAX 919-481-2658. Ed. James Hyatt. adv.; circ. 20,000.
Description: Reports on changes in the automotive industry and their effects on the buying and selling of used cars. Covers the used car operations of franchise dealers and the preparation of cars for resale.

388.3   US   ISSN 1050-5415
USED CAR PRICES - BUYER'S GUIDE REPORTS. 1973. bi-m. $21.95. Pace Publications (Milwaukee), 1020 N. Broadway, Ste. 111, Milwaukee, WI 53202. TEL 414-272-9977. FAX 414-272-9973.
Description: Lists average wholesale and retail prices for all American and foreign cars for the past ten years.

629 658   US
USED CARS INSIDER. 1983. bi-w. $175. Atcom, Inc., Atcom Bldg., 2315 Broadway, New York, NY 10024-4397. TEL 212-873-5900. FAX 212-799-1728. Ed. Steve Byers. circ. 1,500. (reprint service avail. from UMI)
Formerly: Used Cars Today (ISSN 0740-0055)
Description: Newsletter for professionals in the used car business.

796.7   US
V W AUTOIST. 1955. bi-m. $16 ($10 for renewal). Volkswagen Club of America, Box 154, N. Aurora, IL 60542. TEL 708-896-2803. Ed. Fred Ortlip. circ. 1,500. (back issues avail.)
Description: For owners and enthusiasts of Volkswagen and Audi automobiles.

338.476   UK   ISSN 0953-6167
V W MOTORING. 1961. m. £21 (£27 Europe; elsewhere £35). R F W W Publications Ltd., P.O. Box 283, Cheltenham, Glos GL52 3BT, England. TEL 0242-677101. FAX 0242-676020. (Subscr. to: Warners Distribution, The Maltings, Bourne, Lincs. PE10 9PH, England. TEL 0778-393652) Ed. Robin Wager. adv. contact: Bev Cunnington. bk.rev.; charts; illus.; tr.lit.; circ. 25,000. **Indexed:** Ergon.Abstr.
Formerly (until 1985): Safer (Volkswagen) Motoring (ISSN 0036-2417)

TRANSPORTATION — AUTOMOBILES 4705

796.77 US
V W TRENDS. 1983. m. McMullen Publishing, 2145 W. La Palma Ave., Anaheim, CA 92801. TEL 714-635-9040. Ed. Robin Hartfiel. adv.; circ. 95,000.

796.72 917 US
VALLEY MOTORIST. 1936. bi-m. $0.60. Valley Automobile Club, 100 Hazle St., Wilkes-Barre, PA 18702. TEL 717-824-2444. FAX 717-824-9855. Ed. Richard J. Meyers. circ. 51,000. (also avail. in tabloid format)
Formerly: Wyoming Valley Motorist (ISSN 0049-822X)

388 US ISSN 1043-4879
VAN & TRUCK DIGEST. 1983. bi-m. $40. Continental Publishing Company of Indiana, Inc., 58025 C.R. No.9 S., Box 1805, Elkhart, IN 46517. TEL 219-295-1962. FAX 219-295-7574. Ed. Tom Russell. adv.; tr.lit.; circ. 27,346. (reprint service avail.)
Formerly: Van Digest.
Description: For the automotive business professionals actively engaged in the manufacture, distribution, or sales of vans, custom trucks and accessories. Emphasis is on sales, marketing, news and business-oriented features.

388.3 790.13 US ISSN 0884-7231
VAN CONVERSION BLUE BOOK. 4/yr. $40. Maclean Hunter Market Reports, Inc., 29 N. Wacker Dr., Chicago, IL 60606-3297. TEL 312-726-2802. FAX 312-726-2574. (back issues avail.)

388.3 FI ISSN 0355-4295
VAUHDIN MAAILMA. m. FIM 344. Yhtyneet Kuvalehdet Oy, Maistraatinportti 1, 00240 Helsinki, Finland. TEL 0-15661. FAX 0-1566505. TELEX 121364. Ed. Peter Geitel. adv.; circ. 39,177.

388.3 330 US
VEHICLE LEASING TODAY. 1981. bi-m. $29. National Vehicle Leasing Association, 3710 S. Robertson Blvd., Ste. 225, Culver City, CA 90232-2349. TEL 310-838-3170. FAX 310-838-3160. (Subscr. to: Box 34028, Los Angeles, CA 90034-0028) Ed. Rod Couts. adv.; circ. 5,000.

388.1 DK ISSN 0083-5358
VEJTRANSPORTEN I TAL OG TEKST. (Text in Danish; notes in English) 1959. a. DKK 140. Automobil-Importoerernes Sammenslutning, Ryvangs Alle 68, 2900 Hellerup, Denmark. Ed. Kai Noerrung. index, cum.index every 7 yrs.
Description: Covers import and new registration of vehicles, vehicles in use, motor traffic and taxation, road expenditure and traffic accidents.

796.72 AG ISSN 0049-5913
VELOCIDAD. 1950. bi-m. Av. Belgrano 1735, Buenos Aires, Argentina. Ed. Gilberto Julian Riega.

629.2 338 GW
VERBAND DER AUTOMOBILINDUSTRIE. JAHRESBERICHT. (Editions in English, German) a. free. Verband der Automobilindustrie e.V., Westendstr. 61, Postfach 170563, 6000 Frankfurt a.M. 1, Germany. TEL 069-7570-0. FAX 069-7570-261. **Indexed:** Dok.Str.
Formerly: Verband der Automobilindustrie. Taetigkeitsbericht (ISSN 0083-5471)

629.286 GW
VERKEHRSUNFALL UND FAHRZEUGTECHNIK; Verkehrsunfall Fachblatt fuer Kraftfahrzeugsachverstaendige. 1961. m. DM.309.60. Verlag Information Ambs GmbH, Obere Haupstr. 13, Postfach 208, 7634 Kippenheim, Germany. TEL 07825-7114. Ed.Bd. illus.; charts.
Formerly: Verkehrsunfall (ISSN 0341-2210)

629.286 XV
VESTNIK A C; galsilo delavnihljudi W.O. A C. (Text and summaries in Serbo-Croatian, Slovenian) 1962. bi-m. free. W.O. Autocomerce, Trinova 4, Ljubljana, Slovenia. TEL 61 323-046. FAX 061-317-196. TELEX 31299 YUAC. Ed. Miran Juvancic. (back issues avail.)

VETERAN. see *ANTIQUES*

388.3 UK ISSN 0042-4781
VETERAN CAR. 1938. 6/yr. membership. Veteran Car Club of Great Britain, Jessamine House, High St., Ashwell, Hertfordshire SG7 5NL, England. Ed. Michael Brisby. adv.; bk.rev.; charts; illus.; index; circ. 1,500.

VETERANTICS. see *ANTIQUES*

796.77 US ISSN 0199-7890
VETTE. 1976. m. $23.97. C S K Publishing Co., Inc., 299 Market St., Saddle Brook, NJ 07662. TEL 201-712-9300. FAX 201-712-9899. (Subscr. to: Box 1010, Denville, NJ 07834) Ed. D. Randy Riggs. adv.; bk.rev.; circ. 55,000. (back issues avail.)
Description: For enthusiasts who eat and sleep Corvette. Covers legends and meets, the old and new, stock and modified, show and strip, personalities, road tests, and shootouts.

388.3 790.1 SW
VI BILAEGARE. 1929. 21/yr. SEK 224. O K Foerlaget AB, Huvudstagatan 1, S-171 58 Solna, Sweden. TEL 46-8-735-83-55. FAX 46-8-735-22-19. Ed. Nils-Eric Svendin. adv.: B&W page SEK 45800, color page SEK 59800; trim 235 x 325. bk.rev.; charts; illus.; circ. 260,000.
Formed by the merger of: Bilekonomi; Vi Bilaegare; Vi Bilaegare med Hem och Hobby (ISSN 0042-4943)
Description: Directed to car owners. Extends to homes, gardening, traveling and leisure, hunting, boats and fishing.

388.3 IT
VIA!. 1948. m. membership. Automobile Club di Milano, Corso Venezia 43, 20121 Milan, Italy. FAX 2781844. TELEX 312047 ACI MI I. Ed. Paolo Montagna. adv.; bk.rev.; abstr.; illus.; stat.; circ. 180,000.
Formerly: Autoclub and Via (ISSN 0005-0962)

796.77 US
VIALE CIRO MENOTTI; a magazine for Maserati enthusiasts. 1976. q. $50. M I E Corporation, Box 772, Mercer Island, WA 98040. TEL 206-455-4449. FAX 206-646-5458. Ed. Francis G. Mandarano. adv.; bk.rev.; index; circ. 3,500. (back issues avail.)

629.222 US ISSN 0147-9695
TL215.T7
VINTAGE TRIUMPH. 1975. q. $20 (foreign $30). Vintage Triumph Register, 15218 W. Larren Ave., Dearborn, MI 48126. Ed. Chris Hansel. adv.; bk.rev.; circ. 4,500. (back issues avail.)
Description: Contains articles and information which fosters the ownership, operation and preservation of Triumph automobiles.

388.3 FR
VIRAGES. 1952. 6/yr. free. Renault Vehicles Industriels, 129 rue Servient, 69003 Lyon, France. TEL 78-63-71-20. FAX 78-63-72-40. Ed. Madette Odier. charts; illus.; stat.; circ. 45,000.
Former titles (until 1989): Info Renault Vehicules Industriels; Magazine R V I - Info R V I (ISSN 0005-9218)

388.3 796.72 GW
VOILA - RENAULT REVUE; Autos zum Leben. 1956. q. DM.8. Deutsche Renault AG, Koelner Weg 6-10, D-5040 Bruehl, Germany. TEL 0228-351111. Ed. Werner P. Roeser. circ. 100,000. (back issues avail.)

388.3 US
VOLKSWAGEN. 1961. q. free to new VW owners; others $10 for 8 issues. Volkswagen United States, Inc., 3800 Hamlin Rd., Auburn Hills, MI 48326. TEL 313-340-5544. FAX 313-340-5540. Ed. Marlene Goldsmith. adv.; bk.rev.; illus.; circ. 280,000.
Formerly: Volkswagen's World (ISSN 0037-7279)

796.7 UK ISSN 0956-9294
VOLKSWAGEN AUDI CAR. 1953. m. £18. AutoMetrix Publications, 10a High St., Toddington, Dunstable, Bedfordshire LU5 6BY, England. TEL 05255-4019. FAX 05255-5582. Ed. Paul Harris. adv.; bk.rev.; illus.; cum.index; circ. 18,000.
Formerly (until Aug. 1982): Beetling.
Description: For Volkswagen and Audi enthusiasts supplying information on products and services.

388.3 US
W O JEEPSTER NEWSLETTER. 1964. m. $12 (foreign $14). Willys Overland Jeepster Club, Box 12042, Coronado Sta., El Paso, TX 79913. TEL 915-581-2671. FAX 915-581-2671. Ed. J. Sherwin. charts; illus.; stat.; tr.lit.; index; circ. 600. (looseleaf format; back issues avail.)
Description: For owners of 1949-1950 Jeepster convertibles. Provides information on restoration and attempts to promote an understanding and appreciation of this particular car.

388.3 US ISSN 0043-0315
HD9710.U5
WARD'S AUTO WORLD. 1964. m. $45. Ward's Communications (Subsidiary of: Intertec Publishing Corp.), 28 W. Adams St., Detroit, MI 48226. TEL 313-962-4433. FAX 313-962-5593. Ed. Edward K. Miller. adv.; bk.rev.; charts; illus.; stat.; index; circ. 94,000. **Indexed:** Bus.Ind., Mich.Mag.Ind., PROMT, Tr.& Indus.Ind.
Formerly: Ward's Quarterly.
Description: Covers the automotive manufacturing industry. Provides in-depth reporting and analysis on every facet of the manufacturer's business--from components to finished vehicles, design to marketing, people to companies.

629.286 US
WARD'S AUTOMOTIVE INTERNATIONAL. 1986. s-m. $375. Ward's Communications (Subsidiary of: Intertec Publishing Corp.), 28 W. Adams St., Detroit, MI 48226. TEL 313-962-4433. FAX 313-962-4532. TELEX 650-259-9164. Ed. David E. Zoia.
Description: News and analysis of auto industry internationally.

629.286 US
WARD'S AUTOMOTIVE REPORTS. 1924. w. $855 (includes Ward's Automotive Yearbook). Ward's Communications (Subsidiary of: Intertec Publishing Corp.), 28 W. Adams St., Detroit, MI 48226. TEL 313-962-4433. FAX 313-962-4456. Ed. James W. Bush. q.index. **Indexed:** PROMT.
Description: Provides statistics and news on the automotive industry, including production numbers, sales figures and marketing trends.

WARD'S AUTOMOTIVE YEARBOOK. see *TRANSPORTATION — Abstracting, Bibliographies, Statistics*

629.286 US
WARD'S ENGINE UPDATE AND VEHICLE TECHNOLOGY. 1975. s-m. $590. Ward's Communications (Subsidiary of: Intertec Publishing Corp.), 28 W. Adams St., Detroit, MI 48226. TEL 313-962-4532. FAX 313-962-4532. Ed. Joel Pietrangelo.
Former titles: Ward's Engine Update; Ward's Wankel Report.
Description: Provides technical information on the world of automotive technology. Covers the latest developments in engine design, drive trains, materials and components.

338.476 US
WARD'S WHO'S WHO AMONG U.S. MOTOR VEHICLE MANUFACTURERS. 1977. irreg. $29.75. Ward's Communications (Subsidiary of: Intertec Publishing Corp.), 28 W. Adams St., Detroit, MI 48226. TEL 313-962-4433. FAX 313-962-4532. Eds. David C. Smith, Patricia J. Williams. adv.; bk.rev.; charts; illus.; stat.; index; circ. 5,000.

388.3 US ISSN 0043-3977
TL1
WESTERN NEW YORK MOTORIST. 1909. m. $1.50. Automobile Club of Western New York, 100 International Dr., Buffalo, NY 14221. Ed. Earle V. Charles III. abstr.; charts; illus.; stat.; circ. 250,000.
Formerly: Buffalo Motorist.

388.3 US
WESTERN PENNSYLVANIA MOTORIST. 1952. m. membership. West Penn AAA, 202 Penn Circle W., Pittsburgh, PA 15206. TEL 412-362-3300. FAX 412-362-0926. Ed. Ann Reed Rose. adv.; bk.rev.; charts; illus.; stat.; tr.lit.; circ. 300,000. (tabloid format; back issues avail.)
Description: Information for the motorist and traveler.

WESTWAYS. see *TRAVEL AND TOURISM*

TRANSPORTATION — COMPUTER APPLICATIONS

614.86 052   CN
WESTWORLD ALBERTA MAGAZINE. 1926. 6/yr. membership. (Alberta Motor Association) Canada Wide Magazines Ltd., 4180 Lougheed Highway, Ste. 401, Burnaby, B.C. V5C 6A7, Canada. Ed. Robon Roberts. adv.; bk.rev.; charts; illus.; stat.; circ. 275,000.
 Former titles (until 1985): Alberta Motorist (ISSN 0228-1082); Alberta Magazine (ISSN 0002-4856)
 Description: Features automotive-related tips; club news; and general interest, national and international travel articles.

388.3   CN
WESTWORLD SASKATCHEWAN. 1951. q. membership. (C A A Saskatchewan) Canada Wide Magazines Ltd., 401-4180 Lougheed Hwy., Burnaby, B.C. V5C 6A7, Canada. TEL 604-299-9188. FAX 604-949-4461. Ed. Robin Robert. adv.; bk.rev.; illus.; circ. 110,000.
 Formerly: Saskatchewan Motorist (ISSN 0036-4940)

388.3   US
WHALES ON WHEELS. 1981. q. $4. Group Ultra Van, 5537 Pioneer Rd., Boulder, CO 80301. TEL 303-530-1288. Ed. W. Christy Barden. circ. 250.
 Description: Technical information on the ongoing care and maintenance of an ultra van.

629.22   UK   ISSN 0307-2991
WHAT CAR?. m. $81. Haymarket Magazines Ltd., 38-42 Hampton Rd., Teddington, Middx. TW11 0JE, England. TEL 081-943-5000. TELEX 895-2440-HAYMRT-G. Ed. Howard Walker. illus.; circ. 142,086.
 —BLDSC shelfmark: 9309.660000.
 Description: Road tests and evaluations of new cars.

796.77   US   ISSN 0888-1103
WHEEL. 1956. m. $15. (Sports Car Club of America, San Francisco Region) Kelly Communications (Pleasanton), 3609 Virgin Islands Ct., Pleasanton, CA 94588. TEL 510-846-7728. (Subscr. to: 301 Preston Court, Livermore, CA 94550) Ed. John F. Kelly, Jr. adv.; bk.rev.; circ. 6,000. (tabloid format)
 Description: Reports on Sports Car Club of America activities in Northern California.

388.3   JA   ISSN 0049-755X
THE WHEEL EXTENDED; a Toyota quarterly review. (Text in English) 1971. q. free. Toyota Motor Corporation, International Public Affairs Division, 1-4-18, Koraku, Bunkyo-ku, Tokyo 112, Japan. TEL 03-3817-9930. FAX 03-3817-9017. charts; illus.; circ. 13,000.
 Indexed: Fuel & Energy Abstr.
 —BLDSC shelfmark: 9310.650000.

388.3   II
WHEEL FARE. 1976. 6/yr. Rs.20. V. Krishnan, Ed. & Pub., 9 State Bank St., 1st Lane, Mount Rd., Madras 600 002, India. TEL 849305. Ed. V. Krishnan. bk.rev.; circ. 15,500.

629.28   US
WHEELINGS. 1984. 4/yr. $40. Kruza Kaleidoscopix, Inc., Box 389, Franklin, MA 02038. TEL 508-528-6211. Ed. David Ward. adv.; circ. 6,000. (tabloid format)
 Description: For auto paint specialists and manufacturers.

388.3   AT   ISSN 0043-4779
WHEELS. 1953. m. Aus.$59.40. Australian Consolidated Press, 54-58 Park St., Sydney, N.S.W. 2001, Australia. Ed. Phil Scott. adv.; bk.rev.; charts; illus.; index; circ. 61,000. **Indexed:** Aus.Rd.Ind., Pinpointer.

629.2   RH
WHEELS. 1979. q. membership. (Automobile Association of Zimbabwe) Modus Publications, P.O. Box 66070, Kopje, Harare, Zimbabwe. TEL 738722. FAX 707130. TELEX 26334 MODUS ZW. Ed. Vivian Mitchell. adv.; charts; illus.; circ. 50,000.
 Supersedes: Motoring Review; Which was Formerly: Automobile Association of Rhodesia. Bulletin.
 Description: Motoring magazine of general interest to the motorist and up-to-date information for AAZ members.

388.3   UK   ISSN 0263-7081
WHEELS & TRACKS; international historical review of military vehicles. q. $26. Battle of Britain Prints International Ltd., Church House, Church St., Stratford, London E15 3JA, England. (Distr. in U.S. by: Sky Books International Inc., 48 East 50th St., New York, NY 10022) Ed. Bart Vanderveen.
 —BLDSC shelfmark: 9310.669500.

796.77   GW
WHEELS MAGAZINE. 1988. bi-m. DM.60. Verlagsgesellschaft Gruetter, Postfach 910708, 3000 Hannover 91, Germany. TEL 0511-4609302. FAX 0511-4609320. Ed. Darius Klapp. adv.; bk.rev.; index; circ. 55,000. (back issues avail.)

388.3   UK
WHICH CAR?. 1982. 7/yr. $30. Evro Publishing Co. Ltd., 60 Waldegrave Rd., Teddington, Middx. TW11 8LG, England. TEL 081-943-5943. Ed. Andy Pudifoot. circ. 30,000.
 Description: Features test results of cars in England; includes a value index listing vehicles in order with full value money ratings.

388.3   US   ISSN 0736-7988
WISCONSIN AUTO VALUATION GUIDE. 8/yr. $49.50. Maclean Hunter Market Reports, Inc., 29 N. Wacker Dr., Chicago, IL 60606-3297. TEL 312-726-2802. FAX 312-726-2574.

380.5   US   ISSN 1043-979X
WOMEN WITH WHEELS. 1989. q. $15 to individuals; institutions $20. Susan Frissell, Ed. & Pub., 1718A Northfield Sq., Northfield, IL 60093. TEL 708-501-3519. adv.; bk.rev.; circ. 150.
 Description: Published by women for women and their automobiles.

388   US
WORLD AUTO FORECAST REPORT. q. D R I - McGraw-Hill, 24 Hartwell Ave., Lexington, MA 02173. TEL 617-863-5100. FAX 617-860-6332. TELEX 200 284. (back issues avail.)

388.4   US
WORLD AUTOMOTIVE MARKET. 1931. a. $35 (foreign $40). (Auto and Truck International) Johnston International Publishing (Subsidiary of: Hunter Publishing Limited Partnership), 950 Lee St., Des Plaines, IL 60016. TEL 708-296-0770. FAX 708-803-3328. Ed. Jim Halloran. circ. 3,500.

629.2   US   ISSN 0085-8307
HD9710.A1
WORLD MOTOR VEHICLE DATA. a. $35. Motor Vehicle Manufacturers Association of the U.S., Inc., 7430 Second Ave., Ste. 300, Detroit, MI 48202. TEL 313-872-4311. **Indexed:** SRI.
 —BLDSC shelfmark: 9356.720000.

629   CN   ISSN 0824-5487
WORLD OF WHEELS. 1983. 6/yr. Can.$5. World of Wheels Publishing Inc., 2061 McCowan Rd., Ste. 207, Scarborough, Ont. M1S 3Y6, Canada. TEL 416-297-9277. FAX 416-297-9677. Ed. Joe Duarte. adv.; circ. 136,000.

388.3   UK
WORLD SPORTS CARS. bi-m. Hyde Park Group, Mansford Rd., London SW15 2RS, England. FAX 203-348-3555. (Dist. in US by: Hyde Park Group, 2001 W. Main St., Stamford, CT 06902. TEL 203-969-2533) Ed. Daryn Styles.

659.1   UK   ISSN 0958-4013
YORKSHIRE AUTO TRADER. 1982. w. £78. Hurst Publishing, Munro House, Duke St., Leeds LS9 8AL, England. FAX 0532-425417. adv.; circ. 49,000.
 Formerly: Yorkshire Motor Trade.
 Description: Trade and private advertisements of cars, motor bikes, caravans, buying and selling.

629.288   UK   ISSN 0957-6525
YOUR CLASSIC. 1989. m. £21. Haymarket Magazines Ltd., 60 Waldegrave Road, Teddington, Mddx. TW11 8LG, England. TEL 081-943-5000. TELEX 8952440. Ed. Ian Bond. circ. 49,059. (back issues avail.)
 Incorporates: Restoring Classic Cars & Classic Car Mechanics.
 Description: Covers less expensive classic cars and first-time buying and owning, including renovation.

388   NE
ZAKENAUTO; Misset select. 1985. s-a. free to qualified personnel. Uitgeversmaatschappij C. Misset B.V., P.O. Box 4, 7000 BA Doetinchem, Netherlands. TEL 08340-49911. FAX 08340-43839. TELEX 45481. Ed. A.N. Cupedo. adv.: B&W page fl.14780; unit 187 x 257; adv. contact: Cor van Nek. circ. 174,000 (controlled).
 Description: Covers all aspects of purchase, operation and use of passenger cars used for business.

388.3   US
3 & 4 WHEEL ACTION. m. $15.98. Hi-Torque Publications, Inc., 10600 Sepulveda Blvd., Mission Hills, CA 91345. TEL 818-365-6831.

629.286   GR   ISSN 1105-1280
4 TROCHI/4 WHEELS. (Text in Greek) 1970. m. Dr.4000($42.50) Technical Press S.A., 6 Gorgiou St., 11636 Athens, Greece. TEL 01-92-30-832. FAX 01-92-30-836. TELEX 222189 TECH GR. Ed. Costas Cavathas. circ. 95,000.
 Description: Presents new car models, new technologies, environmental issues, and driving tests.

380.5   GR   ISSN 1105-1329
4 TROCHOI TEST/4 WHEELS TEST. (Text in Greek) 1979. a. Technical Press, S.A., 6 Gorgiou St., 11636 Athens, Greece. TEL 01-9230832. FAX 01-9230836. TELEX 222189 TECH GR. Ed. Costas Cavathas. circ. 18,000.
 Description: New car models and driving tests.

388.3
4-W D SPORT UTILITY. bi-m. $2.75 per no. McMullen Publishing, 2145 W. La Palma Ave., Anaheim, CA 92801. TEL 714-635-9040. FAX 714-533-9979.
 Formerly: 4-W D Action.

388.3   UK   ISSN 0267-4629
4X4. 1985. bi-m. £17.70. Sovereign International, Sovereign House, Brentwood, Essex CM14 4SE, England. TEL 0277-219876. (Subscr. to: 45 Union Road, Croydon, Surrey CR0 2XU, England) Ed. Colin Dawson. circ. 25,000.

796.77   US
356 REGISTRY. 1974. bi-m. $20. (356 Registry, Inc.) Three Fifty Six, Inc., Box 1000, Westerville, OH 43081-7000. TEL 614-891-0398. Ed. Jerry Keyser. circ. 5,000. (back issues avail.)
 Description: Central forum for the exchange of ideas, experiences and information of all those interested in the 1948-1965 356-series Porsche automobiles.

796.7   UK   ISSN 0306-6312
750 BULLETIN. 1939. m. £17.50 membership. Seven Fifty Motor Club Ltd., Courthouse, St. Winifreds Rd., Biggin Hill, Kent TN16 3HR, England. TEL 0959-75812. FAX 0959-540094. Ed. David Edroff. adv.; bk.rev.; circ. 2,500.

TRANSPORTATION — Computer Applications

625.7 651.8   US   ISSN 0091-5122
TE5
AMERICAN ASSOCIATION OF STATE HIGHWAY AND TRANSPORTATION OFFICIALS. SUB-COMMITTEE ON COMPUTER TECHNOLOGY. NATIONAL CONFERENCE. PROCEEDINGS. 1983. a. $15. American Association of State Highway and Transportation Officials, U.S. Department of Transportation, 444 N. Capitol St. N.W., Ste. 225, Washington, DC 20001. TEL 202-624-5800. Ed. Keith F. Kohler. circ. controlled. Key Title: Proceedings - Committee on Computer Technology.

380.5 380.5   AT   ISSN 0313-895X
AUSTRALIAN ROAD RESEARCH BOARD. TECHNICAL MANUALS. 1977. irreg. Aus.$23 per copy. Australian Road Research Board, 500 Burwood Highway, Vermont S., Vic. 3133, Australia. TEL 03-881-1555. FAX 03-887-8104. TELEX AA33113. illus.; circ. 350. (also avail. in microfiche; back issues avail.) **Indexed:** Dok.Str.
 Description: Covers operation of software equipment.

385   RU   ISSN 0005-2329
TF615   CODEN: ATSVAG
AVTOMATIKA, TELEMEKHANIKA I SVYAZ'. 1957. m. 16.80 Rub. Izdatel'stvo Transport, Komsomol'skii prosp., 42, 119048 Moscow G-48, Russia. (Co-sponsor: Ministerstvo Putei Soobshcheniya) charts; illus.; index. **Indexed:** Chem.Abstr, Sci.Abstr.
—BLDSC shelfmark: 0001.200000.

380.5   US   ISSN 1057-5618
▼**EN ROUTE TECHNOLOGY**; the newsletter of mobile systems integration. 1991. bi-w. $345 in N. America; Europe £245; elsewhere $495. Waters Information Services, Inc., Box 2248, Binghamton, NY 13902. TEL 607-770-8535. FAX 607-798-1692.

380.5   UK   ISSN 0952-2190
FOCUS ON PHYSICAL DISTRIBUTION AND LOGISTICS MANAGEMENT. 1987. m. $4.50 per no. to non-members. Institute of Logistics and Distribution Management, Douglas House, Queen's Sq., Corby, Northants NN17 1P2, England. TEL 0536-205500. FAX 0536-400979. Ed. Raymond Horsley.
—BLDSC shelfmark: 3964.217500.

380.5   US
I E E E WORKSHOP ON AUTOMOTIVE APPLICATIONS OF ELECTRONICS (PUBLICATION). 1982. biennial. price varies. (I E E E, Industrial Electronics Society) Institute of Electrical and Electronics Engineers, Inc., 345 E. 47th St., New York, NY 10017-2394. TEL 212-705-7900. FAX 212-705-7682. (Subscr. to: Box 1331, 445 Hoes Ln., Piscataway, NJ 08855-1331)
Formerly (until 1986): Automotive Applications on Microprocessors.

352.7 624   UK
PLANNING AND TRANSPORT RESEARCH AND COMPUTATION. SUMMER ANNUAL MEETING. PROCEEDINGS. 1968. a. (approx. 20 vols./yr.). price varies. Planning and Transport Research and Computation International Association, Glenthorne House, Hammersmith Grove, London W6 0LG, England. TEL 081-741-1516. FAX 081-741-5993. TELEX 335269-COMET-G. circ. 350. **Indexed:** HRIS.

625 001.642   SA
SOUTH AFRICA. DIVISION OF ROADS AND TRANSPORT TECHNOLOGY. USER MANUALS AND COMPUTER PROGRAMS/DIVISIE VIR PAD- EN VERVOERTEGNOLOGIE. GEBRUIKERSHANDBOEKE EN REKENAARPROGRAMME. 1976. irreg., latest 1990. price varies. Division of Roads and Transport Technology, Computer Information Centre for Transportation, Box 395, Pretoria 0001, South Africa.
Formerly: National Institute for Transport and Road Research. User Manuals for Computer Programs.

TRANSPORTATION — Railroads

385.2   UK   ISSN 0001-0472
A B C RAIL GUIDE. 1853. m. £72. Reed Travel Group (Subsidiary of: Reed International PLC), Church St., Dunstable, Bedfordshire LU5 4HB, England. TEL 0582-600111. TELEX 82168-AIRABC-G. Ed. C. Hopper. adv.; circ. 15,000.
—BLDSC shelfmark: 0537.757700.
Formerly: A B C or Alphabetical Railway Guide.
Description: Contains UK rail schedules and fares. Focuses on London and Southern England.

A M R A JOURNAL. (Australian Model Railway Association) see HOBBIES

385   UK
A R P S INFORMATION PAPERS. irreg. (Association of Railway Preservation Societies Ltd.) A R P S Ltd., c/o J.C. Jeffery, 42 North St., Oundle, Peterborough PE8 4AL, England. TEL 733-582129.

385   SA
A S A MAGAZINE/A P V TYDSKRIF. (Text in Afrikaans and English) 1934. m. membership. (Artisan Staff Association) Leon Maister (Pty) Ltd., Langham House, 59 Long St, P.O. Box 4385, Cape Town, South Africa. Ed. W. Van Der Merwe. adv.; bk.rev.; charts; illus.; stat.; circ. 21,500 (controlled).
Former titles: A S A Journal; Artisan Staff Association Magazine (ISSN 0004-3869)

625.1   US   ISSN 1054-0253
TF858.A2
A S M E - I E E E JOINT RAILROAD CONFERENCE. I E E E TECHNICAL PAPERS. a. price varies. Institute of Electrical and Electronics Engineers, Inc, 345 E. 47th St., New York, NY 10017-2394. TEL 212-705-7366. FAX 212-705-7682. (Subscr. to: Box 1331, 445 Hoes Ln., Piscataway, NJ 08855-1331. TEL 908-562-3871) Key Title: I E E E Technical Papers Presented at the A S M E - I E E E Joint Railroad Conference (1989).
Former titles (until 1986): Joint A S M E - I E E E Railroad Conference. I E E E Technical Papers (ISSN 0885-3800); (1977-1981): Joint A S M E - I E E E - A A R Railroad Conference. I E E E Technical Papers (ISSN 0885-3819) Joint A S M E - I E E E Railroad Technical Conference. I E E E Papers; (until 1975): Joint Railroad Conference. I E E E Papers; Joint Railroad Conference Record; Which supersedes: Joint Railroad Technical Conference. Preprint (ISSN 0075-3998).
Description: Design and technical characteristics of current hardware used to improve the operation of systems in the railroad or transit industries.

385.264   II
AIR CARGO AGENTS ASSOCIATION OF INDIA. NEWS. bi-m. Air Cargo Agents Association of India, 28-B Nariman Bhavan, Nariman Point, 400 021 Bombay, India.

625.1   US
AMERICAN RAILWAY ENGINEERING ASSOCIATION. PROCEEDINGS. a. $78. American Railway Engineering Association, 50 F St., N.W., Ste. 7702, Washington, DC 20001. TEL 202-639-2190. Ed. Louis Cerny. (reprint service avail. from UMI) **Indexed:** Geotech.Abstr.
Former titles: American Railway Engineering Association. Proceedings, Technical Conference (ISSN 0271-4450); American Railway Engineering Association. Proceedings of the Annual Convention.
Description: Reports of technical committees, proposed changes to AREA Manual for Railway Engineering and Portfolio of Trackwork Plans, results of research, papers on various phases of railway engineering construction and maintenance.

625.1   US   ISSN 0003-0694
AMERICAN RAILWAY ENGINEERING ASSOCIATION BULLETIN. Short title: A R E A Bulletin. 1900. 5/yr. $77. American Railway Engineering Association, 50 F St., N.W., Ste. 7702, Washington, DC 20001. TEL 202-639-2190. Ed. Thomas P. Smithberger. adv.; bibl.; charts; index; cum.index; circ. 4,000. (also avail. in microform from UMI; reprint service avail. from UMI) **Indexed:** Br.Rail.Bd., Chem.Abstr., Eng.Ind., Geotech.Abstr.
—BLDSC shelfmark: 6849.668600.

385   US   ISSN 0097-7039
HE2791
AMTRAK ANNUAL REPORT. 1971. a. National Railroad Passenger Corporation, 400 North Capitol St., N.W., Washington, DC 20001. TEL 202-383-3000. circ. 15,000.

AMTRAK EXPRESS. see TRAVEL AND TOURISM — Airline Inflight And Hotel Inroom

385   GW   ISSN 0179-7824
AMTSBLATT DER DEUTSCHEN BUNDESBAHN. 1946. w. DM.175. Deutsche Bundesbahn Zentrale, Presse und Oeffentlichkeitsarbeit, Rhabanusstr. 3, D-6500 Mainz, Germany. TEL 06131-15-498. FAX 06131-15-5490. TELEX 4187732-DBD. adv.; bk.rev.; circ. 29,400.

385   BL
ANUARIO DAS ESTRADAS DE FERRO. 1945. a. Empresa Jornalistica dos Transportes Ltda., Rua Mexico 41, s-904, Rio de Janeiro, Brazil. Ed. Manuel de Moraes Gomes. circ. 10,000.

385   BL
ANUARIO ESTATISTICO DAS FERROVIAS DO BRASIL. 1977. a. free. Rede Ferroviaria Federal, S.A., Gerencia de Estatistica, Pca. Procopio Ferreira 86 s - 1014, 20224 Rio de Janeiro, RJ, Brazil. adv.; circ. 1,200.

625.1   GW   ISSN 0341-0463
ARCHIV FUER EISENBAHNTECHNIK. 1952. a. DM.48. Hestra-Verlag, Holzhofallee 33, Postfach 4244, 6100 Darmstadt 1, Germany. adv. **Indexed:** B.C.I.R.A., Fuel & Energy Abstr., Sci.Abstr.

385   AG
ASOCIACION DEL CONGRESO PANAMERICANO DE FERROCARRILES. BOLETIN. 1916. bi-m. membership. Asociacion del Congreso Panamericano de Ferrocarriles - Pan-American Railway Congress Association, Av. 9 de Julio 1925, Piso 13, 1332 Buenos Aires, Argentina. TEL 38-4625. FAX 54-1-814-1823. Ed. Juan Carlos de Marchi. adv.; bk.rev.; charts; stat.; circ. 800.

385   UK
ASSOCIATED SOCIETY OF LOCOMOTIVE ENGINEERS AND FIREMEN. ANNUAL REPORT AND BALANCE SHEET. 1880. a. membership only. Associated Society of Locomotive Engineers and Firemen, 9 Arkwright Rd., Hampstead, London NW3 6AB, England. circ. controlled.

ASSOCIATION OF PRIVATE POSTAL SYSTEMS. DIRECTORY. see COMMUNICATIONS — Postal Affairs

ASSOCIATION OF PRIVATE POSTAL SYSTEMS. UPDATE. see COMMUNICATIONS — Postal Affairs

ASSOCIATION OF RAILROAD ADVERTISING AND MARKETING. NEWSLETTER. see ADVERTISING AND PUBLIC RELATIONS

625.1   US
ASSOCIATION OF RAILROAD EDITORS. PROOF. m. Association of Railroad Editors, c/o J Ronald Shumate, Association of American Railroads, 50 F St., N.W., Washington, DC 20001. TEL 202-639-2562.

385   UK
ASSOCIATION OF RAILWAY PRESERVATION SOCIETIES. JOURNAL. 1979. q. A R P S Ltd., c/o J.C. Jeffery, 42 North St., Oundle, Peterborough PE8 4AL, England. TEL 733-582129. Ed. Rodney Pitt. adv.; circ. 1,000.
Description: Provides news, comment and articles on subjects of special interest to the railway preservation movement, and details ARPS meetings and seminars.

385.264   IT
ASSOCIAZIONE ITALIANA INGEGNERI DEL TRAFFICO. BOLLETINO. q. Associazione Italiana Ingegneri del Traffico, c/o Facolta di Ingegneria, Via Marzola 9, I-35100 Padova, Italy. TEL 049-831510.

385.264   IT
ASSOCIAZIONE NAZIONALE AUTOSERVIZI IN CONCESSIONE. INFORMA. m. Associazione Nazionale Autoservizi in Concessione, Piazza dell'Esquilino 29, I-00185 Rome, Italy. TEL 06-4820531. FAX 06-4821204.

385   CN   ISSN 0004-7376
AU FIL DU RAIL. 1966. m. (10/yr.). Canadian National Railways, P.O. Box 8100, Montreal, Que. H3C 3N4, Canada. TEL 514-399-8041. FAX 514-399-5344. Ed. Louise Verge. circ. 16,700 (controlled). (tabloid format)
Description: Covers news and events of interest to active and retired employees of Canadian National Railways.

AUSTRALIAN MODEL RAILWAY MAGAZINE. see HOBBIES

385   AT   ISSN 0005-0105
AUSTRALIAN RAILWAY HISTORICAL SOCIETY. BULLETIN. 1937. m. Aus.$20. Australian Railway Historical Society, P.O. Box E129, St. James, N.S.W., 2000, Australia. Ed. A. Bisits. bk.rev.; film rev.; charts; illus.; stat.; index; circ. 3,000. (also avail. in microfiche)

AUSTRALIAN RAILWAYS UNION. FEDERAL OFFICE NEWS. see LABOR UNIONS

385.264   IT
AUTOBUS OGGI. bi-m. Associazione Nazionale Autoservizi in Concessione, Piazza dell'Esquilino 29, I-00185 Rome, Italy. TEL 06-4820531. FAX 06-4821204.

385   US   ISSN 0362-2711
TF25.B8
B & M BULLETIN. 1971. irreg. membership. Boston & Maine Railroad Historical Society, Inc., Box 2936, Woburn, MA 01888. TEL 617-628-4053. Ed. John Alan Roderick. bk.rev.; charts; illus.; circ. 2,700.
Description: Historical record of the B&M and its predecessor railroads.

TRANSPORTATION — RAILROADS

385　　　　　　　　GW
B D E F - JAHRBUCH. 1982. a. DM.15. (Bund Deutscher Eisenbahn-Freunde) Uhle & Kleimann, Pettenpohlstr. 17, 4990 Luebbecke 1, Germany.
TEL 05741-7209. FAX 05741-90224. circ. 3,000. (back issues avail.)

B M W E RAILWAY JOURNAL. (Brotherhood of Maintenance of Way Employes) see *LABOR UNIONS*

385　　　　　　　　US
B N NEWS. 1970. q. Burlington Northern Railroad, 2900 Continental Plaza, 777 Main St., Fort Worth, TX 76102. TEL 817-878-3046.
FAX 817-878-7997. Ed. Susan Green. cum.index: 1970-1990; circ. 55,000 (controlled). (back issues avail.)
Description: Covers news pertaining to Burlington Northern, industry and related subjects.

385　　　　　　　　SW
BENELUX RAIL. (Text in Dutch and French) 1981. s-a. SEK 85($13) Frank Stenvalls Foerlag, Foereningsgatan 67, S-211 52 Malmoe, Sweden.
TEL 040-127703. Ed. Marcel Vleugels. illus. (back issues avail.)

385.264　　　　　　　　NE
BEROEPSVERVOER; wekelijks magazine voor transportondernemigen. 1948. w. (Nationale Organisatie voor het Beroepsgoederenvervoer Wegtransport) S C T Informatiendiensten B.V., P.O. Box 726, 2700 AS Zoetermeer, Netherlands.
TEL 079-683342. FAX 079-683325.

385.264　　　　　　　　BE
BINNENVAART. 1913. s-a. Belgische Transportarbeidersbond, Paardenmark 66, B-2000 Antwerpen, Belgium. TEL 03-224-34-11.
FAX 03-234-01-49.

385　　　　　　　　UK　　ISSN 0263-0125
BLASTPIPE. 1981. irreg. £0.10 per no. Fakenham and Dereham Railway Society, c/o I Jowett, Market Place, East Harling, Norfolk NOR 12X, England. illus.

385　　　　　　　　IT
BOLLETTINO UFFICIALE DELLE FERROVIE DELLO STATO. PARTE PRIMA E SECONDA. bi-w. L.20700. Azienda Autonoma delle Ferrovie dello Stato, Centro di Documentazione, Piazza Croce Rossa, 00100 Rome, Italy.

385　　　　　　　　IT
BOLLETTINO UFFICIALE DELLE FERROVIE DELLO STATO. PARTE TERZA. m. L.11500. Azienda Autonoma delle Ferrovie dello Stato, Centro di Documentazione, Piazza Croce Rossa, 00100 Rome, Italy.

385　　　　　　　　UK
BRANCH LINE NEWS. 1955. s-m. £16.50 (effective through Dec.1991). Branch Line Society, Hon. General Secretary N.J. Hill, 73 Norfolk Park Ave., Sheffield S2 2RB, England. Ed. A.M. Jervis. adv.; bk.rev.; index; circ. 1,200.
Description: General information on British and some overseas railroad branch lines, openings, closings, and local developments.

BRITAIN BY BRITRAIL; how to tour Britain by train. see *TRAVEL AND TOURISM*

385　　　　　　　　UK
BRITISH COAL GUIDE TO STEAM TRAINS IN THE BRITISH ISLES. 1973. a. free. (Association of Railway Preservation Societies Ltd.) A R P S Ltd., c/o J.C. Jeffery, Ed., 42 North St., Oundle, Peterborough PE8 4AL, England. TEL 733-582129. FAX 733-582800. TELEX 32501 PERKOIL G. circ. 350,000.
Formerly (until 1987): Guide to Steam Trains in the British Isles (ISSN 0262-3943)
Description: Provides details of addresses, locations, telephone numbers, facilities, dates and times of opening and special events for 140 railways, museums and other centers where steam trains may be seen.

385.264　　　　　　　　UK
BRITISH INTERNATIONAL FREIGHT ASSOCIATION. YEARBOOK. 1944. a. £28.50. British International Freight Association, Redfern House, Browells Lane, Feltham, Middx. TW13 7EP, England.
FAX 081-890-5546. adv.; circ. 6,000.
Formerly: Institute of Freight Forwarders. Yearbook.

385.1　　　　　　　　UK　　ISSN 0305-1420
BRITISH RAILWAYS BOARD. ANNUAL REPORT AND ACCOUNTS. 1963. a. price varies. British Railways Board, Euston House, P.O. Box 100, London NW1 1DZ, England. TELEX 299431-BRHQLN-G. (Dist. by: H.M.S.O., c/o Liason Officer, Atlantic House, London EC1P 1BW, England)
Formerly: British Railways Board. Report and Statement of Accounts (ISSN 0068-242X)
Description: Annual statement of accounts and business report.

BULLETIN DES TRANSPORTS. see *LAW*

385　　　　　　　　GW　　ISSN 0007-5876
DIE BUNDESBAHN. 1924. m. DM.187.20. (Deutsche Bundesbahn) Hestra-Verlag, Holzhofallee 33, Postfach 4244, 6100 Darmstadt 1, Germany. adv.; bibl.; charts; illus.; index; circ. 10,000. (back issues avail.) **Indexed:** Excerp.Med., HRIS.
—BLDSC shelfmark: 2930.110000.

385.1　　　　　　　　CM
CAMEROON. REGIE NATIONALE DES CHEMINS DE FER. COMPTE RENDU DE GESTION. a. Regie Nationale des Chemins de Fer, Douala, Cameroon.

385　　　　　　　　CM
CAMEROON. REGIE NATIONALE DES CHEMINS DE FER. STATISTIQUES. irreg. Regie Nationale des Chemins de Fer, Douala, Cameroon. illus.

385　　　　　　　　CN　　ISSN 0008-4875
CANADIAN RAIL/RAIL CANADIEN. (Text in English, French) 1949. bi-m. Can.$30($26) Canadian Railroad Historical Association, Box 22, Sta. B, Montreal, Que. H3B 3J5, Canada. Eds. Frederick F. Angus, Douglas N.W. Smith. bk.rev.; illus.; index; circ. 1,600 (controlled).

385　　　　　　　　CN　　ISSN 0226-157X
CANADIAN RAILWAY CLUB. NEWSLETTER. 1908. 3/yr. Can.$15 membership. Canadian Railway Club, Inc., Box 162, Station A, Montreal, Que. H3C 1C5, Canada. Ed. J.H. Glatzmayer. adv.; circ. 1,500.
Formerly (until 1978): Canadian Railway Club. Official Proceedings (ISSN 0008-4883)
Description: Concerned with the construction, operation and maintenance of railroads and railroad equipment.

625.2　　　　　　　　US
CAR AND LOCOMOTIVE CYCLOPEDIA. 1879. irreg. $69.95. Simmons-Boardman Publishing Corporation, 1809 Capitol Ave., Omaha, NE 10014. TEL 402-346-4300. Ed. K. Ellsworth. adv.; bibl.; charts; illus.; circ. 6,500.

625　　　　　　　　US　　ISSN 0069-1623
CENTRAL ELECTRIC RAILFANS' ASSOCIATION. BULLETIN. 1938. irreg., no.127, 1989. membership. Central Electric Railfans' Association, Box 503, Chicago, IL 60690. TEL 312-346-3723. Ed.Bd. circ. 2,000.
Description: List of books and publications pertaining to the history of electric-powered trolleys, streetcars, and railroad systems.

385　　　　　　　　UK
CHANNEL TUNNEL BULLETIN. 1963. s-a. £5($8) Channel Tunnel Association, 44 Westbourne Terrace, London W2 3UH, England. TEL 071-402-4452. TELEX 269935. Ed. C. Fox. bk.rev.; circ. 150.

CHEMINOT. see *LABOR UNIONS*

CHEMINOT DE FRANCE. see *LABOR UNIONS*

CHEMINOT RETRAITE. see *LABOR UNIONS*

385　　　　　　　　FR　　ISSN 0009-2924
CHEMINS DE FER. 1937. bi-m. 310 F. Association Francaise des Amis des Chemins de Fer, Gare de l'Est, 75475 Paris Cedex 10, France. Ed. Bernard Porcher. adv.; bk.rev.; charts; illus.; circ. 5,000.
Description: Discusses worldwide railways of yesterday, today and the future.

385　　　　　　　　US　　ISSN 0886-6287
CHESAPEAKE AND OHIO HISTORICAL MAGAZINE. 1969. m. $17. Chesapeake and Ohio Historical Society, Inc., Box 79, Clifton Forge, VA 24422.
TEL 703-862-2210. Ed. Donald R. Traser. bk.rev.; charts; illus.; circ. 2,500. (also avail. in microfilm from UMI; reprint service avail. from UMI)
Formerly (until 1986): Chesapeake and Ohio Historical Newsletter (ISSN 0883-587X)

385　　　　　　　　US　　ISSN 0193-3477
CLEAR TRACK; railroad construction letter. 1977. 24/yr. National Railroad Construction and Maintenance Association, Inc., 10765 Woodwater Cir., Eden Prairie, MN 55347. FAX 612-942-8947. Ed. Daniel Foth. adv.; bk.rev.; stat.; tr.lit.; index; circ. 1,500 (controlled). (back issues avail.)

385 531.64　　　　　　　　US　　ISSN 0732-8397
COAL TRANSPORTATION REPORT. 1982. fortn. $495 (effective Jan. 1992). Fieldston Publications, Inc., 1920 N St., N.W., Ste. 210, Washington, DC 20036. TEL 202-775-0240. FAX 202-872-8045. Ed. James Heller. bk.rev.
Description: Studies all aspects of coal transportation and railroad legislation and regulation.

385.1　　　　　　　　US　　ISSN 0069-6048
COLORADO RAIL ANNUAL. 1963. irreg. (approx. biennial). price varies. (Colorado Railroad Historical Foundation, Inc.) Colorado Railroad Museum, Box 10, Golden, CO 80402. TEL 303-279-4591. Ed. Cornelius W. Hauck. adv.; bk.rev.; index; circ. 4,500.

385.264　　　　　　　　US
COMMON, CARRIER CONFERENCE-IRREGULAR ROUTE. NEWSLETTER. 1941. bi-m. Common, Carrier Conference-Irregular Route, 2200 Mill Rd., Ste.600, Alexandria, VA 22314. TEL 703-838-1950.

385　　　　　　　　FR　　ISSN 0222-4844
CONNAISSANCE DU RAIL. 1979. m. 310 F. Editions de l'Ormet, Valignat, 03330 Bellenaves, France. adv.; bk.rev.; bibl.; cum.index; circ. 10,000. (back issues avail.)

385　　　　　　　　CN
COUPLER. 1957. bi-m. free. B C Rail Ltd., P.O. Box 8770, Vancouver, B.C. V6B 4X6, Canada.
TEL 604-984-5248. FAX 604-984-5090. Ed. K. Korbin. circ. 4,000.

625.143　　　　　　　　US　　ISSN 0097-4536
CROSSTIES. 1919. bi-m. $25. (Railway Tie Association) Industrial Reporting, Inc., 1893-D1 Billingsgate Cir., Richmond, VA 23233. TEL 804-740-1567.
FAX 804-740-2826. Ed. Ed Brindley, Jr. adv.; charts; illus.; stat.; index; circ. 2,500. **Indexed:** Chem.Abstr.
Formerly: Cross Tie Bulletin (ISSN 0011-197X)
Description: Covers all aspects of the railroad crosstie industry, including forest management, timber processing, worker safety, legislative and engineering issues.

385　　　　　　　　GW
D B. (Deine Bahn); Zeitschrift fuer das Bildungswesen der deutschen Bundesbahn. 1973. m. DM.45.60. (Deutsche Bundesbahn) Eisenbahn-Fachverlag, Postfach 2330, 6500 Mainz, Germany. (Organ of: Verband Deutscher Eisenbahn-Fachschulen) Ed. Alfred Huethig. adv.; bk.rev.; charts; illus.
Supersedes: Eisenbahner. Ausgabe A & B (ISSN 0013-2802); **Incorporates:** Eisenbahnfachmann.

385　　　　　　　　GW　　ISSN 0011-4758
D B - KUNDENBRIEF. 1955. m. free. Deutsche Bundesbahn, Werbe- und Auskunftsamt fuer den Personen- und Gueterverkehr, Gueterstr. 9, 6000 Frankfurt 1, Germany. Ed. Hans Herrmann Waitz. adv.; bk.rev.; charts; illus.; stat.; index; circ. 60,000.

625.1　　　　　　　　GW　　ISSN 0072-1549
HE3071
D B REPORT. 1965. a. DM.33.60. (Deutsche Bundesbahn) Hestra-Verlag, Holzhofallee 33, Postfach 4244, 6100 Darmstadt 1, Germany. adv

385　　　　　　　　GW　　ISSN 0722-0170
D G E G-NACHRICHTEN. 1969. bi-m. DM.24. Deutsche Gesellschaft fuer Eisenbahngeschichte e.V., Postfach 1111, 4711 Selm, Germany. TEL 02592-62040. (Subscr. to: DGEG- Schriftenversand, Gerhard Peterhaensel, Sebastianusweg 11, 5253 Lindlar-Schmitzhoehe, Germany) Ed. Guenter Krause. adv.; bk.rev.; charts; illus.; circ. 2,500. (back issues avail.)

385　　　　　　　　GW　　ISSN 0933-7598
TF3
DAMPF UND REISE; Bahnerlebnisse rund um die Welt - Ueberseeische Bahnen. 1986. 6/yr. DM.62. Roehr-Verlag GmbH, Brandenburgerstr. 10, 4150 Krefeld 12, Germany. TEL 02151-501033. Ed. Gustav F. Roehr.
Incorporates: Verkehr in Afrika.

TRANSPORTATION — RAILROADS

385 UK ISSN 0309-1465
DEVELOPING RAILWAYS. 1966. a. £20. Reed Business Publishing Group (Subsidiary of: Reed International PLC), Quadrant House, The Quadrant, Sutton, Surrey SM2 5AS, England. TEL 081-652-8608. FAX 081-652-8986. Ed. Richard Hope. circ. 8,910. (reprint service avail. from UMI)
 Former titles: International Railway Progress (ISSN 0074-7572); Overseas Railways.

621.2 US ISSN 0070-4830
DIESEL LOCOMOTIVE QUESTION & ANSWER MANUAL.* 1950. irreg. $8. International Association of Railway Operating Officers, 1 Leo Dr., Bloomington, IL 61701-7732.
 Formerly: Diesel Electric Locomotive Examination Book.

385 GW
DUMJAHN'S JAHRBUCH FUER EISENBAHNLITERATUR; ein kritischer Wegweiser zu lieferbaren, angezeigten und empfehlenswerten Buechern "rund um die Eisenbahn". 1984. a. DM.8. Horst-Werner Dumjahn Verlag, Immenhof 12, Postfach 1746, 6500 Mainz 1, Germany. FAX 6131-35600. Ed. Horst-Werner Dumjahn. (back issues avail.)
 Formerly: Jahrbuch fuer Eisenbahnliteratur.

385 II ISSN 0012-8880
EASTERN RAILWAY MAGAZINE. 1952. bi-m. Rs.12. 14-16 Govt. Place East, Calcutta 1, India. Eds. S.K. Basu, S. Sen. adv.; illus.; circ. 5,000.

385 625.1 AU ISSN 0013-2756
EISENBAHN; Geschichte, Technik, Aktualitaeten. 1948. m. S.833. Bohmann Druck und Verlag GmbH & Co. KG, Leberstr. 122, A-1110 Vienna, Austria. TEL 0222-741595. FAX 0222-741595-183. TELEX 132312. adv.; abstr.; illus.; index; circ. 8,500.

EISENBAHN-AMATEUR; Schweizerische Zeitschrift fuer Eisenbahn- und Modellbaufreunde. see *HOBBIES*

625.1 GW ISSN 0934-5930
EISENBAHN INGENIEUR KALENDER (YEAR). (In two parts: A & B) a. DM.33. Deutscher Verkehrs Verlag, Nordkanalstr. 36, Postfach 101609, 2000 Hamburg 1, Germany. Ed.Bd. adv.; circ. 9,000. (back issues avail.)
 —BLDSC shelfmark: 3666.874000.
 Formerly: Elsners Taschenbuch der Eisenbahntechnik (ISSN 0071-0275)
 Description: Part A covers material required by railway engineers in their daily work; Part B covers building, machine engineering, electrical engineering, signalling and telecommunications.

385 GW ISSN 0720-051X
EISENBAHN-JOURNAL. 1975. m. DM.225. Hermann Merker Verlag GmbH, Rudolf-Diesel-Ring 5, 8080 Fuerstenfeldbruck, Germany. TEL 08141-5048. FAX 08141-44689. Ed. Manfred Grauer. adv.; bk.rev.; bibl.; charts; illus.; stat.; index; circ. 48,000. (back issues avail.)

385 625.19 GW ISSN 0342-1902
EISENBAHN MODELLBAHN MAGAZIN. 1963. m. DM.120. Alba Publikationen Alf Teloeken, Roemerstrasse 9, Postfach 320109, 4000 Duesseldorf 30, Germany. TEL 0211-469010. FAX 0211-484382. Ed. J.M. Hill. adv.; bk.rev.; circ. 85,000 (controlled). (back issues avail.)
 Description: Covers all aspects of rail transport and model railroading.

385 AU ISSN 0013-2799
EISENBAHNER.* 1896. m. S.22 to non-members. Oesterreichischer Gewerkschaftsbund, Gewerkschaft der Eisenbahner, Margaretenstr. 166, A-1050 Vienna, Austria. Ed. Hans Freihsl. adv.; abstr.; charts; illus.; play rev.; circ. 120,000.

385 SZ
EISENBAHNER. w. 36 Fr. (foreign 42 Fr.). Schweizer Eisenbahner Verband, Steinerstr. 35, Postfach 186, CH-3000 Bern 16, Switzerland. Ed. Rene Bauer.

625.1 GW ISSN 0013-2810
   CODEN: ESBGAP
DER EISENBAHNINGENIEUR; Fachzeitschrift fuer Eisenbahntechnik. 1949. m. DM.128.40. (Verband Deutscher Eisenbahningenieure) Deutscher Verkehrs Verlag, Nordkanalstr. 36, Postfach 101609, 2000 Hamburg 1, Germany. Ed. Dieter Stuewe. adv.; bk.rev.; bibl.; charts; illus.; pat.; index; circ. 11,500. (back issues avail.) **Indexed:** Excerp.Med., Sci.Abstr.
 Incorporates: Schienenfahrzeuge (ISSN 0036-6021) & Eisenbahnpraxis.
 Description: Complete railway engineering including specialized branches such as building, building construction, surveying, signalling, telecommunications, machines, and electrical engineering.

385 625.1 GW ISSN 0013-2845
EISENBAHNTECHNISCHE RUNDSCHAU; Zeitschrift fuer die gesamte Eisenbahntechnik. (Text in German; summaries in English, French, Spanish) 1952. m. DM.211.20. Hestra-Verlag, Holzhofallee 33, Postfach 4244, 6100 Darmstadt 1, Germany. Ed.Bd. adv.; bk.rev.; abstr.; bibl.; charts; illus.; index; circ. 6,050. **Indexed:** Excerp.Med., Geotech.Abstr., HRIS, INIS Atomind.
 —BLDSC shelfmark: 3668.000000.

385 UK ISSN 0013-4147
ELECTRIC RAILWAY SOCIETY. JOURNAL. 1956. bi-m. £5.75. Electric Railway Society, 14 Askerfield Ave., Allestree, Derby DE3 2ST, England. TEL 0332-550786. Ed. J.A. Rosser. adv.; bk.rev.; index; circ. 400.
 Description: Articles on electric railways worldwide.

385 621.38 GW ISSN 0013-5437
TF701   CODEN: ELBAAQ
ELEKTRISCHE BAHNEN; Zeitschrift fuer Elektrotechnik im Verkehrswesen. 1903. m. DM.242.60. R. Oldenbourg Verlag GmbH, Rosenheimerstr. 145, 8000 Munich 80, Germany. adv.; abstr.; bibl.; charts; illus.; index; circ. 2,000. (also avail. in microform from UMI; reprint service avail. from UMI) **Indexed:** Br.Rail.Bd., Eng.Ind., INIS Atomind., Sci.Abstr.
 —BLDSC shelfmark: 3711.000000.
 Description: Latest developments of the use of electronics in railroads and tramways. Focus on high speed engineering, efficiency and automatic controls.

625.1 US ISSN 0013-8142
ENGINEERS AND ENGINES MAGAZINE. 1955. bi-m $15 (foreign $18). Donald D. Knowles, Ed. & Pub., 1118 N. Raynor Ave., Joliet, IL 60435. TEL 815-727-1830. adv.; charts; illus.; circ. 9,500.

EURAIL GUIDE; how to travel Europe and all the world by train. see *TRAVEL AND TOURISM*

EUROPE BY EURAIL; how to tour Europe by train. see *TRAVEL AND TOURISM*

385.1 SZ ISSN 0071-2264
EUROPEAN COMPANY FOR THE FINANCING OF RAILWAY ROLLING STOCK. ANNUAL REPORT. Short title: EUROFIMA Annual Report. (Text in English, French and German) 1957. a. free. European Company for the Financing of Railway Rolling Stock (EUROFIMA), Rittergasse 20, CH-4001 Basel, Switzerland. FAX 2724105. TELEX 962999. circ. 4,000.
 Description: For the business year of Eurofima.

EXPRESS. see *TRAVEL AND TOURISM — Airline Inflight And Hotel Inroom*

385 US ISSN 0014-1380
EXTRA 2200 SOUTH; locomotive news magazine. vol.6, 1968. q. $13.75. Doug Cummings, Ed. & Pub., Box 8110-820, Blaine, WA 98230. bk.rev.; charts; illus.; stat.; tr.lit.; cum.index; circ. 10,000. (back issues avail.)

F E L A REPORTER & RAILROAD LIABILITY MONITOR. (Federal Employees Liability Act) see *LAW*

385.264 GW
FACHVEREINIGUNG GUTERFERNVERKEHR HAMBURG. MITTEILUNGEN. 1948. m. Fachvereinigung Guterfernverkehr Hamburg, Bullerdeich 36, Postfach 261861, 2000 Hamburg 26, Germany. TEL 257272. TELEX 212442.

385.264 GW
FACHVEREINIGUNG GUTERFERNVERKEHR SCHLESWIG-HOLSTEIN. NACHRICHTENDIENST. m. Fachvereinigung Guterfernverkehr Schleswig-Holstein, Ilsahl 1-3, D-2350 Neumunster, Germany. TEL 04321-31081. TELEX 299637.

385 GW ISSN 0014-6846
FAHRT FREI; Zeitung der Eisenbahner. 1948. fortn. DM.22.10. (Ministerium fuer Verkehrswesen) Transpress Verlagsgesellschaft mbH, Franzoesische Str. 13-14, Postfach 1235, 1086 Berlin, Germany. TEL 203410. Ed. Wolfgang Kroker. illus. (newspaper; reprint service avail. from UMI)

385 AG ISSN 0046-3698
FERROCARRILES ARGENTINOS.* 1971. m. Avda. Ramos Mejia 1302, Buenos Aires, Argentina. Ed.Bd. adv.; charts; illus.; stat.

385 MX ISSN 0015-0207
FERRONALES.* (Supplement avail.) 1930. m. Mex.$20.($2.) Ferrocarriles Nacionales de Mexico, Gerencia Comunicacion Social, Av. Jesus Garcia Corona no. 140, 120 Piso, Ala C, Col. Buenavista, 06358 Mexico. TEL 547-6068. Ed. Ruben Gonzalez Lechuga. adv.; chart.; illus.; stat.; circ. 25,000.

FERROVIERE. see *LABOR UNIONS*

385 UK ISSN 0015-0355
FESTINIOG RAILWAY MAGAZINE. 1958. q. £12 to non-members. Festiniog Railway Society Ltd., c/o P. Johnson, Ed., 12 Maplewell Dr., Leicester LE4 1BD, England. TEL 0533-357268. FAX 0533-357268. Ed. Peter Johnson. adv.; bk.rev.; charts; illus.; circ. 6,000.

385 GW ISSN 0015-2862
FISCHERS TARIF NACHRICHTEN FUER EISENBAHN UND KRAFTWAGEN; Informationen fuer den Gueterverkehr. 1941. m. DM.30.70. Verkehrs-Verlag J. Fischer, Paulusstr. 1, Postfach 140265, 4000 Duesseldorf 4, Germany. TEL 0211-673056. Ed. Paul Urban. adv.; bk.rev.; charts; illus.; circ. 5,000.

385 UK
FIVE FOOT THREE. 1966. s-a. £0.60. Railway Preservation Society of Ireland, Whitehead Excursion Station, Whitehead, Co. Antrim, N. Ireland. Ed. A. Edgar. adv.; bk.rev.; illus.; circ. 1,500.

FOOTPLATE/VOETPLAAT. see *LABOR UNIONS*

FRACHT - DIENST. see *TRANSPORTATION — Ships And Shipping*

385 US ISSN 0742-9355
TF470.A1
FREIGHT CARS JOURNAL; history, modeling, news. 1983. q. $20 (foreign $35). Society of Freight Car Historians, Box 2480, Monrovia, CA 91017. Ed. David G. Casdorph. bk.rev.; circ. 1,000. (back issues avail.)
 Description: Original articles on the history and development of American railway freight cars and related subjects.

385 US ISSN 0016-8866
GERMANA ESPERANTA FERVOJISTA ASOCIO. BULTENO. (Text in Esperanto; summaries in German) 1952. bi-m. DM.6($2) Vereinigung Deutscher Eisenbahner-Esperantisten im Bundesbahn-Sozialwerk, D-8620 Lichtenfels, Germany. Ed. Wilhelm Grass. bk.rev.; illus.; circ. 700.

385 GW
GEWERKSCHAFT DEUTSCHER LOKOMOTIVFUEHRER UND ANWAERTER. VORAUS. 1863. m. DM.15. Gewerkschaft Deutscher Lokomotivfuehrer und Anwaerter, Westendstr. 50, Postfach 97 01 06, 6000 Frankfurt a.M. 97, Germany. TEL 069-724646. FAX 069-729632. adv.; bk.rev.; circ. 45,000.

385 UK ISSN 0307-3319
GREAT NORTH REVIEW. 1964. q. £5. Great North of Scotland Railway Association, c/o J. Gough, 28 East Glebe, Stonehaven AV3 2HW, Scotland. TEL 0569-63139. Ed.Bd. adv.; illus.; cum.index; circ. 195.

TRANSPORTATION — RAILROADS

385   UK
GREAT WESTERN ECHO. 1963. q. £10. Great Western Society Ltd., Didcot, Oxfordshire, England. Ed. Michael Baker. adv.; bk.rev.; bibl.; charts; illus.; tr.lit.; circ. 5,000.

315   US
GREEN BLOCK. 1965. m. $3 to non-members. National Railway Historical Society, Inc., Central New York Chapter, Box 229, Marcellus, NY 13108. Ed. Charles Abbott. bk.rev.

385.5   RU
GUDOK. d. Railway Transport Worker's Union - Gewerkschaft der Arbeiter des Eisenbahnwesens und Transportwegebaus, 21 Sadova - Spasskaya Ul., 107217 Moscow, Russia. **Indexed:** Curr.Dig.Sov.Press.

385.264   BE
HAVEN. 1913. s-a. Belgische Transportarbeidersbond, Paardenmarkt 66, B-2000 Antwerpen, Belgium. TEL 03-224-34-11. FAX 03-234-01-49.

385.264   GW
HESSISCHER VERKEHRSSPIEGEL. m. Fachverband Guterfernverkehr der Vereinigung des Verkehrsgewerbes in Hessen, Konigsberger Str 1-3, D-6000 Frankfurt 90, Germany. TEL 774935. TELEX 12175.

385   US
HIGH SPEED RAIL YEARBOOK. 1984. a. $100. High Speed Rail Association, 206 Valley Court, Ste. 800, Pittsburg, PA 15237. TEL 412-366-8698. FAX 412-369-8698. Ed. Robert J. Casey. circ. 5,000.
    Description: Covers proceedings of the convention, High Speed Rail directory and information about new transportation modes and the industry of high speed rail.

385.22 790   US   ISSN 1055-3967
HOBO TIMES. 6/yr. $18. National Hobo Association, World Way Center, Box 9043, Los Angeles, CA 90009.

HOOFLIG/HEADLIGHT. see *LABOR UNIONS*

HORSE BRASS. see *HOBBIES*

385   AU   ISSN 0005-0504
I F E F, AUSTRIA SEKCIO. BULTENO. (Federacio Esperantista Fervojista) (Text in Esperanto, German) 1956. 4/yr. free. Oesterreichischer Eisenbahner Esperant Verband, Postfach 117, A-1103 Vienna, Austria. Ed. Leopold Patek. illus.

385 387.7
INDIAN BRADSHAW. (Text in English) 1866. m. Rs.294. W. Newman & Co., Ltd., G.P.O. Box 76, 3 Old Court House St., Calcutta 700 069, India. TEL 28-9436. Ed. Milan Chandra Paul. adv.; circ. 80,000.
    Description: Guide for rail and air travel in India.

385   II   ISSN 0019-6258
INDIAN RAILWAY GAZETTE; India's premier railway journal. (Text in English) 1903. m. Rs.15($3.16) Thornes (Private) Ltd., 13 Ezra Mansions, Box 2361, Calcutta 1, India. Ed. L.K. Padmanabhan. adv.; bk.rev.; charts; illus.; stat.; circ. 7,618. (also avail. in microform from UMI; reprint service avail. from UMI)

625.1   II   ISSN 0019-6266
INDIAN RAILWAY TECHNICAL BULLETIN.* (Text in English) 1964. q. Rs.5. Research Designs and Standards Organization, Alambagh, Lucknow 5, India. abstr.; charts; illus.; stat.; circ. 1,500. **Indexed:** Br.Rail.Bd.

385   II   ISSN 0019-6274
INDIAN RAILWAYS; devoted to railway affairs in India and abroad. (Text in English) 1956. m. Rs.100($7.62) Ministry of Railways (Railway Board), c/o Railway Board, Box 467, New Delhi 110 001, India. TEL 11-383522. TELEX 031-66061. Ed. M.D. Banerjee. adv.; bk.rev.; charts; illus.; stat.; tr.lit.; circ. 10,000.

385   II
INDIAN RAILWAYS SAFETY PERFORMANCE - A REVIEW. (Text in English) 1957. a. Railway Board, Directorate of Safety, New Delhi 110001, India.
    Formerly: Review of Accidents on Indian Government Railways (ISSN 0080-1933)

385 625.1   UK
INDUSTRIAL LOCOMOTIVE. 1947. q. £5. Industrial Locomotive Society, Gilfachddu, Llanberis, Gwynedd, Wales LL55 4TY, England. Ed. V.J. Bradley. adv.; bk.rev.; bibl.; illus.; circ. controlled.
    Formerly: Industrial Locomotive Society Journal.

385   US
INFO MAGAZINE. 1968. m. Union Pacific Railroad, Employee Communications Department, 1416 Dodge St., Omaha, NE 68179. Ed. J.H. Beck. circ. 78,000 (controlled).
    Formerly: Infonews.

INFORMATION EISENBAHN; Dokumentation des Fachschrifttums. see *TRANSPORTATION — Abstracting, Bibliographies, Statistics*

385 625.1   IT   ISSN 0020-0956
                                     CODEN: INFEAE
INGEGNERIA FERROVIARIA; rivista di tecnica ed economia dei trasporti. (Text in Italian; summaries in English, French, German) 1904. m. $90. Collegio Ingegneri Ferroviari Italiani, Via Giolitti 34, 00185 Rome, Italy. TEL 06-4827116. FAX 06-47306454. Ed. Giuseppe R. Corazza. adv.; bk.rev.; abstr.; bibl.; charts; illus.; index. **Indexed:** C.I.S. Abstr., Chem.Abstr., Eng.Ind., Geotech.Abstr.
    —BLDSC shelfmark: 4501.000000.

385   II   ISSN 0020-3114
HE3291
INSTITUTE OF RAIL TRANSPORT. JOURNAL. (Text in English) 1965. q. Rs.10. Institute of Rail Transport, Rm. 264, Rail Bhavan, Raisina Rd., New Delhi, India. Ed.Bd. adv.; bk.rev.; charts; circ. 1,250.

385   UK   ISSN 0954-4097
TF1   CODEN: PMFTEV
INSTITUTION OF MECHANICAL ENGINEERS. PROCEEDINGS. PART F: JOURNAL OF RAIL AND RAPID TRANSIT. 2/yr. £68($129) for part F; £748($1420) for parts A-I. Mechanical Engineering Publications Ltd., Northgate Ave., Bury St. Edmunds, Suffolk IP32 6BW, England. TEL 0284-763277. FAX 0284-704006. TELEX 817376. Ed. D.J.W. Sough. circ. 888. **Indexed:** Br.Tech.Ind.
    —BLDSC shelfmark: 6724.900850.
    Description: Covers railway and rapid transit systems and rolling stock.

625.1 385   UK   ISSN 0073-9839
                                    CODEN: PRWEAY
INSTITUTION OF RAILWAY SIGNAL ENGINEERS. PROCEEDINGS. 1912. a. £12. Institution of Railway Signal Engineers, 1 Badlake Close, Badlake Hill, Dawlish, Devon EX7 9JA, England. TEL 0626-888096. Ed. R.L. Weedon. adv.; circ. 2,000.
    Description: Contains papers on modern railway signaling and telecommunications developments.

385.264   SZ
INTERCONTAINER. 3/yr. International Company for the Transport by Transcontainers, Margarethenstr 38, CH-4008 Basel, Switzerland. TEL 061-452525. TELEX 62298.

385.264   US
INTERNATIONAL AIRFORWARDER AND AGENTS ASSOCIATION. UPDATE. 1958. m. International Airforwarder and Agents Association, Box 627, Rockville Centre, NY 11571. TEL 516-536-6229. Dir. Stephen R. Morgan.

387.164   UK   ISSN 0260-1087
INTERNATIONAL BULK JOURNAL. 1981. m. £160($300) I B J Associates, Ranmore House, Ranmore Rd., Dorking, Surrey RH4 1HE, England. TEL 0306-740447. FAX 0306-883650. Ed. Richard G. Peckham. adv.; bk.rev.; circ. 7,000. **Indexed:** Fluidex.
    —BLDSC shelfmark: 4537.678000.

385.204   CS
INTERNATIONAL GUETERKURSBUCH. a. European Goods Trains Timetable Conference, c/o Ustredni Reditelstvi CSD, Nabrezi L. Svobody 12, 110 15 Prague, Czechoslovakia.

385   US   ISSN 0744-5326
TF1
INTERNATIONAL RAILWAY JOURNAL AND RAPID TRANSIT REVIEW. (Text in English; summaries in French, German, Spanish) 1960. m. $33. Simmons-Boardman Publishing Corporation, 345 Hudson St., New York, NY 10014. TEL 212-620-7200. Ed. Mike Knutton. adv.; charts; illus.; stat.; tr.lit.; index; circ. 9,101. (also avail. in microform from UMI; reprint service avail. from UMI)
    Indexed: Br.Rail.Bd., Excerp.Med.
    —BLDSC shelfmark: 4545.605000.
    Formerly: International Railway Journal (ISSN 0020-8450)

INTERNATIONAL RAILWAY STATISTICS. STATISTICS OF INDIVIDUAL RAILWAYS. see *TRANSPORTATION — Abstracting, Bibliographies, Statistics*

INTERNATIONAL RAILWAY TRAVELER. see *TRAVEL AND TOURISM*

INTERNATIONALES VERKEHRSWESEN; Fachzeitschrift fuer Information und Kommunikation im Verkehr. see *TRANSPORTATION — Roads And Traffic*

385   IT   ISSN 0021-3128
ITALY. AZIENDA AUTONOMA DELLE FERROVIE DELLO STATO. INFORMAZIONI DOC. 1961. m. L.8000. Azienda Autonoma delle Ferrovie Dello Stato, Centro di Documentazione, Piazza Croce Rossa, 00100 Rome, Italy. abstr.; bibl.; index; circ. 2,500.

625.1   GW   ISSN 0075-2479
HE3071
JAHRBUCH DES EISENBAHNWESENS. 1950. a. DM.39.60. (Deutsche Bundesbahn) Hestra-Verlag, Holzhofallee 33, Postfach 4244, 6100 Darmstadt 1, Germany. adv.

385.264   GW
JAHRBUCH FUER DAS BAYERISCHE TRANSPORTGEWERBE. a. Fachvereinigung Guterfernverkehr im Landesverband Bayerischer Transportunternehmen, Leonrodstr. 48, Postfach 184, D-8000 Munich 19, Germany. TEL 089-1292096. TELEX 22461.

385.1   UK
TA1215
JANE'S CONTAINERISATION DIRECTORY. 1968. a. £135($210) Jane's Information Group, Sentinel House, 163 Brighton Rd., Coulsdon, Surrey CR5 2NH, England. TEL 081-763-1030. FAX 081-763-1005. TELEX 916907 JANES G. (U.S. & Can. order from: Dept. DSM, 1340 Braddock Pl., Ste. 300, Box 1436, Alexandria, VA 22314-1651) Ed. Patrick Hicks. adv.; index.
    Formerly: Jane's Freight Containers (ISSN 0075-3033)
    Description: Overview of all aspects of the containerisation market worldwide; covers ports and terminals and their facilities, containers operators, handling systems, leasing services, computer systems and containers, and components manufacturers.

385.1 625.1   UK   ISSN 0075-3084
TF1
JANE'S WORLD RAILWAYS. 1950. a. £135($210) Jane's Information Group, Sentinel House, 163 Brighton Rd., Coulsdon, Surrey CR5 2NH, England. TEL 081-763-1030. FAX 081-763-1005. TELEX 916907 JANES G. (U.S. & Can. order from: Dept. DSM, 1340 Braddock Pl., Ste. 300, Box 1436, Alexandria, VA 22314-1651) Ed. Geoffrey Freeman Allen. adv.; index.
    Description: Covers trends and dvelopments of the rail industry worldwide; includes a country-by-country survey of railway systems and equipment manufacturers.

385   DK   ISSN 0107-3702
JERNBANEN.* 1961. bi-m. DKK 175. Dansk Jernbane-Klub - Danish Railway Club, Kalvebod Brygge 40, DK-1560 Copenhagen V, Denmark. TEL 02-308222. Eds. Jan Koed, Jens Koefoed. adv.; bk.rev.; circ. 2,500.

385   CN
KEEPING TRACK. 1966. 10/yr. Canadian National Railways, P.O. Box 8100, Montreal, Que. H3C 3N4, Canada. TEL 514-399-8041. FAX 514-399-5344. Ed. Louise Verge. circ. 83,200. (tabloid format)
    Description: For active and retired employees of CN. Covers news and events about the company.

385　　　MY　　ISSN 0047-3375
KERETAPI. (Text in English, Malay) 1957. q. M.$0.60 per no. Malaya Railway Administration - Pertadbiran Keretapi Tawah Malaya, Box 1, Kuala Lumpur, Malaysia. Ed.Bd. charts; illus.; stat.; circ. 2,400.

KEY, LOCK AND LANTERN. see *ANTIQUES*

385　　　NE　　ISSN 0023-3870
KOPPELING. 1962. w. fl.38. N.V. Nederlandse Spoorwegen - Netherlands Railways Ltd., Postbus 2025, 3500 HA Utrecht, Netherlands. Ed. Jan Stellingwerf. bk.rev.; illus.; circ. 40,000. (tabloid format)

385　　　GW
KURSBUCH DER DEUTSCHEN MUSEUMS - EISENBAHNEN. 1978. a. DM.5. Verlag Uhle & Kleimann, Pettenpohlstr. 17, 4990 Luebbecke 1, Germany. TEL 05741-7209. FAX 05741-90224. Ed. Bernhard Uhle. circ. 15,000. (back issues avail.)

385　　　GW　　ISSN 0344-7146
L O K REPORT; Nachrichtenmagazin fuer Eisenbahnfreunde. 1972. 10/yr. DM.89. Arbeitsgruppe L O K Report e.V., Postfach 1280, 4400 Muenster, Germany. Ed.Bd. adv.; bk.rev.; illus.; stat.; circ. 5,800. (back issues avail.)

385　　　GW　　ISSN 0170-4621
L O K REPORT REISEFUEHRER; Europa-Reisefuehrer fuer Eisenbahnfreunde. 1978. a. DM.26. Arbeitsgruppe L O K Report e.V., Postfach 1280, 4400 Muenster, Germany. adv.; illus.; stat.; index; circ. 3,600. (back issues avail.)

LETTRE CONFIDENTIELLE DES TRANSPORTS. see *TRANSPORTATION — Air Transport*

385 622　　　AT　　ISSN 0155-2260
LIGHT RAILWAY NEWS. 1977. bi-m. Aus.$31.50. Light Railway Research Society of Australia Inc., P.O. Box 21, Surrey Hills, Vic. 3127, Australia. TEL 03-808-6601. Eds. Geoff Hayes, Peg Hayes. circ. 600. (back issues avail.)
　　Description: News and research on operating light railways.

385 622　　　AT　　ISSN 0727-8101
LIGHT RAILWAYS. 1962. q. Aus.$31.50. Light Railway Research Society of Australia Inc., P.O. Box 321, Surrey Hills, Vic. 3127, Australia. TEL 03-808-6601. Ed. Bob McKillop. circ. 800. (back issues avail.)
　　Description: History of light railways in Australasia.

385　　　GW
DIE LINIE. 1930. 6/yr. Uestra Hannoversche Verkehrsbetriebe AG, Am Hohen Ufer 6, 3000 Hannover 1, Germany. TEL 0511-1668519. FAX 0511-1668666. circ. 5,000.

385　　　UK　　ISSN 0142-7326
LIVE RAIL. 1970. bi-m. £8.50. Southern Electric Group, 32 Crowthorne Rd., Sandhurst, Camberley, Surrey GU17 8EP, England. (Subscr. to: 12 Dorchester Gardens, Grand Ave., Worthing, W. Sussex BN11 5Ay, England) Ed. D. Brown. adv.; bk.rev.; index; circ. controlled.
　　—BLDSC shelfmark: 5279.500000.
　　Description: History and developments in the southern region of British Railways.

LOCO-REVUE; pour les modelistes et amateurs de chemins de fer. see *HOBBIES*

385　　　US　　ISSN 0891-7647
LOCOMOTIVE & RAILWAY PRESERVATION. 1986. bi-m. $21.50. Locomotive & Railway Preservation, Box 246, Richmond, VT 05477. TEL 802-434-2351. Ed. Mark Smith. adv.; bk.rev.; circ. 16,000.
　　Description: Articles and photographs depicting the history and preservation of railroads. Covers the history and restoration of railroads, locomotives, streetcars and more.

331.88　　　US　　ISSN 0024-5747
HD6350.R32
LOCOMOTIVE ENGINEER NEWSLETTER. 1867. m. membership only. Brotherhood of Locomotive Engineers, 1370 Ontario St., Mezzanine, Cleveland, OH 44113-1701. TEL 216-241-2630. Ed. S.W. Fitzgerald. circ. 50,000.

331.8 385　　　US　　ISSN 0894-3605
LOCOMOTIVE ENGINEERS JOURNAL. 1987. q. $8 to non-members. Brotherhood of Locomotive Engineers, 1370 Ontario St., Mezzanine, Cleveland, OH 44113-1701. TEL 216-241-2630. Ed. S.W. Fitzgerald. circ. 51,000.

385　　　UK
LOCOMOTIVE JOURNAL. 1888. m. membership. Associated Society of Locomotive Engineers and Firemen, 9 Arkwright Rd., Hampstead, London NW3 6AB, England. Ed. D.F. Fullick. adv.; bk.rev.; illus.; circ. 23,000. (tabloid format)

625.26　　　US　　ISSN 0076-0285
LOCOMOTIVE MAINTENANCE OFFICERS ASSOCIATION. ANNUAL PROCEEDINGS.* 1940. a. $6 (or $10 for both preconvention report and the annual proceedings). Locomotive Maintenance Officers Association, c/o Ron Pondel, Sec.-Tres., 6047 S. Mobile Ave., Chicago, IL 60638-4226. index.

625.26　　　US　　ISSN 0076-0293
TJ675
LOCOMOTIVE MAINTENANCE OFFICERS ASSOCIATION. PRECONVENTION REPORT;* full text of all seven technical committee reports on diesel locomotive and M.U. train maintenance. a. $10 for both preconvention report and the annual proceedings. Locomotive Maintenance Officers Association, 6047 S. Mobile Ave., Chicago, IL 60638-4226. Ed. C.M. Lipcomb. index.

385　　　UK　　ISSN 0307-1804
LOCOMOTIVES ILLUSTRATED; their life and time. 1974. bi-m. £14.50. Ian Allan Ltd., Terminal House, Station Approach, Shepperton, Surrey TW17 8AS, England. TEL 0932-228950. Ed. Chris Leish. adv.; bk.rev.; charts; illus.; circ. 15,000. (reprint service avail. from UMI)
　　—BLDSC shelfmark: 5292.070000.
　　Description: Illustrated histories of the most important steam locomotive classes to have operated on Britain's railways.

385　　　GW　　ISSN 0458-1822
LOK MAGAZIN; eisenbahn gestern, heute, morgen. 1962. bi-m. DM.81.60. Franckh-Kosmos Verlags-GmbH und Co., Pfizerstr. 5-7, Postfach 106011, 7000 Stuttgart 1, Germany. TEL 0711-2191-332. FAX 0711-2191-350. Ed. Horst J. Obermayer. circ. 6,000.
　　Description: Magazine for railroad enthusiasts. Features the history, the present state and future development of steam engines. Includes national and international news, list of exhibitions, and special trips.

385　　　GW　　ISSN 0170-379X
DIE LOKRUNDSCHAU. 1969. bi-m. DM.43.50. Arbeitsgemeinschaft Lokrundschau e.V., Postfach 800107, 2050 Hamburg 80, Germany. TEL 04151-82889. adv.; bk.rev.; circ. 3,200. (back issues avail.)

LUPTA C F R. see *LABOR UNIONS*

M A R T A RIDER'S DIGEST. (Metropolitan Atlanta Rapid Transit Authority) see *GENERAL INTEREST PERIODICALS — United States*

MAERKLIN-MAGAZIN; Zeitschrift fuer grosse und kleine Modell-Eisenbahner. see *HOBBIES*

385　　　UK　　ISSN 0264-7028
MAIN LINE. 1969. q. £8. Great Central Railway, Main Line Steam Trust, Great Central Rd., Loughborough, Leics LE11 1RW, England. TEL 0509-230726. Ed. Melville T. Holley. adv.; bk.rev.; circ. 3,500. (back issues avail.)
　　Description: Publication of Great Central Railway, (a preserved steam railway), includes historical articles.

385　　　MW　　ISSN 0076-3330
MALAWI RAILWAYS. ANNUAL REPORTS AND ACCOUNTS. Title varies: Malawi Railways. Directors' Reports and Accounts. 1932. a. free. Malawi Railways, Ltd., P.O. Box 5144, Limbe, Malawi. circ. 500.

MINITURBAHNEN M I B A. see *HOBBIES*

MODEL RAILWAYS. see *HOBBIES*

621.2　　　US
MODERN LOCOMOTIVE HANDBOOK.* 1950. irreg. $8. International Association of Railway Operating Officers, Box 1189, Champaign, IL 61820-1189.

385 625.2　　　UK　　ISSN 0026-8356
CODEN: MORABC
MODERN RAILWAYS. 1946. m. £29. Ian Allan Ltd., Terminal House, Station Approach, Shepperton, Surrey TW17 8AS, England. TEL 0932-228950. Ed. Ken Cordner. adv.; bk.rev.; charts; illus.; circ. 32,000. (also avail. in microform from UMI; reprint service avail. from UMI) **Indexed**: Br.Rail.Bd., Br.Tech.Ind., HRIS.
　　—BLDSC shelfmark: 5894.900000.
　　Incorporates: Locomotive, Railway Carriage & Wagon Review.
　　Description: News and features covering railways worldwide.

388.4 625　　　UK　　ISSN 0144-1655
TF701
MODERN TRAMWAY AND LIGHT RAIL TRANSIT. 1938. m. £26. (Light Rail Transit Association) Ian Allan Ltd., Terminal House, Station Approach, Shepperton, Surrey TW17 8AS, England. TEL 0932-228950. Ed. W.J. Wyse. adv.; bk.rev.; charts; illus.; index; circ. 7,250. (reprint service avail. from UMI) **Indexed**: Br.Tech.Ind.
　　Former titles: Modern Tramway and Rapid Transit Review; Modern Tramway and Light Railway Review (ISSN 0026-850X)
　　Description: Development of tramways and rapid systems worldwide.

385　　　UK
MOTIVE POWER MONTHLY. 1979. m. £29. Ian Allan Ltd., Terminal House, Station Approach, Shepperton, Surrey TW17 8AS, England. TEL 0932-228950. Ed. Hugh Madgin. adv.; bk.rev.; charts; illus.; circ. 17,000. (reprint service avail. from UMI)
　　Formerly: Modern Railways Pictorial (ISSN 0144-0292)
　　Description: News and features on locomotives, rolling stock and operations of British rail.

385　　　UK
MOTIVE POWER REVIEW. 1986. a. price varies. Ian Allan Ltd., Terminal House, Station Approach, Shepperton, Surrey TW17 8AS, England. TEL 0932-228950. Ed. Brian Morrison. bk.rev. (back issues avail.; reprint service avail. from UMI)
　　Formerly: Motive Power Annual (Year).
　　Description: Annual collection of articles on modern British railways.

385　　　CN
MOVIN'. 1968. 6/yr. Canadian National Railways, P.O. Box 8100, Montreal, Que. H3C 3N4, Canada. TEL 514-399-5822. Ed. Patricia Tokai. circ. 25,000.

385　　　GW　　ISSN 0936-4609
MUSEUMS - EISENBAHN; Zeitschrift fuer Freunde der Dampf-Eisenbahn. 1966. q. DM.25. Deutscher Eisenbahn-Verein e.V., Postfach 1106, 2814 Bruchhausen-Vilsen, Germany. TEL 04252-2626. FAX 04252-3581. Ed. Wolfram Baeumer. adv.; bk.rev.

385　　　US　　ISSN 0740-672X
HE2791
MUTUAL MAGAZINE. 1915. m. $1.20. Mutual Beneficial Association of Rail Transportation Employees, Inc., 1617 JFK Blvd., Ste. 366, Philadelphia, PA 19103-1822. Ed. Stephen M. Santarlasci. adv.; circ. 9,000.
　　Description: Serves as a railroad fraternal monitor. Also covers insurance-related news.

NARROW GAUGE & SHORT LINE GAZETTE. see *HOBBIES*

385　　　UK　　ISSN 0142-5595
NARROW GAUGE NEWS. 1953. bi-m. membership. Narrow Gauge Railway Society, c/o Brian Gent, 38 Stone Chat Close, Petersfield, Hampshire GU31 2RE, England. adv.; bk.rev.; illus.; tr.lit. (back issues avail.)
　　Description: News items and articles on current developments in gauge-rail transportation, focusing on old, present and operational systems, contractors and builders of locomotives and other stock, and miniature and model construction.

TRANSPORTATION — RAILROADS

385.264 US
NATIONAL ASSOCIATION OF FREIGHT TRANSPORTATION CONSULTANTS. PROFESSIONAL DIRECTORY. (Supplement avail.) 1959. a. membership only. National Association of Freight Transportation Consultants, Box 21418, Albuquerque, NM 87154. Dir. Donna F. Behme.

385.264 US
NATIONAL ASSOCIATION OF FREIGHT TRANSPORTATION CONSULTANTS. PROFESSIONAL DIRECTORY. SUPPLEMENT. 1959. m. membership only. National Association of Freight Transportation Consultants, Box 21418, Albuquerque, NM 87154. Dir. Donna F. Behme.

385 US ISSN 0739-3490
NATIONAL ASSOCIATION OF RAILROAD PASSENGERS NEWS. 1969? 11/yr. $20 membership. National Association of Railroad Passengers, 900 Second St., N.E., Ste. 308, Washington, DC 20002-3557. TEL 202-408-8362. Ed. Ross Capon. circ. 14,000. (back issues avail.)
Description: News and advocacy articles on rail passenger and transit service.

385 US ISSN 0077-3387
HE2715
NATIONAL ASSOCIATION OF REGULATORY UTILITY COMMISSIONERS. PROCEEDINGS. a. $35. National Association of Regulatory Utility Commissioners, 1102 Interstate Commerce Commission Bldg., Box 684, Washington, DC 20044-0684. TEL 202-898-2200. FAX 202-898-2213.
Formerly: National Association of Railroad and Utilities Commissioners. Proceedings.

385.264 US
NATIONAL EXPORT TRAFFIC LEAGUE. BULLETIN. 1946. m. National Export Traffic League, 234 5th Ave., New York, NY 10001. TEL 212-697-5895.

NATIONAL MODEL RAILROAD ASSOCIATION. BULLETIN.
see *HOBBIES*

385 970 US
NATIONAL RAILWAY BULLETIN. 1935. bi-m. $15. National Railway Historical Society, Box 58153, Philadelphia, PA 19102. Ed. Frank G. Tatnall. bk.rev.; illus.; circ. 17,000.
Description: Covers US railroads in the early to mid-twentieth century.

385 BE ISSN 0771-517X
NATIONALE MAATSCHAPPIJ VAN BELGISCHE SPOORWEGEN. DOCUMENTATIEBULLETIN. Cover title: Documentation. French edition: Societe Nationale des Chemins de Fer Belges. Bulletin de Documentation (ISSN 0771-5129) (Editions in Dutch, English, French, German) 1947. m. Nationale Maatschappij der Belgische Spoorwegen, Bureau 01-012, Section 80-1 - Societe Nationale des Chemins de Fer Belges, 85 rue de France, B-1070 Brussels, Belgium. TEL 02-525-3530. FAX 02-525-4045. bk.rev.; abstr.; bibl.; circ. 345.
Formerly: Societe Nationale des Chemins de Fer Belges. Documentaire (ISSN 0012-4567)
Description: Catalog of articles of periodicals and books especially on railway transport.

385 AT ISSN 0159-7302
TF121
NETWORK (MELBOURNE); the railways of Australia quarterly. 1964. q. Aus.$20 (foreign Aus.$25). Railways of Australia (Services) Pty. Ltd., Level 4, 85 Queen St., Melbourne, Vic. 2000, Australia. TEL 03-608-0811. FAX 03-670-8808. TELEX AA 31109. Ed. Maurice Reeves. circ. 10,750. (back issues avail.)

385 625.1 AU
NEUE BAHN; oesterreichische Fachzeitschrift fuer modernen Eisenbahntechnik und umweltbewusste Verkehrspolitik. 1966. q. S.295. Bohmann Druck und Verlag GmbH & Co. KG, Leberstr. 122, A-1110 Vienna, Austria. TEL 0222-74095. FAX 0222-74095-183. TELEX 132312. Ed. Josef Mueller. adv.; abstr.; illus.; index; circ. 2,500.
Indexed: Br.Rail.Bd.
Formerly: Eisenbahntechnik (ISSN 0013-2829)

385 US
NEW ELECTRIC RAILWAY JOURNAL. 1988. q. $20. (George Mason University) Free Congress Foundation, 717 Second St., N.E., Washignton, DC 20002. TEL 202-546-3000. FAX 202-543-8425. (Co-publisher: Education Foundation) Ed. Richard Kunz. circ. 5,000.

385 NZ
NEW ZEALAND RAIL LTD. ANNUAL REPORT. 1880? a. free. New Zealand Rail Ltd., Private Bag, Wellington, New Zealand. TEL 04-4725-599. FAX 04-498-3259. illus.; stat.; circ. 750.
Former titles (until 1991): New Zealand. Railways Corporation. Annual Report; New Zealand. Railways Department. Annual Report.

385 NZ ISSN 0028-8624
NEW ZEALAND RAILWAY OBSERVER. 1944. q. NZ.$40. New Zealand Railway & Locomotive Society, Inc., P.O. Box 5134, Wellington, New Zealand. TEL 4-566-2248. Ed. T.A. McGavin. adv.; bk.rev.; charts; illus.; maps; index; circ. 1,400.
Description: Provides information on the design, construction, operation, development and history of railways in New Zealand.

385 ZR
NJANJA. m. Societe Nationale des Chemins de Fer Zairois, Lubumbashi, P.O.B. 297, BP 10597, Kinshasa, Zaire.

385 SW
NORDENS JAERNVAEGAR. (Text in English and Swedish) 1966. a. SEK 85($13) Frank Stenvalls Foerlag, Foereningsgatan 67, S-211 52 Malmoe, Sweden. Ed. Frank Stenvall. illus.; circ. 250. (back issues avail.)

385 SW ISSN 0029-1382
NORDISK JAERNBANE TIDSKRIFT. (Text in Danish, Finnish, Norwegian and Swedish; occasionally in English and German) 1874. bi-m. SEK 60. Nordisk Jearnbane, c/o T G O F A-B, 631 92 Eskilstuna, Sweden. adv.; bk.rev.; charts; illus.; index; circ. 2,200.

385.264 GW
NORDRHEIN VERKEHR. m. Fachvereinigung Guternahverkehr Nordrhein, Engelbertstr 11, D-4000 Dusseldorf 1, Germany. TEL 0211-7335491.

385 US
NORFOLK SOUTHERN WORLD. 1982. m. free to qualified personnel. Norfolk Southern Corporation, Public Relations Department, 8 North Jefferson St., Roanoke, VA 24042. (Co-sponsors: Norfolk and Western Railway Company; Southern Railway System) Ed. Rebecca Burcher. bk.rev.; illus.; circ. 57,000.
Formed by the merger of: Norfolk and Western (ISSN 0029-1633) & Southern Railway System.

385 II ISSN 0029-3210
NORTHERN RAILWAY NEWSLETTER. (Text in English, Hindi) vol.17, 1968. m. free to qualified personnel. Northern Railway, Public Relations Office Bldg., State Entry Rd., New Delhi, India. Ed. O.P. Chopra. adv.; charts; illus.; circ. 2,000.

385 US ISSN 0894-0800
NORTHWESTERNER. 1987. s-a. membership. Northwestern Pacific Railroad Historical Society, Box 667, Santa Rosa, CA 95402-0667. TEL 415-459-7082. Ed. Frederick P. Codoni. adv.; bk.rev.; circ. 500. (back issues avail.)
Description: Information on the history of the Redwood Empire Route.

385.2 331.8 AG ISSN 0029-7658
OBRERO FERROVIARIO.* (Technical supplement) 1912. m. free. Union Ferroviaria, c/o Adolfo Medina, Independencia 2880, Buenos Aires, Argentina. Ed. Hugo Leguizamon. illus.; circ. 140,000.
Description: Covers various topics on the Argentinian railway system. Includes the operators rights, present and future plans to make it more efficient and the railway's faults.

385 340 SZ
OFFICE CENTRAL DES TRANSPORTS INTERNATIONAUX FERROVIAIRES. BULLETIN. (Text in French and German) 1893. bi-m. 30 Fr. Office Central des Transports Internationaux Ferroviaires - Zentralamt fuer den Internationalen Eisenbahnverkehr, Gryphenhuebeliweg 30, Thunplatz, CH-3006 Bern, Switzerland. FAX 4131-431164. TELEX 912063-OCTI-CH. circ. 800.

385 US ISSN 0030-0373
OFFICIAL RAILWAY EQUIPMENT REGISTER. 1886. q. $125. K - III Press, Inc., 424 W. 33rd St., New York, NY 10001. TEL 800-221-5488. FAX 212-695-5025. circ. 7,000. (also avail. in magnetic tape)
Description: Contains complete descriptions of freight cars operated by railroads and private companies in N.A. including series numbers, dimensions and capacities.

380.5 US ISSN 0190-6704
OFFICIAL RAILWAY GUIDE. NORTH AMERICAN FREIGHT SERVICE EDITION. 1868. bi-m. $104. K - III Press, Inc., 424 W. 33rd St., New York, NY 10001. TEL 800-221-5488. FAX 212-695-5025. Ed. Richard Parolisi. adv.; circ. 6,000.
Formerly: Official Guide of the Railways and Steam Navigation Lines of the United States, Puerto Rico, Canada, Mexico and Cuba, Airline Schedules (ISSN 0030-0322)
Description: Contains maps, contact personnel, intermodal terminal locations, freight schedules and route profiles for all railroads.

385 US ISSN 0273-9658
HE2727
OFFICIAL RAILWAY GUIDE. NORTH AMERICAN TRAVEL EDITION. 4/yr. $66. K - III Press, Inc., 424 W. 33rd St., New York, NY 10001. TEL 800-221-5488. FAX 212-695-5025. Ed. Frank Coyle. adv.; circ. 8,500. (also avail. in magnetic tape)
Formerly: Official Railway Guide. North American Passenger Travel Edition (ISSN 0094-5218)

385 US
PACIFIC RAIL NEWS; your Western news source. 1964. m. $30. Interurban Press, Box 6128, Glendale, CA 91225. TEL 818-240-4777. Ed. Don Gulbrandsen. adv.; bk.rev.; charts; illus.; stat.; circ. 11,500. (back issues avail.)
Formerly: Pacific News (ISSN 0030-879X)

385 NZ
PANTOGRAPH. 1956. bi-m. NZ.$45 (foreign NZ.$65). Silver Stream Railway Inc., P.O. Box 30-786, Lower Hutt, New Zealand. TEL 637-348. Ed. A. Collins. bk.rev.; circ. 120.
Former titles: Smokebox; Pantograph (ISSN 0031-1014)

385 US ISSN 0160-6913
HE2583
PASSENGER TRAIN JOURNAL. Short title: P T J. 1968. m. $30 (foreign $36). Interurban Press, Box 6128, Glendale, CA 91225. Ed. Carl Swanson. adv.; bk.rev.; illus.; circ. 11,500. (back issues avail.)
Formerly: P T J. Passenger Train Journal (ISSN 0160-6352)
Description: Covers inter-urban and mainline railroading in the United States.

385 UK ISSN 0031-5524
PERMANENT WAY INSTITUTION. JOURNAL AND REPORT OF PROCEEDINGS. 1884. 3/yr. £10.50. Permanent Way Institution, 4 Reginald Rd., Wombwell, Barnsley, S. Yorks S73 0HP, England. TEL 0226-752605. Ed. A. Blower. adv.; bk.rev.; abstr.; charts; illus.; stat.; index; circ. 8,500. *Indexed:* Br.Rail.Bd., Br.Tech.Ind

385 UK ISSN 0143-8875
PLATFORM (SUTTON-ON-CRAVEN). 1978. q. £7.50. Lancashire & Yorkshire Railway Society, 26 The Hawthorns, Sutton-on-Craven, Keighley BD20 8BP, England. Ed. B.C. Lane. circ. 450.
Description: Devoted to the history of the Lancashire and Yorkshire Railway, including articles, photos, and scale drawings (all pre 1923).

TRANSPORTATION — RAILROADS

385   US   ISSN 0032-1826
HE2723
POCKET LIST OF RAILROAD OFFICIALS; contains listing of over 20,000 officials of railroads, private car companies, etc. (Includes Buyer's Guide) 1895. q. $64. K - III Press, Inc., 424 W. 33rd St., New York, NY 10001. TEL 800-221-5488. FAX 212-695-5025. adv.; circ. 5,600.
   Description: Lists over 30,000 officials in the freight railroad, rail transit and rail supply industries in North America.

385   US
POCKET LIST OF RAILROAD OFFICIALS INTERNATIONAL EDITION. (Includes Buyer's Guide) a. $55 (foreign $66). K - III Press, Inc., 424 W. 33rd St., New York, NY 10001. TEL 800-221-5488. FAX 212-695-5025.
   Description: Provides detailed corporate listings for freight and passenger railroads, rail transit, rail supply companies and related organizations outside N. America.

385   US
PRESIDENT TRANSPORT WORLD. 1979. 4/yr. $12. International Railroad and Transportation Postcard Collectives Club, Box 6782, Providence, RI 02940. Ed. R.J. Andrews. adv.; bk.rev.; circ. 500. (back issues avail.; reprint service avail.)

385   US
PRIVATE VARNISH. 1985. bi-m. $22 (foreign $25). (American Association of Private Car Owners, Inc.) Interurban Press, Box 6128, Glendale, CA 91225. TEL 818-240-9130. Ed. John Kuehl. circ. 3,200.

385   US   ISSN 0033-0817
PROGRESSIVE RAILROADING. 1958. m. $40 (free to qualified personnel). Murphy-Richter Publishing Co., 230 W. Monroe, Ste. 2210, Chicago, IL 60606. TEL 312-454-9155. Ed. Tom Judge. adv.; illus.; tr.lit.; circ. 18,000. **Indexed:** Br.Rail.Bd.
   —BLDSC shelfmark: 6924.665500.

385   RU   ISSN 0033-4715
PUT' I PUTEVOE KHOZYAISTVO. 1957. m. 16.80 Rub. Ministerstvo Putei Soobshcheniya, Krasnoprudnaya 22-24, 107140 Moscow, Russia. (Subscr. to: Mezhdunarodnaya Kniga, Moscow, G-200, Russia) Ed. L.F. Troitskii. bk.rev.; circ. 25,000. **Indexed:** Ref.Zh.
   —BLDSC shelfmark: 0135.421000.

R F F S A. ANUARIO ESTATISTICO. (Rede Ferroviaria Federal, S.A.) see *TRANSPORTATION — Abstracting, Bibliographies, Statistics*

385   GW
R T F. (Revista Tecnica de los Ferrocarriles) 1952. a. DM.24.20. Hestra-Verlag GmbH, Holzhofallee 33, Postfach 4244, 6100 Darmstadt, Germany. TEL 06151-33481. FAX 06151-33485. Ed. Willy Wassmuth. adv.; bk.rev.; circ. 4,787.

625.1   GW
R T UND G T. (Rangiertechnik und Gleisanschlusstechnik) a. DM.22. Hestra-Verlag, Holzhofallee 33, Postfach 4244, 6100 Darmstadt 1, Germany.

385   FR
LE RAIL. (Text in French; summaries in English) 1954. bi-m. (plus 2 special issues). 355 F. I.A. Diffusion, 3 Ave. Hoche, 75008 Paris, France. TEL 46-22-53-71. FAX 40-54-98-93. Ed. Christian Scasso. adv.; bk.rev.; circ. 18,000.
   Former titles (until 1988): Le Rail et le Monde (ISSN 0181-1878); (until no.286, 1979): Vie du Rail Outremer (ISSN 0049-6278)

385   UK
RAIL. 1981. fortn. £39.40. Frontline Ltd. (Subsidiary of: E M A P - Haymarket Ltd.), Park House, 117 Park Rd., Peterborough PE1 2TR, England. Ed. Murray Brown. adv.; bk.rev.; circ. 43,767.
   Formerly: Rail Enthusiast.

385   US
RAIL AND WIRE. 1957. a. $30. Illinois Railway Museum, Inc., Box 427, Union, IL 60180. TEL 815-923-4391. Ed. Walter Weart. circ. 2,500. (looseleaf format)

385   US
RAIL CARRIER SERVICE. 1927. 10 base vols. (plus m. suppl.). $280. Hawkins Publishing Co., Inc., Box 480, Mayo, MD 21106. TEL 301-798-1677. Ed. Carl R. Eyler. cum.index; circ. 500. (looseleaf format; back issues avail.)

385   US
RAIL CLASSICS. bi-m. Challenge Publications, Inc., 7950 Deering Ave., Canoga Park, CA 91304. TEL 818-887-0550. FAX 818-883-3019. Ed. Ed Stauss.

625.1   UK   ISSN 0048-6612
RAIL ENGINEERING INTERNATIONAL. 1971. q. £7.50. Broadfields (Technical Publishers) Ltd., Little Leighs, Chelmsford, Essex CM3 1PF, England. Ed.Bd. adv.; bk.rev.; charts; illus.; circ. 2,550. **Indexed:** Br.Rail.Bd., Eng.Ind., Excerp.Med., ISMEC.

385   BE   ISSN 0020-8442
TF1   CODEN: RAIIAF
RAIL INTERNATIONAL/SCHIENEN DER WELT. (Editions in English, French, German) 1970. m. 3200 BEF. International Railway Congress Association, 85 rue de France, Sect. 10, B-1020 Brussels, Belgium. TEL 02-5207831. FAX 02-5254084. adv.; bk.rev.; bibl.; charts; illus.; stat.; index; circ. 3,400. **Indexed:** Br.Rail.Bd., C.I.S. Abstr., Eng.Ind., Sci.Abstr.
   —BLDSC shelfmark: 7242.840000.
   Formerly: International Railway Congress Association. Monthly Bulletin.
   Description: Covers technical and managerial information related to the railway business.

385   II
RAIL MAZDOOR. m. South Central Railway Mazdoor Union, 7-c Railway Bldg., Accounts Office Compound, Secunderabad 500 025, India. TEL 77823. TELEX 6994-CA-RAILWAYMEN.

RAIL SYNDICALISTE. see *LABOR UNIONS*

385   US   ISSN 0896-4440
RAIL TRAVEL NEWS. 1970. s-m. $25. Message Media, Box 9007, Berkeley, CA 94709. Ed. James Russell. adv.; bk.rev.; illus.; circ. 2,000.

385   US   ISSN 0163-7266
TF1
RAILFAN & RAILROAD. 1974. m. $25. Carstens Publications, Inc., Box 700, Newton, NJ 07860. TEL 201-383-3355. FAX 201-383-4064. Ed. James Boyd. bk.rev.; circ. 52,000. (back issues avail.)
   Formerly: Railfan (Newton) (ISSN 0098-0714); Incorporates (in 1979): Railroad Magazine (ISSN 0033-8761); Which was formerly: Railroad Man's Magazine; And (beginning 1906): Railroad Stories.

385   UK   ISSN 0033-8745
RAILNEWS. (One National Edition) 1963. m. price varies. British Railways Board, Euston House, P.O. Box 100, London NW1 1DZ, England. Ed. S. Knight. adv.; bk.rev.; charts; illus.; circ. 175,000. **Indexed:** Br.Tech.Ind.
   Description: Newspaper of the British Railways Board.

385   US
RAILPACE NEWSMAGAZINE. m. 210 Perrine Ave., Piscataway, NJ 08854-4628. TEL 908-463-1091. Ed. Thomas Nemeth. adv.; circ. 8,500.

385   UK   ISSN 0262-8805
RAILPOWER. 1963. 4/yr. free to qualified personnel. Railway Industry Association of Great Britain, 6 Buckingham Gate, London SW1E 6JP, England. FAX 01-821-1640. TELEX 297304-RIA-G. Ed. Roger Ford. circ. 2,500.

385   US
RAILROAD ENTHUSIASTS. NEW YORK DIVISION. BULLETIN.* 1957. m. $8. Railroad Enthusiasts, New York Division, Inc., Box 1318 Grand Central Sta., New York, NY 10017. Ed. W.S. Webber. bk.rev.; illus.; circ. 500.

385   US   ISSN 0090-7847
TF1
RAILROAD HISTORY. 1921. s-a. $25 to libraries; free to members. Railway & Locomotive Historical Society (Akron), c/o Ed. H. Roger Grant, Dept. of History, Univ. of Akron, Akron, OH 44325-1902. adv.; bk.rev.; bibl.; charts; illus.; cum.index 1921-1984; then every 2 yrs.; circ. 4,100. (also avail. in microform from UMI; reprint service avail. from UMI) **Indexed:** Amer.Hist.& Life, Hist.Abstr.
   —BLDSC shelfmark: 7242.930000.
   Formerly: Railway and Locomotive Historical Society. Bulletin (ISSN 0033-8842)

RAILROAD MODEL CRAFTSMAN. see *HOBBIES*

RAILROAD NEWSLETTER. see *OCCUPATIONAL HEALTH AND SAFETY*

385   US
RAILROAD STATION HISTORICAL SOCIETY. BULLETIN. 1968. bi-m. $9 (foreign $12). J-B Publishing Co., 430 Ivy Ave., Crete, NE 68333. TEL 402-826-3356. Ed. William F. Rapp. adv.; bk.rev.; abstr.; charts; illus.; stat.; index; circ. 500. **Indexed:** Avery Ind.Architt.Per.

385.26   US
RAILROAD STATION HISTORICAL SOCIETY. RAILROAD STATION MONOGRAPH. 1970. a. free to members. J-B Publishing Co., 430 Ivy Ave., Crete, NE 68333. TEL 402-826-3356. Ed.Bd. bibl.; illus.; circ. 500.

385   NZ   ISSN 0110-6155
RAILS. 1971. m. NZ.$36($39.60) Southern Press Ltd., Box 50-134, Porirua, Wellington, New Zealand. TEL 04-239-9063. FAX 04-239-9063. Ed. Robert Stott. adv.; bk.rev.; bibl.; illus.; circ. 4,600.

385   UK   ISSN 0267-5943
RAILWATCH. 1978. q. £3.30 to non-members. Railway Development Society, 48 the Park, Great Bookham, Surrey KT23 3LS, England. TEL 0372-452863. Eds. R. King, G.F.D. Cooper. adv.; bk.rev.; circ. 3,000. (processed)
   Former titles: Railway Development News; Railway Invigoration Society. Progress Reports.
   Description: Contains reports on railways and rail user groups.

657 385   US
RAILWAY ACCOUNTING RULES. base vol. (plus s-a. updates). price varies. Association of American Railroads, Economics and Finance Department, 50 F St., N.W., Washington, DC 20001. TEL 202-639-2304.

385   AT   ISSN 0033-8818
RAILWAY ADVOCATE. vol.42, no.23, 1981. m. Aus.$0.25 per no. National Union of Rail Workers of Australia, 399 Illawarra Rd., Marrickville, Sydney, N.S.W. 2204, Australia. FAX 558-2113. Ed. B. Paterson. adv.; circ. 2,500.

385 625.1   US   ISSN 0033-8826
TF1   CODEN: RAAGA3
RAILWAY AGE. 1856. m. $35 (free to railroad personnel). Simmons-Boardman Publishing Corporation, 345 Hudson St., New York, NY 10014. TEL 212-620-7200. Ed. Luther Miller. adv.; circ. 18,153. (also avail. in microform from UMI; reprint service avail. from UMI) **Indexed:** B.P.I., Br.Rail.Bd., Bus.Ind., Energy Info.Abstr., Environ.Abstr., Fluidex, Key to Econ.Sci., Mag.Ind., P.A.I.S., PROMT, Sci.Abstr., SRI, Tr.& Indus.Ind.
   Incorporates (in Jun. 1991): Modern Railroads; Which was formerly: M R. Modern Railroads - Rail Transit; Modern Railroads (ISSN 0026-8348) Incorporates: Railway Control Systems; Railway Locomotives and Cars (ISSN 0033-7102).

385   UK   ISSN 0033-8834
RAILWAY AND CANAL HISTORICAL SOCIETY JOURNAL. 1954. 3/yr. membership. Railway and Canal Historical Society, Fawnog, Hafod Rd., Gwermynynydd, Clwyd CH7 5JS, Wales. Ed. H.P. White. adv.; bk.rev.; bibl.; charts; index; circ. 800. (also avail. in microform from UMI)
   —BLDSC shelfmark: 4845.400000.

385   US
RAILWAY & LOCOMOTIVE HISTORICAL SOCIETY NEWSLETTER. 1981. s-a. membership. Railway & Locomotive Historical Society, 115 "I" St., Sacramento, CA 95814-2204. (Ed. addr.: 4605 Fourth Rd. N., Arlington, VA 22203-2347) Ed. Bruce Heard. circ. 7,000.

TRANSPORTATION — RAILROADS

385   AT   ISSN 0157-2431
RAILWAY DIGEST. 1963. m. Aus.$13. Australian Railway Historical Society, New South Wales Division, Box E129, St. James, N.S.W., Australia. Ed. I. Fathers. circ. 2,200. (also avail. in microfiche)

385   UK   ISSN 0048-6647
RAILWAY DIGEST INTERNATIONAL. 1971. bi-m. £2.50. Maple Cottage, Ashburnum Ave., Harrow-on-the-Hill, Middlesex HA1 2JO, England. Ed. J.H. Court. adv.; bk.rev.; bibl.; charts; illus.

385   UK   ISSN 0079-9513
HE1009
RAILWAY DIRECTORY AND YEARBOOK. a. $110. Reed Business Publishing Group, Enterprise Division (Subsidiary of: Reed International PLC), Quadrant House, The Quadrant, Sutton, Surrey SM2 5AS, England. TEL 081-652-8608. FAX 081-652-8986. (Subscr. to: Oakfield House, Perrymount Rd., Haywards Heath, W. Sussex RH16 3DH, England. TEL 444-445566) Ed. Chris Bushell. (reprint service avail. from UMI)

385   US   ISSN 0079-9521
TF501
RAILWAY FUEL AND OPERATING OFFICERS ASSOCIATION. PROCEEDINGS.* a. $15. International Association of Railway Operating Officers, Box 1189, Champaign, IL 61820-1189.

625.1   UK   ISSN 0373-5346
TF1   CODEN: RWGIAN
RAILWAY GAZETTE INTERNATIONAL; a journal of management, engineering and operation. (Supplements avail.) 1835. m. £61.20. Reed Business Publishing Group, Enterprise Division (Subsidiary of: Reed International PLC), Quadrant House, The Quadrant, Sutton, Surrey SM2 5AS, England. TEL 081-652-8608. FAX 081-652-8986. (Subscr. to: Oakfield House, Perrymount Rd., Haywards Heath, W. Sussex RH16 3DH, England) Ed. Murray Hughes. adv.; bk.rev.; charts; illus.; stat.; tr.lit.; index; circ. 9,107. (also avail. in microform from UMI; reprint service avail. from UMI) **Indexed:** Br.Rail.Bd., Br.Tech.Ind., C.I.S. Abstr., Eng.Ind., HRIS, Intl.Civil Eng.Abstr., Met.Abstr., Sci.Abstr., Soft.Abstr.Eng., World Alum.Abstr.
—BLDSC shelfmark: 7247.500000.
Formerly: Railway Gazette (ISSN 0033-8907)

385   US   ISSN 0093-8505
TF15
RAILWAY HISTORY MONOGRAPH. (Some Bound volumes avail.) 1972. q. $15. J-B Publishing Co., 430 Ivy Ave., Crete, NE 68333. TEL 402-826-3356. Ed. William F. Rapp. illus.; index; circ. 100. (looseleaf format)
—BLDSC shelfmark: 7247.800000.

385   US
RAILWAY LINE CLEARANCES. 1897. a. $63 (foreign $69). K - III Press, Inc., 424 W. 33rd St., New York, NY 10001. TEL 800-221-5488. FAX 212-695-5025. Ed. Peter Coleman. adv.; circ. 900.
Description: Contains vertical and horizontal clearances and weight limitations for nearly 300 North American railroads.

385   UK   ISSN 0033-8923
TF1
RAILWAY MAGAZINE. 1897. m. $32. I P C Magazine Ltd., Prospect Magazines (Subsidiary of: Reed Business Publishing Ltd.), Prospect House, 9-13 Ewell Rd., Cheam, Surrey SM1 4QQ, England. TEL 081-661-6600. TELEX 892084-REEDBP-G. (Subscr. to: Reed Business Publishing Ltd., 205 E. 42nd St., New York, NY 10017, U.S.A.) Ed. Peter Kelly. adv.; bk.rev.; charts; illus.; index; circ. 35,972. (also avail. in microform from UMI; reprint service avail. from UMI) **Indexed:** Br.Hum.Ind., Br.Tech.Ind.
—BLDSC shelfmark: 7248.150000.
Description: Information on all facets of steam, diesel and electric locomotives.

385   US   ISSN 0094-2278
TF455
RAILWAY PASSENGER CAR ANNUAL. 1974. a. price varies. R P C Publications, Box 296, Godfrey, IL 62035. Ed. W. David Randall. circ. 1,500.
Description: Compilation of photographs of passenger cars taken when they were built. Shows exteriors, interiors, and mechanical details.

625.1   JA   ISSN 0033-9008
TF1   CODEN: QRTIA8
RAILWAY TECHNICAL RESEARCH INSTITUTE. QUARTERLY REPORT. (Text in English) 1960. q. $180. Ken-yusha, Inc., 1-4-5-6, Hikari-cho, Kokubunji-shi, Tokyo, Japan. FAX 0425-73-7255. Ed. Shin'ichi Tanaka. charts; illus.; index; circ. 700. (back issues avail.) **Indexed:** Appl.Mech.Rev., Br.Rail.Bd., Eng.Ind., HRIS, JTA, Sci.Abstr.
—BLDSC shelfmark: 7201.855000.

625.1   GW   ISSN 0079-9548
RAILWAY TECHNICAL REVIEW. (Text in English) 1952. a. DM.24.20. Hestra-Verlag, Holzhofallee 33, Postfach 4244, 6100 Darmstadt 1, Germany. adv. **Indexed:** Br.Rail.Bd.

625.1   US   ISSN 0033-9016
     CODEN: RTSTAR
RAILWAY TRACK & STRUCTURES. 1885. m. $16 ($9 to qualified railroad personnel). Simmons-Boardman Publishing Corporation, 345 Hudson St., New York, NY 10014. TEL 212-620-7200. Ed. Robert Tuzik. adv.; illus.; index; circ. 7,629. (also avail. in microform from UMI; reprint service avail. from UMI) **Indexed:** Br.Rail.Bd., Chem.Abstr., Eng.Ind., HRIS.
—BLDSC shelfmark: 7250.000000.
Formerly: Railway Engineering and Maintenance (ISSN 0097-6687)

385   UK   ISSN 0033-9032
RAILWAY WORLD. 1939. m. £28.50. Ian Allan Ltd., Terminal House, Station Approach, Shepperton, Surrey TW17 8AS, England. TEL 0932-228950. Ed. Handel Kardas. adv.; bk.rev.; film rev.; record rev.; charts; illus.; circ. 37,000. (reprint service avail. from UMI) **Indexed:** Br.Tech.Ind.
—BLDSC shelfmark: 7250.142000.
Description: Features and preservation articles relating to British railways.

385   UK
RAILWAY WORLD YEARBOOK. 1947. a. price varies. Ian Allan Ltd., Terminal House, Station Approach, Shepperton, Surrey TW17 8AS, England. TEL 0932-228950. circ. 8,500. (reprint service avail. from UMI)
Former titles: Railway World Annual (ISSN 0082-5891); Trains Annual; Trains Illustrated Annual.
Description: Annual collection of articles on railway subjects.

RAILWAYS. see TRAVEL AND TOURISM

625.1   SA
RAILWAYS IN SOUTHERN AFRICA. Short title: Railways. (Text in English) 1957. bi-m. R.30 (foreign R.70)(effective 1992). Target Communications - Kommunikasies CC, P.O. Box 3445, 2125 Randburg, Transvaal, South Africa. TEL 011-787-3115. FAX 011-787-3112. Ed. Ron E. Bull. adv.; bk.rev.; charts; illus.; tr.lit.; circ. 2,200 (controlled). (back issues avail.) **Indexed:** Ind.S.A.Per., Sci.Abstr.
Formerly: S.A. Railway Engineering (ISSN 0033-8885)
Description: Covers developments, opinions, and news on the railroad industry.

385   AT   ISSN 0033-9040
RAILWAYS INSTITUTE MAGAZINE. 1897. m. Aus.$5.60. Railways Institute Council, 605 Wellington St., Perth, W.A. 6000, Australia. TEL 322-1348. Ed. T. Jones. adv.; bk.rev.; illus.; circ. 7,400.

385   UK
RAILWAYS RESTORED. 1980. a. £5.95. (Association of Railway Preservation Societies Ltd.) A R P S Ltd., c/o J.C. Jefferey, 42 North St., Oundle, Peterborough PE8 4AL, England. TEL 0932-228950. FAX 0932-232366. TELEX 929806 IALLAN G. (And: Ian Allan Ltd., Coombelands House, Addlestone, Weybridge, Surrey KT15 1HY) Ed. Allan Butcher. circ. 6,000.
Description: Gives details of over 100 railways, museums and steam centers including locomotives, rolling stock and associated organizations.

385   UK   ISSN 0265-0231
RAILWAYS TODAY. 1983. q. Goodhead Publications, 27 Murdock Rd., Bicester, Oxon. OX6 7RG, England. Ed. John Nelson. adv.

385   FI   ISSN 0048-6833
RAUTATIELIIKENNE. 1943. m. (11/yr.). Fmk.30. Rautatievirkamiesliitto - Union of Railway Officials, Rautatiehallitus, Vilhonkatu 13, 00100 Helsinki 10, Finland. Ed. T.P. Elomaa. adv.; bk.rev.; bibl.; charts; illus.; stat.; index; circ. 3,800.

RECHTE LIJN. see LABOR UNIONS

385   CK
REIL. 1961. m. Calle 13, No. 18-24, Bogota, Colombia. adv.; circ. 13,500.

385   US
RENMIN TIEDAO/PEOPLE'S RAILWAY. (Text in Chinese) 4/w. $152. China Books & Periodicals, Inc., 2929 24th St., San Francisco, CA 94110. TEL 415-282-2994. FAX 415-282-0994. (newspaper)

385   BL   ISSN 0034-950X
REVISTA FERROVIARIA. (Yearbook avail.) 1939. m. $50. Empresa Jornalistica dos Transportes, Rua Mexico 41-S-904, Rio de Janeiro, Brazil. TEL 021-532-0260. FAX 021-240-0139. Ed. Gerson Toller Gomes. adv.; bk.rev.; charts; illus.; stat.; circ. 10,000.
Description: Covers the economics, politics and technology of the railway world in Brazil and abroad.

385   FR   ISSN 0035-3183
     CODEN: RGCFAI
REVUE GENERALE DES CHEMINS DE FER. (Supplements avail.: Le Rail; Le Monde) 1885. 11/yr. 700 F. (Societe Nationale des Chemins de Fer Francais) Dunod, 15 rue Gossin, 92543 Montrouge Cedex, France. TEL 33-1-40-92-65-00. FAX 33-1-40-92-65-97. TELEX 270 004. (Subscr. to: Centrale des Revues, 11 rue Gossin, 92543 Montrouge Cedex, France. TEL 33-1-46-56-52-66) Ed. J.P. Bernard. adv.; bk.rev.; abstr.; bibl.; charts; illus.; stat.; index; circ. 3,250. (also avail. in microfilm from UMI) **Indexed:** Br.Rail.Bd., Eng.Ind., Excerp.Med., HRIS.
Description: Covers technical aspects of railway transportation -- materials, trains and underground systems, networks, impact studies, technical difficulties, and new technologies.

385   US   ISSN 0035-7898
ROLL SIGN. 1964. 6/yr. $8. Boston Street Railway Association, Inc., Box 181037, Boston, MA 02118-1037. Ed. Daniel T. Lenihan. bk.rev.; illus.; index; circ. 1,200. (reprint service avail. from UMI)

385   SW   ISSN 0037-5985
S J-NYTT. 1943. m. SEK 120. Statens Jaernvaegars Huvudkontor - State Railways Head Office, S-105 50 Stockholm, Sweden. Ed. Gunnel Sundbom. bk.rev.; illus.

SEASHORE TROLLEY MUSEUM DISPATCH. see MUSEUMS AND ART GALLERIES

385   CC   ISSN 1000-1913
SHANGHAI TIEDAO XUEYUAN XUEBAO/SHANGHAI RAILROAD INSTITUTE. JOURNAL. (Text in Chinese) q. Shanghai Tiedao Xueyuan, 1 Zhennan Lu, Shanghai 200333, People's Republic of China. TEL 2506344. Ed. Xia Jianxin.

385   US   ISSN 0199-4050
THE SHORT LINE; the journal of short line railroads. 1973. bi-m. $17. Box 607, Pleasant Garden, NC 27313. Ed. Garreth M. McDonald. bk.rev.; index, cum.index: (vols.1-60); circ. 1,600. (back issues avail.)
Description: Reviews short line railroad activity from historic to current lines; emphasizes newly created short lines, their management, operations, and equipment.

614.8   AU   ISSN 0037-4539
SICHERHEIT ZUERST. 1958. q. free. Versicherungsanstalt der Oesterreichischen Eisenbahnen, Unfallverhuetungsdienst, Linke Wienzeile 48-52, A-1060 Vienna, Austria. Ed. Max Winter. circ. 20,000. **Indexed:** C.I.S. Abstr.

TRANSPORTATION — RAILROADS

385 GW ISSN 0037-4997
CODEN: SIGDAN
SIGNAL UND DRAHT;* Zeitschrift fuer Informationstechnik im Eisenbahnwesen. 1906. m. DM.153.60. Deutsche Verkehrs Verlag GmbH, Nordkanalstr. 36, Postfach 101609, 2000 Hamburg 1, Germany. Ed. L. Wehner. adv.; bk.rev.; abstr.; bibl.; charts; illus.; pat.; tr.lit.; tr.mk.; index; circ. 3,000. **Indexed:** HRIS.
—BLDSC shelfmark: 8276.000000.
Incorporates: Signal und Schiene (ISSN 0037-5004)
Description: Computer technology used in railway engineering including signalling and telecommunications, data processing, and data processing equipment for office use and selling.

385 BL ISSN 0102-5694
SINTESE FERROVIARIA BRASILEIRA. 1981. irreg. free. Rede Ferroviaria Federal, S.A., Departamento Geral de Estatistica, Rio de Janeiro, Brazil.

385.314 BL
SISTEMA FERROVIARIO R F F S A. 1962. irreg. free. Rede Ferroviaria Federal, S.A., Departamento Geral de Estatistica, Rio de Janeiro, Brazil. adv.; illus.; circ. 1,200. (also avail. in microfiche)

385 US
SMOKE AND CINDERS. 1961. bi-m. $25. Tennessee Valley Railroad Museum, Inc., 4119 Cromwell Rd., Chattanooga, TN 37421. TEL 615-875-2475. Ed. James Baird. bk.rev.; circ. 850.

385 BE ISSN 0081-119X
SOCIETE NATIONALE DES CHEMINS DE FER BELGES. RAPPORT ANNUEL. 1926. a. Societe Nationale des Chemins de Fer Belges - Nationale Maatschappij de Belgischen Spoorwegen, Fonsnylaan 47B, Bureau 40-231, B-1060 Brussels, Belgium. circ. controlled.

385 US ISSN 0038-3805
SOUTHERN AND SOUTHWESTERN RAILWAY CLUB. PROCEEDINGS.* 1890. q. $3. Southern & Southwestern Railway Club, 717 Pinecliffe Dr., Chesapeake, VA 23320. adv.; charts; illus.; circ. 500.

385 US
SOUTHERN PACIFIC BULLETIN. 1913. m. free to libraries; single copies avail. upon request. Southern Pacific Transportation Co., Southern Pacific Bldg., One Market Plaza, San Francisco, CA 94105. TEL 415-541-1656. Ed. Robert B. Hoppe. bk.rev.; illus.; circ. 80,000.

385 II ISSN 0038-450X
SOUTHERN RAILWAYS. (Text in English) 1949. m. $0.25. c/o T.S. Rao, 2235 Bhut Gosami Vattaram, Manojiappa St., Tanjore S., India. Ed. Tanjore Swamirao Krisnakao. circ. 9,000.

385.264 US
SOUTHERN TRAFFIC LIGHT. 1918. w. 225. Southern Transportation League, Inc, 3426 N. Washington Blvd., Arlington, VA 22201. TEL 703-525-4050.

385 US
SPEEDLINES. 1984. m. $55. High Speed Rail Association, 206 Valley Court, Ste. 800, Pittsburgh, PA 15237. TEL 412-366-6887. FAX 412-366-8698. Ed. Robert J. Casey. adv.; circ. 10,000.
Description: News about new transportation mode and industry of high speed rail.

385 BE ISSN 0773-5901
HET SPOOR. French edition: Le Rail (ISSN 0033-8729) 1956. m. 400 Fr. Nationale Maatschappij der Belgische Spoorwegen - Societe Nationale des Chemins de Fer Belges, 85 rue de France, Bureau 05-322, B-1070 Brussels, Belgium. FAX 525-2501. Ed. M. Bouquiaux. bk.rev.; charts; illus.; tr.lit.; circ. 107,000.

385 069.9 DK ISSN 0106-6927
SPORVEJSMUSEET SKJOLDENAESHOLM. AARSBERETNING. 1979. a. DKK 28. Sporvejshistorisk Selskab, Valloevej 24, 2700 Broenshoej, Denmark. Ed. Per Soegaard. illus.; circ. 1,500.

385 AU ISSN 0038-870X
DER SPURKRANZ; Unabhaengige Zeitschrift fuer Verkehrspolitik. 1967. m. S.108. Verein zur Foerderung des Schienenverkehrs, Oldenburggasse 73, A-1232 Vienna, Austria. Ed. Friedrich Rodt. circ. 1,100. (processed)

385 UK
STEAM DAYS. 1971. bi-m. £14. Ian Allan Ltd., Coombelands House, Addlestone, Weybridge, Surrey KT15 1HY, England. TEL 0932-228950. Ed. Chris Leigh. bk.rev.; charts; illus.; circ. 18,000. (reprint service avail. from UMI)
Former titles: Steam Train; Trains Illustrated - Railway Heritage; Trains Illustrated - Railway Preservation; Trains Illustrated - Express Trains (ISSN 0141-9935)
Description: Illustrated feature articles on steam railways.

385.1 US ISSN 0081-542X
TF6.U5
STEAM PASSENGER SERVICE DIRECTORY. 1966. a. $8.95 (effective Jan. 1992; typically set in Nov.). Empire State Railway Museum, c/o Locomotive & Railway Preservation, Ltd., Box 599, Richmond, VT 05477. TEL 802-434-2351. Ed. Mark Smith. adv.; circ. 16,000. (back issues avail.)

385 UK
STEAM RAILWAY. m. £21.50. Frontline Ltd. (Subsidiary of: E M A P - Haymarket Ltd.), Park House, 117 Park Rd., Peterborough PE1 2TR, England. TEL 0733-555161. FAX 62788. TELEX 329292 FRONT G. Ed. David Wilcock. adv.; bk.rev.; illus.; tr.lit.; circ. 39,295.

385.262 GW
STEIG EIN. 1980. irreg. Rheinische Bahngesellschaft AG, Hansaallee 1, 4000 Duesseldorf 11, Germany. TEL 0211-58201. FAX 0211-5821966. circ. 75,000.

385 UK ISSN 0039-1190
STEPHENSON LOCOMOTIVE SOCIETY JOURNAL. 1924. bi-m. £12. Stephenson Locomotive Society, 25 Regency Close, Chigwell, Essex IG7 5NY, England. TEL 0334-776656. Ed. Bruce I. Nathan. adv.; bk.rev.; charts; illus.; stat.; circ. 1,300.

385 NE
STOOMTRACTIE. q. fl.30. Stoom Stichting Nederland, Postbus 541, 2600 AM Delft, Netherlands. adv.; bk.rev.; circ. 1,000.

385 GW ISSN 0340-7071
STRASSENBAHN MAGAZIN; elektrischer Naverkehr - gestern, heute, morgen. 1970. 4/yr. DM.78. Franckh-Kosmos Verlags-GmbH und Co., Pfizerstr. 5-7, Postfach 106011, 7000 Stuttgart 1, Germany. TEL 0711-2191-332. FAX 0711-2191-350. Ed.Bd. bk.rev.; illus.; maps; circ. 3,300.
Description: Publication devoted to the history and the present state of the tramway in Germany and other European countries.

385.264 SZ
STRASSENTRANSPORT. fortn. Schweizerischer Nutzfahrzeugverband, Weissenbuehlweg 3, CH-3007 Bern, Switzerland. TEL 031-452661. TELEX 33670.

385.264 GW
SUEDDEUTSCHER VERKEHRSKURIER. m. Fachvereinigung Guterfernverkehr im Landesverband Bayerischer Transportunternehmen, Leonrodstr 48, Postfach 184, D-8000 Munich 19, Germany. TEL 089-1292096. TELEX 215102.

SUVREMENI PROMET, see *TRANSPORTATION — Air Transport*

385 350.1 SW
SVENSKA JAERNVAEGSTIDNINGEN. m. Jaernvaeg Statstjaenstemannafoerbundet, Box 5308, 102 46 Stockholm, Sweden. adv.; circ. 2,923.

385 SW ISSN 0081-9964
SVERIGES JAERNVAEGAR/RAILWAYS OF SWEDEN. (Subseries of: Sveriges Officiella Statistik: Transport- och Kommunikationsvaesen) 1953. a. SEK 25. Statens Jaernvaegars Huvudkontor - State Railways Head Office, S-105 50 Stockholm, Sweden. circ. 1,000.
Supersedes: Allmaen Jaernvaegsstatistik; Statens Jaernvaegar.

385.264 SZ
SWISS CAMION. 1959. m. 55 Fr. Routiers Suisses, Rue de la Chocolatiere 26, CH-1026 Echandens, Switzerland. TEL 021-7014224. FAX 021-7010037. adv.

385 SW ISSN 0039-8683
TAAG/TRAINS. 1966. m. (10/yr.) SEK 200. Svenska Jaernvaegsklubben - Swedish Railway Club, Box 124, S-101 22 Stockholm, Sweden. Ed. Lars Tornqvist. adv.; bk.rev.; charts; illus.; cum.index; circ. 5,400.

TABI TO TETSUDO. see *TRAVEL AND TOURISM*

385 CH
TAIWAN RAILWAY. (Text in Chinese and English) 1963. irreg. Taiwan Railway Administration, Taipei, Taiwan, Republic of China. Ed. J. Fan. illus.; circ. 2,000.

385 UK ISSN 0300-3272
TALYLLYN NEWS. 1953. q. £12. Talyllyn Railway Preservation Society, Flat One, 25 Gwendolen Ave., London SW15 6ET, England. Ed. J.N. Slater. adv.; bk.rev.; illus.; circ. 2,300.

385 TZ
TANZANIA RAILWAYS CORPORATION. HABARI ZA RELI. (Text in Kiswahili) 1977. m. Sh.12 per no. Tanzania Railways Corporation, Box 468, Dar es Salaam, Tanzania. TELEX 41308 TRC DSM. Ed. Winston Makamba. adv.; bk.rev.; circ. 10,000.
Supersedes in part: Sikio (ISSN 0037-5136)

625.1 AU
TECHNISCHE UNIVERSITAET WIEN. INSTITUT FUER EISENBAHNWESEN. ARBEITEN. 1971. irreg. Technische Universitaet Wien, Institut fuer Eisenbahnwesen, Karlsplatz 13, A-1040 Vienna, Austria. Ed. Edwin Engel.
Formerly (until 1991): Technische Universitaet Wien. Institut fuer Eisenbahnwesen, Spezialbahnen und Verkehrswirtschaft. Arbeiten.

625.1 IT
TECNICA PROFESSIONALE. 1933. m. L.10000. Collegio Ingegneri Ferroviari Italiani, Via Giolitti 34, 00185 Rome, Italy. TEL 06-47307724. FAX 06-47305454. Ed. Antonio Lagani. adv.; bk.rev.; bibl.; charts; illus.

385 JA ISSN 0040-4047
TETSUDO PIKUTORIARU/RAILWAY PICTORIAL. (Text in Japanese) 1951. m. 3480 Yen($9.70) Tetsudo Toshokankai, New Kokusai Bldg., 3-4-1 Marunouchi, Chiyoda-ku, Tokyo 100, Japan. Ed. Ryuzo Tanaka. adv.; charts; illus.; stat.

385 UK ISSN 0144-2708
TIDDLY DYKE. 1978. q. Swindon & Cricklade Railway Society, 36 Parklands Rd., Swindon, Wiltshire, England.

625.1 CC
TIEDAO JIANZHU/RAILWAY CONSTRUCTION. (Text in Chinese) m. Tiedao-bu, Keji Qingbao-suo - Ministry of Railway, Science and Technology Information Institute, Daliushu Beizhan, Xizhimenwai, Beijing 100081, People's Republic of China. TEL 8996445. Ed. Shao Genda.

385 CC
TIEDAO XUEBAO/CHINA RAILWAY SOCIETY. JOURNAL. (Text in Chinese) q. $3.50 per no. Zhongguo Tiedao Xuehui - China Railway Society, 10 Fuxing Lu, Beijing 100844, People's Republic of China. TEL 8645861. (Dist. overseas by: China International Book Trading Corp., P.O. Box 399, Beijing, P.R.C.) Ed. Qing Jingxian.

385 CC
TIEDAO YUNSHU YU JINGJI/RAILWAY TRANSPORTATION AND ECONOMICS. (Text in Chinese) m. Tiedaobu Kexue Yanjiuyuan, Yunshu yu Jingji Yanjiusuo - Science Academy of the Railway Ministry, Institute of Transportation and Economics, 22 Daliushu Beicun, Xizhimenwai, Beijing 100081, People's Republic of China. TEL 8996538. Ed. Wu Jiahao.

TRANSPORTATION — RAILROADS

385   CC   ISSN 1000-0372
TIEDAO ZHISHI/RAILWAY KNOWLEDGE. 1980. bi-m. Y6($5) China Railway Society - Zhongguo Tiedao Xuehui, 10 Fuxing Lu, Beijing 100844, People's Republic of China. TEL 8645861. (Dist. overseas by: China International Book Trading Corp., P.O. Box 339, Beijing, P.R.C.) Ed. Gao Yurui. adv.; circ. 80,000.
    Description: News about China railway construction and international railroad developments.

385.264   CN
TIPS AND TOPICS. m. Atlantic Provinces Transportation Commission, 236 St. George St., Ste.210, P.O.B. 577, Moncton, N.B. E1C 8L9, Canada. TEL 506-857-2820.

385.264 388.324   JA
TORAKKU YUSO JOHO. 1948. 3/mo. Japan Trucking Association, Torakku Kaikan 2, Yotsuya 3-chome, Shinjuku-ku, Tokyo, Japan. TEL 03-357-6271.

385   CN   ISSN 0040-9553
TORONTO RAILWAY CLUB. OFFICIAL PROCEEDINGS. 1931. 3/yr. membership only. Toronto Railway Club, Box 114, Union Station, Toronto, Ont. M5J 1E6, Canada. Ed. V.J. Macciocchi. adv.; charts; illus.; circ. 1,200.

625.1   US
TRACK YEARBOOK. 1982. a. $50. Murphy-Richter Publishing Co., 2 N. Riverside Plaza, Rm. 1825, Chicago, IL 60606. TEL 312-454-1823. Ed. Tom Morgan. adv.; circ. 6,000.

TRAIN COLLECTORS QUARTERLY. see *HOBBIES*

TRAIN DISPATCHER. see *LABOR UNIONS*

385.22   US   ISSN 0896-4424
TRAIN RIDER MAGAZINE. 1986. bi-m. $6. Message Media, Box 9007, Berkeley, CA 94709. Ed. James Russell. illus.; circ. 750.
    Formerly: Train Rider Monthly.

385   ISSN 0041-0926
TRAINMASTER. 1956. m. $27 membership. National Railway Historical Society, Pacific Northwest Chapter, Rm. 1, Union Sta., 800 N.W. Sixth Ave., Portland, OR 97209-3715. TEL 503-226-6747. Ed. Michael Callanan. bk.rev.; circ. 600. (processed)
    Description: Contains information on chapter business and activities, original material by members pertaining to railroad history and preservation.

385   US   ISSN 0041-0934
TF1
TRAINS; the magazine of railroading. 1940. m. $28.95 (foreign $34.95). Kalmbach Publishing Co., Box 1612, Waukesha, WI 53187. TEL 414-796-8776. FAX 414-796-0126. Ed. J. David Ingles. adv.; charts; illus.; stat.; index; circ. 93,000. **Indexed:** Mag.Ind.
    Description: Recalls the romance and glory of railroading's past, and explores the railroads of today. Emphasis on North American railroading, but coverage is worldwide.

385.3   US   ISSN 0041-0845
TRAINSHEET. (Contains occasional supplements) 1965. m. (except Jul. & Aug.) $5 to libraries. National Railway Historical Society, Tacoma Chapter, Box 340, Tacoma, WA 98401. TEL 206-537-1865. (Subscr. to: Rudy Jaskar 17313 22nd Ave. Tacoma, WA 98445) Ed. Rudy Jaskar. bk.rev.; illus.; circ. 275. (processed; also avail. in microform from UMI)

385 625.1   AT   ISSN 0818-5204
TRANSIT AUSTRALIA; the Australian urban transit magazine. 1946. m. Aus.$50 to individuals; institutions Aus.$64. Transit Australia Publishing, G.P.O. Box 1017, Sydney, N.S.W. 2001, Australia. TEL 02-949-4424. Ed. Ian R. Hammond. adv.; bk.rev.; charts; illus.; stat.; index; circ. 1,000. (back issues avail.) **Indexed:** Aus.Rd.Ind.
    Formerly: Electric Traction (ISSN 0013-4163)

385   US
TRANSIT TIMES (ATLANTA). 1949. m. free. Metropolitan Atlanta Rapid Transit Authority, Public Information Division, 2424 Peidmont Rd., N.E., Atlanta, GA 30324. TEL 404-848-5157. Ed. Judith Weisberg. adv.; bk.rev.; illus.; circ. 5,000.

385   SW   ISSN 0348-3118
TRANSPORT-JOURNALEN. 1955. 4/yr. free. Statens Jaernvaegars Huvudkontor, Godstransportdivisionen - State Railways Head Office, S-105 50 Stockholm, Sweden. Ed. Christee Beijbom. bk.rev.; charts; illus.; circ. 60,000.

385   UK
TRANSPORT REVIEW. 1880. fortn. £12. Rail, Maritime & Transport Union, 205 Euston Rd., London N.W.1, England. Ed. J. Finney. adv.; bk.rev.; illus.; stat.; circ. 50,000. (newspaper)
    Formerly: Railway Review (ISSN 0033-8974)

385   CN
TRANSPORT 2000 CANADA. NEWS BULLETIN. 1977. 4/yr. free. Box 3594, Regina, Sask. S4P 3L7, Canada. TEL 306-565-6291. Ed. J. Strother-Stewart. circ. 400 (controlled).
    Formerly: Saskatchewan Rail Committee. News Bulletin (ISSN 0708-028X)

385   RU   ISSN 0041-1701
TRANSPORTNOE STROITEL'STVO. 1951. m. 22.20 Rub. Izdatel'stvo Transport, Komsomol'skii prosp., 42, 119048 Moscow G-48, Russia. (Dist. by: Mezhdunarodnaya Kniga, Moscow, G-200, Russia) bk.rev.; bibl.; charts; illus.; index. **Indexed:** Geotech.Abstr.

385.1   NO
TRANSPORTOEKONOMISK INSTITUTT. AARSBERETNING. 1965. a. free. Transportoekonomisk Institutt - Institute of Transport Economics, P.O. Box 6110 Etterstad, 0602 Oslo 6, Norway. Ed. Harald Aas.
    Formerly: Norges Teknisk-Naturvitenskapelige Forskningsraad. Transportoekonomisk Institutt. Aarsberetning (ISSN 0078-124X)

385.264   BE
TRANSPORTROUTIER. every 3/wks. Federation Nationale Belge des Transportateurs Routiers, Rue Picard 69, B-1020 Brussels, Belgium. TEL 428-1160.

385 790.13 900   IT   ISSN 0392-4602
TRENI OGGI. 1980. m. L.68000 (foreign L.84000). Editrice Trasporti su Rotaie soc.coop.r.l., Piazza Vittorio Emanuele II, 42C, 25087 Salo (Brescia), Italy. FAX 0365-41092. Ed. Erminio Mascherpa. adv.; bk.rev.; illus.; circ. 14,000. (back issues avail.)
    Description: Covers railroads, railroad history and railway modelling.

TROLLEY FARE. see *MUSEUMS AND ART GALLERIES*

TUSSEN DE RAILS. see *TRAVEL AND TOURISM*

385   US   ISSN 0275-3758
U S RAIL NEWS. 1978. fortn. $352.04 (effective Sep. 1992). Business Publishers, Inc., 951 Pershing Dr., Silver Spring, MD 20910-4464. TEL 301-587-6300. FAX 301-585-9075. Ed. Steve Lash. (looseleaf format)
    ●Also available online. Vendor(s): NewsNet (TS11).
    Description: Provides objective views of laws and new technologies affecting rail transport business, both passenger and goods transport.

385.264   NE
UITVAARTWEZEN.* bi-m. Nederlandse Unie van Ondernemers in het Uitvaartverzorgingsbedrijf, c/o N U V U, Nassauplein 27, 2885 The Hague, Netherlands.

331.88 385   MX
UNIFICACION.* vol.4, 1974. m. Sindicato de Trabajadores Ferrocarrileros de la Republica Mexicana, Calzada de Nonolco No. 206, Mexico D.F., Mexico. Ed.Bd. charts; illus.; circ. 60,000.

385   US   ISSN 0163-4674
HE1780
U.S. FEDERAL RAILROAD ADMINISTRATION. OFFICE OF SAFETY. ACCIDENT - INCIDENT BULLETIN. no.144, 1975. a. free. U.S. Federal Railroad Administration, Office of Safety, Washington, DC 20590. TEL 202-366-0881. Key Title: Accident - Incident Bulletin.
    Formerly: U.S. Federal Railroad Administration. Office of Safety. Accident Bulletin (ISSN 0092-1645)

V R - EXPRESS. see *TRAVEL AND TOURISM*

385   HU   ISSN 0133-0314
VAROSI KOZLEKEDES/URBAN TRANSPORT. (Text in Hungarian; summaries in English (in special issues)) 1968. bi-m. 180 Ft.($25.50) Petofi Lap- es Konyvkiado Kft., Szabadsag ter la, 6001 Kecskemet, Hungary. TEL 36-76-27611. Ed. Rudolf Nagy. adv.; bk.rev.; charts; illus.; maps; stat.; index; circ. 1,200.
    Description: Covers urban public and individual transport; includes national and international information.

385.264   GW
VERBAND DES WURTTEMBERGISCHEN VERKEHRSGEWERBES. SUEDDEUTSCHER VERKEHRSURIER. m. Verband des Wurttembergischen Verkehrsgewerbes, Hedelfinger Str. 25, Postfach 600569, D-7000 Stuttgart 60, Germany. TEL 0711-423066. TELEX 22846.

385.204   GW
VERBUNDFAHRPLAN U - S. 1986. s-a. DM.3. Muenchner Verkehrs- und Tarifverbund GmbH, Thierschstr. 2, 8000 Munich 22, Germany. TEL 089-23803-0. FAX 089-238083-282. circ. 35,000. (back issues avail.)

385   GW   ISSN 0232-9042
VERKEHRSGESCHICHTLICHE BLAETTER. 1974. bi-m. DM.24. Verkehrsgeschichtliche Blaetter e.V., Postfach 104, 1020 Berlin, Germany. bk.rev.; index; circ. 1,300.

385.264   GW
VERKEHRSGEWERBE.* m. Hahn Verlag, Im Moore 17, Postfach 2427, 3000 Hannover 1, Germany.

385.264   GW
VERKEHRSGEWERBE FUER NIEDERSACHSEN UND BREMEN. m. Fachvereinigung Guterfernverkehr im Gesamtverband Verkehrsgewerbe Niedersachsen, Lortzingstr. 1, Postfach 6160, D-3000 Hannover 1, Germany. TEL 6262273. TELEX 22461.

385   FR   ISSN 0042-5478
VIE DU RAIL. 1946. w. 473 F. 11 rue de Milan, 75440 Paris cedex 09, France. (U.S. addr.: French National Railroads, 610 Fifth Ave., New York, NY 10020) Ed. Paul Delacroix. adv.; bk.rev.; film rev.; circ. 300,000.
    Description: Technical and general railroad information including tourism and travel by rail.

385   US
VIEWS AND NEWS. 1933. w. membership only. American Short Line Railroad Association, 2000 Massachusetts Ave., N.W., Washington, DC 20036. TEL 202-785-2250. FAX 202-887-0275. Ed. T.C. Dorsey. circ. 1,000.

385   IT
VOCI DELLA ROTAIA. 1955. m. L.10000 (foreign L.20000). Voci Della Rotaia, Piazza Croce Rossa, 1, 00161 Rome, Italy. TEL 06-8415667. FAX 06-8831108. Ed. Francesco Pellegrini. index; circ. 160,000.
    Description: Features articles on the Italian railway system. Includes articles on innovations in technology and transportation.

625.1   RU
VSESOYUZNYI NAUCHNO-ISSLEDOVATEL'SKII INSTITUT VAGONOSTROENIYA. TRUDY. 1966. irreg. 1.30 Rub. Vsesoyuznyi Nauchno-Issledovatel'skii Institut Vagonostroeniya, Moscow, Russia. illus.

385   RU   ISSN 0042-4749
VSESOYUZNYI NAUCHNO-ISSLEDOVATEL'SKII INSTITUT ZHELEZNODOROZHNOGO TRANSPORTA. VESTNIK. 1942. 8/yr. 27.60 Rub.($13.60) Vsesoyuznyi Nauchno-Issledovatelskii Institut Zheleznodorozhnogo Transporta, Moscow, Russia. index. **Indexed:** Chem.Abstr.

380.3   CS
VYZKUMNY USTAV SPOJU. SBORNIK PRACI. (Text in Czech; summaries in English, French, German, Russian) 1974. irreg. (2-3/yr.) 10 Kcs. per no. Nakladatelstvi Dopravy a Spoju, Hybernska 5, 115 78 Prague 1, Czechoslovakia. (Dist. by: Artia, Ve Smeckach 30, 111 27 Prague 1, Czechoslovakia) Ed. Milos Matura. charts; illus.

385 US ISSN 0897-7577
WAYBILL. 1970. q. $4. Mystic Valley Railway Society, Box 486, Hyde Park, MA 02136-0486. TEL 617-361-4445. Ed. W. Russell Rylko. adv.; circ. 14,000. (tabloid format)
  Description: Provides education in the field of railroad transportation.

385.264 BE
WEGWIJS - U B O T EN ROUTE. bi-m. Belgische Transportarbeidersbond, Pardenmarkt 66, B-2000 Antwerpen, Belgium. TEL 03-224-34-11. FAX 03-234-01-49.

385.264 GW
WERKVERKEHR UND VERLADER. 1955. q. Bundesverband Werkverkehr und Verlader, Lengsdorfer Haupstr. 73, 160108, D-5300 Bonn 1, Germany. TEL 0228-253034. TELEX 8869366.

385 CN ISSN 0085-8188
WESTERN CANADIAN STEAM LOCOMOTIVE DIRECTORY. 1969. biennial. $1. Richard L. Coulton, Ed. & Pub., Bentley, Alta. TOC 0J0, Canada. circ. 100.

WESTERN GRAPE REPORT. see *BUSINESS AND ECONOMICS — Marketing And Purchasing*

385 US
TF23.6
WESTERN RAILROADER. 1937. q. $25. Railway & Locomotive Historical Society, Pacific Coast Chapter, 115 "I" St., Sacramento, CA 95814-2204. Ed. Alan Hardy. bk.rev.; charts; illus.; maps; circ. 1,000. (also avail. in microform from UMI)
  Former titles: Western Railroader and Western Railfan (ISSN 0149-4996); Western Railroader (ISSN 0043-4108)

385 US ISSN 0043-4744
WHEEL CLICKS. 1938. m. $20. Pacific Railroad Society, Inc., Box 80726, San Marino, CA 91118-8726. TEL 213-283-0087. Ed. Tom Nelson. bk.rev.; charts; illus.; index; circ. 1,000.
  Description: Details railway construction and operation. Covers Amtrak, SPT & ATSF, Peninsula CalTrain and West Coast rail transit, commuter and tourist lines.

385.264 GW
WIENER FUHRWERKERZEITUNG. m. Fachgruppe Guterbeforderungsgewerbe fuer Wien, Colloredogasse 24, A-1180 Wien, Germany. TEL 345121.

385 NZ ISSN 0044-023X
Y A R N. (Your Auckland Railway News) 1952. 11/yr. NZ.$40 membership. Auckland Railway Enthusiasts Society, Inc., P.O. Box 2429, Auckland, New Zealand. FAX 09-833-6005. Ed. M. Ross. adv.; bk.rev.; circ. 680.

385.264 BE
ZEE. s-a. Belgische Transportarbeidersbond, Paardenmarkt 66, B-2000 Antwerpen, Belgium. TEL 03-224-34-11. FAX 03-234-01-49.

385 SZ
ZEITSCHRIFT FUER DEN INTERNATIONALEN EISENBAHNVERKEHR. 1892. q. Zentralamt fuer den Internationalen Eisenbahnverkehr, Gryphenhuebeliweg 30, CH-3006 Bern, Switzerland. TEL 031-431762. FAX 031-431164. TELEX 912063-OCTI-CH. bk.rev.

625.1 385 CS ISSN 0513-9295
ZELEZNICNI TECHNIKA. (Text in Czech or Slovak; summaries in French, German and Russian) 1972. bi-m. $27. (Federalni Ministerstvo Dopravy) Nakladatelstvi Dopravy a Spoju, Hybernska 5, 115 78 Prague 1, Czechoslovakia. (Dist. by: Artia, Ve Smeckach 30, 111 27 Prague 1, Czechoslovakia) Ed. Margita Crkonova. index.

385 RU ISSN 0044-4448
ZHELEZNODOROZHNYI TRANSPORT. 1919. m. 27.60 Rub. Izdatel'stvo Transport, Komsomol'skii prosp., 42, 119048 Moscow G-48, Russia. (Co-sponsor: Ministerstvo Putei Soobshcheniya) Ed. G.E. Sorokin. adv.; bk.rev.; abstr.; bibl.; charts; illus.; stat.; index; circ. 14,325. **Indexed:** C.I.S. Abstr., Chem.Abstr.
  —BLDSC shelfmark: 0057.550000.

625.1 CC ISSN 1001-4632
ZHONGGUO TIEDAO KEXUE/CHINA RAILWAY SCIENCE. (Text in Chinese) s-a. (Tiedao-bu, Kexue Yanjiuyuan - Ministry of Railway, Science Academy) Zhongguo Tiedao Kexue Bianjibu, Daliushu Beizhan, Xizhimenwai, Beijing 100081, People's Republic of China. TEL 8996577. Ed. Tan Licheng.

625.1 CC ISSN 1001-683X
ZHONGGUO TIELU/CHINA RAILROAD. (Text in Chinese) bi-m. Tiedao-bu, Keji Qingbao-suo - Ministry of Railway, Science and Technology Information Institute, Daliushu Beizhan, Xizhimenwai, Beijing 100081, People's Republic of China. TEL 8317379. Ed. Xie Wenbin.

TRANSPORTATION — Roads And Traffic

see also Engineering–Civil Engineering

A A S H T O QUARTERLY MAGAZINE. (American Association of State Highway and Transportation Officials) see *ENGINEERING — Civil Engineering*

A D A C ATLAS DEUTSCHLAND - EUROPA. (Allgemeiner Deutscher Automobil Club e.V.) see *TRAVEL AND TOURISM*

388.1 IT ISSN 0044-975X
A I S C A T INFORMAZIONI. 1966. q. free. Associazione Italiana Societa Concessionarie Autostrade e Trafori, Via Sardegna 40, 00187 Rome, Italy. FAX 6-4746968. Ed. Vito Rocco. bk.rev.; charts; stat.; circ. 4,500. **Indexed:** Dok.Str.

388.411 AT ISSN 0314-2205
A R R B REGIONAL SYMPOSIUM; program and papers. 1971. irreg. Australian Road Research Board, 500 Burwood Hwy., Vermont Sth., Vic. 3133, Australia. TEL 03-881-1555. FAX 03-887-8104. TELEX AA33113. illus.; circ. 350. (also avail. in microform)
  —BLDSC shelfmark: 1696.540000.

388.31 US
A R T B A NEWSLETTER. 1902. 26/yr. $50 to non-members. American Road & Transportation Builders Association, 501 School St., S.W., 8th Fl., Washington, DC 20024. TEL 202-488-2722. FAX 202-488-3631. circ. 5,000.

624 690 US ISSN 0360-6996
A R T B A OFFICIALS AND ENGINEERS DIRECTORY, TRANSPORTATION AGENCY PERSONNEL. a. $35. American Road and Transportation Builders Association, 501 School St., S.W., 8th Fl., Washington, DC 20024. TEL 202-488-2722. FAX 202-488-3631.

388.312 US
AMERICAN ASSOCIATION OF STATE HIGHWAY AND TRANSPORTATION OFFICIALS. PROCEEDINGS. a. $10. American Association of State Highway and Transportation Officials, 444 N. Capitol St. N.W., Ste. 225, Washington, DC 20001. TEL 202-624-5800. **Indexed:** HRIS.

388.312 GW
DIE ANTWORT. 1985. q. DM.6. Rettungsstiftung Juergen Pegler e.V., Schellengasse 8, D-7100 Heilbronn, Germany. TEL 07131-80080. FAX 07131-81219. circ. 50,000. (back issues avail.)

388.1 US ISSN 0403-1792
ARKANSAS HIGHWAYS. 1954? q. free. State Highway and Transportation Department, Public Affairs Office, Box 2261, Little Rock, AR 72203. TEL 501-569-2000. Ed. Bill Stanton. charts; illus.; circ. controlled.

388.1 US ISSN 0004-4954
TN853
ASPHALT. 1949. 3/yr. free. Asphalt Institute, Box 14052, Lexington, KY 40512-4052. FAX 606-288-4999. Ed. John Davis. illus.; circ. 16,000 (controlled).
  Formerly (until 1986): Asphaltnews; Supersedes (in 1976): Asphalt Institute. Newsletter.

665.5 US
ASPHALT EMULSION MANUFACTURERS ASSOCIATION. NEWSLETTER. 1973. q. membership. Asphalt Emulsion Manufacturers Association, 3 Church Circle, Ste. 250, Annapolis, MD 21401. TEL 410-267-0023. adv.; circ. 1,200.

388.31 AT
AUSTRALIAN ROAD RESEARCH BOARD. BRIEFING. 1989. m. free. Australian Road Research Board, 500 Burwood Hwy., Vermont S., Vic. 3133, Australia. TEL 03-881-1555. FAX 03-887-8104. TELEX AA33113. circ. 1,700. (back issues avail.)

388 625.7 AT ISSN 0572-1431
AUSTRALIAN ROAD RESEARCH BOARD. PROCEEDINGS. 1962. biennial. Australian Road Research Board, 500 Burwood Hwy., Vermont Sth., Vic. 3133, Australia. TEL 03-881-1555. FAX 03-887-8104. TELEX AA33113. **Indexed:** Dok.Str., Eng.Ind., Geotech.Abstr., HRIS, Noise Pollut.Publ.Abstr.
  —BLDSC shelfmark: 6656.200000.

388.411 388.3 AT
AUSTRALIAN ROAD RESEARCH BOARD. RESEARCH REPORT. 1975. irreg. Aus.$23 per no. Australian Road Research Board, 500 Burwood Rd., Vermont S., Vic. 3133, Australia. TEL 03-881-1555. FAX 03-887-8104. TELEX AA33113. circ. 350. (back issues avail.) **Indexed:** Dok.Str.

380.5 388.3 AT ISSN 0572-144X
AUSTRALIAN ROAD RESEARCH BOARD. SPECIAL REPORT. 1966. irreg. Aus.$43 per no. Australian Road Research Board, 500 Burwood Highway, Vermont S., Vic. 3133, Australia. TEL 03-881-1555. FAX 03-887-8104. TELEX AA33113. circ. 350. (also avail. in microfiche; back issues avail.)
  —BLDSC shelfmark: 8386.550000.

AUSTRALIAN ROAD RESEARCH BOARD. TECHNICAL MANUALS. see *TRANSPORTATION — Computer Applications*

AUSTROPACK; Zeitschrift fuer alle Gebiete des Verpackungswesens fuer Transport und Verkehr. see *PACKAGING*

AUTO. see *TRANSPORTATION — Automobiles*

AUTOKAMPIOEN. see *TRANSPORTATION — Automobiles*

AUTOREVUU. see *TRANSPORTATION — Automobiles*

BETTER ROADS. see *ENGINEERING — Civil Engineering*

BIL. see *TRANSPORTATION — Automobiles*

388.31 US
BOHMAN TRAFFIC NEWS SUMMARY. m. $29.95. Bohman Industrial Traffic Consultants, Inc., 32 Pleasant St., Box 889, Gardner, MA 01440. TEL 617-632-1913. Ed. Raynard R. Bohman, Jr.

388 BL
BRASILIA. DEPARTAMENTO DE ESTRADAS DE RODAGEM DO DISTRITO FEDERAL. DIRETORIA GERAL. RELATORIO DE ATIVIDADES. 1978. a. free. Departamento de Estrados de Rodagem do Distrito Federal, Divisao de Programacao, 70000 Brasilia, DF, Brazil. circ. 300.
  Formerly: Brasilia. Departamento de Estradas de Rodagem do Distrito Federal. Diretoria Geral. Relatorio Anual.

BUTTERWORTHS ROAD TRAFFIC SERVICE. see *LAW*

388.411 CN
C U T A - A C T U FORUM. (Text in English and French) 1977. m. Canadian Urban Transit Association - Association Canadienne de Transit Urbain, 55 York St., Ste. 901, Toronto, Ont. M5J 1R7, Canada. TEL 416-365-9800. FAX 416-365-1295. Ed. David Onodera. circ. 600.
  Formerly: Transit Topics.

388.1 FR
CAISSE NATIONALE DES AUTOROUTES. RAPPORT ANNUEL. 1963. a. free. Caisse Nationale des Autoroutes, 56 rue de Lille, 75356 Paris, France. TEL 47-53-85-11. FAX 47-53-98-61. circ. 2,000.
  Description: Report by the board of directors on the activities for the year of the Caisse Nationale des Autoroutes.

TRANSPORTATION — ROADS AND TRAFFIC

388.31   CN   ISSN 0826-8770
CANADIAN INDUSTRIAL TRANSPORTATION LEAGUE. TRANSPORT INFO. 1926. 24/yr. Can.$300 to non-members; free to members. Canadian Industrial Transportation League, Ste. 706, 480 University Ave., Toronto, Ont. M5G 1V2, Canada. TEL 416-596-7833. FAX 596-1272. Ed. Stewart Wallace. adv.; bk.rev.; circ. 1,000.
   Formerly: Canadian Industrial Traffic League. Traffic Notes (ISSN 0045-4974)
   Description: Purpose is to bring Canadian shippers the most useful and timely information available on the transportation industry. Informs members of both legislative and policy changes as they relate to transportation.

388.1   US   ISSN 0008-6789
HE356.S5
CAROLINA HIGHWAYS. 1949. bi-m. free to qualified personnel. Department of Highways and Public Transportation, Box 191, Columbia, SC 29202. TEL 803-758-2102. Ed. James L. Walker, Jr. illus.; circ. 9,000.

388   UN
CENSUS OF MOTOR TRAFFIC ON MAIN INTERNATIONAL TRAFFIC ARTERIES. (Text in English and French) quinquennial; latest 1985. Economic Commission for Europe (ECE), Palais des Nations, 1211 Geneva 10, Switzerland. TEL 734-6011. FAX 733-9879. TELEX 412962. (Or: United Nations Publications, Room DC2-853, New York, NY 10017) (also avail. in microfiche)
   Formerly: Census of Traffic on Main International Traffic Arteries (ISSN 0566-7631)

388.411   II   ISSN 0069-1690
CENTRAL ROAD RESEARCH INSTITUTE, NEW DELHI. ROAD RESEARCH PAPER. (Text in English) 1956. irreg., no.223, 1989. free. Central Road Research Institute, P.O. Central Road Research Institute, New Delhi 110020, India. TEL 6832274. TELEX 31-75369-CRRI-IN. (Affiliate: Council of Scientific and Industrial Research) circ. controlled. **Indexed:** Chem.Abstr., Eng.Ind.

CESTE I MOSTOVI/ROADS AND BRIDGES. see ENGINEERING — Civil Engineering

388.31   UK   ISSN 0009-8698
CLEARWAY; traffic magazine of the metropolitan police. 1967. s-a. free. Metropolitan Police, Traffic Division, c/o The Editor, 1 Area Traffic H.Q., 11 Grove Rd., Chadwell Heath, Essex RM6 4AG, England. TEL 0708-29338. FAX 01-599-7856. Ed.Bd. adv.; bk.rev.; charts; illus.; circ. 3,000.

388.1   II
COMMERCE YEARBOOK OF ROAD TRANSPORT. (Text in English) a. Rs.35. Commerce Publications Limited, NKM International House, 178 Backbay Reclamation, Bombay 400020, India.

CONSTRUCTION INDUSTRIES OF MASSACHUSETTS DIRECTORY; a directory and catalog of highway and heavy construction in New England. see BUSINESS AND ECONOMICS — Trade And Industrial Directories

THE CONTROLLER; journal of air traffic control. see AERONAUTICS AND SPACE FLIGHT

388.1   CR
COSTA RICA. MINISTERIO DE OBRAS PUBLICAS Y TRANSPORTES. MEMORIAS. irreg. Ministerio de Obras Publicas y Transportes, San Jose, Costa Rica.
   Formerly: Costa Rica. Ministerio de Transportes. Memoria (ISSN 0589-8617)

COVJEK I PROMET. see PUBLIC HEALTH AND SAFETY

CYCLING WORLD; the Australian bicycling magazine. see SPORTS AND GAMES — Bicycles And Motorcycles

388.31   US
D R I - MCGRAW-HILL MONTHLY TRAFFIC MONITOR. m. D R I - McGraw-Hill, 24 Hartwell Ave., Lexington, MA 02173. TEL 617-863-5100. FAX 617-860-6332. TELEX 200 284. (back issues avail.)

624 388.1   AG   ISSN 0011-5177
D.V.B.A. PUBLICACIONES TECNICAS. 1957. 10/yr. free. Direccion de Vialidad, Calle 7 No. 1175, 1900 la Plata, Argentina. charts; illus.; stat.; circ. 1,500. (tabloid format)

388.31   GW
D V R REPORT. 1969. 4/yr. Deutscher Verkehrssicherheitsrat e.V., Obere Wilhelmstr. 32, 5300 Bonn 3, Germany. circ. 11,500.
   Formerly: Partner Report.

338.31   GW   ISSN 0012-0901
D V Z. (Deutsche Verkehrs - Zeitung) 1947. 3/wk. DM.372. Deutscher Verkehrs-Verlag GmbH, Nordkanalstr. 36, 2000 Hamburg 1, Germany. TEL 040-23714155. FAX 040-23714-123. Ed. Frank Schnell. adv. contact: Werner Holders. bk.rev.; charts; illus.; circ. 18,250.
   Description: International trade journal for transport and logistics, transport policy, forwarding, warehousing and transhipment.

388.1 352.7   DK   ISSN 0107-0134
DANMARKS TEKNISKE HOEJSKOLE. INSTITUTET FOR VEJE, TRAFIK OG BYPLAN. NOTAT/TECHNICAL UNIVERSITY OF DENMARK. INSTITUTE OF ROADS, TRANSPORT AND TOWN PLANNING. PAPER. 1976. irreg. price varies. Danmarks Tekniske Hoejskole, Institutet for Veje, Trafik og Byplan, Bygning 115, 2800 Lyngby, Denmark. illus.; circ. 100.

388   US   ISSN 0070-329X
DELAWARE. DEPARTMENT OF HIGHWAYS AND TRANSPORTATION. TRAFFIC SUMMARY. 1957. a. $10. Department of Transportation, Bureau of Traffic, Box 778, Dover, DE 19901. TEL 302-739-3304. Ed. James Ho. circ. 400.

388.1   DK   ISSN 0106-312X
DENMARK. STATENS VEJLABORATORIUM. LABORATORIERAPPORT. No.52, 1981. irreg. Statens Vejlaboratorium, Postboks 235, Elisagaardsvej 5-7, DK-4000 Roskilde, Denmark. **Indexed:** Dok.Str.
   Description: Research results, or new techniques of interest to road research workers and road engineers.

388.1   DK   ISSN 0109-5315
DENMARK. STATENS VEJLABORATORIUM. NOTAT. irreg. Statens Vejlaboratorium, Postboks 235, Elisagardsvej 5-7, DK-4000 Roskilde, Denmark.

388.1   DK   ISSN 0109-2405
DENMARK. VEJDIREKTORATET. AARSBERETNING. 1983. a. free. Vejdirektoratet, Copenhagen, Denmark. illus.
   Formerly: Denmark. Vejdirektoratet. Aarsrapport.

388.31   DK
DENMARK. VEJDIREKTORATET. OEKONOMISK-STATISTISK AFDELING. TRAFIKRAPPORT. 1975. a. Vejdirektoratet, Oekonomisk Statistisk Afdeling, Copenhagen, Denmark. illus.
   Formerly: Denmark. Vejdirektoratet. Trafikrapport (ISSN 0106-7389)

388.1   DK   ISSN 0108-1306
DETAILFORSKRIFTER FOR KOERETOEJER/DETAILED REGULATIONS FOR VEHICLES. 1977. a. DKK 100. Justitsministeriet, Faerdselssikkerhedsafdelingen, P.O. Box 2131, DK-1015 Copenhagen K, Denmark. FAX 33-93-22-92. (Subscr. to: Schultz Boghandel, Moentergade 1C, DK-1116 Copenhagen K, Denmark; FAX 36-44-01-41)

388.31   GW   ISSN 0012-0804
DER DEUTSCHE STRASSENVERKEHR. 1952. m. T und M Verlagsgesellschaft mbH, Otto-Grotewohl-Str. 19D, 1086 Berlin, Germany. TEL 030-22512003. adv.; bk.rev.; abstr.; charts; illus.; stat.

388.314   SP
DISMODA; lineas y tendencias del caldoza. 2/yr. 4000 ptas. Pedeca Sociedad Cooperativa, Ltda., Maria Auxiliadora 5, 28040 Madrid, Spain. TEL 459 60 00.

DIXON & MCVEAGH'S ROAD TRAFFIC LAW. see LAW

388.413   US
DRIVE SAFELY. 1989. m. $10.20. Bureau of Business Practice, 24 Rope Ferry Rd., Waterford, CT 06386. TEL 203-442-4365. FAX 203-434-3341. TELEX 966420. Ed. Mary Schantz.

388.31   GW   ISSN 0014-6803
FAHR MIT UNS; Hamburger illustrierte Nahverkehrszeitschrift. 1954. q. DM.10. Hamburger Hochbahn Aktiengesellschaft, Postfach 102720, Steinstr. 20, 2000 Hamburg 1, Germany. FAX 040-326406. Ed. Joachim Haeger. illus.; stat.; circ. 16,000. (also avail. in microform; back issues avail.)

388.1   US   ISSN 0732-9792
HE5614.2
FATAL ACCIDENT REPORTING SYSTEM. 1975. a. U.S. Department of Transportation, National Highway and Traffic Safety Administration, National Center for Statistics and Analysis, 400 Seventh St., S.W., Washington, DC 20590. TEL 202-366-5820. FAX 202-366-7078. (Subscr. to: 400 7th St., S.W., Washington, DC 20590) circ. 8,000. (also avail. in microfiche)
   Formerly (until 1979): Fatal Accident Reporting System. Annual Report (ISSN 0147-6939)
   Description: Presents descriptions of all fatal accidents reported within the 50 states, the District of Columbia, and Puerto Rico, with coded data elements that characterize the accident, the vehicles, and the persons involved.

388.413   US
FLORIDA TRAFFIC & D U I PRACTICE. 2 base vols. (plus suppl. 4-5/yr.). $160. Butterworth Legal Publishers (Salem) (Subsidiary of: Reed International PLC), 90 Stiles Rd., Salem, NH 03079. TEL 800-548-4001. FAX 603-898-9858. Ed. Marcia MacConnell. (looseleaf format)
   Description: Covers all applicable law and procedure, including recent legislative changes regarding drunk driving.

DER FLUGLEITER. see TRANSPORTATION — Air Transport

388   GW
FORSCHUNGSGESELLSCHAFT FUER STRASSEN- UND VERKEHRSWESEN. ARBEITSGRUPPE MINERALSTOFFE IM STRASSENBAU. 1977. irreg. price varies. (Forschungsgesellschaft fuer Strassen- und Verkehrswesen) Kirschbaum Verlag GmbH, Siegfriedstr. 28, Postfach 210209, 5300 Bonn 2, Germany. TEL 0228-343057. FAX 0228-857145. TELEX 889596-KIRVL-D.

388.31   US   ISSN 0749-2774
FROM THE STATE CAPITALS. TRANSPORTATION POLICIES. 1946. 12/yr. $145 (foreign $155)(effective Dec. 1990). Wakeman-Walworth, Inc., 300 N. Washington St., Alexandria, VA 22314. TEL 703-549-8606. FAX 703-549-1372. (processed)
   Incorporates: From the State Capitals. Urban Transit (ISSN 0741-3564); Former titles: From the State Capitals. Parking Regulations (ISSN 0741-3513); From the State Capitals. Off-Street Parking (ISSN 0016-1829)
   Description: Latest information on mass transit funding, urban transit fare structure, commuter lines, financing and grants for roadway and airport construction.

388.3   US
GARDEN STATE PARKWAY TRAFFIC REPORT. 1972. m. free. Highway Authority, Garden State Parkway, Traffic Division, Woodbridge, NJ 07095. TEL 201-442-8600. Ed. Jude T. Depko. charts; illus.; circ. 750. (also avail. in microfilm)
   Formerly: Garden State Parkway Quarterly Report.

388   GW
GERMANY. (FEDERAL REPUBLIC). BUNDESMINISTERIUM FUER VERKEHR. STRASSENBAUBERICHT. 1971. a. DM.15. (Bundesministerium fuer Verkehr) Verlag Ed. Hans Heger, Herderstr. 56, Postfach 200821, 5300 Bonn 2, Germany. illus.; circ. 1,500.

388   CC   ISSN 0451-0712
GONG LU/ROADS. (Text in Chinese) m. Jiaotong-bu, Gonglu Guihua Shejiyuan - Ministry of Communications and Transportation, Road Planning and Designing Institute, 33 Qianchaomian Hutong, Dongsi, Beijing 100010, People's Republic of China. TEL 5125565. Ed. He Xiumei.

GRANT ALERT. see BUSINESS AND ECONOMICS — Public Finance, Taxation

TRANSPORTATION — ROADS AND TRAFFIC

388.31 US
H E R P I C C POTHOLE GAZETTE. 1982. bi-m. free. (Highway Extension and Research Program, Indiana Counties and Cities) Federal Highway Administration, Rm. 254, Federal Bldg., 575 Pennsylvania, Indianapolis, IA 46204. TEL 317-226-7475. Ed. William B. McDermott. circ. 3,500. (back issues avail.)
  Description: Covers maintenance techniques, management, engineering and design for local roads and streets.

388.312 US
H M A T. (Hot Mix Asphalt Technology) 1964. q. free to qualified personnel. National Asphalt Pavement Association, N.A.P.A. Bldg. 5100 Forbes Blvd., Lanham, MD 20706-4413. TEL 301-731-4748. FAX 301-731-4621. Ed. George C. Goggin. adv.; bk.rev.; circ. 25,000 (controlled).
  Supersedes (in 1986): National Asphalt Pavement Association. Paving Forum (ISSN 0048-3079)

388.31 IT ISSN 0391-2019
H P TRASPORTI. 1974. m. L.50000($50) (Automobile Club d'Italia) Editrice dell' Automobile s.r.l., Viale Regina Margherita 290, I-00198 Rome, Italy. TEL (06) 4402061. FAX 06-8440926. Ed. Fabio Montanaro. adv.; bk.rev.; bibl.; charts; illus.; stat.; circ. 25,000.
  Formerly: H P Energia Trasporti; *Supersedes:* Segnalazioni Stradali (ISSN 0037-0959)

HIGHWAY & HEAVY CONSTRUCTION PRODUCTS. see *ENGINEERING — Civil Engineering*

264 UK
HIGHWAY CODE. irreg. H.M.S.O., St. Crispin's, Duke St., Norwich NR3 1 PD, England.

HIGHWAY RESEARCH RECORD; general report on road research work done in India during (year). see *ENGINEERING — Civil Engineering*

388 US
HIGHWAY SAFETY DIRECTIONS. 1970. q. free. University of North Carolina at Chapel Hill, Highway Safety Research Center, 134 1-2 E. Franklin St., CB 3430, Chapel Hill, NC 27599-3430. TEL 919-962-2202. FAX 919-962-8710. Ed. Jeffrey C. Lowrance. circ. 4,500.
  Formed by the 1987 merger of: Totline (Chapel Hill) & Highway Safety Highlights (ISSN 0162-6205)
  Description: Reports on research being conducted by the university on alcohol and highway safety, roadway alignment and engineering, accident investigation and analysis, driver behavior, education and licensing, adult and child passenger safety, seat belts and child car seats. Looks at passenger protection laws, injury prevention, and North Carolina passenger and highway safety efforts.

HIGHWAYS AND TRANSPORTATION. see *ENGINEERING — Civil Engineering*

388.31 GW
HOCHSCHULE FUER VERKEHRSWESEN "FRIEDRICH LIST". VERKEHRSWISSENSCHAFT AKTUELL - WISSENSCHAFTLICHE ZEITSCHRIFT. 1952. 6/yr. DM.10. Hochschule fuer Verkehrswesen "Friedrich List", Friedrich-List-Platz 1, 8010 Dresden, Germany. Ed. M. Zschweigert. adv.; bibl.; charts; illus.; index; circ. 1,200. Indexed: Dok.Str., Math.R.
  Formerly: Hochschule fuer Verkehrswesen "Friedrich List". Wissenschaftliche Zeitschrift (ISSN 0043-6844)
  Description: Devoted to scientific studies conducted at the Hochschule fuer Verkehrswesen "Friedrich List" Dresden. Covers transport and operation economy, technical traffic cybernetics, vehicle engineering, transport construction and mathematics, traffic safety, tourism, telecommunications.

HUNGARY. KOZPONTI STATISZTIKAI HIVATAL. KOZLEKEDESI EVKONYV. see *TRANSPORTATION — Abstracting, Bibliographies, Statistics*

388.1 II
I R C SPECIAL PUBLICATION. 1966. irreg. Indian Roads Congress, Jamnagar House, Shahjahan Rd., New Delhi 110 011, India. TEL 381649. bibl.; charts.

388.31 US ISSN 0162-8178
HE331 CODEN: ITEJDZ
I T E JOURNAL. 1930. m. $50. Institute of Transportation Engineers, 525 School St., S.W., Ste. 410, Washington, DC 20024. TEL 202-554-8050. Ed. Kathy Harrington-Hughes. adv.; bk.rev.; circ. 11,200. (also avail. in microfilm from UMI; reprint service avail. from UMI) Indexed: A.S.& T.Ind., CAD CAM Abstr., Cadscan, Curr.Cont., Dok.Str., Energy Info.Abstr., Eng.Ind., Environ.Abstr., Environ.Per.Bibl., Excerp.Med., Fluidex, Geo.Abstr., Geotech.Abstr., HRIS, INIS Atomind., Intl.Civil Eng.Abstr., Lead Abstr., P.A.I.S, Petrol.Abstr., Risk Abstr., Sage.Urb.Stud.Abstr., Soft.Abstr.Eng., Zincscan.
  —BLDSC shelfmark: 4588.550000.
  Former titles: Transportation Engineering (ISSN 0148-0170); (1933-1977): Traffic Engineering (ISSN 0041-0675)

625.7 US ISSN 0019-1175
IDAHO TRANSPORTATION DEPARTMENT. HIGHWAY INFORMATION. 1920. bi-m. free. Transportation Department, Box 7129, Boise, ID 83707-1129. TEL 208-334-8000. TELEX 334-3858. Ed. Barbara Babic. charts; illus.; stat.; circ. 1,500.
  Formerly: Idaho Department of Highways. Highway Information.

388 II ISSN 0376-4788
CODEN: HREBDK
INDIAN ROADS CONGRESS. HIGHWAY RESEARCH BOARD BULLETIN. (Text in English) 3/yr. Rs.16 per no. Indian Roads Congress, Jamnagar House, Shahjahan Rd., New Delhi 110 011, India. TEL 381649. circ. 6,600. Indexed: HRIS.
  Supersedes (1975): Indian Roads Congress. Road Research Bulletin.

624 II ISSN 0258-0500
CODEN: JIRCAA
INDIAN ROADS CONGRESS. JOURNAL. (Text in English) 1934. q. $20. Indian Roads Congress, Jamnagar House, Shahjahan Rd., New Delhi 110 011, India. TEL 381649. circ. 6,500. Indexed: Dok.Str., Eng.Ind., Geotech.Abstr., HRIS.
  —BLDSC shelfmark: 4429.370000.

388 US ISSN 1054-2647
▼**INSIDE I V H S;** intelligent vehicle - highway systems update. 1991. bi-w. $345 in N. America; Europe $245; elsewhere $495. Waters Information Services, Inc., Box 2248, Binghamton, NY 13902. TEL 607-770-8535. FAX 607-798-1692. charts.

388.413 GW ISSN 0341-5805
INSTITUT FUER STADTBAUWESEN. VEROEFFENTLICHUNGEN. 1967. irreg. (approx. 2/yr.). Institut fuer Stadtbauwesen, T U Braunschweig, Postfach 3329, 3300 Braunschweig, Germany. TEL 0531-391-7920. cum.index; circ. 250.

INSTYTUT BADAWCZY DROG I MOSTOW. PRACE. see *ENGINEERING*

INSURANCE INSTITUTE FOR HIGHWAY SAFETY. STATUS REPORT. see *PUBLIC HEALTH AND SAFETY*

388.31 US
INTERNATIONAL BRIDGE, TUNNEL AND TURNPIKE ASSOCIATION. REPORT OF THE ANNUAL MEETING. 1962. a. price varies. International Bridge, Tunnel and Turnpike Association, 2120 L St., N.W., Ste. 305, Washington, DC 20037. TEL 202-659-4620. FAX 202-6590500. TELEX 275445 TSI UR. Dir. Neil D. Schuster. circ. 2,000.

625.7 US ISSN 0074-3348
INTERNATIONAL CONFERENCE ON THE STRUCTURAL DESIGN OF ASPHALT PAVEMENTS. PROCEEDINGS. 1963. quinquennial. price varies. International Society for Asphalt Pavement, c/o Texas Research and Development Foundation, 2602 Dellana Lane, Austin, TX 78746. TEL 512-327-4211. FAX 512-328-7246. Ed. Morris C. Reinhardt.

388.31 US
INTERNATIONAL FORUM ON TRAFFIC RECORDS SYSTEMS PROCEEDINGS. 1976. a. $10. National Safety Council, Industrial Section, 444 N. Michigan Ave., Chicago, IL 60611. TEL 800-621-7619. Ed. Ted Dudzik. circ. 600.
  Description: Covers all highway traffic records.

388.1 625.7 FR ISSN 0074-7815
INTERNATIONAL ROAD CONGRESSES. PROCEEDINGS. (Editions in English, French) quadrennial since 1964; 19th 1991, Marrakesh. Permanent International Association of Road Congresses, 27 rue Guenegaud, 75006 Paris, France.

388.3 GW ISSN 0020-9511
HE5
INTERNATIONALES VERKEHRSWESEN; Fachzeitschrift fuer Information und Kommunikation im Verkehr. (Supplement avail.: Internationales Verkehrswesen) 1949. m. DM.128. (Deutsche Verkehrswissenschaftliche Gesellschaft) Deutscher Verkehrs-Verlag GmbH, Nordkanalstr. 36, Postfach 101609, 2000 Hamburg 1, Germany. TEL 06151-380-313. FAX 040-23714-236. adv.: B&W page DM.3800; trim 252 x 180; adv. contact: Werner Holders. bk.rev.; abstr.; bibl.; charts; illus.; index; circ. 5,715. Indexed: Dok.Str., Excerp.Med., HRIS, Key to Econ.sci., SCIMP (1991-).
  —BLDSC shelfmark: 4557.185000.
  Incorporates: DDR Verkehr (ISSN 0011-4820);
  Formerly: Internationales Archiv fuer Verkehrswesen.
  Description: Technical and scientific publication covering all fields of traffic and transport, including traffic policy, transport, traffic legislation, and traffic related technology.

388 RU ISSN 0234-4742
HE5614
ITOGI NAUKI I TEKHNIKI. ORGANIZATSIYA I BEZOPASNOST' DOROZHNOGO DVIZHENIYA; auvomatiairovannye sistemy upravleniya dorozhnym dvizheniem. 1978. a. 0.75 Rub. Vsesoyuznyi Institut Nauchno-Tekhnicheskoi Informatsii (VINITI), Baltiiskaya ul. 14, Moscow A-219, Russia. TEL 238-46-00. (Subscr. to: Mezhdunarodnaya Kniga, Dimitrova ul. 39, 113095 Moscow, Russia) Ed. A.G. Romanov.
  —BLDSC shelfmark: 0128.184000.

ITOGI NAUKI I TEKHNIKI: AVTOMOBIL'NYI I GORODSKOI TRANSPORT. see *ENGINEERING — Civil Engineering*

JOURNAL OF TRAFFIC MEDICINE; an international journal of traffic safety. see *MEDICAL SCIENCES — Orthopedics And Traumatology*

388.1 AU ISSN 0075-7306
KURATORIUM FUER VERKEHRSSICHERHEIT. KLEINE FACHBUCHREIHE. (Text in German; summaries in English, French) 1959. irreg., no.20, 1984. price varies. (Kuratorium fuer Verkehrssicherheit) Literas Universitaetsverlag, Berggasse 4, A-1030 Vienna, Austria. Ed.Bd. cum.index: 1959-1971.; circ. 1,300. Indexed: Dok.Str., Hwy.Res.Abstr., Psychol.Abstr., Psychopharmacol.Abstr.

388.1 DK ISSN 0109-6044
LAENGDEN AF OFFENTLIGE VEJE. 1983. a. free. Vejdirektoratet - Ministry of Public Works, Transport Dept., Frederiksholm Kanal 27, 1220 Copenhagen K, Denmark.

LINKS UND RECHTS DER AUTOBAHN; der Reisefuehrer und Reiseatlas speziell fuer die Autobahn. see *HOTELS AND RESTAURANTS*

LOCAL - STATE FUNDING REPORT. see *BUSINESS AND ECONOMICS — Public Finance, Taxation*

388.312 692.8 US ISSN 0024-7030
LOW BIDDER. 1928. bi-m. $25. Associated General Contractors of America, N.Y. State Chapter, 1900 Western Ave., Albany, NY 12203. TEL 518-456-1134. FAX 518-456-1198. Ed. Lois A. Mignand. adv.; illus.; mkt.; circ. 1,600.
  Description: Provides highway contracting technical and news information.

MARTIN AND MORLEY MOTOR VEHICLE LAW (QUEENSLAND). see *LAW*

388.3 US ISSN 0094-6265
HE371.M3
MARYLAND. STATE HIGHWAY ADMINISTRATION. TRAFFIC TRENDS. 1963. a. free. State Highway Administration, Department of Transportation, Box 717, 300 W. Preston St., Baltimore, MD 21203. TEL 410-787-4050. FAX 301-553-6399. Ed. P. Edman. stat.; circ. 200. Key Title: Traffic Trends.

MASKINKONTAKT. see *MACHINERY*

MELYEPITESTUDOMANYI SZEMLE. see *ENGINEERING — Civil Engineering*

TRANSPORTATION — ROADS AND TRAFFIC

388 US
MISSOURI. DIVISION OF HIGHWAY SAFETY. HIGHWAY SAFETY PLAN. 1971. triennial. Division of Highway Safety, Box 104808, Jefferson City, MO 65110-4808. TEL 314-751-4161. FAX 314-634-5977. Ed. Vicky S. Williams. circ. controlled.
Former titles: Missouri's Annual Highway Safety Program; Missouri Annual Highway Safety Work Program (ISSN 0091-1097)

MOT - BAU; Fachzeitschrift fuer Strassenbau und Verkehr. see *ENGINEERING — Civil Engineering*

MOTOR & TRAFFIC LAW SERVICE - VICTORIA. see *LAW — Civil Law*

MOTOR VEHICLE LAW S.A. see *LAW — Civil Law*

625.7 388.31 US ISSN 0077-5614
TE7 CODEN: NCHRDA
NATIONAL COOPERATIVE HIGHWAY RESEARCH PROGRAM REPORTS. 1964. irreg., no.335, 1990. price varies. National Research Council, Transportation Research Board, 2101 Constitution Ave., N.W., Washington, DC 20418. TEL 202-334-3214. FAX 202-334-2519. TELEX 248664 NASWUR. circ. 3,000. (also avail. in microfiche) Indexed: Dok.Str.
—BLDSC shelfmark: 6021.863000.
Description: Formal reports issued at the conclusion of NCHRP research projects.

380.5 US ISSN 0547-5554
TE1
NATIONAL COOPERATIVE HIGHWAY RESEARCH PROGRAM RESEARCH RESULTS DIGEST. 1969. irreg., no.177, 1990. price varies. National Research Council, Transportation Research Board, 2101 Constitution Ave., N.W., Washington, DC 20418. TEL 202-334-3214. FAX 202-334-2519. circ. 4,200. Indexed: Dok.Str.
—BLDSC shelfmark: 7769.587500.
Description: Informal reports providing early awareness of results of NCHRP research projects.

625.7 US ISSN 0547-5570
CODEN: NCHSBB
NATIONAL COOPERATIVE HIGHWAY RESEARCH PROGRAM SYNTHESIS OF HIGHWAY PRACTICE. 1969. irreg., no.170, 1990. price varies. National Research Council, Transportation Research Board, 2101 Constitution Ave., N.W., Washington, DC 20418. TEL 202-334-3214. FAX 202-334-2519. (Co-sponsor: American Association of State Highway & Transportation Officials) circ. 2,500. (also avail. in microfiche) Indexed: Dok.Str.
—BLDSC shelfmark: 6021.866000.
Description: Studies current practices in the field.

388.3 UK ISSN 0260-7735
NATIONAL COUNCIL ON INLAND TRANSPORTATION. NEWSLETTER. 1978. 2/yr. membership. National Council on Inland Transportation, 7 Barnsley Rd., Scawsby, South Yorks, Doncaster DN5 8QJ, England. Ed. R.S.S. Luffman. circ. 200.
Formerly: Civilised Transport.

NEBRASKA. DEPARTMENT OF ROADS. NEBRASKA SELECTED STATISTICS. see *TRANSPORTATION — Abstracting, Bibliographies, Statistics*

388 US ISSN 0091-844X
HE371.N25
NEBRASKA. DEPARTMENT OF ROADS. TRAFFIC ANALYSIS UNIT. CONTINUOUS TRAFFIC COUNT DATA AND TRAFFIC CHARACTERISTICS ON NEBRASKA STREETS AND HIGHWAYS. 1968. a. free. Department of Roads, Transportation Planning Division, 1500 Nebraska Hwy. 2, Box 94759, Lincoln, NE 68509-4759. TEL 402-471-4567. FAX 402-479-4325. circ. controlled.
Description: Contains traffic data from permanent counter, organized by day, hour, and vehicle type.

388.31 US
NEBRASKA HIGHWAY PROGRAM. 1970. a. Department of Roads, 1500 N.E. Hwy. 2, Box 94759, Lincoln, NE 68509-4759. TEL 402-479-4316. FAX 402-479-4325. charts; illus.; stat.; circ. controlled. (processed)
Former titles: Challenge of the 80's; Focus on Nebraska Highways.

388.31 GW
NETZ WERK MAGAZIN. 1985. q. free. Versorgungs und Verkehrgesellschaft Saabruecken, Hohnzollernstr. 104-106, 6600 Saarbruecken, Germany. TEL 0681-587-0. FAX 0681-587-2203. TELEX 4-428623-VVS. Ed. Siggi Petto. circ. 3,000.

NEW ENGLAND JOURNAL OF TRANSPORTATION. see *TRANSPORTATION*

625.7 388.31 US ISSN 0028-5242
NEW HAMPSHIRE HIGHWAYS. vol.25, 1970. m. $25. New Hampshire Good Roads Association, Inc., Box 331, Concord, NH 03302-0331. TEL 603-224-1823. FAX 603-224-9399. adv.; bk.rev.; bibl.; charts; illus.; stat.; tr.lit.; circ. 1,500.

338.413 BE
NIEUWSBRIEF VERKEERSPECIALIST. (Supplement avail.) (Text in Flemish) s-m. 3948 Fr. C E D Samson (Subsidiary of: Wolters Samson Belgie n.v.), Louizalaan 485, B-1050 Brussels, Belgium. TEL 02-7231111. FAX 02-6498480. TELEX CEDSAM 64130.
Description: Provides information on traffic legislation and technical aspects of traffic control.

388 614 US
NORTH DAKOTA'S HIGHWAY SAFETY PLAN. 1967. a. free to qualified personnel. Department of Transportation, Driver's License and Traffic Safety, Traffic Safety Programs Section, 608 E. Blvd. Ave., Bismarck, ND 58505-0700. TEL 701-224-2600. FAX 701-224-4545. circ. 150 (controlled). (looseleaf format)
Formerly: North Dakota's Highway Safety Work Programs.

388.3 AU
OESTERREICHISCHE VERKEHRSWISSENSCHAFTLICHE GESELLSCHAFT. MITTEILUNGEN.* (Text in German; summaries in French, English) 1951. Oesterreichische Verkehrswissenschaftliche Gesellschaft, Gauermanngasse 4, Vienna, Austria. Ed. Otto Seidelmann. adv.; bk.rev.; bibl.; charts.

388.1 US
OKLAHOMA. DEPARTMENT OF TRANSPORTATION. SUFFICIENCY RATING REPORT AND NEEDS STUDY: OKLAHOMA STATE TRANSPORTATION. 1966. biennial. free. Department of Transportation, Planning Division, 200 N.E. 21st., Oklahoma City, OK 73105. TEL 405-521-2579. FAX 405-521-2524. illus.; circ. 200.
Formerly: Oklahoma. Department of Highways. Sufficiency Rating Report and Needs Study: Oklahoma State Highways (ISSN 0094-6230)

388.31 US
OKLAHOMA TURNPIKE AUTHORITY. ANNUAL REPORT TO THE GOVERNOR. 1954. a. free. Turnpike Authority, 3500 Martin Luther King Blvd., Box 11357, Oklahoma City, OK 73136-0357. TEL 405-425-3600. FAX 405-427-8246. charts; stat.; circ. 1,000.

388.31 US
OKLAHOMA TURNPIKE AUTHORITY. REPORT TO BONDHOLDERS. a. Turnpike Authority, 3500 Martin Luther King Blvd., Box 11357, Oklahoma City, OK 73136-0357. TEL 405-425-3600. FAX 405-427-8246.

388.1 II
ORISSA STATE ROAD TRANSPORTATION CORPORATION. ANNUAL ADMINISTRATION REPORT. (Text in English) 1974. a. State Road Transportation Corporation, Cuttack 753001, India. stat.

PAVEMENT MAINTENANCE. see *ENGINEERING — Civil Engineering*

388.411 US
PEDESTRIAN RESEARCH. 1966. q. $5 (foreign $8). American Pedestrian Association, Dorchester Century Village, Bldg. A, Apt. 12A, W. Palm Beach, FL 33417. Ed. L. Wilensky. charts; circ. 275.
Description: Advocates increased penalties, taxes, and tolls on motorists. Works to defend the pedestrian environment and interests against vehicular encroachments.

625.7 US ISSN 0079-8142
PURDUE UNIVERSITY. ROAD SCHOOL. PROCEEDINGS OF ANNUAL ROAD SCHOOL. (Subseries of: Engineering Bulletin. Engineering Extension Series) 1924. a. Purdue University, School of Civil Engineering, West Lafayette, IN 47907. TEL 317-494-2211. FAX 317-496-1105. Ed. K.C. Sinha. circ. 2,500.

625.7 388.1 BU ISSN 0204-6350
PUTISHTA/ROADS. (Text in Bulgarian; summaries in English and Russian) 1961. m. 15 lv.($10) Ministerstvo na Transporta, Glavno Upravlenie na P'tishchata, 3, D. Blagoev Bvrd., 1606 Sofia, Bulgaria. TEL 521354. TELEX 22679 GUP BG. (Dist. by: Hemus, 6, Rouski Blvd., 1000 Sofia, Bulgaria) (Co-sponsor: Nauchno-Tekhnicheski Saiuz po Transporta i Stroitelsvoto) Ed. Tanya Kremencka. adv.; bk.rev.; circ. 1,200. Indexed: BSL Geo.
Description: Scientific and technical magazine highlighting problems in the field of research, design, construction, repair, maintenance and operation of roads, bridges and tunnels, as well as of road construction equipment.

388.1 US
QUARTERLY TRANSPORTATION ACTIVITY REPORT. 1975. q. free. Department of Transportation, Transportation Information Office, Transportation Bldg. KF-01, Olympia, WA 98504-7322. TEL 206-753-2150. FAX 206-586-3593. Ed. Harold R. Garrett. charts; circ. 200.
Former titles: Transportation System Motorists Information Report; Highway and Ferry System Motorists Information Report; (Until Sep. 1975): Highway Construction Bulletin.

388.1 DK ISSN 0105-6956
RAPPORT FRA S T I K K; trafikuhled i Storkoebenhavn. 1977. a. free. Samarbejdsgruppen for Trafiksikkerhed i Kommuneerne i Koebenhavns-Omraadet, Gentofte Kommunes Tekniske Forvaltning, Sekretariat, Raadhuset, 2920 Charlottenlund, Denmark. illus.; circ. 3,000.

388.1 BL
REVISTA RODOVIARIA. 1972. m. Departamento Autonomo del Estradas de Rodagem, Divisao de Servicos Especiais, Av. Borges de Medeiros No 1555, Porto Alegre, Brazil. illus.

387.73 FR ISSN 0035-3191
REVUE GENERALE DES ROUTES ET DES AERODROMES. (Text in French; summaries in English, French, German and Spanish) 1926. 11/yr. 760 F. 9 rue Magellan, 75008 Paris, France. TEL 4720-1857. FAX 49-52-01-80. Dir. B. Dollon. adv.; bk.rev.; abstr.; charts; illus.; index; circ. 5,000. Indexed: Dok.Str., Excerp.Med., Geotech.Abstr., Int.Aerosp.Abstr., Intl.Civil Eng.Abstr., Soft.Abstr.Eng.

385.1 388 UK ISSN 0307-6822
ROAD ACCIDENTS IN GREAT BRITAIN. (Joint publication with Scottish Development Department and the Welsh Office) 1969. a. price varies. H.M.S.O., P.O. Box 276, London SW8 5DT, England.

ROAD DOCUMENTATION FOR DEVELOPING COUNTRIES. see *TRANSPORTATION*

ROAD LAW. see *LAW*

388.1 UK ISSN 0306-5286
ROAD TRAFFIC REPORTS. 1970. 10/yr. £70. Kenneth Mason Publications Ltd., 12 North St., Emsworth, Hants. PO10 7DQ, England. TEL 0243-377977. FAX 0243-379136. Ed. L.N. Williams. cum.index.
●Also available online. Vendor(s): Mead Data Central.
—BLDSC shelfmark: 7997.130000.

388.1 CN ISSN 0319-3780
ROUTES ET TRANSPORTS. (Text in French) 1971. 4/yr. Can.$50($10) Association Quebecoise du Transport et des Routes Inc., 6455 Christophe-Colomb, Montreal, Que. H2S 2G5, Canada. FAX 514-274-9608. Ed. Guy Pare. adv.; bk.rev.; circ. 2,000. (back issues avail.) Indexed: Pt.de Rep. (1983-).
Formerly: Routes du Quebec.

ROUTES - ROADS. see *ENGINEERING — Civil Engineering*

LES ROUTIERS. see *TRANSPORTATION — Trucks And Trucking*

TRANSPORTATION — ROADS AND TRAFFIC

388.31 SA
S A R F NEWSLETTER. (Text in Afrikaans, English) 1955. q. free. Southern Africa Road Federation, P.O. Box 8189, Johannesburg 2000, South Africa. FAX 011-337-5713. Ed. K.P. Gregg. adv.; circ. 1,200.

388.3 CN
S G I - AUTO FUND. ANNUAL REPORT. 1946. a. free. SaskAuto, Saskatchewan Government Insurance, 2260 11th Ave., Regina, Sask. S4P 0J9, Canada. TEL 306-565-1200. FAX 306-757-7477. TELEX 306-071-2417. circ. 2,500.
Former titles: SaskAuto Annual Report; Saskatchewan. Government Insurance Office. Province of Saskatchewan Motor Vehicle Traffic Accidents. Annual Report.

388.31 NO ISSN 0332-8988
SAMFERDSEL. 1925. 10/yr. NOK 375. Transportoekonomisk Instituttt - Institute of Transport Economics, P.O. Box 6110 Etterstad, 0602 Oslo, Norway. TEL 47-2-57-38-00. FAX 47-2-57-02-90. Ed. Harald Aas. adv.; bk.rev.; charts; illus.; tr.lit.; index; circ. 3,400. Indexed: Dok.Str.
Formerly: Norsk Veitidsskrift.

388.31 YU ISSN 0558-6208
SAOBRACAJ. (Issued also as part of Tehnika (ISSN 0350-2597)) (Text in Serbo-Croatian; summaries in English, Russian) vol.28, 1981. m. $50. Savez Inzenjera i Tehnicara Jugoslavije, Kneza Milosa 9, Box 187, 11000 Belgrade, Yugoslavia. Ed. Jovan Rados. adv.; bk.rev.; circ. 3,000.

SAVREMENI VOZAC. see TRANSPORTATION — Automobiles

388.413 DK ISSN 0107-5179
SIKKERHEDSMAESSIG VURDERING OG PRIORITERING AF MINDRE ANLAEGSARBEJDER PAA HOVEDLANDEVEJE. 1975. a. free. Vejdirektoratet - Ministry of Public Works, Transport Dept., Frederiksholm Kanal 27, 1220 Copenhagen K, Denmark. illus.
Formerly: Denmark. Vejdirektoratet. Black-Spotundersoegelse paa Hovedlandeveje.

SILNICNI OBZOR; mesicnik pro technicke, technologicke a ekonomicke otazky automobilove a mestske dopravy a silnichniho hospodarstvi. see TRANSPORTATION — Automobiles

625 SA
SOUTH AFRICA. DEPARTMENT OF TRANSPORT. TECHNICAL METHODS FOR HIGHWAYS. (Text in Afrikaans or English) 1978. irreg., no.3, 1988. price varies. Department of Transport, Private Bag X193, Pretoria 0001, South Africa.
Former titles: South Africa. Division of Road and Transport Technology. Technical Methods for Highways; South Africa. National Institute for Transport and Road Research. Technical Methods for Highways.

388.312 SA
SOUTH AFRICA. DEPARTMENT OF TRANSPORT. TECHNICAL RECOMMENDATIONS FOR HIGHWAYS. (Text in Afrikaans or English) 1970. irreg., no.17, 1984. price varies. Department of Transport, Private Bag X193, Pretoria 0001, South Africa. Indexed: Dok.Str.
Former titles: South Africa. Division of Roads and Transport Technology. Technical Recommendations for Highways; South Africa. National Institute for Transport and Road Research. Technical Recommendations for Highways.

388.1 SA
SOUTH AFRICA. DIVISION OF ROADS AND TRANSPORT TECHNOLOGY. BULLETINS. Alternative title: C S I R Research Reports. (Text in Afrikaans or English) 1956. irreg., no.19, 1987. price varies. Division of Roads and Transport Technology, Box 395, Pretoria 0001, South Africa. Indexed: Chem.Abstr., Deep Sea Res.& Oceanogr.Abstr.
Formerly: National Institute for Transport and Road Research. Bulletins.

388.1 SA
SOUTH AFRICA. DIVISION OF ROADS AND TRANSPORT TECHNOLOGY. P A D SERIES. Alternate title: C S I R Special Reports. (Text in Afrikaans or English) irreg., no.70, 1989. Division of Roads and Transport Technology, Box 395, Pretoria 0001, South Africa. FAX 8413232. TELEX 3-213125A.
Formerly: National Institute for Transport and Road Research. P A D Series.

388.1 DK ISSN 0106-7540
STOPINTERVIEWANALYSE. irreg. Vejdirektoratet - Ministry of Public Works, Transport Dept., Frederiksholm Kanal 27, 1220 Copenhagen K, Denmark. illus.
Formerly: Trafikanalyse.

388.31 GW ISSN 0039-2219
HE363.G29 CODEN: SVKTAC
STRASSENVERKEHRSTECHNIK. (Summaries in English, French and German) 1965. bi-m. DM.78. (Forschungsgesellschaft fuer Strassen- und Verkehrswesen) Kirschbaum Verlag GmbH, Siegfriedstr. 28, Postfach 210209, 5300 Bonn 2, Germany. TEL 0228-343057. FAX 0228-857145. TELEX 889596-KIRVL-D. Ed. Klaus Kirschbaum. adv.; bk.rev.; charts; illus.; tr.lit.; index; circ. 2,500. Indexed: Dok.Str., Eng.Ind., Excerp.Med., Intl.Civil Eng.Abstr., Soft.Abstr.Eng.

388.411 GW
STRASSENWAERTER. m. Verband Deutscher Strassenwaerter, Roesrather Str. 569, Postfach 95 01 67, D-5000 Cologne 91, Germany. TEL 864224.

354.485 SW ISSN 0282-5996
SWEDEN. STATENS VAEG- OCH TRAFIKINSTITUT. VERKSAMHETSBERAETTELSE. English edition: Swedish Road and Traffic Research Institute. Annual Report (ISSN 0347-6057) a. Statens Vaeg- och Trafikinstitut - Swedish Road and Traffic Research Institute, S-581 01 Linkoeping, Sweden.

388.413 SW ISSN 0281-4447
SWEDISH ROAD SAFETY OFFICE. ANALYSIS SECTION REPORT. (Text in Swedish, summaries in English) 1968. irreg. Swedish Road Safety Office, S-78186 Borlaenge, Sweden.

690 FR ISSN 0397-6513
T E C. (Transport Environnement Circulation) 1973. bi-m. 450 F. Association pour le Developpement des Techniques de Transport, d'Environnement et de Circulation (ATEC), 38 av. Emile Zola, 75015 Paris, France. FAX 45-79-52-86. Eds. Andre Imbert, Sylvie Blesson. adv.; bk.rev.; index; circ. 3,000. Indexed: Dok.Str., Excerp.Med.
—BLDSC shelfmark: 9025.602000.

388.411 DK ISSN 0105-5119
TECHNICAL UNIVERSITY OF DENMARK. INSTITUTE OF ROADS, TRANSPORT AND TOWN PLANNING. PAPERS AND REPORTS. (Text in Danish and English; summaries in English) 1937. irreg. Technical University of Denmark, Institute of Roads, Transport and Town Planning, Building 115, DK-2800 Lyngby, Denmark. circ. 50. (back issues avail.)

388.314 333.77 DK
TECHNICAL UNIVERSITY OF DENMARK. INSTITUTE OF ROADS, TRANSPORT AND TOWN PLANNING. REPORT. 1976. irreg., no. 19, 1978. Polytekniske Laereanstalt, Danmarks Tekniske Hoejskole, Instituttet for Vejbygning, Trafikteknik og Byplanlaegning, Bygning 115, DK-2800 Lyngby, Denmark. circ. 250.

353.9 US ISSN 0095-1994
HE5614.3.T2
TENNESSEE. DEPARTMENT OF SAFETY. ANNUAL REPORT. 1971. a. free to qualified personnel. Dept. of Safety, 1150 Foster Ave., Nashville, TN 37210. TEL 615-251-5229. FAX 615-244-7502. circ. 500. Key Title: Annual Report - Department of Safety.

TIE JA LIIKENNE. see ENGINEERING — Civil Engineering

TIJDSCHRIFT LANDINRICHTING. see AGRICULTURE — Crop Production And Soil

388 382.7 US
TOLLWAYS. m. membership. International Bridge, Tunnel & Turnpike Association, 2120 L St. N.W., Ste. 305, Washington, DC 20037. TEL 202-659-4620. FAX 202-659-0500. TELEX 275-445 TSI UR. Ed. Neil D. Schuster. circ. 1,700. (looseleaf format)
Description: Monthly bulletin of the International Bridge, Tunnel and Turnpike Association.

TOW TIMES; the international communications medium for the towing and recovery industry. see TRANSPORTATION — Trucks And Trucking

388.31 US
TRAFFIC AUDIT BUREAU. ANNUAL REPORT. a. Traffic Audit Bureau, 114 E. 32nd St., New York, NY 10016. TEL 212-213-9640.
Description: For outdoor advertisers.

388.31 US
TRAFFIC AUDIT BUREAU. NEWSLETTER. irreg. Traffic Audit Bureau, 114 E. 32nd St., New York, NY 10016. TEL 212-213-9640.
Description: For outdoor advertising industry.

388.413 CN
TRAFFIC CONTROL MANUAL FOR WORK ON ROADWAYS. base vol. (plus irreg. updates). Can.$42. Ministry of Transportation and Highways, Parliament Bldgs., Victoria, B.C. V8V 1X4, Canada. (Subscr. to: Crown Publications, 546 Yates St., Victoria, B.C. V8W 1K8, Canada. TEL 604-386-4636)

388.31 UK ISSN 0041-0683
HE331 CODEN: TENCA4
TRAFFIC ENGINEERING & CONTROL. 1960. m. £42($98) Printerhall Ltd., 29 Newman St., London W1P 3PE, England. TEL 071-636-3956. FAX 071-436-7016. TELEX 8813271 G. Ed. Keith Lumley. adv.; bk.rev.; charts; illus.; index; circ. 5,400. (also avail. in microform from UMI) Indexed: Br.Rail.Bd., Br.Tech.Ind., Dok.Str., Eng.Ind., Ergon.Abstr., Excerp.Med., Geo.Abstr., HRIS, I D A, Intl.Civil Eng.Abstr., Mid.East: Abstr.& Ind., Sci.Abstr., Soft.Abstr.Eng.
—BLDSC shelfmark: 8882.100000.

388 US ISSN 0082-5859
TRAFFIC LAWS COMMENTARY. 1963. irreg., latest 1982. price varies. National Committee on Uniform Traffic Laws and Ordinances, 405 Church St., Box 1409, Evanston, IL 60204.

380.5 US ISSN 0041-0705
TRAFFIC MANAGER. 1925. bi-m. $6. Daily Journal of Commerce, Box 10127, Portland, OR 97210. TEL 503-226-1311. Ed. Victor Graf. adv.; charts; illus.; stat.; circ. 7,112. (also avail. in microform from UMI)

614.86 US ISSN 0041-0721
HV675.A1
TRAFFIC SAFETY (CHICAGO). 1927. bi-m. $24 to non-members; members $19. National Safety Council, Industrial Section, 444 N. Michigan Ave., Chicago, IL 60611. TEL 800-621-7619. Ed. Dawn DeLong. adv.; bibl.; illus.; stat.; tr.lit.; index; circ. 20,000. (also avail. in microfiche from UMI) Indexed: ASCA, C.I.S. Abstr., CJPI.
—BLDSC shelfmark: 8882.190000.

388.1 US
TRAFFIC SAFETY (WASHINGTON); a report on activities under the Highway Safety Act of 1966. 1966. a. U.S. National Highway Traffic Safety Administration, 400 Seventh St., N.W., Washington, DC 20590. (Co-sponsor: U.S. Federal Highway Administration) Indexed: CJPI.

388.31 US
TRAFFIC SAFETY SERIES. irreg. (2-3/yr.). $19.95. Transaction Publishers, Transaction Periodicals Consortium, Department 3092, Rutgers University, New Brunswick, NJ 08903. TEL 908-932-2280. FAX 908-932-3138. Eds. Peter J. Cooper, J. Peter Rothe.
Description: Deals with issues ranging from drunk driving to seat belt use.

388.1 330 DK ISSN 0106-1852
TRAFIKOEKONOMISKE ENHEDSPRISER. 1977. a. free. Vejdirektoratet, Oekonomisk-Statistik Afdelning, Copenhagen, Denmark.

388.1 NZ ISSN 1170-7321
▼**TRANSEARCH.** 1990. irreg. (2-3/yr.). free. Transit New Zealand, Research and Development Section, P.O. Box 5084, Wellington, New Zealand. TEL 04-4996600. FAX 04-4966666. Ed. T. Roodra. circ. 1,800.
Description: Provides information on road, traffic, safety, and land transport studies.

T

TRANSPORTATION — ROADS AND TRAFFIC

388.31 355   US   ISSN 0041-1639
UC270
TRANSLOG; journal of military transportation management. 1970. m. $24. U.S. Military Traffic Management Command, Washington, DC 20315. TEL 202-545-6700. FAX 202-289-2040. (Orders to: Supt. of Documents, Washington, DC 20402) charts; illus.; circ. 29,000. (also avail. in microform from MCA,MIM,UMI) **Indexed:** Air Un.Lib.Ind., Ind.U.S.Gov.Per.
  Formerly: Transportation Proceedings.

388.1   SA   ISSN 0379-4792
TRANSPORT AND ROAD DIGEST/VERVOER- EN PADOORSIG. 1977. irreg., no.50, 1985. Division of Roads and Transport Technology - Divisie vir Pad- en Vervoertegnologie, Box 395, Pretoria 0001, South Africa. FAX 012-841-3232. TELEX 3-21312 SA. Ed. D. Cadle. circ. 3,000. **Indexed:** HRIS.
  Description: Summaries of research projects giving the backround and main results.

388 625.7   UK
TRANSPORT AND ROAD RESEARCH LABORATORY. RESEARCH REPORTS. 1985. irreg. Transport and Road Research Laboratory, Old Wokingham Rd., Crowthorne, Berks. RG1 6AU, England. TEL 0334-770758. FAX 0344-770198. TELEX 848272 TRRLCR G. **Indexed:** Dok.Str.
  Supersedes (as of 1985): Road Notes (ISSN 0080-3294) & Transport and Road Research; Which was formerly: Road Research (ISSN 0080-3308)

TRANSPORT STATISTICS GREAT BRITAIN. see *TRANSPORTATION — Abstracting, Bibliographies, Statistics*

625.7 690   US   ISSN 1043-4054
TE1
TRANSPORTATION BUILDER. 1923. 6/yr. $50. American Road & Transportation Builders Association, 501 School St., S.W., Washington, DC 20024. TEL 202-488-2722. FAX 202-488-3631. Ed. Meg Willett. adv.; bk.rev.; charts; illus.; index; circ. 5,000. **Indexed:** HRIS.
  Former titles: American Transportation Builder (ISSN 0149-4511); American Road Builder (ISSN 0003-0856)
  Description: For transportation construction professionals.

388.413   US
TRANSPORTATION IMPROVEMENT PROGRAM. a. $10. Omaha - Council Bluffs Metropolitan Area Planning Agency, 2222 Cuming St., Omaha, NE 68102-4328. TEL 402-444-6866. FAX 402-342-0949. circ. 500.
  Description: Identifies all transportation capital and service improvement projects scheduled for the following 6 years in Douglas, Sarpy, and Washington counties in Nebraska, and Mills and Pottawatamie counties in Iowa.

TRANSPORTATION JOURNAL. see *TRANSPORTATION*

625.7 388   US   ISSN 0360-859X
CODEN: SRTBDC
TRANSPORTATION RESEARCH BOARD SPECIAL REPORT. 1952. irreg., no.229, 1990. price varies. National Research Council, Transportation Research Board, 2101 Constitution Ave., N.W., Washington, DC 20418. TEL 202-334-3214. FAX 202-334-2519. circ. 3,250. (also avail. in microfiche) **Indexed:** Concr.Abstr., Dok.Str., GeoRef., Geotech.Abstr., HRIS.
  —BLDSC shelfmark: 8401.007800.
  Formerly (until no.144, 1974): Highway Research Board Special Publication (ISSN 0077-5622)
  Description: Addresses transportation policy issues of national significance.

625.7 388   US   ISSN 0361-1981
TE7   CODEN: TRREDM
TRANSPORTATION RESEARCH RECORD. 1963. irreg., no.1290, 1991. $865 to N. America; elsewhere $900. National Research Council, Transportation Research Board, 2101 Constitution Ave., N.W., Washington, DC 20418. TEL 202-334-3218. FAX 202-334-2519. circ. 3,250. (also avail. in microfiche) **Indexed:** Chem.Abstr., Dok.Str., GeoRef., Geotech.Abstr., Intl.Civil Eng.Abstr., Noise Pollut.Publ.Abstr., Ocean.Abstr., Pollut.Abstr., Sel.Water Res.Abstr., Soft.Abstr.Eng., W.R.C.Inf.
  —BLDSC shelfmark: 9026.275000.
  Formerly (until 1974): Highway Research Record (ISSN 0073-2206)
  Description: Presents technical research papers. *Refereed Serial*

388.31   US
TRANSPORTATION TOPICS. 1960. m. free. Transportation Department, Public Affairs Office, Box 1708, Cheyenne, WY 82002-9019. TEL 307-777-4437. FAX 307-777-4289. Ed. Keith Rounds. circ. 600.
  Formerly: Road Construction News.

388   CN   ISSN 0581-8079
TRAVEL ON SASKATCHEWAN HIGHWAYS. 1958. biennial. free. Department of Highways and Transportation, Design and Traffic Safety, 1855 Victoria Ave., Regina, Sask. S4P 3V5, Canada. TEL 306-787-4800. FAX 306-787-1007. Ed. Jon J. Wyatt. circ. 1,000.

UEBER BERG UND TAL. see *PUBLIC ADMINISTRATION*

388.3   US   ISSN 0277-2310
HE5614.2
U.S. DEPARTMENT OF TRANSPORTATION. HIGHWAY SAFETY STEWARDSHIP REPORT. 1974. a. U.S. Department of Transportation, 400 Seventh St. N.W., Washington, DC 20590. TEL 202-655-4000. (Order from: Supt. of Documents, Washington, DC 20402) stat.
  Former titles: Highway Safety Improvement Programs & Annual Report on Highway Safety Improvement Programs (ISSN 0098-3209)

625.7   US   ISSN 0361-4204
TE192
U.S. FEDERAL HIGHWAY ADMINISTRATION. FEDERALLY COORDINATED PROGRAM OF HIGHWAY RESEARCH AND DEVELOPMENT. 1975. a. U.S. Federal Highway Administration, Dept. of Transportation, Washington, DC 20590. TEL 202-426-0600. (Orders to: Supt. of Documents, Washington, DC 20402) illus. Key Title: Federally Coordinated Program of Highway Research and Development.
  Formerly: U.S. Federal Highway Administration. Research and Development Program.

388.413   GW
UNIVERSITAET MUENSTER. INSTITUT FUER VERKEHRSWISSENSCHAFT. BEITRAEGE. 1954. irreg. price varies. (Universitaet Muenster, Institut fuer Verkehrswissenschaft) Vandenhoeck & Ruprecht, Robert-Bosch-Breite 6, Postfach 3753, 3400 Goettingen, Germany. Ed. Helmut Seidenfuess. (back issues avail.)

388.1   DK   ISSN 0108-0385
V D L NYT. 1982. q. free. Vejdatalaboratoriet, Stationsalleen 42, 2730 Herlev, Denmark. illus.
  Formed by the merger of: T P S Nyt & Terminal-Nyt.

388.31   SW   ISSN 0283-7021
V T I ANNUAL REPORT. 1971. a. free. Statens Vaeg- och Trafikinstitut - Swedish Road and Traffic Research Institute, S-581 01 Linkoeping, Sweden. TEL 13204000. FAX 13141436. TELEX 50125-VTISGI-S. charts; circ. 2,000. **Indexed:** Dok.Str.
  —BLDSC shelfmark: 9258.903000.

338.1   SW   ISSN 0347-6049
V T I MEDDELANDE. (Text in Swedish; summaries in English) 1976. irreg. (50-60/yr.). free. Statens Vaeg- och Trafikinstitut - Swedish Road and Traffic Research Institute, S-581 01 Linkoeping, Sweden. **Indexed:** Dok.Str., HRIS.
  —BLDSC shelfmark: 5450.950000.

338.1   SW   ISSN 0347-6030
V T I RAPPORT. (Text in English and Swedish; summaries in English) 1971. irreg. (15-20/yr.). free. Statens Vaeg- och Trafikinstitut - Swedish Road and Traffic Research Institute, S-581 01 Linkoeping, Sweden. circ. 800.
  —BLDSC shelfmark: 9258.905000.

V W-AUTOGRAMM. see *BUSINESS AND ECONOMICS — Labor And Industrial Relations*

388 310   GW   ISSN 0083-5021
V W Z. (Verkehrswirtschaftliche Zahlen) 1954. a. free. Bundesverband des Deutschen Gueterfernverkehrs e.V., Haus des Strassenverkehrs, Postfach 930260, 6000 Frankfurt a.M. 93, Germany. TEL 069-7919-0. FAX 069-7919227. circ. 5,000. **Indexed:** Dok.Str.

VAROSI KOZLEKEDES/URBAN TRANSPORT. see *TRANSPORTATION — Railroads*

388.1   DK   ISSN 0107-0614
VEJDATALABORATORIET. RAPPORT. 1965. irreg. free. Vejdatalaboratoriet, Stationsalleen 42, 2730 Herlev, Denmark. illus.

388.312   SZ
VEREINIGUNG SCHWEIZERISCHER STRASSENFACHLEUTE. FORSCHUNGSBERICHTE. vol.5, 1974. irreg. price varies. Vereinigung Schweizerischer Strassenfachleute, Seefeldstr. 9, CH-8008 Zurich, Switzerland. TEL 01-2516914. FAX 01-2523130. charts; stat.; circ. 140.
  Former titles: Vereinigung Schweizerischer Strassenfachleute. Versuchsberichte; Vereinigung Schweizerischer Strassenfachmaenner. Versuchsbericht.

388.31   NE
VERKEERSKUNDE. 1949. 11/yr. fl.112 to non-members. Koninklijke Nederlandse Toeristenbond ANWB, Wassenaarseweg 220, Postbus 93200, 2509 BA The Hague, Netherlands. Ed. R. Hendriks. adv.; bk.rev.; illus.; circ. 2,500. **Indexed:** Dok.Str., Excerp.Med., Key to Econ.Sci.
  Formerly (until 1975): Verkeerstechniek (ISSN 0042-3998)

VERKEERSRECHT; juridical monthly for the road traffic, liability, damage and insurance. see *LAW*

388   AU
VERKEHR; internationale Fachzeitung fuer Verkehrswirtschaft. 1945. w. S.3400. Bohmann Druck und Verlag GmbH & Co. KG, Leberstr. 122, A-1110 Vienna, Austria. TEL 0222-74095. FAX 0222-74095-183. TELEX 132312. adv.; circ. 4,100. **Indexed:** Dok.Str.

388   GW   ISSN 0340-4536
TF3
VERKEHR UND TECHNIK; Zeitschrift fuer Verkehrstechnik, Verkehrspolitik, Verkehrswirtschaft. 1948. m. DM.175.20. Erich Schmidt Verlag GmbH & Co. (Bielefeld), Viktoriastr. 44A, Postfach 7330, 4800 Bielefeld 1, Germany. TEL 0521-583080. adv.; bk.rev.; charts; illus.; pat.; stat.; index; circ. 2,100. **Indexed:** Dok.Str., Excerp.Med.

VERKEHRS RUNDSCHAU. see *TRANSPORTATION*

388.31   GW   ISSN 0042-4013
VERKEHRSBLATT. 1947. bi-m. DM.129.60 (Europe DM.144; elsewhere DM.154.80). (Bundesministerium fuer Verkehr) Verkehrsblattverlag, Hohe Str. 39, Postfach 100555, 4600 Dortmund 1, Germany. FAX 0231-125640. adv.; bk.rev.; bibl.; illus.; index, cum.index; circ. 10,000 (controlled). (also avail. in microform from BHP) **Indexed:** Dok.Str.

388.413   GW
VERKEHRSDIENST. m. DM.133.20 (foreign DM.137.40). Heinrich Vogel Fachzeitschriften GmbH, Neumarkterstr. 18, Postfach 802020, 8000 Munich 80, Germany. TEL 089-43180-0. FAX 089-4312837.

VERKEHRSGESCHICHTLICHE BLAETTER. see *TRANSPORTATION — Railroads*

388.31   AU   ISSN 0042-4048
VERKEHRSPSYCHOLOGISCHER INFORMATIONSDIENST. 1962. a. free. Kuratorium fuer Verkehrssicherheit, Verkehrspsychologisches Institut, Oelzeltgasse 3, A-1031 Vienna, Austria. TEL 0222-71770171. FAX 0222-717709. TELEX 3222195. circ. 1,500. **Indexed:** Dok.Str.

625.7   SA   ISSN 0042-4978
VIA. 1960. 3-yr. free. Division of Roads and Transport Technology - Divisie vir Pad- en Vervoertegnologie, Box 395, Pretoria 0001, South Africa. FAX 012-841-3232. TELEX 3-21312 SA. Ed. D. Cadle. abstr.; circ. 8,000. **Indexed:** Dok.Str. **Description:** Gives information about current and completed research.

388.411   UK
VINTAGE ROADSCENE. 1984. q. £9. Ian Allan Ltd., Terminal House, Station Approach, Surrey TW17 8AS, England. TEL 0932-228950. Ed. S.W. Stevens-Stratten. bk.rev.; charts; illus.; circ. 18,000. (reprint service avail. from UMI) **Description:** News and features from the field of historic road transport.

388.1   US
VIRGINIA DEPARTMENT OF TRANSPORTATION BULLETIN. 1934. m. free to qualified personnel and libraries. Department of Transportation, 1401 E. Broad St., Richmond, VA 23219. TEL 804-786-4243. FAX 804-786-6250. Ed. Charles M. Armstrong. illus.; circ. 16,000. **Former titles:** Virginia Department of Highways and Transportation Bulletin; (until 1974): Virginia Highway Bulletin (ISSN 0042-6547)

614.86   UK   ISSN 0144-2694
WALK. 1950. 3/yr. $13.50. Pedestrians Association, 1-5 Wandsworth Rd., London SW8 2XX, England. TEL 01-735 3270. Ed. Ronald Binns. adv.; bk.rev.; abstr.; charts; illus.; index; circ. 1,200.
—BLDSC shelfmark: 9261.474400.
Former titles (until Nov. 1979): Arrive (ISSN 0031-3874); Pedestrian.

WEGEN; maandblad voor verkeer, grond-, water- en wegenbouw. see *ENGINEERING — Civil Engineering*

WISCONSIN. DEPARTMENT OF TRANSPORTATION. DIVISION OF PLANNING AND BUDGET. HIGHWAY MILEAGE DATA. see *TRANSPORTATION — Abstracting, Bibliographies, Statistics*

388.1   UK   ISSN 0043-8529
WORLD HIGHWAYS. 1950. 9/yr. $5. (International Road Federation, US) Route One Publishing Ltd., Vigilant House, 120 Wilton Rd., London SW1V 1JZ, England. FAX 202-479-0828. Ed. Hugh M. Gillespie. bk.rev.; charts; illus.; stat.; circ. 5,000. (also avail. in microform from UMI; reprint service avail. from UMI) **Indexed:** Dok.Str., HRIS.

388.413   US   ISSN 0511-0440
WYOMING TRUCKER. 1952. bi-m. free. Wyoming Trucking Association, Inc., Box 1909, Casper, WY 82602. TEL 307-234-1579. Ed. Sharon D. Nichols. adv.; circ. 4,200. (back issues avail.)

388.1   GW   ISSN 0341-2334
ZEITSCHRIFT FUER VERKEHRSERZIEHUNG. 1955. 4/yr. DM.25. Rot-Gelb-Gruen Lehrmittel GmbH, Theodor-Heuss-Str. 3, 3300 Braunschweig, Germany. TEL 0531-809070. FAX 0531-8090721. TELEX 952357. Ed. D. Hohenadel. adv.; bk.rev.; circ. 5,000. (controlled). **Formerly:** Schulverkehrswacht. **Description:** Features traffic safety and education for children. Deals with risks, bicycles, traffic rules, and accidents. Includes statistics and charts.

388.31   GW   ISSN 0044-3654
HE331
ZEITSCHRIFT FUER VERKEHRSSICHERHEIT. (Occasional articles in English) 1955. q. DM.136. Verlag T U V Rheinland GmbH, Am grauen Stein, 5000 Cologne 91, Germany. TEL 0221-8393-0. FAX 0221-8873-659. Ed. C. Graf Hoyos. adv.; bk.rev.; abstr.; bibl.; charts; illus.; index; circ. 1,400. **Indexed:** Dok.Str., Ergon.Abstr., Ger.J.Psych.

380.5   GW   ISSN 0044-3670
HE5
ZEITSCHRIFT FUER VERKEHRSWISSENSCHAFT. 1921. q. DM.74.40. Verkehrs-Verlag J. Fischer, Paulusstr. 1, Postfach 140265, 4000 Duesseldorf 4, Germany. TEL 0211-673056. Ed. Rainer Willeke. adv.; bk.rev.; circ. 800. **Indexed:** Dok.Str., Key to Econ.Sci., P.A.I.S.For.Lang.Ind.

338.31   CC   ISSN 1001-7372
ZHONGGUO GONGLU XUEBAO/CHINA ROAD JOURNAL. (Text in Chinese) q. Zhongguo Gonglu Xuehui - China Road Society, 48 Beisanhuan Zhonglu, Beijing 100088, People's Republic of China. TEL 2013399. Ed. Chen Binglin.
—BLDSC shelfmark: 3180.182000.

TRANSPORTATION — Ships And Shipping

387   UK
A B C CAR FERRY GUIDE. 1979. a. £20. Reed Travel Group (Subsidiary of: Reed International PLC), Church St., Dustable, Bedfordshire LU5 4HB, England. TEL 0582-600111. TELEX 82168-AIRABC-G. Ed. Alison Barker. adv.; circ. 5,000 (controlled). **Formerly:** St. James Press Car Ferry Guide.

387.4   UK
A B C PASSENGER SHIPPING GUIDE. 1952. m. £105. Reed Travel Group (Subsidiary of: Reed International PLC), Church St., Dunstable, Bedfordshire LU5 4HB, England. TEL 0582-600111. TELEX 82168-AIRABC-G. Ed. A. Baties. adv.; index; circ. 6,500. **Formerly:** A B C Shipping Guide (ISSN 0001-0480) **Description:** Contains time-tables.

387   UK
A B O I CATALOGUE. 1974. a. Association of British Oceanic Industries, 32-38 Leman St., London W18 EW, England.

387   AT
A B ORGANISATION MARINE PORTFOLIO. a. A.B. Organisation Pty. Ltd., P.O. Box 319, Avalon Beach, N.S.W. 2107, Australia. TEL 02-918-8322. FAX 02-918-8884. **Description:** Deals with Australian Marine industry with details of related magazines published by the A.B. Organisation.

359.97   FR   ISSN 0373-9090
VK1000
A I S M. BULLETIN/I A L A BULLETIN. (Text in English, French) 1958. q. 100 Fr. Association Internationale de Signalisation Maritime - International Association of Lighthouse Authorities, 20 ter, rue Schnapper, 78100 Saint Germain en Laye, France. TEL 33-1-34-51-70-01. FAX 33-1-34-51-82-05. TELEX 695 499 F. Ed. P. Ridgway. adv.; bk.rev.; circ. 600. Key Title: Bulletin de l'A.I.S.M. **Description:** Technical papers and general information articles on aids to navigation technique and history.

387   UY
A L A M A R INFORMATIVO. 1975. w. $100. Asociacion Latinoamericana de Armadores, Rio Negro 1394-Of. 502, Casilla de Correo 767, Montevideo, Uruguay. TEL 2-987449. FAX 05982-920732. TELEX 26431-ALAMAR-UY. adv.; bk.rev.

387   US
A W O LETTER. 1944. bi-w. $75. American Waterways Operators, 1600 Wilson Blvd., Ste. 1000, Arlington, VA 22209. TEL 703-841-9300. FAX 703-841-0389. Ed. Thia Fisk. circ. 1,500. **Formerly:** A W O Weekly Letter.

A W T A O ANNUAL REPORT. (Association of Water Transportation Accounting Officers) see *BUSINESS AND ECONOMICS — Accounting*

A W T A O BULLETIN. (Association of Water Transportation Accounting Officers) see *BUSINESS AND ECONOMICS — Accounting*

387   NE
DE AAN- EN AFVOER OVER ZEE IN DE NEDERLANDSE ZEEHAVENS. 1982. q. Nationale Havenraad, Kneuterdijk 6, 2514 EN Gravenhage, Netherlands. TEL 070-618757. FAX 070-614600. (back issues avail.)

ABERDEEN PORT HANDBOOK. see *BUSINESS AND ECONOMICS — Trade And Industrial Directories*

387.109   BE
ACADEMIE ROYALE DE MARINE DE BELGIQUE. COMMUNICATIONS/KONINKLIJKE BELGISCHE MARINE ACADEMIE. MEDEDELINGEN. (Text in Dutch, French; summaries in English, French) 1936. irreg. (approx. a.). 720 BEF to individuals; institutions exchange basis. Nationaal Scheepvaartmuseum, Steinplein 1, B-2000 Antwerp, Belgium. TEL 03-232-0850. Ed. G. Asaert. adv.; bibl.; illus. (back issues avail.) **Formerly (until 1986):** Academie de Marine. Communications - Marine Academie. Mededelingen. **Description:** Dedicated to the study of shipping and maritime history, including shipbuilding, navigation, and maritime economics, mainly in Belgium and Zaire (the former Belgian Congo).

387   PO
ADMINISTRACAO DO PORTO DE LISBOA. RELATORIO E CONTAS. 1935. a. free. Administracao do Porto de Lisboa, Divisao de Marketing e Relacoes Publicas, Rua da Junqueira, 94, 1300 Lisbon, Portugal. TEL 1-3637151. FAX 1-646900. TELEX 18529-PORLI. circ. 1,000. **Former titles:** Administracao do Porto de Lisboa. Relatorio; Administracao Geral do Porto de Lisboa. Relatorio.

387   IT
AGENDA NAUTICA. 1955. a. L.28000. Istituto Idrografico della Marina, Passo Osservatorio, 4, 16134 Genoa, Italy. TEL 10-265451. FAX 10-266428. TELEX 270435 MARIDR I. Ed.Bd. circ. 22,000. **Description:** Provides seaman and navigation information. Contains Medieval nautical charts, anecdotes about Columbus, and historical articles.

387   US
AMERICAN BUREAU OF SHIPPING. RECORD. 1869. a. (plus supplement). $520. American Bureau of Shipping, 2 World Trade Center, 106th Fl., New York, NY 10048. TEL 212-839-5000. FAX 212-839-5130. TELEX 232099 ABNY UR. Ed. William R. Hartman. circ. 209. **Indexed:** BMT.

387   US
AMERICAN CANALS. 1972. q. $14. American Canal Society, 809 Rathton Rd., York, PA 17403. TEL 717-843-4035. Ed. David F. Ross. circ. 850. **Description:** For canal buffs, professional planners, historians and archeologists. Covers canal news, history, activities and practical information from the US and around the world.

387   US
AMERICAN INSTITUTE FOR SHIPPERS ASSOCIATIONS. NEWS. m. American Institute for Shippers Associations, Box 33457, Washington, DC 20033. TEL 202-628-0933.

623.87   US   ISSN 0002-9866
VM1
AMERICAN MARINE ENGINEER.* 1906. m. National Marine Engineers Beneficial Association, 444 N. Capitol, Ste. 800, Washington, DC 20001. Ed. Victor Rollo. charts; illus.

AMERICAN MARITIME OFFICER. see *LABOR UNIONS*

387.5   US   ISSN 0364-7374
HE745
AMERICAN MERCHANT MARINE CONFERENCE. PROCEEDINGS. 1935. a. $20. Propeller Club of the United States, 3927 Old Lee Hwy., No. 101A, Fairfax, VA 22030. TEL 703-691-2777. FAX 703-691-4173.

380.5   US   ISSN 0160-225X
HF1
AMERICAN SHIPPER; ports, transportation and industry. 1959. m. $30. Howard Publications, Inc., 33 S. Hogan St., Ste. 230, Box 4728, Jacksonville, FL 32201. TEL 904-355-2601. Ed. David A. Howard. adv.; charts; illus.; mkt.; stat.; circ. 10,180. (also avail. in microform from UMI; reprint service avail. from UMI) **Indexed:** B.P.I., Bus.Ind., P.A.I.S., Tr.& Indus.Ind.
—BLDSC shelfmark: 0857.100000.
Former titles (until 1976): Florida Journal of Commerce - American Shipper (ISSN 0097-6237); (until 1974): Florida Journal of Commerce (ISSN 0015-413X)

TRANSPORTATION — SHIPS AND SHIPPING

387   US
ANCHOR NEWS. 1969. bi-m. Manitowoc Maritime Museum, 75 Maritime Dr., Manitowoc, WI 54220. Ed. Bonnie Spencer. adv.; bk.rev.; circ. 2,400.
Indexed: Amer.Hist.& Life, Hist.Abstr.
Description: Includes articles on the history of the Upper Great Lakes, primarily Lake Superior and Lake Michigan.

387   FR   ISSN 0066-2550
ANNUAIRE DE LA MARINE MARCHANDE. 1904. a. 440 F. Comite Central des Armateurs de France, 73 Bld. Haussmann, 75008 Paris, France. FAX 42-65-71-89. adv.; circ. 650.
—BLDSC shelfmark: 1070.800000.

623.89   AT   ISSN 1035-6878
VK927
ANNUAL AUSTRALIAN NOTICES TO MARINERS. 1933. a. free. Department of Defence, Hydrographic Service, Sydney, Australia. FAX 02-925-4835. Ed. M. Bolger. illus.; index; circ. 3,200.
Formerly: Annual Summary of Australian Notices to Mariners (ISSN 0727-2405)

623.82   JA   ISSN 0448-3294
ANNUAL STATISTICS OF MARITIME SAFETY. (Text in Japanese) 1950. a. Kaijo Hoan-cho - Maritime Safety Agency, 1-3, Kasumigaseki 2-chome, Chiyoda-ku, Tokyo 100, Japan. stat.

387 620   UK   ISSN 0261-2720
ANNUAL SUMMARY OF MERCHANT SHIPS COMPLETED IN THE WORLD. 1892. a. free. Lloyd's Register of Shipping, 71 Fenchurch St., London EC3M 4BS, England. TEL 071-709-9166. (US subscr. addr.: Lloyd's Register of Shipping, 17 Battery Place, New York, NY 10004)
Formerly: Annual Summary of Merchant Ships Launched, Completed in the World; Annual Summary of Merchant Ships Launched in the World (ISSN 0066-4391)
Description: Statistical summary of world completions and launches for all merchant ships of 100 gross tonnage and above.

387.164 381   FR
L'ANTENNE. 1946. d. 2390 F. Smei l'Antenne, 17 rue Venture, P.O. Box 1811, F-13221 Marseille cedex 1, France. FAX 91-55-58-97. TELEX 400 865. adv.; circ. 10,000.

387 623.8   GW
ANTRIEB; Fachzeitschrift fuer Schiffstechnik und Seeverkehrswirtschaft. 1955. bi-m. DM.42($12) Verein der Schiffsingenieure in Bremen e.V., Geeren 26-28, 2800 Bremen 1, Germany. Ed. Herwig Pollem. adv.; bk.rev.; stat.; tr.lit.; circ. 4,000.

ANTWERP PORT ANNUAL. see *BUSINESS AND ECONOMICS — Trade And Industrial Directories*

386   BL
ANUARIO DE PORTOS E NAVIOS. a. $30. Revista Tecnica e Informativa Ltda., Rua Leandro Martins 10, Caixa Postal 2791, Rio de Janeiro, Brazil. Ed. Brasilio Accioly. adv.; charts; stat.

621.8 658   HU   ISSN 0003-6242
ANYAGMOZGATAS-CSOMAGOLAS. (Text in Hungarian; summaries in English, German, Russian) 1956. m. $28. (Muszaki es Termeszettudomanyi Egyesuletek Szovetsege) Lapkiado Vallalat, Lenin korut 9-11, 1073 Budapest 7, Hungary. TEL 1-222-408. (Subscr. to: Kultura, Box 149, H-1389 Budapest, Hungary) (Co-sponsor: Anyagmozgatasi es Csomagolasi Intezet) Ed. Laszlo Felfoldi. adv.; bk.rev.; bibl.; charts; illus.; circ. 1,600. *Indexed:* Food Sci.& Tech.Abstr., Hung.Build.Bull, Packag.Sci.Tech.

387   US
ARBITRATOR. q. free. Society of Maritime Arbitrators, 61 Broadway, Ste. 1650, New York, NY 10006-2701. TEL 212-483-0616. FAX 212-480-3320. circ. 500.

387 971   CN
ARGONAUTA. (Text in English, French) 1984. Can.$25 to individuals; institutions Can.$50. Memorial University of Newfoundland, Maritime Studies Research Unit, St. John's, Nfld. K2A 3Z6, Canada. TEL 709-737-8424. FAX 709-737-8424. TELEX 016-4677. (Subscr. to: Canadian Nautical Research Society, P.O. Box 7008, Sta. J, Ottawa, Ont. K2A 3Z6, Canada) Eds. Lewis R. Fischer, Gerald E. Panting. adv.; bk.rev.; circ. 300.
Description: Publishes articles, news and information on publications and conferences of interest to Canadian maritime historians.

387.54   UK
ARROWSMITH'S BRISTOL CHANNEL TIDE TABLE. 1835. a. £2.40. J.W. Arrowsmith Ltd., Winterstoke Rd., Bristol BS3 2NT, England. adv.; circ. 5,000.

L'ART ET LA MER. see *ART*

387   HK
ASIAN SHIPPING. (Text in English) 1978. m. $50. Asia Trade Journals Ltd., Box 20014, Hennessy Rd., Hong Kong. FAX 5278753. Ed. A.G. Barnett. adv.; charts; illus.; circ. 6,700.

387 380   UK   ISSN 0262-1630
HE557.G7
ASSOCIATED BRITISH PORTS HANDBOOK. 1982. a. £10. Charter International Publications Ltd., Castle Chambers, Castle Acre, King's Lynn, Norfolk PE32 2BQ, England. TEL 07605-634. FAX 07605-625. TELEX 817440. Ed. James P. Moriarty. adv.; circ. 12,000.

387   UK
ASSOCIATED BRITISH PORTS HOLDINGS PLC. ANNUAL REPORT AND ACCOUNTS. 1963. a. free. Associated British Ports Holdings PLC, 150 Holborn, London EC1N 2LR, England.
Formerly: British Transport Docks Board. Annual Report and Accounts (ISSN 0068-2659)

387 623.8 629.1   FR   ISSN 0066-9814
                       CODEN: BATMA8
ASSOCIATION TECHNIQUE MARITIME ET AERONAUTIQUE, PARIS. BULLETIN. (Text in French; summaries in English and French) 1890. a. 450 F. to non-members. Association Technique Maritime et Aeronautique, 47 rue de Monceau, 75008 Paris, France. Ed.Bd. index; circ. 1,000. (back issues avail.)
Indexed: Appl.Mech.Rev.

387   AT   ISSN 0314-0377
AUSTRALASIAN SHIPPING RECORD. 1970. bi-m. Aus.$18 (foreign Aus.$20). Australasian Maritime Historical Society, P.O. Box 89, Lobethal, S.A. 5241, Australia. TEL 389-4292. Ed. Ronald H. Parsons. bk.rev.; index. (back issues avail.)

387   AT   ISSN 1031-3516
AUSTRALIA AND THE SEA. 1988. a. free to qualified personnel. Baird Publications Pty. Ltd., 10 Oxford St., South Yarra, Vic. 3141, Australia. TEL 03-826-8741. FAX 03-827-0704. Ed. Neil Baird. adv.; circ. 8,000.
Description: For overseas companies, individuals and government agencies who are likely to purchase marine products.

387 639.2   AT
AUSTRALIAN CENTRE FOR MARITIME STUDIES. OCCASIONAL PAPERS IN MARITIME AFFAIRS. 1982. a. Aus.$35 to individuals (foreign Aus.$50); institutions Aus.$60 (foreign Aus.$75); corporates Aus.$250 (foreign Aus.$265)(includes Maritime Studies)(effective 1991-92). Australian Centre for Maritime Studies, P.O. Box E20, Queen Victoria Terrace, Canberra, A.C.T. 2600, Australia. Eds. M. Ward, W.S. Bateman. circ. 500. (back issues avail.)

AUSTRALIAN SEA HERITAGE. see *MUSEUMS AND ART GALLERIES*

387 551.46   IT   ISSN 0392-2294
AUTOMAZIONE NAVALE; Tecnologie per il Mare. 1969. m. L.100000. P.O. Box 7463, 16167 Genoa Nervi, Italy. TEL 010-3724340. FAX 010-326447. TELEX NAVAUT 281148. Ed. Decio Lucano. adv.; bk.rev.; circ. 8,000. (back issues avail.)
Description: Deals with ships, ports, shipyards, maritime communication, offshore activities and marine operators. Includes informative articles on development and progress in boating technology.

623.89   FR   ISSN 0180-9938
VK798
AVIS AUX NAVIGATEURS. 1886. w. 772 F. Service Hydrographique et Oceanographique de la Marine, 3 av. Octave Greard, 00300 Armees, France. TEL 98-22-10-80. FAX 98-43-18-11. TELEX HYDRO 940568. (Subscr. to: EPSHOM, B.P. 426, 29275 Brest Cedex, France) illus.

387   DK
B I M C O BULLETIN. bi-m. Baltic and International Maritime Conference, Bagsvaerdvej 161, DK 2880 Bagsvaerd, Denmark. TEL 4544-444500. FAX 4544-444450. TELEX 19086. adv.; bk.rev.; index; circ. 3,000.
Description: Articles on developments affecting the shipping industry at large.

B M T ABSTRACTS. (British Maritime Technology Ltd.) see *TRANSPORTATION — Abstracting, Bibliographies, Statistics*

387   BF
BAHAMAS. MINISTRY OF TRANSPORT. PORT AND MARINE DEPARTMENT. ANNUAL REPORT. a. Ministry of Transport, Port and Marine Department, P.O. Box N-8175, Nassau N.P., Bahamas.
FAX 809-322-5545.

387   SP
BARCELONA PORT; guia de servicios del puerto de Barcelona. 1978. a. 1300 ptas. Publicaciones Men-Car, S.A., Paseo de Colon 24, 08002 Barcelona, Spain. TEL 93-301-5516. FAX 93-318-6645. Eds. Juan Cardona, Manuel Cardona. adv.; circ. 15,000.
Formerly: Port (Year).

387   UK
BARROW AND SILLOTH DOCKS TIDAL PREDICTIONS. a. Associated British Ports, Port Office, Ramsden Dock Rd., Barrow in Furness, Cumbria LA14 2TW, England. TEL 0229-22911. FAX 0229-35822.

BASIC PORT STATISTICS OF INDIA. see *TRANSPORTATION — Abstracting, Bibliographies, Statistics*

387   BE
BELGIUM. ADMINISTRATION DES AFFAIRES MARITIMES ET DE LA NAVIGATION. RAPPORT ANNUEL SUR L'EVOLUTION DE LA FLOTTE DE PECHE. a. Administration des Affaires Maritimes et de la Navigation, 104 rue d'Arlon, 1040 Brussels, Belgium. TEL 02-233-12-11. FAX 02-230-30-02. TELEX 61880 VERTRA B.
Former titles: Belgium. Administration de la Marine et de la Navigation Interieure. Rapport Annuel sur l'Evoltuion de la Flotte de Peche; Belgium. Administration de la Marine. Rapport Annuel sur l'Evolution de la Flotte de Peche.

BENEDICT ON ADMIRALTY. see *LAW — International Law*

BERICHTEN AAN ZEEVARENDEN. see *GEOGRAPHY*

387 623.8   NE   ISSN 0006-4661
BLAUWE WIMPEL; maandblad voor scheepvaart en scheepsbouw in de lage landen. 1946. m. fl.90. C. de Boer Jr. N.V., Postbus 507, 1200 AM Hilversum, Netherlands. Ed. Ineke van Haga. adv.; bk.rev.; charts; illus.; index; circ. 8,000.

BOATBUILDER'S INTERNATIONAL DIRECTORY; the boatbuilder's source book of designers, kit makers and suppliers. see *SPORTS AND GAMES — Boats And Boating*

BOATING INDUSTRY MARINE BUYERS' GUIDE. see *BUSINESS AND ECONOMICS — Trade And Industrial Directories*

387   US
BOHMAN OCEAN SHIPPING NEWS SUMMARY. 1982. m. $29.95. Bohman Industrial Traffic Consultants, Inc., 32 Pleasant St., Box 889, Gardner, MA 01440. TEL 617-632-1913. Ed. Raynard F. Bohman, Jr.

387   PO   ISSN 0006-596X
BOLETIM DO PORTO DE LISBOA. 1951. q. free. Administracao do Porto de Lisboa, Divisao de Marketing e Relacoes Publicas, Rua da Junqueira, 94, 1300 Lisbon, Portugal. illus.; stat.; circ. 2,000.

TRANSPORTATION — SHIPS AND SHIPPING

387　　　　　　　　　AG
BOLETIN MARITIMO DE LA EXPORTACION ARGENTINA. 1918. s-w. $744. Editorial Boletin Maritimo S.C.A., Aguero 892, 1171 Buenos Aires, Argentina. Ed. Luis Kramer. adv.; circ. 3,500.

BOSTON SEA AND AIR PORT HANDBOOK. see *BUSINESS AND ECONOMICS — Trade And Industrial Directories*

387　　　　　　　　　UK
THE BRISTOL PORT COMPANY. 1886. a. free to qualified personnel. The Bristol Port Company, St. Andrews Rd., Avonmouth, Bristol BS11 9DQ, England. TEL 0272-820000. FAX 0272-820698. TELEX 44240. Ed. Julie Gough. adv.; circ. 3,000.
　　Former titles: Port of Bristol Authority; Port of Bristol. Handbook.

387　380　　UK　　ISSN 0265-8178
BRITISH COLUMBIA PORTS HANDBOOK 1984. 1984. biennial. £10. Charter International Publications Ltd., Castle Chambers, Castle Acre, King's Lynn, Norfolk PE32 2BQ, England. TEL 07605-634. FAX 07605-625. TELEX 817440. Ed. James P. Moriarty. adv.; circ. 6,000.

623.82　　　　　　　UK
BRITISH MARINE INDUSTRIES FEDERATION HANDBOOK. 1947. a. £5. British Marine Industries Federation, Boating Industry House, Vale Rd., Weybridge, Surrey KT13 9NS, England. TEL 0932-854511. FAX 0932-852874. TELEX 885471. Ed. Susan Grant. adv.; circ. 1,500.
　　Formerly: Ship and Boat Builders National Federation Handbook.

387　　　　　　　　　UK
BRITISH MARITIME TECHNOLOGY NEWS. 1980. 3/yr. free. British Maritime Technology Ltd., Orlando House, 1 Waldegrove Rd., Teddington, Middlesex TW11 8LZ, England. charts; illus.; circ. 7,000.
　　Formerly: N M I News (ISSN 0260-4817).

386　　　　　UK　　ISSN 0068-2683
HE663
BRITISH WATERWAYS BOARD. ANNUAL REPORT AND ACCOUNTS. 1963. a. price varies. British Waterways Board, Greycaine Rd., Watford, Hertfordshire WD2 4JR, England. TEL 0923-226422. FAX 0923-226081.

623.8　　　　　CI　　ISSN 0007-215X
BRODOGRADNJA. (Text in Croatian or Serbian; summaries in English, German, Russian) 1950. bi-m. $100. (Ministarstvo Znanosti, Tehnologije i Informatike Republike Hrvatske) Hrvatsko Brodogradevno Drustvo "Jadranbroad", V. Holjevca 20, 41020 Zagreb, Croatia. TEL 041-528-699. FAX 41-527-469. TELEX YUBROD-21266. Ed. Dragan Stulhofer. adv. contact: B&W page $700. bk.rev.; abstr.; bibl.; illus.; index; circ. 800. Indexed: BMT.
　　—BLDSC shelfmark: 2349.200000.
　　Description: Publishes original scientific papers and professional papers on all aspects of shipbuilding in Yugoslavia.

623.8　　　　　PL　　ISSN 0007-2990
BUDOWNICTWO OKRETOWE. (Text in various languages) 1956. m. $51. (Stowarzyszenie Inzynierow i Technikow Mechanikow Polskich) Oficyna Wydawnicza SIMP Press, Ltd., Ul. Zurawia 22, 00-515 Warsaw, Poland. (Dist. in UK by: Earlscourt Publications Ltd., 129 Chiswick High Rd., London W4 1PP, England) Ed. Zbigniew Grzywaczewski. adv.; bk.rev.; illus.; index; circ. 700. Indexed: ISMEC.

BULK CARRIER REGISTER. see *PETROLEUM AND GAS*

BULLETIN FROM JOHNNY CAKE HILL. see *HISTORY — History Of North And South America*

387.5　　　　　　　FR
BULLETIN OFFICIEL DE LA MARINE MARCHANDE. irreg.? Imprimerie Nationale, Service des Ventes, 59128 Flers en Escrebieux, France.

BULLINGER'S POSTAL AND SHIPPERS GUIDE FOR THE UNITED STATES AND CANADA. see *COMMUNICATIONS — Postal Affairs*

623.8　　　　　FR　　ISSN 0007-5752
TJ2
BUREAU VERITAS. BULLETIN TECHNIQUE. (Editions in English and French) 1919. 6/yr. 255 F. Bureau Veritas, Cedex 44, 92077 Paris la Defense, France. Ed. Philippe Boisson. bk.rev.; bibl.; illus.; stat.; index; circ. 2,500 (Fr.ed.); 3,500 (Eng.ed.). Indexed: Excerp.Med., INIS Atomind.
　　—BLDSC shelfmark: 2911.000000.

387　　　　　　　　　US
C I B DAILY MARITIME NEWS BULLETIN. 1897. d. $1260 (foreign $1670). Congressional Information Bureau, Inc., 1325 G St., N.W., Ste. 1005, Washington, DC 20005. TEL 202-347-2275. FAX 202-347-2278. Ed. R. Cazalas. cum.index. (back issues avail.)
　　Description: Maritime news, including regulation, promotion, congressional activities, courts, steamship lines, legal matters, conventions and seminars.

387　　　　　　　　　SW
C M I NEWS LETTER. 1975. q. (International Maritime Committee - Comite Maritime International) Almquist & Wiksell International, P.O. Box 638, S-101 28 Stockholm, Sweden. circ. 2,500.
　　Supersedes in part (since 1978): International Maritime Committee. Documentation (ISSN 0538-8643)

387　　　　　　　　　SW
C M I YEAR BOOK. 1978. a. (International Maritime Committee - Comite Maritime International) Almquist & Wiksell International, P.O. Box 638, S-101 28 Stockholm, Sweden. circ. 2,500.
　　Supersedes in part (since 1978): International Maritime Committee. Documentation (ISSN 0538-8643)

CANADIAN SHIPPER. see *TRANSPORTATION — Trucks And Trucking*

623.87　　　　CN　　ISSN 0008-4980
CANADIAN SHIPPING AND MARINE ENGINEERING. 1911. m. Can.$30. Arthurs Publications Ltd., 5805 Whittle Rd., Ste.208, Mississauga, Ont. L4Z 2J1, Canada. TEL 416-568-4131. Ed. Gary Arthurs. adv.; bk.rev.; circ. 3,276. Indexed: BMT, Can.B.P.I., Pollut.Abstr.
　　—BLDSC shelfmark: 3044.709000.

CANAL SOCIETY OF OHIO. NEWSLETTER. see *HISTORY — History Of North And South America*

387　　　　　　　　　US
CANAL TIMES. 1989. q. donation. P.O. Box 4346, Clifton Park, NY 12065. FAX 518-457-6506.
　　Description: To bring various users, workers, and organizations closer together toward a common goal of enhancing the canal systems.

387　380　　UK　　ISSN 0263-7073
CANARY ISLANDS SHIPPING HANDBOOK 1983. 1980. a. £10. Charter International Publications Ltd., Castle Chambers, Castle Acre, King's Lynn, Norfolk PE32 2BQ, England. TEL 07605-634. FAX 07605-625. TELEX 817440. Ed. James P. Moriarty. adv.; circ. 6,000.

623.89　　　　　　　AT
CAPE HORNER JOURNAL. 1960. q. Aus.$2. Cape Horners - Australia Inc., c/o James Hopton, 63 Hurtle Sq., Adelaide, SA 5000, Australia. TEL 81 232-1110. Ed. Jason Hopton. adv.; bk.rev.; circ. 250.
　　Formerly: Cape Horners - Australia. Newsletter.

387　380　　CN　　ISSN 0318-3742
CAPTAIN LILLIE'S COAST GUIDE AND RADIOTELEPHONE DIRECTORY. 1936. biennial. Can.$16. Progress Publishing Co. Ltd., 1765 Bellevue Ave., West Vancouver, B.C. V7V 1A8, Canada. TEL 604-922-6717. FAX 604-922-1739.

387.164　　　　　　　HK
CARGO CLAN. (Text in English) 1976. q. free. Emphasis HK Ltd., 10-F, Wilson House, 19-27 Wyndham St., Central, Hong Kong. TEL 521-5392. FAX 810-6738. Ed. Geraldine Moor. adv.: B&W page $550, color page $850; trim 305 x 223; adv. contact: Cecilia Clinch. circ. 10,000 (controlled). (back issues avail.)
　　Description: Features cargo news of the Cathay Pacific Airways and topics of general interest to the airfreight industry.

387　　　　　　　　　HK　　ISSN 0252-9610
CARGONEWS ASIA. (Text in English) 1977. s-m. $25.50 in Southeast Asia; elsewhere $59.50. Far East Trade Press Ltd., 2-F Kai Tak Commercial Bldg., 317 Des Voeux Rd., Central, Hong Kong. TEL 5453028. FAX 5446979. Ed. Martin Savery. adv.; circ. 12,840.
　　Description: Provides the region's freight professionals with news and future coverage about the freighting business.

387.164　　　　　　　UK
CARGOWARE INTERNATIONAL. 1989. m. National Magazine Co. Ltd., 72 Broadwick St., London W1V 2BP, England. TEL 071-439-5000. FAX 071-439-5602. Ed. Andrew Foxcroft. adv.; circ. 8,600.
　　Description: Information on container box and handling equipment and hardware.

387　　　　　GW　　ISSN 0172-9314
VM1
CARGOWORLD; Europe's transport newsletter. (Text in English) 1956. w. DM.564 (foreign DM.612). Deutscher Verkehrs-Verlag GmbH, Nordkanalstr. 36, 2000 Hamburg 1, Germany. TEL 040-23714165. FAX 040-23714-123. Ed. Alison Bailey. adv.: B&W page DM.3050; trim 260 x 170. bk.rev.; circ. 18,000.
　　Description: Covers developments in all fields of the international transportation industry.

387　　　　　　　　　JM
CARIBBEAN PORTS HANDBOOK. a. (Caribbean Shipping Association) Creative Communications, Inc., Ltd., P.O. Box 105, Kingston 10, Jamaica, W.I. TEL 809-92-74271. FAX 809-92-62217. Ed. Angela deFreitas.

387　　　　　UK　　ISSN 0268-0815
HE565.A3
CASUALTY RETURN. 1891. a. $110. Lloyd's Register of Shipping, 71 Fenchurch St., London EC3M 4BS, England. TEL 071-709-9166. (Subscr. address in US: Lloyd's Register of Shipping, 17 Battery Place, New York, NY 10004)
　　Former titles: Casualty Return Statistical Summary of Merchant Ships Totally Lost, Broken Up, Etc (ISSN 0261-2712); Casualty Return Statistical Summary (ISSN 0008-7572); Merchant Ships Totally Lost, Broken Up, Etc.
　　Description: Annual statistical summary and listing of all merchant ships lost or reported broken up.

387　　　　　　　　　AG
CENTRO DE NAVEGACION TRANSATLANTICA. C.N.T. HANDBOOK. RIVER PLATE HANDBOOK FOR SHIPOWNERS AND AGENTS. Cover title: Centro de Navegacion Transatlantica. C.N.T. Year Book; Ship Owners' and Agents' Handbook, River Plate Ports. (Text in English) 1972. every 3 years. $42. Centro de Navegacion Transatlantica, Maipu 521, 1006 Buenos Aires, Argentina. Ed. Victor L.M. Fricker. adv.; circ. 2,000.
　　Supersedes a similar publication issued 1933-1966 as: M A R Year Book.

387　　　　　　　　　CE
CEYLON SHIPPING CORPORATION. ANNUAL REPORT & STATEMENT OF ACCOUNTS. (Text in English) a. Ceylon Shipping Corporation, Box 1718, Colombo, Sri Lanka.

387　　　　　　　　　US
CHARTERING ANNUAL. 1954. a. $95. Maritime Research, Inc., 499 Ernston Rd., Box 805, Parlin, NJ 08859. TEL 201-727-8040. adv.; abstr.; charts; index.
　　Description: Offers the shipping industry a yearly listing of charter fixture information.

CHERBOURG PORT HANDBOOK. see *BUSINESS AND ECONOMICS — Trade And Industrial Directories*

387　　　　　　　　　CH
CHINESE SEAMEN'S NEWS. m. National Chinese Seamen's Union, 2nd Fl., No. 115, Changchow S. Rd. Sec.1, Taipei, Taiwan, Republic of China.

387.54　　　　　　　BG
CHITTAGONG PORT AUTHORITY. PORT FOLIO, PORT OF CHITTAGONG. (Text in English) m. Chittagong Port Authority, Box 2013, Chittagong, Bangladesh.
　　Supersedes: Chittagong Port Authority. Monthly Bulletin.

TRANSPORTATION — SHIPS AND SHIPPING

387   BG
CHITTAGONG PORT AUTHORITY. YEARBOOK. (Text in English) a. Chittagong Port Authority, Box 2013, Chittagong, Bangladesh.
Formerly: Chittagong Port Trust. Yearbook of Information (ISSN 0069-3723)

623.82   CC   ISSN 1000-6982
CHUANBO GONGCHENG/SHIP ENGINEERING. (Text in Chinese; abstracts in English) 1979. bi-m. $2 per no. Zhongguo Zaochuan Gongcheng Xuehui - Chinese Society of Naval Architecture and Marine Engineering, 71 Sipailou Lu, P.O. Box 040-002, Shanghai 200010, People's Republic of China. TEL 3203055. FAX 86-21-3290929. (Dist. overseas by: Guoji Shudian - China International Book Trading Corporation, P.O. Box 399, Beijing, P.R.C.) Ed. Yu Fengchang. adv.
—BLDSC shelfmark: 8258.600000.

387   CC   ISSN 1001-4624
CHUANBO SHEJI TONGXUN. (Text in Chinese) q. Shanghai Chuanbo Yanjiu Shejiyuan - Shanghai Ship Design Institute, 221 Zhaojiabang Lu, Shanghai 200032, People's Republic of China. TEL 4313600. Ed. Zhang Ruiliang.

387   US
CHUANBO SHIJIE/SHIP WORLD. (Text in Chinese) w. $29.20. China Books & Periodicals, Inc., 2929 24th St., San Francisco, CA 94110. TEL 415-282-2994. FAX 415-282-0994. (newspaper)

387.164   UK   ISSN 0269-381X
COALTRANS. vol.3, 1981. bi-m. $110. CoalTrans Publishing Ltd., 42 Rutherwyke, Epsom, Surrey KT17 2NB, England. FAX 081-786-8175. Ed. Norman Penwarden. adv.; bk.rev.; circ. 8,000. **Indexed:** Fluidex.
—BLDSC shelfmark: 3292.216000.
Formerly (until 1986): Bulk Systems International (ISSN 0143-7852)
Description: Information on the international coal market: mined product trading, transportation, end user technology.

387   US
COAST MARINE AND TRANSPORTATION DIRECTORY. a. $54 (foreign $60). K - III Press, Inc, 424 W. 33rd St., New York, NY 10001. TEL 800-221-5488. FAX 212-695-5025.

359.97   UK
COASTGUARD. 1946. q. free. Department of Transport, H.M. Coastguard, Rm. S13-19 2, Marsham St., London SW1P 3EB, England. TEL 01-276-5082. FAX 01-276-5179. TELEX 22221. Ed. Ian Fraser. adv.; bk.rev.; film rev.; illus.; stat.; circ. 15,000 (controlled).

387.5   FR   ISSN 0069-5815
COLLOQUES INTERNATIONAUX D'HISTOIRE MARITIME. TRAVAUX.* 1957. irreg., 9th, 1967. price varies. Ecole Pratique des Hautes Etudes, 45-47 rue des Ecoles, 75005 Paris, France.

387.5   UK
COMECON MERCHANT SHIPS. 1978. triennial. £14.95. Kenneth Mason Publications Ltd., 12 North St., Emsworth, Hants. PO10 7DQ, England. TEL 0243-377977. FAX 0243-379136. Ed. Ambrose Greenway.

387   BE
COMITE DES ASSOCIATIONS D'ARMATEURS DES COMMUNAUTES EUROPEENS. ANNUAL REPORT.* a. Comite des Associations d'Armateurs des Communautes Europeens, 45 rue Ducale, B-1000 Brussels, Belgium. TEL 2306250.

387   II
COMMERCE YEARBOOK OF PORTS, SHIPPING AND SHIPBUILDING. (Text in English) 1974. a. Rs.50. Commerce Publications Limited, NKM International House, 178 Backbay Reclamation, Bombay 40020, India. Ed. Subhash Chandra Sarker. illus.; stat.
Continues: Commerce Yearbook of Shipping and Shipbuilding.

COMMERCIAL TRANSPORT AND TRANSPORT MANAGERS JOURNAL. see *TRANSPORTATION — Trucks And Trucking*

387   US
CONNECTIONS (TOLEDO, 1956). 1956. q. free. Toledo-Lucas County Port Authority, One Maritime Plaza, 7th Fl., Toledo, OH 43604-1866. TEL 419-243-8251. FAX 419-243-1835. Ed. T. Mark Sweeney. charts; illus.; circ. 10,000.
Formerly (until 1989): Port of Toledo News (ISSN 0032-4868)
Description: News and information on the Port of Toledo, area airports and economic development.

CONSTITUTION CHRONICLE. see *MILITARY*

354.44 623.8   FR
CONSTRUCTION NAVALE. 1919. a. free. Chambre Syndicale des Constructeurs de Navires, 47 rue de Monceau, 75008 Paris, France. FAX 42-89-25-32. TELEX NAVIR 651 756. Ed. P. Castanie. circ. 700.
Former titles: Evolution de la Construction Navale; Construction Navale.

387.164   UK   ISSN 0269-7726
CONTAINER MANAGEMENT. 1984. m. $210. Baltic Publishing Ltd., Great West Road, Brentford, Middlesex TW8 9BU, England. TEL 081-847-2446. FAX 081-569-8688. Ed. Rachael White. circ. 8,000. (back issues avail.)
Description: Addresses cargo handling issues.

387   IT   ISSN 0010-9193
CORRIERE DEI TRASPORTI; settimanale indipendente di informazioni. 1958. w. L.60000 (foreign L.120000). Corriere dei Trasporti, s.a.s., Salita Viale 1-21, 16128 Genoa, Italy. TEL 10-566678. FAX 10-564962. Ed. Virgilio Dardani. adv.; illus.; stat.; circ. 7,500. (tabloid format)

COSTRUZIONI; tecnica ed organizzazione dei cantieri. see *ENGINEERING — Civil Engineering*

387   BE
COURTIER NAUTIQUE. (Text in Flemish and French) 1970. m. 8 rue du Sceptre, B-1040 Brussels, Belgium. adv.; circ. 13,400.

387   UK   ISSN 0070-1629
CRONER'S WORLD DIRECTORY OF FREIGHT CONFERENCES. 1954. m. £97 (effective 1992). Croner Publications Ltd., Croner House, London Road, Kingston, Surrey KT2 6SR, England. TEL 081-547-3333. FAX 081-547-2637. TELEX 267778. Ed. Colin Clark. (looseleaf format)
Description: Contains current information on the world's freight conferences and agreements.

CRUISE DIGEST REPORTS. see *TRAVEL AND TOURISM*

CRUISE INDUSTRY NEWS. see *TRAVEL AND TOURISM*

CRUISE INDUSTRY NEWS ANNUAL. see *TRAVEL AND TOURISM*

CRUISE INDUSTRY NEWS QUARTERLY. see *TRAVEL AND TOURISM*

387   GW
D A G - SCHIFFAHRT; Zeitschrift fuer Seeleute. 1947. 8/yr. DM.55 (free to members). Deutsche Angestellten-Gewerkschaft, Postfach 301230, 2000 Hamburg 36, Germany. TEL 040-34915238. FAX 040-349-15-400. TELEX 211642-AGHV-D. Ed. Klaus-Dieter Schwettscher. bk.rev.; circ. 12,500.

387 551.3   DK   ISSN 0905-3549
D M I NEWS. 1979. irreg. free. Danish Maritime Institute, Hjortekaersvej 99, 2800 Lyngby, Denmark. TEL 45-45879325. FAX 45-45-87-93-33. TELEX 37223-SHILAB-DK. Ed. Arne Hasle Nielsen. bk.rev.; illus.; circ. 1,200.
Former titles: D M I Update (ISSN 0903-112X) & Vind - Nyt (ISSN 0109-2049)

387   BL
DADOS ESTATISTICOS DA MOVIMENTACAO DE CARGA E PASSAGEIROS. Cover title: Dados Estatisticos da Navegacao. a. Empresa de Navegacao de Amazonia, S.A. Setor de Processamento de Dados Estatisticos, Av. Presidente Vargas 41, Belem, Para, Brazil. stat.

387.164   US
DAILY SHIPPING NEWS. d. 7831 S.E. Stark St., Ste. 200, Portland, OR 97215-2357. TEL 503-255-2142. FAX 503-255-2735. Ed. Philip Moore. circ. 1,000.

387   DK   ISSN 0107-8011
DANSK ILLUSTRERET SKIBSLISTE. 1980. a. DKK 280. Seapress, Postboks 288, 8100 Aarhus C, Denmark. Eds. Per Rungholm, Bent Mikkelsen. adv.; illus.; circ. 3,500.

DENMARK. MILJOESTYRELSEN. HAVFORURENINGSLABORATORIUM. REPORT OF THE MARINE POLLUTION LABORATORY. see *ENVIRONMENTAL STUDIES*

623.89 621.38   JA
DENPA KOHO/ELECTRONIC NAVIGATION REVIEW. (Text in Japanese) 1960. m. Japanese Committee for Radio Aids to Navigation - Denpa Koho Kenkyukai, c/o Kaijo Hoan-cho Todai-bu, 2-1-3 Kasumigaseki, Chiyoda-ku, Tokyo 100, Japan. adv.; charts; illus.; stat. **Indexed:** JTA.

DETROIT NEWSPAPER AGENCY. TRAVEL DIRECTORY. see *TRANSPORTATION — Air Transport*

387   GW
DEUTSCHE KUESTENSCHIFFAHRT. m. DM.108. (Verband Deutscher Kuestenschiffseigner) Verlag Paul-Gerhard Kuhls, Maria-Louisen-Stieg 29, 2000 Hamburg 60, Germany. TEL 040-462623. FAX 040-6567901. adv.: B&W page DM.2700; trim 177 x 257. bk.rev.; circ. 3,250.

387   GW   ISSN 0343-3668
DEUTSCHES SCHIFFAHRTSARCHIV. 1975. a. DM.38. (Deutsches Schiffahrtsmuseum Bremerhaven) Ernst Kabel Verlag GmbH, Heubergredder 12-14, 2000 Hamburg 60, Germany. TEL 040-5112951. FAX 040-51129129. Ed. Uwe Schnall. circ. 250.

DEVONPORT NEWS; H.M. Naval Base newspaper. see *MILITARY*

387   UK
DIRECTORY OF SHIPOWNERS AND SHIPBUILDING. 1902. a. $125. Reed Business Publishing Group, Enterprise Division (Subsidiary of: Reed International PLC), Quadrant House, The Quadrant, Sutton, Surrey SM2 5AS, England. TEL 081-652-8183. FAX 081-652-8986. (Subscr. to: Oakfield House, Perrymount Rd., Haywards Heath, W. Sussex RH16 3DH, England. TEL 444-445566) Ed. Paul Doughty. index; circ. 2,750.
Formerly: Directory of Shipowners, Shipbuilders and Marine Engineers (ISSN 0070-6310)

DIRITTO MARITTIMO; rivista trimestrale di dottrina giurisprudenza legislazione italiana e straniera. see *LAW*

387   UK   ISSN 0012-4419
TC1   CODEN: DHBAAL
DOCK AND HARBOUR AUTHORITY. 1921. 10/yr. £45($100) Foxlow Publications Ltd., 20 Harcourt St., London W1H 2AX, England. TEL 071-402-5237. FAX 01-402-5236. TELEX 291829 TLX G. Ed. Bill Reid. adv.: B&W page $720, color page $1170. bk.rev.; charts; illus.; index; circ. 2,176. (also avail. in microform from UMI; reprint service avail.) **Indexed:** BMT, Br.Tech.Ind., Eng.Ind., Excerp.Med., Fluidex, Geotech.Abstr., Intl.Civil Eng.Abstr., J.of Ferroc., Key to Econ.Sci., Ocean.Abstr., P.A.I.S., Pollut.Abstr., Soft.Abstr.Eng.
—BLDSC shelfmark: 3606.000000.

387.1   AT
DOG WATCH. 1943. a. Aus.$9. (Shiplovers' Society of Victoria) Research Publications Pty., G.P.O. Box 1169K, Melbourne, Vic. 3001, Australia. Ed. T.E. Goldfinch. adv.; bk.rev.; circ. 1,000.
Formerly: Annual Dog Watch (ISSN 0066-3921)

387   US
DOMESTIC WATERBORNE TRADE OF THE UNITED STATES. a. U.S. Maritime Administration, Office of Domestic Shipping, MAR-810, Rm. 7301, Washington, DC 20590. TEL 202-366-4374. (Orders to: Supt. of Documents, Washington, DC 20402)
Supersedes: Domestic Oceanborne and Great Lakes Commerce of the United States (ISSN 0070-7058)
Description: Shows the flow of domestic waterborne commerce in the U.S., with the purpose of promoting awareness of the scale, diversity, and vitality of that commerce.

TRANSPORTATION — SHIPS AND SHIPPING 4727

387 380 UK ISSN 0265-1165
DOVER PORT HANDBOOK. 1983. a. £10. Charter International Publications Ltd., Castle Chambers, Castle Acre, King's Lynn, Norfolk PE32 2BQ, England. TEL 07605-634. FAX 07605-625. TELEX 817440. Ed. James P. Moriarty. adv.; circ. 6,000.

387 623.8 UK
DREDGING & PORT CONSTRUCTION. m. $149. International Trade Publications Ltd., Queensway House, 2 Queensway, Redhill, Surrey RH1 1QS, England. TEL 0737-768611. FAX 0737-761989. TELEX 948669-TOPJNL-G. Ed. Derek North. circ. 4,562. **Indexed:** BMT, Excerp.Med., Fluidex, Key to Econ.Sci.

623.82 UK ISSN 0143-5000
DRYDOCK; international journal of ship repair & maintenance. 1979. q. £12 (effective June 1991). Marine Publications International Ltd., 4 Hubbard Rd., Houdmills, Basingstoke, Hampshire RG21 2UH, England. TEL 0256-840444. FAX 0256-817877. Ed. Derek Deere. adv.; illus.; circ. 8,502. **Indexed:** Biodet.Abstr., BMT, Br.Tech.Ind., Excerp.Med., Fluidex, World Surf.Coat.
—BLDSC shelfmark: 3630.225000.

387.5 IO
DUNIA MARITIM.* vol.22, 1972. m. rps. 800. Directorate General of Sea Communication - Direktorat Jenderal Perhubungan Laut, Jl. Merdeka Timur 5, Jakarta, Indonesia. Ed.Bd. adv.; charts; illus.

E P E. see ENGINEERING — Electrical Engineering

387 UK
EAST ANGLICAN SHIP AND BOAT BUILDERS EMPLOYERS ASSOCIATION. QUARTERLY NEWSLETTER. q. East Anglican Ship and Boat Builders Employers Association, 17 Museum St., Ipswich IP1 1HF, England.

387 330.9 IO
ECONOMIC & SHIPPING REVIEW. 1979. m. Rps.7500. Indonesian Shipowners Association, Jalan Bungur Besar 54, Jakarta, Indonesia.

386 UA
EGYPT. SUEZ CANAL AUTHORITY. MONTHLY REPORT. m. Suez Canal Authority, Information Center, Ismailia 41515, Egypt. FAX 64-320784. TELEX 63543 SUCAN UN.

ELECTRONAUT. see COMMUNICATIONS

387 BL
EMPRESA DE NAVEGACAO DA AMAZONIA. ESTATISTICA DA NAVEGACAO. a. Empresa de Navegacao da Amazonia, Av. Presidente Vargas 41, Belem, Para, Brazil. Dir. Eugenio Marques Frazao. charts.

387 FR
ESCALE; revue de personnel du Port Autonome du Havre. 1949. m. free. Port Autonome du Havre, B.P. 1413, Terre-Plein de la Barre, 76067 Le Havre Cedex, France. Ed. Michel Lamglet. charts; illus.; stat.; circ. 4,200.
Formerly: Havre (ISSN 0023-9534)

387 UK
F I D I FOCUS. (Text in English, French, German) 1982. 8/yr. £40. (Federation Internationale des Demenageurs Internationaux - International Federation of International Furniture Removals) Quarrington-Curtis Ltd., 15 Canute Rd., Southampton SO1 1FJ, England. TEL 0703-635438. FAX 0703-632198. TELEX 477704-QCPR. Ed. Colin Quarrington. circ. 2,200.
Description: News items, feature articles, photography, and classified advertisements pertaining to the activities of this organization for overseas furniture moving and storage facilities.

387 UK ISSN 0307-0220
HE561
FAIRPLAY INTERNATIONAL SHIPPING WEEKLY. (Includes: q. Newbuildings (Formerly: World Ships on Order)) 1883. w. £105($200) Fairplay Publications Ltd., 20 Ullswater Crescent, Ullswater Business Park, Coulsdon, Surrey CR5 2HR, England. Ed. C. Hewer. adv.; charts; illus.; mkt.; pat.; tr.lit.; stat.; circ. 5,660. **Indexed:** Fluidex, Key to Econ.Sci.
Formerly: Fairplay Shipping Journal (ISSN 0014-6986)

387 338 UK ISSN 0267-0879
FAIRPLAY MARINE COMPUTING GUIDE. 1984. a. £43($86) Fairplay Publications Ltd., 20 Ullswater Crescent, Ullswater Buisness Park, Coulsdon, Surrey CR5 2HR, England. Ed. P. Malpas.
—BLDSC shelfmark: 3865.507700.

387 UK ISSN 0261-2356
FAIRPLAY WORLD PORTS DIRECTORY. 1869. a. £99($198) Fairplay Publications Ltd., 20 Ullswater Crescent, Ullswater Business Park, Coulsdon, Surrey CR5 2HR, England.

387 UK ISSN 0140-5047
HE561
FAIRPLAY WORLD SHIPPING DIRECTORY. a. £53($106) Fairplay Publications Ltd., 20 Ullswater Crescent, Ullswater Business Park, Coulsdon, Surrey CR5 2HR, England. Ed. P. Malpas.
Formerly: Fairplay World Shipping Year Book.

387 380 UK ISSN 0260-9282
FALMOUTH PORT AND INDUSTRY HANDBOOK 1984. 1981. a. Charter International Publications Ltd., Castle Chambers, Castle Acre, King's Lynn, Norfolk PE32 2BQ, England. TEL 07605-634. FAX 07605-625. TELEX 817440. Ed. James P. Moriarty. adv.; circ. 6,000.

629.3 UK ISSN 0954-3988
VM362 CODEN: FFINE5
FAST FERRY INTERNATIONAL. 1961. 10/yr. £25($50) 24 Leaf Close, Northwood, Middlesex HA6 2YY, England. TEL 09274-27262. FAX 0923-835278. TELEX 291561-VIASOS-G. Ed. Alan Blunden. adv.; bk.rev.; charts; illus.; pat. **Indexed:** Appl.Mech.Rev., BMT, Br.Rail.Bd., Br.Tech.Ind., Met.Abstr., Ocean.Abstr., Pollut.Abstr., World Alum.Abstr.
—BLDSC shelfmark: 3897.170000.
Formerly (until 1989): High-Speed Surface Craft (ISSN 0144-7823); **Incorporates:** Hovering Craft and Hydrofoil (ISSN 0018-6775)

FATHOM; surface ship and submarine safety review. see MILITARY

387 NO
FEARNLEYS MID-WEEK REPORT. w. $300. Fearnleys A-S, Raadhusgaten 27, P.O. Box 1158 Sentrum, N-0107 Oslo, Norway. TEL 47-2-41-70-00. FAX 47-2-41-18-80.
Description: Provides updated information on world economy, chartering markets, sale and purchase, contracting, demolition and more.

387 NO
FEARNLEYS MONTHLY REPORT. m. $290. Fearnleys A-S, Raadhusgaten 27, P.O. Box 1158 Sentrum, N-0107 Oslo 1, Norway. TEL 47-2-41-70-00. FAX 47-2-41-18-80. TELEX 74607 FADM. (back issues avail.)
Description: Provides updated information on world economy, chartering markets, sale and purchase, contracting, demolition, etc.

387 NO ISSN 0801-5589
FEARNLEYS REVIEW. a. $180. Fearnleys A-S, Raadhusgaten 27, Box 1158-Sentrum, 0107 Oslo 1, Norway. TEL 02-417000. FAX 02-411818. (back issues avail.)
Formerly: Fearnly and Egers Chartering Co. Review.
Description: Provides a comprehensive survey of freight markets, sale and purchase, contracting, etc. during the preceeding year.

387 FR ISSN 0223-5358
FEUX ET SIGNAUX DE BRUME. 1950. irreg. Service Hydrographique et Oceanographique de la Marine, 3 av. Octave Greard, 00300 Armees, France. TEL 98-22-10-80. FAX 98-43-18-11. TELEX HYDRO 940568. (Subscr. to: EPSHOM, BP 426, 29275 Brest Cedex, France)

387 UK
FINANCIAL TIMES WORLD SHIPPING YEARBOOK. a. £14($42) Financial Times Business Information Ltd., Tower House, Southampton St., London WC2E 7HA, England. TEL 01-240-9391. FAX 071-240-7946. ●Also available online. Vendor(s): DIALOG.

387 US ISSN 0884-8548
FLORIDA SHIPPER. 1975. w. $35 (Can.$40; foreign $50). S.F.S. Corp., Box 371305, Miami, FL 33137-1305. TEL 305-576-6766. FAX 305-576-6759. Ed. Alinda Montfort. adv.; circ. 1,680.

FORD'S DECK PLAN GUIDE. see TRAVEL AND TOURISM

FORD'S FREIGHTER TRAVEL GUIDE AND WATERWAYS OF THE WORLD. see TRAVEL AND TOURISM

FORD'S INTERNATIONAL CRUISE GUIDE. see TRAVEL AND TOURISM

387 380 UK ISSN 0262-8880
FORTH PORTS HANDBOOK 1984. 1982. a. £10. Charter International Publications Ltd., Castle Chambers, Castle Acre, King's Lynn, Norfolk PE32 2BQ, England. TEL 07605-634. FAX 07605-625. TELEX 817440. Ed. James P. Moriarty. adv.; circ. 6,000.

387 GW ISSN 0939-7965
FRACHT - DIENST. 1945. m. DM.48 (foreign DM.78). Postfach 3240, 3300 Braunschweig, Germany. TEL 0531-340954. FAX 0531-340950. Ed. Andreas Klose. adv.; bk.rev.; circ. 8,000. (back issues avail.)

387 NO ISSN 0015-9352
FRAKTEMANN. 1935. 5/yr. NOK 60.($3.50) Fraktefartoyenes Rederiforening, P.O. Box 2020 Nordnes, N-5024 Bergen, Norway. Ed. Einar Haakon Kirkefjord. adv.; circ. 1,000.

387 FR
FRANCE. COMMISSION CENTRALE POUR LA NAVIGATION DU RHIN. RAPPORT ANNUEL. 1835. a. 70 F. Commission Centrale pour la Navigation du Rhin, Palais du Rhin, 67082 Strasbourg Cedex, France. TEL 88-32-35-84. FAX 88-32-10-72. Ed. Robert M. van Kooy. charts; stat.; circ. 500.

387.1 AT
FREMANTLE PORT NEWS. 1961. 3/yr. Fremantle Port Authority, P.O. Box 95, Fremantle, W.A. 6160, Australia. TEL 09-430-4911. FAX 09-430-4112. Ed. Carolyn Waghorn. adv.; bk.rev.; illus.; circ. 4,200 (controlled).
Formerly: Port of Fremantle.
Description: Explores port development, export trade and shipping lines. Includes staff appointments and activities.

387.54 UK
GARSTON DOCKS TIDE TABLE. a. free. Associated British Ports, Port Office, Garston, Liverpool L19 2JW, England.

GENOA PORT AND SHIPPING HANDBOOK. see BUSINESS AND ECONOMICS — Trade And Industrial Directories

387 US ISSN 0016-8149
HE554.A3
GEORGIA ANCHORAGE. 1955. q. free. Georgia Ports Authority, Box 2406, Savannah, GA 31402. TEL 912-964-3811. FAX 912-964-3903. Ed. Amy Rhodes. adv.; charts; illus.; circ. 12,500.
Description: News articles on the export and import trade and shipping industry in the state, as well as news on the activities of State's Ports Authority.

387 GW ISSN 0178-2495
GERMAN MARITIME INDUSTRY JOURNAL. (Text in English) 1985. bi-m. DM.50($25) Seehafen Verlag GmbH, Wandalenweg 1, 2000 Hamburg 1, Germany. TEL 040-2371402. FAX 040-23714154. Ed. Hans Juergen Witthoeft. adv.; circ. 3,500. (back issues avail.)

387 GW ISSN 0070-4148
GERMAN MERCHANT FLEET; die Deutsche Handelsflotte. 1954. a. DM.529. Seehafen-Verlag Erik Blumenfeld GmbH und Co., Nordkanalstr. 36, Postfach 105605, 2000 Hamburg 1, Germany. adv.

387 380 UK ISSN 0262-1622
GOOLE PORT HANDBOOK. 1982. biennial. £10. Charter International Publications Ltd., Castle Chambers, Castle Acre, King's Lynn, Norfolk PE32 2BQ, England. TEL 07605-634. FAX 07605-625. TELEX 817440. Ed. James P. Moriarty. adv.; illus.; circ. 6,000.

THE GREAT CIRCLE. see HISTORY

387 CN
GREAT LAKES NAVIGATION. 1917. a. Anchor Press, 1056 Chemin du Golf, Nun's Island, Verdun, Que. H3E 1H4, Canada. TEL 514-766-8650. FAX 514-766-5559. Ed. O.J. Silva. adv.

T

TRANSPORTATION — SHIPS AND SHIPPING

386   US   ISSN 0072-7318
GREAT LAKES RED BOOK. 1901. a. $6.75. Freshwater Press, Inc., 1700 E 13th St., Ste. 3R-E, Cleveland, OH 44114. TEL 216-241-0373. Ed. John O. Greenwood. adv.; index; circ. 2,000.

387 380   UK   ISSN 0260-9517
GREAT YARMOUTH PORT AND INDUSTRY HANDBOOK. 1980. a. £10. Charter International Publications Ltd., Castle Chambers, Castle Acre, King's Lynn, Norfolk PE32 2BQ, England. TEL 07605-634. FAX 07605-625. TELEX 817440. Ed. James P. Moriarty. adv.; illus.; circ. 6,000.

386   US   ISSN 0072-7490
HE630.G7
GREENWOOD'S GUIDE TO GREAT LAKES SHIPPING. 1958. a. $58.42. Freshwater Press, Inc., 1700 E. 13th St., Ste. 3R-E, Cleveland, OH 44114. TEL 216-241-0373. Ed. John O. Greenwood. adv.; circ. 3,700.

359.97   IT
GUARDIA COSTIERA. bi-m. L.50000 (foreign L.60000). Via Buonzino 11, Milan, Italy. TEL 02-228881. FAX 02-225125.

387   GW
GUETERTRANSPORT IN SEEVERKEHR. 1954. a. DM.59.81. K.O. Storck Verlag, Stahltwiete 7, 2000 Hamburg 50, Germany. TEL 040-850-0071. FAX 040-850-7758. TELEX 17403448. Ed. H. Meder.
   Formerly: Fracht-Schiffahrts-Konferenzen.

387   PO
GUIA DO PORTO DE LISBOA. 1965. a. free. Administracao do Porto de Lisboa, Divisao de Marketing e Relacoes Publicas, Rua da Junqueira, 94, 1300 Lisbon, Portugal. circ. 3,000.

387   UK
GUIDE TO PORT ENTRY (YEAR). 1971. biennial. £180($360) Shipping Guides Ltd., 75 Bell St., Reigate, Surrey RH2 7AN, England. TEL 0737-242255. FAX 0737-222449. TELEX 917070-SHIPG-G. Ed. Robert Pedlow.
   Description: Detailed port information including port plans, mooring diagrams, regulations, maximum size, port restrictions, port access, required documentation, customs allowances, berthing times and availability for masters and owners.

387   JA
GUIDE TO THE PORT OF YOKOHAMA. (Includes Map) (Text in English and Japanese) a. free. Port and Harbor Bureau, Industry and Trade Center Bldg., 2 Yamashita-cho, Naka-ku, Yokohama, Japan. FAX 45-671-7158.

387   GW
H H L A REPORT. 1974. q. free. Hamburger Hafen- und Lagerhaus-Aktiengesellschaft, Bei St. Annen 1, 2000 Hamburg 11, Germany. FAX 040-30883355. TELEX 2161209. Ed. Gerhard Angerer. circ. 4,500.

623.82   NE   ISSN 0923-666X
VM77
H S B INTERNATIONAL. 1951. m. fl.92.50($65) (foreign fl. 135). Uitgeverij Radius, Grote Kerksplein 5, 3311 CC Dordrecht, Netherlands. TEL 078-131598. FAX 078-311421. (Orders to: Uitgeverij Radius, Postbus 277, 3300 AG Dordrecht, Netherlands) Eds. K. Glas, I. McMillan Marshall. adv.; bk.rev.; charts; illus.; mkt.; pat.; tr.lit.; circ. 7,341. **Indexed:** BMT, Eng.Ind., Fluidex, Key to Econ.Sci., Ocean.Abstr., Pollut.Abstr.
   Former titles: Holland Shipbuilding; Holland Shipbuilding, Marine Engineering and Shipping Herald (ISSN 0018-3571)
   Description: Covers shipbuilding, dredging, engineering, oil and gas industry, ports and shipping, industry, maintenence and corrosion prevention.

387   IS
HADASHOT SAPANUT VETEUFAH - YIDION; shipping and aviation news. (Text in Hebrew) m. Haifa University, Wydra Shipping and Aviation Research Institute, Suite 2318, Eshkol Tower, Haifa 31999, Israel. TEL 04-240186. FAX 04-348908. Ed. M. Ofek.
   Formerly: Israel Shipping and Aviation Research Institute. Yidion.
   Description: News and statistics on shipping and aviation.

387   JA
HAKUYO KOGYO. bi-m. Ship-Machinery Manufacturers' Association of Japan, Senpaku-Shinko Bldg., 1-15-16, Toranomon, Minato-ku, Tokyo 105, Japan.

387   GW
HAMBURG THE QUICK PORT; also Bremen and Weserports. (Text in English) 1958. a. DM.29.91. K.O. Storck Verlag, Stahltwiete 7, 2000 Hamburg 50, Germany. TEL 040-850-0071. FAX 040-850-7758. TELEX 17403448. Ed. H. Meder.

387.54   GW   ISSN 0341-0862
HAMBURGER HAFEN - NACHRICHTEN. 1947. w. DM.230.40. Sehafen-Verlag Erik Blumenfeld GmbH und Co., Postfach 105605, 2000 Hamburg 1, Germany. Ed. Klaus Heims. adv.; charts; illus.; circ. 7,000.
   Formerly: Hamburger Hafen-Nachrichten und Schiffsabfahrten (ISSN 0017-694X)
   Description: Contains timetables.

948   DK   ISSN 0085-1418
HANDELS- OG SOEFARTSMUSEET PAA KRONBORG. AARBOG. (Text in Danish; summaries in English or German) 1942. a. DKK 200 for non-members; members DKK 140. Handels- og Soefartsmuseet paa Kronborg, DK-3000 Helsingoer, Denmark. FAX 49-21-34-40. Ed. Hans Jeppesen. adv.; illus.; cum.index; circ. 2,000.

387   UK   ISSN 0017-7423
HANDY SHIPPING GUIDE. 1887. w. £105. Wilkinson Bros. Ltd., 230-234 Long Lane, London SE1 4QE, England. FAX 071-403-0233. TELEX 8956660-HANDYS-G. Ed. A. Amin. adv.; bk.rev.; circ. controlled.

387   CC   ISSN 1000-0356
HANG HAI. (Text in Chinese) bi-m. Shanghai Hanghai Xuehui, No.2, Alley 590, Room 1001, Yuanping Nanlu, Shanghai 200030, People's Republic of China. TEL 4385774. Ed. Zhou Yiheng.

387   CC
HANGHAI JISHU/OCEAN SHIPPING TECHNOLOGY. (Text in Chinese) bi-m. Zhongguo Hanghai Xuehui, Aijian Dasha, 2nd Fl., Rm. 1005, 590 Yuanping Nanlu, Shanghai 200030, People's Republic of China. TEL 4385457. Ed. Zhou Yiheng.

387   CC   ISSN 1000-4688
HANGHAI KEJI DONGTAI. (Text in Chinese) m. Jiaotong-bu, Shanghai Chuanbo Yunshu Kexue Yanjiusuo - Ministry of Transportation, Shanghai Institute of Shipping Transportation Science, 200 Minsheng Lu, Shanghai 200135, People's Republic of China. TEL 8840438. (Co-sponsor: Zhongguo Hanghai Xuehui) Ed. Lu Wenbiao.

623.8   GW   ISSN 0017-7504
VK3
HANSA; Zeitschrift fuer Schiffahrt, Schiffbau, Hafen. (Summaries in English) 1864. fortn. DM.292.75. Schiffahrts-Verlag Hansa C. Schroedter GmbH und Co. KG, Stubbenhuk 10, 2000 Hamburg 11, Germany. Ed. Gerhard Bollmann. adv.; bk.rev.; abstr.; bibl.; charts; illus.; stat.; index; circ. 6,100. **Indexed:** BMT, C.I.S. Abstr., Excerp.Med., INIS Atomind., Key to Econ.Sci., Met.Abstr., World Alum.Abstr.
—BLDSC shelfmark: 4262.250000.

387   CC   ISSN 1000-1875
HARBIN CHUANBO GONGCHENG XUEYUAN XUEBAO/HARBIN INSTITUTE OF SHIPPING ENGINEERING. JOURNAL. (Text in Chinese) q. Harbin Chuanbo Gongcheng Xueyuan, Xuebao Bianjibu, 31 Lou, Wenmiao Jie, Nangang-qu, Harbin, Heilongjiang 150001, People's Republic of China. Ed. Lu Zhonglu.

387   CN   ISSN 0017-7636
HARBOUR AND SHIPPING. 1918. m. Can.$36($46) Progress Publishing Co. Ltd., 1765 Bellevue Ave., West Vancouver B.C. V7V 1A8, Canada. TEL 604-922-6717. FAX 604-922-1739. adv.; illus.; tr.lit.; circ. 2,000. **Indexed:** BMT, Fluidex.

387   NE
HAVEN AMSTERDAM. bi-m. free outside the Netherlands. Amsterdam Ports Association, Het Havengebouw, 13e etage, De Ruyterkade 7, 1013 AA Amsterdam, Netherlands. TEL 020-6273706. Ed. J. Moes.

387   NE
HAVENNIEUWS.* 8/yr. Scheepvaart Vereniging Zuid Rotterdam - Port Industries Association, Postbus 4222, 3006 AE Rotterdam, Netherlands. TEL 760600.

387   FR
HAVRE PORT. 1981. m. Port Autonome du Havre, B.P. 1413, 76067 le Havre cedex, France. circ. 4,300.

387   BE   ISSN 0018-1978
HINTERLAND; periodical of the port of Antwerp. (Text in Dutch, English, French, German) 1950. q. 360 Fr. (Port of Antwerp Promotion Association) Publitra B.V.B.A., Brouwersvliet 33, B-2000 Antwerp, Belgium. FAX 03-231-27-52. TELEX 33069 B. adv.; charts; illus.; stat.; circ. 16,000. **Indexed:** Avery Ind.Archit.Per.
—BLDSC shelfmark: 4315.170000.

387   GW   ISSN 0323-8725
V3
HOCHSCHULE FUER SEEFAHRT WARNEMUENDE-WUSTROW. WISSENSCHAFTLICHE ZEITSCHRIFT. 1974. q. DM.40 (foreign DM.84). Hochschule fuer Seefahrt Warnemuende-Wustrow, Richard-Wagner-Str. 31, Rastock-Warnemuende, Germany. Ed. Eckhard Moeck. abstr.; bibl.; illus.; index; circ. 650. (back issues avail.)
   Formerly (until 1989): Hochschule fuer Seefahrt Warnemuende-Wustrow. Wissenschaftliche Beitraege.

HOLLAND'S EXPORT MAGAZINE. see BUSINESS AND ECONOMICS — International Commerce

HONG KONG. CENSUS AND STATISTICS DEPARTMENT. SHIPPING STATISTICS. see TRANSPORTATION — Abstracting, Bibliographies, Statistics

387   UK   ISSN 0018-4675
HONOURABLE COMPANY OF MASTER MARINERS. JOURNAL. 1933. q. membership. Honourable Company of Master Mariners, c/o H.Q.S. Wellington, Temple Stairs, Victoria Embankment, London WC2R 2PN, England. Ed.Bd. adv.; bk.rev.; illus.; cum.index every 3 yrs.

629.324   UK   ISSN 0018-6767
HOVERFOIL NEWS. (Includes: New Transport Technology) 1966. m. £115($215) Ferndown Publications, 302 Bramhill Lane S., Bramhill, Stockport SK7 3DL, England. TEL 061-439-4926. Ed. P. Smith. adv.; bk.rev.; illus.; index.
   Description: New technology and information about hovercraft and hoverfoil.

387.2   UN
I M O NEWS. 1977. 4/yr. free. International Maritime Organization, 4 Albert Embankment, London SE1 7SR, England. TEL 071-735-7611. FAX 071-587-3210. TELEX 23588. Ed. Roger Kohn. adv.; bk.rev.; illus.; circ. 10,000. **Indexed:** Deep Sea Res.& Oceanogr.Abstr.
   Former titles: I M C O News; I M C O Bulletin (ISSN 0047-0422)

387   II
INDIAN SHIPPING. (Text in English) 1949. m. Rs.110($24) Indian National Shipowners' Association, 22 Maker Tower F, Cuffe Parade, Bombay 400 005, India. TELEX 011-4611-INSA-IN. Ed. B.V. Nilkund. adv.; bk.rev.; circ. 1,000. **Indexed:** BMT.

387 623.82   II
INDIAN SHIPPING AND SHIPBUILDING. (Text in English) m. Rs.100. V.S. Chhabra, 5 B Bakhtavar, Nariman Point, Bombay 400021, India.

387   AG
INDUSTRIA NAVAL; e intereses maritimos argentinos. w. Blumenau S.A.C.I.F.I.A., Lavalle 1672, Buenos Aires, Argentina. Ed. Ricardo L. Ramsay. illus.

387.1   FR   ISSN 0073-7720
INDUSTRIE DE LA MANUTENTION DANS LES PORTS FRANCAIS. 1964. a. Union Nationale des Industries de la Manutention dans les Ports Francais, 76 Av. Marceau, 75008 Paris, France.

387.5   IT
INFORMARE. bi-m. Media Angle S.r.l., Via M. Mellon 17, 20129 Milan, Italy. TEL 02-7385934. FAX 02-714067. Ed. Gabriele Pardanori.

387　　　　　　　　　UY
INFORMATIVO ALAMAR. 1976. m. Asociacion Latinoamericana de Armadores, Rio Negro 1394 - Of.502, Casilla de Correo 767, Montevideo, Uruguay. TEL 2-98-74-49. FAX 05982-920732. TELEX 26431-ALAMAR-UY. circ. 400.

623.8　　　　SP　　ISSN 0020-1073
INGENIERIA NAVAL. 1929. m. 7200 ptas. Asociacion de Ingenieros Navales de Espana, Castello 66, Madrid 28001, Spain. TEL 575-10-24. FAX 577167975. TELEX 43582 INAV E. Dir. Juan A. Alcaraz Infante. adv.; bk.rev.; abstr.; illus.; index; circ. 2,300. **Indexed:** BMT, Chem.Abstr., Ind.SST.

386　　　　　　　　　US
INLAND RIVER GUIDE. 1972. a. $50. Waterways Journal, Inc., 319 N. Fourth St., 666 Security Bldg., St. Louis, MO 63102. TEL 314-241-7354. FAX 314-241-4207. Ed. Dan Owen. adv.; circ. 4,500.

386　　　　　　　　　US
INLAND RIVER RECORD. 1945. a. $32. Waterways Journal, Inc., 319 N. Fourth St., 666 Security Bldg., St. Louis, MO 63102. TEL 314-241-7354. FAX 314-241-4207. Ed. Dan Owen. adv.; circ. 3,800.

INLAND SEAS. see HISTORY — History Of North And South America

386　　　　　　　　　UK
INLAND WATERWAYS GUIDE. 1972. a. £1.45. (Inland Waterways Association) Archway Nicholas Publications, Faber House, 6 Eastern Rd., Romford, Essex RM1 3PJ, England. TEL 0708-20011. Ed. Michael Faulkner.

387　　　　JA　　ISSN 0386-1198
INSTITUTE FOR SEA TRAINING. JOURNAL. (Text in Japanese, summaries in English) 1951. irreg. free. Ministry of Transport, Institute for Sea Training, 2-1-3 Kasumigaseki, Chiyoda-ku, Tokyo 100, Japan. TEL 81-3-3580-4190. FAX 81-3-3580-4492. Ed.Bd. circ. 300.
Description: Covers navigation, equipment and outfit of ships, marine engineering, and education for seafarers.

387　　　　UK　　ISSN 0267-2006
INSTITUTE OF CHARTERED SHIPBROKERS. REFERENCE BOOK AND LIST OF MEMBERS (YEAR). 1983. a. £25. Millbank Publications Ltd., 25 Catherine St., London WC2B 5JW, England. TEL 071-379-3036. FAX 071-240-6840. adv.; circ. 4,000.

623.89　　　　　　　US
INSTITUTE OF NAVIGATION. PROCEEDINGS OF THE ANNUAL MEETING. a. $60 to non-members. Institute of Navigation, 1026 16th St., N.W., Ste. 104, Washington, DC 20036. TEL 202-783-4121. FAX 202-347-4698.

623.8　　　　UK　　ISSN 0020-3289
INSTITUTION OF ENGINEERS AND SHIPBUILDERS IN SCOTLAND. TRANSACTIONS.* 1857. 7/yr. £6.30. Institution of Engineers and Shipbuilders in Scotland, 10 Elmbank Gardens, Glasgow G2 4HT, Scotland. Ed. W. McLaughlin. adv.; charts; illus.; index. cum.index: vols.1-100; circ. 1,900. **Indexed:** BMT, Chem.Abstr., Eng.Ind., Met.Abstr., Ocean.Abstr., Pollut.Abstr., Sci.Abstr.

623.8　　　　II　　ISSN 0020-3475
INSTITUTION OF MARINE TECHNOLOGISTS. JOURNAL. (Text in English) 1956. s-a. Rs.7.50($1) Institution of Marine Technologists, c/o Ericson & Richards, 32 Nicol Rd., Ballard Estate, Bombay 400038, India. Ed. J.S. Bhatti. adv.; bk.rev.; circ. 700.

387　　　　FR　　ISSN 0223-534X
INSTRUCTIONS NAUTIQUES. 1902. irreg. price varies. Service Hydrographique et Oceanographique de la Marine, 3 av. Octave Greard, 00300 Armees, France. TEL 98-22-10-80. FAX 98-43-18-11. TELEX HYDRO 940568. (Subscr. to: EPSHOM, BP 426, 29275 Brest Cedex, France).

387　　　　HK　　ISSN 1015-2253
INTERMODAL ASIA. q. $50. Lloyd's of London Press (Far East) Ltd., Rm. 1101, Hollywood Centre, 233 Hollywood Rd., Hong Kong. TEL 854-3222. FAX 854-1538.

387　　　　UK　　ISSN 0954-5964
VK235
INTERNATIONAL CARGO HANDLING COORDINATION ASSOCIATION. BUYERS' GUIDE TO MANUFACTURERS. 1984. a. £25. Millbank Publications Ltd., 25 Catherine St., London WC2B 5JW, England. TEL 071-379-3036. FAX 071-240-6840. adv.; illus.; circ. 3,500.

385　　　　　　　　　FR
INTERNATIONAL COMMISSION OF MARITIME HISTORY. COLLOQUES. ACTES. 1957. irreg. Service d'Edition et de Vente des Publications de l'Education Nationale, 13 rue du Four, 75006 Paris, France.

623.89　　　　FR　　ISSN 0538-6128
INTERNATIONAL CONFERENCE ON LIGHTHOUSES AND OTHER AIDS TO NAVIGATION. REPORTS. (Includes: "Discussion Reports" which are in English; occasionally in French) 1929. every 4 yrs. 200 Fr. Association Internationale de Signalisation Maritime - International Association of Lighthouse Authorities, 20 ter, rue Schnapper, 78100 Saint Germain en Laye, France. TEL 33-1-34-51-70-01. FAX 33-1-34-51-82-05. TELEX 695 499 F.
Description: Small booklets, some with photographs and-or drawings covering the conferences.

387 910.09　　　UK　　ISSN 0957-7696
INTERNATIONAL CRUISE AND FERRY REVIEW. 1989. q. £50. Contract Communications Limited, Refuge House, 9-10 River Front, Enfield EN1 3SZ, England. TEL 081-367-3939. FAX 081-366-9091. TELEX 927828-CONTCO-G. circ. 7,000. (back issues avail.)
Description: Reviews developments affecting the international cruise and ferry industry.

387　　　　　　　　UK
INTERNATIONAL FEDERATION OF SHIPMASTERS ASSOCIATIONS. ANNUAL REPORT. a. International Federation of Shipmasters Associations, 202 Lambeth Rd., London SE1 7JY, England. TEL 071-261-0450. TELEX 934089-MARSOC-G.

387　　　　　　　　UK
INTERNATIONAL FEDERATION OF SHIPMASTERS ASSOCIATIONS. NEWSLETTER. q. International Federation of Shipmasters Associations, 202 Lambeth Rd., London SE1 7JY, England. TEL 071-261-0450. FAX 071-401-2537. TELEX 934089 MARSOC G.

387 971　　　CN　　ISSN 0843-8714
INTERNATIONAL JOURNAL OF MARITIME HISTORY. 1989. $45. Memorial University of Newfoundland, Maritime Studies Research Unit, St. John's, Nfld. A1C 5S7, Canada. TEL 709-737-8424. FAX 709-737-4569. TELEX 016-4677. (Co-Sponsor: Maritime Economic History Group) Eds. Lewis R. Fischer, Helge W. Nordvik. adv.; bk.rev.; circ. 500. (also avail. in microform)
—BLDSC shelfmark: 4542.329500.
Description: Publishes scholarly articles, notes, and reviews on maritime economic and social history.
Refereed Serial

623.89　　　　　　　BE
INTERNATIONAL NAVIGATION CONGRESS. PAPERS. (Text in English or French; summaries in English or French) quadrennial, 27th, 1990, Brussels. 8000 Fr. Permanent International Association of Navigation Congresses, 155 rue de la Loi, Boite 9, B-1040 Osaka, Belgium. TEL 02-733-96-70. FAX 02-736-08-04. TELEX 23542 OW SGB.

380.5 623.89　　　　BE
INTERNATIONAL NAVIGATION CONGRESS. PROCEEDINGS. (Text in English or French) 1961, 20th, Baltimore. quadrennial. Permanent International Association of Navigation Congresses, 155 rue de la Loi, Boite 9, B-1040 Brussels, Belgium. TEL 02-733-96-70. FAX 02-736-08-04. TELEX 23542 OW SGB. circ. 4,000.

387　　　　CN　　ISSN 0835-6955
INTERNATIONAL NEWSLETTER OF MARITIME HISTORY. (Text in English, French, German, Spanish) 1989. s-a. Memorial University of Newfoundland, Maritime Studies Research Unit, St. John's, Nfld. A1C 5S7, Canada. TEL 709-737-8424. FAX 709-737-4569. TELEX 016-4677. Eds. Lewis R. Fischer, Helge W. Nordvik. adv.; circ. 500. (also avail. in microform)
Description: Publishes extensive information on news, publications and conferences of interest to maritime historians.
Refereed Serial

387　　　　　　　　UK
INTERNATIONAL OFFSHORE CRAFT CONFERENCE. PROCEEDINGS. irreg., 2nd 1977; 3rd 1979. $50. Thomas Reed Publications Ltd., Weir House, Hurst Rd., E. Molesey, Surrey KT8 9AQ, England. TEL 081-941-8090. FAX 081-941-8046. TELEX 883526-REED-G. Ed. Kenneth D. Troup.

INTERNATIONAL OMEGA ASSOCIATION. PROCEEDINGS OF ANNUAL MEETING. see AERONAUTICS AND SPACE FLIGHT

INTERNATIONAL OMEGA ASSOCIATION NEWSLETTER. see TRANSPORTATION — Air Transport

623.82　　　　NE　　ISSN 0020-868X
　　　　　　　　　　　　CODEN: ISBPAS
INTERNATIONAL SHIPBUILDING PROGRESS. q. fl.214. Delft University Press, Stevinweg 1, 2628 CN Delft, Netherlands. TEL 015-783254. FAX 015-781661.
—BLDSC shelfmark: 4549.300000.

387　　　　　　　　UK
INTERNATIONAL TUG CONVENTION PROCEEDINGS. 1969. biennial. $85. Thomas Reed Publications Ltd., Weir House, Hurst RD., E. Molesey, Surrey KT8 9AQ, England. TEL 081-941-80909. FAX 081-941-8046. TELEX 883526-REED-G. Ed. Ken Troup. adv.; circ. 1,000.

INTERNATIONALE TRANSPORT-ZEITSCHRIFT/JOURNAL POUR LE TRANSPORT INTERNATIONAL/INTERNATIONAL TRANSPORT JOURNAL-OVERSEAS DIGEST. see TRANSPORTATION

387 380　　　UK　　ISSN 0260-924X
HE557.I75
IRELAND PORTS & SHIPPING HANDBOOK. 1981. a. £10. Charter International Publications Ltd., Castle Chambers, Castle Acre, King's Lynn, Norfolk PE32 2BQ, England. TEL 07605-634. FAX 07605-625. TELEX 817440. Ed. James P. Moriarty. adv.; illus.; circ. 6,000.

IRISH SKIPPER. see FISH AND FISHERIES

623.89 550　　　　　　　IT
ISTITUTO UNIVERSITARIO NAVALE. FACOLTA DI SCIENZE NAUTICHE. NAPLES. ANNALI. (Text in English and Italian) 1932. a. free. Istituto Universitario Navale, Via Ammiraglio Acton 38, 80133 Naples, Italy. TEL (81) 5524342. circ. 600. (back issues avail.)
Formerly: Facolta di Scienze Nautiche. Annali.
Description: Covers a wide variety of disciplines related to modern navigation and earth sciences.

ITALY. ISTITUTO CENTRALE DI STATISTICA. STATISTICHE DELLA NAVIGAZIONE MARITTIMA. see TRANSPORTATION — Abstracting, Bibliographies, Statistics

386　　　　RU　　ISSN 0202-7879
TC1
ITOGI NAUKI I TEKHNIKI: VODNYI TRANSPORT. 1966. irreg., latest vol.14-15, 1989. 5.40 Rub. Vsesoyuznyi Institut Nauchno-Tekhnicheskoi Informatsii (VINITI), Baltiiskaya ul. 14, Moscow A-219, Russia. (Subscr. to: Mezhdunarodnaya Kniga, Dimitrova ul. 39, 113095 Moscow, Russia)
—BLDSC shelfmark: 0040.920000.

387　　　　JA　　ISSN 0913-5480
J A M R I REPORT. (Text in English) 1984. irreg. free. Japan Maritime Research Institute - Kaiji Sangyo Kenkyujo, Kaiun Bldg., 2-6-4 Hirakawa-cho, Chiyoda-ku, Tokyo 102, Japan. TEL 03-3265-5231. FAX 03-3265-5035. Ed. Hideo Kuroda. circ. 700. (back issues avail.)

4730 TRANSPORTATION — SHIPS AND SHIPPING

387   JM
JAMAICA PORT NEWS. 1968. q. Port Authority, 15-17 Duke St., Kingston, Jamaica, W.I. TEL 809-922-0290. FAX 809-924-9437. TELEX 2386-PORTOPS. Ed. Jennifer McDonald. circ. 700.
 Description: Highlights shipping and cruise line innovations. Lists promotions and appointments.

JANE'S FIGHTING SHIPS. see *MILITARY*

387   UK
VM363
JANE'S HIGH-SPEED MARINE CRAFT; hydrofoils, builders of air-cushion vehicles and other civil and military vessels, civil operators, engineering components, associations. 1967. a. £135($210) Jane's Information Group, Sentinel House, 163 Brighton Rd., Coulsdon, Surrey CR5 2NH, England. TEL 081-763-1030. FAX 081-763-1005. TELEX 916907 JANES G. (U.S. & Can. order from: Dept. DSM, 1340 Braddock Pl., Ste. 300, Box 1436, Alexandria, VA 22314-1651) Ed. Robert Trillo. adv.; index.
 Former titles (until 1989): Jane's High-Speed Marine Craft and Air Cushion Vehicles (ISSN 0951-3124); (until 1986): Jane's Surface Skimmers (ISSN 0075-305X)

387   JA   ISSN 0447-3728
JAPAN. MARITIME SAFETY AGENCY. HYDROGRAPHIC DEPARTMENT. NOTICES TO MARINERS/SUIRO TSUHO. (Text in English) 1889. w. exchange basis. Kaijo Hoan-cho, Suiro-bu - Maritime Safety Agency, Hydrographic Department, 3-1, Tsukiji 5-chome, Chuo-ku, Tokyo 104, Japan. FAX 03-545-2885. TELEX 2522452 HDJODC J. Ed. Takahiro Sato. stat.

387   551.46 629.1   JA   ISSN 0388-7405
JAPAN INSTITUTE OF NAVIGATION. JOURNAL/NIHON KOKAI GAKKAI RONBUNSHU. (Text in English, Japanese; summaries in English) 1949. s-a. 3000 Yen($21) per no. Japan Institute of Navigation - Nihon Kokai Gakkai, c/o Tokyo University of Mercantile Marine, 2-1-6 Echujima, Koto-ku, Tokyo 135, Japan. Ed. K. Honda. circ. 1,700. (back issues avail.) Indexed: JTA.
 —BLDSC shelfmark: 4805.300000.

387   JA
JAPAN PORT INFORMATION. (Text in English) 1969. biennial. 2000 Yen. (Japan Association of Foreign Ship Agencies) Japan Press Ltd., C.P.O. Box 6, Tokyo 100-91, Japan. TEL 03-3404-5161. FAX 03-3423-2358. TELEX 242-5374 JPRESS J. (Subscr. to: 2-12-8 Kita Aoyama, Minato-ku, Tokyo 107, Japan) Ed. Yoshio Wada.

623.82 359   CC   ISSN 1000-7148
JIANCHUAN ZHISHI. (Text in Chinese) 1979. m. $0.40 per no. (Zhongguo Zaochuan Gongcheng Xuehui - Chinese Ship Engineering Society) Jianchuan Zhishi Bianjibu, 70 Xueyuan Nanlu, Beijing 100081, People's Republic of China. TEL 8315522. Ed. Yang Pu.

387   CC   ISSN 1001-5388
JIANGSU CHUANBO. (Text in Chinese) q. Jiangsu Sheng Chuanbo Sheji Yanjiusuo, 440 Jiefang Lu, Zhenjiang, Jiangsu 212001, People's Republic of China. TEL 232820. Ed. Zhu Minhu.

387   CC   ISSN 1000-4696
JIAOTONGBU SHANGHAI CHUANBO YUNSHU KEXUE YANJIUSUO XUEBAO. (Text in Chinese) s-a. Jiaotong-bu, Shanghai Chuanbo Yunshu Kexue Yanjiusuo - Ministry of Transportation. Shanghai Institute of Shipping Transportation Science, 200 Minsheng Lu, Shanghai 200135, People's Republic of China. TEL 8840438. Ed. Lu Fusheng.

387.5   FR   ISSN 0983-0537
JOURNAL DE LA MARINE MARCHANDE ET DU TRANSPORT MULTIMODAL. 1919. w. 3070 F. (foreign 3240 F.). Moreux, 190 bd. Haussmann, 75008 Paris, France. TEL 1-45-63-11-55. FAX 1-42-89-08-72. TELEX 290 131. adv.; bk.rev.; abstr.; charts; illus.; stat.; circ. 14,500. Indexed: BMT, Excerp.Med., Key to Econ.Sci.
 Incorporates: Marine Marchande (ISSN 0294-8508); Former titles (until 1986): Journal de la Marine Marchande (ISSN 0762-3151); (until 1982): Journal de la Marine Marchande et de la Navigation Aerienne (ISSN 0397-6467); (until 1938): Journal de la Marine Marchande (ISSN 0021-7786)

JOURNAL OF MARITIME LAW AND COMMERCE. see *LAW — Maritime Law*

623.8   UK   ISSN 0373-4633
VK1   CODEN: JONVAL
JOURNAL OF NAVIGATION. 1947. 3/yr. £59($129) (Royal Institute of Navigation) Cambridge University Press, Edinburgh Bldg., Shaftesbury Rd., Cambridge CB2 2RU, England. TEL 0223-312393. FAX 0223-315052. (N. American addr.: Cambridge University Press, 40 W. 20th St., New York, NY 10011-4211. TEL 212-924-3900) Ed. J.F. Kemp. adv.; bk.rev.; charts; illus.; maps; index. cum.index every 15 yrs.; circ. 6,000. (back issues avail.) Indexed: BMT, Br.Tech.Ind., Curr.Cont., Deep Sea Res.& Oceanogr.Abstr., Ergon.Abstr., Excerp.Med., Fluidex, Geo.Abstr., Int.Aerosp.Abstr., Ocean.Abstr., Pollut.Abstr., Sci.Abstr.
 Formerly: Institute of Navigation. Journal (ISSN 0020-3009)
 Description: Presents papers on every aspect of navigation - air, land, sea and space - and papers on every type - scientific, historical and narrative.

623.8   US   ISSN 8756-1417
JOURNAL OF SHIP PRODUCTION. 1985. q. $60. Society of Naval Architects and Marine Engineers, 601 Pavonia Ave., Jersey City, NJ 07306-2907. TEL 201-798-4800. illus.; index; circ. 1,750.
 —BLDSC shelfmark: 5064.350000.

623.8   US   ISSN 0022-4502
VM1   CODEN: JSRHAR
JOURNAL OF SHIP RESEARCH. 1957. q. $70. Society of Naval Architects and Marine Engineers, 601 Pavonia Ave., Jersey City, NJ 07306-2907. charts; illus.; stat.; index; circ. 2,800. Indexed: Appl.Mech.Rev., BMT, Curr.Cont., Eng.Ind., Fluidex, Ocean.Abstr., Pollut.Abstr., Sh.& Vib.Dig.
 —BLDSC shelfmark: 5064.400000.

387   PK
K P T NEWS BULLETIN. (Text in English) 1966. fortn. Rs.2.40 per no. Karachi Port Trust, Post Box 4725, Pakistan. TEL 201305. FAX 2415567. TELEX 2739 KPT PK. Ed. Kafil Ahmed Khan. charts; illus.; stat.; circ. 2,000.

387   JA   ISSN 0286-9152
KAIJI SANGYO KENKYUJOHO/JAPAN MARITIME RESEARCH INSTITUTE. BULLETIN. (Text in Japanese) 1966. m. 10500 Yen. Japan Maritime Research Institute - Kaiji Sangyo Kenkyujo, Kaiun Bldg., 2-6-4 Hirakawa-cho, Chiyoda-ku, Tokyo 102, Japan. TEL 03-3265-5231. FAX 03-3265-5035. Ed. Noburo Kameyama. bk.rev.; index; circ. 1,300. (back issues avail.)
 Description: Journal of shipping, shipbuilding and port research.

KAIJO HOAN-CHO. SUIRO-BU KANSOKU HOKOKU. EISEI SOKUCHI HEN/DATA REPORT OF HYDROGRAPHIC OBSERVATIONS. SERIES OF SATELLITE GEODESY. see *EARTH SCIENCES — Geophysics*

387   JA   ISSN 0022-7803
KAIUN/SHIPPING. (Text in Japanese) 1922. m. 14,400 Yen. Japan Shipping Exchange, Inc. - Nihon Kaiun Shukaijo, Mitsuirokugokan 3-16 Muromachi 2-chome, Nihonbashi, Chuo-ku, Tokyo, Japan. FAX 03-3279-2785. TELEX 02222140 SHIPEX. Ed. Tadashi Inoue. adv.; bk.rev.; stat.; index; circ. 8,000. (looseleaf format)

387.164   BG
KARNAPHULI SHIPPING NEWS. (Text in English) 1977. s-w. 88 Ghat Farhadbag, Kazem Ali Rd., Chittagong 4000, Bangladesh. TEL 31-220366. FAX 880-31-225204. TELEX 66483 RAS BJ. Ed. F. Karim. circ. 10,000.

387   GW   ISSN 0176-473X
KEHRWIEDER. 1957. m. DM.24. Verband Deutscher Reeder e.V., Esplanade 6, Postfach 305580, 2000 Hamburg 36, Germany. TEL 040-350970. FAX 040-35097211. adv.; bk.rev.; circ. 9,000.

KINGS POINTER. see *COLLEGE AND ALUMNI*

387   DK   ISSN 0023-2629
KOEBENHAVNS HAVNEBLAD/PORT OF COPENHAGEN REVIEW. (Text in Danish; summaries in English) 1948. 10/yr. free. Faellesrepraesentationen for Funktionaerer ved Koebenhavns Havnevaesen, Nordre Toldbod 7, Postboks 2083, 1013 Copenhagen K, Denmark. TEL 33 14 43 40, local 310. FAX 33-93-23-40. Eds. John Pri, Per Hagelund. adv.; bk.rev.; illus.; circ. 4,400 (controlled).
 Description: Features articles and news items related to the Port of Copenhagen and its role in international commerce. Includes timetables of scheduled departures from the port.

387   GW   ISSN 0075-6474
KOEHLERS FLOTTENKALENDER. JAHRBUCH FUER SCHIFFAHRT UND HAEFEN. 1901. a. DM.19.80. Koehlers Verlagsgesellschaft mbH, Steintorwall 17, Postfach 2352, 4900 Herford, Germany. TEL 5221-59910. FAX 5221-599125. adv.; bk.rev.; abstr.; charts; illus.; stat.; circ. 20,000.

387   JA   ISSN 0450-660X
KOKAI/NAVIGATION. (Text in Japanese; titles, authors in English) 1954. q. 2000 Yen($14) per no. Japan Institute of Navigation - Nihon Kokai Gakkai, c/o Tokyo Institute of Mercantile Marine, 2-1-6 Echujima, Koto-ku, Tokyo 135, Japan. Ed. A. Sugiura. circ. 1,900. (back issues avail.) Indexed: JTA.
 —BLDSC shelfmark: 6067.100000.

KONKYLIEN. see *WOMEN'S INTERESTS*

623.8 386   BU
KORABOSTROENE I KORABOPLAVANE/SHIPBUILDING AND SHIPPING. (Text in Bulgarian; summaries in English) 1956. m. $11. Ministerstvo na Transporta, Sofia, Bulgaria. (Dist. by: Hemus, 6, Rouski Blvd., 1000 Sofia, Bulgaria) (Co-sponsor: Bulgaria. Ministerstvo na Mashinostroeneto i Metalurgiiata) Ed. S. Popov. circ. 2,017. Indexed: BMT.

387   KO
KOREA SHIPPING GAZETTE. (Text in English, Korean) 1971. w. 34000 Won($550) (Korea Maritime Research Institute) Korea Shipping Gazette Co., Ltd., 43-1 Tongeni-dong, Jongro-ku, C.P.O. Box 3198, Seoul, S. Korea. Ed. Jong Ok Lee. adv.; bk.rev.; illus.; circ. 5,000.

627.2   JA
KOWAN GIJUTSU KENKYUJO. GAIDO/PORT AND HARBOUR RESEARCH INSTITUTE. GUIDE. irreg. exchange basis. Un'yu-sho, Kowan Gijutsu Kenkyujo - Ministry of Transportation, Port and Harbour Research Institute, 1-1, 3-chome, Nagase, Yokosuka, Kanagawa 239, Japan. illus. Indexed: Geotech.Abstr.
 Formerly: Port and Harbour Technical Research Institute. Guide.

386   US   ISSN 0075-7748
HE564.A4
LAKE CARRIERS' ASSOCIATION. ANNUAL REPORT. 1885. a. $20. Lake Carriers' Association, 915 Rockefeller Bldg., Cleveland, OH 44113-1383. TEL 216-621-1107. FAX 216-241-8262. Ed. Glen G. Nekvasil. index; circ. 1,500.

387.5   IT   ISSN 0024-032X
LEGA NAVALE. 1897. m. L.22000. Lega Navale Italiana, Via 24 Maggio 11, 00187 Rome, Italy. Ed. Claudio Ressmann. adv.; bk.rev.; illus.; stat.; circ. 28,000.
 Description: Covers the merchant marine.

LETTRE CONFIDENTIELLE DES TRANSPORTS. see *TRANSPORTATION — Air Transport*

287   UK
LIBERIAN SHIPPING JOURNAL. 1957. m. Arthur H. Thrower Ltd., 44-46 S. Ealing Rd., London W5, England. Ed. A. Thrower. adv.

LIQUID GAS CARRIER REGISTER. see *PETROLEUM AND GAS*

387   UK   ISSN 0260-7387
HE565.A3
LIST OF SHIPOWNERS. 1955. a. $200. Lloyd's Register of Shipping, 71 Fenchurch St., London EC3M 4BS, England. (Subscr. address in US: Lloyd's Register of Shipping, 17 Battery Place, New York, NY 10004)
 Description: Approximately 40,000 shipowners, managers and managing agents: addresses, telephone, telex and fax numbers, and fleet lists.

387   FR
LISTE DES SIGNAUX DISTINCTIFS ET INDICATIFS INTERNATIONAUX DES STATIONS FRANCAISES (NAVIRES, STATIONS TERRESTRES).. 1941. a. price varies. Service Hydrographique et Oceanographique de la Marine, 3 av. Octave Greard, 00300 Armees, France. TEL 98-22-10-80. FAX 98-43-18-11. TELEX HYDRO 940568. (Subscr. to: EPSHOM, B.P. 426, 29275 Brest Cedex, France) Ed.Bd. circ. 1,500. (also avail. in magnetic tape)

387.2   BE
LISTE OFFICIELLE DES NAVIRES DE MER BELGES ET DE LA FLOTTE DE LA FORCE NAVALE. a. Administration des Affaires Maritimes et de la Navigation, 104 rue d'Arlon, 1040 Brussels, Belgium. TEL 02-233-12-11. FAX 02-230-30-02. TELEX 61880 VERTRA B. illus.

387   UK
LLOYD'S A S E A N SHIPPING DIRECTORY. (Association of South East Asian Nations) a. $60. Lloyd's of London Press Ltd., Sheepen Place, Colchester, Essex CO3 3LP, England. TEL 0206-529-9500, 0206-77227. FAX 0206-46273. TELEX 987321 LLOYDS G. (U.S. addr.: Lloyd's of London Press Inc., 611 Broadway, Ste. 523, New York, NY 10012) adv.; tr.lit. (back issues avail.)

387   UK
LLOYD'S INTERNATIONAL MARINE EQUIPMENT GUIDE (YEAR). a. $140. Lloyd's of London Press Ltd., Sheepen Place, Colchester, Essex CO3 3LP, England. TEL 0206-772277. FAX 0206-46273. TELEX 987321 LLOYDS G. (In US, subscr. to: Lloyd's of London Press Inc., 611 Broadway, Ste. 308, NY 10012. TEL 212-529-9500) Ed. Suzanne Hooke. adv.
    Formerly (until 1988): Lloyd's Marine Equipment Guide (ISSN 0268-3253)
    Description: For international buyers and sellers of marine and offshore equipment and services. Provides world-wide list of marine equipment manufacturers available. Contains over 40,000 product entries, 6,300 company listings.

387 368.2   UK
LLOYD'S LIST INTERNATIONAL. 1734. 6/w (Mon.-Sat.). £343($1395) Lloyd's of London Press Ltd., Sheepen Place, Colchester, Essex CO3 3LP, England. TEL 0206-772277. FAX 0206-46273. (US subscr. to: 611 Broadway, Ste. 308, New York, NY 10012. TEL 212-529-9500) Ed. David Gilbertson. adv.; bk.rev.; circ. 14,650.
    Description: Information about shipping, insurance, energy, transportation and finance, with special reports on selected business topics.

387   UK   ISSN 0144-6681
LLOYD'S LOADING LIST. (Free supplements avail.) w. $950. Lloyd's of London Press Ltd., Sheepen Place, Colchester, Essex CO3 3LP, England. TEL 0206-77227. FAX 0206-46273. TELEX 987321. (US subscr. to: 611 Broadway, Ste. 308, New York, NY 10012. TEL 212-529-9500)
    Description: Provides coverage of freighting services by sea, road, rail and air from the UK to over 1000 destinations in all parts of the world.

LLOYD'S MARITIME & COMMERCIAL LAW QUARTERLY. see *LAW — Maritime Law*

387   HK   ISSN 1015-227X
LLOYD'S MARITIME ASIA. (Text in English) 1980. m. HK.$640 (Asia $110; elsewhere $145). Lloyd's of London Press (Far East) Ltd., Rm. 1101, Hollywood Centre, 233 Hollywood Rd., Hong Kong. TEL 854-3222. FAX 854-1538. Ed. Kevin Chinnery. adv.; bk.rev.; chart.; illus.; stat.; tra.lit.; circ. 7,000.

387   UK   ISSN 0076-020X
G1060
LLOYD'S MARITIME ATLAS. 1951. biennial. $90. Lloyd's of London Press Ltd., Sheepen Place, Colchester, Essex CO3 3LP, England. TEL 0206-772277. FAX 0206-46273. TELEX 987321 LLOYDS G. (US subscr. to: 611 Broadway, Ste. 308, New York, NY 10012. TEL 212-529-9500) index; circ. 14,000.
    Description: Gives reference to over 10,000 ports and shipping places around the world. Includes maps, economic information, distance tables, text and other shipping information.

387   UK   ISSN 0268-327X
HE951
LLOYD'S MARITIME DIRECTORY (YEAR); international shipping & shipbuilding directory. 1982. a. $265. Lloyd's of London Press Ltd., Sheepen Place, Colchester, Essex CO3 3LP, England. TEL 0206-772277. FAX 0206-46273. TELEX 987321 LLOYDS G. (US subscr. to: 611 Broadway, Ste. 308, New York, NY 10012. TEL 212-529-9500) Ed. Chris Emery. adv.
    Description: Provides names and addresses of over 5,500 shipowners, managers and agents arranged in alphabetical order under countries, details of the 34,000 vessels under their control, with listings of maritime service industry firms, from shipbuilding to salvage.

LLOYD'S MARITIME LAW NEWSLETTER. see *LAW — Maritime Law*

387   UK   ISSN 0266-6189
LLOYD'S MONTHLY LIST OF LAID UP VESSELS. m. $520. Lloyd's of London Press Ltd., Sheepen Place, Colchester, Essex CO3 3LP, England. TEL 0206-772277. FAX 0206-46273. TELEX 987321. (US subscr. to: 611 Broadway, Ste. 308, New York, NY 10012. TEL 212-529-9500) Ed. C.J. Fairweather. circ. 260.
    Description: Report on the constantly changing record of vessels laid up, with analyses of the listed vessels by type, flag and age.

387   UK   ISSN 0952-5394
LLOYD'S NAUTICAL YEAR BOOK. 1892. a. $65. Lloyd's of London Press Ltd., Sheepen Place, Colchester, Essex CO3 3LP, England. TEL 0206-772277. FAX 0206-46273. TELEX 987321 LLOYDS G. (US subscr. to: 611 Broadway, Ste. 308, New York, NY 10012. TEL 212-529-9500) Ed. Paul Cuny. adv.; circ. 10,000.
    —BLDSC shelfmark: 5287.280000.
    Former titles: Lloyd's Nautical Yearbook and Calendar; Lloyd's Calendar and Nautical Yearbook (ISSN 0076-0196)
    Description: Information on shipping regulations, legislation, and statistics, for companies and individuals involved with shipping ashore or afloat.

387   US
LLOYD'S PASSENGER SHIPPING INTERNATIONAL. 1989. m. $395. Lloyd's of London Press, Inc., 611 Broadway, Ste. 308, New York, NY 10012-2608. TEL 212-529-9500. FAX 212-529-9826. Ed. Jeff Myhre.
    Description: Covers all practical aspects of the dynamic shipping industry. Combines worldwide cruise and ferry news with data on passenger shipping demand and supply, international rules and regulations, port developments, vessel sale and purchase.

387   UK   ISSN 0266-6197
LLOYD'S PORTS OF THE WORLD (YEAR). 1982. a. $240. Lloyd's of London Press Ltd., Sheepen Place, Colchester, Essex CO9 3LP, England. TEL 0206-772277. FAX 0206-46273. TELEX 987321 LLOYDS G. (US subscr. to: 611 Broadway, Ste. 308, New York, NY 10012. TEL 212-529-9500) Ed. Brian Pinchin.
    Description: Lists 2,700 ports worldwide, with name and address of the relevant port authority, approach hazards, and facilities for anyone involved in international trade.

387   UK   ISSN 0261-6688
LLOYD'S REGISTER OF CLASSED YACHTS. 1981. a. $40. Lloyd's Register of Shipping, 71 Fenchurch St., London EC3M 4BS, England. TEL 071-709-0166. (Subscr. address in US: Lloyd's Register of Shipping, 17 Battery Place, New York, NY 10004)
    —BLDSC shelfmark: 5287.287000.
    Supersedes: Lloyd's Register of Yachts.
    Description: Details of all yachts classed with Lloyd's Register of Shipping.

387   UK   ISSN 0076-0234
HE563.A3
LLOYD'S REGISTER OF SHIPPING. STATISTICAL TABLES. 1878. a. $110. Lloyd's Register of Shipping, 71 Fenchurch St., London EC3M 4BS, England. TEL 071-709-0166. (In US, subscr. to: Lloyd's Register of Shipping, 17 Battery Place, New York, NY 10004)
    —BLDSC shelfmark: 5287.600000.
    Description: World merchant fleet broken down by registration, size, age and ship-type.

387   UK   ISSN 0141-4909
HE565.A3
LLOYD'S REGISTER OF SHIPS. (In three volumes) 1764. a. (with m. supplements). $865. Lloyd's Register of Shipping, 71 Fenchurch St., London EC3M 4BS, England. TEL 071-709-9166. (In US, subscr. to: Lloyd's Register of Shipping, 17 Battery Place, New York, NY 10004)
    Description: Information on over 77,000 merchant ships, listed in alphabetical order by ship-name.

387   US
LLOYD'S SHIP ARREST INTERNATIONAL; a confidential worldwide report on detained ships and cargoes. 1989. m. $395. Lloyd's of London Press, Inc., 611 Broadway, Ste. 308, New York, NY 10012-2608. TEL 212-529-9500. FAX 212-529-9826. Ed. Jeff Myhre.
    Description: Covers all aspects of ship and cargo arrest worldwide. Contains news, analysis, views, and features on the detention of ocean-going vessels as well as a data-base report of recent ship arrests compiled from a maritime intelligence network.

387   UK   ISSN 0265-2455
LLOYD'S SHIP MANAGER. vol.2, 1978. m. $275. Lloyd's of London Press Ltd., Sheepen Place, Colchester, Essex CO3 3LP, England. TEL 0206-772277. FAX 0206-46273. TELEX 987321. (US subscr. to: 611 Broadway, Ste. 308, New York, NY 10012. TEL 212-529-9500) Ed. Paul Gunton. adv.; bk.rev.; illus.; circ. 8,500.
    Indexed: BMT, Fluidex.
    —BLDSC shelfmark: 5287.735000.
    Incorporates: Shipping News International & Shipbuilding and Marine Engineering International; **Formerly:** Nautical Review (ISSN 0309-6254)
    Description: Provides monthly information service on all management, technical and operational aspects relating to the safe and profitable operation of ocean-going tonnage.

387   NO
HE561
LLOYD'S SHIP MANAGER. SHIPPING NEWS INTERNATIONAL. (Text in English and Norwegian) 1945. 12/yr. £95. Selvig Publishing A-S, Box 9070 Vaterland, 0134 Oslo 1, Norway. TEL 02-364440. FAX 02-360550. Ed. adv.; bk.rev.; charts; illus.; mkt.; circ. 11,000. **Indexed:** BMT, Key to Econ.Sci., P.A.I.S.
    Former titles: Shipping News International; Norwegian Shipping News (ISSN 0029-3709)

387   UK   ISSN 0144-6673
LLOYD'S SHIPPING ECONOMIST. 1979. m. $995. Lloyd's of London Press Ltd., Sheepen Place, Colchester, Essex CO3 3LP, England. TEL 0206-772277. FAX 0206-46273. TELEX 987321 LLOYDS G. (US subscr. to: 611 Broadway, Ste. 308, New York, NY 10012. TEL 212-529-9500) Ed. Deborah Seyman.
    —BLDSC shelfmark: 5287.743000.
    Description: Provides information, analysis and comment upon supply and demand factors in the international shipping markets.

387   UK   ISSN 0144-4549
LLOYD'S SHIPPING INDEX. 1882. d. $1950. Lloyd's of London Press Ltd., Sheepen Place, Colchester, Essex CO3 3LP, England. TEL 0206-772277. FAX 0206-46273. TELEX 987321 LLOYDS G. (US subscr. to: 611 Broadway, Ste. 308, New York, NY 10012. TEL 212-529-9500) Ed. T.C. Bird. circ. 5,500.
    Description: Presents the current voyages, latest reported movements and vital particulars of 23,000 merchant ships, together with any casualty or other information reported.

387   UK
LLOYD'S SURVEY HANDBOOK. a. $65. Lloyd's of London Press Ltd., Sheepen Place, Colchester, Essex CO3 3LP, England. TEL 0206-77227. FAX 0206-46273. TELEX 987321 LLOYDS G. (US subscr. to: 611 Broadway, Ste. 308, New York, NY 10012. TEL 212-529-9500) tr.lit. (back issues avail.)
    Description: References packing stowage, transportation, and commodity storage for cargo surveyors, loss adjusters, and insurers; also covers general causes of damage and problems associated with transporting goods, plus information about handling hazardous cargoes.

TRANSPORTATION — SHIPS AND SHIPPING

387   UK   ISSN 0144-4557
HE730
LLOYD'S VOYAGE RECORD. 1946. w. $2285. Lloyd's of London Press Ltd., Sheepen Place, Colchester, Essex CO3 3LP, England. TEL 0206-772277. FAX 0206-46273. TELEX 987321 LLOYDS G. (US subscr. to: 611 Broadway, Ste. 308, New York, NY 10012. TEL 212-529-9500) Ed. M.D.S. Rodger. adv.; circ. 1,000. (also avail. in microfiche)
Description: Records vessels' movements chronologically, providing details of the last four ports of call for tankers, six for bulk carriers and eight for dry cargo vessels.

LLOYD'S WEEKLY CASUALTY REPORTS. see INSURANCE

387   AT   ISSN 0815-0052
LOG. 1954. q. Aus.$20 (foreign Aus.$25). Nautical Association of Australia, P.O. Box 4114, Melbourne, Vic. 3001, Australia. Ed. W.G. Volum. adv.; bk.rev.; illus.; index; circ. 600. (back issues avail.)

387   SW
LOGGEN MAGAZINE. (Text in English and Swedish) 1981. bi-m. SEK 150($7) Loggen Magazine, Roekullagatan 10 B, 252 57 Helsingborg, Sweden. Ed. Lennart Hellstroem. adv.; bk.rev.; charts; illus.; circ. 2,500.
Formerly: Loggen (ISSN 0280-8234)

387   UK   ISSN 0260-8839
LONDON PORT HANDBOOK 1984. 1981. a. £10. Charter International Publications Ltd., Castle Chambers, Castle Acre, King's Lynn, Norfolk PE32 2BQ, England. TEL 07605-634. FAX 07605-625. TELEX 817440. Ed. James P. Moriarty. adv.; circ. 6,000.

LOOKOUT (NEW YORK). see RELIGIONS AND THEOLOGY

387 380   UK   ISSN 0266-0644
LOS ANGELES PORT AND SHIPPING HANDBOOK. 1984. a. Charter International Publications Ltd., Castle Chambers, Castle Acre, King's Lynn, Norfolk PE32 2BQ, England. TEL 07605-634. FAX 07605-625. TELEX 817440. Ed. James P. Moriarty. adv.; circ. 6,000.

387   US
HE745
M A R A D (YEAR). 1950. a. U.S. Maritime Administration, Washington, DC 20590. TEL 202-426-5812. (Orders to: Supt. of Documents, Washington, DC 20402)
Formerly: U.S. Maritime Administration. Annual Report (ISSN 0083-1670)
Description: Incorporates reports by the Congress on the following topics: acquisition of obsolete vessels in exchange for vessel trade-in credit; war-risk insurance activities; scrapping or removal of obsolete vessels owned by the U.S.; and U.S.-flag carriage of government-sponsored cargoes. Includes information on the state of the maritime industry, as well as other MARAD activities.

387   SP
MADRID TRANS-PORT. 1983. a. 650 ptas. Publicaciones Men-Car, S.A., Paseo de Colon 24, 08002 Barcelona, Spain. TEL 93-301-5516. FAX 93-318-6645. Eds. Juan Cardona, Manuel Cardona. adv.; circ. 15,000.

387   TS
AL-MAJALLAH AL-BAHRIYYAH/MARITIME MAGAZINE. (Text in Arabic) 1981. q. exchange basis. Arab Maritime Transport Academy, P.O. Box 1552, Sharjah, United Arab Emirates. TEL 358866. FAX 372869. TELEX 68167 ACAD EM. Ed. Abd al-Wahhab al-Diwani. circ. 500.
Description: News and activities of the academy.

387   CL   ISSN 0047-5866
MAR. 1914. a. Liga Maritima de Chile, Errazurriz 471, Casilla 117-V, Valparaiso, Chile. TEL 255179. Dir. Alejandro Navarette Torres. adv.; charts; illus.; circ. 2,000. (controlled)

MARCOM; a business guide to the application of advanced electronics, information systems and computers in shipping. see ENGINEERING — Computer Applications

387 948   GW   ISSN 0542-6758
MARE BALTICUM. (Text in German, Polish, Scandinavian languages) 1965. a. DM.20. Ostseegesellschaft e.V., Europaweg 3, 2400 Luebeck-Travemuende, Germany. FAX 04502-803131. adv.; bk.rev.; bibl.; charts; illus.; index; circ. 3,000. (back issues avail.)

LE MARIN. see FISH AND FISHERIES

387   IT   ISSN 0025-309X
MARINA ITALIANA; Rassegna delle Industrie del Mare. 1902. 10/yr. L.80000 (foreign L.140000). Associazione Italiana di Tecnica Navale, Lungo Bisagno Istria, 34c, 16141 Genoa, Italy. TEL 852151. FAX 010-8355055. TELEX 272372. (Centro Studi Tecnica Navale) adv.; bibl.; illus.; stat.; index; circ. 4,750. **Indexed:** BMT, C.I.S. Abstr. —BLDSC shelfmark: 5373.600000.

387.5   IT   ISSN 0025-3103
HE839
MARINA MERCANTILE. (Summaries in English and Italian) 1947. m. L.12000. Silvio Basile, Lungo Bisagno Istria, 34, 16141 Genoa, Italy. Ed. Ugo Marchese. adv.; bk.rev.; abstr.; bibl.; charts; illus.; pat.; stat.; tr.lit.; index; circ. 6,000. **Indexed:** BMT. —BLDSC shelfmark: 5373.603000.

387   AT
MARINE BOARD OF HOBART. ANNUAL REPORT. 1858. a. Marine Board of Hobart, Franklin Wharf, Tas. 7000, Australia. FAX 61-02-310693. TELEX MARHOB AA58319. Ed. H.C. Knoop. circ. 600.

387   US
HE561
MARINE DIGEST AND TRANSPORTATION NEWS. 1922. m. $28. Marine Publishing Inc., 1201 1st Ave. S., no.305, Box 3905, Seattle, WA 98124. TEL 206-682-3607. FAX 206-682-4023. Ed. Theresa Morrow. adv.; bk.rev.; circ. 4,500.
Formerly: Marine Digest (ISSN 0025-3197)

387   AT
MARINE ENGINE GUIDE. a. A.B. Organisation Pty. Ltd., P.O. Box 319, Avalon Beach, N.S.W. 2107, Australia. TEL 02-918-8322. FAX 02-918-8884.
Description: Lists all the inboard, outboard, stern drive, diesel and petrol engines available in Australia and New Zealand.

623.87   UK   ISSN 0047-5955
VM1   CODEN: MRERBJ
MARINE ENGINEERS REVIEW. 1970. m. £48($96) (Institute of Marine Engineers) Marine Management Holdings Ltd., 76 Mark Lane, London EC3R 7JN, England. (Dist. in N. America by: Learned Information, Inc., 143 Old Marlton Pike, Medford, NJ 08055-8750. TEL 609-654-6266) Ed. John Butchers. adv.; bk.rev.; abstr.; charts; illus.; tr.lit.; index; circ. 16,300. **Indexed:** API Abstr., API Catal., API Hlth.& Environ., API Oil., API Pet.Ref., API Pet.Subst., API Transport., BMT, Br.Tech.Ind., Chem.Abstr., Energy Info.Abstr., Eng.Ind., Excerp.Med., Fluidex, ISMEC, Met.Abstr., Ocean.Abstr., Pollut.Abstr., World Alum.Abstr. —BLDSC shelfmark: 5375.260000.

623.81   US
MARINE EQUIPMENT CATALOG. 1984. a. $65. Maritime Activity Reports, 118 E. 25th St., New York, NY 10010. TEL 212-477-6700. Ed. Laura Ann Sciame. adv.; circ. 12,000.

387   CN
MARINE EQUIPMENT DIRECTORY. 1917. a. Can.$10. Anchor Press, 1056 Chemin du Golf, Nun's Island, Verdun, Que. H3E 1H4, Canada. TEL 514-766-8650. FAX 514-766-5559. Ed. O. J. Silva. adv.

387   AT
MARINE INDUSTRY NEWS; Australia's boating business magazine. m. Aus.$32 (foreign Aus.$80)(effective Apr. 1992). Yaffa Publishing Group, 17-21 Bellevue St., Surry Hills, N.S.W. 2010, Australia. TEL 02-271-2233. FAX 02-281-2750. adv.: B&W page Aus.$1025, color page Aus.$1370; trim 273 x 210. circ. 3,510 (controlled).
Description: For manufacturers, suppliers, distributors and retailers of pleasure boats, boating equipment and components and for marina operators throughout Australia.

MARINE INDUSTRY RETAILER. see BUSINESS AND ECONOMICS — Marketing And Purchasing

623.87   US   ISSN 0897-0491
VM1
MARINE LOG. 1878. m. $35 (foreign $60). Simmons-Boardman Publishing Corporation, 345 Hudson St., New York, NY 10014. TEL 212-620-7200. Ed. Nicholas Blenkey. adv.; bk.rev.; charts; illus.; stat.; tr.lit.; index; circ. 19,041. (also avail. in microform from UMI) **Indexed:** A.S.& T.Ind., Corros.Abstr., Curr.Cont., DM & T, Energy Info.Abstr., Eng.Ind, Environ.Abstr., Excerp.Med., Ocean.Abstr., Pollut.Abstr., PROMT, Risk Abstr.
●Also available online. Vendor(s): Mead Data Central.
—BLDSC shelfmark: 5376.030000.
Formerly (until 1987): Marine Engineering - Log (ISSN 0025-3219)
Description: Highlights shipbuilding and ship operations.

387   UK   ISSN 0025-3243
MARINE NEWS. 1947. m. £17. World Ship Society, 28 Natland Rd., Kendal LA9 7LT, England. Ed. Michael Crowdy. adv.; bk.rev.; charts; illus.; index; circ. 4,200. (also avail. in microfiche; back issues avail.) —BLDSC shelfmark: 5376.700000.

623.8   UK   ISSN 0143-3709
    CODEN: MPRIEC
MARINE PROPULSION INTERNATIONAL. 1981. 6/yr. $134. International Trade Publications Ltd., Queensway House, 2 Queensway, Redhill, Surrey RH1 1QS, England. TEL 737-768611. FAX 0737-761989. TELEX 948669-TOPJNL-G. Ed. Chris Wilbur. adv.; illus.

387 355   GW   ISSN 0025-3294
V3
MARINE-RUNDSCHAU.* 1890. m. DM.90. (Arbeitskreis fuer Wehrforschung) Bernard und Graefe Verlag, Karl-Mand-Str. 2, Postfach 2060, 5400 Koblenz, Germany. Ed. Juergen Friese. adv.; bk.rev.; charts; illus.; stat.; index; circ. 2,500. **Indexed:** Abstr.Mil.Bibl., Amer.Hist.& Life, Hist.Abstr.

623.8   US   ISSN 0025-3316
VM1   CODEN: MARTA4
MARINE TECHNOLOGY. 1964. 6/yr. $60 to non-members. Society of Naval Architects and Marine Engineers, 601 Pavonia Ave., Jersey City, NJ 07306-2907. charts; illus.; index; circ. 12,000. **Indexed:** A.S.& T.Ind., API Abstr., API Catal., API Hlth.& Environ., API Oil., API Pet.Ref., API Pet.Subst., API Transport., BMT, Chem.Abstr., Curr.Cont., Eng.Ind., Excerp.Med., Geo.Abstr., Ocean.Abstr., Pollut.Abstr., Risk Abstr.
—BLDSC shelfmark: 5378.500000.
Description: Focuses on naval architecture. Refereed Serial

387   GW   ISSN 0172-8539
MARINEFORUM. 1925. 10/yr. DM.92. Verlag E.S. Mittler und Sohn GmbH, Steintorwall 17, Postfach 2352, 4900 Herford, Germany. Eds. Capt. Z. See, Erhard Rosenkranz. adv.; bk.rev.; abstr.; charts; illus.; stat.; circ. 7,000.

387   SP
MARITIMAS INFORMACION COMERCIAL. 1948. d. 23000 ptas. Diario Maritimas, S.A., Paseo de Colon 24, 08002 Barcelona, Spain. TEL 93-301-5646. FAX 93-318-6645. Eds. Juan Cardona, Manuel Cardona. adv.; illus.; circ. 8,700. (back issues avail.)

MARITIME ABSTRACTS. see TRANSPORTATION — Abstracting, Bibliographies, Statistics

387 343.09   US   ISSN 0894-6698
KF1097
MARITIME ADVISOR ARBITRATION AWARD DIGEST. 1981. m. $295. Maritime Advisory Services Inc., 10 Signal Rd., Stamford, CT 06902-7909. TEL 203-975-7070. FAX 203-975-7002. Ed. George Tsagaris. circ. 250. (back issues avail.)
Description: North American arbitration decisions affecting the shipping industry.

387 343.09   US
MARITIME ADVISOR MARINE OPERATIONS REPORTER. 1981. m. $250. Maritime Advisory Services Inc., 10 Signal Rd., Stamford, CT 06902-7909. TEL 203-975-7070. FAX 203-975-7002. Ed. Sherry Stossel. circ. 200. (back issues avail.)
Description: Professional guide to U.S. state and federal regulations affecting ship operations and navigation.

TRANSPORTATION — SHIPS AND SHIPPING

387 US
MARITIME ASSOCIATION OF THE PORT OF NEW YORK - NEW JERSEY. NEWSLETTER. 1973. fortn. membership. Maritime Association of the Port of New York - New Jersey, 17 Battery Place, Ste. 1006, New York, NY 10004. adv.; bk.rev.; charts; illus.; stat; circ. 1,500.
  Formerly: Maritime Association of the Port of New York. Newsletter; *Supersedes:* Maritime Exchange Bulletin (ISSN 0025-3421)

387 UK ISSN 0264-6420
HE561
MARITIME GUIDE. 1984. a. $205. Lloyd's Register of Shipping, 71 Fenchurch St., London EC3M 4BS, England. TEL 071-709-9166. (In US, subscr. to: Lloyd's Register of Shipping, 17 Battery Place, New York, NY 10004)
  —BLDSC shelfmark: 5381.352950.
  Formerly: Appendix (ISSN 0261-1821)
  Description: Mainly covers ports facilities (wet and dry docks) worldwide.

387 NE ISSN 0920-1610
MARITIME INFORMATION REVIEW. (Text in English) 1976. m. fl.310. Netherlands Maritime Information Centre, P.O. Box 21873, 3001 AW Rotterdam, Netherlands. TEL 010-4130960.
FAX 010-4112857. TELEX 26585 CMO NL.
  ●Also available online.

387 US ISSN 0161-9373
HE730
MARITIME NEWSLETTER. 1967. m. $2.50. A F L - C I O, Maritime Trades Department, 815 16th St., N.W., Rm. 510, Washington, DC 20006.
TEL 202-628-6300. Ed. Jean F. Ingrao. charts; illus.; stat.
  Formerly: Maritime (ISSN 0025-3391)

387 343.09 US ISSN 0894-5713
KF1107.A59
MARITIME PERSONAL INJURY REPORT. 1986. m. $195. Maritime Advisory Services Inc., 10 Signal Rd., Stamford, CT 06902-7909. TEL 203-975-7070. FAX 203-975-7002. Ed. Chris Dupin. circ. 150. (back issues avail.)
  Description: Covers court cases, insurance reviews and maintenance care.

387 UK ISSN 0308-8839
HC92
MARITIME POLICY AND MANAGEMENT. 1973. q. £154($264) Taylor & Francis Ltd., Rankine Rd., Basingstoke, Hants RG24 0PR, England.
TEL 0256-840366. FAX 0256-479438. TELEX 858540. Ed. J. Evans. adv.; bk.rev. (back issues avail.) Indexed: BMT, C.I.S. Abstr., C.R.E.J., Deep Sea Res.& Oceanogr.Abstr., Fluidex, Mar.Aff.Bibl., Ocean.Abstr., Pollut.Abstr.
  —BLDSC shelfmark: 5381.358000.
  Formerly: Maritime Studies and Management.
  Description: Emphasis is placed on organizational, economic, socio-legal and management topics at port, community, shipping company and shipboard levels.
  Refereed Serial

387 CN
▼**MARITIME REPORT.** 1990. bi-m.
Can.$21.40($37.45) (foreign Can.$58.85). Laurentian Business Publishing, 140 Baig Blvd., Moncton, N.B. E1E 1C8, Canada.
TEL 506-857-9696. FAX 506-859-7395. Ed. Linda MacGibbon. adv.; illus.; circ. 17,000 (controlled). (tabloid format)
  Description: Includes business articles on people and issues in the Maritimes.

623.8 387 US ISSN 0025-3448
VM1
MARITIME REPORTER AND ENGINEERING NEWS. 1939. m. $44. Maritime Activity Reports, 118 E. 25th St., New York, NY 10010. TEL 212-477-6700. Ed. Charles O'Malley. adv.; bk.rev.; illus.; circ. 25,000. Indexed: Tr.& Indus.Ind.

387 US
MARITIME RESEARCH CHARTER NEWSLETTER. 1953. w. $240 (foreign $260). Maritime Research, Inc., Box 805, Parlin, NJ 08859. TEL 908-727-8040.
FAX 908-727-0243. TELEX 4993951. Ed. Jay Lillianthal. adv.; index; circ. 5,000. (back issues avail.)
  Description: Contains a listing of all charter fixtures reported worldwide in the tramp charter market.

387 639.2 AT ISSN 0726-6472
MARITIME STUDIES. 1983. bi-m. Aus.$35 to individuals (foreign Aus.$50); institutions Aus.$60 (foreign Aus.$75); corporates Aus.$250 (foreign Aus.$265)(includes Occasional Papers in Maritime Affairs)(effective 1991-92). Australian Centre for Maritime Studies, P.O. Box E20, Queen Victoria Terrace, Canberra, A.C.T. 2600, Australia.
TEL 062-95-0056. Ed. R.W. Galloway. bk.rev.; circ. 350. (back issues avail.) Indexed: Aus.P.A.I.S.
  Description: Covers all aspects of marine affairs relevant to Australia and its region.

387 AT ISSN 0025-3464
MARITIME WORKER. 1938. 11/yr. Aus.$15. Waterside Workers Federation of Australia, 2nd Floor, 365-375 Sussex St., Sydney, N.S.W. 200, Australia.
TEL 02-267-9134. FAX 02-261-3481. Ed. T. Bull. adv.; bk.rev.; play rev.; illus.; stat.; circ. 9,000. (tabloid format)
  Description: Union journal covering stevedoring and industrial issues.

623.8 SW ISSN 0025-4622
MASKINBEFAELET. 1891. 8/yr. SEK 110. Svenska Maskinbefaelsfoerbundet - Swedish Engineer Officers' Association, Box 12100, S-102 23 Stockholm, Sweden. TEL 08-6520120.
FAX 08-652-4085. TELEX 14364. Ed. Benkt Lundgren. adv.; bk.rev.; charts; illus.; index; circ. 4,918.
  —BLDSC shelfmark: 5386.000000.
  Description: Technical and trade magazine for Swedish marine engineers.

MAST; for mailing and shipping professionals. *see* COMMUNICATIONS — Postal Affairs

387.2 US ISSN 0025-6129
MAY DAY PICTORIAL NEWS;* the west coast's best monthly maritime magazine. 1961. m. $11. (May Day Pictorial News) Wion Publications, 201 Astrid Dr., Pleasant Hill, CA 94523-4305.
TEL 415-947-2138. Ed. Helen Wion. adv.; tr.lit.; circ. 5,298 (controlled).
  Description: News, articles, and announcements on issues that affect maritime activities on the West Coast.

387 UK ISSN 0261-281X
MEDWAY PORTS SHIPPING HANDBOOK. 1981. irreg. £1050. Charter International Publications Ltd., Castle Chambers, Castle Acre, King's Lynn, Norfolk PE32 2BQ, England. Ed. James P. Moriarty. illus.

MELBOURNE PORT AND SHIPPING HANDBOOK. *see* BUSINESS AND ECONOMICS — Trade And Industrial Directories

387 UK ISSN 0261-1848
MERCHANT SHIPBUILDING RETURN. 1888. q. free. Lloyd's Register of Shipping, 71 Fenchurch St., London EC3M 4BS, England. TEL 071-709-9166. (In US, subscr. to: Lloyd's Register of Shipping, 17 Battery Pl., New York, NY 10004)
  Description: Statistical summary of all self-propelled ships of 100 gross tonnage and above which are under construction or on order including analyses by country of build, size, type and registration.

387 UK ISSN 0265-1173
MERSEY PORTS HANDBOOK (YEAR). 1983. a. £10. Charter International Publications Ltd., Castle Chambers, Castle Acre, King's Lynn, Norfolk PE32 2BQ, England. TEL 07605-634. FAX 07605-625. TELEX 817440. Ed. James Moriarty. adv.; circ. 6,000.

623.8 JA ISSN 0026-6825
MITSUI ZOSEN GIHO/MITSUI ZOSEN TECHNICAL REVIEW. (Text in Japanese; summaries in English, Japanese) 1952. q. free to qualified organizations or personnel. Mitsui Engineering & Shipbuilding Co., Ltd., Corporate Technical Research & Development Headquarters - Mitsui Zosen K.K. Gijutsu Soukatsu Honbu, 6-4, Tsukiji 5-chome, Chuo-ku, Tokyo, Japan. Ed. T. Ohi. bk.rev.; abstr.; bibl.; charts; illus.; cum.index; circ. 1,900. (also avail. in microfilm) Indexed: BMT, Chem.Abstr., Sci.Abstr.
  —BLDSC shelfmark: 5829.833000.
  Description: Examines the computer applications as well as latest developments and research in engineering and shipbuilding.

MODELE REDUIT DE BATEAU. *see* HOBBIES

387 CN
MONTREAL PORT GUIDE & DIRECTORY. 1970. a. Anchor Press, 1056 Chemin du Golf, Nun's Island, Verdun, Que. H3E 1H4, Canada. TEL 514-766-8650.
FAX 514-766-5559.

387 CN
MONTREAL PORT GUIDE & TRANSPORTATION REGISTER. a. Anchor Press, 1056 Chemin du Golf, Nun's Island, Verdun, Que. H3E 1H4, Canada.
TEL 514-766-8650. FAX 514-766-5559. adv.

387 MJ
MONTSERRAT. PORT AUTHORITY. ANNUAL REPORT. a. Port Authority, Plymouth, Montserrat, W. Indies.

387 RU ISSN 0027-1217
MORSKOI FLOT; journal of U.S.S.R. merchant marine. (Text in Russian; summaries in English) 1886. m. 30.60 Rub. (Ministerstvo Kommercheskogo Flota) Izdatel'stvo Transport, Komsomol'skii prosp., 42, 119048 Moscow G-48, Russia. (Dist. by: Mezhdunarodnaya Kniga, Moscow, G-200, Russia) Ed. A.V. Klementiev. adv.; bk.rev.; abstr.; bibl.; charts; illus.; stat.; index; circ. 70,550. (microform) Indexed: BMT, Chem.Abstr., Ref.Zh.

387 PL
MORZE. 1924. m. Ul. Widok 10, 00-024 Warsaw, Poland. TEL 48-22-273551. Ed. Janusz Wolniewicz. illus.; circ. 60,000.
  Description: Covers maritime affairs.

623.82 UK ISSN 0027-2000
VM1 CODEN: MOSHA3
MOTOR SHIP. 1920. m. $121. Reed Business Publishing Group, Enterprise Division (Subsidiary of: Reed International PLC), Quadrant House, The Quadrant, Sutton, Surrey SM2 5AS, England.
TEL 081-652-8183. FAX 081-652-8986. (Subscr. to: Oakfield House, Perrymount Rd., Haywards, Heath, W. Sussex RH16 3DH, England. TEL 444-445566) Ed. Paul Doughty. adv.; bk.rev.; charts; illus.; tr.lit.; index; circ. 8,088. (also avail. in microform from UMI; back issues avail.) Indexed: BMT, Br.Tech.Ind., Bus.Ind., Eng.Ind., Excerp.Med., Sci.Abstr., Tr.& Indus.Ind.
  —BLDSC shelfmark: 5975.540000.
  Description: Focuses on shipbuilding.

N K K NEWS; steelmaking, engineering, construction & shipbuilding, advanced materials, electronics, urban development, biotechnology. *see* ENGINEERING — Mechanical Engineering

387 NR
N P A ANNUAL REPORT. a. Nigerian Ports Authority, Public Relations Department, 26-28 Marina, PMB 12588, Lagos, Nigeria.

387 NR ISSN 0794-3008
N P A BULLETIN. q. free. Nigerian Ports Authority, Public Relations Department, 26-28 Marina, P.M.B. 12588, Lagos, Nigeria. TELEX 21500 ONPNPA NG.

387 NR ISSN 0547-0730
N P A NEWS. 1973. q. free. Institute of Transport, Nigerian Ports Authority, Headquarters, 26-28 Marina, Lagos, Nigeria. Ed. Agidi Ovurevu. illus.

387 GW ISSN 0027-7444
NACHRICHTEN FUER SEEFAHRER. 1849. w. DM.178.20. Deutsches Hydrographisches Institut, Bernhard-Nocht-Str. 78, 2000 Hamburg 36, Germany. TEL 040-3190-1. FAX 040-3190-5150. TELEX 211138-BMVHH-D. index; circ. 3,100.

387 GR ISSN 0047-861X
NAFTIKA CHRONIKA. (Text in English and Greek) 1931. s-m. $100. Naftika Chronika Ltd., P.O. Box 80076, 185 10 Piraeus, Greece. FAX 417-2268. TELEX 212845. Ed. D. Rigas-Cottakis. adv.; bk.rev.; illus.; stat.; circ. 4,000.

387 GR
NAFTILIAKI GREEK SHIPPING REVIEW. (Supplement avail: Newsfront Greek Shipping Intelligence) (Text in English, Greek) 1957. q. $250 includes Newsfront - Greek Shipping Intelligence. Diorama Publishers Ltd., 4-6 Efplias St., 185 37 Piraeus, Greece.
TEL 01-4125005. FAX 01-4510805. TELEX 212310NAFT. Ed. David Glass. adv.; bk.rev.; index; circ. 4,000. (back issues avail.)
  Description: News and analysis of Greek merchant shipping and shipping-related business.

TRANSPORTATION — SHIPS AND SHIPPING

387 UK ISSN 0077-5185
NATIONAL MARITIME BOARD. (GREAT BRITAIN) YEAR BOOK.* 1922. a. 50p. National Maritime Board, St. Mary Ave., Rms. 30-32, London EC3A 8ET, England.

387.5 PK
NATIONAL SHIPPING CORPORATION. REPORT AND ACCOUNTS. (Text in English) a. National Shipping Corporation, N S C Bldg., Moulvi Tamizuddin Khan Rd., Karachi, Pakistan.

387 NE
NATIONALE HAVENRAAD. JAARVERSLAG (YEAR). 1970. a. free. Nationale Havenraad, Kneuterdijk 6, 2514 EN Gravenhage, Netherlands. TEL 070-618757. FAX 070-614600. (back issues avail.)
Supersedes: Netherlands. Provisional National Ports Council. Jaarverslag; Formerly: Netherlands. Commissie Zeehavenoverleg. Jaarverslag (ISSN 0077-7552)

623.89 UK ISSN 0077-619X
NAUTICAL ALMANAC. 1960. a. price varies. (Royal Greenwich Observatory) Her Majesty's Stationery Office (H.M.S.O.), 51 Nine Elms Lane, London SW8 5DR, England. (Co-sponsors: H.M. Nautical Almanac Office; U.S. Naval Observatory, Washington, D.C.)

387.2 UK ISSN 0028-1336
NAUTICAL MAGAZINE; for those interested in ships and the sea. 1832. m. £28. Brown, Son and Ferguson, Ltd., 4-10 Darnley St., Glasgow G41 2SD, Scotland. FAX 041-420-1694. Ed. L. Ingram-Brown. adv.; bk.rev.; s-a. index; circ. 1,600. (also avail. in microfiche from BHP)
Description: Discusses nautical arts and science.

387 623.82 US ISSN 0738-7245
V1
NAUTICAL RESEARCH JOURNAL. 1949. q. $25 (effective 1992). Nautical Research Guild, Inc., 26 Bass Ave., Gloucester, MA 01930. Ed. Erik A.R. Ronnberg, Jr. adv.; bk.rev.; illus.; index; circ. 1,500. (also avail. in microfilm; microform from UMI; reprint service avail. from UMI) **Indexed:** Amer.Hist.& Life, Hist.Abstr.
—BLDSC shelfmark: 6063.000000.
Description: For marine artists, model builders, and those interested in marine history. Provides information on maritime lore and model building.

387 GW
NAUTICUS. 1896. irreg. DM.49.80. Verlag E.S. Mittler und Sohn GmbH, Steintorwall 17, Postfach 2352, 4900 Herford, Germany. Ed. Viceadmiral Kampe. adv.; abstr.; charts; illus.; stat.; circ. 1,500.

387 SW ISSN 0028-1379
VK4
NAUTISK TIDSKRIFT. 1908. 8/yr. SEK 80. Sveriges Fartygsbefaelsfoerening - Swedish Ship Officers' Association, Box 12100, S-102 23 Stockholm, Sweden. FAX 8-503493. Ed. Manfred Spanner. adv.; bk.rev.; charts; illus.; tr.lit.; index; circ. 8,079.

623.81 UK ISSN 0306-0209
CODEN: NVARA3
NAVAL ARCHITECT. (Supplement avail.: Small Craft) 1971. 10/yr. £58 to non-members. Royal Institution of Naval Architects, 10 Upper Belgrave St., London SW1X 8BQ, England. TEL 071-235-4622. FAX 071-245-6959. TELEX 265844-SINAI-G. Ed. Mike Wake. adv.; bk.rev.; bibl.; charts; illus.; circ. 8,000. **Indexed:** Appl.Mech.Rev., BMT, Br.Tech.Ind., Curr.Cont., Eng.Ind., Excerp.Med., Ocean.Abstr., Pollut.Abstr.
—BLDSC shelfmark: 6063.850000.
Description: News items and research articles on legislation, architectural and technological developments, and products and services pertaining to the construction and operation of ocean-going vessels.

623.89 FR ISSN 0028-1530
VK2 CODEN: NVGNAL
NAVIGATION; revue technique de navigation maritime aerienne et spatiale. 1953. q. 250 F. Institut Francais de Navigation, 3 av. Octave Greard, 75007 Paris, France. Ed. P. Mannevy. adv.; bk.rev.; abstr.; illus.; index. cum.index every 5 yrs.; circ. 1,200.
Indexed: Bibl.Cart., Deep Sea Res.& Oceanogr.Abstr., Int.Aerosp.Abstr., Sci.Abstr.
—BLDSC shelfmark: 6067.000000.

387 623.89 DK ISSN 0107-4806
NAVIGATOER. (Text in Danish; summaries in English) 1907. 10/yr. DKK 270($45) Navigatoerenes Faellesforening - Danish Navigators Association, Navigatoerenes Hus, 55 Havnegade, DK-1058 Copenhagen K, Denmark. FAX 45-33-129385. TELEX 21025 HAVHUS. Ed. Capt. K. Mols Soerensen. adv.; bk.rev.; index; circ. 5,800.
Former titles: Navigatoer Nyt; Navigatoer (ISSN 0028-1565) Dansk Havneblad; Dansk Lodstidende.

387.5 BL ISSN 0100-1248
F2522
NAVIGATOR. 1970. s-a. $6. Ministerio da Marinha, Servico de Documentacao Geral da Marinha, Rua Dom Manuel 15, 20010 Rio de Janeiro RJ, Brazil. Ed. Max Justo Guedes. bk.rev.; illus.; circ. 3,000.

387 IT
NAVIGAZIONE INTERNA. 1974. q. L.25,000. Unione di Navigazione Interna Italiana, Comunita Padana delle Camere di Commercio, Via Baldesio, 8, 26100 Cremona, Italy. Ed. Camillo Genzini. adv.

387.5 FR ISSN 0028-159X
VM2
NAVIRES PORTS & CHANTIERS. 1949. m. 1355 F. (foreign 1470 F.). Moreux, 190 bd. Haussmann, 75008 Paris, France. TEL 1-45-63-11-55. TELEX 290 131. adv.; bk.rev.; abstr.; charts; illus.; stat.; circ. 13,000. **Indexed:** BMT, C.I.S. Abstr.
Description: Consists of articles about navigation, the newest technical advances and products, port news and news from abroad.

387 FR ISSN 0077-6270
NAVIS; annuaire de la marine marchande, de la construction navale et des ports. 1942. a. 500 F. Moreux, 190 bd. Haussmann, 75008 Paris, France. TEL 45-63-11-55. TELEX NAVIMAR 290131F. index.

623.8 AG
NAVITECNIA Y COMERCIO MARITIMO. 1947. m. $25. Navitecnia S.A.P.E.C.I.M.F., Alsina 1170, 1088 Buenos Aires, Argentina. TEL 1-37-2795. Ed. Ernest Potthoff. adv.; bk.rev.; illus.; index; circ. 2,500.
Formerly: Navitecnia (ISSN 0028-1611)

387 BE ISSN 0028-2790
NEPTUNUS; info marine. (Text in Dutch and French) 1952. bi-m. 200 Fr. Force Navale - Belgische Zeemacht, Postbus 17, Oostende 1, Belgium. Ed. J.C. Lienart. adv.; bk.rev.; charts; illus.; circ. 2,500.

387 NE ISSN 0168-5422
HE845
NETHERLANDS. CENTRAAL BUREAU VOOR DE STATISTIEK. STATISTIEK VAN DE ZEEVAART/STATISTICS OF SEABORNE SHIPPING. (Text in Dutch and English) 1948. a. Centraal Bureau voor de Statistiek, Prinses Beatrixlaan 428, Voorburg, Netherlands. (Dist. by: SDU - Publishers, Christoffel Plantijnstraat, The Hague, Netherlands)

386 314 NE ISSN 0168-5376
NETHERLANDS. CENTRAAL BUREAU VOOR DE STATISTIEK. STATISTIEK VAN DE INTERNATIONALE BINNENVAART/STATISTICS OF THE INTERNATIONAL INLAND SHIPPING. (Text in Dutch and English) 1948. a. Centraal Bureau voor de Statistiek, Prinses Beatrixlaan 428, Voorburg, Netherlands. (Dist. by: SDU - Publishers, Christoffel Plantijnstraat, The Hague, Netherlands)

387.5 NE
NETHERLANDS. CENTRAAL BUREAU VOOR DE STATISTIEK. STATISTIEK VAN DE KOOPVAARDIJVLOOT. STATISTICS OF THE MERCHANT MARINE. (Text in Dutch and English) 1949. a. Centraal Bureau voor de Statistiek, Prinses Beatrixlaan 428, Voorburg, Netherlands. (Orders to: SDU - Publishers, Christoffel Plantijnstraat, The Hague)

386 NE ISSN 0168-5325
HE69
NETHERLANDS. CENTRAAL BUREAU VOOR DE STATISTIEK VAN HET BINNENLANDS GOEDERENVERVOER. STATISTICS OF INTERNAL GOODS TRANSPORT IN THE NETHERLANDS. (Text in Dutch, English) 1948. a. Centraal Bureau voor de Statistiek, Prinses Beatrixlaan 428, Voorburg, Netherlands. (Orders to: Staatsuitgeverij, Christoffel Plantijnstraat, The Hague, Netherlands)

NEW ENGLAND JOURNAL OF TRANSPORTATION. see *TRANSPORTATION*

NEW SOUTH WALES PORTS HANDBOOK. see *BUSINESS AND ECONOMICS — Trade And Industrial Directories*

387 665.5 US ISSN 0953-9336
NEW WORLDWIDE TANKER NOMINAL FREIGHT SCALE; code name worldscale. 1969. a. $1325 (typically set in Sep.). Worldscale Association (NYC), Inc., 17 Battery Pl., New York, NY 10004. TEL 212-422-2786. FAX 212-344-4169. TELEX 62351 WSCALE UW. (U.K. address: 64 Queen St., London EC4R 1AD, England) Eds. Thelma Issman, Robert Porter. circ. 1,200. (back issues avail.)
Formerly (until Jul. 1988): Worldwide Tanker Nominal Freight Scale (ISSN 0267-1913)

387 NZ ISSN 0549-0502
NEW ZEALAND MARINE NEWS. 1949. q. NZ.$25. New Zealand Ship and Marine Society, P.O. Box 5104, Wellington, New Zealand. TEL 64-04-377-0362. FAX 64-04-471-1373. Ed. D.F. Gardner. bk.rev.; circ. 600. (back issues avail.)
Description: For laypersons interested in historical and general aspects of shipping and nautical matters, particularly in reference to New Zealand.

387 NZ ISSN 0545-7866
HE932.5
NEW ZEALAND SHIPPING DIRECTORY. 1962. a. $13.50. Mercantile Gazette Marketing, Box 20-034, Christchurch 5, New Zealand. FAX 03-584-490. Ed. B.M. Stoop. adv.; illus.

387 NZ ISSN 0027-724X
NEW ZEALAND SHIPPING GAZETTE. w. NZ.$95. Mercantile Gazette Marketing, Box 20-034, Christchurch 5, New Zealand. FAX 03-584-490.

387 UK
NEWBUILDINGS. (Supplement to: Fairplay International Shipping Weekly) 1964. q. included with subscription to Fairplay. Fairplay Publications Ltd., 20 Ullswater Crescent, Ullswater Business Park, Coulsdon, Surrey CR5 2HR, England. Ed. C. Hewer. stat.; circ. 5,666.
Formerly: World Ships on Order (ISSN 0043-9010)

387 GR
NEWSFRONT - GREEK SHIPPING INTELLIGENCE. (Text in English) 1984. s-m. $250 includes Naftiliaki Greek Shipping Review. Diorama Publishers Ltd., 4-6 Efplias St., 185 37 Piraeus, Greece. TEL 01-4125005. FAX 01-4510805. TELEX 212310NAFT. Ed. David Glass. adv.; bk.rev.; circ. 4,000. (back issues avail.)
Description: Provides market information and analysis of Greek merchant shipping and shipping-related business.

NIHON SHOSEN SENPUKU TOKEI. see *TRANSPORTATION — Abstracting, Bibliographies, Statistics*

NIKKEI LOGISTICS. see *BUSINESS AND ECONOMICS — Personnel Management*

387 JA
NIPPON YUSEN. ANNUAL REPORT. a. Nippon Yusen K.K., Kohoshitsu, 2-3-2 Marunouchi, Chiyoda-ku, Tokyo 100, Japan. TEL 03-3284-5192. FAX 03-3284-6361.

NOR'EASTER (DULUTH). see *HISTORY — History Of North And South America*

623.82 NO
NORSK BAATINDUSTRI. bi-m. Norsk Baatinformasjon, Postboks 317, 1601 Fredrikstad, Norway. adv.; circ. 4,000.

623.87 NO ISSN 0333-0192
VM4
NORSK MASKIN-TIDENDE/NORWEGIAN MARINE ENGINEERS' MAGAZINE. 1895. m. NOK 220. Norske Maskinistforbund, Arbinsgate 11, 0203 Oslo 2, Norway. TEL 02-446024. FAX 02-449871. TELEX 72962 SKIBF N. Ed. F. Gross. adv.; charts; illus.; tr.lit.; circ. 15,000.
Description: For marine personnel at sea, onshore and in the offshore industry. Contains trade information, nautical and technical news, and topics of general interest.

TRANSPORTATION — SHIPS AND SHIPPING 4735

387 331.8   NO   ISSN 0029-2079
NORSK SJOEMANNSFORBUND. MEDLEMSBLAD. 1910. m. (11/yr.). free to qualified personnel. Norsk Sjoemannsforbund, Grev Wedels Plass 7, Oslo 1, Norway. Ed. Henrik Aasaroed. adv.; bk.rev.; charts; illus.; circ. 17,000.

387   NO   ISSN 0048-0606
NORSK SKIBSFOERERTIDENDE. 1898. m. NOK 120($20) Norges Skibsfoererforbund - Norwegian Shipmasters' Association, Hafrsfjordgate 11, Oslo 2, Norway. Ed. Gudmund Aasheim. adv.; bk.rev.; charts; illus.; stat.; index; circ. 4,000.

387   NO
NORSK SKIBSFOERERTIDENDE. MASKIN-TIDENDE STYRMANSBLAD. 1912. m. (11/yr.). NOK 170. Norsk Styrmandsforening, P.B. 1936, Vika, 0125 Oslo 1, Norway. Ed. Kjell Kjus. adv.; circ. 16,000 (controlled).
   Former titles: Norsk Maskin-Tidende Styrmansblad (ISSN 0801-1400); Norsk Styrmansblad (ISSN 0029-215X)

NORTH AMERICAN SOCIETY FOR OCEANIC HISTORY. NEWSLETTER. see *HISTORY* — History Of North And South America

NORTH EAST COAST INSTITUTION OF ENGINEERS AND SHIPBUILDERS. TRANSACTIONS. see *ENGINEERING*

O A G WORLDWIDE CRUISE & SHIPLINE GUIDE. (Official Airline Guides, Inc.) see *TRAVEL AND TOURISM*

387   FR   ISSN 0474-5884
HE821
O E C D. MARITIME TRANSPORT COMMITTEE. MARITIME TRANSPORT. 1954. a. price varies. Organization for Economic Cooperation and Development, 2 rue Andre-Pascal, 75775 Paris Cedex 16, France. TEL 45-24-82-00. FAX 45-24-85-00. (U.S. orders to: O.E.C.D. Publications and Information Center, 2001 L St., N.W., Ste. 700, Washington, D.C. 20036-4910. TEL 202-785-6323) (also avail. in microfiche from OEC) **Indexed:** IIS.

OAKLAND PORT AND SHIPPING HANDBOOK. see *BUSINESS AND ECONOMICS* — Trade And Industrial Directories

387 910.09   US
OCEAN & CRUISE NEWS. 1980. m. $24. World Ocean & Cruise Liner Society, Box 92, Stamford, CT 06904. TEL 203-329-2787. FAX 203-329-2787. Ed. George C. Devol, III. circ. 5,000. (back issues avail.)
   Description: Covers the latest news about cruises and cruise ships.

387 301.6   UK   ISSN 0261-6777
VK562
OCEAN VOICE; maritime information technology and electronics. 1981. q. free. International Maritime Satellite Organization, 40 Melton St., London NW1 2EQ, England. TEL 01-387-9089. FAX 01-387-6703. TELEX 297201. Ed. Lee Adamson. adv.; bk.rev.; illus.; charts; circ. 18,684 (controlled).
   —BLDSC shelfmark: 6231.396000.

387   II   ISSN 0029-8123
OCEANITE; the maritime magazine of India. (Text in English) 1945. q. Rs.12($2.50) Maritime Union of India, Udyog Bhavan, 4th Fl., 29 Walchand Hirachand Marg, Ballard Estate, Bombay 400 038, India. TEL 26-3052. Ed. K.E. Sukhia. adv.; bk.rev.; illus.; circ. 15,000.
   Description: Includes information for the International Transportworkers' Federation. Covers fuels, repairs, provisions, and job opportunities in the Indian shipping industry.

386.8   US   ISSN 0093-1799
HE550
OFFICIAL PORT OF DETROIT WORLD HANDBOOK. 1973. a. $6. Fourth Seacoast Publishing Co., Inc., 25200 Little Mack, St. Clair Shores, MI 48081. TEL 313-779-5570. FAX 313-779-5547. (Subscr. to: Box 145, St. Clair Shores, MI 48080) Ed. Roger J. Buysse. adv.; illus.; circ. 10,000.

OFFICIAL SHIPPERS GUIDE - ST. LOUIS MOTOR FREIGHT DIRECTORY. see *TRANSPORTATION* — Trucks And Trucking

387.1   US   ISSN 0094-8454
HE554.A6
OFFICIAL SOUTHERN CALIFORNIA PORTS MARITIME DIRECTORY AND GUIDE.* 1974. a. $10. Civic - Data Corp., 941 W. Bay Ave., Balboa Island, CA 92661-1012. illus.

387.54   US   ISSN 0030-0381
OFFICIAL STEAMSHIP GUIDE. Variant title: Official S S Guide. 1932. m. $70. Transportation Guides, Inc., 111 Cherry St., Ste. 205, New Canaan, CT 06840. TEL 203-226-7928. Ed. Bruce Kennedy. adv.; illus.; circ. 9,000.
   Description: Contains time tables.

OFFSHORE FLEET ECONOMICS. see *PETROLEUM AND GAS*

OFFSHORE SERVICE VESSEL REGISTER. see *PETROLEUM AND GAS*

387   CI   ISSN 0030-0713
OGLAS ZA POMORCE/NOTICES TO MARINERS. (Text in Serbo-Croatian) 1924. m. $15. Hidrografski Institut Jugoslavenske Ratne Mornarice, 58000 Split, Croatia. FAX 058-47045. TELEX 26270. bk.rev.

387   US   ISSN 0093-2124
VK1323
ON SCENE. 1971. q. U.S. Coast Guard, Office of Navigation Safety and Waterway Services, 2100 Second St., S.W., Washington, DC 20593-0001. TEL 202-267-1943. bibl.; charts; illus. (also avail. in microform from UMI; reprint service avail. from UMI)
   Formerly: National Maritime S A R Review (ISSN 0047-8946)

P & I INTERNATIONAL; monthly review of mutual insurance. (Protection & Indemnity) see *INSURANCE*

387   US   ISSN 0741-7586
PACIFIC MARITIME MAGAZINE. 1983. m. $12. R.H. Philips Co., 1818 Westlake Ave. N., No.430, Seattle, WA 98109-2707. TEL 206-284-8285. FAX 206-284-0391. Ed. Richard H. Philips. adv.; bk.rev.; circ. 5,788. (back issues avail.)
   Formerly (until 1984): Port Reporter.
   Description: Geared toward owner-operators of steamship lines, their agents and representatives, tug and barge lines, terminal operators, stevedores and port and harbor operations executives in the Pacific.

387   US   ISSN 0030-8900
PACIFIC SHIPPER. 1926. w. $85 (foreign $105). K - III Press, Inc., 424 W. 33rd St., New York, NY 10001. TEL 800-221-5488. FAX 212-695-5025. adv.; circ. 6,300.

387   UK
PADDLE WHEELS. 1959. q. membership. Paddle Steamer Preservation Society, 39 Ellwood Ave., Peterborough, Cambs. PE2 8LX, England. Ed. Russell Plummer. adv.; bk.rev.; illus.; circ. 2,500.

387 380   UK   ISSN 0263-4260
PANAMA HANDBOOK 1983. 1982. a. £10. Charter International Publications Ltd., Castle Chambers, Castle Acre, King's Lynn, Norfolk PE32 2BQ, England. TEL 07605-634. FAX 07605-625. TELEX 817440. Ed. James P. Moriarty. adv.; circ. 6,000.

387.2   AT   ISSN 0814-9089
PANORAMA (MELBOURNE). 1949. 6/yr. free. Port of Melbourne Authority, P.O. Box 4721, Melbourne, Vic. 3001, Australia. FAX 611-1905. Ed. N. Wall. bk.rev.; circ. 8,000. **Indexed:** Aus.P.A.I.S.
   Formerly: Port Panorama; Which supersedes: Port of Melbourne Quarterly (ISSN 0048-4865); Port Gazette.

387   NE   ISSN 0031-4099
PEILING. 1966. m. fl.25 (foreign fl.32.50). (Algemene Vereniging van Zeevarenden) Federatie van Werknemersorganisaties in de Zeevaart, Postbox 25131, 3001 HC Rotterdam, Netherlands. FAX 010-4773846. TELEX 25526. Ed.Bd. adv.; bk.rev.; charts; illus.; stat.; index; circ. 4,000.

PENANG PORT HANDBOOK. see *BUSINESS AND ECONOMICS* — Trade And Industrial Directories

331.8 623.8   UK   ISSN 0048-3400
PERISCOPE; Chatham Naval Base newspaper. 1965. m. 60p. Ministry of Defence, Dockyard Department, Room 211, Carpenter House, Broad Quay, Bath, Avon BA1 5AB, England. Ed. D. Moore. adv.; bk.rev.; charts; illus.; circ. 3,000. (tabloid format)

623.89   BE   ISSN 0480-0516
PERMANENT INTERNATIONAL ASSOCIATION OF NAVIGATION CONGRESSES. BULLETIN. 1926; N.S. 1961; N.S. 1968. 4/yr. 1200 Fr. Permanent International Association of Navigation Congresses, 155 rue de la Loi, Boite 9, B-1040 Brussels, Belgium. TEL 02-733-96-70. FAX 02-736-08-04. TELEX 23542 OW SGB. (back issues avail.) **Indexed:** BMT.

623.89   UK
PILOT (WESTMINSTER). 1887. q. membership. United Kingdom Pilots' Association (Marine), Transport House, Smith Square, Westminster, London SW1P 3JB, England. TEL 01-828-7788. Ed. David Colver. bk.rev.; index; circ. 1,250.

387.5   NO
PLATOU REPORT. 1947. a. free. R. S. Platou A-S, Fjordveien 1, P.O. Box 10, N-1322 Hoevik, Norway. Ed. Johan Aabyholm. illus.; circ. 3,000.

387   SP
PLAYAMAR; revista tecnica de actualidad nautica. m. 2200 ptas. Editorial Borrmart, S.A., Ramon de la Cruz 68, Madrid 1, Spain. adv.; bk.rev.; play rev.; bibl.; illus.; tr.lit.; index; circ. 19,500.

623.8   PL   ISSN 0373-868X
POLITECHNIKA GDANSKA. ZESZYTY NAUKOWE. BUDOWNICTWO OKRETOWE. (Text in English, Polish; summaries in Russian and one West-European language) 1957. irreg. price varies. Politechnika Gdanska, Majakowskiego 11-12, 81-952 Gdansk 6, Poland. (Dist. by: Osrodek Rozpowszechniania Wydawnictw Naukowych PAN, Palac Kultury i Nauki, 00-901 Warsaw, Poland) bibl.; charts; illus.
   Description: Reasearch on ship design and equipment, steam and gas turbines, mechanics and hydromechanics of structures and power installations.

387   UK
POOLE HANDBOOK. 1979. a. £10. Charter International Publications Ltd., Castle Chambers, Castle Acre, King's Lynn, Norfolk PE32 2BQ, England. TEL 07605-8634. FAX 07605-625. TELEX 817440. Ed. James P. Moriarty. adv.; circ. 6,000.
   Formerly: Poole - Commercial Users Handbook (ISSN 0260-2547)

387   UK   ISSN 0032-4809
PORT. 1967. m. £5. Port Publishing Co. Ltd., Focal House, 18-19 Sheds, Tilbury Dock, Tilbury, Essex RM18 7ND, England. Ed. Michael Guy. adv.; bk.rev.; illus.; circ. 10,000. (tabloid format)

387   FR   ISSN 0396-4388
PORT AUTONOME DU HAVRE. BULLETIN ANALYTIQUE DE DOCUMENTATION GENERALE. 1971. m. free on exchange basis. Port Autonome du Havre, Centre de Documentation, B.P. 1413, 76067 Le Havre Cedex, France. Ed. E. Berthoud. circ. 150.

387   FR   ISSN 0396-4396
PORT AUTONOME DU HAVRE. BULLETIN ANALYTIQUE DE DOCUMENTATION TECHNIQUE. 1966. m. free on exchange basis. Port Autonome du Havre, Centre de Documentation, B.P. 1413, 76067 Le Havre Cedex, France. Ed. E. Berthoud. circ. 150.

387   JM
PORT BUSTAMANTE HANDBOOK. 1972. a. free. Shipping Association of Jamaica, Confederation Life Building, 5-7 King Street, P.O. Box 40, Kingston 15, Jamaica. (Co-sponsor: Port Authority of Jamaica) Ed. T.A. Gambrill. circ. 1,700.
   Formerly (until 1977): Port of Kingston Handbook.

623.89   UK   ISSN 0267-4823
PORT DEVELOPMENT INTERNATIONAL. 1985. m. £85($180) Mundy Perry Ltd., 8A West Smithfield, London EC1A 9JR, England. TEL 071-236-0246. FAX 071-248-3336. TELEX 922015-PDI-G. Ed. Alistair Osborne. adv.; bk.rev.; circ. 9,500.
   —BLDSC shelfmark: 6555.260000.
   Description: Covers all critical aspects of port development: port planning, infrastructure development, cargo handling, computerization.

T

TRANSPORTATION — SHIPS AND SHIPPING

387 380   AT   ISSN 0266-3856
PORT KELANG SHIPPING HANDBOOK. 1984. a. Charter Pacific Publications Pty. Ltd., 723 D. Centre Rd., P.O. Box 252, Bentleight East, Vic. 3155, Australia. TEL 03-579-4333. FAX 03-579-4677. Ed. Gerry Cansdale. adv.; circ. 6,000.

387   US
PORT OF BALTIMORE MAGAZINE. 1946. m. free. Maryland Port Administration, World Trade Center Baltimore, Baltimore, MD 21202. TEL 301-333-4550. FAX 301-333-1126. Ed. Jim Gring. adv.; circ. 14,000.
    Formerly: Port of Baltimore Handbook (ISSN 0079-3981)

380   US   ISSN 0032-4825
HE554.H65
PORT OF HOUSTON MAGAZINE. 1959. m. free. Port of Houston Authority, Box 2562, Houston, TX 77252. TEL 713-670-2594. FAX 713-670-2564. Ed. Ann Bordelon. adv.; charts; illus.; circ. 14,000.

387   FR
PORT OF LE HAVRE FLASHES. 1972. m. free. Port Autonome du Havre - Port of Le Havre Authority, Terre Plein de la Barre, 76067 Le Havre, France. TEL 35-21-74-00. (U.S. orders to: Port of Le Havre Authority, One World Trade Center, Ste. 2551, New York, N.Y. 10048) Ed. Patrick Cornet. circ. 7,800.
    Description: Covers news of interest concerning the Port of le Havre Authority.

387   UK   ISSN 0030-8064
HE558.L8
PORT OF LONDON. 1925. q. £7 (foreign £10). Port of London Authority, World Trade Centre, London E1 9AA, England. TEL 071-481-8484. FAX 071-481-2458. TELEX 941-3062. Ed. Roger Mutton. adv.; bk.rev.; illus.; index; circ. 6,000.
    Indexed: Fluidex, Geo.Abstr., W.R.C.Inf.
    Formerly: P L A Monthly.

387   JA
PORT OF OSAKA/OSAKA-KO. (Text in English and Japanese) 1955. a. free. Port and Harbour Bureau - Osaka-shi Kowan-Kyoku, 2-8-24 Chikko, Minato-ku, Osaka 552, Japan. FAX 06-572-0554. TELEX 525-6320. stat.

387   GR
PORT OF PIRAEUS AUTHORITY. ANNUAL REPORT. a. Port of Piraeus Authority, Akti Miaouli II, Merarchias Corner, Piraeus, Greece.

387   GR
PORT OF PIRAEUS AUTHORITY. QUARTERLY REPORT. q. Port of Piraeus Authority, Akti Miaouli II, Merarchias Corner, Piraeus, Greece.

387   GR
PORT OF PIRAEUS AUTHORITY. STATISTICAL REPORT. (Text in English and Greek) 1913. m. Port of Piraeus Authority, Akti Miaouli II, Merarchias Corner, Piraeus, Greece. adv.; circ. 4,000.
    Supersedes: Port of Piraeus Authority. Statistical Bulletin (ISSN 0079-399X)

387   NE   ISSN 0922-7148
HE558.R75
PORT OF ROTTERDAM MAGAZINE. (Editions in Dutch, English and German) 1962. bi-m. (Port of Rotterdam, Municipal Port Management) Wyt · Publishers, Postbus 268, 3000 AG Rotterdam, Netherlands. TEL 010-4762566. FAX 010-4762315. TELEX 21403-WYT-NL. Ed. Willem C.N. van Horssen. adv.; bk.rev.; illus.; stat.; circ. 12,500 (controlled). **Indexed:** Excerp.Med., Fluidex, Key to Econ.Sci.
    —BLDSC shelfmark: 6555.382000.
    Formerly (until 1988): Rotterdam Europoort Delta (ISSN 0035-8487)
    Description: Magazine for port, transport and logistics.

387.1   JA
PORT OF TOKYO; a hand book. 1951. a. free. Tokyo Metropolitan Government, Port and Harbor Bureau, 8-1 Marunouchi 3-chome, Chiyoda-ku, Tokyo 100-81, Japan. TEL 03-3211-7949. TELEX 33346 PORTOKYO J. illus.; circ. 7,000.

315.2   JA
PORT OF YOKOHAMA. ANNUAL REPORT. (Text in Chinese, English and Japanese) a. free. Port and Harbor Bureau, Industry and Trade Center Bldg., 2 Yamashita-cho, Naka-ku, Yokohama, Japan. FAX 45-671-7158. stat.

387 380   UK   ISSN 0266-3848
PORT RASHID: DUBAI SHIPPING HANDBOOK. (Text in Arabic and English) 1984. a. Charter International Publications Ltd., Castle Chambers, Castle Acre, King's Lynn, Norfolk PE32 2BQ, England. TEL 07605-634. FAX 07605-625. TELEX 817440. Ed. James P. Moriarty. adv.; circ. 6,000.

387   SA   ISSN 0032-4892
PORTCULLIS. 1966. q. membership. (Institute of Shipping and Forwarding Agents of Southern Africa) Charter Registrars (Pty) Ltd., Box 1568, Port Elizabeth, South Africa. Ed. A. Gochin. bk.rev.; circ. 500.

387   IT   ISSN 0032-4957
IL PORTO DI SAVONA; rivista mensile dell'Ente autonomo del porto di Savona. (Includes English supplement) 1956. m. L.25000 (foreign L.50000). Ente Autonomo del Porto di Savona, Via Gramsci 14, 17100 Savona, Italy. TEL 019-802021. FAX 19827399. TELEX 271462 EAP SV. Dir. Giovanni Bono. adv./ bk.rev.; charts; illus.; stat.; index; circ. 6,500.
    Description: Covers shipping activities and statistics in the port of Savona.

387   BL   ISSN 0032-4973
PORTOS E NAVIOS; revista tecnica e informativa. 1958. m. Revista Tecnica e Informativa Ltda., Rua Leandro Martins 10, andar 9, Conj. 901-ZC 05, 20080 Rio de Janeiro, RJ, Brazil. Ed. Brasilo Accioly. adv.; abstr.; bibl.; charts; illus.; stat.; index. cum.index; circ. 20,000. **Indexed:** BMT.

387.1   CN
PORTS ANNUAL. 1972. a. Anchor Press, 1056 Chemin du Golf, Nun's Island, Verdun, Que. H3E 1H4, Canada. TEL 514-766-8650. FAX 514-766-5559. illus.

387   NE
PORTS MAGAZINE. bi-m. fl.48. Internationale Publiciteits Diensten, Postbus 317, 4530 AH Terneuzen, Netherlands. adv.; circ. 25,000.

387   SA
PORTS OF SOUTH AFRICA. 1948. a. R.30. Industrial Publishing Co. (Pty) Ltd., P.O. Box 825, Florida 1710, South Africa. adv.; circ. 3,500.

387   US   ISSN 0048-489X
PORTSIDE. 1971. q. free. Port of Portland, Box 3529, Portland, OR 97208. TEL 503-231-5000. Ed. R.G. Montgomery. circ. 12,000.
    Description: News of the Port of Portland marine cargo aviation, land development and ship repair activities.

387.5   PO
PORTUGAL. DIRECCAO GERAL DE MARINHA DO COMERCIO. BOLETIM. 1945. s-a. free. Direccao-Geral da Marinha do Comercio, Praca Luis de Camoes 22-1 Dt., 1200 Lisbon, Portugal. bibl.; charts; stat.; circ. 450.
    Formerly: Junta Nacional da Marinha Mercante. Boletim (ISSN 0022-6742)

387   US   ISSN 0048-5551
PROPELLER CLUB QUARTERLY. 1972. 4/yr. membership. Propeller Club of the United States, 3927 Old Lee Hwy, Ste. 101A, Fairfax, VA 22030. TEL 703-691-2777. FAX 703-691-4173. Ed. J. Daniel Smith. illus.; circ. 14,000.

387.5   PO
PROPULSOR. 1971. bi-m. free. Centro Cultural dos Oficiais e Engenheiros Maquinistas da Marinha Mercante, Avda. D. Carlos I No. 10, 1 Esq., 1200 Lisbon, Portugal. Ed.Bd. adv.; bk.rev.; charts; illus.; circ. 1,750.

PUERTO RICO. PORTS AUTHORITY. OFFICE OF ECONOMIC RESEARCH. STATISTICAL REPORT. see
TRANSPORTATION — Air Transport

QUARTERDECK. see MUSEUMS AND ART GALLERIES

RADIO AIDS TO MARINE NAVIGATION. see
COMMUNICATIONS — Television And Cable

RAILWAY AND CANAL HISTORICAL SOCIETY JOURNAL. see TRANSPORTATION — Railroads

387   RU   ISSN 0034-1290
    CODEN: RETRAN
RECHNOI TRANSPORT. 1941. m. 16.80 Rub. Izdatel'stvo Transport, Komsomol'kii prosp., 42, 119048 Moscow G-48, Russia. (Co-sponsor: Ministerstvo Rechnogo Flota) Ed. M.S. Nazarov. bk.rev.; bibl.; charts; illus.; stat.; index; circ. 15,490.
    Indexed: Chem.Abstr.
    —BLDSC shelfmark: 0154.000000.

347.75   GW   ISSN 0034-1320
RECHT DER SCHIFFAHRT/MARITIME LAW REVIEW; a card index periodical of the international shipping law. (Text in English and German) 1957. bi-m. DM.1280. Alfred Metzner Verlag, Postfach 970148, 6000 Frankfurt a.M. 97, Germany. TEL 069-793009-0. TELEX 4189621-KOMED. Ed. Hans Dabelstein. bk.rev.; circ. 400.

623.89   UK
REED'S COMMERCIAL SALVAGE PRACTICE. (In 2 vols. plus 3 annual supplements) 1987. every 5 yrs. £700 includes 3 annual reviews. Thomas Reed Publications Ltd., Weir House, Hurst RD., E. Molesey, Surrey KT8 9AQ, England. TEL 081-941-8090. FAX 081-941-8046. TELEX 883526-REED-G. Ed. David Hancox. circ. 700.

623.89   UK   ISSN 0263-3620
REED'S MEDITERRANEAN NAVIGATOR. 1983. a. $21. Thomas Reed Publications Ltd., Weir House, Hurst Rd., E. Molesey, Surrey KT8 9AQ, England. TEL 081-941-8090. FAX 081-941-8046. TELEX 883526-REED-G. Ed. Jean Fowler. adv.; circ. 5,000.
    —BLDSC shelfmark: 7331.410000.

623.89   UK
REED'S OCEAN NAVIGATOR. 1969. irreg. Thomas Reed Publications Ltd., Weir House, Hurst Rd., E. Molesey, Surrey KT8 9AQ, England. TEL 081-941-8090. FAX 081-941-8046. TELEX 883526-REED-G. circ. 5,000.

387   UK
REGISTER OF OFFSHORE UNITS, SUBMERSIBLES AND UNDERWATER SYSTEMS. 1976. a. $185. Lloyd's Register of Shipping, 71 Fenchurch St., London EC3M 4BS, England. (Subscr. address in US: Lloyd's Register of Shipping, 17 Battery Place, New York, NY 10004)
    Formerly: Register of Offshore Units, Submersibles and Diving Systems (ISSN 0141-4143)
    Description: Technical information on mobile drilling rigs, submersibles, diving systems and work units. Includes owners' names and addresses.

387   FR
REGISTRE MARITIME. 1829. a. (with q. suppl.). 1000 F. Bureau Veritas, Service Maritime, 17 bis, Place des Reflets, La Defense 2, 92400 Courbevoie, France. FAX 42-91-52-98. TELEX 612440F BVDSM. Ed. Berger Levrault. circ. 800. (also avail. in microfilm)
    Supersedes in part: Registre International de Classification de Navires et d'Aeronefs (ISSN 0080-0678)

RENENG DONGLI GONGCHENG/HEAT DYNAMICS ENGINEERING. see ENGINEERING — Mechanical Engineering

387.2   UN   ISSN 0085-560X
REVIEW OF MARITIME TRANSPORT. Arabic edition (ISSN 0252-5437); Chinese edition (ISSN 0252-5445); French edition (ISSN 0252-5429); Russian edition (ISSN 0252-5453); Spanish edition (ISSN 0252-5410) 1968. a. price varies. (United Nations Conference on Trade and Development (UNCTAD)) United Nations Publications, Room DC2-853, New York, NY 10017. TEL 212-963-8300. FAX 212-963-3489. (Or: Palais des Nations, 1211 Geneva, Switzerland) **Indexed:** IIS.

TRANSPORTATION — SHIPS AND SHIPPING

623.8   FR   ISSN 0767-094X
HE387.R5
REVUE DE LA NAVIGATION FLUVIALE EUROPEENNE, PORTS ET INDUSTRIES. Short title: Navigation, Ports and Industries. 1922. fortn. $195. Editions de la Navigation du Rhin, 7 Quai du General Koenig, 67085 Strasbourg Cedex, France. FAX 88-37-04-82. Ed. Maurice Ruscher. adv.; bk.rev.; charts; illus.; bibl.; index; circ. 2,500. **Indexed:** Excerp.Med.
   Description: Covers current events in navigation such as productivity, port traffic as well as various projects and developments taking place in ports world-wide.

387   NE
RHINE SHIPS REGISTER. 1879. a. fl.435. Internationale Vereniging het Rijnschepenregister (IVR) - International Association for the Rhine Ships Register, Vasteland 12E, Postbus 23210, 3001 KE Rotterdam, Netherlands. TEL 010-4116070. FAX 010-4129091.
   Description: Contains data on ships from Switzerland, France, Germany, Holland, Belgium, and Luxembourg, that sail on the Rhine River.

387   FR
RIVAGES. irreg. Universite de Montpellier (Universite Paul Valery), Laboratoire Amenagement des Littoraux et Organisation de l'Espace, B.P. 5043, 43032 Montpellier Cedex 1, France. TEL 67-14-20-00. Eds. Christian Verlaque, Jean-Marie Miossec.

359.97   US   ISSN 0145-0689
VG53
RIVER CURRENTS. 1947. m. free. U.S. Coast Guard, Public Information Office, 1430 Olive St., St. Louis, MO 63103. TEL 314-425-4627. Ed. Reginald V. Reese. charts; illus.; circ. 1,500. (also avail. in microform from UMI; reprint service avail. from UMI)

387   IT   ISSN 0035-5925
RIVISTA DEL PORTO DI NAPOLI. 1965. bi-m. L.18000 (foreign L.36000). Consorzio Autonomo del Porto, Molo Pisacane, 80133 Naples, Italy. TEL 266566. TELEX 721271 CAPNA I. Ed. Ernesto Mazzetti. adv.; bk.rev.; charts; illus.; stat.; index; circ. 2,000.
  —BLDSC shelfmark: 7992.730500.
   Description: Features articles on the Port of Naples. Includes information on tourism, import-export and the shipping industry.

ROLL ON ROLL OFF IN EUROPE; international guide for roll-on/roll-off shipping. see BUSINESS AND ECONOMICS — International Commerce

623.82   SP   ISSN 0211-2892
ROTACION; actualidad tecnica de maquinaria y equipos para buques. 1968. m. 5000 ptas. Pedeca Sociedad Cooperativa, Ltda., Maria Auxiliadora 5, 28040 Madrid, Spain. TEL 459 60 00. Ed. Antonio Alarcon Sanchez. adv.; bk.rev.; illus.; tr.lit.; circ. 8,000. **Indexed:** Ind.SST.

ROUEN PORT AND SHIPPING HANDBOOK. see BUSINESS AND ECONOMICS — Trade And Industrial Directories

623.81   UK
ROYAL INSTITUTION OF NAVAL ARCHITECTS. SOFT BACK TRANSACTIONS. PARTS A & B. s-a. £80. Royal Institution of Naval Architects, 10 Upper Belgrave St., London SW1X 8BQ, England. TEL 071-235 4622. FAX 071-245-6959. TELEX 265844-SINAI-G. illus.
   Formerly: Royal Institution of Naval Architects. Supplementary Papers (ISSN 0373-529X)

623.81   UK   ISSN 0035-8967
ROYAL INSTITUTION OF NAVAL ARCHITECTS. TRANSACTIONS. 1860. a. £100 to non-members. Royal Institution of Naval Architects, 10 Upper Belgrave St., London SW1X 8BQ, England. TEL 071-235 4622. FAX 071-245-6959. TELEX 265844-SINAI-G. Ed. P.W. Ayling. circ. 1,000. **Indexed:** BMT, Br.Tech.Ind.

S A R STATISTICS. (Search and Rescue) see TRANSPORTATION — Abstracting, Bibliographies, Statistics

387   MY   ISSN 0080-522X
HE884.6.S22
SABAH. MARINE DEPARTMENT. ANNUAL REPORT. (Text in English) 1961. a. M.$2. Marine Department, Jabatan Laut Sabah, Peti Surat 5, 87008 Labuan, Malaysia. TEL 087-412597. FAX 087-413515. TELEX MARKIN MA 80314.

387   623.888   UK   ISSN 0142-0666
VK200
SAFETY AT SEA. 1967. m. $148. International Trade Publications Ltd., Queensway House, 2 Queensway, Redhill, Surrey RH1 1QS, England. TEL 0737-768611. FAX 0737-761989. TELEX 948669-TOPJNL-G. Ed. R. Allen. adv.; bk.rev.; abstr.; illus.; circ. 3,800. **Indexed:** BMT.
  —BLDSC shelfmark: 8069.130000.
   Formerly (until 1978): Safety at Sea International (ISSN 0036-2441)

387   CN   ISSN 0581-3298
HD1694
SAINT LAWRENCE SEAWAY AUTHORITY. ANNUAL REPORT. (Text in English and French) 1955. a. free. Saint Lawrence Seaway Authority, Constitution Square, 360 Albert St., Ottawa, Ont. K1R 7X7, Canada. TEL 613-598-4614. FAX 613-598-4620. TELEX 053-3322 SLSA OTT. circ. 3,000.

387   IS   ISSN 0334-2751
SAPANUT. (Text in English and Hebrew) 1971. 2/yr. $15. Haifa University, Wydra Shipping and Aviation Research Institute, Ste. 2318, Eshkol Tower, Haifa 31999, Israel. TEL 04-240186. FAX 04-348908. Ed. A.M. Goldstein. abstr.; stat.; cum.index; circ. 600. **Indexed:** BMT, Ind.Heb.Per., Ocean.Abstr.
  —BLDSC shelfmark: 8075.730000.
   Formerly: Israel Shipping Research Institute. Journal (ISSN 0047-1593)
   Description: Summaries of institute research in international shipping and port topics. Includes Israeli shipping.

387   IS
HASAPANUT HAYISRAELIT. (Text in Hebrew; summaries in English) a. $20. Haifa University, Wydra Shipping and Aviation Research Institute, Ste. 2318, Eshkol Tower, Haifa 31999, Israel. TEL 04-240186. FAX 04-348908. Ed. M. Ofek.
   Description: Description and analysis of world developments in shipping and ports; with a detailed survey of Israeli developments; comprehensive statistical appendix.

387   UK   ISSN 0955-4408
SCANDANAVIAN AND EUROPEAN SHIPPING REVIEW; quarterly review of ship technology & services. 1989. q. £50. Contract Communcications Limited, Refuge House, 9-10 River Front, Enfield EN1 3SZ, England. TEL 081-367-3939. FAX 081-366-9091. TELEX 927826-CONTCO-G. Ed. Bill Wilson. circ. 10,000. (back issues avail.)

387   DK   ISSN 0036-5629
SCANDINAVIAN SHIPPING GAZETTE;* the international review. (Text in English) 1917. m. $15. Nautisk Forlag, Bentzonsvej 54, P.B. 1462, 2000 Copenhagen K, Denmark. Ed. P.E. Nygaard. adv.; charts; illus.; stat.; circ. 4,000 (controlled).

623.82   GW   ISSN 0938-1643
VM3   CODEN: SHASEZ
SCHIFF UND HAFEN. (Text in Chinese) 1988. s-a. Seehafen Verlag GmbH, Wandalenweg 1, Postfach 105605, 2000 Hamburg 1, Germany. TEL 040-23714-02. FAX 040-23714-154. Ed. Hans Juergen Witthoft. adv.; illus.; circ. 2,500 (controlled).
  —BLDSC shelfmark: 8088.706000.

623.8   627.2   GW
SCHIFF UND HAFEN - KOMMANDOBRUECKE. (Text in English and German) 1976. m. DM.247.20. (Schiffbautechnische Gesellschaft e.V.) Seehafen Verlag, Postfach 105605, 2000 Hamburg 1, Germany. adv.; bk.rev.; charts; illus.; index; circ. 5,500. **Indexed:** BMT, C.I.S. Abstr., Chem.Abstr., Excerp.Med., Fluidex, Met.Abstr., World Alum.Abstr.
   Formed by the merger of: Schiff und Hafen (ISSN 0036-603X) & Kommandobruecke.

387.2   GW
SCHIFF UND ZEIT. 1973. irreg., vol.27, 1988. DM.24.80. (Deutsche Gesellschaft fuer Schiffahrts-und Marinegeschichte e. V.) Koehlers Verlagsgesellschaft mbH, Steintorwall 17, Postfach 2352, 4900 Herford, Germany. TEL 5221-59910. FAX 5221-599125. Ed. Jochen Brennecke. illus.

623.8   GW   ISSN 0342-491X
SCHIFFAHRT INTERNATIONAL. 1949. m. DM.110.40. Koehlers Verlagsgesellschaft mbH, Steintorwall 17, Postfach 2352, 4900 Herford, Germany. TEL 5221-59910. FAX 5221-599125. Ed. Garrit Leemreijze. adv.; bk.rev.; abstr.; charts; illus.; stat.; index; circ. 9,000. **Indexed:** BMT.
   Former titles: Schiffahrt International mit Seekiste und Nautilus; Schiffahrt International - Seekiste (ISSN 0037-0843)

387   AU
SCHIFFAHRT UND STROM. bi-m. S.300. Oesterreichischer Wasserstrassen- und Schiffahrtsverein - Austrian Navigation and Waterways Association, Leberstr. 122, A-1110 Vienna, Austria. FAX 0222-74095-183. adv.; bk.rev.

623.8   GW   ISSN 0036-6056
VM156
SCHIFFBAUFORSCHUNG; wissenschaftlich-technische Mitteilungen. (Text in German; contents page and summaries in English, German, Russian, and Spanish) 1962. q. DM.96 (foreign DM.112). (Universitaet Rostock, Fachbereich Maschinenbau und Schiffstechnik) Ingenieurzentrum Schiffbau GmbH, Carl-Hopp-Str. 19a, 2510 Rostock 5, Germany. FAX 815209. Ed. Karla Apitz. bk.rev.; charts; illus.; circ. 450. **Indexed:** BMT.
  —BLDSC shelfmark: 8088.740000.

623.82   US   ISSN 0374-1222
VM3
SCHIFFBAUTECHNISCHEN GESELLSCHAFT. JAHRBUCH. a. price varies. Springer-Verlag, 175 Fifth Ave, New York, NY 10010. TEL 212-460-1500. (Also Berlin, Heidelberg, Tokyo and Vienna) (reprint service avail. from ISI)

387   GW
SCHIFFS-INGENIEUR JOURNAL. bi-m. Verein der Schiffs-Ingenieur zu Hamburg, Gurlittstr. 32, D-2000 Hamburg 1, Germany. TEL 040-2803883.

387   621.9   GW   ISSN 0177-1116
SCHIFFSBETRIEBSTECHNIK FLENSBURG. 1954. q. DM.25 membership. Schiffsbetriebstechnische Gesellschaft, Kanzleistr. 91-93, 2390 Flensburg, Germany. TEL 0461-29222. Ed.Bd. adv.; bk.rev.; circ. 1,500. (back issues avail.)
   Description: Trade publication for the shipbuilding industry. Features the latest technology, marketing, industry and trade school information. Includes list of events and exhibitions.

387   GW
SCHIFFSLISTE; Verzeichnis der deutschen Reedereien & ihre Schiffe. 1902. a. DM.53. Eckardt & Messtorff GmbH, Roedingsmarkt 16, 2000 Hamburg 11, Germany. FAX 040-373028. Ed. G.U. Detlefsen. adv.; circ. 3,000.

623.8   GW   ISSN 0036-6064
                                    CODEN: SCFTAO
SCHIFFSTECHNIK; Forschungshefte fuer Schiffbau und Schiffsmaschinenbau. 1952. 4/yr. DM.123.60. Schiffahrts-Verlag Hansa C. Schroedter GmbH und Co. KG, Stubbenhuk 10, 2000 Hamburg 11, Germany. adv.; charts; circ. 1,000 (approx.). **Indexed:** Appl.Mech.Rev., BMT, Deep Sea Res.& Oceanogr.Abstr., Eng.Ind.

623.8   NE   ISSN 0036-6099
VM4
SCHIP EN WERF. 1934. fortn. fl.60. (Nederlandsche Vereniging van Technici Op Scheepvaartgebied - Dutch Corporation of Ship-Building Engineers) Wijt en Zn. B.V., Box 268, Rotterdam, Netherlands. (Co-sponsors: Centrale Bond van Scheepsbouwmeesters in Nederland; National Instituut voor Scheepvaart en Scheepsbouw; Nederlandsch Scheepsbouwkundig Proefstation) adv.; index; circ. 3,700. **Indexed:** BMT, C.I.S. Abstr., Excerp.Med., Key to Econ.Sci.

TRANSPORTATION — SHIPS AND SHIPPING

387   UK
SEA. 1974. bi-m. £1.50. Missions to Seamen, St. Michael Paternoster Royal, College Hill, London EC4R 2RL, England. TEL 071-248-5202. FAX 071-248-4761. Ed. Gillian Ennis. circ. 13,000. (tabloid format)

387   UK   ISSN 0036-9977
HE753.P32
SEA BREEZES; the magazine of ships and the sea. 1919. m $61. Jocast Ltd., 202 Cotton Exchange Bldg., Old Hall St., Liverpool L3 9LA, England. Ed. C.H. Milsom. adv.; bk.rev.; charts; illus.; index.
—BLDSC shelfmark: 8213.560000.

387 970   US   ISSN 0582-3471
SEA CHEST. 1967. q. $35. Puget Sound Maritime Historical Society, 1216 Broadway, Bremerton, WA 98310-1669. Ed. Michael Jay Mjelde. bk.rev.; illus.; index; circ. 750. (back issues avail.) **Indexed:** Hist.Abstr.

387   US   ISSN 0146-9312
VK23
SEA HISTORY. 1971. q. $30 (foreign $40). National Maritime Historical Society, 5 John Walsh Blvd., Charles Point, Peekskill, NY 10566-5324. TEL 914-737-7878. Ed. Peter Stanford. adv.; bk.rev.; circ. 20,000. **Indexed:** Bk.Rev.Ind. (1990-), Child.Bk.Rev.Ind. (1990-), Hist.Abstr.
—BLDSC shelfmark: 8213.633000.
Description: Features articles on maritime history and related subjects.

387   US   ISSN 0896-1646
VK23
SEA HISTORY GAZETTE. 1987. m. $18.75 (foreign $28.75). National Maritime Historical Society, 5 John Walsh Blvd., Charles Point, Peekskill, NY 10566-5324. TEL 914-271-2177. Ed. Kevin F. Haydon. circ. 1,000.
Description: Digest of maritime heritage news.

SEA HISTORY'S GUIDE TO AMERICAN & CANADIAN MARITIME MUSEUMS. see *MUSEUMS AND ART GALLERIES*

387   US   ISSN 0732-6882
SEA LETTER. 1961. s-a. membership. National Maritime Museum Association, Presidio of San Francisco Bldg. 275, Crissy Field, San Francisco, CA 94129. TEL 415-929-0202. Ed. Stephen A. Haller. bk.rev.; illus.; circ. 2,000.
Formerly: San Francisco Maritime Museum. Sea Letter (ISSN 0037-0010)

SEA POWER. see *MILITARY*

387 796.95   SA   ISSN 1015-6488
SEA RESCUE. (Text in English) 1981. q. (National Sea Rescue Institute) Yachting News (Pty) Ltd., P.O. Box 3473, Cape Town 8000, South Africa. TEL 021-4617472. FAX 021-4613758. Ed. Anna Tanneberger. adv.; bk.rev.; circ. 10,000 (controlled). (back issues avail.)

387   UK
SEABORNE TRADE AND TRANSPORT REPORTS. 1972. 9/yr. £850. Drewry Shipping Consultants Ltd., 11 Heron Quay, London E14 4JF, England. TEL 071-538 0191. FAX 071-987-9396. TELEX 21167 HPDLDN G. Ed. A.B. Carpenter.
Former titles: Seaborne Trade and Transport; (until 1986): Shipping Studies.
Description: Aimed at those involved in the worldwide bulk shipping industry. Provides coverage of the outlook for international seaborne bulk trade, for ship employment, market balances, and for profitability.

370   UK   ISSN 0037-007X
VK1
SEAFARER. 1934. q. £7($14) to individuals; institutions £9($18). Marine Society, 202 Lambeth Rd., London SE1 7JW, England. TEL 071-261 9535. FAX 071-401-2537. TELEX 934089-MARSOC-G. Ed. Michael Moore. adv.; bk.rev.; illus.; circ. 2,500.
—BLDSC shelfmark: 8213.720000.
Description: Short fiction, poetry, historical vignettes, and informational articles pertaining to British seafaring, with news and announcements about the Society, a maritime charity.

SEAFARERS LOG. see *LABOR UNIONS*

SEAMAN. see *LABOR UNIONS*

387   AT
SEAMEN'S JOURNAL. 1915. m. free. Seamen's Union of Australia, 289A Sussex St., Sydney, N.S.W. 2000, Australia. FAX 02-261-5897. Ed. P. Kingswood. bk.rev.; circ. 4,000.

387   US   ISSN 0743-6246
SEAPORT: NEW YORK'S HISTORY MAGAZINE. 1967. q. $25. South Street Seaport Museum, 207 Front St., New York, NY 10038. TEL 212-669-9400. FAX 212-732-5168. Ed. Madeline Rogers. adv.; bk.rev.; illus.; cum.index; circ. 21,000. (tabloid format) **Indexed:** Avery Ind.Archit.Per.
Former titles: Seaport Magazine; (until vol.12, Oct. 1978): South Street Reporter (ISSN 0038-3538)

387   CN   ISSN 0037-0150
HE561
SEAPORTS AND THE SHIPPING WORLD; voice of the shipping/marine industry in Canada. 1937. m. Can.$40 (foreign Can.$54). Gallery Publications Ltd., 4634 St. Catherine St. W., Montreal, Que. H3Z 1S3, Canada. TEL 514-934-0373. FAX 514-937-4250. Ed. Brian Gallery. adv.; illus.; stat.; tr.lit.; circ. 3,000. (back issues avail.) **Indexed:** Can.B.P.I.
Description: Covers seaway tolls, pilotage, pollution, productivity shipbuilding subsidies.

387 382   CN   ISSN 0080-8423
SEAPORTS AND THE SHIPPING WORLD. ANNUAL ISSUE. 1957. a. Gallery Publications Ltd., 4634 St. Catherine St. W., Montreal, Que. H3Z 1S3, Canada. TEL 514-934-0373. FAX 514-937-4250. Ed. Brian Gallery. adv.; circ. 1,200.

SEATRADE REVIEW. see *BUSINESS AND ECONOMICS — International Commerce*

387   UK
SEATRADE WEEK. 1982. w. $575 includes Seatrade Review. Seatrade Publications Ltd., Seatrade House, 42-48 North Station Rd., Colchester CO1 1RB, England. TEL 0206-45121. FAX 0206-45190. TELEX 98517-DISOP-G. (N. American subscr. to: 125 Village Blvd., Ste. 220, Princeton Forrestal Village, Princeton, NJ 08540-5703. TEL 609-452-9414) Ed. Ian Middleton. adv.; bk.rev.; circ. 3,500.
Description: Shipping news and market data.

387   US   ISSN 0037-0487
HE381.A2
SEAWAY REVIEW. 1970. q. $20. Harbor House Publishers, Inc., 221 Water St., Boyne City, MI 49712. TEL 616-582-2814. FAX 616-582-3392. Ed. Michelle Cortright. adv.; bk.rev.; charts; illus.; stat.; circ. 9,000. (also avail. in microfilm from UMI) **Indexed:** BMT, Mich.Mag.Ind.
Incorporates (as of vol.6, 1977): Limnos (ISSN 0024-3604)
Description: Edited for the bi-national transportation industry and infrastructure in the Great Lakes - St. Lawrence transportation system. Articles concern international trade, port development, shipbuilding, shipping, economics, maritime technology and hardware, ship maintenance, foreign and U.S. liner services and cargo handling.

387   UK   ISSN 0144-1019
SEAWAYS. 1980. m. £45($72) Nautical Institute, 202 Lambeth Rd., London SE1 7LQ, England. Ed. David J. Sanders. adv.; bk.rev.; charts; illus.; index; circ. 5,305. (back issues avail.)
—BLDSC shelfmark: 8216.055600.

623.8   GW   ISSN 0037-0886
SEEWIRTSCHAFT; Fachzeitschrift fuer Schiffahrt, Schiffbau, Seefischerei, Meerestechnik. (Text in German; contents page in English, German and Russian) 1969. m. DM.102 (foreign DM.135.60). Seehafen Verlag GmbH, Wandalenweg 1, 2000 Hamburg 1, Germany. Ed. Juergen Menke. adv.; bk.rev.; bibl.; charts; illus.; pat.; index; circ. 4,500. **Indexed:** BMT, Excerp.Med., Ocean.Abstr., Pollut.Abstr.
Supersedes: Schiffbautechnik.
Description: Technical journal of shipbuilding, sea fisheries and maritime technology.

SEFUNIM. see *ARCHAEOLOGY*

387   SP   ISSN 0211-304X
SERNAVAL. (Servicio Informacion Naval); informe mensual sobre la actividad naval y maritima. (Text in English and Spanish) 1972. m. 40000 ptas. Pedeca Sociedad Cooperativa, Ltda., Maria Auxiliadora 5, 28040 Madrid, Spain. TEL 459 60 00. Ed. Bernardo Moll. stat.; circ. 1,000. (back issues avail.)

387   SZ
SEXTANT. (Text in French and German) 1974. q. Schweizerischer Bootbauer-Verband, Gemeindehaus, Postfach 74, CH-8117 Faellanden, Switzerland. TEL 01-825-0388. FAX 01-825-2256. adv.

387   CC
SHANGHAI HAIYUN XUEYUAN XUEBAO. (Text in Chinese) q. Shanghai Haiyun Xueyuan, 1550 Pudong Dadao, Shanghai 200135, People's Republic of China. TEL 8848911. Ed. Fu Xianghao.

SHARJAH PORTS HANDBOOK. see *BUSINESS AND ECONOMICS — Trade And Industrial Directories*

387   UK
SHIPBUILDING NEWS. 1977. m. £3. 113-115 The Broadway, Leigh-on-Sea, Essex, England. Ed. Michael Guy. adv.; circ. 55,000.

623.8   UK
SHIPCARE & MARITIME MANAGEMENT. 1968. 6/yr. $117. International Trade Publications Ltd., Queensway House, 2 Queensway, Redhill, Surrey RH1 1QS, England. TEL 0737-768611. FAX 0737-761989. TELEX 948669-TOPJNL-G. Ed. Anthony Farrar. adv.; abstr.; illus.; stat.; circ. 2,084. **Indexed:** API Abstr., API Catal., API Hlth.& Environ., API Oil., API Pet.Ref., API Pet.Subst., API Transport., BMT, Br.Tech.Ind., Excerp.Med., Ocean.Abstr.
Formed by the merger of: Shipcare International & Maritime Management (ISSN 0140-8461); **Formerly:** Ship Repair and Maintenance (ISSN 0049-0369)

387   HK
SHIPPERS TODAY. (Text in Chinese, English) 1978. bi-m. HK.$100 (foreign HK.$250). Hong Kong Shippers Council, Rm. 2707A, Office Tower, Convention Plaza, 1 Harbour Rd., Wanchai, Hong Kong. TEL 852-824-1228. FAX 852-824-0394. Ed. Jacqueline E. F. Chu. adv.; circ. 6,000.
Description: Covers international trade and transportation topics of interest to shippers in Hong Kong.

387   GR
SHIPPING; international monthly review. 1957. m. Dr.2500($70) E. Dimopoulou and Co., 89 Kolokotroni St., Piraeus, Greece. Ed. Letta Dimopoulou. adv.; bk.rev.; circ. 2,500.

SHIPPING AND AVIATION STATISTICS OF THE MALTESE ISLANDS. see *TRANSPORTATION — Abstracting, Bibliographies, Statistics*

387.5 639.2 551.46 II   ISSN 0970-0285
HE561
SHIPPING AND MARINE INDUSTRIES JOURNAL; devoted to shipping and shipbuilding industries, fisheries and oceanography. (Text in English) 1972. q. Rs.110($25) V.J. Joseph, Ed. & Pub., 3 Radhe Nivas, 36th Rd., Bandra, Bombay 400 050, India. TEL 6427281-273187. adv.; charts, illus, stat. (reprint service avail.) **Indexed:** BMT.

387 910.09   GR
▼**SHIPPING AND TOURISM.** (Supplement to: Epilogi) 1991. a. Dr.1000. Electra Press, 4 Stadiou St., 10564 Athens, Greece. TEL 01-32-33-203. FAX 01-32-35-160. TELEX 210564. Ed. Christos Papaioannou. adv.; circ. 9,000.

387 382   JA
SHIPPING AND TRADE NEWS. (Text in English) 1949. d. 42900 Yen. Tokyo News Service Ltd., Tsukiji Hamarikyu Bldg., 3-3 Tsukiji, 5-chome, Chuo-ku, Tokyo 104, Japan. TEL 03-3542-8521. Ed. Chiaki Sakurai. circ. 15,000.

TRANSPORTATION — SHIPS AND SHIPPING

387   BA
SHIPPING & TRANSPORT NEWS INTERNATIONAL. (Text in English) m. $115. Al Hilal Publishing & Marketing Group, P.O. Box 224, Manama, Bahrain. TEL 293131. FAX 293400. TELEX 8981 HILAL BN. (In Singapore: Al Hilal Publishing (Far East) Pte Ltd, 50 Jalan Sultan, 20-06 Jalan Sultan Centre, Singapore 0719. TEL 2939233) Ed. Saby Ganguly. adv.; circ. 5,600.
     Formerly: Shipping and Transport News; **Incorporates:** Gulf Shipping and Transport.
     Description: For senior management personnel in the shipping and transport industries of the Middle East and Far East, including air cargo, marine transport, airlines, import - export, and shipping agencies.

387   DK   ISSN 0108-8912
SHIPPING-BLADET. 1982. 24/yr. Nautisk Forlag, Postbox 1462, 2000 Copenhagen F, Denmark. (Co-publisher: Provins-Trykkeriet)

387   US   ISSN 0037-3893
HE561
SHIPPING DIGEST; for export and transportation executives. 1923. w. $38. Geyer-McAllister Publications, Inc., 51 Madison Ave., New York, NY 10010. TEL 212-689-4411. (Subscr. to: Box 1129, Dover, NJ 07801) adv.; circ. 4,900. (back issues avail.)

387   US
SHIPPING DIGEST SHIPPING LINES AND AGENTS DIRECTORY ISSUE. s-a. Geyer-McAllister Publications, Inc., 51 Madison Ave., New York, NY 10010. TEL 212-689-4411. adv.; circ. 4,900.

387   US
SHIPPING DIGEST'S HANDBOOK FOR INTERNATIONAL TRADE. 2/yr. 51 Madison Ave., New York, NY 10010. TEL 212-689-4411. FAX 212-683-7929. adv.; circ. 4,884.
     Description: Shipping industry reference guide containing export documentation requirements for well over 100 countries, a glossary of shipping terms, port cross-references, pier information, intermodal schedules and trade routes.

387   JA   ISSN 0037-3915
SHIPPING GAZETTE; weekly digest of shipping schedules and news. (Text in English and Japanese) 1951. w. 24000 Yen. Japan Press, Ltd., C.P.O. Box 6, Tokyo 100-91, Japan. TEL 03-3404-5151. FAX 03-3423-2358. TELEX 242-5374 JPRESS J. (Subscr. to: 2-12-8 Kita Aoyama, Minato-ku, Tokyo 107, Japan) Ed. Yoshio Wada. adv.; circ. 23,000.

387   II
SHIPPING INFORMATION SERVICES. m. South-Western India Shippers Association, Cochin Chamber Bldg., Bristow Road, Willingdon Island, Cochin 682 003, India. TEL 0484-6349.

623.8   CN   ISSN 0037-3923
SHIPPING REGISTER AND SHIPBUILDER. (Annual Number) 1917. bi-m. Can.$10. Anchor Press, 1056 Chemin du Golf, Nun's Island, Verdun, Que. H3E 1H4, Canada. TEL 514-766-8650. FAX 514-766-5559. Ed. O.J. Silva. adv.; illus.; circ. 5,000.

623.82   UK   ISSN 0037-3931
CODEN: SWSBA5
SHIPPING WORLD & SHIPBUILDER. 1883. m. £30 (foreign £40)(effective Jan. 1991). Marine Publications International Ltd., 4 Hubbard Rd., Houndmills, Basingstoke, Hampshire RG21 2UH, England. TEL 0256 840444. FAX 0256-817877. Ed. Derek Deere. adv.; bk.rev.; illus.; circ. 4,621. (also avail. in microform from UMI; reprint service avail.) Indexed: Appl.Mech.Rev., BMT, Br.Tech.Ind., C.I.S. Abstr., Eng.Ind., Fluidex, Key to Econ.Sci., Ocean.Abstr., Pollut.Abstr., World Surf.Coat.
     —BLDSC shelfmark: 8263.300000.
     Incorporates: Syren and Shipping.

387   AT   ISSN 1032-3449
SHIPS & PORTS. 1988. m. Aus.$50. Baird Publications Pty. Ltd., 10 Oxford St., South Yarra, Vic. 3141, Australia. TEL 03-240-8741. FAX 03-241-0704. Ed. Neil Baird. adv.; circ. 3,000.
     Description: Newsmagazine of the ports and shipping industry in Australia and the South West Pacific.

387   UK   ISSN 0037-394X
VM1
SHIPS MONTHLY. 1966. m. £19.20 (foreign £26.90). Waterway Productions Ltd., Kottingham House, Dale St., Burton-on-Trent, Staffs DE14 3TD, England. TEL 0283-64290. Ed. Robert Shopland. adv.; bk.rev.; charts; illus.; stat.; index; circ. 21,663.
     —BLDSC shelfmark: 8266.150000.

623.82   US
SHIPYARD BULLETIN. 1927. m. free. Newport News Shipbuilding, Newport News, VA 23607. TEL 804-380-2342. FAX 804-380-3867. Ed. Pam Curley. circ. 30,000 (controlled). (tabloid format)
     Description: Includes news on company business as well as employee features.

387   US
SHIPYARD CHRONICLE. 1975. bi-w. $125. Shipbuilders Council of America, 4301 N. Fairfax Dr., Arlington, VA 22203. TEL 703-276-1700. FAX 703-276-1707. Ed. Carol Pardon. bk.rev.; stat.; circ. 3,000.
     Formerly: Shipyard Weekly.

SHIPYARD LOG. see *MILITARY*

387   UK   ISSN 0265-8291
SHIPYARD ORDERS. WEEKLY REPORT. 1984. w. £760. Lloyd's Register of Shipping, 71 Fenchurch St., London EC3M 4BS, England. TEL 071-709-9166.
     Description: Reports of shipyard orders and cancellations worldwide for ships of 100 gross tons and above.

623.8   II   ISSN 0037-3958
SHIPYARD REVIEW. (Text in English and Telugu) 1959. q. Rs.4. Hindustan Shipyard Ltd., Visakhapatnam 5, India. Ed. K.M. Reddy. adv.; bk.rev.; illus.; circ. 5,000.

386   CC   ISSN 1001-3962
TC160
SHUILI SHUIYUN KEXUE YANJIU. (Text in Chinese) q. Nanjing Shuili Kexue Yanjiuyuan, 34 Hujuguan, Nanjing, Jiangsu 210024, People's Republic of China. TEL 637430. Ed. Liu Jinpei.

387 658   CC   ISSN 1000-8799
SHUIYUN GUANLI/WATER TRANSPORTATION MANAGEMENT. (Text in Chinese) bi-m. Shanghai Haiyun Xueyuan, 1550 Pudong Dadao, Shanghai 200135, People's Republic of China. TEL 8840911. Ed. Su Peiji.

SIGNALS. see *MUSEUMS AND ART GALLERIES*

387   SI
SINGAPORE. NATIONAL MARITIME BOARD. REPORT. (Text in English) 1974. q. National Maritime Board, Singapore, Singapore.

SINGAPORE SHIPPING & CARGO STATISTICS. see *TRANSPORTATION — Abstracting, Bibliographies, Statistics*

387   SP
SINGULADURAS. 1969. w. 12000 ptas. (elsewhere L.15000). Antonio Aysa Rodriguez, Ed. & Pub., Ercilla 24-4, Bilbao 48011, Spain. FAX 94-4163797. Ed. M. Martin Pagazaurtundua. adv.; bk.rev.; circ. 1,500.
     Formerly: Bilbao Maritimo.

387   DK
SKANDINAVISK SKIBSFARTS TEKNISKE AARSHEFTE. a. Nautisk Forlag, Bentzonsvej 54, Box 1462, 2000 Copenhagen F, Denmark. adv.; circ. 3,000.

387   NO   ISSN 0800-1235
HE563.N8
SKANDINAVISKE SKIPSREDERIER/YEARBOOK OF SCANDINAVIAN SHIPOWNERS. (Text in English) 1936. a. NOK 300. Maritime Year Books AS, P.O. Box 9156 Vaterland, 0134 Oslo 1, Norway. adv.

623.82   DK
SKIBS OG BAADEBYGNING. 10/yr. (Foreningen af Skibs- og Baadebyggere i Danmark) A. og B. Mogensen ApS, Hambros Alle 3, 2900 Hellerup, Denmark. adv.; circ. 800.

387 623.8   NO   ISSN 0300-3310
SKIP; maritimt/teknisk tidsskrift. (Text in Danish, Norwegian and Swedish) 1962. m. (10/yr.). NOK 150. Bjarne H. Reenskaug A-S, P.O. Box 130, 2261 Kirkenaer, Norway. Ed. Odd H. Vanebo. adv.; charts; illus.; circ. 5,140.

387   DK
SKIPPEREN. 1910. m. DKK 100. Rederiforeningen for Mindre Skibe, Valmuevej 4, 9380 Vestbjerg, Denmark. Ed. A. Traumholm. adv.; circ. 1,000.

623.8 387   UK
SMALL SHIPS. bi-m. £146. International Trade Publications, Queensway House, 2 Queensway, Redhill, Surrey RH1 1QS, England. Ed. Chris Wilbur. adv.; circ. 3,500. **Indexed:** BMT.

387   US
SOCIETY OF MARITIME ARBITRATORS. AWARD SERVICE. 1965. a. $495. Society of Maritime Arbitrators, 61 Broadway, Ste. 1650, New York, NY 10006-2701. TEL 212-483-0616. circ. 300.

623.8   US   ISSN 0081-1661
VM1   CODEN: SNAMAL
SOCIETY OF NAVAL ARCHITECTS AND MARINE ENGINEERS. TRANSACTIONS. 1893. a. $60. Society of Naval Architects and Marine Engineers, 601 Pavonia Ave., Jersey City, NJ 07306-2907. index; circ. 7,000. **Indexed:** BMT, Deep Sea Res.& Oceanogr.Abstr., Ocean.Abstr., Petrol.Abstr., Pollut.Abstr.
     —BLDSC shelfmark: 9008.000000.

387   JA
SOCIETY OF NAVAL ARCHITECTS, JAPAN. JOURNAL. s-a. $190. (Society of Naval Architects, Japan) Intercontinental Marketing Corp., I.P.O. Box 5056, Tokyo 100-31, Japan. FAX 81-3-3667-9646.

387   DK   ISSN 0038-0520
SOEFART. 1950. w. membership. Foreningen til Soefartens Fremme - Association for the Promotion of the Danish Merchant Marine, Box 288, DK-8100 Aarhus C, Denmark. Ed. P. Rungholm. adv.; bk.rev.; charts; illus.; circ. 9,500.

387   US
SOUNDINGS. 1983. m. $125. Professional Mariners Alliance, Inc., 370 W. Park Ave., Long Beach, NY 11561-3292. TEL 516-431-4441. FAX 516-889-5111. Ed. Thomas J. O'Hara III. adv.; bk.rev.; cum.index: 1983-1984; circ. 5,000. (back issues avail.)
     Formerly (until 1986): Professional Mariner.

SOUNDINGS (MILWAUKEE). see *HISTORY — History Of North And South America*

387   AG
SOUTH AMERICAN PORTS HANDBOOK. (Text in English) 1974. biennial. $80. Agencia Maritima Internacional S.A., 25 de Mayo 555, piso 20, 1002 Buenos Aires, Argentina. FAX 313-1996. TELEX 21115. illus.; circ. 1,500.
     Formerly (until 1976): Owners, Masters, Brokers and Agents Handbook on South American Caribbean and Pacific Ports in Venezuela, Colombia, Panama, Ecuador, Peru, Bolivia and Chile.

387 382   US   ISSN 0896-2278
WMCL 82/61
SOUTH CAROLINA PORT NEWS. 1947. m. free. Ports Authority, Box 817, Charleston, SC 29402. TEL 803-577-8622. FAX 803-577-8616. TELEX 810-881-1860 SCPORTSAUTH. Ed. Debra Nelson. adv.; charts; illus.; stat.; circ. 11,200.
     Description: Covers news relevant to the port of Charleston; features on customs and stories of general interst to the community.

SOUTHAMPTON PORT HANDBOOK. see *BUSINESS AND ECONOMICS — Trade And Industrial Directories*

4740 TRANSPORTATION — SHIPS AND SHIPPING

387 US
HE554.J3
SOUTHERN SHIPPER. 1952. m. free. Howard Publications, Inc., 33 S. Hogan St., Ste. 230, Box 4728, Jacksonville, FL 32201. TEL 904-355-2601. FAX 904-791-8836. TELEX 70-3471. Ed. Joseph A. Bonney. adv.; circ. 7,321. (also avail. in microform from UMI; reprint service avail. from UMI)
Former titles: Seafarer (ISSN 0882-7788); Which incorporated: Jacksonville Port Handbook (ISSN 0160-2241); Miami Port Handbook; South Florida Ports Handbook; Georgia Port Handbook; Savannah Port Handbook; Jacksonville Seafarer (ISSN 0447-2462).

387.5 UK
SOVIET MERCHANT SHIPS. 1969. triennial. £16.95. Kenneth Mason Publications Ltd., 12 North St., Emsworth, Hants. PO10 7DQ, England. TEL 0243-377977. FAX 0243-379136. Ed. Ambrose Greenway.

387 RU ISSN 0203-3933
CODEN: SOVSEJ
SOVIET SHIPPING. (Text in English) 1981. q. free. Association of Soviet Shipowners, 4 Rakhmanovsky, Moscow, GSP-4 101412, Russia. Ed. K.A. Ivanov.
—BLDSC shelfmark: 8359.915480.

SPINDRIFT (PHILADELPHIA). see *MUSEUMS AND ART GALLERIES*

SPOTLIGHT (BATH). see *MILITARY*

387 US ISSN 0039-0844
VM1
STEAMBOAT BILL; relating primarily to steam and other power vessels, past and present. 1940. q. $25. Steamship Historical Society of America, Inc., c/o Barry W. Eager, Secy., 300 Ray Dr., Ste. No. 4, Providence, RI 02906. Ed. William M. Rau. charts; illus.; cum.index: 1940-1974; circ. 3,400. (also avail. in microform from UMI; reprint service avail. from UMI)
—BLDSC shelfmark: 8460.975000.

STEAMBOATING. see *SPORTS AND GAMES — Boats And Boating*

387.164 GW
STOWAGE AND SEGREGATION TO I M D G CODE. 1973. a. DM.100.93. K.O. Storck Verlag, Stahltwiete 7, 2000 Hamburg 50, Germany. TEL 040-850-0071. FAX 040-850-7758. TELEX 17403448. Ed. H. Meder.

387 SZ ISSN 0039-2510
STROM & SEE; Zeitschrift fuer Schiffahrt und Weltverkehr. 1906. 7/yr. membership. Schweizerische Schiffahrtsvereinigung - Swiss Shipping Association, Suedquaistr. 14, CH-4019 Basel, Switzerland. Ed. Juergen Zimmermann. adv.; bk.rev.; charts; illus.; tr.lit.; index; circ. 2,100.

387 IT ISSN 0392-5021
STUDI MARITTIMI; economia, diritto e tecnica della navigazione dei porti. 1978. q. L.30000. Consorzio Autonomo del Porto, Piazzale Pisacane, 80133 Naples, Italy. TEL 081-266566. TELEX 721271 CAPNA I. Ed. Ernesto Mazzetti. stat.; charts.
Description: Features maritime and naval studies. Includes navigation, economics, law and technology.

623.8 RU ISSN 0039-4580
CODEN: SUDOAN
SUDOSTROENIE. 1898. m. 37.20 Rub. (Nauchno-tekhnicheskoe Obshchestvo Sudostroietel'noi Promyshlennosti im. A.N. Krylova) Izdatel'stvo Sudostroenie, Ul. Gogolya, 8, St. Petersburg D-65, Russia. (Co-sponsor: Ministerstvo Sudostroeniya) Ed. G.G. Pulyaevskii. bibl.; charts; illus.; tr.lit.; circ. 12,000. (also avail. in microform from MIM) **Indexed:** Appl.Mech.Rev., C.I.S. Abstr., Chem.Abstr.

SUVREMENI PROMET. see *TRANSPORTATION — Air Transport*

387 SW ISSN 0039-6702
VK4
SVENSK SJOEFARTS TIDNING/SCANDINAVIAN SHIPPING GAZETTE. (Text in English and Swedish) 1905. w. SEK 575($100) Sveriges Redarefoerening - Swedish Shipowners' Association, Box 53090, S-400 14 Goeteborg, Sweden. TEL 31-178540. FAX 31-115418. TELEX 20746 SWESHIP S. Ed. Thorsten Rinman. adv.; bk.rev.; illus.; index; circ. 7,901. **Indexed:** BMT.

SVEUCILISTE U ZAGREBU. FAKULTET STROJARSTVA I BRODOGRADNJE. ZBORNIK RADOVA. see *ENGINEERING — Mechanical Engineering*

387 GW
TAEGLICHER HAFENBERICHT. 1947. d. DM.199.50 per month. Sehafen-Verlag Erik Blumenfeld GmbH und Co., Wandalenwes 1, Postfach 105605, 2000 Hamburg 1, Germany. Ed. Jens Meyer. adv.; bk.rev.; charts; illus.; stat.; circ. 1,300.

387 GW
TAEGLICHER HAFENBERICHT. JAHRESAUSGABE. a. DM.27.80. Sehafen-Verlag Erik Blumenfeld GmbH und Co., Postfach 105605, 2000 Hamburg 1, Germany. charts; stat.

387 UK ISSN 0959-6089
▼**TANK CONTAINER WORLD.** 1990. bi-m. $170. Baltic Publishing Ltd., Great West Rd., Brentford, Middlesex TW8 9BU, England. TEL 081-847-2446. FAX 081-569-8688. Ed. Rachael White.

TANKER REGISTER. see *PETROLEUM AND GAS*

387 PL ISSN 0040-1137
TECHNIKA I GOSPODARKA MORSKA. (Text in Polish; summaries and contents page in English) 1951. m. 26000 Zl.($1360) (Ministerstwo Kultury i Sztuki - Ministry of Culture and Arts) Wydawnictwo Morskie, Szeroka 38-40, 80-835 Gdansk, Poland. (Dist. by: Ars Polona-Ruch, Krakowskie Przedmiescie 7, Warsaw, Poland) Ed. Stanislaw A. Szwankowski. adv.; bk.rev.; stat.; index; circ. 3,000. **Indexed:** Packag.Sci.Tech.

387 380 UK ISSN 0265-1181
TEES AND HARTLEPOOL PORTS. 1983. a. £5. Charter International Publications Ltd., Castle Chambers, Castle Acre, King's Lynn, Norfolk PE32 2BQ, England. TEL 07605-634. FAX 07605-625. TELEX 817440. Ed. James P. Moriarty. adv.; circ. 6,000.

387 UK ISSN 0040-2575
TELEGRAPH. 1969. m. National Union of Marine Aviation and Shipping Transport Officers (NUMAST), Oceanair House, 750-760 High Rd., Leytonstone, London E11 3BB, England. TEL 081-989-6677. FAX 081-530-1051. TELEX 892648-NUMAST-G. Ed. Andrew Linington. adv.; bk.rev.; charts; illus.; stat.; circ. 20,500. (tabloid format) **Indexed:** BMT.
Supersedes: Merchant Navy Journal; Ships' Telegraph.

387.1 NE ISSN 0376-6411
TC187 CODEN: TEAQEJ
TERRA ET AQUA. 1972. 3/yr. free. International Association of Dredging Companies, Duinweg 21, 2585 JV The Hague, Netherlands. TEL 070-3523334. FAX 070-3512654. TELEX 31102 DUNE NL. Ed. M. Purvis. charts; illus.; stat.; circ. 3,200. **Indexed:** BMT, Curr.Tit.Ocean., Fluidex.
Formerly (until 1972): Terra.
Description: Aimed at individuals and organizations with a professional interest in development of ports and waterways; particularly dredging work.

387 NE ISSN 0167-9988
TIJDSCHRIFT VOOR ZEEGESCHIEDENIS. (Text in Dutch, English, German) 1961. s-a. fl.52 to domestic members; foreign members fl.65. Nederlandse Vereniging voor Zeegeschiedenis - Dutch Society for Maritime History, Onafhankelijkheidsweg 29, NE-2332 ZN Leiden, Netherlands. adv.; bk.rev.; abstr.; bibl.; cum.index; circ. 700. **Indexed:** E.I.
Formerly: Nederlandse Vereniging voor Zeegeschiedenis. Mededelingen (ISSN 0028-2340)

387 UK
TIME CHARTERS. 1987. irreg. latest 3rd ed. Lloyd's of London Press Ltd., Sheepen Place, Colchester, Essex CO3 3LP, England. TEL 0206-772277. FAX 0206-46273. TELEX 987321-LLOYDS-G. (US subscr. to: 611 Broadway, Ste. 523, New York, NY 10012. TEL 212-529-9500)
Description: Provides current reference to law and arbitration on the chartering and operation of ships on both sides of the Atlantic.

387 US ISSN 0040-8182
TITANIC COMMUTATOR. 1963. q. membership. Titanic Historical Society, Inc., Box 51053, Indian Orchard, MA 01151-0053. Ed.Bd. adv.; bk.rev.; charts; illus.; circ. 4,200.
Description: Articles on the Titanic and other White Star and North Star Atlantic liners. Includes biographies from survivors and others, maritime art, photographs and deck plans. Many accounts contain the results of original research about the liners of the past, the people who built and sailed in them as well as contemporary issues on the subject.

TOKYO SHOSEN DAIGAKU KENKYU HOKOKU. SHIZEN KAGAKU/TOKYO UNIVERSITY OF MERCANTILE MARINE. JOURNAL. NATURAL SCIENCES. see *SCIENCES: COMPREHENSIVE WORKS*

TOWPATHS. see *HISTORY — History Of North And South America*

387.5 JA
TOYAMA SHOSEN KOTO SENMON GAKKO KENKYU SHUROKU/TOYAMA MERCANTILE MARINE COLLEGE. JOURNAL. (Text in Japanese; some articles in English) 1968. a. Toyama Shosen Koto Senmon Gakko - Toyama Mercantile Marine College, 1-2 Ebie Neriai, Shin-Minato, Toyama 933-02, Japan. Ed. Henshu Iinkai. illus.; circ. 140.

387 AT
TRADE-A-BOAT. 1977. m. Aus.$45. Rollocorp No. 39 Pty. Ltd., 122 Ormond Rd., Elwood, Vic. 3184, Australia. TEL 03-525-6033. FAX 03-531-5788. (Or: P.O. Box 86, Elwood, Vic. 3184, Australia) Ed. M. Morton. adv.; circ. 28,300.

TRAFALGAR HOUSE NEWS. see *BUILDING AND CONSTRUCTION*

387 US ISSN 0082-5867
TRAFFIC REPORT OF THE ST. LAWRENCE SEAWAY. a. U.S. Saint Lawrence Seaway Development Corporation, 400 7th St., S.W., Rm. 5424, Box 44090, Washington, DC 20026-4090. TEL 202-366-0091.

387 GW
TRANSPORT-DIENST & WIRTSCHAFTSCORRESPONDENT. 1950. w. DM.148.30. Schiffahrts-Verlag Hansa C. Schroedter GmbH und Co. KG, Stubbenhuk 10, 2000 Hamburg 11, Germany. adv.; bk.rev.; illus.; index; circ. 3,000.
Formerly: Transport-Dienst (ISSN 0041-1426)

TRANSPORT MARITIME: ETUDES ET STATISTIQUES. see *TRANSPORTATION — Abstracting, Bibliographies, Statistics*

387 SW ISSN 0041-1523
TRANSPORT-NYTT. (Text in Scandinavian languages) 1958. 10/yr. SEK 380. Transport-Nytt Foerlags AB, Box 3044, S-122 03 Enskede, Sweden. TEL 46-8-81-12-80. FAX 46-8-81-16-75. Ed. Christer Hillerstroem. adv.; bk.rev.; charts; illus.; circ. 6,000.
Description: Directed to: users of trucks, lifters, warehouse equipment, as well as persons involved in shipping and air cargo.

TRANSPORTATION & DISTRIBUTION. see *TRANSPORTATION*

387 DK ISSN 0109-128X
TRANSPORTNYT; orientering for transportkoebere om transport og Kommunikation. 1982. m. DKK 525. Danish Shippers' Council - Erhvervenes Transport Udvalg, H.C. Andersens Boulevard 18, 1553 Copenhagen V, Denmark. FAX 45-33155928. Ed. Palle Egebjerg. circ. 600.
Formerly: Fragtnyt.

TRAVLTIPS. see *TRAVEL AND TOURISM*

TRANSPORTATION — SHIPS AND SHIPPING

623.8 UK ISSN 0049-4690
TRIDENT; Portsmouth Naval Base newspaper. 1969. m. 60p. Ministry of Defence, Dockyard Department, Rm. 211, Carpenter House, Broad Quay, Bath, Avon BA1 5AB, England. Ed. D. Moore. adv.; bk.rev.; charts; illus.; circ. 2,500. (tabloid format)

387 UK
TUG WORLD NEWSLETTER. (Includes annual supplement: Reed's Tugworld Annual Review) 1984. q. (with a. supplement). $60. Thomas Reed Publications Ltd., Weir House, Hurst Rd., E. Molesey, Surrey KT8 9AQ, England. TEL 081-941-8090. FAX 081-941-8046. TELEX 883526-REED-G. Ed. Kenneth D. Troup. bk.rev.; circ. 2,500 (controlled).
   Description: Covers the design, construction, operation and economics of the vessels employed in the international towage and marine salvage industry.

TUNISIA. OFFICE DES PORTS NATIONAUX. BULLETIN ANNUEL DES STATISTIQUES. see *TRANSPORTATION — Abstracting, Bibliographies, Statistics*

387.1 TI
TUNISIA. OFFICE DES PORTS NATIONAUX. BULLETIN TRIMESTRIEL. q. Office des Ports Nationaux, Tunis, Tunisia. charts, stat.

387 380 UK ISSN 0265-8194
TURKEY PORT AND SHIPPING HANDBOOK (YEAR). 1984. a. £10. Charter International Publications Ltd., Castle Chambers, Castle Acre, King's Lynn, Norfolk PE32 2BQ, England. TEL 07605-634. FAX 07605-625. TELEX 817440. Ed. James P. Moriarty. adv.; circ. 6,000.

U M T R I RESEARCH REVIEW. (University of Michigan, Transportation Research Institute) see *TRANSPORTATION — Automobiles*

387.5 US
U S S REPORTS. 1942. s-a. free. United Seamen's Service, American Merchant Marine Library Association, One World Trade Center, Ste. 2161, New York, NY 10048. FAX 212-432-5492. TELEX 222146 UNS UR. Ed. Jeannine M. Russell. circ. 5,000.
   Description: Reports on USS and its affiliate AMMLA activities.

U S S ST. LOUIS HUBBLE BUBBLE. see *MILITARY*

387 NE ISSN 0041-588X
UIT EUROPOORTKRINGEN; magazine voor het bedrijfsleven in Rotterdam/Botlek/Europoort/Delta. 1962. 20/yr. fl.100. Uitgeversmaatschappij L.A. van Beek B.V., Postbus 53, 2650 AB Berkel, South Holland, Netherlands. TEL 12955. FAX 01891-18401. Ed.Bd. adv.; bk.rev.; charts; illus.; stat.; circ. 4,400.

623.81 SW
UNDER SVENSK FLAGG. (Text in Swedish) 1905. m. SEK 275 (foreign SEK 325). Foreningen Sveriges Sjoefart och Sjoefoersvar - Swedish Maritime League, Amiralitetshuset, Skeppsholmen, S-111 49 Stockholm, Sweden. FAX 08-207660. Ed. Nils Hellstroem. adv.; bk.rev.; illus.; index; circ. 5,000.
   Formerly: Sveriges Flotta (ISSN 0039-6966)

UNDERWATER MAGAZINE. see *BUSINESS AND ECONOMICS — Marketing And Purchasing*

387 623.888 US ISSN 0364-0981
VK23
U.S. COAST GUARD MARINE SAFETY COUNCIL. PROCEEDINGS. 1944. m. free. U.S. Coast Guard, Commandant G-LRA-Z, 2100 Second St. S.W., Washington, DC 20593-0001. TEL 202-267-1483. Ed. Sharon Chapman. circ. 7,000. **Indexed:** BMT, Ind.U.S.Gov.Per. Key Title: Proceedings of the Marine Safety Council.
   Formerly: U.S. Coast Guard. Merchant Marine Council. Proceedings (ISSN 0041-7564)

287 US ISSN 0083-0755
U.S. FEDERAL MARITIME COMMISSION. ANNUAL REPORT. 1962. a. free. U.S. Federal Maritime Commission, 1100 L St. N.W., Washington, DC 20573. TEL 202-523-5707.

387 US ISSN 0083-3207
U.S. SAINT LAWRENCE SEAWAY DEVELOPMENT CORPORATION. ANNUAL REPORT. 1954. a. U.S. Saint Lawrence Seaway Development Corporation, 400 7th St., S.W., Rm. 5424, Box 44090, Washington, DC 20026-4090. TEL 202-366-0091. FAX 202-366-7147. TELEX EASYLINK 510-100-4787.

387 PL ISSN 0208-483X
UNIWERSYTET GDANSKI. WYDZIAL EKONOMIKI TRANSPORTU. ZESZYTY NAUKOWE. EKONOMIKA TRANSPORTU MORSKIEGO. (Text in Polish; summaries in English and Russian) 1971. irreg. price varies. Uniwersytet Gdanski, Wydzial Ekonomiki Transportu, c/o Biblioteka Glowna, Ul. Armii Krajowej 110, 81-824 Sopot, Poland. TEL 51-0061. TELEX 051-2247 BMOR PL. (Dist. by: Ars Polona-Ruch, Krakowskie Przedmiescie 7, 00-680 Warsaw, Poland) circ. 300.
   Description: Covers shipping and seaport policy, the role of shipping and seaports in national economy, economic and financial system of the maritime transport enterprises, international freight market, etc.

386 333.91 SP
VALENCIA PORT; guia del servicios del puerto de Valencia. 1978. a. 1300 ptas. Publicaciones Men-Car, S.A., Paseo de Colon 24, 08002 Barcelona, Spain. TEL 93-301-5516. FAX 93-318-6645. Eds. Juan Cardona, Manuel Cardona. adv.; circ. 15,000.

387 UK ISSN 0264-5661
VANCOUVER PORT HANDBOOK. 1983. biennial. £10. Charter International Publications Ltd., Castle Chambers, Castle Acre, King's Lynn, Norfolk PE32 2BQ, England. TEL 07605-634. FAX 07605-625. TELEX 817440. Ed. James P. Moriarty. adv.; circ. 6,000.

623.82 GW
VERBAND FUER SCHIFFBAU UND MEERESTECHNIK. JAHRESBERICHT. 1962. a. free. Verband fuer Schiffbau und Meerestechnik e.V., An der Alster 1, 2000 Hamburg 1, Germany. TEL 040-246205. FAX 040-246287. TELEX 2162496-VDS-D. bk.rev.; stat.; circ. 1,750.
   Formerly (until 1987): Deutscher Shiffbau.
   Description: Comprehensive report covering current situation, development, industry, political and technical questions.

387 900 NE ISSN 0922-1891
VEREENIGING NEDERLANDSCH HISTORISCH SCHEEPVAART MUSEUM TE AMSTERDAM. JAARVERSLAG. 1917. a. membership. Vereeniging Nederlandsch Historisch Scheepvaart Museum, Kattenburgerplein 1, 1018 KK Amsterdam, Netherlands. TEL 020-52323111. Ed. H.H. Roelfzema. adv.; cum.index: 1917-1980; circ. 1,700.

387 US
VESSEL INVENTORY REPORT. 1938. s-a. free. U.S. Department of Transportation, General Services Administration, Mar. 573, Rm. 8117, 400 7th St., S.W., Washington, DC 20590. TEL 202-366-2267. Ed. R. Brown. stat.; circ. 500. (processed)

387 US
VIA PORT OF NEW YORK - NEW JERSEY. 1949. m. $36 (free to export-import shippers). Port Authority of New York and New Jersey, One World Trade Ctr., Rm. 64E, New York, NY 10048. TEL 212-466-8282. FAX 212-466-9448. Ed. Daniel E. Keough. adv.; bk.rev.; illus.; circ. 30,000. **Indexed:** P.A.I.S.
   Formerly: Via Port of New York (ISSN 0042-5001)

387 VI
VIRGIN ISLANDS PORT AUTHORITY. ANNUAL REPORT. 1968. a. Virgin Islands Port Authority, Box 1707, St. Thomas, VI 00803-1707. TEL 809-774-3140. FAX 809-774-0025. Ed. Jean M. Bozzuto. circ. 500. (reprint service avail.)

387 VI
VIRGIN ISLANDS PORT AUTHORITY DIRECTORY. 1988. irreg. (every 2-3 yrs.), latest 1991. free. Virgin Islands Port Authority, Box 1707, St. Thomas, VI 00803-1707. TEL 809-774-3140. FAX 809-774-0025.
   Description: Provides complete description of cruise shipping, marine cargo and airport facilities and the companies that provide various services to their operations throughout the territory.

387 US
VIRGINIA MARITIMER. 6/yr. free. Port Authority, 600 World Trade Center, Norfolk, VA 23510. TEL 804-683-8000. FAX 804-683-8500. Ed. Tina Dulong. adv.; illus.; circ. 8,000 (controlled).
   Former titles: Ports of Virginia; Port of Hampton Roads Monthly Log; (until Oct. 1981): Virginia Ports.
   Description: International trade development news and information about Virginia's ports, public and private sector.

VIRGINIA PORTS AND SHIPPING HANDBOOK. see *BUSINESS AND ECONOMICS — Trade And Industrial Directories*

387 US
W W S - WORLD WIDE SHIPPING. 1914. 8/yr. $30. World Wide Shipping Guide, Inc., 205 Delaware Dr., Nyack, NY 10960. TEL 914-358-3813. FAX 914-358-3854. Ed. Lee di Paci. adv.; illus.; circ. 15,000. **Indexed:** Ocean.Abstr., Pollut.Abstr.
   Former titles (until 1985): W W S - World Ports (ISSN 0278-6664); (until 1981): American Seaport (ISSN 0161-6323); (until 1978): World Ports - American Seaport; World Ports (ISSN 0043-888X); World Ports and Marine News.

WARSHIP INTERNATIONAL. see *MILITARY*

387 IO ISSN 0125-9229
HE563.I6
WARTA EKONOMI MARITIM REVIEW FOR ENTREPRENEURS; * the monthly independent business magazine. Variant title: Entrepreneur W E M Review. (Text in English) 1968. m. Rps.7500. Maritime Press Foundation, Suryopranotonod, Jakarta-Barat, Indonesia. Ed. Bachtiar Ilyas. adv.; charts; illus.; circ. 16,500.
   Formerly (until 1979): Warta Ekonomi Maritim Review.

WATER TRANSPORT STATISTICS OF INDIA. see *TRANSPORTATION — Abstracting, Bibliographies, Statistics*

387 US ISSN 0083-7725
HE563.U5
WATERBORNE COMMERCE OF THE UNITED STATES. 1952. a. (in 5 separate parts). price varies. U.S. Army Corps of Engineers, Water Resources Support Center, Box 61280, New Orleans, LA 70161. TEL 504-862-2715. FAX 504-862-1091. (Subscr. to: U.S. Army Engineer District, New Orleans, Attn.: CELMN-ED-SX, Box 60267, New Orleans, LA 70160-0267) Ed. Carla Spence. circ. 1,100.
   Description: Part 1: Atlantic Coast; Part 2: Gulf Coast, Mississippi River System and Antilles (Puerto Rico and Virgin Islands); Part 3: The Great Lakes; Part 4: Pacific Coast, Alaska and Hawaii; Part 5: National summary of data published in the other four volumes.

387 US ISSN 0043-1524
HE623
WATERWAYS JOURNAL; devoted to the marine profession and commercial interest of all inland waterways. (Annual Review Number) 1887. w. $26. Waterways Journal, Inc., 319 N. Fourth St., 666 Security Bldg., St. Louis, MO 63102. TEL 314-241-7354. FAX 314-241-4207. Ed. Jack R. Simpson. adv.; bk.rev.; charts; illus.; tr.lit.; circ. 8,500.

387 UK ISSN 0309-1422
WATERWAYS WORLD. 1972. m. £19.20 (foreign £19.20). Waterway Productions Ltd., Kottingham House, Dale St., Burton-on-Trent, Staffs. DE14 3TD, England. TEL 0283-42721. Ed. Hugh Potter. adv.; bk.rev.; charts; illus.; stat.; index; circ. 18,905.

387 US
WEEKLY COMMERCIAL NEWS AND SHIPPING GUIDE. w. C A Page Publishing Company, 1117 W. Manchester, Ste. A, Inglewood, CA 90301-1500. TEL 213-568-4560. FAX 213-568-4567. Ed. Andres Moura. circ. 2,000.

TRANSPORTATION — TRUCKS AND TRUCKING

DIE WESER. see *ENVIRONMENTAL STUDIES*

387   GW   ISSN 0043-2857
WESERLOTSE; Bremer Wirtschafts- und Hafendienst. 1948. m. DM.25. (Bremische Hafenvertretung e.V.) W. Waechter GmbH, Elsasserstr. 41, 2800 Bremen 1, Germany. FAX 0421-344009. Ed. Werner Sauermilch. adv.; bk.rev.; illus.; circ. 5,300.

387.5   AT
WESTERN AUSTRALIAN COASTAL SHIPPING COMMISSION. ANNUAL REPORT. a. free. Coastal Shipping Commission, P.O. Box 394, Fremantle, Australia. stat.; circ. controlled.

387   NO   ISSN 0800-1200
WHERE TO BUILD - WHERE TO REPAIR. (Text in English) 1952. a. NOK 300. Maritime Year Books AS, P.O. Box 9156 Vaterland, 0134 Oslo 1, Norway. adv.

387 380.1   GW
WIE ERREICHE ICH WEN?. 1958. a. DM.26.17. K.O. Storck Verlag, Stahltwiete 7, 2000 Hamburg 50, Germany. TEL 040-850-0071. FAX 040-850-7758. TELEX 17403448. Ed. H. Meder.

387   AT
WORK BOAT WORLD. 1982. m. £35($65) Baird Publications Pty. Ltd., 10 Oxford St., South Yarra, Vic. 3141, Australia. TEL 03-240-8741. FAX 03-241-0704. Ed. Neil Baird. adv.; circ. 4,500.
 Former titles: Work and Patrol Boat World (ISSN 0812-1648); (until 1983): Asia-Pacific Work and Patrol Boat (ISSN 0726-3724)
 Description: International business magazine of the work boat industry.

387   US   ISSN 0043-8014
VK1
WORKBOAT. 1943. bi-m. $20 (foreign $35). Journal Publications (Rockland), Box 908, Rockland, ME 04841. TEL 207-594-6222. Ed. Don Nelson. adv.; bk.rev.; charts; illus.; stat.; circ. 12,500. **Indexed:** Ocean.Abstr., Pollut.Abstr.
 —BLDSC shelfmark: 9348.130000.
 Description: For owners, operators, builders and designers of U.S. commercial vessels. Contains trade-related news, waterway development, economic trends and new legislation.

387   US
▼**WORKBOAT DIRECTORY.** 1992. a. $59. Journal Publications (Mandeville), 3500 Hwy. 190, No. 205, Mandeville, LA 70448. TEL 504-626-0298. FAX 504-624-4801. adv.: B&W & color, B&W page $1790; trim 8 1/8 x 10 7/8. circ. 2,000.
 Description: Documents, indexes and cross-references every business component of the coastal and inland marine industry.

387   UK
WORKBOAT INTERNATIONAL. 1985. 10/yr. Rushton Marine Press Ltd., Woodside, Burnhams Rd., Little Bookham, Leatherhead, Surrey KT23 3BA, England. TEL 0372-453316. FAX 0372-459974. Ed. Carol Fulford. circ. 6,000 (controlled).
 Description: News items on legislation, technological developments, products and services, and contracts pertaining to the marine trade industry worldwide, oriented toward builders and architects, equipment manufacturers, repairers, owners and operators, and governmental authorities.

387   NO   ISSN 0801-5007
WORLD BULK FLEET. 1960. s-a. $290 (includes World Bulk Trades). Fearnleys A-S, Raadhusgaten 27, P.O. Box 1158 Sentrum, N-0107 Oslo 1, Norway. TEL 02-41-7000. FAX 47-02-411880. TELEX 74607 FADM. stat.
 Description: Provides details on the total world fleet of tankers, bulk carriers and combined carriers, existing and on order as well as estimated future fleet.

387   NO   ISSN 0801-4086
WORLD BULK TRADES. a. $290 (includes World Bulk Fleet). Fearnleys A-S, Raadhusgaten 27, P.O. Box 1158 Sentrum, N-0107 Oslo 1, Norway. TEL 47-2-41-70-00. FAX 02-411818. charts; stat.
 Description: Provides a comprehensive review of the total seaborne trade and cargo movements by tankers, combined carriers and bulk carriers.

WORLD DIRECTORY OF LINER SHIPPING AGENTS. see *BUSINESS AND ECONOMICS — Trade And Industrial Directories*

387   UK   ISSN 0046-5046
WORLD FREIGHT.* 1979. m. £18. (Institute of Freight Forwarders Ltd.) Thomas Reed Publications Ltd., 38 S. John St., London EC1M 4AY, England. Ed. Giles Large. adv.; bk.rev.; circ. 10,000.
 Formerly: Freight Forwarding.

WORLD METEOROLOGICAL ORGANIZATION. COMMISSION FOR MARINE METEOROLOGY. ABRIDGED FINAL REPORT OF THE (NO.) SESSION. see *METEOROLOGY*

387   UK
WORLD PORT CONSTRUCTION & OCEAN TECHNOLOGY. bi-m. General Publishing Ltd., Station House, Cross Rd., Tadworth, Surrey KT20 5SP, England. TEL 0737-814757. FAX 0737-814154. TELEX 46690-ICCX-G. Ed. Norman Penwarden.

387   UK   ISSN 0049-8157
WORLD TANKER FLEET REVIEW. 1921. s-a. £250($450) John I. Jacobs PLC, 9 Mandeville Pl., London W1M 5LB, England. TEL 071-486-3000. FAX 071-486-1937. Ed. David G. Barker-Benfield. charts; stat.; circ. 600.
 —BLDSC shelfmark: 9360.068000.

387.164   US   ISSN 0162-0088
HE561
WORLD WIDE SHIPPING GUIDE. 1976. a. $85. World Wide Shipping Guide, Inc., 20 South Delaware Dr., Nyack, NY 10960. TEL 914-358-3813. FAX 914-358-3854. adv.; circ. 12,500.

387.5   PL
WYZSZA SZKOLA MORSKA. ZESZYTY NAUKOWE. irreg. 103 Zl. Wyzsza Szkola Morska w Gdyni - Merchant Marine Academy, Czerwonych Kosynierow 83, 81-225 Gdynia, Poland. (Dist. by: Ars Polona-Ruch, Krakowskie Przedmiescie 7, Warsaw, Poland) Ed. Bozena Sobolewska.

387   JA
YOKOHAMA PORT NEWS. (Text in English) s-a. Port and Harbor Bureau, Industry & Trade Center Bldg., 2 Yamashita-cho, Nakaku, Yokohama, Japan. FAX 45-671-6158.
 Description: Covers current activities as well as future plans of the port of Yokohama.

387   CC   ISSN 1000-3878
ZAOCHUAN JISHU. (Text in Chinese) m. Zhongguo Chuanbo Gongye Zong Gongsi, Chuanbo Gongyi Yanjiusuo, P.O. Box 032-201, Shanghai 200032, People's Republic of China. TEL 4399626. Ed. Fang Zuying.
 —BLDSC shelfmark: 5012.035000.

387 623.8   NE   ISSN 0165-8182
ZEEWEZEN; opinieblad: marine, koopvaardij, zeetechniek en havens. 1911. m. fl.47.50 membership. Koninklijke Nederlandse Vereniging Onze Vloot - Royal Netherlands Navy League, 381 Spechtlaan, 2261 BK Leidschendam, Netherlands. TEL 070-3497692. (Subscr. to: Postbus 16350, 2500 BJ The Hague, Netherlands) Ed. G.J. van Nimwegen. adv.; bk.rev.; illus.; circ. 6,500.
 —BLDSC shelfmark: 9440.240000.
 Formerly: Ons Zeewezen (ISSN 0030-2791)
 Description: Examines the Navy, the Merchant Navy, shipbuilding, national and international harbor services and offshore activities.

386   GW   ISSN 0930-7370
HE669
ZEITSCHRIFT FUER BINNENSCHIFFAHRT UND WASSERSTRASSEN. m. DM.106.80 6/yr. Schiffahrts-Verlag Hansa, Elbchausee 277, 2000 Hamburg 52, Germany. TEL 040-822807-0. FAX 040-822807-52. TELEX 213075-HANSA-D. (Co-sponsor: C. Schroedter & Co. (GmbH & Co. KG)) Ed.Bd. adv.

387   CC   ISSN 1000-5765
ZHENJIANG CHUANBO XUEYUAN XUEBAO. (Text in Chinese) q. Zhenjiang Chuanbo Xueyuan, 2 Huancheng Lu, Zhenjiang, Jiangsu 212003, People's Republic of China. TEL 232290. Ed. Ye Zuyin.

387   CC
ZHONGGUO GANGKOU/CHINESE HARBOR. (Text in Chinese) bi-m. Zhongguo Gangkou Xiehui - Chinese Harbor Society, 12 Zhongshan 2 Lu, Room 415, Shanghai 200002, People's Republic of China. TEL 3280010. Ed. Tang Shaowu.

387   CC
ZHONGGUO HAIYUAN/CHINESE SEAMEN. (Text in Chinese) bi-m. Zhongguo Haiyuan Gonghui - China Seamen's Union, 1441 Changyang Lu, Shanghai 200090, People's Republic of China. TEL 5462878. Ed. Tong Menghou.

387   HK   ISSN 0258-3240
ZHONGGUO HAIYUN/MARITIME CHINA. (Text in Chinese and English) 1983. q. HK.$190($55) (China Ocean Shipping Co., CC - Zhongguo Yuanyang Yunshu Gongsi) Maritime China Ltd. - Zhongguo Haiyun Youxian Gongsi, 4306 China Resources Bldg., 26 Harbour Rd., Hong Kong. TEL 5-8913831. TELEX 68444-HKTF-HX. (Co-sponsor: Seatrade - Haimao Chuban Gongsi) Ed. Oliver Wong. adv.; bk.rev.; illus.; circ. 6,000.

387   CC   ISSN 1000-4653
ZHONGGUO HANGHAI/CHINESE NAVIGATION. (Text in Chinese) s-a. Jiaotong-bu, Shanghai Chuanbo Yunshu Kexue Yanjiusuo - Ministry of Transportation, Shanghai Institute of Shipping Transportation Science, 200 Minsheng Lu, Shanghai 200135, People's Republic of China. TEL 8840348. (Co-sponsor: Zhongguo Hanghai Xuehui) Ed. Qiu Min.

387   CC   ISSN 1001-8328
ZHONGGUO XIUCHUAN/CHINA SHIPREPAIR. (Text in Chinese) 1987. q. Zhongguo Chuanbo Zonggongsi, Yanhai Xiuchuan Keji Qingbaowang - Shiprepairing Technology Research Institute of Tianjin, CSSC, P.O. Box 562, Tanggu, Tianjin 300456, People's Republic of China. TEL 974559. FAX 022-981838. TELEX 23166 TJSIC CN. Ed. Gao Lianze.

387   UK   ISSN 0266-8971
VM1
100A1. 1962. q. free. Lloyd's Register of Shipping, 71 Fenchurch St., London EC3M 4BS, England. TEL 071-709-9166. illus.; circ. 28,000. **Indexed:** Met.Abstr.
 Formerly: Lloyds Register World.
 Description: Articles of general and technical interest to those involved in marine, industrial and offshore activities, likely to use LR services.

TRANSPORTATION — Trucks And Trucking

388.324   UK   ISSN 0308-9304
A B C FREIGHT GUIDE. 1953. a. £29.50. Centaur Communications Ltd., 50 Poland St., London W1V 4AX, England. adv.; circ. 8,000.
 Incorporates: A B C Truck Breakdown Guide; A B C Guide to Recovery Services; **Formerly:** A B C Goods Transport Guide (ISSN 0001-0421)
 Description: Reference source covering road haulage, storage and distribution, driver agencies, international services, heavy haulage and tankers.

388.24   CN   ISSN 1181-7941
▼**A.P.C.R.I.Q. BULLETIN D'INFORMATION**; Quebec's owners - operators association's magazine. (Text in French) 1990. bi-m. Communications J.S.S.R., 3775 bvd. Industriel, Ste. 200, Montreal-Nord, Que. H1H 2Y8, Canada. TEL 514-328-3485. FAX 514-328-9737. Ed. Jean Raymond. circ. 5,000. (back issues avail.)
 Description: Covers new laws and regulations concerning the trucking industry, congress of the Association, truck shows and rodeos.

388.324   SW   ISSN 0348-0356
AAKERI & TRANSPORT. 1938. m. (8/yr.). SEK 220. Aakeriaegarnas Centralfoerbund, 598 10 Vimmerby, Sweden. Ed. Alf Wesik. adv.; bk.rev.; charts; illus.; circ. 26,000.
 Formerly: Aakerifoeretagaren-Transportoeren (ISSN 0001-298X)

AIR CONDITIONING & HEATING SERVICE & REPAIR - DOMESTIC CARS, LIGHT TRUCKS & VANS. see *TRANSPORTATION — Automobiles*

AIR CONDITIONING & HEATING SERVICE & REPAIR - IMPORTED CARS & TRUCKS. see *TRANSPORTATION — Automobiles*

388.3   US
ALLEGHENY TRUCKER; merchandising everything for the trucking industry. 1978. m. $12. Allied Publications, 7355 N. Woodland, Box 603, Indianapolis, IN 46206-0603. TEL 317-297-5500. FAX 317-299-1356. adv.; circ. 20,950.

TRANSPORTATION — TRUCKS AND TRUCKING   4743

388.324 US
ALLIED TRUCKING PUBLICATIONS. m. Box 603, Indianapolis, IA 46206-0603. TEL 317-297-5500. FAX 317-299-1356. circ. 517,452.

388.3 US ISSN 0065-7271
AMERICAN ASSOCIATION OF MOTOR VEHICLE ADMINISTRATORS. ANNUAL CONFERENCE. PROCEEDINGS. 1957. a. American Association of Motor Vehicle Administrators, 4200 Wilson Blvd., Ste. 600, Arlington, VA 22203. TEL 703-522-4200. FAX 703-522-1553. Ed. Jennifer Cagan Thompson. circ. 300.

388.324 US
AMERICAN MOTOR CARRIER DIRECTORY: NORTH AMERICAN EDITION. s-a. $185 (foreign $258). K - III Press, Inc., 424 W. 33rd St., New York, NY 10001. TEL 800-221-5488. FAX 212-695-5025.
 Incorporates: American Motor Carrier Directory: Specialized Services Edition (ISSN 0569-6364); Formerly: American Motor Carrier Directory: National Edition (ISSN 0569-6356)

388.324 US
AMERICAN MOVER. 1936. m. $35 (Canada and Mexico $45; elsewhere $70). American Movers Conference, 1611 Duke St., Alexandria, VA 22314. TEL 703-683-7410. FAX 703-683-7527.
 Former titles: Movers Journal & In the Van.

388.324 US
AMERICAN TRUCKER MAGAZINE.* m. American Trucking Marketing, 7355 N. Woodland Dr., Indianapolis, IN 46278. adv.

AMERICAN TRUCKING ASSOCIATIONS. CURRENT ECONOMIC BULLETIN. see *TRANSPORTATION — Abstracting, Bibliographies, Statistics*

388.4 US
AMERICAN TRUCKING TRENDS (YEAR). 1942. a. $20. American Trucking Associations, Inc., Statistical Analysis Department, 2200 Mill Rd., Alexandria, VA 22314. TEL 703-838-1792. FAX 703-838-1992. Dir. Russell B. Capelle, Jr. illus. stats.; index; circ. 1,500. Indexed: SRI.
 Former titles (until 1986): American Trucking Trends. Statistical Report; American Trucking Associations Report (ISSN 0066-0892)
 Description: Profiles the industry from 1980 to present; equipment and employment, financial state of industry, and taxes.

388.324 FI ISSN 0355-7286
AMMATTIAUTOILIJA. (Text in Finnish and Swedish) 1945. m. FIM 450. Suomen Kuorma-autoliitto r.y., Nuijamiestentie 7, 00400 Helsinki, Finland. TEL 90-578-500. FAX 358-0-578520. TELEX 19100648 VDX SF. Ed. Juha Norppa-Rahkola. adv.; circ. 15,500.

388.324 US
ANTIQUE TRUCK REGISTRY. 1985. biennial. $10. American Truck Historical Society, Box 531168, Birmingham, AL 35253. TEL 205-870-0566. FAX 205-870-3069.
 Description: Lists nearly 13,000 trucks, tractors and trailers, representing nearly 400 manufacturers, owned by over 4,000 members of the society.

388.324 US
ARKANSAS MOTOR CARRIER. q. Arkansas Motor Carriers Association, 2020 W. Third St., No. 515, Little Rock, AR 72205-4466. TEL 501-372-3462. FAX 501-376-1810. Ed. Mary Gwin. circ. 475.

388.324 CN ISSN 0830-1808
ATLANTIC TRUCKING. 1956. 4/yr. Can.$18. Atlantic Provinces Trucking Association, 1 Trites Rd., Ste. 14, Riverview, N.B. E1B 2V5, Canada. TEL 506-387-4413. FAX 506-387-7424. Ed. Dale Elliott. adv.; illus.; circ. 2,000.
 Former titles: Atlantic Truck Transport Review (ISSN 0004-6868); Maritime Truck Transport Review.

AUSTRALIAN FLEET MAGAZINE. see *TRANSPORTATION — Automobiles*

AUTOMOTIVE REPAIR & RE-MANUFACTURE. see *TRANSPORTATION — Automobiles*

AUTOSPARK. see *TRANSPORTATION — Automobiles*

B C I NEWS. (Battery Council International) see *TRANSPORTATION — Automobiles*

388.324 GW
B D G NACHRICHTEN. 1983. s-m. free. Bundesverbaende des Deutschen Gueterkraftverkehrs, Breitenbachstr. 1, Postfach 930260, 6000 Frankfurt a.M. 93, Germany. TEL 069-7919264. FAX 069-7919265. circ. 1,200.

388.324 US
BADGER TRUCKER; merchandising everything for the trucking industry. 1980. m. $12. Allied Publications, 7355 N. Woodland, Box 603, Indianapolis, IN 46206-0603. TEL 317-297-5500. FAX 317-299-1356. adv.; circ. 19,200.
 Formerly: Badger Truck Exchange.

388.324 GW
BESTAND AN KRAFTFAHRZEUGEN UND KRAFTFAHRZEUGANHAENGERN. 1948. a. DM.47. (Kraftfahrt - Bundesamt) Kirschbaum Verlag GmbH, Siegfriedstr. 28, Postfach 210209, 5300 Bonn 2, Germany. TEL 0228-343057. FAX 0228-857145. TELEX 889596-KIRVL-D.

388.324 CN ISSN 0707-5014
BRITISH COLUMBIA MOTOR TRANSPORT DIRECTORY. 1978. a. Can.$39.95. British Columbia Trucking Association, P.O. Box 381, Port Coquitlam, B.C. V3C 4K6, Canada. TEL 604-299-7407. FAX 604-299-0586. adv.; circ. 850.

388.3 US
BUCKEYE TRUCKER; merchandising everything for the trucking industry. 1976. m. $12. Allied Publications, 7355 N. Woodland, Box 603, Indianapolis, IN 46206-0603. TEL 317-297-5500. FAX 317-299-1356. adv.; circ. 28,250.

388.3 US
CALIFORNIA TRUCKER; merchandising everything for the trucking industry. 1979. m. $12. Allied Publications, 7355 N. Woodland, Box 603, Indianapolis, IN 46206-0603. TEL 317-297-5500. FAX 317-299-1356. adv.; circ. 28,250.

388.324 US
CALTRUX. Represents: California Trucking Association. Newsletter. 1949. w. membership. California Trucking Association, 1251 Beacon Blvd., West Sacramento, CA 95691. TEL 916-329-3554. Ed. Deborah B. Smith. adv.; charts; illus.; circ. 4,500.

388.324 IT ISSN 0008-2252
CAMION;* la voce degli autotrasportatori professionali. vol.25, 1970. m. L.1000. Assistenza Sindacale per gli Auto Trasportatori, Via Ovidio 32, 00186 Rome, Italy. Ed. Italo Danese. adv.; illus.

388.324 CN
CANADIAN SHIPPER. bi-m. (Canadian Industrial Transportation League) Naylor Communications Ltd., 920 Yonge St., 6th Fl., Toronto, Ont. M4W 3C7, Canada. TEL 416-961-1028. FAX 416-924-4408. Ed. Will Oliver.

388.324 US
CARGO TANK HAZARDOUS MATERIAL REGULATIONS. a. $40 to non-members; members $35. National Tank Truck Carriers, Inc., 2200 Mill Rd., Alexandria, VA 22314-4677. TEL 703-838-1960. FAX 703-684-5753. circ. 3,000.

388.423 US
CASCADE TRUCKER; merchandising everything for the trucking industry. 1980. m. $12. Allied Publications, 7355 N. Woodland, Box 603, Indianapolis, IN 46206-0603. TEL 317-297-5500. FAX 317-299-1356. adv.; circ. 21,350.

CATALOGO MOTORISTICO. see *TRANSPORTATION — Automobiles*

388.324 US
CENTRAL STATES TRUCKER; merchandising everything for the trucking industry. 1980. m. $12. Allied Publications, 7355 N. Woodland, Box 603, Indianapolis, IN 46206-0603. TEL 317-297-5500. FAX 317-299-1356. adv.; circ. 27,500.

388.324 US ISSN 0734-1423
TL1
CHILTON'S COMMERCIAL CARRIER JOURNAL; for fleet management. 1911. m. $40. Chilton Co., 1 Chilton Way, Radnor, PA 19089. TEL 215-964-4000. FAX 215-964-4512. (Subscr. to: Box 2045, Radnor, PA 19089) Ed. Gerald Standley. adv.; bk.rev.; charts; illus.; stat.; tr.lit.; index; circ. 83,042. (also avail. in microfilm from UMI; reprint service avail. from UMI) Indexed: P.A.I.S., SRI.
 Former titles (until 1982): Chilton's C C J (ISSN 0193-628X); Commercial Car Journal (ISSN 0010-292X)
 Description: Covers truck and bus fleets.

CHINA AUTOMOTIVE JOURNAL/XIANDAI QICHE; an automotive journal for P.R. China. see *TRANSPORTATION — Automobiles*

388.324 US
CLASSIC TRUCKS. 1981. bi-m. $20. Light Commercial Vehicle Association, Box 1162, Big Rapids, MI 49307. TEL 617-796-1197. FAX 616-592-2990. Ed. Tom Brownell. adv.; bk.rev.; index; circ. 900. (tabloid format; back issues avail.)
 Formerly: Plugs 'n Points.
 Description: Mechanical and repair data for light trucks. Includes the history of light trucks.

388.324 US
COME BACK SAFELY. 1988. m. $7.08. Bureau of Business Practice, 24 Rope Ferry Rd., Waterford, CT 06386. TEL 203-442-4365. FAX 203-434-3341. TELEX 966420. Ed. Linda Mileski. illus.

388.324 UK ISSN 0010-3063
COMMERCIAL MOTOR. 1905. w. $244.71. Reed Business Publishing Group, Enterprise Division (Subsidiary of: Reed International PLC), Quadrant House, The Quadrant, Sutton, Surrey SM2 5AS, England. TEL 081-652-3302. FAX 081-652-8986. (Subscr. to: Oakfield House, Perrymount Rd., Haywards Heath, W. Sussex, RH16 3DH, England. TEL 444-445566) Ed. Brian Weatherley. adv.; bk.rev.; charts; illus.; mkt.; stat.; s-a. index; circ. 33,688. (also avail. in microform from UMI) Indexed: Br.Tech.Ind., C.I.S. Abstr., HRIS.

380.5 SA
COMMERCIAL TRANSPORT. 1945. m. R.64 (foreign R.89)(effective 1992). Thomson Publications (Subsidiary of: Times Media Ltd.), P.O. Box 56182, Pinegowrie 2123, South Africa. TEL 011-789-2144. FAX 011-789-3196. Ed. Udo Rypstra. adv.; bk.rev.; charts; illus.; mkt.; tr.lit.; circ. 7,309. Indexed: Ind.S.A.Per.
 Supersedes in part: Commercial Transport and Freight; Which was formed by the merger of: Commercial Transport (ISSN 0036-2107); Freight (ISSN 0016-0857)

388.324 387 IE
COMMERCIAL TRANSPORT AND TRANSPORT MANAGERS JOURNAL. 1971. m. £35. Media 2000, 24 Thomas St., Dublin 8, Ireland. TEL 01-535335. FAX 01-535401. Ed. Triana Gavin. adv.; bk.rev.; circ. 17,760.
 Formerly (until 1976): Commercial Transport.

388.324 SA
COMMERCIAL VEHICLE DATA DIGEST. a. R.37. Mead & McGrouther (Pty) Ltd., 327 Surrey Ave., Box 1240, Ferndale, Randburg 2125, South Africa. adv.; circ. 4,667.

388.324 SA
COMMERCIAL VEHICLE DEALERS' GUIDE. 1978. bi-m. R.57.90. Mead & McGrouther (Pty) Ltd., 327 Surrey Ave., Box 1240, Ferndale, Randburg 2125, South Africa. Ed. O. Peruch. circ. 3,412.
 Formerly: Commercial Vehicle Dealers' Digest.

388.324 US
CONNECTICUT MOTOR TRANSPORT NEWS.* 1932. q. $2. Motor Transport Association of Connecticut, 60 Forest St., Hartford, CT 06105-3204. TEL 203-289-9576. Ed. John McLeod. adv.; bk.rev.; circ. 5,000.

TRANSPORTATION — TRUCKS AND TRUCKING

388.3 UK ISSN 0070-1610
CRONER'S ROAD TRANSPORT OPERATION. 1977. m. £87.30 (effective 1992). Croner Publications Ltd., Croner House, London Rd., Kingston, Surrey KT2 6SR, England. TEL 081-547-3333. FAX 081-547-2637. TELEX 267778. Ed. Colin Clark. (looseleaf format)
   Description: Provides information on United Kingdom and European legislation affecting operators of commercial vehicles.

388.3 NE
D A F MAGAZINE. (Editions in Dutch, English, French, German, Italian, Spanish) 1952. 3/yr. free. DAF, Postbus 90065, 5600 PT Eindhoven, Netherlands. Ed. Jan van der Pol. bk.rev.; illus.; circ. 51,000.
   Formerly (until 1989): D A F Trucks Magazine (ISSN 0011-5282)

388.324 US
D E S MAGAZINE. m. Business Journals, Inc., 50 Day St., Norwalk, CT 06854. TEL 203-853-6015. FAX 203-852-8175. Ed. James Jones. adv.; circ. 23,000.

388.324 US
D R I - McGRAW-HILL COMMERCIAL TRUCK MONITOR. m. D R I - McGraw-Hill, 24 Hartwell Ave., Lexington, MA 02173. TEL 617-863-5100. FAX 617-860-6332. TELEX 200 284.

388.324 DK ISSN 0011-6629
DANSKE VOGNMAEND. 1948. m. DKK 350. Danske Vognmaend Hovedorganisationen, Gammeltorv 18, 1457 Copenhagen K, Denmark. adv.; charts; illus.; mkt.; stat.; index; circ. 6,750 (controlled).

388.324 AT
DEALS ON WHEELS. 1983. m. Aus.$60. Rollocorp No. 39 Pty. Ltd., 122 Ormond Rd., Elwood, Vic. 3184, Australia. TEL 03 525 6033. FAX 03-531-5788. (Or: P.O. Box 86, Elwood, Vic. 3184, Australia) adv.; circ. 27,000.
   Description: Listing of used trucks and earthmoving equipment for sale.

388.324 IT
DELIVERY TRASPORTI COMMERCIALI. 1981. bi-m. L.35000. Edizioni Andrea Latorre s.a.s., Via G. Rotondi 3, Milan, Italy. TEL 02-462538. FAX 02-4697561. Ed. Carlo Latorre. adv.; bk.rev.; circ. 25,000.

388.324 621.436 US ISSN 0012-2610
TJ795.A1
DIESEL EQUIPMENT SUPERINTENDENT; the information source for truck fleet equipment managers. 1923. m. $30. Business Journals, 50 Day St., Box 5550, Norwalk, CT 06856. TEL 203-853-6015. Ed. David Lee Cullen. adv.; charts; illus.; stat.; tr.lit.; circ. 23,000. (also avail. in microform from UMI; reprint service avail. from UMI) **Indexed:** A.S.& T.Ind., ISMEC.

388.324 US ISSN 0092-7449
HF5487
DIRECTION (ALEXANDRIA); for the moving and storage industry. 1920. m. $50 to non-members; members $30. National Moving & Storage Association, 1500 Beauregard St., Alexandria, VA 22311-1715. TEL 703-671-8813. FAX 703-671-6712. Ed. Joyce McDowell. adv.; bk.rev.; charts; illus.; tr.lit.; index, cum.index; circ. 3,100.
   Formerly: Furniture Warehouseman (ISSN 0016-3082)
   Description: Articles relating to all aspects of the moving and storage industry, labor relations, equipment and warehousing. Also features management and diversification issues.

388.324 US
DIRECTORY OF MOVERS. 1936. a. membership. American Movers Conference, 1611 Duke St., Alexandria, VA 22314. TEL 703-683-7410. FAX 703-683-7527.

388.324 CN
DRIVER - OWNER. (Text in English) 1972. 8/yr. Can.$21. Southam Business Communications Inc. (Subsidiary of: Southam Inc.), 1450 Don Mills Rd., Don Mills, Ont. M3B 2X7, Canada. TEL 416-445-6641. FAX 416-442-2261. Ed. John Howarth. adv.; charts; illus.; tr.lit. **Indexed:** Can.B.P.I.
   Formerly: Canadian Driver - Owner.
   Description: Professional magazine for owner - operators and small fleets.

388.324 CN ISSN 0705-7040
L'ECHO DU TRANSPORT. (Text in French) 1976. 10/yr. Can.$35($45) Editions Bomart Ltee., 7493 TransCanada Hwy., Ste. 103, St. Laurent, Que. H4T 1T3, Canada. TEL 514-337-9043. FAX 514-337-1862. Ed. Jean Roch Savard. adv.; bk.rev.; circ. 22,000.
   Description: Covers all areas of local, national and international road transportation industry.

336 US ISSN 1043-6820
ECONOMIC AND TAX REPORT. 1987. m. $50. American Trucking Associations, Inc., 2200 Mill Rd., Alexandria, VA 22314-4677. TEL 800-ATA-LINE. FAX 703-684-5720. Ed. Ken Simonson.
   Description: Covers tax legislation and economic developments that affect the trucking industry.

ELECTRICAL COMPONENT LOCATOR - DOMESTIC CARS, LIGHT TRUCKS & VANS. see *TRANSPORTATION — Automobiles*

ELECTRICAL COMPONENT LOCATOR - IMPORTED CARS, LIGHT TRUCKS & VANS. see *TRANSPORTATION — Automobiles*

388.324 US
EUROPEAN TRUCKS FORECAST REPORT. s-a. D R I - McGraw-Hill, 24 Hartwell Ave., Lexington, MA 02173. TEL 617-863-5100. FAX 617-860-6332. TELEX 200 284. (back issues avail.)

388.324 US
EXCISE TAX QUARTERLY. 1979. q. $6 to non-members; members $3. National Truck Equipment Association, 38705 Seven Mile Rd., No. 345, Livonia, MI 48152-1057. TEL 313-462-2190. FAX 313-462-2108. Ed. Joan Christophersen-Call. circ. 1,600. (looseleaf format; back issues avail.)
   Description: Review of I.R.S. releases and court cases concerning federal excise tax on motor vehicles.

385.324 IT
F A I. 1964. m. Federazione Autotraportatori Italiani, Via Panama 62, 00198 Rome, Italy. Ed. Renato Bertacci. adv.; circ. 34,000.

388.324 GW
FAHRERPOST. bi-m. Iveco Magirus AG, Robert-Schumann-Str. 1, 8044 Munich-Unterschleissheim, Germany. TEL 089-31771120. FAX 089-31771452. circ. 45,000.

388.324 659.1 US
FASTLINE FOR DIXIE TRUCKERS. 1981. m. $12. Fastline Publications, Inc., 4900 Fox Run Rd., Buckner, KY 40010. TEL 502-222-0146. FAX 502-222-9874. circ. 21,564.
   Former titles: Dixie Trucker; Dixie Truck Trader.

388.324 US
FASTLINE FOR FLORIDA TRUCKERS. 1980. m. $12. Fastline Publications, Inc., 4900 Fox Run Rd., Buckner, KY 40010. TEL 502-222-0146. FAX 502-222-9874. Ed. William G. Howard. circ. 20,625.
   Formerly: Florida Trucker.

388.324 US
FASTLINE FOR GEORGIA TRUCKERS. 1979. m. $12. Fastline Publications, Inc., 4900 Fox Run Rd., Buckner, KY 40010. TEL 502-222-0146. FAX 502-222-9874. Ed. William G. Howard. circ. 20,937.
   Formerly: Georgia Trucker.

388.324 US
FASTLINE FOR KENTUCKY TRUCKERS. 1978. m. $12. Fastline Publications, Inc., 4900 Fox Run Rd., Buckner, KY 40010. TEL 502-222-0146. FAX 502-222-9874. Ed. William G. Howard. adv.; circ. 17,988.
   Formerly: Bluegrass Trucker.

388.324 659.1 US
FASTLINE FOR TENNESSEE TRUCKERS. 1979. m. $12. Fastline Publications, Inc., 4900 Fox Run Rd., Buckner, KY 40010. TEL 502-222-0146. FAX 502-222-9874. circ. 17,121.
   Formerly: Tennessee Trucker.

388.324 GW
FERNFAHRER; Magazin fuer L K W-Fahrer im Nah- und Fernverkehr. 1983. m. 50 Fr. Vereinigte Fachverlage, Lise-Meitner-Str. 2, 6500 Mainz, Germany. TEL 06131-99202. Ed. Thomas Blohm. adv.; bk.rev.; circ. 50,000.
   Description: Publication of interest to truckers. Features travel reports, technical information, new truck designs, road testing, traffic and transportation, new product information. Includes reports and calendar of events, readers' letters, classified adds.

388.324 US ISSN 0015-0819
FIFTH WHEEL. 1945. q. $9 to non-members. Indiana Motor Truck Association, Inc., 1 N. Capitol Ave., Ste. 460, Indianapolis, IN 46204. TEL 317-630-4682. Ed. Judith K. Spencer. circ. 2,000.

388.324 US ISSN 0747-2544
TL230.2
FLEET EQUIPMENT. 1974. 12/yr. $80. Maple Publishing, 134 W. Slade St., Palatine, IL 60067. TEL 708-359-6100. FAX 708-359-6420. Ed. Thomas A. Gelinas. adv.; circ. 68,256. **Indexed:** ABI Inform.
—BLDSC shelfmark: 3950.321800.
   Formerly (until 1984): Fleet Maintenance and Specifying (ISSN 0095-3245)

388.324 US
FLEET OWNER. 1928. m. $40 (Canada $50; elsewhere $70; free to qualified personnel). F M Business Publications, Inc., 707 Westchester Ave., Ste. 101, White Plains, NY 10604. TEL 914-949-8500. Ed. Tom Duncan. adv.; bk.rev.; illus.; tr.lit.; circ. 100,000 (controlled). (also avail. in microform from UMI; reprint service avail. from UMI) **Indexed:** ABI Inform., B.P.I., Bus.Ind., Chem.Abstr., Tr.& Indus.Ind.
   Formerly: Fleet Owner: Big Fleet Edition; Superseded in part: Fleet Owner (ISSN 0731-9622)

388.324 US ISSN 0015-4334
FLORIDA TRUCK NEWS. 1946. m. $14. Florida Trucking Association, Inc., 350 E. College Ave., Tallahassee, FL 32301. TEL 904-222-9900. FAX 904-222-9363. Ed. Tom B. Webb, Jr. adv.; bk.rev.; illus.; circ. 2,300.

388.324 AT
FREIGHT CARRIERS. vol.23, 1973. m. Aus.$1.20. (New South Wales Road Transport Association) Percival Publishing Co. Pty. Ltd., 862-870 Elizabeth St., Waterloo, N.S.W. 2017, Australia. adv.; charts; illus.; circ. 1,500.
   Formerly: Master Carriers Journal (ISSN 0025-5009)

388.324 US
FURNITURE TRANSPORTER.* 1965. s-m. $49. Bohman Industrial Traffic Consultants, Inc., Box 889, Gardner, MA 01440. TEL 617-632-1913. Ed. Raynard F. Bohman Jr.

388.324 US ISSN 0738-5935
TL230.A1
GO WEST. 1941. m. $30. Motor Transport Management Group, 1251 Beacon Blvd., West Sacramento, CA 95691. TEL 916-373-3510. FAX 916-373-3631. Ed. Bill Fitzgerald. adv.; charts; illus.; mkt.; stat.; tr.lit.; circ. 46,238 (controlled).
   Formerly: Go (Burlingame) (ISSN 0017-1433)
   Description: Focuses on serving the managerial needs of operators of diesel trucks with routes in or through the fastest growing regions of the United States--the Pacific, Mountain, Southwestern and Central states.

388.324 UK
GOOD VAN GUIDE. 1986. bi-m. $25. Evro Publishing Co. Ltd., 60 Waldegrave Rd., Teddington, Middx. TW11 8LG, England. TEL 081-943-5943. Ed. Alan Anderson. circ. 40,000. (back issues avail.)
   Description: Includes test reports of vans on the market, value index, and a van facts checklist.

388.324 US ISSN 0738-3096
GOVERNMENT TENDER REPORT. d. (5/w.). $350 (including Government Traffic Bulletin $450). American Trucking Associations, Inc., Statistical Analysis Department, 2200 Mill Rd., Alexandria, VA 22314. TEL 703-838-1794. FAX 703-684-5720. Ed. Emry Williams.
   Description: Summary of tenders submitted to the ICC by motor carriers.

TRANSPORTATION — TRUCKS AND TRUCKING

388.324 US ISSN 0738-310X
GOVERNMENT TRAFFIC BULLETIN. w. $150 (including Government Tender Report $450). American Trucking Associations, Inc., Statistical Analysis Department, 2200 Mill Rd., Alexandria, VA 22314. TEL 703-838-1792. FAX 703-838-1992. Ed. Sheri Johnson.
 Description: Reports on the transportation needs of major US government shippers, with emphasis on motor carrier traffic information.

388.324 GW ISSN 0017-5137
GUETERVERKEHR. 1951. m. DM.42. (Bundesverband des Deutschen Gueternah- und Gueterfernverkehrs) Kirschbaum Verlag GmbH, Siegfriedstr. 28, Postfach 210209, 5300 Bonn 2, Germany. TEL 0228-343057. FAX 0228-857145. TELEX 889596-KIRVL-D. adv.; bk.rev.; charts; illus.; index; circ. 25,000. (back issues avail.)

388.324 CN
GUIDE DU TRANSPORT PAR CAMION. a. Editions Bomart Ltee., 7493 TransCanada Hwy., Ste. 103, St. Laurent, Que. H4T 1T3, Canada. TEL 514-337-9043. FAX 514-337-1862. adv.; circ. 5,000.
 Description: Lists Canadian and American cities serviced by road carriers from Montreal, including terminal telephone numbers.

388.324 UK
HAULAGE MANUAL. 1970. biennial. Road Haulage Association, 35 Monument Hill, Weybridge KT13 8RN, England. TEL 0932-841515. Ed. Sydney Balgarnie. adv.; stat.; index; circ. 12,000.

HAZARDOUS COMMODITY HANDBOOK. see ENVIRONMENTAL STUDIES — Waste Management

388.324 US ISSN 0017-9434
HE5601
HEAVY DUTY TRUCKING. 1922. m. $45 (foreign $90). Newport Publications (Subsidiary of: H.I.C. Corporation), Box W, Newport Beach, CA 92658. TEL 714-261-1636. Ed. Doug Condra. adv.; illus.; circ. 100,000.

388.324 US ISSN 0018-1706
HIGHWAY COMMON CARRIER NEWSLETTER. 1948. fortn. $15. Regular Common Carrier Conference, 2200 Mill Rd., Ste. 350, Alexandria, VA 22314-4677. TEL 703-898-1970. Ed. Shawn Fields. bk.rev.; circ. 1,500. (looseleaf format; back issues avail.)
 Description: Summarizes the legislative and regulatory developments affecting the general freight trucking industry.

629.2 SZ
I N U F A KATALOG; internationales Jahrwerk fuer die Nutzfahrzeugindustrie und Transportbranche. 1958. a. 45 Fr. Vogt-Schild AG, Zuchwilerstr. 21, CH-4501 Solothurn 1, Switzerland. TEL 065-247247. FAX 065-247335. TELEX 934646. Ed. Andre Vollmar. adv.; bk.rev.; circ. 5,500.
 Formerly: I N U F A: Internationaler Nutzfahrzeug-Katalog - International Catalogue for Commercial Vehicles (ISSN 0073-4292)

388.324 AU ISSN 0019-0845
I T R. (International Transport Revue) 1962. 14/yr. S.560. Technopress Fachzeitschriften Verlagsgesellschaft mbH, Felix-Mottl-Str. 12, 1190 Vienna, Austria. TEL 0222-322551. Ed. Dr. Helmut Tober. adv.; bk.rev.; illus.; circ. 14,000 (controlled). (tabloid format) **Indexed:** C.I.S. Abstr.

388.324 US ISSN 0019-2309
ILLINOIS TRUCK NEWS. 1935. q. Illinois Trucking Association, 2000 N. 5th Ave., River Grove, IL 60171-1907. FAX 708-452-3508. Ed. Julie McGowen. adv.; bk.rev.; circ. 5,326 (controlled).
 Description: Includes items on election issues, safety and maintenance, legislation and management.

388.3 US
ILLINOIS TRUCKER; merchandising everything for the trucking industry. 1977. m. $12. Allied Publications, 7355 N. Woodland, Box 603, Indianapolis, IN 46206-0603. TEL 317-297-5500. FAX 317-299-1356. adv.; circ. 21,500.

IMPORTED CARS, LIGHT TRUCKS & VANS SERVICE & REPAIR. see TRANSPORTATION — Automobiles

388.3 US
INDIANA TRUCKER; merchandising everything for the trucking industry. 1975. m. $12. Allied Publications, 7355 N. Woodland, Box 603, Indianapolis, IN 46206-0603. TEL 317-297-5500. FAX 317-299-1356. adv.; circ. 20,000.
 Formerly: Indiana Truck Exchange.

INDUSTRY STATISTICS (YEAR). see TRANSPORTATION — Abstracting, Bibliographies, Statistics

388 FR
INFORMATION ROUTIERE ET TOURISTIQUE. 1946. m. 48 F. S E D I T, 48 rue de la Bienfaisance, 75008 Paris, France. Ed. Jean Charrier. adv.; circ. 3,000.

388.324 US
INNOVATIONS IN RELOCATION MANAGEMENT. q. Allied Van Lines, Inc., 300 Park Plaza, Naperville, IL 60563-8457. TEL 708-717-3627. Ed. Paula Riebe. circ. 3,500.

388.324 UK ISSN 0960-0035
HF5415.7 CODEN: IPDMEC
INTERNATIONAL JOURNAL OF PHYSICAL DISTRIBUTION & LOGISTICS MANAGEMENT. 1970. 9/yr. $1779.95. M C B University Press Ltd., 62 Toller Ln., Bradford, W. Yorks BD8 9BY, England. TEL 0274-499821. FAX 0274-547143. TELEX 51317 MCBUNI G. Ed. James Stock. bk.rev.; index. (reprint service avail. from SWZ) **Indexed:** ABI Inform., Account.& Data Proc.Abstr., BPIA, Bus.Ind., Cont.Pg.Manage., Curr.Cont., Excerp.Med., Int.Abstr.Oper.Res., Key to Econ.Sci., Manage.Cont., SCIMP, SSCI.
 Formerly: International Journal of Physical Distribution and Materials Management; Supersedes (with vol.8, 1977): International Journal of Physical Distribution (ISSN 0020-7527)
 Description: Covers transport and inventory management, materials purchasing management, distribution planning and costs, customer service policy and order processing systems.

388.324 UK ISSN 0262-6195
INTERNATIONAL ROAD HAULAGE BY UNITED KINGDOM REGISTERED VEHICLES. 1979. a. £16.50. H.M.S.O., St. Crispin's, Duke St., Norwich NR3 1PD, England. Ed. A.K. Pepper. circ. 180.
 ●Also available online.
 Formerly (until 1980): International Road Haulage by British Registered Vehicles (ISSN 0262-4508)

388.324 US ISSN 0884-8394
INTERSTATE INFORMATION REPORT; a monthly bulletin for motor carrier executives. 1977. m. $55. American Trucking Associations, Inc., State Laws Department, 2200 Mill Rd., Alexandria, VA 22314-4677. TEL 800-ATA-LINE. FAX 703-838-1992. Ed. Jan Balkin. circ. 1,000.
 Description: Compilation of currently enacted state legislation having direct impact on vehicle operations, fuel taxes, sizes and weights and other areas of interest to the trucking industry.

388.324 US
IOWA TRUCKING LIFELINER. 1943. m. $4. Iowa Motor Truck Association, Capital Center One, 600 E. Court, Ste. D, Des Moines, IA 50309-2020. TEL 515-244-5193. FAX 515-244-2204. Ed. Brenda Neville. adv.; illus.; circ. 3,187 (controlled).
 Former titles: Lifeliner (Des Moines); Motor Truck News (ISSN 0027-2116)

388.324 GW ISSN 0341-9681
K F Z ANZEIGER; die Deutsche Fachzeitschrift fuer Transport, Nutzfahrzeug und Werkstatt. 1947. s-m. DM.126. Stuenings Verlagsgesellschaft mbH, Luisenstr. 100-104, Postfach 2980, 4150 Krefeld, Germany. TEL 02151-853-0. FAX 02151-853103. TELEX 172151305-WISTU. Ed. Lothar Neumann. adv.; bk.rev.; circ. 31,124.
 Formerly: Kraftfahrzeug Anzeiger.

388.324 US
KEEP ON TRUCKIN' NEWS. 1974. m. membership only. Mid-West Truckers Association, Inc., 2715 N. Dirksen Parkway, Springfield, IL 62702. TEL 217-525-0310. FAX 217-525-0342. Ed. Robert Jasmon. adv.; circ. 3,500.
 Description: Information on activities in the trucking industry.

388.324 US
KEYSTONE - JERSEY TRUCK EXCHANGE; merchandising everything for the trucking industry. 1980. m. $12. Allied Publications, 7355 N. Woodland, Box 603, Indianapolis, IN 46206-0603. TEL 317-297-5500. FAX 317-299-1356. adv.; circ. 25,000.
 Formerly: Keystone - Jersey Trucker.

KITCHIN'S ROAD TRANSPORT LAW. see LAW

388.324 US
L M T A NEWS. 1944. 6/yr. $7. (Louisiana Motor Transport Association, Inc.) Deep South Communications, Inc., 3626 Seneca St., Box 3694, Baton Rouge, LA 70821. TEL 504-346-1875. Ed. Betty Lawrence. adv.; circ. 1,700.

388.324 US ISSN 0279-6503
LAND LINE MAGAZINE; the business magazine of owner-operator truckers. 1975. bi-m. $14. Owner-Operator Independent Drivers Association of America, Box L, Grain Valley, MO 64029. FAX 816-229-0518. Ed. Todd Spencer. adv.; bk.rev.; circ. 82,500 (controlled).
 Description: For the small business men and women of commercial trucking. Provides news for the serious decision-makers in this segment of the industry.

388.324 GW
LASTAUTO OMNIBUS KATALOG. 1970. a. DM.22. Motor-Presse Stuttgart, Leuschnerstr. 1, Postfach 106036, 7000 Stuttgart 10, Germany. TEL 0711-18201. FAX 0711-1821669. chart.; illus.; circ. 26,000.

388.324 SW ISSN 0023-8678
LASTBILEN. 1931. 15/yr. SEK 430. Aakerifoerlaget AB, Box 508, 182 15 Danderyd, Sweden. FAX 46-08-755-88-95. TELEX 13653. Ed. Eric Bjoerklund. adv.; bk.rev.; illus.; stat.; circ. 21,000.

388.324 NO ISSN 0023-8686
LASTEBILEN. m. (11/yr.) Norges Lastebileier-Forbund - Norwegian Truck-Owners' Assocation, Chr. Krohgsgt. 32A, Postboks 4658 Sofienberg, Oslo 5, Norway. Ed. Karl J. Bjerklund. adv.; charts; circ. 14,000.

388.324 690 US
LIFTING & TRANSPORTATION INTERNATIONAL. 1953. m. $58 (foreign $120). Leo Douglas, Inc., 9607 Gayton Rd. Ste.201, Richmond, VA 23233. TEL 804-741-6704. FAX 703-573-7273. adv.; bk.rev.; circ. 22,108.
 Formerly: Transportation Engineer (ISSN 0041-1604)

388.3 US
M C D'S WAREHOUSING DISTRIBUTION DIRECTORY. (Motor Carrier Directory) 1963. a. $75. K - III Press, Inc., 424 W. 33rd St., New York, NY 10001. TEL 212-714-3100. Ed. David Wise. adv.; circ. 20,000.
 Former titles: National Distribution Directory of Local Cartage-Short Haul Carriers Warehousing (ISSN 0364-9539); National Distribution Directory (ISSN 0077-4219)

388.324 US
▼**M M C A NEWS.** 1990. m. $12.50. (Montana Motor Carriers Association, Inc.) Motor Carrier Service Inc., Box 1714, Helena, MT 59624. TEL 406-442-6600. Ed. B.G. Havdahl.

388.324 FI ISSN 0024-8819
MAARAKENNUS JA KULJETUS/EARTH CONSTRUCTION AND TRANSPORT. 1963. 8/yr. Fmk.130. Maarakentajain Kustannus Oy, Arkadiankatu 16 B, 00100 Helsinki 10, Finland. Ed. Heikki Saarento. adv.; charts; circ. 6,188.

388.324 US
MAINE MOTOR TRANSPORT NEWS. 1946. 10/yr. $25. Maine Motor Transport Association, Inc., 524 Western Ave., Augusta, ME 04330. TEL 207-623-4128. FAX 207-623-4096. Ed. Richard C. Jones. adv. (reprint service avail.)
 Description: Covers the trucking industry.

TRANSPORTATION — TRUCKS AND TRUCKING

388.324 US
MAINTENANCE. m. $75. American Trucking Associations, Inc., 2200 Mill Rd., Alexandria, VA 22314. TEL 800-ATA-LINE. FAX 703-684-5720.
Formed by the 1988 merger of: Maintenance (Newsletter for Professional Truck Equipment Managers) (ISSN 0890-1775) & Maintenance (Newsletter for Professional Truck Equipment Supervisors) (ISSN 0890-1783) & Maintenance (Newsletter for Professional Truck Equipment Executives) (ISSN 0890-1767) & Maintenance (Newsletter for Professional Truck Driver-Owner) (ISSN 0890-1791)

388.324 US
MAINTENANCE: MANAGERS. 1988. q. membership. American Trucking Associations, Inc., 2200 Mill Rd., Alexandria, VA 22314. TEL 800-ATA-LINE. FAX 703-684-5720. Ed. Carl Kirk.
Description: Focuses on current equipment management issues, new equipment and products, and management training.

388.324 CN ISSN 0380-4852
MANITOBA HIGHWAY NEWS. 1971. 6/yr. Manitoba Trucking Association, 25 Bunting St., Winnipeg, Man. R2X 2P5, Canada. Ed. A. Harris. adv.; circ. 7,500.

388.324 CN ISSN 0713-8776
MANITOBA SHIP BY TRUCK DIRECTORY. 1958. a. Can.$23. Manitoba Trucking Association, 25 Bunting St., Winnipeg, Man. R2X 2P5, Canada. Ed. George Gamurelis. adv.; circ. 1,600.
Formerly: M T A Ship by Truck Directory.

388.324 US
MAYFLOWER WAREHOUSEMAN. 1955. 10/yr. $12. 9247 N. Meridian St., Ste. 120, Indianapolis, IN 46260. TEL 317-844-6226. Ed. Julie McLaughlin Foster. circ. 2,000.
Description: Magazine for moving and storage industry.

388.324 US
MICHIGAN TRUCK EXCHANGE; merchandising everything for the trucking industry. 1989. bi-w. $12. Allied Publications, 7355 N. Woodland, Box 603, Indianapolis, IN 46206-0603. TEL 317-297-5500. FAX 317-299-1356. adv.; circ. 20,000.

388.324 US
MID-AMERICA TRANSPORTER. 1946. 11/yr. $12. Kansas Motor Carriers Association, 2900 S. Topeka Blvd., Box 1673, Topeka, KS 66601. TEL 913-267-1641. FAX 913-266-6551. Ed. Carl Hill. adv.; illus.; tr.lit.; circ. 4,500.
Formerly (until 1984): Kansas Transporter (ISSN 0022-8842).

388.324 US
MID SOUTH TRUCKING NEWS. fortn. 9 Lucy Lane, Sherwood, AR 72120. TEL 501-834-8600. FAX 501-985-0026. Ed. Orval Faubus.

388.324 US ISSN 0026-3427
MIDWEST MOTOR TRANSPORT NEWS. 1935. 16/yr. membership only. Minnesota Trucking Association, 1821 University Ave., St. Paul, MN 55104. TEL 612-646-7351. Ed. Andy Piilola. adv.; stat.; tr.lit.; circ. 950.
Description: Provides members of the Minnesota Trucking Association with information regarding rules, regulations, laws and events that affect the trucking industry.

388.324 US
MILK AND LIQUID FOOD TRANSPORTER. 1960. m. $12. Brady Co., Inc., N80 W12878 Fond du Lac Ave., Box 878, Menomonee Falls, WI 53052-0878. TEL 414-255-0108. Ed. Charles Wilshire. adv.; circ. 6,000. (back issues avail.)

388.324 US
MINI TRUCKIN'. q. $2.95 per no. McMullen Publishing, 2145 W. La Palma Ave., Anaheim, CA 92801. TEL 714-635-9040.

388.324 US ISSN 0031-6431
TN860
MODERN BULK TRANSPORTER. 1937. m. $25 (foreign $40)(free to qualified personnel). Tunnell Publications, Inc., Box 66010, Houston, TX 77266. TEL 713-523-8124. FAX 713-523-8384. Ed. Charles Wilson. adv.; charts; illus.; stat.; tr.lit.; circ. 16,000.
—BLDSC shelfmark: 5883.760000.
Formerly: Petroleum and Chemical Transporter.
Description: Serves the tank truck industry that transport petroleum and petroleum products, chemicals, milk, other food products, and other types of liquid and dry commodities in bulk form.

338.324 330 US
MODERN TRUCKSTOP NEWS. bi-m. G C I Publishing, Inc., 1801 Rockville Pike, No. 330, Rockville, MD 20852-1633. TEL 301-984-7333. FAX 301-984-7340. Ed. Louise Classon. adv.; circ. 10,500.

388.3 US
MONTHLY TRUCK TONNAGE REPORT. m. $35. American Trucking Associations, Inc., Statistical Analysis Department, 2200 Mill Rd., Alexandria, VA 22314. TEL 703-838-1799. FAX 703-838-1992. Indexed: SRI.
Description: Tonnage reports from ongoing survey of Class I and II general freight carriers; comparisons with other economic indicators.

388.324 US
MOTOR CARRIER - FREIGHT FORWARDER SERVICE. 1940. 4 base vols. (plus m. suppl.). $280. Hawkins Publishing Co., Inc., Box 480, Mayo, MD 21106-0480. TEL 301-798-1677. Ed. Carl R. Eyler. circ. 500. (back issues avail.)

388.324 CN
MOTOR CARRIER MANAGER. 1983. 6/yr. membership. Naylor Communications Ltd., 920 Yonge St., 6th Fl., Toronto, Ont. M4W 3C7, Canada. TEL 416-961-1028. FAX 416-924-4408. Ed. John Howarth. adv.

388.324 US
MOTOR CARRIER SAFETY REPORT. m. $90. J.J. Keller & Associates, Inc., 3003 W. Breezewood Lane, Box 368, Neenah, WI 54957-0368. TEL 414-722-2848. FAX 414-727-7516. Ed.Bd.
Description: Reports on motor carrier safety and trucking safety.

MOTOR FLEET SUPERVISION; principles and practices. see BUSINESS AND ECONOMICS — Personnel Management

388.324 US
MOTOR FREIGHT CONTROLLER. bi-m. American Trucking Association, 2200 Mill Rd., Alexandria, VA 22304. TEL 703-838-1700.

388.324 UK ISSN 0027-206X
MOTOR TRANSPORT. 1905. w. Reed Business Publishing Group, Enterprise Division (Subsidiary of: Reed International PLC), Quadrant House, The Quadrant, Sutton, Surrey SM2 5AS, England. TEL 081-652-3284. FAX 081-652-3925. (Subscr. to: c/o Computer Action Ltd., 27 Park St., Croydon, Surrey CR0 1YO, England. TEL 081-681-0753) Ed. Geoff Hadwick. adv.; bk.rev.; illus.; circ. 44,697 (controlled). Indexed: C.I.S. Abstr.
—BLDSC shelfmark: 5975.610000.

388.324 CN ISSN 0027-2108
MOTOR TRUCK. 1934. m. Can.$32.10 (foreign $47). Southam Business Communications Inc., 1450 Don Mills Rd., Don Mills, Ont. M3B 2X7, Canada. TEL 416-445-6641. FAX 416-442-2261. Ed. Barry Holmes. adv.; illus.; stat.; tr.lit.; circ. 29,800. Indexed: Can.B.P.I.

388.324 US
MOUNTAIN AMERICA TRUCK TRADER; merchandising everything for the trucking industry. 1983. m. Allied Publications, 7355 N. Woodland, Box 603, Indianapolis, IN 46206-0603. TEL 317-297-5500. FAX 317-299-1356. adv.; circ. 28,500.

338.324 US
MOVERS NEWS. m. N Y S Movers & Warehousemen's Association, 132 State St., Albany, NY 12207-1610. TEL 518-449-3946. FAX 518-449-8981. Ed. Donald J. Boyle. circ. 600.

388.324 US
MOVIN' OUT. 1975. m. Pollock Enterprises, Ltd., 118 1-2 Franklin St., Box 97, Slippery Rock, PA 16057. TEL 412-794-6857. FAX 412-794-1314. adv.; circ. 50,000.
Description: Contains trucking news on a national and local level. Includes new product information.

380.14 US ISSN 0192-7027
MY LITTLE SALESMAN TRUCK CATALOG. 1958. m. $12. Industrial Publishing Co., Box 70208, Eugene, OR 97401. TEL 503-342-1201. FAX 503-342-3307. adv.; B&W page $810; adv. contact: John Hallberg. circ. 60,000.
Description: Provides information to those buying or selling trucks and trucking equipment.

388.324 US
N A T S O TRUCKERS NEWS. m. $0.25 per no. (National Association of Truck Stop Operators) Newport Publications, Box 23128, Toledo, OH 43623. TEL 419-882-1145. FAX 419-885-5895. Ed. Jack Thiessen. circ. 200,000. (tabloid format; back issues avail.)
Description: Covers trucks, trucking and truck stops.

388.324 US ISSN 0077-586X
NATIONAL TANK TRUCK CARRIER DIRECTORY. 1954. a. $36 to non-members; members $27. National Tank Truck Carriers, Inc., 2200 Mill Rd., Alexandria, VA 22314-4677. TEL 703-838-1960. FAX 703-684-5753. Ed. Patricia Whiting. adv.; circ. 2,000.

388.324 US
NATIONAL TRUCK EQUIPMENT ASSOCIATION. LEGISLATIVE REPORT. 1979. m. $4 to non-members; members $2. National Truck Equipment Association, 38705 Seven Mile Rd., No. 345, Livonia, MI 48152-1057. TEL 313-462-2190. FAX 313-462-2108. Ed. Joan Christophersen-Call. circ. 1,600. (looseleaf format; back issues avail.)
Description: Discussion of legislative activities, includes updates in Congressional committee action and pending Congressional bills.

388.324 US
NATIONAL TRUCK EQUIPMENT ASSOCIATION. REGULATIONS REPORT. 1979. m. $4 per no. to non-members; members $2. National Truck Equipment Association, 38705 Seven Mile Rd., No. 345, Livonia, MI 48152-1057. TEL 313-462-2190. FAX 313-462-2108. Ed. Joan Christophersen-Call. circ. 1,600. (looseleaf format; back issues avail.)
Description: Current federal and state regulatory activities affecting the truck equipment industry.

388.324 US
NEBRASKA TRUCKER. 1940. m. $16. Nebraska Motor Carriers' Association, 1701 K St., Box 81010, Lincoln, NE 68508. TEL 402-476-7822. FAX 402-476-0579. Ed. Nance Kirk. adv.; circ. 3,309. (also avail. on diskette)
Formerly: Midwestern Trucker and Shipper.

388.324 GW
NEUZULASSUNGEN BESITZUMSCHREIBUNGEN LOESCHUNGEN VON KRAFTFAHRZEUGEN UND KRAFTFAHRZEUGENANHAENGERN. 1958. a. DM.47. (Kraftfahr - Bundesamt) Kirschbaum Verlag GmbH, Siegfriedstr. 28, Postfach 210209, 5300 Bonn 2, Germany. TEL 0228-343057. FAX 0228-857145. TELEX 889596-KIRVL-D.

388.324 US
NEW ENGLAND TRUCK EXCHANGE; merchandising everything for the trucking industry. 1984. m. $12. Allied Publications, 7355 N. Woodland, Box 603, Indianapolis, IN 46206-0603. TEL 317-297-5500. FAX 317-299-1356. adv.; circ. 25,000.

388.324 US ISSN 0028-5838
NEW JERSEY MOTOR TRUCK ASSOCIATION. BULLETIN. 1964. m. $25. New Jersey Motor Truck Association, 160 Tices Ln., E. Brunswick, NJ 08816. TEL 908-254-5000. FAX 908-613-1745. Ed. Russell Roemmele. adv.; bk.rev.; illus.; circ. 2,100.

388.324 US
NEW YORK TRUCK EXCHANGE; merchandising everything for the trucking industry. 1977. m. $12. Allied Publications, 7355 N. Woodland, Box 603, Indianapolis, IN 46206-0603. TEL 317-297-5500. FAX 317-299-1356. Ed. Robert W. Poorman, Jr. adv.; circ. 25,000.

TRANSPORTATION — TRUCKS AND TRUCKING

NISSAN DIESEL TECHNICAL REVIEW. see *TRANSPORTATION — Automobiles*

NOTIZIARIO MOTORISTICO/MOTOR NEWS/MOTOR-NACHRICHTEN/BULLETIN MOTORISTIQUE; autoattrezzature-impiantistica. see *TRANSPORTATION — Automobiles*

388.324   GW   ISSN 0029-6686
NUTZFAHRZEUG; Das LKW-Magazin. 1948. m. DM.88.80 (foreign DM 97.80). Heinrich Vogel Fachzeitschriften GmbH, Neumarkter Str. 18, Postfach 802020, 8000 Munich 80, Germany. TEL 089-43180-0. Ed. Graf von Sauring-Jeltsch. bk.rev.; bibl.; illus.; pat.; stat.; index; circ. 5,371 (controlled).

388.324   US
OFFICIAL MOTOR CARRIER DIRECTORY. 1958. s-a. $32. Official Motor Freight Guide, Inc., 1130 S. Canal St., Chicago, IL 60607. TEL 312-939-1434. FAX 312-939-2910. Ed. Edward K. Koch. adv.; charts; circ. 5,200.

388.324   US   ISSN 0030-0357
OFFICIAL MOTOR FREIGHT GUIDE. (Published in 3 Regional Editions) 1932. s-a. $25. Official Motor Freight Guide, Inc., 1130 S. Canal St., Chicago, IL 60607. TEL 312-939-1434. Ed. Eugene M. Ornstein. adv.; circ. 63,107.

388.324   US
OFFICIAL SHIPPERS GUIDE - NEW YORK MOTOR EXPRESS GUIDE. 1872. s-a. $35. Official Motor Freight Guide, Inc., 1130 S. Canal St., Chicago, IL 60607. TEL 312-030-1434. Ed. E. Eric Robison. adv.; charts.

388.324   US
OFFICIAL SHIPPERS GUIDE - ST. LOUIS MOTOR FREIGHT DIRECTORY. 1872. s-a. $35. Official Motor Freight Guide, Inc., 1130 S. Canal St., Chicago, IL 60607. TEL 312-939-1434. Ed. Eugene M. Ornstein.

629.2 380.5   FR
OFFICIEL DES TRANSPORTS; l'hebdomadaire du transport routier. 1925. w. 650 F. (foreign 795 F.). Compagnie Generale de Developpement, 11 rue Godefroy Cavaignac, 75541 Paris Cedex 11, France. Ed. Jean Furet. adv.; circ. 24,500.
Formerly: Officiel des Transporteurs (ISSN 0754-4618)

OHIO GOVERNMENT DIRECTORY - OHIO TRUCKING TIMES. see *PUBLIC ADMINISTRATION*

388.324   US   ISSN 0736-6124
OLDER CAR RED BOOK. 4/yr. $68. Maclean Hunter Market Reports, Inc., 29 N. Wacker Dr., Chicago, IL 60606-3297. TEL 312-726-2802. FAX 312-726-2574. (also avail. on diskette; back issues avail.)

ONTARIO SHIP-BY-TRUCK DIRECTORY. see *BUSINESS AND ECONOMICS — Trade And Industrial Directories*

388.324   US
OVER THE ROAD. m. Ramp Publishing Group, 610 Colonial Park Dr., Roswell, GA 30075-3746. TEL 404-587-0311. FAX 404-642-8874. Ed. Ken Kent. circ. 102,000.

388.324   US
OWNER AND OPERATOR DIRECTORY.* 1977. bi-m. Ramp Enterprises, Inc., 610 Colonial Park Dr., Roswell, GA 30075-3746. TEL 404-587-0338. Ed. Penny Shefsky. adv.

388.324   US   ISSN 0475-2112
HE5601
OWNER OPERATOR. 1970. 9/yr. $16. Chilton Co., Chilton Way, Radnor, PA 19089. TEL 215-964-4264. Ed. Leon Witconis. adv.; bk.rev.; charts; illus.; tr.lit.; circ. 101,500. (also avail. in microfilm from UMI; microfiche from UMI; back issues avail.; reprint service avail. from UMI)

388.324   US
OWNER - OPERATOR NEWS. bi-m. Box 88, Oak Grove, MO 64075-0088. TEL 816-229-5791. FAX 816-229-0518. Ed. Todd Spencer. circ. 16,000.

388.324   US
P & D MAGAZINE. (Pickup & Delivery) bi-m. Motor Transport Management Group, 1251 Beacon Blvd., West SacRamento, CA 95691-3461. TEL 916-373-3508. FAX 916-373-3631. Ed. Jim Beach. adv.; circ. 40,000.

388.324   US
PENNTRUX. 1933. m. membership only. Pennsylvania Motor Truck Association, Linda Lane, Box 128, Camp Hill, PA 17001-0128. TEL 717-761-7122. FAX 717-761-8434. Ed. William F. Sperry. adv.; index; circ. 2,500 (controlled).
Description: Covers developments affecting the trucking industry, with emphasis on Pennsylvania.

PRICE GUIDE PRESENTS. see *TRANSPORTATION — Automobiles*

388.324   US   ISSN 0032-8871
HE5623.A1
PRIVATE CARRIER. 1963. m. National Private Truck Council, Private Carrier Conference, 1320 Braddock Pl., Ste. 720, Alexandria, VA 22314. TEL 703-683-1300. FAX 703-683-1217. Ed. Donald E. Tepper. adv.; bk.rev.; charts; illus.; stat.; tr.lit.; circ. 20,000 (controlled). (back issues avail.)

388.324   US
PRIVATE LINE. 1983. m. National Private Truck Council, 1320 Braddock Pl., Ste. 720, Alexandria, VA 22314. TEL 703-683-1300. FAX 703-683-1217. Ed. Donald E. Tepper. adv.; bk.rev.; circ. 12,500 (controlled).

388.324   US
PRO TRUCKER.* 1988. m. Ramp Enterprises, Inc., 610 Colonial Park Dr., Roswell, GA 30075-3746. TEL 404-587-0338. FAX 404-462-8874. Ed. Ryan Rees. adv.; circ. 50,000.
Formerly (until 1988): Pro Driver.
Description: For professional truck drivers, owner operators, fleet owners and drivers in the trucking industry. Covers industry news, and new products.

388.324   AT
QUEENSLAND TRANSPORT NEWS; the management magazine for transport operators. 1985. m. (except Dec.). Aus.$40($70) Publishing Services (Qld.) Pty. Ltd., 244 St. Paul's Terrace, Spring Hill, Brisbane, Qld. 4000, Australia. TEL 617 854 1286. Ed. Andrew Stewart. circ. 11,200. (back issues avail.)

QUICK CALLER: BOSTON AREA AIR CARGO DIRECTORY. see *TRANSPORTATION — Air Transport*

QUICK CALLER: CHICAGO AREA AIR CARGO DIRECTORY. see *TRANSPORTATION — Air Transport*

QUICK CALLER: DETROIT AREA AIR CARGO DIRECTORY. see *TRANSPORTATION — Air Transport*

QUICK CALLER: LOS ANGELES AREA AIR CARGO DIRECTORY. see *TRANSPORTATION — Air Transport*

QUICK CALLER: MIAMI AREA AIR CARGO DIRECTORY. see *TRANSPORTATION — Air Transport*

QUICK CALLER: NEW YORK METRO AREA AIR CARGO DIRECTORY. see *TRANSPORTATION — Air Transport*

QUICK CALLER: SAN FRANCISCO BAY AREA AIR CARGO DIRECTORY. see *TRANSPORTATION — Air Transport*

388.324   US   ISSN 0745-0389
R V TRADE DIGEST. (Recreational Vehicle) m. $24. Continental Publishing Company of Indiana, Inc., 58025 C.R. No.9 S., Box 1805, Elkhart, IN 46517. TEL 219-295-1962. FAX 219-295-7574. Ed. Thomas A. Russell. circ. 19,100.
Description: For business professionals actively engaged in the manufacture, distribution, or sales of RV's and accessories with emphasis on sales, marketing, and business-oriented features.

388.324   US
RAND MCNALLY MOTOR CARRIERS' ROAD ATLAS. a. $16.95. Rand McNally & Co., 8255 N. Central Pk. Ave., Skokie, IL 60076. TEL 708-673-9100. (Orders to: Box 7600, Chicago, IL 60680)

388.324   US   ISSN 0034-3129
REFRIGERATED TRANSPORTER. 1964. m. $25 (foreign $40)(free to qualified personnnel). Tunnell Publications, Inc., Box 66010, Houston, TX 77266. TEL 713-523-8124. FAX 713-523-8384. Ed. Gary Macklin. adv.; illus.; circ. 15,000. **Indexed:** Tr.& Indus.Ind.
—BLDSC shelfmark: 7333.900000.
Description: Serves the operators and shippers of transportation and distribution services concerned with the handling of temperature-controlled commodities.

388.324   US
ROAD KING; the magazine for the professional driver. 1963. bi-m. $12. (Union Oil Company of California (UNOCAL)) William A. Coop, Inc., Box 250, Park Forest, IL 60466. TEL 708-481-9240. FAX 708-481-1063. Ed. George Friend. adv.; bk.rev.; circ. 215,604.

388.324   UK   ISSN 0035-7316
ROAD WAY. 1935. m. £18. Road Haulage Association, 35 Monument Hill, Weybridge KT13 8RN, England. TEL 0932-841515. Ed. Steve Gray. adv.; bk.rev.; illus.; stat.; circ. 14,000.

388.324   US
ROADWISE. 1949. s-a. $12.50. (Montana Motor Carriers Association, Inc.) Motor Carrier Service Inc., Box 1714, Helena, MT 59624. TEL 406-442-6600. Ed. B.G. Havdahl. adv.; circ. 3,500.

388.324 388.312
LES ROUTIERS. 1934. m. 190 Fr. (foreign 380 F.). S E J T, 6 rue d'Isly, 75008 Paris, France. TEL 43-87-61-68. FAX 43-87-50-46. Ed. Patrice de Saulieu. adv.; bk.rev.; circ. 45,000.

388.324   US
S C & R A NEWSLETTER. w. membership. Specialized Carriers & Rigging Association, 2200 Mill Rd., Ste. 616, Alexandria, VA 22314. TEL 703-838-1980. circ. 775.
Description: Industry news on legislation, industrial relations, management and safety.

388.324   US
S C T A HI-LIGHTS. 1937. m. $5. South Carolina Trucking Association, Inc., 2425 Devine St., Box 50166, Columbia, SC 29250-0166. TEL 803-799-4306. FAX 803-254-7148. Ed. J. Richards Todd. adv.; bk.rev.; illus.; circ. 2,504.
Formerly: Motor Transportation Hi-Lights (ISSN 0027-2078)

388.324   US
SAFETY, INDUSTRIAL RELATIONS, AND GOVERNMENT AFFAIRS SPECIAL REPORT. m. membership. Specialized Carriers & Rigging Association, 2200 Mill Rd., Ste. 616, Alexandria, VA 22314. TEL 703-838-1890. circ. 775.
Description: For transportation, crane, millwrighting and rigging professionals.

388.324   CN
SASKATCHEWAN TRUCKING. 1980. q. ProWest Publications, No. 208, 438 Victoria Ave. E., Regina, Sask. S4N 0N7, Canada. TEL 306-352-3400. FAX 306-525-0960. adv.; circ. 4,795.

388.324   CN
SASKATCHEWAN TRUCKING - SHIP BY TRUCK DIRECTORY. 1973. a. Can.$11. Saskatchewan Trucking Association, 1335 Wallace St., Regina, Sask. S4N 3Z5, Canada. TEL 306-569-9696. adv.; circ. 2,000.
Formerly: Saskatchewan Motor Transport Guide (ISSN 0707-0365)

SAVREMENI VOZAC. see *TRANSPORTATION — Automobiles*

388.324   US
SOUTH DAKOTA TRUCKING NEWS. m. South Dakota Trucking Association, Box 89008, Sioux Falls, SD 57105. TEL 605-334-8871.

388.324   US   ISSN 0038-4372
TL230.A1
SOUTHERN MOTOR CARGO; truck equipment magazine of the South. 1945. m. $30. Southern Motor Cargo, Inc., Box 40169, Memphis, TN 38174. FAX 901-276-5400. Ed. Randy Duke. adv.; illus.; circ. 58,000. (also avail. in microform from UMI; reprint service avail. from UMI)

TRANSPORTATION — TRUCKS AND TRUCKING

SOUTHERN TRAFFIC LIGHT. see *TRANSPORTATION — Railroads*

796   US   ISSN 1044-7903
SPORT TRUCK. 1988. m. $17.94. Petersen Publishing Co., 8490 Sunset Blvd., Los Angeles, CA 90069. TEL 213-854-2470. Ed. Hoyt Vandenberg. adv.; circ. 131,000.
  Incorporates (in 1991): Hot Truck.
  Description: Puts trucks in a social context, providing evaluations of the latest trucks and truck products, addresses the truck owners for whom the truck represents a lifestyle.

388.324   US
STATE MOTOR CARRIER GUIDE. 2 base vols. (plus fortn. reports). $1650. Commerce Clearing House, Inc., 4025 W. Peterson Ave., Chicago, IL 60646. TEL 312-583-8500.

388.324   US   ISSN 0039-1298
STEERING WHEEL. 1936. bi-m. $10. Texas Motor Transportation Association, Box 1669, 700 E. 11th, Austin, TX 78767. TEL 512-478-2541. Ed. Cathey Brandewie. adv.; illus.; circ. 3,500 (controlled).

388.324   AT
STOCK HAUL; the management magazine for livestock carriers. 1982. bi-m. Aus.$20($35) Publishing Services (Qld.) Pty. Ltd., 244 St. Paul's Terrace, Spring Hill, Brisbane, Qld. 4000, Australia. TEL 61 7 854 1286. Ed. Mark Stegman. circ. 1,712. (back issues avail.)

621   US   ISSN 0161-6080
SUCCESSFUL DEALER. 1978. bi-m. $50 (foreign $60). Kona Communications, Inc., 707 Lake Cook Rd., Ste. 300, Deerfield, IL 60015. TEL 708-498-3180. FAX 708-498-3197. Ed. Denise Rondini. adv.; charts; illus.; stat.; circ. 19,000.
  Description: For dealer organizations selling medium- and heavy-duty trucks, construction equipment, industrial trucks and diesel engines.

388.324   US
T E NEWS. (Truck Equipment) m. $48 to non-members; members $24. National Truck Equipment Association, 38705 Seven Mile Rd., No. 345, Livonia, MI 48152-1057. TEL 313-462-2190. FAX 313-462-2108. Ed. Joan Christophersen-Call. circ. 1,600. (back issues avail.)
  Description: Truck body and equipment industry newsletter.

388.324   NE
T T M - TRUCK EN TRANSPORT MANAGEMENT. 1985. m. fl.197. Uitgeversmaatschappij C. Misset, Hanzestr. 1, 7006 RH Doetinchem, Netherlands. TEL 8340-49527. FAX 8340-461522. TELEX 45481 NL. (Subscr. to: Postbus 4, 7000 BA Doetinchem, Netherlands) Ed. P.C. Wieman. adv.; bk.rev.; circ. 13,500.
  Description: Journal for officials responsible for the management of road haulage companies and, in conjunction, for the purchase, operation and control of road transport vehicles in the road haulage industry as well as in industrial enterprises with own vehicle fleets.

388.324   US   ISSN 0039-968X
TARHEEL WHEELS. 1944. 4/yr. $3.14. North Carolina Trucking Association, Inc., Box 2977, Raleigh, NC 27602. TEL 919-834-0387. FAX 919-832-0390. Ed. Elbert L. Peters. adv.; illus.; circ. 4,500.
  Description: Information on trucking operations and personalities involved in trucking. Includes announcements of meetings of interest to truckers.

388.324   US
TENNESSEE TRUCKING NEWS. 6/yr. $25. Tennessee Trucking Association, Box 2847, Nashville, TN 37219. TEL 615-255-0558. FAX 615-244-0495. adv.; circ. 1,000 (controlled).
  Formerly: Transport News of Tennessee.
  Description: Covers various topics in transportation.

388.3   US
TEXAS - LOUISIANA TRUCKER; merchandising everything for the trucking industry. 1975. m. Allied Publications, 7355 N. Woodland, Box 603, Indianapolis, IN 46206-0603. TEL 317-297-5500. FAX 317-299-1356. adv.; circ. 28,200.
  Former titles: Texas Truck Trader - Louisiana Trucker - Oklahoma Trucker; Texas Truck Trader - Louisiana Trucker; Texas Truck Trader.

TORAKKU YUSO JOHO. see *TRANSPORTATION — Railroads*

388.324   US
TOW-AGE. 1974. 9/yr. Kruza Kaleidoscopix, Inc., Box 389, Franklin, MA 02038. TEL 308-528-6211. Ed. J.A. Kruza. adv.; bk.rev.; illus.; stat.; tr.lit.; circ. 10,000.
  Formerly: Tow-Line.
  Description: For towing and road service personnel who recover vehicles.

388   US
TOW TIMES; the international communications medium for the towing and recovery industry. 1983. m. $34. T T Publications, Inc., 398 N. Freeman St., Longwood, FL 32750. TEL 407-260-0712. FAX 407-260-1486. (Subscr. to: Box 52-2020, Longwood, FL 32752-2020) Ed. Tim Jackson. adv.; tr.lit.; circ. 30,000 (controlled). (back issues avail.)
  Description: Covers all aspects of the towing industry: economics and law, new products, technical data, recovery reviews, and company profiles.

TRACTOR DIGEST. see *AGRICULTURE — Agricultural Equipment*

388.324   US   ISSN 0041-0772
TRAILER-BODY BUILDERS. 1959. m. $25 (foreign $40)(free to qualified personnel). Tunnell Publications, Inc., Box 66010, Houston, TX 77266. TEL 713-523-8124. FAX 713-523-8384. Ed. Paul Schenck. adv.; illus.; circ. 14,000 (controlled).
  Description: Serves the truck body and trailer manufacturing industry, including tank, van containers, school buses, mobile homes and truck equipment.

388.324   CN
TRANSPORT ELECTRONIC NEWS. q. Truckworld Publications Ltd., 3-1610 Kebet Way, Port Coquitlam, B.C. V3C 5W9, Canada. TEL 604-942-2305. FAX 604-942-4312. Ed. Rob Robertson. adv.; circ. 12,000.

388.324   US
TRANSPORT FLEET NEWS. 1980. m. $15. Transport Publishing Co., 1300 W. Exchange Ave., Chicago, IL 60609. TEL 312-523-6669. FAX 312-523-9062. Ed. Phillip Scopelite. adv.; bk.rev.; film rev.; play rev.; circ. 10,500. (back issues avail.)
  Description: Covers industry news and offers product information for the industry for fleet supervisory personnel.

388.3   SA
TRANSPORT MANAGER'S HANDBOOK AND TRUCKER'S GUIDE. 1978. a. R.154.55. (Federation of Road Transport Associations) Thomson Publications (Subsidiary of: Times Media Ltd.), P.O. Box 56182, Pinegowrie 2123, South Africa. TEL 011-789-2144. FAX 011-789-3196. adv.; circ. 3,014.
  Formerly: Transport Manager's Handbook; Incorporates: Commercial Transport Equipment Index; Supersedes (1964-1978): Commercial Transport Handbook and Buyer's Guide for S A (ISSN 0069-6676)

388.324   UK
TRANSPORT OF GOODS BY ROAD IN GREAT BRITAIN. 1972. a. £9.95. (Department of Transport, Statistics Transport Division) H.M.S.O, PO Box 276, London SW8 5DT, England. FAX 01-276-8690. Ed. R. Garland. charts; stat.; circ. 250. (looseleaf format; back issues avail.)
  Description: Data on goods carried, mileages, output per vehicle, etc. for trucks in the UK.

388.324   UK   ISSN 0267-8411
TRANSPORT OPERATOR. 1955. m. £30 (foreign £40). A.G.B. Hulton Ltd., Warwick House, Azalea Dr., Sanley, Kent BR8 8JR, England. TEL 0322-60411. Ed. Mark Robinson. circ. 20,000.
  Description: Management information supplied to individuals responsible for HGV fleets and workshops.

629.2   SZ   ISSN 0255-6871
TRANSPORT RUNDSCHAU; Unabhaengige Zeitschrift fuer Nutzfahrzeuge, Garageneinrichtungen und Strassentransporte. m. 90 Fr. Vogt-Schild AG, Zuchwilerstr. 21, CH-4501 Solothurn 1, Switzerland. TEL 065-247247. FAX 065-247335. TELEX 934646. Ed. Andre Vollmar. adv.; illus.; circ. 12,000.
  Formerly: I N U F A Rundschau.

388.324   US   ISSN 0041-1558
HE5601
TRANSPORT TOPICS; national newspaper of the trucking industry. 1935. w. $59. American Trucking Associations, Inc., 2200 Mill Rd., Alexandria, VA 22314. TEL 703-838-1770. FAX 703-838-1777. Ed. Oliver Patton. adv.; charts; illus.; stat.; circ. 30,868. (processed; also avail. in microform from UMI)
  Description: Emphasizes trucking industry business, regulation, economics, maintenance, equipment, data processing. Covers all segments of for-hire and private trucking.

388.324 658   US   ISSN 0897-8077
TRANSPORTATION EXECUTIVE UPDATE. 1987. bi-m. $48. Regular Common Carrier Conference, 2200 Mill Rd., Ste. 350, Alexandria, VA 22314-4654. TEL 703-838-1970. Ed. Shawn Fields. circ. 2,000.
  Description: For upper level management of the general freight trucking industry.

TRANSPORTATION LAW INSTITUTE PAPERS AND PROCEEDINGS. see *LAW*

388.324   UK
TRUCK. 1974. m. £18.50 (foreign £22.50). Village Publishing Ltd, 10A London Mews, Paddington, London W2 1HY, England. TEL 071-224-9242. FAX 071-402-3994. Ed. George Bennett.
  Incorporates: Truck & Driver.

388.324 621   UK   ISSN 0263-6263
TRUCK AND BUS BUILDER; the international newsletter of commercial vehicle manufacturing, developments. 1978. m. £114($228) A.J.P. Wilding, Truck & Bus Builder, P.O. Box 2503, Ealing, London W5 2TR, England. TEL 081-997-6946. FAX 081-575-7531. Ed. Eric Gibbins. circ. 1,000. (back issues avail.)
  Description: News briefs and graphical presentations on national and international technical, commercial and marketing developments in truck and bus manufacturing.

388.324   SA   ISSN 0258-9281
TRUCK & BUS, SOUTH AFRICA. 1980. m. R.40. Titan Publications (Pty) Ltd., Rodland House, 382 Jan Smuts Av., Craighall 2196, South Africa. Eds. John Marsh, Justin Haler. illus.; circ. 4,000. **Indexed:** Ind.S.A.Per.

388.324   AT   ISSN 0041-3380
TRUCK AND BUS TRANSPORTATION; Australia's leading national road transport fleetowner monthly. 1936. m. Aus.$23 (New Zealand Aus.$47; elsewhere Aus.$53). Shennen Publishing & Publicity Co. Pry. Ltd., 64 Kippax St., Surry Hills, N.S.W. 2010, Australia. TEL 02-211-3411. FAX 02-281-1691. Ed. G.L. Johnson. adv.; bk.rev.; illus.; tr.lit.; index; circ. 15,000. (back issues avail.) **Indexed:** Aus.Rd.Ind., HRIS.

388.324   US
TRUCK & COMMERCE. 1937. q. $4. Associated Motor Carriers of Oklahoma, Inc., Box 14620, Oklahoma City, OK 73113. TEL 405-843-9488. FAX 405-843-7310. Ed. Vince Robison. adv.; charts; illus.; stat.; circ. 3,800 (controlled).
  Formerly: Oklahoma Motor Carrier.

683.88   US
TRUCK & OFF-HIGHWAY INDUSTRIES. 1979. bi-m. $55. Chilton Co., One Chilton Way, Radnor, PA 19089. TEL 215-964-4255. (Subscr. to: Box 2092, Radnor, PA 19089) Ed. John McElroy. adv.; charts; illus.; stat.; circ. 33,000. (also avail. in microfilm from UMI; microfiche from UMI; reprint service avail. from UMI) **Indexed:** ISMEC.
  Formerly: Chilton's Truck and Off-Highway Industries (ISSN 0194-1410)

388.324   CN
TRUCK & TRAILER. 1987. m. Can.$28. New Communications Group, 452 Attwell Dr., Ste. 100, Etobicoke, Ont. M9W 5C3, Canada. TEL 416-798-2977. FAX 416-798-3017. adv.; circ. 39,000.
  Description: Catalog of new and used trucks and trailers available for sale.

388.324   US   ISSN 8756-4041
TRUCK BLUE BOOK LEASE GUIDE. q. $120 includes Truck Identification Book. Maclean Hunter Market Reports, Inc., 29 N. Wacker Dr., Chicago, IL 60606-3297. TEL 312-726-2802. FAX 312-726-2574. (also avail. on diskette; back issues avail.)

TRANSPORTATION — TRUCKS AND TRUCKING

388.324   CN   ISSN 0564-3392
TRUCK DATA BOOK; identification data for all makes and models of trucks found in Canada. 1949. a. Can.$34. Sanford Evans Communications Ltd., 1700 Church Ave., Box 6900, Winnipeg, Man. R3C 3B1, Canada. TEL 204-694-2022. FAX 204-694-3040. Ed. Gary Henry.
   Description: Nine model years listed. Identification and registration data includes, GVW and curb weight, wheelbase, engine stats and vehicle identification number for light, medium and heavy duty trucks. MSR price for light trucks featured.

388.324   US
TRUCK FACTS. bi-m. $3.95 per no. Pace Publications (Milwaukee), 1020 N. Broadway, Ste. 111, Milwaukee, WI 53202. TEL 414-272-8877. FAX 414-272-9973.

388.324   CN
TRUCK FLEET. 1925. m. Can.$26. Southam Business Communications Inc. (Subsidiary of: Southam Inc.), 1450 Don Mills Road, Don Mills, Ont. M3B 2X7, Canada. TEL 416-445-6641. Ed. John Howarth. adv.; illus.; stat.; tr.lit.; circ. 35,000. (also avail. in microform from UMI) **Indexed:** Can.B.P.I.
   Formerly: Bus and Truck Transport (ISSN 0007-635X)
   Description: Information for both for-hire and private trucking companies.

388.324   US   ISSN 0889-3888
TL230.A1
TRUCK IDENTIFICATION BOOK. a. $15. Maclean Hunter Market Reports, Inc., 29 N. Wacker Dr., Chicago, IL 60606-3297. TEL 312-726-2802. FAX 312-726-2574.

388   US
TRUCK NEWS.* m. $7. New York State Motor Truck Association, c/o Motor Carrier NY Welfare Trust, Box 2275, Fort Lee, NJ 07024-0497. circ. 1,800.

388.324   CN   ISSN 0712-2683
TRUCK NEWS. 1980. m. Can.$21.40 (foreign $40). Southam Business Communications Ltd., 1450 Don Mills Rd., Don Mills, Ont. M3B 2X7, Canada. TEL 416-445-6641. FAX 416-461-6243. circ. 40,000.
   Incorporates: Eastern Trucker; Which was formerly: Eastern Western Trucker.
   Description: Covers Canadian truck operators' concerns: regulations, products, events.

388.324   US
TRUCK PAPER. 1981. w. $47. Peed Corporation, Box 85010, Lincoln, NE 68501. TEL 402-477-8900. Ed. Lee Chapin. circ. 550,000. (tabloid format)

388.324   US   ISSN 0895-3856
TRUCK PARTS & SERVICE. 1966. m. $50 (foreign $60). Kona Communications, Inc., 707 Lake Cook Rd., Ste. 300, Deerfield, IL 60015. TEL 708-498-3180. FAX 708-498-3197. Ed. David Zaritz. adv.; circ. controlled.
   Former titles (until Aug. 1987): Heavy-Duty Distribution (ISSN 0191-6777) & Fleet Distribution.
   Description: Covers the truck parts and service market.

338.3 658.8   US
TRUCK SALES & LEASING MAGAZINE. 1983. 6/yr. $30 (free to qualified personnel). Newport Communications East, Inc., 1045 Taylor Ave., Ste. 214, Baltimore, MD 21204. TEL 301-828-1092. FAX 301-828-4099. Ed. David A. Kolman. adv.; bk.rev.; tr.lit.; circ. 20,000.
   Formerly: Heavy Truck Salesman.
   Description: Intended for truck dealer salespersons and leasing company specialists.

388.324   US   ISSN 1047-4366
TRUCK TRADER - CENTERLINE. w. $59. Heartland Communications Group, Inc., 900 Central Ave., Box 916, Fort Dodge, IA 50501. TEL 515-955-1600. FAX 800-247-2000.
   Formerly: Truck Trader.
   Description: Provides communications link between buyers and sellers to provide timely, current information on personnel and equipment supply and demand within the trucking industry.

388.324   US   ISSN 0049-478X
TRUCK TRENDS.* 1963. m. $15. c/o Paul, 5115 N. First St., DeKalb, IL 60115. adv.; stat; circ. 9,500 (controlled).

388.324   CN
▼**TRUCK WEST**. 1990. m. Can.$19.90($39.90) (foreign Can.$49.90). Southam Business Communications Inc. (Winnipeg) (Subsidiary of: Southam Inc.), 1555 Dublin Ave., No.9, Winnipeg, Man. R3E 3M8, Canada. Ed. Andy Zielinski. adv.; circ. 22,000. (tabloid format)

388.324   CN
TRUCK WORLD & WESTERN TRUCKING NEWS. 1984. m. Can.$24. Global Trade Publications Ltd., 11-106 E. 14th St., North Vancouver, B.C. V7L 2N3, Canada. TEL 604-984-2002. FAX 604-984-2820. Ed. Rob Robertson. circ. 30,000. (tabloid format; back issues avail.)
   Formed by the merger of: Truck World; Western Trucking News.

388.324   US
TRUCKERS DIGEST. m. Interface Publishing, Inc., Box 577, Birmingham, AL 35201-0577. TEL 205-822-8035. FAX 205-822-8135.

388.324   US
TRUCKER'S NEWS. 6/yr. National Association of Truck Stop Operators, Box 1285, Alexandria, VA 22313. TEL 703-549-2100.
   Description: Features news and articles of interest to professional truck drivers.

388.324   US
TRUCKERS - U S A. 1984. m. $29. B P S Inc., 1416 Greensboro Ave., Tuscaloosa, AL 35401. TEL 205-758-3070. Ed. Dave Adams. adv.; circ. 75,000.
   Description: Covers manufacturing and industry news and new products.

388.324   US
TRUCKIN'. m. $15. McMullen Publishing, 2145 W. La Palma Ave., Anaheim, CA 92801. TEL 714-635-9040. Ed. Steve Stillwell. adv.; bk.rev.; charts; illus.; circ. 79,312.

388.324   AT   ISSN 0155-9648
TRUCKIN' LIFE; the voice of the Australian truck driver. 1976. m. Aus.$47. Federal Publishing Company, 180 Bourke Rd., Alexandria, N.S.W. 2015, Australia. TEL 07-854-1119. FAX 07-252-3692. Ed. Mark Gibson. adv.; bk.rev.; circ. 31,700. (back issues avail.)
   Description: Highlights innovations in the trucking industry, freight rates and new motor truck models.

388.3   US
TRUCKING PERMIT & TAX BULLETIN. m. $90. J.J. Keller & Associates, Inc., 3003 W. Breezewood Lane, Box 368, Neenah, WI 54957-0368. TEL 414-722-2848. FAX 414-727-7516. Ed.Bd.
   Description: Covers operating authority, vehicle registration and taxes.

388.324   US
TRUCKING PERMIT GUIDE. 1974. irreg., no.78, 1987. $155. J.J. Keller and Associates, Inc., 3003 W. Breezewood Lane, Box 368, Neenah, WI 54957-0368. TEL 800-558-5011. FAX 414-727-7516. Ed. George B. McDowell.
   Description: Descriptions of the Federal Heavy Vehicle Use Tax.

388.324   US
TRUCKING SAFETY GUIDE. 1974. irreg., no.54, 1986. $155. J.J. Keller and Associates, Inc., 3003 W. Breezewood Lane, Box 368, Neenah, WI 54957-0368. TEL 800-558-5011. Ed. George B. McDowell.
   Description: Reference to federal and state safety requirements.

388.324   US   ISSN 0884-8947
TRUCKS. 1986. 6/yr. $17.50. Trucks Magazine Inc., 765 Churchville Rd., Southampton, PA 18966. TEL 215-355-1034. FAX 215-691-1191. Ed. John Stevens. circ. 100,000.
   Description: Dedicated to those who make a living driving long-haul trucks or own fleets of these trucks. Articles focus on health, safety, profitability, government regulations, image, new products and technology.

TRUCKSTOP WORLD. see BUSINESS AND ECONOMICS — Small Business

388.324   US
TRUX. 1949. q. $3. Georgia Motor Trucking Association, 500 Piedmont Ave., N.E., Atlanta, GA 30308. TEL 404-876-4313. Ed. Ernest Quickel. adv.; illus.; circ. 5,000.

388   US
TRUXBOOK. 1947. a. Can.$35. Alberta Trucking Association, P.O. Box 5520, Station A, Calgary, Alta. T2H 1X9, Canada. TEL 403-253-8401. Ed. Chere Ketcheson. adv.; bk.rev.; circ. 1,500.
   Former titles: Alberta Motor Transport Directory; Alberta Shippers Guide.

388.324   CN
TRUXPRESS. 1978. 10/yr. membership. Alberta Trucking Association, Box 5520, Station "A", Calgary, Alta. T2H 1X9, Canada. TEL 403-253-8401. adv.; circ. 800 (controlled).
   Former titles: Pyramid (ISSN 0709-4272); A T A News Bulletin (ISSN 0380-8920); A M T A News Bulletin (ISSN 0044-7161)

388.324   IT
TUTTOTRASPORTI. 11/yr. $40. Editoriale Domus, Via Grandi 5-7, 20089 Rozzano (MI), Italy. TEL 02 82472527. FAX 02-8255033.

U M T R I RESEARCH REVIEW. (University of Michigan, Transportation Research Institute) see TRANSPORTATION — Automobiles

388.324   US
ULTRA TRUCK. q. McMullen Publishing, 2145 W. La Palma Ave., Anaheim, CA 92801. TEL 714-635-9040.

388.324   CN
UPDATE (REXDALE). 1957. bi-w. Can.$400 to non-members. Ontario Trucking Association, 555 Dixon Rd., Rexdale, Ont. M9W 1H8, Canada. TEL 416-249-7401. FAX 416-245-6152. Ed. Rebecka Freels-Torn. adv.; bk.rev.; stat.; tr.lit.; circ. 1,300. (processed)
   Formerly: O T A News Round-up.
   Description: Provides Ontario Trucking Association members, government and industry with weekly information on Ontario truck transport industry.

388.324   US
UTILITY FLEET MANAGEMENT. 1982. 8/yr. $15 (free to qualified utility personnel). Public Utilities Reports, Inc., 2111 Wilson Blvd., Ste. 200, Arlington, VA 22201. TEL 703-243-7000. FAX 703-527-5829. Ed. Nancy Coe Bailey. adv.; bk.rev.; circ. 5,100.
   Formerly: Electric Utility Fleet Management (ISSN 0744-3501)
   Description: Provides information for specifying, purchasing, operating and maintaining cars, trucks, construction and maintenance equipment and tools for the electric, gas, telephone and water utilities.

388.324   US
VEHICLE SIZES AND WEIGHTS MANUAL. 1974. irreg., no.26, 1987. $95. J.J. Keller and Associates, Inc., 3003 W. Breezewood Lane, Box 368, Neenah, WI 54957-0368. TEL 800-558-5011. Ed. George B. McDowell.
   Description: Federal, state and Canadian requirements for overdimensional movements.

388.324   CN   ISSN 0838-5610
VEHICULE DES CONDUCTEURS PROPRIETAIRES. 1986. 10/yr. Can.$35($45) Editions Bomart Ltee., 7493 TransCanada Hwy., Ste. 103, St. Laurent, Que. H4T 1T3, Canada. TEL 514-337-9043. FAX 514-337-1862. Ed. Julie Calve. adv.; circ. 14,580 (controlled). (back issues avail.)
   Description: Offers articles of general scope as well as diversified and practical columns addressing topics of great interest to owner operators.

388.324   US
WEST VIRGINIA TRANSPORTER. vol.29, 1972. m. membership. West Virginia Motor Truck Association, Box 5187, Charleston, WV 25311. TEL 304-345-2800. Ed. Robert E. Stanley. adv.; circ. 1,450.

WESTERN GRAPE REPORT. see BUSINESS AND ECONOMICS — Marketing And Purchasing

WESTERN TRANSPORT. see TRANSPORTATION

TRAVEL AND TOURISM

388.324 629.222 US ISSN 0738-565X
TL230.A1
WHEELS OF TIME. 1980. bi-m. $20 membership. American Truck Historical Society, Box 531168, Birmingham, AL 35253. TEL 205-870-0566. FAX 205-870-3069. adv.; bk.rev.; circ. 13,500.
  Description: Covers the history of trucks, the trucking industry, and its pioneers.

388.324 621 NO
YRKESBIL. 1980. 15/yr. NOK 216. Fagbladforlaget AS, Urtgaten 9, P.O. Box 9247, Vaterland, 0134 Oslo, Norway. TEL 02-680313. FAX 02-682085. Ed. Jorgen Seemann Berg. circ. 32,000.

388.324 PL ISSN 0514-809X
Z M P D. KWARTALNY BIULETYN INFORMACYJNY. 1965. q. free. Zrzeszenie Miedzynarodowych Przewoznikow Drogowych, Grojecka 17, 02-021 Warsaw, Poland. Ed. Boleslaw Rajkowski. circ. controlled. (processed)

TRAVEL AND TOURISM

see also Travel and Tourism—Airline Inflight and Hotel Inroom

910 US
A A A GOING PLACES. 1982. bi-m. membership. Automobile Association of America, A A A Auto Club South, 1515 N. Westshore Blvd., Box 31087, Tampa, FL 33607. TEL 813-289-5923. Ed. Phyllis W. Zeno. adv.; bk.rev.; circ. 850,000. (back issues avail.)
  Description: Directed to AAA members, with AAA news, legislation affecting motorists and travel articles.

910.09 US
A A A MOTORIST OF NORTHEASTERN PENNSYLVANIA. bi-m. American Automobile Association of Northeastern Pennsylvania, 1035 N. Washington Ave., Scranton, PA 18509-2917. TEL 717-348-2513. Ed. Craig H. Smith. circ. 92,000.

910.202 388.3 US ISSN 1051-3701
A A A TODAY (CINCINNATI). 1923. bi-m. membership. American Automobile Association, Cincinnati Division, 15 W. Central Parkway, Cincinnati, OH 45202. FAX 513-762-8741. Ed. Mark Brackney. circ. 170,000.
  Formerly: Motour.

910.09 US
A A A TODAY (POTTSTOWN). bi-m. American Automobile Association, East Penn Motor Club, 95 S. Hanover St., Pottstown, PA 19464. TEL 215-323-6300. FAX 215-323-6684. Ed. Franklin Mann. circ. 32,500.

A A A TODAY MAGAZINE. (American Automobile Association) see TRANSPORTATION — Automobiles

910.09 US
A A A TRAVEL TOPICS. 5/yr. American Automobile Association, Central Pennsylvania Automobile Club, 2023 Market St., Harrisburg, PA 17103-2531. TEL 717-236-4021. Ed. Thomas G. Miller. circ. 80,000.

614.86 388.3 US
A A A TRAVELER (YORK). 1930. q. $6. A A A Southern Pennsylvania, Mid-State Auto Club, 118 E. Market St., Box 2387, York, PA 17405. TEL 717-845-7676. Ed. Kevin A. Forsythe. adv.; illus.; circ. 124,000.
  Former titles: Motorist; Johnstown Motorist (ISSN 0047-2042); White Rose Motorist. South Penn Traveler (US 0273-8147); South Penn Motorist (US 0038-3503).

A A A WORLD (HEATHROW). (American Automobile Association) see TRANSPORTATION — Automobiles

796.7 US ISSN 0277-1004
A A A WORLD: WISCONSIN EDITION. 1937. bi-m. $4 to non-members (foreign $7). American Automobile Association, A A A Wisconsin, Box 33, Madison, WI 53701-0033. TEL 608-828-2486. FAX 608-828-2443. Ed. Ernest Stetenfeld. adv.; bk.rev.; charts; illus.; circ. 251,335.
  Former titles: A A A Traveler (Madison) (ISSN 0162-3591); Wisconsin A A A Motor News (ISSN 0043-6348).

910 UK
A B C AIR TRAVEL ATLAS. 1979. s-a. £23. Reed Travel Group (Subsidiary of: Reed International PLC), Church St., Dunstable, Bedfordshire LU5 4HB, England. TEL 0582-600111. TELEX 82168-AIRABC-G. Ed. Mary Marchant. adv.; charts; circ. 15,000.
  Description: Maps of major domestic and international flights, time zones, country, city and state codes and airline designators.

910 UK ISSN 0141-6278
A B C GUIDE TO INTERNATIONAL TRAVEL. q. £30. Reed Travel Group (Subsidiary of: Reed International PLC), Church St., Dunstable, Bedfordshire LU5 4HB, England. TEL 0582-600111. TELEX 82168-AIRABC-G. Ed. Ken Smith. adv.; circ. 8,000. —BLDSC shelfmark: 0537.756900.
  Description: Focuses on passport controls, visa regulations, vaccination requirements, currency regulation and import allowances.

910 UK
A B C HOLIDAY GUIDE. 1970. a. Reed Travel Group (Subsidiary of: Reed International PLC), Church St., Dustable, Bedfordshire LU5 4HB, England. TEL 0582-600111. TELEX 82168-AIRABC-G. Ed. Piero Selo.
  Formerly (until 1972): Holiday Guide.

910.09 UK
A B C STAR SERVICE. 1960. base vol. (plus q. supplements). £165. Reed Travel Group (Subsidiary of: Reed International PLC), Church St., Dunstable, Bedfordshire LU5 4HB, England. TEL 0582-600111. TELEX 82168-AIRABC-G. Ed. Steven R. Gordon. circ. 8,000. (looseleaf format)
  Formerly: S T A R Service.
  Description: Provides critical reviews of hotel properties and cruise ships throughout the world written by independent travel writers.

910.09 UK
A B C TRAVEL DIRECTORY. 2/yr. £55. Reed Travel Group (Subsidiary of: Reed International PLC), Church St., Dunstable, Bedfordshire LU5 4HB, England. TEL 0582-600111. TELEX 82168-AIRABC-G. Ed. Alison Barker.
  Formerly: Travel Directory.

A B C WORLD AIRWAYS GUIDE. see TRANSPORTATION — Air Transport

A C E LENKRAD. (Auto Club Europa e.V.) see TRANSPORTATION — Automobiles

A C T A OFFICIAL ANNUAL DIRECTORY. (Allied Canadian Travel Agents) see BUSINESS AND ECONOMICS — Trade And Industrial Directories

910.202 GW
A D A C ATLAS DEUTSCHLAND - EUROPA. a. DM.48. (Allgemeiner Deutscher Automobil-Club e.V.) A D A C Verlag GmbH, Am Westpark 8, Postfach 700126, 8000 Munich 70, Germany. TEL 089-7676-0.

A D A C CAMPINGFUEHRER. BAND 1: SUEDEUROPA. (Allgemeiner Deutscher Automobil-Club e.V.) see SPORTS AND GAMES — Outdoor Life

A D A C CAMPINGFUEHRER. BAND 2: DEUTSCHLAND, MITTEL- UND NORDEUROPA. (Allgemeiner Deutscher Automobil-Club e.V.) see SPORTS AND GAMES — Outdoor Life

A D A C HANDBUCH: REISERECHT ENTSCHEIDUNGEN. (Allgemeiner Deutscher Automobil-Club e.V.) see LAW

A D A C HANDBUCH: UNFALL IM AUSLAND - SCHADENSREGULIERUNG. see LAW

A D A C HANDBUCH: UNFALL RATGEBER. see LAW

A D A C MOTORWELT. see TRANSPORTATION — Automobiles

910.202 GW
A D A C SKIATLAS. a. DM.48. (Allgemeiner Deutscher Automobil Club e.V.) A D A C Verlag GmbH, Am Westpark 8, Postfach 700126, 8000 Munich 70, Germany. TEL 089-7676-0.

910.4 MX
A I M. (Adventures in Mexico Newsletter); a newsletter on retirement and travel in Mexico. 1974. bi-m. $16. AIM, S.A., Apdo. Postal 31-70, Guadalajara, Jalisco, Mexico. Ed. J.W. Wilkins. circ. 2,000.

387.7 US
A P A HOLIDAY.* 1970. 6/yr. $1. (Airline Passengers Association) Curtis Publishing Co., 1000 Waterway Blvd., Indianapolis, IA 46202-2191. TEL 317-634-1100. Ed. Carole Story. adv.; charts; illus.; circ. 75,000.
  Former titles (until fall 1976): APAce; (until spring 1976): Airline Passengers Association News (ISSN 0044-7013)

910 US
A S U TRAVEL GUIDE. (Airline Service Unlimited); the airline employee's discount directory. 1970. q. $31.95. A S U Travel Guide, Inc., 1525 E. Francisco Blvd., San Rafael, CA 94901. TEL 415-459-0300. FAX 415-459-0494. Ed. Christopher Gil. adv.; circ. 61,000.
  Formerly: Interline Tour Guide.

910.4 AU
A T P; Branchen und Presseinformationsdienst. 1975. bi-w. S.390. A T P Zeitungsverlags GmbH, Seidengasse 32-1-17, 1070 Vienna, Austria. TEL 936386. FAX 5266116. circ. 2,000.

A V D AUTO BORDBUCH. see TRANSPORTATION — Automobiles

910.202 US
A Y H DISCOVERY TOURS. 1984. a. free. American Youth Hostels, Inc., Box 37613, Washington, DC 20013-7613. TEL 202-783-6161. FAX 202-783-6171. circ. 100,000.
  Formerly: World Adventure Trip Catalogue.
  Description: Provides complete information (price, itineraries, departures) of 30 different cycling, hiking and motor trips offered by AYH.

910.09 GW ISSN 0935-0454
A Z U R CAMPING MAGAZIN. 1987. s-a. free. A Z U R Freizeit GmbH, Rohrackerstr. 272, 7000 Stuttgart 61, Germany. TEL 0711-427023. FAX 0711-427030. adv.; bk.rev.; index; circ. 70,000. (back issues avail.)
  Description: News about camping in Europe, about campers and carvans.

910.09 GW ISSN 0176-5388
ABENTEUER & REISEN; Das Erlebnis-Magazin. 1981. m. DM.79.60 (foreign DM.96). W D V Wirtschaftsdienst, Lange Strasse 13, 6000 Frankfurt a.M. 1, Germany. TEL 069-29907-0. Ed. Wolfgang C. Ehrnsperger. circ. 100,000.

914.204 UK
ABOUT LONDON. 1976. m. free. About London Publications, 60-62 Westbourne Terrace, London W2 3UJ, England. Ed. Vass Anderson. adv.

917 UK
ABROAD; the P & O European ferries magazine. Variant title: All Abroad with P & O European Ferries. 1982. 3/yr. Media Mart Publishing International Ltd., 35 Greese St., Rathbone Pl., London W1P 1PN, England. TEL 071-580-3105. Ed. Beverly Howell. adv.; circ. 1,500,000.
  Formerly: All Abroad.
  Description: Shipboard magazine with news about ships and travel features.

915.6 TS
ABU DHABI NEWS. (Text in English) w. Department of Information and Tourism, Abu Dhabi, United Arab Emirates.

910.2 MC ISSN 0001-4060
ACADEMIE INTERNATIONALE DU TOURISME. REVUE. 1951. q. 120 F.($12) Academie Internationale du Tourisme, 9, rue Princess Marie de Lorraine, Monte Carlo, Monaco. (Co-sponsor: Editions Nagel (Geneva)) adv.; bk.rev.; illus.; circ. 1,000.

917.204 US
ACAPULCO (YEAR). a. $10. Harper Collins Publishers, Birnbaum Travel Guides, 10 E. 53rd St., New York, NY 10022-5299. TEL 212-207-7000. illus.; index.

TRAVEL AND TOURISM

910.4   SI   ISSN 0217-5851
ACCENT. (Text in English) 1983. m. free. World Publishing Pte Ltd., 119 Tong Xing Complex, Ubi Ave. 4, Singapore 1440, Singapore. TEL 65-747-8088. FAX 65-747-9119. Ed. Teng Juat Leng. adv.; bk.rev.; film rev.; play rev.; abstr. (back issues avail.)
    Description: Covers executive lifestyle, arts, gourmet, sports and management topics.

910.09   US
ACCENT WEST AMARILLO; chronicle of the Southwestern lifestyle. m. $14.98. Accent West, Inc., Box 1504, Amarillo, TX 79105. TEL 806-359-6801. Ed. Don Cantrell.
    Description: Covers city and regional issues for Amarillo and Texas, focusing on the lifestyle of middle to upper income adults.

647   AT
ACCOMMODATION AUSTRALIA. 1984. s-a. Aus.$10 to non members; members Aus.$4. R A C V, 550 Princes Highway, Noble Park, Vic. 3174, Australia. TEL 03-790-2646. FAX 03-790-2844. Ed. A. Bowes. circ. 90,000.
    Formerly: Australian National Tourguide.

919.4   AT
ACCOMMODATION DIRECTORY. 1957. s-a. membership. National Roads and Motorists Association, 151 Clarence St., Sydney N.S.W. 2000, Australia.

ACCOMMODATOR; the magazine of Ontario's hospitality industry. see *HOTELS AND RESTAURANTS*

910.09   PL   ISSN 0860-1119
ACTA UNIVERSITATIS LODZIENSIS: TURYZM. (Text in Polish; summaries in English, French) 1985; N.S. 1988. irreg. Wydawnictwo Uniwersytetu Lodzkiego, Ul. Jaracza 34, Lodz, Poland. (Dist. by: Ars Polona-Ruch, Krakowskie Przedmiescie 7, Warsaw, Poland)

ADIRONDACK LIFE. see *SPORTS AND GAMES — Outdoor Life*

910.202   UK   ISSN 0143-389X
GV191.35
ADVENTURE HOLIDAYS. 1978. a. $12.95. Vacation-Work, 9 Park End St., Oxford OX1 1HJ, England. (Dist. in U.S. by: Peterson's Guides, 202 Carnegie Ctr., Princeton, NJ 08543-2123) Ed. Victoria Pybus. circ. 10,000.

333.78   ISSN 0001-8805
ADVENTURE ROAD. 1964. q. $5 to non-members. Amoco Enterprises, Inc., Amoco Motor Club, 200 E. Randolph Dr., Chicago, IL 60601-0607. TEL 312-856-2583. FAX 312-856-2379. Ed. Marilyn Holstein. adv.; bk.rev.; illus.; tr.lit.; circ. 1,500,000 (controlled).

910.09   US
ADVENTURE TRAVEL. 1987. s-a. $3.95 per no. Rodale Press, Inc., 33 E. Minor St., Emmaus, PA 18098. TEL 215-967-5171. Ed. Bob Woodward. circ. 160,000.

910   US
ADVENTURE TRAVEL NORTH AMERICA. 1972. biennial. $18. Adventure Guides, Inc., Box 698, Newfoundland, NJ 07438. TEL 602-596-0226. FAX 201-697-1520. Ed. Pat Dickerman. **Indexed:** Access.
    Former titles: Adventure Travel (New York) (ISSN 0195-8445); (until 1976): Adventure Trip Guide (ISSN 0084-5965)

910.202   US
ADVISOR (MITCHELL). w. M. Johnson, Ed. & Pub., Box 343, Mitchell, SD 57301. TEL 605-996-8916.

AFANGAR; outdoor living and Icelandic nature. see *SPORTS AND GAMES — Outdoor Life*

968.9 916   RH
AFRICA CALLS WORLDWIDE. 1961. bi-m. Z.$20($22.50) Modus Publications, P.O. Box 66070, Kopje, Harare, Zimbabwe. TEL 738722. FAX 707130. TELEX 26334 MODUS ZW. Ed. Jethro Goko. adv.; bk.rev.; illus.; circ. 6,000.
    Formerly: Africa Calls From Zimbabwe; Africa Calls; Rhodesia Calls (ISSN 0035-4708)

910   US   ISSN 0194-4584
AFRICA UPDATE; the international business and travel magazine. 1978. s-a. $10. c/o Africa Travel Association, 347 Fifth Ave., Ste. 610, New York, NY 10016. Eds. Karen Hoffman, Frank Rossi.

910.09   CN
AGENDA WORLD. 1989. q. $175 (foreign $200). Agenda World, P.O. Box 146, Pointe-Claire, Que. H9R 4N9, Canada. TEL 514-694-8908. FAX 514-426-8447. adv.; circ. 10,000.
    Formerly (until July 1990): World Agenda.
    Description: Lists 1500 events, organizers and locations of congresses, conferences, conventions, exhibitions, fairs and trade shows.

917.1   CN   ISSN 0834-0471
AGENT CANADA; a weekly travel & tourism trade magazine. 1978. w. Can.$47.30($69.10) Agent West Group, 1534 W.Second Ave., Ste. 300, Vancouver, B.C. V6J 1H2, Canada. TEL 604-731-0481. Ed. Douglas W. Keough. adv.; bk.rev.; circ. 13,000.
    Former titles: Agent West Weekly (ISSN 0225-4565); Agent West Traveletter.

AGENT DE VOYAGES; defense et soutien de la profession. see *OCCUPATIONS AND CAREERS*

910.202   CN
AGENT ONTARIO. w. Agent West Group, 1534 W. Second Ave., Ste. 300, Vancouver, B.C. V6J 1H2, Canada. TEL 604-731-0481. Ed. Geoff Deane. circ. 4,732.

AGENT'S HOTEL GAZETTEER: AMERICA. see *HOTELS AND RESTAURANTS*

AGENT'S HOTEL GAZETTEER: RESORTS OF EUROPE. see *HOTELS AND RESTAURANTS*

910   SP
AGENTTRAVEL. (Supplement avail. m.: Empresas y Empresarios) 1987. m. 10000 ptas.($130) (effective 1991). Ediciones Jaguar, C. Conde de Romanones, 9, 28012 Madrid, Spain. adv.; index; circ. 10,000.

910.2   IT   ISSN 0002-0869
AGENZIA DI VIAGGI; quotidiano di notizie di interesse professionale. 1965. 6/w. L.50000($33) Editrice Turistica s.r.l., Via Rasella, 155, 00187 Rome, Italy. TEL 4821539. FAX 4826721. TELEX 621684 ADUGAU. Ed. Alberto Garlanda. adv.; illus.; circ. 12,000. (tabloid format)

910.2   IT   ISSN 0002-0893
AGENZIA NAZIONALE INFORMAZIONI TURISTICHE. 1954. w. L.50000($80) Alberto Calcagno, Ed. & Pub., Viale Somalia 9, Rome, Italy. circ. 950.

910.09   US
AIR TRAVEL JOURNAL. 1971. s-m. $40. Air Travel Publications, One Harborside Dr. E., Boston, MA 02128. TEL 617-561-4000. Ed. Robert H. Weiss. adv.; circ. 15,000.
    Description: Covers news of Logan International Airport in Boston. Includes news of the Massachusetts port authority, airlines and regional events.

917.904   US
AIRCAL. 1967. m. $36. (Air California) Halsey Publishing Co., 12955 Biscayne Blvd., No. 202, No. Miami, FL 33181. TEL 305-893-1520. Ed. Steve Winston. adv.; bk.rev.; illus.; circ. 60,000.
    Former titles: AirCal Magazine (ISSN 0733-4567) & Air California Magazine (ISSN 0195-8062)

387.7 910.202   US   ISSN 0894-1513
AIRPORT POCKET GUIDE; a publication to aid air travelers. 1985. q. $45.95 (Mexico and Canada $43.95; elsewhere $59.95). A M Data Services, Inc., 67 S. Bedford St., Ste. 400W, Burlington, MA 01803. TEL 617-229-5853. FAX 617-272-0558. TELEX 948230. Ed. Andy Migliorini. illus.; circ. 2,000.
    Description: Information resource of 200 US airports; includes airport terminal diagram for 82 of the busiest airports. Diagrams show gate assignments, location of airport services and other helpful travel information.

AKTUEL BILSPORT. see *TRANSPORTATION — Automobiles*

910.202   US
ALABAMA BOOK OF SURPRISES. q. free. Bureau of Tourism and Travel, 401 Adam Ave., Box 4309, Montgomery, AL 36103-4309. FAX 205-242-4554.

910.202   US
ALABAMA TOURIST GUIDE. q. Bureau of Tourism and Travel, 401 Adam Ave., Box 4309, Montgomery, AL 36103-4309. FAX 205-242-4554.
    Formerly: Travel in Alabama.

ALASKA ALMANAC. see *ENCYCLOPEDIAS AND GENERAL ALMANACS*

910.202   US   ISSN 0888-8884
F902.3
ALASKA WILDERNESS MILEPOST. 1986. biennial. $14.95. Alaska Northwest Books (Subsidiary of: G T E Discovery Publications), Box 3007, Bothell, WA 98041. TEL 206-487-6100. FAX 206-486-7296. Ed. Kris Valencia. adv.; charts; illus.; stat.; circ. 15,000.
    Description: Travel guide to those parts of Alaska not accessible by road.

917.9   US
ALL ABOUT ARIZONA, THE HEALTHFUL STATE. biennial. $5.95. Harian Publications, One Vernon Ave., Floral Park, NY 11001. TEL 516-437-3440. Ed. Thomas B. Lesure.

910.202   HK   ISSN 0072-4939
DS504
ALL-ASIA GUIDE. 1961. biennial, latest 15th ed. $19.50. Review Publishing Co. Ltd., G.P.O. Box 160, Hong Kong. TEL 852-832-8300. FAX 852-834-6051. TELEX 62497 REVAD HX. Ed. Mitchell A. Klaif. adv.
    Formerly: Golden Guide to South and East Asia.
    Description: Covers custom and visa procedures, hotels, restaurants, and history and culture of Asian countries.

910.09 917   US   ISSN 0533-0653
ALL OF MEXICO AT LOW COST. biennial. $3.45. Harian Publications, One Vernon Ave., Floral Park, NY 11001. TEL 516-437-3440. Ed. Norman D. Ford. charts.

919.4   AT
ALL STATES TOURIST PARK GUIDE. 1948. a. Aus.$3.25. Syme Magazines (Subsidiary of: Syme Media Pty. Ltd.), G.P.O. Box 628E, Melbourne, Vic. 3000, Australia.

ALLES UEBER WEIN. see *FOOD AND FOOD INDUSTRIES*

914.404   FR
ALLIER MAGAZINE; magazines de France. 1967. m. 280 F. Editions Rene Dessagne, 11 rue Pierre Leroux, B.P. 90, 87000 Limoges cedex, France. TEL 55-77-25-97. Ed. Rene Dessagne. adv.

914.4   FR
ALLO PARIS. 1957. w. B.I.E.P., 3, rue Tronchet, 75008, Paris, France. adv.; circ. 35,000.

915   US   ISSN 0147-5436
DU620
ALOHA; the magazine of Hawaii and the Pacific. 1977. bi-m. $17.97. Davick Publications, Inc., 49 S. Hotel St., St. 309, Honolulu, HI 96313. TEL 808-523-9871. FAX 808-533-2055. Ed. C. Tsutsumi. adv.; bk.rev.; circ. 65,000. (also avail. in microform from UMI)
    Formerly: Pacific.

388   FR   ISSN 0767-8444
ALSACE AUTOMOBILE. 1927. m. 55 F. to non-members; members 35 F. Automobile-Club d'Alsace, 5 av. de la Paix, 67000 Strasbourg, France. TEL 88-360-434. FAX 88-36-00-63. Ed. R. Braun. adv.; bk.rev.; illus.; circ. 55,000.
    Description: Covers all aspects of vehicular transportation, including profiles of cars, car insurance, recreational driving, etc.

AM-CAN REPORT; marketing & trade journal. see *BUSINESS AND ECONOMICS — Marketing And Purchasing*

917   US   ISSN 0569-1966
AMERICA BY CAR. 1958. biennial. $4.95. Harian Publications, One Vernon Ave., Floral Park, NY 11001. TEL 516-437-3440. Ed. Norman D. Ford.

4752 TRAVEL AND TOURISM

917.304 US
AMERICAN HOLIDAY AND LIFE. bi-m. A T L Publishing, Inc., 237 E. 39th St., New York, NY 10016. TEL 212-983-6100. Ed. Louis Montesano. adv.: B&W page $4400; color page $5650; trim 8 3/4 x 11 1/2. circ. 100,000.

910.09 US ISSN 0098-4981
DP501
AMERICAN PORTUGUESE SOCIETY. JOURNAL. 1966. 2/yr. free. American Portuguese Society, Inc., 555 Madison Ave., New York, NY 10022. Ed.Bd. adv.; bk.rev.; circ. 1,000. Key Title: Journal of the American Portuguese Society.
  Formerly: American Portuguese Cultural Society. Journal (ISSN 0003-0570)

910.202 US
AMERICAN URBAN GUIDENOTES; the newsletter of guidebooks. 1979. q. $10. American Urban Guides, Box 186, Washington, DC 20044. TEL 202-667-1357. Ed. John Fondersmith. bk.rev.; circ. 200. (back issues avail.) **Indexed:** Avery Ind.Archit.Per.

AMERICA'S CUP DEFENSE. see SPORTS AND GAMES

910.202 917.04 US
AMERICA'S FAVORITE NATIONAL PARKS. a. $4.95. Prentice Hall Press (Subsidiary of: Simon & Schuster), One Gulf & Western Plaza, New York, NY 10023. TEL 212-373-8500. illus.

AMISTAD. see HISTORY — History Of North And South America

910.09 US
AMOCO TRAVELER. 1981. q. membership. (Amoco Travel Club) Amoco Enterprises, Inc., 200 E. Randolph Dr., Chicago, IL 60601. TEL 212-303-6987. FAX 312-856-2379. Ed. Marilyn Holstein. circ. 75,000 (controlled).

910 US ISSN 0884-7622
ANDREW HARPER'S HIDEAWAY REPORT; a connoisseur's guide to peaceful and unspoiled places. 1979. 12/yr. $90. Harper Associates, Inc., Box 50, Sun Valley, ID 83353. TEL 208-622-3183. (Subscr. to: Box 300, Whitefish, MT 59937) Ed. Andrew Harper. bk.rev.; illus.; index; circ. 16,500. (back issues avail.)

915.9 PH
ANG PHILIPINAS: YOUR TOURIST MAGAZINE.* 4/yr. Bureau of Tourism Promotion, Ministry of Tourism, Tourism Bldg. 3F, TM Kalaw St. Ermita, Manila, Philippines.

914.2 IE
ANGLING HOLIDAYS IN IRELAND. (Text in English and French) 1986. a. $5. Libra House Ltd., P.O. Box 1127, Dublin 8, Ireland. TEL 01-542717. Ed. Cathal Tyrrell. illus.; circ. 15,440.
  Description: Details of facilities and species of fish available at locations throughout Ireland.

910.09 US ISSN 0160-7383
G155.A1
ANNALS OF TOURISM RESEARCH; a social sciences journal. (Text in English; summaries in French) 1982. q. £140 (effective 1992). Pergamon Press, Inc., Journals Division, 660 WHite Plains Rd., Tarrytown, NY 10591-5153. TEL 914-524-9200. FAX 914-333-2444. (And: Headington Hill Hall, Oxford OX3 0BW, England. TEL 0865-794141) Ed. Jafar Jafari. adv.; bk.rev.; film rev.; index; circ. 1,200. (also avail. in microform; back issues avail.) **Indexed:** Abstr.Anthropol., Commun.Abstr., Curr.Cont., E.I., Geo.Abstr., I D A, P.A.I.S., Rural Recreat.Tour.Abstr., Sociol.Abstr., Sportsearch (1979-), SSCI, World Agri.Econ.& Rural Sociol.Abstr. —BLDSC shelfmark: 1044.800000.
  Description: Provides a forum for academic perspectives on tourism.
  Refereed Serial

ANNUAIRE SOUVENIR NORMAND. see HISTORY — History Of Europe

914.504 IT
ANNUARIO GENERALE DELLE IMPRESE DI VIAGGIO E TURISMO. 1970. a. L.8000. Advertising Master Publisher (A.M.P.), Giacomo Spartaco Bertoletti & C. s.a.s., Via Natale Battaglia 27, 20127 Milan, Italy. adv.; circ. 10,000.

ANTARCTIC; a news bulletin. see GEOGRAPHY

914 UK
APARTMENT GAZETTEER (EUROPE). a. £17. C.H.G. Travel Publications, Waterside House, West Common, Gerrards Cross, Bucks, England.

APPALACHIAN HERITAGE; a magazine of southern Appalachian life and culture. see GENERAL INTEREST PERIODICALS — United States

917.204 HO
AQUI Y AHORA. 1976. q. Secretaria de Cultura, Turismo e Informacion, Oficina Central de Informacion, Tegucigalpa, Honduras. illus. (tabloid format)

910 959.9 PH
ARCHIPELAGO. 1974. m. P.100($12.50) Department of Public Information, c/o Bureau of National and Foreign Information, U P L Building, Box 3396, Intramuros, Manila, Philippines. Ed. Lorenzo B. Cruz. adv.; illus.; circ. 5,000.

910 CU
ARENATURIST. 1972. a. free. Arenaturist, Pula, Croatia. Ed. Marijan Fistrovic.

388.3 US
ARIZONA A A A HIGHROADS. 1968. bi-m. $2 to non-members. Arizona Automobile Association, Box 33119, Phoenix, AZ 85067. TEL 602-274-1116. FAX 602-277-1194. Ed. Rebecca Zheng. adv.; circ. 210,000.

917 US ISSN 0004-1521
TE24.A6 CODEN: AZHIAW
ARIZONA HIGHWAYS. 1925. m. $17 (foreign $21). Department of Transportation, 2039 W. Lewis Ave., Phoenix, AZ 85009. TEL 602-258-6641. FAX 602-254-4505. Ed. Robert J. Early. bk.rev.; circ. 420,000. **Indexed:** Access (1975-), Chic.Per.Ind., GeoRef., Mag.Ind., PMR. —BLDSC shelfmark: 1668.438000.
  Description: Encourages tourist travel throughout Arizona. Contains articles on Southwest history, nature, travel, personalities, Native American art and archeology.

338.4 US
ARKANSAS TRAVEL AND TOURISM REPORT. 1972. a. free. Department of Parks and Tourism, Tourism Division, One Capitol Mall, Little Rock, AR 72201. TEL 501-682-7777. Ed. Charles McLemore. illus.; circ. 900.
  Formerly: Tourism in Arkansas. Activity Report.

910.202 HK
▼**ARRIVAL.** 1990. 12/yr. $65 for Asia; elsewhere $75. Far East Trade Press Ltd., Kai Tak Commercial Bldg., 2nd Fl., 717 Des Voeux Rd., Central, Hong Kong. TEL 545-3028. FAX 544-6979. Ed. Renate Boerner. circ. 28,027.
  Description: Corporate business travel magazine.

910.09 US
ARRIVE. q. $12.50. Arrive Publications, Inc., 985 Lincoln Ave., Benicia, CA 94510. Ed. Shirley G. Ray.

910.09 US ISSN 1045-3881
DS10
▼**ASIA PACIFIC TRAVEL;** your guide to Asia & the Pacific Rim. 1990. bi-m. $15 (foreign $30). Publishing Today (Subsidiary of: Health World Magazine, Inc.), 1540 Gilbreth Rd., Burlingame, CA 94010. TEL 415-697-8038. FAX 415-697-7937.

915.04 SI ISSN 0255-7320
ASIA TRAVEL TRADE. 1969. m. $40. Interasia Publications, Ltd., 190 Middle Rd., No.11-01 Fortune Centre, Singapore 0718, Singapore. TEL 339-7622. FAX 339-8521. TELEX RS 36252 RSASIA. (And: 200 Lockhart Rd., 14th Fl., Hong Kong. TEL 852-74-9317) Ed. Hwu Chen Ju. adv.; bk.rev.; illus.; circ. 15,000 (paid); 14,300(controlled).
  Description: Covers the economics and politics of tourism in the Asia-Pacific region.

910.202 US
AT THE PARK. m. Yellow Dot Publishing, Box 597783, Chicago, IL 60659-7783. TEL 312-564-4880. Ed. Allen Ambrosini.

914.9 410 GR ISSN 1011-8993
ATHENIAN; Greece's English language monthly. (Text in English) 1974. m. $38. Athenian Press Ltd., 4 Peta St., Plaka, 105 58 Athens, Greece. TEL 322-2802. FAX 322-3052. Ed. Sloane Elliott. adv.; bk.rev.; film rev.; play rev.; bibl.; illus.; circ. 10,000. (back issues avail.)
  Description: Provides coverage of cultural and political events, as well as information of interest to tourists.

ATLANTE. see GEOGRAPHY

ATLANTIC CITY MAGAZINE. see GENERAL INTEREST PERIODICALS — United States

910 FR
ATLAS - AIR FRANCE; geographie physique et humaine - decouverte de l'homme et de la nature. (Text in English, French) 1982? m. 99 F. Editions Atlas, 89 rue de Boetie, 75008 Paris, France. TEL 45-63-04-14. Ed. Guy Gouezel. adv.; circ. 730,000.
  Former titles: Atlas (Paris, 1960) (ISSN 0004-6922); Atlas Histoire (ISSN 0519-3273)

663.2 US ISSN 0739-3733
ATTERBURY LETTER - WINE, DINING & TRAVEL. 1977. 6/yr. $15. Atterbury Letter, Box 1197, Bethel Is., CA 94511. TEL 415-684-3142. Ed. Kirby Atterbury. bk.rev.; circ. 1,000. (looseleaf format)
  Description: Recommendations, reviews and anecdotes on food, wine and travel.

647 AT
ATTRACTIONS AUSTRALIA. 1988. a. Aus.$6 to non-members; members Aus.$3. R A C V, 550 Princess Highway, Noble Park, VIC 3174, Australia. TEL 03-790-2646. FAX 03-790-2844. TELEX AA 30788. Ed. A. Bowes. adv.; circ. 80,000.
  Formerly: R A C V's Out and About.

910 IT
ATTRAVERSO IL MONDO. q. L.14000. Fouring Periodici s.r.l., Corso Italia 10, Milan, Italy. TEL 02-852673. FAX 02-58300315. TELEX 312476 TCIADM1. Ed. Raffaella Fiory Ceccopieri.

910.2 FR ISSN 0004-7392
AUBERGE DE LA JEUNESSE. 1932. m. 2.50 F. Ligue Francaise pour les Auberges de la Jeunesse, 38 Bd. Raspail, 75007 Paris, France. TEL 1-45-48-69-84.

914 GW ISSN 0004-7961
AUGSBURGER KULTURNACHRICHTEN. 1948. m. DM.30. Kulturreferat, Maximilianstr. 4, 8900 Augsburg, Germany. FAX 0821-324-2765. adv.; illus.; circ. 13,000. (also avail. in microform)

AUSTRALASIAN BUS AND COACH; the management magazine for bus and coach operators. see TRANSPORTATION

919.4 AT
AUSTRALIAN ACCOMMODATION GUIDE. 1963. a. $1. Royal Automobile Association of South Australia Inc., 41 Hindmarsh Sqe., Adelaide, S.A. 5000, Australia. (Co-sponsor: Royal Automobile Club of Victoria) adv.; circ. 120,000.
  Formerly: Royal Automobile Association of South Australia. Accommodation Guide (ISSN 0085-5782)

AUSTRALIAN-AMERICAN NEWS N.S.W. ANNUAL EDITION. see POLITICAL SCIENCE — International Relations

388.346 AT
AUSTRALIAN CARAVAN WORLD AND OUTDOOR LIFE. 1970. m. Aus.$28.60. Syme Magazines (Subsidiary of: Syme Media Pty. Ltd.), G.P.O. Box 628E, Melbourne, Vic. 3000, Australia. TEL 03-601-4222. Ed. Gwen Hasler. adv.; charts; illus.; circ. 20,000.
  Former titles: Australian Caravan World and Camper Trailering; Australian Caravan World.
  Description: News about driving and camping in Australia.

910.09 US
AUSTRALIAN EXPATRIATE. 1989. bi-m. $13.50. 143 S. Cedros Ave., Ste. B202, Solana Beach, CA 92075. TEL 619-793-3694. FAX 619-793-7736. Ed. Elizabeth Kemmis. adv.; bk.rev.; film rev.illus.; circ. 8,000.
  Description: Covers subjects about Australia relating to current events, travel, immigration, economics, art, theatre, music and sports.

TRAVEL AND TOURISM

AUSTRALIAN HOTELIER. see *HOTELS AND RESTAURANTS*

919.4   AT
AUSTRALIAN TOURIST COMMISSION. ANNUAL REPORT. 1968. a. free. Australian Tourist Commission, Level 3, 80 William St., Woolloomooloo, Sydney, N.S.W. 2011, Australia. TEL 02 360 1111. FAX 02-331-4809. TELEX 22322. adv.; bk.rev.; illus.; stat.

AUSTRALIAN WAY. see *TRANSPORTATION — Air Transport*

990.04   AT
AUSTRALIEN KURIER; Australische Monatszeitung. (Text in German) 1984. m. Aus.$32. Europa Kurier Publishing Group, 1-3 Seddon St., Bankstown, N.S.W. 2200, Australia. TEL 02-707-4999. FAX 02-708-6025. (Dist. by: Unipress GmbH, Rosental 3, 8000 Munich 2, Germany. TEL 089-2609014) Ed. John Jakobi. adv.: B&W page Aus.$1600. bk.rev.; circ. 5,000. (back issues avail.)
   Description: Current information about Australia.

796.5 910.202   IT
AUTO CARAVAN NOTIZIE. 1975. m. L.32000 (foreign L.60000). Crisalide Editrice, Via Brusuglio 66, 20161 Milan, Italy. TEL 6464663. Ed. Bianca Carretto. adv.; bk.rev.; circ. 60,000.
   Formerly: Caravan Notizie.

AUTO-JOURNAL. see *TRANSPORTATION — Automobiles*

AUTO TOURING; die Oesterreichische Kraftfahrzeug-Zeitung. see *TRANSPORTATION — Automobiles*

910.2   GW   ISSN 0045-1010
AUTO UND REISE. 1953. m. DM.30. Auto und Reise GmbH Verlag und Wirtschaftsdienst, Oberntieferstr. 20, Postfach 440, 8532 Bad Windsheim, Germany. TEL 09841-409-0. FAX 09841-7033. TELEX 61876-KVDB-D. Ed. Josef Harrer. adv.; bk.rev.; illus.; stat.; tr.lit.; circ. 120,000.
   Formerly: Kraftfahrervereinigung Deutscher Beamter E.V. K V D B Mitteilungen.

910   FI   ISSN 0355-2896
AUTOLLA ULKOMAILLE. 1965. a. FIM 30. Autoliitto - Automobile and Touring Club of Finland, Kansakoulukatu 10, 00100 Helsinki, Finland. Ed. Reijo Kaukinen. adv.; circ. 10,000.
   Formerly: Kansainvalinen Automatkailu (ISSN 0075-4900)

910.09   UK
AUTOMOBILE ASSOCIATION MEMBERS HANDBOOK. biennial. free to AA members. Automobile Association, Fanum House, Basingstoke, Hants RG21 2EA, England. TEL 0256-20123. FAX 0256-22575. circ. 4,000,000.
   Description: Covers services offered by the association, garage and hotel facilities, road-maps and more for members only.

910.09 614.86   FR   ISSN 0758-6957
AUTOMOBILE MAGAZINE. (Supplements avail.) 1945. m. 200 F. Societe des Editions Techniques et Touristiques de France, 60-62 rue Danjou, 92100 Boulogne, France. TEL 46-09-95-96. FAX 46-09-99-85. TELEX 633 055 F. adv.; illus.; circ. 500,000.

914.4   FR
AUTOMOBILISME ARDENNAIS. 1901. q. 45 Fr. Automobile Club Ardennais, 10 Cours A. Briand, 08107 Charleville Mezieres, France. FAX 24-56-29-66. adv.

917.104   CN
AUTOROUTE. 4/yr. Morris Marketing and Media Services, Inc., 366 Adelaide St. W., No. 606, Toronto, Ont. M5V 1R9, Canada. TEL 416-599-9900. FAX 416-599-9700. Ed. Brian Barber. circ. 212,000.

AUVERGNE MAGAZINE; magazines de France. see *GENERAL INTEREST PERIODICALS — France*

AVIATION & SPACE JOURNAL. see *TRANSPORTATION — Air Transport*

910.202   IE
AVIS - PERSONALLY YOURS. (Text in English) 1984. a. free to qualified personnel. International Fairs & Exhibitions Ltd., Belgrave House, 15 Belgrave Rd., Rathmines, Dublin 6, Ireland. TEL 965711. FAX 964142. Ed. Michael Flood. circ. 50,000.

910.202   IT
AVVENTURA. 4/yr. Marco Manicini Editore, Via San Simpliciano, 20121 Milan, Italy. adv.; circ. 86,000.

910.09   IT
AVVENTURE NEL MONDO. 1972. bi-m. L.10000($15) (foreign L.20000). Viaggi nel Mondo, Via Cino da Pistoia, 7, 00152 Rome, Italy. TEL 5891400. Ed.Bd. circ. 100,000.
   Description: Reports on adventure trips internationally.

910.202   US
B & B SHOPTALK.* (Bed & Breakfast) 1981. bi-m. $56. American Bed & Breakfast Association, 1407 Huguenot Rd., Midlothian, VA 23113-2644. TEL 301-261-0180. circ. 3,000. (looseleaf format; back issues avail.)
   Description: For operators of bed and breakfast guesthouses and inns.

910.09   UK
B H & H P A JOURNAL. 1958. bi-m. membership. British Holiday & Home Parks Association Ltd., 31 Park Rd., Gloucester GL1 1LH, England. TEL 0452-526911. FAX 0452-307226. Ed. R.A. Pritchard. adv.; stat.; tr.lit.; circ. 3,000.
   Formerly: N F S O Journal (National Federation of Site Operations).
   Description: Provides information on the holiday and home park industry, including reports on legislation and regulations affecting parks. Geared toward commercial operators of caravan park owners in the UK.

B INTERNATIONAL. see *GENERAL INTEREST PERIODICALS — Hong Kong*

B W I A SUNJET. (British West Indies Airways) see *TRANSPORTATION — Air Transport*

647.94   GW
BAD ABBACHER KUR- UND GESCHAEFTSANZEIGER. 1974. m. DM.66. Roter Brachweg 72a, 8400 Regensburg, Germany. Ed. Annelore Olbrich. index; circ. 3,000. (back issues avail.)

941.3   GW   ISSN 0404-6307
BADEN - WUERTTEMBERG. 1961. s-a. DM.49.20. Verlag G. Braun GmbH, Karl-Friedrich-Str. 14-18, Postfach 1709, 7500 Karlsruhe 1, Germany. circ. 13,000. **Indexed:** GeoRef.
   Formerly: Welt am Oberrhein.

917.204   US
BAHAMAS (YEAR) INCLUDING TURKS & CAICOS. a. $10. Harper Collins Publishers, Birnbaum Travel Guides, 10 E. 53rd St., New York, NY 10022-5299. TEL 212-207-7000. illus.; index.
   Supersedes in part: Caribbean, Bermuda, and the Bahamas (Year).

BAHAMAS DATELINE. see *BUSINESS AND ECONOMICS — Investments*

917.2   BF
BAHAMAS FAMILY ISLANDS TRAVEL GUIDE. 1972. a. $1. (Bahamas Family Islands Promotion Board) Star Publishers Ltd., P.O. Box 4855, Nassau, Bahamas. TEL 809-322-4527. Ed. Paul Bower. adv.; illus.; circ. 200,000.
   Former titles (until 1977): Bahamas Out Islands Travel Guide; Bahama Out Islands Tourist News.

910.202   BA
BAHRAIN TOURISM DIRECTORY. (Text in Arabic, English) 1988. a. $50. Al- Kanary Services and Public Relations, P.O. Box 604, Manama, Bahrain. TEL 256575. FAX 277825. TELEX 7151 NANA BN. adv.; circ. 30,000.

910.202   US
▼**BAJA EXPLORER.** 1991. bi-m. $16. ALTI Corporation, 4180 La Jolla Village Dr., La Jolla, CA 92037. TEL 619-546-8700. Ed. Landon Crumpton. circ. 80,000.
   Description: Promotes the Baja California Peninsula.

910.202   US
BAJA TIMES. (Text in English) 1978. m. $14.95. Editorial Playas de Rosarito, S.A., Box 5577, Chula Vista, CA 91912. TEL 01152-661-21244. FAX 01152-611-22366. Ed. John Utley. adv.; bk.rev.; circ. 65,000. (tabloid format)
   Description: Dedicated to promoting tourism in Baja California, Mexico.

BARBADOS. BOARD OF TOURISM. ANNUAL REPORT. see *TRAVEL AND TOURISM — Abstracting, Bibliographies, Statistics*

919.704   BB
BARBADOS TOURIST BOARD. ANNUAL REPORT. no.14, 1972. a. $3. Barbados Tourist Board, Bridgewater, Barbados, W.I. charts; illus.

914.604   US
BARCELONA (YEAR). a. $10. Harper Collins Publishers, Birnbaum Travel Guides, 10 E. 53rd St., New York, NY 10022-5299. TEL 212-207-7000. illus.; index.

BARCOS. see *SPORTS AND GAMES — Boats And Boating*

910.202   GW
BAYERN ZEITUNG; Nachrichten, Tips und Information aus dem Urlaubsland Bayern. 1983. q. free. M T M Muenchen, Poccistr. 7, 8000 Munich 2, Germany. TEL 089-776019. FAX 089-7250981. Eds. Karl Stankiewitz, W.E. Matthaeus. adv.; circ. 100,000. (back issues avail.)
   Description: Information about tourism in Bavaria.

914.6   IS
BAZAK GUIDE TO SPAIN.* (Text in English) irreg. $4.95. Bazak Israel Guidebook Publishers Ltd., P.O. Box 4471, Jerusalem, Israel. (Dist. in U.S. by: Harper & Row, 60 E. 42nd St., Ste. 411, New York, NY 10017) illus.

917   CN   ISSN 0005-7460
BEAUTIFUL BRITISH COLUMBIA MAGAZINE. 1959. q. Can.$15.95. Beautiful British Columbia Magazine Ltd., 929 Ellery St., Victoria, B.C. V9A 7B4, Canada. TEL 604-384-5456. FAX 604-384-2812. adv.; illus.; index; circ. 242,590. **Indexed:** CMI.
   Description: Devoted to travel and geography of B C.

910.3   UK   ISSN 0267-3436
BED AND BREAKFAST IN BRITAIN. 1955. a. F.H.G. Publications Ltd., Abbey Mill Centre, Seedhill, Paisley PA1 1JN, Scotland. TEL 041-887 0428. Ed. Peter Clark.
   Formed by the merger of: Bed and Breakfast in South and Southwest England (ISSN 0067-4761) & Bed and Breakfast in Wales, Northern England and Scotland (ISSN 0067-477X)

910.22   US
BED & BREAKFAST NORTH AMERICA; a national directory for B & B travel. irreg., latest 5th ed. $15.95. Betsy Ross Publications, 24406 S. Ribbonwood Dr., Sun Lakes, AZ 85248. TEL 602-895-2795. illus.
   Description: Features historic Victorian Inns, intimate urban hotels, country inns, guesthouses and reservation services with details on prices, amenities, facilities, and attractions.

914.2   UK   ISSN 0267-3363
BED & BREAKFAST STOPS. 1975. a. £2.50. F.H.G. Publications Ltd., Abbey Mill Business Centre, Seedhill, Paisley PA1 1JN, Scotland. TEL 041-887 0428.

910.202   US
BED AND BREAKFAST U S A; guide to tourist homes and guest houses. 1977. a. $14 (typically set in Jan.). Penguin Books U S A, Inc., 375 Hudson St., New York, NY 10014. TEL 212-366-2582. FAX 212-366-2888. Ed. Carole DeSanti. circ. 43,000.
   Formerly: Guide to Tourist Homes and Guest Houses.

914.2   UK
BED, BREAKFAST & EVENING MEAL. 1963. a. £2.95. Pastime Publications Ltd., 15 Dublin Street Lane South, Edinburgh EH1 3PX, Scotland. TEL 031-556-1105. FAX 031-556-1129. adv.; circ. 60,000.

TRAVEL AND TOURISM

910.09 055.1   IT
BELL' ITALIA; alla scoperta del paese piu bello del mondo. 1986. m. L.53000 (foreign L.89000). Giorgio Mondadori e Associati S.p.A., Via Cadore, 19, 20135 Milan, Italy. TEL 02-5456421. FAX 02-5469150. Ed. Ettore Mocchetti.

910.202   US
BERKSHIRE RESTAURANT & ENTERTAINMENT GUIDE. 1970. s-a. $1. Ski America Enterprises, Inc., Riverside Rd., Box 737, Lenox, MA 01240. TEL 413-637-9810. Ed. Barry Hollister. adv.; circ. 30,000.

BERLIN & EX-DDR VON HINTEN; das Schwule Reisebuch. see HOMOSEXUALITY

914   GW   ISSN 0005-9250
BERLIN PROGRAMM. (Text in English and German) 1951. m. DM.2.50. (Verkehrsamt) Rimbach Verlag GmbH, Hohenzollerndamm 89, Postfach 330520, 1000 Berlin 33, Germany. FAX 030-8266215. adv.; illus.; circ. 55,000.

910.09   SZ
BERLITZ CRUISE GUIDES. 1984. a. Berlitz Guides, 61 Ave. d'Ouchy, 1000 Lausanne 6, Switzerland. TEL 41-21-27-75-61. FAX 021-26-12-57. adv.; circ. 2,000,000.
    Description: Provides information on ports-of-call, shore excursions, ships services and the voyage for passengers of cruise ships.

914.204   US
BERMUDA (YEAR). a. $10. Harper Collins Publishers, Birnbaum Travel Guides, 10 E. 53rd St., New York, NY 10022-5299. TEL 212-207-7000. illus.; index.
    Supersedes in part: Caribbean, Bermuda, and the Bahamas (Year).

910.09   US
BERMUDA SHORTS. 1986. q. Bermuda Department of Tourism, 310 Madison Ave., Ste. 201, New York, NY 10017. TEL 212-818-9800. Ed. Mario Almonte. (back issues avail.)
    Description: Relates to Bermuda and the travel industry.

914   SZ   ISSN 0005-9412
BERNER WOCHEN BULLETIN/THIS WEEK IN BERNE/SEMAINE A BERNE. (Text in English, French & German) 1943. w. 21 Fr. (Verkehrsverein der Stadt Bern) Buri Druck und Verlag, Eigerstr. 71, 3001 Berne, Switzerland. adv.; illus.

BERTRAND VACANCES. see REAL ESTATE

912   US   ISSN 1054-4089
BEST BED & BREAKFAST IN ENGLAND, SCOTLAND & WALES. a. Globe Pequot Press, 138 W. Main St., Box Q, Chester, CT 06412. TEL 203-526-9571. FAX 203-526-5748.
    Formerly: Best Bed and Breakfast in the World (ISSN 1057-5472)

387.7   US   ISSN 8750-2410
BEST FARES; Texas report. m. $75. Box 170129, Arlington, TX 76003. TEL 817-261-6114. circ. 10,000.
    Description: Covers discount airfares.

BEST GUIDE TO AMSTERDAM & THE BENELUX; for gay men and lesbians, with country and city maps. see HOMOSEXUALITY

BEST GUIDE TO ASIA, AUSTRALASIA, AND SOUTH PACIFIC ISLANDS; for gay men, with country and city maps. see HOMOSEXUALITY

BEST GUIDE TO CARIBBEAN, CENTRAL AND SOUTH AMERICAN LANDS; for gay men, with country and city maps. see HOMOSEXUALITY

BEST GUIDE TO FRANCE, SPAIN, AND PORTUGAL; for gay men, with country and city maps. see HOMOSEXUALITY

BEST GUIDE TO GREAT BRITAIN; for gay men, with city maps. see HOMOSEXUALITY

BEST GUIDE TO MEDITERRANEAN LANDS; for gay men, with country and city maps. see HOMOSEXUALITY

BEST GUIDE TO THE NORTH PACIFIC AND ORIENT; for gay men, with country and city maps. see HOMOSEXUALITY

917.904   US
▼**THE BEST OF EUROPE.** 1990. a. $24 includes European Travel & Life. Murdoch Magazines (Subsidiary of: News America Publishing, Inc.), 200 Madison Ave., New York, NY 10016. TEL 800-627-2557. FAX 212-447-4778. circ. 310,000. (reprint service avail. from UMI)
    Description: Lists practical country information by country and features a destination on the cover of each issue.

910.202   US
BEST OF LAUDERDALE AND THE GOLD COAST. 1980. q. $7.95. Best of Broward, Inc., 11 N. E. 12th Ave., Fort Lauderdale, FL 33301. TEL 305-523-2378. Ed. Yolanda Maurer. adv.; circ. 14,739.

910.09   US
BEST OF MAUI; best of Maui sports, recreation, dining and shopping. 1988. a. $12. Sandwich Islands Publishing Co., Box 10669, Lahaina, Maui, HI 96761. TEL 808-661-5844. FAX 808-661-9878. Ed. Joe Harabin. adv.; bk.rev.; circ. 20,000. (back issues avail.)

917.504   US
▼**BEST OF THE BEACH.** 1991. a. First Publishing Inc., 2100 Riverchase Ctr., Ste. 110, Birmingham, AL 35244. TEL 205-733-1970. FAX 205-733-1974.
    Description: Profiles the Alabama - Florida Gulf Coast tourism industry.

917.404   US
BEST READ GUIDE. 1988. 7/yr. $12. Box 1958, 77 Finlay Rd., Orleans, MA 02653. TEL 508-240-1212. FAX 508-240-2912. Ed. Walter Brooks. adv.; maps; circ. 1,300,000.
    Description: Contains a calendar of events, listings of attractions and restaurants, and ideas for vacationers and travelers.

910.202   IT
BIBIONE VACANZE. (Text in German, Italian) 1968. w. during summer. L.12000($5.50) Pubblistudio de Zorzi Casa Editrice s.a.s., Via Marinoni 53, Udine, Italy. TEL 0432-508243. FAX 0432-508243. adv.; circ. 10,000. (back issues avail.)
    Description: Guide for tourists in Bibione.

910.202   US
BIENVENIDOS PUERTO RICO;* the shining star of the Caribbean. (Puerto Rico Hotel and Tourism Association) Ulrich Communications Corp., 1995 N.E. 150th St., Ste. 107, N. Miami, FL 33181. TEL 305-945-7403. FAX 305-947-6410. Ed. Robert L. Ulrich.

BIKEREPORT. see SPORTS AND GAMES — Bicycles And Motorcycles

796.95 914.2   UK
BLAKES BOATING ABROAD. 1989. a. free. Blakes Holidays Ltd., Wroxham, Norwich NR12 8DH, England. TEL 0603-782141. circ. 200,000.
    Supersedes in part: Blakes Boating Holidays.

796.95 914.2   UK
BLAKES BOATING IN BRITAIN. 1974. a. free. Blakes Holidays Ltd., Wroxham, Norwich NR12 8DH, England. TEL 0603-782141. TELEX 97114. Ed. T.E. Howes. circ. 400,000.
    Supersedes in part: Blakes Boating Holidays; Which superseded: Blakes Boating in Britain; Blakes Boating in Europe. Blakes Boating in Britain & Blakes Boating in Europe superseded in part: Blakes Holidays Afloat; Which was formed by the merger of: Blakes International Holidays Afloat & Norfolk Broads Holidays Afloat (ISSN 0078-1142).

BOATING IN THE SAN JUAN ISLANDS. see SPORTS AND GAMES — Boats And Boating

910.09 301.415   US
BOB DAMRON'S ADDRESS BOOK. 1964. a. $12.95. Damron Company, Inc., P.O. Box 42-2458, San Francisco, CA 94142-2458. TEL 415-255-0404. FAX 415-703-9049. Eds. Dan Delbex, Gina Gatta. adv.; circ. 100,000.
    Description: Gay pocket guide for U.S., Canada, Mexico and the Caribbean.

BOCA RATON MAGAZINE. see GENERAL INTEREST PERIODICALS — United States

918   BO   ISSN 0006-6540
BOLIVIA.* 1969. bi-m. Bol.$6. Ministerio de Cultura, Informacion y Turismo, Av. Camacho 1394, La Paz, Bolivia. Ed. Juan Siles Guevaro. bk.rev.; film rev.; bibl.; charts; illus.

910.09 663.2   US
BON VIVANT. 1975. 6/yr. $10. 138 Lake View Dr. N., Macon, GA 31210-8638. TEL 416-741-3057. Ed. J.D. Shortt. bk.rev.

BONNE TABLE ET TOURISME; revue de la gastronomie et du tourisme dans le monde. see FOOD AND FOOD INDUSTRIES

910.202   SZ
BORDBUCH/LOGBOOK. (Text in English and German) 6/yr. (Deutsche Lufthansa) A L A S AG, Business Centre, Schoengrund 1, CH-6343 Rotkreuz, Switzerland. TEL 042-642964. FAX 042-644535. Ed. Andre Lehman. adv.; circ. 630,000.

917.404   US
BOSTON (YEAR). a. $10. Harper Collins Publishers, Birnbaum Travel Guides, 10 E. 53rd St., New York, NY 10022-5299. TEL 212-207-7000. illus.; index.

910.2   BE   ISSN 0006-8616
BRABANT TOURISME. (Editions in Dutch and French) 1938. 4/yr. 450 Fr. Federation Touristique du Brabant, 61 rue du Marche-aux-Herbes, B-1000 Brussels, Belgium. FAX 02-513-8803. TELEX 63245 B BRUB. Ed. G. Menne. adv.; bk.rev.; bibl.; illus.; circ. 450.
    Former titles: Brabant; Brabant-Tourisme.

BRASILIANS JOURNAL. see ETHNIC INTERESTS

910.09   BL
BRASILTURIS JOURNAL. bi-w. Av. Pacaembir 1400, CEP 01234 Sao Paulo SP, Brazil. TEL 11-825-6811. TELEX 011-37124 SETL BR. Ed. Horacio Neves. circ. 10,000.

918.1   UK
BRAZIL NEWS UPDATE. 1942. q. £15. Brazilian Chamber of Commerce, 32 Green St., London W1Y 3FD, England. TEL 01-499-0186. TELEX 25814 BRASTC G. Ed. Dionisio A. de Castro Cerqueira. bk.rev.; circ. 700.
    Formerly (until 1988): Brazil Journal.

910.202   US
BREAKER'S GUIDE.* 1987. a. O P Publishing, Inc., 10151 University Blvd., No. 199, Orlando, FL 32817-1904. adv.; circ. 700,000.
    Description: Travel information for students planning their annual spring break vacation.

910.09   US
BRIO. 3/yr. Cruise Passenger Network, 2001 W. Main St., Ste. 245, Stamford, CT 06902-4501. TEL 203-359-8626. FAX 203-327-5062. Ed. Barbara Coats. circ. 170,000.

942   US
BRITAIN BY BRITRAIL; how to tour Britain by train. 1980. biennial. Globe Pequot Press, 138 W. Main St., Box Q, Chester, CT 06412. TEL 203-526-9571. FAX 203-526-9571.

914.2   UK
BRITAIN: HOTELS & RESTAURANTS.* 1955. a. free to qualified personnel. British Tourist Authority, Thames Tower, Blacks Rd., London W6 9EL, England. TEL 01-846-9000. adv.

914.2   UK   ISSN 0267-1468
BRITAIN'S BEST HOLIDAYS - A QUICK REFERENCE GUIDE. 1968. a. £2.40. F.H.G. Publications Ltd., Abbey Mill Business Centre, Seedhill, Paisley PA1 1JN, Scotland. TEL 041-887 0428.
    Formerly: Guide to Britain's Best Holidays.

BRITISH AIRWAYS EXECUTIVE. see TRANSPORTATION — Air Transport

BRITISH HERITAGE; a window on the British world. see HISTORY — History Of Europe

914.2   UK   ISSN 0068-2616
BRITISH TOURIST AUTHORITY. DIGEST OF TOURIST STATISTICS. 1969. irreg. £40. British Tourist Authority, Thames Tower, Black's Road, London W6 9EL, England.
—BLDSC shelfmark: 3588.325500.

TRAVEL AND TOURISM

910.202   VB
BRITISH VIRGIN ISLANDS WELCOME TOURIST GUIDE; the welcome. 1971. bi-m. $24 (foreign $38). Island Publishing, P.O. Box 133, Road Town - Tortola, British Virgin Islands, W.I. TEL 809-494-2413. FAX 809-494-4413. Ed. Claudia Colli. circ. 20,000.
  Description: Articles on history, people and locales of BVI; plus information on accomodations, charterboats, dining and shopping.

BRITISH WATERWAYS BOARD. ANNUAL REPORT AND ACCOUNTS. see TRANSPORTATION — Ships And Shipping

BUITENSPOOR. see SPORTS AND GAMES — Outdoor Life

916.8 778.5   RH
BULAWAYO THIS MONTH. 1972. m. free. Modern Publications, P.O. Box 1183, Bulawayo, Zimbabwe. Ed. Les Broughton. adv.; illus.; circ. 2,500.

BULLETIN EKONOMI INDONESIA. see BUSINESS AND ECONOMICS — Domestic Commerce

910   CN
BULLETIN VOYAGES. (Text in French) 1978. w. Can.$47. Editions Acra Ltee., C.P. 85, Succursale "E", Montreal, Que. H2T 3A5, Canada. TEL 514-287-9773. FAX 514-842-6180. Ed. Etienne Ozan-Groulx. adv.; circ. 6,946. (back issues avail.)

910.202   UK
BURKE'S GUIDE TO COUNTRY HOUSES. 1977. irreg. £27.50. Burke's Peerage, 12 Rickett St., London SW6 1RU, England.

388.3   GW   ISSN 0341-5244
BUS-FAHRT; internationale Fachzeitschrift fuer Omnibusverkehr. 1952. m. DM.106. Stuenings Verlagsgesellschaft mbH, Luisenstr. 100-104, Postfach 2980, 4150 Krefeld 1, Germany. TEL 02151-853-0. FAX 02151-853103. TELEX 172151305-WISTU. Ed. Lothar Neumann. adv.; bk.rev.; charts; illus.; stat.; circ. 5,431.
  Description: Focuses on bus travel and tourism.

910.09   GW
BUS TOURIST; Fachmagazin fur international Bustouristik. 1981. bi-m. DM.7.50. Suedwestdeutsche Verlagsanstalt, Presseham am Marktplatz, D-6800 Mannheim 1, Germany. TEL 06-21-17-02-460. circ. 8,500.

BUS TOURS MAGAZINE. see TRANSPORTATION

BUS WORLD; magazine of buses and bus systems. see TRANSPORTATION — Automobiles

910.202   HK
▼**BUSINESS ENTERTAINMENT GUIDE.** (Text in English, Japanese) 1986. m. G-F, Cheung Kong Bldg., 661 King's Rd., Quarry Bay, Hong Kong. TEL 5651313. FAX 5658217. Ed. Jane Puranananda. circ. 146,000.
  Description: Provides information for tourists and visiting executives.

BUSINESS OF TOURISM. see HOTELS AND RESTAURANTS

BUSINESS TRAVEL INTERNATIONAL; quarterly review of international business travel, conferencing and incentive. see MEETINGS AND CONGRESSES

BUSINESS TRAVEL MANAGEMENT. see BUSINESS AND ECONOMICS — Management

910.202   US
BUSINESS TRAVEL NEWS; the newspaper of the business travel industry. 1984. 36/yr. C M P Publications, Inc., 600 Community Dr., Manhasset, NY 11030. TEL 516-562-5000. FAX 516-365-4601. TELEX 647035 CMP PUB MAHA. adv.; circ. 52,000.
  ●Also available online. Vendor(s): Data-Star, DIALOG.

910.09 330   US
BUSINESS TRAVELER INTERNATIONAL. 1988. m. $36. Perry Publications Ltd., 41 E. 42nd St., Ste. 1512, New York, NY 10017. TEL 212-697-1700. FAX 212-697-1005. Ed. Mary Hunt. adv.; bk.rev.

910.2   US
BUSINESS TRAVELER MAGAZINE. 1980. q. $24. National Association of Business Travel Agents, 3255 Wilshire Blvd., Ste. 1514, Los Angeles, CA 90010. TEL 213-382-3335. Ed. Stuart J. Faber. circ. 34,000.
  Description: Informs business travelers on the best hotels, cities, airlines and auto rental centers.

910.202   US
BUSINESS TRAVELER'S AIRPORT HOTEL DIRECTORY. 1987. s-a. $14. National Association of Business Travel Agents, 3255 Wilshire Blvd., Ste. 1514, Los Angeles, CA 90010. TEL 213-382-3335. Ed. Stuart J. Faber. adv.; circ. 10,000.
  Formerly: Business Traveler's America's Greatest Cities.
  Description: Describes hotels near airports.

910.202 647.94   US
BUSINESS TRAVELER'S HOTEL GUIDE. 1987. s-a. National Association of Business Travel Agents, 3255 Wilshire Blvd., Ste. 1514, Los Angeles, CA 90010. TEL 213-382-3335. Ed. Stuart J. Faber. adv.; circ. 39,000.
  Former titles: Business Traveler's Greatest Hotels; Business Traveler's Greatest Hotels and Restaurants.

330   UK   ISSN 0309-9334
BUSINESS TRAVELLER. 1976. m. £33($41) Perry Publications (Holdings) PLC, 388-396 Oxford St., London W1N 9HE, England. TEL 071-629-4688. FAX 071-629-6572. Ed. Gillian Upton. adv.; illus.; index; circ. 42,000. Indexed: BMT.
  Description: Europes leading independent magazine for people who travel on business. Provides information for the regular traveller on every aspect of service provided by the travel industry.

910.202   HK   ISSN 0255-7312
BUSINESS TRAVELLER ASIA-PACIFIC. 1982. m. $50. Interasia Publications, 200 Lockhart Rd., 13th Fl., Hong Kong. TEL 574-9317. FAX 572-6846. TELEX 62107. Ed. Vijay Verghese. circ. 22,599.
  —BLDSC shelfmark: 2934.901000.

910.09 330   US
BUSINESS TRAVELLER INTERNATIONAL. 1988. m. $36. Perry Publications PLC, (Subsidiary of: Perry Publications PLC), 41 E. 42nd St., Ste. 1512, New York, NY 10017. TEL 212-697-1700. FAX 212-697-1005. (In UK: 338-396 Oxford St., London W1N 9HE, England) Ed. Kate Rice. adv.; bk.rev.; illus.; circ. 42,000. (back issues avail.)
  Description: Provides travel tips, feature articles for the international business traveller.

910.09   US
BYWAYS (FAIRFAX). 1984. 6/yr. $17.95. National Motorcoach Network, Inc., Patriot Sq., 10527-C Braddock Rd., Fairfax, VA 22032. TEL 703-250-7897. FAX 703-250-1477. adv.; circ. 37,000 (controlled).
  Description: Features travel destinations in U.S. and Canada.

910.09   IE
C I E TRAVEL EXPRESS. 1972. m. free. (Covas Iompair Eireann) Marine and General Publicity Ltd., 127 Lower Baggot St., Dublin 2, Ireland. Ed. Cyril Ferris. adv.; circ. 110,000.

914.504   IT   ISSN 0394-1434
C I R V I BOLLETTINO. (Text in English, French and Italian) 1980. s-a. L.30000 (foreign L.38000)(effective 1992). Centro Interuniversitario di Ricerche sul Viaggio in Italia, Str. Rivigliasco 6, 10024 Moncalieri, Italy. TEL 011-6407488. bk.rev.

914.7 658   US   ISSN 1059-4957
C I S SOVIET TRAVEL NEWSLETTER. (Commonwealth Independent States) 1979. w. $62. International Intertrade Index, Box 636 Federal Sq., Newark, NJ 07101. TEL 908-686-2382. Ed. John E. Felber. (looseleaf format; back issues avail.)
  Description: News on travel, transportation, hotels, restaurants, marketing and media.

918   AG   ISSN 0007-8859
C O T A L; la revista del turismo total. (Supplement avail.) (Text in English, Spanish; occasionally in Portuguese.) 1961. m. membership. (Confederacion de Organizaciones Turisticas de la America Latina) M. Seoane y Cia., S.A., Lavalle 357, 12th Fl., Ste. 124, Buenos Aires, 1047, Argentina. TEL 541-393-5598. FAX 541-111253. TELEX 23385 COTAL AR. Ed. Mario Seoane. adv.; abstr.; bibl.; illus.; stat.; index, cum.index; circ. 10,000.

910.202   US
C T P A NEWS. 1975. m. membership. California Travel Parks Association, Inc., Box 5648, Auburn, CA 95604. TEL 916-885-1624. FAX 916-823-6331. Ed. Judy Miller. adv.; circ. 900. (back issues avail.)
  Description: News of California, Nevada and Oregon RV park and campground industry.

916.8 647   SA
C V R HOTEL GUIDE TO SOUTHERN AFRICA. (Text in Afrikaans and English) 1966. a. R.16.50. Chris van Rensburg Publications (Pty) Ltd., PO Box 29159, Melville, 2109, South Africa.
  Former Titles: C V R Travel and Hotel Guide to Southern Africa; Guide to Hotels in South Africa (ISSN 0533-5450)

914   FR   ISSN 0068-5151
CAHIERS DU TOURISME. SERIE A: FRANCE. 1963. irreg., no.270, 1990. price varies. Universite d'Aix-Marseille III (Universite de Droit, d'Economie et des Sciences), Centre des Hautes Etudes Touristiques, Fondation Vasarely, 1 Av. Marcel Pagnol, 13090 Aix-en-Provence, France. TEL 42-20-09-73. FAX 42-20-50-98. circ. 140. **Indexed:** World Agri.Econ.& Rural Sociol.Abstr.

910.09   FR   ISSN 0768-3162
CAHIERS DU TOURISME. SERIE B: ETRANGER. 1966. irreg. price varies. Universite d'Aix-Marseille III (Universite de Droit, d'Economie et des Sciences), Centre des Hautes Etudes Touristiques, Fondation Vasarely, 1 Av. Marcel Pagnol, 13090 Aix-en-Provence, France. TEL 42-20-09-73. FAX 42-20-50-98. (back issues avail.)

910.09   FR   ISSN 0768-0279
CAHIERS DU TOURISME. SERIE C: RECHERCHE FONDAMENTALE ET APPLIQUEE - METHODOLOGIE. 1963. irreg. price varies. Universite d'Aix-Marseille III (Universite de Droit, d'Economie et des Sciences), Centre des Hautes Etudes Touristiques, Fondation Vasarely, 1 Av. Marcel Pagnol, 13090 Aix-en-Provence, France. TEL 42-20-09-73. FAX 42-20-50-98.
  —BLDSC shelfmark: 9101.579000.

910.09 340   FR   ISSN 0767-2667
CAHIERS DU TOURISME. SERIE E: LEGISLATION. irreg. price varies. Universite d'Aix-Marseille III (Universite de Droit, d'Economie et des Sciences), Centre des Hautes Etudes Touristiques, Fondation Vasarely, 1 Av. Marcel Pagnol, 13090 Aix-en-Provence, France. TEL 42-20-09-73. FAX 42-20-50-98.

918.104   BL
CALENDARIO CULTURAL DO BRASIL.* 1976. a. Conselho Federal de Cultura, Palacio da Cultura, Rua da Imprensa, 2000 Rio de Janeiro, Brazil. illus.

971   CN
CALGARY CITY. 1982. a. free. Maclean-Hunter Ltd. (Calgary), Ste. 200, 1015 Centre St. N., Calgary, Alta. T2E 2P8, Canada. TEL 403-276-7881. FAX 403-276-5026. Ed. David Coll. circ. 100,000.
  Formerly: Calgary Visitors Guide.

CALIFORNIA EVENTS ANNUAL. see TRANSPORTATION — Automobiles

917.904   US
CALIFORNIA HIGHWAYS. 1988. bi-m. $16.50. S & K Marketing, Inc., 8306 Wilshire Blvd., Ste. 7002, Beverly Hills, CA 90211. TEL 213-935-3107. adv.: B&W page $2675, color page $3680; trim 9 x 12. circ. 30,000.
  Description: Focuses on the beauty and splendor of the state through pictorials and journalism. Includes history, architecture, culture and travel.

CALIFORNIA INNTOUCH. see HOTELS AND RESTAURANTS

TRAVEL AND TOURISM

917 796.5   US
CALIFORNIA - NEVADA CAMPBOOK. Cover title: R V and Tent Sites in California, Nevada. a. membership. American Automobile Association, 1000 AAA Dr., Heathrow, FL 32746-5063. TEL 407-444-7962. FAX 407-444-7380. circ. 509,852.
Formerly (until 1980): California-Nevada Camping.

910.202   US
CALIFORNIA R V & CAMPING GUIDE. 1975. a. $3 (foreign 7) per no. (California Travel Parks Association) Executive Services Group, Box 5578, Auburn, CA 95604-5648. TEL 916-823-1076. FAX 916-823-6331. Ed. Judy Miller. adv.; circ. 225,000.

910.09   IT
CAMMELLO. 1972. q. L.14000 membership. Cammello Club, Via Roma 366, 10121 Turin, Italy. adv.

796.5   US   ISSN 0744-8120
CAMPERWAYS;* the Middle Atlantic campers' newspaper. 11/yr. $15. Compass Publishing, Box 5000, Lake Forest, IL 60045-5000.

910.09   UK   ISSN 0266-4437
CAMPING AND CARAVAN SITE SELECTOR. 1965. a. £2. Stone Leisure Group Ltd., 2a Granville Rd., Sidcup, Kent DA14 4BN, England. TEL 081-302-6150. FAX 081-302-1813. Ed. Bob Griffiths. adv.; circ. 35,000.

CAMPING & WALKING. see *SPORTS AND GAMES — Outdoor Life*

910.202   IT
CAMPING IN ITALY. (Text in English, French, German, Spanish) 1985. q. free. Editoriale Eurocamp s.r.l., Via Durini n.3, 20122 Milan, Italy. TEL 02-76022377. FAX 02-76022430. Ed. Maria Paola Canegrati. adv.; bk.rev.; charts; illus.; circ. 50,000.

CAMPING REVUE; Magazin des Oesterreichischen Camping Clubs. see *SPORTS AND GAMES*

CAMPITUR: CAMPING, CARAVANING, VILLAGGI TURISTICI. see *SPORTS AND GAMES — Outdoor Life*

917.104   US   ISSN 0749-2561
CANADA (YEAR). a. $17. Harper Collins Publishers, Birnbaum Travel Guides, 10 E 53rd St., New York, NY 10022-5299. TEL 212-207-7000. Ed. Stephen Birnbaum.

917   CN
CANADA'S WEST. 1989. a. free. Wake Holdings Ltd., 999 8th St., S.W., Ste. 222, Calgary, Alta. T2R 1J5, Canada. FAX 403-229-2470.

917.1   CN
CANADIAN TOURIST TRAVEL GUIDE OF CANADA. 1983. a. free. Armadale Publications Inc., Box 1193, MPO, Edmonton, Alta. T5J 2M4, Canada. TEL 403-429-1073. FAX 403-425-5844. Ed. Winston Mohabir. adv.; circ. 30,000.
Description: Describes places of interest in Canada; lists hotels and restaurants from Nova Scotia to Vancouver. Includes border US.

917   CN   ISSN 0319-7107
CANADIAN TRAVEL NEWS. fortn. Can.$33($42) Southam Business Communications Inc., 1450 Don Mills Rd., Don Mills, Ont. M3B 2X7, Canada. TEL 416-445-6641. FAX 416-442-2261. Ed. Doug McArthur. adv.; illus.

917   CN   ISSN 0831-9138
CANADIAN TRAVEL PRESS WEEKLY. 1968. w. Can.$45. Baxter Publishing Co., 310 Dupont St., Toronto, Ont. M5R 1V9, Canada. TEL 416-968-7252. FAX 416-968-2377. TELEX 065-28085. Ed. Edith Baxter. adv.; bk.rev.; circ. 14,062.
Formerly: Canadian Travel Press (ISSN 0045-5490)

917.204   US
CANCUN, COZUMEL, AND ISLA MUJERES. a. $10. Harper Collins Publishers, Birnbaum Travel Guides, 10 E. 53rd St., New York, NY 10022-5299. TEL 212-207-7000. illus.; index.

917.204   MX
CANCUN TIPS. (Text in English) 1987. q. $12. Cancun Tips S.A., Av. Tulum no.29 S.M. 5, Ste. 102, Cancun, Q. Roo, Mexico C.P. 77500, Mexico. TEL 988-4-40-44. (US addr.: 12403 Nacogdoches St., Ste. 110, San Antonio, TX 78217) Ed. Victor Vera. circ. 90,000. (tabloid format; back issues avail.)
Formerly: Cancun Scene.
Description: Tourist information and tips on vacationing in Cancun and surrounding areas.

910.4   US
CAPE COD AND ISLANDS ATLAS AND GUIDE BOOK. a. $12.95. Butterworth Company of Cape Cod, Inc., 703 Main St., Harwich Center, Harwichport, MA 02646-1817. TEL 508-432-8200. Ed. Rod Schou. adv.; circ. 30,000.
Description: Complete detailed maps and guide information for all Cape Cod towns and the islands of Martha's Vineyard and Nantucket, plus sections on Cape Cod living, the national seashore, outdoor activities and 80 fresh water fishing maps.

917.4   US
CAPE COD GUIDE. 1946. 24/yr. $24. Prescott Visitor Magazines, 495 Station Ave., So. Yarmonth, MA 02664. TEL 508-760-2027. adv.

910.2 917   US   ISSN 1045-7771
CAPE COD HOME & GARDEN.* 1947-1966; N.S. 1990. 4/yr. $15. Cove Communications Corp., Box 1059, Barnstable, MA 02630-0997. TEL 508-945-3542. Ed. John C. Whitmarsh. adv.; circ. 20,000.
Formerly: Cape Cod Compass (ISSN 0069-021X)
Description: Features articles about fine homes and gardens on Cape Cod, Martha's Vineyard and Nantucket.

974   US
CAPE COD RESORT DIRECTORY. 1921. a. free. Cape Cod Chamber of Commerce Inc., Routes 6 and 132, Hyannis, MA 02601. TEL 508-362-3225. adv.; circ. 250,000.

917.504   US
CAPITAL MAGAZINE. 1974. m. $12. Cappub, Inc., 300 Mill St., Vienna, VA 22180-4524. FAX 703-938-4562. adv.; circ. 70,000 (controlled).

918   VE
CARACAS. (Text in English and Spanish) 1965. a. $6. Elaboraciones Venezuela, Apdo. del Este 60182, Caracas, Venezuela. TEL 2835237. Ed. Lynn Grossberg. adv.; bk.rev.; circ. 10,000.
Incorporates: Ve Venezuela (ISSN 0042-2932); Which was formerly: Caribbean Connexion.

910.2   UK   ISSN 0269-8730
CARAVAN & CHALET PARKS GUIDE. a. £3. Haymarket Magazines Ltd., 38-42 Hampton Rd., Teddington, Middx. TW11 0JE, England. TEL 081-943-5000. TELEX 895-2440-HAYMRT-G. circ. 30,000.
Formerly: Caravan and Chalet Sites Guide (ISSN 0069-0317)
Description: Lists over 3,000 caravan and chalet sites.

914   UK   ISSN 0268-5558
CARAVAN BUSINESS PLUS CARAVAN INDUSTRY. 1969. m. £14 includes Directory (foreign £17)(effective 1992). A.E. Morgan Publications Ltd., Stanley House, 9 West St., Epsom, Surrey KT18 7RL, England. TEL 0372-741411. FAX 0372-744493. Ed. G.D. Ritchie. adv.; bk.rev.
Formed by the 1985 merger of: Caravan Business; Caravan Industry and Park Operator (ISSN 0045-5725)
Description: Trade magazine for the caravan market, developments, advice and special features for park operators, dealers and manufacturers.

910.202   AT
CARAVAN BUYERS MANUAL. 1946. a. Aus.$3.25. Syme Magazines (Subsidiary of: Syme Media Pty. Ltd.), G.P.O. Box 628E, Melbourne, Vic. 3000, Australia.

914 388.3   UK
CARAVAN HOLIDAYS. 1980. q. £5. Gildea & Co. Ltd., Ste. 14D, Monkscoole House, Rathcoole, Co. Antrim BT37 9DA, N. Ireland. Ed. Andrew Gildea.

914.2   UK   ISSN 0268-0440
CARAVAN MAGAZINE. 1933. m. £33.20. Link House Magazines Ltd., Link House, Dingwall Ave., Croydon, Surrey CR9 2TA, England. TEL 01-686-2599. FAX 01-760-0973. TELEX 947709. Ed. Barry Williams. adv.; bk.rev.; charts; illus.; circ. 29,037.
Formerly: Caravan (ISSN 0008-6142); Incorporates: Caravanning Monthly; Which incorporates (in Feb. 1978): Modern Caravanning; Which was formerly: Modern Caravan (ISSN 0026-7554)
Description: Informational and feature articles pertaining to touring trailer and motorized caravans, with reviews of products and equipment, technical advice, and ratings of sites.

910.2 914   UK
CARAVAN SITES. 1955. m. £2.75. Link House Magazines Ltd., Link House, Dingwall Ave., Croydon, Surrey CR9 2TA, England. TEL 01-686-2599. FAX 01-760-0973. TELEX 947709. (Subscr. to: U M S, Stephenson House, 1st Fl., Brunel Centre, Bletchley, Milton Keynes, MK2 2EW) Ed. B. Williams.
Formerly: Caravan Sites and Mobile Home Parks (ISSN 0069-0309)
Description: Lists caravan sites in Great Britain for trailer caravans, motor caravans, caravan holiday homes, and mobile homes.

910.202   AT
CARAVAN TEST. 1970. s-a. Aus.$2.75. Syme Magazines (Subsidiary of: Syme Media Pty. Ltd.), G.P.O. Box 628E, Melbourne, Vic. 3000, Australia.

796.5 910.202   IT
CARAVANING; vacanze turismo auto. 1975. m. L.80000. Edigamma s.r.l., Piazza dei Sanniti 9, 00185 Rome, Italy. TEL 06-4928412. FAX 06-4940719. Ed. Maurizio Testa. adv.; circ. 105,000.

388.3   US   ISSN 0008-6193
CARAVANNER. 1954. q. free to qualified personnel. Airstream, Inc., 419 W. Pike St., Jackson Center, OH 45334. TEL 513-596-6111. FAX 614-596-6092. illus.; circ. 3 (paid); 350,000 (controlled).

919.704   US
CARIBBEAN (YEAR). a. $10. Harper Collins Publishers, Birnbaum Travel Guides, 10 E. 53rd St., New York, NY 10022-5299. TEL 212-207-7000. Ed. Stephen Birnbaum.
Supersedes in part: Caribbean, Bermuda, and the Bahamas (Year).

CARIBBEAN AVIATION AND TOURISM NEWS/NOTICIERO AERONAUTICO Y TURISMO CARIBENSE. see *AERONAUTICS AND SPACE FLIGHT*

CARIBBEAN DATELINE. see *BUSINESS AND ECONOMICS — Investments*

917.2   BB
CARIBBEAN TOURISM. 1977. q. Caribbean Tourism Research and Development Centre, Mervue, Marine Gardens, Christ Church, Barbados, W.I. circ. 2,000.
Supersedes (1977-1981): Caribbean Tourism Research Centre. Newsletter.

919.704   BB
CARIBBEAN TOURISM STATISTICAL REPORT. 1978. a. $50. Caribbean Tourism Organization, Mervue, Marine Gardens, Christ Church, Barbados, W.I. FAX 809-429-3065. TELEX 2488. circ. 1,000.
Formerly: Caribbean Tourism Statistics.

910.09 F2171.3   US   ISSN 0891-9496
CARIBBEAN TRAVEL AND LIFE. 1986. bi-m. $19.95. Caribbean Travel and Life, Inc., 8403 Colesville Rd., Ste. 830, Silver Spring, MD 20910. TEL 301-588-2300. FAX 301-588-2256. Ed. Veronica Gould Stoddart. adv.; bk.rev.; circ. 100,000.
Description: Targeted toward a sophisticated, up-scale audience. Articles and photographs devoted to the unique vacation, recreational, cultural opportunities available throughout the island chain of the Caribbean, the Bahamas, and Bermuda.

TRAVEL AND TOURISM

910.202   US   ISSN 0890-796X
CARIBBEAN TREASURES. 1986. m. $54. Close Communications, Box 1290, Keene, NH 03431. TEL 603-352-3691. FAX 603-357-2450. Ed. David Lord. bk.rev.; illus.; circ. 2,500. (looseleaf format; back issues avail.)
   Description: Provides informational and objective reporting on the best in hotels, restaurants in the Caribbean.

910.09 640   CN
CARIBOO CHILCOTIN TRAVEL GUIDE. 1963. a. Cariboo Tourist Association, P.O. Box 4900, Willians Lake, B.C. V2G 2V8, Canada. TEL 604-392-2226. FAX 604-392-2838. adv.; circ. 70,000.

910.09   US
CARNIVAL CURRENTS. 3/yr. Cruise Passenger Network, 2001 W. Main St., Stamford, CT 06902-4501. TEL 203-359-8626. FAX 203-327-5062. Ed. Barbara Coats. adv.; circ. 619,133.

914   PO
CARTAZ;* revista mensal de cultura e informacao e turismo. vol. 6, 1970. m. Avenida de Roma 72, 1 Esq. Frente, Lisbon, Portugal. Ed. A. Borges Pires. adv.; charts; illus.

CASINO DIGEST. see SPORTS AND GAMES

CASINO WORLD; casino industry newsletter. see HOTELS AND RESTAURANTS

910   SP
CATALOGO AUTOMOVILES TURISMOS. a. 1250 ptas. Tecnipublicaciones, S.A., Fernando VI, 27, 28004 Madrid, Spain. TEL 91-319-7889. FAX 91-319-7089. TELEX 43905 YEBE E.

CATALOGUE OF CANADIAN RECREATION AND LEISURE RESEARCH. see LEISURE AND RECREATION

910.09 282   US
CATHOLIC TRAVELER. 1960. q. $3. Box 786, Port Washington, NY 11050. TEL 516-883-1889. Ed. G. Robert Hewitt. adv.

910.09   US
CAVES AND CAVERNS; national caves association directory. 1973. a. free. National Caves Association, Rt. 9, Box 106, McMinnville, TN 37110. TEL 615-668-3925. Ed. Barbara Munson. circ. 600,000.
   Description: Includes name, address and phone number of current NCA members. Supplies locator map and many pictures.

910.202   UY
CENTAUR. 1977. a. Centro Automovilista del Uruguay, Artigas 1773, Montevideo, Uruguay. Ed. Ever Cabrera Tornielli. adv. Indexed: Anim.Breed.Abstr.

914.704   US
CENTRAL WISCONSIN RESORTER. 1965. w. Box 838, Wautoma, WI 54982. TEL 414-787-3334. Ed. Arlene Buttles. adv.; circ. 11,000.

CENTUR. see TRANSPORTATION — Automobiles

910.04   GW   ISSN 0934-5140
CHECK-IN; das Magazin fuer Geschaeftsreisende Business & Pleasure. bi-m. DM.42 (foreign DM.48). Verlag Industriemagazin, Ingolstaedter Str. 22, 8000 Munich 45, Germany. TEL 089-35093160. FAX 089-352286. TELEX 5215777. Ed. Gerd Otto-Rieke. adv.; bk.rev.; circ. 80,000. (back issues avail.)
   Formerly (until March, 1988): Fliegen.
   Description: Magazine for business travelers.

914.2   UK
CHERWELL GUIDE TO OXFORD. 1948. a. £3. Oxford Student Publications Ltd., Frewin Court, New Inn Hall St., Oxford OX1 3HZ, England. TEL 0865-246464. FAX 0865-200321. circ. 3,000.

CHESAPEAKE BAY MAGAZINE. see SPORTS AND GAMES — Boats And Boating

910.202   US   ISSN 0886-5418 E158
CHEVRON U S A ODYSSEY. 1969. q. membership. (Chevron Travel Club) Ortho Information Services, 6001 Bollinger Canyon Rd., Rm. TB-120, San Ramon, CA 94583. TEL 415-842-5512. FAX 415-842-5518. Ed. Sally W. Smith. bk.rev.; circ. 450,000.
   Formerly: Chevron U S A (ISSN 0199-5707)

917   US   ISSN 0362-4595 F548.1
CHICAGO. 1952. m. $19.90. Chicago Publishing, Inc., 414 N. Orleans, Chicago, IL 60610. TEL 312-222-8999. Ed. Richard Babcock. adv.; bk.rev.; illus.; circ. 200,360. (also avail. in microform from BLH,UMI; microfiche from UMI)
   Indexed: Access (1975-), Art & Archaeol.Tech.Abstr., Mag.Ind.
   Former titles: Chicago Guide (ISSN 0042-9651); W F M T Guide.

917.704   US
CHICAGO (YEAR). a. $10. Harper Collins Publishers, Birnbaum Travel Guides, 10 E. 53rd St., New York, NY 10022-5299. TEL 212-207-7000. illus.; index.

CHICAGO ARCHITECTURE FOUNDATION NEWS. see ARCHITECTURE

910.09   US
CHICAGO MOTOR CLUB HOME & AWAY. bi-m. American Automobile Association, Chicago Motor Club, 999 E. Touhy, Des Plains, IL 60018-2798. TEL 708-390-9000. FAX 708-390-9112. Ed. G. Lionel Kramer. adv.; circ. 353,793.

910 917.7   US
CHICAGOLAND DINING GUIDE. 1981. a. $1.50. P B Communications, Inc., 874 Green Bay Rd., Winnetka, IL 60093. TEL 708-441-7892. Ed. Asher J. Birnbaum. adv.; illus.; circ. 55,000.
   Former titles: Chicagoland Dining and Nightlife Guide; North Shore Dining Guide.
   Description: Guide to Chicago area nightlife and dining.

910.2 914   UK
CHILDREN WELCOME! FAMILY HOLIDAY GUIDE. 1952. a. £2.99. F.H.G. Publications Ltd., Abbey Mill Business Centre, Seedhill, Paisley PA1 1JN, Scotland. TEL 041-887-0428. FAX 041-889-7204. Ed. Peter Clark. adv.; index.
   Formerly: Family Holiday Guide (ISSN 0071-3740); Formed by merger of: Children Welcome (ISSN 0069-3456) & Holiday Guide.
   Description: Holiday guidebook covering hotels and guesthouses where children are welcome.

CHINA GUIDEBOOK. see GENERAL INTEREST PERIODICALS — China

951.04   HK
CHINA TOURISM. French Edition: Voyage en Chine. Chinese edition: Zhongguo Luyou. (Editions in Chinese, English, French) Chinese & English ed. 1980; French ed. 1984. m. HK.$250($62) for English or French eds.; Chinese $55. Hong Kong China Tourism Press, 17th Fl., V. Heun Bldg., 138 Queen's Rd. Central, Hong Kong. TEL 852-5411331. FAX 852-8541721. TELEX 822225-HKCTP-HX. (US subscr. to: China Books & Periodicals, 2929 24th St, San Francisco, CA 94110) adv.; illus.; cum.index; circ. 80,000. (back issues avail.)
   Former titles: Culture, Arts and Crafts; China Tourism Pictorial.
   Description: Contains feature articles on sights, scenery, customs, travel experiences, recent archeological discoveries, and places of historical interest. Also contains regular articles on hotels and shopping.

910.202   HK
CHINA TRAVEL PRESS. (Text in English) m. $12. Ismay Publications Co., C.C. Wu Bldg. 812, 302-308 Hennessy Rd., Wanchai, Hong Kong. TEL 5752270. FAX 8345647. Ed. Jill Hunt.

910.4   US
CHINCOTEAGUE BEACHCOMBER. 1959. 20/yr. free. Box 249, Onley, VA 23418-0249. TEL 804-787-1200. FAX 804-787-9567. Ed. Bill Sterling. circ. 10,000.

910.4   IT
CIOCIARIA; ieri, oggi, domani. (Special editions avail.) vol.7, 1987. bi-m? Ente Provinciale per il Turismo di Frosinone, Piazzale de Matthaeis, Grattacielo L'Edera, Frosinone, Italy. TEL (0775)872525. Ed. Mario Grieco. adv.; charts; illus.
   Description: Features information on tourism, art and culture.

910.09   US
CITY GUIDE; New York's weekly visitors and convention guide. w. $29. Bill of Fare, Inc., 853 Seventh Ave., Ste. 1-A, New York, NY 10019-5215. TEL 212-315-0800. FAX 212-397-9513. Ed. Peter Insalaco. adv.; circ. 42,532.
   Description: Visitors and convention guide to New York.

051 792   US
CITY GUIDE - BROADWAY MAGAZINE. 1982. w. $29. Bill of Fare Inc., 853 7th Ave., Ste. 1-A, New York, NY 10019-5215. FAX 212-397-9513. Ed. Peter Insalaco. adv.; circ. 42,532.
   Former titles: Broadway, Bill of Fare; Bill of Fare.

910   US   ISSN 0277-0342
CITYGUIDE - THE SAN FRANCISCO BAY AREA AND NORTHERN CALIFORNIA. 1978. a. $9.95. Danella Publications, Box 9, Sausalito, CA 94966. TEL 415-332-9601. FAX 415-388-4235. Ed. Bella Whelan. adv.; circ. 60,000. (back issues avail.)
   Description: Contains restaurant menus and reviews and photo-reviews of shops, services, entertainment spots and attractions.

CLUB DE GOURMETS; gastronomy & travel magazine - gastronomia y viajes. see HOTELS AND RESTAURANTS

910.2   UK
COACHES & PARTIES WELCOME. 1977. a. free to qualified personnel. Lewis Productions Ltd., Unit 3, River Gardens Bus. Centre, Spur Rd., Feltham, Middx TW14 OSN, England. Ed. Jonathan Lewis. adv.; circ. 40,000.

910.09   UK
COACHMART. irreg. (approx. q.). £2.50 per no. E M A P Response Publishing, Wentworth House, Wentworth St., Peterborough PE1 1DS, England. TEL 0733-63100. FAX 0733-62656. Ed. Mark Williams.
   Formerly (until 1990): Day Trips and Short Breaks; Which incorporated: Tours and Excursions.
   Description: Provides the coach (bus) operator with current information every week from industry news to second-hand vehicles, parts accessories and support services.

COASTAL CRUISING. see SPORTS AND GAMES — Boats And Boating

910.4   GW
COLOGNE. TRAVEL-REPORT; information for travel agents. (Text in English, French, German, Italian and Spanish) a. free. Verkehrsamt der Stadt Koeln, Unter Fettenhennen 19, 5000 Cologne 1, Germany. TEL 0221-221-3345. FAX 0221-221-3320. TELEX 8883-421-TOC-D. Ed.Bd. circ. 50,000.

910   CK
COLOMBIA. CORPORACION NACIONAL DE TURISMO. BOLETIN INFORMATIVO C E N T U R. 1978. q. free. Corporacion Nacional de Turismo, Centro de Informacion Turistico, Calle 28, 13A-15, Piso 17, Apdo. Aereo 8400, Bogota, Colombia. TEL 2843049. TELEX 441350 COTUR. circ. 700.

910   CK   ISSN 0121-1870
COLOMBIA. CORPORACION NACIONAL DE TURISMO. CATALOGO NACIONAL DE TESIS DE TURISMO Y HOTELERIA. 1988. a. free. Corporacion Nacional de Turismo, Centro de Informacion y Turistica, Calle 28, 13A-15, Piso 17, Apdo. Aereo 8400, Bogota, Colombia. TEL 2843049. TELEX 441350 COTUR. bibl.; circ. 500.
   Description: Bibliography of graduate study works done by hotel and tourism students in Colombia.

910   CK   ISSN 0121-1889
COLOMBIA. CORPORACION NACIONAL DE TURISMO. CATALOGO TURISTICO. 1987. a. free. Corporacion Nacional de Turismo, Centro de Informacion Turistica, Calle 28, 13A-15, Piso 17, Apdo. Aereo 8400, Bogota, Colombia. TEL 2843049. TELEX 441350 COTUR. bibl.; circ. 500.

TRAVEL AND TOURISM

910   CK
COLOMBIA. CORPORACION NACIONAL DE TURISMO. CRONICA TURISTICA. 1988. q. free. Corporacion Nacional de Turismo, Centro de Informacion Turistica, Calle 28, 13A-15, Piso 17, Apdo. Aereo 8400, Bogota, Colombia. TEL 2843049. TELEX 441350 COTUR. circ. 700.

910.09   US
COLORADO DIRECTORY OF CAMPING, LODGES, CABINS, FUN THINGS TO DO. 1980. a. free. (Colorado Campground Association) Colorado Campground & CabinResort Agency, Inc., 5101 Pennsylvania Ave., Boulder, CO 80303. TEL 303-499-9343. Ed. Hilton Fitt-Peaster. adv.; circ. 400,000. (back issues avail.)
    Former titles: Colorado Directory of Camping, R Vs, Cabins, Fun Things to Do; Colorado Directory of Camping, Cabins, Rafting, Fun Things to Do.

917.88   US   ISSN 0146-9991
COLORADO EXPRESS. 1972. s-a. $20 for 2 yrs. Box 18214, Capitol Hill Station, Denver, CO 80218. TEL 303-320-6976. Ed. Karl Kocivar. adv.; bk.rev.; bibl.; charts; illus.; cum.index for vols. 1-13 in vol. 13; circ. 18,000. (back issues avail.)
    Description: Explores alternative cultures.

917.804   US
COLORADO OFFICIAL STATE VACATION GUIDE. 1988. a. Tourism Board, 1625 Broadway, Ste. 1700, Denver, CO 80202. TEL 303-592-5410. FAX 303-592-5406. adv.; circ. 1,000,000.
    Description: Provides information for planning a Colorado vacation with details on lodging, resorts, attractions, transportation, parks and events.

917.904   US
▼**COLUMBIA GORGE MAGAZINE.** 1990. a. $3.95. Gorge Publishing, Inc., 500 Morton Rd., Box 918, Hood River, OR 97031. TEL 503-386-7440. FAX 503-386-7480. circ. 60,000.
    Description: Visitor and recreation guide to the Columbia River Gorge.

COMMERCIO TURISMO. see *BUSINESS AND ECONOMICS — Domestic Commerce*

910.09   US
CONDE NAST TRAVELER; the truth in travel. 1954. m. $15 (Canada $27; elsewhere $31). Conde Nast Publications Inc., Conde Nast Traveler Magazine, 360 Madison Ave., New York, NY 10017. TEL 800-777-0700. FAX 212-880-2190. Ed. Thomas J. Wallace. adv.; bk.rev.; illus.; circ. 757,000. (also avail. in microform from UMI) Indexed: R.G.
    Formerly (until 1987): Signature (ISSN 0037-5039)

910.09   UK
CONFERENCE & INCENTIVE TRAVEL. m. £40 (foreign £50). Haymarket Business Publications Ltd., 30 Lancaster Gate, London W2 3LP, England. Ed. Sara White. adv. contact: Nick Stimpson.

914.406   FR   ISSN 0336-9455
CONNAISSANCE DU PAYS D'OC. (Text in French and Occitan) 1973-1983; N.S. 1984. bi-m. 110 F. Editions de la Source, B.P. 1034, 34006 Montpellier Cedex, France. Ed. Jean Boekholt. adv.; bk.rev.; illus.

910.09   CN
CONNAISSONS NOS VOISINS. (Text in English, French) 1980. q. $8. Communication 75 Corp., C.P. 416, Sta. H, Montreal, Que. H3G 2L1, Canada. TEL 514-989-0398. Ed. J. Noel Parenteau. circ. 12,200.

917.404   US
CONNECTICUT TRAVELER. 1983. m. $11. Connecticut Motor Club, Inc., 2276 Whitney Ave., Hamden, CT 06518. TEL 203-288-7441. adv.; circ. 143,335.
    Description: Covers vacationing, weekending, recreation and entertainment.

974   US
CONNECTICUT VACATION GUIDE. 1968. a. free. Department of Economic Development, 865 Brook St., Rocky Hill, CT 06067. TEL 203-258-4238. Ed. Anthony Davenport. circ. 250,000.

917   US
CONNECTICUT WEST. 1970. a. $2. Foothills Trader, Inc., 85 River Rd., Collinsville, CT 06022-1226. TEL 203-693-2990. FAX 203-693-2875. Ed. James Timpano. adv.; bibl.; circ. 20,000.

910.09   US
CONNECTIONS (BOSTON, 1989). 1989. bi-m. $14.95. Saga International Holidays, Ltd., 120 Boylston St., Boston, MA 02116. TEL 617-451-6808. Ed. Rodica Iliescu-Stahl. circ. 300,000.
    Description: Provides articles on healthy traveling, cruise connections, currency news and travel features. For seniors 60 years of age and older with an interest in traveling.

658.8   NE
CONSUMENTEN REISGIDS. 1973. q. fl.23. Consumentenbond, Leeghwaterplein 26, 2521 CV The Hague, Netherlands. FAX 070-3847413. TELEX 33713. charts; illus.; circ. 61,000. Indexed: Rural Recreat.Tour.Abstr., World Agri.Econ.& Rural Sociol.Abstr.
    Description: Evaluation of trips and tourist attractions in all parts of the world. Covers hotel accomodation, transportation, sights, prices, and organized trips. Includes travel guide evaluation and maps.

910.202 640.73   US   ISSN 0887-8439
                               CODEN: CRTLE3
CONSUMER REPORTS TRAVEL LETTER. 1985. m. $37 (foreign $43). Consumers Union of United States, Inc., 101 Truman Ave., Yonkers, NY 10703-1057. TEL 914-378-2000. FAX 914-378-2906. (Subscr. to: Box 53629, Boulder, CO 80322-3629) Ed. Ed Perkins. circ. 60,000. (back issues avail.)
• Also available online. Vendor(s): DIALOG (File no.646).

CONTINENTAL (DALLAS). see *GENERAL INTEREST PERIODICALS — United States*

914.7 388   UK
CONTINENTAL MOTORING HOLIDAYS. 1972. a. £50. Contemporary Press Ltd., 21A Alma Square, London NW8 9QA, England. Ed. Brian Hedges.

914   UK
CONTINENTAL MOTORING NEWS. m. £50. Travel Publications Ltd., 23 Elizabeth St., London SW1W 9RW, England. Ed. David Wickers. adv.; circ. 45,000.

COOL TRAVELER; literary publication about "place". see *LITERATURE*

914   DK
COPENHAGEN - THIS WEEK. m. Politikens Service Selskab A-S, Vestergade 24, 1456 Copenhagen K, Denmark. FAX 45-33-328674. Ed. John Jensen. adv.; circ. 110,000.

914.2   UK
CORNWALL BLUE BOOK GUIDE AND COUNTY HANDBOOK. 1927. a. E.J. Hubber, Ed.& Pub., Carnmellyn, Newquay, Cornwall, Trenhaile TR8 5JL, England. adv.; circ. 30,000.

910.9   US   ISSN 0739-1587
CORPORATE & INCENTIVE TRAVEL. 1983. m. $55. Coastal Communications Corporation, 488 Madison Ave., New York, NY 10022. TEL 212-888-1500. FAX 212-888-8008. Ed. Harvey Grotsky. adv.; circ. 51,029.
    Description: Covers corporate meetings and incentive travel planners.

910.09   US
CORPORATE CRUISE NEWS. bi-m. Landry & Kling, Inc., 1390 S. Dixie Hwy., Ste. 1207, Coral Gables, FL 33146-2943. TEL 305-661-1880. Ed. Josephine King.

910   US   ISSN 0882-8709
CORPORATE TRAVEL; news and ideas for business travel management. 1985. m. $65. Miller Freeman Inc. (New York) (Subsidiary of: United Newspapers Group), 1515 Broadway, New York, NY 10036. TEL 212-869-1300. FAX 212-302-6273. adv.; circ. 45,000. (tabloid format; back issues avail.)

CORREZE MAGAZINE; magazines de France. see *GENERAL INTEREST PERIODICALS — France*

CORRIERE DEL MEZZOGIORNO; Giornale indipendente di informazioni. see *POLITICAL SCIENCE*

914   IT   ISSN 0045-8716
COSMORAMA; viaggi e turismo. 1960. q. L.3000. Compagnia Italiana Turismo, Piazza della Repubblica 68, Rome, Italy. adv.; bk.rev.; illus.

914.502   IT
COSTA SMERALDA MAGAZINE. (Text and summaries in English and Italian) 1975. bi-m. L.50000. (Consorzio Costa Smeralda) Servizi Marketing Costa Smeralda, 07020 Porto Cervo, Sardinia, Italy. Ed. Claudio Miorelli. adv.; bk.rev.; circ. 40,000. (back issues avail.)

COUNTRY HOMES & INTERIORS. see *INTERIOR DESIGN AND DECORATION*

330   US   ISSN 0898-560X
TX901
COUNTRY INNS, BED & BREAKFAST. 1986. bi-m. $15. Country Inns Publications, Inc., Box 182, S. Orange, NJ 07079-0182. TEL 201-762-7090. FAX 201-762-1491. Ed. Gail Rudder Kent. adv.; bk.rev.; circ. 200,000.
    Description: Covers country inns and bed and breakfast across the United States, international features, interior design, and gourmet dining.

910.202   CN   ISSN 0709-2679
COUP D'OEIL SUR LE SAGUENAY-LAC-SAINT-JEAN. 1978. q. Can.$5. Promotions Gaston Maziade Enr., 623 Louis-Hemon, Chicoutimi, Que. G7H 3W2, Canada. TEL 418-545-7919. Ed. Gaston Maziade. circ. 22,500.

910.09   US
COURIER (LEXINGTON). m. National Tour Association, Inc., 546 E. Main St., Lexington, KY 40508-2342. TEL 606-253-1036. FAX 606-231-9837. Ed. William A. Bowden. adv.; circ. 5,200.

910.09   AT
CRESCENT CHATTER. 1973. w. Crescent Head Country Club Ltd., 1 Rankine St., Crescent Head, N.S.W. 2440, Australia. Ed. Brian Bowyer. bk.rev.; circ. 500.

910.09   US
CRUISE AND VACATION VIEWS. bi-m. Orban Communications, Inc., 60 E. 42nd St., Ste. 905, New York, NY 10165-0905. TEL 212-867-7470. FAX 212-682-4437. Ed. Michael Brown. adv.; circ. 33,000.

910.202   US   ISSN 0886-5604
CRUISE DIGEST REPORTS. 1982. bi-m. $35 (foreign $40). International Cruise Passengers Association, 1521 Alton Rd., Ste. 350, Miami Beach, FL 33139-3301. TEL 305-374-2224. Ed. Douglas Ward. adv.; bk.rev.; circ. 30,000. (tabloid format)
    Description: Presents in-depth reports and reviews on cruise ships, and industry news.

917.14   US   ISSN 0893-1240
CRUISE INDUSTRY NEWS. 1985. s-m. $485. Nissen-Lie Communications, Inc., 441 Lexington Ave., Ste. 1209 A, New York, NY 10017. TEL 212-986-1025. FAX 212-986-1033. Ed. Oivind Mathisen. circ. 2,000. Key Title: Cruise Industry News (Newsletter).
    Description: Inside news report of the cruise shipping industry in North America.

917.04   US   ISSN 1047-3378
CRUISE INDUSTRY NEWS ANNUAL. 1988. a. $445. Nissen-Lie Communications, Inc., 441 Lexington Ave., Ste. 1209 A, New York, NY 10017. TEL 212-986-1025. FAX 212-986-1033. Ed. Oivind Mathisen. circ. 1,100.
    Former titles: Cruise Industry Annual (Year); North American Cruise Industry (Year).
    Description: Covers the cruise shipping industry worldwide.

917.14   US
CRUISE INDUSTRY NEWS QUARTERLY. 1985. q. $20. Nissen-Lie Communications, Inc., 441 Lexington Ave., Ste. 1209 A, New York, NY 10017. TEL 212-986-1025. FAX 212-986-1033. circ. 10,000.
    Description: For cruise industry professionals.

910.09   US
CRUISE TRADE. m. Travel Trade Publications, 15 W. 44th St., New York, NY 10036. TEL 212-730-6600. FAX 212-730-7137. Ed. Joel M. Abels. adv.; circ. 36,983.
    Description: Provides cruise sellers with news and marketing tools.

TRAVEL AND TOURISM

910.09 US ISSN 0199-5111
CRUISE TRAVEL; ships, ports, schedules, prices. 1979. bi-m. $18. World Publishing Co. (Subsidiary of Century Publishing Company), 990 Grove St., Evanston, IL 60201. TEL 708-491-6440. FAX 718-491-0459. (Subscr. to: Box 342, Mt. Morris, IL 61054-0342) Ed. Robert Meyers. adv.; charts; illus.; stat.; circ. 160,000. (also avail. in microfiche; reprint service avail. from UMI)

910.09 US
▼**CRUISES AND TOURS**. 1992. q. $11.80. Vacation Publications, Inc., 2411 Fountain View, Ste. 201, Houston, TX 77057. TEL 713-974-6903. FAX 713-974-0445. adv.; circ. 50,000.
  Incorporates: Cruise Vacations.

910.202 CU
CUBA NOTICIAS TURISTICAS. m. Instituto Nacional del Turismo, Malecon y G, Vedado, Havana, Cuba.

910.09 US
CURRENTS (STAMFORD). 3/yr. Cruise Passenger Network, 2001 W. Main St., Ste. 245, Stamford, CT 06902-4501. TEL 203-359-8626. FAX 203-327-5062. Ed. Barbara Coats. circ. 580,000.

910.4 382 CY
CYPRUS. TOURISM ORGANISATION. ANNUAL REPORT. a. Tourism Organisation, Nicosia, Cyprus. charts; stat.

910.4 338 CY ISSN 0256-1069
CYPRUS TIME OUT; tourist and business guide. (Text in English) 1978. m. $48. Comarts, 2 Pygmalionos & Ledras St., Christophides Bldg., 2nd Fl., A.P. 9, P.O. Box 3697, Nicosia, Cyprus. FAX 360668. Ed. Ellada A. Sophocleous. adv.; bk.rev.; circ. 4,000. (back issues avail.)

910.2 GW ISSN 0078-3943
D C C - CAMPING FUEHRER EUROPA. 1950. a. DM.29.80. (Deutscher Camping Club e.V.) D C C-Wirtschaftsdienst und Verlag GmbH, Postfach 400428, 8000 Munich 40, Germany. TEL 089-334021. FAX 089-334737. TELEX 5215974. adv.; circ. 100,000.

796.5 GW
D C C - TOURISTIK SERVICE. a. (Deutscher Camping Club e.V.) D C C - Wirtschaftsdienst und Verlag GmbH, Postfach 400428, 8000 Munich 40, Germany. TEL 089-334021. FAX 089-334737. TELEX 5215974. adv.

910.2 NE ISSN 0012-4109
D I T. (Documentatie en Informatie over Toerisme); vakblad voor de reiswereld. 1959. fortn. fl.165. Nijgh Periodieken, DIT, P.O. Box 122, 3100 AC Schiedam, Netherlands. TEL 010-427-1400. FAX 010-473-9911. TELEX 22680 NIJGHP. Ed. Peter Uinken. adv.; bk.rev.; illus.; stat.; circ. 3,300.
  Indexed: Key to Econ.Sci.

647.94 GW
D J H; Informationen Meinungen Berichte. 1951. bi-m. DM.18. Deutsches Jugend - Herbergswerk, Bismarckstr. 8, Postfach 1455, 4930 Detmold, Germany. TEL 05231-74010. FAX 05231-740167. Ed. Bert Pichel. bk.rev.; illus.; circ. 4,000.

910.09 GW
D L T FLUGZEIT. (Text in English and German) 4/yr. free on board Lufthansa flights. (D L T Luftverkehrsgesellschaft mbH) Koesler Verlag GmbH, Von-Werth-Str. 44, 5000 Cologne 1, Germany. TEL 0221-131366. FAX 0221-137541. TELEX 889990-RSB-D. circ. 40,000.

DAMPF UND REISE; Bahnerlebnisse rund um die Welt - Ueberseeische Bahnen. see *TRANSPORTATION — Railroads*

910.202 US
DAMRON ROAD ATLAS. 1989. biennial. $12.95. Damron Company, Inc., P.O. Box 42-2458, San Francisco, CA 94142-2458. TEL 415-255-0404. FAX 415-703-9049. Ed. Gina Gatta. adv.; illus.; circ. 50,000.
  Description: Atlas for gay and lesbians highlighting gay locations and tourist attractions in major North American metropolitan areas.

914.8 DK ISSN 0109-6125
DANMARKS TURIST VEJVISER. (Text in Danish, English and German) 1984. a. DKK 40.10. Glumsoe Bogtrykkeri, Noeddevej 10, 4171 Glumsoe, Denmark. illus.

914.8 DK ISSN 0109-6486
DANSK FAELLESREJSE FORENING. MEDLEMSBLAD. 1982. 3/yr. Dansk Faellerejse Forening, c/o Knud Noerr, Sct. Laurentiivej 114, 9990 Skagen, Denmark. illus.

914 DK ISSN 0904-1796
DANSK TURISME. 1982. 10/yr. DKK 300. Danmarks Turistraad - Danish Tourist Board, Vesterbrogade 6 D, 1620 Copenhagen V, Denmark. FAX 33-931416. TELEX 27586. Ed. Lone Zilstorff. adv.; bk.rev.; illus.; circ. 10,000.
  Formerly: D T Forum (ISSN 0108-190X)

919.4 AT
DAWSONS GUIDE - AUSTRALIAN & WORLDWIDE HOTELS. (In two editions: Domestic Consultants and International Consultants) 1951. s-a. Aus.$69.50. Dawson Magazines Pty. Ltd., Tramore Places, Killarney Heights, Sydney, N.S.W. 1087, Australia. adv.; circ. 2,000.
  Formerly (until 1968): Dawsons Guide to Hotels, Motels and Resorts.

910.202 AT ISSN 0815-6794
DAWSONS VENUE DIRECTORY. 1984. s-a. Aus.$35. Dawson Magazines Pty. Ltd., Tramore House, Killarney Heights, Sydney, N.S.W. 1087, Australia. TEL 452 1777. (Subscr. to: P.O. Box 173, 2086 Frenchs Forest, Australia) Ed. Genevieve Rush. adv.; index; circ. 6,388.
  Description: Directory of meetings places, executive retreats and incentive resorts throughout Australasia.

DECCAN GEOGRAPHER. see *GEOGRAPHY*

917.4 US ISSN 1052-4592
DELAWARE VALLEY; magazine of suburban living. 1981. m. $19. Pleasure Hunt Magazine Inc., 2260 Cabot Blvd. W., No. 2264, Langhorne, PA 19047. TEL 215-750-7840. FAX 215-750-7992. Ed. Jodie Green. adv.; bk.rev.; circ. 185,000.
  Formerly: Pleasure Hunt Magazine (ISSN 0883-2382)

914 US
DEPARTURES. (Editions avail. for the United Kingdom, Europe, Australia, and Japan) 1984. bi-m. £18. American Express Publishing Corp., 1120 Ave. of the Americas, New York, NY 10036. TEL 212-382-5600. Ed. Gary Walther. circ. 471,000.

917.104 CN
DESTINATION CALGARY. 1987. bi-m. membership. Calgary Convention and Visitors Bureau, 237 8th Ave., S.E., Calgary, Alta. T2E 0K8, Canada. TEL 403-263-8510. FAX 403-262-3809. Ed. Angela Martin. circ. 1,050 (controlled). (tabloid format; back issues avail.)

917.904 US
DESTINATION WASHINGTON. 1987. a. $4.95. (Washington (State) Tourism Development Division) G T E Discovery Publications, Inc., 22026 20th Ave., S.E., Ste. 101, Bothell, WA 98021. TEL 800-331-3510. FAX 206-486-7296. adv.; circ. 350,000.
  Description: Features outdoor recreation information, a calendar of events, and a profile of the state's tourism regions.

910.09 CN
DESTINATIONS. q. Globe and Mail Ltd., 444 Front St. W., Toronto, Ont. M5V 2S9, Canada. TEL 416-585-5348. FAX 416-585-5705. TELEX 06-219629. Ed. Catherine Bradbury.
  Description: National consumer travel and leisure magazine featuring explore activity-based travel such as hiking, scuba diving, mountain biking, sailing and golf, as well as holiday packages that cater to specific hobbies such as wine, art and wildlife.

910.202 US
▼**DESTINATIONS (ALEXANDRIA)**. 1990. q. $24. Destination Media Productions, 5704-H General Washington Dr., Alexandria, VA 22312. TEL 703-941-1796. Ed. Al Waldack. circ. 45,000.
  Description: For affluent travelers who have a yen for exotic or luxurious vacations. Covers vacation sites and rental properties.

910.4 US ISSN 0279-8468
DESTINATIONS (WASHINGTON). 1979. m. membership. American Bus Association, 1015 15th St., N.W., Ste. 250, Washington, DC 20005. TEL 202-842-1645. FAX 202-842-0850. Ed. Mark Beavers. adv.; illus.; tr.lit.; circ. 5,000. (back issues avail.)

DETROIT NEWSPAPER AGENCY. TRAVEL DIRECTORY. see *TRANSPORTATION — Air Transport*

914.8 DK ISSN 0107-8720
DEUTSCHER VOLKSKALENDER NORDSCHLESWIG. 1924. a. DKK 30. Deutscher Schul- und Sprachverein fuer Nordschleswig, Joergensgaard 5, P.O. Box 242, DK-6200 Aabenraa, Denmark. TEL 45-74624103. FAX 74-62-73-61. Ed. Franz Christiansen. bk.rev.; illus.; circ. 2,500.

910.4 UK ISSN 0269-0551
DEVON TOURISM REVIEW. 1981. a. £5. Devon County Council, Property Department, Amenities and Countryside Division, County Hall, Topsham Rd., Exeter EX2 4QQ, England. FAX 0392-272301. TELEX 42626-DCDBEX-G. Ed. Lesley Garlick. illus.; charts; circ. 1,000.
  —BLDSC shelfmark: 3579.110100.
  Former titles (until 1985): Devon. Property Department. Tourism and Recreation. Topic Report; Devon County Planning Department. Tourism and Recreation. Topic Report (ISSN 0261-2445)
  Description: Reports on the characteristics and trends of the county's tourist industry. Includes details of recent developments in investment, marketing and other related visitor services.

THE DIABETIC TRAVELER. see *PHYSICAL FITNESS AND HYGIENE*

918 AG
DINERS. 9/yr. Lugones, Lanusse, y Asociados, San Martin 232, 2nd Fl., No. 228, 1004 Buenos Aires, Argentina. circ. 110,000.

910.202 AG
DINERS CLUB. m. (Diners Club (Argentina)) Editorial Alton Nivel, S.A.L., Carlos Pellegrini 1023, 9 No. Piso, Buenos Aires, Argentina. adv.; circ. 100,000.

910.202 GW
DINERS CLUB MAGAZINE. (Text in German) 1968. m. DM.6. Gong Verlag, Postfach 400548, 8000 Munich 40, Germany. FAX 089-27270485. Ed. Karin Felix. adv.; bk.rev.; circ. 145,000.

910.09 US
DIRECTORY OF FREE VACATION & TRAVEL INFORMATION. 1977. irreg., latest ed. 1991. $4.95. Pilot Books, 103 Cooper St., Babylon, NY 11702. TEL 516-422-2225. FAX 516-422-2227. Ed. Raymond Carlson.
  Formerly (until 1985): National Directory of Free Vacation and Travel Information.
  Description: Shows where to obtain brochures, maps, events calenders and other useful facts covering recreational areas and landmarks in the U.S. and Canada.

790 US
DIRECTORY OF FUNPARKS & ATTRACTIONS. Variant title: Amusement Business's Funparks Directory. 1961. a. $48. B P I Communications, Inc., Amusement Business Division, Box 24970, Nashville, TN 37202. TEL 615-321-4250. FAX 615-327-1575. Ed. Tom Powell. adv.; circ. 6,000. (also avail. in microfilm)
  Former titles: Funparks Directory; Funspots Directory (ISSN 0071-9951)
  Description: Complete guide to over 2,500 amusement and theme parks, water parks, tourist attractions, zoos and family entertainment centers in the US, Canada and overseas.

T

TRAVEL AND TOURISM

910.09   US   ISSN 0732-6572
HD5260
DIRECTORY OF INCENTIVE TRAVEL INTERNATIONAL. 1977. a. $50. Avanstar Communications, Inc., 7500 Old Oak Blvd., Cleveland, OH 44130. TEL 216-826-2839. FAX 216-891-2726. (Subscr. to: 1 E. First Ave., Duluth, MN 55802) Ed. Connie Goldstein. adv.; bk.rev.; circ. 40,061.
   Former titles: Incentive Travel International; Directory of Incentive Travel International.
   Description: Annual guide to incentive destinations and suppliers worldwide.

910   US
DIRECTORY OF LOW COST VACATIONS WITH A DIFFERENCE. 1986. irreg., latest 1989. $5.95. Pilot Books, 103 Cooper St., Babylon, NY 11702. TEL 516-422-2225. FAX 516-422-2227. Ed. J. Crawford.
   Description: Guide to alternatives to the ordinary vacation such as student exchange, bed and breakfast and work-study programs.

910.202   US
DIRECTORY OF THEME & AMUSEMENT PARKS. 1978. irreg., latest 1992. $5.95. Pilot Books, 103 Cooper St., Babylon, NY 11702. TEL 516-422-2225. FAX 516-422-2227. Eds. Raymond Carlson, Eleanor Popelka.
   Formerly (until 1992): National Directory of Theme Parks and Amusement Areas.
   Description: State by state listing of parks, kiddielands, amusement areas and zoos. Entries include major attractions, address and telephone number.

910.09   US
DISCERNING TRAVELER. 8/yr. Lida Limited, 504 W. Mermaid Lane, Philadelphia, PA 19118. TEL 215-247-5578.

910.09   US
DISCOVER (PALO ALTO); peninsula & silicon valley. 1974. m. $12.50. Latimer Publications, 318 Town & Country Village, Palo Alto, CA 94301. TEL 415-324-1570. FAX 415-324-4220. Ed. Merlyn Holmes. adv.; circ. 30,000. (back issues avail.)
   Description: Visitor's guide to restaurants, shopping and entertainment.

914.7   BU   ISSN 0204-8418
DISCOVER BULGARIA. (Text in Bulgarian, English, French, German, Russian) 1959. bi-m. $17. Balkantourist, Vitosha Bldv. No.1, 1050 Sofia, Bulgaria. TEL 88-49-61. (Subscr. addr.: Lenin Sq., No.1, 1000 Sofia, Bulgaria) Ed. Liliya Gerasimova. circ. 47,000.

910.09   US
DISCOVER COSTA RICA. (Text in English, Spanish) 1989. a. North-South Net, Inc., 100 Almeria Ave., Ste. 220, Coral Gables, FL 33134. TEL 305-441-9744. FAX 305-441-9739. charts; illus.
   Description: Informs travelers about Costa Rica and supplies useful information.

918.04   US
▼**DISCOVER ECUADOR.** (Text in English, Spanish) 1990. a. North-South Net, Inc., 100 Almeria Ave., Ste. 220, Coral Gables, FL 33134. TEL 305-441-9744. FAX 305-441-9739. charts; illus.
   Description: Provides useful information for travellers to Ecuador.

910.09   US
DISCOVER GUATEMALA. (Text in English, Spanish) 1989. a. North-South Net, Inc., 100 Almeria Ave., Ste. 200, Coral Gables, FL 33134. TEL 305-441-9744. FAX 305-441-9739. charts; illus.
   Description: Informs travelers about Guatemala, and supplies useful information.

910.09   US
DISCOVER HAWAII SALES PLANNER; the travel professional's guide to the island. 1975. s-a. $30. Hawaii Business Publishing Corp., Box 913, Honolulu, HI 96814. TEL 808-946-3978. Ed. Michael J. Flynn. circ. 40,000.
   Formerly: Discover Hawaii.

918.04   US
▼**DISCOVER HONDURAS.** (Text in English, Spanish) 1990. a. North-South Net, Inc., 100 Almeria Ave., Ste. 220, Coral Gables, FL 33134. TEL 305-441-9744. FAX 305-441-9739.
   Description: Provides useful information for travellers to Honduras.

917   UK   ISSN 0951-8126
DISCOVER NORTH AMERICA. 1981. a. free to qualified personnel. Phoenix Publishing & MediA Ltd., 10-20 Scrutton St., London EC2A 4RT, England. TEL 071-247-0537. FAX 071-371-2741. (U.S. addr.: 21787 Ventura Blvd., No. 251, Woodland Hills, California) Ed. Stewart Wild. circ. 75,000. (back issues avail.)
   Former titles (until 1986): Holiday U.S.A. and Canada Magazine; Holiday U.S.A.

DISCOVER NORTH AMERICA TRAVEL INDUSTRY DIRECTORY. see BUSINESS AND ECONOMICS — Trade And Industrial Directories

910.09   US
DISCOVER THE PLATINUM COAST. 1986. bi-m. Pacetta Enterprises, Inc., 666 11th Ave., S., Naples, FL 33940. TEL 813-263-1633. Ed. B. Jane Pinel. circ. 150,000.

910.202   HK
DISCOVERY. (Text in English) m. (Cathay Pacific Airways) Emphasis HK Ltd., 10th Fl., Wilson House, 19-27 Wyndham Street, Central, Hong Kong, Hong Kong. FAX 810-6738. TELEX 74523-EMPAS-HX. Ed. Derek Davies. circ. 140,000.

910.2   US   ISSN 0012-3641
GV1024
DISCOVERY (CHICAGO). 1961. q. $8 to non-members. (Allstate Motor Club) Hill and Knowlton, Inc., One Illinois Center, 111 E. Wacker Dr., Ste. 1700, Chicago, IL 60601. TEL 312-565-1200. FAX 312-565-5923. (Subscr. to: 1500 W. Shure Dr., Arlington Heights, IL 60004) Ed. Scott Powers. adv.; bk.rev.; illus.; circ. 1,700,000. (also avail. in microform from UMI; back issues avail.; reprint service avail. from UMI)
   Description: Explores the world by emphasizing sightseeing by car.

916.2   UK
DISCOVERY GUIDE TO CAIRO. 1985. irreg. £7.95. Immel Publishing Ltd., 20 Berkeley St., Berkeley Sq., London N1X 5AE, England. TEL 0403-710971. FAX 0403-711143. TELEX 265871. (Subscr. to: Biblios PDS Ltd., Star Road, Partridge Green, West Sussex RH13 8LD, England)
   Description: Serves the historically-minded traveler and the demanding egyptologist alike.

916.2   UK
DISCOVERY GUIDE TO EGYPT. 1981. irreg. £12.95. Immel Publishing Ltd., 20 Berkeley St., Berkeley Sq., London N1X 5AE, England. TEL 0403-710971. FAX 0403-711143. TELEX 265-871. (Subscr. to: Biblios PDS Ltd., Star Road, Partridge Green, West Sussex, West Sussex RH13 8LD, England)
   Formerly: Travelaid Guide to Egypt.

910.4   JA
▼**DISNEY FAN.** (Text in Japanese) 1990. bi-m. Kodansha Ltd., International Division, 12-2 Otowa 2-chome, Bunkyo-ku, Tokyo 112, Japan. TEL 03-3945-1111. FAX 03-3943-7815. TELEX J34509 KODANSHA. Ed. Masataka Ono. circ. 150,000.
   Description: Provides Disneyland information for the Disney fan.

917.904   US
DISNEYLAND (YEAR). a. $9.95. Houghton Mifflin Co., One Beacon St., Boston, MA 02107. TEL 617-725-5000. (Dist. by: Avon Books, Box 767, Dresden, TN 38225) Ed. Stephen Birnbaum.

DIVER MAGAZINE. see SPORTS AND GAMES

910.09   US
DIVERSION (TAPPAN). 1986. m. $36. Corporacion Editorial, S.A., Box 70, c/o Gretta Alison Int'l, Inc., Tappan, NY 10983. TEL 914-359-6928. FAX 914-359-3986. adv.: B&W page $1621, color page $2586; trim 8 1/4 x 10 7/8. circ. 15,723.
   Description: Directed to Mexican physicians.

910.2   AE   ISSN 0012-4311
DJEZAIR. 1965. s-a. free. Ministere du Tourisme, Office National de l'Animation, de la Promotion et de l'Information Touristique, 27 rue Khelifa Boukhalfa, Algiers, Algeria. Ed. Hafida Chaouch. bk.rev.; charts; illus.

910.09   CN   ISSN 0821-5758
DOCTOR'S REVIEW; leisure-time journal for physicians. 1983. m. Can.$40. Parkhurst Publishing, 400 McGill St., 3rd Fl., Montreal, Que. H2Y 2G1, Canada. FAX 514-397-0228. Ed. David Elkins. circ. 36,950.

DOMOVA POKLADNICA. see LITERATURE

910.4   US
DUDE RANCHER MAGAZINE - DIRECTORY. 1930. a. $3. Dude Ranchers Association, Box 471, LaPorte, CO 80535. TEL 303-223-8440. Ed. Amey Grubbs. adv.; bk.rev.; illus.; circ. 18,000. (back issues avail.)
   Formed by the merger of: Dude Rancher & Dude Rancher Directory.
   Description: Provides descriptions of the association's members and activities.

914   GW   ISSN 0012-7027
DUESSELDORFER HEFTE. 1955. s-m. DM.50. Triltsch Druck und Verlag GmbH und Co. KG, Herzogstr. 53, 4000 Duesseldorf, Germany. adv.; bk.rev.

914.2   UK
EAST ANGLIA GUIDE. 1973. a. £2.50. East Anglia Tourist Board, Toppesfield Hall, Hadleigh, Suffolk, England. FAX 0473-823060. TELEX 987447 EATB G. Ed. E. Woolnough. adv.; circ. 45,000.

917 796.5   US   ISSN 0363-2091
GV191.46.M4
EASTERN CANADA CAMPBOOK. Cover title: R V and Tent Sites in New Brunswick, Newfoundland, Nova Scotia, Ontario, Prince Edward Island, Quebec. a. membership. American Automobile Association, 1000 AAA Dr., Heathrow, FL 32746-5063. TEL 407-444-7962. FAX 407-444-7380. adv.; illus.; circ. 223,204.
   Formerly (until 1980): Eastern Canada Camping.

914.704   US
EASTERN EUROPE (YEAR). a. $17. Harper Collins Publishers, Birnbaum Travel Guides, 10 E. 53rd St., New York, NY 10022-5299. TEL 212-207-7000. illus.; index.

910.09   FR
ECHO TOURISTIQUE. 1933. w. 490 F. (foreign 723 F.)(effective Jan. 1991). (Editions Touristiques Internationales) Groupe L S A, 6 rue Marius Aufan, 92300 Levallois Perret, France. TEL 47-58-20-00. FAX 47-58-77-00. Ed. Anne Gillet. adv.; circ. 9,200.

914   IT   ISSN 0012-9488
ECO DELLA RIVIERA. 1915. s-w. L.14000. Giacomo Gandolfi S.p.A., Corso Mombello 54, 18038 San Remo, Italy. adv.; circ. 8,600. (looseleaf format; also avail. in cards)

910.202 910.03   US
ECONOMIC IMPACT OF THE NEGRO TRAVELER. 1963. biennial. $102.50. Travelers' Research Publishing Co., Inc., 11717 S. Vincennes Ave., Chicago, IL 60643. TEL 312-881-3712. Ed. Clarence M. Markham, Jr. stat.; circ. 10,000. (tabloid format; back issues avail.) **Indexed:** World Bank.Abstr.
   Formerly: Impact of the Negro Traveler.

910.09   US   ISSN 0733-642X
G155.U6
ECONOMIC REVIEW OF TRAVEL IN AMERICA. a. $60. U S Travel Data Center, Two Lafayette Ctr., 1133 21st St., N.W., Washington, DC 20036. TEL 202-293-1040. (reprint service avail. from CIS) **Indexed:** SRI.
   Description: Analysis of travel data presented in tables and charts.

910.09   US
ECOSPHERE. 1965. q. $12. (International Ecosystems University) Forum International, Inc., 91 Gregory Lane, Ste. 21, Pleasant Hill, CA 94523. TEL 415-671-2900. FAX 415-946-1500. Ed. Nicolas D. Hetzer. adv.; bk.rev.; abstr.; bibl.; illus.; circ. 6,000. (tabloid format)

TRAVEL AND TOURISM

910.202 EC
ECUADOR GUIA TURISTICA. (Text in English and Spanish) 1969. irreg. Prensa Informative Turistica, Edificio Brauer, Meja 438, Ofc. 43, Quito, Ecuador. Ed. Jorge Vaca O. adv.; circ. 30,000.

914.6 SP ISSN 0422-6186
EDITUR; semanario de informacion y documentacion turistica. 1960. m. 24300 ptas. Ediciones Turisticas, S. A., Gran via Carlos III 86, Barcelona 28, Spain. Ed. Jaime Arias Zimmermann. circ. 3,000.

910.09 US
EDUCATED TRAVELER. 10/yr. Box 220822, Chantilly, VA 22022. TEL 703-471-1063. FAX 703-471-4439. Ed. Ann H. Waigand. circ. 1,500.

910.202 371.8 CN ISSN 1183-1308
EDUCATIONAL TRAVEL PLANNER; the original guide to adult learning vacations around the world. X. a. Can.$12.95 (effective Jan. 1992). Athabasca University, P.O. Box 10,000, Athabasca, Alta. T0G 2R0, Canada. TEL 403-675-6369. FAX 403-675-6467. Ed. Vicky Busch. adv.; circ. 3,500. (back issues avail.)
 Description: Features descriptions of study tours, language schools, cooking schools and alternative vacation ideas around the world.

EGON RONAY'S GUIDE TO 500 GOOD RESTAURANTS IN MAJOR CITIES OF EUROPE. see *HOTELS AND RESTAURANTS*

910.2 UA ISSN 0013-2381
EGYPT TRAVEL MAGAZINE.* no.156, 1971. q. Ministry of Tourism, 5 Sh. Adly, Cairo, Egypt.

EMPLOYEE SERVICES MANAGEMENT; the journal of employee services, recreation, health and education. see *BUSINESS AND ECONOMICS — Management*

918.1 BL
EMPRESA BRASILEIRA DE TURISMO. ANUARIO ESTATISTICO. 1970. a. (with supplement). price varies. Empresa Brasileira de Turismo, Rua Mariz e Barros 13, Rio de Janeiro 20270, Brazil. stat.
 Description: Details balance of payments, domestic tourism, international, national and EMBRATUR statistics.

918.104 BL
EMPRESA BRASILEIRA DE TURISMO. CALENDARIO TURISTICO. English edition: Empresa Brasileira de Turismo. Tourist Calendar. a. free. Empresa Brasileira de Turismo, Rua Mariz e Barros 13, Rio de Janeiro 20270, Brazil. TEL 55-21-273-2212. FAX 55-21-273-9290. TELEX 38-21-21066 ETUR.

910.202 CN ISSN 0826-7731
EN VILLE. (Text in English, French) 1985. a. Les Publications En Ville Ltee., 8270 Mountain Sights, Ste. 201, Montreal, Que. H4P 2B7, Canada. TEL 514-731-9471. FAX 514-731-7459. adv.; circ. 300,000 (controlled).
 Description: Information on shopping, dining and nightlife in Montreal.

917.704 US
ENCOUNTER INDIANAPOLIS. 1989. m. $20. Encounter Publications Inc., 2105 N. Meridian, Ste. 202, Indianapolis, IN 46202. TEL 317-923-8868. FAX 317-923-8571. Ed. Richard L. Schillen. adv.; circ. 20,000.
 Description: Provides tourists, business professionals, and relocators with greater access to the city by offering a calendar of events, restaurants, reviews and sporting events.

910.09 US ISSN 0279-4853
TX907
ENDLESS VACATION. 1975. m. $59. Endless Vacation Publications, Box 80260, Indianapolis, IN 46280-0260. TEL 317-871-9504. FAX 317-871-9507. Ed. W. O'Guinn. adv.; bk.rev.; circ. 811,256.
 Description: Gives vacation ideas for avid travelers.

914.2 US ISSN 1042-8399
DA650
ENGLAND ON FIFTY DOLLARS A DAY. 1980. a. $14.95. Frommer Books (Subsidiary of: Simon & Schuster, Inc.), 15 Columbus Circle, New York, NY 10023. TEL 212-373-8125. Eds. S. Haggart, D. Porter.
 Former titles: England on Forty Dollars a Day; England and Scotland on Twenty-Five Dollars a Day; England and Scotland on Twenty Dollars a Day (ISSN 0271-3977); Supersedes: England on Fifteen Dollars a Day.

910.09 UK
ENGLISH TOURIST BOARD. ANNUAL REPORT. 1971. a. £5. English Tourist Board, Black's Rd., Hammersmith, London W6 9EL, England. TEL 081-846-9000. FAX 081-563-0302. Ed. John Ison.

910.09 330 CN ISSN 0703-0312
ENROUTE. (Text in English and French) 1973. m. Can.$24. (Air Canada) Southam Printing Limited, Airmedia Division, 150 St. John St., Ste. 900, Toronto, Ont. M5V 3E3, Canada. TEL 416-591-1551. FAX 416-591-3511. Ed. Karen Hanley. adv.; bibl.; illus.; circ. 120,000. (back issues avail.) Indexed: Can.Per.Ind.

910.09 US
ENTREE; an uncompromising and confidential traveler's newsletter. 1982. m. $59. Entree Travel, 1470 E. Valley Rd., Ste. W, Santa Barbara, CA 93108. TEL 805-969-5848. FAX 805-966-7095. (Subscr. to: Box 5148, Santa Barbara, CA 93150) Ed. William Tomicki. bk.rev.; circ. 6,000. (back issues avail.)
 Description: Hotel and restaurant critiques; an insider's look at travel and eating; books spas, cruises, shopping reviews.

EPICUREAN REVUE; a confidential gastronomical & tourism letter. see *HOTELS AND RESTAURANTS*

910 CN ISSN 0710-9911
G1
EQUINOX; the magazine of Canadian discovery. (Text in English) 1982. bi-m. Can.$19.98. Telemedia Publishing Inc., 7 Queen Victoria Rd., Camden East, Ont. K0K 1J0, Canada. TEL 613-378-6661. (Subscr. to: 797 Don Mills Rd., 13th fl., Don Mills, Ont. M3C 1V2, Canada) Ed. Bart Robinson. adv.; bk.rev.; circ. 168,000. (back issues avail.) Indexed: CMI.

910.09 US
ERIE MOTORIST. bi-m. American Automobile Association, Eire County Motor Club, 420 W. Sixth St., Erie, PA 16507-1216. TEL 814-454-0123. FAX 814-455-5688. Ed. Jim Brown. circ. 29,000.

ESCAPEES. see *TRANSPORTATION — Automobiles*

910 647.9 SP
ESPANA HOSTELERA Y TURISTICA. 1950. m. 3000 ptas.($85) Padre Jesus Ordeonez, 10 bajo, 28002 Madrid, Spain. TEL 262-95-49. FAX 262-00-35. Ed. Juan Romero Calvillo. adv.; circ. 17,000.

914.604 SP ISSN 0423-5037
ESTUDIOS TURISTICOS. 1963. q. 2250 ptas. (foreign 3250 ptas.). Ministerio de Industria, Comercio y Turismo, Subdireccion General de Plaificacion y Prospectiva Turisticas, Almagro, 36, 3o, 28010 Madrid, Spain. TEL 308-23-49. Dir. Eduardo Fayos Sola. stat. **Indexed:** Rural Recreat.Tour.Abstr., World Agri.Econ.& Rural Sociol.Abstr.
—BLDSC shelfmark: 3812.816550.

ESTUDOS DE GEOGRAFIA HUMANA E REGIONAL. see *GEOGRAPHY*

914 385 US ISSN 0085-0330
HE3004
EURAIL GUIDE; how to travel Europe and all the world by train. 1971. a. $14.95. Eurail Guide Annual, 27540 Pacific Coast Highway, Malibu, CA 90265. TEL 213-457-7286. Eds. Kathryn S. Turpin, Marvin L. Saltzman.
—BLDSC shelfmark: 3828.087000.
 Description: Contains information about every train ride in the world a tourist might want to take. Includes departure and arrival times, as well as on-board services (eating, sleeping and air-conditioning facilities).

914 AU
EURO-CITY; the Austrian travel magazine. 1928. 6/yr. S.228. Bohmann Druck und Verlag GmbH & Co. KG, Leberstr. 122, A-1110 Vienna, Austria. TEL 0222-74095. FAX 0222-74095-138. TELEX 132312. circ. 70,000.
 Former titles (until 1991): Reiseland Oesterreich (ISSN 0254-5292); Fremdenverkehr-Reiseland-Oesterreich (ISSN 0016-0954)

910.09 GW
EUROKUNST: BESSER REISEN & MEHR ERLEBEN; Magazin fuer Urlaub und Freiheit. (Text in English, German) 1968. q. DM.18. Eurokunstverlag A.R. Purtauf, Postfach 2332, 6200 Wiesbaden, Germany. Ed.Bd. circ. 15,100.
 Former titles: Eurokunst; Eurokunst Magazin Reisen (ISSN 0177-4557)

EUROPA CAMPING UND CARAVANING. INTERNATIONALER FUEHRER. see *SPORTS AND GAMES — Outdoor Life*

914 US
EUROPE (YEAR). a. $17. Harper Collins Publishers, Birnbaum Travel Guides, 10 E. 53rd St., New York, NY 10022-5299. TEL 212-270-7000. Ed. Stephen Birnbaum. **Indexed:** ABI Inform, INIS Atomind., P.A.I.S., Tel.Abstr.

910 US
EUROPE BY EURAIL; how to tour Europe by train. 1976. biennial. Globe Pequot Press, 138 W. Main St., Box Q, Chester, CT 06412. TEL 203-526-9571. FAX 203-526-9571.

914 US
EUROPE FOR BUSINESS TRAVELERS. a. $12. Harper Collins Publishers, Birnbaum Travel Guides, 10 E. 53rd St., New York, NY 10022-5299. TEL 212-270-7000. Ed. Stephen Birnbaum.

910.202 US
D909
EUROPE ON FORTY DOLLARS A DAY. a. $15.95. Frommer Books (Subsidiary of: Simon & Schuster, Inc.), 15 Columbus Circle, New York, NY 10023. TEL 212-373-8125.
 Former titles: Europe on Thirty Dollars a Day (ISSN 0730-1510); Europe on Twenty-Five Dollars a Day; Europe on Fifteen Dollars a Day.

914.04 917.904 US
EUROPEAN TRAVEL AND ENTERTAINMENT MAGAZINE. 1969. m. Box 14545, Phoenix, AZ 85063. TEL 602-233-2342. circ. 5,000.

914.004 940 US ISSN 0882-7737
D923
EUROPEAN TRAVEL & LIFE. 1985. 10/yr. $24 includes a. supplement: Best of Europe. Murdoch Magazines (Subsidiary of: News America Publishing, Inc.), 200 Madison Ave., New York, NY 10016. TEL 800-627-2557. FAX 212-447-4778. adv.; circ. 420,000. (reprint service avail. from UMI)
 Description: Covers European cultural life and events for American Europhiles.

910.09 US
▼**EVENTS - U S A.** 1992. bi-m. Viare Publishing Co., 902 Broadway, New York, NY 10010. TEL 212-477-2200. FAX 212-599-3176. adv.
 Description: Covers upcoming events in the US of interest to vacationers and tourists.

910.09 US ISSN 0890-9911
EXCHANGE BOOK; home exchange directory. 1960. s-a. $50. (Directory Group Association) Vacation Exchange Club, Inc., Box 820, Haleiwa, HI 96712-0820. TEL 800-638-3841. FAX 808-638-5184. Ed. D.J. Costabel. adv.; illus.; circ. 15,000.
 Formerly: Home Exchange Directory.

914.2 UK
EXCLUSIVE LONDON. 1978. q. Exclusive Publications Ltd., 11 Dalmore Rd., London SE21 8HD, England. Ed. Robert Redman. adv.

TRAVEL AND TOURISM

910.09 — **CN**
EXCURSIONS EN AUTOCAR. English edition: Tours on Motorcoach. 1988. m. Can.$40 (effective Jan. 1991). (Bus Owners Association) Publicom Inc., 1055 Beaver Hall, Ste. 400, Montreal, Que. H2Z 1S5, Canada. TEL 514-874-0874. FAX 514-878-9779. TELEX 055-61866. Ed. Francois Marquis. adv.; circ. 5,729 (controlled).
   Description: Trade publication for group tour organizers.

910.202 — **UK** — **ISSN 0263-7685**
EXECUTIVE TRAVEL. 1979. m. £25.50 (foreign £36.50). Reed Travel Group (London) (Subsidiary of: Reed International PLC), Francis House, 11 Francis St., London SW1P 1BZ, England. TEL 071-828-8989. FAX 071-798-9710. Ed. Mike Toynbee. adv.; circ. 40,000 (controlled).
   Formerly: Executive Travel and Leisure.
   Description: For the frequent travelers.

EXHIBITION BULLETIN. see *MEETINGS AND CONGRESSES*

910.202 — **FR**
EXPANSION VOYAGES. 1981. q. Groupe Expansion, 67 av. de Wagram, 75017 Paris, France.

910.09 — **US**
EXPEDITION WORLD. bi-m. 33 Ludlow St., Stamford, CT 06912-0076. TEL 203-967-2900. FAX 203-325-3670. Ed. Candra Carr. circ. 100,000.

EXPLORATION; journal on the literature of exploration and travel. see *LITERATURE*

EXPLORE; Canada's magazine of adventure travel. see *SPORTS AND GAMES — Outdoor Life*

917.704 — **US**
EXPLORE MINNESOTA BED AND BREAKFAST - HISTORIC INNS. a. free. Office of Tourism, 375 Jackson St., Ste. 250, St. Paul, MN 55101. circ. 50,000.

EXPLORE MINNESOTA BIKING. see *SPORTS AND GAMES — Bicycles And Motorcycles*

917 796.5 — **US**
EXPLORE MINNESOTA CAMPGROUND GUIDE. (Former name of issuing body: Minnesota Office of Tourism) 1984. a. free. Minnesota Association of Campground Operators, 1000 E 146th St., Ste. 121, Burnsville, MN 55337. TEL 612-432-2228. FAX 612-432-1204. Ed. Al Brodie. circ. 200,000.
   Former titles: Explore Minnesota Campgrounds; Camping Guide.

EXPLORE MINNESOTA CROSS-COUNTRY SKIING. see *SPORTS AND GAMES — Outdoor Life*

EXPLORE MINNESOTA DOWNHILL SKIING. see *SPORTS AND GAMES — Outdoor Life*

917.704 796 — **US**
EXPLORE MINNESOTA HIKING. biennial. free. Office of Tourism, 375 Jackson St., Ste. 250, St. Paul, MN 55101. circ. 20,000.
   Formerly: Explore Minnesota Canoeing, Backpacking and Hiking.

647.94 — **US**
EXPLORER (WASHINGTON). q. $5. American Youth Hostels, Inc., Box 37613, Washington, DC 20013-7613. TEL 202-783-6161. FAX 202-783-6171. TELEX 384777 AYHINC UD. Ed. Tom Keen.
   Formerly (until 1990): American Youth Hostels Knapsack.

910.09 — **AT**
EXPLORER NEWS. 1982. q. Aus.$8. Barossa News Pty. Ltd., 27 Murray St., Tanunda, S.A. 5352, Australia. TEL 085-632041. (Subscr. to: Box 43, Tanunda, S.A. 5453, Australia) circ. 30,000.
   Description: Covers Barossa and Clare Valleys.

914.4 — **UK**
EXPLORING FRANCE. 1981. irreg. £6.95. Jarrold Publishing, Barrack St., Norwich NR3 1TR, England. TEL 0603-763300. FAX 0603-662748. TELEX 97497. Ed. Peter Titchmarsh.
   Description: Includes 30 maps and over 1,000 illustrations for a comprehensive guide for the English speaking visitor.

EXPRESS. see *TRAVEL AND TOURISM — Airline Inflight And Hotel Inroom*

914.504 — **SP** — **ISSN 1130-3751**
EXPRESS; ihre Urlaubszeitung. (Text in German) 1988. s-m. 1000 ptas. Alantas, Calle Gerona 20, 17600 Figueras, Spain. Ed. H. Kaibach. adv.; bk.rev.; illus.

910.09 — **GW**
F V W INTERNATIONAL. 1967. bi-w. DM.225. Verlag Dieter Niedecken GmbH, Jungfrauenthal 20, 2000 Hamburg 13, Germany. TEL 040-441873-0. FAX 040-44187329. TELEX 211140. Ed. Dieter Niedecken. adv.; circ. 20,571.

910.09 — **US** — **ISSN 0429-9639**
FABULOUS MEXICO; where everything costs less. biennial. $2.50. Harian Publications, One Vernon Ave., Floral Park, NY 11001. TEL 516-437-3440.

917.98 F902.3 — **US** — **ISSN 1051-5623**
FACTS ABOUT ALASKA: ALASKA ALMANAC. 1976. a. $7.95. Alaska Northwest Books (Subsidiary of: G T E Discovery Publications), Box 3007, Bothell, WA 98041. TEL 206-487-6100. FAX 206-486-7296. charts; illus.
   Former titles: Alaska Almanac - Facts About Alaska (ISSN 0270-5370); Facts About Alaska (ISSN 0361-7823)
   Description: General facts on and pertaining to Alaska and the Arctic Circle.

FACTS AND ADVICE FOR AIRLINE PASSENGERS. see *TRANSPORTATION — Air Transport*

914.806 — **GW**
FAHREN IN EUROPA. (Editions avail.: Germany, Switzerland, Austria, Netherlands-Belgium, France) 1983. a. DM.20. Fie Verlag GmbH, Postfach 106104, Spaldingstr. 210, 2000 Hamburg 1, Germany. TEL 040-230173. circ. 44,500.

919.7 F3031 — **UK** — **ISSN 0256-1824**
FALKLAND ISLANDS JOURNAL. (Text in English) 1967. a. price varies. Queen's University of Belfast, Department of Agricultural Botany, Newforge Lane, Belfast BT9 5PX, N. Ireland. TEL 0232-661166. FAX 0232-669551. Ed. J.H. McAdam. illus.; circ. 400.
   Description: Includes general material on all aspects of the history, geography and natural history of the Falkland Islands.

910.202 — **UK**
FAMILY GUIDE ON WHERE TO GO. 1976. a. £3.95. Jarrold Publishing, Barrack St., Norwich NR3 1TR, England. TEL 0603-763300. FAX 0603-662748. TELEX 97497. Ed. Peter Titchmarsh. circ. 10,000.
   Description: Includes 5 maps and over 400 illustrations and descriptions of 800 places to visit in England and Wales.

FAMILY MOTOR COACHING. see *TRANSPORTATION*

910.09 — **US**
FAMILY TRAVEL TIMES. 1984. 10/yr. $35. Travel With Your Children (TWYCH) (Subsidiary of: Dorthy Jordan & Associates), 45 W. 18th St., 7th Fl., New York, NY 10011. TEL 212-206-0688. Eds. Dorothy Jordon, Carol Eannarino. bk.rev.; circ. 2,500. (back issues avail.)
   Description: Contains news and features about family travel around the US and around the world.

915.204 — **JA**
FAR EAST TRAVELER. (Text in English) vol.4, 1972. m. $132 (effective Aug. 1991). Far East Reporters Inc., 1F Palace Nishi-Azabu, 3-17-40 Nishi-Azabu, Minato-ku, Tokyo 106, Japan. TELEX 242-4972. Ed. Nicholas Kosar. adv.; bk.rev.; charts; illus.; circ. 25,000.
   Incorporates (in 1968): Far East Reporter (ISSN 0425-7170)

914.2 — **UK**
FARM & COUNTRY HOLIDAYS. 1969. a. £2.95. Pastime Publications Ltd., 15 Dublin Street Lane South, Edinburgh EH1 3PX, Scotland. TEL 031-556-1105. FAX 031-556-1129. adv.; circ. 40,000.

914.2 — **UK**
FARM HOLIDAY GUIDE (ENGLAND, WALES & IRELAND). 1946. a. £2.99. F.H.G. Publications Ltd., Abbey Mill Business Centre, Seedhill, Paisley PA1 1JN, Scotland. TEL 041-887 0428.
   Formed by the merger of: Farm Holiday Guide (England Edition) (ISSN 0267-2871); Farm Holiday Guide (Wales Edition) (ISSN 0267-2898)

914.1 — **UK** — **ISSN 0267-288X**
FARM HOLIDAY GUIDE (SCOTLAND EDITION). a. £2.50. F.H.G. Publications Ltd., Abbey Mill Business Centre, Seedhill, Paisley PA1 1JN, Scotland. TEL 041-887 0428.

914.2 — **IE**
FARM HOLIDAYS IN IRELAND. 1970. a. $5. Libra House Ltd., 4 St. Kevin's Terrace, Dublin 8, Ireland. TEL 01-542717. Ed. Cathal Tyrrell. adv.; illus.; circ. 89,875.
   Description: List about 420 houses providing meals and accomodation in the countryside and coastal areas.

796 TX907 — **US** — **ISSN 0195-8437**
FARM, RANCH AND COUNTRY VACATIONS. 1949. irreg. (every 2 or 3 years). $12. Adventure Guides, Inc., Box 698, Newfoundland, NJ 07438. TEL 602-596-0226. FAX 201-697-1520. Ed. Pat Dickerman.
   Former titles: Country Vacations U.S.A. (ISSN 0147-3867); Farm, Ranch and Country Vacations; Farm, Ranch and Countryside Guide; Farm and Ranch Vacation Guide (ISSN 0085-0438)

910.4 — **CC**
FENGJING MINGSHENG/SCENIC SPOTS AND HISTORICAL SITES. (Text in Chinese) bi-m. Hangzhou Yuanlin Wenwu Guanliju - Hangzhou Municipal Administration of Gardens and Cultural Relics, 12 Jiangyuan Nong, Xiaoying Xiang, Hangzhou, Zhejiang 310003, People's Republic of China. TEL 20273. Ed. Chen Hanmin.

910.202 — **NO** — **ISSN 0801-5880**
FERIEFORUM; magasin for reiseliv og turisme. (Text in Norwegian) 1983. q. NOK 80($16) Skogveien 85A, N-1320 Stabekk, Norway. TEL 02-534773. Ed. Reidar Nordheim. circ. 20,000.

914.34 — **GW**
FERIEN MAGAZIN ST. PETER - ORDING. a. (Fremdenverkehrsgemeinschaft Eiderstedt e.V.) Westholsteinische Verlagsanstalt Boyens und Co., Wulf-Isebrand-Platz, 2240 Heide, Germany. TEL 0481-691-0.

910.202 — **GW**
FERNREISEN. 1982. m. DM.48. S-P Verlag, Westendstr. 52, D-6000 Frankfurt, Germany. TEL 069-723145. Ed. Hansjoerg Schoen. circ. 13,300.
   Description: Travel and tourism in non-European regions.

917.904 — **US**
FERRY TRAVEL GUIDE. 1984. 3/yr. $7. Olympic Publishing, Inc., 7450 Oak Bay Rd., Port Ludlow, WA 98365-9411. TEL 206-437-2277. FAX 206-437-9503. Ed. Dan Youra. adv.; circ. 100,000. (back issues avail.)
   Former titles: Olympic Travel Guide (ISSN 0897-9618); Olympic Magazine.
   Description: Travel information for Washington State and British Columbia with maps, ferry schedules, resorts, cities and attractions.

949.3 — **BE** — **ISSN 0015-0363**
FESTIVAL. (Text and summaries in Dutch and French) 1947. w. 1500 Fr. Editions E R E L B.V.B.A., 16 St. Sebastiaanstraat, B-8400 Oostende, Belgium. TEL 059-701308. FAX 059-803451. Ed. Monique Lanoye. adv.; bk.rev.; illus.; circ. 20,000. (tabloid format)

FETES ET FESTIVALS. see *BUSINESS AND ECONOMICS — Marketing And Purchasing*

970 F1632 — **US** — **ISSN 0739-0769**
FIELDING'S BERMUDA AND THE BAHAMAS. 1983. a. $9.95. Fielding Travel Books (Subsidiary of: William Morrow and Company, Inc.), 105 Madison Ave., New York, NY 10016. TEL 212-889-3050. Ed. Randy Ladenheim-Gil. index.

TRAVEL AND TOURISM

910.2 US
D909
FIELDING'S BUDGET EUROPE. 1967. a. $9.95. Fielding Travel Books (Subsidiary of: William Morrow and Company, Inc.), 105 Madison Ave., New York, NY 10016.
Former titles: Fielding's Economy Europe (ISSN 0739-0785); Fielding's Low-Cost Europe (ISSN 0095-6406)

910.2 US
FIELDING'S CARIBBEAN. 1968. a. $13.95. Fielding Travel Books (Subsidiary of: William Morrow and Company, Inc.), 105 Madison Ave., New York, NY 10016. TEL 212-889-3050. index.

910.2 US ISSN 0192-5326
D909
FIELDING'S EUROPE. 1948. a. $13.95. Fielding Travel Books (Subsidiary of: William Morrow and Company, Inc.), 105 Madison Ave., New York, NY 10016. TEL 212-889-3050. index.
Formerly: Fielding's Travel Guide to Europe (ISSN 0071-4801)

972 US ISSN 0739-0793
F1209
FIELDING'S MEXICO. 1983. a. $12.95. Fielding Travel Books (Subsidiary of: William Morrow and Company, Inc.), 105 Madison Ave., New York, NY 10016. TEL 212-889-3050. index.

910.2 US ISSN 0071-478X
HF5341
FIELDING'S SELECTIVE SHOPPING GUIDE TO EUROPE. 1957. a. $9.95. Fielding Travel Books (Subsidiary of: William Morrow and Company, Inc.), 105 Madison Ave., New York, NY 10016. TEL 212-889-3050. index.

910.202 FJ
FIJI BEACH PRESS. (Text in English) fortn; overseas ed. s-a. free. P.O. Box 2193, Government Bldgs., Suva, Fiji. TEL 313755. Ed. Mere Momoivalu. circ. 48,000.

910.4 FJ
FIJI MAGIC. (Text in English) m. George Rubine Ltd., P.O. Box 12511, Suva, Fiji. TEL 313944. Ed. Gabriel Singh. circ. 10,000.

FINANCIAL TIMES INTERNATIONAL YEAR BOOKS: WORLD HOTEL DIRECTORY. see *HOTELS AND RESTAURANTS*

910.09 GW
FLIEGEN UND SPAREN; das Magazin fuer clevere Urlauber. 1986. s-a. DM.20($20) Markt Control, Postfach 110431, 4100 Duisburg 11, Germany. TEL 0203-54248. FAX 0203-57970. Eds. Juergen Zupancic, Wolfgang Grahl. adv.; bk.rev.; circ. 52,000.

910.202 GW
FLIEGENDE BLAETTER. 1971. q. free. (Condor Airlines) Koesler Verlag GmbH, Von-Werth Strasse 44, Postfach 19 03 66, 5000 Cologne, Germany. TEL 0221-131366. FAX 0221-137541. TELEX 889990-RSB-D. adv.; circ. 300,000.

629.132 US ISSN 0194-9039
FLIGHT REPORTS. 1978. m. $36. Peter Katz Productions, Inc., 5 Odell Plaza, Yonkers, NY 10701. TEL 914-423-6000. Ed. Peter Katz. bk.rev.

914.504 US
FLORENCE (YEAR). a. $10. Harper Collins Publishers, Birnbaum Travel Guides, 10 E. 53rd St., New York, NY 10022-5299. TEL 212-207-7000. illus.; index.

917.504 US
▼**FLORIDA WORLD MAGAZINE**. (Text in Japanese) 1991. q. Dave Gemma, Ed. & Pub., 816 S.W. First Ave., Portland, OR 97204. TEL 503-274-7640. FAX 503-243-1851. adv.; circ. 25,000.
Description: Includes tips on lodging, dining, transportation, recreation, sightseeing, shopping, currency exchange, climate, and real estate.

338.4 US
FLORIDA'S VISITORS. 1973? a. Department of Commerce, Division of Tourism, 107 W. Gaines St., Tallahassee, FL 32304. TEL 904-488-7300.
Formerly: Florida Tourist Study (ISSN 0430-6953)

FLYER INTERNATIONAL; aviation and tourism. see *TRANSPORTATION — Air Transport*

910.09 CN
FOCUS ON FESTIVALS. 1980. q. Can.$20 membership. Associated Manitoba Arts Festivals, Inc., 205 - 180 Market Ave. E., Winnipeg, Man. R3B 0P7, Canada. TEL 204-945-4578. FAX 204-948-2073. Ed. Karen Oliver. adv.; circ. 500. (back issues avail.)
Description: News about Manitoba's 38 local community arts festivals, the Manitoba Community Arts Development, and provincial festival events.

915.47 PK
FOCUS ON PAKISTAN. (Text in English) 1971-1973; resumed 1976. s-a. Rs.100($10) Pakistan Tourism Development Corporation, House No. 2, Street 61, F-7-4, P.O. Box 1465, Islambad 44000, Pakistan. TEL 811001. TELEX 54356 PTDC PK. Ed. Ashab Naqvi. adv.; circ. 5,000 (controlled).
Description: Articles on the culture, customs, heritage and tourist attractions of Pakistan.

918.6 PN
FOCUS ON PANAMA. (Editions in English and Spanish) 1971. s-a. $5 per no. (free in Panama). Focus Publications (Int.) S.A., Apdo. 6-3287, El Dorado, Panama, Panama. TEL 69-6595. FAX 23-8316. Ed. Kenneth J. Jones. adv.; circ. 70,000.
Description: Full color guide for visitors emphasizing both tourist attractions, business facilities and culture.

917.204 US
FODOR'S ACAPULCO, IXTAPA, ZIHUATANIJO. irreg. $9. Fodor's Travel Publications, Inc. (Subsidiary of: Random House, Inc.), 201 E. 50th St., New York, NY 10022. TEL 800-733-3000. (Dist. by: Random House, Inc., 400 Hahn Dr., Westminster, MD 21157) Ed. Craig Seligman.
Formerly: Fodor's Fun in Acapulco.

914.04 US
D909
FODOR'S AFFORDABLE EUROPE. 1972. a. $12.95. Fodor's Travel Publications, Inc. (Subsidiary of: Random House, Inc.), 201 E. 50th St., New York, NY 10022. TEL 800-733-3000. (Dist. by: Random House, Inc., 400 Hahn Rd., Westminster, MD 21157) Ed. Paula Rackow.
Former titles: Fodor's Budget Europe (ISSN 0197-4998); (until 1979): Fodor's Europe on a Budget (ISSN 0276-0738)

914.404 US
FODOR'S AFFORDABLE FRANCE. 1980. a. $14. Fodor's Travel Publications, Inc. (Subsidiary of: Random House, Inc.), 201 E. 50th St., New York, NY 10022. TEL 800-733-3000. (Dist. by: Random House, Inc., 400 Hahn Rd., Westminster, MD 21157) Ed. Jillian Magalaner.
Former titles: Fodor's Great Travel Values: France; Fodor's Budget Travel France; Fodor's Budget France (ISSN 0194-4150)

914.304 US
FODOR'S AFFORDABLE GERMANY. 1979. a. $15. Fodor's Travel Publications, Inc. (Subsidiary of: Random House, Inc.), 201 E. 50th St., New York, NY 10022. TEL 800-733-3000. (Dist. by: Random House, Inc., 400 Hahn Rd., Westminster, MD 21157) Ed. Carolyn Price.
Former titles: Fodor's Great Travel Values: Germany; Fodor's Budget Travel Germany; Fodor's Budget Germany (ISSN 0193-9033)

914.204 US
FODOR'S AFFORDABLE GREAT BRITAIN. 1979. a. $14. Fodor's Travel Publications, Inc. (Subsidiary of: Random House, Inc.), 201 E. 50th St., New York, NY 10022. TEL 800-733-3000. (Dist. by: Random House, Inc., 400 Hahn Rd., Westminster, MD 21157) Ed. Alison Hoffman.
Former titles: Fodor's Great Travel Values: Britain; Fodor's Budget Travel Britain; Fodor's Budget Britain (ISSN 0193-2381)

914.504 US
FODOR'S AFFORDABLE ITALY. a. $15. Fodor's Travel Publications, Inc. (Subsidiary of: Random House, Inc.), 201 E. 50th St., New York, NY 10022. TEL 800-733-3000. (Dist. by: Random House, Inc., 400 Hahn Rd., Westminster, MD 21157) Ed. Paula Consolo.
Former titles: Fodor's Great Travel Values: Italy; Fodor's Budget Travel Italy; Fodor's Budget Italy (ISSN 0270-787X)

917.9804 US ISSN 0271-2776
F902.3
FODOR'S ALASKA. 1979. a. $14. Fodor's Travel Publications, Inc. (Subsidiary of: Random House, Inc.), 201 E. 50th St., New York, NY 10022. TEL 800-733-3000. (Dist. by: Random House, Inc., 400 Hahn Rd., Westminster, MD 21157) Ed. Suzanne DeGalan.

917.904 US
FODOR'S ARIZONA. a. $13. Fodor's Travel Publications, Inc. (Subsidiary of: Random House, Inc.), 201 E. 50th St., New York, NY 10022. TEL 800-733-3000. (Dist. by: Random House, Inc., 400 Hahn Rd., Westminster, MD 21157) Ed. Jillian Magalaner.

919.04 US
DU95
FODOR'S AUSTRALIA AND NEW ZEALAND. a. $18. Fodor's Travel Publications, Inc. (Subsidiary of: Random House, Inc.), 201 E. 50th St., New York, NY 10022. TEL 800-733-3000. (Dist. by: Random House, Inc., 400 Hahn Rd., Westminster, MD 21157) Ed. Craig Seligman. illus.
Formerly: Fodor's Australia, New Zealand and the South Pacific (ISSN 0191-2321)

914.3604 US ISSN 0071-6340
DB16
FODOR'S AUSTRIA. 1951. a. $16. Fodor's Travel Publications, Inc. (Subsidiary of: Random House, Inc.), 201 E. 50th St., New York, NY 10022. TEL 800-733-3000. (Dist. by: Random House, Inc., 400 Hahn Rd., Westminster, MD 21157) Ed. Craig Seligman.

919.704 US
FODOR'S BAHAMAS. a. $11. Fodor's Travel Publications, Inc. (Subsidiary of: Random House, Inc.), 201 E. 50th St., New York, NY 10022. TEL 800-733-3000. (Dist. by: Random House, Inc., 400 Hahn Rd., Westminster, MD 21157) Ed. Julie Tomasz.
Supersedes in part: Fodor's Caribbean and Bahamas (ISSN 0271-4760)

917.204 US
FODOR'S BAJA AND MEXICO'S PACIFIC COAST RESORTS. irreg. $11. Fodor's Travel Publications, Inc. (Subsidiary of: Random House, Inc.), 201 E. 50th St., New York, NY 10022. TEL 800-733-3000. (Dist. by: Random House, Inc., 400 Hahn Rd., Westminster, MD 21157) Ed. Carolyn Price.
Formerly: Fodor's Mexico's Baja.

917.2904 US
FODOR'S BARBADOS. irreg. $8. Fodor's Travel Publications, Inc. (Subsidiary of: Random House, Inc.), 201 E. 50th St., New York, NY 10022. TEL 800-733-3000. (Dist. by: Random House, Inc., 400 Hahn Rd., Westminster, MD 21157) Ed. Caroline Haberfeld.
Formerly: Fodor's Fun in Barbados.

917.404 US
FODOR'S BED AND BREAKFASTS AND COUNTRY INNS AND OTHER WEEKEND PLEASURES: NEW ENGLAND. irreg. $14. Fodor's Travel Publications, Inc. (Subsidiary of: Random House, Inc.), 201 E. 50th St., New York, NY 10022. TEL 800-733-3000. (Dist. by: Random House, Inc., 400 Hahn Rd., Westminster, MD 21157) Ed. Conrad Paulus.

917.04 US
FODOR'S BED AND BREAKFASTS AND COUNTRY INNS AND OTHER WEEKEND PLEASURES: THE MID-ATLANTIC REGION. irreg. $14. Fodor's Travel Publications, Inc. (Subsidiary of: Random House, Inc.), 201 E. 50th St., New York, NY 10022. TEL 800-733-3000. (Dist. by: Random House, Inc., 400 Hahn Rd., Westminster, MD 21157) Ed. Conrad Paulus.

917.04 US
FODOR'S BED AND BREAKFASTS AND COUNTRY INNS AND OTHER WEEKEND PLEASURES: THE SOUTH. irreg. $15. Fodor's Travel Publications, Inc. (Subsidiary of: Random House, Inc.), 201 E. 50th St., New York, NY 10022. TEL 800-733-3000. (Dist. by: Random House, Inc., 400 Hahn Rd., Westminster, MD 21157) Ed. Conrad Paulus.

TRAVEL AND TOURISM

917.904 US
FODOR'S BED AND BREAKFASTS AND COUNTRY INNS AND OTHER WEEKEND PLEASURES: THE WEST COAST. irreg. $15. Fodor's Travel Publications, Inc. (Subsidiary of: Random House, Inc.), 201 E. 50th St., New York, NY 10022. TEL 800-733-3000. (Dist. by: Random House, Inc., 400 Hahn Rd., Westminster, MD 21157) Ed. Paula Rackow.

914.9304 US ISSN 0071-6359
FODOR'S BELGIUM AND LUXEMBOURG. 1951. biennial. $16. Fodor's Travel Publications, Inc. (Subsidiary of: Random House, Inc.), 201 E. 50th St., New York, NY 10022. TEL 800-733-3000. (Dist. by: Random House, Inc., 400 Hahn Rd., Westminster, MD 21157) Ed. Nancy van Itallie.

914.304 US
FODOR'S BERLIN. a. $10. Fodor's Travel Publications, Inc. (Subsidiary of: Random House, Inc.), 201 E. 50th St., New York, NY 10022. TEL 800-733-3000. (Dist. by: Random House, Inc., 400 Hahn Rd., Westminster, MD 21157) Ed. Julie Tomasz.

919.704 US
FODOR'S BERMUDA. 1979. a. $11. Fodor's Travel Publications, Inc. (Subsidiary of: Random House, Inc.), 201 E. 50th St., New York, NY 10022. TEL 800-733-3000. (Dist. by: Random House, Inc., 400 Hahn Rd., Westminster, MD 21157) Ed. Julie Tomasz.

917.404 US
FODOR'S BOSTON. 1984. a. $10. Fodor's Travel Publications, Inc. (Subsidiary of: Random House, Inc.), 201 E. 50th St., New York, NY 10022. TEL 800-733-3000. (Dist. by: Random House, Inc., 400 Hahn Rd., Westminster, MD 21157) Ed. Jillian Magalaner.

918.104 US ISSN 0163-0628
F2509.5
FODOR'S BRAZIL. 1978. irreg. $11. Fodor's Travel Publications, Inc. (Subsidiary of: Random House, Inc.), 201 E. 50th St., New York, NY 10022. TEL 800-733-3000. (Dist. by: Random House, Inc., 400 Hahn Rd., Westminster, MD 21157) Ed. Paula Consolo.

910.09 US
FODOR'S BUDAPEST. irreg. $11. Fodor's Travel Publications, Inc. (Subsidiary of: Random House, Inc.), 201 E. 50th St., New York, NY 10022. TEL 800-733-3000. (Dist. by: Random House, Inc., 400 Hahn Rd., Westminster, MD 21157) Ed. Christopher Billy.
Supersedes: Fodor's Hungary.

917.904 US ISSN 0192-9925
F859.3
FODOR'S CALIFORNIA. a. $16. Fodor's Travel Publications, Inc. (Subsidiary of: Random House, Inc.), 201 E. 50th St., New York, NY 10022. TEL 800-733-3000. (Dist. by: Random House, Inc., 400 Hahn Rd., Westminster, MD 21157) Ed. Larry Peterson.

917.104 US ISSN 0160-3906
F1009
FODOR'S CANADA. 1978. a. $16. Fodor's Travel Publications, Inc. (Subsidiary of: Random House, Inc.), 201 E. 50th St., New York, NY 10022. TEL 800-733-3000. (Dist. by: Random House, Inc., 400 Hahn Rd., Westminster, MD 21157) Ed. Conrad Paulus.

917.104 US
FODOR'S CANADA'S GREAT COUNTRY INNS BY ANITA STEWART. irreg. $13. Fodor's Travel Publications, Inc. (Subsidiary of: Random House, Inc.), 201 E. 50th St., New York, NY 10022. TEL 800-733-3000. (Dist. by: Random House, Inc., 400 Hahn Rd., Westminster, MD 21157) Ed. Michael Spring.

917.204 US
FODOR'S CANCUN, COZUMEL & THE YUCATAN PENINSULA. a. $11. Fodor's Travel Publications, Inc. (Subsidiary of: Random House, Inc.), 201 E. 50th St., New York, NY 10022. TEL 800-733-3000. (Dist. by: Random House, Inc., 400 Hahn Rd., Westminster, MD 21157) Ed. Carolyn Price.
Formerly: Fodor's Cancun, Cozumel, Merida and the Yucatan.

917.404 US
FODOR'S CAPE COD. 1982. a. $12. Fodor's Travel Publications, Inc. (Subsidiary of: Random House, Inc.), 201 E. 50th St., New York, NY 10022. TEL 800-733-3000. (Dist. by: Random House, Inc., 400 Hahn Rd., Westminster, MD 21157) Ed. Jillian Magalaner.

917.2904 US
FODOR'S CARIBBEAN. 1962. a. $16. Fodor's Travel Publications, Inc. (Subsidiary of: Random House, Inc.), 201 E. 50th St., New York, NY 10022. TEL 800-733-3000. (Dist. by: Random House, Inc., 400 Hahn Rd., Westminster, MD 21157) Ed. Caroline Haberfield.
Supersedes in part: Fodor's Caribbean and Bahamas (ISSN 0271-4760); Former titles: Fodor's Caribbean, Bahamas and Bermuda (ISSN 0098-2547); Fodor's Guide to the Caribbean, Bahamas and Bermuda (ISSN 0071-6561)

917.504 US
FODOR'S CAROLINAS & THE GEORGIA COAST. a. $11. Fodor's Travel Publications, Inc. (Subsidiary of: Random House, Inc.), 201 E. 50th St., New York, NY 10022. TEL 800-733-3000. (Dist. by: Random House, Inc., 400 Hahn Rd., Westminster, MD 21157) Ed. Andrew Collins.

917.204 US ISSN 0270-8183
F1429
FODOR'S CENTRAL AMERICA; Belize, Costa Rica, El Salvador, Guatemala, Honduras, Nicaragua, Panama. irreg., latest 1993 ed. $15. Fodor's Travel Publications, Inc. (Subsidiary of: Random House, Inc.), 201 E. 50th St., New York, NY 10022. TEL 800-733-3000. (Dist. by: Random House, Inc., 400 Hahn Rd., Westminster, MD 21157) Ed. Carolyn Price.

917.704 US
FODOR'S CHICAGO. 1982. a. $11. Fodor's Travel Publications, Inc. (Subsidiary of: Random House, Inc.), 201 E. 50th St., New York, NY 10022. TEL 800-733-3000. (Dist. by: Random House, Inc., 400 Hahn Rd., Westminster, MD 21157) Ed. Suzanne DeGalan.
Formerly: Fodor's Chicago and the Great Lakes.

915.104 US
DS712
FODOR'S CHINA. 1979. a. $19. Fodor's Travel Publications, Inc. (Subsidiary of: Random House, Inc.), 201 E. 50th St., New York, NY 10022. TEL 800-733-3000. (Dist. by: Random House, Inc., 400 Hahn Rd., Westminster, MD 21157) Ed. Craig Seligman.
Formerly: Fodor's People's Republic of China (ISSN 0192-2378)

915.104 US
FODOR'S CHINA'S GREAT CITIES. irreg. $9.95. Fodor's Travel Publications, Inc. (Subsidiary of: Random House, Inc.), 201 E. 50th St., New York, NY 10022. TEL 800-733-3000. (Dist. by: Random House, Inc., 400 Hahn Rd., Westminster, MD 21157) Ed. Vernon Nahrgang.
Formerly: Fodor's Beijing, Guangzhou and Shanghai.

914.704 US
DK16
FODOR'S COMMONWEALTH OF INDEPENDENT STATES AND THE BALTIC COUNTRIES. 1975. a. $18. Fodor's Travel Publications, Inc. (Subsidiary of: Random House, Inc.), 201 E. 50th St., New York, NY 10022. TEL 800-733-3000. (Dist. by: Random House, Inc., 400 Hahn Rd., Westminster, MD 21157) Ed. Christopher Billy. illus.
Formerly: Fodor's Soviet Union (ISSN 0095-1358)

914.204 US
FODOR'S COTTAGES, BED AND BREAKFASTS AND COUNTRY INNS OF ENGLAND AND WALES BY ELIZABETH GUNDRY. irreg. $15. Fodor's Travel Publications, Inc. (Subsidiary of: Random House, Inc.), 201 E. 50th St., New York, NY 10022. TEL 800-733-3000. (Dist. by: Random House, Inc., 400 Hahn Rd., Westminster, MD 21157) Ed. Michael Spring.

910.202 US
FODOR'S CRUISES AND PORTS OF CALL. a. $17. Fodor's Travel Publications, Inc. (Subsidiary of: Random House, Inc.), 201 E. 50th St., New York, NY 10022. TEL 800-733-3000. (Dist. by: Random House, Inc., 400 Hahn Rd., Westminster, MD 21157) Ed. Andrew Collins.

910.2 US ISSN 0071-6367
FODOR'S CZECHOSLOVAKIA. 1970-19?? irreg. $12. Fodor's Travel Publications, Inc. (Subsidiary of: Random House, Inc.), 201 E. 50th St., New York, NY 10022. TEL 800-733-3000. (Dist. by: Random House, Inc., 400 Hahn Rd., Westminster, MD 21157) Ed. Christopher Billy.

917.504 US
FODOR'S DISNEY WORLD & THE ORLANDO AREA. a. $10. Fodor's Travel Publications, Inc. (Subsidiary of: Random House, Inc.), 201 E. 50th St., New York, NY 10022. TEL 800-733-3000. (Dist. by: Random House, Inc., 400 Hahn Rd., Westminster, MD 21157) Ed. Alison Hoffman.
Formerly: Fodor's Fun in Disney World and the Orlando Area.

914.704 US
FODOR'S EASTERN EUROPE. 1980. a. $17. Fodor's Travel Publications, Inc. (Subsidiary of: Random House, Inc.), 201 E. 50th St., New York, NY 10022. TEL 800-733-3000. (Dist. by: Random House, Inc., 400 Hahn Rd., Westminster, MD 21157) Ed. Christopher Billy.

916.204 US ISSN 0147-8176
DT45
FODOR'S EGYPT. 1977. biennial. $14. Fodor's Travel Publications, Inc. (Subsidiary of: Random House, Inc.), 201 E. 50th St., New York, NY 10022. TEL 800-733-3000. (Dist. by: Random House, Inc., 400 Hahn Rd., Westminster, MD 21157) Ed. Edie Jarolim. illus.

914.404 US
FODOR'S EURO DISNEY. a. $10. Fodor's Travel Publications, Inc. (Subsidiary of: Random House, Inc.), 201 E. 50th St., New York, NY 10022. TEL 800-733-3000. (Dist. by: Random House, Inc., 400 Hahn Rd., Westminster, MD 21157) Ed. Paula Consolo.

914.04 US ISSN 0362-0204
D909
FODOR'S EUROPE. 1959. a. $18. Fodor's Travel Publications, Inc. (Subsidiary of: Random House, Inc.), 201 E. 50th St., New York, NY 10022. TEL 800-733-3000. (Dist. by: Random House, Inc., 400 Hahn Rd., Westminster, MD 21157) Ed. Paulu Rackow.
Formerly: Fodor's Guide to Europe (ISSN 0071-6375)

914.04 US
FODOR'S EUROPE'S GREAT CITIES. a. $14. Fodor's Travel Publications, Inc. (Subsidiary of: Random House, Inc.), 201 E. 50th St., New York, NY 10022. TEL 800-733-3000. (Dist. by: Random House, Inc., 400 Hahn Rd., Westminster, MD 21157) Ed. Paula Rackow.

917.504 US ISSN 0193-9556
F309.3
FODOR'S FLORIDA. a. $15. Fodor's Travel Publications, Inc. (Subsidiary of: Random House, Inc.), 201 E. 50th St., New York, NY 10022. TEL 800-733-3000. (Dist. by: Random House, Inc., 400 Hahn Rd., Westminster, MD 21157) Ed. Alison Hoffman.

914.404 US ISSN 0071-6383
FODOR'S FRANCE. 1951. a. $16. Fodor's Travel Publications, Inc. (Subsidiary of: Random House, Inc.), 201 E. 50th St., New York, NY 10022. TEL 800-733-3000. (Dist. by: Random House, Inc., 400 Hahn Rd., Westminster, MD 21157) Ed. Jillian Magalaner.

914.304 US
FODOR'S GERMANY. 1951. a. $17. Fodor's Travel Publications, Inc. (Subsidiary of: Random House, Inc.), 201 E. 50th St., New York, NY 10022. TEL 800-733-3000. (Dist. by: Random House, Inc., 400 Hahn Rd., Westminster, MD 21157) Ed. Christopher Billy.
Former titles: Fodor's Germany: West and East (ISSN 0192-0952); Fodor's Germany (ISSN 0071-6391)

914.304   US
FODOR'S GREAT AMERICAN VACATIONS. irreg. $14.
Fodor's Travel Publications, Inc. (Subsidiary of:
Random House, Inc.), 201 E. 50th St., New York,
NY 10022. TEL 800-733-3000. (Dist. by: Random
House, Inc., 400 Hahn Rd., Westminster, MD
21157) Ed. Jillian Magalaner.

914.104   US   ISSN 0071-6405
DA650
FODOR'S GREAT BRITAIN. 1951. a. $16. Fodor's Travel
Publications, Inc. (Subsidiary of: Random House,
Inc.), 201 E. 50th St., New York, NY 10022.
TEL 800-733-3000. (Dist. by: Random House, Inc.,
400 Hahn Rd., Westminster, MD 21157) Ed.
Caroline Haberfeld.

914.9504   US   ISSN 0071-6413
DF716
FODOR'S GREECE. 1951. biennial. $16. Fodor's Travel
Publications, Inc. (Subsidiary of: Random House,
Inc.), 201 E. 50th St., New York, NY 10022.
TEL 800-733-3000. (Dist. by: Random House, Inc.,
400 Hahn Rd., Westminster, MD 21157) Ed.
Conrad Paulus.

919.6904   US   ISSN 0071-6421
DU622
FODOR'S HAWAII. 1961. a. $15. Fodor's Travel
Publications, Inc. (Subsidiary of: Random House,
Inc.), 201 E. 50th St., New York, NY 10022.
TEL 800-733-3000. (Dist. by: Random House, Inc.,
400 Hahn Rd., Westminster, MD 21157) Ed. Larry
Peterson.

910.202 613.7   US
FODOR'S HEALTHY ESCAPES. irreg. $15. Fodor's Travel
Publications, Inc. (Subsidiary of: Random House,
Inc.), 201 E. 50th St., New York, NY 10022.
TEL 800-733-3000. (Dist. by: Random House, Inc.,
400 Hahn Rd., Westminster, MD 21157) Ed.
Carolyn Price.

914.9204   US   ISSN 0071-643X
DJ16
FODOR'S HOLLAND. 1951. biennial. $14. Fodor's Travel
Publications, Inc. (Subsidiary of: Random House,
Inc.), 201 E. 50th St., New York, NY 10022.
TEL 800-733-3000. (Dist. by: Random House, Inc.,
400 Hahn Rd., Westminster, MD 21157) Ed. Nancy
van Itallie.

915.1204   US
FODOR'S HONG KONG. 1984. a. $12. Fodor's Travel
Publications, Inc. (Subsidiary of: Random House,
Inc.), 201 E. 50th St., New York, NY 10022.
TEL 800-733-3000. (Dist. by: Random House, Inc.,
400 Hahn Rd., Westminster, MD 21157) Ed.
Caroline Haberfeld.
   Formerly: Fodor's Hong Kong and Macau.

915.404   US
DS406
FODOR'S INDIA. 1963. biennial. $19. Fodor's Travel
Publications, Inc. (Subsidiary of: Random House,
Inc.), 201 E. 50th St., New York, NY 10022.
TEL 800-733-3000. (Dist. by: Random House, Inc.,
400 Hahn Rd., Westminster, MD 21157) Ed. Paula
Consolo.
   Former titles: Fodor's India and Nepal (ISSN
0276-5500); Fodor's India (ISSN 0362-0212);
Which supersedes: Fodor's Guide to India (ISSN
0071-6456)

914.1504   US   ISSN 0071-6464
FODOR'S IRELAND. 1968. a. $16. Fodor's Travel
Publications, Inc. (Subsidiary of: Random House,
Inc.), 201 E. 50th St., New York, NY 10022.
TEL 800-733-3000. (Dist. by: Random House, Inc.,
400 Hahn Rd., Westminster, MD 21157) Ed.
Andrew Collins.

915.6904   US   ISSN 0071-6588
DS103
FODOR'S ISRAEL. 1967. a. $16. Fodor's Travel
Publications, Inc. (Subsidiary of: Random House,
Inc.), 201 E. 50th St., New York, NY 10022.
TEL 800-733-3000. (Dist. by: Random House, Inc.,
400 Hahn Rd., Westminster, MD 21157) Ed. Paula
Rackow.

914.504   US   ISSN 0071-6472
FODOR'S ITALY. 1951. a. $17. Fodor's Travel
Publications, Inc. (Subsidiary of: Random House,
Inc.), 201 E. 50th St., New York, NY 10022.
TEL 800-733-3000. (Dist. by: Random House, Inc.,
400 Hahn Rd., Westminster, MD 21157) Ed. Holly
Hughes.

914.504   US
FODOR'S ITALY'S GREAT CITIES. a. $11. Fodor's Travel
Publications, Inc. (Subsidiary of: Random House,
Inc.), 201 E. 50th St., New York, NY 10022.
TEL 800-733-3000. (Dist. by: Random House, Inc.,
400 Hahn Rd., Westminster, MD 21157) Ed. Holly
Hughes.
   Formerly: Fodor's Florence and Venice.

915.204   US
FODOR'S JAPAN. 1962. a. $19. Fodor's Travel
Publications, Inc. (Subsidiary of: Random House,
Inc.), 201 E. 50th St., New York, NY 10022.
TEL 800-733-3000. (Dist. by: Random House, Inc.,
400 Hahn Rd., Westminster, MD 21157) Ed. Paula
Consolo.
   Supersedes in part: Fodor's Japan and Korea (ISSN
0098-1613); Fodor's Japan and East Asia (ISSN
0071-6480)

916.7604   US
FODOR'S KENYA & TANZANIA. irreg. $16. Fodor's Travel
Publications, Inc. (Subsidiary of: Random House,
Inc.), 201 E. 50th St., New York, NY 10022.
TEL 800-733-3000. (Dist. by: Random House, Inc.,
400 Hahn Rd., Westminster, MD 21157) Ed.
Conrad Paulus.
   Formerly: Fodor's Kenya.

915.104   US
FODOR'S KOREA. a. $14. Fodor's Travel Publications,
Inc. (Subsidiary of: Random House, Inc.), 201 E.
50th St., New York, NY 10022.
TEL 800-733-3000. (Dist. by: Random House, Inc.,
400 Hahn Rd., Westminster, MD 21157) Ed. Julie
Tomasz.
   Supersedes in part: Fodor's Japan and Korea (ISSN
0098-1613); Fodor's Japan and East Asia (ISSN
0071-6480)

917.904   US
FODOR'S LAS VEGAS, RENO, TAHOE. a. $12. Fodor's
Travel Publications, Inc. (Subsidiary of: Random
House, Inc.), 201 E. 50th St., New York, NY 10022.
TEL 800-733-3000. (Dist. by: Random House, Inc.,
400 Hahn Rd., Westminster, MD 21157) Ed. Jillian
Magalaner.
   Formerly: Fodor's Fun in Las Vegas.

914.2104   US   ISSN 0071-6596
FODOR'S LONDON. 1971. a. $11. Fodor's Travel
Publications, Inc. (Subsidiary of: Random House,
Inc.), 201 E. 50th St., New York, NY 10022.
TEL 800-733-3000. (Dist. by: Random House, Inc.,
400 Hahn Rd., Westminster, MD 21157) Ed. Craig
Seligman.

917.904   US
FODOR'S LOS ANGELES. a. $12. Fodor's Travel
Publications, Inc. (Subsidiary of: Random House,
Inc.), 201 E. 50th St., New York, NY 10022.
TEL 800-733-3000. (Dist. by: Random House, Inc.,
400 Hahn Rd., Westminster, MD 21157) Ed. Larry
Peterson.

914.604   US
FODOR'S MADRID AND BARCELONA. a. $11. Fodor's
Travel Publications, Inc. (Subsidiary of: Random
House, Inc.), 201 E. 50th St., New York, NY 10022.
TEL 800-733-3000. (Dist. by: Random House, Inc.,
400 Hahn Rd., Westminster, MD 21157) Ed.
Suzanne DeGalan.
   Formerly: Fodor's Madrid.

917.404   US
FODOR'S MAINE, VERMONT, NEW HAMPSHIRE. irreg.
$10. Fodor's Travel Publications, Inc. (Subsidiary of:
Random House, Inc.), 201 E. 50th St., New York,
NY 10022. TEL 800-733-3000. (Dist. by: Random
House, Inc., 400 Hahn Rd., Westminster, MD
21157) Ed. Jillian Magalaner.

917.2904   US
FODOR'S MAUI. a. $9. Fodor's Travel Publications, Inc.
(Subsidiary of: Random House, Inc.), 201 E. 50th
St., New York, NY 10022. TEL 800-733-3000.
(Dist. by: Random House, Inc., 400 Hahn Rd.,
Westminster, MD 21157) Ed. Larry Peterson.
   Formerly: Fodor's Fun in Maui.

917.204   US   ISSN 0071-6499
FODOR'S MEXICO. 1972. a. $16. Fodor's Travel
Publications, Inc. (Subsidiary of: Random House,
Inc.), 201 E. 50th St., New York, NY 10022.
TEL 800-733-3000. (Dist. by: Random House, Inc.,
400 Hahn Rd., Westminster, MD 21157) Ed.
Carolyn Price.

917.504   US
FODOR'S MIAMI & THE KEYS. a. $10. Fodor's Travel
Publications, Inc. (Subsidiary of: Random House,
Inc.), 201 E. 50th St., New York, NY 10022.
TEL 800-733-3000. (Dist. by: Random House, Inc.,
400 Hahn Rd., Westminster, MD 21157) Ed. Alison
Hoffman.
   Formerly: Fodor's Greater Miami and the Gold
Coast.

917.104   US
FODOR'S MONTREAL & QUEBEC CITY. a. $12. Fodor's
Travel Publications, Inc. (Subsidiary of: Random
House, Inc.), 201 E. 50th St., New York, NY 10022.
TEL 800-733-3000. (Dist. by: Random House, Inc.,
400 Hahn Rd., Westminster, MD 21157) Ed.
Conrad Paulus.
   Formerly: Fodor's Fun in Montreal.

916.104   US
FODOR'S MOROCCO. 1980. irreg. $16.95. Fodor's
Travel Publications, Inc. (Subsidiary of: Random
House, Inc.), 201 E. 50th St., New York, NY 10022.
TEL 800-733-3000. (Dist. by: Random House, Inc.,
400 Hahn Rd., Westminster, MD 21157) Ed. Paula
Consolo.
   Formerly: Fodor's North Africa.

914.304   US
FODOR'S MUNICH. 1984. irreg. $11. Fodor's Travel
Publications, Inc. (Subsidiary of: Random House,
Inc.), 201 E. 50th St., New York, NY 10022.
TEL 800-733-3000. (Dist. by: Random House, Inc.,
400 Hahn Rd., Westminster, MD 21157) Ed. Larry
Peterson.

917.804   US
FODOR'S NATIONAL PARKS OF THE WEST. irreg. $17.
Fodor's Travel Publications, Inc. (Subsidiary of:
Random House, Inc.), 201 E. 50th St., New York,
NY 10022. TEL 800-733-3000. (Dist. by: Random
House, Inc., 400 Hahn Rd., Westminster, MD
21157) Ed. Paula Consolo.

917.404   US   ISSN 0192-3412
F2.3
FODOR'S NEW ENGLAND. 1975. a. $16. Fodor's Travel
Publications, Inc. (Subsidiary of: Random House,
Inc.), 201 E. 50th St., New York, NY 10022.
TEL 800-733-3000. (Dist. by: Random House, Inc.,
400 Hahn Rd., Westminster, MD 21157) Ed. Jillian
Magalaner. illus.

917.604   US
FODOR'S NEW ORLEANS. a. $11. Fodor's Travel
Publications, Inc. (Subsidiary of: Random House,
Inc.), 201 E. 50th St., New York, NY 10022.
TEL 800-733-3000. (Dist. by: Random House, Inc.,
400 Hahn Rd., Westminster, MD 21157) Ed. Nancy
van Itallie.

917.404   US
FODOR'S NEW YORK CITY. 1975. a. $13. Fodor's Travel
Publications, Inc. (Subsidiary of: Random House,
Inc.), 201 E. 50th St., New York, NY 10022.
TEL 800-733-3000. (Dist. by: Random House, Inc.,
400 Hahn Rd., Westminster, MD 21157) Ed.
Suzanne DeGalan. illus.
   Former titles: Fodor's New York; Fodor's New York
and New Jersey.

919.304   US
FODOR'S NEW ZEALAND. a. $9. Fodor's Travel
Publications, Inc. (Subsidiary of: Random House,
Inc.), 201 E. 50th St., New York, NY 10022.
TEL 800-733-3000. (Dist. by: Random House, Inc.,
400 Hahn Rd., Westminster, MD 21157) Ed. Craig
Seligman.

917.404   US
FODOR'S NORWAY. irreg. $10. Fodor's Travel
Publications, Inc. (Subsidiary of: Random House,
Inc.), 201 E. 50th St., New York, NY 10022.
TEL 800-733-3000. (Dist. by: Random House, Inc.,
400 Hahn Rd., Westminster, MD 21157) Ed. Nancy
van Itallie.

917.104 US
FODOR'S NOVA SCOTIA, PRINCE EDWARD ISLAND AND NEW BRUNSWICK. irreg. $9. Fodor's Travel Publications, Inc. (Subsidiary of: Random House, Inc.), 201 E. 50th St., New York, NY 10022. TEL 800-733-3000. (Dist. by: Random House, Inc., 400 Hahn Rd. Westminster, MD 21157) Ed. Edie Jarolim.
Formerly: Fodor's Canada's Maritime Provinces.

917.904 US
FODOR'S PACIFIC NORTH COAST. 1984. a. $16. Fodor's Travel Publications, Inc. (Subsidiary of: Random House, Inc.), 201 E. 50th St., New York, NY 10022. TEL 800-733-3000. (Dist. by: Random House, Inc., 400 Hahn Rd., Westminster, MD 21157) Ed. Larry Peterson.

914.404 US ISSN 0149-1288
DC708
FODOR'S PARIS. 1973. a. $12. Fodor's Travel Publications, Inc. (Subsidiary of: Random House, Inc.), 201 E. 50th St., New York, NY 10022. TEL 800-733-3000. (Dist. by: Random House, Inc., 400 Hahn Rd., Westminster, MD 21157) Ed. Paula Consolo.

917.404 US
FODOR'S PHILADELPHIA & THE PENNSYLVANIA DUTCH COUNTRY. irreg. $11. Fodor's Travel Publications, Inc. (Subsidiary of: Random House, Inc.), 201 E. 50th St., New York, NY 10022. TEL 800-733-3000. (Dist. by: Random House, Inc., 400 Hahn St., Westminster, MD 21157) Ed. Caroline Haberfeld.
Formerly: Fodor's Philadelphia.

917.2904 US
FODOR'S POCKET JAMAICA. a. $7. Fodor's Travel Publications, Inc. (Subsidiary of: Random House, Inc.), 201 E. 50th St., New York, NY 10022. TEL 800-733-3000. (Dist. by: Random House, Inc., 400 Hahn Rd., Westminster, MD 21157) Ed. Caroline Haberfeld.
Formerly: Fodor's Fun in Jamaica.

914.2104 US
FODOR'S POCKET LONDON. a. $8. Fodor's Travel Publications, Inc. (Subsidiary of: Random House, Inc.), 201 E. 50th St., New York, NY 10022. TEL 800-733-3000. (Dist. by: Random House, Inc., 400 Hahn Rd., Westminster, MD 21157) Ed. Craig Seligman.
Formerly: Fodor's Fun in London.

917.404 US
FODOR'S POCKET NEW YORK CITY. a. $8. Fodor's Travel Publications, Inc. (Subsidiary of: Random House, Inc.), 201 E. 50th St., New York, NY 10022. TEL 800-733-3000. (Dist. by: Random House, Inc., 400 Hahn Rd., Westminster, MD 21157) Ed. Suzanne DeGalan.
Formerly: Fodor's Fun in New York City.

914.404 US
FODOR'S POCKET PARIS. a. $8. Fodor's Travel Publications, Inc. (Subsidiary of: Random House, Inc.), 201 E. 50th St., New York, NY 10022. TEL 800-733-3000. (Dist. by: Random House, Inc., 400 Hahn Rd., Westminster, MD 21157) Ed. Paula Consolo.
Formerly: Fodor's Fun in Paris.

917.204 US
FODOR'S POCKET PUERTO RICO. a. $7. Fodor's Travel Publications, Inc. (Subsidiary of: Random House, Inc.), 201 E. 50th St., New York, NY 10022. TEL 800-733-3000. (Dist. by: Random House Inc, 400 Hahn Rd., Westminster, MD 21157) Ed. Andrew Collins.

917.904 US
FODOR'S POCKET SAN FRANCISCO. a. $8. Fodor's Travel Publications, Inc. (Subsidiary of: Random House, Inc.), 201 E. 50th St., New York, NY 10022. TEL 800-733-3000. (Dist. by: Random House, Inc., 400 Hahn Rd., Westminster, MD 21157) Ed. Larry Peterson.
Formerly: Fodor's Fun in San Francisco.

917.504 US
FODOR'S POCKET WASHINGTON. a. $8. Fodor's Travel Publications, Inc. (Subsidiary of: Random House, Inc.), 201 E. 50th St., New York, NY 10022. TEL 800-733-3000. (Dist. by: Random House, Inc., 400 Hahn Rd., Westminster, MD 21157) Ed. Suzanne DeGalan.

914.6904 US ISSN 0071-6510
DP516
FODOR'S PORTUGAL. 1951. a. $17. Fodor's Travel Publications, Inc. (Subsidiary of: Random House, Inc.), 201 E. 50th St., New York, NY 10022. TEL 800-733-3000. (Dist. by: Random House, Inc., 400 Hahn Rd., Westminster, MD 21157) Ed. Alison Hoffman.

914.504 US ISSN 0276-2560
DG804
FODOR'S ROME. 1979. a. $13. Fodor's Travel Publications, Inc. (Subsidiary of: Random House, Inc.), 201 E. 50th St., New York, NY 10022. TEL 800-733-3000. (Dist. by: Random House, Inc., 400 Hahn Rd., Westminster, MD 21157) Ed. Julie Tomasz.

917.904 US
FODOR'S SAN DIEGO. a. $11. Fodor's Travel Publications, Inc. (Subsidiary of: Random House, Inc.), 201 E. 50th St., New York, NY 10022. TEL 800-733-3000. (Dist. by: Random House, Inc., 400 Hahn Rd., Westminster, MD 21157) Ed. Larry Peterson.

917.904 US
FODOR'S SAN FRANCISCO. 1982. a. $11. Fodor's Travel Publications, Inc. (Subsidiary of: Random House, Inc.), 201 E. 50th St., New York, NY 10022. TEL 800-733-3000. (Dist. by: Random House, Inc., 400 Hahn Rd., Westminster, MD 21157) Ed. Larry Peterson.

917.804 US
FODOR'S SANTA FE, TAOS, ALBUQUERQUE. a. $12. Fodor's Travel Publications, Inc. (Subsidiary of: Random House, Inc.), 201 E. 50th St., New York, NY 10022. TEL 800-733-3000. (Dist. by: Random House, Inc., 400 Hahn Rd., Westminster, MD 21157) Ed. Julie Tomasz.
Formerly: Fodor's New Mexico.

914.804 US ISSN 0071-6529
FODOR'S SCANDINAVIA. 1951. a. $19. Fodor's Travel Publications, Inc. (Subsidiary of: Random House, Inc.), 201 E. 50th St., New York, NY 10022. TEL 800-733-3000. (Dist. by: Random House, Inc., 400 Hahn Rd., Westminster, MD 21157) Ed. Nancy van Itallie.

914.804 US
FODOR'S SCANDINAVIAN CITIES. irreg. $9. Fodor's Travel Publications, Inc. (Subsidiary of: Random House, Inc.), 201 E. 50th St., New York, NY 10022. TEL 800-733-3000. (Dist. by: Random House, Inc., 400 Hahn Rd., Westminster, MD 21157) Ed. Nancy van Itallie.
Formerly: Fodor's Stockholm, Copenhagen, Oslo, Helsinki and Reykjavik.

914.104 US
FODOR'S SCOTLAND. a. $16. Fodor's Travel Publications, Inc. (Subsidiary of: Random House, Inc.), 201 E. 50th St., New York, NY 10022. TEL 800-733-3000. (Dist. by: Random House, Inc., 400 Hahn Rd., Westminster, MD 21157) Ed. Caroline Haberfeld.

917.904 US
FODOR'S SEATTLE AND VANCOUVER. irreg. $10. Fodor's Travel Publications, Inc. (Subsidiary of: Random House, Inc.), 201 E. 50th St., New York, NY 10022. TEL 800-733-3000. (Dist. by: Random House, Inc., 400 Hahn Rd., Westminster, MD 21157) Ed. Alison Hoffman.

915.9504 US
FODOR'S SINGAPORE. irreg. $13. Fodor's Travel Publications, Inc. (Subsidiary of: Random House, Inc.), 201 E. 50th St., New York, NY 10022. TEL 800-733-3000. (Dist. by: Random House, Inc., 400 Hahn Rd., Westminster, MD 21157) Ed. Craig Seligman.

917.04 796.93 US
FODOR'S SKIING IN THE U S A & CANADA. irreg. $15. Fodor's Travel Publications, Inc. (Subsidiary of: Random House, Inc.), 201 E. 50th St., New York, NY 10022. TEL 800-733-3000. (Dist. by: Random House, Inc., 400 Hahn Rd., Westminster, MD 21157)
Formerly: Fodor's Ski Resorts of North America.

918.04 US ISSN 0071-6537
F2211
FODOR'S SOUTH AMERICA. 1966. a. $17. Fodor's Travel Publications, Inc. (Subsidiary of: Random House, Inc.), 201 E. 50th St., New York, NY 10022. TEL 800-733-3000. (Dist. by: Random House, Inc., 400 Hahn Rd., Westminster, MD 21157) Ed. Julie Tomasz.

919.604 US
FODOR'S SOUTH PACIFIC. irreg. $12. Fodor's Travel Publications, Inc. (Subsidiary of: Random House, Inc.), 201 E. 50th St., New York, NY 10022. TEL 800-733-3000. (Dist. by: Random House, Inc., 400 Hahn Rd., Westminster, MD 21157) Ed. Craig Seligman.

915.904 US ISSN 0160-8991
DS504
FODOR'S SOUTHEAST ASIA. 1975. a. $18. Fodor's Travel Publications, Inc. (Subsidiary of: Random House, Inc.), 201 E. 50th St., New York, NY 10022. TEL 800-733-3000. (Dist. by: Random House, Inc., 400 Hahn Rd., Westminster, MD 21157) Ed. Craig Seligman.
Supersedes in part: Fodor's Japan and East Asia (ISSN 0071-6480)

914.604 US ISSN 0071-6545
FODOR'S SPAIN. 1955. a. $16. Fodor's Travel Publications, Inc. (Subsidiary of: Random House, Inc.), 201 E. 50th St., New York, NY 10022. TEL 800-733-3000. (Dist. by: Random House, Inc., 400 Hahn Rd., Westminster, MD 21157) Ed. Suzanne DeGalan.

FODOR'S SPORTS: CYCLING. see SPORTS AND GAMES — Bicycles And Motorcycles

FODOR'S SPORTS: HIKING. see SPORTS AND GAMES — Outdoor Life

FODOR'S SPORTS: RUNNING. see SPORTS AND GAMES — Outdoor Life

FODOR'S SPORTS: SAILING. see SPORTS AND GAMES — Boats And Boating

917.404 US
FODOR'S SUNDAY IN NEW YORK. irreg. $11. Fodor's Travel Publications, Inc. (Subsidiary of: Random House, Inc.), 201 E. 50th St., New York, NY 10022. TEL 800-733-3000. (Dist. by: Random House, Inc., 400 Hahn Rd., Westminster, MD 21157) Eds. David Low, Andrew Anspach.

914.8504 US
FODOR'S SWEDEN. irreg. $9. Fodor's Travel Publications, Inc. (Subsidiary of: Random House, Inc.), 201 E. 50th St., New York, NY 10022. TEL 800-733-3000. (Dist. by: Random House, Inc., 400 Hahn Rd., Westminster, MD 21157) Ed. Nancy van Itallie.

914.9404 US ISSN 0071-6553
DQ16
FODOR'S SWITZERLAND. 1951. a. $17. Fodor's Travel Publications, Inc. (Subsidiary of: Random House, Inc.), 201 E. 50th St., New York, NY 10022. TEL 800-733-3000. (Dist. by: Random House, Inc., 400 Hahn Rd., Westminster, MD 21157) Ed. Karen Cure.

915.9304 US
FODOR'S THAILAND. irreg. $12. Fodor's Travel Publications, Inc. (Subsidiary of: Random House, Inc.), 201 E. 50th St., New York, NY 10022. TEL 800-733-3000. (Dist. by: Random House, Inc., 400 Hahn Rd., Westminster, MD 21157) Ed. Conrad Paulus.

917.504 US
FODOR'S THE CHESAPEAKE REGION. irreg. $8.95. Fodor's Travel Publications, Inc. (Subsidiary of: Random House, Inc.), 201 E. 50th St., New York, NY 10022. TEL 800-733-3000. (Dist. by: Random House, Inc., 400 Hahn Rd., Westminster, MD 21157) Ed. Vernon Nahrgang.
Formerly: Fodor's Chesapeake.

TRAVEL AND TOURISM 4767

917.04 US ISSN 0147-8680
F207.3
FODOR'S THE SOUTH. 1975. a. $15. Fodor's Travel Publications, Inc. (Subsidiary of: Random House, Inc.), 201 E. 50th St., New York, NY 10022. TEL 800-733-3000. (Dist. by: Random House, Inc., 400 Hahn Rd., Westminster, MD 21157) Ed. Andrew Collins. illus.

914.404 440 US
FODOR'S THREE-IN-ONE: FRANCE; guidebook, language cassette and phrase book. irreg. $27.50. Fodor's Travel Publications, Inc. (Subsidiary of: Random House, Inc.), 201 E. 50th St., New York, NY 10022. TEL 800-733-3000. (Dist. by: Random House, Inc., 400 Hahn Rd., Westminster, MD 21157)

914.304 430 US
FODOR'S THREE-IN-ONE: GERMANY; guidebook, language cassette and phrase book. irreg. $27.50. Fodor's Travel Publications, Inc. (Subsidiary of: Random House, Inc.), 201 E. 50th St., New York, NY 10022. TEL 800-733-3000. (Dist. by: Random House, Inc., 400 Hahn Rd., Westminster, MD 21157)

914.504 450 US
FODOR'S THREE-IN-ONE: ITALY; guidebook, language cassette and phrase book. irreg. $27.50. Fodor's Travel Publications, Inc. (Subsidiary of: Random House, Inc.), 201 E. 50th St., New York, NY 10022. TEL 800-733-3000. (Dist. by: Random House, Inc., 400 Hahn Rd., Westminster, MD 21157)

917.204 460 US
FODOR'S THREE-IN-ONE: MEXICO; guidebook, language cassette and phrase book. irreg. $27.50. Fodor's Travel Publications, Inc. (Subsidiary of: Random House, Inc.), 201 E. 50th St., New York, NY 10022. TEL 800-733-3000. (Dist. by: Random House, Inc., 400 Hahn Rd., Westminster, MD 21157)

914.604 460 US
FODOR'S THREE-IN-ONE: SPAIN; guidebook, language cassette and phrase book. irreg. $27.50. Fodor's Travel Publications, Inc. (Subsidiary of: Random House, Inc.), 201 E. 50th St., New York, NY 10022. TEL 800-733-3000. (Dist. by: Random House, Inc., 400 Hahn Rd., Westminster, MD 21157)

915.204 US
FODOR'S TOKYO. irreg. $12. Fodor's Travel Publications, Inc. (Subsidiary of: Random House, Inc.), 201 E. 50th St., New York, NY 10022. TEL 800-733-3000. (Dist. by: Random House, Inc., 400 Hahn Rd., Westminster, MD 21157) Ed. Paula Consolo.

917.104 US
FODOR'S TORONTO. a. $12. Fodor's Travel Publications, Inc. (Subsidiary of: Random House, Inc.), 201 E. 50th St., New York, NY 10022. TEL 800-733-3000. (Dist. by: Random House, Inc., 400 Hahn Rd., Westminster, MD 21157) Ed. Jillian Magalaner.

914.04 US
FODOR'S TOURING EUROPE. irreg. $14. Fodor's Travel Publications, Inc. (Subsidiary of: Random House, Inc.), 201 E. 50th St., New York, NY 10022. TEL 800-733-3000. (Dist. by: Random House, Inc., 400 Hahn Rd., Westminster, MD 21157) Ed. Nancy van Itallie.

917.304 US
FODOR'S TOURING U S A: EASTERN EDITION. irreg. $16. Fodor's Travel Publications, Inc. (Subsidiary of: Random House, Inc.), 201 E. 50th St., New York, NY 10022. TEL 800-733-3000. (Dist. by: Random House, Inc., 400 Hahn Rd., Westminster, MD 21157) Ed. Holly Hughes.

917.804 US
FODOR'S TOURING U S A: WESTERN EDITION. irreg. $16. Fodor's Travel Publications, Inc. (Subsidiary of: Random House, Inc.), 201 E. 50th St., New York, NY 10022. TEL 800-733-3000. (Dist. by: Random House, Inc., 400 Hahn Rd., Westminster, MD 21157) Ed. Craig Seligman.

915.6104 US ISSN 0071-6618
DR416
FODOR'S TURKEY. 1969. a. $17. Fodor's Travel Publications, Inc. (Subsidiary of: Random House, Inc.), 201 E. 50th St., New York, NY 10022. TEL 800-733-3000. (Dist. by: Random House, Inc., 400 Hahn Rd., Westminster, MD 21157) Ed. Karen Cure.

917.304 US ISSN 0147-8745
E158
FODOR'S U S A. 1976. a. $18. Fodor's Travel Publications, Inc. (Subsidiary of: Random House, Inc.), 201 E. 50th St., New York, NY 10022. TEL 800-733-3000. (Dist. by: Random House, Inc., 400 Hahn Rd., Westminster, MD 21157) Ed. Nancy van Itallie. illus.

919.704 US
FODOR'S U S & BRITISH VIRGIN ISLANDS. a. $12. Fodor's Travel Publications, Inc. (Subsidiary of: Random House, Inc.), 201 E. 50th St., New York, NY 10022. TEL 800-733-3000. (Dist. by: Random House, Inc., 400 Hahn St., Westminster, MD 21157) Ed. Suzanne DeGalan.
  Formerly: Fodor's Virgin Islands.

917.404 US
FODOR'S VACATIONS IN NEW YORK STATE. irreg. $14.95. Fodor's Travel Publications, Inc. (Subsidiary of: Random House, Inc.), 201 E. 50th St., New York, NY 10022. TEL 800-733-3000. (Dist. by: Random House, Inc., 400 Hahn Rd., Westminster, MD 21157)
  Formerly: Fodor's New York State.

917.404 US
FODOR'S VACATIONS ON THE NEW JERSEY SHORE. irreg. $11. Fodor's Travel Publications, Inc. (Subsidiary of: Random House, Inc.), 201 E. 50th St., New York, NY 10022. TEL 800-733-3000. (Dist. by: Random House, Inc., 400 Hahn Rd., Westminster, MD 21157)
  Formerly: Fodor's Atlantic City and the New Jersey Shore.

914.304 US
FODOR'S VIENNA AND THE DANUBE VALLEY. 1984. irreg. $10. Fodor's Travel Publications, Inc. (Subsidiary of: Random House, Inc.), 201 E. 50th St., New York, NY 10022. TEL 800-733-3000. (Dist. by: Random House, Inc., 400 Hahn Rd., Westminster, MD 21157) Ed. Jillian Magalaner.
  Formerly: Fodor's Vienna.

917.504 US
FODOR'S VIRGINIA & MARYLAND. irreg. $12. Fodor's Travel Publications, Inc. (Subsidiary of: Random House, Inc.), 201 E. 50th St., New York, NY 10022. TEL 800-733-3000. (Dist. by: Random House, Inc., 400 Hahn Rd., Westminster, MD 21157) Ed. Alison Hoffman.
  Formerly: Fodor's Virginia.

919.6904 US
FODOR'S WAIKIKI. irreg. $9. Fodor's Travel Publications, Inc. (Subsidiary of: Random House, Inc.), 201 E. 50th St., New York, NY 10022. TEL 800-733-3000. (Dist. by: Random House, Inc., 400 Hahn Rd., Westminster, MD 21157) Ed. Jillian Magalaner.
  Formerly: Fodor's Fun in Waikiki.

917.504 US
FODOR'S WASHINGTON, D.C. a. $11. Fodor's Travel Publications, Inc. (Subsidiary of: Random House, Inc.), 201 E. 50th St., New York, NY 10022. TEL 800-733-3000. (Dist. by: Random House, Inc., 400 Hahn Rd., Westminster, MD 21157) Ed. Suzanne DeGalan.

914.9704 US ISSN 0071-657X
DR304.5
FODOR'S YUGOSLAVIA. 1951. irreg. $16. Fodor's Travel Publications, Inc. (Subsidiary of: Random House, Inc.), 201 E. 50th St., New York, NY 10022. TEL 800-733-3000. (Dist. by: Random House, Inc., 400 Hahn Rd., Westminster, MD 21157) Ed. Nancy van Itallie.

387.2 US ISSN 0096-1353
VM381
FORD'S DECK PLAN GUIDE. Short title: Deck Plan Guide. 1974. a. $75. Ford's Travel Guides, 19448 Londelius St., Northridge, CA 91324. TEL 818-701-7414. Ed. Judith A. Howard. illus.; circ. 5,000.

910.2 US
FORD'S FREIGHTER TRAVEL GUIDE AND WATERWAYS OF THE WORLD. 1952. s-a. $20. Ford's Travel Guides, 19448 Londelius St., Northridge, CA 91324. TEL 818-701-7414. Ed. Judith A. Howard. adv.; illus.; circ. 12,408.
  Formerly: Ford's Freighter Travel Guide (ISSN 0015-7058)

910.2 US ISSN 0015-7066
HE568
FORD'S INTERNATIONAL CRUISE GUIDE. 1970. q. $40. Ford's Travel Guides, 19448 Londelius St., Northridge, CA 91324. TEL 818-701-7414. Ed. Judith A. Howard. adv.; illus.; circ. 12,000.

914.404 US
FRANCE (YEAR). a. $17. Harper Collins Publishers, Birnbaum Travel Guides, 10 E. 53rd St., New York, NY 10022-5299. TEL 212-420-5800. Ed. Stephen Birnbaum.

910.2 FR ISSN 0071-8734
FRANCE EN POCHE. TOTAL GUIDE.* 1970. a. Editions Vrille-Copalic, 32 Boulevard Flandrin, Paris 16e, France.

910.202 US
FRANCE TRAVEL NEWS. vol.2, 1989. m. free. French Government Tourist Office, 610 Fifth Ave., New York, NY 10020. TEL 212-757-1125.
  Description: Provides travel news and information to various destinations in France.

FRANKFURT - RHEIN MAIN NECKAR SAAR VON HINTEN. see *HOMOSEXUALITY*

914 GW
FRANKFURTER WOCHE. 1935. s-m. Verlag Bodet & Partner, Speyererstr. 2-4, 6000 Frankfurt a.M. 1, Germany. TEL 069-730536. FAX 069-735536. film rev.; play rev.; tr.lit.; circ. 20,000.
  Formerly: Frankfurter Wochenschau (ISSN 0016-0024)

910.2 US ISSN 0016-089X
FREIGHTER TRAVEL NEWS. 1958. m. $18. Freighter Travel Club of America, 3524 Harts Lake Rd., Roy, WA 98580. Ed. Leland J. Pledger. adv.; bk.rev.; illus.; index; circ. 3,000.
  Description: Information on the opportunities, services, and facilities available for traveling by ocean-going freighters and other unique forms of water transportation.

FREIZEIT - CARAVAN - CAMPING MAGAZIN. see *SPORTS AND GAMES — Outdoor Life*

910 AU ISSN 0071-948X
FREMDENVERKEHR IN OESTERREICH. (Subseries of: Beitraege zur Oesterreichischen Statistik) 1956. a. S.570. (Oesterreichisches Statistisches Zentralamt) Oesterreichische Staatsdruckerei, Rennweg 12a, 1037 Vienna, Austria. circ. 600.

914 UK
FRENCH FARM AND VILLAGE HOLIDAY GUIDE. 1976. a. £6.99($12.95) F.H.G. Publications Ltd., Abbey Mill Business Centre, Seedhill, Paisley PA1 1JN, Scotland. TEL 041-887 0428. adv.; illus.; circ. 12,000.

917 US ISSN 0734-1199
FROM THE STATE CAPITALS. TOURIST BUSINESS PROMOTION. 1946. w. $215 (foreign $235)(effective Dec. 1990). Wakeman-Walworth, Inc., 300 N. Washington St., Alexandria, VA 22314. TEL 703-549-1372. FAX 703-549-1372. (processed)
  Description: State and municipal action in the US to promote vacation-travel trade.

917.404 US ISSN 1056-5787
F2.3
FROMMER'S COMPREHENSIVE TRAVEL GUIDE. NEW ENGLAND. 1978. a. $14.95. Frommer Books (Subsidiary of: Simon & Schuster, Inc.), 15 Columbus Circle, New York, NY 10023. TEL 212-373-8125.
  Former titles (until 1991): Frommer's New England (ISSN 1044-2286); Frommer's Dollarwise Guide to New England.

TRAVEL AND TOURISM

916.204 US ISSN 1044-226X
DT45
FROMMER'S EGYPT. 1980. biennial. $14.95. Frommer Books (Subsidiary of: Simon & Schuster), 15 Columbus Circle, New York, NY 10023. TEL 212-373-8125.
  Formerly: Frommer's Dollarwise Guide to Egypt.

914.3 US ISSN 1044-2405
DD16
FROMMER'S GERMANY. a. $14.95. Frommer Books (Subsidiary of: Simon & Schuster, Inc.), 15 Columbus Circle, New York, NY 10023. TEL 212-373-8125. Ed. D. Porter.
  Former titles: Frommer's Dollarwise Guide to Germany (ISSN 0731-4442); Arthur Frommer's Dollarwise Guide to Germany (ISSN 0272-0035)

914.509 US ISSN 1044-2170
DG416
FROMMER'S ITALY. 1969. a. $14.95. Frommer Books (Subsidiary of: Simon & Schuster, Inc.), 15 Columbus Circle, New York, NY 10023. TEL 212-373-8125.
  Formerly: Frommer's Dollarwise Guide to Italy (ISSN 0899-336X)

910.09 US
FUNWORLD. 1983. m. $30 (members $25). International Association of Amusement Parks & Attractions, 1448 Duke St., Alexandria, VA 22314-3403. TEL 703-671-5800. FAX 703-824-8365. TELEX 853-485 IAAPA. Ed. Rick Henderson. adv.; bk.rev.; stat.; circ. 5,600. (back issues avail.)
  Description: Statistical and analytical information for members of the association on the amusement industry.

910.4 SA
G S A TRAVEL MARKETING MAGAZINE. (Text in English) 1980. m. R.120. G S A Marketing Pty. Ltd., P.O. Box 3239, Capetown 8000, South Africa. TEL 021-419-1671. FAX 021-419-4851. Ed. Jeff Hawthorne. adv.; circ. 3,400. (back issues avail.)

910.09 GW
GAESTE JOURNAL. 1979. 6/yr. free. (Turistik Zentrale) Wilhelm Bing Verlag, Lengefelderstr. 6, 3540 Korbach, Germany. TEL 05631-56000. FAX 05631-6994. Ed. Arthur Cromm. adv.; bk.rev.; circ. 25,000.
  Formerly (until 1990): Ferienpost.

GAIA'S GUIDE. see *HOMOSEXUALITY*

910.4 MP
▼**GAL/FIRE.** (Text in Mongolian) 1991. bi-m. Mongolian Cultural Foundation, P.O. Box 527, Ulan Bator, Mongolia. TEL 210611. Ed. Y. Baatar.
  Description: Covers non-political, cultural affairs.

910.09 US
GARDENS AND COUNTRYSIDES. 10/yr. Travel Publications, Inc. (San Antonio), 401 Austin Hwy., No. 209, San Antonio, TX 78209. TEL 512-826-5222. FAX 512-826-8996. Ed. Peter C. Selig.

910.202 664 641.5 SZ
GASTRONOMIE & TOURISME. (Text and summaries in French, German, Italian) 1973. bi-m. 42 Fr. (foreign 60 Fr.). Gastronomie & Tourisme SA, Casella Postale 2507, CH-6901 Lugano, Switzerland. TEL 091-528548. FAX 091-524920. Ed. A. Dell'Acqua. circ. 20,000.
  Description: Covers international tourism and gastronomy.

910.202 FR
GAULT - MILLAU MAGAZINE. 1969. m. 250 F.($55) Jour-Azur S.A., 22 bis, rue des Volontaires, 75015 Paris, France. FAX 42-73-04-50. TELEX 203561. Ed. Yves Bridault. adv.; bk.rev.; illus.; charts; circ. 160,000. (back issues avail.)
  Formerly: Nouveau Guide Gault-Millau (ISSN 0399-8223)

917 MX ISSN 0016-5379
GAZER/MIRON. 1950. w. $30. Editorial Monex S. de R.L. y C.V., Ave. Insurgentes Centro 132-204, Mexico 06030, D.F., Mexico. Ed. Raul Esquivel. adv.; charts; illus.; stat.; circ. 25,000.
  Description: Description and travel information on Mexico.

914 FR ISSN 0016-5573
GAZETTE OFFICIELLE DU TOURISME; bulletin d'information et de documentation sur le tourisme. w. 1300 F. Office des Nouvelles Internationales, 18 rue de Folin, 64200 Biarritz, France. TEL 59-41-08-78. FAX 59-41-03-36. TELEX 570061F. Ed. Jacques Darrigrand.

910.09 IT
GENTE VIAGGI. 1979. m. L.57600 (foreign L.100000). Rusconi Editori Associati S.p.a, Servizio Abbonamenti, Via Vitruvio 43, 20124 Milan, Italy. TEL 02-67561. FAX 67562732. Ed. Giuseppe Alberto Orefice. circ. 160,000.

GEO. see *ENVIRONMENTAL STUDIES*

918.304 CL ISSN 0431-1930
F3064 CODEN: GCHLAE
GEOCHILE. 1951. irreg. (Sociedad Geografica de Chile) Lord Cochrane S.A., Providencia 711, Santiago, Chile. illus. **Indexed:** GeoRef.

910.9 IT
GEODES;* la terra che vive. 1978. m. L.52000. Edizioni Purana, Via Borgo Palazzo 226, 24100 Gergamo, Italy. TEL 02-29404473. FAX 02-2948031. Ed. Riccardo Venchiarutti. adv.; bk.rev.; circ. 44,000. (also avail. in microform)

910.09 GW
TI GESCHAEFTSREISE. 1981. s-m. DM.93. Deutscher Verkehrs-Verlag GmbH, Nordkanalstr. 36, 2000 Hamburg 1, Germany. TEL 040-23714165. FAX 040-23714123. Ed. Hans-Juergen Klesse. adv. contact: Werner Holders. circ. 10,300.
  Description: Provides information for travel agencies and business travel departments.

910.202 UK ISSN 0954-0369
GETTING ABOUT BRITAIN; for the independent traveller. 1988. 3/yr. £7 europe £9; elsewhere £10. (British Tourist Authority) Drumport Ltd., 21 Church Walk, Thames Ditton, Surrey KT7 ONP, England. TEL 4481-398-8332. Ed. Clive Lewis. adv.; circ. 40,000 (controlled).
  —BLDSC shelfmark: 4165.228000.
  Description: Details destinations by bus, train, plane and ferry.

910.202 UK
GETTING AROUND THE HIGHLANDS AND ISLANDS. 1978. s-a. F.H.G. Publications Ltd., Abbey Mill Business Centre, Seedhill, Paisley PA1 1JN, Scotland. TEL 041-887-0428. adv.

GIORNALE DEI GELATIERI. see *BUSINESS AND ECONOMICS — Chamber Of Commerce Publications*

GIORNALE DEL COMMERCIO TURISMO. see *BUSINESS AND ECONOMICS — Domestic Commerce*

GLOBE. see *CLUBS*

910.202 SZ
GLOBO; das Reisemagazin. (Text in German) 12/yr. 7.80 Fr. Verlag C.J. Bucher AG, Zurichstr. 5, 6002 Lucerne, Switzerland. adv.; bk.rev.; circ. 35,000.
  Formerly (until 1989): Diners Club Magazine.

796.7 US ISSN 0017-1441
GO (CHARLOTTE). 1923. bi-m. membership. American Automobile Association, Carolina Motor Club, Box 30008, 720 E. Morehead St., Charlotte, NC 28230. TEL 704-377-3600. FAX 704-358-1585. Ed. Quentin Anderson, Jr. adv.; bk.rev.; charts; illus.; stat.; circ. 309,000.
  Description: Gives description and travel information.

914.2 UK
GOFF'S GUIDE TO CATER YOURSELF HOLIDAYS. 1977. a. 50p. Eastern Counties Newspaper Ltd., Prospect House, Rouen Rd., Norwich NR1 1RE, England. Ed. R. De Young.

910.09 US
GOING PLACES (CHICAGO);* the newsletter of international travel. 1980. m. $12. (Wards Wide World of Travel) Signature Publications, 200 N. Martingale Dr., Schaumburg, IL 60173-2096. Ed. Susan Bayer Ward. circ. 125,000.

910.09 US
GOING PLACES (MINOT). m. D D Schmidt Enterprises, 2010 Fourth Ave., N.W., Minot, ND 58701. TEL 701-839-0809. FAX 701-839-0408. Ed. Debbie Schmidt.

910.09 US
GOING PLACES (SCHAUMBURG). 1948. s-a. membership only. Signature Group, 200 N. Martingale Rd., Schaumburg, IL 60173-2096. FAX 312-605-7478. Ed. Ann Cade. circ. 10,000.
  Description: Presents special tips opportunities, travel tips and special city feature stories and destinations.

910.09 UK
GOING PLACES INTERNATIONAL; Britain's premier travel magazine. 1984. q. £2($5.25) Pericles Press, 38 Buckingham Palace Rd., London SW1 WORE, England. TEL 071-486-5353. FAX 071-486-2094. TELEX 27659. Ed. Daphne Aldis. adv.; bk.rev.; circ. 40,000.
  Formerly: Going Places.

GOING PLACES MAGAZINE. see *TRANSPORTATION — Automobiles*

910.202 UK
GOLDEN FALCON. (Text in Arabic and English) m. (Gulf Air) Bryan Richardson & Associates, Parkway House, Sheen Lane, London SW14 8LS, England. Ed. Joanna Donaldson. adv.; circ. 20,000.

910.202 647.94 UK
GOLDEN KEYS MAGAZINE. 1979. q. £6. Tempest Publications Ltd., 94 Gray's Inn Rd., London WC1X 8AA, England. TEL 01-242-5621. FAX 01-242-4132. Ed. Miranda Moore. adv.; bk.rev.; play rev.; circ. 10,000. (back issues avail.)
  Formerly: I Guide (ISSN 0261-4359)

910.202 US
GOLDEN STATE; the magazine of California. 1984. q. $12. (R H L-Golden State) Golden State Publishing, 80 S. Lake Ave., No. 818, Pasadena, CA 91101. TEL 818-584-9703. FAX 818-584-9719. Ed. Tom Lombardi. adv.; circ. 3,125,000 (controlled).
  Description: Distributed to out-of-state motorists at agricultural checkpoints in the state, with articles on site and events, as well as auto-travel tips.

GOLF JOURNAL. see *SPORTS AND GAMES — Ball Games*

GOLFER'S TRAVEL GUIDE. see *SPORTS AND GAMES — Ball Games*

796.5 UK ISSN 0142-5978
GOOD CAMPS GUIDE BRITAIN (YEAR). (Sub-series of: Alan Rogers Good Camps Guide) 1968. a. £3.25 paperback. Deneway Guides and Travel Ltd. (Subsidiary of: Response Marketing Initiatives Limited), Chesil Lodge, W. Bexington, Dorset DT2 9DG, England. TEL 0308-897809. Eds. Clive Edwards, Sue Smart. adv.; circ. 25,000.

796.54 UK
GOOD CAMPS GUIDE EUROPE (YEAR). (Sub-series of: Alan Rogers Good Camps Guide) 1968. a. £5.25. Deneway Guides and Travel Ltd. (Subsidiary of: Response Marketing Initiatives Limited), Chesil Lodge, W. Bexington, Dorset DT2 9DG, England. TEL 0308-897809. Ed.Bd. adv.; illus.; circ. 20,000.
  Formerly: Selected Sites for Caravanning and Camping in Europe (ISSN 0065-5686)
  Description: Provides information for campers, caravaners and motor caravaners regarding location, sanitary facilities, amenities, costs, cleanliness, and maintenance.

796.5 UK
GOOD CAMPS GUIDE FRANCE (YEAR). (Sub-series of: Alan Rogers Good Camps Guide) 1985. a. £3.25. Deneway Guides and Travel Ltd. (Subsidiary of: Response Marketing Initiatives Limited), Chesil Lodge, W. Bexington, Dorset DT2 9DG, England. TEL 0308-879809. Eds. Lois Broughton Edwards, Graham Colborne. illus.; circ. 20,000.
  Description: Covers specially selected nature sights in France for the discerning camper.

910.202 UK
GOOD HOLIDAY MAGAZINE. 1980. q. £9.95. Hill Publications, 1-2 Dawes Court, 93 High St., Esher, Surrey KT10 8QA, England. TEL 0372-69799. Ed. John Hill. circ. 250,000. (back issues avail.)

GOURMED; magazine for doctors. see MEDICAL SCIENCES

GOURMET; the magazine of good living. see FOOD AND FOOD INDUSTRIES

GOURMETOUR; gastronomy & tourist guide. see HOTELS AND RESTAURANTS

910.09 US
GRACIOUS STAYS AND SPECIAL PLACES. q. Person to Person Travel Prod., Inc., 2856 Hundred Oaks, Baton Rouge, LA 70808-1533. TEL 504-346-1928. FAX 504-343-0672. Ed. Helen Heath. circ. 2,500.

914.204 US ISSN 0896-8683
DA650
GREAT BRITAIN (YEAR). a. $17. Harper Collins Publishers, Birnbaum Travel Guides, 10 E 53rd St., New York, NY 10022-5299. TEL 212-207-7000. Ed. Stephen Birnbaum.
  Supersedes (in 1990): Great Britain and Ireland (Year).

910.5 US ISSN 0706-7682
GREAT EXPEDITIONS; the journal of adventure and off the beaten path trips. 1978. 5/yr. $18. Great Expeditions, Inc., Box 18036, Raliegh, NC 27619. TEL 919-872-6684. FAX 919-876-0952. Ed. George W. Kane. adv.; bk.rev.; circ. 7,000. (back issues avail.)
  Description: Emphasizes independent, socially responsible travel outside the usual tourist areas.

910.202 US
GREAT LAKES CAMPBOOK. a. membership. American Automobile Association, 1000 AAA Dr., Heathrow, FL 32746-5063. TEL 407-444-7962. FAX 407-444-7380. adv.; illus.; circ. 300,325.
  Formerly (until 1980): Great Lakes Camping.

919.404 AT
GREAT LAKES ENTERTAINER. 1989. w. Aus.$26. Regional Publishers (N.S.W.) Pty. Ltd., 31 Helen St., Forster, N.S.W. 2423, Australia. TEL 065-546688. FAX 065-556399.
  Description: Features tourist information, fishing, entertainment, leisure.

917.704 US
GREAT LAKES GETAWAY. 1985. 9/yr. $18. Farmers' Advance News, Inc., 130 S. Main St., Box 8, Camden, MI 49232-0008. TEL 517-368-5201. FAX 517-368-5131. Ed. John Snyder. adv.; circ. 130,000 (controlled).
  Description: Travel and tourism guide to the Great Lakes area.

917.7 US ISSN 0887-6223
GREAT LAKES TRAVEL & LIVING. 1986. 8/yr. $17.90. Great Lakes Publishing Co. (Port Clinton), 108 W. Perry St., Port Clinton, OH 43452. TEL 419-734-5774. (Subscr. to: Box 423, Mt. Morris, IL 61054) Ed. David G. Brown. adv.; circ. 40,000. (back issues avail.)
  Description: General interest magazine covering Minnesota, Wisconsin, Illinois, Michigan, Indiana, Ohio, Pennsylvania and New York.

914.95 GR ISSN 0432-6105
DF727
GREECE. (Text in English) 1950. a. National Tourist Organisation of Greece, General Direction of Promotion, Odos Amerikis 2, Athens, Greece. illus.

910.202 GR
GREEK TRAVEL PAGES. 1975. m. $177. International Publications Ltd., 6 Psylla & Filellinon Streets, 10557 Athens, Greece. FAX 3247511. TELEX 3249996. Ed. Eleftherios Theofanopoulos. adv.; bk.rev.; circ. 10,000.

DER GROSSE A D A C SKI ATLAS (YEAR). (Allgemeiner Deutscher Automobil-Club e.V.) see SPORTS AND GAMES — Outdoor Life

914.204
GROSVENOR GUIDE TO LONDON. 1982. a. Grosvenor Press International, Holford Mews, Cruiskshank St., London WC1X 9HD, England. TEL 01-2783000. FAX 01-2782674. TELEX 23931 GPI G. Ed. Ken Gleeson.

910.09 CN ISSN 0711-6136
GROUP TRAVEL/VOYAGE EN GROUPE. (Text in English, French) 1981. bi-m. Can.$8. Voyage en Groupe, 425 Harris St., St-Laurent, Que. H4N 2G8. TEL 514-744-3867. Ed. A. Quesnel. adv.; bk.rev.; circ. 10,000. (back issues avail.)

910.09 601.435 US
▼**GROUP TRAVEL LEADER**. 1991. m. $39. Group Travel Leader, Inc., 340 S. Broadway, Lexington, KY 40508. TEL 606-253-0455. FAX 606-253-0499. adv.; circ. 30,000 (controlled).
  Description: Contains industry news, destination features, and educational articles and information on group travel for seniors.

380.5 PE
GUIA AEREA Y MARITIMA. 1962. m. $60 (S. America $130; N. America $160; elsewhere $215). Lima Editora, S.A., Av. Canaval y Moreyra, 340, p. 12, Lima 27, Peru. TEL 4069930. FAX 407543. Ed. Jose Luis Arrarte. adv.; circ. 2,200. (back issues avail.)
  Description: Covers the travel and airline industries.

GUIA AEREA Y MARITIMA DE VENEZUELA C.A.; Aruba, Curacao y Bonaire. see TRANSPORTATION

GUIA AERONAUTICO. see TRANSPORTATION — Air Transport

918 BL
GUIA BRASIL. (Text in Portuguese; summaries in English, Spanish) 1966. a. price varies. Editora Abril, S.A., Rua Geraldo Flausino Gomes, 61 11 andar, 04575 Sao Paulo, Brazil. TEL 011-5345344. FAX 5221504. TELEX 01124134. Ed. Henri Kobata. charts; illus.; circ. 275,000.
  Description: Details information on 744 cities, as well as various hotels, restaurants, and tourist attractions.

910.202 CU
GUIA DEL SOL. s-a. Instituto Nacional del Turismo, Malecon y G, Vadedo, Havana, Cuba.

910.202 AG
GUIA INTERNACIONAL DE TRAFICO. 1963. m. $180 in America; elsewhere $240. Suipacha 207, Piso 3, Ofc. 316, 1008 Buenos Aires, Argentina. TEL 541-354893. FAX 541-355146. TELEX 25955 ARVIL AR. (U.S. address: c/o Ms. Patricia Carman, Market Links, Dupont Plaza Center 723, 300 Biscayne Blvd. Way, Miami, FL 33131. TEL 305-374-1634) Ed. Alan Rodrigue. adv.; circ. 10,000.
  Formerly: Guia Internacional de Trafico - Division Viajes.
  Description: Airline guide providing international travel information and news.

917.204 HO
GUIA OFICIAL DE CENTRO-AMERICA. 1922. irreg. Apartado 494, Tegucigalpa, Honduras.

910.09 BL ISSN 0102-3225
GUIA PANROTAS. 1972. m. $180. Panrotas Editora Ltda., Av. Jabaquara, 1761, CEP 04045, Sao Paulo, S.P., Brazil. TEL 011-2750211. FAX 011-276-1602. TELEX (11) 56693. Ed. Jose Guillermo Condomi Alcorta. adv.; circ. 11,000.

910.202 BL ISSN 0533-473X
F2509.5
GUIA QUATRO RODAS. BRAZIL. 1969. a. Editora Abril, S.A., R. Geraldo Flausino Gomes, 61, 02909 Sao Paulo, Brazil. FAX 011-522-1504. TELEX 11-24134. Ed. Victor Civita. adv.; charts; illus.; stat.; circ. 276,800.

910.202 796.5 BL
GUIA QUATRO RODAS. CAMPING. 1980. a. Editora Abril, S.A., R. Geraldo Flausino Gomes, 61, 02909 Sao Paulo, Brazil. FAX 011-522-1504. TELEX 11-24134. Ed. Victor Civita. adv.; charts; illus.; stat.; circ. 36,800.

910.202 BL
GUIA QUATRO RODAS. RIO DE JANEIRO. 1973. a. Editora Abril, S.A., R. Geraldo Flausino Gomes, 61, 04575 Sao Paulo, Brazil. FAX 011-522-1504. TELEX 11-24134. Ed. Victor Civita. adv.; charts; illus.; stat.; circ. 39,000.

910.202 BL
GUIA QUATRO RODAS. RODOVIARIO. 1974. a. Editora Abril, S.A., R. Geraldo Flausino Gomes, 61, 40575 Sao Paulo, Brazil. TEL 5345344. FAX 011-522-1504. TELEX 11-24134. Ed. Victor Civita. adv.; charts; illus.; stat.; circ. 110,000.

910.202 BL
GUIA QUATRO RODAS. SAO PAULO. 1973. a. Editora Abril, S.A., R. Geraldo Flausino Gomes, 61, 04575 Sao Paulo, Brazil. TEL 5345344. FAX 011-522-1504. TELEX 11-24134. Ed. Victor Civita. adv.; charts; illus.; stat.; circ. 105,000.

910.202 BL
GUIA QUATRO RODAS. SUL. 1975. a. Editora Abril, S.A., R. Geraldo Flausino Gomes, 61, 04575 Sao Paulo, Brazil. FAX 011-522-1504. TELEX 11-24134. Ed. Victor Civita. adv.; charts; illus.; stat.; circ. 38,000.

918.104 AG
GUIA TURISTICA DE ROSARIO Y SANTE FE. vol.13, 1975. irreg. Talleres Graficos Amalevi, Calle Mendoza 1851, Rosario, Santa Fe, Argentina. Ed. Rafael Vinas Paris. adv.; illus.

910.202 IT
GUIDA EUROCAMPING EUROPA. q. L.21000. Editoriale Eurocamp s.r.l., Via Durini, n.3, 20122 Milan, Italy. TEL 02-76022377. FAX 02-76022430. Ed. Maria Paola Canegrati. adv.; charts; illus.

910.202 IT
GUIDA EUROCAMPING ITALIA E CORSICA. q. L.21000. Editoriale Eurocamp s.r.l., Via Durini, n.3, 20122 Milan, Italy. TEL 02-76022377. FAX 02-76022430. Ed. Maria Paola Canegrati. adv.; charts; illus.

910.202 IT
GUIDA VIAGGI. 1973. s-m. L.120000. G I V I, s.r.l., Via Larga, 2, 20122 Milan, Italy. TEL 876936. FAX 02-866561. Ed. R. Reale. circ. 7,000.

910.202 IT
GUIDE A P A. 18/yr. L.48000. Zanfi Editori s.r.l., Via Ganaceto 121, P.O. Box 433, Italy. TEL 059-222292. FAX 059-225719. TELEX 522272 ZANFI I. circ. 10,000.

910.202 CN ISSN 0838-0023
GUIDE DE LA ROUTE: L'ONTARIO. (Text in French) 1988. a. membership. Canadian Automobile Association, 1775 Courtwood Cres., Ottawa, Ont. K2C 3J2, Canada. TEL 613-226-7631. FAX 613-225-7383. TELEX 053-4440.
  Description: Lists accomodations, sites to see in the province of Ontario.

910.202 CN ISSN 0838-0015
GUIDE DE LA ROUTE: LA FLORIDE. French translation of: American Automobile Association, Florida TourBook. (Text in French) 1987. a. membership. Canadian Automobile Association, 1775 Courtwood Cres., Ottawa, Ont. K2C 3J2, Canada. TEL 613-226-7631. FAX 613-225-7383. TELEX 053-4440. adv.
  Description: Listing accommodation, sites to see, things to do in the state of Florida.

910.202 CN
▼**GUIDE DE LA ROUTE: LE MAINE, LE NEW HAMPSHIRE, ET LE VERMONT**. (Text in French) 1991. a. membership. Canadian Automobile Association, 1775 Courtwood Cres., Ottawa, Ont. K2C 3J2, Canada. TEL 613-226-7631. FAX 613-225-7383.
  Description: Tourbook listing accommodations, sites to see, and things to do in Maine, New Hampshire and Vermont.

910.202 CN
GUIDE DE LA ROUTE: LES PROVINCES DE L'ATLANTIQUE ET LE QUEBEC. (Text in French) 1978. a. membership. Canadian Automobile Association, 1775 Courtwood Cres., Ottawa, Ont. K2C 3J2, Canada. TEL 613-226-7631. FAX 613-225-7383. adv.
  Description: Tourbook listing accommodations, sites to see, things to do in the province of Quebec and the maritime provinces.

910.202 DK ISSN 0106-3022
GUIDE I JYLLAND. 1979. a. DKK 28.50. Bureau Vildmosen, Solvej 5, 9293 Kongerslev, Denmark. illus.

TRAVEL AND TOURISM

910.202   MG
GUIDE ROUTIER ET TOURISTIQUE: MADAGASCAR, REUNION, MAURICE, COMORES ET SEYCHELLES. a. Automobile Club de Madagascar, Service du Guide Routier, B.P. 571, Antananarivo, Malagasy Republic. illus.

796.5   UK   ISSN 0267-3355
GUIDE TO CARAVAN AND CAMPING HOLIDAYS. 1975. a. £2.40. F.H.G. Publications Ltd., Abbey Mill Business Centre, Seedhill, Paisley PA1 1JN, Scotland. TEL 041-887 0428.

910.09   US
GUIDE TO CHARLESTON'S ISLANDS MAGAZINE. 1987. a. free. Ravenel Associates, Inc., 2 Beachwalker Office Park, Kiawah Island, SC 29455. TEL 803-768-2304. FAX 803-768-9386. adv.; tr.lit.; circ. 100,000. (back issues avail.)
  Formerly: Islands Magazine.

GUIDE TO CRUISING THE CHESAPEAKE BAY. see SPORTS AND GAMES — Boats And Boating

910.09   US
GUIDE TO THE QUEEN CHARLOTTES. biennial. $10.95. Alaska Northwest Books (Subsidiary of: G T E Discovery Publications, Inc.), Box 3007, Bothell, WA 98041-3007. TEL 800-331-3510. FAX 206-486-7296.

647 970   US
GUIDE TO THE RECOMMENDED COUNTRY INNS OF ARIZONA, NEW MEXICO, AND TEXAS. biennial. Globe Pequot Press, 138 W. Main St., Box Q, Chester, CT 06412. TEL 203-526-9571. FAX 203-526-9571.

647 970   US
GUIDE TO THE RECOMMENDED COUNTRY INNS OF THE MIDWEST. biennial. Globe Pequot Press, 138 W. Main St., Box Q, Chester, CT 06412. TEL 203-526-9571. FAX 203-526-9571.

647 970   US
GUIDE TO THE RECOMMENDED COUNTRY INNS OF THE ROCKY MOUNTAIN REGION. biennial. Globe Pequot Press, 138 W. Main St., Box Q, Chester, CT 06412. TEL 203-526-9571. FAX 203-526-9571.

647 970   US
GUIDE TO THE RECOMMENDED COUNTRY INNS OF THE SOUTH. biennial. Globe Pequot Press, 138 W. Main St., Box Q, Chester, CT 06412. TEL 203-526-9571. FAX 203-526-9571.

647 970   US
GUIDE TO THE RECOMMENDED COUNTRY INNS OF THE WEST COAST. biennial. Globe Pequot Press, 138 W. Main St., Box Q, Chester, CT 06412. TEL 203-526-9571. FAX 203-526-9571.

647 970   US
GUIDE TO THE RECOMMENDED INNS OF THE MID-ATLANTIC STATES. biennial. Globe Pequot Press, 138 W. Main St., Box Q, Chester, CT 06412. TEL 203-526-9571. FAX 203-526-9571.

917.204   MX
GUIS DE VIAJES. m. free. Editorial This Is Mexico, Calle Londres 166, Apdo. 6-728, 06600 Mexico, D.F., Mexico. FAX 915-208-38. TELEX 017-71-881. illus.; circ. 20,000.
  Former titles: Visitors' Guide to Mexico; Now in Mexico.

910.09   BA
▼**GULF TOURISM DIRECTORY**. (Text in English) 1990. a? P.O. Box 859, Manama, Bahrain. TEL 731224. FAX 731067. Ed. Rashid Bin Muhammad al-Khalifa.

GUT ESSEN/EATS & TREATS; hospitality in Frankfurt and Rhine Main Area. see HOTELS AND RESTAURANTS

H O R E S C A - INFORMATIONS. (Federation Nationale des Hoteliers, Restaurateurs et Cafetiers du Grand-Duche de Luxembourg) see HOTELS AND RESTAURANTS

526 910   US
HAGSTROM MAP AND TRAVEL NEWSLETTER. 1986. q. free. Hagstrom Map and Travel, 57 W. 43rd St., New York, NY 10036. TEL 212-398-1222. Ed. Douglas B. Rose. bk.rev.; circ. 15,780.
  Formerly: Hagstrom Map and Travel Center Newsletter.

HAMBURG - NORDDEUTSCHLAND VON HINTEN; das schwule Reisebuch. see HOMOSEXUALITY

914.04   GW
HAMBURGER TOP INFO FOR VISITORS. (Text in English) 1984. m. DM.46. Hamburg Fuehrer Verlag GmbH, Rothenbaumchaussee 195, 2000 Hamburg 13, Germany. TEL 040-458555. Ed. Katja Kosanke. adv.; illus. (back issues avail.)

915.1   KO
HANDBOOK OF KOREA. 1978. a. Korean Overseas Information Service, Ministry of Culture and Information, Sejongno 1, Seoul, S. Korea.

910.09   GW
HANSESTADT LUEBECK TRAVEMUENDE AKTUELL; das offizielle Programm der Hansestadt Luebeck. 1951. m. DM.6. Schmidt-Roemhild Verlag, Mengstr. 16, 2400 Luebeck 1, Germany. TEL 0451-1605-0. FAX 0451-1605233. TELEX 26536-MSRD. adv.; circ. 9,000.

919.604   US
HAWAII (YEAR). a. $17. Harper Collins Publishers, Birnbaum Travel Guides, 10 E 53rd St., New York, NY 10022-5244. TEL 212-270-7000. Ed. Stephen Birnbaum.

910.202   US
HAWAII DRIVE GUIDES. 1974. 3/yr. Honolulu Publishing Company, Ltd., 36 Merchant St., Honolulu, HI 96813. TEL 808-524-7400. FAX 808-531-2306. Ed. Brett Uprichard. circ. 45,500.
  Description: Touring guides for Oahu, Maui, Hawaii and Kauai, with detailed maps and descriptions of scenic and historical sites, visitor attractions, selected restaurants, shops and centers, things to do, sports and other information for the independent traveller.

919.69   US
HAWAII HOTEL NETWORK. (In 7 editions for 45 hotels) 1973. 3/yr. free in Waikiki and neighbor island hotels of Hawaii. Spotlight Hawaii Publishing, 532 Cummins St., Honolulu, HI 96814. TEL 808-524-8404. FAX 808-537-2121. Ed. Camie Foster. adv.; circ. 580,000.
  Formerly: Here's Hawaii.
  Description: Presents feature articles on a range of subjects for the first-time and repeat visitor. Includes calendar, and directory information.

910.09   US   ISSN 0892-0990
HAWAII MAGAZINE; gateway to the Pacific. 1982. bi-m. $11.99. Fancy Publications, Inc., Box 6050, Mission Viejo, CA 92690. TEL 714-855-8822. FAX 714-855-3045. (Subscr. to: Box 485, Mt. Morris, IL 61054-0485) Ed. Dennis Shattuck. adv.; bk.rev.; index; circ. 63,000. (also avail. in microfilm)

919   US
HAWAII ON 60 DOLLARS A DAY. a. $14.95. Frommer Books (Subsidiary of: Simon & Schuster, Inc.), 15 Columbus Circle, New York, NY 10023. TEL 212-373-8125.
  Former titles: Hawaii on 35 Dollars a Day (ISSN 8755-9250); Hawaii on 30 Dollars a Day (issue avail.); Hawaii on 25 Dollars a Day (ISSN 0197-8527); Hawaii on 20 Dollars a Day.

917.904   US
HAWAII: THE BIG ISLAND, A PARADISE GUIDE. (Supplement avail.: Hawaii: The Big Island Update) biennial. Paradise Publications, 8110 S.W. Wareham, Portland, OR 97223. TEL 503-246-1555.
  Description: Guide to beaches, restaurants, budget travel, and resorts.

917.904   US   ISSN 1042-8046
HAWAII: THE BIG ISLAND UPDATE. (Supplement to: Hawaii: The Big Island, a Paradise Guide) 1989. q. $6. Paradise Publications, 8110 S.W. Wareham, Portland, OR 97223. TEL 503-246-1555. Ed. John Penisten. circ. 2,000.
  Description: Information for tourists and island residents on restaurants, tourist attractions, airlines and hotels.

919.69   US   ISSN 0066-412X
HAWAII VISITORS BUREAU. ANNUAL RESEARCH REPORT. 1953. a. $100 to non-members. Hawaii Visitors Bureau, 2270 Kalakaua Ave., Honolulu, HI 96815. TEL 808-923-1811. FAX 808-922-8991. Ed. Alvin H. Katahara. circ. 4,000.

910.09   US
HEARTLAND ADVENTURES. 7/yr. Rubber Meets the Road Publishing, 635-5 Chicago Ave., Ste. 125, Evanston, IL 60202. TEL 708-328-9474. FAX 708-328-1374. Ed. Joanne Y. Cleaver.

910.202   IS
HELLO ISRAEL. 1972. w. Tourguide Ltd., P.O. Box 3656, Tel Aviv 61036, Israel. FAX 03-5403082. Ed. I. Tamir. adv.; circ. 15,000.

HERALD CARAVANNING GUIDE. see SPORTS AND GAMES — Outdoor Life

210.202   US   ISSN 0741-1952
HIDEAWAYS GUIDE. 1981. 2/yr. $79 includes membership. Hideaways International, 15 Goldsmith St., Box 1270, Littleton, MA 01460. TEL 508-486-8955. FAX 508-486-8525. Ed. Michael F. Thiel. adv.; bk.rev.; circ. 11,000. (back issues avail.)
  Description: Lists villa rentals worldwide, especially Caribbean, Mexico, Hawaii, and Europe. Includes articles about out-of-the-ordinary vacations.

910.202   US
HIDEAWAYS NEWSLETTER. 1983. 4/yr. membership. Hideaways International, 15 Goldsmith St., Box 1270, Littleton, MA 01460. TEL 508-486-8955. FAX 508-486-8525. Ed. Michael F. Thiel. adv.; circ. 11,000. (back issues avail.)
  Description: Lists villa rentals worldwide, especially Caribbean, Mexico, Hawaii, and Europe.

HILTON INTERNATIONAL (U.K.) MAGAZINE. see HOTELS AND RESTAURANTS

HOER ZU. see GENERAL INTEREST PERIODICALS — Germany

910.202   GW
HOLIDAY. 1988. bi-m. DM.39. Burda Verlag GmbH, Arabellastr. 23, Postfach 810164, 8000 Munich 81, Germany. TEL 089-9250-0. (Subscr. to: Holiday Abonnenten Service, Senefelderstr. 4, 7600 Offenburg, Germany) Ed. Lothar Strobach. (back issues avail.)

914.204   UK   ISSN 0073-3016
HOLIDAY HAUNTS IN GREAT BRITAIN. a. £1.45. Archway Nicholas Publications, Faber House, 6 Easter Rd., Romford, Essex RM1 3PJ, England. TEL 0708-2001. Ed. Michael Faulkner.

910.2   UK
HOLIDAY HINTS HANDBOOK. 1960. a. Hoseasons Holidays, Sunway House, Oulton Broad, Lowestoft, Suffolk NR32 3LT, England. TEL 0502-500500. FAX 0502-584962. TELEX 975189-HOSEAS-G.
  Former titles: Norfolk Holiday Handbook (ISSN 0078-1150); Norfolk Holiday Hints Handbook.

914.204   UK
HOLIDAY ISLANDER. 1976. a. free. Portsmouth Publishing, Box 1, Hayling Island PO11 9RL, England. Ed. Pat Holt. adv.; bk.rev.; circ. 10,000.
  Former titles: Hayling Islander; (until 1984): Hayling Island Magazine.

919   AT
HOLIDAY WESTERN AUSTRALIA. TRAVEL NEWS. 1980. bi-m. free. Western Australia Tourism Commission, P.O. Box X2261, Perth, W.A. 6000, Australia. FAX 09-2201702. Ed. Graeme Cocks. circ. 2,500.
  Supersedes: Travel News from Western Australia.

910.202   UK
HOLIDAY WHICH?. 4/yr. £67 avail. only with "Which?". Consumers' Association, 2 Marylebone Rd., London NW1 4DF, England. TEL 071-486-5544. (Subscr. addr.: Consumer's Association, Castlemead, Gascoyne Way, Hertford. SG14 1LH, England) Ed. Patricia Yaks. circ. 176,000.

910.09   SA
▼**HOLIDAYMAKER**. 1990. m. free. Thomson Publications (Subsidiary of: Times Media Ltd.), P.O. Box 56182, Pinegowrie 2123, South Africa. TEL 011-789-2144. FAX 011-789-3196. Ed. Frances Paine. circ. 200,000.

910.09   UK
HOLIDAYS & BUSINESS TRAVEL. 1980. q. £0.85 per no. Lylereed Ltd., 27 Belsize Lane, London NW3, England. Ed. C.G. Thomas. adv.
  Formerly: Holidays and Travel.

TRAVEL AND TOURISM   4771

914   UK   ISSN 0073-3024
HOLIDAYS IN BRITAIN. 1924. a. £1.45. Archway Nicholas Publications, Faber House, 6 Eastern Rd., Romford, Essex RM1 3PJ, England. TEL 0708-20011. Ed. Michael Faulkner. index.

914   RM   ISSN 0018-3555
HOLIDAYS IN ROMANIA. Rumanian edition: Romania Pitoreasca. (Editions in English, French, German, Rumanian) 1958. m. $27. Ministerul Turismului - Ministry of Tourism, Gabriel Peri Str. 8, 70148 Bucharest, Rumania. TEL 597893. (Subscr. to: ROMPRESFILATELIA Sectorul Export-Import Presa, POB.12-201, Calea Grvitei nr. 64-66, Rumania) Ed. Simion Pop. adv.; bk.rev.; illus.; circ. 22,000.
 Formerly: Romania for Tourists.

HOLLAND HERALD; magazine of the Netherlands. see *GENERAL INTEREST PERIODICALS — Netherlands*

HOLY PLACES OF PALESTINE. see *RELIGIONS AND THEOLOGY*

910.202   US   ISSN 8750-5649
HOME & AWAY. 1913. bi-m. $6. (Automobile Association of America) A A A Hoosier Motor Club, Box 88505, Indianapolis, IN 46208-0505. Ed. Hugh F. Orr. adv.; circ. 185,000.
 Formerly: Hoosier Motorist.
 Description: Travel and safety oriented magazine for AAA members in Central Indiana; promotes member services.

910.09   US
HOME & AWAY MINNESOTA. bi-m. American Automobile Association, Minnesota State Automobile Association, Seven Travelers Trail, Burnsville, MN 55337. TEL 612-890-2500. FAX 612-894-4079. Ed. Ronald R. Siegmund. adv.; circ. 222,430.

910.09   US
HOME & AWAY OHIO. bi-m. American Automobile Association, Ohio Auto Club, 90 E. Wilson Bridge Rd., Worthington, OH 43085-2325. TEL 614-431-7919. Ed. William J. Purpura. adv.; circ. 379,475.

HOMES ABROAD. see *REAL ESTATE*

919.404   AT
HOMESTAY EASTERN AUSTRALIA; a guide to accommodation & travel - cities - farms - outback. 1989. a. Aus.$22($18) Sydney's Good Accommodation & Travel Guide Pty. Ltd., P.O. Box 1222, Bathurst, N.S.W. 2795, Australia. FAX 063-37-3558. Ed. W. L. Ogilvie.
 Formerly (until 1991): Homestay Australia.

910.09   HO
HONDURAS. CONSEJO SUPERIOR DE PLANIFICACION ECONOMICA. PLAN OPERATIVO ANUAL. SECTOR TURISMO. a. Consejo Superior de Planificacion Economica, Secretaria Tecnica, Tegucigalpa, Honduras.

910.202   HK
HONG KONG FOR THE BUSINESS VISITOR. (Editions in Chinese, Dutch, English, French, German, Italian, Japanese, Spanish) 1967. a. Hong Kong Trade Development Council, 36-39th Fl., Office Tower, Convention Plaza, 1 Harbour Rd., Wanchai, Hong Kong. TEL 584-4333. FAX 824-0249. Ed. Saul Lockhart. circ. 85,000.
 Description: Hong Kong guidebook aimed specifically at business people.

915   HK
HONG KONG GUIDE - STREETS AND PLACES. (Text in Chinese and English) 1978. irreg. (approx. 2/yr.). HK.$37 (effective Feb. 1991). Principal Government Land Surveyor, Survey and Mapping Office, Buildings and Lands Department, Murray Building, Garden Road, Hong Kong. FAX 521-8726. Ed. Leung Pui-lam. circ. 36,000.
 Formerly (until 1988): Hong Kong Streets and Places.
 Description: Comprehensive directory with maps for the Territory of Hong Kong.

915   HK   ISSN 0018-4616
HONG KONG TRAVEL BULLETIN. (Text in English) 1959. m. free. Hong Kong Tourist Association, Box 2597, Hong Kong. TEL 8017111. FAX 8104877. TELEX 74720-HX. Ed. Penelope Byrne. adv.; charts; illus.; circ. 20,000.

910.202 915.04   HK
052
HONG KONG VISITOR. (Text in English, Japanese) 1984. m. South China Morning Post Publishers Ltd., 6-F, South China Morning Post Bldg., Tong Chong Street 57, Quarry Bay, Hong Kong. TEL 5652430. FAX 5658961. Ed. Deirbhile O'Grady. circ. 50,000 (controlled).
 Formerly: Hong Kong and Guangzhou Visitor.
 Description: Guide and social calender for tourists.

HOSEASONS BOATING HOLIDAYS. see *SPORTS AND GAMES — Boats And Boating*

910.202   UK
HOSEASONS HOLIDAY-HOMES IN U.K.. 1946. a. free. (Hoseasons Holidays) Sunway House, Oulton Broad, Lowestoft, Suffolk NR32 3LT, England. TEL 0502-500-505. FAX 0502-514298. TELEX 975189 HOSWAS G. Ed. James Hoseason. circ. 1,300,000.
 Formerly (until 1970): Hoseasons Holiday-Homes.

HOSPITALITY & TOURISM EDUCATOR. see *EDUCATION — Adult Education*

910.4   AT
HOSTEL TRAVEL. 1949. q. Aus.$20. Youth Hostels Association of N.S.W Inc., G.P.O. Box 5276, Sydney, N.S.W. 2001, Australia. FAX 02-2611969. Ed. Paul Page. adv.; bk.rev.; circ. 40,000.
 Former titles: Y H A Hostel Yarn; Hostel Yarn (ISSN 0156-0115); Y H A Hostel Yarn.

919   AT   ISSN 0157-3977
HOSTELLER. 1949. 3/yr. Aus.$9 to non-members. Youth Hostels Association of Victoria, 205 King St., Melbourne. Vic. 3000, Australia. TEL 03-670-7991. FAX 03-670-9840. Ed. Michele Tardini. adv.; bk.rev.; circ. 31,000.

919   AT   ISSN 0725-8968
HOSTELLING. 1969. q. Aus.$8. Youth Hostels Association of South Australia, Inc., 38 Sturt St., Adelaide, S.A. 500, Australia. FAX 08-231-4219. Ed. E. Ahrens. adv.; bk.rev.; circ. 5,000.

910.1 647.94   US
HOSTELLING NORTH AMERICA; a directory of hostels in the Canada and the United States. 1934. a. $7 to non-members. American Youth Hostels, Inc., Box 37613, Washington, DC 20013-7613. TEL 202-783-6161. FAX 202-783-6171. TELEX 384777 AYHINC UD. adv.; circ. 300,000.
 Former titles: North American Hostels Handbook; American Youth Hostels Handbook; American Youth Hostels Guide and Handbook (ISSN 0066-1201)
 Description: Directory of more than 300 hostels in USA and Canada, including location maps and travel information.

915.204   JA
HOTEL. (Text in Japanese) m. 6000 Yen($100) Ohta Publications Co., Ltd., Dame Ginza Bldg., 7-18 Ginza, 6-chome, Chuo-ku, Tokyo 104, Japan. TEL 03-3571-1181. FAX 03-3574-1650. Ed. Minoru Murakami. adv.; circ. 160,000.
 Description: Offers information on luxury hotels worldwide, and includes detailed coverage of special events, fairs, conventions, seminars, entertainment, arts, and fashion.

910.4   II
HOTEL & TOURISM DEVELOPMENT REPORT. 1979. w. $85. International Press Cutting Service, Box 63, Allahabad 211001, India. Ed. Nandi Khanna. (looseleaf format)

HOTEL AND TRAVEL INDEX; the world wide hotel directory. see *HOTELS AND RESTAURANTS*

HOTEL & TOURISTIK. see *HOTELS AND RESTAURANTS*

HOTEL UND TOURISTIK REVUE. see *HOTELS AND RESTAURANTS*

647   US
HOTELS & TOURISM: LATIN AMERICAN INDUSTRIAL REPORT. (Avail. for each of 22 Latin American countries) 1985. a. $435 per country report. Aquino Productions, Box 15760, Stamford, CT 06901. TEL 203-325-3138. Ed. Andres C. Aquino.

919   BF
HOTELS, MOTELS AND GUESTHOUSES AND RESTAURANTS: NEW PROVIDENCE, PARADISE ISLAND AND GRAND BAHAMA. 1980. a. B.$2. Ministry of Finance, Department of Statistics, Box N 3904, Nassau, Bahamas. Ed.Bd.
 Formerly: Hotels, Motels and Guest Houses in New Providence and Paradise Island.

917   US   ISSN 0272-8060
HOUSTON MONTHLY MAGAZINE.* m. free. Houston Monthly Magazine, Inc., Box 58248, Houston, TX 77258-8248. TEL 713-480-6618. Ed. Janet Henke. adv.

917.504   US
HUMM'S GUIDE TO THE FLORIDA KEYS. 1972. q. $2 per no. Crain Associated Enterprises, 740 Rush St., Chicago, IL 60611. TEL 312-649-5303. adv.
 Description: Covers marinas, fishing, diving, camping, motels, resorts, restaurants, the arts, fashion, homes and gardens.

914.04   GW   ISSN 0343-5555
HUSUMER MONATSHEFTE; Informationen, Fahrplaene, Veranstaltungen. m. DM.28. Husum Druck- und Verlagsgesellschaft mbH, Nordbahnhofstr. 2, Postfach 1480, 2250 Husum, Germany. TEL 04841-6081. Ed. Alfred Lorenzen. adv.; circ. 8,000.

338.4   US
I C T A DIRECTORY. 1969. a. membership. Institute of Certified Travel Agents, 148 Linden St., Box 82-56, Wellesley, MA 02181. TEL 617-237-0280. FAX 617-237-3860. Ed. Patricia Kane. circ. 16,000.
 Formerly: I C T A Roster (ISSN 0094-3517)

374 910.202   US
I C T A NEWS. m. free to members. Institute of Certified Travel Agents, 148 Linden St., Box 82-56, Wellesley, MA 02181. TEL 617-237-0280. FAX 617-237-3860. Ed. Dawn Ringel. circ. 16,000. (back issues avail.)
 Description: Focuses on ICTA activities and programs, including members' accomplishments and management ideas.

I F L NIEUWS. (International Friendship League) see *CLUBS*

917.04   US
I LOVE NEW YORK: THE FINGER LAKES TRAVEL GUIDE. 1951. a. free. Finger Lakes Association, Inc., 309 Lake Street, Penn Yan, NY 14527. TEL 315-536-7488. FAX 315-536-0226. Ed. Jack Kidd. adv.; circ. 65,000.
 Formerly: Finger Lakes Travel Guide.

910.09   PL
I M T SWIATOWID. (Ilustrowany Magazyn Turystyczny) 1952. m. Ul. Nowogrodzka 49, 00-695 Warsaw, Poland. TEL 48-22-212376. Ed. Robert Makowski. illus.; circ. 50,000.

ICI NEW YORK; journal de New York en francais. see *GENERAL INTEREST PERIODICALS — United States*

910.09   US   ISSN 1055-8314
▼**IDEAL TRAVELLER.** (Supplement avail.) 1991. a. $23.99. Publishing & Business Consultants, 951 S. Oxford, No. 109, Los Angeles, CA 90006. TEL 213-732-3477. (Subscr. to: Box 75392, Los Angeles, CA 90075) Ed. Atia Napoleon. adv.; circ. 100,000.
 Previously announced as: Vacation Overseas.
 Description: Provides information on popular vacation destinations, and advice for travelers.

910.09   GW
IHRE FERIENWOHNUNG; das ganzjaehrige Urlaubsmagazin. 1984. a. DM.14.50($8) Touristikverlag H.U.B. GmbH und Co. KG, Stepahienstr. 6, D-7800 Freiburg, Germany. TEL 0761-709693. Eds. W. Bachelle, W. Schwoerer. circ. 40,000. (back issues avail.)

ILLINOIS GOLFER'S TRAVEL GUIDE. see *SPORTS AND GAMES — Ball Games*

ILLINOIS MAGAZINE. see *HISTORY — History Of North And South America*

TRAVEL AND TOURISM

910.09 US ISSN 0730-9813
G155.U6
IMPACT OF TRAVEL ON STATE ECONOMIES. 1976. a. $70. U S Travel Data Center, Two Lafayette Ctr., 1133 21st St., N.W., Washington, DC 20036. TEL 202-293-1040. (reprint service avail. from CIS) **Indexed:** SRI.
Description: Traveler expenditures in various travel industry sectors.

914 UK ISSN 0019-3143
DA650
IN BRITAIN. 1930. m. $39.95. British Tourist Authority, Thames Tower, Blacks Rd., London W6 9EL, England. TEL 081-846-9000. (Subscr. to: Headway Publications, Greater London House, Hampstead Rd., London NW1 7QQ, England) Ed. Sandra Harris.

IN CORNWALL MAGAZINE. see *GENERAL INTEREST PERIODICALS — Great Britain*

IN MOTION (EUREKA). see *SPORTS AND GAMES*

910.09 US
IN - S I T E MAGAZINE. 1987. 3/yr. Society of Incentive Travel Executives, 21 W. 38th St., 10th Fl., New York, NY 10018. TEL 212-575-0910. FAX 212-575-1838. adv.: B&W page $1000, color page $1750; trim 8 3/8 x 10 7/8. circ. 4,000.
Description: Covers incentive travel as a tool to increase productivity in business.

INDEPENDENT NATIONAL EDITION; a monthly journal for thoughtful Canadians. see *ENVIRONMENTAL STUDIES*

INDIANA GOLFER'S TRAVEL GUIDE. see *SPORTS AND GAMES — Ball Games*

917 US ISSN 0019-7777
INDUSTRIA TURISTICA. (Text in Spanish) 1957. m. free. Charles Francis Publications, Inc., Box 52-1898, Miami, FL 33152-1898. TEL 305-592-3168. Eds. Charles Francis, Lucky Francis. adv.; bk.rev.; stat.; tr.lit.; circ. 6,000 (controlled).
Former titles: Industria and Mundo Turistico; Industria Turistica.

910.4 SZ ISSN 0253-8539
INDUSTRIEARCHAEOLOGIE; zeitschrift fuer industrielle Kulturgueter, Montau und Reisen. (Text mainly in German, occasionally in English and French) 1977. q. 59 Fr. c/o Oskar Baldinger, Ed. & Pub., Aarestr. 83, CH-5222 Umiken, Switzerland. TEL 056-410043. FAX 056-414854. adv.; bk.rev.; illus.; circ. 1,100.

INFORMATION ROUTIERE ET TOURISTIQUE. see *TRANSPORTATION — Trucks And Trucking*

INFORMATORE DEI COMMERCIANTI. see *BUSINESS AND ECONOMICS — Chamber Of Commerce Publications*

914 IT ISSN 0020-076X
INFORMATORE TURISTICO; agenzia settimanale di notizie. 1963. w. free. Comitato Nazionale per il Turismo, Viale dell'Astronomia 30, 00144 Rome, Italy. Dir. Guido Zirano. bk.rev.; stat.; circ. 2,000. (looseleaf format)

INN BUSINESS REVIEW NEWSLETTER; country inns, small hotels and bed & breakfasts. see *HOTELS AND RESTAURANTS*

INN PLACES (YEAR). see *HOMOSEXUALITY*

917 US
INNER - VIEW. m. Inner - View Publishing Co., Inc., Box 66156, Houston, TX 77266. TEL 713-523-8352.

INQUILINE WORLDWIDE HOME EXCHANGES AND RENTALS; professional executive homes. see *REAL ESTATE*

910.4 US
INSIDE TRAVEL NEWS. 1971. m. $9. 6229 Bristol Pkwy., Culver City, CA 90230. TEL 213-296-8858. Ed. Lozetta Slaton. adv.; circ. 6,000.

914.604 SP
INSPAIN. (Text in English) 1985. m. 2500 ptas.($21) InSpain Magazine, Dr. Esquerdo 35, 1F, 28028 Madrid, Spain. TEL 256-1779. FAX 256-1779. Ed. George C. Hall. adv.; bk.rev.; circ. 15,000 (controlled).
Description: For native English speakers living in Spain. Covers culture, travel, and sports.

914.2 388 UK
INSPECTED BED & BREAKFAST IN BRITAIN. a. £7.99. Automobile Association, Fanum House, Basingstoke, Hants RG21 2EA, England. TEL 0256-20123. FAX 0256-22575. adv.
Former titles: Guesthouses, Farmhouses and Inns in Britain; Automobile Association. Budget Guide.

917.204 CR
INSTITUTO COSTARRICENSE DE TURISMO. MEMORIA ANUAL. 1955. a. Instituto Costarricense de Turismo, San Jose, Costa Rica. FAX 23-54-52. TELEX 2281 INSTUR. illus.

INTERMAGAZINE. see *BUSINESS AND ECONOMICS*

917.29 BF
INTERNATIONAL BAHAMA LIFE. m. $16. Johnson Publications, P.O. Box N-1505, Nassau, Bahamas.

INTERNATIONAL CRUISE AND FERRY REVIEW. see *TRANSPORTATION — Ships And Shipping*

INTERNATIONAL EMPLOYMENT HOTLINE. see *OCCUPATIONS AND CAREERS*

910.2 BE ISSN 0074-5979
INTERNATIONAL FEDERATION OF JOURNALISTS AND TRAVEL WRITERS. OFFICIAL LIST/REPERTOIRE OFFICIEL. (Text in English and French) 1965. q. 75 Fr. International Federation of Journalists and Travel Writers, Zavelstraat 62, B-3071 Kortenberg, Belgium. adv.; bk.rev.; circ. 2,500.

917 642.5 CN
INTERNATIONAL GUIDE. 1977. a. Can.$6.95. I G Publications Ltd., 999 8th St., S.W., Ste. 222, Calgary, Alta. T2R 1J5, Canada. FAX 403-229-2470. Ed. S.K. Bell. adv.; circ. 125,000.

910.09 647 US ISSN 0278-4319
TX911.3.M27 CODEN: IJHMDN
INTERNATIONAL JOURNAL OF HOSPITALITY MANAGEMENT. 1982. q. £130 (effective 1992). (International Association of Hotel Management Schools) Pergamon Press, Inc., Journals Division, 660 White Plains Rd., Tarrytown, NY 10591-5153. TEL 914-524-9200. FAX 914-333-2444. (And: Headington Hill Hall, Oxford OX3 0BW, England. TEL 0865-794141) Ed. John O'Connor. adv. (also avail. in microform from UMI; reprint service avail. from UMI) **Indexed:** Account.& Data Proc.Abstr.
—BLDSC shelfmark: 4542.283000.
Formerly: International Journal of Hospitality. *Refereed Serial*

910.4 US ISSN 0277-2442
INTERNATIONAL LIVING. 1981. m. $48. Agora, Inc., 824 E. Baltimore St., Baltimore, MD 21202. TEL 301-234-0515. Ed. Kathleen Peddicond. adv.; bk.rev.; circ. 50,000. (back issues avail.)

910.202 UK ISSN 0268-5671
INTERNATIONAL MEETING PLACE; a guide to international conference & exhibition locations. 1986. a. £25. Millbank Publications, 25 Catherine St., London WC2B 5JW, England. TEL 071-379-3036. FAX 071-240-6840. adv.; charts; illus.; circ. 5,000.

385 910.09 US ISSN 0891-7655
INTERNATIONAL RAILWAY TRAVELER. 1983. bi-m. $24. Hardy Publishing Co., Inc., The Belknap Bldg., 1810 Sils Ave., Ste. 306B, Louisville, KY 40205. TEL 502-454-0277. FAX 502-454-1542. (Subscr. to: Fulco, 30 Broad St., Denville, NJ 07834) Ed. Owen Hardy. adv.; bk.rev.; charts; illus.; tr.lit.; circ. 5,000. (back issues avail.)
Description: For all who love to travel by trains, whether by Amtrak or the East African Railway.

910.202 UK ISSN 0269-3747
G155.A1
INTERNATIONAL TOURISM REPORTS. 1971. q. £265($495) (Economist Intelligence Unit) Business International Ltd., 40 Duke St., London W1A 1DW, England. TEL 71-499 2278. FAX 71-499-9767. TELEX 266353 EIUG. (US addr.: Business International Corp., 215 Park Ave. S., New York, NY 10003. TEL 212-460-0600) charts; stat. **Indexed:** Cont.Pg.Manage., Key to Econ.Sci., Rural Recreat.Tour.Abstr., World Agri.Econ.& Rural Sociol.Abstr.
—BLDSC shelfmark: 4551.222000.
Formerly: International Tourism Quarterly (ISSN 0306-4336).
Description: Explores national tourism markets worldwide. Includes country reports with forecasts.

910.202 CN
▼**INTERNATIONAL TRAVEL GUIDE/GUIDE INTERNATIONAL DU VOYAGE.** (Text in English, French) 1992. a. Can.$15. Editions Guide Annuel, 5144 bvd. St-Laurent, Ste. 200, Montreal, Que. H2T 1R8, Canada. TEL 514-278-7788. FAX 514-272-0672. adv.; circ. 40,000.

910 US
INTERNATIONAL TRAVEL NEWS. 1976. m. $16. Martin Publications Inc., 2120 28th St., Sacramento, CA 95818. TEL 916-457-3643. Ed. David Tykol. adv.; bk.rev.; illus.; tr.lit.; circ. 40,000.
Description: Contains reader-written, consumer-oriented information for overseas travelers, including appraisals of tours, cruises and airlines.

914.94 796.552 SZ
INTERNATIONAL UNION OF ALPINE ASSOCIATIONS. BULLETIN/UNION INTERNATIONALE DES ASSOCIATIONS D'ALPINISME. BULLETIN. (Text in English, French or German) 1934. q. 25 Fr. International Union of Alpine Associations, Case Postale 237, 1211 Geneva 11, Switzerland. Ed. Adalbert Fontana. adv.; bk.rev.; circ. 700.

INTERP CENTRAL CLEARINGHOUSE NEWSLETTER. see *ENVIRONMENTAL STUDIES*

910 US
INTERVAC U S; international holiday. 1953. 3/yr. $45. International Home Exchange Service, 30 San Fernando Ct., Tiburon, CA 94920. TEL 415-435-3497. (Subscr. to: Box 190070, San Francisco, CA 94119) Ed. Paula Jaffe. adv.; circ. 8,300.

910.09 US
INTERVAL INTERNATIONAL TRAVELER. q. Interval International, Inc., 6262 Sunset Dr., Miami, FL 33143-8800. TEL 305-666-1861. FAX 305-665-2546. Ed. Edrea Kaiser. adv.; circ. 282,000.

910.202 US
▼**IRELAND (YEAR).** 1990. a. $14.95. Houghton Mifflin Co., 215 Park Ave. S., New York, NY 10003. TEL 212-420-5800.

914.104 US
IRELAND (YEAR). a. $17. Harper Collins Publishers, Birnbaum Travel Guides, 10 E. 53rd St., New York, NY 10022-5299. TEL 212-207-7000. illus.; index.

914 IE ISSN 0021-0943
IRELAND OF THE WELCOMES. 1952. bi-m. $18. Bord Failte - Irish Tourist Board, Baggot St. Bridge, Dublin 2, Ireland. TEL 765871. FAX 764765. Ed. Peter Harbison. adv.; bk.rev.; illus.; circ. 93,000. (also avail. in microform from UMI; reprint service avail. from UMI)

910.09 IT
ISCHIA MONDO. 1972. fortn. L.25000. Lubranopublicitas, Via Roma, 139 T, Ischia, Italy. Ed. Vittorio A. Caravaglios. adv.; bk.rev.; circ. 15,000. (also avail. in microfilm)

910.09 US
ISLAND ESCAPES. bi-m. Islands Publishing Company, 3886 State St., Santa Barbara, CA 93105. TEL 805-682-7177. FAX 805-569-0349. Ed. Joan Tapper.

TRAVEL AND TOURISM 4773

975   US
ISLAND LIFE; featuring the enchanting islands of Florida's Gulf Coast. 1982. s-a. $11 for 4 nos. West Coast Publications, Inc., Box 929, Sanibel Island, FL 33957. TEL 813-337-0010. Ed. Van B. Hooper. adv.; bk.rev.; circ. 12,000.

917   US   ISSN 1051-7898
ISLANDER; serving Hilton Head Island and the southeastern coastal region since 1965. 1965. m. $28.50 (foreign $41). Hilton Head Islander, Inc., Box 5950, Hilton Head Island, SC 29938. TEL 803-785-3613. FAX 803-785-4345. Ed. Lois Claus. adv.; bk.rev.; film rev.; play rev.; circ. 10,000.
    Former titles (until 1988): Hilton Head Islander (ISSN 0749-3517); Islander (ISSN 0021-1869)

051   US
ISLANDS' SOUNDER; serving all of San Juan County. 1964. 52/yr. $22 for countyresidents; state residents $30; elswhere in U.S. $35. Box 758, Eastsound, WA 98245. bk.rev.; illus.; circ. 5,400.
    Formerly: Orcas Island Booster.

790   IS
ISRAEL INFORMATION LETTER. (Text in English) 1962. m. free. Ministry of Tourism, Information Centre, P.O. Box 1018, Jerusalem 91009, Israel. TEL 02-237311. FAX 02-250890. Ed. Ruth Eilat. adv.; circ. 3,000. (processed)
    Former titles: Israel. Tourism News. Information Letter; Tourism Administration. Information Letter; Israel. Ministry of Tourism. Tourist Promotion Department. Information Letter.

380.1   IS
ISRAEL TRAVEL NEWS. (Text in English) 1979. m. $40. Israel Travel News Ltd., P.O. Box 50265, Tel Aviv 61 500, Israel. TEL 03-7517427. circ. 10,900. (back issues avail.)

910.202   TU
ISTANBUL KEY. (Text in English, Turkish) 1968. biennial. Turk Turing Turizm Isletmeciligi Vakfi, Sisli Meydani no.364, 80222 Istanbul, Turkey. FAX 148-96-61. TELEX 27800 TR RING. Ed. Celik Gulersoy. adv.; circ. 5,000.
    Formerly: Istanbul: Handbook for Tourists.

914   IT
ITALIA TURISTICA; rivista di cultura e turismo delle regioni italiane. (Text in English, German, Italian) 1962. bi-m. L.40000 (foreign L.80000). (Italia Turistica) Editrice Ituri s/r.l., Via C. Anti, 9, Casella Postale 1060-8, 35124 Padua, Italy. TEL 049-8011180. FAX 049-8011182. Dir. Antonio Ravazzolo. adv.; bk.rev.; film rev.; illus.; circ. 140,000. (back issues avail.)
    Formerly: Venezie e l'Italia; Incorporates: Turismo in Italia (ISSN 0042-336X)
    Description: Features articles on the various regions of Italy. Includes the "hot spots", culture and food of Italy.

910.09   IT
ITALIA VIAGGIA. 1988. m. L.60000. Editrice Portoria S.r.l., Via Chiossetto, 1, 20122 Milan, Italy. TEL 02-783541. FAX 02-782601. adv.; bk.rev.; circ. 120,000.

914.504   US
ITALY (YEAR). a. $17. Harper Collins Publishers, Birnbaum Travel Guides, 10 E. 53rd St., New York, NY 10022-5299. TEL 212-207-7000. illus.; index.

914.504   IT
ITALY ITALY. 1983. bi-m. L.30000($30) Italy Italy Corp. s.r.l., Via Michele Mercati 51, 00197 Rome, Italy. TEL 039-06-3221150. FAX 039-06-3223869. Ed. Barbara Walsh. adv.
    Description: Guide to Italian people, places, and things.

910.09 362.4   US   ISSN 0743-5223
ITINERARY (BAYONNE); the magazine for travelers with physical disabilities. 1981. 6/yr. $10. Box 2012, Bayonne, NJ 07002-7012. TEL 201-858-3400. Eds. Robert Zywicki, Elizabeth Zywicki. adv.; bk.rev.; circ. 10,400.

917.204   US
IXTAPA & ZIHUATANEJO (YEAR). a. $10. Harper Collins Publishers, Birnbaum Travel Guides, 10 E. 53rd St., New York, NY 10022-5299. TEL 212-207-7000. illus.; index.

914   SP   ISSN 0021-3810
JACETANIA. 1966. bi-m. 600 ptas. Centro de Iniciativa y Turismo, Aptdo. 110, Jaca (Huesca), Spain. adv.; illus.

910.2   GW   ISSN 0075-2150
JAEGER'S INTERTRAVEL; world guide to travel agencies, tour operators, countries, towns and hotels. (Text in English) 1959. a. DM.115. Jaeger Verlag GmbH, Holzhofallee 38, Postfach 110452, 6100 Darmstadt, Germany. TEL 06151-391-0. FAX 06151-391200. TELEX 419548-DAV-D. adv.

382   GW   ISSN 0075-2649
JAHRBUCH FUER FREMDENVERKEHR. 1950. a. DM.50. Deutsches Wirtschaftswissenschaftliches Institut fuer Fremdenverkehr, Hermann-Sack-Str. 2, Postfach 264, 8000 Munich 33, Germany. TEL 089-267091. FAX 089-267613. Ed. Manfred Zeiner. bk.rev.; circ. 500.
    —BLDSC shelfmark: 4631.462000.

910.09   US
JAPANESE CITY GUIDE. (Text in Japanese) 1988. bi-m. $24 (foreign $44). Bill of Fare Inc., 853 Seventh Ave., Ste. 1-A, New York, NY 10019-5215. TEL 212-315-0800. FAX 212-397-9513. adv.; circ. 40,000.
    Description: Articles cover what is and what will be going on in New York over a two month period.

910.202   US
JAPANESE GUIDE TO HAWAII. (Text in Japanese) 1980. bi-m. Honolulu Publishing Company, Ltd., 36 Merchant St., Honolulu, HI 96813. TEL 808-524-7400. FAX 808-531-2306. Ed. Yukie Anthony. adv.; circ. 37,000.
    Description: Serves as the island's Japanese language visitor publication.

910   US   ISSN 0279-7984
JAX FAX TRAVEL MARKETING MAGAZINE; the official reference directory of charters and inclusive tour schedules. 1973. m. $12. Jet Airtransport Exchange, Inc. (JAX), 397 Post Rd., Darien, CT 06820-1413. TEL 203-655-8746. FAX 203-655-6257. (Subscr. to: Box 4013, Darien, CT 06820) Ed. Julie Barton. adv.; circ. 28,000. (back issues avail.)
    Formerly: Jax Fax (ISSN 0148-9542)
    Description: For travel agents.

910.09   UI
JERSEY HOLIDAY POST. 1975. w. (30/yr.). Michael Stanley Publishers, 1 Britannia Pl., Bath St., St. Helier, Jersey, Channel Islands, England. TEL 0534-25517. Ed. Rob Shipley.
    Description: Holiday information for people in Jersey.

JETSTREAM AIR NEWS; Swiss aviation magazine. see TRANSPORTATION — Air Transport

910.2   FR   ISSN 0021-616X
JEUNES DES AUBERGES.* 1956. q. $2.60 to non-members. Federation Unie des Auberges de Jeunesse, 10 rue N-D de Lorette, 75009 Paris, France. charts; illus.; play rev.; stat.; index.

910.2   UK   ISSN 0075-3750
JEWISH TRAVEL GUIDE. 1950. a. $11.50. Jewish Chronicle Publications Ltd., 25 Furnival St., London EC4A 1JT, England. FAX 071-405-9040. TELEX 940-114115. (Dist. in N.America by: Sepher Hermon Press, Inc., 1265 46th St., Brooklyn, New York, NY 11219) Ed. S.W. Massil. adv.; index; circ. 10,000.

910.4   CR   ISSN 1018-1253
JOIN US...COSTA RICA AWAITS YOU. (Text in English) 1989. bi-m. Col.2675($20) (effective 1992). Ediciones Creativas de Costa Rica, S.A., Urb. Jose Maria Zeledon, P.O. Box 146-2300, Curridabat, San Jose, Costa Rica. TEL 506-24-7930. FAX 506-24-9086. Alfonso Ruiz Bolanos. adv.; circ. 30,000.
    Description: General information for tourists visiting Costa Rica including time zones, banking, medical services, lodging, car renting, souvenirs, and tours.

910.09   BE
JOURNAL DE TOURING SECOURS. (Text in Dutch and French) bi-m. 1895 Fr. Touring Club of Belgium, Rue de la Loi 44, 1040 Brussels, Belgium. TEL 02-233-22-11. circ. 770,000.

796 917.1   CN   ISSN 0843-9117
JOURNAL OF APPLIED RECREATION RESEARCH. 1971. q. $35 membership. University of Waterloo Press, Waterloo, Ont. N2L 3G1, Canada. TEL 519-885-1211. FAX 519-747-4606. Ed. Bryan J.A. Smale. bk.review. **Indexed**: Rural Recreat.Tour.Abstr., Sportsearch (1989-), World Agri.Econ.& Rural Sociol.Abstr.
    —BLDSC shelfmark: 4947.028000.
    Formerly (until vol.14, no.4, 1989): Recreation Research Review (ISSN 0702-9284)

JOURNAL OF SAFETY RESEARCH. see TRANSPORTATION

910.202   US   ISSN 1054-8408
                            CODEN: JTTMET
▼**JOURNAL OF TRAVEL & TOURISM MARKETING**. 1992. q. $18 to individuals; institutions $24; libraries $32. Haworth Press, Inc., 10 Alice St., Binghamton, NY 13904-1580. TEL 800-342-9678. FAX 607-722-1424. TELEX 4932599. Ed. Kaye S. Chon. (also avail. in microform from HAW; reprint service avail. from HAW)
    Description: Includes travel services, tourism management organizations, meetings and convention services, and transportation services.
    Refereed Serial

910.2   US   ISSN 0047-2875
G155.A1
JOURNAL OF TRAVEL RESEARCH. 1962. q. $75 to non-members. University of Colorado, Business Research Division, Campus Box 420, Boulder, CO 80309. TEL 303-492-8227. (Co-sponsor: Travel and Tourism Research Association) Ed. Charles R. Goeldner. bk.rev.; circ. 1,600. **Indexed**: ABI Inform, B.P.I., Rural Recreat.Tour.Abstr., World Agri.Econ.& Rural Sociol.Abstr.
    —BLDSC shelfmark: 5070.550000.
    Formerly: Travel Research Bulletin (ISSN 0147-2399)

910.2   GW   ISSN 0022-5932
JUGENDHERBERGE. 1920; N.S. 1951. bi-m. membership only. Hauptverband fuer Jugendwandern und Jugendherbergen e.V., Postfach 1455, 4930 Detmold 1, Germany. TEL 05231-7401-0. Ed. Bert Pichel. adv.; bk.rev.; illus.; circ. 900,000.

910.2   YU   ISSN 0022-605X
JUGOSLAWISCHE TOURISTENZEITUNG/YUGOSLAV TOURIST NEWS. (Editions in English, French and German) 1963. m. $10. Turisticka Stampa, Knez Mihailova 21, Belgrade, Yugoslavia. Ed. Dobrivoje Djokovic.

919   II   ISSN 0047-2999
JUNGLE; a journal for promotion of tourism and nature study. (Text in English) 1971. bi-m. Rs.12. Wild Life Camp, A-268 Defence Colony, New Delhi 3, India. Ed. Priti Debnath. adv.; bibl.; charts; illus.

910.09   US
JUST GO!. q. 1095 Market St., Ste. 812, San Francisco, CA 94103. TEL 415-255-5951. FAX 415-621-4946. Ed. Lisa Tabb. circ. 20,000.

KAKTUSBLUETE. see CHILDREN AND YOUTH — About

910   NE
KAMPEER EN CARAVANKAMPIOEN. 1941. m. fl.85.50 to non-members. Koninklijke Nederlandse Toeristenbond ANWB - Royal Dutch Touring Club, Wassenaarseweg 220, Postbus 93200, 2509 BA The Hague, Netherlands. Ed. F. Voorbergen. adv.; illus.; circ. 140,000. **Indexed**: Key to Econ.Sci.

910.2   NE   ISSN 0022-8265
DJ1
KAMPIOEN. 1885. m. fl.31 to non-members. Koninklijke Nederlandse Toeristenbond ANWB - Royal Dutch Touring Club, Postbus 93200, Wassenaarseweg 220, 2509 BA the Hague, Netherlands. Ed. H.W. van Drunen. adv.; bk.rev.; charts; illus.; index; circ. 2,600,000. **Indexed**: Key to Econ.Sci.

KARATE AND ORIENTAL ARTS. see SPORTS AND GAMES

960   KE
KARIBU. (Text in English) 1977. m. EAs.360($25) Oryx Publications Limited, P.O. Box 40106, Nairobi, Kenya. Peter Moll. adv.; illus.; circ. 5,000.

TRAVEL AND TOURISM

910.202 — II
KARNATAKA. DEPARTMENT OF TOURISM. ANNUAL REPORT. (Text in English) 1975. a. Department of Information and Tourism, 5 Infantry Rd., Bangalore, India.

917.904 — US
KAUAI, A PARADISE GUIDE. (Supplement avail.: Kauai Update) biennial. Paradise Publications, 8110 S.W. Wareham, Portland, OR 97223. TEL 503-246-1555.
Description: Guide to beaches, restaurants, and accomodations.

917.904 — US   ISSN 0898-1418
KAUAI UPDATE. (Supplement to: Kauai, a Paradise Guide) 1988. q. $6. Paradise Publications, 8110 S.W. Wareham, Portland, OR 97223. TEL 503-246-1555. Ed. Christie Stilson. circ. 2,000.
Description: Provides an overview of island events and happenings for tourists and island residents.

914.304 — GW
KAUPERTS DEUTSCHLAND REISEFUEHRER. 1950. a. DM.19.50. Adressbuch-Gesellschaft Berlin mbH, Friedrichstr. 210, 1000 Berlin 61, Germany. Eds. E. Spitzing-Pistorius, C. Georgi-Polotzek. adv.; circ. 8,500.
Formerly: Kauperts Deutschland Staedte-, Hotel-, und Reisefuehrer.

KENTUCKY EXPLORER; featuring things about Kentucky and its history. see *HISTORY — History Of North And South America*

916.04 — KE
KENYA TOURIST DEVELOPMENT CORPORATION. REPORT AND ACCOUNTS. (Text in English) a. Kenya Tourist Development Corporation, Box 42013, Nairobi, Kenya. TEL 330820. TELEX 23009.

KEY INTERNATIONAL GUIDE. see *HOMOSEXUALITY*

917.904 — US
KEY MAGAZINE. CARMEL & MONTEREY PENINSULA. 1969. m. $15. Tri-County Publications, Box 223859, Carmel, CA 93922-3859. adv.; circ. 37,000.

917 — US   ISSN 0040-6279
KEY MAGAZINE. THIS WEEK IN CHICAGO. 1920. w. $52. This Week in Chicago, Inc., 904 W. Blackhawk, 2nd Fl., Chicago, IL 60622-2518. FAX 312-664-6113. Ed. Alexis H. Sakisian. adv.; circ. 20,000.
Formerly: This Week in Chicago.

917 — US
KEY MAGAZINE. THIS WEEK IN LOS ANGELES AND SOUTHERN CALIFORNIA; the leading weekly magazine of Southern entertainment & dining. 1936. w. $22. Falcon Publications, 8432 Steller Dr., Culver City, CA 90232. TEL 310-949-5111. Ed. George Falcon. adv.; bk.rev.; charts; illus.
Formerly: Key (Los Angeles); Incorporates: Information Los Angeles (ISSN 0020-0131)

917 — US
KEY MAGAZINE. THIS WEEK IN SAN FRANCISCO. 1933. w. $54. L. Publishing Co., Inc., 1508 Fillmore St., San Francisco, CA 94115. TEL 415-202-1900. FAX 415-931-1508. Ed. Stephen M.H. Braitman. adv.; circ. 22,000. (back issues avail.)
Description: Visitor's guide to San Francisco and Bay Area activities. Also available at hotels, shops, galleries and tourist oriented points of interest.

919 — CJ
KEY TO CAYMAN. 1978. s-a. free. Cayman Free Press Ltd., Box 1365, Grand Cayman, Cayman Islands, British W.I. TEL 809-949-5111. adv.; circ. 130,000.
Formerly (until Dec. 1989): Tourist Weekly.

910.09 — CN   ISSN 0710-9628
KEY TO KINGSTON. 1980. m. Can.$15($8) Kingston Publications, P.O. Box 1352, 6 Princess St., Kingston, Ont. K7L 5C6, Canada. Ed. K. Wright. adv.; charts; illus.; play rev.; circ. 16,000. (back issues avail)

910.202 — US
KEYS GUIDE. 1988. irreg. (approx. 1-4/m.). free. Prescott Visitor Magazines (Sarasota), 3675 Clark Rd., Sarasota, FL 34233-2358. TEL 813-922-3575. Ed. Lorin Oberweger.

KEYSTONE A A A MOTORIST. see *TRANSPORTATION — Automobiles*

910.202 — GW
KOELN. VERKEHRSAMT. MONATSVORSCHAU. (Text in German; summaries in English, French) 1958. m. DM.24. Cologne Tourist Office, Unter Fettenhennen 19, 5000 Cologne 1, Germany. TEL 0221-221-3343. FAX 0221-221-3320. TELEX 8883421-TOC-D. circ. 12,500.

910.09 — GW
KOELN - REISE - REPORT. (Text in English, French, German, Italian) a. Verkehrsamt der Stadt Koeln, Unter Fettenhennen 19, 5000 Cologne 1, Germany. TEL 0221-2213345. FAX 0221-2213320. TELEX 8883421-TOC-D.

KOELN - RHEINLAND VON HINTEN; das schwule Reisebuch. see *HOMOSEXUALITY*

KOELNER KONGRESS REPORT. see *MEETINGS AND CONGRESSES*

KONCIZE. see *MEETINGS AND CONGRESSES*

910.4 — KN
KOREA. (Editions in Chinese, English, French, Korean, Russian, Spanish) 1956. m. Pyongyang, N. Korea. illus.

KULTURNOPOLITICKY KALENDAR. see *MEETINGS AND CONGRESSES*

943 — GW
KURJOURNAL - BAD TOELZ. (Text in English, German) 1950. m. DM.24. Staedtische Kurverwaltung, Ludwigstr. 11, 8170 Bad Toelz, Germany. TEL 08041-70071. FAX 08041-70075. Ed. Harry E. Haeusser. adv.; play rev.; circ. 2,500.
Description: Information for visitors to Bad Toelz: icluding local events, health treatments.

910.09 — GW
KURZEITUNG GRONENBACH. 1976. m. DM.12. Kurverwaltung Gronenbach, Marktplatz, Postfach 1110, 8944 Gronenbach, Germany. TEL 08334-7711. circ. 850.

L S A NEWSLETTER. (Leisure Studies Association) see *LEISURE AND RECREATION*

LAKE SUPERIOR MAGAZINE. see *HISTORY — History Of North And South America*

910.4 — LS
LAOS. (Editions in English and Lao) q. 80 rue Sethathirath, BP 310, Vientiane, Laos. TEL 2405. Eds. V. Phomchanheuang, O. Phrakhamsay. illus.

910.202 790.1 — US   ISSN 0271-0145
LAS VEGAS INSIDER. 1973. m. $42. Lucky Publishing Co., Box 29274, La Vegas, NV 89126. TEL 602-636-1649. Ed. Donald Currier. adv.; cum.index: 1973-1988; circ. 5,100. (back issues avail.)
Description: Contains the latest gaming, tournament and travel information. Includes tourist tips, freebies, and discounts.

910.09 — US   ISSN 1052-1011
▼**LATITUDES SOUTH.** (Text in English, Spanish) 1991. bi-m. (American Eagle Airlines) Caribbean Travel and Life, Inc., 8403 Colesville Rd., Ste. 830, Silver Spring, MD 20910. TEL 301-588-2300. FAX 301-588-2256. Ed. Sharon Jaffe. adv.
Description: Inflight magazine.

917.104 — CN
LAURENTIAN: SPRING - SUMMER - FALL EDITION; mountains of fun north of Montreal. (Text in English and French) 1976. a. free in hotels, motels, restaurants and boutiques in the Laurentians. Association Touristique des Laurentides, 14142 rue de Lachapelle, R.R. 1, St. Jerome, Que. J7Z 5T4, Canada. TEL 514-436-8532. FAX 514-436-5309. Ed. Andre Goyer. adv.; circ. 100,000.

910.09 — CN   ISSN 0829-8033
LES LAURENTIDES/LAURENTIANS: MOUNTAINS OF FUN NORTH OF MONTREAL. (Text in English, French) 1976. a. free in hotels, motels, restaurants and boutiques in the Laurentians. Association Touristique des Laurentides, 14142 rue de Lachapelle, R.R. 1, St. Jerome, Que. J7Z 5T4, Canada. TEL 514-436-8532. FAX 514-436-5309. Ed. Andre Goyer. adv.; circ. 50,000.

914 — IT   ISSN 0047-4231
LAZIO IERI E OGGI; rivista mensile di cultura, arte, turismo. 1965. m. L.13500. Via Taranto 178, 00182 Rome, Italy. Dir. Willy Pocino. bk.rev.; illus.; index.

LEISURE WORLD. see *LEISURE AND RECREATION*

910.2 914 — US   ISSN 0163-4585
D909
LET'S GO: THE BUDGET GUIDE TO EUROPE.. 1960. a. $9.95. St. Martin's Press, 175 Fifth Ave., New York, NY 10010. TEL 212-674-5151. adv.; circ. 60,000.
Formerly: Let's Go: The Student Guide to Europe (ISSN 0075-8868)

938 956 — US
LET'S GO: THE BUDGET GUIDE TO GREECE, ISRAEL AND EGYPT - INCLUDING CYPRUS & TURKISH COAST. a. $8.95. St. Martin's Press, 175 Fifth Ave., New York, NY 10010. Ed. Scott W. Pink.
Formerly: Let's Go: The Budget Guide to Greece, Israel and Egypt (ISSN 0276-6779)

917.04 — US   ISSN 0192-2920
DG416
LET'S GO: THE BUDGET GUIDE TO ITALY. 1981. a. $8.95. St. Martin's Press, 175 Fifth Ave., New York, NY 10010. TEL 212-674-5151. Ed. Jeremy Metz.

917.04 — US
LET'S GO: U S A. 1973. a. $9.95. St. Martin's Press, 175 Fifth Ave., New York, NY 10010. TEL 212-674-5151. illus.
Formerly: Let's Go: The Student Guide to the United States and Canada (ISSN 0090-788X)

LIAT ISLANDER. see *TRANSPORTATION — Air Transport*

354 — LB
LIBERIA. MINISTRY OF INFORMATION, CULTURAL AFFAIRS & TOURISM. ANNUAL REPORT TO THE SESSION OF THE LEGISLATURE.* (Text in English) a. Ministry of Information, Cultural Affairs and Tourism, Monrovia, Liberia.

910.2 960 — UK
LIBYA PAST AND PRESENT SERIES. 1970. irreg. (approx. 2/yr.). price varies. Oleander Press, 17 Stansgate Ave., Cambridge CB2 2QZ, England. (U.S. addr.: 80 Eighth Ave., Ste. 303, New York, NY 10011) Ed. Philip Ward.
Formerly: Libyan Travel Series (ISSN 0075-9309)

LIMOUSIN MAGAZINE; magazines de France. see *GENERAL INTEREST PERIODICALS — France*

LINKS UND RECHTS DER AUTOBAHN; der Reisefuehrer und Reiseatlas speziell fuer die Autobahn. see *HOTELS AND RESTAURANTS*

914 — AU   ISSN 0024-4147
LINZER WOCHE. 1963. m. S.42. (Magistrat) Rudolf Trauner Verlag, Koeglstr. 14, A-4020 Linz-Donau, Austria. Ed. Dr. Walter Knoglinger. circ. 45,000.

LIVABILITY DIGEST. see *HOUSING AND URBAN PLANNING*

910.202 640.73 — UK
LIVING AND RETIRING ABROAD; the Daily Telegraph guide. irreg. £7.99. Kogan Page Ltd., 120 Pentonville Rd., London N1 9JN, England. TEL 071-278-0483. FAX 071-837-6348.

910.09 — VE
LIVING IN VENEZUELA. (Text in English) 1980. a. Bs.1000($50) Venezuelan-American Chamber of Commerce and Industry - Camara Venezolano Americana de Comercio e Industria, Apdo. 5181, Caracas 1010A, Venezuela. TELEX 28399. adv.; index; circ. 5,000. (back issues avail.)
Formerly: VenAmCham's Executive Newcomers Guide.

910.09 — US
LODGING BRIEFING. m. Walter Matthews Assoc., Inc., Box 889, New York, NY 10018-0968. TEL 212-869-4683. Ed. Walter Matthews.

914.204 — US
LONDON (YEAR). a. $10. Harper Collins Publishers, Birnbaum Travel Guides, 20 E. 53rd St., New York, NY 10022-5299. TEL 212-207-7000. illus.; index.

952

952 UK
LONDON DAYORI; the Japanese journal of London. 1974. m. £15. Dayori of London Publishing Ltd., 7 Wind Mill St., London W1P 1HF, England. FAX 01-580-4844. Ed. Yuriko Akishima. adv.; film rev.; play rev.; illus.; circ. 20,000. (back issues avail.)

910.202 CN
LONDON MAGAZINE GUIDEBOOK. 1989. q. Can.$10. Blackburn Group, 540 York St., London, Ont. N6B 1R5, Canada. TEL 519-679-4901. FAX 519-434-7842. Ed. Jackie Skender. circ. 40,000.
Formerly: London Guide.

910.202 UK
LONDON'S BEST BED & BREAKFAST HOTELS. 1989. a. £2.95. F.H.G. Publications Ltd., Abbey Mill Business Centre, Seedhill, Paisley PA1 1JN, Scotland. TEL 041-887-0428.

914.804 059.945 FI ISSN 0024-6379 DK445
LOOK AT FINLAND. (Text in English) 1964. q. $15. Finnish Tourist Board, P.O. Box 625, 00101 Helsinki, Finland. FAX 0-40301333. TELEX 122690. (Co-sponsor: Finnish Ministry of Foreign Affairs, Press and Cultural Development) Eds. Bengt Pihlstroem, Ann-Mari Pihlstroem. adv.; bk.rev.; abstr.; bibl.; charts; illus.; stat.; circ. 35,000. **Indexed**: P.A.I.S.
—BLDSC shelfmark: 5294.507000.

915 TH
LOOKEAST. (Text in English) 1969. m. Advertising and Media Consultants Ltd., Silom Condominium, 12th Fl., 52-38 Soi Saladaeng 2, Bangkok, Thailand. TEL 2333401. FAX 2366764. TELEX 82463 LOOKEAS TH. Ed. Satish Sehgal. adv.; bk.rev.; charts; illus.; circ. 15,000.

917.904 US
LOS ANGELES (YEAR). a. Harper Collins Publishers, Birnbaum Travel Guides, 10 E. 53rd St., New York, NY 10022-5299. TEL 212-270-7000. illus.; index.

LOUSIANA LIFE. see *GENERAL INTEREST PERIODICALS — United States*

910.4 CC
LU CHAO. (Text in Chinese) bi-m. Guangdong Luyou Chubanshe, No. 42, Taojin Kangkeng, Huanshi Donglu, Guangzhou, Guangdong 510060, People's Republic of China. TEL 750375. Ed. Li Yajun.

910.202 GW
LUFTVERKEHR. 1950. q. free. Flughafen Hannover-Langenhagen GmbH, Postfach 420280, 3000 Hannover 42, Germany. TEL 0511-977-0. adv.; circ. 20,000. (back issues avail.)

910.202 CC
LUXINGJIA/TRAVELLERS. (Text in Chinese) 1955. m. Luxingjia Zazhishe, 23A Dongjiaominxiang, Beijing, People's Republic of China. TEL 01-552631.
Description: Introduces Chinese scenery, customs and culture.

910.202 CC ISSN 1000-7253
LUYOU/TOURISM. (Text in Chinese) 1979. m. $36.80. (Beijing Luyou Shiye Guanliju - Beijing Tourism Management Bureau) Luyou Zazhishe, Chongwenmen Hotel, 11th Fl., Beijing 100062, People's Republic of China. TEL 5122211. (Dist. in US by: China Books & Periodicals, Inc., 2929 24th St., San Francisco, CA 94110. TEL 415-282-2994) Ed. Pan Chao.

915.1 CC
LUYOU TIANDI/TRAVELLING SCOPE. (Text in Chinese) bi-m. $24.30. Shanghai Wenhua Chubanshe, 74 Shaoxing Lu, Shanghai 200020, People's Republic of China. TEL 4372608. (Dist. in US by: China Books & Periodicals, Inc., 2929 24th St., San Francisco, CA 94110. TEL 415-282-2994)

910.4 CC
LUYOU XUEKAN/JOURNAL OF TOURISM. (Text in Chinese) q. Beijing Lianhe Daxue, Luyou Xueyuan, 1, Panjiapo, Chaowai, Beijing 100020, People's Republic of China. TEL 5024956. Ed. Zhao Kefei.

M & C. (Meeting & Congressi) see *MEETINGS AND CONGRESSES*

910.202 UK
M E E D PRACTICAL GUIDE. JORDAN. 1983. irreg. £9.95($20) per no. Middle East Economic Digest Ltd., 21 John St., London WC1N 2BP, England. TEL 071-404-5513. (Distr. in U.S. by: Lynne Rienner Publishers Inc., 948 North St., No.8, Boulder, CO 80302) Ed. Jonn Whelan. adv.; bibl.; illus.; stat.; index.
Description: Guide for tourists and business people on where to stay and what to see in Jordan.

910.202 UK
M E E D PRACTICAL GUIDE. QATAR. 1983. irreg. £9.95($20) per. Middle East Economic Digest Ltd., 21 John St., London WC1N 2BP, England. TEL 071-404-5513. (Distr. in U.S. by: Lynne Rienner Publishers Inc., 948 North St., no.8, Boulder, CO 80302) Ed. John Whelan. adv.; bibl.; illus.; stat.; index.
Description: Guide for business people and tourists on where to stay and what to see in Qatar.

910.202 CN
M F V A BROCHURE. 1972. a. free. Manitoba Farm Vacations Association, 525 Kylemore Ave., Winnipeg, Man. R3L 1B5, Canada. TEL 204-475-6624. FAX 204-475-0292. Ed. Irv Kroeker. adv.; circ. 15,000.

910.4 GW ISSN 0178-1529
M I S - MOTOR IM SCHNEE. 1970. 8/yr. DM.92. Stein Verlag GmbH, Josef-Hermann-Str. 1-3, 7557 Iffezheim - Baden-Baden, Germany. TEL 07229-606-0. Ed. Wilhelm Joesch. circ. 4,000. (back issues avail.)

MACAO. DIRECCAO DOS SERVICOS DE ESTATISTICA E CENSOS. ESTATISTICAS DO TURISMO/MACAO. CENSUS AND STATISTICS DEPARTMENT. TOURISM STATISTICS. see *TRAVEL AND TOURISM — Abstracting, Bibliographies, Statistics*

MACAO. DIRECCAO DOS SERVICOS DE ESTATISTICA E CENSOS. ESTATISTICAS DO TURISMO (RELATORIO ANUAL)/MACAO. CENSUS AND STATISTICS DEPARTMENT. TOURISM STATISTICS (ANNUAL REPORT). see *TRAVEL AND TOURISM — Abstracting, Bibliographies, Statistics*

MAENNER AKTUELL. see *HOMOSEXUALITY*

917.404 US
MAINE INVITES YOU. 1930. a. free. Maine Publicity Bureau, Inc., 209 Maine Ave., Box 2300, Farmingdale, ME 04344. TEL 207-582-9300. Ed. Lynn Verrill. adv.; circ. 135,000.

791 YU ISSN 0025-1178
MALA UKRSTENICA. 1956. m. 240 din.($3.15) Enigmatski Klub, Bulevar Vojvode Misica 67, Box 219, Belgrade, Yugoslavia. Ed. Vlasta Pavlovic.

916 MW
MALAWI: A GUIDE FOR THE VISITOR. (Text in English) 1983. a. free. Department of Tourism, P.O. Box 402, Blantyre, Malawi. FAX 620947. TELEX 44645.

MALTA YEARBOOK. see *POLITICAL SCIENCE*

MAN TO MAN GUIDE; gay-lesbian guide to Holland. see *HOMOSEXUALITY*

917.104 CN
MANITOBA VACATION PLANNER. 1972. a. free. Department of Industry, Trade and Tourism, 155 Carlton St., 7th Fl., Winnipeg, Man. R3C 3H8, Canada. TEL 800-665-0040. FAX 204-945-2302. adv.; illus.
Former titles: Manitoba Vacation Guide, Canada; Manitoba Vacation Handbook.

MANUFACTURED HOME NEWS. see *HOUSING AND URBAN PLANNING*

910.202 HK
MARCO POLO NEWS. (Text in English) 6/yr. (Cathay Pacific Airways) Emphasis HK Ltd., Wilson House, 10th Fl., 19-27 Wyndham St., Central, Hong Kong. FAX 810-6738. TELEX 74523-EMPAS-HX. Ed. Derek Davies. adv.; circ. 32,500.
Formerly: Marco Polo.

910.4 FI ISSN 0784-5480
MARINA. (Text in Finnish, Swedish, plus a supplement in German) 3/yr. Erikoislehdet Oy Business Publications, P.O. Box 16, SF-00381 Helsinki, Finland. Ed. Marketta Rentola. circ. 10,000.

TRAVEL AND TOURISM 4775

910.202 US
MARYLAND MOTORIST. 1920. every 45 days. $1. Automobile Club of Maryland, 1401 Mt. Royal Ave., Baltimore, MD 21217. TEL 301-462-4000. FAX 301-523-0380. Ed. William F. Zorzi. bk.rev.; circ. 230,000.

910.202 US
MARYLAND TRAVELGRAM. 1961. m. free to qualified personnel. Department of Economic and Employment Development, Office of Tourism Development, 217 E. Redwood St., Baltimore, MD 21202. TEL 301-333-6611. FAX 301-757-3809. Ed. Gwen Willis. illus.; circ. 6,000.
Formerly: Maryland Travel Scene (ISSN 0300-7502)
Description: Covers Maryland tourism industry.

910.09 IS
MASA ACHER. (Text in Hebrew) 1987. bi-m. $45. Masa Acher Inc., P.O. Box20493, Tel Aviv 61204, Israel. TEL 03-383898. FAX 03-379-455. TELEX 381528-GILAD. Eds. Gil El-Ami, Moshe Gilad. circ. 32,000.
Description: Dedicated to the topics of geography and travel.

916.8 RH
MASVINGO DIARY. (Text in English) 1963. m. free. Masvingo Great Zimbabwe Publicity Association, P.O. Box 340, Masvingo, Zimbabwe. Ed. Mrs. B. Kanjanga. adv.; illus.; circ. 2,500.
Formerly: Fort Victoria Diary.

910.09 TS
MATAR ABU DHABI AL-DAWLI/SHOPTALK - ABU DHABI DUTY FREE GUIDE. (Text in Arabic, English) 1988. q. free. Motivate Publishing (Abu Dhabi), P.O. Box 7441, Abu Dhabi, United Arab Emirates. TEL 311666. FAX 311888. Eds. Ubaid Hamid al-Tayir, Chuck Grieve. circ. 20,000.
Description: Tourist and duty free information regarding Abu Dhabi and its airport.

910.09 TS
MATAR DUBAI AL-DAWLI/DUBAI INTERNATIONAL AIRPORT. (Text in Arabic, English) 1987. q. free. Motivate Publishing, P.O. Box 2331, Dubai, United Arab Emirates. TEL 246060. FAX 245270. TELEX 48366 MAM EM. Ed. Obaid Humaid al-Tayer. circ. 4,000.
Description: For airline passengers using Dubai airport.

914 796.5 FI
MATKAILU/TOURISM. (Text in Finnish; summaries in Swedish) 1936. 6/yr. Fmk.120. Suomen Matkailuliitto - Finnish Travel Association, Mikonkatu 25, 00100 Helsinki 10, Finland. FAX 0-654358. TELEX 122619-FTATA-ST. Ed. Antero Tuomisto. adv.; bk.rev.; bibl.; illus.; circ. 37,500. (also avail. in microfilm)
Formerly (until 1990): Suomen Matkailu - Tourism of Finland (ISSN 0359-0607); Formed by the merger of: Leirinta ja Retkeily (ISSN 0356-0805) & Matkailumaailma (ISSN 0025-5963); Which were originally titled: Leirintasanomat; Matkailu ja Retkeily.

910.09 US
▼**MATURE GROUP TRAVELER**. 1991. q. $12. Meetings Info-Resources, Inc., 1 Atlantic St., No.413, Stamford, CT 06901. TEL 203-975-1416. FAX 203-975-1418. Ed. George Lowden. adv.; circ. 13,600 (controlled).
Description: Includes feature articles and relevant information about destinations, attractions and other travel services of interest to the senior travel market.

910.09 US ISSN 1043-2280
MATURE TRAVELER; travel bonanzas for 49-ers-plus. 1984. m. $24.50. G E M Publishing Group, 250 E. Riverview Circle, Reno, NV 89509. TEL 702-786-7419. (Subscr. to: Box 50820, Reno, NV 89513-0820) Ed. Gene E. Malott. adv.; bk.rev.; index; circ. 2,200. (back issues avail.)
Description: News about discounts and trips for senior citizens, travel tips, cruise news and senior-friendly destinations.

917.904 US
MAUI, A PARADISE GUIDE. (Supplement avail.: Maui Update) biennial. Paradise Publications, 8110 S.W. Wareham, Portland, OR 97223. TEL 503-246-1555.
Description: Guide to beaches, restaurants, accomodations, and attractions.

T

4776 TRAVEL AND TOURISM

917.904 US ISSN 0895-9390
MAUI UPDATE. (Supplement to: Maui, a Paradise Guide) 1987. q. $6. Paradise Publications, 8110 S.W. Wareham, Portland, OR 97223. TEL 503-246-1555. Ed. Christie Stilson. adv.; bk.rev.; circ. 2,000. (back issues avail.)
  Description: Provides an overview of current island events of particular interest to the vacationer traveling to Maui, Hawaii.

916.1 NO
MED BIL I EUROPA. 1951. a. membership. Norges Automobil-Forbund, Storgaten 2, Postboks 494, Oslo 1, Norway.

MEETING COMMUNICATIONS. see *MEETINGS AND CONGRESSES*

914.204 UK
MEETING IN LONDON. q. World Trade Magazines Ltd., World Trade House, 49 Dartford Rd., Sevenoaks, Kent TN13 3TE, England. TEL 0732-458144. FAX 0732-456295. adv. (reprint service avail. from UMI)
  Formerly: Destination London.

614.86 GW
MEINE GESUNDHEIT "REISEAPOTHEKE". 1981. a. Otto Hoffmanns Verlag GmbH, Platenstr. 6, 8000 Munich 2, Germany. TEL 089-774096. circ. 1,350,000.

647.94 IT
MERIDIANI. 1988. bi-m. L.48000($64) Editoriale Domus, Via Achille Grandi 5-7, 20089 Rozzano (MI), Italy. TEL 02-824721. Andreina Vanni. circ. 70,000.

915.6 IQ
MESOPOTAMIA. m. Department of Tourism Services, Baghdad, Iraq.

METRO MAN. see *HOMOSEXUALITY*

917.204 US ISSN 0884-1209 F1209
MEXICO (YEAR). a. $17. Harper Collins Publishers, Birnbaum Travel Guides, 10 E. 53rd St., New York, NY 10022-5299. TEL 212-270-7000. Ed. Stephen Birnbaum.

917.204 647 MX
MEXICO CITY DAILY BULLETIN. (Text in English) 1936. d. free. Edit, S.A, Gomez Farias 41, Col. San Rafael, 06470 Mexico, D.F, Mexico. TEL 905-546-5115. FAX 905-535-6060. Ed. C.P. Raul Paredes Parra. circ. 10,000. (back issues avail.)
  Description: Provides English-speaking visitors information of major international happenings as well as information on sites of interest in their own language. Includes local news.

056.1 MX ISSN 0462-1069
MEXICO NEWS. 1962. m. $200. (Mexican Journalist Association) Editorial Bonanza, S. de R.L., Ninos Heroes 105, Dr. Velasco Bldg. 5, Ste. 203, 06040 Mexico DF, Mexico. TEL 593-87-20. FAX 705-24-92. Ed. Mario Perez Morales. adv.; bk.rev.; circ. 10,000.

917 US ISSN 0889-7107
MEXICO WEST; Baja California, Sea of Cortez, Mexico's West Coast. 1976. m. $35. Mexico West Travel Club, Inc., P.O. Box 1646, Bonita, CA 91908. TEL 619-585-3033. FAX 619-422-2671. adv.; bk.rev.; circ. 3,500. (back issues avail.)
  Description: Articles, news, and announcements on vacations and travel to the Pacific West Coast area of the country.

917.504 US
MIAMI (YEAR). a. $10. Harper Collins Publishers, Birnbaum Travel Guides, 10 E. 53rd St., New York, NY 10022-5299. TEL 212-207-7000. illus.; index.

914.404 FR
MICHELIN GREEN GUIDE SERIES: ALPES DU NORD. 1978. irreg., latest 1988. $14.95 per no. Michelin, Services de Tourisme, 46 av. de Breteuil, 75341 Paris Cedex 7, France. (Dist. in U.S. by: Michelin Travel Publications, P.O. Box 19001, Greenville, SC 29602-9001. TEL 800-423-0485)
  Supersedes in part: Michelin Green Guide Series: Alpes.

914.404 FR
MICHELIN GREEN GUIDE SERIES: ALPES DU SUD. irreg., latest 1988. $14.95 per no. Michelin, Services de Tourisme, 46 av. de Breteuil, 75341 Paris Cedex 7, France. (Dist. in US by: Michelin Travel Publications, Box 19001, Greenville, SC 29602-9001. TEL 800-423-0485)
  Supersedes in part: Michelin Green Guide Series: Alpes.

914.404 FR
MICHELIN GREEN GUIDE SERIES: ALSACE ET LORRAINE (VOSGES). irreg., latest 1989. $14.95. Michelin, Services de Tourisme, 46 av. de Breteuil, 75341 Paris Cedex 7, France. (Dist. in U.S. by: Michelin Travel Publications, P.O. Box 19001, Greenville, SC 29602-9001. TEL 800-423-0485)
  Formerly: Michelin Green Guide Series: Vosges.

914.36 FR
MICHELIN GREEN GUIDE SERIES: AUSTRIA. (Text in English) irreg., latest 1986. $14.95 per no. Michelin, Services de Tourisme, 46 av. de Breteuil, 75341 Paris Cedex 7, France. (Dist. in U.S. by: Michelin Travel Publications, P.O. Box 19001, Greenville, SC 29602-9001. TEL 800-423-0485)

914.404 FR
MICHELIN GREEN GUIDE SERIES: AUVERGNE. 1977. irreg., latest 1988. $14.95. Michelin, Services de Tourisme, 46 av. de Breteuil, 75341 Paris Cedex 7, France. (Dist. in U.S. by: Michelin Travel Publications, P.O. Box 19001, Greenville, SC 29602-9001. TEL 800-423-0485)

914.404 FR
MICHELIN GREEN GUIDE SERIES: BELGIQUE - LUXEMBOURG. (Text in French) irreg., latest 1988. $14.95 per no. Michelin, Services de Tourisme, 46 av. de Breteuil, 75341 Paris Cedex 7, France. (Dist. in U.S. by: Michelin Travel Publications, P.O. Box 19001, Greenville, SC 29602-9001. TEL 800-423-0485)

914.404 FR
MICHELIN GREEN GUIDE SERIES: BERRY-LIMOUSIN. (Text in French) irreg., latest 1987. $14.95. Michelin, Services de Tourisme, 46 av. de Breteuil, 75341 Paris Cedex 7, France. (Dist. in U.S. by: Michelin Travel Publications, P.O. Box 19001, Greenville, SC 29304-9001. TEL 800-423-0485)

914.404 FR
MICHELIN GREEN GUIDE SERIES: BOURGOGNE. (Text in French) irreg., latest 1988. $14.95. Michelin, Services de Tourisme, 46 av. de Breteuil, 75341 Paris Cedex 7, France. (Dist. in U.S. by: Michelin Travel Publications, P.O. Box 19001, Greenville, SC 29602-9001. TEL 800-423-0485)

914.4 FR
MICHELIN GREEN GUIDE SERIES: BRITTANY. (Editions in English, French) irreg., latest 1987. $14.95 per no. Michelin, Services de Tourisme, 46 av. de Breteuil, 75341 Paris Cedex 7, France. (Dist. in U.S. by: Michelin Travel Publications, P.O. Box 19001, Greenville, SC 29602-9001. TEL 800-423-0485)

914.404 FR
MICHELIN GREEN GUIDE SERIES: BURGUNDY. (Text in English) irreg., latest 1988. $14.95. Michelin, Services de Tourisme, 46 av. de Breteuil, 75346 Paris Cedex 7, France. (Dist. in U.S. by: Michelin Travel Publications, P.O. Box 19001, Greenville, SC 29602-9001. TEL 800-423-0485)

917.104 FR
MICHELIN GREEN GUIDE SERIES: CANADA. (Editions in English, French) irreg., latest 1989. $14.95. Michelin, Services de Tourisme, 46 av. de Breteuil, 75346 Paris Cedex 7, France. (Dist. in U.S. by: Michelin Travel Publications, P.O. Box 19001, Greenville, SC 29602-9001. TEL 800-423-0485)

914.404 FR
MICHELIN GREEN GUIDE SERIES: CHAMPAGNE-ARDENNES. (Text in French) irreg., latest 1989. $14.95. Michelin, Services de Tourisme, 46 av. de Breteuil, 75346 Paris Cedex 7, France. (Dist. in U.S. by: Michelin Travel Publications, P.O. Box 19001, Greenville, SC 29602-9001. TEL 800-423-0485)

914.4 FR
MICHELIN GREEN GUIDE SERIES: CHATEAUX OF THE LOIRE. (Editions in English, French) irreg., latest 1989. $14.95 per no. Michelin, Services de Tourisme, 46 av. de Breteuil, 75341 Paris Cedex 7, France. (Dist. in U.S. by: Michelin Travel Publications, P.O. Box 19001, Greenville, SC 29602-9001. TEL 800-423-0485)

914.404 FR
MICHELIN GREEN GUIDE SERIES: CORSE. irreg., latest 1989. $14.95. Michelin, Services de Tourisme, 46 av. de Breteuil, 755346 Paris Cedex 7, France. (Dist. in U.S. by: Michelin Travel Publications, P.O. Box 19001, Greenville, SC 29602-9001. TEL 800-423-0485)

914.4 FR
MICHELIN GREEN GUIDE SERIES: COTE D'AZUR. irreg. $14.95. Michelin, Services de Tourisme, 46 av. de Breteuil, 75341 Paris Cedex 7, France. (Dist. in U.S. by: Michelin Travel Publications, P.O. Box 19001, Spartanburg, SC 29602-9001. TEL 800-432-0485)

914.4 FR
MICHELIN GREEN GUIDE SERIES: DORDOGNE. English edition: Michelin Green Guide Series: Perigord. (Editions in English, French) irreg., latest 1987. $14.95. Michelin, Services de Tourisme, 46 av. de Breteuil, 75346 Paris Cedex 7, France. (Dist. in U.S. by: Michelin Travel Publications, P.O. Box 19001, Greenville, SC 29602-9001. TEL 800-423-9001)

914.204 FR
MICHELIN GREEN GUIDE SERIES: ENGLAND, THE WEST COUNTRY. irreg., latest 1990. $14.95. Michelin, Services de Tourisme, 46 av. de Breteuil, 75346 Paris Cedex 7, France. (Dist. in U.S. by: Michelin Travel Publications, P.O. Box 19001, Greenville, SC 29602-9001. TEL 800-423-0485)

914.404 FR
MICHELIN GREEN GUIDE SERIES: FLANDRES, ARTOIS, PICARDIE. (Text in French) irreg., latest 1988. $14.95. Michelin, Services de Tourisme, 46 av. de Breteuil, 75346 Paris Cedex 7, France. (Dist. in U.S. by: Michelin Travel Publications, P.O. Box 19001, Greenville, SC 29602-9001. TEL 800-423-0485)
  Formerly: Michelin Green Guide Series: Nord de la France.

914.4 FR
MICHELIN GREEN GUIDE SERIES: FRANCE. (Editions in English, French) irreg., latest 1991. $14.95. Michelin, Services de Tourisme, 46 av. de Breteuil, 75341 Paris Cedex 7, France. (Dist. in U.S. by: Michelin Travel Publications, P.O. Box 3305, Spartanburg, SC 29304-3305. TEL 800-423-0485)

914.4 FR
MICHELIN GREEN GUIDE SERIES: FRENCH RIVIERA. (Text in English) irreg., latest 1988. $14.95 per no. Michelin, Services de Tourisme, 46 av. de Breteuil, 75341 Paris Cedex 7, France. (Dist. in U.S. by: Michelin Travel Publications, P.O. Box 19001, Greenville, SC 29602-9001. TEL 800-423-0485)

914.3 FR
MICHELIN GREEN GUIDE SERIES: GERMANY. (Text in English) irreg., latest 1987. $14.95 per no. Michelin, Services de Tourisme, 46 av. de Breteuil, 75341 Paris Cedex 7, France. (Dist. in U.S. by: Michelin Travel Publications, P.O. Box 19001, Greenville, SC 29602-9001. TEL 800-423-0485)

914.4 FR
MICHELIN GREEN GUIDE SERIES: GORGES DU TARN. irreg. $14.95. Michelin, Services de Tourisme, 46 av. de Breteuil, 75341 Paris Cedex 7, France. (Dist. in U.S. by: Michelin Travel Publications, Box 19001, Spartanburg, SC 29602-9001. TEL 800-423-0485)

914.2 FR
MICHELIN GREEN GUIDE SERIES: GREAT BRITAIN. irreg., latest 1991. $14.95. Michelin, Services de Tourisme, 46 av. de Breteuil, 75341 Paris Cedex 7, France. (Dist. in U.S. by: Michelin Travel Publications, P.O. Box 3305, Spartanburg, SC 29304-3305. TEL 800-423-0485)

TRAVEL AND TOURISM   4777

914.9   FR
MICHELIN GREEN GUIDE SERIES: GREECE. irreg. $14.95. Michelin, Services de Tourisme, 46 av. de Breteuil, 75341 Paris Cedex 7, France. (Dist. in U.S. by: Michelin Travel Publications, P.O. Box 3305, Spartanburg, SC 29304-3305. TEL 800-423-0485)

914.904   FR
MICHELIN GREEN GUIDE SERIES: HOLLANDE. irreg., latest 1988. $14.95. Michelin, Services de Tourisme, 46 av. de Breteuil, 75341 Paris Cedex 7, France. (Dist. in U.S. by: Michelin Travel Publications, P.O. Box 19001, Greenville, SC 29602-9001. TEL 800-423-0485)

914.404   FR
MICHELIN GREEN GUIDE SERIES: ILE DE FRANCE. (Editions in English, French) irreg., latest 1990. $14.95. Michelin, Services de Tourisme, 46 av. de Breteuil, 75346 Paris Cedex 7, France. (Dist. in U.S by: Michelin Travel Publications, P.O. Box 19001, Greenville, SC 29602-9001. TEL 800-423-0485)
  Supersedes: Michelin Green Guide Series: Environs de Paris.

914.5   FR
MICHELIN GREEN GUIDE SERIES: ITALY. (Text in English) irreg., latest 1989. $14.95 per no. Michelin, Services de Tourisme, 46 av. de Breteuil, 75346 Paris Cedex 7, France. (Dist. in U.S by: Michelin Travel Publications, P.O. Box 19001, Greenville, SC 29602-9001. TEL 800-423-0485)

914.404   FR   ISSN 0293-9436
MICHELIN GREEN GUIDE SERIES: JURA. irreg., latest 1987. $14.95. Michelin, Services de Tourisme, 46 av. de Breteuil, 75341 Paris Cedex 7, France. (Dist. in U.S. by: Michelin Travel Publications, P.O. Box 19001, Greenville, SC 29602-9001. TEL 800-423-0485)

914.204   FR
MICHELIN GREEN GUIDE SERIES: LONDON. (Text in English) irreg., latest 1990. $14.95. Michelin, Services de Tourisme, 46 av. de Breteuil, 75341 Paris Cedex 7, France. (Dist. in U.S. by: Michelin Travel Publications, P.O. Box 19001, Greenville, SC 29602-9001. TEL 800-423-0485)

916.4   FR
MICHELIN GREEN GUIDE SERIES: MAROC. (Text in French) irreg., latest 1988. $14.95 per no. Michelin, Services de Tourisme, 46 av. de Breteuil, 75346 Paris Cedex 7, France. (Dist. in U.S. by: Michelin Travel Publications, P.O. Box 19001, Greenville, SC 29602-9001. TEL 800-423-0485)

917.204   FR
MICHELIN GREEN GUIDE SERIES: MEXICO. (Editions in English, Spanish) irreg., latest 1990. $14.95. Michelin, Services de Tourisme, 46 av. de Breteuil, 75341 Paris Cedex 7, France. (Dist. in U.S. by: Michelin Travel Publications, P.O. Box 19001, Greenville, SC 29602-9001. TEL 800-423-0485)

914.9   FR
MICHELIN GREEN GUIDE SERIES: NETHERLANDS. irreg. $14.95. Michelin, Services de Tourisme, 46 av. de Breteuil, 75341 Paris Cedex 7, France. (Dist. in U.S. by: Michelin Travel Publications, P.O. Box 3305, Spartanburg, SC 29304-0485) TEL 800-423-0485)

917.404   FR
MICHELIN GREEN GUIDE SERIES: NEW ENGLAND. (Editions in English, French) irreg., latest 1988. $14.95. Michelin, Services de Tourisme, 46 av. de Breteuil, 73546 Paris Cedex 7, France. (Dist. in U.S. by: Michelin Travel Publications, P.O. Box 19001, Greenville, SC 29602-9001. TEL 800-423-0485)

917.4   FR
MICHELIN GREEN GUIDE SERIES: NEW YORK (CITY). (Text in English, French) irreg., latest 1988. $14.95 per no. Michelin, Services de Tourisme, 46 av. de Breteuil, 75341 Paris Cedex 7, France. (Dist. in U.S. by: Michelin Travel Publications, P.O. Box 19001, Greenville, SC 29602-9001. TEL 800-423-0485)

914.404   FR
MICHELIN GREEN GUIDE SERIES: NORMANDY, COTENTIN. (Editions in English, French) irreg., latest 1989. $14.95. Michelin, Services de Tourisme, 46 av. de Breteuil, 75341 Paris Cedex 7, France. (Dist. in U.S. by: Michelin Travel Publications, P.O. Box 3305, Spartanburg SC 19001, Greenville, SC 29602-9001. TEL 800-423-0485)

914.404   FR
MICHELIN GREEN GUIDE SERIES: NORMANDY, VALLEY SEINE. (Editions in English, French) irreg., latest 1989. $14.95. Michelin, Services de Tourisme, 46 av. de Breteuil, 75346 Paris Cedex 7, France. (Dist. in U.S. by: Michelin Travel Publications, P.O. Box 19001, Greenville, SC 29602-9001. TEL 800-423-0485)

914.4   FR
MICHELIN GREEN GUIDE SERIES: PARIS. (Editions in English, French) irreg., latest 1990. $14.95 per no. Michelin, Services de Tourisme, 46 av. de Breteuil, 75341 Paris Cedex 7, France. (Dist. in U.S. by: Michelin Travel Publications, P.O. Box 19001, Greenville, SC 29602-9001. TEL 800-423-0485)

914.404   FR
MICHELIN GREEN GUIDE SERIES: PERIGORD-QUERCY. (Text in French) irreg., latest 1986. $14.95. Michelin, Services de Tourisme, 46 av. de Breteuil, 75346 Paris Cedex 7, France. (Dist. in U.S. by: Michelin Travel Publications, P.O. Box 19001, Greenville, SC 29602-9001. TEL 800-423-0485)

914.404   FR
MICHELIN GREEN GUIDE SERIES: POITOU-VENDEE-CHARENTES. (Text in French) irreg., latest 1987. $14.95. Michelin, Services de Tourisme, 46 av. de Breteuil, 75346 Paris Cedex 7, France. (Dist. in U.S. by: Michelin Travel Publications, P.O. Box 19001, Greenville, SC 29602-9001. TEL 800-423-0485)

914.69   FR
MICHELIN GREEN GUIDE SERIES: PORTUGAL. (Editions in English and Spanish) irreg., latest 1989. $14.95 per no. Michelin, Services de Tourisme, 46 av. de Breteuil, 75346 Paris Cedex 7, France. (Dist. in U.S. by: Michelin Travel Publications, P.O. Box 19001, Greenville, SC 29602-9001. TEL 800-423-0485)

914.404   FR
MICHELIN GREEN GUIDE SERIES: PROVENCE. (Editions in English, French) 1980. irreg., latest 1989. $14.95. Michelin, Services de Tourisme, 46 av. de Breteuil, 75346 Paris Cedex 7, France. (Dist. in U.S. by: Michelin Travel Publications, P.O. Box 19001, Greenville, SC 29602-9001. TEL 800-423-0485)

914.404   FR
MICHELIN GREEN GUIDE SERIES: PYRENEES AQUITAINE. irreg., latest 1989. $14.95. Michelin, Services de Tourisme, 46 av. de Breteuil, 75341 Paris Cedex 7, France. (Dist. in U.S. by: Michelin Travel Publications, P.O Box 19001, Greenville, SC 29602-9001. TEL 800-423-0485)
  Supersedes: Michelin Green Guide Series: Pyrenees.

914.404   FR
MICHELIN GREEN GUIDE SERIES: PYRENEES ROUSSILLON. irreg., latest 1989. $14.95. Michelin, Services de Tourisme, 46 av. de Breteuil, 75346 Paris Cedex 7, France. (Dist. in U.S. by: Michelin Travel Publications, P.O. Box 19001, Greenville, SC 29602-9001)

914.404   FR
MICHELIN GREEN GUIDE SERIES: ROME. (Text in English, French) irreg., latest 1985. $14.95. Michelin, Services de Tourisme, 46 de Breteuil, 75341 Paris Cedex 7, France. (Dist. in U.S. by: Michelin Travel Publications, P.O. Box 19001, Greenville, SC 29602-9001. TEL 800-423-0485)

914.104   FR
MICHELIN GREEN GUIDE SERIES: SCOTLAND. irreg., latest 1990. $14.95. Michelin, Services de Tourisme, 46 av. de Breteuil, 75341 Paris Cedex 7, France. (Dist. in U.S. by: Michelin Travel Publications, P.O. Box 19001, Greenville, SC 29602-9001. TEL 800-423-0485)

914.6   FR
MICHELIN GREEN GUIDE SERIES: SPAIN. (Editions in English, Spanish) irreg., latest 1987. $14.95 per no. Michelin, Services de Tourisme, 46 av. de Breteuil, 75341 Paris Cedex 7, France. (Dist. in U.S. by: Michelin Travel Publications, P.O. Box 19001, Greenville, SC 29602-9001. TEL 800-423-0485)

914.94   FR
MICHELIN GREEN GUIDE SERIES: SWITZERLAND. (Editions in English, French) irreg., latest 1988. $14.95 per no. Michelin, Services de Tourisme, 46 av. de Breteuil, 75346 Paris Cedex 7, France. (Dist. in U.S. by: Michelin Travel Publications, Box 19001, Greenville, SC 29602-9001. TEL 800-423-0485)

914.404   FR
MICHELIN GREEN GUIDE SERIES: VALLEE DU RHONE. irreg., latest 1989. $14.95. Michelin, Services de Tourisme, 46 av. de Breteuil, 75346 Paris Cedex 7, France. (Dist. in U.S. by: Michelin Travel Publications, P.O. Box 19001, Greenville, SC 29602-9001. TEL 800-423-0485)

917.4   FR
MICHELIN GREEN GUIDE SERIES: WASHINGTON, D.C.. irreg., latest 1991. $14.95. Michelin, Services de Tourisme, 46 av. de Breteuil, 75341 Paris Cedex 7, France. (Dist. in U.S. by: Michelin Travel Publications, P.O. Box 3305, Spartansburg, SC 29304-3305. TEL 800-423-0485)

910.2 914   FR   ISSN 0076-7743
MICHELIN RED GUIDE SERIES: BENELUX. a. $19.95. Michelin, Services de Tourisme, 46 av. de Breteuil, 75346 Paris Cedex 7, France. (Dist. in U.S. by: Michelin Travel Publications, P.O. Box 19001, Greenville, SC 29602-9001. TEL 800-423-0485)

910.2 914   FR
MICHELIN RED GUIDE SERIES: CAMPING, FRANCE. (Text in Dutch, English, French, German) a. $14.95. Michelin, Services de Tourisme, 46 av. de Breteuil, 75346 Paris Cedex 7, France. (Dist. in U.S. by: Michelin Travel Publications, Box 19001, Greenville, SC 29602-9001. TEL 800-423-0485)
  Formerly: Camping, Caravaning in France (ISSN 0076-7735)

910.2 914   FR
MICHELIN RED GUIDE SERIES: DEUTSCHLAND. (Text in German) a. $19.95. Michelin, Services de Tourisme, 46 av. de Breteuil, 75346 Paris Cedex 7, France. (Dist. in U.S. by: Michelin Travel Publications, Box 19001, Greenville, SC 29602-9001. TEL 800-423-0485)
  Formerly: Michelin Red Guide Series: Germany (ISSN 0076-7751)

910.2 914   FR   ISSN 0076-776X
MICHELIN RED GUIDE SERIES: ESPANA & PORTUGAL. a. $19.95. Michelin, Services de Tourisme, 46 av. de Breteuil, 75346 Paris Cedex 7, France. (Dist. in U.S. by: Michelin Travel Publications, P.O. Box 19001, Greenville, SC 29602-9001. TEL 800-423-0485)

914.04   FR
MICHELIN RED GUIDE SERIES: EUROPE, MAIN CITIES. (Text in English) 9. $19.95. Michelin, Services de Tourisme, 46. av. de Breteuil, 75346 Paris Cedex 7, France. (Dist. in U.S. by: Michelin Travel Publications, P.O. Box 19001, Greenville, SC 29602-9001. TEL 800-423-0485)

910.2 914   FR   ISSN 0076-7778
MICHELIN RED GUIDE SERIES: FRANCE. a. $19.95. Michelin, Services de Tourisme, 46 av. de Breteuil, 75346 Paris Cedex 7, France. (Dist. in U.S. by: Michelin Travel Publications, P.O. Box 19001, Greenville, SC 29602-9001. TEL 800-423-0485)

914.204   FR
MICHELIN RED GUIDE SERIES: GREAT BRITAIN AND IRELAND. a. $19.95. Michelin, Services de Tourisme, 46 av. de Breteuil, 75346 Paris Cedex 7, France. (Dist. in U.S. by: Michelin Travel Publications, P.O. Box 19001, Greenville, SC 29602-9001. TEL 800-423-0485) illus.

914.21   FR
MICHELIN RED GUIDE SERIES: GREATER LONDON. (Text in English) a. $6.95. Michelin, Services de Tourisme, 46 av. de Breteuil, 75346 Paris Cedex 7, France. (Dist. in U.S. by: Michelin Travel Publications, P.O. Box 19001, Greenville, SC 29602-9001. TEL 800-423-0485) illus.

TRAVEL AND TOURISM

914   FR   ISSN 0076-7786
MICHELIN RED GUIDE SERIES: ITALY. (Text in English, French, German, Italian) a. $19.95. Michelin, Services de Tourisme, 46 av. de Breteuil, 75341 Paris Cedex 7, France. (Dist. in U.S. by: Michelin Travel Publications, P.O. Box 3305, Spartanburg, SC 29304-3305. TEL 800-423-0485)

910.2 914   FR   ISSN 0076-7794
MICHELIN RED GUIDE SERIES: PARIS. (Text in French) a. $8.95. Michelin, Services de Tourisme, 46 av. de Breteuil, 75346 Paris Cedex 7, France. (Dist. in U.S. by: Michelin Travel Publications, P.O. Box 19001, Greenville, SC 29602-9001. TEL 800-423-0485)

MICHIGAN GOLFER'S MAP & GUIDE. see SPORTS AND GAMES — Ball Games

MICHIGAN GOLFER'S TRAVEL GUIDE. see SPORTS AND GAMES — Ball Games

796.7   US
MICHIGAN LIVING. 1918. m. $9. Automobile Club of Michigan, One Auto Club Dr., Dearborn, MI 48126. TEL 313-336-1211. Ed. Leonard R. Barnes. adv.; bk.rev.; illus.; circ. 1,013,880. **Indexed:** Mich.Mag.Ind.
    Former titles: Michigan Living - A A A Motor News; Motor News (ISSN 0027-1934)
    Description: Includes description and travel information.

917 796.5   US   ISSN 0734-2705
GV191.42.A84
MIDEASTERN CAMPBOOK. Cover title: R V and Tent Sites in Delaware, District of Columbia, Maryland, New Jersey, Pennsylvania, Virginia, West Virginia. a. membership. American Automobile Association, 1000 AAA Dr., Heathrow, FL 32746-5063. TEL 407-444-7962. FAX 407-444-7380. adv.; illus.; circ. 315,700.
    Formerly (until 1980): Mideastern Camping (ISSN 0147-7285)

MIDWEST MOTORIST. see TRANSPORTATION — Automobiles

910   US   ISSN 0361-1361
GV1024
MILEPOST; all-the-north-travel-guide. 1948. a. $16.95. Alaska Northwest Books (Subsidiary of: G T E Discovery Publications), Box 3007, Bothell, WA 98041. TEL 206-487-6100. FAX 206-486-7296. Ed. Kris Valencia. adv.; charts; illus.; stat.; circ. 80,000.
    Description: Travel guide on the Yukon and Northwest Territories, British Columbia and Alaska.

MILITARY LIVING'S R & R REPORT; the voice of the military traveler. see MILITARY

910.202 355   US
MILITARY TRAVEL GUIDE. m. American City Business Journals, Inc. (Arlington), 2000 14th St. N., Ste. 500, Arlington, VA 22201. TEL 703-875-2200.

910.09 353   US
MILITARY TRAVEL NEWS. 1970. bi-m. $6.95. Connie Gibson Wehrman Connor, 1530 Key Blvd., Ste. 230, Arlington, VA 22209-1534. TEL 703-281-9323. Ed. Ed Wojtas. adv.; circ. 7,500.
    Description: Contains travel bargains and space "A" information for the military traveler, both active duty and retired.

977   US
MINNESOTA EXPLORER; newspaper. 4/yr. free. Office of Tourism, 375 Jackson St., Ste. 250, St. Paul, MN 55101. circ. 500,000.
    Former titles: Explore Minnesota; Incorporating: Minnesota Fall Color Guide and Calendar of Events; Minnesota Spring-Summer Calendar of Events; Minnesota Winter Sports Guide and Calendar of Events.

MINNESOTA - WISCONSIN GOLFER'S TRAVEL GUIDE. see SPORTS AND GAMES — Ball Games

915   RU   ISSN 0868-9547
MIR PUTESHESTVII. 1929. m. 2.50 Rub. per issue (typically set in July). B. Kharitonʹevskii per. 14, 107078 Moscow, Russia. TEL 921-13-90. FAX 095-975-23-20. Ed. Boris V. Moskvin. illus.; circ. 40,000.
    Formerly (until 1991): Turist (ISSN 0041-4182)

917.704   US
MISSOURI WINE COUNTRY JOURNAL. 3/yr. Wein Press, Inc., 514 Wein St., Hermann, MO 65041-1088. TEL 314-486-5522. FAX 314-486-3126. Ed. Sandy Barks. circ. 10,000.

910.09   US
MOBIL MOTORIST. 1981. q. $2. (Mobil Auto Club) Signature Publications, 200 N. Martingale Rd., Schaumburg, IL 60173-2096. Ed. Bruce Gorman. adv.

910.202   GW
MONATSMAGAZIN. Cover title: Das aktuelle Monatsmagazin. m. DM.24. (Arbeitsgemeinschaft der Verkehrsvereine der Staedte Nuernberg, Fuerth, Erlangen und Schwabach) Omnia Druck und Verlag, Pretzfelderstr. 7-11, 8500 Nuernberg, Germany. TEL 0911-3409-100. Ed. Herbert Walchshoefer. adv. contact: Elvira Hirsing. circ. 30,000.

910.09 388.3   FR
MONDE DU CAMPING CAR. 10/yr. 175 F. (foreign 220 F.). Editions Lariviere, 15-17 Quai de l'Oise, 75166 Paris Cedex 19, France. TEL 1-40-34-22-07. FAX 1-40-35-84-41. TELEX 211 678 F.

910.09   US   ISSN 0899-6059
MONK. 1986. q. $10 (foreign $15). Michael Lane and Jim Crotty, Eds. & Pubs., 175 Fifth Ave., Ste. 2322, New York, NY 10010. TEL 212-465-3231. adv.; bk.rev.; circ. 29,000. (also avail. in microfilm)
    Description: Irreverent and humorous look at the odd and notorious in all corners of the U.S.A.

MONTHLY REPORT ON TOURISM - REPUBLIC OF CHINA/KUAN KUANG TZU LIAO. see TRAVEL AND TOURISM — Abstracting, Bibliographies, Statistics

910.09   IS   ISSN 0334-9748
MORESHET DERECH. 1982. 6/yr. IS.58. (Association of Tour Guides in Israel) Eretz Magazine, P.O. Box 565, Givatayim 53104, Israel. TEL 03-5712681. FAX 03-5714184. Ed. Yadin Roman. adv.; bk.rev.; circ. 4,000.

910.202   KO
MORNING CALM. 1977. m. Korean Air, c/o Choong Hoon Cho, Chairman, 41-3 Seosomun-dong, Chung-ku, Seoul, S. Korea. Ed. Choong Kun Cho. adv.; circ. 120,000.

916   MR   ISSN 0027-1160
MOROCCO TOURISM. (Editions in English, French and German) no.49, 1968. q. DH.20.($4.) National Moroccan Tourist Office, 22 rue d'Alger, Rabat 10013, Morocco. Ed. Girard Guibert. adv.; charts; illus.; stat.; circ. 35,000.

910.202   GR
MOTION/KINISI. (Text in English, Greek) 1969. a. free. Olympic Airways S.A., 120 Syngrou Ave., 2nd Fl., 117 41 Athens, Greece. TEL 923-0040. FAX 921-6080. TELEX 215823 OAGR. Ed. M. Gourmeli. adv.; circ. 500,000.
    Formerly: Your Air Companion.

MOTOR. see TRANSPORTATION — Automobiles

388.3   US   ISSN 0463-6457
MOTOR CLUB NEWS. vol.30, 1974. q. membership. Motor Club of America, c/o Marlene Timm, Ed., 484 Central Ave., Newark, NJ 07107. adv.; bk.rev.; charts; illus.; stat.; circ. 130,000 (controlled). (tabloid format; back issues avail.)

MOTORCARAVAN & MOTORHOME MONTHLY. see SPORTS AND GAMES — Outdoor Life

MOTORCYCLIST. see SPORTS AND GAMES — Bicycles And Motorcycles

MOTORING & LEISURE. see TRANSPORTATION — Automobiles

796.7   US   ISSN 0899-7578
MOTORIST (SEATTLE). 1915. m. $3. Automobile Club of Washington, 330 6th Ave. N., Seattle, WA 98109. TEL 206-448-5353. FAX 206-448-8627. Ed. Janet Ray. adv.; bk.rev.; illus.; circ. 250,000. (tabloid format)
    Formerly: Washington Motorist (ISSN 0043-0641)

388.3   US   ISSN 0027-2310
MOTORLAND. 1917. bi-m. $3. California State Automobile Association, 150 Van Ness Ave., San Francisco, CA 94101. TEL 415-565-2451. FAX 415-552-5825. Ed. Lynn L. Ferrin. adv.; charts; illus.; circ. 2,100,000.

915 796.93   AT
MOUNT BULLER NEWS. 1983. w. Mansfield Newspapers Pty. Ltd., 96 High St., Mansfield, Vic. 3722, Australia. TEL 057-752115. FAX 057-751580. Ed. Ray Robinson. adv.; bk.rev.; circ. 8,000.
    Formerly: Mount Buller Guide.

910.4   US
MOUNTAIN TIMES (KILLINGTON). 1971. w. $49. B R D Corp., Box 183, Killington, VT 05751. TEL 802-773-6970. FAX 802-773-4482. circ. 11,350 (controlled). (tabloid format; back issues avail.)
    Description: Central Vermont's news, arts and events; includes a resort and tourist guide.

917 796   US   ISSN 0027-2612
MOUNTAIN VISITOR. 1964. w. free. Mountain Press (Sevierville), Box 4810, Sevierville, TN 37864. TEL 615-428-0746. Ed. Lynn Perella. adv.; charts; illus.; maps; circ. 20,000. (tabloid format; also avail. in microfilm)

MOVING TO & AROUND ALBERTA. see REAL ESTATE

MOVING TO & AROUND MARITIMES & NEWFOUNDLAND. see REAL ESTATE

MOVING TO & AROUND SASKATCHEWAN. see REAL ESTATE

MOVING TO & AROUND SOUTHWESTERN ONTARIO. see REAL ESTATE

MOVING TO & AROUND TORONTO & AREA. see REAL ESTATE

MOVING TO & AROUND VANCOUVER & B.C.. see REAL ESTATE

MOVING TO & AROUND WINNIPEG & MANITOBA. see REAL ESTATE

MOVING TO OTTAWA - HULL. see REAL ESTATE

MPLS. - ST. PAUL MAGAZINE. see GENERAL INTEREST PERIODICALS — United States

910.202   KE
MSAFIRI.* 1980. q. (Kenya Airways) Transportation Displays International (Africa) Ltd., P.O. Box 47188, Nairobi, Kenya. Ed. Eric Hanna. adv.; circ. 30,000.

MUENCHEN & BAYERN VON HINTEN; das schwule Reisebuch. see HOMOSEXUALITY

MULTINATIONAL EXECUTIVE TRAVEL COMPANION. see BUSINESS AND ECONOMICS — International Commerce

915.3   QA
AL-MURSHID/GUIDE. (Text in Arabic, English) 1983. bi-m. Dallah Advertising Agency, P.O. Box 8545, Doha, Qatar. TEL 429920. FAX 447793. TELEX 4420. Ed. Rashid Muhammad al-Noaimi. circ. 15,000.
    Description: Information for business visitors and tourists.

059.9204   BA
AL-MUSAFIR AL-ARABI/ARAB TRAVELLER. 1984. bi-m. Falcon Publishing, P.O. Box 5028, Manama, Bahrain. TEL 253162. FAX 259694. TELEX 8917 FALPUB BN. Ed. Muhammad as-Said.

910.202 780   GW
MUSIKSTADT COLOGNE; Musik-Termine. 1983. s-a. Cologne Tourist Office, Unter Fettenhennen 19, 5000 Cologne 1, Germany. TEL 0221-221-3343. FAX 0221-221-3320. TELEX 8883-321-TOC-D. (Co-sponsor: Presse- und Informationsamt, Kulturamt) circ. 30,000.

N.A.D.A. MOBILE - MANUFACTURED HOUSING APPRAISAL GUIDE. (National Automobile Dealers Association) see BUILDING AND CONSTRUCTION

TRAVEL AND TOURISM

910.09 658 US
N C A CAVE TALK. 1972. bi-m. membership. National Caves Association, Rt. 9, Box 106, McMinnville, TN 37110. TEL 615-668-3925. Ed. Barbara Munson. circ. 115.
Description: For show cave industry personnel on tourism events and ideas.

910 US
N C I V NEWSLETTER. 1956. q. free. National Council for International Visitors, 1420 K St., N.W., Ste. 800, Washington, DC 20005-2401. TEL 202-842-1414. FAX 202-289-4625. TELEX 7660165 NCI UC. Ed. Claire P. Burke. bk.rev.; circ. 8,000.
Formerly (until 1979): C O S E R V Newsletter (National Council for Community Services to International Visitors) (ISSN 0547-5619)

791 NE ISSN 0027-6766
N K B. 1923. s-m. fl.35($10) Nederlandse Kermisbond, Oudegracht 186, Alkmaar, Netherlands. **Indexed:** Key to Econ.Sci.
Formerly: Komeet.

910.09 SI
N T U C LIFESTYLE. (Text in Chinese, English) 1987. bi-m. 1 New Industrial Rd., Times Centre, Singapore 1953, Singapore. TEL 2848844. FAX 2881186. TELEX 25713. Ed. Michael Cheah. circ. 150,000.
Description: Covers travel and leisure.

919.304 NZ
N Z T COMMITTEE - DEPARTMENTAL REPORT SERIES. 1982. irreg., latest 1989. price varies. Tourism Department, Research Services, P.O. Box 95, Wellington, New Zealand. TEL 04-4728-860. FAX 04-4781-736. stat.
Formerly: N Z T P Committee - Departmental Report Series (ISSN 0112-9821)

910.4 NZ ISSN 0112-9724
N Z T P OVERSEAS MARKET RESEARCH SERIES. 1980. irreg., latest 1988. price varies. Tourist and Publicity Department, Market Stategies Division, P.O. Box 95, Wellington, New Zealand. TEL 04-728-860. TELEX 3941. (U.S. addr.: Ste. 530, 630 Fifth Ave., New York, NY 10111. TEL 212-586-0060) stat.

910.09 SA
NANA NO PASUPORTO/SOUTHERN AFRICA PASSPORT. (Text in Japanese; occasionally in English) 1982. a. R.1($1.92) Media Link (Pty.) Ltd., 55 Minors St., Yeoville, Johannesburg, South Africa. Ed. Godfrey Sheldon Busscham. adv.; circ. 8,000. (back issues avail.)

917.604 US
NASHVILLE TRAVEL GUIDE. 1986. a. $3.50. Tom Jackson & Associates, Inc., 1210 Eighth Ave., S., Nashville, TN 37203. TEL 615-242-7747. FAX 615-259-2042. adv.; circ. 45,000.
Description: Lists regional cultural and recreational attractions, annual events, lodging, dining, nightlife, shopping, leisure opportunities, convention services and tours.

917.6 US
NASHVILLE VISITOR. 1974. a. $3.95. Southeast Magazines, Inc., 545 Mainstream Dr., Ste. 101, Nashville, TN 37228. TEL 615-242-6992. FAX 615-242-2248. (Subscr. to: Box 24649, Nashville, TN 37202-4649) Ed. Steve Rogers. circ. 19,000.

910.202 US
NASHVILLE VISITOR'S GUIDE. 1973. a. $2.95. Southeast Magazines, Inc., 545 Mainstream Dr., Ste. 101, Nashville, TN 37228. TEL 615-242-6992. FAX 615-242-2248. (Subscr. to: Box 24649, Nashville, TN 37202-4649) Ed. Steve Rogers. circ. 38,000.

917 BF
NASSAU CABLE BEACH AND PARADISE ISLAND. TOURIST NEWS. 1962. q. $6. (Nassau Cable Beach and Paradise Island Promotion Board) Star Publishers Ltd., Box 4855, Nassau, Bahamas. TEL 809-322-4527. Ed. Paul Bower. adv.; illus.; circ. 52,000. (tabloid format)
Former titles: Nassau and Paradise Island. Tourist News; (until 1971): Bahamas Weekly and Nassau Tourist News (ISSN 0005-3961); (until 1968): Bahamas Weekly.

NATIONAL DIRECTORY OF FREE TOURIST ATTRACTIONS. see BUSINESS AND ECONOMICS — Trade And Industrial Directories

910.202 US ISSN 0747-0932
G1
NATIONAL GEOGRAPHIC TRAVELER. 1984. bi-m. $17.95. National Geographic Society, 17th & M Sts., N.W., Washington, DC 20036. TEL 202-857-7000. Ed. Richard Busch. adv.; maps; circ. 700,000. **Indexed:** Access (1983-).
Description: Offers articles on vacation places in the US and Canada, plus popular spots abroad. Includes columns on photography, weekend destinations, and learning vacations, as well as a regional calendar of events in the US, Canada, Mexico, and the Caribbean.

910.09 388.3 US ISSN 0279-3083
NATIONAL MOTORIST. 1924. bi-m. membership. National Automobile Club, 188 The Embarcadero, San Francisco, CA 94105. TEL 415-777-4000. FAX 415-882-2141. Ed. Jane M. Offers. adv.; bk.rev.; circ. 125,000.
Description: Covers domestic and international travel and transportation plus automotive topics.

910.09 US ISSN 0737-2620
G155.U6
NATIONAL TRAVEL SURVEY. 1979. q. $100 per season. U S Travel Data Center, Two Lafayette Ctr., 1133 21st St., N.W., Washington, DC 20036. TEL 202-293-1040. (reprint service avail. from CIS) **Indexed:** SRI.
Description: Travel information obtained from monthly telephone interviews.

NATIONWIDE OVERNIGHT STABLING DIRECTORY & EQUESTRIAN VACATION GUIDE. see SPORTS AND GAMES — Horses And Horsemanship

910.2 SZ ISSN 0028-0925
NATURFREUND/AMI DE LA NATURE. (Text in French and German) 1962. bi-m. 30 Fr. Naturfreunde Schweiz - Federation Suisse des Amis de la Nature, Muehlemattstr. 31, CH-3000 Bern 14, Switzerland. TEL 031-456004. adv.; bk.rev.; abstr.; charts; illus.; stat.

910.202 BE
NATURISM; world handbook - guide mondiale - f.k.k. weltfuerer. (Text in Dutch, English, French, German) 1952. biennial. fl.26.90($14) (International Naturist Federation) Kluwer, N.V., Box 007, Desguinlei 7, 2000 Antwerp, Belgium. (Subscr. to: I N F, St. Hubertusstr. 3, B-2600 Berchem - Antwerp, Belgium) Ed. Geert Bovenhuis. adv.; charts; illus.; circ. 30,000.
Description: Lists vacation centers and club grounds as well as activies, clubs and guides for the naturist.

915.4 320 II
NAVE PARVA. (Text in English, Konkani or Marathi) 1965. q. Rs.10. Department of Information and Publicity, Panaji, Goa, India. Ed. N. Rajasekhar. bk.rev.; illus.; circ. 2,500.
Formerly: New Era (ISSN 0548-4537)

910.202 US
NETWORK BED & BREAKFAST DIRECTORY. 1985. a. $29.95. Kib Communications, Box 1676, Humble, TX 77396-1676. TEL 713-590-1139. Ed. Veal Johnson. adv.; circ. 200.
Former titles: Network Bed and Breakfast Registry; Bare Texan.
Description: Travel accommodations for the nudist.

917 US ISSN 0199-1248
F836
NEVADA. 1936. 6/yr. $13.50. State of Nevada, 1800 Hwy. 50 E., Ste. 200, Carson City, NV 89710. FAX 702-687-6159. Ed. Dave Moore. adv.; bk.rev.; illus.; circ. 110,000. (also avail. in microform from UMI; reprint service avail. from UMI) **Indexed:** Access (1975-), Amer.Hist.& Life, Hist.Abstr.
Formerly: Nevada Highways and Parks (ISSN 0028-405X)

917.904 US
NEVADA EVENTS. bi-m. 1800 Hwy. 50 E., No. 200, Carson City, NV 89710. TEL 702-687-5416. FAX 702-687-5416. Ed. Kirk Whisler. adv.; circ. 220,000.

917.404 US ISSN 0893-1089
NEW ENGLAND GETAWAYS. 1985. m. $39. New England Publishing Group, Inc., 215 Newbury St., Peabody, MA 01960. TEL 617-535-4186. Ed. Jane Lindley. adv.; bk.rev.; circ. 20,000.
Description: Where to go and what to do in New England each month. Complete calendar of events listed by state and type of events. Includes inn and hotel reviews, and the history of New England.

910 US
NEW JERSEY GOODLIFE. 1983. 12/yr. $24. Publishing Management Group, Inc., 1711 S. Second St., Piscataway, NJ 08854. TEL 201-753-6100. Ed. Rnen Belak Timpone. adv.; circ. 80,000.

917 US ISSN 0028-6249
F791
NEW MEXICO MAGAZINE. 1923. m. $19.95. Tourism Department, 1100 St. Francis Dr., Santa Fe, NM 87503. TEL 505-827-6217. Ed. Emily Drabanski. adv.; bk.rev.; illus.; circ. 95,000. (also avail. in microform from NYT) **Indexed:** Access (1975-), Chic.Per.Ind.

NEW MEXICO SKIERS' GUIDE. see SPORTS AND GAMES — Outdoor Life

910.2 915.2 JA ISSN 0077-8591
DS805.2
NEW OFFICIAL GUIDE: JAPAN. (Text in English) 1952. irreg., 1991. 12000 Yen. (Japan National Tourist Organization) Japan Travel Bureau Inc., Publishing Division, Shibuya Nomura Bldg., 7F, 1-10-8, Dogenzaka, Shibuya-ku, Tokyo 150, Japan. TEL 03-3477-9529. FAX 03-3477-9587. index.
Formerly: Japan: the Official Guide.

910.4 US ISSN 0897-8174
F379.N5
NEW ORLEANS MAGAZINE. 1966. m. $16.95. New Orleans Publishing Group, 111 Veterans Blvd., Ste. 1810, Metairie, LA 70005. TEL 504-831-3731. FAX 504-837-2258. circ. 33,275. **Indexed:** Hlth.Ind., Mag.Ind.
Former titles (until 1987): New Orleans (ISSN 0897-8166); (until 1987): New Orleans Magazine (ISSN 0894-4555); (until 1981): New Orleans (ISSN 0192-804X); (until 1975): Metro New Orleans (ISSN 0300-7251)
Description: Explores life in New Orleans. Contains features on family dynasties, local politics, traditions and social trends.

917.53 US ISSN 0097-8213
F192.3
NEW SETTLER'S GUIDE FOR WASHINGTON, D.C. AND COMMUNITIES IN NEARBY MARYLAND AND VIRGINIA. 1972. a. $6.75. Robco, Inc., 8824 Tuckerman Lane, Potomac, MD 20854. TEL 301-299-7507. Ed. Robert B. Minogue. adv.; illus.; circ. 15,000.
Description: Contains comprehensive information on relocating to metropolitan Washington, including community profiles, a real estate agency directory, public and private school and day care listings, and information for newcomers on shopping, recreation, dining, and cultural attractions in the region.

917.404 US
NEW YORK (YEAR). a. $10. Harper Collins Publishers, Birnbaum Travel Guides, 10 E. 53rd St., New York, NY 10022-5299. TEL 212-207-7000. illus.; index.

917 US ISSN 0028-7288
NEW YORK CONVENTION & VISITORS BUREAU. QUARTERLY CALENDAR OF EVENTS. 1947. 4/yr. free. New York Convention & Visitors Bureau, Inc., 2 Columbus Circle, New York, NY 10019. Ed. Barbara Rugowski. circ. 250,000.

900 US
NEW YORK JOURNAL JAPAN.* 1973. m. $10. c/o Waldorf Astoria, Ste. 1852, 301 Park Ave., New York, NY 10022-6897. Ed. J. Benjamin. adv.; bk.rev.; circ. 201,000.

NEW YORK MOTORIST. see TRANSPORTATION — Automobiles

974 US
NEW YORK STATE FAIR MAGAZINE. 1955. a. $2. New York State Fair, State Fairgrounds, Syracuse, NY 13209. FAX 518-487-9260. Ed. Joseph J. LaGuardia. adv.; circ. 32,500.
Formerly: New York State FairGround.

TRAVEL AND TOURISM

917.4   US
NEW YORK'S NIGHTLIFE.* 1979. m. $15. M.J.C. Publishers, Inc., 770 Grand Blvd. K, Ste. 10, Deer Park, NY 11729-5725. TEL 516-242-7722. Ed. Bill Ervolini. adv.; bk.rev.; circ. 175,062.
    Former titles: New York's and Long Island's Nightlife; Long Island's Nightlife (ISSN 0744-7590)

919.304   NZ
NEW ZEALAND TOURISM DEPARTMENT. DOMESTIC RESEARCH SERIES. 1981. irreg., latest 1991. price varies. Tourism Department, Research Services, P.O. Box 95, Wellington, New Zealand. TEL 04-4728-860. FAX 04-4781-736.
    Formerly: N Z T P Domestic Research Series (ISSN 0112-9767)

NEW ZEALAND TOURISM DEPARTMENT. ECONOMIC RESEARCH SERIES. see *BUSINESS AND ECONOMICS*

919.304   NZ
NEW ZEALAND TOURISM DEPARTMENT. IMPLICATIONS OF TOURISM GROWTH SERIES. 1988. irreg., latest 1989. price varies. Tourism Department, Research Services, P.O. Box 95, Wellington, New Zealand. TEL 04-4728-860. FAX 04-4781-736.
    Formerly: N Z T P Implications of Tourism Growth Series (ISSN 0114-0353)

919.304   NZ
NEW ZEALAND TOURISM DEPARTMENT. REGIONAL RESEARCH SERIES. 1988. irreg., latest 1991. price varies. Tourism Department, Research Services, P.O. Box 95, Wellington, New Zealand. TEL 04-4728-860. FAX 04-4781-736.
    Formerly: N Z T P Regional Research Series (ISSN 0112-9783)

NEW ZEALAND TOURISM DEPARTMENT. SOCIAL RESEARCH SERIES. see *SOCIOLOGY*

919.304   NZ
NEW ZEALAND TOURISM DEPARTMENT. TOURISM INCENTIVES SERIES. 1982. irreg., latest 1988. price varies. Tourism Department, Research Services, P.O. Box 95, Wellington, New Zealand. TEL 04-4728-860. FAX 04-4781-736. TELEX 3941.
    Formerly: N Z T P Tourism Incentives Series (ISSN 0112-9686)

NEWCOMER; an introduction to life in Belgium. see *GENERAL INTEREST PERIODICALS — Belgium*

910.202   US
NEWPORT DINING GUIDE. 1974. q. free. Newport This Week, Box 159, Newport, RI 02840-0002. FAX 401-846-4974.

NIAGARA PARKS COMMISSION. ANNUAL REPORT. see *CONSERVATION*

916.69   NR
NIGERIA TOURIST GUIDE/GUIDE DU TOURISME NIGERIEN. Variant title: National Tourist Guide of Nigeria. 1969. irreg. Nigerian Tourist Board, 47 Marina, P.O. Box 2944, Lagos, Nigeria. adv.; illus.

NIKKEI EVENTS. see *MEETINGS AND CONGRESSES*

658   JA
NIKKEI RESORT. (Text in Japanese) 1989. fortn. 25000 Yen. Nikkei Business Publications, Inc., 3-3-23, Misakicho, Chiyoda-ku, Tokyo 101, Japan. TEL 03-5210-8502. FAX 03-5210-8119. Junichi Ogino. adv.; circ. 15,588.
    Description: Provides data and behind-the-scenes coverage of Japan's fast-growing resort industry. Covers resort construction, development, and management.

NIX WIE WEG; Mitfahrzentralen in Deutschland and aller Welt. see *TRANSPORTATION*

NORDIC NETWORK. see *SPORTS AND GAMES — Outdoor Life*

917.5   US   ISSN 0546-3432
F306
NORMAN FORD'S FLORIDA. biennial. $4.95. Harian Publications, One Vernon Ave., Floral Park, NY 11001. TEL 516-437-3440. Ed. Norman D. Ford. charts; illus.

917.04   US
NORTH AMERICAN GUIDE TO NUDE RECREATION. 1966. a. $21.95. American Sunbathing Association, 1703 N. Main St., Kissimmee, FL 34744. TEL 800-879-6833. FAX 407-933-7577. Eds. Arne Eriksen, Julie Bagby. illus.; circ. 30,000.
    Formerly: Nudist Park Guide.

917 796.5   US   ISSN 0147-8613
GV198.65.N67
NORTH CENTRAL CAMPBOOK. Cover title: R V and Tent Sites in Iowa, Minnesota, Nebraska, North Dakota, South Dakota. a. membership. American Automobile Association, 1000 AAA Dr., Heathrow, FL 32746-5063. TEL 407-444-7962. FAX 407-444-7380. adv.; illus.; circ. 268,5,500.
    Formerly (until 1980): North Central Camping.

974 910.09   US   ISSN 8756-9256
NORTH GEORGIA JOURNAL. 1984. 4/yr. $15. Legacy Communications, Inc., 110 Hunters Mill, Woodstock, GA 30188. TEL 404-928-7739. Ed. Olin Jackson. adv.; bk.rev.; circ. 10,000. (back issues avail.)
    Description: Covers travel opportunities, history, lifestyles and real estate in North Georgia.

647.94   US   ISSN 0732-7315
GV191.42.N74
NORTHEASTERN CAMPBOOK; including location maps. Cover title: R V and Tent Sites in Connecticut, Maine, Massachusetts, New Hampshire, New York, Rhode Island, Vermont. a. American Automobile Association, 1000 AAA Dr., Heathrow, FL 32746-5063. TEL 407-444-7962. FAX 407-444-7380. adv.; illus.; circ. 292,197.
    Former titles (until 1980): Northeastern Camping (ISSN 0196-6456); Northeastern Camping and Trailering.

910.202   US   ISSN 1052-6722
F852.3
NORTHWEST MILEPOSTS. 1986. biennial. $14.95. Alaska Northwest Books (Subsidiary of: G T E Discovery Publications), Box 3007, Bothell, WA 98041. TEL 206-487-6100. FAX 206-486-7296. Ed. Kris Valencia. adv.; charts; illus.; stat.; circ. 30,000.
    Description: Mile-by-mile travel guide to Idaho, Oregon, Washington, western Montana and southwestern Canada.

910.202   US   ISSN 0892-8363
NORTHWEST PALATE; wine, food, & lifestyles of the Pacific Northwest. 1983. bi-m. $21. Box 10860, Portland, OR 97210. TEL 503-228-4897. Ed. Judy Peterson-Nedry. adv.; bk.rev.; circ. 12,000.
    Formerly (until 1987): Oregon Wine Review (ISSN 0736-8496)
    Description: Includes wine reviews in the form of rated tasting notes of new releases, food and wine feature articles, recipes, restaurant and lodging information, wine-maker and chef profiles.

910.202   US
▼**NORTHWEST TRAVEL.** 1991. bi-m. $12.95. Spooner Industries, Box 18000, Florence, OR 97439. TEL 503-997-8401. Ed. Rob Spooner. illus.; circ. 25,000.
    Description: For active as well as armchair travelers; contains travel tips on Washington, Oregon and Idaho.

917.8   US
NORTHWESTERN CAMPBOOK; including location maps. Cover title: R V and Tent Sites in Idaho, Montana, Oregon, Washington, Wyoming. a. membership. American Automobile Association, 1000 AAA Dr., Heathrow, FL 32746-5063. TEL 407-444-7962. FAX 407-444-7380. adv.; illus.; circ. 380,396.
    Former titles (until 1980): Northwestern Camping (ISSN 0095-4411); Northwestern Camping and Trailering.

914   FR   ISSN 0048-0843
NOS MAISONS FAMILIALES DE VACANCES. 1954. q. 27.50 F. Federation des Maisons Familiales de Vacances, 28 place St-Georges, 75442 Paris 9, France. circ. controlled.

NOUVELLE FIPREGAZETTE. see *FOOD AND FOOD INDUSTRIES*

914.3   GW
NUERNBERG HEUTE. 1964. s-a. free. Stadt Nuernberg, Presse- und Informationsamt, Rathausplatz 2, 8500 Nuernberg 1, Germany. TEL 0911-2312252. FAX 0911-2313660. Ed. Norbert Schuergers. adv.; bk.rev.; charts; illus.; circ. 35,000.
    Description: News about the city of Nuremberg.

917   US   ISSN 1053-0002
TX907   CODEN: OBTEE2
O A G BUSINESS TRAVEL PLANNER. NORTH AMERICAN EDITION. 1958. q. $105. Official Airline Guides, Inc., 2000 Clearwater Dr., Oak Brook, IL 60521. TEL 708-574-6000. FAX 708-574-6667. TELEX 2101421. adv.; circ. 66,000.
    Former titles: O A G Travel Planner Hotel and Motel Guide Redbook. North American Edition (ISSN 0894-1726); O A G Travel Planner and Hotel-Motel Guide. North American Edition (ISSN 0193-3299); Supersedes in part: O A G Travel Planner and Hotel-Motel Guide (ISSN 0090-0869); Which was formerly: O A G Travel Planner (ISSN 0048-1246)
    Description: Reference guide for business travelers and those planning travel within North America. Includes listings for over 25,000 hotels, city data and maps, ground and air transportation information, with basic information for travel to Central and South America.

914.04   US   ISSN 0894-1718
TX907.5.E85   CODEN: OTHEEY
O A G TRAVEL PLANNER HOTEL & MOTEL REDBOOK. EUROPEAN EDITION. 1978. q. $105. Official Airline Guides, Inc., 2000 Clearwater Dr., Oak Brook, IL 60521. TEL 708-574-6000. FAX 708-574-6667. TELEX 210144. adv.; circ. 21,100.
    Formerly: O A G Travel Planner and Hotel-Motel Guide. European Edition (ISSN 0162-735X)
    Description: Reference guide for those planning travel within Europe. Includes hotel listings, city data and maps, ground and air transportation information, basic travel information, with additional information for travel to the Middle East and Africa.

910   US   ISSN 0894-1734
TX907.5.P33   CODEN: OPAEE5
O A G TRAVEL PLANNER HOTEL & MOTEL REDBOOK. PACIFIC ASIA EDITION. 1985. q. $105. Official Airline Guides, Inc., 2000 Clearwater Dr., Oak Brook, IL 60521. TEL 708-574-6000. FAX 708-574-6667. TELEX 210144. adv.; circ. 13,700.
    Formerly: O A G Travel Planner and Hotel-Motel Guide. Pacific Area Edition (ISSN 8750-8672); Supersedes (1957-1985): Pacific Hotel Directory and Travel Guide (ISSN 0479-0790)
    Description: Reference guide for those planning travel within the Pacific Asia area. Includes hotel listings, city data, ground and air transportation information, country travel "basics," maps and airport diagrams.

910 387   US   ISSN 0097-8779
HE568
O A G WORLDWIDE CRUISE & SHIPLINE GUIDE. 1975. 6/yr. $97. Official Airline Guides, Inc., 2000 Clearwater Dr., Oak Brook, IL 60521. TEL 708-574-6000. FAX 708-574-6667. TELEX 210144. circ. 9,000.
    Description: Includes individual cruise listings, organized by geographical area and departure date, as well as worldwide ferry schedules, which are displayed on a to-from basis. Also features listings of cruise and ferry operations, port diagrams, and ship profiles.

382   FR
O E C D. TOURISM COMMITTEE. TOURISM POLICY AND INTERNATIONAL TOURISM IN O E C D MEMBER COUNTRIES. a. price varies. Organization for Economic Cooperation and Development, 2 rue Andre-Pascal, 75775 Paris Cedex 16, France. TEL 45-24-82-00. FAX 45-24-85-00. (Dist. in U.S. by: O.E.C.D. Publications and Information Center, 2001 L St., N.W., Ste. 700, Washington D.C. 20036-4910. TEL 202-785-6323) (also avail. in microfiche from OEC; back issues avail.) **Indexed:** IIS.
    Formerly: International Tourism Policy in O E C D Member Countries.

TRAVEL AND TOURISM 4781

910.202   US
OAHU DRIVE GUIDE. 1974. 3/yr. free. Honolulu Publishing Company, Ltd., 36 Merchant St., Honolulu, HI 96813. TEL 808-524-7400. FAX 808-531-2306. Ed. Brett Uprichard.
   Description: For visitors; includes road maps of the island, restaurant guide, places of interest, travel information, and history.

OCEAN & CRUISE NEWS. see *TRANSPORTATION — Ships And Shipping*

917.504   US
OCEANA MAGAZINE. 1978. w. free. Independent Publishers Group, Inc., Box 1943, Ocean City, MD 21842. TEL 302-539-6313. FAX 302-539-6815. Ed. Elizabeth Brownell. adv. (tabloid format; back issues avail.)
   Description: Contains general information on resorts, beaches, tourism, and sports.

ODYSSEUS; an accommodations & travel guide for the gay community, USA & international. see *HOMOSEXUALITY*

OESTERREICHISCHE GASTGEWERBE- UND HOTELZEITUNG. see *HOTELS AND RESTAURANTS*

910.2   AU   ISSN 0048-1483
OESTERREICHISCHE TOURISTENZEITUNG. 1888. m. membership. Oesterreichischer Touristenklub, Baeckerstr. 16, A-1010 Vienna, Austria. Ed. Guenther J. Wolf. bk.rev.; film rev.; illus.; circ. 20,000.

910.2   US   ISSN 1043-1195
TX907.2
OFFICIAL GUIDE TO AMERICAN HISTORIC INNS; 6,000 bed & breakfast and country inns. 1987. a. $14.95. Association of American Historic Inns, Box 336, Dana Point, CA 92629. TEL 800-397-INNS. FAX 714-499-4022. Eds. Timothy J. Sakach, Deborah Edwards Sakach. circ. 2,000.
   Former titles: Official Guide to American Historic Bed and Breakfast Inns and Guesthouses; (until 1988): Official Guide to American Bed and Breakfast Inns and Guesthouses.
   Description: Offers travellers a complete listing of historic inns, bed and breakfasts, and guesthouses built prior to 1940.

OFFICIAL HOTEL GUIDE. see *HOTELS AND RESTAURANTS*

OFFICIAL RAILWAY GUIDE. NORTH AMERICAN TRAVEL EDITION. see *TRANSPORTATION — Railroads*

OFFICIAL STEAMSHIP GUIDE. see *TRANSPORTATION — Ships And Shipping*

917.504   US
OFFICIAL VISITORS GUIDE TO CENTRAL FLORIDA. 1985. s-a. free. Orlando - Orange County Convention and Visitors Bureau, Inc., 7208 Sandlake Rd., Ste. 300, Orlando, FL 32819. TEL 407-363-5800. adv.; circ. 1,000,000 (controlled).
   Description: Lists accommodations, attractions, restaurants and other categories.

914   FR   ISSN 0030-0500
OFFICIEL DES SPECTACLES; cette semaine. 1946. w. 480 F. 100 Champs-Elysees, 75008 Paris, France. FAX 45-61-04-00. Ed. J. P. Richemond. adv.; film rev.; play rev.; illus.; circ. 185,000.
   Description: Paris entertainment guide.

OHIO GOLFER'S TRAVEL GUIDE. see *SPORTS AND GAMES — Ball Games*

796.7   US   ISSN 0030-0985
OHIO MOTORIST. 1909. m. $1.50. American Automobile Association, Ohio Motorists Association, Box 6150, Cleveland, OH 44101. TEL 216-361-6216. Ed. F. Jerome Turk. adv.; bk.rev.; illus.; circ. 385,000. (tabloid format)

910   UK
OLEANDER TRAVEL BOOKS SERIES. a. Oleander Press, 17 Stansgate Ave., Cambridge CB2 2QZ, England. (U.S. address: 80 Eighth Ave., Ste. 303, New York, NY 10011)

647.94   AT
ON THE GO; YHA's budget travel magazine. 1963. q. membership. Youth Hostels Association of Queensland, G.P.O. Box 1128, Brisbane, Qld. 4001, Australia. TEL 07-236-1680. FAX 07-236-1702. Ed. Helen Wicks. adv.; circ. 10,000. (back issues avail.)
   Formely: Queensland Hosteller (ISSN 0818-4380)

ONTARIO BED & BREAKFAST GUIDE. see *HOTELS AND RESTAURANTS*

917.1   CN
ONTARIO MOTOR COACH ASSOCIATION RESOURCES. 1986. a. Naylor Communications Ltd., 920 Yonge St., 6th fl., Toronto, Ont. M4W 3C7, Canada. TEL 416-961-1028. FAX 416-924-4408. adv.

917.1   CN
ONTARIO MOTOR COACH ASSOCIATION YEARBOOK. 1981. a. Naylor Communications Ltd., 920 Yonge St., 6th fl., Toronto, Ont. M4W 3C7, Canada. TEL 416-961-1028. FAX 416-924-4408. Ed. John Howarth. adv.

910.202   CN   ISSN 0707-1442
ONTARIO TOURISM NEWS. 1978. q. Ministry of Tourism and Recreation, 77 Bloor St. W., 7th Fl., Toronto, Ont. M7A 2R9, Canada. TEL 416-965-7680.

917.404   US   ISSN 0734-4066
F1.3
ORIGINAL NEW ENGLAND GUIDE.* 1957. a. $3.95. New England Lifestyle Publications, Inc., Box 1059, Barnstable, MA 02630-0997. Ed. Catherine Smith. adv.; circ. 200,000.
   Supersedes: New England Guide (ISSN 0077-8222)

917.5   US   ISSN 0279-1323
ORLANDO MAGAZINE. 1946. m. $24.95. Orlando Media Affiliates (Subsidiary of: Micromedia Affiliates), 341 Maitland Ave., Maitland, FL 32751. TEL 407-539-3939. FAX 407-539-0533. (Subscr. to: Box 2207, Orlando, FL 32802. TEL 800-669-1002) Ed. Randy Noles. adv.; illus.; tr.lit.; circ. 36,799.
   Incorporates: Central Florida Magazine; (1986-1988): Orbus (ISSN 0890-6432); Which was formerly: Orlando-Land (ISSN 0145-6431)

910.09 296   US
OSCAR ISRAELOWITZ'S GUIDE TO JEWISH NEW YORK CITY. 1987. a. $9.95. Oscar Israelowitz, Ed. & Pub., Box 228, Brooklyn, NY 11229. TEL 718-951-7072. adv.; bibl.; circ. 5,000.

914   NO
OSLO CITY GUIDE. m. Per Sletholt og Co., Boks 57, Tveita, Oslo 6, Norway. adv.

OUR WORLD; the international gay travel magazine. see *HOMOSEXUALITY*

917.504   US
OUT AND ABOUT SMITH MOUNTAIN LAKE. 1989. 3/yr. Rte. 1, Box 437, Moneta, VA 24121. TEL 703-297-6444. Eds. Anne Kidd, Barbie White. adv.; circ. 40,000 (controlled).
   Description: Provides information on accommodations, restaurant locations and shopping centers.

918   US   ISSN 0899-1413
OUT WEST. 1988. q. $8. Out West Publishing (Grass Valley), 10522 Brunswick Rd., Grass Valley, CA 95945. TEL 916-477-9378. Ed. Chuck Woodbury. bk.rev.; circ. 11,000. (tabloid format; back issues avail.)
   Description: Covers travel and the "back roads" of Americas West, includes reports on the various findings.

OUTDOOR; das andere Reisemagazin. see *SPORTS AND GAMES — Outdoor Life*

OUTDOOR ACTION. see *SPORTS AND GAMES — Outdoor Life*

OUTDOOR & TRAVEL PHOTOGRAPHY. see *PHOTOGRAPHY*

OUTDOOR CANADA. see *SPORTS AND GAMES — Outdoor Life*

910.09   US
OUTLOOK FOR TRAVEL AND TOURISM. a. $125 per issue. U S Travel Data Center, Two Lafayette Ctr., 1133 21st St., N.W., Washington, DC 20036. TEL 202-293-1040. charts. (reprint service avail. from CIS)
   Formerly: Travel Outlook Forum Proceedings (ISSN 0160-4651)
   Description: Verbatim account of travel industry experts forecasts on economic developments, demographic lifestyle changes, market segmentation, and other issues affecting U.S. travel and tourism.

OVER THE RAINBOW. see *EDUCATION — Special Education And Rehabilitation*

910.2   UK   ISSN 0030-7424
OVERSEAS. 1915. q. membership. Royal Over-Seas League, Over-Seas House, Park Place, St. James's St., London SW1A 1LP, England. TEL 071-408-0214. FAX 071-499-6738. TELEX 268995 ROSL G. Ed. Pat Treasure. adv.; illus.; circ. 25,000. (tabloid format)

910.09 327   US   ISSN 0882-8938
OVERSEAS LIVING.* 1985. bi-m. $36. International Orientation Service, Box 1611, Cullowhee, NC 28723-1611. Ed. Adele Landsman. adv.; bk.rev. (back issues avail.)
   Description: Covers topics and issues of concern to expatriate residents in business and the military, as well as missionaries and academic professionals.

OWEN'S AFRICA BUSINESS DIRECTORY. see *BUSINESS AND ECONOMICS — International Commerce*

917   US   ISSN 0030-7769
F417.09
OZARKS MOUNTAINEER; the Ozarkswide bi-monthly periodical. 1952. bi-m. $9.50. HCR 3, Box 868, Kirbyville, MO 65679. TEL 417-546-5390. Ed. Clay Anderson. adv.; bk.rev.; charts; illus.; tr.lit.; circ. 33,000.

919   IO   ISSN 0048-2625
P A T A INDONESIA.* 1971. bi-m. free. Pacific Area Travel Association, Indonesia Chapter, Jalan Kramat Raya 81, Jakarta, Indonesia. Ed. J.W. Adnan. adv.; charts; illus.

PACIFIC BOATING ALMANAC. NORTHERN CALIFORNIA & NEVADA. see *SPORTS AND GAMES — Boats And Boating*

PACIFIC BOATING ALMANAC. OREGON, WASHINGTON, BRITISH COLUMBIA & SOUTHEASTERN ALASKA. see *SPORTS AND GAMES — Boats And Boating*

PACIFIC BOATING ALMANAC. SOUTHERN CALIFORNIA, ARIZONA, BAJA. see *SPORTS AND GAMES — Boats And Boating*

917.904   US
PACIFIC COMPANION. (Text in Japanese) 1983. q. Japan Pacific Publications, Inc., 419 Occidental Ave., Ste. 509, Seattle, WA 98104. TEL 206-622-7443. FAX 206-621-1786. Ed. Junko Yajima. adv.; circ. 15,000.
   Description: Provides local information and events for tourists and visitors.

917   CN   ISSN 0030-8692
PACIFIC HOSTELLER. 1964. q. membership. Canadian Hostelling Association, B.C. Region, 1515 Discovery St., Vancouver, B.C. V6R 4K5, Canada. TEL 604-224-7177. FAX 604-224-4852. adv.; bk.rev.; illus.; circ. 10,000 (controlled).

919   FJ   ISSN 0030-8722
DU1
PACIFIC ISLANDS MONTHLY. 1930. m. $45. Fiji Times Ltd., P.O. Box 1167, Suva, Fiji. TEL 30-32-44. FAX 30-38-09. Ed. Jale Moala. adv.; bk.rev.; charts; illus.; mkt.; stat.; index; circ. 9,500. Indexed: So.Pac.Per.Ind.
—BLDSC shelfmark: 6329.840000.

PACIFIC NORTHWEST; the travel and lifestyle magazine of the Northwest. see *GENERAL INTEREST PERIODICALS — United States*

PACIFIC TRAVEL DIRECTORY. see *BUSINESS AND ECONOMICS — Trade And Industrial Directories*

TRAVEL AND TOURISM

919.6   HK
PACIFIC TRAVELLER. 6/yr. $30. Sky Trend Development Ltd., Mezzanine FL., 20-22 Old Bailey St., Central, Hong Kong. TEL 5220037. FAX 5267488. Ed. Derek Maitland.
Description: Covers hotel news and prices. Aims at the frequent business traveller.

943.04   GW
PADERBORN VON ZU TAG; der Kump. 1973. m. DM.21. Verkehrsverein Paderborn - Tourist Information Office, Marienplatz 2a, D-4790 Paderborn, Germany. TEL 05251-26461. FAX 05251-22884. adv.; bk.rev.; circ. 8,000.

910.09 647.9   PK   ISSN 0250-3662
PAKISTAN HOTEL AND TRAVEL REVIEW. (Text in English) 1978. m. Rs.500($42) Maulai Enterprise, J-6-2, al-Naseer, Federal B Area, Blk. No. 1, Karachi 75900, Pakistan. TEL 682764. Ed. Syed Wali Ahmad Maulai. adv.; stat.; circ. 5,000. (back issues avail.)

910.202   PK
PAKISTAN HOTELS & TOURISM. 1975. a. Rs.5. Bhatti Publications, 103-B Gulberg, Lahore, Pakistan. Ed. Mukhtar Bhatti. adv.

917.8   US   ISSN 0031-0425
PALM SPRINGS LIFE. 1947. m. $38. Desert Publications Inc., 303 N. Indian Canyon Dr., Box 2724, Palm Springs, CA 92263. TEL 619-325-2333. FAX 619-325-7008. Ed. Jamie Lee Pricer. adv.; bk.rev.; film rev.; circ. 20,923. (also avail. in microfiche from UMI)
Description: Covers events in and around Palm Springs.

917.904   US
PALM SPRINGS LIFE DESERT GUIDE. 1967. m. Desert Publications, Inc., 303 N. Indian Canyon Dr., Box 2724, Palm Springs, CA 92263. TEL 619-325-2333. FAX 619-325-7008. Ed. Donna Curran. circ. 76,325.

910.4   US   ISSN 0553-0601
PAN AM WORLD GUIDE;* encyclopedia of travel. a. $9.95. Pan American World Airways, c/o East-West Network, Inc., 5900 Willshire Blvd., Los Angeles, CA 90036. adv.; charts; illus.; circ. 50,000.

PANAMA NOW. see *BUSINESS AND ECONOMICS — Domestic Commerce*

917   US   ISSN 0048-282X
PANORAMA (BOSTON); Boston's official bi-weekly visitor guide. 1951. fortn. $50. Jerome Press, 332 Congress St., Boston, MA 02210. TEL 617-423-3400. FAX 617-423-7108. Ed. Robin Koppernaes. adv.; film rev.; play rev.; charts; illus.; circ. 55,156. Indexed: Int.Packag.Abstr.
Incorporates: Cityguide.

910.2   AT
PAPUA NEW GUINEA HANDBOOK. 1954. irreg., 11th ed., 1985. Aus.$14.95. Pacific Publications (Australia) Pty. Ltd., G.P.O. Box 4245, Sydney, N.S.W. 2001, Australia. Ed. John Hunter. adv.; index.
Formerly: Handbook of Papua and New Guinea (ISSN 0072-9868)

910.202   PP
PARADISE. 1976. 6/yr. $24 (typically set in Jan). Air Nuigini, P.O. Box 7186, Boroko, Papua New Guinea. FAX 273-416. Ed. Geoff McLaughlin. adv.; circ. 50,000.

914.404   US
PARIS (YEAR). a. $10. Harper Collins Publishers, Birnbaum Travel Guides, 10 E. 53rd St., New York, NY 10022-5299. TEL 212-207-7000. illus.; index.

910.202   US
PARTNERS-IN-TRAVEL. 1981. bi-m. $45. Box 491145, Los Angeles, CA 90049. TEL 213-476-4869. Ed. Miriam E. Tobolowsky. circ. 700. (tabloid format)
Description: Offers cost-cutting tips and information relating to the needs and interests of the single traveler.

914.504   IT
PASSEGGIATE NEL LAZIO. 1977. irreg. price varies. (Regione Lazio, Assessorato al Turismo) Bulzoni Editore, Via dei Liburni, 00185 Rome, Italy.

917.1   CN   ISSN 0835-4162
PASSION MAGAZINE. 1987. q. Can.$10. Titan Publishing Inc. (Guelph), 291 Woodlawn Rd. W., Unit 7, Guelph, Ont. N1H 7A1, Canada. TEL 519-763-5058. Ed. Karen Mantel. circ. 25,000.
Description: Dedicated to entertainment and dining in the Guelph, Kitchener-Waterloo, and Cambridge areas.

910.2   US   ISSN 0031-272X
PASSPORT; the newsletter for the discriminating international traveler. 1965. m. $65. Remy Publishing Co., 350 W. Hubbard St., No. 440, Chicago, IL 60610-4011. TEL 312-464-0300.

910.202   JA
PASSPORT. 1958. m. Japan Tourist Bureau Inc., 1-6-4 Marunouchi, Chiyoda-Ku, Tokyo, Japan. Ed. Herbert Slew Sai. adv.; circ. 100,000.

910.09   HK
▼**PATA TRAVEL NEWS AMERICAS.** Short title: P T N Americas. (Text in English) 1990. m. Asian Business Press (Hong Kong) Ltd. (Subsidiary of: Asian Business Press Group), 1302 East Point Ctr., 555 Hennessy Rd., Causeway Bay, Hong Kong, Hong Kong. TEL 5-8335022. Ed. Yeoh Siew Hoon. adv.; circ. 25,000.

910.09   HK
PATA TRAVEL NEWS ASIA - PACIFIC. Short title: P T N Asia - Pacific. (Text in English) 1987. m. $33 in Asia; elsewhere $54. Asian Business Press (Hong Kong) Ltd. (Subsidiary of: Asian Business Press Group), 1302 East Point Centre, 555 Hennessy Rd., Causeway Bay, Hong Kong, Hong Kong. TEL 5-8335022. FAX 5-8345132. TELEX HX-63393-ABPHK. Ed. Yeoh Siew Hoon. adv.; circ. 13,751.
Description: Trade information for Asia's travel and tourism industries.

910.4   HK
▼**PATA TRAVEL NEWS EUROPE.** Short title: P T N Europe. (Text in English) 1990. m. Asian Business Press (Hong Kong) Ltd. (Subsidiary of: Asian Business Press Group), 1302 East Point Centre, 555 Hennessy Rd., Causeway Bay, Hong Kong, Hong Kong. TEL 5-8335022. FAX 5-8345132. TELEX HX-63393-ABPHK. Ed. Yeoh Siew Hoon. adv.

910.09   US
▼**PAUL EDWARDS' TRAVEL CONFIDENTIAL.** 1991. m. $195. Lowell Communications, Inc., 88 Bleecker St., New York, NY 10012. TEL 212-254-1069. Ed. Paul L. Edward.
Formerly: Travel Smarter.
Description: Covers low cost travel for individuals and groups.

915.94   HK
PENINSULA GROUP MAGAZINE. 1974. 3/yr. free to qualified personnel. Peninsula Group, St. George's Bldg., 8th Fl., 2 Ice House Street, Central, Hong Kong. TEL 840-7211. FAX 845-5512. TELEX 74509-KREM-HX. Ed. Liam Fitzpatrick. adv.; circ. 53,000.

PENINSULAGUEST. see *GENERAL INTEREST PERIODICALS — United States*

941.04   UK   ISSN 0261-2836
PENNINE MAGAZINE. 1979. bi-m. £9 (foreign £10). Pennine Heritage Ltd., Birchcliffe Centre, Hebden Bridge, West Yorkshire HX7 8DG, England. Ed. Hilary Darby. adv.; bk.rev.; circ. 8,000. (back issues avail.)

PENNSYLVANIA MAGAZINE. see *GENERAL INTEREST PERIODICALS — United States*

910.09   US
PENTON EXECUTIVE NETWORK. (Includes supplement: Executives on the Go) 1969. m. (avail. only with subscr. to selected Penton magazines). Penton Publishing (Subsidiary of: Pittway Company), 1100 Superior Ave., Cleveland, OH 44114-2543. TEL 216-696-7000. FAX 216-696-8765. (Subscr. to: Box 95759, Cleveland, OH 44101) adv.; illus.; circ. 1,600,000. (reprint service avail. from UMI)
Former titles: Management Personal Time Network; Management Personal Time; Management Leisure Time; Management Time and Leisure.
Description: Provides a channel of communication to upscale managers and professionals.

917.7   US
PEORIA TODAY. 1965. q. Walfred Co., Inc., 1625 W. Candletree Dr., Peoria, IL 61614-1556. TEL 309-692-4910. Ed. David Pfanschmidt.

PERIGORD MAGAZINE; magazines de France. see *GENERAL INTEREST PERIODICALS — France*

917   CN   ISSN 0048-3451
PERSONNEL GUIDE TO CANADA'S TRAVEL INDUSTRY. 1969. s-a. Can.$40. Baxter Publishing Co., 310 Dupont St., Toronto, Ont. M5R 1V9, Canada. TEL 416-968-7252. FAX 416-968-2377. Ed. Wendy Baxter-McClung. adv.; circ. 5,000.

371.42   US   ISSN 0894-9417
GV186
PETERSON'S SUMMER OPPORTUNITIES FOR KIDS AND TEENAGERS (YEAR). 1983. a. $17.95. Peterson's Guides, Inc., 202 Carnegie Center, Box 2123, Princeton, NJ 08543-2123. TEL 609-243-9111. FAX 609-243-9150. circ. 10,000.
Description: Covers more than 1200 summer programs for young people, including those offered by private schools, colleges, camps, religious organizations and travel and sports groups.

910.2 914   UK   ISSN 0079-130X
PETS WELCOME; animal lovers' holiday guide. 1961. a. £2.99. F.H.G. Publications Ltd., Abbey Mill Business Centre, Seedhill, Paisley PA1 1JN, Scotland. TEL 041-887 0428. Ed. Peter Clark.

PHILIPPINES TRANSPORTATION. see *TRANSPORTATION*

910.202   US   ISSN 0745-4554
PHYSICIANS' TRAVEL & MEETING GUIDE. 1982. m. $60 to individuals; US physicians $40; foreign $100. Cahners Publishing Company (New York), Medical-Health Care Group (Subsidiary of: Reed International PLC), Division of Reed Publishing (USA) Inc., 249 W. 17th St., New York, NY 10011. TEL 212-645-0067. FAX 212-242-6987. Ed. Bea Riemschneider. adv.; tr.lit.; circ. 113,335.
Description: For physicians to help them plan their attendance at medical meetings and their personal and business travel.

299 910   US
PILGRIM'S GUIDE TO PLANET EARTH.* 1974. irreg. $8.95. Arcline Publishing, c/o Highpoint Type-Graphics, 131 Springs St., Claremont, CA 91711-4930. TEL 714-623-1738. Ed. Parmatma Singh Khalsa. circ. 17,500.

791   YU   ISSN 0031-9880
PINGRIN;* nedeljni ilustrovani zabavnik. 1966. w. 50 din. Napred, Valjevo, Vuka Karadzica 26, Fah 62, Valjevo, Yugoslavia. Ed. Bronislav Nikolic.

PINK PAGES; Scotland's premier guide to food and drink. see *HOTELS AND RESTAURANTS*

910.4 621.381   US
PINKERTON EYE ON TRAVEL. 1987. m. $129. Pinkerton Risk Assessment Services, 1600 Wilson Blvd., Ste. 901, Arlington, VA 22209-2507. TEL 703-525-6111. FAX 703-525-2454. Ed. E. Mastroangelo. circ. 1,000.
●Also available on CD-ROM.
Formerly: International Travel Briefing Service.
Description: Covers travel briefing, printed on IBM PC-XT-AT computers. Includes full text advisories.

614.86
PINKERTON WORLD STATUS MAP. 1983. bi-m. $36. Pinkerton Risk Assessment Services, 1600 Wilson Blvd., Ste. 901, Arlington, VA 22209-2507. TEL 703-525-6111. FAX 703-525-2454. Ed. E. Mastroangelo. circ. 1,700.
Formerly: World Status Map (ISSN 0887-9559)
Description: Provides danger-medical warnings for international travelers.

910.09   US
PINNACLE. (International ed. avail.) bi-m. Kelly Communications (Charlottesville), 410 E. Water St., Charlottesville, VA 22901. TEL 804-296-5676. Ed. Margaret Mucklo. circ. 2,193,156.

PLACES FOR MEN (YEAR). see *HOMOSEXUALITY*

PLACES OF INTEREST (YEAR); atlas of gay travel. see *HOMOSEXUALITY*

PLACES OF INTEREST TO WOMEN: USA AND WORLDWIDE. see *HOMOSEXUALITY*

TRAVEL AND TOURISM

PLAISIRS. see *HOTELS AND RESTAURANTS*

918 BF
POCKET GUIDE TO THE BAHAMAS. 1947. s-a. Cartwright Publications, Box N494, Nassau, Bahamas. Ed. Kevin B. Cartwright. circ. 150,000.

910.09 IT
POLITICA DEL TURISMO; rivista bimestrale di studi e documentazione. 1984. bi-m. L.120000 (effective 1992). Maggioli Editore, Via Crimea, 1, Casella Postale 290, 47037 Rimini, Italy. TEL 0541-626777. FAX 0541-622020. Ed. Emilio Becheri.

914
PONENTE. fortn. L.10000. Ilio Masprone Societa Editrice IL Ponente s.a.s., Via Grande Albergo, 6, Saremo (IM), Italy. TEL 0184-266433.

914.2 UK
PORTLAND SOUVENIR MAGAZINE. 1971. a. £0.25. Royal Naval Association, Portland Branch, 2 Clarence Rd., Portland, Dorset, England. Ed. John Barnes.

914.904 US
PORTUGAL (YEAR). a. $17. Harper Collins Publishers, Birnbaum Travel Guides, 10 E. 53rd St., New York, NY 10022-5299. TEL 212-207-7000. illus.; index.

914.604 PO
PORTUGAL TURISMO ACTUALIDADE. 1980. m. Rua Joaquim Antonio de Aguiar 45-5o, Esq., 1000 Lisbon, Portugal. TEL 01-557175. FAX 01-557667. circ. 40,000.

914 PL ISSN 0032-6151
POZNAJ SWOJ KRAJ; miesiecznik krajoznawczo-turystyczny. 1958. m. 2400 Zl.($9) Instytut Wydawniczy "Nasza Ksiegarnia", Ul. Spasowskiego 4, 00-389 Warsaw, Poland. TEL 48 22 26-24-31. (Dist. by: Ars Polona-Ruch, Krakowskie Przedmiescie 7, Warsaw, Poland) Ed. Andrzej Gordon. adv.; bk.rev.; illus.; index; circ. 25,000.

910.202 US
PRAIRIE PROFILE. w. 312 Fifth Ave., Box 177, Brookings, SD 57006. TEL 605-692-6271. Ed. Kristin Anderson.

910.202 CN
PRESENTER'S HANDBOOK/GUIDE DU DIFFUSEUR. (Editions in English, French) 1975. irreg., latest Dec., 1991. Can.$11($16) (foreign $25). Canada Council, Touring Office, P.O. Box 1047, 99 Metcalfe St., Ottawa, Ont. K1P 5V8, Canada. TEL 613-598-4392. FAX 613-598-4404.
Former titles: Sponsors' Handbook for the 80's - Guide du Commanditaire; Sponsors' Handbook for Touring Attractions.

PRESIDENTS' JOURNAL. see *HISTORY — History Of North And South America*

910.202 CN
PRESSE VOYAGES; magazine en tourisme. 1989. s-m. Can.$23($19) (effective Jan. 1990). P.O. Box 591, Brossard, Que. J4Z 3R1, Canada. TEL 514-678-9918. FAX 514-678-4471. Ed. Mayelinne De Lara. circ. 5,000. (back issues avail.)

917 BM ISSN 0048-5268
PREVIEW BERMUDA. 1959. m. $30. Preview of Bermuda, Ltd., P.O. Box HM 266, Hamilton HMAX, Bermuda. TEL 809-292-4155. FAX 809-295-4724. Eds. Ann Brown, Roxana Kaufmann. adv.; charts; illus.
Description: Complete guide for the Bermuda visitor.

PREVISIONS GLISSANTES DETAILLEES EN PERSPECTIVES SECTORIELLES (VOL.34): TOURISME, HOTELLERIE, RESTAURATION, LOISIRS. see *BUSINESS AND ECONOMICS — Economic Situation And Conditions*

PRIMI PIANI. see *MUSIC*

PRISM; quarterly of Egyptian culture. see *GENERAL INTEREST PERIODICALS — Egyptian Arab Republic*

910.09 GW ISSN 0932-4631
▼**PROFITRAVEL**; das internationale Geschaeftsreise-Magazin. 1987. bi-m. DM.36. Gesellschaft fuer Wirtschaftspublizistik (GWP) mbH, Kasernenstr. 67, Postfach 37 34, 4000 Dusseldorf 1, Germany. TEL 0211-887-2501. FAX 0211-326943. TELEX 17211308-HBL. Ed. Thomas Michael Schweizer. adv.; circ. 181,000. (back issues avail.)

914 AU
PROGRAMM WIEN; events-manifestations. (Text in English, French, German, Italian) 1957. m. S.115. Vienna Tourist Board, Obere Augartenstr. 40, A-1025 Vienna, Austria. Ed.Bd. adv.; circ. 120,000.
Formerly: Wien-Veranstaltungen.

910.09 UK ISSN 0952-5424
G155.A1
PROGRESS IN TOURISM, RECREATION AND HOSPITALITY MANAGEMENT. 1989. a. £39 (typically set in June). Belhaven Press, 25 Floral St., London WC2E 9DS, England. TEL 071-240-9233. FAX 071-379-5553. Ed. C.P. Cooper. bk.rev.; bibl.; index; circ. 1,200.
—BLDSC shelfmark: 6924.608300.
Description: Review of research in tourism and related fields, with emphasis on the fields rapidly advancing and of international importance.

PROMENADE. see *GENERAL INTEREST PERIODICALS — United States*

PROMOBIL. see *TRANSPORTATION — Automobiles*

910.4 PO
PUBLITURIS; jornal da industria do turismo. 1968. s-m. Esc.2,000($35) Publiotel Ltd, Rua Marechal Sandanha, 4-1, 1200 Lisbon, Portugal. TEL 3475201. FAX 327718. TELEX 64440 NEWS P. Ed. Belmiro Santos. adv.; circ. 7,500.
Description: Covers various areas of travel and tourism, includes air transport, hotels, meetings and incentives.

PUERTO RICO LIVING. see *GENERAL INTEREST PERIODICALS — Puerto Rico*

910.09 US ISSN 1053-3842
PUNCH IN INTERNATIONAL TRAVEL AND ENTERTAINMENT MAGAZINE. 1970. m. $100 (prices set in Nov.). Enterprises Publishing, 400 E. 59th St., Ste. 9F, New York, NY 10022. TEL 212-755-4563. Ed. Jerome Walman. circ. 650,000. (back issues avail.)
●Also available online.
Also available on CD-ROM.

PUNGOLO DEL SUD; periodico di cronache mediterranee. see *GENERAL INTEREST PERIODICALS — Italy*

Q T DIRECTORY. (Quality Travel) see *BUSINESS AND ECONOMICS — Trade And Industrial Directories*

QUADERNI DE "LA TERRA SANTA". see *RELIGIONS AND THEOLOGY*

910.9 IT
QUALITYTRAVEL MAGAZINE; rivista di congressi - viaggi - incentive per l'uomo d'affari. 1986. bi-m. L.60000. A P I Editrice srl., Via Pezzotti, 4, 20141 Milan, Italy. TEL 02-832-1087. FAX 02-8323710. Ed. Claudia Levizzani. circ. 10,000.

388.3 796.7 BL ISSN 0033-5908
QUATRO RODAS. 1960. m. $120. Editora Abril, S.A., R. Geraldo Flausino Gomes, 61, 04575 Sao Paulo, Brazil. TEL 011-8239222. FAX 011-8643796. TELEX 011-80360 EDAB BR. (Subscr. to: Rua do Curtume, 769 CEP 05065 Lapa, Sao Paulo, Brazil.) Ed. Victor Civita. adv.; charts; illus.; mkt.; stat.; index; circ. 191,515.
Description: For the auto enthusiast, contains exclusive tests, future advances, price tables for new and used cars, insurance information, competition news and maps.

917 PR
QUE PASA; official visitors guide to Puerto Rico. 1948. q. free. Tourism Company of Puerto Rico, Box 4435, Old San Juan Sta., San Juan, PR 00905. FAX 809-725-4417. Ed. Mary Anne Hopgood. adv.; charts; illus.; circ. 150,000.
Formerly: Que Pasa in Puerto Rico (ISSN 0048-623X)

QUE SAVOIR; industrie-commerce-tourisme. see *BUSINESS AND ECONOMICS*

910.2 AT
QUEENSLAND TOURIST AND TRAVEL CORPORATION. ANNUAL REPORT. 1980. a. free. Queensland Tourist and Travel Corporation, 123 Eagle St., G.P.O. Box 328, Brisbane, Qld. 4001, Australia. illus.; circ. 400.

QUERCY MAGAZINE; magazines de France. see *GENERAL INTEREST PERIODICALS — France*

910.2 FR ISSN 0048-6450
QUEYRAS. 1971. 3/yr. 24 F. Courier du Queyras, Route de la Gare, 05600 Guillestre, France. Dir. Philippe Lamour. adv.; bk.rev.; charts; illus.

910.2 IT ISSN 0042-546X
QUI TOURING. 1971. m. L.3800 to non-members; membership. (Touring Club Italiano) Touring Periodici s.r.l., Corso Italia 10, 20122 Milan, Italy. TEL 02-85261. TELEX 321160. Ed. Giuseppe Bozzini. adv.; bk.rev.; circ. 510,000.
Supersedes: Vie d'Italia.

R A C B ROYAL AUTO. (Koninklijke Automobiel Club van Belgie) see *TRANSPORTATION — Automobiles*

910.202 UK
R A C EUROPEAN HOTEL GUIDE. 1932. a. £7.95. (Royal Automobile Club) R A C Publishing, Box 100, R A C House, Brighton Rd., South Croydon CR2 6XW, England. TEL 01-686-0088. FAX 01-688-2882. adv.
Former titles: R A C Continental Hotel Guide; (until 1986): R A C Continental Handbook and Hotel Guide; R A C Continental Motoring Guide; (until 1982): R A C Continental Handbook.

796.77 UK
R A C HOTEL GUIDE GREAT BRITAIN & IRELAND. 1904. a. £12.99. (Royal Automobile Club) R A C Publishing, Box 100, R A C House, Brighton Rd., South Croydon CR2 6XW, England. TEL 01-686-0088. FAX 01-688-2882.
Former titles: R A C Hotel Guide; (until 1986): R A C Handbook and Hotel Guide; (until 1985): R A C Guide and Handbook.

R A C MOTOR SPORT YEAR BOOK. see *SPORTS AND GAMES*

910.4 GW
R B HOTEL MARKETING. 1967. 60/yr. DM.360. R B Redaktions Buero, Schraemelstr. 126, 8000 Munich 60, Germany. TEL 089-88888888. FAX 089-882686. Ed. H.N. Nechleba.

910.4 GW
R B LUFTFAHRT MARKETING. 1967. 60/yr. DM.360($290) R B Redaktions Buero, Schraemelstr. 126, 8000 Munich 60, Germany. TEL 089-88888888. FAX 089-882686. Ed. Hans Nechleba. circ. 1,150. (looseleaf format; back issues avail.)

910.09 GW
R B MARKETING. 1967. 60/yr. DM.360($200) R B Marketing Der Graue Dienst, Schraemelstr. 126, 8000 Munich 60, Germany. TEL 089-88888888. FAX 089-882686. Ed. Hans N. Nechleba. adv.; bk.rev.; circ. 1,100. (looseleaf format)

796.6 CN
R V TIMES. (Recreational Vehicle) 5/yr. Can.$13.86. Sheila Jones Publishing Ltd., 32512 Beaver Dr., Mission, B.C. V2V 5T4, Canada. TEL 604-826-4249. FAX 604-826-1999. Ed. Sheila Jones. adv.; bk.rev.; circ. 30,000.
Description: Includes events of interest in BC and Washington state, camping stories, repair tips and general RV and camping information.

910.202 388.2 US
R V WEST. 1981. m. $12. PresComm Media, Inc., 4133 Mohr Ave., Ste. I, Pleasanton, CA 94566. TEL 510-426-3200. FAX 510-426-1422. Ed. Cheryl R. Morriston. adv.; circ. 90,000. (back issues avail.)
Former titles (until Nov. 1988): Western R V Traveler; (until 1986): California Traveler.
Description: Dedicated to recreational vehicle lifestyle.

TRAVEL AND TOURISM

910.09 385.26   US
RAILWAYS. q. Parlor Car Press, Box 10396, Glendale, CA 91209-3396. TEL 818-500-0542. FAX 818-247-9671. Ed. Vincent Prest. circ. 1,100.

910.09   IO
RAJAWALI. m. Jakarta, Indonesia. Ed. Karyono Adhy.

910.202 330   US
RAND MCNALLY BUSINESS TRAVELER'S ROAD ATLAS; and guide to major cities. a. $16.95. Rand McNally & Co., 8255 N. Central Park, Skokie, IL 60076. TEL 708-673-9100. (Subscr. to: Box 7600, Chicago, IL 60680) Ed. Virginia O'Neill.

RAND MCNALLY FISHING HOTSPOTS: MIDWEST. see *SPORTS AND GAMES — Outdoor Life*

910.202   US
RAND MCNALLY ROAD ATLAS. 1924. a. $7.95. Rand McNally & Co., 8255 N. Central Park Ave., Skokie, IL 60076. TEL 708-673-9100. (Subscr. to: Box 7600, Chicago, IL 60680) Ed. Virginia O'Neill. adv.

910.202 914.04   US
RAND MCNALLY ROAD ATLAS & CITY GUIDE OF EUROPE. a. $18.95. Rand McNally & Co., 8255 N. Central Park, Skokie, IL 60076. TEL 708-673-9100. (Subscr. to: Box 7600, Chicago, IL 60680)

910.202   US
RAND MCNALLY ROAD ATLAS & VACATION GUIDE; United States, Canada, Mexico. a. $16.95. Rand McNally & Co., 8255 N. Central Park, Skokie, IL 60076. TEL 708-673-9100. (Subscr. to: Box 7600, Chicago, IL 60680) Ed. Virginia O'Neill.

910.202 914.204   US
RAND MCNALLY ROAD ATLAS OF BRITAIN; the ultimate road atlas for travel in England, Scotland, and Wales. a. $18.95. Rand McNally & Co., 8255 N. Central Park, Skokie, IL 60076. TEL 708-673-9100. (Subscr. to: Box 7600, Chicago, IL 60680)

910.202 914.04   US
RAND MCNALLY ROAD ATLAS OF EUROPE. a. $9.95. Rand McNally & Co., 8255 N. Central Park, Skokie, IL 60076. TEL 708-673-9100. (Subscr. to: Box 7600, Chicago, IL 60680) Ed. Virginia O'Neill. illus.

910.202 917.04   US
RAND MCNALLY VACATION PLACES RATED. 1986. irreg. $12.95. Prentice Hall Press (Subsidiary of: Simon & Schuster), One Gulf & Western Plaza, New York, NY 10023. TEL 212-373-8500.

910.09   US
READING - BERKS AUTO CLUB MAGAZINE. bi-m. (American Automobile Association, Reading-Berks Auto Club) Roberts & Company, 920 Van Reed Rd., Wyomissing, PA 19610-1716. TEL 215-375-4525. Ed. Bob Gerhart. circ. 75,500.

917.   US
RECOMMEND: MAGAZINE. 1967. m. $48. Worth International Communications Corp., 5979 N.W. 151st St., Ste. 120, Miami Lakes, FL 33014. TEL 800-447-0123. FAX 305-826-6950. adv.; circ. 43,000. (processed)
Formerly: Recommend: Florida (ISSN 0034-1452)

910.2 914   UK   ISSN 0267-3428
RECOMMENDED COUNTRY HOTELS OF BRITAIN. 1973. a. £3.50. F.H.G. Publications Ltd., Abbey Mill Business Centre, Seedhill, Paisley PA1 1JN, Scotland. TEL 041-887 0428. Ed. Peter Clark.

914   UK
RECOMMENDED SHORT BREAK HOLIDAYS. a. £3.50. F.H.G. Publications Ltd., Abbey Mill Business Centre, Seedhill, Paisley PA1 1JN, Scotland. TEL 041-887 0428. Ed. Peter Clark.
Formerly: Mini-Break Holidays in Britain (ISSN 0267-341X)

910.2 914   UK   ISSN 0080-0252
RECOMMENDED WAYSIDE INNS OF BRITAIN. 1962. a. £2.99. F.H.G. Publications Ltd., Abbey Mill Business Centre, Seedhill, Paisley PA1 1JN, Scotland. TEL 041-887 0428. Ed. Peter Clark.

910.09   US
RECREATION ADVISOR. 1984. bi-m. $15. (International Family Recreation Association) Recreational World Services, Inc., Box 17148, Pensacola, FL 32522. TEL 904-477-2123. Ed. K.W. Stephens. adv.; bk.rev.; charts; illus.; stat.; tr.; lit.; circ. 13,000. (tabloid format)

910.202   AU
REISE UND CAMPING. 4/yr. W. Rothmueller, Lerchenfelderquertel 25, 1160 Vienna, Austria. adv.; circ. 25,000.

910.202   GW   ISSN 0932-4186
REISE UND PREISE; magazine of air travel and vacation planning. 1987. q. DM.27.20. Reise und Preise Verlags GmbH, Lutherallee 10, 2150 Buxtehude, Germany. TEL 04161-87500. FAX 04161-80131. Ed. Oliver Kuehn. adv.; bk.rev.; circ. 32,000. (back issues avail.)

910.09   GW
REISEBUERO BULLETIN; weekly news for the German travel trade. 1967. w. DM.72. Bulletin Verlag GmbH, Roentgenstr. 80, 6100 Darmstadt 12, Germany. TEL 06151-374066. FAX 06151-370114. Ed. Michael Knuth. adv.; circ. 13,370. (back issues avail.)
Description: Features all aspects of travel such as hotels, tourism, airline information, travel agency news and events.

910.09   GW   ISSN 0177-4050
REISEFIEBER; das nuetzliche Reisemagazin. 1985. bi-m. DM.27. Hayit Verlag GmbH, Hansaring 82, 5000 Cologne 1, Germany. TEL 0221-123088. FAX 0221-132967. Ed. Ertay Hayit. adv.; bk.rev.; circ. 47,000. (back issues avail.)
Description: Provides practical and useful information on travel to destinations throughout the world.

910.202   GW
REISEFUHRER - WOHIN IN BERLIN; internationaler Fremdenverkehr. 1950. a. B. Friedrich Commerzia Verlag Werbung und Vertrieb GmbH, Buhrowwstr. 5, 1000 Berlin 41, Germany. TEL 030-7968871. Ed. Horst Borchardt.

914   NO
REISELIV. 1922. m. (10/yr.). NOK 70. Landslaget for Reiselivet i Norge - Norway Travel Association, H. Heyerdahlsgt 1, Oslo 1, Norway. (Co-sponsor: Norske Reisebyraaforening) Ed. Oddvar Hegge. adv.; bk.rev.; charts; illus.; circ. 3,300.
Formerly: Reiseliv i Norge (ISSN 0034-3676)

910.202   GW   ISSN 0177-2953
REISEN IN DEUTSCHLAND: REISEFUEHRER. 1949. a. DM.43. Jaeger Verlag GmbH, Holzhofallee 38, Postfach 11 04 52, 6100 Darmstadt, Germany. TEL 06151-391-0. FAX 06151-391200. TELEX 419548-DAV-D. Ed. Guenter Hulwa. circ. 15,000.

910.2   GW
REISEN IN DEUTSCHLAND: ZIMMERKATALOG. 1925. a. (in 2 vols.). DM.39. Jaeger Verlag GmbH, Holzhofallee 38, Postfach 110452, 6100 Darmstadt, Germany. TEL 06151-391-0. FAX 06151-391200. TELEX 419548-DAV-D. adv.
Former titles: Zimmerkatalog; Reisen in Deutschland; Deutsches Handbuch fuer Fremdenverkehr: Volume 2 (ISSN 0177-2961)

388.3   GW
REISEN MIT DEM AUTO. 1952. s-a. A V D Verlag GmbH, Lyonerstr. 16, 6000 Frankfurt a.M. 71, Germany. TEL 069-66060. circ. 10,000.
Formerly: Reisen mit dem Auto durch Europa.

910.202   GW   ISSN 0936-627X
REISEN UND LEBEN. 1980. s-a. DM.18. Verlag Ursula Hinrichsen, Ziegeleistr. 7, 3457 Stadtoldendorf, Germany. FAX 05531-7290. Ed. Alex W. Hinrichsen. adv.; bk.rev.; circ. 500.
Description: Looks at the history of tourism and of tour guides.

914.806   GW
REISEWEGE NACH SKANDINAVIEN. 1954. a. DM.7.50. Fie Verlag GmbH, Postfach 106104, Spaldingstr. 210, 2000 Hamburg 1, Germany. TEL 040-230173. FAX 040-234613. adv.; circ. 60,000.
Formerly: Fahren nach Skandinavien.

910.09   GW
REISEZIELE; Landkarten, Reisefuehrer, Bildbaende, mit vielen touristischen Tips. 1970. a. GeoCenter Verlagsvertrieb GmbH, Neumarkter Str. 18, 8000 Munich 80, Germany. TEL 089-43189-505. FAX 089-43189555.

910   NE
REIZEN. 1937. m. fl.90 to non-members. Koninklijke Nederlandse Toeristenbond ANWB - Royal Dutch Touring Club, Wassenaarseweg 220, Postbus 93200, 2509 BA The Hague, Netherlands. Ed. M. Bisschops. adv.; illus.; circ. 35,000. **Indexed:** Key to Econ.Sci.
Formerly (until 1986): Toeristenkampoeien.

910.09   DK   ISSN 0108-6812
REJSEBOGEN (YEAR); muligheder for ophold i udlandet af kortere eller laengere varighed. 1983. a. DKK 97. Forlaget Nuna, Fasanvej 3, 9670 Loegstoer, Denmark. Ed. Georg Harmsen. adv.; bk.rev.; circ. 8,000.

915.1   JA
REKISHI TO TABI/HISTORY AND TRAVEL. (Text in Japanese) 1974. m. 5400 Yen. Akita Shoten Publishing Co. Ltd., 10-8, 2-chome, Iidabashi, Tokyo 102, Japan. Ed. Toru Suzuki.

910.202   FR
RELAIS ROUTIERS. 1934. m. 85 Fr. Societe d'Exploitation de Journeaux Techniques, 6 rue de l'Isly, 75008 Paris, France. TEL 43-87-61-68. FAX 43-87-50-46. Ed. Patrice de Saulieu. adv.; bk.rev.; circ. 4,500.

910.09   US
RELAX; the travel magazine for practicing physicians. 1985. m. $24. Physicians Publications Limited Partnership, 2333 Waukegan Rd., Ste., S-280, Bannockburn, IL 60015. TEL 312-940-8333. Ed. Mary Kaye Stray. index; circ. 120,000.

RELEVE. see *POLITICAL SCIENCE*

910.09 268   US   ISSN 1050-2742
RELIGIOUS CONFERENCE MANAGER. 1972. q. $18 (foreign $28). Laux Company, Inc., 63 Great Rd., Maynard, MA 01754. TEL 508-897-5552. FAX 508-897-6824. Ed. Betsy Bair Cassidy. adv.; circ. 1,434.
Description: Provides religious planners with information to help them in arranging for and conducting meetings and conventions.

917.1   CN
RENDEZ-VOUS CANADA. 1981. a. $15. Baxter Publishing Co., 310 Dupont St., Toronto, Ont. M5R 1V9, Canada. TEL 416-968-7252. FAX 416-968-2377. TELEX 065-28085. Ed. Edith Baxter. adv.

910.2   FR   ISSN 0034-4575
REPERTOIRE DES VOYAGES/TRAVEL TRADE REPERTORY; international travel trade magazine. (Text in French) 1948. Editions Touristiques Internationales, 1 cite Bergere, 75009 Paris, France. adv.; circ. 8,300.

910   II   ISSN 0378-7478
RESEARCH IN TOURISM. q. Rs.400($80) K.K. Roy (Private) Ltd., 55 Gariahat Rd., P.O. Box 10210, Calcutta 700 019, India. Ed. Kuldip Kumar Roy.

910.09   US
RESORTS AND GREAT HOTELS. 1987. a. $15. R & R Publishing Co., 123 W. Padre St., Santa Barbara, CA 93105. TEL 805-687-1422. FAX 805-682-8634. Ed. Annette Burden. adv.; illus.; circ. 89,000. (back issues avail.)
Description: Covers luxury hotels and resorts around the world.

910.09   US
RETIREMENT PARADISES OF THE WORLD. biennial. $4.95. Harian Publications, One Vernon Ave, Floral Park, NY 11001. TEL 516-437-3440. Ed. Norman D. Ford. illus.
Supersedes: Bargain Paradises of the World (ISSN 0408-568X)

REVISTA CATALANA DE GEOGRAFIA. see *GEOGRAPHY*

| 918 | EC |

REVISTA DINERS. 1979. m. $40. (Ecuadorian Diners Club) Dinediciones S.A., 12 de Octubre 1764 y Lizardo Garcia, Quito, Ecuador. TEL 504910. FAX 565477. Ed. Fidel Egas Grijalva. adv.; bk.rev.; circ. 45,000.

| 791.4 | LU | ISSN 0035-0729 |

REVUE; Letzeburger illustreiert (Luxembourg's weekly magazine). (Incl. supplement Revue Agenda) (Text in German) 1945. w. 2200 Fr. Editions Revue S.A., Boite Postale 2755, 1027 Luxembourg, Luxembourg. TEL 45-41-51. FAX 45-88-74. Ed. Yolande Kieffer. adv.; bk.rev.; film rev.; abstr.; illus.; stat.; circ. 24,000.

| 919 | MG |

REVUE LITTERAIRE ET CULTURELLE DE L'OCEAN INDIEN. (Text in French) 1981. q. $29. Communication et Media Ocean Indien, Rue H. Rabesahala, B.P. 46, Antsakaviro, 101 Antananarivo, Malagasy Republic. TEL 22536. FAX 34534. TELEX 22225. Ed. Henriette Rasendralisoa. adv.; bk.rev.; circ. 3,000.

| 971 | CN |

RICE LAKE VACATION GUIDE. 1956. a. Can.$3. Clay Publishing Co. Ltd., One Oak St., Bewdley, Ont. KOL 1E0, Canada. TEL 416-797-2281. Ed. Charlotte Clay. adv. (back issues avail.)

| 914 DC1 | FR | ISSN 0035-5097 |

RICHESSES DE FRANCE;* revue du tourisme, de l'economie et des arts. 1949. q. 312.50 F. Editions J. Delmas et Cie, 48 bd. Gouvion St. Cyr 17e, 75006 Paris, France. Ed. Claude Breteau. illus.; circ. 8,000.

RIDER; motorcycle touring & commuting. see *SPORTS AND GAMES — Bicycles And Motorcycles*

| 910 | IT |

RIVIERA ECO. 1962. w. free. Viale dei Mille 14, Riccione, Italy. Ed. Costantino Zangheri. adv.; circ. 100,000.

ROAD AHEAD. see *TRANSPORTATION — Automobiles*

ROAD RIDER; America's first motorcycle touring magazine. see *SPORTS AND GAMES — Bicycles And Motorcycles*

ROBERT NOAH'S PARIS EN CUISINE NEWSLETTER; the insider's guide to gastronomic news of France. see *FOOD AND FOOD INDUSTRIES*

| 910 | US |

ROCKY MOUNTAIN MOTORIST. 1926. m. membership. (American Automobile Association) Rocky Mountain Motorists, Inc., 4100 E. Arkansas Ave., Denver, CO 80222. TEL 303-753-8800. FAX 303-758-8515. Ed. Barbara Bauerle. adv.; circ. 224,000.

| 790.13 | US | ISSN 0896-7261 |

ROLLER COASTER!. 1978. q. $50. American Roller Coaster Enthusiasts, Box 352, Penfield, NY 14526. TEL 716-381-6829. Ed. Paul L. Ruben. adv.; bk.rev.; charts; illus.; cum.index: 1978-1988; circ. 4,000. (back issues avail.)
Description: Contains roller coaster-related articles, pictures, history, and news.

| 914.7 | RM |

ROMANIA PITOREASCA. English edition: Holidays in Romania. (Editions in English, French, German, Romanian) 1958. m. 60 lei($20) Ministerul Turismului - Ministry of Tourism, Gabriel Peri Str. 8, 70148 Bucharest, Rumania. TEL 597893. (Subscr. to: ROMPRE SFILATELIA Sectorul Export-Import Presa, POB.12-201, Calea Grivitei nr. 64-66, Rumania) Ed. Pop Simion. adv.; charts; illus.; circ. 32,000.

| 910.09 | US | ISSN 1053-0177 |

ROMANTIC TRAVELING. 1989. q. $15. Winterbourne Press, 236 W. Portal Ave., Ste. 237, San Francisco, CA 94127. TEL 415-566-9309. FAX 415-731-8239. Ed. Elaine O'Gara. bk.rev.; circ. 4,000. (back issues avail.)
Formerly (until 1990): Travel Publishing News (ISSN 1043-6138)
Description: Helps couples intensify their relationship through travel destinations covered throughout the world.

| 914.504 | US |

ROME (YEAR). a. $10. Harper Collins Publishers, Birnbaum Travel Guides, 10 E. 53rd St., New York, NY 10022-5299. TEL 212-207-7000. illus.; index.

ROUERGUE MAGAZINE; magazines de France. see *GENERAL INTEREST PERIODICALS — France*

ROYAL TEHRAN HILTON. see *HOTELS AND RESTAURANTS*

ROYALAUTO. see *TRANSPORTATION — Automobiles*

| 910.09 | US |

RUNAWAY. 1971. q. Travel Publications, Inc., Box 610, Alta Loma, CA 91701. Ed. Robert R. Hill. adv.; bk.rev.; circ. 356,000 (controlled).

RUNZHEIMER ON CARS & LIVING COSTS. see *TRANSPORTATION — Automobiles*

RUNZHEIMER REPORTS ON RELOCATION. see *BUSINESS AND ECONOMICS — Labor And Industrial Relations*

| 910.09 658 | US | ISSN 0730-8663 |

RUNZHEIMER REPORTS ON TRAVEL MANAGEMENT. 1981. m. $295. Runzheimer International, Runzheimer Park, Rochester, WI 53167. TEL 414-534-3121. (Subscr. to: 555 Skokie Blvd., Ste. 340, Northbrook, IL 60062. TEL 800-942-9949) Ed. Ralph McDarmont. (looseleaf format; back issues avail.)

| 388.3 HE5623.A1 | US | ISSN 0036-0171 |

RUSSELL'S OFFICIAL NATIONAL MOTOR COACH GUIDE; official publications of bus lines for United States and Canada. Title varies: Official Bus Guide. 1908. m. $88.70. Russell's Guides, Inc., 834 Third Ave., S.E., Box 278, Cedar Rapids, IA 52403. TEL 319-364-6138. FAX 319-364-4853. Ed. Tom Whitters. adv.; charts; maps; circ. 14,000.

S F E; going places with the arts. (Santa Fe East) see *ART*

S J-NYTT. (Statens Jaernvaegars Huvudkontor) see *TRANSPORTATION — Railroads*

| 914.604 387.7 | SP | ISSN 0036-1852 |

S P I C; revista de turismo. 1966. fortn. 7500 ptas.($200) in America; Europe $150; elsewhere $250. S P I C Ediciones S.A., Sanchez Barcaiztegui 38, 28007 Madrid, Spain. TEL 1-551-0126. FAX 1-433-8354. TELEX 46322 SPIC E. Ed. Lorenzo Herranz Garcia. adv.; bk.rev.; illus.; circ. 11,500.

| 916 DT421 | KE | ISSN 0036-2352 |

SAFARI; tourist magazine for East Africa. 1969. bi-m. EAs.260($30) News Publishers Ltd., Box 30339, Nairobi, Kenya. Ed. Clive Mutiso. adv.; circ. 2,500.

| 910.202 | VI |

ST. CROIX THIS WEEK. 1960. m. This Week Publishing, Inc., P.O. Box 1627, St. Thomas, VI 00804. TEL 809-774-2500.
Description: For the tourist market.

| 914 | SZ | ISSN 0036-2832 |

ST. GALLEN; offizielles St. Galler Wochenprogramm. (Text in German) 1946. w. 30 Fr.($2) Verkehrsbuero St. Gallen, Postfach 476, Bahnhofplatz 1a, CH-9001 St. Gallen, Switzerland. FAX 071-234304. TELEX 883633. adv.; circ. 5,500 (controlled).

| 914.604 | US |

▼**ST. PETERSBURG NEWS.** (Text in English; summaries in Russian) 1990. q. (Aeroflot, SW) Nielson Communications Ltd., 128 Warncke Rd., Wilton, CT 06897. adv.; circ. 50,000.
Formerly: Leningrad News.
Description: Focuses on Soviet foreign trade and international business. Covers hotels, restaurants, recreation and culture in St. Petersburg.

| 910.202 | VI |

ST. THOMAS THIS WEEK. 1960. w. This Week Publishing, Inc., P.O. Box 1627, St. Thomas, VI 00804. TEL 809-774-2500. Ed. Margot Macdonald Bachman.
Description: For the tourist market.

TRAVEL AND TOURISM   4785

| 914.04 | GW |

SALES GUIDE TO GERMANY. (Editions in English and Japanese) 1971. a. (German National Tourist Office) Redaktion fuer Wirtschaftspublizistik, Heidelbergerstr. 33, 6100 Darmstadt, Germany. TEL 06151-33527. FAX 06151-33529.

| 914.2 | UK |

SALISBURY; Salisbury for all seasons. (Text in English, French, German) 1983. a. free. Salisbury District Council, Publicity Office, Bourne Hill, Salisbury SP1 3UZ, England. TEL 0722-334956. FAX 0722-335855. (Subscr. to: Tourist Information Centre, Fish Row, Salisbury SP1 1EJ, England) Ed. John S. Guthrie. adv.; maps; circ. 30,000.
Former titles (until 1989): Touring from Salisbury; (until 1987): Touring in Historic Wessex.
Description: Promotional brochure for prospective visitors to Salisbury area.

| 910.4 | GW |

SAMMLUNG DENKWUERDIGER REISEN. 1988. a. DM.29.80. Edition Temmen, Hohenlohestr. 21, 2800 Bremen 1, Germany. TEL 0421-344280. FAX 0421-348094.

| 917.904 | US |

SAN DIEGAN. 1969. a. $2.95. San Diego Guide, Inc., Box 99127, San Diego, CA 92109. TEL 619-275-2213. Ed. D. Craig. adv.; cum.index; circ. 175,000.
Description: Covers San Diego and Baja California, Mexico.

| 917.904 | US |

SAN FRANCISCO (YEAR). a. $10. Harper Collins Publishers, Birnbaum Travel Guides, 10 E. 53rd St., New York, NY 10022-5299. TEL 212-207-7000. illus.; index.

| 917.904 | US |

SAN FRANCISCO BOOK. 1984. q. San Francisco Convention & Visitors Bureau, 201 Third St., Ste. 900, San Francisco, CA 94103. TEL 415-974-6900. FAX 415-227-2602. TELEX 797810 SFCUB. Ed. Cynthia W. Hu. adv.; circ. 600,000.
Description: Provides information on the San Francisco Bay area: sightseeing, restaurants, retail and events.

| 910.09 | US |

SAN JUANS BECKON; & Fidalgo Islands, Sidney, B.C. 1964. 2/yr. $20 in Washington (State); other states $24. Islanders' Sounder, Box 758, Eastsound, WA 98245. FAX 206-376-4501. circ. 4,600.

| 910.09 | US |

SANDWICH ISLANDS MAGAZINE. 1986. q. $16. Resort Publications, Inc., Box 748, Kilauea, Kauai, HI 96754. TEL 808-828-1125. FAX 808-828-1266. Ed. Patricia Ewing. adv.; circ. 20,000 (controlled).
Incorporates (in 1990): North Shore; Which was formerly: Hawaiian North Shore.
Description: Regional magazine covering the history and ecology of Kauai Island.

| 791 | FR | ISSN 0036-5793 |

SCENES ET PISTES. 1954. 8/yr. 85 F. Manita Carrington, Pub., 127 rue Saint-Germain, 27400 Louviers, France. Ed. Pierre Balancia. adv.; illus.; circ. 4,000.

| 914.904 | SZ |

SCHWEIZER TOURISTIK; Switzerland's leading travel trade magazine. (Text in German) 1983. w. 145 SFr. (foreign 165 SFr.). Schweizer Touristik AG, Forchstr. 60, CH-8008 Zuerich, Switzerland. TEL 01-3822380. FAX 01-3822388. TELEX 812105. Ed. Hans Stocker. adv.; circ. 6,000.
Description: Each issue focuses on a specific area.

SCI; rivista degli sport invernali. see *SPORTS AND GAMES — Outdoor Life*

| 914.2 | UK |

SCOTLAND. 1972. a. free. Scottish Tourist Board, 23 Ravelston Terrace, Edinburgh EH4 3EU, Scotland. TEL 031-332-2433. FAX 031-343-1513. TELEX 72272. charts; illus.; circ. 750,000.
Former titles: Scotland's for Me; Enjoy Scotland; Scotland: A World of Difference.

TRAVEL AND TOURISM

914.1 UK
SCOTLAND: BED AND BREAKFAST. a. £3.25. Scottish Tourist Board, 23 Ravelston Terr., Edinburgh EH4 3EU, Scotland. TEL 031-332-2433. FAX 031-343-1513. TELEX 72272. circ. 45,000.
  Former titles: Scotland: Where to Stay, Bed and Breakfast; Where to Stay in Scotland. Bed and Breakfast; Supersedes in part: Where to Stay in Scotland (ISSN 0083-9221)

914.1 UK
SCOTLAND: CAMPING AND CARAVAN PARKS. 1960. a. £3.25. Scottish Tourist Board, 23 Ravelston Terr., Edinburgh EH4 3EU, Scotland. TEL 031-332-2433. FAX 031-343-1513. TELEX 72272. adv.; circ. 25,000.
  Former titles: Scotland: Camping and Caravan Sites; Scotland for Touring Caravans; Scotland for Caravan Holidays.

914.104 UK
▼**SCOTLAND FOR OUTDOOR ACTIVITIES.** 1992. a. £4.90. Pastime Publications Ltd., 15 Dublin Street Ln., S., Edinburgh EH1 3PX, Scotland. TEL 031-556-1105. FAX 031-556-1129. adv.; circ. 10,000.

914.1 UK
SCOTLAND FOR THE MOTORIST. 1970. a. £2.95. Pastime Publications Ltd., 15 Dublin Street Ln., S., Edinburgh EH1 3PX, Scotland. TEL 031-556-1105. FAX 031-556-1129. adv.; circ. 20,000.

914.1 UK
SCOTLAND: HOTELS AND GUEST HOUSES. 1947. a. £4.95. Scottish Tourist Board, 23 Ravelston Terr., Edinburgh EH4 3EU, Scotland. TEL 031-332-2433. FAX 031-343-1513. TELEX 72272. circ. 32,000.
  Former titles: Scotland: Where to Stay, Hotels and Guest Houses & Where to Stay in Scotland. Hotels and Guest Houses; Supersedes in part: Where to Stay in Scotland (ISSN 0083-9221)

914.2 UK
SCOTLAND: SELF-CATERING ACCOMMODATION. 1971. a. £4.50. Scottish Tourist Board, 23 Ravelston Terr., Edinburgh EH4 3EU, Scotland. TEL 031-332-2433. FAX 031-343-1513. TELEX 72272. charts; circ. 20,000.

910.2 UK
SCOTLAND: 1001 THINGS TO SEE. 1970. irreg. £3.75. Scottish Tourist Board, 23 Ravelston Terr., Edinburgh EH4 3EU, Scotland. TEL 031-332-2433. FAX 031-343-1513. TELEX 72272.
  Former titles: Scotland: 600 Things to See; Scottish Castles and Historic Houses (ISSN 0080-7931); Scotlands Castles.

914.1 UK ISSN 0961-6608
SCOTLAND'S WHAT'S ON. 1975. m. £11 (Europe £16; overseas £35). What's on Publications, 9A St. Bernards Cresc., Edinburgh EH4 1NR, Scotland. TEL 031-332-0471. FAX 031-343-1573. Ed. Alistair H.N. Stein. adv.; bk.rev.; circ. 30,000.
  Former titles: What's On Scotland; What's On - Key to Scotland; (until June 1985): What's on Across Scotland; (until June 1980): What's on in and Around Edinburgh.
  Description: Guide to leisure and tourism in Scotland.

910.09 381 UK
SCOTTISH COMMERCIAL TRAVELLERS' ASSOCIATION. NEWSCALL. a. £16. Scottish Commercial Travellers' Association, 20 Anderson St., Airdrie ML6 OAA, Scotland. TEL 0236-56161. FAX 0236-66149. circ. 600.

910.202 US
SEA BREEZE. 1977. bi-m. $10. Wachters' Organic Sea Products Corporation, 360 Shaw Rd., South San Francisco, CA 94080. FAX 415-875-1626. Ed. Joseph Wachter. bk.rev.; circ. 50,000 (controlled).

910.202 AT
SEE AUSTRALIA REGIONAL INFORMATION SERIES. 1980. 2/yr. Aus.$24. Research Publications Pty. Ltd., 27A Boronia Rd., Vermont, Vic. 3133, Australia. TEL 03-873-1450. Ed. Ted Colville. adv.; circ. 3,500.
  Former titles: See Australia (ISSN 0810-2236) & Regional Information Series (ISSN 0159-7485)

917.504 US
SEE DAYTONA BEACH. bi-m. Miles Media Group, Inc., 3675 N. Clark Rd., Sarasota, FL 34233-2358. TEL 813-922-3575. Ed. Patti Pearson. circ. 55,000.

919 II ISSN 0037-0762
SEE INDIA; quarterly compendium of the tourist industry. (Text in English) 1967. q. Rs.20($5) A-47-D, DDA Flats, Munirka, New Delhi 110067, India. Ed. J.M.L. Bhatnagar. illus.; circ. 2,000.

914.2 UK ISSN 0267-4599
SELF-CATERING AND FURNISHED HOLIDAYS. 1968. a. £2.50. F.H.G. Publications Ltd., Abbey Mill Business Centre, Seedhill, Paisley PA1 1JN, Scotland. TEL 041-887-0428.
  Formed by the merger of: Self-Catering Holiday Homes, Caravans & Boats; *Formerly:* Furnished Holidays in Britain.

910.4 UK
SELF CATERING HOLIDAYS. 1959. a. £2.95. Pastime Publications Ltd., 15 Dublin Street Ln., S., Edinburgh EH1 3PX, Scotland. TEL 031-556-1105. FAX 031-556-1129. adv.; circ. 45,000.

910 US
SENIOR CITIZEN'S GUIDE TO BUDGET TRAVEL IN THE UNITED STATES AND CANADA. 1983. irreg. $4.95. Pilot Books, 103 Cooper St., Babylon, NY 11702. TEL 516-422-2225. FAX 516-422-2227. Ed. Paige Palmer.
  Description: How to find low cost transportation, accommodations, restaurants, and tours all over the U.S. and Canada.

910.202 CC
SHANDONG LUYOU/TRAVEL IN SHANDONG. (Text in Chinese) bi-m. Shandong Sheng Luyou Ju - Shandong Provincial Bureau of Tourism, No. 26, Jing 10 Lu, Jinan, Shandong 250014, People's Republic of China. TEL 615858. Ed. Sun Chuanyuan.

916.8 SA
SHELL TOURIST GUIDE TO SOUTH AFRICA. a. R.4.40. Chris van Rensburg Publications (Pty) Ltd., Box 25272, Marshalltown 2107, South Africa. adv.

SHIPPING AND TOURISM. see *TRANSPORTATION — Ships And Shipping*

914.1 UK
SHOPPING IN EDINBURGH. 1981. a. £1. Pastime Publications Ltd., 15 Dublin Street Ln., S., Edinburgh EH1 3PX, Scotland. TEL 031-556-1105. FAX 031-556-1129. adv.; circ. 50,000.

914.104 UK
SHOPPING IN GLASGOW. 1987. a. £1. Pastime Publications Ltd., 15 Dublin Street Ln., S., Edinburgh EH1 3PX, Scotland. TEL 031-556-1105. FAX 031-556-1129. adv.; circ. 30,000.

910.4 SA
SIGNATURE. (Text in Afrikaans, English) 1968. 6/yr. R.12. Diners Club S.A. (Pty) Ltd., Box 10727, Johannesburg 2000, South Africa. Ed. Jack Fisch. adv.; bk.rev.; circ. 41,000.

910.202 II
SIGNATURE. 1977. 12/yr. Rs.130. Parsiana Publications Pvt. Ltd., c/o H.L. Rochat & Co., Navsari Chambers, A.K. Nayak Marg, Fort, Bombay 400 001, India. TEL 22-2042624. FAX 22-2042922. TELEX 11-5710 RABO IN. Ed. Jehangir R. Patel. adv.; bk.rev.; circ. 40,000.
  Description: Citibank Diner Club magazine focussing primarily on travel.

910.202 JA
SIGNATURE. (Text in Japanese) 1961. m. 4800 Yen. Diners Club of Japan, Senshu Bldg., 13-7 Shibuya 1-chome, Shibuya-ku, Tokyo, Japan. TEL 03-356-6131. FAX 03-352-6415. TELEX 242-2704. Ed. Yoichiro Akashi. adv.; bk.rev.; circ. 350,000.

910.202 SI
SIGNATURE. (Text in English) m. Signature Publishing Pty. Ltd., 2-201 Merlin Place, Beach Rd., Singapore 7, Singapore. Ed. Filipina Elizabeth Reyes. adv.; circ. 32,000.

910.202 BE
SIGNATURE. (Editions in Dutch, French) 1963. q. 680 Fr. Diners Club, 36 rue Ravenstein, B-1000 Brussels, Belgium. TEL 02-5159525. FAX 02-5136652. Ed.Bd. adv.; bk.rev.; circ. 130,000.

916 KE
SIGNATURE. (Text in English) 1982. bi-m. EAs.55. Signature, Diners Club Africa, Box 30403, Nairobi, Kenya. TEL 727-2438. FAX 723747. TELEX 22554. Ed. Carole McNab. adv.; bk.rev.; illus.; cum.index; circ. 8,000.

910.202 GR
SIGNATURE EXCLUSIVE. (Text in Greek) bi-m. membership. Diners Club of Greece, S.A., P.O. Box 10, Athens, Greece. adv.; circ. 100,000 (controlled).
  Formerly (until 1989): Signature.

SIGNPOST FOR NORTHWEST TRAILS. see *SPORTS AND GAMES — Outdoor Life*

SILENCE COURIER; Gaestezeitschrift der Silencehotels Deutschland. see *GENERAL INTEREST PERIODICALS — Germany*

919 SI ISSN 0129-5020
SINGAPORE TRAVEL. 1964. bi-m. free. Singapore Tourist Promotion Board, Raffles City Tower No. 36-04, 250 North Bridge Road, Singapore 0617, Singapore. TEL 3396622. FAX 65-3399423. TELEX STBSIN RS 33375. Ed. Georgette Tan. adv.; illus.; circ. 22,000.
  Formerly (until 1978): Singapore Travel News (ISSN 0037-5713)

910.202 SI
SINGAPORE VISITOR. Japanese edition: Japanese Singapore Visitor. (Text in English) Eng.ed. 1970; Jap. ed. 1981. w. free. Creations and Communications Pte. Ltd., 38 Duxton Hill, Singapore 0208, Singapore. FAX 221-3530. Ed. Susan A. Gallagher. adv.; circ. English ed. 18,000; Japanese ed. 12,000.
  Description: Contains information on places of interest, nightlife, shopping, and restaurants for tourists visiting Singapore.

SKI DIRECTORY. see *SPORTS AND GAMES*

SKI SCOTLAND. see *SPORTS AND GAMES — Outdoor Life*

SKI TRAVEL. see *SPORTS AND GAMES — Outdoor Life*

910.202 US
SOBEK'S EXCEPTIONAL ADVENTURES. 1983. a. membership. Mountain Travel - Sobek, 6420 Fairmount Ave., El Cerrito, CA 94530. Ed. John Yost. adv.; illus.; index; circ. 160,000 (controlled). (back issues avail.)
  Former titles: Sobek's Adventure Annual & Sobek's Adventure Vacation; Adventure Book.
  Description: Descriptive listing of adventure travel vacations with dates and costs.

914.6 388.3 SP
SOCIEDAD ESPANOLA DE AUTOMOVILES DE TURISMO. MEMORIA Y BALANCE. 1953. a. free. Sociedad Espanola de Automoviles de Turismo, S.A., Paseo Castellana, 278, Madrid 16, Spain. charts; stat.; circ. 1,000.

SOFIA NEWS; weekly for politics, economics, culture, tourism and sport. see *POLITICAL SCIENCE*

910.09 US
SOJOURNS. q. Journal Communications Inc., 5123 Paddock, No. C-23, Brentwood, TN 37027. TEL 615-371-0010. FAX 615-371-0258. Ed. Barry Parker. circ. 750,000.

910.09 CU
SOL DE CUBA. (Editions in English, French, Spanish) 1983. q. Instituto Nacional del Turismo, Malecon y G, Vedado, Havana, Cuba. TEL 7-32-9881. TELEX 511955. Ed. Doris Velez. circ. 200,000.

915.404 II
SOMA; magazine for Oberoi Hotels International. (Text in English) 1971. q. $20. East India Hotels Ltd., Oberoi Towers, Nariman Point, Bombay 400 021, India. TEL 2025757. FAX 2043282. TELEX 84153-OBBY-IN. Ed. Gouri Wagadarikar. adv.; bk.rev.; illus.; circ. 10,000.

910.202 236   US
SOPHISTICATED LEISURE TRAVEL DIRECTORY. 1985. a. $8.95. Schueler Communications, Inc., 208 N. Townsend St., Syracuse, NY 13203. TEL 315-472-6948. Ed. Bruce Coville. adv.; index; circ. 400,000.
  Formerly (until 1986): Seniority Travel Directory.

647.94   US   ISSN 0278-4378
SOURCE I; news items and features for vacation travel newsletters. 1981. bi-m. $60. Travel Marketing, 19235 Village 19, Camarillo, CA 93012. Ed. Evelyn Reichman.

647.94   US   ISSN 0278-4386
SOURCE II; news items and features for business travel newsletters. bi-m. $60. Travel Marketing, 19235 Village 19, Camarillo, CA 93012. TEL 805-987-0563. Ed. Evelyn Reichman. **Indexed:** Sage Pub.Admin.Abstr.

918   US   ISSN 0193-7944
F2211
SOUTH AMERICA (NEW YORK). 1980. a. $17. Harper Collins Publihsers, Birnbaum Travel Guides, 10 E. 53rd St., New York, NY 10022-5299. TEL 212-420-5800. FAX 212-420-5855. Ed. Stephen Birnbaum. circ. 10,000.

918   US   ISSN 0889-7891
F2224
SOUTH AMERICAN EXPLORER. (Text in English) 1977. q. $30 membership. South American Explorers Club, Box 18327, Denver, CO 80218. TEL 303-320-0388. (Alt. addr.: Avda. Republica de Portugal 416, Brana, Lima, Peru. TEL 31-44-80) Ed. Don Montague. adv.; bk.rev.; illus.; circ. 5,000. (back issues avail.)
  Description: Explores various field sciences in Latin America.

SOUTH AUSTRALIAN MOTOR. see *TRANSPORTATION — Automobiles*

917 796.5   US
SOUTH CENTRAL CAMPBOOK. Cover title: R V and Tent Sites in Arkansas, Kansas, Missouri, Oklahoma, Texas. a. membership. American Automobile Association, 1000 AAA Dr., Heathrow, FL 32746-5063. TEL 407-444-7961. FAX 407-444-7380. adv.; illus.; circ. 253,652.
  Formerly (until 1980): South Central Camping (ISSN 0364-7161)

910.202   SI   ISSN 0218-0553
SOUTH EAST ASIA TRAVELLER; the complete ASEAN travel magazine. (Text in English) 1985. bi-m. S.$113 for 18 nos. Compass Publishing Private Ltd., 336 Smith St., No.04-303, New Bridge Centre, Singapore 0105, Singapore. TEL 2211111. FAX 222-5251. Ed. Julia Goh. adv.; circ. 21,000. (back issues avail.)
  Description: Travel news and information for South East Asia.

910.09   US
SOUTHEAST TRAVEL PROFESSIONAL. m. Florida Travel Professional, 1200 N.W. 78th Ave., No. 201, Miami, FL 33126-1817. TEL 305-592-6133. FAX 305-592-9741. Ed. Lawrence Cafiero. adv.; circ. 10,000.

917 796.5   US   ISSN 0731-5112
GV191.42.S83
SOUTHEASTERN CAMPBOOK. Cover title: R V and Tent Sites in Alabama, Florida, Georgia, Kentucky, Louisiana, Mississippi, North Carolina, South Carolina, Tennessee. a. membership. American Automobile Association, 1000 AAA Dr., Heathrow, FL 32746-5063. TEL 407-444-7962. FAX 407-444-7380. adv.; illus.; circ. 372,075.
  Formerly (until 1980): Southeastern Camping (ISSN 0162-9166)

916.8 916.9   SA
SOUTHERN AFRICA AND THE INDIAN OCEAN ISLANDS TRAVEL TRADE DIRECTORY. 1974. a. $15. Da Gama Publishers (Pty) Ltd., 4th Fl., Cavendish Chambers, 183 Jeppe St., P.O. Box 3910, Johannesburg 2000, South Africa. Ed. June Wickham. adv.; circ. 3,000.

910   SA
SOUTHERN AFRICA'S TRAVEL NEWS WEEKLY. (Text in English) 1970. w. R.140. Travel and Trade Publishing (Pty) Ltd., 12 Loveday Street, P.O. Box 6202, Johannesburg 2000, South Africa. TEL 011-833-1030. FAX 011-834-6889. Ed. Leona Marsh. adv.; circ. 8,500 (controlled).
  Formerly: Southern Africa's Travel News.
  Description: Provides timely news and information of relevance to the Southern African travel industry.

917   US   ISSN 0038-3902
SOUTHERN CALIFORNIA GUIDE; the current directory of restaurants, art galleries, hotels, motels, entertainment, shopping, sightseeing, tourist attractions. (Text in English and Japanese) 1919. m. Westworld Publishing Corp., 11385 Exposition Bl., No. 102, Los Angeles, CA 90064. TEL 213-391-8255. Ed. Valerie Summers. adv.; bk.rev.; circ. 28,000 (controlled).

SOUTHERN LINKS. see *SPORTS AND GAMES — Ball Games*

910.09 051   US   ISSN 1041-3642
SOUTHERN LIVING TRAVEL SOUTH. 1984. q. $12 (effective Jan. 1992). Southern Progress Corp. (Subsidiary of: Time, Inc. Magazine Co.), c/o H. Jahnson, V.P. Circulation, 2100 Lakeshore Dr., Birmingham, AL 35209. TEL 205-877-6000. (Subscr. to: P.O Box 830611, Birmingham, AL 35201) adv.; charts; illus.; tr.lit.; circ. 200,000. (back issues avail.)
  Formerly (until 1988): Southern Travel; **Supersedes** (in 1986): Travel South (ISSN 0743-6629)
  Description: Travel magazine for tourists visiting the Southern United States.

910.202   AT
SOUTHERN SUN. 1985. m. Aus.$10. Southern Publishers, 34 Auckland St., Bega, N.S.W., Australia. TEL 044-725-342. (Subscr. to: P.O. Box 411, Batemans Bay, N.S.W. 2536, Australia) circ. 30,000. (back issues avail.)

917 796.5   US   ISSN 0731-8103
GV191.42.A165
SOUTHWESTERN CAMPBOOK. Cover title: R V and Tent Sites in Arizona, Colorado, New Mexico, Utah. a. membership. American Automobile Association, 1000 AAA Dr., Heathrow, FL 32746-5063. TEL 407-444-7962. FAX 407-444-7380. adv.; illus.; circ. 353,625.
  Formerly (until 1980): Southwestern Camping (ISSN 0094-2855)

SOUVENIR. see *GIFTWARE AND TOYS*

910.09   CN
SPA DESTINATIONS/DESTINATIONS SPA. (Editions in English, French) 1989. q. Can.$20($40) Publicom Inc., 1055 Beaver Hall, Ste. 200, Montreal, Que. H2Z 1S5, Canada. TEL 514-874-0874. FAX 514-866-3839. Ed. Ann Bolduc. adv.; circ. 11,579.

SPA FINDER. see *PHYSICAL FITNESS AND HYGIENE*

SPA VACATIONS. see *PHYSICAL FITNESS AND HYGIENE*

914.604   US
SPAIN (YEAR). a. $17. Harper Collins Publishers, Birnbaum Travel Guides, 10 E. 53rd St., New York, NY 10022-5299. TEL 212-207-7000. illus.; index.

SPARTACUS INTERNATIONAL GAY GUIDE. see *HOMOSEXUALITY*

SPELEO. see *EARTH SCIENCES*

915.404   CE
SPICY ISLE.* (Text in English) 1971. q. 23 Rajamalwatte Rd., Colombo 15, Sri Lanka. Ed.Bd. adv.; illus.

SPORTACCOM; magazine voor realisatie, beheer en onderhoud van sportsaccomodaties. see *SPORTS AND GAMES*

SPOTLIGHT (ROBBINSVILLE). see *TRANSPORTATION — Automobiles*

TRAVEL AND TOURISM   **4787**

915.04   CE
SRI LANKA ACCOMMODATION GUIDE. (Text in English, French, German) s-a. free. Ceylon Tourist Board, P.O. Box 1504, Colombo 3, Sri Lanka. adv.; charts; circ. 10,000.
  Formerly: Welcome to Sri Lanka.

910.202   CE
SRI LANKA OFFICIAL TOURIST HANDBOOK. (Text in English, French, German) s-a. Ceylon Tourist Board, P.O. Box 1504, Colombo 3, Sri Lanka. Ed. Florence Ratwalte. circ. 100,000.
  Formerly: Sri Lanka Tourist Information.

910.4   CE
SRI LANKA TODAY. (Text in English) q. Government Department of Information, 7 Sir Baron Jayatilaka Mawatha, Colombo 1, Sri Lanka. TEL 1-28376. Ed. Manel Abhayaratne. circ. 80,000.

914   DK
STADTFUHER KOPENHAGEN. (Text in German) a. Politikens Service Selskab A-S, Vestergade 24, 1456 Copenhagen K, Denmark. FAX 45-33-328674. adv.; circ. 200,000.

STAR INTERNATIONAL. see *SPORTS AND GAMES*

974.9   US
STATE AND NATIONAL REGISTERS OF HISTORIC PLACES. 1977. a. free. Department of Environmental Protection, Division of Parks and Forestry, Office of New Jersey Heritage, CN 404, Trenton, NJ 08625. TEL 609-292-2023. Ed. Susan Pringle. circ. 2,000.
  Description: Lists names and addresses of properties designated "historic places".

914   IT   ISSN 0039-1131
STELUTIS ALPINIS. 1955. m. membership. Unione Operaia Escursionisti Italiani, Sezione di Udine, Via Grazzano N. 7, 33100 Udine, Italy. Dir. Enzo Driussi. adv.; abstr.; illus.; stat.; circ. 3,500. (tabloid format)

STI OG VARDE. see *SPORTS AND GAMES — Outdoor Life*

910.09   IT
STRALIGNANO. (Text in German, Italian) 1956. w. during summer. L.12000($6) Pubblistudio de Zorzi Casa Editrice s.a.s., Via Marinoni 53, 33100 Udine, Italy. TEL 0432-508243. FAX 0432-508243. Ed.Bd. adv.; circ. 10,000. (back issues avail.)

910.202   GW
STRASSEN. 1962. a. DM.14.80. Ravenstein Verkag GmbH, Auf der Krautweide 24, 6232 Bad Soden, Germany. TEL 06196-609630. FAX 06196-27450. TELEX 4072538-HACO-D.

STRATEGIC INFORMATION ON U S AIR TRAVEL. see *TRANSPORTATION — Air Transport*

STUDENT TRAVELS. see *EDUCATION — International Education Programs*

910.09   US   ISSN 0095-3482
G155.U6
SUMMARY AND ANALYSIS OF INTERNATIONAL TRAVEL IN THE U.S. 1983. m. $250. U.S. Travel & Tourism Administration, Main Commerce Bldg., Washington, DC 20230. FAX 202-377-8887. (Subscr. to: 14th St. & Constitution Ave., N.W., Rm. 1516, Washington, DC 20230) Ed. Ron Erdmann. stat.

910.09   SA
SUN. (Text in English) 1985. m. Metromedia Pty. Ltd., P.O. Box 65663, Benmore 2010, South Africa. Ed. Nelia van Velden. adv.; circ. 45,000. (back issues avail.)

919   CJ
SUN LIVING. q. free. Cayman News, Ltd., Box 764, Grand Cayman, Cayman Islands. Ed. Mike Cross. adv.

SURVEY OF OVERSEAS VISITORS TO SINGAPORE. see *TRAVEL AND TOURISM — Abstracting, Bibliographies, Statistics*

T

4788 TRAVEL AND TOURISM

910.09   US
SURVEY OF STATE TRAVEL OFFICES. 1973. a. $75. U S Travel Data Center, Two Lafayette Ctr., 1133 21st St., N.W., Washington, DC 20036.
TEL 202-293-1040. (reprint service avail. from CIS)
    Description: State-by-state analysis of official government agencies responsible for travel promotion.

910.2   CN
T I A C NEWSLETTER. 1946. bi-m. free. Tourism Industry Association of Canada, 130 Albert St., Ste. 1016, Ottawa, Ont. K1P 5G4, Canada.
TEL 613-238-3883. FAX 613-238-3878. Ed. Debra Berk. circ. 2,000.

910.09   GW
T I D TOURISTIK KONTAKT. 1965. a. DM.40. TourCon Hannelore Niedecken GmbH, Postfach 323462, 2000 Hamburg 13, Germany. TEL 040-44187341. FAX 040-44187348. TELEX 211140 NIEDD.

910.09   JA
T M. (Travel Management) (Text in English, Japanese) 1978. s-m. 28700 Yen (foreign 8700 Yen). Travel Consultants of Japan, Ltd., Kono Bldg., 1-23-9 Nishi-Shinbashi, Minato-ku, Tokyo 105, Japan.
TEL 03-3595-0621. FAX 03-3580-5619. TELEX J25279-HTLINDEX. Ed. Masato Toyoda. circ. 9,754. (back issues avail.)

910.09   US   ISSN 0893-1259
T M S - LETTER. (Travel Marketing and Sales Newsletter) 1987. s-m. $120. Nissen-Lie Communications, Inc., 441 Lexington Ave., Ste. 1209 A, New York, NY 10017.
TEL 212-986-1025. FAX 212-986-1033. Ed. Angela Reale Mathisen. adv.; bk.rev.; circ. 1,500.
    Description: News report and digest on travel marketing, sales, advertising and public relations.

910.2   US   ISSN 0039-8454
T.P.A. TRAVELERS. 1965. q. $0.40 to non-members. Travelers Protective Association of America, 3755 Lindell Blvd., St. Louis, MO 36108.
TEL 314-371-0533. Ed. Nick Moser. illus.; circ. 188,000. (processed)

910.09   US
T T R A NEWSLETTER. 6/yr. membership. (Travel and Tourism Research Association) University of Utah, Bureau of Economic & Business Research, Box 58066, Salt Lake City, UT 84158.
TEL 801-581-3363. FAX 801-581-3354. Ed. Jan Crispin-Little. adv.; circ. 1,100 (controlled). (back issues avail.)

910   JA
TABI NI DEYO. 1973. bi-m. 2700 Yen. Mainichi Newspapers, 1-1-1, Hitotsubashi, Chiyoda-ku, Tokyo 100-51, Japan. TEL 03-3212-0321.
FAX 03-3211-0895. TELEX 22324. Ed. Reimi Yamazaki. circ. 130,000.

910.202 385   JA
TABI TO TETSUDO. 1971. 4/yr. 770 Yen. Tetsudo Journal Sha, Iidabashi 4-8-6, Chiyoda-ku, Tokyo, Japan. FAX 03-265-3597. Ed. Toshimoto Takeshima. adv.; bk.rev.; circ. 130,000.

910.202   FP   ISSN 1157-349X
TAHITI BEACH PRESS. w. Tahiti Publications Touristiques, B.P. 887, Papeete, Tahiti.
FAX 689-435184.

910.202   FP
TAHITI SUN PRESS. (Text in English) 1980. m. $50. Tahiti Publications Touristiques, B.P. 887, Papeete, Tahiti. FAX 689-435184. Eds. Al Prince, Gerard Warti. adv.; circ. 3,000.
    Formerly: Update Tahiti (ISSN 0766-3269)

915.4   II
TAJ MAGAZINE. (Text in English) 1972. q. Rs.220($24) (Taj Group of Hotels) Indian Hotels Company Ltd., Apollo Bunder, Bombay 400 039, India. TEL 22-2023366. FAX 022-2872711. TELEX 11-82442 TAJB IN. Ed. Camellia Panjabi. adv.; charts; illus.; circ. 25,000.
    Description: News about India for tourists.

910.2   DK   ISSN 0107-1270
TAKE OFF; travel trade magazine for Scandinavian agents, tourist offices, airlines. 1957. m. DKK 350 (foreign DKK 450). Skandinavisk Bladforlag A-S, Frederiksberg Alle 3, DK-1621 Copenhagen V, Denmark. TEL 45-31-238099. FAX 45-31237042. adv.; bk.rev.; illus.; stat.; circ. 6,000 (controlled).

338.7
TAMIL NADU TOURISM DEVELOPMENT CORPORATION. ANNUAL REPORT.* (Text in English) a. Tamil Nadu Tourism Development Corporation, V.S.T. Motor Bldgs., 34 Mount Rd., Madras 600008, India.

910.09   AT
TASMANIAN TRAVELWAYS. 1960. bi-m. free. (Department of Tourism) Creative Publications Pty., Ltd., 72 Charles St., Launceston, Tas. 7250, Australia. Ed.Bd. adv.; charts; illus.; stat.; circ. 78,000.

914.2   UK
TASTE OF SCOTLAND GUIDE (YEAR). 1972. a. £3.25($18) Taste of Scotland Scheme Ltd., 33 Melville St., Edinburgh EH3 7JF, Scotland.
TEL 031-220 1900. FAX 031-220-6102. Ed. Nancy K. Campbell. adv.; illus.; circ. 50,000.
    Formerly: Taste of Scotland.

TEACHERS' GUIDE TO OVERSEAS TEACHING; a complete and comprehensive guide of English-language schools and colleges overseas. see EDUCATION — International Education Programs

910.202   US
TEACHERS TRAVEL GAZETTE. q? Teachers Travel, Box 5513, Santa Monica, CA 90405.

910.4   AT
TEMPO AUSTRALIA. 1983. bi-m. Aus.$30. Unimedia Publications Pty. Ltd., 272 Elgin St., Carlton, Vic. 3053, Australia. TEL 03-347-3422.
FAX 03-347-5769. Ed. Ettore Flacco. circ. 35,000. (back issues avail.)
    Formerly: Australian Tempo Libero.

910.202   CN   ISSN 0823-5708
TEMPS LIBRE. 1983. 3/yr. Can.$10 (foreign Can.$16). Regroupement Tourisme Jeunesse, 4545 Pierre de Coubertin Av., Sta. M, Box 1000, Montreal, Que. H1V 3R2, Canada. TEL 514-252-3117.
FAX 514-252-3119. TELEX 05-829647. adv.; circ. 50,000.
    Description: Covers youth tourism, foreign exchange programs, travel tips, youth hostels.

917.604   US
TENNESSEE TRAVEL GUIDE. 1983. a. Tom Jackson & Associates, Inc., 1210 Eighth Ave., S., Nashville, TN 37203. TEL 615-242-7747. FAX 615-259-2042. adv.; circ. 40,000.
    Description: Lists lodging, dining, attractions, tours, shopping and airline services statewide.

917.604   US
TENNESSEE VISITOR GUIDE. 1947. m. Tom Jackson & Associates, Inc., 1210 Eighth Ave., S., Nashville, TN 37203. TEL 615-242-7747. FAX 615-259-2042. adv.; circ. 400,000.
    Description: Lists tourist attractions and events in five geographic areas of the state. Includes feature articles covering different events.

910   CN   ISSN 0712-8657
TEOROS. 1982. q. Can.$15 (foreign Can.$18). Universite du Quebec a Montreal, Service des Publications, C.P. 8888, Succ. "A", Montreal, Que. H3C 3P8, Canada. TEL 514-987-7747. Ed. Jean Stafford. (back issues avail.) **Indexed:** Pt.de Rep. (1991-).

914   IT   ISSN 0040-3652
TERAMO; le notizie del turismo. (Text in English, French, German and Italian) 1959. irreg. free. Ente Provinciale per Il Turismo di Teramo, Via del Castello,10, 64100 Teramo, Italy.
TEL 0861-54243. Dir. Giammario Sgattoni. bk.rev.; charts; illus.; tr.lit.; circ. 10,000.
    Description: Forum covering news from the region of Teramo.

TERRA GRISCHUNA - GRAUBUENDEN; Zeitschrift fuer buendner Natur, Kultur, Tourismus, Verkehr. see ENVIRONMENTAL STUDIES

917   SZ
TERRA PLANA.* no.6, 1972. s-a. 6 Fr. Sarganserlaendische Buchdruckerei AG, 8887 Mels, Switzerland. Ed. A. Stucky.

625.7   US   ISSN 0040-4349
TE24.T4
TEXAS HIGHWAYS. 1974. m. $12.50 (foreign $20). Texas Department of Transportation, Travel and Information Division, Box 141009, Austin, TX 78714-1009. TEL 512-483-3675.
FAX 512-483-3672. Ed. Tommie Pinkard. bk.rev.; illus.; circ. 430,000. (back issues avail.)
—BLDSC shelfmark: 8798.870000.

917.604   US
TEXAS PEOPLE AND PLACES. m. Huckaby Communications, Box 810, Joshua, TX 76058. TEL 817-556-3605. Ed. Billy J. Huckaby. adv.; circ. 30,000.

910.202   US
THE TEXAS SURVEYOR. bi-m. Texas Society of Porfessional Surveyors, 400 E. Anderson Lane, No. 340, Austin, TX 78752-3824. TEL 512-834-1275. FAX 512-834-1277.

917.604   US
▼**TEXAS TOUR AND MEETING GUIDE.** 1990. a. Publishing Partnership (Subsidiary of: Texas Monthly, Inc.), Box 1569, Austin, TX 78767. TEL 512-320-6900. adv.; circ. 52,355.
    Description: Provides travel information on the seven regions of Texas. Covers cities, attractions, events, weather, ranches, wineries, and golf courses.

910.2 914   UK   ISSN 0082-3805
THAMES BOOK. 1966. a. £3.50. Link House Magazines Ltd., Link House, Dingwall Ave., Croydon, Surrey CR9 2TA, England. TEL 01-686-2599.
FAX 01-760-0973. TELEX 947709. (Subscr. to: U M S, Stephenson House, 1st Fl., Brunel Centre, Bletchley, Milton Keynes, MK2 2EW) maps; illus.
    Description: Guide to the River Thames, from its source to its estuary. Covers boating, fishing and mooring, with photography, operational and regulatory information.

914   UK   ISSN 0040-6171
THIS ENGLAND. 1968. q. £14.50($29) This England Ltd., Box 52, Cheltenham, Gloucestershire, England. TEL 0242-577775. FAX 0242-222034. Ed. Roy Faiers. adv.; bk.rev.; illus.; circ. 182,252. **Indexed:** Child.Lit.Abstr.

916.7   BS
THIS IS BOTSWANA. 1987. irreg. free. Information and Broadcasting, Private Bag 0060, Gaborone, Botswana. Ed. Tom Okoyo. circ. 10,000.
    Description: Presents travel and tourism features for travelers and business people. Highlights the natural wonders and potential for develpment in tourism and related industries.

918.604   EC
THIS IS ECUADOR. (Text in English) 1968. m. La Nina 55 y Avda. Amazonas, Quito, Ecuador. Dir. Gustavo Vallejo.

917.704   US
▼**THIS IS INDIANAPOLIS.** 1990. s-a. Indianapolis Convention and Visitors Association, One Hoosier Dome, Ste. 100, Indianapolis, IN 46225.
TEL 317-639-4282. FAX 317-639-5273. Ed. Betsy A. Kranz. adv.; circ. 150,000.
    Description: For business and pleasure travelers and convention delegates staying at ICVA member hotels. Covers area leisure interests, travel-related services and city information.

914   UK   ISSN 0040-6198
THIS IS LONDON; the weekly magazine for visitors. 1956. w. £28. This is London Magazine Ltd., 3 Heddon St., London W1R 7LE, England.
TEL 071-434-1281. FAX 071-287-0592. Ed. Sue Webster. adv.; bk.rev.; film rev.; play rev.; illus.; circ. 10,250.

910.09   MX
THIS IS MEXICO; Mexico's weekly visitor's pocket guide. 1960. w. free. Editorial This is Mexico, Calle Londres 166, Apdo 6-728, 06600 Mexico, D.F., Mexico.
TEL 533-15-40. FAX 915-208-28-38. TELEX 017-71-881. Ed. Jesus Maldonado. adv.; charts; illus.; circ. 20,000.

915.3   QA
THIS IS QATAR. (Text in English) 1978. q. Gulf Publica Relations (Qatar), P.O. Box 4015, Doha, Qatar. TEL 413813. FAX 413814. TELEX 4787. Ed. Yousuf Qassim Darwish. adv.; circ. 5,000.

THIS IS VIETNAM. see *BUSINESS AND ECONOMICS*

910.202   US
THIS WEEK BIG ISLAND. 1966. w. free. Hagadone Hawaii, Inc., This Week Magazines, 715 S. King St., Ste. 325, Honolulu, HI 96813. TEL 808-526-1702. FAX 808-533-0471. Ed. Simone Grandmain. circ. 18,500.
    Description: Includes information, maps and coupons for the visitor.

919 910.202   AT
THIS WEEK IN ADELAIDE. w. Peter Isaacson Publications Pty. Ltd., 45-50 Porter St., Prahran, Vic. 3181, Australia. TEL 03-520-5555. FAX 03-521-3647. Ed. Robert Gibson. circ. 7,095.
    Description: General information for travel in Adelaide.

919 910.202   AT
THIS WEEK IN BRISBANE. w. Peter Isaacson Publications Pty. Ltd., 45-50 Porter St., Prahran, Vic. 3181, Australia. TEL 03-520-5555. FAX 03-521-3647. Ed. Robert Gibson. circ. 7,156.
    Description: General information for travel in Brisbane.

919 910.202   AT
THIS WEEK IN CANBERRA. w. Peter Isaacson Publications Pty. Ltd., 45-50 Porter St., Prahran, Vic. 3181, Australia. TEL 03-520-5555. FAX 03-521-3647. Ed. Robert Gibson. circ. 7,079.
    Description: Travel information on sightseeing, shopping, entertainment, and dining out in Canberra.

919 910.202   AT
THIS WEEK IN DARWIN. w. Peter Isaacson Publications Pty. Ltd., 45-50 Porter St., Prahran, Vic. 3181, Australia. TEL 03-520-5555. FAX 03-521-3647. Ed. Robert Gibson. circ. 6,319.
    Description: Travel information on sightseeing, shopping, entertainment, accommodations and dining out in Darwin.

919 910.202   AT
THIS WEEK IN MELBOURNE. w. Peter Isaacson Publications Pty. Ltd., 45-50 Porter St., Prahran, Vic. 3181, Australia. TEL 03-520-5555. FAX 03-521-3647. Ed. Robert Gibson. circ. 10,457.
    Description: Travel information on sightseeing, shopping, entertainment, accommodations, and dining out in Melbourne.

919 910.202   AT
THIS WEEK IN PERTH. w. Peter Isaacson Publications Pty. Ltd., 45-50 Porter St., Prahran, Vic. 3181, Australia. TEL 03-520-5555. FAX 03-521-3647. Ed. Robert Gibson. circ. 7,688.
    Description: Tourist information on accommodations, sightseeing, shopping, entertainment, and dining out in Perth.

919 910.202   AT
THIS WEEK IN SYDNEY. w. Peter Isaacson Publications Pty. Ltd., 45-50 Porter St., Prahran, Vic. 3181, Australia. TEL 03-520-5555. FAX 03-521-3647. Ed. Robert Gibson. circ. 10,840.
    Description: Tourist information on sightseeing, shopping, entertainment, dining out and accommodations in Sydney.

919 910.202   AT
THIS WEEK IN TASMANIA. w. Peter Isaacson Publications Pty. Ltd., 45-50 Porter St., Prahran, Vic. 3181, Australia. TEL 03-520-5555. FAX 03-529-3647. Ed. Robert Gibson. circ. 9,117.

910.09   US
THIS WEEK IN THE PIEDMONT TRIAD. 1960. w. $24. Box 8278, Greensboro, NC 27419. TEL 919-854-3033. Ed. Richard Crotners. adv.; circ. 7,000.

917.4   US
THIS WEEK IN THE POCONOS. 1932. 29/yr. $52. Printing Craftsmen, Inc., Pocono Pines, PA 18350. TEL 717-839-7103. FAX 717-646-5315. Ed. Peggy Bancroft. adv.; circ. 248,000.

910.2   US
THIS WEEK IN WESTERN NORTH CAROLINA. 1930. w. $20. Mountain Meadows Publications, 959 Merrimon Ave., Box 1513, Asheville, NC 28802. TEL 704-253-9299. Ed. Bobbi Cannon. adv.; charts; illus.; circ. 8,000.
    Formerly: This Week (ISSN 0040-6309)
    Description: Informs the local resident, newcomer and tourist about things to do and see in western North Carolina.

910.202   US
THIS WEEK KAUAI. 1966. w. free. Hagadone Hawaii, Inc., This Week Magazines, 715 S. King St., Ste. 325, Honolulu, HI 96813. TEL 808-526-1702. FAX 808-533-0471. Ed. Simone Grandmain. circ. 17,500.
    Description: Provides information, maps and coupons for the visitor.

910.202   US
THIS WEEK MAUI. 1966. w. free. Hagadone Hawaii, Inc., This Week Magazines, 715 S. King St., Ste. 325, Honolulu, HI 96813. TEL 808-526-1702. FAX 808-879-1846. Ed. Simone Grandmain. circ. 25,500.
    Description: Provides information, maps and coupons for the visitor.

910.202   US
THIS WEEK OAHU. 1966. w. free. Hagadone Hawaii, Inc., This Week Magazines, 715 S. King St., Ste. 325, Honolulu, HI 96813. TEL 808-526-1702. FAX 808-533-0471. Ed. Simone Grandmain. circ. 42,000.
    Description: Provides information, maps and coupons for the visitor.

910.202   SI
THIS WEEK SINGAPORE; newspaper for travelers. 1977. w. Asian Business Press Pte. Ltd. (Subsidiary of: Asian Business Press Group), 100 Beach Rd., 26-00 Shaw Towers, Singapore 0718, Singapore. TEL 294-3366. FAX 298-5534. TELEX RS-25280-ABPSIN. Ed. Gaynor Thomas. adv.; circ. 17,500.
    Formerly (until 1989): Lion City (ISSN 0129-4822)

910.2 919   US
THRUM'S ALL ABOUT HAWAII. 1970. a. $3.50. S B Printers, Inc., Box 100, Honolulu, HI 96810-0100. TEL 808-537-5353. Ed. Arlene King Duncan. adv.; circ. 25,000.
    Former titles: Almanac of the Pacific (ISSN 0065-6461); All About Hawaii.

917.1   CN
THUNDER BAY GUEST; visitor's magazine. 1963. m. free. Algoma Publishers Ltd., 1126 Roland St., Thunder Bay, Ont. P7B 5M4, Canada. TEL 807-623-4424. FAX 807-622-3140. Ed. Lorraine Deck. adv.; circ. 160,000.

910.202   CN
THUNDER BAY LIFE. 1985. 12/yr. Can.$15($15) North Superior Publishing Inc., 1145 Barton St., Thunder Bay, Ont. P7B 5N3, Canada. TEL 807-623-2348. FAX 807-623-7515. Ed. Scott A. Sumner. circ. 5,000. (back issues avail.)
    Formerly: Thunder Bay Destinations.

TIBET SOCIETY BULLETIN. see *ETHNIC INTERESTS*

910.2   SZ
TICKET. (Editions in French and German) 1930. 6/yr. 20 Fr. membership. Schweizerische Jugendherbergen - Swiss Youth Hostel Association, Engestr. 9, Postfach 85, CH-3000 Bern 26, Switzerland. FAX 031-233231. adv.; bk.rev.; illus.; circ. 120,000.
    Formerly: Jugi - Ajiste (ISSN 0022-6009)

TICKET; tips and travel. see *MILITARY*

910.09   SP
TIEMPO DE VIAJAR. m. Ediciones Zeta, O'Donnell 12, 28009 Madrid, Spain. TEL 91-5781572. FAX 91-5775400. Dir. Emilio Rey.

910.2 917   US   ISSN 1054-5034
TIM BELL'S ALASKA TRAVEL GUIDE. 1960. a. $11.95. Box 65504, Salt Lake City, UT 84165. Ed. Tim Bell. adv.; bk.rev.; circ. 60,000.
    Formerly: Alaska Travel Guide (ISSN 0065-5848)

TRAVEL AND TOURISM   4789

914   UK   ISSN 0049-3910
TIME OUT; London's biggest selling magazine listing London's events plus news & reviews. 1968. w. £1.20. Time Out Magazine Ltd., Tower House, Southampton St., London WC2E 7HD, England. FAX 071-836-4411. (Subscr. to: Unit 8, Grove Ash, Bletchley, Milton Keynes MK1 1BZ, England) Ed. John Morrish. adv.; bk.rev.; film rev.; play rev.; illus.; circ. 88,000.
    —BLDSC shelfmark: 8852.150000.

915.204   JA
TOKYO CITY GUIDE TOUR COMPANION. 24/yr. Tokyo News Service Ltd., Tsukiji Hamarikyu Bldg., 5-3-3 Tsukiji, Chuo-ku, Tokyo 104, Japan. TEL 03-3542-6511.

915.2   JA
TOKYO JOURNAL. m. Intercontinental Marketing Corp., I.P.O. Box 5056, Tokyo 100-31, Japan. TEL 03-661-8373. FAX 03-667-9646.
    Description: Useful news for the foreign resident or traveler.

919.04   AT   ISSN 0725-5365
TOOWOOMBA AND GOLDEN WEST VISITORS' GUIDE. s-a. Toowoomba and Golden West Regional Tourist Association Ltd., P.O. Box 3090, Town Hall, Toowoomba, Qld. 4350, Australia. TEL 076-321988. FAX 076-324404. adv.; circ. 35,000.
    Description: Regional information for tourists and travellers to this area.

TOOWOOMBA - QUEENSLAND'S GROWTH CENTRE. see *BUSINESS AND ECONOMICS — Production Of Goods And Services*

914   IT
TOSCANA QUI. m. L.50000 (foreign L.100000). Casa Editrice Bonechi, Via Cairoli, 18-A, Florence, Italy. TEL 055-576841.

910.202   US
TOUR & TRAVEL MARKETPLACE. 6/yr. C M P Publications, Inc., 600 Community Dr., Manhasset, NY 11030. TEL 516-562-5000. FAX 516-365-4601. TELEX 647035-CMP-PUB-MAHA. adv.; circ. 51,000.

910.09   US
TOUR AND TRAVEL NEWS. 1985. m. C M P Publications, Inc., 600 Community Dr., Manhasset, NY 11030. TEL 516-562-5000. FAX 516-365-4601. TELEX 647035-CMP-PUB-MAHA. Ed. Jim Alkon. circ. 41,190.
    ●Also available online. Vendor(s): Data-Star, DIALOG, NewsNet.

910   JA
TOUR COMPANION. (Text in English) 1973. fortn. free. Tokyo News Service Ltd. - Tokyo Nyusu Tsushinsha, Tsukiji Hamarikyu Bldg., 10th Fl., 3-3 Tsukiji 5-chome, Chuo-ku, Tokyo 104, Japan. TEL 03-3542-6511. Ed. Takashi Takeda. adv.; bk.rev.; charts; illus.; circ. 80,000.
    Description: Provides all foreigners in the Tokyo vicinity, whether tourists or residents, with the most up-to-date information concerning events, shopping, dining, night-life and other topics of interest.

917.1   CN
TOUR HEBDO. (Text in English, French) 1986. w. $16. Tour Hebdo M.D. Inc., 1224 Stanley St., Rm. 313, Montreal, Que. H3B 2S7, Canada. TEL 514-397-1344. FAX 514-397-1764. Ed. Didier Montrevel. adv.; circ. 4,413. (tabloid format)

190.202   CN
TOUR ORGANIZERS' HANDBOOK/GUIDE DU DIRECTEUR DE TOURNEES DE SPECTACLES. (Text in English, French) 1977. irreg., latest May, 1981. Can.$11($16) (foreign Can.$25). Canada Council, Touring Office, Box 1047, 99 Metcalfe St., Ottawa, Ont. K1P 5V8, Canada. TEL 613-598-4392. FAX 613-598-4404.

910.09   US
TOUR TRADE. m. Travel Trade Publications, 15 W. 44th St., New York, NY 10036. TEL 212-730-6600. FAX 212-730-7137. adv.; circ. 69,983.
    Description: Provides travel agency personnel with news and features on the North American tour and travel market.

TRAVEL AND TOURISM

TOURARTS. see BUSINESS AND ECONOMICS — Trade And Industrial Directories

917.6 US ISSN 0361-4948
F324.3
TOURBOOK: ALABAMA, LOUISIANA, MISSISSIPPI. Cover title: Alabama, Louisiana, Mississippi TourBook. a. membership. American Automobile Association, 1000 AAA Dr., Heathrow, FL 32746-5063. TEL 407-444-4300. FAX 407-444-7380. adv.; illus.; circ. 881,912.

917.89 US ISSN 0362-3599
F809.3
TOURBOOK: ARIZONA, NEW MEXICO. Cover title: Arizona, New Mexico TourBook. a. membership. American Automobile Association, 1000 AAA Dr., Heathrow, FL 32746-5063. TEL 407-444-4300. FAX 407-444-7380. adv.; illus.; circ. 1,339,656.

917.6 US
TOURBOOK: ARKANSAS, KANSAS, MISSOURI, OKLAHOMA. Cover title: Arkansas, Kansas, Missouri, Oklahoma TourBook. a. membership. American Automobile Association, 1000 AAA Dr., Heathrow, FL 32746-5063. TEL 407-444-4300. FAX 407-444-7380. adv.; illus.; circ. 1,162,175.

917.15 US ISSN 0363-1788
F1035.8
TOURBOOK: ATLANTIC PROVINCES AND QUEBEC. Cover title: Atlantic Provinces and Quebec; New Brunswick Newfoundland, Nova Scotia, Prince Edward Island, Quebec TourBook. a. membership. American Automobile Association, 1000 AAA Dr., Heathrow, FL 32746-5063. TEL 407-444-4300. FAX 407-444-7380. (Co-sponsor: Canadian Automobile Association) adv.; illus.; circ. 648,281.
Formerly: Eastern Canada Tour Book (ISSN 0569-2857)

917.9 US
TOURBOOK: CALIFORNIA, NEVADA. Cover title: California, Nevada TourBook. a. membership. American Automobile Association, 1000 AAA Dr., Heathrow, FL 32746-5053. TEL 407-444-4300. FAX 407-444-7380. adv.; illus.; circ. 3,084,480.

917.8 US ISSN 0362-9821
F774.3
TOURBOOK: COLORADO, UTAH. Cover title: Colorado, Utah TourBook. a. membership. American Automobile Association, 1000 AAA Dr., Heathrow, FL 32746-5063. TEL 407-444-4300. FAX 407-444-7380. adv.; illus.; circ. 1,097,196.

917.4 US
TOURBOOK: CONNECTICUT, MASSACHUSETTS, RHODE ISLAND. Cover title: Connecticut, Massachusetts, Rhode Island TourBook. a. membership. American Automobile Association, 1000 AAA Dr., Heathrow, FL 32746-5063. TEL 407-444-4300. FAX 407-444-7380. adv.; illus.; circ. 1,281,720.
Supersedes in part: Northeastern Tour Book (ISSN 0468-6853)

917.59 US ISSN 0516-9674
GV1024
TOURBOOK: FLORIDA. Cover title: Florida TourBook. 1965. a. membership. American Automobile Association, 1000 AAA Dr., Heathrow, FL 32746-5063. TEL 407-444-4300. FAX 407-444-7380. adv.; illus.; circ. 2,518,692.

917.5 US ISSN 0361-4956
F284.3
TOURBOOK: GEORGIA, NORTH CAROLINA, SOUTH CAROLINA. Cover title: Georgia, North Carolina, South Carolina TourBook. a. membership. American Automobile Association, 1000 AAA Dr., Heathrow, FL 32746-5063. TEL 407-444-4300. FAX 407-444-7380. adv.; illus.; circ. 2,330,669.

917 US
TOURBOOK: HAWAII. Cover title: Hawaii TourBook. a. membership. American Automobile Association, 1000 AAA Dr., Heathrow, FL 32746-5063. TEL 407-444-4300. FAX 407-444-7380. adv.; illus.; circ. 405,332.

917.9 US ISSN 0363-2695
F744.3
TOURBOOK: IDAHO, MONTANA, WYOMING. Cover title: Idaho, Montana, Wyoming TourBook. a. membership. American Automobile Association, 1000 AAA Dr., Heathrow, FL 32746-5063. TEL 407-444-4300. FAX 407-444-7380. adv.; illus.; circ. 877,910.
Supersedes in part: Northwestern Tour Book (ISSN 0094-078X); Continues: Northwestern States.

917 US
TOURBOOK: ILLINOIS, INDIANA, OHIO. Cover title: Illinois, Indiana, Ohio TourBook. a. membership. American Automobile Association, 1000 AAA Dr., Heathrow, FL 32746-5063. TEL 407-444-4300. FAX 407-444-7380. adv.; illus.; circ. 1,961,004.

917.68 US ISSN 0361-4964
F449.3
TOURBOOK: KENTUCKY, TENNESSEE. Cover title: Kentucky, Tennessee TourBook. a. membership. American Automobile Association, 1000 AAA Dr., Heathrow, FL 32746-5063. TEL 407-444-4300. FAX 407-444-7380. adv.; illus.; circ. 1,588,020.

917.4 US
TOURBOOK: MAINE, NEW HAMPSHIRE, VERMONT. Cover title: Maine, New Hampshire, Vermont TourBook. a. membership. American Automobile Association, 1000 AAA Dr., Heathrow, FL 32746-5063. TEL 407-444-4300. FAX 407-444-7380. adv.; illus.; circ. 1,044,435.
Supersedes in part: Northeastern Tour Book (ISSN 0468-6853)

917 US
TOURBOOK: MICHIGAN, WISCONSIN. Cover title: Michigan, Wisconsin TourBook. a. membership. American Automobile Association, 1000 AAA Dr., Heathrow, FL 32746-5063. TEL 407-444-4300. FAX 407-444-7380. adv.; illus.; circ. 1,001,640.

917 US ISSN 0364-0086
F106
TOURBOOK: MID-ATLANTIC. Cover title: Mid-Atlantic-Delaware, District of Columbia, Maryland, Virginia, West Virginia TourBook. a. membership. American Automobile Association, 1000 AAA Dr., Heathrow, FL 32746-5063. TEL 407-444-4300. FAX 407-444-7380. adv.; illus.; circ. 2,372,245.

917 US
TOURBOOK: NEW JERSEY, PENNSYLVANIA. Cover title: New Jersey, Pennsylvania TourBook. a. membership. American Automobile Association, 1000 AAA Dr., Heathrow, FL 32746-5063. TEL 407-444-4300. FAX 407-444-7380. adv.; illus.; circ. 1,962,072.

917 US ISSN 0363-1540
F117.3
TOURBOOK: NEW YORK. Cover title: New York TourBook. a. membership. American Automobile Association, 1000 AAA Dr., Heathrow, FL 32746-5063. TEL 407-444-4300. FAX 407-444-7380. adv.; illus.; circ. 1,565,832.

917 US
TOURBOOK: NORTH CENTRAL. Cover title: North Central-Iowa, Minnesota, Nebraska, North Dakota, South Dakota Tourbook. a. membership. American Automobile Association, 1000 AAA Dr., Heathrow, FL 32746-5063. TEL 407-444-4300. FAX 407-444-7380. adv.; illus.; circ. 926,220.
Formerly: North Central Tour Book (ISSN 0733-835X)

917 US
TOURBOOK: ONTARIO. Cover title: Ontario TourBook. a. membership. American Automobile Association, 1000 AAA Dr., Heathrow, FL 32746-5063. TEL 407-444-4300. FAX 407-444-7380. adv.; illus.; circ. 861,924.

918 US
TOURBOOK: OREGON, WASHINGTON. Cover title: Oregon, Washington TourBook. a. membership. American Automobile Association, 1000 AAA Dr., Heathrow, FL 32746-5063. FAX 407-444-7380. adv.; illus.; circ. 1,131,725.

917 US
TOURBOOK: TEXAS. Cover title: Texas TourBook. a. membership. American Automobile Association, 1000 AAA Dr., Heathrow, FL 32746-5063. TEL 407-444-4300. FAX 407-444-7380. adv.; illus.; circ. 987,828.

917.12 US ISSN 0362-3602
F1060.4
TOURBOOK: WESTERN CANADA AND ALASKA. Cover title: Western Canada and Alaska, Alberta, British Columbia, Manitoba, Saskatchewan, Northwest Territories, Yukon Territory and Alaska TourBook. a. membership. American Automobile Association, 1000 AAA Dr., Heathrow, FL 32746-5063. TEL 407-444-4300. FAX 407-444-7380. adv.; illus.; circ. 853,020.

TOURING. see TRANSPORTATION — Automobiles

914 SZ ISSN 0040-9758
TOURING. (Editions in French, German and Italian) 1936. fortn. 35 Fr. Druck- und Verlags Konsortium Touring, c/o Zollikofer AG, Fuerstenlandstr. 122, CH-9001 St. Gallen, Switzerland. FAX 31-250226. Ed. Christian E. Ziegler. adv.; bk.rev.; illus.; stat.; circ. 1,200,000. (newspaper)

910.202 FR
TOURING. 1980. m. Touring Club de France, 6 rue Firmin Gillot, 75737 Paris Cedex 15, France. adv.; circ. 207,000.

917.304 US ISSN 1055-6850
▼**TOURING AMERICA.** 1991. bi-m. $15. Fancy Publications, Inc., Box 57900, Los Angeles, CA 90057. TEL 213-385-2222. FAX 213-385-8565. Ed. Gene Booth. adv.; circ. 95,000.

388.3 796.7 BE
TOURING CLUB MAGAZINE. (Text in Dutch, French) 1895. m. 1055 Fr. Touring Club of Belgium, Rue de la Loi 44, 1040 Brussels, Belgium. TEL 02-233-22-11. adv.; bk.rev.; bibl.; illus.; index; circ. 70,000.
Formerly: Autotouring (ISSN 0045-1126)

TOURING GIOVANI. see CHILDREN AND YOUTH — For

910.09 CN
TOURING M. s-m. 606 Cathcart St., Ste. 200, Montreal, Que. H3B 1K9, Canada. TEL 514-392-0014. FAX 514-393-9324. Ed. Denis Duquet. circ. 400,000.

919.404 658 AT
TOURISM AND TRAVEL MANAGEMENT. 1989. m. Aus.$74 (effective May 1991). P O L Concepts Pty. Ltd., 125-127 Little Eveleigh St., Redfern, N.S.W. 2016, Australia. TEL 02-318-0500. FAX 02-318-1140. Ed. Eileen Prehn. adv.; circ. 9,000.

910.09 II
TOURISM AND WILDLIFE. (Text in English) 1972. q. Rs.32($16) G.C. Verma, Ed. & Pub., 24 Gola Market, Netaji Subash Marg, New Delhi 110 002, India. adv.; bk.rev.; charts; illus.; circ. 20,000.
Description: For the tourist industry as well as educational institutions. Covers various tourist and wildlife attractions, in addition to art and cultural events.

910.09 UK
THE TOURISM INDUSTRY. a. £15. The Tourism Society, 26 Grosvenor Gardens, London SW1W 0DU, England. TEL 071-730-4380. Ed. Helen Cameron.

910 UK ISSN 0261-5177
G155.A1
TOURISM MANAGEMENT. 1980. 4/yr. £138 in UK & Europe; elsewhere £150. Butterworth - Heinemann Ltd. (Subsidiary of: Reed International PLC), Linacre House, Jordan Hill, Oxford OX2 8DP, England. TEL 0865-310366. FAX 0865-310898. TELEX 83111 BHPOXF G. (Subscr. to: Turpin Transactions Ltd., Distribution Centre, Blackhorse Rd., Letchworth, Herts SG6 1HN, England. TEL 0462-672555) Ed. Frances Brown. abstr.; charts; illus. (also avail. in microform from UMI; back issues avail.) **Indexed:** Cont.Pg.Manage., I D A.
—BLDSC shelfmark: 8870.920970.
Description: Publishes original research in tourism, analysis of current trends, and information on the planning and management of all aspects of travel and tourism.
Refereed Serial

TRAVEL AND TOURISM 4791

915.4 II ISSN 0250-8281
TOURISM RECREATION RESEARCH. (Special issues avail.) (Text in English) 1976. s-a. Rs.500($75) Centre for Tourism Research, A 965-6 Indira Nagar, Lucknow 226 016, India. TEL 71586. FAX 091-0522-234023. Ed. Tej vir Singh. adv.; bk.rev.; bibl.; illus.; circ. 1,500. (back issues avail.) **Indexed:** Rural Recreat.Tour.Abstr., Sportsearch (1981-), World Agri.Econ.& Rural Sociol.Abstr. —BLDSC shelfmark: 8870.922350.

910.4 FR ISSN 0751-6657
TOURISME; courrier des affaires touristiques. 1971. w. 500 F. 58, rue Saint Georges, 75009 Paris, France. FAX 1-40-23-98-18. TELEX 281 078. Ed. Odile Dechelotte. adv.; illus.; circ. 8,500.

910.202 CN ISSN 0836-205X
TOURISME PLUS, LE JOURNAL DES VOYAGES. (Text in French) 1980. w. (46/yr.). Can.$48. Publications Transcontinental Inc., 465 St. Jean St., 9th Fl., Montreal, Que. H2Y 3S4, Canada. TEL 514-842-6491. FAX 514-842-8557. TELEX 055-61971. Ed. Michel Villeneuve. circ. 6,500. (back issues avail.)
Formed by the 1986 merger of: Tourisme Plus (ISSN 0226-6601); Journal des Voyages (ISSN 0225-0462)
Description: Trade information for travel agents, wholesalers, airlines, cruises, and hotels.

910.09 380.6 011 IT ISSN 0394-8536
TOURISPRESS ITALIA; giornale d'informazione turistica. 1985. s-m. L.90000. Travelpress Italia s.r.l., Via Valperga Caluso 15, 10125 Turin, Italy. TEL 011-669-85-59-62. FAX 011-657058. TELEX 224468 TPS I. Ed. Paola Segre. circ. 9,679. (back issues avail.)
Description: Worldwide travel trade information.

910.202 658 US
TOURIST ATTRACTIONS AND PARKS. 1972. 7/yr. $25. Kane Communications, Inc., 7000 Terminal Square, Ste. 210, Upper Darby, PA 19082. TEL 215-734-2420. Ed. Charles Tooley. adv.; circ. 21,500.
Incorporates: American Showman.
Description: For the management personnel of theme, water, and amusement parks, zoos, museums and arcades.

910.09 GW ISSN 0936-3637
TOURIST AUF REISEN; Tourist-Information fuer Gruppen- und Einzelreisen. 1989. a. DM.7.50. Stuenings Verlag, Postfach 2980, 4150 Krefeld, Germany. TEL 021521-8530. circ. 50,000. (back issues avail.)

971.04 CN
TOURIST GUIDE BOOK OF ONTARIO. 1921. a. free. C A A Auto Club & Travel Agency, 1215 Ouellette Ave., P.O. Box 580, Windsor, Ont. N9A 6N3, Canada. TEL 519-255-1212. FAX 519-977-1197. Ed. Douglas O'Neil. adv.; circ. 150,000.

TOURIST MAGAZINE. see SPORTS AND GAMES — Outdoor Life

910.202 AT
TOURIST PARK GUIDE. 1946. a. Aus.$3.25. Syne Magazines (Subsidiary of: Syme Media Pty. Ltd.), 603-611 Little Lonsdale St., Melbourne, Vic. 3000, Australia. TEL 03-605-4222. FAX 03-670-9096. Ed. Gwen Haslar. adv.; circ. 30,000.

910.2 GW ISSN 0049-4283
TOURISTIK AKTUELL; the Travel Trade Report. 1970. w. DM.94. Jaeger Verlag GmbH, Holzhofallee 38, Postfach 110452, 6100 Darmstadt, Germany. TEL 06151-391-0. FAX 06151-391200. TELEX 419548-DAV-D. adv.; bk.rev.; abstr.; illus.; stat.; circ. 11,604.

910.09 GW ISSN 0173-606X
TOURISTIK R.E.P.O.R.T.. 1980. fortn. DM.72($36) W D V Wirtschaftsdienst, Lange Str. 13, Postfach 112041, 6000 Frankfurt a.M. 1, Germany. TEL 069-29907-0. FAX 069-29907-499. Ed. Heiner Berninger. circ. 16,128.

910.202 CY
TOURISTIKA CHRONIKA/TOURISM CHRONICLE. 1986. bi-m. POB 7083, Nicosia, Cyprus. TEL 02-443240. Ed. A. Karouzis. circ. 2,000.

910.09 US
TOURS!. 1987. q. $12. National Tour Marketing Services, Inc., 546 E. Main St., Lexington, KY 40508. TEL 606-253-1036. FAX 606-233-1099. adv.; circ. 100,000.
Description: Focuses on destinations and attractions in North America that appeal to escorted group tour travelers.

910.202 US ISSN 0890-2852
TOURS & RESORTS. 1985. bi-m. $18. World Publishing Co. (Subsidiary of: Century Publishing Company), 990 Grove St., Evanston, IL 60201. TEL 708-491-6440. FAX 718-491-0459. (Subscr. to: Box 400, Mt Morris, IL 61054-0400) Ed. Robert Meyers. adv.; charts; illus.; tr.lit.; circ. 225,000. (also avail. in microform)

910.202 US ISSN 0278-467X T49.5
TOURS AND VISITS DIRECTORY. irreg., 2nd ed., 1981. $120. Gale Research Inc., 835 Penobscot Bldg., Detroit, MI 48226. TEL 313-961-2242. FAX 313-961-6083. TELEX 810-221-7086.
Formerly: Behind the Scenes (ISSN 0270-3416)

917.1 CN
TOURS ON MOTORCOACH. French edition: Excurions en Autocar. 1988. m. (Bus Owners Association) Publicom Inc., 1055 Beaver Hall, Ste. 200, Montreal, Que. H2Z 1S5, Canada. TEL 514-874-0874. FAX 514-878-9779. TELEX 055-61866. Ed. Ray Dulude. adv.; circ. 12,127 (controlled).
Description: Travel trade publication for group tour organizers.

TOUTES LES NOUVELLES DE L'HOTELLERIE ET DU TOURISME. see HOTELS AND RESTAURANTS

914.3 AU
TRACHTLER.* 1974. 3/yr. Landesverband der Heimat und Trachtenvereine fuer Tirol, Langstrasse 46, A-6020 Innsbruck, Austria. Ed. Hans Glatzl. adv.; illus.

330 US
TRADESHOW & CONVENTION GUIDE. 1964. a. $85. B P I Communications, Inc., Amusement Business Division, Box 24970, Nashville, TN 37202. TEL 615-321-4250. FAX 615-327-1575. Ed. Tom Powell. adv.; circ. 6,000.
Description: Sourcebook for those planning trade shows and conventions, corporate or association meetings and exhibits. Includes dates and data for conventions and trade shows for up to the next 5 years. Also lists hotels, auditoriums, convention centers and facilities servicing the industry.

TRADESHOW DIRECTORY. see BUSINESS AND ECONOMICS — Trade And Industrial Directories

910.202 US
TRADEWIND MAGAZINE. (Text in English, Spanish) 1978. q. (A L M Antillean Airlines) Caribbean Travel and Life, Inc., 8403 Colesville Rd., Ste. 830, Silver Spring, MD 20910. TEL 301-588-2300. FAX 301-588-2256. Ed. Norie Quintos. adv.; bk.rev.; circ. 250,000 (controlled).
Description: Showcases the vacation, recreation and cultural opportunities throughout the Carribean and South America.

910.09 PE
TRAFICO; directorio informativo y mensual de transporte y turismo. 1972. m. Trafico S.A., Av. Nicolas de Pierola 742, Of. 506, Lima, Peru. TEL 31-3820. Ed. Alberto G. Castro. circ. 3,500.

910.09 US
TRAILBLAZER. 1978. m. $24. Thousand Trails, Inc. (Subsidiary of: Southmark Corp.), 1000 124th Ave., N.E., Bellevue, WA 98005. FAX 206-646-1378. Ed. Tim Burns. adv.; tr.lit.; circ. 250,000.
Description: For RV travelers and resort camping enthusiasts.

TRAILER LIFE CAMPGROUND AND R V SERVICES DIRECTORY. see SPORTS AND GAMES — Outdoor Life

TRAILER LIFE'S RECREATIONAL VEHICLE CAMPGROUND AND SERVICES DIRECTORY. see BUSINESS AND ECONOMICS — Trade And Industrial Directories

910.202 UK
TRAILFINDER. 1970. 3/yr. £8 (foreign £12). Trailfinders Ltd., 42-50 Earls Court Rd., London W8 6EJ, England. TEL 071-937-7933. FAX 071-937-9294. TELEX 919670. Ed. Gabrielle Hunt. adv.; circ. 200,000.
Description: Travel articles on non-European destinations, especially Australia, Asia and North America. Section on latest flight prices worldwide.

TRAILS-A-WAY. see SPORTS AND GAMES — Outdoor Life

TRANSPORT; guia ecuatoriana de transporte y turismo. see TRANSPORTATION

TRANSPORT AND TOURISM JOURNAL. see TRANSPORTATION

914 BE ISSN 0041-1442
TRANSPORT ET TOURISME/TRANSPORT EN TOERISME. (Editions in Dutch, French) 1928. m. 7250 Fr. Federation Belge des Exploitants d'Autobus et d'Autocars, 4 Leon Lepagestraat, B-1000 Brussels, Belgium. TEL 02-512-23-33. FAX 051-22-9273. TELEX 22781. Ed. P. Laeremans. adv.; illus.; circ. 450 (French ed.); 600 (Dutch ed.).

910.202 MX
TRANSPORTES Y TURISMO. 1935. m. Insurgentes Norte No. 696, Mexico 4, DF, Mexico. Dir. Prof. Dolores Marquez V. de Mejia. adv.; circ. 4,000.

910.09 CN ISSN 0836-7353
TRAVEL A LA CARTE. 1988. 6/yr. Can.$11.97($18) (foreign $22). Interpress, Inc., 136 Walton St., Port Hope, Ont. L1A 1N5, Canada. TEL 416-444-3633. FAX 416-444-3931. Ed. Heather Kerrigan. adv.; circ. 145,000.
Description: National travel and leisure magazine. Features articles focusing on domestic and international travel.

910.2 UK ISSN 0041-1981
TRAVEL AGENCY; Britain's monthly business, marketing and sales publication for the travel trade. 1925. m. £50. Maclean Hunter Ltd., Maclean Hunter House, Chalk Lane, Cockfosters Rd., Barnet, Hersts EN4 0BU, England. TEL 081-975-9759. FAX 081-440-1796. TELEX 299072 MACHUN G. Ed. Andrew McGeehan. adv.; charts; illus.; mkt.; stat.; tr.lit.; index; circ. 11,310.

910.09 MY
TRAVEL AGENCY.* vol.5, 1978. m. Aus.$20. Phoenix Enterprise, KTM Godown No. 2A, Jalan Tun Sambanthan, 50470 Kuala Lumpur, Malaysia. adv.; illus.

910.09 US
TRAVEL AGENCY REFERENCE & PROFILE DIRECTORY. 1970. q. $115 per no. World Travel Communications Inc., 911 W. Moana Ln., Ste. 11830, Reno, NV 89503. TEL 702-795-2411. FAX 702-795-8473. Ed. Julie Jackson. circ. 5,000.
Incorporates (in 1991): Travel Agency Communications Reports - Eastern Edition; Which was formerly: Eastern Travel Sales Guide; Incorporates (in 1991): Travel Agency Communications Reports - North American Edition; (in 1991): Travel Agency Communications Reports - Western Edition; Which was formerly: Western Travel Sales Guide.

910.2 US ISSN 0041-199X
TRAVEL AGENT.* 1930. s-w. $12. American Traveler, Inc. (Subsidiary of: Fairchild Publications), 7 W. 34th St., New York, NY 10001. TEL 212-630-4000. Ed. Richard S. Kahn. adv.; bk.rev.; film rev.; charts; illus.; mkt.; circ. 42,532. **Indexed:** P.A.I.S., Tr.& Indus.Ind.

910.09 US
TRAVEL AGENT MAGAZINE.* 1978. q. $79 (foreign $149); free to qualified personnel. Travel Agent Magazine, 801 Second Ave., New York, NY 10017-4706. TEL 215-887-1900. FAX 212-887-1865. Ed. Mikki Dorsey. adv.; circ. 55,000.
Former titles (until 1988): Travel Agent Domestic Tour Manual; Official Sales Guide Motorcoach Tours of North America; Motorcoach Tour Mart.

TRAVEL AND TOURISM

914   CN
TRAVEL AGENTS GUIDE TO EUROPE. (Text English, French) 1988. a. Motivations International Inc., 14 Ronan Ave., Toronto, Ont. M4N 2X9, Canada. TEL 416-481-6384. Ed. John Stephenson. adv.; circ. 10,000.

910.2   US   ISSN 0041-2007
G149
TRAVEL & LEISURE. (In 6 regional eds., and 1 demographic ed.) 1971. m. $32. American Express Publishing Corp., 1120 Ave. of the Americas, New York, NY 10036. TEL 212-382-5600. Ed. Ila Stanger. adv.; bk.rev.; illus.; tr.lit.; circ. 1,200,000. (also avail. in microform from UMI) **Indexed:** Access (1975-), Mag.Ind., PMR.
    Formerly: Travel and Camera (ISSN 0049-4542)

TRAVEL AND TOURISM - ABSTRACTING, BIBLIOGRAPHIES, STATISTICS. see *TRAVEL AND TOURISM — Abstracting, Bibliographies, Statistics*

910.202   UK   ISSN 0269-3755
G155.A1
TRAVEL & TOURISM ANALYST. bi-m. £495($945) (Economist Intelligence Unit) Business International Ltd., 40 Duke St., London W1A 1DW, England. TEL 71-493-6711. FAX 71-499-9767. TELEX 266353 EIUG. (US addr.: Business International Corp., 215 Park Ave. S., New York, NY 10003. TEL 212-460-0600)
    —BLDSC shelfmark: 9045.450900.
    Description: News and forecasts for all sectors of the industry: airlines, travel agents, hotels and accommodations.

350   US
TRAVEL & TOURISM EXECUTIVE REPORT. 1979. m. $85 to non-members. (Association of Travel Marketing Executives) Leisure Industry - Recreation News, Box 43563, Washington, DC 20010. TEL 202-232-7107. Ed. Marj Jensen. adv.; charts; stat.; circ. 4,000.
    Formerly (until 1981): Travel and Tourism Newsletter; **Supersedes:** Travel Marketing News.
    Description: Focuses on the marketing and promotion of travel destination products. Presents information and data on trends and demographics.

910.202   BA
TRAVEL & TOURISM NEWS INTERNATIONAL. (Text in English) m. $90. Al Hilal Publishing & Marketing Group, P.O. Box 224, Manama, Bahrain. TEL 293131. FAX 293400. TELEX 8981 HILAL BN. (In Singapore: Al Hilal Publishing (Far East) Pte Ltd, 50 Jalan Sultan, 20-06 Jalan Sultan Centre, Singapore 0719. TEL 2939233) Ed. Frankie Fernandez. adv.; circ. 5,200.
    Incorporates: Arab Travel Magazine.
    Description: For travel industry professionals, including travel and tour agents, airline and airport personnel, government tourist offices.

910.09   US   ISSN 0276-8968
G149.5
TRAVEL AND TOURISM RESEARCH ASSOCIATION. PROCEEDINGS OF THE ANNUAL CONFERENCE. 1970. a. $75. University of Utah, Bureau of Economic and Business Research, David Eccles School of Business, KDG Bldg., Rm. 401, Salt Lake City, UT 84112. TEL 801-581-6333. FAX 801-581-3354. Ed. Mari Lou Wood. charts; illus.; circ. 900.
    —BLDSC shelfmark: 6840.428450.

990   AT
TRAVEL AUSTRALIA. 1986. s-a. Aus.$50. Australian Tourism Magazine, G.P.O. Box 7039, Sydney, N.S.W. 2000, Australia. TEL 02-233-7516. FAX 02-233-7604. TELEX AA10718892. Ed. Shamoli Dutt. adv.; bk.rev.; circ. 6,000.
    Description: Promotes Australia as a destination and Australian tourist products.

910.22 330.9   HK   ISSN 1011-7768
TRAVEL BUSINESS ANALYST. 1981. m. $300. Travel Business Analyst, 200 Lockhart Rd., 14th Fl., P.O. Box 12761, Hong Kong. TEL 5749310. FAX 8344620. TELEX 62107-HX. (Also: 10 Rue Auguste Vitu, 75015 Paris, France. TEL 1-45-78-6422) Ed. Murray Bailey. bk.rev.; charts; stat. (back issues avail.)

914   BE
TRAVEL CHECK; the Benelux buyer's guide to business & incentive travel. (Text in English) 1982. m. Travel Check, Keesinglaan 19, 2100 Antwerp, Belgium. TEL 323-325-2235. circ. 13,850. (back issues avail.)

915.104   CN   ISSN 0834-258X
TRAVEL CHINA NEWSLETTER. 1986. m. $87. Blendon Information Services, 126 Willowdale Ave., No. 1, Willowdale, Ont. M2N 4Y2, Canada. TEL 416-223-5397. FAX 416-223-5397. Ed. Ruth Lor Malloy. (back issues avail.)

910.09   US   ISSN 1040-0001
TRAVEL COLLECTOR. 1988. m. $11.95. Box 40, Manawa, WI 54949-0040. FAX 414-596-1944. Ed. Dick Sherry. adv.; bk.rev.; circ. 5,000.
    Description: Contains features and news for collectors of virtually anything -- for travelers who collect, and collectors who travel.

910.09   US
▼**TRAVEL COUNSELOR.** 1991. q. (Institute of Certified Travel Agents) C M P Publications, Inc., 600 Community Dr., Manhasset, NY 11030. TEL 516-562-5000. FAX 516-562-5465. adv.; circ. 28,000.
    Description: For certified travel counselors and career travel agents.

917   CN   ISSN 1182-9699
TRAVEL COURIER. 1965. w. Can.$35($40) Baxter Publishing Co., 310 Dupont St., Toronto, Ont. M5R 1V9, Canada. TEL 416-968-7252. FAX 416-968-2377. TELEX 06-528085 BAXPUB CIP. Ed. David Meyler. adv.; charts; illus.; stat.; circ. 6,654. (also avail. in microform from UMI) **Indexed:** Can.B.P.I.
    Formerly (until 1982): Canadian Travel Courier (ISSN 0008-5219)
    Description: Profiles, surveys and articles in the tourist trade.

914.04   GW
TRAVEL DIARY. 1977. a. DM.32. Bulletin Verlag GmbH, Roentgenstr. 80, 6100 Darmstadt 12, Germany. TEL 06151-374066. FAX 06151-370114. Ed. Michael Knuth. circ. 7,500.

910.202   HK   ISSN 0256-4203
TRAVEL DIRECTORY. 1977. a. $25. Interasia Publications, 200 Lockhart Rd., 13th Fl., Hong Kong. Ed. Murray Bailey. adv.; bk.rev.; illus.; circ. 6,000.
    Formerly: Asia Travel Trade Directory.

910.202   SI   ISSN 0218-236X
TRAVEL DIRECTORY (YEAR). (Text in English) 1977. a. $50. Interasia Publications Ltd., Fortune Centre 11-01, 190 Middle Rd., Singapore 0718, Singapore. TEL 3397622. FAX 3398521. adv.; circ. 3,700 (controlled).
    Description: Reference for Asian and Pacific's travel industry professionals and business travellers.

914   CN
TRAVEL EUROPE. 1988. s-a. Motivations International Inc., 14 Ronan Ave., Toronto, Ont. M4N 2X9, Canada. TEL 416-481-6384. Ed. John Stephenson. adv.; circ. 5,000.

910.09   CN
TRAVEL EXCHANGE. 1980. w. Traveltrade Canada Inc., 210-1015 Burrard St., Vancouver, B.C. V62 1Y5, Canada. TEL 604-669-7737. FAX 604-684-2562. Ed. M. Prupas. circ. 12,000.

914.2   UK
TRAVEL G.B.I.; the trade journal of British Isles tourism, transport services and business travel. 1978. m. £28. Travelscope Travel Publications, Foundation House, 3rd Fl., Perseverance Works, 38 Kingsland Rd., London E2 8DD, England. TEL 071-729-5171. FAX 071-729-1716. Ed. Bob MacBeth-Seath. adv.; bk.rev.; illus.; circ. 21,000.
    Description: Covers tourism and travel exclusively in the British Isles. Contains color photographs.

910   SA
TRAVEL GUIDE, S.A. a. R.13.90. Promco (Pty) Ltd., 1202 Radio City, Tulbagh Square, Cape Town 8001, South Africa. Ed. L.D. Solomon. adv.

914.1   US
TRAVEL GUIDE TO EUROPE. a. $8.95. American Automobile Association, 1000 AAA Dr., Heathrow, FL 32746-5063. TEL 407-444-4300. FAX 407-444-7380. adv.; illus.; circ. 286,184.
    Formed by the merger of: British Isles and Ireland Travel Guide (ISSN 0095-1579); Central Europe and Scandinavia Travel Guide (ISSN 0094-3657); Eastern Europe Travel Guide (ISSN 0094-8632); Southern Europe Travel Guide (ISSN 0094-3614)

919
TRAVEL GUIDE TO THE CARIBBEAN. a. $6.95. American Automobile Association, 1000 AAA Dr., Heathrow, FL 32746-5063. TEL 407-444-4300. FAX 407-444-7380. adv.; illus.; circ. 238,152.

917   US
TRAVEL - HOLIDAY. 1901. m. $11. Reader's Digest Association, Inc., Pleasantville, NY 10570. TEL 914-241-5700. Ed. Meggie Simmons. adv.; bk.rev.; dance rev.; film rev.; play rev.; rec.rev.; s-a. index; circ. 775,000. (also avail. in microform from UMI; reprint service avail. from UMI) **Indexed:** Acad.Ind., Bk.Rev.Ind. (1965-), Child.Bk.Rev.Ind. (1965-), Mag.Ind., PMR, R.G., TOM.
    Incorporates (in Jan. 1979): Travel Advisor; **Formerly:** Travel (ISSN 0161-7184); **Formed by the Nov. 1977 merger of:** Travel (ISSN 0041-1965); Holiday (ISSN 0018-3520)

914.95   GR
TRAVEL IN GREECE. (Text in Greek) 1970. a. Dr.450($3.30) Hellenews Ltd., 39 Amaroussiou-Halandriou Rd., Amaroussion, Athens, Greece. Ed. D.G. Kalofolias.

TRAVEL INDUSTRY PERSONNEL DIRECTORY. see *BUSINESS AND ECONOMICS — Trade And Industrial Directories*

TRAVEL INDUSTRY WORLD YEARBOOK; the big picture. see *TRAVEL AND TOURISM — Abstracting, Bibliographies, Statistics*

910.202   BE   ISSN 0771-937X
TRAVEL JOURNALIST/JOURNALISTE DE TOURISME. (Text in English and French) 1977. q. 320 Fr. Centre International de Documentation Touristique, Avenue Brugmann 29-23, B-1060 Brussels, Belgium. TEL 2-5387599. FAX 2-539-40-57. (Co-sponsor: Federation Internationale des Journalistes et Ecrivains du Tourisme) Ed. Marton Payrits. adv.; stat.; circ. 3,200. (back issues avail.)
    —BLDSC shelfmark: 9045.452450.
    Description: Studies made by experts in tourism worldwide.

910.202   US
TRAVEL LIFE. bi-m. Whittle Communications L.P., 333 Main Ave., Knoxville, TN 37902. TEL 615-595-5300. FAX 615-595-5670. Paula Spencer.
    Description: Serves and informs travel agency owners, managers, agents and entertain travel planning professionals.

910.202   LE
TRAVEL MAGAZINE. m. Picot St., Nassau Bldg., P.O. Box 2323, Beirut, Lebanon. adv.; circ. 4,000.

910.2   US   ISSN 0041-2015
TRAVEL MANAGEMENT DAILY. 1970. 5/w. £485. Official Airline Guides, Inc. (New York), Travel Magazines Division, 1775 Broadway, 19th Fl., New York, NY 10019. TEL 212-237-3070. FAX 212-237-3007. (Subscr. to: Official Airline Guides, 2000 Clearwater Dr., Oak Brook, IL 60521) Ed. Jim Glab.

910.202   UK   ISSN 0952-0899
TRAVEL MANAGEMENT INTERNATIONAL; the comprehensive guide to world business travel. 1982. a. £25. Millbank Publications Ltd., 25 Catherine St., London WC2B 5JW, England. TEL 071-379-3036. FAX 071-240-6840. adv.; illus.; circ. 4,000.
    Formerly (until 1985): Travel Managers Reference Book (ISSN 0264-7664)

910.202   US
TRAVEL MANAGEMENT NEWSLETTER. 1965. 2/w. $295. Official Airline Guides, Inc. (New York), 1775 Broadway, 19th fl., New York, NY 10019. TEL 212-237-3070. FAX 212-237-3007. (Subscr. to: Official Airline Guides, 2000 Clearwater Dr., Oak Brook, IL 60521) Ed. Jim Glab. (tabloid format)

TRAVEL AND TOURISM

910.09 US ISSN 0275-3545
TRAVEL MARKETING AND AGENCY MANAGEMENT GUIDELINES; travel management advisory newsletter. 1973. bi-m. $35. Travel Marketing, 19235 Village 19, Camarillo, CA 93012. TEL 805-987-0563. Ed. Evelyn Reichman. bk.rev.

TRAVEL MEDICINE ADVISOR. see *MEDICAL SCIENCES*

612 616.98 UK
TRAVEL MEDICINE INTERNATIONAL. 1983. q. £75 (foreign £100). Mark Allen Publishing Ltd., 288 Croxted Rd., London SE24 9DA, England. TEL 081-671-7521. FAX 081-671-1722. Ed. Dr. Hugh L'Etang. Indexed: Abstr.Hyg.
Formerly: Travel and Traffic Medicine International.

917.404 US
TRAVEL NEW ENGLAND. m. Robert Weiss Associates, 1 Harborside Dr., East Boston, MA 02128-2901. TEL 617-561-4000. Ed. Robert H. Weiss. circ. 5,500.

910.09 US
TRAVEL NEWS. 1970. 4/yr. $7.95. Connie Gibson Wehrman Connor, 1530 Key Blvd., Ste. 230, Arlington, VA 22209-1534. TEL 703-281-9323. Ed. Ed Wojtas. circ. 750.
Description: Contains information on travel bargains for hotels, motels, air fares, and cruise lines.

915 HK ISSN 0252-9629
TRAVEL NEWS ASIA. 1974. fortn. HK.$100($20) in Southeast Asia; elsewhere HK.$200($30). Far East Trade Press Ltd., 2-F Kai Tak Commercial Bldg., 317 Des Voeux Rd., Central, Hong Kong. TEL 5453028. FAX 544-6979. Ed. Mike Sullivan. adv.; circ. 17,843.
Description: News magazine covering developments in Southeast Asia's travel industry.

910.202 US
TRAVEL PEOPLE. 1988. m. C M P Publications, Inc., 600 Community Dr., Manhasset, NY 11030. TEL 516-562-5000. FAX 516-365-4601. TELEX 647035-CMP-PUB-MAHA. Ed. Linda Ball. adv.
Description: Profiles influential people in the travel industry, provides information on travel discounts, travel directories and other publications. Includes a calendar of events.

910.09 US
TRAVEL PLANNER. 1981. bi-m. Hearst Professional Magazines, Inc., 60 E. 42nd St., New York, NY 10165. TEL 212-682-3710. Ed. Stephen Birnbaum. adv.; circ. 93,429.
Description: Details meeting destinations for physicians.

917.3 US
TRAVEL PRINTOUT; research news from the U S Travel Data Center. 1972. m. $75 (foreign $85). U S Travel Data Center, Two Lafayette Ctr., 1133 21st St., N.W., Washington, DC 20036. TEL 202-293-1040. charts; stat.; circ. 500. (reprint service avail. from CIS) Indexed: SRI.
Description: Reports on trends in the travel industry.

910.09 US ISSN 1053-1998
▼**TRAVEL REVIEW.** 1990. bi-m. $27. Box 414, Glen Echo, MD 20812. illus.; maps.
Description: Contains travel articles selected from U.S. and world press.

910.09 CN ISSN 0822-9228
TRAVEL SCOOP. 1983. 10/yr. Can.$39. 411 Annette St., Toronto, Ont. M6P 1R7, Canada. (Subscr. to: 2 Bloor St. W., Ste. 100, Toronto, Ont. M4W 3E2, Canada. TEL 416-975-1726) Ed. Joe Harris. bk.rev.; circ. 12,500.
Description: Information to help Canadians make informed decisions about travel.

910.09 US ISSN 0741-5826
TRAVEL SMART. 1976. m. $44. Communications House Inc., 40 Beechdale Rd., Dobbs Ferry, NY 10522. TEL 914-693-8300. Ed. H.J. Teison. bk.rev.; charts; stat.; tr.lit.; index; circ. 11,000. (back issues avail.)
Incorporates (in 1983): Joy of Travel (ISSN 0277-7738); Which was formerly (1969-1983): Joyer Travel Report (ISSN 0145-9473)
Description: Articles, tips on travel.

916 SA ISSN 0041-204X
TRAVEL TIMES. 1965. m. $25. Da Gama Publishers (Pty) Ltd., 4th Fl., Cavendish Chambers, 183 Jeppe St., P.O. Box 3910, Johannesburg 2000, South Africa. Ed. Colleen Broadley. adv.; bk.rev.; illus.; stat.; circ. 7,200. (tabloid format)
Incorporates: Travelgram (ISSN 0300-3108)

910.09 JA
TRAVEL TIMES. (Text in Japanese) s-m. 16000 Yen($195) Ohta Publications Co., Ltd., Dame Ginza Bldg., 7-18 Ginza, 6-chome, Chuo-ku, Tokyo 104, Japan. TEL 03-3571-1181. FAX 03-3574-1650. Ed. Hiroyuki Takagishi. stat.; circ. 8,300.
Description: Travel and tourism marketing magazine. Offers market analyses and surveys, practical tips on how to cope with emerging trends and consumer preferences, new tour possibilities, profitable auxiliary services, and information on industry activities and events.

910.09 US
TRAVEL TIPS. bi-m. 5281 Scotts Valley Dr., Scotts Valley, CA 95066-3514. TEL 408-438-6150. FAX 408-438-4705. Ed. Elana Anderson. circ. 3,600.

910.2 US ISSN 0041-2066
CODEN: TRTRD3
TRAVEL TRADE;* the business paper of the travel industry. 1929. w. $10. Travel Trade Publications, 15 W. 44th St., 6th fl., New York, NY 10036. TEL 212-730-6600. FAX 212-730-7020. Ed. Joel M. Abels. adv.; illus.; circ. 35,053.

910.09 AT
TRAVEL TRADE. 1964. fortn. Aus.$35. Reed Business Publishing Pty. Ltd., 1-5 Railway St., Chatswood, N.S.W. 2067, Australia. TEL 02-372-5222. FAX 02-419-7533. Ed. Michael Woolley. adv.; illus.; circ. 7,900. (tabloid format)

917.1 CN
TRAVEL TRADE CANADA. 1985. fortn. $20. Travel Trade Canada Ltd., 210-1015 Burrard St., Vancouver, B.C. V6Z 1Y5, Canada. TEL 604-669-7737. FAX 604-684-2562. TELEX 04-508799. Ed. Marilynne Prupas. adv.; circ. 13,280.

TRAVEL TRADE DIRECTORY. see *BUSINESS AND ECONOMICS — Trade And Industrial Directories*

TRAVEL TRADE DIRECTORY, U K AND IRELAND. see *BUSINESS AND ECONOMICS — Trade And Industrial Directories*

901.09 SI
TRAVEL TRADE GAZETTE ASIA. Short title: T T G Asia. (Text in English) 1974. w. $45 in Asia; elsewhere $75. Asian Business Press Pte. Ltd. (Subsidiary of: Asian Business Press Group), 100 Beach Rd., 26-00 Shaw Towers, Singapore 0718, Singapore. TEL 294-3366. Ed. Yeoh Siew Hoon. adv.; circ. 14,500. (tabloid format; back issues avail.)

914 UK
TRAVEL TRADE GAZETTE EUROPA. Short title: T T G Europa. 1968. bi-w. $75 (free in continental Europe). Morgan-Grampian (Publishers) Ltd., Morgan Grampian House, Calderwood St., Woolwich, London SE18 6QH, England. TEL 01-855-7777. FAX 01-854-7476. TELEX 896284. Ed. Ian Ainsworth. adv.; circ. 16,002. (tabloid format)
Formerly: T T G International (ISSN 0039-8500)

914 UK
TRAVEL TRADE GAZETTE U K & IRELAND. Short title: T T G - U K & Ireland. w. $75 (free in the U.K.). Morgan-Grampian (Publishers) Ltd., 30 Calderwood St., Woolwich, London SE18 6QH, England. TEL 01-855-7777. FAX 01-854-7476. TELEX 896284. Ed. Nigel Coombs. adv.; circ. 24,866.

910.09 KO
TRAVEL TRADE JOURNAL; inbound & outbound tourism business. 1986. m. $95. Business Korea Co., Ltd., Yoido P.O. Box 273, Seoul 150-602, S. Korea. TEL 02-784-4010. FAX 02-784-1915. Ed. Kim Kyong-Hae. adv.

910.09 US
TRAVEL TRADE NEWS EDITION. w. Travel Trade Publications, 15 W. 44th St., New York, NY 10036. TEL 212-730-6600. FAX 212-730-7020. Ed. Joel M. Abels.

910.202 TH
TRAVEL TRADE REPORTER - ASIA. 1978. w. $70. Orient Pacific Enterprises Ltd., Asia Bldg., 6th Fl., 294-1 Phya Thai Rd., Bangkok 10400, Thailand. TEL 2-215-4685. FAX 2-216-6599. Ed. Don Ross. adv.; circ. 8,500(controlled).
Description: Covers travel industry, with product news on destinations marketed in Asia.

910 AT
TRAVEL TRADE YEARBOOK. 1965. s-a. Aus.$27. Reed Business Publishing Pty. Ltd., 1-5 Railway St., Chatswood, N.S.W. 2067, Australia. TEL 02-372-5222. FAX 02-419-7533. Ed. Kaye Tanner. circ. 4,200.

910 US
TRAVEL TRENDS IN THE UNITED STATES AND CANADA. 1960. irreg., latest ed. 1984. $45. University of Colorado, Business Research Division, Campus Box 420, Boulder, CO 80309. TEL 303-492-8227. Ed. Charles R. Goeldner. circ. 1,100.
Formerly: Travel Trends in the United States and Canadian Provinces (ISSN 0082-6200)

910.202 GW
TRAVEL TRIBUNE. 1982. w. DM.456. M. Schweizer, Ed. & Pub., Schweizerstr. 14, 6000 Frankfurt a.M. 70, Germany. TEL 069-625024. FAX 069-625026. circ. 1,500.

910.202 SA
TRAVEL VALUE REPORT. 1982. m. R.119($76) Prescon Publishing Corporation, P.O. Box 84004, Greenside 2034, Johannesburg 2001, South Africa. TEL 011-646-9750. FAX 011-646-4617. Ed. Marjorie Dean. adv.; bk.rev.; circ. 4,500. (back issues avail.)
Formerly: Travel World.
Description: Covers Southern African and international travel.

910.2 US ISSN 0041-2082
G155.A1
TRAVEL WEEKLY. 1958. s-w. $26 to individuals; travel agents $19.50. Reed Travel Group (Subsidiary of: Reed International PLC), 500 Plaza Dr., Secaucus, NJ 07096. TEL 201-902-2000. (UK addr.: Church St., Dunstable, Bedfordshire LU5 4HB, England. TEL 0582-600111) adv.; bk.rev.; charts; illus.; mkt.; stat.; circ. 39,000. (tabloid format) Indexed: Bus.Ind., Tr.& Indus.Ind.
●Also available online. Vendor(s): DIALOG.
Incorporates (1969-1991): Travel News (ISSN 0049-4577)

TRAVEL WEEKLY'S WORLD TRAVEL DIRECTORY; official guide to the worldwide travel industry. see *BUSINESS AND ECONOMICS — Trade And Industrial Directories*

910.09 US
TRAVEL WORLD NEWS. m. Travel Industry Network, One Morgan Ave., Norwalk, CT 06851-5006. TEL 203-853-4955. FAX 203-866-1153. Ed. Sara Southworth. circ. 35,706.

TRAVEL WRITER. see *JOURNALISM*

910.202 301.435 US ISSN 1049-6211
▼**TRAVEL 50 & BEYOND.** 1990. q. $11.80. Vacation Publications, Inc., 2411 Fountain View, Houston, TX 77057. TEL 713-974-0445. FAX 713-974-0445. Ed. Alan Fox. adv.; circ. 50,000.
Description: For travelers aged 50 and over. Gives practical tips and recommendations for finding the best values.

917.204 US
TRAVELAGE CARIBBEAN. m. Official Airline Guides, Inc. (New York), 1775 Broadway, New York, NY 10019-1903. TEL 212-237-3000. FAX 212-237-3667. Ed. Ed Sullivan.

910.2 US ISSN 0041-2104
TRAVELAGE EAST. Issued with: TravelAge Europe and TravelAge Caribbean. 1967. w. free to travel agents within region. Official Airline Guides, Inc. (New York), 1775 Broadway, 19th Fl., New York, NY 10019. TEL 212-237-3000. FAX 212-237-3007. (Subscr. to: Circulation Dept., 2000 Clearwater Dr., Oak Brook, IL 60521) Ed. Martin B. Deutsch. adv.; illus.; circ. controlled.
Incorporates (1976-1988?): TravelAge Southeast.

TRAVEL AND TOURISM

914.04   US
TRAVELAGE EUROPE. m. Official Airline Guides, Inc. (New York), 1775 Broadway, New York, NY 10019-1903. TEL 212-237-3000. FAX 212-237-3667. Ed. Ed Sullivan.

910.09   US
TRAVELAGE MID-AMERICA. Issued with: TravelAge Europe and TravelAge Caribbean. 1975. w. $25 (free to travel agents within region). Official Airline Guides, Inc. (Chicago), 320 N. Michigan, Ste. 601, Chicago, IL 60601-5901. TEL 312-346-4952. FAX 312-346-5034. (Subscr. to: Circulation Dept., 1775 Broadway, New York, NY 10019) Ed. Karen Goodwin. adv.; circ. 20,000. (also avail. in microfiche)

917   US   ISSN 0041-1973
TRAVELAGE WEST; the weekly newspaper for the travel agency sales forces in the West. Issued with: TravelAge Europe, TravelAge Caribbean & TravelAge Asia Pacific. 1969. w. $25 (free to travel agents within region). Official Airline Guides, Inc. (San Francisco), 49 Stevenson, No. 460, San Francisco, CA 94105-2909. TEL 415-905-1155. FAX 415-905-1145. Ed. Robert Carlsen. adv.; bk.rev.; illus.; tr.lit.; circ. 34,277 (controlled).
    Description: Regional and national news and destination feature material primarily to help travel agents sell.

919.404   AT
TRAVELEISURE.* 1986. q. Aus.$10. Australasian Holiday Passport Pty. Ltd., P.O. Box 6495, Gold Coast Mail Centre, Surfers Paradise, Qld. 4217, Australia. TEL 075-911-466. Ed. Alexander McRobbie. adv.; bk.rev.; circ. 50,000. (back issues avail.)
    Formerly (until Mar. 1989): Australian Holiday.

917   US
TRAVELER & CONVENTIONEER. 1942. bi-m. $7.50. Travelers' Research Publishing Co., Inc., 11717 S. Vincennes Ave., Chicago, IL 60643. TEL 312-881-3712. Ed. C. M. Markham, Jr. adv.; bk.rev.; stat.; circ. 72,000. (also avail. in microform from UMI)
    Former titles: Negro Traveler and Conventioneer (ISSN 0028-2537); Negro Travel.

917.204   MX
TRAVELERS GUIDE TO MEXICO. (Text in English) 1969. a. $17.95. Prometur, S.A. de C.V., Apdo. 6-1007, 06600 Mexico, D.F., Mexico. TEL 905-271-4736. FAX 905-272-5942. Ed. Wendy Luft. adv.; circ. 3,600,000.
    Description: Guide book to Mexico placed in first class hotel rooms in major resorts and sold in the gift shops of these hotels.

647.94   CN
TRAVELLER. vol.4, 1970. q. membership. Canadian Hostelling Association, Northern Alberta District, 10926-88 Ave., Edmonton, Alta. T6G 0Z1, Canada. TEL 403-432-7798. Ed. Stephen Edgerton. adv.; bk.rev.; circ. 40,000. (processed)
    Formerly: Pathfinder (ISSN 0031-2940)

910.09   UK   ISSN 0262-2726
TRAVELLER. 1970. 4/yr. £36.83 (foreign £46.91). Wexas Ltd., 45 Brompton Rd., London SW3 1DE, England. TEL 071-581-4130. FAX 071-581-1375. TELEX 297155-WEXAS-G. Ed. Caroline Brandenburger. adv.; bk.rev.; charts; illus.; circ. 35,359.
    Formerly: Expedition.
    Description: Travel-related articles, letters, and equipment reviews.

916.7   UK   ISSN 0144-7661
TRAVELLER'S GUIDE TO CENTRAL AND SOUTHERN AFRICA. 1978. irreg. £10.95($19.95) I.C. Publications Ltd., Box 261, Carlton House, 69 Gt. Queen St., London WC2B 5BN, England. TEL 071-404-4333. FAX 071-404-5336. TELEX 8811757 ARABY G. Ed. Alan Rake. (back issues avail.)
    Description: Covers facilities, customs regulations, currencies, climate, health, economy, culture, politics and people.

916.7   UK   ISSN 0144-7653
TRAVELLER'S GUIDE TO EAST AFRICA AND THE INDIAN OCEAN. 1978. irreg. £10.95($19.95) I.C. Publications Ltd., Box 261, Carlton House, 69 Gt. Queen St., London WC2B 5BN, England. TEL 071-404-4333. FAX 071-404-5336. TELEX 8811757 ARABY G. Ed. Alan Rake. (back issues avail.)
    Description: Covers facilities, customs regulations, currencies, climate, health, economy, culture, politics and people.

917.204   MX
TRAVELLERS GUIDE TO MEXICO. 1969. a. $17.95. Promociones de Mercados Turisticos, S.A., Gen. Juan Cano 68, Col. San Miguel Chapultepec, Apdo. 6-1007, 11850 Mexico D.F. TEL 525-5150925. FAX 525-272-5942. Ed. Wendy Luft. adv.; circ. 3,500,000 (controlled).

916.1   UK   ISSN 0144-7637
TRAVELLER'S GUIDE TO NORTH AFRICA. 1978. irreg. £10.95($19.95) I.C. Publications Ltd., Box 261, Carlton House, 69 Gt. Queen St., London WC2B 5BN, England. TEL 071-404-4333. FAX 071-404-5336. TELEX 8811757 ARABY G. Ed. Linda Van Buren.
    Description: Covers facilities, customs regulations, currencies, climate, health, economy, culture, politics and people.

915.6   UK   ISSN 0140-1319
TRAVELLER'S GUIDE TO THE MIDDLE EAST. 1978. irreg. £10.95($19.95) I.C. Publications Ltd., Box 261, Carlton House, 69 Gt. Queen St., London WC2B 5BN, England. TEL 071-404-4333. FAX 071-404-5336. TELEX 8811757 ARABY G. Ed. Pat Lancaster. maps; illus.
    Description: Covers facilities, customs regulations, currencies, climate, health, economy, culture, politics and people.

916.6   UK   ISSN 0144-7645
TRAVELLER'S GUIDE TO WEST AFRICA. 1978. irreg. £10.95($19.95) I.C. Publications Ltd., Box 261, Carlton House, 69 Gt. Queen St., London WC2B 5BN, England. TEL 071-404-4333. FAX 071-404-5336. TELEX 8811757 ARABY G. Ed. Alan Rake. illus. (back issues avail.)
    Description: Covers facilities, customs regulations, currencies, climate, health, economy, culture, politics and people.

910.4   HK
TRAVELLING MAGAZINE/LU HSING TSA CHIH; the first Chinese language travel magazine. (Text in Chinese; captions in English) m. HK.$10 per no. Rm.903, Yat Fat Bldg., 44 Des Voeux Rd., Central, Hong Kong. TEL 5-247738. FAX 5-218390. Ed. Tien-Pei Hsu. adv.; illus.
    Description: Covers travel to all parts of the world.

TRAVELODGE AND VISCOUNT HOTELS NORTH AMERICAN TRAVEL DIRECTORY. see BUSINESS AND ECONOMICS — Trade And Industrial Directories

917   US
TRAVELOG. 1960. a. $2. Meridian Publishing, Inc., Box 10010, Ogden, UT 84409. TEL 801-394-9446. Ed. Marjorie Rice. adv.; illus.; circ. 125,000.

910.09   US   ISSN 0270-2398
TRAVELORE REPORT. Running title: T R Report. 1971. m. $30 (foreign $48). T R Report, 1512 Spruce St., Philadelphia, PA 19102. TEL 215-735-3838. FAX 215-545-7976. Ed. Theodore Barkus. bk.rev.; circ. 25,000.
    Description: Reports and appraises domestic and international travel and tourism.

910.202   CN
TRAVELSAVELIFE. q. 1300 Don Mills Td., Don Mills, Ont. M3B 2W6, Canada. TEL 416-449-9440. FAX 416-441-9754. Ed. William Maki. circ. 75,000.

910.2   AT
TRAVELWEEK; fortnightly newspaper of the travel industry. 1961. fortn. Aus.$35. Peter Isaacson Publications Pty. Ltd., 45-50 Porter St., Prahran, Vic. 3181, Australia. TEL 03-520-5555. FAX 03-521-3647. Ed. Ian McMahon. adv.; bk.rev.; illus.; stat.; circ. 5,053. (tabloid format)
    Former titles: International Travelweek; International Travel (ISSN 0020-9015)

910.202   CN
TRAVELWEEK BULLETIN. 1973. s-w. Can.$44.94($75) (typically set in Jul.). Concepts Travel Media, Ltd., 553 Church St., Toronto, Ont. M4Y 2E2, Canada. FAX 416-924-5721. Ed. Patrick Dineen. adv.; circ. 7,000.
    Formerly: C T M Weekly Bulletin (ISSN 0380-2019)

TRAVELWRITER MARKETLETTER. see JOURNALISM

910.2   US   ISSN 0162-9816
TRAVLTIPS. 1967. bi-m. $15. TravLtips Inc., Box 188, Flushing, NY 11358. TEL 718-939-2400. Ed. Edmund M. Kirk. adv.; illus.; circ. 26,000. (tabloid format)
    Formerly: TravLtips Freighter Bulletin (ISSN 0049-4585)
    Description: Accounts of freighter and other unusual cruises.

914   BE
TREKKERSKRANT. 1945. bi-m. 200 Fr. to non-members. Vlaamse Jeugdherbergcentrale, Van Stralenstraat 40, B-2000 Antwerp, Belgium. Ed. E. De Roover. adv.; circ. 20,000.
    Formerly: Trekker (ISSN 0041-2260)
    Description: News concerning hostels.

910.2   UK
TRIANGLE. 1972. 3/yr. £6 to non-members. Youth Hostels Association (England and Wales), Trevelyan House, St. Albans, Herts AL1 2DY, England. TEL 0727-55215. FAX 0727-44126. Ed. Hellen Barnes. adv.; bk.rev.; illus.; circ. 320,000. **Indexed:** Sci.Abstr.
    Former titles: Hostelling News (ISSN 0267-9353); Hostelling News (ISSN 0306-8927); Supersedes: Youth Hosteller (ISSN 0044-1228)

917   US   ISSN 0041-2619
TRIANGLE POINTER. 1961. w. $27. Village Companies, Inc., Box 2777, Chapel Hill, NC 27515. Ed. Sue Chen Reeder. adv.; charts; circ. 13,000.

TRILOGY. see SPORTS AND GAMES — Outdoor Life

910.09   UK
TRIP OUT. 1977. biennial. £4.25. G.P. Hamer, Ed. & Pub., 77 St. Mary's Grove, London W4 3LW, England. (back issues avail.)

910.09   GW
DER TROTTER. 1975. q. DM.40 membership. Deutsche Zentrale fuer Globetrotter e.V., c/o Hans Michael Buer, Birkenweg 19, 2359 Henstedt-Ulzburg, Germany. TEL 04193-3914. bk.rev.; abstr.; charts; illus.; stat.; index; circ. 1,400. (back issues avail.)
    Formerly: Globetrotter.
    Description: Magazine for world travellers with travel accounts, information, tips, personal stories, and reader's letters.

TUEBINGER BLAETTER. see COLLEGE AND ALUMNI

917   PN
TURISGUIA. (Text in English, Spanish) 1964. m. $36. Apdo. Postal 9525, Panama 4, Panama. TEL 25-8486. Ed. Roy Tasco Wesley. adv.; circ. 10,000.

917   IT
TURISMO D'AFFARI. 8/yr. L.20000. Ediman s.r.l., Via S. Simpliciano 4, 20121 Milan, Italy. adv.; circ. 30,000.

910.202   IT
TURISMO D'ITALIA. 1988. m. L.60000 to non-members; members L.30000. (Federazione delle Associazioni Italiane Alberghi e Turismo) Ediman Due, Via S. Simpliciano 4, 20121 Milan, Italy. TEL 02-869-0587. adv.

910.202   IT
TURISMO GRADESE. (Text in German, Italian) 1960. w. during summer. L.12000($5.50) Pubblistudio de Zorzi Casa Editrice s.a.s., Via Marinoni 53, Udine, Italy. TEL 0432-508243. FAX 0432-508243. adv.; circ. 7,000. (back issues avail.)
    Description: Guide for tourists to Grado.

914.504   IT
TURISMO VENETO. 1980. m. L.20000. Editrice Turismo Triveneto, Via Torino 61, 30172 Mestre, Italy. Ed. Pierluigi Violin. adv.; circ. 20,000.

TRAVEL AND TOURISM

910.09   BL
TURISPRESS. m. Hotelnews Ediciões e Promoções Ltda., Rua Camuiramo 36, CEP 22270 Rio de Janeiro RJ; 4/91 input 91094(DL), Brazil. TEL 21-286-2218. TELEX 21-34148. Ed. Marcos Milone.

914   SW   ISSN 0041-4190
TURIST. 1933. 6/yr. membership. Svenska Turistfoereningen - Swedish Touring Club, Drottninggatan 33, Box 25, 101 20 Stockholm, Sweden. Ed. Cenneth Sparby. adv.; bk.rev.; illus.; index; circ. 250,000.

TURIST- OG RUTEBILBLADET. see *TRANSPORTATION — Automobiles*

910.09   DK   ISSN 0108-8734
TURISTFOERER. Variant title: Turistfoererforeningen. Medlemliste. 1975. a. free. (Turistfoererforeningen) Scan-ide Publishing ApS, Gersonsvej 33, DK-2900 Hellerup, Denmark. TEL 31-62-73-10. Ed. Robert Bachmann. adv.; circ. 3,500.

914   YU   ISSN 0041-4204
TURISTICKE NOVINE. 1952. w. 300 din. Turisticka Stampa, Knez Mihailova 21, Belgrade, Yugoslavia. Ed. Dobrivoje Djokovic. adv.; bk.rev.; abstr.; bibl.; charts; illus.; index.

910.09   HU
TURIZMUS. m. $21. Muzeum u. 11, 1088 Budapest, Hungary. TEL 138-4638. TELEX 22-5297. Ed. Zsolt Szebeni. circ. 8,000.

TURKISH TREASURES; culture-art-tourism magazine. see *ART*

914   NE   ISSN 0041-4379
TUSSEN DE RAILS. 1951. m. fl.62.50. Annoventura, P.O. Box 152, 1000 AD Amsterdam, Netherlands. Ed. C. Bauer. adv.; rec.rev.; illus.; tr.lit.

910.09   IT
TUTTOTURISMO. 11/yr. $60. Editorale Domus, Via Grandi 5-7, 20089 Rozzano (MI), Italy. TEL 02-82472266. FAX 02-8255033.

914.9   BE
U I T - MAGAZINE. 1986. m. 990 Fr. Vlaamse Toeristenbond, Vlaamse Automobilistenbond, Sint-Jakobsmarkt 45-47, B-2000 Antwerp, Belgium. TEL 22-03-400. FAX 234-05-98. TELEX 31679. circ. 210,000.
Description: Travel reports, tips for weekend traveling, consumers' information, tests of food products, restaurant reports and road tests.

U J Q. (Uncle Jam Quarterly) see *LITERARY AND POLITICAL REVIEWS*

941.04   UK
U K HOLIDAY GUIDE. 1979. q. £5.45. Archway Nicholas Publications, Faber House, 6 Eastern Road, Romford, Essex RM1 3PJ, England. TEL 0708-20011. Ed. Michael Faulkner. (back issues avail.)

917   US
U S A FOR BUSINESS TRAVELERS. a. $12. Harper Collins Publishers, Birnbaum Travel Guides, 10 E. 53rd St., New York, NY 10022-5299. TEL 212-270-7000. Ed. Stephen Birnbaum.

914   CI   ISSN 0041-557X
U T; revija za ugostiteljstvo i turizam. (Text in Croatian) 1952. m. $60. Ugostiteyski i Turisticki Marketing, d.o.o., Trg Mazuravica 5-2, Zabreg, Croatia. TEL 041-440-049. Ed. Drago Ferencic. index; circ. 20,000.
Formerly: Ugostiteljstvo i Turizam.
Description: Covers the catering and tourist trade.

914   FR   ISSN 0049-5190
UNE SEMAINE DE PARIS-PARISCOPE. Variant title: Pariscop. 1923. w. 340 F. (foreign 500 F.). Publications Filipacchi, 65 av. des Champs-Elysees, 75008 Paris, France. TEL 42-56-72-72. TELEX 290294. (Subscr. to: 99 rue d'Amsterdam, 75008 Paris, France) film rev.; play rev.

910.202   US
UNIQUE & EXOTIC TRAVEL REPORTER. 1982. m. $36. 6716 Eastside Dr. N.E., No.12, Tacoma, WA 98422-1114. TEL 206-927-1688. Ed. Pat Chesebro. adv.; bk.rev. (back issues avail.)
Description: Provides information about unique and special interest travel opportunities throughout the world.

719.32   US   ISSN 0083-2316
U.S. NATIONAL PARK SERVICE. HISTORICAL HANDBOOK SERIES. 1950. irreg. U.S. National Park Service, Interior Bldg., Washington, DC 20240. TEL 202-343-1100. (Orders to: Supt. of Doc., Washington, DC 20402)

917   US
UNITED STATES (YEAR). a. $17. Harper Collins Publishers, Birnbaum Travel Guides, 10 E 53rd St., New York, NY 10022-5299. TEL 212-207-7000. Ed. Stephen Birnbaum.

914   FR   ISSN 0395-8086
UNIVERSITE D'AIX-MARSEILLE 3. CENTRE DES HAUTES ETUDES TOURISTIQUES. COLLECTION "ESSAIS". 1976. irreg., no.431, 1991. 50 F. Universite d'Aix-Marseille III (Universite de Droit, d'Economie et des Sciences), Centre des Hautes Etudes Touristiques, Fondation Vasarely, 1 av. Marcel Pagnol, 13090 Aix-en-Provence, France. TEL 42-20-09-73. FAX 42-20-50-98. **Indexed:** Rural Recreat.Tour.Abstr., World Agri.Econ.& Rural Sociol.Abstr.

914   FR   ISSN 0065-4965
UNIVERSITE D'AIX-MARSEILLE 3. CENTRE DES HAUTES ETUDES TOURISTIQUES. ETUDES ET MEMOIRES. 1963. irreg., no.172, 1991. price varies. Universite d'Aix-Marseille III (Universite de Droit, d'Economie et des Sciences), Centre des Hautes Etudes Touristiques, Fondation Vasarely, 1 av. Marcel Pagnol, 13090 Aix-en-Provence, France. TEL 42-20-09-73. FAX 42-20-50-98. (back issues avail.)

919.09 338   PL
UNIWERSYTET GDANSKI. WYDZIAL EKONOMIKI PRODUKCJI. ZESZYTY NAUKOWE. EKONOMIKA I ORGANIZACJA TURYSTYKI I USLUG. (Text in Polish; summaries in English, Russian) 1985. irreg. price varies. Uniwersytet Gdanski, Wydzial Ekonomiki Produkcji, c/o Biblioteka Glowna, Ul. Armii Krajowej 110, 81-824 Sopot, Poland. TEL 51-0061. TELEX 051 2247 BMOR PL. Ed. Wladyslaw Gaworecki. circ. 250.
Description: Covers the economics of consumption, services, trade, small manufacturers, and organization of tourism and tourist enterprises.

910.202   CN   ISSN 0828-4253 F1060.A1
UP HERE; life in Canada's North. 1984. bi-m. Can.$21 (foreign Can.$30). Outcrop Ltd., P.O. Box 1350, Yellowknife, N.W.T. X1A 2N9, Canada. TEL 403-920-4652. FAX 403-873-2844. Ed. Rosemary Allerston. adv.; bk.rev.; film rev.; play rev.; circ. 37,000. (also avail. in microfiche from MML) **Indexed:** Can.Per.Ind.
Description: Lifestyles, travel and issues in Canada's Northwest Territories and the Yukon.

UPSTATE MAGAZINE. see *GENERAL INTEREST PERIODICALS — United States*

910.4 385.23   FI   ISSN 0358-7711
V R - EXPRESS. q. Erikoislehdet Oy Business Publications, P.O. Box 16, SF-00381 Helsinki, Finland. Ed. Marketta Rentola. circ. 100,000.

910.09   US
VACATION REVIEWS. q. Glen Ivy Financial Group, 268 N. Lincoln Ave., No.11, Corona, CA 91720-7164. TEL 714-371-5131. Ed. Sue Nitti. adv.; circ. 55,000.

910.202   US
VACATION WEEK. 1953. m. 330 W. Division St., Box 1929, Eagle River, WI 54521. TEL 715-479-4421. Ed. Kurt Krueger. adv.; circ. 16,000.

910.09   US   ISSN 0894-9093
VACATIONS. 1987. q. $11.80. Vacation Publications, Inc., 2411 Fountain View, Ste. 201, Houston, TX 77057. TEL 713-974-6903. Ed. R. Alan Fox. adv.; circ. 260,000.

910.222   CN
VANCOUVER VISITOR NEWS. 1985. 18/yr. Can.$30 (typically set in Dec.). Vancouver Visitor News Ltd., P.O. Box 5217, 109-1161 Melville St., Vancouver, B.C. V6B 4B3, Canada. TEL 604-683-4871. Ed. Toni Dabbs. adv.; circ. 22,000.
Description: Information about events, attractions and services for visitors to the greater Vancouver area.

VANUATU IN FACTS AND FIGURES. see *TRAVEL AND TOURISM — Abstracting, Bibliographies, Statistics*

VARTA - FUEHRER; ausgewaehlte Hotels und Restaurants in der Bundesrepublik Deutschland. see *HOTELS AND RESTAURANTS*

910.09   CU
VEA. s-a. Instituto Nacional del Turismo, Malecon y G, Vedado, Havana, Cuba.

VEGETARIAN HANDBOOK. see *NUTRITION AND DIETETICS*

910.202   UK   ISSN 0144-4751
VENEZUELA. 1978. m. (Venezuelan Embassy) Hunter Bureau of Communications, Drayton House, Gordon St., London WC1, England.

914.504   US
VENICE (YEAR). a. $10. Harper Collins Publishers, Birnbaum Travel Guides, 10 E. 53rd St., New York, NY 10022-5299. TEL 212-207-7000. illus.; index.

910.4   US
VERMONT VACATION. 3/yr. Travel Routes, Inc., 86 Canal St., Brattleboro, VT 05301. FAX 802-254-2372. adv.; maps; circ. 150,000.
Description: Provides tourist information. Includes calendar of events.

VIA!. see *TRANSPORTATION — Automobiles*

917.1   CN
VIA MAGAZINE. (Text in English and French) q. Maclean Hunter Ltd., 2 Place Ville Marie, 6th Fl., Montreal, Que. H3C 3N3, Canada. TEL 514-596-6000. FAX 514-861-6463. TELEX 05-268530. Ed. Rene Homier-Roy.
Description: Distributed aboard all Via train across Canada. Aims to promote tourism in Canada and provide passengers with interesting reading.

910   IT
VIAGGIANDO IN AUTOSTRADE. m. L.27500 (foreign L.55000). Autostrade - Concessioni e Costruzioni Autostrade S.p.A., Via A. Bergammi, 50, 00159 Rome, Italy. TEL 0643631. Ed. Giuseppe Fedi. (back issues avail.)

910.09   US
VIAJANDO/TRAVELING. (Text in English, Spanish) 1989. m. Global Magazines, Inc., 6355 N.W. 36th St., Virginia Gardens, FL 33166. TEL 305-871-6400. TELEX 441094. Ed. Cristina J. Arencibia. adv.; circ. 20,000.
Description: Contains general interest for frequent airline travelers.

910.202   BL
VIAJE BEM. 1961. 6/yr. Grupo Editorial Spagat Ltda., Rua Prof. Artur Ramos 183, Andar 10, CEP 01454 Sao Paulo, SP, Brazil. TEL 0110-813-4455. Ed. Carlos Andre Spagat. adv.; circ. 100,000.

919.3   AT
VICTORIA A - Z. irreg., approx. every 2 yrs. Research Publications Pty. Ltd., 27A Boronia Rd., Vermont, Vic. 3133, Australia. TEL 03-873-1450. circ. 12,000.
Description: Tourism magazine emphasising local attractions throughout various regions in Victoria.

917.104   CN
VICTORIA CLIPPER. s-a. Smart Publishing Group Ltd., 1368 Hampshire Rd., Victoria, B.C. V8V 3L1, Canada. TEL 604-386-1433. FAX 604-386-3664.

914   IT   ISSN 0042-7292
VIDA ITALIANA; documentos e informaciones. (Text in Spanish) 1952. q. L.26000. Presidenza del Consiglio dei Ministri - Presidencia del Consejo de Ministros, Via Po, 14, 00198 Rome, Italy. Ed. Italo Borzi. adv.; charts; illus.; stat.; cum.index: 1964-1976.
Formerly: Hoy en Italia.

4796 TRAVEL AND TOURISM

910.09 **IT**
VIE DEL MONDO. 1987. m. L.58000. Touring Periodici s.r.l., Corso Italia 10, Milan, Italy. TEL 02-58300527. FAX 02-58300315. TELEX 312476 TCIADM 1. Ed. Raffaella Fiory Ceccopieri.

614.7 **FR**
VIE MANCELLE; revue mensuelle de l'Association Culturelle et Touristique du Maine. 1959. m. 120 F. Association Culturelle et Touristique du Mans et de la Sarthe, 64, rue de la Pelouse, 72000 Le Mans, France. Ed. J.P. Martin. bk.rev.

910.202 **MR**
VIE TOURISTIQUE. (Text in French) w. 142 bd. Mohamed V, Casablanca, Morocco. Ed. Mohamed Zghari. adv.

917 **CN** **ISSN 0049-6448**
VIKING. 1968. a. free to hotels and tourist agencies. Fundy Group Publications, Box 128, 2 Second St., Yarmouth. N.S., Canada. TEL 902-742-7111. adv.; illus.; circ. 17,500. **Indexed:** Geo.Abstr.

910.202 **CN**
VIKING TOURIST GUIDE. 6/yr. Cameron Publications, 2 Second St., P.O. Box 128, Yarmouth, N.S. B5A 4B1, Canada. TEL 902-742-7111. FAX 902-742-2311. Ed. Fred A. Hatfield. circ. 15,000.

910.202 **VI**
VIRGIN ISLANDS PLAYGROUND. a. free. Island Media, Inc., P.O. Box 10563, St. Thomas, VI 00801. TEL 809-776-3646. Ed. Frances E. Newbold.
  Description: Includes restaurant directory, shopping guide, island map.

917 **US**
VISIT U S A GUIDE.* 1979. m. Travel Trade Publishing Co., 15 West 44th St., New York, NY 10036. TEL 212-883-1110. Eds. Nanette Lind, Lewis Abels. adv.; circ. 16,000.

910.202 **JM**
VISITOR. 1980. w. Jam.$137.50($30) Western Publishers Ltd., P.O. Box 1258, Montego Bay, No. 1, Jamaica, W.I. TEL 952-5253. FAX 952-6513. Ed. Lloyd B. Smith. circ. 10,000.
  Description: Contains travel and tourist news, tips on where to shop, what to buy, what to see, villas, restaurants, hotels, and tours.

VISITOR BEHAVIOR. see *PSYCHOLOGY*

917 **CN**
▼**VISITORS CHOICE.** 1992. s-a. free. I G Publications Ltd., 999 8th St., S.W., Ste. 222, Calgary, Alta. T2R 1J5, Canada. FAX 403-229-2470.

917.1 **CN** **ISSN 0839-1335**
VISITOR'S MAGAZINE. 1978. 5/yr. Can.$10 (effective Jan. 1991). Janne Dean, Ed. & Pub., 215 Fairway Rd., Kitchener, Ont. N2G 4E5, Canada. TEL 519-894-1630. FAX 519-894-2173. adv.; circ. 50,000. (back issues avail.)
  Formerly: Waterloo Region Visitor's Guide.
  Description: Lists dining, accomodations, shopping and tourist information in the Kitchener, Waterloo, Cambridge, Guelph and Stratford areas.

917.704 **US**
▼**VISITOR'S POCKET GUIDE TO ST. LOUIS.** 1991. s-a. Pocket Guide Publications, Inc., 8630 Delmar, No. 215, St. Louis, MO 63124. TEL 314-991-5222. adv.: B&W page $4800, color page $5000; trim 4 x 5 1/2. circ. 100,000.
  Description: Lists places to go, things to do, history and significant information about the area.

917.504 **US**
VISTA MAGAZINE. 1980. m. Horizon, 999 Ponce de Leon Blvd., Ste. 600, Coral Gables, FL 33134. TEL 305-442-2462. FAX 305-443-7650. adv.; circ. 20,000. (back issues avail.)
  Formerly: Vista Magazine Miami Metro Guide (ISSN 0743-5738)
  Description: Information and entertainment for Hispanic Americans from different countries of origin and geographic locations.

917 790.13 051 **US**
VISTA U S A. 1965. q. $3. Exxon Travel Club, Inc., Box 161, Convent Sta., NJ 07961. TEL 201-538-7600. FAX 201-538-9509. (Alt. addr.: 3550 Dacoma, Houston, TX 77092) Ed. Martha J. Mendez. adv.; bk.rev.; circ. 875,000.
  Formerly: Vista (ISSN 0507-1577)

914 **DK**
VOGNMANDEN. 1951. m. DKK 270. Turistvognmaendenes Landsforening - Danish Coach Owners Association, Carit Etlars Vej 3, DK-1814 Frederiksberg C, Denmark. TEL 31-211888. FAX 31-211901. Ed. Michael Brandt-Nielsen. adv.; circ. 1,500.

910.202 **CN**
▼**VOIR AILLEURS**; le travail a l'etranger rendu facile. 1991. a. Can.$14.95. Regroupement Tourisme Jeunesse, 4545 Pierre de Coubertin Av., Sta. M, Box 1000, Montreal, Que. H1V 3R2, Canada. TEL 514-252-3117. FAX 514-252-3119. TELEX 05-829647. Eds. Anne Marie Parent, Anne-Marie Poitras.
  Description: A guide for working abroad, with information regarding working permits, exchange programs and helpful organizations.

910.09 **US** **ISSN 1040-8541**
VOYAGER INTERNATIONAL. 1984. m. $38. Argonaut Enterprises, Inc., 7 Northgate, Box 2777, Westport, CT 06880. TEL 203-226-1647. FAX 203-846-2796. Ed. Jason N. Fisher. bk.rev.; film rev.; cum.index: 1987-1991; circ. 20,000. (back issues avail.)
  Description: Evaluates the world for the discerning traveller.

917.1 **CN**
VOYAGEUR MAGAZINE. (Text in English or French) 1984. q. Publications Vacances Quebec, Inc., 615, Grande Allee est, Quebec City, Que. G1R 2K4, Canada. TEL 418-523-9577. FAX 418-681-7477. Ed. Jo Ouellet. adv.; circ. 75,000.
  Description: For passengers on the Voyageur colonial bus networks across Quebec and Ontario. Contains articles of general interest, includes features on wine and cuisine, word games, and quizzes.

914 **CV**
VOZ DO POVO. 1962. 3/wk. Direccao Nacional de Informacao, Caixa Postal 118, Praia, Sao Tiago, Cape Verde Islands. Ed. Alfredo Simao Carvalho Santos. circ. 3,000. **Indexed:** Bio-Contr.News & Info.
  Supersedes: Arquipelago (ISSN 0004-2668)

VYSOKE TATRY. see *GENERAL INTEREST PERIODICALS — Czechoslovakia*

919.6 **US**
WAIKIKI NEWS. 1971. m. $16. Fred C. Pugarelli, Ed. & Pub., Box 89133, Honolulu, HI 96830-9133. adv.; bk.rev.; illus.; circ. 1,000.

914.2 **UK**
WALES BEST HOLIDAYS. 1974-199? a. £1.25. F.H.G. Publications Ltd., Abbey Mill Business Centre, Seedhill, Paisley PA1 1JN, Scotland. TEL 041-887 0428.
  Formerly: Holidays in Wales (ISSN 0267-3401)

914.04 **US**
WALL STREET JOURNAL GUIDE TO BUSINESS TRAVEL: EUROPE. irreg. $50. Fodor's Travel Publications, Inc. (Subsidiary of: Random House, Inc.), 201 E. 50th St., New York, NY 10022. TEL 800-733-3000. (Dist. by: Random House, Inc., 400 Hahn Rd., Westminster, MD 21157) Ed. Edie Jarolim.

915.04 **US**
WALL STREET JOURNAL GUIDE TO BUSINESS TRAVEL: PACIFIC RIM. irreg. $20. Fodor's Travel Publications, Inc. (Subsidiary of: Random House, Inc.), 201 E. 50th St., New York, NY 10022. TEL 800-733-3000. (Dist. by: Random House, Inc., 400 Hahn Rd., Westminster, MD 21157) Ed. Edie Jarolim.

917.04 **US**
WALL STREET JOURNAL GUIDE TO BUSINESS TRAVEL: U S A & CANADA. irreg. $20. Fodor's Travel Publications, Inc. (Subsidiary of: Random House, Inc.), 201 E. 50th St., New York, NY 10022. TEL 800-733-3000. (Dist. by: Random House, Inc., 400 Hahn Rd., Westminster, MD 21157) Ed. Edie Jarolim.

910.202 **SZ**
WALLIS. 1980. 6/yr. price varies. (Vereinigung Oberwalliser Verkehrsinteressenten) Rotten-Verlags AG, Leser-Dienst, Terbinerstr. 2, CH-3930 Visp, Switzerland. Ed. Armin Karlen. adv.

917.504 **US**
WALT DISNEY WORLD (YEAR). a. Hearst Corporation, Walt Disney World, 250 W. 55th St., 11th Fl., New York, NY 10019. TEL 212-903-5190. Ed. Stephen Birnbaum.
  ●Also available online.

915.4 **II**
WARRIOR. (Text in English) 1971. m. free. Director of Information and Public Relations, Kohima, Nagaland, India. Ed. Chipeni Merry. stat.; circ. 4,000.

917.504 **US**
WASHINGTON, D.C. VISITOR'S GUIDE. a. Bell Atlantic Specialty Guides, 6701 Democracy Blvd., 9th Fl., Bethesda, MD 20817. TEL 301-493-3258. circ. 315,000.
  Description: Lists business and leisure services and facilities in and around D.C. Features articles on transportation services, sightseeing, performing arts and special events.

917.504 **US**
WASHINGTON ENTERTAINMENT MAGAZINE. bi-m. T A D Publishing Co., Inc., Box 894, Vienna, VA 22180. TEL 703-281-3400. Ed. Carol Eicher. circ. 50,000.

917.504 **US** **ISSN 1046-3089**
WASHINGTON FLYER MAGAZINE. 1989. bi-m. $15. Ackerly Airport Advertising, Inc., 11 Canal Center Plaza, Ste. 111, Alexandria, VA 22314. TEL 703-739-9292. FAX 703-683-2848. adv.
  Description: Focuses on travel, transportation, trade and communication, hospitality and business. Contains information for travelers on the nation's capital.

910.09 **US** **ISSN 1051-0257**
WASHINGTON INTERNATIONAL; discovering destinations, cultures and our international community. 1986. bi-m. $12. 1019 19th St., N.W., Ste. 900, Washington, DC 20036. TEL 202-223-3180. (Subscr. to: Box 18031, Washington, DC 20036) Ed. Patricia Keegan. adv.; circ. 25,000. (tabloid format; back issues avail.)
  Description: Contains diplomatic news and travel articles directed toward the international, travel, and cultural community of Washington DC. Includes interviews with Washington personalities, features international hotel spotlights, and calendar of cultural events.

WASSERSKI MAGAZIN. see *SPORTS AND GAMES — Boats And Boating*

WATERFRONT NEWS; South Florida's nautical newspaper. see *SPORTS AND GAMES — Boats And Boating*

914.5 **IT**
WEEKEND VIAGGI. 1973. m. L.63000 (foreing L.125000). Arianna S.p.A., Piazza Aspromonte 13-A, 20131 Milan, Italy. TEL 02-706421. FAX 02-70638544. (back issues avail.)

914 **CY** **ISSN 0044-0698**
WELCOME TO CYPRUS. 1959. m. 20s.($3.) PAN Publishing House, Corner Makarios-Xenopoullos Sts., Box 1209, Nicosia, Cyprus. Ed. P. Kokkinos. adv.; circ. 4,500.
  Formerly: You Are Welcome Sir, to Cyprus.

914.37 **CS** **ISSN 0043-2210**
WELCOME TO CZECHOSLOVAKIA. French edition: Soyez les Bienvenus en Tchecoslovaquie. German edition: Willkommen in der Tschechoslowakei. Russian edition: Dobro Pozhalovat v Chekhoslovakiyu. 1965. q. 48 Kcs.($8.80) (Czech Governmental Committee for Tourism) Orbis Oress Agency, Vinohradska 46, 120 41 Prague 2, Czechoslovakia. (Co-sponsor: Slovak Committee for Tourism) Ed. Vit Suchy. illus.; circ. 36,000.

910.202 **LE**
WELCOME TO LEBANON & THE MIDDLE EAST. 1959. m. Tourist Information and Advertising Bureau, Starco Centre, N. Block 711, P.O. Box 4204, Beirut, Lebanon. Ed. Souhaji Toufik Abou-Jamra. adv.; circ. 6,000.

917.504 **US**
WEST VIRGINIA - IT'S YOU. 1989. a. $3.95. Bell Atlantic Specialty Guides, 6701 Democracy Blvd., 9th Fl., Bethesda, MD 20817. TEL 301-493-3258. FAX 301-493-3833. Ed. Debra Auerback-Deutsch. adv.; circ. 265,000.

TRAVEL AND TOURISM

917.12 US
WESTERN CANADA ALASKA CAMPBOOK. Cover title: R V and Tent Sites in Alberta, British Columbia, Manitoba, Northwest Territories, Saskatchewan, Yukon Territory and Alaska. a. membership. American Automobile Association, 1000 AAA Dr., Heathrow, FL 32746-5063. TEL 407-444-4300. FAX 407-444-7380. adv.; illus.; circ. 281,900. Key Title: CampBook. Western Canada and Alaska.
  Formerly: Western Canada. Alaska Camping.

914.004 US
WESTERN EUROPE (YEAR). a. $17. Harper Collins Publishers, Birnbaum Travel Guides, 10 E. 53rd St., New York, NY 10022-5299. TEL 212-207-7000. illus.; index.

WESTERN LINKS. see SPORTS AND GAMES — Ball Games

796.7 US ISSN 0043-4434
WESTWAYS. 1909. m. $11 to non-members; members $8; foreign $11. Automobile Club of Southern California, Box 2890, Los Angeles, CA 90051. TEL 213-741-4760. FAX 213-741-3069. Ed. Mary Ann Fisher. bk.rev.; illus.; circ. 475,000. **Indexed:** Access (1975-), Cal.Per.Ind. (1978-), Hist.Abstr.

WESTWORLD SASKATCHEWAN. see TRANSPORTATION — Automobiles

914.2 UK
WHAT TO DO IN THE NORFOLK BROADS. 1927. a. £3.50. Jarrold Publishing, Barrack St., Norwich NR3 1TR, England. TEL 0603-763300. FAX 0603-662748. TELEX 97497. maps; illus.; charts.
  Description: Includes 20 maps and over 25 illustrations, tide tables and distance charts.

914 UK
WHAT'S ON IN ABERDEEN. 1945. m. £30. Aberdeen Tourist Board, St. Nicholas House, Broad St., Aberdeen AB9 1DE, Scotland. TEL 0224-632727. FAX 0224-644822. TELEX 73366. Ed. Brenda Jenkins. adv.; circ. 162,500.
  Former titles: What's on and Where to Shop in Aberdeen & What's on in Aberdeen (ISSN 0043-4639)

919.4 AT
WHAT'S ON IN ADELAIDE AND SOUTH AUSTRALIA;* what's on and where to go in Adelaide this month. 1958. m. free. (South Australian Government Tourist Bureau) John Carroll & Associates Pty. Ltd., P O Box 54, Burnside, S.A. 5066, Australia. Ed. Nicholas Carroll. adv.; circ. 10,100.

914.204 UK
WHAT'S ON IN AND AROUND MANCHESTER. 1971. m. free. Intercity Publications (N.W.) Ltd., 21 Roebuck Lane, Sale, Cheshire M33 1SY, England. Ed. Dennis Haines. adv.; bk.rev.; circ. 16,000.

914.204 UK
WHAT'S ON IN AVON. 1976. m. £0.20 per no. Newswest International, Foxlark, Smitham Hill, E. Harptree, Bristol BS18 6BZ, England. Ed. Tony Ferrand. adv.

919 II ISSN 0043-4647
WHAT'S ON IN CALCUTTA; city's entertainment & tourist guide. 1965. fortn. Rs.300($100) India-International News Service, 12 India Exchange Place, Calcutta 700 001, India. Ed. H. Kothari. adv.; film rev.; mkt.; play rev.

914.2 UK
WHAT'S ON IN EAST ANGLIA. 1969. m. £7.50. Profile Publishing, 101 Thunder Lane, Norwich NR7 0JG, England. Ed. Stephen Ford. adv.; bk.rev.; circ. 26,000.
  Description: Leisure guide for East Anglia.

914 UK ISSN 0043-4671
WHAT'S ON IN LONDON (LONDON, 1935). 1935. w. £30. Webster's Publications Ltd., Onslow House, 60-66 Saffron Hill, London EC1N 8AY, England. Ed. Kenneth Hurren. adv.; bk.rev.; film rev.; play rev.; illus.; circ. 25,000.

914 792 UK
WHAT'S ON IN LONDON (LONDON, 1966). 1966. w. £56.16. Where to Go Ltd., 182 Pentonville Rd., London N1 9LB, England. TEL 01-278-4393. FAX 01-837-5838. Ed. David Parkes-Bristow. adv.; bk.rev.; film rev.; play rev.; circ. 40,000.
  Former titles: What's on & Where to go (ISSN 0264-3227); Where to Go in London and Around (ISSN 0043-4817)
  Description: Guide to London's mainstream and fringe theatre, cinema, opera, ballet, classical, jazz and popular music, art galleries, museums, restaurants, pageantry, entertainment and leisure.

915.9 PH
WHAT'S ON IN MANILA. 26/yr. Western Communications, Inc., Pacific Bldg., no.403, Ayala Ave., Makati MM, Philippines. TEL 8150659.

914 IT
WHAT'S ON IN MILAN. m. Garp - Spd, Piazza San Simpliciano, 7, 20121 Milan, Italy. TEL 02-870078. Ed. Marina Saccheri Borri. circ. 10,000.

910.09 AT ISSN 0812-2040
WHAT'S ON IN VICTORIA. 1983. q. Aus.$12($14.80) Life Be in It Australia, Batmar Ave., Melbourne, Vic. 3004, Australia. FAX 03-654-4973. Eds. Wilma Bedford, Jenny Robinson. adv.; circ. 20,000. (back issues avail.)

914.204 UK
WHAT'S ON NORTH WEST. a. free. Intercity Publications (N.W.) Ltd., 21 Roebuck Lane, Sale, Cheshire M33 1SY, England. adv.; illus.; circ. 100,000.

796 US
WHEELERS R V RESORT AND CAMPGROUND GUIDE: NORTH AMERICAN EDITION. 1972. a. $10.95. Print Media Services, Ltd., 1310 Jarvis Ave., Elk Grove Village, IL 60007. TEL 708-981-0100. FAX 708-981-0106. adv.; circ. 180,000.
  Supersedes regional editions of: Wheelers Recreational Vehicle Resort and Campground Guide; Which was formerly titled: Wheelers Trailer Resort and Campground Guide (ISSN 0090-600X)

910.202 TH
WHERE. m. B.20($0.85) per no. Media Transasia (Thailand) Ltd., 14th Fl., Orakarn Bldg., 26 Chidlom Rd., Bangkok 10330, Thailand. FAX 2535335. TELEX 84003-MEDTRAN-TH. Ed. Kelvin Rugg. adv.; circ. 25,940.
  Description: Tourist guide to Thailand aimed at affluent travelers.

914 UK ISSN 0143-2478
WHERE (LONDON, 1975); your best guide to: shopping, dining, sightseeing and entertainment. 1975. m. £24 (foreign £36). Where Publications, 26-27 Market Place, London W1N 7AL, England. TEL 071-436-5553. FAX 071-436-4507. Ed. Maureen Mills. adv.; circ. 60,000.
  Description: Guide to London for high-earning and free-spending visitors.

910.09 US
WHERE (NEW YORK). (Various city editions avail.) 1934. m. $32. 600 Third Ave., 15th Fl., New York, NY 10016. TEL 212-687-4646. Ed. Michael Kelly Tucker. adv.; circ. 128,000 (paid); 128,000.
  Description: Distributed to hotels for out-of-town visitors.

910.202 CN
WHERE CALGARY; visitors' magazine. 1981. m. Can.$20 (foreign Can.$25). Key West Publishers Ltd., 250, 125 9th Ave. S.E., Calgary, Alta. T2G 0P6, Canada. TEL 403-266-5085. FAX 403-290-0573. Ed. Jennifer Mac Leod. adv.; circ. 29,000.
  Formerly: Key to Calgary.
  Description: Information and maps about things to see and do in Calgary.

917.704 US
WHERE CHICAGO. m. 1165 N. Clark St., Chicago, IL 60610-2845. TEL 312-642-1896. FAX 312-642-5467. Ed. Margaret Doyle. circ. 100,000.

917 US
WHERE NEW ORLEANS. (Text in English, Spanish) 1968. m. $15 (hotels free). V.I.P., 921 Canal St., Ste. 703, New Orleans, LA 70112. TEL 504-522-6468. Ed. Linda Bays Powers. adv.; circ. 70,000. (back issues avail.)
  Description: Information for visitors: maps, dining, shopping, nightlife, points of interest.

910.202 CN
WHERE ROCKY MOUNTAINS. 1978. s-a. Can.$4($4) R M V Publications Ltd., Ste. 250, One Palliser Sq., 125 Ninth Ave. S.E., Calgary, Alta. T2G 0P6, Canada. TEL 403-266-5085. FAX 403-290-0573. Ed. Jack Newton. adv.; circ. 360,000 (controlled).
  Formerly: Rocky Mountain Visitor.
  Description: Information for visitors to the Canadian Rocky Mountains.

WHERE TO EAT IN BERKSHIRE. see HOTELS AND RESTAURANTS

WHERE TO EAT IN BRISTOL, BATH & AVON. see HOTELS AND RESTAURANTS

WHERE TO EAT IN CANADA. see HOTELS AND RESTAURANTS

WHERE TO EAT IN CORNWALL. see HOTELS AND RESTAURANTS

WHERE TO EAT IN DEVON. see HOTELS AND RESTAURANTS

WHERE TO EAT IN DORSET AND SOUTH WILTSHIRE. see HOTELS AND RESTAURANTS

WHERE TO EAT IN GLOUCESTERSHIRE, OXFORDSHIRE AND THE COTSWOLDS. see HOTELS AND RESTAURANTS

WHERE TO EAT IN HAMPSHIRE. see HOTELS AND RESTAURANTS

WHERE TO EAT IN KENT. see HOTELS AND RESTAURANTS

WHERE TO EAT IN NORTH WEST ENGLAND. see HOTELS AND RESTAURANTS

WHERE TO EAT IN SOMERSET. see HOTELS AND RESTAURANTS

WHERE TO EAT IN SURREY. see HOTELS AND RESTAURANTS

WHERE TO EAT IN SUSSEX. see HOTELS AND RESTAURANTS

WHERE TO EAT IN THE CHANNEL ISLANDS. see HOTELS AND RESTAURANTS

WHERE TO EAT IN WALES. see HOTELS AND RESTAURANTS

914.2 UK
WHERE TO GO IN THE THAMES AND CHILTERNS. 1980. a. £1.95. Thames & Chilterns Tourist Board, Mount House, Church Green, Witney, Oxfordshire OX8 6DZ, England. TEL 0993-778800. FAX 0993-779152. TELEX 83343-ABTELEX-G. (Dist. by: Automobile Association, Fanum House, Basingstoke RG21 2EA, England) Ed. Stan Bowes. adv.; circ. 25,000.
  Description: Guide to tourist attractions and accommodation in the five-county region: Buckinghamshire, Berkshire, Oxfordshire, Bedfordshire and Hertfordshire.

914.2 UK
WHERE TO GO, WHAT TO DO IN THE SOUTH. a. £1.35. James Dunning Publications, 20 Riverside Gardens, Romsey, Hants. SO51 8HN, England. TEL 0794-523039. FAX 0794-513081. Ed. J. Dunning. adv.; circ. 20,000.
  Description: Details over 1000 places to visit in Hampshire, Wiltshire, Dorset, Sussex and the Isle of Wight.

917 CN
WHERE TORONTO. 1954. m. Can.$25($30) Key Publishers Co. Ltd., 6 Church St., 2nd fl., Toronto, Ont. M5E 1M1, Canada. TEL 416-364-3333. Ed. Christopher Loudon. adv.; illus.; circ. 90,000 (controlled).
  Formerly: Key to Toronto (ISSN 0023-0863)

TRAVEL AND TOURISM — ABSTRACTING, BIBLIOGRAPHIES, STATISTICS

917.704 US
WHERE TWIN CITIES. m. Toma Publishing, 33 S. Fifth St., Minneapolis, MN 55402. TEL 512-375-9929. Ed. Lisa Holmberg. play rev. (back issues avail.)

918 PE
WHERE, WHEN, HOW.... m. Peruvian Times, S.A., Apartado 2484, Lima, Peru. Ed. Anne Arrarte. circ. 25,000.

WHO'S WHO IN AMERICA'S RESTAURANTS; encyclopedia of America's dining establishments. see ENCYCLOPEDIAS AND GENERAL ALMANACS

WIESBADENER LEBEN. see GENERAL INTEREST PERIODICALS — Germany

917.1 051 CN ISSN 0318-2460
WINDSOR THIS MONTH. 1976. 12/yr. Can.$21.40 (foreign Can.$25). Controlled Publications, Box 1029, Sta. A, Windsor, Ont. N9A 6P4, Canada. TEL 519-977-0007. FAX 519-977-1403. Ed. Betty Strosberg. adv.; bk.rev.; circ. 24,000.

WINESTATE. see BEVERAGES

WINGS OF ALOHA. see TRANSPORTATION — Air Transport

WINGS WEST; the Western aviation magazine. see TRANSPORTATION — Air Transport

917.904 US
WINSTON'S TRAVEL DELUXE. bi-m. Box 9, Sausalito, CA 94966-0009. TEL 415-332-9612. Ed. Isabella Winston.

914.04 GW
WIR; in Nieder-Erlenbach. 1970. m. Sozialdemokratische Partei Deutschlands, Ortsverein Nieder - Erlenbach, Bornweg 30, 6000 Frankfurt 56, Germany. TEL 06101-43434. circ. 1,500.

WISCONSIN WEST MAGAZINE. see HISTORY — History Of North And South America

910.09 053.931 NE ISSN 0043-7212
WOLKENRIDDER. (Editions in Dutch, English) 1946. fortn. fl.40. K L M Royal Dutch Airlines, Public Relations Bureau, Postbus 7700, 1117 ZL Schiphol, Netherlands. FAX 020-6488200. Ed. Marjolein Gelderman. adv.; bk.rev.; illus.; circ. 30,000. (tabloid format)
Description: Internal company publication.

910.09 US ISSN 1055-1905
E158
WOMEN'S TRAVELLER. 1989. a. $10. Damron Company, Inc., Box 42-2458, San Francisco, CA 94142-2458. TEL 415-255-0404. FAX 415-703-9049. Ed. Gina M. Gatta. circ. 50,000.
Description: Complete travel guide and atlas for women. Provides information on women's accommodations.

WORDS OF WISDOM. see ETHNIC INTERESTS

WORKAMPER NEWS; America's guide to working while camping. see OCCUPATIONS AND CAREERS

WORKING ABROAD (LONDON). see BUSINESS AND ECONOMICS — Labor And Industrial Relations

910.09 UK
WORKING HOLIDAYS (YEAR). 1952. a. £7.95. Central Bureau, Seymour Mews Hosue, London W1H 9PE, England. TEL 071-486-5101. circ. 10,000.
Description: Guide published by the Central Bureau, the UK National office responsible for the provision of information and advice on all forms of educational visits and exchanges.

910 709
WORLD CULTURAL GUIDES.* irreg. Holt, Rinehart and Winston, Inc., c/o Harcourt Brace Jovanovich, 6277 Sea Harbor Dr., Orlando, FL 32887. TEL 407-345-2500.

910.202 US
WORLD HOLIDAY AND TIME GUIDE. 1982. a. Morgan Guaranty Trust Company of New York, 23 Wall St., New York, NY 10015. TEL 212-483-2323.

WORLD HOTEL AND CONVENTION DIRECTORY. see HOTELS AND RESTAURANTS

WORLD LEISURE AND RECREATION. see LEISURE AND RECREATION

910.09 639.9 UK ISSN 0951-2195
GF1
WORLD MAGAZINE; the magazine of mankind. 1987. m. £24($48) World Publications Ltd., Hyde Park House, 5 Manfred Rd., Putney SW15 2RS, England. TEL 081-877-1080. FAX 081-874-1845. (Subscr. to: Punch Subscriptions, Stephenson Hse., Brunel Ctr., Bletcheley, Milton Keynes, London MK2 2EW, England) Ed. Peter Crookston. adv.; bk.rev.; circ. 60,000. (also avail. in microfilm from UMI) Indexed: Mag.Ind.
Description: Combines photography with writing to tell stories of the Earth's people, places and the marvels of its geography.

910.09 BA
▼**WORLD OF TOURISM/ALAM AL-SIYAHA.** (Text in Arabic, English) 1990. m. $3 per issue. Al- Kanary Publishing and Public Relations, P.O. Box 604, Manama, Bahrain. TEL 294601. FAX 294757. TELEX 7151 NANA BN. (Or: 9 Highshore Rd., London SE15 5AA, England. TEL 081-732-7625) Ed. Abdu Bushara. adv.; illus.; stat.; tr.; lit. (back issues avail.)
Description: Covers the tourist industry throughout the world, with a focus on events and issues affecting tourism in the Middle East.

910.09 US ISSN 0163-1780
WORLD TRAVELING. 1978. bi-m. $12. Midwest News Service, Inc., 30943 Club House Lane, Farmington Hills, MI 48018. Ed. Theresa Mitan. adv.; bk.rev.; circ. 60,000.

910.09 US ISSN 1051-6247
G149
▼**WORLDWIDE TRAVEL INFORMATION CONTACT BOOK.** 1991. a. Gale Research Inc., 835 Penobscot Bldg., Detroit, MI 48226. TEL 313-961-2242. FAX 313-961-6083.

915.13 CC
XINAN LUYOU/SOUTHWEST TOURISM. (Text in Chinese) bi-m. $20.70. Sichuan Renmin Chubanshe, 3, Yandao Jie, Chengdu, Sichuan 610016, People's Republic of China. TEL 664570. (Dist. in US by: China Books & Periodicals, Inc., 2929 24th St., San Francisco, CA 94110. TEL 415-282-2994) Ed. Deng Hongping.
Description: Covers tourism in southwestern China.

XTRA!; your free gay guide to Toronto. see HOMOSEXUALITY

649.94 AT
Y H A HOSTELS IN AUSTRALIA. 1957. a. Aus.$1.50. (Australian Youth Hostels Association Incorporated) Kingsgrove Press Pty. Ltd., 43 Kingsway, Kingsgrove NSW 2208, Australia. Ed. P. Carter. adv.; circ. 150,000.
Formerly: Australian Youth Hostels Handbook (ISSN 0156-0107)
Description: Hostel information, addresses, maps of locations state by state, booking information, regional descriptions, holidays, festival dates, concessions.

YACHTSMAN'S GUIDE TO THE BAHAMAS. see SPORTS AND GAMES — Boats And Boating

917.4 US ISSN 1055-226X
F2.3
YANKEE MAGAZINE'S TRAVEL GUIDE TO NEW ENGLAND, NEW YORK & EASTERN CANADA. 1972. a. $4.95. Yankee Publishing, Inc., 33 Union St., Boston, MA 02108. TEL 617-723-4309. Ed. Janice Brand. adv.; circ. 210,000. (reprint service avail. from UMI)
Former titles: Yankee Magazine's Travel Guide to New England and its Neighbors (ISSN 1055-2251); Yankee Magazine's Travel Guide to New England (ISSN 0740-6215); Yankee Magazine's Guide to New England; Yankee Guide to the New England Countryside.

919 II ISSN 0049-8289
YATRI; a bimonthly newsletter of Indian tourism. (Text in English) no. 27, 1971. bi-m. free. India Tourism Development Corporation, Himalaya House, 6th Fl., 23 Kasturba Gandhi Marg, New Delhi 110001, India. Ed. Chandni Luthra. illus.; circ. 10,000.

910.202 NP
YETI. 2/yr. Royal Nepal Airlines, Public Relations & Publicity Service, Kanti Path, Kathmandu, Nepal. Ed. I.K. Pradhan. adv.; circ. 20,000.

647.94 UK
YOUTH HOSTELS ASSOCIATION (ENGLAND AND WALES) ACCOMMODATION GUIDE. 1931. a. £4.99. Youth Hostels Association (England and Wales), Trevelyan House, St. Albans AL1 2DY, England. TEL 0727-55215. FAX 0727-44126. Ed. Hellen Barnes. adv.; circ. 320,000.
Former titles: Youth Hostels Association (England and Wales) Guide & Youth Hostels Association (England and Wales) Handbook.

910.09 NE
ZAKENREIS/BUSINESS TRAVEL. 1969. m. fl.25. Esdoornhof 20, 3831 XX Leusden, Netherlands. TEL 033-941368. FAX 033-943366. TELEX 43776. Ed. C.G. Hundenpool. adv.; bk.rev.; circ. 12,000.

914 SZ ISSN 0044-2755
ZEITSCHRIFT FUER FREMDENVERKEHR/REVUE DE TOURISME/TOURIST REVIEW. (Text in English, French, German, Italian and Spanish) 1946. q. 52 Fr.($37) (International Association of Scientific Experts in Tourism) Staempfli und Cie AG, Postfach, CH-3001 Berne, Switzerland. FAX 031-276699. TELEX 911987. (Co-sponsors: University of Berne, Tourist Research Institute; University of St. Gallen, Institute for Tourism and Transport Economy) Ed. C. Kaspar. adv.; bk.rev.; bibl.; stat. Indexed: Key to Econ.Sci., P.A.I.S.For.Lang.Ind., Rural Recreat.Tour.Abstr., World Agri.Econ.& Rural Sociol.Abstr.
—BLDSC shelfmark: 8870.925000.

614.86 387.742 CC ISSN 1001-2079
ZHONGGUO MINHANG BAO/CIVIL AVIATION ADMINISTRATION OF CHINA. JOURNAL. (Text in Chinese) bi-m. Zhongguo Minhang Baoshe, 155 Dongsi Xidajie, Beijing 100710, People's Republic of China. TEL 4012233. Ed. Yu Quanfu.
Description: In-house publication of CAAC.

2 C PLEIN AIR. see SPORTS AND GAMES — Outdoor Life

4 TAXIS. see ART

800 & FAX TRAVEL DIRECTORY. see BUSINESS AND ECONOMICS — Trade And Industrial Directories

914.2 UK
2000 DAYS OUT IN BRITAIN. a. £3.99. Automobile Association, Fanum House, Basingstoke, Hants. RG21 2EA, England. TEL 0256-20123. FAX 0256-22575. adv.
Former titles: 2000 Places to Visit in Britain; Stately Homes, Museums, Castles and Gardens in Britain; Stately Homes, Museums, Castles and and Gardens; Britain's Heritage.

TRAVEL AND TOURISM — Abstracting, Bibliographies, Statistics

ARTICLES IN HOSPITALITY AND TOURISM. see HOTELS AND RESTAURANTS — Abstracting, Bibliographies, Statistics

914 AU
AUSTRIA. BUNDESKAMMER DER GEWERBLICHEN WIRTSCHAFT. FREMDENVERKEHR IN ZAHLEN; Oesterreichische und internationale Fremdenverkehrs- und Wirtschaftsdaten. 1965. bi-m. free. (Bundeskammer der Gewerblichen Wirtschaft, Sektion Fremdverkehr) Ungar-Druckerei GmbH, Nikolsdorfer Gasse 7-11, A-1050 Vienna, Austria. illus.; stat.; circ. 350.
Formerly: Austria. Bundeskammer der Gewerblichen Wirtschaft. Statistik und Dokummentation. Information (ISSN 0039-0585)

910.202 BB
BARBADOS. BOARD OF TOURISM. ANNUAL REPORT. 1972. a. Board of Tourism, Harbour Rd., P.O. Box 242, Bridgetown, Barbados, W.I. TEL 809-427-2623. FAX 809-426-4080. TELEX WB 2420.
Description: Records the Board's function, structure, achievements and undertakings.

TRAVEL AND TOURISM — ABSTRACTING, BIBLIOGRAPHIES, STATISTICS

319 BB
BARBADOS. STATISTICAL SERVICE. DIGEST OF TOURISM STATISTICS.. a. Statistical Service, National Insurance Building, 3rd Fl., Fairchild St., Bridgetown, Barbados, W.I.

910.2 BE ISSN 0067-5547
BELGIUM. INSTITUT NATIONAL DE STATISTIQUE. STATISTIQUE DU TOURISME ET DE L'HOTELLERIE. (Text in Dutch, French) a. 52 Fr. (foreign 95 Fr.). Institut National de Statistique, 44 rue de Louvain, B-1000 Brussels, Belgium.

BELGIUM. INSTITUT NATIONAL DE STATISTIQUE. STATISTIQUES DU COMMERCE EXTER. see *TRANSPORTATION — Abstracting, Bibliographies, Statistics*

011 US
BIBLIOGRAPHY OF TOURISM AND TRAVEL RESEARCH STUDIES, REPORTS AND ARTICLES. 1980. irreg. $60 for 9 vols. University of Colorado, Business Research Division, Campus Box 420, Boulder, CO 80309. TEL 303-492-8227. Ed. Charles R. Goeldner. circ. 500.

959 016 SI ISSN 0068-0176
Z3248.S5
BOOKS ABOUT SINGAPORE. (Text in English) 1963. biennial. free. National Library, Stamford Rd., Singapore 0617, Singapore. TEL 3377355. FAX 3309611. TELEX RS-26620-NATLIB. circ. 1,500.
 Formerly: Books About Malaysia.

916.8 316 BS
BOTSWANA. CENTRAL STATISTICS OFFICE. TOURIST STATISTICS. 1974. a. P.1. Central Statistics Office, Ministry of Finance and Development Planning, Private Bag 0024, Gaborone, Botswana. (Orders to: Government Printer, Box 87, Gaborone, Botswana) charts; stat.
 Description: Information on travelers, length of stay and residence permit issues.

910.09 FR ISSN 0294-6831
CAHIERS DU TOURISME. SERIE D: STATISTIQUES. 1981. irreg. price varies. Universite d'Aix-Marseille III (Universite de Droit, d'Economie et des Sciences), Centre des Hautes Etudes Touristiques, Fondation Vasarely, 1 av. Marcel Pagnol, 13090 Aix-en-Provence, France. TEL 42-20-09-73. FAX 42-20-50-98.

910.09 FR
▼**CAHIERS DU TOURISME. SERIE F: BANQUE DE DONNEES STATISTIQUES.** 1990. irreg. 750 F. per no. Universite d'Aix-Marseille III (Universite de Droit, d'Economie et des Sciences), Centre des Hautes Etudes Touristiques, Fondation Vasarely, 1 av. Marcel Pagnol, 13090 Aix-en-Provence, France. TEL 42-20-09-73. FAX 42-20-50-98.

338.4 CN ISSN 0838-3952
G155.C3
CANADA. STATISTICS CANADA. INTERNATIONAL TRAVEL. (Catalogue 66-001) (Text in English and French) 1931. q. Can.$154($185) (foreign $216). Statistics Canada, Publications Sales and Services, Ottawa, Ont. K1A 0T6, Canada. TEL 613-951-7277. FAX 613-951-1584. (also avail. in microform from MML)
 Formerly: Canada. Statistics Canada. Travel Between Canada and Other Countries (ISSN 0317-6738)
 Description: Shows province of entry, transportation and country of residence of visitors as well as estimates of the travel account for the balance of payments both seasonally and not seasonally adjusted.

910.09 CE
CEYLON TOURIST BOARD. ANNUAL STATISTICAL REPORT. 1968. a. $10. Ceylon Tourist Board, Research Department, P.O. Box 1504, Colombo 3, Sri Lanka. circ. 1,000.

910.09 CE
CEYLON TOURIST BOARD. MONTHLY BULLETIN ON THE PERFORMANCE OF THE TOURISM SECTOR. m. $10. Ceylon Tourist Board, Research Department, P.O. Box 1504, Colombo 3, Sri Lanka.

915 310 CH
CHINA, REPUBLIC OF. REPORT ON TOURISM. STATISTICS (YEAR). a. Tourism Bureau, 9/F, 280 Chunghsiao E. Rd, Sec. 4, P.O. Box 1490, Taipei, Taiwan, Republic of China. TEL 02-721-8541. FAX 02-781-5399. TELEX 26408 ROCTB.

910.202 CK
COLOMBIA. CORPORACION NACIONAL DE TURISMO. BOLETIN DE ESTADISTICA TURISTICA. (YEAR). 1970. irreg., latest no.22, 1989. free. Corporacion Nacional de Turismo, Oficina de Planeacion, Calle 28 No. 13A-15, Piso 1, Local 3, Apdo. Aereo 8400, Bogota, Colombia. TEL 2839466. FAX 2843818. TELEX 441350 COTUR. (Co-sponsor: Ministerio de Desarrollo Economico) bk.rev.; charts; stat.; circ. 2,500.
 Formerly: Colombia. Corporacion Nacional de Turismo. Boletin de Investigaciones e Informacion Turistica.
 Description: Presents general information on Colombian tourism. Provides details on airlines, makes various distinctions between towns and regions and looks at Colombia's role in the evolution of world travel.

301.32 312 CY ISSN 0253-8709
CYPRUS. DEPARTMENT OF STATISTICS AND RESEARCH. TOURISM, MIGRATION AND TRAVEL STATISTICS. (Text in English) 1973. a. £C4. Ministry of Finance, Department of Statistics and Research, Nicosia, Cyprus.
 Description: Movements of travelers, departures and returns of permanent residents, emigrants and immigrants.

997 DQ
DOMINICA. QUARTERLY BULLETIN OF TOURISM STATISTICS. 1978. q. $16. Ministry of Finance, Statistical Division, 22 Bath Rd., Roseau, Dominica.

016 940 US ISSN 0070-8097
EAST EUROPE IN GERMAN BOOKS; a bulletin listing new books on East Europe published in the German language. 1971. irreg. v.5, 1977. Park College, Governmental Research Bureau, Kansas City, MO 64152. TEL 816-741-2000. Ed. Jerzy Hauptmann.

916 UA ISSN 0041-4948
EGYPT. MINISTRY OF TOURISM. STATISTICAL BULLETIN.* q. free. Ministry of Tourism, Under-Secretariat for Planning and Follow-up, General Directorate for Research and Statistics, 5 Adly St., Cairo, Egypt. (processed)

319 FJ
FIJI. BUREAU OF STATISTICS. TOURISM AND MIGRATION STATISTICS. 1973. a. $5. Bureau of Statistics, Box 2221, Suva, Fiji.
 Supersedes: Statistical Report on Tourism in Fiji.

914.94 SZ
FREMDENVERKEHRSBILANZ DER SCHWEIZ/BALANCE TOURISTIQUE DE LA SUISSE. (Text in French and German) 1967. a. 6 Fr. Bundesamt fuer Statistik, Hallwylstr. 15, CH-3003 Bern, Switzerland. TEL 031-618836. FAX 031-617856.

916.6 316 GM
GAMBIA. CENTRAL STATISTICS DEPARTMENT. CONSUMER PRICE INDEX. (Formerly issued by Central Statistics Division) m. D.12. Central Statistics Department, Wellington St., Banjul, Gambia.

339 GM
GAMBIA. CENTRAL STATISTICS DEPARTMENT. SUMMARY OF TOURIST STATISTICS. (Formerly issued by Central Statistics Division) m. D.12. Central Statistics Department, Wellington St., Banjul, Gambia.

312.8 910 GM
GAMBIA. CENTRAL STATISTICS DEPARTMENT. TOURIST STATISTICS. (Formerly issued by Central Statistics Division) a. D.12. Central Statistics Department, Wellington St., Banjul, Gambia.

GEO KATALOG (YEAR). VOLUME 1. TOURISTISCHE VEROEFFENTLICHUNGEN. see *GEOGRAPHY*

910.09 316 GH
GHANA. TOURIST CONTROL BOARD. BI-ANNUAL STATISTICS ON TOURISM. 1974. s-a. Tourist Board, Box 3106, Accra, Ghana.
 Formerly (until 1975): Ghana. Tourist Control Board. Quarterly Statistics on Tourism.

HOSPITALITY INDEX; an index for the hotel, foodservice and travel industries. see *HOTELS AND RESTAURANTS — Abstracting, Bibliographies, Statistics*

914.704 314 HU ISSN 0230-4414
G155.H9
HUNGARY. KOZPONTI STATISZTIKAI HIVATAL. IDEGENFORGALMI EVKONYV. a. 408 Ft. Statisztikai Kiado Vallalat, Kaszasdulo u. 2, P.O.Box 99, 1300 Budapest 3, Hungary. TEL 1-688-635. TELEX 22-6699. (Subscr. to: Kultura, Box 149, H-1389 Budapest, Hungary) circ. 800.
 —BLDSC shelfmark: 4362.418400.
 Supersedes: Idegenforgalmi Statisztika (ISSN 0209-4819)

INTERNATIONAL RARE BOOK PRICES - VOYAGES, TRAVEL & EXPLORATION. see *PUBLISHING AND BOOK TRADE — Abstracting, Bibliographies, Statistics*

915.69 IS ISSN 0075-1405
ISRAEL TOURIST STATISTICS/TAYARUT BE-YISRAEL. (Subseries of the Bureau's Special Series) (Text in English and Hebrew) irreg., latest no. 732, 1982. $8 price varies. Central Bureau of Statistics, Box 13015, Jerusalem, Israel.

915.6 JO
JORDAN. MINISTRY OF TOURISM AND ANTIQUITIES. TOURIST ARRIVALS IN NUMBERS. Variant title: Jordan. Ministry of Tourism and Antiquities. Travel Statistics. (Editions in Arabic and English) a. Ministry of Tourism & Antiquities, Jordan tourism authority, Box 224, Amman, Jordan. circ. 1,000.

338.4 KE
KENYA. CENTRAL BUREAU OF STATISTICS. MIGRATION AND TOURISM STATISTICS. 1971. irreg., latest 1978. Central Bureau of Statistics, Ministry of Planning and National Development, Box 30266, Nairobi, Kenya. (Dist. by: Government Printing and Stationery Office, Box 30128, Nairobi, Kenya)

910 016 UK ISSN 0261-1392
GV191.6
LEISURE, RECREATION AND TOURISM ABSTRACTS. 1976. q. £109($198) C.A.B. International, Wallingford, Oxon OX10 8DE, England. TEL 0491-32111. FAX 0491-33508. TELEX 847964 COMAGG G. (U.S. subscr. to: C.A.B. International, North American Office, 845 N. Park Ave., Tucson, AZ 85719. TEL 800-528-4841) circ. 350. (also avail. in microfiche; also avail. on floppy disk; back issues avail.)
 ●Also available online. Vendor(s): BRS (TOUR), CISTI, DIMDI, DIALOG, European Space Agency (File nos.16 & 124/CAB).
 —BLDSC shelfmark: 5182.267000.
 Formerly: Rural Recreation and Tourism Abstracts (ISSN 0308-0137)
 Description: Presents information on the many aspects of leisure for those interested in research and strategic development of leisure, recreation, sport, tourism and hospitality activities, facilities, products and services.

910.4 MH
MACAO. DIRECCAO DOS SERVICOS DE ESTATISTICA E CENSOS. ESTATISTICAS DO TURISMO/MACAO. CENSUS AND STATISTICS DEPARTMENT. TOURISM STATISTICS. (Text in Chinese, English, Portuguese) 1988. m. free. Direccao dos Servicos de Estatistica e Censos, Rua Inacio Baptista, No.4D-6, P.O. Box 3022, Macao. TEL 550935. FAX 561884.
 Description: Presents monthly data on visitor arrivals and occupancy rates among hotels and other establishments of accomodation.

910.4 MH
MACAO. DIRECCAO DOS SERVICOS DE ESTATISTICA E CENSOS. ESTATISTICAS DO TURISMO (RELATORIO ANUAL)/MACAO. CENSUS AND STATISTICS DEPARTMENT. TOURISM STATISTICS (ANNUAL REPORT). (Text in English, Portuguese) 1986. a. free. Direccao dos Servicos de Estatistica e Censos, Rua Inacio Baptista, No.4D-6, P.O. Box 3022, Macao. TEL 550935. FAX 561884.
 Description: Presents data on visitors arrivals, number of hotels and other accommodation establishments, room occupancy rates.

4800 TRAVEL AND TOURISM — ABSTRACTING, BIBLIOGRAPHIES, STATISTICS

916   MW
MALAWI TOURISM REPORT. 1970. a. K.2($2.50) National Statistical Office, Box 333, Zomba, Malawi. stat. (processed)
  Formerly: Malawi. National Statistical Office. Tourist Report (ISSN 0085-302X)

338.4   MF
MAURITIUS. CENTRAL STATISTICAL OFFICE. INTERNATIONAL TRAVEL AND TOURISM STATISTICS. 1974. a. Rs.75. Central Statistical Office, Port-Louis, Mauritius. (Subscr. to: G.P.O., La Tour Koenig, Port-Louis, Mauritius)
  Formerly: Mauritius. Central Statistical Office. International Travel and Tourism.

915.1   CH
MINISTRY OF COMMUNICATION. TOURISM BUREAU. ANNUAL REPORT. (Text in English) 1972. a. free. Ministry of Communications, Tourism Bureau, Box 1490, Taipei, Taiwan, Republic of China. FAX 02-7735487. TELEX 26408. Ed. Mao Chi-Kuo. illus.; circ. 2,500.
  Annual Report on Tourism Statistics, Republic of China.

915 915   CH
MONTHLY REPORT ON TOURISM - REPUBLIC OF CHINA/KUAN KUANG TZU LIAO. (Text in Chinese and English) 1968. m. free. Ministry of Communications, Tourism Bureau - Chiao T'ung Pu, Kuan Kuang Chu, Ta Lu Bldg., 9th Fl., 280 Chung Hsiao E. Rd. Sec. 4, Taipei, Taiwan, Republic of China. TEL 02-721-8541. FAX 02-7815399. TELEX 26408 ROTCB. (Subscr. to: P.O. Box 1490, Taipei, Taiwan, R.O.C.) Ed. Lin Ch'ing-Shih. charts; stat.; circ. 3,500. (looseleaf format)
  Description: Statistics of tourism in Taiwan, broken down by country of origin, nationality, sex, age.

997   MJ
MONTSERRAT. STATISTICS OFFICE. TOURISM REPORT. irreg. Statistics Office, Government Headquarters, Plymouth, Montserrat.

910 310   NE   ISSN 0168-5538
NETHERLANDS. CENTRAAL BUREAU VOOR DE STATISTIEK. STATISTIEK VREEMDELINGENVERKEER.. (Text in Dutch and English) 1952. a. Centraal Bureau voor de Statistiek, Prinses Beatrixlaan 428, Voorburg, Netherlands. (Orders to: SDU - Publishers, Christoffel Plantijnstraat, The Hague)

910.2   NE   ISSN 0168-3411
G155.N2
NETHERLANDS. CENTRAAL BUREAU VOOR DE STATISTIEK. VAKANTIEONDERZOEK. (Text in Dutch and English) 1954. a. Centraal Bureau voor de Statistiek, Prinses Beatrixlaan 428, Voorburg, Netherlands. (Orders to: SDU - Publishers, Christoffel Plantijnstraat, The Hague)
  Formerly: Vakantiebesteding van de Nederlandse Bevolking (ISSN 0077-7501)

910.4   NZ
NEW ZEALAND TOURISM DEPARTMENT. INTERNATIONAL VISITORS RESEARCH SERIES. 1982. irreg., no.22, 1989. price varies. Tourism Department, Research Services, P.O. Box 95, Wellington, New Zealand. TEL 04-4728-860. FAX 04-4781-736.
  Formerly: N Z T P International Visitors Research Series (ISSN 0112-983X)

647.94   NZ
NEW ZEALAND TOURISM DEPARTMENT. PRODUCT RESEARCH SERIES. 1980. irreg., latest 1989. price varies. Tourism Department, Research Services, P.O. Box 95, Wellington, New Zealand. TEL 04-4728-860. FAX 04-4781-736.
  Formerly: N Z T P Product Research Series (ISSN 0112-9589)

919.3   NZ
NEW ZEALAND TOURISM DEPARTMENT. VISITOR STATISTICS RESEARCH SERIES. 1973. a. price varies. Tourist Department, Research Services, P.O. Box 95, Wellington, New Zealand. TEL 04-728-860. FAX 04-781-736. adv.
  Formerly: N Z T P Visitor Statistics Research Series (ISSN 0112-9732)
  Description: Provides information on visitor arrivals in New Zealand; statistical tables including summary data, historical series, country profiles and department information.

332.1 314   NO   ISSN 0333-208X
NORWAY. STATISTISK SENTRALBYRAA. REISELIVSTATISKK/STATISTICS ON TRAVEL. (Subseries of its Norges Offisielle Statistikk) (Text in Norwegian and English) 1977. a. NOK 55. Statistisk Sentralbyraa, Box 8131 Dep., 0033 Oslo 1, Norway. TEL 02-864500. FAX 02-864973. stat.; circ. 800.

910.09   US
P A T A RESEARCH. ANNUAL STATISTICAL REPORT. 1967. a. $120 to non-members; members $80. Pacific Asia Travel Association, Telesis Tower, Ste. 1750, One Montgomery St., San Francisco, CA 94104. TEL 415-986-4646. Ed. Low Poh Gek. circ. 500.
  Description: Report that includes data on visitor arrivals in PATA destinations, outbound travel statistics from PATA countries, and other tourism-related statistics.

910 314   PL
POLAND. GLOWNY URZAD STATYSTYCZNY. TURYSTYKA. (Subseries of: Statystyka Polski) 1969. irreg., latest 1988. 10 Zl. Glowny Urzad Statystyczny, Al. Niepodleglosci 208, 00-925 Warsaw, Poland. TEL 22-25-03-45.

914.69   PO   ISSN 0377-2306
G155.P75
PORTUGAL. INSTITUTO NACIONAL DE ESTATISTICA. ESTATISTICAS DO TURISMO. CONTINENTE, ACORES E MADEIRA. 1969. a. Esc.5200. Instituto Nacional de Estatistica, Av. Antonio Jose de Almeida, 1078 Lisbon Codex, Portugal. (Orders to: Imprensa Nacional, Casa da Moeda, Direccao Comercial, rua D. Francisco Manuel de Melo 5, 1000 Lisbon, Portugal)
  Formerly: Portugal. Instituto Nacional de Estatistica. Estatisticas do Turismo.

914.94   SZ
REISEVERKEHR DER SCHWEIZER IM AUSLAND/TOURISTES SUISSES A L'ETRANGER. (Text in French and German) 1984. a. 6 Fr. Bundesamt fuer Statistik, Hallwylstr. 15, CH-3003 Bern, Switzerland. TEL 031-618836. FAX 031-617856.

910.09   TZ   ISSN 0564-836X
REPORT ON TOURISM STATISTICS IN TANZANIA. 1968. irreg. Bureau of Statistics, Box 796, Dar es Salaam, Tanzania. (Orders to: Government Publications Agency, Box 1801, Dar es Salaam, Tanzania)

ST. LUCIA. STATISTICAL DEPARTMENT. ANNUAL MIGRATION AND TOURISM STATISTICS. see POPULATION STUDIES — Abstracting, Bibliographies, Statistics

ST. LUCIA. STATISTICAL DEPARTMENT. QUARTERLY MIGRATION & TOURISM STATISTICS. see POPULATION STUDIES — Abstracting, Bibliographies, Statistics

914.94   SZ
SCHWEIZER TOURISMUS IN ZAHLEN/TOURISME SUISSE EN CHIFFRES. (Text in French and German) 1988. a. Bundesamt fuer Statistik, Hallwylstr. 15, CH-3003 Bern, Switzerland. TEL 031-618836. FAX 031-617856.

310   SE
SEYCHELLES. DEPARTMENT OF FINANCE. VISITOR SURVEY. a. R.5. Department of Finance, Statistics Division, P.O.Box 206, Independence House, Victoria, Seychelles.

960 316   SE
SEYCHELLES. PRESIDENT'S OFFICE. STATISTICS DIVISION. MIGRATION AND TOURISM STATISTICS. a. Rs.15. President's Office, Department of Finance, Statistics Division, Box 206, Mahe, Seychelles.
  Formerly: Seychelles. President's Office. Statistics Division. Tourism and Migration Report.

910.4 310   SE
SEYCHELLES. PRESIDENT'S OFFICE. STATISTICS DIVISION. TOURISM. 1982. m. Rs.5.00. President's Office, Department of Finance, Statistics Division, Box 206, Mahe, Seychelles.

915.95   SI
SINGAPORE ANNUAL REPORT ON TOURISM STATISTICS. 1969. a. S.$30. Singapore Tourist Promotion Board, Market Planning Department, Raffles City Tower No. 36-04, 250 North Bridge Road, Singapore 0617, Singapore. TEL 3396622. FAX 3399423. TELEX STBSIN-RS-33375. charts; stat.; circ. 1,500. (tabloid format)
  Formerly: Singapore Tourist Promotion Board. Annual Statistical Report on Visitor Arrivals.

915.9   SI
SINGAPORE MONTHLY REPORT ON TOURISM STATISTICS. (Supplement avail.) 1973. m. S.$81 (foreign S$.96). Singapore Tourist Promotion Board, Market Planning Department, Raffles City Tower No. 36-04, 250 N. Bridge Rd., Singapore 0617, Singapore. TEL 3396622. FAX 3399423. TELEX STBSIN RS 33375. charts; stat.; circ. 1,000.
  Formerly: Singapore Tourist Promotion Board. Monthly Statistical Report on Visitor Arrivals.
  Description: Brings out statistical information on visitor arrivals by country of residence, nationality and travel characteristics.

SOUTH AFRICA. CENTRAL STATISTICAL SERVICE. TOURISM AND MIGRATION. see POPULATION STUDIES — Abstracting, Bibliographies, Statistics

914.6   SP   ISSN 0212-5773
SPAIN. MINISTERIO DE TRANSPORTES, TURISMO Y COMUNICACIONES. SECRETARIA GENERAL DE TURISMO. ANUARIO DE ESTADISTICAS DE TURISMO. 1964. a. free. Ministerio de Transportes, Turismo y Comunicaciones, Direccion General de Aviacion Civil, Gabinete de Planificacion, Jefe Administracion base de datos-estadistica, C. Josefa Valcarcel 52, 28071 Madrid, Spain. Key Title: Anuario de Estadisticas de Turismo.
  Former titles: Spain. Ministerio de Comercio y Turismo. Estadisticas de Turismo; (until 1975): Spain. Ministerio de Informacion y Turismo. Estadisticas de Turismo (ISSN 0081-346X)

SPECIALTY TRAVEL INDEX; directory of special interest travel. see BUSINESS AND ECONOMICS — Trade And Industrial Directories

STATISTICAL OFFICE OF THE EUROPEAN COMMUNITIES. TRANSPORT, COMMUNICATIONS, TOURISME - ANNUAIRE STATISTIQUE. see TRANSPORTATION — Abstracting, Bibliographies, Statistics

338.4   IO
STATISTICAL REPORT ON VISITOR ARRIVALS TO INDONESIA. (Text in English) 1975. a. free. Department of Tourism, Post, and Telecommunications, Research and Development Centre, Jalan Kebon Sirih, No.36, Jakarta, Indonesia. TEL 021-347611. FAX 021-375409. TELEX 45157. bk.rev.; circ. 500 (controlled).
  Former titles (until 1983): Statistics of Incoming Visitors; (until 1978): Indonesia Tourist Statistics.

915.1   HK
STATISTICAL REVIEW OF TOURISM IN HONG KONG. (Text in English) 1974. a. HK.$100($20) Hong Kong Tourist Association, Research Department, G.P.O. Box 2597, Hong Kong. TEL 8017111. FAX 8104877. TELEX 74720-HX. Ed.Bd. circ. 6,000.
  Supersedes: Hong Kong Tourist Association. Digest of Annual Statistics.

310   IS   ISSN 0334-2476
STATISTICS OF TRAVEL AND TOURISM/TAYARUT V'SHERUTEI HA-ARAHA. (Text in English and Hebrew) q. $30. Central Bureau of Statistics, Box 13015, Jerusalem, Israel. TEL 02-533400.
  Description: Data on tourists and tourism services in Israel.

919   SI
SURVEY OF OVERSEAS VISITORS TO SINGAPORE. (Text in English) 1975. a. S.$30. Singapore Tourist Promotion Board, Market Planning Department, Raffles City Tower No. 36-04, 250 N. Bridge Rd., Singapore 0617, Singapore. TEL 3396622. FAX 3399423. TELEX STBSIN RS 33375. charts.
  Description: Visitor expenditure data, lead times, visit impressions, ratings of facilities and activities during visit.

338.4   VB
TOURISM IN THE BRITISH VIRGIN ISLANDS. 1973. a. $3. Statistics Office, Finance Department, Road Town, Tortola, British Virgin Islands. stat.

TRAVEL AND TOURISM — AIRLINE INFLIGHT AND HOTEL INROOM

917.29   PR
TOURISM INDUSTRY OF PUERTO RICO. SELECTED STATISTICS. 1970. a. free. Tourism Company of Puerto Rico, Office of Statistics and Economic Studies, P.O. Box 4435, Old San Juan Sta., San Juan, PR 00905. FAX 809-722-6352. Ed. Maria I. Aponte. stat.; circ. 1,250. (processed)

917   CN
TOURISM ROOM REVENUES. 12/yr. Can.$60. Ministry of Finance and Corporate Relations, 1405 Douglas St., 2nd Fl., Victoria, B.C. V8V 1X4, Canada. TEL 604-387-0327. FAX 604-387-0329.
   Description: Details revenues received from room rentals by type of accomodation, with a geographic breakdown by development region.

914.94   SZ
TOURISMUS IN DER SCHWEIZ/TOURISME EN SUISSE. (Text in French and German) 1974. a. 28 Fr. Bundesamt fuer Statistik, Hallwylstr. 15, CH-3003 Bern, Switzerland. TEL 031-618836. FAX 031-617856.

310   IS
TRAVEL AND TOURISM - ABSTRACTING, BIBLIOGRAPHIES, STATISTICS. (Text in English and Hebrew) q. $30. Central Bureau of Statistics, Box 13015, Jerusalem 91 130, Israel. TEL 02-553400.

910   US   ISSN 1040-8142
Z6004.T6
TRAVEL & TOURISM INDEX. 1984. q. (plus a. cum.). $50. Brigham Young University, Hawaii Campus, Business Division, Box 1773, Laie, HI 96762. FAX 808-293-3645. Ed. Gerald V. Bohnet. circ. 500.
   Description: Indexes articles by subject/title from periodicals in the travel and tourism field.

910.09   US   ISSN 0738-9515
G155.A1
TRAVEL INDUSTRY WORLD YEARBOOK; the big picture. 1956. a. $79 (foreign $89). Child & Waters, Inc., 516 Fifth Ave., New York, NY 10036. TEL 212-840-1935. Ed. Somerset Waters. (back issues avail.) **Indexed:** SRI.
—BLDSC shelfmark: 2057.271000.
   Description: Information and statistics pertaining to trends in and prospects for the international and national tourism industry, with industry trends for motels-hotels, travel agents, food services, and supplemental amenities.

917.1   CN   ISSN 0713-2840
TRAVEL-LOG. 1982. q. Can.$42($50) (foreign $59). Statistics Canada, Publications Division, Ottawa, Ont. K1A 0T6, Canada. TEL 613-951-7277. FAX 613-951-1584.
   Description: Presents a diverse range of tourism topics in an easy-to-read format drawing together data from several tourism-related surveys conducted by Statistics Canada.

910 310   TR   ISSN 0082-6537
TRINIDAD AND TOBAGO. CENTRAL STATISTICAL OFFICE. INTERNATIONAL TRAVEL REPORT. 1955. a., latest 1981. T.T.$5. Central Statistical Office, 23 Park St., P.O. Box 98, Port-of-Spain, Trinidad & Tobago, W.I. TEL 809-62-53705. (Dist. by: Government Printing Office, 110 Henry St., Port-of-Spain, Trinidad & Tobago, W.I.)

910.09   TR
TRINIDAD AND TOBAGO. CENTRAL STATISTICAL OFFICE. QUARTERLY TRAVEL. 1955; N.S. 1965. q. T.T.$3 per no. Central Statistical Office, 23 Park St., P.O. Box 98, Port-of-Spain, Trinidad & Tobago, W.I. TEL 809-62-53705. (Dist. by: Government Printing Office, 110 Henry St., Port-of-Spain, Trinidad & Tobago, W.I.) stat.
   Formerly: Trinidad and Tobago. Central Statistical Office. Monthly Travel.

919.604   NN
VANUATU IN FACTS AND FIGURES. (Text in English and French) 1975. a. free. Statistics Office, Private Mail Bag 19, Port-vila, Vanuatu. stat.; circ. 500.
   Former titles: Vanuatu in Figures; New Hebrides. Bureau of Statistics. Some Facts and Figures about the New Hebrides.

910.2   SP
YEARBOOK OF TOURISM STATISTICS. (Text in English, French and Spanish) 1953. a. $33. World Tourism Organization, Capitan Haya 42, 28020 Madrid, Spain. (looseleaf format)
   Former title: World Tourism Statistics; International Travel Statistics (ISSN 0074-9184)

910.09   YU
YUGOSLAVIA. SAVEZNI ZAVOD ZA STATISTIKU. TURIZAM. (Subseries of its Statisticki Bilten). a. 30 din.($1.67) Savezni Zavod za Statistiku, Kneza Milosa 20, Belgrade, Yugoslavia. TEL 11-681-999. stat.

910.09 316   RH
ZIMBABWE. CENTRAL STATISTICAL OFFICE. MONTHLY MIGRATION AND TOURIST STATISTICS. m. Rhod.$0.45. Central Statistical Office, Box 8063, Causeway, Harare, Zimbabwe. circ. 220.

TRAVEL AND TOURISM — Airline Inflight And Hotel Inroom

056.1 051   US
ABOARD AVIATECA. (Text in English, Spanish) 1987. bi-m. free to airline passengers. North-South Net, Inc., 100 Almeria Ave., Ste. 220, Coral Gables, FL 33134. TEL 305-441-9744. FAX 305-441-9739. Ed. Gloria Shanahan. bk.rev.; illus.; circ. 10,000.
   Description: General interest articles for travelers into and out of Latin America. Includes information on tourist attractions.

056.1 051   US
ABOARD DOMINICANA. (Text in English, Spanish) 1983. bi-m. free to airline passengers. North-South Net, Inc., 100 Almeria Ave., Ste. 220, Coral Gables, FL 33134. TEL 305-441-9744. FAX 305-441-9739. Ed. Gloria Shanahan. bk.rev.; illus.; circ. 6,000.
   Description: General interest articles for travelers into and out of Latin America. Includes information on tourist attractions.

056.1 051   US
ABOARD ECUATORIANA. (Text in English, Spanish) 1983. bi-m. free to airline passengers. North-South Net, Inc., 100 Almeria Ave., Ste. 220, Coral Gables, FL 33134. TEL 305-441-9744. FAX 305-441-9739. Ed. Gloria Shanahan. bk.rev.; illus.; circ. 10,000.
   Description: General interest articles for travellers to and from Latin America, with information on tourist attractions.

056.1 051   US
ABOARD L A B AIRLINES. (Lloyd Aero Boliviano) (Text in English, Spanish) 1977. bi-m. free to airline passengers. North-South Net, Inc., 100 Almeria Ave., Ste. 220, Coral Gables, FL 33134. TEL 305-441-9744. FAX 305-441-9739. Ed. Gloria Shanahan. bk.rev.; illus.; circ. 14,000.
   Description: Features general interest articles for travelers into and out of Latin America. Includes information on tourist attractions.

056.1 051   US
ABOARD LAN-CHILE. (Text in English, Spanish) 1976. bi-m. free to airline passengers. North-South Net, Inc., 100 Almeria Ave., Ste. 220, Coral Gables, FL 33134. TEL 305-441-9744. FAX 305-441-9739. Ed. Gloria Shanahan. bk.rev.; illus.; circ. 23,000.
   Description: Features general interest articles for travelers into and out of Latin America. Includes information on tourist attractions.

056.1 051   US
ABOARD TACA; international airlines. (Text in English, Spanish) 1981. bi-m. free to airline passengers. North-South Net, Inc., 100 Almeria Ave., Ste. 220, Coral Gables, FL 33134. TEL 305-441-9744. FAX 305-441-9739. Ed. Gloria Shanahan. bk.rev.; illus.; circ. 14,000.
   Description: Features general-interest articles for travelers into and out of Latin America. Includes information on tourist attractions.

056.1 051   US
ABOARD VIASA; la linea aerea de Venezuela. (Text in English, Spanish) 1977. bi-m. free to airline passengers. North-South Net, Inc., 100 Almeria Ave., Ste. 220, Coral Gables, FL 33134. TEL 305-441-9744. FAX 305-441-9739. Ed. Cristina Juri Arencibia. circ. 18,000.
   Description: Features general interest articles for travelers into and out of Latin America. Includes information on tourist attractions.

056.1 051   MX
▼**AEROMEXICO ESCALA.** (Text in English and Spanish) 1990. m. (AeroMexico) Impresiones Aereas, S.A. de C.V., Arquimedes, 5, Col. Polanco C.P., 11560 Mexico D.F., Mexico. TEL 250-58-79. adv.; circ. 100,000.

051 059.927   SU
AHLAN WASAHLAN/HELLO, WELCOME. (Text in Arabic and English) 1977. 12/yr. Saudi Arabian Airlines, P.O. Box 620, Jeddah 21231, Saudi Arabia. TEL 02-686-2349. FAX 02-814-5877. TELEX 847031 ARBIA G. Ed. Yarub A. Balkhair. adv.; circ. 150,000.
   Description: In-flight magazine.

051 054   FR
AIR FRANCE MADAME. (Text in English, French) 6/yr. Air France, 71 rue Desnouettes, Paris 75015, France. TEL 48-28-40-58. FAX 48-28-39-50. adv.
   Description: Covers personalities, culture, fashion, and travel.

051   US
AIR WISCONSIN - AIR DESTINATIONS.* m. (United Express System) Stout Publishing Corp., 6006 S. Holly St., Ste. 123, Englewood, CO 80111-4200. TEL 303-399-3000. Ed. Rod Manuel. adv.
   Description: In-flight magazine.

051 387.7   US
ALASKA AIRLINES MAGAZINE. 1977. m. $30. Paradigm Press, 2701 1st Ave., Ste. 250, Seattle, WA 98121. TEL 206-441-5871. FAX 206-448-6939. Ed. Paul Temple. adv.; bk.rev.; circ. 40,000 (controlled).
   Formerly: Alaskafest (ISSN 0199-0586)
   Description: General interest publication for business and leisure travellers.

051   US
AMERICA WEST AIRLINES MAGAZINE. 1986. m. $29. Skyword Marketing, Inc., 7500 N. Dreamy Draw Dr., Ste. 240, Phoenix, AZ 85020. TEL 602-997-7200. Ed. Michael Derr. adv.; bk.rev.; bibl.; charts; illus.; circ. 125,000.

051   US   ISSN 0003-1518
AMERICANWAY. 1966. s-m. $72 (free to American Airlines and American Eagle passengers). (American Airlines, Inc.) A A Magazine Publications, Box 619640, Dallas-Ft. Worth Airport, Dallas, TX 75261-9640. TEL 817-967-1804. FAX 817-967-1571. Ed. Doug Crichton. adv.; bk.rev.; illus.; circ. 300,000. (also avail. in microform from UMI)

056.1 051   US
AMIGOS VOLANDO. (Text in English, Spanish) 1983. m. (Avianca Airlines) Carvajal International, Inc., 717 Ponce de Leon Blvd., Ste. 304, Coral Gables, FL 33134. TEL 305-448-6875. FAX 305-448-9942. Ed. Gustavo M. Garcia Arena. circ. 90,000.
   Description: For passengers of Avianca Airlines to read during flights.

385.23 051   US   ISSN 1040-1776
AMTRAK EXPRESS. 1981. bi-m. $18. (National Railroad Passenger Corporation) Pace Communications Inc., 1301 Carolina St., Greensboro, NC 27401. TEL 919-378-6065. FAX 919-275-2864. Ed. Melinda L. Stovall. adv. contact: Maryann Earley. circ. 253,000 (controlled).
   Description: General interest articles on life in the U.S., with travel and railroad-related features.

051   IS
ARKIA IN-FLIGHT MAGAZINE. (Text in English) s-a. P.O. Box 7052, Jerusalem 91 070, Israel. TEL 02-234131. circ. 15,000.

TRAVEL AND TOURISM — AIRLINE INFLIGHT AND HOTEL INROOM

051 US
ARRIVED. q. Russ Moore & Associates Inc., 4151 Knob Dr., Ste. 200, Eagan, MN 55122. TEL 612-452-0571. Ed. Diane Steen. circ. 200,000 (controlled).
Description: In-room magazine distributed to guests at Carlson Hospitality Group hotels located in the United States, Mexico, Canada and the Caribbean. Covers exotic locations, tips for business travelers, personality profiles, and the hospitality industry.

051 KO
ASIANA. m. Asiana Airlines, Asiana Bldg., 10-1 Hoehyon-dong 2 ga, Chung-gu, Seoul, Korea. TEL 82-2-758-8452. FAX 82-2-758-8008. Ed. Sam-Koo Park. adv.; circ. 100,000.
Description: Airline inflight magazine on Korea, Japan, Hong Kong, Tapei, Bangkok and Singapore.

051 US
ASPEN AIRWAYS - AIR DESTINATIONS.* 1984. m. $9.95. (United Express System) Stout Publishing Corp., 6006 S. Holly St., Ste. 123, Englewood, CO 80111-4200. TEL 303-399-3000. Ed. Kristi Theis.
Description: In-flight magazine for Aspen Airways, focusing on Colorado, Wyoming and New Mexico.

052 IC
ATLANTICA. (Text in English) 1976. 5/yr. (Icelandair) Iceland Review, Box 8576, Reykjavik, Iceland. Ed. Haraldur J. Hamar. adv.; circ. 55,000. **Indexed:** Deep Sea Res.& Oceanogr.Abstr.
Description: Icelandair in-flight magazine.

052 AU
AUSTRIAN AIRLINES SKYLINES. bi-m. Osterreichische Luftverkehrs, A.G., Vienna A1107, Austria. TEL 43-222-68-35-11. Ed. Nicole Schmidt. adv.: B&W page S.7254; color page S.11606; trim 7 1/8 x 9 1/8. circ. 150,000.
Description: Airline inflight magazine.

917.04 US
BIENVENIDOS A MIAMI. (Text in Spanish) 1975. fortn. free to visitors in hotels & motels. Welcome Publications, Inc., Box 630-518, 1751 NE 162nd St., Miami, FL 33163. TEL 305-944-9444. Ed. Mona K. Levine. adv.; circ. 13,000.
Formerly: Bienvenidos a Miami y a la Florida.

052 FI ISSN 0358-7703
BLUE WINGS; Finnair's in-flight magazine. (Text in English) 1980. bi-m. Erikoislehdet Oy Business Publications, Box 16, SF-00381 Helsinki, Finland. Ed. Marketta Rentola. adv.; circ. 92,000.

051 CN
CANADIAN (VERNON). 1978. m. (Canadian Airlines International) Synergism Marketing & Communications Inc., 111 Avenue Rd., Ste. 801, Toronto, Ont. M5R 3J8, Canada. TEL 416-962-9184. FAX 416-962-2380. Ed. Kathleen Hurd. adv.; bk.rev.; circ. 141,000. **Indexed:** Can.Per.Ind.
Description: In-flight magazine.

052 IE ISSN 0008-6088
CARA; inflight magazine of Aer Lingus. 1968. 6/yr. £12($30) Aer Lingus, Publicity Department, Box 180, Dublin Airport PA7, Dublin, Ireland. FAX 01-426-998. Ed. Bernard Share. adv.; bk.rev.; circ. 330,000.
Description: Publication for passengers on all Aer Lingus flights: scheduled, charter, and commuter.

051 US ISSN 1051-7383
COMPASS READINGS. 1989. m. $36. (Northwest Airlines) Skies America Publishing Company, 7730 S.W. Mohawk, Tualatin, OR 97062. TEL 503-691-1955. FAX 503-691-1275. Ed. Terri J. Wallo. circ. 400,000.
Description: Inflight magazine.

051 US
CONTINENTAL PROFILES. 1968. m. (Continental Airlines) Publishing Images, 34 E. 51st St., New York, NY 10022. TEL 212-888-5900. FAX 212-752-0521. adv.; circ. 394,972.
Description: In-flight magazine for the business traveler.

052 UK
DUTY FREE MAGAZINE. s-a. free. (Sealink Stena Line) Illustrated London News, 20 Upper Ground, London SE1 9PF, England. TEL 071-928-2111. FAX 071-620-1594. Ed. Alison Booth. circ. 350,000.
Formerly: Connections (London).
Description: In-flight magazine providing travel information. Includes tips on duty and tax-free shopping.

052 CH
DYNASTY. (Text in Chinese and English) 1969. 6/yr. free. China Airlines Ltd. - Chung Hua Hang K'ung Kung Ssu, 131 Nanking E. Rd. Sec. 3, Taipei, Taiwan, Republic of China. Ed. Wu I-Shou. adv.; circ. 60,000.

910.09 CH
EVA AIRWAYS VERVE. m. Eva Airways Corp., 7-F, 330 Minsheng East Rd., Taipei, Taiwan, Republic of China. TEL 02-505-7766. adv.; circ. 17,000.

051 910.4 US
EXPRESS. 1981. bi-m. $12 (free to qualified personnel). Amtrak, c/o Paul Podgus, Box 0, Huntington, NY 11743. TEL 516-385-9299. Ed. Christopher Podgus. adv.; bk.rev.; circ. 160,000. **Indexed:** Avery Ind.Archit.Per.
Description: For Amtrak riders. Covers a broad spectrum of topics, including places of interest, interviews, and current events.

051 054 LU
FLYDOSCOPE; magazine de bord de Luxair. (Text in English, French, German) 1975. 3/yr. free to passengers. Luxair, B.P. 2203, L-2987 Luxembourg, Luxembourg. TEL 4798-2221. FAX 43-63-44. TELEX 2372 LGDDAP LU. adv.; circ. 40,000 (controlled).
Description: Consists of feature articles on aviation, art, culture travel and places of interest to those who fly Luxair.

051 NE
FLYING DUTCHMAN DIRECTIONS. (Text in English) 1981. 6/yr. free to qualified personnel. (K L M - Royal Dutch Airlines) Multi Media International, P.O. Box 469, 1180 AL Amstelveen, Netherlands. TEL 020-5473550. FAX 020-6438581. adv.; illus.; circ. 100,000 (controlled). **Indexed:** Key to Econ.Sci.
Former titles (until 1992): Flying Dutchman International; Flying Dutchman.
Description: Short informative articles for KLM frequent flyers.

910.202 SA
FLYING SPRINGBOK/VLIEENDE SPRINGBOK. 1961. q. (South African Airways) Springbok Publishing Co. (Pty) Ltd., P.O. Box 3734, Randburg 2125, South Africa. Ed. Ernest Webb-Stock. adv.; bk.rev.; circ. 50,000. (also avail. in microfiche)

051 059.992 IO
GARUDA MAGAZINE. (Text in English and Indonesian) 1971. bi-m. free. (Garuda Indonesia) P.T. Travia Duta, 3rd Fl., Hotel Borobudur Inter-Continental, Jalan Lapangan Bateng Selatan, Jakarta 10220, Indonesia. TEL 21-3809595. FAX 21-359-741. TELEX 44156-BDOIHC-IA. Ed. Daisy Hadmoko. adv.; charts; illus.; circ. 150,000 (controlled).
Formerly (until 1981): Garuda Indonesia Airways Magazine (ISSN 0046-5453)
Description: In-flight magazine for passengers of Garuda Indonesia.

917.304 US
GUEST INFORMANT. (In 39 U.S. city editions.) 1937. a. Guest Informant, 21200 Erwin St., Woodland Hills, CA 91367. TEL 818-716-7484. adv.
Description: Hotel inroom publication that acquaints travelers with the city their hotel is in. Covers shopping, dining, history, culture, sights and recreation.

910.4 US
GUEST INFORMANT - ATLANTA. (In 36 editions) 1982. a. L I N Cellular Communications Corp., 21200 Irwin St., Woodland Hills, CA 91367. TEL 818-716-7484. Ed. Andrea Zwerdling. circ. 2,730,000.
Formerly: Leisureguide - Atlanta.

917.4 US
GUEST INFORMANT - BOSTON. 1978. a. L I N Cellular Communications Corp., 21200 Irwin St., Woodland hills, CA 91367. TEL 818-716-7484. Ed. Andrea Zwerdling. adv.; circ. 2,979,000.
Formerly: Leisureguide - Boston.

917 US
GUEST INFORMANT - CHICAGO. 1971. a. L I N Cellular Communications Corp., 21200 Irwin St., Woodland Hills, CA 91367. TEL 818-716-7484. Ed. Andrea Zwerdling. adv.; circ. 3,800,000.
Formerly: Leisureguide - Chicago.

917 US
GUEST INFORMANT - HOUSTON. 1978. a. L I N Cellular Communications Corp., 21200 Irwin St., Woodland Hills, CA 91367. TEL 818-716-7484. Ed. Andrea Zwerdling. adv.; circ. 3,186,000.
Formerly: Leisureguide - Houston.

910.4 US
GUEST INFORMANT - KANSAS CITY. 1982. a. L I N Cellular Communications Corp., 21200 Irwin St., Woodland Hills, CA 91367. TEL 818-716-7484. Ed. Andrea Zwerdling. circ. 1,740,000.
Formerly: Leisureguide - Kansas City.

910.4 US
GUEST INFORMANT - NEW ORLEANS. 1982. a. L I N Cellular Communications Corp., 21200 Irwin St., Woodland Hills, CA 91367. TEL 818-716-7484. Ed. Andrea Zwerdling. circ. 1,980,000.
Formerly: Leisureguide - New Orleans.

917.5 US
GUEST INFORMANT - ORLANDO. 1980. a. L I N Cellular Communications Corp., 21200 Irwin St., Woodland Hills, CA 91367-7356. TEL 818-716-7484. Ed. Andrea Zwerdling. adv.; circ. 3,100,000.
Formerly: Leisureguide - Orlando.

917.2 US
GUEST INFORMANT - PUERTO RICO. 1980. a. L I N Cellular Communications Corp., 21200 Irwin St., Woodland Hills, CA 91367. TEL 818-716-7484. Ed. Andrea Zwerdling. adv.; circ. 3,045,000.
Formerly: Leisureguide - Puerto Rico.

917 US
GUEST INFORMANT - THE FLORIDA GOLD COAST. 1974. a. L I N Cellular Communications Corp., 21200 Irwin St., Woodland Hills, CA 91367. TEL 818-716-7484. Ed. Andrea Zwerdling. adv.; circ. 5,590,000.
Formerly: Leisureguide - The Florida Gold Coast.

910.4 US
GUEST INFORMANT - TWIN CITIES. 1982. a. L I N Cellular Communications Corp., 21200 Irwin St., Woodland Hills, CA 91367. TEL 818-716-7484. Ed. Andrea Zwerdling. circ. 1,800,000.
Formerly: Leisureguide - Twin Cities.

051 US
HAWAIIAN AIRLINES MAGAZINE. 1989. m. Hawaii Business Publishing Corp., Box 913, 825 Keeaumoku St., Honolulu, HI 96814. TEL 808-946-3978. FAX 808-947-8498. Ed. Michael Flynn. adv.; circ. 85,000.
Description: Covers events, activities, attractions, arts, business and personalities.

052 UK
HIGH LIFE. 1974. m. £18 (foreign £20; free to qualified personnel). (British Airways) Headway Publications Ltd. (Subsidiary of: Maxwell Consumer Publishing and Communications Ltd.), Greater London House, Hampstead Rd., London NW1 7QQ, England. TEL 071-377-3171. FAX 071-387-9518. TELEX 269470. Ed. Willian Davis. adv.; charts; illus.; tr.lit.; circ. 215,000.
Description: Inflight magazine featuring current travel news and information.

051 US ISSN 1050-2440
HORIZON AIR MAGAZINE. 1979. m. Paradigm Press, 2701 First Ave., Ste. 250, Seattle, WA 98121. TEL 206-441-5871. Ed. Paul Temple. adv.; tr.lit.; circ. 20,000 (controlled).
Description: Aimed at business travelers in the Northwest and includes regional business, travel and general interest topics.

TRAVEL AND TOURISM — AIRLINE INFLIGHT AND HOTEL INROOM

052 UK ISSN 0952-7974
HOT AIR; Virgin Atlantic Airways in-flight magazine. 1983. bi-m. John Brown Publishing Ltd., The Boathouse, Crabtree Lane, London SW6 8NJ, England. TEL 01-381-6007. FAX 01-381-3930. Ed. Caroline Wheal. adv.; bk.rev.; circ. 200,000.

910.202 TH
HUMSAFAR. 1980. 6/yr. $29. (Pakistan International Airlines) Media Transasia (Thailand) Ltd., 14th Fl., Orakarn Bldg., 26 Chidlom Rd., Ploenchit, Bangkok 10330, Thailand. FAX 2535335. TELEX 84003-MEDTRAN-TH. Ed. X. Colaco. adv.; circ. 70,000.
  Description: Inflight publication of Pakistan International Airlines. Focuses on travel and tourism.

051 BL
ICARO. 1983. m. (Varig Airlines) Icaro Editora Ltd., Rua Vieria de Morais, 1928, CEP 04617 Sao Paulo, Brazil. adv.; circ. 130,000.
  Description: Inflight magazine covering business, cultural and international topics on Brazil and on Varig's destinations.

051 059.927 TS
AL-IMARAT FIL-AJWA/EMIRATES IN FLIGHT. (Text in Arabic, English) 1987. m. free. (Emirates Airlines) Motivate Publishing, P.O. Box 2331, Dubai, United Arab Emirates. TEL 246060. FAX 214820. TELEX 48366 MAM EM. Ed. Obaid Humaid al-Tayer. circ. 1,000.
  Description: In-flight magazine.

910.202 US
INN ROOM MAGAZINE. 1977. m. free. In Room Publications, 210 S. Juniper, Ste. 215, Escondido, CA 92025. TEL 619-489-5252. Ed. Donna Abate. adv.; bk.rev.; circ. 90,025.

059.956 US
K L M WINDMILL. (Text in Japanese) m. (K L M Royal Airlines) Multi Media International, P.O. Box 469, 1180 Amstelveen, Netherlands. TEL 31-020-5473550. FAX 31-020-6438581. Ed. Ken Wilkie. adv.; circ. 90,000.

057.85 PL
KALEIDOSCOPE. 1979. q. (L O T Polish Airlines) A G P O L, Ul. Sienkiewicza 12, P.O. Box 136, 00-950 Warsaw, Poland. adv.; circ. 80,000.

051 056.1 US
LASCA'S WORLD. (Text in English, Spanish) 1985. bi-m. $25. E R Publishing, 1911 N.W. 114th St., Pembroke Lakes, FL 33026. TEL 305-431-0161. FAX 305-431-4661. Ed. Manja Rippen. circ. 20,000. (back issues avail.)
  Description: Covers leisure activities, business trends, travel and dining, and travel destinations in the United States, Caribbean, Central and South America.

051 PH ISSN 0217-6998
MABUHAY; the inflight magazine of Philippine Airlines. (Text in English) 1981. m. P.100($3.50) per no. (Philippine Airlines) Eastgate Publishing Corporation, Attn: Ms. Jing Sanchez-Lagandaon, Rms.603-604 Emerald Bldg., Emerald Ave., Pasig, Metro Manila, Philippines. TEL 6312921. FAX 632-6312992. TELEX 43162 VAFOC PM. Ed. Max V. Soliven. adv.; circ. 82,000. (back issues avail.)

051 US
MESA CONNECTION.* 1987. bi-m. (Mesa Airlines) Stout Publishing Corp., 6006 S. Holly St., Ste. 123, Englewood, CO 80111-4200. TEL 303-399-3000. Ed. Kristi Theis. adv.; circ. 10,000.

051 056.1 CK
EL MUNDO AL VUELO - INFLIGHT NOTES. (Text in English and Spanish) 1972. 12/y. $40. (Avianca) Caravajal S.A., Apdo. 53550, Bogota, Colombia. Ed. Maria Christina Lamus. adv.; bk.rev.; circ. 90,000.
  Formerly: Apuntes de Abordo - Inflight Notes.
  Description: For passengers on Avianca's domestic and international flights, also sent to important commercial and tourist organizations.

051 US
N P A - AIR DESTINATIONS.* bi-m. (United Express System) Stout Publishing Corp., 6006 S. Holly St., Ste. 123, Englewood, CO 80111-4200. TEL 303-399-3000. Ed. Kristi Theis. adv.
  Description: In-flight magazine.

052 II
NAMASKAAR. (Text in English) 1980. 6/yr. (Air India) Asia Publishing House, Bhogilal Hargobindas Bldg., 18-20 K Dubash Marg, Bombay 400 023, India. TEL 225353. FAX 010-9122-225685. Ed. Homi J. Vakeel. adv.; circ. 45,000.

051 US ISSN 0029-327X
NORTHLINER MAGAZINE;* news and features for passengers of North Central Airlines. 1969. q. free to airline passengers. (North Central Airlines) Dorn Communications, Inc., 15 5th St. S., Ste. 900, Minneapolis, MN 55402. Ed. James Carney. adv.; bk.rev.; charts; illus.; circ. 80,000.

051 CN
NORTHWEST EXPLORER MAGAZINE. 1981. 6/yr. Outcrop Ltd., P.O. Box 1350, Yellowknife, N.W.T. X1A 2N9, Canada. TEL 403-920-4652. FAX 403-873-2844. Ed. Rosemary Allerston. adv.; circ. 26,180.
  Description: In-flight magazine.

051 US
NORTHWEST ORIENT. 1969. m. $24 (free to passengers). (Northwest Orient Airlines) East-West Network, Inc. (New York), 34 E. 51st St., New York, NY 10022. TEL 212-888-5900. Ed. Bill McCoy. adv.; bk.rev.; illus.; circ. 175,000.
  Formerly (until 1983): Passages.

052 AT
PANORAMA (SYDNEY); Ansett Airlines' inflight magazine. 1958. m. Aus.$28. (Ansett Airlines of Australia) Australian Consolidated Press, 54 Park St., Sydney, N.S.W. 2000, Australia. Ed. Fenelia Souter. adv.; bk.rev.; circ. 75,600.

917.04 US
PORTLAND AND THE PACIFIC NORTHWEST. 1975. a. $12. Fox Publishing Co., 320 S.W. Stark, Ste. 519, Portland, OR 97204. TEL 503-223-0051. FAX 503-225-1245. Ed. Susan Monti. adv.; circ. 18,500.
  Description: In-room guidebook.

051 US
PRESIDENTIAL - AIR DESTINATIONS.* bi-m. (United Express System) Stout Publishing Corp., 6006 S. Holly St., Ste. 123, Englewood, CO 80111-4200. TEL 303-399-3000. Ed. Rod Manuel. adv.
  Description: In-flight magazine.

051 056.1 SP
RONDA IBERIA. (Text in English, Spanish) 1974. m. free. (Iberia Airlines) Ediciones Reunidas, S.A., O'Donnell, 12, 28009 Madrid, Spain. TEL 91-522-0072. FAX 91-541-03-75. TELEX 41969 EDIT E. bk.rev.; circ. 220.
  Description: Provides useful information for Iberia passengers and reports on various national and international destinations. Includes articles on nature and sports activities.

052 BE ISSN 0036-2158
SABENA REVUE. (Text in English) 1935. q. 200 Fr. (Sabena Belgian World Airlines) International Publications, Boechoutlaan 55 (bus 5), B-1853 Strombeek-Bever, Belgium. FAX 02-460-1332. TELEX 23785. Ed. J. Sparrow. adv.; bk.rev.; charts; illus.; circ. 50,000.

050 BE
SABENA SPHERE. m. (Sabena Belgian World Airlines) International Publications, Boechoutlaan 55, Bus 5, 1853 Strombeek-Bever, Belgium. TEL 32-2-640-59-99. FAX 32-2-640-13-32. Ed. George McDonald. adv.; circ. 78,000.

052 HK
SAWASDEE. 1971. m. $70. (Thai Air International) Travel & Trade Publishing (Asia) Ltd., 16-F, Capitol Centre, 5-19 Jardine's Bazaar, Causeway Bay, Hong Kong. TEL 890-3067. FAX 895-2375. TELEX 76591-TPAL-HX. Ed. Julia Birch. adv.; circ. 100,000.
  Description: In-flight magazine.

052 SW
SCANORAMA. (Text in English) 1972. 10/yr. $70. S A S Media Partner, Gaevlegatan 18B, S-11330 Stockholm, Sweden. TEL 46-8-7297575. FAX 46-8-7288524. Ed. Lars Bringert. adv.; bk.rev.; charts; illus.; tr.lit.; circ. 140,000.
  Description: In-flight magazine.

052 HK
SERENDIB. (Text in English) 1982. 6/yr. free. (Air Lanka) Emphasis HK Ltd., Wilson House, 10th Fl., 19-27 Wyndam St., Central, Hong Kong, Hong Kong. TEL 5-215392. FAX 810-6738. TELEX 74523-EMFAS-HX. Ed. Alan Moores. adv.; circ. 25,000.
  Description: In-flight magazine on travel in Sri Lanka.

051 US
SHUTTLE QUARTERLY. 1988. q. Shuttle Quarterly, Inc., 50 Freedom Hollow, Ste. 401, Salem, MA 01970. TEL 508-745-1874. adv.; circ. 30,000.
  Description: In-flight magazine for passengers of the Pan-Am and Trump shuttles between Boston, New York and Washington D.C.

052 HK
▼**SILKROAD.** 1991. bi-m. Dragon Airlines Ltd., 12-f Tower 6, 33 Canton Rd., Kowloon, Hong Kong, Hong Kong. TEL 738-3394. FAX 738-0833. adv.; circ. 33,000.
  Description: Inflight magazine.

052 SI ISSN 0129-606X
SILVER KRIS; Singapore Airlines inflight magazine. (Text in English) 1976. m. (Singapore International Airlines) M P H Magazines Pty. Ltd., Pan-I Warehouse Complex 03-21, 601 Sims Drive, Singapore 1438, Singapore. FAX 7440620. TELEX 35853 MPHMAG. Ed. Arthur Hullett. adv.; circ. 250,000.

051 US
SKY MAGAZINE. 1972. m. free. (Delta Airlines) Halsey Publishing Co., 600 Corporate Dr., Ft. Lauderdale, FL 33334. TEL 305-776-0066. FAX 305-493-8969. Ed. Lidia DeLeon. adv.; circ. 500,000.
  Description: Provides articles that entertain and inform on such subjects as business, sports, the arts, personalities, foreign and domestic travel and human interest topics.

052 JM
SKYWRITINGS. 1973. q. (Air Jamaica) Creative Communications, Inc., Ltd., Box 105, Kingston 10, Jamaica, W.I. TEL 809-92-74271. FAX 809-92-62217. Ed. Angela deFreitas. adv.; circ. 30,000.

051 US
SOUTHWEST SPIRIT. 1972. m. (SouthWest Airlines) Publishing Images, 34 E. 51st St., New York, NY 10022. Ed. Gabrielle Cosgriff. adv.; bk.rev.; circ. 140,000.
  Formerly: Southwest Airlines Spirit.
  Description: Inflight magazine.

051 US
SPIRIT OF ALOHA. 1976. m. (Aloha Airlines) Honolulu Publishing Company, Ltd., 36 Merchant St., Honolulu, HI 96813. TEL 808-524-7400. FAX 808-531-2306. Ed. Pat Pitzer. adv.; circ. 65,000.
  Description: Inflight magazine of Aloha Airlines and Aloha Island Air.

052 CY ISSN 1011-1727
SUNJET; Cyprus Airways in-flight magazine. (Text in English) 1973. q. $30. Action Publications Ltd., P.O. Box 4676, Nicosia, Cyprus. TEL 444104. FAX 450048. Ed. Tony Christodoulou. adv.; bk.rev.; circ. 75,000.

052 059.927 UK
SUNRISE. (Text in Arabic and English) 1980. m. (Kuwait Airways) Bryan Richardson & Associates, Parkway House, Sheen Lane, London SW14 8LS, England. adv.; circ. 20,000.

052 053 054 SZ
SWISSAIR GAZETTE. (Text in English, French and German) m. Swissair A.G., Rudigerstrasse 10, CH-8045 Zurich, Switzerland. TEL 1455-83324. FAX 1281-2018. Ed. Viviane Egli. adv.; circ. 470,000.
  Description: Airline publication devoted to news and features about Switzerland and other parts of the world. Also includes Swiss culture, travel, education, products, and hotel guide.

UROLOGY AND NEPHROLOGY

051 US ISSN 0039-8632
T W A AMBASSADOR. 1968. m. free. (Trans World Airlines) Halsey Publishing Co., 12955 Biscayne Blvd., Ste. 202, N. Miami, FL 33181. TEL 305-893-1520. adv.; bk.rev.; illus.; tr.lit.; circ. 305,246.
Description: In-flight magazine for passengers on TWA, with articles on a variety of topics of interest to travelers.

051 US
U S AIR MAGAZINE. 1973. m. $50. Pace Communications Inc., 1301 Carolina St., Greensboro, NC 27401. TEL 919-378-6065. FAX 919-275-2864. Ed. Terri Barnes. adv.; bk.rev.; tr.lit.; circ. 425,000.
Formerly (until 1979): Pace.
Description: In-flight magazine.

052 054 FR
U T A FRENCH AIRLINES: DISTANCE. (Text in English, French) 1973. 6/yr. 120 F. (foreign 160 F.). Union de Transports Aeriens, 3 bd. Malesherbes, 75008 Paris, France. FAX 47-76-52-13. TELEX 610692 F. Ed. Claude Schmit. adv.; bk.rev.; circ. 110,000.

051 US
VIS A VIS. 1957. m. $36. (United Airlines) Pace Communications Inc., 1301 Carolina St., Greensboro, NC 27401. TEL 919-378-6065. FAX 919-275-2864. adv.; bk.rev.; illus.; circ. 400,000.
Former titles: United; United Mainliner; Mainliner (ISSN 0025-083X)
Description: Inflight magazine.

052 059.956 JA
WINDS. (Text in English, Japanese) 1979. m. 6000 Yen($31) (Japan Air Lines Co. Ltd.) Emphasis, Inc., Central Roppongi Bldg., 1-4-27 Roppongi, Minato-ku, Tokyo 106, Japan. FAX 03-3585-1596. Ed. Tom Chapman. adv.; circ. 490,000.
Description: Inflight magazine of Japan Air Lines.

052 MY ISSN 0126-5393
WINGS OF GOLD. 1975. m. M.$5 per no. (free on MAS flights). Malaysia Airlines, Public Relations Department, 32nd Fl., MAS Bldg., Jalan Sultan Ismail, 50250 Kuala Lumpur, Malaysia. TEL 03-2610555. FAX 6-03-2624010. TELEX LAYANG-MA-37614. Ed. Khalilah Talha. adv.; bk.rev.; circ. 600,000.
Description: In-flight magazine. Contains general interest articles, particularly on Malaysia and on travel in general.

UROLOGY AND NEPHROLOGY

see Medical Sciences-Urology and Nephrology

VETERINARY SCIENCE

636.089 AT ISSN 1034-9219
A A H L BIENNIAL REPORT. biennial. Australian Animal Health Laboratory, P.O. Bag 24, Geelong, Vic. 3220, Australia. TEL 052-265222. Ed. Niall Byrne.

636.089 AT
A A H L NEWSLETTER. irreg. Australian Animal Health Laboratory, P.O. Bag 24, Geelong, Vic. 3220, Australia. TEL 052-265222. FAX 052-23-1424. Ed. Niall Byrne.

636.089 US
A V E A NEWSLETTER. 1936. q. membership. American Veterinary Exhibitors Association, Box 6842, Santa Barbara, CA 93160. TEL 805-683-0489. Ed. Fred Hamlin. circ. 200. (tabloid format)
Description: Concerns exhibiting at veterinary conventions.

636.089 FR ISSN 0001-4192
CODEN: BAVFAV
ACADEMIE VETERINAIRE DE FRANCE. BULLETIN. 1844. 4/yr. 600 F. (effective Jan. 1992). Academie Veterinaire de France, 60, blvd. Latour-Maubourg, 75007 Paris, France. FAX 20-87-79-06. TELEX 820 187 F. Ed. Catsaras. adv.; bk.rev.; abstr.; bibl.; charts; illus.; stat.; index; circ. 800. **Indexed:** Anim.Breed.Abstr., Biol.Abstr., Biotech.Abstr., Chem.Abstr., Curr.Adv.Ecol.Sci., Curr.Cont., Dairy Sci.Abstr., Food Sci.& Tech.Abstr., Helminthol.Abstr., Ind.Vet., Nutr.Abstr., Poult.Abstr., Rev.Plant Path., Vet.Bull.
—BLDSC shelfmark: 2378.000000.

636.089 PL ISSN 0860-2840
CODEN: AAAVEZ
ACTA ACADEMIAE AGRICULTURAE AC TECHNICAE OLSTENENSIS. VETERINARIA - VETERINARY MEDICINE. (Text in Polish; summaries in English and Russian) 1972. irreg. price varies. (Akademia Rolniczo-Techniczna im. M. Oczapowskiego 12) Wydawnictwo A R T Olsztyn, Blok 21, 10-957 Olsztyn-Kortowo, Poland. TEL 48-89-273310. TELEX 0526419. (Dist. by: Ars Polona-Ruch, Krakowskie Przedmiescie 7, 00-901 Warsaw, Poland. TEL 48-22-265334) illus.; charts; bibl.; circ. 210 (controlled). **Indexed:** Chem.Abstr., Curr.Cont., Dairy Sci.Abstr., Ind.Vet., Pig News & Info., Ref.Zh., Vet.Bull.
Formerly: Akademia Rolniczo-Techniczna. Zeszyty Naukowe. Weterynaria (ISSN 0324-9220).

636.089 IT ISSN 0001-6136
CODEN: AMVEAX
ACTA MEDICA VETERINARIA. (Text in Italian; summaries in English, French, German and Spanish) 1955. bi-m. $10. Facolta di Medicina Veterinaria, Via Veterinaria 1, 80137 Naples, Italy. bk.rev.; charts; illus.; tr.lit.; index. **Indexed:** Anim.Breed.Abstr., Biol.Abstr., Chem.Abstr., Dairy Sci.Abstr., Excerp.Med., Food Sci.& Tech.Abstr., Herb.Abstr., Ind.Med., Ind.Vet., Nutr.Abstr., Pig News & Info., Protozool.Abstr., Rev.Med.& Vet.Mycol., Small Anim.Abstr., Vet.Bull.
—BLDSC shelfmark: 0635.500000.

636.089 CS ISSN 0001-7213
CODEN: ACVTB9
ACTA VETERINARIA. (Text in English; summaries in Czech, English, Russian) 1922. q. 70 Kcs.($10) (Vysoka Skola Veterinarni, Brno) Statni Pedagogicke Nakladatelstvi, Ostrovni 30, 113 01 Prague 1, Czechoslovakia. (Subscr. to: c/o Eva Baranyiova, Vysoka Skola Vaterinarni, Palackiho 1-3, 612 42 Brno, Czechoslovakia) Ed. A. Holub. bk.rev.; bibl.; charts; illus.; index. cum.index; circ. 700. **Indexed:** Anim.Breed.Abstr., Biol.Abstr., Chem.Abstr., Curr.Adv.Ecol.Sci., Curr.Cont., Dairy Sci.Abstr., Excerp.Med., Food Sci.& Tech.Abstr., Helminthol.Abstr., Ind.Vet., Nutr.Abstr., Pig News & Info., Poult.Abstr., Protozool.Abstr., Sci.Cit.Ind, Vet.Bull.
—BLDSC shelfmark: 0670.890000.
Formerly: Acta Universitatis Agriculturae. Facultas Veterinaria: Rada B.

636.089 HU ISSN 0236-6290
CODEN: AVHUEA
ACTA VETERINARIA HUNGARICA. (Text in English, French, German, Russian) 1951. q. $62. (Magyar Tudomanyos Akademia) Akademiai Kiado, Publishing House of the Hungarian Academy of Sciences, P.O. Box 24, H-1363 Budapest, Hungary. Eds. J. Meszaros, A. Szekely. adv.; bk.rev.; bibl.; charts; illus.; index. **Indexed:** Anim.Breed.Abstr., ASCA, Biol.Abstr., Biotech.Abstr., Chem.Abstr., Curr.Adv.Ecol.Sci., Curr.Cont., Dairy Sci.Abstr., Excerp.Med., Helminthol.Abstr., Ind.Med., Ind.Vet., INIS Atomind., Nutr.Abstr., Pig News & Info., Poult.Abstr., Protozool.Abstr., Rev.Plant Path, Sci.Cit.Ind, Soils & Fert., Vet.Bull.
—BLDSC shelfmark: 0670.980000.
Formerly: Academia Scientiarum Hungarica. Acta Veterinaria (ISSN 0001-7205).

636.089 DK ISSN 0044-605X
CODEN: AVSCA7
ACTA VETERINARIA SCANDINAVICA.* (Text in English; summaries in Danish and English) q. DKK 410 (incl. supplements). (Societatum Veteranariarum Scandanivacarum) Danske Dyrlaegeforening, Rosenlunds Alle 8, DK 2720 Vanloese, Denmark. TEL 31-71-08-88. FAX 31-71-03-22. Ed. Dr. H.C. Adler. bibl.; charts; illus. **Indexed:** Anim.Breed.Abstr., Biol.Abstr., Biotech.Abstr., Chem.Abstr., Curr.Adv.Ecol.Sci., Curr.Cont., Dairy Sci.Abstr., Excerp.Med., Food Sci.& Tech.Abstr., Helminthol.Abstr., Ind.Med., Ind.Sci.Rev., Ind.Vet., INIS Atomind., Nutr.Abstr., Pig News & Info., Poult.Abstr., Protozool.Abstr., Rev.Plant Path., Sci.Cit.Ind, Small Anim.Abstr., Soils & Fert., Triticale Abstr., Vet.Bull.
—BLDSC shelfmark: 0671.300000.

636.089 DK ISSN 0065-1699
SF604 CODEN: AVSPAC
ACTA VETERINARIA SCANDINAVICA. SUPPLEMENTUM. (Text in English, French or German; summaries in English and German) 1961. irreg. DKK 800 (incl. main vols.). (Societatum Veteranariarum Scandanivacarum) Danske Dyrlaegeforening, Rosenlunds Alle 8, DK-2720 Vanloese, Denmark. TEL 31-71-08-88. FAX 31-71-03-22. **Indexed:** Biol.Abstr., Dairy Sci.Abstr., Food Sci.& Tech.Abstr., Ind.Med., INIS Atomind., Nutr.Abstr.

ACTA ZOOLOGICA ET PATHOLOGICA ANTVERPIENSIA. see BIOLOGY — Zoology

636.089 FR ISSN 0001-7523
ACTION VETERINAIRE.* 1946. w. 430 F. Societe S P I, 35 rue de Chaillot, 75116 Paris, France. Ed. Didier Lefay. **Indexed:** Ind.Vet., Vet.Bull.

636.089 MX
ACTUALIDAD VETERINARIA. 1976. 6/yr. Via Gustavo Baz No. 118, Bosques de Echegaray, Naucalpan, Edo. de Mexico, Mexico. Ed. Alfonso Ortega Said. circ. 5,000.

ADELAIDE. INSTITUTE OF MEDICAL AND VETERINARY SCIENCE. ANNUAL REPORT OF THE COUNCIL. see MEDICAL SCIENCES

ADVANCES IN ANIMAL WELFARE SCIENCE. see ANIMAL WELFARE

636.089 US ISSN 1041-7826
ADVANCES IN SMALL ANIMAL MEDICINE AND SURGERY; a monthly review of current developments in veterinary medicine. 1988. m. $42 (foreign $56). John Colet Press, Inc., 31 St. James Ave., Boston, MA 02116-4101. TEL 617-426-2303. FAX 617-426-9767. Ed. Rhea V. Morgan.
Refereed Serial

636.089 GW ISSN 0301-2794
CODEN: AVYMAX
ADVANCES IN VETERINARY MEDICINE/FORTSCHRITTE DER VETERINAERMEDIZIN. (Supplement to: Advances in Veterinary Medicine, Series A, Anatomia; Serie B, Histologie; and Series C, Embryologia) 1958. irreg. price varies. Verlag Paul Parey (Berlin), Seelbuschring 9-17, 1000 Berlin 42, Germany. TEL 030-70784-0. FAX 030-70784199. (U.S. address: Paul Parey Scientific Publishers, 150 E. 27th St., No.1A, New York, NY 10016) bibl.; illus.; index. **Indexed:** Biol.Abstr., Chem.Abstr, Excerp.Med., Food Sci.& Tech.Abstr., Ind.Sci.Rev., Ind.Vet., Sci.Cit.Ind, Small Anim.Abstr., Vet.Bull.
—BLDSC shelfmark: 0711.770000.

636.089 US ISSN 0065-3519
SF745 CODEN: AVSCB8
ADVANCES IN VETERINARY SCIENCE AND COMPARATIVE MEDICINE. 1953. irreg., vol.35, 1990. Academic Press, Inc., 1250 Sixth Ave., San Diego, CA 92101. TEL 619-231-0926. FAX 619-699-6715. Eds. Charles E. Cornelius, Charles F. Simpson. index. (reprint service avail. from ISI) **Indexed:** Anim.Breed.Abstr., Biol.Abstr., Biotech.Abstr., Dairy Sci.Abstr., Dent.Ind., Excerp.Med., Helminthol.Abstr., Ind.Med., Ind.Sci.Rev., Ind.Vet., Nutr.Abstr., Pig News & Info., Protozool.Abstr., Sci.Cit.Ind, Vet.Bull.
—BLDSC shelfmark: 0711.820000.
Refereed Serial

AGBIOTECHNOLOGY NEWS; agricultural research - business. see BIOLOGY — Biotechnology

VETERINARY SCIENCE

636.089   US   ISSN 0745-452X
AGRI-PRACTICE; the journal of medicine and surgery for the food animal practitioner. 1980. 10/yr. $36 (effective 1992). Veterinary Practice Publishing Co., 7 Ashley Ave. S., Santa Barbara, CA 93103-9989. TEL 805-965-1028. FAX 805-965-0722. (Subscr. addr.: Box 4457, Santa Barbara, CA 93140-4457) Ed.Bd. adv.; bk.rev.; abstr.; charts; illus.; stat.; tr.lit.; index; circ. 5,500. (also avail. in microform from UMI; reprint service avail. from UMI) **Indexed:** Anim.Breed.Abstr., Curr.Adv.Ecol.Sci., Dairy Sci.Abstr., Ind.Vet., Pig News & Info., Rev.Med.& Vet.Mycol., Vet.Bull.
—BLDSC shelfmark: 0764.155000.
Formerly (until 1982): Bovine Practice (ISSN 0199-5456)
Description: Professional journal devoted to food animals including cattle and swine, with topics important to the food animal practitioner.
Refereed Serial

590 636.089   IT
ALLEVATORE. 1945. w. L.5000. Associazione Italiana Allevatori, Via Tomassetti 9, 00161 Rome, Italy. Ed. Carlo Venino. adv.; circ. 40,000.

636.089   US   ISSN 0164-1999
CODEN: SPAHDN
AMERICAN ANIMAL HOSPITAL ASSOCIATION. ANNUAL MEETING SCIENTIFIC PROCEEDINGS. a. $42 to non-members. American Animal Hospital Association, Box 150899, Denver, CO 80215-0899. TEL 303-279-2500. FAX 303-279-1816.

636.089   US   ISSN 0587-2871
SF601   CODEN: JAAHBL
AMERICAN ANIMAL HOSPITAL ASSOCIATION JOURNAL. 1965. bi-m. $97 (foreign $110). American Animal Hospital Association, Box 150899, Denver, CO 80215-0899. TEL 303-279-2500. FAX 303-729-1816. Ed. Dr. Jill Ellen Frucci. adv.; bk.rev.; abstr.; charts; illus.; tr.lit.; circ. 12,500. (also avail. in microform from UMI; reprint service avail. from UMI) **Indexed:** Anim.Breed.Abstr., Biol.Abstr., Biol.& Agr.Ind., Chem.Abstr, Curr.Cont., Excerp.Med., Helminthol.Abstr., Ind.Sci.Rev., Ind.Vet., Protozool.Abstr., Rev.Plant Path., Small Anim.Abstr., Vet.Bull. Key Title: Journal of the American Animal Hospital Association.
—BLDSC shelfmark: 4683.790000.
Formerly: American Animal Hospital Association Bulletin (ISSN 0002-7251)
Description: Clinical manuscripts relating to animal care.
Refereed Serial

636.089   US   ISSN 0065-7182
AMERICAN ASSOCIATION OF EQUINE PRACTITIONERS. PROCEEDINGS OF THE ANNUAL CONVENTION.* 2nd convention, 1956. a. $25. American Association of Equine Practitioners, 4075 Iron Works Rd., Lexington, KY 40511-8434. Ed. Mary Royer. circ. 5,000. (also avail. in microfilm from UMI; back issues avail.) **Indexed:** Helminthol.Abstr., Ind.Vet., Vet.Bull.

636.087 636.8
AMERICAN ASSOCIATION OF FELINE PRACTITIONERS. JOURNAL. 1983? s-a. American Association of Feline Practitioners, 10707 N. 51st Ave., Glendale, AZ 85304. Ed. Dr. R.L. Kritsberg. adv.
Description: Covers feline medicine, research and surgery. Contains news of the association and meeting announcements.

636.089   US
AMERICAN FUND FOR ALTERNATIVES TO ANIMAL RESEARCH. NEWS ABSTRACTS. 1977. 3/yr. $10. American Fund for Alternatives to Animal Research, 175 W. 12th St., Ste. 16G, New York, NY 10011. Ed. Ethel Thurston. adv.; bk.rev.; circ. 7,000. (back issues avail.)
Description: Provides finance for scientific programs to develop or teach alternatives to animals in research, testing, validation and education.

636.089   US
AMERICAN HEARTWORM SOCIETY. BULLETIN.* 1974. q. $30. American Heartworm Society, 161 S. Lincolnway, Ste. 302, N. Aurora, IL 60542. TEL 708-844-9676. Ed. Dr. Mark D. Soll. adv.; circ. 1,200.
Description: Keeping up on current research and commercial development on the prevention and treatment of heartworm disease in dogs.

636.089   US
AMERICAN HEARTWORM SOCIETY. SYMPOSIUM PROCEEDINGS.* 1977. triennial. price varies. American Heartworm Society, 161 S. Lincolnway, Ste. 302, N. Aurora, IL 60542. TEL 708-844-9676.

636.087   US
AMERICAN HOLISTIC VETERINARY MEDICAL ASSOCIATION. JOURNAL. 1982. q. $40 includes membership. American Holistic Veterinary Medical Association, 2214 Old Emmorton Rd., Bel Air, MD 21015. FAX 410-515-7774. adv.
Formerly (until Sep. 1989): American Holistic Veterinary Medical Association. Newsletter.
Description: Promotes natural healing, preventive health care, nutrition and avoidance of drugs and medication.

636.089   US   ISSN 0002-9645
SF601   CODEN: AJVRAH
AMERICAN JOURNAL OF VETERINARY RESEARCH.* 1940. m. $105 (foreign $125). American Veterinary Medical Association, 1931 N. Meacham Rd., Ste. 100, Schaumburg, IL 60173-4360. TEL 708-605-8070. FAX 708-330-2862. Ed. Dr. Albert Koltveit. adv.; bk.rev.; charts; illus.; stat.; index; circ. 7,900. (also avail. in microform from UMI,PMC) **Indexed:** Anim.Breed.Abstr., Biol.Abstr., Biol.& Agr.Ind, Biotech.Abstr., Chem.Abstr., Curr.Adv.Cancer Res., Curr.Adv.Ecol.Sci., Curr.Cont., Dairy Sci.Abstr., Dent.Ind., Excerp.Med., Food Sci.& Tech.Abstr., Helminthol.Abstr., Herb.Abstr., Ind.Med., Ind.Sci.Rev., Ind.Vet., INIS Atomind., Maize Abstr., Nutr.Abstr., Pig News & Info., Poult.Abstr., Protozool.Abstr., Rev.Appl.Entomol., Rev.Med.& Vet.Mycol., Sci.Cit.Ind, Small Anim.Abstr., Vet.Bull., Weed Abstr.
—BLDSC shelfmark: 0840.000000.
Refereed Serial

636   US   ISSN 0569-7832
CODEN: PMWSA7
AMERICAN SOCIETY OF ANIMAL SCIENCE. WESTERN SECTION PROCEEDINGS. 1949. a. $18. American Society of Animal Science, Western Section, 309 W. Clark St., Champaign, IL 61820. TEL 217-356-3182. FAX 217-398-4119. circ. 600. **Indexed:** Food Sci.& Tech.Abstr.

636.089   US   ISSN 0066-1147
SF611
AMERICAN VETERINARY MEDICAL ASSOCIATION. DIRECTORY.* 1920. a. $60. American Veterinary Medical Association, 1931 N. Meacham Rd., Ste. 100, Schaumburg, IL 60173-4360. TEL 708-605-8070. FAX 708-330-2862. Ed. Mrs. J. La Frana. adv.; circ. 50,000. **Indexed:** Curr.Adv.Ecol.Sci.

636.089   US   ISSN 0003-1488
SF601   CODEN: JAVMA4
AMERICAN VETERINARY MEDICAL ASSOCIATION. JOURNAL.* 1877. s-m. $70 (foreign $90). American Veterinary Medical Association, 1931 N. Meacham Rd., Ste. 100, Schaumburg, IL 60173-4360. TEL 708-605-8070. FAX 708-330-2862. Ed. Dr. Albert Koltveit. adv.; bk.rev.; charts; illus.; s-a. index; circ. 52,000. (also avail. in microform from UMI; microfiche from BHP) **Indexed:** Anim.Breed.Abstr., Biol.Abstr., Biol.& Agr.Ind., Biotech.Abstr., Chem.Abstr., Curr.Adv.Cancer Res., Curr.Cont., Dairy Sci.Abstr., Dent.Ind., Excerp.Med., Food Sci.& Tech.Abstr., Helminthol.Abstr., Herb.Abstr., Ind.Med., Ind.Vet., INIS Atomind., Nutr.Abstr., Pig News & Info., Poult.Abstr., Protozool.Abstr., Rev.Appl.Entomol., Rev.Plant Path., Small Anim.Abstr., Soils & Fert., Vet.Bull., World Agri.Econ.& Rural Sociol.Abstr.
—BLDSC shelfmark: 4695.000000.
Refereed Serial

636.089   AG
ANALECTA VETERINARIA. (Text in Spanish; summaries in English, French or German) 1969. 3/yr. $21. Universidad Nacional de la Plata, Facultad de Ciencias Veterinarias, Calle 60 y 118, 1900 La Plata, Argentina. circ. 800. (back issues avail.) **Indexed:** Biol.Abstr., Chem.Abstr., Food Sci.& Tech.Abstr., Ind.Vet., Vet.Bull.

636.089   SP   ISSN 0213-5434
CODEN: AVMAE9
ANALES DE VETERINARIA DE MURCIA. (Text in Spanish and English) 1985. a. 1500 ptas. Universidad de Murcia, Secretariado de Publicaciones e Intercambio Cientifico, Santo Cristo, 1, 30001 Murcia, Spain. TEL 3468-239450. Ed. Jose Serrano Merino. bk.rev.; abstr.; circ. 300.
Description: Contains original researches and advances in all fields of veterinary science.

636.089   GW   ISSN 0340-2096
CODEN: AHEMA5
ANATOMIA, HISTOLOGIA, EMBRYOLOGIA. SERIES C. (Supplement: Advances in Veterinary Medicine) (Text in English and German) 1972. q. DM.588($338) (World Association of Veterinary Anatomists) Verlag Paul Parey (Berlin), Seelbuschring 9-17, 1000 Berlin 42, Germany. TEL 030-70784-0. FAX 030-70784199. (U.S. address: Paul Parey Scientific Publishers, 150 E. 27th St., No.1A, New York, NY 10016) Eds. J. Breazile, B. Vollmerhaus. bk.rev.; illus.; stat. (back issues avail.) **Indexed:** Biol.Abstr., Biol.& Agr.Ind., Curr.Adv.Ecol.Sci., Curr.Cont., Dairy Sci.Abstr., Dent.Ind., Excerp.Med., Helminthol.Abstr., Ind.Med., Ind.Vet., Nutr.Abstr., Sci.Cit.Ind., Vet.Bull.
—BLDSC shelfmark: 0897.960000.

ANIMAL BEHAVIOUR. see *BIOLOGY — Zoology*

636.089   UK   ISSN 0144-3879
ANIMAL DISEASE OCCURRENCE. Short title: A.D.O. (Former name of issuing body: Commonwealth Agricultural Bureaux) 1980-1989; resumed 1991. s-a. £35($52) C.A.B. International, Wallingford, Oxon OX10 8DE, England. TEL 800-528-4841, 0491 32111. FAX 0491-33508. TELEX 847964 COMAGG G. (U.S. subscr. to: C.A.B. International, North American Office, 845 N. Park Ave., Tucson, AZ 85719) Ed. G.D. Phillips. circ. 1,000. (also avail. in microfiche) **Indexed:** Vet.Bull.
●Also available online. Vendor(s): BRS (VETR), CISTI, DIMDI, DIALOG, European Space Agency (File nos.16 & 124/CAB).
Description: Covers the world literature on bacterial, viral, fungal and protozoal diseases, as well as nutritional and metabolic disorders.

636.089   US
ANIMAL FEEDING AND NUTRITION. 1977. irreg., vol.11, 1990. Academic Press, Inc., 1250 Sixth Ave., San Diego, CA 92101. TEL 619-231-6616. FAX 619-699-6715. Ed. Tony J. Cunha. (back issues avail.)
Refereed Serial

636.089   UG
ANIMAL HEALTH RESEARCH CENTRE. ANNUAL REPORT. (Text in English) a. Animal Health Research Centre, Box 24, Entebbe, Uganda. **Indexed:** Rev.Appl.Entomol.

636.089   UK   ISSN 0142-6591
ANIMAL HEALTH TRUST. ANNUAL REPORT. 1963. a. £4.50. Animal Health Trust, P.O. Box 5, Newmarket, Suffolk CB8 7DW, England. FAX 0638-665789. TELEX 818418 (ANHLTH G). (And: 122 E. 55th St., New York, N.Y. 10022) Ed.Bd. adv.; bk.rev.; charts; illus.; index; circ. 3,500. **Indexed:** Biol.Abstr.
—BLDSC shelfmark: 1107.011000.
Formerly: Animal Health (ISSN 0003-3502)

636.089   UN   ISSN 0066-1872
ANIMAL HEALTH YEARBOOK. (Text in English, French and Spanish) 1957. a. $55. Food and Agriculture Organization of the United Nations, c/o UNIPUB, 4611-F Assembly Dr., Lanham, MD 20706-4391. FAX 301-459-0056. **Indexed:** Dairy Sci.Abstr., Helminthol.Abstr., Nutr.Abstr.
—BLDSC shelfmark: 0904.010000.

ANIMAL HUSBANDRY AND BREEDING. see *AGRICULTURE — Poultry And Livestock*

ANIMAL MODELS OF PSYCHIATRIC DISORDERS. see *MEDICAL SCIENCES — Psychiatry And Neurology*

VETERINARY SCIENCE

636.089   UK   ISSN 0262-2238
ANIMAL PHARM; world animal health and nutrition news. 1982. s-m. £270($530) P J B Publications Ltd., 18-20 Hill Rise, Richmond, Surrey TW10 6UA, England. TEL 081-948-3262. FAX 081-948-6866. TELEX 8951042. Ed. J. Marchant. adv.; bk.rev.; circ. 1,400. **Indexed:** ABC, PROMT.
●Also available online. Vendor(s): BRS, Data-Star, DIALOG.
—BLDSC shelfmark: 0905.030000.
Description: Includes regulations, companies, livestock and market trends, product news (introductions, R&D) and environmental issues.

636.089   UK   ISSN 0264-4754
ANIMAL TECHNOLOGY. 1950. 3/yr. £25. Institute of Animal Technology of Great Britain, c/o Geoffrey E. Ward, Ed., Department of Biochemistry, University College, Box 78, Cathays Park, Cardiff, Wales. (Subscr. addr.: c/o John A. Gregory, Zoology Department, Royal Postgraduate Medical School, Ducane Rd., London W12 0HS, England) adv.; bk.rev.; charts; illus.; circ. 1,500. **Indexed:** Anim.Breed.Abstr., Bio-Contr.News & Info., Biol.Abstr., Ind.Vet., Nutr.Abstr., Protozool.Abstr., Rev.Med.& Vet.Mycol., Vet.Bull.
—BLDSC shelfmark: 0905.125000.
Formerly: Institute of Animal Technicians. Journal (ISSN 0020-2711)

636.089   TU   ISSN 0003-3685
CODEN: VTFDAQ
ANKARA UNIVERSITESI. VETERINER FAKULTESI. DERGISI. (Text in Turkish; summaries in English, French or German) 1954. q. $10. University of Ankara, Faculty of Veterinary Medicine, Ankara, Turkey. Ed.Bd. bk.rev.; bibl.; charts; illus.; circ. 750. **Indexed:** Anim.Breed.Abstr., Bio-Contr.News & Info., Biol.Abstr., Chem.Abstr., Dairy Sci.Abstr., Helminthol.Abstr., Ind.Vet., INIS Atomind., Nutr.Abstr., Poult.Abstr., Protozool.Abstr., Small Anim.Abstr., Soyabean Abstr., Triticale Abstr., Vet.Bull.

636.089   BE   ISSN 0003-4118
CODEN: AMVRA4
ANNALES DE MEDECINE VETERINAIRE. 1849. 8/yr. 1200 Fr. Imprimerie Bietlot, 20 Bd. de Colonster, B42, B-4000 Sart Tilman, Liege, Belgium. FAX 02-520-89-61. Ed. F. Lomba. adv.; bk.rev.; charts; illus.; index; circ. 1,500. **Indexed:** Agri.Eng.Abstr., Anim.Breed.Abstr., Biol.Abstr., Biotech.Abstr., Chem.Abstr., Curr.Adv.Ecol.Sci., Curr.Adv.Genetics & Molec.Biol., Curr.Cont., Dairy Sci.Abstr., Helminthol.Abstr., Ind.Med., Ind.Sci.Rev., Ind.Vet., Pig News & Info., Poult.Abstr., Protozool.Abstr., Rev.Plant Path., Sci.Cit.Ind, Small Anim.Abstr., Vet.Bull.
—BLDSC shelfmark: 0982.000000.

636.089   FR   ISSN 0003-4193
CODEN: ARCVBP
ANNALES DE RECHERCHES VETERINAIRES/ANNALS OF VETERINARY RESEARCH. (Text mainly in French; summaries in English, French) 1972. 4/yr. 700 F. (foreign 820 F.)(effective 1992). Institut National de la Recherche Agronomique, 29 rue Buffon, 75005 Paris, France. TEL 47-07-11-22. FAX 43-36-80-93. TELEX 202400F. Ed.Bd. adv.; circ. 2,000. (also avail. in microform; reprint service avail. from ISI) **Indexed:** Anim.Breed.Abstr., Bibl.Agri., Biol.Abstr., Biotech.Abstr., Chem.Abstr., Curr.Adv.Ecol.Sci., Curr.Cont., Dairy Sci.Abstr., Dent.Ind., Excerp.Med., Field Crop Abstr, Helminthol.Abstr., Herb.Abstr., Ind.Med., Ind.Sci.Rev., Ind.Vet., Nutr.Abstr., Pig News & Info., Poult.Abstr., Protozool.Abstr., Rev.Plant Path, Sci.Cit.Ind, Vet.Bull.
—BLDSC shelfmark: 0995.350000.
Formerly: Recherches Veterinaires.
Description: Covers all scientific aspects of veterinary and comparitive medicine and related subjects. The principal areas of interest are: immunology, virology, parasitology, physiology, biochemistry and nutrition.

639.089   PL   ISSN 0301-7737
CODEN: ACDDA6
ANNALES UNIVERSITATIS MARIAE CURIE-SKLODOWSKA. SECTIO DD. MEDICINA VETERINARIA. (Text in Polish or English; summaries in English) 1949. a. price varies. Uniwersytet Marii Curie-Sklodowskiej, Wydawnictwo, Pl. M. Curie-Sklodowskiej 5, 20-031 Lublin, Poland. Ed. Zdzislaw Glinski. circ. 500. **Indexed:** Anim.Breed.Abstr., Biol.Abstr., Chem.Abstr., Ind.Vet., Landwirt.Zentralbl., Rev.Med.& Vet.Mycol., Vet.Bull.
—BLDSC shelfmark: 0959.000000.

636.089   PL   ISSN 0239-4243
SF84   CODEN: AUEZE3
ANNALES UNIVERSITATIS MARIAE CURIE-SKLODOWSKA. SECTIO EE. ZOOTECHNIKA. (Text in English or Polish; summaries in English) 1983. a. price varies. Uniwersytet Marii Curie-Sklodowskiej, Wydawnictwo, Pl. M. Curie-Sklodowskieg 5, 20-031 Lublin, Poland. TEL 48-81-375304. FAX 48-81-336699. TELEX 0643223. Ed. Marian Budzynski. circ. 650.
—BLDSC shelfmark: 0961.010000.

636.089   US   ISSN 0887-7386
CODEN: AHPDE3
APIS; the international journal bulletin for specialty livestock and pet-animal product development. 1989. 4/yr. $165. C I T A International (USA), Industrial Journals Division, Box 70, Phoenix, AZ 85001. TEL 602-234-2642. FAX 602-878-9616. Ed. E.M. Morsy. adv.; bibl.; charts; illus.; index; circ. 2,000. (back issues avail.)
Description: Covers research and development, manufacture, chemistry formulation and raw materials for veterinary products, animal health and allied industries.

636.089   UA   ISSN 0003-746X
ARAB VETERINARY MEDICAL ASSOCIATION. JOURNAL. (Text in Arabic and English) vol.14, 1964. q. $10. Arab Veterinary Medical Association, 8 Sh 26 July, Cairo, Egypt. Ed. K.N. Soliman. bk.rev.; charts; illus.

ARANETA RESEARCH JOURNAL. see *AGRICULTURE*

636.089   GW   ISSN 0003-9055
CODEN: AXVMAW
ARCHIV FUER EXPERIMENTELLE VETERINAERMEDIZIN.* (Summaries in English and Russian) 1950. 6/yr. DM.204. (Akademie der Landwirtschaftswissenschaften) Terra-Druck, Krausenstr. 38-39, 1086 Berlin, Germany. Ed. J. Beer. adv.; bk.rev.; charts; illus.; index. cum.index. (reprint service avail. from ISI) **Indexed:** Anim.Breed.Abstr., Biodet.Abstr., Biol.Abstr., Biotech.Abstr., Chem.Abstr., Curr.Adv.Biochem., Curr.Adv.Ecol.Sci., Curr.Cont., Dairy Sci.Abstr., Excerp.Med., Food Sci.& Tech.Abstr., Helminthol.Abstr., Ind.Med., Ind.Vet., INIS Atomind., Nutr.Abstr., Pig News & Info., Poult.Abstr., Protozool.Abstr., Triticale Abstr., Vet.Bull., Weed Abstr.
Description: Covers biology and biotechnology of reproduction, anatomy, embryology, clinical veterinary medicine, biochemistry, endocrinology, immunology, infectology, reproduction disorders, breeding hygiene, virology, and toxicology.

636.089   GW   ISSN 0003-942X
CODEN: ARTIA2
ARCHIVES OF ANIMAL NUTRITION/ARCHIV FUER TIERERNAEHRUNG. (Text and summaries in English, German) 1951. m. DM.380.40. Akademie-Verlag Berlin, Leipziger Str. 3-4, 1086 Berlin, Germany. Ed. H. Bergner. bk.rev.; charts; illus.; index. **Indexed:** Anim.Breed.Abstr., Biodet.Abstr., Biol.Abstr., Biotech.Abstr., Chem.Abstr., Curr.Adv.Ecol.Sci., Curr.Cont., Excerp.Med., Food Sci.& Tech.Abstr., Helminthol.Abstr., Ind.Med., Ind.Vet., INIS Atomind.. Maize Abstr., Nutr.Abstr., Pig News & Info., Poult.Abstr., Protozool.Abstr., Rice Abstr., Sci.Cit.Ind, Soils & Fert., Soyabean Abstr., Triticale Abstr., Vet.Bull.
—BLDSC shelfmark: 1631.227000.

636.089   IT   ISSN 0004-0479
CODEN: AVEIAN
ARCHIVIO VETERINARIO ITALIANO. (Text in English, Italian; summaries in English, French, German) 1950. bi-m. L.50000 (foreign L.70000). (Universita degli Studi di Milano, Facolta di Veterinaria) Edizioni Citta Studi, P. Leonardo da Vinci 7, 20133 Milan, Italy. TEL 02-70634844. FAX 02-2367642. TELEX 326593 CLUP I. (Co-sponsor: Istituto di Ispezione degli Alimenti di Origine Animale, Facolta Medica Veterinaria) Dir. Carlo Cantoni. adv.; bk.rev.; abstr.; charts; illus.; index; circ. 1,000. (also avail. in microfilm from PMC) **Indexed:** Agri.Eng.Abstr., Anim.Breed.Abstr., Biol.Abstr., Biotech.Abstr., Curr.Adv.Ecol.Sci., Curr.Cont., Dairy Sci.Abstr., Food Sci.& Tech.Abstr., Helminthol.Abstr., Ind.Sci.Rev., Ind.Vet., Nutr.Abstr., Vet.Bull.
—BLDSC shelfmark: 1648.900000.

ARCHIVOS DE ZOOTECNIA. see *AGRICULTURE — Poultry And Livestock*

636.089   IT
ARGOS (MILAN). m. L.48000 (foreign L.71000). Giorgio Mondadori e Associati S.p.A., Via Cadore, 19, 20135 Milan, Italy. TEL 02-545641. FAX 5469150. Ed. Luca Sprea. circ. 68,870.

636.089   BL   ISSN 0102-0935
CODEN: ABMZDB
ARQUIVO BRASILEIRO DE MEDICINA VETERINARIA E ZOOTECNIA. (Text in Portuguese; summaries in English) 1943. bi-m. $100. Universidade Federal de Minas Gerais, Escola de Veterinaria, Av. Antonio Carlos, 6627, C.P. 567, 30.161 Belo Horizonte, Minas Gerais, Brazil. TEL 031-448-1536. FAX 031-441-9918. TELEX 0312308 UFMG. Ed. Hamilton Carmelio Machado da Silva. circ. 1,500. (also avail. in microform; reprint service avail. from ISI) **Indexed:** Agrindex, Anim.Breed.Abstr., Bibl.Agri., Biodet.Abstr., Biol.Abstr., Chem.Abstr., Dairy Sci.Abstr., Food Sci.& Tech.Abstr., Helminthol.Abstr., Herb.Abstr., Ind.Med., Ind.Vet., Nutr.Abstr., Poult.Abstr., Poult.Abstr., Protozool.Abstr., Ref.Zh, Soyabean Abstr., Vet.Bull.
—BLDSC shelfmark: 1695.100000.
Formerly (until vol.35, 1983): Universidade Federal de Minas Gerais. Escola de Veterinaria. Arquivos (ISSN 0076-8863)
Description: Contains articles on veterinary medicine, animal science, technology and inspection of products of animal origin.

636.089   BL   ISSN 0102-6380
ARS VETERINARIA. (Text in Portuguese; summaries in English) 1985. s-a. $30 exchange basis. (Faculdade de Ciencias Agrarias e Veterinarias, Departamento de Patologia Veterinaria) Editora U N E S P, Rodovia Carlos Tonanni, km 5, 14870 Jaboticabal S.P., Brazil. TEL 0163-224000. TELEX 111-9016 UJMF. Ed. Bd. charts; illus.; stat. **Indexed:** Anim.Breed.Abstr., Biodet.Abstr., Biol.Abstr., Dairy Sci.Abstr., Ind.Vet., Vet.Bull.
—BLDSC shelfmark: 1697.885000.

636.089   UA   ISSN 1012-5973
ASSIUT VETERINARY MEDICAL JOURNAL. (Text and summaries in Arabic and English) 1974. 4/yr. ££10($20) Assiut University, Faculty of Veterinary Medicine, Assiut, Egypt. TELEX 92863 UN. Ed. Ahmed A. Aamer. charts; illus.; stat.; circ. 30. **Indexed:** Agri.Eng.Abstr., Anim.Breed.Abstr., Biodet.Abstr., Dairy Sci.Abstr., Helminthol.Abstr., Ind.Vet., Nutr.Abstr., Poult.Abstr., Protozool.Abstr., Rev.Med.& Vet.Mycol., Rice Abstr., Small Anim.Abstr., Vet.Bull.
—BLDSC shelfmark: 1746.672100.

636.087   US   ISSN 0892-9904
CODEN: AAVTEW
ASSOCIATION OF AVIAN VETERINARIANS. JOURNAL. (Text in English; summaries in French, German, Spanish) 1980. q. $20. Association of Avian Veterinarians, 5770 Lake Worth Rd., Lake Worth, FL 33463-3299. Ed. Linda R. Harrison. bk.rev.; abstr.; illus. **Indexed:** Bibl.Agri., Helminthol.Abstr., Ind.Vet., Protozool.Abstr., Small Anim.Abstr.
Former titles (until 1989): A A V Today; (until 1987): A A V Newsletter.
Description: Addresses avian research, pet bird medicine and surgery, conservation, aviculture, pharmaceuticals and biologicals and veterinary medical education.

636.089   IT   ISSN 0004-5977
ASSOCIAZIONE ITALIANA VETERINARI PER PICCOLI ANIMALI. BOLLETTINO. 1961. q. membership. Cartografica Artigiana, Via Bela Bartok 21-23, 44100 Ferrara I-AIVPA, Italy. FAX 0532-92668. Ed. Cesare Pareschi. adv.; bk.rev.; abstr.; illus.; charts; illus.; stat.; tr.lit.; index; circ. 300. **Indexed:** Anim.Breed.Abstr., Ind.Vet., Small Anim.Abstr., Vet.Bull.

AUSTRALIAN JOURNAL OF EXPERIMENTAL AGRICULTURE. see *AGRICULTURE — Crop Production And Soil*

636.089   AT
AUSTRALIAN VETERINARY ASSOCIATION. ANNUAL REPORT. a. Aus.$20 (effective 1992). Australian Veterinary Association, 134-136 Hampden Rd., Artarmon, N.S.W. 2064, Australia. TEL 02-411-2733. FAX 02-411-5089.
Formerly: Australian Veterinary Association. Year Book (ISSN 0812-9169)

VETERINARY SCIENCE

636.089   AT
AUSTRALIAN VETERINARY ASSOCIATION CONFERENCE HANDBOOK. 1981. a. Aus.$20 to non-members (effective 1992). Australian Veterinary Association, 134-136 Hampden Rd., Artarmon, N.S.W. 2064, Australia. TEL 02-411-2733. FAX 02-411-5089. Ed. P.E. Greenwood. circ. 4,000.
    Formerly: Australian Advances in Veterinary Science (ISSN 0728-8425)

636.089   AT   ISSN 0005-0423
CODEN: AUVJA2
AUSTRALIAN VETERINARY JOURNAL. 1925. m. Aus.$235. Australian Veterinary Association, 272 Brunswick St., Brunswick, Vic. Aus. TEL 02-411-2733. FAX 03-3872982. Ed. Dr. K.L. Hughes. adv.; bk.rev.; index; circ. 4,500. (back issues avail.) **Indexed:** Abstr.Hyg., Agroforest.Abstr., Anim.Breed.Abstr., Bio-Contr.News & Info., Biol.Abstr., Biol.& Agr.Ind., Biotech.Abstr., Cadscan., Chem.Abstr., Curr.Adv.Ecol.Sci., Curr.Cont., Dairy Sci.Abstr., Dent.Ind., Excerp.Med., Field Crop Abstr., Helminthol.Abstr., Herb.Abstr., Ind.Med., Ind.Sci.Rev., Ind.Vet., Key Word Ind.Wildl.Res., Lead Abstr., Nutr.Abstr., Ornam.Hort., Pig News & Info., Poult.Abstr., Protozool.Abstr., Rev.Appl.Entomol., Rev.Med.& Vet.Mycol., Rev.Plant Path., Risk Abstr., Sci.Cit.Ind, Small Anim.Abstr., So.Pac.Per.Ind., Soils & Fert., Soyabean Abstr., Triticale Abstr., Trop.Dis.Bull., Vet.Bull., Weed Abstr., Zincscan.
    —BLDSC shelfmark: 1824.000000.

636   AT   ISSN 0310-138X
AUSTRALIAN VETERINARY PRACTITIONER. 1971. q. Aus.$70 (foreign Aus.$75). Australian Small Animal Veterinary Association, P.O. Box 371, Artarmon, N.S.W. 2026, Australia. FAX 02-360-7184. Ed. R.E. Atwell. adv.; bk.rev.; circ. 1,200. **Indexed:** Anim.Breed.Abstr., Biol.Abstr., Curr.Adv.Ecol.Sci., Curr.Cont., Helminthol.Abstr., Ind.Sci.Rev., Ind.Vet., Protozool.Abstr., Sci.Cit.Ind, Small Anim.Abstr., Vet.Bull.
    —BLDSC shelfmark: 1824.100000.

636.089   US   ISSN 0005-2086
CODEN: AVDIAI
AVIAN DISEASES. 1957. q. $60 (foreign $70). American Association of Avian Pathologists, Inc., University of Pennsylvania, New Bolton Center, Kennett Square, PA 19348-1692. TEL 215-444-4282. FAX 215-444-5387. Ed. Dr. D.P. Anderson. adv.; bibl.; charts; illus.; index; circ. 1,900. (also avail. in microform from UMI; microfilm from WSH,PMC; back issues avail.) **Indexed:** Anim.Breed.Abstr., Biol.Abstr., Biotech.Abstr., Chem.Abstr., Curr.Adv.Cancer Res., Curr.Adv.Ecol.Sci., Curr.Cont., Helminthol.Abstr., Ind.Med., Ind.Sci.Rev., Ind.Vet., Poult.Abstr., Protozool.Abstr., Rev.Med.& Vet.Mycol., Rev.Plant Path., Sci.Cit.Ind, Small Anim.Abstr., Vet.Bull.
    —BLDSC shelfmark: 1837.890000.
    Refereed Serial

636.089   UK   ISSN 0307-9457
CODEN: AVPADN
AVIAN PATHOLOGY. (Text in English; summaries in French, German and Spanish) 1972. q. $84 to individuals; institutions $168. (World Veterinary Poultry Association) Carfax Publishing Co., P.O. Box 25, Abingdon, Oxfordshire OX14 3UE, England. TEL 0235-555335. FAX 0235-553559. TELEX 329154 HPRS. (U.S. subscr. addr.: Carfax Publishing Co., Box 2025, Dunnellon, FL 32630) Ed. L.N. Payne. adv.; bk.rev.; circ. 700. (back issues avail.) **Indexed:** Anim.Breed.Abstr., Biol.Abstr., Biotech.Abstr., Curr.Adv.Ecol.Sci., Helminthol.Abstr., Ind.Sci.Rev., Ind.Vet., Poult.Abstr., Protozool.Abstr., Rev.Med.& Vet.Mycol., Sci.Cit.Ind, Small Anim.Abstr., Vet.Bull.
    —BLDSC shelfmark: 1837.891000.

BANGLADESH JOURNAL OF ANIMAL SCIENCE. see *AGRICULTURE — Poultry And Livestock*

636.089   BG
BANGLADESH VETERINARY JOURNAL. 1967. q. $10. Bangladesh Veterinary Association, Bangladesh Agricultural University, Mymensingh, Bangladesh. Ed. M.L. Dewan. adv.; bk.rev.; charts; illus.; circ. 1,000. **Indexed:** Anim.Breed.Abstr., Ind.Vet., Vet.Bull.
    Formerly (until 1969): Pakistan Journal of Veterinary Science (ISSN 0030-9915)

BEITRAEGE ZUR TROPISCHEN LANDWIRTSCHAFT UND VETERINAERMEDIZIN. see *AGRICULTURE*

636.089   GW   ISSN 0005-9366
CODEN: BEMTAM
BERLINER UND MUENCHENER TIERAERZTLICHE WOCHENSCHRIFT. (Text in German; summaries in English and German) 1888. s-m. DM.378($217) Verlag Paul Parey (Berlin), Seelbuschring 9-17, 1000 Berlin 42, Germany. TEL 030-70784-00. FAX 030-70784199. (U.S. address: Paul Parey Scientific Publishers, 150 E. 27th St., No.1A, New York, NY 10016) Ed.Bd. adv.; bk.rev.; abstr.; illus.; stat.; index. (back issues avail.) **Indexed:** Anim.Breed.Abstr., Biodet.Abstr., Biol.Abstr., Biotech.Abstr., Chem.Abstr., Curr.Adv.Ecol.Sci., Curr.Cont., Dairy Sci.Abstr., Dent.Ind., Field Crop Abstr., Food Sci.& Tech.Abstr., Helminthol.Abstr., Herb.Abstr., Ind.Med., Ind.Sci.Rev., Ind.Vet., INIS Atomind., Key Word.Ind.Wildl.Res., Nutr.Abstr., Pig News & Info., Poult.Abstr., Protozool.Abstr., Rev.Plant Path., Sci.Cit.Ind, Small Anim.Abstr., Soils & Fert., Vet.Bull.
    —BLDSC shelfmark: 1941.360000.

636.089   BL   ISSN 0029-6953
BIOLOGICO. (Text in Portuguese; summaries in English) 1935. s-a. Cr.$1260($12) Instituto Biologico, Av. Rodrigues Alves 1252, C.P. 4185, Sao Paulo, Brazil. TEL 572-9822. Ed.Bd. bibl.; illus.; index. cum.index; circ. 2,000. **Indexed:** Bio-Contr.News & Info., Biol.Abstr., Biotech.Abstr., Chem.Abstr., Field Crop Abstr., Forest.Abstr., Helminthol.Abstr., Herb.Abstr., Hort.Abstr., Ind.Vet., Plant Breed.Abstr., Rev.Appl.Entomol., Rev.Plant Path., Seed Abstr., Triticale Abstr., Trop.Oil Seeds Abstr., Vet.Bull., Weed Abstr.
    —BLDSC shelfmark: 2082.000000.

636.089   GW   ISSN 0723-6212
BIOLOGISCHE TIERMEDIZIN. q. DM.16. Aurelia Verlag GmbH, Ruhrstr. 14, Postfach 115, 7570 Baden-Baden, Germany. TEL 07221-50102. circ. 15,000.

636 615.1   CS   ISSN 0139-8571
CODEN: BCZVDE
BIOLOGIZACE A CHEMIZACE ZIVOCISNE VYROBY - VETERINARIA/BIOLOGICAL AND CHEMICAL FACTORS IN ANIMAL PRODUCTION - VETERINARIA /BIOLOGISATION UND CHEMISATION DER TIERERZEUGUNG - VETERINARIA/FACTEURS BIOLOGIQUES ET CHIMIQUES DANS LA PRODUCTION DES ANIMAUX - VETERINARIA /FACTORES BIOLOGICOS Y QUIMICOS DE LA PRODUCTION ANIMAL - VETERINARIA. (Text in Czech or Slovak; summaries in English, French, German, Russian and Spanish) 1964. bi-m. 54 Kcs.($26.20) (SPOFA, Spojene Podniky pro Zdravotnickou Vyrobu, Vyzkumny Ustav pro Biofaktory a Veterinarni Leciva, Odbor Vedeckych Informaci) Statni Zemedelske Nakladatelstvi, Vaclavske nam. 47, 113 11 Prague, Czechoslovakia. TEL 26 59 51. (Subscr. to: Artia, ve Smeckach 30, 11127 Prague 1, Czechoslovakia) Ed. Bohumil Sevcik. adv.; bk.rev.; bibl.; charts; illus.; stat. (reprint service avail. from ISI) **Indexed:** Anim.Breed.Abstr., Cadscan, Chem.Abstr., Curr.Adv.Ecol.Sci., Curr.Cont., Dairy Sci.Abstr., Excerp.Med., Helminthol.Abstr., Ind.Sci.Rev., Ind.Vet., Lead Abstr., Nutr.Abstr., Pig News & Info., Poult.Abstr., Protozool.Abstr., Sci.Cit.Ind, Vet.Bull., Zincscan.
    —BLDSC shelfmark: 2089.353600.

BLAA STJAERNAN. see *PETS*

636.089   UK
BLACK'S VETERINARY DICTIONARY. 1928. irreg., (every 2-3 yrs.). £18. A & C Black (Publishers) Ltd., Howard Rd., Eaton Socon, Huntingdon,Cambs PE19 3EZ, England. TEL 0480-21666. FAX 0480-40514. TELEX 32524-ACBLAC. Ed. Geoffrey P. West.
    Description: Comprehensive veterinary dictionary for veterinary and agricultural students, vets and farmers. Covers related fields.

BOLLETTINO DELL'AGRICOLTURA. see *AGRICULTURE*

636.089   US   ISSN 0524-1685
CODEN: BOVPBO
BOVINE PRACTITIONER. 1969. a. $20 (foreign $25). American Association of Bovine Practitioners, c/o Dr. Eric I. Williams, Ed., 1226 N. Lincoln, Stillwater, OK 74075. FAX 405-372-0939. adv.; bk.rev.; circ. 5,000. **Indexed:** Dairy Sci.Abstr., Protozool.Abstr.
    —BLDSC shelfmark: 2264.630000.

636.089 615   UK
BRITISH PHARMACOPOEIA (VETERINARY). 1977. irreg. £35. British Pharmacopoeia Commission, Market Towers, 1 Nine Elms Lane, London SW8 5NQ, England. (Subscr. to: H.M.S.O., P.O. Box 276, London SW8 5DT, England)

636.089   UK   ISSN 0007-1935
CODEN: BVJOA9
BRITISH VETERINARY JOURNAL. 1875. bi-m. $166. Bailliere Tindall, 24-28 Oval Rd., London NW1 7DX, England. Ed. A.J. Higgins. adv.; bk.rev.; abstr.; charts; illus.; stat.; index. (also avail. in microform from UMI,PMC; reprint service avail. from UMI) **Indexed:** Anim.Breed.Abstr., Biol.Abstr., Biotech.Abstr., C.I.S. Abstr., Chem.Abstr., Curr.Adv.Ecol.Sci., Curr.Cont., Dairy Sci.Abstr., Excerp.Med., Food Sci.& Tech.Abstr., Helminthol.Abstr., Ind.Med., Ind.Sci.Rev., Ind.Vet., Nutr.Abstr., Pig News & Info., Poult.Abstr., Protozool.Abstr., Rev.Appl.Entomol., Rev.Plant Path., Risk Abstr., Sci.Cit.Ind, Small Anim.Abstr., Vet.Bull.
    —BLDSC shelfmark: 2347.000000.
    Description: Publishes worldwide contributions on all aspects of veterinary science and its related subjects.

BULLETIN OF ANIMAL HEALTH AND PRODUCTION IN AFRICA/BULLETIN DES SANTE ET PRODUCTION ANIMALES EN AFRIQUE. see *AGRICULTURE — Poultry And Livestock*

636.089   US   ISSN 0008-1612
CALIFORNIA VETERINARIAN. 1947. bi-m. $35 (foreign $55). California Veterinary Medical Association, 5231 Madison Ave., Sacramento, CA 95841. Ed. Kathleen M. Edwards. adv.; illus.; index; circ. 3,800. (also avail. in microform from UMI; back issues avail.) **Indexed:** Biotech.Abstr., Chem.Abstr., Ind.Vet., Small Anim.Abstr., Vet.Bull.
    —BLDSC shelfmark: 3015.350000.
    Description: Professional, scientific and business-oriented articles for doctors of veterinary medicine.

CANADIAN HORSEMAN. see *SPORTS AND GAMES — Horses And Horsemanship*

636.089 610   CN   ISSN 0830-9000
CODEN: CJVRE9
CANADIAN JOURNAL OF VETERINARY RESEARCH/REVUE CANADIENNE DE RECHERCHE VETERINAIRE. (Text in English and French) 1937. q. Can.$70 (foreign Can.$85). Canadian Veterinary Medical Association, 339 Booth St., Ottawa, Ont. K1R 7K1, Canada. TEL 613-236-1162. FAX 613-236-9681. Ed. Dr. Joren Rosendal. bibl.; charts; illus.; index; circ. 2,000. **Indexed:** Anim.Breed.Abstr., Biol.Abstr., Biotech.Abstr., Chem.Abstr., Curr.Adv.Ecol.Sci., Curr.Cont., Dairy Sci.Abstr., Dent.Ind., Excerp.Med., Food Sci.& Tech.Abstr., Helminthol.Abstr., Ind.Med., Ind.Sci.Rev., Ind.Vet., Med.Care Rev., Nutr.Abstr., Pig News & Info., Poult.Abstr., Protozool.Abstr., Sci.Cit.Ind, Small Anim.Abstr., Vet.Bull.
    —BLDSC shelfmark: 3036.700000.
    Former titles: Canadian Journal of Comparative Medicine (ISSN 0008-4050); Canadian Journal of Comparative Medicine and Veterinary Science.

636.089   CN   ISSN 0825-754X
CANADIAN VET SUPPLIES. 1984. 6/yr. Can.$10($18) Selc Publishing Inc., 1 Philipsburg St., C.P. 1320, Bedford, Que. J0J 1A0, Canada. TEL 514-248-3356. FAX 514-248-2195. Ed. Mario Martel. adv.; circ. 4,172. (tabloid format)

636.089   CN   ISSN 0008-5286
CODEN: CNVJA9
CANADIAN VETERINARY JOURNAL/REVUE VETERINAIRE CANADIENNE. (Text in English and French) 1960. m. Can.$80 (foreign Can.$90). Canadian Veterinary Medical Association, 339 Booth St., Ottawa, Ont. K1R 7K1, Canada. TEL 613-236-1162. FAX 613-236-9681. Ed. Dr. Doug Hare. adv.; bk.rev.; abstr.; charts; illus.; index; circ. 5,500. (also avail. in microform from UMI,PMC) **Indexed:** Agri.Eng.Abstr., Anim.Breed.Abstr., Biol.Abstr., Biotech.Abstr., Chem.Abstr., Curr.Adv.Ecol.Sci., Curr.Cont., Dairy Sci.Abstr., Excerp.Med., Helminthol.Abstr., Ind.Med., Ind.Sci.Rev., Ind.Vet., INIS Atomind., Nutr.Abstr., Pig News & Info., Poult.Abstr., Protozool.Abstr., Rev.Appl.Entomol., Sci.Cit.Ind, Small Anim.Abstr., Vet.Bull.
    —BLDSC shelfmark: 3046.100000.

VETERINARY SCIENCE

636.089   IT
CANI, GATTI E COMPAGNIA. 1987. q. L.15000 (foreign L.20000) or free to qualified personnel. Editore S.C.I.V.A.C., Via Pallavicino, 26, Cremona, Italy. TEL 0372-23501. Ed. Antonio Manfredi. circ. 80,000.

636.089   US   ISSN 1057-6622
SF991   CODEN: CPRAEE
CANINE PRACTICE; the journal of canine medicine & surgery for the practitioner. 1974. bi-m. $28. Veterinary Practice Publishing Co., 7 Ashley Ave. S., Santa Barbara, CA 93103-9989. TEL 805-965-1028. (Subscr. addr.: Box 4457, Santa Barbara, CA 93140-4457) Ed. Dr. Joseph Alexander. adv.; bk.rev.; illus.; index; circ. 7,500. (also avail. in microform from UMI) **Indexed:** Curr.Adv.Ecol.Sci., Ind.Vet., Small Anim.Abstr., Soyabean Abstr., Vet.Bull.
Former titles: Companion to Animal Pratice (ISSN 0094-4904); Canine Practice.
Description: Written for practitioners of canine medicine and surgery.

636.089   UN
CENTRO PANAMERICANO DE ZOONOSIS. NOTAS TECNICAS. (Text in Spanish) 1971. irreg. Centro Panamericano de Zoonosis, Casilla 3092, 1000 Buenos Aires, Argentina. TEL 792-4047-49. TELEX 24577 AR CPZ. (Affiliate: World Health Organization)

636.089   UN
CENTRO PANAMERICANO DE ZOONOSIS. PUBLICACIONES ESPECIALES. (Text in Spanish) 1974. irreg. Centro Panamericano de Zoonosis, Casilla 3092, 1000 Buenos Aires, Argentina. FAX 792-4047-49. TELEX 24577 AR CPZ. (Affiliate: World Health Organization)

636.089   II   ISSN 0379-542X
CODEN: CHRNAR
CHEIRON; Tamil Nadu journal of veterinary science and animal husbandry. (Text in English) 1972. bi-m. Rs.40($20) Tamil Nadu Veterinary & Animal Science University, Madras-600007, India. TEL 581-506. FAX 044-560114. Ed. M. Mohamed Habibulla Khan. adv.: B&W page Rs.1000. index; circ. 750. (back issues avail.) **Indexed:** Agri.Eng.Abstr., Anim.Breed.Abstr., Biodet.Abstr., Biol.Abstr., Chem.Abstr., Curr.Adv.Ecol.Sci., Dairy Sci.Abstr., Food Sci.& Tech.Abstr., Helminthol.Abstr., Herb.Abstr., Ind.Vet., Nutr.Abstr., Poult.Abstr., Protozool.Abstr., Rev.Appl.Entomol., Trop.Oil Seeds Abstr., Vet.Bull., World Agri.Econ.& Rural Sociol.Abstr.
—BLDSC shelfmark: 3133.430000.

636.089   CU
CIENCIA Y TECNICA EN LA AGRICULTURA. SERIE: VETERINARIA. (Table of contents and abstracts in English) 1978. 2/yr. $14 in N. and S. America; Europe $16; others $17; or exchange basis. Centro de Informacion y Documentacion Agropecuario, Gaveta Postal 4149, Havana 4, Cuba. (Dist. by: Ediciones Cubanas, Obispo No. 527, Apdo. 605, Havana, Cuba) **Indexed:** Agrindex, Ind.Vet., Vet.Bull.

636.089   IT   ISSN 0009-9082
CODEN: CLVEAE
CLINICA VETERINARIA. (Text in Italian; summaries in English) 1878. m. L.20000. Istituto Sieroterapico Milanese, Via Darwin 20, Milan, Italy. adv.; bk.rev.; bibl.; illus.; index; circ. 2,800. **Indexed:** Anim.Breed.Abstr., Biol.Abstr., Biotech.Abstr., Chem.Abstr., Dairy Sci.Abstr., Excerp.Med., Food Sci.& Tech.Abstr., Helminthol.Abstr., Ind.Vet., Nutr.Abstr., Pig News & Info., Poult.Abstr., Protozool.Abstr., Small Anim.Abstr., Vet.Bull.
—BLDSC shelfmark: 3286.242000.

636.089   AT   ISSN 1031-1580
COMMONWEALTH SCIENTIFIC AND INDUSTRIAL RESEARCH ORGANIZATION. DIVISION OF ANIMAL HEALTH. REPORT. 1966. biennial. C.S.I.R.O., Division of Animal Health, Private Bag No. 1, Parkville, Vic. 3052, Australia. TEL 03-342-9700. FAX 03-347-4042. TELEX 32677. circ. 1,000 (controlled). **Indexed:** Biol.Abstr., Ind.Vet., Rev.Appl.Entomol., Vet.Bull.
—BLDSC shelfmark: 7411.359310.
Former titles (until 1983): Commonwealth Scientific and Industrial Research Organization. Division of Animal Health. Research Report (ISSN 0812-7336); (until 1982): Commonwealth Scientific and Industrial Research Organization. Division of Animal Health. Annual Report (ISSN 0069-7273)
Description: Discusses various aspects of research projects: management, resources, finances and end results.

COMPARATIVE ANIMAL NUTRITION. see *BIOLOGY — Zoology*

COMPARATIVE IMMUNOLOGY, MICROBIOLOGY AND INFECTIOUS DISEASES; the international journal for medical and veterinary researchers and practitioners. see *BIOLOGY — Microbiology*

636.089   US   ISSN 0193-1903
COMPENDIUM ON CONTINUING EDUCATION FOR THE PRACTICING VETERINARIAN. 1979. m. $52 to individuals (foreign $83); libraries $70 (foreign $96). Veterinary Learning Systems, 425 Phillips Blvd., Ste. 100, Trenton, NJ 08618. TEL 609-882-5600. FAX 609-882-6357. Ed.Bd. adv.; index; circ. 27,500. (also avail. in microform from UMI; back issues avail.) **Indexed:** Agri.Eng.Abstr., Anim.Breed.Abstr., Curr.Cont., Dairy Sci.Abstr., Herb.Abstr., Pig News & Info., Protozool.Abstr., Small Anim.Abstr., Vet.Bull.
Formerly: Compendium on Continuing Education for the Small Animal Practitioner (ISSN 0164-5455)

COMPLETING THE INTERNAL MARKET OF THE EUROPEAN COMMUNITY: 1992 LEGISLATION - VETERINARY & PHYTOSANITARY CONTROLS. see *LAW — International Law*

636.089   US   ISSN 0010-8901
CODEN: COVEAZ
CORNELL VETERINARIAN. 1911. q. $30 (foreign $35). Cornell Veterinarian, Inc., Ithaca, NY 14853. Ed. Dr. Maurice White. adv.; bk.rev.; abstr.; charts; illus.; index; circ. 1,000. **Indexed:** Anim.Breed.Abstr., Biol.Abstr., Biol.& Agr.Ind., Biotech.Abstr., Cadscan, Chem.Abstr., Curr.Adv.Ecol.Sci., Curr.Cont., Dairy Sci.Abstr., Dent.Ind., Excerp.Med., Food Sci.& Tech.Abstr., Helminthol.Abstr., Ind.Med., Ind.Sci.Rev., Ind.Vet., Lead Abstr., Nutr.Abstr., Pig News & Info., Protozool.Abstr., Rev.Plant Path., Sci.Cit.Ind., Small Anim.Abstr., Vet.Bull., Zincscan.
—BLDSC shelfmark: 3470.970000.
Description: Presents original research papers and case reports in veterinary medicine.
Refereed Serial

636.089   CN   ISSN 0843-5634
CREST. 1989. q. Ontario Veterinary College, Alumni Association, University of Guelph, Guelph, Ont. N1G 2W1, Canada. TEL 519-823-8800. FAX 519-837-3230. Ed. Martha Leibbrandt. illus.; circ. 5,000.
Description: News of OVC's people, events and programs.

636.089   CU   ISSN 0138-8134
CUBA. CENTRO DE INFORMACION Y DOCUMENTACION AGROPECUARIO. BOLETIN DE RESENAS. SERIE: VETERINARIA. (Abstracts in English) 1974. irreg. exchange basis. Centro de Informacion y Documentacion Agropecuario, Gaveta Postal 4149, Havana 4, Cuba. TEL 292227. (Dist. by: Ediciones Cubana, Obispo No. 461, Apdo. 605, Havana, Cuba) stat. **Indexed:** Agrindex.
Formerly: Cuba. Centro de Informacion y Divulgacion Agropecuario. Boletin de Resenas. Serie: Veterinaria.

636.089   GW   ISSN 0341-6593
CODEN: DDTWDG
D T W - DEUTSCHE TIERAERZTLICHE WOCHENSCHRIFT. (Text in German; summaries in English) 1893. 12/yr. DM.265 (foreign DM.280). Verlag M. und H. Schaper, Kalandstr. 4, Postfach 1642, 3220 Alfeld, Germany. adv.; bk.rev.; abstr.; bibl.; charts; illus.; index; circ. 1,500. **Indexed:** Agri.Eng.Abstr., Anim.Breed.Abstr., Biol.Abstr., Biotech.Abstr., Chem.Abstr., Curr.Adv.Ecol.Sci., Curr.Cont., Dairy Sci.Abstr., Dent.Ind., Excerp.Med., Field Crop Abstr., Food Sci.& Tech.Abstr., Helminthol.Abstr., Herb.Abstr., Ind.Med., Ind.Sci.Rev., Ind.Vet., Ind.Vet., INIS Atomind., Key Word Ind.Wildl.Res., Maize Abstr., Nutr.Abstr., Pig News & Info., Potato Abstr., Poult.Abstr., Protozool.Abstr., Rev.Plant Path., Risk Abstr., Sci.Cit.Ind, Small Anim.Abstr., Soils & Fert., Soyabean Abstr., Triticale Abstr., Vet.Bull.
—BLDSC shelfmark: 3574.000000.
Former title: Deutsche Tieraerztliche Wochenschrift (ISSN 0012-0847)

636.089 658   US
D V M MANAGEMENT. (Doctor of Veterinary Medicine); the business newsletter for the practicing veterinarian. 10/yr. $92 (foreign $102). American Veterinary Publications, Inc., 5782 Thornwood Dr., Goleta, CA 93117-3896. TEL 805-967-5988. (looseleaf format)

636.089   US   ISSN 0012-7337
D V M NEWSMAGAZINE. 1970. m. $24. Avanstar Communications, Inc., 7500 Old Oak Blvd., Cleveland, OH 44130. TEL 216-826-2839. FAX 216-891-2726. (Subscr. to: 1 E. First St., Duluth, MN 55802) Ed. Maureen Hrehocik. adv.; bk.rev.; abstr.; illus.; tr.lit.; circ. 35,707.
Description: Covers news and trends for veterinarians.

DAIRY INDIA YEARBOOK. see *AGRICULTURE — Dairying And Dairy Products*

636.089   DK   ISSN 0106-6854
DANSK VETERINAERTIDSSKRIFT/DANISH VETERINARY JOURNAL. 1918. s-m. DKK 480. Danske Dyrlaegeforening - Danish Veterinary Association, Rosenlunds Alle 8, DK-2720 Vanloese, Denmark. TEL 31-71-08-88. FAX 31-71-03-22. Ed. Bent Christensen. adv.; bk.rev.; circ. 3,200. **Indexed:** Agri.Eng.Abstr., Anim.Breed.Abstr., Biodet.Abstr., Biol.Abstr., Dairy Sci.Abstr., Food Sci.& Tech.Abstr., Ind.Vet., Nutr.Abstr., Pig News & Info., Protozool.Abstr., Small Anim.Abstr., Vet.Bull., World Agri.Econ.& Rural Sociol.Abstr.
—BLDSC shelfmark: 3533.035000.
Formerly: Danske Dyrlaegeforening. Medlemsblad (ISSN 0011-6564)

636.089   FR   ISSN 0180-3573
DEPECHE VETERINAIRE. 1977. 44/yr. 530 F. (typically set in Jan.). Syndicat National des Veterinaires de France, 10 Place Leon Blum, 75011 Paris, France. FAX 43-79-76-96. Ed. Pierre Royer. adv.

636.089   GW   ISSN 0340-1898
DEUTSCHES TIERAERZTEBLATT. 1949. m. DM.170 (foreign DM.194). (Deutsche Tieraerzteschaft e.V.) Schluetersche Verlagsanstalt GmbH und Co., Georgswall 4, Postfach 5440, 3000 Hannover 1, Germany. TEL 0511-1236-0. Ed. Dr. Hans-Ludwig Schlegel. adv.; bk.rev.; stat.; circ. 25,342. **Indexed:** Ind.Vet., Vet.Bull.
—BLDSC shelfmark: 3578.160000.

636.089   NE
DEVELOPMENTS IN ANIMAL AND VETERINARY SCIENCES. 1976. irreg., vol.25, 1991. price varies. Elsevier Science Publishers B.V., Books Division, P.O. Box 211, 1000 AE Amsterdam, Netherlands. TEL 020-5803911. FAX 020-5803705. TELEX 18582 ESPA NL. (Subscr. in U.S. and Canada to: Elsevier Science Publishing Co., Inc., Box 882, Madison Sq. Sta., New York, NY 10159. TEL 212-989-5800) (back issues avail.)
Refereed Serial

VETERINARY SCIENCE 4809

636.089 NE ISSN 0920-2412
DIER - EN - ARTS/VETERINARIAN; wetenschappelijke praktijkgerichte informatie. (Text in Dutch) 1986. 9/yr. fl.85.50 (students fl.45)(foreign fl.125)(free to qualified personnel). Transmondial, Baron van Nagellstr. 27, 3781 AP Voorthuizen, Netherlands. TEL 03429-3135. FAX 03429-3154. Ed.Bd. adv.; bk.rev.; abstr.; bibl.; charts; illus.; stat. (back issues avail.)
●Also available online.
—BLDSC shelfmark: 3580.557000.
Description: Provides information for practicing veterinary surgeons and includes examples of practical solutions to problems encountered in daily practice.

636.089 FR ISSN 1012-5329
DISEASE INFORMATION. (Text in English, French, Spanish) 1988. w. 340 F.($60) (effective 1992). Office International des Epizooties, 12, rue de Prony, 75017 Paris, France. TEL 44-15-18-88. FAX 42-67-09-87. TELEX EPIZOTI 642 285 F. (U.S. Subscr. to: Scientific, Medical Publications of France, 100 East 42nd St., Ste 1002, New York, NY 10017. TEL 212-983-6278) Ed. J. Blancon. (back issues avail.)
Description: Updates reports on outbreaks of emergency animal diseases.

636 TU ISSN 1010-7592
DOGA TURKISH JOURNAL OF VETERINARY AND ANIMAL SCIENCES/DOGA TURK VETERINERLIK VE HAYVANCILIK DERGISI. (Text in English, Turkish) 1976. 3/yr. $20. Scientific and Technical Research Council of Turkey - Turkiye Bilimsel ve Teknik Arastirma Kurumu, Ataturk Bulvari, No. 221, Kavaklidere, 06100 Ankara, Turkey. TEL 1673657. FAX 1277489. TELEX 43186 BTAK TR. Ed. Dr. Huseyin Kerim Urman. **Indexed:** Anim.Breed.Abstr., Biol.Abstr., Chem.Abstr, Dairy Sci.Abstr., INIS Atomind., Maize Abstr.
—BLDSC shelfmark: 3614.642540.
Formerly: Doga Bilim Dergisi. Series D: Veterinary and Animal Sciences.

DOMESTIC ANIMAL ENDOCRINOLOGY. see *MEDICAL SCIENCES — Endocrinology*

DROBIARSTWO/POULTRY INDUSTRY. see *AGRICULTURE — Poultry And Livestock*

636.089 DK
DYRENES RET. 1975. q. Landsforeningen Komiteen mod Dyreforsoeg, Valdemarsgade 67, 5.tv., P.O. Box 228, DK-1502 Copenhagen V, Denmark. TEL 31-22-41-15. Ed.Bd. bk.rev.; circ. 2,000.
Formerly: Komiteen mod Dyreforsoeg, Fonden til Sygdomsbekaempelse uden Dyreforsoeg (ISSN 0109-3878)

636 UA ISSN 1110-0222
EGYPTIAN JOURNAL OF VETERINARY SCIENCE. (Text in English; summaries in Arabic and English) 1964. s-a. $30. (Arabic Veterinary Medical Association) National Information and Documentation Centre (NIDOC), Tahrir St., Dokki, Awqaf P.O., Cairo, Egypt. Ed. M.R. Shalash. circ. 1,500. **Indexed:** Anim.Breed.Abstr., Biol.Abstr., Chem.Abstr., Curr.Adv.Ecol.Sci., Excerp.Med., Ind.Vet., Vet.Bull.
Formerly (until vol. 9, 1972): United Arab Republic Journal of Veterinary Science (ISSN 0041-7165)

EMBRYO TRANSFER NEWSLETTER. see *BIOLOGY — Zoology*

636.089 UN
EPIDEMIOLOGICAL SURVEILLANCE OF RABIES FOR THE AMERICAS. Spanish Edition: Vigilancia Epidemiologica de la Rabia para las Americas. 1969. s-a. Centro Panamericano de Zoonosis, Casilla 3092, 1000 Buenos Aires, Argentina. TEL 792-4047-49. TELEX 24577 AR CPZ. (Affiliate: World Health Organization) Ed. Eduardo Guarnera. circ. 1,400 (950 Span. ed.; 450 Eng. ed.).

636.089 GR
EPISTIMONIKI EPITERIS KTENIATRIKIS SCHOLIS. (Text in Greek; summaries in English) 1952. irreg. Aristotelian University of Thessaloniki, Faculty of Veterinary Medicine, Thessaloniki, Greece. Ed. A.G. Spais. circ. 500. **Indexed:** Biol.Abstr.

636 US ISSN 1047-8620
EQUINE ATHLETE; the equine sportsmedicine news journal for trainers and veterinarians. 1988. bi-m. $44.50. Veterinary Practice Publishing Co., 7 Ashley Ave. S., Santa Barbara, CA 93103-9989. TEL 805-965-1028. FAX 805-965-0722. (Subscr. addr.: Box 4457, Santa Barbara, CA 93140-4457) Ed. Dr. Jerry R. Gillespie. adv.; charts; illus.; circ. 6,500.

636.089 US
EQUINE MEDICINE. 1977. m. $108. Audio Veterinary Medicine, 810 S. Myrtle Ave., Monrovia, CA 91016. TEL 818-303-2531. FAX 818-303-2534. (Subscr. to: Box 1729, Monrovia, CA 91017-5729) Ed. Anthony C. Crum, II. circ. 280. (audio cassette; back issues avail.)

636.089 US ISSN 0162-8941
SF951 CODEN: EQPRDF
EQUINE PRACTICE; journal of equine medicine and surgery for the practitioner. 1979. 10/yr. $36 to individuals; students $20; Canada and Mexico $42; elsewhere $50. Veterinary Practice Publishing Co., 7 Ashley Ave. S., Santa Barbara, CA 93103-9989. TEL 805-965-1028. FAX 805-965-0722. (Subscr. addr.: Box 4457, Santa Barbara, CA 93140-4457) Ed. Dr. Charles Vail. adv.; bk.rev.; illus.; index; circ. 4,500. (also avail. in microform from UMI; reprint service avail. from UMI) **Indexed:** Anim.Breed.Abstr., Curr.Adv.Ecol.Sci., Dairy Sci.Abstr., Ind.Vet., Protozool.Abstr., Rice Abstr., Vet.Bull.
—BLDSC shelfmark: 3794.518000.
Incorporates: Journal of Equine Medicine and Surgery (ISSN 0147-0833)
Description: Directed to the equine segment of the veterinary clinical market.
Refereed Serial

636.089 CN ISSN 0835-5509
EQUINE RESEARCH CENTRE NEWSLETTER. 1986. q. free. Equine Research Centre, University of Guelph, Guelph, Ont. N1G 2W1, Canada. TEL 519-837-0061. FAX 519-767-1081. Ed. Gabrielle M. Neff. cum.index 1986-1991; circ. 5,000. (back issues avail.)
Description: Articles on equine research written for the horse owner, educator and equine veterinary practitioner.

636.089 US ISSN 0739-9065
EQUINE VETERINARY DATA. 1980. s-m. $120 to individuals; institutions $150; foreign $150. William E. Jones, Ed. & Pub., Box 1209, Wildomar, CA 92395. TEL 714-678-1083. index. (back issues avail.) **Indexed:** Ind.Vet.
—BLDSC shelfmark: 3794.519000.
Description: Professional newsletter for DVM equine practitioners.

636.087 375 UK ISSN 0957-7734
EQUINE VETERINARY EDUCATION. 1989. 6/yr. £72 (foreign £84). R & W Publications (Newmarket) Ltd., Goodwin House, Willie Snaith Rd., Newmarket, Suffolk CB8 7SQ, England. TEL 638-667600. FAX 638-667229. Ed. I.G. Mayhew. illus.; circ. 1,000.
—BLDSC shelfmark: 3794.519400.
Description: Covers continuing education for equine veterinarians.

636.089 UK ISSN 0425-1644
CODEN: EQVJAI
EQUINE VETERINARY JOURNAL. 1968. bi-m. £58 (foreign £78). (British Equine Veterinary Association) R & W Publications (Newmarket) Ltd., Goodwin House, Willie Snaith Rd., Newmarket, Suffolk CB8 7SQ, England. TEL 638-667600. FAX 638-667229. Ed. P.D. Rossdale. adv.; bk.rev.; abstr.; charts; illus.; stat.; index; circ. 2,300. (reprint service avail. from UMI) **Indexed:** Agri.Eng.Abstr., Anim.Breed.Abstr., Biol.Abstr., Curr.Adv.Ecol.Sci., Curr.Cont., Dent.Ind., Helminthol.Abstr, Ind.Med., Ind.Sci.Rev., Ind.Vet., Nutr.Abstr., Protozool.Abstr., Rev.Plant Path., Sci.Cit.Ind, Vet.Bull.
—BLDSC shelfmark: 3794.520000.

EQUINEWS; serving the horse industry - all breeds, all disciplines. see *SPORTS AND GAMES — Horses And Horsemanship*

EQUUS. see *SPORTS AND GAMES — Horses And Horsemanship*

636.089 GW ISSN 0138-5003
ERKRANKUNGEN DER ZOOTIERE. (Text in English, French, German) 1967. a. (Akademie der Wissenschaften der DDR) Akademie-Verlag Berlin, Leipziger Str. 3-4, 1086 Berlin, Germany. TELEX 114420-AVERL-DD.
—BLDSC shelfmark: 3810.200000.
Description: Proceedings of international conferences on zoo animal diseases.

636.08 PK
▼**FARM SCIENTIST.** (Text in English, Urdu) 1990. m. $3 per no. Press Corporation of Pakistan, P.O. Box 3138, Karachi 754000, Pakistan. TEL 21-455-3703. FAX 21-7736198. Ed. Dr. M.S. Jaffery. circ. 5,000.

636.039 628 US ISSN 0164-6257
FEDERAL VETERINARIAN. 1922. m. $30 (foreign $50). National Association of Federal Veterinarians, 1023 15th St., N.W., Ste. 300, Washington, DC 20005-2602. TEL 202-289-6334. Ed. Dr. Edward L. Menning. adv.; bk.rev.; circ. 2,000. (tabloid format; back issues avil.)
Description: Federal regulatory news about veterinary drugs, meat inspection, animal disease control, human disease from animals and federal personnel issues.

636.089 US
FELINE HEALTH TOPICS. 1981. q. $25. Cornell Feline Health Center, Cornell University, College of Veterinary Medicine, Ithaca, NY 14853-6401. TEL 607-253-3414. FAX 607-253-3419. Ed. June Tuttle. circ. 25,000. (back issues avail.)
Description: For veterinary professionals.

636.8 US ISSN 1057-6614
SF985 CODEN: FELPEJ
FELINE PRACTICE; the journal of feline medicine & surgery for the practitioner. 1971. bi-m. $28. Veterinary Practice Publishing Co., 7 Ashley Ave. S., Santa Barbara, CA 93103-9989. TEL 805-965-1028. FAX 805-965-0722. (Subscr. addr.: Box 4457, Santa Barbara, CA 93140-4457) Ed. Dr. Fred Scott. adv.; bk.rev.; illus.; index; circ. 7,500. (also avail. in microform from UMI; reprint service avail. from UMI) **Indexed:** Curr.Adv.Ecol.Sci., Ind.Vet., Small Anim.Abstr.
Formerly: Companion Animal Practice (ISSN 0046-3639)
Description: Focuses on feline medicine and surgery. Official journal of the American Association of Feline Practitioners.
Refereed Serial

636.089 GW
FLEISCH- UND LEBENSMITTELHYGIENE. 1948. m. DM.67. Kommunalschriften-Verlag J. Jehle Muenchen GmbH, Kirschstr. 14, 8000 Munich 40, Germany. Eds. Peter Habit, Josef Pueschner. adv.; bk.rev.; circ. 3,000. (back issues avail.)
Formerly (until 1987): Fleisch und Lebensmittelkontrolle (ISSN 0341-4558)

636.089 634.9 CS
FOLIA VENATORIA; pol'ovnicky zbornik. (Text in Czech, Slovak; summaries in English, German, Russian) 1971. a. price varies. (Forest Research Institute, Federal Committee of Hunting Associations in the CSSR) Priroda, Krizkova 9, 815 34 Bratislava, Czechoslovakia. TEL 472-41-45. Ed. Pavel Hell. bk.rev.; charts; illus.; cum.index. **Indexed:** Biol.Abstr.

636.089 CS ISSN 0015-5748
CODEN: FVMCAW
FOLIA VETERINARIA. (Text and summaries in English) 1955. s-a. 20 Kcs. Vysoka Skola Veterinarska v Kosiciach, c/o Dir. Marta Prosbova, Central Library and Information Centre, College of Veterinary Medicine, Komenskeho 73, 041 81 Kosice, Czechoslovakia. TEL 321-11-15. FAX 42-95-767675. TELEX 77322. Ed. Dusan Magic. adv.; bk.rev.; abstr.; bibl.; index; cum.index; circ. 550. **Indexed:** Agri.Eng.Abstr., Biol.Abstr., Chem.Abstr., Dairy Sci.Abstr., Ind.Vet., Nutr.Abstr., Pig News & Info., Poult.Abstr., Protozool.Abstr., Small Anim.Abstr., Soyabean Abstr., Vet.Bull.
—BLDSC shelfmark: 3974.310000.

VETERINARY SCIENCE

636.089   CC   ISSN 1003-4331
FUJIAN XUMU SHOUYI/FUJIAN JOURNAL OF VETERINARY AND ANIMAL HUSBANDRY. (Text in Chinese; abstracts and table of contents in English) 1979. q. Y12. Fujina Xumu Shouyi Bianjibu, Pudang, Fuzhou Shijiao (Suburb), Fuzhou, Fujian 350013, People's Republic of China. (Dist. overseas by: Jiangsu Publications Import & Export Corp., 56 Gao Yun Ling, Nanjing, Jiangsu, P.R.C.)

636.089   FR
G T V BULLETIN. 1974. 6/yr. 700 F. Groupements Techniques Veterinaires, Syndicat National des Veterinaires Practiciens Francais (SNVPF), 10 Place Leon Blum, 75011 Paris, France. FAX 43-79-32-14. adv.; bk.rev.; circ. 3,900. **Indexed:** Agri.Eng.Abstr., Anim.Breed.Abstr., Biodet.Abstr., Chem.Abstr, Dairy Sci.Abstr., Ind.Vet., Protozool.Abstr., Vet.Bull.

GANAGRINCO; ganaderia-agricultura-industria-comercio. see *AGRICULTURE*

636.089   US
GRAYSON GRAM. 1984. q. free. Grayson Foundation, Inc., 1718 Alexandria Dr., Box 4158, Lexington, KY 40544. TEL 606-278-5243. Ed. Edward S. Ford. circ. 3,500.

636.089   IT   ISSN 0391-1918
GUIDA DI VETERINARIA E ZOOTECNIA; Italian directory of veterinary drugs, feed additives and manufacturers. 1966. biennial. L.93000 (foreign L.120000). Organizzazione Editoriale Medico-Farmaceutica, Via Edolo 42, Box 10434, 20125 Milan, Italy. (U.S. dist.: Drug Intelligence & Clinical Pharmacy, Box 42435, Cincinnati, OH 45242) Ed. Carlo Marini.

GUOWAI XUMU KEJI/FOREIGN ANIMAL HUSBANDRY SCIENCE AND TECHNOLOGY. see *AGRICULTURE — Poultry And Livestock*

HARYANA AGRICULTURAL UNIVERSITY. JOURNAL OF RESEARCH. see *AGRICULTURE*

636.089   II   ISSN 0033-4359
HARYANA VETERINARIAN. (Text in English) vol.10, 1971. s-a. Rs.20($12) Haryana Agricultural University, College of Veterinary Sciences, Hissar 125 004, Haryana, India. Ed. Dr. A.R. Rao. adv.; bk.rev.; abstr.; charts; illus.; stat.; circ. 500. **Indexed:** Dairy Sci.Abstr., Ind.Vet., Poult.Abstr., Vet.Bull.
Formerly: Punjab Veterinarian.

636.089   GR   ISSN 0257-2354
HELLENIC VETERINARY MEDICAL SOCIETY. BULLETIN/DELTIO TIS ELLINIKIS KTINIATRIKIS ETERIAS. (Text in Greek; summaries in English) 1924. q. Dr.2,000($30) Hellenic Veterinary Medical Society, P.O. Box 18281, 116 10 Athens, Greece. (Subscr. to: Olga Sabatakou, P.O. Box 3546, 102 10 Athens) Ed. Dr. A. Tsagarakis. adv.; bk.rev.; circ. 1,000. **Indexed:** Biodet.Abstr., Biol.Abstr., Ind.Vet., Vet.Bull.

636.089   UK   ISSN 0268-4276
HENSTON VETERINARY VADE MECUM (LARGE ANIMALS). 1984. a. £24 (foreign £27). Reed Business Publishing Group, Carew Division (Subsidiary of: Reed International PLC), Quadrant House, The Quadrant, Sutton, Surrey SM2 5AS, England. TEL 081-661-3500. Ed. Dr. J.M. Evans. adv.; index; circ. 5,000. (back issues avail.)
—BLDSC shelfmark: 4295.815500.
Description: For veterinary surgeons or similarly qualified personnel. Covers diseases, conditions, and symptoms of large animals, as well as therapeutic products.

636.089   UK   ISSN 0268-4268
HENSTON VETERINARY VADE MECUM (SMALL ANIMALS). 1982. a. £24 (foreign £27). Reed Business Publishing Group, Carew Division (Subsidiary of: Reed International PLC), Quadrant House, The Quadrant, Sutton, Surrey SM2 5AS, England. TEL 081-661-3500. Ed. Dr. J.M. Evans. adv.; index; circ. 5,000. (back issues avail.)
—BLDSC shelfmark: 4295.816000.
Description: For veterinary surgeons or similarly qualified personnel. Covers diseases, conditions, and symptoms of small animals, as well as therapeutic products.

HIMACHAL JOURNAL OF AGRICULTURAL RESEARCH. see *AGRICULTURE*

636.089   DK   ISSN 0105-1423
SF615
HISTORIA MEDICINAE VETERINARIAE. (Text and summaries in English, French and German) 1976. q. DKK 320($47) (typically set in Jan.). Historia Medicinae Veterinariae, Soendergade 39, 4130 Viby Sjaelland, Denmark. Ed. Ivan Katic. adv.; bk.rev.; illus.; index. cum.index; circ. 330. **Indexed:** Ind.Vet., Vet.Bull.
—BLDSC shelfmark: 4316.056500.

636.089   UK   ISSN 0263-841X
                         CODEN: IPRCDH
IN PRACTICE. bi-m. £29.50. British Veterinary Association, 7 Mansfield St., London W1M 0AT, England. TEL 01-636 6541. Ed. Edward Boden. adv.; circ. 10,000. **Indexed:** Anim.Breed.Abstr., Biol.Abstr., Biol.& Agr.Ind., Dairy Sci.Abstr., Dent.Ind., Excerp.Med., Food Sci.& Tech.Abstr., Ind.Med., Ind.Vet., Pig News & Info., Small Anim.Abstr., Vet.Bull.
—BLDSC shelfmark: 4372.411000.

636.089   II   ISSN 0019-5057
                         CODEN: IJAHA4
INDIAN JOURNAL OF ANIMAL HEALTH. (Text in English) 1960. s-a. $35. 61-4 Belgachia Rd., Calcutta 700037, India. Ed. Dilip K. Ray. adv.; bk.rev.; abstr.; bibl.; charts; illus.; stat.; circ. 2,000. **Indexed:** Anim.Breed.Abstr., Biol.Abstr., Chem.Abstr., Curr.Cont., Dairy Sci.Abstr., Food Sci.& Tech.Abstr., Helminthol.Abstr., Hort.Abstr., Ind.Vet., Nutr.Abstr., Protozool.Abstr., Rev.Plant Path., Vet.Bull.

INDIAN JOURNAL OF ANIMAL NUTRITION. see *AGRICULTURE — Poultry And Livestock*

INDIAN JOURNAL OF ANIMAL RESEARCH; half-yearly research journal of animal, food and zoological sciences. see *AGRICULTURE — Poultry And Livestock*

636.089   II
INDIAN JOURNAL OF ANIMAL SCIENCES. 1931. m. Rs.480($110) Indian Society of Agricultural Engineers, Satya Mansion, Flat No.s 305-306, Community Centre, Ranjit Nagar, New Delhi 100 008, India. Ed. R.R. Lokeshwar. adv.; bk.rev.; charts; illus.; index; circ. 2,000. (also avail. in microform from UMI; reprint service avail. from UMI) **Indexed:** Agrindex, Agroforest.Abstr., Anim.Breed.Abstr., Biol.Abstr., Biotech.Abstr., Chem.Abstr., Curr.Adv.Ecol.Sci., Curr.Adv.Genetics & Molec.Biol., Curr.Cont., Dairy Sci.Abstr., Excerp.Med., Field Crop Abstr., Food Sci.& Tech.Abstr., Forest.Abstr., Helminthol.Abstr., Herb.Abstr., Ind.Sci.Rev., Ind.Vet., INIS Atomind., Nutr.Abstr., Pig News & Info., Poult.Abstr., Protozool.Abstr., Rev.Appl.Entomol., Rev.Plant Path., Rice Abstr., Rural Recreat.Tour.Abstr., Sci.Cit.Ind, Small Anim.Abstr., Sorghum & Millets Abstr., Soyabean Abstr., Triticale Abstr., Vet.Bull., Weed Abstr., World Agri.Econ.& Rural Sociol.Abstr.
Formerly: Indian Journal of Veterinary Science and Animal Husbandry (ISSN 0019-5715)

636.089 611   II   ISSN 0971-1937
INDIAN JOURNAL OF VETERINARY ANATOMY. (Text and summaries in English) s-a. Rs.150($30) Indian Association of Veterinary Anatomists (IAVA), c/o R.P. Saigal, Secr., Dept. of Veterinary Anatomy and Histology, Punjab Agricultural University, Ludhiana 141 004, India. (Affiliate: World Association of Veterinary Anatomists) Ed. Dwarika Nath Sharma. adv.; bk.rev.
Description: Publishes the original research articles, short communications, reviews and comments on experimental and applied anatomy.

INDIAN POULTRY INDUSTRY YEARBOOK. see *AGRICULTURE — Poultry And Livestock*

INDIAN POULTRY REVIEW. see *AGRICULTURE — Poultry And Livestock*

636.089   II   ISSN 0019-6479
SF604   CODEN: IVEJAC
INDIAN VETERINARY JOURNAL; a monthly record of veterinary science. (Text in English) 1924. m. $30. Indian Veterinary Association, 7, Chamiers Rd., Madras 600 035, India. TEL 451006. Ed. Dr. V.S. Alwar. adv.; bk.rev.; abstr.; illus.; stat.; index; circ. 4,500. (reprint service avail. from ISI) **Indexed:** Anim.Breed.Abstr., Biol.Abstr., Biotech.Abstr., Chem.Abstr, Curr.Adv.Cancer Res., Curr.Adv.Ecol.Sci., Curr.Adv.Genetics & Molec.Biol., Curr.Cont., Dairy Sci.Abstr., Field Crop Abstr., Food Sci.& Tech.Abstr., Helminthol.Abstr., Herb.Abstr., Hort.Abstr., Ind.Med., Ind.Sci.Rev., Ind.Vet., Maize Abstr., Nutr.Abstr., Pig News & Info., Poult.Abstr., Protozool.Abstr., Rev.Appl.Entomol., Rev.Plant Path., Sci.Cit.Ind, Small Anim.Abstr., Soyabean Abstr., Trop.Oil Seeds Abstr., Vet.Bull.
—BLDSC shelfmark: 4431.000000.

590   II   ISSN 0250-5266
                         CODEN: IVMJDL
INDIAN VETERINARY MEDICAL JOURNAL. (Text in English; association news in English and Hindi) 1977. q. Rs.30($50) to individuals; institutions Rs.50; foreign $60 (typically set in Jan.). Uttar Pradesh Veterinary Association, c/o Institute of Veterinary Biologicals, Badshahbagh, Lucknow 226007, India. Ed. J.N.S. Yadava. adv.; bk.rev.; bibl.; circ. 2,500. **Indexed:** Anim.Breed.Abstr., Biol.Abstr., Chem.Abstr., Dairy Sci.Abstr., Helminthol.Abstr., Hort.Abstr., Ind.Vet., Poult.Abstr., Protozool.Abstr., Small Anim.Abstr., Vet.Bull.
Supersedes: U P Veterinary Journal.

636.089   II   ISSN 0304-7067
SF779.M78
INDIAN VETERINARY RESEARCH INSTITUTE. ANNUAL REPORT. (Text in English) 1947. a. exchange basis. Indian Veterinary Research Institute, Mukteswar-Kumaon, Izatnagar 243122, Uttar Pradesh, India. circ. 1,500. **Indexed:** Anim.Breed.Abstr.
Formerly: Muktesar, India. Imperial Veterinary Research Institute. Report.

636.089   CU   ISSN 0138-7235
INFORMACION EXPRESS. SERIE: VETERINARIA. 1977. 4/yr. $9 in N. America; S. America $11; Europe $13; others $18; or exchange basis. Centro de Informacion y Documentacion Agropecuario, Gaveta Postal 4149, Havana 4, Cuba. (Dist. by: Ediciones Cubanas, Obispo No. 527, Apdo. 605, Havana, Cuba) **Indexed:** Agrindex.

636.089   FR   ISSN 0246-2303
INSTITUT D'ELEVAGE ET DE MEDECINE VETERINAIRE DES PAYS TROPICAUX. RAPPORT D'ACTIVITE. 1954. a. Institut d'Elevage et de Medecine Veterinaire des Pays Tropicaux, 10 rue Pierre Curie, 94704 Maisons Alfort Cedex, France. Ed.Bd. bibl.; circ. 400. (back issues avail.) **Indexed:** Biol.Abstr.

636.089   BL   ISSN 0020-3653
INSTITUTO BIOLOGICO. ARQUIVOS. (Text in Portuguese; summaries in English) 1928. s-a. Cr.$1890($18) Instituto Biologico, Av. Rodrigues Alves 1252, C.P. 4185, Sao Paulo, Brazil. TEL 572-98-22. Ed. Manuel A.S.C. Portugal. illus.; index. (also avail. in microfilm) **Indexed:** Biol.Abstr., Chem.Abstr., Curr.Adv.Ecol.Sci., Dairy Sci.Abstr., Excerp.Med., Helminthol.Abstr., Hort.Abstr., Ind.Med., Ind.Vet., Rev.Appl.Entomol., Seed Abstr., Sorghum & Millets Abstr., Trop.Oil Seeds Abstr., Vet.Bull.
—BLDSC shelfmark: 1687.000000.

INSTITUTO COLOMBIANO AGROPECUARIO. REVISTA I C A. (Instituto Colombiano Agropecuario) see *AGRICULTURE*

636.089   BL
INSTITUTO DE PESQUISAS VETERINARIAS DESIDERIO FINAMOR. BOLETIM. (Text in Portuguese; summaries in English) 1972. a. exchange basis only. Instituto de Pesquisas Veterinarias Desiderio Finamor, Caixa Postal 2076, 90000 Porto Alegre, RS, Brazil. adv.; circ. 1,000. **Indexed:** Biol.Abstr., Dairy Sci.Abstr., Pig News & Info., Protozool.Abstr., Vet.Bull.

VETERINARY SCIENCE 4811

636.089　　　　PE　　ISSN 0020-3963
INSTITUTO DE ZOONOSIS E INVESTIGACION PECUARIA REVISTA. (Text in Spanish; summaries in English) 1950. s-a. donations. Ministerio de Salud, Instituto de Zoonosis e Investigacion Pecuaria, Bibliotecaria, Apartado 1128, Lima, Peru. bk.rev.; abstr.; circ. 1,000.
　Formerly: Instituto de Investigaciones Pecuarias Revista.

636.089 636.089　　　　SP
INSTITUTO DE ZOOTECNIA. FACULTAD DE VETERINARIA. CATALOGO DE PUBLICACIONES. 1961. a. exchange basis. Consejo Superior de Investigaciones Cientificas, Instituto de Zootecnia, Facultad de Veterinaria, Av. de Medina Azahara, 9, 14005 Cordoba, Spain. TEL 957-237589. FAX 957-413903. bibl.; circ. 700.

INSTITUTUL AGRONOMIC CLUJ-NAPOCA. BULETINUL. SERIA ZOOTEHNIE SI MEDICINA VETERINARA. see *AGRICULTURE — Poultry And Livestock*

INSTITUTUL AGRONOMIC ION IONESCU DE LA BRAD. LUCRARI STIINTIFICE, SERIA ZOOTECHNIE - MEDICINA VETERINARIA. see *AGRICULTURE — Poultry And Livestock*

636.089　　　　SW
INTERNATIONAL CONGRESS ON ANIMAL REPRODUCTION. PROCEEDINGS. 1948. quadrennial, 11th, 1988, Dublin. $60. International Standing Committee on International Congress on Animal Reproduction, c/o Prof. Stig Einarsson, Dept. of Obstetrics and Gynaecology, Swedish University of Agricultural Sciences, P.O. Box 7039, S-750 07 Uppsala, Sweden. circ. 2,000. **Indexed:** Biol.Abstr.
　Formerly: International Congress on Animal Reproduction and Artificial Insemination. Proceedings (ISSN 0074-4026)

636.089　　　　KE
INTERNATIONAL SCIENTIFIC COUNCIL FOR TRYPANOSOMIASIS RESEARCH AND CONTROL. (Text in English or French) 1951. biennial. price varies. (Interafrican Bureau for Animal Resources) Eleza Services Ltd., P.O. Box 30786, Nairobi, Kenya. Ed. K.M. Katondo. circ. 1,000. (back issues avail.)
Indexed: Biol.Abstr.

636.7　　　　US
INTERNATIONAL SYMPOSIUM ON CANINE HEARTWORM DISEASE. PROCEEDINGS. 1969. irreg., 2d, Jacksonville, 1971. $12. University of Florida, Institute of Food and Agricultural Sciences, Department of Veterinary Science, Gainesville, FL 32611. TEL 904-392-1733. Ed. Richard E. Bradley. bibl.; illus.

636.089　　　　US　　ISSN 0099-5851
IOWA STATE UNIVERSITY VETERINARIAN. 1938. s-a. $10 to non-members. (American Veterinary Medical Association, Iowa State University Chapter) Iowa State University, College of Veterinary Medicine, Ames, IA 50011. TEL 515-294-0867. Ed. J.H. Greve. adv.; bk.rev.; index; circ. 2,500. (also avail. in microfiche from UMI; reprint service avail. from UMI) **Indexed:** Dairy Sci.Abstr., Ind.Vet., Pig News & Info., Small Anim.Abstr., Vet.Bull.

636.089　　　　IE　　ISSN 0368-0762
　　　　　　　　　　CODEN: IVTJAJ
IRISH VETERINARY JOURNAL. vol.34, 1980. m. £6. (Irish Veterinary Association) Britmark Ltd., 7 Berkeley Rd., Phibsboro, Dublin 7, Ireland. TEL 01-685263. FAX 604345. Ed. Dr. P.J. Hartigan. adv.; bk.rev.; abstr.; circ. 1,300. **Indexed:** Agri.Eng.Abstr., Anim.Breed.Abstr., Chem.Abstr, Curr.Cont., Dairy Sci.Abstr., Excerp.Med., Helminthol.Abstr., Ind.Sci.Rev., Ind.Vet., INIS Atomind., Pig News & Info., Poult.Abstr., Protozool.Abstr., Rev.Plant Path., Sci.Cit.Ind, Small Anim.Abstr., Vet.Bull.
　—BLDSC shelfmark: 4575.000000.

636.089　　　　IE　　ISSN 0332-236X
IRISH VETERINARY NEWS. 1979. m. I£25. Jude Publications Ltd., 2-6 Tara St., Dublin 2, Ireland. Ed. Maria Farren. illus. **Indexed:** Dairy Sci.Abstr., Ind.Vet., Pig News & Info., Protozool.Abstr., Small Anim.Abstr., Vet.Bull.
　—BLDSC shelfmark: 4575.020000.

ISRAEL INSTITUTE OF ANIMAL SCIENCE. SCIENTIFIC ACTIVITIES. see *MEDICAL SCIENCES — Experimental Medicine, Laboratory Technique*

636.089　　　　IS　　ISSN 0334-9152
ISRAEL JOURNAL OF VETERINARY MEDICINE. (Text in English and Hebrew) 1943. q. $44. Israel Veterinary Medical Association, P.O. Box 3076, Rishon Le-Zion 75130, Israel. FAX 3-9681753. Ed.Bd. adv.; bk.rev.; charts; illus.; circ. 1,200. **Indexed:** Biol.Abstr., Biotech.Abstr., Chem.Abstr., Curr.Cont., Dairy Sci.Abstr., Excerp.Med., Food Sci.& Tech.Abstr., Helminthol.Abstr., Ind.Vet., Pig News & Info., Poult.Abstr., Protozool.Abstr., Rev.Appl.Entomol., Small Anim.Abstr., Soyabean Abstr., Vet.Bull.
　Formerly (until 1986): Refuah Veterinarith (ISSN 0034-3153)

ISTITUTO SUPERIORE DI SANITA. ANNALI. see *PUBLIC HEALTH AND SAFETY*

J N K V V NEWS. (Jawaharlal Nehru Krishi Vishwa Vidyalaya) see *AGRICULTURE*

636.089　　　　AU　　ISSN 0075-2606
JAHRBUCH FUER DEN OESTERREICHISCHEN TIERARZT. 1950. a. S.378. Alois Goeschl und Co., Trummelhofgasse 12, A-1190 Vienna, Austria. Ed. Hiltraud Lechner. adv.

636.089　　　　JA　　ISSN 0388-7421
SF917　　　　　　　　CODEN: DIKNAA
JAPAN. MINISTRY OF AGRICULTURE, FORESTRY AND FISHERIES. NATIONAL VETERINARY ASSAY LABORATORY. ANNUAL REPORT. (Text and summaries in English, Japanese) 1960. a. free. Ministry of Agriculture, Forestry and Fisheries, National Veterinary Assay Laboratory, 1-15-1, Tokura, Kokubunji, Tokyo 185, Japan. TEL 423-21-1841. FAX 423-21-1769. Ed.Bd. circ. 800. (back issues avail.) **Indexed:** Ind.Vet., Poult.Abstr., Vet.Bull.
　—BLDSC shelfmark: 1369.500000.

636　　　　JA　　ISSN 0388-2403
　　　　　　　　　　CODEN: NSKHD5
JAPAN. NATIONAL INSTITUTE OF ANIMAL HEALTH. BULLETIN/NORIN SUISAN-SHO KACHIKU EISEI SHIKENJO KENKYU HOKOKU. (Text in Japanese; summaries in European languages) 1918. s-a. exchange basis. Norinsuisan-sho, Kachiku Eisei Shikenjo - Ministry of Agriculture, Forestry and Fisheries, National Institute of Animal Health, 1-1 Kannondai 3-chome, Tsukuba-shi, Ibaraki-ken 305, Japan. FAX 02975-6-7880. Ed. Tomoo Itabisashi. circ. 2,050. **Indexed:** Ind.Vet.
　—BLDSC shelfmark: 2640.030000.

JAPANESE JOURNAL OF SANITARY ZOOLOGY/EISEI DOBUTSU. see *BIOLOGY — Zoology*

636.089　　　　JA　　ISSN 0047-1917
　　　　　　　　　　CODEN: JJVRAE
JAPANESE JOURNAL OF VETERINARY RESEARCH. (Text in English and European languages) 1954. q. exchange basis. Hokkaido University, Faculty of Veterinary Medicine - Hokkaido Daigaku Juigakubu, Nishi-9-chome, Kita-18-jo, Sapporo 060, Japan. FAX 011-717-7569. Ed. Masao Kamiga. bk.rev.; illus.; circ. 650. (also avail. in microfilm; microfiche) **Indexed:** Anim.Breed.Abstr., Biol.Abstr., Chem.Abstr., Curr.Cont., Dairy Sci.Abstr., Excerp.Med., Helminthol.Abstr., Ind.Med., Ind.Sci.Rev., Ind.Vet., Nutr.Abstr., Pig News & Info., Protozool.Abstr., Sci.Cit.Ind., Vet.Bull.
　—BLDSC shelfmark: 4659.090000.
　Formerly: Juigaku Kenkyu.

636.089　　　　UK　　ISSN 0021-9975
　　　　　　　　　　CODEN: JCVPAR
JOURNAL OF COMPARATIVE PATHOLOGY. 1888. 8/yr (2 vols./yr.). $326. Academic Press Ltd., 24-28 Oval Rd., London NW1 7DX, England. TEL 071-267-4466. FAX 071-482-2293. TELEX 25775 ACPRES G. Ed. E.J.H. Ford. adv.; bibl.; charts; illus.; index. (reprint service avail. from KTO) **Indexed:** Anim.Breed.Abstr., Biol.Abstr., Biotech.Abstr., Chem.Abstr., Curr.Cont., Dairy Sci.Abstr., Dent.Ind., Excerp.Med., Helminthol.Abstr., Ind.Med., Ind.Sci.Rev., Ind.Vet., Nutr.Abstr., Pig News & Info., Poult.Abstr., Protozool.Abstr., Rev.Plant Path., Sci.Cit.Ind., Small Anim.Abstr., Soyabean Abstr., Vet.Bull.
　—BLDSC shelfmark: 4962.800000.
　Description: Directed to workers in veterinary and medical science who investigate dieseases of all vertebrate animals, including domesticated zoo, wild and marine species, and man.

636.089　　　　US　　ISSN 0737-0806
JOURNAL OF EQUINE VETERINARY SCIENCE. 1981. bi-m. $40 to individuals; institutions $60; foreign $60. William E. Jones, Ed. & Pub., Box 1209, Wildomar, CA 92395. TEL 714-678-1889. adv.; bk.rev.; circ. 3,175. **Indexed:** Anim.Breed.Abstr., Dairy Sci.Abstr., Ind.Vet., Vet.Bull.
　—BLDSC shelfmark: 4979.492000.
　Incorporates: Equine Sportsmedicine News.

636.089　　　　JA
JOURNAL OF REPRODUCTION AND DEVELOPMENT. (Text in English) 1955. q. 6000 Yen. Japanese Society of Animal Reproduction, c/o Dept. of Veterinary Physiology, University of Tokyo, 1-1-1 Yayoi, Bunkyo-ku, Tokyo 113, Japan. TEL 81-3-3812-2111. FAX 81-3-3815-4266. Ed. Dr. Michio Takahashi. adv.; bk.rev. (back issues avail.) **Indexed:** Anim.Breed.Abstr., Dairy Sci.Abstr., Ind.Vet., INIS Atomind., Pig News & Info., Vet.Bull.
　Formerly (until Feb. 1992): Japanese Journal of Animal Reproduction (ISSN 0385-9932)

636.089　　　　UK　　ISSN 0022-4510
　　　　　　　　　　CODEN: JAPRAN
JOURNAL OF SMALL ANIMAL PRACTICE. 1960. m. £88($220) British Veterinary Association, 7 Mansfield St., London W1M OAT, England. TEL 01-637 0620. Ed. W.D Taverner. adv.; bk.rev.; bibl.; charts; illus.; index; circ. 3,500. (back issues avail.; reprint service avail. from ISI) **Indexed:** Anim.Breed.Abstr., Biol.Abstr., Biotech.Abstr., Chem.Abstr, Curr.Adv.Ecol.Sci., Curr.Cont., Dairy Sci.Abstr., Excerp.Med., Helminthol.Abstr., Ind.Med., Ind.Sci.Rev., Ind.Vet., Protozool.Abstr., Rev.Plant Path., Rice Abstr., Small Anim.Abstr., Vet.Bull.
　—BLDSC shelfmark: 5064.700000.

636.089　　　　US
▼**JOURNAL OF SMALL EXOTIC ANIMAL MEDICINE.** 1991. q. $50. Kathy Lyon, Ed. & Pub., 11552 Hartsook St., Box 70, N. Hollywood, CA 91603. TEL 818-769-6111. FAX 818-766-0046.

636.089　　　　II　　ISSN 0971-0701
　　　　　　　　　　CODEN: KJVSAS
JOURNAL OF VETERINARY AND ANIMAL SCIENCES. 1970. s-a. Rs.40($25) (effective 1990). Kerala Agricultural University, Faculty of Veterinary and Animal Sciences, Trichur, Kerala, India. TELEX 887-268 KAU IN. Ed. A. Rajan. circ. 1,000. **Indexed:** Anim.Breed.Abstr., Biol.Abstr., Chem.Abstr., Dairy Sci.Abstr., Helminthol.Abstr., Ind.Vet., Nutr.Abstr., Rural Ext.Educ.& Tr.Abstr., Rural Recreat.Tour.Abstr., Vet.Bull., World Agri.Econ.& Rural Sociol.Abstr.
　Formerly (until vol.20, 1991): Kerala Journal of Veterinary Science (ISSN 0374-8774)

636.087　　　　US　　ISSN 0898-7564
JOURNAL OF VETERINARY DENTISTRY. (Includes: Animal Health Technician Dental Newsletter) 1984. q. $30. American Veterinary Dental Society, c/o Dr. Colin E. Harvey, 3850 Spruce St., Philadelphia, PA 19104. Ed. Dr. Jean Hawkins.
　Formerly, until 1987: Veterinary Dentistry.
　Description: Covers crowns and restorations, bleaching, periodontal disease, oral surgery and root canals.

636.089　　　　US　　ISSN 1040-6387
JOURNAL OF VETERINARY DIAGNOSTIC INVESTIGATION. 1989. q. $50 (foreign $60). American Association of Veterinary Laboratory Diagnosticians, c/o H.S. Gosser, Sec.-Treas., Box 6023, Columbia, MO 65205. TEL 314-882-6811. FAX 314-882-1411. Ed. Lenn R. Harrison. adv.
　—BLDSC shelfmark: 5072.360000.
　Description: Covers molecular biology, immunology, microbiology, clinical pathology, parasitology, anatomical pathology, toxicology, computer science and public health.

636.089 617.1　　　US　　ISSN 1056-6392
▼**JOURNAL OF VETERINARY EMERGENCY AND CRITICAL CARE.** 1991. 2/yr. $22. Veterinary Practice Publishing Co., 7 Ashley Ave. S., Santa Barbara, CA 93103-9989. TEL 805-965-1028. FAX 805-965-0722. (Subscr. addr.: Box 4457, Santa Barbara, CA 93140-4457) Ed. Dr. William W. Muir. circ. 700.
　Description: Covers clinical and nonclinical problems and solutions, case reports and guest editorials.

VETERINARY SCIENCE

636.089   US   ISSN 0891-6640
CODEN: JVIMEM
JOURNAL OF VETERINARY INTERNAL MEDICINE. 1987. bi-m. $40 to individuals (foreign $55); institutions $55 (foreign $65). (American College of Veterinary Internal Medicine) J.B. Lippincott Co., E. Washington Sq., Philadelphia, PA 19105. TEL 215-238-4200. Ed. Dr. Alfred M. Legendre. illus.; index; circ. 6,000. (also avail. in microform from UMI) **Indexed:** Curr.Cont., Ind.Med., Ind.Vet., Small Anim.Abstr., Vet.Bull.
—BLDSC shelfmark: 5072.365000.
Description: Covers small and large animal internal medicine, cardiology, neurology, pathophysiology and the disease process.
Refereed Serial

636.089 378   US   ISSN 0748-321X
NOT IN LC
JOURNAL OF VETERINARY MEDICAL EDUCATION. 1974. 2/yr. $20 to individuals; institutions and foreign $30. Association of American Veterinary Medical Colleges, c/o Richard B. Talbot, Ed., Virginia-Maryland Regional College of Veterinary Medicine, Virginia Polytechnic Institute and State University, Blacksburg, VA 24061.
TEL 703-231-7666. adv.; bk.rev.; circ. 3,400. (also avail. in microform from UMI; reprint service avail. from UMI) **Indexed:** C.I.J.E., Cont.Pg.Educ.
—BLDSC shelfmark: 5072.370000.

636.089   JA   ISSN 0916-7250
CODEN: JVMSEQ
JOURNAL OF VETERINARY MEDICAL SCIENCE. (Text in English) 1939. 6/yr. Japanese Society of Veterinary Science - Nihon Juigakkai, c/o Dept. of Veterinary Pharmacology, Faculty of Agriculture, University of Tokyo, 1-1-1 Yayoi, Bunkyo-ku, Tokyo 113, Japan. (Overseas dist. by: Maruzen Co., Ltd., Maruzen Bldg. No.3 Nihonbashi, Chuo-ku, Tokyo 103, Japan) Ed. Hideaki Karaki. adv.; circ. 5,000. **Indexed:** Anim.Breed.Abstr., Biol.Abstr., Biotech.Abstr., Chem.Abstr., Curr.Cont., Dairy Sci.Abstr., Dent.Ind., Helminthol.Abstr., Ind.Med., Ind.Vet., Nutr.Abstr., Pig News & Info., Poult.Abstr., Protozool.Abstr., Sci.Cit.Ind., Small Anim.Abstr., Soils & Fert., Vet.Bull., Weed Abstr.
—BLDSC shelfmark: 5072.375000.
Formerly (until 1991): Japanese Journal of Veterinary Science (ISSN 0021-5295)
Description: International journal on basic and applied veterinary medical sciences

636.089   GW   ISSN 0931-184X
JOURNAL OF VETERINARY MEDICINE. SERIES A; animal physiology, pathology, and clinical veterinary medicine. (Supplement: Advances in Veterinary Medicine/Fortschritte der Veterinaermedizin) (Text in English, French, German or Spanish; summaries in each language) 1953. m. (10/yr.).
DM.1098($629) Verlag Paul Parey (Berlin), Seelbuschring 9-17, 1000 Berlin 42, Germany. TEL 030-70784-0. FAX 030-70784199. (U.S. address: Paul Parey Scientific Publishers, 150 E. 27th St., No.1A, New York, NY 10016) Ed.Bd. bk.rev.; illus.; index. cum.index. (back issues avail.) **Indexed:** Anim.Breed.Abstr., Biol.Abstr., Biotech.Abstr., Chem.Abstr., Curr.Adv.Biochem., Curr.Adv.Ecol.Sci., Curr.Cont., Dairy Sci.Abstr., Food Sci.& Tech.Abstr., Helminthol.Abstr., Ind.Med., Ind.Vet., Nutr.Abstr., Pig News & Info., Poult.Abstr., Sci.Cit.Ind., Small Anim.Abstr., Triticale Abstr., Vet.Bull.
—BLDSC shelfmark: 5072.385000.
Formerly: Zentralblatt fuer Veterinaermedizin. Series A (ISSN 0300-8711); Supersedes in part (1953-1969): Zentralblatt fuer Veterinaermedizin (ISSN 0044-4294)

636.089   GW   ISSN 0931-1793
JOURNAL OF VETERINARY MEDICINE. SERIES B; infectious diseases, immunology, fovel hygiene, veterinary, public health. (Supplement: Advances in Veterinary Medicine) (Text in English, French, German or Spanish; summaries in English, French, German and Spanish) 1963. 10/yr.
DM.1098($629) Verlag Paul Parey (Berlin), Seelbuschring 9-17, 1000 Berlin 42, Germany. TEL 030-70784-0. FAX 030-70784199. (U.S. address: Paul Parey Scientific Publishers, 150 E. 27th St., No.1A, New York, NY 10016) bk.rev.; illus.; stat.; index; cum.index. (back issues avail.) **Indexed:** Biol.Abstr., Biotech.Abstr., Chem.Abstr., Curr.Adv.Ecol.Sci., Curr.Cont., Dairy Sci.Abstr., Food Sci.& Tech.Abstr., Helminthol.Abstr., Ind.Med., Ind.Vet., Nutr.Abstr., Pig News & Info., Poult.Abstr., Protozool.Abstr., Rev.Plant Path., Sci.Cit.Ind., Vet.Bull.
—BLDSC shelfmark: 5072.386000.
Formerly: Zentralblatt fuer Veterinaermedizin. Series B (ISSN 0514-7166); Supersedes in part (1953-1963): Zentralblatt fuer Veterinaermedizin (ISSN 0044-4294)

JOURNAL OF VETERINARY PHARMACOLOGY AND THERAPEUTICS. see *PHARMACY AND PHARMACOLOGY*

636.089   US   ISSN 0090-3558
CODEN: JWIDAW
JOURNAL OF WILDLIFE DISEASES. 1965. q. $80. Wildlife Disease Association, Inc., 224 S.E. 16th St., Box 886, Ames, IA 50010. TEL 515-233-1931. adv.; bk.rev.; abstr.; charts; illus.; index; circ. 1,350. (back issues avail.) **Indexed:** Bio-Contr.News & Info., Biol.Abstr., Biol.Dig., Chem.Abstr., Curr.Adv.Ecol.Sci., Curr.Cont., Dairy Sci.Abstr., Dent.Ind., Environ.Per.Bibl., Helminthol.Abstr., Ind.Med., Ind.Sci.Rev., Ind.Vet., INIS Atomind., Ocean.Abstr., Pig News & Info., Pollut.Abstr., Poult.Abstr., Protozool.Abstr., Rev.Appl.Entomol., Rev.Plant Path., Small Anim.Abstr., Soils & Fert., Vet.Bull., Wild Life Rev.
—BLDSC shelfmark: 5072.620000.
Former titles: Wildlife Disease Association. Journal (ISSN 0043-5473); Wildlife Disease Association. Bulletin.
Refereed Serial

636   US   ISSN 1042-7260
CODEN: JZWMEI
JOURNAL OF ZOO AND WILDLIFE MEDICINE. 1971. q. $100 (foreign $110). American Association of Zoo Veterinarians, 3400 Girard Ave., Philadelphia, PA 19104-1196. TEL 215-387-9094.
FAX 215-387-8733. Ed. James Carpenter. adv.; bk.rev.; charts; illus.; stat.; cum.index: 1970-1987; circ. 1,000. (processed; back issues avail.) **Indexed:** Curr.Adv.Ecol.Sci., Curr.Cont., Dairy Sci.Abstr., Helminthol.Abstr., Ind.Sci.Rev., Ind.Vet., Small Anim.Abstr., Vet.Bull.
—BLDSC shelfmark: 5072.765000.
Formerly: Journal of Zoo Animal Medicine (ISSN 0093-4526)
Description: Publishes original research findings and clinical observations as well as case reports in the field of veterinary medicine dealing with captive and free-ranging wild animals.
Refereed Serial

636.089   MY
JURNAL VETERINAR MALAYSIA. 1989. s-a. Veterinary Association of Malaysia (VAM), Faculty of Veterinary Medicine and Animal Science, Universiti Pertanian Malaysia, 43400 UPM, Serdang, Selangor, Malaysia. TEL 03-9486101-110. FAX 03-9482507. TELEX UNIPER-MA-37454. Ed. Dr. Tan Hock Seng. abstr.
Description: Publishes research papers on various aspects of veterinary medicine and animal science. Includes articles and short communications.

636.089   KE
KENYA AGRICULTURAL RESEARCH INSTITUTE. VETERINARY RESEARCH DEPARTMENT. ANNUAL REPORT. (Text in English) 1977. a. Kenya Agricultural Research Institute, Box 30148, Nairobi, Kenya. **Indexed:** Field Crop Abstr., Herb.Abstr., Rev.Appl.Entomol., Weed Abstr.

636.089   KE
KENYA VETERINARIAN. (Text in English) 1977. s-a. $10. Kenya Veterinary Association, Box 29089, Nairobi, Kenya. Ed. Dr. Thomas T. Dolan. adv.; circ. 500. **Indexed:** Ind.Vet., Soils & Fert., Vet.Bull.

636.089   GW   ISSN 0023-2076
KLEINTIER-PRAXIS; Archiv fuer kleine Haus- und Nutztiere sowie Laboratoriums- und Zoo-Tiere. (Text in German; summaries in English) 1956. 12/yr. DM.165 (foreign DM.180). (World Small Animal Veterinary Association, Deutsche Gruppe) Verlag M. und H. Schaper, Kalandstr. 4, Postfach 1642, 3220 Alfeld, Germany. adv.; bk.rev.; bibl.; charts; illus.; index.; circ. 3,500. **Indexed:** Anim.Breed.Abstr., Biol.Abstr., Biotech.Abstr., Chem.Abstr., Curr.Adv.Ecol.Sci., Curr.Cont., Dairy Sci.Abstr., Helminthol.Abstr., Ind.Sci.Rev., Ind.Vet., Nutr.Abstr., Rev.Plant Path., Small Anim.Abstr., Soils & Fert., Vet.Bull.
—BLDSC shelfmark: 5099.121000.

KONGELIGE VETERINAER- OG LANDBOHOEJSKOLE. HAANDBOG. see *AGRICULTURE*

636.089 630   DK   ISSN 0106-8261
KONGELIGE VETERINAER OG LANDBOHOEJSKOLE. SKOVBRUGINSTITUTET. MEDDELELSER. 1975. irreg., no.17, 1984. Kongelige Veterinaer og Landbohoejskole, Skovbruginstitutet - Royal Veterinary and Agricultural University, Dept. of Forestry, Thorvaldsensvej 57, 1871 Frederiksberg C, Denmark. illus.

LARGE ANIMAL VETERINARIAN. see *AGRICULTURE — Poultry And Livestock*

636.089   US
▼**LARGE ANIMAL VETERINARY REPORT.** 1990. m. $48 to individuals; institutions $60; foreign $60. William E. Jones, Ed. & Pub., Box 1209, Wildomar, CA 92395. TEL 714-678-1083.

LIVESTOCK ADVISER; an English monthly dedicated to improve the animal wealth of India. see *AGRICULTURE — Poultry And Livestock*

LLAMAS MAGAZINE; information for Camelid lovers everywhere. see *BIOLOGY — Zoology*

636.089   HU   ISSN 0025-004X
CODEN: MGALA5
MAGYAR ALLATORVOSOK LAPJA/JOURNAL OF HUNGARIAN VETERINARY SCIENCE. (Text in Hungarian; table of contents and summaries in English, German and Russian) 1946. m. 1440 Ft.($42) (Mezogazdasagi es Elelmezesugyi Miniszterium) Agroinform, Atilla ut 93, 1253, 1021 Budapest 1, Hungary. TEL 156-8211. FAX 156-8846. TELEX 224717 AGINF H. (Subscr. to: Kultura, Box 149, H-1389 Budapest, Hungary) Ed. Ferenc Hollo. adv.; bk.rev.; abstr.; bibl.; charts; illus.; index; circ. 4,300. **Indexed:** Agri.Eng.Abstr., Anim.Breed.Abstr., Biol.Abstr., Biotech.Abstr., Chem.Abstr., Curr.Adv.Ecol.Sci., Curr.Cont., Dairy Sci.Abstr., Food Sci.& Tech.Abstr., Helminthol.Abstr., Ind.Sci.Rev., Ind.Vet., INIS Atomind., Maize Abstr., Nutr.Abstr., Pig News & Info., Poult.Abstr., Protozool.Abstr., Rev.Plant Path., Small Anim.Abstr., Soyabean Abstr., Vet.Bull.
—BLDSC shelfmark: 5340.300000.

636.089   MW   ISSN 0076-3365
MALAWI. DEPARTMENT OF VETERINARY SERVICES AND ANIMAL INDUSTRY. ANNUAL REPORT. a. K.1.50. Government Printer, P.O. Box 37, Zomba, Malawi. **Indexed:** Anim.Breed.Abstr., Field Crop Abstr., Herb.Abstr.

636.089   CN   ISSN 0225-9591
CODEN: MVEQDC
MEDECIN VETERINAIRE DU QUEBEC. (Text in French) 1971. q. Can.$30($40) Corporation Professionelle des Medecins Veterinaires du Quebec - Corporation of Veterinarians of Quebec, 795, av. du Palais, Ste. 200, Saint Hyacinthe, Que. J2S 5C6, Canada. TEL 514-774-1423. FAX 514-774-7635. Ed. Guy-Pierre Martineau. adv.; circ. 2,050. **Indexed:** Biol.Abstr., Dairy Sci.Abstr., Helminthol.Abstr., Ind.Vet., Pt.de Rep. (1983-), Small Anim.Abstr., Vet.Bull.
—BLDSC shelfmark: 5487.670000.

636.089   CU
MEDIVET. s-m. Ministerio de la Agricultura, Instituto de Medicina Veterinaria, Paseo 604th, 25 y 27 Valdado, Havana 4, Cuba.

VETERINARY SCIENCE

636.089   PL   ISSN 0025-8628
CODEN: MDWTAG
MEDYCYNA WETERYNARYJNA. (Text in Polish; summaries in English) 1945. m. $75. (Polskie Towarzystwo Nauk Weterynaryjnych - Polish Society of Veterinary Sciences) Medycyna Weterynaryjna - Redakcja, Ul. Akademicka 12, 20-033 Lublin, Poland. TEL 48-81-329-12. FAX 48-81-335-49. TELEX 643176 ARPL. Ed. Prof. Dr. Edmund Prost. adv.; bk.rev.; abstr.; bibl.; charts; illus.; mkt.; index. cum.index; circ. 3,300. **Indexed:** Agri.Eng.Abstr., Anim.Breed.Abstr., Biol.Abstr., Chem.Abstr., Dairy Sci.Abstr., Excerp.Med., Food Sci.& Tech.Abstr., Helminthol.Abstr., Ind.Vet., INIS Atomind., Nutr.Abstr., Pig News & Info., Poult.Abstr., Protozool.Abstr., Rev.Appl.Entomol., Rev.Plant Path., Small Anim.Abstr., Vet.Bull.
—BLDSC shelfmark: 5536.050000.
Description: Devoted to the problems of veterinary science and practice.

636.089   US   ISSN 0076-6542
SF748
MERCK VETERINARY MANUAL: A HANDBOOK OF DIAGNOSIS AND THERAPY FOR THE VETERINARIAN. 1955. irreg., 6th ed., 1986. $19. Merck and Co., Inc., Attn: Michele Stotz, FTA-230, Box 2000, Rahway, NJ 07065. TEL 201-855-4558. Ed. Clarence Fraser.

636.089 616.01   DK
MIKROBIOLOGI-NYT. 1983. q. $10. Mikrobiologisk Gruppe-Levnedsmiddelselskabet, Ingenioerhuset, Vester Farimagsgade 29, DK-1606 Copenhagen V, Denmark. FAX 02-88-4774. TELEX 37529 DTHDIA. Ed. Lone Gram. adv.; bk.rev. (looseleaf format)
Formerly: Hurtigmetode-nyt (ISSN 0109-0763)

636.089   US   ISSN 0362-8140
CODEN: MVPRAX
MODERN VETERINARY PRACTICE. 1920. 12/yr. $42 (Canada $49; foreign $66). American Veterinary Publications, Inc., 5782 Thornwood Dr., Goleta, CA 93117-3896. TEL 805-967-5988. Ed. Dr. P.W. Pratt. adv.; bk.rev.; bibl.; charts; illus.; circ. 3,000. **Indexed:** Anim.Breed.Abstr., Biol.Abstr., Biotech.Abstr., Chem.Abstr., Curr.Adv.Ecol.Sci., Curr.Cont., Dairy Sci.Abstr., Dent.Ind., Helminthol.Abstr., Ind.Med., Ind.Sci.Rev., Ind.Vet., Poult.Abstr., Protozool.Abstr., Rev.Plant Path., Small Anim.Abstr., Vet.Bull.
—BLDSC shelfmark: 5900.020000.
Incorporates (1983-1986): Veterinary Computing (ISSN 8755-0946)
Description: Abstracts of clinically oriented articles from worldwide veterinary literature.

636.089   GW   ISSN 0026-9263
SF603   CODEN: MVMZA8
MONATSHEFTE FUER VETERINAERMEDIZIN. (Text in German; summaries in English and German) 1946. s-m. $120. Gustav Fischer Verlag Jena, Villengang 2, Postfach 176, 6900 Jena, Germany. TEL 03778-27332. FAX 03778-22638. TELEX 18069-588676. Eds. O. Dietz, E. Wiesner. adv.; bk.rev.; abstr.; bibl.; charts; illus.; index. (reprint service avail. from ISI) **Indexed:** Agri.Eng.Abstr., Anim.Breed.Abstr., Bio-Contr.News & Info., Biol.Abstr., Biotech.Abstr., Chem.Abstr., Curr.Adv.Ecol.Sci., Curr.Cont., Dairy Sci.Abstr., Excerp.Med., Field Crop Abstr., Food Sci.& Tech.Abstr., Helminthol.Abstr., Herb.Abstr., Ind.Sci.Rev., Ind.Vet., Nutr.Abstr., Pig News & Info., Poult.Abstr., Protozool.Abstr., Ref.Zh., Rev.Plant Path., Small Anim.Abstr., Soils & Fert., Soyabean Abstr., Vet.Bull., World Agri.Econ.& Rural Sociol.Abstr.
—BLDSC shelfmark: 5906.000000.

636.089 574.524   PL   ISSN 0540-6722
MONOGRAFIE PARAZYTOLOGICZNE. 1959. irreg., vol.10, 1985. price varies. Polskie Towarzystwo Parazytologiczne, Norwida 29, 50-375 Wroclaw, Poland. (Distb. by: Ars Polona, Krakowskie Przedmiescie 7, 00-068 Warsaw, Poland) Ed. Leszek Grzywinski. bibl.; illus.; circ. 400. (back issues avail.) **Indexed:** Biol.Abstr.

NAUKA U PRAKSI. see AGRICULTURE

636.089   US   ISSN 0277-3015
NEW METHODS; the journal of animal health technology. 1977-1984 (Jan.); resumed Nov. 1984. irreg. $29. New Methods Co., Box 22605, San Francisco, CA 94122-0605. TEL 415-664-3469. Ed. Ronald S. Lippert. adv.; bk.rev.; bibl.; charts; illus.; index; circ. 6,000 (controlled). (back issues avail.)
Formerly: Methods: The Journal of Animal Health Technology.
Description: Information source that represents basic interests in the animal health profession.

636.089   NZ   ISSN 0048-0169
CODEN: NEZTAF
NEW ZEALAND VETERINARY JOURNAL. 1952. q. NZ.$160 (foreign NZ.$175). New Zealand Veterinary Association, P.O. Box 27-499, Wellington, New Zealand. TEL 64-4-384-3632. FAX 64-4-384-3631. Ed. A. W. Keber. adv.; bk.rev.; illus.; circ. 1,750. **Indexed:** Anim.Breed.Abstr., Biol.Abstr., Biotech.Abstr., Cadscan, Chem.Abstr., Curr.Adv.Ecol.Sci., Curr.Cont., Dairy Sci.Abstr., Excerp.Med., Field Crop Abstr., Helminthol.Abstr., Herb.Abstr., Ind.Med., Ind.Sci.Rev., Ind.Vet., Lead Abstr., Maize Abstr., Nutr.Abstr., Pig News & Info., Poult.Abstr., Protozool.Abstr., Rev.Appl.Entomol., Rev.Plant Path., Small Anim.Abstr., Soils & Fert., Vet.Bull., Zincscan.
—BLDSC shelfmark: 6099.900000.
Description: Publishes original research and clinical observations in all aspects of veterinary science.
Refereed Serial

NIGERIA. NATIONAL ANIMAL PRODUCTION RESEARCH INSTITUTE. JOURNAL. see AGRICULTURE — Poultry And Livestock

630 636.089   JA   ISSN 0373-8361
CODEN: NJDKAF
NIPPON JUI CHIKUSAN DAIGAKU KENKYU HOKOKU/NIPPON VETERINARY AND ANIMAL SCIENCE UNIVERSITY. BULLETIN. (Text in English or Japanese; summaries in English) 1953. a. 2000 Yen or exchange basis. Nippon Jui Chikusan Daigaku - Nippon Veterinary and Animal Science University, 1-7-1 Kyonan-cho, Musashino-shi, Tokyo 180, Japan. TEL 422-31-4151. FAX 422-33-2035. Ed.Bd. circ. 500 (controlled). (reprint service avail.) **Indexed:** Anim.Breed.Abstr., Biol.Abstr., Dairy Sci.Abstr., Helminthol.Abstr., Ind.Vet., Protozool.Abstr., Vet.Bull.
Formerly: Nippon Jui Chikusan Daigaku Kiyo (ISSN 0078-0839)

636.089   NO   ISSN 0078-6721
NORGES VETERINAERHOEGSKOLE. PUBLIKASJONER/NORWEGIAN COLLEGE OF VETERINARY MEDICINE. PUBLICATIONS. 1981. a. free or on exchange basis. Norges Veterinaerhoegskole, P.O. Box 8146 Dep., 0033 Oslo 1, Norway. circ. 1,500.

636.089   NO   ISSN 0029-2273
CODEN: NOVDAH
NORSK VETERINAERTIDSSKRIFT. 1888. m. NOK 540 (free to qualified personnel). Norske Veterinaerforening, Sognsveien 4, Oslo 4, Norway. TEL 02-567650. FAX 02-690450. Ed. Ulf Erik Gustavsen. adv.; bk.rev.; charts; illus.; index; circ. 1,956. (reprint service avail.) **Indexed:** Anim.Breed.Abstr., Biol.Abstr., Biotech.Abstr., Dairy Sci.Abstr., Food Sci.& Tech.Abstr., Helminthol.Abstr., Ind.Vet., Landwirt.Zentralbl., Pig News & Info., Protozool.Abstr., Ref.Zh., Small Anim.Abstr., Vet.Bull.
Description: Prints information of interest to veterinarians and others with interest in public health, hygiene and meat control.

636.089 578   FR   ISSN 0300-9823
SF781   CODEN: OTEBA6
O.I.E. BULLETIN. (Text in English, French, Spanish) m. 490 F.($88) (effective 1992). Office International des Epizooties, 12 rue de Prony, 75017 Paris, France. TEL 44-15-18-88. FAX 42-67-09-87. TELEX EPIZOTI 642 285 F. (U.S. Subscr. to: Scientific, Medical Publications of France, 100 East 42nd St., Ste 1002, New York, NY 10017. TEL 212-983-6278) Ed. J. Blancon. **Indexed:** Ind.Vet., Vet.Bull.
—BLDSC shelfmark: 2663.000000.
Description: Presents monthly evolution of the major epizootic diseases throughout the world.

636.089 578   FR   ISSN 0253-1933
SF781   CODEN: RTOEDX
O.I.E. REVUE SCIENTIFIQUE ET TECHNIQUE/O.I.E. SCIENTIFIC AND TECHNICAL REVIEW. (Text in English, French or Spanish; summaries in English, French, Spanish) 1982. q. 590 F.($108) (effective 1992). Office International des Epizooties, 12 rue de Prony, 75017 Paris, France. TEL 44-15-18-88. FAX 42-67-09-87. TELEX EPIZOTI 642 285 F. (U.S. Subscr. to: Scientific, Medical Publications of France, 100 East 42nd St., Ste. 1002, New York, NY 10017. TEL 212-983-6278) Ed. J. Blancon. **Indexed:** Bio-Contr.News & Info., Dairy Sci.Abstr., Ind.Vet., Pig News & Info., Protozool.Abstr., Small Anim.Abstr., Vet.Bull.
—BLDSC shelfmark: 7950.029000.
Description: Promotes experimental or other research work on diagnosis and control of contagious diseases of livestock. Also circulates all facts and documents of general interest to the world medical and veterinary scientific communities.

636.089   IT   ISSN 0392-1913
OBIETTIVI E DOCUMENTI VETERINARI. Short title: O D V. 1980. m. L.77000 (foreign L.110000). Edagricole S.p.A., Via Emilia Levante 31, 40139 Bologna, Italy. TEL 051-492211. FAX 051-493660. Ed. Giovanni Ballarini. circ. 14,830. **Indexed:** Dairy Sci.Abstr., Ind.Vet., Protozool.Abstr., Small Anim.Abstr., Vet.Bull.
—BLDSC shelfmark: 6196.955000.
Description: Covers the veterinary sciences. Provides professional training information.

636.089   AU   ISSN 0048-1475
OESTERREICHISCHE TIERAERZTEZEITUNG. 1949. m. S.430. Bundeskammer der Tieraerzte Oesterreichs, Biberstr. 22, A-1010 Vienna, Austria. Ed. Dr. Guenther Gebauer. adv.; bk.rev.; circ. 2,100. **Indexed:** Ind.Vet., Pig News & Info., Vet.Bull.

636.089   AU   ISSN 0029-9766
OESTERREICHISCHER KLEINTIERZUECHTER; Fachblatt fuer die gesamte Kleintierzucht. 1946. m. S.250. Rassezuchtverband Oesterreichischer Kleintierzuechter, Postfach 14, A-4910 Ried im Innkreis, Austria. Ed. Karl Rudinger. adv.; bk.rev.; illus.; circ. 6,000.

636.089   US
OHIO VETERINARY MEDICAL ASSOCIATION. NEWSLETTER. 1952. m. $2 membership. Ohio Veterinary Medical Association, 1350 W. Fifth Ave., Columbus, OH 43212. TEL 614-486-7253. FAX 614-486-1325. Ed. George Kukor. adv.; illus.; circ. 1,930.
Formerly (until 1970): Ohio Veterinarian (ISSN 0030-1213)

636.089   JA   ISSN 0911-5137
OKINAWA-KEN KACHIKU EISEI SHIKENJO NENPO. (Text in Japanese; summaries in English) 1958. a. free. Okinawa-ken Kachiku Eisei Shikenjo - Okinawa Prefectural Institute of Animal Health, 112 Kohagura, Naha-shi, Okinawa-ken 900, Japan. TEL 0988-32-1515. circ. 300. (back issues avail.)
Description: Covers research on animal diseases.

636.089   SA   ISSN 0030-2465
SF601   CODEN: OJVRAZ
ONDERSTEPOORT JOURNAL OF VETERINARY RESEARCH. 1933. q. R.12.50 per no. Department of Agricultural Development, Private Bag X144, Pretoria 0001, South Africa. TEL 012-2062181. FAX 012-3232156. Ed. D.W. Verwoerd. bibl.; charts; illus.; index. cum.index; circ. 1,500. (also avail. in microform from UMI; reprint service avail. from UMI) **Indexed:** Abstr.Hyg., Agri.Eng.Abstr., Anim.Breed.Abstr., Biol.Abstr., Biol.& Agr.Ind., Biotech.Abstr., Chem.Abstr., Curr.Adv.Ecol.Sci., Curr.Cont., Dairy Sci.Abstr., Field Crop Abstr., Food Sci.& Tech.Abstr., Helminthol.Abstr., Herb.Abstr., Ind.Med., Ind.S.A.Per., Ind.Vet., Nutr.Abstr., Pig News & Info., Poult.Abstr., Protozool.Abstr., Rev.Appl.Entomol., Rev.Plant Path., Trop.Dis.Bull., Vet.Bull.
—BLDSC shelfmark: 6258.000000.

VETERINARY SCIENCE

636.089 SP
ONE. 1979. bi-m. 8500 ptas. (effective 1992). Ediciones y Textos, S.A., Roger de Flor, 222 bis, 1o 5a, 08013 Barcelona, Spain. TEL 93-459-00-55. FAX 93-459-41-36. Ed. Dr. Jordi Serratosa. adv.; abstr.; bibl.; charts; illus.; circ. 10,000. **Indexed:** Anim.Breed.Abstr., Ind.Vet., Pig News & Info., Poult.Abstr., Protozool.Abstr., Small Anim.Abstr., Vet.Bull.
Description: Covers recent research in the veterinary sciences.

ONS VEE; maandblad voor de veehouderij. see AGRICULTURE — Poultry And Livestock

636.089 CN ISSN 0821-6320
ONTARIO VETERINARY ASSOCIATION. UPDATE. 1983. bi-m. $25. Ontario Veterinary Association, 340 Woodlawn Rd., Unit 24-25, Guelph, Ont. N1H 2X1, Canada. FAX 519-824-6497. Ed. O. Osborne. circ. 3,000.

PAKISTAN JOURNAL OF AGRICULTURE, AGRICULTURAL ENGINEERING AND VETERINARY SCIENCES. see AGRICULTURE

PAKISTAN JOURNAL OF ANIMAL SCIENCES. see AGRICULTURE — Poultry And Livestock

636.089 PK
PAKISTAN VETERINARIAN; animal sciences. (Text in English) 1988. m. $5 per no. Press Corporation of Pakistan, P.O. Box 3138, Karachi 75400, Pakistan. TEL 21-455-3703. FAX 21-7736198. Ed. Saeed Hafeez. circ. 5,000.

636.089 PK
PAKISTAN VETERINARY INDEX. (Text in English) 1985. a. $15. Press Corporation of Pakistan, P.O. Box 3138, Karachi 75400, Pakistan. TEL 21-455-3703. FAX 21-7736198. Ed. Saeed Hafeez. circ. 5,000.

636.089 PK ISSN 0253-8318
CODEN: PVJODU
PAKISTAN VETERINARY JOURNAL. (Text in English) 1981. q. Rs.100($30) University of Agriculture, Faculty of Veterinary Science, Faisalabad, Pakistan. Ed. Mohammed Nawaz. adv.; bk.rev.; circ. 600. **Indexed:** Anim.Breed.Abstr., Biol.Abstr., Chem.Abstr., Dairy Sci.Abstr., Ind.Vet., Poult.Abstr., Protozool.Abstr., Small Anim.Abstr., Vet.Bull.

636.089 SP ISSN 0210-1017
PANORAMA VETERINARIO; edicion Espanola de tierarztliche umschau. 1965. m. 750 ptas.($11) Editorial ECO, S.A., Calle de la Cruz 44, Barcelona 34, Spain. Eds. J.M. Gomis, M. Luera. adv.; charts; illus.; stat.; circ. 8,000.

PARASITOLOGY TODAY; international review journal in the field of medical and veterinary parasites. see MEDICAL SCIENCES

636.089 IE
PEGASUS. 1954. a. £1. Veterinary Students Union of Ireland, Veterinary College of Ireland, Ballsbridge, Dublin, 4, Ireland. Eds. Donal Sammin, Brendan Fee. adv.; bk.rev.; circ. 1,500.
Fomerly: A V S Journal (ISSN 0066-9768)
Description: Concerned with up-to-date developments and opportunities for recent graduates in Ireland and the world.

591 US
PERSPECTIVES IN ETHOLOGY. 1973. irreg., vol.9, 1991. Plenum Publishing Corp., 233 Spring St., New York, NY 10013-1578. TEL 212-620-8000. FAX 212-463-0742. TELEX 23-421139. Eds. P.P.G. Bateson, P.H. Klopfer. (back issues avail.)
Refereed Serial

PET FOCUS; practical information for people who love pets. see PETS

636 US ISSN 1043-7533
PET VETERINARIAN. 1989. bi-m. $24. Watt Publishing Co., 122 S. Wesley Ave., Mt. Morris, IL 60154-1497. TEL 815-734-4171. Ed. Dr. Tim Phillips. circ. 30,000.
Description: Directed to the small animal practitioner focusing on marketing, client education and science summaries.

636.089 GW ISSN 0177-7726
PFERDEHEILKUNDE; zeitschrift fuer wissenschaft und praxis. (Text in German; summaries in English and German) 1985. bi-m. DM.260 (foreign DM.272). Hippiatrika Verlag GmbH, Buehlstr. 5, 7265 Neubulach, Germany. TEL 7053-3261. Ed. Eva Pietschmann. (back issues avail.)
—BLDSC shelfmark: 6437.519000.

636.089 PH ISSN 0115-2173
CODEN: PJVSDI
PHILIPPINE JOURNAL OF VETERINARY AND ANIMAL SCIENCES. (Text and summaries in English) 1975. q. P.80($20) Philippine Society of Animal Sciences, c/o Institute of Animal Science, University of the Philippines, College of Agriculture, Los Banos, Laguna 3720, Phillipines. Ed. Dr. Cefeino P. Maala. adv.; circ. 1,100. **Indexed:** Biol.Abstr., Chem.Abstr., Dairy Sci.Abstr., Food Sci.& Tech.Abstr., Nutr.Abstr.
Formerly: Philippine Journal of Animal Science.

636.089 PH ISSN 0031-7705
CODEN: PJVMAV
PHILIPPINE JOURNAL OF VETERINARY MEDICINE. 1962. s-a. $30. University of the Philippines, College of Veterinary Medicine, Los Banos, Laguna 3720, Philippines. Ed. Elito F. Landicho. adv.; bk.rev.; bibl.; charts; illus.; circ. 1,000. **Indexed:** Biol.Abstr., Chem.Abstr., Curr.Cont., Helminthol.Abstr., Ind.Vet., Vet.Bull.
—BLDSC shelfmark: 6456.050000.

636.089 UK ISSN 0956-0939
PIG VETERINARY JOURNAL. 1976. s-a. £18 (foreign £20). Burlington Press Ltd., Foxton, Cambridge CB2 6SW, England. TEL 0666-822967. FAX 0666-822009. (Subscr. to: The Grove Centre, Corston, Malmesbury, Wilts. SN16 OHL, England) Ed. D. Basinger. bk.rev.; circ. 900. **Indexed:** Agri.Eng.Abstr., Anim.Breed.Abstr., Ind.Vet., Vet.Bull.
—BLDSC shelfmark: 6500.129700.
Formerly: Pig Veterinary Society. Proceedings.
Description: Papers given at pig veterinary national and international meetings.

636.089 FR
POINT VETERINAIRE. 1973. 8/yr. 765 F. Editions du Point Veterinaire S.A., 25 rue Bourgelat, B.P. 233, 94702 Maisons-Alfort Cedex, France. TEL 43-53-20-01. Ed. Philippe Devisme. adv.; bk.rev. **Indexed:** Agri.Eng.Abstr., Bio-Contr.News & Info., Dairy Sci.Abstr., Ind.Vet., Pig News & Info., Poult.Abstr., Protozool.Abstr., Small Anim.Abstr., Vet.Bull., Weed Abstr.

636.089 PL ISSN 0079-3647
CODEN: PARWAC
POLSKIE ARCHIWUM WETERYNARYJNE/ARCHIWUM VETERINARIUM POLONICUM. (Text in Polish and English; summaries in English, Polish and Russian) 1951. irreg., vol.28, 1988. price varies. (Polska Akademia Nauk, Komitet Nauk Weterynaryjnych) Panstwowe Wydawnictwo Naukowe, Miodowa 10, 00-251 Warsaw, Poland. (Dist. by: Osrodek Rozpowszechniania Wydawnictw Naukowych PAN ORPAN, Palac Kultury i Nauki, 00-901 Warsaw, Poland) Ed. Piotr Wyrost. abstr.; charts; illus.; circ. 400. **Indexed:** Anim.Breed.Abstr., Biol.Abstr., Chem.Abstr., Dairy Sci.Abstr., Excerp.Med., Field Crop Abstr., Food Sci.& Tech.Abstr., Herb.Abstr., Ind.Med., Ind.Vet., Nutr.Abstr., Pig News & Info., Rev.Plant Path., Vet.Bull.
—BLDSC shelfmark: 6546.600000.

POULTRY ADVISER; English monthly dedicated to poultry development. see AGRICULTURE — Poultry And Livestock

636.089 GW ISSN 0032-681X
CODEN: PRTIAV
DER PRAKTISCHE TIERARZT. 1921. 13/yr. DM.208. (Bundesverbandes praktischer Tieraerzte e.V.) Schluetersche Verlagsanstalt GmbH und Co., Georgswall 4, Postfach 5440, 3000 Hannover 1, Germany. TEL 0511-1236-0. Ed. Dr. H. Hagenlocher. adv.; bk.rev.; charts; illus.; index; circ. 8,980. **Indexed:** Agri.Eng.Abstr., Anim.Breed.Abstr., Biotech.Abstr., Chem.Abstr., Curr.Adv.Cancer Res., Curr.Adv.Ecol.Sci., Curr.Cont., Dairy Sci.Abstr., Helminthol.Abstr., INIS Atomind., Pig News & Info., Protozool.Abstr., Small Anim.Abstr., Vet.Bull.
—BLDSC shelfmark: 6601.200000.

636.089 FR
PRATIQUE MEDICALE ET CHIRURGICALE DE L'ANIMAL DE COMPAGNIE. 1966. 7/yr. 1111.65 F. Conference Nationale des Veterinaires Specialises en Petits Animaux, 82, av. de Villiers, 75017 Paris, France. TEL 42-67-72-96. FAX 42-67-51-76. Ed. Dr. Pages. adv.; bk.rev.; circ. 3,000.
Formerly: Animal de Compagnie.

636.089 NE ISSN 0167-5877
PREVENTIVE VETERINARY MEDICINE; an international journal on research and development in veterinary epidemiology, animal disease prevention and control, and animal health economics. (Text in English) 1982. 12/yr. (in 3 vols., 4 nos./vol.). fl.903 (effective 1992). Elsevier Science Publishers B.V., P.O. Box 211, 1000 AE Amsterdam, Netherlands. TEL 020-5803911. FAX 020-5803598. TELEX 18582 ESPA NL. (Subscr. in U.S. and Canada to: Elsevier Science Publishing Co., Inc., Box 882, Madison Sq. Sta., New York, NY 10159. TEL 212-989-5800) Eds. H.N. Erb, I.R. Dohoo. bk.rev.; illus.; index; circ. 800. (back issues avail.) **Indexed:** Anim.Breed.Abstr., Biol.Abstr., Curr.Adv.Ecol.Sci., Curr.Cont., Dairy Sci.Abstr., Ind.Vet., Pig News & Info., Poult.Abstr., Protozool.Abstr., Rev.Appl.Entomol., Small Anim.Abstr., Vet.Bull.
—BLDSC shelfmark: 6612.795000.
Description: Aims to disseminate, on a worldwide basis, information and reports of significance in the field of animal (mammalian, aquatic and avian) health programmes and preventive veterinary medicine.
Refereed Serial

PRIMATES; journal of primatology. see BIOLOGY — Zoology

636.089 US ISSN 1041-0228
PROBLEMS IN VETERINARY MEDICINE. 1989. q. $75 to individuals (foreign $95); institutions $95 (foreign $110). J.B. Lippincott Co., E. Washington Sq., Philadelphia, PA 19105. TEL 215-238-4295. (Subscr to: Downsville Pike, Rte. 3, Box 20-B, Hagerstown, MD 21740) Eds. Dr. William J. Kay, Dr. Nancy O. Brown, (also avail. in microform from UMI) **Indexed:** Ind.Vet., Small Anim.Abstr., Vet.Bull.
—BLDSC shelfmark: 6617.941800.
Description: Focuses on clinical problems encountered by the veterinarian in daily practice.

636.089 617.7 US
▼PROGRESS IN VETERINARY & COMPARATIVE OPHTHALMOLOGY; an international journal of clinical and investigational ophthalmology. 1991. q. $50 (effective 1992). Veterinary Practice Publishing Co., 7 Ashley Ave. S., Santa Barbara, CA 93103-9989. TEL 805-965-1028. FAX 805-965-0722. (Subscr. addr.: Box 4457, Santa Barbara, CA 93140-4457) Ed. Dr. Robert L. Peiffer. circ. 2,500.
Refereed Serial

636.087 US
▼PROGRESS IN VETERINARY NEUROLOGY; an international journal of veterinary neurology and neurosurgery. 1990. q. $50 (effective 1992). Veterinary Practice Publishing Co., 7 Ashley Ave., S., Santa Barbara, CA 93103-9989. TEL 805-965-1028. FAX 805-965-0722. (Subscr. to: Box 4457, Santa Barbara, CA 93140-4457) Ed. Dr. Alan J. Parker. bk.rev.; circ. 2,500.
Refereed Serial

636.089 MX
PRONTUARIO DE ESPECIALIDADES VETERINARIAS. 1971. a. Ediciones P L M, S.A. de C.V., San Bernadino 17, Col. del Valle, 03100 Mexico D.F., Mexico. TEL 687-1766. FAX 536-5027. Ed. Luis Hochenstein. circ. 5,000.

636.089 614 GW ISSN 0178-2010
R F L - RUNDSCHAU FLEISCHHYIENE UND LEBENSMITTELUEBERWACHUNG. 1949. 11/yr. DM.99 (foreign DM.114). Verlag M. und H. Schaper, Kalandstr. 4, Postfach 1642, 3220 Alfeld, Germany. adv.; bk.rev.; bibl.; illus.; index; circ. 2,700. **Indexed:** Ind.Vet., Vet.Bull.
Formerly: Rundschau fuer Fleischuntersuchung und Lebensmittelueberwachung (ISSN 0341-0668)

RASSEGNA DI DIRITTO, LEGISLAZIONE E MEDICINA LEGALE VETERINARIA. see LAW

VETERINARY SCIENCE

636.089   FR   ISSN 0034-1843
CODEN: RMVEAG
RECUEIL DE MEDECINE VETERINAIRE D'ALFORT.
(Summaries in English, Spanish) 1824. 9/yr. 700 F. Association pour la Publications du Recueil de Medecine Veterinaire, Ecole Nationale Veterinaire Alfort, 7 av. du General de Gaulle, 94704 Maisons Alfort, France. TEL 1-43-96-71-76. FAX 1-43-75-12-10. Ed. M. Paragon. adv.; bk.rev.; abstr.; illus.; index; circ. 25,000. (reprint service avail. from UMI) **Indexed:** Anim.Breed.Abstr., Biol.Abstr., Chem.Abstr., Curr.Adv.Ecol.Sci., Curr.Cont., Excerp.Med., Food Sci.& Tech.Abstr., Helminthol.Abstr., Ind.Vet., Maize Abstr., Nutr.Abstr., Poult.Abstr., Protozool.Abstr., Vet.Bull.
—BLDSC shelfmark: 7329.000000.

636.089   UK
REGISTERS & DIRECTORY OF VETERINARY SURGEONS.
1870. a. £17. Royal College of Veterinary Surgeons, 32 Belgrave Square, London SW1X 8QP, England. TEL 071-235-4971. FAX 071-245-6100. Ed. B. Needham. adv.; circ. 14,500.

636.089   GW   ISSN 0936-6768
S494   CODEN: RDANEF
REPRODUCTION IN DOMESTIC ANIMALS; Physiology, Pathology, Biotechnology, Zuchthygiene. (Text in German; summaries in English and German) 1966. 6/yr. DM.378($217) per vol. Verlag Paul Parey (Berlin), Seelbuschring 9-17, 1000 Berlin 42, Germany. TEL 030-70784-0. FAX 030-70784199. (U.S. address: Paul Parey Scientific Publishers, 150 E. 27th St., No.1A, New York, NY 10016) Ed.Bd. adv.; bk.rev.; illus.; stat.; index. (back issues avail.) **Indexed:** Anim.Breed.Abstr., Biol.Abstr., Biotech.Abstr., Chem.Abstr., Curr.Adv.Cell & Devel.Biol., Curr.Adv.Ecol.Sci., Curr.Adv.Genetics & Molec.Biol., Curr.Cont., Dairy Sci.Abstr., Ind.Vet., Pig News & Info., Vet.Bull.
—BLDSC shelfmark: 7713.599600.
Formerly: Zuchthygiene (ISSN 0044-5371)

636.089   UK   ISSN 0034-5288
SF601   CODEN: RVTSA9
RESEARCH IN VETERINARY SCIENCE. 1960. bi-m. £103.50 (foreign £166). British Veterinary Association, 7 Mansfield St, London W1M OAT, England. TEL 01-636 6541. Ed. E.N. Boden. adv.; bibl.; charts; illus.; index; circ. 945. (also avail. in microform from UMI; reprint service avail. from UMI) **Indexed:** Anim.Breed.Abstr., Biol.Abstr., Biotech.Abstr., Chem.Abstr., Curr.Adv.Ecol.Sci., Curr.Cont., Dairy Sci.Abstr., Dent.Ind., Excerp.Med., Food Sci.& Tech.Abstr., Helminthol.Abstr., Ind.Med., Ind.Vet., Nutr.Abstr., Pig News & Info., Protozool.Abstr., Rev.Appl.Entomol., Rev.Plant Path., Risk Abstr., Soils & Fert., Soyabean Abstr., Vet.Bull.
—BLDSC shelfmark: 7774.100000.

REVISTA CERES; orgao de divulgacao tecnico-cientifica em ciencias agrarias. see *AGRICULTURE*

636.089   CU   ISSN 0048-7678
REVISTA CUBANA DE CIENCIAS VETERINARIAS. (Text in Spanish; summaries in Spanish and English) 1970. 4/yr. $16 in N. America; S. America $17; Europe $19; others $21 or exchange basis. (Consejo Cientifico Veterinario) Ediciones Cubanas, Obispo No. 527, Aptdo. 605, Havana, Cuba. bk.rev.; bibl.; charts; illus.; circ. 3,000. (also avail. in microfilm) **Indexed:** Anim.Breed.Abstr., Biol.Abstr., Dairy Sci.Abstr., Helminthol.Abstr., Ind.Vet., Maize Abstr., Nutr.Abstr., Pig News & Info., Poult.Abstr., Protozool.Abstr., Vet.Bull.
—BLDSC shelfmark: 7852.098000.

636.089   PE
REVISTA DE INVESTIGACIONES PECUARIAS. (Text in English; summaries in English) 1972. s-a. $5. Universidad Nacional Mayor de San Marcos, Instituto Veterinario de Investigaciones Tropicales y de Altura, Aptdo. 4270, Lima, Peru. Ed. C. Novoa. circ. 1,500. **Indexed:** Vet.Bull.

636.089   CU
REVISTA DE SALUD ANIMAL. (Text in Spanish; summaries in English) 1979. 4/yr. $21 in N. and S. America; Europe $26. (Centro Nacional de Sanidad Agropecuaria) Ediciones Cubanas, Obispo No. 527, Apdo. 605, Havana, Cuba. charts; bibl. **Indexed:** Agri.Eng.Abstr., Anim.Breed.Abstr., Biol.Abstr., Bull.Signal., Chem.Abstr., Dairy Sci.Abstr., Food Sci.& Tech.Abstr., Helminthol.Abstr., Herb.Abstr., Ind.Vet., Pig News & Info., Poult.Abstr., Protozool.Abstr., Ref.Zh., Soyabean Abstr., Vet.Bull.

636.089   PO   ISSN 0035-0389
REVISTA PORTUGUESA DE CIENCIAS VETERINARIAS.
1902. q. Esc.4500 (typically set in Jan.). Sociedade Portuguesa de Ciencias Veterinarias, Rua D. Dinis 2-A, 1200 Lisbon, Portugal. Ed. Maria C. Peleteiro. adv.; bk.rev.; abstr.; bibl.; index; circ. 1,100. **Indexed:** Anim.Breed.Abstr., Biol.Abstr., Dairy Sci.Abstr., Helminthol.Abstr., Ind.Vet., Nutr.Abstr., Vet.Bull.
—BLDSC shelfmark: 7869.880000.
Description: Papers from Portuguese researchers on all areas of veterinary science.

REVISTA THEOBROMA. see *AGRICULTURE*

636.089   VE
REVISTA VETERINARIA VENEZOLANA. 1956. m. Federacion de Colegios de Medicos Veterinarios de Venezuela, Qta. Marilina, Av. Paez, Calle Stolk, El Paraiso, Apdo. 2921, Caracas 102, Venezuela. Ed. Dr. C. Ruiz Martinez.

591 636.089   CK   ISSN 0120-4114
REVISTA VETERINARIA Y ZOOTECNICA DE CALDAS.
1982. 2/yr. Col.2000($5) University of Caldas, School of Veterinary Medicine & Animal Husbandry, Apdo. Aereo 275, Manizales, Colombia. TEL 968-852139. Ed. Rodrigo Hoyos. adv.; circ. 600. (back issues avail.)
Description: Contains research articles on animal medicine and husbandry.

636.089   FR   ISSN 0035-1865
REVUE D'ELEVAGE ET DE MEDECINE VETERINAIRE DES PAYS TROPICAUX. (Text in English, French; summaries in English, French, Spanish) 1947. q. 275 F. (foreign 450 F.)(effective 1992). (Institut d'Elevage et de Medecine Veterinaire des Pays Tropicaux) Expansion Scientifique, 15 rue Saint Benoit, 75278 Paris Cedex 06, France. Ed. A.H. Robinet. adv.; bk.rev.; abstr.; bibl.; charts; index. cum.index: 1947-1977; circ. controlled. (also avail. in microfiche) **Indexed:** Anim.Breed.Abstr., Biol.Abstr., Biotech.Abstr., Curr.Adv.Ecol.Sci., Curr.Cont., Dairy Sci.Abstr., Excerp.Med., Field Crop Abstr., Helminthol.Abstr., Herb.Abstr., Ind.Med., Ind.Vet., Irr.& Drain.Abstr., Nutr.Abstr., Pig News & Info., Poult.Abstr., Protozool.Abstr., Rev.Appl.Entomol., Rev.Plant Path., So.Pac.Per.Ind., Trop.Oil Seeds Abstr., Vet.Bull.
—BLDSC shelfmark: 7900.000000.

636.089   FR   ISSN 0035-1555
CODEN: RVMVAH
REVUE DE MEDECINE VETERINAIRE. (Text in French; summaries in English, German, Spanish) 1838. m. 790 F. Ecole Nationale Veterinaire, 23 Chemin des Capelles, 31076 Toulouse Cedex, France. TEL 61-49-11-40. FAX 61-31-00-36. Ed. A. Milon. adv.; bk.rev.; abstr.; illus.; index; circ. 3,300. (reprint service avail. from ISI, UMI) **Indexed:** Anim.Breed.Abstr., Biol.Abstr., Biotech.Abstr., Bull.Signal., Chem.Abstr., Curr.Adv.Ecol.Sci., Curr.Cont., Dairy Sci.Abstr., Excerp.Med., Helminthol.Abstr., Ind.Vet., Nutr.Abstr., Pig News & Info., Poult.Abstr., Protozool.Abstr., Psychol.Abstr., Rev.Plant Path., Small Anim.Abstr., Vet.Bull.
—BLDSC shelfmark: 7932.000000.

636.089   IT   ISSN 0016-5700
RILANCIO; agricultural veterinary zootechnical magazine. 1969. irreg. (9-12/yr.). free. Carlo Erba S.p.A., Via Carlo Imbonati 24, 20159 Milan, Italy. Ed. Prof. Bruno Mainardi. adv.; abstr.; index; circ. 35,000.

RIVISTA DI ZOOTECNIA E VETERINARIA; rassegna di informazione e aggiornamento. see *AGRICULTURE — Poultry And Livestock*

636.089   UK   ISSN 0952-7222
ROWETT RESEARCH INSTITUTE REPORT. a. Rowett Research Institute, Greenburn Rd., Bucksburn, Aberdeen AB2 9SB, Scotland. TEL 0224-712751. FAX 0224-712751. TELEX 739988-ROWETT-G.

636.089   SZ   ISSN 0036-7281
CODEN: SATHAA
SCHWEIZER ARCHIV FUER TIERHEILKUNDE. 10/yr. 154 SFr. (foreign 172 SFr.). (Gesellschaft Schweizerischer Tieraerzte) Orell Fuessli Graphische Betriebe AG, Dietzingerstr. 3, CH-8036 Zurich, Switzerland. adv.; circ. 1,600. **Indexed:** Anim.Breed.Abstr., ASCA, Biol.Abstr., Biotech.Abstr., Chem.Abstr., Curr.Adv.Ecol.Sci., Curr.Cont., Dairy Sci.Abstr., Excerp.Med., Food Sci.& Tech.Abstr., Helminthol.Abstr., Ind.Med., Ind.Vet., Nutr.Abstr., Pig News & Info., Poult.Abstr., Protozool.Abstr., Rev.Plant Path., Small Anim.Abstr., Soils & Fert., Vet.Bull.
—BLDSC shelfmark: 8110.000000.

636.089   FR
SCIENCES VETERINAIRES - MEDECINE COMPAREE. BULLETIN. 1898. 4/yr. 475 F. (effective 1992). Societe des Sciences Veterinaires et de Medecine Comparee de Lyon, Ecole Nationale Veterinaire de Lyon, B.P. 83, 69280 Marcy l'Etoile, France. TEL 78-87-25-25. FAX 78-87-82-62. adv.; bk.rev. **Indexed:** Biol.Abstr., Chem.Abstr., Ind.Vet., Nutr.Abstr., Poult.Abstr., Vet.Bull.
Formerly: Societe des Sciences Veterinaires et de Medecine Comparee de Lyon. Bulletin (ISSN 0750-7682)

SCIENTIA AGRICULTURAE BOHEMOSLOVACA. see *AGRICULTURE*

636.089 574   IT   ISSN 0392-9639
SCIENZA VETERINARIA E BIOLOGIA ANIMALE. 1982. bi-m. L.24000 (foreign L.48000). Edi. Ermes, Via Timavo 12, 20124 Milan, Italy. TEL 02-66984715. FAX 02-66800773. Ed. Raffaele Grandi. adv.; bk.rev.; cum.index; circ. 13,500. (back issues avail.) **Indexed:** Ind.Vet., Small Anim.Abstr.
Description: Features research articles on veterinary science and animal biology. Includes articles on animal alimentation, animal hunters and animal surgery.

636.089   IT   ISSN 0037-1521
CODEN: SVETDJ
SELEZIONE VETERINARIA. 1960. m. L.60000 (effective Jan. 1992). Istituto Zooprofilattico Sperimentale della Lombardia e dell' Emilia, Via A. Bianchi 7, 25100 Brescia, Italy. FAX 030-225613. Eds. G.L. Gualandi, G.F. Panina. bk.rev.; circ. 3,000. (reprint service avail.) **Indexed:** Anim.Breed.Abstr., Dairy Sci.Abstr., Ind.Vet., Pig News & Info., Poult.Abstr., Protozool.Abstr., Vet.Bull.
—BLDSC shelfmark: 8235.340000.
Description: Articles on veterinary sciences with emphasis on infectious diseases, microbiology, parasitology, reproduction and breeding.

636.089   FR   ISSN 0396-5015
SEMAINE VETERINAIRE. 1976. 40/yr. 800 F. Editions du Point Veterinaire S.A., 25 rue Bourgelat, B.P. 233, 94702 Maisons-Alfort Cedex, France. Ed. Philippe Devigne. adv.; circ. 5,000.

636.089   US
▼**SEMINARS IN AVIAN AND EXOTIC PET MEDICINE.**
1992. q. W.B. Saunders Co. (Subsidiary of: Harcourt Brace Jovanovich, Inc.), Curtis Bldg., Independence Sq. W., Philadelphia, PA 19106. TEL 215-238-7800. Ed. Dr. Alan M. Fudge. adv.; circ. 2,000.
Description: Covers a single topic in avian and exotic pet medicine in each issue.

636.089   US   ISSN 0882-0511
CODEN: SVMSEN
SEMINARS IN VETERINARY MEDICINE AND SURGERY: SMALL ANIMAL. (Translated into Spanish) 1986. q. $57 to individuals; institutions $81; foreign $96. W.B. Saunders Co. (Subsidiary of: Harcourt Brace Jovanovich, Inc.), Curtis Center, Independence Square W., Philadelphia, PA 19106. TEL 215-238-7800. Ed. Dr. Robert J. Murtaugh. adv.; bibl.; charts; illus.; index. **Indexed:** Curr.Cont., Ind.Med., Ind.Vet., Small Anim.Abstr., Vet.Bull.
—BLDSC shelfmark: 8239.487000.
Description: Contains a specific theme of interest to small animal veterinarians in each issue.
Refereed Serial

VETERINARY SCIENCE

636.089   CC   ISSN 1000-7725
SHANGHAI XUMU SHOUYI TONGXUN/SHANGHAI BULLETIN OF VETERINARY SCIENCE. (Text in Chinese) 1956. bi-m. Y4.80. Shanghai Nongye Kexueyuan, Xumu Shouyi Yanjiusuo - Shanghai Academy of Agricultural Science, Institute of Veterinary Science, 2451 Xietu Lu, Shanghai 200030, People's Republic of China. TEL 4383161. Ed. Liu Ruisan. adv.; bk.rev.

SINGAPORE JOURNAL OF PRIMARY INDUSTRIES. see *AGRICULTURE*

636.089   US
SMALL ANIMAL PRACTICE. 1976. m. $108. Audio Veterinary Medicine, 810 S. Myrtle Ave., Monrovia, CA 91016. TEL 818-303-2531. FAX 818-303-2534. (Subscr. to: Box 1729, Monrovia, CA 91017-5729) Ed. Anthony C. Crum, II. circ. 100. (also avail. in audio cassette; back issues avail.)

SMALL RUMINANT RESEARCH. see *AGRICULTURE — Poultry And Livestock*

636.089 637   BL   ISSN 0100-4859
CODEN: RSBZBM
SOCIEDADE BRASILEIRA DE ZOOTECNIA. REVISTA. (Text in Portuguese; summaries in English) 1972. bi-m. $50. Sociedade Brasileira de Zootecnia, Departamento de Zootecnia, Universidade Federal de Vicosa, 36570 Vicosa MG, Brazil. FAX 031-891-1903. TELEX 031-1587. Ed. Jose Brandao Fonseca. circ. 2,000. (back issues avail.) **Indexed:** Anim.Breed.Abstr., Biol.Abstr., Dairy Sci.Abstr., Field Crop Abstr., Maize Abstr., Poult.Abstr., Sorghum & Millets Abstr., Soyabean Abstr.
—BLDSC shelfmark: 7834.455000.

SODOBNO KMETIJSTVO. see *AGRICULTURE*

636.089   SA
CODEN: JAVTAP
SOUTH AFRICAN VETERINARY ASSOCIATION. SCIENTIFIC JOURNAL. 1929. q. $250. South African Veterinary Association, P.O. Box 25033, Monument Park, 0105 Pretoria, South Africa. TEL 012-3461150. FAX 012-3462929. Ed. J. van Heerden. adv.; bk.rev.; charts; illus.; index; circ. 1,600. (back issues avail.) **Indexed:** Anim.Breed.Abstr., Bio-Contr.News & Info., Biotech.Abstr., Chem.Abstr., Curr.Adv.Ecol.Sci., Curr.Cont., Dairy Sci.Abstr., Dent.Ind., Excerp.Med., Field Crop Abstr., Helminthol.Abstr., Herb.Abstr., Ind.Med., Ind.S.A.Per., Ind.Vet., INIS Atomind., Nutr.Abstr., Protozool.Abstr., Rev.Appl.Entomol., Small Anim.Abstr., Vet.Bull., Weed Abstr.
Former titles: South African Veterinary Association. Journal (ISSN 0301-0732); South African Veterinary Medical Association. Journal (ISSN 0038-2809)

SPAIN. INSTITUTO NACIONAL DE INVESTIGACIONES AGRARIAS. COMUNICACIONES. SERIE: HIGIENE Y SANIDAD. see *AGRICULTURE — Poultry And Livestock*

636.089   CE
SRI LANKA VETERINARY JOURNAL. (Text in English) 1953. s-a. $10. Veterinary Research Institute, Peradeniya, Sri Lanka. Ed. Prof. S.T. Fernando. adv.; bk.rev.; abstr.; charts; illus.; index; circ. 1,000. (tabloid format) **Indexed:** Anim.Breed.Abstr., Biol.Abstr., Chem.Abstr., Dairy Sci.Abstr., Field Crop Abstr., Helminthol.Abstr., Herb.Abstr., Ind.Vet., Nutr.Abstr., Pig News & Info., Poult.Abstr., Protozool.Abstr., Rev.Appl.Entomol., Small Anim.Abstr., Soils & Fert., Sri Lanka Sci.Ind., Vet.Bull.
Formerly (until 1982): Ceylon Veterinary Journal (ISSN 0009-0891)

636.089   FI   ISSN 0039-5501
SUOMEN ELAINLAAKARILEHTI/FINSK VETERINARTIDSKRIFT. (Text in Finnish and Swedish; summaries in English) 1892. m. Fmk.400. Suomen Elainlaakariliitto - Finnish Veterinary Association, Akavatalo, Rautatielaisenkatu 6, 00520 Helsinki 52, Finland. Ed. M. Haemaelainen. adv.; bk.rev.; bibl.; charts; illus.; circ. 1,550. **Indexed:** Anim.Breed.Abstr., Biol.Abstr., Dairy Sci.Abstr., Food Sci.& Tech.Abstr., Helminthol.Abstr., Ind.Vet., Nutr.Abstr., Pig News & Info., Poult.Abstr., Protozool.Abstr., Small Anim.Abstr., Vet.Bull.
—BLDSC shelfmark: 8541.800000.

636.089   SW   ISSN 0346-2250
SVENSK VETERINAERTIDNING. 1949. 15/yr. Kr.600 (typically set in Jan.). Sveriges Veterinaerfoerbund - Swedish Veterinary Association, Kungsholms Hamnplan 7, S-112 20 Stockholm, Sweden. TEL 08-654-2480. FAX 08-6517082. Ed. Johan Beck-Friis. adv.; bk.rev.; circ. 2,429 (controlled). **Indexed:** Anim.Breed.Abstr., Dairy Sci.Abstr., Food Sci.& Tech.Abstr., Helminthol.Abstr., Ind.Vet., Nutr.Abstr., Pig News & Info., Protozool.Abstr., Vet.Bull., World Agri.Econ.& Rural Sociol.Abstr.
—BLDSC shelfmark: 8562.598000.
Description: Articles of interest to veterinarians and news about the association.

636.089   US
SWINE PRACTITIONER. 1988. q. $20. Vance Publishing Corporation, 7950 College Blvd., Shawnee Mission, KS 66210. TEL 913-451-2200. Ed. Thomas Quaife. circ. 4,000.

636.089   US   ISSN 0040-4756
TEXAS VETERINARY MEDICAL JOURNAL. 1939. bi-m. $50 to individuals; institutions $30 (Can. & Mexico $40; elsewhere $55). Texas Veterinary Medical Association, 6633 Hwy., 290 E., No. 201, Austin, TX 78723-1134. TEL 512-452-4224. Ed. Donald M. Ward. adv.; bk.rev.; charts; illus.; stat.; circ. 3,000.

636.089   US   ISSN 0093-691X
CODEN: THGNBO
THERIOGENOLOGY; an international journal of animal reproduction. 1974. m. (2 vols./yr.). $280 (foreign $360). Butterworth - Heinemann Ltd. (Subsidiary of: Reed International PLC), 80 Montvale Ave., Stoneham, MA 02180. TEL 617-438-8464. FAX 617-438-1479. TELEX 880052. Ed. Victor Shille. (also avail. in microfiche from UMI; back issues avail.) **Indexed:** Anim.Breed.Abstr., ASCA, Bibl.Repro., Biol.Abstr., Chem.Abstr., Curr.Adv.Cell & Devel.Biol., Curr.Adv.Ecol.Sci., Curr.Adv.Genetics & Molec.Biol., Curr.Cont., Dairy Sci.Abstr., Helminthol.Abstr., Ind.Vet., Nutr.Abstr., Pig News & Info., Poult.Abstr., Small Anim.Abstr., Vet.Bull.
—BLDSC shelfmark: 8814.773000.
Description: Forum for information on the reproduction of domestic and wild animals. *Refereed Serial*

636.089   GW   ISSN 0303-6286
CODEN: TAZPB8
TIERAERZTLICHE PRAXIS; Zeitschrift fuer den Tierarzt. 6/yr. DM.276($186) to individuals; institutions DM.339($222). F.K. Schattauer Verlagsgesellschaft mbH, Postfach 104545, 7000 Stuttgart 10, Germany. TEL 0711-22987-0. FAX 0711-22987-50. **Indexed:** Anim.Breed.Abstr., Ind.Vet., Poult.Abstr., Protozool.Abstr., Small Anim.Abstr., Vet.Bull.
—BLDSC shelfmark: 8831.800000.

636.089   GW   ISSN 0049-3864
TIERAERZTLICHE UMSCHAU; Zeitschrift fuer alle Gebiete der Veterinaermedizin. 1946. m. DM.172. Terra Verlag GmbH, Neuhauser Str. 21, Postfach 102144, 7750 Konstanz, Germany. TEL 07531-54041. FAX 07531-50083. Ed. O.C. Straub. adv.; bk.rev.; circ. 8,600. **Indexed:** Agri.Eng.Abstr., Anim.Breed.Abstr., ASCA, Biol.Abstr., Biotech.Abstr., Chem.Abstr., Curr.Adv.Ecol.Sci., Curr.Cont., Dairy Sci.Abstr., Food Sci.& Tech.Abstr., Helminthol.Abstr., Ind.Vet., Nutr.Abstr., Poult.Abstr., Protozool.Abstr., Rev.Plant Path., Small Anim.Abstr., Soils & Fert., Vet.Bull.
—BLDSC shelfmark: 8832.000000.

636.089   NE   ISSN 0040-7453
CODEN: TIDIAY
TIJDSCHRIFT VOOR DIERGENEESKUNDE/NETHERLANDS JOURNAL OF VETERINARY SCIENCE. (Titles and summaries in Dutch and English) 1863. 24/yr. fl.295. Koninklijke Nederlandse Maatschappij voor Diergeneeskunde - Royal Netherlands Veterinary Association, Julianalaan 10, Box 14031, 3508 SB Utrecht, Netherlands. TEL 030-510111. FAX 030-511787. Ed.Bd. adv.; bk.rev.; abstr.; bibl.; charts; illus.; index; circ. 4,500. **Indexed:** Abstr.Hyg., Agri.Eng.Abstr., Anim.Breed.Abstr., ASCA, Bibl.Agri., Biol.Abstr., Chem.Abstr., Curr.Adv.Cancer Res., Curr.Adv.Ecol.Sci., Curr.Cont., Dairy Sci.Abstr., Dairy Sci.Abstr., Food Sci.& Tech.Abstr., Helminthol.Abstr., Ind.Med., Ind.Vet., Landwirt.Zentralbl., Nutr.Abstr., Pig News & Info., Poult.Abstr., Protozool.Abstr., Rev.Plant Path., Rural Recreat.Tour.Abstr., Small Anim.Abstr., Trop.Dis.Bull., Vet.Bull., World Agri.Econ.& Rural Sociol.Abstr.
—BLDSC shelfmark: 8838.000000.

636.089   US
TOPICS IN VETERINARY MEDICINE. 1926. 3/yr. free to qualified personnel. SmithKline Beecham Animal Health, 812 Springdale Dr., Exton, PA 19341-2803. TEL 215-363-3100. FAX 215-363-3284. Ed. Kathleen M. Etchison. adv.; circ. 50,000. **Indexed:** Ind.Vet., Vet.Bull.
Formerly (until 1990): Norden News.

636.089   US   ISSN 0883-1696
TRENDS MAGAZINE. 1985. bi-m. $60 (foreign $70). American Animal Hospital Association, Denver Office Park, Box 150899, Denver, CO 80215-0899. TEL 303-279-2500. FAX 303-279-1816. Ed. Marilyn Bergquist. circ. 10,900.

636.089   US
U.S. DEPARTMENT OF AGRICULTURE. ANIMAL AND PLANT HEALTH INSPECTION SERVICE. REPORTED ARTHROPOD-BORNE ENCEPHALITIDES IN HORSES AND OTHER EQUIDAE. 1966. a. free. U.S. Animal and Plant Health Inspection Service, Federal Building, Hyattsville, MD 20782. TEL 301-436-8645. illus.; stat. **Indexed:** Bibl.Agri.

636.089 SF601   US   ISSN 0082-8750
UNITED STATES ANIMAL HEALTH ASSOCIATION. PROCEEDINGS OF THE ANNUAL MEETING.* no.73, 1969. a. $20. United States Animal Health Association, Box K227, Richmond, VA 23288-0001. circ. 1,200. (back issues avail.) **Indexed:** Ind.Med., Ind.Vet., Pig News & Info., Vet.Bull.
Supersedes: United States Livestock Sanitary Association. Proceedings.

636.089   VE
UNIVERSIDAD CENTRAL DE VENEZUELA. FACULTAD DE CIENCIAS VETERINARIAS. REVISTA. (Text in Spanish; summaries mainly in English and Spanish) 1939. 4/yr. free to qualified personnel. Universidad Central de Venezuela, Facultad de Ciencias Veterinarias, Apdo. de Correos 4563, Maracay-Edo. Aragua, Venezuela. Eds. Dr. Haroldo Mayaudon Tarbes, Dr. Arnaldo Leon D'Alessandro. circ. 1,800. **Indexed:** Biol.Abstr., Chem.Abstr., Ind.Vet., Protozool.Abstr., Rev.Appl.Entomol., Vet.Bull.
Formerly: Revista de Medicina Veterinaria y Parasitologia (ISSN 0048-7724)

636.089   GT
UNIVERSIDAD DE SAN CARLOS DE GUATEMALA. FACULTAD DE MEDICINA VETERINARIA Y ZOOTECNIA REVISTA. (Text in Spanish; summaries in English and Spanish) 1962. irreg. exchange basis. Universidad de San Carlos de Guatemala, Facultad de Medicina Veterinaria y Zootecnia, Ciudad Universitaria, Zona 12, Guatemala. TEL 760790. **Indexed:** Biol.Abstr.

636   CN   ISSN 0383-8455
UNIVERSITE DE MONTREAL. FACULTE DE MEDECINE VETERINAIRE. ANNUAIRE. 1968. a. free. Universite de Montreal, Faculte de Medecine Veterinaire, C.P. 6128, succ. A, Montreal, Que. H3C 3J7, Canada. TEL 514-343-6111. FAX 514-773-2161.
Formerly: Ecole de Medecine Veterinaire, Saint-Hyacinthe, Quebec. Annuaire (ISSN 0383-8447)

UNIVERSITY OF DAR ES SALAAM. FACULTY OF AGRICULTURE, FORESTRY AND VETERINARY SCIENCE. ANNUAL RECORD OF RESEARCH. see *AGRICULTURE*

VETERINARY SCIENCE

636.089   TU
UNIVERSITY OF ISTANBUL. FACULTY OF VETERINARY MEDICINE. JOURNAL. (Text in Turkish; summaries in English, French and German) 1975. 2/yr. $6. University of Istanbul, Faculty of Veterinary Medicine, Avcilar Campus, 34851 Avcilar - Istanbul, Turkey. FAX 5916991. Ed. Dr. M. Ercan Artan. circ. 750. **Indexed:** Biol.Abstr., Ind.Vet.

636   US   ISSN 0076-9711
UNIVERSITY OF MISSOURI, COLUMBIA. VETERINARY MEDICAL DIAGNOSTIC LABORATORY. ANNUAL REPORT. 1967. a. $5. University of Missouri, Columbia, Veterinary Medical Diagnostic Laboratory, Box 6023, Columbia, MO 65205. TEL 314-882-6811. FAX 314-882-1411. Ed. H.S. Gosser. circ. 800.

636.089   XV
UNIVERZA V LJUBLJANI. VETERINARSKA FAKULTETA. ZBORNIK. 1960. s-a. 800 din.($15) Univerza v Ljubljani, Veterinarska Fakulteta, Gerbiceva 60, 61115 Ljubljana, Slovenia. FAX 061-218-005. circ. 500. **Indexed:** Biol.Abstr., Hort.Abstr., Maize Abstr., Nutr.Abstr., Pig News & Info., Soyabean Abstr., Triticale Abstr.
Formerly (until 1990): Univerza E. Kardelja v Ljubljani. Biotehnicki Fakultet. Zbornik.

636.089   UK   ISSN 0268-2877
V.C.F. NEWSLETTER. 1963. bi-m. free. Veterinary Christian Fellowship, 2 Saxon Close, Godmanchester, Cambs PG18 8JL, England. TEL 0480-52601. Ed. John Brown. bk.rev.; circ. 420 (controlled).
Description: General interest veterinary material for Christians.

636.089   GW   ISSN 0083-5862
CODEN: VMZNA5
VETERINAER-MEDIZINISCHE NACHRICHTEN. 1953. 4/yr. DM,6. N.G. Elwert Verlag, Reitgasse 7-9, Postfach 1128, 3550 Marburg, Germany. adv.; circ. 10,000. **Indexed:** Dairy Sci.Abstr., Ind.Vet., Vet.Bull.

636.089   SP
VETERINARIA;* revista tecnica. (Text mainly in Spanish; occasionally in English or French) bi-m. 750 ptas.($15) Editorial Veterinaria, S.A., Maria Auxiliadora 19, Salamanca, Spain.

636.089   BN   ISSN 0372-6827
CODEN: VTRNAE
VETERINARIA. (Text in Serbo-Croatian; summaries in English) 1951. q. $40. University of Sarajevo, Veterinary Faculty, V. Putnika 134, 71000 Sarajevo, Bosnia Hercegovina. TEL 071 655-922. adv.; bk.rev.; index. (back issues avail.) **Indexed:** Ind.Vet., Maize Abstr., Pig News & Info., Small Anim.Abstr., Vet.Bull.
—BLDSC shelfmark: 9223.000000.
Description: Covers the field of animal production.

636.089   AG   ISSN 0326-4629
VETERINARIA ARGENTINA. 1984. m. (10/yr.). Arg.$60($90) Veterinaria Argentina S.R.L., Viamonte 494, 1053 Buenos Aires, Argentina. Dir. Jose A. Carrazzoni. adv.; bk.rev.; abstr.; bibl.; illus.; pat.; index. cum.index; circ. 7,000. **Indexed:** Agri.Eng.Abstr., Anim.Breed.Abstr., Biol.Abstr., Chem.Abstr., Dairy Sci.Abstr., Helminthol.Abstr., Ind.Vet., Protozool.Abstr., Rev.Plant Path., Small Anim.Abstr., Vet.Bull.
—BLDSC shelfmark: 9223.350000.
Supersedes (1939-1984): Gaceta Veterinaria (ISSN 0367-3812)

636   BL   ISSN 0102-5716
CODEN: VEZOEO
VETERINARIA E ZOOTECNIA. (Text in Portuguese; summaries in English, Portuguese) 1985; ceased same yr.; resumed (vol.2). a. $30 or exchange basis. Universidade Estadual Paulista, Av. Vicente Ferreira 1278, Caixa Postal 603, 17500 Marilia SP, Brazil. TEL 0144-33-1844. FAX 0144-22-2504. TELEX 1119016 UJME BR. Ed.Bd.
Description: Original papers in veterinary medicine and zoological research.
Refereed Serial

636.089   MX   ISSN 0301-5092
CODEN: VTERBU
VETERINARIA MEXICO. (Text in Spanish; summaries in English) 1970. bi-m. Mex.$40000($20) Universidad Nacional Autonoma de Mexico, Facultad de Medicina Veterinaria y Zootecnia, Ciudad Universitaria, Deleg. Coyoacan, 04510 Mexico, D.F., Mexico. TEL 550-52-15-4925. FAX 548-48-09. Ed. M.V.Z. Raymundo Martinez Pena. adv.; bk.rev.; charts; illus.; stat.; index; circ. 2,000. (back issues avail.) **Indexed:** Anim.Breed.Abstr., Biol.Abstr., Chem.Abstr., Dairy Sci.Abstr., Helminthol.Abstr., Herb.Abstr., Ind.Vet., Nutr.Abstr., Pig News & Info., Poult.Abstr., Protozool.Abstr., Rural Recreat.Tour.Abstr., Small Anim.Abstr., Vet.Bull., World Agri.Econ. & Rural Sociol.Abstr.
—BLDSC shelfmark: 9222.940000.
Formerly (until 1975): Veterinaria.
Description: Original research articles in the general field of veterinary and animal science, with emphasis on topics of local and national interest. Includes summaries of student theses.

636.089   VE
VETERINARIA TROPICAL. (Text in Spanish; summaries in English and Spanish) 1976. a. Bs.40($8) or exchange basis. Fondo Nacional de Investigaciones Agropecuarias, Apdo. 2103, Maracay 2101, Venezuela. Ed.Bd. bibl.; charts; illus.; circ. 800. **Indexed:** Helminthol.Abstr., Ind.Vet., Pig News & Info., Poult.Abstr., Protozool.Abstr., Vet.Bull.
Formerly (until 1976): Instituto de Investigaciones Veterinarias. Boletin.

636.089   CN   ISSN 0849-5009
VETERINARIAN MAGAZINE. 1989. 6/yr. Can.$30 (foreign $50). H G K Communications, Inc., 15596 Dufferin St., Inglewood, Ont. L0N 1K0, Canada. TEL 416-838-3861. FAX 416-838-3709. Ed. Anne-Lise Gasser. adv.; circ. 4,600. (back issues avail.)
Description: Professional information for veterinarians across Canada about companion animals, food animals, research, nutrition, new procedures and clinical management.

636.089   CN
VETERINARIUS. (Text in French) 1984. 6/yr. $20. Corporation Professionelle des Medecins Veterinaires du Quebec, 795 Av. du Palais, Ste. 200, St. Hyacinthe, Que. J2S 5C6, Canada. TEL 514-774-1427. FAX 514-774-7635. adv.; circ. 1,900.

636.089   RU   ISSN 0042-4846
CODEN: VETNAL
VETERINARIYA. 1924. m. $13.20. Agropromizdat, Sadovo-Spasskaya, 18, 107807 Moscow, Russia. (Co-sponsor: Ministerstvo Sel'skogo Khozyaistva S.S.S.R.) Ed. L.I. Bespalov. bk.rev.; bibl.; illus.; index. **Indexed:** Agri.Eng.Abstr., Anim.Breed.Abstr., Biol.Abstr., Biotech.Abstr., Chem.Abstr., Dairy Sci.Abstr., Food Sci.& Tech.Abstr., Helminthol.Abstr., Ind.Med., Ind.Vet., Maize Abstr., Nutr.Abstr., Pig News & Info., Poult.Abstr., Protozool.Abstr., Rev.Appl.Entomol., Small Anim.Abstr., Soyabean Abstr., Triticale Abstr., Vet.Bull., Weed Abstr.
—BLDSC shelfmark: 0038.000000.

636   CS   ISSN 0375-8427
VETERINARNI MEDICINA/VETERINARY MEDICINE; vedecky casopis. (Text and summaries in Czech or Slovak and English) 1928. m. $88. Ustav Vedeckotechnickych Informaci pro Zemedelstvi, Slezska 7, 120 56 Prague 2, Czechoslovakia. (Dist. by: Artia-Pegas-Press, Tiskarska 6, 108 00 Prague 10, Czechoslovakia) Ed. Z. Radosova. adv.; bibl.; charts; illus.; stat.; circ. 1,130. **Indexed:** Anim.Breed.Abstr., Biol.Abstr., Chem.Abstr., Curr.Adv.Ecol.Sci., Curr.Cont., Dairy Sci.Abstr., Excerp.Med., Field Crop Abstr., Food Sci.& Tech.Abstr., Helminthol.Abstr., Herb.Abstr., Ind.Med., Ind.Vet., Maize Abstr., Nutr.Abstr., Pig News & Info., Poult.Abstr., Protozool.Abstr., Rev.Plant Path., Rice Abstr., Small Anim.Abstr., Triticale Abstr., Vet.Bull.
—BLDSC shelfmark: 9225.550000.

636.089 597   CI   ISSN 0372-5480
CODEN: VEARA6
VETERINARSKI ARHIV. (Text in Croatian, English) 1931. bi-m. 500 din. to individuals; institutions 2000 din.; students 50 din. (foreign $50). Sveuciliste u Zagrebu, Veterinarski Fakultet - University of Zagreb, Veterinary Faculty, Heinzelova 55, P.O. Box 190, 41001 Zagreb, Croatia. TEL 041-290-111. Ed. Dubravko Timet. index; cum.index; circ. 900. (back issues avail.) **Indexed:** Anim.Breed.Abstr., Biol.Abstr., Biotech.Abstr., Chem.Abstr., Helminthol.Abstr., Herb.Abstr., Ind.Vet., Nutr.Abstr., Pig News & Info., Poult.Abstr., Protozool.Abstr., Ref.Zh., Small Anim.Abstr., Soyabean Abstr., Vet.Bull.
—BLDSC shelfmark: 9226.100000.
Description: Scientific journal of veterinary and related sciences: microbiology, immunology, parasitology, clinical sciences, animal science, physiology, anatomy.

636.089   YU   ISSN 0350-2457
VETERINARSKI GLASNIK. (Text in Serbo-Croatian; summaries in English, Russian) 1947. m. 900 din.($100) (effective Jan. 1990). Savez Veterinara i Veterinarskih Tehnicara, Bulevar JNA 18, 11000 Belgrade, Yugoslavia. TEL 011 684-597. (Dist. by: Jugoslovenska Knjiga, Trg. Republike 5-5, 11000 Belgrade, Yugoslavia) Ed. Dr. Bozidar Markovic. adv.; bk.rev.; index; circ. 2,500. (back issues avail.) **Indexed:** Anim.Breed.Abstr., Dairy Sci.Abstr., Forest Prod.Abstr., Herb.Abstr., Ind.Vet., Maize Abstr., Pig News & Info., Poult.Abstr., Protozool.Abstr., Small Anim.Abstr., Triticale Abstr., Vet.Bull.
—BLDSC shelfmark: 9226.400000.

636.089   GW   ISSN 0932-0814
SF910.5
VETERINARY AND COMPARATIVE ORTHOPAEDICS AND TRAUMATOLOGY. Short title: V.C.O.T. (Text in English) 1988. q. DM.232($144) to individuals; institutions DM.284($174.80). F.K. Schattauer Verlagsgesellschaft mbH, Postfach 104545, 7000 Stuttgart 10, Germany. TEL 0711-22987-0. FAX 0711-22987-50. (Co-sponsors: Veterinary Orthopedic Society (North America), European Society of Veterinary Orthopaedics and Traumatology) Ed. G. Sumner-Smith. bk.rev.; abstr. **Indexed:** Bibl.Agri., Ind.Vet., Small Anim.Abstr., Vet.Bull.
—BLDSC shelfmark: 9226.600000.
Refereed Serial

VETERINARY AND HUMAN TOXICOLOGY. see *ENVIRONMENTAL STUDIES — Toxicology And Environmental Safety*

636.089   UK   ISSN 0083-5870
SF601
VETERINARY ANNUAL. 1959. a. £45. Blackwell Scientific Publications Ltd., Osney Mead, Oxford OX2 0EL, England. (also avail. in microform from UMI; back issues avail.) **Indexed:** Anim.Breed.Abstr., Biol.Abstr., Dairy Sci.Abstr., Ind.Vet., Nutr.Abstr., Pig News & Info., Vet.Bull.
—BLDSC shelfmark: 9226.850000.

636 660   FR   ISSN 1018-533X
▼**VETERINARY BIOTECHNOLOGY NEWSLETTER.** (Text in English, French, Spanish) 1991. a. 150 F.($26) (effective 1992). Office International des Epizooties, 12 rue de Prony, 75017 Paris, France. TEL 44-15-18-88. (U.S. subscr. to: Scientific, Medical Publications of France, 100 East 42nd St., Ste. 1002, New York, NY 10017. TEL 212-983-6278) Ed. J. Blancon.
Description: Inventories the major developments in biotechnology applicable to animal health and production: monoclonal antibodies, nucleic acid probes, genetically-engineered vaccines, resistance marker genes.

636.089   US
VETERINARY CLINICAL PATHOLOGY. 1977. q. $28. (American Society for Veterinary Clinical Pathology) Veterinary Practice Publishing Co., 7 Ashley Ave. S., Santa Barbara, CA 93103-9989. TEL 805-965-1028. FAX 805-965-0722. (Subscr. addr.: Box 4457, Santa Barbara, CA 93140-4457) Ed. Dr. Alan Rebar. bk.rev.; abstr.; circ. 1,500. (also avail. in microfilm from UMI; reprint service avail. from UMI) **Indexed:** Chem.Abstr., Ind.Vet., Small Anim.Abstr., Vet.Bull.
Former titles: American Society for Veterinary Clinical Pathology. Journal; American Society of Veterinary Clinical Pathologists. Bulletin.

VETERINARY SCIENCE

636.089 US ISSN 0749-0739
VETERINARY CLINICS OF NORTH AMERICA: EQUINE PRACTICE. 1985. 3/yr. $66. W.B. Saunders Co., Curtis Center, Independence Square W., Philadelphia, PA 19106. TEL 215-238-7800. (Subscr. to: Journals 6277 Sea Harbor Dr., 4th Fl, Orlando FL 32891) Ed. Ruth Savitz. circ. 2,400. (also avail. in microfilm; back issues avail.) **Indexed:** Curr.Adv.Ecol.Sci., Ind.Vet., Protozool.Abstr.
—BLDSC shelfmark: 9227.017800.

636.089 US ISSN 0749-0720
VETERINARY CLINICS OF NORTH AMERICA: FOOD ANIMAL PRACTICE. 1985. 3/yr. $43. W.B. Saunders Co., Curtis Center, Independence Square W., Philadelphia, PA 19106. TEL 215-238-7800. (Subscr. to: Journals 6277 Sea Harbor Dr., 4th Fl., Orlando FL 32891) Ed. Ruth Savitz. circ. 1,800. (also avail. in microfilm; back issues avail.) **Indexed:** Agri.Eng.Abstr., Anim.Breed.Abstr., Curr.Adv.Ecol.Sci., Ind.Vet., Pig News & Info., Poult.Abstr., Vet.Bull.
—BLDSC shelfmark: 9227.017900.

636.089 US ISSN 0195-5616
CODEN: VNAPDW
VETERINARY CLINICS OF NORTH AMERICA: SMALL ANIMAL PRACTICE. 1971. 6/yr. $79. W.B. Saunders Co., Curtis Center, Independence Square W., Philadelphia, PA 19106. TEL 215-238-7800. Ed. Ruth Savitz. illus.; index. (also avail. in microform from MIM,UMI; reprint service avail. from UMI, ISI) **Indexed:** Anim.Breed.Abstr., Biol.Abstr., Curr.Adv.Ecol.Sci., Curr.Cont., Dent.Ind., Excerp.Med., Helminthol.Abstr., Ind.Med., Ind.Vet., Poult.Abstr., Protozool.Abstr., Small Anim.Abstr., Vet.Bull.
—BLDSC shelfmark: 9227.020000.
Supersedes in part (1971-1979): Veterinary Clinics of North America (ISSN 0091-0279)

636.089 US
VETERINARY DERMATOLOGY; an international journal. 1990. 6/yr. £130 (effective 1992). (European Society of Veterinary Dermatology) Pergamon Press, Inc., Journals Division, 660 White Plains Rd., Tarrytown, NY 10591-5153. TEL 914-524-9200. FAX 914-333-2444. (And: Headington Hill Hall, Oxford OX3 0BW, England. TEL 0865-794141) (Co-sponsor: American College of Veterinary Dermatology) Ed. Carol Foil. (also avail. in microform; back issues avail.)
Description: Research papers on all aspects of the skin of mammals, birds, reptiles, amphibians and fish.
Refereed Serial

636.089 FR ISSN 1010-3538
VETERINARY DRUG REGISTRATION NEWSLETTER. (Text in English, French, Spanish) 1987. s-a. 330 F.($55) (effective 1992). Office International des Epizooties, 12, rue de Prony, 75017 Paris, France. TEL 44-15-18-88. FAX 42-67-09-87. TELEX EPIZOTI 642 285 F. (U.S. Subscr. to: Scientific, Medical Publications of France, 100 East 42nd St., Ste. 1002, New York, NY 10017. TEL 212-983-6278) Ed. J. Blancon.
Description: Features information on international meetings, procedures for registering veterinary drugs, registration of new veterinary drugs, quality of pharmaceutical products, industry news and new developments.

636.089 US ISSN 0042-4862
VETERINARY ECONOMICS; the veterinarian's business magazine. 1960. m. (free to practicing veterinarians in the U.S.). Veterinary Medicine Publishing Co., 9073 Lenexa Dr., Lenexa, KS 66215. TEL 913-492-4300. Ed. Rebecca R. Turner. adv.; bk.rev.; charts; illus.; stat.; tr.lit.; index; circ. 40,000. (also avail. in microform from UMI) **Indexed:** Account.Ind. (1974-), Helminthol.Abstr., Ind.Vet., Vet.Bull.
—BLDSC shelfmark: 9227.070000.

636.087 CN
VETERINARY FOCUS. 1989. 4/yr. $26. Arthurs Publications Ltd., 5200 Dixie Rd., Ste. 204, Mississauga, Ontario L4W 1E4, Canada. Ed. Linda Wright.
Description: Covers a specific topic in small animal veterinary medicine in each issue.
Refereed Serial

636.089 US
VETERINARY FORUM. 1982. m. $30 (free to qualified personnel). Forum Publications, Inc., 1610-A Frederica Rd., St. Simons Island, GA 31522-2509. TEL 912-638-4848. FAX 912-634-0768. Ed. Michael D. Sollars. adv.; bk.rev.; tr.lit.; circ. 42,000 (controlled).
Formerly: Veterinary Classified.
Description: Created to educate readers on the various ways they can offer more services and products to their clients. Provides a ready reference in medical and practical management.

636.089 UK ISSN 0301-6943
VETERINARY HISTORY. 1978. s-a. £4 (foreign £6) individuals; £6(foreign £8) institutions. Veterinary History Society, c/o E. Barbour-Hill, Tan-Y-Coed, High St., Penlon, Bangor, Gwynedd LL57 1PX, Wales. Ed. A.W. Johnson. adv.; bk.rev.; circ. 200. **Indexed:** Ind.Vet.

636.089 NE ISSN 0165-2427
CODEN: VIIMDS
VETERINARY IMMUNOLOGY AND IMMUNOPATHOLOGY; an international journal of comparative immunology. (Text in English) 1980. 16/yr.(in 4 vols.; 4 nos./vol.). fl.1124 (effective 1992). Elsevier Science Publishers B.V., P.O. Box 211, 1000 AE Amsterdam, Netherlands. TEL 020-5803911. FAX 020-5803598. TELEX 18582 ESPA NL. (Subscr. in U.S. and Canada to: Elsevier Science Publishing Co., Inc., Box 882, Madison Sq. Sta., New York, NY 10159. TEL 212-989-5800) Eds. J. Goudswaard, S. Krakowka. adv.; bk.rev.; illus.; index. (also avail. in microform from RPI; back issues avail.) **Indexed:** Anim.Breed.Abstr., Biol.Abstr., Chem.Abstr., Curr.Adv.Ecol.Sci., Curr.Cont., Dairy Sci.Abstr., Excerp.Med., Helminthol.Abstr., Ind.Med., Ind.Vet., Pig News & Info., Poult.Abstr., Protozool.Abstr., Small Anim.Abstr., Vet.Bull.
—BLDSC shelfmark: 9228.200000.
Description: Deals with the study of veterinary immunology and immunopathology as applied to domestic animals, laboratory animals and other species that are useful to man.
Refereed Serial

636.089 PL ISSN 0042-4870
CODEN: BVIPA7
VETERINARY INSTITUTE, PULAWY. BULLETIN. (Text and summaries in English) 1957. a. $50 or exchange basis. Instytut Weterynarii, c/o Krystyna Ciemiega-Wilczynska, Sec., Al. Partyzantow 55, 24-100 Pulawy, Poland. TEL 30-51. TELEX 642401 IWET PL. Ed. Marian Grundboeck. circ. 500. **Indexed:** Anim.Breed.Abstr., Biol.Abstr., Chem.Abstr., Curr.Adv.Ecol.Sci., Dairy Sci.Abstr., Food Sci.& Tech.Abstr., Helminthol.Abstr., Ind.Vet., Landwirt.Zentralbl., Nutr.Abstr., Pig News & Info., Poult.Abstr., Ref.Zh., Small Anim.Abstr., Vet.Bull.
—BLDSC shelfmark: 2805.300000.
Description: Publishes original scientific papers of research performed in the institute.

636.089 US
VETERINARY MEDICAL REVIEW. 1971; N.S. 1980. s-a. free. University of Missouri, Columbia, College of Veterinary Medicine, Veterinary Medical Library, W218 Veterinary Medicine, Columbia, MO 65211. TEL 314-882-2461. Ed. Deborah Beroset Diamond. charts; illus.; stat.; circ. 3,000. (back issues avail.) **Indexed:** Anim.Breed.Abstr., Biotech.Abstr., Chem.Abstr., Dairy Sci.Abstr., Helminthol.Abstr., Ind.Vet., Protozool.Abstr., Vet.Bull.
Incorporates (1950-1979): Missouri Veterinarian (ISSN 0540-4517); Which was formerly: Veterinary Scope.
Description: For alumni, faculty and students, as well as other practicing veterinarians in Missouri.

636.089 US ISSN 8750-7943
VETERINARY MEDICINE. 1905. m. $41.95. Veterinary Medicine Publishing Co., 9073 Lenexa Dr., Lenexa, KS 66215. TEL 913-492-4300. Ed. Dr. Tracy Revoir. adv.; bk.rev.; abstr.; bibl.; charts; illus.; stat.; tr.lit.; index; circ. 25,000. (also avail. in microform from UMI) **Indexed:** Anim.Breed.Abstr., Biol.Abstr., Biol.& Agr.Ind., Biotech.Abstr., Curr.Adv.Ecol.Sci., Curr.Cont., Dairy Sci.Abstr., Helminthol.Abstr., Herb.Abstr., Ind.Med., Ind.Vet., Nutr.Abstr., Pig News & Info., Protozool.Abstr., Rev.Plant Path., Risk Abstr., Small Anim.Abstr., Vet.Bull.
Formerly (until 1985): Veterinary Medicine - Small Animal Clinician (ISSN 0042-4889)
Refereed Serial

VETERINARY MEDICINE GUIDANCE MANUAL. see *PUBLIC HEALTH AND SAFETY*

636 593 578 NE ISSN 0378-1135
CODEN: VMICDQ
VETERINARY MICROBIOLOGY; an international journal. (Text in English) 1976. 16/yr.(in 4 vols.; 4 nos./vol.). fl.1144 (effective 1992). Elsevier Science Publishers B.V., P.O. Box 211, 1000 AE Amsterdam, Netherlands. TEL 020-5803911. FAX 020-5803598. TELEX 18582 ESPA NL. (Subscr. in U.S. and Canada to: Elsevier Science Publishing Co., Inc., Box 882, Madison Sq. Sta., New York, NY 10159. TEL 212-989-5800) Eds. P.B. Spradbrow, A.J. Frost. adv.; bk.rev.; bibl.; illus.; index. (also avail. in microform from RPI) **Indexed:** Abstr.Hyg., Biol.Abstr., Chem.Abstr., Curr.Adv.Ecol.Sci., Curr.Cont., Dairy Sci.Abstr., Dent.Ind., Excerp.Med., Helminthol.Abstr., Ind.Med., Ind.Vet., Microbiol.Abstr., Pig News & Info., Poult.Abstr., Ref.Zh., Small Anim.Abstr., Trop.Dis.Bull., Vet.Bull.
—BLDSC shelfmark: 9229.120000.
Description: Concerned with microgiological diseases of all animals that are useful to man. Publishes information on pathogeneses, host responses, immunology, epidemiology, disease prevention, treatment, control and comparative studies of diseases affecting man and animals, as well as laboratory studies of the causal agents of diseases of animals.
Refereed Serial

636.089 NE ISSN 0304-4017
CODEN: VPARDI
VETERINARY PARASITOLOGY; an international scientific journal. (Text in English) 1975. 16/yr.(in 4 vols.; 4 nos./vol.). fl.1204 (effective 1992). Elsevier Science Publishers B.V., P.O. Box 211, 1000 AE Amsterdam, Netherlands. TEL 020-5803911. FAX 020-5803598. TELEX 18582 ESPA NL. (Subscr. in U.S. and Canada to: Elsevier Science Publishing Co., Inc., Box 882, Madison Sq. Sta., New York, NY 10159. TEL 212-989-5800) Ed. S.M. Gaafar. (also avail. in microform from RPI) **Indexed:** Abstr.Hyg., Biol.Abstr., Chem.Abstr., Curr.Adv.Ecol.Sci., Curr.Cont., Dairy Sci.Abstr., Dent.Ind., Excerp.Med., Helminthol.Abstr., Ind.Med., Ind.Vet., Pig News & Info., Poult.Abstr., Protozool.Abstr., Ref.Zh., Rev.Appl.Entomol., Small Anim.Abstr., Trop.Dis.Bull., Vet.Bull.
—BLDSC shelfmark: 9229.163000.
Description: Publishes papers dealing with all aspects of disease prevention, pathology, treatment, epidemiology, and control of parasites in all animals which can be regarded as being useful to man.
Refereed Serial

636.089 US ISSN 0300-9858
SF769 CODEN: VTPHAK
VETERINARY PATHOLOGY. (Text in English and German) 1964. bi-m. $60. (American College of Veterinary Pathologists) Waverly Press, Inc. (Subsidiary of: Williams & Wilkins), 428 E. Preston St., Box 64025, Baltimore, MD 21202. TEL 301-528-4000. Ed.Bd. adv.; bk.rev.; bibl.; charts; illus.; index; circ. 1,200. **Indexed:** Biol.Abstr., Biotech.Abstr., Chem.Abstr., Curr.Adv.Cancer Res., Curr.Adv.Ecol.Sci., Curr.Cont., Dairy Sci.Abstr., Dent.Ind., Excerp.Med., Helminthol.Abstr., Herb.Abstr., Ind.Med., Ind.Vet., Nutr.Abstr., Pig News & Info., Poult.Abstr., Protozool.Abstr., Rev.Plant Path., Small Anim.Abstr., So.Pac.Per.Ind., Vet.Bull.
—BLDSC shelfmark: 9229.165000.
Formerly: Pathologia Veterinaria (ISSN 0031-2975)
Refereed Serial

636.089 UK ISSN 0042-4897
VETERINARY PRACTICE. 1966. s-m. £22 (foreign £25.40)(effective Jan. 1992). A.E. Morgan Publications Ltd., Stanley House, 9 West St., Epsom, Surrey KT18 7RL, England. TEL 0372-741411. FAX 0372-744493. Ed. C. Cattrall. adv.; bk.rev.; abstr.; charts; illus. (tabloid format; also avail. in microform from UMI) **Indexed:** Ind.Vet., Small Anim.Abstr., Vet.Bull.
Formerly: Veterinary News.
Description: News and articles on products and developments in the veterinary profession.

636.089 US ISSN 1047-8639
VETERINARY PRACTICE STAFF; current ideas and new information. 1989. bi-m. $28. Veterinary Practice Publishing Co., 7 Ashley Ave. S., Santa Barbara, CA 93103-9989. TEL 805-965-1028. FAX 805-965-0722. (Subscr. addr.: Box 4457, Santa Barbara, CA 93140-4457) Ed. Dr. Donald Applegate. circ. 16,000.
 Description: Targeted towards employees of the veterinary clinic, including technicians, assistants, office personnel, and receptionists.

636.089 AT ISSN 0157-3136
VETERINARY PRESCRIBERS INDEX. 1979. a. Aus.$36. P V P Publications Pty Ltd., Box 278, Balgowlah, NSW 2093, Australia. circ. 3,000.

636.089 US
VETERINARY PRODUCT NEWS. Short title: V P N. 1987. 8/yr. $30 ($62 in N. America; elsewhere $98)(effective 1992). Enterprise Communications Inc., 1483 Chain Bridge Rd., Ste. 202, McLean, VA 22101. TEL 703-448-0336. FAX 703-448-0270. (Subscr. to: 1165 Northchase Pkwy., N.E., Ste. 350, Marietta, GA 30067. TEL 404-988-9558) Ed. Lynn E. Densford. adv.; circ. 41,500.

636.089 NE ISSN 0165-2176
CODEN: VEQUDU
VETERINARY QUARTERLY. (Text in English) 1979. q. fl.162($92) (Koninklijke Nederlandse Maatschappij voor Diergeneeskunde - Royal Netherlands Veterinary Association) Kluwer Academic Publishers, Postbus 17, 3300 AA Dordrecht, Netherlands. TEL 078-334911. FAX 078-334254. TELEX 29245. (Dist. by: Kluwer Academic Publishers Group, P.O. Box 322, 3300 AH Dordrecht, Netherlands; N. America dist. addr.: Box 358, Accord Station, Hingham, MA 02018-0358. TEL 617-871-6600) Ed. J. Goudswaard. adv. (back issues avail.; reprint service avail. from SWZ) **Indexed:** Anim.Breed.Abstr., Bibl.Agri., Biol.Abstr., Biotech.Abstr., Chem.Abstr., Curr.Adv.Ecol.Sci., Curr.Cont., Dairy Sci.Abstr., Food Sci.Abstr., Helminthol.Abstr., Ind.Med., Ind.Vet., Pig News & Info., Poult.Abstr., Protozool.Abstr., Small Anim.Abstr., Vet.Bull.
—BLDSC shelfmark: 9229.270000.

636.089 US ISSN 1058-8183
SF757.8
VETERINARY RADIOLOGY & ULTRASOUND. 1960. bi-m. $72 to individuals (foreign $82); institutions $92 (foreign $102). American College of Veterinary Radiology, c/o Lucinda Ayres, 2520 Beechridge Rd., Raleigh, NC 27608. TEL 919-881-4165. FAX 919-821-9578. (Co-sponsor: International Veterinary Radiology Association) Ed. Dr. Donald E. Thrall. adv.; illus.; index; circ. 700. (also avail. in microform from UMI) **Indexed:** Biol.Abstr., Helminthol.Abstr., Ind.Vet., Small Anim.Abstr., Vet.Bull.
 Former titles (until 1992): Veterinary Radiology (ISSN 0196-3627); (until 1980): American Veterinary Radiology Society. Journal (ISSN 0066-1155)
 Description: Presents articles of interest to the practicing veterinarian. Covers radiologic and ultrasound techniques, diagnostic interpretation, radiologic therapy and current advances in the field.
Refereed Serial

636.089 UK ISSN 0042-4900
CODEN: VETRAX
VETERINARY RECORD. 1888. w. £100 (foreign £138.50). British Veterinary Association, 7 Mansfield St., London W1M 0AT, England. TEL 01-636 6541. Ed. Edward Boden. circ. 10,000. (also avail. in microform from UMI; reprint service avail. from UMI) **Indexed:** Anim.Breed.Abstr., Biol.Abstr., Biol.& Agr.Ind., Biotech.Abstr., Chem.Abstr., Curr.Adv.Biochem., Curr.Adv.Cancer Res., Curr.Adv.Ecol.Sci., Curr.Cont., Dairy Sci.Abstr., Dent.Ind., Excerp.Med., Food Sci.& Tech.Abstr., Helminthol.Abstr., Herb.Abstr., Ind.Med., Ind.Vet., Nutr.Abstr., Pig News & Info., Poult.Abstr., Protozool.Abstr., Rev.Appl.Entomol., Rev.Plant Path., Risk Abstr., Vet.Bull., W.R.C.Inf., Weed Abstr., World Agri.Econ. & Rural Sociol.Abstr.
—BLDSC shelfmark: 9230.000000.

636.089 NE ISSN 0165-7380
CODEN: VRCODX
VETERINARY RESEARCH COMMUNICATIONS; an international journal publishing topical reviews and research articles on all aspects of the veterinary sciences. 1977. 6/yr. fl.307($174) Kluwer Academic Publishers, Postbus 17, 3300 AA Dordrecht, Netherlands. TEL 078-334911. FAX 078-334254. TELEX 29245. (Dist. by: Kluwer Academic Publishers Group, P.O. Box 322, 3300 AH Dordrecht, Netherlands; N. America dist. addr.: Box 358, Accord Station, Hingham, MA 02018-0358. TEL 617-871-6600) Ed. M.M.H. Sewell. adv.; bk.rev.; abstr.; bibl.; charts; illus.; index. cum.index; circ. 600. (also avail. in microform from RPI; back issues avail.; reprint service avail. from SWZ) **Indexed:** Anim.Breed.Abstr., Biol.Abstr., Chem.Abstr., Curr.Adv.Ecol.Sci., Curr.Cont., Dairy Sci.Abstr., Excerp.Med., Helminthol.Abstr., Ind.Med., Ind.Vet., Nutr.Abstr., Pig News & Info., Poult.Abstr., Protozool.Abstr., Small Anim.Abstr., Soyabean Abstr., Vet.Bull.
—BLDSC shelfmark: 9230.200000.
 Formerly: Veterinary Science Communications (ISSN 0378-4312)
 Description: Forum for current research in all disciplines of veterinary sciences.

636 NZ
VETERINARY SURGEONS IN NEW ZEALAND; registered under the Veterinary Surgeons Act 1956 & persons entitled to use the title or description of veterinary practitioner. 1957. a. price varies. Government Printing Office, Private Bag, Wellington, New Zealand. circ. 1,000.

636.089 US ISSN 0161-3499
SF911 CODEN: VESUD6
VETERINARY SURGERY. 1972. bi-m. $65 to individuals (foreign $80); institutions $95 (foreign $100). (American College of Veterinary Surgeons, Inc.) J.B. Lippincott Co., East Washington Sq., Philadelphia, PA 19105. TEL 215-238-4200. (Co-sponsor: American College of Veterinary Anesthesiologists) Ed. Ghery D. Pettit, D.V.M. adv.; illus.; index; circ. 2,300. (reprint service avail. from UMI) **Indexed:** Biol.Abstr., Ind.Vet., Pig News & Info., Small Anim.Abstr., Vet.Bull.
—BLDSC shelfmark: 9231.037000.
 Formerly: Journal of Veterinary Surgery.
 Description: Covers clinical and research topics of interest to veterinary surgeons and anesthesiologists.
Refereed Serial

636.089 US ISSN 8750-8990
VETERINARY TECHNICIAN. 1980. 10/yr. $31. Veterinary Learning Systems, 425 Phillips Blvd., Ste. 100, Trenton, NJ 08618. TEL 609-882-5600. FAX 609-882-6357. Ed. Richard B. Ford, DVM. adv.; index; circ. 20,000. **Indexed:** Dairy Sci.Abstr., Ind.Vet., Protozool.Abstr., Small Anim.Abstr.
—BLDSC shelfmark: 9231.038000.

636.089 UK
VETERINARY TIMES. 1972. m. £36 (foreign £44)(free to qualified personnel). Veterinary Business Development Ltd., Olympus House, Werrington Centre, Peterborough PE4 6NA, England. TEL 733-325522. FAX 733-325512. Ed. D. Ritchie. adv.; bk.rev.; circ. 7,000. (tabloid format) **Indexed:** Agri.Eng.Abstr., Ind.Vet., Pig News & Info., Small Anim.Abstr.
 Formerly (until Sep. 1984): Veterinary Drug.
 Description: Covers new products, new techniques and news.

636.089 IE
VETERINARY UPDATE. 1984. bi-m. Jude Publications Ltd., 2-6 Tara St., Dublin 2, Ireland. Ed. Maria Farren. **Indexed:** Ind.Vet.

636.089 UN
VIGILANCIA EPIDEMIOLOGICA DE LA RABIA PARA LAS AMERICAS. English edition: Epidemiological Surveillance of Rabies for the Americas. 1969. m. free. Centro Panamericano de Zoonosis, Casilla 3092, 1000 Buenos Aires, Argentina. (Affiliate: World Health Organization) Ed. Eduardo Guarnera. circ. 950 (Spanish ed.); 450 (English ed.).
 Supersedes in part (since vol.7, no.4, 1978): Vigilancia Epidemiologica.

636.089 BE ISSN 0303-9021
CODEN: VDTIAX
VLAAMS DIERGENEESKUNDIG TIJDSCHRIFT/FLEMISH VETERINARY JOURNAL. (Text in Dutch and English; summaries in English) 1932. bi-m. 1000 BEF. Natuur- en Geneeskundige Vennootschap, Krijgslaan 281 S.8, B-9000 Ghent, Belgium. Ed. M. Pensaert. adv.; bk.rev.; abstr.; charts; illus.; index; circ. 1,550. **Indexed:** Anim.Breed.Abstr., Biol.Abstr., Biotech.Abstr., Chem.Abstr., Curr.Adv.Ecol.Sci., Curr.Cont., Dairy Sci.Abstr., Helminthol.Abstr., Ind.Vet., Pig News & Info., Protozool.Abstr., Rev.Plant Path., Small Anim.Abstr., Vet.Bull.
—BLDSC shelfmark: 9246.000000.

636.089 PL
CODEN: AWAMDP
WARSAW AGRICULTURAL UNIVERSITY. S G G W. ANNALS. VETERINARY MEDICINE. (Text mainly in English; occasionally in French, German or Russian; summaries in Polish) 1957. irreg. $6. Szkola Glowna Gospodarstwa Wiejskiego (SGGW) - Warsaw Agricultural University, Ul. Nowoursynowska 166, 02-766 Warsaw, Poland. (Dist. by: Ars Polona-Ruch, Krakowskie Przedmiescie 7, 00-068 Warsaw, Poland) Ed. T. Roskosz. **Indexed:** Chem.Abstr., Food Sci.& Tech.Abstr., Ind.Vet., Vet.Bull.
 Former titles: Warsaw Agricultural University. S G G W - A R. Annals. Veterinary Medicine (ISSN 0208-5763); (until 1980): Akademia Rolnicza, Warsaw. Zeszyty Naukowe. Weterynaria (ISSN 0324-9085)

636.089 AU ISSN 0043-535X
CODEN: WTMOA3
WIENER TIERAERZTLICHE MONATSSCHRIFT. (Text in German; summaries in English) vol.72, 1985. m. S.1100. (Oesterreichische Tieraerzteschaft) Ostag Weiss und Co., Wickenburggasse 17, A-1082 Vienna, Austria. TEL 0222-427573. FAX 0222-488292. (Co-sponsor: Oesterreichische Gesellschaft der Tieraerzte) Ed.Bd. adv.; bk.rev.; abstr.; bibl.; charts; illus.; index; circ. 1,500. **Indexed:** Anim.Breed.Abstr., Biol.Abstr., Biotech.Abstr., Chem.Abstr., Curr.Adv.Ecol.Sci., Curr.Cont., Dairy Sci.Abstr., Excerp.Med., Food Sci.& Tech.Abstr., Helminthol.Abstr., Ind.Vet., Nutr.Abstr., Pig News & Info., Poult.Abstr., Protozool.Abstr., Rev.Plant Path., Small Anim.Abstr., Soils & Fert., Soyabean Abstr., Vet.Bull.
—BLDSC shelfmark: 9316.000000.

WILDLIFE DISEASE REVIEW. see *MEDICAL SCIENCES*

WILDLIFE JOURNAL. see *BIOLOGY*

636.089 639.9 US ISSN 1044-2618
WILDLIFE REHABILITATION TODAY. 1989. q. $15. Coconut Creek Publishing Co., 2201 N.W. 40th Terrace, Coconut Creek, FL 33066-2032. TEL 305-972-6092. adv.; bk.rev.; circ. 7,509. (back issues avail.)
 Description: Contains non-technical veterinary and wildlife care, and educational articles.

WILDLIFE RESCUE NEWS. see *ANIMAL WELFARE*

636.089 FR ISSN 1017-3102
WORLD ANIMAL HEALTH. (Text in English, French, Spanish) a. 250 F.($60) Office International des Epizooties, 12, rue de Prony, 75017 Paris, France. TEL 44-15-18-88. FAX 42-67-09-87. TELEX EPIZOTI 642 285 F. (U.S. Subscr. to: Scientific, Medical Publications of France, 100 East 42nd St., Ste. 1002, New York, NY 10017. TEL 212-983-6278) Ed. J. Blancon. (back issues avail.)
—BLDSC shelfmark: 9352.912250.
 Description: Disease status of over 100 countries for 105 diseases of animals and fish.

WORLD ANIMAL SCIENCE. see *BIOLOGY — Zoology*

636.089 BE
WORLD BUIATRICS CONGRESS. (Each report published in the host country) (Text in English, French, German and Spanish) 1960. biennial. World Association for Buiatrics, c/o P. Lekeux, Sec., Faculte de Medecine Veterinaire, Bat B42, Sart Tilman, B-4000 Liege, Belgium. TEL 32-41-564030. FAX 32-41-562935.
 Formerly: International Meeting on Cattle Diseases. Reports. (ISSN 0074-6975)

VETERINARY SCIENCE

636.089   SP   ISSN 0084-2443
WORLD VETERINARY CONGRESS. PROCEEDINGS. 1863. quadrennial, 21st, 1979, Moscow; 22nd, 1983, Perth; 23rd, 1987, Montreal; 24th, 1991, Rio de Janeiro. price varies. World Veterinary Association, C. Principe de Vergara, 276, piso 6, apdo. E, 28016 Madrid, Spain. TEL 458-29-09. FAX 458-29-38. Ed.Bd. bibl.; circ. 5,000. **Indexed:** Anim.Breed.Abstr.

636.089 636   CC   ISSN 0366-6964
XUMU SHOUYI XUEBAO/ACTA VETERINARIA ET ZOOTECHNICA SINICA. (Text in Chinese) q. $1.80 per no. Zhongguo Nongye Kexueyuan, Xumu Yanjiusuo - Chinese Academy of Agriculture, Institute of Animal Husbandry, Ma Lian Wa, Haidian Qu, Beijing 100094, People's Republic of China. TEL 2581177. Ed. Dong Wei. **Indexed:** Anim.Breed.Abstr., Biol.Abstr., Curr.Leather Lit., Ind.Vet., Nutr.Abstr., Pig News & Info., Poult.Abstr., Protozool.Abstr., Rev.Med.& Vet.Mycol., Vet.Bull. —BLDSC shelfmark: 0670.900000.

636.089   ZA
ZAMBIA. DEPARTMENT OF VETERINARY AND TSETSE CONTROL SERVICES. ANNUAL REPORT. (Text in English) a. 1 n. Government Printer, Box 30136, Lusaka, Zambia.
Description: Annual paper of veterinary research and diagnostic work in the identification of disease in Zambia.

636.089   NR
ZARIYA VETERINARIAN. (Text in English) s-a. £N40 (foreign $50). Ahmadu Bello University, Faculty of Veterinary Medicine, Zaria, Kaduna State, Nigeria. Ed. J.B. Adeyanju. circ. 1,000. (back issues avail.)

636.089   GW
ZEITSCHRIFT FUER GANZHEITLICHE TIERMEDIZIN. q. DM.56 (students DM.36). (Deutsche Gesellschaft fuer Biologische Veterinaer-Medizin e.V.) Karl F. Haug Verlag GmbH, Fritz-Frey-Str. 21, Postfach 102840, 6900 Heidelberg 1, Germany. TEL 06221-4062-0. FAX 06221-400727. TELEX 461683-HVVFMD. Ed. Dr. H. Krueger.
Formerly: Deutsche Zeitschrift fuer Biologische Veterinaermedizin (ISSN 0179-714X)

ZENTRALINSTITUT FUER VERSUCHSTIERZUCHT. JAHRESBERICHT. see *BIOLOGY*

ZHONGGUO RENSHOU GONGHUANBING ZAZHI. see *BIOLOGY — Microbiology*

636.089   CC
ZHONGGUO SHOUYI ZAZHI/CHINESE JOURNAL OF VETERINARY MEDICINE. (Text in Chinese) m. $0.80 per no. Guoji Shudian, Qikan Bu, Chegongzhuang Xilu 21, P.O. Box 399, Beijing 100044, People's Republic of China. **Indexed:** Anim.Breed.Abstr., Ind.Vet., Pig News & Info., Poult.Abstr., Protozool.Abstr., Vet.Bull.

636.089   CC   ISSN 0258-7033
CODEN: ZXZADM
ZHONGGUO XUMU ZAZHI/CHINESE JOURNAL OF ANIMAL SCIENCE. (Text in Chinese) 1963. bi-m. $0.70 per no. Zhongguo Xumu Shouyi Xuehui - Chinese Society of Animal Husbandry and Veterinary Science, 33 Nong Feng Li, Dongdaqiao, Chaoyangqu, Beijing 100020, People's Republic of China. TEL 5002288. Ed. Feng Yanglian. **Indexed:** Chem.Abstr., Ind.Vet., Maize Abstr., Pig News & Info., Poult.Abstr., Soyabean Abstr., Trop.Oil Seeds Abstr.

636.089   RH
ZIMBABWE VETERINARY JOURNAL. (Text and summaries in English) 1970. q. $50. Zimbabwe Veterinary Association, P.O. Box A195, Avondale, Harare, Zimbabwe. TEL 725743. Ed. G. Hill. adv.; bk.rev.; abstr.; index; circ. 350. (back issues avail.) **Indexed:** Field Crop Abstr., Ind.Vet., Rev.Appl.Entomol., Vet.Bull.
Formerly (until 1980): Rhodesian Veterinary Journal.
Description: Contains original and review papers on all aspects of animal health in Zimbabwe and SADCC countries, including articles by non-veterinarians.

VETERINARY SCIENCE — Abstracting, Bibliographies, Statistics

636.097 016   JA   ISSN 0001-7221
ACTA VETERINARIA JAPONICA. (Text in English and European languages) 1956. q. exchange basis. Nihon University, Research Institute for Veterinary Science - Nihon Daigaku Juigaku Kenkyujo, Shimouma, Setagaya-ku, Tokyo 154, Japan. Ed. Ushio Tanaka. bk.rev.; index; circ. 650.

AGRICULTURAL AND VETERINARY PRODUCT INDEX. see *AGRICULTURE — Abstracting, Bibliographies, Statistics*

AGROINDEX - AUTOMATED INFORMATION SYSTEM; bibliographic and abstracting journal. see *AGRICULTURE — Abstracting, Bibliographies, Statistics*

636.089 016   GW   ISSN 0233-2809
AGROSELEKT. REIHE 4: VETERINAERMEDIZIN; an agricultural abstracting journal. 1956. m. DM.453.60. (Akademie der Landwirtschaftswissenschaften der DDR, Institut fuer Landwirtschaftliche Information und Dokumentation) Akademie-Verlag Berlin, Leipziger Str. 3-4, 1086 Berlin, Germany. Ed. W. Kleeberg. bk.rev.; index. cum.index; circ. 650. **Indexed:** Ind.Vet., Vet.Bull.
Formerly: Landwirtschaftliches Zentralblatt. Abteilung 4: Veterinaermedizin (ISSN 0023-821X)

636.089   UN
CENTRO PANAMERICANO DE ZOONOSIS. SERIE DE BIBLIOGRAFIAS. 1982. irreg. Centro Panamericano de Zoonosis, Casilla 3092, 1000 Buenos Aires, Argentina. TEL 792-4047-49. TELEX 24577 AR CPZ. (Affiliate: World Health Organization)

636.089 016   SA   ISSN 0019-0918
I V S. (Index of Veterinary Specialists) 1962. q. M.I.M.S. (Subsidiary of: Times Media Ltd.), P.O. Box 2059, Pretoria 0001, South Africa. TEL 012-3485010. FAX 012-477716. Ed. Dr. A. Immelman. adv.; index; cum.index; circ. 2,044. (back issues avail.)
Description: Indexes veterinary medicines available in South Africa in alphabetical and pharmacological order.

636.089 016   UK   ISSN 0019-3941
INDEX OF VETERINARY SPECIALITIES. 1961. bi-m. £18 (foreign £19)(effective Jan. 1992). A.E. Morgan Publications Ltd., Stanley House, 9 West St., Epsom, Surrey KT18 7RL, England. TEL 0372-741411. FAX 0372-744493. Ed. C. Cattrall. adv.; circ. 3,700. (also avail. in microform from UMI; reprint service avail. from UMI)
Description: Articles and news of products and developments in the veterinary field.

636.089   AT   ISSN 1033-2863
INDEX OF VETERINARY SPECIALTIES. 1980. a. Aus.$35. M I M S Australia, 48 Albany St., Crows Nest, N.S.W. 2065, Australia. TEL 02-438-3588. Ed. Linda H. Bodewitz-Dodd. circ. 3,500.
Description: Classified listing of all veterinary drugs available in Australia.

636 016   UK   ISSN 0019-4123
Z6674
INDEX VETERINARIUS; a classified subject and author index produced by computer processes of current literature on veterinary science with approximately 23,000 titles. 1933. m. (with annual cumulation). £432($802) C.A.B. International, Wallingford, Oxon OX10 8DE, England. TEL 0491 32111. FAX 0491-33508. TELEX 847964 COMAGG G. (U.S. subscr. to: C.A.B. International, North American Office, 845 N. Park Ave., Tucson, AZ 85719. TEL 800-528-4841) bibl.; circ. 750. (also avail. on floppy disk; back issues avail.) **Indexed:** Dairy Sci.Abstr., Helminthol.Abstr., Nutr.Abstr., Rev.Appl.Entomol., Rev.Plant Path.
●Also available online. Vendor(s): BRS (VETR), CISTI, DIMDI, DIALOG, European Space Agency (File nos.16 & 124/CAB).
—BLDSC shelfmark: 4390.000000.

636.089   II   ISSN 0254-4105
CODEN: IJVSD9
INDIAN JOURNAL OF VETERINARY SURGERY. (Text in English) 1980. s-a. Rs.75($40) Indian Society for Veterinary Surgery, Department of Surgery & Radiology, College of Veterinary Sciences, Pantnagar, Nainital (U.P.) 263145, India. Ed. Dr. Amresh Kumar. adv.; bk.rev.; circ. 500. **Indexed:** Biol.Abstr., Ind.Vet., Indian Sci.Abstr., Vet.Bull.
Description: Publishes research results, clinical and review articles in Indian and foreign veterinary surgery and related subjects.

595.7 016   UK   ISSN 0957-6770
REVIEW OF MEDICAL AND VETERINARY ENTOMOLOGY. 1913. m. £149($274) C.A.B. International, Wallingford, Oxon OX10 8DE, England. TEL 0491-32111. FAX 0491-33508. TELEX 847964 COMAGG G. (U.S. subscr. to: C.A.B. International, North American Office, 845 N. Park Ave., Tucson, AZ 85719. TEL 800-528-4841) Ed.Bd. adv.; bk.rev.; abstr.; index; circ. 1,250. (also avail. on floppy disk; back issues avail.) **Indexed:** Abstr.Hyg., Chem.Abstr., Helminthol.Abstr., Poult.Abstr., Rev.Appl.Entomol., Trop.Dis.Bull., Vet.Bull.
●Also available online. Vendor(s): BRS (VETR), CISTI, DIMDI, DIALOG, European Space Agency (File nos.16 & 124/CAB).
Formerly: Review of Applied Entomology. Series B: Medical and Veterinary (ISSN 0305-0084)
Description: Deals with insects and other arthropods which transmit diseases or are otherwise injurious to man and to animals of significance to man.

REVIEW OF MEDICAL AND VETERINARY MYCOLOGY. see *BIOLOGY — Abstracting, Bibliographies, Statistics*

636 016   UK   ISSN 0961-3501
SMALL ANIMALS. 1975. a. £47($87) C.A.B. International, Wallingford, Oxon OX10 8DE, England. TEL 0491 32111. FAX 0491-33508. TELEX 847964 COMAGG G. (U.S. subscr. to: C.A.B. International, North American Office, 845 N. Park Ave., Tucson, AZ 85719. TEL 800-528-4841) circ. 250. (back issues avail.) **Indexed:** Rev.Appl.Entomol.
●Also available online. Vendor(s): BRS (VETR), CISTI, DIMDI, DIALOG, European Space Agency (File nos.16 & 124/CAB).
Formerly (until 1991): Small Animal Abstracts (ISSN 0306-7580)
Description: Covers the research literature on diseases, physiology, reproduction, nutrition and behavior of dogs, cats and other pets.

636.089   UK   ISSN 0042-4854
SF601
VETERINARY BULLETIN; a monthly abstract journal on veterinary science. 1931. m. £351($639) C.A.B. International, Wallingford, Oxon OX10 8DE, England. TEL 0491-32111. FAX 0491-33508. TELEX 847964-COMAGG-G. (U.S. subscr. to: C.A.B. International, North American Office, 845 N. Park Ave., Tucson, AZ 85719. TEL 800-528-4841) Ed. R. Mack. adv.; bk.rev.; abstr.; circ. 1,900. (also avail. on floppy disk; back issues avail.) **Indexed:** Abstr.Hyg., Anim.Breed.Abstr., Biotech.Abstr., Chem.Abstr., Dairy Sci.Abstr., Field Crop Abstr., Helminthol.Abstr., Herb.Abstr., Ind.Vet., Nutr.Abstr., Rev.Appl.Entomol., Trop.Dis.Bull.
●Also available online. Vendor(s): BRS (VETR), CISTI, DIMDI, DIALOG, European Space Agency (File nos.16 & 124/CAB).
—BLDSC shelfmark: 9227.000000.
Description: Presents abstracts of the core literature in the whole field of animal health.

636.089   US
VETERINARY UPDATE CLINICAL ABSTRACT SERVICE. (In 2 editions: Small Animal, Large Animal) 1960. q. $112 for each edition; $189 combined. American Veterinary Publications, Inc., 5782 Thornwood Dr., Goleta, CA 93117-3896. TEL 805-967-5988. Ed. Dr. P.W. Pratt. circ. 3,000. (avail. on diskette) **Indexed:** Biol.Abstr., Chem.Abstr.
Formerly: Update Veterinary Reference Service.
Description: Abstracts of clinically oriented articles from worldwide veterinary literature.

VETERINARY SCIENCE — Computer Applications

056.1 051 US
ABOARD TAN SAHSA; the international airlines of Honduras. (Text in English, Spanish) 1986. bi-m. free to airline passengers. North-South Net, Inc., 100 Almeria Ave., Ste. 220, Coral Gables, FL 33134. TEL 305-441-9744. FAX 305-441-9739. Ed. Gloria Shanahan. bk.rev.; illus.; circ. 10,000.
 Description: Features general-interest articles for travelers into and out of Latin America. Includes information on tourist attractions.

VIDEO

see Communications–Video

VISUALLY IMPAIRED

see Handicapped–Visually Impaired

WASTE MANAGEMENT

see Environmental Studies–Waste Management

WATER RESOURCES

see also Environmental Studies

333.91 US
A S D W A UPDATE. 1986. bi-m. $40 to non-members. Association of State Drinking Water Administrators, 1911 N. Fort Myer Dr., Arlington, VA 22209. TEL 703-524-2428. FAX 703-524-1453. Ed. Vanessa M. Leiby. bk.rev.; circ. 400.
 Description: Examines issues related to the protection of public health through the assurance of high quality drinking water.

A W T; Abfalltechnik und Recycling. (Abwassertechnik) see *ENVIRONMENTAL STUDIES*

333.91 US ISSN 0273-3218
A W W A MAINSTREAM. 1955. m. membership. American Water Works Association, 6666 W. Quincy Ave., Denver, CO 80235. TEL 303-794-7711. Ed. Mary Parmelee. charts; illus.; tr.lit.; circ. 40,000.
 Incorporates: Willing Water (Denver) (ISSN 0149-8037)

333.19 639.2 PL ISSN 0860-2611
 CODEN: ATOPEG
ACTA ACADEMIAE AGRICULTURAE AC TECHNICAE OLSTENENSIS. PROTECTIO AQUARUM ET PISCATORIA - WATER CONSERVATION AND INLAND FISHERIES. (Supplement avail.: Protectio Aquarum et Piscatoria) (Text in English, Polish; summaries in English, Russian) 1956. irreg. price varies. (Akademia Rolniczo-Techniczna im. M. Oczapowskiego) Wydawnictwo A R T Olsztyn, Blok 21, 10-957 Olsztyn-Kortowo, Poland. TEL 48-89-273310. TELEX 0526419. (Dist. by: Ars Polona-Ruch, Krakowskie Przedmiescie 7, 00-901 Warsaw, Poland. TEL 48-22-265334) illus.; charts; bibl.; circ. 280 (controlled). **Indexed:** Chem.Abstr., Potato Abstr., Ref.Zh.
 Formerly: Akademia Rolniczo-Techniczna. Zeszyty Naukowe. Ochrona Wod i Rybactwo Srodladowe (ISSN 0324-9190)

333.7 628 US
ADVANCED WATER CONFERENCE. PROCEEDINGS.. irreg., 3rd, 1971. price varies. Oklahoma State University, College of Engineering, Engineering Extension, 512 Engineering North, Stillwater, OK 74078. TEL 405-624-5033.

551.4 333.91 UK ISSN 0309-1708
TC1 CODEN: AWREDI
ADVANCES IN WATER RESOURCES. 1978. 6/yr. £191 (effective 1992). Elsevier Science Publishers Ltd., Crown House, Linton Rd., Barking, Essex IG11 8JU, England. TEL 081-594-7272. FAX 081-594-5942. TELEX 896950 APPSCI G. (Subscr. in U.S. and Canada to: Elsevier Science Publishing Co., Inc., Box 882, Madison Sq. Sta., New York, NY 10159. TEL 212-989-5800) Eds. W.G. Gray, M.A. Celia. (back issues avail.) **Indexed:** Appl.Mech.Rev., Curr.Tit.Ocean, Eng.Ind., Environ.Abstr., Environ.Per.Bibl., Excerp.Med., Fluidex, GeoRef, Intl.Civil Eng.Abstr., Irr.& Drain.Abstr., Sci.Abstr., Sel.Water Res.Abstr., Soft.Abstr.Eng., Soils & Fert., W.R.C.Inf.
 —BLDSC shelfmark: 0712.120000.
 Incorporates (in 1991): Hydrosoft (ISSN 0268-6856)
 Description: For engineers or scientists interested in theoretical and computational aspects of water resources engineering: groundwater hydrology, water quality, surface water hydrology and stochastic hydrology.
 Refereed Serial

333.91 FR
AGENCES DE L'EAU. a. 240 F. (foreign 228.84 F.). Pierre Johanet et ses Fils, 7 av. Franklin Roosevelt, 75008 Paris, France. TEL 33-1-43-59-08-91. FAX 33-1-42-25-59-47. TELEX 649712.

AGRICULTURAL RESEARCH DEPARTMENT. WINAND STARING CENTRE FOR INTEGRATED LAND, SOIL AND WATER RESEARCH. REPORTS. see *AGRICULTURE — Crop Production And Soil*

AGRICULTURAL WATER MANAGEMENT; an international journal. see *AGRICULTURE — Crop Production And Soil*

333.91 US
ALASKA SNOW SURVEYS - BASIN OUTLOOK REPORTS. 1962. 4/yr. free. U.S. Soil Conservation Service (Anchorage), 201 E. 9th Ave., No. 300, Anchorage, AK 99501-3687. TEL 907-271-2424. FAX 907-868-2424. Ed. George P. Clagett. charts; stat.; index; circ. 500. (tabloid format; back issues avail.)
 ●Also available online.
 Former titles: Alaska Snow Surveys; (until 1985): Snow Surveys and Water Supply Outlook for Alaska (ISSN 0731-8499); (until 1981): Federal-State-Private Snow Surveys and Water Supply Outlook for Alaska.
 Description: Focuses on seasonal snow depth, snow-water content, accumulated water-year precipitation statistics from a network of 200 data sites and selected streamflow facts.

133.3 US
AMERICAN DOWSER. 1961. q. $25 includes membership. American Society of Dowsers, Inc., Danville, VT 05828. TEL 802-684-3417. Ed.Bd. bk.rev.; cum.index every 5 yrs.; circ. 3,500.
 Supersedes: American Society of Dowsers. Quarterly Digest.

627 551.4 US
AMERICAN INSTITUTE OF HYDROLOGY. BULLETIN. 1983. q. $16. American Institute of Hydrology, 3416 University Ave., S.E., Ste. 200, Minneapolis, MN 55414-3328. TEL 612-379-1030. adv.; bk.rev.; circ. 800. (tabloid format; back issues avail.)
 Description: Newsletter regarding activities and members of institute.

AMERICAN SHORE AND BEACH PRESERVATION ASSOCIATION. NEWSLETTER. see *ENVIRONMENTAL STUDIES*.

333.91 US
AMERICAN WATER RESOURCES ASSOCIATION. MONOGRAPHS. irreg., no.6, 1991. price varies. American Water Resources Association, 5410 Grosvenor Lane, Ste. 220, Bethesda, MD 20814-2192. TEL 301-493-8600. FAX 301-493-5844.

333.91 US
AMERICAN WATER RESOURCES SYMPOSIA. ANNUAL PROCEEDINGS. 1965. a., latest 1990, Denver, Colorado. $35.95 to non-members; members $29.95. American Water Resources Association, 5410 Grosvenor Ln., Ste. 220, Bethesda, MD 20814. TEL 301-493-8600. FAX 301-493-5844. **Indexed:** GeoRef.
 Formerly: American Water Resources Conferences. Annual Proceedings (ISSN 0066-1171)

628 US ISSN 0003-150X
TD201 CODEN: JAWWA5
AMERICAN WATER WORKS ASSOCIATION. JOURNAL. 1914. m. $85 to libraries and governmental agencies only. American Water Works Association, 6666 W. Quincy Ave., Denver, CO 80235. TEL 303-794-7711. Ed. Nancy M. Zeilig. adv.; bk.rev.; abstr.; bibl.; charts; illus.; stat.; tr.lit.; index. cum.index 1946-1980 (5 vols.); circ. 38,500. (also avail. in microfilm from UMI,PMC; microfiche from UMI; back issues avail., reprint service avail. from UMI, BLH) **Indexed:** A.S.& T.Ind., Abstr.Bull.Inst.Pap.Chem., Acid Pre.Dig., Acid Rain Abstr., Acid Rain Ind., AESIS, Anal.Abstr., Biol.Abstr., Cadscan, Chem.Abstr., Copper Abstr., Corros.Abstr., Curr.Cont., Deep Sea Res.& Oceanogr.Abstr., Dok.Arbeitsmed., Eng.Ind., Environ.Abstr., Environ.Per.Bibl., Excerp.Med., Food Sci.& Tech.Abstr., Geo.Abstr., GeoRef, INIS Atomind., Intl.Civil Eng.Abstr., Lead Abstr., Met.Abstr., Ocean.Abstr., Pollut.Abstr., Sci.Cit.Ind., Sel.J.Water, Sel.Water Res.Abstr., Soft.Abstr.Eng., Zincscan.
 —BLDSC shelfmark: 4696.000000.

628 US ISSN 0360-814X
TD201 CODEN: PWACDO
AMERICAN WATER WORKS ASSOCIATION. PROCEEDINGS, A W W A ANNUAL CONFERENCE. a. American Water Works Association, 6666 W. Quincy Ave., Denver, CO 80235. TEL 303-794-7711. illus. **Indexed:** GeoRef. Key Title: Proceedings, A W W A Annual Conference.
 —BLDSC shelfmark: 1082.452000.

627 BL
ANAIS HIDROGRAFICOS. 1933. a. free. Ministerio da Marinha, Diretoria de Hidrografia e Navegacao, Rio de Janeiro, Brazil. charts; illus.; stat.; circ. controlled.

333.91 US ISSN 0161-4924
GB705.N6
ANNUAL NEW MEXICO WATER CONFERENCE. PROCEEDINGS. 1956. a. $5.25. New Mexico Water Resources Research Institute, Box 30001, Dept. 3167, New Mexico State University, Las Cruces, NM 88003-0001. TEL 505-646-4337. FAX 505-646-6418. Ed. Cathy Ortega Klett. circ. 500 (controlled).

333.91 UK ISSN 0003-7214
TD201 CODEN: AQUAAA
AQUA. (Text in English and French) 1951. bi-m. £96($179.50) (International Water Supply Association) Blackwell Scientific Publications Ltd., Osney Mead, Oxford OX2 0EL, England. TEL 0865-240201. FAX 0865-721205. TELEX 833355-MEDBOK-G. Ed. M. Bernhardt. adv.; bk.rev.; abstr.; charts; illus.; circ. 4,500. (also avail. in microform from MIM,UMI) **Indexed:** Chem.Abstr., Curr.Adv.Ecol.Sci., Environ.Per.Bibl., Fluidex, GeoRef, I D A, W.R.C.Inf.
 —BLDSC shelfmark: 1581.860000.
 Description: Concerned with water supply for domestic, agricultural and industrial purposes and the safeguarding, control and provision of the necessary water resources.

331.91 FI ISSN 0356-7133
GB727.4 CODEN: AQFEDI
AQUA FENNICA. (Text in English; summaries in Finnish) 1971. s-a. FIM 120($40) Aqua Fennica Publishing Board, P.O. Box 436, 00101 Helsinki 10, Finland. FAX 0-73144188. Ed. Pertti Seuna. adv.; bk.rev.; charts; illus.; circ. 350. (back issues avail.) **Indexed:** Chem.Abstr., Curr.Adv.Ecol.Sci., Curr.Cont., Deep Sea Res.& Oceanogr.Abstr., Pollut.Abstr., Sel.Water Res.Abstr., W.R.C.Inf.
 —BLDSC shelfmark: 1581.863000.

WATER RESOURCES

333.91 US ISSN 1048-8111
AQUA TERRA; water concepts for the ecological society. 1985. s-a. $5.95. (National Water Center) Waterworks Publishing, Rte. 3, Box 716, Eureka Springs, AR 72632. TEL 501-253-9431. FAX 501-253-8280. Ed. Jacqueline Froelich. adv.; bk.rev.; circ. 2,000. (back issues avail.)
   Formerly (until 1991): Water Center News.
   Description: Information on technical and metaphysical ways of keeping waste out of water. Also features poetry and interviews.

AQUARICULTURE AND AQUATIC SCIENCES. JOURNAL. see *BIOLOGY*

627 UK ISSN 0261-5355
AQUATECHNIC INTERNATIONAL. 1981. 10/yr. £75. D.J.L. Marketing Ltd., 47 Burney St., Greenwich, London SE10 8EX, England. FAX 081-853-4079. Ed. David Longhurst. adv.; bk.rev.; circ. 13,000. (back issues avail.) **Indexed:** Fluidex.

333.91 US ISSN 0092-0622
AQUEDUCT. 1934. 3/yr. free to qualified personnel. Metropolitan Water District of Southern California, Box 54153, Los Angeles, CA 90054. TEL 213-250-6000. Ed. Joann Lundgren. illus.; circ. 40,000.
   Former titles: Aqueduct News (ISSN 0003-7338); Colorado River Aqueduct News.

333.91 CY ISSN 0255-8580
ARAB WATER WORLD. (Text in Arabic, English) 1977. 6/yr. $40. Chatila Publishing House, P.O. Box 5122, Limassol, Cyprus. TEL 357-2-476353. FAX 357-2-456252. TELEX 4990FLY CY. (Or P.O. Box 135121, Chouran, Beirut, Lebanon.) Ed. Fathi Chatila. adv.; bk.rev.; circ. 16,448. **Indexed:** Fluidex, W.R.C.Inf.
   —BLDSC shelfmark: 1583.298000.

627 PL
TC1 CODEN: AHDRAF
ARCHIVES OF HYDROTECHNIC. (Text in English; summaries in English, Polish) q. $44. Polska Akademia Nauk, Instytut Budownictwa Wodnego, Ul. Koscierska 7, 80-952 Gdansk-Oliwa, Poland. (Dist. by: Ars Polona-Ruch, Krakowskie Przedmiescie 7, 00-068 Warsaw, Poland) Ed. Ryszard Zeidler. illus.; charts; index; circ. 500. **Indexed:** Appl.Mech.Rev., Fluidex, Geotech.Abstr., Sel.Water Res.Abstr.
   Formerly (until no.3-4, 1990): Archiwum Hydrotechniki (ISSN 0004-0789)

ARID LANDS NEWSLETTER. see *AGRICULTURE*

331.91 US
ARIZONA. DEPARTMENT OF WATER RESOURCES. OPEN-FILE REPORT. 1986. irreg. $3. Department of Water Resources, Basic Data Section, 2810 S. 24th St., Ste. 122, Phoenix, AZ 85034. TEL 602-255-1543.
   Description: Covers water resources of Arizona.

333.91 US ISSN 0571-0278
ARKANSAS. GEOLOGICAL COMMISSION. WATER RESOURCES CIRCULARS. 1955. irreg., no.12, 1975. price varies. Geological Commission, Vardelle Parham Geology Center, 3815 West Roosevelt Rd., Little Rock, AR 72204. TEL 501-663-9714. (back issues avail.) **Indexed:** GeoRef.

ASIAN ENVIRONMENT; journal of environmental science and technology for balanced development. see *ENVIRONMENTAL STUDIES*

ASIAN WATER & SEWAGE. see *ENVIRONMENTAL STUDIES*

ATTENDERINGSBULLETIN STARING-GEBOUW: LAND, BODEM, WATER. see *ENVIRONMENTAL STUDIES — Abstracting, Bibliographies, Statistics*

333.9 US ISSN 0067-043X
AUBURN UNIVERSITY. WATER RESOURCES RESEARCH INSTITUTE. ANNUAL REPORT. 1965. a. free. Auburn University, Water Resources Research Institute, 202 Hargis Hall, Auburn, AL 36849. TEL 205-826-5075. Eds. Joseph F. Judkins, Jr., Dennis H. Block. circ. 600.

627 AT ISSN 1037-3535
AUSTRALIAN DRILLING. 1972. bi-m. Aus.$50. Australian Drilling Industry Association, P.O. Box 279, Mentone, Vic. 3194, Australia. TEL 613-793-1735. FAX 613-793-1741. Ed. Graeme Wakeling. adv.; bk.rev.; charts; illus.; circ. 6,000. (back issues avail.) **Indexed:** AESIS.
   Former titles (until 1992): Water and Mineral Development (ISSN 0811-5931); (until 1982): National Water Well Association. Journal (ISSN 0310-3625)
   Description: Provides information on technical advances, new equipment and product news.

614 AT
AUSTRALIAN FLUORIDATION NEWS. AQUA-PURA. 1963. bi-m. $15 membership. Anti-Fluoridation Association of Victoria, Box C9, P.O. Box Clarence St., Sydney, N.S.W. 2000, Australia. TEL 03-592-5088. Ed. G. Walker. bk.rev.; circ. 2,000.
   Formerly: Aqua Pura.

333.91 AT ISSN 0811-5397
AUSTRALIAN WATER RESOURCES COUNCIL. WATER RESOURCES SERIES. irreg. Department of Primary Industries and Energy, Australian Water Resources Council, G.P.O. Box 858, Canberra, A.C.T. 2601, Australia. **Indexed:** AESIS.

627 600 GW ISSN 0937-3756
B B R. (Brunnenbau, Bau von Wasserwerk, Rohrleitungsbau); Wasser und Rohrbau. 1949. m. DM.160 (foreign DM.172). Verlagsgesellschaft Rudolf Mueller, Stolberger Str. 84, Postfach 410949, 5000 Cologne 41, Germany. TEL 0221-5497-0. Ed. Rudolf Bleser. adv.; bk.rev.; circ. 3,133. **Indexed:** Chem.Abstr., INIS Atomind.
   —BLDSC shelfmark: 1871.366070.
   Formerly: Brunnenbau, Bau von Wasserwerk, Rohrleitungsbau (ISSN 0340-3874)

BEITRAEGE ZUR HYDROLOGIE. see *EARTH SCIENCES — Hydrology*

628 II ISSN 0006-0461
TC903
BHAGIRATH; irrigation and power quarterly. (Editions in English and Hindi) 1954. q. Rs.5($2) (Ministry of Irrigation & Power, Central Water Commission) India. Ministry of Information and Broadcasting, Publications Division, Patiala House, Tilak Marg, New Delhi 110001, India. (U.S. subscr. address: M/S Inter Culture Associates, Thompson, CT 06277) Ed. M.S. Ramchander. adv.; bk.rev.; charts; illus.; index; circ. 5,000. **Indexed:** INIS Atomind.

628 MW ISSN 0084-7925
BLANTYRE WATER BOARD. ANNUAL REPORT AND STATEMENT OF ACCOUNTS. 1967. a. Blantyre Water Board, Box 30369, Chichiri, Blantyre 3, Malawi. stat.; circ. 500.

BRITISH COLUMBIA. MINISTRY OF ENVIRONMENT. ANNUAL REPORT. see *CONSERVATION*

627 631 GR
BULLETIN G C I D. (Text in Greek; summaries in English) 1962. s-a. Dr.300. International Commission on Irrigation and Drainage, Greek National Committee, 13 Tsakona St., Psychico, Athens, Greece. Ed. George Papadopoulos. adv.; bk.rev.; bibl.; charts; illus.; stat.; tr.lit.; circ. 4,000.
   Former titles: G C I D Scientific Bulletin; G C I D Information Letter; International Committee on Irrigation and Drainage. Greek National Committee. Bulletin (ISSN 0011-8109)

354.66 631.7 UV
BURKINA FASO. DIRECTION DE L'HYDRAULIQUE ET DE L'EQUIPEMENT RURAL. SERVICE I.R.H. RAPPORT D'ACTIVITES. irreg. Direction de l'Hydraulique et de l'Equipement Rural, Service I.R.H., Ministere du Plan, du Developpement Rural, de l'Environnement et du Tourisme, Ouagadougou, Burkina Faso.
   Formerly: Upper Volta. Direction de l'Hydraulique et de l'Equipement Rural. Service I.R.H. Rapport d'Activites.

627 UV
BURKINA FASO. MINISTERE DE L'EAU. ANNUAIRE HYDROLOGIQUE DU BURKINA. a. Ministere de l'Eau, Direction de l'Inventaire des Ressources Hydrauliques, B.P. 7025, Ouagadougou 03, Burkina Faso. TEL 30-80-35.

627 UV
BURKINA FASO. MINISTERE DE L'EAU. BULLETIN HYDROLOGIQUE DU BURKINA. m. Ministere de l'Eau, Direction de l'Inventaire des Ressources Hydrauliques, B.P. 7025, Ouagadougou 03, Burkina Faso. TEL 30-80-35.

333.91 US
C R A NEWSLETTER. q. Colorado River Association, 417 S. Hill St., Los Angeles, CA 90013. FAX 213-628-4910. Ed. Pat Messigian.

333.9 US ISSN 0084-8263
CODEN: CAWRAF
CALIFORNIA. DEPARTMENT OF WATER RESOURCES. BULLETIN. (Issued in several sub-series) a. price varies. Department of Water Resources, Box 924836, Sacramento, CA 94236-0001. TEL 916-445-9248. circ. controlled. **Indexed:** GeoRef.

333.91 US
CALIFORNIA DIRECTORY OF WATER RESOURCES EXPERTISE. 1975. biennial. free. University of California, Riverside, Water Resources Center, Rubidoux Hall, Riverside, CA 92521. TEL 714-787-4327. FAX 714-787-5295. Ed. Rex J. Woods. circ. 1,750.

614.772 US ISSN 0008-1620
CALIFORNIA WATER POLLUTION CONTROL ASSOCIATION. BULLETIN. 1964. q. $25 or membership. California Water Pollution Control Association, Inc., 3050 Citrus Cir., Ste. 225, Walnut Creek, CA 94598-2628. FAX 510-938-0182. Ed. Linda S. Brewer. adv.; bk.rev.; bibl.; charts; illus.; circ. 7,000 (controlled). **Indexed:** Biol.Abstr., Ocean.Abstr., Pollut.Abstr.

333.91 US ISSN 0575-4941
GB705.C2 CODEN: CUWCA8
CALIFORNIA WATER RESOURCES CENTER. CONTRIBUTION. irreg., no.199, 1989. Water Resources Center, University of California, Rubidoux Hall, 4501 Glenwood Dr., Riverside, CA 92521. TEL 714-787-4327. Eds. Ben J. Tsuang, John A. Dracup. bibl.; charts; circ. 265. **Indexed:** GeoRef.
   —BLDSC shelfmark: 3457.250000.

333.91 US
CALIFORNIA WATER RESOURCES DIRECTORY; a guide to organizations and information resources. 1984. irreg., 2nd ed. 1991. $25. California Institute of Public Affairs, Box 189040, Sacramento, CA 95818. TEL 916-442-CIPA. FAX 916-442-2478. (Affiliate: The Claremont Graduate School) Ed. Roberta Childers. circ. 750.
   Description: Comprehensive guide to the nearly 1,000 governmental and non-governmental organizations in the state that deal with water policy, development, supply, and conservation, as well as related health, environmental protection, energy, and economic aspects.

CANADA. AGRICULTURE CANADA. ANNUAL REPORT OF PRAIRIE FARM REHABILITATION ADMINISTRATION. see *AGRICULTURE — Crop Production And Soil*

354 CN ISSN 0701-6786
VK597.C2
CANADA. HYDROGRAPHIC SERVICE. ACTIVITY REPORT/CANADA. SERVICE HYDROGRAPHIQUE. RAPPORT DES ACTIVITES. (Text in English and French) a. free. Department of Fisheries & Oceans, 200 Kent St., Ottawa, Ont. K1A 0E6, Canada. TEL 613-995-4031. illus.
   Formed by the merger of: Canada. Hydrographic Service. Annual Report (ISSN 0704-3139) & Canada. Service Hydrographique. Rapport Annuel (ISSN 0704-3147)

333.91 CN
CANADIAN WATER AND WASTEWATER ASSOCIATION. BULLETIN/ASSOCIATION CANADIENNE DES EAUX POTABLES ET USEES. BULLETIN. (Text in English, French) 1987. 10/yr. membership. Canadian Water and Wastewater Association, 24 Clarence St., 3rd Fl., Ottawa, Ont. K1N 5P3, Canada. TEL 613-238-5692. FAX 613-237-2965. Ed. Steve Bonk. bk.rev.; circ. 1,500.
   Formerly: Canadian Water and Wastewater Association. Newsletter.

333.91   CN   ISSN 0701-1784
CANADIAN WATER RESOURCES JOURNAL/REVUE CANADIENNE DES RESSOURCES EN EAU. (Text in English and French) 1976. q. Can.$55. Canadian Water Resources Association - Association Canadienne des Ressources Hydriques, c/o Faculty of Engineering, University of Saskatchewan, Saskatchewan, Sask. S7N 0W0, Canada. TEL 306-966-5335. FAX 306-966-5334. Ed. Jon A. Gillies. adv.: page Can.$600; trim 5 x 7 1/2. bk.rev.; circ. 900.
—BLDSC shelfmark: 3046.135000.
Formerly: Reclamation.
Refereed Serial

333.91 631   CN   ISSN 1180-050X
CANADIAN WATER WELL. 1978. 4/yr. Can.$22. A I S Communications Ltd., 145 Thames Rd. W., Exeter, Ont. NOM 1S3, Canada. TEL 519-235-2400. FAX 519-235-0798. Ed. Scott Hill. adv.; illus.; circ. 3,741. (back issues avail.)

333.91 016   NE   ISSN 0920-9786
CATALOGUS VAN NEDERLANDSE ZEEKAARTEN EN ANDERE HYDROGRAFISCHE PUBLIKATIES/CATALOG OF CHARTS AND OTHER HYDROGRAPHIC PUBLICATIONS. (Text in Dutch, English) 1874. a. free. (Ministerie van Defensie) Hydrographic Service, P.O. Box 90704, 2509 LS The Hague, Netherlands. TEL 070-3162800. FAX 070-3162843. Ed.Bd. circ. 800.
Formerly: Netherlands. Departement van Marine. Catalogus van Nederlandse Zeekaarten en Boekwerken.

628   SW   ISSN 0280-4026
                         CODEN: PCTHET
CHALMERS UNIVERSITY OF TECHNOLOGY. DEPARTMENT OF SANITARY ENGINEERING. PUBLICATIONS; current reports on research in water supply and sewage disposal. (Text in Swedish; summaries in English) 1962. irreg. price varies. Chalmers University of Technology, Department of Sanitary Engineering - Chalmers Tekniska Hoegskolan, S-412 96 Goeteborg 5, Sweden. FAX 46-31-722128. Ed. Torsten Hedberg. charts; illus.; circ. 100.

333.91   US
CLEAN WATER ACTION NEWS.* 1976. 4/yr. $24 to members; institutions $40. Clean Water Action Project, 1320 18th St. N.W., 3rd fl., Washington, DC 20035-1811. TEL 202-547-1196. Ed. David Zwick. adv.; circ. 60,000.
Description: News articles on the legislative, policy, and environmental efforts at the federal and state levels to control pollution and contamination.

CLEARWATERS. see *ENVIRONMENTAL STUDIES — Pollution*

333.91   US   ISSN 0069-4657
HD1694.S6   CODEN: CUWRBK
CLEMSON UNIVERSITY. WATER RESOURCES RESEARCH INSTITUTE. REPORT. 1967. irreg., no.67, 1977. free. Clemson University, Water Resources Research Institute, Clemson, SC 29634-2900. TEL 803-656-2698. FAX 803-656-4780. circ. 200 (paid); controlled. *Indexed:* Pollut.Abstr., Water Resour.Abstr.

333.9   US   ISSN 0360-6864
TC425.C7
COLUMBIA RIVER WATER MANAGEMENT REPORT. 1971. a. free. U.S. Army Corps of Engineers, CENPD-PE-WM, Box 2870, Portland, OR 97208-2870. TEL 503-221-6021. illus.
Description: Reviews the annual operation of the major dams and powerhouses in the Columbia Basin and the North West

COMISION DE INTEGRACION ELECTRICA REGIONAL. RECURSOS ENERGETICOS DE LOS PAISES DE LA C I E R. see *PETROLEUM AND GAS*

333.91   UN
CONFLUENCE. (Text in English) 1982. s-a. United Nations Economic and Social Commission for Asia and the Pacific (ESCAP), Natural Resources Division, Water Resources Section, United Nations Bldg., Rajadamnern Nok Ave., Bangkok 10200, Thailand. TEL 2-2829161-170. circ. 600. (back issues avail.)
Description: Aids information exchange between government programs and agencies engaged in water resources development in ESCAP member countries. Covers the range of technological, managerial, and conceptual information.

627   BL   ISSN 0589-3305
CONGRESSO LATINOAMERICANO DE HIDRAULICA (PAPERS).* irreg. Associacao Internacional de Pesquisas Hidraulicas, Av. Bento Goncalves 10600, Porto Allegre, Brazil.

CONSERVATION VOTER. see *ENVIRONMENTAL STUDIES*

333.91   FR   ISSN 1146-5786
▼**COURANTS;** revue de l'eau et de l'amenagement. 1990. 6/yr. 405 F. (foreign 510 F.). P Y C Edition, B.P. 105, 5, av. de Verdun, 94208 Ivry sur Seine Cedex, France. TEL 1-49-60-86-36. FAX 1-46-72-41-85. TELEX 263 424. adv.; bk.rev.; abstr.; charts; illus.; circ. 5,000.

COVICRIER. see *ENVIRONMENTAL STUDIES*

627   AT
CROSSCURRENT. m. Australian Water & Wastewater Association, P.O. Box 388, Artarmon, N.S.W. 2064, Australia. TEL 02-413-1288. FAX 02-413-1047. Ed. Bell Rees. adv.
Description: Contains news updates, articles and papers about water and its use.

333.91   US
DELAWARE RIVER BASIN BIENNIAL WATER RESOURCES CONFERENCE. PROCEEDINGS. 1962. biennial. membership. Water Resources Association of the Delaware River Basin, Box 867, Davis Rd., Valley Forge, PA 19481. TEL 215-783-0634. FAX 215-783-0635.
Formerly: Delaware River Basin Water Resources Conference. Proceedings.

628   NE   ISSN 0011-8079
DELTAWERKEN. 1957. q. fl.30.75. Staatsuitgeverij, Christoffel Plantijnstraat 1, The Hague, Netherlands. (Prepared by: Deltadienst Rijkswaterstaat) circ. 5,500. *Indexed:* Excerp.Med., Key to Econ.Sci.

628   NE   ISSN 0011-9164
TD478   CODEN: DSLNAH
DESALINATION; the international journal on the science and technology of desalting and water purification. (Text in English, French, German) 1966. 15/yr.(in 5 vols.; 3 nos./vol.). fl.1855 (fl.4522 combined subscr. with Journal of Membrane Science)(effective 1992). Elsevier Science Publishers B.V., P.O. Box 211, 1000 AE Amsterdam, Netherlands. TEL 020-5803911. FAX 020-5803598. TELEX 18582 ESPA NL. (Subscr. in U.S. and Canada to: Elsevier Science Publishing Co., Inc., Box 882, Madison Sq. Sta., New York, NY 10159. TEL 212-989-5800) Ed. M. Balaban. adv.; bk.rev.; charts; illus.; pat.; stat.; tr.mk.; index. (also avail. in microform from RPI) *Indexed:* AESIS, Biol.Abstr., Chem.Abstr., Chem.Eng.Abstr., Curr.Cont., Energy Ind., Energy Info.Abstr., Energy Rev., Eng.Ind., Environ.Abstr., Environ.Per.Bibl., Excerp.Med., Fluidex, Food Sci.& Tech.Abstr., Foul.Prev.Res.Dig., Ind.Sci.Rev., Ocean.Abstr., Pollut.Abstr., Sci.Abstr., Sel.Water Res.Abstr., T.C.E.A., W.R.C.Inf.
—BLDSC shelfmark: 3555.700000.
Description: Covers all desalting fields - distillation, membranes, reverse osmosis, electrodialysis, ion exchange, freezing and water purification.
Refereed Serial

628.167   IS
DESALINATION DIRECTORY; desalination and water reuse. (Text in English) 1981. a. $210 to non-members; members $140. Balaban Publishers, International Science Services, P.O. Box 2039, Rehovot 76120, Israel. TEL 8-476216. FAX 8-467632. (And: Kiebitzrain 84, 3000 Hanover 51, Germany)
Description: Guide to academic, government and private institutions, organizations, companies and individuals concerned with desalination and water reuse.

WATER RESOURCES 4823

627 551.4   GW   ISSN 0012-0235
GB651   CODEN: DGMTAO
DEUTSCHE GEWAESSERKUNDLICHE MITTEILUNGEN; Mitteilungsblatt der gewaesserkundlichen Dienststellen des Bundes und der Laender. (Summaries in English) 1957. bi-m. DM.50. Bundesanstalt fuer Gewaesserkunde, Kaiserin-Augusta-Anlagen 15-17, P.O. Box 309, 5400 Koblenz, Germany. TEL 1306-O. Ed. Hans-Juergen Liebscher. bk.rev.; abstr.; bibl.; charts; illus.; maps; tr.lit.; index; circ. 1,600. *Indexed:* Biol.Abstr., Chem.Abstr., Excerp.Med., Geo.Abstr., GeoRef, INIS Atomind., Pollut.Abstr., Sel.Water Res.Abstr., W.R.C.Inf.
Description: Reports on quantitative and qualitative hydrology, water resources management and water protection.

551.4 627   GW   ISSN 0340-5176
DEUTSCHES GEWAESSERKUNDLICHES JAHRBUCH. DONAUGEBIET. 1898. a. exchange basis. Bayerisches Landesamt fuer Wasserwirtschaft, Lazarettstr. 67, 8000 Munich 19, Germany. TEL (089)1259-203. charts; stat.; circ. 500. *Indexed:* GeoRef.

551.4 627   GW   ISSN 0340-5184
DEUTSCHES GEWAESSERKUNDLICHES JAHRBUCH. KUESTENGEBIET DER NORD- UND OSTSEE. 1941. a. DM.40. Landesamt fuer Wasserhaushalt und Kuesten, Saarbrueckenstr. 38, 2300 Kiel 1, Germany. FAX 0431-61955. Ed. Mr. Benn. stat.; index, cum.index; circ. controlled.
Description: Hydrological statistics of German coasts.

551 627   GW   ISSN 0173-7260
DEUTSCHES GEWAESSERKUNDLICHES JAHRBUCH. RHEINGEBIET TEIL 2: MAIN. 1898. a. exchange basis. Bayerisches Landesamt fuer Wasserwirtschaft, Lazarettstr. 67, 8000 Munich 19, Germany. TEL (089)1259-203. charts; stat.; circ. 500.

DEVELOPING HYDROPOWER IN WASHINGTON STATE; a guide to permits, licenses, and incentives. see *ENGINEERING — Hydraulic Engineering*

333.91   UK
DEVELOPING WORLD WATER. 1985. a. Grosvenor Press International, Holford Mews, Cruickshack St., London WC1X 9HD, England. TEL 01-2783000. FAX 01-2781674. TELEX 23931 GPI G. Ed. John Pickford. adv.; circ. 15,000.

DIENST LANDBOUWKUNDIG ONDERZOEK. STARING CENTRUM, INSTITUUT VOOR ONDERZOEK VAN HET LANDELIJKE GEBIED. JAARVERSLAG. see *AGRICULTURE — Crop Production And Soil*

DIENST LANDBOUWKUNDIG ONDERZOEK. STARING CENTRUM, INSTITUUT VOOR ONDERZOEK VAN HET LANDELIJK GEBIED. RAPPORTEN. see *AGRICULTURE — Crop Production And Soil*

628   GW   ISSN 0012-5156
Z7935
DOKUMENTATION WASSER. 1960. 9/yr. DM.268.20. (Umwelt Bundesamt, Dokumentationszentrale Wasser) Erich Schmidt Verlag GmbH & Co. (Bielefeld), Viktoriastr.44a, Postfach 7330, 4800 Bielefeld 1, Germany. TEL 0521-583080. (back issues avail.)

627 620   US
DREDGING SEMINAR. PROCEEDINGS. 1968. a. price varies. Texas A & M University, Center for Dredging Studies, College Station, TX 77843-3136. TEL 409-845-4516. FAX 409-845-6156. Ed. Dr. John B. Herbich. charts; circ. 800.

333.91   US   ISSN 1055-9140
▼**DRINKING WATER RESEARCH.** 1991. bi-m. $40. American Water Works Association, Research Foundation, 6666 W. Quincy Ave., Denver, CO 80235-3098. TEL 303-794-7711. Ed. Marianne Prekker.
Description: Describes the activities of the AWWA Research Foundation; reports on results of research programs.

WATER RESOURCES

333.91 631.7   US
DROUGHT NETWORK NEWS. 1989. 3/yr. free. International Drought Information Center, 241 L.W. Chase Hall, University of Nebraska, Box 830728, Lincoln, NE 68583-0728. TEL 402-472-6707. FAX 402-472-6614. TELEX UNL COMM LCN 484340. (Co-sponsor: National Oceanic and Atmospheric Administration) illus.; circ. 1,000. (back issues avail.)
Description: Provides information on current episodes of drought, response, mitigation and planning of activities, new technologies relating to planning and management.

627 628.167   II
DRYLAND RESOURCES AND TECHNOLOGY ANNUAL (YEAR). a. $50. Divyajyoti Prakashan, 5 Bhagat-ki-kothi, Jodhpur 342 003, India. (Co-sponsor: Geo-Environ Academia) Eds. Alam Singh, G.R. Chowdhary.
Former titles: Current Practices in Dryland Resources and Technology; Dryland Resources and Technology (ISSN 0254-8305); (until 1984): Desert Resources and Technology.

333.7 338   FR
L'EAU, L'INDUSTRIE, LES NUISANCES. 1975. m. 530 F. Pierre Johanet et ses Fils, 7 av. Franklin-D.-Roosevelt, 75008 Paris, France. TEL 33-1-43-59-08-91. FAX 33-1-42-25-59-47. TELEX 649712. adv.; illus.; circ. 6,000. **Indexed:** Chem.Abstr., Excerp.Med., W.R.C.Inf.
Formerly: Eau et l'Industrie (ISSN 0755-5016)

333.91   FR   ISSN 0424-2033
EAU PURE.* bi-m. 45 F. Association Nationale pour la Protection des Eaux, 4, rue Nenard, 78000 Versailles, France. Ed. Jacques Vrignaud. **Indexed:** Pollut.Abstr.

ECOALERT. see ENVIRONMENTAL STUDIES

EFFLUENT AND WATER TREATMENT JOURNAL. see ENVIRONMENTAL STUDIES — Pollution

627   US
ENGINEERING COMMITTEE ON OCEANIC RESOURCES. PROCEEDINGS OF THE GENERAL ASSEMBLY. irreg., 2nd, 1975, Tokyo. Engineering Committee on Oceanic Resources, 2101 Constitution Ave. N.W., Washington, DC 20418. TEL 202-334-2000.

ENVIRONMENTAL TOXICOLOGY AND WATER QUALITY; an international journal. see ENVIRONMENTAL STUDIES — Toxicology And Environmental Safety

EUROPEAN WATER POLLUTION CONTROL. see ENVIRONMENTAL STUDIES — Pollution

627   UN   ISSN 0254-5284
F A O IRRIGATION AND DRAINAGE PAPERS. (Editions in English, French, Spanish) 1971. irreg., no.45, 1989. price varies. Food and Agriculture Organization of the United Nations, c/o UNIPUB, 4611-F Assembly Dr., Lanham, MD 20706-4391. FAX 301-459-0056. **Indexed:** Excerp.Med.

333.91   US   ISSN 0046-306X
FACETS OF FRESHWATER. 1976. m. $25 membership. Freshwater Foundation, 725 County Rd. 6, Waynata, MN 55391. TEL 612-449-0092. FAX 617-449-0592. Ed. Barbara Nicol. bibl.; charts; illus.; circ. controlled.

627   FI   ISSN 0355-0982
GB747.F5   CODEN: VSMJA4
FINLAND. VESTIENTUTKIMUSLAITOS. JULKAISUJA/FINLAND. WATER RESEARCH INSTITUTE. PUBLICATIONS. (Text in Finnish; summaries in English) 1972. irreg. price varies. Valtion Painatuskeskus - Government Printing Centre, Annankatu 44, 00100 Helsinki 10, Finland. illus.

333.91   US   ISSN 0896-1794
TD485
FLORIDA WATER RESOURCES JOURNAL; the overflow. 1949. m. $24. (Florida Water & Pollution Control Operator's Association, Inc.) Florida Water Resources Journal, Inc., Box 1702-518, Gainesville, FL 32602-1702. TEL 904-374-4946. FAX 904-372-6229. (Subscr. to: Box 7068, Gainesville, FL 32606) (Co-sponsors: American Water Works Association, Florida Station; Florida Pollution Control Association) Ed. John D. Crane. adv.; circ. 8,000.
Description: Covers water supply, treatment, and distribution; includes waste water collection, treatment and disposal.

333.91 614.7   CN   ISSN 0832-6673
FOCUS ON INTERNATIONAL JOINT COMMISSION ACTIVITIES. 1974. 3/yr. free. International Joint Commission, Great Lakes Regional Office, 100 Ouellette Ave., 8th Fl., Windsor, Ont. N9A 6T3, Canada. TEL 519-256-7821. FAX 519-256-7791. (Or: Box 32869, Detroit, MI 48232) Ed. Sally Cole-Misch. bk.rev.; bibl.; illus.; circ. 14,000. (also avail. in microform from UMI) **Indexed:** Energy Ind., Energy Info.Abstr., Environ.Abstr.
Former titles (until vol.11, no.2, 1986): Focus on Great Lakes Water Quality (ISSN 0711-0855); (until vol.7, 1981): Great Lakes Focus on Water Quality.

333.91   US
FOCUS ON WATER. 1980. bi-m. free to qualified personnel. Metropolitan Water District of Southern California, Box 54153, Los Angeles, CA 90054. TEL 213-250-6000. Ed. Garry Hofer. circ. 40,000. (back issues avail.)
Supersedes (1974-1979): Meter.

FORCES. see GENERAL INTEREST PERIODICALS — Canada

333.91 352   US   ISSN 0734-1237
FROM THE STATE CAPITALS. WATER SUPPLY. 1946. w. $215 (foreign $235)(effective Dec. 1990). Wakeman-Walworth, Inc., 300 N. Washington St., Alexandria, VA 22314. TEL 703-549-8606. FAX 703-549-1372. (processed)
Description: State and local action in the US with respect to water conservation and supply development problems.

G W A/G E E U - GAZ EAUX EAUX USEES. see PETROLEUM AND GAS

GAS - ERDGAS - G W F; das Gas- und Wasserfach. see PETROLEUM AND GAS

333.7 333.7   GW
GERMANY (FEDERAL REPUBLIC, 1949-). BUNDESANSTALT FUER GEWAESSERKUNDE. JAHRESBERICHT. 1949-1962; resumed 1974. a. Bundesanstalt fuer Gewaesserkunde, Kaisern-Augusta-Anlagen 15-17, P.O. Box 309, 5400 Koblenz, Germany. TEL 1306-0. illus.
Description: Working report on scientific and technical projects.

621.312   RU   ISSN 0016-9714
CODEN: GTSTA8
GIDROTEKHNICHESKOE STROITEL'STVO. 1930. m. 31.80 Rub. Ministerstvo Goryuchego i Energetiki Rosii - Ministry of Fuel and Energetics of Russia, Bol'shoi Cherkasskii Per., 2-10, 103012 Moscow, Russia. adv.; bk.rev.; abstr.; bibl.; charts; illus.; stat.; index; circ. 6,400. **Indexed:** Appl.Mech.Rev., Chem.Abstr., Eng.Ind., Fluidex, Geotech.Abstr., Intl.Civil Eng.Abstr., Sci.Abstr., Soft.Abstr.Eng. —BLDSC shelfmark: 0050.000000.

627   RU   ISSN 0016-9722
TC1   CODEN: GIMEAQ
GIDROTEKHNIKA I MELIORATSIYA. (Contents page in English) 1949. m. $18.60. Agropromizdat, Sadovo-Sasskaya, 18, 107807 Moscow, Russia. (Co-sponsor: Ministerstvo Sel'skogo Khozyaistva S.S.S.R.) Ed. E.A. Nesterov. adv.; bk.rev.; bibl.; charts; illus.; maps; stat.; circ. 36,500. **Indexed:** Chem.Abstr., Field Crop Abstr., Geotech.Abstr., Herb.Abstr., Soils & Fert.

628 551.4   PL   ISSN 0017-2448
CODEN: GOWOAC
GOSPODARKA WODNA. (Text in Polish; contents page in English) 1935. m. $51. Wydawnictwo Czasopism i Ksiazek Technicznych SIGMA - NOT, Ul. Biala 4, P.O. Box 1004, 00-950 Warsaw, Poland. (Dist. by: SIGMA NOT Ltd., Ul. Bartycka 20, 00-716 Warsaw, Poland) Ed. Marian Chudzynski. bk.rev.; charts; illus.; maps; stat.; index; circ. 2,250. **Indexed:** Chem.Abstr., Geotech.Abstr., W.R.C.Inf.

333.9   UK   ISSN 0072-7253
GREAT BRITAIN. WATER RESOURCES BOARD. REPORT. 1963. a. price varies. (Water Resources Board) H.M.S.O., Atlantic House, Holborn Viaduct, London EC1P 1BN, England.

977 016   US   ISSN 0072-7326
GREAT LAKES RESEARCH CHECKLIST. 1959. s-a. free. Great Lakes Commission, 400 Fourth St., Ann Arbor, MI 48103. TEL 313-665-9135. FAX 313-665-4370. Ed. Albert G. Ballert. bk.rev.; circ. 800. (also avail. in microfilm from UMI; reprint service avail. from UMI)
Description: Bibliography of current Great Lakes related journals, articles, books and documents. Includes news notes.

363.6   CN   ISSN 0710-8702
TD223.3
GREAT LAKES SCIENCE ADVISORY BOARD. REPORT. 1975. biennial. free. International Joint Commission, Great Lakes Regional Commission, 100 Ouellette Ave., 8th Fl., Windsor, Ont. N9A 6T3, Canada. TEL 519-256-7821. FAX 519-256-7791. Ed.Bd. circ. 8,000 (controlled). (also avail. in microfilm from UMI; reprint service avail. from UMI) **Indexed:** Environ.Abstr., Sel.Water Res.Abstr.
Formerly: Great Lakes Research Advisory Board. Annual Report.

333.91   US   ISSN 0046-645X
TD403   CODEN: GWAGD5
GROUND WATER AGE. 1969. m. $39. National Trade Publications, Inc., 13 Century Hill, Latham, NY 12110-2197. TEL 518-783-1281. Ed. Greg Norton. adv.; bk.rev.; charts; illus.; pat.; tr.lit.; circ. 29,000. (also avail. in microfilm from UMI; reprint service avail. from UMI) **Indexed:** Excerp.Med., W.R.C.Inf.

333.91 614.7   US   ISSN 0882-6188
CODEN: GWMOEM
GROUND WATER MONITOR; legislation, regulation, litigation, technology. 1985. fortn. $474.54 (effective Sep. 1992). Business Publishers, Inc., 951 Pershing Dr., Silver Spring, MD 20910-4464. TEL 301-587-6300. FAX 301-585-9075. Ed. Michael Carolan. (looseleaf format; back issues avail.)
●Also available online. Vendor(s): Data-Star (PTBN), DIALOG, NewsNet (EV18).
Description: News from Congress, EPA and states on cleanup of ground water contamination across the U.S.

GROUND WATER MONITORING REVIEW. see EARTH SCIENCES — Hydrology

GROUNDWATER POLLUTION NEWS. see ENVIRONMENTAL STUDIES — Pollution

333.91   FR
GUIDE DE L'EAU. a. 975 F. (foreign 829.15 F.). Pierre Johanet et ses Fils, 7, av. Franklin Roosevelt, 75008 Paris, France. TEL 33-1-43-59-08-91. FAX 33-1-142-25-59-47. TELEX 649712.

333.91   GW
HAMBURGER WASSERWERKE. FACHLICHE BERICHTE. 1982. s-a. free to qualified personnel. Hamburger Wasserwerke GmbH, Billhorner Deich 2, 2000 Hamburg 26, Germany. TEL 040-7888-2483. FAX 040-7888-2513. circ. 1,000.

HEDESELSKABETS TIDSSKRIFT; tidsskrift for grundforbedring og skovbrug. see FORESTS AND FORESTRY

551.49　　　　　HU　　ISSN 0018-1323
　　　　　　　　　　　CODEN: HIDRAV
HIDROLOGIAI KOZLONY. (Text in Hungarian; contents page and summaries in English) 1918. bi-m. 300 Ft.($27.50) Magyar Hidrologiai Tarsasag, H-1027 Budapest, Fo u.68, Hungary. (Subscr. to: Kultura, Box 149, H-1389 Budapest, Hungary) Ed. A. Szollosi-Nagy. adv.; bk.rev.; abstr.; bibl.; charts; illus.; index. cum.index; circ. 1,150. **Indexed:** Appl.Mech.Rev., Chem.Abstr., Fluidex, Geotech.Abstr., Meteor.& Geoastrophys.Abstr., Sel.Water Res.Abstr.

627 551.5　　　　　RM
HIDROTEHNICA. (Text in Rumanian; summaries in English, French, German and Russian) 1956. m. 144 lei to individuals; institutions 192 lei. Consiliul National al Apelor, Institutul de Meteorologie si Hidrologie, Str. Negustori nr. 3, Bucharest, Rumania. (Subscr. to: ILEXIM, Str. 13 Decembrie Nr. 3, P.O. Box 136-137, Bucharest, Rumania) bk.rev.; abstr.; bibl.; charts; illus.; index; circ. 2,000. **Indexed:** Chem.Abstr., Deep Sea Res.& Oceanogr.Abstr., Field Crop Abstr., Geotech.Abstr., Herb.Abstr., INIS Atomind., Meteor.& Geoastrophys.Abstr., W.R.C.Inf.
　Formerly: Hidrotehnica, Gospodarirea Apelor, Meteorologia (ISSN 0018-134X)
　Description: Covers mathematics, atmospheric physics and atmospheric electricity.

620 551.4 333.91　　FR　　ISSN 0018-6368
TC1　　　　　　　　　　CODEN: HOBLAB
HOUILLE BLANCHE; revue internationale de l'eau. (Text in English or French; summaries in English, French, German, Spanish) 1946. 8/yr. 920 Fr. (Societe Hydrotechnique de France) Revue Generale de l'Electricite S.A., 48 rue de la Procession, 75724 Paris Cedex 15, France. FAX 40-65-92-29. TELEX SEE 200565F. Ed. J. Valembois. adv.; bk.rev.; abstr.; bibl.; charts; illus.; index; circ. 4,000. (back issues avail.) **Indexed:** Appl.Mech.Rev., Chem.Abstr., Deep Sea Res.& Oceanogr.Abstr., Eng.Ind., Excerp.Med., Fluidex, Fuel & Energy Abstr., Geotech.Abstr., INIS Atomind., Math.R., Meteor.& Geoastrophys.Abstr., Sci.Abstr., Sel.Water Res.Abstr.
　—BLDSC shelfmark: 4334.000000.
　Description: Covers a range of preoccupations of engineers interested in water problems: fluid mechanics, hydraulic theory and its applications, river and maritime engineering works, water resources and their management, waters treatment.

HUNTER VALLEY RESEARCH FOUNDATION. WORKING PAPERS. see *STATISTICS*

333.91　　　　　　US
HYDATA - NEWS AND VIEWS. 1988. bi-m. $22 (foreign $28). American Water Resources Association, 5410 Grosvenor Ln., Ste. 220, Bethesda, MD 20814. TEL 301-493-8600. FAX 301-493-5844.
　Description: Disseminates information relating to water resources science and monitors news affecting the water resources profession.

333.91 551.4 614.7
620　　　　　　　US　　ISSN 0887-686X
GB651
HYDROLOGICAL SCIENCE AND TECHNOLOGY. 1985. q. $75. American Institute of Hydrology, 3416 University Ave., S.E., Ste. 200, Minneapolis, MN 55414-3328. TEL 612-379-1030. adv.; circ. 350. (back issues avail.)
　—BLDSC shelfmark: 4347.627000.
　Description: Papers communicating new ideas, findings, methods and techniques in all aspects of hydrology, hydrogeology and water resources.

551.4　　　　　　FR　　ISSN 0246-1528
GB651　　　　　　　　　CODEN: HYCOEV
HYDROLOGIE CONTINENTALE. (Text in French; summaries in English) 1964. s-a. 215 F. (Institut Francais de Recherche Scientifique pour le Developpement en Cooperation) Editions de l' O R S T O M, 72 Route d'Aulnay, 93143 Bondy Cedex, France. TEL 48-47-31-95. FAX 48-47-30-88. circ. 1,000. (back issues avail.) **Indexed:** Biol.Abstr., Deep Sea Res.& Oceanogr.Abstr., Geo.Abstr., I D A, INIS Atomind.
　—BLDSC shelfmark: 4347.880000.
　Supersedes: Cahiers O R S T O M Serie Hydrologie (ISSN 0008-0381)

331.91　　　　　　FR
HYDROPLUS; magazine international de l'eau - international water review. (Text in English, French) m. Hydrocom, 13 rue Saint-Florentin, 75008 Paris, France. TEL 1-47-03-33-13. FAX 1-40-15-05-79. adv.: B&W page 12000 F., color page 16000 F.; trim 210 x 297. circ. 12,000.
　Description: Listens to and informs water industrial professionals and provides a forum for reflection in the international water market.

627　　　　　　　　NE
H2O; tijdschrift voor watervoorziening en afvalwaterbehandeling. 1968. s-m. fl.150. Vereniging van Exploitanten van Waterleidingbedrijven in Nederland, Postbus 70, 2280 AB Rijswijk, Netherlands. FAX 070-3953420. Ed. G.B. Vinke. adv.; bk.rev.; circ. 4,400. **Indexed:** Excerp.Med.

I C A S A L S NEWSLETTER. (International Center for Arid and Semiarid Land Studies) see *AGRICULTURE*

I C I D BULLETIN. (International Commission on Irrigation and Drainage) see *AGRICULTURE*

628.167　　　　　　US
I D A NEWSLETTER. m. International Desalination Association, Box 387, Topsfield, MA 01938-0387. TEL 508-356-2727. FAX 508-356-9964. Ed. Patricia Burke.

I G W M C GROUND WATER MODELING NEWSLETTER. (International Ground Water Modeling Center) see *EARTH SCIENCES — Hydrology*

333.91　　　　　　IS　　ISSN 0333-5194
I O L R COLLECTED REPORTS. (Text in English) 1971. a. free. Israel Oceanographic and Limnological Research Ltd., P.O. Box 8030, Haifa 31080, Israel. TEL 04-515202. FAX 04-511911. TELEX 371704.

333.91　　　　　　UK
I W S A YEAR BOOK. (Text in English and French) 1979. a. £30. International Water Supply Association, c/o L.R. Bays, Sec. Gen., 1 Queen Anne's Gate, London SW1H 9BT, England. TEL 01-222-8111. FAX 01-222-7243. Ed. L.R. Bays. adv.; circ. 5,000.
　Formerly: International Who's Who in Water Supply (ISSN 0260-4604)
　Description: General information about the association, directory of members, standing committees, and regional associations. Includes a buyer's guide.

IDAHO CLEAN WATER. see *ENVIRONMENTAL STUDIES — Pollution*

627　　　　　　　　IT
IDROTECNICA; l'acqua nell'agricoltura, nell'igiene, nell'industria. 1930. bi-m. L.120000 (effective 1992). (Associazione Idrotecnica Italiana) Maggioli Editore, Via Crimea, 1, Casella Postale 290, 47037 Rimini, Italy. TEL 0541-626777. FAX 0541-622020. Ed. Umberto Messina.

628.167 333.91
IN THE ANACOSTIA WATERSHED. q. free. Interstate Commission on the Potomac River Basin, 6110 Executive Blvd., Ste. 300, Rockville, MD 20852-3909. TEL 301-984-1908. Ed. Beverly Bandler. illus.; circ. 9,000.

627　　　　　　　　II　　ISSN 0019-5537
TC1　　　　　　　　　　CODEN: IJPRA7
INDIAN JOURNAL OF POWER AND RIVER VALLEY DEVELOPMENT. 1950. m. $48. Books & Journals Private Ltd., 6-2 Madan St., Calcutta 700 072, India. Ed. P.K. Menon. adv.; bk.rev.; abstr.; charts; illus.; circ. 2,662. (also avail. in microform from UMI; reprint service avail. from UMI) **Indexed:** Eng.Ind., Fluidex, Geotech.Abstr., Rural Recreat.Tour.Abstr., Sci.Abstr., Soils & Fert., World Agri.Econ.& Rural Sociol.Abstr.
　—BLDSC shelfmark: 4420.200000.

333.91　　　　　　PK　　ISSN 0537-4715
INDUS. (Text in English) 1960. q. Rs.150. Water and Power Development Authority, WAPDA House, Shara-e-Quaid-e-Azam, Lahore, Pakistan. TEL 212900. TELEX 44869 WAPDA PK. Ed. Raziuddin Shaikh. adv.; illus.
　Description: Articles on water and power resources of the country and technical information on completed and on-going projects.

627　　　　　　　　US
▼**INDUSTRIAL WATER TREATMENT.** 1990. bi-m. Tall Oaks Publishing, Inc., 10394 W. Chatfield Ave., Ste. 108, Littleton, CO 80162. TEL 303-973-6700. FAX 303-973-5327. adv.: B&W page $2400; trim 8 1/2 x 10 3/4. circ. 11,000.
　Description: For operators of boilers, cooling systems, and industrial processes using chemically treated water.

333.91　　　　　　FR　　ISSN 0012-9003
INFORMATION EAUX. 1949. 11/yr. 1170 F.($240) Office International de l'Eau, Direction de la Documentation et des Donnees, Rue Edouard Chamberland, 87065 Limoges Cedex. bk.rev.; charts. **Indexed:** GeoRef., W.R.C.Inf.
　●Also available online. Vendor(s): European Space Agency (File no.73/AFEE).
　—BLDSC shelfmark: 4493.565000.
　Formerly: Eaux et Industries.

INGEGNERIA AMBIENTALE. see *PUBLIC HEALTH AND SAFETY*

INGEGNERIA AMBIENTALE QUADERNI. see *PUBLIC HEALTH AND SAFETY*

627　　　　　　　　MX　　ISSN 0186-4076
TC28
INGENIERIA HIDRAULICA EN MEXICO. (Supplement avail.) (Summaries in English, French and Portuguese) 1930. 3/yr. Mex.$10,000($25) Comision Nacional del Agua, Apdo. Postal No. 202, C.P. 65500, CIVAC, Morelos, Mexico. (Co-sponsor: Instituto Mexicano de Tecnologia del Agua) Ed. Marta Hernandez R. abstr.; charts; illus.; circ. 2,500. (back issues avail.) **Indexed:** GeoRef, Soils & Fert.
　Former titles (until 1978): Recursos Hidraulicos (ISSN 0020-1057); (until 1972): Ingenieria Hidraulica en Mexico; (until 1947): Irrigacion en Mexico.
　Description: Covers all aspects of hydraulic engineering, especially as it relates to agriculture.

333.91 551.4　　　　GW　　ISSN 0343-8090
INSTITUT FUER WASSERWIRTSCHAFT, HYDROLOGIE UND LANDWIRTSCHAFTLICHEN WASSERBAU. MITTEILUNGEN. 1958. irreg. DM.50 per no. Institut fuer Wasserwirtschaft, Hydrologie und landwirtschaftlichen Wasserbau, University of Hannover, Appelstr. 9A, 3000 Hannover 1, Germany. FAX 0511-762-3731. TELEX 0923868-UNIHN-D. (back issues avail.)

INSTITUTION OF ENGINEERS (INDIA). ENVIRONMENTAL ENGINEERING DIVISION. JOURNAL. see *PUBLIC HEALTH AND SAFETY*

333.91　　　　　　UK　　ISSN 0951-7359
TD201
INSTITUTION OF WATER AND ENVIRONMENTAL MANAGEMENT. JOURNAL. 1987. bi-m. £95 to non-members; Journal and Newsletter to non-members £110. Institution of Water and Environmental Management, 15 John St., London WC1N 2EB, England. TEL 071-831-3110. FAX 071-405-4967. Eds. M.D.F. Haigh, C.P. James. adv.; bk.rev.; charts; illus.; index; circ. 12,500. (back issues avail.) **Indexed:** Br.Tech.Ind., Energy Info.Abstr., Environ.Per.Bibl.
　—BLDSC shelfmark: 9267.575000.
　Description: Water, including water resources, river management, pollution control, fisheries, sewerage, navigation.

333.91　　　　　　UK
INSTITUTION OF WATER AND ENVIRONMENTAL MANAGEMENT. NEWSLETTER. 1967. bi-m. £25 to non-members; Newsletter and Journal to non-members £110. Institution of Water and Environmental Management, 15 John St., London WC1N 2EB, England. TEL 071-831-3110. FAX 071-405-4967. Ed. P.A. Walters. circ. 12,500. (back issues avail.)
　Formerly: I W P C Newsletter (ISSN 0143-960X)

333.91　　　　　　RM
INSTITUTUL DE STUDII CERCETARI SI PROIECTARI PENTRU GOSPODARIREA APELOR. STUDII DE ECONOMIA APELOR.. Continues a publication with the same title issued by: Institutul de Studii si Cercetari Pentru Imbunatatiri Funciare si Gospodarirea Apelor. (Text in Rumanian; summaries in English, French and Russian) 1972. irreg. Institutul de Studii Cercetari si Proiectari Pentru Gospodarirea Apelor, Splaiul Indepentei 294, Sector 6, Bucharest 17, Rumania. illus.

WATER RESOURCES

INSTYTUT METEOROLOGII I GOSPODARKI WODNEJ. WIADOMOSCI/INSTITUTE OF METEOROLOGY AND WATER MANAGEMENT. REPORTS. see *METEOROLOGY*

333.91 551.4 UV
INTERAFRICAN COMMITTEE FOR HYDRAULIC STUDIES. LIAISON BULLETIN. French edition: Comite Interafricain d'Etudes Hydrauliques. Bulletin de Liaison. 1970. q. 7000 Fr.CFA. Interafrican Committee for Hydraulic Studies, B.P. 369, Ouagadougou 01, Burkina Faso. TEL 30-71-12. TELEX 5277 BF. adv.; bk.rev.; bibl.; circ. 700.

631.6 II ISSN 0538-5768
INTERNATIONAL COMMISSION ON IRRIGATION AND DRAINAGE. REPORT. (Text in English and French) 1951. a. International Commission on Irrigation and Drainage - Commission Internationale des Irrigations et du Drainage, 48 Nyaya Marg, Chanakyapuri, New Delhi 110021, India. TEL 3016837. circ. 1,000(controlled).
Description: Contains administrative matters of the council meeting. For internal use only.

INTERNATIONAL JOURNAL OF CLIMATOLOGY. see *METEOROLOGY*

333.91 UK ISSN 0790-0627
INTERNATIONAL JOURNAL OF WATER RESOURCES DEVELOPMENT. 1983. q. £135 in UK & Europe; elsewhere £150. Butterworth - Heinemann Ltd. (Subsidiary of: Reed International PLC), Linacre House, Jordan Hill, Oxford OX2 8DP, England. TEL 0865-310366. FAX 0865-310898. TELEX 83111 BHPOXF G. (Subscr. to: Turpin Transactions Ltd., Distribution Centre, Blackhorse, Letchworth, Herts SG6 1HN, England. TEL 0462-672555) Ed. Asit K. Biswas. (also avail. in microform from UMI; back issues avail.) **Indexed:** Agri.Eng.Abstr., Energy Rev., Environ.Abstr., Environ.Per.Bibl., Irr.& Drain.Abstr., Rice Abstr., Soils & Fert.
—BLDSC shelfmark: 9273.883800.
Description: Covers all aspects of water development and management in both industrialized and third world countries.
Refereed Serial

333.91 628.44 CN
INTERNATIONAL SYMPOSIUM ON WASTEWATER TREATMENT. (Text in English, French) a. free. Environment Canada, E P Publications, Ottawa, Ont. K1A 0H3, Canada. FAX 819-953-9029. circ. 1,000.

333.91 US ISSN 0074-9575
TD201 CODEN: PWWPAY
INTERNATIONAL WATER CONFERENCE. PROCEEDINGS. 1941. a. $45 (foreign $53). Engineers' Society of Western Pennsylvania, International Water Conference, 337 Fourth Ave., Pittsburgh, PA 15222-2097. TEL 412-261-0710. FAX 412-261-1606. adv.; cum.index: 1940-1974; circ. 1,700. **Indexed:** Chem.Abstr.
—BLDSC shelfmark: 6847.040000.
Description: Provides current technological updates and case studies dealing with industrial water treatment, use and reuse for both industrial and engineering purposes.

627.8 UK ISSN 0306-400X
TK1081 CODEN: IWPCDM
INTERNATIONAL WATER POWER AND DAM CONSTRUCTION. 1949. m. $226. Reed Business Publishing Group, Electrical - Electronic Press Division (Subsidiary of: Reed International PLC), Quadrant House, The Quadrant, Sutton, Surrey SM2 5AS, England. TEL 081-652-8815. FAX 081-652-8986. TELEX 892084-REEDBP-G. (Subscr. to: Oakfield House, 35 Perrymount Rd., Haywards Heath, W. Sussex RH19 3DH, England. TEL 444-445566) Ed. Alison Bartle. adv.; bk.rev.; abstr.; charts; illus.; index; circ. 4,032. (also avail. in microform from UMI; reprint service avail. from UMI) **Indexed:** Abstr.J.Earthq.Eng., Br.Tech.Ind., Energy Info.Abstr., Eng.Ind., Environ.Abstr., Fluidex, Fuel & Energy Abstr., Geotech.Abstr., Intl.Civil Eng.Abstr., ISMEC, Sci.Abstr., Sel.Water Res.Abstr., Soft.Abstr.Eng., W.R.C.Inf.
—BLDSC shelfmark: 4551.705000.
Formerly: Water Power (ISSN 0043-1338)
Description: Practical and theoretical articles and news concerning all aspects of hydro-electric developments and large dam construction throughout the world. Coverage of research into hydraulics, hydraulic machinery, wave and tidal power.

333.91 US
INTERNATIONAL WATER REPORT. 1978. 4/yr. $37. Water Information Center, Inc., 125 E. Bethpage Rd., Plainview, NY 11803. TEL 516-249-7634. FAX 516-249-7610. Ed. Judith M. Schoeck. bk.rev.

333.91 US ISSN 0535-4676
INTERSTATE COMMISSION ON THE POTOMAC RIVER BASIN. PROCEEDINGS. a. Interstate Commission on the Potomac River Basin, 6110 Executive Blvd., Ste. 300, Rockville, MD 20852. TEL 301-984-1908.
Description: Proceedings of meetings on water resources topics.

620 II ISSN 0021-1664
IRRIGATION AND POWER. (Text in English) 1943. q. Rs.85($20) Central Board of Irrigation and Power, c/o Member Secretary, Malcha Marg, Chanakyapuri, New Delhi 110 021, India. TEL 11-3015984. TELEX 31-66415 CBIP IN. (Subscr. to: Department of Publication, Civil Lines, Delhi 110 054) Ed. C.V.J. Varma. adv.; bk.rev.; charts; illus.; index; circ. 4,500. (reprint service avail. from UMI) **Indexed:** Agri.Eng.Abstr., Chem.Abstr., Eng.Ind., Fluidex, Geotech.Abstr., Herb.Abstr., Rice Abstr.

IRRIGATION JOURNAL (VAN NUYS). see *AGRICULTURE — Crop Production And Soil*

627 630 UK ISSN 0265-5136
IRRIGATION NEWS. 1981. 2/yr. £20. U.K. Irrigation Association, c/o Silsoe College, Silsoe, Bedford MK45 4DT, England. TEL 0525-60428. FAX 0525-61527. TELEX 26581-MONREF-GEUM. Ed. M.K.V. Carr. adv.; bk.rev.; charts; illus.; index; circ. 1,000. (back issues avail.)
—BLDSC shelfmark: 4580.969000.

627 PK
IRRIGATION RESEARCH INSTITUTE, LAHORE. REPORT. 1973. irreg. Irrigation Research Institute, The Mall, Lahore, Pakistan.

IRRIGATION SCIENCE. see *AGRICULTURE*

631 627 IT ISSN 0021-1680
IRRIGAZIONE E DRENAGGIO. (Summaries in English) 1954. q. L.65000 (foreign L.80000). (Centro Internazionale Studi sull'Irrigazione) Edagricole S.p.A., Via Emilia Levante 31, 40139 Bologna, Italy. TEL 051-492211. FAX 051-493660. Ed. Ariosto Degan. adv.; bk.rev.; charts; illus.; index; circ. 18,920. **Indexed:** Agri.Eng.Abstr., Field Crop Abstr., Hort.Abstr., Irr.& Drain.Abstr., Rural Recreat.Tour.Abstr., Soils & Fert., Soyabean Abstr., World Agri.Econ.& Rural Sociol.Abstr.
Formerly: Irrigazione

ISRAEL. METEOROLOGICAL SERVICE. RAINFALL SEASON. see *METEOROLOGY*

JOURNAL OF AGRICULTURE AND WATER RESEARCH. PLANT PRODUCTION. see *AGRICULTURE*

JOURNAL OF AGRICULTURE AND WATER RESOURCES RESEARCH. ANIMAL PRODUCTION. see *AGRICULTURE*

JOURNAL OF AGRICULTURE AND WATER RESOURCES RESEARCH. SOIL AND WATER RESOURCES. see *AGRICULTURE*

JOURNAL OF AQUATIC ECOSYSTEM HEALTH. see *ENVIRONMENTAL STUDIES*

JOURNAL OF HYDRAULIC RESEARCH. see *ENGINEERING — Hydraulic Engineering*

JOURNAL OF SOIL AND WATER CONSERVATION. see *AGRICULTURE — Crop Production And Soil*

JOURNAL OF SOIL AND WATER CONSERVATION IN INDIA. see *CONSERVATION*

JOURNAL OF WATER RESOURCES. see *EARTH SCIENCES — Hydrology*

333.91 US
KANSAS. WATER OFFICE. ANNUAL REPORT ON WATER-RELATED STUDIES-RESEARCH IN KANSAS. 1984. a. free. Water Office, 109 S.W. Ninth St., Ste. 300, Topeka, KS 66612-1249. TEL 913-296-3187. FAX 913-296-0878. abstr.; bibl.; stat.; circ. 200.
Formerly: Kansas. Water Office. Semi-Annual Report on Water-Related Studies-Research in Kansas.
Description: Covers various research in water resources.

333.91 US
KANSAS. WATER OFFICE. FACT SHEET. s-m. Water Office, 109 S.W. 9th St., Ste. 300, Topeka, KS 66612-1249. TEL 913-296-3185. FAX 913-296-0878.

333.91 US
KANSAS WATER PLAN. a. Water Office, 109 S.W. Ninth St., Ste. 300, Topeka, KS 66612-1249. TEL 913-296-3187. FAX 913-296-0878. Dir. Stephen A. Hurst.

333.91 US ISSN 0160-2659
TC424.K2
KANSAS WATER RESOURCES RESEARCH INSTITUTE. ANNUAL REPORT. 1964. a. free. Kansas Water Resources Research Institute, 144 Waters Hall, Kansas State Univ., Manhattan, KS 66506-4007. Ed. Hyde S. Jacobs. circ. 65. **Indexed:** GeoRef.

KORRESPONDENZ ABWASSER; Wasser - Abwasser - Abfall. see *ENVIRONMENTAL STUDIES*

333.91 US
LAKE AND RESERVOIR MANAGEMENT. 1987. 2/yr. $35 membershi only. North American Lake Management Society, One Progress Blvd., Box 27, Alachua, FL 32615-9536. TEL 904-462-2554. FAX 904-462-2568. Ed. Roger Bachman. circ. 2,000. **Indexed:** Environ.Abstr.

LANDSCAPE & IRRIGATION. see *AGRICULTURE — Crop Production And Soil*

LES. see *FORESTS AND FORESTRY*

333.91 FR
LEXIQUE TRILINGUE DE L'EAU. a. 350 F. (foreign 333.27 F.). Pierre Johanet et ses Fils, 7, av. Franklin Roosevelt, 75008 Paris, France. TEL 33-1-43-59-08-91. FAX 33-1-42-25-59-47. TELEX 649712.

LITERATURBERICHTE UEBER WASSER, ABWASSER, LUFT UND FESTE ABFALLSTOFFE. see *ENVIRONMENTAL STUDIES — Pollution*

628 551.4 US
LOUISIANA WATER RESOURCES RESEARCH INSTITUTE. ANNUAL REPORT. 1965. a. $10. Louisiana Water Resources Research Institute, 3418 Ceba Bldg., Louisiana State University, Baton Rouge, LA 70803. FAX 504-388-5990. (Co-sponsor: U.S. Department of Interior) circ. controlled. (reprint service avail. from NTI) **Indexed:** GeoRef.

MAGYAR VIZGAZDALKODAS/HUNGARIAN WATER SUPPLY. see *ENGINEERING — Hydraulic Engineering*

620 333.91 US ISSN 0025-0805
MAINE WATER UTILITIES ASSOCIATION. JOURNAL. 1924. 6/yr. membership. Maine Water Utilities Association, 225 Douglass St., Portland, ME 04104. Ed. J. Ronald Caron. adv.; circ. 400.

MAJI REVIEW. see *ENERGY*

333.91 US ISSN 0090-5968
TC424.C2
MANAGEMENT OF THE CALIFORNIA STATE WATER PROJECT. (Subseries of California. Dept. of Water Resources. Bulletin) 1963. a. price varies. Department of Water Resources, Box 942836, Sacramento, CA 94236-0001. TEL 916-445-9248. illus.; stat.; circ. controlled. (back issues avail.)

354 CN ISSN 0318-3912
TD227.M3
MANITOBA. WATER SERVICES BOARD. ANNUAL REPORT. 1973. a. free. Water Services Board, 2022 Currie Blvd., Brandon, Man. R7A 6A3, Canada. FAX 204-726-6290. circ. 300.

333.91 US ISSN 0076-4817
MARYLAND. GEOLOGICAL SURVEY. WATER RESOURCES BASIC DATA REPORT. 1966. irreg., latest no.18. price varies. Maryland Geological Survey, 2300 St. Paul St., Baltimore, MD 21218. TEL 301-554-5500. FAX 301-554-5502. **Indexed:** GeoRef.

MARYLAND TOMORROW. see *HOUSING AND URBAN PLANNING*

WATER RESOURCES 4827

333.91   IS
MAYIM VE HASHKAIYA. 1975. m. IS.36. Water Works Association, 8 King Saul Blvd., Tel Aviv, Israel. FAX 03-250530. Ed. Yoseff Gur-Arie. adv.

628   US
MICHIGAN STATE UNIVERSITY. INSTITUTE OF WATER RESEARCH. ANNUAL REPORT. 1966. a. price varies. Michigan State University, Institute of Water Research, 334 Natural Resources Bldg., East Lansing, MI 48824. TEL 517-353-3744. Ed. Frank M. D'Itri. illus.; circ. 150. (processed; reprint service avail. from UMI) **Indexed:** GeoRef.

628   US   ISSN 0580-9746
MICHIGAN STATE UNIVERSITY. INSTITUTE OF WATER RESEARCH. TECHNICAL REPORTS. 1968. a. price varies. Michigan State University, Institute of Water Research, 334 Natural Resources Bldg., East Lansing, MI 48824. TEL 517-353-3742. (Dist. by: National Technical Information Service, 5285 Port Royal Rd., Springfield, VA 22151) (back issues avail.; reprint service avail. from UMI) **Indexed:** GeoRef.

333.91   CY
MIDDLE EAST AND WORLD WATER DIRECTORY. (Text in English) 1980. biennial. $80 for two vols.; single vol. $45. Chatila Publishing House, P.O. Box 135121, Chouran, Beirut, Lebanon. TEL 357-2-476353. FAX 357-2-456252. TELEX 4990 FLY CY. Ed. Fathi Chatila. adv.; circ. 5,100.

333.91 551.4   US   ISSN 0076-9614
CODEN: MGWAAE
MISSOURI. DIVISION OF GEOLOGICAL SURVEY AND WATER RESOURCES. WATER RESOURCES REPORT. 1956. irreg., no.36, 1985. price varies. Department of Natural Resources, Division of Geology and Land Survey, Box 250, Rolla, MO 65401. TEL 314-364-1752.

629 333.91   US   ISSN 0275-6633
MONO LAKE COMMITTEE NEWSLETTER. 1978. q. $20. Mono Lake Committee, 1207 W. Magnolia, Ste. D, Burbank, CA 91506. TEL 818-972-2025. (Subscr. to: Box 29, Lee Vining, CA 93541) Ed. Bob Schlichting. adv.; bk.rev.; charts; illus.; stat.; circ. 22,000.
Description: Covers the damaging effects of the excessive diversion of water from Mono Lake, and the struggle, legal and scientific, to protect a valuable and endangered ecosystem.

628   US
MONTANA WATER RESOURCES CENTER. ANNUAL REPORT. 1982. a. Montana Water Resources Center, Montana State University, 208 Cobleigh Hall, Bozeman, MT 59717. TEL 406-994-6690. abstr.
Formerly: Montana Water Resources Research Center. Annual Report.

628   US
MONTANA WATER RESOURCES CENTER. TECHNICAL REPORTS. 1966. 10/yr. Montana Water Resources Center, Montana State University, 208 Cobleigh Hall, Bozeman, MT 59717. TEL 406-994-6690. circ. 125. (processed)
Formerly: Montana Water Resources Research Center. Technical Report.

627   JA
NAGOYA UNIVERSITY. WATER RESEARCH INSTITUTE. ANNUAL REPORT/SUIKEN KAGAKU KENKYUJO NENPO. (Text in Japanese) 1974. a. Nagoya Daigaku, Suishitsu Kagaku Kenkyu Shisetsu - Nagoya University, Water Research Institute, Furo-cho, Chikusa-ku, Nagoya 464, Japan. illus.

627 665.5 622   US   ISSN 0279-7739
NATIONAL DRILLERS BUYERS GUIDE. 1980. m. $50 in N. America; elsewhere $110. National Drillers Buyers Guide, Drawer 400, Hwy. 90 East, Bonifay, FL 32425. TEL 904-547-4244. FAX 904-547-5277. Ed. W.C. Doc Faison. adv.; charts; illus.; tr.lit.; circ. 38,600. (tabloid format)
Description: Provides information for the water monitoring, shallow oil and gas, mining and hydrology industries.

333.9   US
NEBRASKA. NATURAL RESOURCES COMMISSION. STATE WATER PLANNING AND REVIEW PROCESS. irreg. Natural Resources Commission, 301 Centennial Mall South, Box 94876, Lincoln, NE 68509. TEL 402-471-2081. illus.
Formerly: Nebraska. Natural Resources Commission. State Water Plan Publication (Lincoln) (ISSN 0092-6442)
Description: Technical data on title subjects used in future planning of resources.

NEUE D E L I W A - ZEITSCHRIFT; Fachzeitschrift fuer die Energie- und Wasserversorgung. see *ENERGY*

628.1   US   ISSN 0028-4939
TD201   CODEN: JNEWA6
NEW ENGLAND WATER WORKS ASSOCIATION. JOURNAL. 1882. q. $20 (foreign $28). New England Water Works Association, 42A Dilla St., Milford, MA 01757. TEL 508-478-6996. FAX 508-634-8643. Ed. Peter Karalekas, Jr. adv.; bk.rev.; charts; illus.; cum.index every 10 yrs.; circ. 2,200. (also avail. in microform from UMI; reprint service avail. from UMI) **Indexed:** Biol.Abstr., Chem.Abstr., Eng.Ind., Excerp.Med., Fluidex, GeoRef, Ocean.Abstr., Pollut.Abstr., Sel.Water Res.Abstr., W.R.C.Inf.
•Also available on CD-ROM. Producer(s): Dialog Information Services.
—BLDSC shelfmark: 4832.000000.

LE NORD. see *FORESTS AND FORESTRY*

627   US
NORTHWATER; notes on water resources research in Alaska. 1974. s-a. free. University of Alaska, Institute of Northern Engineering, Water Research Center, Fairbanks, AK 99775-1760. TEL 907-474-7775. FAX 907-474-6087. circ. 1,800. (back issues avail.)

333.91   FR
NOUVELLE HYDROLOGIE ALPINE/NEW ALPINE HYDROLOGY/NEUE ALPINE HYDROLOGIE/NUOVA IDROLOGIA ALPINA. (Text in English, French, German, Italian) 1984. biennial. 180 F. (Laboratoire de la Montagne Alpine) Reseau International de Documentation et d'Information de la Montagne Alpine, 17 rue Maurice Gignoux, 38031 Grenoble Cedex, France.

OCEAN SCIENCE, RESOURCES AND TECHNOLOGY. see *EARTH SCIENCES — Oceanography*

OCEAN THERMAL ENERGY CONVERSION WORKSHOP. WORKSHOP PROCEEDINGS. see *ENERGY*

628   US   ISSN 0029-9588
CODEN: OSWAAI
OESTERREICHISCHE WASSERWIRTSCHAFT; Zeitschrift fuer alle wissenschaftlichen, technischen, rechtlichen, und wirtschaftlichen Fragen des gesamten Wasserwesens. (Text in German) 1949. m. DM.136($96) Springer-Verlag, Journals, 175 Fifth Ave., New York, NY 10010. TEL 212-460-1500. (Also Berlin, Heidelberg, Vienna) Ed.Bd. bk.rev.; bibl.; charts; illus.; index. (reprint service avail. from ISI) **Indexed:** Biol.Abstr., Chem.Abstr., Fluidex, Geotech.Abstr., Intl.Civil Eng.Abstr., Sel.Water Res.Abstr., Soft.Abstr.Eng.
—BLDSC shelfmark: 6236.000000.

333.9   US   ISSN 0092-2528
TC424.O5
OKLAHOMA WATER RESOURCES RESEARCH INSTITUTE. ANNUAL REPORT. 1966. a. Oklahoma Water Resources Research Institute, 003 Life Sciences E., Stillwater, OK 74078. TEL 405-744-9994. FAX 405-744-7673. Ed. Carol Engle. illus.; circ. 200. Key Title: Annual Report of the Oklahoma Water Resources Research Institute.

333.9   CN   ISSN 0078-5156
ONTARIO. MINISTRY OF THE ENVIRONMENT. GROUND WATER BULLETIN. 1961. irreg. free. Ministry of the Environment, Water Resources Branch, 1 St. Clair Ave. W., 4th fl., Toronto, Ont. M4V 1K6, Canada. TEL 416-965-6141.

333.91   US   ISSN 0887-2104
OPERATIONS FORUM; a W P C F publication for wastewater professionals. 1984. m. $75 (foreign $99). Water Pollution Control Federation, 601 Wythe St., Alexandria, VA 22314-1994. TEL 703-684-2400. FAX 703-684-2492. Ed. Lisa Preston. adv.; tr.lit.; circ. 20,000. (back issues avail.; reprint service avail.) **Indexed:** Excerp.Med.
—BLDSC shelfmark: 6268.790000.

OPFLOW. see *ENGINEERING*

333.91   JA
OSAKA MUNICIPAL WATER WORKS BUREAU. WATER EXAMINATION LABORATORY. ANNUAL REPORT. (Text in Japanese) 1949. a. free. Osaka Municipal Water Works Bureau, Water Examination Laboratory, 1-3-14 Kunijima, Higasiyodogawa-Ku, Osaka-Shi 533, Japan. FAX 06-320-3259. Ed. Shunichi Tatsumi. circ. 500.

OZONE; science and engineering. see *ENGINEERING — Chemical Engineering*

PASSAIC RIVER REVIEW. see *CONSERVATION*

PENNSYLVANIA STATE UNIVERSITY. ENVIRONMENTAL RESOURCES RESEARCH INSTITUTE. NEWSLETTER. see *CONSERVATION*

PIPES AND PIPELINES INTERNATIONAL; pipes, hoses, tubes, pumps, valves. see *PETROLEUM AND GAS*

POLIMERY V MELIORATSII I VODNOM KHOZYAISTVE. see *ENGINEERING — Hydraulic Engineering*

333.91   PL
POLITECHNIKA KRAKOWSKA. ZESZYTY NAUKOWE. INZYNIERIA SANITARNA I WODNA. (Text in Polish; summaries in English, French, German and Russian) 1957. irreg. price varies. Politechnika Krakowska, Ul. Warszawska 24, 31-155 Krakow, Poland. TEL 48-12-374289. FAX 48-12-335773. TELEX 322468 PK PL. (Dist. by: Ars Polona-Ruch, Krakowskie Przedmiescie 7, 00-068 Warsaw, Poland) bibl.; charts; illus.; circ. 200.
Formerly: Politechnika Krakowska. Zeszyty Naukowe. Budownictwo Wodne i Inzynieria Sanitarna (ISSN 0137-1363)

628   PL   ISSN 0079-3477
POLSKA AKADEMIA NAUK. KOMITET GOSPODARKI WODNEJ. PRACE I STUDIA. 1956. irreg., vol.11, 1972. price varies. Polska Akademia Nauk, Komitet Gospodarki Wodnej, Palac Kultury i Nauki, Pietro XX, pok.20-21, 00-901 Warsaw, Poland. (Dist. by: Ars Polona, Krakowskie Przedmiescie 7, 00-068 Warsaw, Poland)

628.167 333.91   US
POTOMAC BASIN REPORTER. 10/yr. free. Interstate Commission on the Potomac River Basin, 6110 Executive Blvd., Ste. 300, Rockville, MD 20852. TEL 301-984-1908. Ed. Curtis M. Dalpra.
Description: Current events on Potomac River water quality, supply, recreation.

333.91   US
POTOMAC ISSUES. irreg. price varies. Interstate Commission on the Potomac River Basin, 6110 Executive Blvd., Ste. 300, Rockville, MD 20852. TEL 301-984-1908.
Description: Basin water resource issues.

333.91   US
POTOMAC RIVER BASIN WATER QUALITY REPORTS. irreg. Interstate Commission on the Potomac River Basin, 6110 Executive Blvd., Ste. 300, Rockville, MD 20852. TEL 301-984-1908.
Formerly: Potomac River Water Quality Network (ISSN 0539-2047)
Description: Analysis of water quality in the basin.

354.712   CN
PRAIRIE PROVINCES WATER BOARD ANNUAL REPORT. (First report covers period Oct. 30, 1969-Mar. 31, 1972) 1972. a. free. Prairie Provinces Water Board, Rm. 201, 2050 Cornwall St., Regina, Sask. S4P 2K5, Canada. TEL 306-522-6671. circ. 400.

PROBLEMY OSVOENIYA PUSTYN'. see *AGRICULTURE*

U V W X Y Z

WATER RESOURCES

333.7   BW   ISSN 0131-3010
PROBLEMY POLES'YA. (Text in Russian) 1972. biennial. 2.90 Rub. Akademiya Navuk Belarusskoai S.S.R. - B.S.S.R. Academy of Sciences, Leninskii Prospekt 66, 220072 Minsk 72, Byelarus. TEL 39 48 15. TELEX 252277 NAUKA. Ed. E.E. Lishtvan. bibl.; charts; illus.; index; circ. 1,000.
—BLDSC shelfmark: 0133.585000.
Description: Presents papers on scientific problems of environmental protection, rational use of natural resources of Byelorussian region of Poles'e.

PROGRESS IN ENVIRONMENTAL SCIENCE & TECHNOLOGY. see *ENVIRONMENTAL STUDIES*

333.91   US
PURDUE UNIVERSITY. WATER RESOURCES RESEARCH CENTER. ANNUAL REPORT. 1966. a. free. Purdue University, Water Resources Research Center, School of Civil Engineering, W. Lafayette, IN 47907. FAX 317-494-0395. Ed. Jeff R. Wright. circ. 230. (also avail. in microfiche)

333.91   BE
LA RADIOACTIVITE DES PRINCIPALES SOURCES D'EAU MINERALE EN BELGIQUE. ETUDE. (Editions in Flemish, French) a. Ministere de la Sante Publique et de la Famille, Institut d'Hygiene et d'Epidemiologie - Ministerie van Volksgezondheid en van het Gezin, 14 rue Juliette Wytsman, B-1050 Brussels, Belgium. Eds. Dr. P. Binaux, Dr. P. Le Jeune.

333.91   CN
▼**RECLAIM.** 1990. bi-m. Can.$12. Reclaim Publications, 3C-2020 Portage Ave., Winnipeg, Man. R3J 0K4, Canada. TEL 204-885-7798. FAX 204-889-3576. Ed. Craig Kelman. adv.; circ. 6,200.

333.91   AG   ISSN 0048-6981
RECURSOS HIDRICOS. 1971. q. free. Secretaria de Recursos Naturales y Ambiante Humano, Av. Santa Fe 1548, Buenos Aires 1060, Argentina. Ed.Bd. charts; illus.

333.91   II   ISSN 0970-9258
TC503
RIVER BEHAVIOUR AND CONTROL. (Text in English) vol.9, 1976. a. Department of Irrigation & Waterways, River Research Institute, 11-A Mirza Ghalib St., Calcutta 700087, India. circ. 300.
Description: News for research workers and field engineers. Covers hydraulics, hydrology, sedimentation and soil mechanics.

333.91 614.7   US   ISSN 0898-8048
GB1201   CODEN: RIVREV
▼**RIVERS;** studies in the science, environmental policy and law of instream flow. 1990. q. $115. S E L & Associates, 3024 Phoenix Dr., Fort Collins, CO 80525-2517. FAX 303-482-0251. Ed. Susan Lamb. adv.; bk.rev.; circ. 410.
—BLDSC shelfmark: 7977.145000.
Description: Addresses issues of North American, European and Australasian instream flow; covers multiagency actions, water resource planning, fisheries biology, water law, riparian corridor management, and regulations involved with flow usage.

620   PL   ISSN 0035-9394
TC7   CODEN: RZHTAE
ROZPRAWY HYDROTECHNICZNE/HYDROTECHNICAL TRANSACTIONS. (Text in various languages; summaries in English) 1956. irreg., vol.54, 1991. price varies. Polska Akademia Nauk, Instytut Budownictwa Wodnego, Ul. Koscierska 7, 80-952 Gdansk-Oliwa, Poland. (Dist. by: Ars Polona, Krakowskie Przedmiescie 7, 00-068 Warsaw, Poland) Ed. Ryszrd Zeidler. circ. 280. **Indexed:** Chem.Abstr., Fluidex, Geotech.Abstr.
—BLDSC shelfmark: 8035.900000.

614.8 627.5   US   ISSN 0270-4447
T55.A1
SAFETY NEWS (DENVER). 1937. q. membership. Bureau of Reclamation, Safety Office, Box 25007, D-7600 Denver, CO 80225. TEL 303-236-6774. charts; illus.; stat.; circ. 550. **Indexed:** Bibl.Agri, C.I.S. Abstr., Sel.Water Res.Abstr.
Former titles: Reclamation Safety News (ISSN 0034-1436); Reclamation Safety Record.

333.91   YU   ISSN 0408-9936
SAOPSTENJA. 1954. q. 11,000 din.($90) Institut za Vodoprivredu Jaroslav Cerni, Ulica Jaroslava Cernija 80, 11223 Belgrade - Beli Potok, Yugoslavia. circ. 500.

SCAN. see *AGRICULTURE — Crop Production And Soil*

551   GW   ISSN 0172-665X
GB651   CODEN: SBLWEQ
SCHRIFTENREIHE DES BAYERISCHES LANDESAMTES FUER WASSERWIRTSCHAFT. 1975. irreg. (approx. 3/yr.). avail. on exchange. Bayerisches Landesamt fuer Wasserwirtschaft, Lazarettstrasse 67, 8000 Munich 19, Germany. TEL (089)1259-203. circ. 500.

SCIENCES DE L'EAU; journal of water science. see *EARTH SCIENCES — Hydrology*

333.91   CN   ISSN 0823-0269
                       CODEN: STEADG
SCIENCES ET TECHNIQUES DE L'EAU. (Text in French; abstracts in English and French) 1968. q. Can.$40 (US Can.$45, elsewhere Can.$50)(typically set in Sep.). Association Quebecoise des Techniques de l'Eau, 407, bd. St. Laurent, bureau 500, Montreal, Que. H2Y 2Y5, Canada. TEL 514-874-3700. FAX 514-866-4020. Ed. Louis Tremblay. adv.; bk.rev.; index; circ. 4,000. (back issues avail.) **Indexed:** Appl.Ecol.Abstr., Biol.Abstr., Bull.Signal., Chem.Abstr., Energy Ind., Energy Info.Abstr., Eng.Ind., Environ.Abstr., Environ.Per.Bibl., Excerp.Med., Microbiol.Abstr., Pollut.Abstr., Pt.de Rep. (1983-), RADAR.
—BLDSC shelfmark: 8166.515000.
Formerly (until 1985): Eau du Quebec (ISSN 0315-2081)

SCOOP. see *ENVIRONMENTAL STUDIES — Abstracting, Bibliographies, Statistics*

628.167   US   ISSN 0720-0773
TD478
SEAWATER AND DESALTING. 1980. irreg. price varies. Springer-Verlag, 175 Fifth Ave., New York, NY 10010. TEL 212-460-1500. (Also Berlin, Heidelberg, Vienna) (reprint service avail. from ISI)

333.91 639.2   US   ISSN 8755-4682
SEICHE. 1976. q. free. University of Minnesota, Sea Grant Program, 1518 Cleveland Ave., N., St. Paul, MN 55108. TEL 612-625-9790.
FAX 612-625-1263. Ed. Alice Tibbetts. circ. 3,500. (back issues avail.)

628   US
SENSUS WATER JOURNAL; devoted to the operation and management of water works. 1908. 2/yr. free. Sensus Technologies, Inc., Bailey and Gallatin Aves., Box 487, Uniontown, PA 15401.
TEL 412-439-7700. FAX 412-430-3959. Ed. James Shugarts. charts; illus.; circ. 14,500.
Formerly: Rockwell Water Journal (ISSN 0892-9548)

333.91 550   CC   ISSN 0559-9342
SHUILI FADIAN/HYDRO-ELECTRIC POWER. (Text in Chinese) m. $2.50 per no. (Shuili Shuidian Guihua Sheji Guanli-ju - Hydraulic and Hydro-electric Power Planning Administration) Shuili Fadian Bianjibu, 65 Ande Lu, Xicheng-qu, Beijing 100011, People's Republic of China. TEL 4011177. Ed. Zhang Peiji.
—BLDSC shelfmark: 9271.960000.

SOCIETY AND NATURAL RESOURCES. see *ENVIRONMENTAL STUDIES*

333.91   SA
SOUTH AFRICA. WATER RESEARCH COMMISSION. ANNUAL REPORT. (Text in Afrikaans or English) 1971. a. free. Water Research Commission - Waternavorsingskommissie, P.O. Box 824, Pretoria 0001, South Africa. TEL 012-330-0340. FAX 012-705-925. TELEX 32-0464-WATCO-SA. charts; illus.; stat.; circ. 3,200.
Description: Covers the research activities of the commission. Also lists publications issued from research connected with the commission.

627   US   ISSN 0734-1679
TD204
SOVIET JOURNAL OF WATER CHEMISTRY AND TECHNOLOGY. English translation of: Khimiya i Tekhnologiya Vody (UR ISSN 0204-3556) 1981. bi-m. $795. (Russian Academy of Sciences, RU) Allerton Press, Inc., 150 Fifth Ave., New York, NY 10011. TEL 212-924-3950. (Co-sponsor: Ukrainian Academy of Sciences) Ed. A.T. Pilipenko. bk.rev.; charts; illus.; pat. **Indexed:** Sel.J.Water, W.R.C.Inf.
—BLDSC shelfmark: 0423.680000.

627   DK   ISSN 0108-0466
SPILDEVANDSTEKNISK TIDSSKRIFT. 1973. 4/yr. membership. Spildevandsteknisk Forening, c/o Bent Christensen, Egevangen 19, Sig, 6800 Varde, Denmark. Ed. Ole Poulsen. illus.; circ. 1,300.

333.91   UK   ISSN 0307-9074
STREAM. 1974. 10/yr. £3. Severn-Trent Water Authority, Abelson House, 2297 Coventry Rd., Sheldon, Birmingham B26 3PU, England. Ed. Christine Mosley. adv.; circ. 13,000. (tabloid format; back issues avail.)

627   RM
STUDII DE IRIGATII SI DESECARI. (Text in Rumanian; summaries in English and French) a. Academia de Stiinte Agricole si Silvice, Institutul de Cercetari Pentru Imbunatatiri Funciare, B-dul Marasti, 61, Bucharest, Rumania. (Subscr. to: ILEXIM, Str. 13 Decembrie Nr. 3, P.O. Box 136-137, Bucharest, Rumania)

333.91   JA   ISSN 0039-4858
SUIRI KAGAKU/WATER SCIENCE. (Text in Japanese; contents page in English) 1956. bi-m.
3500 Yen($13) Water Utilization Research Institute - Suiri Kagaku Kenkyujo, 7-12 Koraku 1-chome, Bunkyo-ku, Tokyo 112, Japan. Ed. Hirotada Muto. adv.; bk.rev. **Indexed:** Chem.Abstr.

SUO. see *AGRICULTURE*

333.9   US   ISSN 0094-6427
TC425.S8
SUSQUEHANNA RIVER BASIN COMMISSION. ANNUAL REPORT. 1972. a. free. Susquehanna River Basin Commission, 1721 N. Front St., Harrisburg, PA 17102. TEL 717-238-0422. FAX 717-238-2436. illus. Key Title: Annual Report - Susquehanna River Basin Commission.
Description: Describes the work of the commission for the fiscal year. Also contains featured articles about special subjects.

TECHNIQUES - SCIENCES - METHODES. GENIE URBAIN RURAL. see *PUBLIC ADMINISTRATION — Municipal Government*

333   SP   ISSN 0211-8173
TECNOLOGIA DEL AGUA; revista tecnica de la captacion, distribucion, tratamiento, y depuracion del agua. 1980. 14/yr. 11550 ptas.($120) Prensa XXI, S.A., Avda Parallel, 180, Apdo. No. 350 F.D., 08015 Barcelona, Spain. TEL 93-325-53-50.
FAX 93-425-28-80. Ed. Ramon Quevalt Torrell. adv.; bk.rev.; charts; illus.; circ. 10,000. **Indexed:** Fluidex, Ind.SST.

333.91   US
TEXAS. WATER COMMISSION. LIBRARY. BULLETIN..
1969. irreg. Water Commission, Library, Box 13087, Capitol Station, Austin, TX 78711.
TEL 512-463-7834. Ed. Sylvia von Fange. circ. 130.
Former titles (1977-1985): Texas. Department of Water Resources. Library. Bulletin (ISSN 0148-7876); Texas. Water Development Board. Library. Bulletin.
Description: Lists new holdings added to the libarary collection for the period between issues.

627 333.91   US
TEXAS. WATER DEVELOPMENT BOARD. REPORT. 1950. irreg. free. Water Development Board, Box 13231, Capitol Station, Austin, TX 78711.
TEL 512-463-7834. (also avail. in microfiche) **Indexed:** Chem.Abstr., GeoRef, Pollut.Abstr., Sel.Water Res.Abstr.
Former titles (until 1985): Texas. Department of Water Resources. Report; (until 1977): Texas. Water Development Board. Report (ISSN 0082-3562); (until 1965): Texas. Water Commission. Bulletin.

340 333.91   US   ISSN 0197-2340
TEXAS NATURAL RESOURCES REPORTER. 1977. s-m. $495. Research & Planning Consultants, Inc., 3200 Red River, Ste. 302, Austin, TX 78705. TEL 512-472-7765. FAX 512-472-2232. Ed. Gaylon Finklea. circ. 250. (looseleaf format; back issues avail.)

333.91   US
TEXAS WATER RESOURCES. q. Texas Water Resources Institute, College Station, TX 77843. TEL 409-845-8571. FAX 409-845-3932. Ed. Ric Jensen. circ. 10,490.

627 628   US   ISSN 1051-709X
▼**TEXAS WATER UTILITIES JOURNAL.** 1990. m. $15 (foreign $20) (typically set in June). Texas Water Utilities Association, 1106 Clayton Ave., Ste.101 East, Austin, TX 78723-1033. TEL 512-459-3124. FAX 512-459-7124. Ed. Christine Loven. adv.; circ. 9,200. (back issues avail)
   Description: Covers essential information for all individuals working within the water utilities industry in Texas, including rules and regulations, certification, education, and communication.

THALASSIA SALENTINA. see BIOLOGY — Botany

333.91   DK   ISSN 0106-8334
TIDEVANDSTABELLER FOR DANMARK. (Text in Danish and English) 1977. a. price varies. Farvandsvaesenet, Farvandsdirektoratet, P.O. Box 1919, 1023 Copenhagen K, Denmark. TEL 31 57 40 50. FAX 31-57-43-41. TELEX 9 11 44 30. Flemming Skyttedamoe.

TIJDSCHRIFT LANDINRICHTING. see AGRICULTURE — Crop Production And Soil

333.91   BE
TRIBUNE D'EAU; eau, environnement, pollution. 1947. 5/yr. 4600 Fr. (Centre Belge d'Etude et de Documentation de l'Environnement) C E B E D O C S.P.R.L., 2 rue Armand Stevart, 4000 Liege, Belgium. adv.; bk.rev.; abstr.; bibl.; charts; index; circ. 10,000. Indexed: Biol.Abstr., Excerp.Med., Sel.Water Res.Abstr.
   Formerly (until 1988): C E B E D E A U. Tribune (ISSN 0577-1056)

627   II   ISSN 0080-4045
U P IRRIGATION RESEARCH INSTITUTE. GENERAL ANNUAL REPORT.* (Issued in its Technical Memorandum Series) a. U P Irrigation Research Institute, Roorkee, Uttar Pradesh, India.

627   II   ISSN 0080-4053
U P IRRIGATION RESEARCH INSTITUTE. TECHNICAL MEMORANDUM.* (Text in English) irreg. U P Irrigation Research Institute, Roorkee, Uttar Pradesh, India.

627   US
U S C I D NEWSLETTER. 1958. q. membership. United States Committee on Irrigation and Drainage, 1616 17th St., Ste. 483, Denver, CO 80202. TEL 303-628-5430. FAX 303-628-5431. Ed. Larry D. Stephens. bk.rev.; circ. 750.
   Formerly: I.C.I.D. Newsletter.

620   US   ISSN 0041-5480
U S C O L D NEWSLETTER. 1960. 3/yr. membership. U S Committee on Large Dams, (Subsidiary of: International Commission on Large Dams), 1616 Seventeenth Street, Suite 483, Denver, CO 80202. TEL 303-628-5430. FAX 303-628-5431. bk.rev.; circ. 1,500.

333.91   US   ISSN 0749-1980
            CODEN: USWNEP
U S WATER NEWS. 1984. m. $44 (foreign $79). U S Water News, Inc., 230 Main St., Halstead, KS 67056. TEL 316-835-2222. Ed. Steven D. Seibel. adv.; bk.rev.; circ. 25,000. (tabloid format; back issues avail.) Indexed: Environ.Abstr.
   Description: Covers wide range of national news about water resources.

333.91   US   ISSN 0747-8291
            CODEN: ULWAE5
ULTRAPURE WATER. 1984. 9/yr. $18. Tall Oaks Publishing, Inc., 10394 W. Chatfield Ave., Ste. 108, Littleton, CO 80127. TEL 303-973-6700. FAX 303-973-5327. Ed. Mike Henley. adv.; bk.rev.; circ. 13,000. (also avail. in microform from UMI; reprint service avail.) Indexed: Chem.Abstr., Energy Info.Abstr., Environ.Abstr., Telegen.
   —BLDSC shelfmark: 9082.783500.
   Description: Addresses all aspects of high purity water production in the high-pressure boiler industry, electric utilities, semiconductor manufacturing, pharmaceuticals and biotechnology.

333.91   UN
UNITED NATIONS. ECONOMIC AND SOCIAL COMMISSION FOR ASIA AND THE PACIFIC. NATURAL RESOURCES - WATER SERIES. 1964. irreg., no.60, 1985. price varies. Rajademnern Ave., Bangkok 10200, Thailand.
   Formerly: United Nations. Department of International Economic and Social Affairs. Natural Resources - Water Series.

333.91   UN
UNITED NATIONS. ECONOMIC AND SOCIAL COMMISSION FOR ASIA AND THE PACIFIC. WATER RESOURCES SERIES. 1951. irreg., no.63, 1989. price varies. United Nations Economic and Social Commission for Asia and the Pacific (ESCAP), United Nations Bldg., Rajamnern Ave., Bangkok 10200, Thailand. (Dist. by: United Nations Publications, Room DC2-0853, New York, NY 10017; or Distribution and Sales Section, Palais des Nations, CH-1211 Geneva 10, Switzerland) (back issues avail.)
   Former titles: United Nations. Economic and Social Commission for Asia and the Pacific. Water Resources Development Series (ISSN 0082-8130); (until 1964): United Nations. Economic and Social Commission for Asia and the Pacific. Flood Control Series.

U.S. BUREAU OF RECLAMATION. ANNUAL REPORT. see CONSERVATION

U.S. BUREAU OF RECLAMATION. ENGINEERING MONOGRAPH. see ENGINEERING — Hydraulic Engineering

333.91   US
U.S. SOIL CONSERVATION SERVICE. ANNUAL REPORT. a. free. U.S. Soil Conservation Service (Spokane), 360 U.S. Courthouse, Spokane, WA 99201. TEL 206-456-3704. Ed. William F. Weller.

333.91   GW
UNIVERSITAET HANNOVER. INSTITUT FUER SIEDLUNGSWASSERWIRTSCHAFT. VEROEFFENTLICHUNGEN. 1957. irreg., no.50, 1980. price varies. Universitaet Hannover, Institut fuer Siedlungswasserwirtschaft, Welfengarten 1, 3000 Hannover, Germany.
   Formerly: Technische Universitaet Hannover. Institut fuer Siedlungswasserwirtschaft. Veroeffentlichungen (ISSN 0073-0319)

333.91   US
UNIVERSITY OF ALASKA. INSTITUTE OF NORTHERN ENGINEERING. 1975. biennial. free. University of Alaska, Institute of Northern Engineering, Water Research Center, Fairbanks, AK 99775-1760. TEL 907-474-7775. FAX 907-474-6087. circ. 1,800.
   Former titles: University of Alaska. Institute of Water Resources-Engineering Experiment Station. Annual Report; University of Alaska. Institute of Water Resources. Annual Report (ISSN 0065-5953)

333.91   US   ISSN 0068-6301
UNIVERSITY OF CALIFORNIA, DAVIS. WATER RESOURCES CENTER. CONTRIBUTIONS. 1957. irreg. (5-7/yr.). free. University of California, Davis, Water Resources Center, Davis, CA 95616. TEL 916-752-1544. circ. 600. Indexed: Sel.Water Res.Abstr., Soils & Fert.

333.9   US   ISSN 0069-9063
            CODEN: CUWRAJ
UNIVERSITY OF CONNECTICUT. INSTITUTE OF WATER RESOURCES. REPORT SERIES. 1966. irreg., latest 1990. University of Connecticut, Institute of Water Resources, Storrs, CT 06269-4018. TEL 203-486-0335. Indexed: GeoRef.
   Description: Includes chemical, biological, geological, legal, engineering and sociopolitical reports on resources.
   Refereed Serial

333.7   US
UNIVERSITY OF CONNECTICUT. INSTITUTE OF WATER RESOURCES. WETLANDS CONFERENCE. PROCEEDINGS. (Subseries of its Report) 1973. irreg., 3rd, 1976. University of Connecticut, Institute of Water Resources, Box U-18, Storrs, CT 06296-4018. TEL 203-486-0335. charts; illus. (also avail. in microfiche from NTI) Indexed: Sel.Water Res.Abstr.

333.91   US
UNIVERSITY OF HAWAII. WATER RESOURCES RESEARCH CENTER. ANNUAL REPORT. 1966. a. $13. University of Hawaii, Water Resources Research Center, 2540 Dole St., Holmes Hall 283, Honolulu, HI 96822. TEL 808-948-7847. FAX 808-948-5044. Ed. Faith N. Fujimura. circ. 500. (back issues avail.)

333.9 628   US   ISSN 0073-1293
UNIVERSITY OF HAWAII. WATER RESOURCES RESEARCH CENTER. COLLECTED REPRINTS. 1969. biennial. price varies. University of Hawaii, Water Resources Research Center, 2540 Dole St., Honolulu, HI 96822. TEL 808-948-7847. Ed. Faith N. Fujimura. circ. 500. (also avail. in microfiche from NTI)
   Refereed Serial

333.91   US
UNIVERSITY OF HAWAII. WATER RESOURCES RESEARCH CENTER. PROJECT BULLETIN. 1972. irreg. University of Hawaii, Water Resources Research Center, 2540 Dole St., Honolulu, HI 96822. TEL 808-948-7847.

333.91   US
UNIVERSITY OF HAWAII. WATER RESOURCES RESEARCH CENTER. RAIN WATER CISTERN SYSTEMS. 1982. irreg. $25. University of Hawaii, Water Resources Research Center, 2540 Dole St., Honolulu, HI 96822. TEL 808-948-7847. FAX 808-948-5044. Ed. Faith N. Fujimura. charts.

333.9 628   US   ISSN 0073-1307
TC1   CODEN: HUWTAC
UNIVERSITY OF HAWAII. WATER RESOURCES RESEARCH CENTER. TECHNICAL REPORT. 1967. irreg. price varies. University of Hawaii, Water Resources Research Center, 2540 Dole St., Honolulu, HI 96822. TEL 808-948-7847. Ed. Faith N. Fujimura. circ. 300. (also avail. in microfiche from NTI) Indexed: Pollut.Abstr.
   Refereed Serial

333.91   US
UNIVERSITY OF HAWAII. WATER RESOURCES RESEARCH CENTER. WORKSHOP SERIES. 1976. irreg. University of Hawaii, Water Resources Research Center, 2540 Dole St., Honolulu, HI 96822. TEL 808-948-7847.

333.9 627   US   ISSN 0073-4616
TC424.I2
UNIVERSITY OF IDAHO. WATER RESOURCES RESEARCH INSTITUTE. ANNUAL REPORT. 1965. a. free. University of Idaho, Water Resources Research Institute, Moscow, ID 83843. TEL 208-885-6429. Ed. Leland L. Mink. circ. 400.

333.91   US   ISSN 0073-5434
UNIVERSITY OF ILLINOIS AT URBANA-CHAMPAIGN. WATER RESOURCES CENTER. ANNUAL REPORT. 1965. a. $5. University of Illinois at Urbana-Champaign, Water Resources Center, 205 N. Mathews, Urbana, IL 61801. TEL 217-333-0536. FAX 217-244-6633. Ed. Glenn E. Stout. (also avail. in microform from NTI)

333.91   US   ISSN 0073-5442
HD1694   CODEN: IUWRAH
UNIVERSITY OF ILLINOIS AT URBANA-CHAMPAIGN. WATER RESOURCES CENTER. RESEARCH REPORT. 1966. irreg., no.212, 1989. price varies. University of Illinois at Urbana-Champaign, Water Resources Center, 205 N. Mathews, Urbana, IL 61801. TEL 217-333-0536. FAX 217-244-6633. Ed. Glenn E. Stout. (also avail. in microform from NTI) Indexed: Biol.Abstr., Pollut.Abstr.
   Refereed Serial

333.91   US
UNIVERSITY OF ILLINOIS AT URBANA-CHAMPAIGN. WATER RESOURCES CENTER. SPECIAL REPORTS. 1968. irreg., no.17, 1989. price varies. University of Illinois at Urbana-Champaign, Water Resources Center, 205 N. Mathews, Urbana, IL 61801. TEL 217-333-0536. FAX 217-244-6633. Indexed: Biol.Abstr., GeoRef, Pollut.Abstr.

WATER RESOURCES

333.91 634.9   US
UNIVERSITY OF MINNESOTA. CENTER FOR NATURAL RESOURCE POLICY AND MANAGEMENT. WORKING PAPERS. 1984. irreg., latest no.5. University of Minnesota, Center for Natural Resource Policy & Management, 115 Green Hall, Dept. of Forest Resources, St. Paul, MN 55108. TEL 612-624-9796. FAX 612-625-5212. Ed. James Perry. circ. 150.
   Description: Covers water quality, common property and economics of natural resources and forestry research.

333.9   US
UNIVERSITY OF NEBRASKA. WATER CENTER. ANNUAL REPORT OF ACTIVITIES. 1968. a. free. University of Nebraska, Water Center, 103 Natural Resources Hall, Lincoln, NE 68583-0844. circ. 1,500.
   Formerly: Nebraska Water Resources Research Institute. University of Nebraska. Annual Report of Activities (ISSN 0077-6394)

333.91   AT   ISSN 1030-4134
UNIVERSITY OF NEW ENGLAND. CENTRE FOR WATER POLICY RESEARCH. OCCASIONAL PAPERS (NO.). 1987. irreg., no.6, 1990. University of New England, Centre for Water Policy Research, Armidale, N.S.W. 2351, Australia. TEL 61-6773-2420. FAX 61-6773-3237.

627 333.9   AT   ISSN 0077-8818
UNIVERSITY OF NEW SOUTH WALES. WATER RESEARCH LABORATORY, MANLY VALE. LABORATORY RESEARCH REPORTS. 1959. irreg., latest no.173, 1988. price varies. University of New South Wales, Water Research Laboratory, King St., Manly Vale, N.S.W. 2093, Australia. **Indexed:** GeoRef., Sel.Water Res.Abstr.

333.9 628   US
UNIVERSITY OF RHODE ISLAND. WATER RESOURCES CENTER. ANNUAL REPORT. 1965. a. $10 (effective Sep. 1991). Rhode Island Water Resources Center, University of Rhode Island, Kingston, RI 02881. TEL 401-792-2680. FAX 401-782-1066. Ed. Calvin Poon. circ. 800.

333.91   US
UNIVERSITY OF TEXAS AT AUSTIN. CENTER FOR RESEARCH IN WATER RESOURCES. TECHNICAL REPORT SERIES. 1964. irreg., latest no.223. price varies. University of Texas at Austin, Center for Research in Water Resources, Balcones Research Center, Austin, TX 78712. TEL 512-471-3131. FAX 512-471-0072. **Indexed:** Chem.Abstr.
   Description: Summary of research findings resulting from sponsored projects in the water resources area conducted by faculty members of the university.
   Refereed Serial

333.91   US
UNIVERSITY OF TEXAS AT AUSTIN. CENTER FOR RESEARCH IN WATER RESOURCES. WATER RESOURCES SYMPOSIUM SERIES. 1968. irreg. price varies. University of Texas at Austin, Center for Research in Water Resources, 10100 Burnet Rd., Austin, TX 78758-4497. TEL 512-471-3131.
   Former titles: University of Texas at Austin. Center for Research in Water Resources. Symposium Series; University of Texas at Austin. Center for Research in Water Resources. Resource Symposium Series.
   Description: Compilation of papers presented at the latest Water Resources Symposium.

551 623 333.7   US   ISSN 0886-2664
UPWELLINGS. 1977. q. free. Michigan Sea Grant College Program, 4113 Institute of Science & Technology, 2200 Bonisteel Blvd., Ann Arbor, MI 48109. TEL 313-764-1138. FAX 313-747-0036. (Co-sponsors: University of Michigan; Michigan State University) Ed. Carol Allaire. bk.rev.; circ. 5,000. (back issues avail.)
   Description: News, articles, and information on issues related to the Great Lakes.

VALENCIA PORT; guia del servicios del puerto de Valencia. see *TRANSPORTATION — Ships And Shipping*

VANDERBILT UNIVERSITY. DEPARTMENT OF ENVIRONMENTAL AND WATER RESOURCES ENGINEERING. TECHNICAL REPORTS. see *ENVIRONMENTAL STUDIES*

627   DK   ISSN 0106-3677
VANDTEKNIK. 1926. 10/yr. DKK 240 (typically set in Jan.). Dansk Vandteknisk Forening, Vilh. Becks Vej 60, 8260 Viby J, Denmark. TEL 86112333609. Ed. Eva Munck. adv.; circ. 1,525 (controlled).
   Description: Focuses on water resources, groundwater protection, abstraction and administration, water quality, waterworks technique, water distribution, pipelines, domestic installations, consumption and consumer relations.

629 333.91   SW   ISSN 0042-2886
                                  CODEN: VTTNAO
VATTEN/WATER; tidskrift foer vattenvaard/periodical on water conservation. (Text mainly in Swedish, occasional papers in English or German; summaries in English, German) 1945. q. SEK 580. Foereningen foer Vattenhygien - Swedish Association for Water Hygiene, Nyckelkroken 22, S-226 47 Lund, Sweden. Ed. Artur Almestrand. adv.; bk.rev.; bibl.; charts; illus.; index, cum.index; circ. 1,600. **Indexed:** Biol.Abstr., Chem.Abstr., Environ.Per.Bibl., Excerp.Med., Ocean.Abstr., Pollut.Abstr., W.R.C.Inf.
   —BLDSC shelfmark: 9149.680000.
   Formerly: Vattenhygien - Water Hygiene.

VERSORGUNGSWIRTSCHAFT. see *ENGINEERING — Electrical Engineering*

333.91 627   FI   ISSN 0505-3838
VESITALOUS; Finnish journal of water economy, hydraulic and agricultural engineering. (Text in Finnish; summaries in English) 1960. bi-m. Fmk.150. Maa- Ja Vesitekniikan Tuki, Tontunmaentie 33D, 02200 Espoo, Finland. FAX 0-425207. Ed. Marja-Leena Jaarvi. adv.; bk.rev.; charts; illus.; circ. 3,000. **Indexed:** Chem.Abstr., Excerp.Med., W.R.C.Inf.
   —BLDSC shelfmark: 9218.460000.

353.9   US
VIRGINIA. STATE WATER CONTROL BOARD. BASIC DATA BULLETIN. 1930. irreg., no.44, 1975. State Water Control Board, 4900 Cox Road, Glen Allen, VA 23060. TEL 804-527-5215. FAX 804-527-5313.

353.9   US
VIRGINIA. STATE WATER CONTROL BOARD. INFORMATION BULLETIN. no.527, 1977. irreg. State Water Control Board, 4900 Cox Road, Glen Allen, VA 23233. TEL 804-367-0056. FAX 804-367-0067.

353.9   US
VIRGINIA. STATE WATER CONTROL BOARD. PLANNING BULLETIN. no.304, 1976. irreg. State Water Control Board, 4900 Cox Rd., Glen Allen, VA 23233. TEL 804-367-0056. FAX 804-367-0067. **Indexed:** GeoRef.

333.91   US
VIRGINIA. WATER RESOURCES RESEARCH CENTER. BULLETIN. 1965. irreg., latest no.170. free within Virginia; out-of-state $10 per no. Water Resources Research Center, Virginia Polytechnic Institute and State University, 617 N. Main St., Blacksburg, VA 24060. TEL 703-231-8036. abstr.; bibl.; illus.; circ. 250. (also avail. in microfilm from UMI; back issues avail.) **Indexed:** Geo.Abstr., GeoRef.

333.91   US
VIRGINIA. WATER RESOURCES RESEARCH CENTER. WATER NEWS. 1970. m. $15 (free in Virginia; foreign $18). Water Resources Research Center, Virginia Polytechnic Institute and State University, 617 N. Main St., Blacksburg, VA 24060. TEL 703-231-5624. Ed. Elizabeth B. Crumbley.

VODNI HOSPODARSTVI. SERIE A/WATER MANAGEMENT. SERIES A. see *ENGINEERING — Hydraulic Engineering*

333.91 338 627   CS
VODNI HOSPODARSTVI. SERIE B/WATER MANAGEMENT. SERIES B. (Text in Czech; summaries in English and Russian) 1950. m. 60 Kcs.($39.60) (Ministerstvo Lesniho a Vodniho Hospodarstvi Ceske Republiky) Statni Zemedelske Nakladatelstvi, Vaclavske nam. 47, 113 11 Prague 1, Czechoslovakia. TEL 26 59 51. (Subscr. to: Artia, Ve Smeckach 30, 111 27 Prague 1, Czechoslovakia) Ed. Josef Benes. adv.; illus.; circ. 4,000. **Indexed:** Biol.Abstr., Chem.Abstr., Food Sci.& Tech.Abstr., W.R.C.Inf.

627   BU   ISSN 0204-8248
VODNI PROBLEMI. 1975. irreg. 1.40 lv. per no. (Bulgarska Akademiia na Naukite, Institut po Vodni Problemi) Publishing House of the Bulgarian Academy of Sciences, Acad. G. Bonchev St., Bldg. 6, 1113 Sofia, Bulgaria. circ. 480. **Indexed:** BSL Geo.
   —BLDSC shelfmark: 0040.743000.
   Supersedes: Bulgarska Akademiia na Naukite. Institut po Vodni Problemi. Izvestiia.

333.7   RU   ISSN 0321-0596
                                  CODEN: VDRSBK
VODNYE RESURSY. 1972. bi-m. 51.90 Rub. (Akademiya Nauk S.S.S.R., Institut Vodnykh Problem) Izdatel'stvo Nauka, 90 Profsoyuznaya ul., 117864 Moscow, Russia. TEL 234-05-84. (Dist. by: Mezhdunarodnaya Kniga, ul. Dimitrova D.39, 113095 Moscow, Russia) Ed. G.V. Voropaev. bk.rev.; abstr.; charts; illus.; circ. 1,575. **Indexed:** Chem.Abstr., GeoRef.
   —BLDSC shelfmark: 0040.860000.

551.4 628   CS   ISSN 0042-790X
GB772.C95   CODEN: VOCAAZ
VODOHOSPODARSKY CASOPIS/WATER SYSTEM PERIODICAL. (Text in Czech or Slovak; summaries in English, French, German, Russian) 1953. bi-m. 120 Kcs.($38) (Slovenska Akademia Vied) Veda, Publishing House of the Slovak Academy of Sciences, Klemensova 19, 814 30 Bratislava, Czechoslovakia. (Dist. by: Slovart, Nam. Slobody 6, 817 64 Bratislava, Czechoslovakia) (Co-sponsor: Ceskoslovenska Akademie Ved) Ed. Jan Benetin. charts; illus.; index, cum.index: 1953-1968; circ. 1,200. **Indexed:** Chem.Abstr., Fluidex, GeoRef., Geotech.Abstr., Ref.Zh., Soils & Fert.
   Description: Presents news regarding research status in water system regions, information concerning new measurement and computer methods, new devices coming out of congresses and symposia.

VODOSNABZHENIE I SANITARNAYA TEKHNIKA. see *PUBLIC HEALTH AND SAFETY*

VOLUNTAD HIDRAULICA. see *ENGINEERING — Hydraulic Engineering*

608 540   GW   ISSN 0083-6915
TD203   CODEN: VJWWAU
VOM WASSER; ein Fachbuch fuer Wasserchemie und Wasserreinigungstechnik. irreg., vol.72, 1989. price varies. (Gesellschaft Deutscher Chemiker, Fachgruppe Wasserchemie) V C H Verlagsgesellschaft mbH, Postfach 101161, 6940 Weinheim, Germany. TEL 06201-602-0. FAX 06201-602328. TELEX 465516-VCHWH-D. (U.S. addr.: V C H Publishers Inc., 220 E. 23rd St., New York, NY 10010-4606) adv. (reprint service avail. from ISI) **Indexed:** Biol.Abstr., Chem.Abstr., Excerp.Med., W.R.C.Inf.
   —BLDSC shelfmark: 9255.000000.

333.91   PK
W A P D A NEWS. (Text in English) 1978. fortn. Rs.70. Water and Power Development Authority, Public Relations Division, WAPDA House, Shara-e-Quaid-e-Azam, Lahore, Pakistan. TEL 212900. TELEX 44869 WAPDA PK. Ed. Raziuddin Shaikh.
   Description: News coverage of the activities of the authority.

333.9   US   ISSN 0549-799X
HD1694.N8
W R R I NEWS. 1966. bi-m. $10 outside N. Carolina; free to state residents. North Carolina State University, Water Resources Research Institute, Box 7912, Raleigh, NC 27695-7912. TEL 919-515-2815. FAX 919-515-7802. Ed. Jeri Gray. bk.rev.; circ. 150 (controlled). **Indexed:** Pollut.Abstr., Sel.Water Res.Abstr.
   ●Also available online.
   Formerly: North Carolina State University. Water Resources Research Institute. Report (ISSN 0078-1525)

333.91   US   ISSN 0044-9970
W R R I NEWS REPORT. 1971. q. free. Auburn University, Water Resources Research Institute, 202 Hargis Hall, Auburn, AL 36849. TEL 205-826-5075. Eds. Joseph F. Judkins, Jr., Dennis H. Block. circ. 1,100. (processed) **Indexed:** Environ.Abstr., GeoRef.

333.91   GW
WASSER - ABWASSER - G W F; das gas- und wasserfach. 1858. m. DM.308. (Bundesverband der Deutscher Gas- und Wasserwirtschaft) R. Oldenbourg Verlag GmbH, Postfach 801360, Rosenheimerstr. 145, 8000 Munich 80, Germany. (Co-sponsor: Abwassertechnische Vereinigung) **Indexed:** Chem.Abstr., Excerp.Med., INIS Atomind.
Former titles: G W F Gas- und Wasserfach (ISSN 0016-3651); Wasser - Abwasser.
Description: For the water and sewer industry. Publishes information and chemical research on water pollution, quality and treatment of drinking water.

620   SZ
WASSER, ENERGIE, LUFT/EAU, ENERGIE, AIR. (Text mainly in German, partly in French) 1910. 7/yr. 120 Fr. Schweizerischer Wasserwirtschaftsverband, Ruetistrasse 3A, CH-5401 Baden, Switzerland. TEL 056-225069. FAX 056-211083. Ed. Georg Weber. adv.; bk.rev.; charts; illus.; index, cum.index; circ. 3,000. **Indexed:** Eng.Ind., Excerp.Med., Geotech.Abstr., Intl.Civil Eng.Abstr., Sel.Water Res.Abstr., Soft.Abstr.Eng.
Formerly: Wasser und Energiewirtschaft (ISSN 0043-096X)
Description: Trade publication covering water rights and supply, hydraulic construction, water power utilization, protection of waterways, irrigation, drainage, flood protection, and inland navigation. Includes reports and announcements of events.

628.1 333.7   GW   ISSN 0511-3520
TD203   CODEN: WAKADP
WASSER - KALENDER; Jahrbuch fuer das gesamte Wasserfach. 1966. a. price varies. Erich Schmidt Verlag GmbH & Co. (Berlin), Genthiner Str. 30g, 1000 Berlin 30, Germany. Ed. R. Wagner. charts; stat.; circ. 3,000.

WASSER, LUFT UND BODEN; unabhaengige Zeitschrift fuer Wasserwirtschaft, Luftreinhaltung, Abfallverwertung und Umwelttechnik. see *ENVIRONMENTAL STUDIES — Pollution*

333.91   GW
WASSER MAGAZIN; Kundeninformation der Hamburger Wasserwerke. 1981. 2/yr. free. Hamburger Wasserwerke GmbH, Billhorner Deich 2, 2000 Hamburg 26, Germany. TEL 040-7888-2483. FAX 040-7888-2513. Ed. Hans-Werner Krueger. circ. 850,000.

333.7 628.1   GW   ISSN 0512-5030
    CODEN: WAFPDB
WASSER UND ABWASSER IN FORSCHUNG UND PRAXIS. (Text in German; summaries in English and French) 1969. irreg., vol.20, 1987. price varies. Erich Schmidt Verlag GmbH & Co. (Bielefeld), Viktoriastr. 44A, Postfach 7330, 4800 Bielefeld, Germany. TEL 0521-583080. (back issues avail.)

624   GW   ISSN 0043-0951
S605   CODEN: WUBOAN
WASSER UND BODEN; Zeitschrift fuer die gesamte Wasserwirtschaft. 1949. m. DM.160($84) Verlag Paul Parey (Hamburg), Spitalerstr. 12, 2000 Hamburg 1, Germany. TEL 040-33969-0. FAX 040-33969-199. TELEX 2161-391-PARV-D. (U.S. address: Paul Parey Scientific Publishers, 35 West 38th St., No.3W, New York, NY 10018) adv.; bk.rev.; bibl.; charts; illus.; index; circ. 6,000. (reprint service avail. from ISI) **Indexed:** Biol.Abstr., Chem.Abstr., Excerp.Med., GeoRef.

333.7 340 628.1   GW   ISSN 0508-1254
WASSERRECHT UND WASSERWIRTSCHAFT. 1960. irreg., vol.26, 1991. price varies. Erich Schmidt Verlag GmbH & Co. (Berlin), Genthiner Str. 30g, 1000 Berlin 30, Germany. bibl.; charts; illus.; stat. **Indexed:** W.R.C.Inf.

DAS WASSERTRIEBWERK. see *ENERGY*

628   GW   ISSN 0043-0978
    CODEN: WSWTAR
WASSERWIRTSCHAFT; Fachzeitschrift fuer Wasserwesen und Umwelttechnik. 1905. m. DM.164.40. (Deutscher Verband fuer Wasserwirtschaft und Kulturbau e.V.) Franckh-Kosmos Verlags-GmbH und Co., Pfizerstr. 5-7, Postfach 106011, 7000 Stuttgart 1, Germany. TEL 0711-2191-332. FAX 0711-2191-350. Ed. G. Marotz. adv.; bk.rev.; abstr.; bibl.; charts; illus.; index; circ. 3,500. **Indexed:** Appl.Mech.Rev., Chem.Abstr., Excerp.Med., Geo.Abstr., GeoRef., Geotech.Abstr., Intl.Civil Eng.Abstr., Ocean.Abstr., Pollut.Abstr., Sel.Water Res.Abstr., Soft.Abstr.Eng.
Description: Trade publication for the water and sewer industry. Features technology of water purification, ground-water protection, and sewage treatment. Includes industry news, list of events and suppliers.

620   GW   ISSN 0043-0986
TC1   CODEN: WSWSAO
WASSERWIRTSCHAFT - WASSERTECHNIK (W W T); Zeitschrift fuer Technik und Oekonomik der Wasserwirtschaft. 1951. 8/yr. DM.69.60. (Kammer der Technik, Fachverband Wasser) Verlag fuer Bauwesen, Franzosische Str. 13-14, 1086 Berlin, Germany. Ed. Petra Ulbrich. adv.; bk.rev.; abstr.; illus.; index. **Indexed:** Chem.Abstr., Excerp.Med., Fluidex, GeoRef., Geotech.Abstr., Intl.Civil Eng.Abstr., Ocean.Abstr., Pollut.Abstr., Sel.Water Res.Abstr., Soft.Abstr.Eng., W.R.C.Inf.
—BLDSC shelfmark: 9266.500000.

627   AU   ISSN 0043-0994
WASSERWIRTSCHAFTLICHE MITTEILUNGEN. 1964. m. membership. Oesterreichischer Wasserwirtschaftsverband, Marc-Aurel-Strasse 5, A-1010 Vienna, Austria. bk.rev.; circ. 950.

WASTE DISPOSAL AND WATER MANAGEMENT IN AUSTRALIA. see *ENVIRONMENTAL STUDIES — Waste Management*

628.168   CN   ISSN 0829-352X
WASTEWATER TECHNOLOGY CENTRE NEWSLETTER/CENTRE TECHNIQUE DES EAUX USEES. BULLETIN. 1985. 4/yr. free. Environment Canada, Wastewater Technology Centre, P.O. Box 5068, 867 Lakeshore Rd., Burlington, Ont. L7R 4L7, Canada. TEL 416-336-4765. FAX 416-336-4858. circ. 2,000.
—BLDSC shelfmark: 9267.090000.
Description: Focuses on research projects at the facility.

628   US   ISSN 0043-1028
WASTEWATER WORKS NEWS. vol.20, 1964. q. membership. Michigan Water Pollution Control Association, Box 11128, Lansing, MI 48901. (Editorial addr.: 3059 Chicago Dr. S.W., Grandville, MI 49418.) Ed. Dan Wolz. illus.; circ. 1,200.
Description: Deals with water quality issues in Michigan for association members.

627   AT   ISSN 0310-0367
    CODEN: WTRMDP
WATER. 1973. bi-m. Aus.$30. Australian Water and Wastewater Association, P.O. Box 388, Artarmon, N.S.W. 2064, Australia. TEL 02-413-1288. FAX 02-413-1047. Ed. E.A. Swinton. adv.; bk.rev.; circ. 3,300. **Indexed:** Chem.Abstr., W.R.C.Inf.
—BLDSC shelfmark: 9267.454000.
Description: Studies water, water supply and sewerage; treatment, operation, management, administration and environmental aspects.

333.91   SA
WATER. 2/yr. Erudita Publications (Pty) Ltd., Cnr. 11th Ave. & Main Rd., P.O. Box 29159, Melville, Johannesburg 2109, South Africa. adv. **Indexed:** Excerp.Med.

333.91   US
WATER ACTIVITIES TRADE REPORT. 1987. bi-w. $100. American Water Foundation, 1616 17th St., Ste.376, Denver, CO 80215. TEL 303-628-5516. FAX 303-236-5151. Ed. Michael R. Vaughan. bk.rev.; circ. 100. (back issues avail.)
Description: Provides current information on trade opportunities, bids, and tenders in developing countries in the water sector.

WATER RESOURCES   4831

627   IS   ISSN 0334-5807
WATER AND IRRIGATION REVIEW. (Text in English) 1981. q. $54. Subscription Dept., P.O. Box 21051, Tel Aviv 61210, Israel. FAX 03-268665. Ed. Joshua Jacobson. adv.; circ. 8,800. **Indexed:** Irr.& Drain.Abstr.
Description: Articles on all aspects of water and irrigation technology.

628.168   CN
WATER & POLLUTION CONTROL. 1893. 6/yr. Can.$32.10($50) Zanny Publications Ltd., 190 Main St., Unionville, Ont. L3R 2G9, Canada. TEL 416-477-2922. FAX 416-479-4834. Ed. Mary Ellen Jamieson. adv.; circ. 23,355. **Indexed:** Environ.Abstr.

628.1   CN
WATER & POLLUTION CONTROL. DIRECTORY AND BUYERS' GUIDE. (Title varies slightly) 1962. a. Can.$15. Southam Business Communications Inc. (Subsidiary of: Southam Inc.), 1450 Don Mills Road, Don Mills, Ont. M3B 2X7, Canada. TEL 416-445-6641. FAX 416-442-2261. Ed. Tom Davey. adv.; bk.rev.; illus.; circ. 8,238. **Indexed:** W.R.C.Inf.
Former titles: Water and Pollution Control. Directory and Handbook (ISSN 0318-0468); Water and Pollution Control Directory (ISSN 0511-3555)

338.7   II
WATER AND POWER DEVELOPMENT CONSULTANCY SERVICES. ANNUAL REPORT AND STATEMENT OF ACCOUNTS. (Report year ends Mar. 31) (Text in English) a. Water and Power Development Consultancy Services (India) Ltd., Kailash, 26 K. G. Marg, New Delhi 110001, India.

628.1   AT
WATER AND THE ENVIRONMENT. 1959. bi-m. Aus.$100 (includes Research Report Series and Annual Report). Water Research Foundation of Australia, c/o Centre for Resource and Environmental Studies, Australian National University, G.P.O. Box 4, Canberra, A.C.T. 2601, Australia. circ. 1,000. **Indexed:** AESIS.
Formerly: Water Research Foundation of Australia. Newsletter.

628   UK   ISSN 0043-1133
WATER AND WASTE TREATMENT. 1950. m. £47. Faversham House Group Ltd., 111 St. James's Rd., Croydon, Surrey CR9 2TH, England. Ed. John Lambert. adv.; bk.rev.; bibl.; charts; illus.; tr.lit.; circ. 8,644. (also avail. in microform from MIM,UMI) **Indexed:** Biol.Abstr., BMT, Br.Ceram.Abstr., Br.Tech.Ind., Chem.Abstr., Environ.Per.Bibl., Excerp.Med., Intl.Civil Eng.Abstr., Pollut.Abstr., Sel.Water Res.Abstr., Soft.Abstr.Eng., W.R.C.Inf., World Text.Abstr.
—BLDSC shelfmark: 9268.699000.

WATER AND WASTES DIGEST. see *PUBLIC HEALTH AND SAFETY*

333.91   UK   ISSN 0262-9909
TD257
WATER BULLETIN. 1982. w. £45 (foreign £65). Water Services Association of England and Wales, 1 Queen Anne's Gate, London SW1H 9BH, England. TEL 01-222-8111. FAX 01-222-1811. Ed. Paul Garrett. adv.; bk.rev.; charts; illus.; circ. 8,000. **Indexed:** Br.Tech.Ind., Chem.Abstr., Curr.Adv.Ecol.Sci., Fluidex, Geo.Abstr., W.R.C.Inf.
—BLDSC shelfmark: 9269.250000.
Supersedes: Water (ISSN 0305-3105)

628.1   US   ISSN 0746-4029
    CODEN: WCPUEN
WATER CONDITIONING AND PURIFICATION. 1959. m. $34. Publicom Inc., 4651 N. First Ave., Ste. 101, Tucson, AZ 85718. FAX 602-887-2383. Ed. Darlene J. Scheel. adv.; bk.rev.; charts; illus.; index; circ. 14,000 (controlled). **Indexed:** Environ.Abstr.
—BLDSC shelfmark: 9269.450000.
Former titles: Water Conditioning (ISSN 0043-1184); Water Conditioning Sales.

628   US   ISSN 0043-1206
WATER DESALINATION REPORT. 1965. w. $300 (typically set in Dec.). Maria C. Smith, Ed. & Pub., Box 10, Tracey's Landing, MD 20779. TEL 301-261-5010. FAX 301-261-5010. bk.rev.

WATER RESOURCES

628 US ISSN 0273-2238
TD1 CODEN: WENMD2
WATER - ENGINEERING AND MANAGEMENT. 1882. m. $25 (foreign $45). Scranton Gillette Communications, Inc., 380 E. Northwest Hwy., Des Plaines, IL 60016. TEL 312-298-6622. adv.; bk.rev.; abstr.; charts; illus.; stat.; index, cum.index; circ. 30,000. (also avail. in microform from UMI) **Indexed:** A.S.& T.Ind., Abstr.Bull.Inst.Pap.Chem., Acid Pre.Dig., Anal.Abstr., Biol.Abstr., Chem.Abstr., Chem.Eng.Abstr., Curr.Adv.Ecol.Sci., Curr.Cont., Energy Info.Abstr., Eng.Ind., Environ.Abstr., Environ.Per.Bibl., Excerp.Med., Fluidex, Geo.Abstr., GeoRef., Intl.Civil Eng.Abstr., Ocean.Abstr., Pollut.Abstr., PROMT, Sel.J.Water, Sel.Water Res.Abstr., Soft.Abstr.Eng., T.C.E.A., W.R.C.Inf.
—BLDSC shelfmark: 9269.780000.
Formerly (until 1981): Water and Sewage Works (ISSN 0043-1125); **Incorporates (1964-1981):** Water and Wastes Engineering (ISSN 0043-115X); Which was formerly : Water Works and Wastes Engineering (ISSN 0096-6320)
Description: Informational articles pertaining to research on and the application of applied water and wastewater technology, with product and legislative updates.

WATER ENVIRONMENT & TECHNOLOGY. see ENVIRONMENTAL STUDIES

333.91 630 US ISSN 1051-0583
WATER FARMING JOURNAL; America's aquaculture news monthly. 1986. m. $19 (foreign $40). Carroll Trosclair and Associates, Inc., 3400 Neyrey Dr., Metairie, LA 70002. TEL 504-454-8934. FAX 504-488-4135. Ed. Carroll Trosclair. adv.; bk.rev.; charts; illus.; stat.; tr.lit.; circ. 6,000. (back issues avail.)
Description: Covers production, marketing, legislation, new technology, research and equipment relating to aquaculture.

333.91 US
WATER IMPACTS. 1980. m. free. Michigan State University, Institute of Water Research, 334 Natural Resources Bldg., East Lansing, MI 48824-1222. TEL 517-353-3742. FAX 517-353-1812. Ed. Lois G. Wolfson. bk.rev.; index; circ. 2,800. (back issues avail.)

333.91 US ISSN 0250-8060
GB651
WATER INTERNATIONAL. 1975. q. $75. International Water Resources Association, University of Illinois, 205 N. Mathews Ave., Urbana, IL 61801. TEL 217-333-0536. FAX 217-244-6633. TELEX 510011969 UI TELCOM URUD. Ed. Glenn E. Stout. adv.; bk.rev.; bibl.; illus.; circ. 1,800. (back issues avail.) **Indexed:** Abstr.Hyg., AESIS, Energy Ind., Energy Info.Abstr., Environ.Abstr., Environ.Per.Bibl., Geo.Abstr., GeoRef., I D A, Irr.& Drain.Abstr., Rural Devel.Abstr., Sel.Water Res.Abstr.
—BLDSC shelfmark: 9270.400000.
Description: Provides members with news about IWRA, their activities, events in the international water resources field, and reports on water related topics.
Refereed Serial

WATER INVESTMENT NEWSLETTER. see BUSINESS AND ECONOMICS — Investments

628 JA
WATER JAPAN; Japan's water works yearbook. 1906. m. free. Suido Sangyo Shinbun Ltd., Osaka Godo Bldg., 1-5, Doyama-cho, Kita-ku, Osaka-shi 530, Japan. Ed. Hiroshi Ishimaru.
Formerly: Japan Water Works Association. Journal.
Description: Discusses supply systems, quality management, pollution control. Includes international activities and an industry directory.

WATER LAW NEWSLETTER. see LAW

628 GH ISSN 0043-1265
WATER NEWS. 1968. bi-m. free. Ghana Water & Sewerage Corporation, Box M194, Accra, Ghana. Ed. E.Y. Frempong-Mensah. adv.; bk.rev.; circ. 8,000. **Indexed:** AESIS.
Former titles: Sewerage News; Water.

333.91 CN
WATER NEWS/NOUVELLES DE L'EAU. q. Canadian Water Resources Association - Association Canadienne des Ressources Hydriques, c/o Faculty of Engineering, University of Saskatchewan, Saskatchewan, Sask. S7N 0W0, Canada. TEL 306-966-5335. FAX 306-966-5334. adv.
Description: Provides news and information on branch and membership activities and disseminates water resource related information of a regional and national character.

628 333.91 US ISSN 0043-1273
WATER NEWSLETTER; water supply, waste disposal, conservation, pollution. 1958. s-m. $147. Water Information Center, Inc., 125 E. Bethpage Rd., Plainview, NY 11803. TEL 516-249-7634. FAX 516-249-7610. bk.rev.
Incorporates: Research and Development News.

614.7 US
WATER POLLUTION: A SERIES OF MONOGRAPHS. 1974. irreg., no.7, 1984. Academic Press, Inc., 1250 Sixth Ave., San Diego, CA 92101. TEL 619-231-0926. FAX 619-699-6715. Eds. K.S. Speigler, J. Bregman. (reprint service avail. from ISI)
Refereed Serial

WATER POLLUTION CONTROL. see ENVIRONMENTAL STUDIES — Pollution

WATER POLLUTION CONTROL FEDERATION. RESEARCH JOURNAL. see ENVIRONMENTAL STUDIES — Pollution

WATER POLLUTION RESEARCH JOURNAL OF CANADA. see ENVIRONMENTAL STUDIES — Pollution

333.91 CN ISSN 0383-5472
TD227.05
WATER QUALITY DATA FOR ONTARIO STREAMS & LAKES. a. free. Ministry of the Environment, Water Resources Branch, 1 St. Clair Ave. W., 4th Fl., Toronto, Ont. M4V 1P5, Canada. TEL 416-965-6141.

WATER QUALITY INTERNATIONAL. see ENVIRONMENTAL STUDIES — Pollution

627 US ISSN 0043-1354
TD420 CODEN: WATRAG
WATER RESEARCH. 1967. 13/yr. £715 (effective 1992). (International Association on Water Pollution Research and Control) Pergamon Press, Inc., Journals Division, 660 White Plains Rd., Tarrytown, NY 10591-5153. TEL 914-524-9200. FAX 914-333-2444. (And: Headington Hill Hall, Oxford OX3 0BW, England. TEL 0865-794141) Ed. K.J. Ives. adv.; bk.rev.; charts; illus.; stat.; index, cum.index; circ. 3,800. (also avail. in microform from MIM,UMI) **Indexed:** A.S.& T.Ind., Abstr.Bull.Inst.Pap.Chem., Acid Pre.Dig., Acid Rain Abstr., Acid Rain Ind., Biol.Abstr., Biol.& Agr.Ind., Biotech.Abstr., Chem.Abstr., Curr.Adv.Ecol.Sci., Curr.Cont., Deep Sea Res.& Oceanogr.Abstr., Energy Rev., Eng.Ind., Environ.Abstr., Environ.Per.Bibl., Excerp.Med., Food Sci.& Tech.Abstr., Geo.Abstr., GeoRef., Helminthol.Abstr., I D A, Ind.Vet., Int.Abstr.Biol.Sci., Intl.Civil Eng.Abstr., Irr.& Drain.Abstr., Ocean.Abstr., Pig News & Info., Pollut.Abstr., Potato Abstr., Protozool.Abstr., Sci.Abstr., Sel.Water Res.Abstr., Soft.Abstr.Eng., Soils & Fert., Vet.Bull., W.R.C.Inf., Weed Abstr.
—BLDSC shelfmark: 9273.400000.
Description: Covers all aspects of the pollution of marine and fresh water, and the management of water resources and water quality.
Refereed Serial

628.168 UK
WATER RESEARCH CENTRE. ANNUAL REVIEW. 1974. a. free. Water Research Centre, P.O. Box 16, Henley Rd., Medmenham, Marlow, Bucks SL7 2HD, England. circ. 5,000.
Formerly: Water Research Centre. Annual Report (ISSN 0143-2443); Formed by the merger of: Water Research Association. Report; Water Pollution Research.

628.1 AT
WATER RESEARCH FOUNDATION OF AUSTRALIA. ANNUAL REPORT. a. Aus.$100 (includes Research Report Series, Water and the Environment - Newsletter). Water Research Foundation of Australia, c/o Centre for Resource and Environmental Studies, Australian National University, G.P.O. Box 4, Canberra, A.C.T. 2601, Australia.

628.1 AT ISSN 0085-8021
TC521 CODEN: WRARB7
WATER RESEARCH FOUNDATION OF AUSTRALIA. RESEARCH REPORT. 1959. bi-m. Aus.$100 (includes Water and the Environment - Newsletter, and Annual Report). Water Research Foundation of Australia Ltd., c/o Centre for Resource and Environmental Studies, Australian National University, G.P.O. Box 4, Canberra, A.C.T. 2601, Australia. TEL 06-2490651. FAX 06-2490757. circ. 1,000. **Indexed:** Aus.Sci.Ind., Biol.Abstr., GeoRef.
—BLDSC shelfmark: 7629.400000.
Incorporates: Water Research Foundation of Australia. Bulletin (ISSN 0085-8013)

333.91 AT
WATER RESEARCH IN AUSTRALIA: CURRENT PROJECTS. 1982. a. free. Department of Primary Industries and Energy, G.P.O. Box 858, Canberra, A.C.T. 2601, Australia. FAX 062-724526. circ. 1,604. **Indexed:** AESIS.
●Also available online.
Former titles: Water Research in Australia (ISSN 0810-736X); Inventory of Water Resources Research.

553.7 333.9 US ISSN 0097-8078
GB746 CODEN: WARED4
WATER RESOURCES. English translation of: Vodnye Resursy. 1974. bi-m. $765 (foreign $865)(effective 1992). (Russian Academy of Sciences, RU) Plenum Publishing Corp., Consultants Bureau, 233 Spring St., New York, NY 10013-1578. TEL 212-620-8468. FAX 212-463-0742. TELEX 23-421139. Ed. G.V. Voropaev. (also avail. in microfilm from JSC; back issues avil.) **Indexed:** Eng.Ind., Geo.Abstr., Irr.& Drain.Abstr., Saf.Sci.Abstr., Sel.Water Res.Abstr.
—BLDSC shelfmark: 0431.700000.
Refereed Serial

333.91 US
WATER RESOURCES ASSOCIATION OF THE DELAWARE RIVER BASIN. ALERTING BULLETIN. irreg., no.228, 1988. membership. Water Resources Association of the Delaware River Basin, Box 867, Davis Rd., Valley Forge, PA 19481. TEL 215-783-0634. FAX 215-783-0635.

333.91 US
WATER RESOURCES ASSOCIATION OF THE DELAWARE RIVER BASIN. NEWSLETTER. q., with m. supplements. membership. Water Resources Association of the Delaware River Basin, Box 867, Davis Rd., Valley Forge, PA 19481. TEL 215-783-0634. FAX 215-783-0635.

628 333.91 US ISSN 0043-1370
GB651 CODEN: WARBAQ
WATER RESOURCES BULLETIN; a journal of water resources research, planning, development and management. 1965. bi-m. $105 (foreign $125). American Water Resources Association, 5410 Grosvenor Lane, Ste. 220, Bethesda, MD 20814. TEL 301-493-8600. FAX 301-493-5844. Ed. William Lord. bk.rev.; abstr.; charts; illus.; index; circ. 4,000. (also avail. in microform from UMI) **Indexed:** Acid Rain Abstr., Acid Rain Ind., Agri.Eng.Abstr., Biol.Abstr., Chem.Abstr., Crop Physiol.Abstr., Curr.Adv.Ecol.Sci., Curr.Cont., Energy Info.Abstr., Eng.Ind., Environ.Abstr., Environ.Ind., Environ.Per.Bibl., Excerp.Med., Field Crop Abstr., Forest.Abstr., Geo.Abstr., GeoRef., Intl.Civil Eng.Abstr., Irr.& Drain.Abstr., Ocean.Abstr., Pollut.Abstr., Rural Recreat.Tour.Abstr., Sel.J.Water, Sel.Water Res.Abstr., So.Pac.Per.Ind., Soft.Abstr.Eng., Soils & Fert., Soyabean Abstr., W.R.C.Inf., World Agri.Econ.& Rural Sociol.Abstr.
Description: Publishes original papers covering water resources issues. Includes litigation and legislation issues.
Refereed Serial

333.91 US
WATER RESOURCES DEVELOPMENT IN NORTH CAROLINA (YEAR). biennial. free. U.S. Army Corps of Engineers, South Atlantic Division, 77 Forsyth St., S.W., Atlanta, GA 30335-6801. TEL 404-331-6641. FAX 404-331-4837. circ. 2,000.
Description: Summarizes the status of all Corps of Engineers civil works studies and projects within the state of North Carolina.

333.91 UN ISSN 0377-8053
JX1977
WATER RESOURCES JOURNAL. 1949. q. free. United Nations Economic and Social Commission for Asia and the Pacific (ESCAP), United Nations Bldg., Rajadamnern Ave, Bangkok 10200, Thailand. Indexed: GeoRef., IIS, Rural Recreat.Tour.Abstr., World Agri.Econ. & Rural Sociol.Abstr.
Formerly: Flood Control Journal (ISSN 1010-531X)

333.91 NE ISSN 0920-4741
TC401 CODEN: WRMAEJ
WATER RESOURCES MANAGEMENT. (Text in English) 1987. q. fl.256($145.50) (European Committee for Water Resources Management) Kluwer Academic Publishers, Postbus 17, 3300 AA Dordrecht, Netherlands. TEL 078-334911. FAX 078-334254. TELEX 29245. (Dist. by: Kluwer Academic Publishers Group, P.O. Box 322, 3300 AH Dordrecht, Netherlands; N. America dist. addr.: Box 358, Accord Station, Hingham, MA 02018-0358. TEL 617-871-6600) Ed. G. Tsakiris. (reprint service avail. from SWZ) Indexed: Agri.Eng.Abstr., Field Crop Abstr., Irr.& Drain.Abstr., Soils & Fert.
—BLDSC shelfmark: 9273.910000.

333.91 620 US
WATER RESOURCES MONOGRAPHS. 1971. irreg. American Geophysical Union, 2000 Florida Ave. N.W., Washington, DC 20009. TEL 202-462-6900. (reprint service avail. from ISI) Indexed: GeoRef.

333.9 US
WATER RESOURCES REPORT SERIES. irreg. $3. Texas Tech University, Water Resources Center, Box 4630, Lubbock, TX 79409. circ. 600.
Formerly: Civil Engineering Report Series (ISSN 0095-1692)

551.4 US ISSN 0043-1397
GB651 CODEN: WRERAQ
WATER RESOURCES RESEARCH. 1965. m. $505 to non-members (foreign $530); members $84 (foreign $109); students $42 (foreign $67). American Geophysical Union, 2000 Florida Ave. N.W., Washington, DC 20009. TEL 202-462-6900. FAX 202-328-0566. TELEX 710-882-9300. Ed. David Brookshire. abstr.; charts; illus.; index; circ. 4,000. (also avail. in microform from MIM; reprint service avail. from ISI) Indexed: Acid Pre.Dig., Acid Rain Abstr., Acid Rain Ind., AESIS, Agri.Eng.Abstr., Appl.Mech.Rev., Biol.Abstr., Chem.Abstr., Curr.Adv.Ecol.Sci., Curr.Cont., Deep Sea Res.& Oceanogr.Abstr., Energy Ind., Energy Info.Abstr., Environ.Abstr., Environ.Per.Bibl., Excerp.Med., Field Crop Abstr., Fluidex., Forest.Abstr., Forest Prod.Abstr., Geo.Abstr., GeoRef., Geotech.Abstr., Herb.Abstr., I D A, Int.Abstr.Oper.Res., Int.Aerosp.Abstr., Intl.Civil Eng.Abstr., Irr.& Drain.Abstr., J.of Econ.Lit., Ocean.Abstr., Petrol.Abstr., Pollut.Abstr., Risk Abstr., Rural Recreat.Tour.Abstr., Sci.Abstr., Sel.J.Water, Sel.Water Res.Abstr., Soft.Abstr.Eng., Soils & Fert., Triticale Abstr., W.R.C.Inf., World Agri.Econ. & Rural Sociol.Abstr.
—BLDSC shelfmark: 9275.150000.
Description: Provides a comprehensive source for students, scientists, and engineers to obtain the latest ideas conserning hydrologic processes in the environment.

551.4 333.9 US ISSN 0518-6374
TC424.A8 CODEN: AGWAAI
WATER RESOURCES SUMMARY. Continues the publication with the same title issued by the commission under its earlier name: Arkansas Geological and Conservation Commission. 1962. irreg., latest 1973. price varies. Geological Commission, Vardelle Parham Geology Center, 3815 W. Roosevelt Rd, Little Rock, AR 72204. TEL 501-663-9714. illus.

333.9 SA ISSN 0378-4738
TD201 CODEN: WASADV
WATER S.A.. (Text in Afrikaans, English; summaries in English) 1975. q. free. Water Research Commission - Waternavorsingskommissie, P.O. Box 824, Pretoria 0001, South Africa. Ed. Ingrid Buchan. abstr.; bibl.; charts; circ. 2,600. (back issues avail.; reprint service avail. from ISI) Indexed: Abstr.Bull.Inst.Pap.Chem., Acid Rain Abstr., Acid Rain Ind., Agri.Eng.Abstr., Biol.Abstr., Chem.Abstr., Curr.Adv.Ecol.Sci., Curr.Cont., Eng.Ind., Environ.Abstr., Ind.S.A.Per., Irr.& Drain.Abstr., J.of Ferroc., Maize Abstr., Ocean.Abstr., Pollut.Abstr., Sci.Cit.Ind., Sel.J.Water, Sel.Water Res.Abstr., Soils & Fert., W.R.C.Inf., Water Resour.Abstr.
—BLDSC shelfmark: 9275.430000.
Description: Contains original work in all branches of water science, technology, and engineering.

333.91 628.168 US ISSN 0273-1223
TD419 CODEN: WSTED4
WATER SCIENCE AND TECHNOLOGY. 1972. 24/yr. £1115 (combined subscr. with Water Research £1650)(effective 1992). (International Association on Water Pollution Research and Control) Pergamon Press, Inc., Journals Division, 660 White Plains Rd., Tarrytown, NY 10591-5153. TEL 914-524-9200. FAX 914-333-2444. (And: Headington Hill Hall, Oxford OX3 0BW, England. TEL 0865-794141) Ed. Elizabeth Izod. adv.; index. (also avail. in microform from MIM,UMI; back issues avail.) Indexed: Acid Rain Abstr., Acid Rain Ind., Biol.Abstr., Biotech.Abstr., Chem.Abstr., Curr.Adv.Ecol.Sci., Dairy Sci.Abstr., Energy Rev., Environ.Abstr., Environ.Ind., Environ.Per.Bibl., Excerp.Med., Fluidex, Food Sci.& Tech.Abstr., Geo.Abstr., GeoRef., Ocean.Abstr., Pollut.Abstr., Risk Abstr., Sel.J.Water, Sel.Water Res.Abstr., Soils & Fert.
—BLDSC shelfmark: 9275.445000.
Supersedes: International Conference on Water Pollution Research. Proceedings; Which was formerly (until 1981): Progress in Water Technology (ISSN 0306-6746)
Refereed Serial

628 UK ISSN 0301-7028
TD201 CODEN: WTSVAK
WATER SERVICES. 1899. m. $166. International Trade Publications Ltd., Queensway House, 2 Queensway, Redhill, Surrey RH1 1QS, England. TEL 0737-768611. FAX 0737-761989. TELEX 948669-TOPJNL-G. Ed. J. Manson. adv.; bk.rev.; abstr.; illus.; stat.; tr.lit.; index; circ. 8,600. (also avail. in microform from UMI) Indexed: Br.Geol.Lit., Br.Tech.Ind., Chem.Abstr., Curr.Cont., Eng.Ind., Excerp.Med., Fluidex, GeoRef., Intl.Civil Eng.Abstr., Soft.Abstr.Eng., W.R.C.Inf.
—BLDSC shelfmark: 9275.450000.
Formerly: Water and Water Engineering (ISSN 0043-1168)

WATER SEWAGE AND EFFLUENT. see PUBLIC HEALTH AND SAFETY

628.1 UK ISSN 0735-1917
TD201 CODEN: WASUDN
WATER SUPPLY. (Text in English and French) 1983. q. £278($507.50) (International Water Supply Association) Blackwell Scientific Publications Ltd., Osney Mead, Oxford OX2 0EL, England. TEL 0865-240201. FAX 0865-721205. TELEX 833355-MEDBOK-G. Ed. L.R. Bays. adv.; circ. 3,000. (also avail. in microfiche from MIM,UMI) Indexed: Biol.Abstr., Curr.Adv.Ecol.Sci., Curr.Cont., Environ.Abstr., Environ.Per.Bibl., W.R.C.Inf.
—BLDSC shelfmark: 9275.680000.
Incorporates (in 1983): International Water Supply Congress. Proceedings (ISSN 0074-9583)

628 NE ISSN 0169-2577
WATER SUPPLY AND WASTEWATER DISPOSAL - INTERNATIONAL ALMANAC. (Text in English, French, German) 1976. a. $70. International Institute for Water Supply and Wastewater Disposal, Gooiland 11, 2716 BP Zoetermeer, Netherlands. TEL 079-210-126. Eds. A. Kepinski, W.A.S. Kepinski. bk.rev.; circ. 750.

333.91 US
WATER SUPPLY OUTLOOK FOR THE WESTERN UNITED STATES. 6/yr. free. U.S. Soil Conservation Service (Portland), West National Technical Service Center, 511 N.W. Broadway, Rm. 248, Portland, OR 97209-3489. TEL 503-326-2843. Eds. C. Pachecko, J. Matheson. circ. 1,500. Indexed: Amer.Stat.Ind.

333.91 US
WATER SUPPLY OUTLOOK FOR WASHINGTON. 1954. 6/yr. free. U.S. Soil Conservation Service (Spokane), W316 Boone Ave., Rock Point Tower II, Ste. 450, Spokane, WA 99201. TEL 509-353-2341. Ed. William F. Weller. circ. 870. Indexed: Amer.Stat.Ind.

614.7 US
WATER TECHNOLOGY; the magazine for the water treatment professional. 1978. m. $39. National Trade Publications, Inc., 13 Century Hill, Latham, NY 12110-2197. TEL 518-783-1281. Ed. John Keenan. adv.; circ. 17,000. Indexed: Corros.Abstr.

628.167 CC ISSN 0921-2639
TD430 CODEN: WTREE2
WATER TREATMENT. Chinese Edition: Shui Chuli. (Editions in Chinese, English) q. $152 or fl.580 (effective 1991). (Guojia Haiyang-ju, Hangzhou Shui Chuli Jishu Kaifa Zhongxin) China Ocean Press, International Cooperation Department, Haimao Dalou, 1 Fuxingmenwai Dajie, Beijing 100860, People's Republic of China. TEL 868941. FAX 862209. TELEX 22536 NBO CN. Ed. Shi Song. Indexed: Chem.Eng.Abstr., T.C.E.A.
—BLDSC shelfmark: 9278.250000.
Description: Publishes scientific papers, monographs, research reports, and reviews on applied techniques of water treatment. Includes special topics such as membrane separation, desalination, and other treatment techniques using physical chemistry and biochemistry methods.
Refereed Serial

628.1 US ISSN 0043-1443
TD405 CODEN: WWJOA9
WATER WELL JOURNAL. 1946. m. $24 (foreign $48). Water Well Journal Publishing Co., 6375 Riverside Dr., Dublin, OH 43017. TEL 614-761-3222. Ed. Anita B. Stanley. adv.; tr.lit.; index; circ. 41,000. (reprint service avail. from UMI) Indexed: Eng.Ind., Environ.Abstr., Excerp.Med., Geo.Abstr., GeoRef., Sel.Water Res.Abstr.
—BLDSC shelfmark: 9278.500000.

333.91 US ISSN 0894-511X
CODEN: WATME5
WATERMARKS. 1965. irreg. (3-4/yr.). free. University of Texas at Austin, Center for Research in Water Resources, Balcones Research Center, 10100 Burnet Rd., Austin, TX 78712. TEL 512-471-3131. Ed. Michelle Gilson. bk.rev.; circ. 3,000.
Former titles: Center for Research in Water Resources Newsletter; C R W R News (ISSN 0049-3538)
Description: Details current work in progress at the center.

628 NE ISSN 0043-1486
HD1683.N2
WATERSCHAPSBELANGEN; veertiendaags tijdschrift voor waterschapsbestuur en waterschapsbeheer. 1915. s-m. fl.82 (foreign fl.102). Unie van Waterschappen - Association of Waterboards, Johan van Oldenbarneveltlaan 5, P.O. Box 80 200, 2508 GE The Hague, Netherlands. TEL 070-3519751. FAX 070-3544642. Ed.Bd. adv.; bk.rev.; index; circ. 3,400. (processed) Indexed: Excerp.Med., Key to Econ.Sci.
—BLDSC shelfmark: 9279.500000.
Description: Covers current news and information concerning the waterboards. Features studies, laws, safety, new projects, government, technical subjects, and environmental protection. Includes list of events and courses, positions available.

627 US ISSN 0747-9735
TD485
WATERWORLD NEWS. 1984. bi-m. $10. PennWell Publishing Co., Box 1260, Tulsa, OK 74101. TEL 918-835-3161. Ed. Mark Scharfeneker. adv.; tr.lit.; circ. 100,000. (reprint service avail.) Indexed: Energy Rev., Environ.Abstr.

614.7 US
WELL CONNECTED. 3/yr. Water Systems Council, 600 S. Federal St., Ste.400, Chicago, IL 60605-1842. TEL 312-922-6222. FAX 312-922-2734. Ed. Charles Stolberg. circ. 500.

WATER RESOURCES — ABSTRACTING, BIBLIOGRAPHIES, STATISTICS

628.44   CN
WESTERN CANADA WATER AND WASTE WATER ASSOCIATION. BULLETIN. 1949; N.S. 1983. q. Can.$40. Western Canada Water and Waste Water Association, P.O. Box 6168, Postal Station A, Calgary, Alta. T2H 2L4, Canada. TEL 403-259-4041. FAX 403-258-1631. adv.; bk.rev.; circ. 3,000. **Indexed:** Environ.Abstr.
Former titles: Western Canada Water and Sewage Conference. Bulletin; Western Canada Water and Sewage Conference. Papers Presented at Annual Convention (ISSN 0083-8799)

333.9 627   US
WESTERN WATER. vol.25, 1973. bi-m. $22. Water Education Foundation, 717 K St., No. 517, Sacramento, CA 95814-3406. FAX 916-448-7699. Ed. Rita Schmidt Sudman. bk.rev.; illus.; tr.lit.; circ. 15,000. **Indexed:** Environ.Per.Bibl., P.A.I.S.

620.85 331.91   US   ISSN 0277-5212
WETLANDS. 1981. 2/yr. $40 includes membership; libraries $100. Society of Wetlands Scientists, Box 296, Wilmington, NC 28402. Ed. Douglas A. Wilcox. abstr. **Indexed:** Aqua.Sci.& Fish.Abstr., Biol.Abstr., Curr.Cont., Ecol.Abstr., Entomol.Abstr., Ocean.Abstr.
—BLDSC shelfmark: 9306.630800.
Description: Interdisciplinary research on all aspects of freshwater and estuarine wetlands biology, ecology, hydrology, soil and sediment characteristics, as well as management, legal, and regulatory issues.
Refereed Serial

620.85 628.1   NE   ISSN 0923-4861
CODEN: WEMAEU
WETLANDS ECOLOGY AND MANAGEMENT. (Text in English) 1989. 4/yr. $120 (effective 1992). S P B Academic Publishing b.v., P.O. Box 97747, 2509 GC The Hague, Netherlands. Ed. Rebecca R. Sharitz.
—BLDSC shelfmark: 9306.632000.
Description: Publishes research and review papers on fundamental and applied aspects of wetlands of freshwater, brackish or marine origin, as well as contributions on integrated wetlands research and management, and topics including techno-cultural transformations, pollution impact, and environmental conservation.
Refereed Serial

333.91   UK
WHO'S WHO IN THE WATER INDUSTRY. 1975. a. (Water Services Association) Turret Group Plc., Turret House, 171 High St., Rickmansworth, Herts. WD3 1SN, England. TEL 0923-777000. FAX 0923-221346. Ed. Peter Hall. adv.; circ. 4,500.

627 333.91   AU
WIENER MITTEILUNGEN: WASSER, ABWASSER, GEWAESSER. 1968. irreg. price varies. Technische Universitaet Wien, Institut fuer Wasserguete und Landschaftswasserbau, A-1040 Vienna, Austria. FAX 01-5042234. (Co-sponsors: Institute for Hydraulik, Gewaesserkunde und Wasserwirtschaft; Universitaet fuer Bodenkultur) circ. 350. **Indexed:** Chem.Abstr.

628.168   US   ISSN 0362-5354
TD224.W6
WISCONSIN. DEPARTMENT OF NATURAL RESOURCES. ANNUAL WATER QUALITY REPORT TO CONGRESS. biennial. Department of Natural Resources, Box 7921, Madison, WI 53707. TEL 608-267-7610. illus. Key Title: Annual Water Quality Report to Congress.

628.167   UK   ISSN 0140-9050
TD201
WORLD WATER. 1978. m. £69. Thomas Telford Services Ltd., Thomas Telford House, 1 Heron Quay, London E14 4JD, England. TEL 071-987-6999. FAX 071-537-2443. TELEX 298105-CIVILS-G. Ed. Roy Opie. adv.; circ. 14,000. **Indexed:** AESIS, Environ.Per.Bibl., Excerp.Med., Fluidex, Geo.Abstr., GeoRef., Key to Econ.Sci., W.R.C.Inf.
Description: Covers international water and wastewater industry. Oriented toward administrators, engineers, and government officials. Emphasis on European issues.

333.9   US
HC107.W93
WYOMING. WATER QUALITY DIVISION. STATE - E P A AGREEMENT. (Environmental Protection Agency) a. Department of Environmental Quality, Water Quality Division, Cheyenne, WY 82002. TEL 307-777-7781. FAX 307-777-5973.
Formerly: Wyoming. Water Quality Division. Wyoming State Plan (ISSN 0098-0846)

YEARS AHEAD. see *PUBLIC HEALTH AND SAFETY*

ZAHLENTAFELN DER PHYSIKALISCH-CHEMISCHEN UNTERSUCHUNGEN DES RHEINWASSERS/TABLEAUX NUMERIQUES DES ANALYSES PHYSICO-CHIMIQUES DES EAUX DU RHIN. see *ENVIRONMENTAL STUDIES — Pollution*

333.91 627   ZA   ISSN 0084-4705
ZAMBIA. DEPARTMENT OF WATER AFFAIRS. REPORT. 1964. a. 1 n. Government Printer, P.O. Box 136, Lusaka, Zambia.
Description: Review of hydrogeological concerns in Zambia.

628   GW   ISSN 0044-3727
TD203   CODEN: ZWABAQ
ZEITSCHRIFT FUER WASSER- UND ABWASSERFORSCHUNG/JOURNAL FOR WATER AND WASTE WATER RESEARCH. (Text in German and English) 1967. 6/yr. DM.466($215) (Gesellschaft Deutscher Chemiker, Fachgruppe Wasserchemie) V C H Verlagsgesellschaft mbH, Postfach 101161, 6940 Weinheim, Germany. TEL 06201-602-0. FAX 06201-602328. TELEX 465516-VCHWH-D. (U.S. addr.: V C H Publishers Inc., 220 E. 23rd St., New York, NY 10010-4606) Ed. K.-E. Quentin. adv.; bk.rev.; abstr.; charts; illus.; stat.; index; circ. 960. (reprint service avail. from ISI) **Indexed:** Chem.Abstr., Curr.Adv.Ecol.Sci., Curr.Cont., Risk Abstr., Sel.Water Res.Abstr., Soils & Fert., Weed Abstr.
—BLDSC shelfmark: 9491.800000.

628 340   GW   ISSN 0722-8910
ZEITSCHRIFT FUER WASSERRECHT. 1961. 4/yr. (plus 1 special no.). DM.192. Carl Heymanns Verlag KG, Luxemburgerstr. 449, 5000 Cologne 41, Germany. TEL 0221-046010-0. FAX 0221-4601069. Ed. Dr. Manfred Czychowski. adv.; bk.rev.; circ. 500.

WATER RESOURCES — Abstracting, Bibliographies, Statistics

AGRICULTURAL LITERATURE OF CZECHOSLOVAKIA. see *AGRICULTURE — Abstracting, Bibliographies, Statistics*

628.1 614.7 016   UK
AQUALERT; selective dissemination of information. 12/yr. £180 (effective 1992). (Water Research Centre) Pergamon Press plc, Headington Hill Hall, Oxford OX3 0BW, England. TEL 0865-794141. FAX 0865-743911. TELEX 83177 PERGAP. (And: 660 White Plains Rd., Tarrytown, NY 10591-5153. TEL 914-524-9200)
Description: Provides a selection of current abstracts from the Aqualine database on topics of interest to the water industry according to subscriber's specific information needs.

628.1 614.7 016   UK   ISSN 0748-2531
AQUALINE ABSTRACTS. Variant title: Aqualine. 1927. 26/yr. £295 (effective 1992). (Water Research Centre) Pergamon Press plc, Headington Hill Hall, Oxford OX3 0BW, England. TEL 0865-794141. FAX 0865-743911. TELEX 83177 PERGAP. (And: 660 White Plains Rd., Tarrytown, NY 10591-5153. TEL 914-524-9200) Ed. Krystyna Lenik. bibl.; circ. 3,600. (also avail. in microform; reprint service avail. from KTO) **Indexed:** Abstr.Bull.Inst.Pap.Chem., Anal.Abstr., Fluidex, Ind.Vet., Vet.Bull., Weed Abstr., World Text.Abstr.
●Also available online. Vendor(s): DIALOG, European Space Agency, Orbit Information Technologies (AQUALINE), Pergamon Infoline (AQUALINE).
—BLDSC shelfmark: 1581.866240.
Formerly (until 1985): W R C Information (ISSN 0306-6649); **Supersedes:** Water Pollution Abstracts (ISSN 0043-1281)

551.46 639.3 016
333.7   US   ISSN 0140-5373
AQUATIC SCIENCES & FISHERIES ABSTRACTS. PART 1: BIOLOGICAL SCIENCES AND LIVING RESOURCES. 1971. m. $855 (foreign $960). (Food and Agriculture Organization of the U.N.) Cambridge Scientific Abstracts, 7200 Wisconsin Ave., 6th Fl., Bethesda, MD 20814. TEL 301-961-6750. FAX 301-961-6720. TELEX 910 2507547 CAMB MD. (Co-sponsors: U.N. Office for Ocean Affairs and the Law of the Sea; U.N. Environment Programme; Intergovernmental Oceanographic Commission) Ed. R. Pepe. adv.; abstr.; bibl.; index. (also avail. in magnetic tape; back issues avail.) **Indexed:** Cal.Tiss.Abstr., Chemorec.Abstr., Oncol.Abstr., Pollut.Abstr., Weed Abstr.
●Also available online. Vendor(s): BRS (CSAL), CISTI, DIMDI, DIALOG (File no.44), European Space Agency.
Also available on CD-ROM. Producer(s): Cambridge Scientific Abstracts (Compact Cambridge ASFA).
—BLDSC shelfmark: 1582.460000.
Supersedes in part: Aquatic Sciences and Fisheries Abstracts (ISSN 0044-8516); Which was formed by the merger of: Aquatic Biology Abstracts (ISSN 0003-7311); Current Bibliography for Aquatic Sciences and Fisheries (ISSN 0011-3239)
Description: International network of aquatic science centers' studies on marine, freshwater and brackish water organisms.

551.46 639.3 016   US   ISSN 0140-5381
AQUATIC SCIENCES & FISHERIES ABSTRACTS. PART 2: OCEAN TECHNOLOGY, POLICY AND NON-LIVING RESOURCES. 1969. m. $615 (foreign $685). (Food and Agriculture Organization of the U.N.) Cambridge Scientific Abstracts, 7200 Wisconsin Ave., 6th Fl., Bethesda, MD 20814. TEL 301-961-6750. FAX 301-961-6720. TELEX 910 2507547 CAMB MD. (Co-sponsors: U.N. office of Ocean Affairs and the Law of the Sea; U.N. Environment Programme; Intergovernmental Oceanographic Commission) Ed. R. Pepe. adv.; abstr.; bibl.; index. (also avail. in magnetic tape; back issues avail.) **Indexed:** Cal.Tiss.Abstr., Chemorec.Abstr., Comput.& Info.Sys., Oncol.Abstr., Pollut.Abstr., Weed Abstr.
●Also available online. Vendor(s): BRS (CSAL), CISTI, DIMDI, DIALOG (File no.44), European Space Agency.
Also available on CD-ROM. Producer(s): Cambridge Scientific Abstracts (Compact Cambridge ASFA).
—BLDSC shelfmark: 1582.470000.
Supersedes in part: Aquatic Sciences and Fisheries Abstracts (ISSN 0044-8516); Which was formed by the merger of: Aquatic Biology Abstracts (ISSN 0003-7311); Current Bibliography for Aquatic Sciences and Fisheries (ISSN 0011-3239)
Description: International network of aquatic science centers' studies on ocean resources, offshore and coastal structures and oceanography.

333.91 620   PL   ISSN 0239-622X
BIBLIOGRAFIA GOSPODARKI I INZYNIERII WODNEJ/BIBLIOGRAPHY OF WATER MANAGEMENT AND ENGINEERING. (Text in English, French, German, Polish, Russian) 1977. irreg. $75. Instytut Meteorologii i Gospodarki Wodnej - Institute of Meteorology and Water Management, 61 Podlesna St., 01-673 Warsaw, Poland. circ. 150.
Description: Articles on water management, hydraulics, water engineering, water pollution, water resources, water quality, sanitary engineering, and sewage water treatment.

627 016   II   ISSN 0523-302X
BIBLIOGRAPHY ON IRRIGATION, DRAINAGE, RIVER TRAINING AND FLOOD CONTROL/BIBLIOGRAPHIE DE LA C I I D. IRRIGATION, DRAINAGE ET MAITRISE DES CRUES. (Text in English and French) 1954. a. $10 per copy. International Commission on Irrigation and Drainage - Commission Internationale des Irrigations et du Drainage, 48 Nyaya Marg, Chanakyapuri, New Delhi 110021, India. bk.rev.; circ. 1,200. (back issues avail.)

WELDING

see Metallurgy–Welding

WIND ENERGY

see Energy–Wind Energy

WOMEN'S HEALTH

see also Medical Sciences–Obstetrics and Gynecology

A A - B A NEWSLETTER. (American Anorexia - Bulimia Association, Inc.) see PSYCHOLOGY

A N A D: WORKING TOGETHER. (National Association of Anorexia Nervosa and Associated Disorders) see PSYCHOLOGY

A N R E D ALERT. (Anorexia Nervosa & Related Eating Disorders, Inc.) see PSYCHOLOGY

ABORTION BIBLIOGRAPHY. see BIRTH CONTROL — Abstracting, Bibliographies, Statistics

301.426 613.94   US   ISSN 0361-1116
CODEN: ABRNA
ABORTION RESEARCH NOTES. 1972. 3/yr. $25. Transnational Family Research Institute, 8307 Whitman Dr., Bethesda, MD 20817. TEL 301-469-6313. FAX 301-469-0461. Ed. Henry P. David. bk.rev.; circ. 3,600. (back issues avail.)

613.9   UK   ISSN 0262-7299
ABORTION REVIEW. 1981. 4/yr. £10 (typically set in Jan.). Birth Control Trust, 27 Mortimer St., London W1N 7RJ, England. TEL 071-580-9360. FAX 071-637-1378. stat.; circ. 500.
 Description: Round-up of the medical, legal and social aspects of abortion in the UK.

610   II
ASSOCIATION OF MEDICAL WOMEN IN INDIA. JOURNAL. (Text in English) 1920. bi-m. Rs.15. Association of Medical Women in India, IMA Bldg., 16 Haji Ali Park, Keshavrao Khudye Marg, Bombay 400034, India. Ed. Dr. Tara Ramarao. adv.; circ. 500.

BACK TO HEALTH MAGAZINE; your guide to relief recovery and well-being. see PHYSICAL FITNESS AND HYGIENE

BATTERED WOMEN'S DIRECTORY. see WOMEN'S INTERESTS

613.7   US   ISSN 1055-3398
BEST OF HEALTH. 1987. q. $14. Box 40-1232, Brooklyn, NY 11240-1232. TEL 718-756-2245. Ed. Wista Jeanne Johnson. adv.; bk.rev.; circ. 1,000. (back issues avail.)
 Description: Health issues for African-American women.

BREAKING CHAINS. see LAW

BRITISH REVIEW OF BULIMIA AND ANOREXIA NERVOSA. see PSYCHOLOGY

C O H S E JOURNAL. (Confederation of Health Service Employees) see PUBLIC HEALTH AND SAFETY

610   GW   ISSN 0933-0747
CLIO; eine feministische Zeitschrift zur gesundheitlichen Selbsthilfe. 1976. s-a. DM.24($12) for 4 nos. Feministisches Frauen Gesundheitszentrum e.V., Bambergerstr. 51, 1000 Berlin 30, Germany. adv.; bk.rev.; illus.; circ. 5,000. (back issues avail.) **Indexed:** Abstr.Engl.Stud.
 Description: Topics covered include women's health, diseases and feminist critiques of medical care, self-help and reproductive technology.

DONNA MODERNA. see WOMEN'S INTERESTS

EESTI NAINE; a magazine for women. see WOMEN'S INTERESTS

ELLE ITALIA. see WOMEN'S INTERESTS

A FRIEND INDEED. see WOMEN'S INTERESTS

H E R S NEWSLETTER. (Hysterectomy Educational Resources & Services) see WOMEN'S INTERESTS

HANDLING PREGNANCY AND BIRTH CASES. see LAW — Family And Matrimonial Law

HEALTH & FITNESS; magazine for healthy, sound living. see PHYSICAL FITNESS AND HYGIENE

618   US   ISSN 0739-9332
CODEN: HCWIDQ
HEALTH CARE FOR WOMEN, INTERNATIONAL. 1979. q. $95. Hemisphere Publishing Corporation (Subsidiary of: Taylor & Francis Group), 1900 Frost Rd., Ste. 101, Bristol, PA 19007-1598. TEL 215-785-5800. FAX 215-785-5515. Ed. Phyllis Noerager Stern. adv.; bk.rev.; film rev.; bibl.; charts; illus.; index; circ. 400. (back issues avail.; reprint service avail. from UMI) **Indexed:** CINAHL, Int.Nurs.Ind., J.of Abstr.Int.Educ., Lang.& Lang.Behav.Abstr., NRN, Nurs.Abstr., Sage Fam.Stud.Abstr., Sociol.Abstr., Sp.Ed.Needs Abstr., Stud.Wom.Abstr.
 —BLDSC shelfmark: 4274.950600.
 Formerly (until 1983): Issues in Health Care of Women (ISSN 0161-5246)
 Description: Interdisciplinary approach to health care and related topics that concern women.

HEALTH EDUCATION JOURNAL. see PHYSICAL FITNESS AND HYGIENE

HEALTH NOW. see NUTRITION AND DIETETICS

305.412 613.9   CN   ISSN 0226-1510
HEALTHSHARING; a Canadian women's health quarterly. 1979. q. Can.$15($18) to individuals (foreign Can.$19); institutions Can.$28($31)(foreign Can.$32). Women Healthsharing Inc., 14 Skey Lane, Toronto, Ont. M6J 3S4, Canada. TEL 416-532-0812. FAX 416-588-6638. Ed.Bd. adv.; bk.rev.; circ. 5,000. (also avail. in microform from MMI; back issues avail.; reprint service avail. from MML) **Indexed:** Alt.Press Ind., Can.Per.Ind., Can.Wom.Per.Ind., CMI.

HEARTBEAT (ORLANDO). see BIRTH CONTROL

HOT FLASH. see WOMEN'S INTERESTS

INDUCED ABORTION: A WORLD REVIEW. see POPULATION STUDIES

L.E. BEACON. (Lupus Erythematosus) see MEDICAL SCIENCES — Rheumatology

MASSAGE THERAPY JOURNAL. see PHYSICAL FITNESS AND HYGIENE

MATERNITY AND MOTHERCRAFT. see WOMEN'S INTERESTS

613.7   US
MELPOMENE JOURNAL; a journal for women's health research. 1981. 3/yr. $32 to individuals; institutions $50. Melpomene Institute for Women's Health Research, 1010 University Ave. W., Saint Paul, MN 55104-4706. Ed. Judy Remington. illus.; circ. 2,500. (reprint service avail.) **Indexed:** Sportsearch (1988-).
 Formerly: Melpomene Report.
 Description: Research articles with scientific bibliographies, personal profiles, news and updates, providing information about health and physically active women.

MOTHER AND CHILD. see WOMEN'S INTERESTS

MOTHERING. see MEDICAL SCIENCES — Obstetrics And Gynecology

N A A C O G'S WOMEN'S HEALTH NURSING SCAN. (Organization for Obstetric, Gynecologic and Neonatal Nurses) see MEDICAL SCIENCES — Abstracting, Bibliographies, Statistics

NATIONAL WOMEN'S HEALTH NETWORK. see WOMEN'S INTERESTS

WOMEN'S INTERESTS

610 US ISSN 0741-9147
NATIONAL WOMEN'S HEALTH REPORT. 1984. 6/yr. $21 to individuals; institutions and international $30. National Women's Health Resource Center, 2440 M St., N.W., Ste. 201, Washington, DC 20037. TEL 202-293-6045. FAX 202-293-7256. Ed. Yvonne P. Hiott. bk.rev.; index; circ. 30,000. (back issues avail.)
Description: Covers medical and public policy issues relating to women's health.

613.7 301.412 US ISSN 8755-867X
NETWORK NEWSNEWS. 1975. 6/yr. $25. National Women's Health Network, 1325 G St., N.W., Washington, DC 20005. bk.rev.
Former titles (until 1986): National Women's Health Network Newsletter (ISSN 0277-0385); Network News.
Description: For women's health activists. The network is a consciousness-raising political watchdog organization. Covers controversial issues and includes product alerts and interviews.

NEW CLEVELAND WOMAN JOURNAL. see *WOMEN'S INTERESTS*

ON THE ISSUES; the journal of substance for progressive women. see *WOMEN'S INTERESTS*

OUR SPECIAL; magazine devoted to matters of interest to blind women. see *HANDICAPPED — Visually Impaired*

OVULATION METHOD TEACHERS ASSOCIATION (PUBLICATION). see *BIRTH CONTROL*

P M S ACCESS NEWSLETTER. (Premenstrual Syndrome) see *MEDICAL SCIENCES — Obstetrics And Gynecology*

PRO - CHOICE NEWS. see *BIRTH CONTROL*

PULSE (ORLANDO). see *BIRTH CONTROL*

RADIANCE; the magazine for large women. see *WOMEN'S INTERESTS*

SCARLET LETTER. see *WOMEN'S INTERESTS*

SELF. see *WOMEN'S INTERESTS*

SOBERING THOUGHTS. see *DRUG ABUSE AND ALCOHOLISM*

SPECIAL DELIVERY. see *MEDICAL SCIENCES — Obstetrics And Gynecology*

613.7 CN
TURNER'S SYNDROME NEWS. 1982. q. Can.$25 individual membership; institutions Can.$35; students Can.$15. Turner's Syndrome Society, 7777 Keele St., 2nd Fl., Concord, Ont. L4K 1Y7, Canada. TEL 416-660-7766. FAX 416-660-7450. circ. 500.

610 US ISSN 0363-0242
RG1 CODEN: WOHEDI
WOMEN & HEALTH; the journal of women's health care. 1976. q. $36 to individuals; institutions $90; libraries $190. Haworth Press, Inc., 10 Alice St., Binghamton, NY 13904. TEL 800-342-9678. FAX 607-722-1424. TELEX 4932599. Ed. Jeanne Stellman. adv.; bk.rev.; circ. 639. (also avail. in microfiche from HAW; back issues avail.; reprint service avail. from HAW,ISI) Indexed: Abstr.Health Care Manage.Stud., Abstr.Hyg., Adol.Ment.Hlth.Abstr., Alt.Press Ind., Biol.Abstr., Bull.Signal., CINAHL, Curr.Cont., Curr.Lit.Fam.Plan., Excerp.Med., Hlth.Ind., Ind.Med., Lang.& Lang.Behav.Abstr., Med.Care Rev., P.A.I.S., Psychol.Abstr., Risk Abstr., Soc.Work Res.& Abstr., SSCI, Stud.Wom.Abstr., Wom.Stud.Abstr. (1976-). —BLDSC shelfmark: 9343.260000.
Description: Contains information that is useful for all women - consumers as well as providers of health care.
Refereed Serial

613.7 US ISSN 0272-0515
WOMEN & HEALTH ROUNDTABLE REPORTS. 1976. m. $25. Women & Health Roundtable, 1000 Connecticut Ave. N.W., No. 9, Washington, DC 20036. TEL 301-953-4215. Ed. Ruth Pitlick. circ. 130.

WOMEN & THERAPY; a feminist quarterly of research and opinion. see *PSYCHOLOGY*

610 US
WOMEN IN CONTEXT. 1978. irreg., latest 1990. price varies. Plenum Publishing Corp., 233 Spring St., New York, NY 10013-1578. TEL 212-620-8000. FAX 212-463-0742. TELEX 23-421139. Ed.Bd. (back issues avail.)
Formerly: Women in Context: Development and Stresses.
Refereed Serial

610 US ISSN 1049-3867
RG1
▼**WOMEN'S HEALTH ISSUES.** 1991. 4/yr. $78 (foreign $94)(effective 1992). (Jacobs Institute of Women's Health) Elsevier Science Publishing Co., Inc. (New York), 655 Ave. of Americas, New York, NY 10010. TEL 212-989-5800. FAX 212-633-3965. TELEX 420643 AEP UI. Ed. Warren Pearse.
—BLDSC shelfmark: 9343.379010.
Description: For health professionals, social scientists, policy makers, and others concerned with developments affecting health care for women.
Refereed Serial

613.7 US
WOMEN'S PHYSIQUE WORLD. q. $3.50 per no. Women's Physique Magazine, Box 429, Midland Park, NJ 07432. TEL 201-825-7448.

WOMEN'S SPORTS AND FITNESS. see *SPORTS AND GAMES*

305 613 US ISSN 0890-9695
WOMENWISE. 1978. q. $10 to individuals; institutions $20. New Hampshire Federation of Feminist Health Centers, Concord Feminist Health Center, 38 S. Main St., Concord, NH 03301. TEL 603-225-2739. Ed.Bd. adv.; bk.rev.; circ. 5,000. (tabloid format; back issues avail.)
Description: Covers women's health issues with a feminist perspective. Includes political analyses.

WOMEN'S INTERESTS

A A W C J C NEWSLETTER. (American Association of Women in Community and Junior Colleges) see *EDUCATION — Higher Education*

A L F NEWSLETTER. (Association of Libertarian Feminists) see *POLITICAL SCIENCE*

A M B A NEWS. (Australian Multiple Birth Association Inc.) see *CHILDREN AND YOUTH — About*

A U L INSIGHTS. (Americans United for Life) see *LAW*

A U L STUDIES IN LAW, MEDICINE & SOCIETY. (Americans United for Life) see *LAW*

A W C NEWS FORUM. (American Women Composers, Inc.) see *MUSIC*

500 600 US
Q149.U5
A W I S MAGAZINE. 1971. bi-m. $55 to libraries. Association for Women in Science, 1522 K St. N.W., Ste. 820, Washington, DC 20005. TEL 202-408-0742. FAX 202-408-8321. Ed. Dr. Barbara Mandula. adv.; bk.rev.; circ. 4,000.
Former titles: Association for Women in Science. Newsletter (ISSN 0160-256X); A W I S Newsletter (ISSN 0098-6267)
Description: Features articles on the status of women in science and policy issues, listing of current grant and employment opportunities, and news of chapter activities.

A W N Y MATTERS. (Advertising Women of New York) see *ADVERTISING AND PUBLIC RELATIONS*

A W S C P A. NEWSLETTER. (American Women's Society of Certified Public Accountants) see *BUSINESS AND ECONOMICS — Accounting*

301.412 BG
AACHAL. (Text in Bengali) 1985. w. $4. 100B Malibagh Chowdhury Para, Dhaka 1219, Bangladesh. TEL 2-414043. Ed. Ferdousi Begum. adv.; bk.rev.; circ. 25,000.

301.412 CR
ABANICO. (Supplement to: Prensa Libre) w. Calle 4, esq. Avda. 4, Apdo. 10121, San Jose, Costa Rica. TEL 23-6666. Ed. Guiselle Borrase. circ. 50,000.

305.412 CN ISSN 0708-6180
ABOUT WOMEN (WINNIPEG). 1977. 3/yr. free. Manitoba Women's Directorate, 4th floor, 500 Portage Ave., Winnipeg, Man. R3C 3X1, Canada. TEL 204-945-3476. FAX 204-945-0013. Ed. Doris Mae Oulton. bk.rev.; illus.; circ. 5,000.
Description: Bulletin covering topical issues relating to government and women.

640 LE
ACHABAKA. (Text in Arabic) 1976. w. $200. Dar Assayad S.A.L, P.O. Box 1038, Beirut, Lebanon. FAX 4529957. TELEX 44224 SAYYAD LE. (UK addr.: c/o Contact Public Relations, 3 Park Pl., 12 Lawn Ln., London SW8, England. TEL 071-582-2220) Ed. George Ibrahim El Khoury. circ. 102,000.

ACTION ALERT (WASHINGTON, 1980). see *LAW*

301.412 CN
ACTION NOW/A L'ACTION; bulletin. (Text in English and French) 9/yr. National Action Committee on the Status of Women, 57 Mobile Dr, Toronto, Ont. M4A 1H5, Canada. TEL 416-759-5252. FAX 416-759-5370.
Formerly: Action (Toronto) (ISSN 0820-5728)
Description: Published to encourage action in response to legislative issues of concern to the committee.

301.412 GH
AFRICAN WOMAN. m. Ring Rd. West, POB 1496, Accra, Ghana.

301.412 SA ISSN 1013-0950
AGENDA; a journal about women and gender. 1987. 4/yr. R.32. Agenda, P.O. Box 37432, Overport 4067, South Africa. TEL 3054074. FAX 301-6611. Ed.Bd. adv.; bk.rev.; illus. (back issues avail.)
Description: Provides a forum for discussion and debate on all aspects of women's lives in South Africa.

AIR FRANCE MADAME. see *TRAVEL AND TOURISM — Airline Inflight And Hotel Inroom*

ALASKA WOMEN. see *LITERARY AND POLITICAL REVIEWS*

301.412 US
ALERT (WASHINGTON, 1980). 1980. bi-m. membership. Federation of Organizations for Professional Women, 2001 S St., N.W., Ste. 500, Washington, DC 20009-1125. TEL 202-328-1415. FAX 202-462-5241. Ed. Viola M. Young-Horvath. adv.; bk.rev.; circ. 250. (back issues avail.)
Description: Opportunity for organizations and individuals to use their collective power to influence policy and enhance status of professional women.

323.42 AT
ALIVE & W E L. 1972. m. Aus.$40. Women's Electoral Lobby (Vic.), Rm. 503, 328 Flinders St., Melbourne, Vic. 3000, Australia. TEL 03-614-1128. Ed. Valda Byth.

396 PK
ALL PAKISTAN WOMEN'S ASSOCIATION. TRIENNIAL CONFERENCE REPORT. (Text in English) triennial. All Pakistan Women's Association, Information and Research Bureau, 67-B Garden Rd., Karachi 3, Pakistan.

305.412 DK ISSN 0002-6506
ALT FOR DAMERNE. 1946. w. DKK 829.40. Gutenberghus Bladene, Vognmagergade 11, 1148 Copenhagen K, Denmark. Ed. Lone Kuhlmann. adv.; illus.; circ. 110,000.

AMERICAN ASSOCIATION OF WOMEN DENTISTS. CHRONICLE. see *MEDICAL SCIENCES — Dentistry*

AMERICAN BAPTIST WOMAN. see *RELIGIONS AND THEOLOGY*

AMERICAN CATTLEWOMAN. see *AGRICULTURE — Poultry And Livestock*

AMERICAN MEDICAL WOMEN'S ASSOCIATION. JOURNAL. see *MEDICAL SCIENCES*

301.412 US ISSN 1042-5985
▼**AMERICAN UNIVERSITY STUDIES. SERIES 27. FEMINIST STUDIES.** 1990. irreg. Peter Lang Publishing, Inc., 62 W. 45th St., 4th Fl., New York, NY 10036. TEL 212-302-6740. Ed. Kathryn Earle.

WOMEN'S INTERESTS

051 US
▼**AMERICAN WOMAN.** 1990. q. $7.99. G C R Publishing Group, Inc., 1700 Broadway, 34th Fl., New York, NY 10019. Ed. Lynn Varacalli. circ. 130,000. (also avail. in microfilm from KTO)
  Description: Covers relationships, careers and changing lifestyles.

AMERICAN WOMAN MOTORSPORTS. see *SPORTS AND GAMES*

055.1 IT
AMICA. 1962. w. L.93600. Rizzoli Editore-Corriere della Sera, Via A. Rizzoli 2, 20132 Milan, Italy. TEL 02-6339. Ed. P. Pietroni. circ. 211,000.

301.412 BL ISSN 0003-1755
AMIGA. 1970. w. $103. Bloch Editores S.A., Rua do Russell 766-804, 22214 Rio de Janeiro, Brazil. TEL 21-265-2012. TELEX 21-21525. Ed. Moyses Weltman. adv.; circ. 83,000.

059 FR ISSN 0244-0008
AMINA. 1972. m. 280 F. S A P E F, 11 rue Teheran, 75008 Paris, France. Ed. Assiatou Aiallo. adv.; bk.rev.; circ. 85,170.
  Incorporates (in 1985): Wife.

301.4 SG
AMINA. m. B.P. 2120, Dakar, Senegal.

ANCHORA. see *CLUBS*

305.412 PR
ANGELA LUISA. 1967. m. Publicaciones Torregrosa, Apdo. 1807, Hato Rey, PR 00919. Ed. Angela Luisa Torregrosa. adv.; illus.; circ. 20,000.

ANIMA; the journal of human experience. see *NEW AGE PUBLICATIONS*

059.94 FI ISSN 0355-3035
ANNA. 1963. w. FIM 956. Yhtyneet Kuvalehdet Oy, Maistraatinportti 1, 00240 Helsinki, Finland. TEL 0-15661. FAX 01566505. TELEX 121364. Ed. Riitta Tulonen. adv.; illus.; circ. 161,346.

301.412 IT
ANNA. w. Rizzoli Editore-Corriere della Sera, Via A. Rizzoli 2, 20132 Milan, Italy. TEL 02-2588.

052 UK ISSN 0003-3758
ANNABEL; the magazine women really enjoy. 1966. m. D. C. Thomson & Co. Ltd., Albert Square, Dundee DD1 9QJ, Scotland. adv.; bk.rev.; illus.

055.1 IT ISSN 0003-3766
ANNABELLA. 1932. w. L.78000. Rizzoli Editore-Corriere della Sera, Via A. Rizzoli 2, 20132 Milan, Italy. TEL 02-25843213. Ed. M. Venturi. circ. 270,000.

053.1 SZ
ANNABELLE. 1938. fortn. 94 SFr. Conzett & Huber Zeitschriften AG, CH-8036 Zurich, Switzerland. TEL 01-2484611. FAX 01-2911470. Ed. Gina Gysin. adv.; bk.rev.; film rev.; play rev.; bibl.; illus.; circ. 106,293. (tabloid format)
  Former titles: Annabelle-Femina; Annabelle (ISSN 0003-3774)

346.013 US
ANTISEXISM NEWSLETTER. 1984. 4/yr. $15 to non-members. National Lawyers Guild, Anti-Sexism Task Force, c/o Carpenter & Mayfield, 131 George St., San Jose, CA 95110-2116. Eds. Constance Carpenter, Tony Prees. bk.rev.; circ. 800.
  Formerly: Women's Newsletter.

301.412 JA
ANY. (Text in Japanese) 1989. bi-w. S.S. Communications Inc., Cosmo Hirakawacho Bldg., 3-14, Hirakawa-cho 1-chome, Chiyoda-ku, Tokyo 102, Japan. TEL 03-3527-6220. FAX 03-3527-6229. Ed. Yukio Miwa. circ. 380,000.

301.412 323.4 US
APROPOS. 1984. m. $12. Pulse Publications, Inc. (Bellingham), 339 Telegraph Rd., Bellingham, WA 98226. TEL 206-671-3933. adv.; circ. 6,000.
  Description: Informs women of Whatcom County about people, news, trends, and opinions affecting their lives.

301.412 GW ISSN 0178-1073
ARIADNE. 1985. s-a. DM.16. Archiv der Deutschen Frauenbewegung e.V., Sommerweg 1B, 3500 Kassel, Germany. TEL 0561-55600. adv.; bk.rev.; bibl.; illus.; circ. 1,000. (back issues avail.)

301.412 US
ARIZONA WOMEN'S VOICE. 1984. m. $12. 5515 N. 7th St., Ste. 5-173, Phoenix, AZ 85014. TEL 602-279-1347. Ed. Joanne Brickman. adv.; bk.rev.; circ. 17,000. (tabloid format; back issues avail.)
  Description: Purpose is to share information, issues and news items for and about women.

ARTEMIS - ARTISTS AND WRITERS; artists and writers from the Blue Ridge Mountains. see *LITERATURE — Poetry*

618 MY
ASIAN AND PACIFIC WOMEN'S RESOURCE AND ACTION SERIES. (Text in English) 1989. irreg. free. Asian and Pacific Development Centre, P.O. Box 12224, 50770 Kuala Lumpur, Malaysia. TEL 03-2548088. FAX 03-2550316. TELEX MA-30676-APDEC. Ed. Noeleen Heyzerc.
  Description: Provides a forum for women's experiences and thoughts on issues critical to women's health, the environment, work and law from a Third World perspective.
  Refereed Serial

510 376 US
ASSOCIATION FOR WOMEN IN MATHEMATICS. NEWSLETTER. 1971. 6/yr. $20 to individuals; institutions $50. Association of Women in Mathematics, Wellesley College, Box 178, Wellesley, MA 02181. TEL 617-235-0320. Ed. Anne Leggett. adv.; bk.rev.; circ. 2,500.
  Description: Serves and encourages women to study and have active careers in the mathematical sciences.

ASSOCIATION OF MEDICAL WOMEN IN INDIA. JOURNAL. see *WOMEN'S HEALTH*

305.412 RH
ASSOCIATION OF WOMEN'S CLUBS. NEWS. 1964. q. $0.50. Association of Women's Clubs, P.O. Box UA 339, Harare, Zimbabwe. TEL 790339. Ed. F. Samhungu. circ. 1,100.
  Formerly: Federation of African Women's Clubs.

305.412 FI ISSN 0004-6094
ASTRA. 1919. m. FIM 170. Svenska Kvinnofoerbundet, Handelsesplanade 23A, 65100 Vasa, Finland. Ed. Charlotta Oedman. adv.; bk.rev.; circ. 3,000.

305.412 301.4157 US
ATALANTA. 1973. m. $15 to non-members; institutions $25. Atlanta Lesbian Feminist Alliance, Newsletter Committee, Box 5502, Atlanta, GA 30307. Ed.Bd. adv.; bk.rev.; circ. 250.

323.42 649 US ISSN 0896-0631
ATHENA; international newspaper for victory over domestic violence. 1988. s-a. $3 (Canada and Mexico $6; elsewhere $7). Athena Press (Westlake Village), 31220 La Baya Dr., Ste. 110, Westlake Village, CA 91362. TEL 800-343-9444. (Subscr. to: Box 5028, Thousand Oaks, CA 91360) Ed. Ronald K. Jones. adv.; bk.rev.; circ. 10,000. (tabloid format; back issues avail.; reprint service avail.)
  Description: Personal essays and fiction (some poetry) by and about battered women and children.

305.412 US
ATLANTA N O W NEWS.* vol.6, 1973. m. $15. 604, National Organization for Women, Atlanta Chapter, Box 8556, Atlanta, GA 30306-0556. TEL 404-523-1227. FAX 404-688-0869. Ed. Samantha Claar. adv.; bk.rev.; circ. 700 (controlled).
  Formerly: N O W Notes - Atlanta Chapter.

301.412 CN
ATLANTIC WOMAN. q. County Press Ltd., P.O. Box 56, Dartmouth, N.S. B2Y 3Y2, Canada. TEL 902-465-4711. FAX 902-423-9603. Ed. Juan C. Canales.

301.412 323.4 AU
AUF - EINE FRAUENZEITSCHRIFT. 1974. q. S.170. Verein zur Foerderung Feministischer Projekte, Postfach 817, A-1011 Vienna, Austria. adv.; bk.rev.; circ. 2,500.

AURORA (MADISON); S F science fiction-speculative feminism. see *LITERATURE — Science Fiction, Fantasy, Horror*

378 AT
AUSTRALIAN FEDERATION OF UNIVERSITY WOMEN. NEWSLETTER. 1960. q. membership. Australian Federation of University Women, A.F.U.W. Federal Council, P.O. Box 726, Sandy Bay, Tas. 7005, Australia. Ed. M. Coatman. circ. 2,200.

378 900 AT ISSN 0816-4649
HQ1101
AUSTRALIAN FEMINIST STUDIES. 1986. s-a. Aus.$30 to individuals; institutions Aus.$50. Research Centre for Women's Studies, University of Adelaide, G.P.O. Box 498, Adelaide, S.A. 5001, Australia. TEL 61 8 228-5267. FAX 08-224-0464. TELEX UNIVAD 89141. Ed. Susan Magarey. adv.; bk.rev.; circ. 600. (back issues avail.) Indexed: Stud.Wom.Abstr. —BLDSC shelfmark: 1798.923500.
  Description: Publishes both disciplinary and transdisciplinary scholarship and discussion in the fields of feminist research and women's studies courses.

AUSTRALIAN WOMEN'S CHESS BULLETIN. see *SPORTS AND GAMES*

305.412 AT ISSN 0005-0458
AUSTRALIAN WOMEN'S WEEKLY. 1933. m. Aus.$37.20. Australian Consolidated Press, 54-58 Park St., Sydney, N.S.W. 2000, Australia. FAX 02-282-8116. TELEX 120514. Ed. Jennifer Rowe. adv.; bk.rev.; illus.; tele.rev.; circ. 1,167,000.

305.412 NE ISSN 0005-1985
AVENUE. 1965. m. fl.96 includes Intermagazine (effective 1992). Geillustreerde Pers B.V., Stadhouderskade 85, Amsterdam, Netherlands. TEL 20-5734811. FAX 20-5734406. Ed. Rob van Vuure. adv.; bk.rev.; circ. 50,000.

B B W: BIG BEAUTIFUL WOMAN MAGAZINE. see *CLOTHING TRADE — Fashions*

051 CN ISSN 0045-3080
B.C. VOICE. 1963. q. Can.$6 to individuals; institutions $8 (typically set in Jan.). British Columbia Voice of Women, P.O. Box 586, Keremeos, B.C. V0X 1N0, Canada. Ed. Deeno Birmingham. bk.rev.; circ. 400.
  Description: Women's interests, particularly as these relate to world peace and the environment.

301.4 ZR
B E A MAGAZINE DE LA FEMME. fortn. 2 ave Masimanimba, B.P. 113380, Kinshasa I, Zaire. Ed. Mutinga Mutwishayi.

B W P A GAZETTE. (British Women Pilots Association) see *AERONAUTICS AND SPACE FLIGHT*

301.412 GW
BABY; Das Elternmagazin. m. Wort & Bild Verlag Konradshoehe GmbH, Konradshoehe, 8021 Baierbrunn, Germany. TEL 089-72700. FAX 089-7270157. Ed. Dorothee Walzel.

301.412 CN
▼**BABY AND CHILD CARE QUICK REFERENCE ENCYCLOPEDIA.** 1990. s-a. Family Communications, Inc., 37 Hanna Ave., Toronto, Ont. M6K 1X1, Canada. TEL 416-537-2604. FAX 416-538-1794. Ed. Kathy Fremes. adv.; circ. 100,000.

649 618 US
▼**BABY ON THE WAY: BASICS.** 1991. a. free. (American College of Obstetricians and Gynecologists) Time Venture Publishing Inc., Baby Talk, 636 Ave. of the Americas, New York, NY 10011. TEL 212-989-8181. adv. contact: Kevin Walsh. circ. 300,000.
  Description: Information for expectant mothers with low reading ability, in easy-to-read format.

305.412 323.4 US
BACKLASH TIMES. 1983. s-a. $20. Feminists Fighting Pornography, Box 6731, Yorkville Sta., New York, NY 10128. TEL 212-410-5182. Ed. Page Mellish. stat.; circ. 25,250.
  Description: Published data on pornography by anti-porn lobby.

BAD ATTITUDE; a lesbian sex magazine. see *HOMOSEXUALITY*

WOMEN'S INTERESTS

305.412   PH   ISSN 0115-3994
BALIKATANEWS. (Text in English) 1979. irreg. Balikatan sa Kaunlaran, Inc., Malvar Wing, the Philippine Women's University, Taft Avenue, Manila, Philippines. TEL 58-71-75. Eds. Ramona Raneses, Evelyn Alcantara. bk.rev.; circ. 1,000.

059.91   II   ISSN 0005-5573
BANO. (Text in Urdu) 1957. m. Rs.115 (foreign Rs.650). Shama Magazine, 13-14 Asaf Ali Rd., New Delhi 110002, India. TEL 91-11-732666. TELEX 3161601-SHMA-IN. adv.; illus.; circ. 12,700. (tabloid format)

301.42   US
BATTERED WOMEN'S DIRECTORY.* 1975. irreg., latest 1985. $12. c/o Terry Mehlman, 2702 Fairlawn Rd., Durham, NC 27705-2774. adv.; bk.rev.; bibl.; stat.; circ. 2,000. (also avail. in microform)
   Formerly: Working on Wife Abuse.

BEGINNINGS (NEW YORK); pediatrics edition. see MEDICAL SCIENCES — Pediatrics

BEGINNINGS (RALEIGH). see MEDICAL SCIENCES — Nurses And Nursing

301.412   BG
BEGUM. (Text in Bengali) w. 66 Loyal St., Dhaka 1, Bangladesh. TEL 2-233789. Ed. Nurjahan Begum. circ. 25,000.

305.412   GW
BELLA. 1978. w. DM.124.80. Heinrich Bauer Verlag, Burchardstr. 11, 2000 Hamburg 1, Germany. TEL 040-3019-0. FAX 040-326589. Ed. Juergen Pietzker. adv.; illus.; circ. 656,236.
   Description: Concentrates on fashion, cosmetics, home economics, nutrition, advice and entertainment.

055.1   IT   ISSN 0005-8602
BELLA (MILAN, 1947); settimanale di attualita e moda. 1947. w. L.67600. Rizzoli Editore-Corriere della Sera, Via Angelo Rizzoli 2, 20132 Milan, Italy. Ed. Mara Santini. adv.; bk.rev.; illus.
   Incorporates: Buona Tavola.

054 305.412   IT   ISSN 0399-2322
BELLA (MILAN, 1975); le magazine de la femme noire. 1975. m. Rizzoli Editore-Corriere della Sera, Via Angelo Rizzoli 2, 20132 Milan, Italy. Ed. Luciana Omicini. circ. 313,555.

BENISSIMO. see CLOTHING TRADE — Fashions

BERKELEY WOMEN'S LAW JOURNAL. see LAW

BETTER HOMES & DYKES. see HOMOSEXUALITY

BI-LIFESTYLE; devoted to the interests of bisexual swingers. see MEN'S INTERESTS

BIG APPLE PARENTS' PAPER. see CHILDREN AND YOUTH — About

BIRTH NOTES. see MEDICAL SCIENCES — Obstetrics And Gynecology

305.412 910.03   US
BLACK WOMEN'S VOICE.* q. National Council of Negro Women, Inc., 1211 Connecticut Ave. N.W., No. 702, Washington, DC 20036-2701. Ed. Dorothy I. Height. bk.rev.; bibl.

305.412   FR
BONNE SOIREE TELE. 1922. w. 6.50 F. per no. Editions Mondiales, 26 rue le la Tremoille, 75008 Paris, France. FAX 1-40-70-98-93. TELEX 643 932. Ed. M.H. Adler. circ. 234,637.

BOOKWOMAN. see PUBLISHING AND BOOK TRADE

301.412   US
BOSTON WOMAN.* m. Boston Woman, Inc., Box 1260, Brookline, MA 02146-0010. TEL 617-783-8000. adv.
   Description: Features articles about Boston women in business, politics, professions, the creative arts and the community.

BRASIL VOGUE. see CLOTHING TRADE — Fashions

301.412   GW
BRAUT UND BRAEUTIGAM; wissenwertes ueber heiraten und wohnen. 1986. q. DM.40. Christiaan Publishing GmbH, Am Seestern 24, 4000 Duesseldorf 11, Germany. TEL 0211-596716. FAX 0211-591240. Ed. Bert Klomp. adv.; bk.rev.; circ. 53,000. (back issues avail.)
   Formerly: Braut und Braeutigam mit Trachtenmode.

305.412   GW
BRIGITTE. 1886. s-m. DM.78. Gruner und Jahr AG und Co., Am Baumwall 11, 2000 Hamburg 11, Germany. TEL 040-3703-0. FAX 040-37035631. Ed. Anne Volk. circ. 1,234,000. (also avail. in microfilm from UMI; reprint service avail. from UMI)

305.412   NZ   ISSN 0110-8603
BROADSHEET; New Zealand feminist magazine. 1972. 4/yr. NZ.$35. Broadsheet Magazine Ltd., P.O. Box 56-147, Auckland, New Zealand. TEL 09-8343472. adv.; bk.rev.; circ. 4,500. (back issues avail.)
   Indexed: Wom.Stud.Abstr.

305.412   US   ISSN 0883-9611
HQ1059.5.U5
BROOMSTICK; the national magazine by, for, and about women over forty. 1978. q. $15 to individuals; institutions $30. Broomstick, 3543 18th St., No. 3, San Francisco, CA 94110. TEL 415-552-7460. Ed.Bd. adv.; bk.rev.; circ. 5,000. **Indexed:** Alt.Press Ind.

BUSINESS AND PROFESSIONAL WOMAN (CANADA). see OCCUPATIONS AND CAREERS

BUSINESS AND PROFESSIONAL WOMAN (ENGLAND). see OCCUPATIONS AND CAREERS

323.4   CN   ISSN 1188-2654
C A C S W NEWS. 1986. s-a. free. Canadian Advisory Council on the Status of Women - Conseil Consultatif Canadien sur la Situation de la Femme, 110 O'Connor St., 9th Fl., P.O. Box 1541, Station "B", Ottawa, Ont. K1P 5R5, Canada. TEL 613-992-4975. FAX 613-992-1715. bk.rev.; circ. 12,000.
   Former titles (until 1991): Fine Balances - Juste Equilibre; Inside Out.
   Description: Covers recent Council activities, publications, emerging issues for women of Canada.

C A U S NEWSLETTER; color, design, fashion, marketing. (Color Association of the United States) see CLOTHING TRADE

C E D H U. (Centro de Estudios Humanitarios) see LAW

305.412 338.91   US
C E D P A WORLD WIDE. 1984. q. free. Centre for Development and Population Activities, 1717 Massachusetts Ave., N.W., Ste. 202, Washington, DC 20036. TEL 202-667-1142. FAX 202-332-4496. TELEX 440384 CFPA. Eds. Katherine Nutt, Heather Svokos. bk.rev.; circ. 3,600. (back issues avail.)
   Description: News and announcements pertaining to the Centre's mission to provide training and technical assistance to Third World managers of health, population, and development programs.

301.412   CN
C R I A W PAPERS. 1981. irreg. price varies. Canadian Research Institute for the Advancement of Women - Institut Canadien de Recherches sur les Femmes, 151 Slater St., Ste. 408, Ottawa, Ont. K1P 5H3, Canada. TEL 613-563-0681. FAX 613-563-0682.
   Description: Publishes original research papers and review articles drawn from various disciplines, as well as interdisciplinary works, advancing the knowledge and understanding of women's experience.

301.412   FR
C R I F BULLETIN. 1982. irreg. 80 Fr. (foreign 170 F.). Centre de Recherches, de Reflexion et d'Information Feministes, 1 rue des Fosses St. Jacques, 75005 Paris, France. TEL 43-25-63-48. Ed.Bd. bk.rev.; circ. 500. (back issues avail.)
   Description: Analytical texts about feminist theory and politics.

C W A O NEWS. (Coalition of Women's Art Organizations) see ART

305.412   UK
C W L NEWS. 1911. q. £2. Catholic Women's League, 48 Great Peter St., London SW1P 2HP, England.

301.412   UY
LA CACEROLA. 1984. irreg., latest no.8. Urg.$500 per no. Grupo de Estudios Sobre la Condicion de la Mujer en el Uruguay (GRECMU), Miguel del Corro 1474, Casilla de Correos, 11200 Montevideo, Uruguay. TEL 41-64-15.

CADERNOS DE PESQUISA; revista de estudos e pesquisas em educacao. see EDUCATION

301.412 323.4   FR   ISSN 0154-7763
CAHIERS DE FEMINISME. 1977. q. 65 F. Presse Edition Communication, 2 Rue Richard Lenoir, 93108 Montreuil, France. Ed. Isabelle Alleton. illus.; circ. 4,000. (back issues avail.)
   —BLDSC shelfmark: 2948.941400.
   Description: Covers civil rights and equality issues from a feminist perspective.

CALIFORNIA FAMILY LAW MONTHLY. see LAW — Family And Matrimonial Law

305.412   US   ISSN 0008-1663
CALIFORNIA WOMAN. vol.37, 1970. 4/yr. $6. California Federation of Business & Professional Women's Clubs, Inc., 2150 River Plaza Dr., Ste.315, Sacramento, CA 95833-3880. TEL 916-641-2279. adv.; illus.; circ. 6,000.

301.412   US   ISSN 0193-7618
HQ1236.5.U6
CALIFORNIA WOMEN. 1978. q. free. Commission on the Status of Women, 1303 J St., Ste. 400, Sacramento, CA 95814. TEL 916-445-3173. Ed. Nan Smith. **Indexed:** Cal.Per.Ind. (1984-).

CALIFORNIA YOUTH AUTHORITY'S STATUS OF FEMALE EMPLOYEES. REPORT. see BUSINESS AND ECONOMICS — Labor And Industrial Relations

CANADA. WOMEN'S BUREAU. WOMEN IN THE LABOUR FORCE. see BUSINESS AND ECONOMICS — Labor And Industrial Relations

301.412   CN   ISSN 0705-6028
HQ1453
CANADIAN ADVISORY COUNCIL ON THE STATUS OF WOMEN. ANNUAL REPORT - RAPPORT ANNUEL. 1973. a. free. Canadian Advisory Council on the Status of Women - Conseil Consultatif Canadien sur la Situation de la Femme, 110 O'Connor St., 9th Floor, P.O. Box 1541, Station "B", Ottawa, Ont. K1P 5R5, Canada. TEL 613-992-4975. FAX 613-992-1715. Ed. James C. Young. bk.rev.; circ. 10,000.
   Description: Analysis of women's issues plus news of the council.

305.412   CN   ISSN 0229-7256
CANADIAN RESEARCH INSTITUTE FOR THE ADVANCEMENT OF WOMEN. NEWSLETTER/INSTITUT CANADIEN DE RECHERCHES SUR LES FEMMES. BULLETIN. (Text in English and French) 1981. 4/yr. Can.$25. Canadian Research Institute for the Advancement of Women - Institut Canadien de Recherches sur les Femmes, 151 Slater St., Ste. 408, Ottawa, Ont. K1P 5H3, Canada. TEL 613-563-0681. FAX 613-563-0682. Ed. Linda Clippingale. adv.; circ. 1,100.
   Description: Features the latest in research news, print, audio-visual and film resources, employment and funding opportunities.

305.412   US   ISSN 8755-9218
HD6093
CAREER WOMAN MAGAZINE. 1973. 3/yr. $13. Equal Opportunity Publications, Inc., 44 Broadway, Greenlawn, NY 11740. TEL 516-261-8899. FAX 516-261-8935. Ed. Eileen Nester. adv.; bk.rev.; illus.; circ. 10,500.
   —BLDSC shelfmark: 3051.772000.
   Former titles: Collegiate Career Woman Magazine; Collegiate Woman's Career Magazine (ISSN 0095-0653)
   Description: Career magazine for entry-level college graduates.

301.412   BL
CARINHO. m. Bloch Editores S.A., Rua do Russell 766-804, 22214 Rio de Janeiro, Brazil. TEL 21-265-2012. TELEX 21-21525. circ. 65,000.

301.412   CL
CAROLA. fortn. Editorial Antartica S.A., San Francisco 116, Casills 1858, Santiago, Chile. TEL 2-33-6433. TELEX 240656. Dir. Isabel Margarita Aguirre de Maino.

WOMEN'S INTERESTS

301.412 610.73 US
CASSANDRA; radical feminist nurses newsjournal. 1982. 3/yr. $35. Cassandra: Radical Feminist Nurses Network, Box 181039, Cleveland Hts., OH 44118. bk.rev.; circ. 400. (back issues avail.)

CENTER FOR SELF-SUFFICIENCY UPDATE. see *EDUCATION — Adult Education*

CENTRE INTERNATIONAL DE L'ENFANCE. PROGRAMME OF ACTIVITIES. see *CHILDREN AND YOUTH — About*

323.4 PY ISSN 1017-6063
CENTRO DE DOCUMENTACION Y ESTUDIOS. INFORMATIVO MUJER. 1989. m. $35. Centro de Documentacion y Estudios, Pai Perez 737, Asuncion, Paraguay. (Dist. by: D.I.P.P., Box 2507, Asuncion, Paraguay) Ed. Dr. Line Bareiro. circ. 500.

301.412 UK
CHAT. 1985. w. I P C Magazines Ltd., I P C Women's Magazines Group (Subsidiary of: Reed International PLC), Kings Reach Tower, Stamford St., London SE1 9LS, England. TEL 071-261-5000. Ed. Terry Tavner. circ. 568,095.
Description: Entertainment magazine for the 25-34 year old woman; includes a weekly pullout puzzle book.

301.412 051 CN ISSN 0009-1995
AP5
CHATELAINE (ENGLISH EDITION). French edition (ISSN 0317-2635) 1928. m. Can.$17($32) Maclean Hunter Ltd., Maclean Hunter Bldg., 777 Bay St., Toronto, Ont. M5W 1A7, Canada. TEL 416-596-5425. FAX 416-593-3197. TELEX 062-19547. (Subscr. to: Box 4003, Sta. A, Toronto, Ont. M5W 1A7, Canada) Ed. Mildred Istona. adv.; bk.rev.; film.; illus.; circ. 900,000. (also avail. in microform from MIM,UMI) **Indexed**: Can.Lit.Ind., Can.Per.Ind., CMI, Mag.Ind., Pt.de Rep.

301.412 054.1 CN ISSN 0317-2635
CHATELAINE (FRENCH EDITION). English edition (ISSN 0009-1995) 1960. m. Can.$17. Magazines Maclean Hunter Quebec Ltee., 1001 bvd. de Maisonneuve W., Montreal, Que. H3A 3E1, Toronto, Ont. M5W 1A7, Canada. TEL 514-845-5141. FAX 514-845-7393. TELEX 055-60604. Ed. Micheline Lachance. adv.; bk.rev.; film rev.; circ. 201,325. (also avail. in microform from MIM,UMI) **Indexed**: Can.Wom.Per.Ind., Pt.de Rep. (1979-).

301.412 SI
CHERIE MAGAZINE. (Text in English) 1983. bi-m. 12 Everton Road, Singapore 0208, Singapore. TEL 2229733. FAX 2843859. Ed. Josephine Ng. circ. 34,000.

301.412 640 US
CHERITH. (Suppl. to: Cottage Connections) 1981. q. $10 (Canada $12; elsewhere $17; includes m. Cottage Connections). Cottage Cheese, 11113 Radisson Ct., Burnsville, MN 55337. Ed. Mary Morgan Bevis.
Former titles: Cottage Cheese; Homemakers' Journal.
Description: Provides encouragement for the many women in the home. Includes poetry, short stories, articles and essays; features their active involvement in politics, education, writers' clubs, and Christian ministries.

CHILD CARE ACTION NEWS. see *CHILDREN AND YOUTH — About*

CHILD, YOUTH, AND FAMILY FUTURES CLEARINGHOUSE. see *SOCIAL SERVICES AND WELFARE*

305.412 FR
CHOISIR. 1972. 6/yr. 70 F. 102 rue St. Dominique, F-75007 Paris, France. bk.rev.; circ. 6,000. (newspaper) **Indexed**: CERDIC.

CHRISTIAN MOTHER (PITTSBURGH). see *RELIGIONS AND THEOLOGY*

CHRISTIAN WOMAN. see *RELIGIONS AND THEOLOGY*

053.1 GW ISSN 0009-5788
DIE CHRISTLICHE FRAU. 1902. 6/yr. DM.15. Katholischer Deutscher Frauenbund, Kaesenstr. 18, 5000 Cologne 1, Germany. TEL 0221-314930. bk.rev.; circ. 28,000. (back issues avail.)

THE CIVIL WAR LADY; women in reenacting, historical information, research, medical. see *MILITARY*

305.412 AG ISSN 0009-8493
CLAUDIA. 1957. m. $44. Ryela, S.A., Av. Leandro N. Alem 896, Buenos Aires, 1001, Argentina. TEL 1-312-6010. TELEX 9229. Dir. Mercedes Marques. adv.; bk.rev.; abstr.; illus.; circ. 17,100.

056.9 BL ISSN 0009-8507
CLAUDIA. (Supplement avail.: Claudia Cozinha) 1961. m. $150. Editora Abril, S.A., R. Geraldo Flausino Gomes, 61, 04575 Sao Paulo, Brazil. TEL 011-8239222. FAX 011-86437964. TELEX 011-80360 EDAB BR. (Subscr. to: Rua do Curtume, 769 CEP 05065 Lapa, Sao Paulo, Brazil.) Ed. Victor Civita. adv.; bk.rev.; film rev.; play rev.; illus.; circ. 311,979.
Description: For the woman of today, who has both career and home. Contains information on education for children, fashion, beauty, health, decorating, medicine and psychology.

301.412 MX ISSN 0009-8515
CLAUDIA. 1965. m. $67. Editorial Mex-Ameris, S.A., Av. Morelos 16, 4o piso, 06040 Mexico D.F., Mexico. TEL 5-521-4690. Ed. Hilda O'Farrill de Compean. adv.; bk.rev.; bibl.; illus.; circ. 181,170.

CLEAR BEGINNINGS. see *LITERATURE*

052 AT ISSN 0310-1797
CLEO. 1972. m. Aus.$46.20. Australian Consolidated Press, 54-58 Park St., Sydney, N.S.W. 2000, Australia. TEL 02-282-8617. FAX 02-267-2150. TELEX 120514. Ed. Lisa Wilkinson. bk.rev.; film rev.; circ. 293,000.

CLIN D'OEIL. see *CLOTHING TRADE — Fashions*

CLIO; eine feministische Zeitschrift zur gesundheitlichen Selbsthilfe. see *WOMEN'S HEALTH*

301.412 331.11 IT
CLIO NOTIZIE; quadrimestrale di orientamento e informazione al lavoro per le donne. 1989. 3/yr. L.38000 (foreign L.55000)(effective 1992). Franco Angeli Editore, Viale Monza, 106, Casella Postale 17175, 20100 Milan, Italy. TEL 02-2895762.

301.412 JA
CLIQUE. (Text in Japanese) 1989. bi-w. Magazine House, 3-13-10, Ginza, Chuo-ku, Tokyo 104, Japan. TEL 03-3545-7100. FAX 03-3546-0034. Ed. Hitoshi Akiba. circ. 250,000.

CLUBDATE MAGAZINE; magazine of the good life in Cleveland, U.S.A. see *CONSUMER EDUCATION AND PROTECTION*

CO-LABORER. see *RELIGIONS AND THEOLOGY*

COMING CHANGES; newsletter for Florida's lesbian-feminists. see *HOMOSEXUALITY*

COMMON LIVES - LESBIAN LIVES. see *HOMOSEXUALITY*

640 JA
▼**COMO**. (Text in Japanese) 1990. m. 10440 Yen. Shufunotomo Co., Ltd., 2-9 Kanda Surugadai, Chiyoda-ku, Tokyo 101, Japan. Ed. Nobuko Kano. circ. 300,000.

052 305.412 UK ISSN 0141-1144
COMPANY. 1978. m. £15.60. National Magazine Co. Ltd., 72 Broadwick St., London W1V 2BP, England. TEL 071-439-5000. FAX 071-437-6886. Ed. Mandi Norwood. adv.; illus.; circ. 194,791.

301.412 US
COMPLETE WOMAN. bi-m. $13. Associated Publications, 1165 N. Clark St., Ste. 607, Chicago, IL 60610. TEL 312-266-8680.

301.412 SP
COMPLICE. 1985. m. Pedro Teixeira 8, 28020 Madrid, Spain. TEL 91-5560048. Dir. Martha Cardozo. circ. 80,991.

301.412 US ISSN 0147-8311
PS508.W7
CONDITIONS;* a feminist magazine of writing by women, with an emphasis on writing by lesbians. 1977. a. $24 for 3 nos. to individuals; institutions $34. Conditions, Inc., Box 159046, Van Brunt Station, Brooklyn, NY 11215-9046. TEL 718-258-4102. adv.; bk.rev.; circ. 3,000. (back issues avail.) **Indexed**: A.I.P.P., Alt.Press Ind.

055.1 IT
CONFIDENZE. 1946. w. L.93600 (foreign L.126800). Arnoldo Mondadori Editore S.p.A., Casella Postale 1833, 20101 Milan, Italy. TEL 3199345. Ed. Aldo Gustavo Cimarelli. circ. 363,390.

051 US
CONNECTICUT PARENT. 1984. m. $18. 315 Peck St., Box 580, New Haven, CT 06513. TEL 203-782-1420. Ed. Joel D. MacClaren. adv.; bk.rev.; circ. 30,000. (tabloid format; back issues avail.)

CONNECTIONS (SPRINGFIELD). see *OCCUPATIONS AND CAREERS*

305.412 US ISSN 0886-7062
HQ1101
CONNEXIONS (OAKLAND); an international women's quarterly. 1981. 4/yr. $15 to individuals (foreign $17); institutions $24. Peoples Translation Service, 4228 Telegraph Ave., Oakland, CA 94609. TEL 510-654-6725. Ed.Bd. adv.; bk.rev.; circ. 3,000. (back issues avail.) **Indexed**: Alt.Press Ind., Can.Wom.Per.Ind., HR Rep., Left Ind. (1982-), Stud.Wom.Abstr.
Description: Thematic coverage of women's issues, with writings, translations and interviews focusing on women outside the U.S.

305.412 IT
CONSIGLI PRATICI. 1968. m. L.40000 (foreign L.58000). Via Borgogna 5, 20122 Milan, Italy. Ed. Sandra Rudoni.

613.2 US ISSN 0741-7748
CONSUMING PASSIONS.* 1982. bi-m. $18. Fulfillment Etc., Inc., Box 292593, Davie, FL 33329. TEL 203-544-9663. Ed. Barbara May. adv.; bk.rev.; circ. 5,000.

CONTEMPORARY WOMEN WRITERS OF SPAIN. see *LITERATURE*

301.412 US
CONTRA COSTA WOMAN. q. Gretchen Weberling, Ed.& Pub., Box 544, Clayton, CA 94517-0544. TEL 415-672-7899. circ. 12,000.

301.42 US ISSN 0147-104X
CONTRIBUTIONS IN WOMEN'S STUDIES. 1978. irreg., no.129, 1992. price varies. Greenwood Press, Inc. (Subsidiary of: Greenwood Publishing Group Inc.), 88 Post Rd. W., Box 5007, Westport, CT 06881-5007. TEL 203-226-3571. FAX 203-222-1502.
—BLDSC shelfmark: 3461.480000.

CORNERSTONE (ANN ARBOR). see *EDUCATION — Higher Education*

051 US ISSN 0010-9541
AP2
COSMOPOLITAN. 1886. m. $24. Hearst Corporation, Cosmopolitan, 224 W. 57th St., New York, NY 10019. TEL 212-649-2000. Ed. Helen Gurley Brown. adv.; bk.rev.; film rev.; illus.; circ. 2,740,000. (also avail. in microform from UMI) **Indexed**: Access, Biog.Ind., Mag.Ind., Media Rev.Dig., R.G.
Description: For the contemporary woman. Features articles on beauty, health, fashion and social issues affecting today's woman.

305.412 NE
COSMOPOLITAN. 1981. m. fl.82.20. Geillustreerde Pers b.v., Stadhouderskade 85, 1073 AT Amsterdam, Netherlands. TEL 20-5734811. FAX 20-5734406. Ed. Maarten Siffels. adv.; bk.rev.; illus.; circ. 135,000.

305.412 GR
COSMOPOLITAN. 1987. m. P. Rokanas, Leoforos Marathonas 14, Pallini, 153 00 Athens, Greece. TEL 6665706. Ed. K. Kostoulias.
Description: Covers fashion, beauty and health.

054.1 FR
COSMOPOLITAN (FRANCE); magazine de la femme moderne. 1973. m. 121 F. Inter-Edi (Subsidiary of: Groupe Marie-Claire), 11 bis rue Boissy d'Anglas, 75008 Paris, France. Ed. Juliette Boisriveaud. adv.; bk.rev.; circ. 300,000. **Indexed**: PMR.

U
V
W
X
Y
Z

WOMEN'S INTERESTS

301.412 746.96   GW
COSMOPOLITAN (GERMANY). 1980. m. DM.5.80 per no. M V G Medien Verlagsgesellschaft, Arabellastr. 33, D-8000 Munich 81, Germany. FAX 9234202. Ed. Ms. von Hatzfeld, Ms. Geissler. adv.; bk.rev.; circ. 436,809.
    Description: Magazine for modern young women dealing with self-improvement, careers, clothes, health, travel, and entertainment.

055.1   IT
COSMOPOLITAN (ITALY). 1976. m. L.35000. Edizioni S Y D S Italia s.r.l., Viale Stelvio 57, 20159 Milan, Italy. Ed. Giuseppe Della Schiava. adv.; circ. 210,000.

301.412 746.96   JA
COSMOPOLITAN (JAPAN). (Text in Japanese) 1980. m. Shueisha, Inc., 2-5-10 Hitotsubashi, Chiyoda-ku, Tokyo, Japan. Ed. Hiroshi Ohtsuka. adv.; bk.rev.; circ. 300,000.

301.412 746.96   SA
COSMOPOLITAN (SOUTH AFRICA). 1984. m. 2 Long St., 19th Fl., 8001 Cape Town, South Africa. TEL 21-5442. FAX 21-6684. TELEX 5-22991. Ed. Jane Raphaely. adv.; illus.; circ. 97,241.

305.412   US
COSMOPOLITAN EN ESPANOL. (Editions avail. for Central America, Chile, Colombia, Dominican Republic, Ecuador, Mexico, Peru, Puerto Rico, U.S., Venezuela) 1973. m. $22.50. Editorial America, S.A., Vanidades Continental Bldg., 6355 N.W. 36th St., Virginia Gardens, FL 33166. TEL 305-871-6400. FAX 305-871-8769. Ed. Sara M. Castany. circ. 251,760. (also avail. in microform from UMI)

301.412   BL
COSMOPOLITAN NOVA. 1973. m. Cr.$3000($35) Editora Abril, S.A., Geraldo Flausino Gomez, 61, Sao Paulo, 04575, Brazil. TEL 011-534-53-55. (Subscr. to: Rua do Curtume, 665, Bloco G, Sao Paulo 05065, Brazil) Ed. Marcia Neder. adv.; illus.; circ. 290,000.

051   US
COTTAGE CONNECTIONS. (Supplement avail: Cherith) m. $10 (Canada $12; elsewhere $17; includes q. Cherith). Cottage Connections, 11113 Radisson Ct., Burnsville, MN 55337. circ. 1,000 (controlled).
    Description: Keeps networking of outreaches and ministries recommended by members current; features their active involvement in politics, education, writers' clubs, and Christian ministries.

305.412 630   US   ISSN 0892-8525
COUNTRY WOMAN. 1971. bi-m. $16.98. Reiman Publications, Inc., 5400 S. 60th St., Greendale, WI 53129. TEL 414-423-0100. FAX 414-423-1143. (Subscr. to: Box 572, Milwaukee, WI 53201) Ed. Ann Kaiser. circ. 1,100,000.
    Former titles: Farm Woman (ISSN 0888-1472); Farm Wife News.

305.412   UK   ISSN 0011-0302
COUNTRYWOMAN. 1933. q. £15 (effective Jan. 1990). Associated Country Women of the World, Vincent House, Vincent Sq., London SW1P 2NB, England. TEL 071-834-8635. adv.; illus.; circ. 8,000.
    Indexed: New Per.Ind.

700 800   US   ISSN 0736-4733
CREATIVE WOMAN. 1977. 3/yr. $12. Governors State University, University Park, IL 60466. TEL 708-534-5000. Ed. Helen E. Hughes. bk.rev.; film rev.; bibl.; illus.; cum.index every 2 yrs.; circ. 900. Indexed: Stud.Wom.Abstr.
    —BLDSC shelfmark: 3487.249000.
    Description: Articles, poetry, verse, biographical sketches, essays and photographs pertaining to the artistic and scientific endeavors of women.

301.412   BL
CRIATIVA. m. Rua Itapiri 1209, 21251 Rio de Janeiro, Brazil. TEL 21-273-5522. TELEX 21-23365. Dir. Oscar D. Neves. circ. 121,000.

CRITICAL THEORY. see LINGUISTICS

305.412   IT   ISSN 0574-475X
CRONACHE E OPINIONI. Title varies: Cronache. m. free for members. Centro Italiano Femminile, Via Carlo Zucchi 25, 00165 Rome, Italy. FAX 39-6-6621167. Ed. Lilliana Piccinini. adv.; bk.rev.

305.412   DK   ISSN 0109-1476
D K K F - NYT. 1981. bi-m. DKK 30. Dansk Katolsk Kvinde-Forbund, c/o Simone Pedersen, Elbaekvej 16, 8240 Risskov, Denmark. illus.

D M W B E ACTION NEWSLETTER. (Disadvantaged Minority and Women Business Enterprises) see TRANSPORTATION

305.412   US   ISSN 0739-1749
BV4527
DAUGHTERS OF SARAH. 1974. q. $18. 3801 N. Keeler, Chicago, IL 60641-6790. TEL 312-736-3399. Ed. Reta Finger. adv.; bk.rev.; index; circ. 6,200. (also avail. in microfilm from UMI; back issues avail.) Indexed: Rel.Ind.One.
    Description: Christian feminist magazine addressing issues of interest to women in the church: biblical interpretation, poverty, racism, divorce and sexuality. Includes personal stories.

305.412   US
DAWN FOR THE ORANGE COUNTY WOMAN.* 1975. m. $7.50. Jeanne and Gerry Parham, Pubs., 26412 Payaso, Mission Viejo, CA 92691. Ed. Maryann Easley. adv.; bk.rev.; circ. 33,000.

DE TEXTOS. see SOCIOLOGY

DENEUVE. see HOMOSEXUALITY

DIARY. see CLOTHING TRADE — Fashions

A DIFFERENT LIGHT REVIEW; a catalog of gay and lesbian literature. see HOMOSEXUALITY

DINAH. see HOMOSEXUALITY

101   FR
DIPLOMEES. 1952. q. 90 F. Association Francaise des Femmes Diplomees des Universites, 4, rue de Chevreuse, 75006 Paris, France. Ed. Huguette Delavault. adv.; bk.rev.; circ. 2,000.

DIRECTORY OF WOMEN IN BUSINESS, PROFESSIONS & MANAGEMENT. see BUSINESS AND ECONOMICS — Trade And Industrial Directories

305.412   AE
AL-DJEZA'IRIYYAH. (Text in Arabic, French) 1970. m. Union Nationale des Femmes Algeriennes, Villa Joly, 24 av. Franklin Roosevelt, Algiers, Algeria. illus.

301.412   RM
DOLGOZO NO. (Text in Hungarian) 1945. m. National Women's Council, Str. Napoca 16, Cluj-Napoca, Rumania. circ. 106,000.

DOMINATRIX CROSS ROADS. see MEN'S INTERESTS

DONNA; international fashion magazine. see CLOTHING TRADE — Fashions

301.412   IT
DONNA & MAMMA. m. L.38000. Eurotrend S.p.A., Viale Regina Giovanna 39, 20129 Milan, Italy. TEL 02-29405655. FAX 29404868. Ed. Gaetano Manti.

055   IT   ISSN 0046-0591
DONNA DI CASA; rivista mensile femminile. 1959. m. L.140000. Oscar Vona, Ed. & Pub., 44 Via Benedetto Marcello, 20124 Milan, Italy. TEL 02-2047940. adv.; illus.

305.412   IT
DONNA E SOCIETA. 1968. q. L.15000. Corso Rinascimento 113, 00186 Rome, Italy. TEL 656-9166. Ed. Maria Paola Colombo Svevo. adv.; bk.rev.

301.412   IT
DONNA MODERNA. w. L.78000 (foreign L.114400). Arnoldo Mondadori Editore S.p.A., Casella Postale 17135, 20170 Milan, Italy. TEL 3199345. Ed. Edvige Bernasconi.

301.412 746.92   SP
DUNIA. 1976. fortn. 4300 ptas. (Europe 11120 ptas.; elsewhere 16100 ptas.). G & J Espana, S.A. (Subsidiary of: Gruner & Jahr USA Publishing), Marques de Villamagna, 4, 28001 Madrid, Spain. TEL 431-6631. FAX 2767881. TELEX 43419 ORBOSA E. Ed. Mercedes Casanova. adv.; bk.rev.; circ. 112,863.

301.412   IO
DUNIA WANITA. 1949. fortn. Rps.1500 (effective 1991). Jalan Brigjen, Katamso1, Medan, Indonesia. TEL 061-520858. FAX 061-510025. Ed. Rayati Syafrin. adv.; B&W page Rps.500,000, color page Rps.650,000. circ. 10,000.

DYKE DIANNIC WICCA SEPARATIST AMAZON MAGICK. see HOMOSEXUALITY

E K-BLADET. (Erhverskvinders Klub) see BUSINESS AND ECONOMICS

305.412   US   ISSN 0163-0989
PS508.W7
EARTH'S DAUGHTERS; a feminist arts periodical. 1971. 3/yr. $14 to individuals; institutions $22. Box 41, Central Park Sta., Buffalo, NY 14215. TEL 716-886-2636. Ed.Bd. bk.rev.; circ. 1,000.

305.412   GW
ECHO DER FRAU. 1973. w. DM.46.80. Westdeutscher Zeitschriften Verlag Gmbh, Adlerstr. 22, Postfach 8509, 4000 Duesseldorf 1, Germany. Ed. Peter Saller. bk.rev.; circ. 400,000.

EDITH WHARTON REVIEW. see LITERATURE

376   ER   ISSN 0235-7488
EESTI NAINE; a magazine for women. (Text in Estonian) 1924. m. 0.35 Rub. per issue. Estonian Press, Parnu mnt. 67a, 200106 Tallinn, Estonia. TEL 681-310. Ed. Aimi Paalandi. illus.; circ. 207,000.
    Formerly: Noukogude Naine.

305.412   FI   ISSN 0355-2985
EEVA. 1934. m. FIM 420. A-Lehdet Oy, Hitsaajankatu 7, 00810 Helsinki 81, Finland. FAX 0-786-858. Heljae Laukkanen. adv.; bk.rev.; charts; illus.; circ. 108,647.
    Description: For the refined adult woman.

305.412   JA
EF. (Text in Japanese) 1985. m. 11280 Yen. Shufunotomo Co., Ltd., 2-9 Kanda Surugadai, Chiyoda-ku, Tokyo 101, Japan. Ed. Yumiko Koma. circ. 200,000.

301   US   ISSN 0740-8307
EIDOS; sexual freedom and erotic entertainment for women, men and couples. 1984. q. $30. Box 96, Boston, MA 02137-0096. TEL 617-262-0096. Ed. Brenda Loew Tatelbaum. adv.; bk.rev.; film rev.; circ. 10,000. (tabloid format; back issues avail.)
    Formerly: Eidos. Erotica for Women.
    Description: Depicts mutually respectful images of the human form for all sexual orientations, preferences and lifestyles.

053.932   BE
EIGEN AARD. 1911. m. (Katholiek Vormingswerk van Landelijke Vrouwen) Publicarto N.V., Langestraat 170, B-1150 Brussels 15, Belgium. adv.; bk.rev.; illus.; circ. 156,273 (controlled).
    Formerly: Bij de Haard (ISSN 0006-2227)
    Description: Socio-cultural magazine addressed to members of the K.V.L.V. women's organization.

301.412 305.3   BL   ISSN 0531-9153
ELE E ELA; uma revista para ler a dois. 1969. m. $37. Bloch Editores S.A., Rua do Russell 766-804, 22214 Rio de Janeiro, Brazil. TEL 21-265-2012. FAX 21-205-4999. TELEX 21-21525. Ed. Sergio Ryff. adv.; charts; illus.; circ. 150,000.

687   NE
ELEGANCE. 1943. m. fl.99.50. B.V. Uitgeverijmaatschappij Bonaventura, Hoogoorddreef 60, 1101 BE Amsterdam, Netherlands. TEL 20-5674911. FAX 20-5674629. TELEX 14013 BONAV NL. Ed. Rupert Van Woerkom. bk.rev.; illus.; circ. 55,000.

301.412   PO
ELES & ELAS; club. 1983. m. Esc.500($35) Gabinete 1, Imprensa, Promocao e Relacoes Publicas, Ltd., Rua de Sao Bento, 311, 3o Esq., 1200 Lisbon, Portugal. TEL 01-3961771. FAX 01-605688. Dir. Maria da Luz de Braganca. adv.; circ. 64,500. (microform; back issues avail.)
    Supersedes in part: Eles e Elas - a Revista (ISSN 0870-8932)

WOMEN'S INTERESTS

301.412   VE
ELLAS. fortn. Edif. El Bucare, Avda. Federico Solano, Caracas 101, Venezuela. TEL 2-71-2798. Ed. Nery Russo. circ. 30,000.

301.412   US   ISSN 0888-0808
TT500
ELLE. (American Edition) 1985. m. $24. Elle Publishing (Subsidiary of: Hachette Publications), 1633 Broadway, New York, NY 10019. TEL 212-767-5800. FAX 212-489-4216. (Subscr. to: Box 53578, Boulder, CO 80322. TEL 800-876-8775) adv.; bk.rev.; circ. 825,000. **Indexed**: Access (1986-).
Description: International style magazine for the sophisticated, affluent, well traveled woman. Reports on global ideas and trends in fashion, personalities and lifestyles.

301.412   PO
ELLE. 1988. m. Av. 5 de Outubro 204-2o A-B-C, 1200 Lisbon, Portugal. TEL 01-736878. Dir. Maria Teresa Coelho. circ. 40,000.

301.412   SP
ELLE. 1987. m. 3840 ptas. (foreign 5360 ptas.)(effective Jan. 1992). Hachette Publicaciones, Santa Engracia 6, 1o, 28010 Madrid, Spain. TEL 91-593-84-62. FAX 91-446-09-06. (Subscr. to: Cempro, Plaza del Conde Valle Suchill 20, 28015 Madrid, Spain. TEL 593-34-11) Dir. Charo Izquierdo. adv. contact: Alvaro Gomez Acebo. circ. 200,000.

053.1   GW
ELLE. 1988. m. Burda GmbH and F.E.P., Arabella Str. 23, D-8000 Munich, Germany. TEL 49-89-9250-3040. adv.: B&W page DM.20540, color page DM.30840; trim 230 x 285. circ. 173,423.
Description: Covers fashion, books, arts, cuisine, and films.

059.956   JA
ELLE. 1989. fortn. Time - Hachette, Daini Sakae Bld., 11-14 Otawa, 2 Chome, Tokyo 112, Japan. TEL 81-3-5395-2612. adv.: B&W page 1140000 Yen, color page 1720000 Yen; trim 267 x 210. circ. 250,000.
Description: Covers fashion, books, art, cuisine, and films.

052   UK
ELLE. 1985. m. £1.60 per no. Hachette Magazines, Rex House 5-12, Lower Regent St., London SW1Y 4PE, England. TEL 44-71-930-9050. adv.: B&W page £4400, color page £5900; trim 222 x 300. circ. 183,178.
Description: Covers fashion, books, art, cuisine and films.

301.412   BL
ELLE (BRAZIL). 1988. m. $160. Editora Abril, S.A., R. Geraldo Flausino Gomez, 61, 04575 Sao Paulo, Brazil. TEL 011-8239222. FAX 011-8643796. TELEX 011-80360 EDAB BR. bk.rev.; film rev.; circ. 92,540.
Description: Covers fashion, beauty, health, well-being, home decorating, cooking, personalities and travel.

054.1   FR   ISSN 0013-6298
ELLE (FRANCE). 1945. w. 339 F.($70) 6 rue Ancelle, 92521 Neuilly-sur-Seine, France. TEL 1-40-88-60-00. FAX 1-47-45-38-12. TELEX 611 462. Ed. Francois Vincens. adv.; illus.; circ. 395,077.

301.412   IT
ELLE ITALIA. 1987. m. Rizzoli Editore-Corriere della Sera, Via A. Vespucci 2, 20124 Milan, Italy. TEL 392-628-6183. Ed. Daniela Giussani. adv.: color page L.30600000; trim 230 x 287. circ. 110,583.

301.412   CN
EMBER. bi-m. Ember Publications, P.O. Box 328, Sta. A, Newmarket, Ont. L3Y 4X7, Canada. TEL 416-773-2889. FAX 416-836-1528. Ed. Katherine Walker Alleyne. circ. 20,000.

EMERGE!; a journal for Christian Scientists supporting lesbians and gay men. see *HOMOSEXUALITY*

EMERGE PLAYCOUPLE. see *MEN'S INTERESTS*

301.435   TS
EMIRATES WOMAN. (Text in English) 1981. m. Motivate Publishing, P.O. Box 2331, Dubai, United Arab Emirates. TEL 246060. FAX 245270. TELEX 48366 MAM EM. Ed. Fay Yendell. circ. 12,000.
Description: Fashion, health, beauty and other topics of interest to women in the U.A.E.

323.4   GW   ISSN 0721-9741
EMMA; Magazin von Frauen fuer Frauen. 1977. m. DM.72 (Europe DM.81). Emma Frauen-Verlag GmbH, Kolpingplatz 1a, 5000 Cologne 1, Germany. TEL 0221-210282. FAX 0221-218130. (Subscr. to: Zenit Pressevertrieb, Postfach 810640, 7000 Stuttgart 80) Ed. Alice Schwarzer. adv.; bk.rev.; tr.lit.; index; circ. 60,000. (also avail. in microfiche; back issues avail.)

059.8   GR
ENA. 1983. w. $150. Grammi S.A., 15 Voukourestiou Str., 106 71 Athens, Greece. TEL 3643821-4, 3644151-5. Ed. Nikos Simos. adv.; circ. 81,000.

ENDOMETRIOSIS ASSOCIATION NEWSLETTER. see *MEDICAL SCIENCES — Obstetrics And Gynecology*

301.412   CN
ENFANTS. 2/yr. Quebecor Inc., 2 Bates Chemin, Outremont, Que. H2V 1A7, Canada. TEL 514-270-1100. FAX 514-270-4810. Ed. Jean Lessard. circ. 40,000.

ENTREPRENEURIAL WOMAN. see *BUSINESS AND ECONOMICS — Small Business*

323.4   US
EQUAL RIGHTS. 1930. q. $15. National Women's Party, 144 Constitution Ave., N.E., Washington, DC 20002. TEL 202-546-1210. Ed. Sharon Griffith. circ. 3,000. (also avail. in microfilm; back issues avail.)

305.412   US
EQUALITY N O W!. 1972. m. $5. National Organization for Women, Madison Chapter, Box 2512, Madison, WI 53701. TEL 608-255-3911. Ed. Sharyn Gardill. adv.; bk.rev.; circ. 800. (processed) **Indexed**: Build.Manage.Abstr., High.Educ.Curr.Aware.Bull.
Formerly: Madison N O W Chapter Newsletter.

EROTIC WRITER'S AND COLLECTOR'S MARKET. see *PUBLISHING AND BOOK TRADE*

376   BO
ESCOBA. 1986. 4/yr. Centro de Informacion y Desarrollo de la Mujer, Casilla 3961, La Paz, Bolivia.

ESSEN UND TRINKEN. see *FOOD AND FOOD INDUSTRIES*

917.309   US   ISSN 0014-0880
E185.86
ESSENCE (NEW YORK); the magazine for today's black woman. 1970. m. $16. Essence Communications Inc., 1500 Broadway, New York, NY 10036. TEL 212-642-0600. FAX 212-921-5173. Ed. Susan L. Taylor. adv.; bk.rev.; film rev.; charts; illus.; circ. 900,000. (also avail. in microfilm from UMI) **Indexed**: Bk.Rev.Ind. (1984-), Child.Bk.Rev.Ind. (1984-), Curr.Lit.Fam.Plan., Hlth.Ind., Ind.Per.Negroes, Mag.Ind., Media Rev.Dig., PMR, R.G., TOM.
Description: Black women's interests.

301.412 640   UK   ISSN 0953-6337
ESSENTIALS. 1988. m. £18 (overseas £24). I P C Magazines Ltd., Specialist, & Leisure Group (Subsidiary of: Reed International PLC), King's Reach Tower, Stamford St., London S91 9LS, England. TEL 071-261-5000. (Subscr. to: P.O. Box 500, Leicester LE99 0AA, England) Ed. Gilly Cubit. circ. 543,000. (back issues avail.)
Description: Practical women's magazine with cooking, health, beauty and fashion advice.

301.412   CN
L'ESSENTIEL. m. Quebecor Inc., 7 Bates Chemin, Outremont, Que. H2V 1A6, Canada. TEL 514-270-1100. FAX 514-270-4810. Ed. Sylvie Bergeron. circ. 141,000.

301.412   SP
ESTAR VIVA. 1988. w. G & J Espana, S.A. (Subsidiary of: Gruner & Jahr USA Publishing), Marques de Villamagna 4, 28001 Madrid, Spain. TEL 5938462. FAX 5767881. Dir. Ketty Rico. circ. 122,000.

301.412   BO
ESTUDIOS DE PROMOCION FEMENINA. 1978. irreg., no.6, 1985. Centro de Investigaciones Sociales, Casilla 6931 - Correo Central, La Paz, Bolivia.

301.435 915.5   IR
ETTELA'AT BANOVAN. w. Ettela'at Publications, Khayyam Ave., Teheran 11144, Iran. TEL 021-311071. TELEX 212336. Ed. Mrs. Rahnaward. circ. 85,000.

305.412   GW   ISSN 0174-3465
DIE EULE; Diskussionsforum fuer rationalitaetsgenealogische, insbesondere feministische Theorie. 1978. s-a. DM.1 per no. (Arbeitsgruppe fuer Anti-Psychoanalyse) Heide Heinz, Ed.& Pub., Augustastr. 123, 5600 Wuppertal 1, Germany. illus.

056.1   DR   ISSN 0014-3286
EVA. 1967. fortn. RD.$4($17) Publicaciones Ahora, Ave. San Martin 236, Apdo. Postal 1402, Santo Domingo, Dominican Republic. Ed. Magda Florencio.

EVA. see *CLOTHING TRADE — Fashions*

055.1   IT   ISSN 0014-3308
EVA EXPRESS. 1933. w. L.83200 (foreign L.140000). Rusconi Editori Associati S.p.A., Servizio Abbonamenti, Via Vitruvio 43, 20124 Milan, Italy. TEL 02-67561. FAX 67562732. Ed. Mario Palumbo. adv.; bk.rev.; film rev.; illus.; tr.lit.; circ. 280,000.
Formerly: Eva.

052   HK
EVE. 1979. m. HK.$250. Communication Management Ltd., 1811 Hong Kong Plaza, 188 Connaught Rd. W., Hong Kong. TEL 547-7117. FAX 858-2671. Ed. Lina Ross. adv.; circ. 310,920.

301.412   UK   ISSN 0267-2294
EVERYWOMAN; the current affairs magazine for women. 1985. m. £32 (foreign £45). Everywoman Publishing Ltd., 34 Islington Green, London N1 8DU, England. TEL 071-359-5496. Ed. B. Rogers. adv.; bk.rev.; circ. 15,000. (back issues avail.)
Description: Current affairs, reporting and background on issues affecting women.

052   II   ISSN 0014-3812
EVE'S WEEKLY. (Text in English) 1947. w. Rs.470. Eve's Weekly Ltd., J.K. Somani Bldg., Bombay Samachar Marg, Bombay 400 023, India. TEL 22-271444. Ed. Shola Ramachandran. circ. 40,000.

EXEC-U-TARY. see *BUSINESS AND ECONOMICS — Office Equipment And Services*

301   US   ISSN 0199-2880
HF5500.3.U54
EXECUTIVE FEMALE. 1978. bi-m. $29. National Association for Female Executives, 127 W. 24th St., New York, NY 10011. TEL 212-645-0770. FAX 212-633-6489. (Subscr. to: CS 6208, Farmingdale, NY 11736-9908) Ed. Diane P. Burley. adv.; bk.rev.; circ. 250,000. **Indexed**: B.P.I, BPIA, Bus.Ind., Tr.& Indus.Ind.
●Also available online.
Formerly: Executive Female Digest (ISSN 0160-8134)
Description: Focuses on career and financial management topics for upwardly mobile women and entrepreneurs; includes short humor and point-of-view pieces on work-related issues.

EXECUTIVE WOMEN INTERNATIONAL. PULSE. see *BUSINESS AND ECONOMICS*

301.412   UK
EXPLORATIONS IN FEMINISM. no.7, 1981. irreg. Women's Research and Resources Centre, Explorations in Feminism Collective, c/o Silver Moon Women's Bookshop, 68 Charing Cross Rd., London WC2H 0BB, England.

323.4   US
EXPONENT II; a quarterly newspaper concerning Mormon women, published by Mormon women, and of interest to Mormon women and others. 1974. q. $10 (effective 1989). Exponent II, Inc., Box 37, Arlington, MA 02174. TEL 617-862-1928. FAX 617-868-3464. Ed. Susan L. Paxman. bk.rev.; illus.; index; circ. 4,000. (tabloid format)

WOMEN'S INTERESTS

305.412 054 **FR** ISSN 0014-5327
EXPRESSION; revue culturelle feminine internationale. (Text in English, French and German) 1964. a. membership. Editions Expression et Communication, 1 av. de Chatou, 92561 Reuil-Malmaison Cedex, France. Ed. Perigot De LaTour. adv.; illus.; circ. 3,000. (tabloid format)

305.412 **US** ISSN 0895-3619
F E W'S NEWS AND VIEWS. 1969. bi-m. $12. Federally Employed Women Inc., 1400 Eye St., N.W., Ste. 425, Washington, DC 20005. TEL 202-898-0994. FAX 202-898-0998. Ed. Joanne Dumene. adv.; bk.rev.; bibl.; illus.; circ. 7,000.
  Former titles: News and Views from Federally Employed Women (ISSN 0162-2471); F E W's News and Views (ISSN 0046-3477)

305.412 **FR**
F MAGAZINE. 1978. m. 130 F. 65, avenue des Champs-Elysees, 75008 Paris, France. (Subscr. to: 31 Cours des Juilliottes, B.P. 89, 94704 Maisons-Alfort Cedex, France) Dir. Ms. Claude Servan-Schreiber. circ. 230,000.
  Former titles (until 1983): Nouveau F; F Magazine.

FACETS (CHICAGO). see *MEDICAL SCIENCES*

FACETS (PEARLAND). see *JEWELRY, CLOCKS AND WATCHES*

FACTS ON WOMEN AT WORK IN AUSTRALIA. see *BUSINESS AND ECONOMICS — Labor And Industrial Relations*

052 **SA** ISSN 0014-6927
FAIR LADY. 1965. fortn. R.110.10. National Magazines (Subsidiary of: National Media Ltd.), P.O. Box 1802, Cape Town 8000, South Africa. TEL 25-4850. TELEX 5-21125. Ed. Liz Butler. adv.; bk.rev.; film rev.; illus.; circ. 168,786. Indexed: Ind.S.A.Per.

052 **SA**
▼**FAIR LADY JUNIOR.** (Text in English) 1990. fortn. National Magazines (Subsidiary of: National Media Ltd.), P.O. Box 1802, Cape Town 8000, South Africa. TEL 21-25-4850. TELEX 5-21125.
  Description: Intended for readers of Fair Lady who have children under six years of age.

305.312 **US**
FAIRFIELD COUNTY WOMAN. 1983. m. $15. F C W, Inc., 15 Bank St., Stamford, CT 06901. TEL 203-323-3105. Ed. Joan Honig. adv.; circ. 50,000. (tabloid format; back issues avail.)

059.927 **TS**
FAJR AL-JADID/NEW DAWN. (Text in Arabic) 1973. m. Jam'iyyat al-Nisa'iyyah, Umm al-Quwain - Umm al-Quwain Women's Society, P.O. Box 43, Umm al-Quwain, United Arab Emirates. TEL 666455. Ed. Mariam Ali Rashid al-Muala. circ. 1,000.
  Description: Covers the activities of the society, the state of the women's movement in the U.A.E., and women's health issues.

FAMILY AFFAIRS. see *MEN'S INTERESTS*

301.412 640 **US**
FASHION POETRY PATTERNS & RECITALS NEWS. 1986. biennial. $25. Patterns Etc., by Alfreda, c/o Prosperity & Profits Unlimited, Box 570213, Houston, TX 77257. Ed. A.C. Doyle. circ. 1,500. (looseleaf format; also avail. in microfiche; back issues avail.)
  Description: Patterns in poetry form.

FEDERATION FEMININE FRANCO-AMERICAINE. BULLETIN. see *ETHNIC INTERESTS*

301.412 **BE**
▼**FEELING.** (Text in Dutch) 1990. s-m. 4108 Fr. I U M, Jan Blockxtraat 7, Antwerpen 2018, Belgium. TEL 32-3-247-4511. FAX 32-3-237-6136. adv.; circ. 62,861.
  Description: Covers beauty, home and environment, health, cooking, and culture and tourism.

305.412 **MX**
FEM. 1976. m. $60. Difusion Cultural Feminista, A C, Av. Universidad 1855, piso 4, Col. Oxtopulco, C.P. 04310 Mexico, D.F., Mexico. TEL 550-73-06. adv.; bk.rev.; circ. 15,000. Indexed: Chic.Per.Ind., Hisp.Amer.Per.Ind.
  Description: Focuses on the women's liberation movement.

FEMALE BODYBUILDING. see *PHYSICAL FITNESS AND HYGIENE*

055.91 **RM** ISSN 0046-3655
FEMEIA; revista social politica si culturala. 1948. m. 36 lei($8) (Consiliul National al Femeilor din Republica Socialista Romania) Editura Scinteia, Piata Presei Libere 1, 71341 Bucharest, Rumania. (Subscr. to: ILEXIM, Str. 13 Decembrie Nr. 3, P.O. Box 136-137, Bucharest, Rumania) Ed. Constanta Niculescu. adv.; bk.rev.; film rev.; charts; illus.; circ. 475,000.

058.81 **DK** ISSN 0014-9853
FEMINA. 1874. w. DKK 421. Aller Press A-S, Vigerslev Alle 18, 2500 Valby, Denmark. Ed. Jutta Larsen. adv.; bk.rev.; circ. 146,415.

311 **II** ISSN 0430-2990
FEMINA. (Text in English, Gujarati) 1959. fortn. Rs.220($20) Bennett, Coleman & Co., Ltd. (Bombay), Times of India Bldg., Dr. Dadabhai Naoroji Road, Bombay 400 001, India. TEL 22-2620271. TELEX 1182699. (U.S. subscr. address: Ms. Kalpana, 42-75 Main St., Flushing NY 11355) Ed. Vimla Patil. adv.; bk.rev.; illus.

305.412 **SA**
FEMINA. m. R.55 (foreign R.69). Associated Magazines (Pty) Ltd., 2 Long St, 19th fl., Cape Town 8000, South Africa. FAX 021-216684. TELEX 522991. Ed. Jane Raphaely. adv. contact: Volker Kuehnel. bk.rev.; circ. 108,000.
  Formerly (until 1988): Darling.
  Description: Provides general information of interest to women in South Africa.

301.412 **IO**
FEMINA. 1972. w. Blok B, Jalan H.R. Rasuna Said, Kav. 32-33, Jakarta Selatan, Indonesia. TEL 021-513816. FAX 021-513-041. TELEX 62338. circ. 130,000.

305.412 **SW**
FEMINA MAANADENS MAGASIN/FEMINA MONTHLY MAGAZINE. 1981. m. SEK 212. Aller Specialtidningar AB, S-251 85 Helsingborg, Sweden. Ed. Stina Norling. circ. 151,148.
  Incorporates: Mode & Mat och Fest; Supersedes (1944-1981): Femina (ISSN 0014-9861)

301.412 860 **AG**
FEMINARIA. 1988. s-a. $20 to individuals; institutions $40. C.C. 402, 1000 Buenos Aires, Argentina. TEL 568-3029. FAX 541-6242. Ed. Lea Fletcher. circ. 1,000.
  Description: Covers general feminist theory, feminist literary theory and criticism, interviews of and notes about women and their activities, and prose, poetry, humor and artwork created by women.

FEMINISM & PSYCHOLOGY. see *PSYCHOLOGY*

301.412 **US** ISSN 1041-1801
HQ1101
FEMINISMS. 1988. bi-m. $8. Center for Women's Studies, Ohio State University, 207 Dulles Hall, 230 W. 17th Ave., Columbus, OH 43210. Ed. Kim Davies. bk.rev.; circ. 600.

305.412 **GW**
DER FEMINIST; beitraege zur theorie und praxis. 1976. irreg. (1-2/yr.). DM.8.50 per no. Forderkreis Zum Aufbau der Feministischen Partei, Christrosenweg 5, 8000 Munich 70, Germany. Ed. Hannelore Mabry. bk.rev.; circ. 4,000. (back issues avail.)
  Description: Directed to female and male feminists, reports on theory and practice of feminism, criticism of Christianity and theology.

305.42 **CN** ISSN 0831-3377
FEMINIST ACTION/ACTION FEMINISTE. 7/yr. Can.$25 to institutions. National Action Committee on the Status of Women, 57 Mobile Dr., Toronto, Ont. M4A 1H5, Canada. TEL 416-759-5252. FAX 416-757-5370. circ. 3,000. Indexed: Can.Wom.Per.Ind.
  Incorporates: Action Bulletin (ISSN 0832-1418); Which was formerly (until 1985): N A C Memo (ISSN 0712-3183)
  Description: Publication reporting on the status of women and policies that threaten women's rights.

FEMINIST BOOKSTORE NEWS. see *PUBLISHING AND BOOK TRADE*

301.412 **CN**
FEMINIST PERSPECTIVES/PERSPECTIVES FEMINISTES. (Text in English or French) 1985. irreg. (approx. 6/yr.). Can.$3($3) per no. Canadian Research Institute for the Advancement of Women - Institut Canadien de Recherches sur les Femmes, 151 Slater St., Ste. 408, Ottawa, Ont. K1P 5H3, Canada. TEL 613-563-0681. FAX 613-563-0682. (back issues avail.)
  Description: Series of topical, issue-oriented papers exploring women's experience and concerns.

FEMINIST PRAXIS. see *SOCIOLOGY*

305.412 **US**
FEMINIST RENAISSANCE.* bi-m. $10. Feminist Renaissance Publishing Co., c/o Joan Boccafola, 191 Grand St., No. 10, New York, NY 10013. Ed. Fredda S. Pearlson. adv.

301.412 **FR**
FEMME NOUVELLE. 1976. m. Association Francaise et Internationale d'Artisinat d'Art et de Creation, 23 rue des Volontaires, 75015 Paris, France.

300 **CN** ISSN 0838-9446
FEMME PLUS. m. (Quebecor Inc.) Publicor Inc., 7 Chemin Bates, Outremont, Que. H2V 1A6, Canada. TEL 514-270-1100. FAX 514-270-6900. Ed. Sylvie Bergeron. circ. 77,000. Indexed: Pt.de Rep. (1991-).

305.412 **FR** ISSN 0014-9926
FEMME PRATIQUE.* (Text in Belgian and French) 1960. m. 110 F. Editions du Hennin, 34 rue Eugene-Flachat, 75017 Paris, France. TEL 1-42-27-49-49. TELEX 649964. Ed. Michele Butten. adv.; bk.rev.; film rev.; play rev.; bibl.; illus.; pat.; tr.lit.; circ. 380,000. (tabloid format)

305.412 **CN** ISSN 0226-9902
FEMMES D'ACTION. 1970. 5/yr. Can.$12 to individuals; institutions Can.$23. Federation Nationale des Femmes Canadiennes Francaises, 325 Dalhousie Piece 525, Ottawa, Ont. K1N 7G2, Canada. TEL 613-232-5791. Ed. Micheline Piche. adv.; bk.rev.; circ. 2,400. Indexed: Can.Per.Ind., Can.Wom.Per.Ind.

305.412 **BE** ISSN 0014-9950
FEMMES D'AUJOURD'HUI. 1933. w. 290 Fr. (foreign 390 Fr.). Edibel, 9 av. Frans van Kalken, B-1070 Brussels, Belgium. adv.; bk.rev.; film rev.; play rev.; record rev.; bibl.; illus.; mkt.; pat.; tr.mk.; circ. 160,000.

323.4 **CN** ISSN 0705-3851
FEMMES D'ICI. 1977. 5/yr. Can.$15. Association Feminine d'Education et d'Action Sociale, 5999 De Marseille St., Montreal, Que. H1N 1K6, Canada. TEL 514-251-1636. Ed. Huguette Dalpe. adv.; bk.rev.; circ. 30,000.
  Formerly: A.F.E.A.S. Bulletin (ISSN 0044-9458)
  Description: Covers news of the association, profiles of important feminists, reports of congresses and committee activities.

FEMMES EN LITTERATURE. see *LITERATURE*

305.412 **IT**
FEMMINILE. m. San Pantalon 3700, 30100 Venice, Italy. Ed. Luciana Boccardi.

059.3 **SA**
▼**FEMNET.** (Text in Afrikaans, occasionally in English) 1991. q. Femnet: Vroue-organisatie van Transnet - Women's Organization of Transnet, Transnet Park Fase 2, Hillsideweg 8, Parktown 2193, South Africa. Ed. Wilma de Bruin. illus.
  Supersedes: Sasvrou - Sarwoman.

FIGHTING WOMAN NEWS. see *SPORTS AND GAMES*

301.412 **FJ**
FIJI WOMEN. (Text in English) m. George Rubine Ltd., P.O. Box 12511, Suva, Fiji. TEL 313944. Ed. George Matai.

301.412 **PH**
FINA MAGAZINE. 1972. m. P.55. Soller Press & Publishing House, Inc., 45 E. Jacinto St., Expana Extension, Box 121, Quezon City, Philippines. Ed. Franklin Roosevelt C. Cabaluna. adv.; bk.rev.; film rev.; charts; illus.; circ. 30,000.

FINANCIAL WOMAN TODAY. see *BUSINESS AND ECONOMICS — Banking And Finance*

WOMEN'S INTERESTS

FINANCIAL WOMEN'S ASSOCIATION OF NEW YORK NEWSLETTER. see BUSINESS AND ECONOMICS — Banking And Finance

323   SG
FIPPU. 1987. q. Yewwu Yewwi Pour la Liberation des Femmes, Dakar, Senegal. Ed. Fatoumata Sow.

810.8 700   CN   ISSN 0706-3857
FIREWEED; a feminist quarterly. 1978. 4/yr. Can.$4 per no. Fireweed Inc., Box 279, Sta. B, Toronto, Ont. M5T 2W2, Canada. TEL 416-323-9512. Ed.Bd. adv.; bk.rev.; bibl.; film rev.; illus.; circ. 1,500. (back issues avail.) Indexed: Can.Lit.Ind., Can.Wom.Per.Ind.
— BLDSC shelfmark: 3934.411000.

305.412   BE
FLAIR (DUTCH EDITION). 1980. w. 2340 Fr. Tijdschriften Uitgevers Maatschappij-N.V.I.U.M., Jan Blockxstraat 7, 2018 Antwerp, Belgium. (US addr.: Interactive Market System, 55 Fifth Ave., New York, NY 10003) Ed. W. Elbersen. adv.; illus.; circ. 215,000.

301.412   BE
FLAIR (FRENCH EDITION). 1987. w. 2600 Fr. L N P, Av. Brugemann L7 A, 1060 Brussels, Belgium. TEL 32-2-538-8020. adv.; circ. 48,090.

FOCAL POINT. see MEDICAL SCIENCES — Obstetrics And Gynecology

301.412   CN
FOCUS ON WOMEN. 1988. m. Can.$20. Campbell Communications Inc., 1218 Langley St., 3rd Fl., Victoria, B.C. V8W 1W2, Canada. TEL 604-388-7231. FAX 604-383-1140. Ed. Leslie Campbell. adv.; circ. 29,800 (controlled).

FOKUS. see POLITICAL SCIENCE

FORBIDDEN CONNECTIONS; the kinkiest magazine from coast to coast. see MEN'S INTERESTS

FORD FOUNDATION ANNUAL REPORT. see SOCIAL SCIENCES: COMPREHENSIVE WORKS

FORD FOUNDATION REPORT. see SOCIAL SCIENCES: COMPREHENSIVE WORKS

301.412 055.1   IT
FOTOROMANZA. m. (Athena 2001 Coop) Edizioni L.E.T.I. s.r.l., Via E.Q. Visconti 20, 00193 Rome, Italy. TEL 06-314451. Ed. Salvatore Puzzo.

301.412   GW
FRANKFURTER FRAUENBLATT. 1978. bi-m. DM.35. Weibliche Erkenntnisse im Bundesland Hessen e.V., Hamburgerallee 45, 6000 Frankfurt a.M. 90, Germany. TEL 069-7074157. index. (back issues avail.)

301.412   JA
FRAU. 1963. s-m. Kodansha Ltd., International Division, 12-21 Otowa 2-chome, Bunkyo-ku, Tokyo 112, Japan. TEL 03-3945-1111. FAX 03-3943-7815. TELEX J34509 KODANSHA. Ed. Michinori Ihara. circ. 250,000.
    Formerly (until 1991): Young Lady.
    Description: Variety magazine for women 25 to 27 years old.

305.412   AU
FRAU AKTUELL. no.54, 1973. q. Oesterreichische Frauenbewegung, Landesleitung Wien, Falkestr. 3, A-1010 Vienna, Austria. Ed. Barbara Stigmayr. adv.; bk.rev.; charts; illus.
    Formerly (until 1980): Frau in Wien.

305.435   GW
FRAU AKTUELL. 1965. w. DM.52. Westdeutscher Zeitschriften Verlag GmbH, Adlerstr. 22, Postfach 8509, 4000 Duesseldorf 1, Germany. Ed. Dieter Ulrich. adv.; illus.; circ. 600,000.
    Formerly: Frau.

200   GW   ISSN 0016-0148
FRAU IM LEBEN. 1948. m. DM.30. Weltbild - Verlag GmbH, Frauentorstr. 5, D-8900 Augsburg 1, Germany. Ed. Dagmar Kutscher. adv.; bk.rev.; illus.; circ. 330,000.
    Formerly: Katholische Frau.

053   GW   ISSN 0046-497X
FRAU IM SPIEGEL. 1946. w. DM.98.80. Verlag Ehrlich und Sohn KG, Griegstr. 75, Postfach 50 04 25, D-2000 Hamburg 50, Germany. Ed. Klaus Freikamp. illus.; circ. 775,000.

396   GW
FRAU IN UNSERER ZEIT; Materialien zur freiheitlich sozialen Politik. 1971. q. DM.18. (Konrad-Adenauer-Stiftung fuer Politische Bildung und Studienfoerderung e.V.) Ernst Knoth GmbH, Postfach 226, 452 Melle 1, Germany. TEL 05422-2895. FAX 05422-43038. bk.rev.; bibl.; stat.
    Formerly: Frau in der Offenen Gesellschaft (ISSN 0721-6971)

640   GW
FRAU MIT HERZ. 1948. w. DM.1.80 per no. Sonnenverlag GmbH, Bismarckstr. 4, Postfach 720, 7570 Baden-Baden, Germany. Ed. Heinz Gaertner. adv.; circ. 405,399.

301.412   SZ
FRAU OHNE HERZ; eine Zeitschrift fuer Frauen und andere Lesben. 1975. s-a. 20 Fr. for 4 nos. Mattengasse 27, CH-8005 Zurich, Switzerland. circ. 750.

FRAU UND FREIZEIT. see CLOTHING TRADE — Fashions

053.1   GW
FRAU UND KULTUR; Erleben & Gestalten. 1897. s-m. DM.20. Deutscher Verband Frau und Kultur e.V., Winterbergstr. 90, 4973 Vlotho, Germany. TEL 05733-4220. Ed. Irma Hildebrandt. adv.; bk.rev.; illus.; circ. 5,000.
    Formerly: Frauenkulter (ISSN 0016-0245)

305.412   GW   ISSN 0016-0210
DIE FRAU VON HEUTE. 1958. m. free. Ernst Gerdes Verlag, Wakendorfer Str. 61, Posfach 140, 2308 Preetz, Germany. circ. 261,000.

FRAUEN UND FILM. see MOTION PICTURES

376   GW
FRAUENBILDUNGS- UND FERIENHAUS OSTERESCH. 1981. s-a. Frauenbildungs- und Ferienhaus e.V. Osteresch, Zum Osteresch 1, D-4447 Hopsten-Schale, Germany. TEL 05457-1513. (back issues avail.)

301.412   SZ   ISSN 1015-2431
FRAUEZITIG. Short title: FRAZ. 1982. q. 20 Fr. (Europe 32 Fr.; elsewhere 38 Fr.). Postfach 648, CH-8025 Zurich, Switzerland. TEL 01-2727371. adv.; bk.rev.; circ. 4,000.

FREE AZANIA. see POLITICAL SCIENCE

FREE FOCUS. see LITERATURE

329.81   US   ISSN 0272-4367
FREEDOM SOCIALIST; voice of revolutionary feminism. 1966. q. $5 to individuals; institutions $10. Freedom Socialist Party, 5018 Rainier Ave. S., Seattle, WA 98118-1927. TEL 206-722-2453. Ed. Andrea Bauer. bk.rev.; circ. 10,000. (also avail. in microform; back issues avail.) Indexed: Alt.Press Ind., Left Ind. (1984-).

FREUNDIN; Leben im jungen Stil. see HOME ECONOMICS

301.412   CN   ISSN 0824-1961
A FRIEND INDEED. (Text in English or French) 1984. m (10/yr.). $30. A Friend Indeed Publications Inc., Box 515, Place du Parc Station, Montreal, Que. H2W 2P1, Canada. TEL 514-843-5730. FAX 514-843-5681. (US addr.: Box 1710, Champlain, NY 12919-1710) Ed. Janine O'Leary Cobb. bk.rev.; bibl.; cum.index: 1984-87; circ. 4,500. (looseleaf format; back issues avail.) Indexed: Can.Wom.Per.Ind.
    Description: Information, support and exchange for women in menopause or mid-life.

FRIENDLY WOMAN; a journal for exchange of ideas, feelings, hopes and experiences by and among Quaker women. see RELIGIONS AND THEOLOGY — Other Denominations And Sects

FROM THE STATE CAPITALS. WOMEN AND THE LAW. see LAW

FUJIN NO TOMO/WOMEN'S FRIEND. see EDUCATION — Adult Education

FUJINKORON. see LITERATURE

305.412   US
FULL CIRCLE. 1979. m. $10. Box 235, Contoocook, NH 03229. Ed. Elizabeth Alexander. adv.; bk.rev.; circ. 300.

305.412   CC
FUNU/WOMEN. (Text in Chinese) m. $35.90. Funu Zazhishe, 25 Heping Dajie Erduan, Shenyang, Lianning 110002, People's Republic of China. (Dist. in US by: China Books & Periodicals, Inc., 2929 24th St., San Francisco, CA 94110. TEL 415-282-2994)

305.412   CC
FUNU GONGZUO/WOMEN'S AFFAIRS. (Text in Chinese) m. Zhonghua Quanguo Funu Lianhehui - All-China Women's Federation, No. 50, Dengshikou, Beijing 100730, People's Republic of China. TEL 554931. Ed. Wang Shubo.

301.412   CC
FUNU SHENGHUO. (Text in Chinese) m. Y0.80 per no. Funu Shenghuo Zazhishe, 15, Jinshui Lu, Zhengzhou, Henan 450003, People's Republic of China. (Dist. outside China by: China Publications Foreign Trade Corp., P.O. Box 782, Beijing, P.R.C.) Eds. Liu Xuqian, Xu Chunting. adv.
    Description: Covers topics of interest to women. Includes personal ads.

301.412   CC
FUNU ZHI YOU/WOMEN'S FRIEND. (Text in Chinese) m. Heilongjiang Sheng Funu Lianhehui, 11, Ashihe Jie, Nangang-qu, Harbin, Heilongjiang 150001, People's Republic of China. TEL 34059. Ed. Liu Xiangyao.

G F W C CLUBWOMAN. (General Federation of Women's Clubs) see CLUBS

GAEA. see EARTH SCIENCES

GAIA'S GUIDE. see HOMOSEXUALITY

GAME SU. see EDUCATION — Adult Education

LA GAUCHE. see POLITICAL SCIENCE

305.412   CN   ISSN 0704-4550
GAZETTE DES FEMMES. (Text in French) 1979. 6/yr. free. Conseil du Statut de la Femme, 8 rue Cook, 3e Etage, Bur. 300, Quebec, Que. G1R 5J7, Canada. TEL 418-643-4326. FAX 418-643-8926. Ed. Francine Gagnon. bk.rev.; film rev.; circ. 100,000 (controlled). (also avail. on diskette) Indexed: Can.Wom.Per.Ind., Pt.de Rep. (1981-).
    Description: Covers mental and physical health, education, law, labor, economy.

GENERAL COUNCIL OF THE ASSEMBLIES OF GOD. MEMOS; leadership magazine for Women's Ministries Auxiliary. see RELIGIONS AND THEOLOGY — Other Denominations And Sects

GEORGE SAND STUDIES. see LITERATURE

354   GH
GHANA. NATIONAL COUNCIL ON WOMEN AND DEVELOPMENT. ANNUAL REPORT. 1976. a. National Council on Women and Development, Box M.53, Accra, Ghana. TEL 229119. circ. 3,000 (controlled).
    Description: Reports on the activities of the council at all levels as it works to ensure the integration of women in society during the development of the country.

055.1   IT   ISSN 0017-0062
GIOIA. 1938. w. L.104000 (foreign L.260000). Rusconi Editori Associati S.p.A., Servizio Abbonamenti, Via Vitruvio 43, 20124 Milan, Italy. TEL 02-67561. FAX 67562732. Ed. Silvana Giacobini. adv.; bk.rev.; film rev.; play rev.; illus.; circ. 420,000.

055.1   IT
GIOIELLI (MILAN, 1974). 1974. m. L.11800. Rusconi Editori Associati S.p.A., Via Vitruvio 43, 20124 Milan, Italy. Ed. Giuseppe Pardieri. adv.; illus.; circ. 200,000.
    Formerly: Gioielli di Rakam.

GIOVANNI'S ROOM; gay and feminist literature. see HOMOSEXUALITY

WOMEN'S INTERESTS

305.412 — UK
GIRL ABOUT TOWN. 1972. w. Girl About Town Magazine Ltd., 141-143 Drury Lane, London WC2B 5TS, England. FAX 071-836-2618. Ed. Claire Gillman. adv.; bk.rev.; circ. 125,000.

055.1 — IT
GLAMOUR. m. L.48000 (foreign L.96000). Edizioni Conde Nast S.p.A., Piazza Castello 27, 20121 Milan, Italy. FAX 02-870686. Ed. G. D'Annunzio. adv.; circ. 206,618.
Formerly (until 1992): Lei.

300 054.1 — FR
GLAMOUR. 1988. 10/yr. 140 F.($49) (foreign 280 F.)(effective 1991). Publications Conde Nast S.A., 4 place du Palais Bourbon, 75341 Paris Cedex 07, France. (Subscr. to: 60732 Sainte-Genevieve Cedex, France. TEL 16-44-03-44-00; U.S. subscr. to: International Subscriptions Inc., 1305 Paterson Plank Rd., N. Bergen, NJ 07470-1890. TEL 201-867-9381) Ed. Olivier Mayeras. adv.; circ. 107,283.

GLOS POLEK/POLISH WOMENS' VOICE. see *ETHNIC INTERESTS*

305.412 — SI ISSN 0217-765X
GO. 1980. m. S.$73. Times Periodicals Private Ltd., 422 Thomson Rd., Times Industrial Bldg., Singapore 1129, Singapore. TEL 2550011. FAX 2568016. Ed. Sandra Campbell. film rev.; illus.; circ. 20,000.
Supersedes: Fanfare (ISSN 0046-3248)

376 — SW ISSN 0283-2399
GOETEBORG WOMEN'S STUDIES. 1986. irreg. Acta Universitatis Gothoburgensis, P.O. Box 5096, S-402 22 Goeteborg, Sweden.

053 — GW ISSN 0046-6093
DAS GOLDENE BLATT. 1971. w. DM.67.60. Bastei-Verlag Gustav H. Luebbe GmbH und Co., Scheidtbachstr. 23-31, 5060 Bergisch Gladbach 2, Germany. TEL 2202-121-0. Ed. Ernst-Heinz Breil. adv.; bk.rev.; circ. 481,000.

GOLF FOR WOMEN. see *SPORTS AND GAMES — Ball Games*

GOOD HOUSEKEEPING. see *HOME ECONOMICS*

GOOD HOUSEKEEPING. see *HOME ECONOMICS*

GRAPEVINE (SEASIDE). see *HOMOSEXUALITY*

055.1 — IT
GRAZIA. 1938. w. L.130000 (foreign L.232600). Arnoldo Mondadori Editore S.p.A., Casella Postale 1833, 20101 Milan, Italy. TEL 3199345. Ed. Andreina Vanni. illus.; circ. 360,951. (back issues avail.)

GREAT EXPECTATIONS. see *MEDICAL SCIENCES — Obstetrics And Gynecology*

GRECA. see *CLOTHING TRADE — Fashions*

301.412 — II
GRIH SHOBHA. (Editions in Gujarati, Hindi, Marathi) 1979. m. Rs.250 for Hindi ed.; Gujarati ed. Rs.225; Marathi ed. Rs.200. Delhi Press Patra Prakashan Ltd., Delhi Press Bldg., E-3, Jhandewalan Estate, Rani Jhansi Rd., New Delhi 110 055, India. Ed. Vishwa Nath. circ. 370,000.
Description: Includes fiction, recipes, fashion notes and other articles of interest to women of India.

301.412 — GW
GRUENE BLAETTER. 1989. bi-m. Forstr. 93, 7000 Stuttgart 1, Germany. TEL 0711-638140. circ. 7,000.

301.412 — PO
GUIA - REVISTA PRATICA. w. Av. 5 de Outubro 184-8o, Apdo. 1126, Lisbon, Portugal. TEL 01-7939211. FAX 01-768632. TELEX 64991. Ed. Alice Cruz. circ. 80,000.

GUIDE MAGAZINE (SEATTLE). see *HOMOSEXUALITY*

GUIDE TO WOMEN'S ART ORGANIZATIONS; directory for the arts. see *ART*

300 — GV
GUINEENNE. m. Conakry, Guinea.

GULLIVER; German-English Yearbook. see *LINGUISTICS*

305.412 — GR
GYNAIKA. 1950. fortn. $90. E. Ch. Terzopoulos, Ed. & Pub., 7 Frankoglissias St., Paradissos, Maroussi, Athens, Greece. adv.; illus.; circ. 150,000.

301.412 — US
H A N O W HERALD. 1970. m. $3. Houston Area National Organization for Women, Box 66351, Houston, TX 77266. TEL 713-668-9008. bk.rev.; bibl.; circ. 500.
Formerly: Broadside (Houston).

301.412 613.9 — US ISSN 0892-628X
H E R S NEWSLETTER. 1982. q. $20. (Hysterectomy Educational Resources & Services) H E R S Foundation, 422 Bryn Mawr Ave., Bala Cynwyd, PA 19004. TEL 215-667-7757. Ed. Nora W. Coffey. bk.rev.; abstr.; stat.; cum.index; circ. 10,000. (back issues avail.)
Description: Medical and scientific reviews discussing alternatives and consequences of hysterectomies.

HADASSAH HEADLINES. see *ETHNIC INTERESTS*

305.412 — NR
HAPPY HOME. 1971. m. £N6. Punch (Nigeria) Ltd., Kudeti Street, P. M. B. 1204, Ikeja, Lagos, Nigeria. Ed. Sam Amuka. adv.; bk.rev.; illus.; circ. 50,000.
Formerly: Happy Home and Family Health.

305.412 — II
HAREEM. (Text in Urdu) 1931. m. Rs.24. Nasim Book Depot, 25, Latouche Rd., Lucknow 226018, India. Ed. Nasim Inhonvi. adv.; bk.rev.; circ. 2,000.

052 — UK ISSN 0141-0547
HARPERS & QUEEN. 1970. m. £30. National Magazine Co. Ltd., 72 Broadwick St., London W1V 2BP, England. TEL 071-439-5000. FAX 071-437-6886. Ed. Vicki Woods. adv.; bk.rev.; circ. 91,875. (also avail. in microform from UMI; reprint service avail. from UMI)
Incorporates: Queen (ISSN 0033-6009)

HARPER'S BAZAAR EN ESPANOL. see *CLOTHING TRADE — Fashions*

059.92 — UA
HAWA'A/EVE. (Text in Arabic) w. Dar Al-Hilal, 12 Sharia Muhammad Ezz al-Arab, Cairo, Egypt. TELEX 92703. Ed. Suad Ahmad Hilmi. adv.; illus.; circ. 160,837.

346.969 KFH91.W6 — US ISSN 0092-9190
HAWAII. STATE COMMISSION ON THE STATUS OF WOMEN. ANNUAL REPORT. 1972. a. State Commission on the Status of Women, 335 Merchant St., Rm. 253, Honolulu, HI 96813. TEL 808-548-4199. Ed. Kathleen McRae. illus.; circ. 400. Key Title: Annual Report - State of Hawaii. State Commission on the Status of Women.
Description: Sent to government offices, the Governor and Lt. Governor, and legislators.

HE - SHE DIRECTORY. see *MEN'S INTERESTS*

HEADWAY. see *SPORTS AND GAMES*

HEALTH CARE FOR WOMEN, INTERNATIONAL. see *WOMEN'S HEALTH*

HEALTHSHARING; a Canadian women's health quarterly. see *WOMEN'S HEALTH*

HEARTLAND CRITIQUES. see *LITERARY AND POLITICAL REVIEWS*

050 — GW
HEIM UND WELT. 1948. w. DM.124.80. Zeitungs- und Zeitschriften-Verlag Heim und Welt, Am Jungferplan 3, 3000 Hannover 1, Germany. TEL 0511-855757. FAX 0511-854603. Eds. H.G. Bruenemann, J.H. Wuerger. adv.; illus.; circ. 260,000.

305.412 — DK
HENDES VERDEN. 1937. w. DKK 509.60. Gutenberghus Bladene, Vognmagergade 11, 1148 Copenhagen K, Denmark. Ed. Eva Ravn. adv.; circ. 125,000.

HER OWN WORDS; women's history & literature media. see *LITERATURE*

305.412 — SI ISSN 0046-7278
HER WORLD. 1960. m. S.$132. Times Periodicals Private Ltd., 422 Thomson Rd., Times Industrial Bldg., Singapore 1129, Singapore. TEL 2550011. FAX 2568016. Ed. Tan Wang Joo. adv.; bk.rev.; illus.; circ. 60,000.

301.412 — MY
HER WORLD. (Text in English) m. Berita Publishing Snd. Bhd., 22 Jalan Liku, 59100 Kuuala Lumpur, Malaysia. TEL 03-2744322. FAX 03-2740605. Ed. Foong Peto. circ. 30,000.

052 — SI ISSN 0217-1058
HER WORLD ANNUAL. 1976. a. S.$5. Times Periodicals Private Ltd., 422 Thomson Rd., Times Industrial Bldg., Singapore 1129, Singapore. TEL 2550011. FAX 2568016. adv.; bk.rev.; illus.; circ. 30,000.

301.4157 613.7 — US
HERA; Binghamton's women's newspaper. 1981. 10/yr. $6 or donation. Women's Center, Box 354, Binghamton, NY 13902. TEL 607-724-3462. Ed. Teri Walters. adv.; bk.rev.; circ. 1,000. (tabloid format; back issues avail.)
Description: Regional feminist news and analysis.

305.412 — SW ISSN 0018-0912
HERTHA. 1914. bi-m. SEK 150. Fredrika-Bremer Foerbundet, Hornsgatan 52, S-117 21 Stockholm, Sweden. Eds. Carin Mannberg-Zackari, Anita Widen. adv.; bk.rev.; bibl.; illus.; circ. 11,000.

HIGHER EDUCATION OPPORTUNITIES FOR MINORITIES AND WOMEN: ANNOTATED SELECTIONS. see *EDUCATION — Higher Education*

301.412 — II
▼**HIGHLAND BOOKNEWS**; book review magazine. (Text in English and Malayalam) 1990. q. Rs.20($5) Women's Alliance for Publishing, Cheerooth Building, Kodimatha, Kottayam 686 039, India. Ed. Nicyk Runnoose. circ. 2,000. (back issues avai.)

301.435 — TS
HIYA. (Includes children's supplement: Qanadil) 1978. m. Dar al-Suhuf al-Wahda, Majallat Hiya, P.O. Box 26264, Abu Dhabi, United Arab Emirates. TEL 330115. FAX 211386. TELEX 22596. Ed. Mamduh Taha.
Formerly: Samra'a.
Description: Woman's magazine with a family focus.

056.1 — EC ISSN 0018-3210
HOGAR; la revista de la familia ecuatoriana. 1964. m. $50. Editores Nacionales, Aguirre 724 y Boyaca, Apdo. 1239, Guayaquil, Ecuador. TEL 4-327-200. TELEX 3423. Ed. Rosa A. Alvarado. circ. 35,000 (controlled).

056.1 — SP ISSN 0046-7723
HOGAR Y MODA. 1909. w. $64. Hogar y la Moda, S.A., Diputacion, 211, 08011 Barcelona, Spain. TEL 254 10 04. FAX 254-13-22. Ed. Dona Maria Asuncion Baille Brossa. adv.; film rev.; circ. 71,123.

305.412 640 — UK
HOME AND COUNTRY. 1919. m. £9.84. National Federation of Women's Institutes, 104 New Kings Road, Fulham, London SW6 4LY, England. TEL 071-371-5777. FAX 071-736-4061. Ed. Penny Kitchen. adv.; bk.rev.; circ. 100,000. (back issues avail.)

640 301.412 — US
HOME COOKING. 1983. m. $9.95. House of White Birches Publishing, 306 E. Parr Rd., Berne, IN 46711. TEL 219-589-8741. Ed. Judi Merkel. adv.; bk.rev.; charts; illus.; circ. 61,810. (back issues avail.)
Formerly: Women's Circle Home Cooking (ISSN 0195-2439)
Description: Contains 1,000 recipes each year, swaps, contests, low-budget meal ideas and foreign, exotic dishes.

640 — US
HOMEMAKERS NETWORK NEWSLETTER. 1986. bi-m. $4.75. Homemakers Network, c/o Lois Altenkirch, Ed., 340 Caldwell Ave., Paterson, NJ 07501. adv.; bk.rev.; circ. 175.
Description: Offers tips on child care and homemaking to expectant mothers.

WOMEN'S INTERESTS 4845

051 US
HOMESTEAD HOTLINE. 1979. bi-m. $20. 720 Morrow Ave., Clayton, NJ 08312. TEL 609-881-0319. Ed. Manuel Castlewitz. adv.; circ. 6,000.

HOOKS AND LINES. see SPORTS AND GAMES — Outdoor Life

305.412 US
HOT FLASH. 1981. q. $25. National Action Forum for Midlife and Older Women, Box 816, Stonybrook, NY 11790-0609. Ed. Jane Porcino. bk.rev.; circ. 2,000. (back issues avail.)

HOT LETTERS. see MEN'S INTERESTS

305.2 US ISSN 0747-8887
ML82
HOT WIRE; the journal of women's music and culture. 1984. 3/yr. $17 to individuals (Europe $27; Asia & Africa $31); institutions $25. Empty Closet Enterprises, 5210 N. Wayne, Chicago, IL 60640. TEL 312-769-9009. Ed. Toni L. Armstrong, Jr. adv.; circ. 15,000. (back issues avail.) Indexed: Can.Wom.Per.Ind., Music Artic.Guide.
  Description: Focusing on feminist - lesbian music and culture movement; each 64 page issue includes a stereo recording.

HOUSEWIFE - WRITER'S FORUM. see LITERATURE — Poetry

640 JA
HOUSEWIVES AND LIVING. (Text in Japanese) 1946. m. 8380 Yen. Shufu-to-Seikatsusha Ltd., 5-7, 3-chome, Kyobashi, Chuo-ku, Tokyo 104, Japan. Ed. Hiroaki Watari.

HOUSEWIVES' HANDY HINTS, SMALL BUSINESSWOMAN'S NEWSLETTER. see NEEDLEWORK

HUMAN SEXUALITY; opposing viewpoints sources. see PSYCHOLOGY

HUMAN SEXUALITY. see BIOLOGY — Physiology

HUMANSPACE BOOKS. NEWSLETTER. see HOMOSEXUALITY

305.412 US ISSN 0882-7907
HQ1101
HURRICANE ALICE; a feminist quarterly. 1983. 4/yr. $12. Hurricane Alice Foundation, 207 Lind Hall, 207 Church St., S.E., Minneapolis, MN 55455. TEL 612-625-1834. Ed.Bd. adv.; bk.rev.; circ. 1,000.
  Description: Feminist prose, poetry and artwork.

058.69 IC ISSN 0018-7984
HUSFREYJAN. 1949. q. ISK 1500($12) Kvenfelagasamband Islands - Union of Women's Societies, Hallveigarstoedum, Tungotu 14, Reykjavik, Iceland. Ed. Greta E. Palsdottir. adv.; bk.rev.; cum.index; circ. 5,200.

640 NO ISSN 0018-8034
HUSMORBLADET. 1886. m. NOK 20. Norges Husmorforbund, Oskarsgate 43, 0258 Oslo 2, Norway. TEL 02-55-79-07. Ed. Barbro Sveen. adv.; bk.rev.; film rev.; play rev.; illus.; circ. 47,000. (back issues avail.)

301.412 GW
I A F - INFORMATION. 1975. q. DM.17 (foreign DM.20). (Interessengemeinschaft der mit Auslaendern Verheirateten Frauen e.V.) Verband Bi-Nationaler Familien und Partnerschaften, Kasseler Str. 1A, 6000 Frankfurt a.M. 90, Germany. bk.rev.; circ. 2,000. (back issues avail.)

I C A E NEWS. (International Council for Adult Education) see EDUCATION — Adult Education

301 US
I C R W OCCASIONAL PAPER SERIES. 1984. irreg. price varies. International Center for Research on Women, 1717 Massachusetts Ave., N.W., Ste. 302., Washington, DC 20036. FAX 202-797-0020. (back issues avail.)

I L G A BULLETIN. (International Lesbian and Gay Association) see HOMOSEXUALITY

376 UN
I N S T R A W NEWS. (Text in English, French and Spanish) 1984. s-a. free. International Research and Training Institute for the Advancement of Women, P.O. Box 21747, Santo Domingo, Dominican Republic. TEL 809 685-2111. FAX 809-685-2117. TELEX 326-4280 WRASD. bk.rev.; circ. 14,500.
  Description: Presents trends, disseminates training materials, and promotes networking for women concerning development issues at a global level.

I W F A YEARBOOK. (International Women's Fishing Association) see SPORTS AND GAMES — Outdoor Life

052 GH
IDEAL WOMAN/OBAA SIMA; the magazine for the woman who looks ahead. (Text in English) 1971. q. NC.9000($24) Teiba Publications Ltd., Box 5737, Accra, Ghana. Ed. Kate Abbam. adv.; bk.rev.; illus.; circ. 10,000.

301.412 GW
IGITTE; Dortmunder Frauenzeitung. 1987. bi-m. DM.12. Igitte e.V., Adlerstr. 81, 4600 Dortmund 1, Germany. TEL 0231-162366. circ. 2,000.

IMPETUS. see ART

305.412 GW ISSN 0020-0352
INFORMATIONEN FUER DIE FRAU. 1952. m. DM.34($6) Deutscher Frauenrat - National Council of German Women's Organizations, Simrockstr. 5, 5300 Bonn 1, Germany. TEL 0228-223008. FAX 0228-218819. Ed. Hanne E. Pollmann. bk.rev.; index; circ. 2,500. (tabloid format) Indexed: Dok.Arbeitsmed.

640 GW
INGRID. 1977. m. DM.2.80 per no. Sonnenverlag GmbH, Lichtentaler Allee 10, Postfach 720, 7570 Baden-Baden, Germany. Ed. M. Muesch. adv.

INITIATIVES. see EDUCATION — School Organization And Administration

320 AT
INK W E L. 1978. bi-m. Aus.$45 to individuals; institutions Aus.$40. Women's Electoral Lobby A.C.T., 3 Lobelia St., O'Connor, A.C.T. 2601, Australia. Ed. Ann Wentworth. adv.; bk.rev.; circ. 450.
  Formerly: Women's Electoral Lobby. National Bulletin.
  Description: Provides discussion of issues from a feminist perspective.

INTENSIVE CARING UNLIMITED. see CHILDREN AND YOUTH — About

396 US ISSN 0538-2912
INTER-AMERICAN COMMISSION OF WOMEN. NEWS BULLETIN. Spanish edition: Inter-American Commission of Women. Noticiero (ISSN 0538-2920) 1953. irreg., latest no.33. Organization of American States, Department of Publications, 1889 F St., N.W., Washington, DC 20006. TEL 703-941-1617.

396 US ISSN 0538-2920
INTER-AMERICAN COMMISSION OF WOMEN. NOTICIERO. English edition: Inter-American Commission of Women. News Bulletin (ISSN 0538-2912) 1951. irreg., latest no. 33. Organization of American States, 1889 F St., N.W., Washington, DC 20006. TEL 703-941-1617.

INTERNATIONAL FASHION GROUP. ANNUAL REPORT. see CLOTHING TRADE — Fashions

INTERNATIONAL FASHION GROUP. BULLETIN. see CLOTHING TRADE — Fashions

INTERNATIONAL FASHION GROUP. NEWSLETTER. see CLOTHING TRADE — Fashions

INTERNATIONAL SOCIETY OF WOMEN AIRLINE PILOTS NEWSLETTER. see AERONAUTICS AND SPACE FLIGHT

301 FR
INTIMITE. 1949. w. 2 rue des Italiens, 75009 Paris, France. Ed. Antoine de Clermont-Tonnerre. circ. 509,622.

301.412 IT
IO E IL MIO BAMBINO. m. Eurotrend S.p.A., Viale Regina Giovanna 39, 20129 Milan, Italy. TEL 02-29405. Ed. Gaetano Manti.

301.412 IT
IO E MIO FIGLIO. m. Publibaby S.r.l., Via Volta 35-37-39, 20090 Cusago (MI), Italy. TEL 02-9019951. FAX 02-9019953. Ed. Emilio Terzagli.

301.412 US
IOWA IMAGE. 1989. q. Kay Baughman, Ed. & Pub., Box 744, Centerville, OH 52544. TEL 515-437-1143. adv.; circ. 7,000.
  Description: Provides advice on the spiritual, social, mental, financial and physical beauty growth of women using the editor's five-point concept.

IOWA WOMAN. see LITERATURE

301.412 808.8 US ISSN 0896-1301
IRIS: A JOURNAL ABOUT WOMEN. 1980. s-a. $15. University of Virginia, Women's Center, Box 323 HSC, University of Virginia, Charlottesville, VA 22903. TEL 804-924-4500. Eds. Rebecca Hyman. adv.; bk.rev.; film rev.; play rev.; circ. 4,000. (back issues avail.) Indexed: Wom.Stud.Abstr.
  Description: Covers the following by and about women: fiction, poetry, humor and art; also includes information about social, ethnic, and international affairs as they pertain to women.

305.412 296 200 IS
ISHA L'ISHA NEWSLETTER. (Text in Arabic, English, Hebrew) 1973. bi-m. Isha L'isha Haifa Feminist Center, P.O.B. 3610, Haifa, Israel. bk.rev.; circ. 1,000.
  Former titles: Isha l'Isha - Woman to Woman; (until 1984): Haifa Feminist Circle. Newsletter; (until 1977): Haifa Feminist Movement. Journal; (until 1974): Nilham.
  Description: News of current and upcoming projects and activities, writings on women's issues, and news of the lesbian-feminist community.

ISHRAQAT JEEL. see RELIGIONS AND THEOLOGY — Islamic

301.412 IS
ISRAEL WOMEN'S NETWORK. NEWSLETTER. (Text in English) q. $15. Israel Women's Network, P.O. Box 3171, Jerusalem 91031, Israel. TEL 02-690358.

301.412 IS
ISRAEL WOMEN'S NETWORK. YIDION. (Text in Hebrew) q. $15. Israel Women's Network, P.O. Box 3171, Jerusalem 91031, Israel. TEL 02-690358.

ISSUES IN REPRODUCTIVE AND GENETIC ENGINEERING; journal of international feminist analysis. see BIOLOGY — Genetics

ITHACA WOMEN'S ANTHOLOGY. see LITERATURE — Poetry

059.927 915.3 QA
AL-JAWHARA. 1977. m. Al-Ahd Establishment for Journalism, Printing and Publications Ltd., P.O. Box 2531, Doha, Qatar. TEL 414575. TELEX 4920. Ed. Abdullah Yousuf al-Hussaini. circ. 8,000.

JENNY CRAIG'S YOUR BODY, YOUR HEALTH. see PHYSICAL FITNESS AND HYGIENE

JETZT; Ordensfrauen, Ordensleben, Kirche - Information, Konfrontation. see RELIGIONS AND THEOLOGY — Roman Catholic

JIATING/FAMILY. see HOME ECONOMICS

JOURNAL OF COUPLES THERAPY. see PSYCHOLOGY

305.412 340 331 US ISSN 0362-062X
KF478.A45
JOURNAL OF REPRINTS OF DOCUMENTS AFFECTING WOMEN. Variant title: Journal of Reprints Affecting Women's Rights & Opportunities. 1975. q. $40. Today Publications and News Service, Inc., 621 National Press Building, Washington, DC 20045. TEL 202-628-6663. Ed. Myra E. Barrer.

UVWXYZ

WOMEN'S INTERESTS

305.412 200 320   US   ISSN 0888-5621
JOURNAL OF WOMEN AND RELIGION. 1981. a. $15. Center for Women and Religion, Graduate Theological Union, 2400 Ridge Rd., Berkeley, CA 94709. TEL 510-649-2490. FAX 510-649-1417. bk.rev.; circ. 800. (back issues avail.) Indexed: Rel.Ind.One.
   Description: Focuses on transformation and theological education to stop sexism against women.

JOYFUL WOMAN. see *RELIGIONS AND THEOLOGY — Protestant*

305.412   JA
JUNON. (Text in Japanese) 1973. m. 6360 Yen. Shufu-to-Seikatsu Sha Ltd., 5-7, Kyobashi 3-chome, Chuo-ku, Tokyo 104, Japan. TEL 03-3563-5131. FAX 03-3567-7893. Ed. Junichi Hamamoto.
   Description: Covers television and entertainment.

JURISFEMME. see *LAW*

331.4   CN
▼**JUST WAGES**; a bulletin on wage discrimination and pay equity. 1991. q. Can.$10 to individuals; institutions Can.$15; foreign Can.$18. Women's Resource Centre, 101-2245 West Broadway, Vancouver, B.C. V6K 2E4, Canada. (Co-sponsor: Trade Union Research Bureau) Ed. Debra J. Lewis. illus.; stat.

323.4 323.46   IO
K O W A N I NEWS. (Text in English) 3/yr. Kongres Wanita Indonesia - Indonesian Women's Congress, Jl. Imam Bonjol 58, Jakarta Pusat, Indonesia. TEL 364921. Ed.Bd.

KALLIOPE; a journal of women's art. see *LITERATURE*

305.412   II
KALUVABALA; women's fortnightly. fortn. Andhra Patrika, 14-14-21 Mallikarjuna Rao St., Gandhinagar, Vijayawada 520 003, India. TEL 61247. adv.

KELUARGA. see *HOME ECONOMICS*

305.412   VE
KENA.* w. Plaza del Panteon, Torre de la Prensa, piso 11, Caracas, Venezuela. Ed. Maria E. Matheus. circ. 40,000.

KICK IT OVER. see *POLITICAL SCIENCE*

346.013   CN   ISSN 0317-9095
KINESIS; news about women that's not in the dailies. 1972. 10/yr. Can.$20 to individuals (foreign Can.$28); institutions Can.$45 (foreign Can.$53). Vancouver Status of Women, 1720 Grant St., Ste. 301, Vancouver, B.C. V5L 2Y6, Canada. TEL 604-255-5499. Ed. Nancy Pollak. adv.; bk.rev.; film rev.play rev.; circ. 2,500. Indexed: Alt.Press Ind.
   Description: Covers news from a feminist angle. Analyzes government policies, feminist theories and debates within the women's movement.

301.412   US
KINHEART CONNECTION. 1982. 5/yr. membership. Kinheart, 2214 Ridge Ave., Evanston, IL 60201. TEL 708-491-1103. Ed. Mary Jo Osterman. bk.rev.; circ. 1,000.
   Formerly: Kinheart Quarterly.
   Description: Includes calendar of programs groups and special events; news items and an educational article about homophobia or heterosexism.

053.931   NE   ISSN 0023-2289
KNIP. 1969. m. fl.63. Uitgeverij Spaarnestad B.V., Europalaan 93, 3526 KP Utrecht, Netherlands. TEL 030-822511. FAX 030-898388. Ed. Julia Martens. adv.; circ. 197,000.

057.85   PL   ISSN 0023-2548
KOBIETA I ZYCIE. (Supplement avail.: Wykroje i Wzory) 1946. w. $114. Dziennikarska Spoldzielnia Wydawnicza, Ul. Koszykowa 6A, 00-564 Warsaw, Poland. TEL 48-22-214856. (Subscr. to: C.H.S. Ars Polona, 00-950 Warsaw, Poland) Ed. Anna Szymanska-Kwiatkowska. adv.; bk.rev.; illus.; circ. 471,000.

305.412   DK   ISSN 0900-2855
KONKYLIEN. 1977. 10/yr. DKK 80. Soemandskoneforeningen af 1976, c/o Jette Haugaard, Sandbjergvej 7, 3660 Stenloese, Denmark. Ed. Birgit Kjeldsen. adv.; bk.rev.; circ. 1,200.

KOREAN WOMEN. see *POLITICAL SCIENCE*

KOTILIESI. see *HOME ECONOMICS*

301.412   IO
KOWANI NEWS. (Editions in English and Indonesian) 1986 (English ed.). irreg. Kongres Wanita Indonesia - Indonesian Women's Congress, Jl. Imam Bonjol 58, Jakarta Pusat, Indonesia. TEL 21-364921. Ed. Kuraisin Sunhadi (English ed.).
   Formerly: Indonesian Women's Congress. Bulletin - Kongres Wanita Indonesia. Berita.

KVINDER, KVINDER. see *HOMOSEXUALITY*

301.412   DK   ISSN 0108-3961
KVINDESTUDIER VED A U C. AARBOG. (Aalborg Universitetscenter) (Also forms part of: Serie om Kvindeforskning) 1982. a. DKK 132. (Institut for Samfundsudvikling og Planaegning) Aalborg Universitetsforlag, Aalborg, Denmark. illus.

058.82   NO   ISSN 0023-5857
KVINNER OG KLAER/WOMEN & CLOTHES. 1873. w. NOK 1722. A-S Allers Familie-Journal, Persveien 20, Box 250, Oslo 5, Norway. Ed. June Traennes Hansen. adv.; illus.; circ. 97,006.

305.412   SW
KVINNOBULLETINEN. 1970. 4/yr. SEK 130. Grupp 8, Stockholm, Snickarbacken 10, 11139 Stockholm, Sweden. Ed. Si Felicetti. bk.rev.; circ. 2,000.

301.412   CY
KYPRIA/CYPRIOT WOMAN. (Text in Greek) 1984. bi-m. P.O. Box 8506, Nicosia, Cyprus. Ed. Marco Karayianni. circ. 6,000.
   Description: Greek-Cypriot woman's interest review.

L A PARENT; magazine for Southern California families. see *CHILDREN AND YOUTH — About*

L A R C NEWSLETTER. (Radcliffe College, Lesbian Alumni) see *HOMOSEXUALITY*

L E A F LINES. (Women's Legal Education and Action Fund) see *LAW*

L F L REPORTS:. (Libertarians for Life) see *BIRTH CONTROL*

L I P NEWSLETTER. (Lesbian Interest Press) see *HOMOSEXUALITY*

301   US
LABYRINTH; the Philadelphia Women's newspaper. 1983. m. $15. Labyrinth, Inc., 4722 Baltimore Ave., Philadelphia, PA 19143. TEL 215-724-6181. adv.; bk.rev.; film rev.; circ. 10,000. (tabloid format; back issues avail.)
   Description: Coverage of women's issues, news of feminist activities, monthly feminist movie reviews and creative writing by women.

051   US   ISSN 0023-7124
AP2
LADIES HOME JOURNAL (INKPRINT EDITION). 1883. m. $19.97. Meredith Corporation, Special Interest Publications, 1716 Locust St., Des Moines, IA 50336. TEL 515-284-3000. (Or: 100 Park Ave., New York, NY 10017-5599) Ed. Myrna Blyth. adv.; illus.; tr.lit.; circ. 5,118,000. (also avail. in microform from UMI) Indexed: Abr.R.G., Consum.Ind., Hlth.Ind., Mag.Ind., R.G., TOM.
●Also available online. Vendor(s): DIALOG.
   Description: Contains women's issues, cooking recipes, consumer tips, and features about family life.

051   US
▼**LADIES' HOME JOURNAL PARENT'S DIGEST.** 1991. s-a. Meredith Corporation, 1716 Locust St., Des Moines, IA 50336. TEL 515-284-3000.

301.412   US
LADY; the international magazine for today's woman. q. Vivian Seton, Ed. & Pub., 3535 Olympic St., Silver Spring, MD 20906. TEL 301-949-6949. circ. 50,000.

053.1 305.42   GW   ISSN 0343-3366
LADY INTERNATIONAL; die Zeitschrift fuer Damen heute. (Text in German) 1952. 4/yr. DM.45. Terra Verlag GmbH, Neuhauser Str. 21, Postfach 102144, 7750 Konstanz, Germany. TEL 07531-54031. FAX 07531-50083. Ed. Michael R. Schade. adv.; bk.rev.; illus.; circ. 60,000. (tabloid format)
   Formerly: Lady (ISSN 0023-7175)

051   US   ISSN 0023-7191
LADY'S CIRCLE. 1963. bi-m. $11.97. Lopez Publications, Inc., 152 Madison Ave., Ste. 905, New York, NY 10016. TEL 212-689-3933. FAX 212-725-2239. Ed. Mary F. Bemis. adv.; bk.rev.; illus.; circ. 200,000.

305 778   US
LADYSLIPPER CATALOG AND RESOURCE GUIDE OF RECORDS, TAPES, COMPACT DISCS AND VIDEOS BY WOMEN. 1976. a. free. Ladyslipper, Inc., Box 3124, Durham, NC 27715. TEL 919-682-5601. Ed. Laurie Fuchs. adv.; film rev.; index; circ. 250,000. (back issues avail.)

301.412   IS
LAISHA/FOR WOMEN. (Text in Hebrew) 1946. w. Nitzan Ltd., 35 Bnei Brak St., Tel Aviv 66021, Israel. TEL 03-371464. FAX 03-378071. Ed. Zvi Elgat.

301.412 613.7   IT
LAPIS; percorsi della reflessione femminile. no.10, Dec. 1990. q. L.35000 (foreign L.64000). Gruppo Editoriale Faenza Editrice S.p.A., Via Pier. de Crescenzi, 44, 48018 Faenza RA, Italy. TEL 0546-663488. FAX 0546-660440. TELEX 550387 EDITFA I. Ed. Lea Melandri. adv.; circ. 4,000. (back issues avail.)

LAVENDER MORNING; a lesbian newsletter for lesbians. see *HOMOSEXUALITY*

LAVENDER PRAIRIE NEWS. see *HOMOSEXUALITY*

LAW & WOMEN SERIES. see *LAW*

305.412   US   ISSN 0897-0149
HQ1059.4
LEAR'S. 1988. m. $21. Lear Publishing, Inc., 655 Madison Ave., New York, NY 10021. TEL 212-888-0007. FAX 212-888-0087. Ed. Frances Lear. adv.; illus.; circ. 450,000.
   Description: Features information on health and fitness, beauty, fashion, education, career, money, relationships and cultural interests.

305.412   IT
LEGGERE DONNA. 1980. bi-m. L.50000. Centro Documentazione Donna, Via Ticchioni 38-1, 44100 Ferrara, Italy. TEL 0532-53186. FAX 0532-92668. Ed. Luciana Tufani. adv.; bk.rev.; circ. 5,000.

305.412   IS
LEISHA. w. Beit Yediot Acharanot, Derech Petach Tikva 138, Tel Aviv, Israel. TEL 03-378071.

LESBENRUNDBRIEF. see *HOMOSEXUALITY*

LESBENSTICH; das Lesbenmagazin fuer den aufrechten Gang. see *HOMOSEXUALITY*

LESBIAN CENTER NEWS. see *HOMOSEXUALITY*

LESBIAN COMMUNITY NEWS. see *HOMOSEXUALITY*

LESBIAN CONNECTION. see *HOMOSEXUALITY*

LESBIAN ETHICS. see *HOMOSEXUALITY*

305.4157   US
LESBIAN FEMINIST.* m. $3. c/o Lesbian Feminist Liberation, 2170 Broadway, No. 2243, New York, NY 10024-6642.

LESBIAN NEWS. see *HOMOSEXUALITY*

LESBIANS RISING. see *HOMOSEXUALITY*

LETRAS FEMENINAS. see *LITERATURE*

LEX VITAE; the pro-life legislation and litigation summary. see *LAW*

WOMEN'S INTERESTS

053.932 054.1   BE   ISSN 0024-175X
LIBELLE. (Editions in Dutch, French) 1945. w. 2340 Fr. Tijdschriften Uitgevers Maatschappij N.V.I.U.M., Jan Blockxstraat 7, B-2018 Antwerp, Belgium. (US addr.: Interactive Market Systems, 55 Fifth Ave., New York, NY 10003) Ed. M. De Borger. adv.; illus.; circ. 210,000.

LIFE DOCKET. see *LAW*

305.412 296   US   ISSN 0146-2334
BM729.W6
LILITH. 1976. q. $24 to individuals; institutions $20. Lilith Publications, Inc., 250 W. 57th St., Ste. 2432, New York, NY 10107. Ed. Leslie Margulies. adv.; bk.rev.; circ. 10,000. (also avail. in microfilm from UMI) **Indexed:** Ind.Jew.Per., Mid.East: Abstr.& Ind., Wom.Stud.Abstr. (1976-).
Description: Directed to Jewish women, featuring editorials, fiction, poetry, news.

305.412 323.4   UK
LINK (LONDON, 1973). 1973. q. £2.20. Communist Party of Great Britain, 16 St. John St., London EC1M 4AL, England. Ed.Bd. bk.rev.; circ. 2,200. (back issues avail.)

301.412 284   CN   ISSN 0380-4100
LINK & VISITOR; a magazine for Baptist women. 1927. 9/yr. Can.$7 to groups, individuals $10; foreign $14. Baptist Women's Missionary Society of Ontario & Quebec, 217 St. George St., Toronto, Ont. M5R 2M2, Canada. TEL 416-922-5163. Ed. Esther Barnes. adv.; bk.rev.; index; circ. 6,000. (back issues avail.)
Description: Encourages Christian women to create a difference in their world.

051   US   ISSN 0893-8083
LISTEN REAL LOUD; news of women's liberation worldwide. 1979. q. donation. American Friends Service Committee, Inc., Nationwide Women's Program, 1501 Cherry St., Philadelphia, PA 19102. TEL 215-241-7051. FAX 215-864-0104. bk.rev.; circ. 3,000.
Description: Promotes communication and debate among regional, national, overseas staff, and committee members; expands dialogue with other movements involved with AFSC.

301.412   SA
LIVING AND LOVING. m. R.36.60. Republican Press (Pty) Ltd., Box 32083, Mobeni 4060, Natal, South Africa. Ed. Angela Still. circ. 105,000.
Description: Successful parenting for first-time mothers.

LONG ISLAND PARENTING NEWS. see *CHILDREN AND YOUTH — About*

305.412 323.4   NE   ISSN 0165-8042
LOVER; literatuuroverzicht voor de vrouwenbeweging. 1974. q. fl.28.50. Stichting Internationaal Informatiecentrum voor de Vrouwenbeweging - International Information Center and Archive for the Women's Movement, Keizersgracht 10, 1015 CN Amsterdam, Netherlands. TEL 020-277054. FAX 020-233855. adv.; bk.rev.; circ. 3,000.

LOVING MORE. see *SOCIOLOGY*

305.412   CN   ISSN 0704-7886
LUNDI. 1976. w. Can.$69. Quebecor Inc., 7 Chemin Bates, Outrement, Que. H2V 1A6, Canada. TEL 514-270-1100. FAX 514-270-6900. Ed. Michel Choiniere. adv.; illus.; circ. 106,000.

LUST & GRATIE; lesbisch cultureel universeel tijdschrift. see *HOMOSEXUALITY*

LUTHERAN WOMAN TODAY. see *RELIGIONS AND THEOLOGY — Protestant*

LUTHERAN WOMAN'S QUARTERLY; knowing Christ and making Him known. see *RELIGIONS AND THEOLOGY — Protestant*

301.412   GW
LYDIA; die christliche Zeitschrift fur die Frau. 1986. q. DM.17.50($11.65) Lydia Verlag GmbH, Postfach 1222, 6334 Asslar, Germany. TEL 06443-3011. FAX 06443-1707. Ed. Elizabeth Mittelstaedt. (back issues avail.)
Description: Themes covering the interest of Christian women.

M A N A. (Mexican American Women's National Association) see *ETHNIC INTERESTS*

M I D S NEWSLETTER. (Miscarriage, Infant Death, and Stillbirth) see *MEDICAL SCIENCES — Obstetrics And Gynecology*

301.412 618   US
M O M MAGAZINE. 1984. q. $12. Mothers and Others for Midwives, Box 1068, Sugarloaf, CA 92386. TEL 714-585-4175. Ed. Jeriann Fairman. adv.; bk.rev.; circ. 2,000.
Description: Promotes women's choices in health care. Offers alternative birth and parenting information.

305.412   US   ISSN 8756-9965
M O T C'S NOTEBOOK. 1960. q. $15 (foreign $20). National Organization of Mothers of Twins Clubs, Inc., Box 23185, Albuquerque, NM 87192-1188. TEL 505-275-0955. FAX 505-293-8129. Ed. Martha Eicker. adv.; bk.rev.; illus.; circ. 12,000. (tabloid format)
Description: Articles and news to increase the understanding of child development and rearing, especially relating to multiple births.

M S U U NEWSLETTER: GLEANINGS. (Ministerial Sisterhood Unitarian Universalist) see *RELIGIONS AND THEOLOGY — Protestant*

051   US   ISSN 0024-8908
TT500   CODEN: MCCAEQ
McCALL'S. 1876. m. $15.97. McCall's Magazine (Subsidiary of: New York Times Company, Inc.), 110 5th Ave., New York, NY 10011. TEL 800-777-0333. (Subscr. to: P.O. Box 3178, Harlan, IA 51537-0369) Ed. Kate White. adv.; film rev.; illus.; circ. 4,600,000. (also avail. in microform from UMI) **Indexed:** Hlth.Ind., Mag.Ind., Media Rev.Dig., PMR, R.G., TOM.
—BLDSC shelfmark: 5413.417000.
Description: Emphasis on women's home interests: cooking, decorating, and parenting. Includes information and how-to-tips on beauty, health and fashion.

McCALL'S SILVER. see *GERONTOLOGY AND GERIATRICS*

640   US   ISSN 0024-9394
AP2
MADEMOISELLE. 1935. m. $15. Conde Nast Publications Inc., Mademoiselle Magazine, 350 Madison Ave., New York, NY 10017-3704. TEL 212-489-8585. FAX 212-880-8289. Ed. Amy Levin Cooper. adv.; bk.rev.; illus.; circ. 1,298,000. (also avail. in microform from UMI; reprint service avail. from UMI) **Indexed:** Biog.Ind., Consum.Ind., Hlth.Ind., Mag.Ind., Media Rev.Dig., R.G., TOM.
Description: Directed toward young women; includes articles on fashion, beauty, travel, self-help, how-to, travel; also includes fiction excepts.

MADISON GAY LESBIAN RESOURCE CENTER. DIRECTORY; a guide to organizations serving Madison's gay/lesbian/bisexual community. see *BUSINESS AND ECONOMICS — Trade And Industrial Directories*

301.412 649   IT
MADRE. 1988. m. L.35000. Societa Edizioni Madre, Bassiche 47/G, 25122 Brescia, Italy. Ed. Angelo Onger. adv.; bk.rev.; circ. 100,000.

059.94   HU   ISSN 0029-0963
MAGYAR NOK LAPJA. 1949. w. $24. Vico Press R.T., Torokvesz u. 30-A, 1022 Budapest, Hungary. TEL 115-40-37. FAX 115-40-39. TELEX 22-5554. (Subscr. to: Kultura, Box 149, 1389 Budapest, Hungary) Ed. Lili Zetenyi. illus.; circ. 380,000.

MAHJUBAH. see *RELIGIONS AND THEOLOGY — Islamic*

305.412   RH
MAHOGANY; Africa's magazine for women. (Text in English) bi-m. Z.$4.50. Munn Publishing (Pvt.) Ltd., Box UA 589, Union Ave., Harare, Zimbabwe. TEL 700475. Ed. G. Beach. circ. 32,000.

MAINE LESBIAN FEMINIST NEWSLETTER. see *HOMOSEXUALITY*

MALAYSIAN JOURNAL OF REPRODUCTIVE HEALTH. see *BIRTH CONTROL*

301.4   ML
MALI MUSO. q. Union des Femmes du Mali, Bamako, Mali. circ. 5,000.

301   US
MAMA BEARS NEWS AND NOTES. 1983. bi-m. $6. Mama Bears Bookstore Coffeehouse, 6536 Telegraph Ave., Oakland, CA 94609. TEL 415-428-9684. Ed. Alice Molloy. adv.; bk.rev.; circ. 10,000. (tabloid format; back issues avail.)
Description: Articles, features and announcements on feminist and lesbian issues.

305.412   NE   ISSN 0025-2956
MARGRIET. 1939. w. fl.122.20. Geillustreerde Pers B.V., Stadhouderskade 85, 1073 AT Amsterdam, Netherlands. TEL 20-5734811. FAX 20-5734406. Ed. Aty Luitze. adv.; illus.; circ. 550,000.

301.412   PO
MARIA. w. Av. Miguel Bombarda 33-35, 2745 Queluz, Portugal. TEL 964388. Dir. Jaques Rodriques. circ. 369,000.

303   CN
MARIAGE QUEBEC. 1989. 2/yr. Can.$3.95 per no. 360 Ouest Notre-Dame, Ste.G03, Montreal, Que. H2Y 1T9, Canada. TEL 514-849-2625. FAX 514-849-2032. Ed. Suzanne Bouvrette-Hurst. adv.; bk.rev.; circ. 25,000.
Description: A fashion, beauty, lifestyle and travel guide for the bride-to-be, the engaged couple, their bridal party and entourage.

301.412   PO
MARIE CLAIRE. 1989. m. Rua Mouzinho da Silveira 27, 1200 Lisbon, Portugal. TEL 01-526553. Dir. Maria Elisa Domingues. circ. 45,000.

301.412   SP
MARIE CLAIRE 16. 1987. m. Hermanos Garcia Noblejas 39, 3o, 28037 Madrid, Spain. TEL 4072700. FAX 4084944. Dir. Ana Rosa Semprun. circ. 115,000.

055.1   IT
MARIE CLAIRE - DONNAPIU. 1984. m. L.54000 (foregin l.79800). Arnoldo Mondadori Editore S.p.A., Casella Postale 1833, 20101 Milan, Italy. TEL 3199345. Ed. Vera Montanari. circ. 143,684.
Formerly: Donnapiu.

305.412   JA
MARIE CLAIRE JAPON. (Text in Japanese) 1982. m. 6510 Yen. Chuokoron-Sha, Inc., No. 2-8-7 Kyobashi, Chuo-ku, Tokyo, Japan. Ed. Kazuo Matsumura.

059   NE
MARIE CLAIRE - NEDERLANDSE EDITIE. 1990. m. fl.78. Geillustreerde Pers B.V., Stadhouderskade 85, 1073 AT Amsterdam, Netherlands. TEL 20-5734811. FAX 20-5734406. Ed. Renie van Wijk. adv.; illus.; circ. 76,000.

054.1   FR   ISSN 0025-3057
MARIE-FRANCE.* 1944. m. 121 F. Societe de Publications Economiques, Feminines et Familiales, 13 rue Bleue, 75009 Paris, France. TEL 1-40-21-75-32. FAX 1-48-24-06-63. TELEX 281 100. Ed. Michele Faure. adv.; circ. 315,058.

054   MU   ISSN 0047-5920
HQ1804.M38
MARIEMOU; revue de la jeune fille et de la femme Mauritaniennes. (Editions in Arabic and French) 1969. q. B.P. 47, Nouakchott, Mauritania. Ed. Toure Aissata Kane. adv.; bk.rev.; illus.

MARKETING TO WOMEN; lifestyle studies about women in America. see *BUSINESS AND ECONOMICS — Marketing And Purchasing*

MARRIAGE MAGAZINE. see *MATRIMONY*

301.412   CN   ISSN 0836-7515
MATCH NEWS. (Text in English, French) 1976. q. Can.$25 membership. Match International Centre, 1102-200 Elgin St., Ottawa, Ont. K2P 1L5, Canada. TEL 613-238-1312. FAX 613-238-6867. circ. 5,000. (back issues avail.)
Description: News about women and development.

MATERNAL HEALTH NEWS. see *MEDICAL SCIENCES — Nurses And Nursing*

WOMEN'S INTERESTS

305.412 649   UK
MATERNITY AND MOTHERCRAFT. bi-m. (Newbourne Group) Home & Law Publishing Ltd., Greater London House, Hampstead Rd., London NW1 7QQ, England. adv.

MATH SCIENCE NETWORK BROADCAST. see *MATHEMATICS*

301.412   GW
MAXI. 1986. m. DM.42. Heinrich Bauer Verlag, Burchardstr. 11, 2000 Hamburg 1, Germany. TEL 040-3019-0. FAX 040-326589. Ed. Andreas Danch. circ. 503,085.

301.412   BL
MAXIMA. 1989. m. $120. Editora Abril, S.A., R. Geraldo Flausino Gomez, 61, 04575 Sao Paulo, Brazil. TEL 011-8239222. FAX 011-8643796. TELEX 011-80360 EDAB BR. circ. 124,297.

301.412   PO
MAXIMA. 1989. m. Rua Vitor Cordon 37-3o, 1200 Lisbon, Portugal. TEL 01-3423136. Dir. Margarida Maraute. circ. 45,000.

301.412   UK   ISSN 0956-2486
ME MAGAZINE. 1989. w. I P C Magazines, Inc., I P C Woman's Magazine Group (Subsidiary of: Reed Internaitonal P L C), Kings Reach Tower, Stamford St., London SE1 9LS, England. TEL 071-261-6907. Ed. Kay Goddard. adv.; film rev.; circ. 733,412.
Description: Directed to the 18-35 year old woman with a strong emphasis on practicals. Includes a free sewing pattern every week.

059.94   FI   ISSN 0025-6277
AP80
ME NAISET. 1952. w. Fmk.420. (Sanomaprint) Sanoma Corporation, PL. 113, SF-00381 Helsinki, Finland. TEL 358-0-1221. Ed. Ulla-Maija Paavilainen. adv.; circ. 97,274.

305.16   US   ISSN 0145-9651
HQ1402
MEDIA REPORT TO WOMEN. 1972. bi-m. $45. Communication Research Associates, Inc., 10606 Mantz Rd., Silver Spring, MD 20903. TEL 301-445-3230. Ed. Sheila Gibbons. adv.; bk.rev.; cum.index: 1972-1985; circ. 1,000. (back issues avail.) **Indexed:** Chic.Per.Ind., Film Lit.Ind. (1985-), HR Rep., Wom.Stud.Abstr.
Description: Devoted to women in media topics.

051   US
MEDICAL - MRS.; the magazine for doctors' wives. 1977. bi-m. $9.95. Hillbart Publications, Inc., Kirby Lane, Rye, NY 10580. TEL 914-967-7173. Ed. Cynthia S. Smith. adv.; film rev.; circ. 100,000.

301.4   IT
MEDITERRANEA; l'observatorio delle donne. q. L.40000. Editrice Pellegrini, Via Roma 74, Casella Postale 158, 87100 Cosenza, Italy.

301.412   GW   ISSN 0179-8596
MEIN ERLEBNIS; Frauen von heute berichten. 1975. m. DM.25.20. Publica Verlag GmbH, Bismarckstr. 67, 1000 Berlin 12, Germany. TEL 030-3424000. Ed. Karl-Heinz Loeding. adv.; circ. 120,000. (back issues avail.)

301.412   GW
MEIN GEHEIMNIS; moderne Frauen sprechen sich aus. 1977. bi-m. Condor Interpart Verlag GmbH und Co. KG, Bismarckstr. 67, 1000 Berlin 12, Germany. TEL 030-3413070. Ed. Wolfgang M. Biehler.

301.412   GW
MEIN SCHICKSAL; Frauen von heute sprechen sich aus. 1979. bi-m. Condor-Interpart Verlag GmbH und Co. KG, Bismarckstr. 67, 1000 Berlin 12, Germany. TEL 030-3413070. Ed. Wolfgang M. Biehler.

301.412   GW   ISSN 0935-8005
MEINE GESCHICHTE; erlebnis magazin fuer die moderne Frau. 1972. fortn. DM.48.30. Publica Verlag GmbH, Bismarckstr. 67, 1000 Berlin 12, Germany. TEL 030-3424000. Ed. Karl-Heinz Loeding. adv.; circ. 114,000. (back issues avail.)

640   UK   ISSN 0965-7738
MELA. 1978. 12/yr. £8. Stiwdio Mei, 32-36 Stryd y Wyddfa, Penygroes, Caernarfon, Gwynedd LL54 6NG, Wales. TEL 0286-880302. FAX 0286-880302. circ. 5,000.
Formerly: Pais.

920 301.412   FR
MEMOIRE DES FEMMES.* 1978. irreg. price varies. Editions Syros, 6 rue Montmarte, 75001 Paris, France.

305.412   IT   ISSN 0392-4564
HQ1104
MEMORIA; rivista di storia delle donne. 1981. 3/yr. L.44000 (Europe L.60000; elsewhere L.75000). Rosenberg & Sellier, Via Andrea Doria 14, 10123 Turin, Italy. TEL 011-561-39-07. FAX 011-532188. Ed.Bd. adv.; bk.rev.; film rev.; index; circ. 3,000. (back issues avail.)
Description: Examines woman's oppression via marriage, the use of power, dress, and motherhood. Discusses the culture of feminism.

301.412   US
MEN OF THE WEST COAST; a magazine for the single woman, focusing on single men and their lifestyles. vol.1, no.2, 1990. 4/yr. $14.95 in US; Canada $17.95. 3296 S. Mooney Blvd., Ste. 112, Visalia, CA 93277. TEL 209-733-2921. Ed. Nancy Hicks. illus.
Description: Introduces single men for interested single women. Includes photos and addresses.

MEXICO VOGUE. see *CLOTHING TRADE — Fashions*

301.412   LS
MEYING LAO. (Text in Lao) 1980. m. Vientiane, Laos. Ed. Khamphon Phimmaseng. circ. 4,000.

301.412   SP
MIA. 1986. w. 4160 ptas. (Europe 10360 ptas.; elsewhere 21660 ptas.). G & J Espana, S.A., Marques de Villamagna 4, 28001 Madrid, Spain. TEL 91-4356032. FAX 91-5767881. circ. 155,000.

MIDWIFERY TODAY AND CHILDBIRTH EDUCATION. see *MEDICAL SCIENCES — Obstetrics And Gynecology*

MILITARY LIFESTYLE. see *MILITARY*

055.1   IT
MILLE IDEE PER LA DONNA. m. L.36000. Rizzoli Editoriale-Corriere della Sera, Via A. Rizzoli 2, 20132 Milan, Italy. TEL 02-2588. Ed. Maria Santini. adv.; circ. 362,800.

646.7   JA
MINE. (Text in Japanese) 1920. s-m. Kodansha Ltd., International Division, 12-21 Otowa 2-chome, Bunkyo-ku, Tokyo 112, Japan. TEL 03-3945-1111. FAX 03-3943-7815. TELEX J34509 KODANSHA. Ed. Kohjiro Amano. circ. 350,000.
Formerly (until 1987): Fujin Club.
Description: Fashion and variety magazine for young homemakers.

MINERVA; quarterly report on women and the military. see *MILITARY*

MINERVA'S BULLETIN BOARD. see *MILITARY*

659.152   US
MIRABELLA. 1989. m. $12. Murdoch Magazines (Subsidiary of: News America Publishing, Inc.), 200 Madison Ave., New York, NY 10016. TEL 800-888-3927. FAX 212-447-4778. (Subscr. to: Box 10009, Des Moines, IA 50340-0009) Ed. Gay Bryant. (reprint service avail. from UMI) **Indexed:** Access (1990-).
Description: Covers a variety of topics ranging from art and politics to beauty, travel, business and fashion, for the savvy woman.

MIRJAM; Monatszeitschrift der weltoffenen Frau. see *RELIGIONS AND THEOLOGY — Roman Catholic*

MISS MOM - MISTER MOM. see *CHILDREN AND YOUTH — About*

305.412   UK
MIZZ. 1985. fortn. £26 (foreign £32.60). I P C Magazines Ltd., Holborn Group (Subsidiary of: Reed Business Publishing Ltd.), Kings Reach Tower, Stamford St., London SE1 9LS, England. TEL 071-261-5000. Ed. Simon Geller. circ. 180,328.
Description: Fashion and beauty teenage lifestyle magazine.

MODA. see *CLOTHING TRADE — Fashions*

MODE AUSTRALIA. see *CLOTHING TRADE — Fashions*

305.412   NR   ISSN 0047-7761
MODERN WOMAN. 1964. m. £N3.48. Modern Publications Co. Ltd., Box 2583, Lagos, Nigeria. Ed. Romke Bamisebi. adv.; circ. 40,000.

301.412   IE   ISSN 0790-3855
MODERN WOMAN. 1984. m. £9. Meath Chronicle Ltd., Market Square, Navan, Co. Meath, Ireland. TEL 046-21442. FAX 046-23565. Ed. Margot Davis. adv.; circ. 30,000. (tabloid format; back issues avail.)

305.412   US
MOM'S APPLE PIE. 1974. q. $10 to non-members. Lesbian Mothers National Defense Fund, Box 21567, Seattle, WA 98111. TEL 206-325-2643. Ed.Bd. adv.; bk.rev.; bibl.; illus.; circ. 500. (back issues avail.)

305.412   GW   ISSN 0047-7885
MONIKA; Zeitschrift fuer die Frau. 1869. m. DM.25.20. (Paedagogische Stiftung Cassianeum) Verlag Ludwig Auer, Postfach 1152, 8850 Donauwoerth, Germany. Ed. Gerda Roeder. adv.; bk.rev.; circ. 59,000.

301.412   BO
MONOGRAFIAS DE PROMOCION FEMENINA. 1985. irreg. price varies. Centro de Investigaciones Sociales, Casilla 6931 - Correo Central, La Paz, Bolivia.

MONTREAL WOMEN'S DIRECTORY/ANNUAIRE DES FEMMES DE MONTREAL. see *BUSINESS AND ECONOMICS — Trade And Industrial Directories*

301.412 133   US
MOONCIRCLES. 1985. 8/yr. $11. Circles of Exchange, 9594 First Ave., N.E., Ste. 333, Seattle, WA 98115. TEL 206-654-9610. FAX 206-523-7351. Ed. Nan Hawthrone. adv.; bk.rev.; circ. 225. (looseleaf format; also avail. in magnetic tape; back issues avail.)
Description: Newsletter of women's spiritual correspondence and creativity exchange. Includes announcements and members' comments on different themes.

640   JA
MORE. (Text in Japanese) 1977. m. Shueisha Inc., 5-10, 2-chome, Hitotsubashi, Chiyoda-ku, Tokyo 101-50, Japan. TEL 03-3230-6350. Ed. Kouzo Tsuruya.

376   NZ   ISSN 0112-0808
MORE. 1983. m. NZ.$62.40. Australian Consolidated Press (NZ) Ltd., Private Bag, Wellesley St., Auckland, New Zealand. TEL 09-373-5408. FAX 09-309-8718. adv. contact: Sandra Taua. bk.rev.; film rev.; music rev.; circ. 47,000.
Description: New Zealand's glossy for savvy women.

305.412   SW   ISSN 0027-1101
MORGONBRIS. 1904. 8/yr. SEK 50. Sveriges Socialdemokratiska Kvinnofoerbund, Box 11545, S-100 61 Stockholm, Sweden. TEL 08-449580. FAX 08-7029564. Ed. Ulla Kindenberg. adv.; bk.rev.; charts; illus.; circ. 40,000.
Description: Explores the women's liberation movement.

305.4   LI
MOTERIS. 1952. m. Maironio 1, Vilnius 232600, Lithuania. TEL (0122) 610-169. Ed. Regina Paulauskiene.

362   PK
MOTHER AND CHILD. (Text in English) 1965-1972; resumed 1974. q. Rs.25. Maternity & Child Welfare Association of Pakistan, MCH House, 30-F, Gulberg-II, Lahore 54666, Pakistan. TEL 874621. Ed. Akram Sheikh. adv.; bk.rev.; circ. 1,000.

301.412   US   ISSN 0047-830X
MOVING OUT; a feminist literary & arts journal. 1971. irreg. $6 to individuals; libraries $9. Box 21249, Detroit, MI 48221. Ed.Bd. adv.; bk.rev.; illus.; circ. 1,000. (also avail. in microform from UMI; back issues avail.) **Indexed:** A.I.P.P., Wom.Stud.Abstr.

301.412   SP
MUCHO MAS. w. Pedro Teixeira 8, 28020 Madrid, Spain. TEL 91-5560048. Dir. Alicia Otero.

331 323   CL
MUJER - FEMPRESS. 1981. m. Esc.10000($40) in Latin America; U.S. and Canada $60; elsewhere $65. I L E T - Fempress, Callao 3461 Las Condes, Santiago, Chile. TEL 56-2-232-2557. FAX 56-2-232-5000. bk.rev.; circ. 4,000.
Formerly: Mujer I L E T.

056.1   CU   ISSN 0581-2011
MUJERES. 1961. m. $21 in N. America; S. America $27; Europe $30; elsewhere $42. Federacion de Mujeres Cubanas, Editora de la Mujer, Galiano 264 esq. Neptuno, Aptdo. 2545, Havana 2, Cuba. TEL 7-61-5919. (Dist. by: Ediciones Cubanas, Obispo No. 527, Aptdo. 605, Havana, Cuba) Dir. Regla Zulueta. illus.; circ. 270,000.

305.412   AG
MUJERES. 1981. m. Sarmiento 2210, 1 Piso, Buenos Aires, Argentina. Ed. Ana Maria Giacosa.

MUSICAL WOMAN. see *MUSIC*

305.412   UK
MY GUY. 1977. w. I P C Magazines Ltd., Holborn Group (Subsidiary of: Reed Business Publishing Ltd.), Kings Reach Tower, Stamford St., London SE1 9LS, England. TEL 071-404-0700. Ed. Frank Hopkinson. circ. 80,197.
Incorporates: Girl.

301.412   UK
MY GUY MONTHLY. 1984. m. I P C Magazines Ltd., Reed Business Publishing Ltd. (Subsidiary of: Holborn Group), Kings Reach Tower, Stamford St., London SE1 9LS, England. TEL 071-261-5000. Ed. June Smith. adv.; circ. 47,260.

305.412   UK
MY WEEKLY. 1910. w. D.C. Thomson & Co. Ltd., Albert Square, Dundee DD1 9QJ, Scotland.

N A W J COUNTERBALANCE. (National Association of Women Judges) see *LAW*

N C A W E NEWS. (National Council of Administrative Women in Education) see *EDUCATION — School Organization And Administration*

323.4   362.7   US   ISSN 0161-2115
N C J W JOURNAL. 1978. q. $2. National Council of Jewish Women, 53 W. 23rd St., New York, NY 10010. TEL 212-645-4048. Ed. Michele Spirn. adv.; bk.rev.; circ. 100,000.
Formerly: Council Woman.

968   SA   ISSN 0027-6367
N C W NEWS. (Text in Afrikaans, English) 1936. 5/yr. R.10 to non-members. National Council of Women of South Africa - Nasionale Vroueraad van Suid-Afrika, P.O. Box 1242, Johannesburg 2000, South Africa. TEL 011-834-1366. Ed. Mrs. H. Robinson. bk.rev.; circ. 2,000.

N F E - W I D EXCHANGE - ASIA. NEWSLETTER. see *EDUCATION*

323.42   US
N O W NEWS (BOSTON).* vol.4, 1973. m. membership. National Organization for Women, 1000 - 16th St. N.W., Ste.700, Washington, DC 20036. TEL 202-331-0066. Ed. Rosemary Dempsey. adv.; bk.rev.; circ. 600.
Former titles: Boston N O W; National Organization for Women. Eastern Massachusetts Chapter. Newsletter.

301.412   US
N O W SAN DIEGO NEWS. 1971. m. $20. National Organization for Women, San Diego County Chapter, Box 80292, San Diego, CA 92138. TEL 619-237-1824. Ed. Kris Anderson. adv.; bk.rev.; circ. 900. (also avail. in microfilm)

305.412   UK   ISSN 0952-5335
N W R NATIONAL NEWSLETTER. 1965. 2/yr. membership. National Women's Register, National Office, 9 Bank Plain, Norwich, Norfolk NR2 4SL, England. TEL 0603-765392. Ed. Nikki Iles. adv.; bk.rev.; circ. 18,000. **Indexed:** Hum.Ind., Soc.Sci.Ind.
Former titles (until 1987): N H R National Newsletter (ISSN 0142-2146); National Housewives Register. Newsletter.

305.412   IS
NAAMAT; magazine for women-in work, society & family. Issued with: Urim Ia-Orim (ISSN 0042-1073) (Text in Hebrew) 1934. 10/yr. IS.55. Histadrut, Working Women Organization and Volunteers, 93 Arlozorov St., 62 098 Tel Aviv, Israel. TEL 03-431111. TELEX 342-488-HISTD-IL. Ed. Zivya Cohen. adv.; bk.rev.; film rev.; play rev.; illus.; index; circ. 15,000. **Indexed:** Ind.Heb.Per.
Formerly: Dvar Hapoelet.
Description: Studies women's role in work and society, women's status, and legal rights.

NA'AMAT WOMAN. see *RELIGIONS AND THEOLOGY — Judaic*

301.412   327   US
NAJDA NEWSLETTER. 1964. q. $5. Najda: Women Concerned About the Middle East, Box 7152, Berkeley, CA 94707. TEL 415-549-3512. Ed. Alice Kawash. bk.rev.; circ. 700.

305.412   XV
NASA ZENA. (Includes supplement: Krojne Pole) (Text in Slovenian) 1940. w. 1440 din.($32) T.O.Z.D. Delavska Enotnost, N.sol.o. Celovska 43, N.sub.o. CGP Delo, Box 313-VI, 61001 Ljubljana, Slovenia. Ed. Sonja Tramsek.

305.412   US
NASHVILLE WOMEN'S ALLIANCE. NEWSLETTER. 1977. m. $10 contribution. Nashville Women's Alliance, Box 120834, Nashville, TN 37212. TEL 615-726-2716. Ed. Nancy Bolen. adv.; bk.rev.; film rev.; play rev.; illus.; tr.lit.; circ. 525. **Indexed:** Lang.& Lang.Behav.Abstr., Rehabil.Lit.

051   650   US   ISSN 0027-8831
HD6050
NATIONAL BUSINESS WOMAN. 1919. 4/yr. $10. National Federation of Business and Professional Women's Clubs, Inc., 2012 Massachusetts Ave., N.W., Washington, DC 20036. TEL 202-293-1100. FAX 202-861-0298. Ed. Maryanne Sugarman Costa. adv.; illus.; index; circ. 100,000. **Indexed:** Mag.Ind., Pers.Lit., Work Rel.Abstr.
Description: Covers topics of interest to working women, such as economic equality, dependent care, reproductive freedom and women in business.

NATIONAL DIRECTORY OF WOMAN - OWNED BUSINESS FIRMS. see *BUSINESS AND ECONOMICS — Trade And Industrial Directories*

323.42   US   ISSN 0149-4740
NATIONAL N O W TIMES. 1968? 6/yr. $35 to non-members. National Organization for Women, Inc., 1000 16th St., N.W., Ste. 700, Washington, DC 20036-5705. TEL 202-347-2279. Ed. Rosemary Dempsey. adv.; illus.; circ. 200,000. (tabloid format) **Indexed:** Alt.Press Ind., New Per.Ind., PMR.
Formerly: Do It N O W.

301.412   320   US
NATIONAL ORDER OF WOMEN LEGISLATORS NEWS & VIEWS.* q. $25. National Order of Women Legislators, Inc., c/o Sheehan Associates, 727 15th St., N.W., Ste. 1200, Washington, DC 20005. TEL 202-347-0044. Ed. Annie Rhodes.
Description: Promotes and reports on participation of women in public affairs.

346.013   US
NATIONAL PARALEGAL REPORTER. 1975. q. $15. National Federation of Paralegal Associations, 5700 Old Orchard Rd., 1st Fl., Skokie, IL 60077-1057. TEL 708-965-2323. FAX 708-966-7814. Ed. Julia Hosea. adv.; bk.rev.; circ. 17,500. (back issues avail.)
Description: Covers issues concerning the legal assistant and the paralegal profession; includes activites of the federation.

613.7   US
NATIONAL WOMEN'S HEALTH NETWORK. q. National Women's Health Network, 1325 G St., N.W., Washington, DC 20005.

NATIONAL WOMEN'S HEALTH REPORT. see *WOMEN'S HEALTH*

301.412   CC
NEI MENGGU FUNU/INNER MONGOLIAN WOMEN. (Text in Mongolian) m. Nei Menggu Zizhiqu Funu Lianhehui - Inner Mongolian Autonomous Region Women's Association, 9 Zhongshan Donglu, Huhhot, Nei Menggu 010020, People's Republic of China. TEL 662584. Ed. Xi Xingfang.

NETWORK (NEW YORK); an alliance and network for those connected to the written word. see *JOURNALISM*

301.412   US
NETWORK (SALT LAKE CITY). m. Diversified Suburban Newspapers, 155 E. 4905 South, Salt Lake City, UT 84107. TEL 801-262-6682. Ed. Lynne Tempest. circ. 16,000.

NETWORK NEWSNEWS. see *WOMEN'S HEALTH*

323.4   US
NETWORKER: JUSTICE FOR WOMEN AND FAMILIES. 2/yr. price varies. Interfaith Impact for Justice and Peace, 110 Maryland Ave., NE, Washington, DC 20002. TEL 202-543-2800.

305.412   GW
NEUE POST. w. DM.124.80. Heinrich Bauer Verlag, Burchardstr. 11, 2000 Hamburg 1, Germany. TEL 040-3019-0. FAX 040-326589. Ed. Hartmut Klemann. adv.; bk.rev.; film rev.; illus.; circ. 1,826,046. (tabloid format)
Description: Topical reports, background information, entertainment, relaxation, advice and support.

NEW BOOKS ON WOMEN & FEMINISM. see *BIBLIOGRAPHIES*

301.412   US
NEW CLEVELAND WOMAN JOURNAL. 1983. m. $17. 104 E. Bridge St., Berea, OH 44017. TEL 216-243-3740. FAX 216-243-0460. Ed. Melinda Benson. adv.; bk.rev.; circ. 35,000. (tabloid format; back issues avail.)
Description: Offers legal, business, financial, health, fitness, and stress management advice to women.

NEW DAWN. see *HOMOSEXUALITY*

NEW ENGLAND BRIDE. see *MATRIMONY*

NEW FAMILY. see *HOME ECONOMICS*

301.412   US
NEW HAVEN COUNTY WOMAN. m. MacClaren Press, Inc., 315 Peck St., New Haven, CT 06513-2933. TEL 203-782-1420. Ed. Lisa Spooner. adv.; circ. 30,000.

052   AT   ISSN 0819-9981
NEW IDEA. 1902. w. Aus.$93.60 (foreign Aus.$130). Southdown Press, 32 Walsh Street, Melbourne, Vic., 3000, Australia. TEL 03-320-700. FAX 03-320-7410. Ed. D. Boling. adv.; bk.rev.; illus.; circ. 1,003,223.
Description: Articles on homemaking, crafts, cooking, gardening.

301.412   US
NEW JERSEY WOMAN MAGAZINE. 1979. 9/yr. $24. Advantage Publication Services, Inc., 27 McDermott Place, Bergenfield, NJ 07621. TEL 201-384-0201. Ed. Louise Hafesh. adv.; bk.rev.; circ. 15,000. (back issues avail.)
Formerly: Jersey Woman Magazine (ISSN 0197-4610)
Description: Directed toward New Jersey woman of accomplishment and the upscale market.

NEW PARENT. see *MEDICAL SCIENCES — Obstetrics And Gynecology*

305.412   US   ISSN 0028-6974
HQ1101
NEW WOMAN. 1971. m. $16.97 (effective 1992). K-III Magazines, 200 Madison Ave., New York, NY 10016. TEL 212-447-4700. FAX 212-447-4778. (Subscr. to: Box 56229, Boulder, CO 80322. TEL 800-627-2557) Ed. Karen Walden. adv.; bk.rev.; film rev.; circ. 1,260,000. (also avail. in microform from UMI; reprint service avail. from UMI) **Indexed:** PMR.
Description: Covers health, food and diet, fashion, beauty and decorating, love, sex and relationships, psychology, self-improvement and self discovery for the young, professional woman.

WOMEN'S INTERESTS

051   US   ISSN 0149-8452
NEW YORK (CITY). COMMISSION ON THE STATUS OF WOMEN. STATUS REPORT. 1977. irreg., latest 1991. Commission on the Status of Women, 52 Chambers St., Rm. 209, New York, NY 10007. TEL 212-788-2738. Ed. Maxine Gold. bk.rev.; circ. 9,000. (tabloid format)
Description: News articles and listings of publications on current issues pertaining to the rights, roles and activities of women, with announcements of conferences and workshops of interest to women.

052   NZ   ISSN 0028-8829
NEW ZEALAND WOMAN'S WEEKLY. 1932. w. NZ.$210. New Zealand Magazines Ltd., Private Bag, Dominion Rd., Auckland 3, New Zealand. TEL 09-688-105. FAX 09-609-128. Ed. Jenny Lynch. adv.; bk.rev.; illus.; circ. 165,719.

305.412 374   CN
NEWFOUNDLAND AND LABRADOR WOMEN'S INSTITUTES. NEWSLETTER. 1966. q. Can.$3. Newfoundland and Labrador Women's Institutes, P.O. Box 13785, St. John's, Nfld. A1B 4G3, Canada. Ed. Jennifer Perry. bk.rev.; circ. 750. (back issues avail.)

305.412 350   US
NEWS ON WOMEN IN GOVERNMENT. 1978. s-a. Center for Women in Government, SUNY Albany, Draper Hall 310, 1400 Washington Ave., Albany, NY 12222. TEL 518-442-3900. Ed. Audrey Seidman. circ. 20,000.

NEWSLETTER: A LESBIAN POSITION. see *HOMOSEXUALITY*

NIGHTINGALE. see *MEDICAL SCIENCES — Nurses And Nursing*

509.2   JA
NIHON FUJIN KAGAKUSHA NO KAI NYUSU. (Text in Japanese) 1958. irreg. Nihon Fujin Kagakusha no Kai - Association of Japanese Women Scientists, 29-2-203 Koenji kita-4-chome, Suginami-ku, Tokyo 166, Japan.
Description: Contains news of the association.

376 360 369.4   CS
NO. 1951. w. 145.60 Kcs. (Slovak Women's Union) Zivena, Nalepkova 15, 812 64 Bratislava, Czechoslovakia. TEL 33 04 20. (Subscr. to: Slovart, Gottwaldovo n. 6, 810 05 Bratislava, Czechoslovakia) Text in Hungarian. (back issues avail.)

301.412   IS   ISSN 0333-6387
NOGA. 1980. 3/yr. IS.16($14) Lilit, P.O. Box 21376, Tel Aviv 61 213, Israel. TEL 03-227663. Ed. Rachel Ostrawitz. bk.rev.; circ. 2,000. (back issues avail.)

055.1   IT   ISSN 0029-0920
NOI DONNE. 1944. m. L.50000. (Unione Donne Italiane) Cooperativa Libera Stampa, Via della Trinita dei Pellegrini 12, 00186 Rome, Italy. FAX 6-6545380. Ed. Mariella Gramaglia. adv.; bk.rev.; film rev.; play rev.; illus.; tr.lit.; index; circ. 180,000.

NORTH COAST BRIDE AND GROOM. see *MATRIMONY*

NOUNCEMENTS. see *MILITARY*

NOUVELLES PRATIQUES SOCIALES. see *SOCIAL SERVICES AND WELFARE*

305.412   FR
NOUVELLES QUESTIONS FEMINISTES. 1982. q. 260 F. to individuals; institutions 440 F. I R E S C O, c/o C. Delphy, 59-61 rue Pouchet, 75017 Paris, France. Ed.Bd. bk.rev.; circ. 600.

305.412   BL
NOVA; a revista da mulher cada vez mais nova. 1973. m. $110. Editora Abril, S.A., R. Geraldo Flausino Gomes, 61, 04575 Sao Paulo, Brazil. TEL 011-8239222. FAX 011-8643796. TELEX 011-80360 EDAB BR. (Subscr. to: Rua do Curtume, 769 CEP 05065 Lapa, Sao Paulo, Brazil.) Ed. Victor Civita. adv.; illus.; circ. 211,606.
Description: Covers effective living, sexual behavior, fashion, beauty, professional life, health, and leisure.

301.412   IO   ISSN 0853-0300
NOVA; mingguan berita wanita. 1988. w. Rps.33.80. Jl. Kebahagiaan No. 4-14, Jakarta 11140, Indonesia. TEL 021-6297809. FAX 021-5494035. TELEX 073-46327 KOMPAS IA. Ed. Evie Fadjari. adv. contact: Tommy Anwar. circ. 330,000.

055.1   IT
NOVELLA 2000. w. L.62400. Rizzoli Editore-Corriere della Sera, Via A. Rizzoli 2, 20132 Milan, Italy. Ed. F. Andreoli.

NUESTRA VOZ. see *LITERATURE*

301.412   SP
NUEVO ESTILO. m. Axel Springer Verlag, Pedro Teixeira 8, 28020 Madrid, Spain. TEL 91-5560048. FAX 91-5667044. circ. 144,000.

301.412   CC
NUZI SHIJIE/WOMEN'S WORLD. (Text in Chinese) m. Hebei Sheng Funu Lianhehui - Hebei Provincial Women's Association, 244 Nanma Lu, Shijiazhuang, Hebei 050051, People's Republic of China. TEL 27871. Ed. Ding Cong.

058.82   NO   ISSN 0048-122X
DET NYE. 1957. m. NOK 384. Ernst G. Mortensens Forlag A-S, Soerkedalsveien 10 A, 0369 Oslo 3, Norway. TEL 02-603090. FAX 02-692542. Ed. Kristin Ma Berg. illus.; circ. 82,182.

OF A LIKE MIND. see *RELIGIONS AND THEOLOGY*

305.412   IS
OLAM HA-EISHA. 1984. m. Bari Communications (1984) Ltd., P.O. Box 20530, Tel Aviv, Israel. TEL 03-5615677. FAX 03-5611644. TELEX 341759-WISCO. Ed. R. Keinan. adv.; bk.rev.; circ. 50,000.

059.927 915.3   MK
AL-OMANIYYAH. m. P.O. Box 6303, Ruwi, Muscat, Sultanate of Oman. TEL 707849. TELEX 3758. Ed. Saida bint Khatir al-Farisi. circ. 11,500.

ON OUR BACKS; entertainment for the adventurous lesbian. see *HOMOSEXUALITY*

323.4   US   ISSN 0895-6014
RA564.85
ON THE ISSUES; the journal of substance for progressive women. 1983. 4/yr. $9.50. Choices Women's Medical Center, 97-77 Queens Blvd., Forest Hills, NY 11374. TEL 718-275-6020. FAX 718-997-1206. Ed. Merle Hoffman. adv.; bk.rev.; circ. 50,000.
Description: Feminist topics fostering global political consciousness, anti-racism, anti-sexism, anti-speciesism.

051 100   US
ON WINGS. 1983. 8/yr. $16. Women In Constant Creative Action, Box 5080, Eugene, OR 97405. TEL 503-345-6381. Ed. Norma Joyce. bk.rev.

301.41   CN   ISSN 0830-9442
HQ1457
ONTARIO ADVISORY COUNCIL ON WOMEN'S ISSUES. ANNUAL REPORT. 1974. a. free. Ontario Advisory Council on Women's Issues, 880 Bay St., 5th Fl., Toronto, Ont. M7A 1N3, Canada. TEL 416-326-1840. FAX 416-326-1836. Ed. Lydia Oleksyn. illus.; circ. 9,000.
Former titles: Ontario. Advisory Council on Women's Issues. Annual Report on the Status of Women's Issues; Ontario. Status of Women Council. Annual Report.

301.412   CN
ONTARIO WOMAN. q. Can.$20. Merrick Enterprises, 349 Claremont Cres., Oakville, Ont. L6J 6J9, Canada. Ed. John Merrick.

OPEN DOOR INTERNATIONAL FOR THE EMANCIPATION OF THE WOMAN WORKER. REPORT OF CONGRESS. see *BUSINESS AND ECONOMICS — Labor And Industrial Relations*

OPTIONS (WASHINGTON). see *POPULATION STUDIES*

ORAH. see *ETHNIC INTERESTS*

OTHER BLACK WOMAN; an international magazine for women. see *ETHNIC INTERESTS*

OUR SPECIAL; magazine devoted to matters of interest to blind women. see *HANDICAPPED — Visually Impaired*

OUT. see *HOMOSEXUALITY*

OUTLOOK (SEATTLE); drug regulation and reproductive health. see *PUBLIC HEALTH AND SAFETY*

OUTRAGEOUS LETTERS. see *MEN'S INTERESTS*

305.412 323   UK   ISSN 0265-8429
OUTWRITE WOMEN'S NEWSPAPER. 1982. m. £6. Feminist Newspaper Ltd., Oxford House, Derbyshire St., London E2 6HG, England. Ed.Bd. adv.; bk.rev.; film rev.; play rev.; circ. 7,000. (tabloid format; back issues avail.)

305.412   UK
OVER 21. 1972. m. $35. Spotlight Publications Ltd., Greater London House, Hampstead Rd., London NW1 7QZ, England. Ed. Pat Roberts. adv.; bk.rev.; charts; illus.; circ. 92,038.
Description: Fashion topics for young women.

OVER 40. see *MEN'S INTERESTS*

OVULATION METHOD TEACHERS ASSOCIATION (PUBLICATION). see *BIRTH CONTROL*

353.9   US
P C S W ANNUAL REPORT. 1973. a. free. Permanent Commission on the Status of Women, 90 Washington St., Hartford, CT 06106. TEL 203-566-5702. Ed. Fredrica K. Gray.

P M S ACCESS NEWSLETTER. (Premenstrual Syndrome) see *MEDICAL SCIENCES — Obstetrics And Gynecology*

P S A C UNION UPDATE. see *LABOR UNIONS*

P W P NEWSLETTER. (Professional Women Photographers) see *PHOTOGRAPHY*

305 646   VE
PAGINAS. 1948. w. Bs.3.50 per no. Editorial Elite, Torre de la Prensa, Plaza del Panteon, Apdo. Postal 2976, Caracas 101, Venezuela. TEL 2-81-4931. Ed. Miguel Angel Capriles. adv.; illus.; circ. 80,025.

305.412   AG
PARA TI. 1922. w. Editorial Atlantida, S.A., Azopardo 579, 1307 Buenos Aires, Argentina. TEL 33-4591. Ed. Anibal C. Vigil. adv.; illus.; circ. 104,000.

PARENTING MAGAZINE OF ORANGE COUNTY. see *CHILDREN AND YOUTH — About*

305.412   SP
PATRONES. 1982. bi-m. $36.10. Hogar y la Moda, S.A., Diputacion, 211, 08011 Barcelona, Spain. TEL 254 10 04. Ed. Dona Maria Asuncion Batlle Brossa. adv.; film rev.; circ. 87,196.

301.412   CL
PAULA. fortn. Triana 851, Santiago, Chile. TEL 2-225-3447. Dir. Andrea Eluchans. circ. 20,000.

PEACE AND FREEDOM. see *POLITICAL SCIENCE — International Relations*

PEACELINES. see *POLITICAL SCIENCE*

THE PEN WOMAN. see *LITERATURE*

305.412   UK
PEOPLE'S FRIEND. 1869. w. D.C. Thomson & Co. Ltd., Albert Square, Dundee DD1 9QJ, Scotland.

301.412   CR
PERFIL. fortn. Llorente de Tibas, Apdo. 10138, San Jose, Costa Rica. TEL 35-1211. FAX 36-6485. TELEX 2358. Dir. Patricia de Liberman. circ. 24,500.

PERFORMING WOMAN; a national directory of professional women musicians. see *MUSIC*

PETITE; fashion - entertainment - glamour for women. see *CLOTHING TRADE — Fashions*

WOMEN'S INTERESTS

053.1   GW   ISSN 0031-630X
PETRA. 1967. m. DM.84. Jahreszeiten Verlag GmbH, Possmoorweg 5, 2000 Hamburg 60, Germany. TEL 040-27170. FAX 040-27172056. TELEX 213214. adv.; charts; illus.; tr.lit.; circ. 584,000.
   Formerly: Moderne Frau (ISSN 0026-8593)

DIE PHILOSOPHIN; Forum fuer feministische Theorie und Philosophie. see *PHILOSOPHY*

301.412   VN
PHU NU VIET-NAM/VIETNAMESE WOMEN. w. Vietnamese Women's Union, 47 Hang Chuoi, Hanoi, Socialist Republic of Vietnam. TEL 53500. Ed. Phyong Minh.

323.4 355 370   US   ISSN 0556-0152
E839.5
PHYLLIS SCHLAFLY REPORT. 1967. m. $20. Eagle Trust Fund, Box 618, Alton, IL 62002. TEL 618-462-5415. Ed. Phyllis Schlafly. circ. 70,000. (back issues avail.)
   Description: Commentary on women's issues, education, national defense, legal issues, economics and foreign policy.

PILLOW TALK; the journal of sexual fulfillment. see *MEN'S INTERESTS*

PLACES OF INTEREST TO WOMEN: USA AND WORLDWIDE. see *HOMOSEXUALITY*

051   US
PLAYGIRL; entertainment for women. 1973. 13/yr. $21.97 (foreign $46)(effective 1992). Drake Publishers, 801 Second Ave., New York, NY 10017-4706. TEL 212-986-5100. FAX 212-692-9297. (Subscr. to: Box 533, Mt. Morris, IL 61054. TEL 800-877-6139) adv.; bk.rev.; circ. 575,547.
   Description: Focuses on women's sexuality, with centerfolds and pictorials.

301.412   SP
PODER Y LIBERTAD. 1976. irreg. 2250 ptas.($15) Partido Feminista de Espana, Bailen 18, Barcelona, Spain. (Or: Magdalena 29, 1, 28012 Madrid, Spain) Ed. Lidia Falcon. illus.
   Formerly: Vindicacion Feminista (ISSN 0212-324X)

917.309   US   ISSN 0032-3594
POLKA; Polish women's quarterly magazine. 1935. q. $2. National United Women's Societies of the Adoration of the Most Blessed Sacrament, Polish National Catholic Church of U.S. and Canada, 1004 Pittston Ave., Scranton, PA 18505. TEL 717-344-1513. Ed. Cecelia D. Lallo. adv.; circ. 1,200. **Indexed:** CERDIC.

301.412   PO
PORTUGAL. COMISSAO PARA A IGUALDADE E DIREITOS DAS MULHERES. COLECCAO INFORMAR AS MULHERES. 1979. irreg. Comissao para a Igualdade e Direitos das Mulheres, Avda. da Republica 32-1, 1093 Lisbon Codex, Portugal. TEL 797-60-81. FAX 793-76-91.
   Formerly: Portugal. Comissao da Condicao Feminina. Coleccao Informar as Mulheres.
   Description: Covers women's issues: marriage, divorce and separation, children, widowhood, adoption, voluntary work and menopause.

305.412   PO   ISSN 0871-9799
PORTUGAL. COMISSAO PARA A IGUALDADE E DIREITOS DAS MULHERES. INFORMACAO BIBLIOGRAFICA. 1976. bi-m. Comissao para a Igualdade e Direitos das Mulheres, Avda. da Republica 32-1, 1093 Lisbon Codex, Portugal. TEL 797-60-81. FAX 793-76-91.
   Formerly: Portugal. Comissao da Condicao Feminina. Informacao Bibliografica.

301   PO   ISSN 0871-3316
PORTUGAL. COMISSAO PARA A IGUALDADE E DIREITOS DAS MULHERES. NOTICIAS. 1985. q. free. Comissao para a Igualdade e Direitos das Mulheres, Avda. da Republica 32-1, 1093 Lisbon Codex, Portugal. TEL 797-60-81. FAX 793-76-91.
   Formerly: Portugal. Comissao da Condicao Feminina. Noticias.

057.8   YU   ISSN 0032-6747
PRAKTICNA ZENA. 1956. fortn. $96. B I G Z, Bulevar vojvode Misica 17, Belgrade, Yugoslavia. Ed. Olivia Panic.

301.412 800   US   ISSN 0364-7609
PS508.W7
PRIMAVERA (CHICAGO). 1975. a. $7. Box 37-7547, Chicago, IL 60637-7547. TEL 312-324-5920. Ed.Bd. illus.; circ. 1,000. (also avail. in microfilm from UMI; reprint service avail. from UMI) **Indexed:** Amer.Hum.Ind., Ind.Amer.Per.Verse.
   Description: Publishes original fiction, poetry, illustrations, and photography that reflect the experiences of women.

PRO - CHOICE NEWS. see *BIRTH CONTROL*

PROBE (CHICAGO); feminist religious women. see *RELIGIONS AND THEOLOGY — Roman Catholic*

301.412 659.152   US
PROFESSIONAL MODEL NEWSLETTER. m. Professional Model Publications, Inc., 201 N. Wells St., Ste. 410, Chicago, IL 60606-1305. TEL 312-263-3513. FAX 312-236-8870. Ed. Linda Balhorn.

PROFESSIONAL WOMEN AND MINORITIES; a manpower data resource service. see *OCCUPATIONS AND CAREERS*

PROMIN. see *ETHNIC INTERESTS*

301.412 371.42   US
PROWOMAN. bi-m. Matri Media Inc., Box 6957, Portland, OR 97228-6957. TEL 503-452-0121. Ed. Ellen Nichols. circ. 15,000.

301.412 057.85   PL   ISSN 0033-2534
PRZYJACIOLKA. 1948. w. $16.40. Oferta dla Kazdego, Spolka z o.o., Ul. Wiejska 12, 00-490 Warsaw, Poland. TEL 48-22-280583. (Dist. by: Ars Polona-Ruch, Krakowskie Przedmiescie 7, Warsaw, Poland) Ed. Ewa Luszczuk. adv.; illus.; circ. 1,500,000.

PSYCHOLOGIE UND GESELLSCHAFTSKRITIK. see *PSYCHOLOGY*

346.013   PY   ISSN 1017-2815
▼**LA PUERTA.** 1990. q. $10. Centro de Estudios Humanitarios, Azara 3267, Asuncion, Paraguay. (Dist. by: D.I.P.P., Box 2507, Asuncion, Paraguay) Ed. Esther Prieto. circ. 1,000.

301.412 646.7   IT
PUI BELLA. w. Rizzoli Editore-Corriere della Sera, Via A. Rizzoli 2, 20132 Milan, Italy. TEL 02-2588. Ed. Mirella Pallotti.

Q W. (Queer World) see *HOMOSEXUALITY*

305.412   IT   ISSN 0048-6205
QUARTO MONDO. 1971. m. Fronte Italiano di Liberazione Femminile, Piazza Ss. Apostoli 49, 00187 Rome, Italy. Ed. Laura Lilli. bk.rev.; illus.

052   AT   ISSN 0033-6092
QUEENSLAND COUNTRY WOMAN. 1930. m. Aus.$15. Queensland Country Women's Association, 1st Fl., Ruth Fairfax House, 89-95 Gregory Terrace, Brisbane, Qld. 4000, Australia. Ed. M. Marsden. adv.; bk.rev.; circ. 10,000. (tabloid format)

305.412   BU
RABOTNICHKA. 1965. bi-m. 0.30 lv. per issue. Izdatelstvo Profizdat, 82, Dondukov Blvd., Sofia, Bulgaria. circ. 22,425.

RADCLIFFE QUARTERLY. see *COLLEGE AND ALUMNI*

305.412 613.7   US   ISSN 0889-9495
RA778
RADIANCE; the magazine for large women. 1984. q. $15. Alice Ansfield, Ed. & Pub., Box 30246, Oakland, CA 94604. TEL 510-482-0680. adv.; bk.rev.; circ. 30,000. (back issues avail.)

305.412   LE
AL - RAIDA. 1976. q. $25. Beirut University College, Institute for Women's Studies in the Arab World, Box 13-5053, Beirut, Lebanon. TEL 811968. TELEX BUC 23389 LE. (U.S. addr.: 475 Riverside Dr., Rm. 1846, New York, N.Y. 10115) Ed. Randa Abul-Husn. adv.; bk.rev.; circ. 700.
   Description: Brings to the reader the Arab woman today: her role, her status, and current issues related to her. Includes news items on conferences and publications.

055.1   IT   ISSN 0033-9113
RAKAM; mensile di moda e lavori femminili. 1929. m. L.38400 (foreign L.66000). Rusconi Editori Associati S.p.A., Servizio Abbonamenti, Via Vitruvio 43, 20124 Milan, Italy. TEL 02-67561. FAX 67562732. Ed. Anna Tuveri. adv.; illus.; circ. 280,000.

305.412   JA
RAY. (Text in Japanese) 1988. m. 11280 Yen. Shufunotomo Co., Ltd., 2-9 Kanda Surugadai, Chiyoda-ku, Tokyo 101, Japan. Ed. Koichi Murata. circ. 200,000.

REBIRTH OF ARTEMIS. see *LITERATURE — Poetry*

301.412   CN   ISSN 0838-4479
RECHERCHES FEMINISTES; revue interdisciplinaire francophone d'etudes feministes. (Text in French, summaries in English, French) 1988. 2/yr. Can.$22 to individuals (foreign Can.$27); institutions Can.$35 (foreign Can.$39); students Can.$20 (foreign Can.$25). Universite Laval, Groupe de Recherche Multidisciplinaire Feministe, 3e etage, 2336 Chemin Ste-Foy, Quebec, Que. G1K 7P4, Canada. TEL 418-656-5421. FAX 418-656-3266. Ed. Huguette Dagenais. adv.; bk.rev.; circ. 1,000. (back issues avail.) **Indexed:** P.A.I.S.For.Lang.Ind., Pt.de Rep., Wom.Stud.Abstr.
   Description: A source of information on feminist teaching, research and action.
   Refereed Serial

RECIPES FOR SALE. see *FOOD AND FOOD INDUSTRIES*

RED. see *CLOTHING TRADE — Fashions*

REDBOOK. see *GENERAL INTEREST PERIODICALS — United States*

305.412   FI   ISSN 0355-841X
REGINA. s-m. Fmk.374. Kolmiokirja Oy, Box 246, 90101 Oulu, Finland. FAX 358-81-225249. Ed. Eeva Vainikainen. adv.; circ. 57,131.

301.412 305.3   US
RELATIONSHIPS TODAY.* 1988. m. $24. Romantic Lifelines, c/o Jon Anderson, Box 2765, Gainesville, FL 32602. Ed. Lyle Benjamin. circ. 160,000.

RESIST NEWSLETTER. see *POLITICAL SCIENCE — Civil Rights*

305.412   US   ISSN 0894-7597
                                         CODEN: RVWCEE
RESPONSE TO THE VICTIMIZATION OF WOMEN AND CHILDREN. 1976. q. $27.50 to individuals; institutions $50. (Response, Inc.) Guilford Publications, Inc., 72 Spring St., 4th Fl., New York, NY 10012. TEL 212-431-9800. FAX 212-966-6708. Ed. Jane Roberts Chapman. adv.; bk.rev.; play rev.; bibl.; stat.; tr.lit.; circ. 3,000. (back issues avail.) **Indexed:** Psychol.Abstr., Stud.Wom.Abstr.
   —BLDSC shelfmark: 7777.695350.
   Former titles: Response to Violence in the Family and Sexual Assault; Response (Washington); Response to Family Violence and Sexual Assault.
   Description: Latest developments in the advocacy and the treatment and prevention of victims of interpersonal violence.
   Refereed Serial

RESPONSIVE PHILANTHROPY. see *SOCIAL SERVICES AND WELFARE*

RETI - PRATICHE E SAPERI DI DONNE. see *POLITICAL SCIENCE*

054.1   CN
REVUE FERMIERES AUJOURD'HUI. 1974. 5/yr. Can.$12.84. Editions Penelope, 3945 St. Martin Blvd. W., Laval, Que. H7T 1B7, Canada. TEL 514-688-6380. FAX 514-681-1682. Ed. Pierrette Pare Walsh. adv.; bk.rev.; illus.; circ. 81,000.
   Formerly: Revue des Fermieres (ISSN 0381-8225)

641.5   GW
REZEPTE MIT PFIFF. 1975. 6/yr. DM.2.50 per no. Sonnenverlag GmbH, Lichtentaler Allee 10, Postfach 720, 7570 Baden-Baden, Germany. Ed. H.D. Stein. adv.

RICHMOND LESBIAN FEMINIST FLYER. see *HOMOSEXUALITY*

WOMEN'S INTERESTS

376   AT   ISSN 0311-8754
RIGHT TO CHOOSE; a women's health action magazine. 1972. irreg. Aus.$8. Women's Abortion Action Campaign, P.O. Box E233, St. James, N.S.W. 2000, Australia. Ed. Angela Rome. adv.; bk.rev.; index; circ. 1,000. (back issues avail.)

305.412   BE   ISSN 0035-5313
HET RIJK DER VROUW. (Text in Flemish) 1928. w. 2150 Fr. Edibel, 9 Av. Frans van Kalken, B-1070 Brussels, Belgium. adv.; bk.rev.; film rev.; play rev.; record rev.; bibl.; illus.; mkt.; pat.; tr.lit.; circ. 160,000.

055   IT
RIVISTA DELLA DONNA. 1971. q. Istituto Publiaci, Corso Vittorio Emanuele 326, 00186 Rome, Italy. Ed. Marcello Vazio. adv.; circ. 75,000.

305.412   SA   ISSN 0035-8207
ROOI ROSE. (Text in Afrikaans) 1944. fortn. R.89.70. Republican Press (Pty) Ltd., Box 3208, Mobeni 4060, Natal, South Africa. Ed. Irma Louw. adv.; bk.rev.; film rev.; illus.; circ. 170,636. (tabloid format) **Indexed:** Ind.S.A.Per.
    Description: Cookery and homecrafts, fashion and beauty, as well as general interest features.

305.412   US
S F N O W TIMES. Alternate title: N O W. 1971. m. $4.50. National Organization for Women, San Francisco Chapter, P.O. Box 1267, San Francisco, CA 94101. TEL 415-861-8880. Ed. Helen L. Grieco. adv.; bk.rev.; film rev.; illus.; circ. 750.
    Formerly: N O W San Francisco.

305.42   US
S I R O W NEWSLETTER. 1979. 3/yr. free. Southwest Institute for Research on Women, c/o Women's Studies, 102 Douglass Bldg., University of Arizona, Tucson, AZ 85721. TEL 602-621-7338. FAX 602-621-9424. Ed. M.A. Saint-Germain. bk.rev.; circ. 3,000.

301.412   US
SAGE WOMAN; a quarterly magazine of women's spirituality. q. $18. Box 641, Point Arena, CA 95468.

301.412   US
SAGE YEARBOOKS IN WOMEN'S POLICY STUDIES. 1976. a. $36 for hardcover; softcover $17.95. Sage Publications, Inc., 2455 Teller Rd., Newbury Park, CA 91320. TEL 805-499-0721. FAX 805-499-0871. (And: Sage Publications Ltd., 6 Bonhill St., London EC2A, 4PU, England) Ed. Susan Cozzens. (back issues avail.) **Indexed:** ERIC, Sociol.Abstr.
    Formerly: Yearbook in Women's Policy Studies.

051   CN
SALLY ANN; a Christian magazine for women. 1953. m. Can.$6.50($9.50) (Salvation Army, Canada Territorial Headquarters) Triumph Press, 455 North Service Road East, Oakville, Ont. L6H 1A5, Canada. TEL 416-844-2561. bk.rev.; illus.; circ. 11,250.
    Former titles: Home Leaguer; Canadian Home Leaguer (ISSN 0008-3771)

SAN DIEGO PARENT. see *CHILDREN AND YOUTH — About*

323.4 305.412   US
SAN JOAQUIN N O W NEWSLETTER. 1973. m. $10. National Organization for Women, San Joaquin Chapter, Box 4073, Stockton, CA 95204. Ed. Renee LaCouture-Tulloch. circ. 100.

SANDMUTOPIA GUARDIAN & DUNGEON JOURNAL. see *MEN'S INTERESTS*

301.4157 808   US   ISSN 0275-6757
SAPPHIC TOUCH; a journal of lesbian erotica. 1981. irreg. $7 per no. Pamir Productions, Box 40218, San Francisco, CA 94140. Eds. Jeannie Karen, Sue Skope.

052   SA
SARIE. 1949. fortn. R.105.04. National Magazines (Subsidiary of: National Media Ltd.), P.O. Box 1802, Cape Town 8000, South Africa. TEL 25-4850. TELEX 5-21125. Ed. Il de Villiers. adv.; bk.rev.; film rev.; illus.; circ. 204,610. **Indexed:** Ind.S.A.Per.

SASSY (NEW YORK, 1988). see *CHILDREN AND YOUTH — About*

301.412   TH
SATRI SARN. (Text in Thai) 1948. w. 83-35 Arkarnthrithosthep 2, Prachathipatai Rd., Bangkok, Thailand. TEL 02-281-9136. Ed. Nilawan Pintong.

301.435   TS
SAWT AL-MAR'AH/WOMAN'S VOICE. (Text in Arabic) 1976. m. Women's Union Society, Cultural Section - Jam'iyyat al-Ittihad al-Nisa'iyyah, Al-Lajnah al-Thiqafiyyah, P.O. Box 142, Sharjah, United Arab Emirates. TEL 22646. Ed. Fatimah Muhammad Hadi. circ. 1,000.
    Description: Covers women's issues in the U.A.E.

363   AT   ISSN 0311-7057
SCARLET LETTER. 1969. bi-m. Aus.$15. Council for the Single Mothers and their Children, G.P.O. Box 1399 M, Melbourne, Vic. 3001, Australia. FAX 650-4755. Ed. Sharon Good. adv.; bk.rev.; circ. 2,000.
    Formerly (until May 1977): C S M C News.

301.412 320.531   AT   ISSN 0313-4423
SCARLET WOMAN; socialist feminist magazine. 1975. s-a. Aus.$6. Scarlet Woman Collective, P.O. Box A222, Sydney South, N.S.W. 2000, Australia. Ed.Bd. adv.; bk.rev.; circ. 1,500. (back issues avail.)
    Description: For feminists concerning the family, unions, and aboriginal women from a socialist perspective.

053.1 200   GW   ISSN 0036-696X
SCHRIFTENREIHE FUER DIE EVANGELISCHE FRAU.* 1938. 6/yr. DM.19.80. Burckhardthaus-Laetare Verlag GmbH, Schumannstr. 161, 6050 Offenbach, Germany. illus.; circ. 8,000.

053.1   SZ   ISSN 0036-7346
SCHWEIZER FRAUENBLATT; unabhaengiges Informationsorgan fuer Fraueninteressen u. Konsumentenfragen. (Text in German) 1918. s-m. 24 Fr. Verlag Boersig AG, D-8703 Erlenbach, Switzerland. adv.; bk.rev.; illus.; circ. 9,500.

640   UK   ISSN 0036-925X
SCOTTISH HOME AND COUNTRY. 1924. m. £9.60 (foreign £10.60). Scottish Women's Rural Institute, 42a Heriot Row, Edinburgh EH3 6ES, Scotland. TEL 031-225-1934. Ed. Stella Roberts. adv.; bk.rev.; circ. 18,000.
    Description: Contains regular features on handicrafts, cookery, travel, fashion, gardening, floral art, consumer news and country customs. Includes patterns and information on competitions.

SECRETARESSE MAGAZINE: S. see *BUSINESS AND ECONOMICS — Office Equipment And Services*

305.412   US   ISSN 0149-0699
RA778.A1
SELF. 1979. m. $15 (Canada $27; foreign $30). Conde Nast Publications Inc., Self Magazine, 350 Madison Ave., New York, NY 10017. TEL 800-274-6111. FAX 212-880-8110. (Subscr. to: Box 5267, Boulder, CO 80321) Ed. Alexandra Penney. circ. 1,201,000. (also avail. in microform from UMI; reprint service avail. from UMI) **Indexed:** PMR.

SENSATIONS. see *LITERATURE*

SENSUOUS LETTERS. see *MEN'S INTERESTS*

056.1   US
▼**SER PADRES/BEING PARENTS.** (Text in Spanish) 1990. bi-m. $1.95 per no. Gruner & Jahr U.S.A. Publishing, 685 Third Ave., New York, NY 10017. TEL 212-878-8700. Ed. Mirta Rodriguez. circ. 225,000 (controlled).
    Description: For young Hispanic mothers and mothers-to-be. Addresses the day-to-day needs and concerns of Hispanic parents living in the United States.

305.412   PE
SERIE MUJER. 1982. m. Asociacion Amauta, Apto. Postal 982, Cusco, Peru. circ. 2,000.

028.5   US   ISSN 0037-301X
SEVENTEEN. 1944. m. $15.95 (Mexico $22, Canada $26; elsewhere $27). Murdoch Magazines (Subsidiary of: News America Publishing, Inc.), 200 Madison Ave., New York, NY 10016. TEL 800-628-7300. FAX 215-688-3285. (And: Matsonford Rd., Box 500, Radnor, PA 19088) Ed. Midge T. Richardson. adv.; illus.; circ. 1,750,000. (microform; also avail. in microform from UMI; reprint service avail. from UMI) **Indexed:** Abr.R.G., Hlth.Ind., Jun.High.Mag.Abstr., Mag.Ind., Media Rev.Dig., PMR, R.G., TOM.
    Description: Covers fashion and beauty ideas, health and fitness, career topics, and personal relationships as they pertain to young women.

SHAPE; the best information available for your body, mind, spirit and beauty. see *PHYSICAL FITNESS AND HYGIENE*

059.927   SU
AL-SHARQIYYAH ELLE. m. P.O. Box 6, Riyadh, Saudi Arabia. TELEX 40112. Ed. Samira M. Khashaggi.

305.412   UK   ISSN 0037-3370
AP4
SHE. 1955. m. £14.40. National Magazine Co. Ltd., 72 Broadwick St., London W1V 2BP, England. TEL 071-439-5000. FAX 071-437-6886. Ed. Linda Kelsey. adv.; bk.rev.; illus.; circ. 240,621.

301.412   CC
SHIDAI JIEMEI. (Text in Chinese) m. Jilin Sheng Funu Lianhehui - Jilin Women's Federation, 49, Stalin Street, Changchun, Jilin 130051, People's Republic of China. TEL 802316. Ed. Dai Huanmei.

SHORT FICTION BY WOMEN. see *LITERATURE*

305.415   AA
SHQIPTARJA E RE. m. $7.40. Union des Femmes d'Albanie, Tirana, Albania.

640   JA
SHUFU NO TOMO/FRIEND OF HOUSEWIVES. (Text in Japanese) 1917. m. 15000 Yen. Shufunotomo Co. Ltd., 2-9 Kanda Surugadai, Chiyoda-ku, Tokyo 101, Japan. Ed. Sachiko Hayashi. circ. 400,000.

301.412   JA
SHUFU-TO-SEIKATSU. (Text in Japanese) m. Shufu-To-Seikatsu Sha Ltd., 5-7, Kyobashi 3-chome, Chuo-ku, Tokyo 104, Japan. TEL 03-3563-5131. FAX 03-3567-7893. circ. 368,999.

301.412   JA
SHUKAN JOSEI. (Text in Japanese) 1957. w. Shufu-To-Seikatsu Sha Ltd., 507, Kyobashi 3-chome, Chuo-ku, Tokyo 104, Japan. TEL 03-3563-5131. FAX 03-3567-7893. circ. 800,000.

301.412   GW   ISSN 0037-4482
SIBYLLE. 1958. m. DM.46.80. Zeitschriftenverlag fuer die Frau, Friedrich-Ebert-Str. 76-78, 7010 Leipzig, Germany.

305.412   US   ISSN 0097-9740
HQ1101
SIGNS: JOURNAL OF WOMEN IN CULTURE AND SOCIETY. 1975. q. $31 to individuals; institutions $70; students $22. University of Chicago Press, Journals Division, 5720 S. Woodlawn Ave., Chicago, IL 60637. TEL 312-753-3347. FAX 312-702-0694. TELEX 25-4603. (Orders to: Box 37005, Chicago, IL 60637) Eds. Ruth-Sllen Botcher Joeres, Barbara LaSlett. adv.; bk.rev.; circ. 6,100. (also avail. in microform from UMI; reprint service avail. from UMI,ISI) **Indexed:** A.B.C.Pol.Sci., Acad.Ind., Adol.Ment.Hlth.Abstr., Amer.Bibl.Slavic & E.Eur.Stud., Amer.Hist.& Life, Amer.Hum.Ind., ASCA, ASSIA, Bk.Rev.Ind. (1984-), C.I.J.E., CERDIC, Child.Bk.Rev.Ind. (1984-), Commun.Abstr., Curr.Cont., Hist.Abstr., Int.Lab.Doc., Lang.& Lang.Behav.Abstr., M.L.A., Mid.East: Abstr.& Ind., Psychol.Abstr., Soc.Sci.Ind., Sociol.Abstr., SSCI, Stud.Wom.Abstr., Wom.Stud.Abstr. (1975-).
—BLDSC shelfmark: 8276.317000.
    Description: Examines theories and methodologies from a variety of disciplines and provides important links between feminist theory and the realities of women's lives.
    Refereed Serial

305.412   FI   ISSN 0359-0267
SINAMINA. 1983. s-m. Fmk.350. Kolmiokirja Oy, Box 246, 90101 Oulu, Finland. FAX 358-81-225249. Ed. Heidi Niskala. adv.; circ. 51,000.
Formerly: Tarina.

SING HEAVENLY MUSE!; women's poetry and prose. see *LITERATURE*

305.412   301.4157
810   US   ISSN 0196-1853
PS508.W7
SINISTER WISDOM; a journal for the lesbian imagination in the arts and politics. 1976. q. $17 to individuals (foreign $22); institutions $30. Box 3252, Berkeley, CA 94703. Ed. Elana Dykewomon. adv.; bk.rev.; illus.; circ. 5,000. (back issues avail.) **Indexed:** Alt.Press Ind., Stud.Wom.Abstr.

SISTERLIFE JOURNAL. see *POLITICAL SCIENCE — Civil Rights*

SISTERS UNITED. see *HOMOSEXUALITY*

SKIP MAGAZINE; the community service magazine for schools, kids, involved parents. see *EDUCATION — Teaching Methods And Curriculum*

SOBERING THOUGHTS. see *DRUG ABUSE AND ALCOHOLISM*

SOCIAL ANARCHISM; a journal of practice & theory. see *LITERARY AND POLITICAL REVIEWS*

SOCIALIST CHALLENGE. see *POLITICAL SCIENCE*

331.4   UK
SOCIETY FOR PROMOTING TRAINING OF WOMEN. ANNUAL REPORT. 1859. a. free. Society for Promoting Training of Women, The Rectory, Bent Lane, Warburton, Lymn, Chesire WA13 9TQ, England. circ. 50.

323.4   US   ISSN 0191-8699
HQ1402
SOJOURNER; the women's forum. 1975. m. $19 to individuals; institutions $29. Sojourner, Inc., 42 Seaverns Ave., Jamaica Plain, MA 02130-2865. Ed. Karen Kahn. adv.; bk.rev.; film rev.; illus.; circ. 36,000. (tabloid format; also avail. in microfiche; back issues avail.) **Indexed:** Alt.Press Ind., PMR.

SOLIDAIRES (PARIS). see *SOCIAL SERVICES AND WELFARE*

305.412   NQ
SOMOS. 1982. 3/yr. Asociacion de Mujeres Nicaraguenses "Luisa Amanda Espinoza", Apdo. Postal A-238, Managua, Nicaragua. TEL 71661. Ed. Patricia Lindo. bk.rev.; circ. 30,000.

646.7   JA
SOPHIA (TOKYO, 1984). (Text in Japanese) 1984. m. Kodansha Ltd., International Division, 12-21 Otowa 2-chome, Bunkyo-ku, Tokyo 112, Japan. TEL 03-3945-1111. FAX 03-3943-7815. TELEX J34509 KODANSHA. Ed. Hiroshi Ohhira. circ. 220,000.
Description: Life-style magazine for women.

305   US
SOPHIA CIRCLE. 1985. s-a. 8319 Fulham Court, Richmond, VA 23227-1712. TEL 804-266-7400. Ed. Donna Gorman. circ. 313.
Description: Advocates disestablishing patriarchy.

SOUTH AFRICAN BRIDE TO BE: FIRST HOME. see *MATRIMONY*

SOUTHERN ASSOCIATION FOR WOMEN HISTORIANS. NEWSLETTER. see *HISTORY*

301.412   RU   ISSN 0038-5913
SOVETSKAYA ZHENSHCHINA. English edition: Sovet Woman (ISSN 0201-6982) (Former name of issuing body: Komitet Sovetskikh Zhenshchin (Soviet Women's Committee)) (Editions in Bengali, Chinese, English, Finnish, German, Hindi, Russian, Spanish, Vietnamese) 1945. m. Kuznetsky Most 22, 103764 Moscow, Russia. TEL 095-221-0781. (Dist. by: Eastern News Distributors, 155 W. 15th St., New York, NY 10011, U.S.A.) Ed. Valentina Fedotova. bk.rev.; illus.; circ. 1,000,000.
Description: Covers social and political issues as well as literature and art. Features include special reports on current events, interviews with national female leaders, health reports, news from world women's organizations, fashion reports, cooking, crafts and fiction.

305.412   UK   ISSN 0306-7971
SPARE RIB. 1972. m. £17 to individuals; institutions £30. Spare Ribs Ltd., 27 Clerkenwell Close, London EC1R 0AT, England. TEL 01-253-9792. Ed.Bd. adv.; bk.rev.; film rev.; play rev.; illus.; circ. 30,000. (also avail. in microfilm) **Indexed:** Alt.Press Ind., Stud.Wom.Abstr.

SPARTACIST CANADA. see *POLITICAL SCIENCE — International Relations*

821 820 305.412   NZ   ISSN 0110-1145
SPIRAL. 1976. irreg. NZ.$10 per no. Spiral Collectives, c/o Anna Keir, 29 North Terrace, Kelburn, Wellington, New Zealand. Ed.Bd. adv.; bk.rev.; circ. 500. (back issues avail.)

301.412   US
SPOKANE WOMAN. 1989. m. $12. Northwest Business Press, Inc., S. 104 Division, Spokane, WA 99202. TEL 509-456-0203. Ed. Jean Kavanagh. adv.; circ. 20,000.
Description: For women in their mid-20s to mid-50s in the Spokane area.

301.412   CE
SRI. (Text in English) 1963. m. 5 Gunasena Mawatha, Colombo 12, Sri Lanka. TEL 1-23864.

STANFORD GAY AND LESBIAN AWARENESS WEEK PROGRAM. see *HOMOSEXUALITY*

STEPFAMILIES & BEYOND; America's first independent newsletter about remarriage for stepparents and professionals. see *CHILDREN AND YOUTH — About*

STORIA. see *LITERATURE*

646.4   GW
STRICK UND HAEKELMODE. 1975. m. DM.2.80 per no. Sonnenverlag GmbH, Lichtentaler Allee 10, Postfach 720, 7570 Baden-Baden, Germany. Ed. G. Maenner. adv.

STUDIES IN WOMEN AND RELIGION. see *RELIGIONS AND THEOLOGY*

746.96   HK
STYLE. (Text in Chinese and English) 1969. m. HK.$270($88) Thomson Press Hong Kong Ltd., 19-F, Tai Sang Commercial Bldg., 24-34 Hennessy Rd., Hong Kong. TEL 5-283351. FAX 5-8650825. TELEX 61504-THOMS-HX. Ed. Rosamund Chang. adv.; bk.rev.; circ. 32,811.

305.412   330   US
SUCCESSFUL WOMAN IN BUSINESS. 1979. q. $42. American Society of Professional and Executive Women, 1429 Walnut St., Philadelphia, PA 19102. TEL 215-563-4415. Ed. Hennie Shore. adv.; bk.rev.; circ. 32,643. (also avail. in microfiche; back issues avail.)
Former titles: Successful Woman (ISSN 0275-0260); (until 1983): Ascend Report.
Description: Contains ideas and practical strategies for women for achieving career, financial, and management goals.

305.412   EI   ISSN 1012-1935
SUPPLEMENTS OF WOMEN OF EUROPE. 1977. irreg. free. Commission of the European Communities, Directorate General of Information, Communication, Culture, 200 rue de la Loi, B-1049 Brussels, Belgium. TEL 32-2-239-94-11. FAX 32-2-239-92-83. TELEX COMEU B 21877. Ed. Fausta Deshormes. bk.rev.; index; circ. 30,000. **Indexed:** EC Ind.
Supersedes (in 1992): Women of Europe (ISSN 0258-6169)

SURPLUS; tijdschrift over literatuur van vrouwen (women's review of books). see *LITERATURE*

SWINGERS UPDATE. see *MEN'S INTERESTS*

SWINGING TIMES. see *MEN'S INTERESTS*

208   US
T B P'S OCTAVA; a news-journal of women's spirituality and thealogy. 1984. 8/yr. $10. New Moon Collective, Box 8, Clear Lake, WA 98235. Ed. Helen G. Farias. adv.; bk.rev.; play rev.; bibl.; illus.; circ. 500.
Formerly: Beltane Papers.

305.412   BE
T V STORY. (Text in Dutch) 1975. w. 2080 Fr. Tijdschriften Uitgevers Maatschappij N.V.I.U.M., Jan Blockxstraat 7, B-2018 Antwerp, Belgium. (U.S. addr.: Interactive Market Systems, 55 Fifth Ave., New York, NY 10003) Ed. L. van Raak. adv.; circ. 180,500.
Formerly: Story.

TAS TOTS. see *CHILDREN AND YOUTH — For*

TELEWOMAN. see *LITERATURE*

TENPERCENT. see *HOMOSEXUALITY*

301.4   TG
TEV FEMA. (Text in Kabiye) 1977. m. Ministry of Social and Women's Affairs, 19 ave. de la Nouvelle Marche, B.P. 1247, Lome, Togo. TEL 21-37-18. circ. 3,000.

TEXAS JOURNAL OF WOMEN AND THE LAW. see *LAW*

323   US
TEXAS WOMAN'S NEWS.* 1984. m. $13. T W N Communications Inc., HCR 5, Box 574-46, Kerrville, TX 78028-9025. Ed. Lorraine Bruck. adv.; bk.rev.; play rev.; circ. 50,000. (tabloid format; back issues avail.)

TEXTURES; Hadassah National Jewish studies bulletin. see *ETHNIC INTERESTS*

301.412   SA
THANDI. 1985. m. R.14.55. Republican Press (Pty) Ltd., Box 32083, Mobeni 4060, South Africa. Ed. Lorna Nisbet. circ. 34,000.
Description: Lifestyles and aspirational features for young black women.

301.412   CE
THARUNEE. (Text in Sinhala) 1969. w. Lake House, D.R. Wijewardene Mawatha, P.O. Box 248, Colombo 10, Sri Lanka. TEL 1-21181. Ed. Sumana Sapramadu. circ. 95,000.

THESMOPHORIA; voice of the new women's religion. see *RELIGIONS AND THEOLOGY — Other Denominations And Sects*

THIRD WORLD WOMAN'S GAY-ZETTE. see *HOMOSEXUALITY*

TINA. see *HOME ECONOMICS*

051   US
▼**TO US.** 1991. bi-m. $12. Innovisions Unlimited, 5405 Alton Pkwy., Ste. A344, Irvine, CA 92714. TEL 714-733-9150.

301.412   US
TODAY'S ARIZONA WOMAN. m. Publishers West, Inc., 4425 N. Saddlebag Trail, Scottsdale, AZ 85251-3419. TEL 602-945-5000. FAX 602-941-5196. Ed. Becky Kistler. adv.; circ. 40,000.

301.412   US
TODAY'S CHICAGO WOMAN.* 1982. m. Leigh Communications, Inc., 233 E. Ontario St., Ste. 1300, Chicago, IL 60611-3214. TEL 312-951-7600. adv.; circ. 140,000.
Description: Contains personality profiles, career strategies, business trends, health, finance, fitness, fashion and activities for professional women.

TODAY'S CHRISTIAN WOMAN. see *RELIGIONS AND THEOLOGY*

TODAY'S INSURANCE WOMAN. see *INSURANCE*

WOMEN'S INTERESTS

301.412 US
▼**TODAY'S LIFESTYLES**; light and lively. 1990. bi-m. Prestige Publications, Inc., 4151 Knob Dr., St. Paul, MN 55122. TEL 612-452-0571.
FAX 612-454-5791. Ed. Diane Stern. adv.; circ. 60,000.
Description: Covers personal makeovers, meal preparation, and lifestyle trends.

305.412 US
TOGETHER (LOS ANGELES). 6/yr. $18. University of California, Los Angeles, 112 Kerckhoff Hall, Los Angeles, CA 90024. Ed. Theta Pavis-Weil. adv. (tabloid format)
Description: Explores women's issues from a feminist perspective.

331.4 331 US
TRADE TRAX. 1983. m. membership. Tradeswomen, Inc., Box 40664, San Francisco, CA 94140. TEL 415-821-7334. circ. 1,000. (back issues avail.)

331.4 US ISSN 0739-344X
TRADESWOMEN; for women in blue-collar work. 1981. q. membership. Tradeswomen, Inc., Box 40664, San Francisco, CA 94140. TEL 415-821-7334. Eds. Molly Martin, Helen Vozenilek. adv.; bk.rev.; circ. 1,500. (back issues avail.) **Indexed:** Alt.Press Ind.

305.412 UK ISSN 0041-2244
TREFOIL. 1955. q. £5. Trefoil Guild, 17 Buckingham Palace Rd., London SW1W 0PT, England.
FAX 071-828-8317. Ed. Myra Street. adv.; bk.rev.; illus.; circ. 22,000.

305.412 US ISSN 0738-9779
TRIBUNE. Spanish edition: Tribuna (ISSN 0748-4607); French edition: Tribune (ISSN 0748-4593) (Editions in English, French and Spanish) 1976. 4/yr. $12 (free to qualified personnel; foreign $16). International Women's Tribune Centre, 777 United Nations Plaza, New York, NY 10017.
TEL 212-687-8633. FAX 212-661-2704. Ed. Anne S. Walker. circ. 14,000 (6,000 Eng. ed.; 5,000 Sp. ed.; 3,000 Fr. ed.). (back issues avail.) **Indexed:** HR Rep.
Formerly: International Women's Tribune Center. Newsletter.

TRIVIA; a journal of ideas. see LITERARY AND POLITICAL REVIEWS

301.432 910.3 SA
TRUE LOVE AND FAMILY. (Text in English) 1970. m. R.29.60 (foreign R.39.96). Drum Publications, National Magazines (Subsidiary of: National Media Limited), 2nd Fl., Eaton Place, Norwich Park, Sandton 2199, South Africa. TEL 011-783-7227. FAX 011-783-8822. Ed. Barney Cohen. adv.; bk.rev.; circ. 96,000.
Description: For black women. Features news and views on fashion, beauty, and parenting.

TRUE ROMANCE. see LITERATURE — Adventure And Romance

301.412 PN ISSN 0746-9691
TU. (Editions avail. for: Ecuador, Central America, Chile, Colombia, Mexico, Peru, Puerto Rico, U.S., Venezuela) (Text in Spanish) 1980. m. $22.50. Editorial America S.A., 6355 N.W. 36th St., Virginia Gardens, FL 33166. TEL 305-871-6400. (Subscr. to: Box 10950, Des Moines, IA 50347-0950) Ed. Irene Carol. adv.; film rev.; music rev.; illus.; circ. 190,000.
Description: For teens, covers health, beauty, fashion, relationships, entertainment and psychology.

301.412 US
TULSA WOMEN. 1989. q. $8. (Tulsa Women's Foundation) Langdon Publishing Co., 1221 E. 33rd St., Tulsa, OK 74105. TEL 918-747-9924. Ed. Charlotte Stewart. adv.; circ. 30,000.
Description: Provides information on women's issues and activities in Tulsa.

305.412 US ISSN 8756-1697
TURN-OF-THE-CENTURY WOMEN. 1984. s-a. $15 (foreign $17.50). Dept. of English, Georgetown Univ., Washington, DC 20057. TEL 202-625-4949. Ed. Margaret D. Stetz. adv.; bk.rev.; circ. 500.
Indexed: M.L.A.
—BLDSC shelfmark: 9074.550000.
Description: Scholarly journal studying the literary, artistic, political, theatrical and social lives of British and American women in the period 1880-1920.

TWIN CITIES GAZE; the news weekly for the gay and lesbian community. see HOMOSEXUALITY

TWINS. see CHILDREN AND YOUTH — About

649 PL
TWOJE DZIECKO. 1951. m. Ul. Wspolna 41 m.30, 00-519, Poland. TEL 48-22-284412. Ed. Janina Szewczykowska. circ. 250,000.
Description: Women's magazine concerning children's affairs.

U S WOMAN ENGINEER. see ENGINEERING

288 US
U U W F FEDERATION NEWSLETTER. 1976. 5/yr. price varies. Unitarian Universalist Women's Federation, 25 Beacon St., Boston, MA 02108.
TEL 617-742-2100. Ed. Ellen Spencer. circ. 9,000. (back issues avail.)

288 US
U U W F JOURNAL. 1976. 3/yr. membership. Unitarian Universalist Women's Federation, 25 Beacon St., Boston, MA 02108. TEL 617-742-2100. Ed. Ellen Spenser. circ. 150,000. (tabloid format; back issues avail.)
Formerly (until 1983): Kyriokos.

301.412 UG
UGANDA ASSOCIATION OF UNIVERSITY WOMEN. BULLETIN. 1960. N.S. 1987. a. $5. Uganda Association of University Women, c/o Makerere University Library, P.O. Box 7062, Kampala, Uganda. TELEX 62104 MAKU. Ed. Maria G. Musoke. adv.; bk.rev.
Description: Includes articles on and by women, reports from committees, courses, seminars and conferences, research projects by association members, announcements and other items of interest to women in development.

ULSTER BRIDE. see MATRIMONY

UNCENSORED SWINGER. see MEN'S INTERESTS

301.42 001.3 677 970 TT835 US ISSN 0277-0628
UNCOVERINGS; research papers. 1980. a. $18. American Quilt Study Group, 660 Mission St., Ste. 400, San Francisco, CA 94105-4007.
TEL 415-495-0163. Ed. Laurel Horton. illus.; index; circ. 750.
Description: Covers the history of quilts, quiltmaking and textiles. Includes research into women's arts.

UNTER UNS; Zeitschrift fuer Frauen und Maedchen. see HANDICAPPED — Visually Impaired

301.412 GW ISSN 0939-5474
▼**UNTERSCHIEDE**. 1991. q. DM.49.60. (Neue Bildungswege fuer Frauen e.V.) Kleine Verlag GmbH, Postfach 4822, 4800 Bielefeld 1, Germany.
TEL 0521-15811. adv.; circ. 3,000.

305.412 FI ISSN 0500-8476
UUSI NAINEN. 1945. m. Fmk.250. Palmikottry, Vilhonkatu 4C27, 00100 Helsinki 10, Finland.
FAX 90-639100. Ed. Anneli Kanto. adv.; bk.rev.; circ. 12,000.

323.4 ZA
V O W: VOICE OF WOMEN. (Text in English) 1974. bi-m. $10. African National Congress of South Africa, Women's Liberation Movement, Box 31791, Lusaka, Zambia. Ed.Bd. circ. 5,000.
Description: Provides a forum for anti-apartheid and human rights movements.

301.412 US
VALLEY WOMEN'S VOICE; a chronicle of feminist thought and action. 1979. m. $15. University of Massachusetts, 321 Student Union, Amherst, MA 01003. TEL 413-545-2436. Ed.Bd. adv.; bk.rev.; film rev.; play rev.; circ. 6,000. (tabloid format; back issues avail.)
Description: Contains radical feminist news and analysis plus fiction, poetry, graphic and photographic art; also includes an abuse survivor column.

301.412 II
VANITA JYOTI. (Text in Telugu) 1978. m. Rs.54. Labbipet, Vijayawada 520 010, India.
TEL 866-474532. Ed. J Satyanarayana. circ. 30,000.
Description: Provides information regarding women's problems and solutions. Also includes interviews of woman doctors, lawyers, ministers, social workers and world-famous women.

301.412 II
VANITHA. (Text in Malayalam) 1975. fortn. M.M. Publications Pvt. Ltd., P.O. Box 226, Erayilkadavu, Kottayam 686 001, India. TEL 481-3721.
FAX 481-2479. TELEX 888201. Ed. Mrs. K.M. Mathew. circ. 218,206.

301.412 CE
VANITHA VITTI. (Text in Sinhala) 1957. m. Wijeya Publications, 8 Humiptiya Cross Rd., Colombo 2, Sri Lanka. TEL 1-435454. Ed. Anula De Silva. circ. 50,000.

301.412 VE
VARIEDADES. w. Edif. Bloque Dearmas, Final Avda. San Martin cruce con Avda. La Paz, Caracas 1020, Venezuela. TEL 2-572-0322. Ed. Armando de Armas. circ. 58,230.

301.412 US
VENUS. bi-m. Prestige Publications, Inc., 4151 Knob Dr., St. Paul, MN 55122-1876. TEL 800-728-3213. FAX 612-454-5791. Ed. Diane Steen. circ. 100,000.

VIDEO RESERVED COLLECTION. see COMMUNICATIONS — Video

746.96 BE
VIE FEMININE. 1920. m. Publicarto N.V., Langestraat 170, B-1150 Brussels, Belgium.
TEL 02-782-00-00. FAX 02-782-16-16. Vie Feminine (Mouvement Chretien d'Action Culturelle et Sociale). circ. 81,291.
Description: Addressed to members of the Vie Feminine women's organization.

305.412 MF
VIRGINIE; le magazine de la femme Mauricienne. (Text in French) bi-m. Ave. des Azalees, Quatre Bornes, Mauritius.

305.413 200 US ISSN 0164-7288
VIRTUE. 1977. 6/yr. $16.95 (effective Jan. 1992). (Virtue Ministries, Inc.) Good Family Magazine, Box 850, Sisters, OR 97759. TEL 503-549-8261.
FAX 503-549-0153. Ed. Becky Durost Fish. adv.; bk.rev.; circ. 150,000.
Description: For Christian homemakers. Offers articles on creative home management, self-improvement, spiritual enrichment and family relationships.

305.412 NE
VIVA. 1972. w. fl.124.80. Geillustreerde Pers B.V., Stadhouderskade 85, 1073 AT Amsterdam, Netherlands. TEL 20-5734811. FAX 20-5734406. Ed. Tineke Verhoeven. adv.; illus.; circ. 135,000.

305.412 KE
VIVA; the magazine for Kenya women. (Text in English) 1974. m. Viva Publishers Ltd., Box 51951, Nairobi, Kenya. Ed. Horace Awdri. adv.; bk.rev.; circ. 28,000.

305.412 PE
VIVA (LIMA). 1984. q. $30 in Latin America; elsewhere $45 (typically set in Mar.). Centro de la Mujer Peruana "Flora Tristan", P.O. Box 0415, Lima 14, Peru. TEL 51-14-330694. FAX 51-14-339060. Ed. Mariella Sala. adv.; circ. 2,000.

VIVE LA DIFFERENCE. see SOCIOLOGY

646.7 JA
VIVI. (Text in Japanese) 1983. m. Kodansha Ltd., International Division, 12-21 Otowa 2-chome, Bunkyo-yu, Tokyo 112, Japan. TEL 03-3945-1111. FAX 03-3943-7815. TELEX J34509 KODANSHA. Ed. Masahiro Senda. circ. 550,000.
Description: Fashion and variety magazine for young women.

301.412 SP
VOGUE ESPANA. 1988. m. Serrano 3, 4o, 28001 Madrid, Spain. TEL 91-5783390.
FAX 91-5777783. Ed. Maria Eugenia Alberti. circ. 60,000.

WOMEN'S INTERESTS

301.412 US
VOICE OF GUATEMALAN WOMEN.* 1984. irreg. $10. Women for Guatemala, National Coordinating Office, P.O. Box 232, Gaithersburg, MD 20884-0232. TEL 913-243-1013. Ed. Kay Studer. circ. 700. (back issues avail.)
 Description: Contains information about Guatemalan women and children for North American women.

VOICE OF WORKING WOMEN. see *BUSINESS AND ECONOMICS*

301.412 FR
VOICI. w. 360 F. (foreign 575 F.). Prisma Presse, 6 rue Daru, 75008 Paris, France. TEL 44-03-34-54. Ed. Axel Ganz. circ. 780,000.

301.412 AG
VOSOTRAS. (Includes monthly supplements: Labores, Modas) 1935. w. Avda. Leandro N. Alem 896, 3o, 1001 Buenos Aires, Argentina. TEL 32-6010. Dir. Abel Zanotto. circ. 33,000.

301.412 CN
VOUS. 10/yr. Quebecor Inc., 7 Bates Chemin, Outrement, Que. H2V 1A6, Canada. TEL 514-270-1100. FAX 514-270-7079. circ. 50,000.

746.96 BE
VROUW EN WERELD. 1920. m. 40 Fr. Publicarto N.V., Langestraat 170, B-1150 Brussels, Belgium. TEL 02-782-00-00. FAX 02-782-16-16. adv.; bk.rev.; circ. 321,923 C.
 Description: Addressed to members of the K.A.V. women's organization.

305.412 NE
VROUWENSTUDIES UTRECHT.* q. fl.2.50 per no. Studium Generale, Gen. Foulkesweg 1, 6703 BG Wageningen, Netherlands. bk.rev.; circ. 500.

301.42 US
W A M M NEWSLETTER. 1982. m. $30 to individuals; families $40. Women Against Military Madness, 3255 Hennepin Ave. S., Ste. 125B, Minneapolis, MN 55408. TEL 612-827-5364. FAX 612-827-6433. adv.; circ. 3,000. (back issues avail.)

333.7 US
W A N D BULLETIN. 1982. q. $35. Women's Action for Nuclear Disarmament, Box B, Arlington, MA 02174-0001. TEL 617-643-6740. Ed. Margaret Covert. bk.rev.; charts; illus.; circ. 20,000. (tabloid format)
 Description: Attempts to educate women in political action so that they can work to eliminate weapons of mass destruction and redirect military spending to human and environmental needs.

W C P S QUARTERLY. (Women's Caucus for Political Science) see *POLITICAL SCIENCE*

W F S QUARTERLY. (Women in the Fire Service) see *FIRE PREVENTION*

W I D BULLETIN. (Women and International Development Program) see *POLITICAL SCIENCE — Civil Rights*

W I D FORUM. (Women and International Development Program) see *POLITICAL SCIENCE — Civil Rights*

301.412 940 IS ISSN 0042-9732
W I Z O REVIEW. Spanish edition: Revista W I Z O. (Editions in English, German and Spanish) 1947. q. $5. Women's International Zionist Organization, 38 David Hamelech Blvd., Tel Aviv 64237, Israel. TEL 3-5421717. FAX 3-6958267. Ed. Hillel Schenker. adv.; bk.rev.; illus.; circ. 20,000.

W L D F NEWS. (Women's Legal Defense Fund) see *LAW*

W L W JOURNAL; news, views, reviews for women and libraries. (Women Library Workers) see *LIBRARY AND INFORMATION SCIENCES*

W M A - NOUNCEMENTS. (Women Marines Association) see *MILITARY*

W R E E - VIEW OF WOMEN. (Women for Racial and Economic Equality) see *POLITICAL SCIENCE — Civil Rights*

301.412 US
WASHINGTON EQUAL TIMES.* 1969. m. $10 to non-members. (National Organization for Women, Washington D.C. Metropolitan Chapters) Washington Equal Times, Box 7279, Washington, DC 20044. TEL 202-331-0066. Ed. Bd. adv.; bk.rev.; circ. 12,000. (also avail. in microfiche)
 Formerly: Vocal Majority.

305.412 CN ISSN 0829-5654
WEDDING BELLS MAGAZINE. (Text in English, French) 1985. q. Can.$15. 120 Front St. E., Ste. 200, Toronto, Ont. M4L 4L9, Canada. TEL 416-869-8479. FAX 416-862-2184. Ed. Crys Stewart. adv.; circ. 107,000.

301.412 659.152 CN
WEDDING PAGES. 1989. a. Wedding Pages Inc., 1962 Yonge St., Ste.205, Toronto, Ont. M4S 1Z4, Canada. TEL 416-322-5590. FAX 416-481-6055. adv.; circ. 5,000.

WEIGHT WATCHERS MAGAZINE. see *PHYSICAL FITNESS AND HYGIENE*

155 361.41 US ISSN 8750-9563
WELCOME HOME; a publication in support of mothers who choose to stay at home. 1984. m. $15 (foreign $25). Mothers-at-Home, 8310A Old Courthouse Rd., Vienna, VA 22182. TEL 703-827-5903. Ed. Pam Goresh. bk.rev.; illus.; circ. 15,000.

305.412 US
WHAT SHE WANTS; Cleveland's only women's newspaper. 1973. m. Box 18465, Cleveland Heights, OH 44118. Ed.Bd. adv.; bk.rev.; circ. 1,000.

WHOM NEWSLETTER. see *HISTORY*

WHO'S WHO OF WOMEN IN WORLD POLITICS; biographies of women currently in government legislatures. see *BIOGRAPHY*

301.412 US
WICHITA WOMEN MAGAZINE; to ease, enrich & celebrate the lives of busy women. 1986. m. $15. Watson Wordsmiths, Inc., 400 N. Woodlawn, Ste. 28, Wichita, KS 67208. TEL 316-684-3620. Ed. Kate Watson. adv.; film rev.; illus.; circ. 30,000. (tabloid format; back issues avail.)

650 UK ISSN 0049-7614
HD6050
WIDENING HORIZONS. (Text in English, French and Spanish) 1931. s-a. £3.75($6) International Federation of Business and Professional Women, Studio Sixteen, Cloisters House, Cloisters Business Centre, 8 Battersea Park, London SW8 4BG, England. TEL 01-738-8323. FAX 01-622-8528. Ed. Amanda Hewett. adv.; bk.rev.; illus.; circ. 7,000.
 Description: Provides news of the federation, as well as intergovernmental organizations. Includes profiles.

WIENERIN. see *GENERAL INTEREST PERIODICALS — Austria*

323.4 GW ISSN 0178-6083
WIR FRAUEN. 1982. q. DM.16 (foreign DM.25). Wir Frauen Verein zur Foerderung von Frauenpublizistik, Rochusstr. 43, 4000 Duesseldorf 1, Germany. TEL 0211-4912078. Ed. Florence Herve. adv.; bk.rev.; circ. 4,000.

301.412 US
WISCONSIN WOMAN.* 1987. m. $14.95. E C K Lectic, Inc, Box 10, Menomonee Falls, WI 53052-0010. TEL 414-273-1234. adv.; bk.rev.; circ. 25,000.
 Description: Covers business, law, finance, health, parenting, fashion and travel for professional women.

WISCONSIN WOMEN'S LAW JOURNAL. see *LAW*

305.412 133.4 US ISSN 0883-119X
THE WISE WOMAN. 1980. q. $15. Ann Forfreedom, Ed. & Pub., 2441 Cordova St., Oakland, CA 94602. TEL 510-536-3174. adv.; bk.rev.; illus.
 Description: Focuses on feminist issues, Goddess lore, feminist spirituality, and feminist witchcraft. Includes history, news, analysis, art, poetry, interviews and original research about witch-hunts, women's heritage and women today.

WISHING WELL. see *HOMOSEXUALITY*

646.7 JA
WITH. 1981. m. Kodansha Ltd., International Division, 12-21 Otowa 2-chome, Bunkyo-ku, Tokyo 112, Japan. TEL 03-3945-1111. FAX 03-3943-7815. TELEX J34509 KODANSHA. Ed. Michio Yoshioka. circ. 840,000.
 Description: Fashion and variety magazine for women.

052 UK ISSN 0043-7220
WOMAN. 1937. w. I P C Magazines Ltd., Woman's Magazine Group (Subsidiary of: Reed International PLC), King's Reach Tower, Stamford St., London SE1 9LS, England. TEL 071-261-5000. TELEX 915748-MAGDIV-G. Ed. David Durman. adv.; bk.rev.; film rev.; illus.; circ. 928,170.
 Description: Women's fashion magazine aimed at 20-40 year-old age group with emphasis on celebrities, features and advice.

301.412 CH
THE WOMAN. (Text in Chinese) 1968. m. 3 Lane 52, Nanking E. Rd., Sec.4, Taipei, Taiwan, Republic of China. TEL 02-7524425. FAX 02-7814308. TELEX 11887. Ed. C.Y. Chang. circ. 80,000.

301.412 CH
WOMAN A B C MAGAZINE. (Text in Chinese) 1982. m. Apollo Bldg., 13th Floor, 218-4 Chung Hsiao E. Rd., Sec.4, Taipei, Taiwan, Republic of China. TEL 02-7314625. FAX 02-7314328. circ. 72,000.

WOMAN ACTIVIST; an action bulletin for women's rights from the courthouse to the White House. see *POLITICAL SCIENCE — Civil Rights*

331.4 US
WOMAN & CO.* 1985. m. $18. City Business - LaCrosse, Inc., Box 83, New Albin, IA 52160-0083. Ed. Vickie Lyons. adv.; bk.rev.; circ. 12,000.

331.4 UK
WOMAN AND HOME. 1926. m. I P C Magazines Ltd., Women's Magazines Group (Subsidiary of: Reed International PLC), King's Reach Tower, Stamford St., London SE1 9LS, England. TEL 01-261-5000. FAX 01-261-5997. TELEX 915748 MAGIDV G. Ed. Sue Dobson. circ. 600,100.

WOMAN BOWLER. see *SPORTS AND GAMES — Ball Games*

WOMAN ENGINEER. see *ENGINEERING*

WOMAN ENGINEER. see *ENGINEERING*

331.4 US
WOMAN ENTREPRENEUR.* m. American Woman's Economic Development Corp., 641 Lexington Ave., Ste. 9, New York, NY 10022-4503.

301.412 US ISSN 0195-9743
WOMAN IN HISTORY. 1980. irreg., vol.79, 1989. price varies. Monument Press (Las Colinas), Box 160361, Las Colinas, TX 75016-9998. (Co-publishers: Texas Independent Press; Liberal Press; Tanglewuld Press; Liberal Arts Press) Ed. Samantha Gonzales. circ. 300.

305.412 700 800 US ISSN 0743-2356
HQ1101
WOMAN OF POWER; a magazine of feminism, spirituality, and politics. 1984. q. $26. Woman of Power, Inc., Box 2785, Orleans, MA 02653. TEL 508-240-7877. Ed. Char McKee. adv.; bk.rev.; bibl.; circ. 75,000. (back issues avail.)

WOMAN POET. see *LITERATURE — Poetry*

305.412 US
WOMANEWS. 1979. m. $15. Womanews, Box 220, Village Sta., New York, NY 10014. Ed.Bd. adv.; bk.rev.; circ. 5,000. **Indexed:** Alt.Press Ind.

301.412 SI
WOMAN'S AFFAIR. (Text in English) 1988. 10/yr. 305 UBI Ave., 02-169, Singapore 1648, Singapore. TEL 7472822. FAX 7472811. TELEX 35361. Ed. Gloria Fu. circ. 22,000.

WOMAN'S ART JOURNAL. see *ART*

WOMEN'S INTERESTS

305.412   AT   ISSN 0043-7328
WOMAN'S DAY. 1948. w. Aus.$1.90 per issue. Australian Consolidated Press, 54-58 Park St., Sydney, N.S.W. 2000, Australia. TEL 02-282-8000. FAX 02-267-2150. TELEX 30104. Ed. Nene King. adv.; circ. 1,120,000.
    Incorporates: Woman's World.
    Description: Entertainment, news and features magazine for women.

051   US
WOMAN'S DAY BEAUTIFUL BRIDES. a. $3.95. Hachette Magazines, Inc., Woman's Day Special Publications, 1633 Broadway, 45th Fl., New York, NY 10019. TEL 212-767-6000.

305.412 640   II
WOMAN'S ERA. (Text in English) 1973. fortn. Rs.325. Delhi Press Patra Prakashan Ltd., Delhi Press Bldg., E-3 Jhandewala Estate, New Delhi 110 055, India. TEL 11-526311. TELEX 3163053. Ed. Vishwa Nath. illus.; circ. 115,000.
    Description: Includes fiction, recipes, fashion notes, and other articles of interest to the women of India.

WOMAN'S HEALTH ADVISER. see *MEDICAL SCIENCES*

305.412   UK   ISSN 0043-7344
AP4
WOMAN'S JOURNAL. 1927. m. £22. I P C Magazines Ltd., Women's Monthly Magazines Group (Subsidiary of: Reed International plc.), King's Reach Tower, Stamford St., London SE1 9LS, England. TEL 0580-200657. Ed. Deirdre Vine. adv.; bk.rev.; illus.; circ. 193,003.

305.412   KE
WOMAN'S MIRROR. (Text in English) 1982. m. $230. New Press Publications, P.O. Box 8454, Nairobi, Kenya. Ed. Muli wa Kyendo. adv.; bk.rev.; circ. 17,320.

051   US
WOMAN'S NATIONAL FARM & GARDEN MAGAZINE. 1914. 3/yr. membership. Woman's National Farm & Garden Association, Inc., 531 Clinton Ct., Findlay, OH 45840. TEL 419-422-5972. Ed. Freda Rose. bk.rev.; illus.; circ. 5,500.
    Formerly: Woman's National Magazine (ISSN 0043-7352)

305.412   US
WOMAN'S NEWSPAPER;* for the professional woman. no.56, 1986. m. Woman's Newspaper of Princeton, Inc., 330 Milltown Rd., East Brunswick, NJ 08816-2267. TEL 609-890-0999. (And: Middlesex Publications, Inc., 575 Cranbury Rd., Ste. B5, E. Brunswick, NJ 08816) Ed. Karen Bookmam. adv.; bk.rev.; circ. 30,000.
    Description: Reports on business news, health, home improvements, education, and fashion for the business and professional woman.

052   UK   ISSN 0043-7360
WOMAN'S OWN. 1932. w. I P C Magazines Ltd., Weeklies and Woman & Home Group (Subsidiary of: Reed International PLC), King's Reach Tower, Stamford St., London SE1 9LS, England. TEL 071-261-5000. TELEX 915748-MAGDIV-G. Ed. Keith McNeill. adv.; illus.; circ. 902,165.

052   UK
WOMAN'S OWN HOLIDAY READING. a. £0.90. I P C Magazines Ltd., King's Reach Tower, Stamford St., London SE1 9LS, England. circ. 250,000.

052   UK   ISSN 0043-7387
WOMAN'S REALM. 1958. w. I P C Magazines Ltd., I P C Woman's Magazines Group (Subsidiary of: Reed International PLC), King's Reach Tower, Stamford St., London SE1 9LS, England. TEL 071-261-5000. TELEX 915748-MAGDIV-G. Ed. Ann Wallace. illus.; circ. 483,000.
    Description: Directed to the 30-55 year-old woman emphasizing features, advice and family issues.

WOMAN'S TOUCH; an inspirational magazine for women. see *RELIGIONS AND THEOLOGY — Other Denominations And Sects*

052   SA
WOMAN'S VALUE. 1977. m. R.45.96. National Magazines (Subsidiary of: National Media Ltd.), P.O. Box 1802, Cape Town 8000, South Africa. TEL 25-4850. TELEX 5-21125. Ed. Jane Pryce. adv.; bk.rev.; film rev.; illus.; circ. 219,340.

305.412   BB
WOMAN'S VOICE. 1977. m. $12. (National Organization of Women) Impact Productions Ltd., Bridgetown, Barbados, W.I. Ed. Jeannette Layne-Clarke. adv.; bk.rev.; illus.; circ. 5,000.

301.412   US
WOMAN'S VOICE. m. Shelby J. Hoon, Ed. & Pub., Box 13049, Fairlawn, OH 44334. TEL 216-864-2683. circ. 15,000.

305.412   IE
WOMAN'S WAY; the Voice of Irish Women. 1963. w. £40. Smurfit Publications, 126 Lower Baggot St., Dublin 2, Ireland. TEL 01-608 264. FAX 01-619-486. Ed. Celine Naughton. adv.; bk.rev.; illus.; circ. 68,431.
    Formerly: Woman's Way Weekly (ISSN 0043-7409)

052   UK   ISSN 0043-7417
WOMAN'S WEEKLY. 1911. w. I P C Magazines Ltd., I P C Women's Magazines Group (Subsidiary of: Reed International PLC), King's Reach Tower, Stamford St., London SE1 9LS, England. TEL 071-261-5000. TELEX 915748-MAGDIV-G. Ed. Judith Hall. adv.; illus.; circ. 993,986.

305.412   US
WOMAN'S WORLD; the woman's weekly. 1981. w. $78. Bauer Publishing Company, 270 Sylvan Ave., Englewood Cliffs, NJ 07632. TEL 201-569-6699. FAX 201-569-3584. Ed. Dena Vane. adv.; circ. 1,200,000.

301.412   NR   ISSN 0331-4162
WOMAN'S WORLD. 1965. m. £N36. Daily Times of Nigeria Ltd., Publications Division, New Isheri Rd., Agidingbi - Ikeja, P.M.B. 21340, Lagos, Nigeria. TEL 900850-9. Ed. Toyin Johnson.

305.412   KO
WOMEN/YEO SUNG. (Text in English and Korean) 1964. m. free. Korean National Council of Women, 40-427 3ka Hangangro, Yongsanku, Seoul, S. Korea. Ed. Yo-Shik Lee.

395.412   UK   ISSN 0957-4042
HQ1591
▼**WOMEN: A CULTURAL REVIEW.** 1990. 3/yr. £39($79) Oxford University Press, Oxford Journals, Pinkhill House, Southfield Road, Eynsham, Oxford OX8 1JJ, England. TEL 0865-882283. FAX 0865-882890. TELEX 837330 OXPRES G. (U.S. subscr. to: Journals Fulfillment, 2001 Evans Rd., Cary, NC 27513. TEL 919-677-0977) Eds. Isobel Armstrong, Helen Carr. adv.; bk.rev.; index; circ. 900.
    —BLDSC shelfmark: 9343.223500.
    Description: Explores the past and present role and representation of women in the arts and culture.

051   US
WOMEN AGAINST RAPE NEWSLETTER. 1984. q. $15. Women Against Rape, Box 02084, Columbus, OH 43202. TEL 614-291-9751. adv.; bk.rev.; circ. 5,000.
    Description: Provides rape prevention information to women in the Greater Columbus, Ohio area.

WOMEN AND ENVIRONMENTS. see *WOMEN'S STUDIES*

WOMEN & GUNS. see *SPORTS AND GAMES*

WOMEN & HEALTH ROUNDTABLE REPORTS. see *WOMEN'S HEALTH*

WOMEN AND INTERNATIONAL DEVELOPMENT ANNUAL. see *BUSINESS AND ECONOMICS — International Development And Assistance*

WOMEN AND MINORITIES IN SCIENCE AND ENGINEERING. see *ENGINEERING*

WOMEN & PERFORMANCE: A JOURNAL OF FEMINIST THEORY. see *THEATER*

WOMEN AND POLITICS (WESTPORT). see *POLITICAL SCIENCE*

323.4   US
WOMEN AND REVOLUTION. 1971. irreg. $3 for 3 nos. (Spartacist League, Commission for Work Among Women) Spartacist Publishing Co., Box 1377, New York, NY 10116. TEL 212-732-7861. Ed.Bd. illus.
    Indexed: Alt.Press Ind., Left Ind. (1982-).

WOMEN & WORK. see *BUSINESS AND ECONOMICS — Labor And Industrial Relations*

WOMEN AND WORK (NEWBURY PARK). see *BUSINESS AND ECONOMICS — Labor And Industrial Relations*

WOMEN AND WORK (WASHINGTON); news from the Department of Labor. see *BUSINESS AND ECONOMICS — Labor And Industrial Relations*

WOMEN ARTISTS NEWS. see *ART*

WOMEN DIRECTORS OF THE TOP 1000 CORPORATIONS. see *BUSINESS AND ECONOMICS — Management*

WOMEN IN A CHANGING WORLD. see *RELIGIONS AND THEOLOGY*

301.412   PH
WOMEN IN ACTION. (Text in English) 4/yr. $20 to individuals; institutions $30. Isis International, 85-A E. Maya St., Philamlife Homes, Quezon City 1100, Philippines. FAX 632-99-75-12. **Indexed:** Wom.Stud.Abstr.
    Description: Offers news and information about groups, conferences, events and resources. Keeps readers up-to-date on the women's movement worldwide.

WOMEN IN BROADCAST TECHNOLOGY DIRECTORY. see *COMMUNICATIONS*

WOMEN IN BUSINESS. see *BUSINESS AND ECONOMICS*

WOMEN IN CONTEXT. see *WOMEN'S HEALTH*

301.2   US
WOMEN IN CULTURE AND SOCIETY. 1984. irreg., latest 1986. price varies. University of Chicago Press, 5801 S. Ellis Ave., Chicago, IL 60637. TEL 312-702-7899. (Subscr. to: 11030 Langley Ave., Chicago, IL 60628) Ed. Catharine R. Stimpson.
    Refereed Serial

WOMEN IN LIBRARIES. see *LIBRARY AND INFORMATION SCIENCES*

WOMEN IN MANAGEMENT REVIEW. see *BUSINESS AND ECONOMICS — Management*

WOMEN IN MINING NATIONAL QUARTERLY. see *MINES AND MINING INDUSTRY*

WOMEN IN THE ARTS. see *ART*

WOMEN IN THE ARTS NEWSLETTER. see *ART*

305.412   CC
WOMEN OF CHINA. Chinese edition: Zhongguo Funu. 1956. m. Y13.20($25.50) for English ed.; Chinese ed. $36.80. Zhongguo Funu Zazhishe, A24, Shijia Hutong, Beijing 100010, People's Republic of China. TEL 5126980. (Dist. outside China by: China International Book Trading Corp., P.O. Box 399, Beijing, P.R.C.; Dist. in US by: China Books and Periodicals, Inc., 2929 24th St., San Francisco, CA 94110) Ed. Guo Nanning. adv.; illus.
    Description: Looks at developments and problems in women's economic and political rights, in work, childcare and healthcare, courtship and marriage, and in women's role in Chinese culture.

305.412   VN   ISSN 0512-1825
HQ1750.5
WOMEN OF VIETNAM. (Editions in English and French) 1973. q. $8. Vietnam Women's Union, 39 Hang Chuoi Str., Hanoi, Socialist Republic of Vietnam. TEL 53143. Ed. Duong Thi Duyen. bk.rev.; illus.

WOMEN ON WINE CHAPTER FLYER. see *BEVERAGES*

WOMEN ON WINE NATIONAL NEWS. see *BEVERAGES*

WOMEN OUTDOORS. see *SPORTS AND GAMES — Outdoor Life*

WOMEN STRIKE FOR PEACE. LEGISLATIVE ALERT. see *POLITICAL SCIENCE — Civil Rights*

051   US   ISSN 0043-7506
WOMEN TODAY. 1970. 26/yr. $40. Today Publications and News Service, Inc., 621 National Press Bldg., Washington, DC 20045. TEL 202-628-6999. Ed. Lester A. Barrer. bk.rev.; bibl.; stat.; index.; cum.index. (looseleaf format)
    Formerly: Frontline News for Women.

301.412   US
WOMEN UNLIMITED. 1989. m. $21. Alice Stelzer, Ed. & Pub., 603 Sumner Ave., Springfield, MA 01108. TEL 413-733-1231. FAX 413-737-1008. adv.; circ. 3,000.
   Description: Written for women in northern Connecticut and the Pioneer Valley of Massachusetts.

WOMEN WITH WHEELS. see TRANSPORTATION — Automobiles

WOMEN WRITERS OF ITALY. see LITERATURE

323.42   US
WOMENEWS. 1975. q. free upon request. Commission for Women, 209 Finance Bldg., Box 1326, Harrisburg, PA 17120-0018. TEL 717-787-8128. FAX 717-787-8614. Ed. Elizabeth McInnis. bk.rev.; bibl.; circ. 20,000. (tabloid format; reprint service avail. from UMI)
   Formerly: Pennsylvania Commission for Women News.

WOMEN'S CAUCUS FOR ART. HONOR AWARDS CATALOGUE. see ART

WOMEN'S CAUCUS FOR ART. NATIONAL UPDATE. see ART

305.412   US   ISSN 0509-089X
WOMEN'S CIRCLE. bi-m. $9.95. House of White Birches Publishing, 306 E. Parr Rd., Berne, IN 46711. TEL 219-589-8741. Ed. Marjorie Pearl. illus.; circ. 42,741.
   Description: Contains decorating ideas, craft projects, recipes and advice. Readers share how to turn home hobbies into businesses.

367   IE
WOMEN'S CLUBS MAGAZINE. 1971. q. £1.50 per issue. (Irish Federation of Women's Clubs) Maxwell Publicity, 49 Wainsfort Park, Dublin 6, Ireland. TEL 353-1-904168. FAX 353-1-900834. TELEX 91247 IMILEI. circ. 23,000. (processed)

301.412   US
WOMEN'S COLLECTION NEWSLETTER. 1974. irreg. free. Northwestern University Library, Special Collections Department, 1935 Sheridan Rd., Evanston, IL 60208. TEL 708-491-3635. Ed. Judy Lowman. bk.rev.; abstr.; bibl.; circ. 1,500.

301.412 200   US
WOMEN'S CONCERNS REPORT. 1973. bi-m. donation. Mennonite Central Committee, 21 S. 12th St., Box 500, Akron, PA 17501-0500. TEL 717-859-1151. Ed. Tina Mast Burnett. bibl.; illus.; cum.index (1973-1986); circ. 3,759. (looseleaf format; back issues avail.)
   Description: Information on various women's issues ranging from religious concerns to women in the arts.

376 374   CN   ISSN 0714-9786
WOMEN'S EDUCATION/EDUCATION DES FEMMES. (Text and summaries in English and French) 1982. q. Can.$18.19 to individuals; institutions Can.$30.70. Canadian Congress for Learning Opportunities for Women, 47 Main St., Toronto, Ont. M4E 2V6, Canada. TEL 416-699-1909. FAX 416-699-2145. Ed. Christina Starr. bk.rev.; index; cum.index vols.1-6; circ. 1,600. (back issues avail.) **Indexed:** Can.Wom.Per.Ind.
   Description: Discusses women's access to education and provides a feminist analysis of education and learning.

WOMEN'S ELECTORAL LOBBY (SOUTH AUSTRALIAN) NEWSLETTER. see SOCIAL SERVICES AND WELFARE

WOMEN'S HEALTH ISSUES. see WOMEN'S HEALTH

973   US
WOMEN'S HISTORY NETWORK NEWS. 1983. q. $25. National Women's History Project, 7738 Bell Rd., Windsor, CA 95492. TEL 707-838-6000. FAX 707-838-0478. Ed. Mary Ruthsdotter. bk.rev.; circ. 800. (tabloid format; back issues avail.)

WOMEN'S HISTORY RESOURCE CATALOG. see HISTORY — History Of North And South America

WOMEN'S HISTORY REVIEW. see HISTORY — History Of Europe

640   US   ISSN 0510-7385
WOMEN'S HOUSEHOLD. 1962. m. $12.97. House of White Birches Publishing, 306 E. Parr Rd., Berne, IN 46711. TEL 219-589-8741. Ed. Allison Ballard-Bonfitto. adv.; charts; illus.; circ. 25,736.
   Description: Brings to readers letters, ideas, craft projects, advice, pen pals, "how-to" information, recipes and needlecraft.

301.412 026   SZ
WOMEN'S INFORMATION UPDATES. Variant title: W I C C E Newsletter. (Text in English, French, Spanish) 1976. s-a. 20 Fr. to individuals and groups; institutions 40 Fr. Isis - Women's International Cross-Cultural Exchange, 3, chemin des Campanules, CH-1219 Geneva Aiere, Switzerland. TEL 022-796-44-37. FAX 022-796-06-03. adv.; bk.rev.; bibl.; stat. (also avail. in microfiche)
   Description: Lists new documentation and books at the center as well as in-depth thematic listings of resources, information about new groups, activities, actions, and campaigns.

WOMEN'S LEAGUE OUTLOOK. see RELIGIONS AND THEOLOGY — Judaic

WOMEN'S MUSIC PLUS; directory of resources in women's music & culture. see MUSIC

301.4157 780   US
WOMEN'S NETWORK; national newsletter for women. 1977. s-a. donation. 2137 Quimby Ave., Bronx, NY 10473. TEL 212-597-7091. Ed. Dorothy Feola. adv.; bk.rev.; illus.
   Formerly: Women's Network - Women in Music.

310.412   NL   ISSN 1017-3900
WOMEN'S NEWS. (Text in English or French) 1982. q. South Pacific Commission, B.P. D5, Noumea, Cedex, New Caledonia. TEL 26-2000. FAX 687-263818. TELEX 3139 NM SOPACOM.
   Formerly: Women's Newsletter.

301.412   US
WOMEN'S NEWS. m. Popper - Strong Communications Inc., Box 829, Harrison, NY 10528. TEL 914-835-5400. Ed. Marjorie Roberts. circ. 250,000.

301.412   US
WOMEN'S ORGANIZATIONS: A NATIONAL DIRECTORY. 1986. irreg. (approx. 2-3/yr.). $25. Garrett Park Press, Box 190B, Garrett Park, MD 20896. TEL 301-946-2553. Ed. Martha Merrill Doss.

301.412   US
WOMEN'S ORGANIZATIONS: A NEW YORK CITY DIRECTORY. 1982. irreg. $6.95. Commission on the Status of Women, 52 Chambers St., Rm. 209, New York, NY 10007. TEL 212-788-2738. Ed. Maxine Gold. circ. 5,000.
   Description: Annotated listing of 455 women's business, professional, and advocacy groups in New York City.

301.41   US   ISSN 0092-6639
HQ1883
WOMEN'S ORGANIZATIONS & LEADERS DIRECTORY. 1973. biennial. $65. Today Publications and News Service, Inc., 621 National Press Building, Washington, DC 20045. TEL 202-638-0348. Ed. Lester A. Barrer.

WOMEN'S OUTDOOR JOURNAL. see SPORTS AND GAMES — Outdoor Life

WOMEN'S POLITICAL TIMES. see POLITICAL SCIENCE

305.412   JA
WOMEN'S PUBLIC OPINION/FUJIN KORON. (Text in Japanese) 1916. m. 8950 Yen. Chuokoron-Sha, Inc., No. 2-8-7 Kyobashi, Chuo-ku, Tokyo, Japan. Ed. Toshiaki Matsuda.

301.412   US
WOMEN'S RECORD. 1985. m. $10. J A G Publishers, 55 Northern Blvd., Greenvale, NY 11548-1317. TEL 516-625-3033. FAX 516-625-3411. Ed. Marcia Byalick. adv.; bk.rev.; film rev.; circ. 35,000. (tabloid format; back issues avail.)
   Description: Covers national issues bringing them into regional focus and salutes Long Island women in business.

WOMEN'S INTERESTS 4857

051   US
WOMEN'S RESOURCE & ACTION CENTER. NEWSLETTER. 1971. m. $5. (Women's Resource & Action Center) University of Iowa, 130 N. Madison, Iowa City, IA 52240. TEL 319-335-1486. bk.rev.; bibl.; circ. 1,000.
   Description: Feminist newsletter covering activities and issues of interest to women.

305.412   US
WOMEN'S RIGHTS TO WOMEN LEADERS. vol.12, 1982. q. free. D C Commission for Women, Women's Program Managers Committee, 2000 14th St., N.W., Rm. 354, Washington, DC 20009. TEL 202-939-8083.
   Formerly (until 1987): N A C W Breakthrough (National Association of Commissions for Women).
   Description: Chronology of the DC commission's 20 years as an advocacy agency working on the behalf of women and their families.

WOMEN'S SPORTS AND FITNESS. see SPORTS AND GAMES

WOMEN'S TRAVELLER. see TRAVEL AND TOURISM

640   AT
WOMEN'S VIEW. 1962. q. membership. (View Clubs of Australia) Smith Family, 16 Larkin St., Camperdown, N.S.W. 2050, Australia. TEL 02-550-4422. FAX 02-550-4235. Ed. Bridget Battersby. adv.: B&W page Aus.$1150, color page Aus.$3000; trim 275 x 200; adv. contact: James Tonkin. bk.rev.; circ. 26,000 (controlled).
   Formerly (until Sep. 1991): View World.
   Description: For contemporary women with traditional values.

301.412   KO
WOMEN'S WEEKLY. (Text in English) w. 14 Chunghak-dong, Chongno-ku, Seoul, S. Korea.

305.412 296   US   ISSN 0043-759X
WOMEN'S WORLD. 1951. 4/yr. membership. B'nai B'rith Women, Inc., 1828 L St., N.W., Ste. 250, Washington, DC 20036. TEL 202-857-1320. FAX 202-857-1380. Ed. Susan Tomchin. bk.rev.; charts; illus.; circ. 120,000. (tabloid format) **Indexed:** Mag.Ind.

WOMEN'S YELLOW PAGES. see BUSINESS AND ECONOMICS — Trade And Industrial Directories

WOMEN'S YELLOW PAGES ARIZONA; a directory of women's businesses, services & professions. see BUSINESS AND ECONOMICS — Trade And Industrial Directories

WOMENWISE. see WOMEN'S HEALTH

301.412   US   ISSN 0049-786X
WOMYN'S PRESS; a feminist news journal. 1970. 6/yr. $7 to individuals; institutions $16. Womyn's Press Collective, Box 562, Eugene, OR 97440. TEL 503-343-4311. Ed.Bd. adv.; bk.rev.; film rev.; play rev.; charts; illus.; circ. 2,000. (tabloid format)

305.412   UK   ISSN 0260-6127
WORKERS EDUCATION ASSOCIATION. WOMEN'S STUDIES NEWSLETTER. 1977. s-a. £2.50. Workers' Education Association, 9 Upper Berkeley St., London W1H 8BY, England. TEL 071-402-5608. FAX 071-402-5600. adv.; bk.rev.; illus.; circ. 2,000.

WORKING AT HOME. see BUSINESS AND ECONOMICS — Small Business

640   US   ISSN 0278-193X
HQ759
WORKING MOTHER (NEW YORK). 1978. m. $7.97. Lang Communications, 230 Park Ave., New York, NY 10169. TEL 212-551-9500. Ed. Judson Culdreth. circ. 556,462. (also avail. in microform from UMI) **Indexed:** PMR.
   Incorporates (1986-1988): Baby; McCall's Working Mother (ISSN 0160-6131).

WORKING PAPERS ON WOMEN IN INTERNATIONAL DEVELOPMENT. see BUSINESS AND ECONOMICS — International Development And Assistance

U V W X Y Z

WOMEN'S INTERESTS — ABSTRACTING, BIBLIOGRAPHIES, STATISTICS

305.412   US   ISSN 0145-5761
HQ1101
WORKING WOMAN. 1976. m. $9.97. Lang Communications, 230 Park Ave., New York, NY 10169. TEL 212-309-9800. (Subscr. to: Box 10132, Des Moines, IA 50340) Ed. Lynn Povich. adv.; bk.rev.; illus.; circ. 900,000. (also avail. in microfiche from UMI; reprint service avail. from UMI) **Indexed:** ABI Inform, Acad.Ind., BPIA, Bus.Ind., Curr.Lit.Fam.Plan., Hlth.Ind., Mag.Ind., PMR, PSI, R.G. ●Also available online. Vendor(s): DIALOG.
—BLDSC shelfmark: 9351.213000.

051   US
▼**WORLD CLASS ENTERTAINMENT.** 1990. m. $17.95. Duncan Publications, 621 Renken Rd., Staunton, IL 62088. TEL 618-637-2202. Ed. Susan Duncan. circ. 100,000. (tabloid format)
Description: For upscale women between the ages of 25 and 54. Covers fashion, travel, celebrities and entertainment.

920.72   UK
WORLD WHO'S WHO OF WOMEN. 1973. every 18 mos. price varies. Melrose Press Ltd., 3 Regal Lane, Soham, Ely, Cambridgeshire CB7 5BA, England. TEL 0353-721091. FAX 0353-721839. Ed. Dr. Ernest Kay. illus.

WRITING ABOUT WOMEN: FEMINIST LITERARY STUDIES. see *LITERATURE*

X LETTERS. see *MEN'S INTERESTS*

301.412   CC
XIANDAI FUNU/MODERN WOMEN. (Text in Chinese) m. Xiandai Funu Zazhishe, 213 Minjiaqiao, Lanzhou, Gansu 730000, People's Republic of China. TEL 465667. (Dist. overseas by: Jiangsu Publications Import & Export Corp., 56 Gao Yun Ling, Nanjing, Jiangsu, P.R.C.) Ed. Han Xiangjing.

301.412   CC
XINGFU/HAPPINESS. (Text in Chinese) bi-m. Wuhan Shi Funu Lianhehui - Wuhan Municipal Women's Association, No. 22, Haomengling Lu, Hankou, Wuhan, Hubei 430010, People's Republic of China. TEL 512071. Ed. Yang Fuhua.

301.412   CC
YANBIAN FUNU/YANBIAN WOMEN. (Text in Korean) m. Yanbian Funu Lianhehui, 1 Youyi Lu, Guangming Jie, Yanji, Jilin 133000, People's Republic of China. TEL 518494. Ed. Jin Yangjin.

301.412   US   ISSN 1048-8626
YEARBOOK OF WOMEN'S STUDIES. a. $19.95 to individuals; institutions $29.95. Edwin Mellen Press, 240 Portage Rd., Box 450, Lewiston, NY 14902. TEL 800-753-2788. FAX 716-754-4335. Eds. Kathryn Benzel, Lauren de la Vars.

310.412   SP
YMODA. 1984. bi-m. $20. Hogar y la Moda, S.A., Diputacion, 211, 08011 Barcelona, Spain. TEL 254 10 04. Ed. Dona Maria Asuncion Batlle Brossa. adv.; film rev.; circ. 60,426.

301.412   KO
YOSONG DONG-A. 1933. m. Dong-A Ilbo, 139 Sejongno, Chongno-gu, Seoul, S. Korea. TEL 02-721-7114. Ed. Kwon O-Kie. circ. 237,000.

305.412   SA
YOUR FAMILY. m. R.37.80. Republican Press (Pty) Ltd., Box 32083, Mobeni 4060, Natal, South Africa. Ed. Angela Waller-Paton. circ. 248,000.
Description: Do-it-yourself information on cookery, garment-making, and homecrafts.

Z MAGAZINE. see *POLITICAL SCIENCE*

301.435   TS
ZAHRAT AL-KHALIJ. (Text in Arabic) 1979. w. Al-Ittihad Press, Publishing and Distribution Corp., Zahrat al-Khalij, P.O. Box 3342, Abu Dhabi, United Arab Emirates. TEL 451600. FAX 461801. TELEX 22984 ITTPRESS EM. Ed. Abla Al-Nuwais. circ. 709,900.
Description: Covers issues of interest to Arab women throughout the Gulf and the Arab world.

301.435 915.5   IR
ZAN-E RUZ. 1964. w. Kayhan Publications, Ferdowsi Ave., P.O. Box 11365-9631, Teheran, Iran. TEL 021-310251. TELEX 212467. circ. 100,000.

ZARJA/DAWN. see *ETHNIC INTERESTS*

059.927   SU
ZEINA. 6/yr. P.O. Box 157, Jeddah 21411, Saudi Arabia. TEL 682-7736. circ. 48,260.

640   CI   ISSN 0513-9481
ZENA. 1943. bi-m. $18. Savjet za Pitanja Drustvenog Polozaja Zene PK SSRNH, Vlaska 70a-lll, 41000 Zagreb, Croatia. Ed. Melita Singer. adv.; bk.rev.; circ. 1,700.

323   RU
▼**ZHENSHCHINA: VEK XX.** 1991. m. 1 Rub. per issue. (Komitet Sovetskikh Zhentschin) T.A.S.S., Tverskoi Bul'var, 10-12, 103009 Moscow, Russia. Ed. S.F. Bulantsev. circ. 1,700.

057.1   RU   ISSN 0044-4456
ZHENSHCHINY MIRA. 1958. q. 5.20 Rub. Mezhdunarodnaya Demokraticheskaya Federatsiya Zhenshchin, Moscow, Russia.

305   CN   ISSN 0513-9856
HQ1104
ZHINOCHYI SVIT/WOMAN'S WORLD. (Text in Ukrainian and English) 1950. m. Can.$25 (effective Jan. 1991). Ukrainian Women's Organization, 937 Main St., Winnipeg, Man. R2W 3P2, Canada. TEL 416-943-8230. Ed. Anne Wach. adv.; bk.rev.; illus.; circ. 2,500. **Indexed:** Amer.Bibl.Slavic & E.Eur.Stud.

305.4   CC   ISSN 1000-4157
ZHIYIN/BOSOM FRIEND. (Text in Chinese) 1985. m. $35.90. Hubei Sheng Funu Lianhehui, Shengwei Dayuan, Shuiguo Hu, Wuhan, Hubei 430071, People's Republic of China. TEL 711030. (Dist. in US by: China Books & Periodicals, Inc., 2929 24th St., San Francisco, CA 94110. TEL 415-282-2994) Ed. Hu Xunbi.

301.412   CC
ZHONGWAI FUNU WENZHAI. (Text in Chinese) m. Neimenggu Zizhiqu Funu Lianhehui, 9, Zhongshan Donglu, Huhhot, Neimenggu (Inner Mongolia) 010020, People's Republic of China. Ed. Xi Xingfang.

301.412   US   ISSN 0279-3229
ZONTIAN. (Text in English; summaries in French, German, Japanese, Spanish) 1923. q. $7. Zonta International, 557 W. Randolph St., Chicago, IL 60661-2206. TEL 312-930-5848. FAX 312-930-0951. TELEX 190200. Ed. Dawn M. Olson. circ. 35,000.
Description: Presents articles regarding organization's programs and activities.

323.4   GW
ZWEIWOCHENDIENST FRAUEN UND POLITIK. 1986. m. DM.84 to individuals; institutions DM.156; low income DM.48. Zweiwochendienst Verlag GmbH, Pressehaus I, Room 234, Heussallee 2-10, 5300 Bonn 1, Germany. TEL 0228-217375. FAX 0228-215226. bibl.; stat.
Description: Covers women in politics and provides suggestions on how to better women's chances in education and business. Includes information on equal rights for men and women.

9 TO 5 NEWSLETTER. see *BUSINESS AND ECONOMICS — Labor And Industrial Relations*

13TH MOON; a feminist literary magazine. see *LITERATURE*

052   UK   ISSN 0262-1126
19. 1968. m. £16.40 (foreign £25). I P C Magazines Ltd., Women's Monthly Magazines Group (Subsidiary of: Holborn Publishing Group), King's Reach Tower, Stamford St., London SE1 9LS, England. TEL 071-261 5000. Ed. M. Rice. adv.; bk.rev.; film rev.; circ. 156,340.

054.1   FR
20 ANS. 1967. 12/yr. 176 F. (foreign 279 F.)(effective 1992). Excelsior Publications, 1 rue du Colonel Pierre Avia, 75503 Paris Cedex 15, France. TEL 46-48-48-48. FAX 46-48-46-09. TELEX 631 994 F. Ed. Yveline Dupuy. adv. contact: Gilles de Keranflech. circ. 106,000.

055.1   IT
100 COSE. 1978. m. L.71400. Arnoldo Mondadori Editore S.p.A., Casella Postale 1833, 20101 Milan, Italy. Ed. Kicca Menoni. circ. 117,325.

305.412   FR
100 IDEES. m. 70 F. 11 bis rue Boissy d'Anglas, 75008 Paris, France. Ed. Collette Gouvion. circ. 346,978.

WOMEN'S INTERESTS — Abstracting, Bibliographies, Statistics

305.412 011   CN
CANADIAN WOMEN'S PERIODICALS INDEX. (Text in English and French) 1984. 3/yr. Can.$40 to non-members; members Can.$30; libraries Can.$50. 11019-90 Avenue, University of Alberta, Edmonton, Alta. T6G 2E1, Canada. TEL 403-492-3093. FAX 403-492-1186. (back issues avail.)
Former titles: Canadian Women's Periodicals: Title Word Index (ISSN 0829-9552); Canadian Women's Periodicals: K W I C Index.

301.412 016   GW   ISSN 0344-1415
Z7964.G4
DIE FRAUENFRAGE IN DEUTSCHLAND. BIBLIOGRAPHIE. 1951; N.S. 1981. irreg. price varies. (Deutscher Akademikerinnenbund) K.G. Saur Verlag KG, Ortlerstr. 8, Postfach 701620, 8000 Munich 70, Germany. TEL 089-76902-0. FAX 089-76902150.
Description: Lists women's studies titles written in German and those in other languages concerning women in Germany.

LESBIAN HERSTORY ARCHIVES NEWSLETTER. see *HOMOSEXUALITY*

LESBISCH ARCHIVARIA. see *HOMOSEXUALITY — Abstracting, Bibliographies, Statistics*

WOMEN AND APPROPRIATE TECHNOLOGIES; a bibliography. see *TECHNOLOGY: COMPREHENSIVE WORKS — Abstracting, Bibliographies, Statistics*

WOMEN'S STUDIES

AFFILIA; journal of women and social work. see *SOCIAL SERVICES AND WELFARE*

305.4 327   SJ   ISSN 0255-4070
HQ1793.5
AHFAD JOURNAL; women and change. (Text in English; summaries in Arabic) 1984. s-a. $40. Ahfad University for Women, P.O. Box 167, Omdurman, Sudan. TEL 53363. (Subscr. in U.S.: c/o Dr. Lee G. Burchinal, Ste.1216, 4141 N. Henderson Rd., Ste.1216, Arlington, VA 22203) Ed. Amna El Sadik Badri. adv.; bk.rev.; circ. 400. (also avail. in microform; back issues avail.; reprint service avail. from UMI) **Indexed:** Wom.Stud.Abstr. (1989-).
—BLDSC shelfmark: 0772.281500.
Description: Covers issues affecting women, families and children in developing countries, and role of women in national development.

305.412   CN   ISSN 0702-7818
HQ1180
ATLANTIS; a women's studies journal - revue d'etudes sur la femme. (Text in English and French) 1975. s-a. Can.$20($30) to individuals; institutions Can.$30($40). Mount Saint Vincent University, 166 Bedford Hwy., Halifax, N.S. B3M 2J6, Canada. TEL 902-443-4450. FAX 902-445-3960. Ed. Deborah Poff. adv.; bk.rev.; cum.index; circ. 900. (also avail. in microfilm from MML) **Indexed:** Alt.Press Ind., Amer.Hist.& Life, Can.Lit.Ind., Can.Per.Ind., Can.Wom.Per.Ind., CMI, Hist.Abstr., M.L.A., Stud.Wom.Abstr. (1975-), Wom.Stud.Abstr.
—BLDSC shelfmark: 1765.960000.

BELLES LETTRES; a review of books by women. see *LITERATURE*

305.4   US
C C W H P - C G W H NEWSLETTER. 1969. bi-m. $30. Coordinating Committee on Women in the Historical Profession - Conference Group on Women's History, c/o Barbara Winslow, Dir.-Treas., 124 Park Pl., Brooklyn, NY 11217. TEL 718-638-3227. Eds. Bonnie Gordon, Eileen Boris. adv.; circ. 850. **Indexed:** Wom.Stud.Abstr. (1972-).

CAMERA OBSCURA; a journal of feminism and film theory. see *MOTION PICTURES*

CANADIAN JOURNAL OF WOMEN AND THE LAW/REVUE FEMMES ET DROIT. see *LAW*

WOMEN'S STUDIES

305.412   CN   ISSN 0713-3235
HQ1451
CANADIAN WOMAN STUDIES/CAHIERS DE LA FEMME. (Text in English, French) 1978. q. Can.$30 to individuals; institutions Can.$40 (effective Jun. 1991). Inanna Publications and Education Inc., 212 Founders College, York University, 4700 Keele St., Downsview, Ont. M3J 1P3, Canada. TEL 416-736-5356. Ed. Carol Greene. adv.; bk.rev.; illus.; circ. 5,000. **Indexed:** C.P.I., Can.Per.Ind., CMI, Stud.Wom.Abstr., Wom.Stud.Abstr. (1990-).
—BLDSC shelfmark: 3046.154720.
Formerly (until vol.3, no.2, 1981): Canadian Women's Studies (ISSN 0706-8204)

305.412   US   ISSN 1040-7391
HQ1101   CODEN: DIFFEX
DIFFERENCES; a journal of feminist cultural studies. 1989. 3/yr. $28 to individuals; institutions $48. (Brown University, Pembroke Center) Indiana University Press, Journals Division, 601 N. Morton St., Bloomington, IN 47404. TEL 812-855-9449. Eds. Naomi Schor, Elizabeth Weed. (back issues avail.) **Indexed:** Left Ind. (1989-), Wom.Stud.Abstr. (1989-).
—BLDSC shelfmark: 3584.100000.
Description: Focuses on how concepts and categories of difference (notably but not exclusively gender) operate within a culture. Provides a forum for exchange between cultural studies and feminism.

331.4   UK   ISSN 0261-0159
EQUAL OPPORTUNITIES INTERNATIONAL. 1981. 6/yr. £305.4($323.4) Barmarick Publications, Enholmes Hall, Patrington, Hull HU12 0PR, England. TEL 0964-630033. Ed. Nancy Wise. circ. 200. (back issues avail.; reprint service avail. from SWZ) **Indexed:** ABI Inform., Int.Lab.Doc., Stud.Wom.Abstr.
—BLDSC shelfmark: 3794.504500.
Description: Publishes articles and features on all aspects of women's involvement in the labor force. Outlines the latest international developments within the realm of equal opportunity studies, as well as practical case studies and regular reviews of research projects.

305.4 070.5   US   ISSN 0742-7441
Z688.W65
FEMINIST COLLECTIONS; a quarterly of women's studies resources. 1980. 4/yr. $23 to individuals; institutions $43 (includes New Books on Women & Feminism and Feminist Periodicals). University of Wisconsin System, Women's Studies Librarian, 430 Memorial Library, 728 State St., Madison, WI 53706. TEL 608-263-5754. Eds. Susan E. Searing, Linda Shult. bk.rev.; bibl.; circ. 1,500. **Indexed:** Stud.Wom.Abstr., Wom.Stud.Abstr.
—BLDSC shelfmark: 3905.197200.
Description: Covers feminist publishing, bookselling and distribution, feminist librarianship and resources for feminist research.

305.412   US   ISSN 0270-6679
HQ1101
FEMINIST ISSUES. s-a. $15 to individuals (foreign $25); institutions $34 (foreign $44). (Feminist Forum, Inc.) Transaction Publishers, Transaction Periodicals Consortium, Department 3092, Rutgers University, New Brunswick, NJ 08903. TEL 201-932-2280. FAX 201-932-3138. Eds. Mary Jo Lakeland, Susan Ellis Wolf. adv.; circ. 600. (also avail. in microform from UMI; reprint service avail. from UMI) **Indexed:** Alt.Press Ind., Left Ind. (1982-), Stud.Wom.Abstr., Wom.Stud.Abstr.
—BLDSC shelfmark: 3905.197300.
Description: Devoted to feminist social and political analysis, with emphasis on an international exchange of ideas.

305.4   US   ISSN 0742-7433
Z7963.F44
FEMINIST PERIODICALS; a current listing of contents. 1981. 4/yr. $23 to individuals; institutions $43 (includes Feminist Collections and New Books on Women & Feminism). University of Wisconsin System, Women's Studies Librarian, 430 Memorial Library, 728 State St., Madison, WI 53706. TEL 608-263-5754. Ed. Ingrid Markhardt. circ. 1,500. (back issues avail.) **Indexed:** Stud.Wom.Abstr.
Description: For women's studies scholars, researchers, librarians, and others interested in women's studies. Reproduces the table of contents of major feminist periodicals.

305.4   UK   ISSN 0141-7789
HQ1154
FEMINIST REVIEW. 1979. 3/yr. £36.50($75) (Feminist Review Collective) Routledge, 11 New Fetter Ln., London EC4P 4EE, England. TEL 01-583-9855. (Subscr. to: Routledge Journals Subscription Dept., North Way, Andover Hants SP10 5BE, England) adv.; bk.rev.; circ. 3,500. (back issues avail.) **Indexed:** Alt.Press Ind., ASSIA, Lang.& Lang.Behav.Abstr., Left Ind. (1982-), Mid.East: Abstr.& Ind., Sociol.Abstr., Stud.Wom.Abstr.
—BLDSC shelfmark: 3905.197600.
Description: Articles on socialist-feminist theory. Covers women in history and the Third World, topical political problems, art and literature.

305.4   US   ISSN 0046-3663
HQ1101   CODEN: FMSDA2
FEMINIST STUDIES. 1972. 3/yr. $25 to individuals (foreign $30); institutions $55 (foreign $60). Feminist Studies, Inc., c/o Women's Studies Program, University of Maryland, College Park, MD 20742. TEL 301-405-7415. Ed. Claire Moses. adv.; bk.rev.; illus.; cum.index: 1972-1982; circ. 8,000. (also avail. in microfiche from UMI; reprint service avail. from UMI) **Indexed:** A.I.P.P., Acad.Ind., Adol.Ment.Hlth.Abstr., Alt.Press Ind., Amer.Hist.& Life, ASSIA, Bull.Signal., Curr.Cont., Hist.Abstr., Lang.& Lang.Behav.Abstr., M.L.A., Phil.Ind., Psychol.Abstr., Sage Fam.Stud.Abstr., Soc.Sci.Ind., Sociol.Abstr., SSCI, Stud.Wom.Abstr., Wom.Stud.Abstr. (1972-).
—BLDSC shelfmark: 3905.197800.
Description: Presents scholarly research, essays, art, book reviews, and poetry, fiction, and creative narrative pertaining to the feminist experience in the social sciences, history, politics, and literature.

305.4 371.3   US   ISSN 0882-4843
FEMINIST TEACHER. 1984. 3/yr. $12 to individuals (foreign $17); institutions $20 (foreign $25). Feminist Teacher Editorial Collective, Indiana University, Ballantine 442, Bloomington, IN 47405. Ed.Bd. adv.; bk.rev.; circ. 900. (back issues avail.) **Indexed:** Alt.Press Ind., Cont.Pg.Educ., Stud.Wom.Abstr., Wom.Stud.Abstr. (1984-).
—BLDSC shelfmark: 3905.197900.
Description: Forum for new ideas in the classroom. Includes articles and essays written for teachers and by teachers.

305.4   US   ISSN 0160-9009
FRONTIERS: A JOURNAL OF WOMEN STUDIES. 1975. 3/yr. $20 to individuals; institutions $33. Frontiers Editorial Collective, Mesa Vista Hall 2142, University of New Mexico, Albuquerque, NM 87131. TEL 303-492-3205. Ed. Louise Lamphere. adv.; bk.rev.; film rev.; play rev.; bibl.; charts; illus.; circ. 1,000. (also avail. in microform from UMI; back issues avail.; reprint service avail. from UMI) **Indexed:** Adol.Ment.Hlth.Abstr., Amer.Hist.& Life, Amer.Hum.Ind., Hist.Abstr., Human Resour.Abstr., LCR, M.L.A., P.A.I.S., Soc.Sci.Ind., Sociol.Abstr., Stud.Wom.Abstr., Wom.Stud.Abstr. (1975-).
—BLDSC shelfmark: 4041.400000.
Description: Bridges the gap between the academy and the community. Contains a variety of innovative and traditional feminist work.

GENDER AND EDUCATION. see *EDUCATION*

GENDER AND HISTORY. see *HISTORY*

GENDER AND SOCIETY. see *SOCIOLOGY*

305   US   ISSN 0894-9832
NX1
GENDERS. 1988. 3/yr. $24 to individuals (foreign $29.50); institutions $40 (foreign $45.50). University of Texas Press, Box 7819, Austin, TX 78713. TEL 512-471-7233. FAX 512-320-0668. TELEX 776453-UTEXPRES-AUS. Ed. Ann Kibbey. circ. 900. **Indexed:** Film Lit.Ind. (1989-), Wom.Stud.Abstr. (1988-).
—BLDSC shelfmark: 4096.401800.
Description: Essays in art, literature, film, and history that focus on sexuality and gender. Addresses theoretical issues relating sexuality and gender to social, political, racial, economic, or stylistic concerns.

HARVARD WOMEN'S LAW JOURNAL. see *LAW*

305.4   AT   ISSN 0311-4198
HECATE; women's interdisciplinary journal. 1975. s-a. Aus.$15 to individuals; institutions Aus.$40. Hecate Press, c/o English Dept., Univ. Queensland, St. Lucia, Qld. 4067, Australia. TEL 07-377-4401. FAX 07-371-9578. Ed. Carole Ferrier. adv.; bk.rev.; bibl.; circ. 2,000. (also avail. in microform from UMI; back issues avail.) **Indexed:** Alt.Press Ind., Aus.P.A.I.S., Left Ind. (1982-), Stud.Wom.Abstr., Wom.Stud.Abstr. (1975-).
Description: Perspectives on the status of women from a socialist and women's liberation standpoint. Includes articles, interviews, plays, poems and stories.
Refereed Serial

305.412 700   US   ISSN 0146-3411
HQ1101
HERESIES; a feminist publication on art and politics. 1977. 2/yr. $23 to individuals (foreign $29); institutions $33 (foreign $39) for 4 nos. Heresies Collective, Inc., Box 1306, Canal Street Sta., New York, NY 10013. TEL 212-227-2108. Ed.Bd. adv.; circ. 5,000. **Indexed:** Alt.Press Ind., Artbibl.Mod., Avery Ind.Architl.Per., Mid.East: Abstr.& Ind., Stud.Wom.Abstr., Wom.Stud.Abstr. (1977-).
—BLDSC shelfmark: 4300.025800.

305.4   US   ISSN 0887-5367
HQ1101
HYPATIA; a journal of feminist philosophy. (First 3 issues (1983-1985) published as Special Issues of Women's Studies International Forum) 1986. 4/yr. $32.50 to individuals; institutions $50. Indiana University Press, Journals Division, 601 N. Morton St., Bloomington, IN 47404. TEL 812-855-9449. FAX 812-855-7931. Ed. Linda Lopez McAlister. adv.; bk.rev.; circ. 1,500. (also avail. in microfiche; back issues avail.) **Indexed:** Acad.Ind., Alt.Press Ind., Phil.Ind., Sociol.Abstr., Wom.Stud.Abstr. (1986-).
●Also available online. Vendor(s): DIALOG (File no. 57), Information Access Company.
—BLDSC shelfmark: 4352.621500.
Description: Recognizes the historical roots of feminist philosophy; created to help end sexism and provides a sense of relevency to feminism.

305.4   PH
ISIS INTERNATIONAL WOMEN'S BOOK SERIES. (Text and summaries in English) 1974. 1/yr. $20 to individuals; institutions $30. Isis International, 85-A E. Maya St., Philamlife Homes, Quezon City 1100, Philippines. FAX 632-99-75-12. Ed. Marilee Karl. bk.rev.; film rev.; circ. 4,500. (back issues avail.) **Indexed:** Alt.Press Ind., Int.Lab.Doc., Stud.Wom.Abstr., Wom.Stud.Abstr. (1974-).
Former titles (until 1987): Isis International Women's Journal; Isis Women's International Journal and Supplement; Isis International Bulletin.

305.412 616.89   US   ISSN 0895-2833
RC488.5
JOURNAL OF FEMINIST FAMILY THERAPY. 1989. q. $24 to individuals; institutions $40; libraries $95. Haworth Press, Inc., 10 Alice St., Binghamton, NY 13904. TEL 800-342-9678. FAX 607-722-1424. Ed. Lois Braverman. adv.; bk.rev. (also avail. in microfiche from HAW; reprint service avail. from HAW) **Indexed:** Soc.Work Res.& Abstr., Wom.Stud.Abstr. (1989-).
—BLDSC shelfmark: 4983.937000.
Description: Explores feminist theory in relation to family therapy practice and theory.
Refereed Serial

305.4 200   UK   ISSN 8755-4178
HQ1393
JOURNAL OF FEMINIST STUDIES IN RELIGION. 1985. s-a. £13.95 to individuals; institutions £18.95. T & T Clark, 59 George St., Edingurgh EH2 2LQ, Scotland. TEL 031-225-4703. (Dist. in U.S. by: Scholars Press, Box 15288, Atlanta, GA 30333. TEL 404-636-8301) Eds. E. Fiorenza, J. Plaskow. adv. (back issues avail.) **Indexed:** Rel.& Theol.Abstr. (1985-), Wom.Stud.Abstr. (1985-).
—BLDSC shelfmark: 4983.940000.
Description: Papers on the academic study of religion from a feminist perspective.

WOMEN'S STUDIES

301.412 362.6 US ISSN 0895-2841
HV1457 CODEN: JWAGE5
▼**JOURNAL OF WOMEN AND AGING.** 1991. q. $28 to individuals; institutions $38; libraries $75. Haworth Press, Inc., 10 Alice St., Binghamton, NY 13904. TEL 800-342-9678. FAX 607-722-1424. TELEX 4932599. Ed. J. Dianne Garner. adv.; bk.rev.; circ. 183. (also avail. in microform from HAW; reprint service avail. from HAW) **Indexed:** Soc.Work Res.& Abstr., Wom.Stud.Abstr. (1991-).
—BLDSC shelfmark: 5072.632800.
Description: Designed to enhance the knowledge of a variety of professionals concerned with meeting the social, psychological, and health-care needs of women as they mature.
Refereed Serial

305.412 US ISSN 1042-7961
HQ1101
JOURNAL OF WOMEN'S HISTORY. 1989. 3/yr. $25 to individuals; institutions $45. Indiana University Press, Journals Division, 601 N. Morton St., Bloomington, IN 47404. TEL 812-855-9449. Eds. Christie Farnham, Joan Hoff-Wilson. adv.; circ. 1,500. (also avail. in microfilm; back issues avail.) **Indexed:** Film Lit.Ind. (1989-), Wom.Stud.Abstr. (1989-).
—BLDSC shelfmark: 5072.634500.
Description: Covers new research on women's history. Promotes scholarship about women in all time periods that is broadly representative of national, racial, ethnic, religious, and sexual groupings.

LEGACY (UNIVERSITY PARK); a journal of nineteenth-century American women writers. see *LITERATURE*

MALE - FEMALE ROLES; opposing viewpoints sources. see *ANTHROPOLOGY*

305.412 II ISSN 0257-7305
HQ1104
MANUSHI; a journal about women and society. (Text in English) 1979. bi-m. Rs.60($24) to individuals; institutions Rs.85($36). Manushi Trust, C1 - 202 Lajpat Nagar, New Delhi 110024, India. TEL 6833022. Ed. Madhu Kishwar. adv.; bk.rev.; circ. 10,000. **Indexed:** Alt.Press Ind., HR Rep., Int.Lab.Doc., Stud.Wom.Abstr., Wom.Stud.Abstr. (1990-).
—BLDSC shelfmark: 5368.465000.
Description: Covers human rights issues with an emphasis on women's issues. Examines women's working and living conditions in India, and their struggle for change.

305.4 US ISSN 0047-8318
HQ1101
MS. 1972-1989; resumed July 1990. bi-m. $45. Lang Communications, 230 Park Ave., New York, NY 10169. TEL 212-551-9500. (Subscr. to: Ms., Box 57122, Boulder, CO 80321-7122) Ed. Robin Morgan. adv.; bk.rev.; index; circ. 500,000. (also avail. in microform from UMI,MIM) **Indexed:** Acad.Ind., Bk.Rev.Ind. (1974-), Child.Bk.Rev.Ind. (1974-), Consum.Ind., Curr.Lit.Fam.Plan., Film Lit.Ind. (1974-), Hlth.Ind., Mag.Ind., Media Rev.Dig., Mid.East: Abstr.& Ind., Pers.Lit., PMR, R.G., Stud.Wom.Abstr., TOM, Wom.Stud.Abstr. (1972-1989, 1990-).
—BLDSC shelfmark: 5980.840000.
Description: Contains features about feminist issues and concerns, national and international news concerning women, plus original fiction and poetry.

305.412 US ISSN 1040-0656
CODEN: NWJOEG
N W S A JOURNAL. 1988. 3/yr. $39.50 to individuals; institutions $105. (National Women's Studies Association) Ablex Publishing Corporation, 355 Chestnut St., Norwood, NJ 07648. TEL 201-767-8450. FAX 201-767-6717. TELEX 135-393. Ed. Patrocinio Schweickart. adv.; bk.rev.; abstr.; bibl.; illus.; circ. 1,400. **Indexed:** Left Ind. (1990-), Wom.Stud.Abstr. (1988-).
—BLDSC shelfmark: 6190.647000.
Description: Publishes research linking feminist theory with teaching and activism.

305.4 US
N W S ACTION. 1988. q. membership. National Women's Studies Association, Univ. of Maryland, College Park, MD 20742-1325. TEL 301-404-5573. FAX 301-314-9320. Ed. Debra Humphreys. circ. 4,000. (back issues avail.) **Indexed:** Wom.Stud.Abstr. (1988-).
Description: Articles on women's studies and related subjects for those interested in feminist education.

305.412 US ISSN 0160-1075
NEW DIRECTIONS FOR WOMEN. 1972. bi-m. $12 to individuals; institutions $20. New Directions for Women, Inc., 108 W. Palisade Ave., Englewood, NJ 07631. TEL 201-568-0226. FAX 201-568-6532. Ed. Phyllis Kriegel. adv.; bk.rev.; film rev.; play rev.; illus.; index, cum.index every 10 years; circ. 60,000. (tabloid format; also avail. in microform from UMI; back issues avail.) **Indexed:** Alt.Press Ind., Bk.Rev.Ind. (1984-), Child.Bk.Rev.Ind. (1984-), HR Rep., Stud.Wom.Abstr., Wom.Stud.Abstr. (1972-).
Formerly: New Directions for Women in New Jersey.

305.412 US ISSN 0030-0071
OFF OUR BACKS; a women's news journal. 1970. m. $19 to individuals; institutions $30. Off Our Backs, Inc., 2423 18th St., N.W., Washington, DC 20009-2003. TEL 202-234-8072. Ed.Bd. adv.; bk.rev.; film rev.; play rev.; illus.; index; circ. 22,000. (tabloid format; also avail. in microfilm from UMI; back issues avail.) **Indexed:** Alt.Press Ind., New Per.Ind., Stud.Wom.Abstr., Wom.Stud.Abstr. (1970-).
—BLDSC shelfmark: 6236.527000.
Description: Covers news affecting the women's liberation movement.

ON CAMPUS WITH WOMEN. see *EDUCATION — Higher Education*

PSYCHOLOGY OF WOMEN QUARTERLY. see *PSYCHOLOGY*

305.412 CN ISSN 0707-8412
HQ1101
RESOURCES FOR FEMINIST RESEARCH/DOCUMENTATION SUR LA RECHERCHE FEMINISTE. (Text in English, French) 1972. 4/yr. Can.$25($40) to individuals; Can.$50($65) to institutions. Ontario Institute for Studies in Education, 252 Bloor St. W., Toronto, Ont. M5S 1V6, Canada. TEL 416-923-6641. FAX 416-926-4725. TELEX 06217720. adv.; bk.rev.; abstr.; bibl.; circ. 2,000. (also avail. in microfilm; back issues avail.) **Indexed:** Amer.Hist.& Life, Can.Educ.Ind., Can.Wom.Per.Ind., CMI, Hist.Abstr., Hum.Ind., Lang.& Lang.Behav.Abstr., Sociol.Abstr., Stud.Wom.Abstr., Wom.Stud.Abstr. (1972-).
—BLDSC shelfmark: 7777.608150.
Formerly: Canadian Newsletter of Research on Women (ISSN 0319-4477)
Description: Presents international research on women's studies and feminist theory.

ROOM OF ONE'S OWN; a feminist journal of literature and criticism. see *LITERATURE*

305.4 910.03 US ISSN 0741-8639
E185.86
SAGE: A SCHOLARLY JOURNAL ON BLACK WOMEN. 1984. 2/yr. $15 to individuals; institutions $25. Sage Women's Educational Press, Inc., Box 42741, Atlanta, GA 30311-0741. FAX 404-753-8383. Eds. Patricia Bell-Scott, Beverly Guy-Sheftall. adv.; bk.rev.; film rev.; play rev.; bibl.; circ. 2,000. (back issues avail.) **Indexed:** Alt.Press Ind., Hist.Abstr., Psychol.Abstr., Sociol.Abstr., Stud.Wom.Abstr., Wom.Stud.Abstr. (1984-).
—BLDSC shelfmark: 8069.215400.
Description: Interdisciplinary forum for critical discussion of issues relating to Black women.

SISTERSONG; women across cultures. see *LITERATURE*

STUDIES IN GENDER AND CULTURE. see *SOCIOLOGY*

305.4 UK
TROUBLE AND STRIFE; a radical feminist journal. 1983. 3/yr. £13 to individuals; institutions £30. P.O. Box 8, Diss, Norfolk IP22 3XG, England. adv.; bk.rev.; film rev.; illus.; index; circ. 3,000. **Indexed:** Stud.Wom.Abstr.

TULSA STUDIES IN WOMEN'S LITERATURE. see *LITERATURE*

301.412 US
VOICES FROM THE ATTIC. 2/yr. Women's Studies Research Center, University of Wisconsin, 209 N. Brooks St., Madison, WI 53715. TEL 608-263-2053. FAX 608-265-2409. circ. 1,500.

305.412 US ISSN 0145-7985
HQ1101
W I N NEWS; all the news that is fit to print by, for & about women. 1975. q. $30 to individuals; institutions $40. Women's International Network, 187 Grant St., Lexington, MA 02173. TEL 617-862-9431. Ed. Fran P. Hosken. adv.; bk.rev.; index; circ. 1,150. (also avail. in microform; back issues avail.) **Indexed:** HR Rep., Stud.Wom.Abstr.
—BLDSC shelfmark: 9343.379400.
Description: Reports on the status of women and women's rights around the world.

WOMAN OF MYSTERY. see *LITERATURE*

305 305.4 AT
WOMANSPEAK. 1974. 4/yr. Aus.$10 (foreign Aus.$12) to individuals; institutions and libraries Aus.$12 (foreign Aus.$20). Womanspeak Collective, P.O. Box 103, Spit Junction, Sydney, N.S.W. 2088, Australia. Ed.Bd. adv.; bk.rev.; illus.; circ. 1,500. **Indexed:** HR Rep., Stud.Wom.Abstr.
Description: Provides information on women's involvement in film, art, fiction, theatre, work and domesticity and politics. Discusses a broad range of related issues, especially as they pertain to feminist activism.

WOMEN & CRIMINAL JUSTICE. see *LAW — Criminal Law*

305.412 CN ISSN 0229-480X
WOMEN AND ENVIRONMENTS. 1976. 4/yr. Can.$20 to individuals; institutions Can.$30. Weed Foundation, 736 Bathurst St., Toronto, Ont. M5S 2R4, Canada. TEL 416-516-2379. FAX 416-531-6214. adv.; bk.rev.; abstr.; bibl.; illus.; circ. 1,000. (also avail. in microfilm from CML; back issues avail.) **Indexed:** Alt.Press Ind., Avery Ind.Archit.Per., Can.Per.Ind., I D A, Sage Fam.Stud.Abstr., Soc.Sci.Ind., Stud.Wom.Abstr., Wom.Stud.Abstr. (1976-).
—BLDSC shelfmark: 9343.246000.
Formerly: Women and Environments International Newsletter.
Description: Examines women's relationship to urban, social and natural environments.

WOMEN AND LANGUAGE. see *LINGUISTICS*

WOMEN & LITERATURE; a journal of women writers and the literary treatment of women. see *LITERATURE*

WOMEN & POLITICS. see *POLITICAL SCIENCE*

WOMEN & THERAPY; a feminist quarterly of research and opinion. see *PSYCHOLOGY*

WOMEN WRITING NEWSLETTER. see *LITERATURE*

WOMEN'S REVIEW OF BOOKS. see *LITERARY AND POLITICAL REVIEWS*

305.412 US
WOMEN'S STUDIES (CHAMPAIGN). irreg. University of Illinois Press, 54 E. Gregory Dr., Champaign, IL 61820. TEL 217-333-0950. FAX 217-244-8082. **Indexed:** Acad.Ind.
Refereed Serial

305.412 US
WOMEN'S STUDIES (LEWISTON). 1988. irreg. latest no.6. $39.95 per no. Edwin Mellen Press, 240 Portage Rd., Box 450, Lewiston, NY 14092. TEL 716-754-8566. FAX 716-754-4335.

305.412　　　　US　　ISSN 0049-7878
HQ1101
WOMEN'S STUDIES (NEW YORK). 1972. 4/yr. (in 1 vol., 4 nos./vol.). $85. Gordon and Breach Science Publishers, 270 Eighth Ave., New York, NY 10011. TEL 212-206-8900. FAX 212-645-2459. TELEX 236735 GOPUB UR. (Subscr. to: Box 786, Cooper Sta., New York, NY 10276. TEL 800-545-8398; UK subscr. to: P.O. Box 90, Reading, Berkshire RG1 8JL, England. TEL 0734-560-080) Ed. Wendy Martin. adv.; bk.rev.; illus.; index. (also avail. in microform from MIM; back issues avail.) **Indexed:** Abstr.Anthropol., Abstr.Engl.Stud., Acad.Ind., Amer.Hum.Ind., ASSIA, Br.Hum.Ind., Commun.Abstr., Hum.Ind., Mid.East: Abstr.& Ind., Wom.Stud.Abstr. (1972-).
　—BLDSC shelfmark: 9343.700000.
　Refereed Serial

305.4　　　　US　　ISSN 0749-1409
P96.S48
WOMEN'S STUDIES IN COMMUNICATION. 1977. s-a. $25 to individuals; institutions $40; students $15. Organization for Research on Women and Communication, c/o Roseann M. Mandziuk,m, Ed., Department of Speech Communication, Southwest Texas State University, San Marcos, TX 78666. TEL 512-245-2165. (Subscr. to: Belle Edson, Department of Communication Studies, Hollins College, Box 9588, Roanoke, VA 24020) adv.; bk.rev.; stat.; circ. 450. (back issues avail.) **Indexed:** Wom.Stud.Abstr. (1977-).

305.412　　　　US　　ISSN 0277-5395
HQ1101　　　　　　　　　CODEN: WSINDA
WOMEN'S STUDIES INTERNATIONAL FORUM; a multidisciplinary journal for the rapid publication of research communications and review articles in women's studies. Supplement: Feminist Forum (ISSN 0732-6378) 1978. 6/yr. £115 (effective 1992). Pergamon Press, Inc., Journals Division, 660 White Plains Rd., Tarrytown, NY 10591-5153. TEL 914-524-9200. FAX 914-333-2444. (And: Headington Hill Hall, Oxford OX3 0BW, England. TEL 0865-794141) Ed. Christine Zmroczek. adv.; index; circ. 1,000. (also avail. in microform from MIM,UMI) **Indexed:** Abstr.Anthropol., ASSIA, Can.Wom.Per.Ind., Commun.Abstr., Curr.Cont., Hist.Abstr., Lang.& Lang.Behav.Abstr., Mid.East: Abstr.& Ind., Psychol.Abstr., Sociol.Abstr., Stud.Wom.Abstr., Wom.Stud.Abstr. (1978-).
　—BLDSC shelfmark: 9343.704000.
　Former titles: Women's Studies International Quarterly; (until 1979): Women's Studies (Oxford) (ISSN 0148-0685)
　Refereed Serial

305.412　　　　US　　ISSN 0732-1562
HQ1181.U5
WOMEN'S STUDIES QUARTERLY. (In 2 vols.) 1972. q. $25 to individuals (foreign $33); institutions $35 (foreign $43). Feminist Press at the City University of New York, 311 E. 94th St., New York, NY 10128-5603. TEL 212-360-5790. FAX 212-348-1241. Ed. Nancy Porter. adv.; bk.rev.; bibl.; circ. 3,000. (controlled). (back issues avail.) **Indexed:** Alt.Press Ind., Chic.Per.Ind., Educ.Ind., Wom.Stud.Abstr. (1972-).
　Formerly: Women's Studies Newsletter (ISSN 0363-1133)
　Description: Publishes essays that connect feminist theory and scholarship to teaching and curriculum development, research, or political action in women's studies.

305.412　　　　SZ
WOMEN'S WORLD. French edition: Monde des Femmes. (Supplement avail.: Women's Information Update) (Editions in English, French) 1976. s-a. 20 Fr. to individuals and groups; institutions 40 Fr. Isis - Women's International Cross-Cultural Exchange (WICCE), 3 Chemin des Campanules, CH-1219 Geneva-Aiere 2, Switzerland. TEL 022-796-4437. FAX 796-0603. adv.; bk.rev.; bibl.; circ. 3,000. (also avail. in microform; back issues avail.) **Indexed:** HR Rep., Wom.Stud.Abstr. (1976-).
　Formerly (until 1983): Isis International Bulletin.
　Description: Global vision on the themes of the Isis exchange programs, including theoretical articles, case studies, as well as information about other groups and resources.

YALE JOURNAL OF LAW AND FEMINISM. see *LAW*

WOMEN'S STUDIES — Abstracting, Bibliographies, Statistics

305.412　　　　US　　ISSN 0742-6941
BIBLIOGRAPHIES AND INDEXES IN WOMEN'S STUDIES. 1984. irreg. price varies. Greenwood Press, Inc. (Subsidiary of: Greenwood Publishing Group Inc.), 88 Post Rd. W., Box 5007, Westport, CT 06881-5007. TEL 203-226-3571. FAX 203-222-1502.
　—BLDSC shelfmark: 1993.097580.

CANADIAN WOMEN'S PERIODICALS INDEX. see *WOMEN'S INTERESTS — Abstracting, Bibliographies, Statistics*

016 305.4　　　　SW　　ISSN 0348-7962
HQ1686
NY LITTERATUR OM KVINNOR: EN BIBLIOGRAFI/NEW LITERATURE ON WOMEN: A BIBLIOGRAPHY. (Text in English and Swedish) q. NOK 170. Goeteborgs Universitet, Universitetsbibliotek, Centralbiblioteket, Box 5096, S-402 22 Goeteborg, Sweden.
　●Also available online.
　Formerly: Goeteborgs Universitet. Universitetsbibliotek. Kvinnohistoriskt Arkiv. Foerteckning Oever Nyutkommen Litteratur.

305.412 016　　　　UK　　ISSN 0262-5644
HQ1180
STUDIES ON WOMEN ABSTRACTS. 1983. bi-m. $159 to individuals; institutions $318. Carfax Publishing Co., P.O. Box 25, Abingdon, Oxfordshire OX14 3UE, England. TEL 0235-555335. FAX 0235-553559. (U.S. subscr. addr.: Carfax Publishing Co., Box 2025, Dunnellon, FL 32630) Ed. June Purvis. adv.; bk.rev.; cum.index. (also avail. in microfiche; back issues avail.)
　—BLDSC shelfmark: 8492.006600.

WOMEN AND APPROPRIATE TECHNOLOGIES; a bibliography. see *TECHNOLOGY: COMPREHENSIVE WORKS — Abstracting, Bibliographies, Statistics*

376 800　　　　UK　　ISSN 0957-1663
WOMEN IN B H I. (British Humanities Index) 1989. q. £35($66) in UK & EEC; elsewhere £39. Bowker-Saur Ltd., 59-60 Grosvenor St., London W1X 9DA, England. TEL 071-493-5841. FAX 071-499-1590. (Subscr. to: Bailey Bros. & Swinfen Ltd., Warner House, Bowles Well Gardens, Folkestone, Kent CT19 6PH, England. TEL 0303-850501; N. America susbscr. to: K.G. Saur, A Reed Reference Publishing Company, 121 Chanlon Rd., New Providence, NJ 07974. TEL 908-665-3576) Ed. Lyn Duffus. index.
　Description: Selected records for BHI of specific interest to women's studies.

305.412 016　　　　US　　ISSN 0049-7835
Z7962
WOMEN STUDIES ABSTRACTS. 1972. q. $56 to individuals; institutions $112 (effective 1992). Rush Publishing Co., Inc., Box 1, Rush, NY 14543. TEL 716-624-4418. Ed. Sara Stauffer Whaley. adv.; bk.rev.; index; circ. 1,000. (also avail. in microfilm from UMI; reprint service avail. from UMI)
　—BLDSC shelfmark: 9343.340000.
　Description: Abstracts and listings of scholarly articles from women studies periodicals, from education to employment and interpersonal relations.

305.4　　　　US　　ISSN 1058-6369
Z7962
▼**WOMEN'S STUDIES INDEX (YEAR).** 1990. a. $125 (foreign $150). G.K. Hall & Co., 70 Lincoln St., Boston, MA 02111. TEL 617-423-3990. FAX 617-423-3999. TELEX 94-0037.
　Description: Covers over 100 journals, from popular magazines to scholarly, feminist, and lesbian journals, indexing articles on a broad range of topics in and relevant to the field of women's studies.

WORD PROCESSING

see *Computers–Word Processing*

ZOOLOGY

see *Biology–Zoology*